# presented to

_____

BY _____

_____

_____

ON THE OCCASION OF _____

_____

_____

DATE _____

◆ ISAIAH 40:8

THE GRASS WITHERS AND THE FLOWERS FADE,
BUT THE WORD OF OUR GOD LASTS FOREVER.

# *marriage*

_____

AND _____

WERE UNITED IN MARRIAGE ON

_____

AT _____

BY _____

WITNESSED BY

MAID OF HONOR_____

BEST MAN _____

ATTENDANTS _____

_____

_____

_____

◆ GENESIS 2:24

THIS EXPLAINS WHY A MAN LEAVES HIS FATHER
AND MOTHER AND IS JOINED TO HIS WIFE,
AND THE TWO ARE UNITED INTO ONE.

*births*

| NAME | DATE |
|------|------|

BIRTHPLACE

| NAME | DATE |
|------|------|

BIRTHPLACE

| NAME | DATE |
|------|------|

BIRTHPLACE

| NAME | DATE |
|------|------|

BIRTHPLACE

| NAME | DATE |
|------|------|

BIRTHPLACE

◆ PSALM 127:3

CHILDREN ARE A GIFT FROM THE LORD;
THEY ARE A REWARD FROM HIM.

# *baptisms*

WAS BAPTIZED ON _____

    AT _____

    BY _____


WAS BAPTIZED ON _____

    AT _____

    BY _____


WAS BAPTIZED ON _____

    AT _____

    BY _____


WAS BAPTIZED ON _____

    AT _____

    BY _____

EPHESIANS 4:5

◆ THERE IS ONE LORD,
ONE FAITH, ONE BAPTISM.

# deaths

NAME _____ DATE _____

NAME _____ DATE _____

NAME _____ DATE _____

NAME _____ DATE _____

NAME _____ DATE _____

NAME _____ DATE _____

NAME _____ DATE _____

◆ 1 CORINTHIANS 6:14

AND GOD WILL RAISE US
FROM THE DEAD BY HIS POWER,
JUST AS HE RAISED OUR LORD FROM THE DEAD.

# husband

# THE FAMILY

| NAME | BIRTHPLACE | DATES |
|---|---|---|

BROTHERS AND SISTERS

## PARENTS

### FATHER

NAME

BIRTHPLACE                    DATES

### MOTHER

NAME

BIRTHPLACE                    DATES

## GRANDPARENTS

### PATERNAL

GRANDFATHER

BIRTHPLACE                    DATES

GRANDMOTHER

BIRTHPLACE                    DATES

### MATERNAL

GRANDFATHER

BIRTHPLACE                    DATES

GRANDMOTHER

BIRTHPLACE                    DATES

## GREAT-GRANDPARENTS

### PATERNAL

GRANDFATHER'S FATHER

BIRTHPLACE                    DATES

GRANDFATHER'S MOTHER

BIRTHPLACE                    DATES

GRANDMOTHER'S FATHER

BIRTHPLACE                    DATES

GRANDMOTHER'S MOTHER

BIRTHPLACE                    DATES

### MATERNAL

GRANDFATHER'S FATHER

BIRTHPLACE                    DATES

GRANDFATHER'S MOTHER

BIRTHPLACE                    DATES

GRANDMOTHER'S FATHER

BIRTHPLACE                    DATES

GRANDMOTHER'S MOTHER

BIRTHPLACE                    DATES

*wife*

# TREE

NAME                            BIRTHPLACE                 DATES

BROTHERS AND SISTERS

## PARENTS

**FATHER**                                     **MOTHER**

NAME                                   NAME

BIRTHPLACE         DATES             BIRTHPLACE         DATES

## GRANDPARENTS

**PATERNAL**                                   **MATERNAL**

GRANDFATHER                          GRANDFATHER

BIRTHPLACE         DATES             BIRTHPLACE         DATES

GRANDMOTHER                        GRANDMOTHER

BIRTHPLACE         DATES             BIRTHPLACE         DATES

## GREAT-GRANDPARENTS

**PATERNAL**                                   **MATERNAL**

GRANDFATHER'S FATHER              GRANDFATHER'S FATHER

BIRTHPLACE         DATES             BIRTHPLACE         DATES

GRANDFATHER'S MOTHER              GRANDFATHER'S MOTHER

BIRTHPLACE         DATES             BIRTHPLACE         DATES

GRANDMOTHER'S FATHER              GRANDMOTHER'S FATHER

BIRTHPLACE         DATES             BIRTHPLACE         DATES

GRANDMOTHER'S MOTHER              GRANDMOTHER'S MOTHER

BIRTHPLACE         DATES             BIRTHPLACE         DATES

*special*
*memories*

EVENT
_____

PLACE _____ DATE _____

EVENT
_____

PLACE _____ DATE _____

EVENT
_____

PLACE _____ DATE _____

EVENT
_____

PLACE _____ DATE _____

PSALM 118:29

◆

GIVE THANKS TO THE LORD, FOR HE IS GOOD!
HIS FAITHFUL LOVE ENDURES FOREVER.

# Life Application
## STUDY BIBLE

# APPLICATION®
## Study Bible

### New Living Translation®
SECOND EDITION

Tyndale House Publishers, Inc.
Carol Steam, Illinois

ISBN 978-1-4143-0077-1 Genuine Leather Black
ISBN 978-1-4143-0082-5 Genuine Leather Black Indexed
ISBN 978-1-4143-0078-8 Genuine Leather Burgundy
ISBN 978-0-8423-8497-1 Bonded Leather Black
ISBN 978-0-8423-8508-4 Bonded Leather Black Indexed
ISBN 978-0-8423-8496-4 Bonded Leather Burgundy
ISBN 978-0-8423-8507-7 Bonded Leather Burgundy Indexed
ISBN 978-0-8423-8479-5 Bonded Leather Navy
ISBN 978-0-8423-8493-3 Hardcover
ISBN 978-1-4143-0972-9 Bonded Leather Brown/Ostrich Tan
ISBN 978-1-4143-0973-6 Bonded Leather Burgundy/Cream

ISBN 978-0-8423-8495-7 LeatherLike Black
ISBN 978-0-8423-8499-5 LeatherLike Black Indexed
ISBN 978-0-8423-8494-0 LeatherLike Burgundy
ISBN 978-0-8423-8498-8 LeatherLike Burgundy Indexed
ISBN 978-1-4143-0080-1 LeatherLike Navy
ISBN 978-1-4143-0081-8 LeatherLike Navy Indexed
ISBN 978-1-4143-0212-6 LeatherLike Black/Grey
ISBN 978-1-4143-0211-9 LeatherLike Camel/Camel
ISBN 978-1-4143-0213-3 LeatherLike Tan/Brown

*Life Application Study Bible,* NLT, also available in large print and personal edition sizes.

Printed in South Korea

14   13   12   11   10   09
18   17   16   15   14   13

# CONTENTS

# LIST OF THE BOOKS OF THE BIBLE

## The Old Testament

| | |
|---|---|
| 2 | GENESIS |
| 94 | EXODUS |
| 158 | LEVITICUS |
| 199 | NUMBERS |
| 262 | DEUTERONOMY |
| 311 | JOSHUA |
| 350 | JUDGES |
| 396 | RUTH |
| 404 | 1 SAMUEL |
| 459 | 2 SAMUEL |
| 507 | 1 KINGS |
| 566 | 2 KINGS |
| 618 | 1 CHRONICLES |
| 664 | 2 CHRONICLES |
| 719 | EZRA |
| 741 | NEHEMIAH |
| 767 | ESTHER |
| 783 | JOB |
| 841 | PSALMS |
| 1000 | PROVERBS |
| 1060 | ECCLESIASTES |
| 1075 | SONG OF SONGS |
| 1088 | ISAIAH |
| 1197 | JEREMIAH |
| 1292 | LAMENTATIONS |
| 1306 | EZEKIEL |
| 1374 | DANIEL |
| 1402 | HOSEA |
| 1426 | JOEL |
| 1435 | AMOS |
| 1451 | OBADIAH |
| 1456 | JONAH |
| 1463 | MICAH |
| 1476 | NAHUM |
| 1482 | HABAKKUK |
| 1489 | ZEPHANIAH |
| 1497 | HAGGAI |
| 1501 | ZECHARIAH |
| 1518 | MALACHI |

## The New Testament

| | |
|---|---|
| 1530 | MATTHEW |
| 1610 | MARK |
| 1666 | LUKE |
| 1745 | JOHN |
| 1811 | ACTS |
| 1890 | ROMANS |
| 1925 | 1 CORINTHIANS |
| 1958 | 2 CORINTHIANS |
| 1980 | GALATIANS |
| 1997 | EPHESIANS |
| 2012 | PHILIPPIANS |
| 2025 | COLOSSIANS |
| 2039 | 1 THESSALONIANS |
| 2048 | 2 THESSALONIANS |
| 2054 | 1 TIMOTHY |
| 2066 | 2 TIMOTHY |
| 2075 | TITUS |
| 2081 | PHILEMON |
| 2085 | HEBREWS |
| 2113 | JAMES |
| 2124 | 1 PETER |
| 2137 | 2 PETER |
| 2143 | 1 JOHN |
| 2155 | 2 JOHN |
| 2158 | 3 JOHN |
| 2161 | JUDE |
| 2165 | REVELATION |

The *Holy Bible*, New Living Translation, was first published in 1996. It quickly became one of the most popular Bible translations in the English-speaking world. While the NLT's influence was rapidly growing, the Bible Translation Committee determined that an additional investment in scholarly review and text refinement could make it even better. So shortly after its initial publication, the committee began an eight-year process with the purpose of increasing the level of the NLT's precision without sacrificing its easy-to-understand quality. This second-generation text was completed in 2004 and is reflected in this edition of the New Living Translation. An additional update with minor changes was subsequently introduced in 2007.

The goal of any Bible translation is to convey the meaning and content of the ancient Hebrew, Aramaic, and Greek texts as accurately as possible to contemporary readers. The challenge for our translators was to create a text that would communicate as clearly and powerfully to today's readers as the original texts did to readers and listeners in the ancient biblical world. The resulting translation is easy to read and understand, while also accurately communicating the meaning and content of the original biblical texts. The NLT is a general-purpose text especially good for study, devotional reading, and reading aloud in worship services.

We believe that the New Living Translation—which combines the latest biblical scholarship with a clear, dynamic writing style—will communicate God's word powerfully to all who read it. We publish it with the prayer that God will use it to speak his timeless truth to the church and the world in a fresh, new way.

*The Publishers*
*October 2007*

## Translation Philosophy and Methodology

English Bible translations tend to be governed by one of two general translation theories. The first theory has been called "formal-equivalence," "literal," or "word-for-word" translation. According to this theory, the translator attempts to render each word of the original language into English and seeks to preserve the original syntax and sentence structure as much as possible in translation. The second theory has been called "dynamic-equivalence," "functional-equivalence," or "thought-for-thought" translation. The goal of this translation theory is to produce in English the closest natural equivalent of the message expressed by the original-language text, both in meaning and in style.

Both of these translation theories have their strengths. A formal-equivalence translation preserves aspects of the original text—including ancient idioms, term consistency, and original-language syntax—that are valuable for scholars and professional study. It allows a reader to trace formal elements of the original-language text through the English translation. A dynamic-equivalence translation, on the other hand, focuses on translating the message of the original-language text. It ensures that the meaning of the text is readily apparent to the contemporary reader. This allows the message to come through with immediacy, without requiring the reader to struggle with foreign idioms and awkward syntax. It also facilitates serious study of the text's message and clarity in both devotional and public reading.

The pure application of either of these translation philosophies would create translations at opposite ends of the translation spectrum. But in reality, all translations contain a mixture of these two philosophies. A purely formal-equivalence translation would be unintelligible in English, and a purely dynamic-equivalence translation would risk being unfaithful to the original. That is why translations shaped by dynamic-equivalence theory are usually quite literal when the original text is relatively clear, and the translations shaped by formal-equivalence theory are sometimes quite dynamic when the original text is obscure.

The translators of the New Living Translation set out to render the message of the original texts of Scripture into clear, contemporary English. As they did so, they kept the concerns of both formal-equivalence and dynamic-equivalence in mind. On the one hand, they translated as simply and literally as possible when that approach yielded an accurate, clear, and natural English text. Many words and phrases were rendered literally and consistently into English, preserving essential literary and rhetorical devices, ancient metaphors, and word choices that give structure to the text and provide echoes of meaning from one passage to the next.

On the other hand, the translators rendered the message more dynamically when the literal rendering was hard to understand, was misleading, or yielded archaic or foreign wording. They clarified difficult metaphors and terms to aid in the reader's understanding. The translators first struggled with the meaning of the words and phrases in the ancient context; then they rendered the message into clear, natural English. Their goal was to be both faithful to the ancient texts and eminently readable. The result is a translation that is both exegetically accurate and idiomatically powerful.

## Translation Process and Team

To produce an accurate translation of the Bible into contemporary English, the translation team needed the skills necessary to enter into the thought patterns of the ancient authors and then to render their ideas, connotations, and effects into clear, contemporary English. To begin this process, qualified biblical scholars were needed to interpret the meaning of the original text and to check it against our base English translation. In order to guard against personal and theological biases, the scholars needed to represent a diverse group of Evangelicals who would employ the best exegetical tools. Then to work alongside the scholars, skilled English stylists were needed to shape the text into clear, contemporary English.

With these concerns in mind, the Bible Translation Committee recruited teams of scholars that represented a broad spectrum of denominations, theological perspectives, and backgrounds within the worldwide Evangelical community. (These scholars are listed at the end of this introduction.) Each book of the Bible was assigned to three different scholars with proven expertise in the book or group of books to be reviewed. Each of these scholars made a thorough review of a base translation and submitted suggested revisions to the appropriate Senior Translator. The Senior Translator then reviewed and summarized these suggestions and proposed a first-draft revision of the base text. This draft served as the basis for several additional phases of exegetical and stylistic committee review. Then the Bible Translation Committee jointly reviewed and approved every verse of the final translation.

Throughout the translation and editing process, the Senior Translators and their scholar teams were given a chance to review the editing done by the team of stylists. This ensured that exegetical errors would not be introduced late in the process and that the entire Bible Translation Committee was happy with the final result. By choosing a team of qualified scholars and skilled stylists and by setting up a process that allowed their interaction throughout the process, the New Living Translation has been refined to preserve the essential formal elements of the original biblical texts, while also creating a clear, understandable English text.

The New Living Translation was first published in 1996. Shortly after its initial publication, the Bible Translation Committee began a process of further committee review and translation refinement. The purpose of this continued revision was to increase the level of precision without sacrificing the text's easy-to-understand quality. This second-edition text was completed in 2004, and an additional update with minor changes was subsequently introduced in 2007. This printing of the New Living Translation reflects the updated 2007 text.

## Written to Be Read Aloud
It is evident in Scripture that the biblical documents were written to be read aloud, often in public worship (see Nehemiah 8; Luke 4:16-20; 1 Timothy 4:13; Revelation 1:3). It is still the case today that more people will hear the Bible read aloud in church than are likely to read it for themselves. Therefore, a new translation must communicate with clarity and power when it is read publicly. Clarity was a primary goal for the NLT translators, not only to facilitate private reading and understanding, but also to ensure that it would be excellent for public reading and make an immediate and powerful impact on any listener.

## The Texts behind the New Living Translation
The Old Testament translators used the Masoretic Text of the Hebrew Bible as represented in *Biblia Hebraica Stuttgartensia* (1977), with its extensive system of textual notes; this is an update of Rudolf Kittel's *Biblia Hebraica* (Stuttgart, 1937). The translators also further compared the Dead Sea Scrolls, the Septuagint and other Greek manuscripts, the Samaritan Pentateuch, the Syriac Peshitta, the Latin Vulgate, and any other versions or manuscripts that shed light on the meaning of difficult passages.

The New Testament translators used the two standard editions of the Greek New Testament: the *Greek New Testament,* published by the United Bible Societies (UBS, fourth revised edition, 1993), and *Novum Testamentum Graece,* edited by Nestle and Aland (NA, twenty-seventh edition, 1993). These two editions, which have the same text but differ in punctuation and textual notes, represent, for the most part, the best in modern textual scholarship. However, in cases where strong textual or other scholarly evidence supported the decision, the translators sometimes chose to differ from the UBS and NA Greek texts and followed variant readings found in other ancient witnesses. Significant textual variants of this sort are always noted in the textual notes of the New Living Translation.

*Translation Issues*

The translators have made a conscious effort to provide a text that can be easily understood by the typical reader of modern English. To this end, we sought to use only vocabulary and language structures in common use today. We avoided using language likely to become quickly dated or that reflects only a narrow sub-dialect of English, with the goal of making the New Living Translation as broadly useful and timeless as possible.

But our concern for readability goes beyond the concerns of vocabulary and sentence structure. We are also concerned about historical and cultural barriers to understanding the Bible, and we have sought to translate terms shrouded in history and culture in ways that can be immediately understood. To this end:

- We have converted ancient weights and measures (for example, "ephah" [a unit of dry volume] or "cubit" [a unit of length]) to modern English (American) equivalents, since the ancient measures are not generally meaningful to today's readers. Then in the textual footnotes we offer the literal Hebrew, Aramaic, or Greek measures, along with modern metric equivalents.
- Instead of translating ancient currency values literally, we have expressed them in common terms that communicate the message. For example, in the Old Testament, "ten shekels of silver" becomes "ten pieces of silver" to convey the intended message. In the New Testament, we have often translated the "denarius" as "the normal daily wage" to facilitate understanding. Then a footnote offers: "Greek *a denarius*, the payment for a full day's wage." In general, we give a clear English rendering and then state the literal Hebrew, Aramaic, or Greek in a textual footnote.
- Since the names of Hebrew months are unknown to most contemporary readers, and since the Hebrew lunar calendar fluctuates from year to year in relation to the solar calendar used today, we have looked for clear ways to communicate the time of year the Hebrew months (such as Abib) refer to. When an expanded or interpretive rendering is given in the text, a textual note gives the literal rendering. Where it is possible to define a specific ancient date in terms of our modern calendar, we use modern dates in the text. A textual footnote then gives the literal Hebrew date and states the rationale for our rendering. For example, Ezra 6:15 pinpoints the date when the postexilic Temple was completed in Jerusalem: "the third day of the month Adar." This was during the sixth year of King Darius's reign (that is, 515 B.C.). We have translated that date as March 12, with a footnote giving the Hebrew and identifying the year as 515 B.C.
- Since ancient references to the time of day differ from our modern methods of denoting time, we have used renderings that are instantly understandable to the modern reader. Accordingly, we have rendered specific times of day by using approximate equivalents in terms of our common "o'clock" system. On occasion, translations such as "at dawn the next morning" or "as the sun was setting" have been used when the biblical reference is more general.
- When the meaning of a proper name (or a wordplay inherent in a proper name) is relevant to the message of the text, its meaning is often illuminated with a textual footnote. For example, in Exodus 2:10 the text reads: "The princess named him Moses, for she explained, 'I lifted him out of the water.'" The accompanying footnote reads: "*Moses* sounds like a Hebrew term that means 'to lift out.'"

    Sometimes, when the actual meaning of a name is clear, that meaning is included in parentheses within the text itself. For example, the text at Genesis 16:11 reads: "You are to name him Ishmael (*which means 'God hears'*), for the LORD has heard your cry of distress." Since the original hearers and readers would have instantly understood the meaning of the name "Ishmael," we have provided modern readers with the same information so they can experience the text in a similar way.

- Many words and phrases carry a great deal of cultural meaning that was obvious to the original readers but needs explanation in our own culture. For example, the phrase "they beat their breasts" (Luke 23:48) in ancient times meant that people were very upset, often in mourning. In our translation we chose to translate this phrase dynamically for clarity: "They went home *in deep sorrow*." Then we included a footnote with the literal Greek, which reads: "Greek *went home beating their breasts*." In other similar cases, however, we have sometimes chosen to illuminate the existing literal expression to make it immediately understandable. For example, here we might have expanded the literal phrase to read: "They went home beating their breasts *in sorrow*." If we had done this, we would not have included a textual footnote, since the literal Greek clearly appears in translation.
- Metaphorical language is sometimes difficult for contemporary readers to understand, so at times we have chosen to translate or illuminate the meaning of a metaphor. For example, the ancient poet writes, "Your neck is *like* the tower of David" (Song of Songs 4:4). We have rendered it "Your neck is *as beautiful as* the tower of David" to clarify the intended positive meaning of the simile. Another example comes in Ecclesiastes 12:3, which can be literally rendered: "Remember him . . . when the grinding women cease because they are few, and the women who look through the windows see dimly." We have rendered it: "Remember him before your teeth—your few remaining servants—stop grinding; and before your eyes—the women looking through the windows—see dimly." We clarified such metaphors only when we believed a typical reader might be confused by the literal text.
- When the content of the original language text is poetic in character, we have rendered it in English poetic form. We sought to break lines in ways that clarify and highlight the relationships between phrases of the text. Hebrew poetry often uses parallelism, a literary form where a second phrase (or in some instances a third or fourth) echoes the initial phrase in some way. In Hebrew parallelism, the subsequent parallel phrases continue, while also furthering and sharpening the thought expressed in the initial line or phrase. Whenever possible, we sought to represent these parallel phrases in natural poetic English.
- The Greek term *hoi Ioudaioi* is literally translated "the Jews" in many English translations. In the Gospel of John, however, this term doesn't always refer to the Jewish people generally. In some contexts, it refers more particularly to the Jewish religious leaders. We have attempted to capture the meaning in these different contexts by using terms such as "the people" (with a footnote: Greek *the Jewish people*) or "the religious leaders," where appropriate.
- One challenge we faced was how to translate accurately the ancient biblical text that was originally written in a context where male-oriented terms were used to refer to humanity generally. We needed to respect the nature of the ancient context while also trying to make the translation clear to a modern audience that tends to read male-oriented language as applying only to males. Often the original text, though using masculine nouns and pronouns, clearly intends that the message be applied to both men and women. A typical example is found in the New Testament letters, where the believers are called "brothers" (*adelphoi*). Yet it is clear from the content of these letters that they were addressed to all the believers—male and female. Thus, we have usually translated this Greek word as "brothers and sisters" in order to represent the historical situation more accurately.

We have also been sensitive to passages where the text applies generally to human beings or to the human condition. In some instances we have used plural pronouns (they, them) in place of the masculine singular (he, him). For example, a traditional rendering of Proverbs 22:6 is: "Train up a child in the way he should go, and when he is old he will not turn from it." We have rendered it: "Direct your children onto the right path, and when they are older, they will not leave it." At times, we have also replaced third person pronouns with the second person to ensure clarity. A traditional rendering of Proverbs 26:27 is: "He who digs a pit will fall into it, and he who rolls a stone, it will come back on him." We have rendered it: "If you set a trap for others, you will get caught in it yourself. If you roll a boulder down on others, it will crush you instead."

We should emphasize, however, that all masculine nouns and pronouns used to represent God (for example, "Father") have been maintained without exception. All decisions of this kind have been driven by the concern to reflect accurately the intended meaning of the original texts of Scripture.

## Lexical Consistency in Terminology

For the sake of clarity, we have translated certain original-language terms consistently, especially within synoptic passages and for commonly repeated rhetorical phrases, and within certain word categories such as divine names and non-theological technical terminology (e.g., liturgical, legal, cultural, zoological, and botanical terms). For theological terms, we have allowed a greater semantic range of acceptable English words or phrases for a single Hebrew or Greek word. We have avoided some theological terms that are not readily understood by many modern readers. For example, we avoided using words such as "justification" and "sanctification," which are carryovers from Latin translations. In place of these words, we have provided renderings such as "made right with God" and "made holy."

## The Spelling of Proper Names

Many individuals in the Bible, especially the Old Testament, are known by more than one name (e.g., Uzziah/Azariah). For the sake of clarity, we have tried to use a single spelling for any one individual, footnoting the literal spelling whenever we differ from it. This is especially helpful in delineating the kings of Israel and Judah. King Joash/Jehoash of Israel has been consistently called Jehoash, while King Joash/Jehoash of Judah is called Joash. A similar distinction has been used to distinguish between Joram/Jehoram of Israel and Joram/Jehoram of Judah. All such decisions were made with the goal of clarifying the text for the reader. When the ancient biblical writers clearly had a theological purpose in their choice of a variant name (e.g., Esh-baal/Ishbosheth), the different names have been maintained with an explanatory footnote.

For the names Jacob and Israel, which are used interchangeably for both the individual patriarch and the nation, we generally render it "Israel" when it refers to the nation and "Jacob" when it refers to the individual. When our rendering of the name differs from the underlying Hebrew text, we provide a textual footnote, which includes this explanation: "The names 'Jacob' and 'Israel' are often interchanged throughout the Old Testament, referring sometimes to the individual patriarch and sometimes to the nation."

## The Rendering of Divine Names

All appearances of 'el, 'elohim, or 'eloah have been translated "God," except where the context demands the translation "god(s)." We have generally rendered the tetragrammaton (YHWH) consistently as "the LORD," utilizing a form with small capitals that is common among English translations. This will distinguish it from the name 'adonai, which we render "Lord." When 'adonai and YHWH appear together, we have rendered it "Sovereign LORD." This also distinguishes 'adonai YHWH from cases where YHWH appears with 'elohim, which is rendered "LORD God." When YH (the short form of YHWH) and YHWH appear together, we have rendered it "LORD GOD." When YHWH appears with the term tseba'oth, we have rendered it "LORD of Heaven's Armies" to translate the meaning of the name. In a few cases, we have utilized the transliteration, Yahweh, when the personal character of the name is being invoked in contrast to another divine name or the name of some other god (for example, see Exod 3:15; 6:2-3).

In the New Testament, the Greek word christos has been translated as "Messiah" when the context assumes a Jewish audience. When a Gentile audience can be assumed, christos has been translated as "Christ." The Greek word *kurios* is consistently translated "Lord," except that it is translated "Lᴏʀᴅ" wherever the New Testament text explicitly quotes from the Old Testament, and the text there has it in small capitals.

*Textual Footnotes*

The New Living Translation provides several kinds of textual footnotes, all designated in the text with an asterisk:

- When for the sake of clarity the NLT renders a difficult or potentially confusing phrase dynamically, we generally give the literal rendering in a textual footnote. This allows the reader to see the literal source of our dynamic rendering and how our translation relates to other more literal translations. These notes are prefaced with "Hebrew," "Aramaic," or "Greek," identifying the language of the underlying source text. For example, in Acts 2:42 we translated the literal "breaking of bread" (from the Greek) as "the Lord's Supper" to clarify that this verse refers to the ceremonial practice of the church rather than just an ordinary meal. Then we attached a footnote to "the Lord's Supper," which reads: "Greek *the breaking of bread.*"

- Textual footnotes are also used to show alternative renderings, prefaced with the word "Or." These normally occur for passages where an aspect of the meaning is debated. On occasion, we also provide notes on words or phrases that represent a departure from long-standing tradition. These notes are prefaced with "Traditionally rendered." For example, the footnote to the translation "serious skin disease" at Leviticus 13:2 says: "Traditionally rendered *leprosy.* The Hebrew word used throughout this passage is used to describe various skin diseases."

- When our translators follow a textual variant that differs significantly from our standard Hebrew or Greek texts (listed earlier), we document that difference with a footnote. We also footnote cases when the NLT excludes a passage that is included in the Greek text known as the *Textus Receptus* (and familiar to readers through its translation in the King James Version). In such cases, we offer a translation of the excluded text in a footnote, even though it is generally recognized as a later addition to the Greek text and not part of the original Greek New Testament.

- All Old Testament passages that are quoted in the New Testament are identified by a textual footnote at the New Testament location. When the New Testament clearly quotes from the Greek translation of the Old Testament, and when it differs significantly in wording from the Hebrew text, we also place a textual footnote at the Old Testament location. This note includes a rendering of the Greek version, along with a cross-reference to the New Testament passage(s) where it is cited (for example, see notes on Psalms 8:2; 53:3; Proverbs 3:12).

- Some textual footnotes provide cultural and historical information on places, things, and people in the Bible that are probably obscure to modern readers. Such notes should aid the reader in understanding the message of the text. For example, in Acts 12:1, "King Herod" is named in this translation as "King Herod Agrippa" and is identified in a footnote as being "the nephew of Herod Antipas and a grandson of Herod the Great."

- When the meaning of a proper name (or a wordplay inherent in a proper name) is relevant to the meaning of the text, it is either illuminated with a textual footnote or included within parentheses in the text itself. For example, the footnote concerning the name "Eve" at Genesis 3:20 reads: "*Eve* sounds like a Hebrew term that means 'to give life.' " This wordplay in the Hebrew illuminates the meaning of the text, which goes on to say that Eve "would be the mother of all who live."

AS WE SUBMIT this translation for publication, we recognize that any translation of the Scriptures is subject to limitations and imperfections. Anyone who has attempted to communicate the richness of God's Word into another language will realize it is impossible to make a perfect translation. Recognizing these limitations, we sought God's guidance and wisdom throughout this project. Now we pray that he will accept our efforts and use this translation for the benefit of the church and of all people.

We pray that the New Living Translation will overcome some of the barriers of history, culture, and language that have kept people from reading and understanding God's Word. We hope that readers unfamiliar with the Bible will find the words clear and easy to understand and that readers well versed in the Scriptures will gain a fresh perspective. We pray that readers will gain insight and wisdom for living, but most of all that they will meet the God of the Bible and be forever changed by knowing him.

*The Bible Translation Committee*
*October 2007*

## PENTATEUCH

**Daniel I. Block,** Senior Translator
*Wheaton College*

### GENESIS
**Allen Ross,** *Beeson Divinity School, Samford University*
**Gordon Wenham,** *Trinity Theological College, Bristol*

### EXODUS
**Robert Bergen,** *Hannibal-LaGrange College*
**Daniel I. Block,** *Wheaton College*
**Eugene Carpenter,** *Bethel College, Mishawaka, Indiana*

### LEVITICUS
**David Baker,** *Ashland Theological Seminary*
**Victor Hamilton,** *Asbury College*
**Kenneth Mathews,** *Beeson Divinity School, Samford University*

### NUMBERS
**Dale A. Brueggemann,** *Assemblies of God Division of Foreign Missions*
**R. K. Harrison (deceased),** *Wycliffe College*
**Paul R. House,** *Wheaton College*
**Gerald L. Mattingly,** *Johnson Bible College*

### DEUTERONOMY
**J. Gordon McConville,** *University of Gloucester*
**Eugene H. Merrill,** *Dallas Theological Seminary*
**John A. Thompson (deceased),** *University of Melbourne*

## HISTORICAL BOOKS

**Barry J. Beitzel,** Senior Translator
*Trinity Evangelical Divinity School*

### JOSHUA, JUDGES
**Carl E. Armerding,** *Schloss Mittersill Study Centre*
**Barry J. Beitzel,** *Trinity Evangelical Divinity School*
**Lawson Stone,** *Asbury Theological Seminary*

### 1 & 2 SAMUEL
**Robert Gordon,** *Cambridge University*
**V. Philips Long,** *Regent College*
**J. Robert Vannoy,** *Biblical Theological Seminary*

### 1 & 2 KINGS
**Bill T. Arnold,** *Asbury Theological Seminary*
**William H. Barnes,** *North Central University*
**Frederic W. Bush,** *Fuller Theological Seminary*

### 1 & 2 CHRONICLES
**Raymond B. Dillard (deceased),** *Westminster Theological Seminary*

**David A. Dorsey,** *Evangelical School of Theology*
**Terry Eves,** *Erskine College*

### RUTH, EZRA—ESTHER
**William C. Williams,** *Vanguard University*
**H. G. M. Williamson,** *Oxford University*

## WISDOM BOOKS

**Tremper Longman III,** Senior Translator
*Westmont College*

### JOB
**August Konkel,** *Providence Theological Seminary*
**Tremper Longman III,** *Westmont College*
**Al Wolters,** *Redeemer College*

### PSALMS 1–75
**Mark D. Futato,** *Reformed Theological Seminary*
**Douglas Green,** *Westminster Theological Seminary*
**Richard Pratt,** *Reformed Theological Seminary*

### PSALMS 76–150
**David M. Howard Jr.,** *Bethel Theological Seminary*
**Raymond C. Ortlund Jr.,** *Trinity Evangelical Divinity School*
**Willem VanGemeren,** *Trinity Evangelical Divinity School*

### PROVERBS
**Ted Hildebrandt,** *Gordon College*
**Richard Schultz,** *Wheaton College*
**Raymond C. Van Leeuwen,** *Eastern College*

### ECCLESIASTES, SONG OF SONGS
**Daniel C. Fredericks,** *Belhaven College*
**David Hubbard (deceased),** *Fuller Theological Seminary*
**Tremper Longman III,** *Westmont College*

## PROPHETS

**John N. Oswalt,** Senior Translator
*Wesley Biblical Seminary*

### ISAIAH
**John N. Oswalt,** *Wesley Biblical Seminary*
**Gary Smith,** *Midwestern Baptist Theological Seminary*
**John Walton,** *Wheaton College*

### JEREMIAH, LAMENTATIONS
**G. Herbert Livingston,** *Asbury Theological Seminary*
**Elmer A. Martens,** *Mennonite Brethren Biblical Seminary*

### EZEKIEL
**Daniel I. Block,** *Wheaton College*

*Senior Editorial Team*
Dr. Bruce B. Barton
Ronald A. Beers
Dr. James C. Galvin
LaVonne Neff
Linda Chaffee Taylor
David R. Veerman

*General Editor*
Ronald A. Beers

*Tyndale House Bible Editors*
Philip W. Comfort
Mark R. Norton
Robert K. Brown
Virginia Muir
Del Lankford
Leanne Roberts

*Book Introductions*
David R. Veerman

*Book Outlines, Blueprints, Harmony*
Dr. James C. Galvin

*Megathemes*
Dr. Bruce B. Barton

*Map Development & Computer Operation*
Linda Chaffee Taylor

*Color Map Consultant*
Dr. Barry Beitzel

*Charts & Diagrams*
Neil S. Wilson
Ronald A. Beers
David R. Veerman
Pamela York

*NLT Dictionary/Concordance*
James A. Swanson
Mark R. Norton

*Personality Profiles*
Neil S. Wilson

*Design & Development Team*
Dr. Bruce B. Barton
Ronald A. Beers
Dr. James C. Galvin
David R. Veerman

*Tyndale House Graphic Design*
Timothy R. Botts
Jacqueline Noe

*A Chronology of Bible Events and World Events*
Dr. David Maas

*Theological Reviewers*
Dr. Kenneth S. Kantzer
(deceased)
*General Theological Reviewer*
Dean Emeritus and
Distinguished Professor
of Bible and Systematic
Theology
Trinity Evangelical Divinity
School

Dr. V. Gilbert Beers
President of
Scripture Press Ministries

Dr. Barry Beitzel
Associate Academic Dean
and Professor of Old Testament
and Semitic Languages
Trinity Evangelical Divinity
School

Dr. Edwin A. Blum
Associate Professor of
Historical Theology
Dallas Theological Seminary

Dr. Geoffrey W. Bromiley
Professor
Fuller Theological Seminary

Dr. George K. Brushaber
President
Bethel College & Seminary

Dr. L. Russ Bush
Associate Professor
Philosophy & Religion
Southwestern Baptist
Theological Seminary

C. Donald Cole
Pastor, Moody Radio Network

Mrs. Naomi E. Cole
Speaker & Seminar Leader

Dr. Walter A. Elwell
Dean
Wheaton College Graduate
School

Dr. Gerald F. Hawthorne
Professor Emeritus of Greek
Wheaton College

Dr. Howard G. Hendricks
Professor-at-Large
Chairman
Center for Christian Leadership
Dallas Theological Seminary

Dr. Grant R. Osborne
Professor of New Testament
Trinity Evangelical Divinity
School

A special thanks to the nation-
wide staff of Youth for Christ/
USA for their suggestions and
field testing, and to the follow-
ing additional contributing
writers: V. Gilbert Beers, Neil
Wilson, John Crosby, Joan
Young, Jack Crabtree, Philip
Craven, Bob Black, Bur Shilling,
Arthur Deyo, Annie Lafrentz,
Danny Sartin, William Hanawalt,
William Bonikowsky, Brian
Rathbun, Pamela Barden,
Thomas Stobie, Robert Arnold,
Greg Monaco, Larry Dunn, Lynn
Ziegenfuss, Mitzie Barton,
Mari-jean Hamilton, Larry
Kreider, Gary Dausey, William
Roland, Kathy Howell, Philip
Steffeck, James Coleman, Marty
Grasley, O'Ann Steere, Julia
Amstutz.

A special thanks also to the
following people whose personal
counsel, encouragement, and
determination helped make this
product a reality:

Dr. Kenneth N. Taylor (deceased)
Translator of *The Living Bible*
Chairman of the Board
Tyndale House Publishers, Inc.

Mark D. Taylor
President
Tyndale House Publishers, Inc.

Dr. Wendell C. Hawley
Retired Senior Vice President
Editorial
Tyndale House Publishers, Inc.

Virginia Muir
Retired Assistant
Editor-in-Chief
Tyndale House Publishers, Inc.

Richard R. Wynn
President and CEO of
Emerging Young Leaders

Dr. Jay L. Kesler
President, Taylor University

# A CHRONOLOGY OF
# BIBLE EVENTS AND WORLD EVENTS

THE TIMELINE on the following pages of the introduction gives you a visual overview of events in Bible times as compared to other famous world events. (The timelines in the individual Bible books are different—focusing on the events occurring in the books themselves.) This timeline gives the scope of Bible history from Creation to the resurrection of Christ and the beginnings of the church, along with key events that were occurring in other parts of the world.

| Creation **undated** | Noah builds the ark **undated** | | | Abraham born **2166** | Abraham enters Canaan **2091** |
|---|---|---|---|---|---|

**2500 B.C.**
Egyptians discover papyrus and ink for writing and build the first libraries; iron objects manufactured in the ancient Near East

**2400**
Egyptians import gold from other parts of Africa

**2331**
Semitic chieftain, Sargon, conquers Sumer to become first "world conqueror"

**2300**
Horses domesticated in Egypt; chickens domesticated in Babylon; bows & arrows used in wars

**2100**
Glass made by the Mesopotamians; ziggurats (like the tower of Babel) built in Mesopotamia; earliest discovered drug, ethyl alcohol, used to alleviate pain

# WHY THE
# *LIFE APPLICATION STUDY BIBLE*
# *IS UNIQUE*

Have you ever opened your Bible and asked the following:

- What does this passage really mean?
- How does it apply to my life?
- Why does some of the Bible seem irrelevant?
- What do these ancient cultures have to do with today?
- I love God; why can't I understand what he is saying to me through his Word?
- What's going on in the lives of these Bible people?

Many Christians do not read the Bible regularly. Why? Because in the pressures of daily living, they cannot find a connection between the timeless principles of Scripture and the ever-present problems of day-by-day living.

God urges us to apply his Word (Isaiah 42:23; 1 Corinthians 10:11; 2 Thessalonians 3:4), but too often we stop at accumulating Bible knowledge. This is why the *Life Application Study Bible* was developed—to show how to put into practice what we have learned.

Applying God's Word is a vital part of one's relationship with God; it is the evidence

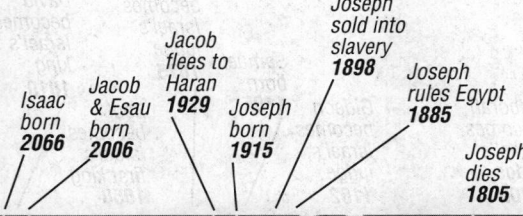

Isaac born **2066**

Jacob & Esau born **2006**

Jacob flees to Haran **1929**

Joseph born **1915**

Joseph sold into slavery **1898**

Joseph rules Egypt **1885**

Joseph dies **1805**

Moses born **1526**

**2000**
Native Americans immigrate to North America from northern Asia; stock breeding and irrigation used in China; Stonehenge, England, a center for religious worship is erected; bellows used in India allowing for higher furnace temperatures

**1900**
Egyptians use irrigation systems to control Nile floods; spoked wheel invented in the ancient Near East; horses used to pull vehicles

**1750**
Babylonian mathematicians already understand cube and square root; Hammurabi of Babylon provides first of all legal codes

**1700**
Egyptian papyrus document describes medical and surgical procedures

**1500**
Sundials used in Egypt; Mexican Sun Pyramid built

that we are obeying him. The difficulty in applying the Bible is not with the Bible itself, but with the reader's inability to bridge the gap between the past and present, the conceptual and practical. When we don't or can't do this, spiritual dryness, shallowness, and indifference are the results.

The words of Scripture itself cry out to us, "Don't just listen to God's word. You must do what it says. Otherwise, you are only fooling yourselves" (James 1:22). The *Life Application Study Bible* does just that. Developed by an interdenominational team of pastors, scholars, family counselors, and a national organization dedicated to promoting God's Word and spreading the gospel, the *Life Application Study Bible* took many years to complete, and all the work was reviewed by several renowned theologians under the directorship of Dr. Kenneth Kantzer.

The *Life Application Study Bible* does what a good resource Bible should—it helps you understand the context of a passage, gives important background and historical information, explains difficult words and phrases, and helps you see the interrelationships within Scripture. But it does much more. The *Life Application Study Bible* goes deeper into God's Word, helping you discover the timeless truth being communicated, see the relevance for your life, and make a personal application. While some study Bibles attempt application, over 75% of this Bible is application-oriented. The notes answer the questions, "So what?" and "What does this passage mean to me, my family, my friends, my job, my neighborhood, my church, my country?"

Imagine reading a familiar passage of Scripture and gaining fresh insight, as if it were the first time you had ever read it. How much richer your life would be if you left each Bible reading with a new perspective and a small change for the better. A small change every day adds up to a changed life—and that is the very purpose of Scripture.

The Exodus from Egypt **1446**

Ten Commandments given **1406**

Hebrews enter Canaan **1406**

Judges begin to rule Israel **1375**

Deborah becomes Israel's judge **1209**

Gideon becomes Israel's judge **1162**

Samuel born **1105**

Samson becomes Israel's judge **1075**

Saul becomes Israel's first king **1050**

David becomes Israel's king **1010**

**1400** First period of Chinese literature; intricate clock used in Egypt

**1380** Palace of Knossos on island of Crete destroyed by earthquake

**1358** Egyptian King Tutankhamen dies and is buried inside an immense treasure-laden tomb

**1250** Silk fabrics manufactured in China

**1200** Labor strike in Thebes; first Chinese dictionary

**1183** Destruction of Troy during Trojan War

The best way to define application is to first determine what it is *not*. Application is *not* just accumulating knowledge. This helps us discover and understand facts and concepts, but it stops there. History is filled with philosophers who knew what the Bible said but failed to apply it to their lives, keeping them from believing and changing. Many think that understanding is the end goal of Bible study, but it is really only the beginning.

Application is *not* just illustration. Illustration only tells us how someone else handled a similar situation. While we may empathize with that person, we still have little direction for our personal situation.

Application is *not* just making a passage "relevant." Making the Bible relevant only helps us to see that the same lessons that were true in Bible times are true today; it does not show us how to apply them to the problems and pressures of our individual lives.

What, then, is application? Application begins by knowing and understanding God's Word and its timeless truths. *But you cannot stop there*. If you do, God's Word may not change your life, and it may become dull, difficult, tedious, and tiring. A good application focuses the truth of God's Word, shows the reader what to do about what is being read,

Solomon becomes Israel's king **970**

Temple in Jerusalem completed **959**

Kingdom of Israel divides **930**

Elijah prophesies in Israel **875**

Ahab becomes Israel's king **874**

Elisha prophesies in Israel **848**

Joash becomes Judah's king **835**

Jonah becomes a prophet **793**

**1000** City of Peking built; Greek mythology fully developed; California Indians build wood-reed houses; Chinese mathematics utilizes root multiplication, geometry, proportions, and theory of motion; glazing of bricks and tiles begins in Near East

**950** Gold vessels and jewelry popular in northern Europe

**900** Celts invade Britain; Assyrians invent inflatable skins for soldiers to cross rivers

**850** Evidence of highly developed metal and stone sculptures in Africa

**814** Founding of Carthage, a Phoenician trading post

**800** Development of caste system in India; Babylonian and Chinese astronomers understand planetary movements; spoked wheels used in Europe; Homer writes Iliad and Odyssey; ice skating a popular sport in northern Europe

**776** First known date of Olympic games

and motivates the reader to respond to what God is teaching. All three are essential to application.

Application is putting into practice what we already know (see Mark 4:24 and Hebrews 5:14) and answering the question, "So what?" by confronting us with the right questions and motivating us to take action (see 1 John 2:5, 6 and James 2:17). Application is deeply personal—unique for each individual. It is making a relevant truth a personal truth, and involves developing a strategy and action plan to live your life in harmony with the Bible. It is the Biblical "how to" of life.

You may ask, "How can your application notes be relevant to my life?" Each application note has three parts: (1) an *explanation* that ties the note directly to the Scripture passage and sets up the truth that is being taught, (2) the *bridge* that explains the timeless truth and makes it relevant for today, (3) the *application* that shows you how to take the timeless truth and apply it to your personal situation. No note, by itself, can apply Scripture directly to your life. It can only teach, direct, lead, guide, inspire, recommend, and urge. It can give you the resources and direction you need to apply the Bible; but only *you* can take these resources and put them into practice.

A good note, therefore, should not only give you knowledge and understanding, but point you to application. Before you buy any kind of resource Bible, you should evaluate the notes and ask the following questions: (1) Does the note contain enough information to help me understand the point of the Scripture passage? (2) Does the note assume I know too much? (3) Does the note avoid denominational bias? (4) Do the notes touch most of life's experiences? (5) Does the note help me *apply* God's Word?

# FEATURES OF THE
# LIFE APPLICATION STUDY BIBLE

## NOTES
In addition to providing the reader with many application notes, the *Life Application Study Bible* also offers several kinds of explanatory notes, which help the reader understand culture, history, context, difficult-to-understand passages, background, places, theological concepts, and the relationship of various passages in Scripture to other passages. Maps, charts, and diagrams are also found on the same page as the passages to which they relate. For an example of an application note, see Mark 15:47. For an example of an explanatory note, see Mark 11:1, 2. The abbreviation *ff* appears in some notes to indicate that the comments apply not only to the verse referenced but to the following passage as well.

## BOOK INTRODUCTIONS
The Book Introductions are divided into several easy-to-find parts:

*Timeline.* This puts the Bible book into its historical setting. It lists the key events of each book and the date when they occurred. (The alternative dates in parentheses are based on a later dating of the Exodus.)

King Nebuchadnezzar of Babylon dies
**562**

Babylon overthrown by Cyrus of Persia
**539**

First Jewish exiles return to Jerusalem
**538**

New Temple completed in Jerusalem
**515**

Esther becomes queen of Persia
**479**

**560**
Aesop writes his fables

**563**
Gautama Buddha, the founder of Buddhism, born in India

**550**
King Cyrus the Great conquers the Medes and founds the Persian Empire; lock & key, water level, and carpenter's square invented

**551**
Confucius, famous Chinese scholar, born

**540**
Horseback postal service in Persian Empire

**534**
Tragedy emerges as a form of Greek drama

**525**
Polo a sport among Persians

**520**
Public libraries open in Athens, Greece

**509**
Rome becomes a republic

**500**
Glass first imported into China from Near East; Indian surgeon Susrata performs cataract operation; origin of Halloween, a Celtic festival

**490**
First time Greek men choose short haircuts

*Vital Statistics.* This is a list of straight facts about the book—those pieces of information you need to know at a glance.

*Overview.* This is a summary of the book with general lessons and applications that can be drawn from the book as a whole.

*Blueprint.* This is the outline of the book. It is printed in easy-to-understand language and is designed for easy memorization. To the right of each main heading is a key lesson that is taught in that particular section.

*Megathemes.* This section gives the main themes of the Bible book, explains their significance, and then tells why they are still important for us today.

*Map.* This shows the key places found in that book and retells the story of the book from a geographical point of view.

## OUTLINE
The *Life Application Study Bible* has a new, custom-made outline that was designed specifically from an application point of view. Several unique features should be noted:

1. To avoid confusion and to aid memory work, each book outline has only three levels for headings. Main outline heads are marked with a capital letter. Subheads are marked by a number. Minor explanatory heads have no letter or number.

2. Each main outline head marked by a letter also has a brief paragraph below it summarizing the content of the following Bible text and offering a general application.

3. Parallel passages are listed where they apply in the Gospels.

## A HARMONY OF THE BOOKS OF KINGS AND CHRONICLES
A harmony of the books of 1 & 2 Kings and 1 & 2 Chronicles was developed to help you understand the interplay between these books. The chart is set up like a timeline,

Ezra returns to Jerusalem
**458**

Nehemiah builds Jerusalem wall
**445**

Malachi becomes a prophet
**430?**

Aramaic begins to replace Hebrew as Jewish language
**390**

**469**
Socrates, philosopher of the ancient world, born

**457**
Golden Age in Athens, Greece begins

**460**
Birth of Democritus, who introduced an atomic theory by arguing that all bodies are made of indivisible and unchangeable atoms

**448**
The Parthenon built on top of Athens' Acropolis

**438**
Greek sculptor Phidias makes a 60-foot-high statue of Zeus—one of the Seven Wonders of the Ancient World

**430**
Romans agree to concept of a dictator in times of military emergency

**399**
Socrates condemned to death by Athenian jury

**384**
Aristotle born

**370**
Plato writes his most famous book, The Republic

providing you with the names of the kings listed chronologically, a brief overview of each king's reign, and where you can read about each king. It also includes the names of all the prophets—as well as when and to whom they prophesied—so you can put their prophecies into context as well. The harmony feature is located between the books of 1 and 2 Kings.

## A HARMONY OF THE GOSPELS

A harmony of the Gospels was developed specifically for this Bible. It is the first harmony that has ever been incorporated into the Bible text. Through a unique and simple numbering system (found both in the harmony feature and parenthesized in the subheads throughout the Gospels), you can read any Gospel account and see just where you are in relation to other events in the life of Christ. The harmony feature is located after the Gospel of John and explained in detail there.

## PERSONALITY PROFILES

Another unique feature of this Bible is the profiles of many Bible people, including their strengths and weaknesses, greatest accomplishments and mistakes, and key lessons from their lives. The profiles of these people are found in the Bible books where their stories occur.

## MAPS

The *Life Application Study Bible* has more maps than any other Bible. A thorough and comprehensive Bible atlas is built right into each Bible book. There are two kinds of maps: (1) A book introduction map, telling the story of that Bible book. (2) Thumbnail maps in the notes, plotting most geographic movements in the Bible. In addition to these numerous black-and-white maps, there is an entirely new and comprehensive set of color maps and diagrams at the back of this Bible.

Temple of
Jerusalem
plundered by
Antiochus IV
**169**

Judas
Maccabeus
begins a
revolt against
Antiochus IV
**165**

**312**
Romans
build first
paved road,
the "Appian
Way," from
Rome to
Capua

**330**
Alexander
the Great
defeats the
Persian
Empire

**241**
Romans
conquer
Sicily and
add their
first
non-Italian
territory to
the Roman
Empire

**255**
Hebrew Old
Testament
translated into
Greek and
called the
Septuagint

**215**
Great Wall
of China
built

**139**
Jews and
astrologers
banished
from Rome

**102**
First Chinese
ships reach
east coast
of India; ball
bearings used
in Danish cart
wheels

**100**
Julius
Caesar,
first
emperor
of Rome,
born

**55**
Romans
conquer
England and
make it part of
Roman Empire
until A.D. 442

**51**
Cleopatra
becomes last
independent
Egyptian
ruler of the
ancient
world

## CHARTS AND DIAGRAMS

Hundreds of charts and diagrams are included to help the reader better visualize difficult concepts or relationships. Most charts not only present the needed information but show the significance of the information as well.

## CROSS-REFERENCES

A carefully organized cross-reference system in the margins of the Bible text helps the reader find related passages quickly. A cross-reference marked by two slashes // indicates that the cross-reference is a parallel passage, largely identical to the identified text in content and wording. A cross-reference marked by a dagger † indicates that the identified text either quotes from the cross-reference or the cross-referenced text quotes the identified text.

## TEXTUAL NOTES AND SECTIONAL HEADINGS

Directly related to the New Living Translation text, the textual notes examine such things as alternate translations, meaning of Hebrew and Greek terms, Old Testament quotations, and variant readings in the ancient biblical manuscripts. The NLT text also contains sectional headings in order to help you more easily understand the subject and content of each section. These headings appear as the third level of the three-level header system. The headings throughout the Gospels also include a parenthesized number, relating each passage to the "Harmony of the Gospels" feature.

## A CHRISTIAN WORKER'S RESOURCE

The Christian Worker's Resource is a special supplement written with you in mind. It includes five articles that you will find useful in your ministry: (1) "How to Become

Herod the Great made king of Judea by the Romans **37**

Mary, Jesus' mother, born **25?**

Herod the Great begins remodeling Temple in Jerusalem **20**

Jesus Christ born **6/5**

Herod the Great dies **4**

Paul born **5?**

Judea becomes a Roman province; Jesus visits Temple as a boy **6/7**

John the Baptist begins his ministry; Pontius Pilate appointed governor **26**

Jesus begins his ministry **26/27**

Jesus crucified; Jesus ascends into heaven; Pentecost; early church beginnings **30**

Paul's conversion on Damascus road **35**

**30** Cleopatra and her lover, Marc Antony, both die by suicide

**23** Sumo wrestling in Japan

**A.D. 1** Saddles first used in Europe

**14** Tiberius succeeds Caesar Augustus as Roman emperor

**46** Julius Caesar becomes dictator for life, then is assassinated two years later

**7** Zealots in Judea rebel against Rome

a Christian" includes the basic steps of becoming a believer, along with Bible verses you can use to guide someone to faith. (2) "How to Follow up with a New Believer" gives you fourteen discussion points to walk through with a new believer over the course of several weeks. These will help him or her to understand the basics of the Christian faith. (3) "Mining the Treasures of the *Life Application Study Bible*" gives you a taste of the depth of the study notes by offering often-asked questions in twenty-five categories (that you probably have been asked from time to time) and sends you to life application notes that help to answer those questions. (4) "So You've Been Asked to Speak" walks you through the process of preparing a talk or Bible study using the many features of the *Life Application Study Bible*. (5) Finally, "Taking the Step to Application" teaches you how to make application a natural part of your personal study, as well as a part of Bible studies you lead or talks you give.

## MASTER INDEX
This Bible contains a complete master index to all the notes, charts, maps, and personality profiles, as well as separate indexes for charts (listed canonically), maps (listed canonically), and personality profiles (listed alphabetically).

## DICTIONARY/CONCORDANCE
A concise concordance identifies terms and proper names of special interest and points to the important occurrences in context. Each word is followed by a brief definition or description.

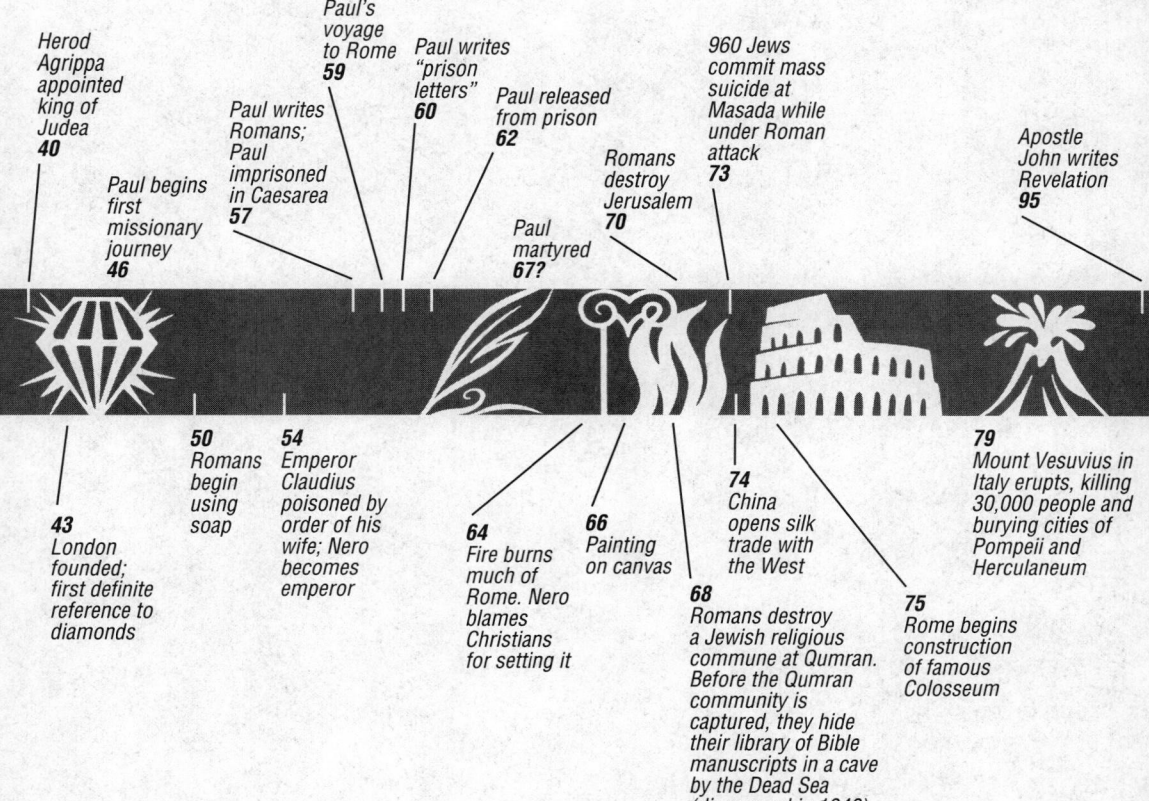

Herod Agrippa appointed king of Judea **40**

Paul begins first missionary journey **46**

Paul writes Romans; Paul imprisoned in Caesarea **57**

Paul's voyage to Rome **59**

Paul writes "prison letters" **60**

Paul released from prison **62**

Paul martyred **67?**

Romans destroy Jerusalem **70**

960 Jews commit mass suicide at Masada while under Roman attack **73**

Apostle John writes Revelation **95**

**43** London founded; first definite reference to diamonds

**50** Romans begin using soap

**54** Emperor Claudius poisoned by order of his wife; Nero becomes emperor

**64** Fire burns much of Rome. Nero blames Christians for setting it

**66** Painting on canvas

**68** Romans destroy a Jewish religious commune at Qumran. Before the Qumran community is captured, they hide their library of Bible manuscripts in a cave by the Dead Sea (discovered in 1948)

**74** China opens silk trade with the West

**75** Rome begins construction of famous Colosseum

**79** Mount Vesuvius in Italy erupts, killing 30,000 people and burying cities of Pompeii and Herculaneum

# *old* TESTAMENT

# GENESIS

## VITAL STATISTICS

**PURPOSE:**
To record God's creation of the world and his desire to have a people set apart to worship him

**AUTHOR:**
Moses

**ORIGINAL AUDIENCE:**
The people of Israel

**DATE WRITTEN:**
1450–1410 B.C.

**WHERE WRITTEN:**
In the wilderness during Israel's wanderings, somewhere in the Sinai peninsula

**SETTING:**
The region presently known as the Middle East

**KEY VERSES:**
"So God created human beings in his own image. In the image of God he created them; male and female he created them" (1:27).
"'I will make you into a great nation. I will bless you and make you famous, and you will be a blessing to others. I will bless those who bless you and curse those who treat you with contempt. All the families on earth will be blessed through you'" (12:2, 3).

**KEY PEOPLE:**
Adam, Eve, Noah, Abraham, Sarah, Isaac, Rebekah, Jacob, Joseph

BEGIN . . . start . . . commence . . . open. . . . There's something refreshing and optimistic about these words, whether they refer to the dawn of a new day, the birth of a child, the prelude of a symphony, or the first miles of a family vacation. Free of problems and full of promise, beginnings stir hope and imaginative visions of the future. *Genesis* means "beginnings" or "origin," and it unfolds the record of the beginning of the world, of human history, of family, of civilization, of salvation. It is the story of God's purpose and plan for his creation. As the book of beginnings, Genesis sets the stage for the entire Bible. It reveals the person and nature of God (Creator, Sustainer, Judge, Redeemer); the value and dignity of human beings (made in God's image, saved by grace, used by God in the world); the tragedy and consequences of sin (the Fall, separation from God, judgment); and the promise and assurance of salvation (covenant, forgiveness, promised Messiah).

God. That's where Genesis begins. All at once we see him creating the world in a majestic display of power and purpose, culminating with a man and woman made like himself (1:26, 27). But before long, sin entered the world, and Satan was unmasked. Bathed in innocence, creation was shattered by the Fall (the willful disobedience of Adam and Eve). Fellowship with God was broken, and evil began weaving its destructive web. In rapid succession, we read how Adam and Eve were expelled from the beautiful garden, their first son turned murderer, and evil bred evil until God finally destroyed everyone on earth except a small family led by Noah, the only godly person left.

As we come to Abraham on the plains of Canaan, we discover the beginning of God's covenant people and the broad strokes of his salvation plan: Salvation comes by faith, Abraham's descendants will be God's people, and the Savior of the world will come through this chosen nation. The stories of Isaac, Jacob, and Joseph that follow are more than interesting biographies. They emphasize the promises of God and the proof that he is faithful. The people we meet in Genesis are simple, ordinary people, yet through them, God did great things. These are vivid pictures of how God can and does use all kinds of people to accomplish his good purposes—even people like you.

Read Genesis and be encouraged. There is hope! No matter how dark the world situation seems, God has a plan. No matter how insignificant or useless you feel, God loves you and wants to use you in his plan. No matter how sinful and separated from God you are, his salvation is available. Read Genesis . . . and hope!

---

## THE BLUEPRINT

**A. THE STORY OF CREATION (1:1—2:4)**

God created the sky, seas, and land. He created the plants, animals, fish, and birds. But he created human beings in his own image. At times, others may treat us disrespectfully. But we can be certain of our dignity and worth because we have been created in the image of God.

| Jacob & Esau born 2006 (1840) | Jacob flees to Haran 1929 (1764) | Joseph born 1915 (1750) | Joseph sold into slavery 1898 (1733) | Joseph rules Egypt 1885 (1720) | Joseph dies 1805 (1640) |
| --- | --- | --- | --- | --- | --- |

B. THE STORY OF ADAM (2:4—5:32)
 1. Adam and Eve
 2. Cain and Abel
 3. Adam's descendants

When Adam and Eve were created by God, they were without sin. But they became sinful when they disobeyed God and ate some fruit from the tree. Through Adam and Eve we learn about the destructive power of sin and its bitter consequences.

C. THE STORY OF NOAH (6:1—11:32)
 1. The Flood
 2. Repopulating the earth
 3. The tower of Babel

Noah was spared from the destruction of the Flood because he obeyed God and built the boat. Just as God protected Noah and his family, he still protects those who are faithful to him today.

D. THE STORY OF ABRAHAM (12:1—25:18)
 1. God promises a nation to Abram
 2. Abram and Lot
 3. God promises a son to Abram
 4. Sodom and Gomorrah
 5. Birth and near sacrifice of Isaac
 6. Isaac and Rebekah
 7. Abraham dies

Abraham was asked to leave his country, wander in Canaan, wait years for a son, and then sacrifice him as a burnt offering. Through these periods of sharp testing, Abraham remained faithful to God. His example teaches us what it means to live a life of faith.

E. THE STORY OF ISAAC (25:19—28:9)
 1. Jacob and Esau
 2. Isaac and Abimelech
 3. Jacob gets Isaac's blessing

Isaac did not demand his own way. He did not resist when he was about to be sacrificed, and he gladly accepted a wife chosen for him by others. Like Isaac, we must learn to put God's will ahead of our own.

F. THE STORY OF JACOB (28:10—36:43)
 1. Jacob starts a family
 2. Jacob returns home

Jacob did not give up easily. He faithfully served Laban for over 14 years. Later, he wrestled with God. Although Jacob made many mistakes, his hard work teaches us about living a life of service for our Lord.

G. THE STORY OF JOSEPH (37:1—50:26)
 1. Joseph is sold into slavery
 2. Judah and Tamar
 3. Joseph is thrown into prison
 4. Joseph is placed in charge of Egypt
 5. Joseph and his brothers meet in Egypt
 6. Jacob's family moves to Egypt
 7. Jacob and Joseph die in Egypt

Joseph was sold into slavery by his brothers and unjustly thrown into prison by his master. Through the life of Joseph, we learn that suffering, no matter how unfair, can develop strong character in us.

## MEGATHEMES

| THEME | EXPLANATION | IMPORTANCE |
| --- | --- | --- |
| Beginnings | Genesis explains the beginning of many important realities: the universe, the earth, people, sin, and God's plan of salvation. | Genesis teaches us that the earth is well made and good. People are special to God and unique. God creates and sustains all life. |
| Disobedience | People are always facing great choices. Disobedience occurs when people choose not to follow God's plan of living. | Genesis explains why people are evil: They choose to do wrong. Even great Bible heroes failed God and disobeyed. |
| Sin | Sin ruins people's lives. It happens when we disobey God. | Living God's way makes life productive and fulfilling. |
| Promises | God makes promises to help and protect people. This kind of promise is called a "covenant." | God kept his promises then, and he keeps them now. He promises to love us, accept us, forgive us. |
| Obedience | The opposite of sin is obedience. Obeying God restores our relationship to him. | The only way to enjoy the benefits of God's promises is to obey him. |
| Prosperity | Prosperity is deeper than mere material wealth. True prosperity and fulfillment come as a result of obeying God. | When people obey God, they find peace with him, with others, and with themselves. |
| Israel | God started the nation of Israel in order to have a dedicated people who would (1) keep his ways alive in the world, (2) proclaim to the world what he is really like, and (3) prepare the world for the birth of Christ. | God is looking for people today to follow him. We are to proclaim God's truth and love to all nations, not just our own. We must be faithful to carry out the mission God has given us. |

# KEY PLACES IN GENESIS

Modern names and boundaries are shown in gray.

God created the universe and the earth. Then he made man and woman, giving them a home in a beautiful garden. Unfortunately, Adam and Eve disobeyed God and were banished from the garden (3:23).

**1 Mountains of Ararat**   Adam and Eve's sin brought sin into the human race. Years later, sin had run rampant and God decided to destroy the earth with a great flood. But Noah, his family, and two of each animal were safe in the boat. When the floods receded, the boat rested on the mountains of Ararat (8:4).

**2 Babel**   People never learn. Again sin abounded, and the pride of the people led them to build a huge tower as a monument to their own greatness—obviously they had no thought of God. As punishment, God scattered the people by giving them different languages (11:8, 9).

**3 Ur of the Chaldeans**   Abram, a descendant of Shem and father of the Hebrew nation, was born in this great city (11:27, 28).

**4 Haran**   Terah, Abram, Lot, and Sarai left Ur and, following the fertile crescent of the Euphrates River, headed toward the land

of Canaan. Along the way, they settled in the village of Haran for a while (11:31).

**5 Shechem**   God urged Abram to leave Haran and go to a place where he would become the father of a great nation (12:1, 2). So Abram, Lot, and Sarai traveled to the land of Canaan and settled near a city called Shechem (12:6).

**6 Hebron**   Abraham moved on to Hebron where he put down his deepest roots (13:18). Abraham, Isaac, and Jacob all lived and were buried here.

**7 Beersheba**   The well at Beersheba was a source of conflict between Abraham and King Abimelech and later became a sign of the oath that they swore there (21:31). Years later, as Isaac was moving from place to place, God appeared to him here and passed on to him the covenant he had made with his father, Abraham (26:23–25).

**8 Bethel**   After deceiving his brother, Jacob left Beersheba and fled to Haran. Along the way, God revealed himself to Jacob in a dream and passed on the covenant he had made with Abraham and Isaac (28:10–22). Jacob lived in Haran, worked for Laban, and married Leah and Rachel (29:15–30). After a tense meeting with his brother, Esau, Jacob returned to Bethel (35:1).

**9 Egypt**   Jacob had 12 sons, including Joseph, Jacob's favorite. Joseph's 10 older brothers grew jealous, until one day the brothers sold him to Ishmaelite traders going to Egypt. Eventually, Joseph rose from Egyptian slave to Pharaoh's "right-hand man," saving Egypt from famine. His entire family moved from Canaan to Egypt and settled there (46:3–7).

## A. THE STORY OF CREATION (1:1—2:4)

We sometimes wonder how our world came to be. But here we find the answer. God created the earth and everything in it, and made humans like himself. Although we may not understand the complexity of just how he did it, it is clear that God did create all life. This shows not only God's authority over humanity, but his deep love for all people.

### The Account of Creation

**1** In the beginning God created the heavens and the earth.* ²The earth was formless and empty, and darkness covered the deep waters. And the Spirit of God was hovering over the surface of the waters.

**1:1** Or *In the beginning when God created the heavens and the earth, . . .* Or *When God began to create the heavens and the earth, . . .*

1:1
Pss 89:11; 102:25
John 1:1-2

1:2
Ps 104:30
Isa 45:18

---

**1:1** The simple statement that God created the heavens and the earth is one of the most challenging concepts confronting the

modern mind. The vast galaxy we live in is spinning at the incredible speed of 490,000 miles an hour. But even at this breakneck

1:3
Pss 33:9; 104:2
2 Cor 4:6
1:6
Job 26:10
Ps 136:5-6
Isa 40:22
1:7
Job 38:8-11
Ps 148:4
1:9
Job 26:7
Ps 95:5
Jer 5:22
2 Pet 3:5
1:10
Pss 33:7; 95:5

³Then God said, "Let there be light," and there was light. ⁴And God saw that the light was good. Then he separated the light from the darkness. ⁵God called the light "day" and the darkness "night."

And evening passed and morning came, marking the first day.

⁶Then God said, "Let there be a space between the waters, to separate the waters of the heavens from the waters of the earth." ⁷And that is what happened. God made this space to separate the waters of the earth from the waters of the heavens. ⁸God called the space "sky."

And evening passed and morning came, marking the second day.

⁹Then God said, "Let the waters beneath the sky flow together into one place, so dry ground may appear." And that is what happened. ¹⁰God called the dry ground "land"

---

**BEGINNINGS**
Origin of the universe

**The Bible** does not discuss the subject of evolution. Rather, its worldview assumes God created the world. The biblical view of creation is not in conflict with science; rather, it is in conflict with any worldview that starts without a creator.

Equally committed and sincere Christians have struggled with the subject of beginnings and come to **differing conclusions.** This, of course, is to be expected because the evidence is very old and, due to the ravages of the ages, quite fragmented. Students of the Bible and of science should avoid polarizations and black/white thinking. Students of the Bible must be careful not to make the Bible say what it doesn't say, and students of science must not make science say what it doesn't say.

The most important aspect of the continuing discussion is not the process of creation, but the origin of creation. **The world is not a product of blind chance and probability; God created it.**

The Bible not only tells us that the world was created by God; more important, it tells us who this God is. It reveals God's personality, his character, and his plan for his creation. It also reveals **God's deepest desire: to relate to and fellowship with the people he created.** God took the ultimate step toward fellowship with us through his historic visit to this planet in the person of his Son Jesus Christ. We can know in a very personal way this God who created the universe.

The heavens and the earth are here. We are here. God created all that we see and experience. The book of Genesis begins, "God created the heavens and the earth."

---

speed, our galaxy still needs 200 million years to make one rotation. And there are over one billion other galaxies just like ours in the universe.

Some scientists say that the number of stars in creation is equal to all the grains of all the sands on all the beaches of the world. Yet this complex sea of spinning stars functions with remarkable order and efficiency. To say that the universe "just happened" or "evolved" requires more faith than to believe that God is behind these amazing statistics. God truly did create a wonderful universe.

God did not *need* to create the universe; he *chose* to create it. Why? God is love, and love is best expressed toward something or someone else—so God created the world and people as an expression of his love. We should avoid reducing God's creation to merely scientific terms. Remember that God created the universe because he loves us.

**1:1ff** The creation story teaches us much about God and ourselves. First, we learn about God: (1) He is creative; (2) as the Creator, he is distinct from his creation; (3) he is eternal and in control of the world. We also learn about ourselves: (1) Since God chose to create us, we are valuable in his eyes; (2) we are more important than the animals. (See 1:28 for more on our role in the created order.)

**1:1ff** Just how did God create the earth? This is still a subject of great debate. Some say that with a sudden explosion, the universe appeared. Others say God started the process and the universe evolved over billions of years. Almost every ancient religion has its own story to explain how the earth came to be. And almost every scientist has an opinion on the origin of the universe. But only the Bible shows one supreme God creating the earth out of his great love and giving all people a special place in it. We will never know all the answers to how God created the earth, but the Bible tells us that God did create it. That fact alone gives worth and dignity to all people.

**1:2** Who created God? To ask that question is to assume there was another creator before God. At some time, however, we are forced to stop asking that question and realize that there had to be something that has always existed. God is that infinite Being who has always existed and who was created by no one. This is difficult to understand because finite minds cannot comprehend the infinite. For example, we can try to think of the highest number, but we can't do it. Likewise, we must not limit the infinite God by our finite understanding.

**1:2** The statement "the earth was formless and empty" provides the setting for the creation narrative that follows. During the second and third days of creation, God gave *form* to the universe; during the next three days, God *filled* the earth with living beings. The "darkness" was dispelled on the first day, when God created light.

**1:2** The image of the Spirit of God hovering over the earth's surface is similar to a mother bird caring for and protecting its young (see Deuteronomy 32:11, 12; Isaiah 31:5). God's Spirit was actively involved in the creation of the world (see Job 33:4; Psalm 104:30). God's care and protection are still active.

**1:3–2:7** How long did it take God to create the world? There are two basic views about the days of creation: (1) Each day was a literal 24-hour period; (2) each day represents an indefinite period of time (even millions of years).

The Bible does not say how long these time periods were. The real question, however, is not how long God took, but how he did it. God created the earth in an orderly fashion (he did not make plants before light), and he created men and women as unique beings capable of communication with him. No other part of creation can claim that remarkable privilege. It is not important how long it took God to create the world, whether a few days or a few billion years, but that he created it just the way he wanted it.

**1:6** The "space between the waters" was a separation between the sea and the mists of the skies.

and the waters "seas." And God saw that it was good. ¹¹Then God said, "Let the land sprout with vegetation—every sort of seed-bearing plant, and trees that grow seed-bearing fruit. These seeds will then produce the kinds of plants and trees from which they came." And that is what happened. ¹²The land produced vegetation—all sorts of seed-bearing plants, and trees with seed-bearing fruit. Their seeds produced plants and trees of the same kind. And God saw that it was good.

¹³And evening passed and morning came, marking the third day.

¹⁴Then God said, "Let lights appear in the sky to separate the day from the night. Let them be signs to mark the seasons, days, and years. ¹⁵Let these lights in the sky shine down on the earth." And that is what happened. ¹⁶God made two great lights—the larger one to govern the day, and the smaller one to govern the night. He also made the stars. ¹⁷God set these lights in the sky to light the earth, ¹⁸to govern the day and night, and to separate the light from the darkness. And God saw that it was good.

¹⁹And evening passed and morning came, marking the fourth day.

²⁰Then God said, "Let the waters swarm with fish and other life. Let the skies be filled with birds of every kind." ²¹So God created great sea creatures and every living thing that scurries and swarms in the water, and every sort of bird—each producing offspring of the same kind. And God saw that it was good. ²²Then God blessed them, saying, "Be fruitful and multiply. Let the fish fill the seas, and let the birds multiply on the earth."

²³And evening passed and morning came, marking the fifth day.

²⁴Then God said, "Let the earth produce every sort of animal, each producing offspring of the same kind—livestock, small animals that scurry along the ground, and wild animals." And that is what happened. ²⁵God made all sorts of wild animals, livestock, and small animals, each able to produce offspring of the same kind. And God saw that it was good.

²⁶Then God said, "Let us make human beings* in our image, to be like us. They will reign over the fish in the sea, the birds in the sky, the livestock, all the wild animals on the earth, and the small animals that scurry along the ground."

**1:26** Or *man;* Hebrew reads *adam.*

**Cross-references (margin):**

1:11 Gen 2:9; Ps 104:14; Matt 6:30

1:14 Pss 74:16; 104:19

1:16 Pss 8:3; 19:1-6; 136:8-9; 1 Cor 15:41

1:18 Jer 33:20, 25

1:20 Gen 2:19; Ps 146:6

1:21 Ps 104:25-28

1:24 Gen 2:19

1:26 Gen 5:1; 9:6; Ps 8:6-8; Acts 17:28-29

---

| | | |
|---|---|---|
| First Day . . . . . . . . . . . . . . | Light (so there was light and darkness) | **DAYS OF CREATION** |
| Second Day . . . . . . . . . . | Sky and water (waters separated) | |
| Third Day . . . . . . . . . . . . | Land and seas (waters gathered); vegetation | |
| Fourth Day . . . . . . . . . . . | Sun, moon, and stars (to govern the day and the night and to mark seasons, days and years) | |
| Fifth Day . . . . . . . . . . . . . | Fish and birds (to fill the waters and the sky) | |
| Sixth Day . . . . . . . . . . . . | Animals (to fill the earth) <br> Man and woman (to care for the earth and to commune with God) | |
| Seventh Day . . . . . . . . . . | God rested and declared all he had made to be very good | |

---

**1:25** God saw that his work was good. People sometimes feel guilty for having a good time or for feeling good about an accomplishment. This need not be so. Just as God felt good about his work, we can be pleased with ours. However, we should not feel good about our work if God would not be pleased with it. What are you doing that pleases both you and God?

**1:26** Why does God use the plural form, "Let *us* make human beings in *our* image"? One view says this is a reference to the Trinity—God the Father, Jesus Christ his Son, and the Holy Spirit—all of whom are God. Another view is that the plural wording is used to denote majesty. Kings traditionally use the plural form in speaking of themselves. From Job 33:4 and Psalm 104:30, we know that God's Spirit was present in the Creation. From Colossians 1:16 we know that Christ, God's Son, was at work in the Creation.

**1:26** In what ways are we made in God's image? God obviously did not create us exactly like himself because God has no physical body. Instead, we are reflections of God's glory. Some feel that our reason, creativity, speech, or self-determination is the image of God. More likely, it is our entire self that reflects the image of God. We will never be totally like God because he is our supreme Creator. But we do have the ability to reflect his character in our love, patience, forgiveness, kindness, and faithfulness.

Knowing that we are made in God's image and thus share many of his characteristics provides a solid basis for self-worth. Human worth is not based on possessions, achievements, physical attractiveness, or public acclaim. Instead, it is based on being made in God's image. Because we bear God's image, we can feel positive about ourselves. Criticizing or downgrading ourselves is criticizing what God has made and the abilities he has given us. Knowing that you are a person of worth helps you love God, know him personally, and make a valuable contribution to those around you.

**1:27**
†Matt 19:4
†Mark 10:6

27 So God created human beings* in his own image.
　　In the image of God he created them;
　　male and female he created them.

28Then God blessed them and said, "Be fruitful and multiply. Fill the earth and govern it. Reign over the fish in the sea, the birds in the sky, and all the animals that scurry along the ground."

**1:29**
Gen 9:3
Pss 104:13; 136:25
**1:30**
Pss 104:14; 145:15

29Then God said, "Look! I have given you every seed-bearing plant throughout the earth and all the fruit trees for your food. 30And I have given every green plant as food for all the wild animals, the birds in the sky, and the small animals that scurry along the ground—everything that has life." And that is what happened.

**1:31**
Ps 104:24

31Then God looked over all he had made, and he saw that it was very good! And evening passed and morning came, marking the sixth day.

**2:2**
Exod 20:11; 31:17
†Heb 4:4
**2:4**
Gen 1:3-31; 5:1;
6:9; 10:1
Job 38:4-11

**2** So the creation of the heavens and the earth and everything in them was completed. 2On the seventh day God had finished his work of creation, so he rested* from all his work. 3And God blessed the seventh day and declared it holy, because it was the day when he rested from all his work of creation.

4This is the account of the creation of the heavens and the earth.

## B. THE STORY OF ADAM (2:4—5:32)

Learning about our ancestors often helps us understand ourselves. Adam and Eve, our first ancestors, were the highlight of God's creation—the very reason God made the world. But they didn't always live the way God intended. Through their mistakes, we can learn important lessons about the way God wants us to live. Adam and Eve teach us much about the nature of sin and its consequences.

### 1. Adam and Eve

**2:5**
Gen 1:11

When the LORD God made the earth and the heavens, 5neither wild plants nor grains were growing on the earth. For the LORD God had not yet sent rain to water the earth, and there were no people to cultivate the soil. 6Instead, springs* came up from the ground and

**1:27** Or *the man;* Hebrew reads *ha-adam.*　**2:2** Or *ceased;* also in 2:3.　**2:6** Or *mist.*

---

| WHAT THE BIBLE SAYS ABOUT MARRIAGE | |
|---|---|
| Genesis 2:18-24 | Marriage is God's idea |
| Genesis 24:58-60 | Commitment is essential to a successful marriage |
| Song of Songs 4:9-10 | Romance is important |
| Jeremiah 7:34 | Marriage holds times of great joy |
| Malachi 2:14, 15 | Marriage creates the best environment for raising children |
| Matthew 5:32 | Unfaithfulness breaks the bond of trust, the foundation of all relationships |
| Matthew 19:6 | Marriage is permanent |
| Romans 7:2, 3 | Ideally, only death should dissolve marriage |
| Ephesians 5:21-33 | Marriage is based on the principled practice of love, not on feelings |
| Ephesians 5:23-32 | Marriage is a living symbol of Christ and the church |
| Hebrews 13:4 | Marriage is good and honorable |

---

**1:27** God made both man and woman in his image. Neither man nor woman is made more in the image of God than the other. From the beginning the Bible places both man and woman at the pinnacle of God's creation. Neither sex is exalted, and neither is depreciated.

**1:28** To "reign over" something is to have absolute authority and control over it. God has ultimate rule over the earth, and he exercises his authority with loving care. When God delegated some of his authority to the human race, he expected us to take responsibility for the environment and the other creatures that share our planet. We must not be careless and wasteful as we fulfill this charge. God was careful how he made this earth. We must not be careless about how we take care of it.

**1:31** God saw that all he had created was excellent in every way. You are part of God's creation, and he is pleased with how

he made you. If at times you feel worthless or of little value, remember that God made you for a good reason. You are valuable to him.

**2:2, 3** We live in an action-oriented world! There always seems to be something to do and no time to rest. Yet God demonstrated that rest is appropriate and right. If God himself rested from his work, we should not be surprised that we also need rest. Jesus demonstrated this principle when he and his disciples left in a boat to get away from the crowds (see Mark 6:31, 32). Our times of rest refresh us for times of service.

**2:3** That God *blessed* the seventh day means that he set it apart for holy use. The Ten Commandments emphasize this distinction by commanding the observance of the Sabbath (Exodus 20:1-17).

watered all the land. [7]Then the LORD God formed the man from the dust of the ground. He breathed the breath of life into the man's nostrils, and the man became a living person.

[8]Then the LORD God planted a garden in Eden in the east, and there he placed the man he had made. [9]The LORD God made all sorts of trees grow up from the ground—trees that were beautiful and that produced delicious fruit. In the middle of the garden he placed the tree of life and the tree of the knowledge of good and evil.

[10]A river flowed from the land of Eden, watering the garden and then dividing into four branches. [11]The first branch, called the Pishon, flowed around the entire land of Havilah, where gold is found. [12]The gold of that land is exceptionally pure; aromatic resin and onyx stone are also found there. [13]The second branch, called the Gihon, flowed around the entire land of Cush. [14]The third branch, called the Tigris, flowed east of the land of Asshur. The fourth branch is called the Euphrates.

[15]The LORD God placed the man in the Garden of Eden to tend and watch over it. [16]But the LORD God warned him, "You may freely eat the fruit of every tree in the garden—[17]except the tree of the knowledge of good and evil. If you eat its fruit, you are sure to die."

[18]Then the LORD God said, "It is not good for the man to be alone. I will make a helper who is just right for him." [19]So the LORD God formed from the ground all the wild animals and all the birds of the sky. He brought them to the man* to see what he would call them, and the man chose a name for each one. [20]He gave names to all the livestock, all the birds of the sky, and all the wild animals. But still there was no helper just right for him.

[21]So the LORD God caused the man to fall into a deep sleep. While the man slept, the LORD God took out one of the man's ribs* and closed up the opening. [22]Then the LORD God made a woman from the rib, and he brought her to the man.

[23]"At last!" the man exclaimed.

> "This one is bone from my bone,
>     and flesh from my flesh!
> She will be called 'woman,'
>     because she was taken from 'man.'"

**2:19** Or *Adam*, and so throughout the chapter.    **2:21** Or *took a part of the man's side.*

**Cross-references (right margin):**

**2:7**
Gen 3:19
Job 33:4
Ps 103:14
John 20:22
†1 Cor 15:45

**2:8**
Gen 3:23; 13:10
Ezek 28:13

**2:9**
Gen 3:22
Ezek 47:12
Rev 2:7; 22:2, 14

**2:10**
Rev 22:1, 17

**2:11**
Gen 25:18

**2:14**
Gen 15:18
Deut 1:7

**2:16**
Gen 3:1-3

**2:17**
Deut 30:15, 19-20
Rom 6:23
Jas 1:15

**2:18**
Gen 3:12
Prov 18:22

**2:22**
1 Cor 11:8-9
1 Tim 2:13

**2:23**
Gen 29:14
Eph 5:28-30

---

**2:7** "From the dust of the ground" implies that there is nothing fancy about the chemical elements making up our bodies. The body is a lifeless shell until God brings it alive with his "breath of life." When God removes his life-giving breath, our bodies once again return to dust. Our life and worth, therefore, come from God's Spirit. Many boast of their achievements and abilities as though they were the originator of their own strengths. Others feel worthless because their abilities do not stand out. In reality, our worth comes not from our achievements but from the God of the universe, who chooses to give us the mysterious and miraculous gift of life. Value life, as he does.

**2:9** The name of the tree of the knowledge of good and evil implies that evil had already occurred, if not in the garden, then at the time of Satan's fall.

**2:9, 16, 17** Were the tree of life and the tree of the knowledge of good and evil real trees? Two views are often expressed: (1) *The trees were real, but symbolic.* Eternal life with God was pictured as eating from the tree of life. (2) *The trees were real, possessing special properties.* By eating the fruit from the tree of life, Adam and Eve could have had eternal life, enjoying a permanent relationship as God's children.

In either case, Adam and Eve's sin separated them from the tree of life and thus kept them from obtaining eternal life. Interestingly, the tree of life again appears in a description in Revelation 22 of people enjoying eternal life with God.

**2:15-17** God gave Adam responsibility for the garden and told him not to eat from the tree of the knowledge of good and evil. Rather than physically preventing him from eating, God gave Adam a choice and, thus, the possibility of choosing wrongly. God still gives us choices, and we, too, often choose wrongly. These wrong choices may cause us pain, but they can help us learn and grow and make better choices in the future. Living with the consequences of our choices teaches us to think and choose more carefully.

**2:16, 17** Why would God place a tree in the garden and then forbid Adam to eat from it? God wanted Adam to obey, but God gave Adam the freedom to choose. Without choice, Adam would have been like a prisoner, and his obedience would have been hollow. The two trees provided an exercise in choice, with rewards for choosing to obey and sad consequences for choosing to disobey. When you are faced with the choice, always choose to obey God.

**2:18-24** God's creative work was not complete until he made woman. He could have made her from the dust of the ground, as he made man. God chose, however, to make her from the man's flesh and bone. In so doing, he illustrated for us that in marriage man and woman symbolically are united into one. This is a mystical union of the couple's hearts and lives. Throughout the Bible, God treats this special partnership seriously. If you are married or planning to be married, are you willing to keep the commitment that makes the two of you one? The goal in marriage should be more than friendship; it should be oneness.

**2:21-23** God forms and equips men and women for various tasks, but all these tasks lead to the same goal—honoring God. Man gives life to woman; woman gives life to the world. Each role carries exclusive privileges; there is no room for thinking that one sex is superior to the other.

**2:24**
†Matt 19:5
†1 Cor 6:16
Eph 5:31

²⁴This explains why a man leaves his father and mother and is joined to his wife, and the two are united into one.

²⁵Now the man and his wife were both naked, but they felt no shame.

**ADAM**

We can hardly imagine what it must have been like to be the first and only person on earth. It's one thing for us to be lonely; it was another for Adam, who had never known another human being. He missed much that makes us who we are—he had no childhood, no parents, no family or friends. He had to learn to be human on his own. Fortunately, God didn't let him struggle too long before presenting him with an ideal companion and mate, Eve. Theirs was a complete, innocent, and open oneness, without a hint of shame.

One of Adam's first conversations with his delightful new companion must have been about the rules of the garden. Before God made Eve, he had already given Adam complete freedom in the garden, with the responsibility to tend and care for it. But one tree was off-limits, the tree of the knowledge of good and evil. Adam would have told Eve all about this. She knew, when Satan approached her, that the tree's fruit was not to be eaten. However, she decided to eat the forbidden fruit. Then she offered some to Adam. At that moment, the fate of creation was on the line. Sadly, Adam didn't pause to consider the consequences. He went ahead and ate.

In that moment of small rebellion something large, beautiful, and free was shattered . . . God's perfect creation. Adam was separated from God by his desire to act on his own. The effect on a plate glass window is the same whether a pebble or a boulder is hurled at it—the thousands of fragments can never be regathered.

In the case of Adam's sin, however, God already had a plan in motion to overcome the effects of the rebellion. The entire Bible is the story of how that plan unfolds, ultimately leading to God's own visit to earth through his Son, Jesus. His sinless life and death made it possible for God to offer forgiveness to all who want it. Our small and large acts of rebellion prove that we are descendants of Adam. Only by asking forgiveness of Jesus Christ can we become children of God.

| | |
|---|---|
| **Strengths and accomplishments** | • The first zoologist—namer of animals<br>• The first landscape architect, placed in the garden to care for it<br>• Father of the human race<br>• The first person made in the image of God, and the first human to share an intimate personal relationship with God |
| **Weaknesses and mistakes** | • Avoided responsibility and blamed others; chose to hide rather than to confront; made excuses rather than admitting the truth<br>• Greatest mistake: teamed up with Eve to bring sin into the world |
| **Lessons from his life** | • As Adam's descendants, we all reflect to some degree the image of God<br>• God wants people who, though free to do wrong, choose instead to love him<br>• We should not blame others for our faults<br>• We cannot hide from God |
| **Vital statistics** | • Where: Garden of Eden<br>• Occupation: Caretaker, gardener, farmer<br>• Relatives: Wife: Eve. Sons: Cain, Abel, Seth. Numerous other children. The only man who never had an earthly mother or father. |
| **Key verses** | "It was the woman you gave me who gave me the fruit, and I ate it" (Genesis 3:12). "Just as everyone dies because we all belong to Adam, everyone who belongs to Christ will be given new life" (1 Corinthians 15:22). |

Adam's story is told in Genesis 1:26–5:5. He is also mentioned in 1 Chronicles 1:1; Luke 3:38; Romans 5:14; 1 Corinthians 15:22, 45; 1 Timothy 2:13, 14.

**2:24** God gave marriage as a gift to Adam and Eve. They were created perfect for each other. Marriage was not just for convenience, nor was it brought about by any culture. It was instituted by God and has three basic aspects: (1) The man leaves his parents and, in a public act, promises himself to his wife; (2) the man and woman are joined together by taking responsibility for each other's welfare and by loving the mate above all others; (3) the two are united into one in the intimacy and commitment of sexual union that is reserved for marriage. Strong marriages include all three of these aspects.

**2:25** Have you ever noticed how a little child can run naked through a room full of strangers without embarrassment? He is not aware of his nakedness, just as Adam and Eve were not

embarrassed in their innocence. But after Adam and Eve sinned, shame and awkwardness followed, creating barriers between themselves and God. We often experience these same barriers in marriage. Ideally a husband and wife have no barriers, feeling no embarrassment in exposing themselves to each other or to God. But, like Adam and Eve (3:7), we put on fig leaves (barriers) because we have areas we don't want our spouse, or God, to know about. Then we hide, just as Adam and Eve hid from God. In marriage, a breakdown of spiritual, emotional, and intellectual intimacy usually precedes a breakdown of physical intimacy. In the same way, when we fail to expose our secret thoughts to God, we break our lines of communication with him.

## The Man and Woman Sin

**3** The serpent was the shrewdest of all the wild animals the LORD God had made. One day he asked the woman, "Did God really say you must not eat the fruit from any of the trees in the garden?"

**3:1**
2 Cor 11:3
Rev 12:9; 20:2

2"Of course we may eat fruit from the trees in the garden," the woman replied. 3"It's only the fruit from the tree in the middle of the garden that we are not allowed to eat. God said, 'You must not eat it or even touch it; if you do, you will die.'"

**3:3**
Gen 2:17

**3:4**
John 8:44
2 Cor 11:3

4"You won't die!" the serpent replied to the woman. 5"God knows that your eyes will be opened as soon as you eat it, and you will be like God, knowing both good and evil."

**3:5**
Isa 14:14
Ezek 28:2

6The woman was convinced. She saw that the tree was beautiful and its fruit looked delicious, and she wanted the wisdom it would give her. So she took some of the fruit and ate it. Then she gave some to her husband, who was with her, and he ate it, too. 7At that moment their eyes were opened, and they suddenly felt shame at their nakedness. So they sewed fig leaves together to cover themselves.

**3:6**
2 Cor 11:3
1 Tim 2:14
Jas 1:14-15
1 Jn 2:16

8When the cool evening breezes were blowing, the man* and his wife heard the LORD

**3:8**
Lev 26:12
Deut 23:14

3:8 Or *Adam*, and so throughout the chapter.

---

**3:1** Disguised as a shrewd serpent, Satan came to tempt Eve. At one time, Satan had been a glorious angel. But in pride, he rebelled against God and was cast out of heaven. As a created being, Satan has definite limitations. Although he is trying to tempt everyone away from God, he will not be the final victor. In 3:14, 15, God promises that Satan will be crushed by one of the woman's offspring, the Messiah.

**3:1-6** Why does Satan tempt us? Temptation is Satan's invitation to give in to his kind of life and give up on God's kind of life. Satan tempted Eve and succeeded in getting her to sin. Ever since then, he's been busy getting people to sin. He even tempted Jesus (Matthew 4:1-11). But Jesus did not sin!

How could Eve have resisted temptation? By following the same guidelines we can follow. First, we must realize that *being tempted* is not a sin. We have not sinned until we *give in* to the temptation. Then, to resist temptation, we must (1) pray for strength to resist, (2) run, sometimes literally, and (3) say no when confronted with what we know is wrong. James 1:12 tells of the blessings and rewards for those who don't give in when tempted.

**3:1-6** The serpent, Satan, tempted Eve by getting her to doubt God's goodness. He implied that God was strict, stingy, and selfish for not wanting Eve to share his knowledge of good and evil. Satan made Eve forget all that God had given her and, instead, focus on what God had forbidden. We fall into trouble, too, when we dwell on what God forbids rather than on the countless blessings and promises God has given us. The next time you are feeling sorry for yourself and what you don't have, consider all you *do* have and thank God. Then your doubts won't lead you into sin.

**3:5** Adam and Eve got what they wanted: an intimate knowledge of both good and evil. But they got it by doing evil, and the results were disastrous. Sometimes we have the illusion that freedom is doing anything we want. But God says that true freedom comes from obedience and knowing what *not* to do. The restrictions he gives us are for our good, helping us avoid evil. We have the freedom to walk in front of a speeding car, but we don't need to be hit to realize it would be foolish to do so. Don't listen to Satan's temptations. You don't have to do evil to gain more experience and learn more about life.

**3:5** Satan used a sincere motive to tempt Eve: "You will be like God." It wasn't wrong of Eve to want to be like God. To become more like God is humanity's highest goal. It is what we are supposed to do. But Satan misled Eve concerning the right way to accomplish this goal. He told her that she could become more like God by defying God's authority, by taking God's place and deciding for herself what was best for her life. In effect, he told her to become her own god.

But to become like God is not the same as trying to become God. Rather, it is to reflect his characteristics and to recognize his authority over your life. Like Eve, we often have a worthy goal but try to achieve it in the wrong way. We act like a political candidate who pays off an election judge to be "voted" into office. When he does this, serving the people is no longer his highest goal.

Self-exaltation leads to rebellion against God. As soon as we begin to leave God out of our plans, we are placing ourselves above him. This is exactly what Satan wants us to do.

**3:6** Satan tried to make Eve think that sin is good, pleasant, and desirable. A knowledge of both good and evil seemed harmless to her. People usually choose wrong things because they have become convinced that those things are good, at least for themselves. Our sins do not always appear ugly to us, and the pleasant sins are the hardest to avoid. So prepare yourself for the attractive temptations that may come your way. We cannot always prevent temptation, but there is always a way of escape (1 Corinthians 10:13). Use God's Word and God's people to help you stand against it.

**3:6, 7** Notice what Eve did: She looked, she took, she ate, and she gave. The battle is often lost at the first look. Temptation often begins by simply seeing something you want. Are you struggling with temptation because you have not learned that looking is the first step toward sin? You would win over temptation more often if you followed Paul's advice to run from those things that produce evil thoughts (2 Timothy 2:22).

**3:6, 7** One of the realities of sin is that its effects spread. After Eve sinned, she involved Adam in her wrongdoing. When we do something wrong, often we try to relieve our guilt by involving someone else. Like toxic waste spilled in a river, sin swiftly spreads. Recognize and confess your sin to God before you are tempted to pollute those around you.

**3:7, 8** After sinning, Adam and Eve felt guilt and embarrassment over their nakedness. Their guilty feelings made them try to hide from God. A guilty conscience is a warning signal God placed inside you that goes off when you've done wrong. The worst step you can take is to eliminate the guilty feelings without eliminating the cause. That would be like using a painkiller but not treating the disease. Be glad those guilty feelings are there. They make you aware of your sin so you can ask God's forgiveness and then correct your wrongdoing.

**3:8** The thought of two humans covered with fig leaves trying to hide from the all-seeing, all-knowing God is humorous. How could they be so silly as to think they could actually hide? Yet we do the same, acting as though God doesn't know what we're doing. Have the courage to share all you do and think with him. And don't try to hide—it can't be done. Honesty will strengthen your relationship with God.

God walking about in the garden. So they hid from the LORD God among the trees. ⁹Then the LORD God called to the man, "Where are you?"

¹⁰He replied, "I heard you walking in the garden, so I hid. I was afraid because I was naked."

¹¹"Who told you that you were naked?" the LORD God asked. "Have you eaten from the tree whose fruit I commanded you not to eat?"

¹²The man replied, "It was the woman you gave me who gave me the fruit, and I ate it."

¹³Then the LORD God asked the woman, "What have you done?"

"The serpent deceived me," she replied. "That's why I ate it."

¹⁴Then the LORD God said to the serpent,

"Because you have done this, you are cursed
    more than all animals, domestic and wild.
You will crawl on your belly,
    groveling in the dust as long as you live.
¹⁵ And I will cause hostility between you and the woman,
    and between your offspring and her offspring.
He will strike* your head,
    and you will strike his heel."

¹⁶Then he said to the woman,

"I will sharpen the pain of your pregnancy,
    and in pain you will give birth.
And you will desire to control your husband,
    but he will rule over you.*"

3:15 Or *bruise;* also in 3:15b.   3:16 Or *And though you will have desire for your husband, / he will rule over you.*

**3:12**
Prov 28:13

**3:13**
2 Cor 11:3
1 Tim 2:14

**3:14**
Deut 28:15
Isa 65:25

**3:15**
John 8:44
Rom 16:20
Heb 2:14

**3:16**
1 Cor 11:3
Eph 5:22
1 Tim 2:15

---

**SATAN'S PLAN AGAINST US**

Doubt . . . . . . . . . . . Makes you question God's Word and his goodness

Discouragement. . . . Makes you look at your problems rather than at God

Diversion . . . . . . . . Makes the wrong things seem attractive so that you will want them more than the right things

Defeat . . . . . . . . . . Makes you feel like a failure so that you don't even try

Delay . . . . . . . . . . . Makes you put off doing something so that it never gets done

---

**3:8, 9** These verses show God's desire to have fellowship with us. They also show why we are afraid to have fellowship with him. Adam and Eve hid from God when they heard him approaching. God wanted to be with them, but because of their sin, they were afraid to show themselves. Sin had broken their close relationship with God, just as it has broken ours. But Jesus Christ, God's Son, opens the way for us to renew our fellowship with him. God longs to be with us. He actively offers us his unconditional love. Our natural response is fear because we feel we can't live up to his standards. But understanding that he loves us, regardless of our faults, can help remove that dread.

**3:11-13** Adam and Eve failed to heed God's warning recorded in 2:16, 17. They did not understand the reasons for his command, so they chose to act in another way that looked better to them. All of God's commands are for our own good, but we may not always understand the reasons behind them. People who trust God will obey because we know God asks them to, whether or not they understand why God commands it.

**3:11-13** When God asked Adam about his sin, Adam blamed Eve. Then Eve blamed the serpent. How easy it is to excuse our sins by blaming someone else or circumstances. But God knows the truth, and he holds each of us responsible for what we do (see 3:14-19). Admit your wrong attitudes and actions and apologize to God. Don't try to get away with sin by blaming someone else.

**3:14ff** Adam and Eve chose their course of action (disobedience), and then God chose his. As a holy God, he could respond only in a way consistent with his perfect moral nature. He could not allow sin to go unchecked; he had to punish it. If the consequences of Adam and Eve's sin seem extreme, remember that their sin set in motion the world's tendency toward disobeying God. That is why we sin today: Every human being ever born, with the exception of Jesus, has inherited the sinful nature of Adam and Eve (Romans 5:12-21). Adam and Eve's punishment reflects how seriously God views sin of any kind.

**3:14-19** Adam and Eve learned by painful experience that because God is holy and hates sin, he must punish sinners. The rest of the book of Genesis recounts painful stories of lives ruined as a result of the Fall. Disobedience is sin, and it breaks our fellowship with God. But, fortunately, when we disobey, God is willing to forgive us and to restore our relationship with him.

**3:15** Satan is our enemy. He will do anything he can to get us to follow his evil, deadly path. The phrase "you will strike his heel" refers to Satan's repeated attempts to defeat Christ during his life on earth. "He will strike your head" foreshadows Satan's defeat when Christ rose from the dead. A strike on the heel is not deadly, but a blow to the head is. Already God was revealing his plan to defeat Satan and offer salvation to the world through his Son, Jesus Christ.

17And to the man he said,

"Since you listened to your wife and ate from the tree
  whose fruit I commanded you not to eat,
the ground is cursed because of you.
  All your life you will struggle to scratch a living from it.
18 It will grow thorns and thistles for you,
  though you will eat of its grains.
19 By the sweat of your brow
  will you have food to eat
until you return to the ground
  from which you were made.
For you were made from dust,
  and to dust you will return."

### Paradise Lost: God's Judgment

20Then the man—Adam—named his wife Eve, because she would be the mother of all who live.* 21And the LORD God made clothing from animal skins for Adam and his wife.

22Then the LORD God said, "Look, the human beings* have become like us, knowing both good and evil. What if they reach out, take fruit from the tree of life, and eat it? Then they will live forever!" 23So the LORD God banished them from the Garden of Eden, and he sent Adam out to cultivate the ground from which he had been made. 24After sending them out, the LORD God stationed mighty cherubim to the east of the Garden of Eden. And he placed a flaming sword that flashed back and forth to guard the way to the tree of life.

## 2. Cain and Abel

**4** Now Adam* had sexual relations with his wife, Eve, and she became pregnant. When she gave birth to Cain, she said, "With the LORD's help, I have produced* a man!" 2Later she gave birth to his brother and named him Abel.

When they grew up, Abel became a shepherd, while Cain cultivated the ground. 3When it was time for the harvest, Cain presented some of his crops as a gift to the LORD. 4Abel also brought a gift—the best of the firstborn lambs from his flock. The LORD accepted Abel and his gift, 5but he did not accept Cain and his gift. This made Cain very angry, and he looked dejected.

6"Why are you so angry?" the LORD asked Cain. "Why do you look so dejected? 7You will

3:20 Eve sounds like a Hebrew term that means "to give life."   3:22 Or the man; Hebrew reads ha-adam.   4:1a Or the man; also in 4:25.   4:1b Or I have acquired. Cain sounds like a Hebrew term that can mean "produce" or "acquire."

**Cross-references (margin):**
3:17 Job 5:7; Eccl 1:3; Rom 8:20-22
3:18 Job 31:40; Heb 6:8
3:19 Gen 2:7; Pss 90:3; 104:29; Eccl 12:7; 1 Cor 15:47
3:20 2 Cor 11:3; 1 Tim 2:13
3:21 2 Cor 5:2-3
3:24 Ezek 10:1; Rev 2:7; 22:2, 14
4:2 Luke 11:50-51
4:3 Lev 2:1-2; Num 18:12
4:4 Exod 13:12; Heb 11:4
4:6 Jon 4:4
4:7 Rom 6:12, 16; Jas 1:15

---

**3:17-19** Adam and Eve's disobedience and fall from God's gracious presence affected all creation, including the environment. Years ago people thought nothing of polluting streams with chemical wastes and garbage. This seemed so insignificant, so small. Now we know that just two or three parts per million of certain chemicals can damage human health. Sin in our lives is similar to pollution in streams. Even small amounts are deadly.

**3:22-24** Life in the Garden of Eden was like living in heaven. Everything was perfect, and if Adam and Eve had obeyed God, they could have lived there forever. But after disobeying, Adam and Eve no longer deserved paradise, and God told them to leave. If they had continued to live in the garden and eat from the tree of life, they would have lived forever. But eternal life in a state of sin would mean forever trying to hide from God. Like Adam and Eve, all of us have sinned and are separated from fellowship with God. We do not have to stay separated, however. God is preparing a new earth as an eternal paradise for his people (see Revelation 21–22).

**3:24** This is how Adam and Eve broke their relationship with God: (1) They became convinced their way was better than God's; (2) they became self-conscious and hid; (3) they tried to excuse and defend themselves. To build a relationship with God we must reverse those steps: (1) We must drop our excuses and self-defenses; (2) we must stop trying to hide from God; (3) we must become convinced that God's way is better than our way.

**4:1** Sexual union means oneness and total knowledge of the other person. Sexual intercourse is the most intimate of acts, sealing a social, physical, and spiritual relationship. That is why God has reserved it for marriage alone.

**4:2** No longer was everything provided for Adam and Eve as it was in the Garden of Eden, where their daily tasks were refreshing and delightful. Now they had to struggle against the elements in order to provide food, clothing, and shelter for themselves and their family. Cain became a farmer, while Abel was a shepherd. In parts of the Middle East today, these ancient occupations are still practiced much as they were in Cain and Abel's time.

**4:3-5** The Bible does not say why God did not accept Cain's gift. Perhaps Cain's attitude was improper, or perhaps his gift was not up to God's standards. Proverbs 21:27 says, "The sacrifice of an evil person is detestable, especially when it is offered with wrong motives." God evaluates both our motives and the quality of what we offer him. When we give to God and others, we should have a joyful heart because of what we are able to give. We should not worry about how much we are giving up, for all things are God's in the first place. Instead, we should joyfully give to God our best in time, money, possessions, and talents.

**4:6, 7** How do you react when someone suggests you have done something wrong? Do you move to correct the mistake or deny that you need to correct it? After Cain's gift was rejected, God gave him the chance to right his wrong and try again. God even encouraged him to do this! But Cain refused, and the rest of his life is a startling example of what happens to those who refuse to

**4:8**
Matt 23:35
1 Jn 3:12

**4:9**
Gen 3:9

**4:10**
Num 35:33
Deut 21:1
Heb 12:24

**4:11**
Deut 27:15-26

be accepted if you do what is right. But if you refuse to do what is right, then watch out! Sin is crouching at the door, eager to control you. But you must subdue it and be its master."

⁸One day Cain suggested to his brother, "Let's go out into the fields."\* And while they were in the field, Cain attacked his brother, Abel, and killed him.

⁹Afterward the LORD asked Cain, "Where is your brother? Where is Abel?"

"I don't know," Cain responded. "Am I my brother's guardian?"

¹⁰But the LORD said, "What have you done? Listen! Your brother's blood cries out to me from the ground! ¹¹Now you are cursed and banished from the ground, which has

**4:8** As in Samaritan Pentateuch, Greek and Syriac versions, and Latin Vulgate; Masoretic Text lacks *"Let's go out into the fields."*

**EVE**

We know very little about Eve, the first woman in the world, yet she is the mother of us all. She was the final piece in the intricate and amazing puzzle of God's creation. Adam now had another human being with whom to fellowship—someone with an equal share in God's image. Here was someone alike enough for companionship, yet different enough for relationship. Together they were greater than either could have been alone.

Eve was approached by Satan in the Garden of Eden, where she and Adam lived. He questioned her contentment. How could she be happy when she was not allowed to eat from one of the fruit trees? Satan helped Eve shift her focus from all that God had done and given to the one thing he had withheld. And Eve was willing to accept Satan's viewpoint without checking with God.

Sound familiar? How often is our attention drawn from the much that is ours to the little that isn't? We get that "I've got to have it" feeling. Eve was typical of us all, and we consistently show we are her descendants by repeating her mistakes. Our desires, like Eve's, can be quite easily manipulated. They are not the best basis for actions. We need to keep God in our decision-making process always. His Word, the Bible, is our guidebook in decision making.

| | |
|---|---|
| **Strengths and accomplishments** | • First wife and mother<br>• First female. As such she shared a special relationship with God, had co-responsibility with Adam over creation, and displayed certain characteristics of God |
| **Weaknesses and mistakes** | • Allowed her contentment to be undermined by Satan<br>• Acted impulsively without talking either to God or to her mate<br>• Not only sinned, but shared her sin with Adam<br>• When confronted, blamed others |
| **Lessons from her life** | • The female shares in the image of God<br>• The necessary ingredients for a strong marriage are commitment to each other, companionship with each other, complete oneness, absence of shame (Genesis 2:24, 25)<br>• The basic human tendency to sin goes back to the beginning of the human race |
| **Vital statistics** | • Where: Garden of Eden<br>• Occupation: Wife, helper, companion, co-manager of Eden<br>• Relatives: Husband: Adam. Sons: Cain, Abel, Seth. Numerous other children. |
| **Key verse** | "Then the LORD God said, 'It is not good for the man to be alone. I will make a helper who is just right for him'" (Genesis 2:18). |

Eve's story is told in Genesis 2:18–4:26. Her death is not mentioned in Scripture.

admit their mistakes. The next time someone suggests you are wrong, take an honest look at yourself and choose God's way instead of Cain's.

**4:7** For Cain to subdue the sin that was waiting to attack and destroy him, he would have to give up his jealous anger so that sin would not find a foothold in his life. Sin is still waiting to attack and destroy us today. Like Cain, we will be victims of sin if we do not master it. But we cannot master sin in our own strength. Instead, we must turn to God to receive faith for ourselves and turn to other believers to receive encouragement and strength. The Holy Spirit will help us master sin. This will be a lifelong battle that will not be over until we are face to face with Christ.

**4:8-10** This is the first murder—taking a life by shedding human blood. Blood represents life (Leviticus 17:10-14). If blood is removed from a living creature, it will die. Because God created life, only God should take life away.

**4:8-10** Adam and Eve's disobedience brought sin into the human race. They may have thought their sin—eating a piece of fruit—wasn't very bad, but notice how quickly their sinful nature developed in their children. Simple disobedience quickly degenerated into outright murder. Adam and Eve acted only against God, but Cain acted against both God and other people. A small sin has a way of growing out of control. Let God help you with your "little" sins before they turn into tragedies.

**4:11-15** Cain was severely punished for this murder. God judges all sins and punishes appropriately, not out of vengeance, but because he desires to correct us and restore our fellowship with him. When you're corrected, don't resent it. Instead, renew your fellowship with God.

swallowed your brother's blood. <sup>12</sup>No longer will the ground yield good crops for you, no matter how hard you work! From now on you will be a homeless wanderer on the earth."

<sup>13</sup>Cain replied to the LORD, "My punishment* is too great for me to bear! <sup>14</sup>You have banished me from the land and from your presence; you have made me a homeless wanderer. Anyone who finds me will kill me!"

<sup>15</sup>The LORD replied, "No, for I will give a sevenfold punishment to anyone who kills you." Then the LORD put a mark on Cain to warn anyone who might try to kill him. <sup>16</sup>So Cain left the LORD's presence and settled in the land of Nod,* east of Eden.

### The Descendants of Cain

<sup>17</sup>Cain had sexual relations with his wife, and she became pregnant and gave birth to Enoch. Then Cain founded a city, which he named Enoch, after his son. <sup>18</sup>Enoch had a son named Irad. Irad became the father of* Mehujael. Mehujael became the father of Methushael. Methushael became the father of Lamech.

<sup>19</sup>Lamech married two women. The first was named Adah, and the second was Zillah. <sup>20</sup>Adah gave birth to Jabal, who was the first of those who raise livestock and live in tents. <sup>21</sup>His brother's name was Jubal, the first of all who play the harp and flute. <sup>22</sup>Lamech's other wife, Zillah, gave birth to a son named Tubal-cain. He became an expert in forging tools of bronze and iron. Tubal-cain had a sister named Naamah. <sup>23</sup>One day Lamech said to his wives,

"Adah and Zillah, hear my voice;
    listen to me, you wives of Lamech.
I have killed a man who attacked me,
    a young man who wounded me.
<sup>24</sup> If someone who kills Cain is punished seven times,
    then the one who kills me will be punished seventy-seven times!"

### The Birth of Seth

<sup>25</sup>Adam had sexual relations with his wife again, and she gave birth to another son. She named him Seth,* for she said, "God has granted me another son in place of Abel, whom Cain killed." <sup>26</sup>When Seth grew up, he had a son and named him Enosh. At that time people first began to worship the LORD by name.

### 3. Adam's descendants
#### From Adam to Noah

**5** This is the written account of the descendants of Adam. When God created human beings,* he made them to be like himself. <sup>2</sup>He created them male and female, and he blessed them and called them "human."

**4:12**
Deut 28:15-24

**4:14**
Gen 9:6
Job 15:22

**4:17**
Ps 49:11

**4:23**
Lev 19:18
Deut 32:35

**4:25**
Gen 4:8; 5:3
1 Chr 1:1
Luke 3:38

**4:26**
Gen 12:8
1 Kgs 18:24
Joel 2:32
Zeph 3:9
Acts 2:21

**5:1**
Gen 1:26; 6:9
1 Chr 1:1

**5:2**
Gen 1:27
†Matt 19:4
†Mark 10:6

**4:13** Or *My sin.*   **4:16** *Nod* means "wandering."   **4:18** Or *the ancestor of,* and so throughout the verse.   **4:25** *Seth* probably means "granted"; the name may also mean "appointed."   **5:1** Or *man;* Hebrew reads *adam;* similarly in 5:2.

---

**4:14** We have heard about only four people so far—Adam, Eve, Cain, and Abel. Two questions arise: Why was Cain worried about being killed by others, and where did he get his wife (see 4:17)?

Adam and Eve had numerous children; they had been told to "fill the earth" (1:28). Cain's guilt and fear over killing his brother was heavy, and he probably feared repercussions from his family. If he was capable of killing, so were they. The wife Cain chose may have been one of his sisters or a niece. The human race was still genetically pure, and there was no fear of side effects from marrying relatives.

**4:15** The expression "sevenfold punishment" means that the person's punishment would be complete, thorough, and much worse than that received by Cain for his sin.

**4:19-26** Unfortunately, when left to themselves, people tend to get worse instead of better. This short summary of Lamech's family shows us the variety of talent and ability God gives humans. It also presents the continuous development of sin as time passes. Another killing occurred, presumably in self-defense. Violence was on the rise. Two distinct groups were emerging: (1) those who showed indifference to sin and evil, and (2) those who worshiped the Lord (the descendants of Seth, 4:26). Seth would take Abel's place as leader of a line of God's faithful people.

**5:1ff** The Bible contains several lists of ancestors, called genealogies. Two basic views concerning these lists include: (1) They are complete, recording the entire history of a family, tribe, or nation; or (2) they are not intended to be exhaustive and may include only famous people or the heads of families. "He became the father of" could refer not just to a son, but also to a more distant descendant.

Why are genealogies included in the Bible? The Hebrew people passed on their beliefs through oral tradition. For many years in many places, writing was primitive or nonexistent. Stories were told to children who passed them on to their children. Genealogies gave a skeletal outline that helped people remember the stories. For centuries these genealogies were added to and passed down from family to family. Even more important than preserving family tradition, genealogies were included to confirm the Bible's promise that the coming Messiah, Jesus Christ, would be born into the line of Abraham.

Genealogies point out that people are important to God as individuals. Therefore, God refers to people by name, mentioning their life span and descendants. The next time you feel overwhelmed in a vast crowd, remember that the focus of God's attention and love is on the individual—and on you!

5:3
Gen 1:26; 4:25
1 Cor 15:49
5:4
1 Chr 1:1
5:5
Gen 2:17
Heb 9:27
5:6
1 Chr 1:1
Luke 3:38
5:9
1 Chr 1:2
Luke 3:37
5:12
1 Chr 1:2
Luke 3:37
5:15
1 Chr 1:2
Luke 3:37
5:18
1 Chr 1:3
Luke 3:37
Jude 1:14
5:21
1 Chr 1:3
Luke 3:37
5:24
2 Kgs 2:1, 11
Ps 73:24
Heb 11:5
5:25
1 Chr 1:3
Luke 3:36

³When Adam was 130 years old, he became the father of a son who was just like him—in his very image. He named his son Seth. ⁴After the birth of Seth, Adam lived another 800 years, and he had other sons and daughters. ⁵Adam lived 930 years, and then he died.

⁶When Seth was 105 years old, he became the father of* Enosh. ⁷After the birth of* Enosh, Seth lived another 807 years, and he had other sons and daughters. ⁸Seth lived 912 years, and then he died.

⁹When Enosh was 90 years old, he became the father of Kenan. ¹⁰After the birth of Kenan, Enosh lived another 815 years, and he had other sons and daughters. ¹¹Enosh lived 905 years, and then he died.

¹²When Kenan was 70 years old, he became the father of Mahalalel. ¹³After the birth of Mahalalel, Kenan lived another 840 years, and he had other sons and daughters. ¹⁴Kenan lived 910 years, and then he died.

¹⁵When Mahalalel was 65 years old, he became the father of Jared. ¹⁶After the birth of Jared, Mahalalel lived another 830 years, and he had other sons and daughters. ¹⁷Mahalalel lived 895 years, and then he died.

¹⁸When Jared was 162 years old, he became the father of Enoch. ¹⁹After the birth of Enoch, Jared lived another 800 years, and he had other sons and daughters. ²⁰Jared lived 962 years, and then he died.

²¹When Enoch was 65 years old, he became the father of Methuselah. ²²After the birth of Methuselah, Enoch lived in close fellowship with God for another 300 years, and he had other sons and daughters. ²³Enoch lived 365 years, ²⁴walking in close fellowship with God. Then one day he disappeared, because God took him.

²⁵When Methuselah was 187 years old, he became the father of Lamech. ²⁶After the

**5:6** Or *the ancestor of;* also in 5:9, 12, 15, 18, 21, 25.   **5:7** Or *the birth of this ancestor of;* also in 5:10, 13, 16, 19, 22, 26.

---

**ABEL**

Abel was the second child born into the world, but the first one to obey God. All we know about this man is that his parents were Adam and Eve, he was a shepherd, he presented pleasing offerings to God, and his short life was ended at the hands of his jealous older brother, Cain.

The Bible doesn't tell us why God liked Abel's gift and disliked Cain's, but both Cain and Abel knew what God expected. Only Abel obeyed. Throughout history, Abel is remembered for his obedience and faith (Hebrews 11:4), and he is called "righteous" (Matthew 23:35).

The Bible is filled with God's general guidelines and expectations for our lives. It is also filled with more specific directions. Like Abel, we must obey regardless of the cost and trust God to make things right.

| Strengths and accomplishments | • First member of the Hall of Faith in Hebrews 11<br>• First shepherd<br>• First martyr for truth (Matthew 23:35) |
|---|---|
| Lessons from his life | • God hears those who come to him<br>• God recognizes the innocent person and sooner or later punishes the guilty |
| Vital statistics | • Where: Just outside of Eden<br>• Occupation: Shepherd<br>• Relatives: Parents: Adam and Eve. Brother: Cain. |
| Key verse | "It was by faith that Abel brought a more acceptable offering to God than Cain did. Abel's offering gave evidence that he was a righteous man, and God showed his approval of his gifts. Although Abel is long dead, he still speaks to us by his example of faith" (Hebrews 11:4). |

Abel's story is told in Genesis 4:1-8. He is also mentioned in Matthew 23:35; Luke 11:51; Hebrews 11:4 and 12:24.

---

**5:3-5** All human beings are related, going back to Adam and Eve. All people form a family that shares one flesh and blood. Remember this when prejudice enters your mind or hatred invades your feelings. Each person is a valuable and unique creation of God.

**5:25-27** How did these people live so long? Some believe that the ages listed here were lengths of family dynasties rather than ages of individual men. Those who think these were actual ages

offer three explanations: (1) The human race was more genetically pure in this early time period with less disease to shorten life spans; (2) no rain had yet fallen on the earth, and the expanse of "the waters of the heavens" (1:7) kept out harmful cosmic rays and shielded people from environmental factors that hasten aging; (3) God gave people longer lives so they would have time to "fill the earth" (1:28).

birth of Lamech, Methuselah lived another 782 years, and he had other sons and daughters. 27Methuselah lived 969 years, and then he died.

28When Lamech was 182 years old, he became the father of a son. 29Lamech named his son Noah, for he said, "May he bring us relief* from our work and the painful labor of farming this ground that the LORD has cursed." 30After the birth of Noah, Lamech lived another 595 years, and he had other sons and daughters. 31Lamech lived 777 years, and then he died.

32By the time Noah was 500 years old, he was the father of Shem, Ham, and Japheth.

## C. THE STORY OF NOAH (6:1—11:32)

Earth was no longer the perfect paradise that God had intended. It is frightening to see how quickly all of humanity forgot about God. Incredibly, in all the world, only one man and his family still worshiped God. That man was Noah. Because of his faithfulness and obedience, God saved him and his family from a vast flood that destroyed every other human being on earth. This section shows us how God hates sin and judges those who enjoy it.

### 1. The Flood

**6** Then the people began to multiply on the earth, and daughters were born to them. 2The sons of God saw the beautiful women* and took any they wanted as their wives. 3Then the LORD said, "My Spirit will not put up with* humans for such a long time, for they are only mortal flesh. In the future, their normal lifespan will be no more than 120 years."

4In those days, and for some time after, giant Nephilites lived on the earth, for whenever the sons of God had intercourse with women, they gave birth to children who became the heroes and famous warriors of ancient times.

5The LORD observed the extent of human wickedness on the earth, and he saw that everything they thought or imagined was consistently and totally evil. 6So the LORD was sorry he had ever made them and put them on the earth. It broke his heart. 7And the LORD said, "I will wipe this human race I have created from the face of the earth. Yes, and I will destroy every living thing—all the people, the large animals, the small animals that scurry along the ground, and even the birds of the sky. I am sorry I ever made them." 8But Noah found favor with the LORD.

### The Story of Noah

9This is the account of Noah and his family. Noah was a righteous man, the only blameless person living on earth at the time, and he walked in close fellowship with God. 10Noah was the father of three sons: Shem, Ham, and Japheth.

11Now God saw that the earth had become corrupt and was filled with violence. 12God observed all this corruption in the world, for everyone on earth was corrupt. 13So God said to Noah, "I have decided to destroy all living creatures, for they have filled the earth with violence. Yes, I will wipe them all out along with the earth!

14"Build a large boat* from cypress wood* and waterproof it with tar, inside and out.

**5:29** *Noah* sounds like a Hebrew term that can mean "relief" or "comfort."   **6:2** Hebrew *daughters of men;* also in 6:4.   **6:3** Greek version reads *will not remain in.*   **6:14a** Traditionally rendered *an ark.*   **6:14b** Or *gopher wood.*

**5:29**
Gen 3:17
1 Chr 1:3
Luke 3:36
Rom 8:20

**5:32**
Gen 7:6; 9:18

**6:1**
Gen 1:28

**6:3**
Ps 78:39
1 Pet 3:20

**6:4**
Num 13:33

**6:5**
Ps 14:1-3

**6:6**
Exod 32:14
1 Sam 15:11, 35

**6:7**
Deut 29:20

**6:8**
Exod 33:17

**6:9**
Job 1:1
Ezek 14:14

**6:11**
Deut 31:29
Judg 2:19
Ezek 8:17

**6:12**
Ps 14:1-3

**6:13**
Isa 34:1-4
Ezek 7:2-3

**6:14**
Exod 2:3
1 Pet 3:20

---

**6:1-4** Some people have thought that the "sons of God" were fallen angels. But the "sons of God" were probably not angels, because angels do not marry or reproduce (Matthew 22:30; Mark 12:25). Some scholars believe this phrase refers to the descendants of Seth who intermarried with Cain's evil descendants. This would have weakened the good influence of the faithful and increased moral depravity in the world, resulting in an explosion of evil.

**6:3** "Their normal lifespan will be no more than 120 years" has been interpreted by some commentators to mean that God was allowing the people of Noah's day 120 years to change their sinful ways. God shows us his great patience with us as well. He is giving us time to quit living our way and begin living his way, the way he shows us in his Word. While 120 years seems like a long time, eventually the time ran out, and the floodwaters swept across the earth. Your time also may be running out. Turn to God to forgive your sins. You can't race the stopwatch of God's patience, and there is no bargaining for additional time.

**6:4** These "giant Nephilites" were people probably nine or ten feet tall. This same Hebrew term was used to name a tall race

of people in Numbers 13:33. Goliath, who was nine feet tall, appears in 1 Samuel 17. The giants used their physical advantage to oppress the people around them.

**6:6, 7** Does this mean that God regretted creating humanity? Was he admitting he made a mistake? No, God does not change his mind (1 Samuel 15:29). Instead, he was expressing sorrow for what the people had done to themselves, as a parent might express sorrow over a rebellious child. God was sorry that the people chose sin and death instead of a relationship with him.

**6:6-8** The people's sin grieved God. Our sins break God's heart as much as sin did in Noah's day. Noah, however, pleased God, although he was far from perfect. We can follow Noah's example and find "favor with the LORD" in spite of the sin that surrounds us.

**6:9** Saying that Noah was "righteous" and "blameless" does not mean that he never sinned (the Bible records one of his sins in 9:20ff). Rather, it means that Noah wholeheartedly loved and obeyed God. For a lifetime he walked step by step in faith as a living example to his generation. Like Noah, we live in a world filled with evil. Are we influencing others or being influenced by them?

Then construct decks and stalls throughout its interior. ¹⁵Make the boat 450 feet long, 75 feet wide, and 45 feet high.* ¹⁶Leave an 18-inch opening* below the roof all the way around the boat. Put the door on the side, and build three decks inside the boat—lower, middle, and upper.

¹⁷"Look! I am about to cover the earth with a flood that will destroy every living thing that breathes. Everything on earth will die. ¹⁸But I will confirm my covenant with you. So enter the boat—you and your wife and your sons and their wives. ¹⁹Bring a pair of every kind of animal—a male and a female—into the boat with you to keep them alive during the flood. ²⁰Pairs of every kind of bird, and every kind of animal, and every kind of small animal that scurries along the ground, will come to you to be kept alive. ²¹And be sure to take on board enough food for your family and for all the animals."

²²So Noah did everything exactly as God had commanded him.

**6:15** Hebrew *300 cubits* [138 meters] *long, 50 cubits* [23 meters] *wide, and 30 cubits* [13.8 meters] *high.*
**6:16** Hebrew *an opening of 1 cubit* [46 centimeters].

**6:17**
Ps 29:10
2 Pet 2:5
**6:18**
Gen 9:9-16; 17:7;
19:12
**6:20**
Gen 7:3
**6:21**
Gen 1:29
**6:22**
Gen 7:5
Exod 40:16

---

In spite of parents' efforts and worries, conflicts between children in a family seem inevitable. Sibling relationships allow both competition and cooperation. In most cases, the mixture of loving and fighting eventually creates a strong bond between brothers and sisters. It isn't unusual, though, to hear parents say, "They fight so much I hope they don't kill each other before they grow up." In Cain's case, the troubling potential became a reality. And while we don't know many details of this first child's life, his story can still teach us.

Cain got angry. Furious. Both he and his brother Abel had given offerings to God, and his had been rejected. Cain's reaction gives us a clue that his attitude was probably wrong from the start. Cain had a choice to make. He could correct his attitude about his offering to God, or he could take his anger out on his brother. His decision is a clear reminder of how often we are aware of opposite choices, yet choose the wrong one just as Cain did. We may not be choosing to murder, but we are still intentionally choosing what we shouldn't.

The feelings motivating our behavior can't always be changed by simple thought-power. But here we can begin to experience God's willingness to help. Asking for his help to do what is right can prevent us from setting into motion actions that we will later regret.

| | |
|---|---|
| **Strengths and accomplishments** | • First human child<br>• First to follow in father's profession, farming |
| **Weaknesses and mistakes** | • When disappointed, reacted in anger<br>• Took the negative option even when a positive possibility was offered<br>• Was the first murderer |
| **Lessons from his life** | • Anger is not necessarily a sin, but actions motivated by anger can be sinful. Anger should be the energy behind good action, not evil action<br>• What we offer to God must be from the heart—the best we are and have<br>• The consequences of sin may last a lifetime |
| **Vital statistics** | • Where: Near Eden, which was probably located in present-day Iraq or Iran<br>• Occupation: Farmer, then wanderer<br>• Relatives: Parents: Adam and Eve. Brothers: Abel, Seth, and others not mentioned by name. |
| **Key verse** | "You will be accepted if you do what is right. But if you refuse to do what is right, then watch out! Sin is crouching at the door, eager to control you. But you must subdue it and be its master" (Genesis 4:7). |

Cain's story is told in Genesis 4:1-17. He is also mentioned in Hebrews 11:4; 1 John 3:12; Jude 1:11.

---

**6:15** The boat Noah built was no canoe! Picture yourself building a boat the length of one and a half football fields and as high as a four-story building. The boat was exactly six times longer than it was wide—the same ratio used by modern shipbuilders. This huge boat was probably built miles from any body of water by only a few faithful men who believed God's promises and obeyed his commands.

**6:18** When God said, "I will confirm my covenant," he was making a promise. This is a familiar theme in Scripture—God making covenants with his people. How reassuring it is to know God's covenant is established with us. He is still our salvation, and we are kept safe through our relationship with him. For more on covenants, see 9:8-17; 12:1-3; and 15:17-21.

**6:22** Noah got right to work when God told him to build the huge boat. Other people must have been warned about the coming disaster (1 Peter 3:20), but apparently they did not expect it to happen. Today things haven't changed much. Each day thousands of people are warned of God's inevitable judgment, yet most of them don't really believe it will happen. Don't expect people to welcome or accept your message of God's coming judgment on sin. Those who don't believe in God will deny his judgment and try to get you to deny God as well. But remember God's promise to Noah to keep him safe. This can inspire you to trust God for deliverance in the judgment that is sure to come.

## The Flood Covers the Earth

**7** When everything was ready, the LORD said to Noah, "Go into the boat with all your family, for among all the people of the earth, I can see that you alone are righteous. ²Take with you seven pairs—male and female—of each animal I have approved for eating and for sacrifice,* and take one pair of each of the others. ³Also take seven pairs of every kind of bird. There must be a male and a female in each pair to ensure that all life will survive on the earth after the flood. ⁴Seven days from now I will make the rains pour down on the earth. And it will rain for forty days and forty nights, until I have wiped from the earth all the living things I have created."

⁵So Noah did everything as the LORD commanded him.

⁶Noah was 600 years old when the flood covered the earth. ⁷He went on board the boat to escape the flood—he and his wife and his sons and their wives. ⁸With them were all the various kinds of animals—those approved for eating and for sacrifice and those that were not—along with all the birds and the small animals that scurry along the ground. ⁹They entered the boat in pairs, male and female, just as God had commanded Noah. ¹⁰After seven days, the waters of the flood came and covered the earth.

¹¹When Noah was 600 years old, on the seventeenth day of the second month, all the underground waters erupted from the earth, and the rain fell in mighty torrents from the sky. ¹²The rain continued to fall for forty days and forty nights.

¹³That very day Noah had gone into the boat with his wife and his sons—Shem, Ham, and Japheth—and their wives. ¹⁴With them in the boat were pairs of every kind of animal—domestic and wild, large and small—along with birds of every kind. ¹⁵Two by two they came into the boat, representing every living thing that breathes. ¹⁶A male and female of each kind entered, just as God had commanded Noah. Then the LORD closed the door behind them.

¹⁷For forty days the floodwaters grew deeper, covering the ground and lifting the boat high above the earth. ¹⁸As the waters rose higher and higher above the ground, the boat floated safely on the surface. ¹⁹Finally, the water covered even the highest mountains on the earth, ²⁰rising more than twenty-two feet* above the highest peaks. ²¹All the living things on earth died—birds, domestic animals, wild animals, small animals that scurry along the ground, and all the people. ²²Everything that breathed and lived on dry land died. ²³God wiped out every living thing on the earth—people, livestock, small animals that scurry along the ground, and the birds of the sky. All were destroyed. The only people who survived were Noah and those with him in the boat. ²⁴And the floodwaters covered the earth for 150 days.

## The Flood Recedes

**8** But God remembered Noah and all the wild animals and livestock with him in the boat. He sent a wind to blow across the earth, and the floodwaters began to recede. ²The underground waters stopped flowing, and the torrential rains from the sky were stopped. ³So the floodwaters gradually receded from the earth. After 150 days, ⁴exactly five months from the time the flood began,* the boat came to rest on the mountains of Ararat. ⁵Two and

7:2 Hebrew *of each clean animal;* similarly in 7:8.   7:20 Hebrew *15 cubits* [6.9 meters].   8:4 Hebrew *on the seventeenth day of the seventh month;* see 7:11.

| Reference |
|---|
| 7:1 Gen 6:18; Matt 24:38; Luke 17:26-27; Heb 11:7; 1 Pet 3:20 |
| 7:2 Lev 11:1-47; Deut 14:3-20; Ezek 44:23 |
| 7:4 Gen 6:7, 13 |
| 7:6 Gen 5:32 |
| 7:7 Gen 6:18 |
| 7:9 Gen 6:22 |
| 7:11 Ps 78:23; Ezek 26:19; Mal 3:10 |
| 7:13 1 Pet 3:20; 2 Pet 2:5 |
| 7:15 Gen 6:19; 7:9 |
| 7:19 Ps 104:6 |
| 7:20 2 Pet 3:6 |
| 7:23 Matt 24:38-39; Luke 17:26-27; 1 Pet 3:20; 2 Pet 2:5 |
| 7:24 Gen 8:3 |
| 8:1 Gen 19:29; 30:22; Exod 2:24; 14:21; Job 12:15; Isa 44:27 |
| 8:2 Gen 7:4, 12 |
| 8:4 Gen 7:20 |

**MOUNTAINS OF ARARAT**   The boat touched land in the mountains of Ararat, located in present-day Turkey. There it rested for almost eight months before Noah, his family, and the animals stepped onto dry land.

**7:1ff**   Pairs of every animal joined Noah in the boat; seven pairs were taken of those animals used for sacrifice. Scholars have estimated that almost 45,000 animals could have fit into the boat.

**7:16**   Many have wondered how this animal kingdom roundup happened. Did Noah and his sons spend years collecting all the animals? In reality the creation, along with Noah, was doing just as God had commanded. There seemed to be no problem gathering the animals—God took care of the details of that job while Noah was doing his part by building the boat. Often we do just the opposite of Noah. We worry about details over which we have no control, while neglecting specific areas (such as attitudes, relationships, responsibilities) that *are* under our control. Like Noah, concentrate on what God has given you to do, and leave the rest to God.

**7:17-24**   Was the Flood a local event, or did it cover the entire earth? A universal flood was certainly possible. Enough water exists in the oceans to cover all dry land (the earth began that way; see 1:9, 10). Afterward God promised never again to destroy the earth with a flood. Thus, this Flood must have either covered the entire earth or destroyed all the inhabitants of the earth. Remember, God's reason for sending the Flood was to a half months later,* as the waters continued to go down, other mountain peaks became visible.

8:7
Lev 11:15
Deut 14:14
1 Kgs 17:4
Luke 12:24
8:8
Isa 60:8
Hos 11:11
Matt 10:16

6After another forty days, Noah opened the window he had made in the boat 7and released a raven. The bird flew back and forth until the floodwaters on the earth had dried up. 8He also released a dove to see if the water had receded and it could find dry ground. 9But the dove could find no place to land because the water still covered the ground. So it returned to the boat, and Noah held out his hand and drew the dove back inside. 10After waiting another seven days, Noah released the dove again. 11This time the dove returned to him in the evening with a fresh olive leaf in its beak. Then Noah knew that the floodwaters were almost gone. 12He waited another seven days and then released the dove again. This time it did not come back.

8:13
Gen 5:32

13Noah was now 601 years old. On the first day of the new year, ten and a half months after the flood began,* the floodwaters had almost dried up from the earth. Noah lifted back the covering of the boat and saw that the surface of the ground was drying. 14Two more months went by,* and at last the earth was dry!

8:16
Gen 7:13
8:17
Gen 1:22

15Then God said to Noah, 16"Leave the boat, all of you—you and your wife, and your sons and their wives. 17Release all the animals—the birds, the livestock, and the small animals that scurry along the ground—so they can be fruitful and multiply throughout the earth."

18So Noah, his wife, and his sons and their wives left the boat. 19And all of the large and small animals and birds came out of the boat, pair by pair.

**8:5** Hebrew *On the first day of the tenth month;* see 7:11 and note on 8:4.   **8:13** Hebrew *On the first day of the first month;* see 7:11.   **8:14** Hebrew *The twenty-seventh day of the second month arrived;* see note on 8:13.

---

**NOAH**

The story of Noah's life involves not one, but two great and tragic floods. The world in Noah's day was flooded with evil. The number of those who remembered the God of creation, perfection, and love had dwindled to one. Of God's people, only Noah was left. God's response to the severe situation was a 120-year-long last chance, during which he had Noah build a graphic illustration of the message of his life. Nothing like a huge boat on dry land to make a point! For Noah, obedience meant a long-term commitment to a project.

Many of us have trouble sticking to any project, whether or not it is directed by God. It is interesting that the length of Noah's obedience was greater than the life span of people today. The only comparable long-term project is our very lives. But perhaps this is one great challenge Noah's life gives us—to live, in acceptance of God's grace, an entire lifetime of obedience and gratitude.

| | |
|---|---|
| **Strengths and accomplishments** | • Only follower of God left in his generation<br>• Second father of the human race<br>• Man of patience, consistency, and obedience<br>• First major shipbuilder |
| **Weakness and mistake** | • Got drunk and embarrassed himself in front of his sons |
| **Lessons from his life** | • God is faithful to those who obey him<br>• God does not always protect us from trouble, but cares for us in spite of trouble<br>• Obedience is a long-term commitment<br>• We may be faithful, but our sinful nature always travels with us |
| **Vital statistics** | • Where: We're not told how far from the Garden of Eden people had settled<br>• Occupation: Farmer, shipbuilder, preacher<br>• Relatives: Grandfather: Methuselah. Father: Lamech. Sons: Ham, Shem, and Japheth. |
| **Key verse** | "So Noah did everything exactly as God had commanded him" (Genesis 6:22). |

Noah's story is told in Genesis 5:28–10:32. He is also mentioned in 1 Chronicles 1:3, 4; Isaiah 54:9; Ezekiel 14:14, 20; Matthew 24:37, 38; Luke 3:36; 17:26, 27; Hebrews 11:7; 1 Peter 3:20; 2 Peter 2:5.

---

destroy all the earth's wickedness. It would have taken a major flood to accomplish this.

**8:6-16** Occasionally Noah would send a bird out to test the earth and see if it was dry. But Noah didn't get out of the boat until God told him to. He was waiting for God's timing. God knew that even

though the water was gone, the earth was not dry enough for Noah and his family to venture out. What patience Noah showed, especially after spending an entire year inside his boat! We, like Noah, must trust God to give us patience during those difficult times when we must wait.

<sup>20</sup>Then Noah built an altar to the LORD, and there he sacrificed as burnt offerings the animals and birds that had been approved for that purpose.* <sup>21</sup>And the LORD was pleased with the aroma of the sacrifice and said to himself, "I will never again curse the ground because of the human race, even though everything they think or imagine is bent toward evil from childhood. I will never again destroy all living things. <sup>22</sup>As long as the earth remains, there will be planting and harvest, cold and heat, summer and winter, day and night."

**8:20**
Gen 4:4; 12:7;
13:18; 22:2

**8:21**
Gen 3:17
Exod 29:18, 25
Lev 1:9, 13
Isa 54:9

**8:22**
Ps 74:17

## 2. Repopulating the earth
### God Confirms His Covenant

**9** Then God blessed Noah and his sons and told them, "Be fruitful and multiply. Fill the earth. <sup>2</sup>All the animals of the earth, all the birds of the sky, all the small animals that scurry along the ground, and all the fish in the sea will look on you with fear and terror. I have placed them in your power. <sup>3</sup>I have given them to you for food, just as I have given you grain and vegetables. <sup>4</sup>But you must never eat any meat that still has the lifeblood in it.

<sup>5</sup>"And I will require the blood of anyone who takes another person's life. If a wild animal kills a person, it must die. And anyone who murders a fellow human must die. <sup>6</sup>If anyone takes a human life, that person's life will also be taken by human hands. For God made human beings* in his own image. <sup>7</sup>Now be fruitful and multiply, and repopulate the earth."

<sup>8</sup>Then God told Noah and his sons, <sup>9</sup>"I hereby confirm my covenant with you and your descendants, <sup>10</sup>and with all the animals that were on the boat with you—the birds, the livestock, and all the wild animals—every living creature on earth. <sup>11</sup>Yes, I am confirming my covenant with you. Never again will floodwaters kill all living creatures; never again will a flood destroy the earth."

<sup>12</sup>Then God said, "I am giving you a sign of my covenant with you and with all living creatures, for all generations to come. <sup>13</sup>I have placed my rainbow in the clouds. It is the sign of my covenant with you and with all the earth. <sup>14</sup>When I send clouds over the earth, the rainbow will appear in the clouds, <sup>15</sup>and I will remember my covenant with you and with all living creatures. Never again will the floodwaters destroy all life. <sup>16</sup>When I see the rainbow in the clouds, I will remember the eternal covenant between God and every living creature on earth." <sup>17</sup>Then God said to Noah, "Yes, this rainbow is the sign of the covenant I am confirming with all the creatures on earth."

**9:1**
Gen 1:22

**9:2**
Gen 1:26-29

**9:4**
Lev 3:17; 7:26;
17:10
Deut 12:16

**9:5**
Exod 21:28-32

**9:6**
Exod 20:13; 21:12
Num 35:33

**9:11**
Isa 24:5

**9:12**
Gen 17:11

**9:13**
Ezek 1:28

**9:15**
Deut 7:9

### Noah's Sons

<sup>18</sup>The sons of Noah who came out of the boat with their father were Shem, Ham, and Japheth. (Ham is the father of Canaan.) <sup>19</sup>From these three sons of Noah came all the people who now populate the earth.

<sup>20</sup>After the flood, Noah began to cultivate the ground, and he planted a vineyard. <sup>21</sup>One day he drank some wine he had made, and he became drunk and lay naked inside his tent. <sup>22</sup>Ham, the father of Canaan, saw that his father was naked and went outside and told his brothers. <sup>23</sup>Then Shem and Japheth took a robe, held it over their shoulders, and backed into the tent to cover their father. As they did this, they looked the other way so they would not see him naked.

**9:21**
Gen 19:35

**9:22**
Hab 2:15

**8:20** Hebrew *every clean animal and every clean bird.*    **9:6** Or *man;* Hebrew reads *ha-adam.*

---

**8:21, 22** Countless times throughout the Bible we see God showing his love and patience toward men and women in order to save them. Although he realizes that their hearts are evil, he continues to try to reach them. When we sin or fall away from God, we surely deserve to be destroyed by his judgment. But God has promised never again to destroy everything on earth until the judgment day when Christ returns to destroy evil forever. Now every change of season is a reminder of his promise.

**9:5** God will require each person to account for his or her actions. We cannot harm or kill another human being without answering to God. A penalty must be paid. Justice will be served.

**9:5, 6** Here God explains why murder is so wrong: To kill a person is to kill one made in God's image. Because all human beings are made in God's image, all people possess the qualities that distinguish them from animals: morality, reason, creativity,

and self-worth. When we interact with others, we are interacting with beings made by God, beings to whom God offers eternal life. God wants us to recognize his image in all people.

**9:8-17** Noah stepped out of the boat onto an earth devoid of human life. But God gave him a reassuring promise. This covenant had three parts: (1) Never again will a flood do such destruction; (2) as long as the earth remains, the seasons will always come as expected; (3) a rainbow will be visible when it rains as a sign to all that God will keep his promises. The earth's order and seasons are still preserved, and rainbows still remind us of God's faithfulness to his word.

**9:20-27** Noah, the great hero of faith, got drunk—a poor example of godliness to his sons. Perhaps this story is included to show us that even godly people can sin and that their bad influence affects their families. Although the wicked people had all been killed, the possibility of evil still existed in the hearts of Noah and his family. Ham's mocking attitude revealed a severe lack of respect for his father and for God.

**9:25**
Deut 27:16

24When Noah woke up from his stupor, he learned what Ham, his youngest son, had done. 25Then he cursed Canaan, the son of Ham:

"May Canaan be cursed!
May he be the lowest of servants to his relatives."

**9:26**
Gen 14:20

26Then Noah said,

"May the LORD, the God of Shem, be blessed,
and may Canaan be his servant!

**9:27**
Gen 10:2-5
Isa 66:19

27 May God expand the territory of Japheth!
May Japheth share the prosperity of Shem,*
and may Canaan be his servant."

**9:29**
Gen 2:17

28Noah lived another 350 years after the great flood. 29He lived 950 years, and then he died.

**10:1**
Gen 9:18
1 Chr 1:4

**10** This is the account of the families of Shem, Ham, and Japheth, the three sons of Noah. Many children were born to them after the great flood.

### Descendants of Japheth

**10:2**
1 Chr 1:5-7
Isa 66:19
Ezek 27:13;
38:2-3, 6
**10:4**
1 Chr 1:6-7

2The descendants of Japheth were Gomer, Magog, Madai, Javan, Tubal, Meshech, and Tiras. 3The descendants of Gomer were Ashkenaz, Riphath, and Togarmah. 4The descendants of Javan were Elishah, Tarshish, Kittim, and Rodanim.* 5Their descendants became the seafaring peoples that spread out to various lands, each identified by its own language, clan, and national identity.

### Descendants of Ham

**10:6**
1 Chr 1:8-10
**10:7**
Isa 43:3
Ezek 27:15, 20, 22

6The descendants of Ham were Cush, Mizraim, Put, and Canaan. 7The descendants of Cush were Seba, Havilah, Sabtah, Raamah, and Sabteca. The descendants of Raamah were Sheba and Dedan.

8Cush was also the ancestor of Nimrod, who was the first heroic warrior on earth. 9Since he was the greatest hunter in the world,* his name became proverbial. People would say, "This man is like Nimrod, the greatest hunter in the world." 10He built

**10:10**
Gen 11:9
**10:11**
Mic 5:6

his kingdom in the land of Babylonia,* with the cities of Babylon, Erech, Akkad, and Calneh. 11From there he expanded his territory to Assyria,* building the cities of Nineveh, Rehoboth-ir, Calah, 12and Resen (the great city located between Nineveh and Calah).

**10:13**
Jer 46:9
**10:14**
1 Chr 1:12
**10:15**
Gen 15:20; 23:3
1 Chr 1:13
Jer 47:4
**10:16**
Gen 15:18-21

13Mizraim was the ancestor of the Ludites, Anamites, Lehabites, Naphtuhites, 14Pathrusites, Casluhites, and the Caphtorites, from whom the Philistines came.* 15Canaan's oldest son was Sidon, the ancestor of the Sidonians. Canaan was also the ancestor of the Hittites,* 16Jebusites, Amorites, Girgashites, 17Hivites, Arkites, Sinites, 18Arvadites, Zemarites, and Hamathites. The Canaanite clans eventually spread out, 19and the territory of Canaan extended from Sidon in the north to Gerar and Gaza in the south, and east as far as Sodom, Gomorrah, Admah, and Zeboiim, near Lasha.

**10:19**
Gen 14:2

**9:27** Hebrew *May he live in the tents of Shem.* **10:4** As in some Hebrew manuscripts and Greek version (see also 1 Chr 1:7); most Hebrew manuscripts read *Dodanim.* **10:9** Hebrew *a great hunter before the LORD;* also in 10:9b. **10:10** Hebrew *Shinar.* **10:11** Or *From that land Assyria went out.* **10:14** Hebrew *Casluhites, from whom the Philistines came, and Caphtorites.* Compare Jer 47:4; Amos 9:7. **10:15** Hebrew *ancestor of Heth.*

| BIBLE NATIONS DESCENDED FROM NOAH'S SONS | Shem | Ham | Japheth | |
|---|---|---|---|---|
| | Hebrews | Canaanites | Greeks | Shem's descendants were called Semites. Abraham, David, and Jesus descended from Shem. Ham's descendants settled in Canaan, Egypt, and the rest of Africa. Japheth's descendants settled for the most part in Europe and Asia Minor. |
| | Chaldeans | Egyptians | Thracians | |
| | Assyrians | Philistines | Scythians | |
| | Persians | Hittites | | |
| | Arameans (Syrians) | Amorites | | |

**9:25** This verse has been wrongly used to support racial prejudice and even slavery. Noah's curse, however, wasn't directed toward any particular race, but rather at the Canaanite nation—a nation God knew would become wicked. The curse was fulfilled when the Israelites entered the Promised Land and drove the Canaanites out (see the book of Joshua).

**10:8, 9** Who was Nimrod? Not much is known about him except that he was a heroic warrior. But people with great gifts can become proud, and that is probably what happened to Nimrod. Some consider him the founder of the great, godless Babylonian Empire.

20These were the descendants of Ham, identified by clan, language, territory, and national identity.

## Descendants of Shem

21Sons were also born to Shem, the older brother of Japheth.* Shem was the ancestor of all the descendants of Eber.

22The descendants of Shem were Elam, Asshur, Arphaxad, Lud, and Aram. 23The descendants of Aram were Uz, Hul, Gether, and Mash. 24Arphaxad was the father of Shelah,* and Shelah was the father of Eber. 25Eber had two sons. The first was named Peleg (which means "division"), for during his lifetime the people of the world were divided into different language groups. His brother's name was Joktan.

26Joktan was the ancestor of Almodad, Sheleph, Hazarmaveth, Jerah, 27Hadoram, Uzal, Diklah, 28Obal, Abimael, Sheba, 29Ophir, Havilah, and Jobab. All these were descendants of Joktan. 30The territory they occupied extended from Mesha all the way to Sephar in the eastern mountains.

31These were the descendants of Shem, identified by clan, language, territory, and national identity.

## Conclusion

32These are the clans that descended from Noah's sons, arranged by nation according to their lines of descent. All the nations of the earth descended from these clans after the great flood.

### 3. The tower of Babel

**11** At one time all the people of the world spoke the same language and used the same words. 2As the people migrated to the east, they found a plain in the land of Babylonia* and settled there.

3They began saying to each other, "Let's make bricks and harden them with fire." (In this region bricks were used instead of stone, and tar was used for mortar.) 4Then they said, "Come, let's build a great city for ourselves with a tower that reaches into the sky. This will make us famous and keep us from being scattered all over the world."

5But the LORD came down to look at the city and the tower the people were building. 6"Look!" he said. "The people are united, and they all speak the same language. After this, nothing they set out to do will be impossible for them! 7Come, let's go down and confuse the people with different languages. Then they won't be able to understand each other."

8In that way, the LORD scattered them all over the world, and they stopped building the city. 9That is why the city was called Babel,* because that is where the LORD confused the people with different languages. In this way he scattered them all over the world.

**10:22**
2 Kgs 15:29
Isa 66:19

**10:23**
Job 1:1

**10:24**
Luke 3:35

**10:32**
Gen 9:19; 10:1

**11:2**
Gen 10:10; 14:1
Isa 11:11

**11:3**
Gen 14:10

**11:4**
2 Sam 8:13

**11:5**
Gen 18:21
Exod 19:11

**11:6**
Gen 9:19; 11:1

**11:7**
Gen 1:26

**11:8**
Gen 9:19

**11:9**
Gen 10:10

**10:21** Or *Shem, whose older brother was Japheth.* **10:24** Greek version reads *Arphaxad was the father of Cainan, Cainan was the father of Shelah.* Compare Luke 3:36. **11:2** Hebrew *Shinar.* **11:9** Or *Babylon. Babel* sounds like a Hebrew term that means "confusion."

**THE TOWER OF BABEL** The plain between the Tigris and Euphrates Rivers offered a perfect location for the city and tower "that reaches into the sky."

**11:3** The brick used to build this tower was man made and not as hard as stone.

**11:3, 4** The tower of Babel was most likely a ziggurat, a common structure in Babylonia at this time. Most often built as temples, ziggurats looked like pyramids with steps or ramps leading up the sides. Ziggurats stood as high as 300 feet and were often just as wide; thus they were the focal point of the city. The people in this story built their tower as a monument to their own greatness, something for the whole world to see.

**11:4** The tower of Babel was a great human achievement, a wonder of the world. But it was a monument to the people themselves rather than to God. We may build monuments to ourselves (expensive clothes, big house, fancy car, important job) to call attention to our achievements. These may not be wrong in themselves, but when we use them to give us identity and self-worth, they take God's place in our lives. We are free to develop in many areas, but we are not free to think we have replaced God. What "towers" have you built in your life?

## From Shem to Abram

**11:10**
Gen 10:22-25
Luke 3:36

¹⁰This is the account of Shem's family.

Two years after the great flood, when Shem was 100 years old, he became the father of* Arphaxad. ¹¹After the birth of* Arphaxad, Shem lived another 500 years and had other sons and daughters.

**11:12**
Luke 3:36

**11:13**
1 Chr 1:17

¹²When Arphaxad was 35 years old, he became the father of Shelah. ¹³After the birth of Shelah, Arphaxad lived another 403 years and had other sons and daughters.*

**11:14**
Luke 3:35

¹⁴When Shelah was 30 years old, he became the father of Eber. ¹⁵After the birth of Eber, Shelah lived another 403 years and had other sons and daughters.

**11:16**
Luke 3:35

¹⁶When Eber was 34 years old, he became the father of Peleg. ¹⁷After the birth of Peleg, Eber lived another 430 years and had other sons and daughters.

**11:18**
Luke 3:35

¹⁸When Peleg was 30 years old, he became the father of Reu. ¹⁹After the birth of Reu, Peleg lived another 209 years and had other sons and daughters.

**11:20**
Luke 3:35

²⁰When Reu was 32 years old, he became the father of Serug. ²¹After the birth of Serug, Reu lived another 207 years and had other sons and daughters.

**11:22**
Luke 3:34

²²When Serug was 30 years old, he became the father of Nahor. ²³After the birth of Nahor, Serug lived another 200 years and had other sons and daughters.

**11:24**
Josh 24:2
Luke 3:34

²⁴When Nahor was 29 years old, he became the father of Terah. ²⁵After the birth of Terah, Nahor lived another 119 years and had other sons and daughters.

**11:26**
Gen 22:20
1 Chr 1:26-27
Luke 3:34

²⁶After Terah was 70 years old, he became the father of Abram, Nahor, and Haran.

## The Family of Terah

²⁷This is the account of Terah's family. Terah was the father of Abram, Nahor, and Haran; and Haran was the father of Lot. ²⁸But Haran died in Ur of the Chaldeans, the land of his birth, while his father, Terah, was still living.

**11:29**
Gen 17:15;
20:11-12; 22:20

²⁹Meanwhile, Abram and Nahor both married. The name of Abram's wife was Sarai, and the name of Nahor's wife was Milcah. (Milcah and her sister Iscah were daughters of Nahor's brother Haran.)

**11:30**
Gen 16:1; 18:11;
25:21
1 Sam 1:5
Luke 1:7

³⁰But Sarai was unable to become pregnant and had no children.

**11:31**
Gen 27:43
Josh 24:2
Acts 7:4

³¹One day Terah took his son Abram, his daughter-in-law Sarai (his son Abram's wife), and his grandson Lot (his son Haran's child) and moved away from Ur of the Chaldeans. He was headed for the land of Canaan, but they stopped at Haran and settled there. ³²Terah lived for 205 years* and died while still in Haran.

## D. THE STORY OF ABRAHAM (12:1—25:18)

Despite God's swift judgment of sin, most people ignored him and continued to sin. But a handful of people really tried to follow him. One of these was Abraham. God appeared to Abraham one day and promised to make his descendants into a great nation. Abram's

**11:10** Or *the ancestor of;* also in 11:12, 14, 16, 18, 20, 22, 24.   **11:11** Or *the birth of this ancestor of;* also in 11:13, 15, 17, 19, 21, 23, 25.   **11:12-13** Greek version reads ¹²*When Arphaxad was 135 years old, he became the father of Cainan.* ¹³*After the birth of Cainan, Arphaxad lived another 430 years and had other sons and daughters, and then he died. When Cainan was 130 years old, he became the father of Shelah. After the birth of Shelah, Cainan lived another 330 years and had other sons and daughters, and then he died.* Compare Luke 3:35-36.   **11:32** Some ancient versions read *145 years;* compare 11:26 and 12:4.

---

**11:10-27** Here and in 10:22-31 appears a list of Shem's descendants, who were blessed (9:26). Because of that blessing, from Shem's line came Abram and the entire Jewish nation, which would eventually conquer the land of Canaan in the days of Joshua.

**11:27-28** Abram grew up in Ur of the Chaldeans, an important city in the ancient world. Archaeologists have discovered evidence of a flourishing civilization there in Abram's day. The city carried on an extensive trade with its neighbors and had a vast library. Growing up in Ur, Abram was probably well educated.

**11:31** Terah left Ur to go to Canaan but settled in Haran instead. Why did he stop halfway? It may have been his health, the climate, or even fear. But this did not change Abram's calling ("the LORD had said to Abram," 12:1). He had respect for his father's leadership, but when Terah died, Abram moved on to Canaan. God's will may come in stages. Just as the time in Haran was a transition period for Abram, so God may give us transition periods and times of waiting to help us depend on him and trust his timing. If we patiently do his will during the transition times, we will be better prepared to serve him as we should when he calls us.

**ABRAM'S JOURNEY TO CANAAN** Abram, Sarai, and Lot traveled from Ur of the Chaldeans to Canaan by way of Haran. Though indirect, this route followed the rivers rather than attempting to cross the vast desert.

part of the agreement was to obey God. Through sharp testing and an incident that almost destroyed his family, Abraham remained faithful to God. Throughout this section we discover how to live a life of faith.

## 1. God promises a nation to Abram

### The Call of Abram

**12** The LORD had said to Abram, "Leave your native country, your relatives, and your father's family, and go to the land that I will show you. [2]I will make you into a great nation. I will bless you and make you famous, and you will be a blessing to others. [3]I will bless those who bless you and curse those who treat you with contempt. All the families on earth will be blessed through you."

[4]So Abram departed as the LORD had instructed, and Lot went with him. Abram was seventy-five years old when he left Haran. [5]He took his wife, Sarai, his nephew Lot, and all his wealth—his livestock and all the people he had taken into his household at Haran—and headed for the land of Canaan. When they arrived in Canaan, [6]Abram traveled through the land as far as Shechem. There he set up camp beside the oak of Moreh. At that time, the area was inhabited by Canaanites.

[7]Then the LORD appeared to Abram and said, "I will give this land to your descendants.*" And Abram built an altar there and dedicated it to the LORD, who had appeared to him. [8]After that, Abram traveled south and set up camp in the hill country, with Bethel to the west and Ai to the east. There he built another altar and dedicated it to the LORD, and he worshiped the LORD. [9]Then Abram continued traveling south by stages toward the Negev.

### Abram and Sarai in Egypt

[10]At that time a severe famine struck the land of Canaan, forcing Abram to go down to Egypt, where he lived as a foreigner. [11]As he was approaching the border of Egypt, Abram

**12:7** Hebrew *seed.*

**12:1**
Gen 15:7
†Acts 7:3
Heb 11:8

**12:2**
Gen 13:16; 15:5;
17:4; 18:18; 22:17
Zech 8:13

**12:3**
Gen 22:18; 26:4
Exod 23:22
†Gal 3:8

**12:6**
Gen 33:18; 35:4
Deut 11:30

**12:7**
Gen 13:15
†Gal 3:16

**12:8**
Gen 4:26; 8:20;
22:9

**12:9**
Gen 13:1; 20:1

**12:10**
Gen 26:1; 42:5

**12:11**
Gen 29:17

---

**12:1-3** When God called him, Abram moved out in faith from Ur to Haran and finally to Canaan. God then established a covenant with Abram, telling him that he would found a great nation. Not only would this nation be blessed, God said, but the other nations of the earth would be blessed through Abram's descendants. Israel, the nation that would come from Abram, was to follow God and influence those with whom it came in contact. Through Abram's family tree, Jesus Christ was born to save humanity. Through Christ, people can have a personal relationship with God and be blessed beyond measure.

**12:2** God promised to bless Abram and make him famous, but God had one condition: Abram had to do what God wanted him to do. This meant leaving his home and friends and traveling to a new land where God promised to build a great nation from

Abram's family. Abram obeyed, walking away from his home for God's promise of even greater blessings in the future. God may be trying to lead you to a place of greater service and usefulness for him. Don't let the comfort and security of your present position make you miss God's plan for you.

**12:5** God planned to develop a nation of people he would call his own. He called Abram from the godless, self-centered city of Ur to a fertile region called Canaan, where a God-centered, moral nation could be established. Though small in dimension, the land of Canaan was the focal point for most of the history of Israel as well as for the rise of Christianity. This small land given to one man, Abram, has had a tremendous impact on world history.

**12:7** Abram built an altar to the Lord. Altars were used in many religions, but for God's people, altars were more than places of sacrifice. For them, altars symbolized communion with God and commemorated notable encounters with him. Built of rough stones and earth, altars often remained in place for years as continual reminders of God's protection and promises.

Abram regularly built altars to God for two reasons: (1) for prayer and worship, and (2) as reminders of God's promise to bless him. Abram couldn't survive spiritually without regularly renewing his love and loyalty to God. Building altars helped Abram remember that God was at the center of his life. Regular worship helps us remember what God desires and motivates us to obey him.

**12:10** When famine struck, Abram went to Egypt where there was food. Why would God allow a famine in the land where he had just called Abram? This was a test of Abram's faith, and Abram passed. He didn't question God's leading when facing this difficulty. Many believers find that when they determine to follow God, they immediately encounter great obstacles. The next time you face such a test, don't try to second-guess what God is doing. Use the intelligence God gave you, as Abram did when he temporarily moved to Egypt, and wait for new opportunities.

**12:11-13** Abram, acting out of fear, asked Sarai to tell a half-truth by saying she was his sister. She *was* his half sister (see 20:12), but she was also his wife.

**ABRAM'S JOURNEY TO EGYPT**
A famine could cause the loss of a shepherd's wealth. So Abram traveled through the Negev to Egypt, where there was plenty of food and good land for his flocks.

N

Mediterranean Sea

CANAAN
Bethel • Ai
**Jerusalem**•
(Salem)

EGYPT     THE NEGEV

Nile River

Mount Sinai

0   50 Mi.
0   50 Km.      Red Sea

| | |
|---|---|
| **12:12**<br>Gen 20:11 | said to his wife, Sarai, "Look, you are a very beautiful woman. ¹²When the Egyptians see you, they will say, 'This is his wife. Let's kill him; then we can have her!' ¹³So please tell them you are my sister. Then they will spare my life and treat me well because of their interest in you." |
| | ¹⁴And sure enough, when Abram arrived in Egypt, everyone noticed Sarai's beauty. |
| **12:16**<br>Gen 20:14; 24:35 | ¹⁵When the palace officials saw her, they sang her praises to Pharaoh, their king, and Sarai was taken into his palace. ¹⁶Then Pharaoh gave Abram many gifts because of her—sheep, goats, cattle, male and female donkeys, male and female servants, and camels. |
| **12:17**<br>1 Chr 16:21<br>Ps 105:14 | ¹⁷But the LORD sent terrible plagues upon Pharaoh and his household because of Sarai, Abram's wife. ¹⁸So Pharaoh summoned Abram and accused him sharply. "What have you done to me?" he demanded. "Why didn't you tell me she was your wife? ¹⁹Why did you say, |
| **12:18**<br>Gen 20:9-10 | 'She is my sister,' and allow me to take her as my wife? Now then, here is your wife. Take her |
| **12:19**<br>Gen 20:5; 26:9 | and get out of here!" ²⁰Pharaoh ordered some of his men to escort them, and he sent Abram out of the country, along with his wife and all his possessions. |
| **13:1**<br>Gen 12:9 | **2. Abram and Lot** |
| **13:2**<br>Gen 12:5 | *Abram and Lot Separate* |
| **13:3**<br>Gen 12:8-9 | **13** So Abram left Egypt and traveled north into the Negev, along with his wife and Lot and all that they owned. ²(Abram was very rich in livestock, silver, and gold.) ³From |

Some people simply drift through life. Their choices, when they can muster the will to choose, tend to follow the course of least resistance. Lot, Abram's nephew, was such a person.

While still young, Lot lost his father. Although this must have been hard on him, he was not left without strong role models in his grandfather Terah and his uncle Abram, who raised him. Still, Lot did not develop their sense of purpose. Throughout his life he was so caught up in the present moment that he seemed incapable of seeing the consequences of his actions. It is hard to imagine what his life would have been like without Abram's careful attention and God's intervention.

By the time Lot drifted out of the picture, his life had taken an ugly turn. He had so blended into the sinful culture of his day that he did not want to leave it. His drifting finally took him in a very specific direction—destruction. Then his daughters committed incest with him.

Lot, however, is called "righteous" in the New Testament (2 Peter 2:7, 8). Ruth, a descendant of Moab, was an ancestor of Jesus, even though Moab was born as a result of Lot's incestuous relationship with one of his daughters. Lot's story gives hope to us that God forgives and often brings about positive circumstances from evil.

What is the direction of your life? Are you headed toward God or away from him? If you're a drifter, the choice for God may seem difficult, but it is the one choice that puts all other choices in a different light.

| | |
|---|---|
| **Strengths and accomplishments** | • He was a successful businessman<br>• Peter calls him a righteous man (2 Peter 2:7, 8) |
| **Weaknesses and mistakes** | • When faced with decisions, he tended to put off deciding, then chose the easiest course of action<br>• When given a choice, his first reaction was to think of himself |
| **Lesson from his life** | • God wants us to do more than drift through life; he wants us to be an influence for him |
| **Vital statistics** | • Where: Lived first in Ur of the Chaldeans, then moved to Canaan with Abram. Eventually he moved to the wicked city of Sodom<br>• Occupation: Wealthy sheep and cattle rancher; also a city official<br>• Relatives: Father: Haran. Adopted by Abram when his father died. The name of his wife, who turned into a pillar of salt, is not mentioned |
| **Key verse** | "When Lot still hesitated, the angels seized his hand and the hands of his wife and two daughters and rushed them to safety outside the city, for the LORD was merciful" (Genesis 19:16). |

Lot's story is told in Genesis 11–14; 19. He is also mentioned in Deuteronomy 2:9; Luke 17:28-32; 2 Peter 2:7, 8.

Abram's intent was to deceive the Egyptians. He feared that if they knew the truth, they would kill him to get Sarai. She would have been a desirable addition to Pharaoh's harem because of her wealth, beauty, and potential for political alliance. As Sarai's brother, Abram would have been given a place of honor. As her husband, however, his life would be in danger because Sarai could not enter Pharaoh's harem unless Abram was dead. So Abram lost faith in God's protection, even after all God had promised him, and

told a half-truth. This shows how lying compounds the effects of sin. When he lied, Abram's problems multiplied.

**13:1, 2** In Abram's day, sheep and cattle owners could acquire great wealth. Abram's wealth not only included silver and gold, but also livestock. These animals were a valuable commodity used for food, clothing, tent material, and sacrifices. They were often traded for other goods and services. Abram was able to watch his wealth grow and multiply daily.

the Negev, they continued traveling by stages toward Bethel, and they pitched their tents between Bethel and Ai, where they had camped before. 4This was the same place where Abram had built the altar, and there he worshiped the LORD again.

5Lot, who was traveling with Abram, had also become very wealthy with flocks of sheep and goats, herds of cattle, and many tents. 6But the land could not support both Abram and Lot with all their flocks and herds living so close together. 7So disputes broke out between the herdsmen of Abram and Lot. (At that time Canaanites and Perizzites were also living in the land.)

8Finally Abram said to Lot, "Let's not allow this conflict to come between us or our herdsmen. After all, we are close relatives! 9The whole countryside is open to you. Take your choice of any section of the land you want, and we will separate. If you want the land to the left, then I'll take the land on the right. If you prefer the land on the right, then I'll go to the left."

10Lot took a long look at the fertile plains of the Jordan Valley in the direction of Zoar. The whole area was well watered everywhere, like the garden of the LORD or the beautiful land of Egypt. (This was before the LORD destroyed Sodom and Gomorrah.) 11Lot chose for himself the whole Jordan Valley to the east of them. He went there with his flocks and servants and parted company with his uncle Abram. 12So Abram settled in the land of Canaan, and Lot moved his tents to a place near Sodom and settled among the cities of the plain. 13But the people of this area were extremely wicked and constantly sinned against the LORD.

14After Lot had gone, the LORD said to Abram, "Look as far as you can see in every direction—north and south, east and west. 15I am giving all this land, as far as you can see, to you and your descendants* as a permanent possession. 16And I will give you so many descendants that, like the dust of the earth, they cannot be counted! 17Go and walk through the land in every direction, for I am giving it to you."

18So Abram moved his camp to Hebron and settled near the oak grove belonging to Mamre. There he built another altar to the LORD.

### Abram Rescues Lot

**14** About this time war broke out in the region. King Amraphel of Babylonia,* King Arioch of Ellasar, King Kedorlaomer of Elam, and King Tidal of Goiim 2fought against King Bera of Sodom, King Birsha of Gomorrah, King Shinab of Admah, King Shemeber of Zeboiim, and the king of Bela (also called Zoar).

3This second group of kings joined forces in Siddim Valley (that is, the valley of the Dead Sea*). 4For twelve years they had been subject to King Kedorlaomer, but in the thirteenth year they rebelled against him.

**13:15** Hebrew *seed;* also in 13:16.   **14:1** Hebrew *Shinar;* also in 14:9.   **14:3** Hebrew *Salt Sea.*

**13:5** Gen 12:5

**13:6** Gen 12:5; 36:7

**13:7** Gen 12:6; 26:20

**13:8** Prov 15:18; 20:3

**13:9** Gen 20:15

**13:10** Gen 2:8-10

**13:13** Gen 18:20; Num 32:23; Isa 1:10; 3:9; 2 Pet 2:8

**13:14** Gen 28:14; Deut 3:27; 34:1-4

**13:15** †Gal 3:16; Gen 12:2, 7; 15:18; 17:7-8

**13:16** Num 23:10

**13:17** Num 13:17-25

**13:18** Gen 14:13; 18:1

**14:1** Gen 10:10; 11:2

**14:2** Gen 10:19; 13:10; Deut 29:23

**14:3** Num 34:3, 12; Deut 3:17; Josh 3:16

---

**13:5-9** Facing a potential conflict with his nephew Lot, Abram took the initiative in settling the dispute. He gave Lot first choice, even though Abram, being older, had the right to choose first. Abram also showed a willingness to risk being cheated. Abram's example shows us how to respond to difficult family situations: (1) Take the initiative in resolving conflicts; (2) let others have first choice, even if that means not getting what we want; (3) put family peace above personal desires.

**13:7, 8** Surrounded by hostile neighbors, the herdsmen of Abram and Lot should have pulled together. Instead, they let petty jealousy tear them apart. Similar situations exist today. Christians often bicker while Satan is at work all around them.

Rivalries, arguments, and disagreements among believers can be destructive in three ways: (1) They damage goodwill, trust, and peace—the foundations of good human relations; (2) they hamper progress toward important goals; (3) they make us self-centered rather than love-centered. Jesus understood how destructive arguments among brothers could be. In his final prayer before being betrayed and arrested, Jesus asked God that his followers be "one" (John 17:21).

**13:10, 11** Lot's character is revealed by his choices. He took the best share of the land even though it meant living near Sodom, a city known for its sin. He was greedy, wanting the best for himself, without thinking about his uncle Abram's needs or what was fair.

Life presents a series of choices. We, too, can choose the best while ignoring the needs and feelings of others. But this kind of choice, as Lot's life shows, leads to problems. When we stop making choices in God's direction, our only option is to make choices in the wrong direction.

**13:12, 13** Good pasture and available water seemed like a wise choice to Lot at first. But he failed to recognize that wicked Sodom could provide temptations strong enough to destroy his family. Have you chosen to live or work in a "Sodom"? Even though you may be strong enough to resist the temptations, other members of your family may not. While God commands us to reach people in the "Sodom" near us, we must be careful not to become like the very people we are trying to reach.

**14:4-16** Who was Kedorlaomer, and why was he important? In Abram's time, most cities had their own kings. Wars and rivalries among kings were common. A conquered city paid tribute to the victorious king. Nothing is known about Kedorlaomer except what we read in the Bible, but apparently he was quite powerful. Five cities including Sodom had paid tribute to him for 12 years. The five cities formed an alliance and rebelled by withholding tribute. Kedorlaomer reacted swiftly and reconquered them all. When he defeated Sodom, he captured Lot, his family, and his possessions. Abram, with only 318 men, chased Kedorlaomer's army and attacked him near Damascus. With God's help, he defeated them and recovered Lot, his family, and their possessions.

**14:5**
Gen 15:20
Deut 1:4; 2:10, 20;
3:11
Josh 13:19

**14:7**
Gen 16:14; 20:1
Num 13:26
Deut 1:4
2 Chr 20:2

**14:12**
Gen 11:27

**14:13**
Gen 10:16; 13:18;
39:14

**14:14**
Gen 12:5
Deut 34:1

**14:15**
Gen 15:2

**14:17**
2 Sam 18:18

**14:18**
Heb 5:6, 10; 7:1

**14:19**
Gen 27:25; 48:9
Mark 10:16

⁵One year later Kedorlaomer and his allies arrived and defeated the Rephaites at Ashte-roth-karnaim, the Zuzites at Ham, the Emites at Shaveh-kiriathaim, ⁶and the Horites at Mount Seir, as far as El-paran at the edge of the wilderness. ⁷Then they turned back and came to En-mishpat (now called Kadesh) and conquered all the territory of the Amalekites, and also the Amorites living in Hazazon-tamar.

⁸Then the rebel kings of Sodom, Gomorrah, Admah, Zeboiim, and Bela (also called Zoar) prepared for battle in the valley of the Dead Sea.* ⁹They fought against King Kedorlaomer of Elam, King Tidal of Goiim, King Amraphel of Babylonia, and King Arioch of Ellasar—four kings against five. ¹⁰As it happened, the valley of the Dead Sea was filled with tar pits. And as the army of the kings of Sodom and Gomorrah fled, some fell into the tar pits, while the rest escaped into the mountains. ¹¹The victorious invaders then plundered Sodom and Gomor-rah and headed for home, taking with them all the spoils of war and the food supplies. ¹²They also captured Lot—Abram's nephew who lived in Sodom—and carried off every-thing he owned.

¹³But one of Lot's men escaped and reported everything to Abram the Hebrew, who was living near the oak grove belonging to Mamre the Amorite. Mamre and his relatives, Eshcol and Aner, were Abram's allies.

¹⁴When Abram heard that his nephew Lot had been captured, he mobilized the 318 trained men who had been born into his household. Then he pursued Kedorlaomer's army until he caught up with them at Dan. ¹⁵There he divided his men and attacked during the night. Kedorlaomer's army fled, but Abram chased them as far as Hobah, north of Damas-cus. ¹⁶Abram recovered all the goods that had been taken, and he brought back his nephew Lot with his possessions and all the women and other captives.

### Melchizedek Blesses Abram

¹⁷After Abram returned from his victory over Kedorlaomer and all his allies, the king of Sod-om went out to meet him in the valley of Shaveh (that is, the King's Valley).

¹⁸And Melchizedek, the king of Salem and a priest of God Most High,* brought Abram some bread and wine. ¹⁹Melchizedek blessed Abram with this blessing:

"Blessed be Abram by God Most High,
    Creator of heaven and earth.

**14:8** Hebrew *Siddim Valley* (see 14:3); also in 14:10.   **14:18** Hebrew *El-Elyon;* also in 14:19, 20, 22.

---

**14:12** Lot's greedy desire for the best of everything led him into sinful surroundings. His burning desire for possessions and success cost him his freedom and enjoyment. As a captive to Kedorlaomer, he faced torture, slavery, or death. In much the same way, we can be enticed into doing things or going places we shouldn't. The prosperity we long for is captivating; it can both entice us and enslave us if our motives are not in line with God's desires.

**14:14-16** These incidents portray two of Abram's characteristics: (1) He had courage that came from God; facing a powerful foe, he attacked. (2) He was prepared; he had taken time to train his men for a potential conflict. We never know when we will be called upon to complete difficult tasks. Like Abram, we should prepare for those times and take courage from God when they come.

**14:14-16** When Abram learned that Lot was a captive, he immediately tried to rescue his nephew. It would have been easier and safer not to become involved. But with Lot in serious trouble, Abram acted at once. Sometimes we must get involved in a messy or painful situation in order to help others. We should be willing to act immediately when others need our help.

**14:18** Who was Melchizedek? He was obviously a God-fearing man, for his name means "king of righteousness," and king of Salem means "king of peace." He was a "priest of God Most High" (Hebrews 7:1, 2). He recognized God as Creator of heaven and earth. What else is known about him? Four main theories have been suggested: (1) Melchizedek was a respected king of that region. Abram was simply showing him the respect he deserved. (2) The name Melchizedek may have been a standing title for all the kings of Salem. (3) Melchizedek was a type of Christ (Hebrews

7:3). A type is an Old Testament event or teaching that is so closely related to what Christ did that it illustrates a lesson about Christ. (4) Melchizedek was the appearance on earth of the preincarnate Christ in a temporary bodily form.

**LOT'S RESCUE**
Having conquered Sodom, Kedor-laomer left for his home country, taking many captives with him. Abram learned what had happened and chased Kedor-laomer past Dan and beyond Damascus. There he defeated the king and rescued the captives, among them Lot.

20 And blessed be God Most High,
      who has defeated your enemies for you."

14:20
Gen 9:26; 24:27
†Heb 7:1-2

Then Abram gave Melchizedek a tenth of all the goods he had recovered.

21The king of Sodom said to Abram, "Give back my people who were captured. But you may keep for yourself all the goods you have recovered."

22Abram replied to the king of Sodom, "I solemnly swear to the LORD, God Most High, Creator of heaven and earth, 23that I will not take so much as a single thread or sandal thong from what belongs to you. Otherwise you might say, 'I am the one who made Abram rich.' 24I will accept only what my young warriors have already eaten, and I request that you give a fair share of the goods to my allies—Aner, Eshcol, and Mamre."

14:22
Gen 1:1
14:23
2 Kgs 5:16
14:24
Gen 14:13

## 3. God promises a son to Abram
*The LORD's Covenant Promise to Abram*

**15** Some time later, the LORD spoke to Abram in a vision and said to him, "Do not be afraid, Abram, for I will protect you, and your reward will be great."

15:1
Gen 21:17; 26:24
Deut 33:29
Ps 3:3

2But Abram replied, "O Sovereign LORD, what good are all your blessings when I don't even have a son? Since you've given me no children, Eliezer of Damascus, a servant in my household, will inherit all my wealth. 3You have given me no descendants of my own, so one of my servants will be my heir."

4Then the LORD said to him, "No, your servant will not be your heir, for you will have a son of your own who will be your heir." 5Then the LORD took Abram outside and said to him, "Look up into the sky and count the stars if you can. That's how many descendants you will have!"

15:4
†Gal 4:28
15:5
Gen 12:2; 22:17;
32:13
†Rom 4:18

6And Abram believed the LORD, and the LORD counted him as righteous because of his faith.

15:6
Ps 106:31
†Rom 4:3, 9, 22
†Gal 3:6

7Then the LORD told him, "I am the LORD who brought you out of Ur of the Chaldeans to give you this land as your possession."

15:7
Gen 12:1; 13:17
Acts 7:2-4

8But Abram replied, "O Sovereign LORD, how can I be sure that I will actually possess it?"

15:8
Luke 1:18

9The LORD told him, "Bring me a three-year-old heifer, a three-year-old female goat, a three-year-old ram, a turtledove, and a young pigeon." 10So Abram presented all these to him and killed them. Then he cut each animal down the middle and laid the halves side by side; he did not, however, cut the birds in half. 11Some vultures swooped down to eat the carcasses, but Abram chased them away.

15:9
Lev 1:14
15:12
Gen 2:21; 28:11

12As the sun was going down, Abram fell into a deep sleep, and a terrifying darkness came down over him. 13Then the LORD said to Abram, "You can be sure that your descendants will be strangers in a foreign land, where they will be oppressed as slaves for 400 years. 14But I will punish the nation that enslaves them, and in the end they will come away

15:13
Exod 12:40
†Acts 7:6
Gal 3:17
15:14
Exod 6:5

---

**14:20ff** Abram gave a tenth of the goods he recovered to Melchizedek. Even in some pagan religions, it was traditional to give a tenth of one's earnings to the gods. Abram followed accepted tradition; however, he refused to take any of the recovered goods from the king of Sodom. Even though this huge amount would significantly increase what he could have given to God, he chose to reject it for more important reasons—he didn't want the ungodly king of Sodom to say, "I am the one who made Abram rich." Instead, Abram wanted him to say, "God has made Abram rich." In this case, accepting the gifts would have focused everyone's attention on Abram or the king of Sodom rather than on God, the giver of victory. When people look at us, they need to see what God has accomplished in our lives.

**15:1** Why would Abram be afraid? Perhaps he feared revenge from the kings he had just defeated (14:15). God gave him two good reasons for courage: (1) He promised to protect Abram, and (2) he promised a great reward to Abram. When you fear what lies ahead, remember that God will stay with you through difficult times and that he has promised you great blessings.

**15:2, 3** Eliezer was Abram's most trusted servant, acting as household administrator. According to custom, if Abram were to die without a son, his eldest servant would become his heir. Although Abram loved his servant, he wanted a son to carry on the family line.

**15:5** Abram wasn't promised wealth or fame; he already had that. Instead, God promised descendants like the stars in the sky or the grains of sand on the seashore (22:17), too numerous to count. To appreciate the vast number of stars scattered through the sky, you need to be, like Abram, away from any distractions. Or pick up a handful of sand and try to count the grains—it can't be done! Just when Abram was despairing of ever having an heir, God promised descendants too numerous to imagine. God's blessings are beyond our imagination!

**15:6** Although Abram had been demonstrating his faith through his actions, it was his belief in the Lord, not his actions, that made Abram right with God (Romans 4:1-5). We, too, can have a right relationship with God by trusting him. Our outward actions—church attendance, prayer, good deeds—will not by themselves make us right with God. A right relationship is based on faith—the heartfelt inner confidence that God is who he says he is and does what he says he will do. Right actions will follow naturally as by-products.

**15:8** Abram was looking for confirmation and assurance that he was doing God's will. We also want assurance when we ask for guidance. But we can know for sure that what we are doing is right if we do what the Bible says. Abram didn't have the Bible—we do.

**15:13, 14** The book of Exodus tells the story of the enslavement and miraculous deliverance of Abram's descendants.

**15:15**
Gen 25:8

**15:16**
Exod 12:40

**15:17**
Jer 34:18-19

**15:18**
Num 34:1-15
Deut 1:7-8

**15:19**
Num 24:21

with great wealth. 15 (As for you, you will die in peace and be buried at a ripe old age.) 16After four generations your descendants will return here to this land, for the sins of the Amorites do not yet warrant their destruction."

17After the sun went down and darkness fell, Abram saw a smoking firepot and a flaming torch pass between the halves of the carcasses. 18So the Lord made a covenant with Abram that day and said, "I have given this land to your descendants, all the way from the border of Egypt* to the great Euphrates River—19the land now occupied by the Kenites, Kenizzites, Kadmonites, 20Hittites, Perizzites, Rephaites, 21Amorites, Canaanites, Girgashites, and Jebusites."

**15:18** Hebrew *the river of Egypt*, referring either to an eastern branch of the Nile River or to the Brook of Egypt in the Sinai (see Num 34:5).

**MELCHIZEDEK**

Do you like a good mystery? History is full of them! They usually involve people. One of the most mysterious people in the Bible is the king of peace, Melchizedek. He appeared one day in the life of Abraham (then Abram) and was never heard from again. What happened that day, however, was to be remembered throughout history and eventually became a subject of a New Testament letter (Hebrews).

This meeting between Abram and Melchizedek was most unusual. Although the two men were strangers and foreigners to each other, they shared a most important characteristic: Both worshiped and served the one God who made heaven and earth.

This was a great moment of triumph for Abram. He had just defeated an army and regained the freedom of a large group of captives. If there was any doubt in his mind about whose victory it was, Melchizedek set the record straight by reminding Abram, "And blessed be God Most High, who has defeated your enemies for you" (Genesis 14:20). Abram recognized that this man worshiped the same God he did.

Melchizedek was one of a small group of God-honoring people throughout the Old Testament who came in contact with the Jews (Israelites) but were not Jews themselves. This indicates that the requirement to be a follower of God is not genetic but is based on faithfully obeying his teachings and recognizing his greatness.

Do you let God speak to you through other people? In evaluating others, do you consider God's impact on their lives? Are you aware of the similarities between yourself and others who worship God, even if their form of worship is quite different from yours? Do you know the God of the Bible well enough to know if you truly worship him? Allow Melchizedek, Abraham, David, and Jesus, along with many other persons in the Bible, to show you this great God, Creator of heaven and earth. He wants you to know how much he loves you; he wants you to know him personally.

| | |
|---|---|
| **Strengths and accomplishments** | • The first priest/king of Scripture—a leader with a heart tuned to God<br>• Good at encouraging others to serve God wholeheartedly<br>• A man whose character reflected his love for God<br>• A person in the Old Testament who reminds us of Jesus and who some believe really was Jesus |
| **Lesson from his life** | • Live for God and you're likely to be at the right place at the right time. Examine your heart: To whom or what is your greatest loyalty? If you can honestly answer *God*, you are living for him |
| **Vital statistics** | • Where: Ruled in Salem, site of the future Jerusalem<br>• Occupation: King of Salem and priest of God Most High |
| **Key verses** | "This Melchizedek was king of the city of Salem and also a priest of God Most High. When Abraham was returning home after winning a great battle against the kings, Melchizedek met him and blessed him. . . . Consider then how great this Melchizedek was. Even Abraham, the great patriarch of Israel, recognized this by giving him a tenth of what he had taken in battle" (Hebrews 7:1, 4). |

Melchizedek's story is told in Genesis 14:17-20. He is also mentioned in Psalm 110:4; Hebrews 5–7.

**15:16** The Amorites were one of the nations living in Canaan, the land God promised Abram. God knew the people would grow more wicked and would someday need to be punished. Part of that punishment would involve taking away their land and giving it to Abram's descendants. God in his mercy was giving the Amorites plenty of time to repent, but he already knew they would not. At the right time, they would have to be punished. Everything God does is true to his character. He is merciful, knows all, and acts justly—and his timing is perfect.

**15:17** Why did God send this strange vision to Abram? God's

covenant with Abram was serious business. It represented an incredible promise from God and a huge responsibility for Abram. To confirm his promise, God gave Abram a sign—the smoking firepot and a flaming torch. The fire and smoke suggest God's holiness, his zeal for righteousness, and his judgment on all the nations. God took the initiative, gave the confirmation, and followed through on his promises. God's passing through the pieces was a visible assurance to Abram that the covenant God had made was real.

## The Birth of Ishmael

**16** Now Sarai, Abram's wife, had not been able to bear children for him. But she had an Egyptian servant named Hagar. ²So Sarai said to Abram, "The LORD has prevented me from having children. Go and sleep with my servant. Perhaps I can have children through her." And Abram agreed with Sarai's proposal. ³So Sarai, Abram's wife, took Hagar the Egyptian servant and gave her to Abram as a wife. (This happened ten years after Abram had settled in the land of Canaan.)

⁴So Abram had sexual relations with Hagar, and she became pregnant. But when Hagar knew she was pregnant, she began to treat her mistress, Sarai, with contempt. ⁵Then Sarai said to Abram, "This is all your fault! I put my servant into your arms, but now that she's pregnant she treats me with contempt. The LORD will show who's wrong—you or me!"

⁶Abram replied, "Look, she is your servant, so deal with her as you see fit." Then Sarai treated Hagar so harshly that she finally ran away.

⁷The angel of the LORD found Hagar beside a spring of water in the wilderness, along the road to Shur. ⁸The angel said to her, "Hagar, Sarai's servant, where have you come from, and where are you going?"

"I'm running away from my mistress, Sarai," she replied.

⁹The angel of the LORD said to her, "Return to your mistress, and submit to her authority." ¹⁰Then he added, "I will give you more descendants than you can count."

¹¹And the angel also said, "You are now pregnant and will give birth to a son. You are to name him Ishmael (which means 'God hears'), for the LORD has heard your cry of distress. ¹²This son of yours will be a wild man, as untamed as a wild donkey! He will raise his fist against everyone, and everyone will be against him. Yes, he will live in open hostility against all his relatives."

¹³Thereafter, Hagar used another name to refer to the LORD, who had spoken to her. She said, "You are the God who sees me."* She also said, "Have I truly seen the One who sees me?" ¹⁴So that well was named Beer-lahai-roi (which means "well of the Living One who sees me"). It can still be found between Kadesh and Bered.

¹⁵So Hagar gave Abram a son, and Abram named him Ishmael. ¹⁶Abram was eighty-six years old when Ishmael was born.

## Abram Is Named Abraham

**17** When Abram was ninety-nine years old, the LORD appeared to him and said, "I am El-Shaddai—'God Almighty.' Serve me faithfully and live a blameless life. ²I will make a covenant with you, by which I will guarantee to give you countless descendants."

16:13 Hebrew *El-roi*.

**16:1-3** Sarai gave Hagar to Abram as a substitute wife, a common practice of that time. A married woman who could not have children was shamed by her peers and was often required to give a female servant to her husband in order to produce heirs. The children born to the servant woman were considered the children of the wife. Abram was acting in line with the custom of the day, but his action showed a lack of faith that God would fulfill his promise.

**16:3** Sarai took matters into her own hands by giving Hagar to Abram. Like Abram she had trouble believing God's promise that was apparently directed specifically toward Abram and Sarai. Out of this lack of faith came a series of problems. This invariably happens when we take over for God, trying to make his promise come true through efforts that are not in line with his specific directions. In this case, time was the greatest test of Abram and Sarai's willingness to let God work in their lives. Sometimes we too must simply wait. When we ask God for something and have to wait, we can be tempted to take matters into our own hands and interfere with God's plans.

**16:5** Although Sarai arranged for Hagar to have a child by Abram, she later blamed Abram for the results. It is often easier to strike out in frustration and accuse someone else than to admit an error and ask forgiveness. (Adam and Eve did the same thing in 3:12, 13.)

**16:6** Sarai was angry with Abram, but she took it out on Hagar, and her treatment was harsh enough to cause Hagar to run away. Anger, especially when it arises from our own shortcomings, can be dangerous.

**16:8** Hagar was running away from her mistress and her problem. The angel of the Lord gave her this advice: (1) to return and face Sarai, the cause of her problem, and (2) to submit to her. Hagar needed to work on her attitude toward Sarai, no matter how justified it may have been. Running away from problems rarely solves them. It is wise to return to our problems, face them squarely, accept God's promise of help, correct our attitudes, and act as we should.

**16:13** We have watched three people make serious mistakes: (1) Sarai, who took matters into her own hands and gave her servant to Abram; (2) Abram, who went along with the plan but, when circumstances began to go wrong, refused to help solve the problem; and (3) Hagar, who ran away from the problem. In spite of this messy situation, God demonstrated his ability to work in all things for good (Romans 8:28). Sarai and Abram still received the son they so desperately wanted, and God solved Hagar's problem despite Abram's refusal to get involved. No problem is too complicated for God if you are willing to let him help you.

**17:1** The Lord told Abram, "I am El-Shaddai—'God Almighty.' Serve me faithfully and live a blameless life." God has the same message for us today. We are to obey the Lord in every respect because he is God—that is reason enough. If you don't think the benefits of obedience are worth it, consider who God is—the only one with the power and ability to meet your every need.

**17:2-8** Why did God repeat his covenant to Abram? Twice before, he had mentioned this agreement (Genesis 12 and 15).

16:1 Gen 11:30; Gal 4:24-25
16:2 Gen 30:3
16:3 Gen 12:4-5
16:4 Gen 16:15
16:5 Gen 31:53
16:7 Gen 21:17; 22:11, 15
16:9 Eph 6:5; Titus 2:9
16:10 Gen 17:20
16:11 Gen 16:15; Exod 3:7-8
16:12 Job 39:5-8
16:13 Gen 32:30
16:14 Gen 14:7
16:15 Gen 21:9; 25:12
16:16 Gen 12:4; 16:3
17:1 Gen 12:7; 28:3; 35:11; 48:3; Deut 18:13; Matt 5:48
17:2 Gen 12:2; 15:18

**17:3**
Gen 17:17; 18:2

**17:5**
Neh 9:7
†Rom 4:17

**17:6**
Gen 35:11

**17:7**
Gen 15:18
Lev 11:45; 26:12
Ps 105:8-11
†Gal 3:16

³At this, Abram fell face down on the ground. Then God said to him, ⁴"This is my covenant with you: I will make you the father of a multitude of nations! ⁵What's more, I am changing your name. It will no longer be Abram. Instead, you will be called Abraham,* for you will be the father of many nations. ⁶I will make you extremely fruitful. Your descendants will become many nations, and kings will be among them!

⁷"I will confirm my covenant with you and your descendants* after you, from generation to generation. This is the everlasting covenant: I will always be your God and the God of your descendants after you. ⁸And I will give the entire land of Canaan, where you now live

**17:5** *Abram* means "exalted father"; *Abraham* sounds like a Hebrew term that means "father of many." **17:7** Hebrew *seed*; also in 17:7b, 8, 9, 10, 19.

---

**ISHMAEL**

Have you ever wondered if you were born into the wrong family? We don't know much about how Ishmael viewed life, but that question must have haunted him at times. His life, his name, and his position were bound up in a conflict between two jealous women. Sarah (Sarai), impatient with God's timetable, had taken matters into her own hands, deciding to have a child through another woman. Hagar, servant that she was, submitted to being used this way. But her pregnancy gave birth to strong feelings of superiority toward Sarah. Into this tense atmosphere, Ishmael was born.

For 13 years Abraham thought Ishmael's birth had fulfilled God's promise. He was surprised to hear God say that the promised child would be Abraham and Sarah's very own. Sarah's pregnancy and Isaac's birth must have had a devastating impact on Ishmael. Until then he had been treated as a son and heir, but this late arrival made his future uncertain. During Isaac's weaning celebration, Sarah caught Ishmael teasing his half brother. As a result, Hagar and Ishmael were permanently expelled from Abraham's family.

Much of what happened throughout his life cannot be blamed on Ishmael. He was caught in a process much bigger than he was. However, his own actions showed that he had chosen to become part of the problem and not part of the solution. He chose to live under his circumstances rather than above them.

The choice he made is one we must all make. There are circumstances over which we have no control (heredity, for instance), but there are others that we can control (decisions we make). At the heart of the matter is the sin-oriented nature we have all inherited. It can be partly controlled, although not overcome, by human effort. In the context of history, Ishmael's life represents the mess we make when we don't try to change the things we could change. The God of the Bible has offered a solution. His answer is not control but a changed life. To have a changed life, turn to God, trust him to forgive your sinful past, and begin to change your attitude toward him and others.

| | |
|---|---|
| **Strengths and accomplishments** | • One of the first to experience the physical sign of God's covenant, circumcision<br>• Known for his ability as an archer and hunter<br>• Fathered 12 sons who became leaders of warrior tribes |
| **Weakness and mistake** | • Failed to recognize the place of his half brother, Isaac, and mocked him |
| **Lesson from his life** | • God's plans incorporate people's mistakes |
| **Vital statistics** | • Where: Canaan and Egypt<br>• Occupation: Hunter, archer, warrior<br>• Relatives: Parents: Hagar and Abraham. Half brother: Isaac. |
| **Key verses** | "But God heard the boy crying, and the angel of God called to Hagar from heaven, 'Hagar, what's wrong? Do not be afraid! God has heard the boy crying as he lies there. Go to him and comfort him, for I will make a great nation from his descendants'" (Genesis 21:17, 18). |

Ishmael's story is told in Genesis 16–17; 21:8-20; 25:12-18; 28:8, 9; 36:1-3. He is also mentioned in 1 Chronicles 1:28-31; Romans 9:7-9; Galatians 4:21-31.

---

Here, however, God was bringing it into focus and preparing to carry it out. He revealed to Abram several specific parts of his covenant: (1) God would give Abram many descendants; (2) many nations would descend from him; (3) God would maintain his covenant with Abram's descendants; (4) God would give Abram's descendants the land of Canaan.

**17:5** In the Bible, people's names were very important—a name described a person's character or experience. Therefore, shortly before the promised son was conceived, God changed Abram's name (which meant "exalted father" to Abraham (which meant "father of many"). From this point on, the Bible calls him Abraham.

**17:5-14** God was making a covenant, or contract, between himself and Abraham. The terms were simple: Abraham would obey God and circumcise all the males in his household; God's part was to give Abraham heirs, property, power, and wealth. Most contracts are even trades: We give something and, in turn, receive something of equal value. But when we become part of God's covenant family, the blessings we receive far outweigh what we must give up.

as a foreigner, to you and your descendants. It will be their possession forever, and I will be their God."

### The Mark of the Covenant

9Then God said to Abraham, "Your responsibility is to obey the terms of the covenant. You and all your descendants have this continual responsibility. 10This is the covenant that you and your descendants must keep: Each male among you must be circumcised. 11You must cut off the flesh of your foreskin as a sign of the covenant between me and you. 12From generation to generation, every male child must be circumcised on the eighth day after his birth. This applies not only to members of your family but also to the servants born in your household and the foreign-born servants whom you have purchased. 13All must be circumcised. Your bodies will bear the mark of my everlasting covenant. 14Any male who fails to be circumcised will be cut off from the covenant family for breaking the covenant."

**17:10**
Acts 7:8
**17:11**
Exod 12:48
Deut 10:16
**17:12**
Lev 12:3
Luke 1:59; 2:21
**17:14**
Exod 30:33
Lev 7:20

### Sarai Is Named Sarah

15Then God said to Abraham, "Regarding Sarai, your wife—her name will no longer be Sarai. From now on her name will be Sarah.* 16And I will bless her and give you a son from her! Yes, I will bless her richly, and she will become the mother of many nations. Kings of nations will be among her descendants."

**17:15**
Gen 17:5
**17:16**
Gen 18:10

17Then Abraham bowed down to the ground, but he laughed to himself in disbelief. "How could I become a father at the age of 100?" he thought. "And how can Sarah have a baby when she is ninety years old?" 18So Abraham said to God, "May Ishmael live under your special blessing!"

**17:17**
Gen 17:3; 18:11-13

19But God replied, "No—Sarah, your wife, will give birth to a son for you. You will name him Isaac,* and I will confirm my covenant with him and his descendants as an everlasting covenant. 20As for Ishmael, I will bless him also, just as you have asked. I will make him extremely fruitful and multiply his descendants. He will become the father of twelve princes, and I will make him a great nation. 21But my covenant will be confirmed with Isaac, who will be born to you and Sarah about this time next year." 22When God had finished speaking, he left Abraham.

**17:19**
Gen 21:2; 26:2-5
**17:20**
Gen 25:12-16
**17:21**
Gen 18:10, 14
**17:22**
Gen 18:33; 35:13

23On that very day Abraham took his son, Ishmael, and every male in his household, including those born there and those he had bought. Then he circumcised them, cutting off their foreskins, just as God had told him. 24Abraham was ninety-nine years old when he was circumcised, 25and Ishmael, his son, was thirteen. 26Both Abraham and his son, Ishmael, were circumcised on that same day, 27along with all the other men and boys of the household, whether they were born there or bought as servants. All were circumcised with him.

**17:23**
Gen 14:14
**17:24**
Rom 4:11
**17:25**
Gen 16:16

## 4. Sodom and Gomorrah
### A Son Is Promised to Sarah

**18** The LORD appeared again to Abraham near the oak grove belonging to Mamre. One day Abraham was sitting at the entrance to his tent during the hottest part of the day. 2He looked up and noticed three men standing nearby. When he saw them, he ran to meet them and welcomed them, bowing low to the ground.

**18:1**
Gen 12:7; 13:18
**18:2**
Gen 32:24
Josh 5:13
Judg 13:6-11

17:15 *Sarai* and *Sarah* both mean "princess"; the change in spelling may reflect the difference in dialect between Ur and Canaan.   17:19 *Isaac* means "he laughs."

---

**17:9, 10** Why did God require circumcision? (1) As a sign of obedience to him in all matters. (2) As a sign of belonging to his covenant people. Once circumcised, the man would be identified as one of God's chosen people (eventually the Jews) forever. (3) As a symbol of "cutting off" the old life of sin, purifying one's heart, and dedicating oneself to God. (4) Possibly as a health measure.
   Circumcision more than any other practice separated God's people from their pagan neighbors. In Abraham's day, this was essential to develop the pure worship of the one true God.

**17:17-27** How could Abraham doubt God? It seemed incredible that he and Sarah in their advanced years could have a child. Abraham, the man God considered righteous because of his faith, had trouble believing God's promise to him. Despite his doubts, however, Abraham followed God's commands (17:22-27). Even people of great faith may have doubts. When God seems to want

the impossible and you begin to doubt his leading, be like Abraham. Focus on God's commitment to fulfill his promises to you, and then continue to obey.

**17:20** God did not forget Ishmael. Although he was not to be Abraham's heir, he would also be the father of a great nation. Regardless of your circumstances, God has not forgotten you. Obey him and trust in his plan.

**18:2-5** Abraham was eager to show hospitality to these three visitors, as was Lot (19:2). In Abraham's day, a person's reputation was largely connected to his hospitality—the sharing of home and food. Even strangers were to be treated as highly honored guests. Meeting another's need for food or shelter was and still is one of the most immediate and practical ways to obey God. It is also a time-honored relationship builder. Hebrews 13:2 suggests that we, like Abraham, might actually entertain angels. This thought should be on our minds the next time we have the opportunity to meet a stranger's needs.

18:4
Gen 19:2; 24:32

18:5
Judg 6:18-19;
13:15-16

3"My lord," he said, "if it pleases you, stop here for a while. 4Rest in the shade of this tree while water is brought to wash your feet. 5And since you've honored your servant with this visit, let me prepare some food to refresh you before you continue on your journey."

"All right," they said. "Do as you have said."

6So Abraham ran back to the tent and said to Sarah, "Hurry! Get three large measures* of your best flour, knead it into dough, and bake some bread." 7Then Abraham ran out to the herd and chose a tender calf and gave it to his servant, who quickly prepared it. 8When the food was ready, Abraham took some yogurt and milk and the roasted meat, and he served it to the men. As they ate, Abraham waited on them in the shade of the trees.

9"Where is Sarah, your wife?" the visitors asked.

"She's inside the tent," Abraham replied.

18:10
†Rom 9:9

18:11
Gen 17:17

18:12
1 Pet 3:6

10Then one of them said, "I will return to you about this time next year, and your wife, Sarah, will have a son!"

Sarah was listening to this conversation from the tent. 11Abraham and Sarah were both very old by this time, and Sarah was long past the age of having children. 12So she laughed silently to herself and said, "How could a worn-out woman like me enjoy such pleasure, especially when my master—my husband—is also so old?"

13Then the LORD said to Abraham, "Why did Sarah laugh? Why did she say, 'Can an old

18:6 Hebrew *3 seahs*, about 15 quarts or 18 liters.

---

**ABRAHAM**

We all know that there are consequences to any action we take. What we do can set into motion a series of events that may continue long after we're gone. Unfortunately, when we are making a decision, most of us think only of the immediate consequences. These are often misleading because they are short-lived.

Abraham had a choice to make. His decision was between setting out with his family and belongings for parts unknown or staying right where he was. He had to decide between the security of what he already had and the uncertainty of traveling under God's direction. All he had to go on was God's promise to guide and bless him. Abraham could hardly have been expected to visualize how much of the future was resting on his decision of whether to go or stay, but his obedience affected the history of the world. His decision to follow God set into motion the development of the nation that God would eventually use as his own when he visited earth himself. When Jesus Christ came to earth, God's promise was fulfilled; through Abraham the entire world was blessed.

You probably don't know the long-term effects of most decisions you make. But shouldn't the fact that there will be long-term results cause you to think carefully and seek God's guidance as you make choices and take action today?

| | |
|---|---|
| **Strengths and accomplishments** | • His faith pleased God<br>• Became the founder of the Jewish nation<br>• Was respected by others and was courageous in defending his family at any cost<br>• Was not only a caring father to his own family, but practiced hospitality to others<br>• Was a successful and wealthy rancher<br>• Usually avoided conflicts, but when they were unavoidable, he allowed his opponent to set the rules for settling the dispute |
| **Weakness and mistake** | • Under direct pressure, he distorted the truth |
| **Lessons from his life** | • God desires dependence, trust, and faith in him—not faith in our ability to please him<br>• God's plan from the beginning has been to make himself known to all people |
| **Vital statistics** | • Where: Born in Ur of the Chaldeans; spent most of his life in the land of Canaan<br>• Occupation: Wealthy livestock owner<br>• Relatives: Brothers: Nahor and Haran. Father: Terah. Wife: Sarah. Nephew: Lot. Sons: Ishmael and Isaac.<br>• Contemporaries: Abimelech, Melchizedek |
| **Key verse** | "And Abram believed the LORD, and the LORD counted him as righteous because of his faith" (Genesis 15:6). |

Abraham's story is told in Genesis 11–25. He is also mentioned in Exodus 2:24; Matthew 1:1, 2; Luke 3:34; Acts 7:2-8; Romans 4; Galatians 3; Hebrews 2; 6–7; 11.

woman like me have a baby?' ¹⁴Is anything too hard for the LORD? I will return about this time next year, and Sarah will have a son."

18:14
Gen 18:10
Jer 32:17, 27
†Rom 9:9

¹⁵Sarah was afraid, so she denied it, saying, "I didn't laugh."

But the LORD said, "No, you did laugh."

## Abraham Intercedes for Sodom

¹⁶Then the men got up from their meal and looked out toward Sodom. As they left, Abraham went with them to send them on their way.

18:16
Gen 18:22; 19:1

¹⁷"Should I hide my plan from Abraham?" the LORD asked. ¹⁸"For Abraham will certainly become a great and mighty nation, and all the nations of the earth will be blessed through him. ¹⁹I have singled him out so that he will direct his sons and their families to keep the way of the LORD by doing what is right and just. Then I will do for Abraham all that I have promised."

18:18
Gen 12:2-3
†Gal 3:18
18:19
Neh 9:7

²⁰So the LORD told Abraham, "I have heard a great outcry from Sodom and Gomorrah, because their sin is so flagrant. ²¹I am going down to see if their actions are as wicked as I have heard. If not, I want to know."

18:20
Gen 19:13
18:21
Gen 11:5
Exod 3:8

²²The other men turned and headed toward Sodom, but the LORD remained with Abraham. ²³Abraham approached him and said, "Will you sweep away both the righteous and the wicked? ²⁴Suppose you find fifty righteous people living there in the city—will you still sweep it away and not spare it for their sakes? ²⁵Surely you wouldn't do such a thing, destroying the righteous along with the wicked. Why, you would be treating the righteous and the wicked exactly the same! Surely you wouldn't do that! Should not the Judge of all the earth do what is right?"

18:22
Gen 18:16; 19:1
18:23
Exod 23:7
18:25
Deut 1:16-17; 32:4
Ps 58:11

²⁶And the LORD replied, "If I find fifty righteous people in Sodom, I will spare the entire city for their sake."

²⁷Then Abraham spoke again. "Since I have begun, let me speak further to my Lord, even though I am but dust and ashes. ²⁸Suppose there are only forty-five righteous people rather than fifty? Will you destroy the whole city for lack of five?"

18:27
Gen 2:7
Job 30:19; 42:6

And the LORD said, "I will not destroy it if I find forty-five righteous people there."

²⁹Then Abraham pressed his request further. "Suppose there are only forty?"

And the LORD replied, "I will not destroy it for the sake of the forty."

³⁰"Please don't be angry, my Lord," Abraham pleaded. "Let me speak—suppose only thirty righteous people are found?"

18:30
Exod 32:32

And the LORD replied, "I will not destroy it if I find thirty."

³¹Then Abraham said, "Since I have dared to speak to the Lord, let me continue—suppose there are only twenty?"

And the LORD replied, "Then I will not destroy it for the sake of the twenty."

---

**18:14** "Is anything too hard for the LORD?" The obvious answer is, "Of course not!" This question reveals much about God. Make it a habit to insert your specific needs into the question. "Is this day in my life too hard for the Lord?" "Is this habit I'm trying to break too hard for him?" "Is the communication problem I'm having too hard for him?" Asking the question this way reminds you that God is personally involved in your life and nudges you to ask for his power to help you.

**18:15** Sarah lied because she was afraid of being discovered. Fear is the most common motive for lying. We are afraid that our inner thoughts and emotions will be exposed or our wrongdoings discovered. But lying causes greater complications than telling the truth and brings even more problems. You will be far better off telling the truth right from the start.

**18:20-33** Did Abraham change God's mind? Of course not. The more likely answer is that God changed Abraham's mind. Abraham knew that God is just and that he punishes sin, but he may have wondered about God's mercy. Abraham seemed to be probing God's mind to see how merciful he really was. He left his conversation with God convinced that God was both kind and fair. Our prayers won't change God's mind, but they may change ours just as Abraham's prayer changed his. Prayer helps us better understand the mind of God.

**18:20-33** Why did God let Abraham question his justice and intercede for a wicked city? Abraham knew that God must punish

sin, but he also knew from experience that God is merciful to sinners. God knew there were not 10 innocent people in the city, but he was merciful enough to allow Abraham to intercede. He was also merciful enough to help Lot, Abraham's nephew, get out of Sodom before it was destroyed. God does not take pleasure in destroying the wicked, but he must punish sin. He is both just and merciful. We should be thankful that God's mercy extends to us.

**18:21** God gave the men of Sodom a fair test. He was not ignorant of the city's wicked practices, but in his fairness and patience he gave the people of Sodom one last chance to repent. God is still waiting, giving people the opportunity to turn to him (2 Peter 3:9). Those who are wise will turn to him before his patience wears out.

**18:25** Was God being unfair to the people of Sodom? Did he really plan to destroy the innocent with the guilty? On the contrary, God's fairness stood out. (1) He agreed to spare the entire city if only 10 innocent people lived there. (2) He showed great mercy toward Lot, apparently the only man in the city who had any kind of relationship with him (and even that was questionable). (3) He showed great patience toward Lot, almost forcing him to leave Sodom before it was destroyed. Remember God's patience when you are tempted to think he is unfair. Even the most godly people deserve his justice. We should be glad God doesn't direct his justice toward us as he did toward Sodom.

³²Finally, Abraham said, "Lord, please don't be angry with me if I speak one more time. Suppose only ten are found there?"

And the LORD replied, "Then I will not destroy it for the sake of the ten."

**18:33**
Gen 17:22; 35:13

³³When the LORD had finished his conversation with Abraham, he went on his way, and Abraham returned to his tent.

### Sodom and Gomorrah Destroyed

**19:1**
Gen 18:2

**19:2**
Gen 18:4

**19:3**
Gen 18:6-8

**19:4**
Gen 13:13; 18:20

**19** That evening the two angels came to the entrance of the city of Sodom. Lot was sitting there, and when he saw them, he stood up to meet them. Then he welcomed them and bowed with his face to the ground. ²"My lords," he said, "come to my home to wash your feet, and be my guests for the night. You may then get up early in the morning and be on your way again."

"Oh no," they replied. "We'll just spend the night out here in the city square."

³But Lot insisted, so at last they went home with him. Lot prepared a feast for them, complete with fresh bread made without yeast, and they ate. ⁴But before they retired for the

**T**here probably isn't anything harder to do than wait, whether we are expecting something good, something bad, or an unknown.

One way we often cope with a long wait (or even a short one) is to begin helping God get his plan into action. Sarah tried this approach. She was too old to expect to have a child of her own, so she thought God must have something else in mind. From Sarah's limited point of view, this could only be to give Abraham a son through another woman—a common practice in her day. The plan seemed harmless enough. Abraham would sleep with Sarah's servant, who would then give birth to a child. Sarah would take the child as her own. The plan worked beautifully—at first. But as you read about the events that followed, you will be struck by how often Sarah must have regretted the day she decided to push God's timetable ahead.

Another way we cope with a long wait is to gradually conclude that what we're waiting for is never going to happen. Sarah waited 90 years for a baby! When God told her she would finally have one of her own, she laughed, not so much from a lack of faith in what God could do, but from doubt about what he could do *through her*. When confronted about her laughter, she lied—as she had seen her husband do from time to time. She probably didn't want her true feelings to be known.

What parts of your life seem to be on hold right now? Do you understand that this may be part of God's plan for you? The Bible has more than enough clear direction to keep us busy while we're waiting for some particular part of life to move ahead.

**SARAH**

| | |
|---|---|
| **Strengths and accomplishments** | • Was intensely loyal to her own child<br>• Became the mother of a nation and an ancestor of Jesus<br>• Was a woman of faith, the first woman listed in the Hall of Faith in Hebrews 11 |
| **Weaknesses and mistakes** | • Had trouble believing God's promises to her<br>• Attempted to work problems out on her own, without consulting God<br>• Tried to cover her faults by blaming others |
| **Lessons from her life** | • God responds to faith even in the midst of failure<br>• God is not bound by what usually happens; he can stretch the limits and cause unheard-of events to occur |
| **Vital statistics** | • Where: Married Abram in Ur of the Chaldeans, then moved with him to Canaan<br>• Occupation: Wife, mother, household manager<br>• Relatives: Father: Terah. Husband: Abraham. Half brothers: Nahor and Haran. Nephew: Lot. Son: Isaac. |
| **Key verse** | "It was by faith that even Sarah was able to have a child, though she was barren and was too old. She believed that God would keep his promise" (Hebrews 11:11). |

Sarah's story is told in Genesis 11–25. She is also mentioned in Isaiah 51:2; Romans 4:19; 9:9; Hebrews 11:11; 1 Peter 3:6.

**18:33** God showed Abraham that asking for anything is allowed, with the understanding that God's answers come from God's perspective. They are not always in harmony with our expectations, for only he knows the whole story. Are you missing God's answer to a prayer because you haven't considered any possible answers other than the one you expect?

**19:1** The entrance of the city was the meeting place for city officials and other men to discuss current events and transact business. It was a place of authority and status where a person could see and be seen. Evidently Lot held an important position in the government or associated with those who did because the angels found him at the city's entrance. Perhaps Lot's status in Sodom was one reason he was so reluctant to leave (19:16, 18-22).

night, all the men of Sodom, young and old, came from all over the city and surrounded the house. ⁵They shouted to Lot, "Where are the men who came to spend the night with you? Bring them out to us so we can have sex with them!"

⁶So Lot stepped outside to talk to them, shutting the door behind him. ⁷"Please, my brothers," he begged, "don't do such a wicked thing. ⁸Look, I have two virgin daughters. Let me bring them out to you, and you can do with them as you wish. But please, leave these men alone, for they are my guests and are under my protection."

⁹"Stand back!" they shouted. "This fellow came to town as an outsider, and now he's acting like our judge! We'll treat you far worse than those other men!" And they lunged toward Lot to break down the door.

¹⁰But the two angels* reached out, pulled Lot into the house, and bolted the door. ¹¹Then they blinded all the men, young and old, who were at the door of the house, so they gave up trying to get inside.

¹²Meanwhile, the angels questioned Lot. "Do you have any other relatives here in the city?" they asked. "Get them out of this place—your sons-in-law, sons, daughters, or anyone else. ¹³For we are about to destroy this city completely. The outcry against this place is so great it has reached the LORD, and he has sent us to destroy it."

¹⁴So Lot rushed out to tell his daughters' fiancés, "Quick, get out of the city! The LORD is about to destroy it." But the young men thought he was only joking.

¹⁵At dawn the next morning the angels became insistent. "Hurry," they said to Lot. "Take your wife and your two daughters who are here. Get out right now, or you will be swept away in the destruction of the city!"

¹⁶When Lot still hesitated, the angels seized his hand and the hands of his wife and two daughters and rushed them to safety outside the city, for the LORD was merciful. ¹⁷When they were safely out of the city, one of the angels ordered, "Run for your lives! And don't look back or stop anywhere in the valley! Escape to the mountains, or you will be swept away!"

¹⁸"Oh no, my lord!" Lot begged. ¹⁹"You have been so gracious to me and saved my life, and you have shown such great kindness. But I cannot go to the mountains. Disaster would catch up to me there, and I would soon die. ²⁰See, there is a small village nearby. Please let me go there instead; don't you see how small it is? Then my life will be saved."

²¹"All right," the angel said, "I will grant your request. I will not destroy the little village. ²²But hurry! Escape to it, for I can do nothing until you arrive there." (This explains why that village was known as Zoar, which means "little place.")

²³Lot reached the village just as the sun was rising over the horizon. ²⁴Then the LORD

19:10 Hebrew *men;* also in 19:12, 16.

**Cross-references (right margin):**

19:5 Lev 18:22; Judg 19:22
19:8 Deut 23:17
19:9 Exod 2:14
19:10 Gen 19:1
19:11 Deut 28:28-29; 2 Kgs 6:18; Acts 13:11
19:13 Gen 18:20; 1 Chr 21:15; Jude 1:7
19:14 Exod 9:21; Jer 5:12; 43:1-2
19:17 Gen 13:10; 19:26; Jer 48:6
19:22 Gen 13:10
19:24 Luke 17:29; Jude 1:7

---

**19:8** How could any father give his daughters to be ravished by a mob of perverts, just to protect two strangers? Possibly Lot was scheming to save both the girls and the visitors, hoping the girls' fiancés would rescue them or that the homosexual men would be disinterested in the girls and simply go away. Although it was the custom of the day to protect guests at any cost, this terrible suggestion reveals how deeply sin had been absorbed into Lot's life. He had become hardened to evil acts in an evil city. Whatever Lot's motives were, we see here an illustration of Sodom's terrible wickedness—a wickedness so great that God had to destroy the entire city.

**19:13** God promised to spare Sodom if only 10 innocent people lived there (18:32). Obviously not even 10 could be found, because the angels arrived to destroy the city. Archaeological evidence points to an advanced civilization in this area during Abraham's day. Most researchers also confirm some kind of sudden and devastating destruction. It is now widely thought that the buried city lies beneath the waters of the southern end of the Dead Sea. The story of Sodom reveals that the people of Lot's day had to deal with the same kinds of repulsive sins the world faces today. We should follow Abraham's example of trusting God. His selfless faith contrasts with the self-gratifying people of Sodom.

**19:14** Lot had lived so long and was so contented among ungodly people that he was no longer a believable witness for God. He had allowed his environment to shape him, rather than he shaping his environment. Do those who know you see you as a witness for God, or are you just one of the crowd, blending in unnoticed? Lot had compromised to the point that he was almost useless to God. When he finally made a stand, nobody listened. Have you, too, become useless to God because you are too much like your environment? To make a difference, you must first decide to be different in your faith and your conduct.

**19:16** Lot hesitated, so the angel seized his hand and rushed him to safety. Lot did not want to abandon the wealth, position, and comfort he enjoyed in Sodom. It is easy to criticize Lot for being hypnotized by Sodom when the choice seems so clear to us. To be wiser than Lot, we must see that our hesitation to obey stems from the false attractions of our culture's pleasures.

**19:16-29** Notice how God's mercy toward Abraham extended to Lot and his family. Because Abraham pleaded for Lot, God was merciful and saved Lot from the fiery destruction of Sodom. A righteous person can often affect others for good. James says that the "earnest prayer of a righteous person has great power" (James 5:16). All Christians should follow Abraham's example and pray for others to be saved.

**19:24** In the story of Sodom and Gomorrah, we see two facets of God's character: his great patience (agreeing to spare a wicked city for 10 good people) and his fierce anger (destroying both cities). As we grow spiritually, we should find ourselves

**19:25**
Deut 29:23
Isa 13:19
2 Pet 2:6

**19:26**
Gen 19:17
Luke 17:32

**19:28**
Rev 9:2

**19:29**
Deut 7:8; 9:5
2 Pet 2:7-8

rained down fire and burning sulfur from the sky on Sodom and Gomorrah. ²⁵He utterly destroyed them, along with the other cities and villages of the plain, wiping out all the people and every bit of vegetation. ²⁶But Lot's wife looked back as she was following behind him, and she turned into a pillar of salt.

²⁷Abraham got up early that morning and hurried out to the place where he had stood in the LORD's presence. ²⁸He looked out across the plain toward Sodom and Gomorrah and watched as columns of smoke rose from the cities like smoke from a furnace.

²⁹But God had listened to Abraham's request and kept Lot safe, removing him from the disaster that engulfed the cities on the plain.

**ISAAC**

A name carries great authority. It sets you apart. It triggers memories. The sound of it calls you to attention anywhere.

Many Bible names accomplished even more. They were often descriptions of important facts about one's past and hopes for the future. The choice of the name *Isaac*, "he laughs," for Abraham and Sarah's son must have created a variety of feelings in them each time it was spoken. At times it must have recalled their shocked laughter at God's announcement that they would be parents in their old age. At other times, it must have brought back the joyful feelings of receiving their long-awaited answer to prayer for a child. Most important, it was a testimony to God's power in making his promise a reality.

In a family of forceful initiators, Isaac was the quiet, mind-my-own-business type unless he was specifically called on to take action. He was the protected only child from the time Sarah got rid of Ishmael until Abraham arranged his marriage to Rebekah.

In his own family, Isaac had the patriarchal position, but Rebekah had the power. Rather than stand his ground, Isaac found it easier to compromise or lie to avoid confrontations.

In spite of these shortcomings, Isaac was part of God's plan. The model his father gave him included a great gift of faith in the one true God. God's promise to create a great nation through which he would bless the world was passed on by Isaac to his twin sons.

It is usually not hard to identify with Isaac in his weaknesses. But consider for a moment that God works through people in spite of their shortcomings and often through their short-comings. As you pray, put into words your desire to be available to God. You will discover that his willingness to use you is even greater than your desire to be used.

| | |
|---|---|
| **Strengths and accomplishments** | • He was the miracle child born to Sarah and Abraham when she was 90 years old and he was 100<br>• He was the first descendant in fulfillment of God's promise to Abraham<br>• He seems to have been a caring and consistent husband, at least until his sons were born<br>• He demonstrated great patience |
| **Weaknesses and mistakes** | • Under pressure he tended to lie<br>• In conflict he sought to avoid confrontation<br>• He played favorites between his sons and alienated his wife |
| **Lessons from his life** | • Patience often brings rewards<br>• Both God's plans and his promises are larger than people<br>• God keeps his promises! He remains faithful though we are often faithless<br>• Playing favorites is sure to bring family conflict |
| **Vital statistics** | • Where: Various places in the southern part of Palestine, including Beersheba (Genesis 26:23)<br>• Occupation: Wealthy livestock owner<br>• Relatives: Parents: Abraham and Sarah. Half brother: Ishmael. Wife: Rebekah. Twin sons: Jacob and Esau. |
| **Key verse** | "But God replied, 'No—Sarah, your wife, will give birth to a son for you. You will name him Isaac, and I will confirm my covenant with him and his descendants as an everlasting covenant'" (Genesis 17:19). |

Isaac's story is told in Genesis 17:15–35:29. He is also mentioned in Romans 9:7-10; Hebrews 11:17-20; James 2:21.

developing not only a deeper respect for God because of his anger toward sin but also a deeper love for God because of his patience when we sin.

**19:26** Lot's wife turned back to look at the smoldering city of Sodom. Clinging to the past, she was unwilling to turn completely away. Are you looking back longingly at sin while trying to move

forward with God? You can't make progress with God as long as you are holding on to pieces of your old life. Jesus said it this way in Matthew 6:24: "No one can serve two masters."

## Lot and His Daughters

30Afterward Lot left Zoar because he was afraid of the people there, and he went to live in a cave in the mountains with his two daughters. 31One day the older daughter said to her sister, "There are no men left anywhere in this entire area, so we can't get married like everyone else. And our father will soon be too old to have children. 32Come, let's get him drunk with wine, and then we will have sex with him. That way we will preserve our family line through our father."

33So that night they got him drunk with wine, and the older daughter went in and had intercourse with her father. He was unaware of her lying down or getting up again.

34The next morning the older daughter said to her younger sister, "I had sex with our father last night. Let's get him drunk with wine again tonight, and you go in and have sex with him. That way we will preserve our family line through our father." 35So that night they got him drunk with wine again, and the younger daughter went in and had intercourse with him. As before, he was unaware of her lying down or getting up again.

36As a result, both of Lot's daughters became pregnant by their own father. 37When the older daughter gave birth to a son, she named him Moab.* He became the ancestor of the nation now known as the Moabites. 38When the younger daughter gave birth to a son, she named him Ben-ammi.* He became the ancestor of the nation now known as the Ammonites.

## Abraham Deceives Abimelech

**20** Abraham moved south to the Negev and lived for a while between Kadesh and Shur, and then he moved on to Gerar. While living there as a foreigner, 2Abraham introduced his wife, Sarah, by saying, "She is my sister." So King Abimelech of Gerar sent for Sarah and had her brought to him at his palace.

3But that night God came to Abimelech in a dream and told him, "You are a dead man, for that woman you have taken is already married!"

4But Abimelech had not slept with her yet, so he said, "Lord, will you destroy an innocent nation? 5Didn't Abraham tell me, 'She is my sister'? And she herself said, 'Yes, he is my brother.' I acted in complete innocence! My hands are clean."

6In the dream God responded, "Yes, I know you are innocent. That's why I kept you from sinning against me, and why I did not let you touch her. 7Now return the woman to her husband, and he will pray for you, for he is a prophet. Then you will live. But if you don't return her to him, you can be sure that you and all your people will die."

8Abimelech got up early the next morning and quickly called all his servants together. When he told them what had happened, his men were terrified. 9Then Abimelech called for Abraham. "What have you done to us?" he demanded. "What crime have I committed that deserves treatment like this, making me and my kingdom guilty of this great sin? No one should ever do what you have done! 10Whatever possessed you to do such a thing?"

19:37 *Moab* sounds like a Hebrew term that means "from father." 19:38 *Ben-ammi* means "son of my kinsman."

**Cross-references (right margin):**

**19:30**
Gen 13:10

**19:33**
Gen 9:21

**19:37**
Gen 36:35
Exod 15:15
Num 21:29
Deut 2:9
Ruth 1:1
**19:38**
Num 21:24
Deut 2:19

**20:1**
Gen 14:7; 18:1;
26:1
**20:2**
Gen 12:13
**20:3**
Gen 28:12; 31:24;
37:5
**20:4**
Gen 18:23-25
**20:5**
Gen 12:19
1 Kgs 9:4
Pss 7:8; 26:6
**20:7**
1 Sam 7:5
Job 42:8

**20:9**
Gen 12:18

---

**19:30-38** In this pitiful sequel to the story of the destruction of Sodom, we see two women compelled to preserve their family line. They were driven not by lust but by desperation—they feared they would never marry. Lot's tendency to compromise and refusal to act reached its peak. He should have found right partners for his daughters long before this; Abraham's family wasn't far away. Now the two daughters stooped to incest, showing their acceptance of the morals of Sodom. We are most likely to sin when we are desperate for what we feel we must have.

**19:30-38** Why doesn't the Bible openly condemn these sisters for what they did? In many cases, the Bible does not judge people for their actions. It simply reports the events. However, incest is clearly condemned in other parts of Scripture (Leviticus 18:6-18; 20:11, 12, 17, 19-21; Deuteronomy 22:30; 27:20-23; Ezekiel 22:11; 1 Corinthians 5:1). Perhaps the consequence of their action—Moab and Ammon became enemies of Israel—was God's way of judging their sin.

**19:37, 38** Moab and Ben-ammi were the products of incest. They became the fathers of two of Israel's greatest enemies, the Moabites and the Ammonites. These nations settled east of the Jordan River, and Israel never conquered them. Because

of the family connection, Moses was forbidden to attack them (Deuteronomy 2:9). Ruth, great-grandmother of David and an ancestor of Jesus, was from Moab.

**20:2** Abraham had used this same trick before to protect himself (12:11-13). Although Abraham is one of our heroes of faith, he did not learn his lesson well enough the first time. In fact, by giving in to the temptation again, he risked turning a sinful act into a sinful pattern of lying whenever he suspected his life was in danger.

No matter how much we love God, certain temptations are especially difficult to resist. These are the vulnerable spots in our spiritual armor. As we struggle with these weaknesses, we can be encouraged to know that God is watching out for us just as he did for Abraham.

**20:6** Abimelech had unknowingly taken a married woman to be his wife and was about to commit adultery. But God somehow prevented him from touching Sarah and held him back from sinning. What mercy on God's part! How many times has God done the same for us, holding us back from sin in ways we can't even detect? We have no way of knowing—we just know from this story that he can. God works just as often in ways we can't see as in ways we can.

**20:11**
Gen 12:12; 42:18

**20:13**
Gen 12:1

**20:14**
Gen 12:16

**20:16**
Gen 23:15

**20:17**
Num 12:13; 21:7
**20:18**
Gen 12:17

**21:2**
Gen 18:10
Gal 4:22
Heb 11:11
**21:4**
Gen 17:10, 12
**21:5**
Heb 6:15
**21:6**
Isa 54:1
**21:7**
Gen 18:13

**21:8**
1 Sam 1:23
**21:9**
Gal 4:29
**21:10**
†Gal 4:30
**21:12**
†Rom 9:7
†Heb 11:18
**21:13**
Gen 16:10; 21:18;
25:12-18
**21:14**
Gen 16:1

**21:16**
Jer 6:26

**21:17**
Exod 3:7
Deut 26:7
Ps 6:8

11Abraham replied, "I thought, 'This is a godless place. They will want my wife and will kill me to get her.' 12And she really is my sister, for we both have the same father, but different mothers. And I married her. 13When God called me to leave my father's home and to travel from place to place, I told her, 'Do me a favor. Wherever we go, tell the people that I am your brother.'"

14Then Abimelech took some of his sheep and goats, cattle, and male and female servants, and he presented them to Abraham. He also returned his wife, Sarah, to him. 15Then Abimelech said, "Look over my land and choose any place where you would like to live. 16And he said to Sarah, "Look, I am giving your 'brother' 1,000 pieces of silver* in the presence of all these witnesses. This is to compensate you for any wrong I may have done to you. This will settle any claim against me, and your reputation is cleared."

17Then Abraham prayed to God, and God healed Abimelech, his wife, and his female servants, so they could have children. 18For the LORD had caused all the women to be infertile because of what happened with Abraham's wife, Sarah.

### 5. Birth and near sacrifice of Isaac
#### The Birth of Isaac

**21** The LORD kept his word and did for Sarah exactly what he had promised. 2She became pregnant, and she gave birth to a son for Abraham in his old age. This happened at just the time God had said it would. 3And Abraham named their son Isaac. 4Eight days after Isaac was born, Abraham circumcised him as God had commanded. 5Abraham was 100 years old when Isaac was born.

6And Sarah declared, "God has brought me laughter.* All who hear about this will laugh with me. 7Who would have said to Abraham that Sarah would nurse a baby? Yet I have given Abraham a son in his old age!"

#### Hagar and Ishmael Are Sent Away

8When Isaac grew up and was about to be weaned, Abraham prepared a huge feast to celebrate the occasion. 9But Sarah saw Ishmael—the son of Abraham and her Egyptian servant Hagar—making fun of her son, Isaac.* 10So she turned to Abraham and demanded, "Get rid of that slave woman and her son. He is not going to share the inheritance with my son, Isaac. I won't have it!"

11This upset Abraham very much because Ishmael was his son. 12But God told Abraham, "Do not be upset over the boy and your servant. Do whatever Sarah tells you, for Isaac is the son through whom your descendants will be counted. 13But I will also make a nation of the descendants of Hagar's son because he is your son, too."

14So Abraham got up early the next morning, prepared food and a container of water, and strapped them on Hagar's shoulders. Then he sent her away with their son, and she wandered aimlessly in the wilderness of Beersheba.

15When the water was gone, she put the boy in the shade of a bush. 16Then she went and sat down by herself about a hundred yards* away. "I don't want to watch the boy die," she said, as she burst into tears.

17But God heard the boy crying, and the angel of God called to Hagar from heaven,

**20:16** Hebrew *1,000 [shekels] of silver*, about 25 pounds or 11.4 kilograms in weight. **21:6** The name *Isaac* means "he laughs." **21:9** As in Greek version and Latin Vulgate; Hebrew lacks *of her son, Isaac.* **21:16** Hebrew *a bowshot.*

**20:11-13** Because Abraham mistakenly assumed that Abimelech was a wicked man, he made a quick decision to tell a half-truth. Abraham thought it would be more effective to deceive Abimelech than to trust God to work in the king's life. Don't assume that God will not work in a situation that has potential problems. You may not completely understand the situation, and God may intervene when you least expect it.

**20:17, 18** Why did God punish Abimelech when he had no idea Sarah was married? (1) Even though Abimelech's intentions were good, as long as Sarah was living in his harem he was in danger of sinning. A person who eats a poisonous toadstool, thinking it's a harmless mushroom, no doubt has perfectly good intentions—but will still suffer. Sin is a poison that damages us and those around us, whatever our intentions. (2) The punishment, striking all the women of Abimelech's household with infertility, lasted only as long as Abimelech was in danger of sleeping with Sarah.

It was meant to change the situation, not to harm Abimelech. (3) The punishment clearly showed that Abraham was in league with almighty God. This incident may have made Abimelech respect and fear Abraham's God.

**21:1-7** Who could believe that Abraham would have a son at 100 years of age—and live to raise him to adulthood? But doing the impossible is everyday business for God. Our big problems won't seem so impossible if we let God handle them.

**21:7** After repeated promises, a visit by two angels, and the appearance of the Lord himself, Sarah finally cried out with surprise and joy at the birth of her son. Because of her doubt, worry, and fear, she had forfeited the peace she could have felt in God's wonderful promise to her. The way to bring peace to a troubled heart is to focus on God's promises. Trust him to do what he says.

"Hagar, what's wrong? Do not be afraid! God has heard the boy crying as he lies there. 18Go to him and comfort him, for I will make a great nation from his descendants."

19Then God opened Hagar's eyes, and she saw a well full of water. She quickly filled her water container and gave the boy a drink.

20And God was with the boy as he grew up in the wilderness. He became a skillful archer, 21and he settled in the wilderness of Paran. His mother arranged for him to marry a woman from the land of Egypt.

### Abraham's Covenant with Abimelech

22About this time, Abimelech came with Phicol, his army commander, to visit Abraham. "God is obviously with you, helping you in everything you do," Abimelech said. 23"Swear to me in God's name that you will never deceive me, my children, or any of my descendants. I have been loyal to you, so now swear that you will be loyal to me and to this country where you are living as a foreigner."

24Abraham replied, "Yes, I swear to it!" 25Then Abraham complained to Abimelech about a well that Abimelech's servants had taken by force from Abraham's servants.

26"This is the first I've heard of it," Abimelech answered. "I have no idea who is responsible. You have never complained about this before."

27Abraham then gave some of his sheep, goats, and cattle to Abimelech, and they made a treaty. 28But Abraham also took seven additional female lambs and set them off by themselves. 29Abimelech asked, "Why have you set these seven apart from the others?"

30Abraham replied, "Please accept these seven lambs to show your agreement that I dug this well." 31Then he named the place Beersheba (which means "well of the oath"), because that was where they had sworn the oath.

32After making their covenant at Beersheba, Abimelech left with Phicol, the commander of his army, and they returned home to the land of the Philistines. 33Then Abraham planted a tamarisk tree at Beersheba, and there he worshiped the LORD, the Eternal God.* 34And Abraham lived as a foreigner in Philistine country for a long time.

### Abraham's Faith Tested

**22** Some time later, God tested Abraham's faith. "Abraham!" God called.
"Yes," he replied. "Here I am."

2"Take your son, your only son—yes, Isaac, whom you love so much—and go to the land of Moriah. Go and sacrifice him as a burnt offering on one of the mountains, which I will show you."

3The next morning Abraham got up early. He saddled his donkey and took two of his ser-

**21:33** Hebrew *El-Olam.*

---

**21:18**
Gen 26:24

**21:20**
Gen 28:15

**21:21**
Gen 25:18

**21:22**
Gen 26:26

**21:23**
Gen 24:2

**21:25**
Gen 26:15

**21:27**
Gen 26:31

**21:30**
Gen 31:44

**21:31**
Gen 21:14; 26:33

**21:33**
1 Sam 22:6; 31:13
Ps 90:2
Isa 9:6; 40:28

**22:1**
Exod 15:25; 16:4
Deut 8:2, 16

**22:2**
2 Chr 3:1
John 3:16

---

**21:18** What happened to Ishmael, and who are his descendants? Ishmael became ruler of a large tribe or nation. The Ishmaelites were nomads living in the wilderness of Sinai and Paran, south of Israel. One of Ishmael's daughters married Esau, Ishmael's nephew (28:9). The Bible pictures the Ishmaelites as hostile to Israel and to God (Psalm 83:5, 6).

**21:31** Beersheba, the southernmost city of Israel, lay on the edge of a vast desert that stretched as far as Egypt to the southwest and Mount Sinai to the south. The area described as being from Dan in the north to Beersheba in the south was often used to describe the traditional boundaries of the Promised Land (2 Chronicles 30:5). Beersheba's southern location and the presence of several wells in the area may explain why Abraham settled there. Beersheba was also the home of Isaac, Abraham's son.

**22:1** God tested Abraham, not to trip him and watch him fall, but to deepen his capacity to obey God and thus to develop his character. Just as fire refines ore to extract precious metals, God refines us through difficult circumstances. When we are tested, we can complain, or we can try to see how God is stretching us to develop our character.

**22:3** That morning Abraham began one of the greatest acts of obedience in recorded history. He traveled 50 miles to Mount Moriah near the site of Jerusalem. Over the years he had learned many tough lessons about the importance of obeying God. This time his obedience was prompt and complete. Obeying God is often a struggle because it may mean giving up something we truly want. We should not expect our obedience to God to be easy or to come naturally.

**ABRAHAM'S TRIP TO MOUNT MORIAH**
Abraham and Isaac traveled the 50 or 60 miles from Beersheba to Mount Moriah in about three days. This was a very difficult time for Abraham, who was on his way to sacrifice his beloved son, Isaac.

Mediterranean Sea

Sea of Galilee

N

Jordan River

Mount Moriah
**Jerusalem** (Salem)

Dead Sea

Beersheba

0   20 Mi.
0   20 Km.

vants with him, along with his son, Isaac. Then he chopped wood for a fire for a burnt offering and set out for the place God had told him about. 4On the third day of their journey, Abraham looked up and saw the place in the distance. 5"Stay here with the donkey," Abraham told the servants. "The boy and I will travel a little farther. We will worship there, and then we will come right back."

**22:6**
John 19:17

**22:7**
Gen 8:20
Exod 29:38-42
John 1:29, 36
Rev 13:8

6So Abraham placed the wood for the burnt offering on Isaac's shoulders, while he himself carried the fire and the knife. As the two of them walked on together, 7Isaac turned to Abraham and said, "Father?"

"Yes, my son?" Abraham replied.

"We have the fire and the wood," the boy said, "but where is the sheep for the burnt offering?"

8"God will provide a sheep for the burnt offering, my son," Abraham answered. And they both walked on together.

**22:9**
Heb 11:17-19
Jas 2:21

**22:11**
Gen 16:7; 21:17

9When they arrived at the place where God had told him to go, Abraham built an altar and arranged the wood on it. Then he tied his son, Isaac, and laid him on the altar on top of the wood. 10And Abraham picked up the knife to kill his son as a sacrifice. 11At that moment the angel of the LORD called to him from heaven, "Abraham! Abraham!"

---

**HAGAR**

Escape of some kind is usually the most tempting solution to our problems. In fact, it can become a habit. Hagar was a person who used that approach. When the going got tough, she usually got going—in the other direction.

However, it is worthwhile to note that the biggest challenges Hagar faced were brought on by *other* people's choices. Sarah chose her to bear Abraham's child, and Hagar probably had little to say in the matter.

It isn't hard to understand how Hagar's pregnancy caused her to look down on Sarah. But that brought on hard feelings, and Sarah consequently punished Hagar. This motivated her first escape. When she returned to the family and gave birth to Ishmael, Sarah's continued barrenness must have contributed to bitterness on both sides.

When Isaac was finally born, Sarah looked for any excuse to have Hagar and Ishmael sent away. She found it when she caught Ishmael teasing Isaac. In the wilderness, out of water and facing the death of her son, Hagar once again tried to escape. She walked away so she wouldn't have to watch her son die. Once again, God graciously intervened.

Have you noticed how patiently God operates to make our escape attempts fail? Have you begun to learn that escape is only a temporary solution? God's continual desire is for us to face our problems with his help. We experience his help most clearly in and through conflicts and difficulties, not away from them. Are there problems in your life for which you've been using the "Hagar solution"? Choose one of those problems, ask for God's help, and begin to face it today.

| | |
|---|---|
| **Strength and accomplishment** | • Mother of Abraham's first child, Ishmael, who became founder of the Arab nations |
| **Weaknesses and mistakes** | • When faced with problems, she tended to run away<br>• Her pregnancy brought out strong feelings of pride and arrogance |
| **Lessons from her life** | • God is faithful to his plan and promises, even when humans complicate the process<br>• God shows himself as one who knows us and wants to be known by us<br>• The New Testament uses Hagar as a symbol of those who would pursue favor with God by their own efforts, rather than by trusting in his mercy and forgiveness |
| **Vital statistics** | • Where: Canaan and Egypt<br>• Occupation: Servant, mother<br>• Relatives: Son: Ishmael |
| **Key verse** | "The angel of the LORD said to her, 'Return to your mistress, and submit to her authority'" (Genesis 16:9). |

Hagar's story is told in Genesis 16; 21. She is also mentioned in Galatians 4:24.

---

**22:6** We don't know how Abraham carried the fire. Perhaps he carried a live coal or a flint to start a fire.

**22:7, 8** Why did God ask Abraham to perform human sacrifice? Pagan nations practiced human sacrifice, but God condemned this as a terrible sin (Leviticus 20:1-5). God did not want Isaac to die, but he wanted Abraham to sacrifice Isaac in his heart so it

would be clear that Abraham loved God more than he loved his promised and long-awaited son. God was testing Abraham. The purpose of testing is to strengthen our character and deepen our commitment to God and his perfect timing. Through this difficult experience, Abraham strengthened his commitment to obey God. He also learned about God's ability to provide.

"Yes," Abraham replied. "Here I am!"

[12] "Don't lay a hand on the boy!" the angel said. "Do not hurt him in any way, for now I know that you truly fear God. You have not withheld from me even your son, your only son."

[13] Then Abraham looked up and saw a ram caught by its horns in a thicket. So he took the ram and sacrificed it as a burnt offering in place of his son. [14] Abraham named the place Yahweh-Yireh (which means "the LORD will provide"). To this day, people still use that name as a proverb: "On the mountain of the LORD it will be provided."

[15] Then the angel of the LORD called again to Abraham from heaven. [16] "This is what the LORD says: Because you have obeyed me and have not withheld even your son, your only son, I swear by my own name that [17] I will certainly bless you. I will multiply your descendants* beyond number, like the stars in the sky and the sand on the seashore. Your descendants will conquer the cities of their enemies. [18] And through your descendants all the nations of the earth will be blessed—all because you have obeyed me."

[19] Then they returned to the servants and traveled back to Beersheba, where Abraham continued to live.

[20] Soon after this, Abraham heard that Milcah, his brother Nahor's wife, had borne Nahor eight sons. [21] The oldest was named Uz, the next oldest was Buz, followed by Kemuel (the ancestor of the Arameans), [22] Kesed, Hazo, Pildash, Jidlaph, and Bethuel. [23] (Bethuel became the father of Rebekah.) In addition to these eight sons from Milcah, [24] Nahor had four other children from his concubine Reumah. Their names were Tebah, Gaham, Tahash, and Maacah.

### The Burial of Sarah

**23** When Sarah was 127 years old, [2] she died at Kiriath-arba (now called Hebron) in the land of Canaan. There Abraham mourned and wept for her.

[3] Then, leaving her body, he said to the Hittite elders, [4] "Here I am, a stranger and a foreigner among you. Please sell me a piece of land so I can give my wife a proper burial."

[5] The Hittites replied to Abraham, [6] "Listen, my lord, you are an honored prince among us. Choose the finest of our tombs and bury her there. No one here will refuse to help you in this way."

[7] Then Abraham bowed low before the Hittites [8] and said, "Since you are willing to help me in this way, be so kind as to ask Ephron son of Zohar [9] to let me buy his cave at Machpe-

22:17 Hebrew *seed;* also in 22:17b, 18.

**22:12**
Heb 11:17
**22:13**
Gen 8:20
**22:14**
Gen 22:7-8
**22:16**
†Heb 6:13-14
**22:17**
Gen 12:2; 15:5;
26:4
†Heb 6:14
**22:18**
†Acts 3:25
†Gal 3:8, 16
**22:19**
Gen 21:14
**22:20**
Gen 11:29
**22:23**
Gen 24:15
**23:2**
Josh 14:15
**23:3**
Gen 10:15
**23:4**
Lev 25:23
1 Chr 29:15
Ps 39:12
Heb 11:9
**23:6**
Gen 14:14-16
**23:8-9**
Gen 25:9

---

**22:12** It is difficult to let go of what we deeply love. What could be more proper than to love your only child? Yet when we do give to God what he asks, he returns to us far more than we could dream. The spiritual benefits of his blessings far outweigh our sacrifices. Have you withheld your love, your children, or your time from him? Trust him to provide (22:8).

**22:13** Notice the parallel between the ram offered on the altar as a substitute for Isaac and Christ offered on the cross as a substitute for us. Whereas God stopped Abraham from sacrificing his son, God did not spare his own Son, Jesus, from dying on the cross. If Jesus had lived, the rest of humankind would have died. God sent his only Son to die for us so that we could be spared from the eternal death we deserve and instead receive eternal life (John 3:16).

**22:15-18** Abraham received abundant blessings because he obeyed God. God promised to give Abraham's descendants the ability to conquer their enemies. In addition, God promised Abraham children and grandchildren who would in turn bless the whole earth. People's lives would be changed as a result of knowing of the faith of Abraham and his descendants. We often think of blessings as gifts that we will enjoy. But when God blesses us, his blessings may also overflow to others—today and into eternity.

**23:1-4** In Abraham's day, death and burial were steeped in ritual and traditions. Failing to honor a dead person demonstrated the greatest possible lack of respect. An improper burial was the equivalent of a curse. Mourning was an essential part of the death ritual. Friends and relatives would cry loudly for the whole neighborhood to hear. Because there were no funeral homes or undertakers, these same friends and relatives would help prepare the body for burial, which usually would take place on the same day because of the warm climate.

**23:4-6** Abraham was in a foreign land looking for a place to bury his wife. Strangers offered to help him because he was "an honored prince," and they respected him. Although Abraham had not put down roots in the area, his reputation was above reproach. Those who invest their time and money in serving God often earn a pleasant return on their investment—a good reputation and the respect of others.

**CAVE OF MACHPELAH**
Sarah died in Hebron. Abraham bought the cave of Machpelah, near Hebron, as her burial place. Abraham was also buried there, as were his son and grandson, Isaac and Jacob.

Mediterranean Sea

Sea of Galilee

Jordan River

N

Jerusalem (Salem)

Hebron

Dead Sea

Cave of Machpelah

0    20 Mi.

0    20 Km.

lah, down at the end of his field. I will pay the full price in the presence of witnesses, so I will have a permanent burial place for my family."

<sup>10</sup>Ephron was sitting there among the others, and he answered Abraham as the others listened, speaking publicly before all the Hittite elders of the town. <sup>11</sup>"No, my lord," he said to Abraham, "please listen to me. I will give you the field and the cave. Here in the presence of my people, I give it to you. Go and bury your dead."

<sup>12</sup>Abraham again bowed low before the citizens of the land, <sup>13</sup>and he replied to Ephron as everyone listened. "No, listen to me. I will buy it from you. Let me pay the full price for the field so I can bury my dead there."

<sup>14</sup>Ephron answered Abraham, <sup>15</sup>"My lord, please listen to me. The land is worth 400 pieces* of silver, but what is that between friends? Go ahead and bury your dead."

<sup>16</sup>So Abraham agreed to Ephron's price and paid the amount he had suggested—400 pieces of silver, weighed according to the market standard. The Hittite elders witnessed the transaction.

<sup>17</sup>So Abraham bought the plot of land belonging to Ephron at Machpelah, near Mamre. This included the field itself, the cave that was in it, and all the surrounding trees. <sup>18</sup>It was transferred to Abraham as his permanent possession in the presence of the Hittite elders at the city gate. <sup>19</sup>Then Abraham buried his wife, Sarah, there in Canaan, in the cave of Machpelah, near Mamre (also called Hebron). <sup>20</sup>So the field and the cave were transferred from the Hittites to Abraham for use as a permanent burial place.

## 6. Isaac and Rebekah

**24** Abraham was now a very old man, and the LORD had blessed him in every way. <sup>2</sup>One day Abraham said to his oldest servant, the man in charge of his household, "Take an oath by putting your hand under my thigh. <sup>3</sup>Swear by the LORD, the God of heaven and earth, that you will not allow my son to marry one of these local Canaanite women. <sup>4</sup>Go instead to my homeland, to my relatives, and find a wife there for my son Isaac."

**23:15** Hebrew *400 shekels*, about 10 pounds or 4.6 kilograms in weight; also in 23:16.

**Side references (left margin):**
23:10 — Ruth 4:1, 11
23:15 — Exod 30:13
23:16 — Jer 32:9
23:17-18 — Gen 25:9; 49:29-30; 50:13
24:1 — Gen 12:2; 24:35
24:2 — Gen 47:29
24:3 — Gen 14:19
24:4 — Gen 12:1

---

**ELIEZER: PROFILE OF A TRUE SERVANT**

Have you ever approached a responsiblity with this kind of single-mindedness and careful planning, while ultimately depending on God?

| | |
|---|---|
| Accepted the challenge | 24:3, 9 |
| Examined alternatives | 24:5 |
| Promised to follow instructions | 24:9 |
| Made a plan | 24:12-14 |
| Submitted the plan to God | 24:12-14 |
| Prayed for guidance | 24:12-14 |
| Devised a strategy with room for God to operate | 24:12-14 |
| Waited | 24:21 |
| Watched closely | 24:21 |
| Accepted the answer thankfully | 24:26 |
| Explained the situation to concerned parties | 24:34-49 |
| Refused unnecessary delay | 24:56 |
| Followed through with entire plan | 24:66 |

---

**23:10-16** The polite interchange between Abraham and Ephron was typical of bargaining at that time. Ephron graciously offered to give his land to Abraham at no charge; Abraham insisted on paying for it; Ephron politely mentioned the price but said, in effect, that it wasn't important; Abraham paid the 400 shekels of silver. Both men knew what was going on as they went through the bargaining process. If Abraham had accepted the land as a gift when it was offered, he would have insulted Ephron, who then would have rescinded his offer. Many Middle Eastern shopkeepers still follow this bargaining ritual with their customers.

**23:16** Four hundred pieces of silver was a high price for the piece of property Abraham bought. The Hittites weren't thrilled about foreigners buying their property, so Abraham had little bargaining leverage.

Ephron asked an outrageous price. The custom of the day was to ask double the fair market value of the land, fully expecting the buyer to offer half the stated price. Abraham, however, did not bargain. He simply paid the initial price. He was not trying to take anything he didn't deserve. Even though God had promised the land to Abraham, he did not just take it away from Ephron.

**24:4** Abraham wanted Isaac to marry within the family. This was a common and acceptable practice at this time that had the added advantage of avoiding intermarriage with pagan neighbors. A son's wife was usually chosen by the parents. It was common for a woman to be married in her early teens, although Rebekah was probably older.

5The servant asked, "But what if I can't find a young woman who is willing to travel so far from home? Should I then take Isaac there to live among your relatives in the land you came from?"

6"No!" Abraham responded. "Be careful never to take my son there. 7For the LORD, the God of heaven, who took me from my father's house and my native land, solemnly promised to give this land to my descendants.* He will send his angel ahead of you, and he will see to it that you find a wife there for my son. 8If she is unwilling to come back with you, then you are free from this oath of mine. But under no circumstances are you to take my son there."

9So the servant took an oath by putting his hand under the thigh of his master, Abraham. He swore to follow Abraham's instructions. 10Then he loaded ten of Abraham's camels with all kinds of expensive gifts from his master, and he traveled to distant Aram-naharaim. There he went to the town where Abraham's brother Nahor had settled. 11He made the camels kneel beside a well just outside the town. It was evening, and the women were coming out to draw water.

12"O LORD, God of my master, Abraham," he prayed. "Please give me success today, and show unfailing love to my master, Abraham. 13See, I am standing here beside this spring, and the young women of the town are coming out to draw water. 14This is my request. I will ask one of them, 'Please give me a drink from your jug.' If she says, 'Yes, have a drink, and I will water your camels, too!'—let her be the one you have selected as Isaac's wife. This is how I will know that you have shown unfailing love to my master."

15Before he had finished praying, he saw a young woman named Rebekah coming out with her water jug on her shoulder. She was the daughter of Bethuel, who was the son of Abraham's brother Nahor and his wife, Milcah. 16Rebekah was very beautiful and old enough to be married, but she was still a virgin. She went down to the spring, filled her jug, and came up again. 17Running over to her, the servant said, "Please give me a little drink of water from your jug."

18"Yes, my lord," she answered, "have a drink." And she quickly lowered her jug from her shoulder and gave him a drink. 19When she had given him a drink, she said, "I'll draw water for your camels, too, until they have had enough to drink." 20So she quickly emptied her jug into the watering trough and ran back to the well to draw water for all his camels.

21The servant watched her in silence, wondering whether or not the LORD had given him success in his mission. 22Then at last, when the camels had finished drinking, he took out a gold ring for her nose and two large gold bracelets* for her wrists.

23"Whose daughter are you?" he asked. "And please tell me, would your father have any room to put us up for the night?"

24"I am the daughter of Bethuel," she replied. "My grandparents are Nahor and Milcah. 25Yes, we have plenty of straw and feed for the camels, and we have room for guests."

**24:7** Hebrew *seed;* also in 24:60.   **24:22** Hebrew *a gold nose-ring weighing a half shekel* [0.2 ounces or 6 grams] *and two gold bracelets weighing 10 shekels* [4 ounces or 114 grams].

**Cross-references (side column):**

**24:5** Gen 24:39

**24:7** Gen 12:1, 7; 16:7; 22:11 / Rom 4:13 / †Gal 3:16

**24:10** Gen 11:29 / Deut 23:4

**24:11** Gen 24:42

**24:12** Gen 24:27, 48

**24:14** Judg 6:17 / 1 Sam 14:10

**24:15** Gen 22:20-24

**24:16** Gen 12:11; 29:17

**24:17** 1 Kgs 17:10 / John 4:7

**24:19** Gen 24:14

**24:22** Gen 24:47

**24:24** Gen 24:15

---

**24:6** Abraham wanted Isaac to stay in Canaan, but he didn't want him to marry one of the local girls. This contrasts to the way Hagar selected a wife for Ishmael in 21:21. To have Isaac stay and marry a woman from Canaan would have been easier. But Abraham wanted to obey God in the *who* as well as in the *where*. Make your obedience full and complete.

**24:11** The well, the chief source of water for an entire village, was usually located outside town along the main road. Many people had to walk a mile or more for their water. They could use only what they could carry home. Farmers and shepherds would come from nearby fields to draw water for their animals. The well was a good place to meet new friends or to chat with old ones. Rebekah would have visited the well twice daily to draw water for her family.

**24:12** Abraham's servant asked God for guidance in this very important task. Obviously Eliezer (see 15:2) had learned much about faith and about God from his master. What are your family members, friends, and associates learning about God from watching you? Be like Abraham, setting an example of dependent faith. And be like Eliezer, asking God for guidance before any venture.

**24:14** Was it right for Abraham's servant to ask God for such a specific sign? The sign he requested was only slightly out of the ordinary. The hospitality of the day required women at the well to offer water to weary travelers, but not to their animals. Eliezer was simply asking God to show him a woman with an attitude of service—someone who would go beyond the expected. An offer to water his camels would indicate that kind of attitude. Eliezer did not ask for a woman with good looks or wealth. He knew the importance of finding a woman with the right heart, and he asked God to help him with this task.

**24:15, 16** Rebekah had physical beauty, but the servant was looking for a sign of inner beauty. Appearance is important to us, and we spend time and money improving it. But how much effort do we put into developing our inner beauty? Patience, kindness, and joy are the beauty treatments that help us become truly lovely—on the inside.

**24:18-21** Rebekah's servant spirit was clearly demonstrated as she willingly and quickly drew water for Eliezer and his camels. The pots used for carrying water were large and heavy. A thirsty camel drinks a lot of water—up to 25 gallons after a week's travel. Seeing Rebekah go to work, Eliezer knew this was a woman with a heart for doing far more than the bare minimum. Do you have a servant spirit? When asked to help or when you see a need, go beyond the minimum.

**24:26**
Exod 4:31

**24:27**
Gen 14:20;
24:12, 48

**24:28**
Gen 29:12

**24:29**
Gen 25:20; 29:5

**24:30**
Gen 24:10

**24:31**
Gen 26:29

**24:34**
Gen 24:1

**24:35**
Gen 12:2

<sup>26</sup>The man bowed low and worshiped the LORD. <sup>27</sup>"Praise the LORD, the God of my master, Abraham," he said. "The LORD has shown unfailing love and faithfulness to my master, for he has led me straight to my master's relatives."

<sup>28</sup>The young woman ran home to tell her family everything that had happened. <sup>29</sup>Now Rebekah had a brother named Laban, who ran out to meet the man at the spring. <sup>30</sup>He had seen the nose-ring and the bracelets on his sister's wrists, and had heard Rebekah tell what the man had said. So he rushed out to the spring, where the man was still standing beside his camels. <sup>31</sup>Laban said to him, "Come and stay with us, you who are blessed by the LORD! Why are you standing here outside the town when I have a room all ready for you and a place prepared for the camels?"

<sup>32</sup>So the man went home with Laban, and Laban unloaded the camels, gave him straw for their bedding, fed them, and provided water for the man and the camel drivers to wash their feet. <sup>33</sup>Then food was served. But Abraham's servant said, "I don't want to eat until I have told you why I have come."

"All right," Laban said, "tell us."

<sup>34</sup>"I am Abraham's servant," he explained. <sup>35</sup>"And the LORD has greatly blessed my master; he has become a wealthy man. The LORD has given him flocks of sheep and goats, herds of cattle, a fortune in silver and gold, and many male and female servants and camels and donkeys.

---

## REBEKAH

Some people are initiators. They help get the ball rolling. Rebekah would easily stand out in this group. Her life was characterized by initiative. When she saw a need, she took action, even though the action was not always right.

It was Rebekah's initiative that first caught the attention of Eliezer, the servant Abraham sent to find a wife for Isaac. It was common courtesy to give a drink to a stranger, but it took added character to also fetch water for ten thirsty camels. Later, after hearing the details of Eliezer's mission, Rebekah was immediately willing to be Isaac's bride.

Several later events help us see how initiative can be misdirected. Rebekah was aware that God's plan would be channeled through Jacob, not Esau (Genesis 25:23). So not only did Jacob become her favorite; she actually planned ways to ensure that he would overshadow his older twin. Meanwhile, Isaac preferred Esau. This created a conflict between the couple. She felt justified in deceiving her husband when the time came to bless the sons, and her ingenious plan was carried out to perfection.

Most of the time we try to justify the things we choose to do. Often we attempt to add God's approval to our actions. While it is true that our actions will not spoil God's plan, it is also true that we are responsible for what we do and must always be cautious about our motives. When thinking about a course of action, are you simply seeking God's stamp of approval on something you've already decided to do? Or are you willing to set the plan aside if the principles and commands of God's Word are against the action? Initiative and action are admirable and right when they are controlled by God's wisdom.

| | |
|---|---|
| **Strengths and accomplishments** | • When confronted with a need, she took immediate action<br>• She was accomplishment oriented |
| **Weaknesses and mistakes** | • Her initiative was not always balanced by wisdom<br>• She favored one of her sons<br>• She deceived her husband |
| **Lessons from her life** | • Our actions must be guided by God's Word<br>• God even makes use of our mistakes in his plan<br>• Parental favoritism hurts a family |
| **Vital statistics** | • Where: Haran, Canaan<br>• Occupation: Wife, mother, household manager<br>• Relatives: Grandparents: Nahor and Milcah. Father: Bethuel. Husband: Isaac. Brother: Laban. Twin sons: Esau and Jacob. |
| **Key verses** | "And Isaac brought Rebekah into his mother Sarah's tent, and she became his wife. He loved her deeply, and she was a special comfort to him after the death of his mother" (Genesis 24:67). "Isaac loved Esau because he enjoyed eating the wild game Esau brought home, but Rebekah loved Jacob" (Genesis 25:28). |

Rebekah's story is told in Genesis 24–27. She is also mentioned in Romans 9:10.

---

**24:26, 27** As soon as Abraham's servant knew that God had answered his prayer, he thanked God for his goodness and guidance. God will also use and lead us if we are available like Eliezer. Our first response should be praise and thanksgiving that God would choose to work in and through us.

36"When Sarah, my master's wife, was very old, she gave birth to my master's son, and my master has given him everything he owns. 37And my master made me take an oath. He said, 'Do not allow my son to marry one of these local Canaanite women. 38Go instead to my father's house, to my relatives, and find a wife there for my son.'

39"But I said to my master, 'What if I can't find a young woman who is willing to go back with me?' 40He responded, 'The LORD, in whose presence I have lived, will send his angel with you and will make your mission successful. Yes, you must find a wife for my son from among my relatives, from my father's family. 41Then you will have fulfilled your obligation. But if you go to my relatives and they refuse to let her go with you, you will be free from my oath.'

42"So today when I came to the spring, I prayed this prayer: 'O LORD, God of my master, Abraham, please give me success on this mission. 43See, I am standing here beside this spring. This is my request. When a young woman comes to draw water, I will say to her, "Please give me a little drink of water from your jug." 44If she says, "Yes, have a drink, and I will draw water for your camels, too," let her be the one you have selected to be the wife of my master's son.'

45"Before I had finished praying in my heart, I saw Rebekah coming out with her water jug on her shoulder. She went down to the spring and drew water. So I said to her, 'Please give me a drink.' 46She quickly lowered her jug from her shoulder and said, 'Yes, have a drink, and I will water your camels, too!' So I drank, and then she watered the camels.

47"Then I asked, 'Whose daughter are you?' She replied, 'I am the daughter of Bethuel, and my grandparents are Nahor and Milcah.' So I put the ring on her nose, and the bracelets on her wrists.

48"Then I bowed low and worshiped the LORD. I praised the LORD, the God of my master, Abraham, because he had led me straight to my master's niece to be his son's wife. 49So tell me—will you or won't you show unfailing love and faithfulness to my master? Please tell me yes or no, and then I'll know what to do next.'

50Then Laban and Bethuel replied, "The LORD has obviously brought you here, so there is nothing we can say. 51Here is Rebekah; take her and go. Yes, let her be the wife of your master's son, as the LORD has directed."

52When Abraham's servant heard their answer, he bowed down to the ground and worshiped the LORD. 53Then he brought out silver and gold jewelry and clothing and presented them to Rebekah. He also gave expensive presents to her brother and mother. 54Then they ate their meal, and the servant and the men with him stayed there overnight.

But early the next morning, Abraham's servant said, "Send me back to my master."

55"But we want Rebekah to stay with us at least ten days," her brother and mother said. "Then she can go."

56But he said, "Don't delay me. The LORD has made my mission successful; now send me back so I can return to my master."

57"Well," they said, "we'll call Rebekah and ask her what she thinks." 58So they called Rebekah. "Are you willing to go with this man?" they asked her.

And she replied, "Yes, I will go."

59So they said good-bye to Rebekah and sent her away with Abraham's servant and his men. The woman who had been Rebekah's childhood nurse went along with her. 60They gave her this blessing as she parted:

"Our sister, may you become
    the mother of many millions!
May your descendants be strong
    and conquer the cities of their enemies."

61Then Rebekah and her servant girls mounted the camels and followed the man. So Abraham's servant took Rebekah and went on his way.

62Meanwhile, Isaac, whose home was in the Negev, had returned from Beer-lahai-roi. 63One evening as he was walking and meditating in the fields, he looked up and saw the camels coming. 64When Rebekah looked up and saw Isaac, she quickly dismounted

**24:36** Gen 21:1-7; 25:5
**24:37** Gen 24:2-4
**24:40** Gen 24:7
**24:45** 1 Sam 1:13
**24:47** Gen 24:23-24
**24:49** Gen 47:29
**24:50** Ps 118:23
**24:52** Gen 24:26
**24:54** Gen 30:25
**24:55** Judg 19:4
**24:59** Gen 35:8
**24:60** Gen 17:16; 22:17
**24:62** Gen 16:14
**24:63** Ps 119:15, 27, 48

---

**24:42, 48** When Eliezer told his story to Laban, he spoke openly of God and his goodness. Often we do the opposite, afraid that we will be misunderstood, rejected, or seen as too religious. Instead, we should share openly what God is doing for us.

**24:64, 65** When Rebekah learned that the man coming to greet them was Isaac, her husband-to-be, she followed two Oriental customs. She dismounted from her camel to show respect, and she placed a veil over her face as a bride.

from her camel. 65"Who is that man walking through the fields to meet us?" she asked the servant.

And he replied, "It is my master." So Rebekah covered her face with her veil. 66Then the servant told Isaac everything he had done.

67And Isaac brought Rebekah into his mother Sarah's tent, and she became his wife. He loved her deeply, and she was a special comfort to him after the death of his mother.

### 7. Abraham dies

**25** Abraham married another wife, whose name was Keturah. 2She gave birth to Zimran, Jokshan, Medan, Midian, Ishbak, and Shuah. 3Jokshan was the father of Sheba and Dedan. Dedan's descendants were the Asshurites, Letushites, and Leummites. 4Midian's sons were Ephah, Epher, Hanoch, Abida, and Eldaah. These were all descendants of Abraham through Keturah.

5Abraham gave everything he owned to his son Isaac. 6But before he died, he gave gifts to the sons of his concubines and sent them off to a land in the east, away from Isaac.

7Abraham lived for 175 years, 8and he died at a ripe old age, having lived a long and satisfying life. He breathed his last and joined his ancestors in death. 9His sons Isaac and Ishmael buried him in the cave of Machpelah, near Mamre, in the field of Ephron son of Zohar the

**24:67**
Gen 23:1-2; 25:20;
29:18

**25:1-4**
//1 Chr 1:32-33

**25:5**
Gen 24:35-36
**25:7**
Gen 12:4
**25:9-10**
Gen 23:17-18;
49:29; 50:13

**ESAU**

Common sense isn't all that common. In fact, the common thread in many decisions is that they don't make sense. Esau's life was filled with choices he must have regretted bitterly. He appears to have been a person who found it hard to consider consequences, reacting to the need of the moment without realizing what he was giving up to meet that need. Trading his birthright for a bowl of stew was the clearest example of this weakness. He also chose wives in direct opposition to his parents' wishes. He learned the hard way.

What are you willing to trade for the things you want? Do you find yourself, at times, willing to negotiate *anything* for what you feel you need *now*? Does your family, spouse, integrity, body, or soul get included in these deals? Do you sometimes feel that the important parts of life escaped while you were grabbing for something else?

If so, your initial response, like Esau's, may be deep anger. In itself that isn't wrong, as long as you direct the energy of that anger toward a solution and not toward yourself or others as the cause of the problem. Your greatest need is to find a focal point other than "what I need now." The only worthy focal point is God. A relationship with him will not only give an ultimate purpose to your life; it will also be a daily guideline for living. Meet him in the pages of the Bible.

| | |
|---|---|
| **Strengths and accomplishments** | • Ancestor of the Edomites<br>• Known for his archery skill<br>• Able to forgive after explosive anger |
| **Weaknesses and mistakes** | • Tended to choose according to the immediate need rather than the long-range effect when faced with important decisions<br>• Angered his parents by poor marriage choices |
| **Lessons from his life** | • God allows certain events in our lives to accomplish his overall purposes, but we are still responsible for our actions<br>• Consequences are important to consider<br>• It is possible to have great anger and yet not sin |
| **Vital statistics** | • Where: Canaan<br>• Occupation: Skillful hunter<br>• Relatives: Parents: Isaac and Rebekah. Brother: Jacob. Wives: Judith, Basemath, and Mahalath. |
| **Key verses** | "Work at living in peace with everyone, and work at living a holy life, for those who are not holy will not see the Lord. Look after each other so that none of you fails to receive the grace of God. Watch out that no poisonous root of bitterness grows up to trouble you, corrupting many. Make sure that no one is immoral or godless like Esau, who traded his birthright as the firstborn son for a single meal. You know that afterward, when he wanted his father's blessing, he was rejected. It was too late for repentance, even though he begged with bitter tears" (Hebrews 12:14-17). |

Esau's story is told in Genesis 25–36. He is also mentioned in Malachi 1:2, 3; Romans 9:13; Hebrews 12:16, 17.

---

**25:1-6** Abraham took another wife, Keturah, after Sarah died. Although the sons and grandson of Abraham and Keturah received many gifts from Abraham, all his property and authority went to Isaac, his principal heir.

Hittite. [10]This was the field Abraham had purchased from the Hittites and where he had buried his wife Sarah. [11]After Abraham's death, God blessed his son Isaac, who settled near Beer-lahai-roi in the Negev.

25:11
Gen 12:2; 24:62

### Ishmael's Descendants

[12]This is the account of the family of Ishmael, the son of Abraham through Hagar, Sarah's Egyptian servant. [13]Here is a list, by their names and clans, of Ishmael's descendants: The oldest was Nebaioth, followed by Kedar, Adbeel, Mibsam, [14]Mishma, Dumah, Massa, [15]Hadad, Tema, Jetur, Naphish, and Kedemah. [16]These twelve sons of Ishmael became the founders of twelve tribes named after them, listed according to the places they settled and camped. [17]Ishmael lived for 137 years. Then he breathed his last and joined his ancestors in death. [18]Ishmael's descendants occupied the region from Havilah to Shur, which is east of Egypt in the direction of Asshur. There they lived in open hostility toward all their relatives.*

25:12-16
//1 Chr 1:29-31

25:17
Gen 25:8
25:18
Gen 16:12; 20:1

## E. THE STORY OF ISAAC (25:19—28:9)
Isaac inherited everything from his father, including God's promise to make his descendants into a great nation. As a boy, Isaac did not resist as his father prepared to sacrifice him, and as a man, he gladly accepted the wife that others chose for him. Through Isaac, we learn how to let God guide our life and place his will ahead of our own.

### 1. Jacob and Esau
[19]This is the account of the family of Isaac, the son of Abraham. [20]When Isaac was forty years old, he married Rebekah, the daughter of Bethuel the Aramean from Paddan-aram and the sister of Laban the Aramean.

[21]Isaac pleaded with the LORD on behalf of his wife, because she was unable to have children. The LORD answered Isaac's prayer, and Rebekah became pregnant with twins. [22]But the two children struggled with each other in her womb. So she went to ask the LORD about it. "Why is this happening to me?" she asked.

25:21
Gen 21:2

[23]And the LORD told her, "The sons in your womb will become two nations. From the very beginning, the two nations will be rivals. One nation will be stronger than the other; and your older son will serve your younger son."

25:23
Gen 17:2-4; 27:29;
48:19
Num 20:14
Deut 2:4, 8
†Rom 9:11-12

[24]And when the time came to give birth, Rebekah discovered that she did indeed have twins! [25]The first one was very red at birth and covered with thick hair like a fur coat. So they named him Esau.* [26]Then the other twin was born with his hand grasping Esau's heel. So they named him Jacob.* Isaac was sixty years old when the twins were born.

25:25
Gen 27:11
25:26
Hos 12:3

### Esau Sells His Birthright
[27]As the boys grew up, Esau became a skillful hunter. He was an outdoorsman, but Jacob had a quiet temperament, preferring to stay at home. [28]Isaac loved Esau because he enjoyed eating the wild game Esau brought home, but Rebekah loved Jacob.

[29]One day when Jacob was cooking some stew, Esau arrived home from the wilderness exhausted and hungry. [30]Esau said to Jacob, "I'm starved! Give me some of that red stew!" (This is how Esau got his other name, Edom, which means "red.")

25:30
Gen 36:1, 8

[31]"All right," Jacob replied, "but trade me your rights as the firstborn son."

[32]"Look, I'm dying of starvation!" said Esau. "What good is my birthright to me now?"

25:31
Deut 21:16-17
1 Chr 5:1-2

25:18 The meaning of the Hebrew is uncertain.   25:25 *Esau* sounds like a Hebrew term that means "hair."
25:26 *Jacob* sounds like the Hebrew words for "heel" and "deceiver."

---

25:21  As Isaac pleaded with God for children, so the Bible encourages us to ask and even plead for our most personal and important requests. God wants to grant our requests, but he wants us to ask him. Even then, as Isaac learned, God may decide to withhold his answer for a while in order to (1) deepen our insight into what we really need, (2) broaden our appreciation for his answers, or (3) allow us to mature so we can use his gifts more wisely.

25:31  A birthright was a special honor given to the firstborn son. It included a double portion of the family inheritance along with the honor of one day becoming the family's leader. The oldest son could sell his birthright or give it away if he chose, but in so doing, he would lose both material goods and his leadership position. By trading his birthright, Esau showed complete disregard for the spiritual blessings that would have come his way if he had kept it.

25:32, 33  Esau traded the lasting benefits of his birthright for the immediate pleasure of food. He acted on impulse, satisfying his immediate desires without pausing to consider the long-range consequences of what he was about to do. We can fall into the same trap. When we see something we want, our first impulse is to get it. At first we feel intensely satisfied and sometimes even powerful because we have obtained what we set out to get. But immediate pleasure often loses sight of the future. We can avoid making Esau's mistake by comparing the short-term satisfaction with its long-range consequences before we act.

Esau exaggerated his hunger. "I'm dying of starvation!" he said. This thought made his choice much easier because if he was starving, what good was an inheritance anyway? The pressure of the moment distorted his perspective and made his

25:33
Gen 27:36
Heb 12:16

³³But Jacob said, "First you must swear that your birthright is mine." So Esau swore an oath, thereby selling all his rights as the firstborn to his brother, Jacob.

³⁴Then Jacob gave Esau some bread and lentil stew. Esau ate the meal, then got up and left. He showed contempt for his rights as the firstborn.

---

**JACOB**

Abraham, Isaac, and Jacob are among the most significant people in the Old Testament. It is important to realize that this significance is not based upon their personal characters, but upon the character of God. They were all men who earned the grudging respect and even fear of their peers; they were wealthy and powerful, and yet each was capable of lying, deceit, and selfishness. They were not the perfect heroes we might have expected; instead, they were just like us, trying to please God, but often falling short.

Jacob was the third link in God's plan to start a nation from Abraham. The success of that plan was more often in spite of than because of Jacob's life. Before Jacob was born, God promised that his plan would be worked out through Jacob and not his twin brother, Esau. Although Jacob's methods were not always respectable, his skill, determination, and patience have to be admired. As we follow him from birth to death, we are able to see God's work.

Jacob's life had four stages, each marked by a personal encounter with God. In the first stage, Jacob lived up to his name, which means "he grasps the heel" (figuratively, "he deceives"). He grabbed Esau's heel at birth, and by the time he fled from home, he had also grabbed his brother's birthright and blessing. During his flight, God first appeared to him. Not only did God confirm to Jacob his blessing, but he awakened in Jacob a personal knowledge of himself. In the second stage, Jacob experienced life from the other side, being manipulated and deceived by Laban. But there is a curious change: The Jacob of stage one would simply have left Laban, whereas the Jacob of stage two, after deciding to leave, waited six years for God's permission. In the third stage, Jacob was in a new role as grabber. This time, by the Jordan River, he grabbed on to God and wouldn't let go. He realized his dependence on the God who had continued to bless him. His relationship to God became essential to his life, and his name was changed to Israel, "he struggles with God." Jacob's last stage of life was to *be* grabbed—God achieved a firm hold on him. In responding to Joseph's invitation to come to Egypt, Jacob was clearly unwilling to make a move without God's approval.

Can you think of times when God has made himself known to you? Do you allow yourself to meet him as you study his Word? What difference have these experiences made in your life? Are you more like the young Jacob, forcing God to track you down in the desert of your own plans and mistakes? Or are you more like the older Jacob who presented his desires and plans before God for his approval before taking any action?

| | |
|---|---|
| **Strengths and accomplishments** | • Father of the 12 tribes of Israel<br>• Third in the Abrahamic line of God's plan<br>• Determined and willing to work long and hard for what he wanted<br>• Good businessman |
| **Weaknesses and mistakes** | • When faced with conflict, relied on his own resources rather than going to God for help<br>• Tended to accumulate wealth for its own sake |
| **Lessons from his life** | • Security does not lie in the accumulation of goods<br>• All human intentions and actions—for good or evil—are woven by God into his ongoing plan |
| **Vital statistics** | • Where: Canaan<br>• Occupation: Shepherd, livestock owner<br>• Relatives: Parents: Isaac and Rebekah. Brother: Esau. Father-in-law: Laban. Wives: Rachel and Leah. Offspring: Twelve sons and one daughter are mentioned in the Bible. |
| **Key verse** | "What's more, I am with you, and I will protect you wherever you go. One day I will bring you back to this land. I will not leave you until I have finished giving you everything I have promised you" (Genesis 28:15). |

Jacob's story is told in Genesis 25–50. He is also mentioned in Hosea 12:2-5; Matthew 1:2; 22:32; Acts 7:8-16; Romans 9:11-13; Hebrews 11:9, 20, 21.

---

decision seem urgent. We often experience similar pressures. For example, when we feel sexual pressure, a marriage vow may seem unimportant. We might feel such great pressure in one area that nothing else seems to matter and we lose our perspec-

tive. Getting through that short, pressure-filled moment is often the most difficult part of overcoming a temptation.

## 2. Isaac and Abimelech
### Isaac Deceives Abimelech

**26** A severe famine now struck the land, as had happened before in Abraham's time. So Isaac moved to Gerar, where Abimelech, king of the Philistines, lived. ²The LORD appeared to Isaac and said, "Do not go down to Egypt, but do as I tell you. ³Live here as a foreigner in this land, and I will be with you and bless you. I hereby confirm that I will give all these lands to you and your descendants,* just as I solemnly promised Abraham, your father. ⁴I will cause your descendants to become as numerous as the stars of the sky, and I will give them all these lands. And through your descendants all the nations of the earth will be blessed. ⁵I will do this because Abraham listened to me and obeyed all my requirements, commands, decrees, and instructions." ⁶So Isaac stayed in Gerar.

⁷When the men who lived there asked Isaac about his wife, Rebekah, he said, "She is my sister." He was afraid to say, "She is my wife." He thought, "They will kill me to get her, because she is so beautiful." ⁸But some time later, Abimelech, king of the Philistines, looked out his window and saw Isaac caressing Rebekah.

⁹Immediately, Abimelech called for Isaac and exclaimed, "She is obviously your wife! Why did you say, 'She is my sister'?"

"Because I was afraid someone would kill me to get her from me," Isaac replied.

¹⁰"How could you do this to us?" Abimelech exclaimed. "One of my people might easily have taken your wife and slept with her, and you would have made us guilty of great sin."

¹¹Then Abimelech issued a public proclamation: "Anyone who touches this man or his wife will be put to death!"

### Conflict over Water Rights

¹²When Isaac planted his crops that year, he harvested a hundred times more grain than he planted, for the LORD blessed him. ¹³He became a very rich man, and his wealth continued to grow. ¹⁴He acquired so many flocks of sheep and goats, herds of cattle, and servants that the Philistines became jealous of him. ¹⁵So the Philistines filled up all of Isaac's wells with dirt. These were the wells that had been dug by the servants of his father, Abraham.

¹⁶Finally, Abimelech ordered Isaac to leave the country. "Go somewhere else," he said, "for you have become too powerful for us."

¹⁷So Isaac moved away to the Gerar Valley, where he set up their tents and settled down. ¹⁸He reopened the wells his father had dug, which the Philistines had filled in after Abraham's death. Isaac also restored the names Abraham had given them.

26:3 Hebrew *seed*; also in 26:4, 24.

**26:1** Gen 12:10; 20:1-2
**26:2** Gen 12:1, 7
**26:3** Gen 12:7; 15:15, 18
**26:4** Gen 15:5; 22:17 Exod 32:13 †Acts 3:25 †Gal 3:8
**26:7** Gen 12:11-13; 20:2, 12
**26:10** Gen 20:7-10
**26:12** Gen 26:3
**26:13** Gen 24:35; 25:5
**26:15** Gen 21:25
**26:16** Exod 1:9

---

**26:1** The Philistines would become some of Israel's fiercest enemies. The Philistines were one group of a number of migrating sea peoples from the Aegean Sea who had settled in Palestine. They arrived by way of Crete and Cyprus and were used as mercenaries by Canaanite rulers. These people, living along the southwest coast, were few but ferocious in battle. Although friendly to Isaac, this small group was the forerunner of the nation that would plague Israel during the time of Joshua, the judges, and David. This King Abimelech was not the same Abimelech that Abraham encountered (chapters 20–21). *Abimelech* may have been a dynastic name of the Philistine rulers.

**26:7-11** Isaac was afraid that the men in Gerar would kill him to get his beautiful wife, Rebekah. So he lied, claiming that Rebekah was his sister. Where did he learn that trick? He may have known about the actions of his father, Abraham (see 12:10-13 and 20:1-5). Parents help shape the world's future by the way they shape their children's values. The first step toward helping children live right is for the parents to live right. Your actions are often copied by those closest to you. What kind of example are you setting for your children?

**26:12-16** God kept his promise to bless Isaac. The neighboring Philistines grew jealous because everything Isaac did seemed to go right. So they filled his wells with dirt and tried to get rid of him. Jealousy is a dividing force strong enough to tear apart the mightiest of nations or the closest of friends. It forces you to separate yourself from what you were longing for in the first place. When you find yourself becoming jealous of others, try thanking God for their good fortune. Before striking out in anger, consider what you could lose—a friend, a job, a spouse?

**26:17, 18** The desolate Gerar area was located on the edge of a desert. Water was as precious as gold. A person who dug a well was staking a claim to the land. Some wells had locks to keep thieves from stealing the water. To fill in someone's well with dirt was an act of war; it was one of the most serious crimes in the land. Isaac had every right to fight back when the

**ISAAC'S MOVE TO GERAR**
Isaac had settled near Beer-lahai-roi ("the well of the Living One who sees me"), where his sons, Jacob and Esau, were born. A famine drove him to Gerar. But when he became wealthy, his jealous neighbors asked him to leave. From Gerar he moved to Beersheba.

26:19
John 4:10-11

19Isaac's servants also dug in the Gerar Valley and discovered a well of fresh water. 20But then the shepherds from Gerar came and claimed the spring. "This is our water," they said, and they argued over it with Isaac's herdsmen. So Isaac named the well Esek (which means "argument"). 21Isaac's men then dug another well, but again there was a dispute over it. So Isaac named it Sitnah (which means "hostility"). 22Abandoning that one, Isaac moved on and dug another well. This time there was no dispute over it, so Isaac named the place Rehoboth (which means "open space"), for he said, "At last the LORD has created enough space for us to prosper in this land."

26:22
Pss 4:1; 18:19
Isa 54:2

26:23
Gen 22:19
26:24
Gen 17:7; 22:17
Exod 3:6
26:25
Gen 12:7-8; 13:4

23From there Isaac moved to Beersheba, 24where the LORD appeared to him on the night of his arrival. "I am the God of your father, Abraham," he said. "Do not be afraid, for I am with you and will bless you. I will multiply your descendants, and they will become a great nation. I will do this because of my promise to Abraham, my servant." 25Then Isaac built an altar there and worshiped the LORD. He set up his camp at that place, and his servants dug another well.

### Isaac's Covenant with Abimelech

26:26
Gen 21:22
26:27
Gen 26:16
26:28
Gen 21:22-23

26One day King Abimelech came from Gerar with his adviser, Ahuzzath, and also Phicol, his army commander. 27"Why have you come here?" Isaac asked. "You obviously hate me, since you kicked me off your land."

28They replied, "We can plainly see that the LORD is with you. So we want to enter into a sworn treaty with you. Let's make a covenant. 29Swear that you will not harm us, just as we have never troubled you. We have always treated you well, and we sent you away from us in peace. And now look how the LORD has blessed you!"

26:30
Gen 31:54
26:31
Gen 21:31
26:33
Gen 21:31
26:34
Gen 28:8
26:35
Gen 27:46

30So Isaac prepared a covenant feast to celebrate the treaty, and they ate and drank together. 31Early the next morning, they each took a solemn oath not to interfere with each other. Then Isaac sent them home again, and they left him in peace.

32That very day Isaac's servants came and told him about a new well they had dug. "We've found water!" they exclaimed. 33So Isaac named the well Shibah (which means "oath"). And to this day the town that grew up there is called Beersheba (which means "well of the oath").

34At the age of forty, Esau married two Hittite wives: Judith, the daughter of Beeri, and Basemath, the daughter of Elon. 35But Esau's wives made life miserable for Isaac and Rebekah.

### 3. Jacob gets Isaac's blessing

27:1
Gen 25:25; 48:10

**27** One day when Isaac was old and turning blind, he called for Esau, his older son, and said, "My son."

"Yes, Father?" Esau replied.

27:2
Gen 47:29
27:3
Gen 25:27
27:4
Gen 24:60; 27:19;
48:9
27:5-6
Gen 25:27-28
27:8
Gen 27:13, 43

2"I am an old man now," Isaac said, "and I don't know when I may die. 3Take your bow and a quiver full of arrows, and go out into the open country to hunt some wild game for me. 4Prepare my favorite dish, and bring it here for me to eat. Then I will pronounce the blessing that belongs to you, my firstborn son, before I die."

5But Rebekah overheard what Isaac had said to his son Esau. So when Esau left to hunt for the wild game, 6she said to her son Jacob, "Listen. I overheard your father say to Esau, 7'Bring me some wild game and prepare me a delicious meal. Then I will bless you in the LORD's presence before I die.' 8Now, my son, listen to me. Do exactly as I tell you. 9Go out to the

---

Philistines ruined his wells, yet he chose to keep the peace. In the end, the Philistines respected him for his patience.

**26:17-22** Three times Isaac and his men dug new wells. When the first two disputes arose, Isaac moved on. Finally room was available for everyone. Rather than start a huge conflict, Isaac compromised for the sake of peace. Would you be willing to forsake an important position or valuable possession to keep peace? Ask God for the wisdom to know when to withdraw and when to stand and fight.

**26:26-31** With his enemies wanting to make a peace treaty, Isaac was quick to respond, turning the occasion into a celebration. We should be just as receptive to those who want to make peace with us. When God's influence in our lives attracts people—even enemies—we must take the opportunity to reach out to them with God's love.

**26:34, 35** Esau married pagan women, and this upset his

parents greatly. Most parents can be a storehouse of good advice, because they have a lifetime of insight into their children's character. You may not agree with everything your parents say, but at least talk with them and listen carefully. This will help avoid the hard feelings Esau experienced.

**27:5-10** When Rebekah learned that Isaac was preparing to bless Esau, she quickly devised a plan to trick him into blessing Jacob instead. Although God had already told her that Jacob would become the family leader (25:23), Rebekah took matters into her own hands. She resorted to doing something wrong to try to bring about what God had already said would happen. For Rebekah, the end justified the means. No matter how good we think our goals are, we should not attempt to achieve them by doing what is wrong. Would God approve of the methods you are using to accomplish your goals?

flocks, and bring me two fine young goats. I'll use them to prepare your father's favorite dish. 10Then take the food to your father so he can eat it and bless you before he dies."

11"But look," Jacob replied to Rebekah, "my brother, Esau, is a hairy man, and my skin is smooth. 12What if my father touches me? He'll see that I'm trying to trick him, and then he'll curse me instead of blessing me."

13But his mother replied, "Then let the curse fall on me, my son! Just do what I tell you. Go out and get the goats for me!"

14So Jacob went out and got the young goats for his mother. Rebekah took them and prepared a delicious meal, just the way Isaac liked it. 15Then she took Esau's favorite clothes, which were there in the house, and gave them to her younger son, Jacob. 16She covered his arms and the smooth part of his neck with the skin of the young goats. 17Then she gave Jacob the delicious meal, including freshly baked bread.

18So Jacob took the food to his father. "My father?" he said.

"Yes, my son," Isaac answered. "Who are you—Esau or Jacob?"

19Jacob replied, "It's Esau, your firstborn son. I've done as you told me. Here is the wild game. Now sit up and eat it so you can give me your blessing."

20Isaac asked, "How did you find it so quickly, my son?"

"The LORD your God put it in my path!" Jacob replied.

21Then Isaac said to Jacob, "Come closer so I can touch you and make sure that you really are Esau." 22So Jacob went closer to his father, and Isaac touched him. "The voice is Jacob's, but the hands are Esau's," Isaac said. 23But he did not recognize Jacob, because Jacob's hands felt hairy just like Esau's. So Isaac prepared to bless Jacob. 24"But are you really my son Esau?" he asked.

"Yes, I am," Jacob replied.

25Then Isaac said, "Now, my son, bring me the wild game. Let me eat it, and then I will give you my blessing." So Jacob took the food to his father, and Isaac ate it. He also drank the wine that Jacob served him. 26Then Isaac said to Jacob, "Please come a little closer and kiss me, my son."

27So Jacob went over and kissed him. And when Isaac caught the smell of his clothes, he was finally convinced, and he blessed his son. He said, "Ah! The smell of my son is like the smell of the outdoors, which the LORD has blessed!

28 "From the dew of heaven
    and the richness of the earth,
may God always give you abundant harvests of grain
    and bountiful new wine.
29 May many nations become your servants,
    and may they bow down to you.
May you be the master over your brothers,
    and may your mother's sons bow down to you.
All who curse you will be cursed,
    and all who bless you will be blessed."

30As soon as Isaac had finished blessing Jacob, and almost before Jacob had left his father, Esau returned from his hunt. 31Esau prepared a delicious meal and brought it to his father. Then he said, "Sit up, my father, and eat my wild game so you can give me your blessing."

**27:11**
Gen 25:25
**27:12**
Gen 9:25; 27:21-22
**27:13**
Gen 27:8

**27:15**
Gen 27:27

**27:19**
Gen 27:31

**27:21**
Gen 27:12
**27:23**
Gen 27:16

**27:25**
Gen 27:4

**27:27**
Ps 65:10
Heb 11:20

**27:28**
Deut 7:13;
33:13, 28
Zech 8:12

**27:29**
Gen 9:25-27; 12:3
Isa 45:14

**27:31**
Gen 27:4

---

**27:11, 12** How we react to a moral dilemma often exposes our real motives. Frequently we are more worried about getting caught than about doing what is right. Jacob did not seem concerned about the deceitfulness of his mother's plan; instead he was afraid of getting in trouble while carrying it out. If you are worried about getting caught, you are probably in a position that is less than honest. Let your fear of getting caught be a warning to do right. Jacob paid a huge price for carrying out this dishonest plan.

**27:11-13** Jacob hesitated when he heard Rebekah's deceitful plan. Although he questioned it for the wrong reason (fear of getting caught), he protested and thus gave her one last chance to reconsider. But Rebekah had become so wrapped up in her plan that she no longer saw clearly what she was doing. Sin had trapped her and was degrading her character. Correcting yourself in the middle of doing wrong may bring hurt and disappointment, but it also will bring freedom from sin's control.

**27:24** Although Jacob got the blessing he wanted, deceiving his father cost him dearly. These are some of the consequences of that deceit: (1) He never saw his mother again; (2) his brother wanted to kill him; (3) he was deceived by his uncle, Laban; (4) his family became torn by strife; (5) Esau became the founder of an enemy nation; (6) he was exiled from his family for years. Ironically, Jacob would have received the birthright and blessing anyway (25:23). Imagine how different his life would have been had he and his mother waited for God to work his way, in his time!

**27:32**
Gen 27:18

<sup>32</sup>But Isaac asked him, "Who are you?"

Esau replied, "It's your son, your firstborn son, Esau."

**27:33**
Gen 27:35

<sup>33</sup>Isaac began to tremble uncontrollably and said, "Then who just served me wild game? I have already eaten it, and I blessed him just before you came. And yes, that blessing must stand!"

**27:34**
Heb 12:17

<sup>34</sup>When Esau heard his father's words, he let out a loud and bitter cry. "Oh my father, what about me? Bless me, too!" he begged.

**27:35**
Gen 27:19
**27:36**
Gen 25:26

<sup>35</sup>But Isaac said, "Your brother was here, and he tricked me. He has taken away your blessing."

<sup>36</sup>Esau exclaimed, "No wonder his name is Jacob, for now he has cheated me twice.* First he took my rights as the firstborn, and now he has stolen my blessing. Oh, haven't you saved even one blessing for me?"

**27:37**
Gen 27:28-29

<sup>37</sup>Isaac said to Esau, "I have made Jacob your master and have declared that all his brothers will be his servants. I have guaranteed him an abundance of grain and wine—what is left for me to give you, my son?"

**27:38**
Heb 12:17

<sup>38</sup>Esau pleaded, "But do you have only one blessing? Oh my father, bless me, too!" Then Esau broke down and wept.

**27:39**
Heb 11:20

<sup>39</sup>Finally, his father, Isaac, said to him,

"You will live away from the richness of the earth,
  and away from the dew of the heaven above.

**27:40**
2 Kgs 8:20-22

<sup>40</sup> You will live by your sword,
  and you will serve your brother.
But when you decide to break free,
  you will shake his yoke from your neck."

### Jacob Flees to Paddan-Aram

**27:41**
Gen 32:3-11; 37:4

<sup>41</sup>From that time on, Esau hated Jacob because their father had given Jacob the blessing. And Esau began to scheme: "I will soon be mourning my father's death. Then I will kill my brother, Jacob."

**27:43**
Gen 27:8
**27:44**
Gen 31:41

<sup>42</sup>But Rebekah heard about Esau's plans. So she sent for Jacob and told him, "Listen, Esau is consoling himself by plotting to kill you. <sup>43</sup>So listen carefully, my son. Get ready and flee to my brother, Laban, in Haran. <sup>44</sup>Stay there with him until your brother cools off. <sup>45</sup>When he calms down and forgets what you have done to him, I will send for you to come back. Why should I lose both of you in one day?"

**27:46**
Gen 26:34-35

<sup>46</sup>Then Rebekah said to Isaac, "I'm sick and tired of these local Hittite women! I would rather die than see Jacob marry one of them."

**28:1**
Gen 24:3
**28:2**
Gen 25:20
**28:3**
Gen 17:16; 35:11
**28:4**
Gen 12:1-3; 15:7;
35:11

**28** So Isaac called for Jacob, blessed him, and said, "You must not marry any of these Canaanite women. <sup>2</sup>Instead, go at once to Paddan-aram, to the house of your grandfather Bethuel, and marry one of your uncle Laban's daughters. <sup>3</sup>May God Almighty* bless you and give you many children. And may your descendants multiply and become many nations! <sup>4</sup>May God pass on to you and your descendants* the blessings he promised to Abraham. May you own this land where you are now living as a foreigner, for God gave this land to Abraham."

**27:36** *Jacob* sounds like the Hebrew words for "heel" and "deceiver."   **28:3** Hebrew *El-Shaddai.*   **28:4** Hebrew *seed;* also in 28:13, 14.

---

**27:33** In ancient times, a person's word was binding (much like a written contract today), especially when it was a formal oath. This is why Isaac's blessing was irrevocable.

**27:33-37** Before the father died, he performed a ceremony of blessing, in which he officially handed over the birthright to the rightful heir. Although the firstborn son was entitled to the birthright, it was not actually his until the blessing was pronounced. Before the blessing was given, the father could take the birthright away from the oldest son and give it to a more deserving son. But after the blessing was given, the birthright could no longer be taken away. This is why fathers usually waited until late in life to pronounce the blessing. Although Jacob had been given the birthright by his older brother years before, he still needed his father's blessing to make it binding.

**27:41** Esau was so angry at Jacob that he failed to see his own wrong in giving away the birthright in the first place. Jealous anger blinds us from seeing the benefits we have and makes us dwell on what we don't have.

**27:41** When Esau lost the valuable family blessing, his future suddenly changed. Reacting in anger, he decided to kill Jacob. When you lose something of great value, or if others conspire against you and succeed, anger is the first and most natural reaction. But you can control your feelings by (1) recognizing your reaction for what it is, (2) praying for strength, and (3) asking God for help to see the opportunities that even your bad situation may provide.

5So Isaac sent Jacob away, and he went to Paddan-aram to stay with his uncle Laban, his mother's brother, the son of Bethuel the Aramean.

6Esau knew that his father, Isaac, had blessed Jacob and sent him to Paddan-aram to find a wife, and that he had warned Jacob, "You must not marry a Canaanite woman." 7He also knew that Jacob had obeyed his parents and gone to Paddan-aram. 8It was now very clear to Esau that his father did not like the local Canaanite women. 9So Esau visited his uncle Ishmael's family and married one of Ishmael's daughters, in addition to the wives he already had. His new wife's name was Mahalath. She was the sister of Nebaioth and the daughter of Ishmael, Abraham's son.

**28:6**
Gen 28:1

**28:8**
Gen 26:35

**28:9**
Gen 36:2

## F. THE STORY OF JACOB (28:10—36:43)
Jacob did everything, both right and wrong, with great zeal. He deceived his own brother, Esau, and his father Isaac. He wrestled with an angel and worked fourteen years to marry the woman he loved. Through Jacob we learn how a strong leader can also be a servant. We also see how wrong actions will always come back to haunt us.

### 1. Jacob starts a family
*Jacob's Dream at Bethel*

10Meanwhile, Jacob left Beersheba and traveled toward Haran. 11At sundown he arrived at a good place to set up camp and stopped there for the night. Jacob found a stone to rest his head against and lay down to sleep. 12As he slept, he dreamed of a stairway that reached from the earth up to heaven. And he saw the angels of God going up and down the stairway.

**28:10**
Gen 26:23

**28:12**
Gen 20:3
Num 12:6
†John 1:51

13At the top of the stairway stood the LORD, and he said, "I am the LORD, the God of your grandfather Abraham, and the God of your father, Isaac. The ground you are lying on belongs to you. I am giving it to you and your descendants. 14Your descendants will be as numerous as the dust of the earth! They will spread out in all directions—to the west and the east, to the north and the south. And all the families of the earth will be blessed through you and your descendants. 15What's more, I am with you, and I will protect you wherever you go. One day I will bring you back to this land. I will not leave you until I have finished giving you everything I have promised you."

**28:14**
Gen 12:2; 13:14;
22:17

**28:15**
Gen 48:21
Deut 7:9; 31:6, 8

16Then Jacob awoke from his sleep and said, "Surely the LORD is in this place, and I wasn't even aware of it!" 17But he was also afraid and said, "What an awesome place this is! It is none other than the house of God, the very gateway to heaven!"

**28:17**
Exod 3:5
Ps 68:35

18The next morning Jacob got up very early. He took the stone he had rested his head against, and he set it upright as a memorial pillar. Then he poured olive oil over it. 19He named that place Bethel (which means "house of God"), although it was previously called Luz.

**28:18**
Gen 35:14

**28:19**
Gen 12:8; 35:6;
48:3

20Then Jacob made this vow: "If God will indeed be with me and protect me on this journey, and if he will provide me with food and clothing, 21and if I return safely to my father's home, then the LORD will certainly be my God. 22And this memorial pillar I have set up will

**28:21**
Exod 15:2

**28:22**
Gen 14:20; 35:7
Deut 14:22

---

**28:9** Ishmael was Isaac's half brother, the son of Abraham and Hagar, Sarah's maidservant (16:1-4, 15). After marrying two foreign girls (26:34), Esau hoped his marriage into Ishmael's family would please his parents, Isaac and Rebekah.

**28:10-15** God's covenant promise to Abraham and Isaac was offered to Jacob as well. But it was not enough to be Abraham's grandson; Jacob had to establish his own personal relationship with God. God has no grandchildren; each person must have a personal relationship with him. It is not enough to hear wonderful stories about Christians in your family. You need to become part of the story yourself (see Galatians 3:6, 7).

**28:19** Bethel was about ten miles north of Jerusalem and 60 miles north of Beersheba, where Jacob left his family. This was where Abraham made one of his first sacrifices to God when he entered the land. At first, Bethel became an important center for worship; later it was a center of idol worship. The prophet Hosea condemned its evil practices.

**28:20-22** Was Jacob trying to bargain with God? It is possible that he, in his ignorance of how to worship and serve God, treated God like a servant who would perform a service for a tip. More likely, Jacob was not bargaining but pledging his future to God. He may have been saying, in effect, "Because you have blessed me, I will follow you." Whether Jacob was bargaining or pledging, God blessed him. But God also had some difficult lessons for Jacob to learn.

**JACOB'S TRIP TO HARAN**   After deceiving Esau, Jacob ran for his life, traveling more than 400 miles to Haran, where an uncle, Laban, lived. In Haran, Jacob married and started a family.

become a place for worshiping God, and I will present to God a tenth of everything he gives me."

## Jacob Arrives at Paddan-Aram

**29** Then Jacob hurried on, finally arriving in the land of the east. ²He saw a well in the distance. Three flocks of sheep and goats lay in an open field beside it, waiting to be watered. But a heavy stone covered the mouth of the well.

³It was the custom there to wait for all the flocks to arrive before removing the stone and watering the animals. Afterward the stone would be placed back over the mouth of the well. ⁴Jacob went over to the shepherds and asked, "Where are you from, my friends?"

"We are from Haran," they answered.

⁵"Do you know a man there named Laban, the grandson of Nahor?" he asked.

"Yes, we do," they replied.

⁶"Is he doing well?" Jacob asked.

"Yes, he's well," they answered. "Look, here comes his daughter Rachel with the flock now."

⁷Jacob said, "Look, it's still broad daylight—too early to round up the animals. Why don't you water the sheep and goats so they can get back out to pasture?"

⁸"We can't water the animals until all the flocks have arrived," they replied. "Then the shepherds move the stone from the mouth of the well, and we water all the sheep and goats."

⁹Jacob was still talking with them when Rachel arrived with her father's flock, for she was a shepherd. ¹⁰And because Rachel was his cousin—the daughter of Laban, his mother's brother—and because the sheep and goats belonged to his uncle Laban, Jacob went over to the well and moved the stone from its mouth and watered his uncle's flock. ¹¹Then Jacob kissed Rachel, and he wept aloud. ¹²He explained to Rachel that he was her cousin on her father's side—the son of her aunt Rebekah. So Rachel quickly ran and told her father, Laban.

¹³As soon as Laban heard that his nephew Jacob had arrived, he ran out to meet him. He embraced and kissed him and brought him home. When Jacob had told him his story, ¹⁴Laban exclaimed, "You really are my own flesh and blood!"

## Jacob Marries Leah and Rachel

After Jacob had stayed with Laban for about a month, ¹⁵Laban said to him, "You shouldn't work for me without pay just because we are relatives. Tell me how much your wages should be."

¹⁶Now Laban had two daughters. The older daughter was named Leah, and the younger one was Rachel. ¹⁷There was no sparkle in Leah's eyes,* but Rachel had a beautiful figure and a lovely face. ¹⁸Since Jacob was in love with Rachel, he told her father, "I'll work for you for seven years if you'll give me Rachel, your younger daughter, as my wife."

¹⁹"Agreed!" Laban replied. "I'd rather give her to you than to anyone else. Stay and work with me." ²⁰So Jacob worked seven years to pay for Rachel. But his love for her was so strong that it seemed to him but a few days.

²¹Finally, the time came for him to marry her. "I have fulfilled my agreement," Jacob said to Laban. "Now give me my wife so I can sleep with her."

²²So Laban invited everyone in the neighborhood and prepared a wedding feast. ²³But that night, when it was dark, Laban took Leah to Jacob, and he slept with her. ²⁴(Laban had given Leah a servant, Zilpah, to be her maid.)

**29:17** Or *Leah had dull eyes,* or *Leah had soft eyes.* The meaning of the Hebrew is uncertain.

Marginal references:
- 29:1 Judg 6:3, 33
- 29:2 Gen 24:10-11
- 29:4 Gen 28:10
- 29:5 Gen 11:29
- 29:6 Exod 2:16
- 29:10 Exod 2:17
- 29:11 Gen 33:4
- 29:12 Gen 28:5
- 29:14 Judg 9:2; 2 Sam 5:1
- 29:15 Gen 30:28; 31:7, 41
- 29:16 Gen 29:25-26
- 29:17 Gen 12:11
- 29:18 Gen 24:67; Hos 12:12
- 29:20 Song 8:7
- 29:22 Judg 14:10
- 29:23 Gen 24:65; 38:14
- 29:24 Gen 30:9

**29:18-27** It was the custom of the day for a man to present a dowry, or substantial gift, to the family of his future wife. This was to compensate the family for the loss of the girl. Jacob's dowry was not a material possession, for he had none to offer. Instead, he agreed to work seven years for Laban. But there was another custom of the land that Laban did not tell Jacob. The older daughter had to be married first. By giving Jacob Leah and not Rachel, Laban tricked him into promising another seven years of hard work.

**29:20-28** People often wonder if working a long time for something they desire is worth it. Jacob worked seven years to marry Rachel. After being tricked, he agreed to work seven more years for her (although he did get to marry Rachel shortly after he married Leah)! The most important goals and desires are worth working for and waiting for. Movies and television have created the illusion that people have to wait only about an hour to solve their problems or get what they want. Don't be trapped into thinking the same is true in real life. Patience is hardest when we need it the most, but it is the key to achieving our goals.

**29:23-25** Jacob was enraged when he learned that Laban had tricked him. The deceiver of Esau was now deceived himself. How natural it is for us to become upset at an injustice done to us while closing our eyes to the injustices we do to others. Sin has a way of coming back to haunt us.

²⁵But when Jacob woke up in the morning—it was Leah! "What have you done to me?" Jacob raged at Laban. "I worked seven years for Rachel! Why have you tricked me?"

²⁶"It's not our custom here to marry off a younger daughter ahead of the firstborn," Laban replied. ²⁷"But wait until the bridal week is over, then we'll give you Rachel, too—provided you promise to work another seven years for me."

²⁸So Jacob agreed to work seven more years. A week after Jacob had married Leah, Laban gave him Rachel, too. ²⁹(Laban gave Rachel a servant, Bilhah, to be her maid.) ³⁰So Jacob slept with Rachel, too, and he loved her much more than Leah. He then stayed and worked for Laban the additional seven years.

### Jacob's Many Children

³¹When the LORD saw that Leah was unloved, he enabled her to have children, but Rachel could not conceive. ³²So Leah became pregnant and gave birth to a son. She named him Reuben,* for she said, "The LORD has noticed my misery, and now my husband will love me."

³³She soon became pregnant again and gave birth to another son. She named him Simeon,* for she said, "The LORD heard that I was unloved and has given me another son."

³⁴Then she became pregnant a third time and gave birth to another son. She named him Levi,* for she said, "Surely this time my husband will feel affection for me, since I have given him three sons!"

³⁵Once again Leah became pregnant and gave birth to another son. She named him Judah,* for she said, "Now I will praise the LORD!" And then she stopped having children.

**30** When Rachel saw that she wasn't having any children for Jacob, she became jealous of her sister. She pleaded with Jacob, "Give me children, or I'll die!"

²Then Jacob became furious with Rachel. "Am I God?" he asked. "He's the one who has kept you from having children!"

³Then Rachel told him, "Take my maid, Bilhah, and sleep with her. She will bear children

**29:25** Gen 12:18
**29:27** Judg 14:12
**29:29** Gen 30:3
**29:30** Gen 29:16
**29:31** Deut 21:15-17
**29:32** Gen 30:23; 37:21; 46:8
**29:33** Deut 21:15
**29:34** Gen 49:5
**29:35** Gen 49:8; Matt 1:2-3
**30:1** 1 Sam 1:5-6
**30:2** Gen 20:18; 29:31
**30:3-4** Gen 16:2-4

**29:32** *Reuben* means "Look, a son!" It also sounds like the Hebrew for "He has seen my misery." **29:33** *Simeon* probably means "one who hears." **29:34** *Levi* sounds like a Hebrew term that means "being attached" or "feeling affection for." **29:35** *Judah* is related to the Hebrew term for "praise."

JACOB *m* ZILPAH ———— GAD
         (Leah's ———— ASHER
         servant)

      *m* LEAH ——— REUBEN
              ——— SIMEON
              ——— LEVI
              ——— JUDAH
                    ——— ISSACHAR
                    ——— ZEBULUN
                    ——— DINAH (only daughter)

      *m* RACHEL ——————— JOSEPH
                  ——————— BENJAMIN

      *m* BILHAH ——— DAN
         (Rachel's ——— NAPHTALI          *m: married*
         servant)

**JACOB'S CHILDREN**
This chart shows from left to right Jacob's children in the order in which they were born.

Jacob's many wives (two wives and two "substitute" wives) led to sad and bitter consequences among the children. Anger, resentment, and jealousy were common among Jacob's sons. It is interesting to note that the worst fighting and rivalry occured between Leah's children and Rachel's children, and among the tribes that descended from them.

**29:28-30** Although Jacob was tricked by Laban, he kept his part of the bargain. There was more at stake than just Jacob's hurt. There was Rachel to think about, as well as God's plan for his life. When we are tricked by others, keeping our part of the bargain may still be wise. Nursing our wounds or plotting revenge makes us unable to see from God's perspective.

**29:32** Today parents usually give their children names that sound good or have sentimental appeal. But the Old Testament portrays a more dynamic use of names. Parents often chose names that reflected the situation at the time of the birth. They sometimes hoped their children would fulfill the meaning of the

names given them. Later the parents could look back and see if their grown children had lived up to their names. Sometimes a person's name was changed because his or her character and name did not match. This happened to Jacob ("he grasps the heel," figuratively, "he deceives"), whose name was changed to Israel ("one who struggles with God"). Jacob's character had changed to the point that he was no longer seen as a deceiver, but as a God-honoring man.

**30:3** Each of the three great patriarchs (Abraham, Isaac, and Jacob) had wives who had difficulty conceiving children. It is interesting to note how each man reacted to his wife's predicafor me,* and through her I can have a family, too." 4So Rachel gave her servant, Bilhah, to Jacob as a wife, and he slept with her. 5Bilhah became pregnant and presented him with a son. 6Rachel named him Dan,* for she said, "God has vindicated me! He has heard my request and given me a son." 7Then Bilhah became pregnant again and gave Jacob a second son. 8Rachel named him Naphtali,* for she said, "I have struggled hard with my sister, and I'm winning!"

9Meanwhile, Leah realized that she wasn't getting pregnant anymore, so she took her servant, Zilpah, and gave her to Jacob as a wife. 10Soon Zilpah presented him with a son. 11Leah named him Gad,* for she said, "How fortunate I am!" 12Then Zilpah gave Jacob a second son. 13And Leah named him Asher,* for she said, "What joy is mine! Now the other women will celebrate with me."

**30:6**
Gen 30:23

**30:8**
Gen 32:28

**30:11**
Gen 35:26; 46:16; 49:19

**30:3** Hebrew *bear children on my knees.*  **30:6** *Dan* means "he judged" or "he vindicated."  **30:8** *Naphtali* means "my struggle."  **30:11** *Gad* means "good fortune."  **30:13** *Asher* means "happy."

---

**RACHEL**

History seems to repeat itself here. Twice a town well at Haran was the site of significant events in one family's story. It was here that Rebekah met Eliezer, Abraham's servant, who had come to find a wife for Isaac. Some 40 years later, Rebekah's son Jacob returned the favor by serving his cousin Rachel and her sheep from the same well. The relationship that developed between them not only reminds us that romance is not a modern invention but also teaches us a few lessons about patience and love.

Jacob's love for Rachel was both patient and practical. Jacob had the patience to wait seven years for her, but he kept busy in the meantime. His commitment to Rachel kindled a strong loyalty within her. In fact, her loyalty to Jacob got out of hand and became self-destructive. She was frustrated by her barrenness and desperate to compete with her sister for Jacob's affection. She was trying to gain from Jacob what he had already given: devoted love.

Rachel's attempts to earn the unearnable are a picture of a much greater error we can make. Like her, we find ourselves trying somehow to earn love—God's love. But apart from his Word, we end up with one of two false ideas. Either we think we've been good enough to deserve his love or we recognize that we aren't able to earn his love and assume that it cannot be ours. If the Bible makes no other point, it shouts this one: God loves us! His love had no beginning and is incredibly patient. All we need to do is respond, not try to earn what is freely offered. God has said in many ways, "I love you. I have demonstrated that love to you by all I've done for you. I have even sacrificed my Son, Jesus, to pay the price for what is unacceptable about you—your sin. Now, live because of my love. Respond to me; love me with your whole being; give yourself to me in thanksgiving, not as payment." Live life fully, in the freedom of knowing you are loved.

| | |
|---|---|
| **Strengths and accomplishments** | • She showed great loyalty to her family<br>• She gave birth to Joseph and Benjamin after being barren for many years |
| **Weaknesses and mistakes** | • Her envy and competitiveness marred her relationship with her sister, Leah<br>• She was capable of dishonesty when she took her loyalty too far<br>• She failed to recognize that Jacob's devotion was not dependent on her ability to have children |
| **Lessons from her life** | • Loyalty must be controlled by what is true and right<br>• Love is accepted, not earned |
| **Vital statistics** | • Where: Haran<br>• Occupation: Shepherd, wife, mother, household manager<br>• Relatives: Father: Laban. Aunt: Rebekah. Sister: Leah. Husband: Jacob. Sons through Bilhah: Dan and Naphtali. Natural Sons: Joseph and Benjamin. |
| **Key verse** | "So Jacob worked seven years to pay for Rachel. But his love for her was so strong that it seemed to him but a few days" (Genesis 29:20). |

Rachel's story is told in Genesis 29:1–35:20. She is also mentioned in Ruth 4:11.

---

ment. Abraham had relations with Sarah's servant in order to have his own child, thus introducing bitterness and jealousy into his family. Isaac, by contrast, prayed to God when his wife was barren. God eventually answered his prayers, and Rebekah had twin sons. Jacob, however, followed his grandfather's example and had children by his wives' servants, leading to sad and sometimes bitter consequences.

**30:4-13** Rachel and Leah were locked in a cruel contest. In their race to have more children, they both gave their servants to Jacob as concubines. Jacob would have been wise to refuse, even though this was an accepted custom of the day. The fact that a custom is socially acceptable does not mean it is wise or right. You will be spared much heartbreak if you look at the potential consequences, to you or others, of your actions. Are you doing anything now that might cause future problems?

¹⁴One day during the wheat harvest, Reuben found some mandrakes growing in a field and brought them to his mother, Leah. Rachel begged Leah, "Please give me some of your son's mandrakes."

¹⁵But Leah angrily replied, "Wasn't it enough that you stole my husband? Now will you steal my son's mandrakes, too?"

Rachel answered, "I will let Jacob sleep with you tonight if you give me some of the mandrakes."

¹⁶So that evening, as Jacob was coming home from the fields, Leah went out to meet him. "You must come and sleep with me tonight!" she said. "I have paid for you with some mandrakes that my son found." So that night he slept with Leah. ¹⁷And God answered Leah's prayers. She became pregnant again and gave birth to a fifth son for Jacob. ¹⁸She named him Issachar,* for she said, "God has rewarded me for giving my servant to my husband as a wife." ¹⁹Then Leah became pregnant again and gave birth to a sixth son for Jacob. ²⁰She named him Zebulun,* for she said, "God has given me a good reward. Now my husband will treat me with respect, for I have given him six sons." ²¹Later she gave birth to a daughter and named her Dinah.

²²Then God remembered Rachel's plight and answered her prayers by enabling her to have children. ²³She became pregnant and gave birth to a son. "God has removed my disgrace," she said. ²⁴And she named him Joseph,* for she said, "May the LORD add yet another son to my family."

### Jacob's Wealth Increases
²⁵Soon after Rachel had given birth to Joseph, Jacob said to Laban, "Please release me so I can go home to my own country. ²⁶Let me take my wives and children, for I have earned them by serving you, and let me be on my way. You certainly know how hard I have worked for you."

²⁷"Please listen to me," Laban replied. "I have become wealthy, for* the LORD has blessed me because of you. ²⁸Tell me how much I owe you. Whatever it is, I'll pay it."

²⁹Jacob replied, "You know how hard I've worked for you, and how your flocks and herds have grown under my care. ³⁰You had little indeed before I came, but your wealth has increased enormously. The LORD has blessed you through everything I've done. But now, what about me? When can I start providing for my own family?"

³¹"What wages do you want?" Laban asked again.

Jacob replied, "Don't give me anything. Just do this one thing, and I'll continue to tend and watch over your flocks. ³²Let me inspect your flocks today and remove all the sheep and goats that are speckled or spotted, along with all the black sheep. Give these to me as my wages. ³³In the future, when you check on the animals you have given me as my wages, you'll see that I have been honest. If you find in my flock any goats without speckles or spots, or any sheep that are not black, you will know that I have stolen them from you."

³⁴"All right," Laban replied. "It will be as you say." ³⁵But that very day Laban went out and removed the male goats that were streaked and spotted, all the female goats that were speckled and spotted or had white patches, and all the black sheep. He placed them in the care of his own sons, ³⁶who took them a three-days' journey from where Jacob was. Meanwhile, Jacob stayed and cared for the rest of Laban's flock.

³⁷Then Jacob took some fresh branches from poplar, almond, and plane trees and peeled off strips of bark, making white streaks on them. ³⁸Then he placed these peeled branches in the watering troughs where the flocks came to drink, for that was where they mated. ³⁹And when they mated in front of the white-streaked branches, they gave birth to young that were streaked, speckled, and spotted. ⁴⁰Jacob separated those lambs from Laban's flock.

30:14 Song 7:13
30:17 Gen 25:21
30:18 Gen 49:14
30:22 1 Sam 1:19-20
30:23 Luke 1:25
30:24 Gen 35:17
30:26 Gen 29:18 Hos 12:12
30:27 Gen 18:3; 39:2-5
30:28 Gen 29:15; 31:7
30:32 Gen 31:8, 12

30:18 *Issachar* sounds like a Hebrew term that means "reward."   30:20 *Zebulun* probably means "honor."
30:24 *Joseph* means "may he add."   30:27 Or *I have learned by divination that.*

30:22-24 Eventually God answered Rachel's prayers and gave her a child of her own. In the meantime, however, she had given her servant to Jacob. Trusting God when nothing seems to happen is difficult. But it is harder still to live with the consequences of taking matters into our own hands. Resist the temptation to think God has forgotten you. Have patience and courage to wait for God to act.

30:37-43 It is unclear what this method was or how it worked. Some say that there was a belief among herdsmen that vivid impressions at mating time influenced the offspring. Most likely, the selective breeding and God's promise of provision were the main reasons that Jacob's flocks increased.

And at mating time he turned the flock to face Laban's animals that were streaked or black. This is how he built his own flock instead of increasing Laban's.

⁴¹Whenever the stronger females were ready to mate, Jacob would place the peeled branches in the watering troughs in front of them. Then they would mate in front of the branches. ⁴²But he didn't do this with the weaker ones, so the weaker lambs belonged to Laban, and the stronger ones were Jacob's. ⁴³As a result, Jacob became very wealthy, with large flocks of sheep and goats, female and male servants, and many camels and donkeys.

**30:43**
Gen 13:2; 24:35;
26:13

## 2. Jacob returns home
*Jacob Flees from Laban*

**31** But Jacob soon learned that Laban's sons were grumbling about him. "Jacob has robbed our father of everything!" they said. "He has gained all his wealth at our father's expense." ²And Jacob began to notice a change in Laban's attitude toward him.

**31:3**
Gen 28:15; 32:9

³Then the Lᴏʀᴅ said to Jacob, "Return to the land of your father and grandfather and to your relatives there, and I will be with you."

⁴So Jacob called Rachel and Leah out to the field where he was watching his flock. ⁵He said to them, "I have noticed that your father's attitude toward me has changed. But the God of my father has been with me. ⁶You know how hard I have worked for your father, ⁷but he has cheated me, changing my wages ten times. But God has not allowed him to do me any

**31:6**
Gen 30:29
**31:7**
Gen 29:25; 31:41

---

**LABAN**

We're all selfish, but some of us have a real corner on the market. Laban's whole life was stamped by self-centeredness. His chief goal was to look out for himself. The way he treated others was controlled by that goal. He made profitable arrangements for his sister Rebekah's marriage to Isaac and used his daughters' lives as bargaining chips. Jacob eventually outmaneuvered Laban, but the older man was unwilling to admit defeat. His hold on Jacob was broken, but he still tried to maintain some kind of control by getting Jacob to promise to be gone for good. He realized that Jacob and Jacob's God were more than he could handle.

On the surface, we may find it difficult to identify with Laban. But his selfishness is one point we have in common. Like him, we often have a strong tendency to control people and events to our benefit. Our "good" reasons for treating others the way we do may simply be a thin cover on our self-centered motives. We may not even recognize our own selfishness. One way to discover it is to examine our willingness to admit we're wrong. Laban could not bring himself to do this. If you ever amaze yourself by what you say and do to avoid facing up to wrong actions, you are getting a glimpse of your selfishness in action. Recognizing selfishness is painful, but it is the first step on the road back to God.

| | |
|---|---|
| **Strengths and accomplishments** | • Controlled two generations of marriages in the Abrahamic family (Rebekah, Leah, Rachel)<br>• Quick-witted |
| **Weaknesses and mistakes** | • Manipulated others for his own benefit<br>• Unwilling to admit wrongdoing<br>• Benefited financially by using Jacob, but never fully benefited spiritually by knowing and worshiping Jacob's God |
| **Lessons from his life** | • Those who set out to use people will eventually find themselves used<br>• God's plan cannot be blocked |
| **Vital statistics** | • Where: Haran<br>• Occupation: Wealthy sheep breeder<br>• Relatives: Father: Bethuel. Sister: Rebekah. Brother-in-law: Isaac. Daughters: Rachel and Leah. Son-in-law: Jacob. |
| **Key verse** | "In fact, if the God of my father had not been on my side—the God of Abraham and the fearsome God of Isaac—you would have sent me away empty-handed. But God has seen your abuse and my hard work. That is why he appeared to you last night and rebuked you!" (Genesis 31:42). |

Laban's story is told in Genesis 24:1–31:55.

---

**31:1, 2** Jacob's wealth made Laban's sons jealous. It is sometimes difficult to be happy when others are doing better than we are. To compare our success with that of others is a dangerous way to judge the quality of our lives. By comparing ourselves to others, we may be giving jealousy a foothold. We can avoid jealousy by rejoicing in others' successes (see Romans 12:15).

**31:4-13** Although Laban treated Jacob unfairly, God still increased Jacob's prosperity. God's power is not limited by lack of fair play. He has the ability to meet our needs and make us thrive even though others mistreat us. To give in and respond unfairly is to be no different from your enemies.

harm. 8For if he said, 'The speckled animals will be your wages,' the whole flock began to produce speckled young. And when he changed his mind and said, 'The striped animals will be your wages,' then the whole flock produced striped young. 9In this way, God has taken your father's animals and given them to me.

**31:8**
Gen 30:32

10"One time during the mating season, I had a dream and saw that the male goats mating with the females were streaked, speckled, and spotted. 11Then in my dream, the angel of God said to me, 'Jacob!' And I replied, 'Yes, here I am.'

**31:11**
Gen 16:7-11;
22:11, 15

12"The angel said, 'Look up, and you will see that only the streaked, speckled, and spotted males are mating with the females of your flock. For I have seen how Laban has treated you. 13I am the God who appeared to you at Bethel,* the place where you anointed the pillar of stone and made your vow to me. Now get ready and leave this country and return to the land of your birth.'"

**31:12**
Gen 30:32
Exod 3:7
**31:13**
Gen 28:10-22

14Rachel and Leah responded, "That's fine with us! We won't inherit any of our father's wealth anyway. 15He has reduced our rights to those of foreign women. And after he sold us, he wasted the money you paid him for us. 16All the wealth God has given you from our father legally belongs to us and our children. So go ahead and do whatever God has told you."

**31:15**
Gen 29:20, 27

17So Jacob put his wives and children on camels, 18and he drove all his livestock in front of him. He packed all the belongings he had acquired in Paddan-aram and set out for the land of Canaan, where his father, Isaac, lived. 19At the time they left, Laban was some distance away, shearing his sheep. Rachel stole her father's household idols and took them with her. 20Jacob outwitted Laban the Aramean, for they set out secretly and never told Laban they were leaving. 21So Jacob took all his possessions with him and crossed the Euphrates River,* heading for the hill country of Gilead.

**31:18**
Gen 25:20
**31:19**
Judg 17:5
**31:20**
Gen 31:27
**31:21**
Gen 37:25
Num 32:1

### Laban Pursues Jacob

22Three days later, Laban was told that Jacob had fled. 23So he gathered a group of his relatives and set out in hot pursuit. He caught up with Jacob seven days later in the hill country of Gilead. 24But the previous night God had appeared to Laban the Aramean in a dream and told him, "I'm warning you—leave Jacob alone!"

**31:22**
Gen 30:36
**31:24**
Gen 25:20

25Laban caught up with Jacob as he was camped in the hill country of Gilead, and he set up his camp not far from Jacob's. 26"What do you mean by deceiving me like this?" Laban demanded. "How dare you drag my daughters away like prisoners of war? 27Why did you slip away secretly? Why did you deceive me? And why didn't you say you wanted to leave? I would have given you a farewell feast, with singing and music, accompanied by tambourines and harps. 28Why didn't you let me kiss my daughters and grandchildren and tell them good-bye? You have acted very foolishly! 29I could destroy you, but the God of your father appeared to me last night and warned me, 'Leave Jacob alone!' 30I can understand your feeling that you must go, and your intense longing for your father's home. But why have you stolen my gods?"

**31:28**
Gen 31:55

31"I rushed away because I was afraid," Jacob answered. "I thought you would take your

**31:31**
Gen 20:11

**31:13** As in Greek version and an Aramaic Targum; Hebrew reads *the God of Bethel.*    **31:21** Hebrew *the river.*

---

**31:14, 15** Leaving home was not difficult for Rachel and Leah because their father had treated them as poorly as he had Jacob. According to custom, they were supposed to receive the benefits of the dowry Jacob paid for them, which was 14 years of hard work. When Laban did not give them what was rightfully theirs, they knew they would never inherit anything from their father. Thus, they wholeheartedly approved of Jacob's plan to take the wealth he had gained and leave.

**31:19** Many people kept small wooden or metal idols ("household idols") in their homes. These idols were called *teraphim,* and they were thought to protect the home and offer advice in times of need. They had legal significance as well, for when they were passed on to an heir, the person who received them could rightfully claim the greatest part of the family inheritance. No wonder Laban was concerned when he realized his idols were missing (31:30). Most likely Rachel stole her father's idols because she was afraid Laban would consult them and learn where she and Jacob had gone, or perhaps she wanted to claim the family inheritance.

**JACOB'S RETURN TO CANAAN**   God told Jacob to leave Haran and return to his homeland. Jacob took his family, crossed the Euphrates River, and headed first for the hill country of Gilead. Laban caught up with him there.

31:32
Gen 44:9
daughters from me by force. 32But as for your gods, see if you can find them, and let the person who has taken them die! And if you find anything else that belongs to you, identify it before all these relatives of ours, and I will give it back!" But Jacob did not know that Rachel had stolen the household idols.

33Laban went first into Jacob's tent to search there, then into Leah's, and then the tents of the two servant wives—but he found nothing. Finally, he went into Rachel's tent. 34But Rachel had taken the household idols and hidden them in her camel saddle, and now she was sitting on them. When Laban had thoroughly searched her tent without finding them, 35she said to her father, "Please, sir, forgive me if I don't get up for you. I'm having my monthly period." So Laban continued his search, but he could not find the household idols.

36Then Jacob became very angry, and he challenged Laban. "What's my crime?" he demanded. "What have I done wrong to make you chase after me as though I were a criminal?
31:37
Gen 31:33
37You have rummaged through everything I own. Now show me what you found that belongs to you! Set it out here in front of us, before our relatives, for all to see. Let them judge between us!
31:38
Gen 27:44
31:39
Exod 22:10-13
38"For twenty years I have been with you, caring for your flocks. In all that time your sheep and goats never miscarried. In all those years I never used a single ram of yours for food. 39If any were attacked and killed by wild animals, I never showed you the carcass and asked you to reduce the count of your flock. No, I took the loss myself! You made me pay for every stolen animal, whether it was taken in broad daylight or in the dark of night.
31:41
Gen 29:30

31:42
Gen 29:32
40"I worked for you through the scorching heat of the day and through cold and sleepless nights. 41Yes, for twenty years I slaved in your house! I worked for fourteen years earning your two daughters, and then six more years for your flock. And you changed my wages ten times! 42In fact, if the God of my father had not been on my side—the God of Abraham and the fearsome God of Isaac*—you would have sent me away empty-handed. But God has seen your abuse and my hard work. That is why he appeared to you last night and rebuked you!"

### Jacob's Treaty with Laban

31:44
Gen 21:27, 30
43Then Laban replied to Jacob, "These women are my daughters, these children are my grandchildren, and these flocks are my flocks—in fact, everything you see is mine. But what can I do now about my daughters and their children? 44So come, let's make a covenant, you and I, and it will be a witness to our commitment."
31:45
Gen 28:18
Josh 24:26-27
45So Jacob took a stone and set it up as a monument. 46Then he told his family members, "Gather some stones." So they gathered stones and piled them in a heap. Then Jacob and Laban sat down beside the pile of stones to eat a covenant meal. 47To commemorate the event, Laban called the place Jegar-sahadutha (which means "witness pile" in Aramaic), and Jacob called it Galeed (which means "witness pile" in Hebrew).
31:48
Gen 21:30
48Then Laban declared, "This pile of stones will stand as a witness to remind us of the covenant we have made today." This explains why it was called Galeed—"Witness Pile."
31:49
Judg 10:17; 11:29
31:50
Judg 11:10
1 Sam 12:5
Jer 29:23; 42:5
49But it was also called Mizpah (which means "watchtower"), for Laban said, "May the LORD keep watch between us to make sure that we keep this covenant when we are out of each other's sight. 50If you mistreat my daughters or if you marry other wives, God will see it even if no one else does. He is a witness to this covenant between us.
31:52
Gen 31:29, 42
31:53
Gen 24:12
51"See this pile of stones," Laban continued, "and see this monument I have set between us. 52They stand between us as witnesses of our vows. I will never pass this pile of stones to harm you, and you must never pass these stones or this monument to harm me. 53I call on the God of our ancestors—the God of your grandfather Abraham and the God of my grandfather Nahor—to serve as a judge between us."

So Jacob took an oath before the fearsome God of his father, Isaac,* to respect the

31:42 Or and the Fear of Isaac.    31:53 Or the Fear of his father, Isaac.

---

31:32 Do you remember feeling absolutely sure about something? Jacob was so sure that no one had stolen Laban's idols that he vowed to kill the offender. Because Rachel took them, this statement put her safety in serious jeopardy. Even when you are absolutely sure about a matter, avoid rash statements. Someone may hold you to them.

31:38-42 Jacob made it a habit to do more than was expected of him. When his flocks were attacked, he took the losses rather than splitting them with Laban. He worked hard even after several

pay cuts. His diligence eventually paid off; his flocks began to multiply. Making a habit of doing more than expected can pay off. It (1) pleases God, (2) earns recognition and advancement, (3) enhances your reputation, (4) builds others' confidence in you, (5) gives you more experience and knowledge, and (6) develops your spiritual maturity.

31:49 To be binding, an agreement had to be witnessed by a third party. In this case, Jacob and Laban used God as their witness that they would keep their word.

boundary line. 54Then Jacob offered a sacrifice to God there on the mountain and invited everyone to a covenant feast. After they had eaten, they spent the night on the mountain.

55*Laban got up early the next morning, and he kissed his grandchildren and his daughters and blessed them. Then he left and returned home.

**32** 1*As Jacob started on his way again, angels of God came to meet him. 2When Jacob saw them, he exclaimed, "This is God's camp!" So he named the place Mahanaim.*

### Jacob Sends Gifts to Esau

3Then Jacob sent messengers ahead to his brother, Esau, who was living in the region of Seir in the land of Edom. 4He told them, "Give this message to my master Esau: 'Humble greetings from your servant Jacob. Until now I have been living with Uncle Laban, 5and now I own cattle, donkeys, flocks of sheep and goats, and many servants, both men and women. I have sent these messengers to inform my lord of my coming, hoping that you will be friendly to me.'"

6After delivering the message, the messengers returned to Jacob and reported, "We met your brother, Esau, and he is already on his way to meet you—with an army of 400 men!" 7Jacob was terrified at the news. He divided his household, along with the flocks and herds and camels, into two groups. 8He thought, "If Esau meets one group and attacks it, perhaps the other group can escape."

9Then Jacob prayed, "O God of my grandfather Abraham, and God of my father, Isaac— O LORD, you told me, 'Return to your own land and to your relatives.' And you promised me, 'I will treat you kindly.' 10I am not worthy of all the unfailing love and faithfulness you have shown to me, your servant. When I left home and crossed the Jordan River, I owned nothing except a walking stick. Now my household fills two large camps! 11O LORD, please rescue me from the hand of my brother, Esau. I am afraid that he is coming to attack me, along with my wives and children. 12But you promised me, 'I will surely treat you kindly, and I will multiply your descendants until they become as numerous as the sands along the seashore—too many to count.'"

13Jacob stayed where he was for the night. Then he selected these gifts from his possessions to present to his brother, Esau: 14200 female goats, 20 male goats, 200 ewes, 20 rams, 1530 female camels with their young, 40 cows, 10 bulls, 20 female donkeys, and 10 male donkeys. 16He divided these animals into herds and assigned each to different servants. Then he told his servants, "Go ahead of me with the animals, but keep some distance between the herds."

17He gave these instructions to the men leading the first group: "When my brother, Esau, meets you, he will ask, 'Whose servants are you? Where are you going? Who owns these animals?' 18You must reply, 'They belong to your servant Jacob, but they are a gift for his master Esau. Look, he is coming right behind us.'"

19Jacob gave the same instructions to the second and third herdsmen and to all who followed behind the herds: "You must say the same thing to Esau when you meet him. 20And be sure to say, 'Look, your servant Jacob is right behind us.'"

Jacob thought, "I will try to appease him by sending gifts ahead of me. When I see him in person, perhaps he will be friendly to me." 21So the gifts were sent on ahead, while Jacob himself spent that night in the camp.

### Jacob Wrestles with God

22During the night Jacob got up and took his two wives, his two servant wives, and his eleven sons and crossed the Jabbok River with them. 23After taking them to the other side, he sent over all his possessions.

**31:54**
Exod 18:12

**31:55**
Gen 31:28

**32:1**
Gen 16:11
2 Kgs 6:16-17

**32:2**
Josh 13:26; 21:38
2 Sam 2:8

**32:3**
Gen 27:41-42

**32:4**
Gen 31:41

**32:7**
Gen 33:1

**32:9**
Gen 28:13-15;
31:13

**32:10**
Gen 24:27

**32:11**
Gen 27:41

**32:12**
Gen 28:14

**32:18**
Gen 32:13

**32:20**
1 Sam 25:19

**32:22**
Deut 3:16
Josh 12:2

---

**31:55** Verse 31:55 is numbered 32:1 in Hebrew text.    **32:1** Verses 32:1-32 are numbered 32:2-33 in Hebrew text.
**32:2** Mahanaim means "two camps."

---

**32:1** Why did angels of God meet Jacob? In Bible times, angels often intervened in human situations. Although angels usually would appear in human form, these angels must have looked different, for Jacob recognized them at once. The reason these angels met Jacob is unclear; but because of their visit, Jacob knew God was with him.

**32:3** The last time Jacob had seen Esau, his older brother had been ready to kill him for stealing the family blessing (25:29–

27:42). Esau was so angry he had vowed to kill Jacob as soon as their father, Isaac, died (27:41). Fearing their reunion, Jacob sent a messenger ahead with gifts. He hoped to buy Esau's favor.

**32:9-12** How would you feel if you knew you were about to meet the person you had cheated out of his most precious possession? Jacob had taken Esau's birthright (25:33) and his blessing (27:27-40). Now he was about to meet this brother

32:24
Gen 18:2

32:26
Hos 12:3-4

²⁴This left Jacob all alone in the camp, and a man came and wrestled with him until the dawn began to break. ²⁵When the man saw that he would not win the match, he touched Jacob's hip and wrenched it out of its socket. ²⁶Then the man said, "Let me go, for the dawn is breaking!"

But Jacob said, "I will not let you go unless you bless me."

²⁷"What is your name?" the man asked.

**LEAH**

How do we respond when life seems set against us? Leah faced a blunt and painful world. She observed it with sad eyes. Women in her day were considered property. Daughters were traded by their fathers in business deals. Leah's father Laban gave her to a man who did not love her. Perhaps it would be more fair to say that Jacob didn't love her as much as he loved her younger sister Rachel. But God loved her.

Leah apparently could not see very well, but her sister looked great! In fact, Jacob agreed to work seven years for Rachel's hand in marriage. Jacob kept his end of the contract, but Laban deceived his future son-in-law. He substituted Leah for Rachel under the wedding veil. By the time Jacob knew a switch had been made, he was already married. Laban excused his deception by citing a local custom that a younger daughter could not marry ahead of an older one. After a brief confrontation, Laban agreed to give Rachel to Jacob in exchange for another seven years of work. And although Leah was not his first choice, Jacob accepted her as his wife.

Leah revealed how she felt toward Jacob in the name she gave their first son, Reuben. The name expressed her desire to be noticed by her husband. Because Leah and Rachel competed for Jacob's attention, there was constant friction in the family. They measured their worth against each other by their ability to bear children. Leah was winning the fertility contest handily when Rachel died bearing her second child, Benjamin. Leah's victory carried little satisfaction. The scriptures mention no more children born to Jacob. Ironically, the greatest honor Jacob finally gave Leah was to bury her with his parents and grandparents in the cave at Machpelah (Genesis 49:31).

When we fail to live at peace with the important people in our lives, we leave a tragic legacy. Although God loved Leah, we are not told of her response to him. Her inability to appreciate God's love also made her unable to love others. When we struggle to love others, we can be helped by reflecting on the fact that God loves us. If God's love doesn't free us, we need to think again!

| | |
|---|---|
| **Strengths and accomplishments** | • Bore Jacob six sons and one daughter<br>• Collaborated with Jacob and Rachel to outwit Laban's ruthless manipulation<br>• Is honored as one of the mothers of Israel (Ruth 4:11)<br>• Stands in the lineage of Jesus through her son Judah |
| **Weaknesses and mistakes** | • Envied her sister Rachel over Jacob's love<br>• Competed with Rachel for Jacob's attention and respect |
| **Lessons from her life** | • Even wrong motives can't entirely cover the truth—Leah gave God specific credit in the birth of five of her sons<br>• Opportunities for joy can be missed through wrong motives toward others<br>• God has a way of using unexpected people to accomplish his purposes and plans |
| **Vital statistics** | • Where: Paddan-aram<br>• Occupation: Wife and mother<br>• Relatives: Father: Laban. Sister: Rachel. Husband: Jacob. Daughter: Dinah. Sons through Zilpah: Gad and Asher. Natural Sons: Reuben, Simeon, Levi, Judah, Issachar, and Zebulun. |
| **Key verse** | "She named him Zebulun, for she said, 'God has given me a good reward. Now my husband will treat me with respect, for I have given him six sons'" (Genesis 30:20). |

Leah's story is told in Genesis 29—35. She is also mentioned in Genesis 46:15, 18, 31 and Ruth 4:11.

for the first time in 20 years, and he was frantic with fear. He collected his thoughts, however, and decided to pray. When we face a difficult conflict, we can run about frantically or we can pause to pray. Which approach will be more effective?

**32:26** Jacob continued this wrestling match all night just to be blessed. He was persistent. God encourages persistence in all areas of our lives, including the spiritual. Where in your spiritual life do you need more persistence? Strong character develops as you struggle through tough conditions.

**32:27-29** God gave many Bible people new names (Abraham, Sarah, Peter). Their new names were symbols of how God had changed their lives. Here we see how Jacob's character had changed. Jacob, the ambitious deceiver, became Israel, the one who struggles with God and overcomes.

He replied, "Jacob."

28"Your name will no longer be Jacob," the man told him. "From now on you will be called Israel,* because you have fought with God and with men and have won."

29"Please tell me your name," Jacob said.

"Why do you want to know my name?" the man replied. Then he blessed Jacob there.

30Jacob named the place Peniel (which means "face of God"), for he said, "I have seen God face to face, yet my life has been spared." 31The sun was rising as Jacob left Peniel,* and he was limping because of the injury to his hip. 32(Even today the people of Israel don't eat the tendon near the hip socket because of what happened that night when the man strained the tendon of Jacob's hip.)

### Jacob and Esau Make Peace

**33** Then Jacob looked up and saw Esau coming with his 400 men. So he divided the children among Leah, Rachel, and his two servant wives. 2He put the servant wives and their children at the front, Leah and her children next, and Rachel and Joseph last. 3Then Jacob went on ahead. As he approached his brother, he bowed to the ground seven times before him. 4Then Esau ran to meet him and embraced him, threw his arms around his neck, and kissed him. And they both wept.

5Then Esau looked at the women and children and asked, "Who are these people with you?"

"These are the children God has graciously given to me, your servant," Jacob replied. 6Then the servant wives came forward with their children and bowed before him. 7Next came Leah with her children, and they bowed before him. Finally, Joseph and Rachel came forward and bowed before him.

8"And what were all the flocks and herds I met as I came?" Esau asked.

Jacob replied, "They are a gift, my lord, to ensure your friendship."

9"My brother, I have plenty," Esau answered. "Keep what you have for yourself."

10But Jacob insisted, "No, if I have found favor with you, please accept this gift from me. And what a relief to see your friendly smile. It is like seeing the face of God! 11Please take this gift I have brought you, for God has been very gracious to me. I have more than enough." And because Jacob insisted, Esau finally accepted the gift.

12"Well," Esau said, "let's be going. I will lead the way."

13But Jacob replied, "You can see, my lord, that some of the children are very young, and the flocks and herds have their young, too. If they are driven too hard, even for one day, all

**32:28**
Gen 35:10
1 Kgs 18:31

**32:29**
Exod 3:13
Judg 13:17

**32:30**
Gen 16:13
Exod 24:10; 33:20
Num 12:8
Deut 5:24; 34:10
Judg 6:22
John 1:18

**33:1**
Gen 32:6-7

**33:3**
Gen 18:2; 42:6
**33:4**
Gen 45:14-15
**33:5**
Gen 48:9

**33:8**
Gen 32:14-16

**33:9**
Gen 27:39

---

**32:28** *Jacob* sounds like the Hebrew words for "heel" and "deceiver." *Israel* means "God fights."   **32:31** Hebrew *Penuel,* a variant spelling of Peniel.

---

**33:1-11** Jacob must have been amazed to see Esau's change of heart when the two brothers met again (33:10). Esau was no

**JACOB'S JOURNEY TO SHECHEM**
After a joyful reunion with his brother, Esau (who journeyed from Edom), Jacob set up camp in Succoth. Later he moved on to Shechem where his daughter, Dinah, was raped and two of his sons took revenge on the city.

*Map labels: Mediterranean Sea; Sea of Galilee; JACOB'S ROUTE; Jordan River; Shechem; Succoth; Jabbok River; Jerusalem; Dead Sea; ESAU'S ROUTE; LAND OF EDOM; N; 0 20 Mi.; 0 20 Km.*

longer bitter over losing his birthright and blessing (27:36-41); instead, he was content with what he had.

Life can bring us some bad situations. We can feel cheated, as Esau did, but we don't have to remain bitter. We can remove bitterness from our lives by honestly expressing our feelings to God, forgiving those who have wronged us, and being content with what we have.

**33:3** Bowing to the ground seven times was the sign of respect given to a king. Jacob was taking every precaution as he met Esau, hoping to dispel any thoughts of revenge.

**33:4** Esau greeted his brother, Jacob, with a great hug. Imagine how difficult this must have been for a man who once had actually plotted his brother's death (27:41). But time away from each other allowed the bitter wounds to heal. With the passing of time, each brother was able to see that their relationship was more important than their real estate.

**33:11** Why did Jacob send gifts ahead for Esau? In Bible times, gifts were given for several reasons. (1) This may have been a bribe. Gifts are still given to win someone over or buy his or her support. Esau may first have refused Jacob's gifts (33:9) because he didn't want or need a bribe. He had already forgiven Jacob, and he had ample wealth of his own. (2) This may have been an expression of affection. (3) It may have been the customary way of greeting someone before an important meeting. Such gifts were often related to a person's occupation. This explains why Jacob sent Esau, who was a herdsman, sheep, goats, and cattle.

the animals could die. ¹⁴Please, my lord, go ahead of your servant. We will follow slowly, at a pace that is comfortable for the livestock and the children. I will meet you at Seir."

¹⁵"All right," Esau said, "but at least let me assign some of my men to guide and protect you."

Jacob responded, "That's not necessary. It's enough that you've received me warmly, my lord!"

¹⁶So Esau turned around and started back to Seir that same day. ¹⁷Jacob, on the other hand, traveled on to Succoth. There he built himself a house and made shelters for his livestock. That is why the place was named Succoth (which means "shelters").

¹⁸Later, having traveled all the way from Paddan-aram, Jacob arrived safely at the town of Shechem, in the land of Canaan. There he set up camp outside the town. ¹⁹Jacob bought the plot of land where he camped from the family of Hamor, the father of Shechem, for 100 pieces of silver.* ²⁰And there he built an altar and named it El-Elohe-Israel.*

## Revenge against Shechem

**34** One day Dinah, the daughter of Jacob and Leah, went to visit some of the young women who lived in the area. ²But when the local prince, Shechem son of Hamor the Hivite, saw Dinah, he seized her and raped her. ³But then he fell in love with her, and he tried to win her affection with tender words. ⁴He said to his father, Hamor, "Get me this young girl. I want to marry her."

⁵Soon Jacob heard that Shechem had defiled his daughter, Dinah. But since his sons were out in the fields herding his livestock, he said nothing until they returned. ⁶Hamor, Shechem's father, came to discuss the matter with Jacob. ⁷Meanwhile, Jacob's sons had come in from the field as soon as they heard what had happened. They were shocked and furious that their sister had been raped. Shechem had done a disgraceful thing against Jacob's family,* something that should never be done.

⁸Hamor tried to speak with Jacob and his sons. "My son Shechem is truly in love with your daughter," he said. "Please let him marry her. ⁹In fact, let's arrange other marriages, too. You give us your daughters for our sons, and we will give you our daughters for your sons. ¹⁰And you may live among us; the land is open to you! Settle here and trade with us. And feel free to buy property in the area."

¹¹Then Shechem himself spoke to Dinah's father and brothers. "Please be kind to me, and let me marry her," he begged. "I will give you whatever you ask. ¹²No matter what dowry or gift you demand, I will gladly pay it—just give me the girl as my wife."

¹³But since Shechem had defiled their sister, Dinah, Jacob's sons responded deceitfully to Shechem and his father, Hamor. ¹⁴They said to them, "We couldn't possibly allow this, because you're not circumcised. It would be a disgrace for our sister to marry a man like you! ¹⁵But here is a solution. If every man among you will be circumcised like we are, ¹⁶then we will give you our daughters, and we'll take your daughters for ourselves. We will live among you and become one people. ¹⁷But if you don't agree to be circumcised, we will take her and be on our way."

¹⁸Hamor and his son Shechem agreed to their proposal. ¹⁹Shechem wasted no time in acting on this request, for he wanted Jacob's daughter desperately. Shechem was a highly respected member of his family, ²⁰and he went with his father, Hamor, to present this proposal to the leaders at the town gate.

²¹"These men are our friends," they said. "Let's invite them to live here among us and trade freely. Look, the land is large enough to hold them. We can take their daughters as wives and let them marry ours. ²²But they will consider staying here and becoming one people with us only if all of our men are circumcised, just as they are. ²³But if we do this, all their livestock and possessions will eventually be ours. Come, let's agree to their terms and let them settle here among us."

33:19 Hebrew *100 kesitahs;* the value or weight of the kesitah is no longer known.   33:20 *El-Elohe-Israel* means "God, the God of Israel."   34:7 Hebrew *a disgraceful thing in Israel.*

---

33:14-17 Why did Jacob imply that he was going to Seir but then stop at Succoth? We don't know the answer, but perhaps Jacob decided to stop there as they journeyed because Succoth is a beautiful site on the eastern side of the Jordan River. Whatever the reason, Jacob and Esau parted in peace. Then they lived fairly close to each other until after their father's death (36:6-8).

34:1-4 Shechem may have been a victim of "love at first sight," but his actions were impulsive and evil. Not only did he sin against Dinah; he sinned against the entire family (34:6, 7). The consequences of his deed were severe both for his family and for Jacob's (34:25-31). Even Shechem's declared love for Dinah could not excuse the evil he did by raping her. Don't allow sexual passion to boil over into evil actions. Passion must be controlled.

24So all the men in the town council agreed with Hamor and Shechem, and every male in the town was circumcised. 25But three days later, when their wounds were still sore, two of Jacob's sons, Simeon and Levi, who were Dinah's full brothers, took their swords and entered the town without opposition. Then they slaughtered every male there, 26including Hamor and his son Shechem. They killed them with their swords, then took Dinah from Shechem's house and returned to their camp.

27Meanwhile, the rest of Jacob's sons arrived. Finding the men slaughtered, they plundered the town because their sister had been defiled there. 28They seized all the flocks and herds and donkeys—everything they could lay their hands on, both inside the town and outside in the fields. 29They looted all their wealth and plundered their houses. They also took all their little children and wives and led them away as captives.

30Afterward Jacob said to Simeon and Levi, "You have ruined me! You've made me stink among all the people of this land—among all the Canaanites and Perizzites. We are so few that they will join forces and crush us. I will be ruined, and my entire household will be wiped out!"

31"But why should we let him treat our sister like a prostitute?" they retorted angrily.

### Jacob's Return to Bethel

**35** Then God said to Jacob, "Get ready and move to Bethel and settle there. Build an altar there to the God who appeared to you when you fled from your brother, Esau."

2So Jacob told everyone in his household, "Get rid of all your pagan idols, purify yourselves, and put on clean clothing. 3We are now going to Bethel, where I will build an altar to the God who answered my prayers when I was in distress. He has been with me wherever I have gone."

4So they gave Jacob all their pagan idols and earrings, and he buried them under the great tree near Shechem. 5As they set out, a terror from God spread over the people in all the towns of that area, so no one attacked Jacob's family.

6Eventually, Jacob and his household arrived at Luz (also called Bethel) in Canaan. 7Jacob built an altar there and named the place El-bethel (which means "God of Bethel"), because God had appeared to him there when he was fleeing from his brother, Esau.

8Soon after this, Rebekah's old nurse, Deborah, died. She was buried beneath the oak tree in the valley below Bethel. Ever since, the tree has been called Allon-bacuth (which means "oak of weeping").

9Now that Jacob had returned from Paddan-aram, God appeared to him again at Bethel.

**34:24** Gen 28:15

**34:25** Gen 49:5-7 Josh 5:8

**34:28** Gen 43:18

**34:30** Gen 13:7; 49:5-7 Exod 5:21 2 Sam 10:6 1 Chr 16:19

**35:1** Gen 12:8; 28:19

**35:2** Gen 31:19

**35:3** Gen 28:15-22

**35:4** Exod 32:3 Judg 8:24 Hos 2:13

**35:5** Exod 15:16

**35:6** Gen 28:19

**35:7** Gen 28:19

**35:8** Gen 24:59

**35:9** Gen 28:13

---

**34:25-31** Why did Simeon and Levi take such harsh action against the city of Shechem? Jacob's family saw themselves as set apart from others. God wanted them to remain separate from their pagan neighbors. But the brothers wrongly thought that being set apart also meant being better. This arrogant attitude led to the terrible slaughter of innocent people.

**JACOB'S JOURNEY BACK TO HEBRON**
After Jacob's sons Simeon and Levi destroyed Shechem, God told Jacob to move to Bethel, where God reminded him that his name had been changed to Israel. He then traveled to Hebron, but along the way, his dear wife Rachel died near Ephrath (Bethlehem).

**34:27-29** When Shechem raped Dinah, the consequences were far greater than he could have imagined. Dinah's brothers were outraged and took revenge. Pain, deceit, and murder followed. Sexual sin is devastating because its consequences are so far-reaching.

**34:30, 31** In seeking revenge against Shechem, Simeon and Levi lied, stole, and murdered. Their desire for justice was right, but their ways of achieving it were wrong. Because of their sin, their father cursed them with his dying breath (49:5-7). Generations later, their descendants lost the part of the Promised Land allotted to them. When tempted to return evil for evil, leave revenge to God and spare yourself the dreadful consequences of sin.

**35:2** Why did the people have these idols? Idols were sometimes seen more as good luck charms than as gods. Some Israelites, even though they worshiped God, had idols in their homes, just as some Christians today own good luck trinkets. Jacob believed that idols should have no place in his household. He wanted nothing to divert his family's spiritual focus.

Jacob ordered his household to get rid of their idols. Unless we remove idols from our lives, they can ruin our faith. What idols do we have? An idol is anything we put before God. Idols don't have to be physical objects; they can be thoughts or desires. Like Jacob, we should get rid of anything that could stand between us and God.

**35:4** Why did the people give Jacob their earrings? Jewelry in itself was not evil, but in Jacob's day earrings were often worn as good luck charms to ward off evil. The people in his family had to cleanse themselves of all pagan influences, including reminders of foreign gods.

35:10
Gen 32:28
35:11
Gen 12:2; 17:1, 6
35:12
Gen 13:15; 28:13
35:13
Judg 6:21; 13:20
35:14
Gen 28:18-19

35:16
Ruth 4:11
35:17
Gen 30:22-24

God blessed him, [10]saying, "Your name is Jacob, but you will not be called Jacob any longer. From now on your name will be Israel."* So God renamed him Israel.

[11]Then God said, "I am El-Shaddai—'God Almighty.' Be fruitful and multiply. You will become a great nation, even many nations. Kings will be among your descendants! [12]And I will give you the land I once gave to Abraham and Isaac. Yes, I will give it to you and your descendants after you." [13]Then God went up from the place where he had spoken to Jacob.

[14]Jacob set up a stone pillar to mark the place where God had spoken to him. Then he poured wine over it as an offering to God and anointed the pillar with olive oil. [15]And Jacob named the place Bethel (which means "house of God"), because God had spoken to him there.

### The Deaths of Rachel and Isaac

[16]Leaving Bethel, Jacob and his clan moved on toward Ephrath. But Rachel went into labor while they were still some distance away. Her labor pains were intense. [17]After a very hard

35:10 *Jacob* sounds like the Hebrew words for "heel" and "deceiver." *Israel* means "God fights."

**DINAH**

As far as we know, Dinah was Jacob's only daughter. She lived among ten older and two younger brothers. She grew up in a family rocked by struggle between two sisters married to the same man. Dinah's mother, Leah, knew that Jacob loved her sister and rival Rachel. We don't know how the bitterness and jealousy between these women affected the only girl child in the family. By the time Dinah was a teenager, her family was living in Shechem, a town north of Bethel and Jerusalem in the Promised Land.

Apparently no one really paid much attention to Dinah until she went out for a walk in town one day. She was noticed and raped by Shechem, the son of the ruler of the city. Violated and shamed, Dinah found herself in the center of a family crisis. Shechem asked his father to arrange a marriage with Dinah. But in Jacob's and his sons' eyes, Dinah had been damaged and their family had been insulted. Jacob failed to provide any fatherly leadership in this situation and his sons took matters into their own hands. The results were treacherous and bloody.

In all of this, the victim was overlooked. Dinah was neither comforted nor consulted. Instead, she was treated with almost as much disrespect by her family as she had been by Shechem. By handing her over to Shechem, they used Dinah as bait in a trap that led to the murder of all the men in Shechem's village. Dinah's brothers profited from the massacre of Shechem. Jacob was angry at his sons for their actions, but did nothing. Meanwhile, Dinah slipped back into oblivion. Her story reminds us of the tragedies that occur when family members are careless with each other. Someone ends up paying a high price.

You probably know someone who can identify closely with Dinah. Perhaps you have experienced that same anonymity as a victim who was unnoticed or forgotten. Remember several glimmers of hope: Even when everyone else forgets, God doesn't; when no one seems to notice, God sees; when no one seems to care, God cares; when you feel all alone, you aren't. And one of the first lessons God will teach you as you depend on him is that there are others who also care and are willing to help. Begin to speak to God today in prayer about your past.

| | |
|---|---|
| **Strengths and accomplishments** | • Jacob's only daughter |
| **Lessons from her life** | • Thoughtless avengers often hurt the original victims a second time<br>• Family members can be trampled in the rush for family honor |
| **Vital statistics** | • Where: Paddan-aram<br>• Relatives: Parents: Jacob and Leah. Siblings: Twelve brothers. Aunt: Rachel. Grandparents: Isaac and Rebekah, Laban. Uncle: Esau. |
| **Key verse** | "Later she gave birth to a daughter and named her Dinah" (Genesis 30:21). |

Dinah's story is told in Genesis 34. Her birth is mentioned in Genesis 30:21; she is last mentioned in Genesis 46:15.

35:10 God reminded Jacob of his new name, Israel, which meant "one who struggles with God." Although Jacob's life was littered with difficulties and trials, his new name was a tribute to his desire to stay close to God despite life's disappointments.

Many people believe that Christianity should offer a problem-free life. Consequently, as life gets tough, they draw back disappointed. Instead, they should determine to prevail with God through life's storms. Problems and difficulties are painful but inevitable; you might as well see them as opportunities for growth. You can't prevail with God unless you have troubles to prevail over.

35:13, 14 This oil used to anoint the pillar was olive oil of the finest grade of purity. It was expensive, so using it showed the high value placed on the anointed object. Jacob was showing the greatest respect for the place where he had met with God.

delivery, the midwife finally exclaimed, "Don't be afraid—you have another son!" [18]Rachel was about to die, but with her last breath she named the baby Ben-oni (which means "son of my sorrow"). The baby's father, however, called him Benjamin (which means "son of my right hand"). [19]So Rachel died and was buried on the way to Ephrath (that is, Bethlehem). [20]Jacob set up a stone monument over Rachel's grave, and it can be seen there to this day.

[21]Then Jacob* traveled on and camped beyond Migdal-eder. [22]While he was living there, Reuben had intercourse with Bilhah, his father's concubine, and Jacob soon heard about it.

These are the names of the twelve sons of Jacob:

[23]The sons of Leah were Reuben (Jacob's oldest son), Simeon, Levi, Judah, Issachar, and Zebulun.
[24]The sons of Rachel were Joseph and Benjamin.
[25]The sons of Bilhah, Rachel's servant, were Dan and Naphtali.
[26]The sons of Zilpah, Leah's servant, were Gad and Asher.
These are the names of the sons who were born to Jacob at Paddan-aram.

[27]So Jacob returned to his father, Isaac, in Mamre, which is near Kiriath-arba (now called Hebron), where Abraham and Isaac had both lived as foreigners. [28]Isaac lived for 180 years. [29]Then he breathed his last and died at a ripe old age, joining his ancestors in death. And his sons, Esau and Jacob, buried him.

### Descendants of Esau

**36** This is the account of the descendants of Esau (also known as Edom). [2]Esau married two young women from Canaan: Adah, the daughter of Elon the Hittite; and Oholibamah, the daughter of Anah and granddaughter of Zibeon the Hivite. [3]He also married his cousin Basemath, who was the daughter of Ishmael and the sister of Nebaioth. [4]Adah gave birth to a son named Eliphaz for Esau. Basemath gave birth to a son named Reuel. [5]Oholibamah gave birth to sons named Jeush, Jalam, and Korah. All these sons were born to Esau in the land of Canaan.

[6]Esau took his wives, his children, and his entire household, along with his livestock and cattle—all the wealth he had acquired in the land of Canaan—and moved away from his brother, Jacob. [7]There was not enough land to support them both because of all the livestock and possessions they had acquired. [8]So Esau (also known as Edom) settled in the hill country of Seir.

[9]This is the account of Esau's descendants, the Edomites, who lived in the hill country of Seir.

[10]These are the names of Esau's sons: Eliphaz, the son of Esau's wife Adah; and Reuel, the son of Esau's wife Basemath.
[11]The descendants of Eliphaz were Teman, Omar, Zepho, Gatam, and Kenaz. [12]Timna, the concubine of Esau's son Eliphaz, gave birth to a son named Amalek. These are the descendants of Esau's wife Adah.
[13]The descendants of Reuel were Nahath, Zerah, Shammah, and Mizzah. These are the descendants of Esau's wife Basemath.
[14]Esau also had sons through Oholibamah, the daughter of Anah and granddaughter of Zibeon. Their names were Jeush, Jalam, and Korah.

**35:21** Hebrew *Israel;* also in 35:22a. The names "Jacob" and "Israel" are often interchanged throughout the Old Testament, referring sometimes to the individual patriarch and sometimes to the nation.

**35:18** Gen 49:27
**35:19** Gen 48:7
**35:22** Gen 49:4 / Lev 18:8 / 1 Chr 5:1
**35:23-26** //1 Chr 2:1-2
**35:23** Gen 29:31-35; 30:18-20
**35:24** Gen 30:24
**35:25** Gen 30:5-8
**35:26** Gen 30:10-13
**35:27** Gen 13:18; 23:2
**35:28** Gen 25:7-8, 20
**36:1** Gen 25:30
**36:2** Gen 26:34 / 1 Chr 1:40
**36:3** Gen 25:13
**36:4** 1 Chr 1:35
**36:5** Gen 36:18
**36:7** Gen 13:6
**36:8** Gen 14:6; 25:30
**36:9** Gen 36:43
**36:10-14** //1 Chr 1:35-37

---

**35:22** Reuben's sin was costly, although not right away. As the oldest son, he stood to receive a double portion of the family inheritance and a place of leadership among his people. Reuben may have thought he had gotten away with his sin. No more is mentioned of it until Jacob, on his deathbed, assembled his family for the final blessing. Suddenly Jacob took away Reuben's double portion and gave it to someone else. The reason? "You went to bed with my wife; you defiled my marriage couch" (49:4).

Sin's consequences can plague us long after the sin is committed. When we do something wrong, we may think we can escape unnoticed, only to discover later that the sin has been quietly breeding serious consequences.

**36:9** The Edomites were descendants of Esau who lived south and east of the Dead Sea. The country featured rugged mountains and desolate wilderness. Several major roads led through Edom because it was rich in natural resources. During the Exodus, God told Israel to leave the Edomites alone (Deuteronomy 2:4, 5) because they were "relatives." But Edom refused to let them enter the land, and later they became bitter enemies of King David. The nations of Edom and Israel shared the same ancestor, Isaac, and the same border. Israel looked down on the Edomites because they had intermarried with the Canaanites.

[15]These are the descendants of Esau who became the leaders of various clans:

The descendants of Esau's oldest son, Eliphaz, became the leaders of the clans of Teman, Omar, Zepho, Kenaz, [16]Korah, Gatam, and Amalek. These are the clan leaders in the land of Edom who descended from Eliphaz. All these were descendants of Esau's wife Adah.

[17]The descendants of Esau's son Reuel became the leaders of the clans of Nahath, Zerah, Shammah, and Mizzah. These are the clan leaders in the land of Edom who descended from Reuel. All these were descendants of Esau's wife Basemath.

[18]The descendants of Esau and his wife Oholibamah became the leaders of the clans of Jeush, Jalam, and Korah. These are the clan leaders who descended from Esau's wife Oholibamah, the daughter of Anah.

**36:19**
1 Chr 1:35

[19]These are the clans descended from Esau (also known as Edom), identified by their clan leaders.

### Original Peoples of Edom

**36:20-28**
//1 Chr 1:38-42
**36:20**
Gen 14:6
Deut 2:12, 22

[20]These are the names of the tribes that descended from Seir the Horite. They lived in the land of Edom: Lotan, Shobal, Zibeon, Anah, [21]Dishon, Ezer, and Dishan. These were the Horite clan leaders, the descendants of Seir, who lived in the land of Edom.

[22]The descendants of Lotan were Hori and Hemam. Lotan's sister was named Timna.
[23]The descendants of Shobal were Alvan, Manahath, Ebal, Shepho, and Onam.
[24]The descendants of Zibeon were Aiah and Anah. (This is the Anah who discovered the hot springs in the wilderness while he was grazing his father's donkeys.)

**36:25**
Gen 36:2, 5, 14, 18
1 Chr 1:41
**36:27**
1 Chr 1:38, 42

[25]The descendants of Anah were his son, Dishon, and his daughter, Oholibamah.
[26]The descendants of Dishon* were Hemdan, Eshban, Ithran, and Keran.
[27]The descendants of Ezer were Bilhan, Zaavan, and Akan.
[28]The descendants of Dishan were Uz and Aran.

**36:29-30**
Gen 36:20

[29]So these were the leaders of the Horite clans: Lotan, Shobal, Zibeon, Anah, [30]Dishon, Ezer, and Dishan. The Horite clans are named after their clan leaders, who lived in the land of Seir.

### Rulers of Edom

**36:31-43**
//1 Chr 1:43-54

[31]These are the kings who ruled in the land of Edom before any king ruled over the Israelites*:

[32]Bela son of Beor, who ruled in Edom from his city of Dinhabah.
[33]When Bela died, Jobab son of Zerah from Bozrah became king in his place.
[34]When Jobab died, Husham from the land of the Temanites became king in his place.
[35]When Husham died, Hadad son of Bedad became king in his place and ruled from the city of Avith. He was the one who defeated the Midianites in the land of Moab.
[36]When Hadad died, Samlah from the city of Masrekah became king in his place.
[37]When Samlah died, Shaul from the city of Rehoboth-on-the-River became king in his place.
[38]When Shaul died, Baal-hanan son of Acbor became king in his place.
[39]When Baal-hanan son of Acbor died, Hadad* became king in his place and ruled from the city of Pau. His wife was Mehetabel, the daughter of Matred and granddaughter of Me-zahab.

[40]These are the names of the leaders of the clans descended from Esau, who lived in the places named for them: Timna, Alvah, Jetheth, [41]Oholibamah, Elah, Pinon, [42]Kenaz, Teman, Mibzar, [43]Magdiel, and Iram. These are the leaders of the clans of Edom, listed according to their settlements in the land they occupied. They all descended from Esau, the ancestor of the Edomites.

## G. THE STORY OF JOSEPH (37:1—50:26)

Joseph, one of Jacob's 12 sons, was obviously the favorite. Hated by his brothers for this, Joseph was sold to slave traders only to emerge as ruler of all Egypt. Through Joseph, we learn how suffering, no matter how unfair, develops strong character and deep wisdom.

**36:26** Hebrew *Dishan*, a variant spelling of Dishon; compare 36:21, 28.   **36:31** Or *before an Israelite king ruled over them.*   **36:39** As in some Hebrew manuscripts, Samaritan Pentateuch, and Syriac version (see also 1 Chr 1:50); most Hebrew manuscripts read *Hadar.*

## 1. Joseph is sold into slavery

### Joseph's Dreams

**37** So Jacob settled again in the land of Canaan, where his father had lived as a foreigner. ²This is the account of Jacob and his family. When Joseph was seventeen years old, he often tended his father's flocks. He worked for his half brothers, the sons of his father's wives Bilhah and Zilpah. But Joseph reported to his father some of the bad things his brothers were doing.

³Jacob* loved Joseph more than any of his other children because Joseph had been born to him in his old age. So one day Jacob had a special gift made for Joseph—a beautiful robe.* ⁴But his brothers hated Joseph because their father loved him more than the rest of them. They couldn't say a kind word to him.

⁵One night Joseph had a dream, and when he told his brothers about it, they hated him more than ever. ⁶"Listen to this dream," he said. ⁷"We were out in the field, tying up bundles of grain. Suddenly my bundle stood up, and your bundles all gathered around and bowed low before mine!"

⁸His brothers responded, "So you think you will be our king, do you? Do you actually think you will reign over us?" And they hated him all the more because of his dreams and the way he talked about them.

⁹Soon Joseph had another dream, and again he told his brothers about it. "Listen, I have had another dream," he said. "The sun, moon, and eleven stars bowed low before me!"

¹⁰This time he told the dream to his father as well as to his brothers, but his father scolded him. "What kind of dream is that?" he asked. "Will your mother and I and your brothers actually come and bow to the ground before you?" ¹¹But while his brothers were jealous of Joseph, his father wondered what the dreams meant.

¹²Soon after this, Joseph's brothers went to pasture their father's flocks at Shechem. ¹³When they had been gone for some time, Jacob said to Joseph, "Your brothers are pasturing the sheep at Shechem. Get ready, and I will send you to them."

"I'm ready to go," Joseph replied.

¹⁴"Go and see how your brothers and the flocks are getting along," Jacob said. "Then come back and bring me a report." So Jacob sent him on his way, and Joseph traveled to Shechem from their home in the valley of Hebron.

¹⁵When he arrived there, a man from the area noticed him wandering around the countryside. "What are you looking for?" he asked.

¹⁶"I'm looking for my brothers," Joseph replied. "Do you know where they are pasturing their sheep?"

¹⁷"Yes," the man told him. "They have moved on from here, but I heard them say, 'Let's go on to Dothan.'" So Joseph followed his brothers to Dothan and found them there.

**37:1** Gen 17:8; 28:4
**37:2** Gen 35:22-26; 41:46
**37:3** Gen 37:23, 32; 44:20
**37:4** Gen 27:41
**37:5** Gen 28:12 Num 12:6 Dan 2:1
**37:7** Gen 42:6, 9; 43:26
**37:8** Deut 33:16
**37:10** Gen 27:29
**37:11** Luke 2:19, 51 Acts 7:9
**37:13** Gen 33:19
**37:14** Gen 35:27
**37:17** 2 Kgs 6:13

**37:3a** Hebrew *Israel;* also in 37:13. See note on 35:21.   **37:3b** Traditionally rendered *a coat of many colors.* The exact meaning of the Hebrew is uncertain.

---

**37:3** In Joseph's day, everyone had a robe or cloak. Robes were used for warmth, to bundle up belongings for a trip, to wrap babies, to sit on, or even to serve as security for a loan. Most robes were knee length, short sleeved, and plain. In contrast, Joseph's robe was probably of the kind worn by royalty—long sleeved, ankle length, and colorful. The robe became a symbol of Jacob's favoritism toward Joseph, and it aggravated the already strained relations between Joseph and his brothers. Favoritism in families may be unavoidable, but its divisive effects should be minimized. Parents may not be able to change their feelings toward a favorite child, but they can change their actions toward the others.

**37:6-11** Joseph's brothers were already angry over the possibility of being ruled by their little brother. Joseph then fueled the fire with his immature attitude and boastful manner. No one enjoys a braggart. Joseph learned this the hard way. His angry brothers sold him into slavery to get rid of him. After several years of hardship, Joseph learned an important lesson: Because our talents and knowledge come from God, it is more appropriate to thank him for them than to brag about them. Later Joseph gave God the credit (41:16).

**JOSEPH GOES TO MEET HIS BROTHERS**
Jacob asked Joseph to go find his brothers, who were grazing their flocks near Shechem. When Joseph arrived, he learned that his brothers had gone on to Dothan, which lay along a major trade route to Egypt. There the jealous brothers sold Joseph as a slave to a group of Ishmaelite traders on their way to Egypt.

### Joseph Sold into Slavery

**37:20**
Gen 37:33

**37:21**
Gen 42:22

**37:22**
Gen 37:29

**37:23**
Gen 37:3

**37:24**
Jer 38:6; 41:7

**37:25**
Gen 31:21; 37:28
Jer 8:22; 46:11

¹⁸When Joseph's brothers saw him coming, they recognized him in the distance. As he approached, they made plans to kill him. ¹⁹"Here comes the dreamer!" they said. ²⁰"Come on, let's kill him and throw him into one of these cisterns. We can tell our father, 'A wild animal has eaten him.' Then we'll see what becomes of his dreams!"

²¹But when Reuben heard of their scheme, he came to Joseph's rescue. "Let's not kill him," he said. ²²"Why should we shed any blood? Let's just throw him into this empty cistern here in the wilderness. Then he'll die without our laying a hand on him." Reuben was secretly planning to rescue Joseph and return him to his father.

²³So when Joseph arrived, his brothers ripped off the beautiful robe he was wearing. ²⁴Then they grabbed him and threw him into the cistern. Now the cistern was empty; there was no water in it. ²⁵Then, just as they were sitting down to eat, they looked up and saw a caravan of camels in the distance coming toward them. It was a group of Ishmaelite traders taking a load of gum, balm, and aromatic resin from Gilead down to Egypt.

²⁶Judah said to his brothers, "What will we gain by killing our brother? We'd have to cover up the crime.* ²⁷Instead of hurting him, let's sell him to those Ishmaelite traders. After all, he is our brother—our own flesh and blood!" And his brothers agreed.

**37:26** Hebrew *cover his blood.*

---

**JOSEPH**

As a youngster, Joseph was overconfident. His natural self-assurance—increased by being Jacob's favorite son and by knowing of God's designs on his life—was unbearable to his ten older brothers, who eventually conspired against him. But this self-assurance, molded by pain and combined with a personal knowledge of God, allowed him to survive and prosper where most would have failed. He added quiet wisdom to his confidence and won the hearts of everyone he met—Potiphar, the prison warden, other prisoners, the pharaoh, and, after many years, even those ten brothers.

Perhaps you can identify with one or more of these hardships Joseph experienced: He was betrayed and deserted by his family, exposed to sexual temptation, and punished for doing the right thing; he endured a long imprisonment and was forgotten by those he helped. As you read his story, note what Joseph did in each case. His positive response transformed each setback into a step forward. He didn't spend much time asking why. His approach was "What shall I do now?" Those who met Joseph were aware that wherever he went and whatever he did, God was with him. When you're facing a setback, the beginning of a Joseph-like attitude is to acknowledge that God is with you. There is nothing like his presence to shed new light on a dark situation.

| | |
|---|---|
| **Strengths and accomplishments** | • Rose in power from slave to ruler of Egypt<br>• Was known for his personal integrity<br>• Was a man of spiritual sensitivity<br>• Prepared a nation to survive a famine |
| **Weakness and mistake** | • His youthful pride caused friction with his brothers |
| **Lessons from his life** | • What matters is not so much the events or circumstances of life, but our response to them<br>• With God's help, any situation can be used for good, even when others intend it for evil |
| **Vital statistics** | • Where: Canaan, Egypt<br>• Occupation: Shepherd, slave, convict, ruler<br>• Relatives: Parents: Jacob and Rachel. Siblings: Eleven brothers and one sister. Wife: Asenath. Sons: Manasseh and Ephraim. |
| **Key verse** | "So Pharaoh asked his officials, 'Can we find anyone else like this man so obviously filled with the spirit of God?'" (Genesis 41:38). |

Joseph's story is told in Genesis 30—50. He is also mentioned in Hebrews 11:22.

---

**37:19, 20** Could jealousy ever make you feel like killing someone? Before saying, "Of course not," look at what happened in this story. Ten men were willing to kill their younger brother over a robe and a few reported dreams. Their deep jealousy had grown into ugly rage, completely blinding them to what was right. Jealousy can be difficult to recognize because our reasons for it seem to make sense. But left unchecked, jealousy grows quickly and leads to serious sins. The longer you cultivate jealous feelings, the harder it is to uproot them. The time to deal with

jealousy is when you notice yourself keeping score of others' recognition, awards, and achievements.

**37:26, 27** The brothers were worried about bearing the guilt of Joseph's death. Judah suggested an option that was not right but would leave them innocent of murder. Sometimes we jump at a solution because it is the lesser of two evils but still is not the right action to take. When someone proposes a seemingly workable solution, first ask, "Is it right?"

²⁸So when the Ishmaelites, who were Midianite traders, came by, Joseph's brothers pulled him out of the cistern and sold him to them for twenty pieces* of silver. And the traders took him to Egypt.

²⁹Some time later, Reuben returned to get Joseph out of the cistern. When he discovered that Joseph was missing, he tore his clothes in grief. ³⁰Then he went back to his brothers and lamented, "The boy is gone! What will I do now?"

³¹Then the brothers killed a young goat and dipped Joseph's robe in its blood. ³²They sent the beautiful robe to their father with this message: "Look at what we found. Doesn't this robe belong to your son?"

³³Their father recognized it immediately. "Yes," he said, "it is my son's robe. A wild animal must have eaten him. Joseph has clearly been torn to pieces!" ³⁴Then Jacob tore his clothes and dressed himself in burlap. He mourned deeply for his son for a long time. ³⁵His family all tried to comfort him, but he refused to be comforted. "I will go to my grave* mourning for my son," he would say, and then he would weep.

³⁶Meanwhile, the Midianite traders* arrived in Egypt, where they sold Joseph to Potiphar, an officer of Pharaoh, the king of Egypt. Potiphar was captain of the palace guard.

## 2. Judah and Tamar

**38** About this time, Judah left home and moved to Adullam, where he stayed with a man named Hirah. ²There he saw a Canaanite woman, the daughter of Shua, and he married her. When he slept with her, ³she became pregnant and gave birth to a son, and he named the boy Er. ⁴Then she became pregnant again and gave birth to another son, and she named him Onan. ⁵And when she gave birth to a third son, she named him Shelah. At the time of Shelah's birth, they were living at Kezib.

⁶In the course of time, Judah arranged for his firstborn son, Er, to marry a young woman named Tamar. ⁷But Er was a wicked man in the LORD's sight, so the LORD took his life. ⁸Then Judah said to Er's brother Onan, "Go and marry Tamar, as our law requires of the brother of a man who has died. You must produce an heir for your brother."

⁹But Onan was not willing to have a child who would not be his own heir. So whenever he had intercourse with his brother's wife, he spilled the semen on the ground. This prevented her from having a child who would belong to his brother. ¹⁰But the LORD considered it evil for Onan to deny a child to his dead brother. So the LORD took Onan's life, too.

**37:28** Hebrew *20 shekels*, about 8 ounces or 228 grams in weight.   **37:35** Hebrew *go down to Sheol*.
**37:36** Hebrew *the Medanites*. The relationship between the Midianites and Medanites is unclear; compare 37:28. See also 25:2.

**37:28**
Gen 39:1; 45:4-5
Lev 27:5
Judg 8:22-24
Acts 7:9

**37:29**
Gen 37:34; 44:13
Num 14:6

**37:30**
Gen 42:13, 36

**37:32**
Luke 15:30

**37:33**
Gen 37:20; 44:28

**37:34**
Gen 37:29

**37:35**
Gen 44:29
2 Sam 12:17
Ps 77:2

**37:36**
Gen 39:1; 40:3

**38:1**
Josh 15:35
1 Sam 22:1

**38:2**
Gen 24:3; 34:2;
38:12

**38:3**
Gen 46:12
Num 26:19

**38:6**
Matt 1:3

**38:7**
Gen 6:5; 13:13;
19:13; 38:10
1 Chr 2:3

**38:8**
Lev 18:15
Num 36:8
Deut 25:5-10
†Mark 12:19
Matt 22:24

**37:28** Although Joseph's brothers didn't kill him outright, they wouldn't expect him to survive for long as a slave. They were quite willing to let cruel slave traders do their dirty work for them. Joseph faced a 30-day journey through the desert, probably chained and on foot. He would be treated like baggage and, once in Egypt, would be sold as a piece of merchandise. His brothers thought they would never see him again. But God was in control of Joseph's life and had other plans.

**37:29, 30** Reuben returned to the cistern to find Joseph, but his little brother was gone. His first response, in effect, was "What will happen to me?" rather than "What will happen to Joseph?" In a tough situation, are you usually concerned first about yourself? Consider the person most affected by the problem, and you will be more likely to find a solution for it.

**37:31-35** To cover their evil action, Jacob's sons deceived their father into thinking Joseph was dead. Jacob himself had deceived others many times (including his own father; 27:35). Even though he didn't know it at this point, Jacob was learning by hard experience the painfulness and destructive consequences of deceit.

**37:34** Tearing one's clothes and wearing burlap (sometimes called sackcloth) were signs of mourning, much like wearing black today.

**37:36** Imagine the culture shock Joseph experienced upon arriving in Egypt. Joseph had lived as a nomad, traveling the countryside with his family, caring for sheep. Suddenly he was thrust into the world's most advanced civilization with great pyramids, beautiful homes, sophisticated people, and a new language. While Joseph saw Egypt's skill and intelligence at their best, he also saw the Egyptians' spiritual blindness. They worshiped countless gods related to every aspect of life.

**38:1ff** This chapter vividly contrasts the immoral character of Judah with the moral character of Joseph. Judah's lack of integrity resulted in family strife and deception. Chapter 39 shows how Joseph's integrity and wise choices reflect his godly character. His faithfulness was rewarded with blessings greater than he could imagine, both for himself and for his family.

**38:8-10** This law about marrying a widow in the family is explained in Deuteronomy 25:5-10. Its purpose was to ensure that a childless widow would have a son who would receive her late husband's inheritance and who, in turn, would care for her. Because Judah's son (Tamar's husband) had no children, there was no family line through which the inheritance and the blessing of the covenant could continue. God killed Onan

**38:11**
Ruth 1:13

¹¹Then Judah said to Tamar, his daughter-in-law, "Go back to your parents' home and remain a widow until my son Shelah is old enough to marry you." (But Judah didn't really intend to do this because he was afraid Shelah would also die, like his two brothers.) So Tamar went back to live in her father's home.

**38:12**
Gen 31:19
Josh 15:10, 57

¹²Some years later Judah's wife died. After the time of mourning was over, Judah and his friend Hirah the Adullamite went up to Timnah to supervise the shearing of his sheep. ¹³Someone told Tamar, "Look, your father-in-law is going up to Timnah to shear his sheep."

**38:14**
Josh 15:34

¹⁴Tamar was aware that Shelah had grown up, but no arrangements had been made for her to come and marry him. So she changed out of her widow's clothing and covered herself with a veil to disguise herself. Then she sat beside the road at the entrance to the village of Enaim, which is on the road to Timnah. ¹⁵Judah noticed her and thought she was a prostitute,

---

**REUBEN**

Parents are usually the best judges of their children's character. Jacob summarized the personality of his son Reuben by comparing him to water. Except when frozen, water has no stable shape of its own. It always shapes itself to its container or environment. Reuben usually had good intentions, but he seemed unable to stand against a crowd. His instability made him hard to trust. He had both private and public values, but these contradicted each other. He went along with his brothers in their action against Joseph while hoping to counteract the evil in private. The plan failed. Compromise has a way of destroying convictions. Without convictions, lack of direction will destroy life. Reuben's sleeping with one of his father's wives showed how little he had left of the integrity he had displayed earlier in life.

How consistent are your public and private lives? We may want to think they are separate, but we can't deny that they affect each other. What convictions are present in your life at all times? How closely does Jacob's description of his son—"unruly as a flood"— describe your life?

| | |
|---|---|
| **Strengths and accomplishments** | • Saved Joseph's life by talking the other brothers out of murder<br>• Showed intense love for his father by offering his own sons as a guarantee that Benjamin's life would be safe |
| **Weaknesses and mistakes** | • Gave in quickly to group pressure<br>• Did not directly protect Joseph from his brothers, although as oldest son he had the authority to do so<br>• Slept with one of his father's wives |
| **Lessons from his life** | • Public and private integrity must be the same, or one will destroy the other<br>• Punishment for sin may not be immediate, but it is certain |
| **Vital statistics** | • Where: Canaan, Egypt<br>• Occupation: Shepherd<br>• Relatives: Parents: Jacob and Leah. Siblings: Eleven brothers, one sister. |
| **Key verses** | "Reuben, you are my firstborn, my strength, the child of my vigorous youth. You are first in rank and first in power. But you are as unruly as a flood, and you will be first no longer. For you went to bed with my wife; you defiled my marriage couch" (Genesis 49:3, 4). |

Reuben's story is told in Genesis 29—50.

---

because he refused to fulfill his obligation to his brother and to Tamar.

**38:15-23** It may seem strange that prostitution is written about in such a matter-of-fact way here. Prostitutes were common in pagan cultures such as Canaan. Public prostitutes served Canaanite goddesses and were common elements of the religious cults. Fornication was encouraged to improve fertility in crops and flocks. Public prostitutes were more highly respected than private prostitutes, who were sometimes punished when caught. Tamar was driven to seduce Judah because of her intense desire to have children and be the matriarch of Judah's line; Judah was driven by his lust. Neither case was justified.

**38:15-24** Why was Judah so open about his relations with a prostitute, yet ready to execute his daughter-in-law for being one? To understand this apparent contradiction, we must understand the place of women in Canaan. A woman's most important function was bearing children who would perpetuate the family line. To ensure that children belonged to the husband, the bride was expected to be a virgin, and the wife was expected to have

relations only with him. If a wife committed adultery, she could be executed. Some women, however, did not belong to families. They might serve as shrine prostitutes supported by offerings or common prostitutes supported by the men who used their services. Their children were nobody's heirs, and men who hired them adulterated no one's bloodlines.

Judah saw no harm in hiring a prostitute for a night; after all, he was more than willing to pay. He was ready to execute Tamar, however, because if she was pregnant as a result of prostitution, his grandchild would not be part of his family line. Apparently the question of sexual morality never entered Judah's mind; his concern was for keeping his inheritance in the family. Ironically, it was Tamar, not Judah, who acted to provide him with legal heirs. By seducing him, she acted more in the spirit of the law than he did when he refused to send his third son to her.

This event in no way implies that God thinks lightly of prostitution. Throughout Scripture, prostitution is condemned as a serious sin. If the story has a moral, it is that faithfulness to family obligations is important. Incidentally, Judah and Tamar are direct ancestors of Jesus Christ (see Matthew 1:1-6).

since she had covered her face. <sup>16</sup>So he stopped and propositioned her. "Let me have sex with you," he said, not realizing that she was his own daughter-in-law.

"How much will you pay to have sex with me?" Tamar asked.

<sup>17</sup>"I'll send you a young goat from my flock," Judah promised.

"But what will you give me to guarantee that you will send the goat?" she asked.

<sup>18</sup>"What kind of guarantee do you want?" he replied.

She answered, "Leave me your identification seal and its cord and the walking stick you are carrying." So Judah gave them to her. Then he had intercourse with her, and she became pregnant. <sup>19</sup>Afterward she went back home, took off her veil, and put on her widow's clothing as usual.

<sup>20</sup>Later Judah asked his friend Hirah the Adullamite to take the young goat to the woman and to pick up the things he had given her as his guarantee. But Hirah couldn't find her. <sup>21</sup>So he asked the men who lived there, "Where can I find the shrine prostitute who was sitting beside the road at the entrance to Enaim?"

"We've never had a shrine prostitute here," they replied.

<sup>22</sup>So Hirah returned to Judah and told him, "I couldn't find her anywhere, and the men of the village claim they've never had a shrine prostitute there."

<sup>23</sup>"Then let her keep the things I gave her," Judah said. "I sent the young goat as we agreed, but you couldn't find her. We'd be the laughingstock of the village if we went back again to look for her."

<sup>24</sup>About three months later, Judah was told, "Tamar, your daughter-in-law, has acted like a prostitute. And now, because of this, she's pregnant."

"Bring her out, and let her be burned!" Judah demanded.

<sup>25</sup>But as they were taking her out to kill her, she sent this message to her father-in-law: "The man who owns these things made me pregnant. Look closely. Whose seal and cord and walking stick are these?"

<sup>26</sup>Judah recognized them immediately and said, "She is more righteous than I am, because I didn't arrange for her to marry my son Shelah." And Judah never slept with Tamar again.

<sup>27</sup>When the time came for Tamar to give birth, it was discovered that she was carrying twins. <sup>28</sup>While she was in labor, one of the babies reached out his hand. The midwife grabbed it and tied a scarlet string around the child's wrist, announcing, "This one came out first." <sup>29</sup>But then he pulled back his hand, and out came his brother! "What!" the midwife exclaimed. "How did you break out first?" So he was named Perez.* <sup>30</sup>Then the baby with the scarlet string on his wrist was born, and he was named Zerah.*

### 3. Joseph is thrown into prison
*Joseph in Potiphar's House*

**39** When Joseph was taken to Egypt by the Ishmaelite traders, he was purchased by Potiphar, an Egyptian officer. Potiphar was captain of the guard for Pharaoh, the king of Egypt.

<sup>2</sup>The LORD was with Joseph, so he succeeded in everything he did as he served in the

**38:29** *Perez* means "breaking out." **38:30** *Zerah* means "scarlet" or "brightness."

**Marginal references:**
- **38:16** 2 Sam 13:11
- **38:17** Gen 38:20
- **38:18** Gen 41:42; Hos 4:11
- **38:24** Lev 20:10; 21:9
- **38:26** 1 Sam 24:17
- **38:27** Gen 25:24
- **38:29** Gen 46:12; Num 26:20-21; Ruth 4:12; 1 Chr 2:4; Matt 1:3; Luke 3:33
- **39:1** Gen 37:25

---

**38:18** This identification seal was used to authenticate legal documents. Usually a unique design carved in stone and worn on a ring or necklace inseparable from its owner, the seal was used by the wealthy and powerful to mark clay or wax. Because Tamar had Judah's seal, she could prove beyond a doubt that he had been with her.

**38:24-26** When Tamar revealed she was pregnant, Judah, who unknowingly had gotten her pregnant, moved to have her killed. Judah had concealed his own sin, yet he came down harshly on Tamar. Often the sins we try to cover up are the ones that anger us most when we see them in others. If you become indignant at the sins of others, you may have a similar tendency to sin that you don't wish to face. When we admit our sins and ask God to forgive us, forgiving others becomes easier.

**39:1** The date of Joseph's arrival in Egypt is debatable. Many believe he arrived during the period of the Hyksos rulers, foreigners who came from the region of Canaan. They invaded Egypt and controlled the land for almost 150 years. If Joseph arrived during their rule, it is easy to see why he was rapidly promoted up the royal ladder. Because the Hyksos were foreigners themselves, they would not hold this brilliant young foreigner's ancestry against him.

**39:1** *Pharaoh* was the general name for all the kings of Egypt. It was a title like "king" or "president" used to address the country's leader. The pharaoh who placed Joseph in charge of Egypt was a different person from the pharaoh who turned against the Hebrews in the book of Exodus.

**39:1** Ancient Egypt was a land of great contrasts. People were either rich beyond measure or poverty stricken. There wasn't much middle ground. Joseph found himself serving Potiphar, an extremely rich officer in Pharaoh's service. Rich families like Potiphar's had elaborate homes two or three stories tall with beautiful gardens and balconies. They enjoyed live entertainment at home as they chose delicious fruit from expensive bowls. They surrounded themselves with alabaster vases, paintings, beautiful rugs, and hand-carved chairs. Dinner was served on golden table-

**39:2**
Acts 7:9

**39:4**
Gen 40:4
Prov 22:29

**39:5**
Deut 28:3-4, 11

**39:6**
Gen 29:17
1 Sam 16:12, 18
Acts 7:20

**39:7**
Prov 7:15-20

**39:8**
Gen 39:5
Prov 6:23-24

home of his Egyptian master. ³Potiphar noticed this and realized that the LORD was with Joseph, giving him success in everything he did. ⁴This pleased Potiphar, so he soon made Joseph his personal attendant. He put him in charge of his entire household and everything he owned. ⁵From the day Joseph was put in charge of his master's household and property, the LORD began to bless Potiphar's household for Joseph's sake. All his household affairs ran smoothly, and his crops and livestock flourished. ⁶So Potiphar gave Joseph complete administrative responsibility over everything he owned. With Joseph there, he didn't worry about a thing—except what kind of food to eat!

Joseph was a very handsome and well-built young man, ⁷and Potiphar's wife soon began to look at him lustfully. "Come and sleep with me," she demanded.

⁸But Joseph refused. "Look," he told her, "my master trusts me with everything in his entire household. ⁹No one here has more authority than I do. He has held back nothing from

## POTIPHAR & HIS WIFE

Potiphar, the captain of Pharaoh's royal guard, had a large household and a wife with too much time on her hands. One day he purchased Joseph from some Midianite slave traders and put him to work in his home. This was the best decision Potiphar ever made. Not only was Joseph talented, but God was also with him. Because of Joseph, Potiphar began to prosper greatly.

While Potiphar was benefiting from Joseph's good work ethic, Potiphar's wife was noticing Joseph's good looks. Soon she moved from looking to seducing, but Joseph continually resisted her advances. Denied the thrill of chasing and capturing her prey, of feeling a few moments of illicit pleasure, Potiphar's wife became angry and hurt. One day, after she had been scorned by Joseph, she accused Joseph of attempted rape. Since she couldn't have Joseph, she decided to punish him.

Potiphar had Joseph thrown into prison. We don't know if Potiphar ever realized what was going on in his house, but he sided with his wife. Because he listened to a faithless woman, Potiphar jailed an innocent man and got rid of the best household overseer in all of Egypt. Had Potiphar been more observant, he would have seen that Joseph was not merely an administrative windfall, he was also a young man of integrity. Perhaps he did see Joseph's character but didn't have enough himself to face the truth. In any case, Potiphar and his wife deserved each other.

Although Potiphar recognized talent when he saw it, he wasn't quite as good a judge of character. Both qualities are important, but character matters far more in the long run. Selfishness, faithlessness, and deceit have no place in a person who wants to develop character. Potiphar and his wife show us that anyone can be a judge of talent, but it takes insight and courage to be a judge of character.

| | |
|---|---|
| **Strengths and accomplishments** | • Potiphar reached a high rank in Pharaoh's court<br>• Both enjoyed the temporary blessing of having Joseph, God's servant, as their slave<br>• Potiphar was a good judge of talent |
| **Weaknesses and mistakes** | • Neither recognized the amazing person who lived in their house<br>• Both failed in judging character—Potiphar toward his wife and Joseph, his wife toward Joseph<br>• Falsely accused and imprisoned Joseph, their faithful servant |
| **Lessons from their lives** | • A lasting marriage requires faithfulness and hard work<br>• God can accomplish his purposes through other's mistakes and sins<br>• God blesses many people who clearly don't deserve his grace and help<br>• One person with character stands out among those who possess little of it |
| **Vital statistics** | • Where: Egypt<br>• Occupation: Potiphar: Palace official. Potiphar's wife: wife. |
| **Key verse** | "From the day Joseph was put in charge of his master's household and property, the LORD began to bless Potiphar's household for Joseph's sake. All his household affairs ran smoothly, and his crops and livestock flourished" (Genesis 39:5). |

The story of Potiphar and his wife is told in Genesis 37:36 and Genesis 39.

ware, and the rooms were lighted with gold lampstands. Servants, like Joseph, worked on the first floor, while the family occupied the upper stories.

**39:9** Potiphar's wife failed to seduce Joseph, who resisted this temptation by saying it would be a sin against God. Joseph didn't say, "I'd be hurting you," or "I'd be sinning against Potiphar," or "I'd be sinning against myself." Under pressure, such excuses are easily rationalized away. Remember that sexual sin is not just between two consenting adults. It is an act of disobedience against God.

me except you, because you are his wife. How could I do such a wicked thing? It would be a great sin against God."

¹⁰She kept putting pressure on Joseph day after day, but he refused to sleep with her, and he kept out of her way as much as possible. ¹¹One day, however, no one else was around when he went in to do his work. ¹²She came and grabbed him by his cloak, demanding, "Come on, sleep with me!" Joseph tore himself away, but he left his cloak in her hand as he ran from the house.

¹³When she saw that she was holding his cloak and he had fled, ¹⁴she called out to her servants. Soon all the men came running. "Look!" she said. "My husband has brought this Hebrew slave here to make fools of us! He came into my room to rape me, but I screamed. ¹⁵When he heard me scream, he ran outside and got away, but he left his cloak behind with me."

¹⁶She kept the cloak with her until her husband came home. ¹⁷Then she told him her story. "That Hebrew slave you've brought into our house tried to come in and fool around with me," she said. ¹⁸"But when I screamed, he ran outside, leaving his cloak with me!"

### Joseph Put in Prison

¹⁹Potiphar was furious when he heard his wife's story about how Joseph had treated her. ²⁰So he took Joseph and threw him into the prison where the king's prisoners were held, and there he remained. ²¹But the Lord was with Joseph in the prison and showed him his faithful love. And the Lord made Joseph a favorite with the prison warden. ²²Before long, the warden put Joseph in charge of all the other prisoners and over everything that happened in the prison. ²³The warden had no more worries, because Joseph took care of everything. The Lord was with him and caused everything he did to succeed.

### Joseph Interprets Two Dreams

**40** Some time later, Pharaoh's chief cup-bearer and chief baker offended their royal master. ²Pharaoh became angry with these two officials, ³and he put them in the prison where Joseph was, in the palace of the captain of the guard. ⁴They remained in prison for quite some time, and the captain of the guard assigned them to Joseph, who looked after them.

⁵While they were in prison, Pharaoh's cup-bearer and baker each had a dream one night, and each dream had its own meaning. ⁶When Joseph saw them the next morning, he noticed that they both looked upset. ⁷"Why do you look so worried today?" he asked them.

⁸And they replied, "We both had dreams last night, but no one can tell us what they mean."

"Interpreting dreams is God's business," Joseph replied. "Go ahead and tell me your dreams."

⁹So the chief cup-bearer told Joseph his dream first. "In my dream," he said, "I saw a grapevine in front of me. ¹⁰The vine had three branches that began to bud and blossom, and soon it produced clusters of ripe grapes. ¹¹I was holding Pharaoh's wine cup in my hand, so I took a cluster of grapes and squeezed the juice into the cup. Then I placed the cup in Pharaoh's hand."

**39:10**
1 Thes 5:22

**39:12**
Prov 7:13
2 Tim 2:22

**39:17**
Exod 20:16; 23:1
Ps 55:3

**39:20**
Gen 40:1-3, 15;
41:10
Ps 105:18

**39:21**
Ps 105:19
Acts 7:9

**39:23**
Gen 39:3

**40:1**
Neh 1:11

**40:4**
Gen 37:36; 39:4

**40:5**
Gen 20:3; 41:11

**40:8**
Gen 41:15-16
Dan 2:27-28

---

**39:10-15** Joseph avoided Potiphar's wife as much as possible. He refused her advances and finally *ran* from her. Sometimes merely trying to avoid temptation is not enough. We must turn and run from them, especially when the temptations seem very strong, as is often the case in sexual temptations.

**39:20** Prisons were grim places with vile conditions. They were used to house forced laborers or, like Joseph, the accused who were awaiting trial. Prisoners were guilty until proven innocent, and there was no right to a speedy trial. Many prisoners never made it to court because trials were held at the whim of the ruler. Joseph was in prison a long time before he appeared before Pharaoh, and then he was called out to interpret a dream, not to stand trial.

**39:21-23** As a prisoner and slave, Joseph could have seen his situation as hopeless. Instead, he did his best with each small task given him. His diligence and positive attitude were soon noticed by the warden, who promoted him to prison administrator. Are you facing a seemingly hopeless predicament? At work, at home, or at

school, follow Joseph's example by taking each small task and doing your best. Remember how God turned Joseph's situation around. He will see your efforts and can reverse even overwhelming odds.

**40:1-3** The cup-bearer and the chief baker were two of the most trusted men in Pharaoh's kingdom. The baker was in charge of making the Pharaoh's food, and the cup-bearer tasted all of Pharaoh's food and drink before giving it to him, in case any of it was contaminated or poisoned. These trusted men must have been suspected of a serious wrong, perhaps of conspiring against Pharaoh. Later the cup-bearer was released and the baker executed.

**40:8** When the subject of dreams came up, Joseph focused everyone's attention on God. Rather than using the situation to make himself look good, he turned it into a powerful witness for the Lord. One secret of effective witnessing is to recognize opportunities to relate God to the other person's experience. When the opportunity arises, we must have the courage to speak, as Joseph did.

**40:12**
Gen 41:12

**40:13**
Gen 40:19-20

**40:14**
1 Sam 20:14

**40:15**
Gen 37:26-28;
39:20

¹²"This is what the dream means," Joseph said. "The three branches represent three days. ¹³Within three days Pharaoh will lift you up and restore you to your position as his chief cup-bearer. ¹⁴And please remember me and do me a favor when things go well for you. Mention me to Pharaoh, so he might let me out of this place. ¹⁵For I was kidnapped from my homeland, the land of the Hebrews, and now I'm here in prison, but I did nothing to deserve it."

¹⁶When the chief baker saw that Joseph had given the first dream such a positive interpretation, he said to Joseph, "I had a dream, too. In my dream there were three baskets of white pastries stacked on my head. ¹⁷The top basket contained all kinds of pastries for Pharaoh, but the birds came and ate them from the basket on my head."

**40:18**
Gen 40:12

**40:19**
Deut 21:22-23

**40:20**
2 Kgs 25:27
Jer 52:31

¹⁸"This is what the dream means," Joseph told him. "The three baskets also represent three days. ¹⁹Three days from now Pharaoh will lift you up and impale your body on a pole. Then birds will come and peck away at your flesh."

²⁰Pharaoh's birthday came three days later, and he prepared a banquet for all his officials and staff. He summoned* his chief cup-bearer and chief baker to join the other officials.

**40:22**
Gen 40:19

**40:23**
Gen 40:14

²¹He then restored the chief cup-bearer to his former position, so he could again hand Pharaoh his cup. ²²But Pharaoh impaled the chief baker, just as Joseph had predicted when he interpreted his dream. ²³Pharaoh's chief cup-bearer, however, forgot all about Joseph, never giving him another thought.

### 4. Joseph is placed in charge of Egypt
*Pharaoh's Dreams*

**41:2**
Isa 19:6-7

**41** Two full years later, Pharaoh dreamed that he was standing on the bank of the Nile River. ²In his dream he saw seven fat, healthy cows come up out of the river and begin grazing in the marsh grass. ³Then he saw seven more cows come up behind them from the Nile, but these were scrawny and thin. These cows stood beside the fat cows on the riverbank. ⁴Then the scrawny, thin cows ate the seven healthy, fat cows! At this point in the dream, Pharaoh woke up.

**41:5**
2 Kgs 4:42

**41:6**
Ezek 19:12

⁵But he fell asleep again and had a second dream. This time he saw seven heads of grain, plump and beautiful, growing on a single stalk. ⁶Then seven more heads of grain appeared, but these were shriveled and withered by the east wind. ⁷And these thin heads swallowed up the seven plump, well-formed heads! Then Pharaoh woke up again and realized it was a dream.

**41:8**
Exod 7:11-12
Dan 2:1-3; 4:5

**41:9**
Gen 40:14

**41:10**
Gen 40:2

**41:11**
Gen 40:5

**41:12**
Gen 40:12

**41:13**
Gen 40:22

⁸The next morning Pharaoh was very disturbed by the dreams. So he called for all the magicians and wise men of Egypt. When Pharaoh told them his dreams, not one of them could tell him what they meant.

⁹Finally, the king's chief cup-bearer spoke up. "Today I have been reminded of my failure," he told Pharaoh. ¹⁰"Some time ago, you were angry with the chief baker and me, and you imprisoned us in the palace of the captain of the guard. ¹¹One night the chief baker and I each had a dream, and each dream had its own meaning. ¹²There was a young Hebrew man with us in the prison who was a slave of the captain of the guard. We told him our dreams, and he told us what each of our dreams meant. ¹³And everything happened just as he had predicted. I was restored to my position as cup-bearer, and the chief baker was executed and impaled on a pole."

**41:14**
Ps 105:20

¹⁴Pharaoh sent for Joseph at once, and he was quickly brought from the prison. After he

**40:20** Hebrew *He lifted up the head of.*

---

**40:23** When Pharaoh's cup-bearer was freed from prison, he forgot about Joseph. Two full years passed before another opportunity to be freed (41:1). Yet Joseph's faith was deep, and he would be ready when the next chance came. When we feel passed by, overlooked, or forgotten, we shouldn't be surprised that people are often ungrateful. In similar situations, we should trust God as Joseph did. More opportunities may be waiting.

**41:8** Magicians and wise men were common in the palaces of ancient rulers. Their job description included studying sacred arts and sciences, reading the stars, interpreting dreams, predicting the future, and performing magic. These men had power (see Exodus 7:11, 12), but their power was satanic. They were unable to interpret Pharaoh's dream, but God had revealed it to Joseph in prison.

**41:14** Our most important opportunities may come when we least expect them. Joseph was brought hastily from the dungeon and pushed before Pharaoh. Did he have time to prepare? Yes and no. He had no warning that he would be suddenly pulled from prison and questioned by the king. Yet Joseph was ready for almost anything because of his right relationship with God. It was not Joseph's knowledge of dreams that helped him interpret their meaning. It was his knowledge of God. Be ready for opportunities by staying close to God. Then, when he calls you to a task, you'll be ready.

shaved and changed his clothes, he went in and stood before Pharaoh. [15]Then Pharaoh said to Joseph, "I had a dream last night, and no one here can tell me what it means. But I have heard that when you hear about a dream you can interpret it."

[16]"It is beyond my power to do this," Joseph replied. "But God can tell you what it means and set you at ease."

[17]So Pharaoh told Joseph his dream. "In my dream," he said, "I was standing on the bank of the Nile River, [18]and I saw seven fat, healthy cows come up out of the river and begin grazing in the marsh grass. [19]But then I saw seven sick-looking cows, scrawny and thin, come up after them. I've never seen such sorry-looking animals in all the land of Egypt. [20]These thin, scrawny cows ate the seven fat cows. [21]But afterward you wouldn't have known it, for they were still as thin and scrawny as before! Then I woke up.

[22]"Then I fell asleep again, and I had another dream. This time I saw seven heads of grain, full and beautiful, growing on a single stalk. [23]Then seven more heads of grain appeared, but these were blighted, shriveled, and withered by the east wind. [24]And the shriveled heads swallowed the seven healthy heads. I told these dreams to the magicians, but no one could tell me what they mean."

[25]Joseph responded, "Both of Pharaoh's dreams mean the same thing. God is telling Pharaoh in advance what he is about to do. [26]The seven healthy cows and the seven healthy heads of grain both represent seven years of prosperity. [27]The seven thin, scrawny cows that came up later and the seven thin heads of grain, withered by the east wind, represent seven years of famine.

[28]"This will happen just as I have described it, for God has revealed to Pharaoh in advance what he is about to do. [29]The next seven years will be a period of great prosperity throughout the land of Egypt. [30]But afterward there will be seven years of famine so great that all the prosperity will be forgotten in Egypt. Famine will destroy the land. [31]This famine will be so severe that even the memory of the good years will be erased. [32]As for having two similar dreams, it means that these events have been decreed by God, and he will soon make them happen.

[33]"Therefore, Pharaoh should find an intelligent and wise man and put him in charge of the entire land of Egypt. [34]Then Pharaoh should appoint supervisors over the land and let them collect one-fifth of all the crops during the seven good years. [35]Have them gather all the food produced in the good years that are just ahead and bring it to Pharaoh's storehouses. Store it away, and guard it so there will be food in the cities. [36]That way there will be enough to eat when the seven years of famine come to the land of Egypt. Otherwise this famine will destroy the land."

### Joseph Made Ruler of Egypt

[37]Joseph's suggestions were well received by Pharaoh and his officials. [38]So Pharaoh asked his officials, "Can we find anyone else like this man so obviously filled with the spirit of God?" [39]Then Pharaoh said to Joseph, "Since God has revealed the meaning of the dreams to you, clearly no one else is as intelligent or wise as you are. [40]You will be in charge of my court, and all my people will take orders from you. Only I, sitting on my throne, will have a rank higher than yours."

[41]Pharaoh said to Joseph, "I hereby put you in charge of the entire land of Egypt." [42]Then Pharaoh removed his signet ring from his hand and placed it on Joseph's finger. He dressed him in fine linen clothing and hung a gold chain around his neck. [43]Then he had Joseph ride in the chariot reserved for his second-in-command. And wherever Joseph went, the command was shouted, "Kneel down!" So Pharaoh put Joseph in charge of all

Cross references: 41:15 Dan 2:25; 41:16 Gen 40:8; 41:17 Gen 41:1; 41:27 2 Kgs 8:1; 41:29 Gen 41:47; 41:30 Gen 47:13; 41:33 Gen 41:39; 41:36 Gen 47:14; 41:38 Dan 4:8, 18; 5:11, 14; 41:39 Gen 41:33; 41:40 Gen 39:9; Acts 7:10; 41:41 Esth 8:2; Dan 6:3; 41:42 Esth 3:10; 6:8

**41:16** Joseph made sure that he gave the credit to God. We should be careful to do the same. To take the honor for ourselves is a form of stealing God's honor. Don't be silent when you know you should be giving glory and credit to God.

**41:28-36** After interpreting Pharaoh's dream, Joseph gave the king a survival plan for the next 14 years. The only way to prevent starvation was through careful planning; without a famine plan Egypt would have turned from prosperity to ruin. Many had detailed planning boring and unnecessary. But planning is a responsibility, not an option. Joseph was able to save a nation by translating God's plan for Egypt into practical actions (implementation).

**41:38** Pharaoh recognized that Joseph was a man "filled with the spirit of God." You probably won't get to interpret dreams for a king, but those who know you should be able to see God in you, through your kind words, merciful acts, and wise advice. Do your relatives, neighbors, and co-workers see you as a person in whom the Spirit of God lives?

**41:39, 40** Joseph rose quickly to the top, from prison walls to Pharaoh's palace. His training for this important position involved being first a slave and then a prisoner. In each situation he learned the importance of serving God and others. Whatever your situation, no matter how undesirable, consider it part of your training program for serving God.

**41:44**
Gen 45:8
Ps 105:22

**41:45**
Ezek 30:17

**41:46**
Gen 37:2

**41:51**
Gen 48:1
Deut 33:17

**41:52**
Gen 17:6

**41:54**
Gen 41:30
Ps 105:16
Acts 7:11

**41:55**
Gen 41:41

**41:57**
Gen 42:5; 47:15
Ps 105:16

**42:1**
Acts 7:12

**42:2**
Gen 43:2, 4

**42:3**
Gen 43:20

**42:4**
Gen 35:24

**42:5**
Gen 41:57
Acts 7:11

**42:6**
Ps 105:16-21

**42:7**
Gen 42:30

Egypt. ⁴⁴And Pharaoh said to him, "I am Pharaoh, but no one will lift a hand or foot in the entire land of Egypt without your approval."

⁴⁵Then Pharaoh gave Joseph a new Egyptian name, Zaphenath-paneah.* He also gave him a wife, whose name was Asenath. She was the daughter of Potiphera, the priest of On.* So Joseph took charge of the entire land of Egypt. ⁴⁶He was thirty years old when he began serving in the court of Pharaoh, the king of Egypt. And when Joseph left Pharaoh's presence, he inspected the entire land of Egypt.

⁴⁷As predicted, for seven years the land produced bumper crops. ⁴⁸During those years, Joseph gathered all the crops grown in Egypt and stored the grain from the surrounding fields in the cities. ⁴⁹He piled up huge amounts of grain like sand on the seashore. Finally, he stopped keeping records because there was too much to measure.

⁵⁰During this time, before the first of the famine years, two sons were born to Joseph and his wife, Asenath, the daughter of Potiphera, the priest of On. ⁵¹Joseph named his older son Manasseh,* for he said, "God has made me forget all my troubles and everyone in my father's family." ⁵²Joseph named his second son Ephraim,* for he said, "God has made me fruitful in this land of my grief."

⁵³At last the seven years of bumper crops throughout the land of Egypt came to an end. ⁵⁴Then the seven years of famine began, just as Joseph had predicted. The famine also struck all the surrounding countries, but throughout Egypt there was plenty of food. ⁵⁵Eventually, however, the famine spread throughout the land of Egypt as well. And when the people cried out to Pharaoh for food, he told them, "Go to Joseph, and do whatever he tells you." ⁵⁶So with severe famine everywhere, Joseph opened up the storehouses and distributed grain to the Egyptians, for the famine was severe throughout the land of Egypt. ⁵⁷And people from all around came to Egypt to buy grain from Joseph because the famine was severe throughout the world.

## 5. Joseph and his brothers meet in Egypt
### Joseph's Brothers Go to Egypt

**42** When Jacob heard that grain was available in Egypt, he said to his sons, "Why are you standing around looking at one another? ²I have heard there is grain in Egypt. Go down there, and buy enough grain to keep us alive. Otherwise we'll die."

³So Joseph's ten older brothers went down to Egypt to buy grain. ⁴But Jacob wouldn't let Joseph's younger brother, Benjamin, go with them, for fear some harm might come to him. ⁵So Jacob's* sons arrived in Egypt along with others to buy food, for the famine was in Canaan as well.

⁶Since Joseph was governor of all Egypt and in charge of selling grain to all the people, it was to him that his brothers came. When they arrived, they bowed before him with their faces to the ground. ⁷Joseph recognized his brothers instantly, but he pretended to be a stranger and spoke harshly to them. "Where are you from?" he demanded.

"From the land of Canaan," they replied. "We have come to buy food."

**41:45a** *Zaphenath-paneah* probably means "God speaks and lives." **41:45b** Greek version reads *of Heliopolis;* also in 41:50. **41:51** *Manasseh* sounds like a Hebrew term that means "causing to forget." **41:52** *Ephraim* sounds like a Hebrew term that means "fruitful." **42:5** Hebrew *Israel's.* See note on 35:21.

**41:45** Pharaoh may have been trying to make Joseph more acceptable by giving him an Egyptian name and wife. He probably wanted to (1) play down the fact that Joseph was a nomadic shepherd, an occupation disliked by the Egyptians, (2) make Joseph's name easier for Egyptians to pronounce and remember, and (3) show how highly he was honored by giving him the daughter of a prominent Egyptian official.

**41:46** Joseph was 30 years old when he became second-in-command in Egypt. At age 17, he had been sold into slavery by his brothers. Thus he had spent 13 years as an Egyptian slave and as a prisoner.

**41:54** Famine was a catastrophe because ancient peoples relied almost exclusively on their own crops for food. Almost perfect conditions were needed to produce good crops because there were no chemical fertilizers or pesticides. Any variances in rainfall or insect activity could cause crop failure and great hunger. Lack of storage, refrigeration, or transportation turned a moderate famine into a desperate situation. The famine Joseph prepared

for was especially severe because seven years of famine came one right after the other. Without God's intervention, the Egyptian nation would have crumbled.

**42:1, 2** Why was grain so valuable in those days? As a food source it was universal and used in nearly everything eaten. It could be dried and stored much longer than any vegetables, milk products, or meat. It was so important that it was even used as money.

**42:4** Jacob was especially fond of Benjamin because he was Joseph's only full brother and—as far as Jacob knew—the only surviving son of his beloved wife, Rachel. Benjamin was Jacob's youngest son and a child of his old age.

**42:7** Joseph could have revealed his identity to his brothers at once. But Joseph's last memory of them may well have been staring in horror at their faces as slave traders carried him away. Were his brothers still evil and treacherous, or had they changed over the years? Joseph decided to put them through a few tests to find out.

8Although Joseph recognized his brothers, they didn't recognize him. 9And he remembered the dreams he'd had about them many years before. He said to them, "You are spies! You have come to see how vulnerable our land has become."

10"No, my lord!" they exclaimed. "Your servants have simply come to buy food. 11We are all brothers—members of the same family. We are honest men, sir! We are not spies!"

12"Yes, you are!" Joseph insisted. "You have come to see how vulnerable our land has become."

13"Sir," they said, "there are actually twelve of us. We, your servants, are all brothers, sons of a man living in the land of Canaan. Our youngest brother is back there with our father right now, and one of our brothers is no longer with us."

14But Joseph insisted, "As I said, you are spies! 15This is how I will test your story. I swear by the life of Pharaoh that you will never leave Egypt unless your youngest brother comes here! 16One of you must go and get your brother. I'll keep the rest of you here in prison. Then we'll find out whether or not your story is true. By the life of Pharaoh, if it turns out that you don't have a younger brother, then I'll know you are spies."

17So Joseph put them all in prison for three days. 18On the third day Joseph said to them, "I am a God-fearing man. If you do as I say, you will live. 19If you really are honest men, choose one of your brothers to remain in prison. The rest of you may go home with grain for your starving families. 20But you must bring your youngest brother back to me. This will prove that you are telling the truth, and you will not die." To this they agreed.

21Speaking among themselves, they said, "Clearly we are being punished because of what we did to Joseph long ago. We saw his anguish when he pleaded for his life, but we wouldn't listen. That's why we're in this trouble."

22"Didn't I tell you not to sin against the boy?" Reuben asked. "But you wouldn't listen. And now we have to answer for his blood!"

23Of course, they didn't know that Joseph understood them, for he had been speaking to them through an interpreter. 24Now he turned away from them and began to weep. When he regained his composure, he spoke to them again. Then he chose Simeon from among them and had him tied up right before their eyes.

25Joseph then ordered his servants to fill the men's sacks with grain, but he also gave secret instructions to return each brother's payment at the top of his sack. He also gave them supplies for their journey home. 26So the brothers loaded their donkeys with the grain and headed for home.

27But when they stopped for the night and one of them opened his sack to get grain for his donkey, he found his money in the top of his sack. 28"Look!" he exclaimed to his brothers. "My money has been returned; it's here in my sack!" Then their hearts sank. Trembling, they said to each other, "What has God done to us?"

29When the brothers came to their father, Jacob, in the land of Canaan, they told him everything that had happened to them. 30"The man who is governor of the land spoke very harshly to us," they told him. "He accused us of being spies scouting the land. 31But we said, 'We are honest men, not spies. 32We are twelve brothers, sons of one father. One brother is no longer with us, and the youngest is at home with our father in the land of Canaan.'

33"Then the man who is governor of the land told us, 'This is how I will find out if you are honest men. Leave one of your brothers here with me, and take grain for your starving families and go on home. 34But you must bring your youngest brother back to me. Then I will know you are honest men and not spies. Then I will give you back your brother, and you may trade freely in the land.'"

35As they emptied out their sacks, there in each man's sack was the bag of money he had paid for the grain! The brothers and their father were terrified when they saw the bags of money. 36Jacob exclaimed, "You are robbing me of my children! Joseph is gone! Simeon is gone! And now you want to take Benjamin, too. Everything is going against me!"

**42:8**
Gen 37:2
**42:9**
Gen 42:16, 30-34
**42:10**
Gen 37:6-9
**42:11**
Gen 42:19, 31-34
**42:13**
Gen 37:30-33; 44:20; 46:31
**42:14**
Gen 42:9
**42:17**
Gen 40:4
**42:18**
Gen 20:11
Lev 25:43
**42:20**
Gen 42:34; 43:15
**42:21**
Gen 37:23-28; 45:3-5
**42:22**
Gen 9:6; 37:21-22
**42:24**
Gen 43:14, 23
**42:25**
Gen 44:1
**42:28**
Gen 43:23
**42:30**
Gen 42:7
**42:31**
Gen 42:11
**42:32**
Gen 42:13
**42:34**
Gen 34:10
**42:35**
Gen 43:12, 15, 18
**42:36**
Gen 43:14; 44:20-22

---

**42:8, 9** Joseph remembered his dreams about his brothers bowing down to him (37:6-9). Those dreams were coming true! As a young boy, Joseph had been boastful about his dreams. As a man, he no longer flaunted his superior status. He did not feel the need to say, "I told you so." It was not yet time to reveal his identity, so he kept quiet. Sometimes it is best to remain quiet, even when we would like to have the last word.

**42:15** Joseph was testing his brothers to make sure they had not been as cruel to Benjamin as they had been to him. Benjamin was his only full brother, and he wanted to see him face to face.

**42:22** Reuben couldn't resist saying, "I told you so." He thought they were being punished by God for what they had done to Joseph. Apparently the intervening years had not lessened their guilt. Selling Joseph into slavery amounted to death in their minds, for they surely never expected to see him again.

**42:37**
Gen 43:9; 44:32

**42:38**
Gen 37:35;
44:29, 34

37Then Reuben said to his father, "You may kill my two sons if I don't bring Benjamin back to you. I'll be responsible for him, and I promise to bring him back."

38But Jacob replied, "My son will not go down with you. His brother Joseph is dead, and he is all I have left. If anything should happen to him on your journey, you would send this grieving, white-haired man to his grave.*"

## The Brothers Return to Egypt

**43:1**
Gen 41:56-57

**43:2**
Gen 42:25

**43:3**
Gen 42:15; 44:23

**43** But the famine continued to ravage the land of Canaan. 2When the grain they had brought from Egypt was almost gone, Jacob said to his sons, "Go back and buy us a little more food."

3But Judah said, "The man was serious when he warned us, 'You won't see my face again unless your brother is with you.' 4If you send Benjamin with us, we will go down and buy more food. 5But if you don't let Benjamin go, we won't go either. Remember, the man said, 'You won't see my face again unless your brother is with you.'"

6"Why were you so cruel to me?" Jacob* moaned. "Why did you tell him you had another brother?"

**43:7**
Gen 42:13; 43:27

7"The man kept asking us questions about our family," they replied. "He asked, 'Is your father still alive? Do you have another brother?' So we answered his questions. How could we know he would say, 'Bring your brother down here'?"

**43:8**
Gen 42:2

**43:9**
Gen 42:37
Phlm 1:18-19

8Judah said to his father, "Send the boy with me, and we will be on our way. Otherwise we will all die of starvation—and not only we, but you and our little ones. 9I personally guarantee his safety. You may hold me responsible if I don't bring him back to you. Then let me bear the blame forever. 10If we hadn't wasted all this time, we could have gone and returned twice by now."

**43:11**
Gen 32:13; 37:25

**43:12**
Gen 42:25, 35

**43:13**
Gen 43:3

**43:14**
Gen 42:24
Ps 106:46

**43:16**
Gen 44:1

11So their father, Jacob, finally said to them, "If it can't be avoided, then at least do this. Pack your bags with the best products of this land. Take them down to the man as gifts—balm, honey, gum, aromatic resin, pistachio nuts, and almonds. 12Also take double the money that was put back in your sacks, as it was probably someone's mistake. 13Then take your brother, and go back to the man. 14May God Almighty* give you mercy as you go before the man, so that he will release Simeon and let Benjamin return. But if I must lose my children, so be it."

15So the men packed Jacob's gifts and double the money and headed off with Benjamin. They finally arrived in Egypt and presented themselves to Joseph. 16When Joseph saw Benjamin with them, he said to the manager of his household, "These men will eat with me this noon. Take them inside the palace. Then go slaughter an animal, and prepare a big feast." 17So the man did as Joseph told him and took them into Joseph's palace.

**43:18**
Gen 42:28, 35

18The brothers were terrified when they saw that they were being taken into Joseph's house. "It's because of the money someone put in our sacks last time we were here," they said. "He plans to pretend that we stole it. Then he will seize us, make us slaves, and take our donkeys."

## A Feast at Joseph's Palace

**43:21**
Gen 42:25, 35;
43:12

19The brothers approached the manager of Joseph's household and spoke to him at the entrance to the palace. 20"Sir," they said, "we came to Egypt once before to buy food. 21But as

**42:38** Hebrew *to Sheol.*   **43:6** Hebrew *Israel;* also in 43:11. See note on 35:21.   **43:14** Hebrew *El-Shaddai.*

---

**43:1** Jacob and his sons had no relief from the famine. They could not see God's overall plan of sending them to Egypt to be reunited with Joseph and fed from Egypt's storehouses. If you are praying for relief from suffering or pressure and God is not bringing it as quickly as you would like, remember that God may be leading you to special treasures.

**43:9** Judah accepted full responsibility for Benjamin's safety. He did not know what that might mean for him, but he was determined to do his duty. In the end, Judah's stirring words caused Joseph to break down with emotion and reveal himself to his brothers (44:18-34). Accepting responsibilities is difficult, but it builds character and confidence, earns others' respect, and motivates us to complete our work. When you have been given an assignment to complete or a responsibility to fulfill, commit yourself to seeing it through.

**43:11** These gifts of balm, honey, gum, aromatic resin, pistachio nuts, and almonds were highly valuable specialty items not common in Egypt. Because of the famine, they were even more rare.

**43:12** Joseph's brothers arrived home from Egypt only to find in their grain sacks the money they had used to pay for the grain (42:35). Some months later, when it was time to return to Egypt for more food, Jacob instructed them to take extra money so they could pay for the previous purchase as well as for additional grain. Jacob did not try to get away with anything. He was a man of integrity who paid for what he bought, whether he had to or not. We should follow his example and guard our integrity. A reputation for honesty is worth far more than the money we might gain by compromising it.

we were returning home, we stopped for the night and opened our sacks. Then we discovered that each man's money—the exact amount paid—was in the top of his sack! Here it is; we have brought it back with us. 22We also have additional money to buy more food. We have no idea who put our money in our sacks."

23"Relax. Don't be afraid," the household manager told them. "Your God, the God of your father, must have put this treasure into your sacks. I know I received your payment." Then he released Simeon and brought him out to them.

24The manager then led the men into Joseph's palace. He gave them water to wash their feet and provided food for their donkeys. 25They were told they would be eating there, so they prepared their gifts for Joseph's arrival at noon.

26When Joseph came home, they gave him the gifts they had brought him, then bowed low to the ground before him. 27After greeting them, he asked, "How is your father, the old man you spoke about? Is he still alive?"

28"Yes," they replied. "Our father, your servant, is alive and well." And they bowed low again.

29Then Joseph looked at his brother Benjamin, the son of his own mother. "Is this your youngest brother, the one you told me about?" Joseph asked. "May God be gracious to you, my son." 30Then Joseph hurried from the room because he was overcome with emotion for his brother. He went into his private room, where he broke down and wept. 31After washing his face, he came back out, keeping himself under control. Then he ordered, "Bring out the food!"

32The waiters served Joseph at his own table, and his brothers were served at a separate table. The Egyptians who ate with Joseph sat at their own table, because Egyptians despise Hebrews and refuse to eat with them. 33Joseph told each of his brothers where to sit, and to their amazement, he seated them according to age, from oldest to youngest. 34And Joseph filled their plates with food from his own table, giving Benjamin five times as much as he gave the others. So they feasted and drank freely with him.

### Joseph's Silver Cup

**44** When his brothers were ready to leave, Joseph gave these instructions to his palace manager: "Fill each of their sacks with as much grain as they can carry, and put each man's money back into his sack. 2Then put my personal silver cup at the top of the youngest brother's sack, along with the money for his grain." So the manager did as Joseph instructed him.

3The brothers were up at dawn and were sent on their journey with their loaded donkeys. 4But when they had gone only a short distance and were barely out of the city, Joseph said to his palace manager, "Chase after them and stop them. When you catch up with them, ask them, 'Why have you repaid my kindness with such evil? 5Why have you stolen my master's silver cup,* which he uses to predict the future? What a wicked thing you have done!'"

6When the palace manager caught up with the men, he spoke to them as he had been instructed.

7"What are you talking about?" the brothers responded. "We are your servants and would never do such a thing! 8Didn't we return the money we found in our sacks? We brought it back all the way from the land of Canaan. Why would we steal silver or gold from your master's house? 9If you find his cup with any one of us, let that man die. And all the rest of us, my lord, will be your slaves."

10"That's fair," the man replied. "But only the one who stole the cup will be my slave. The rest of you may go free."

11They all quickly took their sacks from the backs of their donkeys and opened them.

44:5 As in Greek version; Hebrew lacks this phrase.

Cross-references:
43:22 Gen 42:28
43:23 Gen 42:24
43:24 Gen 18:4; 24:32
43:27 Gen 43:7; 45:3
43:28 Exod 18:7
43:29 Num 6:25; Ps 67:1
43:30 Gen 42:24; 45:2, 14-15; 46:29
43:31 Gen 45:1
43:32 Gen 46:34; Exod 8:26
43:33 Gen 44:12
44:1 Gen 42:25; 43:16
44:4 Prov 17:13
44:5 Gen 30:27; Lev 19:26; Deut 18:10-14
44:8 Gen 43:21
44:9 Gen 31:32

**43:23** How did the money get into the sacks? Most likely, Joseph instructed his household manager to replace the money and then explain it with this response. Note that the household manager credited their God, not some Egyptian deity.

**43:32** Joseph ate by himself because he was following the laws of the Egyptians' caste system. Egyptians considered themselves highly intelligent and sophisticated. They looked upon shepherds and nomads as uncultured and even vulgar. As a Hebrew, Joseph could not eat with Egyptians even though he outranked them. As foreigners and shepherds, his brothers were lower in rank than any Egyptian citizens, so they had to eat separately, too.

**44:2** Joseph's silver cup was a symbol of his authority. It was thought to have supernatural powers, and to steal it would be a serious crime. Such goblets were used for predicting the future. A person poured water into the cup and interpreted the reflections, ripples, and bubbles. Joseph wouldn't have needed his cup, since God told him everything he needed to know about the future.

**44:12**
Gen 44:2
**44:13**
Gen 37:29, 34

¹²The palace manager searched the brothers' sacks, from the oldest to the youngest. And the cup was found in Benjamin's sack! ¹³When the brothers saw this, they tore their clothing in despair. Then they loaded their donkeys again and returned to the city.

**44:15**
Gen 44:5

¹⁴Joseph was still in his palace when Judah and his brothers arrived, and they fell to the ground before him. ¹⁵"What have you done?" Joseph demanded. "Don't you know that a man like me can predict the future?"

**44:16**
Gen 42:11; 43:18

¹⁶Judah answered, "Oh, my lord, what can we say to you? How can we explain this? How can we prove our innocence? God is punishing us for our sins. My lord, we have all returned to be your slaves—all of us, not just our brother who had your cup in his sack."

¹⁷"No," Joseph said. "I would never do such a thing! Only the man who stole the cup will be my slave. The rest of you may go back to your father in peace."

### Judah Speaks for His Brothers

**44:18**
Gen 37:7-8

¹⁸Then Judah stepped forward and said, "Please, my lord, let your servant say just one word to you. Please, do not be angry with me, even though you are as powerful as Pharaoh himself.

**44:19**
Gen 42:11; 43:7

¹⁹"My lord, previously you asked us, your servants, 'Do you have a father or a brother?' ²⁰And we responded, 'Yes, my lord, we have a father who is an old man, and his youngest son is a child of his old age. His full brother is dead, and he alone is left of his mother's children, and his father loves him very much.'

**44:21**
Gen 42:11, 15
**44:23**
Gen 43:3
**44:24**
Gen 42:29-34
**44:25**
Gen 42:2
**44:26**
Gen 43:5
**44:27**
Gen 46:19
**44:28**
Gen 37:33
**44:29**
Gen 42:38
**44:30**
1 Sam 18:1
**44:32**
Gen 43:9

²¹"And you said to us, 'Bring him here so I can see him with my own eyes.' ²²But we said to you, 'My lord, the boy cannot leave his father, for his father would die.' ²³But you told us, 'Unless your youngest brother comes with you, you will never see my face again.'

²⁴"So we returned to your servant, our father, and told him what you had said. ²⁵Later, when he said, 'Go back again and buy us more food,' ²⁶we replied, 'We can't go unless you let our youngest brother go with us. We'll never get to see the man's face unless our youngest brother is with us.'

²⁷"Then my father said to us, 'As you know, my wife had two sons, ²⁸and one of them went away and never returned. Doubtless he was torn to pieces by some wild animal. I have never seen him since. ²⁹Now if you take his brother away from me, and any harm comes to him, you will send this grieving, white-haired man to his grave.*'

³⁰"And now, my lord, I cannot go back to my father without the boy. Our father's life is bound up in the boy's life. ³¹If he sees that the boy is not with us, our father will die. We, your servants, will indeed be responsible for sending that grieving, white-haired man to his grave. ³²My lord, I guaranteed to my father that I would take care of the boy. I told him, 'If I don't bring him back to you, I will bear the blame forever.'

³³"So please, my lord, let me stay here as a slave instead of the boy, and let the boy return with his brothers. ³⁴For how can I return to my father if the boy is not with me? I couldn't bear to see the anguish this would cause my father!"

### Joseph Reveals His Identity

**45:1**
Gen 43:31
Acts 7:13

**45** Joseph could stand it no longer. There were many people in the room, and he said to his attendants, "Out, all of you!" So he was alone with his brothers when he told them

**44:29** Hebrew *to Sheol;* also in 44:31.

---

**44:13** Tearing clothes was an expression of deep sorrow, a customary manner of showing grief. The brothers were terrified that Benjamin might be harmed.

**44:16-34** When Judah was younger, he had showed no regard for his brother Joseph or his father, Jacob. First he had convinced his brothers to sell Joseph as a slave (37:27); then he had joined his brothers in lying to his father about Joseph's fate (37:32). But what a change had taken place in Judah! The man who had sold one favored little brother into slavery now offered to become a slave himself to save another favored little brother. He was so concerned for his father and younger brother that he was willing to die for them. When you are ready to give up hope on yourself or someone else, remember that God can work a complete change in even the most selfish personality.

**44:18-34** Judah finally could take no more and stepped forward to plead their case. This was risky because Joseph could have had him killed. But Judah courageously defended himself and his brothers and pleaded for mercy. And he offered to put himself in

Benjamin's place. At times we should be silent, but at times we should speak up, even if there could be serious repercussions. When faced with a situation that needs a strong voice and courageous action, remember Judah and speak up.

**44:32, 33** Judah had promised Jacob that he would guarantee young Benjamin's safety (43:9). Now Judah had a chance to keep that promise. Becoming a slave was a terrible fate, but Judah was determined to keep his word to his father. He showed great courage in carrying out his promise. Accepting a responsibility means carrying it out with determination and courage, regardless of the personal sacrifice.

**44:33** Joseph wanted to see if his brothers' attitudes had changed for the better, so he tested the way they treated each other. Judah, the brother who had stepped forward with the plan to sell Joseph (37:27), now stepped forward to take Benjamin's punishment so that Benjamin could return to their father. This courageous act convinced Joseph that his brothers had dramatically changed for the better.

who he was. [2]Then he broke down and wept. He wept so loudly the Egyptians could hear him, and word of it quickly carried to Pharaoh's palace.

[3]"I am Joseph!" he said to his brothers. "Is my father still alive?" But his brothers were speechless! They were stunned to realize that Joseph was standing there in front of them. [4]"Please, come closer," he said to them. So they came closer. And he said again, "I am Joseph, your brother, whom you sold into slavery in Egypt. [5]But don't be upset, and don't be angry with yourselves for selling me to this place. It was God who sent me here ahead of you to preserve your lives. [6]This famine that has ravaged the land for two years will last five more years, and there will be neither plowing nor harvesting. [7]God has sent me ahead of you to keep you and your families alive and to preserve many survivors.* [8]So it was God who sent me here, not you! And he is the one who made me an adviser* to Pharaoh—the manager of his entire palace and the governor of all Egypt.

[9]"Now hurry back to my father and tell him, 'This is what your son Joseph says: God has made me master over all the land of Egypt. So come down to me immediately! [10]You can live in the region of Goshen, where you can be near me with all your children and grandchildren, your flocks and herds, and everything you own. [11]I will take care of you there, for there are still five years of famine ahead of us. Otherwise you, your household, and all your animals will starve.'"

[12]Then Joseph added, "Look! You can see for yourselves, and so can my brother Benjamin, that I really am Joseph! [13]Go tell my father of my honored position here in Egypt. Describe for him everything you have seen, and then bring my father here quickly." [14]Weeping with joy, he embraced Benjamin, and Benjamin did the same. [15]Then Joseph kissed each of his brothers and wept over them, and after that they began talking freely with him.

### Pharaoh Invites Jacob to Egypt

[16]The news soon reached Pharaoh's palace: "Joseph's brothers have arrived!" Pharaoh and his officials were all delighted to hear this.

[17]Pharaoh said to Joseph, "Tell your brothers, 'This is what you must do: Load your pack animals, and hurry back to the land of Canaan. [18]Then get your father and all of your families, and return here to me. I will give you the very best land in Egypt, and you will eat from the best that the land produces.'"

[19]Then Pharaoh said to Joseph, "Tell your brothers, 'Take wagons from the land of Egypt to carry your little children and your wives, and bring your father here. [20]Don't worry about your personal belongings, for the best of all the land of Egypt is yours.'"

[21]So the sons of Jacob* did as they were told. Joseph provided them with wagons, as Pharaoh had commanded, and he gave them supplies for the journey. [22]And he gave each of them new clothes—but to Benjamin he gave five changes of clothes and 300 pieces* of silver. [23]He also sent his father ten male donkeys loaded with the finest products of Egypt, and ten female donkeys loaded with grain and bread and other supplies he would need on his journey.

[24]So Joseph sent his brothers off, and as they left, he called after them, "Don't quarrel about all this along the way!" [25]And they left Egypt and returned to their father, Jacob, in the land of Canaan.

[26]"Joseph is still alive!" they told him. "And he is governor of all the land of Egypt!" Jacob was stunned at the news—he couldn't believe it. [27]But when they repeated to Jacob every-

**45:3** Gen 43:7
**45:4** Gen 37:28
**45:5** Gen 50:20
**45:6** Gen 41:30
**45:8** Gen 41:41; Judg 17:10
**45:9** Acts 7:14
**45:10** Gen 46:28, 34
**45:11** Gen 47:12
**45:13** Acts 7:14
**45:14** Gen 45:2
**45:16** Acts 7:13
**45:17** Gen 42:26
**45:18** Gen 27:28
**45:19** Gen 45:27; 46:5
**45:20** Gen 46:6
**45:22** Gen 24:53; 2 Kgs 5:5
**45:23** Gen 43:11
**45:24** Gen 42:21-22
**45:26** Gen 37:31-35
**45:27** Gen 45:19

**45:7** Or and to save you with an extraordinary rescue. The meaning of the Hebrew is uncertain. **45:8** Hebrew a father. **45:21** Hebrew Israel; also in 45:28. See note on 35:21. **45:22** Hebrew 300 shekels, about 7.5 pounds or 3.4 kilograms in weight.

**45:4-8** Although Joseph's brothers had wanted to get rid of him, God used even their evil actions to fulfill his ultimate plan. He had sent Joseph ahead to preserve their lives, save Egypt, and prepare the way for the beginning of the nation of Israel. God is sovereign. His plans are not dictated by human actions. When others intend evil toward you, remember that they are only God's tools. As Joseph said to his brothers, "You intended to harm me, but God intended it all for good. He brought me to this position so I could save the lives of many people" (50:20).

**45:17-20** Joseph had been rejected, kidnapped, enslaved, and imprisoned. Although his brothers had been unfaithful to him, he graciously forgave them and shared his prosperity. Joseph demonstrated how God forgives us and showers us with goodness even though we have sinned against him. The same forgiveness and blessings are ours if we ask for them.

**45:26, 27** Jacob needed some evidence before he could believe the incredible news that Joseph was alive. Similarly, Thomas refused to believe that Jesus had risen from the dead until he could see and touch him (John 20:25). It is hard to change what you believe without all the facts—or sometimes even with the facts. Good news can be difficult to believe. Don't ever give up hope that God has a wonderful future in store for you.

thing Joseph had told them, and when he saw the wagons Joseph had sent to carry him, their father's spirits revived.

**45:28**
Gen 44:28

28Then Jacob exclaimed, "It must be true! My son Joseph is alive! I must go and see him before I die."

### 6. Jacob's family moves to Egypt

*Jacob's Journey to Egypt*

**46:1**
Gen 21:14; 26:24;
28:13; 31:42
**46:2**
Gen 22:11; 31:11
Num 12:6
**46:3**
Gen 17:1; 26:2
**46:4**
Gen 28:13;
Exod 3:8

**46** So Jacob* set out for Egypt with all his possessions. And when he came to Beersheba, he offered sacrifices to the God of his father, Isaac. 2During the night God spoke to him in a vision. "Jacob! Jacob!" he called.

"Here I am," Jacob replied.

3"I am God,* the God of your father," the voice said. "Do not be afraid to go down to Egypt, for there I will make your family into a great nation. 4I will go with you down to Egypt, and I will bring you back again. You will die in Egypt, but Joseph will be with you to close your eyes."

**46:1** Hebrew *Israel*; also in 46:29, 30. See note on 35:21.    **46:3** Hebrew *I am El.*

---

**JUDAH**

People who are leaders stand out. They don't necessarily look or act a certain way until the need for their action is apparent. Among their skills are outspokenness, decisiveness, action, and control. These skills can be used for great good or great evil. Jacob's fourth son, Judah, was a natural leader. The events of his life provided many opportunities to exercise those skills. Unfortunately Judah's decisions were often shaped more by the pressures of the moment than by a conscious desire to cooperate with God's plan. But when he did recognize his mistakes, he was willing to admit them. His experience with Tamar and the final confrontation with Joseph are both examples of Judah's willingness to bear the blame when confronted. It was one of the qualities he passed on to his descendant David.

Whether or not we have Judah's natural leadership qualities, we share with him a tendency to be blind toward our own sin. Too often, however, we don't share his willingness to admit mistakes. From Judah we can learn that it is not wise to wait until our errors force us to admit to wrongdoing. It is far better to admit our mistakes openly, to shoulder the blame, and to seek forgiveness.

| | |
|---|---|
| **Strengths and accomplishments** | • Was a natural leader—outspoken and decisive<br>• Thought clearly and took action in high-pressure situations<br>• Was willing to stand by his word and put himself on the line when necessary<br>• Was the fourth son of 12 through whom God would eventually bring David and Jesus, the Messiah |
| **Weaknesses and mistakes** | • Suggested to his brothers they sell Joseph into slavery<br>• Failed to keep his promise to his daughter-in-law, Tamar |
| **Lessons from his life** | • God is in control, far beyond the immediate situation<br>• Procrastination often makes matters worse<br>• Judah's offer to substitute his life for Benjamin's is a picture of what his descendant Jesus would do for all people |
| **Vital statistics** | • Where: Canaan and Egypt<br>• Occupation: Shepherd<br>• Relatives: Parents: Jacob and Leah. Siblings: Eleven brothers and one sister mentioned in the Bible. Wife: Bathshua (1 Chronicles 2:3). Daughter-in-law: Tamar. Sons: At least five. |
| **Key verses** | "Judah, your brothers will praise you. You will grasp your enemies by the neck. All your relatives will bow before you. Judah, my son, is a young lion that has finished eating its prey. Like a lion he crouches and lies down; like a lioness—who dares to rouse him? The scepter will not depart from Judah, nor the ruler's staff from his descendants, until the coming of the one to whom it belongs, the one whom all nations will honor" (Genesis 49:8-10). |

Judah's story is told in Genesis 29:35–50:26. He is also mentioned in 1 Chronicles 2–4.

---

**46:3, 4** The Israelites did become a great nation, and Jacob's descendants eventually returned to Canaan. The book of Exodus recounts the story of Israel's slavery in Egypt for 400 years (fulfilling God's words to Abraham in 15:13-16), and the book of Joshua gives an exciting account of the Israelites entering and conquering Canaan, the Promised Land.

**46:3, 4** God told Jacob to leave his home and travel to a strange and faraway land. But God reassured him by promising to go with

him and take care of him. When new situations or surroundings frighten you, recognize that experiencing fear is normal. To be paralyzed by fear, however, is an indication that you question God's ability to take care of you.

**46:4** Jacob never returned to Canaan, but God promised that his descendants would return. That Jacob would die in Egypt with Joseph at his side was God's promise to Jacob that he would never know the pain of being lonely again.

⁵So Jacob left Beersheba, and his sons took him to Egypt. They carried him and their little ones and their wives in the wagons Pharaoh had provided for them. ⁶They also took all their livestock and all the personal belongings they had acquired in the land of Canaan. So Jacob and his entire family went to Egypt—⁷sons and grandsons, daughters and granddaughters— all his descendants.

⁸These are the names of the descendants of Israel—the sons of Jacob—who went to Egypt:

Reuben was Jacob's oldest son. ⁹The sons of Reuben were Hanoch, Pallu, Hezron, and Carmi.

¹⁰The sons of Simeon were Jemuel, Jamin, Ohad, Jakin, Zohar, and Shaul. (Shaul's mother was a Canaanite woman.)

¹¹The sons of Levi were Gershon, Kohath, and Merari.

¹²The sons of Judah were Er, Onan, Shelah, Perez, and Zerah (though Er and Onan had died in the land of Canaan). The sons of Perez were Hezron and Hamul.

¹³The sons of Issachar were Tola, Puah,* Jashub,* and Shimron.

¹⁴The sons of Zebulun were Sered, Elon, and Jahleel.

¹⁵These were the sons of Leah and Jacob who were born in Paddan-aram, in addition to their daughter, Dinah. The number of Jacob's descendants (male and female) through Leah was thirty-three.

¹⁶The sons of Gad were Zephon,* Haggi, Shuni, Ezbon, Eri, Arodi, and Areli.

¹⁷The sons of Asher were Imnah, Ishvah, Ishvi, and Beriah. Their sister was Serah. Beriah's sons were Heber and Malkiel.

¹⁸These were the sons of Zilpah, the servant given to Leah by her father, Laban. The number of Jacob's descendants through Zilpah was sixteen.

¹⁹The sons of Jacob's wife Rachel were Joseph and Benjamin.

²⁰Joseph's sons, born in the land of Egypt, were Manasseh and Ephraim. Their mother was Asenath, daughter of Potiphera, the priest of On.*

²¹Benjamin's sons were Bela, Beker, Ashbel, Gera, Naaman, Ehi, Rosh, Muppim, Huppim, and Ard.

²²These were the sons of Rachel and Jacob. The number of Jacob's descendants through Rachel was fourteen.

²³The son of Dan was Hushim.

²⁴The sons of Naphtali were Jahzeel, Guni, Jezer, and Shillem.

²⁵These were the sons of Bilhah, the servant given to Rachel by her father, Laban. The number of Jacob's descendants through Bilhah was seven.

²⁶The total number of Jacob's direct descendants who went with him to Egypt, not counting his sons' wives, was sixty-six. ²⁷In addition, Joseph had two sons* who were born in Egypt. So altogether, there were seventy* members of Jacob's family in the land of Egypt.

### Jacob's Family Arrives in Goshen

²⁸As they neared their destination, Jacob sent Judah ahead to meet Joseph and get directions to the region of Goshen. And when they finally arrived there, ²⁹Joseph prepared his chariot and traveled to Goshen to meet his father, Jacob. When Joseph arrived, he embraced his father and wept, holding him for a long time. ³⁰Finally, Jacob said to Joseph, "Now I am ready to die, since I have seen your face again and know you are still alive."

³¹And Joseph said to his brothers and to his father's entire family, "I will go to Pharaoh and tell him, 'My brothers and my father's entire family have come to me from the land of

**46:5**
Gen 45:19
**46:6**
Num 20:15
Deut 26:5
Acts 7:15
**46:8**
Gen 29:32; 35:26
**46:9**
1 Chr 5:3
**46:10**
1 Chr 4:24
**46:11**
1 Chr 6:16
**46:12**
1 Chr 2:3
**46:13**
1 Chr 7:1
**46:14**
Gen 30:20
**46:15**
Gen 30:21
**46:16**
Gen 30:11
Num 26:15
**46:17**
Gen 30:13
**46:19**
Gen 44:27
**46:20**
Gen 41:45, 50-52
**46:21**
Num 26:38-41
1 Chr 7:6-12
**46:22**
Gen 35:24
**46:23**
Gen 30:6
Num 26:42
**46:24**
Gen 30:8
**46:25**
Gen 35:2
**46:27**
Exod 1:5
Deut 10:22
Acts 7:14
**46:28**
Gen 43:3; 45:10
**46:29**
Gen 45:14-15
**46:30**
Gen 44:28
**46:31**
Gen 47:1

**46:13a** As in Syriac version and Samaritan Pentateuch (see also 1 Chr 7:1); Hebrew reads *Puvah*. **46:13b** As in some Greek manuscripts and Samaritan Pentateuch (see also Num 26:24; 1 Chr 7:1); Hebrew reads *Iob*. **46:16** As in Greek version and Samaritan Pentateuch (see also Num 26:15); Hebrew reads *Ziphion*. **46:20** Greek version reads *of Heliopolis*. **46:27a** Greek version reads *nine sons*, probably including Joseph's grandsons through Ephraim and Manasseh (see 1 Chr 7:14-20). **46:27b** Greek version reads *seventy-five*; see note on Exod 1:5.

---

**46:31-34** Jacob moved his whole family to Egypt, but they wanted to live apart from the Egyptians. To ensure this, Joseph told them to let Pharaoh know they were shepherds. Although Pharaoh may have been sympathetic to shepherds (for he was probably descended from the nomadic Hyksos line), the Egyptian culture would not willingly accept shepherds among them. The strategy worked, and Jacob's family was able to benefit from Pharaoh's generosity as well as from the Egyptians' prejudice.

**46:32**
Gen 37:2; 47:3
**46:33**
Gen 47:3
**46:34**
Gen 13:7; 26:20;
37:2

Canaan. 32These men are shepherds, and they raise livestock. They have brought with them their flocks and herds and everything they own.'"

33Then he said, "When Pharaoh calls for you and asks you about your occupation, 34you must tell him, 'We, your servants, have raised livestock all our lives, as our ancestors have always done.' When you tell him this, he will let you live here in the region of Goshen, for the Egyptians despise shepherds."

**47:1**
Gen 46:31

### Jacob Blesses Pharaoh

**47** Then Joseph went to see Pharaoh and told him, "My father and my brothers have arrived from the land of Canaan. They have come with all their flocks and herds and possessions, and they are now in the region of Goshen."

**47:2**
Gen 43:15
**47:3**
Gen 46:32-33
**47:4**
Gen 46:34

2Joseph took five of his brothers with him and presented them to Pharaoh. 3And Pharaoh asked the brothers, "What is your occupation?"

They replied, "We, your servants, are shepherds, just like our ancestors. 4We have come to live here in Egypt for a while, for there is no pasture for our flocks in Canaan. The famine is very severe there. So please, we request permission to live in the region of Goshen."

**47:6**
Gen 45:18
Exod 18:21, 25

5Then Pharaoh said to Joseph, "Now that your father and brothers have joined you here, 6choose any place in the entire land of Egypt for them to live. Give them the best land of Egypt. Let them live in the region of Goshen. And if any of them have special skills, put them in charge of my livestock, too."

**47:7**
Gen 47:10
2 Sam 14:22
1 Kgs 8:66
**47:10**
Gen 14:19

7Then Joseph brought in his father, Jacob, and presented him to Pharaoh. And Jacob blessed Pharaoh.

8"How old are you?" Pharaoh asked him.

9Jacob replied, "I have traveled this earth for 130 hard years. But my life has been short compared to the lives of my ancestors." 10Then Jacob blessed Pharaoh again before leaving his court.

**47:11**
Exod 1:11; 12:37
**47:12**
Gen 45:11

11So Joseph assigned the best land of Egypt—the region of Rameses—to his father and his brothers, and he settled them there, just as Pharaoh had commanded. 12And Joseph provided food for his father and his brothers in amounts appropriate to the number of their dependents, including the smallest children.

**47:13**
Gen 41:30
Acts 7:11
**47:14**
Gen 41:56
**47:15**
Gen 47:18-19
**47:17**
Exod 14:9

### Joseph's Leadership in the Famine

13Meanwhile, the famine became so severe that all the food was used up, and people were starving throughout the lands of Egypt and Canaan. 14By selling grain to the people, Joseph eventually collected all the money in Egypt and Canaan, and he put the money in Pharaoh's treasury. 15When the people of Egypt and Canaan ran out of money, all the Egyptians came to Joseph. "Our money is gone!" they cried. "But please give us food, or we will die before your very eyes!"

16Joseph replied, "Since your money is gone, bring me your livestock. I will give you food in exchange for your livestock." 17So they brought their livestock to Joseph in exchange for

---

**JACOB MOVES TO EGYPT**
After hearing the joyful news that Joseph was alive, Jacob packed up and moved his family to Egypt. Stopping first in Beersheba, Jacob offered sacrifices and received assurance from God that Egypt was where he should go. Jacob and his family settled in the region of Goshen, in the northeastern part of Egypt.

**47:1-6** Joseph's faithfulness affected his entire family. When he was in the pit and in prison, Joseph must have wondered about his future. Instead of despairing, he faithfully obeyed God and did what was right. Here we see one of the exciting results. We may not always see the effects of our faith, but we can be sure that God will honor faithfulness.

food. In exchange for their horses, flocks of sheep and goats, herds of cattle, and donkeys, Joseph provided them with food for another year.

18But that year ended, and the next year they came again and said, "We cannot hide the truth from you, my lord. Our money is gone, and all our livestock and cattle are yours. We have nothing left to give but our bodies and our land. 19Why should we die before your very eyes? Buy us and our land in exchange for food; we offer our land and ourselves as slaves for Pharaoh. Just give us grain so we may live and not die, and so the land does not become empty and desolate."

20So Joseph bought all the land of Egypt for Pharaoh. All the Egyptians sold him their fields because the famine was so severe, and soon all the land belonged to Pharaoh. 21As for the people, he made them all slaves,* from one end of Egypt to the other. 22The only land he did not buy was the land belonging to the priests. They received an allotment of food directly from Pharaoh, so they didn't need to sell their land.

23Then Joseph said to the people, "Look, today I have bought you and your land for Pharaoh. I will provide you with seed so you can plant the fields. 24Then when you harvest it, one-fifth of your crop will belong to Pharaoh. You may keep the remaining four-fifths as seed for your fields and as food for you, your households, and your little ones."

25"You have saved our lives!" they exclaimed. "May it please you, my lord, to let us be Pharaoh's servants." 26Joseph then issued a decree still in effect in the land of Egypt, that Pharaoh should receive one-fifth of all the crops grown on his land. Only the land belonging to the priests was not given to Pharaoh.

## 7. Jacob and Joseph die in Egypt

27Meanwhile, the people of Israel settled in the region of Goshen in Egypt. There they acquired property, and they were fruitful, and their population grew rapidly. 28Jacob lived for seventeen years after his arrival in Egypt, so he lived 147 years in all.

29As the time of his death drew near, Jacob* called for his son Joseph and said to him, "Please do me this favor. Put your hand under my thigh and swear that you will treat me with unfailing love by honoring this last request: Do not bury me in Egypt. 30When I die, please take my body out of Egypt and bury me with my ancestors."

So Joseph promised, "I will do as you ask."

31"Swear that you will do it," Jacob insisted. So Joseph gave his oath, and Jacob bowed humbly at the head of his bed.*

### Jacob Blesses Manasseh and Ephraim

**48** One day not long after this, word came to Joseph, "Your father is failing rapidly." So Joseph went to visit his father, and he took with him his two sons, Manasseh and Ephraim.

2When Joseph arrived, Jacob was told, "Your son Joseph has come to see you." So Jacob* gathered his strength and sat up in his bed.

3Jacob said to Joseph, "God Almighty* appeared to me at Luz in the land of Canaan and blessed me. 4He said to me, 'I will make you fruitful, and I will multiply your descendants. I will make you a multitude of nations. And I will give this land of Canaan to your descendants* after you as an everlasting possession.'

5"Now I am claiming as my own sons these two boys of yours, Ephraim and Manasseh, who were born here in the land of Egypt before I arrived. They will be my sons, just as Reuben and Simeon are. 6But any children born to you in the future will be your own, and they will inherit land within the territories of their brothers Ephraim and Manasseh.

7"Long ago, as I was returning from Paddan-aram, Rachel died in the land of Canaan. We were still on the way, some distance from Ephrath (that is, Bethlehem). So with great sorrow I buried her there beside the road to Ephrath."

8Then Jacob looked over at the two boys. "Are these your sons?" he asked.

47:19 Neh 5:2; Job 2:4; Lam 1:11 / 47:22 Deut 14:28-29 / 47:24 Gen 41:34 / 47:25 Gen 32:5 / 47:26 Gen 47:22 / 47:27 Exod 1:7 / 47:29 Gen 24:2; 50:24-25 / 47:30 Gen 23:17-20; 25:9; 49:29; Acts 7:15-16 / 47:31 Heb 11:21 / 48:1 Gen 41:51-52; Heb 11:21 / 48:3 Gen 28:13-19; 35:9-12 / 48:5 Gen 29:32-33 / 48:7 Gen 35:19

47:21 As in Greek version and Samaritan Pentateuch; Hebrew reads *he moved them all into the towns.* 47:29 Hebrew *Israel;* also in 47:31b. See note on 35:21. 47:31 Greek version reads *and Israel bowed in worship as he leaned on his staff.* Compare Heb 11:21. 48:2 Hebrew *Israel;* also in 48:8, 10, 11, 13, 14, 21. See note on 35:21. 48:3 Hebrew *El-Shaddai.* 48:4 Hebrew *seed;* also in 48:19.

47:29-31 Jacob had Joseph promise to bury him in his homeland. Few things were written in this culture, so a person's word carried as much force as a written contract does today. People today seem to find it easy to say, "I didn't mean that." God's people, however, are to speak the truth and live the truth. Let your words be as binding as a written contract.
48:8-20 Jacob gave Ephraim, instead of his older brother Manasseh, the greater blessing. When Joseph objected, Jacob

**48:9**
Gen 33:5

⁹"Yes," Joseph told him, "these are the sons God has given me here in Egypt." And Jacob said, "Bring them closer to me, so I can bless them."

**48:10**
Gen 27:1

**48:11**
Gen 44:28

**48:12**
Gen 33:3; 42:6

¹⁰Jacob was half blind because of his age and could hardly see. So Joseph brought the boys close to him, and Jacob kissed and embraced them. ¹¹Then Jacob said to Joseph, "I never thought I would see your face again, but now God has let me see your children, too!" ¹²Joseph moved the boys, who were at their grandfather's knees, and he bowed with his face to the ground. ¹³Then he positioned the boys in front of Jacob. With his right hand he directed Ephraim toward Jacob's left hand, and with his left hand he put Manasseh at Jacob's

**48:14**
Gen 41:51-52

right hand. ¹⁴But Jacob crossed his arms as he reached out to lay his hands on the boys' heads. He put his right hand on the head of Ephraim, though he was the younger boy, and his

**48:15**
Gen 17:1; 49:24

left hand on the head of Manasseh, though he was the firstborn. ¹⁵Then he blessed Joseph and said,

> "May the God before whom my grandfather Abraham
> and my father, Isaac, walked—
> the God who has been my shepherd
> all my life, to this very day,

**48:16**
Gen 22:11;
28:13-15; 31:11
†Heb 11:21

> ¹⁶ the Angel who has redeemed me from all harm—
> may he bless these boys.
> May they preserve my name
> and the names of Abraham and Isaac.
> And may their descendants multiply greatly
> throughout the earth."

¹⁷But Joseph was upset when he saw that his father placed his right hand on Ephraim's head. So Joseph lifted it to move it from Ephraim's head to Manasseh's head. ¹⁸"No, my

**48:19**
Gen 28:14; 46:3

father," he said. "This one is the firstborn. Put your right hand on his head." ¹⁹But his father refused. "I know, my son; I know," he replied. "Manasseh will also become

---

**PARALLELS BETWEEN JOSEPH AND JESUS**
Genesis
37—50

| Joseph | Parallels | Jesus |
|---|---|---|
| 37:3 | Their fathers loved them dearly | Matthew 3:17 |
| 37:2 | Shepherds of their fathers' sheep | John 10:11, 27 |
| 37:13, 14 | Sent by father to brothers | Hebrews 2:11 |
| 37:4 | Hated by brothers | John 7:5 |
| 37:20 | Others plotted to harm them | John 11:53 |
| 39:7 | Tempted | Matthew 4:1 |
| 37:25 | Taken to Egypt | Matthew 2:14, 15 |
| 37:23 | Robes taken from them | John 19:23 |
| 37:28 | Sold for the price of a slave | Matthew 26:15 |
| 39:20 | Bound in chains | Matthew 27:2 |
| 39:16-18 | Falsely accused | Matthew 26:59, 60 |
| 40:2, 3 | Placed with two other prisoners, one who was saved and the other lost | Luke 23:32 |
| 41:46 | Both 30 years old at the beginning of public recognition | Luke 3:23 |
| 41:41 | Exalted after suffering | Philippians 2:9-11 |
| 45:1-15 | Forgave those who wronged them | Luke 23:34 |
| 45:7 | Saved their nation | Matthew 1:21 |
| 50:20 | What people did to hurt them God turned to good | 1 Corinthians 2:7, 8 |

---

refused to listen because God had told him that Ephraim would become greater. God often works in unexpected ways. When he chooses people to fulfill his plans, he always goes deeper than appearance, tradition, or position. He sometimes surprises us by choosing the less obvious person, at least by human reasoning. God can use you to carry out his plans, even if you don't think you have all the qualifications.

**48:11** When Joseph became a slave, Jacob thought he was dead and wept in despair (37:34). But eventually God's plan allowed Jacob to regain not only his son but his grandchildren as well. Circumstances are never so bad that they are beyond God's help. Jacob regained his son. Job got a new family (Job 42:10-17).

Mary regained her brother, Lazarus (John 11:1-44). We need never despair because we belong to a loving God. We don't yet know what good he may bring out of a seemingly hopeless situation.

**48:15** Jacob spoke of God as his shepherd throughout his life. In his old age, he could clearly see his dependence upon God. This marks a total attitude change from that of his scheming and dishonest youth. To develop an attitude like Jacob's, let God shepherd you as you trust in his provision and care. When people chase after what they want with no thought of God, they are willing to do anything, even what is wrong, in order to get it. It is far better to trust God and realize that all good things come from his hand.

a great people, but his younger brother will become even greater. And his descendants will become a multitude of nations."

²⁰So Jacob blessed the boys that day with this blessing: "The people of Israel will use your names when they give a blessing. They will say, 'May God make you as prosperous as Ephraim and Manasseh.'" In this way, Jacob put Ephraim ahead of Manasseh.

²¹Then Jacob said to Joseph, "Look, I am about to die, but God will be with you and will take you back to Canaan, the land of your ancestors. ²²And beyond what I have given your brothers, I am giving you an extra portion of the land* that I took from the Amorites with my sword and bow."

## Jacob's Last Words to His Sons

**49** Then Jacob called together all his sons and said, "Gather around me, and I will tell you what will happen to each of you in the days to come.

² "Come and listen, you sons of Jacob;
   listen to Israel, your father.

³ "Reuben, you are my firstborn, my strength,
   the child of my vigorous youth.
   You are first in rank and first in power.

⁴ But you are as unruly as a flood,
   and you will be first no longer.
For you went to bed with my wife;
   you defiled my marriage couch.

⁵ "Simeon and Levi are two of a kind;
   their weapons are instruments of violence.

⁶ May I never join in their meetings;
   may I never be a party to their plans.
For in their anger they murdered men,
   and they crippled oxen just for sport.

⁷ A curse on their anger, for it is fierce;
   a curse on their wrath, for it is cruel.
I will scatter them among the descendants of Jacob;
   I will disperse them throughout Israel.

⁸ "Judah, your brothers will praise you.
   You will grasp your enemies by the neck.
   All your relatives will bow before you.

⁹ Judah, my son, is a young lion
   that has finished eating its prey.
Like a lion he crouches and lies down;
   like a lioness—who dares to rouse him?

¹⁰ The scepter will not depart from Judah,
   nor the ruler's staff from his descendants,*
until the coming of the one to whom it belongs,*
   the one whom all nations will honor.

**48:20** Ruth 4:11
**48:21** Gen 28:15; 46:4; 50:24
**48:22** Josh 24:32; John 4:5
**49:1** Num 24:14
**49:3** Num 26:5; Deut 21:17; Pss 78:51; 105:36
**49:4** Gen 35:22; Deut 27:20
**49:5** Gen 29:33-34; 34:25-30
**49:6** Gen 34:26
**49:7** Josh 19:1, 9; 21:1-42
**49:8** 1 Chr 5:2; Heb 7:14
**49:9** Num 24:9; Mic 5:8
**49:10** Num 24:17; Pss 2:6-9; 60:7

**48:22** Or *an extra ridge of land.* The meaning of the Hebrew is uncertain. **49:10a** Hebrew *from between his feet.* **49:10b** Or *until tribute is brought to him and the peoples obey;* traditionally rendered *until Shiloh comes.*

**48:20-22** Jacob was giving these young boys land occupied by the Philistines and Canaanites. His gift became reality when the tribes of Ephraim and Manasseh occupied the east and west sides of the Jordan River (Joshua 16).

**49:3-28** Jacob blessed each of his sons and then made a prediction about each one's future. The way the men had lived played an important part in Jacob's blessing and prophecy. Our past also affects our present and future. By sunrise tomorrow, our actions of today will have become part of the past. Yet they will already have begun to shape the future. What actions can you choose or avoid that will positively shape your future?

**49:4** The oldest son was supposed to receive a double inheritance, but Reuben lost his special honor. Unruly and untrust-

worthy, especially in his younger days, he had gone so far as to sleep with one of his father's concubines. Jacob could not give the birthright blessing to such a dishonorable son.

**49:8-12** Judah had sold Joseph into slavery and tried to defraud his daughter-in-law. So why did Jacob grant him this blessing? God had chosen Judah to be the ancestor of Israel's line of kings (that is the meaning of "the scepter will not depart from Judah"). This may have been due to Judah's dramatic change of character (44:33, 34). Judah's line would produce the promised Messiah, Jesus.

**49:10** "Until the coming of the one to whom it belongs" may also be translated, "until Shiloh comes." What is *Shiloh?* The meaning of this difficult passage is disputed. *Shiloh* may be

**49:11**
Deut 8:7-8
2 Kgs 18:32

<sup>11</sup> He ties his foal to a grapevine,
    the colt of his donkey to a choice vine.
He washes his clothes in wine,
    his robes in the blood of grapes.
<sup>12</sup> His eyes are darker than wine,
    and his teeth are whiter than milk.

**49:13**
Deut 33:18-19

<sup>13</sup> "Zebulun will settle by the seashore
    and will be a harbor for ships;
    his borders will extend to Sidon.

**49:14**
Judg 5:16
Ps 68:13

<sup>14</sup> "Issachar is a sturdy donkey,
    resting between two saddlepacks.*

**49:15**
Josh 19:17-23

<sup>15</sup> When he sees how good the countryside is
    and how pleasant the land,
he will bend his shoulder to the load
    and submit himself to hard labor.

**49:16**
Deut 33:22
Judg 18:26-27

<sup>16</sup> "Dan will govern his people,
    like any other tribe in Israel.
<sup>17</sup> Dan will be a snake beside the road,
    a poisonous viper along the path
    that bites the horse's hooves
    so its rider is thrown off.
<sup>18</sup> I trust in you for salvation, O LORD!

**49:19**
Deut 33:20

<sup>19</sup> "Gad will be attacked by marauding bands,
    but he will attack them when they retreat.

**49:20**
Deut 33:24-25

<sup>20</sup> "Asher will dine on rich foods
    and produce food fit for kings.

**49:21**
Deut 33:23

<sup>21</sup> "Naphtali is a doe set free
    that bears beautiful fawns.

**49:22**
Deut 33:13-17

<sup>22</sup> "Joseph is the foal of a wild donkey,
    the foal of a wild donkey at a spring—
    one of the wild donkeys on the ridge.*

**49:14** Or *sheepfolds,* or *hearths.*    **49:22** Or *Joseph is a fruitful tree, / a fruitful tree beside a spring. / His branches reach over the wall.* The meaning of the Hebrew is uncertain.

---

**JACOB'S SONS AND THEIR NOTABLE DESCENDANTS**

Jacob's 12 sons were the ancestors of the 12 tribes of Israel. The entire nation of Israel came from these men.

| | |
|---|---|
| REUBEN | none |
| SIMEON | none |
| LEVI | Aaron, Moses, Eli, John the Baptist |
| JUDAH | David, Jesus |
| DAN | Samson |
| NAPHTALI | Barak, Elijah (?) |
| GAD | Jephthah (?) |
| ASHER | none |
| ISSACHAR | none |
| ZEBULUN | none |
| JOSEPH | Joshua, Gideon, Samuel |
| BENJAMIN | Saul, Esther, Paul |

---

another name for the Messiah because its literal meaning is "sent." *Shiloh* might also refer to the Tabernacle set up at the city of Shiloh (Joshua 18:1).

**49:18** In the middle of his prophecy to Dan, Jacob exclaimed, "I trust in you for salvation, O LORD !" He was emphasizing to Dan that he would be a strong leader only if he trusted in God, not in his natural strength or ability. Those who are strong, attractive, or

talented often find it easier to trust in themselves than in God who gave them their gifts. Remember to thank God for what you are and have so your trust does not become misplaced.

**49:22** Joseph would have some heroic descendants. Among them were Joshua, who would lead the Israelites into the Promised Land (Joshua 1:10, 11); and Deborah, Gideon, and Jephthah, judges of Israel (Judges 4:4; 6:11, 12; 11:11).

23 Archers attacked him savagely;
    they shot at him and harassed him.
24 But his bow remained taut,
    and his arms were strengthened
by the hands of the Mighty One of Jacob,
    by the Shepherd, the Rock of Israel.
25 May the God of your father help you;
    may the Almighty bless you
with the blessings of the heavens above,
    and blessings of the watery depths below,
    and blessings of the breasts and womb.
26 May the blessings of your father
    surpass the blessings of the ancient mountains,*
    reaching to the heights of the eternal hills.
May these blessings rest on the head of Joseph,
    who is a prince among his brothers.

27 "Benjamin is a ravenous wolf,
    devouring his enemies in the morning
    and dividing his plunder in the evening."

28These are the twelve tribes of Israel, and this is what their father said as he told his sons good-bye. He blessed each one with an appropriate message.

### Jacob's Death and Burial

29Then Jacob instructed them, "Soon I will die and join my ancestors. Bury me with my father and grandfather in the cave in the field of Ephron the Hittite. 30This is the cave in the field of Machpelah, near Mamre in Canaan, that Abraham bought from Ephron the Hittite as a permanent burial site. 31There Abraham and his wife Sarah are buried. There Isaac and his wife, Rebekah, are buried. And there I buried Leah. 32It is the plot of land and the cave that my grandfather Abraham bought from the Hittites."

33When Jacob had finished this charge to his sons, he drew his feet into the bed, breathed his last, and joined his ancestors in death.

**50** Joseph threw himself on his father and wept over him and kissed him. 2Then Joseph told the physicians who served him to embalm his father's body; so Jacob* was embalmed. 3The embalming process took the usual forty days. And the Egyptians mourned his death for seventy days.

4When the period of mourning was over, Joseph approached Pharaoh's advisers and said, "Please do me this favor and speak to Pharaoh on my behalf. 5Tell him that my father made me swear an oath. He said to me, 'Listen, I am about to die. Take my body back to the land of Canaan, and bury me in the tomb I prepared for myself.' So please allow me to go and bury my father. After his burial, I will return without delay."

6Pharaoh agreed to Joseph's request. "Go and bury your father, as he made you promise," he said. 7So Joseph went up to bury his father. He was accompanied by all of Pharaoh's offi-

**49:23** Gen 37:24
**49:24** Ps 132:2, 5; Isa 41:10; 49:26
**49:25** Gen 28:13
**49:26** Deut 33:15-16
**49:27** Deut 33:12
**49:29** Gen 23:16-20; 25:8-9
**49:31** Gen 23:19; 25:9; 35:29
**49:33** Gen 25:8; Acts 7:15
**50:1** Gen 46:4
**50:2** Gen 50:26
**50:3** Num 20:29; Deut 34:8
**50:5** Gen 47:29-31

**49:26** Or *of my ancestors.*  **50:2** Hebrew *Israel.* See note on 35:21.

---

**49:23, 24** These verses celebrate the times God rescued Joseph when his enemies attacked him. So often we struggle by ourselves, forgetting that God is able to help us fight our battles, whether they are against people with weapons or against spiritual forces. Joseph was able to draw closer to God as adversity mounted. To trust God to rescue you shows great faith. Can you trust him when injury or persecution is directed at you? Such spiritual battles require teamwork between courageous, faithful people and a mighty God.

**50:1-11** When Jacob died at the age of 147, Joseph wept and mourned for months. When someone close to us dies, we need a long period of time to work through our grief. Crying and sharing our feelings with others helps us recover and go on with life. Allow yourself and others the freedom to grieve over the loss of a loved one, and give yourself time enough to complete your grieving process.

**50:2, 3** Embalming was typical for Egyptians but unusual for nomadic shepherds. Believing that the dead went to the next world in their physical bodies, the Egyptians embalmed bodies to preserve them so they could function in the world to come. Jacob's family allowed him to be embalmed as a sign of courtesy and respect to the Egyptians.

**50:5** Joseph had proven himself trustworthy as Pharaoh's adviser. Because of his good record, Pharaoh had little doubt that he would return to Egypt as promised after burying his father in Canaan. Privileges and freedom often result when we have demonstrated our trustworthiness. Since trust must be built gradually over time, take every opportunity to prove your reliability even in minor matters.

**50:8**
Gen 45:10

**50:9**
Gen 41:43

cials, all the senior members of Pharaoh's household, and all the senior officers of Egypt. ⁸Joseph also took his entire household and his brothers and their households. But they left their little children and flocks and herds in the land of Goshen. ⁹A great number of chariots and charioteers accompanied Joseph.

¹⁰When they arrived at the threshing floor of Atad, near the Jordan River, they held a very great and solemn memorial service, with a seven-day period of mourning for Joseph's father. ¹¹The local residents, the Canaanites, watched them mourning at the threshing floor of Atad. Then they renamed that place (which is near the Jordan) Abel-mizraim,* for they said, "This is a place of deep mourning for these Egyptians."

**50:12**
Gen 49:29

**50:13**
Gen 23:16-18

¹²So Jacob's sons did as he had commanded them. ¹³They carried his body to the land of Canaan and buried him in the cave in the field of Machpelah, near Mamre. This is the cave that Abraham had bought as a permanent burial site from Ephron the Hittite.

### Joseph Reassures His Brothers

**50:15**
Gen 42:21-22

**50:16**
Gen 49:29

**50:17**
Gen 45:5, 7
Matt 6:14
Luke 6:27
Rom 12:19

**50:18**
Gen 37:7-10

**50:19**
Gen 30:2

**50:20**
Gen 37:26-27

**50:21**
Gen 45:11

¹⁴After burying Jacob, Joseph returned to Egypt with his brothers and all who had accompanied him to his father's burial. ¹⁵But now that their father was dead, Joseph's brothers became fearful. "Now Joseph will show his anger and pay us back for all the wrong we did to him," they said.

¹⁶So they sent this message to Joseph: "Before your father died, he instructed us ¹⁷to say to you: 'Please forgive your brothers for the great wrong they did to you—for their sin in treating you so cruelly.' So we, the servants of the God of your father, beg you to forgive our sin." When Joseph received the message, he broke down and wept. ¹⁸Then his brothers came and threw themselves down before Joseph. "Look, we are your slaves!" they said.

¹⁹But Joseph replied, "Don't be afraid of me. Am I God, that I can punish you? ²⁰You intended to harm me, but God intended it all for good. He brought me to this position so I could save the lives of many people. ²¹No, don't be afraid. I will continue to take care of you and your children." So he reassured them by speaking kindly to them.

### The Death of Joseph

**50:24**
Gen 13:15; 28:13

**50:25**
Exod 13:19
Josh 24:32
Heb 11:22

**50:26**
Exod 1:6

²²So Joseph and his brothers and their families continued to live in Egypt. Joseph lived to the age of 110. ²³He lived to see three generations of descendants of his son Ephraim, and he lived to see the birth of the children of Manasseh's son Makir, whom he claimed as his own.*

²⁴"Soon I will die," Joseph told his brothers, "but God will surely come to help you and lead you out of this land of Egypt. He will bring you back to the land he solemnly promised to give to Abraham, to Isaac, and to Jacob."

²⁵Then Joseph made the sons of Israel swear an oath, and he said, "When God comes to help you and lead you back, you must take my bones with you." ²⁶So Joseph died at the age of 110. The Egyptians embalmed him, and his body was placed in a coffin in Egypt.

**50:11** *Abel-mizraim* means "mourning of the Egyptians." **50:23** Hebrew *who were born on Joseph's knees.*

---

**50:12, 13** Abraham had purchased the cave in the field of Machpelah as a burial place for his wife Sarah (23:1-9). It was to be a burial place for his entire family. Jacob was Abraham's grandson, and Jacob's sons returned to Canaan to bury him in this cave along with Abraham and Isaac. Their desire to be buried in this cave expressed their faith in God's promise to give their descendants the land of Canaan.

**50:15-21** Now that Jacob (or Israel) was dead, the brothers feared revenge from Joseph. Could he really have forgiven them for selling him into slavery? But to their surprise, Joseph not only forgave them but reassured them, offering to care for them and their families. Joseph's forgiveness was complete. He demonstrated how God graciously accepts us even though we don't deserve it. Because God forgives us even when we have ignored or rejected him, we should graciously forgive others.

**50:20** God brought good from the brothers' evil deed, Potiphar's wife's false accusation, the cup-bearer's neglect, and seven years of famine. The experiences in Joseph's life taught him that God brings good from evil for those who trust him. Do you trust God enough to wait patiently for him to bring good out of bad situations? You can trust him because, as Joseph learned, God can overrule people's evil intentions to bring about his intended results.

**50:24** Joseph was ready to die. He had no doubts that God would keep his promise and one day bring the Israelites back to their homeland. What a tremendous example! The secret of that kind of faith is a lifetime of trusting God. Your faith is like a muscle—it grows with exercise, gaining strength over time. After a lifetime of exercising trust, your faith can be as strong as Joseph's. Then at your death, you can be confident that God will fulfill all his promises to you and to all those faithful to him who may live after you.

**50:24** This verse sets the stage for what would begin to happen in Exodus and come to completion in Joshua. God was going to make Jacob's family into a great nation, lead them out of Egypt, and bring them into the land he had promised them. The nation would rely heavily on this promise, and Joseph emphasized his belief that God would do what he had promised.

**50:26** The book of Genesis gives us rich descriptions of the lives of many great men and women who walked with God. They sometimes succeeded and often failed. Yet we learn much by reading the biographies of these people. Where did they get their motivation and courage? They got it by realizing God was with them despite their inadequacies. Knowing this should encourage us to be faithful to God, to rely on him for guidance, and to utilize the potential he has given us.

Joseph
dies
1805 B.C.
(1640 B.C.)

## VITAL STATISTICS

**PURPOSE:**
To record the events of Israel's deliverance from Egypt and development as a nation

**AUTHOR:**
Moses

**ORIGINAL AUDIENCE:**
The people of Israel

**DATE WRITTEN:**
1450–1410 B.C., approximately the same as Genesis

**WHERE WRITTEN:**
In the wilderness during Israel's wanderings, somewhere in the Sinai peninsula

**SETTING:**
Egypt. God's people, once highly favored in the land, are now slaves. God is about to set them free.

**KEY VERSES:**
"Then the LORD told him, 'I have certainly seen the oppression of my people in Egypt. I have heard their cries of distress because of their harsh slave drivers. Yes, I am aware of their suffering. . . . Now go, for I am sending you to Pharaoh. You must lead my people Israel out of Egypt'" (3:7, 10).

**KEY PEOPLE:**
Moses, Miriam, Pharaoh, Pharaoh's daughter, Jethro, Aaron, Joshua, Bezalel

**KEY PLACES:**
Egypt, Goshen, Nile River, Midian, Red Sea, Sinai peninsula, Mount Sinai

**SPECIAL FEATURES:**
Exodus relates more miracles than any other Old Testament book and is noted for containing the Ten Commandments.

GET UP . . . leave . . . take off—these words sound good to those trapped or enslaved. Some resist their marching orders, however, preferring present surroundings to a new, unknown environment. It's not easy to trade the comfortable security of the known for an uncertain future. But what if God gives the order to move? Will we follow his lead? Exodus describes a series of God's calls and the responses of his people.

Four hundred years had passed since Joseph moved his family to Egypt. These descendants of Abraham had now grown to over two million strong. To Egypt's new pharaoh, the Hebrews were foreigners, and their numbers were frightening. Pharaoh decided to make them slaves so they wouldn't upset his balance of power. As it turned out, that was his biggest mistake, for God then came to the rescue of his people.

Through a series of strange events, a Hebrew boy named Moses became a prince in Pharaoh's palace and then an outcast in a wilderness land. God visited Moses in the mysterious flames of a burning bush, and, after some discussion, Moses agreed to return to Egypt to lead God's people out of slavery. Pharaoh was confronted, and through a cycle of plagues and promises made and broken, Israel was torn from his grasp.

Mobilizing this mass of humanity was no easy task, but they marched out of Egypt, through the Red Sea, and into the wilderness behind Moses and the pillars of cloud and fire. Despite continual evidence of God's love and power, the people complained and began to yearn for their days in Egypt. God provided for their physical and spiritual needs with food and a place to worship, but he also judged their disobedience and unbelief. Then in the dramatic Sinai meeting with Moses, God gave his laws for right living.

God led Moses and the nation of Israel, and he wants to lead us as well. Is he preparing you, like Moses, for a specific task? He will be with you; obey and follow. Is he delivering you from an enemy or a temptation? Trust him, and do what he says. Have you heard his clear moral directions? Read, study, and obey his Word. Is he calling you to true worship? Discover God's presence in your life, in your home, and in the body of assembled believers. Exodus is the exciting story of God's guidance. Read with the determination to follow God wherever he leads.

<table>
<thead>
<tr><th>Moses born 1526 (1350)</th><th>Exodus from Egypt 1446 (1280)</th><th>Ten Commandments given 1445 (1279)</th><th>Israel enters Canaan 1406 (1240)</th><th>Judges begin to rule 1375 (1220)</th></tr>
</thead>
</table>

## THE BLUEPRINT

A. ISRAEL IN EGYPT (1:1—12:30)
   1. Slavery in Egypt
   2. God chooses Moses
   3. God sends Moses to Pharaoh
   4. Plagues strike Egypt
   5. The Passover

When the Israelites were enslaved in Egypt, God heard their cries and rescued them. We can be confident that God still hears the cries of his people. Just as he delivered the Israelites from their captors, he delivers us from sin, death, and evil.

B. ISRAEL IN THE WILDERNESS (12:31—18:27)
   1. The Exodus
   2. Crossing the sea
   3. Complaining in the wilderness

After crossing the Red Sea, the Israelites became quarrelsome and discontent. Like the Israelites, we find it easy to complain and be dissatisfied. Christians still have struggles, but we should never allow difficulties and unpleasant circumstances to turn us away from trusting God.

C. ISRAEL AT SINAI (19:1—40:38)
   1. Giving the law
   2. Tabernacle instructions
   3. Breaking the law
   4. Tabernacle construction

God revealed his law to the Israelites at Sinai. Through the law, they learned more about what God is like and how he expected his people to live. The law is still instructional for us, for it exposes our sin and shows us God's standard for living.

## MEGATHEMES

| THEME | EXPLANATION | IMPORTANCE |
|---|---|---|
| Slavery | During the Israelites 400-year stay in the land of Egypt, they became enslaved to the Egyptians. Pharaoh, the king of Egypt, oppressed them cruelly. They prayed to God for deliverance from this situation. | Like the Israelites, we need both human and divine leadership to escape from the slavery of sin. After their escape, the memory of slavery helped the Israelites learn to treat others generously. We need to stand against those who oppress others. |
| Rescue/ Redemption | God rescued Israel through the leader Moses and through mighty miracles. The Passover celebration was an annual reminder of their escape from slavery. | God delivers us from the slavery of sin. Jesus Christ celebrated the Passover with his disciples at the Last Supper and then went on to rescue us from sin by dying in our place. |
| Guidance | God guided Israel out of Egypt by using the plagues, Moses' heroic courage, the miracle of the Red Sea, and the Ten Commandments. God is a trustworthy guide. | Although God is all-powerful and can do miracles, he normally leads us by wise leadership and team effort. His Word gives us the wisdom to make daily decisions and govern our lives. |
| Ten Commandments | God's law system had three parts. The Ten Commandments were the first part, containing the absolutes of spiritual and moral life. The civil law was the second part, giving the people rules to manage their lives. The ceremonial law was the third part, showing them patterns for building the Tabernacle and for regular worship. | God was teaching Israel the importance of choice and responsibility. When they obeyed the conditions of the law, he blessed them; if they forgot or disobeyed, he punished them or allowed calamities to come. Many great countries of the world base their laws on the moral system set up in the book of Exodus. God's moral law is valid today. |
| The Nation | God founded the nation of Israel to be the source of truth and salvation to all the world. His relationship to his people was loving yet firm. The Israelites had no army, schools, governors, mayors, or police when they left Egypt. God had to instruct them in their constitutional laws and daily practices. He showed them how to worship and how to have national holidays. | Israel's newly formed nation had all the behavioral characteristics of Christians today. We are often disorganized, sometimes rebellious, and sometimes victorious. God's Person and Word are still our only guides. If our churches reflect his leadership, they will be effective in serving him. |

# KEY PLACES IN EXODUS

Modern names and boundaries are shown in gray.

**1 Goshen** This area was given to Jacob and his family when they moved to Egypt (Genesis 47:5, 6). It became the Hebrews' homeland for 400 years and remained separate from the main Egyptian centers, for Egyptian culture looked down upon shepherds and nomads. As the years passed, Jacob's family grew into a large nation (1:7).

**2, 3 Pithom and Rameses** During the Israelites' stay in the land of Egypt, a pharaoh came to the throne who had no respect for these descendants of Joseph and feared their large numbers. He forced them into slavery in order to oppress and subdue them. Out of their slave labor, the supply cities of Pithom and Rameses were built (1:11).

**4 Midian** Moses, an Egyptian prince who was born a Hebrew, killed an Egyptian and fled for his life to Midian. Here he became a shepherd and married a woman named Zipporah. It was while he was

here that God commissioned him for the job of leading the Hebrew people out of Egypt (2:15—4:31).

**5 Baal-zephon** Slavery was not to last because God planned to deliver his people. After choosing Moses and Aaron to be his spokesmen to Pharaoh, God worked a series of dramatic miracles in the land of Egypt to convince Pharaoh to let the Hebrews go (5:1—12:33). When finally freed, the entire nation set out with the riches of Egypt (12:34–36). One of their first stops was at Baal-zephon (14:2), where Pharaoh, who had changed his mind, chased the Hebrews and trapped them against the sea. But God parted the waters and led the people through the sea on dry land. When Pharaoh's army tried to pursue, the waters collapsed around them, and they were drowned (14:5–31).

**6 Marah** Moses now led the people southward. The long trek across the desert brought hot tempers and parched throats for this mass of people. At Marah, the water they found was bitter, but God sweetened it (15:22–25).

**7 Elim** As they continued their journey, the Hebrews (now called Israelites) came to Elim, an oasis with 12 springs (15:27).

**8 Wilderness of Sin** Leaving Elim, the people headed into the Wilderness of Sin. Here the people became hungry, so God provided them with manna that came from heaven and covered the ground each morning (16:1, 13–15). The people ate this manna until they entered the Promised Land.

**9 Rephidim** Moses led the people to Rephidim where they found no water. But God miraculously provided water from a rock (17:1, 5, 6). Here the Israelites encountered their first test in battle: The Amalekites attacked and were defeated (17:9–13). Moses' father-in-law, Jethro, then arrived on the scene with some sound advice on delegating responsibilities (18).

**10 Mount Sinai** God had previously appeared to Moses on this mountain and commissioned him to lead Israel (3:1–10). Now Moses returned with the people God had asked him to lead. For almost a year the people camped at the foot of Mount Sinai. During this time God gave them his Ten Commandments as well as other laws for right living. He also provided the blueprint for building the Tabernacle (19—40). God was forging a holy nation, prepared to live for and serve him alone.

## A. ISRAEL IN EGYPT (1:1—12:30)

Joseph brought his family to Egypt and protected them there. But after Joseph's death, as they multiplied into a nation, they were forced into slavery. God then prepared Moses to free his people from slavery and lead them out of Egypt. To help Moses, God unleashed ten plagues upon the land. After the tenth plague, Pharaoh let the people go. On the night before the great Exodus, God's new nation celebrated the Passover. Just as God delivered Israel from Egypt, he delivers us from sin, death, and evil.

### 1. Slavery in Egypt

**1:1**
Gen 46:8-27

**1:5**
Gen 46:26

**1** These are the names of the sons of Israel (that is, Jacob) who moved to Egypt with their father, each with his family: ²Reuben, Simeon, Levi, Judah, ³Issachar, Zebulun, Benjamin, ⁴Dan, Naphtali, Gad, and Asher. ⁵In all, Jacob had seventy* descendants in Egypt, including Joseph, who was already there.

**1:6**
Gen 50:26
Acts 7:15-16

⁶In time, Joseph and all of his brothers died, ending that entire generation. ⁷But their descendants, the Israelites, had many children and grandchildren. In fact, they multiplied so greatly that they became extremely powerful and filled the land.

**1:7**
Gen 12:2; 35:11;
46:3; 47:27; 48:4
†Acts 7:17

**1:8**
Acts 7:18-19

**1:9**
Ps 105:25

⁸Eventually, a new king came to power in Egypt who knew nothing about Joseph or what he had done. ⁹He said to his people, "Look, the people of Israel now outnumber us and are stronger than we are. ¹⁰We must make a plan to keep them from growing even more. If we don't, and if war breaks out, they will join our enemies and fight against us. Then they will escape from the country.*"

**1:10**
Ps 105:24-25
Acts 7:17-19

**1:11**
Exod 2:11; 3:7

**1:14**
Exod 2:23

¹¹So the Egyptians made the Israelites their slaves. They appointed brutal slave drivers over them, hoping to wear them down with crushing labor. They forced them to build the cities of Pithom and Rameses as supply centers for the king. ¹²But the more the Egyptians oppressed them, the more the Israelites multiplied and spread, and the more alarmed the Egyptians became. ¹³So the Egyptians worked the people of Israel without mercy. ¹⁴They made their lives bitter, forcing them to mix mortar and make bricks and do all the work in the fields. They were ruthless in all their demands.

**1:16**
Acts 7:19

¹⁵Then Pharaoh, the king of Egypt, gave this order to the Hebrew midwives, Shiphrah and Puah: ¹⁶"When you help the Hebrew women as they give birth, watch as they deliver.* If the

**1:5** Dead Sea Scrolls and Greek version read *seventy-five;* see notes on Gen 46:27. **1:10** Or *will take the country.*
**1:16** Hebrew *look upon the two stones;* perhaps the reference is to a birthstool.

---

**1:1** The "sons of Israel" (or Israelites) were the descendants of Jacob, whose name was changed to Israel after he wrestled with the angel (see Genesis 32:24-30). Jacob's family had moved to Egypt at the invitation of Joseph, one of Jacob's sons who had become a great ruler under Pharaoh. Jacob's family grew into a large nation. But as foreigners and newcomers, their lives were quite different from the Egyptians'. The Hebrews worshiped one God; the Egyptians worshiped many gods. The Hebrews were wanderers; the Egyptians had a deeply rooted culture. The Hebrews were shepherds; the Egyptians were builders. The Hebrews were also physically separated from the Egyptians: They lived in Goshen, north of the great Egyptian cultural centers.

**1:9, 10** Pharaoh was afraid the Israelites were becoming so numerous that they would organize and threaten his kingdom, so he made them slaves and oppressed them to kill their spirit and stop their growth. Slavery was an ancient practice used by almost all nations to employ conquered people and other captives. Most likely, the great pyramids of Egypt were built with slave labor. Although Israel was not a conquered nation, the people were foreigners and thus lacked the rights of native Egyptians.

**1:11** There were levels of slavery in Egypt. Some slaves worked long hours in mud pits while others were skilled carpenters, jewelers, and craftsmen. Regardless of their skill or level, all slaves were watched closely by brutal slave drivers, supervisors whose assignment was to keep the slaves working as fast as possible. They were specialists at making a slave's life miserable.

**1:11** Ancient records indicate that these cities were built in 1290 B.C., which is why some scholars believe the Exodus occurred early in the 13th century. Looking at other evidence,

however, other scholars believe the Hebrews left Egypt in 1446 B.C. How could they build two cities 150 years after they left? These scholars suggest that Rameses II, the pharaoh in 1290 B.C., did not build the cities of Pithom and Rameses. Instead, he renamed two cities that actually had been built 150 years previously. It was a common practice for an Egyptian ruler to make improvements on a city and then take credit for building it, thus wiping out all records of previous founders. Also see the second note on 13:17, 18.

**1:12** The Egyptians tried to wear down the Hebrew people by forcing them into slavery and mistreating them. Instead, the Hebrews multiplied and grew stronger. When we are burdened or mistreated, we may feel defeated. But our burdens can make us stronger and develop qualities in us that will prepare us for the future. We cannot be overcomers without troubles to overcome. Be true to God in the hard times because even the worst situations can make us better people.

**1:15-17** Shiphrah and Puah may have been supervisors over the midwives, or else these two were given special mention. Hebrew midwives helped women give birth and cared for the baby until the mother was stronger. When Pharaoh ordered the midwives to kill the Hebrew baby boys, he was asking the wrong group of people. Midwives were committed to helping babies be born, not to killing them. These women showed great courage and love for God by risking their lives to disobey Pharaoh's command.

baby is a boy, kill him; if it is a girl, let her live." 17But because the midwives feared God, they refused to obey the king's orders. They allowed the boys to live, too.

18So the king of Egypt called for the midwives. "Why have you done this?" he demanded. "Why have you allowed the boys to live?"

19"The Hebrew women are not like the Egyptian women," the midwives replied. "They are more vigorous and have their babies so quickly that we cannot get there in time."

20So God was good to the midwives, and the Israelites continued to multiply, growing more and more powerful. 21And because the midwives feared God, he gave them families of their own.

22Then Pharaoh gave this order to all his people: "Throw every newborn Hebrew boy into the Nile River. But you may let the girls live."

**1:19** Josh 2:4-6 2 Sam 17:20
**1:20** Exod 1:12
**1:22** Acts 7:19

## 2. God chooses Moses
### The Birth of Moses

**2** About this time, a man and woman from the tribe of Levi got married. 2The woman became pregnant and gave birth to a son. She saw that he was a special baby and kept him hidden for three months. 3But when she could no longer hide him, she got a basket made of papyrus reeds and waterproofed it with tar and pitch. She put the baby in the basket and laid it among the reeds along the bank of the Nile River. 4The baby's sister then stood at a distance, watching to see what would happen to him.

5Soon Pharaoh's daughter came down to bathe in the river, and her attendants walked along the riverbank. When the princess saw the basket among the reeds, she sent her maid to get it for her. 6When the princess opened it, she saw the baby. The little boy was crying, and she felt sorry for him. "This must be one of the Hebrew children," she said.

7Then the baby's sister approached the princess. "Should I go and find one of the Hebrew women to nurse the baby for you?" she asked.

8"Yes, do!" the princess replied. So the girl went and called the baby's mother.

9"Take this baby and nurse him for me," the princess told the baby's mother. "I will pay you for your help." So the woman took her baby home and nursed him.

**2:1** Exod 6:20 Num 26:59
**2:2** Acts 7:20 Heb 11:23
**2:3** Gen 6:14 Isa 18:2
**2:4** Exod 15:20 Num 26:59
**2:5** Exod 7:15; 8:20 Acts 7:21

**1:17-21** Against Pharaoh's orders, the midwives spared the Hebrew babies. Their faith in God gave them the courage to take a stand for what they knew was right. In this situation, disobeying the authority was proper. God does not expect us to obey those in authority when they ask us to disobey him or his Word. The Bible is filled with examples of those who were willing to sacrifice their very lives in order to obey God or save others. Esther and Mordecai (Esther 3:2; 4:13-16) and Shadrach, Meshach, and Abednego (Daniel 3:16-18) are some of the people who took a bold stand for what was right. Whole nations can be caught up in immorality (racial hatred, slavery, prison cruelty); thus following the majority or the authority is not always right. Whenever we are ordered to disobey God's Word, we must "obey God rather than any human authority" (Acts 5:29).

**1:19-21** Did God bless the Hebrew midwives for lying to Pharaoh? God blessed them not because they lied, but because they saved the lives of innocent children. This doesn't mean that a lie was necessarily the best way to answer Pharaoh. The midwives were blessed, however, for not violating the higher law of God that forbids the senseless slaughter of innocent lives.

**2:1, 2** Although a name is not mentioned yet, the baby in this story was Moses. Moses' mother and father were named Jochebed and Amram. His brother was Aaron and his sister, Miriam.

**2:3** This tiny boat made of papyrus reeds was fashioned by a woman who knew what she was doing. Egyptian riverboats were made with these same reeds and waterproofed with tar. The reeds, which grew as tall as 16 feet, could be gathered in swampy areas along the Nile. Thus a small basket hidden among the reeds would be well insulated from the weather and difficult to see.

**2:3ff** Moses' mother knew how wrong it would be to destroy her child. But there was little she could do to change Pharaoh's new

law. Her only alternative was to hide the child and later place him in a tiny papyrus basket on the river. God used her courageous act to place her son, the Hebrew of his choice, in the house of Pharaoh. Do you sometimes feel surrounded by evil and frustrated by how little you can do about it? When faced with evil, look for ways to act against it. Then trust God to use your effort, however small it seems, in his war against evil.

**2:5** Who was Pharaoh's daughter? There are two popular explanations. (1) Some think that Hatshepsut was the woman who pulled Moses from the river. Her husband was Pharaoh Thutmose II. (This would match the earlier Exodus date.) Apparently Hatshepsut could not have children, so Thutmose had a son by another woman, and this son became heir to the throne. Hatshepsut would have considered Moses a gift from the gods because now she had her own son who would be the legal heir to the throne. (2) Some think the princess who rescued baby Moses was the daughter of Rameses II, an especially cruel Pharaoh who would have made life miserable for the Hebrew slaves. (This would match the later Exodus date.)

**2:7, 8** Miriam, the baby's sister, saw that Pharaoh's daughter had discovered Moses. Quickly she took the initiative to suggest a nurse (her mother) who might care for the baby. The Bible doesn't say if Miriam was afraid to approach the Egyptian princess or if the princess was suspicious of the Hebrew girl. But Miriam did approach her, and the princess bought the services of Miriam and her mother. Their family was reunited. Special opportunities may come our way unexpectedly. Don't let the fear of what might happen cause you to miss an opportunity. Be alert for the opportunities God gives you, and take full advantage of them.

**2:9** Moses' mother was reunited with her baby! God used her courageous act of saving and hiding her baby to begin his plan to rescue his people from Egypt. God doesn't need much from us to accomplish his plan for our lives. Focusing on our human

**2:10**
1 Sam 1:20
2 Sam 22:17

[10]Later, when the boy was older, his mother brought him back to Pharaoh's daughter, who adopted him as her own son. The princess named him Moses,* for she explained, "I lifted him out of the water."

*Moses Escapes to Midian*

**2:11**
Acts 7:23-24
Heb 11:24-26

[11]Many years later, when Moses had grown up, he went out to visit his own people, the Hebrews, and he saw how hard they were forced to work. During his visit, he saw an Egyptian beating one of his fellow Hebrews.

**2:12**
Acts 7:24

[12]After looking in all directions to make sure no one was watching, Moses killed the Egyptian and hid the body in the sand.

**2:13**
Acts 7:26-28

[13]The next day, when Moses went out to visit his people again, he saw two Hebrew men fighting. "Why are you beating up your friend?" Moses said to the one who had started the fight.

**2:14**
†Acts 7:27, 35

[14]The man replied, "Who appointed you to be our prince and judge? Are you going to kill me as you killed that Egyptian yesterday?"

**2:15**
Acts 7:29

Then Moses was afraid, thinking, "Everyone knows what I did." [15]And sure enough, Pharaoh heard what had happened, and he tried to kill Moses. But Moses fled from Pharaoh and went to live in the land of Midian.

**2:16**
Gen 24:11
Exod 3:1; 18:1

When Moses arrived in Midian, he sat down beside a well. [16]Now the priest of Midian had seven daughters who came as usual to draw water and fill the water troughs for their father's flocks.

**2:17**
Gen 29:10

[17]But some other shepherds came and chased them away. So Moses jumped up and rescued the girls from the shepherds. Then he drew water for their flocks.

**2:18**
Num 10:29

[18]When the girls returned to Reuel, their father, he asked, "Why are you back so soon today?"

**2:20**
Gen 18:5

[19]"An Egyptian rescued us from the shepherds," they answered. "And then he drew water for us and watered our flocks."

**2:21**
Exod 4:25; 18:2
Acts 7:29

[20]"Then where is he?" their father asked. "Why did you leave him there? Invite him to come and eat with us."

**2:22**
Gen 23:4
Heb 11:13

[21]Moses accepted the invitation, and he settled there with him. In time, Reuel gave Moses his daughter Zipporah to be his wife. [22]Later she gave birth to a son, and Moses named him Gershom,* for he explained, "I have been a foreigner in a foreign land."

**2:23**
Exod 6:5, 9
Acts 7:34

[23]Years passed, and the king of Egypt died. But the Israelites continued to groan under their burden of slavery. They cried out for help, and their cry rose up to God. [24]God heard

**2:24**
Gen 22:16-18;
26:2-3; 28:13
Ps 105:10, 42

**2:10** *Moses* sounds like a Hebrew term that means "to lift out." **2:22** *Gershom* sounds like a Hebrew term that means "a foreigner there."

---

predicament may paralyze us because the situation may appear humanly impossible. But concentrating on God and his power will help us see the way out. Right now you may feel unable to see through your troubles. Focus instead on God, and trust him for the way out. That is all he needs to begin his work in you.

**2:12-14** Moses tried to make sure no one was watching before he killed the Egyptian. But as it turned out, someone did see, and Moses had to flee the country. Sometimes we mistakenly think we can get away with doing wrong if no one sees or catches us. Sooner or later, however, doing wrong will catch up with us as it did with Moses. Even if we are not caught in this life, we will still have to face God and his evaluation of our actions.

**2:15** To escape punishment for killing the Egyptian, Moses ran away to Midian. He became a stranger in a strange land, separated from his home and family. It took many years after this incident for Moses to be ready to serve God. But he trusted God instead of fearing the king (Hebrews 11:27). We may feel abandoned or isolated because of something we have done. But though we feel afraid and separated, we should not give up. Moses didn't. He trusted God to deliver him, no matter how dark his past or bleak his future.

**2:17** How did Moses handle these shepherds so easily? As an Egyptian prince, Moses would have been well trained in the Egyptian military, the most advanced army in the world. Even a large group of shepherds would have been no match for the sophisticated fighting techniques of this trained warrior.

**2:18** Reuel is also called Jethro in 3:1.

**2:23-25** God's rescue doesn't always come the moment

we want it. God had promised to bring the Hebrew slaves out of Egypt (Genesis 15:16; 46:3, 4). The people had waited a long time for that promise to be kept, but God rescued them when he knew the right time had come. God knows the best time to act. When you feel that God has forgotten you in your troubles, remember that God has a time schedule we can't see.

**MOSES FLEES TO MIDIAN**
After murdering an Egyptian, Moses escaped into Midian. There he married Zipporah and became a shepherd.

their groaning, and he remembered his covenant promise to Abraham, Isaac, and Jacob. 25He looked down on the people of Israel and knew it was time to act.*

## Moses and the Burning Bush

**3** One day Moses was tending the flock of his father-in-law, Jethro,* the priest of Midian. He led the flock far into the wilderness and came to Sinai,* the mountain of God. 2There the angel of the LORD appeared to him in a blazing fire from the middle of a bush. Moses stared in amazement. Though the bush was engulfed in flames, it didn't burn up. 3"This is amazing," Moses said to himself. "Why isn't that bush burning up? I must go see it."

4When the LORD saw Moses coming to take a closer look, God called to him from the middle of the bush, "Moses! Moses!"

"Here I am!" Moses replied.

5"Do not come any closer," the LORD warned. "Take off your sandals, for you are standing on holy ground. 6I am the God of your father*—the God of Abraham, the God of Isaac, and the God of Jacob." When Moses heard this, he covered his face because he was afraid to look at God.

7Then the LORD told him, "I have certainly seen the oppression of my people in Egypt. I have heard their cries of distress because of their harsh slave drivers. Yes, I am aware of their suffering. 8So I have come down to rescue them from the power of the Egyptians and lead them out of Egypt into their own fertile and spacious land. It is a land flowing with milk and honey—the land where the Canaanites, Hittites, Amorites, Perizzites, Hivites, and Jebusites now live. 9Look! The cry of the people of Israel has reached me, and I have seen how harshly the Egyptians abuse them. 10Now go, for I am sending you to Pharaoh. You must lead my people Israel out of Egypt."

11But Moses protested to God, "Who am I to appear before Pharaoh? Who am I to lead the people of Israel out of Egypt?"

12God answered, "I will be with you. And this is your sign that I am the one who has sent you: When you have brought the people out of Egypt, you will worship God at this very mountain."

13But Moses protested, "If I go to the people of Israel and tell them, 'The God of your ancestors has sent me to you,' they will ask me, 'What is his name?' Then what should I tell them?"

---

**3:2**
†Acts 7:30

**3:3**
†Acts 7:31

**3:5**
Gen 28:17
Josh 5:15
†Acts 7:33

**3:6**
†Matt 22:32
†Mark 12:26
†Luke 20:37
†Acts 3:13; 7:32

**3:7**
†Acts 7:34

**3:8**
Gen 15:18-19;
46:4; 50:24
Exod 3:17
Deut 6:3; 8:7-9;
11:9; 26:9

**3:10**
†Acts 7:34

**3:11**
Exod 4:10; 6:12

**3:12**
Exod 4:12; 19:2
†Acts 7:7

**3:13**
Exod 15:3

---

**2:25** Or *and acknowledged his obligation to help them.* **3:1a** Moses' father-in-law went by two names, Jethro and Reuel. **3:1b** Hebrew *Horeb,* another name for Sinai. **3:6** Greek version reads *your fathers.*

---

**3:1** What a contrast between Moses' life as an Egyptian prince and his life as a Midianite shepherd! As a prince he had everything done for him; he was the famous son of an Egyptian princess. As a shepherd he had to do everything for himself; he was holding the very job he had been taught to despise (Genesis 43:32; 46:33, 34), and he lived as an unknown foreigner. What a humbling experience this must have been for Moses! But God was preparing him for leadership. Living the life of a shepherd and nomad, Moses learned about the ways of the people he would be leading and also about life in the wilderness. Moses couldn't appreciate this lesson, but God was getting him ready to free Israel from Pharaoh's grasp.

**3:1** Mount Sinai is the place where God would give the people his revealed law, known today as the Ten Commandments (3:12; 19:1–20:21).

**3:2** God spoke to Moses from an unexpected source: a burning bush. When Moses saw it, he went to investigate. God may use unexpected sources when communicating to us too, whether people, thoughts, or experiences. Be willing to investigate, and be open to God's surprises.

**3:2-4** Moses saw a burning bush and spoke with God. Many people in the Bible experienced God in visible (not necessarily human) form. Abraham saw the smoking firepot and flaming torch (Genesis 15:17); Jacob wrestled with a man (Genesis 32:24-29). When the slaves were freed from Egypt, God led them by pillars of cloud and fire (13:17-22). God made such appearances to encourage his new nation, to guide them, and to prove the reliability of his verbal message.

**3:5, 6** At God's command, Moses removed his sandals and covered his face. Taking off his shoes was an act of reverence, conveying his own unworthiness before God. God is our friend, but he is also our sovereign Lord. To approach him frivolously shows a lack of respect and sincerity. When you come to God in worship, do you approach him casually, or do you come as though you were an invited guest before a king? If necessary, adjust your attitude so it is suitable for approaching a holy God.

**3:8** This "land flowing with milk and honey" is the land of Israel and Jordan today. This was a poetic word picture expressing the beauty and productivity of the Promised Land.

**3:10ff** Moses made excuses because he felt inadequate for the job God asked him to do. It was natural for him to feel that way. He *was* inadequate all by himself. But God wasn't asking Moses to work alone. He offered other resources to help (God himself, Aaron, and the ability to do miracles). God often calls us to do tasks that seem too difficult, but he doesn't ask us to do them alone. God offers us his resources, just as he did to Moses. We should not hide behind our inadequacies, as Moses did, but look beyond ourselves to the great resources available. Then we can allow God to use our unique contributions.

**3:13-15** The Egyptians had many gods by many different names. Moses wanted to know God's name so the Hebrew people would know exactly who had sent him to them. God called himself I AM, a name describing his eternal power and unchangeable character. In a world where values, morals, and laws change constantly, we can find stability and security in our unchanging God. The God who appeared to Moses is the same God who can live in us today. Hebrews 13:8 says Jesus Christ is the same "yesterday, today, and forever." Because God's nature is stable and trustworthy,

**3:14**
Exod 6:3
John 8:58
Rev 1:8; 4:8

**3:15**
Pss 72:17; 102:12;
135:13
†Acts 3:13

**3:16**
Exod 4:29

**3:17**
Exod 3:8
Josh 24:11

**3:18**
Exod 4:23; 5:1, 3
Num 23:4, 16

**3:19**
Exod 5:2; 6:1; 7:4

**3:20**
Exod 11:1;
12:31-33
Neh 9:10
Acts 7:36

**3:21**
Exod 11:3

**3:22**
Exod 11:2; 12:35

**4:1**
Exod 3:15-16, 18

**4:3**
Exod 7:8-12, 15

**4:5**
Exod 4:31; 19:9

¹⁴God replied to Moses, "I AM WHO I AM.* Say this to the people of Israel: I AM has sent me to you." ¹⁵God also said to Moses, "Say this to the people of Israel: Yahweh,* the God of your ancestors—the God of Abraham, the God of Isaac, and the God of Jacob—has sent me to you.

This is my eternal name,
my name to remember for all generations.

¹⁶"Now go and call together all the elders of Israel. Tell them, 'The LORD, the God of your ancestors—the God of Abraham, Isaac, and Jacob—has appeared to me. He told me, "I have been watching closely, and I see how the Egyptians are treating you. ¹⁷I have promised to rescue you from your oppression in Egypt. I will lead you to a land flowing with milk and honey—the land where the Canaanites, Hittites, Amorites, Perizzites, Hivites, and Jebusites now live."'

¹⁸"The elders of Israel will accept your message. Then you and the elders must go to the king of Egypt and tell him, 'The LORD, the God of the Hebrews, has met with us. So please let us take a three-day journey into the wilderness to offer sacrifices to the LORD, our God.'

¹⁹"But I know that the king of Egypt will not let you go unless a mighty hand forces him.* ²⁰So I will raise my hand and strike the Egyptians, performing all kinds of miracles among them. Then at last he will let you go. ²¹And I will cause the Egyptians to look favorably on you. They will give you gifts when you go so you will not leave empty-handed. ²²Every Israelite woman will ask for articles of silver and gold and fine clothing from her Egyptian neighbors and from the foreign women in their houses. You will dress your sons and daughters with these, stripping the Egyptians of their wealth."

### Signs of the LORD's Power

**4** But Moses protested again, "What if they won't believe me or listen to me? What if they say, 'The LORD never appeared to you'?"

²Then the LORD asked him, "What is that in your hand?"

"A shepherd's staff," Moses replied.

³"Throw it down on the ground," the LORD told him. So Moses threw down the staff, and it turned into a snake! Moses jumped back.

⁴Then the LORD told him, "Reach out and grab its tail." So Moses reached out and grabbed it, and it turned back into a shepherd's staff in his hand.

⁵"Perform this sign," the LORD told him. "Then they will believe that the LORD, the God of their ancestors—the God of Abraham, the God of Isaac, and the God of Jacob—really has appeared to you."

**3:14** Or *I WILL BE WHAT I WILL BE*. **3:15** *Yahweh* is a transliteration of the proper name *YHWH* that is sometimes rendered "Jehovah"; in this translation it is usually rendered "the LORD" (note the use of small capitals). **3:19** As in Greek and Latin versions; Hebrew reads *will not let you go, not by a mighty hand*.

---

we are free to follow and enjoy him rather than spend our time trying to figure him out.

**3:14, 15** God reminded Moses of his covenant promises to Abraham (Genesis 12:1-3; 15; 17), Isaac (Genesis 26:2-5), and Jacob (Genesis 28:13-15), and used the name I AM to show his unchanging nature. What God promised to the great patriarchs hundreds of years earlier he would fulfill through Moses. His wisdom spans the ages, and his promises give meaning and direction to our lives.

**3:16, 17** God told Moses to tell the people what he saw and heard at the burning bush. Our God is a God who acts and speaks. One of the most convincing ways to tell others about him is to describe what he has done and how he has spoken to his people. If you are trying to explain God to others, talk about what he has done for you, for people you know, or for people whose stories are told in the Bible.

**3:18-20** The elders (leaders) of Israel would accept God's message, and the leaders of Egypt would reject it. God knew what both reactions would be before they happened. This is more than good psychology—God knows the future. Any believer can trust his or her future to God because God already knows what is going to happen.

**3:22** The jewelry and clothing were not merely borrowed— they were asked for and easily received. The Egyptians were so glad to see the Israelites go that they sent them out with gifts.

These items were used later in building the Tabernacle (35:5, 22). The promise of being able to strip the Egyptians of their wealth seemed impossible to Moses at this time.

**4:1** Moses' reluctance and fear were caused by overanticipation. He was worried about how the people might respond to him. We often build up events in our minds and then panic over what might go wrong. God does not ask us to go where he has not provided the means to help. Go where he leads, trusting him to supply courage, confidence, and resources at the right moment.

**4:2-4** A shepherd's staff was commonly a three- to six-foot wooden rod with a curved hook at the top. The shepherd used it for walking, guiding his sheep, killing snakes, and many other tasks. Still, it was just a stick. But God used the simple shepherd's staff Moses carried as a sign to teach him an important lesson. God sometimes takes joy in using ordinary things for extraordinary purposes. What are the ordinary things in your life—your voice, a pen, a hammer, a broom, a musical instrument? While it is easy to assume God can use only special skills, you must not hinder his use of the everyday contributions you can make. Little did Moses imagine the power his simple staff would wield when it became the staff of God.

⁶Then the LORD said to Moses, "Now put your hand inside your cloak." So Moses put his hand inside his cloak, and when he took it out again, his hand was white as snow with a severe skin disease.* ⁷"Now put your hand back into your cloak," the LORD said. So Moses put his hand back in, and when he took it out again, it was as healthy as the rest of his body.

⁸The LORD said to Moses, "If they do not believe you and are not convinced by the first miraculous sign, they will be convinced by the second sign. ⁹And if they don't believe you or listen to you even after these two signs, then take some water from the Nile River and pour it out on the dry ground. When you do, the water from the Nile will turn to blood on the ground."

¹⁰But Moses pleaded with the LORD, "O Lord, I'm not very good with words. I never have been, and I'm not now, even though you have spoken to me. I get tongue-tied, and my words get tangled."

¹¹Then the LORD asked Moses, "Who makes a person's mouth? Who decides whether people speak or do not speak, hear or do not hear, see or do not see? Is it not I, the LORD? ¹²Now go! I will be with you as you speak, and I will instruct you in what to say."

¹³But Moses again pleaded, "Lord, please! Send anyone else."

¹⁴Then the LORD became angry with Moses. "All right," he said. "What about your brother, Aaron the Levite? I know he speaks well. And look! He is on his way to meet you now. He will be delighted to see you. ¹⁵Talk to him, and put the words in his mouth. I will be with both of you as you speak, and I will instruct you both in what to do. ¹⁶Aaron will be your spokesman to the people. He will be your mouthpiece, and you will stand in the place of God for him, telling him what to say. ¹⁷And take your shepherd's staff with you, and use it to perform the miraculous signs I have shown you."

### Moses Returns to Egypt

¹⁸So Moses went back home to Jethro, his father-in-law. "Please let me return to my relatives in Egypt," Moses said. "I don't even know if they are still alive."

"Go in peace," Jethro replied.

¹⁹Before Moses left Midian, the LORD said to him, "Return to Egypt, for all those who wanted to kill you have died."

²⁰So Moses took his wife and sons, put them on a donkey, and headed back to the land of Egypt. In his hand he carried the staff of God.

²¹And the LORD told Moses, "When you arrive back in Egypt, go to Pharaoh and perform all the miracles I have empowered you to do. But I will harden his heart so he will refuse to let the people go. ²²Then you will tell him, 'This is what the LORD says: Israel is my firstborn son. ²³I commanded you, "Let my son go, so he can worship me." But since you have refused, I will now kill your firstborn son!'"

²⁴On the way to Egypt, at a place where Moses and his family had stopped for the night,

**4:6**
Num 12:10
2 Kgs 5:27

**4:7**
2 Kgs 5:14
Matt 8:3
Luke 17:12-14

**4:9**
Exod 7:17-21

**4:10**
Exod 3:11
Jer 1:6

**4:11**
Ps 94:9
Matt 11:5

**4:12**
Deut 18:15, 18
Matt 10:19-20
Mark 13:11

**4:14**
Exod 4:27

**4:15**
Isa 51:16
Jer 1:9

**4:16**
Exod 7:1; 18:19-20

**4:17**
Exod 14:16; 17:9

**4:19**
Exod 2:15, 23

**4:20**
Exod 18:3
Acts 7:29

**4:21**
Exod 7:3, 13; 9:12
Deut 2:30
John 12:40

**4:22**
Isa 63:16; 64:8
Jer 31:9
Hos 11:1
Rom 9:4

**4:23**
Exod 5:1; 6:11;
7:16

**4:24**
Num 22:22
1 Chr 21:16

**4:6** Or *with leprosy*. The Hebrew word used here can describe various skin diseases.

---

**4:6, 7** This severe skin disease was leprosy, one of the most feared diseases of this time. There was no cure, and a great deal of suffering preceded eventual death. Through this experience, Moses learned that God could cause or cure any kind of problem. He saw that God indeed had all power and was commissioning him to exercise that power to lead the Hebrews out of Egypt.

**4:10-13** Moses pleaded with God to let him out of his mission. After all, he was not a good speaker and would probably embarrass both himself and God. But God looked at Moses' problem quite differently. All Moses needed was some help, and who better than God could help him say and do the right things. God made his mouth and would give him the words to say. It is easy for us to focus on our weaknesses, but if God asks us to do something, then he will help us get the job done. If the job involves some of our weak areas, then we can trust that he will provide words, strength, courage, and ability where needed.

**4:14** God finally agreed to let Aaron speak for Moses. Moses' feelings of inadequacy were so strong that he could not trust even God's ability to help him. Moses had to deal with his deep sense of inadequacy many times. When we face difficult or frightening situations, we must be willing to let God help us.

**4:16** The phrase "you will stand in the place of God for him"

means that Moses would tell Aaron what to say as God was telling him.

**4:17-20** Moses clung tightly to the shepherd's staff as he left for Egypt to face the greatest challenge of his life. The staff was his assurance of God's presence and power. When feeling uncertain, some people need something to stabilize and reassure them. For assurance when facing great trials, God has given promises from his Word and examples from great heroes of faith. Any Christian may cling tightly to these. As we grow in faith, we will outgrow our need for physical or temporary assurances and be able to trust God's Word alone.

**4:24-26** God was about to kill Moses because Moses had not circumcised his son. Why hadn't Moses done this? Remember that Moses had spent half his life in Pharaoh's palace and half his life in the Midianite wilderness. He might not have been too familiar with God's laws, especially since all the requirements of God's covenant with Israel (Genesis 17) had not been actively carried out for over 400 years. In addition, Moses' wife, due to her Midianite background, may have opposed circumcision. But Moses could not effectively serve as deliverer of God's people until he had fulfilled the conditions of God's covenant, and one of those conditions was circumcision. Before they could go any

**4:25-26**
Josh 5:2-3

**4:27**
Exod 4:14

**4:28**
Exod 4:16

**4:29**
Exod 3:16

**4:30**
Exod 4:15

**4:31**
Exod 3:18; 12:27

**5:1**
Exod 3:18; 4:23

**5:2**
Exod 3:19
Job 21:15

**5:3**
Exod 3:18
Deut 28:21

**5:4-5**
Exod 1:11

**5:6**
Exod 3:7; 5:10, 14

**5:7**
Gen 11:13

the LORD confronted him and was about to kill him. ²⁵But Moses' wife, Zipporah, took a flint knife and circumcised her son. She touched his feet* with the foreskin and said, "Now you are a bridegroom of blood to me." ²⁶(When she said "a bridegroom of blood," she was referring to the circumcision.) After that, the LORD left him alone.

²⁷Now the LORD had said to Aaron, "Go out into the wilderness to meet Moses." So Aaron went and met Moses at the mountain of God, and he embraced him. ²⁸Moses then told Aaron everything the LORD had commanded him to say. And he told him about the miraculous signs the LORD had commanded him to perform.

²⁹Then Moses and Aaron returned to Egypt and called all the elders of Israel together. ³⁰Aaron told them everything the LORD had told Moses, and Moses performed the miraculous signs as they watched. ³¹Then the people of Israel were convinced that the LORD had sent Moses and Aaron. When they heard that the LORD was concerned about them and had seen their misery, they bowed down and worshiped.

## 3. God sends Moses to Pharaoh

### Moses and Aaron Speak to Pharaoh

**5** After this presentation to Israel's leaders, Moses and Aaron went and spoke to Pharaoh. They told him, "This is what the LORD, the God of Israel, says: Let my people go so they may hold a festival in my honor in the wilderness."

²"Is that so?" retorted Pharaoh. "And who is the LORD? Why should I listen to him and let Israel go? I don't know the LORD, and I will not let Israel go."

³But Aaron and Moses persisted. "The God of the Hebrews has met with us," they declared. "So let us take a three-day journey into the wilderness so we can offer sacrifices to the LORD our God. If we don't, he will kill us with a plague or with the sword."

⁴Pharaoh replied, "Moses and Aaron, why are you distracting the people from their tasks? Get back to work! ⁵Look, there are many of your people in the land, and you are stopping them from their work."

### Making Bricks without Straw

⁶That same day Pharaoh sent this order to the Egyptian slave drivers and the Israelite foremen: ⁷"Do not supply any more straw for making bricks. Make the people get it themselves!

**4:25** The Hebrew word for "feet" may refer here to the male sex organ.

---

farther, Moses and his family had to follow God's commands completely. Under Old Testament law, failing to circumcise your son was to remove yourself and your family from God's blessings. Moses learned that disobeying God was even more dangerous than tangling with an Egyptian pharaoh.

**4:25, 26** Why did Zipporah perform the circumcision? It may have been Zipporah who, as a Midianite unfamiliar with the circumcision requirement, had persuaded Moses not to circumcise their son. If she prevented the action, now she would have to perform it. It is also possible that Moses became ill as a result of permitting disobedience, and so Zipporah had to perform the circumcision herself to save both her husband and son. This would not have made her happy—hence, her unflattering comment to Moses.

**5:1, 2** Pharaoh was familiar with many gods (Egypt was filled with them), but he had never heard of the God of Israel. Pharaoh assumed that the God of the Hebrew slaves couldn't live very powerful. At first, Pharaoh was not at all worried about Moses' message, for he had not yet seen any evidence of the Lord's power.

**5:3** Pharaoh would not listen to Moses and Aaron because he did not know or respect God. People who do not know God may not listen to his Word or his messengers. Like Moses and Aaron, we need to persist. When others reject you or your faith, don't be surprised or discouraged. Continue to tell them about God, trusting him to open minds and soften stubborn hearts.

**5:4-9** Moses and Aaron took their message to Pharaoh just as God directed. The unhappy result was harder work and more oppression for the Hebrews. Sometimes hardship comes as a result of obeying God. Are you following God but still suffering—

or suffering even worse than before? If your life is miserable, don't assume you have fallen out of God's favor. You may be suffering for doing good in an evil world.

**5:7, 8** Mixing straw with mud made bricks stronger and more durable. Pharaoh had supplied the slaves with straw, but now he made them find their own straw and keep up their production quota as well.

**MOSES RETURNS TO EGYPT**
God appeared to Moses in a mysterious burning bush on Mount Sinai. Later Aaron met Moses at the mountain, and together they returned to Egypt, a 200-mile trip.

8But still require them to make the same number of bricks as before. Don't reduce the quota. They are lazy. That's why they are crying out, 'Let us go and offer sacrifices to our God.' 9Load them down with more work. Make them sweat! That will teach them to listen to lies!"

10So the slave drivers and foremen went out and told the people: "This is what Pharaoh says: I will not provide any more straw for you. 11Go and get it yourselves. Find it wherever you can. But you must produce just as many bricks as before!" 12So the people scattered throughout the land of Egypt in search of stubble to use as straw.

13Meanwhile, the Egyptian slave drivers continued to push hard. "Meet your daily quota of bricks, just as you did when we provided you with straw!" they demanded. 14Then they whipped the Israelite foremen they had put in charge of the work crews. "Why haven't you met your quotas either yesterday or today?" they demanded. **5:14** Isa 10:24

15So the Israelite foremen went to Pharaoh and pleaded with him. "Please don't treat your servants like this," they begged. 16"We are given no straw, but the slave drivers still demand, 'Make bricks!' We are being beaten, but it isn't our fault! Your own people are to blame!"

17But Pharaoh shouted, "You're just lazy! Lazy! That's why you're saying, 'Let us go and offer sacrifices to the Lord.' 18Now get back to work! No straw will be given to you, but you must still produce the full quota of bricks." **5:17** Exod 5:8

19The Israelite foremen could see that they were in serious trouble when they were told, "You must not reduce the number of bricks you make each day." 20As they left Pharaoh's court, they confronted Moses and Aaron, who were waiting outside for them. 21The foremen said to them, "May the Lord judge and punish you for making us stink before Pharaoh and his officials. You have put a sword into their hands, an excuse to kill us!" **5:21** Gen 16:5; 34:30

22Then Moses went back to the Lord and protested, "Why have you brought all this trouble on your own people, Lord? Why did you send me? 23Ever since I came to Pharaoh as your spokesman, he has been even more brutal to your people. And you have done nothing to rescue them!" **5:22** Num 11:11 Jer 4:10 **5:23** Exod 3:8

## Promises of Deliverance

6 Then the Lord told Moses, "Now you will see what I will do to Pharaoh. When he feels the force of my strong hand, he will let the people go. In fact, he will force them to leave his land!" **6:1** Exod 3:19-20; 11:1; 12:31

2And God said to Moses, "I am Yahweh—'the Lord.'* 3I appeared to Abraham, to Isaac, and to Jacob as El-Shaddai—'God Almighty'*—but I did not reveal my name, Yahweh, to them. 4And I reaffirmed my covenant with them. Under its terms, I promised to give them the land of Canaan, where they were living as foreigners. 5You can be sure that I have heard the groans of the people of Israel, who are now slaves to the Egyptians. And I am well aware of my covenant with them. **6:3** Gen 17:1 Ps 83:18 Isa 52:6 **6:4** Gen 15:18 **6:5** Exod 2:23-24

6"Therefore, say to the people of Israel: 'I am the Lord. I will free you from your oppression and will rescue you from your slavery in Egypt. I will redeem you with a powerful arm and great acts of judgment. 7I will claim you as my own people, and I will be your God. Then you will know that I am the Lord your God who has freed you from your oppression in **6:6** Exod 3:17; 13:3, 14 Deut 6:12; 26:8 **6:7** Exod 16:12 Deut 4:20 Isa 60:16

**6:2** Yahweh is a transliteration of the proper name *YHWH* that is sometimes rendered "Jehovah"; in this translation it is usually rendered "the Lord" (note the use of small capitals).   **6:3** El-Shaddai, which means "God Almighty," is the name for God used in Gen 17:1; 28:3; 35:11; 43:14; 48:3.

---

**5:15-21** The foremen were caught in the middle. First they tried to get the people to produce the same amount; then they complained to Pharaoh; finally they turned on Moses. Perhaps you have felt caught in the middle at work, or in relationships in your family or church. Complaining or turning on the leadership does not solve the problem. In the case of these supervisors, God had a larger purpose in mind, just as he might have in your situation. So rather than turning on the leadership when you feel pressured by both sides, turn to God to see what else he might be doing in this situation.

**5:22, 23** Pharaoh had just increased the Hebrews' workload, and Moses protested that God had not rescued his people. Moses expected faster results and fewer problems. When God is at work, suffering, setbacks, and hardship may still occur. In James 1:2-4, we are encouraged to be happy when difficulties come our way. Problems develop our patience and character by teaching us to (1) trust God to do what is best for us, (2) look for ways to honor

God in our present situation, (3) remember that God will not abandon us, and (4) watch for God's plan for us.

**6:6** Small problems need only small answers. But when we face great problems, God has an opportunity to exercise his great power. As the Hebrews' troubles grew steadily worse, God planned to intervene with his mighty power and perform great miracles to deliver them. How big are your problems? Big problems put you in a perfect position to watch God give big answers.

**6:6-8** God's promises in these verses were fulfilled to the letter when the Hebrews left Egypt. He freed them from slavery, became their God, and accepted them as his people. Then he led them toward the land he had promised. When the Hebrews were rescued from slavery, they portrayed the drama of salvation for all of us. When God redeems us from sin, he delivers us, accepts us, and becomes our God. Then he leads us to a new life as we follow him.

**6:8**
Num 14:30
Josh 24:13

**6:11**
Exod 5:1; 7:2

**6:12**
Exod 4:10; 6:30

**6:14**
Gen 46:9
Num 26:5-11

**6:15**
Gen 46:10

**6:16**
Gen 46:11
Num 3:17
1 Chr 6:1, 16-19

**6:17**
Num 3:18-20
1 Chr 6:17

**6:18**
Num 3:25-30
1 Chr 6:2, 18

**6:19**
1 Chr 6:19

**6:20**
Exod 2:1-2
Num 26:59

**6:21**
Num 16:1

**6:22**
Lev 10:4

**6:23**
Ruth 4:19-20

**6:24**
1 Chr 6:22-23, 37

**6:25**
Num 25:7, 11
Josh 24:33

**6:26**
Exod 6:13

**6:29**
Exod 6:2, 6, 8; 7:2

**6:30**
Exod 4:10; 6:12

Egypt. 8I will bring you into the land I swore to give to Abraham, Isaac, and Jacob. I will give it to you as your very own possession. I am the LORD!'"

9So Moses told the people of Israel what the LORD had said, but they refused to listen anymore. They had become too discouraged by the brutality of their slavery.

10Then the LORD said to Moses, 11"Go back to Pharaoh, the king of Egypt, and tell him to let the people of Israel leave his country."

12"But LORD!" Moses objected. "My own people won't listen to me anymore. How can I expect Pharaoh to listen? I'm such a clumsy speaker!*"

13But the LORD spoke to Moses and Aaron and gave them orders for the Israelites and for Pharaoh, the king of Egypt. The LORD commanded Moses and Aaron to lead the people of Israel out of Egypt.

## The Ancestors of Moses and Aaron

14These are the ancestors of some of the clans of Israel:

The sons of Reuben, Israel's oldest son, were Hanoch, Pallu, Hezron, and Carmi. Their descendants became the clans of Reuben.

15The sons of Simeon were Jemuel, Jamin, Ohad, Jakin, Zohar, and Shaul. (Shaul's mother was a Canaanite woman.) Their descendants became the clans of Simeon.

16These are the descendants of Levi, as listed in their family records: The sons of Levi were Gershon, Kohath, and Merari. (Levi lived to be 137 years old.)

17The descendants of Gershon included Libni and Shimei, each of whom became the ancestor of a clan.

18The descendants of Kohath included Amram, Izhar, Hebron, and Uzziel. (Kohath lived to be 133 years old.)

19The descendants of Merari included Mahli and Mushi.

These are the clans of the Levites, as listed in their family records.

20Amram married his father's sister Jochebed, and she gave birth to his sons, Aaron and Moses. (Amram lived to be 137 years old.)

21The sons of Izhar were Korah, Nepheg, and Zicri.

22The sons of Uzziel were Mishael, Elzaphan, and Sithri.

23Aaron married Elisheba, the daughter of Amminadab and sister of Nahshon, and she gave birth to his sons, Nadab, Abihu, Eleazar, and Ithamar.

24The sons of Korah were Assir, Elkanah, and Abiasaph. Their descendants became the clans of Korah.

25Eleazar son of Aaron married one of the daughters of Putiel, and she gave birth to his son, Phinehas.

These are the ancestors of the Levite families, listed according to their clans.

26The Aaron and Moses named in this list are the same ones to whom the LORD said, "Lead the people of Israel out of the land of Egypt like an army." 27It was Moses and Aaron who spoke to Pharaoh, the king of Egypt, about leading the people of Israel out of Egypt.

28When the LORD spoke to Moses in the land of Egypt, 29he said to him, "I am the LORD! Tell Pharaoh, the king of Egypt, everything I am telling you." 30But Moses argued with the LORD, saying, "I can't do it! I'm such a clumsy speaker! Why should Pharaoh listen to me?"

**6:12** Hebrew *I have uncircumcised lips;* also in 6:30.

---

**6:9-12** When Moses gave God's message to the people, they were too discouraged to listen. The Hebrews didn't want to hear any more about God and his promises because the last time they listened to Moses, all they got was more work and greater suffering. Sometimes a clear message from God is followed by a period when no change in the situation is apparent. During that time, seeming setbacks may turn people away from wanting to hear more about God. If you are a leader, don't give up. Keep bringing people God's message as Moses did. By focusing on God, who must be obeyed, rather than on the results to be achieved, good leaders see beyond temporary setbacks and reversals.

**6:10-12** Think how hard it must have been for Moses to bring God's message to Pharaoh when his own people had trouble believing it. Eventually the Hebrews believed that God had sent

Moses, but for a time he must have felt very alone. Moses obeyed God, however, and what a difference it made! When the chances for success appear slim, remember that anyone can obey God when the task is easy and everyone is behind it. Only those with persistent faith can obey when the task seems impossible.

**6:14-25** This genealogy or family tree was placed here to identify more firmly Moses and Aaron. Genealogies were used to establish credentials and authority as well as outlining the history of a family.

**6:26** To bring the Israelites out of Egypt like an army means that they would be brought out in tribes, clans, or family groups.

## Aaron's Staff Becomes a Serpent

**7** Then the LORD said to Moses, "Pay close attention to this. I will make you seem like God to Pharaoh, and your brother, Aaron, will be your prophet. 2Tell Aaron everything I command you, and Aaron must command Pharaoh to let the people of Israel leave his country. 3But I will make Pharaoh's heart stubborn so I can multiply my miraculous signs and wonders in the land of Egypt. 4Even then Pharaoh will refuse to listen to you. So I will bring down my fist on Egypt. Then I will rescue my forces—my people, the Israelites—from the land of Egypt with great acts of judgment. 5When I raise my powerful hand and bring out the Israelites, the Egyptians will know that I am the LORD."

6So Moses and Aaron did just as the LORD had commanded them. 7Moses was eighty years old, and Aaron was eighty-three when they made their demands to Pharaoh.

8Then the LORD said to Moses and Aaron, 9"Pharaoh will demand, 'Show me a miracle.' When he does this, say to Aaron, 'Take your staff and throw it down in front of Pharaoh, and it will become a serpent.*'"

10So Moses and Aaron went to Pharaoh and did what the LORD had commanded them. Aaron threw down his staff before Pharaoh and his officials, and it became a serpent! 11Then Pharaoh called in his own wise men and sorcerers, and these Egyptian magicians did the same thing with their magic. 12They threw down their staffs, which also became serpents! But then Aaron's staff swallowed up their staffs. 13Pharaoh's heart, however, remained hard. He still refused to listen, just as the LORD had predicted.

## 4. Plagues strike Egypt
### A Plague of Blood

14Then the LORD said to Moses, "Pharaoh's heart is stubborn,* and he still refuses to let the people go. 15So go to Pharaoh in the morning as he goes down to the river. Stand on the bank of the Nile and meet him there. Be sure to take along the staff that turned into a snake. 16Then announce to him, 'The LORD, the God of the Hebrews, has sent me to tell you, "Let my people go, so they can worship me in the wilderness." Until now, you have refused to listen to him. 17So this is what the LORD says: "I will show you that I am the LORD." Look! I will strike the water of the Nile with this staff in my hand, and the river will turn to blood. 18The fish in it will die, and the river will stink. The Egyptians will not be able to drink any water from the Nile.'"

19Then the LORD said to Moses: "Tell Aaron, 'Take your staff and raise your hand over the waters of Egypt—all its rivers, canals, ponds, and all the reservoirs. Turn all the water to blood. Everywhere in Egypt the water will turn to blood, even the water stored in wooden bowls and stone pots.'"

20So Moses and Aaron did just as the LORD commanded them. As Pharaoh and all of his officials watched, Aaron raised his staff and struck the water of the Nile. Suddenly, the whole river turned to blood! 21The fish in the river died, and the water became so foul that the Egyptians couldn't drink it. There was blood everywhere throughout the land of Egypt.

7:9 Hebrew *tannin*, which elsewhere refers to a sea monster. Greek version translates it "dragon." 7:14 Hebrew *heavy.*

---

**7:1** God made Moses "seem like God to Pharaoh"—in other words, a powerful person who deserved to be listened to. Pharaoh himself was considered a god, so he recognized Moses as one of his peers. His refusal to give in to Moses shows, however, that he did not feel inferior to Moses.

**7:11** How were these wise men and sorcerers able to duplicate Moses' miracles? Some of their feats involved trickery or illusion, and some may have used satanic power since worshiping gods of the underworld was part of their religion. Ironically, whenever they duplicated one of Moses' plagues, it only made matters worse. If the magicians had been as powerful as God, they would have reversed the plagues, not added to them.

**7:12** God performed a miracle by turning Aaron's staff into a serpent, and Pharaoh's magicians did the same through trickery or sorcery. Although miracles can help us believe, it is dangerous to rely on them alone. Satan can imitate some parts of God's work and lead people astray. Pharaoh focused on the miracle rather than the message. We can avoid this error by letting the Word of God be the basis of our faith. No miracle from God

would endorse any message that is contrary to the teachings of his Word.

**7:17** God dramatically turned the water of the Nile into blood to show Pharaoh who he was. Do you sometimes wish for miraculous signs so you can be sure about God? God has given you the miracle of eternal life through your faith in him, something Pharaoh never obtained. This is a quiet miracle, and though less evident right now, just as extraordinary as water turned to blood. The desire for spectacular signs may cause us to ignore the more subtle miracles God is working every day.

**7:20** Egypt was a large country, but most of the population lived along the banks of the Nile River. This 3,000-mile waterway was truly a river of life for the Egyptians. It made life possible in a land that was mostly desert by providing water for drinking, farming, bathing, and fishing. Egyptian society was a ribbon of civilization lining the banks of this life source, rarely reaching very far into the surrounding desert. Without the Nile's water, Egypt could not have existed. Imagine Pharaoh's dismay when Moses turned this sacred river to blood!

**7:22**
Exod 8:7

22But again the magicians of Egypt used their magic, and they, too, turned water into blood. So Pharaoh's heart remained hard. He refused to listen to Moses and Aaron, just as the LORD had predicted. 23Pharaoh returned to his palace and put the whole thing out of his mind. 24Then all the Egyptians dug along the riverbank to find drinking water, for they couldn't drink the water from the Nile.

25Seven days passed from the time the LORD struck the Nile.

### A Plague of Frogs

**8:1**
Exod 5:1
**8:2**
Ps 105:30

**8** 1*Then the LORD said to Moses, "Go back to Pharaoh and announce to him, 'This is what the LORD says: Let my people go, so they can worship me. 2If you refuse to let them go, I will send a plague of frogs across your entire land. 3The Nile River will swarm with frogs. They will come up out of the river and into your palace, even into your bedroom and onto your bed! They will enter the houses of your officials and your people. They will even jump into your ovens and your kneading bowls. 4Frogs will jump on you, your people, and all your officials.'"

**8:5**
Exod 7:9-20
**8:6**
Pss 78:45; 105:30
**8:7**
Exod 7:11

5*Then the LORD said to Moses, "Tell Aaron, 'Raise the staff in your hand over all the rivers, canals, and ponds of Egypt, and bring up frogs over all the land.'" 6So Aaron raised his hand over the waters of Egypt, and frogs came up and covered the whole land! 7But the magicians were able to do the same thing with their magic. They, too, caused frogs to come up on the land of Egypt.

**8:8**
Exod 9:28; 10:10

8Then Pharaoh summoned Moses and Aaron and begged, "Plead with the LORD to take the frogs away from me and my people. I will let your people go, so they can offer sacrifices to the LORD."

9"You set the time!" Moses replied. "Tell me when you want me to pray for you, your officials, and your people. Then you and your houses will be rid of the frogs. They will remain only in the Nile River."

**8:10**
Exod 9:14; 15:11
Deut 4:35
Isa 46:9

10"Do it tomorrow," Pharaoh said.

"All right," Moses replied, "it will be as you have said. Then you will know that there is no one like the LORD our God. 11The frogs will leave you and your houses, your officials, and your people. They will remain only in the Nile River."

**8:12**
Exod 8:30; 9:33;
10:18

12So Moses and Aaron left Pharaoh's palace, and Moses cried out to the LORD about the frogs he had inflicted on Pharaoh. 13And the LORD did just what Moses had predicted. The frogs in the houses, the courtyards, and the fields all died. 14The Egyptians piled them into great heaps, and a terrible stench filled the land. 15But when Pharaoh saw that relief had come, he became stubborn.* He refused to listen to Moses and Aaron, just as the LORD had predicted.

**8:15**
Exod 7:14
Eccl 8:11

### A Plague of Gnats

**8:16**
Exod 4:2
**8:17**
Ps 105:31

16So the LORD said to Moses, "Tell Aaron, 'Raise your staff and strike the ground. The dust will turn into swarms of gnats throughout the land of Egypt.'" 17So Moses and Aaron did just as the LORD had commanded them. When Aaron raised his hand and struck the ground with his staff, gnats infested the entire land, covering the Egyptians and their animals. All the dust in the land of Egypt turned into gnats. 18Pharaoh's magicians tried to do the same thing with their secret arts, but this time they failed. And the gnats covered everyone, people and animals alike.

**8:18**
Exod 7:11; 9:11

**8:19**
Exod 7:5
1 Sam 6:9

19"This is the finger of God!" the magicians exclaimed to Pharaoh. But Pharaoh's heart remained hard. He wouldn't listen to them, just as the LORD had predicted.

**8:1** Verses 8:1-4 are numbered 7:26-29 in Hebrew text.   **8:5** Verses 8:5-32 are numbered 8:1-28 in Hebrew text.
**8:15** Hebrew *made his heart heavy;* also in 8:32.

---

**8:3ff** Moses predicted that every house in Egypt would be infested with frogs. The poor of Egypt lived in small, mud-brick houses of one or two rooms with palm-trunk roofs. The homes of the rich, however, were often two or three stories high, surrounded by landscaped gardens and enclosed by a high wall. Servants lived and worked on the first floor while the family occupied the upper floors. Thus, if the frogs got into the royal bedrooms, they had infiltrated even the upper floors. No place in Egypt would be safe from them.

**8:15** After repeated warnings, Pharaoh still refused to obey God. He hardened his heart every time there was a break in the plagues. His stubborn disobedience brought suffering upon

himself and his entire country. While persistence is good, stubbornness is usually self-centered. Stubbornness toward God amounts to rebellion against him. Rebellion will not only bring you grief, but it also may affect those who stand with you.

**8:19** Some people think, "If only I could see a miracle, I could believe in God." God gave Pharaoh just such an opportunity. When gnats infested Egypt, even the magicians agreed that this was God's work ("the finger of God")—but still Pharaoh refused to believe. He was stubborn, and stubbornness can blind a person to the truth. When you rid yourself of stubbornness, you may be surprised by abundant evidence of God's work in your life.

*A Plague of Flies*

20Then the LORD told Moses, "Get up early in the morning and stand in Pharaoh's way as he goes down to the river. Say to him, 'This is what the LORD says: Let my people go, so they can worship me. 21If you refuse, then I will send swarms of flies on you, your officials, your people, and all the houses. The Egyptian homes will be filled with flies, and the ground will be covered with them. 22But this time I will spare the region of Goshen, where my people live. No flies will be found there. Then you will know that I am the LORD and that I am present even in the heart of your land. 23I will make a clear distinction between* my people and your people. This miraculous sign will happen tomorrow.'"

24And the LORD did just as he had said. A thick swarm of flies filled Pharaoh's palace and the houses of his officials. The whole land of Egypt was thrown into chaos by the flies.

25Pharaoh called for Moses and Aaron. "All right! Go ahead and offer sacrifices to your God," he said. "But do it here in this land."

26But Moses replied, "That wouldn't be right. The Egyptians detest the sacrifices that we offer to the LORD our God. Look, if we offer our sacrifices here where the Egyptians can see us, they will stone us. 27We must take a three-day trip into the wilderness to offer sacrifices to the LORD our God, just as he has commanded us."

28"All right, go ahead," Pharaoh replied. "I will let you go into the wilderness to offer sacrifices to the LORD your God. But don't go too far away. Now hurry and pray for me."

29Moses answered, "As soon as I leave you, I will pray to the LORD, and tomorrow the swarms of flies will disappear from you and your officials and all your people. But I am warning you, Pharaoh, don't lie to us again and refuse to let the people go to sacrifice to the LORD."

30So Moses left Pharaoh's palace and pleaded with the LORD to remove all the flies. 31And the LORD did as Moses asked and caused the swarms of flies to disappear from Pharaoh, his officials, and his people. Not a single fly remained. 32But Pharaoh again became stubborn and refused to let the people go.

*A Plague against Livestock*

**9** "Go back to Pharaoh," the LORD commanded Moses. "Tell him, 'This is what the LORD, the God of the Hebrews, says: Let my people go, so they can worship me. 2If you continue to hold them and refuse to let them go, 3the hand of the LORD will strike all your livestock—your horses, donkeys, camels, cattle, sheep, and goats—with a deadly plague. 4But the LORD will again make a distinction between the livestock of the Israelites and that of the Egyptians. Not a single one of Israel's animals will die! 5The LORD has already set the time for the plague to begin. He has declared that he will strike the land tomorrow.'"

6And the LORD did just as he had said. The next morning all the livestock of the Egyptians died, but the Israelites didn't lose a single animal. 7Pharaoh sent his officials to investigate, and they discovered that the Israelites had not lost a single animal! But even so, Pharaoh's heart remained stubborn,* and he still refused to let the people go.

*A Plague of Festering Boils*

8Then the LORD said to Moses and Aaron, "Take handfuls of soot from a brick kiln, and have Moses toss it into the air while Pharaoh watches. 9The ashes will spread like fine dust over the whole land of Egypt, causing festering boils to break out on people and animals throughout the land."

10So they took soot from a brick kiln and went and stood before Pharaoh. As Pharaoh watched, Moses threw the soot into the air, and boils broke out on people and animals alike. 11Even the magicians were unable to stand before Moses, because the boils had bro-

**8:20** Exod 7:15
**8:22** Exod 9:4; 10:23
**8:24** Pss 78:45; 105:31
**8:25** Exod 8:8; 10:8
**8:27** Exod 3:18
**8:28** Exod 8:8
**8:30** Exod 8:12
**8:32** Exod 8:8, 15
**9:1** Exod 8:1; 10:3
**9:3** Exod 7:4
**9:4** Exod 8:23; 9:26
**9:7** Exod 7:14; 8:32
**9:9** Lev 13:18; Rev 16:2
**9:11** Exod 8:18

**8:23** As in Greek and Latin versions; Hebrew reads *I will set redemption between.*   **9:7** Hebrew *heavy.*

**8:25-29** Pharaoh wanted a compromise. He would allow the Hebrews to sacrifice, but only if they would do it nearby. God's requirement, however, was firm: The Hebrews had to leave Egypt. Sometimes people urge believers to compromise and give only partial obedience to God's commands. But commitment and obedience to God cannot be negotiated. When it comes to obeying God, half measures won't do.

**8:26** The Israelites would be sacrificing animals that the Egyptians regarded as sacred, and this would be offensive to them. Moses was concerned about a violent reaction to sacrificing these animals near the Egyptians.

**9:1** This was the fifth time God sent Moses back to Pharaoh with the demand "Let my people go." By this time, Moses may have been tired and discouraged, but he continued to obey. Is there a difficult conflict you must face again and again? Don't give up when you know what is right to do. As Moses discovered, persistence is rewarded.

**9:12**
Exod 4:21

ken out on them and all the Egyptians. [12]But the LORD hardened Pharaoh's heart, and just as the LORD had predicted to Moses, Pharaoh refused to listen.

*A Plague of Hail*

**9:13**
Exod 8:20

[13]Then the LORD said to Moses, "Get up early in the morning and stand before Pharaoh. Tell him, 'This is what the LORD, the God of the Hebrews, says: Let my people go, so they can wor-

**9:14**
Exod 8:10; 15:11

ship me. [14]If you don't, I will send more plagues on you* and your officials and your people. Then you will know that there is no one like me in all the earth. [15]By now I could have lifted my hand and struck you and your people with a plague to wipe you off the face of the earth.

**9:16**
Exod 14:4, 17
†Rom 9:17

[16]But I have spared you for a purpose—to show you my power* and to spread my fame throughout the earth. [17]But you still lord it over my people and refuse to let them go. [18]So

**9:18**
Exod 9:23, 24

tomorrow at this time I will send a hailstorm more devastating than any in all the history of Egypt. [19]Quick! Order your livestock and servants to come in from the fields to find shelter.

**9:20**
Prov 13:13

Any person or animal left outside will die when the hail falls.'"

**9:14** Hebrew *on your heart.*   **9:16** Greek version reads *to display my power in you;* compare Rom 9:17.

| THE PLAGUES ON EGYPT | Reference | Plague | What Happened | Result |
|---|---|---|---|---|
| | 7:14-24 | Blood | Fish die, the river smells, the people are without water | Pharaoh's magicians duplicate the miracle by "their magic," and Pharaoh is unmoved |
| | 8:1-15 | Frogs | Frogs come up from the water and completely cover the land | Again Pharaoh's magicians duplicate the miracle by sorcery, and Pharaoh is unmoved |
| | 8:16-19 | Gnats | All the dust of Egypt becomes a massive swarm of gnats | Magicians are unable to duplicate this; they say it is the "finger of God," but Pharaoh's heart remains hard |
| | 8:20-32 | Flies | Swarms of flies cover the land | Pharaoh promises to let the Hebrews go but then hardens his heart and refuses |
| | 9:1-7 | Livestock | All the Egyptian livestock die—but none of Israel's is even sick | Pharaoh still refuses to let the people go |
| | 9:8-12 | Boils | Horrible boils break out on everyone in Egypt | Magicians cannot respond because they are struck down with boils as well—Pharaoh refuses to listen |
| | 9:13-35 | Hail | Hailstorms kill all the slaves and animals left out or unprotected and strip or destroy almost every plant | Pharaoh admits his sin but then changes his mind and refuses to let Israel go |
| | 10:1-20 | Locusts | Locusts cover Egypt and eat everything left after the hail | Everyone advises Pharaoh to let the Hebrews go, but God hardens Pharaoh's heart and he refuses |
| | 10:21-29 | Darkness | Total darkness covers Egypt for three days so no one can even move—except the Hebrews, who have light as usual | Pharaoh again promises to let Israel go but again changes his mind |
| | 11:1–12:33 | Death of Firstborn | The firstborn of all the people and cattle of Egypt die—but Israel is spared | Pharaoh and the Egyptians urge Israel to leave quickly; after they are gone, Pharaoh again changes his mind and chases after them |

**9:12** God gave Pharaoh many opportunities to heed Moses' warnings. But finally God seemed to say, "All right, Pharaoh, have it your way," and Pharaoh's heart became permanently hardened. Did God intentionally harden Pharaoh's heart and overrule his free will? No, he simply confirmed that Pharaoh freely chose a life of resisting God. Similarly, after a lifetime of resisting God, you may find it impossible to turn to him. Don't wait until just the *right* time before turning to God. Do it now while you still have the chance. If you continually ignore God's voice, eventually you will be unable to hear it at all.

20Some of Pharaoh's officials were afraid because of what the LORD had said. They quickly brought their servants and livestock in from the fields. 21But those who paid no attention to the word of the LORD left theirs out in the open.

22Then the LORD said to Moses, "Lift your hand toward the sky so hail may fall on the people, the livestock, and all the plants throughout the land of Egypt."

23So Moses lifted his staff toward the sky, and the LORD sent thunder and hail, and lightning flashed toward the earth. The LORD sent a tremendous hailstorm against all the land of Egypt. 24Never in all the history of Egypt had there been a storm like that, with such devastating hail and continuous lightning. 25It left all of Egypt in ruins. The hail struck down everything in the open field—people, animals, and plants alike. Even the trees were destroyed. 26The only place without hail was the region of Goshen, where the people of Israel lived.

27Then Pharaoh quickly summoned Moses and Aaron. "This time I have sinned," he confessed. "The LORD is the righteous one, and my people and I are wrong. 28Please beg the LORD to end this terrifying thunder and hail. We've had enough. I will let you go; you don't need to stay any longer."

29"All right," Moses replied. "As soon as I leave the city, I will lift my hands and pray to the LORD. Then the thunder and hail will stop, and you will know that the earth belongs to the LORD. 30But I know that you and your officials still do not fear the LORD God."

31(All the flax and barley were ruined by the hail, because the barley had formed heads and the flax was budding. 32But the wheat and the emmer wheat were spared, because they had not yet sprouted from the ground.)

33So Moses left Pharaoh's court and went out of the city. When he lifted his hands to the LORD, the thunder and hail stopped, and the downpour ceased. 34But when Pharaoh saw that the rain, hail, and thunder had stopped, he and his officials sinned again, and Pharaoh again became stubborn.* 35Because his heart was hard, Pharaoh refused to let the people leave, just as the LORD had predicted through Moses.

## A Plague of Locusts

**10** Then the LORD said to Moses, "Return to Pharaoh and make your demands again. I have made him and his officials stubborn* so I can display my miraculous signs among them. 2I've also done it so you can tell your children and grandchildren about how I made a mockery of the Egyptians and about the signs I displayed among them—and so you will know that I am the LORD."

3So Moses and Aaron went to Pharaoh and said, "This is what the LORD, the God of the Hebrews, says: How long will you refuse to submit to me? Let my people go, so they can worship me. 4If you refuse, watch out! For tomorrow I will bring a swarm of locusts on your country. 5They will cover the land so that you won't be able to see the ground. They will devour what little is left of your crops after the hailstorm, including all the trees growing in the fields. 6They will overrun your palaces and the homes of your officials and all the houses in Egypt. Never in the history of Egypt have your ancestors seen a plague like this one!" And with that, Moses turned and left Pharaoh.

7Pharaoh's officials now came to Pharaoh and appealed to him. "How long will you let this man hold us hostage? Let the men go to worship the LORD their God! Don't you realize that Egypt lies in ruins?"

8So Moses and Aaron were brought back to Pharaoh. "All right," he told them, "go and worship the LORD your God. But who exactly will be going with you?"

9Moses replied, "We will all go—young and old, our sons and daughters, and our flocks and herds. We must all join together in celebrating a festival to the LORD."

9:34 Hebrew *made his heart heavy.*  10:1 Hebrew *have made his heart and his officials' hearts heavy.*

**9:22** Rev 16:21

**9:23** Gen 19:24 Josh 10:11 Ps 78:47 Rev 8:7; 16:21

**9:25** Ps 105:32

**9:26** Exod 8:22; 10:23

**9:27** 2 Chr 12:6 Ps 129:4

**9:28** Exod 8:8; 10:16-17

**9:29** Ps 24:1 1 Cor 10:26

**9:30** Exod 8:29

**9:35** Exod 4:21

**10:1** Exod 4:21; 7:14

**10:2** Exod 13:8, 14 Deut 4:9 Ps 44:1

**10:3** Exod 4:23

**10:4** Rev 9:3

**10:5** Exod 9:32 Joel 1:4; 2:25

**10:7** Exod 7:5

**10:8** Exod 8:8, 25

**10:9** Exod 12:37

---

**9:20, 21** If all the Egyptian livestock were killed in the earlier plague (9:6), how could the slaves of Pharaoh bring their livestock in from the fields? The answer is probably that the earlier plague killed all the animals in the fields (9:3) but not those in the shelters.

**9:27-34** After promising to let the Hebrews go, Pharaoh immediately broke his promise and brought even more trouble upon the land. His actions reveal that his repentance was not real. We do damage to ourselves and to others if we pretend to change but don't mean it.

**10:2** God told Moses that his miraculous experiences with Pharaoh should be retold to his descendants. What stories Moses had to tell! Living out one of the greatest dramas in biblical history, he witnessed events few people would ever see. It is important to tell our children about God's work in our past and to help them see what he is doing right now. What are the turning points in your life where God intervened? What is God doing for you now? Your stories will form the foundations of your children's belief in God.

10:10
Gen 50:8
Exod 12:31

10:11
Exod 10:28

10:12
Exod 7:19

10:13
Pss 78:46; 105:34

10:14
Joel 1:4, 7; 2:1-11

10:15
Exod 10:5
Ps 105:35

10:16
Exod 8:8; 9:27

10:17
Exod 8:8, 29
1 Sam 15:25

10:18
Exod 8:30

10:20
Exod 4:21; 11:10

10:21
Deut 28:29

10:22
Ps 105:28

10:23
Exod 8:22

10:24
Exod 8:8, 10

10:26
Exod 10:9

10:27
Exod 4:21; 14:4

10:28
Exod 10:11

10:29
Heb 11:27

11:1
Exod 12:31, 33, 39

11:2
Exod 3:22;
12:35-36

11:3
Exod 3:21; 12:36
Deut 34:10-12

11:4
Exod 12:29

11:5
Exod 12:12, 29
Pss 78:51; 105:36;
135:8; 136:10

10Pharaoh retorted, "The Lord will certainly need to be with you if I let you take your little ones! I can see through your evil plan. 11Never! Only the men may go and worship the Lord, since that is what you requested." And Pharaoh threw them out of the palace.

12Then the Lord said to Moses, "Raise your hand over the land of Egypt to bring on the locusts. Let them cover the land and devour every plant that survived the hailstorm."

13So Moses raised his staff over Egypt, and the Lord caused an east wind to blow over the land all that day and through the night. When morning arrived, the east wind had brought the locusts. 14And the locusts swarmed over the whole land of Egypt, settling in dense swarms from one end of the country to the other. It was the worst locust plague in Egyptian history, and there has never been another one like it. 15For the locusts covered the whole country and darkened the land. They devoured every plant in the fields and all the fruit on the trees that had survived the hailstorm. Not a single leaf was left on the trees and plants throughout the land of Egypt.

16Pharaoh quickly summoned Moses and Aaron. "I have sinned against the Lord your God and against you," he confessed. 17"Forgive my sin, just this once, and plead with the Lord your God to take away this death from me."

18So Moses left Pharaoh's court and pleaded with the Lord. 19The Lord responded by shifting the wind, and the strong west wind blew the locusts into the Red Sea.* Not a single locust remained in all the land of Egypt. 20But the Lord hardened Pharaoh's heart again, so he refused to let the people go.

### A Plague of Darkness

21Then the Lord said to Moses, "Lift your hand toward heaven, and the land of Egypt will be covered with a darkness so thick you can feel it." 22So Moses lifted his hand to the sky, and a deep darkness covered the entire land of Egypt for three days. 23During all that time the people could not see each other, and no one moved. But there was light as usual where the people of Israel lived.

24Finally, Pharaoh called for Moses. "Go and worship the Lord," he said. "But leave your flocks and herds here. You may even take your little ones with you."

25"No," Moses said, "you must provide us with animals for sacrifices and burnt offerings to the Lord our God. 26All our livestock must go with us, too; not a hoof can be left behind. We must choose our sacrifices for the Lord our God from among these animals. And we won't know how we are to worship the Lord until we get there."

27But the Lord hardened Pharaoh's heart once more, and he would not let them go. 28"Get out of here!" Pharaoh shouted at Moses. "I'm warning you. Never come back to see me again! The day you see my face, you will die!"

29"Very well," Moses replied. "I will never see your face again."

### Death for Egypt's Firstborn

**11** Then the Lord said to Moses, "I will strike Pharaoh and the land of Egypt with one more blow. After that, Pharaoh will let you leave this country. In fact, he will be so eager to get rid of you that he will force you all to leave. 2Tell all the Israelite men and women to ask their Egyptian neighbors for articles of silver and gold." 3(Now the Lord had caused the Egyptians to look favorably on the people of Israel. And Moses was considered a very great man in the land of Egypt, respected by Pharaoh's officials and the Egyptian people alike.)

4Moses had announced to Pharaoh, "This is what the Lord says: At midnight tonight I will pass through the heart of Egypt. 5All the firstborn sons will die in every family in Egypt, from the oldest son of Pharaoh, who sits on his throne, to the oldest son of his lowliest servant girl

10:19 Hebrew *sea of reeds.*

---

**10:22** As each gloomy plague descended upon the land, the Egyptian people realized how powerless their own gods were to stop it. Hapi, the god of the Nile River, could not prevent the waters from turning to blood (7:20). Hathor, the crafty cow-goddess, was helpless as Egyptian livestock died in droves (9:6). Amon-Re, the sun-god and chief of the Egyptian gods, could not stop an eerie darkness from covering the land for three full days (10:21, 22). The Egyptian gods were (1) not personal, centering around images like the sun or the river; (2) numerous; (3) not exclusive (any and all could be worshiped). By contrast, the God of the Hebrews was (1) a living personal Being, (2) the only true God, and (3) the only God who should be worshiped. God was proving to both the Hebrews and the Egyptians that he alone is the living and all-powerful God.

**10:27, 28** Why was Pharaoh so reluctant to let the people go? The Hebrews were Egypt's free labor—the builders of their great cities. As Egypt's leader, Pharaoh would not easily let such a great resource go.

who grinds the flour. Even the firstborn of all the livestock will die. ⁶Then a loud wail will rise throughout the land of Egypt, a wail like no one has heard before or will ever hear again. ⁷But among the Israelites it will be so peaceful that not even a dog will bark. Then you will know that the LORD makes a distinction between the Egyptians and the Israelites. ⁸All the officials of Egypt will run to me and fall to the ground before me. 'Please leave!' they will beg. 'Hurry! And take all your followers with you.' Only then will I go!" Then, burning with anger, Moses left Pharaoh.

⁹Now the LORD had told Moses earlier, "Pharaoh will not listen to you, but then I will do even more mighty miracles in the land of Egypt." ¹⁰Moses and Aaron performed these miracles in Pharaoh's presence, but the LORD hardened Pharaoh's heart, and he wouldn't let the Israelites leave the country.

## 5. The Passover

**12** While the Israelites were still in the land of Egypt, the LORD gave the following instructions to Moses and Aaron: ²"From now on, this month will be the first month of the year for you. ³Announce to the whole community of Israel that on the tenth day of this month each family must choose a lamb or a young goat for a sacrifice, one animal for each household. ⁴If a family is too small to eat a whole animal, let them share with another family in the neighborhood. Divide the animal according to the size of each family and how much they can eat. ⁵The animal you select must be a one-year-old male, either a sheep or a goat, with no defects.

⁶"Take special care of this chosen animal until the evening of the fourteenth day of this first month. Then the whole assembly of the community of Israel must slaughter their lamb or young goat at twilight. ⁷They are to take some of the blood and smear it on the sides and top of the doorframes of the houses where they eat the animal. ⁸That same night they must roast the meat over a fire and eat it along with bitter salad greens and bread made without yeast. ⁹Do not eat any of the meat raw or boiled in water. The whole animal—including the head, legs, and internal organs—must be roasted over a fire. ¹⁰Do not leave any of it until the next morning. Burn whatever is not eaten before morning.

¹¹"These are your instructions for eating this meal: Be fully dressed,* wear your sandals,

**12:11** Hebrew *Bind up your loins.*

**11:6**
Exod 12:30
Amos 5:17

**11:7**
Exod 8:22

**11:8**
Exod 12:31-33
Heb 11:27

**11:9**
Exod 7:3-4

**11:10**
Exod 4:21
Rom 2:5; 9:17

**12:2**
Exod 34:18
Deut 16:1

**12:3**
Mark 14:12
1 Cor 5:7

**12:6**
Lev 23:5
Num 9:3
Deut 16:4, 6

**12:7**
Exod 12:22

**12:8**
Exod 34:25
Num 9:11-12
Deut 16:7

**12:10**
Exod 23:18; 34:25

**12:11**
Num 28:16

---

**11:7** Moses told Pharaoh that God made a distinction between Egypt and Israel. At this time the distinction was very clear in God's mind: He knew the Hebrews would become his chosen people. The distinction was taking shape in Moses' mind also. But the Hebrews still saw the distinction only in terms of slave and free. Later, when they were in the wilderness, God would teach them the laws, principles, and values that would make them distinct as his people. Remember that God sees us in terms of what we will become and not just what we are right now.

**11:9, 10** You may wonder how Pharaoh could be so foolish as to see God's miraculous power and still not listen to Moses. But Pharaoh had his mind made up long before the plagues began. He couldn't believe that someone was greater than he. This stubborn unbelief led to a heart so hard that even a major catastrophe couldn't soften it. Finally, it took the greatest of all calamities, the loss of his son, to force him to recognize God's authority. But even then he wanted God to leave, not to rule his country. We must not wait for great calamities to drive us to God but must open our hearts and minds to his direction now.

**11:10** Did God really harden Pharaoh's heart and force him to do wrong? Before the 10 plagues began, Moses and Aaron announced what God would do if Pharaoh didn't let the people go. But their message only made Pharaoh stubborn—he was hardening his own heart. In so doing, he defied both God and his messengers. Through the first six plagues, Pharaoh's heart grew even more stubborn. After the sixth plague, God passed judgment. Sooner or later, evil people will be punished for their sins. When it became evident that Pharaoh wouldn't change, God confirmed Pharaoh's prideful decision and set the painful consequences of his actions in motion. God didn't force Pharaoh to reject him; rather, he gave him every opportunity to change his

mind. In Ezekiel 33:11, God says, "I take no pleasure in the death of wicked people."

**12:1-3** Certain holidays were instituted by God himself. Passover was a holiday designed to celebrate Israel's deliverance from Egypt and to remind the people of what God had done. Holidays can be important today, too, as annual reminders of what God has done for us. Develop traditions in your family to highlight the religious significance of certain holidays. These serve as reminders to the older people and learning experiences for the younger ones.

**12:3ff** For the Israelites to be spared from the plague of death, a lamb with no defects had to be killed and its blood placed on the doorframes of each home. What was the significance of the lamb? In killing the lamb, the Israelites shed innocent blood. The lamb was a sacrifice, a substitute for the person who would have died in the plague. From this point on, the Hebrew people would clearly understand that for them to be spared from death, an innocent life had to be sacrificed in their place.

**12:6-11** The festival of Passover was to be an annual holiday in honor of the night when the Lord "passed over" the homes of the Israelites. The Hebrews followed God's instructions by smearing the blood of a lamb on the doorframes of their homes. That night the firstborn son of every family that did not have blood on the doorframes was killed. The lamb had to be killed in order to get the blood that would protect them. (This foreshadowed the blood of Christ, the Lamb of God, who gave his blood for the sins of all people.) Inside their homes, the Israelites ate a meal of roast lamb, bitter herbs, and bread made without yeast. Unleavened bread could be made quickly because the dough did not have to rise. Thus, they could leave at any time. Bitter herbs signified the bitterness of slavery.

**12:11** Eating the Passover feast while dressed for travel was a sign of the Hebrews' faith. Although they were not yet free, they

**12:12**
Exod 11:4-5
Num 33:4

**12:13**
Heb 11:28

and carry your walking stick in your hand. Eat the meal with urgency, for this is the LORD's Passover. 12On that night I will pass through the land of Egypt and strike down every firstborn son and firstborn male animal in the land of Egypt. I will execute judgment against all the gods of Egypt, for I am the LORD! 13But the blood on your doorposts will serve as a sign, marking the houses where you are staying. When I see the blood, I will pass over you. This plague of death will not touch you when I strike the land of Egypt.

**12:14-20**
//Lev 23:4-8
//Num 28:16-25
//Deut 16:1-8

**12:15**
Exod 23:15; 34:18
Lev 23:5-6
Deut 16:3

**12:16**
Lev 23:7-8

**12:17**
Exod 13:3

14"This is a day to remember. Each year, from generation to generation, you must celebrate it as a special festival to the LORD. This is a law for all time. 15For seven days the bread you eat must be made without yeast. On the first day of the festival, remove every trace of yeast from your homes. Anyone who eats bread made with yeast during the seven days of the festival will be cut off from the community of Israel. 16On the first day of the festival and again on the seventh day, all the people must observe an official day for holy assembly. No work of any kind may be done on these days except in the preparation of food.

**12:18**
Lev 23:5-8
Num 28:16-25

**12:19**
Exod 12:15

17"Celebrate this Festival of Unleavened Bread, for it will remind you that I brought your forces out of the land of Egypt on this very day. This festival will be a permanent law for you; celebrate this day from generation to generation. 18The bread you eat must be made without yeast from the evening of the fourteenth day of the first month until the evening of the twenty-first day of that month. 19During those seven days, there must be no trace of yeast in your homes. Anyone who eats anything made with yeast during this week will be cut off from the community of Israel. These regulations apply both to the foreigners living among

---

**THE HEBREW CALENDAR**

A Hebrew month began in the middle of a month on our calendar today. Crops are planted in November and December and harvested in March and April.

| Month | Today's Calendar | Bible Reference | Israel's Holidays |
|---|---|---|---|
| 1 Abib (Nisan) | March–April | Exodus 13:4; 23:15; 34:18; Deuteronomy 16:1 | Passover (Leviticus 23:5) Unleavened Bread (Leviticus 23:6) First Harvest (Leviticus 23:10) |
| 2 Ziv (Iyyar) | April–May | 1 Kings 6:1, 37 | Second Passover (Numbers 9:10, 11) |
| 3 Sivan | May–June | | Harvest (Pentecost) (Leviticus 23:16) |
| 4 Tammuz | June–July | | |
| 5 Ab | July–August | | |
| 6 Elul | August–September | | |
| 7 Ethanaim (Tishri) | September–October | 1 Kings 8:2 | Trumpets (Numbers 29:1; Leviticus 23:24) Day of Atonement (Leviticus 23:27) Shelters (Leviticus 23:34) |
| 8 Bul (Marcheshvan) | October–November | 1 Kings 6:38 | |
| 9 Kislev | November–December | Nehemiah 1:1 | Dedication (Hanukkah) (John 10:22) |
| 10 Tebeth | December–January | | |
| 11 Shebat | January–February | | |
| 12 Adar | February–March | | Purim (Esther 9:24-32) |

---

were to prepare themselves, for God had said he would lead them out of Egypt. Their preparation was an act of faith. Preparing ourselves for the fulfillment of God's promises, however unlikely they may seem, demonstrates our faith.

**12:17, 23** Passover and the Festival of Unleavened Bread became an annual remembrance of how God delivered the Hebrews from Egypt. Each year the people would pause to remember the day when the death angel passed over their homes. They gave thanks to God for saving them from death

and bringing them out of a land of slavery and sin. Believers today have experienced a day of deliverance as well—the day we were delivered from spiritual death and slavery to sin. The Lord's Supper is our Passover remembrance of our new life and freedom from sin. The next time struggles and trials come, remember how God has delivered you in the past and focus on his promise of new life with him.

you and to the native-born Israelites. 20During those days you must not eat anything made with yeast. Wherever you live, eat only bread made without yeast."

21Then Moses called all the elders of Israel together and said to them, "Go, pick out a lamb or young goat for each of your families, and slaughter the Passover animal. 22Drain the blood into a basin. Then take a bundle of hyssop branches and dip it into the blood. Brush the hyssop across the top and sides of the doorframes of your houses. And no one may go out through the door until morning. 23For the LORD will pass through the land to strike down the Egyptians. But when he sees the blood on the top and sides of the doorframe, the LORD will pass over your home. He will not permit his death angel to enter your house and strike you down.

24"Remember, these instructions are a permanent law that you and your descendants must observe forever. 25When you enter the land the LORD has promised to give you, you will continue to observe this ceremony. 26Then your children will ask, 'What does this ceremony mean?' 27And you will reply, 'It is the Passover sacrifice to the LORD, for he passed over the houses of the Israelites in Egypt. And though he struck the Egyptians, he spared our families.' " When Moses had finished speaking, all the people bowed down to the ground and worshiped.

28So the people of Israel did just as the LORD had commanded through Moses and Aaron. 29And that night at midnight, the LORD struck down all the firstborn sons in the land of Egypt, from the firstborn son of Pharaoh, who sat on his throne, to the firstborn son of the prisoner in the dungeon. Even the firstborn of their livestock were killed. 30Pharaoh and all his officials and all the people of Egypt woke up during the night, and loud wailing was heard throughout the land of Egypt. There was not a single house where someone had not died.

## B. ISRAEL IN THE WILDERNESS (12:31—18:27)

As Egypt buried its dead, the Hebrew slaves left the country, a free people at last. Pharaoh made one last attempt to bring them back, but the people escaped when God miraculously parted the waters of the Red Sea. But on the other side, the people soon became dissatisfied and complained bitterly to Moses and Aaron about their trek through the wilderness. Through these experiences of the Hebrews, we learn that the Christian life is not always trouble-free. We still have struggles and often complain bitterly to God about conditions in our lives.

### 1. The Exodus

31Pharaoh sent for Moses and Aaron during the night. "Get out!" he ordered. "Leave my people—and take the rest of the Israelites with you! Go and worship the LORD as you have requested. 32Take your flocks and herds, as you said, and be gone. Go, but bless me as you leave." 33All the Egyptians urged the people of Israel to get out of the land as quickly as possible, for they thought, "We will all die!"

34The Israelites took their bread dough before yeast was added. They wrapped their kneading boards in their cloaks and carried them on their shoulders. 35And the people of Israel did as Moses had instructed; they asked the Egyptians for clothing and articles of silver and gold. 36The LORD caused the Egyptians to look favorably on the Israelites, and they gave the Israelites whatever they asked for. So they stripped the Egyptians of their wealth!

37That night the people of Israel left Rameses and started for Succoth. There were about

**12:21**
Mark 14:12-16
Heb 11:28

**12:22**
Lev 14:4, 6
Num 19:18
Ps 51:7
Heb 11:28

**12:23**
Exod 12:12
Isa 37:36

**12:24**
Exod 13:4-5, 10

**12:25**
Exod 3:17

**12:26**
Exod 10:2;
13:14-15

**12:27**
Exod 4:31

**12:29**
Exod 4:23; 11:4
Pss 78:51; 105:36

**12:30**
Exod 11:6

**12:31**
Exod 8:8, 25

**12:33**
Exod 10:7; 11:1

**12:35**
Exod 3:22

**12:36**
Exod 3:22

**12:37**
Exod 38:26
Num 1:46

---

**12:29, 30** Every firstborn child of the Egyptians died, but the Israelite children were spared because the blood of the lamb had been smeared on their doorframes. So begins the story of redemption, the central theme of the Bible.

*Redemption* means "to buy back" or "to save from captivity by paying a ransom." One way to buy back a slave was to offer an equivalent or superior slave in exchange. That is the way God chose to buy us back—he offered his Son in exchange for us.

In Old Testament times, God accepted symbolic offerings. Jesus had not yet been sacrificed, so God accepted the life of an animal in place of the life of the sinner. When Jesus came, he substituted his perfect life for our sinful lives, taking the penalty for sin that we deserve. Thus he redeemed us from the power of sin and restored us to God. Jesus' sacrifice made animal sacrifice no longer necessary.

We must recognize that if we want to be freed from the deadly consequences of our sins, a tremendous price must be paid. But

we don't have to pay it. Jesus Christ, our substitute, has already redeemed us by his death on the cross. Our part is to trust him and accept his gift of eternal life. Our sins have been paid for, and the way has been cleared for us to begin a relationship with God (Titus 2:14; Hebrews 9:13-15, 23-26).

**12:34** A kneading board was made of wood, bronze, or pottery and used for kneading dough. Bread was made by mixing water and flour with a small piece of leavened dough saved from the previous day's batch. Bread was the primary food in the Hebrews' diet, and thus it was vital to bring the board along. It could be easily carried on the shoulder.

**12:37, 38** The total number of people leaving Egypt is estimated to have been about two million. The "rabble of non-Israelites" may have been Egyptians and others who were drawn to the Hebrews by God's mighty works and who decided to leave Egypt with them.

**12:38**
Num 11:4

**12:39**
Exod 11:1

**12:40-41**
Gen 15:3, 16
Acts 7:6
Gal 3:17

**12:42**
Exod 3:10
Deut 16:1

**12:43**
Num 9:14

**12:44**
Gen 17:12-13
Lev 22:11

**12:46**
Num 9:12
John 19:33, 36

**12:48**
Num 9:13-14
Gal 3:28

**12:49**
Lev 24:22
Num 15:15-16

**12:50**
Exod 12:28

**13:2**
Exod 13:12-13;
22:29; 34:20
Lev 27:26
Num 3:13
Deut 15:19
†Luke 2:23

**13:3**
Exod 3:20; 6:1

**13:4**
Exod 12:2

**13:5**
Exod 3:8, 17;
12:25-26

**13:6**
Exod 12:15-20

**13:9**
Exod 12:14
Deut 6:8

**13:10**
Exod 12:24-25

**13:12**
Exod 13:2; 22:29
Num 3:13
†Luke 2:23

600,000 men,* plus all the women and children. 38A rabble of non-Israelites went with them, along with great flocks and herds of livestock. 39For bread they baked flat cakes from the dough without yeast they had brought from Egypt. It was made without yeast because the people were driven out of Egypt in such a hurry that they had no time to prepare the bread or other food.

40The people of Israel had lived in Egypt* for 430 years. 41In fact, it was on the last day of the 430th year that all the LORD's forces left the land. 42On this night the LORD kept his promise to bring his people out of the land of Egypt. So this night belongs to him, and it must be commemorated every year by all the Israelites, from generation to generation.

### Instructions for the Passover

43Then the LORD said to Moses and Aaron, "These are the instructions for the festival of Passover. No outsiders are allowed to eat the Passover meal. 44But any slave who has been purchased may eat it if he has been circumcised. 45Temporary residents and hired servants may not eat it. 46Each Passover lamb must be eaten in one house. Do not carry any of its meat outside, and do not break any of its bones. 47The whole community of Israel must celebrate this Passover festival.

48"If there are foreigners living among you who want to celebrate the LORD's Passover, let all their males be circumcised. Only then may they celebrate the Passover with you like any native-born Israelite. But no uncircumcised male may ever eat the Passover meal. 49This instruction applies to everyone, whether a native-born Israelite or a foreigner living among you."

50So all the people of Israel followed all the LORD's commands to Moses and Aaron. 51On that very day the LORD brought the people of Israel out of the land of Egypt like an army.

### Dedication of the Firstborn

**13** Then the LORD said to Moses, 2"Dedicate to me every firstborn among the Israelites. The first offspring to be born, of both humans and animals, belongs to me."

3So Moses said to the people, "This is a day to remember forever—the day you left Egypt, the place of your slavery. Today the LORD has brought you out by the power of his mighty hand. (Remember, eat no food containing yeast.) 4On this day in early spring, in the month of Abib,* you have been set free. 5You must celebrate this event in this month each year after the LORD brings you into the land of the Canaanites, Hittites, Amorites, Hivites, and Jebusites. (He swore to your ancestors that he would give you this land—a land flowing with milk and honey.) 6For seven days the bread you eat must be made without yeast. Then on the seventh day, celebrate a feast to the LORD. 7Eat bread without yeast during those seven days. In fact, there must be no yeast bread or any yeast at all found within the borders of your land during this time.

8"On the seventh day you must explain to your children, 'I am celebrating what the LORD did for me when I left Egypt.' 9This annual festival will be a visible sign to you, like a mark branded on your hand or your forehead. Let it remind you always to recite this teaching of the LORD: 'With a strong hand, the LORD rescued you from Egypt.'* 10So observe the decree of this festival at the appointed time each year.

11"This is what you must do when the LORD fulfills the promise he swore to you and to your ancestors. When he gives you the land where the Canaanites now live, 12you must

**12:37** Or *fighting men;* Hebrew reads *men on foot.* **12:40** Samaritan Pentateuch reads *in Canaan and Egypt;* Greek version reads *in Egypt and Canaan.* **13:4** Hebrew *On this day in the month of Abib.* This first month of the ancient Hebrew lunar calendar usually occurs within the months of March and April. **13:9** Or *Let it remind you always to keep the instructions of the LORD on the tip of your tongue, because with a strong hand, the LORD rescued you from Egypt.*

---

**13:2** *Dedicate* means to sacrifice or to consider something as belonging to God. This dedication practice described in 13:11-16 was to remind the people of their deliverance through God.

**13:6-9** The Festival of Unleavened Bread marked the Hebrews as a unique people—as though they were branded on their hands and foreheads. What do you do that marks you as a follower of God? The way you raise your children, demonstrate love for others, show concern for the poor, and live in devotion to God—these actions will leave visible marks for all to see. While national groups are marked by customs and traditions, Christians are marked by loving one another (John 13:34, 35).

**13:12-14** What did it mean to "buy back every firstborn son"?

During the night the Israelites escaped from Egypt, God spared the oldest son of every house marked with blood on the doorframe. Because God saved the lives of the firstborn, he had a rightful claim to them. But God commanded the Israelites to buy their sons back from him. This ritual served three main purposes: (1) It was a reminder to the people of how God had spared their sons from death and freed them all from slavery; (2) it showed God's high respect for human life in contrast to the pagan gods who, their worshipers believed, demanded human sacrifice; (3) it looked forward to the day when Jesus Christ would buy us back by paying the price for our sin once and for all.

present all firstborn sons and firstborn male animals to the Lord, for they belong to him. ¹³A firstborn donkey may be bought back from the Lord by presenting a lamb or young goat in its place. But if you do not buy it back, you must break its neck. However, you must buy back every firstborn son.

13:13
Exod 34:20
Num 18:15-16

¹⁴"And in the future, your children will ask you, 'What does all this mean?' Then you will tell them, 'With the power of his mighty hand, the Lord brought us out of Egypt, the place of our slavery. ¹⁵Pharaoh stubbornly refused to let us go, so the Lord killed all the firstborn males throughout the land of Egypt, both people and animals. That is why I now sacrifice all the firstborn males to the Lord—except that the firstborn sons are always bought back.' ¹⁶This ceremony will be like a mark branded on your hand or your forehead. It is a reminder that the power of the Lord's mighty hand brought us out of Egypt."

13:14
Exod 12:26-27
Deut 6:20-23

13:15
Exod 12:29

13:16
Exod 13:9
Deut 6:8

## 2. Crossing the sea
### Israel's Wilderness Detour

¹⁷When Pharaoh finally let the people go, God did not lead them along the main road that runs through Philistine territory, even though that was the shortest route to the Promised Land. God said, "If the people are faced with a battle, they might change their minds and return to Egypt." ¹⁸So God led them in a roundabout way through the wilderness toward the Red Sea.* Thus the Israelites left Egypt like an army ready for battle.*

13:17
Exod 14:11
Num 14:1-4
Deut 17:16

¹⁹Moses took the bones of Joseph with him, for Joseph had made the sons of Israel swear to do this. He said, "God will certainly come to help you. When he does, you must take my bones with you from this place."

13:19
Gen 50:24-25
Josh 24:32
Acts 7:16

²⁰The Israelites left Succoth and camped at Etham on the edge of the wilderness. ²¹The Lord went ahead of them. He guided them during the day with a pillar of cloud, and he provided light at night with a pillar of fire. This allowed them to travel by day or by night. ²²And the Lord did not remove the pillar of cloud or pillar of fire from its place in front of the people.

13:20
Exod 12:37
Num 33:6-8

13:21
Exod 14:19, 24
Ps 105:39
1 Cor 10:1

**14** Then the Lord gave these instructions to Moses: ²"Order the Israelites to turn back and camp by Pi-hahiroth between Migdol and the sea. Camp there along the shore, across from Baal-zephon. ³Then Pharaoh will think, 'The Israelites are confused. They are

14:2
Num 33:7-8

**13:18a** Hebrew *sea of reeds.*    **13:18b** Greek version reads *left Egypt in the fifth generation.*

---

**13:17, 18** God doesn't always work in the way that seems best to us. Instead of guiding the Israelites along the direct route from Egypt to the Promised Land, he took them by a longer route to avoid fighting with the Philistines. If God does not lead you along the shortest path to your goal, don't complain or resist. Follow him willingly and trust him to lead you safely around unseen

**THE EXODUS**
The Israelites left Succoth and camped first at Etham before going toward Baal-zephon to camp by the sea (14:2). God miraculously brought them across the sea, into the Desert of Shur (15:22). After stopping at the oasis of Elim, the people moved into the Wilderness of Sin (16:1).

obstacles. He can see the end of your journey from the beginning, and he knows the safest and best route.

**13:17, 18** When did the Hebrews leave Egypt? There are two theories. The *early* theory says the Exodus occurred around 1446–1445 B.C. The *late* theory suggests the Exodus happened between 1300 and 1200 B.C. Those who hold to the earlier date point to 1 Kings 6:1, where the Bible clearly states that Solomon began building the Temple 480 years after the Hebrews left Egypt. Since almost all scholars agree that Solomon began building the Temple in 966, this puts the Exodus in the year 1446. But those who hold to the later date suggest that the 480 years cannot be taken literally. They point to Exodus 1:11, which says that the Hebrews built the store cities of Pithom and Rameses, named after Pharaoh Rameses II, who reigned around 1290 B.C. Regardless of which date is correct, the fact is that God led the Hebrews out of Egypt, just as he had promised. This showed his great power and his great love for his people.

**13:21, 22** God gave the Hebrews a pillar of cloud and a pillar of fire so they would know day and night that God was with them on their journey to the Promised Land. What has God given us so that we can have the same assurance? The Bible—something the Israelites did not have. He also has given us the Holy Spirit to remind us of what the Bible says and to guide us each day (John 14:26). Look to God's Word for reassurance of his presence. As the Hebrews looked to the pillars of cloud and fire, we can look to God's Word day and night to know he is with us, helping us on our journey.

**13:21, 22** The pillars of fire and cloud were examples of *theophany*—God appearing in a physical form. In this form, God lighted Israel's path, protected them from their enemies,

**14:4**
Exod 4:21; 7:5
Rom 9:17, 22-23

trapped in the wilderness!' 4And once again I will harden Pharaoh's heart, and he will chase after you.* I have planned this in order to display my glory through Pharaoh and his whole army. After this the Egyptians will know that I am the LORD!" So the Israelites camped there as they were told.

### The Egyptians Pursue Israel

**14:5**
Ps 105:25
**14:7**
Exod 15:4

5When word reached the king of Egypt that the Israelites had fled, Pharaoh and his officials changed their minds. "What have we done, letting all those Israelite slaves get away?" they asked. 6So Pharaoh harnessed his chariot and called up his troops. 7He took with him

**14:4** Hebrew *after them.*

---

**MOSES**

Some people can't stay out of trouble. When conflict breaks out, they always manage to be nearby. Reaction is their favorite action. This was Moses. He seemed drawn to what needed to be righted. Throughout his life, he was at his finest and his worst responding to the conflicts around him. Even the burning bush experience was an illustration of his character. Having spotted the fire and seen that the bush did not burn, he had to investigate. Whether jumping into a fight to defend a Hebrew slave or trying to referee a struggle between two kinsmen, when Moses saw conflict, he reacted.

Over the years, however, an amazing thing happened to Moses' character. He didn't stop reacting, but rather learned to react correctly. The kaleidoscopic action of each day of leading two million people in the wilderness was more than enough challenge for Moses' reacting ability. Much of the time he served as a buffer between God and the people. At one moment he had to respond to God's anger at the people's stubbornness and forgetfulness. At another moment he had to react to the people's bickering and complaining. At still another moment he had to react to their unjustified attacks on his character.

Leadership often involves reaction. If we want to react with instincts consistent with God's will, we must develop habits of obedience to God. Consistent obedience to God is best developed in times of less stress. Then when stress comes, our natural reaction will be to obey God.

In our age of lowering moral standards, we find it almost impossible to believe that God would punish Moses for the one time he outright disobeyed. What we fail to see, however, is that God did not reject Moses; Moses simply disqualified himself to enter the Promised Land. Personal greatness does not make a person immune to error or its consequences.

In Moses we see an outstanding personality shaped by God. But we must not misunderstand what God did. He did not change who or what Moses was; he did not give Moses new abilities and strengths. Instead, he took Moses' characteristics and molded them until they were suited to his purposes. Does knowing this make a difference in your understanding of God's purpose in your life? He is trying to take what he created in the first place and use it for its intended purposes. The next time you talk with God, don't ask, "What should I change into?" but "How should I use my own abilities and strengths to do your will?"

| | |
|---|---|
| **Strengths and accomplishments** | • Egyptian education; wilderness training<br>• Greatest Jewish leader; set the Exodus in motion<br>• Prophet and lawgiver; recorder of the Ten Commandments<br>• Author of the Pentateuch |
| **Weaknesses and mistakes** | • Failed to enter the Promised Land because of disobedience to God<br>• Did not always recognize and use the talents of others |
| **Lessons from his life** | • God prepares, then uses. His timetable is life-sized<br>• God does his greatest work through frail people |
| **Vital statistics** | • Where: Egypt, Midian, wilderness of Sinai<br>• Occupations: Prince, shepherd, leader of the Israelites<br>• Relatives: Sister: Miriam. Brother: Aaron. Wife: Zipporah. Sons: Gershom and Eliezer. |
| **Key verses** | "It was by faith that Moses, when he grew up, refused to be called the son of Pharaoh's daughter. He chose to share the oppression of God's people instead of enjoying the fleeting pleasures of sin" (Hebrews 11:24, 25). |

Moses' story is told in the books of Exodus through Deuteronomy. He is also mentioned in Acts 7:20–44; Hebrews 11:23–29.

---

provided reassurance, controlled their movements, and inspired the burning zeal that Israel should have for their God.

**14:6-9** Six hundred Egyptian war chariots were bearing down on the helpless Israelites, who were trapped between the mountains and the sea. The war chariots each carried two people—one to drive and one to fight. These chariots were made of a wood or leather cab placed over two wheels, and they were pulled by horses. These were the armored tanks of Bible times. But even their power was no match for God, who destroyed both the chariots and their soldiers.

600 of Egypt's best chariots, along with the rest of the chariots of Egypt, each with its commander. [8]The LORD hardened the heart of Pharaoh, the king of Egypt, so he chased after the people of Israel, who had left with fists raised in defiance. [9]The Egyptians chased after them with all the forces in Pharaoh's army—all his horses and chariots, his charioteers, and his troops. The Egyptians caught up with the people of Israel as they were camped beside the shore near Pi-hahiroth, across from Baal-zephon.

[10]As Pharaoh approached, the people of Israel looked up and panicked when they saw the Egyptians overtaking them. They cried out to the LORD, [11]and they said to Moses, "Why did you bring us out here to die in the wilderness? Weren't there enough graves for us in Egypt? What have you done to us? Why did you make us leave Egypt? [12]Didn't we tell you this would happen while we were still in Egypt? We said, 'Leave us alone! Let us be slaves to the Egyptians. It's better to be a slave in Egypt than a corpse in the wilderness!'"

[13]But Moses told the people, "Don't be afraid. Just stand still and watch the LORD rescue you today. The Egyptians you see today will never be seen again. [14]The LORD himself will fight for you. Just stay calm."

### Escape through the Red Sea

[15]Then the LORD said to Moses, "Why are you crying out to me? Tell the people to get moving! [16]Pick up your staff and raise your hand over the sea. Divide the water so the Israelites can walk through the middle of the sea on dry ground. [17]And I will harden the hearts of the Egyptians, and they will charge in after the Israelites. My great glory will be displayed through Pharaoh and his troops, his chariots, and his charioteers. [18]When my glory is displayed through them, all Egypt will see my glory and know that I am the LORD!"

[19]Then the angel of God, who had been leading the people of Israel, moved to the rear of the camp. The pillar of cloud also moved from the front and stood behind them. [20]The cloud settled between the Egyptian and Israelite camps. As darkness fell, the cloud turned to fire, lighting up the night. But the Egyptians and Israelites did not approach each other all night.

[21]Then Moses raised his hand over the sea, and the LORD opened up a path through the water with a strong east wind. The wind blew all that night, turning the seabed into dry land. [22]So the people of Israel walked through the middle of the sea on dry ground, with walls of water on each side!

[23]Then the Egyptians—all of Pharaoh's horses, chariots, and charioteers—chased them into the middle of the sea. [24]But just before dawn the LORD looked down on the Egyptian army from the pillar of fire and cloud, and he threw their forces into total confusion. [25]He twisted* their chariot wheels, making their chariots difficult to drive. "Let's get out of here—away from these Israelites!" the Egyptians shouted. "The LORD is fighting for them against Egypt!"

14:25 As in Greek version, Samaritan Pentateuch, and Syriac version; Hebrew reads *He removed*.

---

**14:8**
Num 33:3
Acts 13:17

**14:9**
Exod 14:2; 15:9
Josh 24:6

**14:10**
Josh 24:7
Neh 9:9

**14:11**
Exod 5:21; 15:24
Ps 106:7-8

**14:13**
Gen 15:1
Exod 14:30; 15:2

**14:14**
Exod 15:3
Deut 1:30; 3:22
Isa 30:15

**14:15**
Josh 7:10

**14:16**
Exod 4:17, 20
Num 20:8-9, 11

**14:18**
Exod 14:25

**14:19**
Exod 13:21-22

**14:21**
Pss 106:9; 114:3, 5
Isa 63:12-13

**14:22**
Exod 15:19
Neh 9:11
Pss 66:6; 78:13
Heb 11:29

**14:24**
Exod 13:21

---

**14:10, 11** Trapped against the sea, the Israelites faced the Egyptian army sweeping in for the kill. The Israelites thought they were doomed. After watching God's powerful hand deliver them from Egypt, their only response was fear, whining, and despair. Where was their trust in God? Israel had to learn from repeated experience that God was able to provide for them. God has preserved these examples in the Bible so that we can learn to trust him the first time. By focusing on God's faithfulness in the past, we can face crises with confidence rather than with fear and complaining.

**14:11, 12** This is the first instance of grumbling and complaining by the Israelites. Grumbling would become a major problem for the people on this journey. Their lack of faith in God is startling. Yet how often do we find ourselves doing the same thing—complaining over inconveniences or discomforts? The Israelites were about to learn some tough lessons. Had they trusted God, they would have been spared much grief.

**14:13, 14** The people were hostile and despairing, but Moses encouraged them to watch the wonderful way God would rescue them. Moses had a positive attitude! When it looked as if they were trapped, Moses called upon God to intervene. We may not be chased by an army, but we may still feel trapped. Instead of giving

in to despair, we should adopt Moses' attitude to "stand still and watch the LORD rescue" us.

**14:15** The Lord told Moses to stop praying and get moving! Prayer must have a vital place in our lives, but there is also a place for action. Sometimes we know what to do, but we pray for more guidance as an excuse to postpone doing it. If we know what we should do, then it is time to get moving.

**14:21** There was no apparent way of escape, but the Lord opened up a dry path through the sea. Sometimes we find ourselves caught in a problem and see no way out. Don't panic; God can open up a way.

**14:21, 22** Some scholars believe the Israelites did not cross the main body of the Red Sea but one of the shallow lakes or marshes north of it that dry up at certain times of the year, or perhaps it was a smaller branch of the Red Sea where the water would have been shallow enough to wade across. But the Bible clearly states that the Lord "opened up a path through the water with a strong east wind . . . turning the seabed into dry land" (14:21; see also Joshua 3:15, 16; and 2 Kings 2:13, 14). Also, the water was deep enough to cover the chariots (14:28). The God who created the earth and water performed a mighty miracle at exactly the right time to demonstrate his great power and love for his people.

14:26
Exod 14:16

14:27
Exod 15:1, 7
Deut 11:4
Heb 11:29

14:28
Exod 15:19
Neh 9:11
Pss 78:53; 106:11

14:29
Ps 66:6
Isa 11:15

14:30
Ps 106:8
Isa 63:8, 11

14:31
Exod 4:31; 19:9
Ps 106:12

15:1
Ps 106:12
Isa 12:5; 42:10-12
Jer 51:21
Rev 15:3

15:2
Exod 3:15-16
Deut 10:21
2 Sam 22:47
Ps 18:1
Isa 12:2

26When all the Israelites had reached the other side, the LORD said to Moses, "Raise your hand over the sea again. Then the waters will rush back and cover the Egyptians and their chariots and charioteers." 27So as the sun began to rise, Moses raised his hand over the sea, and the water rushed back into its usual place. The Egyptians tried to escape, but the LORD swept them into the sea. 28Then the waters returned and covered all the chariots and charioteers—the entire army of Pharaoh. Of all the Egyptians who had chased the Israelites into the sea, not a single one survived.

29But the people of Israel had walked through the middle of the sea on dry ground, as the water stood up like a wall on both sides. 30That is how the LORD rescued Israel from the hand of the Egyptians that day. And the Israelites saw the bodies of the Egyptians washed up on the seashore. 31When the people of Israel saw the mighty power that the LORD had unleashed against the Egyptians, they were filled with awe before him. They put their faith in the LORD and in his servant Moses.

### A Song of Deliverance

**15** Then Moses and the people of Israel sang this song to the LORD:

"I will sing to the LORD,
  for he has triumphed gloriously;
he has hurled both horse and rider
  into the sea.
2 The LORD is my strength and my song;
  he has given me victory.
This is my God, and I will praise him—
  my father's God, and I will exalt him!

---

| FAMOUS SONGS IN THE BIBLE | Where | Purpose of Song |
|---|---|---|
| | Exodus 15:1-21 | Moses' song of deliverance and praise after God led Israel out of Egypt and saved them by parting the Red Sea; Miriam joined in the singing, too |
| | Numbers 21:17 | Israel's song of praise to God for giving them water in the wilderness |
| | Deuteronomy 32:1-43 | Moses' song of Israel's history with thanksgiving and praise as the Hebrews were about to enter the Promised Land |
| | Judges 5:2-31 | Deborah and Barak's song of praise thanking God for Israel's victory over King Jabin's army at Mount Tabor |
| | 2 Samuel 22:2-51 | David's song of thanks and praise to God for rescuing him from Saul and his other enemies |
| | Song of Songs | Solomon's song of love celebrating the union of husband and wife |
| | Isaiah 26:1 | Isaiah's prophetic song about how the redeemed will sing in the new Jerusalem |
| | Ezra 3:11 | Israel's song of praise at the completion of the Temple's foundation |
| | Luke 1:46-55 | Mary's song of praise to God for the conception of Jesus |
| | Luke 1:68-79 | Zechariah's song of praise for the birth of his son |
| | Acts 16:25 | Paul and Silas sang hymns in prison |
| | Revelation 5:9, 10 | The "new song" of the 24 elders acclaiming Christ as worthy to break the seven seals of God's scroll |
| | Revelation 14:3 | The song of the 144,000 redeemed from the earth |
| | Revelation 15:3, 4 | The song of all the redeemed in praise of the Lamb who redeemed them |

---

**14:27, 28** No evidence of this great Exodus has been discovered in Egyptian historical records. This was because it was a common practice for Egyptian pharaohs not to record their defeats. They even went so far as to take existing records and delete the names of traitors and political adversaries. Pharaoh would have been especially anxious not to record that his great army was destroyed chasing a band of runaway slaves. Since either the Egyptians failed to record the Exodus or the record has not yet been found, it is impossible to place a precise date on the event.

**15:1ff** Music played an important part in Israel's worship and celebration. Singing was an expression of love and thanks, and it was a creative way to pass down oral traditions. Some say this song of Moses is the oldest recorded song in the world. It was a festive epic poem celebrating God's victory, lifting the hearts and voices of the people outward and upward. After having been delivered from great danger, they sang with joy! Psalms and hymns can be great ways to express relief, praise, and thanks when you have been through trouble.

3 The LORD is a warrior;
    Yahweh* is his name!

**15:3**
Exod 14:14
Pss 24:8; 83:18

4 Pharaoh's chariots and army
    he has hurled into the sea.
  The finest of Pharaoh's officers
    are drowned in the Red Sea.*

**15:4**
Exod 14:6-7, 17, 28

5 The deep waters gushed over them;
    they sank to the bottom like a stone.

**15:5**
Exod 14:28
Neh 9:11

6 "Your right hand, O LORD,
    is glorious in power.
  Your right hand, O LORD,
    smashes the enemy.

**15:6**
Exod 3:20
Ps 118:15-16

7 In the greatness of your majesty,
    you overthrow those who rise against you.
  You unleash your blazing fury;
    it consumes them like straw.

**15:7**
Exod 9:16; 14:24
Ps 78:49-50

8 At the blast of your breath,
    the waters piled up!
  The surging waters stood straight like a wall;
    in the heart of the sea the deep waters became hard.

**15:8**
Exod 14:22, 29
Ps 78:13

9 "The enemy boasted, 'I will chase them
    and catch up with them.
  I will plunder them
    and consume them.
  I will flash my sword;
    my powerful hand will destroy them.'

**15:9**
Exod 14:5-9

10 But you blew with your breath,
    and the sea covered them.
  They sank like lead
    in the mighty waters.

**15:10**
Exod 14:27-28

11 "Who is like you among the gods, O LORD—
    glorious in holiness,
  awesome in splendor,
    performing great wonders?

**15:11**
Exod 8:10
Deut 3:24
1 Sam 2:2
2 Sam 7:22
Pss 22:23; 72:18
Isa 6:3
Rev 4:8

12 You raised your right hand,
    and the earth swallowed our enemies.

**15:12**
Exod 15:6

13 "With your unfailing love you lead
    the people you have redeemed.
  In your might, you guide them
    to your sacred home.

**15:13**
Neh 9:12
Ps 77:15, 20

14 The peoples hear and tremble;
    anguish grips those who live in Philistia.

**15:14**
Deut 2:25
Hab 3:7

15 The leaders of Edom are terrified;
    the nobles of Moab tremble.
  All who live in Canaan melt away;

**15:15**
Num 22:3
Deut 2:4
Josh 2:11; 5:1

16   terror and dread fall upon them.
  The power of your arm
    makes them lifeless as stone
  until your people pass by, O LORD,
    until the people you purchased pass by.

17 You will bring them in and plant them on your own
    mountain—
  the place, O LORD, reserved for your own dwelling,
    the sanctuary, O Lord, that your hands have established.

**15:17**
Exod 23:20; 32:34
Pss 2:6; 78:54, 68
Isa 5:2
Jer 2:21

18 The LORD will reign forever and ever!"

**15:18**
Pss 10:16; 29:10
Isa 57:15

**15:3** Yahweh is a transliteration of the proper name YHWH that is sometimes rendered "Jehovah"; in this translation it is usually rendered "the LORD" (note the use of small capitals).  **15:4** Hebrew sea of reeds; also in 15:22.

**15:19**
Exod 14:22, 28

**15:20**
Exod 2:4
Num 26:59
1 Sam 18:6
Pss 30:11; 150:4

**15:21**
Exod 15:1

¹⁹When Pharaoh's horses, chariots, and charioteers rushed into the sea, the LORD brought the water crashing down on them. But the people of Israel had walked through the middle of the sea on dry ground!

²⁰Then Miriam the prophet, Aaron's sister, took a tambourine and led all the women as they played their tambourines and danced. ²¹And Miriam sang this song:

> "Sing to the LORD,
>     for he has triumphed gloriously;
> he has hurled both horse and rider
>     into the sea."

## 3. Complaining in the wilderness
### Bitter Water at Marah

**15:22**
Num 33:8
Pss 77:20; 78:52

**15:23**
Num 33:8
Ruth 1:20

**15:24**
Exod 14:11
Ps 106:13

**15:25**
Exod 14:10; 16:4

**15:26**
Exod 19:5-6
Deut 7:15
Ps 103:3

**15:27**
Num 33:9

²²Then Moses led the people of Israel away from the Red Sea, and they moved out into the desert of Shur. They traveled in this desert for three days without finding any water. ²³When they came to the oasis of Marah, the water was too bitter to drink. So they called the place Marah (which means "bitter").

²⁴Then the people complained and turned against Moses. "What are we going to drink?" they demanded. ²⁵So Moses cried out to the LORD for help, and the LORD showed him a piece of wood. Moses threw it into the water, and this made the water good to drink.

It was there at Marah that the LORD set before them the following decree as a standard to test their faithfulness to him. ²⁶He said, "If you will listen carefully to the voice of the LORD your God and do what is right in his sight, obeying his commands and keeping all his decrees, then I will not make you suffer any of the diseases I sent on the Egyptians; for I am the LORD who heals you."

²⁷After leaving Marah, the Israelites traveled on to the oasis of Elim, where they found twelve springs and seventy palm trees. They camped there beside the water.

### Manna and Quail from Heaven

**16:1**
Exod 17:1
Num 33:11-12

**16:2**
Exod 14:11
1 Cor 10:10

**16:4**
Deut 8:2, 16
Pss 78:24; 105:40
John 6:31
1 Cor 10:3

**16:5**
Exod 16:22

**16** Then the whole community of Israel set out from Elim and journeyed into the wilderness of Sin,* between Elim and Mount Sinai. They arrived there on the fifteenth day of the second month, one month after leaving the land of Egypt.* ²There, too, the whole community of Israel complained about Moses and Aaron.

³"If only the LORD had killed us back in Egypt," they moaned. "There we sat around pots filled with meat and ate all the bread we wanted. But now you have brought us into this wilderness to starve us all to death."

⁴Then the LORD said to Moses, "Look, I'm going to rain down food from heaven for you. Each day the people can go out and pick up as much food as they need for that day. I will test them in this to see whether or not they will follow my instructions. ⁵On the sixth day they will gather food, and when they prepare it, there will be twice as much as usual."

**16:1a** The geographical name *Sin* is related to *Sinai* and should not be confused with the English word *sin*.
**16:1b** The Exodus had occurred on the fifteenth day of the first month (see Num 33:3).

---

**15:20** Miriam was called a prophet not only because she received revelations from God (Numbers 12:1, 2; Micah 6:4) but also because of her musical skill. Prophecy and music were often closely related in the Bible (1 Samuel 10:5; 1 Chronicles 25:1).

**15:23, 27** The water in the oasis of Marah is contrasted with the springs in the oasis of Elim. Marah stands for the unbelieving, grumbling attitude of the people who would not trust God. Elim stands for God's bountiful provision. How easy it is to grumble and complain too quickly, only to be embarrassed by God's help! We must be patient for God's kindness and help. Don't let your negative attitude erode your trust in God.

**15:26** God promised that if the people obeyed him, they would not suffer from the diseases that plagued the Egyptians. Little did they know that many of the moral laws he later gave them were designed to keep them free from sickness. For example, following God's law against prostitution would keep us free of venereal disease. God's laws for us are often designed to keep us from harm. Men and women are complex beings. Our physical, emotional, and spiritual lives are intertwined. Modern medicine is now acknowledging what these laws assumed. If we want God to care for us, we need to submit to his directions for living.

**16:1** The wilderness of Sin was a vast and hostile environment of sand and stone. Its barren surroundings provided the perfect place for God to test and shape the character of his people.

**16:2, 3** It happened again. As the Israelites encountered danger, shortages, and inconvenience, they complained bitterly and longed to be back in Egypt. But as always, God provided for their needs. Difficult circumstances often lead to stress, and complaining is a natural response. The Israelites didn't really want to be back in Egypt; they just wanted life to get a little easier. In the pressure of the moment, they could not focus on the cause of their stress (in this case, lack of trust in God); they could only think about the quickest way of escape. When pressure comes your way, resist the temptation to make a quick escape. Instead, focus on God's power and wisdom to help you deal with the cause of your stress.

**16:4, 5** God promised to meet the Hebrews' need for food in the desert, but he decided to test their obedience. God wanted to see if they would obey his detailed instructions. We can learn to trust him as our Lord only by following. We can learn to obey by taking small steps of obedience.

6So Moses and Aaron said to all the people of Israel, "By evening you will realize it was the Lord who brought you out of the land of Egypt. 7In the morning you will see the glory of the Lord, because he has heard your complaints, which are against him, not against us. What have we done that you should complain about us?" 8Then Moses added, "The Lord will give you meat to eat in the evening and bread to satisfy you in the morning, for he has heard all your complaints against him. What have we done? Yes, your complaints are against the Lord, not against us."

9Then Moses said to Aaron, "Announce this to the entire community of Israel: 'Present yourselves before the Lord, for he has heard your complaining.'" 10And as Aaron spoke to the whole community of Israel, they looked out toward the wilderness. There they could see the awesome glory of the Lord in the cloud.

11Then the Lord said to Moses, 12"I have heard the Israelites' complaints. Now tell them, 'In the evening you will have meat to eat, and in the morning you will have all the bread you want. Then you will know that I am the Lord your God.'"

13That evening vast numbers of quail flew in and covered the camp. And the next morning the area around the camp was wet with dew. 14When the dew evaporated, a flaky substance as fine as frost blanketed the ground. 15The Israelites were puzzled when they saw it. "What is it?" they asked each other. They had no idea what it was.

And Moses told them, "It is the food the Lord has given you to eat. 16These are the Lord's instructions: Each household should gather as much as it needs. Pick up two quarts* for each person in your tent."

17So the people of Israel did as they were told. Some gathered a lot, some only a little. 18But when they measured it out,* everyone had just enough. Those who gathered a lot had nothing left over, and those who gathered only a little had enough. Each family had just what it needed.

19Then Moses told them, "Do not keep any of it until morning." 20But some of them didn't listen and kept some of it until morning. But by then it was full of maggots and had a terrible smell. Moses was very angry with them.

21After this the people gathered the food morning by morning, each family according to its need. And as the sun became hot, the flakes they had not picked up melted and disappeared. 22On the sixth day, they gathered twice as much as usual—four quarts* for each person instead of two. Then all the leaders of the community came and asked Moses for an explanation. 23He told them, "This is what the Lord commanded: Tomorrow will be a day of complete rest, a holy Sabbath day set apart for the Lord. So bake or boil as much as you want today, and set aside what is left for tomorrow."

24So they put some aside until morning, just as Moses had commanded. And in the morning the leftover food was wholesome and good, without maggots or odor. 25Moses said, "Eat this food today, for today is a Sabbath day dedicated to the Lord. There will be no food on the ground today. 26You may gather the food for six days, but the seventh day is the Sabbath. There will be no food on the ground that day."

27Some of the people went out anyway on the seventh day, but they found no food. 28The Lord asked Moses, "How long will these people refuse to obey my commands and instructions? 29They must realize that the Sabbath is the Lord's gift to you. That is why he gives you a two-day supply on the sixth day, so there will be enough for two days. On the Sabbath day you must each stay in your place. Do not go out to pick up food on the seventh day." 30So the people did not gather any food on the seventh day.

31The Israelites called the food manna.* It was white like coriander seed, and it tasted like honey wafers.

32Then Moses said, "This is what the Lord has commanded: Fill a two-quart container with manna to preserve it for your descendants. Then later generations will be able to see the food I gave you in the wilderness when I set you free from Egypt."

16:6 Exod 6:6
16:7 Exod 16:12; Num 14:27; 16:11
16:10 Num 16:19
16:12 Exod 16:7
16:13 Num 11:31; Pss 78:27-28; 105:40
16:14 Num 11:7-9; Deut 8:3
16:15 Exod 16:31; Neh 9:5; John 6:31; 1 Cor 10:3
16:16 Exod 16:33, 36
16:18 †2 Cor 8:15
16:19 Exod 12:10; 23:18
16:22 Exod 16:5; 34:31
16:23 Gen 2:3; Exod 20:8; 23:12; Neh 9:14
16:24 Exod 16:20
16:28 Ps 78:10
16:31 Num 11:7-9; Deut 8:3, 16

16:16 Hebrew *1 omer* [2 liters]; also in 16:32, 33.   16:18 Hebrew *measured it with an omer.*   16:22 Hebrew *2 omers* [4 liters].   16:31 *Manna* means "What is it?" See 16:15.

---

16:14-16 Manna (16:31) appeared on the ground each day as thin flakes like frost. The people gathered it, ground it like grain, and made it into honey-tasting pancakes. For the Israelites the manna was a gift—it came every day and was just what they needed. It satisfied their temporary physical need. In John 6:48-51

Jesus compares himself to manna. Christ is our daily bread who satisfies our eternal, spiritual need.

16:23 The Israelites were not to work on the Sabbath—not even to cook food. Why? God knew that the busy routine of daily living could distract people from worshiping him. It is so easy to let

**16:33**
Heb 9:4
Rev 2:17

**16:34**
Exod 25:16, 21
Num 1:50

**16:35**
Josh 5:12
Neh 9:20-21

³³Moses said to Aaron, "Get a jar and fill it with two quarts of manna. Then put it in a sacred place before the LORD to preserve it for all future generations." ³⁴Aaron did just as the LORD had commanded Moses. He eventually placed it in the Ark of the Covenant—in front of the stone tablets inscribed with the terms of the covenant.* ³⁵So the people of Israel ate manna for forty years until they arrived at the land where they would settle. They ate manna until they came to the border of the land of Canaan.

³⁶The container used to measure the manna was an omer, which was one tenth of an ephah; it held about two quarts.*

### Water from the Rock

**17:1**
Exod 16:1; 19:2
Num 33:15

**17:2**
Exod 14:11-12
Num 20:3
Deut 6:16
1 Cor 10:10

**17:3**
Exod 16:2-3

**17:4**
Num 14:10; 16:19

**17** At the LORD's command, the whole community of Israel left the wilderness of Sin* and moved from place to place. Eventually they camped at Rephidim, but there was no water there for the people to drink. ²So once more the people complained against Moses. "Give us water to drink!" they demanded.

"Quiet!" Moses replied. "Why are you complaining against me? And why are you testing the LORD?"

³But tormented by thirst, they continued to argue with Moses. "Why did you bring us out of Egypt? Are you trying to kill us, our children, and our livestock with thirst?"

⁴Then Moses cried out to the LORD, "What should I do with these people? They are ready to stone me!"

**17:5**
Exod 7:20; 14:16

**17:6**
Num 20:8-10
Pss 78:15-16;
105:41
1 Cor 10:4

**17:7**
Deut 6:16; 9:22
Pss 81:7; 95:8

⁵The LORD said to Moses, "Walk out in front of the people. Take your staff, the one you used when you struck the water of the Nile, and call some of the elders of Israel to join you. ⁶I will stand before you on the rock at Mount Sinai.* Strike the rock, and water will come gushing out. Then the people will be able to drink." So Moses struck the rock as he was told, and water gushed out as the elders looked on.

⁷Moses named the place Massah (which means "test") and Meribah (which means "arguing") because the people of Israel argued with Moses and tested the LORD by saying, "Is the LORD here with us or not?"

**17:8**
Gen 36:12, 16
Num 24:20
Deut 25:17-19

**17:9**
Exod 24:13
Num 11:28

### Israel Defeats the Amalekites

⁸While the people of Israel were still at Rephidim, the warriors of Amalek attacked them. ⁹Moses commanded Joshua, "Choose some men to go out and fight the army of Amalek for us. Tomorrow, I will stand at the top of the hill, holding the staff of God in my hand."

**16:34** Hebrew *He placed it in front of the Testimony;* see note on 25:16.　**16:36** Hebrew *An omer is one tenth of an ephah.*　**17:1** The geographical name *Sin* is related to *Sinai* and should not be confused with the English word *sin.*　**17:6** Hebrew *Horeb,* another name for Sinai.

---

work, family responsibilities, and recreation crowd our schedules so tightly that we don't take time to worship. Carefully guard your time with God.

**16:32** The Hebrews put some manna in a special jar as a reminder of the way God provided for them in the wilderness.

**JOURNEY TO MOUNT SINAI**
God miraculously supplied food and water in the wilderness for the Israelites. In the Wilderness of Sin, he provided manna (16). At Rephidim, he provided water from a rock (17:1–7). Finally God brought them to the foot of Mount Sinai, where he gave them his holy laws.

Symbols have always been an important part of Christian worship also. We use special objects as symbols to remind us of God's work. Such symbols can be valuable aids to our worship as long as we are careful to keep them from becoming objects of worship.

**17:2** Again the people complained about their problem instead of praying. Some problems can be solved by careful thought or by rearranging our priorities. Some can be solved by discussion and good counsel. But some problems can be solved only by prayer. We should make a determined effort to pray when we feel like complaining because complaining only raises our level of stress. Prayer quiets our thoughts and emotions and prepares us to listen.

**17:8** The Amalekites were descendants of Amalek, a grandson of Esau. They were a fierce nomadic tribe that lived in the desert region of the Dead Sea. They made part of their livelihood by conducting frequent raids on other settlements and carrying off plundered goods. They killed for pleasure. One of the greatest insults in Israelite culture was to call someone "a friend of Amalek." When the Israelites entered the region, the warriors of Amalek saw this as a perfect opportunity for both pleasure and profit. But this hostile tribe was moving in on the wrong group—a people led by God. For the Israelite slaves to defeat such a warlike nation was more than enough proof that God was with them as he had promised to be.

**17:9** Here we meet Joshua for the first time. Later he would become the great leader who would bring God's people into the Promised Land. As a general of the Israelite army, he was gaining valuable experience for the greater battles to come.

¹⁰So Joshua did what Moses had commanded and fought the army of Amalek. Meanwhile, Moses, Aaron, and Hur climbed to the top of a nearby hill. ¹¹As long as Moses held up the staff in his hand, the Israelites had the advantage. But whenever he dropped his hand, the Amalekites gained the advantage. ¹²Moses' arms soon became so tired he could no longer hold them up. So Aaron and Hur found a stone for him to sit on. Then they stood on each side of Moses, holding up his hands. So his hands held steady until sunset. ¹³As a result, Joshua overwhelmed the army of Amalek in battle.

¹⁴After the victory, the LORD instructed Moses, "Write this down on a scroll as a permanent reminder, and read it aloud to Joshua: I will erase the memory of Amalek from under heaven." ¹⁵Moses built an altar there and named it Yahweh-nissi (which means "the LORD is my banner"). ¹⁶He said, "They have raised their fist against the LORD's throne, so now* the LORD will be at war with Amalek generation after generation."

## Jethro's Visit to Moses

**18** Moses' father-in-law, Jethro, the priest of Midian, heard about everything God had done for Moses and his people, the Israelites. He heard especially about how the LORD had rescued them from Egypt.

²Earlier, Moses had sent his wife, Zipporah, and his two sons back to Jethro, who had taken them in. ³(Moses' first son was named Gershom,* for Moses had said when the boy was born, "I have been a foreigner in a foreign land." ⁴His second son was named Eliezer,* for Moses had said, "The God of my ancestors was my helper; he rescued me from the sword of Pharaoh.") ⁵Jethro, Moses' father-in-law, now came to visit Moses in the wilderness. He brought Moses' wife and two sons with him, and they arrived while Moses and the people were camped near the mountain of God. ⁶Jethro had sent a message to Moses, saying, "I, Jethro, your father-in-law, am coming to see you with your wife and your two sons."

⁷So Moses went out to meet his father-in-law. He bowed low and kissed him. They asked about each other's welfare and then went into Moses' tent. ⁸Moses told his father-in-law everything the LORD had done to Pharaoh and Egypt on behalf of Israel. He also told about all the hardships they had experienced along the way and how the LORD had rescued his people from all their troubles. ⁹Jethro was delighted when he heard about all the good things the LORD had done for Israel as he rescued them from the hand of the Egyptians.

¹⁰"Praise the LORD," Jethro said, "for he has rescued you from the Egyptians and from Pharaoh. Yes, he has rescued Israel from the powerful hand of Egypt! ¹¹I know now that the LORD is greater than all other gods, because he rescued his people from the oppression of the proud Egyptians."

¹²Then Jethro, Moses' father-in-law, brought a burnt offering and sacrifices to God. Aaron and all the elders of Israel came out and joined him in a sacrificial meal in God's presence.

## Jethro's Wise Advice

¹³The next day, Moses took his seat to hear the people's disputes against each other. They waited before him from morning till evening.

¹⁴When Moses' father-in-law saw all that Moses was doing for the people, he asked, "What are you really accomplishing here? Why are you trying to do all this alone while everyone stands around you from morning till evening?"

**17:16** Or *Hands have been lifted up to the LORD's throne, and now.* **18:3** *Gershom* sounds like a Hebrew term that means "a foreigner there." **18:4** *Eliezer* means "God is my helper."

### Cross-references

**17:10** Exod 24:14; 31:2
**17:12** Isa 35:3
**17:14** Exod 24:4; 34:27 Num 33:2
**17:15** Gen 22:14
**18:1** Exod 2:16, 18; 3:1
**18:2** Exod 2:21; 4:25
**18:3** Exod 2:22 Acts 7:29
**18:4** Gen 49:25
**18:5** Exod 3:1
**18:7** Gen 43:28
**18:8** Exod 15:6, 16 Num 20:14
**18:9** Isa 63:7-14
**18:10** 1 Kgs 8:56 Ps 68:19-20
**18:11** Exod 12:12; 15:11
**18:12** Gen 31:54 Exod 24:5

---

**17:10-13** Aaron and Hur stood by Moses' side and held up his arms to ensure victory against Amalek. We need to "hold up the hands" of our spiritual leaders as well. Shouldering some responsibility, lending a word of encouragement, or offering a prayer are ways of refreshing spiritual leaders in their work.

**18:7** Jethro entered Moses' tent where the two talked. Tents were the homes of shepherds. In shape and design, they resembled the tents of today, but they were very large and made of a thick cloth woven from goat or camel hair. This fabric breathed in warm weather and contracted in stormy weather to offer protection from the winter winds and rains. The floor was often covered with animal-skin rugs, while curtains divided the inside space into rooms.

**18:8-11** Moses told his father-in-law all that God had done, convincing him that the Lord was greater than any other god. Our

relatives are often the hardest people to tell about God. Yet we should look for opportunities to tell them what God is doing in our lives because we can have an important influence on them.

**18:12** This reunion turned into a large celebration. The Israelites frequently shared a sacrificial meal among themselves. A burnt offering was sacrificed to God, and then the meal taken from the sacrifice was dedicated to God and eaten ceremonially as a fellowship dinner.

**18:13-26** Moses was spending so much time and energy hearing the Hebrews' complaints that he could not get to other important work. Jethro suggested that Moses delegate most of this work to others and focus his efforts on jobs only he could do. People in positions of responsibility sometimes feel they are the only ones who can do necessary tasks; but others are capable of handling part of the load. Delegation relieved Moses' stress

**18:15**
Num 9:8
Deut 17:8-13

**18:16**
Exod 24:14

**18:18**
Num 11:14, 17
Deut 1:9

**18:19-20**
Deut 1:18

**18:21**
Deut 1:13, 15
Ps 15:1-5

**18:22**
Num 11:17
Deut 1:17-18

**18:25**
Deut 1:15; 16:18

**18:26**
Deut 16:18

**18:27**
Num 10:29-30

¹⁵Moses replied, "Because the people come to me to get a ruling from God. ¹⁶When a dispute arises, they come to me, and I am the one who settles the case between the quarreling parties. I inform the people of God's decrees and give them his instructions."

¹⁷"This is not good!" Moses' father-in-law exclaimed. ¹⁸"You're going to wear yourself out—and the people, too. This job is too heavy a burden for you to handle all by yourself. ¹⁹Now listen to me, and let me give you a word of advice, and may God be with you. You should continue to be the people's representative before God, bringing their disputes to him. ²⁰Teach them God's decrees, and give them his instructions. Show them how to conduct their lives. ²¹But select from all the people some capable, honest men who fear God and hate bribes. Appoint them as leaders over groups of one thousand, one hundred, fifty, and ten. ²²They should always be available to solve the people's common disputes, but have them bring the major cases to you. Let the leaders decide the smaller matters themselves. They will help you carry the load, making the task easier for you. ²³If you follow this advice, and if God commands you to do so, then you will be able to endure the pressures, and all these people will go home in peace."

²⁴Moses listened to his father-in-law's advice and followed his suggestions. ²⁵He chose capable men from all over Israel and appointed them as leaders over the people. He put them in charge of groups of one thousand, one hundred, fifty, and ten. ²⁶These men were always available to solve the people's common disputes. They brought the major cases to Moses, but they took care of the smaller matters themselves.

²⁷Soon after this, Moses said good-bye to his father-in-law, who returned to his own land.

People such as Jethro and Melchizedek—not Israelites, but nevertheless worshipers of the true God—play an important role in the Old Testament. They remind us of God's commitment to the world. God chose one nation through which to work, but his love and concern are for all nations!

Jethro's religious background prepared him for, rather than prevented him from, responding in faith to God. When he saw and heard what God had done for the Israelites, he worshiped God wholeheartedly. We can guess that for 40 years as Moses' father-in-law, Jethro had been watching God at work, molding a leader. Moses' and Jethro's relationship must have been close, for Moses readily accepted his father-in-law's advice. Each benefited from knowing the other. Jethro met God through Moses, and Moses received hospitality, his wife, and wisdom from Jethro.

The greatest gift one person can give another is an introduction to God. But that gift is hindered if the believer's attitude is, "I have the greatest gift to pass on to you, while you have nothing to give me in return." Real friends give to and receive from each other. The importance of introducing a friend to God does not make the friend's gifts to us insignificant. Rather, the believer is doubly blessed—first by receiving the gifts the friend wishes to give; then by growing in knowledge of the Lord. For we discover that in introducing another person to God, we increase our own awareness of God. As we give God away, he gives himself even more to us.

Is all you know about God a miscellaneous collection of trivia, or do you have a living relationship with him? Only with a vital relationship can you pass on to others the excitement of allowing God to guide your life. Have you reached the point of saying, with Jethro, "I know now that the LORD is greater than all other gods" (Exodus 18:11)?

| | |
|---|---|
| **Strengths and accomplishments** | • As father-in-law to Moses, he came to recognize the one true God<br>• He was a practical troubleshooter and organizer |
| **Lessons from his life** | • Supervision and administration are team efforts<br>• God's plan includes all nations |
| **Vital statistics** | • Where: The land of Midian and the wilderness of Sinai<br>• Occupations: Shepherd, priest<br>• Relatives: Daughter: Zipporah. Son-in-law: Moses. Son: Hobab. |
| **Key verse** | "Jethro was delighted when he heard about all the good things the LORD had done for Israel as he rescued them from the hand of the Egyptians" (Exodus 18:9). |

Jethro's story is told in Exodus 2:15—3:1; 18:1-27. He is also mentioned in Judges 1:16.

and improved the quality of the government. It helped prepare them for the system of government set up in Canaan. Proper delegation can multiply your effectiveness while giving others a chance to grow.

**18:16** Moses not only decided these cases, he also taught the people God's laws. Whenever we help others settle disputes or resolve conflicts, we should also look for opportunities to teach about God.

## C. ISRAEL AT SINAI (19:1—40:38)

After escaping through the Red Sea, the Hebrews traveled through the wilderness and arrived at Sinai, God's holy mountain. There they received the Ten Commandments, as well as instructions for building a Tabernacle as a center of worship. Through Israel's experiences at Mount Sinai, we learn about the importance of obedience in our relationship with God. His laws help expose sin, and they give standards for righteous living.

### 1. Giving the law

*The LORD Reveals Himself at Sinai*

**19** Exactly two months after the Israelites left Egypt,* they arrived in the wilderness of Sinai. ²After breaking camp at Rephidim, they came to the wilderness of Sinai and set up camp there at the base of Mount Sinai.

³Then Moses climbed the mountain to appear before God. The LORD called to him from the mountain and said, "Give these instructions to the family of Jacob; announce it to the descendants of Israel: ⁴'You have seen what I did to the Egyptians. You know how I carried you on eagles' wings and brought you to myself. ⁵Now if you will obey me and keep my covenant, you will be my own special treasure from among all the peoples on earth; for all the earth belongs to me. ⁶And you will be my kingdom of priests, my holy nation.' This is the message you must give to the people of Israel."

⁷So Moses returned from the mountain and called together the elders of the people and told them everything the LORD had commanded him. ⁸And all the people responded together, "We will do everything the LORD has commanded." So Moses brought the people's answer back to the LORD.

⁹Then the LORD said to Moses, "I will come to you in a thick cloud, Moses, so the people themselves can hear me when I speak with you. Then they will always trust you."

Moses told the LORD what the people had said. ¹⁰Then the LORD told Moses, "Go down and prepare the people for my arrival. Consecrate them today and tomorrow, and have them wash their clothing. ¹¹Be sure they are ready on the third day, for on that day the LORD will come down on Mount Sinai as all the people watch. ¹²Mark off a boundary all around the mountain. Warn the people, 'Be careful! Do not go up on the mountain or even touch its boundaries. Anyone who touches the mountain will certainly be put to death. ¹³No hand may touch the person or animal that crosses the boundary; instead, stone them or shoot them with arrows. They must be put to death.' However, when the ram's horn sounds a long blast, then the people may go up on the mountain.*"

¹⁴So Moses went down to the people. He consecrated them for worship, and they washed their clothes. ¹⁵He told them, "Get ready for the third day, and until then abstain from having sexual intercourse."

**19:1** Hebrew *In the third month after the Israelites left Egypt, on the very day,* i.e., two lunar months to the day after leaving Egypt. Compare Num 33:3.   **19:13** Or *up to the mountain.*

**9:1**
Exod 12:51; 16:1
**19:3**
Exod 20:21
Acts 7:38
**19:4**
Deut 29:2
Isa 40:31; 63:9
Rev 12:14
**19:5**
Exod 15:26
Deut 10:14
**19:6**
Lev 11:44-45
Deut 33:3
†1 Pet 2:5, 9
Rev 1:6; 5:10
**19:7**
Exod 4:29-30; 24:9
**19:8**
Exod 24:3, 7
Deut 5:27; 26:17
**19:9**
Exod 19:16; 24:15
Deut 4:11
Ps 99:7
**19:10**
Gen 35:2
Lev 11:44-45
Num 8:7; 19:19
Heb 10:22
Rev 22:14
**19:11**
Exod 19:16
**19:13**
†Heb 12:20
**19:15**
1 Sam 21:4
1 Cor 7:5

---

**19:2, 3** Mount Sinai is one of the most sacred locations in Israel's history. Located in the south-central Sinai peninsula, this mountain is where Moses met God in a burning bush, God made his covenant with Israel, and Elijah heard God in the gentle whisper. Here God gave his people the laws and guidelines for right living. They learned the potential blessings of obedience (34:4-28) and the tragic consequences of disobedience (34:7).

**19:4-6** God had a reason for rescuing the Israelites from slavery. Now he was ready to tell them what it was: Israel was to become a kingdom of priests and a holy nation where anyone could approach God freely. It didn't take long, however, for the people to corrupt God's plan. God then established Aaron's descendants from the tribe of Levi as priests (Leviticus 8–9), representing what the entire nation should have been. But with the coming of Jesus Christ, God has once again extended his plan to all believers. We are to become holy, "royal priests" (1 Peter 2:9). The death and resurrection of Christ has allowed each of us to approach God freely.

**19:5** Why did God choose Israel as his nation? God knew that no nation on earth was good enough to deserve to be called his people, his "special treasure." He chose Israel, not because of anything they had done, but in his love and mercy he chose Israel in spite of the wrong the nation had done and would do. Why did he want to have a special nation on earth? To represent

his way of life, to teach his Word, and to be an agent of salvation to the world. "All the nations of the earth" would be blessed through Abraham's descendants (Genesis 18:18). Gentiles and kings would come to the Lord through Israel, predicted Isaiah (Isaiah 60:3). Through the nation of Israel, the Messiah, God's chosen Son, would be born. God chose one nation and put it through a rigorous training program, so that one day it could be a channel for his blessings to the whole world.

**19:5-8** In Genesis 15 and 17, God made a covenant with Abraham, promising to make his descendants into a great nation. Now that promise was being realized as God restated his agreement with the Israelite nation, the descendants of Abraham. God promised to bless and care for them. The people promised to obey him. The covenant was thus sealed. But the good intentions of the people quickly wore off. Have you made a commitment to God? How are you holding up your end of the bargain?

**19:9-11** Moses was told to consecrate the people. This meant getting them physically and spiritually ready to meet God. The people were to set themselves apart from sin and even ordinary daily routine in order to dedicate themselves to God. The act of washing and preparing served to get their minds and hearts ready. When we meet God for worship, we should set aside the cares and preoccupations of everyday life. Use your time of physical preparation to get your mind ready to meet God.

**19:16**
Exod 9:23; 20:18
Heb 12:18-19

**19:17**
Deut 4:11

**19:18**
Exod 24:17
Deut 5:4
Pss 68:7-8; 104:32

**19:19**
Ps 81:7

**19:20**
Exod 24:12
Neh 9:13

**19:21**
Exod 3:5

**19:22**
Lev 10:3; 21:6-8

**19:24**
Exod 24:1, 9

16On the morning of the third day, thunder roared and lightning flashed, and a dense cloud came down on the mountain. There was a long, loud blast from a ram's horn, and all the people trembled. 17Moses led them out from the camp to meet with God, and they stood at the foot of the mountain. 18All of Mount Sinai was covered with smoke because the LORD had descended on it in the form of fire. The smoke billowed into the sky like smoke from a brick kiln, and the whole mountain shook violently. 19As the blast of the ram's horn grew louder and louder, Moses spoke, and God thundered his reply. 20The LORD came down on the top of Mount Sinai and called Moses to the top of the mountain. So Moses climbed the mountain.

21Then the LORD told Moses, "Go back down and warn the people not to break through the boundaries to see the LORD, or they will die. 22Even the priests who regularly come near to the LORD must purify themselves so that the LORD does not break out and destroy them."

23"But LORD," Moses protested, "the people cannot come up to Mount Sinai. You already warned us. You told me, 'Mark off a boundary all around the mountain to set it apart as holy.'"

24But the LORD said, "Go down and bring Aaron back up with you. In the meantime, do not let the priests or the people break through to approach the LORD, or he will break out and destroy them."

25So Moses went down to the people and told them what the LORD had said.

## Ten Commandments for the Covenant Community

**20:1-17**
//Deut 5:6-21

**20:3**
Exod 15:11; 20:23

**20:4**
Lev 26:1

**20:5**
Exod 23:13, 24
Num 14:18
Deut 4:24

**20:6**
Exod 34:6-7
Deut 7:9

**20:7**
Lev 19:12

**20:8**
Exod 16:23

**20** Then God gave the people all these instructions*:

2"I am the LORD your God, who rescued you from the land of Egypt, the place of your slavery.

3"You must not have any other god but me.

4"You must not make for yourself an idol of any kind or an image of anything in the heavens or on the earth or in the sea. 5You must not bow down to them or worship them, for I, the LORD your God, am a jealous God who will not tolerate your affection for any other gods. I lay the sins of the parents upon their children; the entire family is affected—even children in the third and fourth generations of those who reject me. 6But I lavish unfailing love for a thousand generations on those* who love me and obey my commands.

7"You must not misuse the name of the LORD your God. The LORD will not let you go unpunished if you misuse his name.

8"Remember to observe the Sabbath day by keeping it holy. 9You have six days each week

**20:1** Hebrew *all these words.*   **20:6** Hebrew *for thousands of those.*

---

**19:23** Because God's glory and power were so strong, and because God is completely holy, the people could not come to him. God did this to show that he was not like the idols of Egypt that could be seen and touched. Now, however, we are invited to approach God because of what Christ has done for us (Hebrews 12:18-24). Jesus is superior to Moses because Jesus opens the way for us to come to God with great joy.

**20:1ff** Why were the Ten Commandments necessary for God's new nation? At the foot of Mount Sinai, God showed his people the true function and beauty of his laws. The commandments were designed to lead Israel to a life of practical holiness. In them, people could see the nature of God and his plan for how they should live. The commands and guidelines were intended to direct the community to meet the needs of each individual in a loving and responsible manner. By Jesus' time, however, most people looked at the law the wrong way. They saw it as a means to prosperity in both this world and the next. And they thought that to obey every law was the way to earn God's protection from foreign invasion and natural disaster. Law keeping became an end in itself, not the means to fulfill God's ultimate law of love.

**20:1-6** The Israelites had just come from Egypt, a land of many idols and many gods. Because each god represented a different aspect of life, it was common to worship many gods in order to get the maximum number of blessings. When God told his people to worship and believe in him, that wasn't so hard for them— he was just one more god to add to the list. But when he said, "You must not have any other god but me," that was difficult for

the people to accept. But if they didn't learn that the God who led them out of Egypt was the only true God, they could not be his people—no matter how faithfully they kept the other nine commandments. Thus, God made this his first commandment. Today we can allow many things to become gods to us. Money, fame, work, or pleasure can become gods when we concentrate too much on them for personal identity, meaning, and security. No one sets out with the intention of worshiping these things. But by the amount of time we devote to them, they can grow into gods that ultimately control our thoughts and energies. Letting God hold the central place in our lives keeps these things from turning into gods.

**20:7** God's name is special because it carries his personal identity. Using it frivolously or in a curse is so common today that we may fail to realize how serious it is. The way we use God's name conveys how we really feel about him. We should respect his name and use it appropriately, speaking it in praise or worship rather than in curse or jest. We should not take lightly the abuse or dishonor of his name.

**20:8-11** The Sabbath was a day set aside for rest and worship. God commanded a Sabbath because human beings need to spend unhurried time in worship and rest each week. A God who is concerned enough to provide a day each week for us to rest is indeed wonderful. To observe a regular time of rest and worship in our fast-paced world demonstrates how important God is to us, and it gives us the extra benefit of refreshing our spirits. Don't neglect God's provision.

for your ordinary work, ¹⁰but the seventh day is a Sabbath day of rest dedicated to the LORD your God. On that day no one in your household may do any work. This includes you, your sons and daughters, your male and female servants, your livestock, and any foreigners living among you. ¹¹For in six days the LORD made the heavens, the earth, the sea, and everything in them; but on the seventh day he rested. That is why the LORD blessed the Sabbath day and set it apart as holy.

¹²"Honor your father and mother. Then you will live a long, full life in the land the LORD your God is giving you.

¹³"You must not murder.

¹⁴"You must not commit adultery.

¹⁵"You must not steal.

¹⁶"You must not testify falsely against your neighbor.

¹⁷"You must not covet your neighbor's house. You must not covet your neighbor's wife, male or female servant, ox or donkey, or anything else that belongs to your neighbor."

¹⁸When the people heard the thunder and the loud blast of the ram's horn, and when they saw the flashes of lightning and the smoke billowing from the mountain, they stood at a distance, trembling with fear.

¹⁹And they said to Moses, "You speak to us, and we will listen. But don't let God speak directly to us, or we will die!"

²⁰"Don't be afraid," Moses answered them, "for God has come in this way to test you, and so that your fear of him will keep you from sinning!"

²¹As the people stood in the distance, Moses approached the dark cloud where God was.

### Proper Use of Altars

²²And the LORD said to Moses, "Say this to the people of Israel: You saw for yourselves that I spoke to you from heaven. ²³Remember, you must not make any idols of silver or gold to rival me.

²⁴"Build for me an altar made of earth, and offer your sacrifices to me—your burnt offerings and peace offerings, your sheep and goats, and your cattle. Build my altar wherever I cause my name to be remembered, and I will come to you and bless you. ²⁵If you use stones to build my altar, use only natural, uncut stones. Do not shape the stones with a tool, for that would make the altar unfit for holy use. ²⁶And do not approach my altar by going up steps. If you do, someone might look up under your clothing and see your nakedness.

**20:11**
Gen 2:2-3
†Acts 4:24

**20:12**
†Matt 15:4
†Mark 7:10
†Luke 18:20
†Eph 6:2

**20:13**
†Matt 5:21; 19:18
†Rom 13:9
†Jas 2:11

**20:14**
†Matt 5:27

**20:15**
†Matt 19:18

**20:16**
Matt 19:18

**20:17**
†Rom 7:7

**20:18**
Exod 19:18
Heb 12:18

**20:19**
Deut 5:23-27

**20:21**
Deut 5:22
Ps 97:2

**20:23**
Exod 32:4
Deut 29:17-18

**20:24**
Exod 10:25; 18:12;
24:5
Lev 1:2
Deut 12:5

**20:25**
Deut 27:5-6
Josh 8:31

**20:26**
Exod 28:42

---

**20:12** This is the first commandment with a promise attached. To live in peace for generations in the Promised Land, the Israelites would need to respect authority and build strong families. But what does it mean to "honor" parents? Partly, it means speaking well of them and politely to them. It also means acting in a way that shows them courtesy and respect (but not to obey them if this means disobedience to God). It means following their teaching and example of putting God first. Parents have a special place in God's sight. Even those who find it difficult to get along with their parents are still commanded to honor them.

**20:16** To testify falsely means lying in court. God knew that Israel could not survive unless its system of justice was incorruptible. We should be honest in our private dealings as well as in our public statements. In either situation, we "testify falsely" by leaving something out of a story, telling a half-truth, twisting the facts, or inventing a falsehood. God warns us against deception. Even though deception is a way of life for many people, God's people must not give in to it!

**20:17** To covet is to wish to have the possessions of others. It goes beyond simply admiring someone else's possessions or thinking, "I'd like to have one of those." Coveting includes envy—resenting the fact that others have what you don't. God knows, however, that possessions never make anyone happy for long. Since only God can supply all our needs, true contentment is found only in him. When you begin to covet, try to determine if a more basic need is leading you to envy. For example,

you may covet someone's success, not because you want to take it away from him, but because you would like to feel as appreciated by others as he is. If this is the case, pray that God will help you deal with your resentment and meet your basic needs.

**20:18** Sometimes God speaks to his people with a majestic display of power; at other times he speaks quietly. Why the difference? God speaks in the way that best accomplishes his purposes. At Sinai, the awesome display of light and sound was necessary to show Israel God's great power and authority. Only then would they listen to Moses and Aaron.

**20:20** Throughout the Bible we find this phrase: "Don't be afraid." God wasn't trying to scare the people. He was showing his mighty power so the Israelites would know he was the true God and would therefore obey him. If they would do this, he would make his power available to them. God wants us to follow him out of love rather than fear. To overcome fear, we must think more about his love. First John 4:18 says, "Perfect love expels all fear."

**20:24-26** Why were specific directions given for building altars? God's people had no Bible and few religious traditions to learn from. God had to start from scratch and teach them how to worship him. God gave specific instructions about building altars because he wanted to control the way sacrifices were offered. To prevent idolatry from creeping into worship, God did not allow the altar stones to be cut or shaped into any form. Nor did God let the people build an altar just anywhere. This was designed to prevent them from starting their own religions or making changes in the way God wanted things done. God is not against creativity, but he is against us creating our own religion.

21:1
Deut 4:14

21:2-6
Lev 25:39-41
//Deut 15:12-18

21:2
Jer 34:14

21:5
Deut 15:16

21:6
Exod 22:8-9

21:7
Neh 5:5

21:10
1 Cor 7:3, 5

21:12
Gen 9:6
Lev 24:21

21:13
Num 35:22
Deut 19:4-5
Josh 20:9

## Fair Treatment of Slaves

**21** "These are the regulations you must present to Israel. 2"If you buy a Hebrew slave, he may serve for no more than six years. Set him free in the seventh year, and he will owe you nothing for his freedom. 3If he was single when he became your slave, he shall leave single. But if he was married before he became a slave, then his wife must be freed with him.

4"If his master gave him a wife while he was a slave and they had sons or daughters, then only the man will be free in the seventh year, but his wife and children will still belong to his master. 5But the slave may declare, 'I love my master, my wife, and my children. I don't want to go free.' 6If he does this, his master must present him before God.* Then his master must take him to the door or doorpost and publicly pierce his ear with an awl. After that, the slave will serve his master for life.

7"When a man sells his daughter as a slave, she will not be freed at the end of six years as the men are. 8If she does not satisfy her owner, he must allow her to be bought back again. But he is not allowed to sell her to foreigners, since he is the one who broke the contract with her. 9But if the slave's owner arranges for her to marry his son, he may no longer treat her as a slave but as a daughter.

10"If a man who has married a slave wife takes another wife for himself, he must not neglect the rights of the first wife to food, clothing, and sexual intimacy. 11If he fails in any of these three obligations, she may leave as a free woman without making any payment.

## Cases of Personal Injury

12"Anyone who assaults and kills another person must be put to death. 13But if it was simply an accident permitted by God, I will appoint a place of refuge where the slayer can run for

**21:6** Or *before the judges.*

| THE TEN COMMAND-MENTS AND THE WORDS OF JESUS | The Ten Commandments said . . . | Jesus said . . . |
|---|---|---|
| | Exodus 20:3 "You must not have any other god but me." | Matthew 4:10 "You must worship the LORD your God and serve only him." |
| | Exodus 20:4 "You must not make for yourself an idol." | Luke 16:13 "No one can serve two masters." |
| | Exodus 20:7 "You must not misuse the name of the LORD your God." | Matthew 5:34 "Do not make any vows! Do not say, 'By heaven!' because heaven is God's throne." |
| | Exodus 20:8 "Remember to observe the Sabbath day by keeping it holy." | Mark 2:27, 28 "The Sabbath was made to meet the needs of people, and not people to meet the requirements of the Sabbath. So the Son of Man is Lord, even over the Sabbath!" |
| | Exodus 20:12 "Honor your father and mother." | Matthew 10:37 "If you love your father or mother more than you love me, you are not worthy of being mine." |
| | Exodus 20:13 "You must not murder." | Matthew 5:22 "If you are even angry with someone, you are subject to judgment!" |
| | Exodus 20:14 "You must not commit adultery." | Matthew 5:28 "Anyone who even looks at a woman with lust has already committed adultery with her in his heart." |
| | Exodus 20:15 "You must not steal." | Matthew 5:40 "If you are sued in court and your shirt is taken from you, give your coat, too." |
| | Exodus 20:16 "You must not testify falsely against your neighbor." | Matthew 12:36 "You must give an account on judgment day for every idle word you speak." |
| | Exodus 20:17 "You must not covet." | Luke 12:15 "Guard against every kind of greed." |

**21:1ff** These laws were given because everything we do has consequences. It is vital to think before acting, to consider the effects of our choices. Think of your plans for today and consider what their long-range results will be. As we deal with others, we should keep the principles of these laws in mind. We should act responsibly and justly with all people—friends and enemies alike.

**21:2** The Hebrews, though freed from slavery, had slaves (or servants) themselves. A person could become a slave because of poverty, debt, or even crime. But Hebrew slaves were treated as humans, not property, and were allowed to work their way to freedom. The Bible acknowledges the existence of slavery but never encourages it.

safety. ¹⁴However, if someone deliberately kills another person, then the slayer must be dragged even from my altar and be put to death.

¹⁵"Anyone who strikes father or mother must be put to death.

¹⁶"Kidnappers must be put to death, whether they are caught in possession of their victims or have already sold them as slaves.

¹⁷"Anyone who dishonors* father or mother must be put to death.

¹⁸"Now suppose two men quarrel, and one hits the other with a stone or fist, and the injured person does not die but is confined to bed. ¹⁹If he is later able to walk outside again, even with a crutch, the assailant will not be punished but must compensate his victim for lost wages and provide for his full recovery.

²⁰"If a man beats his male or female slave with a club and the slave dies as a result, the owner must be punished. ²¹But if the slave recovers within a day or two, then the owner shall not be punished, since the slave is his property.

²²"Now suppose two men are fighting, and in the process they accidentally strike a pregnant woman so she gives birth prematurely.* If no further injury results, the man who struck the woman must pay the amount of compensation the woman's husband demands and the judges approve. ²³But if there is further injury, the punishment must match the injury: a life for a life, ²⁴an eye for an eye, a tooth for a tooth, a hand for a hand, a foot for a foot, ²⁵a burn for a burn, a wound for a wound, a bruise for a bruise.

²⁶"If a man hits his male or female slave in the eye and the eye is blinded, he must let the slave go free to compensate for the eye. ²⁷And if a man knocks out the tooth of his male or female slave, he must let the slave go free to compensate for the tooth.

²⁸"If an ox* gores a man or woman to death, the ox must be stoned, and its flesh may not be eaten. In such a case, however, the owner will not be held liable. ²⁹But suppose the ox had a reputation for goring, and the owner had been informed but failed to keep it under control. If the ox then kills someone, it must be stoned, and the owner must also be put to death. ³⁰However, the dead person's relatives may accept payment to compensate for the loss of life. The owner of the ox may redeem his life by paying whatever is demanded.

³¹"The same regulation applies if the ox gores a boy or a girl. ³²But if the ox gores a slave, either male or female, the animal's owner must pay the slave's owner thirty silver coins,* and the ox must be stoned.

³³"Suppose someone digs or uncovers a pit and fails to cover it, and then an ox or a donkey falls into it. ³⁴The owner of the pit must pay full compensation to the owner of the animal, but then he gets to keep the dead animal.

³⁵"If someone's ox injures a neighbor's ox and the injured ox dies, then the two owners must sell the live ox and divide the price equally between them. They must also divide the dead animal. ³⁶But if the ox had a reputation for goring, yet its owner failed to keep it under control, he must pay full compensation—a live ox for the dead one—but he may keep the dead ox.

## Protection of Property

**22** ¹*"If someone steals an ox* or sheep and then kills or sells it, the thief must pay back five oxen for each ox stolen, and four sheep for each sheep stolen.

²*"If a thief is caught in the act of breaking into a house and is struck and killed in the process, the person who killed the thief is not guilty of murder. ³But if it happens in daylight, the one who killed the thief is guilty of murder.

### Marginal cross-references

**21:14** Num 35:30-31; 1 Kgs 2:28-34
**21:16** Deut 24:7
**21:17** Lev 20:9; Deut 5:16; †Matt 15:4; †Mark 7:10
**21:21** Lev 25:44-46
**21:23** Lev 24:19
**21:24** Lev 24:20; †Matt 5:38
**21:26** Job 31:13
**21:28** Gen 9:5
**21:32** Gen 37:28; Zech 11:12-13; Matt 26:15; 27:3, 9
**21:33** Luke 14:5
**22:1** Lev 6:1-7; 2 Sam 12:6; Prov 6:31; Luke 19:8
**22:2** Num 35:26-27
**22:3** Exod 21:2

---

**21:17** Greek version reads *Anyone who speaks disrespectfully of.* Compare Matt 15:4; Mark 7:10. **21:22** Or *so she has a miscarriage;* Hebrew reads *so her children come out.* **21:28** Or *bull,* or *cow;* also in 21:29-36. **21:32** Hebrew *30 shekels of silver,* about 12 ounces or 342 grams in weight. **22:1a** Verse 22:1 is numbered 21:37 in Hebrew text. **22:1b** Or *bull,* or *cow;* also in 22:4, 9, 10. **22:2** Verses 22:2-31 are numbered 22:1-30 in Hebrew text.

---

**21:24, 25** The "eye for an eye" rule was instituted as a guide for judges, not as a rule for personal relationships or to justify revenge. This rule made the punishment fit the crime, thereby preventing the cruel and barbaric punishments that characterized many ancient countries. Jesus used this principle to teach us not to retaliate (Matthew 5:38-48). Judges, parents, teachers, and others who work with people must make wise decisions in order for discipline to be effective. A punishment too harsh is unfair, and one too lenient is powerless to teach. Ask God for wisdom before you judge.

**22:1ff** These are not a collection of picky laws but are case studies of God's principles in action. God was taking potential situations and showing how his laws would work in the Israelites' everyday lives. These case studies had several objectives: (1) to protect the nation, (2) to organize the nation, and (3) to focus the nation's attention on God. The laws listed here do not cover every possible situation but give practical examples that make it easier to decide what God wants.

**22:3ff** Throughout chapter 22 we find examples of the principle of restitution—making wrongs right. For example, if a man stole an animal, he had to repay double the beast's market value. If you have done someone wrong, perhaps you should go beyond what

**22:4**
Prov 6:31
Jer 2:26
John 12:6

**22:5**
Exod 21:34

**22:7**
Lev 6:1-7

**22:8**
Exod 21:6
Deut 17:8-9; 19:17

**22:9**
Deut 25:1

**22:13**
Gen 31:39

**22:16-17**
Deut 22:28-29

**22:18**
Lev 20:27
Deut 18:10

**22:19**
Lev 18:23; 20:15

**22:20**
Exod 32:8; 34:15

**22:21**
Lev 19:33

**22:22**
Deut 24:17-18

**22:25**
Lev 25:35-37
Deut 23:19-20

**22:26**
Deut 24:6, 10-13

"A thief who is caught must pay in full for everything he stole. If he cannot pay, he must be sold as a slave to pay for his theft. ⁴If someone steals an ox or a donkey or a sheep and it is found in the thief's possession, then the thief must pay double the value of the stolen animal.

⁵"If an animal is grazing in a field or vineyard and the owner lets it stray into someone else's field to graze, then the animal's owner must pay compensation from the best of his own grain or grapes.

⁶"If you are burning thornbushes and the fire gets out of control and spreads into another person's field, destroying the sheaves or the uncut grain or the whole crop, the one who started the fire must pay for the lost crop.

⁷"Suppose someone leaves money or goods with a neighbor for safekeeping, and they are stolen from the neighbor's house. If the thief is caught, the compensation is double the value of what was stolen. ⁸But if the thief is not caught, the neighbor must appear before God,* who will determine if he stole the property.

⁹"Suppose there is a dispute between two people who both claim to own a particular ox, donkey, sheep, article of clothing, or any lost property. Both parties must come before God, and the person whom God declares* guilty must pay double compensation to the other.

¹⁰"Now suppose someone leaves a donkey, ox, sheep, or any other animal with a neighbor for safekeeping, but it dies or is injured or gets away, and no one sees what happened. ¹¹The neighbor must then take an oath in the presence of the LORD. If the LORD confirms that the neighbor did not steal the property, the owner must accept the verdict, and no payment will be required. ¹²But if the animal was indeed stolen, the guilty person must pay compensation to the owner. ¹³If it was torn to pieces by a wild animal, the remains of the carcass must be shown as evidence, and no compensation will be required.

¹⁴"If someone borrows an animal from a neighbor and it is injured or dies when the owner is absent, the person who borrowed it must pay full compensation. ¹⁵But if the owner was present, no compensation is required. And no compensation is required if the animal was rented, for this loss is covered by the rental fee.

## Social Responsibility

¹⁶"If a man seduces a virgin who is not engaged to anyone and has sex with her, he must pay the customary bride price and marry her. ¹⁷But if her father refuses to let him marry her, the man must still pay him an amount equal to the bride price of a virgin.

¹⁸"You must not allow a sorceress to live.

¹⁹"Anyone who has sexual relations with an animal must certainly be put to death.

²⁰"Anyone who sacrifices to any god other than the LORD must be destroyed.*

²¹"You must not mistreat or oppress foreigners in any way. Remember, you yourselves were once foreigners in the land of Egypt.

²²"You must not exploit a widow or an orphan. ²³If you exploit them in any way and they cry out to me, then I will certainly hear their cry. ²⁴My anger will blaze against you, and I will kill you with the sword. Then your wives will be widows and your children fatherless.

²⁵"If you lend money to any of my people who are in need, do not charge interest as a money lender would. ²⁶If you take your neighbor's cloak as security for a loan, you must return it before sunset. ²⁷This coat may be the only blanket your neighbor has. How can a

**22:8** Or *before the judges.*   **22:9** Or *before the judges, and the person whom the judges declare.*   **22:20** The Hebrew term used here refers to the complete consecration of things or people to the LORD, either by destroying them or by giving them as an offering.

---

is expected to make things right. This will (1) help ease any pain you've caused, (2) help the other person be more forgiving, and (3) make you more likely to think before you do it again.

**22:18** Why did God's laws speak so strongly against sorcery (Leviticus 19:31; 20:6, 27; Deuteronomy 18:10-12)? Sorcery was punishable by death because it was a crime against God himself. To invoke evil powers violated the first commandment to not worship any other god. Sorcery was rebellion against God and his authority. In essence, it was teaming up with Satan instead of with God.

**22:21** God warned the Israelites not to treat foreigners unfairly because they themselves were once foreigners in Egypt. It is not easy coming into a new environment where you feel alone and out of place. Are there foreigners in your corner of the world? refugees? new arrivals at school? immigrants from another country?

Be sensitive to their struggles, and express God's love by your kindness and generosity.

**22:22-27** The Hebrew law code is noted for its fairness and social responsibility toward the poor. God insisted that the poor and powerless be well treated and given the chance to restore their fortunes. We should reflect God's concern for the poor by giving and by helping those less fortunate than ourselves.

**22:26** Why did the law insist on returning a person's cloak before sunset? The cloak was one of an Israelite's most valuable possessions. Making clothing was difficult and time-consuming. As a result, cloaks were expensive, and most people owned only one. The cloak was used as a blanket, a sack to carry things in, a place to sit, a pledge for a debt, and, of course, clothing.

person sleep without it? If you do not return it and your neighbor cries out to me for help, then I will hear, for I am merciful.

28"You must not dishonor God or curse any of your rulers.

29"You must not hold anything back when you give me offerings from your crops and your wine.

"You must give me your firstborn sons.

30"You must also give me the firstborn of your cattle, sheep, and goats. But leave the newborn animal with its mother for seven days; then give it to me on the eighth day.

31"You must be my holy people. Therefore, do not eat any animal that has been torn up and killed by wild animals. Throw it to the dogs.

## A Call for Justice

**23** "You must not pass along false rumors. You must not cooperate with evil people by lying on the witness stand.

2"You must not follow the crowd in doing wrong. When you are called to testify in a dispute, do not be swayed by the crowd to twist justice. 3And do not slant your testimony in favor of a person just because that person is poor.

4"If you come upon your enemy's ox or donkey that has strayed away, take it back to its owner. 5If you see that the donkey of someone who hates you has collapsed under its load, do not walk by. Instead, stop and help.

6"In a lawsuit, you must not deny justice to the poor.

7"Be sure never to charge anyone falsely with evil. Never sentence an innocent or blameless person to death, for I never declare a guilty person to be innocent.

8"Take no bribes, for a bribe makes you ignore something that you clearly see. A bribe makes even a righteous person twist the truth.

9"You must not oppress foreigners. You know what it's like to be a foreigner, for you yourselves were once foreigners in the land of Egypt.

10"Plant and harvest your crops for six years, 11but let the land be renewed and lie uncultivated during the seventh year. Then let the poor among you harvest whatever grows on its own. Leave the rest for wild animals to eat. The same applies to your vineyards and olive groves.

12"You have six days each week for your ordinary work, but on the seventh day you must stop working. This gives your ox and your donkey a chance to rest. It also allows your slaves and the foreigners living among you to be refreshed.

13"Pay close attention to all my instructions. You must not call on the name of any other gods. Do not even speak their names.

## Three Annual Festivals

14"Each year you must celebrate three festivals in my honor. 15First, celebrate the Festival of Unleavened Bread. For seven days the bread you eat must be made without yeast, just as I commanded you. Celebrate this festival annually at the appointed time in early spring, in the month of Abib,* for that is the anniversary of your departure from Egypt. No one may appear before me without an offering.

**23:15** Hebrew *appointed time in the month of Abib.* This first month of the ancient Hebrew lunar calendar usually occurs within the months of March and April.

22:28 Lev 24:15-16; Acts 23:5
22:29 Exod 13:2; 23:16, 19; 34:20; Deut 26:2
22:30 Gen 17:12; Lev 12:3; 22:27
22:31 Exod 19:6; Lev 7:24; 17:15; 22:8
23:1 Exod 20:16; Ps 35:11
23:2 Deut 1:17; 16:19
23:4-5 Deut 22:1-4
23:6 Exod 23:2-3
23:7 Exod 20:13, 16; Deut 27:25
23:8 Deut 16:19
23:9 Exod 22:21; Lev 19:33-34
23:10 Lev 25:3
23:11 Lev 25:1-7
23:12 Exod 20:8-11
23:13 Deut 4:9, 23
23:14 Exod 34:23-24; Deut 16:16
23:15 Exod 12:15; 13:4; Lev 23:5

**22:29** The Israelites were to be prompt in giving God their offerings and not hold anything back. The first of the harvest was to be dedicated to him. Since God doesn't send payment overdue notices, it is easy to take care of other financial responsibilities while letting our gifts to him slide. Giving to God first out of what he has allowed you to have demonstrates that he has first priority in your life.

**23:1** Making up or spreading false rumors was strictly forbidden by God. Gossip, slander, and false witnessing would undermine families, strain neighborhood cooperation, and make chaos of the justice system. Destructive gossip still causes problems. Even if you do not initiate a lie, you become responsible if you pass it along. Don't circulate rumors; squelch them.

**23:2, 3** Justice is often perverted in favor of the rich. Here the people are warned against twisting justice in favor of the poor.

Justice should be impartial, treating rich and poor alike. Giving special privileges to either rich or poor only makes justice for everyone more unlikely. Withstand the pressure of the crowd to sway your decision about a person. Let the fairness God shows to each of us guide your judgment.

**23:4, 5** The thought of being kind to enemies was new and startling in a world where revenge was the common form of justice. God not only introduced this idea to the Israelites, he made it law! If a man found a lost animal owned by his enemy, he was to return it at once, even if his enemy might use it to harm him. Jesus clearly taught in Luke 10:30-37 to reach out to all people in need, even our enemies. Following the laws of right living is hard enough with friends. When we apply God's laws of fairness and kindness to our enemies, we show how different we are from the world.

**23:16**
Exod 34:22
Lev 23:34
Deut 16:13
**23:17**
Deut 16:16

**23:18**
Exod 12:8; 34:25
Lev 2:11

**23:19**
Exod 22:29
Deut 14:21

**23:20**
Exod 32:34
**23:21**
Exod 3:14; 34:5
Num 14:10-11
**23:22**
Num 24:9
Deut 30:7
**23:23**
Josh 24:8, 11
**23:24**
Exod 20:5; 34:13
**23:25**
Exod 15:26
Lev 26:3-13
Deut 7:12-15;
28:1-14
**23:27**
Gen 35:5
Exod 15:14
Deut 7:23
**23:28**
Deut 7:20
**23:29-30**
Deut 7:22
**23:31**
Gen 15:18
Josh 21:44;
24:12, 18
**23:32**
Deut 7:2
**23:33**
Deut 7:1-5, 16

**24:1**
Exod 6:23; 19:24

**24:2**
Num 12:6-8
**24:3**
Exod 19:8; 24:7
Deut 5:27; 11:1

16"Second, celebrate the Festival of Harvest,* when you bring me the first crops of your harvest.

"Finally, celebrate the Festival of the Final Harvest* at the end of the harvest season, when you have harvested all the crops from your fields. 17At these three times each year, every man in Israel must appear before the Sovereign, the LORD.

18"You must not offer the blood of my sacrificial offerings together with any baked goods containing yeast. And do not leave the fat from the festival offerings until the next morning.

19"As you harvest your crops, bring the very best of the first harvest to the house of the LORD your God.

"You must not cook a young goat in its mother's milk.

### A Promise of the LORD's Presence

20"See, I am sending an angel before you to protect you on your journey and lead you safely to the place I have prepared for you. 21Pay close attention to him, and obey his instructions. Do not rebel against him, for he is my representative, and he will not forgive your rebellion. 22But if you are careful to obey him, following all my instructions, then I will be an enemy to your enemies, and I will oppose those who oppose you. 23For my angel will go before you and bring you into the land of the Amorites, Hittites, Perizzites, Canaanites, Hivites, and Jebusites, so you may live there. And I will destroy them completely. 24You must not worship the gods of these nations or serve them in any way or imitate their evil practices. Instead, you must utterly destroy them and smash their sacred pillars.

25"You must serve only the LORD your God. If you do, I* will bless you with food and water, and I will protect you from illness. 26There will be no miscarriages or infertility in your land, and I will give you long, full lives.

27"I will send my terror ahead of you and create panic among all the people whose lands you invade. I will make all your enemies turn and run. 28I will send terror* ahead of you to drive out the Hivites, Canaanites, and Hittites. 29But I will not drive them out in a single year, because the land would become desolate and the wild animals would multiply and threaten you. 30I will drive them out a little at a time until your population has increased enough to take possession of the land. 31And I will fix your boundaries from the Red Sea to the Mediterranean Sea,* and from the eastern wilderness to the Euphrates River.* I will hand over to you the people now living in the land, and you will drive them out ahead of you.

32"Make no treaties with them or their gods. 33They must not live in your land, or they will cause you to sin against me. If you serve their gods, you will be caught in the trap of idolatry."

### Israel Accepts the LORD's Covenant

**24** Then the LORD instructed Moses: "Come up here to me, and bring along Aaron, Nadab, Abihu, and seventy of Israel's elders. All of you must worship from a distance. 2Only Moses is allowed to come near to the LORD. The others must not come near, and none of the other people are allowed to climb up the mountain with him."

3Then Moses went down to the people and repeated all the instructions and regulations

23:16a Or *Festival of Weeks.* This was later called the Festival of Pentecost (see Acts 2:1). It is celebrated today as Shavuot (or Shabuoth). 23:16b Or *Festival of Ingathering.* This was later called the Festival of Shelters or Festival of Tabernacles (see Lev 23:33-36). It is celebrated today as Sukkot (or Succoth). 23:25 As in Greek and Latin versions; Hebrew reads *he.* 23:28 Often rendered *the hornet.* The meaning of the Hebrew is uncertain. 23:31a Hebrew *from the sea of reeds to the sea of the Philistines.* 23:31b Hebrew *from the wilderness to the river.*

**23:20, 21** Who was this angel that went with the Israelites? Most likely the angel was a manifestation of God. God is not present in all the angels in this way. Angels are God's created messengers (Hebrews 1:14). God chose to make himself known in this special way for a special purpose. God was in the angel in the same way he was present in the pillars of cloud and fire (13:21, 22). "He is my representative" means the essential nature and power of God were made known in this angel.

**23:24, 25** If you're in the furnace, it's easy to catch on fire. God warned the Israelites about their neighbors whose beliefs and actions could turn them away from him. We also live among neighbors whose values may be completely different from ours. We are called to maintain a life-style that shows our faith. This can be a struggle, especially if our Christian life-

style differs from the norm. Our lives should demonstrate that obeying God takes precedence over conforming to our neighbors' way of life. God's Word, not society, dictates how we should live.

**23:29** Not all of God's solutions are instantaneous. Nor does delay justify inaction. In this case, God's cause would require constant cooperation, persistence, and effort by the Israelites. Success would come step by step.

**23:32, 33** God continually warned the people to avoid false religions and false gods. In Egypt they had been surrounded by idols and sorcerers, but leaving that land did not mean they were free from pagan religious influences. The land of Canaan was just as infested with idol worship. God knew his people needed extra strength, so he continually emphasized guarding against the influence of pagan religions.

the LORD had given him. All the people answered with one voice, "We will do everything the LORD has commanded."

4Then Moses carefully wrote down all the LORD's instructions. Early the next morning Moses got up and built an altar at the foot of the mountain. He also set up twelve pillars, one for each of the twelve tribes of Israel. 5Then he sent some of the young Israelite men to present burnt offerings and to sacrifice bulls as peace offerings to the LORD. 6Moses drained half the blood from these animals into basins. The other half he splattered against the altar.

7Then he took the Book of the Covenant and read it aloud to the people. Again they all responded, "We will do everything the LORD has commanded. We will obey."

8Then Moses took the blood from the basins and splattered it over the people, declaring, "Look, this blood confirms the covenant the LORD has made with you in giving you these instructions."

9Then Moses, Aaron, Nadab, Abihu, and the seventy elders of Israel climbed up the mountain. 10There they saw the God of Israel. Under his feet there seemed to be a surface of brilliant blue lapis lazuli, as clear as the sky itself. 11And though these nobles of Israel gazed upon God, he did not destroy them. In fact, they ate a covenant meal, eating and drinking in his presence!

12Then the LORD said to Moses, "Come up to me on the mountain. Stay there, and I will give you the tablets of stone on which I have inscribed the instructions and commands so you can teach the people." 13So Moses and his assistant Joshua set out, and Moses climbed up the mountain of God.

14Moses told the elders, "Stay here and wait for us until we come back. Aaron and Hur are here with you. If anyone has a dispute while I am gone, consult with them."

15Then Moses climbed up the mountain, and the cloud covered it. 16And the glory of the LORD settled down on Mount Sinai, and the cloud covered it for six days. On the seventh day the LORD called to Moses from inside the cloud. 17To the Israelites at the foot of the mountain, the glory of the LORD appeared at the summit like a consuming fire. 18Then Moses disappeared into the cloud as he climbed higher up the mountain. He remained on the mountain forty days and forty nights.

## 2. Tabernacle instructions
### Offerings for the Tabernacle

**25** The LORD said to Moses, 2"Tell the people of Israel to bring me their sacred offerings. Accept the contributions from all whose hearts are moved to offer them. 3Here is a list of sacred offerings you may accept from them:

gold, silver, and bronze;
4 blue, purple, and scarlet thread;
fine linen and goat hair for cloth;
5 tanned ram skins and fine goatskin leather;
acacia wood;
6 olive oil for the lamps;
spices for the anointing oil and the fragrant incense;
7 onyx stones, and other gemstones to be set in the ephod and the priest's chestpiece.

**24:4**
Deut 31:9
**24:5**
Exod 18:12
**24:6**
Heb 9:18
**24:7**
Exod 19:8; 24:3
Heb 9:19
**24:8**
Zech 9:11
Matt 26:28
1 Cor 11:25
†Heb 9:20
**24:10**
Exod 33:20
Num 12:8
Isa 6:5
Ezek 1:26
**24:12**
Jer 31:33
2 Cor 3:3
**24:15**
Exod 19:9
**24:16**
Exod 16:10
Num 14:10
**24:17**
Exod 3:2
Deut 4:24, 36
Heb 12:18, 29
**24:18**
Exod 34:28
Deut 9:9; 10:10
1 Kgs 19:8

**25:1-7**
//Exod 35:4-9
**25:2**
1 Chr 29:2-5
Ezra 2:68
Neh 7:70-72
2 Cor 8:11-12; 9:7

**25:6**
Exod 27:20; 30:23

---

**24:6-8** To understand this unusual covenant ratification ceremony, we need to understand the Bible's view of sin and forgiveness. God is the sovereign Judge of the universe. He is also absolutely holy. As the holy Judge of all, he condemns sin and judges it worthy of death. In the Old Testament God accepted the death of an animal as a substitute for the sinner. The animal's shed blood was proof that one life had been given for another. So on the one hand, blood symbolized the death of the animal, but it also symbolized the life that was spared as a result. Of course the death of the animal that brought forgiveness in the Old Testament was only a temporary provision, looking forward to the death of Jesus Christ (Hebrews 9:9–10:28).

In this ceremony described here, Moses sprinkled half the blood from the sacrificed animals on the altar to show that the sinner could once again approach God because something had died in his place. He sprinkled the other half of the blood on the people to show that the penalty for their sin had been paid and

they could be reunited with God. Through this symbolic act God's promises to Israel were reaffirmed, and lessons are taught to us about the future sacrificial death (or atonement) of Jesus Christ.

**25:1ff** Chapters 25 through 31 record God's directions for building the Tabernacle. Chapters 35 through 39 tell how these instructions were carried out. But what can all these ancient, complicated construction details show us today? First, the high quality of the precious materials making up the Tabernacle shows God's greatness and transcendence. Second, the curtain surrounding the Most Holy Place shows God's moral perfection as symbolized by his separation from the common and unclean. Third, the portable nature of the Tabernacle shows God's desire to be with his people as they traveled. Fourth, the Tabernacle, its furnishings, and the service performed there provide a picture of the atonement that would one day come through Jesus Christ.

25:8
Exod 29:45; 36:1-5
Deut 12:11

8"Have the people of Israel build me a holy sanctuary so I can live among them. 9You must build this Tabernacle and its furnishings exactly according to the pattern I will show you.

## Plans for the Ark of the Covenant

25:10-20
//Exod 37:1-9
25:12
Exod 26:29; 27:7;
37:5; 38:7
25:15
1 Kgs 8:8
25:16
Exod 16:34
Heb 9:4
25:17
Exod 37:6
Lev 16:13
Rom 3:25
Heb 9:5
25:20
1 Kgs 8:7
Heb 9:5
25:21
Exod 26:34
25:22
Exod 30:6, 36
Lev 1:1

10"Have the people make an Ark of acacia wood—a sacred chest 45 inches long, 27 inches wide, and 27 inches high.* 11Overlay it inside and outside with pure gold, and run a molding of gold all around it. 12Cast four gold rings and attach them to its four feet, two rings on each side. 13Make poles from acacia wood, and overlay them with gold. 14Insert the poles into the rings at the sides of the Ark to carry it. 15These carrying poles must stay inside the rings; never remove them. 16When the Ark is finished, place inside it the stone tablets inscribed with the terms of the covenant,* which I will give to you.

17"Then make the Ark's cover—the place of atonement—from pure gold. It must be 45 inches long and 27 inches wide.* 18Then make two cherubim from hammered gold, and place them on the two ends of the atonement cover. 19Mold the cherubim on each end of the atonement cover, making it all of one piece of gold. 20The cherubim will face each other and look down on the atonement cover. With their wings spread above it, they will protect it. 21Place inside the Ark the stone tablets inscribed with the terms of the covenant, which I will give to you. Then put the atonement cover on top of the Ark. 22I will meet with you there and talk to you from above the atonement cover between the gold cherubim that hover over the Ark of the Covenant.* From there I will give you my commands for the people of Israel.

## Plans for the Table

25:23-29
//Exod 37:10-16

23"Then make a table of acacia wood, 36 inches long, 18 inches wide, and 27 inches high.* 24Overlay it with pure gold and run a gold molding around the edge. 25Decorate it with a 3-inch border* all around, and run a gold molding along the border. 26Make four gold rings for the table and attach them at the four corners next to the four legs. 27Attach the rings near the border to hold the poles that are used to carry the table. 28Make these poles from acacia wood, and overlay them with gold. 29Make special containers of pure gold for the table—bowls, pans, pitchers, and jars—to be used in pouring out liquid offerings. 30Place the Bread of the Presence on the table to remain before me at all times.

25:29
Exod 37:16
Num 4:7
25:30
Exod 39:36; 40:23
Lev 24:5-9
Num 4:7

25:10 Hebrew 2.5 cubits [115 centimeters] long, 1.5 cubits [69 centimeters] wide, and 1.5 cubits high.   25:16 Hebrew Place inside the Ark the Testimony; similarly in 25:21. The Hebrew word for "testimony" refers to the terms of the LORD's covenant with Israel as written on stone tablets, and also to the covenant itself.   25:17 Hebrew 2.5 cubits [115 centimeters] long and 1.5 cubits [69 centimeters] wide.   25:22 Or Ark of the Testimony.   25:23 Hebrew 2 cubits [92 centimeters] long, 1 cubit [46 centimeters] wide, and 1.5 cubits [69 centimeters] high.   25:25 Hebrew a border of a handbreadth [8 centimeters].

---

**THEOPHANIES IN THE SCRIPTURE**
Appearances of God

At the foot of Mount Sinai, God appeared to the people of Israel in a physical form. This is called a *theophany.* Here are some of the other times God appeared to Bible people.

| Verse | Theophany |
| --- | --- |
| Genesis 16:7 | The angel of the Lord appeared to Sarah's servant, Hagar, announcing the birth of Abraham's son Ishmael |
| Genesis 18:1-11 | The Lord appeared to Abraham, foretelling Isaac's birth |
| Genesis 22:11, 12 | The angel of the Lord stopped Abraham from sacrificing Isaac |
| Exodus 3:2 | The angel of the Lord appeared to Moses as a blazing fire in a bush |
| Exodus 14:19 | The angel of God appeared to Israel in pillars of cloud and fire to guide them through the wilderness |
| Exodus 33:11 | The Lord spoke to Moses face to face |
| Daniel 3:25 | One "like a god" appeared as the fourth man with Shadrach, Meshach, and Abednego in the fiery furnace |

("Angel of the Lord" is a reverential way to refer to God.)

---

**25:10** Much of the Tabernacle and its furniture was made of acacia wood. Acacia trees flourished in barren regions and were fairly common in Old Testament times. The wood was brownish-orange and very hard, making it an excellent material for furniture. Acacia wood is still used in furniture making today.
**25:17** The cover of the Ark of the Covenant was called the atonement cover. This is where, between the two golden cherubim (mighty angels), the presence of God would dwell in a cloud above their outstretched wings. The atonement cover was where the highest and most perfect act of atonement would be made when the high priest would enter the Most Holy Place on the Day of Atonement to atone for the sins of all the people (30:10).

### Plans for the Lampstand

31"Make a lampstand of pure, hammered gold. Make the entire lampstand and its decorations of one piece—the base, center stem, lamp cups, buds, and petals. 32Make it with six branches going out from the center stem, three on each side. 33Each of the six branches will have three lamp cups shaped like almond blossoms, complete with buds and petals. 34Craft the center stem of the lampstand with four lamp cups shaped like almond blossoms, complete with buds and petals. 35There will also be an almond bud beneath each pair of branches where the six branches extend from the center stem. 36The almond buds and branches must all be of one piece with the center stem, and they must be hammered from pure gold. 37Then make the seven lamps for the lampstand, and set them so they reflect their light forward. 38The lamp snuffers and trays must also be made of pure gold. 39You will need seventy-five pounds* of pure gold for the lampstand and its accessories.

40"Be sure that you make everything according to the pattern I have shown you here on the mountain.

### Plans for the Tabernacle

**26** "Make the Tabernacle from ten curtains of finely woven linen. Decorate the curtains with blue, purple, and scarlet thread and with skillfully embroidered cherubim. 2These ten curtains must all be exactly the same size—42 feet long and 6 feet wide.* 3Join five of these curtains together to make one long curtain, then join the other five into a second long curtain. 4Put loops of blue yarn along the edge of the last curtain in each set. 5The fifty loops along the edge of one curtain are to match the fifty loops along the edge of the other curtain. 6Then make fifty gold clasps and fasten the long curtains together with the clasps. In this way, the Tabernacle will be made of one continuous piece.

7"Make eleven curtains of goat-hair cloth to serve as a tent covering for the Tabernacle. 8These eleven curtains must all be exactly the same size—45 feet long and 6 feet wide.* 9Join five of these curtains together to make one long curtain, and join the other six into a second long curtain. Allow 3 feet of material from the second set of curtains to hang over the front* of the sacred tent. 10Make fifty loops for one edge of each large curtain. 11Then make fifty bronze clasps, and fasten the loops of the long curtains with the clasps. In this way, the tent covering will be made of one continuous piece. 12The remaining 3 feet* of this tent covering will be left to hang over the back of the Tabernacle. 13Allow 18 inches* of remaining material to hang down over each side, so the Tabernacle is completely covered. 14Complete the tent covering with a protective layer of tanned ram skins and a layer of fine goatskin leather.

15"For the framework of the Tabernacle, construct frames of acacia wood. 16Each frame must be 15 feet high and 27 inches wide,* 17with two pegs under each frame. Make all the frames identical. 18Make twenty of these frames to support the curtains on the south side of the Tabernacle. 19Also make forty silver bases—two bases under each frame, with the pegs fitting securely into the bases. 20For the north side of the Tabernacle, make another twenty frames, 21with their forty silver bases, two bases under each frame. 22Make six frames for the rear—the west side of the Tabernacle—23along with two additional frames to reinforce the rear corners of the Tabernacle. 24These corner frames will be matched at the bottom and firmly attached at the top with a single ring, forming a single corner unit. Make both of these corner units the same way. 25So there will be eight frames at the rear of the Tabernacle, set in sixteen silver bases—two bases under each frame.

26"Make crossbars of acacia wood to link the frames, five crossbars for the north side of the Tabernacle 27and five for the south side. Also make five crossbars for the rear of the Tabernacle, which will face west. 28The middle crossbar, attached halfway up the frames, will run all the way from one end of the Tabernacle to the other. 29Overlay the frames with gold, and make gold rings to hold the crossbars. Overlay the crossbars with gold as well.

30"Set up this Tabernacle according to the pattern you were shown on the mountain.

31"For the inside of the Tabernacle, make a special curtain of finely woven linen. Deco-

25:31-39 //Exod 37:17-24
25:31 Exod 37:17; 1 Kgs 7:49; Heb 9:2; Rev 1:12
25:37 Exod 27:21; Zech 4:2; Rev 1:4, 12, 20; 4:5
25:40 Acts 7:44; †Heb 8:5
26:1-37 //Exod 36:8-38
26:3 Exod 36:10
26:5 Exod 36:12
26:7 Exod 36:14
26:11 Exod 36:18
26:14 Exod 36:19
26:15 Exod 36:20-34
26:20 Exod 36:23
26:25 Exod 36:30
26:30 Exod 25:9, 40; Acts 7:44; †Heb 8:5
26:31 Exod 36:35; 2 Chr 3:14; Matt 27:51; Heb 9:3

25:39 Hebrew *1 talent* [34 kilograms].   26:2 Hebrew *28 cubits* [12.9 meters] *long and 4 cubits* [1.8 meters] *wide.*   26:8 Hebrew *30 cubits* [13.8 meters] *long and 4 cubits* [1.8 meters] *wide.*   26:9 Hebrew *Double over the sixth sheet at the front.*   26:12 Hebrew *The half sheet that is left over.*   26:13 Hebrew *1 cubit* [46 centimeters].   26:16 Hebrew *10 cubits* [4.6 meters] *high and 1.5 cubits* [69 centimeters] *wide.*

**26:31-33** This curtain separated the two sacred rooms in the Tabernacle—the Holy Place and the Most Holy Place. The priest entered the Holy Place each day to commune with God and to tend to the incense altar, the lampstand, and the table with the Bread of the Presence. The Most Holy Place was where God himself dwelt, his presence resting on the

**26:33**
Exod 25:16; 40:21
Heb 9:2-3

**26:34**
Exod 25:21; 37:6
Heb 9:5

**26:36**
Exod 40:28
**26:37**
Exod 36:38

**27:1-8**
//Exod 38:1-7
**27:2**
Exod 29:12
Lev 4:7
**27:3**
Num 4:14
**27:6**
Exod 25:13
**27:8**
Exod 25:40; 26:30

**27:9-19**
//Exod 38:9-20
**27:10**
Exod 38:17

**27:14**
Exod 38:15

**27:16**
Exod 36:37

**27:20-21**
//Lev 24:1-3
Zech 4:11-12
**27:21**
Exod 25:22
Lev 3:17; 16:34

rate it with blue, purple, and scarlet thread and with skillfully embroidered cherubim. 32Hang this curtain on gold hooks attached to four posts of acacia wood. Overlay the posts with gold, and set them in four silver bases. 33Hang the inner curtain from clasps, and put the Ark of the Covenant* in the room behind it. This curtain will separate the Holy Place from the Most Holy Place.

34"Then put the Ark's cover—the place of atonement—on top of the Ark of the Covenant inside the Most Holy Place. 35Place the table outside the inner curtain on the north side of the Tabernacle, and place the lampstand across the room on the south side.

36"Make another curtain for the entrance to the sacred tent. Make it of finely woven linen and embroider it with exquisite designs, using blue, purple, and scarlet thread. 37Craft five posts from acacia wood. Overlay them with gold, and hang the curtain from them with gold hooks. Cast five bronze bases for the posts.

### Plans for the Altar of Burnt Offering

**27** "Using acacia wood, construct a square altar 7½ feet wide, 7½ feet long, and 4½ feet high.* 2Make horns for each of its four corners so that the horns and altar are all one piece. Overlay the altar with bronze. 3Make ash buckets, shovels, basins, meat forks, and firepans, all of bronze. 4Make a bronze grating for it, and attach four bronze rings at its four corners. 5Install the grating halfway down the side of the altar, under the ledge. 6For carrying the altar, make poles from acacia wood, and overlay them with bronze. 7Insert the poles through the rings on the two sides of the altar. 8The altar must be hollow, made from planks. Build it just as you were shown on the mountain.

### Plans for the Courtyard

9"Then make the courtyard for the Tabernacle, enclosed with curtains made of finely woven linen. On the south side, make the curtains 150 feet long.* 10They will be held up by twenty posts set securely in twenty bronze bases. Hang the curtains with silver hooks and rings. 11Make the curtains the same on the north side—150 feet of curtains held up by twenty posts set securely in bronze bases. Hang the curtains with silver hooks and rings. 12The curtains on the west end of the courtyard will be 75 feet long,* supported by ten posts set into ten bases. 13The east end of the courtyard, the front, will also be 75 feet long. 14The courtyard entrance will be on the east end, flanked by two curtains. The curtain on the right side will be 22½ feet long,* supported by three posts set into three bases. 15The curtain on the left side will also be 22½ feet long, supported by three posts set into three bases.

16"For the entrance to the courtyard, make a curtain that is 30 feet long.* Make it from finely woven linen, and decorate it with beautiful embroidery in blue, purple, and scarlet thread. Support it with four posts, each securely set in its own base. 17All the posts around the courtyard must have silver rings and hooks and bronze bases. 18So the entire courtyard will be 150 feet long and 75 feet wide, with curtain walls 7½ feet high,* made from finely woven linen. The bases for the posts will be made of bronze.

19"All the articles used in the rituals of the Tabernacle, including all the tent pegs used to support the Tabernacle and the courtyard curtains, must be made of bronze.

### Light for the Tabernacle

20"Command the people of Israel to bring you pure oil of pressed olives for the light, to keep the lamps burning continually. 21The lampstand will stand in the Tabernacle, in front of the

**26:33** Or *Ark of the Testimony;* also in 26:34.    **27:1** Hebrew *5 cubits* [2.3 meters] *wide, 5 cubits long, a square, and 3 cubits* [1.4 meters] *high.*    **27:9** Hebrew *100 cubits* [46 meters]; also in 27:11.    **27:12** Hebrew *50 cubits* [23 meters]; also in 27:13.    **27:14** Hebrew *15 cubits* [6.9 meters]; also in 27:15.    **27:16** Hebrew *20 cubits* [9.2 meters].    **27:18** Hebrew *100 cubits* [46 meters] *long and 50 by 50* [23 meters] *wide and 5 cubits* [2.3 meters] *high.*

atonement cover, which covered the Ark of the Covenant. Only the high priest could enter the Most Holy Place. Even he could do so only once a year (on the Day of Atonement) to make atonement for the sins of the nation as a whole. When Jesus Christ died on the cross, the curtain in the Temple (which had replaced the Tabernacle) tore from top to bottom (Mark 15:38), symbolizing our free access to God because of Jesus' death. No longer did people have to approach God through priests and sacrifices.

**27:1** The altar of burnt offering was the first thing the Israelites saw as they entered the Tabernacle courtyard. Here sacrifices were constantly made. Its vivid presence constantly reminded the people that they could only come to God by means of the sacrifice. It was the only way their sins could be forgiven and taken away. In Hebrews 10:1-18, Jesus Christ is portrayed as the ultimate sacrifice. This teaches that we are not to seek any other means to having a personal relationship with God. No counseling theory, Eastern mysticism, or modern ideas of spirituality can remove our sin. Jesus is our only High Priest today. Put all your confidence in him.

inner curtain that shields the Ark of the Covenant.* Aaron and his sons must keep the lamps burning in the LORD's presence all night. This is a permanent law for the people of Israel, and it must be observed from generation to generation.

## Clothing for the Priests

**28** "Call for your brother, Aaron, and his sons, Nadab, Abihu, Eleazar, and Ithamar. Set them apart from the rest of the people of Israel so they may minister to me and be my priests. 2Make sacred garments for Aaron that are glorious and beautiful. 3Instruct all the skilled craftsmen whom I have filled with the spirit of wisdom. Have them make garments for Aaron that will distinguish him as a priest set apart for my service. 4These are the garments they are to make: a chestpiece, an ephod, a robe, a patterned tunic, a turban, and a sash. They are to make these sacred garments for your brother, Aaron, and his sons to wear when they serve me as priests. 5So give them fine linen cloth, gold thread, and blue, purple, and scarlet thread.

## Design of the Ephod

6"The craftsmen must make the ephod of finely woven linen and skillfully embroider it with gold and with blue, purple, and scarlet thread. 7It will consist of two pieces, front and back, joined at the shoulders with two shoulder-pieces. 8The decorative sash will be made of the same materials: finely woven linen embroidered with gold and with blue, purple, and scarlet thread.

9"Take two onyx stones, and engrave on them the names of the tribes of Israel. 10Six names will be on each stone, arranged in the order of the births of the original sons of Israel. 11Engrave these names on the two stones in the same way a jeweler engraves a seal. Then mount the stones in settings of gold filigree. 12Fasten the two stones on the shoulder-pieces of the ephod as a reminder that Aaron represents the people of Israel. Aaron will carry these names on his shoulders as a constant reminder whenever he goes before the LORD. 13Make the settings of gold filigree, 14then braid two cords of pure gold and attach them to the filigree settings on the shoulders of the ephod.

## Design of the Chestpiece

15"Then, with great skill and care, make a chestpiece to be worn for seeking a decision from God.* Make it to match the ephod, using finely woven linen embroidered with gold and with blue, purple, and scarlet thread. 16Make the chestpiece of a single piece of cloth folded to form a pouch nine inches* square. 17Mount four rows of gemstones* on it. The first row will contain a red carnelian, a pale-green peridot, and an emerald. 18The second row will contain a turquoise, a blue lapis lazuli, and a white moonstone. 19The third row will contain an orange jacinth, an agate, and a purple amethyst. 20The fourth row will contain a blue-green beryl, an onyx, and a green jasper. All these stones will be set in gold filigree. 21Each stone will represent one of the twelve sons of Israel, and the name of that tribe will be engraved on it like a seal.

22"To attach the chestpiece to the ephod, make braided cords of pure gold thread. 23Then make two gold rings and attach them to the top corners of the chestpiece. 24Tie the

**28:1** Exod 24:1, 9; Num 18:7; Ps 99:6; Heb 5:1, 4
**28:2** Exod 29:5, 9; 31:10; Lev 8:7, 30; Num 20:26
**28:5** Exod 25:3-4
**28:6-14** //Exod 39:2-7
**28:12** Exod 39:7
**28:15-28** //Exod 39:8-21
**28:17** Exod 39:10
**28:21** Exod 39:14
**28:24** Exod 39:17

27:21 Hebrew *in the Tent of Meeting, outside the inner curtain that is in front of the Testimony.* See note on 25:16. **28:15** Hebrew *a chestpiece for decision.* **28:16** Hebrew *1 span* [23 centimeters]. **28:17** The identification of some of these gemstones is uncertain.

**28:1ff** God was teaching his people how to worship him. To do so, he needed ministers to oversee the operations of the Tabernacle and to help the people maintain their relationship with God. These men were called priests and Levites, and they could only be members of the tribe of Levi. Chapters 28 and 29 give some details about priests. Not only was a priest from the tribe of Levi, but he also was a descendant of Aaron, Israel's first high priest. Priests had more responsibilities than Levites. As high priest, Aaron was in charge of all the priests and Levites. The priests performed the daily sacrifices, maintained the Tabernacle, and counseled the people on how to follow God. They were the people's representatives before God and thus were required to live worthy of their office. Jesus is now our High Priest (Hebrews 8). Daily sacrifices are no longer required because he sacrificed himself on the cross for our sins. Today ministers no longer sacrifice animals. Instead, ministers lead us in prayer and teach us

about both the benefits and the commandments that characterize our new life as Christians.

**28:3** The tailors who made Aaron's garments were given wisdom by God in order to do their task. All of us have special skills. God wants to fill us with his Spirit so we will use those skills for his glory. Think about your special talents and abilities and the ways you could use them for God's work in the world. As you focus on helping and giving to others, God will show you the best ways to do it and give you wisdom to accomplish the task.

**28:6-13** The ephod was a kind of apron elaborately embroidered with two pieces, back and front, joined at the shoulder with a band at the waist. On each shoulder strap was a stone with 6 of the 12 tribes of Israel engraved on it. The priest symbolically carried the burden of the whole nation on his shoulders as he represented them before God.

two gold cords to the two rings on the chestpiece. 25Tie the other ends of the cords to the gold settings on the shoulder-pieces of the ephod. 26Then make two more gold rings and attach them to the inside edges of the chestpiece next to the ephod. 27And make two more gold rings and attach them to the front of the ephod, below the shoulder-pieces, just above the knot where the decorative sash is fastened to the ephod. 28Then attach the bottom rings of the chestpiece to the rings on the ephod with blue cords. This will hold the chestpiece securely to the ephod above the decorative sash.

29"In this way, Aaron will carry the names of the tribes of Israel on the sacred chestpiece* over his heart when he goes into the Holy Place. This will be a continual reminder that he represents the people when he comes before the LORD. 30Insert the Urim and Thummim into the sacred chestpiece so they will be carried over Aaron's heart when he goes into the LORD's presence. In this way, Aaron will always carry over his heart the objects used to determine the LORD's will for his people whenever he goes in before the LORD.

### Additional Clothing for the Priests

31"Make the robe that is worn with the ephod from a single piece of blue cloth, 32with an opening for Aaron's head in the middle of it. Reinforce the opening with a woven collar* so it will not tear. 33Make pomegranates out of blue, purple, and scarlet yarn, and attach them to the hem of the robe, with gold bells between them. 34The gold bells and pomegranates are to alternate all around the hem. 35Aaron will wear this robe whenever he ministers before the LORD, and the bells will tinkle as he goes in and out of the LORD's presence in the Holy Place. If he wears it, he will not die.

36"Next make a medallion of pure gold, and engrave it like a seal with these words: HOLY TO THE LORD. 37Attach the medallion with a blue cord to the front of Aaron's turban, where it must remain. 38Aaron must wear it on his forehead so he may take on himself any guilt of the people of Israel when they consecrate their sacred offerings. He must always wear it on his forehead so the LORD will accept the people.

39"Weave Aaron's patterned tunic from fine linen cloth. Fashion the turban from this linen as well. Also make a sash, and decorate it with colorful embroidery.

40"For Aaron's sons, make tunics, sashes, and special head coverings that are glorious and beautiful. 41Clothe your brother, Aaron, and his sons with these garments, and then anoint and ordain them. Consecrate them so they can serve as my priests. 42Also make linen undergarments for them, to be worn next to their bodies, reaching from their hips to their thighs. 43These must be worn whenever Aaron and his sons enter the Tabernacle* or approach the altar in the Holy Place to perform their priestly duties. Then they will not incur guilt and die. This is a permanent law for Aaron and all his descendants after him.

### Dedication of the Priests

**29** "This is the ceremony you must follow when you consecrate Aaron and his sons to serve me as priests: Take a young bull and two rams with no defects. 2Then, using choice wheat flour and no yeast, make loaves of bread, thin cakes mixed with olive oil, and wafers spread with oil. 3Place them all in a single basket, and present them at the entrance of the Tabernacle, along with the young bull and the two rams.

4"Present Aaron and his sons at the entrance of the Tabernacle,* and wash them with water. 5Dress Aaron in his priestly garments—the tunic, the robe worn with the ephod, the ephod itself, and the chestpiece. Then wrap the decorative sash of the ephod around him. 6Place the turban on his head, and fasten the sacred medallion to the turban. 7Then anoint him by pouring the anointing oil over his head. 8Next present his sons, and dress them in

**28:26**
Exod 39:17

**28:29**
Exod 28:12

**28:30**
Lev 8:8
Num 27:21

**28:31-43**
//Exod 39:22-31

**28:36**
Exod 39:30-31
Lev 8:9

**28:38**
Lev 10:17; 22:16
Num 18:1
Heb 9:28
1 Pet 2:24

**28:40**
Exod 39:27-29
Lev 8:13

**28:41**
Exod 29:7-9
Lev 8:1-36
Heb 7:28

**28:42**
Lev 6:10; 16:4
Ezek 44:18

**28:43**
Exod 20:26; 27:21

**29:1-37**
//Lev 8:1-36

**29:2**
Lev 6:19-23

**29:4**
Exod 40:12
Heb 10:22

**29:5**
Exod 28:2, 5

**29:6**
Exod 28:36

**29:7**
Exod 28:41
Lev 8:12-13
Ps 133:2

**28:29** Hebrew *the chestpiece for decision;* also in 28:30. See 28:15.   **28:32** The meaning of the Hebrew is uncertain.
**28:43** Hebrew *Tent of Meeting.*   **29:4** Hebrew *Tent of Meeting;* also in 29:10, 11, 30, 32, 42, 44.

---

**28:30** The Urim and the Thummim were used by the priest to make decisions. These names mean "Curses" and "Perfections" and refer to the nature of God whose will they revealed. They were kept in a pocket and taken out or shaken out to get either a yes or no decision.

**29:1ff** Why did God set up the priesthood? God had originally intended that his chosen people be a "kingdom of priests" with both the nation as a whole and each individual dealing directly with God. But the people's sin prevented this from happening because a sinful person is not worthy to approach a perfect God. God then

appointed priests from the tribe of Levi and set up the system of sacrifices to help the people approach him. He promised to forgive the people's sins if they would offer certain sacrifices administered by the priests on behalf of the people. Through these priests and their work, God wished to prepare all people for the coming of Jesus Christ, who would once again offer a direct relationship with God for anyone who would come to him. But until Christ came, the priests were the people's representatives before God. Through this Old Testament system, we can better understand the significance of what Christ did for us (see Hebrews 10:1-14).

their tunics. 9Wrap the sashes around the waists of Aaron and his sons, and put their special head coverings on them. Then the right to the priesthood will be theirs by law forever. In this way, you will ordain Aaron and his sons.

10"Bring the young bull to the entrance of the Tabernacle, where Aaron and his sons will lay their hands on its head. 11Then slaughter the bull in the LORD's presence at the entrance of the Tabernacle. 12Put some of its blood on the horns of the altar with your finger, and pour out the rest at the base of the altar. 13Take all the fat around the internal organs, the long lobe of the liver, and the two kidneys and the fat around them, and burn it all on the altar. 14Then take the rest of the bull, including its hide, meat, and dung, and burn it outside the camp as a sin offering.

15"Next Aaron and his sons must lay their hands on the head of one of the rams. 16Then slaughter the ram, and splatter its blood against all sides of the altar. 17Cut the ram into pieces, and wash off the internal organs and the legs. Set them alongside the head and the other pieces of the body, 18then burn the entire animal on the altar. This is a burnt offering to the LORD; it is a pleasing aroma, a special gift presented to the LORD.

19"Now take the other ram, and have Aaron and his sons lay their hands on its head. 20Then slaughter it, and apply some of its blood to the right earlobes of Aaron and his sons. Also put it on the thumbs of their right hands and the big toes of their right feet. Splatter the rest of the blood against all sides of the altar. 21Then take some of the blood from the altar and some of the anointing oil, and sprinkle it on Aaron and his sons and on their garments. In this way, they and their garments will be set apart as holy.

22"Since this is the ram for the ordination of Aaron and his sons, take the fat of the ram, including the fat of the broad tail, the fat around the internal organs, the long lobe of the liver, and the two kidneys and the fat around them, along with the right thigh. 23Then take one round loaf of bread, one thin cake mixed with olive oil, and one wafer from the basket of bread without yeast that was placed in the LORD's presence. 24Put all these in the hands of Aaron and his sons to be lifted up as a special offering to the LORD. 25Afterward take the various breads from their hands, and burn them on the altar along with the burnt offering. It is a pleasing aroma to the LORD, a special gift for him. 26Then take the breast of Aaron's ordination ram, and lift it up in the LORD's presence as a special offering to him. Then keep it as your own portion.

27"Set aside the portions of the ordination ram that belong to Aaron and his sons. This includes the breast and the thigh that were lifted up before the LORD as a special offering. 28In the future, whenever the people of Israel lift up a peace offering, a portion of it must be set aside for Aaron and his descendants. This is their permanent right, and it is a sacred offering from the Israelites to the LORD.

29"Aaron's sacred garments must be preserved for his descendants who succeed him, and they will wear them when they are anointed and ordained. 30The descendant who succeeds him as high priest will wear these clothes for seven days as he ministers in the Tabernacle and the Holy Place.

31"Take the ram used in the ordination ceremony, and boil its meat in a sacred place. 32Then Aaron and his sons will eat this meat, along with the bread in the basket, at the Tabernacle entrance. 33They alone may eat the meat and bread used for their purification* in the ordination ceremony. No one else may eat them, for these things are set apart and holy. 34If any of the ordination meat or bread remains until the morning, it must be burned. It may not be eaten, for it is holy.

35"This is how you will ordain Aaron and his sons to their offices, just as I have commanded you. The ordination ceremony will go on for seven days. 36Each day you must sacrifice a young bull as a sin offering to purify them, making them right with the LORD.* Afterward, cleanse the altar by purifying it*; make it holy by anointing it with oil. 37Purify

**29:9** Exod 40:15 Num 3:10; 18:7; 25:13 Deut 18:5
**29:10** Lev 1:4; 8:14
**29:12** Exod 27:2 Lev 8:15
**29:13** Lev 3:3-5
**29:14** Lev 4:11-12, 21 Heb 13:11
**29:15** Exod 29:10
**29:18** Gen 8:21
**29:21** Exod 30:25, 31 Heb 9:22
**29:23** Lev 8:26
**29:24** Lev 7:30
**29:26** Lev 7:31, 34; 8:29
**29:27** Lev 7:31, 34 Num 18:11-12 Deut 18:3
**29:29** Num 20:26, 28
**29:30** Lev 8:35
**29:33** Lev 22:10, 13
**29:34-35** Lev 8:32-33
**29:36** Exod 40:10 Heb 10:11
**29:37** Exod 40:10 Matt 23:19

**29:33** Or *their atonement.* **29:36a** Or *to make atonement.* **29:36b** Or *by making atonement for it;* similarly in 29:37.

---

**29:10-41** Why were there such detailed rituals in connection with these sacrifices? Partly it was for quality control. A centralized, standardized form of worship prevented problems of belief which could arise from individuals creating their own worship. Also, it differentiated the Hebrews from the pagan Canaanites they would meet in the Promised Land. By closely following God's instructions, the Hebrews could not possibly join the Canaanites in their immoral religious practices. Finally, it showed Israel that God was serious about his relationship with them.

**29:37** Notice the overwhelming emphasis on the holiness of God. The priests, the clothes, the Tabernacle, and the sacrifices had to be clean and consecrated, prepared to meet God. In contrast, today we tend to take God for granted, rushing into worship and treating him with almost casual disregard. But we worship the almighty Creator and Sustainer of the universe.

29:38
Num 28:3-31;
29:6-38
1 Chr 16:40
Dan 12:11

29:41
2 Kgs 16:15
Ezra 9:4-5
Ps 141:2

29:42
Exod 30:8

29:43
1 Kgs 8:11

29:45
Exod 25:8
Lev 26:12
Num 5:3
Deut 12:11
Ps 68:18
Zech 2:10
2 Cor 6:16
Rev 21:3

29:46
Exod 20:2

30:1-5
//Exod 37:25-28
1 Kgs 6:20
Rev 8:3

30:6
Exod 25:21-22

30:7
Exod 27:21;
30:34-35
1 Sam 2:28
Luke 1:9

30:10
Lev 16:8

30:12
Exod 38:25-26
Num 1:2; 26:2
2 Sam 24:1
Matt 20:28

30:13
Matt 17:24

30:15
Prov 22:2

the altar, and consecrate it every day for seven days. After that, the altar will be absolutely holy, and whatever touches it will become holy.

38"These are the sacrifices you are to offer regularly on the altar. Each day, offer two lambs that are a year old, 39one in the morning and the other in the evening. 40With one of them, offer two quarts of choice flour mixed with one quart of pure oil of pressed olives; also, offer one quart of wine* as a liquid offering. 41Offer the other lamb in the evening, along with the same offerings of flour and wine as in the morning. It will be a pleasing aroma, a special gift presented to the LORD.

42"These burnt offerings are to be made each day from generation to generation. Offer them in the LORD's presence at the Tabernacle entrance; there I will meet with you and speak with you. 43I will meet the people of Israel there, in the place made holy by my glorious presence. 44Yes, I will consecrate the Tabernacle and the altar, and I will consecrate Aaron and his sons to serve me as priests. 45Then I will live among the people of Israel and be their God, 46and they will know that I am the LORD their God. I am the one who brought them out of the land of Egypt so that I could live among them. I am the LORD their God.

## Plans for the Incense Altar

**30** "Then make another altar of acacia wood for burning incense. 2Make it 18 inches square and 36 inches high,* with horns at the corners carved from the same piece of wood as the altar itself. 3Overlay the top, sides, and horns of the altar with pure gold, and run a gold molding around the entire altar. 4Make two gold rings, and attach them on opposite sides of the altar below the gold molding to hold the carrying poles. 5Make the poles of acacia wood and overlay them with gold. 6Place the incense altar just outside the inner curtain that shields the Ark of the Covenant,* in front of the Ark's cover—the place of atonement—that covers the tablets inscribed with the terms of the covenant.* I will meet with you there.

7"Every morning when Aaron maintains the lamps, he must burn fragrant incense on the altar. 8And each evening when he lights the lamps, he must again burn incense in the LORD's presence. This must be done from generation to generation. 9Do not offer any unholy incense on this altar, or any burnt offerings, grain offerings, or liquid offerings.

10"Once a year Aaron must purify* the altar by smearing its horns with blood from the offering made to purify the people from their sin. This will be a regular, annual event from generation to generation, for this is the LORD's most holy altar."

## Money for the Tabernacle

11Then the LORD said to Moses, 12"Whenever you take a census of the people of Israel, each man who is counted must pay a ransom for himself to the LORD. Then no plague will strike the people as you count them. 13Each person who is counted must give a small piece of silver as a sacred offering to the LORD. (This payment is half a shekel,* based on the sanctuary shekel, which equals twenty gerahs.) 14All who have reached their twentieth birthday must give this sacred offering to the LORD. 15When this offering is given to the LORD to purify your lives, making you right with him,* the rich must not give more than the specified

29:40 Hebrew 1/10 of an ephah [2.2 liters] of choice flour . . . 1/4 of a hin [1 liter] of pure oil . . . 1/4 of a hin of wine. 30:2 Hebrew 1 cubit [46 centimeters] long and 1 cubit wide, a square, and 2 cubits [92 centimeters] high. 30:6a Or Ark of the Testimony; also in 30:26. 30:6b Hebrew that covers the Testimony; see note on 25:16. 30:10 Or make atonement for; also in 30:10b. 30:13 Or 0.2 ounces, or 6 grams. 30:15 Or to make atonement for your lives; similarly in 30:16.

---

Remember that profound truth when you pray or worship, and come before him with reverence and repentance.

**29:45, 46** God's action in bringing the Israelites out of Egypt showed his great desire to be with them and protect them. Throughout the Bible, God shows that he is not an absentee landlord. He wants to live among us, even in our hearts. Don't exclude God from your life. Allow him to be your God as you obey his Word and communicate with him in prayer. Let him be your resident landlord.

**30:10** This once-a-year ceremony was called the Day of Atonement. On this day a sacrifice was made for the sins of the entire Israelite nation. This was the only day the high priest could enter the Most Holy Place, the innermost room of the Tabernacle. Here he asked God to forgive the people. The Day of Atonement

served as a reminder that the daily, weekly, and monthly sacrifices could cover sins only temporarily. It pointed toward Jesus Christ, the perfect atonement, who could remove sins forever.

**30:11-16** This money was like a census tax. It continued the principle that all the people belonged to God and therefore needed to be redeemed by a sacrifice. Whenever a census took place, everyone, both rich and poor, was required to pay a ransom. God does not discriminate between people (see Acts 10:34; Galatians 3:28). All of us need mercy and forgiveness because of our sinful thoughts and actions. There is no way the rich person can buy off God, and no way the poor can avoid paying. God's demand is that all of us come humbly before him to be forgiven and brought into his family.

amount, and the poor must not give less. [16]Receive this ransom money from the Israelites, and use it for the care of the Tabernacle.* It will bring the Israelites to the LORD's attention, and it will purify your lives."

## Plans for the Washbasin

[17]Then the LORD said to Moses, [18]"Make a bronze washbasin with a bronze stand. Place it between the Tabernacle and the altar, and fill it with water. [19]Aaron and his sons will wash their hands and feet there. [20]They must wash with water whenever they go into the Tabernacle to appear before the LORD and when they approach the altar to burn up their special gifts to the LORD—or they will die! [21]They must always wash their hands and feet, or they will die. This is a permanent law for Aaron and his descendants, to be observed from generation to generation."

**30:18**
Exod 38:8; 40:7, 30
**30:19**
Exod 40:31-32
**30:21**
Exod 28:43

## The Anointing Oil

[22]Then the LORD said to Moses, [23]"Collect choice spices—12½ pounds of pure myrrh, 6¼ pounds of fragrant cinnamon, 6¼ pounds of fragrant calamus,* [24]and 12½ pounds of cassia*—as measured by the weight of the sanctuary shekel. Also get one gallon of olive oil.* [25]Like a skilled incense maker, blend these ingredients to make a holy anointing oil. [26]Use this sacred oil to anoint the Tabernacle, the Ark of the Covenant, [27]the table and all its utensils, the lampstand and all its accessories, the incense altar, [28]the altar of burnt offering and all its utensils, and the washbasin with its stand. [29]Consecrate them to make them absolutely holy. After this, whatever touches them will also become holy.

[30]"Anoint Aaron and his sons also, consecrating them to serve me as priests. [31]And say to the people of Israel, 'This holy anointing oil is reserved for me from generation to generation. [32]It must never be used to anoint anyone else, and you must never make any blend like it for yourselves. It is holy, and you must treat it as holy. [33]Anyone who makes a blend like it or anoints someone other than a priest will be cut off from the community.'"

**30:25**
Exod 37:29; 40:9
**30:26**
Lev 8:10
Num 7:1
**30:29**
Exod 29:37
**30:30**
Lev 8:2, 12, 30
**30:33**
Gen 17:14
Exod 12:15
Lev 7:20-21

## The Incense

[34]Then the LORD said to Moses, "Gather fragrant spices—resin droplets, mollusk shell, and galbanum—and mix these fragrant spices with pure frankincense, weighed out in equal amounts. [35]Using the usual techniques of the incense maker, blend the spices together and sprinkle them with salt to produce a pure and holy incense. [36]Grind some of the mixture into a very fine powder and put it in front of the Ark of the Covenant,* where I will meet with you in the Tabernacle. You must treat this incense as most holy. [37]Never use this formula to make this incense for yourselves. It is reserved for the LORD, and you must treat it as holy. [38]Anyone who makes incense like this for personal use will be cut off from the community."

**30:36**
Exod 29:42
Lev 2:3

## Craftsmen: Bezalel and Oholiab

**31** Then the LORD said to Moses, [2]"Look, I have specifically chosen Bezalel son of Uri, grandson of Hur, of the tribe of Judah. [3]I have filled him with the Spirit of God, giving him great wisdom, ability, and expertise in all kinds of crafts. [4]He is a master craftsman, expert in working with gold, silver, and bronze. [5]He is skilled in engraving and mounting gemstones and in carving wood. He is a master at every craft!

[6]"And I have personally appointed Oholiab son of Ahisamach, of the tribe of Dan, to be his assistant. Moreover, I have given special skill to all the gifted craftsmen so they can make all the things I have commanded you to make:

**31:2-6**
//Exod 35:30–36:1
1 Chr 2:20
**31:3**
1 Kgs 7:14
**31:6**
Exod 35:34; 36:1

**30:16** Hebrew *Tent of Meeting;* also in 30:18, 20, 26, 36. **30:23** Hebrew *500 shekels* [5.7 kilograms] *of pure myrrh, 250 shekels* [2.9 kilograms] *of fragrant cinnamon, 250 shekels of fragrant calamus.* **30:24a** Hebrew *500 shekels* [5.7 kilograms] *of cassia.* **30:24b** Hebrew *1 hin* [3.8 liters] *of olive oil.* **30:36** Hebrew *in front of the Testimony;* see note on 25:16.

---

**30:34-38** The Israelites often burned incense, but this holy incense could be burned only in the Tabernacle. Here God gave the recipe for this special incense. The sweet-smelling incense was burned in shallow dishes called incense burners and was used to show honor and reverence to God. It was like prayer lifting up to God. It was also a vital part of the sacred ceremony on the Day of Atonement, when the high priest carried his smoking censer into the Most Holy Place. This incense, like the sacred

anointing oil, was so holy that the people were strictly forbidden to copy it for personal use.

**31:1-11** God regards all the skills of his people, not merely those with theological or ministerial abilities. Our tendency is to regard only those who are up front and in leadership roles. God gave Bezalel and Oholiab Spirit-filled abilities in artistic craftsmanship. Take notice of all the abilities God gives his people. Don't diminish your skills if they are not like Moses' and Aaron's.

**31:7**
Exod 37:1-9

⁷ the Tabernacle;*
the Ark of the Covenant;*
the Ark's cover—the place of atonement;
all the furnishings of the Tabernacle;

**31:8**
Exod 37:10-16
Lev 24:4

⁸ the table and its utensils;
the pure gold lampstand with all its accessories;
the incense altar;

⁹ the altar of burnt offering with all its utensils;
the washbasin with its stand;

¹⁰ the beautifully stitched garments—the sacred garments for Aaron the priest, and the
garments for his sons to wear as they minister as priests;

**31:11**
Exod 30:23-32

¹¹ the anointing oil;
the fragrant incense for the Holy Place.

The craftsmen must make everything as I have commanded you."

### Instructions for the Sabbath

**31:13**
Lev 19:3, 30
Ezek 20:12-13

¹²The LORD then gave these instructions to Moses: ¹³"Tell the people of Israel: 'Be careful to keep my Sabbath day, for the Sabbath is a sign of the covenant between me and you from generation to generation. It is given so you may know that I am the LORD, who makes you holy. ¹⁴You must keep the Sabbath day, for it is a holy day for you. Anyone who desecrates it must be put to death; anyone who works on that day will be cut off from the community. ¹⁵You have six days each week for your ordinary work, but the seventh day must be a Sabbath day of complete rest, a holy day dedicated to the LORD. Anyone who works on the Sabbath must be put to death. ¹⁶The people of Israel must keep the Sabbath day by observing it from generation to generation. This is a covenant obligation for all time. ¹⁷It is a permanent sign of my covenant with the people of Israel. For in six days the LORD made heaven and earth, but on the seventh day he stopped working and was refreshed.'"

**31:14**
Exod 16:23; 35:2
John 7:23

**31:16**
Exod 20:8
**31:17**
Gen 2:2-3
Exod 20:11

**31:18**
Exod 24:12;
32:15-16; 34:1, 28

¹⁸When the LORD finished speaking with Moses on Mount Sinai, he gave him the two stone tablets inscribed with the terms of the covenant,* written by the finger of God.

## 3. Breaking the law
### The Gold Calf

**32:1**
Exod 24:18
Deut 9:9-12
†Acts 7:40

**32** When the people saw how long it was taking Moses to come back down the mountain, they gathered around Aaron. "Come on," they said, "make us some gods who can lead us. We don't know what happened to this fellow Moses, who brought us here from the land of Egypt."

**32:2**
Exod 35:22

²So Aaron said, "Take the gold rings from the ears of your wives and sons and daughters, and bring them to me."

³All the people took the gold rings from their ears and brought them to Aaron.

**31:7a** Hebrew *the Tent of Meeting.* **31:7b** Hebrew *the Ark of the Testimony.* **31:18** Hebrew *the two tablets of the Testimony;* see note on 25:16.

**31:12-17** The Sabbath had two purposes: It was a time *to rest* and a time *to remember* what God had done. We need rest. Without time out from the bustle, life loses its meaning. In our day, as in Moses' day, taking time out is not easy. But God reminds us that without Sabbaths we will forget the purpose for all of our activity and lose the balance crucial to a faithful life. Make sure your Sabbath provides a time of both refreshment and remembrance of God.

**31:18** The two stone tablets contained the Ten Commandments. These were not the only code of laws in the ancient world. Other law codes had come into existence when cities or nations decided that there must be standards of judgment, ways to correct specific wrongs. But God's laws for Israel were unique: (1) They alleviated the harsh judgments typical of the day; (2) they were egalitarian—the poor and the powerful received the same punishment; (3) they did not separate religious and social law. All law rested on God's authority.

**32:1-10** Idols again! Even though Israel had seen the invisible God in action, they still wanted the familiar gods they could see and shape into whatever image they desired. How much like them we are! Our great temptation is still to shape God to our liking, to make him convenient to obey or ignore. God responds in great anger when his mercy is trampled on. The gods we create blind us to the love that our loving God wants to shower on us. God cannot work in us when we elevate anyone or anything above him. What false gods in your life are preventing the true God from living in you?

4Then Aaron took the gold, melted it down, and molded it into the shape of a calf. When the people saw it, they exclaimed, "O Israel, these are the gods who brought you out of the land of Egypt!"

32:4
Exod 20:23
Deut 9:16
Ps 106:19
Acts 7:41

5Aaron saw how excited the people were, so he built an altar in front of the calf. Then he announced, "Tomorrow will be a festival to the LORD!"

6The people got up early the next morning to sacrifice burnt offerings and peace offerings. After this, they celebrated with feasting and drinking, and they indulged in pagan revelry.

32:6
Num 25:2
Acts 7:41
†1 Cor 10:7

7The LORD told Moses, "Quick! Go down the mountain! Your people whom you brought from the land of Egypt have corrupted themselves. 8How quickly they have turned away from the way I commanded them to live! They have melted down gold and made a calf, and they have bowed down and sacrificed to it. They are saying, 'These are your gods, O Israel, who brought you out of the land of Egypt.'"

32:7
Exod 19:24; 33:1
Deut 9:12

32:8
Exod 22:20; 34:15
Deut 32:17

9Then the LORD said, "I have seen how stubborn and rebellious these people are. 10Now leave me alone so my fierce anger can blaze against them, and I will destroy them. Then I will make you, Moses, into a great nation."

32:9
Exod 33:5
Num 14:11
Acts 7:51

32:10
Num 14:12
Deut 9:14

11But Moses tried to pacify the LORD his God. "O LORD!" he said. "Why are you so angry with your own people whom you brought from the land of Egypt with such great power and such a strong hand? 12Why let the Egyptians say, 'Their God rescued them with the evil intention of slaughtering them in the mountains and wiping them from the face of the earth'? Turn away from your fierce anger. Change your mind about this terrible disaster you have threatened against your people! 13Remember your servants Abraham, Isaac, and Jacob.* You bound yourself with an oath to them, saying, 'I will make your descendants as numerous as the stars of heaven. And I will give them all of this land that I have promised to your descendants, and they will possess it forever.'"

32:11
Deut 9:18, 26
Ps 106:23

32:12
Num 14:13-16
Deut 9:28

32:13
Gen 15:5; 22:16-18
Heb 6:13

14So the LORD changed his mind about the terrible disaster he had threatened to bring on his people.

32:14
2 Sam 24:16
Ps 106:45

15Then Moses turned and went down the mountain. He held in his hands the two stone tablets inscribed with the terms of the covenant.* They were inscribed on both sides, front and back. 16These tablets were God's work; the words on them were written by God himself.

32:15
Exod 24:18
Deut 9:15

32:16
Exod 31:18

17When Joshua heard the boisterous noise of the people shouting below them, he exclaimed to Moses, "It sounds like war in the camp!"

18But Moses replied, "No, it's not a shout of victory nor the wailing of defeat. I hear the sound of a celebration."

19When they came near the camp, Moses saw the calf and the dancing, and he burned with anger. He threw the stone tablets to the ground, smashing them at the foot of the

32:19
Exod 32:6
Deut 9:16-17

32:13 Hebrew *Israel*. The names "Jacob" and "Israel" are often interchanged throughout the Old Testament, referring sometimes to the individual patriarch and sometimes to the nation.   32:15 Hebrew *the two tablets of the Testimony*; see note on 25:16.

---

**32:4, 5** Two popular Egyptian gods, Hapi (Apis) and Hathor, were thought of as a bull and a heifer. The Canaanites around them worshiped Baal, thought of as a bull. Baal was their sacred symbol of power and fertility and was closely connected to immoral sexual practices. No doubt the Israelites, fresh from Egypt, found it quite natural to make a gold calf to represent the God that had just delivered them from their oppressors. They were weary of a god without a face. But in doing so, they were ignoring the command he had just given them: "You must not make for yourself an idol of any kind" (20:4). They may even have thought they were worshiping God. Their apparent sincerity was no substitute for obedience or excuse for disobedience.

Even if we do not make idols, we are often guilty of trying to make God in our image, molding him to fit our expectations, desires, and circumstances. When we do this, we end up worshiping ourselves rather than the God who created us—and self-worship, today as in the Israelites' time, leads to all kinds of immorality. What is your favorite image of God? Is it biblical? Is it adequate? Do you need to destroy it in order to worship the immeasurably powerful God who delivered you from bondage to sin?

**32:9-14** God was ready to destroy the whole nation because of their sin. But Moses pleaded for mercy, and God spared them.

This is one of the countless examples in the Bible of God's mercy. Although we deserve his anger, he is willing to forgive and restore us to himself. We can receive God's forgiveness from sin by asking him. Like Moses, we can pray that he will forgive others and use us to bring them the message of his mercy.

**32:14** How could God relent? God did not change his mind in the same way that a parent decides not to discipline a child. Instead, God changed his behavior to remain consistent with his nature. When God first wanted to destroy the people, he was acting consistently with his justice. When Moses interceded for the people, God relented in order to act consistently with his mercy. God had often told the people that if they changed their ways, he would not condemn them. They changed, and God forgave them as he had promised.

**32:19, 20** Overwhelmed by the actual sight of the blatant idolatry and revelry, Moses broke the tablets containing the commandments which had already been broken in the hearts and actions of the people. There is a place for righteous anger. However angry Moses might have been, God was angrier still—he wanted to kill all the people. Anger at sin is a sign of spiritual vitality. Don't squelch this kind of anger. But when you are justifiably angry at sin, be careful not to do anything that you will regret later.

**32:20**
Deut 9:21

mountain. 20He took the calf they had made and burned it. Then he ground it into powder, threw it into the water, and forced the people to drink it.

21Finally, he turned to Aaron and demanded, "What did these people do to you to make you bring such terrible sin upon them?"

**32:22**
Deut 9:24

**32:23**
Exod 32:1

22"Don't get so upset, my lord," Aaron replied. "You yourself know how evil these people are. 23They said to me, 'Make us gods who will lead us. We don't know what happened to this fellow Moses, who brought us here from the land of Egypt.' 24So I told them, 'Whoever has gold jewelry, take it off.' When they brought it to me, I simply threw it into the fire—and out came this calf!"

**32:25**
1 Kgs 12:28-30

**32:26**
2 Sam 20:11

25Moses saw that Aaron had let the people get completely out of control, much to the amusement of their enemies.* 26So he stood at the entrance to the camp and shouted, "All of you who are on the LORD's side, come here and join me." And all the Levites gathered around him.

**32:27**
Num 25:5
Deut 33:9

**32:28**
Num 16:32; 25:9

27Moses told them, "This is what the LORD, the God of Israel, says: Each of you, take your swords and go back and forth from one end of the camp to the other. Kill everyone—even your brothers, friends, and neighbors." 28The Levites obeyed Moses' command, and about 3,000 people died that day.

**32:29**
Deut 13:6; 33:9

29Then Moses told the Levites, "Today you have ordained yourselves* for the service of the LORD, for you obeyed him even though it meant killing your own sons and brothers. Today you have earned a blessing."

**32:25** Or *out of control, and they mocked anyone who opposed them.* The meaning of the Hebrew is unclear.
**32:29** As in Greek and Latin versions; Hebrew reads *Today ordain yourselves.*

---

Effective teamwork happens when each team member uses his or her special skills. Ideally each member's strengths will contribute something important to the team effort. In this way, members make up for one another's weaknesses. Aaron made a good team with Moses. He provided Moses with one skill Moses lacked—effective public speaking. But while Aaron was necessary to Moses, he needed Moses as well. Without a guide, Aaron had little direction of his own. There was never any doubt as to who God's chosen and trained leader was. The pliability that made Aaron a good follower made him a weak leader. His major failures were caused by his inability to stand alone. His yielding to public pressure and making an idol was a good example of this weakness.

Most of us have more of the follower than the leader in us. We may even be good followers, following a good leader. But no leader is perfect, and no human deserves our complete allegiance. Only God deserves our complete loyalty and obedience. We need to be effective team members in using the skills and abilities God has given us. But if the team or the leader goes against God's Word, we must be willing to stand alone.

| | |
|---|---|
| **Strengths and accomplishments** | • First high priest of God in Israel<br>• Effective communicator; Moses' mouthpiece |
| **Weaknesses and mistakes** | • Pliable personality; gave in to people's demands for a gold calf<br>• Joined with Moses in disobeying God's orders about the water-giving rock<br>• Joined sister Miriam in complaining against Moses |
| **Lessons from his life** | • God gives individuals special abilities, which he weaves together for his use<br>• The very skills that make a good team player sometimes also make a poor leader |
| **Vital statistics** | • Where: Egypt, wilderness of Sinai<br>• Occupations: Priest, Moses' second in command<br>• Relatives: Brother: Moses. Sister: Miriam. Sons: Nadab, Abihu, Eleazar, and Ithamar. |
| **Key verses** | "Then the LORD became angry with Moses. 'All right,' he said. 'What about your brother, Aaron the Levite? I know he speaks well. And look! He is on his way to meet you now. He will be delighted to see you. . . . Aaron will be your spokesman to the people. He will be your mouthpiece, and you will stand in the place of God for him, telling him what to say'" (Exodus 4:14, 16). |

Aaron's story is told in Exodus—Deuteronomy 10:6. He is also mentioned in Hebrews 7:11.

AARON

---

**32:21-24** Aaron's decision nearly cost him his life. His absurd excuse shows the spiritual decline in his leadership and in the people. Those who function as spokespersons and assistants need to be doubly sure their theology and morality are in tune with God so they will not be influenced by pressure from people. For more information on Aaron, see his Profile above.

## Moses Intercedes for Israel

30The next day Moses said to the people, "You have committed a terrible sin, but I will go back up to the LORD on the mountain. Perhaps I will be able to obtain forgiveness* for your sin."

31So Moses returned to the LORD and said, "Oh, what a terrible sin these people have committed. They have made gods of gold for themselves. 32But now, if you will only forgive their sin—but if not, erase my name from the record you have written!"

33But the LORD replied to Moses, "No, I will erase the name of everyone who has sinned against me. 34Now go, lead the people to the place I told you about. Look! My angel will lead the way before you. And when I come to call the people to account, I will certainly hold them responsible for their sins."

35Then the LORD sent a great plague upon the people because they had worshiped the calf Aaron had made.

**33:31**
Exod 20:23

**32:32**
Dan 12:1
Mal 3:16-17
Phil 4:3
Rev 3:5; 21:27

**32:33**
Deut 29:20
Ps 9:5
Rev 3:5

**32:34**
Exod 3:17; 23:20
Ps 99:8

**33** The LORD said to Moses, "Get going, you and the people you brought up from the land of Egypt. Go up to the land I swore to give to Abraham, Isaac, and Jacob. I told them, 'I will give this land to your descendants.' 2And I will send an angel before you to drive out the Canaanites, Amorites, Hittites, Perizzites, Hivites, and Jebusites. 3Go up to this land that flows with milk and honey. But I will not travel among you, for you are a stubborn and rebellious people. If I did, I would surely destroy you along the way."

4When the people heard these stern words, they went into mourning and stopped wearing their jewelry and fine clothes. 5For the LORD had told Moses to tell them, "You are a stubborn and rebellious people. If I were to travel with you for even a moment, I would destroy you. Remove your jewelry and fine clothes while I decide what to do with you." 6So from the time they left Mount Sinai,* the Israelites wore no more jewelry or fine clothes.

7It was Moses' practice to take the Tent of Meeting* and set it up some distance from the camp. Everyone who wanted to make a request of the LORD would go to the Tent of Meeting outside the camp.

8Whenever Moses went out to the Tent of Meeting, all the people would get up and stand in the entrances of their own tents. They would all watch Moses until he disappeared inside. 9As he went into the tent, the pillar of cloud would come down and hover at its entrance while the LORD spoke with Moses. 10When the people saw the cloud standing at the entrance of the tent, they would stand and bow down in front of their own tents. 11Inside the Tent of Meeting, the LORD would speak to Moses face to face, as one speaks to a friend. Afterward Moses would return to the camp, but the young man who assisted him, Joshua son of Nun, would remain behind in the Tent of Meeting.

**33:1**
Gen 12:7
Exod 32:7, 13

**33:2**
Exod 23:27-31

**33:3**
Exod 3:8, 17;
32:9-10

**33:4**
Num 14:1, 39

**33:5**
Exod 33:3

**33:7**
Exod 29:42-43

**33:8**
Num 16:27

**33:9**
Exod 13:21; 19:9;
25:22
Ps 99:7

**33:11**
Num 12:8
Deut 34:10

## Moses Sees the LORD's Glory

12One day Moses said to the LORD, "You have been telling me, 'Take these people up to the Promised Land.' But you haven't told me whom you will send with me. You have told me, 'I know you by name, and I look favorably on you.' 13If it is true that you look favorably on me, let me know your ways so I may understand you more fully and continue to enjoy your favor. And remember that this nation is your very own people."

14The LORD replied, "I will personally go with you, Moses, and I will give you rest—everything will be fine for you."

15Then Moses said, "If you don't personally go with us, don't make us leave this place. 16How will anyone know that you look favorably on me—on me and on your people—if you

**33:12**
Exod 3:10; 32:34
John 10:14-15
2 Tim 2:19

**33:13**
Exod 34:9
Pss 25:4; 27:11

**33:14**
Exod 13:21
Josh 22:4
Isa 63:9

**33:16**
Exod 34:10
Lev 20:24, 26
Num 14:14

32:30 Or to make atonement.   33:6 Hebrew Horeb, another name for Sinai.   33:7 This "Tent of Meeting" is different from the Tabernacle described in chapters 26 and 36.

---

**33:5, 6** This was not a permanent ban on all jewelry. It was a temporary sign of repentance and mourning. In 35:22 we read that the people still had jewelry.

**33:11** God and Moses talked face to face in the Tent of Meeting, just as friends do. Why did Moses find such favor with God? It certainly was not because he was perfect, gifted, or powerful. Rather, it was because God chose Moses, and

Moses in turn relied wholeheartedly on God's wisdom and direction. Friendship with God was a true privilege for Moses, out of reach for the other Hebrews. But it is not out of reach for us today. Jesus called his disciples—and, by extension, all of his followers—his friends (John 15:15). He has called you to be his friend. Will you accept his invitation to openly communicate with him? He desires this kind of relationship with you.

**33:11** Joshua, Moses' aide, did not leave the Tent of Meeting, probably because he was guarding it. No doubt there were curious people who would have dared to go inside.

**33:17**
Exod 33:12

**33:18**
Exod 33:20, 23

**33:19**
†Rom 9:15

**33:20**
Isa 6:5
John 1:18
1 Tim 6:16

**33:22**
Ps 91:1, 4
Isa 49:2; 51:16

**33:23**
John 1:18

don't go with us? For your presence among us sets your people and me apart from all other people on the earth."

¹⁷The LORD replied to Moses, "I will indeed do what you have asked, for I look favorably on you, and I know you by name."

¹⁸Moses responded, "Then show me your glorious presence."

¹⁹The LORD replied, "I will make all my goodness pass before you, and I will call out my name, Yahweh,* before you. For I will show mercy to anyone I choose, and I will show compassion to anyone I choose. ²⁰But you may not look directly at my face, for no one may see me and live." ²¹The LORD continued, "Look, stand near me on this rock. ²²As my glorious presence passes by, I will hide you in the crevice of the rock and cover you with my hand until I have passed by. ²³Then I will remove my hand and let you see me from behind. But my face will not be seen."

**34:1**
Exod 24:12; 32:19
Deut 10:2, 4

**34:3**
Exod 19:12-13

## A New Copy of the Covenant

**34** Then the LORD told Moses, "Chisel out two stone tablets like the first ones. I will write on them the same words that were on the tablets you smashed. ²Be ready in the morning to climb up Mount Sinai and present yourself to me on the top of the mountain. ³No one else may come with you. In fact, no one is to appear anywhere on the mountain. Do not even let the flocks or herds graze near the mountain."

⁴So Moses chiseled out two tablets of stone like the first ones. Early in the morning he climbed Mount Sinai as the LORD had commanded him, and he carried the two stone tablets in his hands.

**34:5**
Exod 33:19

**34:6**
Num 14:18
Neh 9:17
Pss 86:15; 103:8

⁵Then the LORD came down in a cloud and stood there with him; and he called out his own name, Yahweh.* ⁶The LORD passed in front of Moses, calling out,

"Yahweh!* The LORD!
    The God of compassion and mercy!
I am slow to anger
    and filled with unfailing love and faithfulness.

**34:7**
Exod 20:6-7
Deut 5:10
Nah 1:3

⁷ I lavish unfailing love to a thousand generations.*
    I forgive iniquity, rebellion, and sin.
But I do not excuse the guilty.
    I lay the sins of the parents upon their children and grandchildren;
the entire family is affected—
    even children in the third and fourth generations."

**34:9**
Num 14:19
Deut 4:20; 32:9
Ps 25:11

⁸Moses immediately threw himself to the ground and worshiped. ⁹And he said, "O Lord, if it is true that I have found favor with you, then please travel with us. Yes, this is a stubborn and rebellious people, but please forgive our iniquity and our sins. Claim us as your own special possession."

**34:10**
Deut 5:2-3
Pss 72:18; 136:4

¹⁰The LORD replied, "Listen, I am making a covenant with you in the presence of all your

**33:19** *Yahweh* is a transliteration of the proper name *YHWH* that is sometimes rendered "Jehovah"; in this translation it is usually rendered "the LORD" (note the use of small capitals).    **34:5** *Yahweh* is a transliteration of the proper name *YHWH* that is sometimes rendered "Jehovah"; in this translation it is usually rendered "the LORD" (note the use of small capitals).    **34:6** See note on 34:5.    **34:7** Hebrew *for thousands.*

---

**33:18-23** Moses wanted to see God's glory. He wanted assurance of God's presence with him, Aaron, and Joshua, and also he desired to know that presence experientially. Because we are finite and morally imperfect, we cannot exist and see God as he is. To see God from behind means we can only see where God has passed by. We can only know him by what he does and how he acts. We cannot comprehend God as he really is apart from Jesus Christ (John 14:9). Jesus promised to show himself to those who love him (John 14:21).

**34:6, 7** Moses had asked to see God's glorious presence (33:18), and this was God's response. What is God's glory? It is his character, his nature, his way of relating to his creatures. Notice that God did not give Moses a vision of his power and majesty, but rather of his love. God's glory is revealed in his mercy, grace, compassion, faithfulness, forgiveness, and justice. God's love and mercy are truly wonderful, and we benefit from them. We can respond and give glory to God when our characters resemble his.

**34:6, 7** Many people think the God of the Old Testament is a God of wrath, only to be feared. These words from God revealed to Moses the very heart or essence of God's nature (33:19). What do we learn from these assurances to Moses? God is merciful, gracious, loving, forgiving. Don't accept anyone's argument that the God of the Old Testament is merely vengeful. Instead, remember that God is "slow to anger," and his love cannot be diminished.

**34:7** Why would sins affect children and grandchildren? This is no arbitrary punishment. Children still suffer for the sins of their parents. Consider child abuse or alcoholism, for example. While these sins are obvious, sins like selfishness and greed can be passed along as well. The dire consequences of sin are not limited to the individual family member. Be careful not to treat sin casually, but repent and turn from it. The sin may cause you little pain now, but it could sting in a most tender area of your life later—your children and grandchildren.

people. I will perform miracles that have never been performed anywhere in all the earth or in any nation. And all the people around you will see the power of the LORD—the awesome power I will display for you. ¹¹But listen carefully to everything I command you today. Then I will go ahead of you and drive out the Amorites, Canaanites, Hittites, Perizzites, Hivites, and Jebusites.

**34:11**
Exod 33:2
Deut 6:3

¹²"Be very careful never to make a treaty with the people who live in the land where you are going. If you do, you will follow their evil ways and be trapped. ¹³Instead, you must break down their pagan altars, smash their sacred pillars, and cut down their Asherah poles. ¹⁴You must worship no other gods, for the LORD, whose very name is Jealous, is a God who is jealous about his relationship with you.

**34:12**
Exod 23:32-33

**34:13**
Exod 23:24
Deut 7:5; 12:3;
16:21
2 Chr 34:3-4

¹⁵"You must not make a treaty of any kind with the people living in the land. They lust after their gods, offering sacrifices to them. They will invite you to join them in their sacrificial meals, and you will go with them. ¹⁶Then you will accept their daughters, who sacrifice to other gods, as wives for your sons. And they will seduce your sons to commit adultery against me by worshiping other gods. ¹⁷You must not make any gods of molten metal for yourselves.

**34:14**
Exod 20:3
Deut 4:24

**34:15**
Judg 2:17
Num 25:2

**34:16**
Deut 7:3
Josh 23:12

¹⁸"You must celebrate the Festival of Unleavened Bread. For seven days the bread you eat must be made without yeast, just as I commanded you. Celebrate this festival annually at the appointed time in early spring, in the month of Abib,* for that is the anniversary of your departure from Egypt.

**34:17**
Exod 20:4, 23

**34:18**
Exod 12:2, 15-17

¹⁹"The firstborn of every animal belongs to me, including the firstborn males from your herds of cattle and your flocks of sheep and goats. ²⁰A firstborn donkey may be bought back from the LORD by presenting a lamb or young goat in its place. But if you do not buy it back, you must break its neck. However, you must buy back every firstborn son.

**34:19**
Exod 13:2; 22:29

**34:20**
Exod 13:13, 15
Num 3:45

"No one may appear before me without an offering.

²¹"You have six days each week for your ordinary work, but on the seventh day you must stop working, even during the seasons of plowing and harvest.

**34:21**
Exod 31:15; 35:2

²²"You must celebrate the Festival of Harvest* with the first crop of the wheat harvest, and celebrate the Festival of the Final Harvest* at the end of the harvest season. ²³Three times each year every man in Israel must appear before the Sovereign, the LORD, the God of Israel. ²⁴I will drive out the other nations ahead of you and expand your territory, so no one will covet and conquer your land while you appear before the LORD your God three times each year.

**34:22**
Exod 23:16

**34:23**
Exod 23:14-17
Deut 16:16

**34:24**
Exod 33:2
Josh 11:23

²⁵"You must not offer the blood of my sacrificial offerings together with any baked goods containing yeast. And none of the meat of the Passover sacrifice may be kept over until the next morning.

**34:25**
Exod 12:10; 23:18

²⁶"As you harvest your crops, bring the very best of the first harvest to the house of the LORD your God.

**34:26**
Exod 23:19
Deut 26:2

"You must not cook a young goat in its mother's milk."

²⁷Then the LORD said to Moses, "Write down all these instructions, for they represent the terms of the covenant I am making with you and with Israel."

**34:27**
Exod 17:14; 24:4

²⁸Moses remained there on the mountain with the LORD forty days and forty nights. In all that time he ate no bread and drank no water. And the LORD* wrote the terms of the covenant—the Ten Commandments*—on the stone tablets.

**34:28**
Exod 24:18
Deut 4:13; 10:4

²⁹When Moses came down Mount Sinai carrying the two stone tablets inscribed with the terms of the covenant,* he wasn't aware that his face had become radiant because he had

**34:29**
Exod 32:15
Matt 17:2
2 Cor 3:7, 13

**34:18** Hebrew *appointed time in the month of Abib.* This first month of the ancient Hebrew lunar calendar usually occurs within the months of March and April. **34:22a** Hebrew *Festival of Weeks;* compare 23:16. This was later called the Festival of Pentecost. It is celebrated today as Shavuot (or Shabuoth). **34:22b** Or *Festival of Ingathering.* This was later called the Festival of Shelters or Festival of Tabernacles (see Lev 23:33-36). It is celebrated today as Sukkot (or Succoth). **34:28a** Hebrew *he.* **34:28b** Hebrew *the ten words.* **34:29** Hebrew *the two tablets of the Testimony;* see note on 25:16.

---

**34:12-14** God told the Israelites not to join in religious rites with the sinful people around them, but to give their absolute loyalty and exclusive devotion to him. Pagan worship simply cannot be mixed with the worship of the holy God. As Jesus pointed out, "No one can serve two masters. . . . You cannot serve both God and money" (Luke 16:13). Love of money is the god of this age, and many Christians attempt to make a treaty with this enslaving god. Are you trying to worship two gods at once? Where is your first allegiance?

**34:13** Sacred pillars were wooden poles that stood by Baal's altar (see Judges 6:25). Also called "Asherah poles," they were used to worship the goddess who was the consort (wife) of Baal. She represented fertility and good luck in agriculture.

**34:28-35** Moses' face was radiant after he spent time with God. The people could clearly see God's presence in him. How often do you spend time alone with God? Although your face may not light up a room, time spent in prayer, reading the Bible, and meditating should have such an effect on your life that people will know you have been with God.

spoken to the LORD. [30]So when Aaron and the people of Israel saw the radiance of Moses' face, they were afraid to come near him.

[31]But Moses called out to them and asked Aaron and all the leaders of the community to come over, and he talked with them. [32]Then all the people of Israel approached him, and Moses gave them all the instructions the LORD had given him on Mount Sinai. [33]When Moses finished speaking with them, he covered his face with a veil. [34]But whenever he went into the Tent of Meeting to speak with the LORD, he would remove the veil until he came out again. Then he would give the people whatever instructions the LORD had given him, [35]and the people of Israel would see the radiant glow of his face. So he would put the veil over his face until he returned to speak with the LORD.

## 4. Tabernacle construction
### Instructions for the Sabbath

**35** Then Moses called together the whole community of Israel and told them, "These are the instructions the LORD has commanded you to follow. [2]You have six days each week for your ordinary work, but the seventh day must be a Sabbath day of complete rest, a holy day dedicated to the LORD. Anyone who works on that day must be put to death. [3]You must not even light a fire in any of your homes on the Sabbath."

### Offerings for the Tabernacle

[4]Then Moses said to the whole community of Israel, "This is what the LORD has commanded: [5]Take a sacred offering for the LORD. Let those with generous hearts present the following gifts to the LORD:

gold, silver, and bronze;
[6]blue, purple, and scarlet thread;
fine linen and goat hair for cloth;
[7]tanned ram skins and fine goatskin leather;
acacia wood;
[8]olive oil for the lamps;
spices for the anointing oil and the fragrant incense;
[9]onyx stones, and other gemstones to be set in the ephod and the priest's chestpiece.

[10]"Come, all of you who are gifted craftsmen. Construct everything that the LORD has commanded:

[11]the Tabernacle and its sacred tent, its covering, clasps, frames, crossbars, posts, and bases;
[12]the Ark and its carrying poles;
the Ark's cover—the place of atonement;
the inner curtain to shield the Ark;
[13]the table, its carrying poles, and all its utensils;
the Bread of the Presence;
[14]for light, the lampstand, its accessories, the lamp cups, and the olive oil for lighting;
[15]the incense altar and its carrying poles;
the anointing oil and fragrant incense;
the curtain for the entrance of the Tabernacle;
[16]the altar of burnt offering;
the bronze grating of the altar and its carrying poles and utensils;
the washbasin with its stand;
[17]the curtains for the walls of the courtyard;
the posts and their bases;
the curtain for the entrance to the courtyard;

---

**34:33**
2 Cor 3:13

**34:34**
2 Cor 3:16

**34:35**
2 Cor 3:13

**35:2**
Exod 20:9-10;
23:12; 31:15; 34:21
Num 15:32-36
Deut 5:13-14

**35:3**
Exod 16:23

**35:4-9**
//Exod 25:1-9

**35:10-19**
//Exod 39:32-41
Exod 25:2; 35:5

---

**35:5-21** God did not require these special offerings, but he appealed to people with generous hearts. Only those who were willing to give were invited to participate. God loves people who give cheerfully (2 Corinthians 9:7). Our giving should be from love and generosity, not from a guilty conscience. Review what God has done for you. Has he blessed you with enough to meet your daily needs? Thank him, and then cheerfully give so others' needs can be met. Learn the joy of giving wholeheartedly to God.

**35:10-19** Moses asked people with various abilities to help with the Tabernacle. Every one of God's people has been given special abilities. We are responsible to develop these abilities—even the ones not considered religious—and to use them for God's glory. We can become skilled through study, by watching others, and through practice. Work on your skills or abilities that could help your church or community.

¹⁸ the tent pegs of the Tabernacle and courtyard and their ropes;

¹⁹ the beautifully stitched garments for the priests to wear while ministering in the Holy Place—the sacred garments for Aaron the priest, and the garments for his sons to wear as they minister as priests."

²⁰So the whole community of Israel left Moses and returned to their tents. ²¹All whose hearts were stirred and whose spirits were moved came and brought their sacred offerings to the LORD. They brought all the materials needed for the Tabernacle,* for the performance of its rituals, and for the sacred garments. ²²Both men and women came, all whose hearts were willing. They brought to the LORD their offerings of gold—brooches, earrings, rings from their fingers, and necklaces. They presented gold objects of every kind as a special offering to the LORD. ²³All those who owned the following items willingly brought them: blue, purple, and scarlet thread; fine linen and goat hair for cloth; and tanned ram skins and fine goatskin leather. ²⁴And all who had silver and bronze objects gave them as a sacred offering to the LORD. And those who had acacia wood brought it for use in the project.

²⁵All the women who were skilled in sewing and spinning prepared blue, purple, and scarlet thread, and fine linen cloth. ²⁶All the women who were willing used their skills to spin the goat hair into yarn. ²⁷The leaders brought onyx stones and the special gemstones to be set in the ephod and the priest's chestpiece. ²⁸They also brought spices and olive oil for the light, the anointing oil, and the fragrant incense. ²⁹So the people of Israel—every man and woman who was eager to help in the work the LORD had given them through Moses—brought their gifts and gave them freely to the LORD.

³⁰Then Moses told the people of Israel, "The LORD has specifically chosen Bezalel son of Uri, grandson of Hur, of the tribe of Judah. ³¹The LORD has filled Bezalel with the Spirit of God, giving him great wisdom, ability, and expertise in all kinds of crafts. ³²He is a master craftsman, expert in working with gold, silver, and bronze. ³³He is skilled in engraving and mounting gemstones and in carving wood. He is a master at every craft. ³⁴And the LORD has given both him and Oholiab son of Ahisamach, of the tribe of Dan, the ability to teach their skills to others. ³⁵The LORD has given them special skills as engravers, designers, embroiderers in blue, purple, and scarlet thread on fine linen cloth, and weavers. They excel as craftsmen and as designers.

# 36

"The LORD has gifted Bezalel, Oholiab, and the other skilled craftsmen with wisdom and ability to perform any task involved in building the sanctuary. Let them construct and furnish the Tabernacle, just as the LORD has commanded."

²So Moses summoned Bezalel and Oholiab and all the others who were specially gifted by the LORD and were eager to get to work. ³Moses gave them the materials donated by the people of Israel as sacred offerings for the completion of the sanctuary. But the people continued to bring additional gifts each morning. ⁴Finally the craftsmen who were working on the sanctuary left their work. ⁵They went to Moses and reported, "The people have given more than enough materials to complete the job the LORD has commanded us to do!"

⁶So Moses gave the command, and this message was sent throughout the camp: "Men and women, don't prepare any more gifts for the sanctuary. We have enough!" So the people stopped bringing their sacred offerings. ⁷Their contributions were more than enough to complete the whole project.

35:21 Hebrew *Tent of Meeting*.

**35:23**
Exod 39:1

**35:25**
Exod 28:3

**35:27**
1 Chr 29:6
Ezra 2:68

**35:29**
1 Chr 29:9

**35:30-35**
//Exod 31:2-6

**35:34**
Exod 31:6

**35:35**
Exod 31:3, 6; 35:31
1 Kgs 7:14

**36:1**
Exod 25:8

**36:2**
Exod 35:21, 26
1 Chr 29:5

**36:5**
2 Chr 24:14;
31:6-10
2 Cor 8:2-3

**36:7**
1 Kgs 8:64

---

**35:20-24** Where did the Israelites, who were once Egyptian slaves, get all this gold and jewelry? When the Hebrews left Egypt, they took with them items they requested from the Egyptians. The Egyptians had been so glad for them to go that they readily gave these valuables to the Hebrews (3:22; 12:35, 36). This included gold, silver, jewels, linen, skins, and other valuables.

**35:21, 22** Those whose hearts were stirred gave willingly to the Tent of Meeting (also called the Tabernacle). With great enthusiasm they gave because they knew how important their giving was to the completion of God's house. Moses had care-

fully explained the need and the plans for the Tabernacle, and so many people responded generously. For God to stir our hearts, we must be informed. If your church has a stewardship campaign, get involved and learn all you can. Find out about evangelistic missions and ministries to the poor. God will use this knowledge to stir your heart.

**35:26** Those who spun cloth made a beautiful contribution to the Tabernacle. Good workers take pride in the quality and beauty of their work. God is concerned with the quality and beauty of what you do. Whether you are a corporate executive or a drugstore cashier, your work should reflect the creative abilities God has given you.

### Building the Tabernacle

**36:8-38**
//Exod 26:1-37

8The skilled craftsmen made ten curtains of finely woven linen for the Tabernacle. Then Bezalel* decorated the curtains with blue, purple, and scarlet thread and with skillfully embroidered cherubim. 9All ten curtains were exactly the same size—42 feet long and 6 feet wide.* 10Five of these curtains were joined together to make one long curtain, and the other five were joined to make a second long curtain. 11He made fifty loops of blue yarn and put them along the edge of the last curtain in each set. 12The fifty loops along the edge of one curtain matched the fifty loops along the edge of the other curtain. 13Then he made fifty gold clasps and fastened the long curtains together with the clasps. In this way, the Tabernacle was made of one continuous piece.

**36:14**
Exod 26:7

14He made eleven curtains of goat-hair cloth to serve as a tent covering for the Tabernacle. 15These eleven curtains were all exactly the same size—45 feet long and 6 feet wide.* 16Bezalel joined five of these curtains together to make one long curtain, and the other six were joined to make a second long curtain. 17He made fifty loops for the edge of each large curtain. 18He also made fifty bronze clasps to fasten the long curtains together. In this way, the tent covering was made of one continuous piece. 19He completed the tent covering with a layer of tanned ram skins and a layer of fine goatskin leather.

**36:20-34**
Exod 26:15-29;
40:18-19

20For the framework of the Tabernacle, Bezalel constructed frames of acacia wood. 21Each frame was 15 feet high and 27 inches wide,* 22with two pegs under each frame. All the frames were identical. 23He made twenty of these frames to support the curtains on the south side of the Tabernacle. 24He also made forty silver bases—two bases under each frame, with the pegs fitting securely into the bases. 25For the north side of the Tabernacle, he made another twenty frames, 26with their forty silver bases, two bases under each

**36:8** Hebrew *he;* also in 36:16, 20, 35. See 37:1.   **36:9** Hebrew *28 cubits* [12.9 meters] *long and 4 cubits* [1.8 meters] *wide.*   **36:15** Hebrew *30 cubits* [13.8 meters] *long and 4 cubits* [1.8 meters] *wide.*   **36:21** Hebrew *10 cubits* [4.6 meters] *high and 1.5 cubits* [69 centimeters] *wide.*

| KEY TABERNACLE PIECES | Name | Function and Significance |
|---|---|---|
| | Ark of the Covenant | • A golden rectangular box that contained the Ten Commandments<br>• Symbolized God's covenant with Israel's people<br>• Located in the Most Holy Place |
| | Atonement Cover | • The lid to the Ark of the Covenant<br>• Symbolized the presence of God among his people |
| | Curtain | • The curtain that divided the two sacred rooms of the Tabernacle—the Holy Place and the Most Holy Place<br>• Symbolized how the people were separated from God because of sin |
| | Table | • A wooden table located in the Holy Place of the Tabernacle. The Bread of the Presence and various utensils were kept on this table |
| | Bread of the Presence | • Twelve loaves of baked bread, one for each tribe of Israel<br>• Symbolized the spiritual nourishment God offers his people |
| | Lampstands and Lamps | • A golden lampstand located in the Holy Place, which held seven burning oil lamps<br>• The lampstand lit the Holy Place for the priests |
| | Incense Altar | • An altar in the Holy Place in front of the curtain<br>• Used for burning God's special incense and symbolic of acceptable prayer |
| | Anointing Oil | • A special oil used to anoint the priests and all the pieces in the Tabernacle<br>• A sign of being set apart for God |
| | Altar of Burnt Offering | • The bronze altar outside the Tabernacle used for the sacrifices<br>• Symbolized how sacrifice restored one's relationship with God |
| | Washbasin | • A large washbasin outside the Tabernacle used by the priests to cleanse themselves before performing their duties<br>• Symbolized the need for spiritual cleansing |

**36:8, 9** Making cloth (spinning and weaving) took a great deal of time in Moses' day. To own more than two or three changes of clothes was a sign of wealth. The effort involved in making enough cloth for the Tabernacle was staggering. The Tabernacle would never have been built without tremendous community involvement. Today, churches and neighborhoods often require this same kind of pulling together. Without it, many essential services wouldn't get done.

frame. 27He made six frames for the rear—the west side of the Tabernacle—28along with two additional frames to reinforce the rear corners of the Tabernacle. 29These corner frames were matched at the bottom and firmly attached at the top with a single ring, forming a single corner unit. Both of these corner units were made the same way. 30So there were eight frames at the rear of the Tabernacle, set in sixteen silver bases—two bases under each frame.

31Then he made crossbars of acacia wood to link the frames, five crossbars for the north side of the Tabernacle 32and five for the south side. He also made five crossbars for the rear of the Tabernacle, which faced west. 33He made the middle crossbar to attach halfway up the frames; it ran all the way from one end of the Tabernacle to the other. 34He overlaid the frames with gold and made gold rings to hold the crossbars. Then he overlaid the crossbars with gold as well.

35For the inside of the Tabernacle, Bezalel made a special curtain of finely woven linen. He decorated it with blue, purple, and scarlet thread and with skillfully embroidered cherubim. 36For the curtain, he made four posts of acacia wood and four gold hooks. He overlaid the posts with gold and set them in four silver bases.

36:35-38<br>Exod 26:31-37

37Then he made another curtain for the entrance to the sacred tent. He made it of finely woven linen and embroidered it with exquisite designs using blue, purple, and scarlet thread. 38This curtain was hung on gold hooks attached to five posts. The posts with their decorated tops and hooks were overlaid with gold, and the five bases were cast from bronze.

## Building the Ark of the Covenant

**37** Next Bezalel made the Ark of acacia wood—a sacred chest 45 inches long, 27 inches wide, and 27 inches high.* 2He overlaid it inside and outside with pure gold, and he ran a molding of gold all around it. 3He cast four gold rings and attached them to its four feet, two rings on each side. 4Then he made poles from acacia wood and overlaid them with gold. 5He inserted the poles into the rings at the sides of the Ark to carry it.

37:1-9<br>//Exod 25:10-20<br>37:1<br>Deut 10:3

6Then he made the Ark's cover—the place of atonement—from pure gold. It was 45 inches long and 27 inches wide.* 7He made two cherubim from hammered gold and placed them on the two ends of the atonement cover. 8He molded the cherubim on each end of the atonement cover, making it all of one piece of gold. 9The cherubim faced each other and looked down on the atonement cover. With their wings spread above it, they protected it.

## Building the Table

10Then Bezalel* made the table of acacia wood, 36 inches long, 18 inches wide, and 27 inches high.* 11He overlaid it with pure gold and ran a gold molding around the edge. 12He decorated it with a 3-inch border* all around, and he ran a gold molding along the border. 13Then he cast four gold rings for the table and attached them at the four corners next to the four legs. 14The rings were attached near the border to hold the poles that were used to carry the table. 15He made these poles from acacia wood and overlaid them with gold. 16Then he made special containers of pure gold for the table—bowls, pans, jars, and pitchers—to be used in pouring out liquid offerings.

37:10-16<br>//Exod 25:23-29;<br>40:22

## Building the Lampstand

17Then Bezalel made the lampstand of pure, hammered gold. He made the entire lampstand and its decorations of one piece—the base, center stem, lamp cups, buds, and petals. 18The lampstand had six branches going out from the center stem, three on each side. 19Each of the six branches had three lamp cups shaped like almond blossoms, complete

37:17-24<br>//Exod 25:31-39;<br>40:24<br>37:17<br>Heb 9:2<br>Rev 1:12

---

**37:1** Hebrew *2.5 cubits* [115 centimeters] *long, 1.5 cubits* [69 centimeters] *wide, and 1.5 cubits high.*   **37:6** Hebrew *2.5 cubits* [115 centimeters] *long and 1.5 cubits* [69 centimeters] *wide.*   **37:10a** Hebrew *he;* also in 37:17, 25.
**37:10b** Hebrew *2 cubits* [92 centimeters] *long, 1 cubit* [46 centimeters] *wide, and 1.5 cubits* [69 centimeters] *high.*
**37:12** Hebrew *a border of a handbreadth* [8 centimeters].

---

**36:35** Cherubim are mighty angels.

**37:1** The Ark (also called the Ark of the Covenant) was built to hold the Ten Commandments. It symbolized God's covenant with his people. Two gold angels called cherubim were placed on its top. The Ark was Israel's most sacred object and was kept in the Most Holy Place in the Tabernacle. Only once each year, the high priest entered the Most Holy Place to sprinkle blood on the top of the Ark (called the atonement cover) to atone for the sins of the entire nation.

with buds and petals. ²⁰The center stem of the lampstand was crafted with four lamp cups shaped like almond blossoms, complete with buds and petals. ²¹There was an almond bud beneath each pair of branches where the six branches extended from the center stem, all made of one piece. ²²The almond buds and branches were all of one piece with the center stem, and they were hammered from pure gold.

²³He also made seven lamps for the lampstand, lamp snuffers, and trays, all of pure gold. ²⁴The entire lampstand, along with its accessories, was made from seventy-five pounds* of pure gold.

### Building the Incense Altar

37:25-28
//Exod 30:1-5

37:25
Heb 9:4
Rev 8:3

37:29
Exod 30:22-23;
40:9
Lev 8:10

²⁵Then Bezalel made the incense altar of acacia wood. It was 18 inches square and 36 inches high,* with horns at the corners carved from the same piece of wood as the altar itself. ²⁶He overlaid the top, sides, and horns of the altar with pure gold, and he ran a gold molding around the entire altar. ²⁷He made two gold rings and attached them on opposite sides of the altar below the gold molding to hold the carrying poles. ²⁸He made the poles of acacia wood and overlaid them with gold.

²⁹Then he made the sacred anointing oil and the fragrant incense, using the techniques of a skilled incense maker.

### Building the Altar of Burnt Offering

38:1-7
//Exod 27:1-8;
40:10, 29

**38** Next Bezalel* used acacia wood to construct the square altar of burnt offering. It was 7½ feet wide, 7½ feet long, and 4½ feet high.* ²He made horns for each of its four corners so that the horns and altar were all one piece. He overlaid the altar with bronze. ³Then he made all the altar utensils of bronze—the ash buckets, shovels, basins, meat forks, and firepans. ⁴Next he made a bronze grating and installed it halfway down the side of the altar, under the ledge. ⁵He cast four rings and attached them to the corners of the bronze grating to hold the carrying poles. ⁶He made the poles from acacia wood and overlaid them with bronze. ⁷He inserted the poles through the rings on the sides of the altar. The altar was hollow and was made from planks.

### Building the Washbasin

38:8
Exod 30:18

⁸Bezalel made the bronze washbasin and its bronze stand from bronze mirrors donated by the women who served at the entrance of the Tabernacle.*

### Building the Courtyard

38:9-20
//Exod 27:9-19;
40:8

⁹Then Bezalel made the courtyard, which was enclosed with curtains made of finely woven linen. On the south side the curtains were 150 feet long.* ¹⁰They were held up by twenty posts set securely in twenty bronze bases. He hung the curtains with silver hooks and rings. ¹¹He made a similar set of curtains for the north side—150 feet of curtains held up by twenty posts set securely in bronze bases. He hung the curtains with silver hooks and rings. ¹²The curtains on the west end of the courtyard were 75 feet long,* hung with silver hooks and rings and supported by ten posts set into ten bases. ¹³The east end, the front, was also 75 feet long.

¹⁴The courtyard entrance was on the east end, flanked by two curtains. The curtain on the right side was 22½ feet long* and was supported by three posts set into three bases. ¹⁵The curtain on the left side was also 22½ feet long and was supported by three posts set into three bases. ¹⁶All the curtains used in the courtyard were made of finely woven linen. ¹⁷Each post had a bronze base, and all the hooks and rings were silver. The tops of the posts of the courtyard were overlaid with silver, and the rings to hold up the curtains were made of silver.

¹⁸He made the curtain for the entrance to the courtyard of finely woven linen, and he decorated it with beautiful embroidery in blue, purple, and scarlet thread. It was 30 feet long, and its height was 7½ feet,* just like the curtains of the courtyard walls. ¹⁹It was supported by four posts, each set securely in its own bronze base. The tops of the posts were overlaid with silver, and the hooks and rings were also made of silver.

²⁰All the tent pegs used in the Tabernacle and courtyard were made of bronze.

**37:24** Hebrew *1 talent* [34 kilograms].    **37:25** Hebrew *1 cubit* [46 centimeters] *long and 1 cubit wide, a square, and 2 cubits* [92 centimeters] *high.*    **38:1a** Hebrew *he;* also in 38:8, 9.    **38:1b** Hebrew *5 cubits* [2.3 meters] *wide, 5 cubits long, a square, and 3 cubits* [1.4 meters] *high.*    **38:8** Hebrew *Tent of Meeting;* also in 38:30.
**38:9** Hebrew *100 cubits* [46 meters]; also in 38:11.    **38:12** Hebrew *50 cubits* [23 meters]; also in 38:13.
**38:14** Hebrew *15 cubits* [6.9 meters]; also in 38:15.    **38:18** Hebrew *20 cubits* [9.2 meters] *long and 5 cubits* [2.3 meters] *high.*

## Inventory of Materials

21This is an inventory of the materials used in building the Tabernacle of the Covenant.* The Levites compiled the figures, as Moses directed, and Ithamar son of Aaron the priest served as recorder. 22Bezalel son of Uri, grandson of Hur, of the tribe of Judah, made everything just as the LORD had commanded Moses. 23He was assisted by Oholiab son of Ahisamach, of the tribe of Dan, a craftsman expert at engraving, designing, and embroidering with blue, purple, and scarlet thread on fine linen cloth.

24The people brought special offerings of gold totaling 2,193 pounds,* as measured by the weight of the sanctuary shekel. This gold was used throughout the Tabernacle.

**38:25-26**
Exod 12:37;
30:11-16
Num 1:46; 26:51

25The whole community of Israel gave 7,545 pounds* of silver, as measured by the weight of the sanctuary shekel. 26This silver came from the tax collected from each man registered in the census. (The tax is one beka, which is half a shekel,* based on the sanctuary shekel.) The tax was collected from 603,550 men who had reached their twentieth birthday. 27The hundred bases for the frames of the sanctuary walls and for the posts supporting the inner curtain required 7,500 pounds of silver, about 75 pounds for each base.* 28The remaining 45 pounds* of silver was used to make the hooks and rings and to overlay the tops of the posts.

29The people also brought as special offerings 5,310 pounds* of bronze, 30which was used for casting the bases for the posts at the entrance to the Tabernacle, and for the bronze altar with its bronze grating and all the altar utensils. 31Bronze was also used to make the bases for the posts that supported the curtains around the courtyard, the bases for the curtain at the entrance of the courtyard, and all the tent pegs for the Tabernacle and the courtyard.

## Clothing for the Priests

# 39

The craftsmen made beautiful sacred garments of blue, purple, and scarlet cloth— clothing for Aaron to wear while ministering in the Holy Place, just as the LORD had commanded Moses.

**39:1**
Exod 35:23

## Making the Ephod

2Bezalel* made the ephod of finely woven linen and embroidered it with gold and with blue, purple, and scarlet thread. 3He made gold thread by hammering out thin sheets of gold and cutting it into fine strands. With great skill and care, he worked it into the fine linen with the blue, purple, and scarlet thread.

**39:2-7**
//Exod 28:6-14

4The ephod consisted of two pieces, front and back, joined at the shoulders with two shoulder-pieces. 5The decorative sash was made of the same materials: finely woven linen embroidered with gold and with blue, purple, and scarlet thread, just as the LORD had commanded Moses. 6They mounted the two onyx stones in settings of gold filigree. The stones were engraved with the names of the tribes of Israel, just as a seal is engraved. 7He fastened these stones on the shoulder-pieces of the ephod as a reminder that the priest represents the people of Israel. All this was done just as the LORD had commanded Moses.

## Making the Chestpiece

8Bezalel made the chestpiece with great skill and care. He made it to match the ephod, using finely woven linen embroidered with gold and with blue, purple, and scarlet thread. 9He made the chestpiece of a single piece of cloth folded to form a pouch nine inches* square.

**38:21** Hebrew *the Tabernacle, the Tabernacle of the Testimony.*   **38:24** Hebrew *29 talents and 730 shekels* [994 kilograms]. Each shekel weighed about 0.4 ounces.   **38:25** Hebrew *100 talents and 1,775 shekels* [3,420 kilograms].   **38:26** Or *0.2 ounces,* or *6 grams.*   **38:27** Hebrew *100 talents* [3,400 kilograms] of silver, *1 talent* [34 kilograms] *for each base.*   **38:28** Hebrew *1,775 shekels* [20.2 kilograms].   **38:29** Hebrew *70 talents and 2,400 shekels* [2,407 kilograms].   **39:2** Hebrew *He;* also in 39:8, 22.   **39:9** Hebrew *1 span* [23 centimeters].

---

**38:21** In the building of the Tabernacle, Moses laid out the steps, but Ithamar supervised the project. We all have different talents and abilities. God didn't ask Moses to build the Tabernacle but to motivate the experts to do it. Look for the areas where God has gifted you and then seek opportunities to allow God to use your gifts.

**39:1-21** The priests wore a uniform to the Tabernacle each day. Some of the pieces of their uniform were not only beautiful but also significant. Two parts of the high priest's uniform were the ephod and chestpiece. The ephod looked like a vest and was

worn over the outer clothing. The chestpiece was fitted to the ephod (and sometimes was called the ephod). The chestpiece was made of colored linens about nine inches square. On its front were attached 12 gemstones, each inscribed with the name of a tribe of Israel. This symbolized how the high priest represented all the people before God. The chestpiece also contained pockets that held two stones or plates called the Urim and Thummim. The high priest could determine God's will for the nation by consulting the Urim and Thummim. (See the notes on 28:30 and Leviticus 8:8.)

[39:14
Rev 21:12]

[10]They mounted four rows of gemstones* on it. The first row contained a red carnelian, a pale-green peridot, and an emerald. [11]The second row contained a turquoise, a blue lapis lazuli, and a white moonstone. [12]The third row contained an orange jacinth, an agate, and a purple amethyst. [13]The fourth row contained a blue-green beryl, an onyx, and a green jasper. All these stones were set in gold filigree. [14]Each stone represented one of the twelve sons of Israel, and the name of that tribe was engraved on it like a seal.

[15]To attach the chestpiece to the ephod, they made braided cords of pure gold thread. [16]They also made two settings of gold filigree and two gold rings and attached them to the top corners of the chestpiece. [17]They tied the two gold cords to the rings on the chestpiece. [18]They tied the other ends of the cords to the gold settings on the shoulder-pieces of the ephod. [19]Then they made two more gold rings and attached them to the inside edges of the chestpiece next to the ephod. [20]Then they made two more gold rings and attached them to the front of the ephod, below the shoulder-pieces, just above the knot where the decorative sash was fastened to the ephod. [21]They attached the bottom rings of the chestpiece to the rings on the ephod with blue cords. In this way, the chestpiece was held securely to the ephod above the decorative sash. All this was done just as the LORD had commanded Moses.

### Additional Clothing for the Priests

[39:22-31
//Exod 28:31-43]

[22]Bezalel made the robe that is worn with the ephod from a single piece of blue woven cloth, [23]with an opening for Aaron's head in the middle of it. The opening was reinforced with a woven collar* so it would not tear. [24]They made pomegranates of blue, purple, and scarlet yarn, and attached them to the hem of the robe. [25]They also made bells of pure gold and placed them between the pomegranates along the hem of the robe, [26]with bells and pomegranates alternating all around the hem. This robe was to be worn whenever the priest ministered before the LORD, just as the LORD had commanded Moses.

[39:27
Exod 28:39-40, 42]

[27]They made tunics for Aaron and his sons from fine linen cloth. [28]The turban and the special head coverings were made of fine linen, and the undergarments were also made of finely woven linen. [29]The sashes were made of finely woven linen and embroidered with blue, purple, and scarlet thread, just as the LORD had commanded Moses.

[39:30
Exod 28:36-37]

[30]Finally, they made the sacred medallion—the badge of holiness—of pure gold. They engraved it like a seal with these words: HOLY TO THE LORD. [31]They attached the medallion with a blue cord to Aaron's turban, just as the LORD had commanded Moses.

### Moses Inspects the Work

[39:32-41
//Exod 35:10-19]

[32]And so at last the Tabernacle* was finished. The Israelites had done everything just as the LORD had commanded Moses. [33]And they brought the entire Tabernacle to Moses:

the sacred tent with all its furnishings, clasps, frames, crossbars, posts, and bases;
[34] the tent coverings of tanned ram skins and fine goatskin leather;
the inner curtain to shield the Ark;
[35] the Ark of the Covenant* and its carrying poles;
the Ark's cover—the place of atonement;
[36] the table and all its utensils;
the Bread of the Presence;
[37] the pure gold lampstand with its symmetrical lamp cups, all its accessories, and the olive oil for lighting;
[38] the gold altar;
the anointing oil and fragrant incense;
the curtain for the entrance of the sacred tent;
[39] the bronze altar;
the bronze grating and its carrying poles and utensils;
the washbasin with its stand;
[40] the curtains for the walls of the courtyard;
the posts and their bases;

39:10 The identification of some of these gemstones is uncertain.   39:23 The meaning of the Hebrew is uncertain.   39:32 Hebrew *the Tabernacle, the Tent of Meeting;* also in 39:40.   39:35 Or *Ark of the Testimony.*

**39:32** The Tabernacle was finally complete to the last detail. God was keenly interested in every minute part. The Creator of the universe was concerned about even the little things. Matthew 10:30 says that God knows the number of hairs on our heads. This shows that God is greatly interested in you. Don't be afraid to talk with him about any of your concerns—no matter how small or unimportant they might seem.

the curtain for the entrance to the courtyard;

the ropes and tent pegs;

all the furnishings to be used in worship at the Tabernacle;

41 the beautifully stitched garments for the priests to wear while ministering in the Holy Place—the sacred garments for Aaron the priest, and the garments for his sons to wear as they minister as priests.

42So the people of Israel followed all of the LORD's instructions to Moses. 43Then Moses inspected all their work. When he found it had been done just as the LORD had commanded him, he blessed them.

**39:43**
Lev 9:22-23
Num 6:23-26
1 Kgs 8:14
2 Chr 30:27

### The Tabernacle Completed

**40** Then the LORD said to Moses, 2"Set up the Tabernacle* on the first day of the new year.* 3Place the Ark of the Covenant* inside, and install the inner curtain to enclose the Ark within the Most Holy Place. 4Then bring in the table, and arrange the utensils on it. And bring in the lampstand, and set up the lamps.

**40:2**
Exod 12:2; 19:1;
40:17
Num 1:1

5"Place the gold incense altar in front of the Ark of the Covenant. Then hang the curtain at the entrance of the Tabernacle. 6Place the altar of burnt offering in front of the Tabernacle entrance. 7Set the washbasin between the Tabernacle* and the altar, and fill it with water. 8Then set up the courtyard around the outside of the tent, and hang the curtain for the courtyard entrance.

**40:3**
Exod 26:33;
40:21-30
Num 4:5

**40:4**
Exod 25:30

**40:7**
Exod 30:18

9"Take the anointing oil and anoint the Tabernacle and all its furnishings to consecrate them and make them holy. 10Anoint the altar of burnt offering and its utensils to consecrate them. Then the altar will become absolutely holy. 11Next anoint the washbasin and its stand to consecrate them.

**40:9**
Exod 30:26

12"Present Aaron and his sons at the entrance of the Tabernacle, and wash them with water. 13Dress Aaron with the sacred garments and anoint him, consecrating him to serve me as a priest. 14Then present his sons and dress them in their tunics. 15Anoint them as you did their father, so they may also serve me as priests. With their anointing, Aaron's descendants are set apart for the priesthood forever, from generation to generation."

**40:12**
Lev 8:1-13

**40:15**
Exod 29:9
Num 25:13

16Moses proceeded to do everything just as the LORD had commanded him. 17So the Tabernacle was set up on the first day of the first month of the second year. 18Moses erected the Tabernacle by setting down its bases, inserting the frames, attaching the crossbars, and setting up the posts. 19Then he spread the coverings over the Tabernacle framework and put on the protective layers, just as the LORD had commanded him.

**40:17**
Exod 40:2
Num 7:1

20He took the stone tablets inscribed with the terms of the covenant and placed them* inside the Ark. Then he attached the carrying poles to the Ark, and he set the Ark's cover—the place of atonement—on top of it. 21Then he brought the Ark of the Covenant into the Tabernacle and hung the inner curtain to shield it from view, just as the LORD had commanded him.

**40:20**
Exod 25:16
Deut 10:5
1 Kgs 8:9
2 Chr 5:10
Heb 9:4

22Next Moses placed the table in the Tabernacle, along the north side of the Holy Place, just outside the inner curtain. 23And he arranged the Bread of the Presence on the table before the LORD, just as the LORD had commanded him.

**40:23**
Exod 25:30
Lev 24:5-8

**40:2a** Hebrew *the Tabernacle, the Tent of Meeting;* also in 40:6, 29. **40:2b** Hebrew *the first day of the first month.* This day of the ancient Hebrew lunar calendar occurred in March or April. **40:3** Or *Ark of the Testimony;* also in 40:5, 21. **40:7** Hebrew *Tent of Meeting;* also in 40:12, 22, 24, 26, 30, 32, 34, 35. **40:20** Hebrew *He placed the Testimony;* see note on 25:16.

---

**39:42** Moses had learned his management lesson well. He gave important responsibilities to others and then trusted them to do the job. Great leaders, like Moses, give plans and direction while letting others participate on the team. If you are a leader, trust your assistants with key responsibilities.

**39:43** Moses inspected the finished work, saw that it was done the way God wanted, and then blessed the people. A good leader follows up on assigned tasks and gives rewards for good work. In whatever responsible position you find yourself, follow up to make sure that tasks are completed as intended, and show your appreciation to the people who have helped.

**40:1ff** Moses was careful to obey God's instructions in the smallest detail. Notice that he didn't make a reasonable facsimile of God's description, but an exact copy. We should follow Moses'

example and be fastidious about our obedience. If God has told you to do something, do it, do it right, and do it completely.

**40:16** God told Moses how to build the Tabernacle, and Moses delegated jobs in order to do it. God allows people to participate with him in carrying out his will. Your task is not just to sit and watch God work, but to give your best effort when work needs to be done.

**40:17-33** The physical care of the Tabernacle required a long list of tasks, and each was important to the work of God's house. This principle is important to remember today when God's house is the church. There are many seemingly unimportant tasks that must be done to keep your church building maintained. Washing dishes, painting walls, or shoveling snow may not seem very spiritual. But they are vital to the ministry of the church and are an important part of our worship of God.

24He set the lampstand in the Tabernacle across from the table on the south side of the Holy Place. 25Then he lit the lamps in the LORD's presence, just as the LORD had commanded him. 26He also placed the gold incense altar in the Tabernacle, in the Holy Place in front of the inner curtain. 27On it he burned the fragrant incense, just as the LORD had commanded him.

28He hung the curtain at the entrance of the Tabernacle, 29and he placed the altar of burnt offering near the Tabernacle entrance. On it he offered a burnt offering and a grain offering, just as the LORD had commanded him.

30Next Moses placed the washbasin between the Tabernacle and the altar. He filled it with water so the priests could wash themselves. 31Moses and Aaron and Aaron's sons used water from it to wash their hands and feet. 32Whenever they approached the altar and entered the Tabernacle, they washed themselves, just as the LORD had commanded Moses.

33Then he hung the curtains forming the courtyard around the Tabernacle and the altar. And he set up the curtain at the entrance of the courtyard. So at last Moses finished the work.

**40:31**
Exod 30:19-21

### The LORD's Glory Fills the Tabernacle

**40:34**
Num 9:15-23
1 Kgs 8:11

34Then the cloud covered the Tabernacle, and the glory of the LORD filled the Tabernacle. 35Moses could no longer enter the Tabernacle because the cloud had settled down over it, and the glory of the LORD filled the Tabernacle.

**40:35**
1 Kgs 8:10-11

**40:36**
Num 9:17; 10:11

36Now whenever the cloud lifted from the Tabernacle, the people of Israel would set out on their journey, following it. 37But if the cloud did not rise, they remained where they were until it lifted. 38The cloud of the LORD hovered over the Tabernacle during the day, and at night fire glowed inside the cloud so the whole family of Israel could see it. This continued throughout all their journeys.

**40:37**
Num 9:19-22

**40:38**
1 Cor 10:1

---

**40:34** The Tabernacle was God's home on earth. He filled it with his glory—the overpowering sense of his presence. Almost 500 years later, Solomon built the Temple, which replaced the Tabernacle as the central place of worship. God also filled the Temple with his glory (2 Chronicles 5:13, 14). But when Israel turned from God, his glory and presence departed from the Temple, and it was destroyed by invading armies (2 Kings 25). The Temple was rebuilt in 515 B.C. God's glory returned in even greater splendor nearly five centuries later when Jesus Christ, God's Son, entered it and taught. When Jesus was crucified, God's glory again left the Temple. However, God no longer needed a physical building after Jesus rose from the dead. God's temple now is his church, the body of believers.

**40:38** The Israelites were once Egyptian slaves making bricks without straw. Here they were following the pillar of cloud and the pillar of fire, carrying the Tabernacle they had built for God. Exodus begins in gloom and ends in glory. This parallels our progress through the Christian life. We begin as slaves to sin, are redeemed by God, and end our pilgrimage living with God forever. The lessons the Israelites learned along the way are ones we also need to learn.

# LEVITICUS

SLAVERY IN EGYPT

Joseph
dies
1805 B.C.
(1640 B.C.)

## VITAL STATISTICS

**PURPOSE:**
A handbook for the priests and
Levites outlining their duties
in worship, and a guidebook
of holy living for the Hebrews

**AUTHOR:**
Moses

**ORIGINAL AUDIENCE:**
The people of Israel

**DATE WRITTEN:**
1450–1410 B.C.

**WHERE WRITTEN:**
In the wilderness during Israel's
wanderings, somewhere in the
Sinai peninsula

**SETTING:**
At the foot of Mount Sinai. God
is teaching the Israelites how
to live as holy people.

**KEY VERSE:**
"You must be holy because I, the
LORD your God, am holy" (19:2).

**KEY PEOPLE:**
Moses, Aaron, Nadab, Abihu,
Eleazar, Ithamar

**KEY PLACE:**
Mount Sinai

**SPECIAL FEATURE:**
Holiness is mentioned more times
(152) than in any other book of
the Bible.

"GOD seems so far away . . . if only I could see or hear him." Have you ever felt this way—struggling with loneliness, burdened by despair, riddled with sin, overwhelmed by problems? Made in God's image, we were created to have a close relationship with him; thus, when fellowship is broken, we are incomplete and need restoration. Communion with the living God is the essence of worship. It is vital, touching the very core of our lives. Perhaps this is why a whole book of the Bible is dedicated to worship. After Israel's dramatic exit from Egypt, the nation was camped at the foot of Mount Sinai for two years to listen to God (Exodus 19 to Numbers 10). It was a time of resting, teaching, building, and meeting with him face to face. Redemption in Exodus is the foundation for cleansing, worship, and service in Leviticus.

The overwhelming message of Leviticus is the holiness of God—"You must be holy because I, the LORD your God, am holy" (19:2). But how can unholy people approach a holy God? The answer—first sin must be dealt with. Thus the opening chapters of Leviticus give detailed instructions for offering sacrifices, which were the active symbols of repentance and obedience. Whether bulls, grain, goats, or sheep, the sacrificial offerings had to be perfect, with no defects or bruises—pictures of the ultimate sacrifice to come, Jesus, the Lamb of God. Jesus has come and opened the way to God by giving up his life as the final sacrifice in our place. True worship and oneness with God begin as we confess our sin and accept Christ as the only one who can redeem us from sin and help us approach God.

In Leviticus, sacrifices, priests, and the sacred Day of Atonement opened the way for the Israelites to come to God. God's people were also to worship him with their lives. Thus we read of purity laws (chapters 11—15) and rules for daily living, concerning family responsibilities, sexual conduct, relationships, worldliness (chapters 18—20), and vows (chapter 27). These instructions involve one's holy walk with God, and the patterns of spiritual living still apply today. Worship, therefore, has a horizontal aspect—that is, God is honored by our lives as we relate to others.

The final emphasis in Leviticus is celebration. The book gives instructions for the festivals. These were special, regular, and corporate occasions for remembering what God had done, giving thanks to him, and rededicating lives to his service (chapter 23). Our Christian traditions and holidays are different, but they are necessary ingredients of worship. We, too, need special days of worship and celebration with our spiritual brothers and sisters to remember God's goodness in our lives.

As you read Leviticus, rededicate yourself to holiness, worshiping God in private confession, public service, and group celebration.

## THE BLUEPRINT

A. WORSHIPING A HOLY GOD
   (1:1—17:16)
   1. Instructions for the offerings
   2. Instructions for the priests
   3. Instructions for the people
   4. Instructions for the altar

God provided specific directions for the kind of worship that would be pleasing to him. These instructions teach us about the nature of God and can help us develop a right attitude toward worship. Through the offerings we learn of the seriousness of sin and the importance of bringing our sins to God for forgiveness.

B. LIVING A HOLY LIFE (18:1—27:34)
   1. Standards for the people
   2. Rules for priests
   3. Seasons and festivals
   4. Receiving God's blessing

God gave clear standards to the Israelites for living a holy life. They were to be separate and distinct from the pagan nations around them. In the same way, all believers should be separated from sin and dedicated to God. God still wants to remove sin from the lives of his people.

## MEGATHEMES

| THEME | EXPLANATION | IMPORTANCE |
|---|---|---|
| Sacrifice/Offering | There are five kinds of offerings that fulfill two main purposes: one to show praise, thankfulness, and devotion; the other for atonement, the covering and removal of guilt and sin. Animal offerings demonstrated that the person was giving his or her life to God by means of the life of the animal. | The sacrifices (offerings) were for worship and forgiveness of sin. Through them we learn about the cost of sin, for we see that we cannot forgive ourselves. God's system says that a life must be given for a life. In the Old Testament, an animal's life was given to save the life of a person. But this was only a temporary measure until Jesus' death paid the penalty of sin for all people forever. |
| Worship | Seven festivals were designated as religious and national holidays. They were often celebrated in family settings. These events teach us much about worshiping God in both celebration and quiet dedication. | God's rules about worship set up an orderly, regular pattern of fellowship with him. They allowed times for celebration and thanksgiving as well as for reverence and rededication. Our worship should demonstrate our deep devotion. |
| Health | Civil rules for handling food, disease, and sex were taught. In these physical principles, many spiritual principles were suggested. Israel was to be different from the surrounding nations. God was preserving Israel from disease and community health problems. | We are to be different morally and spiritually from the unbelievers around us. Principles for healthy living are as important today as in Moses' time. A healthy environment and a healthy body make our service to God more effective. |
| Holiness | Holy means "separated" or "devoted." God removed his people from Egypt; now he was removing Egypt from the people. He was showing them how to exchange Egyptian ways of living and thinking for his ways. | We must devote every area of life to God. God desires absolute obedience in motives as well as practices. Though we do not observe all the worship practices of Israel, we are to have the same spirit of preparation and devotion. |
| Levites | The Levites and priests instructed the people in their worship. They were the ministers of their day. They also regulated the moral, civil, and ceremonial laws and supervised the health, justice, and welfare of the nation. | The Levites were servants who showed Israel the way to God. They provide the historical backdrop for Christ, who is our High Priest and yet our Servant. God's true servants care for all the needs of their people. |

## A. WORSHIPING A HOLY GOD (1:1—17:16)

The Israelites have arrived safely at the foot of Mount Sinai, and the Tabernacle has been completed. The people will spend a great deal of time here as God shows them a new way of life with clear instructions on how sinful people can relate to a holy God. These instructions help us avoid taking our relationship with the same holy God too lightly. We learn about the holiness and majesty of the God with whom we are allowed to have a personal relationship.

### 1. Instructions for the offerings
*Procedures for the Burnt Offering*

**1** The LORD called to Moses from the Tabernacle* and said to him, ²"Give the following instructions to the people of Israel. When you present an animal as an offering to the LORD, you may take it from your herd of cattle or your flock of sheep and goats.

³"If the animal you present as a burnt offering is from the herd, it must be a male with no

**1:1** Hebrew *Tent of Meeting;* also in 1:3, 5.

**1:1**
Exod 25:22
Num 7:89
**1:2**
Lev 6:9-13; 17:1-8
**1:3**
Heb 9:14

---

**1:1** The book of Leviticus begins where the book of Exodus ends—at the foot of Mount Sinai. The Tabernacle was just completed (Exodus 35–40), and God was ready to teach the people how to worship there.

**1:1** The "Tabernacle" where God met with Moses was actually the Tent of Meeting, a smaller structure inside the larger Tabernacle. The Tent of Meeting contained the sanctuary in one part and the Most Holy Place with the Ark in another part. These two sections were separated by a curtain. God revealed himself to Moses in the Most Holy Place. Exodus 33:7 mentions a "Tent of Meeting" where Moses met God before the Tabernacle was constructed. Many believe it served the same function as the one described here.

**1:1ff** We may be tempted to dismiss Leviticus as a record of bizarre rituals of a different age. But its practices made sense to the people of the day and offer important insights for us into God's nature and character. Animal sacrifice seems obsolete and repulsive to many people today, but animal sacrifices were practiced in many cultures in the Middle East. God used the form of sacrifice to teach his people about faith. Sin needed to be taken seriously. When people saw the sacrificial animals being killed, they were sensitized to the importance of their sin and guilt. Our culture's casual attitude toward sin ignores the cost of sin and need for repentance and restoration. Although many of the rituals of Leviticus were designed for the culture of the day, their purpose was to reveal a high and holy God who should be loved, obeyed, and worshiped. God's laws and sacrifices were intended to bring out true devotion of the heart. The ceremonies and rituals were the best way for the Israelites to focus their lives on God.

**1:2** Was there any difference between a sacrifice and an offering? In Leviticus the words are interchanged. Usually a specific

sacrifice is called an offering (burnt offering, grain offering, peace offering). Offerings in general are called sacrifices. The point is that each person *offered* a gift to God by *sacrificing* it on the altar. In the Old Testament, the sacrifice was the only way to approach God and restore a relationship with him. There was more than one kind of offering or sacrifice. The variety of sacrifices made them more meaningful because each one related to a specific life situation. Sacrifices were given in praise, worship, and thanksgiving, as well as for forgiveness and fellowship. The first seven chapters of Leviticus describe the variety of offerings and how they were to be used.

**1:2** When God taught his people to worship him, he placed great emphasis on sacrifices. Why? Sacrifices were God's Old Testament way for people to ask for forgiveness for their sins. Since Creation, God has made it clear that sin separates people from him, and that those who sin deserve to die. Because "everyone has sinned" (Romans 3:23), God designed sacrifice as a way to seek forgiveness and restore a relationship with him. Because he is a God of love and mercy, God decided from the very first that he would come into our world and die to pay the penalty for all humans. This he did in his Son, who, while still God, became a human being. In the meantime, before God made this ultimate sacrifice of his Son, he instructed people to kill animals as sacrifices for sin.

Animal sacrifice accomplished two purposes: (1) The animal symbolically took the sinner's place and paid the penalty for sin, and (2) the animal's death represented one life given so that another life could be saved. This method of sacrifice continued throughout Old Testament times. It was effective in teaching and guiding the people and bringing them back to God. But in New Testament times, Christ's death became the last sacrifice needed. He took our punishment once and for all. Animal sacrifice is no longer required. Now any person can be freed from the penalty of sin by simply believing in Jesus, acknowledging Jesus' sacrifice in his or her place, and accepting the forgiveness Jesus offers.

**1:3, 4** The first offering God describes is the burnt offering. A person who had sinned brought an animal with no defects to a priest. The unblemished animal symbolized the moral perfection demanded by a holy God and the perfect nature of the real sacrifice to come—Jesus Christ. The person then laid his hand on the head of the animal to symbolize the person's complete identification with the animal as his substitute. Then he killed the animal, and the priest sprinkled the blood. He symbolically transferred his sins to the animal, and thus his sins were taken away (atonement). Finally the animal (except for the blood and skin) was burned on the altar, signifying the person's complete dedication to God. God required more than a sacrifice, of course. He also asked the sinner to have an attitude of repentance. The outward symbol (the sacrifice) and the inner change (repentance) were to work together. But it is important to remember that neither sacrifice nor repentance actually caused the sin to be taken away. God alone forgives sin. Fortunately for us, forgiveness is part of God's loving nature. Have you responded to God's offer to forgive you?

**1:3ff** What did sacrifices teach the people? (1) By requiring

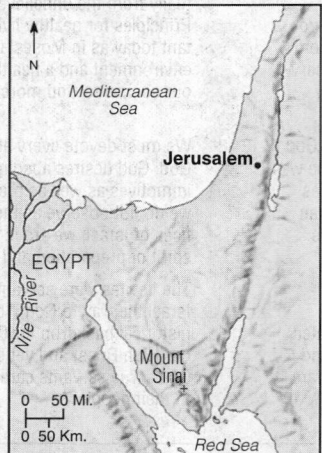

**THE ISRAELITES AT MOUNT SINAI**
Throughout the book of Leviticus, the Israelites were camped at the foot of Mount Sinai. It was time to regroup as a nation and learn the importance of following God as they prepared to march toward the Promised Land.

**1:4**
2 Chr 29:23-24

**1:5**
Lev 1:11; 3:8
Heb 12:24

**1:6**
Lev 7:8

**1:8**
Exod 29:13

**1:9**
Gen 8:21
Exod 29:17
Eph 5:2

**1:14**
Gen 15:9
Lev 12:8

**1:15**
Lev 5:9

defects. Bring it to the entrance of the Tabernacle so you* may be accepted by the LORD. ⁴Lay your hand on the animal's head, and the LORD will accept its death in your place to purify you, making you right with him.* ⁵Then slaughter the young bull in the LORD's presence, and Aaron's sons, the priests, will present the animal's blood by splattering it against all sides of the altar that stands at the entrance to the Tabernacle. ⁶Then skin the animal and cut it into pieces. ⁷The sons of Aaron the priest will build a wood fire on the altar. ⁸They will arrange the pieces of the offering, including the head and fat, on the wood burning on the altar. ⁹But the internal organs and the legs must first be washed with water. Then the priest will burn the entire sacrifice on the altar as a burnt offering. It is a special gift, a pleasing aroma to the LORD.

¹⁰"If the animal you present as a burnt offering is from the flock, it may be either a sheep or a goat, but it must be a male with no defects. ¹¹Slaughter the animal on the north side of the altar in the LORD's presence, and Aaron's sons, the priests, will splatter its blood against all sides of the altar. ¹²Then cut the animal in pieces, and the priests will arrange the pieces of the offering, including the head and fat, on the wood burning on the altar. ¹³But the internal organs and the legs must first be washed with water. Then the priest will burn the entire sacrifice on the altar as a burnt offering. It is a special gift, a pleasing aroma to the LORD.

¹⁴"If you present a bird as a burnt offering to the LORD, choose either a turtledove or a young pigeon. ¹⁵The priest will take the bird to the altar, wring off its head, and burn it on

**1:3** Or *it.*  **1:4** Or *to make atonement for you.*

---

**THE OFFERINGS**
Listed here are the five key offerings the Israelites made to God. They made these offerings in order to have their sins forgiven and to restore their fellowship with God. The death of Jesus Christ made these sacrifices unnecessary. Because of his death, our sins were completely forgiven, and fellowship with God has been restored.

| Offering | Purpose | Significance | Christ, the Perfect Offering |
|---|---|---|---|
| Burnt Offering (Lev. 1—voluntary) | To make payment for sins in general | Showed a person's devotion to God | Christ's death was the perfect offering |
| Grain Offering (Lev. 2—voluntary) | To show honor and respect to God in worship | Acknowledged that all we have belongs to God | Christ was the perfect man, who gave all of himself to God and others |
| Peace Offering (Lev. 3—voluntary) | To express gratitude to God | Symbolized peace and fellowship with God | Christ is the only way to fellowship with God |
| Sin Offering (Lev. 4—required) | To make payment for unintentional sins of uncleanness, neglect, or thoughtlessness | Restored the sinner to fellowship with God; showed seriousness of sin | Christ's death restores our fellowship with God |
| Guilt Offering (Lev. 5—required) | To make payment for sins against God and others. A sacrifice was made to God, and the injured person was repaid or compensated | Provided compensation for injured parties | Christ's death takes away the deadly consequences of sin |

---

perfect animals and holy priests, they taught reverence for a holy God. (2) By demanding exact obedience, they taught true submission to God's laws. (3) By requiring an animal of great value, they showed the high cost of sin and demonstrated the sincerity of the people's commitment to God. (4) By their nature, sacrifices required the use of all the senses in worship, encouraging a whole-person response to God. Some sacrifices were voluntary while others were required. The sacrificial system taught a combination of requirement before God, but also presented opportunities for heartfelt voluntary response to God.

**1:3-13** Why are there such detailed regulations for each offering? God had a purpose in giving these commands. Starting from scratch, he was teaching his people a whole new way of life, cleansing them from the many pagan practices they had learned in Egypt and restoring true worship of himself. The strict details kept Israel from slipping back into their old lifestyle. In addition, each law paints a graphic picture of the seriousness of sin and of God's great mercy in forgiving sinners.

**1:4ff** Israel was not the only nation to sacrifice animals. Many other religions did it as well to try to please their gods. Some cultures even included human sacrifice, which was strictly forbidden by God. However, the meaning of Israel's animal sacrifices was clearly different from that of their pagan neighbors' sacrifices. Israelites sacrificed animals, not just to appease God's wrath, but as a substitute for the punishment they deserved for their sins. A sacrifice showed faith in God and commitment to his laws. Most important, this system foreshadowed the day when the Lamb of God (Jesus Christ) would die and conquer sin once and for all.

**1:13** The "pleasing aroma" is a way of saying that God accepted the sacrifice because of the attitude of the people.

the altar. But first he must drain its blood against the side of the altar. ¹⁶The priest must also remove the crop and the feathers* and throw them in the ashes on the east side of the altar. ¹⁷Then, grasping the bird by its wings, the priest will tear the bird open, but without tearing it apart. Then he will burn it as a burnt offering on the wood burning on the altar. It is a special gift, a pleasing aroma to the LORD.

## Procedures for the Grain Offering

**2** "When you present grain as an offering to the LORD, the offering must consist of choice flour. You are to pour olive oil on it, sprinkle it with frankincense, ²and bring it to Aaron's sons, the priests. The priest will scoop out a handful of the flour moistened with oil, together with all the frankincense, and burn this representative portion on the altar. It is a special gift, a pleasing aroma to the LORD. ³The rest of the grain offering will then be given to Aaron and his sons. This offering will be considered a most holy part of the special gifts presented to the LORD.

⁴"If your offering is a grain offering baked in an oven, it must be made of choice flour, but without any yeast. It may be presented in the form of thin cakes mixed with olive oil or wafers spread with olive oil. ⁵If your grain offering is cooked on a griddle, it must be made of choice flour mixed with olive oil but without any yeast. ⁶Break it in pieces and pour olive oil on it; it is a grain offering. ⁷If your grain offering is prepared in a pan, it must be made of choice flour and olive oil.

⁸"No matter how a grain offering for the LORD has been prepared, bring it to the priest, who will present it at the altar. ⁹The priest will take a representative portion of the grain offering and burn it on the altar. It is a special gift, a pleasing aroma to the LORD. ¹⁰The rest of the grain offering will then be given to Aaron and his sons as their food. This offering will be considered a most holy part of the special gifts presented to the LORD.

¹¹"Do not use yeast in preparing any of the grain offerings you present to the LORD, because no yeast or honey may be burned as a special gift presented to the LORD. ¹²You may add yeast and honey to an offering of the first crops of your harvest, but these must never be offered on the altar as a pleasing aroma to the LORD. ¹³Season all your grain offerings with salt to remind you of God's eternal covenant. Never forget to add salt to your grain offerings.

¹⁴ "If you present a grain offering to the LORD from the first portion of your harvest, bring fresh grain that is coarsely ground and roasted on a fire. ¹⁵Put olive oil on this grain offering, and sprinkle it with frankincense. ¹⁶The priest will take a representative portion of the grain moistened with oil, together with all the frankincense, and burn it as a special gift presented to the LORD.

## Procedures for the Peace Offering

**3** "If you present an animal from the herd as a peace offering to the LORD, it may be a male or a female, but it must have no defects. ²Lay your hand on the animal's head, and slaughter it at the entrance of the Tabernacle.* Then Aaron's sons, the priests, will splatter

**2:1**
Exod 29:2
Lev 6:14-18; 24:7
Num 15:4-21
**2:2**
Lev 5:12-13;
6:15-18
**2:3**
Lev 10:12-13

**2:4**
Exod 29:2
Lev 7:12

**2:9**
Gen 8:21
Lev 2:2; 6:15
**2:10**
Lev 2:3
**2:11**
Lev 6:16-17
**2:12**
Lev 7:13; 23:9-14
**2:13**
Num 18:19
2 Chr 13:5
Ezek 43:24
Mark 9:49
**2:14**
Lev 23:9-14
2 Kgs 4:42
**2:16**
Lev 2:1-2

**3:1**
Lev 1:3; 7:11-21
**3:2**
Exod 29:11
Lev 1:4; 7:14

**1:16** Or *the crop and its contents.* The meaning of the Hebrew is uncertain.   **3:2** Hebrew *Tent of Meeting;* also in 3:8, 13.

---

**2:1ff** The grain offering accompanied all burnt offerings and was a gift of thanks to God. It reminded the people that their food came from God and that they therefore owed their lives to him. Three kinds of grain offerings are listed: (1) fine flour with oil and incense, (2) baked cakes or wafers of fine flour and oil, and (3) roasted kernels of grain (corn) with oil and incense. The absence of yeast symbolized the absence of sin, and the oil symbolized God's presence. Part of the grain offering was burned on the altar as a gift to God, and the rest was eaten by the priests. The offerings helped support them in their work.

**2:11** Why was no yeast allowed in the grain offerings? Yeast is a bacterial fungus or mold and is, therefore, an appropriate symbol for sin. It grows in bread dough just as sin grows in a life. A little yeast will affect the whole loaf, just as a little sin can ruin a whole life. Jesus expanded this analogy by warning about the "yeast of the Pharisees and Sadducees" (Matthew 16:6; Mark 8:15). How do you visualize the effects of sin in your life? What do you do to eliminate sin from your attitudes and actions?

**2:13** The offerings were seasoned with salt as a reminder of the people's covenant (contract) with God. Salt is a good symbol of

God's activity in a person's life because it penetrates, preserves, and aids in healing. God wants to be active in your life. Let him become part of you, penetrating every aspect of your life, preserving you from the evil all around, and healing you of your sins and shortcomings.

**2:13** In ancient Middle Eastern lands, an agreement was sealed with a gift of salt to show the strength and permanence of the contract. Salt also points to the effects of a truthful agreement— it changes behavior. In Matthew 5:13 believers are called "the salt of the earth." Let the salt you use each day remind you that you are now one of God's covenant people, who actively helps preserve and purify the world.

**2:14, 15** Coarsely ground heads of new grain mixed with oil and baked was typical food for the average person. This offering was a token presentation of a person's daily food. In this way, people acknowledged God as provider of their food. Even a poor person could fulfill this offering. God was pleased by the motivation and the dedication of the persons making it.

**3:1ff** A person gave a peace offering as an expression of gratitude and a means of maintaining fellowship between himself and

**3:3**
Exod 29:13, 22
Lev 3:9-11

**3:5**
Num 15:8-10

**3:6**
Lev 3:1

**3:13**
Lev 1:5

**3:15-16**
Lev 4:26; 7:23-25

**3:17**
Lev 7:26-27; 17:10
Deut 12:16
Acts 15:20

**4:2**
Lev 4:22; 22:14
Num 15:22-29

**4:3**
Lev 4:14; 9:2
Ezek 43:19

**4:5**
Lev 4:16; 16:14
**4:7**
Lev 8:15

**4:8**
Lev 3:3

**4:11**
Num 19:5
Heb 13:11

**4:13**
Num 15:23-26
**4:14**
Lev 4:3

its blood against all sides of the altar. ³The priest must present part of this peace offering as a special gift to the LORD. This includes all the fat around the internal organs, ⁴the two kidneys and the fat around them near the loins, and the long lobe of the liver. These must be removed with the kidneys, ⁵and Aaron's sons will burn them on top of the burnt offering on the wood burning on the altar. It is a special gift, a pleasing aroma to the LORD.

⁶"If you present an animal from the flock as a peace offering to the LORD, it may be a male or a female, but it must have no defects. ⁷If you present a sheep as your offering, bring it to the LORD, ⁸lay your hand on its head, and slaughter it in front of the Tabernacle. Aaron's sons will then splatter the sheep's blood against all sides of the altar. ⁹The priest must present the fat of this peace offering as a special gift to the LORD. This includes the fat of the broad tail cut off near the backbone, all the fat around the internal organs, ¹⁰the two kidneys and the fat around them near the loins, and the long lobe of the liver. These must be removed with the kidneys, ¹¹and the priest will burn them on the altar. It is a special gift of food presented to the LORD.

¹²"If you present a goat as your offering, bring it to the LORD, ¹³lay your hand on its head, and slaughter it in front of the Tabernacle. Aaron's sons will then splatter the goat's blood against all sides of the altar. ¹⁴The priest must present part of this offering as a special gift to the LORD. This includes all the fat around the internal organs, ¹⁵the two kidneys and the fat around them near the loins, and the long lobe of the liver. These must be removed with the kidneys, ¹⁶and the priest will burn them on the altar. It is a special gift of food, a pleasing aroma to the LORD. All the fat belongs to the LORD.

¹⁷"You must never eat any fat or blood. This is a permanent law for you, and it must be observed from generation to generation, wherever you live."

### Procedures for the Sin Offering

**4** Then the LORD said to Moses, ²"Give the following instructions to the people of Israel. This is how you are to deal with those who sin unintentionally by doing anything that violates one of the LORD's commands.

³"If the high priest* sins, bringing guilt upon the entire community, he must give a sin offering for the sin he has committed. He must present to the LORD a young bull with no defects. ⁴He must bring the bull to the LORD at the entrance of the Tabernacle,* lay his hand on the bull's head, and slaughter it before the LORD. ⁵The high priest will then take some of the bull's blood into the Tabernacle, ⁶dip his finger in the blood, and sprinkle it seven times before the LORD in front of the inner curtain of the sanctuary. ⁷The priest will then put some of the blood on the horns of the altar for fragrant incense that stands in the LORD's presence inside the Tabernacle. He will pour out the rest of the bull's blood at the base of the altar for burnt offerings at the entrance of the Tabernacle. ⁸Then the priest must remove all the fat of the bull to be offered as a sin offering. This includes all the fat around the internal organs, ⁹the two kidneys and the fat around them near the loins, and the long lobe of the liver. He must remove these along with the kidneys, ¹⁰just as he does with cattle offered as a peace offering, and burn them on the altar of burnt offerings. ¹¹But he must take whatever is left of the bull—its hide, meat, head, legs, internal organs, and dung—¹²and carry it away to a place outside the camp that is ceremonially clean, the place where the ashes are dumped. There, on the ash heap, he will burn it on a wood fire.

¹³"If the entire Israelite community sins by violating one of the LORD's commands, but the people don't realize it, they are still guilty. ¹⁴When they become aware of their sin, the people must bring a young bull as an offering for their sin and present it before the

4:3 Hebrew *the anointed priest;* also in 4:5, 16.   4:4 Hebrew *Tent of Meeting;* also in 4:5, 7, 14, 16, 18.

God. The animal's sacrificed life emphasized the value of gratitude and maintaining harmony with God. Neither peace with God nor thanks to God was to be considered a cheap or unimportant gift. Because it symbolized peace with God, part of the offering could be eaten by the person presenting it.

**4:1ff** Have you ever done something wrong without realizing it until later? Although your sin was unintentional, it was still sin. God's commands served to make the Israelites aware of their sins (even the unintentional ones) so they could be forgiven for them, and to keep the people from repeating those sins. Leviticus 4 and 5 mention some of these unintentional sins and the way the Israel-

ites could be forgiven for them. As you read more of God's laws, keep in mind that they were meant to teach and guide the people. Let them help you become more aware of sin in your life.

**4:3** The sin offering was for those who (1) committed a sin without realizing it or (2) committed a sin out of weakness or negligence as opposed to outright rebellion against God. Both individuals and groups could be guilty of unintentional sin. Different animals were sacrificed for the different kinds of sin. The death of Jesus Christ was the final sin offering in the Bible (Hebrews 9:25-28 tells why).

Tabernacle. ¹⁵The elders of the community must then lay their hands on the bull's head and slaughter it before the Lord. ¹⁶The high priest will then take some of the bull's blood into the Tabernacle, ¹⁷dip his finger in the blood, and sprinkle it seven times before the Lord in front of the inner curtain. ¹⁸He will then put some of the blood on the horns of the altar for fragrant incense that stands in the Lord's presence inside the Tabernacle. He will pour out the rest of the blood at the base of the altar for burnt offerings at the entrance of the Tabernacle. ¹⁹Then the priest must remove all the animal's fat and burn it on the altar, ²⁰just as he does with the bull offered as a sin offering for the high priest. Through this process, the priest will purify the people, making them right with the Lord,* and they will be forgiven. ²¹Then the priest must take what is left of the bull and carry it outside the camp and burn it there, just as is done with the sin offering for the high priest. This offering is for the sin of the entire congregation of Israel.

²²"If one of Israel's leaders sins by violating one of the commands of the Lord his God but doesn't realize it, he is still guilty. ²³When he becomes aware of his sin, he must bring as his offering a male goat with no defects. ²⁴He must lay his hand on the goat's head and slaughter it at the place where burnt offerings are slaughtered before the Lord. This is an offering for his sin. ²⁵Then the priest will dip his finger in the blood of the sin offering and put it on the horns of the altar for burnt offerings. He will pour out the rest of the blood at the base of the altar. ²⁶Then he must burn all the goat's fat on the altar, just as he does with the peace offering. Through this process, the priest will purify the leader from his sin, making him right with the Lord, and he will be forgiven.

²⁷"If any of the common people sin by violating one of the Lord's commands, but they don't realize it, they are still guilty. ²⁸When they become aware of their sin, they must bring as an offering for their sin a female goat with no defects. ²⁹They must lay a hand on the head of the sin offering and slaughter it at the place where burnt offerings are slaughtered. ³⁰Then the priest will dip his finger in the blood and put it on the horns of the altar for burnt offerings. He will pour out the rest of the blood at the base of the altar. ³¹Then he must remove all the goat's fat, just as he does with the fat of the peace offering. He will burn the fat on the altar, and it will be a pleasing aroma to the Lord. Through this process, the priest will purify the people, making them right with the Lord, and they will be forgiven.

³²"If the people bring a sheep as their sin offering, it must be a female with no defects. ³³They must lay a hand on the head of the sin offering and slaughter it at the place where burnt offerings are slaughtered. ³⁴Then the priest will dip his finger in the blood of the sin offering and put it on the horns of the altar for burnt offerings. He will pour out the rest of the blood at the base of the altar. ³⁵Then he must remove all the sheep's fat, just as he does with the fat of a sheep presented as a peace offering. He will burn the fat on the altar on top of the special gifts presented to the Lord. Through this process, the priest will purify the people from their sin, making them right with the Lord, and they will be forgiven.

## Sins Requiring a Sin Offering

**5** "If you are called to testify about something you have seen or that you know about, it is sinful to refuse to testify, and you will be punished for your sin.

²"Or suppose you unknowingly touch something that is ceremonially unclean, such as the carcass of an unclean animal. When you realize what you have done, you must admit your defilement and your guilt. This is true whether it is a wild animal, a domestic animal, or an animal that scurries along the ground.

³"Or suppose you unknowingly touch something that makes a person unclean. When you realize what you have done, you must admit your guilt.

⁴"Or suppose you make a foolish vow of any kind, whether its purpose is for good or for bad. When you realize its foolishness, you must admit your guilt.

**4:20** Or *will make atonement for the people;* similarly in 4:26, 31, 35.

---

**5:4** Have you ever sworn to do or not do something and then realized how foolish your promise was? God's people are called to keep their word, even if they make promises that are tough to keep. Jesus was warning against swearing (in the sense of making vows or oaths) when he said, "Just say a simple, 'Yes, I will,' or 'No, I won't.' Anything beyond this is from the evil one" (Matthew 5:37). Our word should be enough. If we feel we have to strengthen it with an oath, something is wrong with our sincerity. The only promises we ought not to keep are promises that lead to sin. A wise and self-controlled person avoids making rash promises.

Cross-references: 4:15 Lev 8:14; Num 8:10-12; 4:17 Lev 4:6; 4:19 Lev 4:8; 4:20 Num 15:25; 4:21 Lev 4:12; 4:22 Lev 4:2, 13; 4:24 Lev 6:25; 4:25 Lev 4:7; 4:26 Lev 4:19-20; 4:27 Lev 4:2; 4:28 Lev 4:23; 4:30 Lev 4:7; 4:31 Gen 8:21; Exod 29:18; Lev 2:2; 4:8; 6:15; 4:32 Lev 4:28; 4:35 Lev 3:5; 5:1 Prov 29:24; 5:2 Lev 11:4-11, 24-39; Num 19:11-16; Deut 14:3-21; 5:4 Num 30:6-8

**5:5**
Lev 16:21
Num 5:7
Josh 7:19
**5:6**
Lev 4:28, 32
**5:7**
Lev 12:8
Luke 2:24
**5:8**
Lev 1:15, 17
**5:9**
Lev 4:7; 7:2
**5:10**
Lev 1:14-17
**5:11**
Lev 14:21
†Luke 2:24
**5:15**
Exod 30:13
Lev 6:6; 7:1-10;
22:14
**5:16**
Lev 6:5; 22:14
**5:17**
Lev 5:15
**6:2**
Exod 22:7-15
Num 5:6
Col 3:9
**6:3**
Deut 22:1-3
**6:5-6**
Lev 5:15-16
Num 5:8

⁵"When you become aware of your guilt in any of these ways, you must confess your sin. ⁶Then you must bring to the Lord as the penalty for your sin a female from the flock, either a sheep or a goat. This is a sin offering with which the priest will purify you from your sin, making you right with the Lord.*

⁷"But if you cannot afford to bring a sheep, you may bring to the Lord two turtledoves or two young pigeons as the penalty for your sin. One of the birds will be for a sin offering, and the other for a burnt offering. ⁸You must bring them to the priest, who will present the first bird as the sin offering. He will wring its neck but without severing its head from the body. ⁹Then he will sprinkle some of the blood of the sin offering against the sides of the altar, and the rest of the blood will be drained out at the base of the altar. This is an offering for sin. ¹⁰The priest will then prepare the second bird as a burnt offering, following all the procedures that have been prescribed. Through this process the priest will purify you from your sin, making you right with the Lord, and you will be forgiven.

¹¹"If you cannot afford to bring two turtledoves or two young pigeons, you may bring two quarts* of choice flour for your sin offering. Since it is an offering for sin, you must not moisten it with olive oil or put any frankincense on it. ¹²Take the flour to the priest, who will scoop out a handful as a representative portion. He will burn it on the altar on top of the special gifts presented to the Lord. It is an offering for sin. ¹³Through this process, the priest will purify those who are guilty of any of these sins, making them right with the Lord, and they will be forgiven. The rest of the flour will belong to the priest, just as with the grain offering."

### Procedures for the Guilt Offering

¹⁴Then the Lord said to Moses, ¹⁵"If one of you commits a sin by unintentionally defiling the Lord's sacred property, you must bring a guilt offering to the Lord. The offering must be your own ram with no defects, or you may buy one of equal value with silver, as measured by the weight of the sanctuary shekel.* ¹⁶You must make restitution for the sacred property you have harmed by paying for the loss, plus an additional 20 percent. When you give the payment to the priest, he will purify you with the ram sacrificed as a guilt offering, making you right with the Lord, and you will be forgiven.

¹⁷"Suppose you sin by violating one of the Lord's commands. Even if you are unaware of what you have done, you are guilty and will be punished for your sin. ¹⁸For a guilt offering, you must bring to the priest your own ram with no defects, or you may buy one of equal value. Through this process the priest will purify you from your unintentional sin, making you right with the Lord, and you will be forgiven. ¹⁹This is a guilt offering, for you have been guilty of an offense against the Lord."

### Sins Requiring a Guilt Offering

**6** ¹*Then the Lord said to Moses, ²"Suppose one of you sins against your associate and is unfaithful to the Lord. Suppose you cheat in a deal involving a security deposit, or you steal or commit fraud, ³or you find lost property and lie about it, or you lie while swearing to tell the truth, or you commit any other such sin. ⁴If you have sinned in any of these ways, you are guilty. You must give back whatever you stole, or the money you took by extortion, or the security deposit, or the lost property you found, ⁵or anything obtained by swearing falsely. You must make restitution by paying the full price plus an additional 20 percent to the person you have harmed. On the same day you must present a guilt offering. ⁶As a guilt offering

**5:6** Or *will make atonement for you for your sin;* similarly in 5:10, 13, 16, 18.　**5:11** Hebrew *1/10 of an ephah* [2.2 liters]. **5:15** Each shekel was about 0.4 ounces or 11 grams in weight.　**6:1** Verses 6:1-7 are numbered 5:20-26 in Hebrew text.

---

**5:5** The entire system of sacrifices could not help a sinner unless he brought his offering with an attitude of repentance and a willingness to confess sin. Today, because of Christ's death on the cross, we do not have to sacrifice animals. But it is still vital to confess sin, because genuine confession shows realization of sin, awareness of God's holiness, humility before God, and willingness to turn from this sin (Psalm 51:16, 17). Even Jesus' death will be of little value to us if we do not repent and follow him. It is like a vaccine for a dangerous disease—it won't help unless it enters the bloodstream.

**5:14-19** The guilt offering was a way of taking care of sin committed unintentionally. It was for those who sinned in some way against "sacred property"—the Tabernacle or the priest-

hood—as well as for those who unintentionally sinned against someone. In either case, a ram with no defects had to be sacrificed, plus those harmed by the sin had to be compensated for their loss, plus a 20 percent penalty. Even though Christ's death has made guilt offerings unnecessary for us today, we still need to make things right with those we hurt.

**6:1-7** Here we discover that stealing involves more than just taking from someone. Finding something and not returning it or failing to return something borrowed are other forms of stealing. These are sins against God and not just your neighbor, a stranger, or a large business. If you have gotten something deceitfully, then confess your sin to God, apologize to the owner, and return the stolen items—with interest.

to the Lord, you must bring to the priest your own ram with no defects, or you may buy one of equal value. ⁷Through this process, the priest will purify you before the Lord, making you right with him,* and you will be forgiven for any of these sins you have committed."

### Further Instructions for the Burnt Offering
⁸*Then the Lord said to Moses, ⁹"Give Aaron and his sons the following instructions regarding the burnt offering. The burnt offering must be left on top of the altar until the next morning, and the fire on the altar must be kept burning all night. ¹⁰In the morning, after the priest on duty has put on his official linen clothing and linen undergarments, he must clean out the ashes of the burnt offering and put them beside the altar. ¹¹Then he must take off these garments, change back into his regular clothes, and carry the ashes outside the camp to a place that is ceremonially clean. ¹²Meanwhile, the fire on the altar must be kept burning; it must never go out. Each morning the priest will add fresh wood to the fire and arrange the burnt offering on it. He will then burn the fat of the peace offerings on it. ¹³Remember, the fire must be kept burning on the altar at all times. It must never go out.

6:9
Exod 29:38-42
Lev 6:12-13
Num 28:1-25
6:10
Exod 28:39-43

6:12
Lev 3:5

### Further Instructions for the Grain Offering
¹⁴"These are the instructions regarding the grain offering. Aaron's sons must present this offering to the Lord in front of the altar. ¹⁵The priest on duty will take from the grain offering a handful of the choice flour moistened with olive oil, together with all the frankincense. He will burn this representative portion on the altar as a pleasing aroma to the Lord. ¹⁶Aaron and his sons may eat the rest of the flour, but it must be baked without yeast and eaten in a sacred place within the courtyard of the Tabernacle.* ¹⁷Remember, it must never be prepared with yeast. I have given it to the priests as their share of the special gifts presented to me. Like the sin offering and the guilt offering, it is most holy. ¹⁸Any of Aaron's male descendants may eat from the special gifts presented to the Lord. This is their permanent right from generation to generation. Anyone or anything that touches these offerings will become holy."

6:14
Lev 2:1
6:15
Lev 2:1-2, 9

6:16
Lev 10:12-15
Num 18:10
6:17
Lev 2:11; 6:29;
10:17
6:18
Lev 6:29
Num 18:10
1 Cor 9:13

### Procedures for the Ordination Offering
¹⁹Then the Lord said to Moses, ²⁰"On the day Aaron and his sons are anointed, they must present to the Lord a grain offering of two quarts* of choice flour, half to be offered in the morning and half to be offered in the evening. ²¹It must be carefully mixed with olive oil and cooked on a griddle. Then slice* this grain offering and present it as a pleasing aroma to the Lord. ²²In each generation, the high priest* who succeeds Aaron must prepare this same offering. It belongs to the Lord and must be burned up completely. This is a permanent law. ²³All such grain offerings of a priest must be burned up entirely. None of it may be eaten."

6:21
Lev 2:5, 8; 7:9

6:22-23
Exod 29:30

### Further Instructions for the Sin Offering
²⁴Then the Lord said to Moses, ²⁵"Give Aaron and his sons the following instructions regarding the sin offering. The animal given as an offering for sin is a most holy offering, and it must be slaughtered in the Lord's presence at the place where the burnt offerings are slaughtered. ²⁶The priest who offers the sacrifice as a sin offering must eat his portion in a sacred place within the courtyard of the Tabernacle. ²⁷Anyone or anything that touches the sacrificial meat will become holy. If any of the sacrificial blood spatters on a person's clothing, the soiled garment must be washed in a sacred place. ²⁸If a clay pot is used to boil the sacrificial meat, it must then be broken. If a bronze pot is used, it must be scoured and thoroughly rinsed with water. ²⁹Any male from a priest's family may eat from this offering; it is most holy. ³⁰But the offering for sin may not be eaten if its blood was brought into the Tabernacle as an offering for purification* in the Holy Place. It must be completely burned with fire.

6:25
Lev 4:24, 29

6:27
Exod 29:37
6:28
Lev 11:33; 15:12

6:29
Lev 6:18
6:30
Lev 4:1, 18

**6:7** Or *will make atonement for you before the Lord.*   **6:8** Verses 6:8-30 are numbered 6:1-23 in Hebrew text.
**6:16** Hebrew *Tent of Meeting;* also in 6:26, 30.   **6:20** Hebrew *1/10 of an ephah* [2.2 liters].   **6:21** The meaning of this Hebrew term is uncertain.   **6:22** Hebrew *the anointed priest.*   **6:30** Or *an offering to make atonement.*

---

**6:12, 13** While the previous offerings and sacrifices were ones that the people did, the section from 6:8–7:38 deals with general and continual priestly duties. The burnt offering was presented in the morning and evening for the whole nation (see Exodus 29:38-43). The holy fire on the altar had to keep burning because God had started it. This represented God's continual presence in the sacrificial system. It showed the people that only by God's gracious favor could their sacrifices be acceptable. God's fire is present in each believer's life today. He lights the fire when the Holy Spirit comes to live in us, and he tends it so that we will grow in grace as we walk with him. When we are aware that God lives in us, we have confidence to come to him for forgiveness and restoration. We can carry out our work with strength and enthusiasm.

### Further Instructions for the Guilt Offering

**7:1**
Lev 5:14–6:7

**7:2**
Lev 1:11

**7:3**
Lev 3:3, 9

7 "These are the instructions for the guilt offering. It is most holy. ²The animal sacrificed as a guilt offering must be slaughtered at the place where the burnt offerings are slaughtered, and its blood must be splattered against all sides of the altar. ³The priest will then offer all its fat on the altar, including the fat of the broad tail, the fat around the internal organs, ⁴the two kidneys and the fat around them near the loins, and the long lobe of the liver. These are to be removed with the kidneys, ⁵and the priests will burn them on the altar as a special gift presented to the Lord. This is the guilt offering. ⁶Any male from a priest's family may eat the meat. It must be eaten in a sacred place, for it is most holy.

**7:6**
Lev 6:18, 29
Num 18:10

**7:7**
Lev 14:13

**7:9**
Lev 2:5, 8

⁷"The same instructions apply to both the guilt offering and the sin offering. Both belong to the priest who uses them to purify someone, making that person right with the Lord.* ⁸In the case of the burnt offering, the priest may keep the hide of the sacrificed animal. ⁹Any grain offering that has been baked in an oven, prepared in a pan, or cooked on a griddle belongs to the priest who presents it. ¹⁰All other grain offerings, whether made of dry flour or flour moistened with olive oil, are to be shared equally among all the priests, the descendants of Aaron.

### Further Instructions for the Peace Offering

**7:11**
Lev 3:1-17

**7:12**
Lev 2:4
Num 6:15

**7:13**
Lev 2:12; 23:17

**7:15**
Lev 22:29-30

¹¹"These are the instructions regarding the different kinds of peace offerings that may be presented to the Lord. ¹²If you present your peace offering as an expression of thanksgiving, the usual animal sacrifice must be accompanied by various kinds of bread made without yeast—thin cakes mixed with olive oil, wafers spread with oil, and cakes made of choice flour mixed with olive oil. ¹³This peace offering of thanksgiving must also be accompanied by loaves of bread made with yeast. ¹⁴One of each kind of bread must be presented as a gift to the Lord. It will then belong to the priest who splatters the blood of the peace offering against the altar. ¹⁵The meat of the peace offering of thanksgiving must be eaten on the same day it is offered. None of it may be saved for the next morning.

**7:16**
Lev 19:6-8

**7:17**
Exod 12:10

¹⁶"If you bring an offering to fulfill a vow or as a voluntary offering, the meat must be eaten on the same day the sacrifice is offered, but whatever is left over may be eaten on the second day. ¹⁷Any meat left over until the third day must be completely burned up. ¹⁸If any of the meat from the peace offering is eaten on the third day, the person who presented it will not be accepted by the Lord. You will receive no credit for offering it. By then the meat will be contaminated; if you eat it, you will be punished for your sin.

**7:19**
Lev 11:47

**7:20**
Gen 17:14
Lev 22:3-7
Num 19:13

**7:21**
Lev 5:2-3

¹⁹"Meat that touches anything ceremonially unclean may not be eaten; it must be completely burned up. The rest of the meat may be eaten, but only by people who are ceremonially clean. ²⁰If you are ceremonially unclean and you eat meat from a peace offering that was presented to the Lord, you will be cut off from the community. ²¹If you touch anything that is unclean (whether it is human defilement or an unclean animal or any other unclean, detestable thing) and then eat meat from a peace offering presented to the Lord, you will be cut off from the community."

### The Forbidden Blood and Fat

**7:24**
Exod 22:31
Lev 17:15

**7:26**
Gen 9:4
Lev 17:10-14
Acts 15:20, 29

²²Then the Lord said to Moses, ²³"Give the following instructions to the people of Israel. You must never eat fat, whether from cattle, sheep, or goats. ²⁴The fat of an animal found dead or torn to pieces by wild animals must never be eaten, though it may be used for any other purpose. ²⁵Anyone who eats fat from an animal presented as a special gift to the Lord will be cut off from the community. ²⁶No matter where you live, you must never consume the blood of any bird or animal. ²⁷Anyone who consumes blood will be cut off from the community."

**7:7** Or *to make atonement.*

---

**7:11-18** The peace offering was divided into three kinds according to purpose: thanksgiving offering, vow offering, and voluntary offering. A thanksgiving offering was appropriate whenever one wished to show thanks to God, as when recovering from a serious illness, or surviving a dangerous calamity (Psalm 107). A vow offering was given in fulfillment of a vow (2 Samuel 15:7, 8). The voluntary offering, however, needed no special occasion or reason.

**7:22-27** The fat portions were regarded as the best portions; therefore, it was appropriate to dedicate them only to God. Because blood was the river of life, and life was God's gift and his alone, blood had to be returned to God and not used by people.

## A Portion for the Priests

28Then the LORD said to Moses, 29"Give the following instructions to the people of Israel. When you present a peace offering to the LORD, bring part of it as a gift to the LORD. 30Present it to the LORD with your own hands as a special gift to the LORD. Bring the fat of the animal, together with the breast, and lift up the breast as a special offering to the LORD. 31Then the priest will burn the fat on the altar, but the breast will belong to Aaron and his descendants. 32Give the right thigh of your peace offering to the priest as a gift. 33The right thigh must always be given to the priest who offers the blood and the fat of the peace offering. 34For I have reserved the breast of the special offering and the right thigh of the sacred offering for the priests. It is the permanent right of Aaron and his descendants to share in the peace offerings brought by the people of Israel. 35This is their rightful share. The special gifts presented to the LORD have been reserved for Aaron and his descendants from the time they were set apart to serve the LORD as priests. 36On the day they were anointed, the LORD commanded the Israelites to give these portions to the priests as their permanent share from generation to generation."

37These are the instructions for the burnt offering, the grain offering, the sin offering, and the guilt offering, as well as the ordination offering and the peace offering. 38The LORD gave these instructions to Moses on Mount Sinai when he commanded the Israelites to present their offerings to the LORD in the wilderness of Sinai.

**7:29**
Lev 3:1

**7:30**
Exod 29:26-27
Lev 8:29
Num 6:20

**7:31**
Lev 7:34
Num 18:11

**7:32**
Num 18:18

**7:34**
Exod 29:22
Lev 10:15

**7:36**
Exod 29:22-34;
40:13-15

**7:38**
Lev 26:46

## 2. Ordination for the priests
### Ordination of the Priests

**8** Then the LORD said to Moses, 2"Bring Aaron and his sons, along with their sacred garments, the anointing oil, the bull for the sin offering, the two rams, and the basket of bread made without yeast, 3and call the entire community of Israel together at the entrance of the Tabernacle.*"

4So Moses followed the LORD's instructions, and the whole community assembled at the Tabernacle entrance. 5Moses announced to them, "This is what the LORD has commanded us to do!" 6Then he presented Aaron and his sons and washed them with water. 7He put the official tunic on Aaron and tied the sash around his waist. He dressed him in the robe, placed the ephod on him, and attached the ephod securely with its decorative sash. 8Then

**8:2**
Exod 28:1

**8:6**
Exod 29:3-4

**8:8**
Exod 28:30-31
Ezra 2:63

**8:3** Hebrew *Tent of Meeting;* also in 8:4, 31, 33, 35.

---

**7:28-30** God told the people of Israel to bring their peace offerings personally, with their own hands. They were to take time and effort to express thanks to God. You are the best person to express your thankfulness to God and to others. Do you leave it to others to express thanks to someone who has been helpful? Do you rely on the one leading in prayer to thank God for you? Take time to communicate your personal gratitude both to God and to others who have helped and blessed you.

**7:31-36** Part of the offering was designated for the priests. This food helped to care for the priests, who cared for God's house. The New Testament teaches that ministers should be paid by the people they serve (1 Corinthians 9:14). We should give generously to those who minister to us.

**7:37** The ordination offering refers to the offering given at the ceremony when priests were inducted into office (8:22).

**7:38** God gave his people many rituals and instructions to follow. All the rituals in Leviticus were meant to teach the people valuable lessons. But over time, the people became indifferent to the meanings of these rituals, and they began to lose touch with God. When your church appears to be conducting dry, meaningless rituals, instead of criticizing or becoming discouraged, try rediscovering the original meaning and purpose behind each. Your worship will be revitalized.

**8:1ff** Why did Aaron and his sons need to be cleansed and set apart? Although all the men from the tribe of Levi were dedicated for service to God, only Aaron's descendants could be priests. They alone had the honor and responsibility of performing the sacrifices. These priests had to cleanse and dedicate themselves before they could help the people do the same.

The ceremony described in Leviticus 8 and 9 was their ordination ceremony. Aaron and his sons were washed with water (8:6),

clothed with special garments (8:7-9, 13), and anointed with oil (8:12). They placed their hands on a young bull as it was killed (8:14, 15), and on two rams as they were killed (8:18, 19, 22, 23). This showed that holiness came from God alone, not from the priestly role. Similarly, we are not spiritually cleansed because we have a religious position, reputation, or title. Spiritual cleansing comes only from God. No matter how high our position or how long we have held it, we must depend on God for spiritual vitality.

**8:2, 3** Why were priests needed in Israel? In Exodus 19:6, the Israelites were instructed to be a kingdom of priests; ideally they would all be holy and relate to God. But from the time of Adam's fall, sin has separated humans and God, and people have needed mediators to help them find forgiveness. At first, the patriarchs— heads of households like Abraham and Job—were priests of the house or clan and made sacrifices for the family. When the Israelites left Egypt, the descendants of Aaron, from the tribe of Levi, were chosen to serve as priests for the nation. The priests stood in the gap between God and people. They were the full-time spiritual leaders and overseers of offerings. The priestly system was a concession to people's inability, because of sin, to confront and relate to God individually and corporately. In Christ, this imperfect system was transformed. Jesus Christ himself is our High Priest. Now all believers can approach God through him.

**8:8** What were the Urim and Thummim? Little is known about them, but they were probably precious stones or flat objects that God used to give guidance to his people. The high priest kept them in a pocket attached to his chestpiece. Some scholars think the Urim may have been the *no* answer and the Thummim the *yes* answer. After a time of prayer for guidance, the priest would shake the stones and God would cause the proper one to fall out. Another view is that the Urim and Thummim were small flat

| | |
|---|---|
| **8:9**<br>Exod 28:4, 36-38 | Moses placed the chestpiece on Aaron and put the Urim and the Thummim inside it. ⁹He placed the turban on Aaron's head and attached the gold medallion—the badge of holiness—to the front of the turban, just as the Lord had commanded him. |
| **8:10**<br>Exod 30:26-33<br>**8:11**<br>Exod 29:37<br>Lev 16:14<br>**8:12**<br>Exod 28:41; 30:30<br>Lev 21:10-12<br>**8:13**<br>Exod 28:4, 39 | ¹⁰Then Moses took the anointing oil and anointed the Tabernacle and everything in it, making them holy. ¹¹He sprinkled the oil on the altar seven times, anointing it and all its utensils, as well as the washbasin and its stand, making them holy. ¹²Then he poured some of the anointing oil on Aaron's head, anointing him and making him holy for his work. ¹³Next Moses presented Aaron's sons. He clothed them in their tunics, tied their sashes around them, and put their special head coverings on them, just as the Lord had commanded him. |
| **8:14**<br>Exod 29:10-14<br>Lev 4:4<br>**8:15**<br>Lev 4:7 | ¹⁴Then Moses presented the bull for the sin offering. Aaron and his sons laid their hands on the bull's head, ¹⁵and Moses slaughtered it. Moses took some of the blood, and with his finger he put it on the four horns of the altar to purify it. He poured out the rest of the blood at the base of the altar. Through this process, he made the altar holy by purifying it.* ¹⁶Then |
| **8:17**<br>Lev 4:11 | Moses took all the fat around the internal organs, the long lobe of the liver, and the two kidneys and the fat around them, and he burned it all on the altar. ¹⁷He took the rest of the bull, including its hide, meat, and dung, and burned it on a fire outside the camp, just as the Lord had commanded him. |
| **8:18**<br>Exod 29:15-19 | ¹⁸Then Moses presented the ram for the burnt offering. Aaron and his sons laid their hands on the ram's head, ¹⁹and Moses slaughtered it. Then Moses took the ram's blood and splattered it against all sides of the altar. ²⁰Then he cut the ram into pieces, and he burned the head, some of its pieces, and the fat on the altar. ²¹After washing the internal organs and the legs with water, Moses burned the entire ram on the altar as a burnt offering. It was a pleasing aroma, a special gift presented to the Lord, just as the Lord had commanded him. |
| **8:22**<br>Exod 29:31<br>**8:23**<br>Exod 29:20-21 | ²²Then Moses presented the other ram, which was the ram of ordination. Aaron and his sons laid their hands on the ram's head, ²³and Moses slaughtered it. Then Moses took some of its blood and applied it to the lobe of Aaron's right ear, the thumb of his right hand, and the big toe of his right foot. ²⁴Next Moses presented Aaron's sons and applied some of the blood to the lobes of their right ears, the thumbs of their right hands, and the big toes of their right feet. He then splattered the rest of the blood against all sides of the altar. |
| **8:25**<br>Exod 29:22<br>**8:26**<br>Exod 29:23<br>**8:27**<br>Exod 29:24<br>**8:28**<br>Exod 29:25<br>**8:29**<br>Exod 29:26<br>Lev 7:31-34 | ²⁵Next Moses took the fat, including the fat of the broad tail, the fat around the internal organs, the long lobe of the liver, and the two kidneys and the fat around them, along with the right thigh. ²⁶On top of these he placed a thin cake of bread made without yeast, a cake of bread mixed with olive oil, and a wafer spread with olive oil. All these were taken from the basket of bread made without yeast that was placed in the Lord's presence. ²⁷He put all these in the hands of Aaron and his sons, and he lifted them up as a special offering to the Lord. ²⁸Moses then took all the offerings back from them and burned them on the altar on top of the burnt offering. This was the ordination offering. It was a pleasing aroma, a special gift presented to the Lord. ²⁹Then Moses took the breast and lifted it up as a special offering to the Lord. This was Moses' portion of the ram of ordination, just as the Lord had commanded him. |
| **8:30**<br>Exod 29:21 | ³⁰Next Moses took some of the anointing oil and some of the blood that was on the altar, and he sprinkled them on Aaron and his garments and on his sons and their garments. In this way, he made Aaron and his sons and their garments holy. |
| **8:31**<br>Exod 29:31-32<br>**8:32**<br>Exod 29:34<br>**8:33**<br>Exod 29:35<br>**8:34**<br>Heb 7:16 | ³¹Then Moses said to Aaron and his sons, "Boil the remaining meat of the offerings at the Tabernacle entrance, and eat it there, along with the bread that is in the basket of offerings for the ordination, just as I commanded when I said, 'Aaron and his sons will eat it.' ³²Any meat or bread that is left over must then be burned up. ³³You must not leave the Tabernacle entrance for seven days, for that is when the ordination ceremony will be completed. ³⁴Everything we have done today was commanded by the Lord in order to purify |

**8:15** Or *by making atonement for it;* or *that offerings for purification might be made on it.*

objects, each with a *yes* side and a *no* side. The priest spilled both from his pouch. If both landed on their *yes* sides, God's answer was positive. Two *no* sides were negative. A *yes* and a *no* meant no reply. God had a specific purpose for using this method of guidance—he was teaching a nation the principles of following him. Our situation is not the same, however, so we must not invent ways like this for God to guide us.

**8:12** What was the significance of anointing Aaron as high priest? The high priest had special duties that no other priest had. He alone could enter the Most Holy Place in the Tabernacle on the annual Day of Atonement to atone for the sins of the nation. Therefore, he was in charge of all the other priests. The high priest was a picture of Jesus Christ, who is our High Priest (Hebrews 7:26-28).

you, making you right with him.* ³⁵Now stay at the entrance of the Tabernacle day and night for seven days, and do everything the LORD requires. If you fail to do this, you will die, for this is what the LORD has commanded." ³⁶So Aaron and his sons did everything the LORD had commanded through Moses.

**8:35**
Num 3:7; 9:19
Deut 11:1
1 Kgs 2:3
Ezek 48:11

### The Priests Begin Their Work

**9** After the ordination ceremony, on the eighth day, Moses called together Aaron and his sons and the elders of Israel. ²He said to Aaron, "Take a young bull for a sin offering and a ram for a burnt offering, both without defects, and present them to the LORD. ³Then tell the Israelites, 'Take a male goat for a sin offering, and take a calf and a lamb, both a year old and without defects, for a burnt offering. ⁴Also take a bull* and a ram for a peace offering and flour moistened with olive oil for a grain offering. Present all these offerings to the LORD because the LORD will appear to you today.'"

**9:3**
Lev 4:3

**9:4**
Exod 29:43

⁵So the people presented all these things at the entrance of the Tabernacle,* just as Moses had commanded. Then the whole community came forward and stood before the LORD. ⁶And Moses said, "This is what the LORD has commanded you to do so that the glory of the LORD may appear to you."

**9:6**
Lev 9:23

⁷Then Moses said to Aaron, "Come to the altar and sacrifice your sin offering and your burnt offering to purify yourself and the people. Then present the offerings of the people to purify them, making them right with the LORD,* just as he has commanded."

**9:7**
Heb 5:1-3; 7:27

⁸So Aaron went to the altar and slaughtered the calf as a sin offering for himself. ⁹His sons brought him the blood, and he dipped his finger in it and put it on the horns of the altar. He poured out the rest of the blood at the base of the altar. ¹⁰Then he burned on the altar the fat, the kidneys, and the long lobe of the liver from the sin offering, just as the LORD had commanded Moses. ¹¹The meat and the hide, however, he burned outside the camp.

**9:9**
Lev 4:6-7

¹²Next Aaron slaughtered the animal for the burnt offering. His sons brought him the blood, and he splattered it against all sides of the altar. ¹³Then they handed him each piece of the burnt offering, including the head, and he burned them on the altar. ¹⁴Then he washed the internal organs and the legs and burned them on the altar along with the rest of the burnt offering.

¹⁵Next Aaron presented the offerings of the people. He slaughtered the people's goat and presented it as an offering for their sin, just as he had first done with the offering for his own sin. ¹⁶Then he presented the burnt offering and sacrificed it in the prescribed way. ¹⁷He also presented the grain offering, burning a handful of the flour mixture on the altar, in addition to the regular burnt offering for the morning.

**9:15**
Lev 4:27-31; 9:3

**9:16**
Lev 1:3, 10

**9:17**
Lev 2:1-3; 3:5

¹⁸Then Aaron slaughtered the bull and the ram for the people's peace offering. His sons brought him the blood, and he splattered it against all sides of the altar. ¹⁹Then he took the fat of the bull and the ram—the fat of the broad tail and from around the internal organs—along with the kidneys and the long lobes of the livers. ²⁰He placed these fat portions on top of the breasts of these animals and burned them on the altar. ²¹Aaron then lifted up the breasts and right thighs as a special offering to the LORD, just as Moses had commanded.

**9:18**
Lev 3:1-11

**9:19**
Lev 3:9

**9:21**
Lev 7:30, 32

²²After that, Aaron raised his hands toward the people and blessed them. Then, after presenting the sin offering, the burnt offering, and the peace offering, he stepped down from the altar. ²³Then Moses and Aaron went into the Tabernacle, and when they came back out, they blessed the people again, and the glory of the LORD appeared to the whole community. ²⁴Fire blazed forth from the LORD's presence and consumed the burnt offering and the fat on the altar. When the people saw this, they shouted with joy and fell face down on the ground.

**9:22**
Num 6:24-26

**9:23**
Num 16:19, 42

**9:24**
1 Kgs 18:38

**8:34** Or *to make atonement for you.*   **9:4** Or *cow;* also in 9:18, 19.   **9:5** Hebrew *Tent of Meeting;* also in 9:23.
**9:7** Or *to make atonement for them.*

---

**8:36** Aaron and his sons did "everything the LORD had commanded." Considering the many detailed lists of Leviticus, that was a remarkable feat. They knew what God wanted, how he wanted it done, and with what attitude it was to be carried out. This can serve as a model for how carefully we ought to obey God. God wants us to be thoroughly holy people, not a rough approximation of the way his followers should be.

**9:22, 23** In 9:6 Moses said to the people, "This is what the LORD has commanded you to do so that the glory of the LORD may appear to you." Moses, Aaron, and the people then got to work and

followed God's instructions. Soon after, the glory of the Lord appeared. Often we look for God's glorious acts without concern for following his instructions. Do you serve God in the daily routines of life, or do you wait for him to do a mighty act? If you depend on his glorious acts, you may find yourself sidestepping your everyday duty to obey.

**9:24** As a display of his mighty power, God sent fire from the sky to consume Aaron's offering. The people fell to the ground in awe. Some people wonder if God really exists because they don't see his activity in the world. But God is at work in today's world just as

### The Sin of Nadab and Abihu

**10:1**
Exod 6:23
Num 3:2
**10:2**
Num 26:61
**10:3**
Exod 19:22
Ezek 38:16

**10** Aaron's sons Nadab and Abihu put coals of fire in their incense burners and sprinkled incense over them. In this way, they disobeyed the LORD by burning before him the wrong kind of fire, different than he had commanded. ²So fire blazed forth from the LORD's presence and burned them up, and they died there before the LORD.

³Then Moses said to Aaron, "This is what the LORD meant when he said,

'I will display my holiness
   through those who come near me.
I will display my glory
   before all the people.'"

And Aaron was silent.

---

Some brothers, like Cain and Abel or Jacob and Esau, get each other in trouble. Nadab and Abihu got in trouble together.

Although little is known of their early years, the Bible gives us an abundance of information about the environment in which they grew up. Born in Egypt, they were eyewitnesses of God's mighty acts of the Exodus. They saw their father, Aaron, their uncle, Moses, and their aunt, Miriam, in action many times. They had firsthand knowledge of God's holiness as few men have ever had, and, for a while at least, they followed God wholeheartedly (Leviticus 8:36). But at a crucial moment they chose to treat with indifference the clear instructions from God. The consequence of their sin was fiery, instant, and shocking to all.

We are in danger of making the same mistake as these brothers when we treat lightly the justice and holiness of God. We must draw near to God while realizing that there is a proper fear of God. Don't forget that the opportunity to know God personally is based on his gracious invitation to an always unworthy people, not a gift to be taken for granted. Do your thoughts about God include a humble recognition of his great holiness?

**NADAB/ABIHU**

| | |
|---|---|
| **Strengths and accomplishments** | • Oldest sons of Aaron<br>• Primary candidates to become high priest after their father<br>• Involved with the original consecration of the Tabernacle<br>• Commended for doing "everything the LORD had commanded" (Leviticus 8:36) |
| **Weakness and mistake** | • Treated God's direct commands lightly |
| **Lesson from their lives** | • Sin has deadly consequences |
| **Vital statistics** | • Where: The Sinai peninsula<br>• Occupation: Priests-in-training<br>• Relatives: Father: Aaron. Uncle: Moses. Aunt: Miriam. Brothers: Eleazar and Ithamar. |
| **Key verses** | "Aaron's sons Nadab and Abihu put coals of fire in their incense burners and sprinkled incense over them. In this way, they disobeyed the LORD by burning before him the wrong kind of fire, different than he had commanded. So fire blazed forth from the LORD's presence and burned them up, and they died there before the LORD" (Leviticus 10:1, 2). |

The story of Nadab and Abihu is told in Leviticus 8—10. They are also mentioned in Exodus 24:1, 9; 28:1; Numbers 3:2–4; 26:60, 61.

---

he was in Moses' world. Where a large body of believers is active for him, God tends not to display his power in the form of mighty physical acts. Instead, he works to change the world through the work of these believers. When you realize that, you will begin to see acts of love and faith that are just as supernatural.

**10:1** What was the "wrong kind of fire" that Nadab and Abihu offered before the Lord? The fire on the altar of burnt offering was never to go out (6:12, 13), implying that it was holy. It is possible that Nadab and Abihu brought coals of fire to the altar from another source, making the sacrifice unholy. It has also been suggested that the two priests gave an offering at an unprescribed time. Whatever explanation is correct, the point is that Nadab and Abihu abused their office as priests in a flagrant act of disrespect to God, who had just reviewed with them

precisely how they were to conduct worship. As leaders, they had special responsibility to obey God. In their position, they could easily lead many people astray. If God has commissioned you to lead or teach others, never take that role for granted or abuse it. Stay faithful to God and follow his instructions.

**10:2** Aaron's sons were careless about following the laws for sacrifices. In response, God destroyed them with a blast of fire. Performing the sacrifices was an act of obedience. Doing them correctly showed respect for God. It is easy for us to grow careless about obeying God, to live our way instead of God's. But if one way were just as good as another, God would not have commanded us to live his way. He always has good reasons for his commands, and we always place ourselves in danger when we consciously or carelessly disobey them.

⁴Then Moses called for Mishael and Elzaphan, Aaron's cousins, the sons of Aaron's uncle Uzziel. He said to them, "Come forward and carry away the bodies of your relatives from in front of the sanctuary to a place outside the camp." ⁵So they came forward and picked them up by their garments and carried them out of the camp, just as Moses had commanded.

⁶Then Moses said to Aaron and his sons Eleazar and Ithamar, "Do not show grief by leaving your hair uncombed* or by tearing your clothes. If you do, you will die, and the LORD's anger will strike the whole community of Israel. However, the rest of the Israelites, your relatives, may mourn because of the LORD's fiery destruction of Nadab and Abihu. ⁷But you must not leave the entrance of the Tabernacle* or you will die, for you have been anointed with the LORD's anointing oil." So they did as Moses commanded.

*Instructions for Priestly Conduct*

⁸Then the LORD said to Aaron, ⁹"You and your descendants must never drink wine or any other alcoholic drink before going into the Tabernacle. If you do, you will die. This is a permanent law for you, and it must be observed from generation to generation. ¹⁰You must distinguish between what is sacred and what is common, between what is ceremonially unclean and what is clean. ¹¹And you must teach the Israelites all the decrees that the LORD has given them through Moses."

¹²Then Moses said to Aaron and his remaining sons, Eleazar and Ithamar, "Take what is left of the grain offering after a portion has been presented as a special gift to the LORD, and eat it beside the altar. Make sure it contains no yeast, for it is most holy. ¹³You must eat it in a sacred place, for it has been given to you and your descendants as your portion of the special gifts presented to the LORD. These are the commands I have been given. ¹⁴But the breast and thigh that were lifted up as a special offering may be eaten in any place that is ceremonially clean. These parts have been given to you and your descendants as your portion of the peace offerings presented by the people of Israel. ¹⁵You must lift up the thigh and breast as a special offering to the LORD, along with the fat of the special gifts. These parts will belong to you and your descendants as your permanent right, just as the LORD has commanded."

¹⁶Moses then asked them what had happened to the goat of the sin offering. When he discovered it had been burned up, he became very angry with Eleazar and Ithamar, Aaron's remaining sons. ¹⁷"Why didn't you eat the sin offering in the sacred area?" he demanded. "It is a holy offering! The LORD has given it to you to remove the guilt of the community and to purify the people, making them right with the LORD.* ¹⁸Since the animal's blood was not brought into the Holy Place, you should have eaten the meat in the sacred area as I ordered you."

¹⁹Then Aaron answered Moses, "Today my sons presented both their sin offering and their burnt offering to the LORD. And yet this tragedy has happened to me. If I had eaten the people's sin offering on such a tragic day as this, would the LORD have been pleased?" ²⁰And when Moses heard this, he was satisfied.

### 3. Instructions for the people
*Ceremonially Clean and Unclean Animals*

**11** Then the LORD said to Moses and Aaron, ²"Give the following instructions to the people of Israel.

"Of all the land animals, these are the ones you may use for food. ³You may eat any animal that has completely split hooves and chews the cud. ⁴You may not, however, eat the

**10:4** Exod 6:18
**10:6** Lev 21:1-15; Num 1:53; 16:22; Josh 7:1
**10:7** Lev 21:12
**10:9** Ezek 44:21
**10:10** Lev 11:47; Ezek 22:26
**10:11** Deut 33:10
**10:12** Lev 21:22; Num 3:2
**10:14** Lev 7:28-36
**10:15** Lev 7:30-34
**10:16** Lev 9:3
**10:17** Lev 6:24-30
**10:18** Lev 6:30
**10:19** Lev 9:8, 12
**11:1-23** //Deut 14:3-20
**11:4** Acts 10:14

**10:6** Or *by uncovering your heads.* **10:7** Hebrew *Tent of Meeting;* also in 10:9. **10:17** Or *to make atonement for the people before the LORD.*

**10:8-11** The priests were not to drink wine or other alcoholic beverages before going into the Tabernacle. If their senses were dulled by alcohol, they might repeat Nadab and Abihu's sin and bring something unholy into the worship ceremony. In addition, drinking would disqualify them to teach the people God's requirements of self-discipline. Drunkenness was associated with pagan practices and the Jewish priests were supposed to be distinctively different.

**10:10, 11** This passage (along with 19:1, 2) shows the focus of Leviticus. The Ten Commandments recorded in Exodus 20 were God's fundamental laws. Leviticus explained and supplemented those laws with many other guidelines and principles that helped the Israelites put them into practice. The purpose of God's laws

was to teach people how to distinguish right from wrong, the sacred from the common, the clean from the unclean. The nation who lived by God's laws would obviously be set apart, dedicated to his service.

**10:16-20** The priest who offered the sin offering was supposed to eat a portion of the animal and then burn the rest (6:24-30). Moses was angry because Eleazar and Ithamar burned the sin offering but did not eat any of it. Aaron explained to Moses that his two sons did not feel it appropriate to eat the sacrifice after their two brothers, Nadab and Abihu, had just been killed for sacrificing wrongly. Moses then understood that Eleazar and Ithamar were not trying to disobey God. They were simply afraid and upset over what had just happened to their brothers.

following animals* that have split hooves or that chew the cud, but not both. The camel chews the cud but does not have split hooves, so it is ceremonially unclean for you. ⁵The hyrax* chews the cud but does not have split hooves, so it is unclean. ⁶The hare chews the cud but does not have split hooves, so it is unclean. ⁷The pig has evenly split hooves but does not chew the cud, so it is unclean. ⁸You may not eat the meat of these animals or even touch their carcasses. They are ceremonially unclean for you.

⁹"Of all the marine animals, these are ones you may use for food. You may eat anything from the water if it has both fins and scales, whether taken from salt water or from streams. ¹⁰But you must never eat animals from the sea or from rivers that do not have both fins and scales. They are detestable to you. This applies both to little creatures that live in shallow water and to all creatures that live in deep water. ¹¹They will always be detestable to you. You must never eat their meat or even touch their dead bodies. ¹²Any marine animal that does not have both fins and scales is detestable to you.

¹³"These are the birds that are detestable to you. You must never eat them: the griffon vulture, the bearded vulture, the black vulture, ¹⁴the kite, falcons of all kinds, ¹⁵ravens of all kinds, ¹⁶the eagle owl, the short-eared owl, the seagull, hawks of all kinds, ¹⁷the little owl, the cormorant, the great owl, ¹⁸the barn owl, the desert owl, the Egyptian vulture, ¹⁹the stork, herons of all kinds, the hoopoe, and the bat.

²⁰"You must not eat winged insects that walk along the ground; they are detestable to you. ²¹You may, however, eat winged insects that walk along the ground and have jointed legs so they can jump. ²²The insects you are permitted to eat include all kinds of locusts, bald locusts, crickets, and grasshoppers. ²³All other winged insects that walk along the ground are detestable to you.

²⁴"The following creatures will make you ceremonially unclean. If any of you touch their carcasses, you will be defiled until evening. ²⁵If you pick up their carcasses, you must wash your clothes, and you will remain defiled until evening.

²⁶"Any animal that has split hooves that are not evenly divided or that does not chew the cud is unclean for you. If you touch the carcass of such an animal, you will be defiled. ²⁷Of the animals that walk on all fours, those that have paws are unclean. If you touch the carcass of such an animal, you will be defiled until evening. ²⁸If you pick up its carcass, you must wash your clothes, and you will remain defiled until evening. These animals are unclean for you.

²⁹"Of the small animals that scurry along the ground, these are unclean for you: the mole rat, the rat, large lizards of all kinds, ³⁰the gecko, the monitor lizard, the common lizard, the sand lizard, and the chameleon. ³¹All these small animals are unclean for you. If any of you touch the dead body of such an animal, you will be defiled until evening. ³²If such an animal dies and falls on something, that object will be unclean. This is true whether the object is made of wood, cloth, leather, or burlap. Whatever its use, you must dip it in water, and it will remain defiled until evening. After that, it will be ceremonially clean and may be used again.

³³"If such an animal falls into a clay pot, everything in the pot will be defiled, and the pot must be smashed. ³⁴If the water from such a container spills on any food, the food will be defiled. And any beverage in such a container will be defiled. ³⁵Any object on which the carcass of such an animal falls will be defiled. If it is an oven or hearth, it must be destroyed, for it is defiled, and you must treat it accordingly.

**11:7** Isa 65:4; 66:3, 17
**11:8** Heb 9:10
**11:9-10** Deut 14:9-10
**11:13** Deut 14:12-19
**11:22** Matt 3:4; Mark 1:6
**11:25** Lev 11:28, 40; Num 19:11-13
**11:32** Lev 15:12
**11:33** Lev 6:28

11:4 The identification of some of the animals, birds, and insects in this chapter is uncertain.   11:5 Or *coney*, or *rock badger*.

**11:8** God had strictly forbidden eating the meat of certain "unclean" animals; to make sure, he forbade even touching them. He wanted the people to be totally separated from those things he had forbidden. So often we flirt with temptation, rationalizing that at least we are technically keeping the commandment not to commit the sin. But God wants us to separate ourselves completely from all sin and tempting situations. Perhaps this passage has made you aware of areas of your life where you have "technical" innocence but in which you have actually been involved in sin. It's time to cross back over the line and stay there.

**11:25** In order to worship, people need to be prepared. Some acts of disobedience, some natural acts (such as childbirth, menstruation, or sex), or some accidents (such as touching a dead or diseased body) would make people ceremonially unclean (defiled) and thus forbidden to participate in worship. This did not imply that they had sinned or were rejected by God, but it insured that all worship was done decently and in order. This chapter describes many of the intentional or accidental occurrences that would disqualify people from worship until they were "cleansed" or straightened out. Similarly, we need to be *prepared* for worship. We cannot live any way we want during the week and then rush into God's presence on Sunday. We should prepare ourselves through repentance, correction of errors where possible, and thoughtful anticipation of what it will mean to be in God's presence with other believers.

³⁶"However, if the carcass of such an animal falls into a spring or a cistern, the water will still be clean. But anyone who touches the carcass will be defiled. ³⁷If the carcass falls on seed grain to be planted in the field, the seed will still be considered clean. ³⁸But if the seed is wet when the carcass falls on it, the seed will be defiled.

³⁹"If an animal you are permitted to eat dies and you touch its carcass, you will be defiled until evening. ⁴⁰If you eat any of its meat or carry away its carcass, you must wash your clothes, and you will remain defiled until evening.

⁴¹"All small animals that scurry along the ground are detestable, and you must never eat them. ⁴²This includes all animals that slither along on their bellies, as well as those with four legs and those with many feet. All such animals that scurry along the ground are detestable, and you must never eat them. ⁴³Do not defile yourselves by touching them. You must not make yourselves ceremonially unclean because of them. ⁴⁴For I am the LORD your God. You must consecrate yourselves and be holy, because I am holy. So do not defile yourselves with any of these small animals that scurry along the ground. ⁴⁵For I, the LORD, am the one who brought you up from the land of Egypt, that I might be your God. Therefore, you must be holy because I am holy.

⁴⁶"These are the instructions regarding land animals, birds, marine creatures, and animals that scurry along the ground. ⁴⁷By these instructions you will know what is unclean and clean, and which animals may be eaten and which may not be eaten."

### Purification after Childbirth

**12** The LORD said to Moses, ²"Give the following instructions to the people of Israel. If a woman becomes pregnant and gives birth to a son, she will be ceremonially unclean for seven days, just as she is unclean during her menstrual period. ³On the eighth day the boy's foreskin must be circumcised. ⁴After waiting thirty-three days, she will be purified from the bleeding of childbirth. During this time of purification, she must not touch anything that is set apart as holy. And she must not enter the sanctuary until her time of purification is over. ⁵If a woman gives birth to a daughter, she will be ceremonially unclean for two weeks, just as she is unclean during her menstrual period. After waiting sixty-six days, she will be purified from the bleeding of childbirth.

⁶"When the time of purification is completed for either a son or a daughter, the woman must bring a one-year-old lamb for a burnt offering and a young pigeon or turtledove for a purification offering. She must bring her offerings to the priest at the entrance of the Tabernacle.* ⁷The priest will then present them to the LORD to purify her.* Then she will be ceremonially clean again after her bleeding at childbirth. These are the instructions for a woman after the birth of a son or a daughter.

**12:6** Hebrew *Tent of Meeting.*  **12:7** Or *to make atonement for her;* also in 12:8.

**11:40**
Lev 11:25; 17:15
Deut 14:21
Ezek 4:14; 44:31
**11:41**
Lev 11:29
**11:44-45**
Exod 6:7; 19:6
Lev 19:2
1 Thes 4:7
†1 Pet 1:16
**11:47**
Lev 10:10
Ezek 22:26; 44:23
**12:2**
Lev 15:19; 18:19
**12:3**
Gen 17:12-14
**12:6**
Luke 2:22

---

**11:44, 45** There is more to this chapter than eating right. These verses provide a key to understanding all the laws and regulations in Leviticus. God wanted his people to be *holy* (set apart, different, unique), just as he is holy. He knew they had only two options: to be separate and holy, or to compromise with their pagan neighbors and become corrupt. That is why he called them out of idolatrous Egypt and set them apart as a unique nation, dedicated to worshiping him alone and leading moral lives. That is also why he designed laws and restrictions to help them remain separate—both socially and spiritually—from the wicked pagan nations they would encounter in Canaan. Christians also are called to be holy (1 Peter 1:15). Like the Israelites, we should remain spiritually separate from the world's wickedness, even though unlike them, we rub shoulders with unbelievers every day. It is no easy task to be holy in an unholy world, but God doesn't ask you to accomplish this on your own. He has provided help. Through the death of his Son, "you are holy and blameless as you stand before him without a single fault" (Colossians 1:22). With Christ, you can live *in* the world without having to be *of* the world.

**11:47** The designations *clean* and *unclean* were used to define the kind of animals the Israelites could and could not eat. There were several reasons for this restricted diet: (1) To ensure the health of the nation. The forbidden foods were usually scavenging animals that fed on dead animals; thus disease could be transmitted through them. (2) To visibly distinguish Israel from other nations. The pig, for example, was a common sacrifice of pagan religions. (3) To avoid objectionable associations. The creatures that move about on the ground, for example, were reminiscent of serpents, which often symbolized sin.

**12:1-4** Why was a woman considered "ceremonially unclean" after the wonderful miracle of birth? It was due to the bodily emissions and secretions occurring during and after childbirth. These were considered unclean and made the woman unprepared to enter the pure surroundings of the Tabernacle. Her temporary status highlighted her role as a young mother and relieved her of certain duties that probably made the early days with a new baby easier.

**12:1-4** *Unclean* did not mean sinful or dirty. God created us male and female, and he ordered us to be fruitful and multiply (Genesis 1:27, 28). He did not change his mind and say that sex and procreation were now somehow unclean. Instead, he made a distinction between his worship and the popular worship of fertility gods and goddesses. Canaanite religions incorporated prostitution and immoral rites as the people begged their gods to make their crops, herds, and families increase. By contrast, Israel's religion avoided all sexual connotations. By keeping worship and sex entirely separate, God helped the Israelites avoid confusion with pagan rites. The Israelites worshiped God as their loving Creator and Provider, and they thanked him for bountiful crops, marital love, and safe childbirth.

12:8
Lev 5:7
Luke 2:24

8"If a woman cannot afford to bring a lamb, she must bring two turtledoves or two young pigeons. One will be for the burnt offering and the other for the purification offering. The priest will sacrifice them to purify her, and she will be ceremonially clean."

## Serious Skin Diseases

13:2-3
Lev 14:56
Deut 24:8

**13** The LORD said to Moses and Aaron, 2"If anyone has a swelling or a rash or discolored skin that might develop into a serious skin disease,* that person must be brought to Aaron the priest or to one of his sons.* 3The priest will examine the affected area of the skin. If the hair in the affected area has turned white and the problem appears to be more than skin-deep, it is a serious skin disease, and the priest who examines it must pronounce the person ceremonially unclean.

4"But if the affected area of the skin is only a white discoloration and does not appear to be more than skin-deep, and if the hair on the spot has not turned white, the priest will quarantine the person for seven days. 5On the seventh day the priest will make another ex-

13:6
Lev 11:25

amination. If he finds the affected area has not changed and the problem has not spread on the skin, the priest will quarantine the person for seven more days. 6On the seventh day the priest will make another examination. If he finds the affected area has faded and has not spread, the priest will pronounce the person ceremonially clean. It was only a rash. The person's clothing must be washed, and the person will be ceremonially clean. 7But if the rash continues to spread after the person has been examined by the priest and has been pronounced clean, the infected person must return to be examined again. 8If the priest finds that the rash has spread, he must pronounce the person ceremonially unclean, for it is indeed a skin disease.

9"Anyone who develops a serious skin disease must go to the priest for an examination.

13:10
Num 12:10
2 Kgs 5:27

10If the priest finds a white swelling on the skin, and some hair on the spot has turned white, and there is an open sore in the affected area, 11it is a chronic skin disease, and the priest must pronounce the person ceremonially unclean. In such cases the person need not be quarantined, for it is obvious that the skin is defiled by the disease.

12"Now suppose the disease has spread all over the person's skin, covering the body from head to foot. 13When the priest examines the infected person and finds that the disease covers the entire body, he will pronounce the person ceremonially clean. Since the skin has turned completely white, the person is clean. 14But if any open sores appear, the infected person will be pronounced ceremonially unclean. 15The priest must make this pronounce- ment as soon as he sees an open sore, since open sores indicate the presence of a skin dis-

13:16
Luke 5:12-14

ease. 16However, if the open sores heal and turn white like the rest of the skin, the person must return to the priest 17for another examination. If the affected areas have indeed turned white, the priest will then pronounce the person ceremonially clean by declaring, 'You are clean!'

13:18
Exod 9:9

18"If anyone has a boil on the skin that has started to heal, 19but a white swelling or a red- dish white spot develops in its place, that person must go to the priest to be examined. 20If the priest examines it and finds it to be more than skin-deep, and if the hair in the affected area has turned white, the priest must pronounce the person ceremonially unclean. The boil has become a serious skin disease. 21But if the priest finds no white hair on the affected area and the problem appears to be no more than skin-deep and has faded, the priest must quar- antine the person for seven days. 22If during that time the affected area spreads on the skin, the priest must pronounce the person ceremonially unclean, because it is a serious disease. 23But if the area grows no larger and does not spread, it is merely the scar from the boil, and the priest will pronounce the person ceremonially clean.

24"If anyone has suffered a burn on the skin and the burned area changes color, becom- ing either reddish white or shiny white, 25the priest must examine it. If he finds that the hair in the affected area has turned white and the problem appears to be more than skin-deep,

**13:2a** Traditionally rendered *leprosy.* The Hebrew word used throughout this passage is used to describe various skin diseases.   **13:2b** Or *one of his descendants.*

**13:1ff** Leprosy (here called "a serious skin disease") is a name applied to several different diseases and was greatly feared in Bible times. Some of these diseases, unlike the disease we call leprosy or Hansen's disease today, were highly contagious. The worst of them slowly ruined the body and, in most cases, were fatal. Lepers were separated from family and friends and confined outside the camp. Since priests were responsible for the health of the camp, it was their duty to expel and readmit lepers. If someone's leprosy appeared to go away, only the priest could decide if that person was truly cured. Leprosy is often used in the Bible as an illustration of sin because sin is contagious and destructive and leads to separation.

a skin disease has broken out in the burn. The priest must then pronounce the person ceremonially unclean, for it is clearly a serious skin disease. 26But if the priest finds no white hair on the affected area and the problem appears to be no more than skin-deep and has faded, the priest must quarantine the infected person for seven days. 27On the seventh day the priest must examine the person again. If the affected area has spread on the skin, the priest must pronounce that person ceremonially unclean, for it is clearly a serious skin disease. 28But if the affected area has not changed or spread on the skin and has faded, it is simply a swelling from the burn. The priest will then pronounce the person ceremonially clean, for it is only the scar from the burn.

29"If anyone, either a man or woman, has a sore on the head or chin, 30the priest must examine it. If he finds it is more than skin-deep and has fine yellow hair on it, the priest must pronounce the person ceremonially unclean. It is a scabby sore of the head or chin. 31If the priest examines the scabby sore and finds that it is only skin-deep but there is no black hair on it, he must quarantine the person for seven days. 32On the seventh day the priest must examine the sore again. If he finds that the scabby sore has not spread, and there is no yellow hair on it, and it appears to be only skin-deep, 33the person must shave off all hair except the hair on the affected area. Then the priest must quarantine the person for another seven days. 34On the seventh day he will examine the sore again. If it has not spread and appears to be no more than skin-deep, the priest will pronounce the person ceremonially clean. The person's clothing must be washed, and the person will be ceremonially clean. 35But if the scabby sore begins to spread after the person is pronounced clean, 36the priest must do another examination. If he finds that the sore has spread, the priest does not need to look for yellow hair. The infected person is ceremonially unclean. 37But if the color of the scabby sore does not change and black hair has grown on it, it has healed. The priest will then pronounce the person ceremonially clean.

38"If anyone, either a man or woman, has shiny white patches on the skin, 39the priest must examine the affected area. If he finds that the shiny patches are only pale white, this is a harmless skin rash, and the person is ceremonially clean.

40"If a man loses his hair and his head becomes bald, he is still ceremonially clean. 41And if he loses hair on his forehead, he simply has a bald forehead; he is still clean. 42However, if a reddish white sore appears on the bald area at the top or back of his head, this is a skin disease. 43The priest must examine him, and if he finds swelling around the reddish white sore anywhere on the man's head and it looks like a skin disease, 44the man is indeed infected with a skin disease and is unclean. The priest must pronounce him ceremonially unclean because of the sore on his head.

45"Those who suffer from a serious skin disease must tear their clothing and leave their hair uncombed.* They must cover their mouth and call out, 'Unclean! Unclean!' 46As long as the serious disease lasts, they will be ceremonially unclean. They must live in isolation in their place outside the camp.

## Treatment of Contaminated Clothing

47"Now suppose mildew* contaminates some woolen or linen clothing, 48woolen or linen fabric, the hide of an animal, or anything made of leather. 49If the contaminated area in the clothing, the animal hide, the fabric, or the leather article has turned greenish or reddish, it is contaminated with mildew and must be shown to the priest. 50After examining the affected spot, the priest will put the article in quarantine for seven days. 51On the seventh day the priest must inspect it again. If the contaminated area has spread, the clothing or fabric or leather is clearly contaminated by a serious mildew and is ceremonially unclean. 52The priest must burn the item—the clothing, the woolen or linen fabric, or piece of leather—for it has been contaminated by a serious mildew. It must be completely destroyed by fire.

53"But if the priest examines it and finds that the contaminated area has not spread in the clothing, the fabric, or the leather, 54the priest will order the object to be washed and then quarantined for seven more days. 55Then the priest must examine the object again. If he

13:27
Lev 13:5

13:33
Lev 14:9

13:34
Lev 14:8

13:40
2 Kgs 2:23
Isa 15:2
Ezek 29:18
Amos 8:10

13:45
Lam 4:15
Ezek 24:17, 22
Mic 3:7

13:46
Num 5:1-4; 12:14
2 Kgs 7:3; 15:5
Luke 17:12

13:51
Lev 14:44

13:45 Or and uncover their heads.    13:47 Traditionally rendered leprosy. The Hebrew term used throughout this passage is the same term used for the various skin diseases described in 13:1-46.

13:45, 46 A person with a serious skin disease had to perform this strange ritual to protect others from coming too near. Because the disease described in Leviticus was highly contagious, it was important that people stay away from those who had it.

finds that the contaminated area has not changed color after being washed, even if it did not spread, the object is defiled. It must be completely burned up, whether the contaminated spot* is on the inside or outside. [56]But if the priest examines it and finds that the contaminated area has faded after being washed, he must cut the spot from the clothing, the fabric, or the leather. [57]If the spot later reappears on the clothing, the fabric, or the leather article, the mildew is clearly spreading, and the contaminated object must be burned up. [58]But if the spot disappears from the clothing, the fabric, or the leather article after it has been washed, it must be washed again; then it will be ceremonially clean.

[59]"These are the instructions for dealing with mildew that contaminates woolen or linen clothing or fabric or anything made of leather. This is how the priest will determine whether these items are ceremonially clean or unclean."

## Cleansing from Skin Diseases

**14** And the LORD said to Moses, [2]"The following instructions are for those seeking ceremonial purification from a skin disease.* Those who have been healed must be brought to the priest, [3]who will examine them at a place outside the camp. If the priest finds that someone has been healed of a serious skin disease, [4]he will perform a purification ceremony, using two live birds that are ceremonially clean, a stick of cedar,* some scarlet yarn, and a hyssop branch. [5]The priest will order that one bird be slaughtered over a clay pot filled with fresh water. [6]He will take the live bird, the cedar stick, the scarlet yarn, and the hyssop branch, and dip them into the blood of the bird that was slaughtered over the fresh water. [7]The priest will then sprinkle the blood of the dead bird seven times on the person being purified of the skin disease. When the priest has purified the person, he will release the live bird in the open field to fly away.

[8]"The persons being purified must then wash their clothes, shave off all their hair, and bathe themselves in water. Then they will be ceremonially clean and may return to the camp. However, they must remain outside their tents for seven days. [9]On the seventh day they must again shave all the hair from their heads, including the hair of the beard and eyebrows. They must also wash their clothes and bathe themselves in water. Then they will be ceremonially clean.

[10]"On the eighth day each person being purified must bring two male lambs and a one-year-old female lamb, all with no defects, along with a grain offering of six quarts* of choice flour moistened with olive oil, and a cup* of olive oil. [11]Then the officiating priest will present that person for purification, along with the offerings, before the LORD at the entrance of the Tabernacle.* [12]The priest will take one of the male lambs and the olive oil and present them as a guilt offering, lifting them up as a special offering before the LORD. [13]He will then slaughter the male lamb in the sacred area where sin offerings and burnt offerings are slaughtered. As with the sin offering, the guilt offering belongs to the priest. It is a most holy offering. [14]The priest will then take some of the blood of the guilt offering and apply it to the lobe of the right ear, the thumb of the right hand, and the big toe of the right foot of the person being purified.

[15]"Then the priest will pour some of the olive oil into the palm of his own left hand. [16]He will dip his right finger into the oil in his palm and sprinkle some of it with his finger seven times before the LORD. [17]The priest will then apply some of the oil in his palm over the blood from the guilt offering that is on the lobe of the right ear, the thumb of the right hand, and the big toe of the right foot of the person being purified. [18]The priest will apply the oil remaining in his hand to the head of the person being purified. Through this process, the priest will purify* the person before the LORD.

[19]"Then the priest must present the sin offering to purify the person who was cured of the skin disease. After that, the priest will slaughter the burnt offering [20]and offer it on the altar along with the grain offering. Through this process, the priest will purify the person who was healed, and the person will be ceremonially clean.

[21]"But anyone who is too poor and cannot afford these offerings may bring one male lamb for a guilt offering, to be lifted up as a special offering for purification. The person must also bring two quarts* of choice flour moistened with olive oil for the grain offering and a cup of olive oil. [22]The offering must also include two turtledoves or two young pigeons, whichever the person can afford. One of the pair must be used for the sin offering

**14:2** Matt 8:4; Mark 1:40-45; Luke 5:12-14; 17:12-14
**14:3** Lev 13:46
**14:4** Lev 14:6, 49-52; Num 19:6
**14:6** Ps 51:7
**14:8** Lev 14:9; Num 8:7
**14:9** Lev 13:33; 14:8; Num 6:9
**14:10** Lev 23:12-13; Num 6:10; Matt 8:4; Mark 1:44; Luke 5:14
**14:12** Exod 29:24
**14:13** Lev 1:11-13; 6:24–7:10
**14:14** Exod 29:20; Lev 8:23-24
**14:20** Lev 14:8
**14:21** Lev 5:7, 11; 12:8
**14:22** Lev 5:7

**13:55** The meaning of the Hebrew is uncertain. **14:2** Traditionally rendered *leprosy;* see note on 13:2a. **14:4** Or *juniper;* also in 14:6, 49, 51. **14:10a** Hebrew *3/10 of an ephah* [6.6 liters]. **14:10b** Hebrew *1 log* [0.3 liters]; also in 14:21. **14:11** Hebrew *Tent of Meeting;* also in 14:23. **14:18** Or *will make atonement for;* similarly in 14:19, 20, 21, 29, 31, 53. **14:21** Hebrew *1/10 of an ephah* [2.2 liters].

and the other for a burnt offering. 23On the eighth day of the purification ceremony, the person being purified must bring the offerings to the priest in the LORD's presence at the entrance of the Tabernacle. 24The priest will take the lamb for the guilt offering, along with the olive oil, and lift them up as a special offering to the LORD. 25Then the priest will slaughter the lamb for the guilt offering. He will take some of its blood and apply it to the lobe of the right ear, the thumb of the right hand, and the big toe of the right foot of the person being purified.

26"The priest will also pour some of the olive oil into the palm of his own left hand. 27He will dip his right finger into the oil in his palm and sprinkle some of it seven times before the LORD. 28The priest will then apply some of the oil in his palm over the blood from the guilt offering that is on the lobe of the right ear, the thumb of the right hand, and the big toe of the right foot of the person being purified. 29The priest will apply the oil remaining in his hand to the head of the person being purified. Through this process, the priest will purify the person before the LORD.

30"Then the priest will offer the two turtledoves or the two young pigeons, whichever the person can afford. 31One of them is for a sin offering and the other for a burnt offering, to be presented along with the grain offering. Through this process, the priest will purify the person before the LORD. 32These are the instructions for purification for those who have recovered from a serious skin disease but who cannot afford to bring the offerings normally required for the ceremony of purification."

### Treatment of Contaminated Houses

33Then the LORD said to Moses and Aaron, 34"When you arrive in Canaan, the land I am giving you as your own possession, I may contaminate some of the houses in your land with mildew.* 35The owner of such a house must then go to the priest and say, 'It appears that my house has some kind of mildew.' 36Before the priest goes in to inspect the house, he must have the house emptied so nothing inside will be pronounced ceremonially unclean. 37Then the priest will go in and examine the mildew on the walls. If he finds greenish or reddish streaks and the contamination appears to go deeper than the wall's surface, 38the priest will step outside the door and put the house in quarantine for seven days. 39On the seventh day the priest must return for another inspection. If he finds that the mildew on the walls of the house has spread, 40the priest must order that the stones from those areas be removed. The contaminated material will then be taken outside the town to an area designated as ceremonially unclean. 41Next the inside walls of the entire house must be scraped thoroughly and the scrapings dumped in the unclean place outside the town. 42Other stones will be brought in to replace the ones that were removed, and the walls will be replastered.

43"But if the mildew reappears after all the stones have been replaced and the house has been scraped and replastered, 44the priest must return and inspect the house again. If he finds that the mildew has spread, the walls are clearly contaminated with a serious mildew, and the house is defiled. 45It must be torn down, and all its stones, timbers, and plaster must be carried out of town to the place designated as ceremonially unclean. 46Those who enter the house during the period of quarantine will be ceremonially unclean until evening, 47and all who sleep or eat in the house must wash their clothing.

48"But if the priest returns for his inspection and finds that the mildew has not reappeared in the house after the fresh plastering, he will pronounce it clean because the mildew is clearly gone. 49To purify the house the priest must take two birds, a stick of cedar, some scarlet yarn, and a hyssop branch. 50He will slaughter one of the birds over a clay pot filled with fresh water. 51He will take the cedar stick, the hyssop branch, the scarlet yarn, and the live bird, and dip them into the blood of the slaughtered bird and into the fresh water. Then he will sprinkle the house seven times. 52When the priest has purified the house in exactly this way, 53he will release the live bird in the open fields outside the town. Through this process, the priest will purify the house, and it will be ceremonially clean.

**14:34** Traditionally rendered *leprosy;* see note on 13:47.

**Cross references (margin):**

**14:23** Lev 14:11

**14:25** Lev 14:14

**14:34** Gen 17:8; Num 32:22; Deut 7:1

**14:35** Ps 91:10

**14:39** Lev 13:5

**14:45** Lev 14:41-45

**14:49** Lev 14:4; Num 19:6

---

**14:34, 35** This mildew was dry rot or mineral crystals affecting stone walls. These specific cleansing procedures designated for mildewed clothing and buildings were fully required by the law (14:44-57). Why was mildew so dangerous? This fungus could spread rapidly and promote disease. It was therefore important to check its spread as soon as possible. In extreme cases, if the fungus had done enough damage, the clothing was burned or the house destroyed.

<sup>54</sup>"These are the instructions for dealing with serious skin diseases,* including scabby sores; <sup>55</sup>and mildew,* whether on clothing or in a house; <sup>56</sup>and a swelling on the skin, a rash, or discolored skin. <sup>57</sup>This procedure will determine whether a person or object is ceremonially clean or unclean.

"These are the instructions regarding skin diseases and mildew."

*Bodily Discharges*

**15** The LORD said to Moses and Aaron, <sup>2</sup>"Give the following instructions to the people of Israel.

"Any man who has a bodily discharge is ceremonially unclean. <sup>3</sup>This defilement is caused by his discharge, whether the discharge continues or stops. In either case the man is unclean. <sup>4</sup>Any bed on which the man with the discharge lies and anything on which he sits will be ceremonially unclean. <sup>5</sup>So if you touch the man's bed, you must wash your clothes and bathe yourself in water, and you will remain unclean until evening. <sup>6</sup>If you sit where the man with the discharge has sat, you must wash your clothes and bathe yourself in water, and you will remain unclean until evening. <sup>7</sup>If you touch the man with the discharge, you must wash your clothes and bathe yourself in water, and you will remain unclean until evening. <sup>8</sup>If the man spits on you, you must wash your clothes and bathe yourself in water, and you will remain unclean until evening. <sup>9</sup>Any saddle blanket on which the man rides will be ceremonially unclean. <sup>10</sup>If you touch anything that was under the man, you will be unclean until evening. You must wash your clothes and bathe yourself in water, and you will remain unclean until evening. <sup>11</sup>If the man touches you without first rinsing his hands, you must wash your clothes and bathe yourself in water, and you will remain unclean until evening. <sup>12</sup>Any clay pot the man touches must be broken, and any wooden utensil he touches must be rinsed with water.

<sup>13</sup>"When the man with the discharge is healed, he must count off seven days for the period of purification. Then he must wash his clothes and bathe himself in fresh water, and he will be ceremonially clean. <sup>14</sup>On the eighth day he must get two turtledoves or two young pigeons and come before the LORD at the entrance of the Tabernacle* and give his offerings to the priest. <sup>15</sup>The priest will offer one bird for a sin offering and the other for a burnt offering. Through this process, the priest will purify* the man before the LORD for his discharge.

<sup>16</sup>"Whenever a man has an emission of semen, he must bathe his entire body in water, and he will remain ceremonially unclean until the next evening.* <sup>17</sup>Any clothing or leather with semen on it must be washed in water, and it will remain unclean until evening. <sup>18</sup>After a man and a woman have sexual intercourse, they must each bathe in water, and they will remain unclean until the next evening.

<sup>19</sup>"Whenever a woman has her menstrual period, she will be ceremonially unclean for seven days. Anyone who touches her during that time will be unclean until evening.

**Cross-references (left margin):**
**14:56** Lev 13:2
**15:2** Lev 22:4 Num 5:2
**15:12** Lev 6:28; 11:32-33
**15:13** Lev 15:28
**15:15** Lev 14:30-31
**15:16** Lev 22:4 Deut 23:10-11
**15:18** 1 Sam 21:4
**15:19** Lev 12:2

**14:54** Traditionally rendered *leprosy;* see note on 13:2a.   **14:55** Traditionally rendered *leprosy;* see note on 13:47.
**15:14** Hebrew *Tent of Meeting;* also in 15:29.   **15:15** Or *will make atonement for;* also in 15:30.   **15:16** Hebrew *until evening;* also in 15:18.

**14:54-57** God told the Israelites how to diagnose serious skin diseases and mildew so they could avoid them or treat them. These laws were given for the people's health and protection. They helped the Israelites avoid diseases that were serious threats in that time and place. Although they wouldn't have understood the medical reasons for some of these laws, their obedience to them made them healthier. Many of God's laws must have seemed strange to the Israelites. His laws, however, helped them avoid not only physical contamination but also moral and spiritual infection.

The Word of God still provides a pattern for physically, spiritually, and morally healthy living. We may not always understand the wisdom of God's laws, but if we obey them, we will thrive. Does this mean we are to follow the Old Testament health and dietary restrictions? In general, the basic principles of health and cleanliness are still healthful practices, but it would be legalistic, if not wrong, to adhere to each specific restriction today. Some of these regulations were intended to mark the Israelites as different from the wicked people around them. Others were given to prevent God's people from becoming involved in pagan religious practices, one of the most serious problems of the day. Still others related to quarantines in a culture where exact medical diagnosis was impossible. Today, for example, physicians can diagnose the different forms of leprosy, and they know which ones are contagious. Treatment methods have greatly improved, and quarantine for leprosy is rarely necessary.

**15:18** The verses in this section are not implying that sex is dirty or disgusting. God created sex for (a) the enjoyment of married couples, (b) the continuation of the race, and (c) the preservation of the covenant. Everything must be seen and done with a view toward God's love and ultimate authority. Sex is not separate from spirituality and God's care. God is concerned about our sexual habits. He designed us, including our sexuality, as wonderfully complex and unified creations. We tend to separate our physical and spiritual lives, but there is an inseparable intertwining. God must be Lord over our whole selves—including our private lives. In what ways do you acknowledge your relationship with God in your sexuality?

20Anything on which the woman lies or sits during the time of her period will be unclean. 21If any of you touch her bed, you must wash your clothes and bathe yourself in water, and you will remain unclean until evening. 22If you touch any object she has sat on, you must wash your clothes and bathe yourself in water, and you will remain unclean until evening. 23This includes her bed or any other object she has sat on; you will be unclean until evening if you touch it. 24If a man has sexual intercourse with her and her blood touches him, her menstrual impurity will be transmitted to him. He will remain unclean for seven days, and any bed on which he lies will be unclean.

25"If a woman has a flow of blood for many days that is unrelated to her menstrual period, or if the blood continues beyond the normal period, she is ceremonially unclean. As during her menstrual period, the woman will be unclean as long as the discharge continues. 26Any bed she lies on and any object she sits on during that time will be unclean, just as during her normal menstrual period. 27If any of you touch these things, you will be ceremonially unclean. You must wash your clothes and bathe yourself in water, and you will remain unclean until evening.

28"When the woman's bleeding stops, she must count off seven days. Then she will be ceremonially clean. 29On the eighth day she must bring two turtledoves or two young pigeons and present them to the priest at the entrance of the Tabernacle. 30The priest will offer one for a sin offering and the other for a burnt offering. Through this process, the priest will purify her before the LORD for the ceremonial impurity caused by her bleeding.

31"This is how you will guard the people of Israel from ceremonial uncleanness. Otherwise they would die, for their impurity would defile my Tabernacle that stands among them. 32These are the instructions for dealing with anyone who has a bodily discharge—a man who is unclean because of an emission of semen 33or a woman during her menstrual period. It applies to any man or woman who has a bodily discharge, and to a man who has sexual intercourse with a woman who is ceremonially unclean."

## 4. Instructions for the altar
### The Day of Atonement

**16** The LORD spoke to Moses after the death of Aaron's two sons, who died after they entered the LORD's presence and burned the wrong kind of fire before him. 2The LORD said to Moses, "Warn your brother, Aaron, not to enter the Most Holy Place behind the inner curtain whenever he chooses; if he does, he will die. For the Ark's cover—the place of atonement—is there, and I myself am present in the cloud above the atonement cover.

3"When Aaron enters the sanctuary area, he must follow these instructions fully. He must bring a young bull for a sin offering and a ram for a burnt offering. 4He must put on his linen tunic and the linen undergarments worn next to his body. He must tie the linen sash around his waist and put the linen turban on his head. These are sacred garments, so he must bathe himself in water before he puts them on. 5Aaron must take from the community of Israel two male goats for a sin offering and a ram for a burnt offering.

6"Aaron will present his own bull as a sin offering to purify himself and his family, mak-

**15:24**
Lev 18:19; 20:18
Ezek 18:6

**15:25**
Matt 9:20
Mark 5:25
Luke 8:43-44

**15:30**
Lev 5:7; 14:22

**15:31**
Num 5:3; 19:13, 20

**16:1**
Lev 10:1-2
**16:2**
Exod 25:21-22;
30:10
Heb 9:25
**16:3**
Lev 16:6-7
**16:4**
Exod 28:39-43;
39:27-29
Ezek 44:17-18
**16:6**
Lev 9:7
Heb 5:1-3;
7:27-28; 9:7

---

**15:32, 33** God is concerned about health. He upholds the dignity of the person, the dignity of the body, and the dignity of the sexual experience. His commands call the people to avoid unhealthy practices and promote healthy ones with practical instructions. Washing was a God-directed means to maintain physical health; acts of purification or cleansing were God-directed means to preserve spiritual dignity. Millennia before the rise of the AIDS epidemic, God's directions already preserved people from known and unknown dangers. This shows God's high regard for sex and sexuality. In our day, sex has been degraded by shocking media exposure. It has become public domain, not private celebration. We are called to have a high regard for sex, both in good health and in purity. Our deepest form of gratitude to God for the gift of sex is expressed in how we use the gift.

**16:1ff** The Day of Atonement was the greatest day of the year for Israel. The Hebrew word for *atone* means "to cover." Old Testament sacrifices could not actually remove sins, only cover them. On this day, the people confessed their sins as a nation, and the high priest went into the Most Holy Place to make atonement for them. Sacrifices were made and blood was shed so that the people's sins could be "covered" until Christ's sacrifice on the cross would give people the opportunity to have their sin removed forever.

**16:1-25** Aaron had to spend hours preparing himself to meet God. But we can approach God anytime (Hebrews 4:16). What a privilege! We are offered easier access to God than the high priests of Old Testament times! Still, we must never forget that God is holy nor let this privilege cause us to approach God carelessly. The way to God has been opened to us by Christ. But easy access to God does not eliminate our need to prepare our hearts as we draw near in prayer.

**16:5-28** This event with the two goats occurred on the Day of Atonement. The two goats represented the two ways God was dealing with the Israelites' sin: (1) He was forgiving their sin through the first goat, which was sacrificed, and (2) he was removing their guilt through the second goat, the scapegoat, that was sent into the wilderness. The same ritual had to be repeated every year. Jesus Christ's death replaced this system once and for all. We can have our sins forgiven and guilt removed by placing our trust in Christ (Hebrews 10:1-18).

ing them right with the LORD.* [7]Then he must take the two male goats and present them to the LORD at the entrance of the Tabernacle.* [8]He is to cast sacred lots to determine which goat will be reserved as an offering to the LORD and which will carry the sins of the people to the wilderness of Azazel. [9]Aaron will then present as a sin offering the goat chosen by lot for the LORD. [10]The other goat, the scapegoat chosen by lot to be sent away, will be kept alive, standing before the LORD. When it is sent away to Azazel in the wilderness, the people will be purified and made right with the LORD.*

[11]"Aaron will present his own bull as a sin offering to purify himself and his family, making them right with the LORD. After he has slaughtered the bull as a sin offering, [12]he will fill an incense burner with burning coals from the altar that stands before the LORD. Then he will take two handfuls of fragrant powdered incense and will carry the burner and the incense behind the inner curtain. [13]There in the LORD's presence he will put the incense on the burning coals so that a cloud of incense will rise over the Ark's cover—the place of atonement—that rests on the Ark of the Covenant.* If he follows these instructions, he will not die. [14]Then he must take some of the blood of the bull, dip his finger in it, and sprinkle it on the east side of the atonement cover. He must sprinkle blood seven times with his finger in front of the atonement cover.

[15]"Then Aaron must slaughter the first goat as a sin offering for the people and carry its blood behind the inner curtain. There he will sprinkle the goat's blood over the atonement cover and in front of it, just as he did with the bull's blood. [16]Through this process, he will purify* the Most Holy Place, and he will do the same for the entire Tabernacle, because of the defiling sin and rebellion of the Israelites. [17]No one else is allowed inside the Tabernacle when Aaron enters it for the purification ceremony in the Most Holy Place. No one may enter until he comes out again after purifying himself, his family, and all the congregation of Israel, making them right with the LORD.

[18]"Then Aaron will come out to purify the altar that stands before the LORD. He will do this by taking some of the blood from the bull and the goat and putting it on each of the horns of the altar. [19]Then he must sprinkle the blood with his finger seven times over the altar. In this way, he will cleanse it from Israel's defilement and make it holy.

[20]"When Aaron has finished purifying the Most Holy Place and the Tabernacle and the altar, he must present the live goat. [21]He will lay both of his hands on the goat's head and confess over it all the wickedness, rebellion, and sins of the people of Israel. In this way, he will transfer the people's sins to the head of the goat. Then a man specially chosen for the

**16:6** Or *to make atonement for himself and his family;* similarly in 16:11, 17b, 24, 34.   **16:7** Hebrew *Tent of Meeting;* also in 16:16, 17, 20, 23, 33.   **16:10** Or *wilderness, it will make atonement for the people.*   **16:13** Hebrew *that is above the Testimony.* The Hebrew word for "testimony" refers to the terms of the LORD's covenant with Israel as written on stone tablets, which were kept in the Ark, and also to the covenant itself.   **16:16** Or *make atonement for;* similarly in 16:17a, 18, 20, 27, 33.

---

**OLD/NEW SYSTEMS OF SACRIFICE**

| Old System of Sacrifice | New System of Sacrifice |
|---|---|
| Was temporary (Hebrews 8:13) | Is permanent (Hebrews 7:21) |
| Aaron first high priest (Leviticus 16:32) | Jesus only High Priest (Hebrews 4:14) |
| From tribe of Levi (Hebrews 7:5) | From tribe of Judah (Hebrews 7:14) |
| Ministered on earth (Hebrews 8:4) | Ministers in heaven (Hebrews 8:1, 2) |
| Used blood of animals (Leviticus 16:15) | Uses blood of Christ (Hebrews 10:4-12) |
| Required many sacrifices (Hebrews 10:1-3) | Requires one sacrifice (Hebrews 9:28) |
| Needed perfect animals (Leviticus 22:19) | Needs a perfect life (Hebrews 5:9) |
| Required careful approach to Tabernacle (Leviticus 16:2) | Encourages confident approach to throne (Hebrews 4:16) |
| Looked forward to new system (Hebrews 10:1) | Sets aside old system (Hebrews 10:9) |

---

**16:12** An incense burner was a dish or shallow bowl that hung by a chain or was carried with tongs. Inside the burner were placed incense (a combination of sweet-smelling spices) and burning coals from the altar. On the Day of Atonement, the high priest entered the Most Holy Place carrying a smoking incense burner. The smoke shielded him from the Ark of the Covenant and the presence of God—otherwise he would die. Incense may also have had a very practical purpose. The sweet smell drew the people's attention to the morning and evening sacrifices and helped cover the sometimes foul smell.

task will drive the goat into the wilderness. 22As the goat goes into the wilderness, it will carry all the people's sins upon itself into a desolate land.

23"When Aaron goes back into the Tabernacle, he must take off the linen garments he was wearing when he entered the Most Holy Place, and he must leave the garments there. 24Then he must bathe himself with water in a sacred place, put on his regular garments, and go out to sacrifice a burnt offering for himself and a burnt offering for the people. Through this process, he will purify himself and the people, making them right with the LORD. 25He must then burn all the fat of the sin offering on the altar.

26"The man chosen to drive the scapegoat into the wilderness of Azazel must wash his clothes and bathe himself in water. Then he may return to the camp.

27"The bull and the goat presented as sin offerings, whose blood Aaron takes into the Most Holy Place for the purification ceremony, will be carried outside the camp. The animals' hides, internal organs, and dung are all to be burned. 28The man who burns them must wash his clothes and bathe himself in water before returning to the camp.

29"On the tenth day of the appointed month in early autumn,* you must deny yourselves.* Neither native-born Israelites nor foreigners living among you may do any kind of work. This is a permanent law for you. 30On that day offerings of purification will be made for you,* and you will be purified in the LORD's presence from all your sins. 31It will be a Sabbath day of complete rest for you, and you must deny yourselves. This is a permanent law for you. 32In future generations, the purification* ceremony will be performed by the priest who has been anointed and ordained to serve as high priest in place of his ancestor Aaron. He will put on the holy linen garments 33and purify the Most Holy Place, the Tabernacle, the altar, the priests, and the entire congregation. 34This is a permanent law for you, to purify the people of Israel from their sins, making them right with the LORD once each year."

Moses followed all these instructions exactly as the LORD had commanded him.

## Prohibitions against Eating Blood

**17** Then the LORD said to Moses, 2"Give the following instructions to Aaron and his sons and all the people of Israel. This is what the LORD has commanded.

3"If any native Israelite sacrifices a bull* or a lamb or a goat anywhere inside or outside the camp 4instead of bringing it to the entrance of the Tabernacle* to present it as an offering to the LORD, that person will be as guilty as a murderer.* Such a person has shed blood and will be cut off from the community. 5The purpose of this rule is to stop the Israelites from sacrificing animals in the open fields. It will ensure that they bring their sacrifices to the priest at the entrance of the Tabernacle, so he can present them to the LORD as peace offerings. 6Then the priest will be able to splatter the blood against the LORD's altar at the entrance of the Tabernacle, and he will burn the fat as a pleasing aroma to the LORD. 7The people must no longer be unfaithful to the LORD by offering sacrifices to the goat idols.* This is a permanent law for them, to be observed from generation to generation.

8"Give them this command as well. If any native Israelite or foreigner living among you offers a burnt offering or a sacrifice 9but does not bring it to the entrance of the Tabernacle to offer it to the LORD, that person will be cut off from the community.

10"And if any native Israelite or foreigner living among you eats or drinks blood in any form, I will turn against that person and cut him off from the community of your people, 11for the life of the body is in its blood. I have given you the blood on the altar to purify you,

| Reference column |
|---|
| **16:22** Isa 53:12 |
| **16:23** Exod 28:42 Lev 16:4 |
| **16:24** Exod 29:4-9 |
| **16:27** Lev 4:11-12; 6:30 |
| **16:28** Num 19:8, 10 |
| **16:29** Lev 23:26-32 Num 29:7 |
| **16:31** Lev 23:32 Ezra 8:21 |
| **16:34** Lev 23:14, 21, 30-31 Heb 9:7 |
| **17:4** Deut 12:5-21 |
| **17:5** Lev 3:1 Deut 12:4-7 |
| **17:6** Exod 29:18 Num 18:17 |
| **17:7** Exod 22:20; 32:8 Deut 32:17 2 Chr 11:15 1 Cor 10:20 |
| **17:9** Lev 17:4 |
| **17:10** Lev 3:17 Deut 12:16, 23-25 |
| **17:11** Gen 9:4 Lev 17:14 Heb 9:22 |

**16:29a** Hebrew *On the tenth day of the seventh month.* This day in the ancient Hebrew lunar calendar occurred in September or October.   **16:29b** Or *must fast;* also in 16:31.   **16:30** Or *atonement will be made for you, to purify you.*   **16:32** Or *atonement.*   **17:3** Or *cow.*   **17:4a** Hebrew *Tent of Meeting;* also in 17:5, 6, 9.   **17:4b** Hebrew *will be guilty of blood.*   **17:7** Or *goat demons.*

---

**17:1ff** Chapters 17–26 are sometimes called the "holiness code" because they focus on what it means to live a holy life. The central verse is 19:2, "You must be holy because I, the LORD your God, am holy."

**17:3-9** Why were the Israelites prohibited from sacrificing outside the Tabernacle area? God had established specific times and places for sacrifices, and each occasion was permeated with symbolism. If people sacrificed on their own, they might easily add to or subtract from God's laws to fit their own lifestyles. Many pagan religions allowed every individual priest to set his own rules; God's command helped the Israelites resist the temp-

tation to follow the pagan pattern. When the Israelites slipped into idolatry, it was because "all the people did whatever seemed right in their own eyes" (Judges 17:6).

**17:7** The "goat idols" were objects of worship and sacrifice in ancient times, particularly in Egypt from which they had recently escaped. God did not want the people to make this kind of sacrifice in the wilderness or in the Promised Land, where they were heading.

**17:11-14** How does blood make atonement for sin? When offered with the right attitude, the sacrifice and the blood shed from it made forgiveness of sin possible. On the one hand, blood making you right with the LORD.* It is the blood, given in exchange for a life, that makes purification possible. 12That is why I have said to the people of Israel, 'You must never eat or drink blood—neither you nor the foreigners living among you.'

**17:13**
Deut 12:16
Ezek 24:7

**17:14**
Gen 9:4
Lev 17:11

**17:15**
Exod 22:31
Lev 7:24
Deut 14:21

13"And if any native Israelite or foreigner living among you goes hunting and kills an animal or bird that is approved for eating, he must drain its blood and cover it with earth. 14The life of every creature is in its blood. That is why I have said to the people of Israel, 'You must never eat or drink blood, for the life of any creature is in its blood.' So whoever consumes blood will be cut off from the community.

15"And if any native-born Israelites or foreigners eat the meat of an animal that died naturally or was torn up by wild animals, they must wash their clothes and bathe themselves in water. They will remain ceremonially unclean until evening, but then they will be clean. 16But if they do not wash their clothes and bathe themselves, they will be punished for their sin."

## B. LIVING A HOLY LIFE (18:1—27:34)

After the sacrificial system for forgiving sins was in place, the people were instructed on how to live as forgiven people. Applying these standards to our lives helps us grow in obedience and please God.

## 1. Standards for the people

*Forbidden Sexual Practices*

**18:2**
Exod 6:7
Lev 11:44

**18:3**
Exod 23:24
Lev 20:23

**18:5**
Ezek 20:11
Luke 10:28
†Rom 10:5
†Gal 3:12

**18:7**
Lev 20:11

**18:8**
Gen 35:22
Lev 20:11
Deut 27:20

**18:9**
Lev 20:17

**18** Then the LORD said to Moses, 2"Give the following instructions to the people of Israel. I am the LORD your God. 3So do not act like the people in Egypt, where you used to live, or like the people of Canaan, where I am taking you. You must not imitate their way of life. 4You must obey all my regulations and be careful to obey my decrees, for I am the LORD your God. 5If you obey my decrees and my regulations, you will find life through them. I am the LORD.

6"You must never have sexual relations with a close relative, for I am the LORD.

7"Do not violate your father by having sexual relations with your mother. She is your mother; you must not have sexual relations with her.

8"Do not have sexual relations with any of your father's wives, for this would violate your father.

9"Do not have sexual relations with your sister or half sister, whether she is your

**17:11** Or *to make atonement for you.*

---

represented the sinner's life, infected by his sin and headed for death. On the other hand, the blood represented the innocent life of the animal that was sacrificed in place of the guilty person making the offering. The death of the animal (of which the blood was proof) fulfilled the penalty of death. God therefore granted forgiveness to the sinner. It is God who forgives based on the faith of the person doing the sacrificing.

**17:14** Why was eating or drinking blood prohibited? The prohibition against eating blood can be traced all the way back to Noah (Genesis 9:4). God prohibited eating or drinking blood for several reasons: (1) To discourage pagan practices. Israel was to be separate and distinct from the foreign nations around them. Eating blood was a common pagan practice. It was often done in hopes of gaining the characteristics of the slain animal (strength, speed, etc.). God's people were to rely on him, not on ingested blood, for their strength. (2) To preserve the symbolism of the sacrifice. Blood symbolized the life of the animal that was sacrificed in the sinner's place. To drink it would change the symbolism of the sacrificial penalty and destroy the evidence of the sacrifice. (3) To protect the people from infection because many deadly diseases are transmitted through the blood. The Jews took this prohibition seriously, and that is why Jesus' hearers were so upset when Jesus told them to drink his blood (John 6:53-56). However, Jesus, as God himself and the last sacrifice ever needed for sins, was asking believers to identify with him completely. He wants us to take his life into us, and he wants to participate in our lives as well.

**18:3** The Israelites moved from one idol-infested country (Egypt) to another (Canaan). They also had contact with other cultures (Moab). As God helped them form a new culture, he warned them

to leave all aspects of their pagan background and surroundings behind. He also warned them how easy it would be to slip into the pagan culture of Canaan, where they were going. Canaan's society and religions appealed to worldly desires, especially sexual immorality and drunkenness. The Israelites were to keep themselves pure and set apart for God. God did not want his people absorbed into the surrounding culture and environment. Society may pressure us to conform to its way of life and thought, but yielding to that pressure will (1) create confusion as to which side we should be on and (2) eliminate our effectiveness in serving God. Follow God by obeying his Word, and don't let the culture around you mold your thoughts and actions.

**18:6-18** Marrying relatives was prohibited by God for physical, social, and moral reasons. Children born to near relatives may experience serious health problems. Without these specific laws, sexual promiscuity would have been more likely, first in families, then outside. Improper sexual relations destroy family life.

**18:6-27** Several detestable activities are listed here: (1) having sexual relations with close relatives, (2) committing adultery, (3) offering children as sacrifices, (4) having homosexual relations, and (5) having sexual relations with animals. These practices were common in pagan religions and cultures, and it is easy to see why God dealt harshly with those who began to follow them. Such practices lead to disease, deformity, and death. They disrupt family life and society and reveal a low regard for the value of oneself and of others. Society today takes some of these practices lightly, even trying to make them acceptable. But they are still sins in God's eyes. If you consider them acceptable, you are not judging by God's standards.

father's daughter or your mother's daughter, whether she was born into your household or someone else's.

¹⁰"Do not have sexual relations with your granddaughter, whether she is your son's daughter or your daughter's daughter, for this would violate yourself.

¹¹"Do not have sexual relations with your stepsister, the daughter of any of your father's wives, for she is your sister.

¹²"Do not have sexual relations with your father's sister, for she is your father's close relative.

**18:12**
Lev 20:19

¹³"Do not have sexual relations with your mother's sister, for she is your mother's close relative.

¹⁴"Do not violate your uncle, your father's brother, by having sexual relations with his wife, for she is your aunt.

**18:14**
Lev 20:20

¹⁵"Do not have sexual relations with your daughter-in-law; she is your son's wife, so you must not have sexual relations with her.

**18:15**
Lev 20:12
Ezek 22:11

¹⁶"Do not have sexual relations with your brother's wife, for this would violate your brother.

**18:16**
Lev 20:21

¹⁷"Do not have sexual relations with both a woman and her daughter. And do not take* her granddaughter, whether her son's daughter or her daughter's daughter, and have sexual relations with her. They are close relatives, and this would be a wicked act.

**18:17**
Lev 20:14

¹⁸"While your wife is living, do not marry her sister and have sexual relations with her, for they would be rivals.

¹⁹"Do not have sexual relations with a woman during her period of menstrual impurity.

**18:19**
Lev 15:24; 20:18

²⁰"Do not defile yourself by having sexual intercourse with your neighbor's wife.

**18:20**
Exod 20:14
Lev 20:10
Matt 5:27-28
1 Cor 6:9

²¹"Do not permit any of your children to be offered as a sacrifice to Molech, for you must not bring shame on the name of your God. I am the Lᴏʀᴅ.

**18:21**
Lev 19:12; 20:1-5;
21:6
Deut 12:31
2 Kgs 23:10
Mal 1:12

²²"Do not practice homosexuality, having sex with another man as with a woman. It is a detestable sin.

**18:22**
Gen 19:5
Lev 20:13
Rom 1:27

²³"A man must not defile himself by having sex with an animal. And a woman must not offer herself to a male animal to have intercourse with it. This is a perverse act.

**18:23**
Exod 22:19
Lev 20:15-16
Deut 27:21

²⁴"Do not defile yourselves in any of these ways, for the people I am driving out before you have defiled themselves in all these ways. ²⁵Because the entire land has become defiled, I am punishing the people who live there. I will cause the land to vomit them out. ²⁶You must obey all my decrees and regulations. You must not commit any of these detestable sins. This applies both to native-born Israelites and to the foreigners living among you.

**18:24**
Lev 18:3

**18:25**
Lev 20:22-23
Deut 9:5

²⁷"All these detestable activities are practiced by the people of the land where I am taking you, and this is how the land has become defiled. ²⁸So do not defile the land and give it a reason to vomit you out, as it will vomit out the people who live there now. ²⁹Whoever commits any of these detestable sins will be cut off from the community of Israel. ³⁰So obey my instructions, and do not defile yourselves by committing any of these detestable practices that were committed by the people who lived in the land before you. I am the Lᴏʀᴅ your God."

**18:26**
Lev 18:2-3

### Holiness in Personal Conduct

**19** The Lᴏʀᴅ also said to Moses, ²"Give the following instructions to the entire community of Israel. You must be holy because I, the Lᴏʀᴅ your God, am holy.

**19:2**
Exod 19:6
Lev 11:44
1 Pet 1:16

³"Each of you must show great respect for your mother and father, and you must always observe my Sabbath days of rest. I am the Lᴏʀᴅ your God.

**19:3**
Exod 20:8, 12
Lev 11:44

⁴"Do not put your trust in idols or make metal images of gods for yourselves. I am the Lᴏʀᴅ your God.

**19:4**
Exod 20:23
Lev 26:1

⁵"When you sacrifice a peace offering to the Lᴏʀᴅ, offer it properly so you* will be accepted by God. ⁶The sacrifice must be eaten on the same day you offer it or on the next day. Whatever is left over until the third day must be completely burned up. ⁷If any of the sacrifice is eaten on the third day, it will be contaminated, and I will not accept it. ⁸Anyone who eats it on the third day will be punished for defiling what is holy to the Lᴏʀᴅ and will be cut off from the community.

**19:6-7**
Lev 7:16-18

⁹"When you harvest the crops of your land, do not harvest the grain along the edges of

**19:9**
Lev 23:22
Deut 24:19-22

**18:17** Or *do not marry.*   **19:5** Or *it.*

---

**19:9, 10** This law was a protection for the poor and the foreigner and a reminder that God owned the land; the people were only caretakers. Laws such as this showed God's generosity and liberality. As people of God, the Israelites were to your fields, and do not pick up what the harvesters drop. ¹⁰It is the same with your grape crop—do not strip every last bunch of grapes from the vines, and do not pick up the grapes that fall to the ground. Leave them for the poor and the foreigners living among you. I am the LORD your God.

**19:11**
Exod 20:15-16

¹¹"Do not steal.

"Do not deceive or cheat one another.

**19:13**
Exod 22:7-15,
21-27; 23:4-9
Deut 24:14-15
Mal 3:5
Jas 5:4

¹²"Do not bring shame on the name of your God by using it to swear falsely. I am the LORD.
¹³"Do not defraud or rob your neighbor.

"Do not make your hired workers wait until the next day to receive their pay.

**19:14**
Deut 27:18

¹⁴"Do not insult the deaf or cause the blind to stumble. You must fear your God; I am the LORD.

**19:15**
Exod 23:2-3, 6
Deut 1:17
Prov 24:23
Jas 2:1-4

¹⁵"Do not twist justice in legal matters by favoring the poor or being partial to the rich and powerful. Always judge people fairly.

**19:16**
Exod 23:1, 7
Ezek 22:9

¹⁶"Do not spread slanderous gossip among your people.*

"Do not stand idly by when your neighbor's life is threatened. I am the LORD.

**19:17**
Matt 18:15-17
1 Jn 2:9, 11; 3:15

¹⁷"Do not nurse hatred in your heart for any of your relatives.* Confront people directly so you will not be held guilty for their sin.

**19:18**
Ps 103:9
†Matt 19:19; 22:39
†Mark 12:31
†Luke 10:27
†Rom 13:9
†Gal 5:14
†Heb 2:8
†Jas 2:8

¹⁸"Do not seek revenge or bear a grudge against a fellow Israelite, but love your neighbor as yourself. I am the LORD.

¹⁹"You must obey all my decrees.

"Do not mate two different kinds of animals. Do not plant your field with two different kinds of seed. Do not wear clothing woven from two different kinds of thread.

**19:19**
Deut 22:9-11

²⁰"If a man has sex with a slave girl whose freedom has never been purchased but who is committed to become another man's wife, he must pay full compensation to her master. But since she is not a free woman, neither the man nor the woman will be put to death. ²¹The man, however, must bring a ram as a guilt offering and present it to the LORD at the entrance of the Tabernacle.* ²²The priest will then purify him* before the LORD with the ram of the guilt offering, and the man's sin will be forgiven.

**19:20**
Deut 22:23-27

**19:21**
Lev 5:15

²³"When you enter the land and plant fruit trees, leave the fruit unharvested for the first three years and consider it forbidden.* Do not eat it. ²⁴In the fourth year the entire crop must be consecrated to the LORD as a celebration of praise. ²⁵Finally, in the fifth year you may eat the fruit. If you follow this pattern, your harvest will increase. I am the LORD your God.

**19:26**
Deut 18:10-12

²⁶"Do not eat meat that has not been drained of its blood.

"Do not practice fortune-telling or witchcraft.

**19:27**
Lev 21:5

²⁷"Do not trim off the hair on your temples or trim your beards.

**19:28**
Lev 21:5
Deut 14:1
Jer 16:6; 41:5

²⁸"Do not cut your bodies for the dead, and do not mark your skin with tattoos. I am the LORD.

**19:29**
Lev 21:9
Deut 23:17-18

²⁹"Do not defile your daughter by making her a prostitute, or the land will be filled with prostitution and wickedness.

**19:30**
Exod 20:8-11
Lev 26:2

³⁰"Keep my Sabbath days of rest, and show reverence toward my sanctuary. I am the LORD.

**19:31**
Lev 20:6

³¹"Do not defile yourselves by turning to mediums or to those who consult the spirits of the dead. I am the LORD your God.

**19:32**
1 Tim 5:1-2

³²"Stand up in the presence of the elderly, and show respect for the aged. Fear your God. I am the LORD.

**19:16** Hebrew *Do not act as a merchant toward your own people.*   **19:17** Hebrew *for your brother.*   **19:21** Hebrew *Tent of Meeting.*   **19:22** Or *make atonement for him.*   **19:23** Hebrew *consider it uncircumcised.*

---

reflect his nature and characteristics in their attitudes and actions. Ruth and Naomi were two people who benefited from this merciful law (Ruth 2:2).

**19:9, 10** God instructed the Hebrews to provide for those in need. He required that the people leave the edges of their fields unharvested, providing food for travelers and the poor. It is easy to ignore the poor or forget about those who have less than we do. But God desires generosity. In what ways can you leave the "edges of your fields" for those in need?

**19:10-35** "Do not . . ." Some people think the Bible is nothing but a book of don'ts. But Jesus neatly summarized all these rules

when he said to love God with all your heart and your neighbor as yourself. He called these the greatest commandments (or rules) of all (Matthew 22:34-40). By carrying out Jesus' simple commands, we find ourselves following all of God's other laws as well.

**19:32** People often find it easy to dismiss the elderly and avoid taking time to visit with them. But the fact that God commanded the Israelites to show respect for the elderly shows how seriously we should take the responsibility of respecting those older than we are. Their wisdom gained from experience can save us from many pitfalls. How do you show respect and honor to your elders?

33"Do not take advantage of foreigners who live among you in your land. 34Treat them like native-born Israelites, and love them as you love yourself. Remember that you were once foreigners living in the land of Egypt. I am the LORD your God.

35"Do not use dishonest standards when measuring length, weight, or volume. 36Your scales and weights must be accurate. Your containers for measuring dry materials or liquids must be accurate.* I am the LORD your God who brought you out of the land of Egypt.

37"You must be careful to keep all of my decrees and regulations by putting them into practice. I am the LORD."

## Punishments for Disobedience

**20** The LORD said to Moses, 2"Give the people of Israel these instructions, which apply both to native Israelites and to the foreigners living in Israel.

"If any of them offer their children as a sacrifice to Molech, they must be put to death. The people of the community must stone them to death. 3I myself will turn against them and cut them off from the community, because they have defiled my sanctuary and brought shame on my holy name by offering their children to Molech. 4And if the people of the community ignore those who offer their children to Molech and refuse to execute them, 5I myself will turn against them and their families and will cut them off from the community. This will happen to all who commit spiritual prostitution by worshiping Molech.

6"I will also turn against those who commit spiritual prostitution by putting their trust in mediums or in those who consult the spirits of the dead. I will cut them off from the community. 7So set yourselves apart to be holy, for I am the LORD your God. 8Keep all my decrees by putting them into practice, for I am the LORD who makes you holy.

9"Anyone who dishonors* father or mother must be put to death. Such a person is guilty of a capital offense.

10"If a man commits adultery with his neighbor's wife, both the man and the woman who have committed adultery must be put to death.

11"If a man violates his father by having sex with one of his father's wives, both the man and the woman must be put to death, for they are guilty of a capital offense.

12"If a man has sex with his daughter-in-law, both must be put to death. They have committed a perverse act and are guilty of a capital offense.

Marginal references: 19:34 Lev 19:18 / 19:35 Deut 25:13-16 / 19:36 Deut 25:13-15; Prov 20:10 / 20:2 Lev 18:21; 24:14-23 / 20:3 Lev 18:21; Num 19:20; Ezek 5:11 / 20:6 Lev 19:26, 31 / 20:7 Lev 11:44-45; †1 Pet 1:16 / 20:9 Exod 21:17; Deut 27:16; †Matt 15:4 / 20:10 Exod 20:14; Deut 22:22 / 20:11 Lev 18:7-8; Deut 27:20 / 20:12 Lev 18:15

19:36 Hebrew *Use an honest ephah* [a dry measure] *and an honest hin* [a liquid measure]. 20:9 Greek version reads *Anyone who speaks disrespectfully of.* Compare Matt 15:4; Mark 7:10.

**19:33, 34** How do you feel when you encounter foreigners, especially those who don't speak your language? Are you impatient? Do you think or act as if they should go back where they came from? Are you tempted to take advantage of them? God says to treat foreigners as you'd treat fellow countrymen, to love them as you love yourself. In reality, we are all foreigners in this world because it is only our temporary home. View strangers, newcomers, and foreigners as opportunities to demonstrate God's love.

**20:1-3** Sacrificing children to the gods was a common practice in ancient religions. The Ammonites, Israel's neighbors, made child sacrifice to Molech (their national god) a vital part of their religion. They saw this as the greatest gift they could offer to ward off evil or appease angry gods. God made it clear that this practice was detestable and strictly forbidden. In Old Testament times as well as New, his character made human sacrifice unthinkable. (1) Unlike the pagan gods, he is a God of love, who does not need to be appeased (Exodus 34:6). (2) He is a God of life, who prohibits murder and encourages practices that lead to health and happiness (Deuteronomy 30:15, 16). (3) He is God of the helpless, who shows special concern for children (Psalm 72:4). (4) He is a God of unselfishness who, instead of demanding human sacrifices, sacrificed himself for us (Isaiah 53:4, 5).

**20:6** Everyone is interested in what the future holds, and we often look to others for guidance. But God warned about looking to the occult for advice. Mediums and psychics were outlawed because God was not the source of their information. At best, occult practitioners are fakes whose predictions cannot be trusted. At worst, they are in contact with evil spirits and are thus extremely dangerous. We don't need to look to the occult for information about the future. God has given us the Bible so that we may obtain all the information we need—and the Bible's teaching is trustworthy.

**20:10-21** This list of commands against sexual sins includes extremely harsh punishments. Why? God had no tolerance for such acts for the following reasons: (1) they shatter the mutual commitment of married partners; (2) they destroy the sanctity of the family; (3) they twist people's mental well-being; and (4) they spread disease. Sexual sin has always been widely available, but the glorification of sex between people who are not married to each other often hides deep tragedy and hurt behind the scenes. When society portrays sexual sins as attractive, it is easy to forget the dark side. God had good reasons for prohibiting sexual sins: He loves us and wants the very best for us.

**20:10-21** The detestable acts listed here were very common in the pagan nations of Canaan; their religions were rampant with sex goddesses, temple prostitution, and other gross sins. The Canaanites' immoral religious practices reflected a decadent culture that tended to corrupt whoever came in contact with it. By contrast, God was building a nation to make a positive influence on the world. He did not want the Israelites to adopt the Canaanites' practices and slide into debauchery. So he prepared the people for what they would face in the Promised Land by commanding them to steer clear of sexual sins. God still expects those who worship him to maintain sexual purity in their lives.

<sup>13</sup>"If a man practices homosexuality, having sex with another man as with a woman, both men have committed a detestable act. They must both be put to death, for they are guilty of a capital offense.

<sup>14</sup>"If a man marries both a woman and her mother, he has committed a wicked act. The man and both women must be burned to death to wipe out such wickedness from among you.

<sup>15</sup>"If a man has sex with an animal, he must be put to death, and the animal must be killed.

<sup>16</sup>"If a woman presents herself to a male animal to have intercourse with it, she and the animal must both be put to death. You must kill both, for they are guilty of a capital offense.

<sup>17</sup>"If a man marries his sister, the daughter of either his father or his mother, and they have sexual relations, it is a shameful disgrace. They must be publicly cut off from the community. Since the man has violated his sister, he will be punished for his sin.

<sup>18</sup>"If a man has sexual relations with a woman during her menstrual period, both of them must be cut off from the community, for together they have exposed the source of her blood flow.

<sup>19</sup>"Do not have sexual relations with your aunt, whether your mother's sister or your father's sister. This would dishonor a close relative. Both parties are guilty and will be punished for their sin.

<sup>20</sup>"If a man has sex with his uncle's wife, he has violated his uncle. Both the man and woman will be punished for their sin, and they will die childless.

<sup>21</sup>"If a man marries his brother's wife, it is an act of impurity. He has violated his brother, and the guilty couple will remain childless.

<sup>22</sup>"You must keep all my decrees and regulations by putting them into practice; otherwise the land to which I am bringing you as your new home will vomit you out. <sup>23</sup>Do not live according to the customs of the people I am driving out before you. It is because they do these shameful things that I detest them. <sup>24</sup>But I have promised you, 'You will possess their land because I will give it to you as your possession—a land flowing with milk and honey.' I am the LORD your God, who has set you apart from all other people.

<sup>25</sup>"You must therefore make a distinction between ceremonially clean and unclean animals, and between clean and unclean birds. You must not defile yourselves by eating any unclean animal or bird or creature that scurries along the ground. I have identified them as being unclean for you. <sup>26</sup>You must be holy because I, the LORD, am holy. I have set you apart from all other people to be my very own.

<sup>27</sup>"Men and women among you who act as mediums or who consult the spirits of the dead must be put to death by stoning. They are guilty of a capital offense."

## 2. Rules for the priests

**21** The LORD said to Moses, "Give the following instructions to the priests, the descendants of Aaron.

"A priest must not make himself ceremonially unclean by touching the dead body of a relative. <sup>2</sup>The only exceptions are his closest relatives—his mother or father, son or daughter, brother, <sup>3</sup>or his virgin sister who depends on him because she has no husband. <sup>4</sup>But a priest must not defile himself and make himself unclean for someone who is related to him only by marriage.

<sup>5</sup>"The priests must not shave their heads or trim their beards or cut their bodies. <sup>6</sup>They must be set apart as holy to their God and must never bring shame on the name of God. They must be holy, for they are the ones who present the special gifts to the LORD, gifts of food for their God.

<sup>7</sup>"Priests may not marry a woman defiled by prostitution, and they may not marry a woman who is divorced from her husband, for the priests are set apart as holy to their God. <sup>8</sup>You must treat them as holy because they offer up food to your God. You must consider them holy because I, the LORD, am holy, and I make you holy.

**20:13** Lev 18:22
**20:14** Lev 18:17 Deut 27:23
**20:15** Lev 18:23 Deut 27:21
**20:17** Lev 18:9
**20:18** Lev 15:24; 18:19
**20:19** Lev 18:12-13
**20:20** Lev 18:14
**20:21** Lev 18:16
**20:22** Lev 18:28
**20:23** Lev 18:1-3, 24-30
**20:24** Exod 13:5; 33:1-3, 16
**20:25** Lev 11:1-47 Deut 14:3-5
**20:26** Lev 20:24
**20:27** Lev 19:31
**21:1** Lev 19:28 Ezek 44:25
**21:2** Lev 21:11
**21:5** Lev 19:27-28 Deut 14:1 Jer 16:6
**21:6** Lev 10:3
**21:7** Lev 21:14 Ezek 44:22
**21:8** Lev 11:44

**20:22, 23** God gave many rules to his people—but not without reason. He did not withhold good from them; he only prohibited those acts that would bring them to ruin. All of us understand God's physical laws of nature. For example, jumping off a 10-story building means death because of the law of gravity. But some of us don't understand how God's spiritual laws work. God forbids us to do certain things because he wants to keep us from self-destruction. Next time you are drawn to a forbidden physical or emotional pleasure, remind yourself that its consequences might be suffering and separation from God, who is trying to help you.

9"If a priest's daughter defiles herself by becoming a prostitute, she also defiles her father's holiness, and she must be burned to death.

10"The high priest has the highest rank of all the priests. The anointing oil has been poured on his head, and he has been ordained to wear the priestly garments. He must never leave his hair uncombed* or tear his clothing. 11He must not defile himself by going near a dead body. He may not make himself ceremonially unclean even for his father or mother. 12He must not defile the sanctuary of his God by leaving it to attend to a dead person, for he has been made holy by the anointing oil of his God. I am the LORD.

13"The high priest may marry only a virgin. 14He may not marry a widow, a woman who is divorced, or a woman who has defiled herself by prostitution. She must be a virgin from his own clan, 15so that he will not dishonor his descendants among his clan, for I am the LORD who makes him holy."

16Then the LORD said to Moses, 17"Give the following instructions to Aaron: In all future generations, none of your descendants who has any defect will qualify to offer food to his God. 18No one who has a defect qualifies, whether he is blind, lame, disfigured, deformed, 19or has a broken foot or arm, 20or is hunchbacked or dwarfed, or has a defective eye, or skin sores or scabs, or damaged testicles. 21No descendant of Aaron who has a defect may approach the altar to present special gifts to the LORD. Since he has a defect, he may not approach the altar to offer food to his God. 22However, he may eat from the food offered to God, including the holy offerings and the most holy offerings. 23Yet because of his physical defect, he may not enter the room behind the inner curtain or approach the altar, for this would defile my holy places. I am the LORD who makes them holy."

24So Moses gave these instructions to Aaron and his sons and to all the Israelites.

**22** The LORD said to Moses, 2"Tell Aaron and his sons to be very careful with the sacred gifts that the Israelites set apart for me, so they do not bring shame on my holy name. I am the LORD. 3Give them the following instructions.

"In all future generations, if any of your descendants is ceremonially unclean when he approaches the sacred offerings that the people of Israel consecrate to the LORD, he must be cut off from my presence. I am the LORD.

4"If any of Aaron's descendants has a skin disease* or any kind of discharge that makes him ceremonially unclean, he may not eat from the sacred offerings until he has been pronounced clean. He also becomes unclean by touching a corpse, or by having an emission of semen, 5or by touching a small animal that is unclean, or by touching someone who is ceremonially unclean for any reason. 6The man who is defiled in any of these ways will remain unclean until evening. He may not eat from the sacred offerings until he has bathed himself in water. 7When the sun goes down, he will be ceremonially clean again and may eat from the sacred offerings, for this is his food. 8He may not eat an animal that has died a natural death or has been torn apart by wild animals, for this would defile him. I am the LORD.

9"The priests must follow my instructions carefully. Otherwise they will be punished for their sin and will die for violating my instructions. I am the LORD who makes them holy.

10"No one outside a priest's family may eat the sacred offerings. Even guests and hired workers in a priest's home are not allowed to eat them. 11However, if the priest buys a slave for himself, the slave may eat from the sacred offerings. And if his slaves have children, they also may share his food. 12If a priest's daughter marries someone outside the priestly family, she may no longer eat the sacred offerings. 13But if she becomes a widow or is divorced and has no children to support her, and she returns to live in her father's home as in her youth,

21:9
Lev 19:29

21:10
Lev 10:6-7
21:11
Lev 19:28

21:12
Lev 10:7
Num 19:11-13
21:13
Ezek 44:22
21:14
Lev 21:7, 13

21:17
Lev 21:6

21:21
Lev 21:17-21
21:22
1 Cor 9:13
21:23
Lev 21:12

22:3
Lev 7:20-21
Num 19:13

22:4
Lev 11:24, 28, 31,
39-40; 14:1-32

22:5
Lev 11:24-25,
41-44

22:8
Exod 22:31
Lev 17:15
22:9
Exod 28:43
Lev 18:30
Num 18:1-7
22:10
Exod 29:31-34
Lev 22:13
22:11
Gen 17:13
Exod 12:44
22:13
Lev 22:10

21:10 Or *never uncover his head.*   22:4 Traditionally rendered *leprosy;* see note on 13:2a.

---

**21:16-23** Was God unfairly discriminating against handicapped people when he said they were unqualified to offer sacrifices? Just as God demanded that no imperfect animals be used for sacrifice, he required that no handicapped priests offer sacrifices. This was not meant as an insult; rather, it had to do with the fact that the priest must match as closely as possible the perfect God he served. Of course, such perfection was not fully realized until Jesus Christ came. Because they were Levites, the handicapped priests were protected and supported with food from the sacrifices. They were not abandoned; they still had opportunity to perform many essential services within the Tabernacle.

**22:1-9** Why were there so many specific guidelines for the priests? The Israelites would have been quite familiar with priests from Egypt. Egyptian priests were mainly interested in politics. They viewed religion as a way to gain power. Thus, the Israelites would have been suspicious of the establishment of a new priestly order. But God wanted his priests to serve him and the people. Their duties were religious—to help people draw near to God and worship him. They could not use their position to gain power because they were not allowed to own land or take money from anyone. All these guidelines reassured the people and helped the priests accomplish their purpose.

she may eat her father's food again. Otherwise, no one outside a priest's family may eat the sacred offerings.

**22:14**
Lev 5:15-16
**22:15**
Lev 19:8
**22:16**
Lev 22:9

¹⁴"Any such person who eats the sacred offerings without realizing it must pay the priest for the amount eaten, plus an additional 20 percent. ¹⁵The priests must not let the Israelites defile the sacred offerings brought to the LORD ¹⁶by allowing unauthorized people to eat them. This would bring guilt upon them and require them to pay compensation. I am the LORD who makes them holy."

### Worthy and Unworthy Offerings

¹⁷And the LORD said to Moses, ¹⁸"Give Aaron and his sons and all the Israelites these instructions, which apply both to native Israelites and to the foreigners living among you.

**22:19**
Lev 1:3
**22:20**
Lev 1:3
Deut 15:21
Heb 9:14
1 Pet 1:19

"If you present a gift as a burnt offering to the LORD, whether it is to fulfill a vow or is a voluntary offering, ¹⁹you* will be accepted only if your offering is a male animal with no defects. It may be a bull, a ram, or a male goat. ²⁰Do not present an animal with defects, because the LORD will not accept it on your behalf.

²¹"If you present a peace offering to the LORD from the herd or the flock, whether it is to fulfill a vow or is a voluntary offering, you must offer a perfect animal. It may have no defect of any kind. ²²You must not offer an animal that is blind, crippled, or injured, or that has a wart, a skin sore, or scabs. Such animals must never be offered on the altar as special gifts to the LORD. ²³If a bull* or lamb has a leg that is too long or too short, it may be offered as a voluntary offering, but it may not be offered to fulfill a vow. ²⁴If an animal has damaged testicles or is castrated, you may not offer it to the LORD. You must never do this in your own land, ²⁵and you must not accept such an animal from foreigners and then offer it as a sacrifice to your God. Such animals will not be accepted on your behalf, for they are mutilated or defective."

**22:25**
Lev 21:6, 17

²⁶And the LORD said to Moses, ²⁷"When a calf or lamb or goat is born, it must be left with its mother for seven days. From the eighth day on, it will be acceptable as a special gift to the LORD. ²⁸But you must not slaughter a mother animal and her offspring on the same day, whether from the herd or the flock. ²⁹When you bring a thanksgiving offering to the LORD,

**22:28**
Deut 22:6
**22:29**
Lev 7:12

**22:19** Or it.   **22:23** Or cow.

---

**THE FESTIVALS**
Besides enjoying one Sabbath day of rest each week, the Israelites also enjoyed 19 days when national holidays were celebrated.

| Festival | What It Celebrated | Its Importance |
|---|---|---|
| Passover<br>One day<br>(Leviticus 23:5) | When God spared the lives of Israel's firstborn children in Egypt and freed the Hebrews from slavery | Reminded the people of God's deliverance |
| Unleavened Bread<br>Seven days<br>(Leviticus 23:6-8) | The exodus from Egypt | Reminded the people they were leaving the old life behind and entering a new way of living |
| First Harvest<br>One day<br>(Leviticus 23:9-14) | The first crops of the barley harvest | Reminded the people how God provided for them |
| Harvest (Pentecost)<br>One day<br>(Leviticus 23:15-22) | The end of the barley harvest and beginning of the wheat harvest | Showed joy and thanksgiving over the bountiful harvest |
| Trumpets<br>One day<br>(Leviticus 23:23-25) | The beginning of the seventh month (civil new year) | Expressed joy and thanksgiving to God |
| Day of Atonement<br>One day<br>(Leviticus 23:26-32) | The removal of sin from the people and the nation | Restored fellowship with God |
| Shelters<br>Seven days<br>(Leviticus 23:33-43) | God's protection and guidance in the wilderness | Renewed Israel's commitment to God and trust in his guidance and protection |

---

**22:19-25** Animals with defects were not acceptable as sacrifices because they did not represent God's holy nature. Furthermore, the animal had to be without defect in order to foreshadow the perfect, sinless life of Jesus Christ. When we give our best time, talent, and treasure to God rather than what is tarnished or common, we demonstrate the true meaning of worship and testify to God's supreme worth. What kind of quality can people see in your service and giving?

sacrifice it properly so you will be accepted. ³⁰Eat the entire sacrificial animal on the day it is presented. Do not leave any of it until the next morning. I am the LORD.

**22:30**
Lev 7:15

³¹"You must faithfully keep all my commands by putting them into practice, for I am the LORD. ³²Do not bring shame on my holy name, for I will display my holiness among the people of Israel. I am the LORD who makes you holy. ³³It was I who rescued you from the land of Egypt, that I might be your God. I am the LORD."

**22:31**
Lev 19:37
**22:33**
Lev 11:45

## 3. Seasons and festivals

**23** The LORD said to Moses, ²"Give the following instructions to the people of Israel. These are the LORD's appointed festivals, which you are to proclaim as official days for holy assembly.

**23:2**
Lev 23:21
Num 29:39

³"You have six days each week for your ordinary work, but the seventh day is a Sabbath day of complete rest, an official day for holy assembly. It is the LORD's Sabbath day, and it must be observed wherever you live.

**23:3**
Exod 20:8-11;
23:12; 31:15
Deut 5:13-14

⁴"In addition to the Sabbath, these are the LORD's appointed festivals, the official days for holy assembly that are to be celebrated at their proper times each year.

### Passover and the Festival of Unleavened Bread

⁵"The LORD's Passover begins at sundown on the fourteenth day of the first month.* ⁶On the next day, the fifteenth day of the month, you must begin celebrating the Festival of Unleavened Bread. This festival to the LORD continues for seven days, and during that time the bread you eat must be made without yeast. ⁷On the first day of the festival, all the people must stop their ordinary work and observe an official day for holy assembly. ⁸For seven days you must present special gifts to the LORD. On the seventh day the people must again stop all their ordinary work to observe an official day for holy assembly."

**23:5**
Exod 12:3-20
Deut 16:1-8
**23:6**
Exod 12:14-20

### Celebration of First Harvest

⁹Then the LORD said to Moses, ¹⁰"Give the following instructions to the people of Israel. When you enter the land I am giving you and you harvest its first crops, bring the priest a bundle of grain from the first cutting of your grain harvest. ¹¹On the day after the Sabbath, the priest will lift it up before the LORD so it may be accepted on your behalf. ¹²On that same day you must sacrifice a one-year-old male lamb with no defects as a burnt offering to the LORD. ¹³With it you must present a grain offering consisting of four quarts* of choice flour moistened with olive oil. It will be a special gift, a pleasing aroma to the LORD. You must also offer one quart* of wine as a liquid offering. ¹⁴Do not eat any bread or roasted grain or fresh kernels on that day until you bring this offering to your God. This is a permanent law for you, and it must be observed from generation to generation wherever you live.

**23:10**
Exod 23:19; 34:26

**23:13**
Lev 6:20

### The Festival of Harvest

¹⁵"From the day after the Sabbath—the day you bring the bundle of grain to be lifted up as a special offering—count off seven full weeks. ¹⁶Keep counting until the day after the seventh Sabbath, fifty days later. Then present an offering of new grain to the LORD. ¹⁷From wherever you live, bring two loaves of bread to be lifted up before the LORD as a special offering. Make these loaves from four quarts of choice flour, and bake them with yeast. They will be an offering to the LORD from the first of your crops. ¹⁸Along with the bread, present seven

**23:15**
Num 28:26-31
Deut 16:9-12

---

**23:5** This day in the ancient Hebrew lunar calendar occurred in late March, April, or early May.  **23:13a** Hebrew *2/10 of an ephah* [4.4 liters]; also in 23:17.  **23:13b** Hebrew *1/4 of a hin* [1 liter].

---

**23:1ff** Festivals played a major role in Israel's culture. Israel's festivals were different from those of any other nation because, being ordained by God, they were times of celebrating with him, not times of moral depravity. God wanted to set aside special days for the people to come together for rest, refreshment, and remembering with thanksgiving all he had done for them.

**23:1-4** God established several national holidays each year for celebration, fellowship, and worship. Much can be learned about people by observing the holidays they celebrate and the way they celebrate them. Take note of your holiday traditions. What do they say about your values? In what ways do your celebrations and holidays reflect your relationship with God?

**23:6** The Festival of Unleavened Bread reminded Israel of their escape from Egypt. For seven days they ate unleavened bread, just as they had eaten it back then (Exodus 12:14, 15). The

symbolism of this bread made without yeast was important to the Israelites. First, because the bread was unique, it illustrated Israel's uniqueness as a nation. Second, because yeast was a symbol of sin, the yeast-less bread represented Israel's moral purity. Third, the baking method reminded them to obey quickly. Their ancestors left the yeast out of their dough so they could leave Egypt quickly without waiting for the dough to rise.

**23:9-14** The Festival of First Harvest required that the first crops harvested be offered to God. The Israelites could not eat the food from their harvest until they had made this offering. Today God still expects us to set aside his portion first, not last. Giving leftovers to God is no way to express thanks. What does the "first harvest" represent in your life?

**23:15-22** The Festival of Harvest was a festival praising God for a bountiful harvest.

one-year-old male lambs with no defects, one young bull, and two rams as burnt offerings to the LORD. These burnt offerings, together with the grain offerings and liquid offerings, will be a special gift, a pleasing aroma to the LORD. ¹⁹Then you must offer one male goat as a sin offering and two one-year-old male lambs as a peace offering.

²⁰"The priest will lift up the two lambs as a special offering to the LORD, together with the loaves representing the first of your crops. These offerings, which are holy to the LORD, belong to the priests. ²¹That same day will be proclaimed an official day for holy assembly, a day on which you do no ordinary work. This is a permanent law for you, and it must be observed from generation to generation wherever you live.*

²²"When you harvest the crops of your land, do not harvest the grain along the edges of your fields, and do not pick up what the harvesters drop. Leave it for the poor and the foreigners living among you. I am the LORD your God."

### The Festival of Trumpets

²³The LORD said to Moses, ²⁴"Give the following instructions to the people of Israel. On the first day of the appointed month in early autumn,* you are to observe a day of complete rest. It will be an official day for holy assembly, a day commemorated with loud blasts of a trumpet. ²⁵You must do no ordinary work on that day. Instead, you are to present special gifts to the LORD."

### The Day of Atonement

²⁶Then the LORD said to Moses, ²⁷"Be careful to celebrate the Day of Atonement on the tenth day of that same month—nine days after the Festival of Trumpets.* You must observe it as an official day for holy assembly, a day to deny yourselves* and present special gifts to the LORD. ²⁸Do no work during that entire day because it is the Day of Atonement, when offerings of purification are made for you, making you right with* the LORD your God. ²⁹All who do not deny themselves that day will be cut off from God's people. ³⁰And I will destroy anyone among you who does any work on that day. ³¹You must not do any work at all! This is a permanent law for you, and it must be observed from generation to generation wherever you live. ³²This will be a Sabbath day of complete rest for you, and on that day you must deny yourselves. This day of rest will begin at sundown on the ninth day of the month and extend until sundown on the tenth day."

### The Festival of Shelters

³³And the LORD said to Moses, ³⁴"Give the following instructions to the people of Israel. Begin celebrating the Festival of Shelters* on the fifteenth day of the appointed month—five days after the Day of Atonement.* This festival to the LORD will last for seven days. ³⁵On the first day of the festival you must proclaim an official day for holy assembly, when you do no ordinary work. ³⁶For seven days you must present special gifts to the LORD. The eighth day is another holy day on which you present your special gifts to the LORD. This will be a solemn occasion, and no ordinary work may be done that day.

³⁷("These are the LORD's appointed festivals. Celebrate them each year as official days for holy assembly by presenting special gifts to the LORD—burnt offerings, grain offerings, sacrifices, and liquid offerings—each on its proper day. ³⁸These festivals must be observed in addition to the LORD's regular Sabbath days, and the offerings are in addition to your personal gifts, the offerings you give to fulfill your vows, and the voluntary offerings you present to the LORD.)

**23:19** Lev 3:1 Num 28:30
**23:20** Exod 29:24
**23:22** Lev 19:9-10 Deut 24:19-21
**23:24** Num 10:9-10; 29:1
**23:25** Lev 23:7
**23:27** Lev 16:29-30
**23:28** Lev 23:7
**23:29** Gen 17:14
**23:32** Lev 16:31
**23:33-34** Num 29:12-39 Deut 16:13-16 Ezra 3:4 Neh 8:14 Zech 14:16 John 7:2
**23:35** Lev 23:7
**23:36** Num 29:12-38
**23:37** Lev 23:2
**23:38** Num 29:39

**23:21** This celebration, called the Festival of Harvest or the Festival of Weeks, was later called the Festival of Pentecost (see Acts 2:1). It is celebrated today as Shavuot (or Shabuoth). **23:24** Hebrew *On the first day of the seventh month.* This day in the ancient Hebrew lunar calendar occurred in September or October. This festival is celebrated today as Rosh Hashanah, the Jewish new year. **23:27a** Hebrew *on the tenth day of the seventh month;* see 23:24 and the note there. This day in the ancient Hebrew lunar calendar occurred in September or October. It is celebrated today as Yom Kippur. **23:27b** Or *to fast;* similarly in 23:29, 32. **23:28** Or *when atonement is made for you before.* **23:34a** Or *Festival of Booths,* or *Festival of Tabernacles.* This was earlier called the Festival of the Final Harvest or Festival of Ingathering (see Exod 23:16b). It is celebrated today as Sukkot (or Succoth). **23:34b** Hebrew *on the fifteenth day of the seventh month;* see 23:27a and the note there.

**23:23, 24** Most of the trumpets used were rams' horns, although some of the more special trumpets were made of beaten silver. Trumpets were blown to announce the beginning of each month as well as the start of festivals.

**23:33-43** The Festival of Shelters was a special celebration involving the whole family (see 23:34; Exodus 23:16; Deuteronomy 16:13, 14). Like Passover, this festival taught family members of all ages about God's nature and what he had done for them and was a time of renewed commitment to God. Our families also need rituals of celebration to renew our faith and to pass it on to our children. In addition to Christmas and Easter, we should select other special days to commemorate God's goodness.

<sup>39</sup>"Remember that this seven-day festival to the LORD—the Festival of Shelters—begins on the fifteenth day of the appointed month,* after you have harvested all the produce of the land. The first day and the eighth day of the festival will be days of complete rest. <sup>40</sup>On the first day gather branches from magnificent trees*—palm fronds, boughs from leafy trees, and willows that grow by the streams. Then celebrate with joy before the LORD your God for seven days. <sup>41</sup>You must observe this festival to the LORD for seven days every year. This is a permanent law for you, and it must be observed in the appointed month* from generation to generation. <sup>42</sup>For seven days you must live outside in little shelters. All native-born Israelites must live in shelters. <sup>43</sup>This will remind each new generation of Israelites that I made their ancestors live in shelters when I rescued them from the land of Egypt. I am the LORD your God."

<sup>44</sup>So Moses gave the Israelites these instructions regarding the annual festivals of the LORD.

### Pure Oil and Holy Bread

**24** The LORD said to Moses, <sup>2</sup>"Command the people of Israel to bring you pure oil of pressed olives for the light, to keep the lamps burning continually. <sup>3</sup>This is the lampstand that stands in the Tabernacle, in front of the inner curtain that shields the Ark of the Covenant.* Aaron must keep the lamps burning in the LORD's presence all night. This is a permanent law for you, and it must be observed from generation to generation. <sup>4</sup>Aaron and the priests must tend the lamps on the pure gold lampstand continually in the LORD's presence.

<sup>5</sup>"You must bake twelve loaves of bread from choice flour, using four quarts* of flour for each loaf. <sup>6</sup>Place the bread before the LORD on the pure gold table, and arrange the loaves in two rows, with six loaves in each row. <sup>7</sup>Put some pure frankincense near each row to serve as a representative offering, a special gift presented to the LORD. <sup>8</sup>Every Sabbath day this bread must be laid out before the LORD. The bread is to be received from the people of Israel as a requirement of the eternal covenant. <sup>9</sup>The loaves of bread will belong to Aaron and his descendants, who must eat them in a sacred place, for they are most holy. It is the permanent right of the priests to claim this portion of the special gifts presented to the LORD."

### An Example of Just Punishment

<sup>10</sup>One day a man who had an Israelite mother and an Egyptian father came out of his tent and got into a fight with one of the Israelite men. <sup>11</sup>During the fight, this son of an Israelite woman blasphemed the Name of the LORD* with a curse. So the man was brought to Moses for judgment. His mother was Shelomith, the daughter of Dibri of the tribe of Dan. <sup>12</sup>They kept the man in custody until the LORD's will in the matter should become clear to them.

<sup>13</sup>Then the LORD said to Moses, <sup>14</sup>"Take the blasphemer outside the camp, and tell all those who heard the curse to lay their hands on his head. Then let the entire community stone him to death. <sup>15</sup>Say to the people of Israel: Those who curse their God will be punished for their sin. <sup>16</sup>Anyone who blasphemes the Name of the LORD must be stoned to death by the whole community of Israel. Any native-born Israelite or foreigner among you who blasphemes the Name of the LORD must be put to death.

<sup>17</sup>"Anyone who takes another person's life must be put to death.

<sup>18</sup>"Anyone who kills another person's animal must pay for it in full—a live animal for the animal that was killed.

**23:40** Neh 8:15 | **23:43** Deut 16:13-15; Ps 78:1-8 | **23:44** Lev 23:37 | **24:2** Exod 27:20-21 | **24:4** Exod 25:31 | **24:5** Exod 25:30; 40:23; Lev 23:13; Heb 9:2 | **24:9** Lev 6:16-17; Matt 12:4 | **24:11** Exod 22:28; Job 1:11; 2:5; Isa 8:21 | **24:14** Lev 20:2, 27; Deut 13:9; 17:7; 21:21 | **24:15** Exod 22:28 | **24:17** Gen 9:5-6; Exod 21:12, 14; Num 35:30-31; Deut 19:11-12 | **24:18** Lev 24:21

**23:39** Hebrew *on the fifteenth day of the seventh month.*   **23:40** Or *gather fruit from majestic trees.*   **23:41** Hebrew *the seventh month.*   **24:3** Hebrew *in the Tent of Meeting, outside the inner curtain of the Testimony;* see note on 16:13.   **24:5** Hebrew *2/10 of an ephah* [4.4 liters].   **24:11** Hebrew *the Name;* also in 24:16b.

**23:44** Worship involves both celebration and confession. But in Israel's national holidays, the balance seems heavily tipped in favor of celebration—five joyous occasions to two solemn ones. The God of the Bible encourages joy! God does not intend for religion to be only meditation and introspection. He also wants us to celebrate. Serious reflection and immediate confession of sin is essential, of course. But this should be balanced by celebrating who God is and what he has done for his people. What special occasions on your calendar would you describe as times for joy? Which would be times for confession? How are you doing with the five-to-two balance?

**24:14** This punishment for blasphemy (cursing God) seems extreme by modern standards. But it shows how seriously God expects us to take our relationship with him. Often we use his name in swearing, or we act as though he doesn't exist. We should be careful how we speak and act, treating God with reverence. Eventually he will have the last word.

**24:17-22** This was a code for judges, not an endorsement of personal vengeance. In effect, it was saying that the punishment should fit the crime, but it should not go beyond.

**24:20**
Exod 21:24-25
Deut 19:21
Matt 5:38
**24:21**
Lev 24:17-18
**24:22**
Exod 12:49
Num 15:15-16, 29

<sup>19</sup>"Anyone who injures another person must be dealt with according to the injury inflicted—<sup>20</sup>a fracture for a fracture, an eye for an eye, a tooth for a tooth. Whatever anyone does to injure another person must be paid back in kind.

<sup>21</sup>"Whoever kills an animal must pay for it in full, but whoever kills another person must be put to death.

<sup>22</sup>"This same standard applies both to native-born Israelites and to the foreigners living among you. I am the LORD your God."

<sup>23</sup>After Moses gave all these instructions to the Israelites, they took the blasphemer outside the camp and stoned him to death. The Israelites did just as the LORD had commanded Moses.

## The Sabbath Year

**25:2**
Exod 23:11

**25:3**
Exod 23:10
**25:4**
Lev 25:1, 20-23
**25:5**
2 Kgs 19:29
**25:6**
Lev 25:20-21

**25** While Moses was on Mount Sinai, the LORD said to him, <sup>2</sup>"Give the following instructions to the people of Israel. When you have entered the land I am giving you, the land itself must observe a Sabbath rest before the LORD every seventh year. <sup>3</sup>For six years you may plant your fields and prune your vineyards and harvest your crops, <sup>4</sup>but during the seventh year the land must have a Sabbath year of complete rest. It is the LORD's Sabbath. Do not plant your fields or prune your vineyards during that year. <sup>5</sup>And don't store away the crops that grow on their own or gather the grapes from your unpruned vines. The land must have a year of complete rest. <sup>6</sup>But you may eat whatever the land produces on its own during its Sabbath. This applies to you, your male and female servants, your hired workers, and the temporary residents who live with you. <sup>7</sup>Your livestock and the wild animals in your land will also be allowed to eat what the land produces.

## The Year of Jubilee

**25:9**
Num 10:10
**25:10**
Lev 25:8-16, 28-54
Isa 61:1
Jer 34:8, 15, 17
Luke 4:19

<sup>8</sup>"In addition, you must count off seven Sabbath years, seven sets of seven years, adding up to forty-nine years in all. <sup>9</sup>Then on the Day of Atonement in the fiftieth year,* blow the ram's horn loud and long throughout the land. <sup>10</sup>Set this year apart as holy, a time to proclaim freedom throughout the land for all who live there. It will be a jubilee year for you, when each of you may return to the land that belonged to your ancestors and return to your own clan. <sup>11</sup>This fiftieth year will be a jubilee for you. During that year you must not plant your fields or store away any of the crops that grow on their own, and don't gather the grapes from your unpruned vines. <sup>12</sup>It will be a jubilee year for you, and you must keep it holy. But you may eat whatever the land produces on its own. <sup>13</sup>In the Year of Jubilee each of you may return to the land that belonged to your ancestors.

**25:13**
Lev 25:10, 24-31
**25:14**
Lev 25:17

<sup>14</sup>"When you make an agreement with your neighbor to buy or sell property, you must not take advantage of each other. <sup>15</sup>When you buy land from your neighbor, the price you pay must be based on the number of years since the last jubilee. The seller must set the price by taking into account the number of years remaining until the next Year of Jubilee. <sup>16</sup>The more years until the next jubilee, the higher the price; the fewer years, the lower the price. After all, the person selling the land is actually selling you a certain number of harvests. <sup>17</sup>Show your fear of God by not taking advantage of each other. I am the LORD your God.

**25:17**
Lev 25:14-16

<sup>18</sup>"If you want to live securely in the land, follow my decrees and obey my regulations. <sup>19</sup>Then the land will yield large crops, and you will eat your fill and live securely in it. <sup>20</sup>But you might ask, 'What will we eat during the seventh year, since we are not allowed to plant or harvest crops that year?' <sup>21</sup>Be assured that I will send my blessing for you in the sixth year, so the land will produce a crop large enough for three years. <sup>22</sup>When you plant your fields in the eighth year, you will still be eating from the large crop of the sixth year. In fact, you will still be eating from that large crop when the new crop is harvested in the ninth year.

**25:9** Hebrew *on the tenth day of the seventh month, on the Day of Atonement;* see 23:27a and the note there.

---

**25:1-7** The Sabbath year provided one year in seven for the fields to lay fallow (unplowed). This was good management of natural resources and reminded the people of God's control and provision for them.

**25:8-17** The Year of Jubilee was meant to be celebrated every 50 years. It included canceling all debts, freeing all slaves, and returning to its original owners all land that had been sold.

There is no indication in the Bible that the Year of Jubilee was ever carried out. If Israel had followed this practice faithfully, they would have been a society without permanent poverty.

## Redemption of Property

23"The land must never be sold on a permanent basis, for the land belongs to me. You are only foreigners and tenant farmers working for me. 24"With every purchase of land you must grant the seller the right to buy it back. 25If one of your fellow Israelites falls into poverty and is forced to sell some family land, then a close relative should buy it back for him. 26If there is no close relative to buy the land, but the person who sold it gets enough money to buy it back, 27he then has the right to redeem it from the one who bought it. The price of the land will be discounted according to the number of years until the next Year of Jubilee. In this way the original owner can then return to the land. 28But if the original owner cannot afford to buy back the land, it will remain with the new owner until the next Year of Jubilee. In the jubilee year, the land must be returned to the original owners so they can return to their family land.

29"Anyone who sells a house inside a walled town has the right to buy it back for a full year after its sale. During that year, the seller retains the right to buy it back. 30But if it is not bought back within a year, the sale of the house within the walled town cannot be reversed. It will become the permanent property of the buyer. It will not be returned to the original owner in the Year of Jubilee. 31But a house in a village—a settlement without fortified walls— will be treated like property in the countryside. Such a house may be bought back at any time, and it must be returned to the original owner in the Year of Jubilee.

32"The Levites always have the right to buy back a house they have sold within the towns allotted to them. 33And any property that is sold by the Levites—all houses within the Levitical towns—must be returned in the Year of Jubilee. After all, the houses in the towns reserved for the Levites are the only property they own in all Israel. 34The open pastureland around the Levitical towns may never be sold. It is their permanent possession.

## Redemption of the Poor and Enslaved

35"If one of your fellow Israelites falls into poverty and cannot support himself, support him as you would a foreigner or a temporary resident and allow him to live with you. 36Do not charge interest or make a profit at his expense. Instead, show your fear of God by letting him live with you as your relative. 37Remember, do not charge interest on money you lend him or make a profit on food you sell him. 38I am the LORD your God, who brought you out of the land of Egypt to give you the land of Canaan and to be your God.

39"If one of your fellow Israelites falls into poverty and is forced to sell himself to you, do not treat him as a slave. 40Treat him instead as a hired worker or as a temporary resident who lives with you, and he will serve you only until the Year of Jubilee. 41At that time he and his children will no longer be obligated to you, and they will return to their clans and go back to the land originally allotted to their ancestors. 42The people of Israel are my servants, whom I brought out of the land of Egypt, so they must never be sold as slaves. 43Show your fear of God by not treating them harshly.

44"However, you may purchase male and female slaves from among the nations around you. 45You may also purchase the children of temporary residents who live among you, including those who have been born in your land. You may treat them as your property, 46passing them on to your children as a permanent inheritance. You may treat them as slaves, but you must never treat your fellow Israelites this way.

**25:23**
Exod 19:5
1 Chr 29:15

**25:25**
Ruth 2:20; 4:4, 6
Jer 32:7

**25:27**
Lev 25:50-52

**25:28**
Lev 25:10, 13

**25:34**
Num 35:2-5

**25:35**
Deut 15:7-11
Prov 21:26

**25:36**
Exod 22:25
Deut 23:19-20

**25:38**
Lev 11:45

**25:39**
Exod 21:2-11
Deut 15:12-18

**25:40**
Lev 25:53

**25:43**
Col 4:1

**25:46**
Lev 25:40, 53

---

**25:23** The people would one day possess land in Canaan, but in God's plan, only God's ownership was absolute. He wanted his people to avoid greed and materialism. If you have the attitude that you are taking care of the Lord's property, you will make what you have more available to others. This is difficult to do if you have an attitude of ownership. Think of yourself as a manager of all that is under your care, not as an owner.

**25:35ff** The Bible places great emphasis on assisting the poor and helpless, especially orphans, widows, and the handicapped. In Israelite society, no paid work was available to women; thus, a widow and her children had no livelihood. Neither was there work available for the seriously handicapped in this nation of farmers and shepherds. The poor were to be helped without charging any interest. Individual and family responsibility for the poor was crucial since there was no government aid.

**25:35-37** God said that neglecting the poor was a sin. Perma-

nent poverty was not allowed in Israel. Financially secure families were responsible to help and house those in need. Many times we do nothing, not because we lack compassion, but because we are overwhelmed by the size of the problem and don't know where to begin. God doesn't expect you to eliminate poverty, nor does he expect you to neglect your family while providing for others. He does, however, expect that when you see an individual in need, you will reach out with whatever help you can offer, including hospitality.

**25:44** Why did God allow the Israelites to purchase slaves? Under Hebrew laws, slaves were treated differently from slaves in other nations. They were seen as human beings with dignity, and not as animals. Hebrew slaves, for example, took part in the religious festivals and rested on the Sabbath. Nowhere does the Bible condone slavery, but it recognizes its existence. God's laws offered many guidelines for treating slaves properly.

<sup>47</sup>"Suppose a foreigner or temporary resident becomes rich while living among you. If any of your fellow Israelites fall into poverty and are forced to sell themselves to such a foreigner or to a member of his family, <sup>48</sup>they still retain the right to be bought back, even after they have been purchased. They may be bought back by a brother, <sup>49</sup>an uncle, or a cousin. In fact, anyone from the extended family may buy them back. They may also redeem themselves if they have prospered. <sup>50</sup>They will negotiate the price of their freedom with the person who bought them. The price will be based on the number of years from the time they were sold until the next Year of Jubilee—whatever it would cost to hire a worker for that period of time. <sup>51</sup>If many years still remain until the jubilee, they will repay the proper proportion of what they received when they sold themselves. <sup>52</sup>If only a few years remain until the Year of Jubilee, they will repay a small amount for their redemption. <sup>53</sup>The foreigner must treat them as workers hired on a yearly basis. You must not allow a foreigner to treat any of your fellow Israelites harshly. <sup>54</sup>If any Israelites have not been bought back by the time the Year of Jubilee arrives, they and their children must be set free at that time. <sup>55</sup>For the people of Israel belong to me. They are my servants, whom I brought out of the land of Egypt. I am the LORD your God.

## 4. Receiving God's blessing
### Blessings for Obedience

**26** "Do not make idols or set up carved images, or sacred pillars, or sculptured stones in your land so you may worship them. I am the LORD your God. <sup>2</sup>You must keep my Sabbath days of rest and show reverence for my sanctuary. I am the LORD.

<sup>3</sup>"If you follow my decrees and are careful to obey my commands, <sup>4</sup>I will send you the seasonal rains. The land will then yield its crops, and the trees of the field will produce their fruit. <sup>5</sup>Your threshing season will overlap with the grape harvest, and your grape harvest will overlap with the season of planting grain. You will eat your fill and live securely in your own land.

<sup>6</sup>"I will give you peace in the land, and you will be able to sleep with no cause for fear. I will rid the land of wild animals and keep your enemies out of your land. <sup>7</sup>In fact, you will chase down your enemies and slaughter them with your swords. <sup>8</sup>Five of you will chase a hundred, and a hundred of you will chase ten thousand! All your enemies will fall beneath your sword.

<sup>9</sup>"I will look favorably upon you, making you fertile and multiplying your people. And I will fulfill my covenant with you. <sup>10</sup>You will have such a surplus of crops that you will need to clear out the old grain to make room for the new harvest! <sup>11</sup>I will live among you, and I will not despise you. <sup>12</sup>I will walk among you; I will be your God, and you will be my people. <sup>13</sup>I am the LORD your God, who brought you out of the land of Egypt so you would no longer be their slaves. I broke the yoke of slavery from your neck so you can walk with your heads held high.

### Punishments for Disobedience

<sup>14</sup>"However, if you do not listen to me or obey all these commands, <sup>15</sup>and if you break my covenant by rejecting my decrees, treating my regulations with contempt, and refusing to obey my commands, <sup>16</sup>I will punish you. I will bring sudden terrors upon you—wasting diseases and burning fevers that will cause your eyes to fail and your life to ebb away. You will plant your crops in vain because your enemies will eat them. <sup>17</sup>I will turn against you, and you will be defeated by your enemies. Those who hate you will rule over you, and you will run even when no one is chasing you!

**26:1ff** This chapter presents the two paths of obedience and disobedience that God set before the people (see also Deuteronomy 28). The people of the Old Testament were warned over and over against worshiping idols. We wonder how they could deceive themselves with these objects of wood and stone. Yet God could well give us the same warning, for we are prone to put idols before him. Idolatry is making anything more important than God, and our lives are full of that temptation. Money, looks, success, reputation, security—these are today's idols. As you look at these false gods that promise everything you want but nothing you need, does idolatry seem so far removed from your experience?

**26:13** Imagine the joy of a slave set free. God took the children of Israel out of bitter slavery and gave them freedom and dignity. We, too, are set free when we accept Christ's payment that redeems us from sin's slavery. We no longer need to be bogged down in shame over our past sins; we can walk with dignity because God has forgiven them and forgotten them. But just as the Israelites were still in danger of returning to a slave mentality, we need to beware of the temptation to return to our former sinful patterns.

18"And if, in spite of all this, you still disobey me, I will punish you seven times over for your sins. 19I will break your proud spirit by making the skies as unyielding as iron and the earth as hard as bronze. 20All your work will be for nothing, for your land will yield no crops, and your trees will bear no fruit.

21"If even then you remain hostile toward me and refuse to obey me, I will inflict disaster on you seven times over for your sins. 22I will send wild animals that will rob you of your children and destroy your livestock. Your numbers will dwindle, and your roads will be deserted.

23"And if you fail to learn the lesson and continue your hostility toward me, 24then I myself will be hostile toward you. I will personally strike you with calamity seven times over for your sins. 25I will send armies against you to carry out the curse of the covenant you have broken. When you run to your towns for safety, I will send a plague to destroy you there, and you will be handed over to your enemies. 26I will destroy your food supply, so that ten women will need only one oven to bake bread for their families. They will ration your food by weight, and though you have food to eat, you will not be satisfied.

27"If in spite of all this you still refuse to listen and still remain hostile toward me, 28then I will give full vent to my hostility. I myself will punish you seven times over for your sins. 29Then you will eat the flesh of your own sons and daughters. 30I will destroy your pagan shrines and knock down your places of worship. I will leave your lifeless corpses piled on top of your lifeless idols,* and I will despise you. 31I will make your cities desolate and destroy your places of pagan worship. I will take no pleasure in your offerings that should be a pleasing aroma to me. 32Yes, I myself will devastate your land, and your enemies who come to occupy it will be appalled at what they see. 33I will scatter you among the nations and bring out my sword against you. Your land will become desolate, and your cities will lie in ruins. 34Then at last the land will enjoy its neglected Sabbath years as it lies desolate while you are in exile in the land of your enemies. Then the land will finally rest and enjoy the Sabbaths it missed. 35As long as the land lies in ruins, it will enjoy the rest you never allowed it to take every seventh year while you lived in it.

36"And for those of you who survive, I will demoralize you in the land of your enemies. You will live in such fear that the sound of a leaf driven by the wind will send you fleeing. You will run as though fleeing from a sword, and you will fall even when no one pursues you. 37Though no one is chasing you, you will stumble over each other as though fleeing from a sword. You will have no power to stand up against your enemies. 38You will die among the foreign nations and be devoured in the land of your enemies. 39Those of you who survive will waste away in your enemies' lands because of their sins and the sins of their ancestors.

40"But at last my people will confess their sins and the sins of their ancestors for betraying me and being hostile toward me. 41When I have turned their hostility back on them and brought them to the land of their enemies, then at last their stubborn hearts will be humbled, and they will pay for their sins. 42Then I will remember my covenant with Jacob and my covenant with Isaac and my covenant with Abraham, and I will remember the land. 43For the land must be abandoned to enjoy its years of Sabbath rest as it lies deserted. At last the people will pay for their sins, for they have continually rejected my regulations and despised my decrees.

**26:18** Lev 26:21, 24, 28
**26:19** Deut 28:23; Isa 25:11; 26:5
**26:21** Lev 26:18
**26:22** Deut 32:24
**26:23** Jer 2:30; 5:3
**26:25** Deut 28:21-22, 27-29; 32:35
**26:26** Isa 3:1; 9:19-20; Ezek 4:16
**26:29** Deut 28:53-57; 2 Kgs 6:26-30
**26:30** 1 Kgs 13:2; Isa 27:9
**26:31** Ps 74:3; Isa 63:18
**26:32** Jer 12:11; 18:16
**26:33** Deut 28:64-68
**26:34** Lev 26:43; 2 Chr 36:21
**26:36** Ezek 21:7
**26:38** Deut 4:25-27
**26:39** Ezek 33:10
**26:40** Jer 3:12-15; Luke 15:18; 1 Jn 1:9
**26:42** Gen 12:1-3; 15:1-4, 13-16; 26:2-5; 28:13-15
**26:43** Lev 26:34

26:30 The Hebrew term (literally *round things*) probably alludes to dung.

**26:18** If the Israelites obeyed, there would be peace in the land. If they disobeyed, disaster would follow. God used sin's consequences to draw them to repentance, not to get back at them. Today, sin's consequences are not always so apparent. When calamity strikes us, we may not know the reason. It may be (1) the result of our own disobedience, (2) the result of someone else's sin, or (3) the result of natural disaster. Because we don't know, we should search our hearts and be sure we are at peace with God. His Spirit, like a great searchlight, will reveal those areas we need to deal with. Because calamity is not always the result of wrongdoing, we must guard against assigning or accepting blame for every tragedy we encounter. Misplaced guilt is one of Satan's favorite weapons against believers.

**26:33-35** In 2 Kings 17 and 25 the warning pronounced in these verses came true. The people persistently disobeyed, and eventually they were conquered and carried off to the lands of Assyria and Babylonia. The nation was held in captivity for 70 years, making up for all of the years that the Israelites did not observe the law of the Sabbath year (2 Chronicles 36:21).

**26:40-45** These verses show what God meant when he said he is slow to anger (Exodus 34:6). Even if the Israelites chose to disobey and were scattered among their enemies, God would still give them the opportunity to repent and return to him. His purpose was not to destroy them, but to help them grow. Our day-to-day experiences and hardships are sometimes overwhelming; unless we can see that God's purpose is to bring about continual growth in us, we may despair. The hope we need is well expressed in Jeremiah 29:11, 12: "'For I know the plans I have for you,' says the LORD. 'They are plans for good and not for disaster, to give you a future and a hope. In those days when you pray, I will listen.'" To retain hope while we suffer shows we understand God's merciful ways of relating to his people.

**26:44**
Deut 4:29-31
Rom 11:2

**26:45**
Gen 17:7
Exod 6:6-8

**26:46**
Lev 27:34

44"But despite all this, I will not utterly reject or despise them while they are in exile in the land of their enemies. I will not cancel my covenant with them by wiping them out, for I am the LORD their God. 45For their sakes I will remember my ancient covenant with their ancestors, whom I brought out of the land of Egypt in the sight of all the nations, that I might be their God. I am the LORD."

46These are the decrees, regulations, and instructions that the LORD gave through Moses on Mount Sinai as evidence of the relationship between himself and the Israelites.

### Redemption of Gifts Offered to the LORD

**27:3**
Exod 30:13
Lev 5:15; 27:25

**27:6**
Num 3:46-48;
18:14-16

**27:8**
Lev 14:21-22

**27** The LORD said to Moses, 2"Give the following instructions to the people of Israel. If anyone makes a special vow to dedicate someone to the LORD by paying the value of that person, 3 here is the scale of values to be used. A man between the ages of twenty and sixty is valued at fifty shekels* of silver, as measured by the sanctuary shekel. 4A woman of that age is valued at thirty shekels* of silver. 5A boy between the ages of five and twenty is valued at twenty shekels of silver; a girl of that age is valued at ten shekels* of silver. 6A boy between the ages of one month and five years is valued at five shekels of silver; a girl of that age is valued at three shekels* of silver. 7A man older than sixty is valued at fifteen shekels of silver; a woman of that age is valued at ten shekels* of silver. 8If you desire to make such a vow but cannot afford to pay the required amount, take the person to the priest. He will determine the amount for you to pay based on what you can afford.

**27:10**
Lev 27:14-33

9"If your vow involves giving an animal that is acceptable as an offering to the LORD, any gift to the LORD will be considered holy. 10 You may not exchange or substitute it for another animal—neither a good animal for a bad one nor a bad animal for a good one. But if you do exchange one animal for another, then both the original animal and its substitute will be considered holy. 11If your vow involves an unclean animal—one that is not acceptable as an offering to the LORD—then you must bring the animal to the priest. 12He will assess its value, and his assessment will be final, whether high or low. 13If you want to buy back the animal, you must pay the value set by the priest, plus 20 percent.

14"If someone dedicates a house to the LORD, the priest will come to assess its value. The priest's assessment will be final, whether high or low. 15 If the person who dedicated the house wants to buy it back, he must pay the value set by the priest, plus 20 percent. Then the house will again be his.

**27:18**
Lev 25:14-16

16"If someone dedicates to the LORD a piece of his family property, its value will be assessed according to the amount of seed required to plant it—fifty shekels of silver for a field planted with five bushels of barley seed.* 17 If the field is dedicated to the LORD in the Year of Jubilee, then the entire assessment will apply. 18But if the field is dedicated after the Year of Jubilee, the priest will assess the land's value in proportion to the number of years left until the next Year of Jubilee. Its assessed value is reduced each year. 19If the person who dedicated the field wants to buy it back, he must pay the value set by the priest, plus 20 percent. Then the field will again be legally his. 20 But if he does not want to buy it back, and it is sold

**27:21**
Lev 25:8-54
Num 18:14
Ezek 44:29

to someone else, the field can no longer be bought back. 21When the field is released in the Year of Jubilee, it will be holy, a field specially set apart* for the LORD. It will become the property of the priests.

**27:3** Or *20 ounces* [570 grams]. **27:4** Or *12 ounces* [342 grams]. **27:5** Or *A boy . . . 8 ounces* [228 grams] *of silver; a girl . . . 4 ounces* [114 grams]. **27:6** Or *A boy . . . 2 ounces* [57 grams] *of silver; a girl . . . 1.2 ounces* [34 grams]. **27:7** Or *A man . . . 6 ounces* [171 grams] *of silver; a woman . . . 4 ounces* [114 grams]. **27:16** Hebrew *50 shekels* [20 ounces, or 570 grams] *of silver for a homer* [182 liters] *of barley seed.* **27:21** The Hebrew term used here refers to the complete consecration of things or people to the LORD, either by destroying them or by giving them as an offering; also in 27:28, 29.

---

**27:1ff** The Israelites were required to give or dedicate certain things to the Lord and to his service: the first portion of their harvests, firstborn animals, their firstborn sons, a tithe of their increase. Many wished to go beyond this and dedicate themselves or another family member, additional animals, a house, or a field to God. In these cases, it was possible to donate money instead of the actual person, animal, or property. Some people made rash or unrealistic vows. To urge them to think about it first, a 20 percent penalty was put on those items purchased back by money. This chapter explains how valuations were to be made and what to do if a donor later wished to buy back what had been donated to God.

**27:9, 10** God taught the Israelites that when they made a vow to him, they must not go back on their promise even if it turned out to cost more than expected. (This applied to animals; humans could be redeemed or purchased back.) God takes our promises seriously. If you vow to give 10 percent of your income and suddenly some unexpected bills come along, your faithful stewardship will be costly. God, however, expects you to fulfill your vow even if it is difficult to do so.

**27:14-25** Real estate could be given as a voluntary offering in much the same way that today people give property through a will or donate the proceeds from the sale of property to a church or Christian organizations.

22 "If someone dedicates to the LORD a field he has purchased but which is not part of his family property, 23 the priest will assess its value based on the number of years left until the next Year of Jubilee. On that day he must give the assessed value of the land as a sacred donation to the LORD. 24In the Year of Jubilee the field must be returned to the person from whom he purchased it, the one who inherited it as family property. 25 (All the payments must be measured by the weight of the sanctuary shekel,* which equals twenty gerahs.)

26 "You may not dedicate a firstborn animal to the LORD, for the firstborn of your cattle, sheep, and goats already belong to him. 27However, you may buy back the firstborn of a ceremonially unclean animal by paying the priest's assessment of its worth, plus 20 percent. If you do not buy it back, the priest will sell it at its assessed value.

28 "However, anything specially set apart for the LORD—whether a person, an animal, or family property—must never be sold or bought back. Anything devoted in this way has been set apart as holy, and it belongs to the LORD. 29 No person specially set apart for destruction may be bought back. Such a person must be put to death.

30 "One tenth of the produce of the land, whether grain from the fields or fruit from the trees, belongs to the LORD and must be set apart to him as holy. 31If you want to buy back the LORD's tenth of the grain or fruit, you must pay its value, plus 20 percent. 32Count off every tenth animal from your herds and flocks and set them apart for the LORD as holy. 33You may not pick and choose between good and bad animals, and you may not substitute one for another. But if you do exchange one animal for another, then both the original animal and its substitute will be considered holy and cannot be bought back."

34These are the commands that the LORD gave through Moses on Mount Sinai for the Israelites.

**27:24**
Lev 25:28

**27:25**
Exod 30:13
Num 3:47; 18:16
Ezek 45:12

**27:26**
Exod 13:2, 12

**27:28**
Josh 6:17-19

**27:30**
Gen 28:22
Num 18:26
2 Chr 31:5-6
Neh 3:12
Mal 3:8

**27:33**
Lev 27:10

**27:34**
Lev 26:46

27:25 Each shekel was about 0.4 ounces [11 grams] in weight.

---

**27:28, 29** Things set apart (devoted) applies to personal property or persons placed under God's ban, such as captured plunder from idol worshipers or idols themselves. These were to be destroyed and could not be redeemed.

**27:33** Many of the principles regarding sacrifices and tithes were intended to encourage inward attitudes as well as outward actions. If a person gives grudgingly, he shows that he has a stingy heart. God wants us to be cheerful givers (2 Corinthians 9:7), who give with gratitude to him.

**27:34** The book of Leviticus is filled with the commands God gave his people at the foot of Mount Sinai. From these com-

mands we can learn much about God's nature and character. At first glance, Leviticus seems irrelevant to our high-tech world. But digging a little deeper, we realize that the book still speaks to us today—God has not changed, and his principles are for all times. As people and society change, we need constantly to search for ways to apply the principles of God's law to our present circumstances. God was the same in Leviticus as he is today and will be forever (Hebrews 13:8).

# KEY PLACES IN NUMBERS

Modern names and boundaries are shown in gray.

leader from each tribe was sent to spy out the new land. After 40 days they returned, and all but Joshua and Caleb were too afraid to enter. Because of their lack of faith, the Israelites were made to wander in the wilderness for 40 years (12:16—19:22).

**3 Kadesh** With the years of wandering nearing an end, the Israelites set their sights once again on the Promised Land. Kadesh was the oasis where they spent most of their desert years. Miriam died here. And it was here that Moses angrily struck the rock, which kept him from entering the Promised Land (20).

**4 Arad** When the king there heard that Israel was on the move, he attacked, but he was soundly defeated. Moses then led the people southward and eastward around the Dead Sea (21:1–3).

**5 Edom** The Israelites wanted to travel through Edom, but the king of Edom refused them passage (20:14–22). So they traveled around Edom and became very discouraged. The people complained, and God sent poisonous snakes to punish them. Only by looking at a bronze snake on a pole could those bitten be healed (21:4–9).

**6 Ammon** Next, King Sihon of the Amorites refused Israel passage. When he attacked, Israel defeated his army and conquered the territory as far as the border of Ammon (21:21–32).

**7 Bashan** Moses sent spies to Bashan. King Og attacked, but he was also defeated (21:33–35).

**8 Plains of Moab** The people camped on the plains of Moab, east of the Jordan River across from Jericho. They were on the verge of entering the Promised Land (22:1).

**1 Mount Sinai** Numbers begins at Mount Sinai in the wilderness of Sinai with Moses taking a census of the men eligible for battle. As the battle preparations began, the people also prepared for the spiritual warfare they would face. The Promised Land was full of wicked people who would try to entice the Israelites to sin. God, therefore, taught Moses and the Israelites how to live right (1:1—12:15).

**2 Wilderness of Paran** After a full year at Mount Sinai, the Israelites broke camp and began their march toward the Promised Land by moving into the wilderness of Paran. From there, one

**9 Moab** King Balak of Moab, terrified of the Israelites, called upon Balaam, a famous sorcerer, to curse Israel from the mountains above where the Israelites camped. But the Lord caused Balaam to bless them instead (22:2—24:25).

**10 Gilead** The tribes of Reuben and Gad decided to settle in the fertile country of Gilead east of the Jordan River because it was a good land for their sheep. But first they promised to help the other tribes conquer the land west of the Jordan River (32).

# NUMBERS

## VITAL STATISTICS

**PURPOSE:**
To tell the story of how Israel prepared to enter the Promised Land, how they sinned and were punished, and how they prepared to try again

**AUTHOR:**
Moses

**ORIGINAL AUDIENCE:**
The people of Israel

**DATE WRITTEN:**
1450–1410 B.C.

**WHERE WRITTEN:**
In the wilderness during Israel's wanderings, somewhere in the Sinai peninsula

**SETTING:**
The vast desert of the Sinai region, as well as lands just south and east of Canaan

**KEY VERSES:**
"Not one of these people will ever enter that land. They have all seen my glorious presence and the miraculous signs I performed both in Egypt and in the wilderness, but again and again they tested me by refusing to listen to my voice. They will never even see the land I swore to give their ancestors. None of those who have treated me with contempt will ever see it" (14:22, 23).

**KEY PEOPLE:**
Moses, Aaron, Miriam, Joshua, Caleb, Eleazar, Korah, Balaam

**KEY PLACES:**
Mount Sinai, Promised Land (Canaan), Kadesh, Mount Hor, plains of Moab

EVERY parent knows the shrill whine of a young child—a slow, high-pitched complaint that grates on the eardrums and aggravates the soul. The tone of voice is difficult to bear, but the real irritation is the underlying cause—discontentment and disobedience. As the "children" of Israel journeyed from the foot of Mount Sinai to the land of Canaan, they grumbled, whined, and complained at every turn. They focused on their present discomforts. Faith had fled, and they added an extra 40 years to their trip.

Numbers, which records the tragic story of Israel's unbelief, should serve as a dramatic lesson for all of God's people. God loves us and wants the very best for us. He can and should be trusted. Numbers also gives a clear portrayal of God's patience. Again and again he withholds judgment and preserves the nation. But his patience must not be taken for granted. His judgment will come. We must obey.

As Numbers begins, the nation of Israel was camped at the foot of Mount Sinai. The people had received God's laws and were preparing to move. A census was taken to determine the number of men fit for military service. Next, the people were set apart for God. God was making the people, both spiritually and physically, ready to receive their inheritance.

But then the complaining began. First, the people complained about the food. Next, it was over Moses' authority. God punished some people but spared the nation because of Moses' prayers. The nation then arrived at Kadesh, and spies were sent into Canaan to assess its strength. Ten returned with fearful stories of giants. Only Caleb and Joshua encouraged the nation to "go at once to take the land" (13:30). The minority report fell on deaf ears full of the ominous message of the majority. Because of their unbelief, God declared that the present generation would not live to see the Promised Land. Thus the "wanderings" began. These wilderness wanderings featured a continuous pattern of grumbling, defiance, discipline, and death. How much better it would have been to have trusted God and entered his land! Then the terrible waiting began—waiting for the old generation to die off and waiting to see if the new generation could faithfully obey God.

Numbers ends as it begins, with preparation. This new generation of Israelites was numbered and sanctified. After defeating numerous armies, they settled on the east side of the Jordan River. Then they faced their greatest test: to cross the river and possess the beautiful land God had promised to them.

The lesson is clear. God's people must trust him, moving ahead by *faith* if they are to claim his promised land.

## THE BLUEPRINT

A. PREPARING FOR THE JOURNEY (1:1—10:10)
  1. The first census of the nation
  2. The role of the Levites
  3. The purity of the camp
  4. Receiving guidance for the journey

As part of their preparations, the Lord gave strict guidelines to the Israelites regarding purity in the camp. He wanted them to have a lifestyle distinct from the nations around them. He wanted them to be a holy people. Similarly, we should concern ourselves with purity in the church.

B. FIRST APPROACH TO THE PROMISED LAND (10:11—14:45)
  1. The people complain
  2. Miriam and Aaron oppose Moses
  3. The scouts incite rebellion

The Israelites were prevented from entering the Promised Land because of their unbelief. Throughout history, God's people have continued to struggle with lack of faith. We must prevent unbelief from gaining a foothold in our lives, for it will keep us from enjoying the blessings that God has promised.

C. WANDERING IN THE WILDERNESS (15:1—21:35)
  1. Additional regulations
  2. Many leaders rebel against Moses
  3. Duties of priests and Levites
  4. The new generation

When the people complained against God and criticized Moses, they were severely punished. Over 14,000 people died as a result of rebellion against Moses. As a result of Korah's rebellion, Korah, Dathan, and Abiram and their households died, along with 250 false priests. Dissatisfaction and discontent, if allowed to remain in our lives, can easily lead to disaster. We should refrain from complaining and criticizing our leaders.

D. SECOND APPROACH TO THE PROMISED LAND (22:1—36:13)
  1. The story of Balaam
  2. The second census of the nation
  3. Instructions concerning offerings
  4. Vengeance on the Midianites
  5. The Transjordan tribes
  6. Camped on the plains of Moab

The Moabites and Midianites could not get Balaam to curse Israel, but they did get him to give advice on how to draw the Israelites to idol worship. Balaam knew what was right, but he gave in to the temptation of material rewards and sinned. Knowing what is right alone is never enough. We must also do what is right.

## MEGATHEMES

| THEME | EXPLANATION | IMPORTANCE |
|---|---|---|
| Census | Moses counted the Israelites twice. The first census organized the people into marching units to better defend themselves. The second prepared them to conquer the country east of the Jordan River. | People have to be organized, trained, and led to be effective in great movements. It is always wise to count the cost before setting out on some great undertaking. When we are aware of the obstacles before us, we can more easily avoid them. In God's work, we must remove barriers in our relationships with others so that our effectiveness is not diminished. |
| Rebellion | At Kadesh, 12 scouts were sent out into the land of Canaan to report on the fortifications of the enemies. When the scouts returned, 10 said that they should give up and go back to Egypt. As a result, the people refused to enter the land. Faced with a choice, Israel rebelled against God. Rebellion did not start with an uprising, but with griping and murmuring against Moses and God. | Rebellion against God is always a serious matter. It is not something to take lightly, for God's punishment for sin is often very severe. Our rebellion does not usually begin with all-out warfare, but in subtle ways—with griping and criticizing. Make sure your negative comments are not the product of a rebellious spirit. |
| Wandering | Because they rebelled, the Israelites wandered 40 years in the wilderness. This shows how severely God can punish sin. Forty years was enough time for all those who held on to Egypt's customs and values to die off. It gave time to train up a new generation in the ways of God. | God judges sin harshly because he is holy. The wanderings in the wilderness demonstrate how serious God considers flagrant disobedience of his commands. Purging our lives of sin is vital to God's purpose. |

| Canaan | Canaan is the Promised Land. It was the land God had promised to Abraham, Isaac, and Jacob—the land of the covenant. Canaan was to be the dwelling place of God's people, those set apart for true spiritual worship. | Although God's punishment for sin is often severe, he offers reconciliation and hope—his love is truly amazing. Just as God's love and law led Israel to the Promised Land, God desires to give purpose and destiny to our lives. |

## A. PREPARING FOR THE JOURNEY (1:1—10:10)

At Mount Sinai, the Israelites received specific directions for their lifestyle in the new land God would give to them. A census was taken and the second Passover was celebrated, marking one year of freedom from slavery in Egypt. The people were now prepared to continue their journey to the Promised Land. Just as the Lord prepared the Israelites, he prepares us for our journey through life.

### 1. The first census of the nation

**1** A year after Israel's departure from Egypt, the LORD spoke to Moses in the Tabernacle* in the wilderness of Sinai. On the first day of the second month* of that year he said, ²"From the whole community of Israel, record the names of all the warriors by their clans and families. List all the men ³twenty years old or older who are able to go to war. You and Aaron must register the troops, ⁴and you will be assisted by one family leader from each tribe.

⁵"These are the tribes and the names of the leaders who will assist you:

**1:1** Exod 40:2, 17

**1:2** Exod 38:25-26 Num 26:2

**1:4** Exod 18:21 Num 34:18

**1:5** Gen 29:32 Rev 7:5

| Tribe | Leader |
|---|---|
| Reuben. . . . . . . . . . . . . . . . . . . . . . . . . . . . . . . | Elizur son of Shedeur |
| ⁶ Simeon. . . . . . . . . . . . . . . . . . . . . . . . . . . . . . | Shelumiel son of Zurishaddai |
| ⁷ Judah . . . . . . . . . . . . . . . . . . . . . . . . . . . . . . . | Nahshon son of Amminadab |
| ⁸ Issachar . . . . . . . . . . . . . . . . . . . . . . . . . . . . . | Nethanel son of Zuar |
| ⁹ Zebulun . . . . . . . . . . . . . . . . . . . . . . . . . . . . . | Eliab son of Helon |
| ¹⁰ Ephraim son of Joseph. . . . . . . . . . . . . . . . . | Elishama son of Ammihud |
| Manasseh son of Joseph . . . . . . . . . . . . . . | Gamaliel son of Pedahzur |
| ¹¹ Benjamin. . . . . . . . . . . . . . . . . . . . . . . . . . . . | Abidan son of Gideoni |
| ¹² Dan . . . . . . . . . . . . . . . . . . . . . . . . . . . . . . . | Ahiezer son of Ammishaddai |
| ¹³ Asher . . . . . . . . . . . . . . . . . . . . . . . . . . . . . . | Pagiel son of Ocran |
| ¹⁴ Gad . . . . . . . . . . . . . . . . . . . . . . . . . . . . . . . | Eliasaph son of Deuel |
| ¹⁵ Naphtali. . . . . . . . . . . . . . . . . . . . . . . . . . . . | Ahira son of Enan |

**1:7** Ruth 4:20 1 Chr 2:10

**1:14** Num 2:14

¹⁶These are the chosen leaders of the community, the leaders of their ancestral tribes, the heads of the clans of Israel."

¹⁷So Moses and Aaron called together these chosen leaders, ¹⁸and they assembled the whole community of Israel on that very day.* All the people were registered according to their ancestry by their clans and families. The men of Israel who were twenty years old or older were listed one by one, ¹⁹just as the LORD had commanded Moses. So Moses recorded their names in the wilderness of Sinai.

²⁰⁻²¹This is the number of men twenty years old or older who were able to go to war, as their names were listed in the records of their clans and families*:

**1:16** Num 7:2; 16:2; 26:9

**1:18** Num 1:1 Ezra 2:59

**1:20** Num 26:5-11

**1:1a** Hebrew *the Tent of Meeting.*   **1:1b** This day in the ancient Hebrew lunar calendar occurred in April or May.   **1:18** Hebrew *on the first day of the second month;* see 1:1.   **1:20-21a** In the Hebrew text, this sentence (*This is the number of men twenty years old or older who were able to go to war, as their names were listed in the records of their clans and families*) is repeated in 1:22, 24, 26, 28, 30, 32, 34, 36, 38, 40, 42.

**1:1** As the book of Numbers opens, the Israelites had been camped near Mount Sinai for more than a year. There they had received all the laws and regulations recorded in the book of Leviticus. They had been transformed into a new nation and equipped for their task. At this time, they were ready to move out and receive their land. In preparation, Moses and Aaron were told to number all the men who were able to serve in the army. This book is named for this census, or numbering, of the people.

**1:1** The Tabernacle contained the sanctuary (or Holy Place) in one part, and the Most Holy Place with the Ark in another part. These two parts were separated by a curtain. God revealed himself to Moses in the Most Holy Place.

Exodus 33:7 mentions the "Tent of Meeting" as the place where Moses met with God before the Tabernacle was

constructed. Many believe that the Tent of Meeting in Exodus served the same function as the Tabernacle described here.

**1:2-15** Taking a census was long and tedious, but it was an important task. The fighting men had to be counted to determine Israel's military strength before entering the Promised Land. In addition, the tribes had to be organized to determine the amount of land each would need, as well as to provide genealogical records. Without such a census, the task of conquering and organizing the Promised Land would have been more difficult. Whenever we are at a crossroads, it is important to take inventory of our resources. We will serve more effectively if, before plunging in, we set aside time to take a "census" of all we have—possessions, relationships, spiritual condition, time, goals.

**1:20-46** If there were 603,550 men, not counting the Levites

| | Tribe | Number |
|---|---|---|
| **1:22**<br>Num 26:12-14 | Reuben (Jacob's* oldest son) .......................................... | 46,500 |
| **1:24**<br>Num 26:15-18 | 22-23 Simeon............................................................ | 59,300 |
| **1:26**<br>Num 26:19-22 | 24-25 Gad.............................................................. | 45,650 |
| **1:28**<br>Num 26:23-25 | 26-27 Judah............................................................ | 74,600 |
| **1:30**<br>Num 26:26-27 | 28-29 Issachar......................................................... | 54,400 |
| **1:32**<br>Num 26:35-37 | 30-31 Zebulun.......................................................... | 57,400 |
| **1:34**<br>Num 26:28-34 | 32-33 Ephraim son of Joseph........................................... | 40,500 |
| **1:36**<br>Num 26:38-41 | 34-35 Manasseh son of Joseph ......................................... | 32,200 |
| **1:38**<br>Num 26:42-43 | 36-37 Benjamin......................................................... | 35,400 |
| **1:40**<br>Num 26:44-47 | 38-39 Dan.............................................................. | 62,700 |
| **1:42**<br>Num 26:48-50 | 40-41 Asher ........................................................... | 41,500 |
| **1:44**<br>Num 26:64 | 42-43 Naphtali ........................................................ | 53,400 |

**1:46**<br>Num 2:32; 26:51

**1:47**<br>Num 2:33; 26:57

**1:50**<br>Num 3:25-37

**1:51**<br>Num 4:1-33

**1:52**<br>Num 2:2

**1:53**<br>Num 1:50

44These were the men registered by Moses and Aaron and the twelve leaders of Israel, all listed according to their ancestral descent. 45They were registered by families—all the men of Israel who were twenty years old or older and able to go to war. 46The total number was 603,550.

47But this total did not include the Levites. 48For the LORD had said to Moses, 49"Do not include the tribe of Levi in the registration; do not count them with the rest of the Israelites. 50Put the Levites in charge of the Tabernacle of the Covenant,* along with all its furnishings and equipment. They must carry the Tabernacle and all its furnishings as you travel, and they must take care of it and camp around it. 51Whenever it is time for the Tabernacle to move, the Levites will take it down. And when it is time to stop, they will set it up again. But any unauthorized person who goes too near the Tabernacle must be put to death. 52Each tribe of Israel will camp in a designated area with its own family banner. 53But the Levites will camp around the Tabernacle of the Covenant to protect the community of Israel from the LORD's anger. The Levites are responsible to stand guard around the Tabernacle."

54So the Israelites did everything just as the LORD had commanded Moses.

### Organization for Israel's Camp

**2:2**<br>Num 1:52

**2** Then the LORD gave these instructions to Moses and Aaron: 2"When the Israelites set up camp, each tribe will be assigned its own area. The tribal divisions will camp beneath their family banners on all four sides of the Tabernacle,* but at some distance from it.

**2:3**<br>Num 10:14

3-4"The divisions of Judah, Issachar, and Zebulun are to camp toward the sunrise on the east side of the Tabernacle, beneath their family banners. These are the names of the tribes, their leaders, and the numbers of their registered troops:

| | Tribe | Leader | Number |
|---|---|---|---|
| | Judah ..................... | Nahshon son of Amminadab ................. | 74,600 |
| **2:5**<br>Num 1:8 | 5-6 Issachar ................... | Nethanel son of Zuar ...................... | 54,400 |
| **2:9**<br>Num 10:14 | 7-8 Zebulun ................... | Eliab son of Helon ......................... | 57,400 |

9So the total of all the troops on Judah's side of the camp is 186,400. These three tribes are to lead the way whenever the Israelites travel to a new campsite.

**2:10**<br>Num 1:5

10-11"The divisions of Reuben, Simeon, and Gad are to camp on the south side of the Tabernacle, beneath their family banners. These are the names of the tribes, their leaders, and the numbers of their registered troops:

**1:20-21b** Hebrew *Israel's.* The names "Jacob" and "Israel" are often interchanged throughout the Old Testament, referring sometimes to the individual patriarch and sometimes to the nation.   **1:50** Or *Tabernacle of the Testimony;* also in 1:53.   **2:2** Hebrew *the Tent of Meeting;* also in 2:17.

or women and children, the total population must have numbered more than two million Israelites. How could such a large population grow from Jacob's family of 70 who moved down to Egypt? The book of Exodus tells us that the Israelites who descended from Jacob's family "multiplied so greatly that they became extremely powerful and filled the land" (Exodus 1:7). Because they remained in Egypt more than 400 years, they had plenty of time to grow into a large group of people. After leaving Egypt, they were able to survive in the wilderness because God miraculously provided the food and water they needed. The leaders of Moab were terrified because of the large number of Israelites (22:3).

**2:2** The nation of Israel was organized according to tribes for several reasons. (1) It was an effective way to manage and govern a large group. (2) It made dividing the Promised Land easier. (3) It was part of their culture and heritage (people were not known by a last name, but by their family, clan, and tribe). (4) It made it easier to keep detailed genealogies, and genealogies were the only way to prove membership in God's chosen nation. (5) It made travel much more efficient. The people followed the tribe's standard (a kind of flag) and thus stayed together and kept from getting lost.

| Tribe | Leader | Number |
|---|---|---|
| Reuben.................. | Elizur son of Shedeur ........................ | 46,500 |
| 12-13 Simeon.................... | Shelumiel son of Zurishaddai................. | 59,300 |
| 14-15 Gad ...................... | Eliasaph son of Deuel* ...................... | 45,650 |

<sup></sup>

2:12
Num 1:6

2:14
Num 1:14

16So the total of all the troops on Reuben's side of the camp is 151,450. These three tribes will be second in line whenever the Israelites travel.

2:17
Num 1:53

17"Then the Tabernacle, carried by the Levites, will set out from the middle of the camp. All the tribes are to travel in the same order that they camp, each in position under the appropriate family banner.

18-19"The divisions of Ephraim, Manasseh, and Benjamin are to camp on the west side of the Tabernacle, beneath their family banners. These are the names of the tribes, their leaders, and the numbers of their registered troops:

| Tribe | Leader | Number |
|---|---|---|
| Ephraim................... | Elishama son of Ammihud ................... | 40,500 |
| 20-21 Manasseh................. | Gamaliel son of Pedahzur .................... | 32,200 |
| 22-23 Benjamin ................. | Abidan son of Gideoni ...................... | 35,400 |

2:20
Num 1:10

24So the total of all the troops on Ephraim's side of the camp is 108,100. These three tribes will be third in line whenever the Israelites travel.

2:24
Num 10:22

25-26"The divisions of Dan, Asher, and Naphtali are to camp on the north side of the Tabernacle, beneath their family banners. These are the names of the tribes, their leaders, and the numbers of their registered troops:

2:25
Num 1:12

| Tribe | Leader | Number |
|---|---|---|
| Dan ....................... | Ahiezer son of Ammishaddai ................. | 62,700 |
| 27-28 Asher .................... | Pagiel son of Ocran .......................... | 41,500 |
| 29-30 Naphtali.................. | Ahira son of Enan............................ | 53,400 |

2:27
Num 1:13

31So the total of all the troops on Dan's side of the camp is 157,600. These three tribes will be last, marching under their banners whenever the Israelites travel."

2:31
Num 10:25

32In summary, the troops of Israel listed by their families totaled 603,550. 33But as the LORD had commanded, the Levites were not included in this registration. 34So the people of Israel did everything as the LORD had commanded Moses. Each clan and family set up camp and marched under their banners exactly as the LORD had instructed them.

2:32
Exod 38:26
Num 1:45-46

2:33
Num 1:47

## 2. The role of the Levites
### Levites Appointed for Service

**3** This is the family line of Aaron and Moses as it was recorded when the LORD spoke to Moses on Mount Sinai: 2 The names of Aaron's sons were Nadab (the oldest), Abihu, Eleazar, and Ithamar. 3 These sons of Aaron were anointed and ordained to minister as priests. 4But Nadab and Abihu died in the LORD's presence in the wilderness of Sinai when they burned before the LORD the wrong kind of fire, different than he had commanded. Since they had no sons, this left only Eleazar and Ithamar to serve as priests with their father, Aaron.

5Then the LORD said to Moses, 6"Call forward the tribe of Levi, and present them to Aaron the priest to serve as his assistants. 7 They will serve Aaron and the whole community, per-

3:2
Num 26:60

3:3
Exod 28:41

3:4
Lev 10:1-2
Num 26:61

3:6
Num 8:6-22; 18:2-6

3:7
Num 3:11-12, 41;
8:16-18

**2:14-15** As in many Hebrew manuscripts, Samaritan Pentateuch, and Latin Vulgate (see also 1:14); most Hebrew manuscripts read *son of Reuel.*

---

**2:34** This must have been one of the biggest campsites the world has ever seen! It would have taken about 12 square miles to set up tents for just the 600,000 fighting men—not to mention the women and children. Moses must have had a difficult time managing such a group. In the early stages of the journey and at Mount Sinai, the people were generally obedient to both God and Moses. But when the people left Mount Sinai and traveled across the rugged wilderness, they began to complain, grumble, and disobey. Soon problems erupted, and Moses could no longer effectively manage the Israelites. The books of Exodus, Leviticus, and Numbers present a striking contrast between how much we can accomplish when we obey God and how little we can accomplish when we don't.

**3:4** See Leviticus 10:1, 2 for the story of Nadab and Abihu.

**3:5-13** At the time of the first Passover, God instructed every Israelite family to dedicate its firstborn son to him (Exodus 13:2). They were set apart to assist Moses and Aaron in ministering to the people. This was only a temporary measure, however. Here God chose all the men from the tribe of Levi to replace the firstborn sons from every Israelite tribe (3:40-51 and 8:16). These men, called Levites, were set apart to care for the Tabernacle and minister to the people. All the priests had to belong to the tribe of Levi, but not all Levites were priests. The Levites were to be 25 years old before entering service. They probably received five years of on-the-job training before being admitted to full service at age 30.

forming their sacred duties in and around the Tabernacle.* ⁸They will also maintain all the furnishings of the sacred tent,* serving in the Tabernacle on behalf of all the Israelites. ⁹Assign the Levites to Aaron and his sons. They have been given from among all the people of Israel to serve as their assistants. ¹⁰Appoint Aaron and his sons to carry out the duties of the priesthood. But any unauthorized person who goes too near the sanctuary must be put to death."

**3:10**
Num 1:51

¹¹And the LORD said to Moses, ¹²"Look, I have chosen the Levites from among the Israelites to serve as substitutes for all the firstborn sons of the people of Israel. The Levites belong to me, ¹³for all the firstborn males are mine. On the day I struck down all the firstborn sons of the Egyptians, I set apart for myself all the firstborn in Israel, both of people and of animals. They are mine; I am the LORD."

**3:12**
Num 3:41
**3:13**
Exod 13:2, 12, 15
Num 8:17

### Registration of the Levites

¹⁴The LORD spoke again to Moses in the wilderness of Sinai. He said, ¹⁵"Record the names of the members of the tribe of Levi by their families and clans. List every male who is one month old or older." ¹⁶So Moses listed them, just as the LORD had commanded.

**3:15**
Num 1:47

¹⁷Levi had three sons, whose names were Gershon, Kohath, and Merari.

¹⁸The clans descended from Gershon were named after two of his descendants, Libni and Shimei.

¹⁹The clans descended from Kohath were named after four of his descendants, Amram, Izhar, Hebron, and Uzziel.

²⁰The clans descended from Merari were named after two of his descendants, Mahli and Mushi.

These were the Levite clans, listed according to their family groups.

²¹The descendants of Gershon were composed of the clans descended from Libni and Shimei. ²²There were 7,500 males one month old or older among these Gershonite clans. ²³They were assigned the area to the west of the Tabernacle for their camp. ²⁴The leader of the Gershonite clans was Eliasaph son of Lael. ²⁵These two clans were responsible to care for the Tabernacle, including the sacred tent with its layers of coverings, the curtain at its entrance, ²⁶the curtains of the courtyard that surrounded the Tabernacle and altar, the curtain at the courtyard entrance, the ropes, and all the equipment related to their use.

**3:25**
Num 4:24-26

²⁷The descendants of Kohath were composed of the clans descended from Amram, Izhar, Hebron, and Uzziel. ²⁸There were 8,600* males one month old or older among these

**3:27**
Exod 6:18
1 Chr 26:23

**3:7** Hebrew *around the Tent of Meeting, doing service at the Tabernacle.*   **3:8** Hebrew *the Tent of Meeting;* also in 3:25.   **3:28** Some Greek manuscripts read *8,300;* see total in 3:39.

**ARRANGEMENT OF TRIBES AROUND THE TABERNACLE WHILE IN THE WILDERNESS**

DAN

ASHER                    NAPHTALI

BENJAMIN      Merari        ISSACHAR
              (Son of Levi)

EPHRAIM    Gershon    TABERNACLE    Moses    JUDAH
           (Son of Levi)            Aaron
                                    Sons of Aaron

MANASSEH      Kohath        ZEBULUN
              (Son of Levi)

GAD                      SIMEON

REUBEN

**3:10** Aaron and his descendants were appointed to the priesthood. There is a tremendous contrast between the priesthood of Aaron in the Old Testament and the priesthood of Christ in the New Testament. Aaron and his descendants were the only ones who could carry out the duties of the priests and approach God's dwelling place. Now that Christ is our High Priest—our intermediary with God—anyone who follows him is also called a priest (1 Peter 2:5, 9). Now all Christians may come into God's presence without fear because God's own Son encourages his followers to do so. We can put guilt behind us and experience forgiveness when we have a special relationship with God based on what Christ has done for us.

Kohathite clans. They were responsible for the care of the sanctuary, 29and they were assigned the area south of the Tabernacle for their camp. 30The leader of the Kohathite clans was Elizaphan son of Uzziel. 31These four clans were responsible for the care of the Ark, the table, the lampstand, the altars, the various articles used in the sanctuary, the inner curtain, and all the equipment related to their use. 32Eleazar, son of Aaron the priest, was the chief administrator over all the Levites, with special responsibility for the oversight of the sanctuary.

33The descendants of Merari were composed of the clans descended from Mahli and Mushi. 34There were 6,200 males one month old or older among these Merarite clans. 35They were assigned the area north of the Tabernacle for their camp. The leader of the Merarite clans was Zuriel son of Abihail. 36These two clans were responsible for the care of the frames supporting the Tabernacle, the crossbars, the pillars, the bases, and all the equipment related to their use. 37They were also responsible for the posts of the courtyard and all their bases, pegs, and ropes.

38The area in front of the Tabernacle, in the east toward the sunrise,* was reserved for the tents of Moses and of Aaron and his sons, who had the final responsibility for the sanctuary on behalf of the people of Israel. Anyone other than a priest or Levite who went too near the sanctuary was to be put to death.

39When Moses and Aaron counted the Levite clans at the LORD's command, the total number was 22,000 males one month old or older.

### Redeeming the Firstborn Sons

40Then the LORD said to Moses, "Now count all the firstborn sons in Israel who are one month old or older, and make a list of their names. 41The Levites must be reserved for me as substitutes for the firstborn sons of Israel; I am the LORD. And the Levites' livestock must be reserved for me as substitutes for the firstborn livestock of the whole nation of Israel."

42So Moses counted the firstborn sons of the people of Israel, just as the LORD had commanded. 43The number of firstborn sons who were one month old or older was 22,273.

44Then the LORD said to Moses, 45"Take the Levites as substitutes for the firstborn sons of the people of Israel. And take the livestock of the Levites as substitutes for the firstborn livestock of the people of Israel. The Levites belong to me; I am the LORD. 46There are 273 more firstborn sons of Israel than there are Levites. To redeem these extra firstborn sons, 47collect five pieces of silver* for each of them (each piece weighing the same as the sanctuary shekel, which equals twenty gerahs). 48Give the silver to Aaron and his sons as the redemption price for the extra firstborn sons."

49So Moses collected the silver for redeeming the firstborn sons of Israel who exceeded the number of Levites. 50He collected 1,365 pieces of silver* on behalf of these firstborn sons of Israel (each piece weighing the same as the sanctuary shekel). 51And Moses gave the silver for the redemption to Aaron and his sons, just as the LORD had commanded.

### Duties of the Kohathite Clan

**4** Then the LORD said to Moses and Aaron, 2"Record the names of the members of the clans and families of the Kohathite division of the tribe of Levi. 3List all the men between the ages of thirty and fifty who are eligible to serve in the Tabernacle.*

4"The duties of the Kohathites at the Tabernacle will relate to the most sacred objects. 5When the camp moves, Aaron and his sons must enter the Tabernacle first to take down the inner curtain and cover the Ark of the Covenant* with it. 6Then they must cover the inner curtain with fine goatskin leather and spread over that a single piece of blue cloth. Finally, they must put the carrying poles of the Ark in place.

**3:33** Exod 6:19

**3:38** Num 1:51; 3:10

**3:39** Num 26:62

**3:41** Num 3:12, 45

**3:43** Num 3:39

**3:45** Lev 11:44

**3:46** Exod 13:13, 15 Num 18:14-16

**3:47** Exod 30:13 Lev 27:1-8

**3:50** Num 3:46-48

**4:3** Num 4:23; 8:24-25

**4:6** Num 4:25

**3:38** Hebrew *toward the sunrise, in front of the Tent of Meeting.*   **3:47** Hebrew *5 shekels* [2 ounces or 57 grams].
**3:50** Hebrew *1,365 shekels* [34 pounds or 15.5 kilograms].   **4:3** Hebrew *the Tent of Meeting;* also in 4:4, 15, 23, 25, 28, 30, 31, 33, 35, 37, 39, 41, 43, 47.   **4:5** Or *Ark of the Testimony.*

---

**4:2ff** The Kohathites, Gershonites (4:21), and Merarites (4:29) were families of Levites who were assigned special tasks in Israel's worship. For the jobs described in this chapter, a Levite had to be between 30 and 50 years old. He was expected to carry out his duties as described here in every detail. In fact, failure to do so would mean death (4:20). This contrasted greatly from the religious practices of the Egyptians who could purchase amulets and potions. Their idols could be handled. The God of the Hebrews was not to be handled or reduced to common elements. He is greater than anything in his creation. Worshiping our holy God must not be taken lightly.

4:7
Exod 37:10-16
Lev 24:5-8

7"Next they must spread a blue cloth over the table where the Bread of the Presence is displayed, and on the cloth they will place the bowls, pans, jars, pitchers, and the special bread. 8They must spread a scarlet cloth over all of this, and finally a covering of fine goatskin leather on top of the scarlet cloth. Then they must insert the carrying poles into the table.

4:9
Exod 25:37-38

9"Next they must cover the lampstand with a blue cloth, along with its lamps, lamp snuffers, trays, and special jars of olive oil. 10Then they must cover the lampstand and its accessories with fine goatskin leather and place the bundle on a carrying frame.

11"Next they must spread a blue cloth over the gold incense altar and cover this cloth with fine goatskin leather. Then they must attach the carrying poles to the altar. 12They must take all the remaining furnishings of the sanctuary and wrap them in a blue cloth, cover them with fine goatskin leather, and place them on the carrying frame.

13"They must remove the ashes from the altar for sacrifices and cover the altar with a purple cloth. 14All the altar utensils—the firepans, meat forks, shovels, basins, and all the containers—must be placed on the cloth, and a covering of fine goatskin leather must be spread over them. Finally, they must put the carrying poles in place. 15The camp will be ready to move when Aaron and his sons have finished covering the sanctuary and all the sacred articles. The Kohathites will come and carry these things to the next destination. But they must not touch the sacred objects, or they will die. So these are the things from the Tabernacle that the Kohathites must carry.

4:15
Num 4:19-20

4:16
Exod 25:1-7;
30:22-34

16"Eleazar son of Aaron the priest will be responsible for the oil of the lampstand, the fragrant incense, the daily grain offering, and the anointing oil. In fact, Eleazar will be responsible for the entire Tabernacle and everything in it, including the sanctuary and its furnishings."

17Then the LORD said to Moses and Aaron, 18"Do not let the Kohathite clans be destroyed from among the Levites! 19This is what you must do so they will live and not die when they approach the most sacred objects. Aaron and his sons must always go in with them and assign a specific duty or load to each person. 20The Kohathites must never enter the sanctuary to look at the sacred objects for even a moment, or they will die."

## Duties of the Gershonite Clan

21And the LORD said to Moses, 22"Record the names of the members of the clans and families of the Gershonite division of the tribe of Levi. 23List all the men between the ages of thirty and fifty who are eligible to serve in the Tabernacle.

4:23
Num 4:3

4:25
Num 3:25-26

24"These Gershonite clans will be responsible for general service and carrying loads. 25They must carry the curtains of the Tabernacle, the Tabernacle itself with its coverings, the outer covering of fine goatskin leather, and the curtain for the Tabernacle entrance. 26They are also to carry the curtains for the courtyard walls that surround the Tabernacle and altar, the curtain across the courtyard entrance, the ropes, and all the equipment related to their use. The Gershonites are responsible for all these items. 27Aaron and his sons will direct the Gershonites regarding all their duties, whether it involves moving the equipment or doing other work. They must assign the Gershonites responsibility for the loads they are to carry. 28So these are the duties assigned to the Gershonite clans at the Tabernacle. They will be directly responsible to Ithamar son of Aaron the priest.

## Duties of the Merarite Clan

29"Now record the names of the members of the clans and families of the Merarite division of the tribe of Levi. 30List all the men between the ages of thirty and fifty who are eligible to serve in the Tabernacle.

4:30
Num 4:3

31"Their only duty at the Tabernacle will be to carry loads. They will carry the frames of the Tabernacle, the crossbars, the posts, and the bases; 32also the posts for the courtyard walls with their bases, pegs, and ropes; and all the accessories and everything else related to their use. Assign the various loads to each man by name. 33So these are the duties of the Merarite clans at the Tabernacle. They are directly responsible to Ithamar son of Aaron the priest."

---

**4:27, 28** The Gershonites could receive directions from any of Aaron's sons, but they were directly responsible to Ithamar only. The lines of authority and accountability were clearly communicated to all. As you function with others in service to God, make sure the lines of authority between you and those you work with are clearly understood. Good communication builds good relationships.

## Summary of the Registration

34So Moses, Aaron, and the other leaders of the community listed the members of the Kohathite division by their clans and families. 35The list included all the men between thirty and fifty years of age who were eligible for service in the Tabernacle, 36and the total number came to 2,750. 37So this was the total of all those from the Kohathite clans who were eligible to serve at the Tabernacle. Moses and Aaron listed them, just as the LORD had commanded through Moses.

38The Gershonite division was also listed by its clans and families. 39The list included all the men between thirty and fifty years of age who were eligible for service in the Tabernacle, 40and the total number came to 2,630. 41So this was the total of all those from the Gershonite clans who were eligible to serve at the Tabernacle. Moses and Aaron listed them, just as the LORD had commanded.

42The Merarite division was also listed by its clans and families. 43The list included all the men between thirty and fifty years of age who were eligible for service in the Tabernacle, 44and the total number came to 3,200. 45So this was the total of all those from the Merarite clans who were eligible for service. Moses and Aaron listed them, just as the LORD had commanded through Moses.

46So Moses, Aaron, and the leaders of Israel listed all the Levites by their clans and families. 47All the men between thirty and fifty years of age who were eligible for service in the Tabernacle and for its transportation 48numbered 8,580. 49When their names were recorded, as the LORD had commanded through Moses, each man was assigned his task and told what to carry.

And so the registration was completed, just as the LORD had commanded Moses.

## 3. The purity of the camp

**5** The LORD gave these instructions to Moses: 2"Command the people of Israel to remove from the camp anyone who has a skin disease* or a discharge, or who has become ceremonially unclean by touching a dead person. 3This command applies to men and women alike. Remove them so they will not defile the camp in which I live among them." 4So the Israelites did as the LORD had commanded Moses and removed such people from the camp.

5Then the LORD said to Moses, 6"Give the following instructions to the people of Israel: If any of the people—men or women—betray the LORD by doing wrong to another person, they are guilty. 7They must confess their sin and make full restitution for what they have done, adding an additional 20 percent and returning it to the person who was wronged. 8But if the person who was wronged is dead, and there are no near relatives to whom restitution can be made, the payment belongs to the LORD and must be given to the priest. Those who are guilty must also bring a ram as a sacrifice, and they will be purified and made right with the LORD.* 9All the sacred offerings that the Israelites bring to a priest will belong to him. 10Each priest may keep all the sacred donations that he receives."

## Protecting Marital Faithfulness

11And the LORD said to Moses, 12"Give the following instructions to the people of Israel.

"Suppose a man's wife goes astray, and she is unfaithful to her husband 13and has sex with another man, but neither her husband nor anyone else knows about it. She has defiled herself, even though there was no witness and she was not caught in the act. 14If her husband becomes jealous and is suspicious of his wife and needs to know whether or not she has defiled herself, 15the husband must bring his wife to the priest. He must also bring an offering of two quarts* of barley flour to be presented on her behalf. Do not mix it with

**4:46** Num 1:19

**4:49** Num 1:47-49

**5:2** Lev 13:3, 46; 15:2

**5:3** Lev 26:12 2 Cor 6:16

**5:7** Lev 5:5, 16; 6:4-5

**5:9** Lev 6:17

**5:12** Num 5:19-21, 29

**5:15** Ezek 29:16

**5:2** Traditionally rendered *leprosy*. The Hebrew word used here describes various skin diseases. **5:8** Or *bring a ram for atonement, which will make atonement for them.* **5:15** Hebrew *1/10 of an ephah* [2.2 liters].

---

**5:5-8** God included restitution, a unique concept for that day, as part of his law for Israel. When someone was robbed, the guilty person was required to restore the loss to the victim and pay an additional interest penalty. When we have wronged others, we ought to do more than apologize. We should look for ways to set matters right and, if possible, leave the victim even better off than when we harmed him or her. When we have been wronged, we should still seek restoration rather than striking out in revenge.

**5:11-31** This test for adultery served to remove a jealous husband's suspicion. Trust between husband and wife had to be completely eroded for a man to bring his wife to the priest for this type of test. Today priests and pastors help restore marriages by counseling couples who have lost faith in each other. Men and women should strengthen the bond of trust in marriage. Flirtatious and intimate communication with someone you're not married to can build suspicion and weaken trust. Guard your heart and guard your marriage in order to maintain trust and strengthen your bond with your spouse.

olive oil or frankincense, for it is a jealousy offering—an offering to prove whether or not she is guilty.

16"The priest will then present her to stand trial before the LORD. 17He must take some holy water in a clay jar and pour into it dust he has taken from the Tabernacle floor. 18When the priest has presented the woman before the LORD, he must unbind her hair and place in her hands the offering of proof—the jealousy offering to determine whether her husband's suspicions are justified. The priest will stand before her, holding the jar of bitter water that brings a curse to those who are guilty. 19The priest will then put the woman under oath and say to her, 'If no other man has had sex with you, and you have not gone astray and defiled yourself while under your husband's authority, may you be immune from the effects of this bitter water that brings on the curse. 20But if you have gone astray by being unfaithful to your husband, and have defiled yourself by having sex with another man—'

**5:21**
Josh 6:26
1 Sam 4:24
Neh 10:29

21"At this point the priest must put the woman under oath by saying, 'May the people know that the LORD's curse is upon you when he makes you infertile, causing your womb to shrivel* and your abdomen to swell. 22Now may this water that brings the curse enter your body and cause your abdomen to swell and your womb to shrivel.*' And the woman will be required to say, 'Yes, let it be so.' 23And the priest will write these curses on a piece of leather and wash them off into the bitter water. 24He will make the woman drink the bitter water that brings on the curse. When the water enters her body, it will cause bitter suffering if she is guilty.

**5:26**
Lev 2:2
**5:27**
Jer 29:18; 42:18

25"The priest will take the jealousy offering from the woman's hand, lift it up before the LORD, and carry it to the altar. 26He will take a handful of the flour as a token portion and burn it on the altar, and he will require the woman to drink the water. 27If she has defiled herself by being unfaithful to her husband, the water that brings on the curse will cause bitter suffering. Her abdomen will swell and her womb will shrink,* and her name will become a curse among her people. 28But if she has not defiled herself and is pure, then she will be unharmed and will still be able to have children.

**5:29**
Num 5:11

29"This is the ritual law for dealing with suspicion. If a woman goes astray and defiles herself while under her husband's authority, 30or if a man becomes jealous and is suspicious that his wife has been unfaithful, the husband must present his wife before the LORD, and the priest will apply this entire ritual law to her. 31The husband will be innocent of any guilt in this matter, but his wife will be held accountable for her sin."

## Nazirite Laws

**6** Then the LORD said to Moses, 2"Give the following instructions to the people of Israel. "If any of the people, either men or women, take the special vow of a Nazirite, setting themselves apart to the LORD in a special way, 3they must give up wine and other alcoholic drinks. They must not use vinegar made from wine or from other alcoholic drinks, they must not drink fresh grape juice, and they must not eat grapes or raisins. 4As long as they are bound by their Nazirite vow, they are not allowed to eat or drink anything that comes from a grapevine—not even the grape seeds or skins.

**6:2**
Judg 13:4-5; 16:17
Amos 2:11-12
**6:3**
Luke 1:15

5"They must never cut their hair throughout the time of their vow, for they are holy and set apart to the LORD. Until the time of their vow has been fulfilled, they must let their hair grow long. 6And they must not go near a dead body during the entire period of their vow to the LORD. 7Even if the dead person is their own father, mother, brother, or sister, they must not defile themselves, for the hair on their head is the symbol of their separation to God. 8This requirement applies as long as they are set apart to the LORD.

**6:5**
1 Sam 1:11
**6:6**
Lev 21:1-3
Num 19:11-22

9"If someone falls dead beside them, the hair they have dedicated will be defiled. They must wait for seven days and then shave their heads. Then they will be cleansed from their defilement. 10On the eighth day they must bring two turtledoves or two young pigeons to

**6:9**
Num 6:18

5:21 Hebrew *when he causes your thigh to waste away.*   5:22 Hebrew *and your thigh to waste away.*   5:27 Hebrew *and her thigh will waste away.*

---

**6:1, 2** In Moses' day, a personal vow was as binding as a written contract. It was one thing to say you would do something, but it was considered much more serious when you made a solemn vow to do it. God instituted the Nazirite vow for people who wanted to devote some time exclusively to serving him. This vow could be taken for as little as 30 days or as long as a lifetime. It was voluntary, with one exception—parents could take the vow

for their young children, making them Nazirites for life. The vow included three distinct restrictions: (1) He must abstain from wine and fermented drink; (2) the hair could not be cut, and the beard could not be shaved; (3) touching a dead body was prohibited. The purpose of the Nazirite vow was to raise up a group of leaders devoted completely to God. Samson, Samuel, and John the Baptist were probably Nazirites for life.

the priest at the entrance of the Tabernacle.* [11]The priest will offer one of the birds for a sin offering and the other for a burnt offering. In this way, he will purify them* from the guilt they incurred through contact with the dead body. Then they must reaffirm their commitment and let their hair begin to grow again. [12]The days of their vow that were completed before their defilement no longer count. They must rededicate themselves to the LORD as a Nazirite for the full term of their vow, and each must bring a one-year-old male lamb for a guilt offering.

**6:11**
Lev 5:7; 12:6-8

**6:12**
Lev 5:6

[13]"This is the ritual law for Nazirites. At the conclusion of their time of separation as Nazirites, they must each go to the entrance of the Tabernacle [14]and offer their sacrifices to the LORD: a one-year-old male lamb without defect for a burnt offering, a one-year-old female lamb without defect for a sin offering, a ram without defect for a peace offering, [15]a basket of bread made without yeast—cakes of choice flour mixed with olive oil and wafers spread with olive oil—along with their prescribed grain offerings and liquid offerings. [16]The priest will present these offerings before the LORD: first the sin offering and the burnt offering; [17]then the ram for a peace offering, along with the basket of bread made without yeast. The priest must also present the prescribed grain offering and liquid offering to the LORD.

**6:14**
Lev 14:10

**6:15**
Num 15:1-7

[18]"Then the Nazirites will shave their heads at the entrance of the Tabernacle. They will take the hair that had been dedicated and place it on the fire beneath the peace-offering sacrifice. [19]After the Nazirite's head has been shaved, the priest will take for each of them the boiled shoulder of the ram, and he will take from the basket a cake and a wafer made without yeast. He will put them all into the Nazirite's hands. [20]Then the priest will lift them up as a special offering before the LORD. These are holy portions for the priest, along with the breast of the special offering and the thigh of the sacred offering that are lifted up before the LORD. After this ceremony the Nazirites may again drink wine.

**6:18**
Num 6:9

**6:20**
Lev 7:28-34

[21]"This is the ritual law of the Nazirites, who vow to bring these offerings to the LORD. They may also bring additional offerings if they can afford it. And they must be careful to do whatever they vowed when they set themselves apart as Nazirites."

## The Priestly Blessing

[22]Then the LORD said to Moses, [23]"Tell Aaron and his sons to bless the people of Israel with this special blessing:

**6:23**
Deut 21:5
1 Chr 23:13

[24] 'May the LORD bless you
      and protect you.
[25] May the LORD smile on you
      and be gracious to you.
[26] May the LORD show you his favor
      and give you his peace.'

**6:24**
Deut 28:3-6

**6:25**
Ps 80:3, 7, 19

**6:26**
Pss 4:6; 29:11;
44:3

[27]Whenever Aaron and his sons bless the people of Israel in my name, I myself will bless them."

## Offerings of Dedication

**7** On the day Moses set up the Tabernacle, he anointed it and set it apart as holy. He also anointed and set apart all its furnishings and the altar with its utensils. [2]Then the leaders of Israel—the tribal leaders who had registered the troops—came and brought their offerings. [3]Together they brought six large wagons and twelve oxen. There was a wagon for every two leaders and an ox for each leader. They presented these to the LORD in front of the Tabernacle.

**7:1**
Exod 40:9-11

**7:2**
Num 1:2-16

[4]Then the LORD said to Moses, [5]"Receive their gifts, and use these oxen and wagons for

**6:10** Hebrew *the Tent of Meeting;* also in 6:13, 18.   **6:11** Or *make atonement for them.*

---

**6:24-26** A blessing was one way of asking for God's divine favor to rest upon others. The ancient blessing in these verses helps us understand what a blessing was supposed to do. Its five parts conveyed hope that God would (1) bless and protect them; (2) smile on them (be pleased); (3) be gracious (merciful and compassionate); (4) show his favor toward them (give his approval); (5) give peace. When you ask God to bless others

or yourself, you are asking him to do these five things. The blessing you offer will not only help the one receiving it, it will also demonstrate love, encourage others, and provide a model of caring for others.

**7:1ff** After the Tabernacle was set up, anointed, and consecrated, the leaders of the 12 tribes brought gifts and offerings for its use and maintenance. All of the people participated—it was everyone's Tabernacle.

transporting the Tabernacle.* Distribute them among the Levites according to the work they have to do." 6So Moses took the wagons and oxen and presented them to the Levites. 7He gave two wagons and four oxen to the Gershonite division for their work, 8and he gave four wagons and eight oxen to the Merarite division for their work. All their work was done under the leadership of Ithamar son of Aaron the priest. 9But he gave none of the wagons or oxen to the Kohathite division, since they were required to carry the sacred objects of the Tabernacle on their shoulders.

10The leaders also presented dedication gifts for the altar at the time it was anointed. They each placed their gifts before the altar. 11The LORD said to Moses, "Let one leader bring his gift each day for the dedication of the altar."

12On the first day Nahshon son of Amminadab, leader of the tribe of Judah, presented his offering.

13His offering consisted of a silver platter weighing 3¼ pounds and a silver basin weighing 1¾ pounds* (as measured by the weight of the sanctuary shekel). These were both filled with grain offerings of choice flour moistened with olive oil. 14He also brought a gold container weighing four ounces,* which was filled with incense. 15He brought a young bull, a ram, and a one-year-old male lamb for a burnt offering, 16and a male goat for a sin offering. 17For a peace offering he brought two bulls, five rams, five male goats, and five one-year-old male lambs. This was the offering brought by Nahshon son of Amminadab.

18On the second day Nethanel son of Zuar, leader of the tribe of Issachar, presented his offering.

19His offering consisted of a silver platter weighing 3¼ pounds and a silver basin weighing 1¾ pounds (as measured by the weight of the sanctuary shekel). These were both filled with grain offerings of choice flour moistened with olive oil. 20He also brought a gold container weighing four ounces, which was filled with incense. 21He brought a young bull, a ram, and a one-year-old male lamb for a burnt offering, 22and a male goat for a sin offering. 23For a peace offering he brought two bulls, five rams, five male goats, and five one-year-old male lambs. This was the offering brought by Nethanel son of Zuar.

24On the third day Eliab son of Helon, leader of the tribe of Zebulun, presented his offering. 25His offering consisted of a silver platter weighing 3¼ pounds and a silver basin weighing 1¾ pounds (as measured by the weight of the sanctuary shekel). These were both filled with grain offerings of choice flour moistened with olive oil. 26He also brought a gold container weighing four ounces, which was filled with incense. 27He brought a young bull, a ram, and a one-year-old male lamb for a burnt offering, 28and a male goat for a sin offering. 29For a peace offering he brought two bulls, five rams, five male goats, and five one-year-old male lambs. This was the offering brought by Eliab son of Helon.

30On the fourth day Elizur son of Shedeur, leader of the tribe of Reuben, presented his offering.

31His offering consisted of a silver platter weighing 3¼ pounds and a silver basin weighing 1¾ pounds (as measured by the weight of the sanctuary shekel). These were both filled with grain offerings of choice flour moistened with olive oil. 32He also brought a gold container weighing four ounces, which was filled with incense. 33He brought a young bull, a ram, and a one-year-old male lamb for a burnt offering, 34and a male goat for a sin offering. 35For a peace offering he brought two bulls, five rams, five male goats, and five one-year-old male lambs. This was the offering brought by Elizur son of Shedeur.

36On the fifth day Shelumiel son of Zurishaddai, leader of the tribe of Simeon, presented his offering.

37His offering consisted of a silver platter weighing 3¼ pounds and a silver basin weighing 1¾ pounds (as measured by the weight of the sanctuary shekel). These were both filled with grain offerings of choice flour moistened with olive oil. 38He also brought a gold container weighing four ounces, which was filled with incense. 39He

**7:7**
Num 4:26
**7:8**
Num 4:33
**7:9**
Num 4:5-15

**7:13**
Num 3:47

**7:14**
Exod 30:34

**7:16**
Lev 4:3
**7:17**
Lev 3:1

**7:18**
Num 1:8

**7:29**
Lev 7:32

**7:30**
Num 1:5

**7:34**
Heb 10:4

**7:36**
Num 1:6

7:5 Hebrew *the Tent of Meeting;* also in 7:89.   7:13 Hebrew *silver platter weighing 130 shekels* [1.5 kilograms] *and a silver basin weighing 70 shekels* [800 grams]; also in 7:19, 25, 31, 37, 43, 49, 55, 61, 67, 73, 79, 85.
7:14 Hebrew *10 shekels* [114 grams]; also in 7:20, 26, 32, 38, 44, 50, 56, 62, 68, 74, 80, 86.

brought a young bull, a ram, and a one-year-old male lamb for a burnt offering, 40and a male goat for a sin offering. 41For a peace offering he brought two bulls, five rams, five male goats, and five one-year-old male lambs. This was the offering brought by Shelumiel son of Zurishaddai.

42On the sixth day Eliasaph son of Deuel, leader of the tribe of Gad, presented his offering. 43His offering consisted of a silver platter weighing 3¼ pounds and a silver basin weighing 1¾ pounds (as measured by the weight of the sanctuary shekel). These were both filled with grain offerings of choice flour moistened with olive oil. 44He also brought a gold container weighing four ounces, which was filled with incense. 45He brought a young bull, a ram, and a one-year-old male lamb for a burnt offering, 46and a male goat for a sin offering. 47For a peace offering he brought two bulls, five rams, five male goats, and five one-year-old male lambs. This was the offering brought by Eliasaph son of Deuel.

**7:42** Num 1:14

48On the seventh day Elishama son of Ammihud, leader of the tribe of Ephraim, presented his offering. 49His offering consisted of a silver platter weighing 3¼ pounds and a silver basin weighing 1¾ pounds (as measured by the weight of the sanctuary shekel). These were both filled with grain offerings of choice flour moistened with olive oil. 50He also brought a gold container weighing four ounces, which was filled with incense. 51He brought a young bull, a ram, and a one-year-old male lamb for a burnt offering, 52and a male goat for a sin offering. 53For a peace offering he brought two bulls, five rams, five male goats, and five one-year-old male lambs. This was the offering brought by Elishama son of Ammihud.

**7:48** Num 1:10

**7:52** Heb 10:4

54On the eighth day Gamaliel son of Pedahzur, leader of the tribe of Manasseh, presented his offering. 55His offering consisted of a silver platter weighing 3¼ pounds and a silver basin weighing 1¾ pounds (as measured by the weight of the sanctuary shekel). These were both filled with grain offerings of choice flour moistened with olive oil. 56He also brought a gold container weighing four ounces, which was filled with incense. 57He brought a young bull, a ram, and a one-year-old male lamb for a burnt offering, 58and a male goat for a sin offering. 59For a peace offering he brought two bulls, five rams, five male goats, and five one-year-old male lambs. This was the offering brought by Gamaliel son of Pedahzur.

60On the ninth day Abidan son of Gideoni, leader of the tribe of Benjamin, presented his offering. 61His offering consisted of a silver platter weighing 3¼ pounds and a silver basin weighing 1¾ pounds (as measured by the weight of the sanctuary shekel). These were both filled with grain offerings of choice flour moistened with olive oil. 62He also brought a gold container weighing four ounces, which was filled with incense. 63He brought a young bull, a ram, and a one-year-old male lamb for a burnt offering, 64and a male goat for a sin offering. 65For a peace offering he brought two bulls, five rams, five male goats, and five one-year-old male lambs. This was the offering brought by Abidan son of Gideoni.

**7:60** Num 1:11

66On the tenth day Ahiezer son of Ammishaddai, leader of the tribe of Dan, presented his offering. 67His offering consisted of a silver platter weighing 3¼ pounds and a silver basin weighing 1¾ pounds (as measured by the weight of the sanctuary shekel). These were both filled with grain offerings of choice flour moistened with olive oil. 68He also brought a gold container weighing four ounces, which was filled with incense. 69He brought a young bull, a ram, and a one-year-old male lamb for a burnt offering, 70and a male goat for a sin offering. 71For a peace offering he brought two bulls, five rams, five male goats, and five one-year-old male lambs. This was the offering brought by Ahiezer son of Ammishaddai.

**7:66** Num 1:12

**7:70** Heb 10:4

72On the eleventh day Pagiel son of Ocran, leader of the tribe of Asher, presented his offering. 73His offering consisted of a silver platter weighing 3¼ pounds and a silver basin weighing 1¾ pounds (as measured by the weight of the sanctuary shekel). These were both filled with grain offerings of choice flour moistened with olive oil. 74He also brought a gold container weighing four ounces, which was filled with incense. 75He brought a young bull, a ram, and a one-year-old male lamb for a burnt offering, 76and a male goat for a sin offering. 77For a peace offering he brought two bulls, five rams, five male goats, and five one-year-old male lambs. This was the offering brought by Pagiel son of Ocran.

**7:78**
Num 1:15

78On the twelfth day Ahira son of Enan, leader of the tribe of Naphtali, presented his offering.

79His offering consisted of a silver platter weighing 3¼ pounds and a silver basin weighing 1¾ pounds (as measured by the weight of the sanctuary shekel). These were both filled with grain offerings of choice flour moistened with olive oil. 80He also brought a gold container weighing four ounces, which was filled with incense. 81He brought a young bull, a ram, and a one-year-old male lamb for a burnt offering, 82and a male goat for a sin offering. 83For a peace offering he brought two bulls, five rams, five male goats, and five one-year-old male lambs. This was the offering brought by Ahira son of Enan.

**7:84**
Num 7:10

84So this was the dedication offering brought by the leaders of Israel at the time the altar was anointed: twelve silver platters, twelve silver basins, and twelve gold incense containers. 85Each silver platter weighed 3¼ pounds, and each silver basin weighed 1¾ pounds. The total weight of the silver was 60 pounds* (as measured by the weight of the sanctuary shekel). 86Each of the twelve gold containers that was filled with incense weighed four ounces (as measured by the weight of the sanctuary shekel). The total weight of the gold was three pounds.* 87 Twelve young bulls, twelve rams, and twelve one-year-old male lambs were donated for the burnt offerings, along with their prescribed grain offerings. Twelve male goats were brought for the sin offerings. 88Twenty-four bulls, sixty rams, sixty male goats, and sixty one-year-old male lambs were donated for the peace offerings. This was the dedication offering for the altar after it was anointed.

**7:88**
Num 7:1, 10

89 Whenever Moses went into the Tabernacle to speak with the LORD, he heard the voice speaking to him from between the two cherubim above the Ark's cover—the place of atonement—that rests on the Ark of the Covenant.* The LORD spoke to him from there.

**7:89**
Exod 25:21-22;
33:9-11
Pss 80:1; 99:1

## Preparing the Lamps

**8:2**
Exod 25:37

**8** The LORD said to Moses, 2"Give Aaron the following instructions: When you set up the seven lamps in the lampstand, place them so their light shines forward in front of the lampstand." 3 So Aaron did this. He set up the seven lamps so they reflected their light forward, just as the LORD had commanded Moses. 4The entire lampstand, from its base to its decorative blossoms, was made of beaten gold. It was built according to the exact design the LORD had shown Moses.

**8:4**
Exod 25:18,
31-36, 40

## The Levites Dedicated

5Then the LORD said to Moses, 6"Now set the Levites apart from the rest of the people of Israel and make them ceremonially clean. 7Do this by sprinkling them with the water of purification, and have them shave their entire body and wash their clothing. Then they will be ceremonially clean. 8Have them bring a young bull and a grain offering of choice flour moistened with olive oil, along with a second young bull for a sin offering. 9 Then assemble the whole community of Israel, and present the Levites at the entrance of the Tabernacle.* 10When you present the Levites before the LORD, the people of Israel must

**8:7**
Lev 14:8-9
Num 19:9, 17-18
**8:8**
Num 15:3-12

**8:10**
Lev 3:2

7:85 Hebrew *2,400 shekels* [27.6 kilograms].    7:86 Hebrew *120 shekels* [1.4 kilograms].    7:89 Or *Ark of the Testimony.*    8:9 Hebrew *the Tent of Meeting;* also in 8:15, 19, 22, 24, 26.

---

**7:89** Imagine hearing the very voice of God! Moses must have trembled at the sound. Yet we have God's words recorded for us in the Bible, and we should have no less reverence and awe for them. God sometimes spoke directly to his people to tell them the proper way to live. The Bible records these conversations to give us insights into God's character. How tragic when we take these very words of God lightly. Like Moses, we have the privilege of talking to God, but God answers us differently—through his written Word and the guidance of his Holy Spirit.

To receive this guidance, we need to seek to know God as Moses did.

**8:1-4** The lamps provided light for the priests as they carried out their duties. The light was also an expression of God's presence. Jesus said, "I am the light of the world" (John 8:12). The golden lampstand is still one of the major symbols of the Jewish faith.

lay their hands on them. [11]Raising his hands, Aaron must then present the Levites to the LORD as a special offering from the people of Israel, thus dedicating them to the LORD's service.

[12]"Next the Levites will lay their hands on the heads of the young bulls. Present one as a sin offering and the other as a burnt offering to the LORD, to purify the Levites and make them right with the LORD.* [13]Then have the Levites stand in front of Aaron and his sons, and raise your hands and present them as a special offering to the LORD. [14]In this way, you will set the Levites apart from the rest of the people of Israel, and the Levites will belong to me. [15]After this, they may go into the Tabernacle to do their work, because you have purified them and presented them as a special offering.

[16]"Of all the people of Israel, the Levites are reserved for me. I have claimed them for myself in place of all the firstborn sons of the Israelites; I have taken the Levites as their substitutes. [17]For all the firstborn males among the people of Israel are mine, both of people and of animals. I set them apart for myself on the day I struck down all the firstborn sons of the Egyptians. [18]Yes, I have claimed the Levites in place of all the firstborn sons of Israel. [19]And of all the Israelites, I have assigned the Levites to Aaron and his sons. They will serve in the Tabernacle on behalf of the Israelites and make sacrifices to purify* the people so no plague will strike them when they approach the sanctuary."

[20]So Moses, Aaron, and the whole community of Israel dedicated the Levites, carefully following all the LORD's instructions to Moses. [21]The Levites purified themselves from sin and washed their clothes, and Aaron lifted them up and presented them to the LORD as a special offering. He then offered a sacrifice to purify them and make them right with the LORD.* [22]After that the Levites went into the Tabernacle to perform their duties, assisting Aaron and his sons. So they carried out all the commands that the LORD gave Moses concerning the Levites.

[23]The LORD also instructed Moses, [24]"This is the rule the Levites must follow: They must begin serving in the Tabernacle at the age of twenty-five, [25]and they must retire at the age of fifty. [26]After retirement they may assist their fellow Levites by serving as guards at the Tabernacle, but they may not officiate in the service. This is how you must assign duties to the Levites."

### The Second Passover

**9** A year after Israel's departure from Egypt, the LORD spoke to Moses in the wilderness of Sinai. In the first month* of that year he said, [2]"Tell the Israelites to celebrate the Passover at the prescribed time, [3]at twilight on the fourteenth day of the first month.* Be sure to follow all my decrees and regulations concerning this celebration."

[4]So Moses told the people to celebrate the Passover [5]in the wilderness of Sinai as twilight fell on the fourteenth day of the month. And they celebrated the festival there, just as the LORD had commanded Moses. [6]But some of the men had been ceremonially defiled by touching a dead body, so they could not celebrate the Passover that day. They came to Moses and Aaron that day [7]and said, "We have become ceremonially unclean by touching a dead body. But why should we be prevented from presenting the LORD's offering at the proper time with the rest of the Israelites?"

[8]Moses answered, "Wait here until I have received instructions for you from the LORD."

[9]This was the LORD's reply to Moses. [10]"Give the following instructions to the people of Israel: If any of the people now or in future generations are ceremonially unclean at

*Marginal cross-references:*
**8:12** Exod 29:10-14
**8:14** Num 3:12
**8:16** Num 3:13
**8:17** Exod 13:12-13
**8:19** Num 1:53
**8:24** Num 4:3
**9:2** Exod 12:1-6
**9:5** Josh 5:10
**9:6** Num 19:11-22
**9:8** Exod 18:15

**8:12** Or to make atonement for the Levites.   **8:19** Or make atonement for.   **8:21** Or then made atonement for them to purify them.   **9:1** The first month of the ancient Hebrew lunar calendar usually occurs within the months of March and April.   **9:3** This day in the ancient Hebrew lunar calendar occurred in late March, April, or early May.

---

**8:25, 26** Why were the Levites supposed to retire at age 50? The reasons were probably more practical than theological. (1) Moving the Tabernacle and its furniture through the wilderness required strength. The younger men were more suited for the work of lifting the heavy articles. (2) The Levites over 50 did not stop working altogether. They were allowed to assist with various light duties in the Tabernacle. This helped the younger men assume more responsibilities, and it allowed the older men to be in a position to advise and counsel them.

**9:2** This is the second Passover. The first was instituted in Egypt and recorded in Exodus 12. Passover and the Festival

of Unleavened Bread were an eight-day religious observance (Leviticus 23:5, 6) commemorating the Israelites' escape from slavery in Egypt by God's power.

**9:6-12** Several men came to Moses because of the predicament they faced: They were "ceremonially defiled" because of contact with a dead body (or entering the home of a person who had died), and this prevented them from participating in the Passover meal. Notice that God did not adjust the requirements of the Passover. The standards of holiness were maintained, and the men were not allowed to participate. But God did make an exception and allowed the men to celebrate the Passover at a later date.

9:11
Exod 12:8

9:12
Exod 12:10, 43, 46
†John 19:36

9:13
Exod 12:15
Num 15:30-31

9:14
Exod 12:48-49

Passover time because of touching a dead body, or if they are on a journey and cannot be present at the ceremony, they may still celebrate the LORD's Passover. ¹¹They must offer the Passover sacrifice one month later, at twilight on the fourteenth day of the second month.* They must eat the Passover lamb at that time with bitter salad greens and bread made without yeast. ¹²They must not leave any of the lamb until the next morning, and they must not break any of its bones. They must follow all the normal regulations concerning the Passover.

¹³"But those who neglect to celebrate the Passover at the regular time, even though they are ceremonially clean and not away on a trip, will be cut off from the community of Israel. If they fail to present the LORD's offering at the proper time, they will suffer the consequences of their guilt. ¹⁴And if foreigners living among you want to celebrate the Passover to the LORD, they must follow these same decrees and regulations. The same laws apply both to native-born Israelites and to the foreigners living among you."

## 4. Receiving guidance for the journey
### The Fiery Cloud

9:15
Exod 13:21-22;
40:2, 17, 34
Neh 9:12, 19
Ps 78:14

9:17
Exod 40:36-38
Num 10:11, 33-34

9:18
1 Cor 10:1

9:22
Exod 40:36-37

¹⁵On the day the Tabernacle was set up, the cloud covered it.* But from evening until morning the cloud over the Tabernacle looked like a pillar of fire. ¹⁶This was the regular pattern— at night the cloud that covered the Tabernacle had the appearance of fire. ¹⁷Whenever the cloud lifted from over the sacred tent, the people of Israel would break camp and follow it. And wherever the cloud settled, the people of Israel would set up camp. ¹⁸In this way, they traveled and camped at the LORD's command wherever he told them to go. Then they remained in their camp as long as the cloud stayed over the Tabernacle. ¹⁹If the cloud remained over the Tabernacle for a long time, the Israelites stayed and performed their duty to the LORD. ²⁰Sometimes the cloud would stay over the Tabernacle for only a few days, so the people would stay for only a few days, as the LORD commanded. Then at the LORD's command they would break camp and move on. ²¹Sometimes the cloud stayed only overnight and lifted the next morning. But day or night, when the cloud lifted, the people broke camp and moved on. ²²Whether the cloud stayed above the Tabernacle for two days, a month, or a year, the people of Israel stayed in camp and did not move on. But as soon as it lifted, they broke camp and moved on. ²³So they camped or traveled at the LORD's command, and they did whatever the LORD told them through Moses.

### The Silver Trumpets

10:3
Jer 4:5

**10** Now the LORD said to Moses, ²"Make two trumpets of hammered silver for calling the community to assemble and for signaling the breaking of camp. ³When both trumpets are blown, everyone must gather before you at the entrance of the Tabernacle.*

9:11 This day in the ancient Hebrew lunar calendar occurred in late April, May, or early June.   9:15 Hebrew *covered the Tabernacle, the Tent of the Testimony.*   10:3 Hebrew *Tent of Meeting.*

---

This upheld the sacred requirements while allowing the men to participate in the feast—a duty for all Israelite men. Sometimes we face predicaments where the most obvious solution might cause us to compromise God's standards. Like Moses, we should use wisdom and prayer to reach a workable solution.

**9:14** God said regarding foreigners and the Passover, "They must follow these same decrees and regulations." This principle designed for foreigners doesn't mean we mandate our religion to our neighbors, but in our homes we should live out our convictions. When we have guests in our homes, whether visitors or family, we may be tempted to change or water down our Christian practices. If family devotions, attending church, and mealtime prayers are your practices, don't change these when you have guests. Holidays such as Christmas and Easter should not be reduced to nothing more than society's expressions. Further, you should maintain your family standards even when guests visit— for example, unmarried couples who are guests should not be allowed to sleep together. Maintain your Christian standards and principles. You never know what influence you may have on the guests in your home.

**9:15-22** A pillar of cloud by day and a pillar of fire by night guided and protected the Israelites as they traveled across the wilderness. Some have said this pillar may have been a burning bowl of pitch whose smoke was visible during the day and whose fire could be seen at night. However, a bowl of pitch would not have lifted itself up and moved ahead of the people, and the Bible is clear that the cloud and fire moved in accordance with the will of God. The cloud and the fire were not merely natural phenomena; they were the vehicle of God's presence and the visible evidence of his moving and directing his people.

**9:23** The Israelites traveled and camped as God guided. When you follow God's guidance, you know you are where God wants you, whether you're moving or staying in one place. You are physically somewhere right now. Instead of praying, "God, what do you want me to do next?" ask, "God, what do you want me to do while I'm right here?" Direction from God is not just for your next big move. He has a purpose in placing you where you are right now. Begin to understand God's purpose for your life by discovering what he wants you to do now!

**10:1-10** The two silver trumpets were used to coordinate the tribes as they moved through the wilderness. To keep so many people in tight formations required clear communication and control. Trumpet blasts also reminded Israel of God's protection over them.

⁴But if only one trumpet is blown, then only the leaders—the heads of the clans of Israel—must present themselves to you.

⁵"When you sound the signal to move on, the tribes camped on the east side of the Tabernacle must break camp and move forward. ⁶When you sound the signal a second time, the tribes camped on the south will follow. You must sound short blasts as the signal for moving on. ⁷But when you call the people to an assembly, blow the trumpets with a different signal. ⁸Only the priests, Aaron's descendants, are allowed to blow the trumpets. This is a permanent law for you, to be observed from generation to generation.

⁹"When you arrive in your own land and go to war against your enemies who attack you, sound the alarm with the trumpets. Then the LORD your God will remember you and rescue you from your enemies. ¹⁰Blow the trumpets in times of gladness, too, sounding them at your annual festivals and at the beginning of each month. And blow the trumpets over your burnt offerings and peace offerings. The trumpets will remind the LORD your God of his covenant with you. I am the LORD your God."

**10:5**
Num 10:14

**10:7**
Joel 2:1

**10:8**
Num 31:6
Josh 6:3-9
2 Chr 5:11-12

**10:9**
Judg 2:18
Ps 106:4

**10:10**
Lev 23:24
Num 29:1
Ps 81:3-5

## B. FIRST APPROACH TO THE PROMISED LAND (10:11—14:45)

As the Israelites approached the Promised Land, Moses sent leaders to scout out the land and its people. But the scouts returned with a discouraging report—"It is indeed a bountiful country. . . . But the people living there are powerful. . . . We can't go up against them!" Although Joshua and Caleb disagreed, the Israelites had already made up their minds and began to complain. As punishment for their lack of faith, God condemned them to wander in the wilderness for 40 years. Our obedience must be complete and timely.

### 1. The people complain

*The Israelites Leave Sinai*

¹¹In the second year after Israel's departure from Egypt—on the twentieth day of the second month*—the cloud lifted from the Tabernacle of the Covenant.* ¹²So the Israelites set out from the wilderness of Sinai and traveled on from place to place until the cloud stopped in the wilderness of Paran.

¹³When the people set out for the first time, following the instructions the LORD had given through Moses, ¹⁴Judah's troops led the way. They marched behind their banner, and their leader was Nahshon son of Amminadab. ¹⁵They were joined by the troops of the tribe of Issachar, led by Nethanel son of Zuar, ¹⁶and the troops of the tribe of Zebulun, led by Eliab son of Helon.

¹⁷Then the Tabernacle was taken down, and the Gershonite and Merarite divisions of the Levites were next in the line of march, carrying the Tabernacle with them. ¹⁸Reuben's troops went next, marching behind their banner. Their leader was Elizur son of Shedeur. ¹⁹They were joined by the troops of the tribe of Simeon, led by Shelumiel son of Zurishaddai, ²⁰and the troops of the tribe of Gad, led by Eliasaph son of Deuel.

**10:11**
Exod 40:17

**10:12**
Gen 21:20-21
Num 12:16

**10:13**
Deut 1:6

**10:14**
Num 2:3-31

**10:17**
Num 4:21-23

**10:18**
Num 2:10-16

**10:11a** This day in the ancient Hebrew lunar calendar occurred in late April, May, or early June.   **10:11b** Or *Tabernacle of the Testimony.*

---

**10:21** Those who travel, move, or face new challenges know what it is to be uprooted. Life is full of changes, and few things remain stable. The Israelites were constantly moving through the wilderness. They were able to handle change only because God's presence in the Tabernacle was always with them. The portable Tabernacle signified God and his people moving together. For us, stability does not mean lack of change, but moving with God in every circumstance.

**ISRAEL'S DEPARTURE FROM SINAI**
It has been two years since Israel left Egypt. Having received God's travel instructions through Moses, Israel set out from Mount Sinai into the wilderness of Paran on their way toward the Promised Land.

**10:21**
Num 4:1-20

**10:22**
Num 2:3-31

²¹Next came the Kohathite division of the Levites, carrying the sacred objects from the Tabernacle. Before they arrived at the next camp, the Tabernacle would already be set up at its new location. ²²Ephraim's troops went next, marching behind their banner. Their leader was Elishama son of Ammihud. ²³They were joined by the troops of the tribe of Manasseh, led by Gamaliel son of Pedahzur, ²⁴and the troops of the tribe of Benjamin, led by Abidan son of Gideoni.

²⁵Dan's troops went last, marching behind their banner and serving as the rear guard for all the tribal camps. Their leader was Ahiezer son of Ammishaddai. ²⁶They were joined by the troops of the tribe of Asher, led by Pagiel son of Ocran, ²⁷and the troops of the tribe of Naphtali, led by Ahira son of Enan.

²⁸This was the order in which the Israelites marched, division by division.

**10:29**
Exod 2:18-21; 3:1
Judg 4:11

²⁹One day Moses said to his brother-in-law, Hobab son of Reuel the Midianite, "We are on our way to the place the LORD promised us, for he said, 'I will give it to you.' Come with us and we will treat you well, for the LORD has promised wonderful blessings for Israel!"

³⁰But Hobab replied, "No, I will not go. I must return to my own land and family."

**10:32**
Ps 22:27-31

³¹"Please don't leave us," Moses pleaded. "You know the places in the wilderness where we should camp. Come, be our guide. ³²If you do, we'll share with you all the blessings the LORD gives us."

**10:33**
Deut 1:33

**10:34**
Num 9:15-23

**10:35**
Ps 68:1-2

**10:36**
Deut 1:10-11

³³They marched for three days after leaving the mountain of the LORD, with the Ark of the LORD's Covenant moving ahead of them to show them where to stop and rest. ³⁴As they moved on each day, the cloud of the LORD hovered over them. ³⁵And whenever the Ark set out, Moses would shout, "Arise, O LORD, and let your enemies be scattered! Let them flee before you!" ³⁶And when the Ark was set down, he would say, "Return, O LORD, to the countless thousands of Israel!"

### The People Complain to Moses

**11:1**
Lev 10:1-2
Num 14:2; 16:35;
17:5

**11** Soon the people began to complain about their hardship, and the LORD heard everything they said. Then the LORD's anger blazed against them, and he sent a fire to rage among them, and he destroyed some of the people in the outskirts of the camp. ²Then the people screamed to Moses for help, and when he prayed to the LORD, the fire stopped. ³After that, the area was known as Taberah (which means "the place of burning"), because fire from the LORD had burned among them there.

**11:3**
Deut 9:22

**11:4**
Exod 12:38
Lev 24:10-11
Ps 78:18
1 Cor 10:6

⁴Then the foreign rabble who were traveling with the Israelites began to crave the good things of Egypt. And the people of Israel also began to complain. "Oh, for some meat!" they exclaimed. ⁵"We remember the fish we used to eat for free in Egypt. And we had all the cucumbers, melons, leeks, onions, and garlic we wanted. ⁶But now our appetites are gone. All we ever see is this manna!"

**11:6**
Num 21:5

**11:7**
Exod 16:14, 31

⁷The manna looked like small coriander seeds, and it was pale yellow like gum resin. ⁸The people would go out and gather it from the ground. They made flour by grinding it with hand mills or pounding it in mortars. Then they boiled it in a pot and made it into flat

---

**10:29-32** By complimenting Hobab's wilderness skills, Moses let him know he was needed. People cannot know you appreciate them if you do not tell them they are important to you. Complimenting those who deserve it builds lasting relationships and helps people know they are valued. Think about those who have helped you this month. What can you do to let them know how much you need and appreciate them?

**11:1, 6-15** The Israelites complained, and then Moses complained. But God responded positively to Moses and negatively to the rest of the people. Why? The people complained *to one another*, and nothing was accomplished. Moses took his complaint *to God*, who could solve any problem. Many of us are good at complaining to each other. We need to learn to take our problems to the One who can do something about them.

**11:4** The *foreign rabble* refers to a mixed crowd of Egyptians and others who had followed Israel out of Egypt (Exodus 12:38).

**11:4-6** Dissatisfaction comes when our attention shifts from what we have to what we don't have. The people of Israel didn't seem to notice what God was doing for them—setting them free, making them a nation, giving them a new land—because they were so wrapped up in what God wasn't doing for them. They

could think of nothing but the delicious Egyptian food they had left behind. Somehow they forgot that the brutal whip of Egyptian slavery was the cost of eating that food. Before we judge the Israelites too harshly, it's helpful to think about what occupies our attention most of the time. Are we grateful for what God has given us, or are we always thinking about what we would like to have? We should not allow our unfulfilled desires to cause us to forget God's gifts of life, food, health, work, and friends.

**11:4-9** Every morning the Israelites drew back their tent doors and witnessed a miracle. Covering the ground was pale yellow, fluffy manna—food from heaven. But soon that wasn't enough. Feeling it was their right to have more, they forgot what they already had. They didn't ask God to fill their need; instead, they demanded meat, and they stopped trusting God to care for them. "Give us meat to eat!" (11:13) they complained to Moses as they reminisced about the good food they had in Egypt. God gave them what they asked for, but they paid dearly for it when a plague struck the camp (see 11:18-20, 31-34). When you ask God for something, he may grant your request. But if you approach him with a sinful attitude, getting what you want may prove costly.

cakes. These cakes tasted like pastries baked with olive oil. ⁹The manna came down on the camp with the dew during the night.

¹⁰Moses heard all the families standing in the doorways of their tents whining, and the LORD became extremely angry. Moses was also very aggravated. ¹¹And Moses said to the LORD, "Why are you treating me, your servant, so harshly? Have mercy on me! What did I do to deserve the burden of all these people? ¹²Did I give birth to them? Did I bring them into the world? Why did you tell me to carry them in my arms like a mother carries a nursing baby? How can I carry them to the land you swore to give their ancestors? ¹³Where am I supposed to get meat for all these people? They keep whining to me, saying, 'Give us meat to eat!' ¹⁴I can't carry all these people by myself! The load is far too heavy! ¹⁵If this is how you intend to treat me, just go ahead and kill me. Do me a favor and spare me this misery!"

### Moses Chooses Seventy Leaders

¹⁶Then the LORD said to Moses, "Gather before me seventy men who are recognized as elders and leaders of Israel. Bring them to the Tabernacle* to stand there with you. ¹⁷I will come down and talk to you there. I will take some of the Spirit that is upon you, and I will put the Spirit upon them also. They will bear the burden of the people along with you, so you will not have to carry it alone.

¹⁸"And say to the people, 'Purify yourselves, for tomorrow you will have meat to eat. You were whining, and the LORD heard you when you cried, "Oh, for some meat! We were better off in Egypt!" Now the LORD will give you meat, and you will have to eat it. ¹⁹And it won't be for just a day or two, or for five or ten or even twenty. ²⁰You will eat it for a whole month until you gag and are sick of it. For you have rejected the LORD, who is here among you, and you have whined to him, saying, "Why did we ever leave Egypt?"'"

²¹But Moses responded to the LORD, "There are 600,000 foot soldiers here with me, and yet you say, 'I will give them meat for a whole month!' ²²Even if we butchered all our flocks and herds, would that satisfy them? Even if we caught all the fish in the sea, would that be enough?"

²³Then the LORD said to Moses, "Has my arm lost its power? Now you will see whether or not my word comes true!"

²⁴So Moses went out and reported the LORD's words to the people. He gathered the seventy elders and stationed them around the Tabernacle.* ²⁵And the LORD came down in the cloud and spoke to Moses. Then he gave the seventy elders the same Spirit that was upon Moses. And when the Spirit rested upon them, they prophesied. But this never happened again.

²⁶Two men, Eldad and Medad, had stayed behind in the camp. They were listed among the elders, but they had not gone out to the Tabernacle. Yet the Spirit rested upon them as well, so they prophesied there in the camp. ²⁷A young man ran and reported to Moses, "Eldad and Medad are prophesying in the camp!"

²⁸Joshua son of Nun, who had been Moses' assistant since his youth, protested, "Moses, my master, make them stop!"

²⁹But Moses replied, "Are you jealous for my sake? I wish that all the LORD's people were prophets and that the LORD would put his Spirit upon them all!" ³⁰Then Moses returned to the camp with the elders of Israel.

11:16 Hebrew *the Tent of Meeting.* 11:24 Hebrew *the tent;* also in 11:26.

Cross-references:
11:9 Exod 16:13
11:10 Ps 78:21
11:11 Exod 5:22
11:12 Gen 26:3; Exod 13:4-5; Isa 49:23
11:14 Exod 18:18; Deut 1:12
11:15 Exod 32:32
11:16 Exod 24:1, 9
11:17 Exod 34:5-6; Num 11:25; 12:5
11:18 Exod 19:10, 14-15
11:21 Exod 12:37
11:23 Isa 50:2
11:25 Num 11:16-17
11:28 Josh 1:1; Mark 9:38-40

---

**11:21, 22** Moses had witnessed God's power in spectacular miracles, yet at this time he questioned God's ability to feed the wandering Israelites. If Moses doubted God's power, how much easier it is for us to do the same. But completely depending upon God is essential, regardless of our level of spiritual maturity. When we begin to rely on our own understanding, we are in danger of ignoring God's assessment of the situation. By remembering his past works and his present power, we can be sure that we are not cutting off his potential help.

**11:23** How strong is God? It is easy to trust God when we see his mighty acts (the Israelites saw many), but after a while, in the routine of daily life, his strength may appear to diminish. God doesn't change, but our view of him often does. The monotony of day-by-day living lulls us into forgetting how powerful God can be. As Moses learned, God's strength is always available.

**11:26-29** This incident is similar to a story told in Mark 9:38-41. The disciples wanted Jesus to forbid others to drive out demons because they were not part of the disciples' group. But this type of narrow attitude was condemned by both Moses and Jesus. Beware of putting limits on God—he can work through whomever he chooses.

**11:29** Moses was looking forward to the day when all God's people would experience the pouring out of God's Spirit. The prophet Joel recorded God's promise to pour out his Spirit on all believers (Joel 2:28, 29), and this was fulfilled at Pentecost (Acts 2:16-21). Believers today can be sure that they have the Holy Spirit when they become Christians (Romans 8:9). We also can pray to live by the Holy Spirit's power (Galatians 5:16-26). If you wish to have the Holy Spirit's power, pray for him to fill your life with his presence and strengthen you to follow Christ.

### The LORD Sends Quail

**11:31**
Exod 16:13
Pss 78:26-33;
105:40

**11:33**
Num 11:10

**11:34**
Deut 9:22

**11:35**
Num 33:17

31Now the LORD sent a wind that brought quail from the sea and let them fall all around the camp. For miles in every direction there were quail flying about three feet above the ground.* 32So the people went out and caught quail all that day and throughout the night and all the next day, too. No one gathered less than fifty bushels*! They spread the quail all around the camp to dry. 33But while they were gorging themselves on the meat—while it was still in their mouths—the anger of the LORD blazed against the people, and he struck them with a severe plague. 34So that place was called Kibroth-hattaavah (which means "graves of gluttony") because there they buried the people who had craved meat from Egypt. 35From Kibroth-hattaavah the Israelites traveled to Hazeroth, where they stayed for some time.

### 2. Miriam and Aaron oppose Moses

**12:1**
Exod 2:21; 15:20

**12:2**
Num 16:3

**12** While they were at Hazeroth, Miriam and Aaron criticized Moses because he had married a Cushite woman. 2They said, "Has the LORD spoken only through Moses?

**11:31** Or *there were quail 3 feet* [2 cubits or 92 centimeters] *deep on the ground.*   **11:32** Hebrew *10 homers* [1.8 kiloliters].

---

| ISRAEL'S COMPLAINING | | Complaint | Sin | Result |
|---|---|---|---|---|
| | 11:1 | About their hardships | Complained about their problems instead of praying to God about them | Thousands of people were destroyed when God sent a plague of fire to punish them |
| | 11:4 | About the lack of meat | Lusted after things they didn't have | God sent quail; but as the people began to eat, God struck them with a plague that killed many |
| | 14:1-4 | About being stuck in the wilderness, facing the giants of the Promised Land, and wishing to return to Egypt | Openly rebelled against God's leaders and failed to trust in his promises | All who complained were not allowed to enter the Promised Land, being doomed to wander in the wilderness until they died |
| | 16:3 | About Moses' and Aaron's authority and leadership | Were greedy for more power and authority | The families, friends, and possessions of Korah, Dathan, and Abiram were swallowed up by the earth. Fire then burned up the 250 other men who rebelled |
| | 16:41 | That Moses and Aaron caused the deaths of Korah and his conspirators | Blamed others for their own troubles | God began to destroy Israel with a plague. Moses and Aaron made atonement for the people, but 14,700 of them were killed |
| | 20:2, 3 | About the lack of water | Refused to believe that God would provide as he had promised | Moses sinned along with the people. For this he was barred from entering the Promised Land |
| | 21:5 | That God and Moses brought them into the wilderness | Failed to recognize that their problems were brought on by their own disobedience | God sent poisonous snakes that killed many people and seriously injured many others |

---

**11:34** Craving or lusting is more than inappropriate sexual desire. It can be an unnatural or greedy desire for anything (sports, knowledge, possessions, influence over others). In this circumstance, God punished the Israelites for craving good food! Their desire was not wrong; the sin was in allowing that desire to turn into greed. They felt it was their right to have fine food, and they could think of nothing else. When you become preoccupied with something until it affects your perspective on everything else, you have moved from desire to lust.

**12:1** Moses didn't have a Jewish wife because he lived with the Egyptians the first 40 years of his life, and he was in the wilderness the next 40 years. The woman is probably not Zipporah, his first wife, who was a Midianite (see Exodus 2:21). A Cushite was an Ethiopian. There is no explanation given for why Miriam objected to this woman.

**12:1** People often argue over minor disagreements, leaving the real issue untouched. Such was the case when Miriam and Aaron criticized Moses. They represented the priests and the prophets, the two most powerful groups next to Moses. The real issue was their growing jealousy of Moses' position and influence. Since they could not find fault with the way Moses was leading the people, they chose to criticize his wife. Rather than face the problem squarely by dealing with their envy and pride, they chose to create a diversion from the real issue. When you are in a disagreement, stop and ask yourself if you are arguing over the real issue or if you have introduced a smoke screen by attacking someone's character. If you are unjustly criticized, remember that your critics may be afraid to face the real problem. Don't take this type of criticism personally. Ask God to help you identify the real issue and deal with it.

Hasn't he spoken through us, too?" But the LORD heard them. ³(Now Moses was very humble—more humble than any other person on earth.)

⁴So immediately the LORD called to Moses, Aaron, and Miriam and said, "Go out to the Tabernacle,* all three of you!" So the three of them went to the Tabernacle. ⁵Then the LORD descended in the pillar of cloud and stood at the entrance of the Tabernacle.* "Aaron and Miriam!" he called, and they stepped forward. ⁶And the LORD said to them, "Now listen to what I say:

"If there were prophets among you,
   I, the LORD, would reveal myself in visions.
   I would speak to them in dreams.
⁷ But not with my servant Moses.
   Of all my house, he is the one I trust.
⁸ I speak to him face to face,
   clearly, and not in riddles!
   He sees the LORD as he is.
So why were you not afraid
   to criticize my servant Moses?"

⁹The LORD was very angry with them, and he departed. ¹⁰As the cloud moved from above the Tabernacle, there stood Miriam, her skin as white as snow from leprosy.* When Aaron saw what had happened to her, ¹¹he cried out to Moses, "Oh, my master! Please don't punish us for this sin we have so foolishly committed. ¹²Don't let her be like a stillborn baby, already decayed at birth."

¹³So Moses cried out to the LORD, "O God, I beg you, please heal her!"

¹⁴But the LORD said to Moses, "If her father had done nothing more than spit in her face, wouldn't she be defiled for seven days? So keep her outside the camp for seven days, and after that she may be accepted back."

¹⁵So Miriam was kept outside the camp for seven days, and the people waited until she was brought back before they traveled again. ¹⁶Then they left Hazeroth and camped in the wilderness of Paran.

### 3. The scouts incite rebellion

*Twelve Scouts Explore Canaan*

**13** The LORD now said to Moses, ²"Send out men to explore the land of Canaan, the land I am giving to the Israelites. Send one leader from each of the twelve ancestral tribes." ³So Moses did as the LORD commanded him. He sent out twelve men, all tribal leaders of Israel, from their camp in the wilderness of Paran. ⁴These were the tribes and the names of their leaders:

| Tribe | Leader |
| --- | --- |
| Reuben | Shammua son of Zaccur |
| ⁵ Simeon | Shaphat son of Hori |
| ⁶ Judah | Caleb son of Jephunneh |
| ⁷ Issachar | Igal son of Joseph |
| ⁸ Ephraim | Hoshea son of Nun |
| ⁹ Benjamin | Palti son of Raphu |
| ¹⁰ Zebulun | Gaddiel son of Sodi |
| ¹¹ Manasseh son of Joseph | Gaddi son of Susi |

**12:4** Hebrew *the Tent of Meeting*.   **12:5** Hebrew *the tent;* also in 12:10.   **12:10** Or *with a skin disease*. The Hebrew word used here can describe various skin diseases.

**Cross-references (margin):**
12:3 Matt 11:29
12:5 Num 11:25
12:6 Gen 15:1; 31:10-11; 46:2; 1 Kgs 3:5
12:7 Ps 105:26; Heb 3:2, 5
12:8 Exod 33:11, 19; Deut 34:10
12:10 Deut 24:9
12:11 2 Sam 19:19
12:14 Lev 13:46; Num 5:1-3; Deut 25:9
13:2 Deut 1:22-25; Josh 1:3
13:8 Num 13:16

**12:11** Aaron asked that he and Miriam not be punished for their sin. It is easy to look back at our mistakes and recognize their foolishness. It is much harder to recognize foolish plans while we are carrying them out because somehow then they seem appropriate. To get rid of foolish ideas before they turn into foolish actions requires eliminating our wrong thoughts and motives. Failing to do this caused Miriam and Aaron much grief.

**12:14** Spitting in someone's face was considered the ultimate insult and a sign of shame imposed on wrongdoers. The religious leaders spat in Jesus' face to insult him (Matthew 26:67). God punished Miriam for her smug attitude not only toward Moses' authority but also God's. He struck her with leprosy, then ordered her out of the camp for a week. This punishment was actually quite lenient. A week was the length of time she would have been excluded if her father had spit in her face. How much more she deserved for wronging God! Once again, God was merciful while retaining effective discipline.

¹² Dan ........................................................ Ammiel son of Gemalli
¹³ Asher ...................................................... Sethur son of Michael
¹⁴ Naphtali .................................................... Nahbi son of Vophsi
¹⁵ Gad ........................................................ Geuel son of Maki

**13:16**
Num 13:8

**13:17**
Gen 12:9; 13:1
Num 13:21

**13:20**
Deut 1:25

**13:21**
Num 20:1; 27:14
Josh 19:28
Judg 1:31
Amos 6:14

**13:22**
Num 13:33
Josh 11:21; 15:14
Judg 1:20

**13:23**
Num 13:24; 32:9
Deut 1:24-25

¹⁶These are the names of the men Moses sent out to explore the land. (Moses called Hoshea son of Nun by the name Joshua.)

¹⁷Moses gave the men these instructions as he sent them out to explore the land: "Go north through the Negev into the hill country. ¹⁸See what the land is like, and find out whether the people living there are strong or weak, few or many. ¹⁹See what kind of land they live in. Is it good or bad? Do their towns have walls, or are they unprotected like open camps? ²⁰Is the soil fertile or poor? Are there many trees? Do your best to bring back samples of the crops you see." (It happened to be the season for harvesting the first ripe grapes.)

²¹So they went up and explored the land from the wilderness of Zin as far as Rehob, near Lebo-hamath. ²²Going north, they passed through the Negev and arrived at Hebron, where Ahiman, Sheshai, and Talmai—all descendants of Anak—lived. (The ancient town of Hebron was founded seven years before the Egyptian city of Zoan.) ²³When they came to the valley

**MIRIAM**

**A**sk older brothers or sisters what their greatest trial in life is, and they will often answer, "My younger brother [or sister]!" This is especially true when the younger sibling is more successful than the older. The bonds of family loyalty can be strained to the breaking point.

When we first meet Miriam, she is involved in one of history's most unusual baby-sitting jobs. She is watching her infant brother float on the Nile River in a waterproof cradle. Miriam's quick thinking allowed Moses to be raised by his own mother. Her protective superiority, reinforced by that event, must have been hard to give up as she watched her little brother rise to greatness.

Eventually Moses' choice of a wife gave Miriam an opportunity to criticize. It was natural for her insecurity to break out over this issue. With Moses married, Miriam was clearly no longer the most important woman in his life. The real issue, however, was not the kind of woman Moses had married. It was the fact that he was now the most important man in Israel. "Has the LORD spoken only through Moses? Hasn't he spoken through us, too?" No mention is made of Moses' response, but God had a quick answer for Miriam and Aaron. Without denying their role in his plan, God clearly pointed out his special relationship with Moses. Miriam was stricken with leprosy, a deadly disease, as punishment for her insubordination. But Moses, true to his character, intervened for his sister so that God healed Miriam of her leprosy.

Before criticizing someone else, we need to pause long enough to discover our own motives. Failing to do this can bring disastrous results. What is often labeled "constructive criticism" may actually be destructive jealousy, since the easiest way to raise our own status is to bring someone else down. Are you willing to question your motives before you offer criticism? Does the critical finger you point need to be pointed first toward yourself?

| | |
|---|---|
| **Strengths and accomplishments** | • Quick thinker under pressure<br>• Led the people alongside Moses and Aaron<br>• Led the people in praises to God<br>• God's prophet |
| **Weaknesses and mistakes** | • Was jealous of Moses' authority<br>• Openly criticized Moses' leadership |
| **Lesson from her life** | • The motives behind criticism are often more important to deal with than the criticism itself |
| **Vital statistics** | • Where: Egypt, Sinai peninsula<br>• Occupations: Able leader, songwriter, prophet<br>• Relatives: Brothers: Aaron and Moses |
| **Key verses** | "Then Miriam the prophet, Aaron's sister, took a tambourine and led all the women as they played their tambourines and danced. And Miriam sang this song: 'Sing to the LORD, for he has triumphed gloriously; he has hurled both horse and rider into the sea'" (Exodus 15:20, 21). |

Miriam's story is told in Exodus 2; 15; and Numbers 12; 20. She is also mentioned in Deuteronomy 24:9; 1 Chronicles 6:3; Micah 6:4.

**13:17-20** Moses decided what information was needed before the people could enter the Promised Land, and he took careful steps to get that information. When you are making decisions or assuming new responsibilities, remember these two important steps. Ask yourself what you need to know about the opportunity, and then obtain that knowledge. Common sense is a valuable aid in accomplishing God's purposes. See Proverbs 12:15 and 15:22.

of Eshcol, they cut down a branch with a single cluster of grapes so large that it took two of them to carry it on a pole between them! They also brought back samples of the pomegranates and figs. 24That place was called the valley of Eshcol (which means "cluster"), because of the cluster of grapes the Israelite men cut there.

### The Scouting Report

25After exploring the land for forty days, the men returned 26to Moses, Aaron, and the whole community of Israel at Kadesh in the wilderness of Paran. They reported to the whole community what they had seen and showed them the fruit they had taken from the land. 27This was their report to Moses: "We entered the land you sent us to explore, and it is indeed a bountiful country—a land flowing with milk and honey. Here is the kind of fruit it produces. 28But the people living there are powerful, and their towns are large and fortified. We even saw giants there, the descendants of Anak! 29 The Amalekites live in the Negev, and the Hittites, Jebusites, and Amorites live in the hill country. The Canaanites live along the coast of the Mediterranean Sea* and along the Jordan Valley."

30But Caleb tried to quiet the people as they stood before Moses. "Let's go at once to take the land," he said. "We can certainly conquer it!"

31But the other men who had explored the land with him disagreed. "We can't go up against them! They are stronger than we are!" 32 So they spread this bad report about the land among the Israelites: "The land we traveled through and explored will devour anyone who goes to live there. All the people we saw were huge. 33 We even saw giants* there, the descendants of Anak. Next to them we felt like grasshoppers, and that's what they thought, too!"

**13:29** Hebrew *the sea.* **13:33** Hebrew *nephilim.*

**13:26**
Num 12:16; 13:3;
20:1; 32:8

**13:27**
Exod 13:5
Deut 1:25

**13:28**
Num 13:22-23

**13:29**
Num 14:43

**13:30**
Num 14:6, 24

**13:31**
Deut 1:28

**13:32**
Num 14:36

**13:33**
Deut 1:28

---

**13:25-29** God told the Israelites that the Promised Land was rich and fertile. Not only that, he promised that this bountiful land would be theirs. When the scouts reported back to Moses, they gave plenty of good reasons for entering the land, but they couldn't stop focusing on their fear. Talk of giants (descendants of Anak) and fortified cities made it easy to forget about God's promise to help. When facing a tough decision, don't let the negatives cause you to lose sight of the positives. Weigh both sides carefully. Don't let potential difficulties blind you to God's power to help and his promise to guide.

**13:26** Although Kadesh was only an oasis in the wilderness, it was a crossroads in Israel's history. When the scouts returned to Kadesh from scouting the new land, the people had to decide either to enter the land or to retreat. They chose to retreat and were condemned to wander 40 years in the wilderness. It was also at Kadesh that Moses disobeyed God (20:7-12). For this, he, too, was denied entrance into the Promised Land. Aaron and Miriam died there, for they could not enter the new land either. Kadesh was near Canaan's southern borders, but because of the Israelites' lack of faith, they needed more than a lifetime to go from Kadesh to the Promised Land.

**13:27** The Promised Land, also called the land of Canaan, was indeed bountiful, as the 12 scouts discovered. The Bible often calls it the land flowing with milk and honey. Although the land was relatively small—150 miles long and 60 miles wide—its lush hillsides were covered with fig, date, and nut trees. It was the land God had promised to Abraham, Isaac, and Jacob.

**13:28** The "descendants of Anak" were a race of abnormally large people. The family of Goliath may have been descended from these people (see 2 Samuel 21:16-22).

**13:28, 29** The fortified cities the scouts talked about were surrounded by high walls as much as 20 feet thick and 25 feet tall. Guards were often stationed on top, where there was a commanding view of the countryside. Some of the inhabitants, said the scouts, were formidable men—from seven to nine feet tall—so that the Israelites felt like grasshoppers next to them (13:33). The fortified cities and the giants struck fear into the hearts of most of the scouts.

**13:30-32** Imagine standing before a crowd and loudly voicing an unpopular opinion! Caleb was willing to take the unpopular stand to do as God had commanded. To be effective when you go

against the crowd, you must (1) have the facts (Caleb had seen the land himself); (2) have the right attitude (Caleb trusted God's promise to give Israel the land); (3) state clearly what you believe (Caleb said, "We can certainly conquer it!").

**13:33–14:4** The negative opinion of 10 men caused a great rebellion among the people. Because it is human nature to accept opinion as fact, we must be especially careful when voicing our negative opinions. What we say may heavily influence the actions of those who trust us to give sound advice.

**ROUTE OF THE SCOUTS** The scouts traveled from Kadesh at the southernmost edge of the wilderness of Zin to Rehob at the northernmost edge and back, a round trip of about 500 miles.

### The People Rebel

**14** Then the whole community began weeping aloud, and they cried all night. ²Their voices rose in a great chorus of protest against Moses and Aaron. "If only we had died in Egypt, or even here in the wilderness!" they complained. ³"Why is the LORD taking us to this country only to have us die in battle? Our wives and our little ones will be carried off as plunder! Wouldn't it be better for us to return to Egypt?" ⁴Then they plotted among themselves, "Let's choose a new leader and go back to Egypt!"

⁵Then Moses and Aaron fell face down on the ground before the whole community of Israel. ⁶Two of the men who had explored the land, Joshua son of Nun and Caleb son of Jephunneh, tore their clothing. ⁷They said to all the people of Israel, "The land we traveled through and explored is a wonderful land! ⁸And if the LORD is pleased with us, he will bring us safely into that land and give it to us. It is a rich land flowing with milk and honey. ⁹Do not rebel against the LORD, and don't be afraid of the people of the land. They are only helpless prey to us! They have no protection, but the LORD is with us! Don't be afraid of them!"

¹⁰But the whole community began to talk about stoning Joshua and Caleb. Then the glorious presence of the LORD appeared to all the Israelites at the Tabernacle.* ¹¹And the LORD said to Moses, "How long will these people treat me with contempt? Will they never believe me, even after all the miraculous signs I have done among them? ¹²I will disown them and destroy them with a plague. Then I will make you into a nation greater and mightier than they are!"

### Moses Intercedes for the People

¹³But Moses objected. "What will the Egyptians think when they hear about it?" he asked the LORD. "They know full well the power you displayed in rescuing your people from Egypt. ¹⁴Now if you destroy them, the Egyptians will send a report to the inhabitants of this land, who have already heard that you live among your people. They know, LORD, that you have appeared to your people face to face and that your pillar of cloud hovers over them. They know that you go before them in the pillar of cloud by day and the pillar of fire by night. ¹⁵Now if you slaughter all these people with a single blow, the nations that have heard of your fame will say, ¹⁶'The LORD was not able to bring them into the land he swore to give them, so he killed them in the wilderness.'

¹⁷"Please, Lord, prove that your power is as great as you have claimed. For you said, ¹⁸'The LORD is slow to anger and filled with unfailing love, forgiving every kind of sin and rebellion. But he does not excuse the guilty. He lays the sins of the parents upon their children; the entire family is affected—even children in the third and fourth generations.' ¹⁹In keeping with your magnificent, unfailing love, please pardon the sins of this people, just as you have forgiven them ever since they left Egypt."

**14:10** Hebrew *the Tent of Meeting.*

**14:2** Exod 15:24; 16:3 Num 11:1; 16:13; 20:4; 21:5
**14:3** Exod 5:21; 16:3 Num 14:31 Deut 1:39
**14:5** Num 16:22, 45
**14:7** Num 13:27 Deut 1:25
**14:8** Exod 3:8 Num 13:27
**14:9** Deut 1:21, 29; 7:18; 9:7, 23-24
**14:10** Exod 16:7, 10; 17:4; 24:16-17; 32:9-13 Lev 9:23
**14:12** Exod 32:10 Lev 26:25 Deut 28:21
**14:13** Exod 9:28; 32:12
**14:14** Exod 13:21; 33:11 Deut 5:4
**14:16** Exod 32:12 Deut 9:28 Josh 7:7
**14:19** Exod 34:9 Ps 106:45

**14:1-4** When the chorus of despair went up, everyone joined in. Their greatest fears were being realized. Losing their perspective, the people were caught up in the emotion of the moment, forgetting what they knew about God's character. What if the people had spent as much energy moving forward as they did moving back? They could have enjoyed their land—instead they never even entered it. When a cry of despair goes up around you, consider the larger perspective before you join in. You have better ways to use your energy than to complain.

**14:5-9** With great miracles, God had led the Israelites out of slavery, through the desolate wilderness, and up to the very edge of the Promised Land. He had protected them, fed them, and fulfilled every promise. Yet when encouraged to take that last step of faith and enter the land, the people refused. After witnessing so many miracles, why did they stop trusting God? Why did they refuse to enter the Promised Land when that had been their goal since leaving Egypt? They were afraid. Often we do the same thing. We trust God to handle the smaller issues but doubt his ability to take care of the big problems, the tough decisions, the frightening situations. Don't stop trusting God just as you are ready to reach your goal. He brought you this far and won't let you down now. We can continue trusting God by remembering all he has done for us.

**14:6** Tearing clothing was a customary way of showing deep sorrow, mourning, or despair. Joshua and Caleb were greatly distressed by the people's refusal to enter the land.

**14:6-10** Two wise men, Joshua and Caleb, encouraged the people to act on God's promise and move ahead into the land. The people rejected their advice and even talked of stoning them. Don't be too quick to reject advice you don't like. Evaluate it carefully, comparing it to the teaching in God's Word. The advice may be God's message.

**14:17-20** Moses pleaded with God, asking him to forgive his people. His plea reveals several characteristics of God: (1) God is immensely patient; (2) God's love is one promise we can always count on; (3) God forgives again and again; (4) God is merciful, listening to and answering our requests. God has not changed since Moses' day. Like Moses, we can rely on God's love, patience, forgiveness, and mercy.

20Then the LORD said, "I will pardon them as you have requested. 21But as surely as I live, and as surely as the earth is filled with the LORD's glory, 22not one of these people will ever enter that land. They have all seen my glorious presence and the miraculous signs I performed both in Egypt and in the wilderness, but again and again they have tested me by refusing to listen to my voice. 23They will never even see the land I swore to give their ancestors. None of those who have treated me with contempt will ever see it. 24But my servant Caleb has a different attitude than the others have. He has remained loyal to me, so I will bring him into the land he explored. His descendants will possess their full share of that land. 25Now turn around, and don't go on toward the land where the Amalekites and Canaanites live. Tomorrow you must set out for the wilderness in the direction of the Red Sea.*"

### The LORD Punishes the Israelites

26Then the LORD said to Moses and Aaron, 27"How long must I put up with this wicked community and its complaints about me? Yes, I have heard the complaints the Israelites are making against me. 28Now tell them this: 'As surely as I live, declares the LORD, I will do to you the very things I heard you say. 29You will all drop dead in this wilderness! Because you complained against me, every one of you who is twenty years old or older and was included in the registration will die. 30You will not enter and occupy the land I swore to give you. The only exceptions will be Caleb son of Jephunneh and Joshua son of Nun.

31"'You said your children would be carried off as plunder. Well, I will bring them safely into the land, and they will enjoy what you have despised. 32But as for you, you will drop dead in this wilderness. 33And your children will be like shepherds, wandering in the wilderness for forty years. In this way, they will pay for your faithlessness, until the last of you lies dead in the wilderness.

34"'Because your men explored the land for forty days, you must wander in the wilderness for forty years—a year for each day, suffering the consequences of your sins. Then you will discover what it is like to have me for an enemy.' 35I, the LORD, have spoken! I will certainly do these things to every member of the community who has conspired against me. They will be destroyed here in this wilderness, and here they will die!"

36The ten men Moses had sent to explore the land—the ones who incited rebellion against the LORD with their bad report—37were struck dead with a plague before the LORD. 38Of the twelve who had explored the land, only Joshua and Caleb remained alive.

39When Moses reported the LORD's words to all the Israelites, the people were filled with grief. 40Then they got up early the next morning and went to the top of the range of hills. "Let's go," they said. "We realize that we have sinned, but now we are ready to enter the land the LORD has promised us."

14:25 Hebrew sea of reeds.

**14:20** Ps 106:23; Mic 7:18-20
**14:23** Num 26:65; 32:11
**14:24** Num 32:12; Josh 14:6-15
**14:25** Num 13:29
**14:28** Num 14:21; Heb 3:17
**14:29** Num 1:17-19; 26:2
**14:30** Num 14:24, 38
**14:31** Num 14:3
**14:32** Num 26:64-65; 32:13; 1 Cor 10:5
**14:33** Deut 2:7; 8:2
**14:36** Num 13:4-16
**14:39** Exod 33:4
**14:40** Deut 1:41-44

**14:20-23** The people of Israel had a clearer view of God than any people before them, for they had both his laws and his physical presence. Their refusal to follow God after witnessing his miraculous deeds and listening to his words made the judgment against them more severe. Increased opportunity brings increased responsibility. As Jesus said: "When someone has been given much, much will be required in return" (Luke 12:48). How much greater is our responsibility to obey and serve God—we have the whole Bible, and we know God's Son, Jesus Christ.

**14:22** God wasn't exaggerating when he said that the Israelites had "again and again" failed to trust and obey him. Here is a list of their failures: (1) lacking trust at the crossing of the Red Sea (Exodus 14:11, 12); (2) complaining over bitter water at Marah (Exodus 15:24); (3) complaining in the wilderness of Sin (Exodus 16:3); (4) collecting more than the daily quota of manna (Exodus 16:20); (5) collecting manna on the Sabbath (Exodus 16:27-29); (6) complaining over lack of water at Rephidim (Exodus 17:2, 3); (7) engaging in idolatry with a golden calf (Exodus 32:7-10); (8) complaining at Taberah (Numbers 11:1, 2); (9) more complaining over the lack of delicious food (Numbers 11:4); (10) failing to trust God and enter the Promised Land (Numbers 14:1-4).

**14:24** The fulfillment of this verse is recorded in Joshua 14:6-15 when Caleb received his inheritance in the Promised Land. Caleb followed God with all his heart and was rewarded for his obedience. Are you wholehearted in your commitment to obey God?

**14:34** God's judgment came in the form the people feared most. The people were afraid of dying in the wilderness, so God punished them by making them wander in the wilderness until they died. Now they wished they had the problem of facing the giants and the fortified cities of the Promised Land. Failing to trust God often brings even greater problems than those we originally faced. When we run from God, we inevitably run into problems.

**14:35** Was this judgment—wandering 40 years in the wilderness—too harsh? Not compared to the instant death that God first threatened (14:12). Instead, God allowed the people to live. God had brought his people to the edge of the Promised Land, just as he said he would. He was ready to give them the rich land, but the people didn't want it (14:1, 2). By this time, God had put up with a lot. Again and again the people had refused to trust and obey him (14:22). The whole nation (except for Joshua, Caleb, Moses, and Aaron) showed contempt for and distrust of God. But God's punishment was not permanent. In 40 years, a new generation would have a chance to enter Canaan (Joshua 1–3).

**14:40-44** When the Israelites realized their foolish mistake, they were suddenly ready to return to God. But God didn't confuse their admission of guilt with true repentance because he knew their hearts. Sure enough, they soon went their own way again. Sometimes right actions or good intentions come too late. We must not only do what is right, but also do it at the right time. God wants complete and instant obedience.

⁴¹But Moses said, "Why are you now disobeying the Lᴏʀᴅ's orders to return to the wilderness? It won't work. ⁴²Do not go up into the land now. You will only be crushed by your enemies because the Lᴏʀᴅ is not with you. ⁴³When you face the Amalekites and Canaanites in battle, you will be slaughtered. The Lᴏʀᴅ will abandon you because you have abandoned the Lᴏʀᴅ."

⁴⁴But the people defiantly pushed ahead toward the hill country, even though neither Moses nor the Ark of the Lᴏʀᴅ's Covenant left the camp. ⁴⁵Then the Amalekites and the Canaanites who lived in those hills came down and attacked them and chased them back as far as Hormah.

**14:44**
Num 10:33; 31:6
**14:45**
Num 21:3
Judg 1:17

## C. WANDERING IN THE WILDERNESS (15:1—21:35)

After their disobedience and unsuccessful attempt to enter the Promised Land, the Israelites were condemned to wander 40 years in the wilderness. Even in the midst of this punishment, the people continued to rebel, and thus God continued to punish them. But the hearts of the people remained hard and rebellious. Hard hearts toward God may bring similar calamity to us.

### 1. Additional regulations
*Laws concerning Offerings*

**15** Then the Lᴏʀᴅ told Moses, ²"Give the following instructions to the people of Israel. "When you finally settle in the land I am giving you, ³you will offer special gifts as a pleasing aroma to the Lᴏʀᴅ. These gifts may take the form of a burnt offering, a sacrifice to fulfill a vow, a voluntary offering, or an offering at any of your annual festivals, and they may be taken from your herds of cattle or your flocks of sheep and goats. ⁴When you present these offerings, you must also give the Lᴏʀᴅ a grain offering of two quarts* of choice flour mixed with one quart* of olive oil. ⁵For each lamb offered as a burnt offering or a special sacrifice, you must also present one quart of wine as a liquid offering.

**15:3**
Lev 1:1; 2:1-16;
22:21; 23:37-38;
27:2

**15:5**
Num 15:5-10; 28:7

15:4a Hebrew *1/10 of an ephah* [2.2 liters].   15:4b Hebrew *1/4 of a hin* [1 liter]; also in 15:5.

The voice of the minority is not often given a hearing. Nevertheless, truth cannot be measured by numbers. On the contrary, it often stands against majority opinion. Truth remains unchanged because it is guaranteed by the character of God. God is truth; what he says is the last word. At times, a person must even stand alone on the side of truth.

Caleb was not so much a man of great faith as a man of faith in a great God! His boldness rested on his understanding of God, not on his confidence in Israel's abilities to conquer the land. He could not agree with the majority, for that would be to disagree with God.

We, on the other hand, often base our decisions on what everyone else is doing. Few of us are first-order cowards like the 10 scouts. We are more like the people of Israel, getting our cowardice secondhand. Our search for right and wrong usually starts with questions such as "What do the experts say?" or "What do my friends say?" The question we most often avoid is "What does God say?" The principles we learn as we study the Bible provide a dependable road map for life. They draw us into a personal relationship with the God whose Word is the Bible. The God who gave Caleb his boldness is the same God who offers us the gift of eternal life through his Son, Jesus. That's truth worth believing!

| | |
|---|---|
| **Strengths and accomplishments** | • One of the scouts sent by Moses to survey the land of Canaan<br>• One of the only two adults who left Egypt and entered the Promised Land<br>• Voiced the minority opinion in favor of conquering the land<br>• Expressed faith in God's promises, in spite of apparent obstacles |
| **Lessons from his life** | • Majority opinion is not an accurate measurement of right and wrong<br>• Boldness based on God's faithfulness is appropriate<br>• For courage and faith to be effective, they must combine words and actions |
| **Vital statistics** | • Where: From Egypt to the Sinai peninsula to the Promised Land, specifically Hebron<br>• Occupations: Scout, soldier, shepherd |
| **Key verse** | "But my servant Caleb has a different attitude than the others have. He has remained loyal to me, so I will bring him into the land he explored. His descendants will possess their full share of that land" (Numbers 14:24). |

Caleb's story is told in Numbers 13—14 and Joshua 14—15. He is also mentioned in Judges 1 and 1 Chronicles 4:15.

CALEB

6"If the sacrifice is a ram, give a grain offering of four quarts* of choice flour mixed with a third of a gallon* of olive oil, 7and give a third of a gallon of wine as a liquid offering. This will be a pleasing aroma to the LORD.

8"When you present a young bull as a burnt offering or as a sacrifice to fulfill a vow or as a peace offering to the LORD, 9you must also give a grain offering of six quarts* of choice flour mixed with two quarts* of olive oil, 10and give two quarts of wine as a liquid offering. This will be a special gift, a pleasing aroma to the LORD.

11"Each sacrifice of a bull, ram, lamb, or young goat should be prepared in this way. 12Follow these instructions with each offering you present. 13All of you native-born Israelites must follow these instructions when you offer a special gift as a pleasing aroma to the LORD. 14And if any foreigners visit you or live among you and want to present a special gift as a pleasing aroma to the LORD, they must follow these same procedures. 15Native-born Israelites and foreigners are equal before the LORD and are subject to the same decrees. This is a permanent law for you, to be observed from generation to generation. 16The same instructions and regulations will apply both to you and to the foreigners living among you."

17Then the LORD said to Moses, 18"Give the following instructions to the people of Israel. "When you arrive in the land where I am taking you, 19and you eat the crops that grow there, you must set some aside as a sacred offering to the LORD. 20Present a cake from the first of the flour you grind, and set it aside as a sacred offering, as you do with the first grain from the threshing floor. 21Throughout the generations to come, you are to present a sacred offering to the LORD each year from the first of your ground flour.

22"But suppose you unintentionally fail to carry out all these commands that the LORD has given you through Moses. 23And suppose your descendants in the future fail to do everything the LORD has commanded through Moses. 24If the mistake was made unintentionally, and the community was unaware of it, the whole community must present a young bull for a burnt offering as a pleasing aroma to the LORD. It must be offered along with its prescribed grain offering and liquid offering and with one male goat for a sin offering. 25With it the priest will purify the whole community of Israel, making them right with the LORD,* and they will be forgiven. For it was an unintentional sin, and they have corrected it with their offerings to the LORD—the special gift and the sin offering. 26The whole community of Israel will be forgiven, including the foreigners living among you, for all the people were involved in the sin.

27"If one individual commits an unintentional sin, the guilty person must bring a one-year-old female goat for a sin offering. 28The priest will sacrifice it to purify* the guilty person before the LORD, and that person will be forgiven. 29These same instructions apply both to native-born Israelites and to the foreigners living among you.

30"But those who brazenly violate the LORD's will, whether native-born Israelites or foreigners, have blasphemed the LORD, and they must be cut off from the community. 31Since they have treated the LORD's word with contempt and deliberately disobeyed his command, they must be completely cut off and suffer the punishment for their guilt."

## Penalty for Breaking the Sabbath

32One day while the people of Israel were in the wilderness, they discovered a man gathering wood on the Sabbath day. 33The people who found him doing this took him before Moses, Aaron, and the rest of the community. 34They held him in custody because they did not know what to do with him. 35Then the LORD said to Moses, "The man must be put to death! The whole community must stone him outside the camp." 36So the whole community took the man outside the camp and stoned him to death, just as the LORD had commanded Moses.

**15:8**
Lev 3:1; 7:11-18
**15:10**
Num 28:14

**15:15**
Num 9:14; 15:29

**15:19**
Josh 5:11-12

**15:22**
Lev 4:2

**15:25**
Lev 4:20

**15:29**
Num 15:15

**15:30**
Num 14:40-44
Deut 1:43; 17:13

**15:32**
Exod 31:14-15;
35:2-3

**15:35**
Lev 24:14, 23
Deut 21:21

**15:6a** Hebrew 2/10 of an ephah [4.4 liters].   **15:6b** Hebrew 1/3 of a hin [1.3 liters]; also in 15:7.   **15:9a** Hebrew 3/10 of an ephah [6.6 liters].   **15:9b** Hebrew 1/2 of a hin [2 liters]; also in 15:10.   **15:25** Or will make atonement for the whole community of Israel.   **15:28** Or to make atonement for.

---

**15:30, 31** God was willing to forgive those who made unintentional errors if they realized their mistakes quickly and corrected them. However, those who brazenly and deliberately sinned received a harsher judgment. Intentional sin grows out of an improper attitude toward God. A child who knowingly disobeys his parents challenges their authority and dares them to respond. Both the act and the attitude have to be dealt with.

**15:32-36** Stoning a man for gathering wood on the Sabbath seems like a severe punishment, and it was. This act was a deliberate sin, defying God's law against working on the Sabbath. Perhaps the man was taking advantage of everyone else while they were at home resting, in addition to breaking the Sabbath.

## Tassels on Clothing

**15:38**
Lev 3:17
Num 10:8
Deut 22:12
Matt 23:5

**15:40**
Lev 11:44
Rom 12:1
Col 1:22
1 Pet 1:15-16

37 Then the LORD said to Moses, 38 "Give the following instructions to the people of Israel: Throughout the generations to come you must make tassels for the hems of your clothing and attach them with a blue cord. 39 When you see the tassels, you will remember and obey all the commands of the LORD instead of following your own desires and defiling yourselves, as you are prone to do. 40 The tassels will help you remember that you must obey all my commands and be holy to your God. 41 I am the LORD your God who brought you out of the land of Egypt that I might be your God. I am the LORD your God!"

## 2. Many leaders rebel against Moses
### Korah, Dathan, and Abiram

**16:1**
Exod 6:21
Num 26:9
Deut 11:6
Jude 1:11

**16:2**
Num 1:16

**16:3**
Exod 19:6
Num 16:7; 35:34

**16:4**
Num 14:5

**16:5**
Lev 10:3
Num 17:5, 8
Ps 65:4

**16:7**
Num 16:3

**16** One day Korah son of Izhar, a descendant of Kohath son of Levi, conspired with Dathan and Abiram, the sons of Eliab, and On son of Peleth, from the tribe of Reuben. 2 They incited a rebellion against Moses, along with 250 other leaders of the community, all prominent members of the assembly. 3 They united against Moses and Aaron and said, "You have gone too far! The whole community of Israel has been set apart by the LORD, and he is with all of us. What right do you have to act as though you are greater than the rest of the LORD's people?"

4 When Moses heard what they were saying, he fell face down on the ground. 5 Then he said to Korah and his followers, "Tomorrow morning the LORD will show us who belongs to him* and who is holy. The LORD will allow only those whom he selects to enter his own presence. 6 Korah, you and all your followers must prepare your incense burners. 7 Light fires in them tomorrow, and burn incense before the LORD. Then we will see whom the LORD chooses as his holy one. You Levites are the ones who have gone too far!"

**16:10**
Num 3:6-10

**16:11**
Exod 16:7
1 Cor 10:10

8 Then Moses spoke again to Korah: "Now listen, you Levites! 9 Does it seem insignificant to you that the God of Israel has chosen you from among all the community of Israel to be near him so you can serve in the LORD's Tabernacle and stand before the people to minister to them? 10 Korah, he has already given this special ministry to you and your fellow Levites. Are you now demanding the priesthood as well? 11 The LORD is the one you and your followers are really revolting against! For who is Aaron that you are complaining about him?"

**16:13**
Num 11:5; 14:2-3;
20:3-4

**16:14**
Exod 22:5
Num 20:5

12 Then Moses summoned Dathan and Abiram, the sons of Eliab, but they replied, "We refuse to come before you! 13 Isn't it enough that you brought us out of Egypt, a land flowing with milk and honey, to kill us here in this wilderness, and that you now treat us like your subjects? 14 What's more, you haven't brought us into another land flowing with milk and honey. You haven't given us a new homeland with fields and vineyards. Are you trying to fool these men?* We will not come."

**16:15**
Gen 4:4
1 Sam 12:3

15 Then Moses became very angry and said to the LORD, "Do not accept their grain offerings! I have not taken so much as a donkey from them, and I have never hurt a single one of them." 16 And Moses said to Korah, "You and all your followers must come here tomorrow and present yourselves before the LORD. Aaron will also be here. 17 You and each of your

**16:5** Greek version reads *God has visited and knows those who are his.* Compare 2 Tim 2:19.   **16:14** Hebrew *Are you trying to put out the eyes of these men?*

---

**15:39** The tassels were to remind people not to seek after their own lustful desires, but to seek the Lord. Idol worship is self-centered, focusing on what a person can get from serving an idol. Good luck, prosperity, long life, and success in battle were expected from the gods. So were power and prestige. The worship of God is the opposite. Believers are to be selfless rather than self-centered. Instead of expecting God to serve us, we are to serve him, expecting nothing in return. We serve God for who he is, not for what we get from him.

**16:1-3** Korah and his associates had seen the advantages of the priesthood in Egypt. Egyptian priests had great wealth and political influence, something Korah wanted for himself. Korah may have assumed that Moses, Aaron, and his sons were trying to make the Israelite priesthood the same kind of political machine, and he wanted to be a part of it. He did not understand that Moses' main ambition was to serve God rather than to control others.

**16:8-10** Moses saw through their charge to their true motivation—some of the Levites wanted the power of the priesthood. Like Korah, we often desire the special qualities God has given

others. Korah had significant, worthwhile abilities and responsibilities of his own. In the end, however, his ambition for more caused him to lose everything. Inappropriate ambition is greed in disguise. Concentrate on finding the special purpose God has for you instead of wishing you were in someone else's shoes.

**16:13, 14** One of the easiest ways to fall away from following God is to look at our present problems and exaggerate them. Dathan and Abiram did just that when they began to long for better food and more pleasant surroundings. Egypt, the place they had longed to leave, was now looking better and better—not because of slavery and taskmasters, of course, but because of its mouthwatering food! These two men and their followers had completely lost their perspective. When we take our eyes off God and start looking at ourselves and our problems, we begin to lose our perspective as well. Overrating problems can hinder our relationship with God. Don't let difficulties make you lose sight of God's direction for your life.

250 followers must prepare an incense burner and put incense on it, so you can all present them before the LORD. Aaron will also bring his incense burner."

18So each of these men prepared an incense burner, lit the fire, and placed incense on it. Then they all stood at the entrance of the Tabernacle* with Moses and Aaron. 19Meanwhile, Korah had stirred up the entire community against Moses and Aaron, and they all gathered at the Tabernacle entrance. Then the glorious presence of the LORD appeared to the whole community, 20and the LORD said to Moses and Aaron, 21"Get away from all these people so that I may instantly destroy them!"

22But Moses and Aaron fell face down on the ground. "O God," they pleaded, "you are the God who gives breath to all creatures. Must you be angry with all the people when only one man sins?"

23And the LORD said to Moses, 24"Then tell all the people to get away from the tents of Korah, Dathan, and Abiram."

25So Moses got up and rushed over to the tents of Dathan and Abiram, followed by the elders of Israel. 26"Quick!" he told the people. "Get away from the tents of these wicked men, and don't touch anything that belongs to them. If you do, you will be destroyed for their sins." 27So all the people stood back from the tents of Korah, Dathan, and Abiram. Then Dathan and Abiram came out and stood at the entrances of their tents, together with their wives and children and little ones.

28And Moses said, "This is how you will know that the LORD has sent me to do all these things that I have done—for I have not done them on my own. 29If these men die a natural death, or if nothing unusual happens, then the LORD has not sent me. 30But if the LORD does something entirely new and the ground opens its mouth and swallows them and all their belongings, and they go down alive into the grave,* then you will know that these men have shown contempt for the LORD."

31He had hardly finished speaking the words when the ground suddenly split open beneath them. 32The earth opened its mouth and swallowed the men, along with their households and all their followers who were standing with them, and everything they owned. 33So they went down alive into the grave, along with all their belongings. The earth closed over them, and they all vanished from among the people of Israel. 34All the people around them fled when they heard their screams. "The earth will swallow us, too!" they cried. 35Then fire blazed forth from the LORD and burned up the 250 men who were offering incense.

36*And the LORD said to Moses, 37"Tell Eleazar son of Aaron the priest to pull all the incense burners from the fire, for they are holy. Also tell him to scatter the burning coals. 38Take the incense burners of these men who have sinned at the cost of their lives, and hammer the metal into a thin sheet to overlay the altar. Since these burners were used in the LORD's presence, they have become holy. Let them serve as a warning to the people of Israel."

39So Eleazar the priest collected the 250 bronze incense burners that had been used by the men who died in the fire, and he hammered them into a thin sheet to overlay the altar. 40This would warn the Israelites that no unauthorized person—no one who was not a descendant of Aaron—should ever enter the LORD's presence to burn incense. If anyone did, the same thing would happen to him as happened to Korah and his followers. So the LORD's instructions to Moses were carried out.

41But the very next morning the whole community of Israel began muttering again against Moses and Aaron, saying, "You have killed the LORD's people!" 42As the community gathered to protest against Moses and Aaron, they turned toward the Tabernacle and saw that the cloud had covered it, and the glorious presence of the LORD appeared.

**16:19** Lev 9:6; Num 14:10; 16:42; 20:6

**16:21** Exod 32:10

**16:22** Gen 18:23-32

**16:24** Num 16:45

**16:26** Gen 19:12-17

**16:28** Exod 3:12; 4:1-9; 7:9

**16:32** Num 16:30; 26:10

**16:35** Lev 10:2; Num 11:1-3; 26:10

**16:40** Num 1:51; 3:10, 38

**16:41** Num 16:3

**16:42** Exod 40:34; Num 14:10; 16:19

**16:18** Hebrew *the Tent of Meeting;* also in 16:19, 42, 43, 50.   **16:30** Hebrew *into Sheol;* also in 16:33.   **16:36** Verses 16:36-50 are numbered 17:1-15 in Hebrew text.

---

**16:26** The Israelites were told not even to touch the belongings of the wicked rebels. In this case, doing so would have shown sympathy to their cause and agreement with their principles. Korah, Dathan, and Abiram were directly challenging Moses and God. Moses clearly stated what God intended to do to the rebels (16:28-30). He did this so that everyone would have to choose between following Korah or following Moses, God's chosen leader. When God asks us to make a fundamental choice between siding with wicked people or siding with him, we should not hesitate but commit ourselves to be 100 percent on the Lord's side.

**16:27-35** Although the families of Dathan and Abiram were swallowed up, the sons of Korah were not wiped out (see 26:11).

**16:41** Just one day after Korah and his followers were executed for grumbling and complaining against God, the Israelites started

**16:45**
Num 16:21, 24

**16:46**
Lev 10:1, 6
Num 8:19; 18:5;
25:13
Deut 9:22

**16:47**
Num 25:7-8, 13

**16:49**
Num 16:32-35;
25:9

⁴³Moses and Aaron came and stood in front of the Tabernacle, ⁴⁴and the LORD said to Moses, ⁴⁵"Get away from all these people so that I can instantly destroy them!" But Moses and Aaron fell face down on the ground.

⁴⁶And Moses said to Aaron, "Quick, take an incense burner and place burning coals on it from the altar. Lay incense on it, and carry it out among the people to purify them and make them right with the LORD.* The LORD's anger is blazing against them—the plague has already begun."

⁴⁷Aaron did as Moses told him and ran out among the people. The plague had already begun to strike down the people, but Aaron burned the incense and purified* the people. ⁴⁸He stood between the dead and the living, and the plague stopped. ⁴⁹But 14,700 people died in that plague, in addition to those who had died in the affair involving Korah. ⁵⁰Then because the plague had stopped, Aaron returned to Moses at the entrance of the Tabernacle.

**16:46** Or *to make atonement for them.*   **16:47** Or *and made atonement for.*

---

**KORAH**

Some notorious historical figures might have remained anonymous if they hadn't tried to grab on to more than they could hold. But by refusing to be content with what they had, and by trying to get more than they deserved, they ended up with nothing. Korah, one of the Israelite leaders, was one such person.

Korah was a Levite who assisted in the daily functions of the Tabernacle. Shortly after Israel's great rebellion against God (Numbers 13—14), Korah instigated his own mini-rebellion. He recruited a grievance committee and confronted Moses and Aaron. Their list of complaints boils down to three statements: (1) You are no better than anyone else; (2) everyone in Israel has been chosen of the Lord; (3) we don't need to obey you. It is amazing to see how Korah twisted the first two statements—both true—to reach the wrong conclusion.

Moses would have agreed that he was no better than anyone else. He would also have agreed that all Israelites were God's chosen people. But Korah's application of these truths was wrong. Not all Israelites were chosen to lead. Korah's hidden claim was this: "I have as much right to lead as Moses does." His error cost him not only his job—a position of service that he enjoyed—but also his life.

Korah's story gives us numerous warnings: (1) Don't let desire for what someone else has make you discontented with what you already have. (2) Don't try to raise your own self-esteem by attacking someone else's. (3) Don't use part of God's Word to support what you want, rather than allowing its entirety to shape your wants. (4) Don't expect to find satisfaction in power and position; God may want to work through you in the position you are now in.

| | |
|---|---|
| **Strengths and accomplishments** | • Popular leader; influential figure during the Exodus<br>• Mentioned among the chief men of Israel (Exodus 6)<br>• One of the first Levites appointed for special service in the Tabernacle |
| **Weaknesses and mistakes** | • Failed to recognize the significant position God had placed him in<br>• Forgot that his fight was against someone greater than Moses<br>• Allowed greed to blind his common sense |
| **Lessons from his life** | • There is a fine line between goals and greed<br>• If we are discontented with what we have, we may lose it without gaining anything better |
| **Vital statistics** | • Where: Egypt, Sinai peninsula<br>• Occupation: Levite (Tabernacle assistant) |
| **Key verses** | "Then Moses spoke again to Korah: 'Now listen, you Levites! Does it seem insignificant to you that the God of Israel has chosen you from among all the community of Israel to be near him so you can serve in the LORD's Tabernacle and stand before the people to minister to them? Korah, he has already given this special ministry to you and your fellow Levites. Are you now demanding the priesthood as well?'" (Numbers 16:8–10). |

Korah's story is told in Numbers 16:1–40. He is also mentioned in Numbers 26:9; Jude 1:11.

---

all over with more muttering and complaining. Their negative attitude only caused them to rebel even more and to bring about even greater trouble. It eroded their faith in God and encouraged thoughts of giving up and turning back. The path to open rebellion against God begins with dissatisfaction and skepticism, then moves to grumbling about both God and present circumstances.

Next come bitterness and resentment, followed finally by rebellion and open hostility. If you are often dissatisfied, skeptical, complaining, or bitter—beware! These attitudes lead to rebellion and separation from God. Any choice to side against God is a step in the direction of letting go of him completely and making your own way through life.

## The Budding of Aaron's Staff

**17** ¹*Then the LORD said to Moses, ²"Tell the people of Israel to bring you twelve wooden staffs, one from each leader of Israel's ancestral tribes, and inscribe each leader's name on his staff. ³Inscribe Aaron's name on the staff of the tribe of Levi, for there must be one staff for the leader of each ancestral tribe. ⁴Place these staffs in the Tabernacle in front of the Ark containing the tablets of the Covenant,* where I meet with you. ⁵Buds will sprout on the staff belonging to the man I choose. Then I will finally put an end to the people's murmuring and complaining against you."

⁶So Moses gave the instructions to the people of Israel, and each of the twelve tribal leaders, including Aaron, brought Moses a staff. ⁷Moses placed the staffs in the LORD's presence in the Tabernacle of the Covenant.* ⁸When he went into the Tabernacle of the Covenant the next day, he found that Aaron's staff, representing the tribe of Levi, had sprouted, budded, blossomed, and produced ripe almonds!

⁹When Moses brought all the staffs out from the LORD's presence, he showed them to the people. Each man claimed his own staff. ¹⁰And the LORD said to Moses: "Place Aaron's staff permanently before the Ark of the Covenant* to serve as a warning to rebels. This should put an end to their complaints against me and prevent any further deaths." ¹¹So Moses did as the LORD commanded him.

¹²Then the people of Israel said to Moses, "Look, we are doomed! We are dead! We are ruined! ¹³Everyone who even comes close to the Tabernacle of the LORD dies. Are we all doomed to die?"

## 3. Duties of priests and Levites

**18** Then the LORD said to Aaron: "You, your sons, and your relatives from the tribe of Levi will be held responsible for any offenses related to the sanctuary. But you and your sons alone will be held responsible for violations connected with the priesthood.

²"Bring your relatives of the tribe of Levi—your ancestral tribe—to assist you and your sons as you perform the sacred duties in front of the Tabernacle of the Covenant.* ³But as the Levites go about all their assigned duties at the Tabernacle, they must be careful not to go near any of the sacred objects or the altar. If they do, both you and they will die. ⁴The Levites must join you in fulfilling their responsibilities for the care and maintenance of the Tabernacle,* but no unauthorized person may assist you.

⁵"You yourselves must perform the sacred duties inside the sanctuary and at the altar. If you follow these instructions, the LORD's anger will never again blaze against the people of Israel. ⁶I myself have chosen your fellow Levites from among the Israelites to be your special assistants. They are a gift to you, dedicated to the LORD for service in the Tabernacle. ⁷But you and your sons, the priests, must personally handle all the priestly rituals associated with the altar and with everything behind the inner curtain. I am giving you the priesthood as your special privilege of service. Any unauthorized person who comes too near the sanctuary will be put to death."

## Support for the Priests and Levites

⁸The LORD gave these further instructions to Aaron: "I myself have put you in charge of all the holy offerings that are brought to me by the people of Israel. I have given all these consecrated offerings to you and your sons as your permanent share. ⁹You are allotted the portion of the most holy offerings that is not burned on the fire. This portion of all the most

**17:4**
Exod 25:22
Num 17:10

**17:5**
Num 16:5; 17:8

**17:7**
Num 18:2

**17:8**
Num 17:5
Heb 9:4

**17:10**
Num 17:4
Deut 9:7, 24

**17:12**
Isa 6:5

**17:13**
Num 1:51-53

**18:1**
Exod 28:38

**18:2**
Num 3:5-10

**18:5**
Num 16:46

**18:6**
Num 3:9, 12

**18:7**
Exod 29:9
Num 1:51; 3:10

**18:8**
Lev 7:28-34
Deut 12:6

**18:9**
Lev 2:1-16;
6:25-30

---

**17:1** Verses 17:1-13 are numbered 17:16-28 in Hebrew text.   **17:4** Hebrew *in the Tent of Meeting before the Testimony.* The Hebrew word for "testimony" refers to the terms of the LORD's covenant with Israel as written on stone tablets, which were kept in the Ark, and also to the covenant itself.   **17:7** Or *Tabernacle of the Testimony;* also in 17:8.   **17:10** Hebrew *before the Testimony;* see note on 17:4.   **18:2** Or *Tabernacle of the Testimony.* **18:4** Hebrew *the Tent of Meeting;* also in 18:6, 21, 22, 23, 31.

---

**17:5, 10** After witnessing spectacular miracles, seeing the Egyptians punished by the plagues, and experiencing the actual presence of God, the Israelites still complained and rebelled. We wonder how they could be so blind and ignorant, and yet we often repeat this same pattern. We have centuries of evidence, the Bible in many translations, and the convincing results of archaeological and historical studies. But people today continue to disobey God and go their own way. Like the Israelites, we are more concerned about our physical condition than our spiritual condition. We can escape this pattern only by paying attention to all the signs of God's presence that we have been given. Has God guided and protected you? Has he answered your prayers? Do you know people who have experienced remarkable blessings and healings? Do you know Bible stories about the way God has led his people? Focus your thoughts on what God has done, and rebellion will become unthinkable.

holy offerings—including the grain offerings, sin offerings, and guilt offerings—will be most holy, and it belongs to you and your sons. [10]You must eat it as a most holy offering. All the males may eat of it, and you must treat it as most holy.

18:11
Lev 22:2-3, 11-13

[11]"All the sacred offerings and special offerings presented to me when the Israelites lift them up before the altar also belong to you. I have given them to you and to your sons and daughters as your permanent share. Any member of your family who is ceremonially clean may eat of these offerings.

18:12
Exod 23:19
Deut 18:4

[12]"I also give you the harvest gifts brought by the people as offerings to the LORD—the best of the olive oil, new wine, and grain. [13]All the first crops of their land that the people present to the LORD belong to you. Any member of your family who is ceremonially clean may eat this food.

18:14
Lev 27:28

[14]"Everything in Israel that is specially set apart for the LORD* also belongs to you.

[15]"The firstborn of every mother, whether human or animal, that is offered to the LORD will be yours. But you must always redeem your firstborn sons and the firstborn of ceremonially unclean animals. [16]Redeem them when they are one month old. The redemption price is five pieces of silver* (as measured by the weight of the sanctuary shekel, which equals twenty gerahs).

18:19
2 Chr 13:5

[17]"However, you may not redeem the firstborn of cattle, sheep, or goats. They are holy and have been set apart for the LORD. Sprinkle their blood on the altar, and burn their fat as a special gift, a pleasing aroma to the LORD. [18]The meat of these animals will be yours, just like the breast and right thigh that are presented by lifting them up as a special offering before the altar. [19]Yes, I am giving you all these holy offerings that the people of Israel bring to the LORD. They are for you and your sons and daughters, to be eaten as your permanent share. This is an eternal and unbreakable covenant* between the LORD and you, and it also applies to your descendants."

18:20
Deut 10:9; 18:2
Josh 13:33
Ezek 44:28
18:21
Lev 27:30-33

[20]And the LORD said to Aaron, "You priests will receive no allotment of land or share of property among the people of Israel. I am your share and your allotment. [21]As for the tribe of Levi, your relatives, I will compensate them for their service in the Tabernacle. Instead of an allotment of land, I will give them the tithes from the entire land of Israel.

18:23
Num 18:1, 20

[22]"From now on, no Israelites except priests or Levites may approach the Tabernacle. If they come too near, they will be judged guilty and will die. [23]Only the Levites may serve at the Tabernacle, and they will be held responsible for any offenses against it. This is a permanent law for you, to be observed from generation to generation. The Levites will receive no allotment of land among the Israelites, [24]because I have given them the Israelites' tithes, which have been presented as sacred offerings to the LORD. This will be the Levites' share. That is why I said they would receive no allotment of land among the Israelites."

18:26
Num 18:28
Neh 10:38

[25]The LORD also told Moses, [26]"Give these instructions to the Levites: When you receive from the people of Israel the tithes I have assigned as your allotment, give a tenth of the tithes you receive—a tithe of the tithe—to the LORD as a sacred offering. [27]The LORD will consider this offering to be your harvest offering, as though it were the first grain from your own threshing floor or wine from your own winepress. [28]You must present one-tenth of the tithe received from the Israelites as a sacred offering to the LORD. This is the LORD's sacred portion, and you must present it to Aaron the priest. [29]Be sure to give to the LORD the best portions of the gifts given to you.

18:28
Num 18:21

18:31
Matt 10:10
Luke 10:7
1 Cor 9:13
1 Tim 5:18
18:32
Lev 22:2, 15-16

[30]"Also, give these instructions to the Levites: When you present the best part as your offering, it will be considered as though it came from your own threshing floor or winepress. [31]You Levites and your families may eat this food anywhere you wish, for it is your compensation for serving in the Tabernacle. [32]You will not be considered guilty for accepting the LORD's tithes if you give the best portion to the priests. But be careful not to treat the holy gifts of the people of Israel as though they were common. If you do, you will die."

18:14 The Hebrew term used here refers to the complete consecration of things or people to the LORD, either by destroying them or by giving them as an offering.  18:16 Hebrew *5 shekels* [2 ounces or 57 grams] *of silver.*
18:19 Hebrew *a covenant of salt.*

**18:25, 26** Even the Levites, who were ministers, had to tithe to support the Lord's work. No one was exempt from returning to God a portion of what was received. Though the Levites owned no land and operated no great enterprises, they were to treat their income the same as everyone else did by giving a portion to care for the needs of the other Levites and of the Tabernacle. The tithing principle is still relevant. God expects all his followers to supply the material needs of those who devote themselves to meeting the spiritual needs of the community of faith. Ask God to direct you about what you should give and to help you give generously.

## The Water of Purification

**19** The LORD said to Moses and Aaron, 2"Here is another legal requirement commanded by the LORD: Tell the people of Israel to bring you a red heifer, a perfect animal that has no defects and has never been yoked to a plow. 3Give it to Eleazar the priest, and it will be taken outside the camp and slaughtered in his presence. 4Eleazar will take some of its blood on his finger and sprinkle it seven times toward the front of the Tabernacle.* 5As Eleazar watches, the heifer must be burned—its hide, meat, blood, and dung. 6Eleazar the priest must then take a stick of cedar,* a hyssop branch, and some scarlet yarn and throw them into the fire where the heifer is burning.

7"Then the priest must wash his clothes and bathe himself in water. Afterward he may return to the camp, though he will remain ceremonially unclean until evening. 8The man who burns the animal must also wash his clothes and bathe himself in water, and he, too, will remain unclean until evening. 9Then someone who is ceremonially clean will gather up the ashes of the heifer and deposit them in a purified place outside the camp. They will be kept there for the community of Israel to use in the water for the purification ceremony. This ceremony is performed for the removal of sin. 10The man who gathers up the ashes of the heifer must also wash his clothes, and he will remain ceremonially unclean until evening. This is a permanent law for the people of Israel and any foreigners who live among them.

11"All those who touch a dead human body will be ceremonially unclean for seven days. 12They must purify themselves on the third and seventh days with the water of purification; then they will be purified. But if they do not do this on the third and seventh days, they will continue to be unclean even after the seventh day. 13All those who touch a dead body and do not purify themselves in the proper way defile the LORD's Tabernacle, and they will be cut off from the community of Israel. Since the water of purification was not sprinkled on them, their defilement continues.

14"This is the ritual law that applies when someone dies inside a tent: All those who enter that tent and those who were inside when the death occurred will be ceremonially unclean for seven days. 15Any open container in the tent that was not covered with a lid is also defiled. 16And if someone in an open field touches the corpse of someone who was killed with a sword or who died a natural death, or if someone touches a human bone or a grave, that person will be defiled for seven days.

17"To remove the defilement, put some of the ashes from the burnt purification offering in a jar, and pour fresh water over them. 18Then someone who is ceremonially clean must take a hyssop branch and dip it into the water. That person must sprinkle the water on the tent, on all the furnishings in the tent, and on the people who were in the tent; also on the person who touched a human bone, or touched someone who was killed or who died

**19:2**
Lev 22:20-25
Deut 21:3

**19:4**
Lev 4:6, 17; 16:14

**19:6**
Lev 14:4, 6, 49

**19:7**
Lev 11:25;
16:26-28

**19:9**
Num 8:7; 19:13,
20-21

**19:10**
Num 19:7-8, 19

**19:11**
Lev 21:1

**19:12**
Num 19:17-19

**19:13**
Lev 7:20-21; 15:31;
20:3; 22:3

**19:16**
Num 19:11; 31:19

**19:17**
Num 19:9

**19:4** Hebrew *the Tent of Meeting.*   **19:6** Or *juniper.*

---

**19:9, 10** What is the significance of the red heifer's ashes? When a person touched a dead body, he was considered unclean (i.e., unable to approach God in worship). This ritual purified the unclean person so that once again he could offer sacrifices and worship God. Death was the strongest of defilements because it was the final result of sin. Thus, a special sacrifice—a red heifer—was required. It had to be offered by someone who was not unclean. When it had been burned on the altar, its ashes were used to purify water for ceremonial cleansing—not so much physically as symbolically. The unclean person then washed himself, and often his clothes and belongings, with this purified water as an act of becoming clean again.

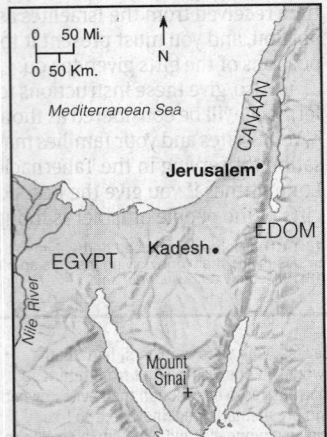

**EVENTS AT KADESH**
After wandering in the wilderness for 40 years, Israel arrived at Kadesh, where Miriam died. There was not enough water, and the people complained bitterly. Moses struck a rock, and it gave enough water for everyone. The king of Edom refused Israel passage through his land, forcing them to travel around his country.

**19:19**
Ezek 36:25-27
Heb 10:22

naturally, or touched a grave. ¹⁹On the third and seventh days the person who is ceremonially clean must sprinkle the water on those who are defiled. Then on the seventh day the people being cleansed must wash their clothes and bathe themselves, and that evening they will be cleansed of their defilement.

**19:20**
Num 19:13

²⁰"But those who become defiled and do not purify themselves will be cut off from the community, for they have defiled the sanctuary of the LORD. Since the water of purification has not been sprinkled on them, they remain defiled. ²¹This is a permanent law for the people. Those who sprinkle the water of purification must afterward wash their clothes, and anyone who then touches the water used for purification will remain defiled until evening. ²²Anything and anyone that a defiled person touches will be ceremonially unclean until evening."

**19:21**
Lev 11:25, 40;
16:26-28
Num 19:7

**19:22**
Lev 5:2-3; 7:21

### 4. The new generation
*Moses Strikes the Rock*

**20:1**
Num 13:21

**20:2**
Exod 17:1

**20:3**
Exod 17:2
Num 14:2-3;
16:31-35

**20** In the first month of the year,* the whole community of Israel arrived in the wilderness of Zin and camped at Kadesh. While they were there, Miriam died and was buried.

²There was no water for the people to drink at that place, so they rebelled against Moses and Aaron. ³The people blamed Moses and said, "If only we had died in the LORD's presence

20:1 The first month of the ancient Hebrew lunar calendar usually occurs within the months of March and April. The number of years since leaving Egypt is not specified.

---

**ELEAZAR**

An understudy must know the lead role completely and be willing to step into it at a moment's notice. Eleazar was an excellent understudy, well trained for his eventual leading role. However, his moments in the spotlight were painful. On one occasion, he watched his two older brothers burn to death for failing to take God's holiness seriously. Later, as his father was dying, he was made high priest, surely one of the most responsible—and therefore potentially most stressful—positions in Israel.

An understudy benefits from having both the script and a human model of the role. Ever since childhood, Eleazar had been able to observe Moses and Aaron. Now he could learn from watching Joshua. In addition, he had God's laws to guide him as he worked as priest and adviser to Joshua.

| | |
|---|---|
| **Strengths and accomplishments** | • Succeeded his father, Aaron, as high priest<br>• Completed his father's work by helping lead the people into the Promised Land<br>• Teamed up with Joshua<br>• Acted as God's spokesman to the people |
| **Lessons from his life** | • Concentrating on our present challenges and responsibilities is the best way to prepare for what God has planned for our future<br>• God's desire is consistent obedience throughout our lives |
| **Vital statistics** | • Where: Wilderness of Sinai, Promised Land<br>• Occupations: Priest and high priest<br>• Relatives: Father: Aaron. Brothers: Nadab, Abihu, and Ithamar. Aunt: Miriam. Uncle: Moses.<br>• Contemporaries: Joshua, Caleb |
| **Key verses** | "There, on the border of the land of Edom, the LORD said to Moses and Aaron, 'The time has come for Aaron to join his ancestors in death. . . . Now take Aaron and his son Eleazar up Mount Hor. There you will remove Aaron's priestly garments and put them on Eleazar, his son'" (Numbers 20:23–26). |

Eleazar is mentioned in Exodus 6:23; Leviticus 10:16–20; Numbers 3:1–4; 4:16; 16:36–40; 20:25–29; 26:1–4, 63; 27:2, 15–23; 32:2; 34:17; Deuteronomy 10:6; Joshua 14:1; 17:4; 24:33.

---

**20:1** It had been 37 years since Israel's first scouting mission into the Promised Land (Numbers 13–14) and 40 years since the Exodus from Egypt. The Bible is virtually silent about those 37 years of aimless wandering. The generation of those who had lived in Egypt had almost died off, and the new generation would soon be ready to enter the land. Moses, Aaron, Joshua, and Caleb were among the few who remained from those who had left Egypt. Once again they camped at Kadesh, the site of the first scouting mission

that had ended in disaster. Moses hoped the people were ready for a fresh start.

**20:3-5** After 37 years in the wilderness, the Israelites forgot that their wanderings were a result of their parents' and their own sin. They could not accept the fact that they brought their problems upon themselves, so they blamed Moses for their condition. Often our troubles result from our own disobedience or lack of faith. We cannot blame God for our sins. Until we face this reality, we will have little peace and no spiritual growth.

with our brothers! 4Why have you brought the congregation of the LORD's people into this wilderness to die, along with all our livestock? 5Why did you make us leave Egypt and bring us here to this terrible place? This land has no grain, no figs, no grapes, no pomegranates, and no water to drink!"

6Moses and Aaron turned away from the people and went to the entrance of the Tabernacle,* where they fell face down on the ground. Then the glorious presence of the LORD appeared to them, 7and the LORD said to Moses, 8"You and Aaron must take the staff and assemble the entire community. As the people watch, speak to the rock over there, and it will pour out its water. You will provide enough water from the rock to satisfy the whole community and their livestock."

9So Moses did as he was told. He took the staff from the place where it was kept before the LORD. 10Then he and Aaron summoned the people to come and gather at the rock. "Listen, you rebels!" he shouted. "Must we bring you water from this rock?" 11Then Moses raised his hand and struck the rock twice with the staff, and water gushed out. So the entire community and their livestock drank their fill.

12But the LORD said to Moses and Aaron, "Because you did not trust me enough to demonstrate my holiness to the people of Israel, you will not lead them into the land I am giving them!" 13This place was known as the waters of Meribah (which means "arguing") because there the people of Israel argued with the LORD, and there he demonstrated his holiness among them.

## Edom Refuses Israel Passage

14While Moses was at Kadesh, he sent ambassadors to the king of Edom with this message:

"This is what your relatives, the people of Israel, say: You know all the hardships we have been through. 15Our ancestors went down to Egypt, and we lived there a long time, and we and our ancestors were brutally mistreated by the Egyptians. 16But when we cried out to the LORD, he heard us and sent an angel who brought us out of Egypt. Now we are camped at Kadesh, a town on the border of your land. 17Please let us travel through your land. We will be careful not to go through your fields and vineyards. We won't even drink water from your wells. We will stay on the king's road and never leave it until we have passed through your territory."

18But the king of Edom said, "Stay out of my land, or I will meet you with an army!"
19The Israelites answered, "We will stay on the main road. If our livestock drink your water, we will pay for it. Just let us pass through your country. That's all we ask."

20But the king of Edom replied, "Stay out! You may not pass through our land." With that he mobilized his army and marched out against them with an imposing force. 21Because Edom refused to allow Israel to pass through their country, Israel was forced to turn around.

## The Death of Aaron

22The whole community of Israel left Kadesh and arrived at Mount Hor. 23There, on the border of the land of Edom, the LORD said to Moses and Aaron, 24"The time has come for Aaron to join his ancestors in death. He will not enter the land I am giving the people of

20:6 Hebrew *the Tent of Meeting.*

**20:12** The Lord had told Moses to speak to the rock; however, Moses struck it, not once, but twice. God did the miracle; yet Moses was taking credit for it when he said, "Must we bring you water from this rock?" (20:10). For this he was forbidden to enter the Promised Land. Was God's punishment of Moses too harsh? After all, the people had nagged him, slandered him, and rebelled against both him and God. Now they were at it again (20:5). But Moses was the leader and model for the entire nation. Because of this great responsibility to the people, he could not be let off lightly. By striking the rock, Moses disobeyed God's direct command and dishonored God in the presence of his people.

**20:14** Two brothers became the ancestors of two nations. The Edomites descended from Esau, the Israelites from Jacob. Thus, the Edomites were "relatives" to the Israelites. Israel sent a brotherly message to Edom requesting passage through their land on the main road, a well-traveled trade route. Israel promised to stay on the road, thus harmlessly bypassing Edom's fields, vineyards,

and wells. The Edomites refused, however, because they did not trust Israel's word. They were afraid that this great horde of people would either attack them or devour their crops (Deuteronomy 2:4, 5). Because brothers should not fight, God told the Israelites to turn back and travel by a different route to the Promised Land.

**20:17** The king's road was an old caravan route. Long before this time it was used as a major public road.

**20:21** Moses tried to negotiate and reason with the Edomite king. When nothing worked, he was left with two choices—force a conflict or avoid it. Moses knew there would be enough barriers in the days and months ahead. There was no point in adding another one unnecessarily. Sometimes conflict is unavoidable. Sometimes, however, it isn't worth the consequences. Open warfare may seem heroic, courageous, and even righteous, but it is not always the best choice. At times, we should follow Moses' example and find another way to solve our problems, even if it is harder for us to do.

Israel, because the two of you rebelled against my instructions concerning the water at Meribah. 25Now take Aaron and his son Eleazar up Mount Hor. 26There you will remove Aaron's priestly garments and put them on Eleazar, his son. Aaron will die there and join his ancestors."

27So Moses did as the LORD commanded. The three of them went up Mount Hor together as the whole community watched. 28At the summit, Moses removed the priestly garments from Aaron and put them on Eleazar, Aaron's son. Then Aaron died there on top of the mountain, and Moses and Eleazar went back down. 29When the people realized that Aaron had died, all Israel mourned for him thirty days.

### Victory over the Canaanites

**21** The Canaanite king of Arad, who lived in the Negev, heard that the Israelites were approaching on the road through Atharim. So he attacked the Israelites and took some of them as prisoners. 2Then the people of Israel made this vow to the LORD: "If you will hand these people over to us, we will completely destroy* all their towns." 3The LORD heard the Israelites' request and gave them victory over the Canaanites. The Israelites completely destroyed them and their towns, and the place has been called Hormah* ever since.

### The Bronze Snake

4Then the people of Israel set out from Mount Hor, taking the road to the Red Sea* to go around the land of Edom. But the people grew impatient with the long journey, 5and they began to speak against God and Moses. "Why have you brought us out of Egypt to die here in the wilderness?" they complained. "There is nothing to eat here and nothing to drink. And we hate this horrible manna!"

6So the LORD sent poisonous snakes among the people, and many were bitten and died. 7Then the people came to Moses and cried out, "We have sinned by speaking against the LORD and against you. Pray that the LORD will take away the snakes." So Moses prayed for the people.

8Then the LORD told him, "Make a replica of a poisonous snake and attach it to a pole. All

**Margin references:**
20:25 Num 3:4; 19:3-4
20:26 Num 20:24
20:28 Num 33:38
21:1 Num 33:40; Josh 12:14; Judg 1:16
21:3 Num 14:45
21:4 Deut 2:8
21:5 Num 11:5-6; 14:2-3; Ps 78:19
21:6 Deut 8:15; 1 Cor 10:9
21:7 Ps 78:34
21:8 Isa 14:29; John 3:14-15

**21:2** The Hebrew term used here refers to the complete consecration of things or people to the LORD, either by destroying them or by giving them as an offering; also in 21:3.　**21:3** *Hormah* means "destruction."　**21:4** Hebrew *sea of reeds.*

**EVENTS IN THE WILDERNESS** Israel next met resistance from the king of Arad but soundly defeated him. The next stop was Mount Hor (where Aaron had died); then they traveled south and east around Edom. After camping at Oboth, they moved toward the Arnon River and onto the plains of Moab near Pisgah Peak.

**20:28** Aaron died just before entering the Promised Land, probably as punishment for his sin of rebellion (Exodus 32; Numbers 12:1-9). This was the first time that a new high priest was appointed. The priestly clothing was removed from Aaron and placed on his son Eleazar, following the commands recorded in the book of Leviticus.

**21:5** In Psalm 78, we learn the sources of Israel's complaining: (1) Their spirits were not faithful to God (78:8); (2) they refused to obey God's law (78:10); (3) they forgot the miracles God had done for them (78:11). Our complaining often has its roots in one of these thoughtless actions and attitudes. If we can deal with the cause of our complaining, it will not take hold and grow in our lives.

**21:6** God used poisonous snakes to punish the people for their unbelief and complaining. The wilderness where they traveled has a variety of snakes. Some hide in the sand and attack without warning. Both the Israelites and the Egyptians had a great fear of snakes. A bite by a poisonous snake often meant a slow death with intense suffering.

**21:8, 9** When the bronze snake was hung on the pole, the Israelites didn't know the fuller meaning Jesus Christ would bring to this event (see John 3:14, 15). Jesus explained that just as the Israelites were healed of their sickness by looking at the snake on the pole, all believers today can be saved from the sickness of sin by looking to Jesus' death on the cross. It was not the snake that healed the people but their belief that God could heal them. This belief was demonstrated by their obedience to God's instructions. In the same way, we should continue to look to Christ (see Hebrews 12:2).

who are bitten will live if they simply look at it!" 9 So Moses made a snake out of bronze and attached it to a pole. Then anyone who was bitten by a snake could look at the bronze snake and be healed!

21:9
2 Kgs 18:4
John 3:14; 12:32

### Israel's Journey to Moab

10The Israelites traveled next to Oboth and camped there. 11Then they went on to Iye-abarim, in the wilderness on the eastern border of Moab. 12From there they traveled to the valley of Zered Brook and set up camp. 13Then they moved out and camped on the far side of the Arnon River, in the wilderness adjacent to the territory of the Amorites. The Arnon is the boundary line between the Moabites and the Amorites. 14For this reason *The Book of the Wars of the LORD* speaks of "the town of Waheb in the area of Suphah, and the ravines of the Arnon River, 15and the ravines that extend as far as the settlement of Ar on the border of Moab."

21:10
Num 33:43

16From there the Israelites traveled to Beer,* which is the well where the LORD said to Moses, "Assemble the people, and I will give them water." 17There the Israelites sang this song:

21:15
Num 21:28
Deut 2:9
21:16
Judg 9:21

> "Spring up, O well!
>     Yes, sing its praises!
> 18 Sing of this well,
>     which princes dug,
> which great leaders hollowed out
>     with their scepters and staffs."

Then the Israelites left the wilderness and proceeded on through Mattanah, 19Nahaliel, and Bamoth. 20After that they went to the valley in Moab where Pisgah Peak overlooks the wasteland.*

### Victory over Sihon and Og

21The Israelites sent ambassadors to King Sihon of the Amorites with this message:

21:21
Deut 2:26-28
Judg 11:19-21
21:22
Num 20:17

22"Let us travel through your land. We will be careful not to go through your fields and vineyards. We won't even drink water from your wells. We will stay on the king's road until we have passed through your territory."

23But King Sihon refused to let them cross his territory. Instead, he mobilized his entire army and attacked Israel in the wilderness, engaging them in battle at Jahaz. 24But the Israelites slaughtered them with their swords and occupied their land from the Arnon River to the Jabbok River. They went only as far as the Ammonite border because the boundary of the Ammonites was fortified.*

21:23
Num 20:21
Deut 2:32
Judg 11:20
21:24
Deut 2:19, 31-37
Josh 12:1-2; 13:10

21:16 *Beer* means "well." 21:20 Or *overlooks Jeshimon.* 21:24 Or *because the terrain of the Ammonite frontier was rugged;* Hebrew reads *because the boundary of the Ammonites was strong.*

---

21:14 There is no other existing record of *The Book of the Wars of the LORD.* Most likely, it was a collection of victory songs or poems.

**BATTLES WITH SIHON AND OG**
King Sihon refused passage to the Israelites through his land, and he attacked Israel at Jahaz. Israel defeated him, occupying the land between the Arnon and Jabbok Rivers, including the capital city, Heshbon. As they moved north, they defeated King Og of Bashan at Edrei.

21:25
Amos 2:10

21:26
Ps 135:11

25So Israel captured all the towns of the Amorites and settled in them, including the city of Heshbon and its surrounding villages. 26Heshbon had been the capital of King Sihon of the Amorites. He had defeated a former Moabite king and seized all his land as far as the Arnon River. 27Therefore, the ancient poets wrote this about him:

> "Come to Heshbon and let it be rebuilt!
> Let the city of Sihon be restored.

21:28
Deut 2:9, 18
Jer 48:45-46

> 28 A fire flamed forth from Heshbon,
> a blaze from the city of Sihon.
> It burned the city of Ar in Moab;
> it destroyed the rulers of the Arnon heights.

21:29
Judg 11:24
1 Kgs 11:7, 33

> 29 What sorrow awaits you, O people of Moab!
> You are finished, O worshipers of Chemosh!
> Chemosh has left his sons as refugees,
> his daughters as captives of Sihon, the Amorite king.
> 30 We have utterly destroyed them,
> from Heshbon to Dibon.
> We have completely wiped them out
> as far away as Nophah and Medeba.*"

21:32
Num 32:1, 35
Jer 48:32

21:33
Deut 3:3-4

31So the people of Israel occupied the territory of the Amorites. 32After Moses sent men to explore the Jazer area, they captured all the towns in the region and drove out the Amorites who lived there. 33Then they turned and marched up the road to Bashan, but King Og of Bashan and all his people attacked them at Edrei. 34The LORD said to Moses, "Do not be afraid of him, for I have handed him over to you, along with all his people and his land. Do the same to him as you did to King Sihon of the Amorites, who ruled in Heshbon." 35And Israel killed King Og, his sons, and all his subjects; not a single survivor remained. Then Israel occupied their land.

## D. SECOND APPROACH TO THE PROMISED LAND (22:1—36:13)

Now the old generation has died and a new generation stands poised at the border, ready to enter the Promised Land. Neighboring nations, however, cause Israel to begin worshiping other gods. Without Moses' quick action, the nation may never have entered Canaan. We must never let down our guard in resisting sin.

### 1. The story of Balaam

*Balak Sends for Balaam*

22:1
Num 33:48-49

22:2
Exod 15:15
Deut 2:25

22:4
Num 22:7;
25:15-18

**22** Then the people of Israel traveled to the plains of Moab and camped east of the Jordan River, across from Jericho. 2Balak son of Zippor, the Moabite king, had seen everything the Israelites did to the Amorites. 3And when the people of Moab saw how many Israelites there were, they were terrified. 4The king of Moab said to the elders of Midian, "This mob will devour everything in sight, like an ox devours grass in the field!"

21:30 Or *until fire spread to Medeba.* The meaning of the Hebrew is uncertain.

---

**THE SNAKE IN THE WILDERNESS**
Compare the texts for yourself:
Numbers 21:7-9 and John 3:14, 15.

| Israelites | Christians |
| --- | --- |
| Bitten by snakes | Bitten by sin |
| Little initial pain, then intense suffering | Little initial pain, then intense suffering |
| Physical death from snakes' poison | Spiritual death from sin's poison |
| Bronze snake lifted up in the wilderness | Christ lifted up on the cross |
| Looking to the snake spared one's life | Looking to Christ saves from eternal death |

---

**21:27-30** Chemosh, the national god of Moab, was worshiped as a god of war. This false god, however, was no help to this nation when it fought against Israel. Israel's God was stronger than any of Canaan's war gods.

**21:34** God assured Moses that Israel's enemy was conquered even before the battle began! God wants to give us victory over our enemies (which are usually problems related to sin rather than armed soldiers). But first we must believe that he can help us. Second, we must trust him to help us. Third, we must take the steps he shows us.

**22:4-6** Balaam was a sorcerer, one called upon to place curses on others. Belief in curses and blessings was common in Old Testament times. Sorcerers were thought to have power with the gods. Thus, the king of Moab wanted Balaam to use his powers with the God of Israel to place a curse on Israel—hoping that, by magic, God would turn against his people. Neither Balaam nor Balak had any idea whom they were dealing with!

So Balak, king of Moab, [5]sent messengers to call Balaam son of Beor, who was living in his native land of Pethor* near the Euphrates River.* His message said:

22:5
Num 23:7
Deut 23:4

"Look, a vast horde of people has arrived from Egypt. They cover the face of the earth and are threatening me. [6]Please come and curse these people for me because they are too powerful for me. Then perhaps I will be able to conquer them and drive them from the land. I know that blessings fall on any people you bless, and curses fall on people you curse."

[7]Balak's messengers, who were elders of Moab and Midian, set out with money to pay Balaam to place a curse upon Israel.* They went to Balaam and delivered Balak's message to him. [8]"Stay here overnight," Balaam said. "In the morning I will tell you whatever the LORD directs me to say." So the officials from Moab stayed there with Balaam.

22:7
Num 23:23

[9]That night God came to Balaam and asked him, "Who are these men visiting you?"

[10]Balaam said to God, "Balak son of Zippor, king of Moab, has sent me this message: [11]'Look, a vast horde of people has arrived from Egypt, and they cover the face of the earth. Come and curse these people for me. Then perhaps I will be able to stand up to them and drive them from the land.'"

[12]But God told Balaam, "Do not go with them. You are not to curse these people, for they have been blessed!"

22:12
Num 23:13-15

[13]The next morning Balaam got up and told Balak's officials, "Go on home! The LORD will not let me go with you."

[14]So the Moabite officials returned to King Balak and reported, "Balaam refused to come with us." [15]Then Balak tried again. This time he sent a larger number of even more distinguished officials than those he had sent the first time. [16]They went to Balaam and delivered this message to him:

"This is what Balak son of Zippor says: Please don't let anything stop you from coming to help me. [17]I will pay you very well and do whatever you tell me. Just come and curse these people for me!"

22:17
Num 22:6

[18]But Balaam responded to Balak's messengers, "Even if Balak were to give me his palace filled with silver and gold, I would be powerless to do anything against the will of the LORD my God. [19]But stay here one more night, and I will see if the LORD has anything else to say to me."

22:18
Num 23:26; 24:13

[20]That night God came to Balaam and told him, "Since these men have come for you, get up and go with them. But do only what I tell you to do."

22:20
Num 22:35;
23:12, 26

### Balaam and His Donkey

[21]So the next morning Balaam got up, saddled his donkey, and started off with the Moabite officials. [22]But God was angry that Balaam was going, so he sent the angel of the LORD to

22:21
2 Pet 2:15

22:5a Or *who was at Pethor in the land of the Amavites.* 22:5b Hebrew *the river.* 22:7 Hebrew *set out with the money of divination in their hand.*

---

**22:9** Why would God speak through a sorcerer like Balaam? God wanted to give a message to the Moabites, and they had already chosen to employ Balaam. So Balaam was available for God to use, much as he used the wicked pharaoh to accomplish his will in Egypt (Exodus 10:1). Balaam entered into his prophetic role seriously, but his heart was mixed. He had some knowledge of God, but not enough to forsake his magic and turn wholeheartedly to God. Although this story leads us to believe he turned completely to God, later passages in the Bible show that Balaam couldn't resist the tempting pull of money and idolatry (31:16; 2 Peter 2:15; Jude 1:11).

**22:20-23** God let Balaam go with Balak's messengers, but he was angry about Balaam's greedy attitude. Balaam claimed that he would not go against God just for money, but his resolve was beginning to slip. His greed for the wealth offered by the king blinded him so that he could not see how God was trying to stop him. Though we may know what God wants us to do, we can become blinded by the desire for money, possessions, or prestige. We can avoid Balaam's mistake by looking past the allure of fame or fortune to the long-range benefits of following God.

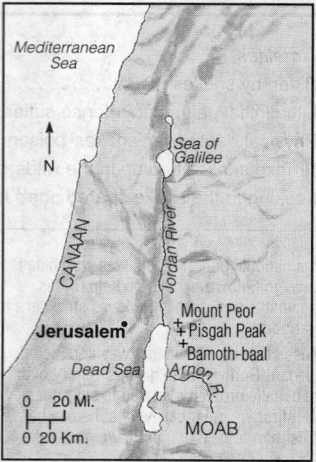

Mediterranean
Sea

N

CANAAN

Sea of
Galilee

Jordan River

**Jerusalem**

Dead Sea

Mount Peor
✝ Pisgah Peak
✝ Bamoth-baal
Arnon

0    20 MI.

0    20 Km.              MOAB

**THE STORY OF BALAAM**
At King Balak's request, Balaam traveled nearly 400 miles to curse Israel. Balak took Balaam to Bamoth-baal ("the high places of Baal"), then to Pisgah Peak, and finally to Mount Peor. Each place looked over the plains of Moab, where the Israelites were camped. But to the king's dismay, Balaam blessed, not cursed, Israel.

stand in the road to block his way. As Balaam and two servants were riding along, 23Balaam's donkey saw the angel of the LORD standing in the road with a drawn sword in his hand. The donkey bolted off the road into a field, but Balaam beat it and turned it back onto the road. 24Then the angel of the LORD stood at a place where the road narrowed between two vineyard walls. 25When the donkey saw the angel of the LORD, it tried to squeeze by and crushed Balaam's foot against the wall. So Balaam beat the donkey again. 26Then the angel of the LORD moved farther down the road and stood in a place too narrow for the donkey to get by at all. 27This time when the donkey saw the angel, it lay down under Balaam. In a fit of rage Balaam beat the animal again with his staff.

**22:28**
2 Pet 2:16

28Then the LORD gave the donkey the ability to speak. "What have I done to you that deserves your beating me three times?" it asked Balaam.

29"You have made me look like a fool!" Balaam shouted. "If I had a sword with me, I would kill you!"

**22:30**
2 Pet 2:16

30"But I am the same donkey you have ridden all your life," the donkey answered. "Have I ever done anything like this before?"

"No," Balaam admitted.

**22:31**
Josh 5:13-15

31Then the LORD opened Balaam's eyes, and he saw the angel of the LORD standing in the roadway with a drawn sword in his hand. Balaam bowed his head and fell face down on the ground before him.

32"Why did you beat your donkey those three times?" the angel of the LORD demanded. "Look, I have come to block your way because you are stubbornly resisting me. 33Three times the donkey saw me and shied away; otherwise, I would certainly have killed you by now and spared the donkey."

**B**alaam was one of those noteworthy Old Testament characters who, though not one of God's chosen people, was willing to acknowledge that Yahweh (the LORD) was indeed a powerful God. But he did not believe in the Lord as the only true God. His story exposes the deception of maintaining an outward facade of spirituality over a corrupt inward life. Balaam was a man ready to obey God's command as long as he could profit from doing so. This mixture of motives—obedience and profit—eventually led to Balaam's death. Although he realized the awesome power of Israel's God, his heart was occupied with the wealth he could gain in Moab. There he returned to die when the armies of Israel invaded.

Eventually, each of us lives through the same process. Who and what we are will somehow come to the surface, destroying any masks we may have put on to cover up our real selves. Efforts spent on keeping up appearances would be much better spent on finding the answer to sin in our lives. We can avoid Balaam's mistake by facing ourselves and realizing that God is willing to accept us, forgive us, and literally make us over from within. Don't miss this great discovery that eluded Balaam.

| | |
|---|---|
| **Strengths and accomplishments** | • Widely known for his effective curses and blessings<br>• Obeyed God and blessed Israel, in spite of Balak's bribe |
| **Weaknesses and mistakes** | • Encouraged the Israelites to worship idols (Numbers 31:16)<br>• Returned to Moab and was killed in war |
| **Lessons from his life** | • Motives are just as important as actions<br>• Your treasure is where your heart is |
| **Vital statistics** | • Where: Lived near the Euphrates River, traveled to Moab<br>• Occupations: Sorcerer, prophet<br>• Relative: Father: Beor<br>• Contemporaries: Balak (king of Moab), Moses, Aaron |
| **Key verses** | "They have wandered off the right road and followed the footsteps of Balaam son of Beor, who loved to earn money by doing wrong. But Balaam was stopped from his mad course when his donkey rebuked him with a human voice" (2 Peter 2:15, 16). |

Balaam's story is told in Numbers 22:1—24:25. He is also mentioned in Numbers 31:7, 8, 16; Deuteronomy 23:4, 5; Joshua 24:9, 10; Nehemiah 13:2; Micah 6:5; 2 Peter 2:15, 16; Jude 1:11; Revelation 2:14.

**22:27** Donkeys were all-purpose vehicles used for transportation, carrying loads, grinding grain, and plowing fields. They were usually highly dependable, which explains why Balaam became so angry when his donkey refused to move.

**22:29** The donkey saved Balaam's life but made him look foolish in the process, so Balaam lashed out at the donkey. We sometimes strike out at blameless people who get in our way because we are embarrassed or our pride is hurt. Lashing out at others can be a sign that something is wrong with us. Don't allow your own hurt pride to lead you to hurt others.

34Then Balaam confessed to the angel of the Lord, "I have sinned. I didn't realize you were standing in the road to block my way. I will return home if you are against my going."

35But the angel of the Lord told Balaam, "Go with these men, but say only what I tell you to say." So Balaam went on with Balak's officials. 36When King Balak heard that Balaam was on the way, he went out to meet him at a Moabite town on the Arnon River at the farthest border of his land.

37"Didn't I send you an urgent invitation? Why didn't you come right away?" Balak asked Balaam. "Didn't you believe me when I said I would reward you richly?"

38Balaam replied, "Look, now I have come, but I have no power to say whatever I want. I will speak only the message that God puts in my mouth." 39Then Balaam accompanied Balak to Kiriath-huzoth, 40where the king sacrificed cattle and sheep. He sent portions of the meat to Balaam and the officials who were with him. 41The next morning Balak took Balaam up to Bamoth-baal. From there he could see some of the people of Israel spread out below him.

## Balaam Blesses Israel

**23** Then Balaam said to King Balak, "Build me seven altars here, and prepare seven young bulls and seven rams for me to sacrifice." 2Balak followed his instructions, and the two of them sacrificed a young bull and a ram on each altar.

3Then Balaam said to Balak, "Stand here by your burnt offerings, and I will go to see if the Lord will respond to me. Then I will tell you whatever he reveals to me." So Balaam went alone to the top of a bare hill, 4and God met him there. Balaam said to him, "I have prepared seven altars and have sacrificed a young bull and a ram on each altar."

5The Lord gave Balaam a message for King Balak. Then he said, "Go back to Balak and give him my message."

6So Balaam returned and found the king standing beside his burnt offerings with all the officials of Moab. 7This was the message Balaam delivered:

"Balak summoned me to come from Aram;
    the king of Moab brought me from the eastern hills.
'Come,' he said, 'curse Jacob for me!
    Come and announce Israel's doom.'
8 But how can I curse those
    whom God has not cursed?
How can I condemn those
    whom the Lord has not condemned?
9 I see them from the cliff tops;
    I watch them from the hills.
I see a people who live by themselves,
    set apart from other nations.
10 Who can count Jacob's descendants, as numerous as dust?
    Who can count even a fourth of Israel's people?
Let me die like the righteous;
    let my life end like theirs."

11Then King Balak demanded of Balaam, "What have you done to me? I brought you to curse my enemies. Instead, you have blessed them!"

12But Balaam replied, "I will speak only the message that the Lord puts in my mouth."

## Balaam's Second Message

13Then King Balak told him, "Come with me to another place. There you will see another part of the nation of Israel, but not all of them. Curse at least that many!" 14So Balak took Balaam to the plateau of Zophim on Pisgah Peak. He built seven altars there and offered a young bull and a ram on each altar.

15Then Balaam said to the king, "Stand here by your burnt offerings while I go over there to meet the Lord."

---

**22:34**
1 Sam 15:24

**22:35**
Num 22:20

**22:37-38**
Num 22:18

**22:41**
Num 21:28; 23:13

**23:1**
Num 22:40

**23:5**
Num 22:20, 35; 23:16

**23:7**
Num 22:6

**23:8**
Num 22:12

**23:9**
Num 22:41

**23:10**
Gen 13:16
Ps 37:37
Isa 57:1

**23:12**
Num 22:20, 38

---

**22:41** Bamoth-baal means the "high places of Baal" near Heshbon and Dibon. It was the first stopping point on the way to the high plains of Moab. From this vantage point, they could see the entire Israelite camp.

**23:1-3** The number seven was sacred among many of the nations and religions at this time.

**23:16**
Num 22:38

16And the Lord met Balaam and gave him a message. Then he said, "Go back to Balak and give him my message."

17So Balaam returned and found the king standing beside his burnt offerings with all the officials of Moab. "What did the Lord say?" Balak asked eagerly.

18This was the message Balaam delivered:

"Rise up, Balak, and listen!
Hear me, son of Zippor.

**23:19**
1 Sam 15:29
Isa 40:8; 55:11

19 God is not a man, so he does not lie.
He is not human, so he does not change his mind.
Has he ever spoken and failed to act?
Has he ever promised and not carried it through?

**23:20**
Isa 43:13

20 Listen, I received a command to bless;
God has blessed, and I cannot reverse it!

**23:21**
Exod 3:12
Deut 31:23

21 No misfortune is in his plan for Jacob;
no trouble is in store for Israel.
For the Lord their God is with them;
he has been proclaimed their king.

**23:22**
Num 24:8

22 God brought them out of Egypt;
for them he is as strong as a wild ox.

**23:23**
Num 22:7

23 No curse can touch Jacob;
no magic has any power against Israel.
For now it will be said of Jacob,
'What wonders God has done for Israel!'

**23:24**
Gen 49:9

24 These people rise up like a lioness,
like a majestic lion rousing itself.
They refuse to rest
until they have feasted on prey,
drinking the blood of the slaughtered!"

**23:26**
Num 22:38

25Then Balak said to Balaam, "Fine, but if you won't curse them, at least don't bless them!"

26But Balaam replied to Balak, "Didn't I tell you that I can do only what the Lord tells me?"

### Balaam's Third Message

27 Then King Balak said to Balaam, "Come, I will take you to one more place. Perhaps it will please God to let you curse them from there."

**23:28**
Num 31:16
Josh 22:17

28So Balak took Balaam to the top of Mount Peor, overlooking the wasteland.* 29Balaam again told Balak, "Build me seven altars, and prepare seven young bulls and seven rams for me to sacrifice." 30So Balak did as Balaam ordered and offered a young bull and a ram on each altar.

**24:1**
Num 23:23, 38

**24:2**
Num 11:25-26
1 Sam 10:10
2 Chr 15:1

**24:3**
Num 23:7-10,
18-24

**24:4**
Num 12:6; 22:20

**24** By now Balaam realized that the Lord was determined to bless Israel, so he did not resort to divination as before. Instead, he turned and looked out toward the wilderness, 2where he saw the people of Israel camped, tribe by tribe. Then the Spirit of God came upon him, 3and this is the message he delivered:

"This is the message of Balaam son of Beor,
the message of the man whose eyes see clearly,
4 the message of one who hears the words of God,
who sees a vision from the Almighty,
who bows down with eyes wide open:

**23:28** Or *overlooking Jeshimon.*

---

**23:27** Balak took Balaam to several places to try to entice him to curse the Israelites. He thought a change of scenery might help change Balaam's mind. But changing locations won't change God's will. We must learn to face the source of our problems. Moving to escape problems only makes solving them more difficult. Problems rooted in us are not solved by a change of scenery. A change in location or job may only distract us from the need for us to change our heart.

**24:1** Because Balaam was a sorcerer, he would look for omens or signs to help him tell the future. In this situation, however, it was clear that God himself was speaking, and so Balaam needed no other signs, real or imagined.

5 How beautiful are your tents, O Jacob;
    how lovely are your homes, O Israel!
6 They spread before me like palm groves,*
    like gardens by the riverside.
  They are like tall trees planted by the LORD,
    like cedars beside the waters.

24:6
Ps 45:8

7 Water will flow from their buckets;
    their offspring have all they need.
  Their king will be greater than Agag;
    their kingdom will be exalted.

24:7
1 Sam 15:8-9
Ps 145:11-13

8 God brought them out of Egypt;
    for them he is as strong as a wild ox.
  He devours all the nations that oppose him,
    breaking their bones in pieces,
    shooting them with arrows.

24:8
Ps 45:5

9 Like a lion, Israel crouches and lies down;
    like a lioness, who dares to arouse her?
  Blessed is everyone who blesses you, O Israel,
    and cursed is everyone who curses you."

24:9
Gen 12:3; 27:29;
49:9
Num 23:24

¹⁰King Balak flew into a rage against Balaam. He angrily clapped his hands and shouted, "I called you to curse my enemies! Instead, you have blessed them three times. ¹¹Now get out of here! Go back home! I promised to reward you richly, but the LORD has kept you from your reward."

24:11
Num 22:17, 37

¹²Balaam told Balak, "Don't you remember what I told your messengers? I said, ¹³'Even if Balak were to give me his palace filled with silver and gold, I would be powerless to do anything against the will of the LORD.' I told you that I could say only what the LORD says! ¹⁴Now I am returning to my own people. But first let me tell you what the Israelites will do to your people in the future."

24:13
Num 22:18, 20

### Balaam's Final Messages

¹⁵This is the message Balaam delivered:

"This is the message of Balaam son of Beor,
    the message of the man whose eyes see clearly,
16 the message of one who hears the words of God,
    who has knowledge from the Most High,
  who sees a vision from the Almighty,
    who bows down with eyes wide open:

24:15
Gen 49:1
Num 24:3-4

17 I see him, but not here and now.
    I perceive him, but far in the distant future.
  A star will rise from Jacob;
    a scepter will emerge from Israel.
  It will crush the foreheads of Moab's people,
    cracking the skulls of the people of Sheth.

24:17
Gen 49:10
Isa 15:1—16:4
Matt 2:2

18 Edom will be taken over,
    and Seir, its enemy, will be conquered,
    while Israel marches on in triumph.

24:18
Amos 9:12

**24:6** Or *like a majestic valley.*

---

**24:7** Who was Agag? *Agag* was the title for the king of the Amalekites, just as *Pharaoh* was the ruler of Egypt. Saul, the first king of Israel, defeated Agag (1 Samuel 15:8). Balaam prophesied correctly the ruin of Israel's oldest enemy (Exodus 17:14-16).

**24:11** Although Balaam's motives were not correct, in blessing Israel he acted with integrity. God's message had so filled him that Balaam spoke the truth. In so doing, he forfeited the reward that had lured him to speak in the first place. Staying true to God's Word may cost us promotions and advantages in the short run,

but those who choose God over money will one day acquire heavenly wealth beyond measure (Matthew 6:19-21).

**24:15-19** The star that will rise from Jacob is often thought to refer to the coming Messiah. It was probably this prophecy that convinced the astrologers to travel to Israel to search for the baby Jesus (see Matthew 2:1, 2). It seems strange that God would use a sorcerer like Balaam to foretell the coming of the Messiah. But this teaches us that God can use anything or anyone to accomplish his plans. By using a sorcerer, God did not make sorcery acceptable; in fact, the Bible condemns it in several places (Exodus 22:18; 2 Chronicles 33:6; Revelation 18:23). Rather, God showed his ultimate sovereignty over good and evil.

**24:19**
Gen 49:10

¹⁹ A ruler will rise in Jacob
  who will destroy the survivors of Ir."

**24:20**
Exod 17:14

²⁰Then Balaam looked over toward the people of Amalek and delivered this message:

"Amalek was the greatest of nations,
  but its destiny is destruction!"

**24:21**
Gen 15:19

²¹Then he looked over toward the Kenites and delivered this message:

"Your home is secure;
  your nest is set in the rocks.

**24:22**
Gen 10:22

²² But the Kenites will be destroyed
  when Assyria* takes you captive."

²³Balaam concluded his messages by saying:

"Alas, who can survive
  unless God has willed it?

**24:24**
Gen 10:4, 21

²⁴ Ships will come from the coasts of Cyprus*;
  they will oppress Assyria and afflict Eber,
  but they, too, will be utterly destroyed."

²⁵Then Balaam and Balak returned to their homes.

### Moab Seduces Israel

**25:1**
Num 33:49
Josh 2:1
**25:2**
Exod 34:15-16
**25:3**
Num 25:5
Deut 4:3-4

**25** While the Israelites were camped at Acacia Grove,* some of the men defiled themselves by having* sexual relations with local Moabite women. ²These women invited them to attend sacrifices to their gods, so the Israelites feasted with them and worshiped the gods of Moab. ³In this way, Israel joined in the worship of Baal of Peor, causing the LORD's anger to blaze against his people.

⁴The LORD issued the following command to Moses: "Seize all the ringleaders and execute them before the LORD in broad daylight, so his fierce anger will turn away from the people of Israel."

⁵So Moses ordered Israel's judges, "Each of you must put to death the men under your authority who have joined in worshiping Baal of Peor."

**25:6**
Num 22:4
**25:7-8**
Ps 106:30

⁶Just then one of the Israelite men brought a Midianite woman into his tent, right before the eyes of Moses and all the people, as everyone was weeping at the entrance of the Tabernacle.* ⁷ When Phinehas son of Eleazar and grandson of Aaron the priest saw this, he jumped up and left the assembly. He took a spear ⁸and rushed after the man into his tent. Phinehas thrust the spear all the way through the man's body and into the woman's stomach. So the plague against the Israelites was stopped, ⁹but not before 24,000 people had died.

**25:9**
†1 Cor 10:8

**24:22** Hebrew *Asshur;* also in 24:24.   **24:24** Hebrew *Kittim.*   **25:1a** Hebrew *Shittim.*   **25:1b** As in Greek version; Hebrew reads *some of the men began having.*   **25:6** Hebrew *the Tent of Meeting.*

---

**25:1** This verse shows the great challenge Israel had to face. The most dangerous problem for Moses and Joshua was not Jericho's hostile army, but the ever-present temptation to compromise with the pagan Canaanite religions and cultures.

**25:1, 2** The Bible doesn't say how the Israelite men got involved in sexual immorality. We do know that sacred prostitution was a common practice among Canaanite religions. At first, they didn't think about worshiping idols; they were just interested in sex. Before long they started attending local feasts and family celebrations that involved idol worship. Soon they were in over their heads, absorbed into the practices of the pagan culture. Their desire for fun and pleasure caused them to loosen their spiritual commitment. Have you relaxed your standards in order to justify your desires?

**25:1-3** This combination of sexual sin and idolatry, it turns out, was Balaam's idea (see 31:16; Revelation 2:14), the same Balaam who had just blessed Israel and who appeared to be on their side. It is easy to see how the Israelites were misled, for Balaam seemed to say and do all the right things—at least for a while (22–24). Not until Balaam had inflicted great damage

on them did the Israelites realize that he was greedy, used sorcery, and was deeply involved in pagan religious practices. We must be careful to weigh both the words and the deeds of those who claim to offer spiritual help.

**25:3** Baal was the most popular god in Canaan, the land Israel was about to enter. Represented by a bull, symbol of strength and fertility, he was the god of the rains and harvest. The Israelites were continually attracted to Baal worship, in which prostitution played a large part, throughout their years in Canaan. Because Baal was so popular, his name was often used as a generic title for all the local gods.

**25:6** That this man "brought a Midianite woman into his tent" meant that she was brought into his tent for sex. Zimri (25:14) so disregarded the law of God that he brought the woman right into the camp.

¹⁰Then the LORD said to Moses, ¹¹"Phinehas son of Eleazar and grandson of Aaron the priest has turned my anger away from the Israelites by being as zealous among them as I was. So I stopped destroying all Israel as I had intended to do in my zealous anger. ¹²Now tell him that I am making my special covenant of peace with him. ¹³In this covenant, I give him and his descendants a permanent right to the priesthood, for in his zeal for me, his God, he purified the people of Israel, making them right with me.*"

25:12
Ps 106:30-31
Isa 54:10

¹⁴The Israelite man killed with the Midianite woman was named Zimri son of Salu, the leader of a family from the tribe of Simeon. ¹⁵The woman's name was Cozbi; she was the daughter of Zur, the leader of a Midianite clan.

25:15
Num 25:18; 31:8
Josh 13:21

¹⁶Then the LORD said to Moses, ¹⁷"Attack the Midianites and destroy them, ¹⁸because they assaulted you with deceit and tricked you into worshiping Baal of Peor, and because of Cozbi, the daughter of a Midianite leader, who was killed at the time of the plague because of what happened at Peor."

25:17
Num 31:2
25:18
Num 23:28

## 2. The second census of the nation

**26** After the plague had ended, the LORD said to Moses and to Eleazar son of Aaron the priest, ²"From the whole community of Israel, record the names of all the warriors by their families. List all the men twenty years old or older who are able to go to war."

26:1
Num 25:6-9
26:2
Num 1:2-15

³So there on the plains of Moab beside the Jordan River, across from Jericho, Moses and Eleazar the priest issued these instructions to the leaders of Israel: ⁴"List all the men of Israel twenty years old and older, just as the LORD commanded Moses."

This is the record of all the descendants of Israel who came out of Egypt.

### The Tribe of Reuben

⁵These were the clans descended from the sons of Reuben, Jacob's* oldest son:

The Hanochite clan, named after their ancestor Hanoch.

The Palluite clan, named after their ancestor Pallu.

⁶ The Hezronite clan, named after their ancestor Hezron.

The Carmite clan, named after their ancestor Carmi.

26:5
Exod 6:14

⁷ These were the clans of Reuben. Their registered troops numbered 43,730.

⁸Pallu was the ancestor of Eliab, ⁹and Eliab was the father of Nemuel, Dathan, and Abiram. This Dathan and Abiram are the same community leaders who conspired with Korah against Moses and Aaron, rebelling against the LORD. ¹⁰But the earth opened up its mouth and swallowed them with Korah, and fire devoured 250 of their followers. This served as a warning to the entire nation of Israel. ¹¹However, the sons of Korah did not die that day.

26:9
Num 16:1
26:10
Num 16:32, 35, 38

### The Tribe of Simeon

¹² These were the clans descended from the sons of Simeon:

The Jemuelite clan, named after their ancestor Jemuel.*

The Jaminite clan, named after their ancestor Jamin.

The Jakinite clan, named after their ancestor Jakin.

¹³ The Zoharite clan, named after their ancestor Zohar.*

The Shaulite clan, named after their ancestor Shaul.

26:12
1 Chr 4:24-43

¹⁴These were the clans of Simeon. Their registered troops numbered 22,200.

### The Tribe of Gad

¹⁵These were the clans descended from the sons of Gad:

The Zephonite clan, named after their ancestor Zephon.

**25:13** Or *he made atonement for the people of Israel.*   **26:5** Hebrew *Israel's*; see note on 1:20-21b.   **26:12** As in Syriac version (see also Gen 46:10; Exod 6:15); Hebrew reads *Nemuelite . . . Nemuel.*   **26:13** As in parallel texts at Gen 46:10 and Exod 6:15; Hebrew reads *Zerahite . . . Zerah.*

---

**25:10, 11** It is clear from Phinehas's story that some anger is proper and justified. Phinehas was angry because of his zeal for the Lord. But how can we know when our anger is appropriate and when it should be restrained? Ask these questions when you become angry: (1) Why am I angry? (2) Whose rights are being violated (mine or another's)? (3) Is the truth (a principle of God) being violated? If only your rights are at stake, it may be wiser to keep angry feelings under control. But if the truth is at stake,

anger is often justified, although violence and retaliation are usually the wrong way to express it (Phinehas's case was unique). If we are becoming more and more like God, we should be angered by sin.

**25:12, 13** Phinehas's act made atonement for the nation of Israel; in effect, what he did averted God's judgment. Because of this, his descendants would become the high priests of Israel. They continued so throughout the history of the Tabernacle and the Temple.

The Haggite clan, named after their ancestor Haggi.
The Shunite clan, named after their ancestor Shuni.
16 The Oznite clan, named after their ancestor Ozni.
The Erite clan, named after their ancestor Eri.
17 The Arodite clan, named after their ancestor Arodi.*
The Arelite clan, named after their ancestor Areli.

18These were the clans of Gad. Their registered troops numbered 40,500.

### The Tribe of Judah

19Judah had two sons, Er and Onan, who had died in the land of Canaan. 20These were the clans descended from Judah's surviving sons:
The Shelanite clan, named after their ancestor Shelah.
The Perezite clan, named after their ancestor Perez.
The Zerahite clan, named after their ancestor Zerah.

21These were the subclans descended from the Perezites:
The Hezronites, named after their ancestor Hezron.
The Hamulites, named after their ancestor Hamul.

22These were the clans of Judah. Their registered troops numbered 76,500.

### The Tribe of Issachar

**26:23**
1 Chr 7:1-5

23These were the clans descended from the sons of Issachar:
The Tolaite clan, named after their ancestor Tola.
The Puite clan, named after their ancestor Puah.*
24 The Jashubite clan, named after their ancestor Jashub.
The Shimronite clan, named after their ancestor Shimron.

25These were the clans of Issachar. Their registered troops numbered 64,300.

### The Tribe of Zebulun

26These were the clans descended from the sons of Zebulun:
The Seredite clan, named after their ancestor Sered.
The Elonite clan, named after their ancestor Elon.
The Jahleelite clan, named after their ancestor Jahleel.

27These were the clans of Zebulun. Their registered troops numbered 60,500.

### The Tribe of Manasseh

**26:28**
Gen 46:19-22

28Two clans were descended from Joseph through Manasseh and Ephraim.

29These were the clans descended from Manasseh:
The Makirite clan, named after their ancestor Makir.
The Gileadite clan, named after their ancestor Gilead, Makir's son.

30These were the subclans descended from the Gileadites:
The Iezerites, named after their ancestor Iezer.
The Helekites, named after their ancestor Helek.
31 The Asrielites, named after their ancestor Asriel.
The Shechemites, named after their ancestor Shechem.
32 The Shemidaites, named after their ancestor Shemida.
The Hepherites, named after their ancestor Hepher.
33 (One of Hepher's descendants, Zelophehad, had no sons, but his daughters' names
were Mahlah, Noah, Hoglah, Milcah, and Tirzah.)

34These were the clans of Manasseh. Their registered troops numbered 52,700.

### The Tribe of Ephraim

**26:35**
1 Chr 7:20

35These were the clans descended from the sons of Ephraim:
The Shuthelahite clan, named after their ancestor Shuthelah.
The Bekerite clan, named after their ancestor Beker.
The Tahanite clan, named after their ancestor Tahan.

**26:17** As in Samaritan Pentateuch and Greek and Syriac versions (see also Gen 46:16); Hebrew reads *Arod*.
**26:23** As in Samaritan Pentateuch, Greek and Syriac versions, and Latin Vulgate (see also 1 Chr 7:1); Hebrew reads
*The Punite clan, named after its ancestor Puvah.*

36This was the subclan descended from the Shuthelahites:
    The Eranites, named after their ancestor Eran.

37These were the clans of Ephraim. Their registered troops numbered 32,500.

26:37
Num 1:33

These clans of Manasseh and Ephraim were all descendants of Joseph.

### The Tribe of Benjamin
38These were the clans descended from the sons of Benjamin:
    The Belaite clan, named after their ancestor Bela.
    The Ashbelite clan, named after their ancestor Ashbel.
    The Ahiramite clan, named after their ancestor Ahiram.
39 The Shuphamite clan, named after their ancestor Shupham.*
    The Huphamite clan, named after their ancestor Hupham.

26:38
Gen 46:21
1 Chr 8:1

40These were the subclans descended from the Belaites:
    The Ardites, named after their ancestor Ard.*
    The Naamites, named after their ancestor Naaman.

26:40
1 Chr 8:3

41These were the clans of Benjamin. Their registered troops numbered 45,600.

### The Tribe of Dan
42These were the clans descended from the sons of Dan:
    The Shuhamite clan, named after their ancestor Shuham.

26:42
Gen 46:23-25

43These were the Shuhamite clans of Dan. Their registered troops numbered 64,400.

### The Tribe of Asher
44These were the clans descended from the sons of Asher:
    The Imnite clan, named after their ancestor Imnah.
    The Ishvite clan, named after their ancestor Ishvi.
    The Beriite clan, named after their ancestor Beriah.

26:44
Gen 46:17

45These were the subclans descended from the Beriites:
    The Heberites, named after their ancestor Heber.
    The Malkielites, named after their ancestor Malkiel.

46Asher also had a daughter named Serah.

47These were the clans of Asher. Their registered troops numbered 53,400.

### The Tribe of Naphtali
48These were the clans descended from the sons of Naphtali:
    The Jahzeelite clan, named after their ancestor Jahzeel.
    The Gunite clan, named after their ancestor Guni.
49 The Jezerite clan, named after their ancestor Jezer.
    The Shillemite clan, named after their ancestor Shillem.

26:48
1 Chr 7:13

50These were the clans of Naphtali. Their registered troops numbered 45,400.

### Results of the Registration
51In summary, the registered troops of all Israel numbered 601,730.
    52 Then the LORD said to Moses, 53"Divide the land among the tribes, and distribute the grants of land in proportion to the tribes' populations, as indicated by the number of names on the list. 54Give the larger tribes more land and the smaller tribes less land, each group receiving a grant in proportion to the size of its population. 55But you must assign the land by lot, and give land to each ancestral tribe according to the number of names on the list. 56Each grant of land must be assigned by lot among the larger and smaller tribal groups."

26:51
Num 1:46

26:54
Num 33:54
26:55
Num 33:54; 34:13

### The Tribe of Levi
57This is the record of the Levites who were counted according to their clans:
    The Gershonite clan, named after their ancestor Gershon.
    The Kohathite clan, named after their ancestor Kohath.
    The Merarite clan, named after their ancestor Merari.

26:57
Gen 46:11
1 Chr 6:1

26:39 As in some Hebrew manuscripts, Samaritan Pentateuch, Greek and Syriac versions, and Latin Vulgate; most Hebrew manuscripts read *Shephupham.*    26:40 As in Samaritan Pentateuch, some Greek manuscripts, and Latin Vulgate; Hebrew lacks *named after their ancestor Ard.*

**26:58**
Num 3:16-35

58The Libnites, the Hebronites, the Mahlites, the Mushites, and the Korahites were all subclans of the Levites.

Now Kohath was the ancestor of Amram, 59and Amram's wife was named Jochebed. She also was a descendant of Levi, born among the Levites in the land of Egypt. Amram and Jochebed became the parents of Aaron, Moses, and their sister, Miriam. 60To Aaron were born Nadab, Abihu, Eleazar, and Ithamar. 61But Nadab and Abihu died when they burned before the LORD the wrong kind of fire, different than he had commanded.

**26:60**
Num 3:2
**26:61**
Lev 10:1-2
Num 3:4
**26:62**
Num 3:39

62The men from the Levite clans who were one month old or older numbered 23,000. But the Levites were not included in the registration of the rest of the people of Israel because they were not given an allotment of land when it was divided among the Israelites.

**26:64**
Num 14:20-43
Deut 2:14-15

63So these are the results of the registration of the people of Israel as conducted by Moses and Eleazar the priest on the plains of Moab beside the Jordan River, across from Jericho. 64Not one person on this list had been among those listed in the previous registration taken by Moses and Aaron in the wilderness of Sinai. 65For the LORD had said of them, "They will all die in the wilderness." Not one of them survived except Caleb son of Jephunneh and Joshua son of Nun.

### The Daughters of Zelophehad

**27:1**
Num 26:28-37;
36:1-4

**27** One day a petition was presented by the daughters of Zelophehad—Mahlah, Noah, Hoglah, Milcah, and Tirzah. Their father, Zelophehad, was a descendant of Hepher son of Gilead, son of Makir, son of Manasseh, son of Joseph. 2These women stood before Moses, Eleazar the priest, the tribal leaders, and the entire community at the entrance of the Tabernacle.* 3"Our father died in the wilderness," they said. "He was not among Korah's followers, who rebelled against the LORD; he died because of his own sin. But he had no sons. 4Why should the name of our father disappear from his clan just because he had no sons? Give us property along with the rest of our relatives."

**27:7**
Num 36:1-4
Josh 17:4

5So Moses brought their case before the LORD. 6And the LORD replied to Moses, 7"The claim of the daughters of Zelophehad is legitimate. You must give them a grant of land along with their father's relatives. Assign them the property that would have been given to their father.

8"And give the following instructions to the people of Israel: If a man dies and has no son, then give his inheritance to his daughters. 9And if he has no daughter either, transfer his inheritance to his brothers. 10If he has no brothers, give his inheritance to his father's brothers. 11But if his father has no brothers, give his inheritance to the nearest relative in his clan. This is a legal requirement for the people of Israel, just as the LORD commanded Moses."

**27:11**
Num 35:29

### Joshua Chosen to Lead Israel

**27:12**
Num 33:47
Deut 32:49
**27:13**
Deut 32:50-51
**27:14**
Num 20:9-13
Deut 32:48-52

12One day the LORD said to Moses, "Climb one of the mountains east of the river,* and look out over the land I have given the people of Israel. 13After you have seen it, you will die like your brother, Aaron, 14for you both rebelled against my instructions in the wilderness of Zin. When the people of Israel rebelled, you failed to demonstrate my holiness to them at the waters." (These are the waters of Meribah at Kadesh* in the wilderness of Zin.)

**27:2** Hebrew *the Tent of Meeting.*   **27:12** Or *the mountains of Abarim.*   **27:14** Hebrew *waters of Meribath-kadesh.*

---

**26:64** A new census for a new generation. Thirty-eight years had elapsed since the first great census recorded in Numbers (see 1:1–2:33). During that time, every Israelite man and woman 20 years old and over—except Caleb, Joshua, and Moses—had died, and yet God's laws and the spiritual character of the nation were still intact. Numbers records some dramatic miracles. This is a quiet but powerful miracle often overlooked: A whole nation moved from one land to another, lost its entire adult population, yet managed to maintain its spiritual direction. Sometimes it may feel like God isn't working dramatic miracles in our lives. But God often works in quiet ways to bring about his long-range purposes.

**27:3** "Died because of his own sin" means that he died a natural death. His death fell under the judgment of the entire nation for believing the faithless scouts.

**27:3, 4** Up to this point, the Hebrew law gave sons alone the right to inherit. The daughters of Zelophehad, having no

brothers, came to Moses to ask for their father's possessions. God told Moses that if a man died without sons, his inheritance would go to his daughters (27:8). But the daughters could keep it only if they married within their own tribe, probably so the territorial lines would remain intact (36:5-12).

15Then Moses said to the LORD, 16"O LORD, you are the God who gives breath to all creatures. Please appoint a new man as leader for the community. 17Give them someone who will guide them wherever they go and will lead them into battle, so the community of the LORD will not be like sheep without a shepherd."

18The LORD replied, "Take Joshua son of Nun, who has the Spirit in him, and lay your hands on him. 19Present him to Eleazar the priest before the whole community, and publicly commission him to lead the people. 20Transfer some of your authority to him so the whole community of Israel will obey him. 21When direction from the LORD is needed, Joshua will stand before Eleazar the priest, who will use the Urim—one of the sacred lots cast before the LORD—to determine his will. This is how Joshua and the rest of the community of Israel will determine everything they should do."

22So Moses did as the LORD commanded. He presented Joshua to Eleazar the priest and the whole community. 23Moses laid his hands on him and commissioned him to lead the people, just as the LORD had commanded through Moses.

## 3. Instructions concerning offerings
### The Daily Offerings

**28** The LORD said to Moses, 2"Give these instructions to the people of Israel: The offerings you present as special gifts are a pleasing aroma to me; they are my food. See to it that they are brought at the appointed times and offered according to my instructions.

3"Say to the people: This is the special gift you must present to the LORD as your daily burnt offering. You must offer two one-year-old male lambs with no defects. 4Sacrifice one lamb in the morning and the other in the evening. 5With each lamb you must offer a grain offering of two quarts* of choice flour mixed with one quart* of pure oil of pressed olives. 6This is the regular burnt offering instituted at Mount Sinai as a special gift, a pleasing aroma to the LORD. 7Along with it you must present the proper liquid offering of one quart of alcoholic drink with each lamb, poured out in the Holy Place as an offering to the LORD. 8Offer the second lamb in the evening with the same grain offering and liquid offering. It, too, is a special gift, a pleasing aroma to the LORD.

### The Sabbath Offerings
9"On the Sabbath day, sacrifice two one-year-old male lambs with no defects. They must be accompanied by a grain offering of four quarts* of choice flour moistened with olive oil, and a liquid offering. 10This is the burnt offering to be presented each Sabbath day, in addition to the regular burnt offering and its accompanying liquid offering.

### The Monthly Offerings
11"On the first day of each month, present an extra burnt offering to the LORD of two young bulls, one ram, and seven one-year-old male lambs, all with no defects. 12These must be accompanied by grain offerings of choice flour moistened with olive oil—six quarts* with each bull, four quarts with the ram, 13and two quarts with each lamb. This burnt offering will be a special gift, a pleasing aroma to the LORD. 14You must also present a liquid offering with each sacrifice: two quarts* of wine for each bull, a third of a gallon* for the ram, and one quart* for each lamb. Present this monthly burnt offering on the first day of each month throughout the year.

**28:5a** Hebrew 1/10 of an ephah [2.2 liters]; also in 28:13, 21, 29. **28:5b** Hebrew 1/4 of a hin [1 liter]; also in 28:7. **28:9** Hebrew 2/10 of an ephah [4.4 liters]; also in 28:12, 20, 28. **28:12** Hebrew 3/10 of an ephah [6.6 liters]; also in 28:20, 28. **28:14a** Hebrew 1/2 of a hin [2 liters]. **28:14b** Hebrew 1/3 of a hin [1.3 liters]. **28:14c** Hebrew 1/4 of a hin [1 liter].

**27:17**
1 Kgs 22:17
Ezek 34:1-24
Zech 10:2
Matt 9:36
†Mark 6:34
**27:18**
Deut 34:9
**27:20**
Josh 1:16-17
**27:21**
Exod 28:30
1 Sam 28:6
**28:3**
Exod 29:38-41
**28:4**
Lev 6:19-20
**28:5**
Num 15:3-12
**28:7**
Exod 29:42
Lev 23:13
**28:11**
Num 10:10; 28:19
Ezek 46:6-7
**28:12**
Num 15:4-12

**27:15-17** Moses asked God to appoint a leader who was capable of directing both external and internal affairs—one who could lead them in battle but who would also care for their needs. The Lord responded by appointing Joshua. Many people want to be known as leaders. Some are very capable of reaching their goals, while others care deeply for the people in their charge. The best leaders are both goal-oriented and people-oriented.

**27:15-21** Moses did not want to leave his work without making sure a new leader was ready to replace him. First, he asked God to help him find a replacement. Then, when Joshua was selected, Moses gave him a variety of tasks to ease the transition into his new position. Moses also clearly told the people that Joshua had the authority and the ability to lead the nation. His display of confidence in Joshua was good for both Joshua and the people. To

minimize leadership gaps, anyone in a leadership position should train others to carry on the duties should he or she suddenly or eventually have to leave. While you have the opportunity, follow Moses' pattern: pray, select, develop, and commission.

**28:1, 2** Offerings had to be brought regularly and presented according to prescribed rituals under the priests' supervision. Following these rituals took time, and this gave the people the opportunity to prepare their hearts for worship. Unless our hearts are ready, worship is meaningless. By contrast, God is delighted, and we get more from it, when our hearts are prepared to come before him in a spirit of thankfulness.

**28:9, 10** Why were extra offerings made on the Sabbath day? The Sabbath was a special day of rest and worship commemorating both creation (Exodus 20:8-11) and the deliverance from

**28:15**
Num 28:3

¹⁵"On the first day of each month, you must also offer one male goat for a sin offering to the LORD. This is in addition to the regular burnt offering and its accompanying liquid offering.

### Offerings for the Passover

**28:16**
Exod 12:6, 18
Lev 23:5-14
Deut 16:1-8

**28:19**
Num 28:11

¹⁶"On the fourteenth day of the first month,* you must celebrate the LORD's Passover. ¹⁷On the following day—the fifteenth day of the month—a joyous, seven-day festival will begin, but no bread made with yeast may be eaten. ¹⁸The first day of the festival will be an official day for holy assembly, and no ordinary work may be done on that day. ¹⁹As a special gift you must present a burnt offering to the LORD—two young bulls, one ram, and seven one-year-old male lambs, all with no defects. ²⁰These will be accompanied by grain offerings of choice flour moistened with olive oil—six quarts with each bull, four quarts with the ram, ²¹and two quarts with each of the seven lambs. ²²You must also offer a male goat as a sin offering to purify yourselves and make yourselves right with the LORD.* ²³Present these offerings in addition to your regular morning burnt offering. ²⁴On each of the seven days of the festival, this is how you must prepare the food offering that is presented as a special gift, a pleasing aroma to the LORD. These will be offered in addition to the regular burnt offerings and liquid offerings. ²⁵The seventh day of the festival will be another official day for holy assembly, and no ordinary work may be done on that day.

### Offerings for the Festival of Harvest

**28:26**
Exod 23:16
Lev 23:9-22
Deut 16:9-12

²⁶"At the Festival of Harvest,* when you present the first of your new grain to the LORD, you must call an official day for holy assembly, and you may do no ordinary work on that day. ²⁷Present a special burnt offering on that day as a pleasing aroma to the LORD. It will consist of two young bulls, one ram, and seven one-year-old male lambs. ²⁸These will be accompanied by grain offerings of choice flour moistened with olive oil—six quarts with each bull, four quarts with the ram, ²⁹and two quarts with each of the seven lambs. ³⁰Also, offer one

**28:31**
Num 28:3

male goat to purify yourselves and make yourselves right with the LORD. ³¹Prepare these special burnt offerings, along with their liquid offerings, in addition to the regular burnt offering and its accompanying grain offering. Be sure that all the animals you sacrifice have no defects.

### Offerings for the Festival of Trumpets

**29:1**
Num 28:26

**29** "Celebrate the Festival of Trumpets each year on the first day of the appointed month in early autumn.* You must call an official day for holy assembly, and you may do no ordinary work. ²On that day you must present a burnt offering as a pleasing aroma to the LORD. It will consist of one young bull, one ram, and seven one-year-old male lambs, all with no defects. ³These must be accompanied by grain offerings of choice flour moistened with olive oil—six quarts* with the bull, four quarts* with the ram, ⁴and two quarts* with each of

**29:6**
Num 28:3

the seven lambs. ⁵In addition, you must sacrifice a male goat as a sin offering to purify yourselves and make yourselves right with the LORD.* ⁶These special sacrifices are in addition to your regular monthly and daily burnt offerings, and they must be given with their prescribed grain offerings and liquid offerings. These offerings are given as a special gift to the LORD, a pleasing aroma to him.

**28:16** This day in the ancient Hebrew lunar calendar occurred in late March, April, or early May. **28:22** Or *to make atonement for yourselves;* also in 28:30. **28:26** Hebrew *Festival of Weeks.* This was later called the Festival of Pentecost (see Acts 2:1). It is celebrated today as Shavuot (or Shabuoth). **29:1** Hebrew *the first day of the seventh month.* This day in the ancient Hebrew lunar calendar occurred in September or October. This festival is celebrated today as Rosh Hashanah, the Jewish new year. **29:3a** Hebrew *3/10 of an ephah* [6.6 liters]; also in 29:9, 14. **29:3b** Hebrew *2/10 of an ephah* [4.4 liters]; also in 29:9, 14. **29:4** Hebrew *1/10 of an ephah* [2.2 liters]; also in 29:10, 15. **29:5** Or *to make atonement for yourselves.*

---

Egypt (Deuteronomy 5:12-15). Because of the significance of this special day, it was only natural to offer extra sacrifices on it.

**29:1ff** God placed many holidays on Israel's calendar. The Festival of Trumpets was one of three great holidays celebrated in the seventh month (the Festival of Shelters and Day of Atonement were the other two). These holidays provided a time to refresh the mind and body and to renew one's commitment to God. If you feel tired or far from God, try taking a "spiritual holiday." Separate yourself from your daily routine and concentrate on renewing your commitment to God.

**29:1, 2** The Festival of Trumpets demonstrated three important principles that we should follow in our worship today: (1) The

people gathered together to celebrate and worship. There is an extra benefit to be gained from worshiping with other believers. (2) The normal daily routine was suspended, and no hard work was done. It takes time to worship, and setting aside the time allows us to adjust our attitudes before and reflect afterward. (3) The people gave God something of value by sacrificing animals as burnt offerings to him. We show our commitment to God when we give something of value to him. God desires wholehearted worship. Our gift of money presented generously to God's work also demonstrates our thanks to him. The best gift, of course, is ourselves.

## Offerings for the Day of Atonement

7 "Ten days later, on the tenth day of the same month,* you must call another holy assembly. On that day, the Day of Atonement, the people must go without food and must do no ordinary work. 8 You must present a burnt offering as a pleasing aroma to the LORD. It will consist of one young bull, one ram, and seven one-year-old male lambs, all with no defects. 9 These offerings must be accompanied by the prescribed grain offerings of choice flour moistened with olive oil—six quarts of choice flour with the bull, four quarts of choice flour with the ram, 10 and two quarts of choice flour with each of the seven lambs. 11 You must also sacrifice one male goat for a sin offering. This is in addition to the sin offering of atonement and the regular daily burnt offering with its grain offering, and their accompanying liquid offerings.

**29:7**
Lev 16:29-34;
23:26-32

**29:11**
Lev 16:1-35

## Offerings for the Festival of Shelters

12 "Five days later, on the fifteenth day of the same month,* you must call another holy assembly of all the people, and you may do no ordinary work on that day. It is the beginning of the Festival of Shelters,* a seven-day festival to the LORD. 13 On the first day of the festival, you must present a burnt offering as a special gift, a pleasing aroma to the LORD. It will consist of thirteen young bulls, two rams, and fourteen one-year-old male lambs, all with no defects. 14 Each of these offerings must be accompanied by a grain offering of choice flour moistened with olive oil—six quarts for each of the thirteen bulls, four quarts for each of the two rams, 15 and two quarts for each of the fourteen lambs. 16 You must also sacrifice a male goat as a sin offering, in addition to the regular burnt offering with its accompanying grain offering and liquid offering.

**29:12**
Lev 23:33-43
Deut 16:13-14

17 "On the second day of this seven-day festival, sacrifice twelve young bulls, two rams, and fourteen one-year-old male lambs, all with no defects. 18 Each of these offerings of bulls, rams, and lambs must be accompanied by its prescribed grain offering and liquid offering. 19 You must also sacrifice a male goat as a sin offering, in addition to the regular burnt offering with its accompanying grain offering and liquid offering.

**29:19**
Num 28:3, 11, 31

20 "On the third day of the festival, sacrifice eleven young bulls, two rams, and fourteen one-year-old male lambs, all with no defects. 21 Each of these offerings of bulls, rams, and lambs must be accompanied by its prescribed grain offering and liquid offering. 22 You must also sacrifice a male goat as a sin offering, in addition to the regular burnt offering with its accompanying grain offering and liquid offering.

**29:22**
Num 28:15

23 "On the fourth day of the festival, sacrifice ten young bulls, two rams, and fourteen one-year-old male lambs, all with no defects. 24 Each of these offerings of bulls, rams, and lambs must be accompanied by its prescribed grain offering and liquid offering. 25 You must also sacrifice a male goat as a sin offering, in addition to the regular burnt offering with its accompanying grain offering and liquid offering.

26 "On the fifth day of the festival, sacrifice nine young bulls, two rams, and fourteen one-year-old male lambs, all with no defects. 27 Each of these offerings of bulls, rams, and lambs must be accompanied by its prescribed grain offering and liquid offering. 28 You must also sacrifice a male goat as a sin offering, in addition to the regular burnt offering with its accompanying grain offering and liquid offering.

29 "On the sixth day of the festival, sacrifice eight young bulls, two rams, and fourteen one-year-old male lambs, all with no defects. 30 Each of these offerings of bulls, rams, and lambs must be accompanied by its prescribed grain offering and liquid offering. 31 You must also sacrifice a male goat as a sin offering, in addition to the regular burnt offering with its accompanying grain offering and liquid offering.

32 "On the seventh day of the festival, sacrifice seven young bulls, two rams, and fourteen one-year-old male lambs, all with no defects. 33 Each of these offerings of bulls, rams, and lambs must be accompanied by its prescribed grain offering and liquid offering. 34 You must also sacrifice one male goat as a sin offering, in addition to the regular burnt offering with its accompanying grain offering and liquid offering.

35 "On the eighth day of the festival, proclaim another holy day. You must do no ordinary work on that day. 36 You must present a burnt offering as a special gift, a pleasing aroma to

**29:35**
Lev 23:36

**29:7** Hebrew *On the tenth day of the seventh month;* see 29:1 and the note there. This day in the ancient Hebrew lunar calendar occurred in September or October. It is celebrated today as Yom Kippur.    **29:12a** Hebrew *On the fifteenth day of the seventh month;* see 29:1, 7 and the notes there. This day in the ancient Hebrew lunar calendar occurred in late September, October, or early November.    **29:12b** Or *Festival of Booths,* or *Festival of Tabernacles.* This was earlier called the Festival of the Final Harvest or Festival of Ingathering (see Exod 23:16b). It is celebrated today as Sukkot (or Succoth).

the Lord. It will consist of one young bull, one ram, and seven one-year-old male lambs, all with no defects. 37Each of these offerings must be accompanied by its prescribed grain offering and liquid offering. 38You must also sacrifice one male goat as a sin offering, in addition to the regular burnt offering with its accompanying grain offering and liquid offering.

39"You must present these offerings to the Lord at your annual festivals. These are in addition to the sacrifices and offerings you present in connection with vows, or as voluntary offerings, burnt offerings, grain offerings, liquid offerings, or peace offerings."

40*So Moses gave all of these instructions to the people of Israel as the Lord had commanded him.

### Laws concerning Vows

**30** 1*Then Moses summoned the leaders of the tribes of Israel and told them, "This is what the Lord has commanded: 2A man who makes a vow to the Lord or makes a pledge under oath must never break it. He must do exactly what he said he would do.

3"If a young woman makes a vow to the Lord or a pledge under oath while she is still living at her father's home, 4and her father hears of the vow or pledge and does not object to it, then all her vows and pledges will stand. 5But if her father refuses to let her fulfill the vow or pledge on the day he hears of it, then all her vows and pledges will become invalid. The Lord will forgive her because her father would not let her fulfill them.

6"Now suppose a young woman makes a vow or binds herself with an impulsive pledge and later marries. 7If her husband learns of her vow or pledge and does not object on the day he hears of it, her vows and pledges will stand. 8But if her husband refuses to accept her vow or impulsive pledge on the day he hears of it, he nullifies her commitments, and the Lord will forgive her. 9If, however, a woman is a widow or is divorced, she must fulfill all her vows and pledges.

10"But suppose a woman is married and living in her husband's home when she makes a vow or binds herself with a pledge. 11If her husband hears of it and does not object to it, her vow or pledge will stand. 12But if her husband refuses to accept it on the day he hears of it, her vow or pledge will be nullified, and the Lord will forgive her. 13So her husband may either confirm or nullify any vows or pledges she makes to deny herself. 14But if he does not object on the day he hears of it, then he is agreeing to all her vows and pledges. 15If he waits more than a day and then tries to nullify a vow or pledge, he will be punished for her guilt."

16These are the regulations the Lord gave Moses concerning relationships between a man and his wife, and between a father and a young daughter who still lives at home.

### 4. Vengeance on the Midianites

**31** Then the Lord said to Moses, 2"On behalf of the people of Israel, take revenge on the Midianites for leading them into idolatry. After that, you will die and join your ancestors."

3So Moses said to the people, "Choose some men, and arm them to fight the Lord's war of revenge against Midian. 4From each tribe of Israel, send 1,000 men into battle." 5So they

**29:40** Verse 29:40 is numbered 30:1 in Hebrew text.   **30:1** Verses 30:1-16 are numbered 30:2-17 in Hebrew text.

---

**30:1, 2** Moses reminded the people that their promises to God and others must be kept. In ancient times, people did not sign written contracts. A person's word was as binding as a signature. To make a vow even more binding, an offering was given along with it. No one was forced by law to make a vow; but once made, vows had to be fulfilled. Breaking a vow meant a broken trust and a broken relationship. Trust is still the basis of our relationships with God and others. A broken promise today is just as harmful as it was in Moses' day.

**30:3-8** Under Israelite law, parents could overrule their children's vows. This helped young people avoid the consequences of making foolish promises or costly commitments. From this law comes an important principle for both parents and children. Young people still living at home should seek their parents' help when they make decisions. A parent's experience could save a child from a serious mistake. Parents, however, should exercise their authority with caution and grace. They should let children learn from their mistakes while protecting them from disaster.

**31:1ff** The Midianites were a nomadic people who descended from Abraham and his second wife, Keturah. The land of Midian lay far to the south of Canaan, but large bands of Midianites roamed many miles from their homeland, searching for grazing areas for their flocks. Such a group was near the Promised Land when the Israelites arrived. When Moses fled from Egypt (Exodus 2), he took refuge in the land of Midian. His wife and father-in-law were Midianites. Despite this alliance, the Israelites and Midianites were always bitter enemies.

chose 1,000 men from each tribe of Israel, a total of 12,000 men armed for battle. ⁶Then
Moses sent them out, 1,000 men from each tribe, and Phinehas son of Eleazar the priest led
them into battle. They carried along the holy objects of the sanctuary and the trumpets for
sounding the charge. ⁷They attacked Midian as the Lord had commanded Moses, and they
killed all the men. ⁸All five of the Midianite kings—Evi, Rekem, Zur, Hur, and Reba—died in
the battle. They also killed Balaam son of Beor with the sword.

⁹Then the Israelite army captured the Midianite women and children and seized their
cattle and flocks and all their wealth as plunder. ¹⁰They burned all the towns and villages
where the Midianites had lived. ¹¹After they had gathered the plunder and captives, both
people and animals, ¹²they brought them all to Moses and Eleazar the priest, and to the
whole community of Israel, which was camped on the plains of Moab beside the Jordan
River, across from Jericho. ¹³Moses, Eleazar the priest, and all the leaders of the community
went to meet them outside the camp. ¹⁴But Moses was furious with all the generals and
captains* who had returned from the battle.

¹⁵"Why have you let all the women live?" he demanded. ¹⁶"These are the very ones who
followed Balaam's advice and caused the people of Israel to rebel against the Lord at Mount
Peor. They are the ones who caused the plague to strike the Lord's people. ¹⁷So kill all the
boys and all the women who have had intercourse with a man. ¹⁸Only the young girls who
are virgins may live; you may keep them for yourselves. ¹⁹And all of you who have killed anyone or touched a dead body must stay outside the camp for seven days. You must purify
yourselves and your captives on the third and seventh days. ²⁰Purify all your clothing, too,
and everything made of leather, goat hair, or wood."

²¹Then Eleazar the priest said to the men who were in the battle, "The Lord has given
Moses this legal requirement: ²²Anything made of gold, silver, bronze, iron, tin, or lead—
²³that is, all metals that do not burn—must be passed through fire in order to be made ceremonially pure. These metal objects must then be further purified with the water of
purification. But everything that burns must be purified by the water alone. ²⁴On the seventh day you must wash your clothes and be purified. Then you may return to the camp."

### Division of the Plunder

²⁵And the Lord said to Moses, ²⁶"You and Eleazar the priest and the family leaders of each
tribe are to make a list of all the plunder taken in the battle, including the people and animals. ²⁷Then divide the plunder into two parts, and give half to the men who fought the
battle and half to the rest of the people. ²⁸From the army's portion, first give the Lord his
share of the plunder—one of every 500 of the prisoners and of the cattle, donkeys, sheep,
and goats. ²⁹Give this share of the army's half to Eleazar the priest as an offering to the
Lord. ³⁰From the half that belongs to the people of Israel, take one of every fifty of the prisoners and of the cattle, donkeys, sheep, goats, and other animals. Give this share to the

**31:6**
Num 10:8-9

**31:8**
Josh 13:21-22

**31:16**
Num 25:1-18
2 Pet 2:15-16

**31:17**
Judg 21:10-12
Deut 7:2; 20:16-18

**31:24**
Lev 11:25; 14:9

**31:27**
Josh 22:8

**31:28**
Num 18:21

**31:29**
Num 18:25-26

**31:14** Hebrew *the commanders of thousands, and the commanders of hundreds;* also in 31:48, 52, 54.

---

**31:14-16** Because Midianites were responsible for enticing
Israel into Baal worship, God commanded Israel to destroy them
(25:16-18). But Israel took the women as captives, rather than
killing them, probably because of the tempting enticements of
the Midianites' sinful lifestyle. When we discover sin in our lives,
we must deal with it completely. When the Israelites later entered
the Promised Land, it was their indifferent attitude to sin that
eventually ruined them. Moses dealt with the sin promptly and
completely. When God points out sin, move quickly to remove
it from your life.

**31:16** Balaam's story (22:1–24:25), taken alone, would lead
us to believe that Balaam was an honest and God-fearing man.
But here is the first of much biblical evidence that Balaam was
not the good man he might appear to be. For more on Balaam,
see the notes on 22:9 and 25:1-3 and Balaam's Profile in ch. 22,
p. 239.

**31:25-30** Moses told the Israelites to give a portion of the war
plunder to God. Another portion was to go to the people who
remained behind. Similarly, the money we earn is not ours alone.
Everything we possess comes directly or indirectly from God
and ultimately belongs to him. We should return a portion to
him and also share a portion with those in need.

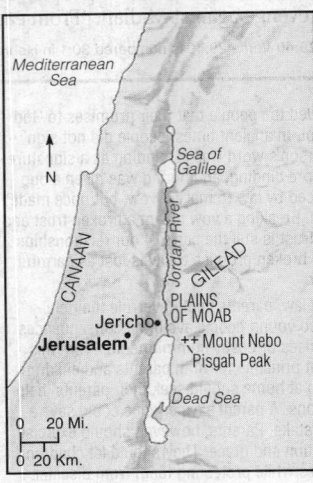

**PREPARING
TO ENTER THE
PROMISED
LAND**
The Israelites
had been camped
in the plains of
Moab, across
from Jericho.
From this position,
they were ready
to enter the
Promised Land.

Levites, who are in charge of maintaining the LORD's Tabernacle." ³¹So Moses and Eleazar the priest did as the LORD commanded Moses.

³²The plunder remaining from everything the fighting men had taken totaled 675,000 sheep and goats, ³³72,000 cattle, ³⁴61,000 donkeys, ³⁵and 32,000 virgin girls.

³⁶Half of the plunder was given to the fighting men. It totaled 337,500 sheep and goats, ³⁷of which 675 were the LORD's share; ³⁸36,000 cattle, of which 72 were the LORD's share; ³⁹30,500 donkeys, of which 61 were the LORD's share; ⁴⁰and 16,000 virgin girls, of whom 32 were the LORD's share. ⁴¹Moses gave all the LORD's share to Eleazar the priest, just as the LORD had directed him.

⁴²Half of the plunder belonged to the people of Israel, and Moses separated it from the half belonging to the fighting men. ⁴³It totaled 337,500 sheep and goats, ⁴⁴36,000 cattle, ⁴⁵30,500 donkeys, ⁴⁶and 16,000 virgin girls. ⁴⁷From the half-share given to the people, Moses took one of every fifty prisoners and animals and gave them to the Levites, who maintained the LORD's Tabernacle. All this was done as the LORD had commanded Moses.

⁴⁸Then all the generals and captains came to Moses ⁴⁹and said, "We, your servants, have accounted for all the men who went out to battle under our command; not one of us is missing! ⁵⁰So we are presenting the items of gold we captured as an offering to the LORD from our share of the plunder—armbands, bracelets, rings, earrings, and necklaces. This will purify our lives before the LORD and make us right with him.*"

⁵¹So Moses and Eleazar the priest received the gold from all the military commanders—all kinds of jewelry and crafted objects. ⁵²In all, the gold that the generals and captains presented as a gift to the LORD weighed about 420 pounds.* ⁵³All the fighting men had taken some of the plunder for themselves. ⁵⁴So Moses and Eleazar the priest accepted the gifts from the generals and captains and brought the gold to the Tabernacle* as a reminder to the LORD that the people of Israel belong to him.

## 5. The Transjordan tribes

**32** The tribes of Reuben and Gad owned vast numbers of livestock. So when they saw that the lands of Jazer and Gilead were ideally suited for their flocks and herds, ²they came to Moses, Eleazar the priest, and the other leaders of the community. They said, ³"Notice the towns of Ataroth, Dibon, Jazer, Nimrah, Heshbon, Elealeh, Sibmah,* Nebo, and Beon. ⁴The LORD has conquered this whole area for the community of Israel, and it is ideally suited for all our livestock. ⁵If we have found favor with you, please let us have this land as our property instead of giving us land across the Jordan River."

⁶"Do you intend to stay here while your brothers go across and do all the fighting?" Moses asked the men of Gad and Reuben. ⁷"Why do you want to discourage the rest of the people of Israel from going across to the land the LORD has given them? ⁸Your ancestors did the same thing when I sent them from Kadesh-barnea to explore the land. ⁹After they went up to the valley of Eshcol and explored the land, they discouraged the people of Israel from entering the land the LORD was giving them. ¹⁰Then the LORD was very angry with them, and he vowed, ¹¹'Of all those I rescued from Egypt, no one who is twenty years old or older will ever see the land I swore to give to Abraham, Isaac, and Jacob, for they have not obeyed me wholeheartedly. ¹²The only exceptions are Caleb son of Jephunneh the Kenizzite and Joshua son of Nun, for they have wholeheartedly followed the LORD.'

**Cross-references (margin):**

31:49
Num 1:19

31:53
Deut 20:14

32:1
Num 21:32

32:3
Num 32:33-42
Josh 13:17
Isa 15:4; 16:9

32:8
Num 13:2-26
Deut 1:19-21

32:9
Num 13:23-24

32:10
Num 14:28-30
Deut 1:34

32:12
Num 14:6, 24, 30
Deut 1:36
Josh 14:8-9

**31:50** Or *will make atonement for our lives before the LORD.* **31:52** Hebrew *16,750 shekels* [191 kilograms]. **31:54** Hebrew *the Tent of Meeting.* **32:3** As in Samaritan Pentateuch and Greek version (see also 32:38); Hebrew reads *Sebam.*

**31:48-50** After carefully accounting for all their men, the officers discovered that not one soldier had been lost in battle. At once they thanked God. After going through tough times, we should be quick to thank God for delivering us and protecting us from severe loss.

**32:1ff** Three tribes (Reuben, Gad, and the half-tribe of Manasseh) wanted to live east of the Jordan River (sometimes referred to as the Transjordan area) on land they had already conquered. Moses immediately assumed they had selfish motives and were trying to avoid helping the others fight for the land across the river. But Moses jumped to the wrong conclusion. In dealing with people, we must find out all the facts before making up our minds. We shouldn't automatically assume that their motives are wrong, even if their plans sound suspicious.

13"The LORD was angry with Israel and made them wander in the wilderness for forty years until the entire generation that sinned in the LORD's sight had died. 14But here you are, a brood of sinners, doing exactly the same thing! You are making the LORD even angrier with Israel. 15If you turn away from him like this and he abandons them again in the wilderness, you will be responsible for destroying this entire nation!"

16But they approached Moses and said, "We simply want to build pens for our livestock and fortified towns for our wives and children. 17Then we will arm ourselves and lead our fellow Israelites into battle until we have brought them safely to their land. Meanwhile, our families will stay in the fortified towns we build here, so they will be safe from any attacks by the local people. 18We will not return to our homes until all the people of Israel have received their portions of land. 19But we do not claim any of the land on the other side of the Jordan. We would rather live here on the east side and accept this as our grant of land."

20Then Moses said, "If you keep your word and arm yourselves for the LORD's battles, 21and if your troops cross the Jordan and keep fighting until the LORD has driven out his enemies, 22then you may return when the LORD has conquered the land. You will have fulfilled your duty to the LORD and to the rest of the people of Israel. And the land on the east side of the Jordan will be your property from the LORD. 23But if you fail to keep your word, then you will have sinned against the LORD, and you may be sure that your sin will find you out. 24Go ahead and build towns for your families and pens for your flocks, but do everything you have promised."

25Then the men of Gad and Reuben replied, "We, your servants, will follow your instructions exactly. 26Our children, wives, flocks, and cattle will stay here in the towns of Gilead. 27But all who are able to bear arms will cross over to fight for the LORD, just as you have said."

28So Moses gave orders to Eleazar the priest, Joshua son of Nun, and the leaders of the clans of Israel. 29He said, "The men of Gad and Reuben who are armed for battle must cross the Jordan with you to fight for the LORD. If they do, give them the land of Gilead as their property when the land is conquered. 30But if they refuse to arm themselves and cross over with you, then they must accept land with the rest of you in the land of Canaan."

31The tribes of Gad and Reuben said again, "We are your servants, and we will do as the LORD has commanded! 32 We will cross the Jordan into Canaan fully armed to fight for the LORD, but our property will be here on this side of the Jordan."

33 So Moses assigned land to the tribes of Gad, Reuben, and half the tribe of Manasseh son of Joseph. He gave them the territory of King Sihon of the Amorites and the land of King Og of Bashan—the whole land with its cities and surrounding lands.

34The descendants of Gad built the towns of Dibon, Ataroth, Aroer, 35Atroth-shophan, Jazer, Jogbehah, 36Beth-nimrah, and Beth-haran. These were all fortified towns with pens for their flocks.

37 The descendants of Reuben built the towns of Heshbon, Elealeh, Kiriathaim, 38Nebo, Baal-meon, and Sibmah. They changed the names of some of the towns they conquered and rebuilt.

39 Then the descendants of Makir of the tribe of Manasseh went to Gilead and conquered it, and they drove out the Amorites living there. 40So Moses gave Gilead to the Makirites, descendants of Manasseh, and they settled there. 41The people of Jair, another clan of the tribe of Manasseh, captured many of the towns in Gilead and changed the name of that region to the Towns of Jair.* 42Meanwhile, a man named Nobah captured the town of Kenath and its surrounding villages, and he renamed that area Nobah after himself.

**32:41** Hebrew *Havvoth-jair.*

**32:13**
Num 14:31-39

**32:15**
Deut 30:17-18

**32:17**
Josh 4:12-13

**32:18-19**
Josh 13:8; 22:4

**32:20**
Deut 3:18

**32:22**
Deut 3:20
Josh 22:4

**32:24**
Num 30:2

**32:33**
Num 21:23-26;
34:14
Deut 3:8-17
Josh 12:1-6

**32:41**
Deut 3:14
Josh 13:30
1 Chr 2:23

**32:16** A simple fold for livestock had four roughly built stone walls, high enough to keep wild animals out. Sometimes the top of the wall was lined with thorns to further discourage predators and thieves. The fold's single entrance made it easier for a shepherd to guard his flock. Often several shepherds used a single fold and took turns guarding the entrance. Mingling the animals was no problem since each flock responded readily to its own shepherd's voice. The three tribes who chose to remain east of the Jordan River wanted to build sheepfolds to protect their flocks, and cities to protect their families before the men crossed the river to help the rest of the tribes conquer the Promised Land.

**32:16-19** The land on the east side of the Jordan had been conquered. The hard work was done by all of the tribes together. But the tribes of Reuben and Gad and the half-tribe of Manasseh did not stop after their land was cleared. They promised to keep working with the others until everyone's land was conquered. After others have helped you, do you make excuses to escape helping them? Finish the whole job, even those parts that may not benefit you directly.

## 6. Camped on the plains of Moab
### *Remembering Israel's Journey*

**33** This is the route the Israelites followed as they marched out of Egypt under the leadership of Moses and Aaron. ²At the LORD's direction, Moses kept a written record of their progress. These are the stages of their march, identified by the different places where they stopped along the way.

**33:3**
Exod 12:33-37

³They set out from the city of Rameses in early spring—on the fifteenth day of the first month*—on the morning after the first Passover celebration. The people of Israel left defiantly, in full view of all the Egyptians. ⁴Meanwhile, the Egyptians were burying all their firstborn sons, whom the LORD had killed the night before. The LORD had defeated the gods of Egypt that night with great acts of judgment!

**33:5**
Exod 13:20

⁵After leaving Rameses, the Israelites set up camp at Succoth.
⁶Then they left Succoth and camped at Etham on the edge of the wilderness.

**33:7**
Exod 14:2, 9

⁷They left Etham and turned back toward Pi-hahiroth, opposite Baal-zephon, and camped near Migdol.

**33:8**
Exod 14:21-22

⁸They left Pi-hahiroth and crossed the Red Sea* into the wilderness beyond. Then they traveled for three days into the Etham wilderness and camped at Marah.

**33:9**
Exod 15:27; 16:1

⁹They left Marah and camped at Elim, where there were twelve springs of water and seventy palm trees.
¹⁰They left Elim and camped beside the Red Sea.*

**33:11**
Exod 16:1; 17:1

¹¹They left the Red Sea and camped in the wilderness of Sin.*
¹²They left the wilderness of Sin and camped at Dophkah.
¹³They left Dophkah and camped at Alush.

**33:14**
Exod 17:1-8

¹⁴They left Alush and camped at Rephidim, where there was no water for the people to drink.

**33:15**
Exod 19:1

¹⁵They left Rephidim and camped in the wilderness of Sinai.

**33:16-17**
Num 11:34-35

¹⁶They left the wilderness of Sinai and camped at Kibroth-hattaavah.
¹⁷They left Kibroth-hattaavah and camped at Hazeroth.
¹⁸They left Hazeroth and camped at Rithmah.
¹⁹They left Rithmah and camped at Rimmon-perez.
²⁰They left Rimmon-perez and camped at Libnah.
²¹They left Libnah and camped at Rissah.
²²They left Rissah and camped at Kehelathah.
²³They left Kehelathah and camped at Mount Shepher.
²⁴They left Mount Shepher and camped at Haradah.
²⁵They left Haradah and camped at Makheloth.
²⁶They left Makheloth and camped at Tahath.
²⁷They left Tahath and camped at Terah.
²⁸They left Terah and camped at Mithcah.
²⁹They left Mithcah and camped at Hashmonah.

**33:30**
Deut 10:6

³⁰They left Hashmonah and camped at Moseroth.
³¹They left Moseroth and camped at Bene-jaakan.
³²They left Bene-jaakan and camped at Hor-haggidgad.

**33:33**
Deut 10:7

³³They left Hor-haggidgad and camped at Jotbathah.
³⁴They left Jotbathah and camped at Abronah.
³⁵They left Abronah and camped at Ezion-geber.

**33:36**
Num 20:1

³⁶They left Ezion-geber and camped at Kadesh in the wilderness of Zin.

**33:38**
Num 20:25-28

³⁷They left Kadesh and camped at Mount Hor, at the border of Edom. ³⁸While they

**33:3** This day in the ancient Hebrew lunar calendar occurred in late March, April, or early May.   **33:8** Hebrew *the sea.*   **33:10** Hebrew *sea of reeds;* also in 33:11.   **33:11** The geographical name *Sin* is related to *Sinai* and should not be confused with the English word *sin.*

**33:1ff** Look at the map in the introduction to the book of Numbers to see the travels of the Israelites.

**33:2** Moses recorded the Israelites' journeys as God instructed him, providing a record of their spiritual as well as geographic progress. Have you made spiritual progress lately? Recording your thoughts about God and lessons you have learned over a period of time can be a valuable aid to spiritual growth. A record of your spiritual pilgrimage

will let you check up on your progress and avoid repeating past mistakes.

**33:4** God "defeated the gods of Egypt" by sending the plagues. See the note on Exodus 10:22 for a further explanation.

were at the foot of Mount Hor, Aaron the priest was directed by the LORD to go up
the mountain, and there he died. This happened in midsummer, on the first day
of the fifth month* of the fortieth year after Israel's departure from Egypt. [39]Aaron was
123 years old when he died there on Mount Hor.

[40]At that time the Canaanite king of Arad, who lived in the Negev in the land of Canaan,
heard that the people of Israel were approaching his land.

**33:40**
Num 21:1

[41]Meanwhile, the Israelites left Mount Hor and camped at Zalmonah.

[42]Then they left Zalmonah and camped at Punon.

[43]They left Punon and camped at Oboth.

**33:43**
Num 21:10-11

[44]They left Oboth and camped at Iye-abarim on the border of Moab.

[45]They left Iye-abarim* and camped at Dibon-gad.

[46]They left Dibon-gad and camped at Almon-diblathaim.

[47]They left Almon-diblathaim and camped in the mountains east of the river,* near
Mount Nebo.

**33:47**
Num 27:12
**33:48**
Num 22:1

[48]They left the mountains east of the river and camped on the plains of Moab beside the
Jordan River, across from Jericho. [49]Along the Jordan River they camped from Beth-
jeshimoth as far as the meadows of Acacia* on the plains of Moab.

**33:49**
Num 25:1

[50]While they were camped near the Jordan River on the plains of Moab opposite Jericho,
the LORD said to Moses, [51]"Give the following instructions to the people of Israel: When you
cross the Jordan River into the land of Canaan, [52]you must drive out all the people living
there. You must destroy all their carved and molten images and demolish all their pagan
shrines. [53]Take possession of the land and settle in it, because I have given it to you to
occupy. [54]You must distribute the land among the clans by sacred lot and in proportion to
their size. A larger portion of land will be allotted to each of the larger clans, and a smaller
portion will be allotted to each of the smaller clans. The decision of the sacred lot is final. In

**33:52**
Exod 23:24; 34:13
Deut 7:2-5, 25-26

**33:54**
Num 26:53-56

**33:38** This day in the ancient Hebrew lunar calendar occurred in July or August.   **33:45** As in 33:44; Hebrew reads
*Iyim,* another name for Iye-abarim.   **33:47** Or *the mountains of Abarim;* also in 33:48.   **33:49** Hebrew *as far as
Abel-shittim.*

---

**33:50-53** God told Moses that before the Israelites settled in
the Promised Land they should drive out the wicked inhabitants
and destroy their idols. In Colossians 3, Paul encourages us
to live as Christians in the same manner: throwing away our
old way of living and moving ahead into our new life of obedience to God and faith in Jesus Christ. Like the Israelites moving
into the Promised Land, we can destroy the wickedness in our
lives, or we can settle down and live with it. To move in and
possess the new life, we must drive out the sinful thoughts and
practices to make room for the new.

**THE BORDERS
OF THE
PROMISED LAND**
The borders of the
Promised Land
stretched from
the wilderness
of Zin and Kadesh-
barnea in the
south to Lebo-
hamath and
Riblah in the
north, and from
the Mediterranean
seacoast on the
west to the Jordan
River on the east.
The land of Gilead
was also included.

**33:50-56** Why were the Israelites told to destroy the people
living in Canaan? God had several compelling reasons for giving
this command: (1) God was stamping out the wickedness of
an extremely sinful group of nations. The Canaanites brought
on their own punishment. Idol worship expressed their deepest
evil desires. It ultimately led to the worship of Satan and the
total rejection of God. (2) God was using Moses and Israel
to judge Canaan for its sins in fulfillment of the prophecy in
Genesis 9:25. (3) God wanted to remove all trace of pagan
beliefs and practices from the land. He did not want his people
to mix or compromise with idolatry in any way. The Israelites
did not fully understand God's reasons, and they did not carry
out his command. This eventually led them to compromise
and corruption. In all areas of life, we should obey God's Word
without question because we know he is just, even if we cannot
fully understand his overall purposes.

**33:55** If you don't do the job right the first time, it often
becomes much more difficult to accomplish. God warned that
if the Israelites did not drive the wicked inhabitants out of the
Promised Land, later these people would become a source
of great irritation. That is exactly what happened. Just as the
Israelites were hesitant to clear out all the wicked people, we
are sometimes hesitant to clear out all the sin in our lives, either
because we are afraid of it (as the Israelites feared the giants),
or because it seems harmless and attractive (as sexual sin
seemed). But Hebrews 12:1 tells us to strip off "the sin that
so easily trips us up." We all have "idols" we don't want to let
go of (a bad habit, an unhealthy relationship, a certain lifestyle).
If we allow these idols to dominate us, they will cause serious
problems later.

33:55
Josh 23:13
Ps 106:34-36

this way, the portions of land will be divided among your ancestral tribes. 55But if you fail to drive out the people who live in the land, those who remain will be like splinters in your eyes and thorns in your sides. They will harass you in the land where you live. 56And I will do to you what I had planned to do to them."

## Boundaries of the Land

34:2
Gen 17:8
Deut 1:7-8
Ezek 47:15
34:3
Josh 15:1-4
34:4
Num 32:8

**34** Then the LORD said to Moses, 2"Give these instructions to the Israelites: When you come into the land of Canaan, which I am giving you as your special possession, these will be the boundaries. 3The southern portion of your country will extend from the wilderness of Zin, along the edge of Edom. The southern boundary will begin on the east at the Dead Sea.* 4It will then run south past Scorpion Pass* in the direction of Zin. Its southernmost point will be Kadesh-barnea, from which it will go to Hazar-addar, and on to Azmon. 5From Azmon the boundary will turn toward the Brook of Egypt and end at the Mediterranean Sea.*

34:6
Josh 15:4
34:7
Ezek 47:15-17

6"Your western boundary will be the coastline of the Mediterranean Sea.

7"Your northern boundary will begin at the Mediterranean Sea and run east to Mount Hor, 8then to Lebo-hamath, and on through Zedad 9and Ziphron to Hazar-enan. This will be your northern boundary.

34:3 Hebrew *Salt Sea;* also in 34:12.  34:4 Or *the ascent of Akrabbim.*  34:5 Hebrew *the sea;* also in 34:6, 7.

| PRIESTS IN ISRAEL'S HISTORY | Priest | Importance | Reference |
|---|---|---|---|
| Numbers 35:25-28 mentions the death of a high priest. Each new high priest had to come from the lineage of Aaron. Listed here are the ones whose stories are told elsewhere in the Bible. | Aaron | Moses' brother and first priest | Exodus 28:1-3 |
| | Eleazar | Watched two of his brothers die in a fire from God because they did not follow God's instructions. He obeyed God and became chief leader of the Tabernacle. | Leviticus 10 Numbers 3:32 |
| | Phinehas | Executed a young Israelite idol worshiper and his Midianite mistress to end a plague. He was then promised that his priestly line would never end. | Numbers 25:1-15 |
| | Ahitub | A priest during King Saul's reign | 1 Samuel 14:3 |
| | Zadok | A faithful high priest under King David. He and Nathan anointed Solomon as the next king. | 2 Samuel 8:17 1 Kings 1:38, 39 |
| | Ahimaaz | Carried the message of Absalom's death to King David but was apparently afraid to tell about it. | 2 Samuel 18:19-29 |
| | Azariah | High priest under King Solomon | 1 Kings 4:2 |
| | Azariah | High priest under Uzziah. He rebuked the king for burning incense himself. | 2 Chronicles 26:17-21 |
| | | When Hezekiah became king, he reopened the Temple. Azariah again served as high priest. | 2 Chronicles 26:17-21 |
| | Amariah | King Jehoshaphat appointed him to judge religious disputes. | 2 Chronicles 19:11 |
| | Hilkiah | Found the Book of the Law during Josiah's reign | 2 Kings 22:3-13 2 Chronicles 34:14-21 |
| | Azariah | Probably one of the first to return to Israel from Babylon | 1 Chronicles 9:10, 11 |
| | Seraiah | The father of Ezra | Ezra 7:1-5 |

**34:1ff** The land was given by God as an inheritance; no tribe was to claim its own land. The boundaries declared by God are larger than the area actually occupied by the Hebrews. The boundaries correspond more to the land conquered by David and to the ideal territory portrayed by Ezekiel (Ezekiel 47–48).

The size of the land portrays God's generosity. He always gives us more than we could ask or think.

¹⁰"The eastern boundary will start at Hazar-enan and run south to Shepham, ¹¹then down to Riblah on the east side of Ain. From there the boundary will run down along the eastern edge of the Sea of Galilee,* ¹²and then along the Jordan River to the Dead Sea. These are the boundaries of your land."

³⁴:¹⁰
Josh 15:5
³⁴:¹¹
2 Kgs 23:33; 25:6
Jer 52:9

¹³Then Moses told the Israelites, "This territory is the homeland you are to divide among yourselves by sacred lot. The LORD has commanded that the land be divided among the nine and a half remaining tribes. ¹⁴The families of the tribes of Reuben, Gad, and half the tribe of Manasseh have already received their grants of land ¹⁵on the east side of the Jordan River, across from Jericho toward the sunrise."

³⁴:¹³
Josh 14:1-2
³⁴:¹⁴
Num 32:33

### Leaders to Divide the Land

¹⁶And the LORD said to Moses, ¹⁷"Eleazar the priest and Joshua son of Nun are the men designated to divide the grants of land among the people. ¹⁸Enlist one leader from each tribe to help them with the task. ¹⁹These are the tribes and the names of the leaders:

³⁴:¹⁸
Num 1:4, 16

| Tribe | Leader |
|---|---|
| Judah | Caleb son of Jephunneh |
| ²⁰ Simeon | Shemuel son of Ammihud |
| ²¹ Benjamin | Elidad son of Kislon |
| ²² Dan | Bukki son of Jogli |
| ²³ Manasseh son of Joseph | Hanniel son of Ephod |
| ²⁴ Ephraim son of Joseph | Kemuel son of Shiphtan |
| ²⁵ Zebulun | Elizaphan son of Parnach |
| ²⁶ Issachar | Paltiel son of Azzan |
| ²⁷ Asher | Ahihud son of Shelomi |
| ²⁸ Naphtali | Pedahel son of Ammihud |

²⁹These are the men the LORD has appointed to divide the grants of land in Canaan among the Israelites."

### Towns for the Levites

**35** While Israel was camped beside the Jordan on the plains of Moab across from Jericho, the LORD said to Moses, ²"Command the people of Israel to give to the Levites from their property certain towns to live in, along with the surrounding pasturelands. ³These towns will be for the Levites to live in, and the surrounding lands will provide pasture for their cattle, flocks, and other livestock. ⁴The pastureland assigned to the Levites around these towns will extend 1,500 feet* from the town walls in every direction. ⁵Measure off 3,000 feet* outside the town walls in every direction—east, south, west, north—with the town at the center. This area will serve as the larger pastureland for the towns.

³⁵:²
Lev 25:32-34
Josh 14:3-4

**34:11** Hebrew *Sea of Kinnereth.*   **35:4** Hebrew *1,000 cubits* [460 meters].   **35:5** Hebrew *2,000 cubits* [920 meters].

---

**34:16-29** In God's plan for settling the land, he (1) explained what to do, (2) communicated this clearly to Moses, and (3) assigned specific people to oversee the apportionment of the land. No plan is complete until each job is assigned and everyone understands his or her responsibilities. When you have a job to do, determine what must be done, give clear instructions, and put people in charge of each part.

**35:2, 3** The Levites were ministers. They were supported by the tithes of the people who gave them homes, flocks, and pasturelands. Likewise, we are responsible to provide for the needs of our ministers and missionaries so they can be free to do their God-ordained work.

**CITIES OF REFUGE**
Six of the Levites' cities were designated as cities of refuge. They were spaced throughout the land and protected those who had accidentally committed a crime or who were awaiting trial.

**35:6**
Josh 20:2-9; 21:3, 13, 21-38

**35:7**
Josh 21:3-42

**35:8**
Num 26:54

6"Six of the towns you give the Levites will be cities of refuge, where a person who has accidentally killed someone can flee for safety. In addition, give them forty-two other towns. 7In all, forty-eight towns with the surrounding pastureland will be given to the Levites. 8These towns will come from the property of the people of Israel. The larger tribes will give more towns to the Levites, while the smaller tribes will give fewer. Each tribe will give property in proportion to the size of its land."

### Cities of Refuge

**35:11**
Num 35:22-25

**35:12**
Josh 20:3

9 The LORD said to Moses, 10"Give the following instructions to the people of Israel.

"When you cross the Jordan into the land of Canaan, 11designate cities of refuge to which people can flee if they have killed someone accidentally. 12 These cities will be places of protection from a dead person's relatives who want to avenge the death. The slayer must not be put to death before being tried by the community. 13Designate six cities of refuge for yourselves, 14three on the east side of the Jordan River and three on the west in the land of Canaan. 15These cities are for the protection of Israelites, foreigners living among you, and traveling merchants. Anyone who accidentally kills someone may flee there for safety.

---

**EIGHT WORDS FOR LAW**

Hebrew law served as the personal and national guide for living under God's authority. It directed the moral, spiritual, and social life. Its purpose was to produce better understanding of God and greater commitment to him.

| Word | Meaning | Examples | Significance |
|------|---------|----------|--------------|
| Torah | Direction, Guidance, Instruction | Exodus 24:12 | Need for law in general; a command from a higher person to a lower |
| Mitswah | Commandment, Command | Genesis 26:5; Exodus 15:26; 20:2-17 | God's specific instruction to be obeyed rather than a general law; used of the Ten Commandments |
| Mishpat | Regulations, Judgment, Ordinance | Genesis 18:19; Deuteronomy 16:18; 17:9 | Refers to the civil, social, and sanitation laws |
| Eduth | Testimony, Truth | Exodus 25:22 | Refers to God's law as he deals with his people |
| Huqqim | Statutes, Laws | Leviticus 18:4; Deuteronomy 4:1 | Dealt with the royal pronouncements; mainly connected to worship and feasts |
| Piqqudim | Orders, Commandments | Psalms 19:8; 103:18 | Used often in the Psalms to describe God's orders and assignments |
| Dabar | Word, Terms | Exodus 34:28; Deuteronomy 4:13 | Used to indicate divine oracles or revelations of God |
| Dath | Royal Edict, Public Law | Ezekiel 7:26; Daniel 6:8, 12 | Refers to a public law or Jewish religious tradition |

---

**35:6** Of the 48 cities given to the Levites, six were cities of refuge. These six cities were probably put under the Levites' supervision because they would be the most impartial judges. Such cities were needed because the ancient customs of justice called for revenge in the event of the death of a relative or loved one (2 Samuel 14:7). The Levites would hold a preliminary hearing outside the gates while the accused person was kept in the city until the time of his trial. If the killing was judged accidental, the person would stay in the city until the death of the high priest. At that time, he would be allowed to go free, and he could start a new life without worrying about avengers. If it was not accidental, the person would be delivered to the slain person's avengers. This system of justice shows how God's law and his mercy go hand in hand.

**35:11-28** If anyone died because of violence, murder was assumed, but the murder suspect was not automatically assumed guilty. The cities of refuge assured the accused that justice would be served. But if that person left the city, then he or she would

be assumed guilty and able to be killed by the avenging party. The people were to be intolerant of the sin yet impartial to the accused so as to have a fair trial. The cities of refuge represented God's concern for justice in a culture that did not always protect the innocent. It is unjust both to overlook wrongdoing and to jump to conclusions about guilt. When someone is accused of wrongdoing, stand up for justice, protect those not yet proven guilty, and listen carefully to all sides of the story.

16"But if someone strikes and kills another person with a piece of iron, it is murder, and the murderer must be executed. 17Or if someone with a stone in his hand strikes and kills another person, it is murder, and the murderer must be put to death. 18Or if someone strikes and kills another person with a wooden object, it is murder, and the murderer must be put to death. 19The victim's nearest relative is responsible for putting the murderer to death. When they meet, the avenger must put the murderer to death. 20So if someone hates another person and pushes him or throws a dangerous object at him and he dies, it is murder. 21Or if someone hates another person and hits him with a fist and he dies, it is murder. In such cases, the avenger must put the murderer to death when they meet.

22"But suppose someone pushes another person without having shown previous hostility, or throws something that unintentionally hits another person, 23or accidentally drops a huge stone on someone, though they were not enemies, and the person dies. 24If this should happen, the community must follow these regulations in making a judgment between the slayer and the avenger, the victim's nearest relative: 25The community must protect the slayer from the avenger and must escort the slayer back to live in the city of refuge to which he fled. There he must remain until the death of the high priest, who was anointed with the sacred oil.

26"But if the slayer ever leaves the limits of the city of refuge, 27and the avenger finds him outside the city and kills him, it will not be considered murder. 28The slayer should have stayed inside the city of refuge until the death of the high priest. But after the death of the high priest, the slayer may return to his own property. 29These are legal requirements for you to observe from generation to generation, wherever you may live.

30"All murderers must be put to death, but only if evidence is presented by more than one witness. No one may be put to death on the testimony of only one witness. 31Also, you must never accept a ransom payment for the life of someone judged guilty of murder and subject to execution; murderers must always be put to death. 32And never accept a ransom payment from someone who has fled to a city of refuge, allowing a slayer to return to his property before the death of the high priest. 33This will ensure that the land where you live will not be polluted, for murder pollutes the land. And no sacrifice except the execution of the murderer can purify the land from murder.* 34You must not defile the land where you live, for I live there myself. I am the LORD, who lives among the people of Israel."

### Women Who Inherit Property

**36** Then the heads of the clans of Gilead—descendants of Makir, son of Manasseh, son of Joseph—came to Moses and the family leaders of Israel with a petition. 2They said, "Sir, the LORD instructed you to divide the land by sacred lot among the people of Israel. You were told by the LORD to give the grant of land owned by our brother Zelophehad to his daughters. 3But if they marry men from another tribe, their grants of land will go with them to the tribe into which they marry. In this way, the total area of our tribal land will be reduced. 4Then when the Year of Jubilee comes, their portion of land will be added to that of the new tribe, causing it to be lost forever to our ancestral tribe."

5So Moses gave the Israelites this command from the LORD: "The claim of the men of the tribe of Joseph is legitimate. 6This is what the LORD commands concerning the daughters of Zelophehad: Let them marry anyone they like, as long as it is within their own ancestral tribe. 7None of the territorial land may pass from tribe to tribe, for all the land given to each tribe must remain within the tribe to which it was first allotted. 8The daughters throughout the tribes of Israel who are in line to inherit property must marry within their tribe, so that all the Israelites will keep their ancestral property. 9No grant of land may pass from one tribe to another; each tribe of Israel must keep its allotted portion of land."

35:33 Or *can make atonement for murder.*

---

35:16
Exod 21:12-14
Lev 24:17

35:30
Deut 17:6-7; 19:15
Matt 18:16
2 Cor 13:1
Heb 10:28

35:34
Lev 18:25

36:1-2
Num 27:1-11

36:8
1 Chr 23:22

---

**36:1-9** Zelophehad had five daughters but no sons. After he died, the daughters made an appeal to Moses. Because the inheritance normally passed only through the male line, the family line of Zelophehad would have disappeared. God told Moses that if a man died without sons, then the inheritance would go to his daughters (27:8). But the question of marriage arose. If the daughters were to marry outside of their tribe, the land would belong to another tribe at the Year of Jubilee. So Moses commanded that in such cases the women should marry men in their own clan and tribe so that each tribe would retain its original inheritance. Later, when the tribes received their land under Joshua, the daughters of Zelophehad received their inheritance as God had instructed (Joshua 17:3-6).

We don't have to look far to find those who want to be considered "special cases" and "exceptions to the rule," but wise leaders will sort out those who have legitimate concerns and make sure that justice is done in these special situations.

**36:11**
Num 26:33; 27:1

¹⁰The daughters of Zelophehad did as the LORD commanded Moses. ¹¹Mahlah, Tirzah, Hoglah, Milcah, and Noah all married cousins on their father's side. ¹²They married into the clans of Manasseh son of Joseph. Thus, their inheritance of land remained within their ancestral tribe.

**36:13**
Lev 7:38; 27:34

¹³These are the commands and regulations that the LORD gave to the people of Israel through Moses while they were camped on the plains of Moab beside the Jordan River across from Jericho.

---

**36:13** The book of Numbers covers 39 years and closes with the Israelites poised near the banks of the Jordan River with the Promised Land in sight. The wanderings in the wilderness have come to an end, and the people are preparing for their next big move—the conquest of the land. The apostle Paul says that the events described in Numbers are examples that warn us and help us avoid the Israelites' mistakes (1 Corinthians 10:1-12). From their experiences we learn that unbelief is disastrous. We also learn not to long for the sinful pleasures of the past, to avoid complaining, and to stay away from all forms of sexual sin. We must not weaken our biblical beliefs by compromising them with our culture's values. If we choose to let God lead our lives, we should not ignore his message in the book of Numbers.

# DEUTERONOMY

| Joseph dies 1805 B.C. (1640 B.C.) | S L A V E R Y   I N   E G Y P T | Exodus from Egypt 1446 (1280) | Ten Commandments given 1445 (1279) |

WILDERNESS WANDERINGS

## VITAL STATISTICS

**PURPOSE:**
To remind the people of what God had done and encourage them to rededicate their lives to him

**AUTHOR:**
Moses (except for the final summary, which was probably written by Joshua after Moses' death)

**ORIGINAL AUDIENCE:**
Israel (the new generation entering the Promised Land)

**DATE WRITTEN:**
About 1407/6 B.C.

**SETTING:**
The east side of the Jordan River, in view of Canaan

**KEY VERSE:**
"Understand, therefore, that the LORD your God is indeed God. He is the faithful God who keeps his covenant for a thousand generations and lavishes his unfailing love on those who love him and obey his commands" (7:9).

**KEY PEOPLE:**
Moses, Joshua

**KEY PLACE:**
The Arabah in Moab

CLASS reunions, photo albums, familiar songs, and old neighborhoods—like long-time friends they awaken our memories and stir our emotions. The past is a kaleidoscope of promises, failures, victories, and embarrassments. Sometimes we want to forget memories that are too painful. As the years pass, however, remembrances of unpleasant events usually fade into our subconscious. But there is a time to remember: Mistakes should not be repeated; commitments made must be fulfilled; and the memory of special events can encourage us and move us to action.

The book of Deuteronomy is written in the form of a treaty between a king and his vassal state typical of the second millennium B.C. It calls Israel to remember who God is and what he has done. Lacking faith, the old generation had wandered for 40 years and had died in the wilderness. They left Egypt behind, but never knew the Promised Land. Then on the east bank of the Jordan River, Moses prepared the sons and daughters of that faithless generation to possess the land. After a brief history lesson emphasizing God's great acts on behalf of his people, Moses reviewed the law. Then he restated the covenant—God's contract with his people.

The lessons are clear. Because of what God has done, Israel should have hope and follow him; because of what he expects, they should listen and obey; because of who he is, they should love him completely. Learning these lessons will prepare them to possess the Promised Land.

As you hear the message of Deuteronomy, remember how God has expressed his kindness in your life, and then commit yourself anew to trust, love, and obey him.

## THE BLUEPRINT

A. WHAT GOD HAS DONE FOR US: MOSES' FIRST ADDRESS (1:1—4:43)

Moses reviewed the mighty acts of God for the nation of Israel. Remembering God's special involvement in our lives gives us hope and encouragement for the future.

B. PRINCIPLES FOR GODLY LIVING: MOSES' SECOND ADDRESS (4:44—29:1)
   1. The Ten Commandments
   2. Love the Lord your God
   3. Laws for proper worship
   4. Laws for ruling the nation
   5. Laws for human relationships
   6. Consequences of obedience and disobedience

Obeying God's laws brought blessings to the Israelites and disobeying brought misfortune. This was part of the written agreement God made with his people. Although we are not part of this covenant, the principle holds true: Obedience and disobedience carry inevitable consequences in this life and the next.

C. A CALL FOR COMMITMENT TO GOD: MOSES' THIRD ADDRESS (29:2—30:20)

Moses called the people to commitment. God still calls us to be committed to love him with all our heart, soul, mind, and strength.

D. THE CHANGE IN LEADERSHIP: MOSES' LAST DAYS (31:1—34:12)

Although Moses made some serious mistakes, he had lived uprightly and carried out God's commands. Moses died with integrity. We too may make some serious mistakes, but that should not stop us from living with integrity and godly commitment.

Moses'
death;
Israelites
enter
Canaan
1406
(1240)

Judges
begin
to rule
1375
(1220)

United
kingdom
under
Saul
1050
(1045)

## MEGATHEMES

| THEME | EXPLANATION | IMPORTANCE |
|---|---|---|
| History | Moses reviewed the mighty acts of God whereby he liberated Israel from slavery in Egypt. He recounted how God had helped them and how the people had disobeyed. | By reviewing God's promises and mighty acts in history, we can learn about his character. We come to know God more intimately through understanding how he has acted in the past. We can also avoid mistakes in our own lives through learning from Israel's past failures. |
| Laws | God reviewed his laws for the people. The legal contract between God and his people had to be renewed by the new generation about to enter the Promised Land. | Commitment to God and his truth cannot be taken for granted. Each generation and each person must respond afresh to God's call for obedience. |
| Love | God's faithful and patient love is portrayed more often than his punishment. God shows his love by being faithful to his people and his promises. In response, God desires love from the heart, not merely a legalistic keeping of his law. | God's love forms the foundation for our trust in him. We trust him because he loves us. Because God loves us, we should maintain justice and respect. |
| Choices | God reminded his people that in order to ratify his covenant, they must choose the path of obedience. A personal decision to obey would bring benefits to their lives; rebellion would bring severe calamity. | Our choices make a difference. Choosing to follow God benefits us and improves our relationships with others. Choosing to abandon God's ways brings harm to ourselves and others. |
| Teaching | God commanded the Israelites to teach their children his ways. They were to use ritual, instruction, and memorization to make sure their children understood God's principles and passed them on to the next generation. | Quality teaching for our children must be a priority. It is important to pass on God's truth to future generations in our traditions. But God desires that his truth be in our hearts and minds and not merely in our traditions. |

## A. WHAT GOD HAS DONE FOR US: MOSES' FIRST ADDRESS (1:1—4:43)

God has led his people out of Egypt and through the great wilderness for 40 years. Now they stand ready to enter the Promised Land. But before the Israelites go into the land, Moses has some important advice to give them. He delivers his advice in three parts. In the first part, Moses reviews the history of God's previous care for the people of Israel. Through God's actions in the past, we can learn about the God we serve today.

### Introduction to Moses' First Address

**1:1**
Deut 2:8, 24; 3:3;
4:1, 44-46

**1** These are the words that Moses spoke to all the people of Israel while they were in the wilderness east of the Jordan River. They were camped in the Jordan Valley* near Suph, between Paran on one side and Tophel, Laban, Hazeroth, and Di-zahab on the other. ²Normally it takes only eleven days to travel from Mount Sinai* to Kadesh-barnea, going

1:1 Hebrew *the Arabah;* also in 1:7.   1:2 Hebrew *Horeb,* another name for Sinai; also in 1:6, 19.

**1:1, 2** The Israelites spent 40 years on a journey that should have lasted 11 days. It wasn't distance that stood between them and the Promised Land. It was the condition of their hearts. God's purpose went deeper than simply transporting a huge group of people to a new land. He was preparing them to live in obedience to him once they arrived. What good was the Promised Land if the Israelites were just as wicked as the nations already living there? The journey was a painful but necessary part of their preparation. Through it God taught the Israelites who he was: the living God, the Leader of their nation. He also taught them who they were: people who were fallen, sinful, prone to rebellion and doubt. He gave his rebellious people the law to

help them understand how to relate to God and to other people. Your spiritual pilgrimage may be lengthy, and you may face pain, discouragement, and difficulties. But remember that God isn't just trying to keep you alive. He wants to prepare you to live for service and devotion to him.

**1:1-5** The 40 years of wilderness wandering come to an end in this book. The events of Deuteronomy cover only a week or two of the 11th month of the 40th year (1:3). The 12th and last month was spent in mourning for Moses (34:8). Then the Israelites entered the Promised Land the first month of the 41st year after the Exodus (Joshua 4:19).

by way of Mount Seir. ³But forty years after the Israelites left Egypt, on the first day of the eleventh month,* Moses addressed the people of Israel, telling them everything the LORD had commanded him to say. ⁴This took place after he had defeated King Sihon of the Amorites, who had ruled in Heshbon, and King Og of Bashan, who had ruled in Ashtaroth and Edrei.

⁵While the Israelites were in the land of Moab east of the Jordan River, Moses carefully explained the LORD's instructions as follows.

### The Command to Leave Sinai

⁶"When we were at Mount Sinai, the LORD our God said to us, 'You have stayed at this mountain long enough. ⁷It is time to break camp and move on. Go to the hill country of the Amorites and to all the neighboring regions—the Jordan Valley, the hill country, the western foothills,* the Negev, and the coastal plain. Go to the land of the Canaanites and to Lebanon, and all the way to the great Euphrates River. ⁸Look, I am giving all this land to you! Go in and occupy it, for it is the land the LORD swore to give to your ancestors Abraham, Isaac, and Jacob, and to all their descendants.'"

### Moses Appoints Leaders from Each Tribe

⁹Moses continued, "At that time I told you, 'You are too great a burden for me to carry all by myself. ¹⁰The LORD your God has increased your population, making you as numerous as the stars! ¹¹And may the LORD, the God of your ancestors, multiply you a thousand times more and bless you as he promised! ¹²But you are such a heavy load to carry! How can I deal with all your problems and bickering? ¹³Choose some well-respected men from each tribe who are known for their wisdom and understanding, and I will appoint them as your leaders.'

¹⁴"Then you responded, 'Your plan is a good one.' ¹⁵So I took the wise and respected men you had selected from your tribes and appointed them to serve as judges and officials over you. Some were responsible for a thousand people, some for a hundred, some for fifty, and some for ten.

¹⁶"At that time I instructed the judges, 'You must hear the cases of your fellow Israelites and the foreigners living among you. Be perfectly fair in your decisions ¹⁷and impartial in

**1:4**
Num 21:24, 33

**1:6**
Num 10:11-13
**1:7**
Gen 15:18-21
Josh 10:5, 40
**1:8**
Gen 12:7; 26:3
Exod 33:1
Num 32:10-11

**1:9**
Exod 18:18, 24
**1:10**
Gen 15:5; 22:17
Deut 10:22; 26:5;
28:62
**1:11**
Deut 1:8, 10
**1:12**
Exod 18:13-14
**1:13**
Exod 18:21-22
Num 11:16-17
**1:16**
Deut 16:18
**1:17**
Exod 18:25-26
Deut 10:17;
16:19; 24:17
Prov 24:23
Jas 2:1, 9

**1:3** Hebrew *In the fortieth year, on the first day of the eleventh month.* This day in the ancient Hebrew lunar calendar occurred in January or February. **1:7** Hebrew *the Shephelah.*

---

**1:6, 7** Notice that Moses' summary of Israel's 40-year journey begins at Mount Sinai, not in Egypt. Why did Moses leave out the first part of the Exodus? Moses was not giving an itinerary—he was summarizing the nation's development. In Moses' mind the nation of Israel began at the base of Mount Sinai, not in

**EVENTS IN DEUTERONOMY**
The book of Deuteronomy opens with Israel camped east of the Jordan River in the land of Moab. Just before the people crossed the river into the Promised Land, Moses delivered an inspirational speech indicating how they were to live.

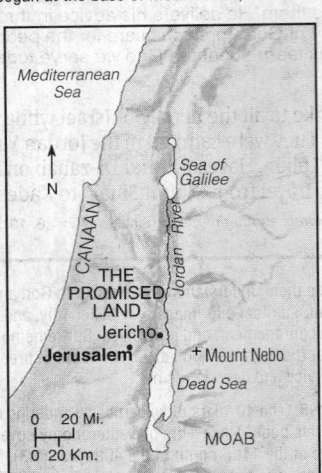

Egypt, for it was at Mount Sinai that God gave his covenant to the people (Exodus 19–20). Along with this covenant came knowledge and responsibility. After the people chose to follow God, they had to know *how* to follow him. Therefore, God gave them a comprehensive set of laws and guidelines that stated how he wanted them to live (these are found in the books of Exodus, Leviticus, and Numbers). The people could no longer say they didn't know the difference between right and wrong. Now that the people had promised to follow God and knew how to follow him, they had a responsibility to do it. When God tells you to break camp and move out to face a challenge he gives you, will you be ready to obey?

**1:9-13** It was a tremendous burden for Moses to lead the nation by himself. He could not accomplish the task single-handedly. As nations, organizations, and churches grow, they become increasingly complex. Conflicting needs and quarrels arise. No longer can one leader make all the decisions. Like Moses, you may have a natural tendency to try to do all the work alone. You may be afraid or embarrassed to ask for help. Moses made a wise decision to share the leadership with others. Rather than trying to handle larger responsibilities alone, look for ways of sharing the load so that others may exercise their God-given gifts and abilities.

**1:13-18** Moses identified some of the inner qualities of good leaders: (1) wisdom, (2) experience, and (3) understanding. These characteristics differ markedly from the ones that often help elect leaders today: good looks, wealth, popularity, willingness to do anything to get to the top. The qualities Moses identified should be evident in us as we lead, and we should look for them in those we elect to positions of leadership.

your judgments. Hear the cases of those who are poor as well as those who are rich. Don't be afraid of anyone's anger, for the decision you make is God's decision. Bring me any cases that are too difficult for you, and I will handle them.'

18"At that time I gave you instructions about everything you were to do.

### Scouts Explore the Land

**1:19**
Deut 1:2; 8:15;
32:10

19"Then, just as the LORD our God commanded us, we left Mount Sinai and traveled through the great and terrifying wilderness, as you yourselves remember, and headed toward the hill country of the Amorites. When we arrived at Kadesh-barnea, 20I said to you, 'You have now reached the hill country of the Amorites that the LORD our God is giving us. 21Look! He has placed the land in front of you. Go and occupy it as the LORD, the God of your ancestors, has promised you. Don't be afraid! Don't be discouraged!'

**1:22-23**
Num 13:1-3

22"But you all came to me and said, 'First, let's send out scouts to explore the land for us. They will advise us on the best route to take and which towns we should enter.'

**1:24**
Num 13:21-25

23"This seemed like a good idea to me, so I chose twelve scouts, one from each of your tribes. 24They headed for the hill country and came to the valley of Eshcol and explored it. 25They picked some of its fruit and brought it back to us. And they reported, 'The land the LORD our God has given us is indeed a good land.'

### Israel's Rebellion against the LORD

**1:26**
Num 14:1-3

**1:27**
Deut 9:28
Ps 106:25

**1:28**
Num 13:28, 33
Deut 9:1-2

**1:29**
Deut 3:22; 7:18

**1:30**
Exod 14:14
Deut 20:4

**1:31**
Deut 32:11
Acts 13:18

**1:33**
Exod 13:21
Num 9:15-23;
10:33-36

**1:34**
Num 14:23; 32:14

**1:36**
Num 14:24
Josh 14:6

**1:37**
Num 20:12; 27:18

**1:38**
Num 34:17
Deut 3:28; 31:7

**1:39**
Num 14:3, 31

**1:40**
Num 14:25

26"But you rebelled against the command of the LORD your God and refused to go in. 27 You complained in your tents and said, 'The LORD must hate us. That's why he has brought us here from Egypt—to hand us over to the Amorites to be slaughtered. 28Where can we go? Our brothers have demoralized us with their report. They tell us, "The people of the land are taller and more powerful than we are, and their towns are large, with walls rising high into the sky! We even saw giants there—the descendants of Anak!"'

29"But I said to you, 'Don't be shocked or afraid of them! 30The LORD your God is going ahead of you. He will fight for you, just as you saw him do in Egypt. 31And you saw how the LORD your God cared for you all along the way as you traveled through the wilderness, just as a father cares for his child. Now he has brought you to this place.'

32"But even after all he did, you refused to trust the LORD your God, 33who goes before you looking for the best places to camp, guiding you with a pillar of fire by night and a pillar of cloud by day.

34"When the LORD heard your complaining, he became very angry. So he solemnly swore, 35'Not one of you from this wicked generation will live to see the good land I swore to give your ancestors, 36except Caleb son of Jephunneh. He will see this land because he has followed the LORD completely. I will give to him and his descendants some of the very land he explored during his scouting mission.'

37"And the LORD was also angry with me because of you. He said to me, 'Moses, not even you will enter the Promised Land! 38Instead, your assistant, Joshua son of Nun, will lead the people into the land. Encourage him, for he will lead Israel as they take possession of it. 39I will give the land to your little ones—your innocent children. You were afraid they would be captured, but they will be the ones who occupy it. 40As for you, turn around now and go on back through the wilderness toward the Red Sea.*'

**1:40** Hebrew *sea of reeds.*

---

**1:22** The scouts had been sent into the land to determine not *whether* they should enter, but *where* they should enter. Upon returning, however, most of the scouts had concluded that the land was not worth the obstacles. God would give the Israelites the power to conquer the land, but they were afraid of the risk and decided not to enter. God gives us the power to overcome our obstacles, but just as the Israelites were filled with fear and skepticism, we often let difficulties control our lives. When we follow God regardless of the difficulties, we demonstrate courageous, overcoming faith.

**1:23-40** Moses retold the story of the scouting mission into the Promised Land (Numbers 13–14). When the scouts returned with reports of giants and walled cities, the people were afraid to move ahead and began to complain about their predicament. But the minority report of Joshua and Caleb pointed out that the land was fertile, the enemy was vulnerable, and God was on their

side. We become fearful and immobile when we focus on the negative aspects of a situation. How much better it is to focus on the positive—God's direction and promises. When you are confronted with an important decision and know what you should do, move out in faith. Focus on the positives while trusting God to overcome the negatives. Problems don't have to rob you of the victory.

**1:28** Canaan was a land with giants and imposing fortresses. The "descendants of Anak" may have been seven to nine feet tall. Many of the land's fortified cities had walls as high as 30 feet. The Israelites' fear was understandable but not justified, for the all-powerful God had already promised them victory.

41"Then you confessed, 'We have sinned against the LORD! We will go into the land and fight for it, as the LORD our God has commanded us.' So your men strapped on their weapons, thinking it would be easy to attack the hill country.

1:41
Num 14:40

42"But the LORD told me to tell you, 'Do not attack, for I am not with you. If you go ahead on your own, you will be crushed by your enemies.'

1:42
Num 14:41-43

43"This is what I told you, but you would not listen. Instead, you again rebelled against the LORD's command and arrogantly went into the hill country to fight. 44But the Amorites who lived there came out against you like a swarm of bees. They chased and battered you all the way from Seir to Hormah. 45Then you returned and wept before the LORD, but he refused to listen. 46So you stayed there at Kadesh for a long time.

1:43
Num 14:44

1:44
Num 14:45

### Remembering Israel's Wanderings

**2** "Then we turned around and headed back across the wilderness toward the Red Sea,* just as the LORD had instructed me, and we wandered around in the region of Mount Seir for a long time.

2:1
Num 21:4

2"Then at last the LORD said to me, 3'You have been wandering around in this hill country long enough; turn to the north. 4Give these orders to the people: "You will pass through the country belonging to your relatives the Edomites, the descendants of Esau, who live in Seir. The Edomites will feel threatened, so be careful. 5Do not bother them, for I have given them all the hill country around Mount Seir as their property, and I will not give you even one square foot of their land. 6If you need food to eat or water to drink, pay them for it. 7For the LORD your God has blessed you in everything you have done. He has watched your every step through this great wilderness. During these forty years, the LORD your God has been with you, and you have lacked nothing."'

2:4
Exod 15:15
Num 20:14

2:5
Deut 23:7
Josh 24:4

2:7
Deut 8:2; 29:5

8"So we bypassed the territory of our relatives, the descendants of Esau, who live in Seir. We avoided the road through the Arabah Valley that comes up from Elath and Ezion-geber.

2:8
Num 20:20

"Then as we turned north along the desert route through Moab, 9the LORD warned us, 'Do not bother the Moabites, the descendants of Lot, or start a war with them. I have given them Ar as their property, and I will not give you any of their land.'"

2:9
Gen 19:37
Deut 2:18, 29

10(A race of giants called the Emites had once lived in the area of Ar. They were as strong and numerous and tall as the Anakites, another race of giants. 11Both the Emites and the Anakites are also known as the Rephaites, though the Moabites call them Emites. 12In earlier times the Horites had lived in Seir, but they were driven out and displaced by the descendants of Esau, just as Israel drove out the people of Canaan when the LORD gave Israel their land.)

2:10
Gen 14:5
Num 13:22, 33

2:12
Gen 14:6
Num 21:25, 35
Deut 2:22

13Moses continued, "Then the LORD said to us, 'Get moving. Cross the Zered Brook.' So we crossed the brook.

14"Thirty-eight years passed from the time we first left Kadesh-barnea until we finally crossed the Zered Brook! By then, all the men old enough to fight in battle had died in the wilderness, as the LORD had vowed would happen. 15The LORD struck them down until they had all been eliminated from the community.

2:14
Num 14:29-35;
26:64-65
Deut 2:7
1 Cor 10:5

2:15
Ps 106:26
Jude 1:5

16"When all the men of fighting age had died, 17the LORD said to me, 18'Today you will cross the border of Moab at Ar 19and enter the land of the Ammonites, the descendants of Lot. But do not bother them or start a war with them. I have given the land of Ammon to them as their property, and I will not give you any of their land.'"

2:18
Num 21:15
Deut 2:9

2:1 Hebrew *sea of reeds.*

---

**2:4-6** When the Israelites passed through Seir, God advised them to be careful. The Israelites were known as warriors, and the descendants of Esau—the Edomites—would be understandably nervous as the great crowd passed through their land. God warned the Israelites not to start a fight, to respect the Edomites' territory, and to pay for whatever they used. God wanted the Israelites to deal justly with these neighbors. We must also act justly in dealing with others. Recognize the rights of others, even your opponents. By behaving wisely and justly you may be able to establish or restore a relationship.

**2:11** Both Moab and Ammon had removed a tall Anakim-like people usually known as the Rephaites, but called Emites by

the Moabites and Zamzummites by the Ammonites (2:20). If our enemies seem overwhelming, we must remember that God can deliver us as he did the Israelites.

**2:14, 15** Israel did not have to spend 40 years on the way to the Promised Land. God sentenced them to wilderness wanderings because they rejected his love, rebelled against his authority, ignored his commands for right living, and willfully broke their end of the agreement made in Exodus 19:8 and 24:3-8. In short, they disobeyed God. We often make life's journey more difficult than necessary by disobedience. Accept God's love, read and follow his commands in the Bible, and make a promise to stick with God whatever your situation. You will find that your life will be less complicated and more rewarding.

2:20
Deut 2:11

2:23
Gen 10:13-14
1 Chr 1:11-12
Jer 47:4
Amos 9:7
2:24
Num 21:13
Judg 11:18
2:25
Exod 15:14-16;
23:27
Deut 11:25
Josh 2:9

2:26
Num 21:21
Deut 20:10
Judg 11:19

2:29
Deut 2:8-9; 23:3

2:30
Exod 4:21
Num 21:23
Josh 11:20

2:33
Num 21:24-30
Deut 3:6; 29:7

2:35
Deut 3:7, 10

2:36
Ps 44:3

2:37
Deut 3:16

3:1
Num 21:33-35
3:2
Num 21:34

3:3
Josh 9:10
3:4
1 Kgs 4:13

3:6
Deut 2:33-34;
20:16
3:7
Deut 2:35

20(That area was once considered the land of the Rephaites, who had lived there, though the Ammonites call them Zamzummites. 21They were also as strong and numerous and tall as the Anakites. But the LORD destroyed them so the Ammonites could occupy their land. 22He had done the same for the descendants of Esau who lived in Seir, for he destroyed the Horites so they could settle there in their place. The descendants of Esau live there to this day. 23A similar thing happened when the Caphtorites from Crete* invaded and destroyed the Avvites, who had lived in villages in the area of Gaza.)

24Moses continued, "Then the LORD said, 'Now get moving! Cross the Arnon Gorge. Look, I will hand over to you Sihon the Amorite, king of Heshbon, and I will give you his land. Attack him and begin to occupy the land. 25Beginning today I will make people throughout the earth terrified because of you. When they hear reports about you, they will tremble with dread and fear.'"

### Victory over Sihon of Heshbon

26Moses continued, "From the wilderness of Kedemoth I sent ambassadors to King Sihon of Heshbon with this proposal of peace:

27'Let us travel through your land. We will stay on the main road and won't turn off into the fields on either side. 28Sell us food to eat and water to drink, and we will pay for it. All we want is permission to pass through your land. 29The descendants of Esau who live in Seir allowed us to go through their country, and so did the Moabites, who live in Ar. Let us pass through until we cross the Jordan into the land the LORD our God is giving us.'

30"But King Sihon of Heshbon refused to allow us to pass through, because the LORD your God made Sihon stubborn and defiant so he could help you defeat him, as he has now done. 31"Then the LORD said to me, 'Look, I have begun to hand King Sihon and his land over to you. Begin now to conquer and occupy his land.'

32"Then King Sihon declared war on us and mobilized his forces at Jahaz. 33But the LORD our God handed him over to us, and we crushed him, his sons, and all his people. 34We conquered all his towns and completely destroyed* everyone—men, women, and children. Not a single person was spared. 35We took all the livestock as plunder for ourselves, along with anything of value from the towns we ransacked.

36"The LORD our God also helped us conquer Aroer on the edge of the Arnon Gorge, and the town in the gorge, and the whole area as far as Gilead. No town had walls too strong for us. 37However, we avoided the land of the Ammonites all along the Jabbok River and the towns in the hill country—all the places the LORD our God had commanded us to leave alone.

### Victory over Og of Bashan

**3** "Next we turned and headed for the land of Bashan, where King Og and his entire army attacked us at Edrei. 2But the LORD told me, 'Do not be afraid of him, for I have given you victory over Og and his entire army, and I will give you all his land. Treat him just as you treated King Sihon of the Amorites, who ruled in Heshbon.'

3"So the LORD our God handed King Og and all his people over to us, and we killed them all. Not a single person survived. 4We conquered all sixty of his towns—the entire Argob region in his kingdom of Bashan. Not a single town escaped our conquest. 5These towns were all fortified with high walls and barred gates. We also took many unwalled villages at the same time. 6We completely destroyed* the kingdom of Bashan, just as we had destroyed King Sihon of Heshbon. We destroyed all the people in every town we conquered—men, women, and children alike. 7But we kept all the livestock for ourselves and took plunder from all the towns.

2:23 Hebrew *from Caphtor.*    2:34 The Hebrew term used here refers to the complete consecration of things or people to the LORD, either by destroying them or by giving them as an offering.    3:6 The Hebrew term used here refers to the complete consecration of things or people to the LORD, either by destroying them or by giving them as an offering; also in 3:6b.

---

2:25 God told Moses he would make the enemy nations terrified of Israel. By worldly standards, Israel's army was not intimidating, but Israel had God on its side. Moses no longer had to worry about his enemies because his enemies were worried about him. God often goes before us in our daily battles, preparing the way and overcoming barriers. We need to follow him wholeheartedly and be alert to his leading.

3:1-3 The Israelites faced a big problem—the well-trained army of Og, king of Bashan. The Israelites hardly stood a chance. But they won because God fought for them. God can help his people regardless of the problems they face. No matter how insurmountable the obstacles may seem, remember that God is sovereign, and he will keep his promises.

8"So we took the land of the two Amorite kings east of the Jordan River—all the way from the Arnon Gorge to Mount Hermon. 9(Mount Hermon is called Sirion by the Sidonians, and the Amorites call it Senir.) 10We had now conquered all the cities on the plateau and all Gilead and Bashan, as far as the towns of Salecah and Edrei, which were part of Og's kingdom in Bashan. 11(King Og of Bashan was the last survivor of the giant Rephaites. His bed was made of iron and was more than thirteen feet long and six feet wide.* It can still be seen in the Ammonite city of Rabbah.)

### Land Division East of the Jordan

12"When we took possession of this land, I gave to the tribes of Reuben and Gad the territory beyond Aroer along the Arnon Gorge, plus half of the hill country of Gilead with its towns. 13Then I gave the rest of Gilead and all of Bashan—Og's former kingdom—to the half-tribe of Manasseh. (This entire Argob region of Bashan used to be known as the land of the Rephaites. 14Jair, a leader from the tribe of Manasseh, conquered the whole Argob region in Bashan, all the way to the border of the Geshurites and Maacathites. Jair renamed this region after himself, calling it the Towns of Jair,* as it is still known today.) 15I gave Gilead to the clan of Makir. 16But I also gave part of Gilead to the tribes of Reuben and Gad. The area I gave them extended from the middle of the Arnon Gorge in the south to the Jabbok River on the Ammonite frontier. 17They also received the Jordan Valley, all the way from the Sea of Galilee down to the Dead Sea,* with the Jordan River serving as the western boundary. To the east were the slopes of Pisgah.

18"At that time I gave this command to the tribes that would live east of the Jordan: 'Although the LORD your God has given you this land as your property, all your fighting men must cross the Jordan ahead of your Israelite relatives, armed and ready to assist them. 19Your wives, children, and numerous livestock, however, may stay behind in the towns I have given you. 20When the LORD has given security to the rest of the Israelites, as he has to you, and when they occupy the land the LORD your God is giving them across the Jordan River, then you may all return here to the land I have given you.'

### Moses Forbidden to Enter the Land

21"At that time I gave Joshua this charge: 'You have seen for yourself everything the LORD your God has done to these two kings. He will do the same to all the kingdoms on the west side of the Jordan. 22Do not be afraid of the nations there, for the LORD your God will fight for you.'

23"At that time I pleaded with the LORD and said, 24'O Sovereign LORD, you have only begun to show your greatness and the strength of your hand to me, your servant. Is there any god in heaven or on earth who can perform such great and mighty deeds as you do? 25Please let me cross the Jordan to see the wonderful land on the other side, the beautiful hill country and the Lebanon mountains.'

26"But the LORD was angry with me because of you, and he would not listen to me. 'That's enough!' he declared. 'Speak of it no more. 27But go up to Pisgah Peak, and look over the land in every direction. Take a good look, but you may not cross the Jordan River. 28Instead, commission Joshua and encourage and strengthen him, for he will lead the people across the Jordan. He will give them all the land you now see before you as their possession.' 29So we stayed in the valley near Beth-peor.

### Moses Urges Israel to Obey

**4** "And now, Israel, listen carefully to these decrees and regulations that I am about to teach you. Obey them so that you may live, so you may enter and occupy the land

---

3:8
Num 32:33-42
Josh 12:1-6;
13:8-13

3:9
Deut 4:48
Josh 11:17
Ps 29:5-6

3:11
Deut 2:11, 20
2 Sam 11:1;
12:26-27
Jer 49:2

3:12
Num 32:33-42
Deut 2:35-36
Josh 13:8-13

3:15
Num 32:40

3:17
Josh 13:27

3:18
Num 32:20
Josh 4:12-13

3:19
Num 32:16
Josh 1:14

3:22
Deut 1:29-30; 20:4

3:24
Ps 86:8

3:26
Deut 1:37; 31:2
3:27
Num 27:12
Deut 1:37
3:28
Num 27:18

4:1
Lev 19:37
Deut 5:32-33; 8:1;
16:20; 30:16
Ezek 20:11
Rom 10:5

---

3:11 Hebrew 9 cubits [4.1 meters] long and 4 cubits [1.8 meters] wide.   3:14 Hebrew Havvoth-jair.   3:17 Hebrew from Kinnereth to the Sea of the Arabah, the Salt Sea.

---

**3:21, 22** What encouraging news for Joshua, who was to lead his men against the persistent forces of evil in the Promised Land! Since God promised to help him win every battle, he had nothing to fear. Our battles may not be against godless armies, but they are just as real as Joshua's. Whether we are resisting temptation or battling fear, God has promised to fight with and for us as we place our hope and confidence in him.

**3:26-28** God had made it clear that Moses would not enter the Promised Land (Numbers 20:12). So God told Moses to commission Joshua as the new leader and encourage him in this new role. This is a good example to churches and organizations who must eventually replace their leaders. Good leaders prepare their people to function without them by discovering those with leadership potential, providing the training they need, and looking for ways to encourage them.

**4:2**
Deut 12:32
Prov 30:6
Matt 5:18

**4:3**
Num 25:1-9

**4:5**
Lev 26:46; 27:34

**4:6**
Ps 19:7-8
Prov 1:7-9

**4:7**
Ps 148:14

**4:8**
Ps 89:14-15

**4:10**
Exod 19:9, 16

**4:11**
Exod 19:18
Heb 12:18

**4:13**
Exod 31:18; 34:28
Deut 10:4

**4:15**
Exod 19:9, 18, 21

**4:16**
Exod 20:4-5; 32:8
Deut 9:12; 31:29

**4:19**
2 Kgs 17:16
Acts 7:43

that the Lord, the God of your ancestors, is giving you. 2Do not add to or subtract from these commands I am giving you. Just obey the commands of the Lord your God that I am giving you.

3"You saw for yourself what the Lord did to you at Baal-peor. There the Lord your God destroyed everyone who had worshiped Baal, the god of Peor. 4But all of you who were faithful to the Lord your God are still alive today—every one of you.

5"Look, I now teach you these decrees and regulations just as the Lord my God commanded me, so that you may obey them in the land you are about to enter and occupy. 6Obey them completely, and you will display your wisdom and intelligence among the surrounding nations. When they hear all these decrees, they will exclaim, 'How wise and prudent are the people of this great nation!' 7For what great nation has a god as near to them as the Lord our God is near to us whenever we call on him? 8And what great nation has decrees and regulations as righteous and fair as this body of instructions that I am giving you today?

9"But watch out! Be careful never to forget what you yourself have seen. Do not let these memories escape from your mind as long as you live! And be sure to pass them on to your children and grandchildren. 10Never forget the day when you stood before the Lord your God at Mount Sinai,* where he told me, 'Summon the people before me, and I will personally instruct them. Then they will learn to fear me as long as they live, and they will teach their children to fear me also.'

11"You came near and stood at the foot of the mountain, while flames from the mountain shot into the sky. The mountain was shrouded in black clouds and deep darkness. 12And the Lord spoke to you from the heart of the fire. You heard the sound of his words but didn't see his form; there was only a voice. 13He proclaimed his covenant—the Ten Commandments*—which he commanded you to keep, and which he wrote on two stone tablets. 14It was at that time that the Lord commanded me to teach you his decrees and regulations so you would obey them in the land you are about to enter and occupy.

### A Warning against Idolatry

15"But be very careful! You did not see the Lord's form on the day he spoke to you from the heart of the fire at Mount Sinai. 16So do not corrupt yourselves by making an idol in any form—whether of a man or a woman, 17an animal on the ground, a bird in the sky, 18a small animal that scurries along the ground, or a fish in the deepest sea. 19And when you look up into the sky and see the sun, moon, and stars—all the forces of heaven—don't be seduced

4:10 Hebrew *Horeb*, another name for Sinai; also in 4:15.   4:13 Hebrew *the ten words.*

**4:2** What is meant by adding to or subtracting from God's commands? These laws were the word of God, and they were complete. How could any human being, with limited wisdom and knowledge, edit God's perfect laws? To add to the laws would make them a burden; to subtract from the laws would make them incomplete. Thus the laws were to remain unchanged. To presume to make changes in God's law is to assume a position of authority over God who gave the laws (Matthew 5:17-19; 15:3-9; Revelation 22:18, 19). The religious leaders at the time of Christ did exactly this; they elevated their own laws to the same level as God's. Jesus rebuked them for this (Matthew 23:1-4).

**4:8** Do the laws God gave to the Israelites still apply to Christians today? God's laws are designed to guide all people toward lifestyles that are healthy, upright, and devoted to God. Their purpose was to point out sin (or potential sin) and show the proper way to deal with that sin. The Ten Commandments, the heart of God's law, are just as applicable today as they were 3,000 years ago because they proclaim a lifestyle endorsed by God. They are the perfect expression of who God is and how he wants people to live.

But God gave other laws besides the Ten Commandments. Are these just as important? God never issued a law that didn't have a purpose. However, many of the laws we read in the Pentateuch were directed specifically to people of that time and culture. Although a specific law may not apply to us, the timeless truth or principle behind the law does.

For example, Christians do not practice animal sacrifice in worship. However, the principles behind the sacrifices—forgiveness for sin and thankfulness to God—still apply. The sacrifices

pointed to the ultimate sacrifice made for us by Jesus Christ. The New Testament says that with the death and resurrection of Jesus Christ the Old Testament laws were fulfilled. This means that while the Old Testament laws help us recognize our sins and correct our wrongdoings, it is Jesus Christ who takes our sins away. Jesus is now our primary example to follow because he alone perfectly obeyed the law and modeled its true intent.

**4:9** Moses wanted to make sure that the people did not forget all they had seen God do, so he urged parents to teach their children about God's great miracles. This helped parents remember God's faithfulness and provided the means for passing on from one generation to the next the stories recounting God's great acts. It is easy to forget the wonderful ways God has worked in the lives of his people. But you can remember God's great acts of faithfulness by telling your children, friends, or associates what you have seen him do.

**4:19** God was not excusing the other nations for their idol worship. He was simply saying that while judgment might be delayed for those other nations, it would be swift and complete for Israel because Israel knew God's laws. We must remember that idol worship was not just keeping statues around the house—harmless lumps of clay, wood, or iron. It was the commitment to the other evil qualities and practices the idol represented (such as murder, prostitution, cruelty in war, or self-centeredness). When the strengths and attributes of powerful humans or animals are revered or the cycles of nature are honored without reference to God who created them, this is idolatry. Because God had so clearly revealed himself in Israel's history, the Israelites had no excuse for worshiping any person or power but the one true God.

into worshiping them. The LORD your God gave them to all the peoples of the earth. [4:20]
20Remember that the LORD rescued you from the iron-smelting furnace of Egypt in order to
make you his very own people and his special possession, which is what you are today.

21"But the LORD was angry with me because of you. He vowed that I would not cross the
Jordan River into the good land the LORD your God is giving you as your special possession.
22You will cross the Jordan to occupy the land, but I will not. Instead, I will die here on the
east side of the river. 23So be careful not to break the covenant the LORD your God has made
with you. Do not make idols of any shape or form, for the LORD your God has forbidden this.
24The LORD your God is a devouring fire; he is a jealous God.

25"In the future, when you have children and grandchildren and have lived in the land a
long time, do not corrupt yourselves by making idols of any kind. This is evil in the sight of
the LORD your God and will arouse his anger.

26"Today I call on heaven and earth as witnesses against you. If you break my covenant,
you will quickly disappear from the land you are crossing the Jordan to occupy. You will live
there only a short time; then you will be utterly destroyed. 27For the LORD will scatter you
among the nations, where only a few of you will survive. 28There, in a foreign land, you will
worship idols made from wood and stone—gods that neither see nor hear nor eat nor smell.
29But from there you will search again for the LORD your God. And if you search for him with
all your heart and soul, you will find him.

30"In the distant future, when you are suffering all these things, you will finally return to
the LORD your God and listen to what he tells you. 31For the LORD your God is a merciful
God; he will not abandon you or destroy you or forget the solemn covenant he made with
your ancestors.

## There Is Only One God

32"Now search all of history, from the time God created people on the earth until now, and
search from one end of the heavens to the other. Has anything as great as this ever been
seen or heard before? 33Has any nation ever heard the voice of God* speaking from fire—as
you did—and survived? 34Has any other god dared to take a nation for himself out of another nation by means of trials, miraculous signs, wonders, war, a strong hand, a powerful
arm, and terrifying acts? Yet that is what the LORD your God did for you in Egypt, right
before your eyes.

35"He showed you these things so you would know that the LORD is God and there is no
other. 36He let you hear his voice from heaven so he could instruct you. He let you see his
great fire here on earth so he could speak to you from it. 37Because he loved your ancestors,
he chose to bless their descendants, and he personally brought you out of Egypt with a great
display of power. 38He drove out nations far greater than you, so he could bring you in and
give you their land as your special possession, as it is today.

39"So remember this and keep it firmly in mind: The LORD is God both in heaven and
on earth, and there is no other. 40If you obey all the decrees and commands I am giving you
today, all will be well with you and your children. I am giving you these instructions so you
will enjoy a long life in the land the LORD your God is giving you for all time."

4:33 Or voice of a god.

### Cross-references
- 4:20 1 Kgs 8:51; Jer 11:4
- 4:21 Num 20:12; Deut 1:37
- 4:23 Exod 20:4-5
- 4:24 Exod 24:17; 34:14; Heb 12:29
- 4:25 Deut 4:16; 31:29
- 4:26 Deut 7:4; 8:19; 31:29
- 4:27 Deut 28:64
- 4:28 Deut 28:36, 64; 29:17; Ps 115:4-8
- 4:29 Deut 6:5; 10:12; 30:1-3; 2 Chr 15:4
- 4:31 Deut 31:6, 8; Josh 1:5; Heb 13:5
- 4:32 Gen 1:27
- 4:33 Exod 20:22; Deut 5:24, 26
- 4:34 Exod 14:30; Deut 5:15; 6:21; 7:19; 33:29
- 4:35 Exod 8:10; 9:14; Deut 4:39; 1 Sam 2:2; †Mark 12:32
- 4:37 Deut 7:8
- 4:38 Num 32:4
- 4:40 Exod 23:26; Deut 4:2; 5:16, 29, 33; 32:47

---

**4:24** God is a devouring fire. Because he is morally perfect, he hates sin and cannot accept those who practice it. Moses' sin kept him from entering the Promised Land, and no sacrifice could remove that judgment. Sin kept us from entering God's presence, but Jesus Christ paid the penalty for our sin and removed God's judgment forever by his death. Trusting in Jesus Christ will save you from God's anger and allow you to begin a personal relationship with him.

**4:24** Jealousy is a demand for someone else's exclusive affec-tion or loyalty. Some jealousy is bad. It is destructive for a person to get upset when his or her spouse talks to someone of the opposite sex. But other jealousy is good. It is right for a man to demand that his wife treat him, and only him, as her husband. Usually we use the word *jealousy* only for the bad reaction. But God's kind of jealousy is appropriate and good. He is defending his word and guarding his high honor. He makes a strong, exclu-sive demand on us: We must treat only the Lord—and no one else in all the universe—as God.

**4:29** Do you want to know God? God promised the Israelites that they would find him when they searched with all their hearts and souls. God is knowable and wants to be known—but we have to want to know him. Acts of service and worship must be accompanied by sincere devotion of the heart. As Hebrews 11:6 says, "Anyone who wants to come to him must believe that God exists and that he rewards those who sincerely seek him." God will reward those who pursue a relationship with him.

**4:32** How tempted we are to look everywhere else but to God for our guidance and leadership! We trust medical doctors, finan-cial advisers, and news commentators, but do we trust God? Get God's advice first (4:39, 40), and recognize his authority over every dimension of life.

**4:40** Was Israel guaranteed prosperity for obeying God's laws? Yes—but we have to look carefully at what that means. God's laws were designed to make his chosen nation devout, healthy, just, and merciful. When the people followed those laws, they prospered. This does not mean, however, that no sickness, no

### Eastern Cities of Refuge

4:41
Num 35:6
Deut 19:1-13

41Then Moses set apart three cities of refuge east of the Jordan River. 42Anyone who killed another person unintentionally, without previous hostility, could flee there to live in safety. 43These were the cities: Bezer on the wilderness plateau for the tribe of Reuben; Ramoth in Gilead for the tribe of Gad; Golan in Bashan for the tribe of Manasseh.

## B. PRINCIPLES FOR GODLY LIVING: MOSES' SECOND ADDRESS (4:44—29:1)

After reviewing the history of Israel's journey, Moses recounts the Ten Commandments and the other laws given to the Israelites at Mount Sinai. He urges them to obey the law and reminds them of the consequences of disobeying God's laws. The Ten Commandments and all of God's laws point out to us where we fall short and show us how we should act as God's people.

### Introduction to Moses' Second Address

44This is the body of instruction that Moses presented to the Israelites. 45These are the laws, decrees, and regulations that Moses gave to the people of Israel when they left Egypt, 46and as they camped in the valley near Beth-peor east of the Jordan River. (This land was formerly occupied by the Amorites under King Sihon, who ruled from Heshbon. But Moses and the Israelites destroyed him and his people when they came up from Egypt. 47Israel took possession of his land and that of King Og of Bashan—the two Amorite kings east of the Jordan. 

4:48
Deut 2:35-36

48So Israel conquered the entire area from Aroer at the edge of the Arnon Gorge all the way to Mount Sirion,* also called Mount Hermon. 49And they conquered the eastern bank of the Jordan River as far south as the Dead Sea,* below the slopes of Pisgah.)

### 1. The Ten Commandments

**5** Moses called all the people of Israel together and said, "Listen carefully, Israel. Hear the decrees and regulations I am giving you today, so you may learn them and obey them!

5:2
Exod 19:5
Mal 4:4
5:4
Num 14:14
5:5
Exod 19:16, 25

2"The LORD our God made a covenant with us at Mount Sinai.* 3The LORD did not make this covenant with our ancestors, but with all of us who are alive today. 4At the mountain the LORD spoke to you face to face from the heart of the fire. 5I stood as an intermediary between you and the LORD, for you were afraid of the fire and did not want to approach the mountain. He spoke to me, and I passed his words on to you. This is what he said:

5:6
Exod 20:2-17
5:7
Exod 20:3
5:8
Exod 20:4
Lev 26:1
Deut 4:16-17
5:9
Exod 34:7, 14

6"I am the LORD your God, who rescued you from the land of Egypt, the place of your slavery.

7"You must not have any other god but me.

8"You must not make for yourself an idol of any kind, or an image of anything in the heavens or on the earth or in the sea. 9You must not bow down to them or worship them, for I, the LORD your God, am a jealous God who will not tolerate your affection for any other gods. I lay the sins of the parents upon their children; the entire family is affected—even children in the third and fourth generations of those who reject me.

**4:48** As in Syriac version (see also 3:9); Hebrew reads *Mount Sion.* **4:49** Hebrew *took the Arabah on the east side of the Jordan as far as the sea of the Arabah.* **5:2** Hebrew *Horeb,* another name for Sinai.

---

sadness, and no misunderstandings existed among them. Rather, it means that as a nation they prospered and that individuals' problems were handled as fairly as possible. Today God's promise of prosperity—his constant presence, comfort, and the resources to live as we should—extends to all believers. We will face trials; Jesus told us that. But we will avoid the misery that directly results from intentional sin, and we will know that a great treasure awaits us in heaven.

**5:1** The people had entered into a covenant with God, and Moses commanded them to hear, learn, and obey his regulations. Christians also have entered into a covenant with God through Jesus Christ and should be responsive to what God expects. Moses' threefold command to the Israelites provides excellent advice for all God's followers. *Listening* is absorbing and accepting information about God. *Learning* is understanding its meaning and implications. *Obeying* is putting into action all we have learned and understood. All three parts are essential to a growing relationship with God.

**5:7** A *god* is whatever people use as a driving force in their lives. Some people literally worship other gods by joining cults or strange religions. In a more subtle way, many of us worship other gods by building our lives around something other than the one true God. If your greatest desire is for popularity, power, or money, you are devoting yourself to something other than God. To put God first, (1) recognize what is taking his place in your life; (2) renounce this substitute god as unworthy of your devotion; (3) ask God for forgiveness; (4) restructure your priorities so that love for God is the motive for everything you do; (5) examine yourself daily to be sure you are giving God first place.

**5:8, 9** How would you feel if someone took a picture of you, framed it, stared at it a lot, showed it to others, but completely ignored the real you? God does not want to be treated this way either. He wants a genuine relationship with us, not mere ritual. He wants us to know him. God knows that if we put anything other than him at the center of our lives, we will not reach our potential and become all that he wants us to be.

¹⁰But I lavish unfailing love for a thousand generations on those* who love me and obey my commands.

¹¹"You must not misuse the name of the Lord your God. The Lord will not let you go unpunished if you misuse his name.

¹²"Observe the Sabbath day by keeping it holy, as the Lord your God has commanded you. ¹³You have six days each week for your ordinary work, ¹⁴but the seventh day is a Sabbath day of rest dedicated to the Lord your God. On that day no one in your household may do any work. This includes you, your sons and daughters, your male and female servants, your oxen and donkeys and other livestock, and any foreigners living among you. All your male and female servants must rest as you do. ¹⁵Remember that you were once slaves in Egypt, but the Lord your God brought you out with his strong hand and powerful arm. That is why the Lord your God has commanded you to rest on the Sabbath day.

¹⁶"Honor your father and mother, as the Lord your God commanded you. Then you will live a long, full life in the land the Lord your God is giving you.

¹⁷"You must not murder.

¹⁸"You must not commit adultery.

¹⁹"You must not steal.

²⁰"You must not testify falsely against your neighbor.

²¹"You must not covet your neighbor's wife. You must not covet your neighbor's house or land, male or female servant, ox or donkey, or anything else that belongs to your neighbor.

²²"The Lord spoke these words to all of you assembled there at the foot of the mountain. He spoke with a loud voice from the heart of the fire, surrounded by clouds and deep darkness. This was all he said at that time, and he wrote his words on two stone tablets and gave them to me.

²³"But when you heard the voice from the heart of the darkness, while the mountain was blazing with fire, all your tribal leaders and elders came to me. ²⁴They said, 'Look, the Lord our God has shown us his glory and greatness, and we have heard his voice from the heart of the fire. Today we have seen that God can speak to us humans, and yet we live! ²⁵But now, why should we risk death again? If the Lord our God speaks to us again, we will certainly die and be consumed by this awesome fire. ²⁶Can any living thing hear the voice of the living God from the heart of the fire as we did and yet survive? ²⁷Go yourself and listen to what the Lord our God says. Then come and tell us everything he tells you, and we will listen and obey.'

²⁸"The Lord heard the request you made to me. And he said, 'I have heard what the people said to you, and they are right. ²⁹Oh, that they would always have hearts like this, that

**5:11** Deut 6:13; 10:20 Matt 5:33
**5:12** Exod 20:8-11
**5:15** Exod 20:11 Deut 15:15; 16:12
**5:16** Exod 20:12; 21:17 †Matt 15:4; 19:9 †Mark 7:10 †Luke 18:20 †Eph 6:2-3 Col 3:20
**5:17** Exod 20:13 †Matt 5:21
**5:18** Exod 20:14 †Mark 10:19 †Luke 18:20 †Rom 13:9 †Jas 2:11
**5:19** Exod 20:15 †Matt 19:19 †Rom 13:9
**5:20** †Matt 19:18 †Mark 10:19 †Luke 18:20
**5:21** †Rom 7:7; 13:9
**5:22** Exod 19:16-19 Deut 4:13
**5:25** Exod 20:18-19 Deut 18:16 Heb 12:19
**5:26** Exod 24:2
**5:28** Deut 18:17
**5:29** Deut 5:16, 33 Ps 81:13 Isa 48:18

**5:10** Hebrew *for thousands of those.*

**5:11** We are familar with the sin to be avoided in this commandment, that we should not misuse the name of the Lord by saying it in an empty or worthless way. But there is also a good work that is commanded: to use God's name to praise him and ascribe to him glory. This is the opposite of misusing his name. While you might be able to keep yourself from swearing, how have you done at finding time to praise God and honor his name?

**5:16** Obeying our parents is our main task when we are young, but honoring them should continue even beyond their death. One way to honor parents is to provide for them in times of financial need or when they are ill and unable to care for themselves. Perhaps the best way to honor them is to pass on their Christ-honoring values to our children. Honoring involves all that sons and daughters do with their lives—the way they work and talk, the values they hold, and the morals they practice. What are you doing to show respect to your parents? Are you living in a way that brings honor to them?

**5:17** "But I don't murder people," you may say. Good. That fulfills the letter of the law. But Jesus explained that hateful anger breaks this commandment (Matthew 5:21, 22). Have you ever been so angry with someone who mistreated you that for a moment you wished that person were dead? Have you ever fantasized that you could get rid of someone? Jesus' teaching concerning this law demonstrates that we are capable of murder

in our hearts. Even if we are legally innocent, we are all morally guilty of murder and need to ask God's forgiveness. We need to commit ourselves to the opposite of hatred and anger—love and reconciliation.

**5:21** To covet means to ardently desire another person's prosperity. We are not to set our desires on anything that belongs to someone else. Not only can such cravings make us miserable, they can also lead us to other sins such as adultery and stealing. Envying others is a useless exercise because God is able to provide everything we really need, even if he does not always give us everything we want. To stop coveting, we need to practice being content with what we have. The apostle Paul emphasizes the significance of contentment in Philippians 4:11, 12. It's a matter of perspective. Instead of thinking about what we don't have, we should thank God for what he has given and strive to be content. After all, our most important possession is free and available to everyone—eternal life through Christ.

**5:29** God told Moses that he wanted the people to incline their hearts to fear him—to *want* to respect and obey him. There is a difference between doing something because it is required and doing something because we want to. God is not interested in forced religious exercises and rule keeping. He wants our hearts and lives completely dedicated to him. If we love him, obedience will follow.

5:31
Exod 24:12

5:32
Deut 17:20
Josh 1:7; 23:6

5:33
Exod 20:12
Deut 4:1, 40

6:2
Deut 4:9; 10:12

6:3
Exod 3:8, 17
Deut 5:33

6:4-5
Deut 4:35, 39
†Matt 22:37
†Mark 12:29-30
Luke 10:27
1 Cor 8:4, 6

6:6
Deut 11:18

they might fear me and obey all my commands! If they did, they and their descendants would prosper forever. [30]Go and tell them, "Return to your tents." [31]But you stand here with me so I can give you all my commands, decrees, and regulations. You must teach them to the people so they can obey them in the land I am giving them as their possession.'"

[32]So Moses told the people, "You must be careful to obey all the commands of the LORD your God, following his instructions in every detail. [33]Stay on the path that the LORD your God has commanded you to follow. Then you will live long and prosperous lives in the land you are about to enter and occupy.

## 2. Love the Lord your God

**6** "These are the commands, decrees, and regulations that the LORD your God commanded me to teach you. You must obey them in the land you are about to enter and occupy, [2]and you and your children and grandchildren must fear the LORD your God as long as you live. If you obey all his decrees and commands, you will enjoy a long life. [3]Listen closely, Israel, and be careful to obey. Then all will go well with you, and you will have many children in the land flowing with milk and honey, just as the LORD, the God of your ancestors, promised you.

[4]"Listen, O Israel! The LORD is our God, the LORD alone.* [5]And you must love the LORD your God with all your heart, all your soul, and all your strength. [6]And you must commit

6:4 Or *The LORD our God is one LORD;* or *The LORD our God, the LORD is one;* or *The LORD is our God, the LORD is one.*

---

**BROKEN COMMAND-MENTS**
The Ten Commandments were God's standard for right living. To obey them was to obey God (5:6-21). Yet throughout the Old Testament, we can see how each commandment was broken. As you read the stories, notice the tragic consequences that occurred as a result of violating God's law.

| Ten Commandments | Notable Violations |
|---|---|
| "You must not have any other god but me." | Solomon (1 Kings 11) |
| "You must not make for yourself an idol of any kind. . . . You must not bow down to them or worship them." | The gold calf-idol incident (Exodus 32); generations after Joshua (Judges 2:10-14; 2 Kings 21:1-15; Jeremiah 1:16) |
| "You must not misuse the name of the LORD your God." | Zedekiah (Ezekiel 17:15-21) |
| "Observe the Sabbath day by keeping it holy." | Judah (2 Chronicles 36:21) |
| "Honor your father and mother." | Eli's sons—Hophni and Phinehas (1 Samuel 2:12, 23-25) |
| "You must not murder." | Hazael (2 Kings 8:15) |
| "You must not commit adultery." | David (2 Samuel 11:2-5) |
| "You must not steal." | Ahab (1 Kings 21:1-19) |
| "You must not testify falsely against your neighbor." | Saul (1 Samuel 15:13-25) |
| "You must not covet your neighbor's wife. You must not covet your neighbor's house or land, . . . or anything else that belongs to your neighbor." | Achan (Joshua 7:19-26) |

---

**6:3** For a nation that had wandered 40 years in a parched wilderness, a land flowing with milk and honey sounded like paradise. It brought to mind rich crops, rushing streams, gentle rains, and lush fields filled with livestock. The Israelites could have had all that 40 years earlier. Numbers 13 and 14 explain how the people missed their chance. Now Moses was determined to help the people avoid the same mistake by whetting their appetite for the beautiful land and then clearly explaining the conditions for entering the land.

**6:4** Monotheism—belief in only one God—was a distinctive feature of Hebrew religion. Many ancient religions believed in many gods. But the God of Abraham, Isaac, and Jacob is the God of the whole earth, the only true God. This was an important insight for the nation of Israel because they were about to enter a land filled with people who believed in many gods. Both then and today, there are people who prefer to place their trust in many different values, belief systems, and "gods." But the day is coming when God will be recognized as the only one. He will be the king over the whole earth (Zechariah 14:9).

**6:4-9** This passage provides the central theme of Deuteronomy. It sets a pattern that helps us relate the Word of God to our daily lives. We are to love God, think constantly about his commandments, teach his commandments to our children, and live each day by the guidelines in his Word. God emphasized the importance of parents teaching the Bible to their children. The church and Christian schools cannot be used to escape from this responsibility. The Bible provides so many opportunities for object lessons and practical teaching that it would be a shame to study it only one day a week. Eternal truths are most effectively learned in the loving environment of a God-fearing home.

**6:5** Jesus said that loving God with all of ourselves is the first and greatest commandment (Matthew 22:37-39). This command, combined with the command to love your neighbor (Leviticus 19:18), encompasses all the other Old Testament laws.

yourselves wholeheartedly to these commands that I am giving you today. 7Repeat them again and again to your children. Talk about them when you are at home and when you are on the road, when you are going to bed and when you are getting up. 8Tie them to your hands and wear them on your forehead as reminders. 9Write them on the doorposts of your house and on your gates.

10"The LORD your God will soon bring you into the land he swore to give you when he made a vow to your ancestors Abraham, Isaac, and Jacob. It is a land with large, prosperous cities that you did not build. 11The houses will be richly stocked with goods you did not produce. You will draw water from cisterns you did not dig, and you will eat from vineyards and olive trees you did not plant. When you have eaten your fill in this land, 12be careful not to forget the LORD, who rescued you from slavery in the land of Egypt. 13You must fear the LORD your God and serve him. When you take an oath, you must use only his name.

14"You must not worship any of the gods of neighboring nations, 15for the LORD your God, who lives among you, is a jealous God. His anger will flare up against you, and he will wipe you from the face of the earth. 16You must not test the LORD your God as you did when you complained at Massah. 17You must diligently obey the commands of the LORD your God— all the laws and decrees he has given you. 18Do what is right and good in the LORD's sight, so all will go well with you. Then you will enter and occupy the good land that the LORD swore to give your ancestors. 19You will drive out all the enemies living in the land, just as the LORD said you would.

20"In the future your children will ask you, 'What is the meaning of these laws, decrees, and regulations that the LORD our God has commanded us to obey?'

21"Then you must tell them, 'We were Pharaoh's slaves in Egypt, but the LORD brought us out of Egypt with his strong hand. 22The LORD did miraculous signs and wonders before our eyes, dealing terrifying blows against Egypt and Pharaoh and all his people. 23He brought us out of Egypt so he could give us this land he had sworn to give our ancestors. 24And the LORD our God commanded us to obey all these decrees and to fear him so he can continue to bless us and preserve our lives, as he has done to this day. 25For we will be counted as righteous when we obey all the commands the LORD our God has given us.'

## The Privilege of Holiness

**7** "When the LORD your God brings you into the land you are about to enter and occupy, he will clear away many nations ahead of you: the Hittites, Girgashites, Amorites, Canaanites, Perizzites, Hivites, and Jebusites. These seven nations are greater and more numerous than you. 2When the LORD your God hands these nations over to you and you conquer them, you must completely destroy* them. Make no treaties with them and show them no mercy. 3You must not intermarry with them. Do not let your daughters and sons marry their sons and daughters, 4for they will lead your children away from me to worship other gods. Then the anger of the LORD will burn against you, and he will quickly destroy

**6:7**
Deut 4:9
Eph 6:4

**6:8**
Exod 13:9

**6:9**
Deut 11:20

**6:10**
Deut 9:1
Josh 24:13

**6:13**
†Matt 4:10
Luke 4:8

**6:15**
Deut 4:24; 5:9

**6:16**
Exod 17:7
†Matt 4:7
†Luke 4:12

**6:17**
Deut 11:22

**6:18**
Deut 4:40

**6:20**
Exod 13:8, 14

**6:24**
Deut 6:17; 10:12

**7:1**
Deut 20:17
Acts 13:19

**7:2**
Exod 23:32

**7:3**
Josh 23:12

**7:2** The Hebrew term used here refers to the complete consecration of things or people to the LORD, either by destroying them or by giving them as an offering; also in 7:26.

---

**6:7** The Hebrews were extremely successful at making religion an integral part of life. The reason for their success was that religious education was life-oriented, not information-oriented. They used the context of daily life to teach about God. The key to teaching your children to love God is stated simply and clearly in these verses. If you want your children to follow God, you must make God a part of your everyday experiences. You must teach your children diligently to see God in all aspects of life, not just those that are church related.

**6:10-13** Moses warned the people not to forget God when they entered the Promised Land and became prosperous. Prosperity, more than poverty, can dull our spiritual vision because it tends to make us self-sufficient and eager to acquire still more of everything—except God. The same thing can happen in our church. Once we become successful in terms of numbers, programs, and buildings, we can easily become self-sufficient and less sensitive to our need for God. This leads us to concentrate on self-preservation instead of thankfulness and service to God.

**6:24** Does the phrase "so he can continue to bless us and preserve our lives" mean that we can expect only good things and no suffering when we obey God? What is promised here is a

right relationship with God for all those who love him with all their heart. It speaks of a good relationship with God and the ultimate benefit of knowing him. It is not blanket protection against poverty, adversity, or suffering. We can have this right relationship with God by obeying his command to love him with all that we are.

**7:2** God told the Israelites to completely destroy their enemies. How can a God of love and mercy wipe out everyone, even children? Although God is loving and merciful, he is also just. These enemy nations were as much a part of God's creation as Israel was, and God does not allow evil to continue unchecked. God had punished Israel by keeping out of the Promised Land all those who had disobeyed. The command to destroy these nations was both a judgment (9:4-6) and a safety measure. On one hand, the people living in the land were being judged for their sin, and Israel was God's instrument of judgment—just as God would one day use other nations to judge Israel for its sin (2 Chronicles 36:17; Isaiah 10:12). On the other hand, God's command was designed to protect the nation of Israel from being ruined by the idolatry and immorality of its enemies. To think that God is too "nice" to judge sin would be to underestimate him.

**7:5**
Exod 23:24

**7:6**
Deut 19:5-6
Deut 14:2; 26:18
1 Pet 2:9

**7:7**
Deut 4:37

**7:9**
Exod 20:6
Deut 4:39; 5:9-10
1 Cor 1:9
1 Thes 5:24
2 Tim 2:13

**7:12**
Lev 26:3
Deut 28:1

**7:13**
Lev 26:9
Deut 28:4; 30:5-6

**7:14**
Exod 23:26

**7:15**
Exod 15:26; 23:26

**7:16**
Exod 23:32
Deut 7:2

**7:17**
Num 33:53

**7:18**
Num 14:9
Deut 1:21, 29

**7:19**
Deut 4:34

you. ⁵This is what you must do. You must break down their pagan altars and shatter their sacred pillars. Cut down their Asherah poles and burn their idols. ⁶For you are a holy people, who belong to the LORD your God. Of all the people on earth, the LORD your God has chosen you to be his own special treasure.

⁷"The LORD did not set his heart on you and choose you because you were more numerous than other nations, for you were the smallest of all nations! ⁸Rather, it was simply that the LORD loves you, and he was keeping the oath he had sworn to your ancestors. That is why the LORD rescued you with such a strong hand from your slavery and from the oppressive hand of Pharaoh, king of Egypt. ⁹Understand, therefore, that the LORD your God is indeed God. He is the faithful God who keeps his covenant for a thousand generations and lavishes his unfailing love on those who love him and obey his commands. ¹⁰But he does not hesitate to punish and destroy those who reject him. ¹¹Therefore, you must obey all these commands, decrees, and regulations I am giving you today.

¹²"If you listen to these regulations and faithfully obey them, the LORD your God will keep his covenant of unfailing love with you, as he promised with an oath to your ancestors. ¹³He will love you and bless you, and he will give you many children. He will give fertility to your land and your animals. When you arrive in the land he swore to give your ancestors, you will have large harvests of grain, new wine, and olive oil, and great herds of cattle, sheep, and goats. ¹⁴You will be blessed above all the nations of the earth. None of your men or women will be childless, and all your livestock will bear young. ¹⁵And the LORD will protect you from all sickness. He will not let you suffer from the terrible diseases you knew in Egypt, but he will inflict them on all your enemies!

¹⁶"You must destroy all the nations the LORD your God hands over to you. Show them no mercy, and do not worship their gods, or they will trap you. ¹⁷Perhaps you will think to yourselves, 'How can we ever conquer these nations that are so much more powerful than we are?' ¹⁸But don't be afraid of them! Just remember what the LORD your God did to Pharaoh and to all the land of Egypt. ¹⁹Remember the great terrors the LORD your God sent against them. You saw it all with your own eyes! And remember the miraculous signs and wonders, and the strong hand and powerful arm with which he brought you out of Egypt. The LORD

---

| **DANGER IN PLENTY** | Person | Reference | Comment |
|---|---|---|---|
| "When you have eaten your fill in this land, be careful not to forget the LORD" (Deuteronomy 6:11, 12). It is often most difficult to follow God when life is easy—we can fall prey to temptation and fall away from God. Here are some notable examples of this truth. | ADAM | Genesis 3 | Adam lived in a perfect world and had a perfect relationship with God. His needs were met; he had everything. But he fell to Satan's deception. |
| | NOAH | Genesis 9 | Noah and his family had survived the Flood, and the whole world was theirs. They were prosperous, and life was easy. Noah shamed himself by becoming drunk and cursed his son Ham. |
| | THE NATION OF ISRAEL | Judges 2 | God had given Israel the Promised Land—rest at last with no more wandering. But as soon as brave and faithful Joshua died, they fell into the idolatrous practices of the Canaanites. |
| | DAVID | 2 Samuel 11 | David ruled well, and Israel was a dominant nation politically, economically, and militarily. In the midst of prosperity and success, he committed adultery with Bathsheba and had her husband, Uriah, murdered. |
| | SOLOMON | 1 Kings 11 | Solomon truly had it all: power, wealth, fame, and wisdom. But his very abundance was the source of his downfall. He loved his pagan, idolatrous wives so much that he allowed himself and Israel to copy their detestable religious rites. |

---

**7:5** Asherah was a Canaanite mother goddess of the sea, associated with Baal. Baal was the most worshiped god of the Canaanites. Most often cast in the form of a bull, he symbolized strength and fertility and was considered the god of agriculture. Asherah was Baal's female consort. She was worshiped by means of wooden pillars (here called "poles").

**7:6-8** How did Israel deserve to be chosen above all of the other nations at that time? It was not a matter of Israel's merit, but of

God keeping his promise to their ancestors. Just as God chose the nation of Israel, he has chosen all believers today to be a part of his treasured possession. Similarly, it is not because of our merit that we have come to faith in Christ. Instead, God chose us out of his goodness and grace.

your God will use this same power against all the people you fear. 20And then the LORD your God will send terror* to drive out the few survivors still hiding from you!

21"No, do not be afraid of those nations, for the LORD your God is among you, and he is a great and awesome God. 22The LORD your God will drive those nations out ahead of you little by little. You will not clear them away all at once, otherwise the wild animals would multiply too quickly for you. 23But the LORD your God will hand them over to you. He will throw them into complete confusion until they are destroyed. 24He will put their kings in your power, and you will erase their names from the face of the earth. No one will be able to stand against you, and you will destroy them all.

25"You must burn their idols in fire, and you must not covet the silver or gold that covers them. You must not take it or it will become a trap to you, for it is detestable to the LORD your God. 26Do not bring any detestable objects into your home, for then you will be destroyed, just like them. You must utterly detest such things, for they are set apart for destruction.

### A Call to Remember and Obey

**8** "Be careful to obey all the commands I am giving you today. Then you will live and multiply, and you will enter and occupy the land the LORD swore to give your ancestors. 2Remember how the LORD your God led you through the wilderness for these forty years, humbling you and testing you to prove your character, and to find out whether or not you would obey his commands. 3 Yes, he humbled you by letting you go hungry and then feeding you with manna, a food previously unknown to you and your ancestors. He did it to teach you that people do not live by bread alone; rather, we live by every word that comes from the mouth of the LORD. 4For all these forty years your clothes didn't wear out, and your feet didn't blister or swell. 5Think about it: Just as a parent disciplines a child, the LORD your God disciplines you for your own good.

6"So obey the commands of the LORD your God by walking in his ways and fearing him. 7For the LORD your God is bringing you into a good land of flowing streams and pools of water, with fountains and springs that gush out in the valleys and hills. 8It is a land of wheat and barley; of grapevines, fig trees, and pomegranates; of olive oil and honey. 9It is a land where food is plentiful and nothing is lacking. It is a land where iron is as common as stone, and copper is abundant in the hills. 10When you have eaten your fill, be sure to praise the LORD your God for the good land he has given you.

11"But that is the time to be careful! Beware that in your plenty you do not forget the LORD

**7:20**
Exod 23:28
Josh 24:12

**7:21**
Exod 29:45

**7:22**
Exod 23:28-30

**7:24**
Deut 11:25
Josh 1:5; 10:8; 23:9

**7:25**
Deut 7:2; 12:3
Josh 7:1, 21

**7:26**
Lev 27:28-29

**8:1**
Lev 26:3
Deut 4:1; 7:11

**8:2**
Exod 15:25
2 Chr 32:31

**8:3**
Ps 78:24
†Matt 4:4
†Luke 4:4

**8:4**
Deut 29:5
Neh 9:21

**8:5**
Prov 3:11-12
Heb 12:6

**8:7**
Deut 11:10-12
Jer 2:7

**8:8**
Deut 32:13

**8:10**
Deut 6:11-12

**8:11**
Deut 4:9

**7:20** Often rendered *the hornet*. The meaning of the Hebrew is uncertain.

---

**7:21-24** Moses told the Israelites that God would destroy Israel's enemies, but not all at once. God had the power to destroy those nations instantly, but he chose to do it in stages, "little by little." In the same way and with the same power, God could miraculously and instantaneously change your life. Usually, however, he chooses to help you gradually, teaching you one lesson at a time. Rather than expecting instant spiritual maturity and solutions to all your problems, slow down and work one step at a time, trusting God to make up the difference between where you should be and where you are now. You'll soon look back and see that a miraculous transformation has occurred.

**7:25, 26** Moses warned Israel against becoming ensnared by the idols of the defeated nations by desiring the silver or gold on them. We may think it's all right to be close to sin as long as we don't participate. "After all," we say, "I won't do anything wrong!" But being close can hurt us as we become attracted and finally give in. Avoid the snare of sin by first reigning in your desires. Then stay as far away from sin as you can.

**8:3** Jesus quoted this verse when the devil tempted him to turn stones into bread (Matthew 4:4). Many people think that life is based on satisfying their appetites. If they can earn enough money to dress, eat, and play in high style, they think they are living "the good life." But such things do not satisfy our deepest longings. In the end they leave us empty and dissatisfied. Real life, according to Moses, comes from total commitment to God

and living by every word that comes from him. How can we live by his word? (1) Recognize our need for it. (2) Agree that God alone can truly satisfy us. (3) Pray for God's presence, wisdom, and direction as we read. (4) Savor the relationship you have with him through Christ. (5) Practice what he teaches you.

**8:4** It's usually easy for us to take God's protection for granted. We seldom take notice or thank God when our car doesn't break down, our clothes don't rip, or our tools don't break. The people of Israel also failed to take notice, it seems, for they didn't even notice that in 40 years of wandering in the wilderness, their clothes didn't wear out and their feet didn't blister or swell. Thus, they did not remember to give thanks to God for these blessings. What has been working well for you? What has been giving you good service? What has been lasting for a long time without breaking down or apart? Remember to thank God for these quiet blessings.

**8:10** This verse is traditionally cited as the reason we say grace before or after meals. Its purpose, however, was to warn the Israelites not to forget God when their needs and wants were satisfied. Let your table prayers serve as a constant reminder of the Lord's goodness to you and your duty to those who are less fortunate.

**8:11-20** In times of plenty, we often take credit for our prosperity and become proud that our own hard work and cleverness have made us rich. It is easy to get so busy collecting and managing wealth that we push God right out of our lives. But it is God who gives us everything we have, and it is God who asks us to manage it for him.

**8:12**
Prov 30:9
Hos 13:6

**8:15**
Exod 17:6
Num 20:11; 21:6
Deut 1:19-21;
32:13
Pss 78:15; 114:8

**8:16**
Exod 16:15
Deut 8:2
John 6:30-31

**8:18**
Prov 10:22
Hos 2:8

**8:19**
Deut 4:26; 30:18

**8:20**
Ezek 5:15-17

your God and disobey his commands, regulations, and decrees that I am giving you today. ¹²For when you have become full and prosperous and have built fine homes to live in, ¹³and when your flocks and herds have become very large and your silver and gold have multiplied along with everything else, be careful! ¹⁴Do not become proud at that time and forget the LORD your God, who rescued you from slavery in the land of Egypt. ¹⁵Do not forget that he led you through the great and terrifying wilderness with its poisonous snakes and scorpions, where it was so hot and dry. He gave you water from the rock! ¹⁶He fed you with manna in the wilderness, a food unknown to your ancestors. He did this to humble you and test you for your own good. ¹⁷He did all this so you would never say to yourself, 'I have achieved this wealth with my own strength and energy.' ¹⁸Remember the LORD your God. He is the one who gives you power to be successful, in order to fulfill the covenant he confirmed to your ancestors with an oath.

¹⁹"But I assure you of this: If you ever forget the LORD your God and follow other gods, worshiping and bowing down to them, you will certainly be destroyed. ²⁰Just as the LORD has destroyed other nations in your path, you also will be destroyed if you refuse to obey the LORD your God.

### Victory by God's Grace

**9:1**
Deut 11:23

**9** "Listen, O Israel! Today you are about to cross the Jordan River to take over the land belonging to nations much greater and more powerful than you. They live in cities with walls that reach to the sky! ²The people are strong and tall—descendants of the famous

**9:3**
Deut 4:24
Heb 12:29

Anakite giants. You've heard the saying, 'Who can stand up to the Anakites?' ³But recognize today that the LORD your God is the one who will cross over ahead of you like a devouring fire to destroy them. He will subdue them so that you will quickly conquer them and drive them out, just as the LORD has promised.

**9:4**
Lev 18:23-30
Deut 7:24; 12:31;
18:9-14

⁴"After the LORD your God has done this for you, don't say in your hearts, 'The LORD has given us this land because we are such good people!' No, it is because of the wickedness of the other nations that he is pushing them out of your way. ⁵It is not because you are so good or have such integrity that you are about to occupy their land. The LORD your God will drive these nations out ahead of you only because of their wickedness, and to fulfill the oath he swore to your ancestors Abraham, Isaac, and Jacob. ⁶You must recognize that the LORD your God is not giving you this good land because you are good, for you are not—you are a stubborn people.

**9:6**
Deut 9:13-14;
10:16; 31:27

**9:7**
Exod 14:11
Num 14:20-22

### Remembering the Gold Calf

**9:8**
Exod 32:7
Ps 106:19-20

⁷"Remember and never forget how angry you made the LORD your God out in the wilderness. From the day you left Egypt until now, you have been constantly rebelling against him. ⁸Even at Mount Sinai* you made the LORD so angry he was ready to destroy you. ⁹This

**9:9**
Exod 24:18
Deut 9:18

**9:8** Hebrew *Horeb,* another name for Sinai.

---

**OBEDIENCE**
Deuteronomy 8:1 tells us to obey God's commandments. We do this by obeying God with . . .

| | |
|---|---|
| OUR HEART . . . . . . . | By loving him more than any relationship, activity, achievement, or possession |
| OUR WILL . . . . . . . . | By committing ourselves completely to him |
| OUR MIND . . . . . . . | By seeking to know him and his Word, so his principles and values form the foundation of all we think and do |
| OUR BODY . . . . . . . | By recognizing that our strengths, talents, and sexuality are given to us by God to be used for pleasure and fulfillment according to his rules, not ours |
| OUR FINANCES . . . | By deciding that all of the resources we have ultimately come from God, and that we are to be managers of them and not owners |
| OUR FUTURE . . . . . | By deciding to make service to God and man the main purpose of our life's work |

---

**9:2, 3** The Anakites were enormous people, some seven to nine feet tall. Goliath, probably a descendant of this race, was over nine feet tall (1 Samuel 17:4-7). Unfortunately, these great men used their stature as a means of intimidation rather than for noble causes. Their appearance alone frightened the Israelite scouts (Numbers 13:28), and their bad reputation may have been the deciding factor that kept the Israelites out of the land 40 years earlier (Numbers 13–14). Moses used all his persuasive power to convince his people that God could handle these bullies. He used the illustration of God as a devouring fire, for not even a giant could stand up to that.

happened when I was on the mountain receiving the tablets of stone inscribed with the words of the covenant that the LORD had made with you. I was there for forty days and forty nights, and all that time I ate no food and drank no water. ¹⁰The LORD gave me the two tablets on which God had written with his own finger all the words he had spoken to you from the heart of the fire when you were assembled at the mountain.

¹¹"At the end of the forty days and nights, the LORD handed me the two stone tablets inscribed with the words of the covenant. ¹²Then the LORD said to me, 'Get up! Go down immediately, for the people you brought out of Egypt have corrupted themselves. How quickly they have turned away from the way I commanded them to live! They have melted gold and made an idol for themselves.'

¹³"The LORD also said to me, 'I have seen how stubborn and rebellious these people are. ¹⁴Leave me alone so I may destroy them and erase their name from under heaven. Then I will make a mighty nation of your descendants, a nation larger and more powerful than they are.'

¹⁵"So while the mountain was blazing with fire I turned and came down, holding in my hands the two stone tablets inscribed with the terms of the covenant. ¹⁶There below me I could see that you had sinned against the LORD your God. You had melted gold and made a calf idol for yourselves. How quickly you had turned away from the path the LORD had commanded you to follow! ¹⁷So I took the stone tablets and threw them to the ground, smashing them before your eyes.

¹⁸"Then, as before, I threw myself down before the LORD for forty days and nights. I ate no bread and drank no water because of the great sin you had committed by doing what the LORD hated, provoking him to anger. ¹⁹I feared that the furious anger of the LORD, which turned him against you, would drive him to destroy you. But again he listened to me. ²⁰The LORD was so angry with Aaron that he wanted to destroy him, too. But I prayed for Aaron, and the LORD spared him. ²¹I took your sin—the calf you had made—and I melted it down in the fire and ground it into fine dust. Then I threw the dust into the stream that flows down the mountain.

²²"You also made the LORD angry at Taberah,* Massah,* and Kibroth-hattaavah.* ²³And at Kadesh-barnea the LORD sent you out with this command: 'Go up and take over the land I have given you.' But you rebelled against the command of the LORD your God and refused to put your trust in him or obey him. ²⁴Yes, you have been rebelling against the LORD as long as I have known you.

²⁵"That is why I threw myself down before the LORD for forty days and nights—for the LORD said he would destroy you. ²⁶I prayed to the LORD and said, 'O Sovereign LORD, do not destroy them. They are your own people. They are your special possession, whom you redeemed from Egypt by your mighty power and your strong hand. ²⁷Please overlook the stubbornness and the awful sin of these people, and remember instead your servants Abraham, Isaac, and Jacob. ²⁸If you destroy these people, the Egyptians will say, "The Israelites died because the LORD wasn't able to bring them to the land he had promised to give them." Or they might say, "He destroyed them because he hated them; he deliberately took them into the wilderness to slaughter them." ²⁹But they are your people and your special possession, whom you brought out of Egypt by your great strength and powerful arm.'

### A New Copy of the Covenant

**10** "At that time the LORD said to me, 'Chisel out two stone tablets like the first ones. Also make a wooden Ark—a sacred chest to store them in. Come up to me on the mountain, ²and I will write on the tablets the same words that were on the ones you smashed. Then place the tablets in the Ark.'

9:22a *Taberah* means "place of burning." See Num 11:1-3.  9:22b *Massah* means "place of testing." See Exod 17:1-7.  9:22c *Kibroth-hattaavah* means "graves of gluttony." See Num 11:31-34.

**9:18** From the record of this event in Exodus 32, it seems as though Moses acted immediately, grinding the gold calf into powder and forcing the people to drink water mixed with it. But evidently, Moses had first spent 40 days and nights interceding for the people.

**9:23** Moses was reminding the people of the nation's unbelief 40 years earlier, when they had been afraid to enter Canaan. The Israelites had not believed God would be able to help them in spite of all he had already done. They refused to follow because they looked only to their own limited resources instead of to God. Unbelief is the root of many sins and problems. When you feel lost, it may be because you're looking everywhere but to God for your help and guidance. (See Psalms 81:6-12; 95:8; 106:13-20; Hebrews 3.)

Marginal references: 9:12 Exod 32:7-8; 9:13 Exod 32:9; 9:15 Exod 32:15; 9:16 Exod 32:19; 9:18 Exod 34:8-9, 28, Deut 9:9; 10:10; 9:19 Exod 32:10-11, †Heb 12:21; 9:21 Exod 32:20; 9:22 Exod 17:7, Num 11:3, 34; 9:24 Exod 32:9, Deut 9:7; 31:27; 9:25 Deut 9:18; 9:26 Exod 32:11-13; 9:27 Exod 32:9; 9:29 Deut 4:34; 10:1 Exod 25:10; 34:1; 10:2 Exod 25:16, Deut 4:13

| | |
|---|---|
| **10:3**<br>Exod 34:4; 37:1 | 3"So I made an Ark of acacia wood and cut two stone tablets like the first two. Then I went |
| **10:4**<br>Exod 34:28<br>Deut 4:13 | up the mountain with the tablets in my hand. 4Once again the LORD wrote the Ten Commandments* on the tablets and gave them to me. They were the same words the LORD had |
| **10:5**<br>Exod 40:20 | spoken to you from the heart of the fire on the day you were assembled at the foot of the mountain. 5Then I turned and came down the mountain and placed the tablets in the Ark of |

3"So I made an Ark of acacia wood and cut two stone tablets like the first two. Then I went up the mountain with the tablets in my hand. 4Once again the LORD wrote the Ten Commandments* on the tablets and gave them to me. They were the same words the LORD had spoken to you from the heart of the fire on the day you were assembled at the foot of the mountain. 5Then I turned and came down the mountain and placed the tablets in the Ark of the Covenant, which I had made, just as the LORD commanded me. And the tablets are still there in the Ark."

**10:6**
Num 20:25-26

6(The people of Israel set out from the wells of the people of Jaakan* and traveled to Moserah, where Aaron died and was buried. His son Eleazar ministered as high priest in his place. 7Then they journeyed to Gudgodah, and from there to Jotbathah, a land with many brooks and streams.

**10:8**
Num 3:6; 18:1
Deut 18:5; 21:5;
31:9

8At that time the LORD set apart the tribe of Levi to carry the Ark of the LORD's Covenant, and to stand before the LORD as his ministers, and to pronounce blessings in his name. These are their duties to this day.

**10:9**
Num 18:20, 24
Deut 18:2
Ezek 44:28

9That is why the Levites have no share of property or possession of land among the other Israelite tribes. The LORD himself is their special possession, as the LORD your God told them.)

**10:10**
Deut 9:18

10"As for me, I stayed on the mountain in the LORD's presence for forty days and nights, as I had done the first time. And once again the LORD listened to my pleas and agreed not to destroy you. 11Then the LORD said to me, 'Get up and resume the journey, and lead the people to the land I swore to give to their ancestors, so they may take possession of it.'

### A Call to Love and Obedience

**10:12**
Deut 6:5
Mic 6:8

12"And now, Israel, what does the LORD your God require of you? He requires only that you fear the LORD your God, and live in a way that pleases him, and love him and serve him with all your heart and soul. 13And you must always obey the LORD's commands and decrees that I am giving you today for your own good.

**10:16**
Lev 26:41-42
Jer 4:4

14"Look, the highest heavens and the earth and everything in it all belong to the LORD your God. 15Yet the LORD chose your ancestors as the objects of his love. And he chose you, their descendants, above all other nations, as is evident today. 16Therefore, change your hearts* and stop being stubborn.

**10:17**
Deut 1:17; 16:19
Ps 136:2

17"For the LORD your God is the God of gods and Lord of lords. He is the great God, the mighty and awesome God, who shows no partiality and cannot be bribed.

**10:18**
Exod 22:22-24
Pss 68:5; 103:6

18He ensures that orphans and widows receive justice. He shows love to the foreigners living among you and gives them food and clothing.

**10:19**
Exod 22:21
Lev 19:34

19So you, too, must show love to foreigners, for you yourselves were once foreigners in the land of Egypt.

**10:20**
Deut 5:11; 6:13

20You must fear the LORD your God and worship him and cling to him. Your oaths must be in his name alone.

**10:21**
Exod 15:2

21He alone is your God, the only one who is worthy of your praise, the one who has done these mighty miracles that you have seen with your own eyes.

**10:22**
Gen 46:27
Deut 1:10

22When your ancestors went down into Egypt, there were only seventy of them. But now the LORD your God has made you as numerous as the stars in the sky!

**10:4** Hebrew *the ten words.*   **10:6** Or *set out from Beeroth of Bene-jaakan.*   **10:16** Hebrew *circumcise the foreskin of your hearts.*

---

**10:5** The tablets of the law were still in the Ark about 500 years later when Solomon put it in his newly built Temple (1 Kings 8:9). The Ark last appears in the Israelites' history during the reign of Josiah, about 300 years after Solomon (2 Chronicles 35:3).

**10:12, 13** Often we ask, What does God expect of me? Here Moses gives a summary that is simple in form and easy to remember. Here are the essentials: (1) Fear God (have reverence for him). (2) Live in a way that pleases him. (3) Love him. (4) Serve him with all your heart and soul. (5) Obey his commands. How often we complicate faith with man-made rules, regulations, and requirements. Are you frustrated and burned out from trying hard to please God? Concentrate on his real requirements and find peace. Respect, follow, love, serve, and obey.

**10:16-19** God required all male Israelites to be circumcised, but he wanted them to go beyond performing the surgery to understanding its meaning. They needed to submit to God inside, in their hearts, as well as outside, in their bodies. Then they could begin to imitate God's love and justice in their relationships with others. If our hearts are right with God, then our relationships

with other people can be made right, too. When your heart has been cleansed and you have been reconciled to God, you will begin to see a difference in the way you treat others.

**10:17** In saying that the Lord is God of gods and Lord of lords, Moses was distinguishing the true God from all the local gods worshiped throughout the land. Then Moses went a step further, calling God "mighty and awesome." He has such awesome power and justice that people cannot stand before him without his mercy. Fortunately, his mercy toward his people is unlimited. When we begin to grasp the extent of God's mercy toward us, we see what true love is and how deeply God loves us. Although our sins deserve severe judgment, God has chosen to show love and mercy to all who seek him.

**10:20** "Your oaths must be in his name alone" means that God alone should have their allegiance.

**11** "You must love the LORD your God and obey all his requirements, decrees, regulations, and commands. ²Keep in mind that I am not talking now to your children, who have never experienced the discipline of the LORD your God or seen his greatness and his strong hand and powerful arm. ³They didn't see the miraculous signs and wonders he performed in Egypt against Pharaoh and all his land. ⁴They didn't see what the LORD did to the armies of Egypt and to their horses and chariots—how he drowned them in the Red Sea* as they were chasing you. He destroyed them, and they have not recovered to this very day!

⁵"Your children didn't see how the LORD cared for you in the wilderness until you arrived here. ⁶They didn't see what he did to Dathan and Abiram (the sons of Eliab, a descendant of Reuben) when the earth opened its mouth in the Israelite camp and swallowed them, along with their households and tents and every living thing that belonged to them. ⁷But you have seen the LORD perform all these mighty deeds with your own eyes!

### The Blessings of Obedience

⁸"Therefore, be careful to obey every command I am giving you today, so you may have strength to go in and take over the land you are about to enter. ⁹If you obey, you will enjoy a long life in the land the LORD swore to give to your ancestors and to you, their descendants—a land flowing with milk and honey! ¹⁰For the land you are about to enter and take over is not like the land of Egypt from which you came, where you planted your seed and made irrigation ditches with your foot as in a vegetable garden. ¹¹Rather, the land you will soon take over is a land of hills and valleys with plenty of rain—¹²a land that the LORD your God cares for. He watches over it through each season of the year!

¹³"If you carefully obey all the commands I am giving you today, and if you love the LORD your God and serve him with all your heart and soul, ¹⁴then he will send the rains in their proper seasons—the early and late rains—so you can bring in your harvests of grain, new wine, and olive oil. ¹⁵He will give you lush pastureland for your livestock, and you yourselves will have all you want to eat.

¹⁶"But be careful. Don't let your heart be deceived so that you turn away from the LORD and serve and worship other gods. ¹⁷If you do, the LORD's anger will burn against you. He will shut up the sky and hold back the rain, and the ground will fail to produce its harvests. Then you will quickly die in that good land the LORD is giving you.

¹⁸"So commit yourselves wholeheartedly to these words of mine. Tie them to your hands and wear them on your forehead as reminders. ¹⁹Teach them to your children. Talk about them when you are at home and when you are on the road, when you are going to bed and when you are getting up. ²⁰Write them on the doorposts of your house and on your gates, ²¹so that as long as the sky remains above the earth, you and your children may flourish in the land the LORD swore to give your ancestors.

²²"Be careful to obey all these commands I am giving you. Show love to the LORD your God by walking in his ways and holding tightly to him. ²³Then the LORD will drive out all the nations ahead of you, though they are much greater and stronger than you, and you will take over their land. ²⁴Wherever you set foot, that land will be yours. Your frontiers will stretch from the wilderness in the south to Lebanon in the north, and from the Euphrates River in the east to the Mediterranean Sea in the west.* ²⁵No one will be able to stand against you, for the LORD your God will cause the people to fear and dread you, as he promised, wherever you go in the whole land.

²⁶"Look, today I am giving you the choice between a blessing and a curse! ²⁷You will be

**11:4** Hebrew *sea of reeds.*    **11:24** Hebrew *to the western sea.*

| | |
|---|---|
| **11:1** | Lev 18:29-30 |
| | Deut 6:5-6; 10:12-13 |
| **11:2** | Deut 5:24 |
| **11:4** | Exod 14:28; 15:4 |
| | Deut 1:40 |
| **11:6** | Num 16:31; 26:10-11 |
| **11:8** | Deut 31:6-7, 23 |
| | Josh 1:6-7 |
| **11:9** | Deut 4:40; 5:33; 9:5 |
| | Prov 10:27 |
| **11:11** | Deut 8:7-9 |
| **11:13** | Deut 4:29; 6:17; 10:12 |
| **11:14** | Lev 26:4-5 |
| | Deut 28:12 |
| **11:15** | Deut 6:10-12 |
| **11:16** | Deut 8:19; 29:18 |
| **11:17** | Deut 4:26; 28:24 |
| **11:18** | Exod 13:9, 16 |
| **11:19** | Deut 4:9; 6:7 |
| **11:22** | Deut 6:17; 10:20 |
| **11:23** | Deut 4:38; 7:1 |
| **11:24** | Gen 15:18 |
| | Exod 23:31 |
| | Deut 1:7-8 |
| | Josh 1:3 |
| **11:25** | Exod 23:27 |
| | Deut 7:24 |
| **11:26** | Deut 30:1, 15-20 |

**11:7** Israel had strong reasons to believe in God and obey his commands. They had witnessed a parade of mighty miracles that demonstrated God's love and care for them. Incredibly, they still had trouble remaining faithful. Because few of us have seen such dramatic miracles, it may seem even more difficult for us to obey God and remain faithful. But we have the Bible, the written record of God's acts throughout history. Reading God's Word gives us a panoramic view of both the miracles Israel saw and others they didn't see. The lessons from the past, the instructions for the present, and the glimpses into the future give us many opportunities to strengthen our faith in God.

**11:26** What is God's curse? It is not a magician's spell. To understand it, we must remember the conditions of the covenant between God and Israel. Both parties had agreed to the terms. The blessings would benefit Israel if they kept their part of the covenant: They would receive the land, live there forever, have fruitful crops, and expel their enemies. The curse would fall on Israel only if they broke their agreement; then they would forfeit God's blessing and be in danger of crop failure, invasion, and expulsion from their land. Joshua later reviewed these blessings and curses with the entire nation (Joshua 8:34).

**11:26** It is amazing that God set before the Israelites a choice between a blessing and a curse. It is even more amazing that most of them, through their disobedience, chose the curse. We have the same fundamental choice today. We can live for ourselves or live in service to God. To choose our own way is to blessed if you obey the commands of the LORD your God that I am giving you today. 28But you will be cursed if you reject the commands of the LORD your God and turn away from him and worship gods you have not known before.

29"When the LORD your God brings you into the land and helps you take possession of it, you must pronounce the blessing at Mount Gerizim and the curse at Mount Ebal. 30(These two mountains are west of the Jordan River in the land of the Canaanites who live in the Jordan Valley,* near the town of Gilgal, not far from the oaks of Moreh.) 31For you are about to cross the Jordan River to take over the land the LORD your God is giving you. When you take that land and are living in it, 32you must be careful to obey all the decrees and regulations I am giving you today.

### 3. Laws for proper worship
*The LORD's Chosen Place for Worship*

**12** "These are the decrees and regulations you must be careful to obey when you live in the land that the LORD, the God of your ancestors, is giving you. You must obey them as long as you live.

2"When you drive out the nations that live there, you must destroy all the places where they worship their gods—high on the mountains, up on the hills, and under every green tree. 3Break down their altars and smash their sacred pillars. Burn their Asherah poles and cut down their carved idols. Completely erase the names of their gods!

4"Do not worship the LORD your God in the way these pagan peoples worship their gods. 5Rather, you must seek the LORD your God at the place of worship he himself will choose from among all the tribes—the place where his name will be honored. 6There you will bring your burnt offerings, your sacrifices, your tithes, your sacred offerings, your offerings to fulfill a vow, your voluntary offerings, and your offerings of the firstborn animals of your herds and flocks. 7 There you and your families will feast in the presence of the LORD your God, and you will rejoice in all you have accomplished because the LORD your God has blessed you.

8"Your pattern of worship will change. Today all of you are doing as you please, 9because you have not yet arrived at the place of rest, the land the LORD your God is giving you as your special possession. 10But you will soon cross the Jordan River and live in the land the LORD your God is giving you. When he gives you rest from all your enemies and you're living safely in the land, 11you must bring everything I command you—your burnt offerings, your sacrifices, your tithes, your sacred offerings, and your offerings to fulfill a vow—to the designated place of worship, the place the LORD your God chooses for his name to be honored.

12"You must celebrate there in the presence of the LORD your God with your sons and daughters and all your servants. And remember to include the Levites who live in your towns, for they will receive no allotment of land among you. 13Be careful not to sacrifice your burnt offerings just anywhere you like. 14You may do so only at the place the LORD will choose within one of your tribal territories. There you must offer your burnt offerings and do everything I command you.

**11:30** Hebrew *the Arabah.*

---

**11:29**
Deut 27:12-26
Josh 8:30-35

**11:30**
Gen 12:6
Josh 4:19

**11:31**
Josh 1:11

**12:1**
Deut 4:9-10; 6:15

**12:2**
2 Kgs 17:10

**12:5**
Exod 20:24
Deut 26:2

**12:6**
Deut 14:22

**12:7**
Deut 12:12, 18;
14:26; 15:20

**12:8**
Judg 17:6

**12:10**
Josh 3:17; 11:23

**12:12**
Deut 10:9; 12:7,
18-19; 26:11

**12:13**
Deut 12:5

---

travel on a dead-end road, but to choose God's way is to receive eternal life (John 5:24).

**12:2, 3** When taking over a nation, the Israelites were supposed to destroy every pagan altar and idol in the land. God knew it would be easy for them to change their beliefs if they started using those altars, so nothing was to remain that might tempt them to worship idols. We, too, should ruthlessly find and remove any centers of false worship in our lives. These may be activities, attitudes, possessions, relationships, places, or habits—anything that tempts us to turn our hearts from God and do wrong. We should never flatter ourselves by thinking we're too strong to be tempted. Israel learned that lesson the hard way.

**12:12, 18** The Hebrews placed great emphasis on family worship. Whether offering a sacrifice or attending a great festival, the family was often together. This gave the children a healthy attitude toward worship, and it put extra meaning into it for the adults. Watching a family member confess his or her sin was just as

important as celebrating a great holiday together. Although there are appropriate times to separate people by ages, some of the most meaningful worship can be experienced only when shared by old and young.

**12:13, 14** While the pagans offered sacrifices to their gods, they offered them in many places. In contrast, the Israelites were only to offer sacrifices in the prescribed manner and in the prescribed places. This restriction was meant to ensure purity of worship for the nation of Israel. Later, they would neglect this injunction and offer sacrifices at the high places where pagan deities were worshiped. (See, for example, 2 Kings 23 where Josiah destroyed the other altars.) We should take steps to safeguard the purity of worship in our congregations. If we all individualized and customized worship to suit our own preferences, we would lose the benefit of worshiping as a body of believers.

15"But you may butcher your animals and eat their meat in any town whenever you want. You may freely eat the animals with which the LORD your God blesses you. All of you, whether ceremonially clean or unclean, may eat that meat, just as you now eat gazelle and deer. 16But you must not consume the blood. You must pour it out on the ground like water.

17"But you may not eat your offerings in your hometown—neither the tithe of your grain and new wine and olive oil, nor the firstborn of your flocks and herds, nor any offering to fulfill a vow, nor your voluntary offerings, nor your sacred offerings. 18You must eat these in the presence of the LORD your God at the place he will choose. Eat them there with your children, your servants, and the Levites who live in your towns, celebrating in the presence of the LORD your God in all you do. 19And be very careful never to neglect the Levites as long as you live in your land.

20"When the LORD your God expands your territory as he has promised, and you have the urge to eat meat, you may freely eat meat whenever you want. 21It might happen that the designated place of worship—the place the LORD your God chooses for his name to be honored—is a long way from your home. If so, you may butcher any of the cattle, sheep, or goats the LORD has given you, and you may freely eat the meat in your hometown, as I have commanded you. 22Anyone, whether ceremonially clean or unclean, may eat that meat, just as you do now with gazelle and deer. 23But never consume the blood, for the blood is the life, and you must not consume the lifeblood with the meat. 24Instead, pour out the blood on the ground like water. 25Do not consume the blood, so that all may go well with you and your children after you, because you will be doing what pleases the LORD.

26"Take your sacred gifts and your offerings given to fulfill a vow to the place the LORD chooses. 27You must offer the meat and blood of your burnt offerings on the altar of the LORD your God. The blood of your other sacrifices must be poured out on the altar of the LORD your God, but you may eat the meat. 28Be careful to obey all my commands, so that all will go well with you and your children after you, because you will be doing what is good and pleasing to the LORD your God.

29"When the LORD your God goes ahead of you and destroys the nations and you drive them out and live in their land, 30do not fall into the trap of following their customs and worshiping their gods. Do not inquire about their gods, saying, 'How do these nations worship their gods? I want to follow their example.' 31You must not worship the LORD your God the way the other nations worship their gods, for they perform for their gods every detestable act that the LORD hates. They even burn their sons and daughters as sacrifices to their gods.

32*"So be careful to obey all the commands I give you. You must not add anything to them or subtract anything from them.

## A Warning against Idolatry

**13** 1*"Suppose there are prophets among you or those who dream dreams about the future, and they promise you signs or miracles, 2and the predicted signs or miracles occur. If they then say, 'Come, let us worship other gods'—gods you have not known

**Cross references (right margin):**

12:15 Deut 12:20-23; 14:3-5
12:16 Lev 17:10-12 Deut 15:23
12:17 Deut 12:26; 14:22-23
12:18 Deut 12:4-5, 26
12:20 Deut 11:24
12:25 Deut 4:40
12:26 Num 5:9-10 Deut 12:17
12:28 Deut 4:40
12:31 Lev 18:21 Deut 9:5; 18:10 Ps 106:37-38
12:32 Deut 4:2
13:1 Matt 24:24 Mark 13:22 2 Thes 2:9

**12:32** Verse 12:32 is numbered 13:1 in Hebrew text.   **13:1** Verses 13:1-18 are numbered 13:2-19 in Hebrew text.

---

**12:16** Eating blood was forbidden for several reasons: (1) It was an integral part of the pagan practices of the land the Israelites were about to enter; (2) it represented life, which is sacred to God; (3) it reminded the people that life and strength come from God, not from drinking or eating blood; (4) it was a symbol of the sacrifice that had to be made for sin. (For more on why eating blood was prohibited, see the note on Leviticus 17:14.)

**12:30, 31** God did not want the Israelites even to ask about the pagan religions surrounding them. Idolatry completely permeated the land of Canaan. It was too easy to get drawn into the subtle temptations of seemingly harmless practices. Sometimes curiosity can cause us to stumble. Knowledge of evil is harmful if the evil becomes too tempting to resist. To resist curiosity about harmful practices shows discretion and obedience.

**13:1-3** Attractive leaders are not always led by God. Moses warned the Israelites against false prophets who encouraged worship of other gods. New ideas from inspiring people may sound good, but we must judge them by whether or not they are consistent with God's Word. When people claim to speak for God today, check them in these areas: Are they telling the truth? Is their focus on God? Are their words consistent with what you already know to be true? Some people speak the truth while directing you toward God, but others speak persuasively while directing you toward themselves. It is even possible to say the right words but still lead people in the wrong direction. God is not against new ideas, but he is for discernment. When you hear a new, attractive idea, examine it carefully before getting too excited. False prophets are still around today. The wise person will carefully test ideas against the truth of God's Word.

**13:2-11** The Israelites were warned not to listen to false prophets or to anyone else who tried to get them to worship other gods—even if this person was a close friend or family member. The temptation to abandon God's commands often sneaks up on us. It may come not with a loud shout but in a whispering doubt. And whispers can be very persuasive, especially if they come from loved ones. But love for relatives should not take before—³do not listen to them. The LORD your God is testing you to see if you truly love him with all your heart and soul. ⁴Serve only the LORD your God and fear him alone. Obey his commands, listen to his voice, and cling to him. ⁵The false prophets or visionaries who try to lead you astray must be put to death, for they encourage rebellion against the LORD your God, who redeemed you from slavery and brought you out of the land of Egypt. Since they try to lead you astray from the way the LORD your God commanded you to live, you must put them to death. In this way you will purge the evil from among you.

⁶"Suppose someone secretly entices you—even your brother, your son or daughter, your beloved wife, or your closest friend—and says, 'Let us go worship other gods'—gods that neither you nor your ancestors have known. ⁷They might suggest that you worship the gods of peoples who live nearby or who come from the ends of the earth. ⁸But do not give in or listen. Have no pity, and do not spare or protect them. ⁹You must put them to death! Strike the first blow yourself, and then all the people must join in. ¹⁰Stone the guilty ones to death because they have tried to draw you away from the LORD your God, who rescued you from the land of Egypt, the place of slavery. ¹¹Then all Israel will hear about it and be afraid, and no one will act so wickedly again.

¹²"When you begin living in the towns the LORD your God is giving you, you may hear ¹³that scoundrels among you are leading their fellow citizens astray by saying, 'Let us go worship other gods'—gods you have not known before. ¹⁴In such cases, you must examine the facts carefully. If you find that the report is true and such a detestable act has been committed among you, ¹⁵you must attack that town and completely destroy* all its inhabitants, as well as all the livestock. ¹⁶Then you must pile all the plunder in the middle of the open square and burn it. Burn the entire town as a burnt offering to the LORD your God. That town must remain a ruin forever; it may never be rebuilt. ¹⁷Keep none of the plunder that has been set apart for destruction. Then the LORD will turn from his fierce anger and be merciful to you. He will have compassion on you and make you a large nation, just as he swore to your ancestors.

¹⁸"The LORD your God will be merciful only if you listen to his voice and keep all his commands that I am giving you today, doing what pleases him.

### Ceremonially Clean and Unclean Animals

**14** "Since you are the people of the LORD your God, never cut yourselves or shave the hair above your foreheads in mourning for the dead. ²You have been set apart as holy to the LORD your God, and he has chosen you from all the nations of the earth to be his own special treasure.

³"You must not eat any detestable animals that are ceremonially unclean. ⁴These are the animals* you may eat: the ox, the sheep, the goat, ⁵the deer, the gazelle, the roe deer, the wild goat, the addax, the antelope, and the mountain sheep.

**13:15** The Hebrew term used here refers to the complete consecration of things or people to the LORD, either by destroying them or by giving them as an offering; similarly in 13:17.   **14:4** The identification of some of the animals and birds listed in this chapter is uncertain.

---

precedence over devotion to God. We can overcome whispered temptations by pouring out our hearts to God in prayer and by diligently studying his Word.

**13:12-16** A town that completely rejected God was to be destroyed so as not to lead the rest of the nation astray. But Israel was not to take action against a town until the rumor about its rejecting God was proven true. This guideline saved many lives when the leaders of Israel wrongly accused three tribes of falling away from their faith (Joshua 22). If we hear of friends who have wandered from the Lord or of entire congregations that have fallen away, we should check the facts and find the truth before doing or saying anything that could prove harmful. There are times, of course, when God wants us to take action—to rebuke a wayward friend, to discipline a child, to reject false teaching—but first we must be sure we have all the facts straight.

**14:1** The actions described here refer to a cult of the dead. Many other religions today have some kind of worship of or service to the dead. But Christianity and Judaism are very different from other religions because they focus on serving God in this life. Don't let concern or worry over the dead distract you from the tasks that God has for you while you are still alive.

**14:3-21** Why was Israel forbidden to eat certain foods? There are several reasons: (1) Predatory animals ate the blood of other animals, and scavengers ate dead animals. Because the people could not eat blood or animals they found dead, they could not eat animals that did these things either. (2) Some forbidden animals had bad associations in the Israelite culture just as bats, snakes, and spiders do for some people today. Some may have been used in pagan religious practices (Isaiah 66:17). To the Israelites, the unclean animals represented sin or unhealthy habits. (3) Perhaps some restrictions were given to Israel just to remind them continually that they were a different and separate people committed to God. Although we no longer must follow these laws about food (Acts 10:9-16), we can still learn from them the lesson that holiness is to be carried into all parts of life. We can't restrict holiness only to the spiritual side; we must be holy in the everyday practical part of life as well. Health practices, finances, use of leisure—all provide opportunities to put holy living into daily living.

6"You may eat any animal that has completely split hooves and chews the cud, 7but if the animal doesn't have both, it may not be eaten. So you may not eat the camel, the hare, or the hyrax.* They chew the cud but do not have split hooves, so they are ceremonially unclean for you. 8And you may not eat the pig. It has split hooves but does not chew the cud, so it is ceremonially unclean for you. You may not eat the meat of these animals or even touch their carcasses.

9"Of all the marine animals, you may eat whatever has both fins and scales. 10You may not, however, eat marine animals that do not have both fins and scales. They are ceremonially unclean for you.

11"You may eat any bird that is ceremonially clean. 12 These are the birds you may not eat: the griffon vulture, the bearded vulture, the black vulture, 13the kite, the falcon, buzzards of all kinds, 14ravens of all kinds, 15the eagle owl, the short-eared owl, the seagull, hawks of all kinds, 16the little owl, the great owl, the barn owl, 17the desert owl, the Egyptian vulture, the cormorant, 18the stork, herons of all kinds, the hoopoe, and the bat.

19"All winged insects that walk along the ground are ceremonially unclean for you and may not be eaten. 20But you may eat any winged bird or insect that is ceremonially clean.

21"You must not eat anything that has died a natural death. You may give it to a foreigner living in your town, or you may sell it to a stranger. But do not eat it yourselves, for you are set apart as holy to the LORD your God.

"You must not cook a young goat in its mother's milk.

## The Giving of Tithes

22"You must set aside a tithe of your crops—one-tenth of all the crops you harvest each year. 23Bring this tithe to the designated place of worship—the place the LORD your God chooses for his name to be honored—and eat it there in his presence. This applies to your tithes of grain, new wine, olive oil, and the firstborn males of your flocks and herds. Doing this will teach you always to fear the LORD your God.

24"Now when the LORD your God blesses you with a good harvest, the place of worship he chooses for his name to be honored might be too far for you to bring the tithe. 25If so, you may sell the tithe portion of your crops and herds, put the money in a pouch, and go to the place the LORD your God has chosen. 26When you arrive, you may use the money to buy any kind of food you want—cattle, sheep, goats, wine, or other alcoholic drink. Then feast there in the presence of the LORD your God and celebrate with your household. 27And do not neglect the Levites in your town, for they will receive no allotment of land among you.

28"At the end of every third year, bring the entire tithe of that year's harvest and store it in the nearest town. 29Give it to the Levites, who will receive no allotment of land among you, as well as to the foreigners living among you, the orphans, and the widows in your towns, so they can eat and be satisfied. Then the LORD your God will bless you in all your work.

## Release for Debtors

**15** "At the end of every seventh year you must cancel the debts of everyone who owes you money. 2 This is how it must be done. Everyone must cancel the loans they have made to their fellow Israelites. They must not demand payment from their neighbors or relatives, for the LORD's time of release has arrived. 3 This release from debt, however, applies only to your fellow Israelites—not to the foreigners living among you.

14:7 Or *coney*, or *rock badger*.

Cross-references: 14:12 Lev 11:13; 14:19 Lev 11:20; 14:21 Exod 23:19; 34:26; Lev 17:15; 22:8; Deut 14:2; Ezek 4:14; 14:22 Deut 12:6, 17; 14:23 Deut 4:10; 12:4; 14:24 Deut 12:5, 21; 14:26 Deut 12:7; 14:27 Num 18:20; Deut 12:12; 14:28 Deut 26:12; 14:29 Deut 16:11; 24:19; 15:1 Deut 31:10-11; 15:3 Deut 23:20

**14:21** This prohibition against cooking a young goat in its mother's milk may reflect a Canaanite fertility rite. Or it may just mean that the Israelites were not to take what was intended to promote life and use it to kill or destroy life. This commandment is also given in Exodus 23:19.

**14:22, 23** The Bible makes the purpose of tithing very clear—to teach us to fear the Lord and to put him first in our lives. We are to give God the first and best of what we earn. For example, what we do first with our money shows what we value most. Giving the first part of our paycheck to God immediately focuses our attention on him. It also reminds us that all we have belongs to him. A habit of regular tithing can keep God at the top of our priority list and give us a proper perspective on everything else we have.

**14:28, 29** The Bible supports an organized system of caring for the poor. God told his people to use their tithe every third year for those who were helpless, hungry, or poor. These regulations were designed to prevent the country from sinking under crushing poverty and oppression. It was everyone's responsibility to care for those less fortunate. Families were to help other family members, and towns were to help members of their community. National laws protected the rights of the poor, but helping the poor was also an active part of religious life. God counts on believers to provide for the needy, and we should use what God has given us to aid those less fortunate. Look beyond your regular giving and think of ways to help the needy. This will help you show your regard for God as Creator of all people, share God's goodness with others, and draw them to him. It is a practical and essential way to make faith work in everyday life.

**15:4**
Deut 28:8

**15:6**
Deut 28:12-13

**15:7**
Deut 15:11
**15:9**
Exod 22:22-23
Deut 15:1;
24:14-15
Job 34:28
**15:10**
2 Cor 9:5, 7
**15:11**
John 12:8

**15:12**
Exod 21:2
Lev 25:39
Jer 34:14

**15:15**
Deut 5:15; 16:12

**15:16**
Exod 21:5-6

**15:19**
Exod 13:2, 12;
34:19
**15:20**
Deut 12:7
**15:21**
Lev 22:19
**15:22**
Deut 12:15
**15:23**
Deut 12:16, 23-24

**16:1-8**
//Exod 12:14-20
//Lev 23:4-8
//Num 28:16-25
**16:1**
Exod 12:2
Num 28:16
**16:2**
Exod 12:5
**16:3**
Exod 12:8, 15;
34:18

4"There should be no poor among you, for the LORD your God will greatly bless you in the land he is giving you as a special possession. 5You will receive this blessing if you are careful to obey all the commands of the LORD your God that I am giving you today. 6The LORD your God will bless you as he has promised. You will lend money to many nations but will never need to borrow. You will rule many nations, but they will not rule over you.

7"But if there are any poor Israelites in your towns when you arrive in the land the LORD your God is giving you, do not be hard-hearted or tightfisted toward them. 8Instead, be generous and lend them whatever they need. 9Do not be mean-spirited and refuse someone a loan because the year for canceling debts is close at hand. If you refuse to make the loan and the needy person cries out to the LORD, you will be considered guilty of sin. 10Give generously to the poor, not grudgingly, for the LORD your God will bless you in everything you do. 11There will always be some in the land who are poor. That is why I am commanding you to share freely with the poor and with other Israelites in need.

### Release for Hebrew Slaves

12"If a fellow Hebrew sells himself or herself to be your servant* and serves you for six years, in the seventh year you must set that servant free.

13"When you release a male servant, do not send him away empty-handed. 14Give him a generous farewell gift from your flock, your threshing floor, and your winepress. Share with him some of the bounty with which the LORD your God has blessed you. 15Remember that you were once slaves in the land of Egypt and the LORD your God redeemed you! That is why I am giving you this command.

16"But suppose your servant says, 'I will not leave you,' because he loves you and your family, and he has done well with you. 17In that case, take an awl and push it through his earlobe into the door. After that, he will be your servant for life. And do the same for your female servants.

18"You must not consider it a hardship when you release your servants. Remember that for six years they have given you services worth double the wages of hired workers, and the LORD your God will bless you in all you do.

### Sacrificing Firstborn Male Animals

19"You must set aside for the LORD your God all the firstborn males from your flocks and herds. Do not use the firstborn of your herds to work your fields, and do not shear the firstborn of your flocks. 20Instead, you and your family must eat these animals in the presence of the LORD your God each year at the place he chooses. 21But if this firstborn animal has any defect, such as lameness or blindness, or if anything else is wrong with it, you must not sacrifice it to the LORD your God. 22Instead, use it for food for your family in your hometown. Anyone, whether ceremonially clean or unclean, may eat it, just as anyone may eat a gazelle or deer. 23But you must not consume the blood. You must pour it out on the ground like water.

### Passover and the Festival of Unleavened Bread

**16** "In honor of the LORD your God, celebrate the Passover each year in the early spring, in the month of Abib,* for that was the month in which the LORD your God brought you out of Egypt by night. 2Your Passover sacrifice may be from either the flock or the herd, and it must be sacrificed to the LORD your God at the designated place of worship—the place he chooses for his name to be honored. 3Eat it with bread made without yeast. For seven days the bread you eat must be made without yeast, as when you escaped from Egypt in such

**15:12** Or *If a Hebrew man or woman is sold to you.*   **16:1** Hebrew *Observe the month of Abib, and keep the Passover unto the LORD your God.* Abib, the first month of the ancient Hebrew lunar calendar, usually occurs within the months of March and April.

**15:7-11** God told the Israelites to help the poor among them when they arrived in the Promised Land. This was an important part of possessing the land. Many people conclude that people are poor through some fault of their own. This kind of reasoning makes it easy to close their hearts and hands to the needy. But we are not to invent reasons for ignoring the poor. We are to respond to their needs no matter who or what was responsible for their condition. Who are the poor in your community? How could your church help them? If your church does not have a program to identify the poor and assist in fulfilling their needs, why not help start one? What can you do to help someone in need?

**15:12-15** The Israelites were to release their servants after six years, sending them away with enough food so that they would be amply supplied until their needs could be met by some other means. This humanitarian act recognized that God created each person with dignity and worth. It also reminded the Israelites that they, too, had once been slaves in Egypt, and that their present freedom was a gift from God. We do not have servants such as these today, but God's instructions still apply to us: We must still be sure to treat our employees with respect and economic fairness.

a hurry. Eat this bread—the bread of suffering—so that as long as you live you will remember the day you departed from Egypt. 4Let no yeast be found in any house throughout your land for those seven days. And when you sacrifice the Passover lamb on the evening of the first day, do not let any of the meat remain until the next morning.

5"You may not sacrifice the Passover in just any of the towns that the LORD your God is giving you. 6You must offer it only at the designated place of worship—the place the LORD your God chooses for his name to be honored. Sacrifice it there in the evening as the sun goes down on the anniversary of your exodus from Egypt. 7Roast the lamb and eat it in the place the LORD your God chooses. Then you may go back to your tents the next morning. 8For the next six days you may not eat any bread made with yeast. On the seventh day proclaim another holy day in honor of the LORD your God, and no work may be done on that day.

### The Festival of Harvest
9"Count off seven weeks from when you first begin to cut the grain at the time of harvest. 10Then celebrate the Festival of Harvest* to honor the LORD your God. Bring him a voluntary offering in proportion to the blessings you have received from him. 11This is a time to celebrate before the LORD your God at the designated place of worship he will choose for his name to be honored. Celebrate with your sons and daughters, your male and female servants, the Levites from your towns, and the foreigners, orphans, and widows who live among you. 12Remember that you were once slaves in Egypt, so be careful to obey all these decrees.

### The Festival of Shelters
13"You must observe the Festival of Shelters* for seven days at the end of the harvest season, after the grain has been threshed and the grapes have been pressed. 14This festival will be a happy time of celebrating with your sons and daughters, your male and female servants, and the Levites, foreigners, orphans, and widows from your towns. 15For seven days you must celebrate this festival to honor the LORD your God at the place he chooses, for it is he who blesses you with bountiful harvests and gives you success in all your work. This festival will be a time of great joy for all.

16"Each year every man in Israel must celebrate these three festivals: the Festival of Unleavened Bread, the Festival of Harvest, and the Festival of Shelters. On each of these occasions, all men must appear before the LORD your God at the place he chooses, but they must not appear before the LORD without a gift for him. 17All must give as they are able, according to the blessings given to them by the LORD your God.

## 4. Laws for ruling the nation
### Justice for the People
18"Appoint judges and officials for yourselves from each of your tribes in all the towns the LORD your God is giving you. They must judge the people fairly. 19You must never twist justice or show partiality. Never accept a bribe, for bribes blind the eyes of the wise and corrupt the decisions of the godly. 20Let true justice prevail, so you may live and occupy the land that the LORD your God is giving you.

21"You must never set up a wooden Asherah pole beside the altar you build for the LORD your God. 22And never set up sacred pillars for worship, for the LORD your God hates them.

**17** "Never sacrifice sick or defective cattle, sheep, or goats to the LORD your God, for he detests such gifts.

**16:4**
Exod 13:7; 34:25

**16:6**
Deut 12:5

**16:7**
2 Chr 35:13

**16:9-12**
//Lev 23:15-22
//Num 28:26-31

**16:9**
Exod 23:16; 34:22
Lev 23:15
Num 28:26

**16:11**
Deut 12:7, 12;
14:29; 24:19

**16:13-17**
//Lev 23:33-43
//Num 29:12-39

**16:13**
Lev 23:16, 40

**16:16**
Exod 23:14-17;
34:20, 22-24

**16:18**
Exod 18:21, 26
Deut 1:16

**16:19**
Exod 23:2-3
Lev 19:15

**16:21**
Exod 34:13
Deut 7:5

**17:1**
Deut 15:21

16:10 Hebrew *Festival of Weeks;* also in 16:16. This was later called the Festival of Pentecost (see Acts 2:1). It is celebrated today as Shavuot (or Shabuoth).    16:13 Or *Festival of Booths,* or *Festival of Tabernacles;* also in 16:16. This was earlier called the Festival of the Final Harvest or Festival of Ingathering (see Exod 23:16b). It is celebrated today as Sukkot (or Succoth).

**16:16, 17** Three times a year every male was to make a journey to the sanctuary in the city that would be designated as Israel's religious capital. At these festivals, each participant was encouraged to give what he could in proportion to what God had given him. God does not expect us to give more than we can, but we will be blessed when we give cheerfully. For some, 10 percent may be a burden. For most of us, that would be far too little. Look at what you have and then give in proportion to what you have been given.

**16:18-20** These verses anticipated a great problem the Israelites would face when they arrived in the Promised Land. Although they had Joshua as their national leader, they failed to complete the task

and choose other spiritual leaders who would lead the tribes, districts, and cities with justice and God's wisdom. Because they did not appoint wise judges and faithful administrators, rebellion and injustice plagued their communities. It is a serious responsibility to appoint or elect wise and just officials. In your sphere of influence—home, church, school, job—are you ensuring that justice and godliness prevail? Failing to choose leaders who uphold justice can lead to much trouble, as Israel would discover.

**17:1** The fact that this command was included probably indicates that some Israelites were sacrificing imperfect or deformed animals to God. Then, as now, it is difficult and expensive to offer

**17:2**
Deut 13:6-11

**17:4**
Deut 13:12-14
**17:5**
Lev 24:14
**17:6**
Num 35:30
Deut 19:15
**17:7**
Lev 24:13-14
Deut 13:9
†1 Cor 5:13
**17:8**
Deut 12:5

**17:11**
Deut 25:1

2"When you begin living in the towns the LORD your God is giving you, a man or woman among you might do evil in the sight of the LORD your God and violate the covenant. 3For instance, they might serve other gods or worship the sun, the moon, or any of the stars—the forces of heaven—which I have strictly forbidden. 4When you hear about it, investigate the matter thoroughly. If it is true that this detestable thing has been done in Israel, 5then the man or woman who has committed such an evil act must be taken to the gates of the town and stoned to death. 6But never put a person to death on the testimony of only one witness. There must always be two or three witnesses. 7The witnesses must throw the first stones, and then all the people may join in. In this way, you will purge the evil from among you.

8"Suppose a case arises in a local court that is too hard for you to decide—for instance, whether someone is guilty of murder or only of manslaughter, or a difficult lawsuit, or a case involving different kinds of assault. Take such legal cases to the place the LORD your God will choose, 9and present them to the Levitical priests or the judge on duty at that time. They will hear the case and declare the verdict. 10You must carry out the verdict they announce and the sentence they prescribe at the place the LORD chooses. You must do exactly what they say. 11After they have interpreted the law and declared their verdict, the sentence they impose must be fully executed; do not modify it in any way. 12Anyone arrogant enough to reject the verdict of the judge or of the priest who represents the LORD your God must die. In this way you will purge the evil from Israel. 13Then everyone else will hear about it and be afraid to act so arrogantly.

## Guidelines for a King

**17:14**
Deut 11:31
Josh 21:43

**17:16**
1 Kgs 4:26
Ezek 17:15
**17:17**
2 Sam 5:13
1 Kgs 11:3-4
**17:18**
Deut 31:9, 24
**17:19**
Deut 4:9-10
Josh 1:8
**17:20**
Deut 5:32

14"You are about to enter the land the LORD your God is giving you. When you take it over and settle there, you may think, 'We should select a king to rule over us like the other nations around us.' 15If this happens, be sure to select as king the man the LORD your God chooses. You must appoint a fellow Israelite; he may not be a foreigner.

16"The king must not build up a large stable of horses for himself or send his people to Egypt to buy horses, for the LORD has told you, 'You must never return to Egypt.' 17The king must not take many wives for himself, because they will turn his heart away from the LORD. And he must not accumulate large amounts of wealth in silver and gold for himself.

18"When he sits on the throne as king, he must copy for himself this body of instruction on a scroll in the presence of the Levitical priests. 19He must always keep that copy with him and read it daily as long as he lives. That way he will learn to fear the LORD his God by obeying all the terms of these instructions and decrees. 20This regular reading will prevent him from becoming proud and acting as if he is above his fellow citizens. It will also prevent him from turning away from these commands in the smallest way. And it will ensure that he and his descendants will reign for many generations in Israel.

---

God our best (i.e., the first part of what we earn). It is always tempting to shortchange God because we think we won't get caught. But our giving shows our real priorities. When we give God the leftovers, it is obvious that he is not at the center of our lives. Give God the honor of having first claim on your money, time, and talents.

**17:6, 7** A person was not put to death on the testimony of only one witness. On the witness of two or three, a person could be condemned and then sentenced to death by stoning. The condemned person was taken outside the city gates, and the witnesses were the first to throw heavy stones down on him or her. Bystanders would then pelt the dying person with stones. This system would "purge the evil" by putting the idolater to death. At the same time, it protected the rights of accused persons two ways. First, by requiring several witnesses, it prevented any angry individual from giving false testimony. Second, by requiring the accusers to throw the first stones, it made them think twice about accusing unjustly. They were responsible to finish what they had started.

**17:14-20** God was not encouraging Israel to appoint a king to rule their nation. He was actually against the idea because he was their King, and the people were to obey and follow him. But God knew that the people would one day demand a king for selfish reasons—they would want to be like the nations around them (1 Samuel 8). If they insisted on having a king, he wanted

to make sure they chose the right person. That is why he included these instructions both for the people's benefit as they chose their king and for the king himself as he sought to lead the nation according to God's laws.

**17:16, 17** Israel's kings did not heed this warning, and their behavior led to their downfall. Solomon had everything going for him, but when he became rich, built up a large army, and married many wives, his heart turned from God (1 Kings 11). Out of Solomon's sin came Israel's disobedience, division, and captivity.

**17:18-20** The king was to be a man of God's Word. He was to (1) make for himself a copy of the law, (2) keep it with him all the time, (3) read from it every day, and (4) obey it completely. Through this process he would learn respect for God, keep himself from feeling more important than others, and avoid neglecting God in times of prosperity. We can't know what God wants except through his Word, and his Word won't affect our lives unless we read and think about it regularly. With the abundant availability of the Bible today, it is not difficult to gain access to the source of the king's wisdom. What is more of a challenge is following its directives.

### Gifts for the Priests and Levites

**18** "Remember that the Levitical priests—that is, the whole of the tribe of Levi—will receive no allotment of land among the other tribes in Israel. Instead, the priests and Levites will eat from the special gifts given to the LORD, for that is their share. [2]They will have no land of their own among the Israelites. The LORD himself is their special possession, just as he promised them.

[3]"These are the parts the priests may claim as their share from the cattle, sheep, and goats that the people bring as offerings: the shoulder, the cheeks, and the stomach. [4]You must also give to the priests the first share of the grain, the new wine, the olive oil, and the wool at shearing time. [5]For the LORD your God chose the tribe of Levi out of all your tribes to minister in the LORD's name forever.

[6]"Suppose a Levite chooses to move from his town in Israel, wherever he is living, to the place the LORD chooses for worship. [7]He may minister there in the name of the LORD his God, just like all his fellow Levites who are serving the LORD there. [8]He may eat his share of the sacrifices and offerings, even if he also receives support from his family.

### A Call to Holy Living

[9]"When you enter the land the LORD your God is giving you, be very careful not to imitate the detestable customs of the nations living there. [10]For example, never sacrifice your son or daughter as a burnt offering.* And do not let your people practice fortune-telling, or use sorcery, or interpret omens, or engage in witchcraft, [11]or cast spells, or function as mediums or psychics, or call forth the spirits of the dead. [12]Anyone who does these things is detestable to the LORD. It is because the other nations have done these detestable things that the LORD your God will drive them out ahead of you. [13]But you must be blameless before the LORD your God. [14]The nations you are about to displace consult sorcerers and fortune-tellers, but the LORD your God forbids you to do such things."

### True and False Prophets

[15]Moses continued, "The LORD your God will raise up for you a prophet like me from among your fellow Israelites. You must listen to him. [16]For this is what you yourselves requested of the LORD your God when you were assembled at Mount Sinai.* You said, 'Don't let us hear the voice of the LORD our God anymore or see this blazing fire, for we will die.'

[17]"Then the LORD said to me, 'What they have said is right. [18]I will raise up a prophet like you from among their fellow Israelites. I will put my words in his mouth, and he will tell the people everything I command him. [19]I will personally deal with anyone who will not listen to the messages the prophet proclaims on my behalf. [20]But any prophet who falsely claims to speak in my name or who speaks in the name of another god must die.'

[21]"But you may wonder, 'How will we know whether or not a prophecy is from the LORD?' [22]If the prophet speaks in the LORD's name but his prediction does not happen or come true, you will know that the LORD did not give that message. That prophet has spoken without my authority and need not be feared.

**18:10** Or *never make your son or daughter pass through the fire.*   **18:16** Hebrew *Horeb*, another name for Sinai.

---

**18:1**
Deut 10:9
1 Cor 9:13
**18:2**
Num 18:20
**18:3**
Lev 7:32
Num 18:11
**18:4**
Exod 22:29
**18:5**
Exod 28:1
Deut 10:8
**18:6**
Num 35:2-3
**18:8**
Lev 27:30
Num 18:21
**18:9**
Deut 9:5; 12:29-30
**18:10**
Exod 22:18
Lev 19:26, 31; 20:6
Deut 12:31
Jer 27:9-10
**18:13**
Gen 6:7-10
Matt 5:48
**18:15**
Luke 24:19
John 1:21, 24-25
†Acts 3:22; 7:37
**18:16**
Deut 5:23-27
**18:18**
†Acts 3:22
**18:19**
Deut 17:12
†Acts 3:22
Heb 12:25
**18:20**
Deut 13:1-4
**18:22**
Jer 28:9

---

**18:1-8** The priests and Levites served much the same function as our ministers today. Their duties included (1) teaching the people about God, (2) setting an example of godly living, (3) caring for the sanctuary and its workers, and (4) distributing the offerings. Because priests and Levites could not own property or pursue outside business interests, God made special arrangements so that people would not take advantage of them. Often churches take advantage of the men and women God has brought to lead them. For example, ministers may not be paid in accordance with their skills or the time they put in. Or pastors may be expected to attend every evening meeting, even if this continual absence is harmful to their families. As you look at your own church in light of God's Word, what ways do you see to honor the leaders God has given you?

**18:10** Child sacrifice and occult practices were strictly forbidden by God. These practices were common among pagan religions. Israel's own neighbors actually sacrificed their children to the god Molech (Leviticus 20:2-5). Other neighboring religions used supernatural means, such as contacting the spirit world, to foretell the future and gain guidance. Because of these wicked practices, God would drive out the pagan nations (Deuteronomy 18:12). The Israelites were to replace their evil practices with the worship of the one true God.

**18:10-13** The Israelites were naturally curious about the occult practices of the Canaanite religions. But Satan is behind the occult, and God flatly forbade Israel to have anything to do with it. Today people are still fascinated by horoscopes, fortune-telling, witchcraft, and bizarre cults. Often their interest comes from a desire to know and control the future. But Satan is no less dangerous today than he was in Moses' time. In the Bible, God tells us all we need to know about what is going to happen. The information Satan offers is likely to be distorted or completely false. With the trustworthy guidance of the Holy Spirit through the Bible and the church, we don't need to turn to occult sources for faulty information.

**18:15** Who is this prophet? Stephen used this verse to support his claim that Jesus Christ is God's Son, the Messiah (Acts 7:37). The coming of Jesus Christ to earth was not an afterthought, but part of God's original plan.

**18:21, 22** As in the days of ancient Israel, some people today

### Cities of Refuge

**19:1**
Deut 6:10-12
**19:2**
Deut 4:41-42
Josh 20:2

**19** "When the LORD your God destroys the nations whose land he is giving you, you will take over their land and settle in their towns and homes. 2 Then you must set apart three cities of refuge in the land the LORD your God is giving you. 3 Survey the territory,* and divide the land the LORD your God is giving you into three districts, with one of these cities in each district. Then anyone who has killed someone can flee to one of the cities of refuge for safety.

**19:4**
Num 35:9-34

4"If someone kills another person unintentionally, without previous hostility, the slayer may flee to any of these cities to live in safety. 5For example, suppose someone goes into the forest with a neighbor to cut wood. And suppose one of them swings an ax to chop down a tree, and the ax head flies off the handle, killing the other person. In such cases, the slayer may flee to one of the cities of refuge to live in safety.

6"If the distance to the nearest city of refuge is too far, an enraged avenger might be able to chase down and kill the person who caused the death. Then the slayer would die unfairly, since he had never shown hostility toward the person who died. 7 That is why I am commanding you to set aside three cities of refuge.

**19:8**
Deut 11:24
**19:9**
Deut 6:5; 11:22
**19:10**
Num 35:33
Deut 21:1-9

8"And if the LORD your God enlarges your territory, as he swore to your ancestors, and gives you all the land he promised them, 9you must designate three additional cities of refuge. (He will give you this land if you are careful to obey all the commands I have given you—if you always love the LORD your God and walk in his ways.) 10That way you will prevent the death of innocent people in the land the LORD your God is giving you as your special possession. You will not be held responsible for the death of innocent people.

**19:13**
Deut 7:2

11"But suppose someone is hostile toward a neighbor and deliberately ambushes and murders him and then flees to one of the cities of refuge. 12In that case, the elders of the murderer's hometown must send agents to the city of refuge to bring him back and hand him over to the dead person's avenger to be put to death. 13Do not feel sorry for that murderer! Purge from Israel the guilt of murdering innocent people; then all will go well with you.

### Concern for Justice

**19:14**
Deut 27:17
Prov 23:10-11
**19:15**
Num 35:30
Deut 17:6
†Matt 18:16
†2 Cor 13:1

14"When you arrive in the land the LORD your God is giving you as your special possession, you must never steal anyone's land by moving the boundary markers your ancestors set up to mark their property.

15"You must not convict anyone of a crime on the testimony of only one witness. The facts of the case must be established by the testimony of two or three witnesses.

**19:16**
Exod 23:1
**19:17**
Deut 17:9; 21:5
**19:19**
†1 Cor 5:13
Prov 19:5
**19:21**
Exod 21:24
Lev 24:20
†Matt 5:38

16"If a malicious witness comes forward and accuses someone of a crime, 17then both the accuser and accused must appear before the LORD by coming to the priests and judges in office at that time. 18The judges must investigate the case thoroughly. If the accuser has brought false charges against his fellow Israelite, 19you must impose on the accuser the sentence he intended for the other person. In this way, you will purge such evil from among you. 20Then the rest of the people will hear about it and be afraid to do such an evil thing. 21You must show no pity for the guilty! Your rule should be life for life, eye for eye, tooth for tooth, hand for hand, foot for foot.

**19:3** Or *Keep the roads in good repair.*

---

claim to have messages from God. God still speaks to his people, but we must be cautious before saying that someone is God's spokesman. How can we tell when people are speaking for the Lord? (1) We can see whether or not their prophecies come true—the ancient test for judging prophets. (2) We can check their words against the Bible. God never contradicts himself, so if someone says something contrary to the Bible, we can know that this is not God's word. (See 13:1-11.)

**19:2-7** Every society must deal with the problem of murder. But how should society treat those who have innocently or accidentally killed someone? God had an answer for the Israelites. Since revenge was common and swift in Moses' day, God had the Israelites set apart several "cities of refuge." Anyone who claimed to have accidentally killed someone could flee to one of these cities until he could have a fair trial. If he was found innocent of intentional murder, he could remain in that city and be safe from those

seeking revenge. This is a beautiful example of how God blended his justice and mercy toward his people. (For more information on cities of refuge, see the note on Numbers 35:6.)

**19:12** The "avenger" was the nearest male relative to the person killed. He acted as the family protector (see Numbers 35:19).

**19:21** This principle was for the judges to use, not a plan for personal vengeance. This attitude toward punishment may seem primitive, but it was actually a breakthrough for justice and fairness in ancient times when most nations used arbitrary methods to punish criminals. This guideline reflects a concern for evenhandedness and justice—ensuring that those who violated the law were not punished more severely than their particular crime deserved. In the same spirit of justice, a false witness was to receive the same punishment the accused person would have suffered. The principle of making the punishment fit the crime should still be observed today.

## Regulations concerning War

**20** "When you go out to fight your enemies and you face horses and chariots and an army greater than your own, do not be afraid. The LORD your God, who brought you out of the land of Egypt, is with you! ²When you prepare for battle, the priest must come forward to speak to the troops. ³He will say to them, 'Listen to me, all you men of Israel! Do not be afraid as you go out to fight your enemies today! Do not lose heart or panic or tremble before them. ⁴For the LORD your God is going with you! He will fight for you against your enemies, and he will give you victory!'

⁵"Then the officers of the army must address the troops and say, 'Has anyone here just built a new house but not yet dedicated it? If so, you may go home! You might be killed in the battle, and someone else would dedicate your house. ⁶Has anyone here just planted a vineyard but not yet eaten any of its fruit? If so, you may go home! You might die in battle, and someone else would eat the first fruit. ⁷Has anyone here just become engaged to a woman but not yet married her? Well, you may go home and get married! You might die in the battle, and someone else would marry her.'

⁸"Then the officers will also say, 'Is anyone here afraid or worried? If you are, you may go home before you frighten anyone else.' ⁹When the officers have finished speaking to their troops, they will appoint the unit commanders.

¹⁰"As you approach a town to attack it, you must first offer its people terms for peace. ¹¹If they accept your terms and open the gates to you, then all the people inside will serve you in forced labor. ¹²But if they refuse to make peace and prepare to fight, you must attack the town. ¹³When the LORD your God hands the town over to you, use your swords to kill every man in the town. ¹⁴But you may keep for yourselves all the women, children, livestock, and other plunder. You may enjoy the plunder from your enemies that the LORD your God has given you.

¹⁵"But these instructions apply only to distant towns, not to the towns of the nations in the land you will enter. ¹⁶In those towns that the LORD your God is giving you as a special possession, destroy every living thing. ¹⁷You must completely destroy* the Hittites, Amorites, Canaanites, Perizzites, Hivites, and Jebusites, just as the LORD your God has commanded you. ¹⁸This will prevent the people of the land from teaching you to imitate their detestable customs in the worship of their gods, which would cause you to sin deeply against the LORD your God.

¹⁹"When you are attacking a town and the war drags on, you must not cut down the trees with your axes. You may eat the fruit, but do not cut down the trees. Are the trees your enemies, that you should attack them? ²⁰You may only cut down trees that you know are not valuable for food. Use them to make the equipment you need to attack the enemy town until it falls.

## 5. Laws for human relationships
### Cleansing for Unsolved Murder

**21** "When you are in the land the LORD your God is giving you, someone may be found murdered in a field, and you don't know who committed the murder. ²In such a case, your elders and judges must measure the distance from the site of the crime to the nearby

**20:17** The Hebrew term used here refers to the complete consecration of things or people to the LORD, either by destroying them or by giving them as an offering.

---

**20:1** Just like the Israelites, we sometimes face overwhelming opposition. Whether at school, at work, or even at home, we can feel outnumbered and helpless. God bolstered the Israelites' confidence by reminding them that he was always with them and that he had already saved them from the potential danger. We, too, can feel secure when we consider that God is able to overcome even the most difficult odds.

**20:13-18** How could a merciful and just God order the destruction of entire population centers? He did this to protect his people from idol worship, which was certain to bring ruin to Israel (20:18). In fact, because Israel did not completely destroy these evil people as God commanded, Israel was constantly oppressed by them and experienced greater bloodshed and

destruction than if they had followed God's instructions in the first place. (See 7:2-6.)

**20:20** Archaeologists have uncovered the remnants of many well-fortified cities in Canaan. Some had tall walls (up to 30 feet high), ramparts, moats, and towers. Accustomed to fighting on the open plains, the Israelites were going to have to learn new battle strategies to conquer these massive fortresses.

**21:1-9** When a crime was committed and the criminal got away, the whole community was held responsible. In much the same way, if a city has a dangerous intersection and someone is killed there, the community may be held responsible for both damages and repairs. God was pointing to the need for the whole community to feel a keen sense of responsibility for what was going on around them and to move to correct any situations that were potentially harmful—physically, socially, or morally.

---

**Cross-references (right margin):**

**20:1** Deut 3:22; 31:6-8
**20:2** Num 10:8; 31:6
**20:3** Josh 23:10
**20:5** Neh 12:27
**20:6** Lev 19:23
**20:7** Deut 24:5
**20:8** Judg 7:3
**20:10** Luke 14:31-32
**20:13** Num 31:7
**20:14** Josh 8:2
**20:16** Exod 23:31; Deut 7:1-2
**20:18** Deut 7:4; 9:5; 12:30

towns. ³When the nearest town has been determined, that town's elders must select from the herd a young cow that has never been trained or yoked to a plow. ⁴They must lead it down to a valley that has not been plowed or planted and that has a stream running through it. There in the valley they must break the young cow's neck. ⁵Then the Levitical priests must step forward, for the LORD your God has chosen them to minister before him and to pronounce blessings in the LORD's name. They are to decide all legal and criminal cases.

⁶"The elders of the town must wash their hands over the young cow whose neck was broken. ⁷Then they must say, 'Our hands did not shed this person's blood, nor did we see it happen. ⁸O LORD, forgive your people Israel whom you have redeemed. Do not charge your people with the guilt of murdering an innocent person.' Then they will be absolved of the guilt of this person's blood. ⁹By following these instructions, you will do what is right in the LORD's sight and will cleanse the guilt of murder from your community.

### Marriage to a Captive Woman

¹⁰"Suppose you go out to war against your enemies and the LORD your God hands them over to you, and you take some of them as captives. ¹¹And suppose you see among the captives a beautiful woman, and you are attracted to her and want to marry her. ¹²If this happens, you may take her to your home, where she must shave her head, cut her nails, ¹³and change the clothes she was wearing when she was captured. She will stay in your home, but let her mourn for her father and mother for a full month. Then you may marry her, and you will be her husband and she will be your wife. ¹⁴But if you marry her and she does not please you, you must let her go free. You may not sell her or treat her as a slave, for you have humiliated her.

### Rights of the Firstborn

¹⁵"Suppose a man has two wives, but he loves one and not the other, and both have given him sons. And suppose the firstborn son is the son of the wife he does not love. ¹⁶When the man divides his inheritance, he may not give the larger inheritance to his younger son, the son of the wife he loves, as if he were the firstborn son. ¹⁷He must recognize the rights of his oldest son, the son of the wife he does not love, by giving him a double portion. He is the first son of his father's virility, and the rights of the firstborn belong to him.

### Dealing with a Rebellious Son

¹⁸"Suppose a man has a stubborn and rebellious son who will not obey his father or mother, even though they discipline him. ¹⁹In such a case, the father and mother must take the son to the elders as they hold court at the town gate. ²⁰The parents must say to the elders, 'This son of ours is stubborn and rebellious and refuses to obey. He is a glutton and a drunkard.' ²¹Then all the men of his town must stone him to death. In this way, you will purge this evil from among you, and all Israel will hear about it and be afraid.

### Various Regulations

²²"If someone has committed a crime worthy of death and is executed and hung on a tree,* ²³the body must not remain hanging from the tree overnight. You must bury the body that same day, for anyone who is hung* is cursed in the sight of God. In this way, you will prevent the defilement of the land the LORD your God is giving you as your special possession.

**22** "If you see your neighbor's ox or sheep or goat wandering away, don't ignore your responsibility.* Take it back to its owner. ²If its owner does not live nearby or you don't know who the owner is, take it to your place and keep it until the owner comes looking for it. Then you must return it. ³Do the same if you find your neighbor's donkey, clothing, or anything else your neighbor loses. Don't ignore your responsibility.

21:22 Or *impaled on a pole;* similarly in 21:23. **21:23** Greek version reads *for everyone who is hung on a tree.* Compare Gal 3:13. **22:1** Hebrew *don't hide yourself;* similarly in 22:3.

**21:5** Deut 10:8; 17:9; 19:17

**21:6** Matt 27:24

**21:8** Num 35:33-34 Jon 1:14
**21:9** Deut 19:13

**21:10** Josh 21:44

**21:12** Lev 14:8-9 Num 6:9
**21:13** Ps 45:10
**21:14** Gen 34:2

**21:17** Gen 49:3

**21:18** Prov 1:8

**21:21** Lev 20:2, 27 Num 15:35

**21:22** Matt 26:65-66
**21:23** John 19:31 †Gal 3:13

**22:1** Exod 23:4

**21:18-21** Disobedient and rebellious children were to be brought before the elders of the city and stoned to death. There is no biblical or archaeological evidence that this punishment was ever carried out, but the point was that disobedience and rebellion were not to be tolerated in the home or allowed to continue unchecked. These principles must never be used to justify or overlook abuse or harsh treatment of children. While firm guidance may be needed with strong consequences for disobedience, the Bible does not condone physical, verbal, or emotional abuse of children.

**22:1-4** The Hebrews were to care for and return lost animals or possessions to their rightful owners. The way of the world, by contrast, is "Finders keepers, losers weepers." To go beyond the finders-keepers rule by protecting and returning the property of others keeps us from being envious and greedy.

4"If you see that your neighbor's donkey or ox has collapsed on the road, do not look the other way. Go and help your neighbor get it back on its feet!

5"A woman must not put on men's clothing, and a man must not wear women's clothing. Anyone who does this is detestable in the sight of the LORD your God.

6"If you happen to find a bird's nest in a tree or on the ground, and there are young ones or eggs in it with the mother sitting in the nest, do not take the mother with the young. 7You may take the young, but let the mother go, so that you may prosper and enjoy a long life.

8"When you build a new house, you must build a railing around the edge of its flat roof. That way you will not be considered guilty of murder if someone falls from the roof.

9"You must not plant any other crop between the rows of your vineyard. If you do, you are forbidden to use either the grapes from the vineyard or the other crop.

10"You must not plow with an ox and a donkey harnessed together.

11"You must not wear clothing made of wool and linen woven together.

12"You must put four tassels on the hem of the cloak with which you cover yourself— on the front, back, and sides.

## Regulations for Sexual Purity

13"Suppose a man marries a woman, but after sleeping with her, he turns against her 14and publicly accuses her of shameful conduct, saying, 'When I married this woman, I discovered she was not a virgin.' 15Then the woman's father and mother must bring the proof of her virginity to the elders as they hold court at the town gate. 16Her father must say to them, 'I gave my daughter to this man to be his wife, and now he has turned against her. 17He has accused her of shameful conduct, saying, "I discovered that your daughter was not a virgin." But here is the proof of my daughter's virginity.' Then they must spread her bed sheet before the elders. 18The elders must then take the man and punish him. 19They must also fine him 100 pieces of silver,* which he must pay to the woman's father because he publicly accused a virgin of Israel of shameful conduct. The woman will then remain the man's wife, and he may never divorce her.

20"But suppose the man's accusations are true, and he can show that she was not a virgin. 21The woman must be taken to the door of her father's home, and there the men of the town must stone her to death, for she has committed a disgraceful crime in Israel by being promiscuous while living in her parents' home. In this way, you will purge this evil from among you.

22"If a man is discovered committing adultery, both he and the woman must die. In this way, you will purge Israel of such evil.

23"Suppose a man meets a young woman, a virgin who is engaged to be married, and he has sexual intercourse with her. If this happens within a town, 24you must take both of them to the gates of that town and stone them to death. The woman is guilty because she did not scream for help. The man must die because he violated another man's wife. In this way, you will purge this evil from among you.

25"But if the man meets the engaged woman out in the country, and he rapes her, then only the man must die. 26Do nothing to the young woman; she has committed no crime worthy of death. She is as innocent as a murder victim. 27Since the man raped her out in the country, it must be assumed that she screamed, but there was no one to rescue her.

**22:19** Hebrew *100 shekels of silver*, about 2.5 pounds or 1.1 kilograms in weight.

---

**22:6** Lev 22:28

**22:9** Lev 19:19
**22:10** 2 Cor 6:14

**22:12** Num 15:37-39
Matt 23:5

**22:13** Deut 24:1

**22:21** Deut 23:17-18

**22:22** Lev 20:10
Ezek 16:38
John 8:5
**22:23** Lev 19:20-22

---

**22:5** This verse commands men and women not to reverse their sexual roles. It is not a statement about clothing styles. Today role rejections are common—there are men who want to become women and women who want to become men. It's not the clothing style that offends God, but using the style to act out a different sex role. God had a purpose in making us uniquely male and female.

**22:8-11** These are practical laws, helpful for establishing good habits for everyday living. Verse 8: Since people used their flat roofs as porches, a railing was a wise safety precaution. Verse 9: If you plant two different crops side by side, one of them will not survive, since the stronger, taller one will block the sunlight and take most of the vital nutrients from the soil. Verse 10: A donkey and an ox, due to differences in strength and size, cannot pull a plow evenly. Verse 11: Two different kinds of thread wear unevenly and wash differently. Combining them reduces the life of the garment. Don't think of God's laws as arbitrary restrictions. Look for the reasons behind the laws. They are made not just to teach or restrict but also to protect and help us.

**22:13-30** Why did God include all these laws about sexual sins? Instructions about sexual behavior would have been vital for three million people on a 40-year camping trip. But they would be equally important when they entered the Promised Land and settled down as a nation. Paul, in Colossians 3:5-8, recognizes the importance of strong rules about sex for believers because sexual sins have the power to disrupt and destroy the church. Sins involving sex are not innocent dabblings in forbidden pleasures, as is so often portrayed, but powerful destroyers of relationships. They confuse and tear down the climate of respect, trust, and credibility that is so essential for solid marriages and secure children.

22:28
Exod 22:16

22:30
Lev 18:8; 20:11
Deut 27:20

23:1
Lev 21:20; 22:24

23:3
Neh 13:1-2

23:4
Num 23:4, 7-10
2 Pet 2:15
Jude 1:11

23:7
Lev 19:34
Deut 10:19

23:11
Lev 15:16

23:14
Lev 26:12

23:15
1 Sam 30:15

23:19
Exod 22:25
Lev 25:36

23:20
Deut 28:12

23:21
Num 30:1-2
Eccl 5:4
Matt 5:33

28"Suppose a man has intercourse with a young woman who is a virgin but is not engaged to be married. If they are discovered, 29he must pay her father fifty pieces of silver.* Then he must marry the young woman because he violated her, and he may never divorce her as long as he lives.

30*"A man must not marry his father's former wife, for this would violate his father.

## Regulations concerning Worship

**23** 1*"If a man's testicles are crushed or his penis is cut off, he may not be admitted to the assembly of the LORD.

2"If a person is illegitimate by birth, neither he nor his descendants for ten generations may be admitted to the assembly of the LORD.

3"No Ammonite or Moabite or any of their descendants for ten generations may be admitted to the assembly of the LORD. 4These nations did not welcome you with food and water when you came out of Egypt. Instead, they hired Balaam son of Beor from Pethor in distant Aram-naharaim to curse you. 5But the LORD your God refused to listen to Balaam. He turned the intended curse into a blessing because the LORD your God loves you. 6As long as you live, you must never promote the welfare and prosperity of the Ammonites or Moabites.

7"Do not detest the Edomites or the Egyptians, because the Edomites are your relatives and you lived as foreigners among the Egyptians. 8The third generation of Edomites and Egyptians may enter the assembly of the LORD.

## Miscellaneous Regulations

9"When you go to war against your enemies, be sure to stay away from anything that is impure.

10"Any man who becomes ceremonially defiled because of a nocturnal emission must leave the camp and stay away all day. 11Toward evening he must bathe himself, and at sunset he may return to the camp.

12"You must have a designated area outside the camp where you can go to relieve yourself. 13Each of you must have a spade as part of your equipment. Whenever you relieve yourself, dig a hole with the spade and cover the excrement. 14The camp must be holy, for the LORD your God moves around in your camp to protect you and to defeat your enemies. He must not see any shameful thing among you, or he will turn away from you.

15"If slaves should escape from their masters and take refuge with you, you must not hand them over to their masters. 16Let them live among you in any town they choose, and do not oppress them.

17"No Israelite, whether man or woman, may become a temple prostitute. 18When you are bringing an offering to fulfill a vow, you must not bring to the house of the LORD your God any offering from the earnings of a prostitute, whether a man* or a woman, for both are detestable to the LORD your God.

19"Do not charge interest on the loans you make to a fellow Israelite, whether you loan money, or food, or anything else. 20You may charge interest to foreigners, but you may not charge interest to Israelites, so that the LORD your God may bless you in everything you do in the land you are about to enter and occupy.

21"When you make a vow to the LORD your God, be prompt in fulfilling whatever you promised him. For the LORD your God demands that you promptly fulfill all your vows, or you will be guilty of sin. 22However, it is not a sin to refrain from making a vow. 23But once you have voluntarily made a vow, be careful to fulfill your promise to the LORD your God.

24"When you enter your neighbor's vineyard, you may eat your fill of grapes, but you

**22:29** Hebrew *50 shekels of silver*, about 1.25 pounds or 570 grams in weight.   **22:30** Verse 22:30 is numbered 23:1 in Hebrew text.   **23:1** Verses 23:1-25 are numbered 23:2-26 in Hebrew text.   **23:18** Hebrew *a dog.*

**23:17, 18** Prostitution was not overlooked in God's law—it was strictly forbidden. To forbid this practice may seem obvious to us, but it may not have been so obvious to the Israelites. Almost every other religion known to them included prostitution as an integral part of its worship services. Prostitution makes a mockery of God's original idea for sex, treating sex as an isolated physical act rather than an act of commitment to another. Outside of marriage, sex destroys relationships. Within marriage, if approached with the right attitude, it can be a relationship builder.

God frequently had to warn the people against the practice of extramarital sex. Today we still need to hear his warnings.

**23:24, 25** This commandment guarded against selfishly holding on to one's possessions. It also ensured that no one had to go hungry. It was not, however, an excuse for taking advantage of one's neighbor. The Pharisees did not interpret this appropriately when they accused Jesus and the disciples of harvesting on the Sabbath (Matthew 12:1, 2).

must not carry any away in a basket. 25And when you enter your neighbor's field of grain, you may pluck the heads of grain with your hand, but you must not harvest it with a sickle.

**23:25**
Matt 12:1-2
Mark 2:23
Luke 6:1

**24** "Suppose a man marries a woman but she does not please him. Having discovered something wrong with her, he writes her a letter of divorce, hands it to her, and sends her away from his house. 2 When she leaves his house, she is free to marry another man. 3But if the second husband also turns against her and divorces her, or if he dies, 4the first husband may not marry her again, for she has been defiled. That would be detestable to the LORD. You must not bring guilt upon the land the LORD your God is giving you as a special possession.

**24:1**
Num 5:12-28
Deut 22:13-21
†Matt 5:31; 19:7
Mark 10:4-5

5"A newly married man must not be drafted into the army or be given any other official responsibilities. He must be free to spend one year at home, bringing happiness to the wife he has married.

**24:5**
Deut 20:7

6"It is wrong to take a set of millstones, or even just the upper millstone, as security for a loan, for the owner uses it to make a living.

7"If anyone kidnaps a fellow Israelite and treats him as a slave or sells him, the kidnapper must die. In this way, you will purge the evil from among you.

8"In all cases involving serious skin diseases,* be careful to follow the instructions of the Levitical priests; obey all the commands I have given them. 9Remember what the LORD your God did to Miriam as you were coming from Egypt.

**24:8**
Lev 13:1, 59
**24:9**
Num 12:10

10"If you lend anything to your neighbor, do not enter his house to pick up the item he is giving as security. 11You must wait outside while he goes in and brings it out to you. 12If your neighbor is poor and gives you his cloak as security for a loan, do not keep the cloak overnight. 13Return the cloak to its owner by sunset so he can stay warm through the night and bless you, and the LORD your God will count you as righteous.

**24:10**
Exod 22:24-26

14"Never take advantage of poor and destitute laborers, whether they are fellow Israelites or foreigners living in your towns. 15You must pay them their wages each day before sunset because they are poor and are counting on it. If you don't, they might cry out to the LORD against you, and it would be counted against you as sin.

**24:14**
Lev 19:13
1 Tim 5:18

16"Parents must not be put to death for the sins of their children, nor children for the sins of their parents. Those deserving to die must be put to death for their own crimes.

**24:16**
2 Kgs 14:6
2 Chr 25:4
Ezek 18:20

17"True justice must be given to foreigners living among you and to orphans, and you must never accept a widow's garment as security for her debt. 18Always remember that you were slaves in Egypt and that the LORD your God redeemed you from your slavery. That is why I have given you this command.

**24:17**
Exod 22:21-22;
23:2-3
Deut 1:17; 10:17
**24:18**
Deut 5:15

19"When you are harvesting your crops and forget to bring in a bundle of grain from your field, don't go back to get it. Leave it for the foreigners, orphans, and widows. Then the LORD your God will bless you in all you do. 20When you beat the olives from your olive trees, don't go over the boughs twice. Leave the remaining olives for the foreigners, orphans, and widows. 21When you gather the grapes in your vineyard, don't glean the vines after they are picked. Leave the remaining grapes for the foreigners, orphans, and widows. 22Remember that you were slaves in the land of Egypt. That is why I am giving you this command.

**24:19**
Lev 19:9-10
Deut 14:28-29
**24:20**
Lev 19:10

**24:8** Traditionally rendered *leprosy.* The Hebrew word used here can describe various skin diseases.

---

**24:1-4** Some think this passage supports divorce, but that is not the case. It simply recognizes a practice that already existed in Israel. All four verses must be read to understand the point of the passage; it certainly is not suggesting that a man divorce his wife on a whim. Divorce was a permanent and final act for the couple. Once divorced and remarried to others, they could never be remarried to each other (24:4). This restriction was to prevent casual remarriage after a frivolous separation. The intention was to make people think twice before divorcing.

**24:5** Newly married couples were to remain together their first year. This was to avoid placing an excessive burden upon a new, unproven relationship and to give it a chance to mature and strengthen before confronting it with numerous responsibilities. A gardener starts a tiny seedling in a small pot and allows it to take root before planting it in the field. Let your marriage grow strong by protecting your relationship from too many outside pressures and distractions—especially in the beginning. And

don't expect or demand so much from newlyweds that they have inadequate time or energy to establish their marriage.

**24:10-22** Throughout the Old Testament God told his people to treat the poor with justice. The powerless and poverty-stricken are often looked upon by some people as incompetent or lazy when, in fact, those facing that situation may be victims of oppression and circumstance. God says we must do all we can to help those who are needy. His justice did not permit the Israelites to insist on profits or quick payment from those who were less fortunate. Instead, his laws gave the poor every opportunity to better their situation, while providing humane options for those who couldn't. None of us is completely isolated from the poor; many of us face needs at one time or another. God wants us to treat each other fairly and do our part to help meet one another's needs.

**24:19-21** God's people were instructed to leave some of their harvest in the fields so travelers and the poor could gather it.

25:1
Deut 17:11

25:3
2 Cor 11:24

25:4
†1 Cor 9:9
†1 Tim 5:18

25:5
†Matt 22:24
Mark 12:19
†Luke 20:28

25:6
Ruth 4:5

25:9-10
Ruth 4:7-8

25:12
Deut 7:2

25:13
Lev 19:35
Prov 11:1; 16:11
Ezek 45:10-11

25:16
Prov 11:1

25:17
Exod 17:8-16

25:19
Deut 14:29

26:2
Exod 22:29;
23:16, 19

**25** "Suppose two people take a dispute to court, and the judges declare that one is right and the other is wrong. ²If the person in the wrong is sentenced to be flogged, the judge must command him to lie down and be beaten in his presence with the number of lashes appropriate to the crime. ³But never give more than forty lashes; more than forty lashes would publicly humiliate your neighbor.

⁴"You must not muzzle an ox to keep it from eating as it treads out the grain.

⁵"If two brothers are living together on the same property and one of them dies without a son, his widow may not be married to anyone from outside the family. Instead, her husband's brother should marry her and have intercourse with her to fulfill the duties of a brother-in-law. ⁶The first son she bears to him will be considered the son of the dead brother, so that his name will not be forgotten in Israel.

⁷"But if the man refuses to marry his brother's widow, she must go to the town gate and say to the elders assembled there, 'My husband's brother refuses to preserve his brother's name in Israel—he refuses to fulfill the duties of a brother-in-law by marrying me.' ⁸The elders of the town will then summon him and talk with him. If he still refuses and says, 'I don't want to marry her,' ⁹the widow must walk over to him in the presence of the elders, pull his sandal from his foot, and spit in his face. Then she must declare, 'This is what happens to a man who refuses to provide his brother with children.' ¹⁰Ever afterward in Israel his family will be referred to as 'the family of the man whose sandal was pulled off'!

¹¹"If two Israelite men get into a fight and the wife of one tries to rescue her husband by grabbing the testicles of the other man, ¹²you must cut off her hand. Show her no pity.

¹³"You must use accurate scales when you weigh out merchandise, ¹⁴and you must use full and honest measures. ¹⁵Yes, always use honest weights and measures, so that you may enjoy a long life in the land the LORD your God is giving you. ¹⁶All who cheat with dishonest weights and measures are detestable to the LORD your God.

¹⁷"Never forget what the Amalekites did to you as you came from Egypt. ¹⁸They attacked you when you were exhausted and weary, and they struck down those who were straggling behind. They had no fear of God. ¹⁹Therefore, when the LORD your God has given you rest from all your enemies in the land he is giving you as a special possession, you must destroy the Amalekites and erase their memory from under heaven. Never forget this!

### Harvest Offerings and Tithes

**26** "When you enter the land the LORD your God is giving you as a special possession and you have conquered it and settled there, ²put some of the first produce from each crop you harvest into a basket and bring it to the designated place of worship—the place the LORD your God chooses for his name to be honored. ³Go to the priest in charge at that time and say to him, 'With this gift I acknowledge to the LORD your God that I have entered the land he swore to our ancestors he would give us.' ⁴The priest will then take the basket from your hand and set it before the altar of the LORD your God.

---

This second gathering, called gleaning, was a way for them to provide food for themselves. Years later, Ruth obtained food for herself and Naomi by gleaning behind the reapers in Boaz's field, picking up the leftovers (Ruth 2:2). Because this law was being obeyed years after it was written, Ruth, a woman in Christ's lineage, was able to find food.

**25:1-3** At first glance these verses appear irrelevant today. But a closer look reveals some important principles about discipline. Are you responsible for the discipline of a child, a student, or an employee? Three important points will help you carry out your responsibility: (1) Let the punishment follow quickly after the offense; (2) let the degree of punishment reflect the seriousness of the offense; and (3) don't overdo the punishment. Discipline is swift, just, and restrained makes its point while preserving the dignity of the offender.

**25:4** What is the point of this Old Testament regulation? Oxen were often used to tread out the grain on a threshing floor. The animal was attached to a large millstone. As it walked around the millstone, its hooves trampled the grain, separating the kernels from the chaff. At the same time, the millstone ground the grain into flour. To muzzle the ox

would prevent it from eating while it was working. Paul used this illustration in the New Testament to argue that people productive in Christian work should not be denied its benefits—they should receive financial support (1 Corinthians 9:9-12; 1 Timothy 5:17, 18). The fact that a person is in Christian ministry doesn't mean he or she should be unfairly paid. There is also a broader application: Don't be stingy with those who work for you.

**25:5-10** This law describes a "levirate" marriage, the marriage of a widow to the brother of her dead husband. The purpose of such a marriage was to carry on the dead man's name and inheritance. Family ties were an important aspect of Israelite culture. The best way to be remembered was through your line of descendants. If a widow married someone outside the family, her first husband's line would come to an end. Tamar fought for this right in Genesis 38.

⁵"You must then say in the presence of the LORD your God, 'My ancestor Jacob was a wandering Aramean who went to live as a foreigner in Egypt. His family arrived few in number, but in Egypt they became a large and mighty nation. ⁶When the Egyptians oppressed and humiliated us by making us their slaves, ⁷we cried out to the LORD, the God of our ancestors. He heard our cries and saw our hardship, toil, and oppression. ⁸So the LORD brought us out of Egypt with a strong hand and powerful arm, with overwhelming terror, and with miraculous signs and wonders. ⁹He brought us to this place and gave us this land flowing with milk and honey! ¹⁰And now, O LORD, I have brought you the first portion of the harvest you have given me from the ground.' Then place the produce before the LORD your God, and bow to the ground in worship before him. ¹¹Afterward you may go and celebrate because of all the good things the LORD your God has given to you and your household. Remember to include the Levites and the foreigners living among you in the celebration.

¹²"Every third year you must offer a special tithe of your crops. In this year of the special tithe you must give your tithes to the Levites, foreigners, orphans, and widows, so that they will have enough to eat in your towns. ¹³Then you must declare in the presence of the LORD your God, 'I have taken the sacred gift from my house and have given it to the Levites, foreigners, orphans, and widows, just as you commanded me. I have not violated or forgotten any of your commands. ¹⁴I have not eaten any of it while in mourning; I have not handled it while I was ceremonially unclean; and I have not offered any of it to the dead. I have obeyed the LORD my God and have done everything you commanded me. ¹⁵Now look down from your holy dwelling place in heaven and bless your people Israel and the land you swore to our ancestors to give us—a land flowing with milk and honey.'

### A Call to Obey the LORD's Commands

¹⁶"Today the LORD your God has commanded you to obey all these decrees and regulations. So be careful to obey them wholeheartedly. ¹⁷You have declared today that the LORD is your God. And you have promised to walk in his ways, and to obey his decrees, commands, and regulations, and to do everything he tells you. ¹⁸The LORD has declared today that you are his people, his own special treasure, just as he promised, and that you must obey all his commands. ¹⁹And if you do, he will set you high above all the other nations he has made. Then you will receive praise, honor, and renown. You will be a nation that is holy to the LORD your God, just as he promised."

## 6. Consequences of obedience and disobedience
### The Altar on Mount Ebal

**27** Then Moses and the leaders of Israel gave this charge to the people: "Obey all these commands that I am giving you today. ²When you cross the Jordan River and enter the land the LORD your God is giving you, set up some large stones and coat them with plaster. ³Write this whole body of instruction on them when you cross the river to enter the land the LORD your God is giving you—a land flowing with milk and honey, just as the LORD, the God of your ancestors, promised you. ⁴When you cross the Jordan, set up these stones at Mount Ebal and coat them with plaster, as I am commanding you today.

⁵"Then build an altar there to the LORD your God, using natural, uncut stones. You must not shape the stones with an iron tool. ⁶Build the altar of uncut stones, and use it to offer burnt offerings to the LORD your God. ⁷Also sacrifice peace offerings on it, and celebrate by feasting there before the LORD your God. ⁸You must clearly write all these instructions on the stones coated with plaster."

**26:5**
Gen 43:1; 46:27
Deut 1:10; 10:22

**26:6**
Exod 1:11-12

**26:8**
Deut 4:34

**26:9**
Exod 3:8, 17

**26:11**
Deut 12:7, 12

**26:12**
Deut 14:28-29
Heb 7:5, 9-10

**26:15**
Zech 2:13

**26:16**
Deut 4:29

**26:17**
Ps 48:14

**26:18**
Deut 7:6

**26:19**
Deut 28:1

**27:2**
Josh 8:30-32

---

**26:5-10** This recitation of God's dealings with his people helped the people remember what God had done for them. What is the history of your relationship with God? Can you put into clear and concise words what God has done for you? Find a friend with whom you can share your spiritual journey. Telling your stories to each other will help you clearly understand your personal spiritual history, as well as encouraging and inspiring you both. Note: *Wandering* can mean lost or dying. Also, Arameans were the people of northern Syria and among the ancestors of Abraham. This is also used as a reference to Jacob, who spent many years there (Genesis 29–31) and got his two wives in Aram.

**26:12** This law is repeated from 14:28-29. The people were to give their tithe to the needy every third year. This amounts to one-third of their giving on a three-year cycle. Though we are not under this law today, the New Testament reminds us not to forget the poor. Consider giving one-third of your annual contribution to overseas ministries, or to relief for the poor, orphans, and widows.

**27:5, 6** The Lord had specified an altar made of natural, uncut stones so that the people would not begin worshiping the altars as idols. To use an iron tool on a stone of the altar would be to profane it (Exodus 20:24-25). Additionally, because the Israelites did not have the capacity to work with iron at this time, using iron tools might mean using the cooperation and expertise of other nations.

**27:9**
Deut 26:17

⁹Then Moses and the Levitical priests addressed all Israel as follows: "O Israel, be quiet and listen! Today you have become the people of the LORD your God. ¹⁰So you must obey the LORD your God by keeping all these commands and decrees that I am giving you today."

### Curses from Mount Ebal

**27:12**
Deut 11:26
Josh 8:33-35

¹¹That same day Moses also gave this charge to the people: ¹²"When you cross the Jordan River, the tribes of Simeon, Levi, Judah, Issachar, Joseph, and Benjamin must stand on Mount Gerizim to proclaim a blessing over the people. ¹³And the tribes of Reuben, Gad, Asher, Zebulun, Dan, and Naphtali must stand on Mount Ebal to proclaim a curse.

¹⁴"Then the Levites will shout to all the people of Israel:

**27:15**
Exod 20:4, 23
Lev 19:4
Deut 4:16; 5:8

¹⁵'Cursed is anyone who carves or casts an idol and secretly sets it up. These idols,
   the work of craftsmen, are detestable to the LORD.'
     And all the people will reply, 'Amen.'

**27:16**
Exod 21:17
Lev 20:9
Ezek 22:7

¹⁶'Cursed is anyone who dishonors father or mother.'
     And all the people will reply, 'Amen.'

**27:17**
Deut 19:14

¹⁷'Cursed is anyone who steals property from a neighbor by moving a boundary marker.'
     And all the people will reply, 'Amen.'

**27:18**
Lev 19:14

¹⁸'Cursed is anyone who leads a blind person astray on the road.'
     And all the people will reply, 'Amen.'

**27:19**
Exod 22:21
Lev 19:33
Deut 10:18

¹⁹'Cursed is anyone who denies justice to foreigners, orphans, or widows.'
     And all the people will reply, 'Amen.'

**27:20**
Lev 18:8; 20:11
Deut 22:30

²⁰'Cursed is anyone who has sexual intercourse with one of his father's wives, for he has
   violated his father.'
     And all the people will reply, 'Amen.'

**27:21**
Exod 22:19
Lev 18:23; 20:15

²¹'Cursed is anyone who has sexual intercourse with an animal.'
     And all the people will reply, 'Amen.'

**27:22**
Lev 18:9; 20:17

²²'Cursed is anyone who has sexual intercourse with his sister, whether she is the
   daughter of his father or his mother.'
     And all the people will reply, 'Amen.'

**27:23**
Lev 18:17; 20:14

²³'Cursed is anyone who has sexual intercourse with his mother-in-law.'
     And all the people will reply, 'Amen.'

**27:24**
Exod 21:12
Lev 24:17
Num 35:30

²⁴'Cursed is anyone who attacks a neighbor in secret.'
     And all the people will reply, 'Amen.'

**27:25**
Exod 23:8
Deut 10:17

²⁵'Cursed is anyone who accepts payment to kill an innocent person.'
     And all the people will reply, 'Amen.'

**27:26**
Deut 28:15
Gal 3:10

²⁶'Cursed is anyone who does not affirm and obey the terms of these instructions.'
     And all the people will reply, 'Amen.'

---

**27:9, 10** Moses was reviewing the law with the new generation of people. When we decide to believe in God, we must also decide to follow his ways. What we do shows what we really believe. Can people tell that you are a member of God's family?

**27:15-26** These curses were a series of oaths, spoken by the priests and affirmed by the people, by which the people promised to stay away from wrong actions. By saying *Amen,* "So be it," the people took responsibility for their actions. Sometimes looking at a list of curses like this gives us the idea that God has a bad temper and is out to crush anyone who steps out of line. But we need to see these restrictions not as threats, but as loving warnings about the plain facts of life. Just as we warn children to stay away from hot stoves and busy streets, God warns us to stay away from dangerous actions. The natural law of his universe makes it clear that wrongdoing toward others or God has tragic consequences. God is merciful enough to tell us this truth plainly. Motivated by love and not anger, his strong words help

us avoid the serious consequences that result from neglecting God or wronging others. But God does not leave us with only curses or consequences. Immediately following these curses, we discover the great blessings (positive consequences) that come from living for God (28:1-14). These give us extra incentive to obey God's laws. While all these blessings may not come in our lifetime on earth, those who obey God will experience the fullness of his blessing when he establishes the new heaven and the new earth.

## Blessings for Obedience

**28** "If you fully obey the LORD your God and carefully keep all his commands that I am giving you today, the LORD your God will set you high above all the nations of the world. 2 You will experience all these blessings if you obey the LORD your God:

3 Your towns and your fields
   will be blessed.
4 Your children and your crops
   will be blessed.
The offspring of your herds and flocks
   will be blessed.
5 Your fruit baskets and breadboards
   will be blessed.
6 Wherever you go and whatever you do,
   you will be blessed.

7 "The LORD will conquer your enemies when they attack you. They will attack you from one direction, but they will scatter from you in seven!

8 "The LORD will guarantee a blessing on everything you do and will fill your storehouses with grain. The LORD your God will bless you in the land he is giving you.

9 "If you obey the commands of the LORD your God and walk in his ways, the LORD will establish you as his holy people as he swore he would do. 10 Then all the nations of the world will see that you are a people claimed by the LORD, and they will stand in awe of you.

11 "The LORD will give you prosperity in the land he swore to your ancestors to give you, blessing you with many children, numerous livestock, and abundant crops. 12 The LORD will send rain at the proper time from his rich treasury in the heavens and will bless all the work you do. You will lend to many nations, but you will never need to borrow from them. 13 If you listen to these commands of the LORD your God that I am giving you today, and if you carefully obey them, the LORD will make you the head and not the tail, and you will always be on top and never at the bottom. 14 You must not turn away from any of the commands I am giving you today, nor follow after other gods and worship them.

## Curses for Disobedience

15 "But if you refuse to listen to the LORD your God and do not obey all the commands and decrees I am giving you today, all these curses will come and overwhelm you:

16 Your towns and your fields
   will be cursed.
17 Your fruit baskets and breadboards
   will be cursed.
18 Your children and your crops
   will be cursed.
The offspring of your herds and flocks
   will be cursed.
19 Wherever you go and whatever you do,
   you will be cursed.

20 "The LORD himself will send on you curses, confusion, and frustration in everything you do, until at last you are completely destroyed for doing evil and abandoning me. 21 The LORD will afflict you with diseases until none of you are left in the land you are about to enter and occupy. 22 The LORD will strike you with wasting diseases, fever, and inflammation, with scorching heat and drought, and with blight and mildew. These disasters will pursue you until you die. 23 The skies above will be as unyielding as bronze, and the earth beneath will be as hard as iron. 24 The LORD will change the rain that falls on your land into powder, and dust will pour down from the sky until you are destroyed.

25 "The LORD will cause you to be defeated by your enemies. You will attack your enemies from one direction, but you will scatter from them in seven! You will be an object of horror to all the kingdoms of the earth. 26 Your corpses will be food for all the scavenging birds and wild animals, and no one will be there to chase them away.

**28:1**
Exod 15:26; 23:22
Lev 26:3
Deut 7:12; 11:13

**28:2**
Jer 32:24

**28:3**
Ps 144:15

**28:4**
Gen 49:25

**28:6**
Ps 121:8

**28:7**
Lev 26:8, 17

**28:8**
Deut 15:4

**28:9**
Exod 19:5

**28:11**
Deut 28:2-6, 8

**28:12**
Lev 26:4
Deut 11:14; 23:20

**28:13**
Deut 28:1, 44

**28:14**
Deut 5:32-33

**28:15**
Lev 26:14
Josh 23:15-16

**28:20**
Deut 8:11; 28:25

**28:21**
Lev 26:25
Num 14:12
Amos 4:10

**28:23**
Lev 26:19

**28:24**
Deut 11:17
1 Kgs 17:1
Jer 14:1

**28:25**
2 Chr 29:8
Isa 30:17
Jer 15:4

**28:26**
Ps 79:2
Jer 7:33; 16:4;
19:7; 34:20

---

28:23, 24 This curse is referring to a drought.

**28:27**
Exod 9:9; 15:26
Deut 7:15
1 Sam 5:6, 9, 12

**28:29**
Exod 10:21
Job 5:14
Isa 59:10

**28:30**
Deut 20:6-7
Job 31:10
Isa 65:22
Amos 5:11

**28:34**
Deut 28:28

**28:35**
Job 2:7

**28:36**
2 Kgs 17:4, 6;
24:12, 14; 25:7, 11

**28:38**
Lev 26:20
Isa 5:10
Mic 6:15

**28:41**
Deut 28:32

**28:42**
Deut 28:38

**28:44**
Deut 28:12-13

**28:45**
Deut 4:25-26

**28:47**
Deut 32:15

**28:49**
Isa 5:26; 7:18
Jer 5:15

**28:52**
Jer 10:17-18
Zeph 1:14-15

**28:53**
Lev 26:29
Jer 19:9
Lam 2:20; 4:10

27"The LORD will afflict you with the boils of Egypt and with tumors, scurvy, and the itch, from which you cannot be cured. 28The LORD will strike you with madness, blindness, and panic. 29 You will grope around in broad daylight like a blind person groping in the darkness, but you will not find your way. You will be oppressed and robbed continually, and no one will come to save you.

30"You will be engaged to a woman, but another man will sleep with her. You will build a house, but someone else will live in it. You will plant a vineyard, but you will never enjoy its fruit. 31Your ox will be butchered before your eyes, but you will not eat a single bite of the meat. Your donkey will be taken from you, never to be returned. Your sheep and goats will be given to your enemies, and no one will be there to help you. 32 You will watch as your sons and daughters are taken away as slaves. Your heart will break for them, but you won't be able to help them. 33A foreign nation you have never heard about will eat the crops you worked so hard to grow. You will suffer under constant oppression and harsh treatment. 34You will go mad because of all the tragedy you see around you. 35The LORD will cover your knees and legs with incurable boils. In fact, you will be covered from head to foot.

36"The LORD will exile you and your king to a nation unknown to you and your ancestors. There in exile you will worship gods of wood and stone! 37 You will become an object of horror, ridicule, and mockery among all the nations to which the LORD sends you.

38"You will plant much but harvest little, for locusts will eat your crops. 39 You will plant vineyards and care for them, but you will not drink the wine or eat the grapes, for worms will destroy the vines. 40You will grow olive trees throughout your land, but you will never use the olive oil, for the fruit will drop before it ripens. 41You will have sons and daughters, but you will lose them, for they will be led away into captivity. 42 Swarms of insects will destroy your trees and crops.

43"The foreigners living among you will become stronger and stronger, while you become weaker and weaker. 44They will lend money to you, but you will not lend to them. They will be the head, and you will be the tail!

45"If you refuse to listen to the LORD your God and to obey the commands and decrees he has given you, all these curses will pursue and overtake you until you are destroyed. 46These horrors will serve as a sign and warning among you and your descendants forever. 47If you do not serve the LORD your God with joy and enthusiasm for the abundant benefits you have received, 48you will serve your enemies whom the LORD will send against you. You will be left hungry, thirsty, naked, and lacking in everything. The LORD will put an iron yoke on your neck, oppressing you harshly until he has destroyed you.

49"The LORD will bring a distant nation against you from the end of the earth, and it will swoop down on you like a vulture. It is a nation whose language you do not understand, 50a fierce and heartless nation that shows no respect for the old and no pity for the young. 51Its armies will devour your livestock and crops, and you will be destroyed. They will leave you no grain, new wine, olive oil, calves, or lambs, and you will starve to death. 52 They will attack your cities until all the fortified walls in your land—the walls you trusted to protect you—are knocked down. They will attack all the towns in the land the LORD your God has given you.

53"The siege and terrible distress of the enemy's attack will be so severe that you will eat the flesh of your own sons and daughters, whom the LORD your God has given you. 54The most tenderhearted man among you will have no compassion for his own brother, his beloved wife, and his surviving children. 55He will refuse to share with them the flesh he is devouring—the flesh of one of his own children—because he has nothing else to eat during the siege and terrible distress that your enemy will inflict on all your towns. 56The most tender and delicate woman among you—so delicate she would not so much as touch the ground with her foot—will be selfish toward the husband she loves and toward her own son or daughter. 57She will hide from them the afterbirth and the new baby she has borne, so that she herself can secretly eat them. She will have nothing else to eat during the siege and terrible distress that your enemy will inflict on all your towns.

---

**28:34** One of the curses for those who rejected God was that they would go mad from seeing all the tragedy around them. Do you ever feel that you will go crazy if you hear about one more rape, kidnapping, murder, or war? Much of the world's evil is a result of people's failure to acknowledge and serve God. When you hear bad news, don't groan helplessly as do unbelievers who

have no hope for the future. Remind yourself that in spite of it all, God has ultimate control and will one day come back to make everything right.

**28:36** This happened when Assyria and Babylonia took the Israelites captive to their lands (2 Kings 17:23; 25:11).

58"If you refuse to obey all the words of instruction that are written in this book, and if you do not fear the glorious and awesome name of the LORD your God, 59then the LORD will overwhelm you and your children with indescribable plagues. These plagues will be intense and without relief, making you miserable and unbearably sick. 60He will afflict you with all the diseases of Egypt that you feared so much, and you will have no relief. 61The LORD will afflict you with every sickness and plague there is, even those not mentioned in this Book of Instruction, until you are destroyed. 62Though you become as numerous as the stars in the sky, few of you will be left because you would not listen to the LORD your God.

63"Just as the LORD has found great pleasure in causing you to prosper and multiply, the LORD will find pleasure in destroying you. You will be torn from the land you are about to enter and occupy. 64For the LORD will scatter you among all the nations from one end of the earth to the other. There you will worship foreign gods that neither you nor your ancestors have known, gods made of wood and stone! 65There among those nations you will find no peace or place to rest. And the LORD will cause your heart to tremble, your eyesight to fail, and your soul to despair. 66Your life will constantly hang in the balance. You will live night and day in fear, unsure if you will survive. 67In the morning you will say, 'If only it were night!' And in the evening you will say, 'If only it were morning!' For you will be terrified by the awful horrors you see around you. 68Then the LORD will send you back to Egypt in ships, to a destination I promised you would never see again. There you will offer to sell yourselves to your enemies as slaves, but no one will buy you."

**28:60**
Deut 28:21, 27

**28:62**
Deut 1:10

**28:63**
Jer 45:4

**28:64**
Lev 26:33
Deut 4:27; 32:17
Neh 1:8

**28:65**
Lam 1:3

**28:66**
Heb 10:27

**29** 1*These are the terms of the covenant the LORD commanded Moses to make with the Israelites while they were in the land of Moab, in addition to the covenant he had made with them at Mount Sinai.*

**29:1**
Lev 27:34
Deut 1:1-5; 5:1

## C. A CALL FOR COMMITMENT TO GOD: MOSES' THIRD ADDRESS (29:2—30:20)

After reviewing God's laws, Moses calls for commitment, urging the people to honor the contract they had previously made with God. Knowing God's Word is not enough; we must obey it.

### Moses Reviews the Covenant

2*Moses summoned all the Israelites and said to them, "You have seen with your own eyes everything the LORD did in the land of Egypt to Pharaoh and to all his servants and to his whole country—3all the great tests of strength, the miraculous signs, and the amazing wonders. 4But to this day the LORD has not given you minds that understand, nor eyes that see, nor ears that hear! 5For forty years I led you through the wilderness, yet your clothes and sandals did not wear out. 6You ate no bread and drank no wine or other alcoholic drink, but he gave you food so you would know that he is the LORD your God.

7"When we came here, King Sihon of Heshbon and King Og of Bashan came out to fight against us, but we defeated them. 8We took their land and gave it to the tribes of Reuben and Gad and to the half-tribe of Manasseh as their grant of land.

9"Therefore, obey the terms of this covenant so that you will prosper in everything you do. 10All of you—tribal leaders, elders, officers, all the men of Israel—are standing today in the presence of the LORD your God. 11Your little ones and your wives are with you, as well as

**29:2**
Exod 19:4
**29:4**
Isa 6:9-10
Acts 28:26
†Rom 11:8
**29:5**
Deut 8:2, 4
**29:7**
Num 21:21
Deut 1:2-5; 2:26
**29:8**
Num 32:31
Deut 3:12
**29:9**
Exod 19:5
Deut 4:6
Josh 1:7
**29:11**
Josh 9:21, 23, 27

**29:1a** Verse 29:1 is numbered 28:69 in Hebrew text.   **29:1b** Hebrew *Horeb*, another name for Sinai.   **29:2** Verses 29:2-29 are numbered 29:1-28 in Hebrew text.

---

**28:64** This severe warning tragically came true when Israel was defeated and carried away into captivity by Assyria (722 B.C.), and Judah to Babylonia (586 B.C.). Later, in A.D. 70, Roman oppression forced many Jews to flee their homeland. Thus, the people were scattered throughout the various nations.

**29:1ff** At Mount Sinai, 40 years earlier, God and Israel had made a covenant (Exodus 19–20). Although there were many parts to the covenant (read the books of Exodus, Leviticus, and Numbers), its purpose can be summed up in two sentences: God promised to bless the Israelites by making them the nation through whom the rest of the world could know God. In return, the Israelites promised to love and obey God in order to receive physical and spiritual blessings. Here Moses reviewed this covenant. God was still keeping his part of the bargain (and he always would), but the Israelites were already neglecting their

part. Moses restated the covenant to warn the people that if they did not keep their part of the agreement, they would experience severe discipline.

**29:5** Just as the people of Israel did not notice God's care for them along their journey, we sometimes do not notice all of the ways that God takes care of us—that all of our daily needs have been supplied and we have been well fed and well clothed. Worse yet, we mistakenly take the credit ourselves for being good providers instead of recognizing God's hand in the process.

**29:9** What is the best way to prosper in life? For the Israelites, their first step was to keep their part of the covenant. They were to love God with all of their heart, soul, and strength (6:4, 5). We, too, are to seek first the Kingdom of God and his righteousness (Matthew 6:33); then true success in life will follow as a blessing from the hand of God.

the foreigners living among you who chop your wood and carry your water. 12You are standing here today to enter into the covenant of the LORD your God. The LORD is making this covenant, including the curses. 13By entering into the covenant today, he will establish you as his people and confirm that he is your God, just as he promised you and as he swore to your ancestors Abraham, Isaac, and Jacob.

14"But you are not the only ones with whom I am making this covenant with its curses. 15I am making this covenant both with you who stand here today in the presence of the LORD our God, and also with the future generations who are not standing here today.

16"You remember how we lived in the land of Egypt and how we traveled through the lands of enemy nations as we left. 17You have seen their detestable practices and their idols* made of wood, stone, silver, and gold. 18I am making this covenant with you so that no one among you—no man, woman, clan, or tribe—will turn away from the LORD our God to worship these gods of other nations, and so that no root among you bears bitter and poisonous fruit.

19"Those who hear the warnings of this curse should not congratulate themselves, thinking, 'I am safe, even though I am following the desires of my own stubborn heart.' This would lead to utter ruin! 20The LORD will never pardon such people. Instead his anger and jealousy will burn against them. All the curses written in this book will come down on them, and the LORD will erase their names from under heaven. 21The LORD will separate them from all the tribes of Israel, to pour out on them all the curses of the covenant recorded in this Book of Instruction.

22"Then the generations to come, both your own descendants and the foreigners who come from distant lands, will see the devastation of the land and the diseases the LORD inflicts on it. 23They will exclaim, 'The whole land is devastated by sulfur and salt. It is a wasteland with nothing planted and nothing growing, not even a blade of grass. It is like the cities of Sodom and Gomorrah, Admah and Zeboiim, which the LORD destroyed in his intense anger.'

24"And all the surrounding nations will ask, 'Why has the LORD done this to this land? Why was he so angry?'

25"And the answer will be, 'This happened because the people of the land abandoned the covenant that the LORD, the God of their ancestors, made with them when he brought them out of the land of Egypt. 26Instead, they turned away to serve and worship gods they had not known before, gods that were not from the LORD. 27That is why the LORD's anger has burned against this land, bringing down on it every curse recorded in this book. 28In great anger and fury the LORD uprooted his people from their land and banished them to another land, where they still live today!'

29"The LORD our God has secrets known to no one. We are not accountable for them, but we and our children are accountable forever for all that he has revealed to us, so that we may obey all the terms of these instructions.

### A Call to Return to the LORD

**30** "In the future, when you experience all these blessings and curses I have listed for you, and when you are living among the nations to which the LORD your God has exiled you, take to heart all these instructions. 2If at that time you and your children return to the LORD your God, and if you obey with all your heart and all your soul all the commands I

29:17 The Hebrew term (literally *round things*) probably alludes to dung.

*Cross references left margin:*
29:13 Gen 17:7; Exod 6:7
29:14 Jer 31:31; Heb 8:7
29:17 Exod 20:23; Deut 4:28; 28:36
29:18 Deut 13:6; 32:32; Heb 12:15
29:20 Deut 9:14; 2 Kgs 14:27; Pss 74:1; 80:4
29:22 Jer 19:8
29:23 Gen 19:24; Isa 1:7; 34:9; 64:11
29:24 1 Kgs 9:8; Jer 22:8-9
29:25 2 Kgs 17:9; 2 Chr 36:13
29:27 Deut 29:20
29:28 1 Kgs 14:15; Ezek 19:12
29:29 John 5:39; Acts 1:7; 17:11
30:1 Lev 26:40-41; Deut 4:30; 11:26
30:2 Deut 4:29-30; Neh 1:9

**29:18** Moses cautioned that the day the Hebrews chose to turn from God, a root would be planted that would produce bitter and poisonous fruit (see Hebrews 12:15). When we decide to do what we know is wrong, we plant an evil seed that begins to grow out of control, eventually yielding a crop of sorrow and pain. But we can prevent those seeds of sin from taking root. If you have done something wrong, confess it to God and others immediately. If the seed never finds fertile soil, its bitter fruit will never ripen.

**29:29** There are some secrets God has chosen not to reveal to us, possibly for the following reasons: (1) Our finite minds cannot fully understand the infinite aspects of God's nature and the universe (Ecclesiastes 3:11); (2) some things are unnecessary for us to know until we are more mature; (3) God is infinite and all-knowing, and we do not have the capacity to know everything he does. This verse shows that although God has not told us everything there is to know about obeying him, he has told us

enough. Thus, disobedience comes from an act of the will, not a lack of knowledge. Through God's Word we know enough about him to be saved by faith and to serve him. We must not use the limitation of our knowledge as an excuse to reject his claim on our life.

**30:1-6** Moses told the Hebrews that when they were ready to return to God, he would be ready to receive them. God's mercy is unbelievable. It goes far beyond what we can imagine. Even if the Jews deliberately walked away from him and ruined their lives, God would still take them back. God would give them inward spiritual renewal. God wants to forgive us and bring us back to himself, too. Some people will not learn this until their world has crashed in around them. Then the sorrow and pain seem to open their eyes to what God has been saying all along. Are you separated from God by sin? No matter how far you have wandered, God promises a fresh beginning if only you will turn to him.

have given you today, [3]then the LORD your God will restore your fortunes. He will have mercy on you and gather you back from all the nations where he has scattered you. [4]Even though you are banished to the ends of the earth, the LORD your God will gather you from there and bring you back again. [5]The LORD your God will return you to the land that belonged to your ancestors, and you will possess that land again. Then he will make you even more prosperous and numerous than your ancestors!

[6]"The LORD your God will change your heart* and the hearts of all your descendants, so that you will love him with all your heart and soul and so you may live! [7]The LORD your God will inflict all these curses on your enemies and on those who hate and persecute you. [8]Then you will again obey the LORD and keep all his commands that I am giving you today.

[9]"The LORD your God will then make you successful in everything you do. He will give you many children and numerous livestock, and he will cause your fields to produce abundant harvests, for the LORD will again delight in being good to you as he was to your ancestors. [10]The LORD your God will delight in you if you obey his voice and keep the commands and decrees written in this Book of Instruction, and if you turn to the LORD your God with all your heart and soul.

### The Choice of Life or Death

[11]"This command I am giving you today is not too difficult for you to understand, and it is not beyond your reach. [12]It is not kept in heaven, so distant that you must ask, 'Who will go up to heaven and bring it down so we can hear it and obey?' [13]It is not kept beyond the sea, so far away that you must ask, 'Who will cross the sea to bring it to us so we can hear it and obey?' [14]No, the message is very close at hand; it is on your lips and in your heart so that you can obey it.

[15]"Now listen! Today I am giving you a choice between life and death, between prosperity and disaster. [16]For I command you this day to love the LORD your God and to keep his commands, decrees, and regulations by walking in his ways. If you do this, you will live and multiply, and the LORD your God will bless you and the land you are about to enter and occupy.

[17]"But if your heart turns away and you refuse to listen, and if you are drawn away to serve and worship other gods, [18]then I warn you now that you will certainly be destroyed. You will not live a long, good life in the land you are crossing the Jordan to occupy.

[19]"Today I have given you the choice between life and death, between blessings and curses. Now I call on heaven and earth to witness the choice you make. Oh, that you would choose life, so that you and your descendants might live! [20]You can make this choice by loving the LORD your God, obeying him, and committing yourself firmly to him. This* is the key to your life. And if you love and obey the LORD, you will live long in the land the LORD swore to give your ancestors Abraham, Isaac, and Jacob."

## D. THE CHANGE IN LEADERSHIP: MOSES' LAST DAYS (31:1—34:12)
Realizing that he is about to die, Moses commissions Joshua, records the laws in a permanent form, and teaches a special song to the Israelites. Thus, Moses prepared the people for his departure. Similarly, we should not allow others to become dependent upon us for their spiritual growth but help them to become dependent upon God.

### Joshua Becomes Israel's Leader

**31** When Moses had finished giving these instructions* to all the people of Israel, [2]he said, "I am now 120 years old, and I am no longer able to lead you. The LORD has told me, 'You will not cross the Jordan River.' [3]But the LORD your God himself will cross over ahead of you. He will destroy the nations living there, and you will take possession of their land. Joshua will lead you across the river, just as the LORD promised.

[4]"The LORD will destroy the nations living in the land, just as he destroyed Sihon and Og,

**30:3**
Gen 28:15
Matt 23:37
John 11:51-52
**30:4**
Isa 43:6
**30:5**
Deut 13:17
Jer 29:14; 30:3
**30:7**
Deut 7:15
**30:9**
Deut 15:10; 29:9
**30:10**
Deut 4:29
**30:11**
Isa 45:19
**30:12-14**
†Rom 10:6-8
**30:15**
Deut 11:26
Jer 21:8
Matt 7:13-14
**30:16**
Deut 4:1; 6:5
**30:18**
Deut 4:26
**30:19**
Deut 4:26; 30:1
**30:20**
Deut 10:20; 13:4
**31:2**
Deut 34:7
**31:3**
Num 27:18

---

**30:6** Hebrew *circumcise your heart.*    **30:20** Or *He.*    **31:1** As in Dead Sea Scrolls and Greek version; Masoretic Text reads *Moses went and spoke.*

---

**30:11-14** God has called us to keep his commands, while reminding us that his laws are not hidden from us or beyond our reach. Have you ever said you would obey God if you knew what he wanted? Have you ever complained that obedience is too difficult for a mere human? These are unacceptable excuses. God's laws are written in the Bible and are clearly evident in the world around us. Obeying them is reasonable, sensible, and beneficial.

The most difficult part of obeying God's laws is simply deciding to start now. Paul refers to this passage in Romans 10:5-8.
**30:19, 20** Moses challenged Israel to choose life, to obey God, and therefore to continue to experience his blessings. God doesn't force his will on anyone. He lets us decide whether to follow him or reject him. This decision, however, is a life-or-death matter. God wants us to realize this, for he would like us all to choose life. Daily, in each new situation, we must affirm and reinforce this commitment.

**31:6**
Deut 20:1
Heb 13:5

**31:7**
Deut 1:38; 3:28

the kings of the Amorites. ⁵The Lᴏʀᴅ will hand over to you the people who live there, and you must deal with them as I have commanded you. ⁶So be strong and courageous! Do not be afraid and do not panic before them. For the Lᴏʀᴅ your God will personally go ahead of you. He will neither fail you nor abandon you."

⁷Then Moses called for Joshua, and as all Israel watched, he said to him, "Be strong and courageous! For you will lead these people into the land that the Lᴏʀᴅ swore to their ancestors he would give them. You are the one who will divide it among them as their grants of land. ⁸Do not be afraid or discouraged, for the Lᴏʀᴅ will personally go ahead of you. He will be with you; he will neither fail you nor abandon you."

### Public Reading of the Book of Instruction

**31:9**
Num 4:5-6
Deut 10:8

**31:10**
Deut 15:1

**31:12**
Deut 4:10

⁹So Moses wrote this entire body of instruction in a book and gave it to the priests, who carried the Ark of the Lᴏʀᴅ's Covenant, and to the elders of Israel. ¹⁰Then Moses gave them this command: "At the end of every seventh year, the Year of Release, during the Festival of Shelters, ¹¹you must read this Book of Instruction to all the people of Israel when they assemble before the Lᴏʀᴅ your God at the place he chooses. ¹²Call them all together—men, women, children, and the foreigners living in your towns—so they may hear this Book of Instruction and learn to fear the Lᴏʀᴅ your God and carefully obey all the terms of these instructions. ¹³Do this so that your children who have not known these instructions will hear them and will learn to fear the Lᴏʀᴅ your God. Do this as long as you live in the land you are crossing the Jordan to occupy."

### Israel's Disobedience Predicted

**31:14**
Num 27:13
Deut 34:5

**31:15**
Exod 33:9

**31:16**
Deut 4:25; 32:50
Judg 2:11; 10:6

**31:17**
Judg 2:12-14

¹⁴Then the Lᴏʀᴅ said to Moses, "The time has come for you to die. Call Joshua and present yourselves at the Tabernacle,* so that I may commission him there." So Moses and Joshua went and presented themselves at the Tabernacle. ¹⁵And the Lᴏʀᴅ appeared to them in a pillar of cloud that stood at the entrance to the sacred tent.

¹⁶The Lᴏʀᴅ said to Moses, "You are about to die and join your ancestors. After you are gone, these people will begin to worship foreign gods, the gods of the land where they are going. They will abandon me and break my covenant that I have made with them. ¹⁷Then my anger will blaze forth against them. I will abandon them, hiding my face from them, and they will be devoured. Terrible trouble will come down on them, and on that day they will say, 'These disasters have come down on us because God is no longer among us!' ¹⁸At that time I will hide my face from them on account of all the evil they commit by worshiping other gods.

**31:20**
Deut 6:10-12; 8:19;
11:16-17

**31:21**
Lev 26:41

¹⁹"So write down the words of this song, and teach it to the people of Israel. Help them learn it, so it may serve as a witness for me against them. ²⁰For I will bring them into the land I swore to give their ancestors—a land flowing with milk and honey. There they will become prosperous, eat all the food they want, and become fat. But they will begin to worship other gods; they will despise me and break my covenant. ²¹And when great disasters come down on them, this song will stand as evidence against them, for it will never be forgotten by their descendants. I know the intentions of these people, even now before they have entered the land I swore to give them."

²²So that very day Moses wrote down the words of the song and taught it to the Israelites.

²³Then the Lᴏʀᴅ commissioned Joshua son of Nun with these words: "Be strong and courageous, for you must bring the people of Israel into the land I swore to give them. I will be with you."

**31:25**
Deut 31:9

²⁴When Moses had finished writing this entire body of instruction in a book, ²⁵he gave

**31:14** Hebrew *Tent of Meeting;* also in 31:14b.

---

**31:10-13** The laws were to be read to the whole assembly so that everyone, including the children, could hear them. Every seven years the entire nation would gather together and listen as a priest read the law to them. There were no books, Bibles, or newsstands to spread God's word, so the people had to rely on word of mouth and an accurate memory. Memorization was an important part of worship because if everyone knew the law, ignorance would be no excuse for breaking it. To fulfill God's purpose and will in our lives, we need the content and substance of his Word in our hearts and minds. For the Hebrews, this process began in childhood. Teaching our children and new believers should be one of our top priorities. Our finest teachers, best resources, and most careful thought should be directed toward showing young believers how to follow God in all life's situations.

**31:23** Joshua had been appointed to take over the leadership of Israel and guide the people into the Promised Land (Moses could not enter the land due to his disobedience—Numbers 20:12). Joshua, first mentioned in Exodus 17:9, had been Moses' assistant for many years (Joshua 1:1). One of his key qualifications was his faith. As one of the 12 scouts to first enter Canaan, only he and Caleb believed that God could help Israel conquer the land (Numbers 13:1–14:30). Moses told Joshua to be strong and courageous twice in this chapter (31:7, 23). Indeed, this was a frightening task with three million people to care for, settle disputes for, and lead into battle. Finding courage would be Joshua's greatest test. He was strong and courageous because he knew God was with him and because he had faith that God would do all he had promised Israel.

this command to the Levites who carried the Ark of the Lord's Covenant: 26"Take this Book of Instruction and place it beside the Ark of the Covenant of the Lord your God, so it may remain there as a witness against the people of Israel. 27For I know how rebellious and stubborn you are. Even now, while I am still alive and am here with you, you have rebelled against the Lord. How much more rebellious will you be after my death!

28"Now summon all the elders and officials of your tribes, so that I can speak to them directly and call heaven and earth to witness against them. 29I know that after my death you will become utterly corrupt and will turn from the way I have commanded you to follow. In the days to come, disaster will come down on you, for you will do what is evil in the Lord's sight, making him very angry with your actions."

## The Song of Moses

30So Moses recited this entire song publicly to the assembly of Israel:

# 32

1"Listen, O heavens, and I will speak!
   Hear, O earth, the words that I say!
2 Let my teaching fall on you like rain;
   let my speech settle like dew.
Let my words fall like rain on tender grass,
   like gentle showers on young plants.
3 I will proclaim the name of the Lord;
   how glorious is our God!
4 He is the Rock; his deeds are perfect.
   Everything he does is just and fair.
He is a faithful God who does no wrong;
   how just and upright he is!

5 "But they have acted corruptly toward him;
   when they act so perversely,
are they really his children?*
   They are a deceitful and twisted generation.
6 Is this the way you repay the Lord,
   you foolish and senseless people?
Isn't he your Father who created you?
   Has he not made you and established you?

7 Remember the days of long ago;
   think about the generations past.
Ask your father, and he will inform you.
   Inquire of your elders, and they will tell you.
8 When the Most High assigned lands to the nations,
   when he divided up the human race,
he established the boundaries of the peoples
   according to the number in his heavenly court.*

9 "For the people of Israel belong to the Lord;
   Jacob is his special possession.
10 He found them in a desert land,
   in an empty, howling wasteland.
He surrounded them and watched over them;
   he guarded them as he would guard his own eyes.*

**32:1** Deut 4:26; Isa 1:2
**32:2** Ps 72:6; Isa 55:10
**32:3** Gen 18:25; Exod 34:5-6; Deut 3:24
**32:4** Gen 49:24; Deut 32:18; 2 Sam 22:2
**32:5** Deut 4:25; 31:27; Matt 17:17
**32:6** Deut 1:31; 32:28
**32:7** Deut 7:18-19
**32:9** 1 Kgs 8:51; Jer 10:16
**32:10** Ps 17:8
**31:27** Deut 9:7, 24
**31:28** Deut 30:19; 32:1
**31:29** Deut 32:5

32:5 The meaning of the Hebrew is uncertain.   32:8 As in Dead Sea Scrolls, which read *the number of the sons of God,* and Greek version, which reads *the number of the angels of God;* Masoretic Text reads *the number of the sons of Israel.*   32:10 Hebrew *as the pupil of his eye.*

**31:27-29** Moses knew that the Israelites, in spite of all they had seen of God's work, were rebellious at heart. They deserved God's punishment, although they often received his mercy instead. We, too, are stubborn and rebellious by nature. Throughout our lives we struggle with sin. Repentance once a month or once a week is not enough. We must constantly turn from our sins to God and let him, in his mercy, save us.

**32:1ff** Moses was not only a great prophet but also a song leader. After three sermons, he changed the form of his message to singing. Sometimes reciting something in a different form makes it easier to remember. This song gives a brief history of Israel. It reminds the people of their mistakes, warns them to avoid repetition of those mistakes, and offers the hope that comes only in trusting God.

**32:10, 11** The Israelites had no excuse for abandoning God. He had shielded them like a kindly shepherd. He had guarded

**32:11**
Exod 19:4
Pss 17:8; 18:10-18

11 Like an eagle that rouses her chicks
   and hovers over her young,
so he spread his wings to take them up
   and carried them safely on his pinions.

**32:12**
Deut 4:35
Isa 43:12

12 The LORD alone guided them;
   they followed no foreign gods.

**32:13**
Job 29:6
Ps 81:16

13 He let them ride over the highlands
   and feast on the crops of the fields.
He nourished them with honey from the rock
   and olive oil from the stony ground.

**32:14**
Ps 147:14

14 He fed them yogurt from the herd
   and milk from the flock,
together with the fat of lambs.
He gave them choice rams from Bashan, and goats,
   together with the choicest wheat.
You drank the finest wine,
   made from the juice of grapes.

**32:15**
Judg 10:6

15 "But Israel* soon became fat and unruly;
   the people grew heavy, plump, and stuffed!
Then they abandoned the God who had made them;
   they made light of the Rock of their salvation.

**32:16**
Pss 78:58; 106:29

16 They stirred up his jealousy by worshiping foreign gods;
   they provoked his fury with detestable deeds.

**32:17**
Lev 17:7
1 Cor 10:20

17 They offered sacrifices to demons, which are not God,
   to gods they had not known before,
to new gods only recently arrived,
   to gods their ancestors had never feared.

**32:18**
Ps 106:21
Deut 8:11; 32:4

18 You neglected the Rock who had fathered you;
   you forgot the God who had given you birth.

**32:19**
Lev 26:30
Ps 106:40

19 "The LORD saw this and drew back,
   provoked to anger by his own sons and daughters.

**32:20**
Deut 32:5

20 He said, 'I will abandon them;
   then see what becomes of them.
For they are a twisted generation,
   children without integrity.

**32:21**
1 Kgs 16:13, 26
†Rom 10:19

21 They have roused my jealousy by worshiping things that are not God;
   they have provoked my anger with their useless idols.
Now I will rouse their jealousy through people who are not even a people;
   I will provoke their anger through the foolish Gentiles.

**32:22**
Lev 26:20
Ps 18:7-8

22 For my anger blazes forth like fire
   and burns to the depths of the grave.*
It devours the earth and all its crops
   and ignites the foundations of the mountains.

**32:15** Hebrew *Jeshurun*, a term of endearment for Israel.   **32:22** Hebrew *of Sheol*.

---

**VARIETY IN WORSHIP**

Israel's worship used all of the senses. They reinforced the meaning of the ceremony. Every sense can be used to worship God.

| | |
|---|---|
| SIGHT | The beauty and symbolism of the Tabernacle; every color and hue had a meaning |
| HEARING | The use of music; there were instructions for the use of a variety of instruments, and the Bible records many songs |
| TOUCH | The head of the animal to be sacrificed was touched, symbolizing the fact that it was taking their place |
| SMELL | The sacrifices were burned, emitting a familiar aroma |
| TASTE | The festivals were celebrations and memorials—much of the food was symbolic |

---

them like a person protects the pupil (apple) of his eye. He had been the encircling protector, like a mother eagle who protects her young. The Lord alone had led them. And he alone leads us. Let us remember to trust in him.

23 I will heap disasters upon them
  and shoot them down with my arrows.
24 I will weaken them with famine,
  burning fever, and deadly disease.
  I will send the fangs of wild beasts
  and poisonous snakes that glide in the dust.
25 Outside, the sword will bring death,
  and inside, terror will strike
  both young men and young women,
  both infants and the aged.
26 I would have annihilated them,
  wiping out even the memory of them.
27 But I feared the taunt of Israel's enemy,
  who might misunderstand and say,
  "Our own power has triumphed!
  The LORD had nothing to do with this!"'

28 "But Israel is a senseless nation;
  the people are foolish, without understanding.
29 Oh, that they were wise and could understand this!
  Oh, that they might know their fate!
30 How could one person chase a thousand of them,
  and two people put ten thousand to flight,
  unless their Rock had sold them,
  unless the LORD had given them up?
31 But the rock of our enemies is not like our Rock,
  as even they recognize.*
32 Their vine grows from the vine of Sodom,
  from the vineyards of Gomorrah.
  Their grapes are poison,
  and their clusters are bitter.
33 Their wine is the venom of serpents,
  the deadly poison of cobras.

34 "The LORD says, 'Am I not storing up these things,
  sealing them away in my treasury?
35 I will take revenge; I will pay them back.
  In due time their feet will slip.
  Their day of disaster will arrive,
  and their destiny will overtake them.'

36 "Indeed, the LORD will give justice to his people,
  and he will change his mind about* his servants,
  when he sees their strength is gone
  and no one is left, slave or free.
37 Then he will ask, 'Where are their gods,
  the rocks they fled to for refuge?
38 Where now are those gods,
  who ate the fat of their sacrifices
  and drank the wine of their offerings?
  Let those gods arise and help you!
  Let them provide you with shelter!
39 Look now; I myself am he!
  There is no other god but me!
  I am the one who kills and gives life;
  I am the one who wounds and heals;
  no one can be rescued from my powerful hand!
40 Now I raise my hand to heaven
  and declare, "As surely as I live,

### Cross-references

**32:23**
Deut 28:15-19
Ps 85:5

**32:24**
Deut 28:53
Ps 91:6

**32:25**
2 Chr 36:17
Lam 1:20; 2:21
Ezek 7:15

**32:26**
Deut 4:27; 28:64

**32:29**
Deut 5:29

**32:30**
Lev 26:7-8
Deut 32:4, 18

**32:32**
Deut 29:18

**32:35**
Jer 23:12
Ezek 7:5
†Rom 12:19

**32:36**
Lev 26:44-45
Deut 30:2-3
†Heb 10:30

**32:37**
Jer 2:28

**32:38**
Num 25:1-2
Jer 11:12

**32:39**
1 Sam 2:6
Ps 50:22
Isa 41:4; 43:10

**32:31** The meaning of the Hebrew is uncertain. Greek version reads *our enemies are fools.* **32:36** Or *will take revenge for.*

32:41
Isa 34:6-8
Jer 12:12; 46:10;
50:28-32

41 when I sharpen my flashing sword
    and begin to carry out justice,
I will take revenge on my enemies
    and repay those who reject me.
42 I will make my arrows drunk with blood,
    and my sword will devour flesh—
the blood of the slaughtered and the captives,
    and the heads of the enemy leaders."'

32:43
†Romans 15:10

43 "Rejoice with him, you heavens,
    and let all of God's angels worship him.*
Rejoice with his people, you nations,
    and let all the angels be strengthened in him.*
For he will avenge the blood of his servants;
    he will take revenge against his enemies.
He will repay those who hate him*
    and cleanse the land for his people."

44So Moses came with Joshua* son of Nun and recited all the words of this song to the people.

32:46
Deut 4:9
Ezek 40:4; 44:5
32:47
Deut 4:40; 8:3;
30:20

45When Moses had finished reciting all these words to the people of Israel, 46he added: "Take to heart all the words of warning I have given you today. Pass them on as a command to your children so they will obey every word of these instructions. 47 These instructions are not empty words—they are your life! By obeying them you will enjoy a long life in the land you will occupy when you cross the Jordan River."

### Moses' Death Foretold

32:49
Num 27:12
Deut 3:27
32:50
Gen 25:8
Num 27:13
32:51
Num 20:12
32:52
Deut 1:37; 3:27

48That same day the LORD said to Moses, 49"Go to Moab, to the mountains east of the river,* and climb Mount Nebo, which is across from Jericho. Look out across the land of Canaan, the land I am giving to the people of Israel as their own special possession. 50Then you will die there on the mountain. You will join your ancestors, just as Aaron, your brother, died on Mount Hor and joined his ancestors. 51For both of you betrayed me with the Israelites at the waters of Meribah at Kadesh* in the wilderness of Zin. You failed to demonstrate my holiness to the people of Israel there. 52 So you will see the land from a distance, but you may not enter the land I am giving to the people of Israel."

### Moses Blesses the People

33:1
Josh 14:6

**33** This is the blessing that Moses, the man of God, gave to the people of Israel before his death:

33:2
Exod 19:18, 20
Judg 5:4
Ps 68:8, 17
Dan 7:10
Hab 3:3
Gal 3:19

2 "The LORD came from Mount Sinai
    and dawned upon us* from Mount Seir;
he shone forth from Mount Paran
    and came from Meribah-kadesh
    with flaming fire at his right hand.*

33:3
Deut 4:37; 6:1-9;
7:6; 14:2

3 Indeed, he loves his people;*
    all his holy ones are in his hands.
They follow in his steps
    and accept his teaching.

33:4
Deut 4:2
Ps 119:111

4 Moses gave us the LORD's instruction,
    the special possession of the people of Israel.*

**32:43a** As in Dead Sea Scrolls and Greek version; Masoretic Text lacks the first two lines. Compare Heb 1:6.
**32:43b** As in Greek version; Hebrew text lacks this line.   **32:43c** As in Dead Sea Scrolls and Greek version;
Masoretic Text lacks this line.   **32:44** Hebrew *Hoshea*, a variant name for Joshua.   **32:49** Hebrew *the mountains
of Abarim.*   **32:51** Hebrew *waters of Meribath-kadesh.*   **33:2a** As in Greek and Syriac versions; Hebrew reads
*upon them.*   **33:2b** Or *came from myriads of holy ones, from the south, from his mountain slopes.* The meaning
of the Hebrew is uncertain.   **33:3** As in Greek version; Hebrew reads *Indeed, lover of the peoples.*   **33:4** Hebrew
*of Jacob.* The names "Jacob" and "Israel" are often interchanged throughout the Old Testament, referring sometimes to the individual patriarch and sometimes to the nation.

**32:46, 47** Moses urged the people to think about God's word and teach it to their children. The Bible can sit on your bookshelf and gather dust, or you can make it a vital part of your life by regularly setting aside time to study it. When you discover the wisdom of God's message, you will want to apply it to your life and pass it on to your family and others. The Bible is not merely good reading—it's real help for real life.

5 The LORD became king in Israel*—
   when the leaders of the people assembled,
   when the tribes of Israel gathered as one."

33:5
Num 23:18-24
Ps 10:16

6 Moses said this about the tribe of Reuben:*

"Let the tribe of Reuben live and not die out,
   though they are few in number."

33:6
Gen 49:3

7 Moses said this about the tribe of Judah:

"O LORD, hear the cry of Judah
   and bring them together as a people.
Give them strength to defend their cause;
   help them against their enemies!"

33:7
Gen 49:8-12

8 Moses said this about the tribe of Levi:

"O LORD, you have given your Thummim and Urim—the sacred lots—
   to your faithful servants the Levites.*
You put them to the test at Massah
   and struggled with them at the waters of Meribah.

33:8
Exod 17:7
Lev 8:8
Num 20:13, 24
Deut 6:16

9 The Levites obeyed your word
   and guarded your covenant.
They were more loyal to you
   than to their own parents.
They ignored their relatives
   and did not acknowledge their own children.

33:9
Exod 32:27
Mal 2:5

10 They teach your regulations to Jacob;
   they give your instructions to Israel.
They present incense before you
   and offer whole burnt offerings on the altar.

33:10
Lev 10:11;
16:12-13
Deut 17:9; 31:9

11 Bless the ministry of the Levites, O LORD,
   and accept all the work of their hands.
Hit their enemies where it hurts the most;
   strike down their foes so they never rise again."

12 Moses said this about the tribe of Benjamin:

"The people of Benjamin are loved by the LORD
   and live in safety beside him.
He surrounds them continuously
   and preserves them from every harm."

33:12
Deut 12:10; 32:8

13 Moses said this about the tribes of Joseph:

"May their land be blessed by the LORD
   with the precious gift of dew from the heavens
   and water from beneath the earth;

33:13
Gen 27:27-29;
49:22

14 with the rich fruit that grows in the sun,
   and the rich harvest produced each month;
15 with the finest crops of the ancient mountains,
   and the abundance from the everlasting hills;
16 with the best gifts of the earth and its bounty,
   and the favor of the one who appeared in the burning bush.
May these blessings rest on Joseph's head,
   crowning the brow of the prince among his brothers.

33:16
Exod 3:2

17 Joseph has the majesty of a young bull;
   he has the horns of a wild ox.

33:17
Num 23:22; 24:8
1 Kgs 22:11

33:5 Hebrew in Jeshurun, a term of endearment for Israel.   33:6 Hebrew lacks Moses said this about the tribe of Reuben.   33:8 As in Greek version; Hebrew lacks the Levites.

33:6-25 Note the difference in blessings God gave each tribe. To one he gave the best land, to another strength, to another safety. Too often we see someone with a particular blessing and think that God must love that person more than others.

He will gore distant nations,
   driving them to the ends of the earth.
This is my blessing for the multitudes of Ephraim
   and the thousands of Manasseh."

**33:18**
Gen 49:13

<sup>18</sup>Moses said this about the tribes of Zebulun and Issachar*:

"May the people of Zebulun prosper in their travels.
   May the people of Issachar prosper at home in their tents.

**33:19**
Pss 4:5; 51:19

<sup>19</sup> They summon the people to the mountain
   to offer proper sacrifices there.
They benefit from the riches of the sea
   and the hidden treasures in the sand."

**33:20**
Gen 49:19

<sup>20</sup>Moses said this about the tribe of Gad:

"Blessed is the one who enlarges Gad's territory!
   Gad is poised there like a lion
   to tear off an arm or a head.

**33:21**
Num 32:1; 34:14
Josh 4:12; 22:1

<sup>21</sup> The people of Gad took the best land for themselves;
   a leader's share was assigned to them.
When the leaders of the people were assembled,
   they carried out the Lord's justice
   and obeyed his regulations for Israel."

**33:22**
Gen 49:16
Ezek 19:2-3

<sup>22</sup>Moses said this about the tribe of Dan:

"Dan is a lion's cub,
   leaping out from Bashan."

**33:23**
Gen 49:21

<sup>23</sup>Moses said this about the tribe of Naphtali:

"O Naphtali, you are rich in favor
   and full of the Lord's blessings;
   may you possess the west and the south."

**33:24**
Gen 49:20
Job 29:6

<sup>24</sup>Moses said this about the tribe of Asher:

"May Asher be blessed above other sons;
   may he be esteemed by his brothers;
   may he bathe his feet in olive oil.

**33:18** Hebrew lacks *and Issachar.*

---

**THE DEATH OF MOSES**
Just before Moses died, he climbed Mount Nebo. Although he could not enter the Promised Land, God showed him its beauty from Mount Nebo's peak.

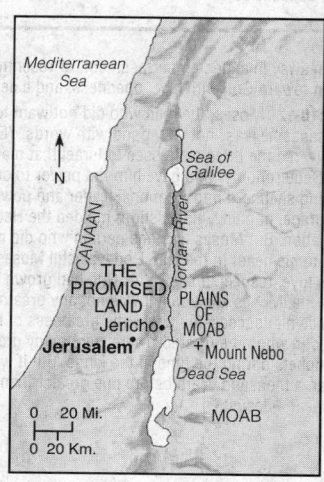

Mediterranean Sea

↑ N

Sea of Galilee

CANAAN

Jordan River

THE PROMISED LAND

PLAINS OF MOAB

Jericho

**Jerusalem**

✝ Mount Nebo

Dead Sea

MOAB

0   20 Mi.

0   20 Km.

Think rather that God draws out in all people their unique talents. All these gifts are needed to complete his plan. Don't be envious of the gifts others have. Instead, look for the gifts God has given you, and resolve to do the tasks he has uniquely qualified you to do.

**33:20, 21** The people of the tribe of Gad received the best of the new land because they obeyed God by punishing Israel's wicked enemies. Punishment is unpleasant for both the giver and the receiver, but it is a necessary part of growth. If you are in a position that sometimes requires you to correct others, don't hold back from fulfilling your task. Understand that realistic discipline is important to character development. Always strive to be both just and merciful, keeping in mind the best interests of the person who must receive the punishment.

**33:24** Bathing feet in oil was a sign of prosperity.

25 May the bolts of your gates be of iron and bronze;
   may you be secure all your days."

26 "There is no one like the God of Israel.*
   He rides across the heavens to help you,
   across the skies in majestic splendor.
27 The eternal God is your refuge,
   and his everlasting arms are under you.
   He drives out the enemy before you;
   he cries out, 'Destroy them!'
28 So Israel will live in safety,
   prosperous Jacob in security,
   in a land of grain and new wine,
   while the heavens drop down dew.
29 How blessed you are, O Israel!
   Who else is like you, a people saved by the LORD?
   He is your protecting shield
   and your triumphant sword!
   Your enemies will cringe before you,
   and you will stomp on their backs!"

### The Death of Moses

**34** Then Moses went up to Mount Nebo from the plains of Moab and climbed Pisgah Peak, which is across from Jericho. And the LORD showed him the whole land, from Gilead as far as Dan; 2all the land of Naphtali; the land of Ephraim and Manasseh; all the land of Judah, extending to the Mediterranean Sea*; 3the Negev; the Jordan Valley with Jericho— the city of palms—as far as Zoar. 4Then the LORD said to Moses, "This is the land I promised on oath to Abraham, Isaac, and Jacob when I said, 'I will give it to your descendants.' I have now allowed you to see it with your own eyes, but you will not enter the land."

5So Moses, the servant of the LORD, died there in the land of Moab, just as the LORD had said. 6The LORD buried him* in a valley near Beth-peor in Moab, but to this day no one knows the exact place. 7Moses was 120 years old when he died, yet his eyesight was clear, and he was as strong as ever. 8The people of Israel mourned for Moses on the plains of Moab for thirty days, until the customary period of mourning was over.

9Now Joshua son of Nun was full of the spirit of wisdom, for Moses had laid his hands on him. So the people of Israel obeyed him, doing just as the LORD had commanded Moses.

10There has never been another prophet in Israel like Moses, whom the LORD knew face to face. 11The LORD sent him to perform all the miraculous signs and wonders in the land of Egypt against Pharaoh, and all his servants, and his entire land. 12With mighty power, Moses performed terrifying acts in the sight of all Israel.

**Cross-references:**
33:25 Ps 147:13
33:26 Exod 15:11; Deut 4:35; Ps 68:33
33:27 Gen 49:24; Deut 7:2; Josh 24:18; Ps 90:1
33:28 Gen 27:27-29, 37; Deut 33:12-13
33:29 Gen 15:1; Deut 4:32; Pss 66:3; 115:11
34:1 Num 21:20; Deut 32:49, 52
34:2 Exod 23:31; Deut 11:24
34:4 Gen 12:7; 26:3
34:5 Num 12:7-8; Deut 32:50
34:6 Deut 3:29; 4:46; Jude 1:9
34:7 Deut 31:2
34:9 Num 27:18; Isa 11:2
34:10 Num 12:8
34:11-12 Deut 4:34

33:26 Hebrew *of Jeshurun*, a term of endearment for Israel.    34:2 Hebrew *the western sea*.    34:6 Hebrew *He buried him*; Samaritan Pentateuch and some Greek manuscripts read *They buried him*.

---

**33:27** Moses' song declares that God is our refuge, our only true security. How often we entrust our lives to other things— perhaps money, career, a noble cause, or a lifelong dream. But our only true refuge is the eternal God, who always holds out his arms to catch us when the shaky supports that we trust collapse and we fall. No storm can destroy us when we take refuge in him. Those without God, however, must forever be cautious. One mistake may wipe them out. Living for God in this world may look like risky business. But it is the godless who are on shaky ground. Because God is our refuge, we can dare to be bold.

**34:4, 10** Moses was the only person who ever spoke with God face to face (Exodus 33:11; Numbers 12:8). He was called Israel's greatest prophet. Yet even this great man was not allowed to enter the Promised Land because he disobeyed God (Numbers 20:12). No matter how good we are or how much we've done for God, we sometimes disobey him. The result of our disobedience is that we will be disciplined. God disciplined Moses severely but still called him his friend. When you experience the sting of God's discipline, respond as Moses did. Don't turn away in anger, embarrassment, or resentment. Instead, turn toward God with love, openness, and a desire to do better.

**34:10-12** Moses, the man who did not want to be sent to Egypt because he was "not very good with words" (Exodus 4:10), delivered the three addresses to Israel that make up the book of Deuteronomy. God gave him the power to develop from a stuttering shepherd into a national leader and powerful orator. His courage, humility, and wisdom molded the Hebrew slaves into a nation. But Moses was one person who did not let success go to his head. In the end, God was still Moses' best friend. His love, respect, and awe for God had grown daily throughout his life. Moses knew that it was not any greatness in himself that made him successful; it was the greatness of the all-powerful God in whom he trusted. There were many great and powerful prophets during the time of the kings. But it would be more than a thousand years before one greater than Moses would appear—Jesus.

# KEY PLACES IN JOSHUA

The broken lines (—·—·) indicate modern boundaries.

**4 Jericho** The walled city of Jericho seemed a formidable enemy. But when Joshua followed God's plans, the great walls were no obstacle. The city was conquered with only the obedient marching of the people (6:1–27).

**5 Ai** Victory could not continue without obedience to God. That is why the disobedience of one man, Achan, brought defeat to the entire nation in the first battle against Ai. But once the sin was recognized and punished, God told Joshua to take heart and try Ai once again. This time the city was taken (7:1—8:29).

**6 The Mountains of Ebal and Gerizim** After the defeat of Ai, Joshua built an altar at Mount Ebal. Then the people divided themselves, half at the foot of Mount Ebal, half at the foot of Mount Gerizim. The priests stood between the mountains holding the Ark of the Covenant as Joshua read God's law to all the people (8:30–35).

**7 Gibeon** It was just after the Israelites reaffirmed their covenant with God that their leaders made a major mistake in judgment: They were tricked into making a peace treaty with the city of Gibeon. The Gibeonites pretended that they had traveled a long distance and asked the Israelites for a treaty. The leaders made the agreement without consulting God. The trick was soon discovered, but because the treaty had been made, Israel could not go back on its word. As a result, the Gibeonites saved their own lives, but they were forced to become Israel's slaves (9:1–27).

**8 Valley of Aijalon** The king of Jerusalem was very angry at Gibeon for making a peace treaty with the Israelites. He gathered armies from four other cities to attack the city. Gibeon summoned Joshua for help. Joshua took immediate action. Leaving Gilgal, he attacked the coalition by surprise. As the battle waged on and moved into the valley of Aijalon, Joshua prayed for the sun to stand still until the enemy could be destroyed (10:1–43).

**1 Acacia Grove** The story of Joshua begins with the Israelites camping at Acacia Grove. The Israelites under Joshua were ready to enter and conquer Canaan. But before the nation moved out, Joshua received instructions from God (1:1–18).

**2 Jordan River** The entire nation prepared to cross this river, which was swollen from spring rains. After the spies returned from Jericho with a positive report, Joshua prepared the priests and people for a miracle. As the priests carried the Ark into the Jordan River, the water stopped flowing, and the entire nation crossed on dry ground into the Promised Land (2:1—4:24).

**3 Gilgal** After crossing the Jordan River, the Israelites camped at Gilgal, where they renewed their commitment to God and celebrated the Passover, the festival commemorating their deliverance from Egypt (see Exodus). As Joshua made plans for the attack on Jericho, an angel appeared to him (5:1–15).

**9 Hazor** Up north in Hazor, King Jabin mobilized the kings of the surrounding cities to unite and crush Israel. But God gave Joshua and Israel victory (11:1–23).

**10 Shiloh** After the armies of Canaan were conquered, Israel gathered at Shiloh to set up the Tabernacle. This movable building had been the nation's center of worship during their years of wandering. The seven tribes who had not received their land were given their allotments (18:1—19:51).

**11 Shechem** Before Joshua died he called the entire nation together at Shechem to remind them that it was God who had given them their land and that only with God's help could they keep it. The people vowed to follow God. As long as Joshua was alive, the land was at rest from war and trouble (24:1–33).

# JOSHUA

| Exodus from Egypt 1446 B.C. (1280 B.C.) | Israelites enter Canaan 1406 (1240) | Judges begin to rule 1375 (1220) |
|---|---|---|

CONQUEST OF CANAAN

## VITAL STATISTICS

**PURPOSE:**
To give the history of Israel's conquest of the Promised Land

**AUTHOR:**
Joshua, except for the ending, which may have been written by the high priest, Phinehas, an eyewitness to the events recounted there

**ORIGINAL AUDIENCE:**
The people of Israel

**SETTING:**
Canaan, also called the Promised Land, which occupied the same general geographical territory of modern-day Israel

**KEY VERSE:**
"'Go through the camp and tell the people to get their provisions ready. In three days you will cross the Jordan River and take possession of the land the LORD your God is giving you'" (1:11).

**KEY PEOPLE:**
Joshua, Rahab, Achan, Phinehas, Eleazar

**KEY PLACES:**
Jericho, Ai, Mount Ebal, Mount Gerizim, Gibeon, Gilgal, Shiloh, Shechem

**SPECIAL FEATURE:**
Out of over a million people, Joshua and Caleb are the only two who left Egypt and entered the Promised Land.

REMEMBER "follow the leader"? The idea was to mimic the antics of the person in front of you in the line of boys and girls winding through the neighborhood. Being a follower was all right, but being leader was the most fun, creating imaginative routes and tasks for everyone else to copy.

In real life, great leaders are rare. Often, men and women are elected or appointed to leadership positions but then falter or fail to act. Others abuse their power to satisfy their egos, crushing their subjects and squandering resources. But without faithful, ethical, and effective leaders, people wander.

For 40 years, Israel had journeyed a circuitous route through the wilderness, but *not* because they were following their leader. Quite the opposite was true—with failing faith, they had refused to obey God and to conquer Canaan. So they wandered. Finally, the new generation was ready to cross the Jordan and possess the land. Having distinguished himself as a man of faith and courage (he and Caleb had given the minority scout report recorded in Numbers 13:30—14:9), Joshua was chosen to be Moses' successor. This book records Joshua's leadership of the people of God as they finished their march and conquered the Promised Land.

Joshua was a brilliant military leader and a strong spiritual influence. But the key to his success was his submission to God. When God spoke, Joshua listened and obeyed. Joshua's obedience served as a model. As a result, Israel remained faithful to God throughout Joshua's lifetime.

The book of Joshua is divided into two main parts. The first narrates the events surrounding the conquest of Canaan. After crossing the Jordan River on dry ground, the Israelites camped near the mighty city of Jericho. God commanded the people to conquer Jericho by marching around the city 13 times, blowing trumpets, and shouting. Because they followed God's unique battle strategy, they won (chapter 6). After the destruction of Jericho, they set out against the small town of Ai. Their first attack was driven back because one of the Israelites (Achan) had sinned (chapter 7). After the men of Israel stoned Achan and his family—purging the community of its sin—the Israelites succeeded in capturing Ai (chapter 8). In their next battle against the Amorites, God even provided extended daylight to aid them in their victory (chapter 10). Finally, after defeating other assorted Canaanites led by Jabin and his allies (chapter 11), they possessed most of the land.

Part two of the book of Joshua records the assignment and settlement of the captured territory (chapters 13—22). The book concludes with Joshua's farewell address and his death (chapters 23—24).

Joshua was committed to obeying God, and this book is about obedience. Whether conquering enemies or settling the land, God's people were required to do it God's way. In his final message to the people, Joshua underscored the importance of obeying God. "So be very careful to love the LORD your God" (23:11), and "choose today whom you will serve. . . . But as for me and my family, we will serve the LORD" (24:15). Read Joshua and make a fresh commitment to obey God today. Decide to follow your Lord wherever he leads and whatever it costs.

United
kingdom
under
Saul
1050
(1045)

David
becomes
king
1010

## THE BLUEPRINT

A. ENTERING THE PROMISED LAND
   (1:1—5:12)
   1. Joshua leads the nation
   2. Crossing the Jordan

Joshua demonstrated his faith in God as he took up the challenge to lead the nation. The Israelites reaffirmed their commitment to God by obediently setting out across the Jordan River to possess the land. As we live the Christian life, we need to cross over from the old life to the new, put off our selfish desires, and press on to possess all God has planned for us. Like Joshua and Israel, we need courageous faith to live the new life.

B. CONQUERING THE PROMISED LAND
   (5:13—12:24)
   1. Joshua attacks the center of the land
   2. Joshua attacks the southern kings
   3. Joshua attacks the northern kings
   4. Summary of conquests

Joshua and his army moved from city to city, cleansing the land of its wickedness by destroying every trace of idol worship. Conflict with evil is inevitable, and we should be as merciless as Israel in destroying sin in our lives.

C. DIVIDING THE PROMISED LAND
   (13:1—24:33)
   1. The tribes receive their land
   2. Special cities are set aside
   3. Eastern tribes return home
   4. Joshua's farewell to Israel

Joshua urged the Israelites to continue to follow the Lord and worship him alone. The people had seen God deliver them from many enemies and miraculously provide for all their needs, but they were prone to wander from the Lord. Even though we may have experienced God at work in our lives, we, too, must continually renew our commitment to obey him above all other authority and to worship him alone.

## MEGATHEMES

| THEME | EXPLANATION | IMPORTANCE |
|---|---|---|
| Success | God gave success to the Israelites when they obeyed his master plan, not when they followed their own desires. Victory came when they trusted in him rather than in their military power, money, muscle, or mental capacity. | God's work done in God's way will bring his success. The standard for success, however, is not to be set by the society around us but by God's Word. We must adjust our minds to God's way of thinking in order to see his standard for success. |
| Faith | The Israelites demonstrated their faith by trusting God daily to save and guide them. By noticing how God fulfilled his promises in the past, they developed strong confidence that he would be faithful in the future. | Our strength to do God's work comes from trusting him. His promises reassure us of his love and that he will be there to guide us in the decisions and struggles we face. Faith begins with believing he can be trusted. |
| Guidance | God gave instructions to Israel for every aspect of their lives. His law guided their daily living, and his specific marching orders gave them victory in battle. | Guidance from God for daily living can be found in his Word. By staying in touch with God, we will have the needed wisdom to meet the great challenges of life. |
| Leadership | Joshua was an example of an excellent leader. He was confident in God's strength, courageous in the face of opposition, and willing to seek God's advice. | To be a strong leader like Joshua, we must be ready to listen and to move quickly when God instructs us. Once we have his instructions, we must be diligent in carrying them out. Strong leaders are led by God. |
| Conquest | God commanded his people to conquer the Canaanites and take all their land. Completing this mission would have fulfilled God's promise to Abraham and brought judgment on the evil people living there. Unfortunately, Israel never finished the job. | The Israelites were faithful in accomplishing their mission at first, but their commitment faltered. To love God means more than being enthusiastic about him. We must complete all the work he gives us and apply his instructions to every corner of our lives. |

## A. ENTERING THE PROMISED LAND (1:1—5:12)

After wandering for 40 years in the wilderness, a new generation is ready to enter Canaan. But first God prepares both Joshua and the nation by teaching them the importance of courageous and consistent faith. The nation then miraculously crosses the Jordan River to begin the long-awaited conquest of the Promised Land. Like Joshua, we, too, need faith to begin and continue living the Christian life.

### 1. Joshua leads the nation

*The LORD's Charge to Joshua*

**1** After the death of Moses the LORD's servant, the LORD spoke to Joshua son of Nun, Moses' assistant. He said, ²"Moses my servant is dead. Therefore, the time has come for you to lead these people, the Israelites, across the Jordan River into the land I am giving them. ³I promise you what I promised Moses: 'Wherever you set foot, you will be on land I have given you—⁴from the Negev wilderness in the south to the Lebanon mountains in the north, from the Euphrates River in the east to the Mediterranean Sea* in the west, including all the land of the Hittites.' ⁵No one will be able to stand against you as long as you live. For I will be with you as I was with Moses. I will not fail you or abandon you.

⁶"Be strong and courageous, for you are the one who will lead these people to possess all the land I swore to their ancestors I would give them. ⁷Be strong and very courageous. Be careful to obey all the instructions Moses gave you. Do not deviate from them, turning either to the right or to the left. Then you will be successful in everything you do. ⁸Study this Book of Instruction continually. Meditate on it day and night so you will be sure to obey everything written in it. Only then will you prosper and succeed in all you do. ⁹This is my command—be strong and courageous! Do not be afraid or discouraged. For the LORD your God is with you wherever you go."

*Joshua's Charge to the Israelites*

¹⁰Joshua then commanded the officers of Israel, ¹¹"Go through the camp and tell the people to get their provisions ready. In three days you will cross the Jordan River and take possession of the land the LORD your God is giving you."

¹²Then Joshua called together the tribes of Reuben, Gad, and the half-tribe of Manasseh.

**1:2** Num 12:7
Deut 34:5

**1:3** Deut 11:24

**1:5** Deut 7:24; 31:6-8
Heb 13:5

**1:7** Deut 5:29, 32;
28:14; 29:9

**1:8** Deut 17:8-9
Ps 1:1-3

**1:9** Deut 31:6-8

**1:10-11** Deut 3:2-4, 15-17

**1:12** Num 32:20-22, 33

**1:4** Hebrew *the Great Sea.*

---

**1:1** As the book of Joshua opens, the Israelites are camped along the east bank of the Jordan River at the very edge of the Promised Land, and they are completing the mourning period for Moses, who has just died (Deuteronomy 34:7, 8). Thirty-nine years earlier (after spending a year at Mount Sinai receiving God's law), the Israelites had an opportunity to enter the Promised Land, but they failed to trust God to give them victory. As a result, God did not allow them to enter the land, but made them wander in the wilderness until the disobedient generation had all died.

During their wilderness wanderings, the Israelites obeyed God's laws. They also taught the new generation to obey God's laws so that they might enter the Promised Land (also called Canaan). As the children grew, they were often reminded that faith and obedience to God brought victory, while unbelief and disobedience brought tragedy. When the last of the older generation had died and the new generation had become adults, the Israelites prepared to make their long-awaited claim on the Promised Land.

**1:1-5** Joshua succeeded Moses as Israel's leader. What qualifications did he have to become the leader of a nation? (1) God appointed him (Numbers 27:18-23). (2) He was one of only two living eyewitnesses to the Egyptian plagues and the Exodus from Egypt. (3) He was Moses' personal aide for 40 years. (4) Of the 12 scouts, only he and Caleb showed complete confidence that God would help them conquer the land.

**1:2** Because Joshua had assisted Moses for many years, he was well prepared to take over the leadership of the nation. Changes in leadership are common in many organizations. At such times, a smooth transition is essential for the establishment of the new administration. This doesn't happen unless new leaders are trained. If you are currently in a leadership position, begin prepar-

ing someone to take your place. Then, when you leave or are promoted, operations can continue to run efficiently. If you want to be a leader, learn from others so that you will be prepared when the opportunity comes.

**1:5** Joshua's new job consisted of leading more than two million people into a strange new land and conquering it. What a challenge—even for a man of Joshua's caliber! Every new job is a challenge. Without God it can be frightening. With God it can be a great adventure. Just as God was with Joshua, he is with us as we face our new challenges. We may not conquer nations, but every day we face tough situations, difficult people, and temptations. God promises, however, that he will never abandon us or fail to help us. By asking God to direct us we can conquer many of life's challenges.

**1:6-8** Many people think that prosperity and success come from having power, influential personal contacts, and a relentless desire to get ahead. But the strategy for gaining prosperity that God taught Joshua goes against such criteria. He said that to succeed Joshua must (1) be strong and courageous because the task ahead would not be easy, (2) obey God's law, and (3) constantly read and study the Book of Instruction—God's Word. To be successful, follow God's words to Joshua. You may not succeed by the world's standards, but you will be a success in God's eyes—and his opinion is most important.

**1:12-15** During the previous year, the tribes of Reuben and Gad and the half-tribe of Manasseh had asked Moses if they could settle just east of the Promised Land. The area was excellent pastureland for their large flocks. Moses agreed to give them the land on one condition—that they help their fellow tribes enter and conquer the Promised Land. Only after the land was conquered could they return to their homes. Now it was time for these three tribes to live up to their agreement.

He told them, 13"Remember what Moses, the servant of the Lord, commanded you: 'The Lord your God is giving you a place of rest. He has given you this land.' 14Your wives, children, and livestock may remain here in the land Moses assigned to you on the east side of the Jordan River. But your strong warriors, fully armed, must lead the other tribes across the Jordan to help them conquer their territory. Stay with them 15until the Lord gives them rest, as he has given you rest, and until they, too, possess the land the Lord your God is giving them. Only then may you return and settle here on the east side of the Jordan River in the land that Moses, the servant of the Lord, assigned to you."

16They answered Joshua, "We will do whatever you command us, and we will go wherever you send us. 17We will obey you just as we obeyed Moses. And may the Lord your God be with you as he was with Moses. 18Anyone who rebels against your orders and does not obey your words and everything you command will be put to death. So be strong and courageous!"

### Rahab Protects the Spies

**2** Then Joshua secretly sent out two spies from the Israelite camp at Acacia Grove.* He instructed them, "Scout out the land on the other side of the Jordan River, especially around Jericho." So the two men set out and came to the house of a prostitute named Rahab and stayed there that night.

**2:1** Hebrew *Shittim.*

**1:13** Deut 3:18-20

**1:15** Josh 22:1-4

**1:16** Num 32:25

**1:17** Josh 1:5, 9

**2:1** Num 25:1 Heb 11:31 Jas 2:25

---

**TAKE THE LAND**
God's Plan for the Promised Land

| | |
|---|---|
| Genesis 12:1-3 | God promised to bless Abraham and make his descendants into a great nation |
| Genesis 15:16 | God would choose the right time for Israel to enter Canaan, because the nations living there then would be wicked and ripe for judgment (their sin would run its course) |
| Genesis 17:7, 8 | God promised to give all the land of Canaan to Abraham's descendants |
| Exodus 33:1-3 | God promised to help the Israelites drive out all the evil nations from Canaan |
| Deuteronomy 4:5-8 | The Israelites were to be an example of right living to the whole world; this would not work if they intermingled with the wicked Canaanites |
| Deuteronomy 7:1-5 | The Israelites were to utterly wipe out the Canaanites because of their wickedness and because of Israel's call to purity |
| Deuteronomy 12:2 | The Israelites were to completely destroy the Canaanite altars so nothing would tempt them away from worshiping God alone |

God told Joshua to lead the Israelites into the Promised Land (also called Canaan) and conquer it. This was not an act of imperialism or aggression but an act of judgment. Here are some of the earlier passages in the Bible where God promised to give this land to the Israelites and the reasons for doing so.

---

**1:13** God was giving the people rest. This was wonderful news to these people who had been on the move for their entire lives. The people who had no land would be given a land of their own, and they would be able to settle and to "rest."

**1:16** If everyone had tried to conquer the Promised Land his own way, chaos would have resulted. In order to complete the enormous task of conquering the land, everyone had to agree to the leader's plan and be willing to support and obey him. If we are going to complete the tasks God has given us, we must fully agree to his plan, pledge ourselves to obey it, and put his principles into action. Agreeing to God's plan means both knowing what the plan is (as found in the Bible) and carrying it out daily.

**1:18** When God commissioned Joshua, he was told three times to be strong and courageous (see 1:6, 7, 9). Here, Joshua was given the same kind of encouragement from the people. Apparently, he took God's message to heart and found the strength and courage he needed in his relationship with God. The next time you are afraid to do what you know is right, remember that strength and courage are readily available from God.

**2:1** Why did Joshua send the spies secretly? As far as he knew, he would be attacking a heavily fortified city using conventional warfare tactics. He needed strategic information about the city for the upcoming battle. But he also knew that this might draw criticism from the other leaders. After all, the last time spies were sent, the report they brought back caused disastrous problems (see Numbers 13:1–14:4). While he did not want to move ahead without information, he also did not want to cause the people to stumble and question his wisdom and ability to lead the nation.

**2:1** Why would the spies stop at the house of Rahab, a prostitute? (1) It was a good place to gather information and have no questions asked in return. (2) Rahab's house was in an ideal location for a quick escape because it was built into the city wall (2:15). (3) God directed the spies to Rahab's house because he knew her heart was open to him and that she would be instrumental in the Israelite victory over Jericho. God often uses people with simple faith to accomplish his great purposes, no matter what kind of past they have had or how insignificant they seem to be. Rahab didn't allow her past to keep her from the new role God had for her.

²But someone told the king of Jericho, "Some Israelites have come here tonight to spy out the land." ³So the king of Jericho sent orders to Rahab: "Bring out the men who have come into your house, for they have come here to spy out the whole land."

⁴Rahab had hidden the two men, but she replied, "Yes, the men were here earlier, but I didn't know where they were from. ⁵They left the town at dusk, as the gates were about to close. I don't know where they went. If you hurry, you can probably catch up with them." ⁶(Actually, she had taken them up to the roof and hidden them beneath bundles of flax she had laid out.) ⁷So the king's men went looking for the spies along the road leading to the shallow crossings of the Jordan River. And as soon as the king's men had left, the gate of Jericho was shut.

⁸Before the spies went to sleep that night, Rahab went up on the roof to talk with them. ⁹"I know the LORD has given you this land," she told them. "We are all afraid of you. Everyone in the land is living in terror. ¹⁰For we have heard how the LORD made a dry path for you through the Red Sea* when you left Egypt. And we know what you did to Sihon and Og, the two Amorite kings east of the Jordan River, whose people you completely destroyed.* ¹¹No wonder our hearts have melted in fear! No one has the courage to fight after hearing such things. For the LORD your God is the supreme God of the heavens above and the earth below.

¹²"Now swear to me by the LORD that you will be kind to me and my family since I have helped you. Give me some guarantee that ¹³when Jericho is conquered, you will let me live, along with my father and mother, my brothers and sisters, and all their families."

¹⁴"We offer our own lives as a guarantee for your safety," the men agreed. "If you don't betray us, we will keep our promise and be kind to you when the LORD gives us the land."

¹⁵Then, since Rahab's house was built into the town wall, she let them down by a rope through the window. ¹⁶"Escape to the hill country," she told them. "Hide there for three days from the men searching for you. Then, when they have returned, you can go on your way."

¹⁷Before they left, the men told her, "We will be bound by the oath we have taken only if you follow these instructions. ¹⁸When we come into the land, you must leave this scarlet rope hanging from the window through which you let us down. And all your family

**2:4**
2 Sam 17:19

**2:6**
Jas 2:25

**2:9**
Exod 23:27
Deut 2:25
Josh 9:24

**2:10**
Exod 14:21
Num 21:21

**2:11**
Deut 4:39

**2:12**
Josh 2:17-18

**2:15**
Josh 2:18, 21

**2:16**
Jas 2:25

2:10a Hebrew *sea of reeds.*   **2:10b** The Hebrew term used here refers to the complete consecration of things or people to the LORD, either by destroying them or by giving them as an offering.

---

**2:4, 5** Was Rahab justified in lying to save the lives of the spies? Although the Bible does not speak negatively about her lie, it is clear that lying is sin. In Hebrews 11:31, however, Rahab is commended for her faith in God. Her lie is not mentioned. Several explanations have been offered: (1) God forgave Rahab's lie because of her faith; (2) Rahab was simply deceiving the enemy, a normal and acceptable practice in wartime; (3) because Rahab was not a Jew, she could not be held responsible for keeping the moral standards set forth in God's law; (4) Rahab broke a lesser principle—telling the truth—to uphold a higher principle—protecting God's people.

There may have been another way to save the lives of the Israelite spies. But under the pressure of the moment, Rahab had to make a choice. Most of us will face dilemmas at one time or another. We may feel that there is no perfect solution to our problem. Fortunately, God does not demand that our judgment be perfect in all situations. He simply asks us to put our trust in him and to do the best we know how. Rahab did that and was commended for her faith.

**2:6** Flax was harvested in the fields and piled high on the rooftops to dry. It was then made into yarn, which was used to make linen cloth. Flax grows to a height of three or four feet. Stacked on the roof, it made an excellent hiding place for the spies.

**2:8-13** Many would assume that Rahab—a pagan, a Canaanite, and a prostitute—would never be interested in God. Yet Rahab was willing to risk everything she had for a God she barely knew. We must not gauge a person's interest in God by his or her background, lifestyle, or appearance. We should let nothing get in the way of our telling people the Good News.

**2:11** Rahab recognized something that many of the Israelites did not—the God of heaven is not an ordinary god! He is all powerful. The people of Jericho were afraid because they had heard the news of God's extraordinary power in defeating the armies across the Jordan River. Today we can worship this same powerful, miracle-working God. He is powerful enough to destroy mighty, wicked armies, as he did in Jericho. He is also powerful enough to save us from certain death, as he did with Rahab.

**2:15** In Joshua's day it was common to build houses on city walls. Many cities had two walls about 12 to 15 feet apart. Houses were built on wooden logs laid across the tops of the two walls. Rahab may have lived in such a house with a window that looked out over the outside wall.

**SPY MISSION
TO JERICHO**
Two spies left the Israelite camp at Acacia Grove, crossed the Jordan River, and slipped into Jericho. The city was built around an oasis in the midst of a hot and desolate valley 840 feet below sea level. Jericho was the first major city the Israelites set out to conquer.

members—your father, mother, brothers, and all your relatives—must be here inside the house. 19If they go out into the street and are killed, it will not be our fault. But if anyone lays a hand on people inside this house, we will accept the responsibility for their death. 20If you betray us, however, we are not bound by this oath in any way."

21"I accept your terms," she replied. And she sent them on their way, leaving the scarlet rope hanging from the window.

22The spies went up into the hill country and stayed there three days. The men who were chasing them searched everywhere along the road, but they finally returned without success.

23Then the two spies came down from the hill country, crossed the Jordan River, and reported to Joshua all that had happened to them. 24"The LORD has given us the whole land," they said, "for all the people in the land are terrified of us."

**2:24**
Josh 2:9; 6:2

## 2. Crossing the Jordan

**3:1**
Josh 2:1

**3:2**
Josh 1:11

**3** Early the next morning Joshua and all the Israelites left Acacia Grove* and arrived at the banks of the Jordan River, where they camped before crossing. 2Three days later the

3:1 Hebrew *Shittim*.

---

One of the greatest challenges facing leaders is to replace themselves, training others to become leaders. Many outstanding accomplishments have been started by someone with great ability whose life or career ended before the vision became reality. The fulfillment of that dream then became the responsibility of that person's successor. Death is the ultimate deadline for leadership. One of the best tests of our leadership is our willingness and ability to train another for our position.

Moses made an excellent decision when he chose Joshua as his assistant. That choice was later confirmed by God himself when he instructed Moses to commission Joshua as his successor (Numbers 27:15–23). Joshua had played a key role in the exodus from Egypt. Introduced as the field general of Israel's army, he was the only person allowed to accompany Moses partway up the mountain when Moses received the law. Joshua and Caleb were the only 2 among the 12 scouts to bring back an encouraging report after being sent into the Promised Land the first time. Other references show him to have been Moses' constant shadow. His basic training was living with Moses—experiencing firsthand what it meant to lead God's people. This was modeling at its best!

Who is your Moses? Who is your Joshua? You are part of the chain of God's ongoing work in the world. You are modeling yourself after others, and others are patterning their lives after you. How important is God to those you want to be like? Do those who are watching you see God reflected in every area of your life? Ask God to lead you to a trustworthy Moses. Ask him to make you a good Joshua.

| | |
|---|---|
| **Strengths and accomplishments** | • Moses' assistant and successor<br>• One of only two adults who experienced Egyptian slavery and lived to enter the Promised Land<br>• Led the Israelites into their God-given homeland<br>• Brilliant military strategist<br>• Faithful to ask God's direction in the challenges he faced |
| **Lessons from his life** | • Effective leadership is often the product of good preparation and encouragement<br>• The persons after whom we pattern ourselves will have a definite effect on us<br>• A person committed to God provides the best model for us |
| **Vital statistics** | • Where: Egypt, the wilderness of Sinai, Canaan (the Promised Land)<br>• Occupations: Special assistant to Moses, warrior, leader<br>• Relative: Father: Nun<br>• Contemporaries: Moses, Caleb, Miriam, Aaron |
| **Key verses** | "So Moses did as the LORD commanded. He presented Joshua to Eleazar the priest and the whole community. Moses laid his hands on him and commissioned him to lead the people, just as the LORD had commanded through Moses" (Numbers 27:22, 23). |

Joshua is also mentioned in Exodus 17:9–14; 24:13; 32:17; 33:11; Numbers 11:28; 13—14; 26:65; 27:18–23; 32:11, 12, 28; 34:17; Deuteronomy 1:38; 3:21, 28; 31:3, 7, 14, 23; 34:9; the book of Joshua; Judges 2:6–9; and 1 Kings 16:34.

---

**3:2-4** The Ark of the Covenant was Israel's most sacred treasure. It was a symbol of God's presence and power. The Ark was a gold rectangular box with two cherubim (angels) facing each other on the lid. Inside the Ark were the tablets of the Ten Commandments Moses received from God, a jar of manna (the bread God miracu- lously sent from heaven during the wilderness wanderings), and Aaron's staff (the symbol of the high priest's authority). According to God's law, only the Levites could carry the Ark. The Ark was constructed at the same time as the Tabernacle (Exodus 37:1-9) and placed in the sanctuary's most sacred room.

Israelite officers went through the camp, ³giving these instructions to the people: "When you see the Levitical priests carrying the Ark of the Covenant of the LORD your God, move out from your positions and follow them. ⁴Since you have never traveled this way before, they will guide you. Stay about a half mile* behind them, keeping a clear distance between you and the Ark. Make sure you don't come any closer."

⁵Then Joshua told the people, "Purify yourselves, for tomorrow the LORD will do great wonders among you."

| | |
|---|---|
| **3:5** | |
| Exod 19:10 | |
| Josh 7:13 | |

⁶In the morning Joshua said to the priests, "Lift up the Ark of the Covenant and lead the people across the river." And so they started out and went ahead of the people.

⁷The LORD told Joshua, "Today I will begin to make you a great leader in the eyes of all the Israelites. They will know that I am with you, just as I was with Moses. ⁸Give this command to the priests who carry the Ark of the Covenant: 'When you reach the banks of the Jordan River, take a few steps into the river and stop there.'"

**3:7**
Josh 4:14
**3:8**
Josh 3:17

⁹So Joshua told the Israelites, "Come and listen to what the LORD your God says. ¹⁰Today you will know that the living God is among you. He will surely drive out the Canaanites, Hittites, Hivites, Perizzites, Girgashites, Amorites, and Jebusites ahead of you. ¹¹Look, the Ark of the Covenant, which belongs to the Lord of the whole earth, will lead you across the Jordan River! ¹²Now choose twelve men from the tribes of Israel, one from each tribe. ¹³The priests will carry the Ark of the LORD, the Lord of all the earth. As soon as their feet touch the water, the flow of water will be cut off upstream, and the river will stand up like a wall."

**3:10**
Deut 7:1
**3:12**
Josh 4:2-4
**3:13**
Exod 15:8

¹⁴So the people left their camp to cross the Jordan, and the priests who were carrying the Ark of the Covenant went ahead of them. ¹⁵It was the harvest season, and the Jordan was overflowing its banks. But as soon as the feet of the priests who were carrying the Ark touched the water at the river's edge, ¹⁶the water above that point began backing up a great distance away at a town called Adam, which is near Zarethan. And the water below that point flowed on to the Dead Sea* until the riverbed was dry. Then all the people crossed over near the town of Jericho.

**3:15**
1 Chr 12:15
**3:16**
Pss 66:6; 74:15;
114:3, 5

¹⁷Meanwhile, the priests who were carrying the Ark of the LORD's Covenant stood on dry ground in the middle of the riverbed as the people passed by. They waited there until the whole nation of Israel had crossed the Jordan on dry ground.

**3:17**
Exod 14:21-22, 29

**3:4** Hebrew *about 2,000 cubits* [920 meters].    **3:16** Hebrew *the sea of the Arabah, the Salt Sea.*

**3:5** Before entering the Promised Land, the Israelites were to perform a purification ceremony. This was often done before making a sacrifice or, as in this case, before witnessing a great act of God. God's law stated that a person could become unclean for many reasons—eating certain foods (Leviticus 11), giving birth (Leviticus 12), dealing with disease (Leviticus 13–14), touching a dead person (Numbers 19:11-22). God used these various outward signs of uncleanness to illustrate a person's inward uncleanness that comes as a result of sin. The purification ceremony pictured the importance of approaching God with a pure heart. Like the Israelites, we need God's forgiveness before we approach him.

**3:9** Just before crossing over into the Promised Land, Joshua gathered the people to hear the words of the Lord. Their excitement was high. No doubt they wanted to rush on, but Joshua made them stop and listen. We live in a fast-paced age where everyone rushes just to keep up. It is easy to get caught up in our tasks, becoming too busy for what God says is most important—listening to his words. Before making your schedule, take time to focus on what God wants from all your activities. Knowing what God has said before you rush into your day can help you avoid foolish mistakes.

**3:10** Why would God help the Israelites drive out these nations from their native land? God had punished Israel first for its disobedience. He then turned to the rest of the nations. Genesis 15:16 implies that the people of Canaan were wicked and deserved to be punished for their terrible sins. Israel was a vehicle for this punishment. More important was the fact that Israel, as a holy nation, could not live among such evil and idolatrous people. To do so would be to invite sin into their lives. The only way to prevent Israel from being infected by evil religions was to drive

out those who practiced them. Israel, however, failed to drive everyone out as God had told them to do. It wasn't long before Israel—the nation God chose to be his holy people—began following the evil practices of the Canaanites.

**3:13, 14** The Israelites were eager to enter the Promised Land, conquer nations, and live peacefully. But first they had to cross the flood-level waters of the Jordan River. God gave them specific instructions: In order to cross, the priests had to step into the water. What if these priests had been afraid to take that first step? Often God provides no solution to our problems until we trust him and move ahead with what we know we should do. What are the rivers, or obstacles, in your life? In obedience to God, take that first step.

**3:13-17** God had parted the waters of the Red Sea to let the people out of Egypt (Exodus 14), and here he parted the Jordan River to let them enter Canaan. These miracles showed Israel that God keeps his promises. God's presence among his people and his faithfulness to them made the entire journey from Egypt to the Promised Land possible. He was with them at the end of their wanderings just as he was with them in the beginning.

**3:15, 16** The Israelites crossed the Jordan River in the spring, when it was overflowing its banks. God chose the time when the river was at its highest to demonstrate his power—parting the waters so that the entire nation could cross on dry ground. Some say that God used a natural occurrence (such as a landslide) to stop the waters of the Jordan; others say he did it by a direct act. In either case, God showed his great power by working a miracle of timing and location to allow his people to cross the river on dry ground. This testimony of God's supernatural power served to build the Israelites' hope in God and to give them a great reputation with their enemies, who greatly outnumbered them.

## Memorials to the Jordan Crossing

**4** When all the people had crossed the Jordan, the LORD said to Joshua, ²"Now choose twelve men, one from each tribe. ³Tell them, 'Take twelve stones from the very place where the priests are standing in the middle of the Jordan. Carry them out and pile them up at the place where you will camp tonight.'"

⁴So Joshua called together the twelve men he had chosen—one from each of the tribes of Israel. ⁵He told them, "Go into the middle of the Jordan, in front of the Ark of the LORD your God. Each of you must pick up one stone and carry it out on your shoulder—twelve stones in all, one for each of the twelve tribes of Israel. ⁶We will use these stones to build a memorial. In the future your children will ask you, 'What do these stones mean?' ⁷Then you can tell them, 'They remind us that the Jordan River stopped flowing when the Ark of the LORD's Covenant went across.' These stones will stand as a memorial among the people of Israel forever."

⁸So the men did as Joshua had commanded them. They took twelve stones from the middle of the Jordan River, one for each tribe, just as the LORD had told Joshua. They carried them to the place where they camped for the night and constructed the memorial there.

⁹Joshua also set up another pile of twelve stones in the middle of the Jordan, at the place where the priests who carried the Ark of the Covenant were standing. And they are there to this day.

¹⁰The priests who were carrying the Ark stood in the middle of the river until all of the LORD's commands that Moses had given to Joshua were carried out. Meanwhile, the people hurried across the riverbed. ¹¹And when everyone was safely on the other side, the priests crossed over with the Ark of the LORD as the people watched.

¹²The armed warriors from the tribes of Reuben, Gad, and the half-tribe of Manasseh led the Israelites across the Jordan, just as Moses had directed. ¹³These armed men—about 40,000 strong—were ready for battle, and the LORD was with them as they crossed over to the plains of Jericho.

¹⁴That day the LORD made Joshua a great leader in the eyes of all the Israelites, and for the rest of his life they revered him as much as they had revered Moses.

¹⁵The LORD had said to Joshua, ¹⁶"Command the priests carrying the Ark of the Covenant* to come up out of the riverbed." ¹⁷So Joshua gave the command. ¹⁸As soon as the priests carrying the Ark of the LORD's Covenant came up out of the riverbed and their feet were on high ground, the water of the Jordan returned and overflowed its banks as before.

¹⁹The people crossed the Jordan on the tenth day of the first month.* Then they camped at Gilgal, just east of Jericho. ²⁰It was there at Gilgal that Joshua piled up the twelve stones taken from the Jordan River.

²¹Then Joshua said to the Israelites, "In the future your children will ask, 'What do these stones mean?' ²²Then you can tell them, 'This is where the Israelites crossed the Jordan on dry ground.' ²³For the LORD your God dried up the river right before your eyes, and he kept it dry until you were all across, just as he did at the Red Sea* when he dried it up until we had all crossed over. ²⁴He did this so all the nations of the earth might know that the LORD's hand is powerful, and so you might fear the LORD your God forever."

**4:16** Hebrew *Ark of the Testimony.* **4:19** This day in the ancient Hebrew lunar calendar occurred in late March, April, or early May. **4:23** Hebrew *sea of reeds.*

Cross-references (left margin):
**4:1** Deut 27:2
**4:2** Josh 3:12
**4:6** Exod 12:26; 13:14
**4:8** Josh 4:20
**4:9** Gen 28:18
**4:12** Num 32:17
**4:14** Josh 3:7
**4:18** Josh 3:15
**4:19** Josh 5:9
**4:22** Josh 3:17
**4:24** 1 Kgs 8:42-43; Ps 89:13

---

**4:1ff** After the people safely crossed the river, what would be next? Conquering the land? Not yet. First, God directed them to build a memorial from 12 stones drawn from the river by 12 men, one from each tribe. This may seem like an insignificant step in their mission of conquering the land, but God did not want his people to plunge into their task unprepared. They were to focus on him and remember who was guiding them. As you are busy doing your God-given tasks, set aside quiet moments, times to build your own memorial to God's power. Too much activity may shift your focus away from God.

**4:14** The Israelites revered Joshua for his role in leading them across the Jordan River. He, like Moses, would receive Israel's praises generation after generation. Although Israel was not a world power at that time, Joshua's reputation for handling his responsibilities God's way brought him greater glory than if he had been a hero in a "superpower" nation. Doing right is more important than doing well.

**4:21-24** The memorial of 12 stones was to be a constant reminder of the day the Israelites crossed the Jordan River on dry ground. Their children would see the stones, hear the story, and learn about God. Do you have traditions—special dates or special places—to help your children learn about God's work in your life? Do you take time to tell them what God has done for you—forgiving and saving you, answering your prayers, supplying your needs? Retelling your story will help keep memories of God's faithfulness alive in your family.

**5** When all the Amorite kings west of the Jordan and all the Canaanite kings who lived along the Mediterranean coast* heard how the LORD had dried up the Jordan River so the people of Israel could cross, they lost heart and were paralyzed with fear because of them.

### Israel Reestablishes Covenant Ceremonies

2At that time the LORD told Joshua, "Make flint knives and circumcise this second generation of Israelites.*" 3 So Joshua made flint knives and circumcised the entire male population of Israel at Gibeath-haaraloth.*

4Joshua had to circumcise them because all the men who were old enough to fight in battle when they left Egypt had died in the wilderness. 5Those who left Egypt had all been circumcised, but none of those born after the Exodus, during the years in the wilderness, had been circumcised. 6The Israelites had traveled in the wilderness for forty years until all the men who were old enough to fight in battle when they left Egypt had died. For they had disobeyed the LORD, and the LORD vowed he would not let them enter the land he had sworn to give us—a land flowing with milk and honey. 7So Joshua circumcised their sons—those who had grown up to take their fathers' places—for they had not been circumcised on the way to the Promised Land. 8After all the males had been circumcised, they rested in the camp until they were healed.

9Then the LORD said to Joshua, "Today I have rolled away the shame of your slavery in Egypt." So that place has been called Gilgal* to this day.

10While the Israelites were camped at Gilgal on the plains of Jericho, they celebrated Passover on the evening of the fourteenth day of the first month.* 11The very next day they began to eat unleavened bread and roasted grain harvested from the land. 12No manna appeared on the day they first ate from the crops of the land, and it was never seen again. So from that time on the Israelites ate from the crops of Canaan.

**5:1** Num 13:29
Josh 2:9-11

**5:2-3** Gen 17:9-10, 23

**5:4** Deut 2:14

**5:6** Num 14:29-35;
26:63-65
Deut 2:7

**5:10** Exod 12:18
Josh 4:19

**5:12** Exod 16:35

### B. CONQUERING THE PROMISED LAND (5:13—12:24)

After crossing the Jordan River, the Israelites begin to conquer Canaan. Jericho is the first to fall. Then Israel suffers its first defeat because of one man's disobedience. After the people remove the sin from their community, they strike again—this time with success. Soon great kings attack from the north and south, but they are defeated because God is with Israel. Evil could not be tolerated in the Promised Land, nor can it be tolerated in our lives. We, like Israel, must ruthlessly remove sin from our lives before it takes control of us.

**5:1** Hebrew *along the sea.*   **5:2** Or *circumcise the Israelites a second time.*   **5:3** *Gibeath-haaraloth* means "hill of foreskins."   **5:9** *Gilgal* sounds like the Hebrew word *galal,* meaning "to roll."   **5:10** This day in the ancient Hebrew lunar calendar occurred in late March, April, or early May.

**5:1** The Amorites and Canaanites were the two major groups living in Canaan at the time of Israel's invasion. The Canaanites worshiped a variety of gods, but Baal was their favorite. Canaanite culture was materialistic, and their religion, sensual. The Israelites continually turned to Baal after entering Canaan. The Amorite gods also infected Israel's worship and turned people away from worshiping the true God. Worshiping these false gods eventually brought about Israel's downfall.

**5:1** The Israelites spent 39 years in the wilderness unnecessarily because they were terrified of the Canaanites. They underestimated God's ability. The Israelites' first attempt to enter the Promised Land had failed (Numbers 13–14). Here Israel saw that the Canaanites were terrified of their army. The Canaanites had heard about Israel's great victories through God (2:9-11), and they hoped that the Jordan River would slow Israel down or discourage them from entering Canaan. But news that the Israelites had crossed the Jordan on dry land caused any courage the Canaanites still had to melt away.

Don't underestimate God. If we are faithful to God, he will cause great opposition to disappear. God can change the attitudes of those who oppose him.

**5:2, 3** The rite of circumcision marked Israel's position as God's covenant people. When God made the original covenant with Abraham, he required that each male be circumcised as a sign of cutting off the old life and beginning a new life with God (Genesis 17:13). Other cultures at that time used circumcision as a sign of entry into adulthood, but only Israel used it as a sign of following God.

**5:8, 9** Located about two miles northeast of Jericho, Gilgal was Israel's base camp and their temporary center of government and

worship during their invasion of Canaan. Here the people renewed their commitment to God and covenant with him before attempting to conquer the new land. At Gilgal the angelic commander of the Lord's army appeared to Joshua with further instructions for battle and encouragement for the conquest (5:13-15). After the conquest, Gilgal continued to be an important place in Israel. It was here that Israel's first king, Saul, was crowned (1 Samuel 11:14, 15).

**5:10** This joyous Passover was the first to be celebrated in the Promised Land and only the third celebrated by Israel since the Exodus from Egypt. The last time was at the foot of Mount Sinai, 39 years earlier. This celebration reminded Israel of God's mighty miracles that brought them out of Egypt. There they had to eat in fear and haste; here they ate in celebration of God's blessings and promises. (See Exodus 12 for a description of the night the angel "passed over" the Israelites' homes.)

**5:11, 12** God supplied manna to the hungry Israelites during their 40 years in the wilderness (Exodus 16:14-31). In the bountiful Promised Land they no longer needed this daily food supply because the land was ready for planting and harvesting. God had miraculously provided food for the Israelites while they were in the wilderness; here he provided food from the land itself. Prayer is not an alternative to preparation, and faith is not a substitute for hard work. God can and does provide miraculously for his people as needed, but he also expects them to use their God-given talents and resources to provide for themselves. If your prayers have gone unanswered, perhaps what you need is within your reach. Pray instead for the wisdom to see it and the energy and motivation to do it.

## 1. Joshua attacks the center of the land

*The LORD's Commander Confronts Joshua*

**5:13**
Gen 18:1-2; 32:24
Exod 23:23
Num 22:31

[13] When Joshua was near the town of Jericho, he looked up and saw a man standing in front of him with sword in hand. Joshua went up to him and demanded, "Are you friend or foe?"

**5:14**
Gen 17:3

[14] "Neither one," he replied. "I am the commander of the LORD's army."

At this, Joshua fell with his face to the ground in reverence. "I am at your command," Joshua said. "What do you want your servant to do?"

[15] The commander of the LORD's army replied, "Take off your sandals, for the place where you are standing is holy." And Joshua did as he was told.

*The Fall of Jericho*

**6:2**
Deut 7:24

**6** Now the gates of Jericho were tightly shut because the people were afraid of the Israelites. No one was allowed to go out or in. [2] But the LORD said to Joshua, "I have given you

---

Rahab was a prostitute in the city of Jericho. As a prostitute, she lived on the edge of society, one stop short of rejection. Her house, built right into the city wall, provided both lodging and favors to travelers. It was a natural place for the Israelite spies to stay, as they would be mistaken for Rahab's customers.

Stories about the Israelites had been circulating for some time, but now it was evident that the Israelites were about to invade. Living on the wall, Rahab felt especially vulnerable. Yet while she shared the general mood of fear with the rest of Jericho's population, she alone turned to the Lord for her salvation. Her faith gave her the courage to hide the spies and lie to the authorities. Rahab knew her position was dangerous; she could have been killed if she had been caught harboring the Israelites. Rahab took the risk, however, because she sensed that the Israelites relied on a God worth trusting. And God rewarded Rahab by promising safety for her and her family.

God works through people—like Rahab—whom we are inclined to reject. God remembers her because of her faith, not her profession. If at times you feel like a failure, remember that Rahab rose above her situation through her trust in God. You can do the same!

| | |
|---|---|
| **Strengths and accomplishments** | • Relative of Boaz, and thus an ancestor of David and Jesus<br>• One of only two women listed in the Hall of Faith in Hebrews 11<br>• Resourceful, willing to help others at great cost to herself |
| **Weakness and mistake** | • She was a prostitute |
| **Lesson from her life** | • She did not let fear affect her faith in God's ability to deliver |
| **Vital statistics** | • Where: Jericho<br>• Occupations: Prostitute/innkeeper, later became a wife<br>• Relatives: Ancestor of David and Jesus (Matthew 1:5)<br>• Contemporary: Joshua |
| **Key verse** | "It was by faith that Rahab the prostitute was not destroyed with the people in her city who refused to obey God. For she had given a friendly welcome to the spies" (Hebrews 11:31). |

Rahab's story is told in Joshua 2 and 6:22, 23. She is also mentioned in Matthew 1:5; Hebrews 11:31; and James 2:25.

---

**5:14, 15** This was an angel of superior rank, the commander of the Lord's army. Some say he was an appearance of God in human form. As a sign of respect, Joshua took off his sandals. Although Joshua was Israel's leader, he was still subordinate to God, the absolute Leader. Awe and respect are the responses due to our holy God. How can we show respect for God? By our attitudes and actions. We should recognize God's power, authority, and deep love, and our actions must model our absolute reverence for God. Respect for God is just as important today as it was in Joshua's day, even though removing shoes is no longer our cultural way of showing it.

**6:1** The city of Jericho, built thousands of years before Joshua was born, was one of the oldest cities in the world. In some places it had fortified walls up to 25 feet high and 20 feet thick. Soldiers standing guard on top of the walls could see for miles. Jericho was a symbol of military power and strength—the Canaanites considered it invincible.

Israel would attack this city first, and its destruction would put the fear of Israel into the heart of every person in Canaan. The Canaanites saw Israel's God as a nature god because he parted the Jordan and as a war god because he defeated Sihon and Og. But the Canaanites did not consider him a fortress god—one who could prevail against a walled city. The defeat of Jericho showed not only that Israel's God was superior to the Canaanite gods but also that he was invincible.

**6:2-5** God told Joshua that Jericho was already delivered into his hands—the enemy was already defeated! What confidence Joshua must have had as he went into battle! Christians also fight against a defeated enemy. Our enemy, Satan, has been defeated by Christ (Romans 8:37-39; Hebrews 2:14, 15; 1 John 3:8). Although we still fight battles every day and sin runs rampant in the world, we have the assurance that the war has already been won. We do not have to be paralyzed by the power of a defeated enemy; we can overcome him through Christ's power.

Jericho, its king, and all its strong warriors. ³You and your fighting men should march
around the town once a day for six days. ⁴Seven priests will walk ahead of the Ark, each carrying a ram's horn. On the seventh day you are to march around the town seven times, with
the priests blowing the horns. ⁵When you hear the priests give one long blast on the rams'
horns, have all the people shout as loud as they can. Then the walls of the town will collapse,
and the people can charge straight into the town."

⁶So Joshua called together the priests and said, "Take up the Ark of the Lord's Covenant,
and assign seven priests to walk in front of it, each carrying a ram's horn." ⁷Then he gave
orders to the people: "March around the town, and the armed men will lead the way in front
of the Ark of the Lord."

⁸After Joshua spoke to the people, the seven priests with the rams' horns started marching in the presence of the Lord, blowing the horns as they marched. And the Ark of the
Lord's Covenant followed behind them. ⁹Some of the armed men marched in front of the
priests with the horns and some behind the Ark, with the priests continually blowing
the horns. ¹⁰"Do not shout; do not even talk," Joshua commanded. "Not a single word from
any of you until I tell you to shout. Then shout!" ¹¹So the Ark of the Lord was carried around
the town once that day, and then everyone returned to spend the night in the camp.

¹²Joshua got up early the next morning, and the priests again carried the Ark of the Lord.
¹³The seven priests with the rams' horns marched in front of the Ark of the Lord, blowing
their horns. Again the armed men marched both in front of the priests with the horns and
behind the Ark of the Lord. All this time the priests were blowing their horns. ¹⁴On the second day they again marched around the town once and returned to the camp. They followed
this pattern for six days.

¹⁵On the seventh day the Israelites got up at dawn and marched around the town as they
had done before. But this time they went around the town seven times. ¹⁶The seventh time
around, as the priests sounded the long blast on their horns, Joshua commanded the people,
"Shout! For the Lord has given you the town! ¹⁷Jericho and everything in it must be completely destroyed* as an offering to the Lord. Only Rahab the prostitute and the others in
her house will be spared, for she protected our spies.

¹⁸"Do not take any of the things set apart for destruction, or you yourselves will be completely destroyed, and you will bring trouble on the camp of Israel. ¹⁹Everything made from
silver, gold, bronze, or iron is sacred to the Lord and must be brought into his treasury."

²⁰When the people heard the sound of the rams' horns, they shouted as loud as they
could. Suddenly, the walls of Jericho collapsed, and the Israelites charged straight into the
town and captured it. ²¹They completely destroyed everything in it with their swords—men
and women, young and old, cattle, sheep, goats, and donkeys.

²²Meanwhile, Joshua said to the two spies, "Keep your promise. Go to the prostitute's
house and bring her out, along with all her family."

²³The men who had been spies went in and brought out Rahab, her father, mother, brothers, and all the other relatives who were with her. They moved her whole family to a safe
place near the camp of Israel.

6:4
Lev 25:9

6:7
Exod 14:15

6:9
Isa 52:12

6:13
Josh 6:4

6:17
Lev 27:28
Deut 20:17

6:18
Deut 20:17
Josh 7:1, 25
6:19
Num 31:21-23
6:20
Heb 11:30
6:21
Deut 20:16
6:22
Josh 2:14
Heb 11:31

6:17 The Hebrew term used here refers to the complete consecration of things or people to the Lord, either
by destroying them or by giving them as an offering; similarly in 6:18, 21.

---

**6:3-5** Why did God give Joshua all these complicated instructions
for the battle? Several answers are possible: (1) God was making
it undeniably clear that the battle would depend upon him, and not
upon Israel's weapons and expertise. This is why priests carrying
the Ark, not soldiers, led the Israelites into battle. (2) God's method
of taking the city accentuated the terror already felt in Jericho (2:9).
(3) This strange military maneuver was a test of the Israelites' faith
and their willingness to follow God completely. The blowing of the
horns had a special significance. They had been instructed to blow
the same horns used in the religious festivals in their battles to
remind them that their victory would come from the Lord, not their
own military might (Numbers 10:9).

**6:21** Why did God demand that the Israelites destroy almost
everyone and everything in Jericho? He was carrying out severe
judgment against the wickedness of the Canaanites. This judgment,
or *ban*, usually required that everything be destroyed (Deuteronomy
12:2, 3; 13:12-18). Because of their evil practices and intense idolatry, the Canaanites were a stronghold of rebellion against God. This

threat to the right kind of living that God required had to be
removed. If not, it would affect all Israel like a cancerous growth
(as it did in the sad story told in the book of Judges). A few people
and some items in Jericho were not destroyed, but these were
special cases. Rahab and her household were saved because she
had faith in God and because she helped the Israelite spies. The
silver and gold and articles of bronze and iron were kept, not to
enrich the people, but to beautify the Tabernacle and its services
(6:24).

God's purpose in all this was to keep the people's faith and
religion uncontaminated. He did not want the plunder to remind
Israel of Canaanite practices.

God also wants us to be pure. He wants us to clean up our
behavior when we begin a new life with him. We must not let the
desire for personal gain distract us from our spiritual purpose.
We must also reject any objects that are reminders of a life of
rebellion against God. (For more information on how Israel
handled its plunder, see the note on Numbers 31:25-30.)

6:25
Josh 2:6
Heb 11:31

6:26
1 Kgs 16:34

6:27
Josh 9:1

7:1
Josh 6:18-19
1 Chr 2:7

7:2
Gen 28:19
Josh 16:2

7:5
Josh 2:11

7:6
Job 2:12; 42:6
Lam 2:10
Rev 18:19

7:7
Exod 5:22

7:9
Exod 32:12
Deut 9:28

24Then the Israelites burned the town and everything in it. Only the things made from silver, gold, bronze, or iron were kept for the treasury of the Lord's house. 25So Joshua spared Rahab the prostitute and her relatives who were with her in the house, because she had hidden the spies Joshua sent to Jericho. And she lives among the Israelites to this day. 26At that time Joshua invoked this curse:

"May the curse of the Lord fall on anyone
   who tries to rebuild the town of Jericho.
At the cost of his firstborn son,
   he will lay its foundation.
At the cost of his youngest son,
   he will set up its gates."

27So the Lord was with Joshua, and his reputation spread throughout the land.

## Ai Defeats the Israelites

7 But Israel violated the instructions about the things set apart for the Lord.* A man named Achan had stolen some of these dedicated things, so the Lord was very angry with the Israelites. Achan was the son of Carmi, a descendant of Zimri* son of Zerah, of the tribe of Judah.

2Joshua sent some of his men from Jericho to spy out the town of Ai, east of Bethel, near Beth-aven. 3When they returned, they told Joshua, "There's no need for all of us to go up there; it won't take more than two or three thousand men to attack Ai. Since there are so few of them, don't make all our people struggle to go up there."

4So approximately 3,000 warriors were sent, but they were soundly defeated. The men of Ai 5chased the Israelites from the town gate as far as the quarries,* and they killed about thirty-six who were retreating down the slope. The Israelites were paralyzed with fear at this turn of events, and their courage melted away.

6Joshua and the elders of Israel tore their clothing in dismay, threw dust on their heads, and bowed face down to the ground before the Ark of the Lord until evening. 7Then Joshua cried out, "Oh, Sovereign Lord, why did you bring us across the Jordan River if you are going to let the Amorites kill us? If only we had been content to stay on the other side! 8Lord, what can I say now that Israel has fled from its enemies? 9For when the Canaanites and all the other people living in the land hear about it, they will surround us and wipe our name off the face of the earth. And then what will happen to the honor of your great name?"

7:1a The Hebrew term used here refers to the complete consecration of things or people to the Lord, either by destroying them or by giving them as an offering; similarly in 7:11, 12, 13, 15.   7:1b As in parallel text at 1 Chr 2:6; Hebrew reads *Zabdi*. Also in 7:17, 18.   7:5 Or *as far as Shebarim*.

---

**6:26** This curse was fulfilled in 1 Kings 16:34 when a man, Hiel, rebuilt Jericho and consequently lost his oldest and youngest sons.

**7:1** The things to be "set apart" refers to all the clothing, cattle, and other plunder that God said Israel should destroy when they conquered Jericho (see 6:17-19). It was not that they found a good use for something that was going to be thrown out anyway. This was a serious offense because it was in direct defiance of an explicit command of God (see Deuteronomy 20:16-18).

**7:1ff** Notice the results of Achan's sin: (1) Many men died (7:5); (2) Israel's army melted in fear (7:5); (3) Joshua questioned God (7:7-9); (4) God threatened to withdraw his presence from the people (7:12); (5) Achan and his family had to be destroyed (7:24-26).

When Israel eliminated the sin from their community, these were the results: (1) God's encouragement (8:1); (2) God's presence in battle (8:1); (3) God's guidance and promise of victory (8:2); (4) God's permission to keep the plunder and livestock from the battle for themselves (8:2). Throughout Israel's history, blessings came when the people got rid of their sin. You will also experience blessings when you turn from your sin and follow God's plan wholeheartedly.

**7:6** Joshua and the leaders tore their clothing and threw dust on their heads as signs of deep mourning before God. They were confused by their defeat at the small city of Ai after the spectacular Jericho victory, so they went before God in deep humility and sorrow to receive his instructions. When our lives fall apart, we also should turn to God for direction and help. Like Joshua and the leaders, we should humble ourselves so that we will be able to hear God's words.

**7:7** When Joshua first went against Ai (7:3), he did not consult God but relied on the strength of his army to defeat the small city. Only after Israel was defeated did they turn to God and ask what happened.

Too often we rely on our own skills and strength, especially when the task before us seems easy. We go to God only when the obstacles seem too great. However, only God knows what lies ahead. Consulting him, even when we are on a winning streak, may save us from grave mistakes or misjudgments. God may want us to learn lessons, remove pride, or consult others before he will work through us.

**7:7-9** Imagine praying this way to God. This is not a formal church prayer; it is the prayer of a man who is afraid and confused by what is happening around him. Joshua poured out his real thoughts to God. Hiding your needs from God is ignoring the only one who can really help. God welcomes your honest prayers and wants you to express your true feelings to him. Any believer can become more honest in prayer by remembering that God is all-knowing and all-powerful and that his love is everlasting.

<sup></sup>¹⁰But the LORD said to Joshua, "Get up! Why are you lying on your face like this? ¹¹Israel has sinned and broken my covenant! They have stolen some of the things that I commanded must be set apart for me. And they have not only stolen them but have lied about it and hidden the things among their own belongings. ¹²That is why the Israelites are running from their enemies in defeat. For now Israel itself has been set apart for destruction. I will not remain with you any longer unless you destroy the things among you that were set apart for destruction.

¹³"Get up! Command the people to purify themselves in preparation for tomorrow. For this is what the LORD, the God of Israel, says: Hidden among you, O Israel, are things set apart for the LORD. You will never defeat your enemies until you remove these things from among you.

¹⁴"In the morning you must present yourselves by tribes, and the LORD will point out the tribe to which the guilty man belongs. That tribe must come forward with its clans, and the LORD will point out the guilty clan. That clan will then come forward, and the LORD will point out the guilty family. Finally, each member of the guilty family must come forward one by one. ¹⁵The one who has stolen what was set apart for destruction will himself be burned with fire, along with everything he has, for he has broken the covenant of the LORD and has done a horrible thing in Israel."

### Achan's Sin

¹⁶Early the next morning Joshua brought the tribes of Israel before the LORD, and the tribe of Judah was singled out. ¹⁷Then the clans of Judah came forward, and the clan of Zerah was singled out. Then the families of Zerah came forward, and the family of Zimri was singled out. ¹⁸Every member of Zimri's family was brought forward person by person, and Achan was singled out.

¹⁹Then Joshua said to Achan, "My son, give glory to the LORD, the God of Israel, by telling the truth. Make your confession and tell me what you have done. Don't hide it from me."

²⁰Achan replied, "It is true! I have sinned against the LORD, the God of Israel. ²¹Among the plunder I saw a beautiful robe from Babylon,* 200 silver coins,* and a bar of gold weighing more than a pound.* I wanted them so much that I took them. They are hidden in the ground beneath my tent, with the silver buried deeper than the rest."

²²So Joshua sent some men to make a search. They ran to the tent and found the stolen goods hidden there, just as Achan had said, with the silver buried beneath the rest. ²³They took the things from the tent and brought them to Joshua and all the Israelites. Then they laid them on the ground in the presence of the LORD.

²⁴Then Joshua and all the Israelites took Achan, the silver, the robe, the bar of gold, his sons, daughters, cattle, donkeys, sheep, goats, tent, and everything he had, and they brought

**7:10** Exod 14:15; 1 Sam 15:24
**7:17** Num 26:20
**7:19** Jer 13:16; John 9:24
**7:24** Josh 15:7

7:21a Hebrew *Shinar.*  7:21b Hebrew *200 shekels of silver,* about 5 pounds or 2.3 kilograms in weight.
7:21c Hebrew *50 shekels,* about 20 ounces or 570 grams in weight.

**7:10-12** Why did Achan's sin bring judgment on the entire nation? Although it was one man's failure, God saw it as national disobedience to a national law. God needed the entire nation to be committed to the job they had agreed to do—conquer the land. Thus, when one person failed, everyone failed. If Achan's sin went unpunished, unlimited looting could break out. The nation as a whole had to take responsibility for preventing this undisciplined disobedience.

Achan's sin was not merely his keeping some of the captured goods (God allowed it in some cases), but his disobeying God's explicit command to destroy everything connected with Jericho. Achan's sin was indifference to the evil and idolatry of the city, not just a desire for money and clothes. God would not protect Israel's army again until the sin was removed and the army returned to obeying him without reservation. God is not content with our doing what is right some of the time. He wants us to do what is right all the time. We are under his orders to eliminate any thoughts, practices, or possessions that hinder our devotion to him.

**7:13** The Israelites had to undergo purification rites like those mentioned in 3:5 when they were preparing to cross the Jordan River. Such rites prepared the people to approach God and constantly reminded them of their sinfulness and his holiness.

**7:24, 25** Achan underestimated God and didn't take his commands seriously (6:18). Taking a robe, along with some silver and gold, may have seemed a small thing to Achan, but the effects of his sin were felt by the entire nation, especially his family. Like Achan, our actions affect more people than just ourselves. Beware of the temptation to rationalize your sins by saying they are too small or too personal to hurt anyone but you.

**7:24-26** Why did Achan's entire family pay for his sin? The biblical record does not tell us if they were accomplices to his crime, but in the ancient world, the family was treated as a whole. Achan, as the head of his family, was like a tribal chief. If he prospered, the family prospered with him. If he suffered, so did they. Many Israelites had already died in battle because of Achan's sin. Now he was to be completely cut off from Israel.

Achan's entire family was to be stoned along with him so that no trace of the sin would remain in Israel. In our permissive and individualistic culture we have a hard time understanding such a decree, but in ancient cultures this punishment was common. The punishment fit the crime: Achan had disobeyed God's command to destroy everything in Jericho; thus, everything that belonged to Achan had to be destroyed. Sin has drastic consequences, so we should take drastic measures to avoid it.

**7:25**
Josh 6:18

**7:26**
Isa 65:10
Hos 2:15

them to the valley of Achor. 25Then Joshua said to Achan, "Why have you brought trouble on us? The LORD will now bring trouble on you." And all the Israelites stoned Achan and his family and burned their bodies. 26They piled a great heap of stones over Achan, which remains to this day. That is why the place has been called the Valley of Trouble* ever since. So the LORD was no longer angry.

### The Israelites Defeat Ai

**8:1**
Deut 1:19-21
Josh 1:9; 6:2; 10:8

**8:2**
Deut 20:14
Josh 8:27

**8**Then the LORD said to Joshua, "Do not be afraid or discouraged. Take all your fighting men and attack Ai, for I have given you the king of Ai, his people, his town, and his land. 2You will destroy them as you destroyed Jericho and its king. But this time you may keep the plunder and the livestock for yourselves. Set an ambush behind the town."

3So Joshua and all the fighting men set out to attack Ai. Joshua chose 30,000 of his best warriors and sent them out at night 4with these orders: "Hide in ambush close behind the town and be ready for action. 5When our main army attacks, the men of Ai will come out to fight as they did before, and we will run away from them. 6We will let them chase us until we have drawn them away from the town. For they will say, 'The Israelites are running away from us as they did before.' Then, while we are running from them, 7you will jump up from

**8:8**
Judg 20:29-38

your ambush and take possession of the town, for the LORD your God will give it to you. 8Set the town on fire, as the LORD has commanded. You have your orders."

9So they left and went to the place of ambush between Bethel and the west side of Ai. But Joshua remained among the people in the camp that night. 10Early the next morning Joshua roused his men and started toward Ai, accompanied by the elders of Israel. 11All the fighting men who were with Joshua marched in front of the town and camped on the north side of Ai, with a valley between them and the town. 12That night Joshua sent 5,000 men to lie in ambush between Bethel and Ai, on the west side of the town. 13So they stationed the main army north of the town and the ambush west of the town. Joshua himself spent that night in the valley.

**8:14**
Deut 1:1
Judg 20:34

14When the king of Ai saw the Israelites across the valley, he and all his army hurried out early in the morning and attacked the Israelites at a place overlooking the Jordan Valley.* But he didn't realize there was an ambush behind the town. 15Joshua and the Israelite army fled toward the wilderness as though they were badly beaten. 16Then all the men in the town were called out to chase after them. In this way, they were lured away from the town. 17There was not a man left in Ai or Bethel* who did not chase after the Israelites, and the town was left wide open.

**7:26** Hebrew *valley of Achor.*  **8:14** Hebrew *the Arabah.*  **8:17** Some manuscripts lack *or Bethel.*

---

**8:1** After Israel had been cleansed from Achan's sin, Joshua prepared to attack Ai again—this time to win. Joshua learned some lessons that we can follow: (1) Confess your sins when God reveals them to you (7:19-21); (2) when you fail, refocus on God, deal with the problem, and move on (7:22-25; 8:1). God wants the cycle of sin, repentance, and forgiveness to strengthen us, not weaken us. The lessons we learn from our failures should make us better able to handle the same situation the second time around. Because God is eager to give us cleansing, forgiveness, and strength, the only way to lose is to give up. We can tell what kind of people we are by what we do on the second and third attempts.

**8:2** Why did God allow the Israelites to keep the plunder and cattle (livestock) this time? Israel's laws for handling the spoils of war covered two situations: (1) Cities like Jericho which were under God's *ban* (judgment for idolatry) could not be looted (see Deuteronomy 20:16-18). God's people were to be kept holy and separate from every influence of idolatry. (2) The distribution of captured goods from cities not under the ban was a normal part of warfare. It provided the army and the nation with the necessary food, flocks, and weapons needed to sustain itself in wartime. Ai was not under the ban. The conquering army needed the food and equipment. Because soldiers were not paid, the plunder was part of their incentive and reward for going to war.

**8:3** The conquest of Ai was very important to the Israelites. Only 11 miles away from Jericho, Ai was a key stronghold for the Canaanites and a buffer fortress for Bethel (8:12). If the Canaanite

kings got wind of an Israelite defeat at Ai, they could unite in a coordinated attack. They did not know that God had restored his power and protection to Joshua's troops. We must depend on God with absolute obedience to be sure of the victory he has promised.

**THE BATTLE FOR AI**
During the night, Joshua sent one detachment of soldiers to the west of Ai to lie in wait. The next morning he led a second group north of Ai. When the army of Ai attacked, the Israelites to the north pretended to scatter, only to turn on the enemy as the men lying in ambush moved in and burned the city.

¹⁸Then the Lord said to Joshua, "Point the spear in your hand toward Ai, for I will hand the town over to you." Joshua did as he was commanded. ¹⁹As soon as Joshua gave this signal, all the men in ambush jumped up from their position and poured into the town. They quickly captured it and set it on fire.

²⁰When the men of Ai looked behind them, smoke from the town was filling the sky, and they had nowhere to go. For the Israelites who had fled in the direction of the wilderness now turned on their pursuers. ²¹When Joshua and all the other Israelites saw that the ambush had succeeded and that smoke was rising from the town, they turned and attacked the men of Ai. ²²Meanwhile, the Israelites who were inside the town came out and attacked the enemy from the rear. So the men of Ai were caught in the middle, with Israelite fighters on both sides. Israel attacked them, and not a single person survived or escaped. ²³Only the king of Ai was taken alive and brought to Joshua.

²⁴When the Israelite army finished chasing and killing all the men of Ai in the open fields, they went back and finished off everyone inside. ²⁵So the entire population of Ai, including men and women, was wiped out that day—12,000 in all. ²⁶For Joshua kept holding out his spear until everyone who had lived in Ai was completely destroyed.* ²⁷Only the livestock and the treasures of the town were not destroyed, for the Israelites kept these as plunder for themselves, as the Lord had commanded Joshua. ²⁸So Joshua burned the town of Ai,* and it became a permanent mound of ruins, desolate to this very day.

²⁹Joshua impaled the king of Ai on a sharpened pole and left him there until evening. At sunset the Israelites took down the body, as Joshua commanded, and threw it in front of the town gate. They piled a great heap of stones over him that can still be seen today.

### The Lord's Covenant Renewed

³⁰Then Joshua built an altar to the Lord, the God of Israel, on Mount Ebal. ³¹He followed the commands that Moses the Lord's servant had written in the Book of Instruction: "Make me an altar from stones that are uncut and have not been shaped with iron tools."* Then on the altar they presented burnt offerings and peace offerings to the Lord. ³²And as the Israelites watched, Joshua copied onto the stones of the altar* the instructions Moses had given them.

³³Then all the Israelites—foreigners and native-born alike—along with the elders, officers, and judges, were divided into two groups. One group stood in front of Mount Gerizim, the other in front of Mount Ebal. Each group faced the other, and between them stood the Levitical priests carrying the Ark of the Lord's Covenant. This was all done according to the commands that Moses, the servant of the Lord, had previously given for blessing the people of Israel.

³⁴Joshua then read to them all the blessings and curses Moses had written in the Book of Instruction. ³⁵Every word of every command that Moses had ever given was read to the entire assembly of Israel, including the women and children and the foreigners who lived among them.

## 2. Joshua attacks the southern kings
### The Gibeonites Deceive Israel

**9** Now all the kings west of the Jordan River heard about what had happened. These were the kings of the Hittites, Amorites, Canaanites, Perizzites, Hivites, and Jebusites, who lived in the hill country, in the western foothills,* and along the coast of the Mediterranean Sea* as far north as the Lebanon mountains. ²These kings combined their armies to fight as one against Joshua and the Israelites.

#### Side references
8:18 Exod 14:16; 17:9-13; Josh 8:26
8:22 Deut 7:2
8:25 Deut 20:16-18
8:26 Exod 17:11-12
8:27 Josh 8:2
8:28 Deut 13:16
8:29 Deut 21:22-23
8:30 Deut 27:2-8
8:31 Exod 20:24-25; Deut 27:5-6
8:33 Deut 27:12-13
8:34 Deut 28:61; 31:11
8:35 Deut 31:12
9:1 Num 13:17; Josh 3:10; 11:19

**8:26** The Hebrew term used here refers to the complete consecration of things or people to the Lord, either by destroying them or by giving them as an offering.  **8:28** Ai means "ruin."  **8:31** Exod 20:25; Deut 27:5-6.  **8:32** Hebrew onto the stones.  **9:1a** Hebrew the Shephelah.  **9:1b** Hebrew the Great Sea.

**8:18, 19** The Lord gave Joshua the city. Yesterday's defeat became today's victory. Once sin is dealt with, forgiveness and victory lie ahead. With God's direction we need not stay discouraged or burdened with guilt. No matter how difficult a setback sin may bring, we must renew our efforts to carry out God's will.

**8:30, 31** The altar was to be built out of uncut stones so it would be holy (see Exodus 20:25). This would prevent the people from worshiping altars like idols, or worshiping the craftsmanship of the workers rather than the great works of God.

**8:32** It was most likely the Ten Commandments (recorded in Exodus 20) that Joshua copied on stones. These were the heart of all God's laws, and are still to be followed today.

**9:1-6** As the news about their victory became widespread, the Israelites experienced opposition in two forms: direct (kings in the area began to unite against them); and indirect (the Gibeonites resorted to deception). We can expect similar opposition as we obey God's commands. To guard against these pressures, we must rely on God and communicate daily with him. He will give us strength to endure the direct and indirect pressures and wisdom to see through deception.

**9:3**
Josh 10:2; 11:19

³But when the people of Gibeon heard what Joshua had done to Jericho and Ai, ⁴they resorted to deception to save themselves. They sent ambassadors to Joshua, loading their donkeys with weathered saddlebags and old, patched wineskins. ⁵They put on worn-out, patched sandals and ragged clothes. And the bread they took with them was dry and moldy. ⁶When they arrived at the camp of Israel at Gilgal, they told Joshua and the men of Israel, "We have come from a distant land to ask you to make a peace treaty with us."

**9:7**
Exod 23:32
Josh 11:19

⁷The Israelites replied to these Hivites, "How do we know you don't live nearby? For if you do, we cannot make a treaty with you."

⁸They replied, "We are your servants."

"But who are you?" Joshua demanded. "Where do you come from?"

**9:9**
Josh 9:16-17
**9:10**
Num 21:24, 33

⁹They answered, "Your servants have come from a very distant country. We have heard of the might of the LORD your God and of all he did in Egypt. ¹⁰We have also heard what he did to the two Amorite kings east of the Jordan River—King Sihon of Heshbon and King Og of Bashan (who lived in Ashtaroth). ¹¹So our elders and all our people instructed us, 'Take supplies for a long journey. Go meet with the people of Israel and tell them, "We are your servants; please make a treaty with us."'

¹²"This bread was hot from the ovens when we left our homes. But now, as you can see, it is dry and moldy. ¹³These wineskins were new when we filled them, but now they are old and split open. And our clothing and sandals are worn out from our very long journey."

**9:14**
Num 27:21

¹⁴So the Israelites examined their food, but they did not consult the LORD. ¹⁵Then Joshua made a peace treaty with them and guaranteed their safety, and the leaders of the community ratified their agreement with a binding oath.

**9:17**
Josh 18:25-28;
15:9, 60

¹⁶Three days after making the treaty, they learned that these people actually lived nearby! ¹⁷The Israelites set out at once to investigate and reached their towns in three days. The names of these towns were Gibeon, Kephirah, Beeroth, and Kiriath-jearim. ¹⁸But the Israelites did not attack the towns, for the Israelite leaders had made a vow to them in the name of the LORD, the God of Israel.

The people of Israel grumbled against their leaders because of the treaty. ¹⁹But the leaders replied, "Since we have sworn an oath in the presence of the LORD, the God of Israel, we cannot touch them. ²⁰This is what we must do. We must let them live, for divine anger would come upon us if we broke our oath. ²¹Let them live." So they made them woodcutters and water carriers for the entire community, as the Israelite leaders directed.

**9:21**
Deut 29:11

²²Joshua called together the Gibeonites and said, "Why did you lie to us? Why did you say that you live in a distant land when you live right here among us? ²³May you be cursed! From now on you will always be servants who cut wood and carry water for the house of my God."

**9:24**
Deut 7:1-2

²⁴They replied, "We did it because we—your servants—were clearly told that the LORD your God commanded his servant Moses to give you this entire land and to destroy all the people living in it. So we feared greatly for our lives because of you. That is why we have done this. ²⁵Now we are at your mercy—do to us whatever you think is right."

**9:27**
Deut 12:5

²⁶So Joshua did not allow the people of Israel to kill them. ²⁷But that day he made the Gibeonites the woodcutters and water carriers for the community of Israel and for the altar of the LORD—wherever the LORD would choose to build it. And that is what they do to this day.

---

**9:14-17** When the leaders sampled these men's provisions, they saw that the bread was dry and moldy, the wineskins were split open, and the clothes and sandals worn out. But they did not see through the deception. After the promise had been made and the treaty ratified, the facts came out—Israel's leaders had been deceived. God had specifically instructed Israel to make no treaties with the inhabitants of Canaan (Exodus 23:32; 34:12; Numbers 33:55; Deuteronomy 7:2; 20:17, 18). As a strategist, Joshua knew enough to talk to God before leading his troops into battle. But the peace treaty seemed innocent enough, so Joshua and the leaders made this decision on their own. By failing to seek God's guidance and rushing ahead with their own plans, they had to deal with angry people and an awkward alliance. Once again, they had forgotten to go to God; yet how often we do the same. A new situation arises, and we forget to seek God's wisdom and guidance. When we learn the lessons of the past and apply them to today, we save ourselves a lot of trouble.

**9:19, 20** Joshua and his advisers had made a mistake. But because they had given an oath to protect the Gibeonites, they would keep their word. The oath was not nullified by the Gibeonites' trickery. God had commanded that oaths be kept (Leviticus 5:4; 27:2, 28), and breaking an oath was serious. This encourages us not to take our promises lightly.

### Israel Defeats the Southern Armies

**10** Adoni-zedek, king of Jerusalem, heard that Joshua had captured and completely destroyed* Ai and killed its king, just as he had destroyed the town of Jericho and killed its king. He also learned that the Gibeonites had made peace with Israel and were now their allies. ²He and his people became very afraid when they heard all this because Gibeon was a large town—as large as the royal cities and larger than Ai. And the Gibeonite men were strong warriors.

³So King Adoni-zedek of Jerusalem sent messengers to several other kings: Hoham of Hebron, Piram of Jarmuth, Japhia of Lachish, and Debir of Eglon. ⁴"Come and help me destroy Gibeon," he urged them, "for they have made peace with Joshua and the people of Israel." ⁵So these five Amorite kings combined their armies for a united attack. They moved all their troops into place and attacked Gibeon.

⁶The men of Gibeon quickly sent messengers to Joshua at his camp in Gilgal. "Don't abandon your servants now!" they pleaded. "Come at once! Save us! Help us! For all the Amorite kings who live in the hill country have joined forces to attack us."

⁷So Joshua and his entire army, including his best warriors, left Gilgal and set out for Gibeon. ⁸"Do not be afraid of them," the LORD said to Joshua, "for I have given you victory over them. Not a single one of them will be able to stand up to you."

⁹Joshua traveled all night from Gilgal and took the Amorite armies by surprise. ¹⁰The LORD threw them into a panic, and the Israelites slaughtered great numbers of them at Gibeon. Then the Israelites chased the enemy along the road to Beth-horon, killing them all along the way to Azekah and Makkedah. ¹¹As the Amorites retreated down the road from Beth-horon, the LORD destroyed them with a terrible hailstorm from heaven that continued until they reached Azekah. The hail killed more of the enemy than the Israelites killed with the sword.

¹²On the day the LORD gave the Israelites victory over the Amorites, Joshua prayed to the LORD in front of all the people of Israel. He said,

"Let the sun stand still over Gibeon,
and the moon over the valley of Aijalon."

¹³So the sun stood still and the moon stayed in place until the nation of Israel had defeated its enemies.

Is this event not recorded in *The Book of Jashar*\*? The sun stayed in the middle of the sky,

**10:1** Josh 8:22-28; 9:15
**10:3** 2 Chr 11:9
**10:5** Num 13:29; Josh 9:2
**10:8** Josh 1:5, 9
**10:10** Deut 7:23
**10:13** 2 Sam 1:18; Isa 38:8

**10:1** The Hebrew term used here refers to the complete consecration of things or people to the LORD, either by destroying them or by giving them as an offering; also in 10:28, 35, 37, 39, 40.  **10:13a** Or *The Book of the Upright.*

**10:5-8** This alliance of enemy kings from the south actually helped Joshua and his army. Because the enemies had united to attack Gibeon, Joshua didn't have to spend the time and resources required to wage separate campaigns against each fortified city represented in the coalition. Joshua confidently confronted this coalition of armies and defeated them in a single battle because he trusted God to give Israel the victory.

**10:6, 7** Joshua's response shows his integrity. After having been deceived by the Gibeonites, Joshua and the leaders could have been slow about their attempt to rescue them. Instead, they immediately responded to their call for help. How willing would you be to help someone who had deceived you, even though you had forgiven him or her? We should take our word as seriously as Joshua did.

**10:12-14** How did the sun stand still? Of course, in relation to the earth the sun always stands still—it is the earth that travels around the sun. But the terminology used in Joshua should not cause us to doubt the miracle. After all, we are not confused when someone tells us the sun rises or sets. The point is that the day was prolonged, not that God used a particular method to prolong it. Two explanations have been given for how this event occurred: (1) A slowing of the earth's normal rotation gave Joshua more time, as the original Hebrew language seems to indicate. (2) Some unusual refraction of the sun's rays gave additional hours of light. Regardless of God's chosen method, the Bible is clear that the day was prolonged by a miracle, and that God's intervention turned the tide of battle for his people.

**10:13** *The Book of Jashar* (also mentioned in 2 Samuel 1:18) was probably a collection of historical events put to music. Many parts of the Bible contain quotations from previous books, songs, poems, or other spoken and written materials. Because God guided the writer of this book to select this material, his message comes with divine authority.

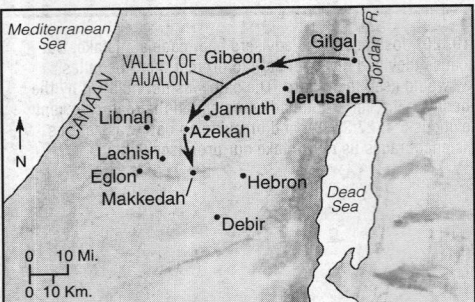

**THE BATTLE FOR GIBEON** Five Amorite kings conspired to destroy Gibeon. Israel came to the aid of the Gibeonites. The Israelites attacked the enemy armies outside of Gibeon and chased them through the valley of Aijalon as far as Makkedah and Azekah.

and it did not set as on a normal day.* ¹⁴There has never been a day like this one before or since, when the LORD answered such a prayer. Surely the LORD fought for Israel that day! ¹⁵Then Joshua and the Israelite army returned to their camp at Gilgal.

### Joshua Kills the Five Southern Kings

¹⁶During the battle the five kings escaped and hid in a cave at Makkedah. ¹⁷When Joshua heard that they had been found, ¹⁸he issued this command: "Cover the opening of the cave with large rocks, and place guards at the entrance to keep the kings inside. ¹⁹The rest of you continue chasing the enemy and cut them down from the rear. Don't give them a chance to get back to their towns, for the LORD your God has given you victory over them."

²⁰So Joshua and the Israelite army continued the slaughter and completely crushed the enemy. They totally wiped out the five armies except for a tiny remnant that managed to reach their fortified towns. ²¹Then the Israelites returned safely to Joshua in the camp at Makkedah. After that, no one dared to speak even a word against Israel.

²²Then Joshua said, "Remove the rocks covering the opening of the cave, and bring the five kings to me." ²³So they brought the five kings out of the cave—the kings of Jerusalem, Hebron, Jarmuth, Lachish, and Eglon. ²⁴When they brought them out, Joshua told the commanders of his army, "Come and put your feet on the kings' necks." And they did as they were told.

²⁵"Don't ever be afraid or discouraged," Joshua told his men. "Be strong and courageous, for the LORD is going to do this to all of your enemies." ²⁶Then Joshua killed each of the five kings and impaled them on five sharpened poles, where they hung until evening.

²⁷As the sun was going down, Joshua gave instructions for the bodies of the kings to be taken down from the poles and thrown into the cave where they had been hiding. Then they covered the opening of the cave with a pile of large rocks, which remains to this very day.

### Israel Destroys the Southern Towns

²⁸That same day Joshua captured and destroyed the town of Makkedah. He killed everyone in it, including the king, leaving no survivors. He destroyed them all, and he killed the king of Makkedah as he had killed the king of Jericho. ²⁹Then Joshua and the Israelites went to Libnah and attacked it. ³⁰There, too, the LORD gave them the town and its king. He killed everyone in it, leaving no survivors. Then Joshua killed the king of Libnah as he had killed the king of Jericho.

³¹From Libnah, Joshua and the Israelites went to Lachish and attacked it. ³²Here again, the LORD gave them Lachish. Joshua took it on the second day and killed everyone in it, just as he had done at Libnah. ³³During the attack on Lachish, King Horam of Gezer arrived with his army to help defend the town. But Joshua's men killed him and his army, leaving no survivors.

³⁴Then Joshua and the Israelite army went on to Eglon and attacked it. ³⁵They captured it that day and killed everyone in it. He completely destroyed everyone, just as he had done at Lachish. ³⁶From Eglon, Joshua and the Israelite army went up to Hebron and attacked it. ³⁷They captured the town and killed everyone in it, including its king, leaving no survivors. They did the same thing to all of its surrounding villages. And just as he had done at Eglon, he completely destroyed the entire population.

³⁸Then Joshua and the Israelites turned back and attacked Debir. ³⁹He captured the town, its king, and all of its surrounding villages. He completely destroyed everyone in it, leaving no survivors. He did to Debir and its king just what he had done to Hebron and to Libnah and its king.

10:13b Or *did not set for about a whole day.*

Cross-references: 10:14 Exod 14:14; Deut 1:30. 10:15 Josh 10:6, 43. 10:16 Josh 10:5. 10:20 Deut 20:16. 10:21 Josh 10:16. 10:22 Deut 7:24. 10:25 Josh 10:8. 10:26 Josh 8:29. 10:27 Deut 21:22-23. 10:29 Num 33:20-21; Josh 15:42. 10:36 Josh 14:13; 15:13.

**10:24** Placing a foot on the neck of a captive was a common military practice in the ancient Near East. It symbolized the victor's domination over his captives. These proud kings had boasted of their power. Now all Israel could see that God was superior to any earthly army.

**10:25** With God's help, Israel won the battle against five Amorite armies. Such a triumph was part of God's daily business as he worked with his people for victory. Joshua told his men never to be afraid because God would give them similar victories over all their enemies. God has often protected us and won victories for us. The same God who empowered Joshua and who has led us in the past will help us with our present and future needs. Reminding ourselves of his help in the past will give us hope for the struggles that lie ahead.

**10:32** Notice that in every Israelite victory, the text gives the credit to the Lord. All of Israel's victories came from God. When we are successful, we may be tempted to take all the credit and glory as though we succeeded by ourselves, in our own strength. In reality, *God* gives us the victories, and he alone delivers us from our enemies. We should give him the credit and praise him for his goodness.

⁴⁰So Joshua conquered the whole region—the kings and people of the hill country, the Negev, the western foothills,* and the mountain slopes. He completely destroyed everyone in the land, leaving no survivors, just as the LORD, the God of Israel, had commanded. ⁴¹Joshua slaughtered them from Kadesh-barnea to Gaza and from the region around the town of Goshen up to Gibeon. ⁴²Joshua conquered all these kings and their land in a single campaign, for the LORD, the God of Israel, was fighting for his people.

**10:40**
Deut 1:7; 7:24;
20:16
**10:41**
Josh 11:16; 15:51
**10:42**
Josh 10:14

⁴³Then Joshua and the Israelite army returned to their camp at Gilgal.

## 3. Joshua attacks the northern kings

**11** When King Jabin of Hazor heard what had happened, he sent messages to the following kings: King Jobab of Madon; the king of Shimron; the king of Acshaph; ²all the kings of the northern hill country; the kings in the Jordan Valley south of Galilee*; the kings in the Galilean foothills*; the kings of Naphoth-dor on the west; ³the kings of Canaan, both east and west; the kings of the Amorites, the Hittites, the Perizzites, the Jebusites in the hill country; and the Hivites in the towns on the slopes of Mount Hermon in the land of Mizpah.

**11:1**
Josh 11:10
**11:2**
Josh 12:3

⁴All these kings came out to fight. Their combined armies formed a vast horde. And with all their horses and chariots, they covered the landscape like the sand on the seashore. ⁵The kings joined forces and established their camp around the water near Merom to fight against Israel.

**11:4**
Judg 7:12

⁶Then the LORD said to Joshua, "Do not be afraid of them. By this time tomorrow I will hand all of them over to Israel as dead men. Then you must cripple their horses and burn their chariots."

**11:6**
Josh 10:8
2 Sam 8:4

⁷So Joshua and all his fighting men traveled to the water near Merom and attacked suddenly. ⁸And the LORD gave them victory over their enemies. The Israelites chased them as far as Greater Sidon and Misrephoth-maim, and eastward into the valley of Mizpah, until not one enemy warrior was left alive. ⁹Then Joshua crippled the horses and burned all the chariots, as the LORD had instructed.

¹⁰Joshua then turned back and captured Hazor and killed its king. (Hazor had at one time been the capital of all these kingdoms.) ¹¹The Israelites completely destroyed* every living thing in the city, leaving no survivors. Not a single person was spared. And then Joshua burned the city.

**11:10**
Judg 4:2
1 Sam 12:9
1 Kgs 9:15
2 Kgs 15:29
**11:11**
Deut 20:16-17

¹²Joshua slaughtered all the other kings and their people, completely destroying them, just as Moses, the servant of the LORD, had commanded. ¹³But the Israelites did not burn any of the towns built on mounds except Hazor, which Joshua burned. ¹⁴And the Israelites took all the plunder and livestock of the ravaged towns for themselves. But they killed all the people, leaving no survivors. ¹⁵As the LORD had commanded his servant Moses, so Moses

**11:14**
Num 31:11-12
**11:15**
Exod 34:11-12

**10:40** Hebrew *the Shephelah.* **11:2a** Hebrew *in the Arabah south of Kinnereth.* **11:2b** Hebrew *the Shephelah;* also in 11:16. **11:11** The Hebrew term used here refers to the complete consecration of things or people to the LORD, either by destroying them or by giving them as an offering; also in 11:12, 20, 21.

---

**THE BATTLE FOR HAZOR**
Kings from the north joined together to battle the Israelites who controlled the southern half of Canaan. They gathered by the water near Merom, but Joshua attacked them by surprise— the enemies' chariots were useless in the dense forests. Hazor, the largest Canaanite center in Galilee, was destroyed.

**10:40-43** God had commanded Joshua to take the leadership in ridding the land of sin so God's people could occupy it. Joshua did his part thoroughly—leading the united army to weaken the inhabitants. When God orders us to stop sinning, we must not pause to debate, consider the options, negotiate a compromise, or rationalize. Instead, like Joshua, our response must be swift and complete. We must be ruthless in avoiding relationships and activities that can lead us into sin.

**11:1-5** Two kings of Hazor were named Jabin. The other, apparently a weak ruler, is mentioned in Judges 4:2, 3. The Jabin of this story was quite powerful because he was able to build an alliance with dozens of kings. By all appearances, Jabin had a clear advantage over Joshua and his outnumbered forces. But those who honor God can be victorious regardless of the odds.

**11:10-13** Victorious invaders usually kept captured cities intact, moving into them and making them centers of commerce and defense. For example, Moses predicted in Deuteronomy 6:10-12 that Israel would occupy cities they themselves had not built. Joshua, however, burned Hazor. As a former capital of the land, Hazor symbolized the wicked culture that Israel had come to destroy. In addition, its capture and destruction broke the backbone of the federation and weakened the will of the people to resist.

**11:15** Joshua carefully obeyed all the instructions given by God.

commanded Joshua. And Joshua did as he was told, carefully obeying all the commands that the LORD had given to Moses.

### 4. Summary of conquests

<sup></sup>

**11:16**
Josh 10:40

**11:17**
Deut 7:24
Josh 12:7

**11:19**
Josh 9:3-15

**11:20**
Exod 14:17
Deut 7:16

**11:21**
Num 13:33
Deut 9:1-2
Josh 14:12; 15:13

**11:23**
Deut 1:38; 12:9-10;
25:19
Heb 4:8

<sup>16</sup>So Joshua conquered the entire region—the hill country, the entire Negev, the whole area around the town of Goshen, the western foothills, the Jordan Valley,* the mountains of Israel, and the Galilean foothills. <sup>17</sup>The Israelite territory now extended all the way from Mount Halak, which leads up to Seir in the south, as far north as Baal-gad at the foot of Mount Hermon in the valley of Lebanon. Joshua killed all the kings of those territories, <sup>18</sup>waging war for a long time to accomplish this. <sup>19</sup>No one in this region made peace with the Israelites except the Hivites of Gibeon. All the others were defeated. <sup>20</sup>For the LORD hardened their hearts and caused them to fight the Israelites. So they were completely destroyed without mercy, as the LORD had commanded Moses.

<sup>21</sup>During this period Joshua destroyed all the descendants of Anak, who lived in the hill country of Hebron, Debir, Anab, and the entire hill country of Judah and Israel. He killed them all and completely destroyed their towns. <sup>22</sup>None of the descendants of Anak were left in all the land of Israel, though some still remained in Gaza, Gath, and Ashdod.

<sup>23</sup>So Joshua took control of the entire land, just as the LORD had instructed Moses. He gave it to the people of Israel as their special possession, dividing the land among the tribes. So the land finally had rest from war.

### Kings Defeated East of the Jordan

**12:1**
Num 32:33
Deut 3:8
Josh 11:1-3

**12:2**
Num 21:23
Deut 2:36

**12:4**
Num 21:33
Josh 13:12

**12:5**
Deut 3:10

**12** These are the kings east of the Jordan River who had been killed by the Israelites and whose land was taken. Their territory extended from the Arnon Gorge to Mount Hermon and included all the land east of the Jordan Valley.*

<sup>2</sup>King Sihon of the Amorites, who lived in Heshbon, was defeated. His kingdom included Aroer, on the edge of the Arnon Gorge, and extended from the middle of the Arnon Gorge to the Jabbok River, which serves as a border for the Ammonites. This territory included the southern half of the territory of Gilead. <sup>3</sup>Sihon also controlled the Jordan Valley and regions to the east—from as far north as the Sea of Galilee to as far south as the Dead Sea,* including the road to Beth-jeshimoth and southward to the slopes of Pisgah.

<sup>4</sup>King Og of Bashan, the last of the Rephaites, lived at Ashtaroth and Edrei. <sup>5</sup>He ruled a territory stretching from Mount Hermon to Salecah in the north and to all of Bashan in the east, and westward to the borders of the kingdoms of Geshur and Maacah. This territory included the northern half of Gilead, as far as the boundary of King Sihon of Heshbon.

<sup>6</sup>Moses, the servant of the LORD, and the Israelites had destroyed the people of King Sihon and King Og. And Moses gave their land as a possession to the tribes of Reuben, Gad, and the half-tribe of Manasseh.

**11:16** Hebrew *the Shephelah, the Arabah.* **12:1** Hebrew *the Arabah;* also in 12:3, 8. **12:3** Hebrew *from the Sea of Kinnereth to the Sea of the Arabah, which is the Salt Sea.*

---

This theme of obedience is repeated frequently in the book of Joshua, partly because obedience is one aspect of life that each individual believer can control. We can't always control our understanding because we may not have all the facts. We can't control what other people do or how they treat us. However, we can control our choice to obey God. Whatever new challenges we may face, the Bible contains relevant instructions that we can choose to ignore or choose to follow.

**11:15** Joshua followed every detail of God's commands to Moses. It is usually difficult to complete someone else's project, but Joshua stepped into Moses' job, building upon what Moses had started, and brought it to completion. A new person starting a new job usually brings a new style and personality to that job. But the church or any other organization cannot work effectively if every change of personnel means starting from scratch. True servants will step in and continue or complete good work that others have begun.

**11:18** The conquest of much of the land of Canaan seems to have happened quickly (we can read about it in one sitting), but it actually took seven years. We often expect quick changes in our lives and quick victories over sin. Our journey with God is a lifelong process, however, and the changes and victories may

take time. It is easy to grow impatient with God and feel like giving up hope because things are moving too slowly. When we are close to a situation, it is difficult to see progress. But when we look back, we can see that God never stopped working.

**11:21, 22** The descendants of Anak were the tribes of giants the Israelite scouts described when they gave their negative report on the Promised Land (Numbers 13–14). This time the people did not let their fear of the giants prevent them from engaging in battle and claiming the land God had promised.

**12:1ff** Chapter 12 is a summary of the first half of the book of Joshua. It lists the kings and nations conquered by Joshua to both the east and the west of the Jordan River. As long as the people trusted and obeyed God, one evil nation after another fell in defeat.

## Kings Defeated West of the Jordan

7 The following is a list of the kings that Joshua and the Israelite armies defeated on the west side of the Jordan, from Baal-gad in the valley of Lebanon to Mount Halak, which leads up to Seir. (Joshua gave this land to the tribes of Israel as their possession, 8including the hill country, the western foothills,* the Jordan Valley, the mountain slopes, the Judean wilderness, and the Negev. The people who lived in this region were the Hittites, the Amorites, the Canaanites, the Perizzites, the Hivites, and the Jebusites.) These are the kings Israel defeated:

9 The king of Jericho
   The king of Ai, near Bethel
10 The king of Jerusalem
   The king of Hebron
11 The king of Jarmuth
   The king of Lachish

**12:8** Hebrew *the Shephelah.*

**12:7**
Josh 11:17

**12:8**
Josh 11:16

**12:9**
Josh 6:2; 8:29

**THE CONQUERED LAND**
Joshua displayed brilliant military strategy in the way he went about conquering the land of Canaan. He first captured the well-fortified Jericho to gain a foothold in Canaan and to demonstrate the awesome might of the God of Israel. Then he gained the hill country around Bethel and Gibeon. From there he subdued towns in the lowlands. Then his army conquered important cities in the north, such as Hazor. In all, Israel conquered land both east (12:1–6) and west (12:7–24) of the Jordan River; from Mount Hermon in the north to beyond the Negev to Mount Halak in the south. Thirty-one kings and their cities had been defeated. The Israelites had overpowered the Hittites, the Amorites, the Canaanites, the Perizzites, the Hivites, and the Jebusites. Other peoples living in Canaan were yet to be conquered.

The broken lines (—·—·—·) indicate modern boundaries.

**12:12**
Josh 10:33

**12:13**
Josh 10:3

12 The king of Eglon
The king of Gezer
13 The king of Debir
The king of Geder
14 The king of Hormah
The king of Arad
15 The king of Libnah
The king of Adullam
16 The king of Makkedah
The king of Bethel
17 The king of Tappuah
The king of Hepher
18 The king of Aphek
The king of Lasharon
19 The king of Madon
The king of Hazor
20 The king of Shimron-meron
The king of Acshaph
21 The king of Taanach
The king of Megiddo
22 The king of Kedesh
The king of Jokneam in Carmel
23 The king of Dor in the town of Naphoth-dor*

**12:24**
Deut 7:24

The king of Goyim in Gilgal*
24 The king of Tirzah.

In all, thirty-one kings were defeated.

## C. DIVIDING THE PROMISED LAND (13:1—24:33)

After seven years of battle, Israel gained control of the land, which was then divided and allotted to the tribes. Joshua dismisses the army, for it was now each tribe's responsibility to clear out the remaining enemies from their own areas. Joshua continues to encourage the people to remain faithful to God so they can remain in the land. The Promised Land was Israel's earthly inheritance. But Israel also had a spiritual inheritance in which we can share when we live a life of faithfulness to God.

### 1. The tribes receive their land
*The Land Yet to Be Conquered*

**13:1**
Josh 14:10

**13:2**
Judg 3:3

**13** When Joshua was an old man, the LORD said to him, "You are growing old, and much land remains to be conquered. 2 This is the territory that remains: all the regions of the Philistines and the Geshurites, 3and the larger territory of the Canaanites, extending from the stream of Shihor on the border of Egypt, northward to the boundary of Ekron. It includes the territory of the five Philistine rulers of Gaza, Ashdod, Ashkelon, Gath, and Ekron. The land of the Avvites 4in the south also remains to be conquered. In the north, the following area has not yet been conquered: all the land of the Canaanites, including Mearah (which belongs to the Sidonians), stretching northward to Aphek on the border of the

12:23a Hebrew *Naphath-dor*, a variant spelling of Naphoth-dor. 12:23b Greek version reads *Goyim in Galilee.*

**13–19** These chapters describe how the Promised Land was to be divided among the 12 tribes. First, the tribe of Levi was not to have any land because they were to spend all their energies serving the people, not their own interests (13:14; 21). Second, the tribes of Reuben and Gad and the half-tribe of Manasseh had already received land east of the Jordan River, which had been given to them by Moses (Numbers 32). Third, the tribes of Judah and Joseph (Ephraim and the other half-tribe of Manasseh) had received land that their ancestor Jacob had promised them 450 years earlier (Genesis 48:22; Joshua 15–17). The rest of the tribes divided up the remaining land by casting sacred lots (chapter 18).

Through Jacob's original blessing of his sons (Genesis 49) and Moses' blessing of the 12 tribes (Deuteronomy 33), the type of land each tribe would receive was already known. The two blessings were prophetic, for although Joshua cast lots to determine the land to be given to each of the remaining tribes, the allotments came out just as Jacob and Moses had predicted.

**13:1** Joshua was getting old—he was between 85 and 100 years of age at this time. God, however, still had work for him to do. Our culture often glorifies the young and strong and sets aside those who are older. Yet older people are filled with the wisdom that comes with experience. They are very capable of serving if given the chance and should be encouraged to do so. Believers are never allowed to retire from God's service. Those past retirement age should not assume that age disqualifies or excuses them from serving God.

Amorites; 5the land of the Gebalites and all of the Lebanon mountain area to the east, from Baal-gad below Mount Hermon to Lebo-hamath; 6and all the hill country from Lebanon to Misrephoth-maim, including all the land of the Sidonians.

13:6
Josh 11:8

"I myself will drive these people out of the land ahead of the Israelites. So be sure to give this land to Israel as a special possession, just as I have commanded you. 7Include all this territory as Israel's possession when you divide this land among the nine tribes and the half-tribe of Manasseh."

### The Land Divided East of the Jordan
8Half the tribe of Manasseh and the tribes of Reuben and Gad had already received their grants of land on the east side of the Jordan, for Moses, the servant of the LORD, had previously assigned this land to them.

13:8
Josh 12:1-6

9 Their territory extended from Aroer on the edge of the Arnon Gorge (including the town in the middle of the gorge) to the plain beyond Medeba, as far as Dibon. 10It also included all the towns of King Sihon of the Amorites, who had reigned in Heshbon, and extended as far as the borders of Ammon. 11It included Gilead, the territory of the kingdoms of Geshur and Maacah, all of Mount Hermon, all of Bashan as far as Salecah, 12and all the territory of King Og of Bashan, who had reigned in Ashtaroth and Edrei. King Og was the last of the Rephaites, for Moses had attacked them and driven them out. 13But the Israelites failed to drive out the people of Geshur and Maacah, so they continue to live among the Israelites to this day.

13:9
Num 32:34

13:12
Num 21:33-35

### An Allotment for the Tribe of Levi
14Moses did not assign any allotment of land to the tribe of Levi. Instead, as the LORD had promised them, their allotment came from the offerings burned on the altar to the LORD, the God of Israel.

13:14
Deut 18:1-2

### The Land Given to the Tribe of Reuben
15Moses had assigned the following area to the clans of the tribe of Reuben.

16Their territory extended from Aroer on the edge of the Arnon Gorge (including the town in the middle of the gorge) to the plain beyond Medeba. 17It included Heshbon and the other towns on the plain—Dibon, Bamoth-baal, Beth-baal-meon, 18Jahaz, Kedemoth, Mephaath, 19Kiriathaim, Sibmah, Zereth-shahar on the hill above the valley, 20Beth-peor, the slopes of Pisgah, and Beth-jeshimoth.

13:16
Josh 12:2

---

**13:7** Much of the land was unconquered at this point, but God's plan was to go ahead and include it in the divisions among the tribes. God's desire was that it would eventually be conquered by the Israelites. God knows the future, and as he leads you he already knows about the victories that lie ahead. But just as the Israelites still had to go to battle and fight, we must still face the trials and fight the battles of our unconquered land.

**THE LAND YET TO BE CONQUERED** Canaan was now controlled by the Israelites, although much land and several cities still needed to be conquered. Joshua told the people to include both conquered and unconquered lands in the territorial allotments (13:7). He was certain the people would complete the conquest as God had commanded.

What are our unconquered lands? They may be overseas missionary territories, new languages in which to translate the Bible, new missionary areas in our neighborhoods, interest groups or institutions that need redemptive work, unchallenged public problems or ethical issues, unconfessed sin in our lives, or underdeveloped talents and resources. What territory has God given you to conquer? This territory is your "Promised Land." Our inheritance will be a new heaven and a new earth (Revelation 21:1) if we fulfill the mission God has given us to do.

**13:13** One reason the Israelites encountered so many problems as they settled the land was that they failed to *fully* conquer the land and drive out all its inhabitants. The cancer-like presence of the remaining pagan peoples of Canaan caused unending difficulties for the Israelites, as the book of Judges records. Just as they failed to remove completely the sin from the land, believers today often fail to remove completely the sin from their lives—also with disastrous results. As a self-test, reread the Ten Commandments in Exodus 20:1-17. Ask yourself, Am I tolerating sinful practices or thoughts? Have I accepted half-measures as good enough? Do I condemn the faults of others but condone my own?

**13:15-23** Because of Joseph's godly character (Genesis 49:22-26), the tribes descended from him—Ephraim and Manasseh—were given the richest, most fertile land in all of Canaan. Judah, who offered himself in exchange for his brother Benjamin's safety (Genesis 44:18-34), received the largest portion of land, which eventually became the southern kingdom and the seat of David's dynasty. Reuben, who slept with one of his father's wives (Genesis 49:4), was given desert land, the region described here. The

13:21-22
Num 31:8

21The land of Reuben also included all the towns of the plain and the entire kingdom of Sihon. Sihon was the Amorite king who had reigned in Heshbon and was killed by Moses along with the leaders of Midian—Evi, Rekem, Zur, Hur, and Reba—princes living in the region who were allied with Sihon. 22The Israelites had also killed Balaam son of Beor, who used magic to tell the future. 23The Jordan River marked the western boundary for the tribe of Reuben. The towns and their surrounding villages in this area were given as a homeland to the clans of the tribe of Reuben.

### The Land Given to the Tribe of Gad

24Moses had assigned the following area to the clans of the tribe of Gad.

13:27
Num 34:11

25Their territory included Jazer, all the towns of Gilead, and half of the land of Ammon, as far as the town of Aroer just west of* Rabbah. 26It extended from Heshbon to Ramath-mizpeh and Betonim, and from Mahanaim to the territory of Lo-debar.* 27In the valley were Beth-haram, Beth-nimrah, Succoth, Zaphon, and the rest of the kingdom of King Sihon of Heshbon. The western boundary ran along the Jordan River, extended as far north as the tip of the Sea of Galilee,* and then turned eastward. 28The towns and their surrounding villages in this area were given as a homeland to the clans of the tribe of Gad.

### The Land Given to the Half-Tribe of Manasseh

29Moses had assigned the following area to the clans of the half-tribe of Manasseh.

13:30
Num 32:41

30Their territory extended from Mahanaim, including all of Bashan, all the former kingdom of King Og, and the sixty towns of Jair in Bashan. 31It also included half of Gilead and King Og's royal cities of Ashtaroth and Edrei. All this was given to the clans of the descendants of Makir, who was Manasseh's son.

13:33
Num 18:20
Josh 13:14

32 These are the allotments Moses had made while he was on the plains of Moab, across the Jordan River, east of Jericho. 33But Moses gave no allotment of land to the tribe of Levi, for the LORD, the God of Israel, had promised that he himself would be their allotment.

### The Land Divided West of the Jordan

14:1
Num 34:16-17

**14** The remaining tribes of Israel received land in Canaan as allotted by Eleazar the priest, Joshua son of Nun, and the tribal leaders. 2 These nine and a half tribes received their grants of land by means of sacred lots, in accordance with the LORD's command through Moses.

14:3
Num 32:33
Josh 13:14

3Moses had already given a grant of land to the two and a half tribes on the east side of the Jordan River, but he had given the Levites no such allotment. 4The descendants of Joseph had become two separate tribes—Manasseh and Ephraim. And the Levites were given no land at all, only towns to live in with surrounding pasturelands for their livestock and all their possessions. 5So the land was distributed in strict accordance with the LORD's commands to Moses.

**13:25** Hebrew *in front of.* **13:26** Hebrew *Li-debir,* apparently a variant spelling of Lo-debar (compare 2 Sam 9:4; 17:27; Amos 6:13). **13:27** Hebrew *Sea of Kinnereth.*

---

blessings Jacob gave to his sons according to their character seem also to be reflected in the characteristics of the land each tribe later received.

**13:29** The tribe of Manasseh was divided into two half-tribes. This occurred when many people from the tribe wanted to settle east of the Jordan River in an area that was especially suited for their flocks (Numbers 32:33). The rest of the tribe preferred to settle west of the Jordan River in the land of Canaan.

**13:33** The tribe of Levi was dedicated to serving God. The Levites needed more time and mobility than a landowner could possibly have. Giving them land would mean saddling them with responsibilities and loyalties that would hinder their service to God. Instead, God arranged for the other tribes to meet the Levites' needs through donations. (See Numbers 35:2-4 for how the Levites were to receive cities within each tribal territory.)

**14:5** The land was divided exactly as God had instructed Moses years before. Joshua did not change a word. He followed God's commands precisely. Often we believe that *almost* is close enough, and this idea can carry over into our spiritual lives. For example, we may follow God's Word as long as we agree with it, but ignore it when the demands seem harsh. But God is looking for people who follow instructions thoroughly.

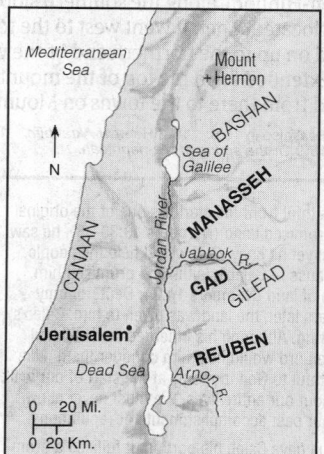

**THE TRIBES EAST OF THE JORDAN** Joshua assigned territory to the tribes of Reuben, Gad, and the half-tribe of Manasseh on the east side of the Jordan where they had chosen to remain because of the wonderful livestock country (Numbers 32:1–5).

## Caleb Requests His Land

⁶A delegation from the tribe of Judah, led by Caleb son of Jephunneh the Kenizzite, came to Joshua at Gilgal. Caleb said to Joshua, "Remember what the LORD said to Moses, the man of God, about you and me when we were at Kadesh-barnea. ⁷I was forty years old when Moses, the servant of the LORD, sent me from Kadesh-barnea to explore the land of Canaan. I returned and gave an honest report, ⁸but my brothers who went with me frightened the people from entering the Promised Land. For my part, I wholeheartedly followed the LORD my God. ⁹So that day Moses solemnly promised me, 'The land of Canaan on which you were just walking will be your grant of land and that of your descendants forever, because you wholeheartedly followed the LORD my God.'

¹⁰"Now, as you can see, the LORD has kept me alive and well as he promised for all these forty-five years since Moses made this promise—even while Israel wandered in the wilderness. Today I am eighty-five years old. ¹¹I am as strong now as I was when Moses sent me on that journey, and I can still travel and fight as well as I could then. ¹²So give me the hill country that the LORD promised me. You will remember that as scouts we found the descendants of Anak living there in great, walled towns. But if the LORD is with me, I will drive them out of the land, just as the LORD said."

¹³So Joshua blessed Caleb son of Jephunneh and gave Hebron to him as his portion of land. ¹⁴Hebron still belongs to the descendants of Caleb son of Jephunneh the Kenizzite because he wholeheartedly followed the LORD, the God of Israel. ¹⁵(Previously Hebron had been called Kiriath-arba. It had been named after Arba, a great hero of the descendants of Anak.)

And the land had rest from war.

## The Land Given to the Tribe of Judah

**15** The allotment for the clans of the tribe of Judah reached southward to the border of Edom, as far south as the wilderness of Zin.

²The southern boundary began at the south bay of the Dead Sea,* ³ran south of Scorpion Pass* into the wilderness of Zin, and then went south of Kadesh-barnea to Hezron. Then it went up to Addar, where it turned toward Karka. ⁴From there it passed to Azmon until it finally reached the Brook of Egypt, which it followed to the Mediterranean Sea.* This was their* southern boundary.

⁵The eastern boundary extended along the Dead Sea to the mouth of the Jordan River.

The northern boundary began at the bay where the Jordan River empties into the Dead Sea, ⁶went up from there to Beth-hoglah, then proceeded north of Beth-arabah to the Stone of Bohan. (Bohan was Reuben's son.) ⁷From that point it went through the valley of Achor to Debir, turning north toward Gilgal, which is across from the slopes of Adummim on the south side of the valley. From there the boundary extended to the springs at En-shemesh and on to En-rogel. ⁸The boundary then passed through the valley of Ben-Hinnom, along the southern slopes of the Jebusites, where the city of Jerusalem is located. Then it went west to the top of the mountain above the valley of Hinnom, and on up to the northern end of the valley of Rephaim. ⁹From there the boundary extended from the top of the mountain to the spring at the waters of Nephtoah,* and from there to the towns on Mount Ephron. Then it turned toward

**14:6** Num 13:30; 14:6, 24, 30
**14:9** Deut 1:36
**14:12** Num 13:33
**14:15** Josh 11:23
**15:1** Num 34:3-4 Deut 32:51
**15:3-4** Num 34:4-5
**15:5-6** Josh 18:15-19
**15:8** Josh 15:63
**15:9** Josh 18:15

**15:2** Hebrew *the Salt Sea;* also in 15:5. **15:3** Hebrew *Akrabbim.* **15:4a** Hebrew *the sea;* also in 15:11. **15:4b** Hebrew *your.* **15:9** Or *the spring at Me-nephtoah.*

**14:6-12** Caleb was faithful from the start. As one of the original scouts sent into the Promised Land (Numbers 13:30-33), he saw great cities and giants, yet he knew God would help the people conquer the land. Because of Caleb's faith, God promised him a personal inheritance of land (Numbers 14:24; Deuteronomy 1:34-36). Here, 45 years later, the land was given to him. Caleb's faith was still unwavering. Although his inherited land still had giants, Caleb knew the Lord would help him conquer them. Like Caleb, we must be faithful to God, not only at the start of our walk with him, but throughout our entire lives. We must never allow ourselves to rest on our past accomplishments or reputations.

**14:6-12** When Joshua gave Caleb his portion, it fulfilled a promise God had made to Caleb 45 years earlier. We expect such integ-

rity and reliability from God, but do we expect the same from his followers? How about you? Is your word this reliable? Would you honor a 45-year-old promise? God would—and does. Even today he is honoring promises he made *thousands* of years ago. In fact, some of his greatest promises are yet to be fulfilled. This gives us much to look forward to. Let your faith grow as you realize that God keeps his word.

**14:15** The descendants of Anak were a race of giants who inhabited parts of the land before Joshua's conquest.

**15:4** Notice that these boundaries and descriptions of the Promised Land are very specific. God was telling Israel exactly what to do, and he was giving them just what they needed. They had no excuse for disobedience.

Baalah (that is, Kiriath-jearim). 10The boundary circled west of Baalah to Mount Seir, passed along to the town of Kesalon on the northern slope of Mount Jearim, and went down to Beth-shemesh and on to Timnah. 11The boundary then proceeded to the slope of the hill north of Ekron, where it turned toward Shikkeron and Mount Baalah. It passed Jabneel and ended at the Mediterranean Sea.

12 The western boundary was the shoreline of the Mediterranean Sea.*

These are the boundaries for the clans of the tribe of Judah.

### The Land Given to Caleb

13 The LORD commanded Joshua to assign some of Judah's territory to Caleb son of Jephunneh. So Caleb was given the town of Kiriath-arba (that is, Hebron), which had been named after Anak's ancestor. 14Caleb drove out the three groups of Anakites—the descendants of Sheshai, Ahiman, and Talmai, the sons of Anak.

15From there he went to fight against the people living in the town of Debir (formerly called Kiriath-sepher). 16Caleb said, "I will give my daughter Acsah in marriage to the one who attacks and captures Kiriath-sepher." 17Othniel, the son of Caleb's brother Kenaz, was the one who conquered it, so Acsah became Othniel's wife.

18When Acsah married Othniel, she urged him* to ask her father for a field. As she got down off her donkey, Caleb asked her, "What's the matter?"

19She said, "Give me another gift. You have already given me land in the Negev; now please give me springs of water, too." So Caleb gave her the upper and lower springs.

### The Towns Allotted to Judah

20This was the homeland allocated to the clans of the tribe of Judah.

21The towns of Judah situated along the borders of Edom in the extreme south were Kabzeel, Eder, Jagur, 22Kinah, Dimonah, Adadah, 23Kedesh, Hazor, Ithnan, 24Ziph, Telem, Bealoth, 25Hazor-hadattah, Kerioth-hezron (that is, Hazor), 26Amam, Shema, Moladah, 27Hazar-gaddah, Heshmon, Beth-pelet, 28Hazar-shual, Beersheba, Biziothiah, 29Baalah, Iim, Ezem, 30Eltolad, Kesil, Hormah, 31Ziklag, Madmannah, Sansannah, 32Lebaoth, Shilhim, Ain, and Rimmon—twenty-nine towns with their surrounding villages.

33 The following towns situated in the western foothills* were also given to Judah: Eshtaol, Zorah, Ashnah, 34Zanoah, En-gannim, Tappuah, Enam, 35Jarmuth, Adullam, Socoh, Azekah, 36Shaaraim, Adithaim, Gederah, and Gederothaim—fourteen towns with their surrounding villages.

37Also included were Zenan, Hadashah, Migdal-gad, 38Dilean, Mizpeh, Joktheel, 39Lachish, Bozkath, Eglon, 40Cabbon, Lahmam, Kitlish, 41Gederoth, Beth-dagon, Naamah, and Makkedah—sixteen towns with their surrounding villages.

42Besides these, there were Libnah, Ether, Ashan, 43Iphtah, Ashnah, Nezib, 44Keilah, Aczib, and Mareshah—nine towns with their surrounding villages.

45The territory of the tribe of Judah also included Ekron and its surrounding settlements and villages. 46From Ekron the boundary extended west and included the towns near Ashdod with their surrounding villages. 47It also included Ashdod with its surrounding settlements and villages and Gaza with its settlements and villages, as far as the Brook of Egypt and along the coast of the Mediterranean Sea.

48Judah also received the following towns in the hill country: Shamir, Jattir, Socoh, 49Dannah, Kiriath-sannah (that is, Debir), 50Anab, Eshtemoh, Anim, 51Goshen, Holon, and Giloh—eleven towns with their surrounding villages.

52Also included were the towns of Arab, Dumah, Eshan, 53Janim, Beth-tappuah, Aphekah, 54Humtah, Kiriath-arba (that is, Hebron), and Zior—nine towns with their surrounding villages.

**Cross-references (left margin):**

15:13 Josh 14:13-15

15:14 Num 13:33 Deut 9:2 Josh 11:21-22

15:17 Judg 1:12-13; 3:9

15:21 Gen 35:21

15:31 1 Sam 27:6

15:33 Judg 13:25; 16:31

15:39 Josh 10:3 2 Kgs 14:19

15:47 Num 34:6

**15:12** Hebrew the Great Sea; also in 15:47.    **15:18** Some Greek manuscripts read he urged her.    **15:33** Hebrew the Shephelah.

15:16-19 Othniel became Israel's first judge after Joshua's death (Judges 1:13; 3:9-11). He played an important role in reforming Israel by chasing away an oppressive enemy army and bringing peace back to the land. Thus Caleb's legacy of faithfulness continued to the next generation.

15:19 Acsah asked Caleb for springs of water because her land was in the south and was very arid. Caleb probably granted her request as a wedding present (see 15:17).

55Besides these, there were Maon, Carmel, Ziph, Juttah, 56Jezreel, Jokdeam, Zanoah, 57Kain, Gibeah, and Timnah—ten towns with their surrounding villages.

58In addition, there were Halhul, Beth-zur, Gedor, 59Maarath, Beth-anoth, and Eltekon—six towns with their surrounding villages.

60There were also Kiriath-baal (that is, Kiriath-jearim) and Rabbah—two towns with their surrounding villages.

61In the wilderness there were the towns of Beth-arabah, Middin, Secacah, 62Nibshan, the City of Salt, and En-gedi—six towns with their surrounding villages.

63But the tribe of Judah could not drive out the Jebusites, who lived in the city of Jerusalem, so the Jebusites live there among the people of Judah to this day.

**15:63**
Judg 1:21
2 Sam 5:6

## The Land Given to Ephraim and West Manasseh

**16** The allotment for the descendants of Joseph extended from the Jordan River near Jericho, east of the springs of Jericho, through the wilderness and into the hill country of Bethel. 2From Bethel (that is, Luz)* it ran over to Ataroth in the territory of the Arkites. 3 Then it descended westward to the territory of the Japhletites as far as Lower Beth-horon, then to Gezer and over to the Mediterranean Sea.*

**16:1**
Josh 8:15; 18:12

**16:2**
Josh 18:13

4This was the homeland allocated to the families of Joseph's sons, Manasseh and Ephraim.

## The Land Given to Ephraim

5The following territory was given to the clans of the tribe of Ephraim.

**16:5**
Josh 18:13

The boundary of their homeland began at Ataroth-addar in the east. From there it ran to Upper Beth-horon, 6then on to the Mediterranean Sea. From Micmethath on the north, the boundary curved eastward past Taanath-shiloh to the east of Janoah. 7From Janoah it turned southward to Ataroth and Naarah, touched Jericho, and ended at the Jordan River. 8From Tappuah the boundary extended westward, following the Kanah Ravine to the Mediterranean Sea. This is the homeland allocated to the clans of the tribe of Ephraim.

**16:6**
Josh 17:7

**16:8**
Josh 17:8-9

9In addition, some towns with their surrounding villages in the territory allocated to the half-tribe of Manasseh were set aside for the tribe of Ephraim. 10They did not drive the Canaanites out of Gezer, however, so the people of Gezer live as slaves among the people of Ephraim to this day.

**16:10**
Josh 15:63;
17:12-13
Judg 1:29
1 Kgs 9:16

## The Land Given to West Manasseh

**17** The next allotment of land was given to the half-tribe of Manasseh, the descendants of Joseph's older son. Makir, the firstborn son of Manasseh, was the father of Gilead. Because his descendants were experienced soldiers, the regions of Gilead and Bashan on the east side of the Jordan had already been given to them. 2So the allotment on the west side of the Jordan was for the remaining families within the clans of the tribe of Manasseh: Abiezer, Helek, Asriel, Shechem, Hepher, and Shemida. These clans represent the male descendants of Manasseh son of Joseph.

**17:1**
Josh 13:8

3However, Zelophehad, a descendant of Hepher son of Gilead, son of Makir, son of Manasseh, had no sons. He had only daughters, whose names were Mahlah, Noah, Hoglah, Milcah, and Tirzah. 4These women came to Eleazar the priest, Joshua son of Nun, and the Israelite leaders and said, "The LORD commanded Moses to give us a grant of land along with the men of our tribe."

**17:3**
Num 26:33; 27:1-7

16:2 As in Greek version (also see 18:13); Hebrew reads From Bethel to Luz.   16:3 Hebrew the sea; also in 16:6, 8.

---

16:1ff Although Joseph was one of Jacob's 12 sons, he did not have a tribe named after him. This was because Joseph, as the oldest son of Jacob's wife Rachel, received a double portion of the inheritance. Joseph's double portion was divided between his two sons, Ephraim and Manasseh, whom Jacob considered as his own (Genesis 48:5). The largest territory and the greatest influence in the northern half of Israel belonged to their tribes.

16:10 Occasionally this short phrase appears: "They did not drive out" the people of the land (see also 15:63; 17:12). This was contrary to God's explicit desire and command (13:1-6). The failure to remove completely the pagan people and their

gods from the land would cause many problems for the nation. The book of Judges records many of these struggles.

17:3, 4 Although women did not traditionally inherit property in Israelite society, Moses put justice ahead of tradition and gave these five women the land they deserved (see Numbers 27:1-11). In fact, God told Moses to add a law that would help other women in similar circumstances inherit property as well. Joshua was now carrying out this law. It is easy to refuse to honor a reasonable request because "we have never done it that way before." But, like Moses and Joshua, we should look carefully at the purpose of the law and the merits of each case before deciding.

So Joshua gave them a grant of land along with their uncles, as the LORD had commanded. ⁵As a result, Manasseh's total allocation came to ten parcels of land, in addition to the land of Gilead and Bashan across the Jordan River, ⁶because the female descendants of Manasseh received a grant of land along with the male descendants. (The land of Gilead was given to the rest of the male descendants of Manasseh.)

17:6
Josh 13:30-31

⁷ The boundary of the tribe of Manasseh extended from the border of Asher to Micmethath, near Shechem. Then the boundary went south from Micmethath to the settlement near the spring of Tappuah. ⁸The land surrounding Tappuah belonged to Manasseh, but the town of Tappuah itself, on the border of Manasseh's territory, belonged to the tribe of Ephraim. ⁹From the spring of Tappuah, the boundary of Manasseh followed the Kanah Ravine to the Mediterranean Sea.* Several towns south of the ravine were inside Manasseh's territory, but they actually belonged to the tribe of Ephraim. ¹⁰In general, however, the land south of the ravine belonged to Ephraim, and the land north of the ravine belonged to Manasseh. Manasseh's boundary ran along the northern side of the ravine and ended at the Mediterranean Sea. North of Manasseh was the territory of Asher, and to the east was the territory of Issachar.

17:11
1 Chr 7:29

¹¹The following towns within the territory of Issachar and Asher, however, were given to Manasseh: Beth-shan,* Ibleam, Dor (that is, Naphoth-dor),* Endor, Taanach, and Megiddo, each with their surrounding settlements.

17:12
Judg 1:27-28

¹²But the descendants of Manasseh were unable to occupy these towns. They could not drive out the Canaanites who continued to live there. ¹³Later, however, when the Israelites became strong enough, they forced the Canaanites to work as slaves. But they did not drive them out of the land.

17:14
Num 26:28-37

¹⁴The descendants of Joseph came to Joshua and asked, "Why have you given us only one portion of land as our homeland when the LORD has blessed us with so many people?"

¹⁵Joshua replied, "If there are so many of you, and if the hill country of Ephraim is not large enough for you, clear out land for yourselves in the forest where the Perizzites and Rephaites live."

17:16
Judg 1:19; 4:3, 13

¹⁶The descendants of Joseph responded, "It's true that the hill country is not large enough for us. But all the Canaanites in the lowlands have iron chariots, both those in Beth-shan and its surrounding settlements and those in the valley of Jezreel. They are too strong for us."

¹⁷Then Joshua said to the tribes of Ephraim and Manasseh, the descendants of Joseph, "Since you are so large and strong, you will be given more than one portion. ¹⁸The forests of the hill country will be yours as well. Clear as much of the land as you wish, and take possession of its farthest corners. And you will drive out the Canaanites from the valleys, too, even though they are strong and have iron chariots."

## The Allotments of the Remaining Land

**18** Now that the land was under Israelite control, the entire community of Israel gathered at Shiloh and set up the Tabernacle.* ²But there remained seven tribes who had not yet been allotted their grants of land.

18:1
Josh 19:51
Judg 21:19
Jer 7:12

17:9 Hebrew *the sea*; also in 17:10.   17:11a Hebrew *Beth-shean*, a variant spelling of Beth-shan; also in 17:16.
17:11b The meaning of the Hebrew here is uncertain.   18:1 Hebrew *Tent of Meeting*.

---

**17:14, 15** Notice the two contrasting attitudes toward settling the Promised Land: Caleb took what God gave him and moved ahead to fulfill God's plan for him (14:12). He was confident that God would help him drive out the wicked inhabitants and that he would soon fully occupy his land (15:14, 15). In contrast, the two tribes of Joseph were given rich land and lots of it, but they were afraid to drive out the inhabitants and take full possession of it. Instead, they begged for more land. But Joshua asked them to prove their sincerity first by clearing the unclaimed forest areas. They agreed, but they failed to carry through (Judges 1:27).

**18:1, 2** With most of the conquest behind them, Israel moved its religious center from Gilgal (see the note on 5:8, 9) to Shiloh. This was probably the first permanent location for the Tabernacle. Its central location in the land made it easier for the people to attend the special worship services and yearly festivals.

The family of Samuel, a great priest and prophet, later would often travel to Shiloh, and Samuel would be taken there when a

small boy (1 Samuel 1:3, 22). The Tabernacle would remain in Shiloh through the period of the judges (about 300 years). Apparently the city was destroyed by the Philistines when the Ark of the Covenant was captured (1 Samuel 4–5). Shiloh never lived up to its reputation as Israel's religious center, for later references in the Bible point to the wickedness and idolatry in the city (Psalm 78:56-60; Jeremiah 7:12-15).

**18:2ff** Seven of the tribes had not yet been assigned their land. They gathered at Shiloh, where Joshua cast lots to determine which areas would be given to them. Using the sacred lottery, God would make the choice, not Joshua or any other human leader.

By this time, the Canaanites were, in most places, so weakened that they were no longer a threat. Instead of fulfilling God's command to destroy the remaining Canaanites, however, these seven tribes would often take the path of least resistance. As nomadic people, they may have been reluctant to settle down, preferring to depend economically on the people they were supposed to

3Then Joshua asked them, "How long are you going to wait before taking possession of the remaining land the LORD, the God of your ancestors, has given to you? 4Select three men from each tribe, and I will send them out to explore the land and map it out. They will then return to me with a written report of their proposed divisions of their new homeland. 5Let them divide the land into seven sections, excluding Judah's territory in the south and Joseph's territory in the north. 6And when you record the seven divisions of the land and bring them to me, I will cast sacred lots in the presence of the LORD our God to assign land to each tribe.

7"The Levites, however, will not receive any allotment of land. Their role as priests of the LORD is their allotment. And the tribes of Gad, Reuben, and the half-tribe of Manasseh won't receive any more land, for they have already received their grant of land, which Moses, the servant of the LORD, gave them on the east side of the Jordan River."

8As the men started on their way to map out the land, Joshua commanded them, "Go and explore the land and write a description of it. Then return to me, and I will assign the land to the tribes by casting sacred lots here in the presence of the LORD at Shiloh." 9The men did as they were told and mapped the entire territory into seven sections, listing the towns in each section. They made a written record and then returned to Joshua in the camp at Shiloh. 10And there at Shiloh, Joshua cast sacred lots in the presence of the LORD to determine which tribe should have each section.

### The Land Given to Benjamin

11The first allotment of land went to the clans of the tribe of Benjamin. It lay between the territory assigned to the tribes of Judah and Joseph.

12The northern boundary of Benjamin's land began at the Jordan River, went north of the slope of Jericho, then west through the hill country and the wilderness of Beth-aven. 13From there the boundary went south to Luz (that is, Bethel) and proceeded down to Ataroth-addar on the hill that lies south of Lower Beth-horon.

14The boundary then made a turn and swung south along the western edge of the hill facing Beth-horon, ending at the village of Kiriath-baal (that is, Kiriath-jearim), a town belonging to the tribe of Judah. This was the western boundary.

15The southern boundary began at the outskirts of Kiriath-jearim. From that western point it ran* to the spring at the waters of Nephtoah,* 16and down to the base of the mountain beside the valley of Ben-Hinnom, at the northern end of the valley of Rephaim. From there it went down the valley of Hinnom, crossing south

**18:3** Judg 18:9
**18:5** Josh 15:1; 16:1-4
**18:7** Num 18:7, 20 Josh 13:33
**18:8** Josh 18:1
**18:10** Num 34:16-29 Josh 19:51
**18:14-15** Josh 15:5-9
**18:16** 2 Kgs 23:10

---

18:15a Or *From there it went to Mozah.* The meaning of the Hebrew is uncertain. 18:15b Or *the spring at Me-nephtoah.*

---

eliminate. Others may have feared the high cost of continued warfare. Trading for goods was easier and more profitable than destroying the suppliers and having to provide for themselves.

**THE TRIBES WEST OF THE JORDAN** Judah, Ephraim, and the other half-tribe of Manasseh were the first tribes to receive land west of the Jordan because of their past acts of faith. The remaining seven tribes—Benjamin, Zebulun, Issachar, Asher, Naphtali, Simeon, and Dan—were slow to conquer and possess the land allotted to them.

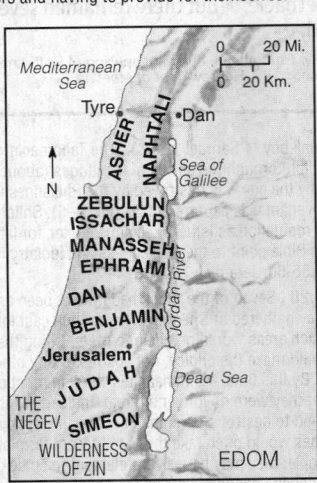

**18:3-6** Joshua asked why some of the tribes were putting off the job of possessing the land. Often we delay doing jobs that seem large, difficult, boring, or disagreeable. But to continue putting them off shows lack of discipline, poor stewardship of time, and, in some cases, disobedience to God. Jobs we don't enjoy require concentration, teamwork, twice as much time, lots of encouragement, and accountability. Remember this when you are tempted to procrastinate.

**18:8** Making decisions by casting lots was a common practice among the Hebrews. Little is known about the actual method used in Joshua's day. A type of dice may have been used. Another possibility is that two urns were used: one containing tribal names; the other, the divisions of the land. Drawing one name from each urn matched a tribe to a region. The Urim and Thummim (explained in the note on Leviticus 8:8) may also have been used. No matter how it was done, the process removed human choice from the decision-making process and allowed God to match tribes and lands as he saw fit.

**18:11** The tribe of Benjamin was given a narrow strip of land that served as a buffer zone between Judah and Ephraim, the two tribes that would later dominate the land.

**18:16** The valley of Hinnom became associated with the worship of Molech (the Ammonite god) in Jeremiah's time. These terrible rites involved the sacrifice of children. Later the valley was used for burning garbage and the corpses of criminals and animals. Thus, the name became a synonym for hell.

of the slope where the Jebusites lived, and continued down to En-rogel. [17]From En-rogel the boundary proceeded in a northerly direction and came to En-shemesh and on to Geliloth (which is across from the slopes of Adummim). Then it went down to the Stone of Bohan. (Bohan was Reuben's son.) [18]From there it passed along the north side of the slope overlooking the Jordan Valley.* The border then went down into the valley, [19]ran past the north slope of Beth-hoglah, and ended at the north bay of the Dead Sea,* which is the southern end of the Jordan River. This was the southern boundary.

[20]The eastern boundary was the Jordan River.

These were the boundaries of the homeland allocated to the clans of the tribe of Benjamin.

### The Towns Given to Benjamin
[21]These were the towns given to the clans of the tribe of Benjamin.

Jericho, Beth-hoglah, Emek-keziz, [22]Beth-arabah, Zemaraim, Bethel, [23]Avvim, Parah, Ophrah, [24]Kephar-ammoni, Ophni, and Geba—twelve towns with their surrounding villages. [25]Also Gibeon, Ramah, Beeroth, [26]Mizpah, Kephirah, Mozah, [27]Rekem, Irpeel, Taralah, [28]Zela, Haeleph, Jebus (that is, Jerusalem), Gibeah, and Kiriath*—fourteen towns with their surrounding villages.

This was the homeland allocated to the clans of the tribe of Benjamin.

### The Land Given to Simeon
**19** The second allotment of land went to the clans of the tribe of Simeon. Their homeland was surrounded by Judah's territory.

[2]Simeon's homeland included Beersheba, Sheba, Moladah, [3]Hazar-shual, Balah, Ezem, [4]Eltolad, Bethul, Hormah, [5]Ziklag, Beth-marcaboth, Hazar-susah, [6]Beth-lebaoth, and Sharuhen—thirteen towns with their surrounding villages. [7]It also included Ain, Rimmon, Ether, and Ashan—four towns with their villages, [8]including all the surrounding villages as far south as Baalath-beer (also known as Ramah of the Negev).

This was the homeland allocated to the clans of the tribe of Simeon. [9]Their allocation of land came from part of what had been given to Judah because Judah's territory was too large for them. So the tribe of Simeon received an allocation within the territory of Judah.

### The Land Given to Zebulun
[10]The third allotment of land went to the clans of the tribe of Zebulun.

The boundary of Zebulun's homeland started at Sarid. [11]From there it went west, going past Maralah, touching Dabbesheth, and proceeding to the brook east of Jokneam. [12]In the other direction, the boundary went east from Sarid to the border of Kisloth-tabor, and from there to Daberath and up to Japhia. [13]Then it continued east to Gath-hepher, Eth-kazin, and Rimmon and turned toward Neah. [14]The northern boundary of Zebulun passed Hannathon and ended at the valley of Iphtah-el. [15]The towns in these areas included Kattath, Nahalal, Shimron, Idalah, and Bethlehem—twelve towns with their surrounding villages.

[16]The homeland allocated to the clans of the tribe of Zebulun included these towns and their surrounding villages.

### The Land Given to Issachar
[17]The fourth allotment of land went to the clans of the tribe of Issachar.

[18]Its boundaries included the following towns: Jezreel, Kesulloth, Shunem, [19]Hapharaim, Shion, Anaharath, [20]Rabbith, Kishion, Ebez, [21]Remeth, En-gannim, En-haddah, and Beth-pazzez. [22]The boundary also touched Tabor, Shahazumah, and Beth-shemesh, ending at the Jordan River—sixteen towns with their surrounding villages.

[23]The homeland allocated to the clans of the tribe of Issachar included these towns and their surrounding villages.

---

**18:18** Hebrew *overlooking the Arabah*, or *overlooking Beth-arabah*.  **18:19** Hebrew *Salt Sea*.  **18:28** Some Greek manuscripts read *Kiriath-jearim*.

18:17
Josh 15:7-8

18:24
Isa 10:29
18:28
Josh 15:8
2 Sam 21:14

19:5
1 Sam 30:1

19:11
Josh 21:34

19:15
Mic 5:2

19:18
1 Sam 28:4

## The Land Given to Asher

24 The fifth allotment of land went to the clans of the tribe of Asher.

25 Its boundaries included these towns: Helkath, Hali, Beten, Acshaph, 26 Allammelech, Amad, and Mishal. The boundary on the west touched Carmel and Shihor-libnath, 27 then it turned east toward Beth-dagon, and ran as far as Zebulun in the valley of Iphtah-el, going north to Beth-emek and Neiel. It then continued north to Cabul, 28 Abdon,* Rehob, Hammon, Kanah, and as far as Greater Sidon. 29 Then the boundary turned toward Ramah and the fortress of Tyre, where it turned toward Hosah and came to the Mediterranean Sea.* The territory also included Mehebel, Aczib, 30 Ummah, Aphek, and Rehob—twenty-two towns with their surrounding villages.

31 The homeland allocated to the clans of the tribe of Asher included these towns and their surrounding villages.

**19:28**
Josh 11:8

**19:30**
Josh 21:31

## The Land Given to Naphtali

32 The sixth allotment of land went to the clans of the tribe of Naphtali.

33 Its boundary ran from Heleph, from the oak at Zaanannim, and extended across to Adami-nekeb, Jabneel, and as far as Lakkum, ending at the Jordan River. 34 The western boundary ran past Aznoth-tabor, then to Hukkok, and touched the border of Zebulun in the south, the border of Asher on the west, and the Jordan River* on the east. 35 The fortified towns included in this territory were Ziddim, Zer, Hammath, Rakkath, Kinnereth, 36 Adamah, Ramah, Hazor, 37 Kedesh, Edrei, En-hazor, 38 Yiron, Migdal-el, Horem, Beth-anath, and Beth-shemesh—nineteen towns with their surrounding villages.

39 The homeland allocated to the clans of the tribe of Naphtali included these towns and their surrounding villages.

**19:34**
Deut 33:23

## The Land Given to Dan

40 The seventh allotment of land went to the clans of the tribe of Dan.

41 The land allocated as their homeland included the following towns: Zorah, Eshtaol, Ir-shemesh, 42 Shaalabbin, Aijalon, Ithlah, 43 Elon, Timnah, Ekron, 44 Eltekeh, Gibbethon, Baalath, 45 Jehud, Bene-berak, Gath-rimmon, 46 Me-jarkon, Rakkon, and the territory across from Joppa.

47 But the tribe of Dan had trouble taking possession of their land,* so they attacked the town of Laish.* They captured it, slaughtered its people, and settled there. They renamed the town Dan after their ancestor.

48 The homeland allocated to the clans of the tribe of Dan included these towns and their surrounding villages.

**19:42**
Judg 1:35

**19:47**
Judg 18:27-31

## The Land Given to Joshua

49 After all the land was divided among the tribes, the Israelites gave a piece of land to Joshua as his allocation. 50 For the LORD had said he could have any town he wanted. He chose Timnath-serah in the hill country of Ephraim. He rebuilt the town and lived there.

51 These are the territories that Eleazar the priest, Joshua son of Nun, and the tribal leaders allocated as grants of land to the tribes of Israel by casting sacred lots in the presence of the LORD at the entrance of the Tabernacle* at Shiloh. So the division of the land was completed.

**19:50**
Josh 24:30

**19:51**
Josh 14:1; 18:10

19:28 As in some Hebrew manuscripts (see also 21:30); most Hebrew manuscripts read *Ebron*. 19:29 Hebrew *the sea*. 19:34 Hebrew *and Judah at the Jordan River*. 19:47a Or *had trouble holding on to their land*. 19:47b Hebrew *Leshem*, a variant spelling of Laish. 19:51 Hebrew *Tent of Meeting*.

---

**19:47, 48** The tribe of Dan found that some of their land was difficult to conquer, so they chose to migrate to Laish, where they knew victory would be easier. Anyone can trust God when the going is easy. It is when everything looks impossible that our faith and courage are put to the test. Have faith that God is great enough to tackle your most difficult situations.

**19:49** There were several good reasons for establishing these well-set boundaries instead of turning the Promised Land into

a single undivided nation. (1) The boundaries gave each tribe ownership of an area, promoting loyalty and unity that would strengthen each tribe. (2) The boundaries delineated areas of responsibility and privilege, which would help each tribe develop and mature. (3) The boundaries reduced conflicts that might have broken out if everyone had wanted to live in the choicest areas. (4) The boundaries fulfilled the promised inheritance to each tribe that began to be given as early as the days of Jacob (Genesis 48:21, 22).

## 2. Special cities are set aside
### The Cities of Refuge

20:2
Num 35:6, 11
Deut 4:41; 19:2

**20** The LORD said to Joshua, [2]"Now tell the Israelites to designate the cities of refuge, as I instructed Moses. [3]Anyone who kills another person accidentally and unintentionally can run to one of these cities; they will be places of refuge from relatives seeking revenge for the person who was killed.

20:4
Ruth 4:1-2

[4]"Upon reaching one of these cities, the one who caused the death will appear before the elders at the city gate and present his case. They must allow him to enter the city and give him a place to live among them. [5]If the relatives of the victim come to avenge the killing, the leaders must not release the slayer to them, for he killed the other person unintentionally and without previous hostility. [6]But the slayer must stay in that city and be tried by the local assembly, which will render a judgment. And he must continue to live in that city until the death of the high priest who was in office at the time of the accident. After that, he is free to return to his own home in the town from which he fled."

20:7
Josh 21:11, 32
1 Chr 6:76
Luke 1:39
20:8
Josh 21:27, 36, 38

[7]The following cities were designated as cities of refuge: Kedesh of Galilee, in the hill country of Naphtali; Shechem, in the hill country of Ephraim; and Kiriath-arba (that is, Hebron), in the hill country of Judah. [8]On the east side of the Jordan River, across from Jericho, the following cities were designated: Bezer, in the wilderness plain of the tribe of Reuben; Ramoth in Gilead, in the territory of the tribe of Gad; and Golan in Bashan, in the land of the tribe of Manasseh. [9]These cities were set apart for all the Israelites as well as the foreigners living among them. Anyone who accidentally killed another person could take refuge in one of these cities. In this way, they could escape being killed in revenge prior to standing trial before the local assembly.

### The Towns Given to the Levites

21:1
Josh 14:1
21:2
Num 35:2

**21** Then the leaders of the tribe of Levi came to consult with Eleazar the priest, Joshua son of Nun, and the leaders of the other tribes of Israel. [2]They came to them at Shiloh in the land of Canaan and said, "The LORD commanded Moses to give us towns to live in and pasturelands for our livestock." [3]So by the command of the LORD the people of Israel gave the Levites the following towns and pasturelands out of their own grants of land.

21:4-39
//1 Chr 6:54-80

[4]The descendants of Aaron, who were members of the Kohathite clan within the tribe of Levi, were allotted thirteen towns that were originally assigned to the tribes of Judah, Simeon, and Benjamin. [5]The other families of the Kohathite clan were allotted ten towns from the tribes of Ephraim, Dan, and the half-tribe of Manasseh.

[6]The clan of Gershon was allotted thirteen towns from the tribes of Issachar, Asher, Naphtali, and the half-tribe of Manasseh in Bashan.

[7]The clan of Merari was allotted twelve towns from the tribes of Reuben, Gad, and Zebulun.

[8]So the Israelites obeyed the LORD's command to Moses and assigned these towns and pasturelands to the Levites by casting sacred lots.

---

**THE CITIES OF REFUGE**
A city of refuge was just that—refuge for someone who committed an unintentional murder that would evoke revenge from the victim's friends and relatives. The six cities of refuge were spaced throughout the land so that a person was never too far from one.

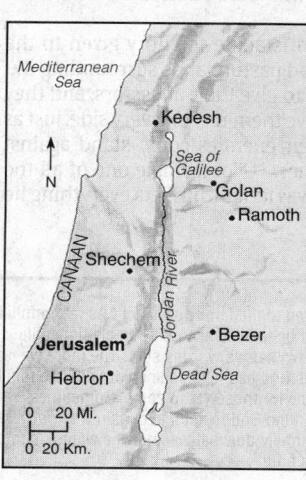

Mediterranean
Sea

Kedesh

Sea of
Galilee

N

Golan

Ramoth

Shechem

CANAAN

Jordan River

Jerusalem

Bezer

Hebron

Dead Sea

0      20 Mi.

0      20 Km.

**20:6** A new nation in a new land needed a new government. Many years earlier God had told Moses how this government should function. One of the tasks God wanted the Israelites to do when they entered the Promised Land was to designate certain cities as "cities of refuge." These were to be scattered throughout the land. Their purpose was to prevent injustice, especially in cases of revenge. For example, if someone accidentally killed another person, he could flee to a city of refuge where he was safe until he could have a fair trial. The Levites were in charge of these cities. They were to ensure that God's principles of justice and fairness were kept. (For more on cities of refuge, see the notes on Numbers 35:6, 11-28.)

**21:2** The Levites were to minister on behalf of all the people, so they were given cities scattered throughout the land. Although Jerusalem was far away from the homes of many Israelites, almost no one lived more than a day's journey from a Levitical city.

⁹ The Israelites gave the following towns from the tribes of Judah and Simeon ¹⁰ to the descendants of Aaron, who were members of the Kohathite clan within the tribe of Levi, since the sacred lot fell to them first: ¹¹Kiriath-arba (that is, Hebron), in the hill country of Judah, along with its surrounding pasturelands. (Arba was an ancestor of Anak.) ¹²But the open fields beyond the town and the surrounding villages were given to Caleb son of Jephunneh as his possession.

¹³ The following towns with their pasturelands were given to the descendants of Aaron the priest: Hebron (a city of refuge for those who accidentally killed someone), Libnah, ¹⁴Jattir, Eshtemoa, ¹⁵Holon, Debir, ¹⁶Ain, Juttah, and Beth-shemesh—nine towns from these two tribes.

¹⁷ From the tribe of Benjamin the priests were given the following towns with their pasturelands: Gibeon, Geba, ¹⁸Anathoth, and Almon—four towns. ¹⁹So in all, thirteen towns with their pasturelands were given to the priests, the descendants of Aaron.

²⁰The rest of the Kohathite clan from the tribe of Levi was allotted the following towns and pasturelands from the tribe of Ephraim: ²¹Shechem in the hill country of Ephraim (a city of refuge for those who accidentally killed someone), Gezer, ²²Kibzaim, and Beth-horon—four towns.

²³ The following towns and pasturelands were allotted to the priests from the tribe of Dan: Eltekeh, Gibbethon, ²⁴Aijalon, and Gath-rimmon—four towns.

²⁵The half-tribe of Manasseh allotted the following towns with their pasturelands to the priests: Taanach and Gath-rimmon—two towns. ²⁶So in all, ten towns with their pasturelands were given to the rest of the Kohathite clan.

²⁷ The descendants of Gershon, another clan within the tribe of Levi, received the following towns with their pasturelands from the half-tribe of Manasseh: Golan in Bashan (a city of refuge for those who accidentally killed someone) and Be-eshterah—two towns.

²⁸From the tribe of Issachar they received the following towns with their pasturelands: Kishion, Daberath, ²⁹Jarmuth, and En-gannim—four towns.

³⁰From the tribe of Asher they received the following towns with their pasturelands: Mishal, Abdon, ³¹Helkath, and Rehob—four towns.

³²From the tribe of Naphtali they received the following towns with their pasturelands: Kedesh in Galilee (a city of refuge for those who accidentally killed someone), Hammoth-dor, and Kartan—three towns. ³³ So in all, thirteen towns with their pasturelands were allotted to the clan of Gershon.

³⁴The rest of the Levites—the Merari clan—were given the following towns with their pasturelands from the tribe of Zebulun: Jokneam, Kartah, ³⁵Dimnah, and Nahalal—four towns.

³⁶From the tribe of Reuben they received the following towns with their pasturelands: Bezer, Jahaz,* ³⁷Kedemoth, and Mephaath—four towns.

³⁸From the tribe of Gad they received the following towns with their pasturelands: Ramoth in Gilead (a city of refuge for those who accidentally killed someone), Mahanaim, ³⁹Heshbon, and Jazer—four towns. ⁴⁰So in all, twelve towns were allotted to the clan of Merari.

⁴¹The total number of towns and pasturelands within Israelite territory given to the Levites came to forty-eight. ⁴²Every one of these towns had pasturelands surrounding it.

⁴³ So the LORD gave to Israel all the land he had sworn to give their ancestors, and they took possession of it and settled there. ⁴⁴And the LORD gave them rest on every side, just as he had solemnly promised their ancestors. None of their enemies could stand against them, for the LORD helped them conquer all their enemies. ⁴⁵Not a single one of all the good promises the LORD had given to the family of Israel was left unfulfilled; everything he had spoken came true.

**21:36** Hebrew *Jahzah*, a variant spelling of Jahaz.

Side references:
**21:11** Josh 15:13-14; 1 Chr 6:55
**21:13** Josh 15:42, 54; 20:7; 1 Chr 6:57
**21:15** Josh 15:49, 51; 1 Chr 6:58
**21:16** Josh 15:10; 1 Chr 6:59
**21:18** 1 Chr 6:60
**21:21** Josh 20:7
**21:32** Josh 20:7
**21:36** Josh 20:8
**21:41** Num 35:7
**21:43** Num 33:53; Deut 11:31; 17:14; 34:4
**21:44** Exod 23:31; Deut 7:24

**21:43-45** God proved faithful in fulfilling every promise he had given to Israel. Fulfillment of some promises took several years, but "not a single one of all the good promises the LORD had given to the family of Israel was left unfulfilled." God's promises will be fulfilled according to his timetable, not ours, but we know that his word is sure. The more we learn of those promises God has fulfilled and continues to fulfill, the easier it is to hope for those yet to come. Sometimes we become impatient, wanting God to act in a certain way *now*. Instead, we should faithfully do what we know he wants us to do and trust him for the future.

### 3. Eastern tribes return home

# 22

Then Joshua called together the tribes of Reuben, Gad, and the half-tribe of Manasseh. ²He told them, "You have done as Moses, the servant of the LORD, commanded you, and you have obeyed every order I have given you. ³During all this time you have not deserted the other tribes. You have been careful to obey the commands of the LORD your God right up to the present day. ⁴And now the LORD your God has given the other tribes rest, as he promised them. So go back home to the land that Moses, the servant of the LORD, gave you as your possession on the east side of the Jordan River. ⁵But be very careful to obey all the commands and the instructions that Moses gave to you. Love the LORD your God, walk in all his ways, obey his commands, hold firmly to him, and serve him with all your heart and all your soul." ⁶So Joshua blessed them and sent them away, and they went home.

⁷Moses had given the land of Bashan, east of the Jordan River, to the half-tribe of Manasseh. (The other half of the tribe was given land west of the Jordan.) As Joshua sent them away and blessed them, ⁸he said to them, "Go back to your homes with the great wealth you have taken from your enemies—the vast herds of livestock, the silver, gold, bronze, and iron, and the large supply of clothing. Share the plunder with your relatives."

⁹So the men of Reuben, Gad, and the half-tribe of Manasseh left the rest of Israel at Shiloh in the land of Canaan. They started the journey back to their own land of Gilead, the territory that belonged to them according to the LORD's command through Moses.

### The Eastern Tribes Build an Altar

¹⁰But while they were still in Canaan, and when they came to a place called Geliloth* near the Jordan River, the men of Reuben, Gad, and the half-tribe of Manasseh stopped to build a large and imposing altar.

¹¹The rest of Israel heard that the people of Reuben, Gad, and the half-tribe of Manasseh had built an altar at Geliloth at the edge of the land of Canaan, on the west side of the Jordan River. ¹²So the whole community of Israel gathered at Shiloh and prepared to go to war against them. ¹³First, however, they sent a delegation led by Phinehas son of Eleazar, the priest, to talk with the tribes of Reuben, Gad, and the half-tribe of Manasseh. ¹⁴In this delegation were ten leaders of Israel, one from each of the ten tribes, and each the head of his family within the clans of Israel.

¹⁵When they arrived in the land of Gilead, they said to the tribes of Reuben, Gad, and the half-tribe of Manasseh, ¹⁶"The whole community of the LORD demands to know why you are betraying the God of Israel. How could you turn away from the LORD and build an altar for yourselves in rebellion against him? ¹⁷Was our sin at Peor not enough? To this day we are not fully cleansed of it, even after the plague that struck the entire community of the LORD. ¹⁸And yet today you are turning away from following the LORD. If you rebel against the LORD today, he will be angry with all of us tomorrow.

¹⁹"If you need the altar because the land you possess is defiled, then join us in the LORD's land, where the Tabernacle of the LORD is situated, and share our land with us. But do not

**22:2**
Num 32:20-22
Josh 1:12-18

**22:4**
Num 32:18
Deut 3:20

**22:5**
Deut 5:10
†Mark 12:32

**22:7**
Num 32:33
Josh 17:1-2

**22:9**
Deut 32:1, 26, 29

**22:11**
Deut 12:5

**22:13**
Num 25:7, 11; 31:6

**22:17**
Num 25:1-9

**22:10** Or *to the circle of stones;* similarly in 22:11.

---

**22:2-4** Before the conquest had begun, these tribes were given land on the east side of the Jordan River. But before they could settle down, they had to first promise to help the other tribes conquer the land on the west side (Numbers 32:20-22). They had patiently and diligently carried out their promised duties. Joshua commended them for doing just that. At last they were permitted to return to their families and build their cities. Follow-through is vital in God's work. Beware of the temptation to quit early and leave God's work undone.

**22:5** Here Joshua briefly restated the central message Moses gave the people in Deuteronomy: Obedience should be based on love for God. Although the Israelites had completed their military responsibility, Joshua reminded them of their spiritual responsibility. Sometimes we think so much about what we are to do that we neglect thinking about who we are to be. If we know we are God's children, we will love him and joyfully serve him. We must not let daily service take away from our love for God.

**22:11-34** When the tribes of Reuben and Gad and the half-tribe of Manasseh built an altar near the Jordan River, the rest of Israel feared that these tribes were starting their own religion and rebel-

ling against God. But before beginning an all-out war, Phinehas led a delegation to learn the truth, following the principle taught in Deuteronomy 13:12-18. He was prepared to negotiate rather than fight if a battle was not necessary. When he learned that the altar was for a memorial rather than for pagan sacrifice, war was averted and unity restored.

As nations and as individuals, we would benefit from a similar approach to resolving conflicts. Assuming the worst about the intentions of others only brings trouble. Israel averted the threat of civil war by asking before assaulting. Beware of reacting before you hear the whole story.

**22:17** For the story of how Israel turned away from God and began to worship Baal at Peor, see Numbers 25:1-18.

rebel against the LORD or against us by building an altar other than the one true altar of the LORD our God. [20]Didn't divine anger fall on the entire community of Israel when Achan, a member of the clan of Zerah, sinned by stealing the things set apart for the LORD*? He was not the only one who died because of his sin."

**22:20**
Josh 7:1-26

[21]Then the people of Reuben, Gad, and the half-tribe of Manasseh answered the heads of the clans of Israel: [22]"The LORD, the Mighty One, is God! The LORD, the Mighty One, is God! He knows the truth, and may Israel know it, too! We have not built the altar in treacherous rebellion against the LORD. If we have done so, do not spare our lives this day. [23]If we have built an altar for ourselves to turn away from the LORD or to offer burnt offerings or grain offerings or peace offerings, may the LORD himself punish us.

**22:22**
Deut 10:17

[24]"The truth is, we have built this altar because we fear that in the future your descendants will say to ours, 'What right do you have to worship the LORD, the God of Israel? [25]The LORD has placed the Jordan River as a barrier between our people and you people of Reuben and Gad. You have no claim to the LORD.' So your descendants may prevent our descendants from worshiping the LORD.

[26]"So we decided to build the altar, not for burnt offerings or sacrifices, [27]but as a memorial. It will remind our descendants and your descendants that we, too, have the right to worship the LORD at his sanctuary with our burnt offerings, sacrifices, and peace offerings. Then your descendants will not be able to say to ours, 'You have no claim to the LORD.'

**22:27**
Josh 24:27

[28]"If they say this, our descendants can reply, 'Look at this copy of the LORD's altar that our ancestors made. It is not for burnt offerings or sacrifices; it is a reminder of the relationship both of us have with the LORD.' [29]Far be it from us to rebel against the LORD or turn away from him by building our own altar for burnt offerings, grain offerings, or sacrifices. Only the altar of the LORD our God that stands in front of the Tabernacle may be used for that purpose."

**22:29**
Deut 12:13

[30]When Phinehas the priest and the leaders of the community—the heads of the clans of Israel—heard this from the tribes of Reuben, Gad, and the half-tribe of Manasseh, they were satisfied. [31]Phinehas son of Eleazar, the priest, replied to them, "Today we know the LORD is among us because you have not committed this treachery against the LORD as we thought. Instead, you have rescued Israel from being destroyed by the hand of the LORD."

**22:31**
Lev 26:11-12
2 Chr 15:2

[32] Then Phinehas son of Eleazar, the priest, and the other leaders left the tribes of Reuben and Gad in Gilead and returned to the land of Canaan to tell the Israelites what had happened. [33]And all the Israelites were satisfied and praised God and spoke no more of war against Reuben and Gad.

[34]The people of Reuben and Gad named the altar "Witness,"* for they said, "It is a witness between us and them that the LORD is our God, too."

**22:34**
Gen 31:47-49

## 4. Joshua's farewell to Israel

**23** The years passed, and the LORD had given the people of Israel rest from all their enemies. Joshua, who was now very old, [2]called together all the elders, leaders, judges, and officers of Israel. He said to them, "I am now a very old man. [3] You have seen everything the LORD your God has done for you during my lifetime. The LORD your God has fought for you against your enemies. [4]I have allotted to you as your homeland all the land of the nations yet unconquered, as well as the land of those we have already conquered—from the Jordan River to the Mediterranean Sea* in the west. [5]This land will be yours, for the LORD your God will himself drive out all the people living there now. You will take possession of their land, just as the LORD your God promised you.

**23:1**
Josh 21:44
**23:2**
Josh 24:1

**23:4**
Exod 23:30

**23:5**
Num 33:53

**22:20** The Hebrew term used here refers to the complete consecration of things or people to the LORD, either by destroying them or by giving them as an offering.    **22:34** Some manuscripts lack this word.    **23:4** Hebrew *the Great Sea.*

**22:20** For the story of Achan, a man who allowed greed to get the best of him, see chapter 7.

**22:26-28** The tribes were concerned that, without some visible sign of unity between the people on the two sides of the Jordan, future generations might see conflict between them. The altar, patterned after the altar of the Lord, was to remind these people that they all worshiped the same God. Often we need to be reminded of the faith of our fathers. What actions demonstrate to your children your reliance on God and remind them of what he has done? Take the time to establish family traditions that will help your children remember.

**23:6**
Deut 5:32
Josh 1:7

**23:7**
Exod 20:5; 23:13
Ps 16:4

**23:8**
Deut 10:20

**23:9**
Deut 7:24

**23:10**
Lev 26:8
Deut 28:7

**23:12**
Deut 7:3-4
Ezra 9:2

**23:13**
Exod 23:33; 34:12
Deut 7:16

**23:15**
Lev 26:14-33
Deut 28:15

**23:16**
Deut 4:25-26

6"So be very careful to follow everything Moses wrote in the Book of Instruction. Do not deviate from it, turning either to the right or to the left. 7Make sure you do not associate with the other people still remaining in the land. Do not even mention the names of their gods, much less swear by them or serve them or worship them. 8Rather, cling tightly to the LORD your God as you have done until now.

9"For the LORD has driven out great and powerful nations for you, and no one has yet been able to defeat you. 10Each one of you will put to flight a thousand of the enemy, for the LORD your God fights for you, just as he has promised. 11So be very careful to love the LORD your God.

12"But if you turn away from him and cling to the customs of the survivors of these nations remaining among you, and if you intermarry with them, 13then know for certain that the LORD your God will no longer drive them out of your land. Instead, they will be a snare and a trap to you, a whip for your backs and thorny brambles in your eyes, and you will vanish from this good land the LORD your God has given you.

14"Soon I will die, going the way of everything on earth. Deep in your hearts you know that every promise of the LORD your God has come true. Not a single one has failed! 15But as surely as the LORD your God has given you the good things he promised, he will also bring disaster on you if you disobey him. He will completely destroy you from this good land he has given you. 16If you break the covenant of the LORD your God by worshiping and serving other gods, his anger will burn against you, and you will quickly vanish from the good land he has given you."

**24:1**
Josh 23:2

**24:2**
Gen 11:27-32

**24:3**
Gen 12:1; 15:5;
21:3; 24:7

**24:4**
Gen 25:25-26;
46:5-7
Deut 2:5

**24:5**
Exod 3:10; 4:14-17

**24:6**
Exod 14:2-22

### The LORD's Covenant Renewed

**24** Then Joshua summoned all the tribes of Israel to Shechem, including their elders, leaders, judges, and officers. So they came and presented themselves to God.

2Joshua said to the people, "This is what the LORD, the God of Israel, says: Long ago your ancestors, including Terah, the father of Abraham and Nahor, lived beyond the Euphrates River,* and they worshiped other gods. 3But I took your ancestor Abraham from the land beyond the Euphrates and led him into the land of Canaan. I gave him many descendants through his son Isaac. 4To Isaac I gave Jacob and Esau. To Esau I gave the mountains of Seir, while Jacob and his children went down into Egypt.

5"Then I sent Moses and Aaron, and I brought terrible plagues on Egypt; and afterward I brought you out as a free people. 6But when your ancestors arrived at the Red Sea,* the

**24:2** Hebrew *the river;* also in 24:3, 14, 15.   **24:6** Hebrew *sea of reeds.*

---

**23:6-13** Joshua knew the nation's weak spots. Before dying, he called the people together and gave commands to help them where they were most likely to slip: (1) Follow all that is written in the Book of Instruction without turning aside; (2) don't associate with the pagan nations or worship their gods; (3) don't intermarry with the pagan nations. These temptations were right in their backyard. Our associations and relationships can be temptations to us as well. It's wise to identify our weak spots before we break down. Then we can develop strategies to overcome these temptations instead of being overcome by them.

**23:8** Joshua was dying, and so he called all the leaders of the nation together to give them his final words of encouragement and instruction. His whole message can be summarized in this verse: "Cling tightly to the LORD your God." Joshua had been a living example of those words, and he wanted that to be his legacy. For what do you want to be remembered, and what do you want to pass on to your children and associates? You can leave them nothing better than the admonition to hold on to God and to the memory of a person who did.

**23:12-16** This chilling prediction about the consequences of intermarriage with the Canaanite nations eventually became a reality. Numerous stories in the book of Judges show what Israel had to suffer because of failure to follow God wholeheartedly. God was supremely loving and patient with Israel, just as he is today. But we must not confuse his patience with us as approval of or indifference to our sin. Beware of demanding your own way because eventually you may get it—along with all its painful consequences.

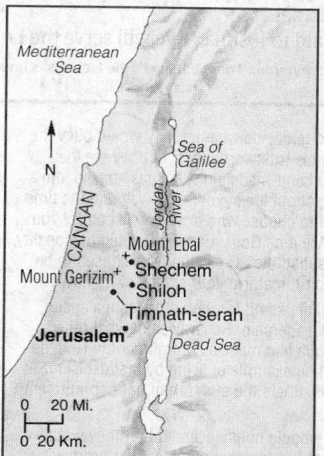

**JOSHUA'S FINAL SPEECH** Joshua called all the Israelites to Shechem to hear his final words. He challenged the people to make a conscious choice to always serve God. Soon afterward, Joshua died and was buried in his hometown of Timnath-serah.

Egyptians chased after you with chariots and charioteers. ⁷When your ancestors cried out to the Lord, I put darkness between you and the Egyptians. I brought the sea crashing down on the Egyptians, drowning them. With your very own eyes you saw what I did. Then you lived in the wilderness for many years.

⁸"Finally, I brought you into the land of the Amorites on the east side of the Jordan. They fought against you, but I destroyed them before you. I gave you victory over them, and you took possession of their land. ⁹Then Balak son of Zippor, king of Moab, started a war against Israel. He summoned Balaam son of Beor to curse you, ¹⁰but I would not listen to him. Instead, I made Balaam bless you, and so I rescued you from Balak.

¹¹"When you crossed the Jordan River and came to Jericho, the men of Jericho fought against you, as did the Amorites, the Perizzites, the Canaanites, the Hittites, the Girgashites, the Hivites, and the Jebusites. But I gave you victory over them. ¹²And I sent terror* ahead of you to drive out the two kings of the Amorites. It was not your swords or bows that brought you victory. ¹³I gave you land you had not worked on, and I gave you towns you did not build—the towns where you are now living. I gave you vineyards and olive groves for food, though you did not plant them.

¹⁴"So fear the Lord and serve him wholeheartedly. Put away forever the idols your ancestors worshiped when they lived beyond the Euphrates River and in Egypt. Serve the Lord alone. ¹⁵But if you refuse to serve the Lord, then choose today whom you will serve. Would you prefer the gods your ancestors served beyond the Euphrates? Or will it be the gods of the Amorites in whose land you now live? But as for me and my family, we will serve the Lord."

¹⁶The people replied, "We would never abandon the Lord and serve other gods. ¹⁷For the Lord our God is the one who rescued us and our ancestors from slavery in the land of Egypt. He performed mighty miracles before our very eyes. As we traveled through the wilderness among our enemies, he preserved us. ¹⁸It was the Lord who drove out the Amorites and the other nations living here in the land. So we, too, will serve the Lord, for he alone is our God."

¹⁹Then Joshua warned the people, "You are not able to serve the Lord, for he is a holy and jealous God. He will not forgive your rebellion and your sins. ²⁰If you abandon the Lord and serve other gods, he will turn against you and destroy you, even though he has been so good to you."

²¹But the people answered Joshua, "No, we will serve the Lord!"

²²"You are a witness to your own decision," Joshua said. "You have chosen to serve the Lord."

"Yes," they replied, "we are witnesses to what we have said."

²³"All right then," Joshua said, "destroy the idols among you, and turn your hearts to the Lord, the God of Israel."

²⁴The people said to Joshua, "We will serve the Lord our God. We will obey him alone."

**24:7**
Exod 14:19-31
Deut 1:46; 2:14

**24:8**
Num 21:21-31

**24:9**
Num 22:2-6

**24:11**
Exod 23:23
Deut 7:1
Josh 3:14-17

**24:12**
Exod 23:28
Deut 7:20
Ps 44:3, 6

**24:13**
Deut 6:10-11

**24:14**
Deut 10:12; 18:13
1 Sam 12:24

**24:15**
Ruth 1:15
1 Kgs 18:21

**24:19**
Exod 20:5; 23:21;
34:14
Lev 19:2; 20:7, 26

**24:20**
Deut 4:25-26
Josh 23:15
1 Chr 28:9
Acts 7:42

**24:24**
Exod 19:8; 24:3, 7
Deut 5:27

**24:12** Often rendered *the hornet*. The meaning of the Hebrew is uncertain.

**24:15** The people had to decide whether they would obey the Lord, who had proven his trustworthiness, or obey the local gods, which were only hand-made idols. It's easy to slip into a quiet rebellion—going about life in your own way. But the time comes when you have to choose who or what will control you. The choice is yours. Will it be God, your own limited personality, or another imperfect substitute? Once you have chosen to be controlled by God's Spirit, reaffirm your choice every day.

**24:15** In taking a definite stand for the Lord, Joshua again displayed his spiritual leadership. Regardless of what others decided, because Joshua had made a commitment to God, he was determined to set an example of living by that decision. The way we live shows others the strength of our commitment to serving God.

**24:16-18, 21** All the people boldly claimed that they would never forsake the Lord. But they did not keep that promise. Very soon God would charge them with breaking their contract with him (Judges 2:2, 3). Talk is cheap. It is easy to say we will

follow God, but it is much more important to live like it. Yet the nation followed God through Joshua's lifetime, a great tribute to Joshua's faith in God and powerful leadership.

**24:23** Joshua told the Israelites to destroy their foreign gods, or idols. To follow God requires destroying whatever gets in the way of worshiping him. We have our own form of idols—greed, wrong priorities, jealousies, prejudices—that get in the way of worshiping God. God is not satisfied if we merely hide these idols. We must completely remove them from our lives.

**24:24-26** The covenant between Israel and God was that the people would worship and obey the Lord alone. Their purpose was to become a holy nation that would influence the rest of the world for God. The conquest of Canaan was a means to achieve this purpose, but Israel became preoccupied with the land and lost sight of the Lord God.

The same can happen in our lives. We can spend so much time on the means that we forget the end—to glorify God. Churches may make this mistake as well. For example, the congregation may pour all of its energies into a new facility, only to become self-satisfied or fearful of letting certain groups use it. If this happens, they have focused on the building and lost sight of its purpose—to bring others to God.

24:25
Exod 24:8

25So Joshua made a covenant with the people that day at Shechem, committing them to follow the decrees and regulations of the LORD. 26Joshua recorded these things in the Book of God's Instructions. As a reminder of their agreement, he took a huge stone and rolled it beneath the terebinth tree beside the Tabernacle of the LORD.

24:27
Josh 22:27

27Joshua said to all the people, "This stone has heard everything the LORD said to us. It will be a witness to testify against you if you go back on your word to God."

28Then Joshua sent all the people away to their own homelands.

### Leaders Buried in the Promised Land

24:29
Judg 2:8
24:30
Josh 19:50

29After this, Joshua son of Nun, the servant of the LORD, died at the age of 110. 30They buried him in the land he had been allocated, at Timnath-serah in the hill country of Ephraim, north of Mount Gaash.

31The people of Israel served the LORD throughout the lifetime of Joshua and of the elders who outlived him—those who had personally experienced all that the LORD had done for Israel.

24:32
Gen 50:24-25
Exod 13:19
John 4:5
Acts 7:16

32 The bones of Joseph, which the Israelites had brought along with them when they left Egypt, were buried at Shechem, in the parcel of ground Jacob had bought from the sons of Hamor for 100 pieces of silver.* This land was located in the territory allotted to the descendants of Joseph.

24:33
Josh 22:13

33Eleazar son of Aaron also died. He was buried in the hill country of Ephraim, in the town of Gibeah, which had been given to his son Phinehas.

24:32 Hebrew *100 kesitahs;* the value or weight of the kesitah is no longer known.

---

**24:29-31** The book of Joshua opens with a new leader being handed a seemingly impossible task—to lead the nation in taking over the land of Canaan. By following God closely, Joshua led the people through military victories and faithful spiritual obedience. In 24:16 we read that the people were sure they would never forsake the Lord. The response of the whole nation during these many years is a tribute both to Joshua's leadership and to the God he faithfully served.

**24:33** Joshua and Eleazar died, but not before laying before the people the fundamentals of what it means to have faith in God. We are to honor and serve the Lord alone (24:14). This is based on a choice: to obey him instead of following other gods (24:15). We are incapable, however, of properly worshiping him because of our rebellion and sins (24:19). By choosing God as Lord, we enter into a covenant with him (24:25) whereby he promises not only to forgive and love us, but also to enable us by his Spirit to do his work here on earth. This covenant requires us to renounce the principles and practices of the culture around us that are hostile to God's plan (24:23). This is not to be done alone, but by binding ourselves together with others who have faith in God. (See Deuteronomy 30:15-20 for a similar message from Moses.)

# JUDGES

## VITAL STATISTICS

**PURPOSE:**
To show that God's judgment against sin is certain, and his forgiveness of sin and restoration to relationship are just as certain for those who repent

**AUTHOR:**
Possibly Samuel

**ORIGINAL AUDIENCE:**
The people of Israel

**SETTING:**
The land of Canaan, later called Israel. God had helped the Israelites conquer Canaan, which had been inhabited by a host of wicked nations. But they were in danger of losing this Promised Land because they compromised their convictions and disobeyed God.

**KEY VERSE:**
"In those days Israel had no king; all the people did whatever seemed right in their own eyes" (17:6).

**KEY PEOPLE:**
Othniel, Ehud, Deborah, Gideon, Abimelech, Jephthah, Samson, Delilah

**SPECIAL FEATURE:**
Records Israel's first civil war

REAL heroes are hard to find these days. Modern research and the media have made the foibles and weaknesses of our leaders very apparent; we search in vain for men and women to emulate. The music, movie, and sports industries produce a steady stream of "stars" who shoot to the top and then quickly fade from view.

Judges is a book about heroes—12 men and women who delivered Israel from its oppressors. These judges were not perfect; in fact, they included an assassin, a sexually promiscuous man, and a person who broke all the laws of hospitality. But they were submissive to God, and God used them.

Judges is also a book about sin and its consequences. Like a minor cut or abrasion that becomes infected when left untreated, sin grows and soon poisons the whole body. The book of Joshua ends with the nation taking a stand for God, ready to experience all the blessings of the Promised Land. After settling in Canaan, however, the Israelites lost their spiritual commitment and motivation. When Joshua and the elders died, the nation experienced a leadership vacuum, leaving them without a strong central government. Instead of enjoying freedom and prosperity in the Promised Land, Israel entered the dark ages of her history.

Simply stated, the reason for this rapid decline was sin—individual and corporate. The first step away from God was incomplete obedience (1:11—2:5); the Israelites refused to eliminate the enemy completely from the land. This led to intermarriage and idolatry (2:6—3:7) and everyone doing "whatever seemed right" (17:6). Before long the Israelites became captives. Out of their desperation they begged God to rescue them. In faithfulness to his promise and out of his loving-kindness, God would raise up a judge to deliver his people, and for a time there would be peace. Then complacency and disobedience would set in, and the cycle would begin again.

The book of Judges spans a period of over 325 years, recording six successive periods of oppression and deliverance, and the careers of 12 deliverers. Their captors included the Mesopotamians, Moabites, Philistines, Canaanites, Midianites, and Ammonites. God used a variety of deliverers—from Othniel to Samson—to lead his people to freedom and true worship. God's deliverance through the judges is a powerful demonstration of his love and mercy toward his people.

As you read the book of Judges, take a good look at these heroes from Jewish history. Note their dependence on God and obedience to his commands. Observe Israel's repeated downward spiral into sin, refusing to learn from history and living only for the moment. But most of all, stand in awe of God's mercy as he delivers his people over and over again.

| Gideon 1162–1122 (1146–1106) | Samuel born 1105 (1083) | Samson 1075–1055 (1083–1063) | Saul anointed king 1050 (1045) | David becomes king 1010 |
| --- | --- | --- | --- | --- |

## THE BLUEPRINT

A. THE MILITARY FAILURE OF ISRAEL (1:1—3:6)
1. Incomplete conquest of the land
2. Disobedience and defeat

The tribes had compromised God's command to drive out the inhabitants of the land. Incomplete removal of evil often means disaster in the end. We must beware of compromising with wickedness.

B. THE RESCUE OF ISRAEL BY THE JUDGES (3:7—16:31)
1. First period: Othniel
2. Second period: Ehud and Shamgar
3. Third period: Deborah and Barak
4. Fourth period: Gideon, Tola, and Jair
5. Fifth period: Jephthah, Ibzan, Elon, and Abdon
6. Sixth period: Samson

Repeatedly we see the nation of Israel sinning against God and God allowing suffering to come upon the land and the people. Sin always has its consequences. Where there is sin we can expect suffering to follow. Rather than living in an endless cycle of abandoning God and then crying out to him for rescue, we should seek to live a consistent life of faithfulness.

C. THE MORAL FAILURE OF ISRAEL (17:1—21:25)
1. Idolatry in the tribe of Dan
2. War against the tribe of Benjamin

Despite the efforts of Israel's judges, the people still would not turn wholeheartedly to God. They all did whatever they thought was best for themselves. The result was the spiritual, moral, and political decline of the nation. Our lives will also fall into decline and decay unless we live by the guidelines God has given us.

## MEGATHEMES

| THEME | EXPLANATION | IMPORTANCE |
| --- | --- | --- |
| Decline/ Compromise | Whenever a judge died, the people faced decline and failure because they compromised their high spiritual purpose in many ways. They abandoned their mission to drive all the people out of the land, and they adopted the customs of the people living around them. | Society has many rewards to offer those who compromise their faith: wealth, acceptance, recognition, power, and influence. When God gives us a mission, it must not be polluted by a desire for approval from society. We must keep our eyes on Christ, who is our Judge and Deliverer. |
| Decay/Apostasy | Israel's moral downfall had its roots in the fierce independence that each tribe cherished. It led to everyone doing whatever seemed right in his own eyes. There was no unity in government or in worship. Law and order broke down. Finally, idol worship and man-made religion led to the complete abandoning of faith in God. | We can expect decay when we value anything more highly than God. If we value our own independence more than dedication to God, we have placed an idol in our hearts. Soon our lives become temples to that god. We must constantly regard God's first claim on our lives and all our desires. |
| Defeat/ Oppression | God used evil oppressors to punish the Israelites for their sin, to bring them to the point of repentance, and to test their allegiance to him. | Rebellion against God leads to disaster. God may use defeat to bring wandering hearts back to him. When all else is stripped away, we recognize the importance of serving only him. |
| Repentance | Decline, decay, and defeat caused the people to cry out to God for help. They vowed to turn from idolatry and to turn to God for mercy and deliverance. When they repented, God delivered them. | Idolatry gains a foothold in our hearts when we make anything more important than God. We must identify modern idols in our hearts, renounce them, and turn to God for his love and mercy. |
| Deliverance/ Heroes | Because Israel repented, God raised up heroes to deliver his people from their path of sin and the oppression it brought. He used many kinds of people to accomplish this purpose by filling them with his Holy Spirit. | God's Holy Spirit is available to all people. Anyone who is dedicated to God can be used for his service. Real heroes recognize the futility of human effort without God's guidance and power. |

# KEY PLACES IN JUDGES

The broken lines (— · — · —) indicate modern boundaries.

**1 Bokim** The book of Judges opens with the Israelites continuing their conquest of the Promised Land. Their failure to obey God and destroy all the evil inhabitants soon came back to haunt them in two ways: (1) The enemies reorganized and counterattacked, and (2) Israel turned away from God, adopting the evil and idolatrous practices of the inhabitants of the land. The angel of the Lord appeared at Bokim to inform the Israelites that their sin and disobedience had broken their agreement with God and would result in punishment through oppression (1:1—3:11).

**2 Jericho** The nation of Moab was one of the first to oppress Israel. Moab's King Eglon conquered much of Israel—including the city of Jericho— and forced the people to pay unreasonable taxes. The messenger chosen to deliver this tax money to King Eglon was named Ehud. But he had more than money to deliver, for he drew his hidden sword and killed the Moabite

king. Ehud then escaped, only to return with an army that chased out the Moabites and freed Israel from its oppressors (3:12–31).

**3 Hazor** After Ehud's death, King Jabin of Hazor conquered Israel and oppressed the people for 20 years. Then Deborah became Israel's leader. She summoned Barak to fight Commander Sisera, the leader of King Jabin's army. Together Deborah and Barak led their army into battle against Jabin's forces in the land between Mount Tabor and the Kishon River and conquered them (4:1—5:31).

**4 Hill of Moreh** After 40 years of peace, the Midianites began to harass the Israelites by destroying their flocks and crops. When the Israelites finally cried out to God, he chose Gideon, a poor and humble farmer, to be their deliverer. After struggling with doubt and feelings of inferiority, Gideon took courage and knocked down his town's altar to Baal, causing a great uproar among the citizens. Filled with the Spirit of God, he attacked the vast army of Midian, which was camped near the Hill of Moreh. With just a handful of men he sent the enemy running away in confusion (6:1—7:25).

**5 Shechem** Even great leaders make mistakes. Gideon's relations with a concubine in Shechem resulted in the birth of a son named Abimelech. Abimelech turned out to be treacherous and power hungry— stirring up the people to proclaim him king. To carry out his plan, he went so far as to kill 69 of his 70 half brothers. Eventually some men of Shechem rebelled against Abimelech, but he gathered together an army and defeated them. His lust for power led him to ransack two other cities, but he was killed by a woman who dropped a millstone onto his head (8:28—9:57).

**6 Land of Ammon** Again Israel turned completely from God; so God turned from them. But when the Ammonites mobilized their army to attack, Israel threw away her idols and called upon God once again. Jephthah, a prostitute's son who had been run out of Israel, was asked to return and lead Israel's forces against the enemy. After defeating the Ammonites, Jephthah became involved in a war with the tribe of Ephraim over a misunderstanding (10:1—12:15).

**7 Timnah** Israel's next judge, Samson, was a miracle child promised by God to a barren couple. He was the one who would begin to free Israel from their next and most powerful oppressor, the Philistines. According to God's command, Samson was to be a Nazirite—one who took a vow to be set apart for special service to God. One of the stipulations of the vow was that Samson's hair could never be cut. But when Samson grew up, he did not always take his special responsibility to God seriously. He even fell in love with a Philistine girl in Timnah and asked to marry her. Before the wedding, Samson held a party for some men in the city, using a riddle to place a bet with them. The men, however, forced Samson's fiancée into giving the answer. Furious at being tricked, Samson paid his bet with the lives of 30 Philistines who lived in the nearby city of Ashkelon (13:1—14:20).

**8 Valley of Sorek** Samson killed thousands of Philistines with his incredible strength. The nation's leaders looked for a way to stop him. They got their chance when another Philistine woman stole Samson's heart. Her name was Delilah, and she lived in the valley of Sorek. In exchange for a great sum of money, Delilah deceived Samson into confiding in her the secret of his strength. One night while he slept, Delilah had his hair cut off. As a result, Samson fell helplessly into the hands of the enemy (15:1—16:20).

**9 Gaza** Samson was blinded and led captive to a prison in Gaza. There his hair began to grow again. After a while, the Philistines held a great festival to celebrate Samson's imprisonment and to humiliate him before the crowds. When he was brought out as the entertainment, he literally brought down the house when he pushed on the main pillars of the banquet hall and killed the thousands trapped inside. The prophecy that he would begin to free Israel from the Philistines had come true (16:21—31).

**10 Hill Country of Ephraim** In the hill country of Ephraim lived a man named Micah. Micah hired his own priest to perform priestly duties in the shrine that housed his collection of idols. He thought he was pleasing God with all his religiosity! Like many of the Israelites, Micah assumed that his own opinions of what was right would agree with God's (17:1—13).

**11 Dan** The tribe of Dan migrated north in order to find new territory. They sent spies ahead of them to scout out the land. One night the spies stopped at Micah's home. Looking for some assurance of victory, the spies stole Micah's idols and priest. Rejoicing the tribe, they came upon the city of Laish and slaughtered the unarmed and innocent citizens, renaming the conquered city Dan. Micah's idols were then set up in the city and became the focal point of the tribe's worship for many years (18:1—31).

**12 Gibeah** The extent to which many people had fallen away from God became clear in Gibeah, a village in the territory of Benjamin. A man and his concubine were traveling north toward the hill country of Ephraim. They stopped for the night in Gibeah, thinking they would be safe. But some perverts in the city gathered around the home where they were staying and demanded that the man come out to have sexual relations with them. Instead, the man and his host pushed the concubine out the door. She was raped and abused all night. When the man found her lifeless body the next morning, he cut it into 12 pieces and sent the parts to each tribe of Israel. This tragic event demonstrated that the nation had sunk to its lowest spiritual level (19:1—30).

**13 Mizpah** The leaders of Israel came to Mizpah to decide how to punish the wicked men from the city of Gibeah. When the city leaders refused to turn the criminals over, the whole nation of Israel took vengeance upon both Gibeah and the tribe of Benjamin where the city was located. When the battle ended, the entire tribe had been destroyed except for a handful of men who took refuge in the hills. Israel had become morally depraved. The stage was now set for the much-needed spiritual renewal that would come under the prophet Samuel (20:1—21:25).

---

## A. THE MILITARY FAILURE OF ISRAEL (1:1—3:6)

By faithfully obeying the Lord, Joshua led the Israelites to military victory. After his death, however, the tribes failed to clear the inhabitants from the land, so the Lord withdrew his promise to help drive the people out and bless the Israelites in battle. The new generation abandoned God and worshiped idols. This part of Judges shows what can happen when we neglect to teach our children to follow the Lord.

### 1. Incomplete conquest of the land
*Judah and Simeon Conquer the Land*

**1:1**
Num 27:21

**1:2**
Gen 49:8

**1** After the death of Joshua, the Israelites asked the LORD, "Which tribe should go first to attack the Canaanites?"

2 The LORD answered, "Judah, for I have given them victory over the land."

---

**1:1** The people of Israel had finally entered and taken control of the land promised to their ancestors (Genesis 12:7; Exodus 3:16, 17). The book of Judges continues the story of this conquest that began in the book of Joshua. Through God's strength, the Israelites had conquered many enemies and overcome many difficulties, but their work was not yet finished. They had effectively met many political and military challenges, but facing spiritual challenges was more difficult. The unholy but attractive lifestyle of the Canaanites proved more dangerous than their military might. The Israelites gave in to the pressure and compromised their faith. If we attempt to meet life's challenges with human effort alone, we will find the pressures and temptations around us too great to resist.

**1:1** Soon after Joshua died, Israel began to lose its firm grip on the land. Although Joshua was a great commander, the people missed his spiritual leadership even more than his military skill, for he had kept the people focused on God and his purposes. Joshua had been the obvious successor to Moses, but there was no obvious successor to Joshua. During this crisis of leadership, Israel had to learn that no matter how powerful and wise the current leader was, their real leader was God. We often focus our hope and confidence on some influential leader, failing to realize that in reality it is God who is in command. Acknowledge God as your commander in chief, and avoid the temptation of relying too heavily on human leaders, regardless of their spiritual wisdom.

**1:1** The Canaanites were all the people who lived in Canaan (the Promised Land). They lived in city-states where each city had its own government, army, and laws. One reason Canaan was so difficult to conquer was that each city had to be defeated individually. There was no single king who could surrender the entire country into the hands of the Israelites.

Canaan's greatest threat to Israel was not its army, but its religion. Canaanite religion idealized evil traits: cruelty in war, sexual immorality, selfish greed, and materialism. It was a "me first, anything goes" society. Obviously, the religions of Israel and Canaan could not coexist.

**1:2** The book of Joshua tells of a swift and thorough conquest of enemy armies and cities, while the book of Judges seems to suggest a more lengthy and gradual conquest. When the Israelites first entered the Promised Land (Joshua 1–12), they united as one army to crush the inhabitants until they were too weak to retaliate. Then, after the land was divided among the 12 tribes (Joshua 13–24), each tribe was responsible for driving out the remaining enemy from its own territory. The book of Judges tells of their failure to do this.

Some tribes were more successful than others. Under Joshua, they all began strong, but soon most were sidetracked by fear, weariness, lack of discipline, or pursuit of their own interests. As a result, their faith began to fade away, and "the people did whatever seemed right in their own eyes" (17:6). In order for our faith to survive, it must be practiced day by day. It must penetrate every aspect of our lives. Beware of starting out strong and then getting sidetracked from your real purpose—loving God and living for him.

3The men of Judah said to their relatives from the tribe of Simeon, "Join with us to fight against the Canaanites living in the territory allotted to us. Then we will help you conquer your territory." So the men of Simeon went with Judah.

1:3
Judg 1:17

4When the men of Judah attacked, the LORD gave them victory over the Canaanites and Perizzites, and they killed 10,000 enemy warriors at the town of Bezek. 5While at Bezek they encountered King Adoni-bezek and fought against him, and the Canaanites and Perizzites were defeated. 6Adoni-bezek escaped, but the Israelites soon captured him and cut off his thumbs and big toes.

1:4
Gen 13:7
1 Sam 11:8

7Adoni-bezek said, "I once had seventy kings with their thumbs and big toes cut off, eating scraps from under my table. Now God has paid me back for what I did to them." They took him to Jerusalem, and he died there.

8The men of Judah attacked Jerusalem and captured it, killing all its people and setting the city on fire. 9Then they went down to fight the Canaanites living in the hill country, the Negev, and the western foothills.* 10Judah marched against the Canaanites in Hebron (formerly called Kiriath-arba), defeating the forces of Sheshai, Ahiman, and Talmai.

1:8
Josh 15:63

1:10-15
//Josh 15:13-19

11From there they went to fight against the people living in the town of Debir (formerly called Kiriath-sepher). 12Caleb said, "I will give my daughter Acsah in marriage to the one who attacks and captures Kiriath-sepher." 13Othniel, the son of Caleb's younger brother, Kenaz, was the one who conquered it, so Acsah became Othniel's wife.

1:13
Judg 3:9

14When Acsah married Othniel, she urged him* to ask her father for a field. As she got down off her donkey, Caleb asked her, "What's the matter?"

15She said, "Let me have another gift. You have already given me land in the Negev; now please give me springs of water, too." So Caleb gave her the upper and lower springs.

16When the tribe of Judah left Jericho—the city of palms—the Kenites, who were descendants of Moses' father-in-law, traveled with them into the wilderness of Judah. They settled among the people there, near the town of Arad in the Negev.

1:16
Deut 34:3
Judg 3:13; 4:11

17Then Judah joined with Simeon to fight against the Canaanites living in Zephath, and they completely destroyed* the town. So the town was named Hormah.* 18In addition, Judah captured the towns of Gaza, Ashkelon, and Ekron, along with their surrounding territories.

1:17
Num 21:3

1:9 Hebrew *the Shephelah.* 1:14 Greek version and Latin Vulgate read *he urged her.* 1:17a The Hebrew term used here refers to the complete consecration of things or people to the LORD, either by destroying them or by giving them as an offering. 1:17b *Hormah* means "destruction."

---

**JUDAH FIGHTS FOR ITS LAND**
The tribe of Judah wasted no time beginning their conquest of the territory allotted to them. With help from the tribe of Simeon, Jerusalem was conquered, as were the Canaanites in the Negev and along the coast. Hebron and Debir fell to Judah, and later Gaza, Ashkelon, and Ekron.

**1:6** The maiming of Adoni-bezek was one example in a long string of actions that demonstrated Israel's tendency to disobey God's instructions by only giving partial obedience. Enemy kings were supposed to be executed, not humiliated. This defeated king recognized God's righteous punishment more clearly than God's people acknowledged God's commands. When we understand what God tells us to do, we run great danger if we don't carry out both the letter and the spirit of his words.

**1:8** Although the Israelites conquered Jerusalem, they did not occupy the city until the days of David (2 Samuel 5:6-10).

**1:12-15** This same event is recorded in Joshua 15:16-19. Caleb was one of the original men who scouted out the Promised Land (Numbers 13–14) and, with Joshua, encouraged the people to conquer it. For his faithfulness, he was given the land of his choice.

**1:17** Why did God order the Israelites to drive the Canaanites from their land? Although the command seems cruel, the Israelites were under God's order to execute judgment on those wicked people. The other nations were to be judged for their sin as God had judged Israel by forcing them to wander for 40 years before they were allowed to enter the Promised Land. Over 700 years earlier, God had told Abraham that when the Israelites entered the Promised Land, the gross evil of the native people would be ready for judgment (Genesis 15:16). But God wasn't playing favorites with the Israelites because eventually they, too, would be severely punished for becoming as evil as the people they were ordered to drive out (2 Kings 17; 25; Jeremiah 6:18, 19; Ezekiel 8). God is not partial; all people are eligible for God's gracious forgiveness as well as for his firm justice.

## Israel Fails to Conquer the Land

1:19
Josh 17:16
Judg 4:3

**19**The LORD was with the people of Judah, and they took possession of the hill country. But they failed to drive out the people living in the plains, who had iron chariots.

1:20
Josh 14:6-9; 15:14

**20**The town of Hebron was given to Caleb as Moses had promised. And Caleb drove out the people living there, who were descendants of the three sons of Anak.

1:21
Josh 15:63

**21**The tribe of Benjamin, however, failed to drive out the Jebusites, who were living in Jerusalem. So to this day the Jebusites live in Jerusalem among the people of Benjamin.

1:22
Gen 28:19
Josh 14:3-4

**22**The descendants of Joseph attacked the town of Bethel, and the LORD was with them. **23**They sent men to scout out Bethel (formerly known as Luz).

1:24
Josh 2:12

**24**They confronted a man coming out of the town and said to him, "Show us a way into the town, and we will have mercy on you."

1:25
Josh 6:25

**25**So he showed them a way in, and they killed everyone in the town except that man and his family. **26**Later the man moved to the land of the Hittites, where he built a town. He named it Luz, which is its name to this day.

1:27
Josh 17:11-13

**27**The tribe of Manasseh failed to drive out the people living in Beth-shan,* Taanach, Dor, Ibleam, Megiddo, and all their surrounding settlements, because the Canaanites were determined to stay in that region. **28**When the Israelites grew stronger, they forced the Canaanites to work as slaves, but they never did drive them completely out of the land.

**1:27** Hebrew *Beth-shean*, a variant spelling of Beth-shan.

---

| THE JUDGES OF ISRAEL | Judge | Years of Judging | Memorable Act(s) | Reference |
|---|---|---|---|---|
| | OTHNIEL | 40 | He captured a powerful Canaanite city | Judges 3:7-11 |
| | EHUD | 80 | He killed Eglon and defeated the Moabites | Judges 3:12-30 |
| | SHAMGAR | unrecorded | He killed 600 Philistines with an ox goad | Judges 3:31 |
| | DEBORAH (w/Barak) | 40 | She defeated Sisera and the Canaanites and later sang a victory song with Barak | Judges 4, 5 |
| | GIDEON | 40 | He destroyed his family idols, used a fleece to determine God's will, raised an army of 10,000, and defeated 135,000 Midianites with 300 soldiers | Judges 6–8 |
| | TOLA | 23 | He judged Israel for 23 years | Judges 10:1, 2 |
| | JAIR | 22 | He had 30 sons | Judges 10:3-5 |
| | JEPHTHAH | 6 | He made a rash vow, defeated the Ammonites, and later battled jealous Ephraim | Judges 10:6–12:7 |
| | IBZAN | 7 | He had 30 sons and 30 daughters | Judges 12:8-10 |
| | ELON | 10 | Unrecorded | Judges 12:11, 12 |
| | ABDON | 8 | He had 40 sons and 30 grandsons, each of whom had his own donkey | Judges 12:13-15 |
| | SAMSON | 20 | He was a Nazirite, killed a lion with his bare hands, burned the Philistine wheat fields, killed 1,000 Philistines with a donkey's jawbone, tore off an iron gate, was betrayed by Delilah, and destroyed thousands of Philistines in one last mighty act | Judges 13–16 |

---

**1:19** Canaanite chariots pulled by horses were among the most sophisticated weapons of the day. Israelite foot soldiers were absolutely powerless when a speeding iron chariot bore down upon them. This is why Israel preferred to fight in the hills where chariots couldn't venture.

**1:21ff** Tribe after tribe failed to drive the evil Canaanites from their land. Why didn't they follow through and completely obey God's commands? (1) They had been fighting for a long time and were tired. Although the goal was in sight, they lacked the discipline and energy to reach it. (2) They were afraid the enemy was too strong—the iron chariots seemed invincible. (3) After Joshua's death, power and authority were decentralized to the tribal leaders, and the tribes were no longer unified in purpose. (4) Spiritual decay had infected them from within. They thought they could handle the temptation and be more prosperous by doing business with the Canaanites.

We, too, often choose to tolerate sin rather than drive it from our lives. We may know what to do but just don't follow through. This results in a gradual deterioration of our relationship with God. In our battles, we may grow tired and want rest, but we need more than a break from our work. We need to know that God loves us and has given us a purpose for life. Victory comes from living according to his purpose and from being willing to fully obey him.

<sup>29</sup>The tribe of Ephraim failed to drive out the Canaanites living in Gezer, so the Canaanites continued to live there among them.

<sup>30</sup>The tribe of Zebulun failed to drive out the residents of Kitron and Nahalol, so the Canaanites continued to live among them. But the Canaanites were forced to work as slaves for the people of Zebulun.

<sup>31</sup>The tribe of Asher failed to drive out the residents of Acco, Sidon, Ahlab, Aczib, Helbah, Aphik, and Rehob. <sup>32</sup>Instead, the people of Asher moved in among the Canaanites, who controlled the land, for they failed to drive them out.

<sup>33</sup>Likewise, the tribe of Naphtali failed to drive out the residents of Beth-shemesh and Beth-anath. Instead, they moved in among the Canaanites, who controlled the land. Nevertheless, the people of Beth-shemesh and Beth-anath were forced to work as slaves for the people of Naphtali.

<sup>34</sup>As for the tribe of Dan, the Amorites forced them back into the hill country and would not let them come down into the plains. <sup>35</sup>The Amorites were determined to stay in Mount Heres, Aijalon, and Shaalbim, but when the descendants of Joseph became stronger, they forced the Amorites to work as slaves. <sup>36</sup>The boundary of the Amorites ran from Scorpion Pass* to Sela and continued upward from there.

### The LORD's Messenger Comes to Bokim

**2** The angel of the LORD went up from Gilgal to Bokim and said to the Israelites, "I brought you out of Egypt into this land that I swore to give your ancestors, and I said I would never break my covenant with you. <sup>2</sup>For your part, you were not to make any covenants with the people living in this land; instead, you were to destroy their altars. But you disobeyed my command. Why did you do this? <sup>3</sup>So now I declare that I will no longer drive out the people living in your land. They will be thorns in your sides,* and their gods will be a constant temptation to you."

<sup>4</sup>When the angel of the LORD finished speaking to all the Israelites, the people wept loudly. <sup>5</sup>So they called the place Bokim (which means "weeping"), and they offered sacrifices there to the LORD.

## 2. Disobedience and defeat
### The Death of Joshua

<sup>6</sup>After Joshua sent the people away, each of the tribes left to take possession of the land allotted to them. <sup>7</sup>And the Israelites served the LORD throughout the lifetime of Joshua and the leaders who outlived him—those who had seen all the great things the LORD had done for Israel.

<sup>8</sup>Joshua son of Nun, the servant of the LORD, died at the age of 110. <sup>9</sup>They buried him in the land he had been allocated, at Timnath-serah* in the hill country of Ephraim, north of Mount Gaash.

1:29 Josh 16:10
1:34 Judg 18:1
1:36 Josh 15:3
2:1 Gen 17:7; Exod 20:2; Judg 6:11
2:2 Exod 23:32; 34:12-13
2:3 Num 33:55
2:5 Josh 7:26
2:6 Josh 24:28-31

1:36 Hebrew *Akrabbim.*   2:3 Hebrew *They will be in your sides;* compare Num 33:55.   2:9 As in parallel text at Josh 24:30; Hebrew reads *Timnath-heres,* a variant spelling of Timnath-serah.

---

**2:1-3** This event marks a significant change in Israel's relationship with God. At Mount Sinai, God made a sacred and binding agreement with the Israelites called a covenant (Exodus 19:5-8). God's part was to make Israel a special nation (see the note on Genesis 12:1-3), to protect them, and to give them unique blessings for following him. Israel's part was to love God and obey his laws. But because they rejected and disobeyed God, the agreement to protect them was no longer in effect. But God wasn't going to abandon his people. They would receive wonderful blessings if they asked God to forgive them and sincerely followed him again.

Although God's agreement to help Israel conquer the land was no longer in effect, his covenant to make Israel a nation through whom the whole world would be blessed (fulfilled in the Messiah's coming) remained valid. God still wanted the Israelites to be a holy people (just as he wants us to be holy), and he often used oppression to bring them back to him, just as he warned he would (Leviticus 26; Deuteronomy 28). The book

of Judges records a number of instances where God allowed his people to be oppressed so that they would repent of their sins and return to him.

Too often people want God to fulfill his promises while excusing themselves from their responsibilities. Before you claim God's promises, ask, Have I done my part?

**2:4** The people of Israel knew they had sinned, and they wept loudly, responding with deep sorrow. Because we have a tendency to sin, only repentance is the true measure of spiritual sensitivity. Repentance means not only confessing sins and asking God to forgive us, but also abandoning our sinful ways. But we cannot do this sincerely unless we are truly sorry for our sinful actions. Tears alone are not enough. When we are aware that we have done wrong, we should admit it plainly to God rather than try to cover it up or hope we can get away with it.

**2:7-9** The account of Joshua's death is found here and at the end of the book of Joshua (24:29). Either this account is a summary of what happened earlier, or the account in the book of Joshua omitted the events in the first chapter of Judges. (For more on Joshua, see his Profile in Joshua 2.)

### Israel Disobeys the LORD

**2:10**
Exod 5:2
1 Sam 2:12

**2:11**
Judg 4:1; 6:1; 8:33;
10:6

**2:12**
Deut 31:16; 32:12
Judg 10:6
Ps 106:40

**2:13**
Judg 10:6

¹⁰After that generation died, another generation grew up who did not acknowledge the LORD or remember the mighty things he had done for Israel.

¹¹The Israelites did evil in the LORD's sight and served the images of Baal. ¹²They abandoned the LORD, the God of their ancestors, who had brought them out of Egypt. They went after other gods, worshiping the gods of the people around them. And they angered the LORD. ¹³They abandoned the LORD to serve Baal and the images of Ashtoreth. ¹⁴This made the LORD burn with anger against Israel, so he handed them over to raiders who stole their possessions. He turned them over to their enemies all around, and they were no longer able to resist them. ¹⁵Every time Israel went out to battle, the LORD fought against them, causing them to be defeated, just as he had warned. And the people were in great distress.

---

**WHY DID ISRAEL WANT TO WORSHIP IDOLS?**

| *Worshiping God* | *Worshiping Idols* |
|---|---|
| Long-range benefits | Short-range benefits |
| Gratification postponed | Self-gratification immediate |
| Morality required | Sensuality approved |
| High ethical standards demanded | Low ethical standards tolerated |
| Neighbors' sins disapproved | Neighbors' sins approved |
| Unseen God worshiped | Visible idols worshiped |
| Unselfishness expected | Selfishness condoned |
| Business relations hindered | Business relations improved |
| Strict religious practices maintained | Religious practices loosely regulated |
| Changed life demanded | Changed life not demanded |
| Ethical stand expected | Compromise and cooperation practiced |
| Concern for others taught | No concern for others expected |

The temptation to follow false gods because of short-term benefits, good feelings, easy "rules," or convenience was always present. *But the benefits were deceptive because the gods were false.* We worship God because he is the one and only true God.

---

**2:10ff** One generation died, and the next did not follow God. Judges 2:10–3:7 is a brief preview of the cycle of sin, judgment, and repentance that Israel experienced again and again. Each generation failed to teach the next generation to love and follow God. Yet this was at the very center of God's law (Deuteronomy 6:4-9). It is tempting to leave the job of teaching the Christian faith to the church or Christian schools. Yet God says that the responsibility for this task belongs primarily to the family. Because children learn so much by our example, the home offers the most effective place to pass on the faith to the next generation.

**2:11-15** Baal was the god of storms and rains; therefore, he was thought to control vegetation and agriculture. Ashtoreth was the mother goddess of love, war, and fertility (she was also called Astarte or Ishtar). Temple prostitution and child sacrifice were a part of the worship of these Canaanite idols. This generation of Israelites abandoned the faith of their parents and began worshiping the gods of their neighbors. Many things can tempt us to abandon what we know is right. The desire to be accepted by our neighbors can lead us into behavior that is unacceptable to God. Don't be lulled into compromise or pressured into disobedience.

**2:12-15** God often saved his harshest criticism and punishment for those who worshiped idols. Why were idols so bad in God's sight? To worship an idol violated the first two of the Ten Commandments (Exodus 20:3-6). The Canaanites had gods for almost every season, activity, or place. To them, the Lord was just another god to add to their collection of gods. Israel, by contrast, was to worship only the Lord. They could not possibly believe that God was the one true God and at the same time bow to an idol. Idol worshipers could not see their god as their creator because they created it. These idols represent sensual, carnal, and immoral aspects of human nature. God's nature is spiritual and moral. Adding the worship of idols to the worship of God could not be tolerated.

**2:15, 16** Despite Israel's disobedience, God showed his great mercy by raising up judges to save the people from their oppressors. Mercy has been defined as "not giving a person what he or she deserves." This is exactly what God did for Israel and what he does for us. Our disobedience demands judgment! But God shows mercy toward us by providing an escape from sin's penalty through Jesus Christ, who alone saves us from sin. When we pray for forgiveness, we are asking for what we do not deserve. Yet when we take this step and trust in Christ's saving work on our behalf, we can experience God's forgiveness.

## The LORD Rescues His People

¹⁶Then the LORD raised up judges to rescue the Israelites from their attackers. ¹⁷Yet Israel did not listen to the judges but prostituted themselves by worshiping other gods. How quickly they turned away from the path of their ancestors, who had walked in obedience to the LORD's commands.

¹⁸Whenever the LORD raised up a judge over Israel, he was with that judge and rescued the people from their enemies throughout the judge's lifetime. For the LORD took pity on his people, who were burdened by oppression and suffering. ¹⁹But when the judge died, the people returned to their corrupt ways, behaving worse than those who had lived before them. They went after other gods, serving and worshiping them. And they refused to give up their evil practices and stubborn ways.

²⁰So the LORD burned with anger against Israel. He said, "Because these people have violated my covenant, which I made with their ancestors, and have ignored my commands, ²¹I will no longer drive out the nations that Joshua left unconquered when he died. ²²I did this to test Israel—to see whether or not they would follow the ways of the LORD as their ancestors did." ²³That is why the LORD left those nations in place. He did not quickly drive them out or allow Joshua to conquer them all.

## The Nations Left in Canaan

**3** These are the nations that the LORD left in the land to test those Israelites who had not experienced the wars of Canaan. ²He did this to teach warfare to generations of Israelites who had no experience in battle. ³These are the nations: the Philistines (those living under the five Philistine rulers), all the Canaanites, the Sidonians, and the Hivites living in the mountains of Lebanon from Mount Baal-hermon to Lebo-hamath. ⁴These people were left to test the Israelites—to see whether they would obey the commands the LORD had given to their ancestors through Moses.

⁵So the people of Israel lived among the Canaanites, Hittites, Amorites, Perizzites, Hivites, and Jebusites, ⁶and they intermarried with them. Israelite sons married their daughters, and Israelite daughters were given in marriage to their sons. And the Israelites served their gods.

**2:16**
Ps 106:43-45

**2:17**
Ps 81:11-12

**2:19**
Judg 4:1; 8:33

**2:21**
Josh 23:13

**3:1**
Judg 1:1; 2:21-22

**3:3**
Josh 13:3

**3:4**
Deut 8:2
Judg 2:22

**3:5**
Ps 106:35

**3:6**
Exod 34:16
Deut 7:3-4

## B. THE RESCUE OF ISRAEL BY THE JUDGES (3:7—16:31)

The Israelites began a series of cycles of sinning, worshiping idols, being punished, crying out for help, being rescued by a judge sent from God, obeying God for a while, then falling back into idolatry. They were conquered by Aram, Moab, Canaan, Midian, Ammon, and Philistia. They even faced the threat of civil war. Just as God sent help to the people when they cried out to him, he will deliver us when we call on him.

**2:16-19** Throughout this period of history Israel went through seven cycles of (1) rebelling against God, (2) being overrun by enemy nations, (3) being delivered by a God-fearing judge, (4) remaining loyal to God under that judge, and (5) again forgetting God when the judge died. We tend to follow the same cycle—remaining loyal to God as long as we are near those who are devoted to him. But when we are on our own, the pressure to be drawn away from God increases. Determine to be faithful to God despite the difficult situations you encounter. Recognize the importance of maintaining contact with other believers.

**2:17** Why would the people of Israel turn away so quickly from their faith in God? Simply put, the Canaanite religion appeared more attractive to the sensual nature and offered more short-range benefits (sexual permissiveness and increased fertility in childbearing and farming). One of its most attractive features was that people could remain selfish and yet fulfill their religious requirements. They could do almost anything they wished and still be obeying at least one of the many Canaanite gods. Male and female prostitution was not only allowed but was encouraged as a form of worship.

Faith in the one true God, however, does not offer short-range benefits that appeal to our sinful human nature. The essence of sin is selfishness; the essence of God's way of life is selflessness. We must seek Christ's help to live God's way.

**3:1-4** We learn from chapter 1 that these enemy nations were still in the land because the Israelites had failed to obey God and

drive them out. Now God would allow the enemies to remain in order to "test" the Israelites; that is, to give them an opportunity to exercise faith and obedience. By now the younger generation that had not fought in the great battles of conquest was coming of age. It was their job to complete the conquest of the land. There were many obstacles yet to be overcome in their new homeland. How they would handle these obstacles would be a test of their faith.

Perhaps God has left obstacles in your life—hostile people, difficult situations, baffling problems—to allow you to develop faith and obedience.

**3:5-7** The Israelites discovered that relationships affect faith. The men and women of the surrounding nations were attractive to the Israelites. Soon they intermarried, and the Israelites accepted their pagan gods. This was clearly prohibited by God (Exodus 34:15-17; Deuteronomy 7:1-4). By accepting these gods into their homes, the Israelites gradually began to accept the immoral practices associated with them. Most Israelites didn't start out determined to be idolaters; they just added the idols to the worship of God. But before long they found themselves absorbed in pagan worship.

A similar danger faces us. We want to befriend those who don't know God, but through those friendships we can become entangled in unhealthy practices. Friendships with unbelievers are important, but we must accept people without compromising or adopting their patterns of behavior.

### 1. First period: Othniel
*Othniel Becomes Israel's Judge*

**3:8**
Judg 2:14

**3:9**
Judg 1:13

**3:10**
Num 11:25-29;
24:2
Judg 6:34; 11:29

**3:11**
Judg 5:31; 8:28

⁷The Israelites did evil in the LORD's sight. They forgot about the LORD their God, and they served the images of Baal and the Asherah poles. ⁸Then the LORD burned with anger against Israel, and he turned them over to King Cushan-rishathaim of Aram-naharaim.* And the Israelites served Cushan-rishathaim for eight years.

⁹But when the people of Israel cried out to the LORD for help, the LORD raised up a rescuer to save them. His name was Othniel, the son of Caleb's younger brother, Kenaz. ¹⁰The Spirit of the LORD came upon him, and he became Israel's judge. He went to war against King Cushan-rishathaim of Aram, and the LORD gave Othniel victory over him. ¹¹So there was peace in the land for forty years. Then Othniel son of Kenaz died.

**3:8** *Aram-naharaim* means "Aram of the two rivers," thought to have been located between the Euphrates and Balih Rivers in northwestern Mesopotamia.

At first glance, Ehud's career as a judge in Israel may not seem relevant to us. He clearly lived in another time. He took radical and violent action to free his people. His murder of Eglon shocks us. His war on Moab was swift and deadly. His life is difficult to relate to. But our commitment to God's Word challenges us not to ignore this leader. As we read about his life, some questions come to mind: (1) When was the last time God showed me something wrong in my life and I took immediate and painful action to correct the error? (2) When was the last time I asked God to show me how he could use something unique about me (as he used Ehud's left-handedness)? (3) When was the last time I made a plan to obey God in some specific area of my life and then followed through on that plan? (4) When was the last time my life was an example to others of obedience to God?

The enemies we face are as real as Ehud's, but they are most often within ourselves. The battles we fight are not against other people but against the power of sin. We need God's help in doing battle against sin. We also need to remember that he has already won the war. He has defeated sin by Jesus' death and resurrection. His help is the cause of each success, and his forgiveness is sufficient for each failure.

| | |
|---|---|
| **Strengths and accomplishments** | • Second judge of Israel<br>• A man of direct action, a frontline leader<br>• Used a perceived weakness (left-handedness) to do a great work for God<br>• Led the revolt against Moabite domination and gave Israel 80 years of peace |
| **Lessons from his life** | • Some conditions call for radical action<br>• God responds to the cry of repentance<br>• God is ready to use our unique qualities to accomplish his work |
| **Vital statistics** | • Where: Born during the last years of the wilderness wanderings or during Israel's early years in the Promised Land<br>• Occupations: Messenger, judge<br>• Relative: Father: Gera<br>• Contemporary: Eglon of Moab |
| **Key verse** | "But when the people of Israel cried out to the LORD for help, the LORD again raised up a rescuer to save them. His name was Ehud son of Gera, a left-handed man of the tribe of Benjamin" (Judges 3:15). |

His story is told in Judges 3:12–30.

**3:7** Baal was the most worshiped god of the Canaanites. Most often cast in the form of a bull, he symbolized strength and fertility and was considered the god of agriculture. Asherah was Baal's female consort, mother goddess of the sea, who was worshiped by means of wooden pillars that substituted for sacred trees. In times of famine, the Canaanites believed Baal was angry with them and was withholding rain as punishment. Archaeologists have uncovered many Baal idols in Israel. It is difficult to imagine the people of Israel trading worship of the Lord for worship of idols of wood, stone, and iron, but we do the same when we forsake worshiping God for other activities, hobbies, or priorities. Our idols are not made of wood or stone, but they are every bit as sinful.

**3:9** Othniel was Israel's first judge. In 1:13 we read that he volunteered to lead an attack against a fortified city. Here he was to lead the nation back to God. Othniel had a rich spiritual heritage—his uncle was Caleb, a man with unwavering faith in God (Numbers 13:30; 14:24). Othniel's leadership brought the people back to God and freed them from oppression. But after Othniel's death, it didn't take the Israelites long to fall back into their neighbors' comfortable but sinful ways.

**3:10** This phrase, "The Spirit of the LORD came upon him," was also spoken of the judges Gideon, Jephthah, and Samson, among others. It expresses a temporary and spontaneous increase of physical, spiritual, or mental strength. This was an extraordinary and supernatural occurrence to prepare a person for a special task. The Holy Spirit is available to all believers today, but he will come upon believers in an extraordinary way for special tasks. We should ask the Holy Spirit's help as we face our daily problems as well as life's major challenges.

## 2. Second period: Ehud and Shamgar

*Ehud Becomes Israel's Judge*

12Once again the Israelites did evil in the LORD's sight, and the LORD gave King Eglon of
Moab control over Israel because of their evil. 13Eglon enlisted the Ammonites and Amalekites as allies, and then he went out and defeated Israel, taking possession of Jericho, the city
of palms. 14And the Israelites served Eglon of Moab for eighteen years.

15But when the people of Israel cried out to the LORD for help, the LORD again raised up a
rescuer to save them. His name was Ehud son of Gera, a left-handed man of the tribe of Benjamin. The Israelites sent Ehud to deliver their tribute money to King Eglon of Moab. 16So
Ehud made a double-edged dagger that was about a foot* long, and he strapped it to his
right thigh, keeping it hidden under his clothing. 17He brought the tribute money to Eglon,
who was very fat.

18After delivering the payment, Ehud started home with those who had helped carry the
tribute. 19But when Ehud reached the stone idols near Gilgal, he turned back. He came to
Eglon and said, "I have a secret message for you."

So the king commanded his servants, "Be quiet!" and he sent them all out of the room.
20Ehud walked over to Eglon, who was sitting alone in a cool upstairs room. And Ehud
said, "I have a message from God for you!" As King Eglon rose from his seat, 21Ehud reached
with his left hand, pulled out the dagger strapped to his right thigh, and plunged it into the
king's belly. 22The dagger went so deep that the handle disappeared beneath the king's fat.
So Ehud did not pull out the dagger, and the king's bowels emptied.* 23Then Ehud closed
and locked the doors of the room and escaped down the latrine.*

24After Ehud was gone, the king's servants returned and found the doors to the upstairs
room locked. They thought he might be using the latrine in the room, 25so they waited. But
when the king didn't come out after a long delay, they became concerned and got a key. And
when they opened the doors, they found their master dead on the floor.

26While the servants were waiting, Ehud escaped, passing the stone idols on his way to
Seirah. 27When he arrived in the hill country of Ephraim, Ehud sounded a call to arms. Then
he led a band of Israelites down from the hills.

28"Follow me," he said, "for the LORD has given you victory over Moab your enemy." So
they followed him. And the Israelites took control of the shallow crossings of the Jordan
River across from Moab, preventing anyone from crossing.

29They attacked the Moabites and killed about 10,000 of their strongest and most able-
bodied warriors. Not one of them escaped. 30So Moab was conquered by Israel that day, and
there was peace in the land for eighty years.

*Shamgar Becomes Israel's Judge*

31After Ehud, Shamgar son of Anath rescued Israel. He once killed 600 Philistines with an
ox goad.

**3:16** Hebrew *gomed*, the length of which is uncertain.  **3:22** Or *and it came out behind.*  **3:23** Or *and went out
through the porch;* the meaning of the Hebrew is uncertain.

Marginal references:

**3:12** Judg 2:11

**3:13** Judg 1:16

**3:15** Judg 20:16; 1 Chr 12:2

**3:24** 1 Sam 24:3

**3:28** Judg 7:24; 12:5

**3:31** Judg 5:6

---

**3:12, 13** The Moabites, Ammonites, and Amalekites were
nomadic tribes that lived near each other east and southeast
of Canaan. These tribes were notorious raiders, possessing
great military skill. This was the first time nations outside
Canaan attacked the Israelites in their own land.

**3:15-30** This unusual story demonstrates how God can use
us just the way he made us. Being left-handed in Ehud's day
was considered an exceptional ability. Many Benjaminites
were left-handed (see 20:16), making them highly specialized
troops, able to use a sling or bow with tactics designed to
repel right-handed warriors. Eglon's bodyguard never checked
Israel's messengers for left-handed weapons. But God used
Ehud's overlooked ability to give Israel victory. Let God use
you the way you are to accomplish his work.

**3:31** To kill 600 Philistines with an ox goad was quite a
feat. An ox goad was a long stick with a small flat piece of
iron on one side and a sharp point on the other. The sharp
side was used to drive the oxen during the times of plowing,
and the flat end was used to clean the mud off the plow.
Eight-foot-long ancient ox goads have been found. In times
of crisis they could easily have been used as spears, as in

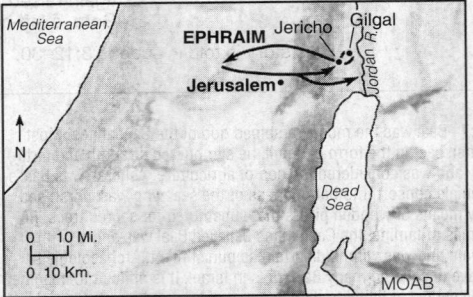

**EHUD FREES ISRAEL FROM MOAB**  When King Eglon of Moab
conquered part of Israel, he set up his throne in the city of Jericho.
Ehud was chosen to take Israel's tribute there. After delivering
Israel's tribute, Ehud killed King Eglon and escaped into the hill
country of Ephraim. From there he gathered together an army to
cut off any Moabites trying to escape across the Jordan River.

## 3. Third period: Deborah and Barak
*Deborah Becomes Israel's Judge*

4:1
Judg 2:19

**4** After Ehud's death, the Israelites again did evil in the LORD's sight. ²So the LORD turned them over to King Jabin of Hazor, a Canaanite king. The commander of his army was Sisera, who lived in Harosheth-haggoyim. ³Sisera, who had 900 iron chariots, ruthlessly oppressed the Israelites for twenty years. Then the people of Israel cried out to the LORD for help.

4:2
Josh 11:1
Ps 83:9

⁴Deborah, the wife of Lappidoth, was a prophet who was judging Israel at that time. ⁵She would sit under the Palm of Deborah, between Ramah and Bethel in the hill country of Ephraim, and the Israelites would go to her for judgment. ⁶One day she sent for Barak son of Abinoam, who lived in Kedesh in the land of Naphtali. She said to him, "This is what the LORD, the God of Israel, commands you: Call out 10,000 warriors from the tribes of Naphtali and Zebulun at Mount Tabor. ⁷And I will call out Sisera, commander of Jabin's army, along with his chariots and warriors, to the Kishon River. There I will give you victory over him."

4:6
1 Sam 12:11
Heb 11:32

4:7
Ps 83:9

⁸Barak told her, "I will go, but only if you go with me."

⁹"Very well," she replied, "I will go with you. But you will receive no honor in this venture, for the LORD's victory over Sisera will be at the hands of a woman." So Deborah went with Barak to Kedesh. ¹⁰At Kedesh, Barak called together the tribes of Zebulun and Naphtali, and 10,000 warriors went up with him. Deborah also went with him.

4:10
Judg 5:18

---

**THE JUDGES' FUNCTIONS**

*Judges of Israel could be*

| | |
|---|---|
| saviors (deliverers) and redeemers (Gideon) . . . . . . . . . . . *or* | mediators and administrators (Tola) |
| providers of rest and peace (Ehud and Jair). . . . . . . . . . . *or* | rude, petty dictators (Jephthah) |
| famous and powerful (Samson) . . . . . . . . . . . . . . . . . . . *or* | hardworking yet unsung (Elon and Abdon) |
| leaders of the nation (Othniel and Deborah). . . . . . . . . . *or* | local heroes (Shamgar and Ibzan) |

Regardless of an individual judge's leadership style, each one demonstrated that God's judgment follows apostasy, while repentance brings restoration.

---

Shamgar's case. Ox goads are still used in the Middle East to drive oxen.

**4:1** Israel sinned "in the LORD's sight." Our sins harm both ourselves and others, but all sin is ultimately against God because it disregards his commands and his authority over us. When confessing his sin, David prayed, "Against you, and you alone, have I sinned; I have done what is evil in your sight" (Psalm 51:4). Recognizing the seriousness of sin is the first step toward removing it from our lives.

**4:2, 3** Nothing more is known about Jabin. Joshua had defeated a king by that name years earlier and burned the city of Hazor to the ground (Joshua 11:1-11). Either the city was rebuilt by this time, or Jabin was hoping to rebuild it.

This is the only time during the period of the judges when the Israelites' enemies came from within their land. The Israelites had failed to drive out all the Canaanites. These Canaanites had regrouped and were attempting to restore their lost power. If the Israelites had obeyed God in the first place and had driven the Canaanites from the land, this incident would not have happened.

**4:2, 3** Chariots were the tanks of the ancient world. Made of iron or wood, they were pulled by one or two horses and were the most feared and powerful weapons of the day. Some chariots even had razor-sharp knives extending from the wheels designed to mutilate helpless foot soldiers. The Canaanite army had 900 iron chariots. Israel was not powerful enough to defeat such an invincible army. Therefore, Jabin and Sisera had no trouble oppressing the people—until a faithful woman named Deborah called upon God.

**4:3** After 20 years of unbearable circumstances, the Israelites finally cried to the Lord for help. But God should be the first place

we turn when we are facing struggles or dilemmas. The Israelites chose to go their own way and got into a mess. We often do the same. Trying to control our own lives without God's help leads to struggle and confusion. By contrast, when we stay in daily contact with the Lord, we are less likely to create painful circumstances for ourselves. This is a lesson the Israelites never fully learned. When struggles come our way, God wants us to come to him first, seeking his strength and guidance.

**4:4ff** The Bible records several women who held national leadership positions, and Deborah was an exceptional woman. Obviously she was the best person for the job, and God chose her to lead Israel. God can choose anyone to lead his people, young or old, man or woman. Don't let your prejudices get in the way of those God may have chosen to lead you.

**4:6-8** Was Barak cowardly or just in need of support? We don't know Barak's character, but we see the character of a great leader in Deborah, who took charge as God directed. Deborah told Barak that God would be with him in battle, but that was not enough for Barak. He wanted Deborah to go with him. Barak's request shows that at heart he trusted human strength more than God's promise. A person of real faith steps out at God's command, even if he or she must do so alone.

**4:9** How did Deborah command such respect? She was responsible for leading the people into battle, but more than that, she influenced them to live for God after the battle was over. Her personality drew people together and commanded the respect of even Barak, a military general. She was also a prophet, whose main role was to encourage the people to obey God. Those who lead must not forget about the spiritual condition of those being led. A true leader is concerned for persons, not just success.

¹¹Now Heber the Kenite, a descendant of Moses' brother-in-law\* Hobab, had moved away from the other members of his tribe and pitched his tent by the oak of Zaanannim near Kedesh.

¹²When Sisera was told that Barak son of Abinoam had gone up to Mount Tabor, ¹³he called for all 900 of his iron chariots and all of his warriors, and they marched from Harosheth-haggoyim to the Kishon River.

¹⁴Then Deborah said to Barak, "Get ready! This is the day the LORD will give you victory over Sisera, for the LORD is marching ahead of you." So Barak led his 10,000 warriors down the slopes of Mount Tabor into battle. ¹⁵When Barak attacked, the LORD threw Sisera and all his chariots and warriors into a panic. Sisera leaped down from his chariot and escaped on foot. ¹⁶Then Barak chased the chariots and the enemy army all the way to Harosheth-haggoyim, killing all of Sisera's warriors. Not a single one was left alive.

¹⁷Meanwhile, Sisera ran to the tent of Jael, the wife of Heber the Kenite, because Heber's family was on friendly terms with King Jabin of Hazor. ¹⁸Jael went out to meet Sisera and said to him, "Come into my tent, sir. Come in. Don't be afraid." So he went into her tent, and she covered him with a blanket.

¹⁹"Please give me some water," he said. "I'm thirsty." So she gave him some milk from a leather bag and covered him again.

²⁰"Stand at the door of the tent," he told her. "If anybody comes and asks you if there is anyone here, say no."

²¹But when Sisera fell asleep from exhaustion, Jael quietly crept up to him with a hammer and tent peg in her hand. Then she drove the tent peg through his temple and into the ground, and so he died.

²²When Barak came looking for Sisera, Jael went out to meet him. She said, "Come, and I will show you the man you are looking for." So he followed her into the tent and found Sisera lying there dead, with the tent peg through his temple.

²³So on that day Israel saw God defeat Jabin, the Canaanite king. ²⁴And from that time on Israel became stronger and stronger against King Jabin until they finally destroyed him.

## The Song of Deborah

**5** On that day Deborah and Barak son of Abinoam sang this song:

> 2 "Israel's leaders took charge,
> and the people gladly followed.
> Praise the LORD!

**4:11** Or *father-in-law.*

---

**Cross-references (margin):**

4:11 Josh 19:33 / Judg 1:16

4:15 Josh 10:10 / Judg 7:21

4:16 Exod 14:28 / Ps 83:9

4:19 Judg 5:25

5:1 Exod 15:1

5:2 Ps 110:3

---

**4:11** Heber was Jael's husband (4:17). He was from the Kenite tribe, descendants of Moses' father-in-law, and longtime allies of Israel. But for some reason, Heber decided to remain neutral in this war, maybe because Jabin's army appeared to have the military advantage. It was probably Heber who told Sisera that the Israelites were camped near Mount Tabor (4:12; see map). Although Heber threw in his lot with Jabin and his forces, his wife, Jael, did not (4:21).

**4:18-21** Sisera couldn't have been more pleased when Jael offered him her tent as a hiding place. First, because Jael was the wife of Heber, a man friendly to Sisera's forces (see the note on 4:11), he thought she could be trusted. Second, because men were never allowed to enter a woman's tent, no one would think to look for Sisera there.

Even though her husband, Heber, apparently sided with Sisera's forces, Jael certainly did not. Because women of that day were in charge of pitching the tents, Jael had no problem driving the tent peg into Sisera's head while he slept. Deborah's prediction was thus fulfilled: The honor of conquering Sisera went to a brave and resourceful woman (4:9).

**5:1ff** Music and singing were a cherished part of Israel's culture. Chapter 5 is a song, sung and possibly composed by Deborah and Barak. It sets to music the story of Israel's great victory recounted in chapter 4. This victory song was accompanied by joyous celebration. It proclaimed God's greatness by giving him credit for the victory. It was an excellent way to preserve and retell this wonderful story from generation to generation. (Other songs in the Bible are listed in the chart in Exodus 15.)

**5:1ff** In victory, Barak and Deborah sang praises to God. Songs of praise focus our attention on God, give us an outlet for spiritual

**KING JABIN IS DEFEATED**
Deborah traveled from her home between Ramah and Bethel to march with Barak and the Israelite army against Hazor. Sisera, commander of Hazor's army, assembled his men at Harosheth-haggoyim. In spite of Sisera's 900 chariots and expertly trained army, Israel was victorious.

Mediterranean Sea

Hazor
Sea of Galilee
Harosheth-haggoyim
Kedesh
Mount Tabor
N
Kishon R.
Jordan R.
Bethel
Ramah
Jerusalem
Dead Sea

0   20 Mi.
0   20 Km.

✴ Battle site

3 "Listen, you kings!
  Pay attention, you mighty rulers!
  For I will sing to the LORD.
  I will make music to the LORD, the God of Israel.

**5:4**
Deut 33:2
Hab 3:6

4 "LORD, when you set out from Seir
  and marched across the fields of Edom,
  the earth trembled,
  and the cloudy skies poured down rain.

**5:5**
Exod 19:18
Pss 97:5; 114:4
Isa 64:3

5 The mountains quaked in the presence of the LORD,
  the God of Mount Sinai—
  in the presence of the LORD,
  the God of Israel.

**5:6**
Judg 3:31; 4:17

6 "In the days of Shamgar son of Anath,
  and in the days of Jael,
  people avoided the main roads,
  and travelers stayed on winding pathways.

7 There were few people left in the villages of Israel*—
  until Deborah arose as a mother for Israel.

**5:8**
Deut 32:17

8 When Israel chose new gods,
  war erupted at the city gates.

5:7 The meaning of the Hebrew is uncertain.

---

**DEBORAH**

Wise leaders are rare. They accomplish great amounts of work without direct involvement because they know how to work through other people. They are able to see the big picture that often escapes those directly involved, so they make good mediators, advisers, and planners. Deborah fit this description perfectly. She had all these leadership skills, and she had a remarkable relationship with God. The insight and confidence God gave this woman placed her in a unique position in the Old Testament. Deborah is among the outstanding women of history.

Her story shows that she was not power hungry. She wanted to serve God. Whenever praise came her way, she gave God the credit. She didn't deny or resist her position in the culture as a woman and wife, but she never allowed herself to be hindered by it either. Her story shows that God can accomplish great things through people who are willing to be led by him.

Deborah's life challenges us in several ways. She reminds us of the need to be available both to God and to others. She encourages us to spend our efforts on what we can do rather than on worrying about what we can't do. Deborah challenges us to be wise leaders. She demonstrates what a person can accomplish when God is in control.

| | |
|---|---|
| **Strengths and accomplishments** | • Fourth and only female judge of Israel<br>• Special abilities as a mediator, adviser, and counselor<br>• When called on to lead, was able to plan, direct, and delegate<br>• Known for her prophetic power<br>• A writer of songs |
| **Lessons from her life** | • God chooses leaders by his standards, not ours<br>• Wise leaders choose good helpers |
| **Vital statistics** | • Where: Canaan<br>• Occupations: Prophet, judge<br>• Relative: Husband: Lappidoth<br>• Contemporaries: Barak, Jael, Jabin of Hazor, Sisera |
| **Key verse** | "Deborah, the wife of Lappidoth, was a prophet who was judging Israel at that time" (Judges 4:4). |

Her story is told in Judges 4—5.

---

celebration, and remind us of God's faithfulness and character. Whether you are experiencing a great victory or a major dilemma, singing praises to God can have a positive effect on your attitude.

**5:8** War was the inevitable result when Israel chose to follow false gods. Although God had given Israel clear directions, the people failed to put his words into practice. Without God at the center of their national life, pressure from the outside soon

became greater than power from within, and they were an easy prey for their enemies. If you are letting a desire for recognition, craving for power, or love of money rule your life, you may find yourself besieged by enemies—stress, anxiety, illness, fatigue. Keep God at the center of your life, and you will have the power you need to fight these destroyers.

Yet not a shield or spear could be seen
    among forty thousand warriors in Israel!
9 My heart is with the commanders of Israel,
    with those who volunteered for war.
    Praise the LORD!

10 "Consider this, you who ride on fine donkeys,
    you who sit on fancy saddle blankets,
    and you who walk along the road.
11 Listen to the village musicians*
    gathered at the watering holes.
They recount the righteous victories of the LORD
    and the victories of his villagers in Israel.
Then the people of the LORD
    marched down to the city gates.

12 "Wake up, Deborah, wake up!
    Wake up, wake up, and sing a song!
Arise, Barak!
    Lead your captives away, son of Abinoam!

13 "Down from Tabor marched the few against the nobles.
    The people of the LORD marched down against mighty warriors.
14 They came down from Ephraim—
    a land that once belonged to the Amalekites;
    they followed you, Benjamin, with your troops.
From Makir the commanders marched down;
    from Zebulun came those who carry a commander's staff.
15 The princes of Issachar were with Deborah and Barak.
    They followed Barak, rushing into the valley.
But in the tribe of Reuben
    there was great indecision.
16 Why did you sit at home among the sheepfolds—
    to hear the shepherds whistle for their flocks?
Yes, in the tribe of Reuben
    there was great indecision.
17 Gilead remained east of the Jordan.
    And why did Dan stay home?
Asher sat unmoved at the seashore,
    remaining in his harbors.
18 But Zebulun risked his life,
    as did Naphtali, on the heights of the battlefield.

19 "The kings of Canaan came and fought,
    at Taanach near Megiddo's springs,
    but they carried off no silver treasures.
20 The stars fought from heaven.
    The stars in their orbits fought against Sisera.
21 The Kishon River swept them away—
    that ancient torrent, the Kishon.
March on with courage, my soul!
22 Then the horses' hooves hammered the ground,
    the galloping, galloping of Sisera's mighty steeds.

5:11 The meaning of the Hebrew is uncertain.

**5:10** Judg 10:4; 12:14

**5:11** Gen 24:11; 1 Sam 12:7

**5:16** Num 32:1-2, 24

**5:17** Josh 13:24-28

**5:19** Josh 11:1-5; Judg 1:27

**5:21** Judg 4:7

**5:22** Job 39:19-25

**5:15-17** Four tribes—Reuben, Gilead (either Gad or Manasseh), Dan, and Asher—were accused of not lending a helping hand in the battle. No reasons are given for their refusal to help their fellow Israelites, but they may be the same ones that stopped them from driving out the Canaanites in the first place: (1) lack of reliance on God for help, (2) lack of effort, (3) fear of the enemy, and (4) fear of antagonizing those with whom they did business and thus from whom they prospered. This disobedience showed both a lack of commitment to God's plan and a weak faith in God's power.

23 'Let the people of Meroz be cursed,' said the angel of the LORD.
    'Let them be utterly cursed,
because they did not come to help the LORD—
    to help the LORD against the mighty warriors.'

**5:24-25**
**Judg 4:17-19**

24 "Most blessed among women is Jael,
    the wife of Heber the Kenite.
May she be blessed above all women who live in tents.
  25 Sisera asked for water,
    and she gave him milk.
In a bowl fit for nobles,
    she brought him yogurt.

**5:26-27**
**Judg 4:21-22**

26 Then with her left hand she reached for a tent peg,
    and with her right hand for the workman's hammer.
She struck Sisera with the hammer, crushing his head.
    With a shattering blow, she pierced his temples.
  27 He sank, he fell,
    he lay still at her feet.
And where he sank,
    there he died.

28 "From the window Sisera's mother looked out.
    Through the window she watched for his return, saying,
'Why is his chariot so long in coming?
    Why don't we hear the sound of chariot wheels?'

29 "Her wise women answer,
    and she repeats these words to herself:

**5:30**
**Exod 15:9**

30 'They must be dividing the captured plunder—
    with a woman or two for every man.
There will be colorful robes for Sisera,
    and colorful, embroidered robes for me.
Yes, the plunder will include
    colorful robes embroidered on both sides.'

**5:31**
**Pss 68:1-2; 92:9**

31 "LORD, may all your enemies die like Sisera!
    But may those who love you rise like the sun in all its power!"

Then there was peace in the land for forty years.

## 4. Fourth period: Gideon, Tola, and Jair
### Gideon Becomes Israel's Judge

**6:1**
**Num 22:4;**
**25:15-18; 31:1-3**
**Judg 2:11**

**6** The Israelites did evil in the LORD's sight. So the LORD handed them over to the Midianites for seven years. 2 The Midianites were so cruel that the Israelites made hiding places for themselves in the mountains, caves, and strongholds.

**6:3**
**Isa 11:14**

3 Whenever the Israelites planted their crops, marauders from Midian, Amalek, and the people of the east would attack Israel, 4 camping in the land and destroying crops as far away as Gaza. They left the

**6:5**
**Judg 7:12**

Israelites with nothing to eat, taking all the sheep, goats, cattle, and donkeys. 5 These enemy hordes, coming with their livestock and tents, were as thick as locusts; they arrived on droves of camels too numerous to count. And they stayed until the land was stripped bare.

**6:6**
**Deut 28:43**

6 So Israel was reduced to starvation by the Midianites. Then the Israelites cried out to the LORD for help.

**6:8**
**Exod 18:9**
**Judg 2:1-2**

7 When they cried out to the LORD because of Midian, 8 the LORD sent a prophet to the Israelites. He said, "This is what the LORD, the God of Israel, says: I brought you up out of

---

**6:2** The Midianites were desert people descended from Abraham's second wife, Keturah (Genesis 25:1, 2). From this relationship came a nation that was always in conflict with Israel. Years earlier the Israelites, while still wandering in the wilderness, battled the Midianites and almost totally destroyed them (Numbers 31:1-20). Because of their failure to completely destroy them, however, the tribe repopulated. Here they were once again oppressing Israel.

**6:6** Again the Israelites hit rock bottom before turning back to God. How much suffering they could have avoided if they had trusted him! Turning to God shouldn't be a last resort; we should look to him for help each day. This isn't to say life will always be easy. There will be struggles, but God will give us the strength to live through them. Don't wait until you're at the end of your rope. Call on God first in every situation.

slavery in Egypt. 9I rescued you from the Egyptians and from all who oppressed you. I drove out your enemies and gave you their land. 10I told you, 'I am the LORD your God. You must not worship the gods of the Amorites, in whose land you now live.' But you have not listened to me."

11Then the angel of the LORD came and sat beneath the great tree at Ophrah, which belonged to Joash of the clan of Abiezer. Gideon son of Joash was threshing wheat at the bottom of a winepress to hide the grain from the Midianites. 12The angel of the LORD appeared to him and said, "Mighty hero, the LORD is with you!"

13"Sir," Gideon replied, "if the LORD is with us, why has all this happened to us? And where are all the miracles our ancestors told us about? Didn't they say, 'The LORD brought us up out of Egypt'? But now the LORD has abandoned us and handed us over to the Midianites."

14Then the LORD turned to him and said, "Go with the strength you have, and rescue Israel from the Midianites. I am sending you!"

15"But Lord," Gideon replied, "how can I rescue Israel? My clan is the weakest in the whole tribe of Manasseh, and I am the least in my entire family!"

16The LORD said to him, "I will be with you. And you will destroy the Midianites as if you were fighting against one man."

17Gideon replied, "If you are truly going to help me, show me a sign to prove that it is really the LORD speaking to me. 18Don't go away until I come back and bring my offering to you."

He answered, "I will stay here until you return."

19Gideon hurried home. He cooked a young goat, and with a basket* of flour he baked some bread without yeast. Then, carrying the meat in a basket and the broth in a pot, he brought them out and presented them to the angel, who was under the great tree.

20The angel of God said to him, "Place the meat and the unleavened bread on this rock, and pour the broth over it." And Gideon did as he was told. 21Then the angel of the LORD touched the meat and bread with the tip of the staff in his hand, and fire flamed up from the rock and consumed all he had brought. And the angel of the LORD disappeared.

22When Gideon realized that it was the angel of the LORD, he cried out, "Oh, Sovereign LORD, I'm doomed! I have seen the angel of the LORD face to face!"

23"It is all right," the LORD replied. "Do not be afraid. You will not die." 24And Gideon built an altar to the LORD there and named it Yahweh-Shalom (which means "the LORD is peace"). The altar remains in Ophrah in the land of the clan of Abiezer to this day.

6:19 Hebrew an ephah [20 quarts or 22 liters].

**6:10**
Josh 24:15

**6:11**
Judg 13:3
Heb 11:32

**6:13**
Deut 31:17
Ps 44:1

**6:15**
Exod 3:11

**6:17**
Isa 38:7

**6:19**
Gen 18:6-8

**6:21**
Lev 9:24

**6:22**
Gen 32:30
Exod 33:20
Judg 13:21-22

---

**6:11** The Old Testament records several appearances of the angel of the Lord: Genesis 16:7; 22:11; 31:11; Exodus 3:2; 14:19; Judges 2:1; 13:3; Zechariah 3:1-6. It is not known whether the same angel appeared in each case. The angel mentioned here appears to be separate from God in one place (6:12) and yet the same as God in another place (6:14). This has led some to believe that the angel was a special appearance of Jesus Christ prior to his mission on earth as recorded in the New Testament. It is also possible that as a special messenger from God, the angel had authority to speak for God. In either case, God sent a special messenger to deliver an important message to Gideon.

**6:11** Threshing was the process of separating the grains of wheat from the useless outer shell called chaff. This was normally done in a large area, often on a hill, where the wind could blow away the lighter chaff when the farmer tossed the beaten wheat into the air. If Gideon had done this, however, he would have been an easy target for the bands of raiders who were overrunning the land. Therefore, he was forced to thresh his wheat in a winepress, a pit that was probably hidden

from view and that would not be suspected as a place to find a farmer's crops.

**6:13** Gideon questioned God about the problems he and his nation faced and about God's apparent lack of help. What he didn't acknowledge was the fact that the people had brought calamity upon themselves when they decided to disobey and neglect God. How easy it is to overlook personal accountability and blame our problems on God and others. Unfortunately, this does not solve our problems. It brings us no closer to God, and it escorts us to the very edge of rebellion and backsliding.

When problems come, the first place to look is within. Our immediate response should be confession to God of sins that may have created our problems.

**6:14-16** "I will be with you," God told Gideon, and God promised to give him the strength he needed to overcome the opposition. In spite of this clear promise for strength, Gideon made excuses. Seeing only his limitations and weaknesses, he failed to see how God could work through him.

Like Gideon, we are called to serve God in specific ways. Although God promises us the tools and strength we need, we often make excuses. But reminding God of our limitations only implies that he does not know all about us or that he has made a mistake in evaluating our character. Don't spend time making excuses. Instead, spend it doing what God wants.

**6:22, 23** Why was Gideon afraid of seeing an angel? The Israelites believed that no one could see God and live (see God's words to Moses in Exodus 33:20). Evidently Gideon thought this also applied to angels.

**6:25**
Exod 34:13
Deut 7:5

²⁵That night the LORD said to Gideon, "Take the second bull from your father's herd, the one that is seven years old. Pull down your father's altar to Baal, and cut down the Asherah pole standing beside it. ²⁶Then build an altar to the LORD your God here on this hilltop sanctuary, laying the stones carefully. Sacrifice the bull as a burnt offering on the altar, using as fuel the wood of the Asherah pole you cut down."

²⁷So Gideon took ten of his servants and did as the LORD had commanded. But he did it at night because he was afraid of the other members of his father's household and the people of the town.

²⁸Early the next morning, as the people of the town began to stir, someone discovered that the altar of Baal had been broken down and that the Asherah pole beside it had been cut down. In their place a new altar had been built, and on it were the remains of the bull that had been sacrificed. ²⁹The people said to each other, "Who did this?" And after asking around and making a careful search, they learned that it was Gideon, the son of Joash.

³⁰"Bring out your son," the men of the town demanded of Joash. "He must die for destroying the altar of Baal and for cutting down the Asherah pole."

³¹But Joash shouted to the mob that confronted him, "Why are you defending Baal? Will you argue his case? Whoever pleads his case will be put to death by morning! If Baal truly is a god, let him defend himself and destroy the one who broke down his altar!" ³²From then on Gideon was called Jerub-baal, which means "Let Baal defend himself," because he broke down Baal's altar.

**GOD USES COMMON PEOPLE**
God uses all sorts of people to do his work—like you and me!

| Person | Known as | Task | Reference |
|---|---|---|---|
| JACOB | A deceiver | To "father" the Israelite nation | Genesis 27–28 |
| JOSEPH | A slave | To save his family | Genesis 39ff |
| MOSES | Shepherd in exile (and murderer) | To lead Israel out of bondage, to the Promised Land | Exodus 3 |
| GIDEON | A farmer | To deliver Israel from Midian | Judges 6:11-14 |
| JEPHTHAH | Son of a prostitute | To deliver Israel from the Ammonites | Judges 11 |
| HANNAH | A homemaker | To be the mother of Samuel | 1 Samuel 1 |
| DAVID | A shepherd boy and last-born of the family | To be Israel's greatest king | 1 Samuel 16 |
| EZRA | A scribe | To lead the return to Judah and to write some of the Bible | Ezra, Nehemiah |
| ESTHER | A slave girl | To save her people from massacre | Esther |
| MARY | A peasant girl | To be the mother of Christ | Luke 1:27-38 |
| MATTHEW | A tax collector | To be an apostle and Gospel writer | Matthew 9:9 |
| LUKE | A Greek physician | To be a companion of Paul and a Gospel writer | Colossians 4:14 |
| PETER | A fisherman | To be an apostle, a leader of the early church, and a writer of two New Testament letters | Matthew 4:18-20 |

**6:25-30** After God called Gideon to be Israel's deliverer, he immediately asked him to tear down the altar of the pagan god Baal—an act that would test Gideon's faith and commitment. Canaanite religion was very political, so an attack on a god was often seen as an attack on the local government supporting that god. If caught, Gideon would face serious social problems and probable physical attack. (For more on Baal and Asherah, see the notes on 2:11-15 and 3:7.)

Gideon took a great risk by following God's higher law, which specifically forbids idol worship (Exodus 20:1-5). After learning what Gideon had done, the townspeople wanted to kill him. Many of those people were fellow Israelites. This shows how immoral God's people had become. God said in Deuteronomy 13:6-11 that idolaters must be stoned to death, but these Israelites wanted to stone Gideon for tearing down an idol and worshiping God! When you begin to accomplish something for God, you may be criticized by the very people who should support you.

## Gideon Asks for a Sign

33 Soon afterward the armies of Midian, Amalek, and the people of the east formed an alliance against Israel and crossed the Jordan, camping in the valley of Jezreel. 34 Then the Spirit of the LORD took possession of Gideon. He blew a ram's horn as a call to arms, and the men of the clan of Abiezer came to him. 35 He also sent messengers throughout Manasseh, Asher, Zebulun, and Naphtali, summoning their warriors, and all of them responded.

36 Then Gideon said to God, "If you are truly going to use me to rescue Israel as you promised, 37 prove it to me in this way. I will put a wool fleece on the threshing floor tonight. If the fleece is wet with dew in the morning but the ground is dry, then I will know that you are going to help me rescue Israel as you promised." 38 And that is just what happened. When Gideon got up early the next morning, he squeezed the fleece and wrung out a whole bowlful of water.

39 Then Gideon said to God, "Please don't be angry with me, but let me make one more request. Let me use the fleece for one more test. This time let the fleece remain dry while the ground around it is wet with dew." 40 So that night God did as Gideon asked. The fleece was dry in the morning, but the ground was covered with dew.

## Gideon Defeats the Midianites

**7** So Jerub-baal (that is, Gideon) and his army got up early and went as far as the spring of Harod. The armies of Midian were camped north of them in the valley near the hill of Moreh. 2 The LORD said to Gideon, "You have too many warriors with you. If I let all of you fight the Midianites, the Israelites will boast to me that they saved themselves by their own strength. 3 Therefore, tell the people, 'Whoever is timid or afraid may leave this mountain* and go home.'" So 22,000 of them went home, leaving only 10,000 who were willing to fight.

4 But the LORD told Gideon, "There are still too many! Bring them down to the spring, and I

**6:33**
Josh 17:16
**6:34**
Judg 3:10
**6:35**
Judg 7:23
**6:36**
Judg 6:14

**6:39**
Gen 18:32

**7:2**
Deut 8:17-18
Isa 10:13
2 Cor 4:7
**7:3**
Deut 20:8
**7:4**
1 Sam 14:6

**7:3** Hebrew *may leave Mount Gilead.* The identity of Mount Gilead is uncertain in this context. It is perhaps used here as another name for Mount Gilboa.

---

**6:33** The armies of Midian and Amalek camped in the valley of Jezreel, the agricultural center for the area. Whoever controlled the valley's rich and fertile land controlled the people who lived in and around it. Because of the valley's vast resources, many major trade routes converged at the pass which led into it. This made it the site of many great battles. Gideon's men attacked the enemy armies from the hills, and the only escape route was through the pass toward the Jordan River. That is why Gideon urged some of his troops to take control of the river's crossing points (7:24).

**GIDEON'S BATTLE**
In spite of Deborah and Barak's victory, the Canaanites still caused trouble in this fertile region. God appeared to Gideon at Ophrah and called him to defeat them. With only 300 fighting men, Gideon routed thousands of Midianites, chasing them to Zererah and Abel-meholah.

**6:37-39** Was Gideon testing God, or was he simply asking God for more encouragement? In either case, though his motive was right (to obey God and defeat the enemy), his method was less than ideal. Gideon seems to have known that his requests might displease God (6:39), and yet he demanded two miracles (6:37, 39), even after witnessing the miraculous fire from the rock (6:21). It is true that to make good decisions, we need facts. Gideon had all the facts, but still he hesitated. He delayed obeying God because he wanted even more proof.

Demanding extra signs was an indication of unbelief. Fear often makes us wait for more confirmation when we should be taking action. Visible signs are unnecessary if they only confirm what we already know is true.

Today the greatest means of God's guidance is his Word, the Bible. Unlike Gideon, we have God's complete, revealed Word. If you want to have more of God's guidance, don't ask for signs; study the Bible (2 Timothy 3:16, 17).

**6:39** After seeing the miracle of the wet fleece, why did Gideon ask for another miracle? Perhaps he thought the results of the first test could have happened naturally. A thick fleece could retain moisture long after the sun had dried the surrounding ground. "Putting out fleeces" is a poor decision-making method. Those who do this put limitations on God. They ask him to fit their expectations. The results of such experiments are usually inconclusive and thus fail to make us any more confident about our choices. Don't let a "fleece" become a substitute for God's wisdom that comes through Bible study and prayer.

**7:2** Self-sufficiency is an handicap when it causes us to believe we can do what needs to be done in our own strength. To prevent this attitude among Gideon's soldiers, God reduced their number from 32,000 to 300. With an army this vastly outnumbered, there could be no doubt that victory was from God. The men could not take the credit. Like Gideon, we must recognize the danger of fighting in our own strength. We can be confident of victory against life's challenges and temptations only if we put our confidence in God and not ourselves.

will test them to determine who will go with you and who will not." 5When Gideon took his warriors down to the water, the LORD told him, "Divide the men into two groups. In one group put all those who cup water in their hands and lap it up with their tongues like dogs. In the other group put all those who kneel down and drink with their mouths in the stream." 6Only 300 of the men drank from their hands. All the others got down on their knees and drank with their mouths in the stream.

7 The LORD told Gideon, "With these 300 men I will rescue you and give you victory over the Midianites. Send all the others home." 8So Gideon collected the provisions and rams' horns of the other warriors and sent them home. But he kept the 300 men with him.

## GIDEON

Most of us want to know God's plan for our lives, but we're not always sure how to find it. One common misunderstanding is the idea that God's guidance will come to us out of the blue, that it has nothing to do with what we're doing now. But if we're always looking around for God's next assignment, we run the risk of ruining whatever we're working on right now. Fortunately, the Bible points to a kind of guidance that does not put our current projects in jeopardy. In the Bible's descriptions of how God guided many people, we can see that often God's call came while people were completely immersed in the challenge of the moment. A good example of this kind of guidance is seen in Gideon's life.

Gideon had a limited vision, but he was committed to it. His challenge was to obtain food for his family even though hostile invaders were making the growing, gathering, and preparation of the food almost impossible. Gideon was resourceful. He put a winepress to double duty by turning it into a sunken threshing floor. It lacked ventilation to blow the chaff away, but at least it was hidden from the Midianites. Gideon was working in his threshing floor when God sent him a messenger with a challenge.

Gideon was surprised by what God told him to do. He did not want to jump into a task for which he was ill prepared. The angel had to overcome three objections before Gideon was convinced: (1) Gideon's feelings of responsibility for his family's welfare, (2) his doubts about the call itself, and (3) his feelings of inadequacy for the job. Once Gideon was convinced, however, he obeyed with zest, resourcefulness, and speed. He dedicated those personality traits to God, with whom he was now personally acquainted.

Gideon had his weak moments and failures, but he was still God's servant. If you can easily relate to Gideon's weakness, can you also see yourself being willing to serve? Remember Gideon as a man who obeyed God by giving his attention to the task at hand. Then give your full attention to believing God will prepare you for tomorrow when it comes.

| | |
|---|---|
| **Strengths and accomplishments** | • Israel's fifth judge. A military strategist who was an expert at surprise<br>• A member of the Hall of Faith in Hebrews 11<br>• Defeated the Midianite army<br>• Was offered a hereditary kingship by the men of Israel<br>• Though slow to be convinced, acted on his convictions |
| **Weaknesses and mistakes** | • Feared that his own limitations would prevent God from working through him<br>• Collected Midianite gold and made a symbol that became an evil object of worship<br>• Through a concubine, fathered a son who would bring great grief and tragedy to both Gideon's family and the nation of Israel<br>• Failed to establish the nation in God's ways; after he died they all went back to idol worship |
| **Lessons from his life** | • God calls in the middle of our present obedience. As we are faithful, he gives us more responsibility<br>• God expands and uses the abilities he has already given us<br>• God uses us in spite of our limitations and failures<br>• Even those who make great spiritual progress can easily fall into sin if they don't consistently follow God |
| **Vital statistics** | • Where: Ophrah, valley of Jezreel, spring of Harod<br>• Occupations: Farmer, warrior, judge<br>• Relatives: Father: Joash. Son: Abimelech.<br>• Contemporaries: Zebah, Zalmunna |
| **Key verses** | "'But Lord,' Gideon replied, 'how can I rescue Israel? My clan is the weakest in the whole tribe of Manasseh, and I am the least in my entire family!' The LORD said to him, 'I will be with you. And you will destroy the Midianites as if you were fighting against one man'" (Judges 6:15, 16). |

His story is told in Judges 6—8. He is also mentioned in Hebrews 11:32.

The Midianite camp was in the valley just below Gideon. ⁹That night the Lᴏʀᴅ said, "Get up! Go down into the Midianite camp, for I have given you victory over them! ¹⁰But if you are afraid to attack, go down to the camp with your servant Purah. ¹¹Listen to what the Midianites are saying, and you will be greatly encouraged. Then you will be eager to attack."

7:9
Josh 2:24; 10:8;
11:6

So Gideon took Purah and went down to the edge of the enemy camp. ¹²The armies of Midian, Amalek, and the people of the east had settled in the valley like a swarm of locusts. Their camels were like grains of sand on the seashore—too many to count! ¹³Gideon crept up just as a man was telling his companion about a dream. The man said, "I had this dream, and in my dream a loaf of barley bread came tumbling down into the Midianite camp. It hit a tent, turned it over, and knocked it flat!"

7:12
Josh 11:4
Judg 6:5; 8:10

¹⁴His companion answered, "Your dream can mean only one thing—God has given Gideon son of Joash, the Israelite, victory over Midian and all its allies!"

¹⁵When Gideon heard the dream and its interpretation, he bowed in worship before the Lᴏʀᴅ.* Then he returned to the Israelite camp and shouted, "Get up! For the Lᴏʀᴅ has given you victory over the Midianite hordes!" ¹⁶He divided the 300 men into three groups and gave each man a ram's horn and a clay jar with a torch in it.

¹⁷Then he said to them, "Keep your eyes on me. When I come to the edge of the camp, do just as I do. ¹⁸As soon as I and those with me blow the rams' horns, blow your horns, too, all around the entire camp, and shout, 'For the Lᴏʀᴅ and for Gideon!'"

¹⁹It was just after midnight,* after the changing of the guard, when Gideon and the 100 men with him reached the edge of the Midianite camp. Suddenly, they blew the rams' horns and broke their clay jars. ²⁰Then all three groups blew their horns and broke their jars. They held the blazing torches in their left hands and the horns in their right hands, and they all shouted, "A sword for the Lᴏʀᴅ and for Gideon!"

²¹Each man stood at his position around the camp and watched as all the Midianites rushed around in a panic, shouting as they ran to escape. ²²When the 300 Israelites blew their rams' horns, the Lᴏʀᴅ caused the warriors in the camp to fight against each other with their swords. Those who were not killed fled to places as far away as Beth-shittah near Zererah and to the border of Abel-meholah near Tabbath.

7:21
2 Kgs 7:7

²³Then Gideon sent for the warriors of Naphtali, Asher, and Manasseh, who joined in chasing the army of Midian. ²⁴Gideon also sent messengers throughout the hill country of Ephraim, saying, "Come down to attack the Midianites. Cut them off at the shallow crossings of the Jordan River at Beth-barah."

7:24
Judg 3:27-28

So all the men of Ephraim did as they were told. ²⁵They captured Oreb and Zeeb, the two Midianite commanders, killing Oreb at the rock of Oreb, and Zeeb at the winepress of Zeeb. And they continued to chase the Midianites. Afterward the Israelites brought the heads of Oreb and Zeeb to Gideon, who was by the Jordan River.

7:25
Judg 8:4
Ps 83:11
Isa 10:26

### Gideon Kills Zebah and Zalmunna

**8** Then the people of Ephraim asked Gideon, "Why have you treated us this way? Why didn't you send for us when you first went out to fight the Midianites?" And they argued heatedly with Gideon.

8:1
Judg 12:1

7:15 As in Greek version; Hebrew reads *he bowed.*   7:19 Hebrew *at the beginning of the second watch.*

---

**7:10, 11** Facing overwhelming odds, Gideon was afraid. God understood his fear, but he didn't excuse Gideon from his task. Instead, he allowed Gideon to slip into the enemy camp and overhear a conversation that would give him courage (7:12-15). Are you facing a battle with internal or external foes that have defeated you in the past or appear invincible today? God can give you the strength you need for any situation. And don't be startled by the way he helps you. Like Gideon, you must listen to God and be ready to take the first step. Only after you begin to obey God will you find the courage to move ahead.

**7:12** Midianites were camel-riding marauders composed of five families linked to Abraham through Midian, the son of Abraham's second wife, Keturah. They inhabited the desert regions from the Dead Sea to the Red Sea.

**7:13** An enemy soldier dreamed of a loaf of barley bread tumbling into camp. Barley grain had only half the value of wheat, and the bread made from it was considered inferior.

In the same way, Israel's tiny band of men was considered inferior to the vast forces of Midian and Amalek. But God would make the underdog Israelites seem invincible.

**7:21** Gideon's warriors simply watched as the army of Midian fell into panic, confusion, and disordered retreat. Not one man had to draw a sword to defeat the enemy. Gideon's small army could never have brought about such a victory in its own strength. God wanted to demonstrate to Israel that victory depends not on strength or numbers but on obedience and commitment to him.

**8:1-3** Ephraim's leaders felt left out because Gideon had not called them to join the battle but had left them in place to "clean up" the escaping Midianites ("leftover grapes"), and so they angrily confronted him. Gideon assured the leaders of Ephraim that their accomplishment was even greater than his own clan's (Abiezer). His diplomatic explanation pointed out that this rear guard had managed to capture the enemy's generals, thus cutting

2But Gideon replied, "What have I accomplished compared to you? Aren't even the left-over grapes of Ephraim's harvest better than the entire crop of my little clan of Abiezer? 3God gave you victory over Oreb and Zeeb, the commanders of the Midianite army. What have I accomplished compared to that?" When the men of Ephraim heard Gideon's answer, their anger subsided.

4Gideon then crossed the Jordan River with his 300 men, and though exhausted, they continued to chase the enemy. 5When they reached Succoth, Gideon asked the leaders of the town, "Please give my warriors some food. They are very tired. I am chasing Zebah and Zalmunna, the kings of Midian."

6But the officials of Succoth replied, "Catch Zebah and Zalmunna first, and then we will feed your army."

7So Gideon said, "After the LORD gives me victory over Zebah and Zalmunna, I will return and tear your flesh with the thorns and briers from the wilderness."

8From there Gideon went up to Peniel* and again asked for food, but he got the same answer. 9So he said to the people of Peniel, "After I return in victory, I will tear down this tower."

10By this time Zebah and Zalmunna were in Karkor with 15,000 warriors—all that remained of the allied armies of the east, for 120,000 had already been killed. 11Gideon circled around by the caravan route east of Nobah and Jogbehah, taking the Midianite army by surprise. 12Zebah and Zalmunna, the two Midianite kings, fled, but Gideon chased them down and captured all their warriors.

13After this, Gideon returned from the battle by way of Heres Pass. 14There he captured a young man from Succoth and demanded that he write down the names of all the seventy-seven officials and elders in the town. 15Gideon then returned to Succoth and said to the leaders, "Here are Zebah and Zalmunna. When we were here before, you taunted me, saying, 'Catch Zebah and Zalmunna first, and then we will feed your exhausted army.'" 16Then Gideon took the elders of the town and taught them a lesson, punishing them with thorns and briers from the wilderness. 17He also tore down the tower of Peniel and killed all the men in the town.

18Then Gideon asked Zebah and Zalmunna, "The men you killed at Tabor—what were they like?"

"Like you," they replied. "They all had the look of a king's son."

19"They were my brothers, the sons of my own mother!" Gideon exclaimed. "As surely as the LORD lives, I wouldn't kill you if you hadn't killed them."

20Turning to Jether, his oldest son, he said, "Kill them!" But Jether did not draw his sword, for he was only a boy and was afraid.

21Then Zebah and Zalmunna said to Gideon, "Be a man! Kill us yourself!" So Gideon killed them both and took the royal ornaments from the necks of their camels.

### Gideon's Sacred Ephod

22Then the Israelites said to Gideon, "Be our ruler! You and your son and your grandson will be our rulers, for you have rescued us from Midian."

8:8 Hebrew *Penuel*, a variant spelling of Peniel; also in 8:9, 17.

**Marginal references:**

8:5 Gen 33:17

8:7 Judg 7:15

8:8 Gen 32:30 1 Kgs 12:25

8:10 Isa 9:4

8:12 Ps 83:11

8:15 Judg 8:6

8:17 Judg 8:8

---

off the leaders from their army. Not every necessary job is a highly visible leadership role. Much of the necessary labor of any effective enterprise is considered by many to be dirty work. But such work is vital to getting any big task done. Engineers and millionaires may design and finance an elegant building, but it is the bricklayers who get the work done. Pride causes us to want recognition. Are you content to be God's bricklayer, or do you resent the work God has given you?

**8:5-9** The leaders of Succoth and Peniel refused to help Gideon, probably fearing Midian's revenge should he fail (Gideon's army was 300 men chasing 15,000). They should have realized that victory was certain because God was with Gideon. But they were so worried about saving themselves that they never thought about God's power to save.

Because of fear for ourselves, we may not recognize God's presence in other people and therefore miss God's victory. Then we must face the often bitter consequences of failing to join forces with those God has chosen to do his work. Because God will prevail with or without you, be quick to join others who

are engaged in his work. Lend support with your time, money, talents, and prayer.

**8:11** The Midianites were escaping into the desert area, where the tent-dwelling nomads lived. They didn't expect Gideon to follow them that far.

**8:15-17** Gideon carried out the threats he had made in 8:7, 9. It is difficult to determine whether this act of revenge was justified or whether he should have left the punishment up to God. Gideon was God's appointed leader, but the officials of Succoth and Peniel refused to help him in any way because they feared the enemy. They showed neither faith nor respect for God or the man God had chosen to save them. We should help others because it is right, regardless of whether we will benefit personally.

**8:20, 21** For a king to be killed by a boy was humiliating because it would look as though he was no match for a boy. The two men wanted to avoid that disgrace as well as the slower and more painful death that an inexperienced swordsman might inflict.

²³But Gideon replied, "I will not rule over you, nor will my son. The LORD will rule over you! ²⁴However, I do have one request—that each of you give me an earring from the plunder you collected from your fallen enemies." (The enemies, being Ishmaelites, all wore gold earrings.)

8:23
1 Sam 12:12

²⁵"Gladly!" they replied. They spread out a cloak, and each one threw in a gold earring he had gathered from the plunder. ²⁶The weight of the gold earrings was forty-three pounds,* not including the royal ornaments and pendants, the purple clothing worn by the kings of Midian, or the chains around the necks of their camels.

²⁷Gideon made a sacred ephod from the gold and put it in Ophrah, his hometown. But soon all the Israelites prostituted themselves by worshiping it, and it became a trap for Gideon and his family.

8:27
Exod 28:6
Judg 17:5

²⁸That is the story of how the people of Israel defeated Midian, which never recovered. Throughout the rest of Gideon's lifetime—about forty years—there was peace in the land.

²⁹Then Gideon* son of Joash returned home. ³⁰He had seventy sons born to him, for he had many wives. ³¹He also had a concubine in Shechem, who gave birth to a son, whom he named Abimelech. ³²Gideon died when he was very old, and he was buried in the grave of his father, Joash, at Ophrah in the land of the clan of Abiezer.

8:30
Judg 9:2, 5
8:31
Judg 9:1

³³As soon as Gideon died, the Israelites prostituted themselves by worshiping the images of Baal, making Baal-berith their god. ³⁴They forgot the LORD their God, who had rescued them from all their enemies surrounding them. ³⁵Nor did they show any loyalty to the family of Jerub-baal (that is, Gideon), despite all the good he had done for Israel.

8:33
Judg 2:11
8:34
Deut 4:9
Judg 3:7

## Abimelech Rules over Shechem

**9** One day Gideon's* son Abimelech went to Shechem to visit his uncles—his mother's brothers. He said to them and to the rest of his mother's family, ²"Ask the leading citizens of Shechem whether they want to be ruled by all seventy of Gideon's sons or by one man. And remember that I am your own flesh and blood!"

9:1
Judg 8:31

**8:26** Hebrew *1,700 shekels* [19.4 kilograms].   **8:29** Hebrew *Jerub-baal;* see 6:32.   **9:1** Hebrew *Jerub-baal's* (see 6:32); also in 9:2, 24.

---

**8:23** The people wanted to make Gideon their king, but Gideon stressed that the Lord was to rule over them. Despite his inconsistencies, Gideon never lost sight of the importance, for both a nation and an individual, of putting God first. Is God first in your life? If he is, he must affect every dimension of your life, not just what you do in church.

**8:26, 27** Those who were very wealthy put ornaments on their camels as a way of displaying their riches. Women wore vast amounts of jewelry as well, often up to 15 pairs of earrings. Jewelry was also worn for good luck. After Gideon's rise to power, he seems to have become carried away with this accumulation of wealth. Eventually it led the Israelites to idolatry.

**ABIMELECH'S FALL**

Gideon's illegitimate son killed 69 of his half brothers in Ophrah and returned to Shechem to be acclaimed king. But three years later, Shechem rebelled. From Arumah, Abimelech attacked Shechem, Beth-millo ("the pillar at Shechem"), and Thebez, where he was killed.

**8:27** An ephod was a linen garment worn by priests over their chests. It was considered holy (Exodus 28:6-35; 39:2-24; Leviticus 8:7, 8). Gideon probably had good motives for making the ephod (a visible remembrance commemorating the victory). Unfortunately, the people began to worship the ephod as an idol. Sadly, many decisions that stem from good motives produce negative results. Perhaps no one stops to ask, "What might go wrong?" or "Is there a possibility of negative consequences?" In your plans and decisions, take time to anticipate how a good idea might lead to a potential problem.

**8:31** This relationship between Gideon and a concubine produced a son who tore apart Gideon's family and caused tragedy for the nation. Gideon's story illustrates the fact that heroes in battle are not always heroes in daily life. Gideon led the nation but could not lead his family. No matter who you are, moral laxness will cause problems. Just because you have won a single battle with temptation does not mean you will automatically win the next one. We need to be constantly watchful against temptation. Sometimes Satan's strongest attacks come after a victory.

**8:33** Baal-berith means "Baal (lord) of the covenant." Worship of the idol may have combined elements of both the Israelite and Canaanite religions.

**9:1-3** With Gideon dead, Abimelech wanted to take his father's place. To set his plan in motion he went to the city of Shechem, his mother's hometown, to drum up support. There he felt kinship with the residents. These relatives were Canaanites and would be glad to unite against Israel. Shechem was an important city, a crossroads for trade routes and a natural link between the coastal plain and the Jordan Valley. Whoever controlled Shechem would dominate the countryside.

**9:2-5** Israel's king was to be the Lord and not a man. But Abimelech wanted to usurp the position reserved for God alone. In his selfish quest, he killed all but one of his 70 half brothers.

**9:4**
Judg 8:33

**9:5**
Judg 6:11; 8:32

³So Abimelech's uncles gave his message to all the citizens of Shechem on his behalf. And after listening to this proposal, the people of Shechem decided in favor of Abimelech because he was their relative. ⁴They gave him seventy silver coins from the temple of Baal-berith, which he used to hire some reckless troublemakers who agreed to follow him. ⁵He went to his father's home at Ophrah, and there, on one stone, they killed all seventy of his half brothers, the sons of Gideon.* But the youngest brother, Jotham, escaped and hid.

⁶Then all the leading citizens of Shechem and Beth-millo called a meeting under the oak beside the pillar* at Shechem and made Abimelech their king.

**9:5** Hebrew *Jerub-baal* (see 6:32); also in 9:16, 19, 28, 57.   **9:6** The meaning of the Hebrew is uncertain.

---

**ABIMELECH**

People who desire power always outnumber those who are able to use power wisely once they have it. Perhaps this is because power has a way of taking over and controlling the person using it. This is especially true in cases of inherited but unmerited power. Abimelech's life shows us what happens when hunger for power corrupts judgment.

Abimelech's position in Gideon's family as the son of a concubine must have created great tension between him and Gideon's many other sons. One against 70: Such odds can either crush a person or make him ruthless. It is obvious which direction Abimelech chose. Gideon's position as warrior and judge had placed Abimelech in an environment of power; Gideon's death provided an opportunity for this son to seize power. Once the process began, the disastrous results were inevitable. A person's thirst for power is not satisfied when he gets power—it only becomes more intense. Abimelech's life was consumed by that thirst. Eventually, he could not tolerate any threat to his power.

By this time, ownership had changed: Abimelech no longer had power—power had him. One lesson we can learn from his life is that our goals control our actions. The amount of control is related to the importance of the goal. Abimelech's most important goal was to have power. His lust for power led him to wipe out not only his brothers but also whole cities that refused to submit to him. Nothing but death could stop his bloodthirsty drive to conquer. How ironic that he was fatally injured by a woman with a farm implement! The contrast between Abimelech and the godly people of the Bible is great. He wanted to control the nation; they were willing to be controlled by God.

| | |
|---|---|
| **Strengths and accomplishments** | • The first self-declared king of Israel<br>• Qualified tactical planner and organizer |
| **Weaknesses and mistakes** | • Power hungry and ruthless<br>• Overconfident<br>• Took advantage of his father's position without imitating his character<br>• Had 69 of his 70 half brothers killed |
| **Vital statistics** | • Where: Shechem, Arumah, Thebez<br>• Occupations: Self-acclaimed king, judge, political troublemaker<br>• Relatives: Father: Gideon. Only surviving half brother: Jotham. |
| **Key verses** | "In this way, God punished Abimelech for the evil he had done against his father by murdering his seventy brothers. God also punished the men of Shechem for all their evil. So the curse of Jotham son of Gideon was fulfilled" (Judges 9:56, 57). |

His story is told in Judges 8:31—9:57. He is also mentioned in 2 Samuel 11:21.

---

People with selfish desires often seek to fulfill them in ruthless ways. Examine your ambitions to see if they are self-centered or God-centered. Be sure you always fulfill your desires in ways that God would approve.

**9:4** Politics played a major part in pagan religions such as the worship of Baal-berith. Governments often went so far as to hire temple prostitutes to bring in additional money. In many cases a religious system was set up and supported by the government so the offerings could fund community projects. Religion became a profit-making business. In Israel's religion, this was strictly forbidden. God's system of religion was designed to come from an attitude of the heart, not from calculated plans and business opportunities. It was also designed to serve people and help those in need, not to oppress the needy. Is your faith genuine and sincere, or is it based on convenience, comfort, and availability?

**9:6** Abimelech was declared ruler of Israel at Shechem, the site of other key Bible events. It was one of Abraham's first stops upon arriving in Canaan (Genesis 12:6, 7). When Jacob lived there, two of his sons killed all the men in Shechem because the prince's son raped their sister (Genesis 34). Joseph's bones were buried in Shechem (Joshua 24:32); Israel renewed its covenant with God there (Joshua 24); and the kingdom of Israel would split apart at this same city (1 Kings 12).

## Jotham's Parable

7When Jotham heard about this, he climbed to the top of Mount Gerizim and shouted,

> "Listen to me, citizens of Shechem!
>   Listen to me if you want God to listen to you!
> 8 Once upon a time the trees decided to choose a king.
>   First they said to the olive tree,
>   'Be our king!'
> 9 But the olive tree refused, saying,
>   'Should I quit producing the olive oil
>     that blesses both God and people,
>     just to wave back and forth over the trees?'
>
> 10 "Then they said to the fig tree,
>   'You be our king!'
> 11 But the fig tree also refused, saying,
>   'Should I quit producing my sweet fruit
>     just to wave back and forth over the trees?'
>
> 12 "Then they said to the grapevine,
>   'You be our king!'
> 13 But the grapevine also refused, saying,
>   'Should I quit producing the wine
>     that cheers both God and people,
>     just to wave back and forth over the trees?'
>
> 14 "Then all the trees finally turned to the thornbush and said,
>   'Come, you be our king!'
> 15 And the thornbush replied to the trees,
>   'If you truly want to make me your king,
>     come and take shelter in my shade.
>   If not, let fire come out from me
>     and devour the cedars of Lebanon.'"

16Jotham continued, "Now make sure you have acted honorably and in good faith by making Abimelech your king, and that you have done right by Gideon and all of his descendants. Have you treated him with the honor he deserves for all he accomplished? 17For he fought for you and risked his life when he rescued you from the Midianites. 18But today you have revolted against my father and his descendants, killing his seventy sons on one stone. And you have chosen his slave woman's son, Abimelech, to be your king just because he is your relative.

19"If you have acted honorably and in good faith toward Gideon and his descendants today, then may you find joy in Abimelech, and may he find joy in you. 20But if you have not acted in good faith, then may fire come out from Abimelech and devour the leading citizens of Shechem and Beth-millo; and may fire come out from the citizens of Shechem and Beth-millo and devour Abimelech!"

21Then Jotham escaped and lived in Beer because he was afraid of his brother Abimelech.

## Shechem Rebels against Abimelech

22After Abimelech had ruled over Israel for three years, 23God sent a spirit that stirred up trouble between Abimelech and the leading citizens of Shechem, and they revolted. 24God was punishing Abimelech for murdering Gideon's seventy sons, and the citizens of

**9:7** Deut 11:29; 27:12 John 4:20

**9:8** 2 Kgs 14:9 Ezek 17:3 Dan 4:10

**9:18** Judg 8:31

**9:23** 1 Sam 16:14
**9:24** Num 35:33 Deut 27:25

---

**9:7-15** In Jotham's parable the trees represented Gideon's 70 sons, and the thornbush represented Abimelech. Jotham's point was this: A productive person would be too busy doing good to want to bother with power politics. A worthless person, on the other hand, would be glad to accept the honor—but he would destroy the people he ruled. Abimelech, like a thornbush, could offer Israel no real protection or security. Jotham's parable came true when Abimelech destroyed the city of Shechem (9:45), burned "the tower of Shechem" (the city of Beth-millo, 9:46-49), and was finally killed at Thebez (9:53, 54).

**9:16** Jotham told the story about the trees in order to help the people set good priorities. He did not want them to appoint a leader of low character. As we serve in leadership positions, we should examine our motives. Do we just want praise, prestige, or power? In the parable, the good trees chose to be productive and to provide benefits to people. Make sure these are your priorities as you aspire to leadership.

**9:22-24** Abimelech was the opposite of what God wanted in a judge, but it was three years before God moved against him, fulfilling Jotham's parable. Those three years must have seemed

Shechem for supporting him in this treachery of murdering his brothers. 25The citizens of Shechem set an ambush for Abimelech on the hilltops and robbed everyone who passed that way. But someone warned Abimelech about their plot.

26One day Gaal son of Ebed moved to Shechem with his brothers and gained the confidence of the leading citizens of Shechem. 27During the annual harvest festival at Shechem, held in the temple of the local god, the wine flowed freely, and everyone began cursing Abimelech. 28"Who is Abimelech?" Gaal shouted. "He's not a true son of Shechem,* so why should we be his servants? He's merely the son of Gideon, and this Zebul is merely his deputy. Serve the true sons of Hamor, the founder of Shechem. Why should we serve Abimelech? 29If I were in charge here, I would get rid of Abimelech. I would say* to him, 'Get some soldiers, and come out and fight!'"

30But when Zebul, the leader of the city, heard what Gaal was saying, he was furious. 31He sent messengers to Abimelech in Arumah,* telling him, "Gaal son of Ebed and his brothers have come to live in Shechem, and now they are inciting the city to rebel against you. 32Come by night with an army and hide out in the fields. 33In the morning, as soon as it is daylight, attack the city. When Gaal and those who are with him come out against you, you can do with them as you wish."

34So Abimelech and all his men went by night and split into four groups, stationing themselves around Shechem. 35Gaal was standing at the city gates when Abimelech and his army came out of hiding. 36When Gaal saw them, he said to Zebul, "Look, there are people coming down from the hilltops!"

Zebul replied, "It's just the shadows on the hills that look like men."

37But again Gaal said, "No, people are coming down from the hills.* And another group is coming down the road past the Diviners' Oak.*"

38Then Zebul turned on him and asked, "Now where is that big mouth of yours? Wasn't it you that said, 'Who is Abimelech, and why should we be his servants?' The men you mocked are right outside the city! Go out and fight them!"

39So Gaal led the leading citizens of Shechem into battle against Abimelech. 40But Abimelech chased him, and many of Shechem's men were wounded and fell along the road as they retreated to the city gate. 41Abimelech returned to Arumah, and Zebul drove Gaal and his brothers out of Shechem.

42The next day the people of Shechem went out into the fields to battle. When Abimelech heard about it, 43he divided his men into three groups and set an ambush in the fields. When Abimelech saw the people coming out of the city, he and his men jumped up from their hiding places and attacked them. 44Abimelech and his group stormed the city gate to keep the men of Shechem from getting back in, while Abimelech's other two groups cut them down in the fields. 45The battle went on all day before Abimelech finally captured the city. He killed the people, leveled the city, and scattered salt all over the ground.

46When the leading citizens who lived in the tower of Shechem heard what had happened, they ran and hid in the temple of Baal-berith.* 47Someone reported to Abimelech that the citizens had gathered in the temple, 48so he led his forces to Mount Zalmon. He took an ax and chopped some branches from a tree, then put them on his shoulder. "Quick, do as I have done!" he told his men. 49So each of them cut down some branches, following Abimelech's example. They piled the branches against the walls of the temple and set them on fire. So all the people who had lived in the tower of Shechem died—about 1,000 men and women.

9:28 Hebrew *Who is Shechem?* 9:29 As in Greek version; Hebrew reads *And he said.* 9:31 Or *in secret;* Hebrew reads *in Tormah;* compare 9:41. 9:37a Or *the center of the land.* 9:37b Hebrew *Elon-meonenim.* 9:46 Hebrew *El-berith,* another name for Baal-berith; compare 9:4.

### Cross-references (margin)

9:27
Judg 8:33

9:33
1 Sam 10:7

9:45
Deut 29:23
9:46
Judg 8:33

9:48
Ps 68:14

---

like forever to Jotham. Why wasn't Abimelech punished sooner for his evil ways?

We are not alone when we wonder why evil seems to prevail (Job 10:3; 21:1-18; Jeremiah 12:1; Habakkuk 1:2-4, 12-17). God promises to deal with sin, but in his time, not ours. Actually it is good news that God doesn't punish *us* immediately because we all have sinned and deserve God's punishment. God, in his mercy, often spares us from immediate punishment and allows us time to turn from our sins and turn to him in repentance. Trusting God for justice means (1) we must first recognize our own sins and repent, and (2) we may face a difficult time of wait-

ing for the wicked to be punished. But in God's time, all evil will be destroyed.

9:23 This "trouble" stirred up was not just an attitude of strife, it was a demon. It was not Satan himself, but one of the fallen angels under Satan's influence. God used this evil spirit to bring about judgment on Shechem. First Samuel 16:14 records how God judged Saul in a similar way.

9:45 To scatter salt over a conquered city was a ritual to symbolize the perpetual desolation of the city. It would not be rebuilt for 150 years.

⁵⁰Then Abimelech attacked the town of Thebez and captured it. ⁵¹But there was a strong tower inside the town, and all the men and women—the entire population—fled to it. They barricaded themselves in and climbed up to the roof of the tower. ⁵²Abimelech followed them to attack the tower. But as he prepared to set fire to the entrance, ⁵³a woman on the roof dropped a millstone that landed on Abimelech's head and crushed his skull.

**9:50**
2 Sam 11:21

**9:53**
2 Sam 11:21

⁵⁴He quickly said to his young armor bearer, "Draw your sword and kill me! Don't let it be said that a woman killed Abimelech!" So the young man ran him through with his sword, and he died. ⁵⁵When Abimelech's men saw that he was dead, they disbanded and returned to their homes.

⁵⁶In this way, God punished Abimelech for the evil he had done against his father by murdering his seventy brothers. ⁵⁷God also punished the men of Shechem for all their evil. So the curse of Jotham son of Gideon was fulfilled.

## Tola Becomes Israel's Judge

**10** After Abimelech died, Tola son of Puah, son of Dodo, was the next person to rescue Israel. He was from the tribe of Issachar but lived in the town of Shamir in the hill country of Ephraim. ²He judged Israel for twenty-three years. When he died, he was buried in Shamir.

## Jair Becomes Israel's Judge

³After Tola died, Jair from Gilead judged Israel for twenty-two years. ⁴His thirty sons rode around on thirty donkeys, and they owned thirty towns in the land of Gilead, which are still called the Towns of Jair.* ⁵When Jair died, he was buried in Kamon.

**10:4**
Num 32:41

## 5. Fifth period: Jephthah, Ibzan, Elon, and Abdon
### The Ammonites Oppress Israel

⁶Again the Israelites did evil in the Lᴏʀᴅ's sight. They served the images of Baal and Ashtoreth, and the gods of Aram, Sidon, Moab, Ammon, and Philistia. They abandoned the Lᴏʀᴅ and no longer served him at all. ⁷So the Lᴏʀᴅ burned with anger against Israel, and he turned them over to the Philistines and the Ammonites, ⁸who began to oppress them that year. For eighteen years they oppressed all the Israelites east of the Jordan River in the land of the Amorites (that is, in Gilead). ⁹The Ammonites also crossed to the west side of the Jordan and attacked Judah, Benjamin, and Ephraim.

**10:6**
Judg 2:11-13

**10:7**
1 Sam 12:9

The Israelites were in great distress. ¹⁰Finally, they cried out to the Lᴏʀᴅ for help, saying, "We have sinned against you because we have abandoned you as our God and have served the images of Baal."

**10:10**
Judg 3:9

**10:4** Hebrew *Havvoth-jair.*

---

**9:53** In times of battle, women were sometimes asked to join the men at the city wall to drop heavy objects on the soldiers below. A millstone would have been an ideal object for this purpose. It was a round stone about 18 inches in diameter with a hole in the center. Millstones were used to grind grain into flour. The grain was placed between two millstones. The top millstone was turned, crushing the grain.

Abimelech's death was especially humiliating: He was killed by a woman, not by fighting; and he was killed by a farm implement instead of a weapon. Abimelech, therefore, asked his armor bearer to stab him with his sword before he died from the blow of the millstone.

**9:56, 57** Gideon, Abimelech's father, succeeded in military battles but sometimes failed in his personal struggles. Gideon was not condemned for taking a concubine (8:31), but the family problems that resulted from this relationship are clearly stated.

In the end, Abimelech killed 69 of his 70 half brothers, tore apart a nation, and then was killed himself. From Gideon's life we learn that no matter how much good we do for God's King-

dom, sin in our lives will still produce powerful, damaging consequences.

**9:56, 57** Jotham's curse is found in 9:16-20.

**10:1-5** In five verses we read about two men who judged Israel for a total of 45 years, yet all we know about them besides the length of their rules is that one had 30 sons who rode around on 30 donkeys. What are you doing for God that is worth noting? When your life is over, will people remember more than just what was in your bank account or the number of years you lived?

**10:6** Baal and Ashtoreth are explained in the notes on 2:11-15 and 3:7. The gods of Aram and Sidon were very similar. The gods of Moab and Ammon were Chemosh and Molech. The Philistine gods were Dagon, Ashtoreth, Asherah, and Baal-zebul.

**10:9, 10** Once again the Israelites suffered for many years before they gave up their sinful ways and called out to God for help (see 4:1-3; 6:1-6). Notice that when the Israelites were at the end of their rope they did not look to their pagan gods for help, but to the only one who was really able to help.

Is God your last resort? So much unnecessary suffering takes place because we don't call on God until we've used up all other resources. Rather than waiting until the situation becomes desperate, turn to God first. He has the necessary resources to meet every kind of problem.

10:11
Exod 14:30
Judg 3:13

10:14
Deut 32:37

10:15
1 Sam 3:18

10:16
Deut 32:36
Josh 24:23
Jer 18:8

11:1
1 Sam 12:11
Heb 11:32

¹¹The Lord replied, "Did I not rescue you from the Egyptians, the Amorites, the Ammonites, the Philistines, ¹²the Sidonians, the Amalekites, and the Maonites? When they oppressed you, you cried out to me for help, and I rescued you. ¹³Yet you have abandoned me and served other gods. So I will not rescue you anymore. ¹⁴Go and cry out to the gods you have chosen! Let them rescue you in your hour of distress!"

¹⁵But the Israelites pleaded with the Lord and said, "We have sinned. Punish us as you see fit, only rescue us today from our enemies." ¹⁶Then the Israelites put aside their foreign gods and served the Lord. And he was grieved by their misery.

¹⁷At that time the armies of Ammon had gathered for war and were camped in Gilead, and the people of Israel assembled and camped at Mizpah. ¹⁸The leaders of Gilead said to each other, "Whoever attacks the Ammonites first will become ruler over all the people of Gilead."

## Jephthah Becomes Israel's Judge

**11** Now Jephthah of Gilead was a great warrior. He was the son of Gilead, but his mother was a prostitute. ²Gilead's wife also had several sons, and when these half brothers grew up, they chased Jephthah off the land. "You will not get any of our father's inheritance,"

### RASH VOWS

Ecclesiastes 5:2 says: "Don't make rash promises, and don't be hasty in bringing matters before God After all, God is in heaven, and you are here on earth. So let your words be few." Scripture records the vows of many men and women. Some of these vows proved to be rash and unwise, and others, though extreme, were kept to the letter by those who made them. Let us learn from the examples in God's Word not to make rash vows.

| Person | Vow | Result | Reference |
|---|---|---|---|
| JACOB | To "choose" the true God and to give back a tenth to him if he kept him safe | God protected Jacob, who kept his vow to follow God | Genesis 28:20 |
| JEPHTHAH | To offer to the Lord whoever came out to meet him after battle (it turned out to be his daughter) | He lost his daughter | Judges 11:30, 31 |
| HANNAH | To give her son back to God if God would give her a son | When Samuel was born, she dedicated him to God | 1 Samuel 1:9-11 |
| SAUL | To kill anyone who ate before evening (Jonathan, his son, had not heard the command and broke it) | Saul would have killed Jonathan if soldiers had not intervened | 1 Samuel 14:24-45 |
| DAVID | To be kind to Jonathan's family | Mephibosheth, Jonathan's son, was treated royally by David | 2 Samuel 9:7 |
| ITTAI | To remain loyal to David | He became one of the great men in David's army | 2 Samuel 15:21 |
| MICAIAH | To say only what God told him to say | He was put in prison | 1 Kings 22:14 |
| JOB | That he was not rebelling against God | His fortunes were restored | Job 42:10 |
| HEROD ANTIPAS | To give Herodias's daughter anything she requested | Herod was forced to order John the Baptist's death | Mark 6:22, 23 |
| PAUL | To offer a sacrifice of thanksgiving in Jerusalem | He made the sacrifice despite the danger | Acts 18:18 |

**10:11-16** These verses show how difficult it can be to follow God over the long haul. The Israelites always seemed to forget God when all was well. But despite being rejected by his own people, God never failed to rescue them when they called out to him in repentance. God never fails to rescue us either. We act just like the Israelites when we put God outside our daily events instead of at the center of them. Just as a loving parent feels rejected when a child rebels, so God feels great rejection when we ignore or neglect him (1 Samuel 8:4-9; 10:17-19; John 12:44-50). We should strive to stay close to God rather than see how far we can go before judgment comes.

**10:17, 18** The power of the Ammonite nation was at its peak during the period of the judges. The people were descendants of Ammon, conceived when Lot's daughter slept with her drunk father (Genesis 19:30-38). The land of Ammon was located just east of the Jordan River across from Jerusalem. South of Ammon lay the land of Moab, the nation conceived when Lot's other daughter slept with her father. Moab and Ammon were usually allies. It was a formidable task to defeat these nations.

**11:1, 2** Jephthah, an illegitimate son of Gilead, was chased out of the country by his half brothers. He suffered as a result of another's decision and not for any wrong he had done. Yet in spite of his brothers' rejection, God used him. If you are suffering from unfair rejection, don't blame others and become discouraged. Remember how God used Jephthah despite his unjust circumstances, and realize that he is able to use you even if you feel rejected by some.

they said, "for you are the son of a prostitute." ³So Jephthah fled from his brothers and lived in the land of Tob. Soon he had a band of worthless rebels following him.

⁴At about this time, the Ammonites began their war against Israel. ⁵When the Ammonites attacked, the elders of Gilead sent for Jephthah in the land of Tob. The elders said, ⁶"Come and be our commander! Help us fight the Ammonites!"

⁷But Jephthah said to them, "Aren't you the ones who hated me and drove me from my father's house? Why do you come to me now when you're in trouble?"

⁸"Because we need you," the elders replied. "If you lead us in battle against the Ammonites, we will make you ruler over all the people of Gilead."

⁹Jephthah said to the elders, "Let me get this straight. If I come with you and if the LORD gives me victory over the Ammonites, will you really make me ruler over all the people?"

¹⁰"The LORD is our witness," the elders replied. "We promise to do whatever you say."

¹¹So Jephthah went with the elders of Gilead, and the people made him their ruler and commander of the army. At Mizpah, in the presence of the LORD, Jephthah repeated what he had said to the elders.

¹²Then Jephthah sent messengers to the king of Ammon, asking, "Why have you come out to fight against my land?"

¹³The king of Ammon answered Jephthah's messengers, "When the Israelites came out of Egypt, they stole my land from the Arnon River to the Jabbok River and all the way to the Jordan. Now then, give back the land peaceably."

¹⁴Jephthah sent this message back to the Ammonite king:

¹⁵"This is what Jephthah says: Israel did not steal any land from Moab or Ammon. ¹⁶When the people of Israel arrived at Kadesh on their journey from Egypt after crossing the Red Sea,* ¹⁷they sent messengers to the king of Edom asking for permission to pass through his land. But their request was denied. Then they asked the king of Moab for similar permission, but he wouldn't let them pass through either. So the people of Israel stayed in Kadesh.

¹⁸"Finally, they went around Edom and Moab through the wilderness. They traveled along Moab's eastern border and camped on the other side of the Arnon River. But they never once crossed the Arnon River into Moab, for the Arnon was the border of Moab.

¹⁹"Then Israel sent messengers to King Sihon of the Amorites, who ruled from Heshbon, asking for permission to cross through his land to get to their destination. ²⁰But King Sihon didn't trust Israel to pass through his land. Instead, he mobilized his army at Jahaz and attacked them. ²¹But the LORD, the God of Israel, gave his people victory over King Sihon. So Israel took control of all the land of the Amorites, who lived in that region, ²²from the Arnon River to the Jabbok River, and from the eastern wilderness to the Jordan.

²³"So you see, it was the LORD, the God of Israel, who took away the land from the Amorites and gave it to Israel. Why, then, should we give it back to you? ²⁴You keep whatever your god Chemosh gives you, and we will keep whatever the LORD our God gives us. ²⁵Are you any better than Balak son of Zippor, king of Moab? Did he try to make a case against Israel for disputed land? Did he go to war against them?

**11:3**
Judg 9:4
2 Sam 10:6, 8

**11:4**
Judg 10:9

**11:10**
Gen 31:50

**11:11**
Judg 10:17

**11:13**
Num 21:24-26

**11:16**
Num 20:1-21

**11:17**
Num 20:14-21
Josh 24:9

**11:18**
Num 21:4
Deut 2:1-9, 18-19

**11:19**
Num 21:21-22

**11:21**
Deut 2:32-34

**11:24**
Num 21:27-30
1 Kgs 11:7

**11:25**
Num 22:2

**11:16** Hebrew *sea of reeds.*

---

**11:3** Circumstances beyond his control forced Jephthah away from his people and into life as an outcast. Today, both believers and nonbelievers may drive away those who do not fit the norms dictated by our society, neighborhoods, or churches. Often, as in Jephthah's case, great potential is wasted because of prejudice— a refusal to look beyond ill-conceived stereotypes. Look around you to see if there are potential Jephthahs being kept out due to factors beyond their control. As a Christian, you know that everyone can have a place in God's family. Can you do anything to help these people gain acceptance for their character and abilities?

**11:11** What does it mean that Jephthah repeated all his words before the Lord? Those making covenants in ancient times often made them at shrines so that they would be witnessed by deities. Often a written copy was also deposited at the shrine. This was much like a coronation ceremony for Jephthah.

**11:14ff** Jephthah sent messengers to the Ammonite king wanting to know why the Israelites in the land of Gilead were being attacked (11:12). The king replied that Israel had stolen this land and he wanted it back (11:13).

Jephthah sent another message to the king (11:14-27). In it he gave three arguments against the king's claim: (1) Gilead was never the king's land in the first place because Israel took it from the Amorites, not the Ammonites (11:16-22); (2) Israel should possess land given by Israel's God, and Ammon should possess land given by Ammon's god; (3) no one had contested Israel's ownership of the land since its conquest 300 years earlier (11:25, 26).

To Jephthah's credit, he tried to solve the problem without bloodshed. But the king of Ammon ignored his message and prepared his troops for battle.

**11:26**
Num 21:25

26"Israel has been living here for 300 years, inhabiting Heshbon and its surrounding settlements, all the way to Aroer and its settlements, and in all the towns along the Arnon River. Why have you made no effort to recover it before now? 27Therefore, I have not sinned against you. Rather, you have wronged me by attacking me. Let the LORD, who is judge, decide today which of us is right—Israel or Ammon."

28But the king of Ammon paid no attention to Jephthah's message.

### Jephthah's Vow

**11:29**
Judg 3:10

29At that time the Spirit of the LORD came upon Jephthah, and he went throughout the land of Gilead and Manasseh, including Mizpah in Gilead, and from there he led an army against the Ammonites. 30And Jephthah made a vow to the LORD. He said, "If you give me victory over the Ammonites, 31I will give to the LORD whatever comes out of my house to meet me when I return in triumph. I will sacrifice it as a burnt offering."

**JEPHTHAH**

It's hard not to admire people whose word can be depended on completely and whose actions are consistent with their words. For such people, talking is not avoiding action; it is the beginning of action. People like this can make excellent negotiators. They approach a conflict with the full intention of settling issues verbally, but they do not hesitate to use other means if verbal attempts fail. Jephthah was this kind of person.

In most of his conflicts, Jephthah's first move was to talk. In the war with the Ammonites, his strategy was negotiation. He clarified the issues so that everyone knew the cause of the conflict. His opponent's response determined his next action.

The fate of Jephthah's daughter is difficult to understand. We are not sure what Jephthah meant by his vow recorded in Judges 11:31. In any case, his vow was unnecessary. We do not know what actually happened to his daughter—whether she was burned as an offering or set apart as a virgin, thus denying Jephthah any hope of descendants since she was his only child. What we do know is that Jephthah was a person of his word, even when it was a word spoken in haste, and even when keeping his word caused him great pain.

How do you approach conflicts? There is a big difference between trying to settle a conflict through words and simply counterattacking someone verbally. How dependable are the statements you make? Do your children, friends, and fellow workers know you to be a person of your word? The measure of your trustworthiness is your willingness to take responsibility, even if you must pay a painful price because of something you said.

| | |
|---|---|
| **Strengths and accomplishments** | • Listed in the Hall of Faith in Hebrews 11<br>• Controlled by God's Spirit<br>• Brilliant military strategist who negotiated before fighting |
| **Weaknesses and mistakes** | • Was bitter over the treatment he received from his half brothers<br>• Made a rash and foolish vow that was costly |
| **Lesson from his life** | • A person's background does not prevent God from working powerfully in his or her life |
| **Vital statistics** | • Where: Gilead<br>• Occupations: Warrior, judge<br>• Relative: Father: Gilead |
| **Key verse** | "So Jephthah led his army against the Ammonites, and the LORD gave him victory" (Judges 11:32). |

His story is told in Judges 11:1—12:7. He is also mentioned in 1 Samuel 12:11 and Hebrews 11:32.

**11:27** Over the years, Israel had many judges to lead them. But Jephthah recognized the Lord as the people's true Judge, the only one who could really lead them and help them conquer the invading enemies.

**11:30, 31** In God's law, a vow was a promise to God that should not be broken (Numbers 30:1, 2; Deuteronomy 23:21-23). It carried as much force as a written contract. Many people made vows in biblical times. Some, like Jephthah's, were very foolish.

**11:30, 31** When Jephthah made his vow, did he stop to consider that a person, not a sheep or goat, might come out to meet him? Scholars are divided over the issue. Those who say Jephthah was considering human sacrifice use the following arguments: (1) He was from an area where pagan religion and human sacrifice were common. In his eyes, it may not have seemed like a

sin. (2) Jephthah may not have had a background in religious law. Perhaps he was ignorant of God's command against human sacrifice.

Those who say Jephthah could not have been thinking about human sacrifice point to other evidence: (1) As leader of the people, Jephthah must have been familiar with God's laws; human sacrifice was clearly forbidden (Leviticus 18:21; 20:1-5). (2) No legitimate priest would have helped Jephthah carry out his vow if a person was to be the sacrifice.

Whatever Jephthah had in mind when he made the vow, did he or did he not sacrifice his daughter? Some think he did, because his vow was to make a burnt offering. Some think he did not, and they offer these two reasons: (1) If the girl was to die, she would not have spent her last two months in the hills. (2) God would not have honored a vow based on a wicked practice.

³²So Jephthah led his army against the Ammonites, and the LORD gave him victory. ³³He crushed the Ammonites, devastating about twenty towns from Aroer to an area near Min-nith and as far away as Abel-keramim. In this way Israel defeated the Ammonites.

³⁴When Jephthah returned home to Mizpah, his daughter came out to meet him, playing on a tambourine and dancing for joy. She was his one and only child; he had no other sons or daughters. ³⁵When he saw her, he tore his clothes in anguish. "Oh, my daughter!" he cried out. "You have completely destroyed me! You've brought disaster on me! For I have made a vow to the LORD, and I cannot take it back."

³⁶And she said, "Father, if you have made a vow to the LORD, you must do to me what you have vowed, for the LORD has given you a great victory over your enemies, the Ammonites. ³⁷But first let me do this one thing: Let me go up and roam in the hills and weep with my friends for two months, because I will die a virgin."

³⁸"You may go," Jephthah said. And he sent her away for two months. She and her friends went into the hills and wept because she would never have children. ³⁹When she returned home, her father kept the vow he had made, and she died a virgin.

So it has become a custom in Israel ⁴⁰for young Israelite women to go away for four days each year to lament the fate of Jephthah's daughter.

### Ephraim Fights with Jephthah

**12** Then the people of Ephraim mobilized an army and crossed over the Jordan River to Zaphon. They sent this message to Jephthah: "Why didn't you call for us to help you fight against the Ammonites? We are going to burn down your house with you in it!"

²Jephthah replied, "I summoned you at the beginning of the dispute, but you refused to come! You failed to help us in our struggle against Ammon. ³So when I realized you weren't coming, I risked my life and went to battle without you, and the LORD gave me victory over the Ammonites. So why have you now come to fight me?"

⁴The people of Ephraim responded, "You men of Gilead are nothing more than fugitives from Ephraim and Manasseh." So Jephthah gathered all the men of Gilead and attacked the men of Ephraim and defeated them.

⁵Jephthah captured the shallow crossings of the Jordan River, and whenever a fugitive from Ephraim tried to go back across, the men of Gilead would challenge him. "Are you a member of the tribe of Ephraim?" they would ask. If the man said, "No, I'm not," ⁶they would tell him to say "Shibboleth." If he was from Ephraim, he would say "Sibboleth," be-cause people from Ephraim cannot pronounce the word correctly. Then they would take him and kill him at the shallow crossings of the Jordan. In all, 42,000 Ephraimites were killed at that time.

**11:34**
Exod 15:20
1 Sam 18:6
Jer 31:4

**11:35**
Num 30:2
Eccl 5:2, 4-5

**11:36**
2 Sam 18:19
Luke 1:38

**12:1**
Judg 8:1

**12:3**
1 Sam 19:5
Job 13:14

**12:5**
Josh 2:7
Judg 3:28; 7:24

---

**JEPHTHAH'S VICTORY**
The Ephraimites mobilized an army because they were angry at not being included in the battle against Ammon. They planned to attack Jephthah at his home in Gilead. Jephthah captured the shallows of the Jordan at the Jabbok River and killed the Ephraimites who tried to cross.

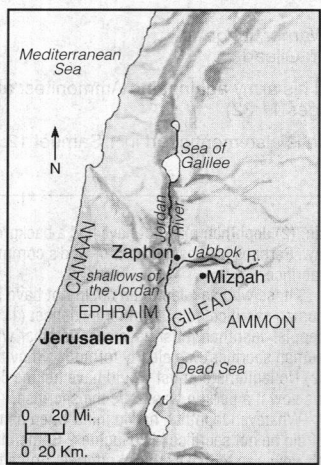

**11:34, 35** Jephthah's rash vow brought him unspeakable grief. In the heat of emotion or personal turmoil it is easy to make fool-ish promises to God. These promises may sound very spiritual when we make them, but they may produce only guilt and frustra-tion when we are forced to fulfill them. Making spiritual "deals" only brings disappointment. God does not want promises for the future, but obedience for today.

**12:1ff** Israel had just won a great battle, but instead of joy, there was pettiness and quarreling. The tribe of Ephraim was angry and jealous that they were not invited to join in the fighting (although Jephthah said he had invited them). The insults of the Ephraimites enraged Jephthah, who called out his troops and killed 42,000 men from Ephraim.

Jephthah usually spoke before he acted, but this time his revenge was swift. It cost Israel dearly, and it might have been avoided. Insulting others and being jealous are not right responses when we feel left out. But seeking revenge for an insult is just as wrong and very costly.

**12:4-7** The men of the tribe of Ephraim caused Jephthah trouble just as they had Gideon (8:1-3). Jephthah captured the shallow crossings of the Jordan, the boundary of Ephraim, and was able to defeat his countrymen as they crossed the river. He used a pronunciation test. *Shibboleth* is the word for "stream." The Ephraimites pronounced "sh" as "s," so Jephthah's army could easily identify them.

12:7
Heb 11:32

⁷Jephthah judged Israel for six years. When he died, he was buried in one of the towns of Gilead.

### Ibzan Becomes Israel's Judge

⁸After Jephthah died, Ibzan from Bethlehem judged Israel. ⁹He had thirty sons and thirty daughters. He sent his daughters to marry men outside his clan, and he brought in thirty young women from outside his clan to marry his sons. Ibzan judged Israel for seven years. ¹⁰When he died, he was buried at Bethlehem.

### Elon Becomes Israel's Judge

¹¹After Ibzan died, Elon from the tribe of Zebulun judged Israel for ten years. ¹²When he died, he was buried at Aijalon in Zebulun.

### Abdon Becomes Israel's Judge

12:14
Judg 5:10

¹³After Elon died, Abdon son of Hillel, from Pirathon, judged Israel. ¹⁴He had forty sons and thirty grandsons, who rode on seventy donkeys. He judged Israel for eight years. ¹⁵When he died, he was buried at Pirathon in Ephraim, in the hill country of the Amalekites.

## 6. Sixth period: Samson
### The Birth of Samson

13:1
Judg 2:11
13:2
Josh 19:41
13:3
Gen 16:7
Judg 6:12
13:4-5
Num 6:1-5
Judg 13:14
Luke 1:15

**13** Again the Israelites did evil in the LORD's sight, so the LORD handed them over to the Philistines, who oppressed them for forty years.

²In those days a man named Manoah from the tribe of Dan lived in the town of Zorah. His wife was unable to become pregnant, and they had no children. ³The angel of the LORD appeared to Manoah's wife and said, "Even though you have been unable to have children, you will soon become pregnant and give birth to a son. ⁴So be careful; you must not drink wine or any other alcoholic drink nor eat any forbidden food.* ⁵You will become pregnant and give birth to a son, and his hair must never be cut. For he will be dedicated to God as a Nazirite from birth. He will begin to rescue Israel from the Philistines."

13:6
1 Sam 2:27

⁶The woman ran and told her husband, "A man of God appeared to me! He looked like one of God's angels, terrifying to see. I didn't ask where he was from, and he didn't tell me his name. ⁷But he told me, 'You will become pregnant and give birth to a son. You must not drink wine or any other alcoholic drink nor eat any forbidden food. For your son will be dedicated to God as a Nazirite from the moment of his birth until the day of his death.'"

⁸Then Manoah prayed to the LORD, saying, "Lord, please let the man of God come back to us again and give us more instructions about this son who is to be born."

⁹God answered Manoah's prayer, and the angel of God appeared once again to his wife as she was sitting in the field. But her husband, Manoah, was not with her. ¹⁰So she quickly ran and told her husband, "The man who appeared to me the other day is here again!"

¹¹Manoah ran back with his wife and asked, "Are you the man who spoke to my wife the other day?"

"Yes," he replied, "I am."

¹²So Manoah asked him, "When your words come true, what kind of rules should govern the boy's life and work?"

**13:4** Hebrew *any unclean thing;* also in 13:7, 14.

---

**12:8-15** There is little else known about these three judges or their importance. The large number of children and donkeys are an indication of the wealth of these men.

**13:1** The Philistines lived on the west side of Canaan, along the Mediterranean seacoast. From Samson's day until the time of David they were the major enemy force in the land and a constant threat to Israel. The Philistines were fierce warriors; they had the advantage over Israel in numbers, tactical expertise, and technology. They knew the secret of making weapons out of iron (1 Samuel 13:19-22). But none of that mattered when God was fighting for Israel.

**13:1ff** Once again the cycle of sin, judgment, and repentance began (3:8, 9, 14, 15; 4:1-4; 6:1-14; 10:6–11:11). The Israelites would not turn to God unless they had been stunned by suffering, oppression, and death. This suffering was not caused by God, but resulted from the fact that the people ignored God, their Judge

and Ruler. What will it take for you to follow God? The warnings in God's Word are clear: If we continue to harden our hearts against God, we can expect the same fate as Israel.

**13:5** Samson was to be a Nazirite—a person who took a vow to be set apart for God's service. Samson's parents made the vow for him. A Nazirite vow was sometimes temporary, but in Samson's case, it was for life. As a Nazirite, Samson could not cut his hair, touch a dead body, or drink anything containing alcohol.

Although Samson often used poor judgment and sinned terribly, he accomplished much when he determined to be set apart for God. In this way he was like the nation Israel. As long as the Israelites remained set apart for God, the nation thrived. But they fell into terrible sin when they ignored God.

13The angel of the LORD replied, "Be sure your wife follows the instructions I gave her. 14She must not eat grapes or raisins, drink wine or any other alcoholic drink, or eat any forbidden food."

15Then Manoah said to the angel of the LORD, "Please stay here until we can prepare a young goat for you to eat."

16"I will stay," the angel of the LORD replied, "but I will not eat anything. However, you may prepare a burnt offering as a sacrifice to the LORD." (Manoah didn't realize it was the angel of the LORD.)

17Then Manoah asked the angel of the LORD, "What is your name? For when all this comes true, we want to honor you."

18"Why do you ask my name?" the angel of the LORD replied. "It is too wonderful for you to understand."

19Then Manoah took a young goat and a grain offering and offered it on a rock as a sacrifice to the LORD. And as Manoah and his wife watched, the LORD did an amazing thing. 20As the flames from the altar shot up toward the sky, the angel of the LORD ascended in the fire. When Manoah and his wife saw this, they fell with their faces to the ground.

21The angel did not appear again to Manoah and his wife. Manoah finally realized it was the angel of the LORD, 22and he said to his wife, "We will certainly die, for we have seen God!"

23But his wife said, "If the LORD were going to kill us, he wouldn't have accepted our burnt offering and grain offering. He wouldn't have appeared to us and told us this wonderful thing and done these miracles."

24When her son was born, she named him Samson. And the LORD blessed him as he grew up. 25And the Spirit of the LORD began to stir him while he lived in Mahaneh-dan, which is located between the towns of Zorah and Eshtaol.

## Samson's Riddle

**14** One day when Samson was in Timnah, one of the Philistine women caught his eye. 2When he returned home, he told his father and mother, "A young Philistine woman in Timnah caught my eye. I want to marry her. Get her for me."

3His father and mother objected. "Isn't there even one woman in our tribe or among all the Israelites you could marry?" they asked. "Why must you go to the pagan Philistines to find a wife?"

But Samson told his father, "Get her for me! She looks good to me." 4His father and mother didn't realize the LORD was at work in this, creating an opportunity to work against the Philistines, who ruled over Israel at that time.

5As Samson and his parents were going down to Timnah, a young lion suddenly attacked Samson near the vineyards of Timnah. 6At that moment the Spirit of the LORD came powerfully upon him, and he ripped the lion's jaws apart with his bare hands. He did it as easily

13:15 Judg 6:19
13:17 Gen 32:29
13:19 Judg 6:20-21
13:22 Gen 32:30; Judg 6:22
13:24 1 Sam 3:19; Luke 1:80; Heb 11:32
13:25 Judg 3:10; 18:11-12; 1 Sam 10:6, 10
14:2 Gen 21:21
14:3 Deut 7:3
14:4 Josh 11:20
14:6 Judg 13:25; 1 Sam 17:34-36

**13:18** Why did the angel keep his name a secret? In those days people believed that if they knew someone's name, they knew his character and how to control him. By not giving his name, the angel was not allowing himself to be controlled by Manoah. He was also saying that his name was a mystery beyond understanding and too wonderful to imagine. Manoah asked the angel for an answer that he wouldn't have understood. Sometimes we ask God questions and then receive no answer. This may not be because God is saying no. We may have asked for knowledge beyond our ability to understand or accept.

**13:19** Manoah sacrificed a grain offering to the Lord. A grain offering was grain, oil, and flour shaped into a cake and burned on the altar along with the *burnt offering* (the young goat). The grain offering, described in Leviticus 2, was offered to God as a sign of honor, respect, and worship. It was an acknowledgment that because the Israelites' food came from God, they owed their lives to him. With the grain offering, Manoah showed his desire to serve God and demonstrated his respect.

**13:25** Samson's tribe, Dan, continued to wander in their inherited land (18:1), which was yet unconquered (Joshua 19:47, 48). Samson must have grown up with his warlike tribe's yearnings for a permanent and settled territory. Thus, his visits to the tribal

army camp stirred his heart, and God's Spirit began preparing him for his role as judge and leader against the Philistines.

Perhaps there are things that stir your heart. These may indicate areas where God wants to use you. God uses a variety of means to develop and prepare us: hereditary traits, environmental influences, and personal experiences. As with Samson, this preparation often begins long before adulthood. Work at being sensitive to the Holy Spirit's leading and the tasks God has prepared for you. Your past may be more useful to you than you imagine.

**14:3** Samson's parents objected to his marrying the Philistine woman for several reasons: (1) It was against God's law (Exodus 34:15-17; Deuteronomy 7:1-4). A stark example of what happened when the Israelites married pagans can be found in 3:5-7. (2) The Philistines were Israel's greatest enemies. Marriage to a hated Philistine would be a disgrace to Samson's family. But Samson's father gave in to Samson's demand and allowed the marriage, even though he had the right to refuse his son.

**14:6** "The Spirit of the LORD came powerfully upon him" refers to the unusual physical strength given him by the Spirit of the Lord. Samson did not seem to be affected in any other way than increased physical strength.

as if it were a young goat. But he didn't tell his father or mother about it. ⁷When Samson arrived in Timnah, he talked with the woman and was very pleased with her.

⁸Later, when he returned to Timnah for the wedding, he turned off the path to look at the carcass of the lion. And he found that a swarm of bees had made some honey in the carcass. ⁹He scooped some of the honey into his hands and ate it along the way. He also gave some to his father and mother, and they ate it. But he didn't tell them he had taken the honey from the carcass of the lion.

¹⁰As his father was making final arrangements for the marriage, Samson threw a party at Timnah, as was the custom for elite young men. ¹¹When the bride's parents* saw him, they selected thirty young men from the town to be his companions.

¹²Samson said to them, "Let me tell you a riddle. If you solve my riddle during these seven days of the celebration, I will give you thirty fine linen robes and thirty sets of festive clothing. ¹³But if you can't solve it, then you must give me thirty fine linen robes and thirty sets of festive clothing."

"All right," they agreed, "let's hear your riddle."

¹⁴So he said:

"Out of the one who eats came something to eat;
out of the strong came something sweet."

**14:12**
Gen 29:27
Ezek 17:2

**14:11** Hebrew *they.*

---

**SAMSON**

It is sad to be remembered for what one might have been. Samson had tremendous potential. Not many people have started life with credentials like his. Born as a result of God's plan in the lives of Manoah and his wife, Samson was to do a great work for God—to rescue Israel from the Philistines. To help him accomplish God's plan, he was given enormous physical strength.

Because Samson wasted his strength on practical jokes and getting out of scrapes, and because he eventually gave it up altogether to satisfy the woman he loved, we tend to see him as a failure. We remember him as the judge in Israel who spent his last days grinding grain in an enemy prison, and we say, "What wasted potential!"

Yes, Samson wasted his life. He could have strengthened his nation. He could have returned his people to the worship of God. He could have wiped out the Philistines. But even though he did none of those things, Samson still accomplished the purpose announced by the angel who visited his parents before his birth. In his final act, Samson began to rescue Israel from the Philistines.

Interestingly, the New Testament does not mention Samson's failures or his heroic feats of strength. In Hebrews 11:33, he is simply listed with others who "overthrew kingdoms, ruled with justice, and received what God had promised them," and in other ways were given superhuman aid. In the end, Samson recognized his dependence on God. When he died, God turned his failures and defeats into victory. Samson's story teaches us that it is never too late to start over. However badly we may have failed in the past, today is not too late for us to put our complete trust in God.

| | |
|---|---|
| **Strengths and accomplishments** | • Dedicated to God from birth as a Nazirite<br>• Known for his feats of strength<br>• Listed in the Hall of Faith in Hebrews 11<br>• Began to free Israel from Philistine oppression |
| **Weaknesses and mistakes** | • Made a vow; violated God's laws on many occasions<br>• Was controlled by sensuality<br>• Confided in the wrong people<br>• Used his gifts and abilities unwisely |
| **Lessons from his life** | • Great strength in one area of life does not make up for great weaknesses in other areas<br>• God's presence does not overwhelm a person's will<br>• God can use a person of faith in spite of his or her mistakes |
| **Vital statistics** | • Where: Zorah, Timnah, Ashkelon, Gaza, valley of Sorek<br>• Occupation: Judge<br>• Relative: Father: Manoah<br>• Contemporaries: Delilah, Samuel (who might have been born while Samson was a judge) |
| **Key verse** | "You will become pregnant and give birth to a son, and his hair must never be cut. For he will be dedicated to God as a Nazirite from birth. He will begin to rescue Israel from the Philistines" (Judges 13:5). |

His story is told in Judges 13—16. He is also mentioned in Hebrews 11:32.

Three days later they were still trying to figure it out. 15On the fourth* day they said to Samson's wife, "Entice your husband to explain the riddle for us, or we will burn down your father's house with you in it. Did you invite us to this party just to make us poor?"

16So Samson's wife came to him in tears and said, "You don't love me; you hate me! You have given my people a riddle, but you haven't told me the answer."

"I haven't even given the answer to my father or mother," he replied. "Why should I tell you?" 17So she cried whenever she was with him and kept it up for the rest of the celebration. At last, on the seventh day he told her the answer because she was tormenting him with her nagging. Then she explained the riddle to the young men.

18So before sunset of the seventh day, the men of the town came to Samson with their answer:

"What is sweeter than honey?
  What is stronger than a lion?"

Samson replied, "If you hadn't plowed with my heifer, you wouldn't have solved my riddle!"

19Then the Spirit of the LORD came powerfully upon him. He went down to the town of Ashkelon, killed thirty men, took their belongings, and gave their clothing to the men who had solved his riddle. But Samson was furious about what had happened, and he went back home to live with his father and mother. 20So his wife was given in marriage to the man who had been Samson's best man at the wedding.

### Samson's Vengeance on the Philistines

**15** Later on, during the wheat harvest, Samson took a young goat as a present to his wife. He said, "I'm going into my wife's room to sleep with her," but her father wouldn't let him in.

2"I truly thought you must hate her," her father explained, "so I gave her in marriage to your best man. But look, her younger sister is even more beautiful than she is. Marry her instead."

3Samson said, "This time I cannot be blamed for everything I am going to do to you Philistines." 4Then he went out and caught 300 foxes. He tied their tails together in pairs, and he fastened a torch to each pair of tails. 5Then he lit the torches and let the foxes run through the grain fields of the Philistines. He burned all their grain to the ground, including the sheaves and the uncut grain. He also destroyed their vineyards and olive groves.

6"Who did this?" the Philistines demanded.

"Samson," was the reply, "because his father-in-law from Timnah gave Samson's wife to be married to his best man." So the Philistines went and got the woman and her father and burned them to death.

7"Because you did this," Samson vowed, "I won't rest until I take my revenge on you!" 8So he attacked the Philistines with great fury and killed many of them. Then he went to live in a cave in the rock of Etam.

9The Philistines retaliated by setting up camp in Judah and spreading out near the town of Lehi. 10The men of Judah asked the Philistines, "Why are you attacking us?"

The Philistines replied, "We've come to capture Samson. We've come to pay him back for what he did to us."

11So 3,000 men of Judah went down to get Samson at the cave in the rock of Etam. They said to Samson, "Don't you realize the Philistines rule over us? What are you doing to us?"

But Samson replied, "I only did to them what they did to me."

12But the men of Judah told him, "We have come to tie you up and hand you over to the Philistines."

**14:15** As in Greek version; Hebrew reads *seventh.*

---

*Marginal cross-references:*

**14:15** Judg 15:6; 16:5

**14:19** Judg 3:10

**14:20** John 3:29

**15:2** Judg 14:20

**15:6** Judg 14:15

**15:11** Judg 13:1; 14:4; 15:20

---

**14:18** "If you hadn't plowed with my heifer" means "If you had not manipulated my wife." If they hadn't threatened his wife, they wouldn't have learned the answer to his riddle.

**14:19** Samson impulsively used the special gift God gave him for selfish purposes. Today, God distributes abilities and skills throughout the church (1 Corinthians 12:1ff). The apostle Paul states that these gifts are to be used "to do his work and build up the church, the body of Christ" (Ephesians 4:12). To use these abilities for selfish purposes is to rob the church and fellow believers of strength. As you use the gifts God has given you, be sure you are helping others, not just yourself.

**15:1ff** Samson's reply in 15:11 tells the story of this chapter: "I only did to them what they did to me." Revenge is an uncontrollable monster. Each act of retaliation brings another. It is a boomerang that cannot be thrown without cost to the thrower. The revenge cycle can be halted only by forgiveness.

"All right," Samson said. "But promise that you won't kill me yourselves."

<sup>13</sup>"We will only tie you up and hand you over to the Philistines," they replied. "We won't kill you." So they tied him up with two new ropes and brought him up from the rock.

<sup>14</sup>As Samson arrived at Lehi, the Philistines came shouting in triumph. But the Spirit of the LORD came powerfully upon Samson, and he snapped the ropes on his arms as if they were burnt strands of flax, and they fell from his wrists. <sup>15</sup>Then he found the jawbone of a recently killed donkey. He picked it up and killed 1,000 Philistines with it. <sup>16</sup>Then Samson said,

> "With the jawbone of a donkey,
>   I've piled them in heaps!
> With the jawbone of a donkey,
>   I've killed a thousand men!"

<sup>17</sup>When he finished his boasting, he threw away the jawbone; and the place was named Jawbone Hill.*

<sup>18</sup>Samson was now very thirsty, and he cried out to the LORD, "You have accomplished this great victory by the strength of your servant. Must I now die of thirst and fall into the hands of these pagans?" <sup>19</sup>So God caused water to gush out of a hollow in the ground at Lehi, and Samson was revived as he drank. Then he named that place "The Spring of the One Who Cried Out,"* and it is still in Lehi to this day.

<sup>20</sup>Samson judged Israel for twenty years during the period when the Philistines dominated the land.

### Samson Carries Away Gaza's Gates

**16** One day Samson went to the Philistine town of Gaza and spent the night with a prostitute. <sup>2</sup>Word soon spread* that Samson was there, so the men of Gaza gathered together and waited all night at the town gates. They kept quiet during the night, saying to themselves, "When the light of morning comes, we will kill him."

<sup>3</sup>But Samson stayed in bed only until midnight. Then he got up, took hold of the doors of the town gate, including the two posts, and lifted them up, bar and all. He put them on his shoulders and carried them all the way to the top of the hill across from Hebron.

### Samson and Delilah

<sup>4</sup>Some time later Samson fell in love with a woman named Delilah, who lived in the valley of Sorek. <sup>5</sup>The rulers of the Philistines went to her and said, "Entice Samson to tell you what makes him so strong and how he can be overpowered and tied up securely. Then each of us will give you 1,100 pieces* of silver."

**Cross-references (left margin):**

15:14 Judg 14:19

15:15 Lev 26:8

15:19 Gen 45:27; 1 Sam 30:12; Isa 40:29

15:20 Judg 13:1; 16:31; Heb 11:32

16:1 Josh 15:47

16:2 Ps 118:10-12

16:5 Judg 14:15

**15:17** Hebrew *Ramath-lehi.* **15:19** Hebrew *En-hakkore.* **16:2** As in Greek and Syriac versions and Latin Vulgate; Hebrew lacks *Word soon spread.* **16:5** Hebrew *1,100 shekels,* about 28 pounds or 12.5 kilograms in weight.

---

**SAMSON'S VENTURES** Samson grew up in Zorah and wanted to marry a Philistine girl from Timnah. Tricked at his own wedding feast, he went to Ashkelon and killed some Philistine men and stole their clothes to pay off a bet. Samson then let himself be captured and brought to Lehi, where he snapped his ropes and killed 1,000 people.

**15:14-17** The Lord's strength came upon Samson, but he was proud and boasted only of his own strength. "With the jawbone of a donkey . . . I've killed a thousand men!" he said. Pride can cause us to take credit for work we've done only because of God's strength.

**15:18** Samson was physically and emotionally exhausted. After a great personal victory, his attitude declined quickly into self-pity—"Must I now die of thirst?" Emotionally, we are most vulnerable after a great effort or when faced with real physical needs. Severe depression often follows great achievements, so don't be surprised if you feel drained after a personal victory.

During these times of vulnerability, avoid the temptation to think that God owes you for your efforts. It was *his* strength that gave you victory. Concentrate on keeping your attitudes, actions, and words focused on God instead of yourself.

**15:20** Apparently Samson was appointed Israel's judge after this victory over the Philistines.

**16:5** The Philistines were ruled by five rulers, not just one. Each ruler ruled from a different city—Ashdod, Ashkelon, Ekron, Gath, or Gaza. Each of these cities was an important center for trade and commerce. Given Delilah's character, it is little wonder that she betrayed Samson when these rich and powerful men paid her a personal visit.

⁶So Delilah said to Samson, "Please tell me what makes you so strong and what it would take to tie you up securely."

⁷Samson replied, "If I were tied up with seven new bowstrings that have not yet been dried, I would become as weak as anyone else."

⁸So the Philistine rulers brought Delilah seven new bowstrings, and she tied Samson up with them. ⁹She had hidden some men in one of the inner rooms of her house, and she cried out, "Samson! The Philistines have come to capture you!" But Samson snapped the bowstrings as a piece of string snaps when it is burned by a fire. So the secret of his strength was not discovered.

¹⁰Afterward Delilah said to him, "You've been making fun of me and telling me lies! Now please tell me how you can be tied up securely."

¹¹Samson replied, "If I were tied up with brand-new ropes that had never been used, I would become as weak as anyone else."

**16:11**
Judg 15:13

¹²So Delilah took new ropes and tied him up with them. The men were hiding in the inner room as before, and again Delilah cried out, "Samson! The Philistines have come to capture you!" But again Samson snapped the ropes from his arms as if they were thread.

¹³Then Delilah said, "You've been making fun of me and telling me lies! Now tell me how you can be tied up securely."

Samson replied, "If you were to weave the seven braids of my hair into the fabric on your loom and tighten it with the loom shuttle, I would become as weak as anyone else."

So while he slept, Delilah wove the seven braids of his hair into the fabric. ¹⁴Then she tightened it with the loom shuttle.* Again she cried out, "Samson! The Philistines have come to capture you!" But Samson woke up, pulled back the loom shuttle, and yanked his hair away from the loom and the fabric.

¹⁵Then Delilah pouted, "How can you tell me, 'I love you,' when you don't share your secrets with me? You've made fun of me three times now, and you still haven't told me what makes you so strong!" ¹⁶She tormented him with her nagging day after day until he was sick to death of it.

**16:15**
Judg 14:16

¹⁷Finally, Samson shared his secret with her. "My hair has never been cut," he confessed, "for I was dedicated to God as a Nazirite from birth. If my head were shaved, my strength would leave me, and I would become as weak as anyone else."

**16:17**
Num 6:2, 5
Judg 13:5

¹⁸Delilah realized he had finally told her the truth, so she sent for the Philistine rulers. "Come back one more time," she said, "for he has finally told me his secret." So the Philistine rulers returned with the money in their hands. ¹⁹Delilah lulled Samson to sleep with his head in her lap, and then she called in a man to shave off the seven locks of his hair. In this way she began to bring him down,* and his strength left him.

**16:13-14** As in Greek version and Latin Vulgate; Hebrew lacks *I would become as weak as anyone else. / So while he slept, Delilah wove the seven braids of his hair into the fabric.* ¹⁴*Then she tightened it with the loom shuttle.*
**16:19** Or *she began to torment him.* Greek version reads *He began to grow weak.*

---

**16:15** Samson was deceived because he wanted to believe Delilah's lies. Although he could strangle a lion, he could not smother his burning lust and see Delilah for who she really was. How can you keep your desire for love and sexual pleasure from deceiving you? (1) You must decide what kind of a person you will love *before* passion takes over. Determine whether a person's character and faith in God are as desirable as his or her physical appearance. (2) Because most of the time you spend with your spouse will *not* involve sex, your companion's personality, temperament, and commitment to solve problems must be as gratifying as his or her kisses. (3) Be patient. Time and observation often reveal what is beneath the pleasant appearance and attentive touch.

**16:16, 17** Delilah kept asking Samson for the secret of his strength until he finally grew tired of hearing her nagging and gave in. This was the second time that Samson allowed himself to be worn down by constant nagging (14:17). What a pitiful excuse for disobedience. Don't allow anyone—no matter how attractive, persuasive, or persistent—to talk you into doing wrong.

**16:19** Delilah was a deceitful woman with honey on her lips and poison in her heart. Cold and calculating, she toyed with Samson, pretending to love him while looking for personal gain. How could Samson be so foolish? Four times Delilah took advantage of him. If he didn't realize what was happening after the first or second experience, surely he should have understood

**SAMSON AND DELILAH**   Samson was seduced by a Philistine woman named Delilah who lived in the valley of Sorek. She betrayed the secret of his strength to the Philistines, who captured him and led him away in chains to Gaza. There he died. His relatives buried him between Zorah and Eshtaol.

**16:20**
1 Sam 16:14; 18:12

²⁰Then she cried out, "Samson! The Philistines have come to capture you!"

When he woke up, he thought, "I will do as before and shake myself free." But he didn't realize the LORD had left him.

²¹So the Philistines captured him and gouged out his eyes. They took him to Gaza, where he was bound with bronze chains and forced to grind grain in the prison.

²²But before long, his hair began to grow back.

### Samson's Final Victory

**16:23**
1 Sam 5:2

²³The Philistine rulers held a great festival, offering sacrifices and praising their god, Dagon. They said, "Our god has given us victory over our enemy Samson!"

²⁴When the people saw him, they praised their god, saying, "Our god has delivered our enemy to us! The one who killed so many of us is now in our power!"

²⁵Half drunk by now, the people demanded, "Bring out Samson so he can amuse us!" So he was brought from the prison to amuse them, and they had him stand between the pillars supporting the roof.

**DELILAH**

**A** person's greatest accomplishment may well be helping others accomplish great things. Likewise, a person's greatest failure may be preventing others from achieving greatness. Delilah played a minor role in Samson's life, but her effect was devastating, for she influenced him to betray his special calling from God. Motivated by greed, Delilah used her persistence to wear down Samson. His infatuation with her made Samson a vulnerable target. For all his physical strength, he was no match for her nagging, and he paid a great price for giving in to her. Delilah is never mentioned again in the Bible. Her unfaithfulness to Samson brought ruin to him and to her people.

Are people helped by knowing you? Do they find that knowing you challenges them to be the best they can be? Even more important, does knowing you help their relationship with God? What do your demands for their time and attention tell them about your real care for them? Are you willing to be God's instrument in the lives of others?

| | |
|---|---|
| **Strength and accomplishment** | • Persistent when faced with obstacles |
| **Weaknesses and mistakes** | • Valued money more than relationships<br>• Betrayed the man who trusted her |
| **Lesson from her life** | • We need to be careful to place our trust only in people who are trustworthy |
| **Vital statistics** | • Where: Valley of Sorek<br>• Contemporary: Samson |
| **Key verses** | "She tormented him with her nagging day after day until he was sick to death of it. Finally, Samson shared his secret with her" (Judges 16:16, 17). |

Her story is told in Judges 16.

the situation by the fourth time! We think Samson is foolish, but how many times do we allow ourselves to be deceived by flattery and give in to temptation and wrong beliefs? Avoid falling prey to deceit by asking God to help you distinguish between deception and truth.

**16:21** Samson, the mighty warrior, became a slave. Rather than kill him, the Philistines preferred to humiliate him by gouging out his eyes and making him grind grain. Samson now had plenty of time to wonder if Delilah's charms were worth spending the rest of his life in humiliation.

Although God did not completely abandon Samson (16:28-30), he allowed Samson's decision to stand, and the consequences of his decision followed naturally. We may choose to be close to God or to go our own way, but there are consequences resulting from our choice. Samson didn't choose to be captured, but he chose to be with Delilah, and he could not escape the consequences of his decision.

**16:21** Blinded and without strength, Samson was taken to Gaza where he would spend the rest of his short life. Gaza was one of the five capital cities of the Philistines. Known for its many wells, Gaza was a vital stop along a great caravan route that connected Egypt to the south with Aram to the north. The Philistines prob-

ably showed off their prize captive, Samson, to many dignitaries passing through.

Ironically, it was in Gaza that Samson had earlier demonstrated his great strength by uprooting the city gates (16:1-3). Now he was an example of weakness.

**16:23, 24** Dagon was the chief god of the Philistines, the god of grain and harvest. Many temples were built to Dagon, and the worship there included human sacrifice. The temples were also the local entertainment centers. Just as people today crowd into theaters, Philistine townspeople crowded into the local temple. They sat on the flat temple roof and looked into the courtyard below. What they often saw was the torture and humiliation of prisoners.

Since the Philistines had control over the Israelites, they thought their god was stronger. But when the Ark of God was placed before Dagon in a similar temple, the idol fell over and broke into pieces (1 Samuel 5:1-7). God's strength goes beyond numbers or physical might.

26Samson said to the young servant who was leading him by the hand, "Place my hands against the pillars that hold up the temple. I want to rest against them." 27Now the temple was completely filled with people. All the Philistine rulers were there, and there were about 3,000 men and women on the roof who were watching as Samson amused them.

28Then Samson prayed to the LORD, "Sovereign LORD, remember me again. O God, please strengthen me just one more time. With one blow let me pay back the Philistines for the loss of my two eyes." 29Then Samson put his hands on the two center pillars that held up the temple. Pushing against them with both hands, 30he prayed, "Let me die with the Philistines." And the temple crashed down on the Philistine rulers and all the people. So he killed more people when he died than he had during his entire lifetime.

31Later his brothers and other relatives went down to get his body. They took him back home and buried him between Zorah and Eshtaol, where his father, Manoah, was buried. Samson had judged Israel for twenty years.

**16:28** Judg 15:18

**16:31** Judg 15:20

## C. THE MORAL FAILURE OF ISRAEL (17:1—21:25)

This section shows Israel falling into idolatry, moral decline, and petty fighting. Israel, the nation that was to set the example for spiritual living, had instead become morally depraved. When Israel did serve God, and that was seldom, it was often from selfish motives. Selfish obedience does not bring us far. Genuine obedience is motivated by a love and reverence for God himself.

### 1. Idolatry in the tribe of Dan

*Micah's Idols*

**17** There was a man named Micah, who lived in the hill country of Ephraim. 2One day he said to his mother, "I heard you place a curse on the person who stole 1,100 pieces* of silver from you. Well, I have the money. I am the one who took it."

"The LORD bless you for admitting it," his mother replied. 3He returned the money to her, and she said, "I now dedicate these silver coins to the LORD. In honor of my son, I will have an image carved and an idol cast."

4So when he returned the money to his mother, she took 200 silver coins and gave them to a silversmith, who made them into an image and an idol. And these were placed in Micah's house. 5Micah set up a shrine for the idol, and he made a sacred ephod and some household idols. Then he installed one of his sons as his personal priest.

6In those days Israel had no king; all the people did whatever seemed right in their own eyes.

7One day a young Levite, who had been living in Bethlehem in Judah, arrived in that area. 8He had left Bethlehem in search of another place to live, and as he traveled, he came to the hill country of Ephraim. He happened to stop at Micah's house as he was traveling through. 9"Where are you from?" Micah asked him.

**17:3** Exod 20:4, 23; 34:17

**17:5** Gen 31:19 Judg 8:27

**17:6** Deut 12:8 Judg 18:1; 19:1; 21:25

**17:7** Judg 19:1 Ruth 1:1-2 Mic 5:2 Matt 2:1

**17:2** Hebrew *1,100 shekels*, about 28 pounds or 12.5 kilograms in weight.

**16:28-30** In spite of Samson's past, God still answered his prayer and destroyed the pagan temple and worshipers. God still loved him. He was willing to hear Samson's prayer of confession and repentance and use him this final time. One of the effects of sin in our lives is to keep us from feeling like praying. But perfect moral behavior is not a condition for prayer. Don't let guilt feelings over sin keep you from your only means of restoration. No matter how long you have been away from God, he is ready to hear from you and restore you to a right relationship. Every situation can be salvaged if you are willing to turn again to him. If God could still work in Samson's situation, he can certainly make something worthwhile out of yours.

**17:2** Micah and his mother seemed to be good and moral and may have sincerely desired to worship God, but they disobeyed God by following their own desires instead of doing what God wanted. The attitude that prevailed in Micah's day was this: "The people did whatever seemed right in their own eyes" (17:6). This is remarkably similar to today's prevailing attitudes. But God has given us standards. He has not left our conduct up to us and our opinions. We can avoid conforming to society's low standards by taking God's commands seriously and applying them to life.

Independence and self-reliance are positive traits, but only within the framework of God's standards.

**17:6** Today, as in Micah's day, everyone seems to put his or her own interests first. Time has not changed human nature. Most people still reject God's right way of living. The people in Micah's time replaced the true worship of God with a homemade version of worship. As a result, justice was soon replaced by revenge and chaos. Ignoring God's direction led to confusion and destruction. Anyone who has not submitted to God will end up doing whatever seems right at the time. This tendency is present in all of us. To know what is really right and to have the strength to do it, we need to draw closer to God and his Word.

**17:7-12** Apparently the Israelites no longer supported the priests and Levites with their tithes because so many of the people no longer worshiped God. The young Levite in this story probably left his home in Bethlehem because the money he received from the people there was not enough to live on. But Israel's moral decay affected even the priests and Levites. This man accepted money (17:10, 11), idols (18:20), and position (17:12) in a way that was inconsistent with God's laws. While Micah revealed the religious downfall of individual Israelites, this priest illustrated the religious downfall of priests and Levites.

He replied, "I am a Levite from Bethlehem in Judah, and I am looking for a place to live."

**17:10**
Judg 18:19

10 "Stay here with me," Micah said, "and you can be a father and priest to me. I will give you ten pieces* of silver a year, plus a change of clothes and your food." 11 The Levite agreed to this, and the young man became like one of Micah's sons.

**17:12**
Num 16:10
Judg 18:1-7

12 So Micah installed the Levite as his personal priest, and he lived in Micah's house. 13 "I know the LORD will bless me now," Micah said, "because I have a Levite serving as my priest."

### Idolatry in the Tribe of Dan

**18:1**
Josh 19:40-48
Judg 17:6; 19:1
**18:2**
Judg 13:25

**18** Now in those days Israel had no king. And the tribe of Dan was trying to find a place where they could settle, for they had not yet moved into the land assigned to them when the land was divided among the tribes of Israel. 2 So the men of Dan chose from their clans five capable warriors from the towns of Zorah and Eshtaol to scout out a land for them to settle in.

When these warriors arrived in the hill country of Ephraim, they came to Micah's house and spent the night there. 3 While at Micah's house, they recognized the young Levite's accent, so they went over and asked him, "Who brought you here, and what are you doing in this place? Why are you here?" 4 He told them about his agreement with Micah and that he had been hired as Micah's personal priest.

**18:4**
Judg 17:10-12

5 Then they said, "Ask God whether or not our journey will be successful."

6 "Go in peace," the priest replied. "For the LORD is watching over your journey."

**18:7**
Josh 19:47

7 So the five men went on to the town of Laish, where they noticed the people living carefree lives, like the Sidonians; they were peaceful and secure.* The people were also wealthy because their land was very fertile. And they lived a great distance from Sidon and had no allies nearby.

8 When the men returned to Zorah and Eshtaol, their relatives asked them, "What did you find?"

**18:10**
Deut 8:9

9 The men replied, "Come on, let's attack them! We have seen the land, and it is very good. What are you waiting for? Don't hesitate to go and take possession of it. 10 When you get there, you will find the people living carefree lives. God has given us a spacious and fertile land, lacking in nothing!"

11 So 600 men from the tribe of Dan, armed with weapons of war, set out from Zorah and Eshtaol. 12 They camped at a place west of Kiriath-jearim in Judah, which is called Mahaneh-dan* to this day. 13 Then they went on from there into the hill country of Ephraim and came to the house of Micah.

**17:10** Hebrew *10 shekels*, about 4 ounces or 114 grams in weight.  **18:7** The meaning of the Hebrew is uncertain.
**18:12** *Mahaneh-dan* means "the camp of Dan."

---

**18:1** The Danites had been assigned enough land to meet their needs (Joshua 19:40-48). However, because they failed to trust God to help them conquer their territory, the Amorites forced them into the hill country and wouldn't let them settle in the plains (Judges 1:34). Rather than fight for their allotted territory, they preferred to look for new land in the north where resistance from the enemy wouldn't be so tough. It was while they were traveling north that some of their men passed Micah's home and stole some of his idols.

**18:4-6** Priests and their assistants were all members of the tribe of Levi (Numbers 3:5-13). They were to serve the people, teach them how to worship God, and perform the rituals involved in the worship services both at the Tabernacle in Shiloh and in the designated cities throughout the land. But this disobedient priest showed disrespect for God because (1) he performed his duties in a house. Priestly duties were to be performed only in the Tabernacle or a designated city. This requirement was intended to prevent God's laws from being changed. (2) He carried idols with him (18:20). (3) He claimed to speak for God when God had not spoken through him (18:6).

**18:11-26** Through this entire incident, no one desired to worship God; instead, they wanted to use God for selfish gain. Today some people go to church to feel better, be accepted, relieve guilt, and gain business contacts or friends. Beware of following God for selfish gain rather than selfless service.

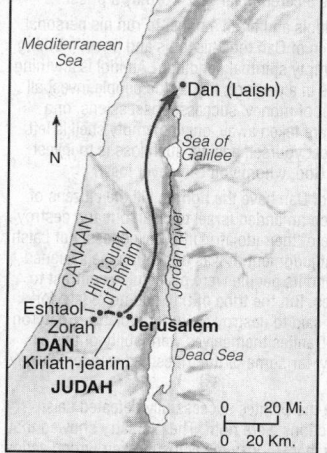

Mediterranean Sea

N

Dan (Laish)

Sea of Galilee

CANAAN

Hill Country of Ephraim

Jordan River

Eshtaol
Zorah  **Jerusalem**
**DAN**
Kiriath-jearim  Dead Sea
**JUDAH**

0          20 Mi.

0          20 Km.

**THE TRIBE OF DAN MOVES NORTH**
Troops from the tribe of Dan traveled from Zorah and Eshtaol into the hill country of Ephraim, where they persuaded Micah's priest to come with them. They continued north to Laish, where they ruthlessly butchered its citizens. The city was renamed Dan, and the priest's idols became the focus of their worship.

¹⁴The five men who had scouted out the land around Laish explained to the others, "These buildings contain a sacred ephod, as well as some household idols, a carved image, and a cast idol. What do you think you should do?" ¹⁵Then the five men turned off the road and went over to Micah's house, where the young Levite lived, and greeted him kindly. ¹⁶As the 600 armed warriors from the tribe of Dan stood at the entrance of the gate, ¹⁷the five scouts entered the shrine and removed the carved image, the sacred ephod, the household idols, and the cast idol. Meanwhile, the priest was standing at the gate with the 600 armed warriors.

¹⁸When the priest saw the men carrying all the sacred objects out of Micah's shrine, he said, "What are you doing?"

¹⁹"Be quiet and come with us," they said. "Be a father and priest to all of us. Isn't it better to be a priest for an entire tribe and clan of Israel than for the household of just one man?"

²⁰The young priest was quite happy to go with them, so he took along the sacred ephod, the household idols, and the carved image. ²¹They turned and started on their way again, placing their children, livestock, and possessions in front of them.

²²When the people from the tribe of Dan were quite a distance from Micah's house, the people who lived near Micah came chasing after them. ²³They were shouting as they caught up with them. The men of Dan turned around and said to Micah, "What's the matter? Why have you called these men together and chased after us like this?"

²⁴"What do you mean, 'What's the matter?'" Micah replied. "You've taken away all the gods I have made, and my priest, and I have nothing left!"

²⁵The men of Dan said, "Watch what you say! There are some short-tempered men around here who might get angry and kill you and your family." ²⁶So the men of Dan continued on their way. When Micah saw that there were too many of them for him to attack, he turned around and went home.

²⁷Then, with Micah's idols and his priest, the men of Dan came to the town of Laish, whose people were peaceful and secure. They attacked with swords and burned the town to the ground. ²⁸There was no one to rescue the people, for they lived a great distance from Sidon and had no allies nearby. This happened in the valley near Beth-rehob.

Then the people of the tribe of Dan rebuilt the town and lived there. ²⁹They renamed the town Dan after their ancestor, Israel's son, but it had originally been called Laish.

³⁰Then they set up the carved image, and they appointed Jonathan son of Gershom, son of Moses,* as their priest. This family continued as priests for the tribe of Dan until the Exile. ³¹So Micah's carved image was worshiped by the tribe of Dan as long as the Tabernacle of God remained at Shiloh.

18:30 As in an ancient Hebrew tradition, some Greek manuscripts, and Latin Vulgate; Masoretic Text reads *son of Manasseh.*

**Cross-references (margin):**
18:14 Judg 17:5
18:19 Judg 17:10
18:27 Josh 19:47
18:28 2 Sam 10:6
18:30 Exod 2:22; 18:3
18:31 Josh 18:1

---

**18:14** An ephod was a ceremonial vest worn by a priest.

**18:24** Micah made idols and hired a priest to run his personal religion. When the men of Dan took his idols and priest, nothing remained. What an empty spiritual condition! An idol is anything that takes God's place in a person's life. Some people invest all their energy in pursuit of money, success, possessions, or a career. If these idols are taken away, only an empty shell is left. The only way to protect yourself against such loss is to invest your life in the living God, whom you can never lose.

**18:27** Did the tribe of Dan have the right to kill the citizens of Laish? No. God had commanded Israel to clean out and destroy certain cities because of their idolatry and wickedness, but Laish did not fall under that judgment. It was not within the assigned boundaries of Dan, and its people were peaceful in contrast to the warlike Canaanites. But the tribe of Dan had no regard for God's law. God's law said to destroy a city for idolatry (Deuteronomy 13:12-15). The Danites themselves were guilty of this sin. This story shows how far some of the tribes had wandered away from God.

**18:27** Just because the Danites successfully defeated Laish doesn't mean their actions were right. Their idolatry showed that God was not guiding them. Today many justify their wrong actions by outward signs of success. They think that wealth, popularity, or lack of suffering is an indication of God's blessing. But many stories in the Bible indicate that evil and earthly success can go hand in hand (see, for example, 2 Kings 14:23-29). Success doesn't indicate God's approval. Don't allow personal success to become a measuring rod of whether or not you are pleasing God.

**18:30, 31** The tribe of Dan had stolen Micah's idols, and now they set them up in Laish. Although the Danites were actually denying God by worshiping these images (Exodus 20:1-5), they probably assumed they were worshiping God through them (see the note on Exodus 32:4, 5). Worshiping images of God is *not* worshiping God, even if it resembles true worship in some ways. People repeat the same mistake today when they claim to be Christians without really believing in God's power or changing their conduct to conform to his expectations. Godliness cannot be merely a claim. It must be a reality in our motives and in our actions.

**18:31** Shiloh was probably destroyed during the events reported in 1 Samuel 4 and 5, not long after the time described here. Because Shiloh was the religious center for Israel, all adult males were required to travel there for certain religious feasts. The tribe of Dan, however, set up idols and priests in the new territory they conquered. The fact that they were over 80 miles away from Shiloh may have been their excuse for not fulfilling the law's requirements. This act was a further demonstration of their disregard for God.

**18:31** The true worship of God should have been maintained through the Levitical priests scattered throughout the land and

## 2. War against the tribe of Benjamin
### The Levite and His Concubine

19:1
Judg 18:1

**19** Now in those days Israel had no king. There was a man from the tribe of Levi living in a remote area of the hill country of Ephraim. One day he brought home a woman from Bethlehem in Judah to be his concubine. 2But she became angry with him* and returned to her father's home in Bethlehem.

19:3
Gen 34:3; 50:21

After about four months, 3her husband set out for Bethlehem to speak personally to her and persuade her to come back. He took with him a servant and a pair of donkeys. When he arrived at* her father's house, her father saw him and welcomed him. 4Her father urged him to stay awhile, so he stayed three days, eating, drinking, and sleeping there.

19:5
Gen 18:5

5On the fourth day the man was up early, ready to leave, but the woman's father said to his son-in-law, "Have something to eat before you go." 6So the two men sat down together and had something to eat and drink. Then the woman's father said, "Please stay another night and enjoy yourself." 7The man got up to leave, but his father-in-law kept urging him to stay, so he finally gave in and stayed the night.

8On the morning of the fifth day he was up early again, ready to leave, and again the woman's father said, "Have something to eat; then you can leave later this afternoon." So they had another day of feasting. 9Later, as the man and his concubine and servant were preparing to leave, his father-in-law said, "Look, it's almost evening. Stay the night and enjoy yourself. Tomorrow you can get up early and be on your way."

19:10
Josh 15:8
1 Chr 11:4-5
19:11
Judg 19:19

10But this time the man was determined to leave. So he took his two saddled donkeys and his concubine and headed in the direction of Jebus (that is, Jerusalem). 11It was late in the day when they neared Jebus, and the man's servant said to him, "Let's stop at this Jebusite town and spend the night there."

12"No," his master said, "we can't stay in this foreign town where there are no Israelites. Instead, we will go on to Gibeah. 13Come on, let's try to get as far as Gibeah or Ramah, and we'll spend the night in one of those towns." 14So they went on. The sun was setting as they came to Gibeah, a town in the land of Benjamin, 15so they stopped there to spend the night. They rested in the town square, but no one took them in for the night.

19:16
Ps 104:23

16That evening an old man came home from his work in the fields. He was from the hill country of Ephraim, but he was living in Gibeah, where the people were from the tribe of Benjamin. 17When he saw the travelers sitting in the town square, he asked them where they were from and where they were going.

19:18
Judg 18:31

18"We have been in Bethlehem in Judah," the man replied. "We are on our way to a remote area in the hill country of Ephraim, which is my home. I traveled to Bethlehem, and now I'm returning home.* But no one has taken us in for the night, 19even though we have everything we need. We have straw and feed for our donkeys and plenty of bread and wine for ourselves."

19:21
Gen 24:32-33

20"You are welcome to stay with me," the old man said. "I will give you anything you might need. But whatever you do, don't spend the night in the square." 21So he took them home with him and fed the donkeys. After they washed their feet, they ate and drank together.

**19:2** Or *she was unfaithful to him.*   **19:3** As in Greek version; Hebrew reads *When she brought him to.*
**19:18** As in Greek version (see also 19:29); Hebrew reads *now I'm going to the Tabernacle of the LORD.*

---

the influence of the Tabernacle in Shiloh. This story shows how pagan influences and moral depravity had crept into every corner of Israelite culture. Although 300 years had passed since they entered the Promised Land, they still had not destroyed the idolatry and evil practices within it.

There may be a tendency in your life to allow "harmless" habits to have their own small corners, but they can become dominating forces. The values, attitudes, and practices you have adopted from the world's system can be exposed by applying the light of God's truth to them. Once you see them for what they are, you can begin to uproot them.

**19:1–21:25** What is the significance of this tragic story? When the Israelites' faith in God disintegrated, their unity as a nation also disintegrated. They could have taken complete possession of the land if they had obeyed God and trusted him to keep his promises. But when they forgot him, they lost their purpose, and

soon "the people did whatever seemed right in their own eyes" (21:25). When they stopped letting God lead them, they became no better than the evil people around them. When they made laws for their own benefit, they set standards far below God's. When you leave God out of your life, you may be shocked at what you are capable of doing (19:30).

**19:1** Having concubines was an accepted part of Israelite society although this is not what God intended (Genesis 2:24). A concubine had most of the duties but only some of the privileges of a wife. Although she was legally attached to one man, she and her children usually did not have the inheritance rights of the legal wife and legitimate children. Her primary purpose was giving the man sexual pleasure, bearing additional children, and contributing more help to the household or estate. Concubines were often foreign prisoners of war. But they could also be Israelites, as was probably the case in this story.

22 While they were enjoying themselves, a crowd of troublemakers from the town surrounded the house. They began beating at the door and shouting to the old man, "Bring out the man who is staying with you so we can have sex with him."

23 The old man stepped outside to talk to them. "No, my brothers, don't do such an evil thing. For this man is a guest in my house, and such a thing would be shameful. 24 Here, take my virgin daughter and this man's concubine. I will bring them out to you, and you can abuse them and do whatever you like. But don't do such a shameful thing to this man."

25 But they wouldn't listen to him. So the Levite took hold of his concubine and pushed her out the door. The men of the town abused her all night, taking turns raping her until morning. Finally, at dawn they let her go. 26 At daybreak the woman returned to the house where her husband was staying. She collapsed at the door of the house and lay there until it was light.

27 When her husband opened the door to leave, there lay his concubine with her hands on the threshold. 28 He said, "Get up! Let's go!" But there was no answer.* So he put her body on his donkey and took her home.

29 When he got home, he took a knife and cut his concubine's body into twelve pieces. Then he sent one piece to each tribe throughout all the territory of Israel.

30 Everyone who saw it said, "Such a horrible crime has not been committed in all the time since Israel left Egypt. Think about it! What are we going to do? Who's going to speak up?"

## Israel's War with Benjamin

**20** Then all the Israelites were united as one man, from Dan in the north to Beersheba in the south, including those from across the Jordan in the land of Gilead. The entire community assembled in the presence of the LORD at Mizpah. 2 The leaders of all the people and all the tribes of Israel—400,000 warriors armed with swords—took their positions in the assembly of the people of God. 3 (Word soon reached the land of Benjamin that the other tribes had gone up to Mizpah.) The Israelites then asked how this terrible crime had happened.

4 The Levite, the husband of the woman who had been murdered, said, "My concubine and I came to spend the night in Gibeah, a town that belongs to the people of Benjamin. 5 That night some of the leading citizens of Gibeah surrounded the house, planning to kill me, and they raped my concubine until she was dead. 6 So I cut her body into twelve pieces and sent the pieces throughout the territory assigned to Israel, for these men have committed a terrible and shameful crime. 7 Now then, all of you—the entire community of Israel—must decide here and now what should be done about this!"

**19:28** Greek version adds *for she was dead.*

Cross-refs: 19:22 Gen 19:4-5; 19:23 Gen 34:7, 2 Sam 13:12; 19:24 Gen 19:8; 19:28 Judg 20:5; 19:29 1 Sam 11:7; 19:30 Judg 20:7; 20:1 1 Sam 7:5; 20:5 Judg 19:22, 25-26; 20:6-7 Judg 19:29-30

**19:24** Nowhere is the unwritten law of hospitality stronger than in the Middle East. Protecting a guest at any cost ranked at the top of a man's code of honor. But here the hospitality code turned to fanaticism. The rape and abuse of a daughter and companion were preferable to the *possibility* of a conflict between a guest and a neighbor. The two men were selfish (they didn't want to get hurt themselves); they lacked courage (they didn't want to face a conflict even when lives were at stake); and they disobeyed God's law (they allowed deliberate abuse and murder). What drastic consequences can result when social protocol carries more authority than moral convictions!

**19:29, 30** Although this was a terrible way to spread the news, it effectively communicated the horror of the crime and called the people to action. Saul used a similar method in 1 Samuel 11:7. Ironically, the man who alerted Israel to the murder of his concubine was just as guilty for her death as the men who actually killed her.

**19:30** The horrible crime described in this chapter wasn't Israel's worst offense. Even worse was the nation's failure to establish a government based upon God's moral principles, where the law of God was the law of the land. As a result, laws were usually not enforced and crime was ignored. Sexual perversion and lawlessness were by-products of Israel's disobedience to God. The Israelites weren't willing to speak up until events had gone too far.

Whenever we get away from God and his Word, all sorts of evil can follow. Our drifting away from God may be slow and almost imperceptible, with the ultimate results affecting a future generation. We must continually call our nation back to God and work toward the establishment of God's moral and spiritual reign in the heart of every person.

**20:1** Dan was the northernmost city in Israel, and Beersheba, the southernmost. The two were often mentioned together as a reference to the entire nation.

**20:5** In reporting the events in Gibeah, the man conveniently left out the fact that he had handed over his concubine to satisfy the mob's demands. He wanted justice for the threats made against himself rather than placing any value on the life of the woman or holding himself partly responsible for her death. How easy it is to give only partial facts or twist events to remove our own culpability when we are seeking to shift blame to someone else. This incident reveals the depths of perversion and violence that develop when a culture abandons God's ways.

8And all the people rose to their feet in unison and declared, "None of us will return home! No, not even one of us! 9Instead, this is what we will do to Gibeah; we will draw lots to decide who will attack it. 10One tenth of the men* from each tribe will be chosen to supply the warriors with food, and the rest of us will take revenge on Gibeah* of Benjamin for this shameful thing they have done in Israel." 11So all the Israelites were completely united, and they gathered together to attack the town.

12The Israelites sent messengers to the tribe of Benjamin, saying, "What a terrible thing has been done among you! 13Give up those evil men, those troublemakers from Gibeah, so we can execute them and purge Israel of this evil."

But the people of Benjamin would not listen. 14Instead, they came from their towns and gathered at Gibeah to fight the Israelites. 15In all, 26,000 of their warriors armed with swords arrived in Gibeah to join the 700 elite troops who lived there. 16Among Benjamin's elite troops, 700 were left-handed, and each of them could sling a rock and hit a target within a hairsbreadth without missing. 17Israel had 400,000 experienced soldiers armed with swords, not counting Benjamin's warriors.

18Before the battle the Israelites went to Bethel and asked God, "Which tribe should go first to attack the people of Benjamin?"

The LORD answered, "Judah is to go first."

19So the Israelites left early the next morning and camped near Gibeah. 20Then they advanced toward Gibeah to attack the men of Benjamin. 21But Benjamin's warriors, who were defending the town, came out and killed 22,000 Israelites on the battlefield that day.

22But the Israelites encouraged each other and took their positions again at the same place they had fought the previous day. 23For they had gone up to Bethel and wept in the presence of the LORD until evening. They had asked the LORD, "Should we fight against our relatives from Benjamin again?"

And the LORD had said, "Go out and fight against them."

24So the next day they went out again to fight against the men of Benjamin, 25but the men of Benjamin killed another 18,000 Israelites, all of whom were experienced with the sword.

26Then all the Israelites went up to Bethel and wept in the presence of the LORD and fasted until evening. They also brought burnt offerings and peace offerings to the LORD. 27The Israelites went up seeking direction from the LORD. (In those days the Ark of the Covenant of God was in Bethel, 28and Phinehas son of Eleazar and grandson of Aaron was the priest.) The Israelites asked the LORD, "Should we fight against our relatives from Benjamin again, or should we stop?"

The LORD said, "Go! Tomorrow I will hand them over to you."

29So the Israelites set an ambush all around Gibeah. 30They went out on the third day and took their positions at the same place as before. 31When the men of Benjamin came out to attack, they were drawn away from the town. And as they had done before, they began to kill the Israelites. About thirty Israelites died in the open fields and along the roads, one leading to Bethel and the other leading back to Gibeah.

32Then the warriors of Benjamin shouted, "We're defeating them as we did before!" But the Israelites had planned in advance to run away so that the men of Benjamin would chase them along the roads and be drawn away from the town.

33When the main group of Israelite warriors reached Baal-tamar, they turned and took up their positions. Meanwhile, the Israelites hiding in ambush to the west* of Gibeah

20:12 Deut 13:14
20:13 1 Cor 5:13
20:16 Judg 3:15
20:18 Num 27:21; Judg 1:1
20:22 Josh 7:6-7
20:26 Judg 21:2-4
20:27 Judg 20:18
20:31 Josh 8:16
20:33 Josh 8:19

20:10a Hebrew 10 men from every hundred, 100 men from every thousand, and 1,000 men from every 10,000. 20:10b Hebrew Geba, in this case a variant spelling of Gibeah; also in 20:33. 20:33 As in Greek and Syriac versions and Latin Vulgate; Hebrew reads hiding in the open space.

20:13 Perhaps the leaders of the tribe of Benjamin had been given distorted facts about the serious crime in their territory, or perhaps they were too proud to admit that some of their people had stooped so low. In either case, they would not listen to the rest of Israel and hand over the accused criminals. They were more loyal to their own tribe than to God's law.

By covering for their kinsmen, the entire tribe of Benjamin sank to a level of immorality as low as that of the criminals. Through this act, we get a glimpse of how thoroughly the nation's moral fabric had unraveled. The time period of the judges ends in a bloody civil war that sets the stage for the spiritual renewal to come under Samuel (see 1 Samuel).

20:27, 28 This is the only place in Judges where the Ark of the Covenant is mentioned. This probably indicates how seldom the people consulted God.

Phinehas the high priest was also the high priest under Joshua (Joshua 22:13). The reference to Phinehas as high priest and the location of the Tabernacle in Bethel instead of Shiloh probably indicate that the events of this story occurred during the early years of the judges.

jumped up to fight. 34There were 10,000 elite Israelite troops who advanced against Gibeah. The fighting was so heavy that Benjamin didn't realize the impending disaster. 35So the LORD helped Israel defeat Benjamin, and that day the Israelites killed 25,100 of Benjamin's warriors, all of whom were experienced swordsmen. 36Then the men of Benjamin saw that they were beaten.

**20:34**
Josh 8:14

**20:36**
Josh 8:15

The Israelites had retreated from Benjamin's warriors in order to give those hiding in ambush more room to maneuver against Gibeah. 37Then those who were hiding rushed in from all sides and killed everyone in the town. 38They had arranged to send up a large cloud of smoke from the town as a signal. 39When the Israelites saw the smoke, they turned and attacked Benjamin's warriors.

**20:37-38**
Josh 8:19-20

By that time Benjamin's warriors had killed about thirty Israelites, and they shouted, "We're defeating them as we did in the first battle!" 40But when the warriors of Benjamin looked behind them and saw the smoke rising into the sky from every part of the town, 41the men of Israel turned and attacked. At this point the men of Benjamin became terrified, because they realized disaster was close at hand. 42So they turned around and fled before the Israelites toward the wilderness. But they couldn't escape the battle, and the people who came out of the nearby towns were also killed.* 43The Israelites surrounded the men of Benjamin and chased them relentlessly, finally overtaking them east of Gibeah.* 44That day 18,000 of Benjamin's strongest warriors died in battle. 45The survivors fled into the wilderness toward the rock of Rimmon, but Israel killed 5,000 of them along the road. They continued the chase until they had killed another 2,000 near Gidom.

**20:40-41**
Josh 8:20-21

**20:42**
Josh 8:15, 24

**20:45**
Judg 21:13

46So that day the tribe of Benjamin lost 25,000 strong warriors armed with swords, 47leaving only 600 men who escaped to the rock of Rimmon, where they lived for four months. 48And the Israelites returned and slaughtered every living thing in all the towns—the people, the livestock, and everything they found. They also burned down all the towns they came to.

### Israel Provides Wives for Benjamin

**21** The Israelites had vowed at Mizpah, "We will never give our daughters in marriage to a man from the tribe of Benjamin." 2Now the people went to Bethel and sat in the presence of God until evening, weeping loudly and bitterly. 3"O LORD, God of Israel," they cried out, "why has this happened in Israel? Now one of our tribes is missing from Israel!"

**21:1**
Judg 21:7, 18
**21:2**
Judg 20:18, 26

4Early the next morning the people built an altar and presented their burnt offerings and peace offerings on it. 5Then they said, "Who among the tribes of Israel did not join us at Mizpah when we held our assembly in the presence of the LORD?" At that time they had taken a solemn oath in the LORD's presence, vowing that anyone who refused to come would be put to death.

**21:4**
Deut 12:5
2 Sam 24:25

6The Israelites felt sorry for their brother Benjamin and said, "Today one of the tribes of Israel has been cut off. 7How can we find wives for the few who remain, since we have sworn by the LORD not to give them our daughters in marriage?"

8So they asked, "Who among the tribes of Israel did not join us at Mizpah when we assembled in the presence of the LORD?" And they discovered that no one from Jabesh-gilead had attended the assembly. 9For after they counted all the people, no one from Jabesh-gilead was present.

**20:42** Or *battle, for the people from the nearby towns also came out and killed them.*    **20:43** The meaning of the Hebrew is uncertain.

---

**20:46-48** The effects of the horrible rape and murder should never have been felt outside the community where the crime happened. The local people should have brought the criminals to justice and corrected the laxness that originally permitted the crime. Instead, first the town and then the entire tribe defended this wickedness, even going to war over it.

To prevent unresolved problems from turning into major conflicts, firm action must be taken quickly, wisely, and forcefully *before* a situation gets out of hand.

**20:48** The tribe of Benjamin eventually recovered from this slaughter. Saul, Israel's first king, was from this tribe (1 Samuel 9:21). So were Queen Esther (Esther 2:5-7) and the apostle Paul (Romans 11:1). But the tribe was always known for being smaller than the rest (as in Psalm 68:27).

**21:8-12** The Israelites moved from one mess to another. Because of a rash vow made in the heat of emotion (21:5), here they destroyed another town. The Israelites probably justified their action with the following arguments: (1) An oath could not be broken, and they had vowed that anyone who did not help them fight the tribe of Benjamin would be killed. (2) Because all the women from Benjamin had been killed, the few remaining men needed wives to prevent the tribe from disappearing. To spare the unmarried women from Jabesh-gilead seemed the right solution.

We do not know all the circumstances behind the brutal massacre at Jabesh-gilead, but it seems that the rest of Israel followed Benjamin's pattern. They put tribal loyalties above God's commands, and they justified wrong actions to correct past mistakes.

21:10
Num 31:17-18

¹⁰So the assembly sent 12,000 of their best warriors to Jabesh-gilead with orders to kill everyone there, including women and children. ¹¹"This is what you are to do," they said. "Completely destroy* all the males and every woman who is not a virgin." ¹²Among the residents of Jabesh-gilead they found 400 young virgins who had never slept with a man, and they brought them to the camp at Shiloh in the land of Canaan.

21:13
Deut 20:10

¹³The Israelite assembly sent a peace delegation to the remaining people of Benjamin who were living at the rock of Rimmon. ¹⁴Then the men of Benjamin returned to their homes, and the 400 women of Jabesh-gilead who had been spared were given to them as wives. But there were not enough women for all of them.

¹⁵The people felt sorry for Benjamin because the LORD had made this gap among the tribes of Israel. ¹⁶So the elders of the assembly asked, "How can we find wives for the few who remain, since the women of the tribe of Benjamin are dead? ¹⁷There must be heirs for the survivors so that an entire tribe of Israel is not wiped out. ¹⁸But we cannot give them our own daughters in marriage because we have sworn with a solemn oath that anyone who does this will fall under God's curse."

21:19
Josh 18:1
Judg 18:31
1 Sam 1:3

21:21
Exod 15:20
Judg 11:34

¹⁹Then they thought of the annual festival of the LORD held in Shiloh, south of Lebonah and north of Bethel, along the east side of the road that goes from Bethel to Shechem. ²⁰They told the men of Benjamin who still needed wives, "Go and hide in the vineyards. ²¹When you see the young women of Shiloh come out for their dances, rush out from the vineyards, and each of you can take one of them home to the land of Benjamin to be your wife! ²²And when their fathers and brothers come to us in protest, we will tell them, 'Please be sympathetic. Let them have your daughters, for we didn't find wives for all of them when we destroyed Jabesh-gilead. And you are not guilty of breaking the vow since you did not actually give your daughters to them in marriage.'"

21:23
Judg 20:48

²³So the men of Benjamin did as they were told. Each man caught one of the women as she danced in the celebration and carried her off to be his wife. They returned to their own land, and they rebuilt their towns and lived in them.

²⁴Then the people of Israel departed by tribes and families, and they returned to their own homes.

²⁵In those days Israel had no king; all the people did whatever seemed right in their own eyes.

21:11 The Hebrew term used here refers to the complete consecration of things or people to the LORD, either by destroying them or by giving them as an offering.

---

21:25 During the time of the judges, the people of Israel experienced trouble because everyone became his own authority and acted on his own opinions of right and wrong. This produced horrendous results. Our world is similar. Individuals, groups, and societies have made themselves the final authorities without reference to God. When people selfishly satisfy their personal desires at all costs, everyone pays the price.

It is the ultimate heroic act to submit all our plans, desires, and motives to God. Men like Gideon, Jephthah, and Samson are known for their heroism in battle. But their personal lives were far from heroic.

To be truly heroic, we must go into battle each day in our home, job, church, and society to make God's Kingdom a reality. Our weapons are the standards, morals, truths, and convictions we receive from God's Word. We will lose the battle if we gather the spoils of earthly treasures rather than seeking the treasures of heaven.

# RUTH

WHEN someone says, "Let me tell you about my mother-in-law," we expect some kind of negative statement or humorous anecdote because the mother-in-law caricature has been a standard centerpiece of ridicule or comedy. The book of Ruth, however, tells a different story. Ruth loved her mother-in-law, Naomi. Recently widowed, Ruth begged to stay with Naomi wherever she went, even though it would mean leaving her homeland. In heartfelt words, Ruth said, "Your people will be my people, and your God will be my God" (1:16). Naomi agreed, and Ruth traveled with her to Bethlehem.

Not much is said about Naomi except that she loved and cared for Ruth. Obviously, Naomi's life was a powerful witness to the reality of God. Ruth was drawn to her—and to the God she worshiped. In the succeeding months, God led this young Moabite widow to a man named Boaz, whom she eventually married. As a result, she became the great-grandmother of David and an ancestor in the line of the Messiah. What a profound impact Naomi's life made!

The book of Ruth is also the story of God's grace in the midst of difficult circumstances. Ruth's story occurred during the time of the judges—a period of disobedience, idolatry, and violence. Even in times of crisis and deepest despair, there are those who follow God and through whom God works. No matter how discouraging or antagonistic the world may seem, there are always people who follow God. He will use anyone who is open to him to achieve his purposes. Ruth was a Moabite, and Boaz was a descendant of Rahab, a former prostitute from Jericho. Nevertheless, their offspring continued the family line through which the Messiah came into our world.

Read this book and be encouraged. God is at work in the world, and he wants to use you. God could use you, as he used Naomi, to bring family and friends to him.

## THE BLUEPRINT

1. Ruth remains loyal to Naomi (1:1–22)
2. Ruth gleans in Boaz's field (2:1–23)
3. Ruth follows Naomi's plan (3:1–18)
4. Ruth and Boaz are married (4:1–22)

When we first meet Ruth, she is a destitute widow. We follow her as she joins God's people, gleans in the grainfields, and risks her honor at the threshing floor of Boaz. In the end, we see Ruth becoming the wife of Boaz. What a picture of how we come to faith in Christ. We begin with no hope and are rebellious aliens with no part in the kingdom of God. Then as we risk everything by putting our faith in Christ, God saves us, forgives us, rebuilds our lives, and gives us blessings that will last through eternity. Boaz's redeeming of Ruth is a picture of Christ redeeming us.

## MEGATHEMES

| THEME | EXPLANATION | IMPORTANCE |
|---|---|---|
| *Faithfulness* | Ruth's faithfulness to Naomi as a daughter-in-law and friend is a great example of love and loyalty. Ruth, Naomi, and Boaz are also faithful to God and his laws. Throughout the story we see God's faithfulness to his people. | Ruth's life was guided by faithfulness toward God and showed itself in loyalty toward the people she knew. To be loyal and loving in relationships, we must imitate God's faithfulness in our relationships with others. |

| | | |
|---|---|---|
| Kindness | Ruth showed great kindness to Naomi. In turn, Boaz showed kindness to Ruth—a despised Moabite woman with no money. God showed his kindness to Ruth, Naomi, and Boaz by bringing them together for his purposes. | Just as Boaz showed his kindness by buying back land to guarantee Ruth and Naomi's inheritance, so Christ showed his kindness by dying for us to guarantee our eternal life. God's kindness should motivate us to love and honor him. |
| Integrity | Ruth showed high moral character by being loyal to Naomi, by her clean break from her former land and customs, and by her hard work in the fields. Boaz showed integrity in his moral standards, his honesty, and by following through on his commitments. | When we have experienced God's faithfulness and kindness, we should respond by showing integrity. Just as the values by which Ruth and Boaz lived were in sharp contrast to those of the culture portrayed in Judges, so our lives should stand out from the world around us. |
| Protection | We see God's care and protection over the lives of Naomi and Ruth. His supreme control over circumstances brings them safety and security. He guides the minds and activities of people to fulfill his purposes. | No matter how devastating our present situation may be, our hope is in God. His resources are infinite. We must believe that he can work in the life of any person— whether that person is a king or a stranger in a foreign land. Trust his protection. |
| Prosperity/Blessing | Ruth and Naomi came to Bethlehem as poor widows, but they soon became prosperous through Ruth's marriage to Boaz. Ruth became the great-grandmother of King David. Yet the greatest blessing was not the money, the marriage, or the child; it was the quality of love and respect between Ruth, Boaz, and Naomi. | We tend to think of blessings in terms of prosperity rather than the high-quality relationships God makes possible for us. No matter what our economic situation, we can love and respect the people God has brought into our lives. In so doing, we give and receive blessings. Love is the greatest blessing. |

## 1. Ruth remains loyal to Naomi

### Elimelech Moves His Family to Moab

**1:1**
Judg 2:16-18
**1:2**
Gen 35:19
Judg 3:30

**1** In the days when the judges ruled in Israel, a severe famine came upon the land. So a man from Bethlehem in Judah left his home and went to live in the country of Moab, taking his wife and two sons with him. ²The man's name was Elimelech, and his wife was Naomi. Their two sons were Mahlon and Kilion. They were Ephrathites from Bethlehem in the land of Judah. And when they reached Moab, they settled there.

³Then Elimelech died, and Naomi was left with her two sons. ⁴The two sons married Moabite women. One married a woman named Orpah, and the other a woman named Ruth. But about ten years later, ⁵both Mahlon and Kilion died. This left Naomi alone, without her two sons or her husband.

### Naomi and Ruth Return

**1:6**
Exod 4:31

⁶Then Naomi heard in Moab that the Lᴏʀᴅ had blessed his people in Judah by giving them good crops again. So Naomi and her daughters-in-law got ready to leave Moab to return to her homeland. ⁷With her two daughters-in-law she set out from the place where she had been living, and they took the road that would lead them back to Judah.

**1:1** The story of Ruth takes place sometime during the period of the rule of the judges. These were dark days for Israel, when "the people did whatever seemed right in their own eyes" (Judges 17:6; 21:25). But during those dark and evil times, there were still some who followed God. Naomi and Ruth are beautiful examples of loyalty, friendship, and commitment—to God and to each other.

**1:1, 2** Moab was the land east of the Dead Sea. It was one of the nations that oppressed Israel during the period of the judges (Judges 3:12ff), so there was hostility between the two nations. The famine must have been quite severe in Israel for Elimelech to move his family there. They were called Ephrathites because Ephrath was an earlier name for Bethlehem. Even if Israel had already defeated Moab, there still would have been tensions between them.

**1:4, 5** Friendly relations with the Moabites were discouraged (Deuteronomy 23:3-6) but probably not forbidden, since the Moabites lived outside the Promised Land. Marrying a Canaanite (and all those living within the borders of the Promised Land), however, was against God's law (Deuteronomy 7:1-4). Moabites were not allowed to worship at the Tabernacle because they had not let the Israelites pass through their land during the exodus from Egypt.

As God's chosen nation, Israel should have set the standards of high moral living for the other nations. Ironically it was Ruth, a Moabitess, whom God used as an example of genuine spiritual character. This shows just how bleak life had become in Israel during those days.

⁸But on the way, Naomi said to her two daughters-in-law, "Go back to your mothers' homes. And may the LORD reward you for your kindness to your husbands and to me. ⁹May the LORD bless you with the security of another marriage." Then she kissed them good-bye, and they all broke down and wept.

¹⁰"No," they said. "We want to go with you to your people."

¹¹But Naomi replied, "Why should you go on with me? Can I still give birth to other sons who could grow up to be your husbands? ¹²No, my daughters, return to your parents' homes, for I am too old to marry again. And even if it were possible, and I were to get married tonight and bear sons, then what? ¹³Would you wait for them to grow up and refuse to marry someone else? No, of course not, my daughters! Things are far more bitter for me than for you, because the LORD himself has raised his fist against me."

¹⁴And again they wept together, and Orpah kissed her mother-in-law good-bye. But Ruth clung tightly to Naomi. ¹⁵"Look," Naomi said to her, "your sister-in-law has gone back to her people and to her gods. You should do the same."

¹⁶But Ruth replied, "Don't ask me to leave you and turn back. Wherever you go, I will go; wherever you live, I will live. Your people will be my people, and your God will be my God. ¹⁷Wherever you die, I will die, and there I will be buried. May the LORD punish me severely if I allow anything but death to separate us!" ¹⁸When Naomi saw that Ruth was determined to go with her, she said nothing more.

¹⁹So the two of them continued on their journey. When they came to Bethlehem, the entire town was excited by their arrival. "Is it really Naomi?" the women asked.

²⁰"Don't call me Naomi," she responded. "Instead, call me Mara,* for the Almighty has made life very bitter for me. ²¹I went away full, but the LORD has brought me home empty. Why call me Naomi when the LORD has caused me to suffer* and the Almighty has sent such tragedy upon me?"

**1:20** *Naomi* means "pleasant"; *Mara* means "bitter." **1:21** Or *has testified against me.*

| Ref | Cross-ref |
|---|---|
| **1:8** | 2 Tim 1:16 |
| **1:9** | Ruth 3:1 |
| **1:11** | Deut 25:5 |
| **1:13** | Judg 2:15 |
| **1:16** | 2 Kgs 2:2 |
| **1:18** | Acts 21:14 |
| **1:20** | Exod 6:3; Job 6:4 |
| **1:21** | Job 1:21 |

---

**1:8, 9** There was almost nothing worse than being a widow in the ancient world. Widows were taken advantage of or ignored. They were almost always poverty stricken. God's law, therefore, provided that the nearest relative of the dead husband should care for the widow; but Naomi had no relatives in Moab, and she did not know if any of her relatives were alive in Israel.

Even in her desperate situation, Naomi had a selfless attitude. Although she had decided to return to Israel, she encouraged Ruth and Orpah to stay in Moab and start their lives over, even though this would mean hardship for her. Like Naomi, we must consider the needs of others and not just our own. As Naomi discovered, when you act selflessly, others are encouraged to follow your example.

**1:11** Naomi's comment here ("sons who could grow up to be your husbands") refers to *levirate marriage*, the obligation of a dead man's brother to care for the widow (Deuteronomy 25:5-10). This law kept the widow from poverty and provided a way for the family name of the dead husband to continue.

Naomi, however, had no other sons for Ruth or Orpah to marry, so she encouraged them to remain in their homeland and remarry. Orpah agreed, which was her right. But Ruth was willing to give up the possibility of security and children in order to care for Naomi.

**1:16** Ruth was a Moabitess, but that didn't stop her from worshiping the true God, nor did it stop God from accepting her worship and blessing her greatly. The Jews were not the only people God loved. God chose the Jews to be the people through whom the rest of the world would come to know him. This was fulfilled when Jesus Christ was born as a Jew. Through him, the entire world can come to know God. Acts 10:35 says that "in every nation he accepts those who fear him and do what is right." God accepts all who worship him; he works through people regardless of their race, sex, or nationality. The book of Ruth is a perfect example of God's impartiality. Although Ruth belonged to a race often despised by Israel, she was blessed because of her faithfulness. She became a great-grandmother of King David and a direct ancestor of Jesus. No one should feel disqualified to serve God because of race, sex, or national background. And God can use every circumstance to build his kingdom.

**1:20, 21** Naomi had experienced severe hardships. She had left Israel married and secure; she returned widowed and poor. Naomi changed her name to express the bitterness and pain she felt. Naomi was not rejecting God by openly expressing her pain. However, it seems she lost sight of the tremendous resources she had in her relationship with Ruth and with God. When you face bitter times, God welcomes your honest prayers, but be careful not to overlook the love, strength, and resources that he provides in your present relationships. And don't allow bitterness and disappointment to blind you to your opportunities.

**SETTING FOR THE STORY**
Elimelech, Naomi, and their sons traveled from Bethlehem to Moab because of a famine. After her husband and sons died, Naomi returned to Bethlehem with her daughter-in-law Ruth.

1:22
Exod 9:31

²²So Naomi returned from Moab, accompanied by her daughter-in-law Ruth, the young Moabite woman. They arrived in Bethlehem in late spring, at the beginning of the barley harvest.

### 2. Ruth gleans in Boaz's field

2:1
Ruth 1:2
2:2
Lev 19:9-10;
23:22

**2** Now there was a wealthy and influential man in Bethlehem named Boaz, who was a relative of Naomi's husband, Elimelech.

²One day Ruth the Moabite said to Naomi, "Let me go out into the harvest fields to pick up the stalks of grain left behind by anyone who is kind enough to let me do it."

Naomi replied, "All right, my daughter, go ahead." ³So Ruth went out to gather grain

**RUTH/NAOMI**

The stories of several people in the Bible are woven together so closely that they are almost inseparable. We know more about their relationship than we know about them as individuals. And in an age that worships individualism, their stories become helpful models of good relationships. Naomi and Ruth are beautiful examples of this blending of lives. Their cultures, family backgrounds, and ages were very different. As mother-in-law and daughter-in-law, they probably had as many opportunities for tension as for tenderness. And yet they were bound to each other.

They shared deep sorrow, great affection for each other, and an overriding commitment to the God of Israel. And yet, as much as they depended on each other, they also gave each other freedom in their commitment to one another. Naomi was willing to let Ruth return to her family. Ruth was willing to leave her homeland to go to Israel. Naomi even helped arrange Ruth's marriage to Boaz although it would change their relationship.

God was at the center of their intimate communication. Ruth came to know the God of Israel through Naomi. The older woman allowed Ruth to see, hear, and feel all the joy and anguish of her relationship to God. How often do you feel that your thoughts and questions about God should be left out of a close relationship? How often do you share your unedited thoughts about God with your spouse or friends? Sharing openly about our relationship with God can bring depth and intimacy to our relationships with others.

| | |
|---|---|
| **Strengths and accomplishments** | • A relationship where the greatest bond was faith in God<br>• A relationship of strong mutual commitment<br>• A relationship in which each person tried to do what was best for the other |
| **Lesson from their lives** | • God's living presence in a relationship overcomes differences that might otherwise create division and disharmony |
| **Vital statistics** | • Where: Moab, Bethlehem<br>• Occupation: Wives, widows<br>• Relatives: Naomi's husband: Elimelech. Ruth's mother-in-law: Naomi. Naomi's sons: Mahlon, Kilion. Naomi's other daughter-in-law: Orpah. Ruth's second husband: Boaz. Ruth's son: Obed. |
| **Key verses** | "But Ruth replied, 'Don't ask me to leave you and turn back. Wherever you go, I will go; wherever you live, I will live. Your people will be my people, and your God will be my God. Wherever you die, I will die, and there I will be buried. May the LORD punish me severely if I allow anything but death to separate us!'" (Ruth 1:16, 17). |

Their story is told in the book of Ruth. Ruth is also mentioned in Matthew 1:5.

---

**1:22** Bethlehem was about five miles southwest of Jerusalem. The town was surrounded by lush fields and olive groves. Its harvests were abundant.

Ruth and Naomi's return to Bethlehem was certainly part of God's plan because in this town David would be born (1 Samuel 16:1), and, as predicted by the prophet Micah (Micah 5:2), Jesus Christ would also be born there. This move, then, was more than mere convenience for Ruth and Naomi. It led to the fulfillment of Scripture.

**1:22** Because Israel's climate is quite moderate, there are two harvests each year, in the spring and in the fall. The barley harvest took place in the spring, and it was during this time of hope and plenty that Ruth and Naomi returned to Bethlehem. Bethlehem was a farming community, and because it was the time of the harvest, there was plenty of leftover grain in the fields. This grain could be collected, or *gleaned*, and then made into food. (See the note on 2:2 for more information on gleaning.)

**2:2** When the wheat and barley were ready to be harvested, harvesters were hired to cut down the stalks and tie them into bundles. Israelite law demanded that the corners of the fields not be harvested. In addition, any grain that was dropped was to be left for poor people, who picked it up (this was called *gleaning*) and used it for food (Leviticus 19:9; 23:22; Deuteronomy 24:19). The purpose of this law was to feed the poor and to prevent the owners from hoarding. This law served as a type of welfare program in Israel. Because she was a widow with no means of providing for herself, Ruth went into the fields to glean the grain.

**2:2, 3** Ruth made her home in a foreign land. Instead of depending on Naomi or waiting for good fortune to happen, she took the initiative. She went to work. She was not afraid of admitting her need or working hard to supply it. When Ruth went out to the fields, God provided for her. If you are waiting for God to provide, consider this: He may be waiting for you to take the first step to demonstrate just how important your need is.

behind the harvesters. And as it happened, she found herself working in a field that belonged to Boaz, the relative of her father-in-law, Elimelech.

⁴While she was there, Boaz arrived from Bethlehem and greeted the harvesters. "The LORD be with you!" he said.

"The LORD bless you!" the harvesters replied.

⁵Then Boaz asked his foreman, "Who is that young woman over there? Who does she belong to?"

⁶And the foreman replied, "She is the young woman from Moab who came back with Naomi. ⁷She asked me this morning if she could gather grain behind the harvesters. She has been hard at work ever since, except for a few minutes' rest in the shelter."

⁸Boaz went over and said to Ruth, "Listen, my daughter. Stay right here with us when you gather grain; don't go to any other fields. Stay right behind the young women working in my field. ⁹See which part of the field they are harvesting, and then follow them. I have warned the young men not to treat you roughly. And when you are thirsty, help yourself to the water they have drawn from the well."

¹⁰Ruth fell at his feet and thanked him warmly. "What have I done to deserve such kindness?" she asked. "I am only a foreigner."

¹¹"Yes, I know," Boaz replied. "But I also know about everything you have done for your mother-in-law since the death of your husband. I have heard how you left your father and mother and your own land to live here among complete strangers. ¹²May the LORD, the God of Israel, under whose wings you have come to take refuge, reward you fully for what you have done."

¹³"I hope I continue to please you, sir," she replied. "You have comforted me by speaking so kindly to me, even though I am not one of your workers."

¹⁴At mealtime Boaz called to her, "Come over here, and help yourself to some food. You can dip your bread in the sour wine." So she sat with his harvesters, and Boaz gave her some roasted grain to eat. She ate all she wanted and still had some left over.

¹⁵When Ruth went back to work again, Boaz ordered his young men, "Let her gather grain right among the sheaves without stopping her. ¹⁶And pull out some heads of barley from the bundles and drop them on purpose for her. Let her pick them up, and don't give her a hard time!"

¹⁷So Ruth gathered barley there all day, and when she beat out the grain that evening, it filled an entire basket.* ¹⁸She carried it back into town and showed it to her mother-in-law. Ruth also gave her the roasted grain that was left over from her meal.

¹⁹"Where did you gather all this grain today?" Naomi asked. "Where did you work? May the LORD bless the one who helped you!"

So Ruth told her mother-in-law about the man in whose field she had worked. She said, "The man I worked with today is named Boaz."

²⁰"May the LORD bless him!" Naomi told her daughter-in-law. "He is showing his kindness to us as well as to your dead husband.* That man is one of our closest relatives, one of our family redeemers."

²¹Then Ruth* said, "What's more, Boaz even told me to come back and stay with his harvesters until the entire harvest is completed."

2:17 Hebrew *it was about an ephah* [20 quarts or 22 liters].   2:20 Hebrew *to the living and to the dead.*
2:21 Hebrew *Ruth the Moabite.*

2:4 Ps 129:8; Luke 1:28
2:6 Ruth 1:22
2:10 1 Sam 25:23
2:12 Ruth 1:16
2:20 Ruth 3:9-10; 4:6

**2:7** Ruth's task, though menial, tiring, and perhaps degrading, was done faithfully. What is your attitude when the task you have been given is not up to your true potential? The task at hand may be all you can do, or it may be the work God wants you to do. Or, as in Ruth's case, it may be a test of your character that can open up new doors of opportunity.

**2:10-12** Ruth's life exhibited admirable qualities: She was hardworking, loving, kind, faithful, and brave. These qualities gained for her a good reputation, but only because she displayed them *consistently* in all areas of her life. Wherever Ruth went or whatever she did, her character remained the same.

Your reputation is formed by the people who watch you at work, in town, at home, in church. A good reputation comes by *consistently* living out the qualities you believe in—no matter what group of people or surroundings you are in.

**2:15, 16** The characters in the book of Ruth are classic examples of good people in action. Boaz went far beyond the intent of the gleaners' law in demonstrating his kindness and generosity. Not only did he let Ruth glean in his field, he also told his workers to let some of the grain fall in her path. Out of his abundance, he provided for the needy. How often do you go beyond the accepted patterns of providing for those less fortunate? Do more than the minimum for others.

**2:19, 20** Naomi had felt bitter (1:20, 21), but her faith in God was still alive, and she praised God for Boaz's kindness to Ruth. In her sorrows, she still trusted God and acknowledged his goodness. We may feel bitter about a situation, but we must never despair. Today is always a new opportunity for experiencing God's care. (For more on a family redeemer, see the note on 3:1-9.)

**2:20** Though Ruth may not have always recognized God's guid-

²²"Good!" Naomi exclaimed. "Do as he said, my daughter. Stay with his young women right through the whole harvest. You might be harassed in other fields, but you'll be safe with him."

²³So Ruth worked alongside the women in Boaz's fields and gathered grain with them until the end of the barley harvest. Then she continued working with them through the wheat harvest in early summer. And all the while she lived with her mother-in-law.

**3:1**
Ruth 1:9

**3:2**
Deut 25:5-10

### 3. Ruth follows Naomi's plan

**3** One day Naomi said to Ruth, "My daughter, it's time that I found a permanent home for you, so that you will be provided for. ²Boaz is a close relative of ours, and he's been very

**BOAZ**

Heroes are easier to admire than to define. They are seldom conscious of their moments of heroism, and others may not recognize their acts as heroic. Heroes simply do the right thing at the right time, whether or not they realize the impact their action will have. Perhaps the one quality they share is a tendency to think of others before they think of themselves.

Boaz was a hero.

In his dealings with other people, he was always sensitive to their needs. His words to his employees, relatives, and others were colored with kindness. He offered help openly, not grudgingly. When he discovered who Ruth was, he took several steps to help her because she had been faithful to his relative Naomi. When Naomi advised Ruth to request his protection, he was ready to marry her if the legal complications could be worked out.

Boaz not only did what was right; he also did it right away. Of course he could not foresee all that his actions would accomplish. He could not have known that the child he would have by Ruth would be an ancestor of both David and Jesus. He only met the challenge of taking the right action in the situation facing him.

We are faced with this challenge in our daily choices. Like Naomi's nearer relative, we are often more concerned with making the easy choice than with making the right one. Yet more often than not, the right choice is clear. Ask God to give you a special awareness in your choices today as well as renewed commitment to make the right ones.

| | |
|---|---|
| **Strengths and accomplishments** | • A man of his word<br>• Sensitive to those in need, caring for his workers<br>• A keen sense of responsibility, integrity<br>• A successful and shrewd businessman |
| **Lessons from his life** | • It can be heroic to do what must be done and to do it right<br>• God often uses little decisions to carry out his big plan |
| **Vital statistics** | • Where: Bethlehem<br>• Occupation: Wealthy farmer<br>• Relatives: Distant cousins: Elimelech, Naomi. Wife: Ruth. Son: Obed. |
| **Key verse:** | "I have acquired Ruth, the Moabite widow of Mahlon, to be my wife. This way she can have a son to carry on the family name of her dead husband and to inherit the family property here in his hometown. You are all witnesses today" (Ruth 4:10). |

His story is told in the book of Ruth. He is also mentioned in Matthew 1:5.

ance, he had been with her every step of the way. She went to glean and "just happened" to end up in the field owned by Boaz who "just happened" to be a close relative. This was more than mere coincidence. As you go about your daily tasks, God is working in your life in ways you may not even notice. We must not close the door on what God can do. Events do not occur by luck or coincidence. We should have faith that God is directing our lives for his purpose.

**3:1-9** As widows, Ruth and Naomi could only look forward to difficult times. (See the note on 1:8, 9 for more on a widow's life.) But when Naomi heard the news about Boaz, her hope for the future was renewed (2:20). Typical of her character, she thought first of Ruth, encouraging her to see if Boaz would take the responsibility of being the "family redeemer" (2:20).

A family redeemer was a relative who volunteered to take responsibility for the extended family. When a woman's husband died, the law (Deuteronomy 25:5-10) provided that she could marry a brother of her dead husband. But Naomi had no more sons. In such a case, the nearest relative to the deceased husband could become a family redeemer and marry the widow. The nearest relative did not have to marry the widow. If he chose not to, the next nearest relative could take his place. If no one chose to help the

widow, she would probably live in poverty the rest of her life, because in Israelite culture the inheritance was passed on to the son or nearest male relative, not to the wife. To take the sting out of these inheritance rules, there were laws for gleaning and family redeemers.

We have a family redeemer in Jesus Christ, who though he was God, came to earth as a man in order to save us. By his death on the cross, he has redeemed us from sin and hopelessness and thereby purchased us to be his own possession (1 Peter 1:18, 19). This guarantees our eternal inheritance.

**3:2** The threshing floor was the place where the grain was separated from the harvested wheat. The wheat stalks were crushed, either by hand or by oxen, and the valuable grain (inner kernels) separated from the worthless chaff (the outside shell). The floor was made from rock or soil and located outside the village, usually on an elevated site where the winds would blow away the lighter chaff when the crushed wheat was thrown into the air (or winnowed). Boaz spent the night beside the threshing floor for two reasons: (1) to prevent theft and (2) to wait for his turn to thresh grain. (Threshing was often done at night because daylight hours were spent harvesting.)

kind by letting you gather grain with his young women. Tonight he will be winnowing barley at the threshing floor. ³Now do as I tell you—take a bath and put on perfume and dress in your nicest clothes. Then go to the threshing floor, but don't let Boaz see you until he has finished eating and drinking. ⁴Be sure to notice where he lies down; then go and uncover his feet and lie down there. He will tell you what to do."

⁵"I will do everything you say," Ruth replied. ⁶So she went down to the threshing floor that night and followed the instructions of her mother-in-law.

⁷After Boaz had finished eating and drinking and was in good spirits, he lay down at the far end of the pile of grain and went to sleep. Then Ruth came quietly, uncovered his feet, and lay down. ⁸Around midnight Boaz suddenly woke up and turned over. He was surprised to find a woman lying at his feet! ⁹"Who are you?" he asked.

"I am your servant Ruth," she replied. "Spread the corner of your covering over me, for you are my family redeemer."

¹⁰"The LORD bless you, my daughter!" Boaz exclaimed. "You are showing even more family loyalty now than you did before, for you have not gone after a younger man, whether rich or poor. ¹¹Now don't worry about a thing, my daughter. I will do what is necessary, for everyone in town knows you are a virtuous woman. ¹²But while it's true that I am one of your family redeemers, there is another man who is more closely related to you than I am. ¹³Stay here tonight, and in the morning I will talk to him. If he is willing to redeem you, very well. Let him marry you. But if he is not willing, then as surely as the LORD lives, I will redeem you myself! Now lie down here until morning."

¹⁴So Ruth lay at Boaz's feet until the morning, but she got up before it was light enough for people to recognize each other. For Boaz had said, "No one must know that a woman was here at the threshing floor." ¹⁵Then Boaz said to her, "Bring your cloak and spread it out." He measured six scoops* of barley into the cloak and placed it on her back. Then he* returned to the town.

¹⁶When Ruth went back to her mother-in-law, Naomi asked, "What happened, my daughter?"

Ruth told Naomi everything Boaz had done for her, ¹⁷and she added, "He gave me these six scoops of barley and said, 'Don't go back to your mother-in-law empty-handed.'"

¹⁸Then Naomi said to her, "Just be patient, my daughter, until we hear what happens. The man won't rest until he has settled things today."

### 4. Ruth and Boaz are married

**4** Boaz went to the town gate and took a seat there. Just then the family redeemer he had mentioned came by, so Boaz called out to him, "Come over here and sit down, friend. I want to talk to you." So they sat down together. ²Then Boaz called ten leaders from the town and asked them to sit as witnesses. ³And Boaz said to the family redeemer, "You know Naomi, who came back from Moab. She is selling the land that belonged to our relative

**3:7**
Judg 19:6, 22
2 Sam 13:28

**3:9**
Ruth 2:20

**3:11**
Prov 12:4; 31:10
**3:12**
Ruth 4:1
**3:13**
Ruth 4:5
Matt 22:24

**3:18**
Ps 37:3-5

**4:1**
Ruth 3:12

**4:3**
Lev 25:25

**3:15a** Hebrew *six measures*, an unknown quantity.    **3:15b** Most Hebrew manuscripts read *he;* many Hebrew manuscripts, Syriac version, and Latin Vulgate read *she*.

---

**3:4** Naomi's advice seems strange, but she was not suggesting a seductive act. In reality, Naomi was telling Ruth to act in accordance with Israelite custom and law. It was common for a servant to lie at the feet of his master and even share a part of his covering. By observing this custom, Ruth would inform Boaz that he could be her family redeemer—that he could find someone to marry her or marry her himself. It was family business, nothing romantic. But the story later became beautifully romantic as Ruth and Boaz developed an unselfish love and deep respect for each other.

**3:5** As a foreigner, Ruth may have thought that Naomi's advice was odd. But Ruth followed the advice because she knew Naomi was kind, trustworthy, and filled with moral integrity. Each of us knows a parent, older friend, or relative who is always looking out for our best interests. Be willing to listen to the advice of a person who is older and wiser than you are. The experience and knowledge of such a person can be invaluable. Imagine what Ruth's life would have been like had she ignored her mother-in-law.

**3:12** Ruth and Naomi must have assumed that Boaz was their closest relative. Boaz, too, must have already considered marrying Ruth because his answer to her shows he had been thinking about it. He couldn't have considered marrying Naomi because she was

probably too old to bear any more children (1:11, 12). One man in the city was a nearer relative than Boaz, and this man had the first right to take Ruth as his wife. If he chose not to, then Boaz could marry Ruth (3:13).

**3:18** Naomi implied that Boaz would follow through with his promise at once. He obviously had a reputation for keeping his word and would not rest until his task was completed. Such reliable people stand out in any age and culture. Do others regard you as one who will do what you say? Keeping your word and following through on assignments should be high on anyone's priority list. Building a reputation for integrity, however, must be done one brick, one act, at a time.

**4:1** Boaz knew he could find his relative at the town gate. This was the center of activity. No one could enter or leave the town without traveling through the gate. Merchants set up their temporary shops near the gate, which also served as "city hall." Here city officials gathered to transact business. Because there was so much activity, it was a good place to find witnesses (4:2) and an appropriate place for Boaz to make his transaction.

**4:3** Boaz cleverly presented his case to the relative. First he brought in new information not yet mentioned in the story—

403                                                                    RUTH 4

**4:4**
Lev 25:25
Jer 32:7-8

Elimelech. [4]I thought I should speak to you about it so that you can redeem it if you wish. If you want the land, then buy it here in the presence of these witnesses. But if you don't want it, let me know right away, because I am next in line to redeem it after you."

The man replied, "All right, I'll redeem it."

**4:5**
Deut 25:5-6

[5]Then Boaz told him, "Of course, your purchase of the land from Naomi also requires that you marry Ruth, the Moabite widow. That way she can have children who will carry on her husband's name and keep the land in the family."

**4:6**
Lev 25:25
Ruth 3:12-13

[6]"Then I can't redeem it," the family redeemer replied, "because this might endanger my own estate. You redeem the land; I cannot do it."

**4:7**
Deut 25:8-10

[7]Now in those days it was the custom in Israel for anyone transferring a right of purchase to remove his sandal and hand it to the other party. This publicly validated the transaction. [8]So the other family redeemer drew off his sandal as he said to Boaz, "You buy the land."

[9]Then Boaz said to the elders and to the crowd standing around, "You are witnesses that today I have bought from Naomi all the property of Elimelech, Kilion, and Mahlon. [10]And with the land I have acquired Ruth, the Moabite widow of Mahlon, to be my wife. This way she can have a son to carry on the family name of her dead husband and to inherit the family property here in his hometown. You are all witnesses today."

**4:11**
Gen 29:25-30

[11]Then the elders and all the people standing in the gate replied, "We are witnesses! May the LORD make this woman who is coming into your home like Rachel and Leah, from whom all the nation of Israel descended! May you prosper in Ephrathah and be famous in Bethle-

**4:12**
Gen 38:29; 46:12

hem. [12]And may the LORD give you descendants by this young woman who will be like those of our ancestor Perez, the son of Tamar and Judah."

### The Descendants of Boaz

**4:13**
Gen 29:31; 33:5

[13]So Boaz took Ruth into his home, and she became his wife. When he slept with her, the LORD enabled her to become pregnant, and she gave birth to a son. [14]Then the women of the

**4:14**
Luke 1:58

town said to Naomi, "Praise the LORD, who has now provided a redeemer for your family! May this child be famous in Israel. [15]May he restore your youth and care for you in your old

**4:15**
Ruth 1:16-17;
2:11-12

age. For he is the son of your daughter-in-law who loves you and has been better to you than seven sons!"

[16]Naomi took the baby and cuddled him to her breast. And she cared for him as if he were her own. [17]The neighbor women said, "Now at last Naomi has a son again!" And they named him Obed. He became the father of Jesse and the grandfather of David.

**4:18-22**
//1 Chr 2:5-15
//Matt 1:3-6
//Luke 3:31-33

[18]This is the genealogical record of their ancestor Perez:

Perez was the father of Hezron.
[19] Hezron was the father of Ram.
Ram was the father of Amminadab.
[20] Amminadab was the father of Nahshon.
Nahshon was the father of Salmon.*
[21] Salmon was the father of Boaz.
Boaz was the father of Obed.
[22] Obed was the father of Jesse.
Jesse was the father of David.

**4:20** As in some Greek manuscripts (see also 4:21); Hebrew reads *Salma*.

---

Elimelech, Naomi's former husband, still had some property in the area that was now for sale. As the nearest relative, this man had the first right to buy the land, which he agreed to do (Leviticus 25:25). But then Boaz said that according to the law, if the relative bought the property he also had to marry the widow (probably because Mahlon, Ruth's former husband and Elimelech's son, had inherited the property). At this stipulation, the relative backed down. He did not want to complicate his inheritance. Whatever his reason, the way was now clear for Boaz to marry Ruth.

**4:15** Ruth's love for her mother-in-law was known and recognized throughout the town. From the beginning of the book of Ruth to the end, her kindness toward others remained unchanged.

**4:15** God brought great blessings out of Naomi's tragedy, even greater than "seven sons." Throughout her tough times, Naomi continued to trust God. And God, in his time, blessed her greatly. Even in our sorrow and calamity, God can bring great blessings.

Instead of asking, "How can God allow this to happen to me?" trust him. He will be with you in the hard times.

**4:16, 17** To some, the book of Ruth may be just a nice story about a girl who was fortunate. But in reality, the events recorded in Ruth were part of God's preparations for the births of David and of Jesus, the promised Messiah. Just as Ruth was unaware of this larger purpose in her life, we will not know the full purpose and importance of our lives until we are able to look back from the perspective of eternity. We must make our choices with God's eternal values in mind. Taking moral shortcuts and living for short-range pleasures are not good ways to move ahead. Because of Ruth's faithful obedience, her life and legacy were significant even though she couldn't see all the results. Live in faithfulness to God, knowing that the significance of your life will extend beyond your lifetime. The rewards will outweigh any sacrifice you may have made.

# 1 SAMUEL

| Judges begin to rule 1375 B.C. (1220 B.C.) | | Samuel born 1105 (1083) | Saul born 1080 |
|---|---|---|---|

"RUNNERS, take your marks," the starter barks his signal, and the crowd turns quiet attention to the athletes walking toward the line. "Get set" . . . in position now, muscles tense, nervously anticipating the sound of the gun. It resounds! And the race begins. In any contest, the start is important, but the finish is even more crucial. Often a front-runner will lose strength and fade to the middle of the pack. And there is the tragedy of the brilliant beginner who sets the pace for a time, but does not even finish. He quits the race burned out, exhausted, or injured.

First Samuel is a book of great beginnings . . . and tragic endings. It begins with Eli as high priest during the time of the judges. As a religious leader, Eli certainly must have begun his life with a close relationship to God. In his communication with Hannah, and in his training of her son Samuel, he demonstrated a clear understanding of God's purposes and call (chapters 1; 3). But his life ended in ignominy as his sacrilegious sons were judged by God, and the sacred Ark of the Covenant fell into enemy hands (chapter 4). Eli's death marked the decline of the influence of the priesthood and the rise of the prophets in Israel.

Samuel was dedicated to God's service by his mother, Hannah. He became one of Israel's greatest prophets. He was a man of prayer who finished the work of the judges, began the school of the prophets, and anointed Israel's first kings. But even Samuel was not immune to finishing poorly. Like Eli's family, Samuel's sons turned away from God, taking bribes and perverting justice. The people rejected the leadership of the judges and priests and clamored for a king "like all the other nations have" (8:5).

Saul also started quickly. A striking figure, this handsome (9:2) and humble (9:21; 10:22) man was God's choice as Israel's first king (10:24). His early reign was marked by leadership (chapter 11) and bravery (14:46–48). But he disobeyed God (chapter 15), became jealous and paranoid (chapters 18—19), and finally had his kingship taken away from him by God (chapter 16). Saul's life continued steadily downward. Obsessed with killing David (chapters 19—30), he consulted a medium (chapter 28) and finally committed suicide (chapter 31).

Among the events of Saul's life stands another great beginner—David. A man who followed God (13:14; 16:7), David ministered to Saul (chapter 16), killed Goliath (chapter 17), and became a great warrior. But we'll have to wait until the book of 2 Samuel to see how David finished.

As you read 1 Samuel, note the transition from theocracy to monarchy; exult in the classic stories of David and Goliath, David and Jonathan, David and Abigail; and watch the rise of the influence of the prophets. But in the midst of reading all the history and adventure, determine to run your race as God's person from start to finish.

## THE BLUEPRINT

A. ELI AND SAMUEL
(1:1—7:17)
   1. Samuel's birth and childhood
   2. War with the Philistines

We see a vivid contrast between young Samuel and Eli's sons. Eli's sons were selfish, but Samuel was helpful. Eli's sons defrauded people, but Samuel grew in wisdom and gave the people messages from God. As an adult, Samuel became a prophet, priest, and judge over Israel. A person's actions reflect his character. This was true of Samuel and of Eli's sons. It is also true of us. Strive, like Samuel, to keep your heart pure before God.

B. SAMUEL AND SAUL
(8:1—15:35)
   1. Saul becomes king of Israel
   2. God rejects Saul for disobedience

Saul showed great promise. He was strong, tall, and modest. God's Spirit came upon him, and Samuel was his counselor. But Saul deliberately disobeyed God and became an evil king. We must not base our hopes or future on our potential. Instead, we must consistently obey God in all areas of life. God evaluates obedience, not potential.

C. SAUL AND DAVID
(16:1—31:13)
   1. Samuel anoints David
   2. David and Goliath
   3. David and Jonathan become friends
   4. Saul pursues David
   5. Saul's defeat and death

David quickly killed Goliath but waited patiently for God to deal with Saul. Although David was anointed to be Israel's next king, he had to wait years to realize this promise. The difficult circumstances in life and the times of waiting often refine, teach, and prepare us for the future responsibilities God has for us.

## MEGATHEMES

| THEME | EXPLANATION | IMPORTANCE |
|---|---|---|
| King | Because Israel suffered from corrupt priests and judges, the people wanted a king. They wanted to be organized like the surrounding nations. Though it was against his original purpose, God chose a king for them. | Establishing a monarchy did not solve Israel's problems. What God desires is the genuine devotion of each person's mind and heart to him. No government or set of laws can substitute for the rule of God in your heart and life. |
| God's Control | Israel prospered as long as the people regarded God as their true king. When the leaders strayed from God's law, God intervened in their personal lives and overruled their actions. In this way, God maintained ultimate control over Israel's history. | God is always at work in this world, even when we can't see what he is doing. No matter what kinds of pressures we must endure or how many changes we must face, God is ultimately in control of our situation. Being confident of God's sovereignty, we can face the difficult situations in our lives with boldness. |
| Leadership | God guided his people using different forms of leadership: judges, priests, prophets, kings. Those whom he chose for these different offices, such as Eli, Samuel, Saul, and David, portrayed different styles of leadership. Yet the success of each leader depended on his devotion to God, not his position, leadership style, wisdom, age, or strength. | When Eli, Samuel, Saul, and David disobeyed God, they faced tragic consequences. Sin affected what they accomplished for God and how some of them raised their children. Being a real leader means letting God guide all aspects of your activities, values, and goals, including the way you raise your children. |
| Obedience | For God, "obedience is better than sacrifice" (15:22). God wanted his people to obey, serve, and follow him with a whole heart rather than to maintain a superficial commitment based on tradition or ceremonial systems. | Although we are free from the sacrificial system of the Jewish law, we may still rely on outward observances to substitute for inward commitment. God desires that all our work and worship be motivated by genuine, heartfelt devotion to him. |
| God's Faithfulness | God faithfully kept the promises he made to Israel. He responded to his people with tender mercy and swift justice. In showing mercy, he faithfully acted in the best interest of his people. In showing justice, he was faithful to his word and perfect moral nature. | Because God is faithful, he can be counted on to be merciful toward us. Yet God is also just, and he will not tolerate rebellion against him. His faithfulness and unselfish love should inspire us to dedicate ourselves to him completely. We must never take his mercy for granted. |

# KEY PLACES IN 1 SAMUEL

LEBANON

N

SYRIA

Mediterranean
Sea

Sea of
Galilee

ISRAEL

Mount
Gilboa

Jordan River

JORDAN

CANAAN

.Ebenezer

Shiloh.

Mizpah.

Gilgal.

Kiriath-jearim.  .Ramah

Jerusalem.

Gath.

VALLEY
OF ELAH

WILDERNESS   Dead
OF ZIPH      Sea

En-gedi.

.Ziklag

WILDERNESS
OF MAON

| 0 | 20 Mi. |
| 0 | 20 Km. |

The broken lines (—·—·) indicate modern boundaries.

**1 Ramah**  Samuel was born in Ramah. Before his birth, Samuel's mother, Hannah, made a promise to God that she would dedicate her son to serve God alongside the priests in the Tabernacle at Shiloh (1:1—2:11).

**2 Shiloh**  The focal point of Israel's worship was at Shiloh, where the Tabernacle and the Ark of the Covenant resided. Eli was the high priest, but his sons, Hophni and Phinehas, were evil men who took advantage of the people. Samuel, however, served God faithfully, and God blessed him as he grew (2:12—3:21).

**3 Kiriath-jearim**  Israel was constantly at odds with the Philistines, and another battle was brewing. Hophni and Phinehas brought the Ark of the Covenant from Shiloh to the battlefield, believing that its mere presence would bring the Israelites victory. The Israelites were defeated by the Philistines at

Ebenezer, and the Ark was captured. However, the Philistines soon found out that the Ark was not quite the great battle trophy they expected. For God sent plagues upon every Philistine city into which the Ark was brought. Finally, the Philistines sent it back to Kiriath-jearim in Israel (4:1—7:1).

**4 Mizpah**  The Israelites' defeat made them realize that God was no longer blessing them. Samuel called the people together at Mizpah and asked them to fast and pray in sorrow for their sins. The assembly at Mizpah was a tempting target for the confident Philistines who advanced for an attack. But God intervened and routed their mighty army. Meanwhile, Samuel was judging cases throughout Israel. But as Samuel grew old, the people came to him at Ramah (his home base) demanding a king in order to be like the other nations. At Mizpah, Saul was chosen by sacred appointment to be Israel's first king with the blessing, but not the approval, of God and Samuel (7:2—10:27).

**5 Gilgal**  A battle with the Ammonites proved Saul's leadership abilities to the people of Israel. He protected the people of Jabesh-gilead and scattered the Ammonite army. Samuel and the people crowned Saul as king of Israel at Gilgal (11:1–15).

**6 Valley of Elah**  Saul won many other battles, but over time he proved to be arrogant, sinful, and rebellious, so God finally rejected him as king. Unknown to Saul, a young shepherd and musician named David was anointed to be Israel's next king. But it would be many years before David sat upon the throne. Ironically, Saul hired David to play the harp in his palace. Saul grew to like David so much that he made him his personal armor bearer. In one particular battle with the Philistines in the valley of Elah, David killed Goliath, the Philistines' mightiest soldier. But this victory was the beginning of the end of Saul's love for David. The Israelites praised David more than Saul, causing Saul to become so jealous that he plotted to kill David (12:1—22:23).

**7 The Wilderness**  Even anointed kings are not exempt from troubles. David literally ran for his life from King Saul, hiding with his band of followers in the wilderness of Ziph (where the men of Ziph constantly betrayed him), the wilderness of Maon, and the wilderness of En-gedi. Though he had opportunities to kill Saul, David refused to do so because Saul was God's anointed king (23:1—26:25).

**8 Gath**  David moved his men and family to Gath, the Philistine city where King Achish lived. Saul then stopped chasing him. The Philistines seemed to welcome this famous fugitive from Israel (27:1–4).

**9 Ziklag**   Desiring privacy in return for his pretended loyalty to King Achish, David asked for a city in which to house his men and family. Achish gave him Ziklag. From there David conducted raids against the cities of the Geshurites, Girzites, and Amalekites, making sure no one escaped to tell the tale (27:5–12). David later conquered the Amalekites after they raided Ziklag (30:1–31).

**10 Mount Gilboa**   War with the Philistines broke out again in the north, near Mount Gilboa. Saul, who no longer relied on God, consulted a medium in a desperate attempt to contact Samuel for help. In the meantime, David was sent back to Ziklag because the Philistine commanders did not trust his loyalty in battle against Israel. The Philistines slaughtered the Israelites on Mount Gilboa, killing King Saul and his three sons, including David's loyal friend Jonathan. Without God, Saul led a bitter and misguided life. The consequences of his sinful actions affected not only him but hurt his family and the entire nation as well (28:1—31:13).

---

## A. ELI AND SAMUEL (1:1—7:17)

Israel has been ruled by judges for over 200 years. Eli and Samuel are the last of those judges. Samuel is born near the end of Eli's life. He grows up in the Tabernacle as a priest-in-training under Eli and is well qualified to serve Israel as both a priest and a judge. Although the nation has fallen away from God, it is clear that God is preparing Samuel from the very beginning to lead the nation back to right living. God is always in control; he is able to bring his people back to him.

### 1. Samuel's birth and childhood
*Elkanah and His Family*

**1:1**
1 Chr 6:22-28,
33-38

**1:2**
Deut 21:15-17

**1:3**
Exod 34:23
Deut 12:4-7
Josh 18:1
Luke 2:41-42

**1:5**
Gen 30:1-2

**1** There was a man named Elkanah who lived in Ramah in the region of Zuph* in the hill country of Ephraim. He was the son of Jeroham, son of Elihu, son of Tohu, son of Zuph, of Ephraim. 2Elkanah had two wives, Hannah and Peninnah. Peninnah had children, but Hannah did not.

3Each year Elkanah would travel to Shiloh to worship and sacrifice to the LORD of Heaven's Armies at the Tabernacle. The priests of the LORD at that time were the two sons of Eli—Hophni and Phinehas. 4On the days Elkanah presented his sacrifice, he would give portions of the meat to Peninnah and each of her children. 5And though he loved Hannah, he would give her only one choice portion* because the LORD had given her no children. 6So Peninnah would taunt Hannah and make fun of her because the LORD had kept her from having children. 7Year after year it was the same—Peninnah would taunt Hannah as they went to the Tabernacle.* Each time, Hannah would be reduced to tears and would not even eat.

**1:1** As in Greek version; Hebrew reads *in Ramathaim-zophim*; compare 1:19.   **1:5** Or *And because he loved Hannah, he would give her a choice portion*. The meaning of the Hebrew is uncertain.   **1:7** Hebrew *the house of the LORD*; also in 1:24.

---

**1:1**   The book of 1 Samuel begins in the days when the judges still ruled Israel, possibly during the closing years of Samson's life. Samuel was Israel's last judge and the first priest and prophet to serve during the time of a king. He was the best example of what a good judge should be, governing the people by God's word and not by his own impulses. Samuel was the man who anointed Saul as Israel's first king.

**1:2**   Although many great Old Testament leaders (such as Abraham, Jacob, and David) had more than one wife, this was not God's original intention for marriage. Genesis 2:24 states that in marriage, two people become one flesh. Why then did polygamy exist among God's people? First, it was to produce more offspring to help in a man's work and to assure the continuation of a man's family line. Numerous children were a symbol of status and wealth. Second, in societies where many young men were killed in battle, polygamy became an accepted way of supporting women who otherwise would have remained unmarried and, very likely, destitute. Nevertheless, polygamy often caused serious family problems, as we see in this story of Hannah and Peninnah.

**1:3**   The Tabernacle was located at Shiloh, the religious center of the nation (see Joshua 18:1). Three times a year all Israelite men were required to attend a religious feast held at the Tabernacle: the Passover with the Festival of Unleavened Bread, the Festival of First Harvest, and the Festival of Shelters (Deuteronomy 16:16). Elkanah made this pilgrimage regularly to fulfill God's commands. (See Exodus 23:14-17 for the regulations concerning the pilgrimage, and see the note on Exodus 40:34 for more on the Tabernacle.)

**1:6**   Hannah had been unable to conceive children, and in Old Testament times, a childless woman was considered a failure. Her barrenness was a social embarrassment for her husband. Children were a very important part of the society's economic structure. They were a source of labor for the family, and it was their duty to care for their parents in their old age. If a wife could not bear children, she was often obligated by ancient Middle Eastern custom to give one of her servant girls to her husband to bear children for her. Although Elkanah could have left Hannah (a husband was permitted to divorce a barren wife), he remained lovingly devoted to her despite social criticism and his rights under civil law.

**1:7**   Part of God's plan for Hannah involved postponing her years of childbearing. While Peninnah and Elkanah looked at Hannah's outward circumstances, God was moving ahead with his plan. Think of those in your world who are struggling with God's timing in answering their prayers and who need your love and help. By supporting those who are struggling, you may help them remain steadfast in their faith and confident in his timing to bring fulfillment to their lives.

8"Why are you crying, Hannah?" Elkanah would ask. "Why aren't you eating? Why be downhearted just because you have no children? You have me—isn't that better than having ten sons?"

## Hannah's Prayer for a Son

9Once after a sacrificial meal at Shiloh, Hannah got up and went to pray. Eli the priest was sitting at his customary place beside the entrance of the Tabernacle.* 10Hannah was in deep anguish, crying bitterly as she prayed to the LORD. 11And she made this vow: "O LORD of Heaven's Armies, if you will look upon my sorrow and answer my prayer and give me a son, then I will give him back to you. He will be yours for his entire lifetime, and as a sign that he has been dedicated to the LORD, his hair will never be cut.*"

12As she was praying to the LORD, Eli watched her. 13Seeing her lips moving but hearing no sound, he thought she had been drinking. 14"Must you come here drunk?" he demanded. "Throw away your wine!"

15"Oh no, sir!" she replied. "I haven't been drinking wine or anything stronger. But I am very discouraged, and I was pouring out my heart to the LORD. 16Don't think I am a wicked woman! For I have been praying out of great anguish and sorrow."

17"In that case," Eli said, "go in peace! May the God of Israel grant the request you have asked of him."

18"Oh, thank you, sir!" she exclaimed. Then she went back and began to eat again, and she was no longer sad.

## Samuel's Birth and Dedication

19The entire family got up early the next morning and went to worship the LORD once more. Then they returned home to Ramah. When Elkanah slept with Hannah, the LORD remembered her plea, 20and in due time she gave birth to a son. She named him Samuel,* for she said, "I asked the LORD for him."

21The next year Elkanah and his family went on their annual trip to offer a sacrifice to the LORD. 22But Hannah did not go. She told her husband, "Wait until the boy is weaned. Then I will take him to the Tabernacle and leave him there with the LORD permanently.*"

23"Whatever you think is best," Elkanah agreed. "Stay here for now, and may the LORD help you keep your promise." So she stayed home and nursed the boy until he was weaned.

1:8 Ruth 4:15
1:9 1 Sam 3:3
1:11 Gen 29:32; Num 6:1-6; 30:6-11; Judg 13:5; Luke 1:15
1:14 Acts 2:13
1:15 Ps 42:4; Lam 2:19
1:17 Ps 20:3-5
1:18 Ruth 2:13
1:19 Gen 21:1-2; 30:22
1:21 Luke 2:22

1:9 Hebrew *the Temple of the LORD.* 1:11 Some manuscripts add *He will drink neither wine nor intoxicants.* 1:20 *Samuel* sounds like the Hebrew term for "asked of God" or "heard by God." 1:22 Some manuscripts add *I will offer him as a Nazirite for all time.*

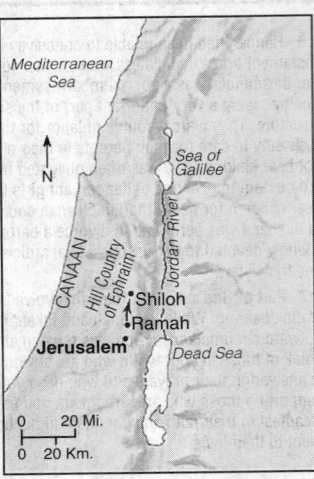

**THE JOURNEY TO SHILOH**
Each year Elkanah and his family traveled from their home at Ramah to Shiloh, where they worshiped and sacrificed at God's Tabernacle.

**1:8** Hannah knew her husband loved her, but even his encouragement could not comfort her. She could not keep from listening to Peninnah's jeers and letting Peninnah's words erode her self-confidence. Although we cannot keep others from unjustly criticizing us, we can choose how we will react to their hurtful words. Rather than dwelling upon our problems, we can enjoy the loving relationships God has given us. By so doing, we can exchange self-pity for hope.

**1:10** Hannah had good reason to feel discouraged and bitter. She was unable to bear children; she shared her husband with a woman who ridiculed her (1:7); her loving husband could not solve her problem (1:8); and even the high priest misunderstood her motives (1:14). But instead of retaliating or giving up hope, Hannah prayed. She brought her problem honestly before God.

Each of us may face times of barrenness when nothing "comes to birth" in our work, service, or relationships. It is difficult to pray in faith when we feel so ineffective. But, as Hannah discovered, prayer opens the way for God to work (1:19, 20).

**1:11** Be careful what you promise in prayer because God may take you up on it. Hannah so desperately wanted a child that she was willing to strike a bargain with God. God took her up on her promise, and to Hannah's credit, she did her part, even though it was painful (1:27, 28).

Although we are not in a position to barter with God, he may still choose to answer a prayer that has an attached promise. When you pray, ask yourself, Will I follow through on any promises I make to God if he grants my request? It is dishonest and dangerous to ignore a promise, especially to God. God keeps his promises, and he expects you to keep yours.

**1:24**
Num 15:8-10

<sup>24</sup>When the child was weaned, Hannah took him to the Tabernacle in Shiloh. They brought along a three-year-old bull* for the sacrifice and a basket* of flour and some wine. <sup>25</sup>After sacrificing the bull, they brought the boy to Eli. <sup>26</sup>"Sir, do you remember me?" Hannah asked. "I am the woman who stood here several years ago praying to the Lord. <sup>27</sup>I asked the Lord to give me this boy, and he has granted my request. <sup>28</sup>Now I am giving him to the Lord, and he will belong to the Lord his whole life." And they* worshiped the Lord there.

**1:24a** As in Dead Sea Scrolls, Greek and Syriac versions; Masoretic Text reads *three bulls.* **1:24b** Hebrew *and an ephah* [20 quarts or 22 liters]. **1:28** Hebrew *he.*

---

**ELKANAH & PENINNAH**

Husbands can be insensitive for many reasons, but often they simply suffer from ignorance. Elkanah had two wives, which doubled his opportunities to seem insensitive. His wife Peninnah was able to give Elkanah many children. The other wife, Hannah, owned Elkanah's heart but was unable to get pregnant. Peninnah, jealous that providing Elkanah with heirs didn't turn his affections toward her, treated Hannah with disdain. Yet Elkanah seemed oblivious to the turmoil around him.

Although the events leading up to the birth of Samuel primarily involved Hannah, both Elkanah and Peninnah played significant roles. Peninnah's competitiveness and derision drove Hannah to prayer; Elkanah's simple love allowed Hannah to entrust their child Samuel into God's care. Elkanah didn't realize how much a little attention toward Peninnah could have cooled the simmering emotions in his home. Nor did he understand that his love for Hannah didn't make up for the emptiness of her womb.

The glimpse God gives us of that tense household provides a helpful backdrop for God's purposes, which are not thwarted by human shortcomings. He worked within the strain and stress of those relationships to bring Samuel into the world—one of the most significant figures in the Old Testament. When our relational systems seem too gnarled to be unraveled or salvaged, we need to remember that God not only displays his creativity by making things from scratch, but also by bringing order and beauty out of messes.

| | |
|---|---|
| **Strengths and accomplishments** | • Elkanah supported Hannah's decision to leave Samuel in Shiloh to be raised as a priest<br>• Regular trips to Shiloh acknowledged God's importance to the entire family |
| **Weaknesses and mistakes** | • Elkanah did not understand what would have helped each of his wives<br>• Peninnah made things worse by taking out her disappointment and anger on Hannah |
| **Lessons from their lives** | • Ignorance is not a good excuse for insensitivity<br>• Jealousy is not a good excuse for bad behavior<br>• God works in the middle of family messes |
| **Vital statistics** | • Where: Ramah<br>• Occupation: Unknown<br>• Relatives: Elkanah and Peninnah had an unknown number of children; Elkanah and Hannah bore two daughters and four sons, including Samuel.<br>• Contemporary: Eli the priest |
| **Key verse** | "'Why are you crying, Hannah?' Elkanah would ask. 'Why aren't you eating? Why be downhearted just because you have no children? You have me—isn't that better than having ten sons?'" (1 Samuel 1:8). |

Their story is told in 1 Samuel 1—2.

---

**1:18** Earlier Hannah had been discouraged to the point of being physically sick and unable to eat. At this point, she returned home well and happy. The change in her attitude may be attributed to three factors: (1) She honestly prayed to God (1:11); (2) she received encouragement from Eli (1:17); (3) she resolved to leave the problem with God (1:18). This is the antidote for discouragement: Tell God how you really feel and leave your problems with him. Then rely upon the support of good friends and counselors.

**1:26-28** To do what she promised (1:11), Hannah gave up what she wanted most—her son—and presented him to Eli to serve in the house of the Lord. In dedicating her only son to God, Hannah was dedicating her entire life and future to God. Because Samuel's life was from God, Hannah was not really giving him up. Rather, she was returning him to God, who had

given Samuel to Hannah in the first place. These verses illustrate the kinds of gifts we should give to God. Do your gifts cost you little (Sunday mornings, a comfortable tithe), or are they gifts of sacrifice? Are you presenting God with tokens, or are you presenting him with your entire life?

**1:28** Samuel was probably three years old—the customary age for weaning—when his mother left him at the Tabernacle. By saying, "I am giving him to the Lord," Hannah meant that she was dedicating Samuel to God for lifetime service. She did not, of course, forget her much-wanted son. She visited him regularly, and each year she brought him a robe just like Eli's (2:19). In later years, Samuel lived in Ramah (7:17), his parents' hometown (1:19, 20).

*Hannah's Prayer of Praise*

**2** Then Hannah prayed:

"My heart rejoices in the LORD!
    The LORD has made me strong.*
Now I have an answer for my enemies;
    I rejoice because you rescued me.

² No one is holy like the LORD!
    There is no one besides you;
    there is no Rock like our God.

³ "Stop acting so proud and haughty!
    Don't speak with such arrogance!
For the LORD is a God who knows what you have done;
    he will judge your actions.
⁴ The bow of the mighty is now broken,
    and those who stumbled are now strong.
⁵ Those who were well fed are now starving,
    and those who were starving are now full.
The childless woman now has seven children,
    and the woman with many children wastes away.
⁶ The LORD gives both death and life;
    he brings some down to the grave* but raises others up.
⁷ The LORD makes some poor and others rich;
    he brings some down and lifts others up.
⁸ He lifts the poor from the dust
    and the needy from the garbage dump.
He sets them among princes,
    placing them in seats of honor.
For all the earth is the LORD's,
    and he has set the world in order.

⁹ "He will protect his faithful ones,
    but the wicked will disappear in darkness.
No one will succeed by strength alone.
¹⁰     Those who fight against the LORD will be shattered.
He thunders against them from heaven;
    the LORD judges throughout the earth.
He gives power to his king;
    he increases the strength* of his anointed one."

¹¹ Then Elkanah returned home to Ramah without Samuel. And the boy served the LORD by assisting Eli the priest.

2:1 Hebrew *has exalted my horn.*    2:6 Hebrew *to Sheol.*    2:10 Hebrew *he exalts the horn.*

---

**Cross References (margin):**

2:1 Luke 1:46-55

2:2 Exod 15:11; Deut 4:35; 32:30-31; 2 Sam 22:32

2:3 1 Sam 16:7; 1 Kgs 8:39; Prov 8:13; 16:2; 24:11-12

2:4 Pss 37:15; 46:7-9

2:5 Ps 113:9; Jer 15:9

2:6 Deut 32:39

2:7 Deut 8:18; Job 1:21; 5:10-11; Ps 75:7

2:8 Job 36:7; 38:4-7; 42:10; Jas 2:5

2:9 Ps 91:11-12; Matt 8:12

2:10 Exod 15:6; 19:16; 1 Sam 7:10; Pss 18:13; 21:1, 7; 89:24; 96:13

2:11 1 Sam 3:1

---

**2:1-10** Hannah praised God for his answer to her prayer for a son. The theme of her poetic prayer is her confidence in God's sovereignty and her thankfulness for everything he had done. Mary, the mother of Jesus, modeled her own praise song, called the Magnificat, after Hannah's prayer (Luke 1:46-55). Like Hannah and Mary, we should be confident of God's ultimate control over the events in our lives, and we should be thankful for the ways God has blessed us. By praising God for all good gifts, we acknowledge his ultimate control over all the affairs of life.

**2:2** Hannah praised God for being a Rock—firm, strong, and unchanging. In our fast-paced world, friends come and go, and circumstances change. It's difficult to find a solid foundation that will not change. Those who devote their lives to achievements, causes, or possessions have as their security that which is finite and changeable. The possessions that we work so hard to obtain will all pass away. But God is always present. Hope in him. He will never fail.

**2:3** No doubt as Hannah said these words, she was thinking of Peninnah's arrogance and chiding. Hannah did not have to get even with Peninnah. She knew that God is all-knowing and that he will judge all sin and pride. Hannah wisely left judgment up to God. Resist the temptation to take justice into your own hands. God will weigh your deeds as well as the deeds of those who have wronged you.

**2:10** Because we live in a world where evil abounds and where war and terrorism always threaten, we may forget that God is in control. Hannah saw God as (1) solid as a rock (2:2), (2) the one who knows what we do (2:3), (3) sovereign over all the affairs of people (2:4-8), and (4) the Supreme Judge who administers perfect justice (2:10). Remembering God's sovereign control helps us put both world and personal events in perspective.

**2:11, 18** Samuel assisted Eli the priest. In this role, Samuel's responsibilities would have included opening the Tabernacle doors each morning (3:15), cleaning the furniture, and sweeping the floors. As he grew older, Samuel would have assisted Eli in offering sacrifices. The fact that he was wearing a linen garment (like the clothing worn only by priests) shows that he was a priest-in-training. Because Samuel was Eli's helper, he was God's helper, too.

### Eli's Wicked Sons

**2:12**
Jer 2:8; 9:3, 6

**2:13**
Lev 7:20, 28-36

**2:15**
Lev 3:2-5

**2:17**
Mal 2:7-9

¹²Now the sons of Eli were scoundrels who had no respect for the LORD ¹³or for their duties as priests. Whenever anyone offered a sacrifice, Eli's sons would send over a servant with a three-pronged fork. While the meat of the sacrificed animal was still boiling, ¹⁴the servant would stick the fork into the pot and demand that whatever it brought up be given to Eli's sons. All the Israelites who came to worship at Shiloh were treated this way. ¹⁵Sometimes the servant would come even before the animal's fat had been burned on the altar. He would demand raw meat before it had been boiled so that it could be used for roasting.

¹⁶The man offering the sacrifice might reply, "Take as much as you want, but the fat must be burned first." Then the servant would demand, "No, give it to me now, or I'll take it by force." ¹⁷So the sin of these young men was very serious in the LORD's sight, for they treated the LORD's offerings with contempt.

**HANNAH**

Hannah's prayer shows us that all we have and receive is on loan from God. Hannah might have had many excuses for being a possessive mother. But when God answered her prayer, she followed through on her promise to dedicate Samuel to God's service.

She discovered that the greatest joy in having a child is to give that child fully and freely back to God. She entered motherhood prepared to do what all mothers must eventually do—let go of their children.

When children are born, they are completely dependent upon their parents for all their basic necessities. This causes some parents to forget that those same children will grow toward independence within the span of a few short years. Being sensitive to the different stages of that healthy process will greatly strengthen family relationships; resisting or denying that process will cause great pain. We must gradually let go of our children in order to allow them to become mature, independent adults.

| | |
|---|---|
| **Strengths and accomplishments** | • Mother of Samuel, Israel's greatest judge<br>• Fervent in worship; effective in prayer<br>• Willing to follow through on even a costly commitment |
| **Weakness and mistake** | • Struggled with her sense of self-worth because she had been unable to have children |
| **Lessons from her life** | • God hears and answers prayer<br>• Our children are gifts from God<br>• God is concerned for the oppressed and afflicted |
| **Vital statistics** | • Where: Ephraim<br>• Occupation: Homemaker<br>• Relatives: Husband: Elkanah. Son: Samuel. Later, three other sons and two daughters.<br>• Contemporary: Eli the priest |
| **Key verses** | "'Sir, do you remember me?' Hannah asked. 'I am the woman who stood here several years ago praying to the LORD. I asked the LORD to give me this boy, and he has granted my request. Now I am giving him to the LORD, and he will belong to the LORD his whole life.' And they worshiped the LORD there" (1 Samuel 1:26–28). |

Her story is told in 1 Samuel 1—2.

When you serve others—even in carrying out ordinary tasks—you are serving God. Because ultimately we serve God, every job has dignity.

**2:12ff** The law stipulated that the needs of all the Levites were to be met through the people's tithes (Numbers 18:20-24; Joshua 13:14, 33). Because Eli's sons were priests, they were to be taken care of this way. But Eli's sons took advantage of their position to satisfy their lust for power, possessions, and control. Their contempt and arrogance toward both people and worship undermined the integrity of the whole priesthood.

Eli knew that his sons were evil, but he did little to correct or stop them, even when the integrity of God's sanctuary was threatened. As the high priest, Eli should have responded by executing his sons (Numbers 15:22-31). No wonder he chose not to confront the situation. But by ignoring their selfish actions, Eli let his sons ruin their own lives and the lives of many others. There are times when serious problems must be confronted, even if the process and consequences could be painful.

**2:13, 14** This fork was a utensil used in the Tabernacle for offering sacrifices. Made of bronze (Exodus 27:3), it usually had three prongs to hook the meat that was to be offered on the altar. Eli's sons used the fork to take more meat from the pot than was due them.

**2:13-17** What were Eli's sons doing wrong? They were taking parts of the sacrifices *before* they were offered to God on the altar. They were also eating meat before the fat was burned off. This was against God's laws (Leviticus 3:3-5). In effect, Eli's sons were treating God's offerings with contempt. Offerings were given to show honor and respect to God while seeking forgiveness for sins, but through their irreverence, Eli's sons were actually sinning while making the offerings. To add to their sins, they were also sleeping with the women who served there (2:22).

Like Eli's sons, some religious leaders look down on the faith of ordinary people and treat their offerings to God casually or even with contempt. God harshly judges those who lead his people astray or scorn what is devoted to him (Numbers 18:32).

18But Samuel, though he was only a boy, served the LORD. He wore a linen garment like that of a priest.* 19Each year his mother made a small coat for him and brought it to him when she came with her husband for the sacrifice. 20Before they returned home, Eli would bless Elkanah and his wife and say, "May the LORD give you other children to take the place of this one she gave to the LORD.*" 21And the LORD gave Hannah three sons and two daughters. Meanwhile, Samuel grew up in the presence of the LORD.

22Now Eli was very old, but he was aware of what his sons were doing to the people of Israel. He knew, for instance, that his sons were seducing the young women who assisted at the entrance of the Tabernacle.* 23Eli said to them, "I have been hearing reports from all the people about the wicked things you are doing. Why do you keep sinning? 24You must stop, my sons! The reports I hear among the LORD's people are not good. 25If someone sins against another person, God* can mediate for the guilty party. But if someone sins against the LORD, who can intercede?" But Eli's sons wouldn't listen to their father, for the LORD was already planning to put them to death.

26Meanwhile, the boy Samuel grew taller and grew in favor with the LORD and with the people.

## A Warning for Eli's Family

27One day a man of God came to Eli and gave him this message from the LORD: "I revealed myself* to your ancestors when the people of Israel were slaves in Egypt. 28I chose your ancestor Aaron* from among all the tribes of Israel to be my priest, to offer sacrifices on my altar, to burn incense, and to wear the priestly vest* as he served me. And I assigned the sacrificial offerings to you priests. 29So why do you scorn my sacrifices and offerings? Why do you give your sons more honor than you give me—for you and they have become fat from the best offerings of my people Israel!

30"Therefore, the LORD, the God of Israel, says: I promised that your branch of the tribe of Levi* would always be my priests. But I will honor those who honor me, and I will despise those who think lightly of me. 31The time is coming when I will put an end to your family, so it will no longer serve as my priests. All the members of your family will die before their time. None will reach old age. 32You will watch with envy as I pour out prosperity on the people of Israel. But no members of your family will ever live out their days. 33Those who survive will live in sadness and grief, and their children will die a violent death.* 34And to prove that what I have said will come true, I will cause your two sons, Hophni and Phinehas, to die on the same day!

2:18 1 Sam 2:11
2:19 1 Sam 1:3
2:21 Gen 21:1; 1 Sam 3:19-21; Luke 2:40
2:22 Exod 38:8
2:23 Num 15:30
2:25 Josh 11:20
2:26 Luke 2:40, 52
2:27 Judg 13:6
2:28 Exod 28:1-4; 30:7-8
2:29 Matt 10:37; Deut 12:5
2:30 Num 25:12-13; Ps 50:23; Mal 2:7-9
2:31 1 Sam 4:11-18; 22:17-20
2:34 1 Sam 4:11, 17; 1 Kgs 13:3

2:18 Hebrew *He wore a linen ephod.* 2:20 As in Dead Sea Scrolls and Greek version; Masoretic Text reads *this one he requested of the LORD.* 2:22 Hebrew *Tent of Meeting.* Some manuscripts lack this entire sentence. 2:25 Or *the judges.* 2:27 As in Greek and Syriac versions; Hebrew reads *Did I reveal myself.* 2:28a Hebrew *your father.* 2:28b Hebrew *an ephod.* 2:30 Hebrew *that your house and your father's house.* 2:33 As in Dead Sea Scrolls, which read *die by the sword;* Masoretic Text reads *die like mortals.*

2:18 Samuel wore a linen garment (also called an ephod). *Ephods,* long sleeveless vests made of plain linen, were worn by all priests. The high priest's ephod carried special significance. It was embroidered with a variety of bright colors. Attached to it was the chestpiece, a bib-like garment with gold embroidered shoulder straps. Twelve precious gemstones were attached to the chestpiece, each stone representing one of the tribes of Israel. A pouch on the ephod held the Urim and the Thummim, two small objects used to determine God's will in certain national matters.

2:21 God honored the desires of faithful Hannah. We never hear about Peninnah or her children again, but Samuel was used mightily by God. God also gave Hannah five children in addition to Samuel. God often blesses us in ways we do not expect. Hannah never expected to have a child at her age, much less six children! Don't resent God's timing. His blessings might not be immediate, but they will come if we are faithful to do what he says in his Word.

2:23-25 Eli's sons knew better, but they continued to disobey God deliberately by cheating, seducing, and robbing the people. Therefore, God planned to kill them. Any sin is wrong, but sin carried out deliberately and deceitfully is the worst kind. When we sin out of ignorance, we deserve punishment. But when we sin intentionally, the consequences will be more severe. Don't ignore God's warnings about sin. Abandon sin before it becomes a way of life.

2:25 Does a loving God really will or want to put people to death?

Consider the situation in the Tabernacle. A person made an offering in order to have his sins forgiven, and Eli's sons stole the offering and made a sham of the person's repentant attitude. God, in his love for Israel, could not permit this situation to continue. He allowed Eli's sons to die as a result of their own boastful presumption. They took the Ark into battle, thinking it would protect them. But God withdrew his protection, and the wicked sons of Eli were killed (4:10, 11).

2:29 Eli had a difficult time rearing his sons. He apparently did not take any strong disciplinary action with them when he became aware of their wrongdoing. But Eli was not just a father trying to handle his rebellious sons; he was the high priest ignoring the sins of priests under his jurisdiction. As a result, the Lord took the necessary disciplinary action that Eli would not.

Eli was guilty of honoring his sons above God by letting them continue in their sinful ways. Is there a situation in your life, family, or work that you allow to continue even though you know it is wrong? If so, you may become as guilty as those engaged in the wrong act.

2:31, 35, 36 For the fulfillment of this prediction see 1 Kings 2:26, 27. This is where Solomon removed Abiathar from his position, thus ending Eli's line. Then God raised up Zadok, a priest under David and then high priest under Solomon. Zadok's line was probably still in place as late as the days of Ezra.

³⁵"Then I will raise up a faithful priest who will serve me and do what I desire. I will establish his family, and they will be priests to my anointed kings forever. ³⁶Then all of your surviving family will bow before him, begging for money and food. 'Please,' they will say, 'give us jobs among the priests so we will have enough to eat.'"

### The Lord Speaks to Samuel

**3:1**
1 Sam 2:11
Ps 74:9
Amos 8:11

**3** Meanwhile, the boy Samuel served the Lord by assisting Eli. Now in those days messages from the Lord were very rare, and visions were quite uncommon. ²One night Eli, who was almost blind by now, had gone to bed. ³The lamp of God had not

**ELI**

Eli was one Old Testament person with a very modern problem. The recognition and respect he earned in public did not extend to his handling of his private affairs. He may have been an excellent priest, but he was a poor parent. His sons brought him grief and ruin. He lacked two important qualities needed for effective parental discipline: firm resolve and corrective action.

Eli responded to situations rather than solving them. But even his responses tended to be weak. God pointed out his sons' errors, but Eli did little to correct them. The contrast between God's dealing with Eli and Eli's dealing with his sons is clear—God gave warning, spelled out the consequences of disobedience, and then acted. Eli only warned. Children need to learn that their parents' words and actions go together. Both love and discipline must be spoken as well as acted out.

But Eli had another problem. He was more concerned with the symbols of his religion than with the God they represented. For Eli, the Ark of the Covenant had become a relic to be protected rather than a reminder of the Protector. His faith shifted from the Creator to the created.

It may be easier to worship things we can see, whether buildings, people, or Scripture itself, but such tangible things have no power in themselves. This book you hold is either merely a respectable religious relic, or it is the sharp and effective Word of God. Your attitude toward it is largely shaped by your relationship to the God from whom it comes. A relic or antique has to be carefully stored away; God's Word has to be used and obeyed. Which attitude accurately describes your approach to the Word of God?

| | |
|---|---|
| **Strengths and accomplishments** | • Judged Israel for 40 years<br>• Spoke with Hannah, the mother of Samuel, and assured her of God's blessing<br>• Reared and trained Samuel, the greatest judge of Israel |
| **Weaknesses and mistakes** | • Failed to discipline his sons or correct them when they sinned<br>• Tended to react to situations rather than take decisive action<br>• Saw the Ark of the Covenant as a relic to be cherished rather than as a symbol of God's presence with Israel |
| **Lessons from his life** | • Parents need to discipline their children responsibly<br>• Life is more than simply reacting; it demands action<br>• Past victories cannot substitute for present trust |
| **Vital statistics** | • Where: Shiloh<br>• Occupations: High priest, judge of Israel<br>• Relatives: Sons: Hophni and Phinehas<br>• Contemporary: Samuel |
| **Key verses** | "Then the Lord said to Samuel, 'I am about to do a shocking thing in Israel. I am going to carry out all my threats against Eli and his family, from beginning to end. I have warned him that judgment is coming upon his family forever, because his sons are blaspheming God and he hasn't disciplined them. So I have vowed that the sins of Eli and his sons will never be forgiven by sacrifices or offerings'" (1 Samuel 3:11–14). |

His story is told in 1 Samuel 1—4. He is also mentioned in 1 Kings 2:26, 27.

**3:1-5** Although God had spoken directly and audibly with Moses and Joshua, his word became rare during the three centuries of rule by judges. By Eli's time, no prophets were speaking God's messages to Israel. Why? Look at the attitude of Eli's sons. They either refused to listen to God or allowed greed to get in the way of any communication with him.

Listening and responding is vital in a relationship with God. Although God does not always use the sound of a human voice, he always speaks clearly through his Word. To receive his messages, we must be ready to listen and to act upon what he tells us. Like Samuel, be ready to say "Here I am" when God calls you to action.

**3:2, 3** The Ark of God was kept in the Most Holy Place, the innermost room of the Tabernacle where only the high priest could enter once a year. In front of the Most Holy Place was the Holy Place, a small room where the other sacred furniture of the Tabernacle was kept (the incense altar, the Bread of the Presence, the lampstand). Just outside the Holy Place was a court with small rooms where the priests were to stay. Samuel probably slept here with the other priests, only a few yards away from the Ark.

yet gone out, and Samuel was sleeping in the Tabernacle* near the Ark of God. ⁴Suddenly the LORD called out, "Samuel!"

"Yes?" Samuel replied. "What is it?" ⁵He got up and ran to Eli. "Here I am. Did you call me?"

"I didn't call you," Eli replied. "Go back to bed." So he did.

⁶Then the LORD called out again, "Samuel!"

Again Samuel got up and went to Eli. "Here I am. Did you call me?"

"I didn't call you, my son," Eli said. "Go back to bed."

⁷Samuel did not yet know the LORD because he had never had a message from the LORD before. ⁸So the LORD called a third time, and once more Samuel got up and went to Eli. "Here I am. Did you call me?"

Then Eli realized it was the LORD who was calling the boy. ⁹So he said to Samuel, "Go and lie down again, and if someone calls again, say, 'Speak, LORD, your servant is listening.'" So Samuel went back to bed.

¹⁰And the LORD came and called as before, "Samuel! Samuel!"

And Samuel replied, "Speak, your servant is listening."

¹¹Then the LORD said to Samuel, "I am about to do a shocking thing in Israel. ¹²I am going to carry out all my threats against Eli and his family, from beginning to end. ¹³I have warned him that judgment is coming upon his family forever, because his sons are blaspheming God* and he hasn't disciplined them. ¹⁴So I have vowed that the sins of Eli and his sons will never be forgiven by sacrifices or offerings."

### Samuel Speaks for the LORD

¹⁵Samuel stayed in bed until morning, then got up and opened the doors of the Tabernacle* as usual. He was afraid to tell Eli what the LORD had said to him. ¹⁶But Eli called out to him, "Samuel, my son."

"Here I am," Samuel replied.

¹⁷"What did the LORD say to you? Tell me everything. And may God strike you and even kill you if you hide anything from me!" ¹⁸So Samuel told Eli everything; he didn't hold anything back. "It is the LORD's will," Eli replied. "Let him do what he thinks best."

¹⁹As Samuel grew up, the LORD was with him, and everything Samuel said proved to be reliable. ²⁰And all Israel, from Dan in the north to Beersheba in the south, knew that Samuel was confirmed as a prophet of the LORD. ²¹The LORD continued to appear at Shiloh and gave messages to Samuel there at the Tabernacle. 4:1And Samuel's words went out to all the people of Israel.

## 2. War with the Philistines

### The Philistines Capture the Ark

**4** At that time Israel was at war with the Philistines. The Israelite army was camped near Ebenezer, and the Philistines were at Aphek. ²The Philistines attacked and defeated the army of Israel, killing 4,000 men. ³After the battle was over, the troops retreated to their camp, and the elders of Israel asked, "Why did the LORD allow us to be defeated by the Philistines?" Then they said, "Let's bring the Ark of the Covenant of the LORD from Shiloh. If we carry it into battle with us, it* will save us from our enemies."

**3:3** Hebrew *the Temple of the LORD.*   **3:13** As in Greek version; Hebrew reads *his sons have made themselves contemptible.*   **3:15** Hebrew *the house of the LORD.*   **4:3** Or *he.*

**Cross-references (margin):**
- **3:7** Amos 3:7
- **3:11** 2 Kgs 21:12
- **3:12** 1 Sam 2:27-36
- **3:14** 1 Sam 2:25
- **3:18** Job 2:10; Isa 39:8
- **3:19** Gen 21:22; Judg 13:24
- **3:20** Judg 20:1
- **4:1** 1 Sam 7:12; 29:1
- **4:3** Num 10:35; Josh 7:7

---

**3:8, 9** One would naturally expect an audible message from God to be given to the priest Eli and not to the child Samuel. Eli was older and more experienced, and he held the proper position. But God's chain of command is based on faith, not on age or position. In finding faithful followers, God may use unexpected channels. Be prepared for the Lord to work at any place, at any time, and through anyone he chooses.

**3:13** Eli had spent his entire life in service to God. His responsibility was to oversee all the worship in Israel. But in pursuing this great mission he neglected the responsibilities in his own home. Don't let your desire to do God's work cause you to neglect your family. If you do, your mission may degenerate into a quest for personal importance, and your family will suffer the consequences of your neglect.

**4:1** The Philistines, descendants of Noah's son Ham, settled along the southeastern Mediterranean coast between Egypt and Gaza. They were originally one of the "Sea Peoples" who had migrated to the Middle East in ships from Greece and Crete. By Samuel's time, these warlike people were well established in five of Gaza's cities in southwest Canaan and were constantly pressing inland against the Israelites. Throughout this time, the Philistines were Israel's major enemy.

**4:3** The Ark of the Covenant contained the Ten Commandments given by God to Moses. The Ark was supposed to be kept in the Most Holy Place, a sacred part of the Tabernacle that only the high priest could enter once a year. Hophni and Phinehas desecrated the room by unlawfully entering it and removing the Ark.

The Israelites rightly recognized the great holiness of the Ark, but they thought that the Ark itself—the wood and metal box—was their source of power. They began to use it as a good luck charm, expecting it to protect them from their enemies. A symbol of God does not guarantee his presence and power.

**4:4**
2 Sam 6:2
Ps 80:1

**4:5**
Josh 6:5

**4:7**
Exod 14:25; 15:14

**4:9**
Judg 13:1

⁴So they sent men to Shiloh to bring the Ark of the Covenant of the LORD of Heaven's Armies, who is enthroned between the cherubim. Hophni and Phinehas, the sons of Eli, were also there with the Ark of the Covenant of God. ⁵When all the Israelites saw the Ark of the Covenant of the LORD coming into the camp, their shout of joy was so loud it made the ground shake!

⁶"What's going on?" the Philistines asked. "What's all the shouting about in the Hebrew camp?" When they were told it was because the Ark of the LORD had arrived, ⁷they panicked. "The gods have* come into their camp!" they cried. "This is a disaster! We have never had to face anything like this before! ⁸Help! Who can save us from these mighty gods of Israel? They are the same gods who destroyed the Egyptians with plagues when Israel was in the wilderness. ⁹Fight as never before, Philistines! If you don't, we will become the Hebrews' slaves just as they have been ours! Stand up like men and fight!"

4:7 Or *A god has.*

| ISRAELITES VERSUS PHILISTINES | Location of the Battle | Winner | Comments | Reference |
|---|---|---|---|---|
| The Israelites and Philistines were archenemies and constantly fought. Here are some of their confrontations, found in 1 and 2 Samuel. When the Israelites trusted God for the victory, they always won. | Aphek to Ebenezer | Philistines | The Ark was captured and Eli's sons killed | 1 Samuel 4:1-11 |
| | Mizpah | Israelites | After the Ark was returned, the Philistines planned to attack again, but God confused them. Israel chased the Philistines back to Beth-car | 1 Samuel 7:7-14 |
| | Geba | Israelites under Jonathan | One detachment destroyed | 1 Samuel 13:3, 4 |
| | Gilgal | A standoff | The Israelites lost their nerve and hid | 1 Samuel 13:6-17 |
| | Micmash | Israelites | Jonathan and his armor bearer said it didn't matter how many enemies there were. If God was with them, they would win. They began the battle, and the army completed it | 1 Samuel 13:23–14:23 |
| | Valley of Elah | Israelites | David and Goliath | 1 Samuel 17:1-58 |
| | ? | Israelites | David killed 200 Philistines to earn a wife | 1 Samuel 18:17-30 |
| | Keilah | Israelites under David | David protected the threshing floors from Philistine looters | 1 Samuel 23:1-5 |
| | Aphek, Jezreel, to Mount Gilboa | Philistines | Saul and Jonathan killed | 1 Samuel 29:1; 31:1-13 |
| | Baal-perazim | Israelites | The Philistines tried to capture King David | 2 Samuel 5:17-25 |
| | Gath | Israelites | There was very little trouble with the Philistines after this defeat | 2 Samuel 8:1 |
| | ? | Israelites | Abishai saved David from a Philistine giant | 2 Samuel 21:15-17 |
| | Gob | Israelites | Other giants were killed, including Goliath's brother | 2 Samuel 21:18-22 |

Their attitude toward the Ark came perilously close to idol worship. When the Ark was captured by their enemies, they thought that Israel's glory was gone (4:19-22) and that God had deserted them (7:1, 2). God uses his power according to his own wisdom and will. He responds to the faith of those who seek him.

**4:4** "The LORD of Heaven's Armies, who is enthroned between the cherubim," conveys that God's presence rested on the Ark of the Covenant between the two gold cherubim (or angels) attached to its lid. The people believed that the Ark would bring victory when Hophni and Phinehas carried it into battle.

**4:5-8** The Philistines were afraid because they remembered stories about God's intervention for Israel when they left Egypt.

But Israel had turned away from God and was clinging to only a form of godliness, a symbol of former victories.

People (and churches) often try to live on the memories of God's blessings. The Israelites wrongly assumed that because God had given them victory in the past, he would do it again, even though they had strayed far from him. Today, as in Bible times, spiritual victories come through a continually renewed relationship with God. Don't live off the past. Keep your relationship with God new and fresh.

<sup>10</sup>So the Philistines fought desperately, and Israel was defeated again. The slaughter was great; 30,000 Israelite soldiers died that day. The survivors turned and fled to their tents. <sup>11</sup>The Ark of God was captured, and Hophni and Phinehas, the two sons of Eli, were killed.

**4:10**
Deut 28:15, 25
**4:11**
1 Sam 2:34
Ps 78:60-61

### The Death of Eli

<sup>12</sup>A man from the tribe of Benjamin ran from the battlefield and arrived at Shiloh later that same day. He had torn his clothes and put dust on his head to show his grief. <sup>13</sup>Eli was waiting beside the road to hear the news of the battle, for his heart trembled for the safety of the Ark of God. When the messenger arrived and told what had happened, an outcry resounded throughout the town.

**4:12**
Josh 7:6
2 Sam 1:2
Neh 9:1

<sup>14</sup>"What is all the noise about?" Eli asked.

The messenger rushed over to Eli, <sup>15</sup>who was ninety-eight years old and blind. <sup>16</sup>He said to Eli, "I have just come from the battlefield—I was there this very day."

**4:15**
Gen 27:1
1 Sam 3:2

"What happened, my son?" Eli demanded.

<sup>17</sup>"Israel has been defeated by the Philistines," the messenger replied. "The people have been slaughtered, and your two sons, Hophni and Phinehas, were also killed. And the Ark of God has been captured."

**4:17**
1 Sam 22:18
Ps 78:61, 64

<sup>18</sup>When the messenger mentioned what had happened to the Ark of God, Eli fell backward from his seat beside the gate. He broke his neck and died, for he was old and overweight. He had been Israel's judge for forty years.

<sup>19</sup>Eli's daughter-in-law, the wife of Phinehas, was pregnant and near her time of delivery. When she heard that the Ark of God had been captured and that her father-in-law and husband were dead, she went into labor and gave birth. <sup>20</sup>She died in childbirth, but before she passed away the midwives tried to encourage her. "Don't be afraid," they said. "You have a baby boy!" But she did not answer or pay attention to them.

**4:20**
Gen 35:17-18

<sup>21</sup>She named the child Ichabod (which means "Where is the glory?"), for she said, "Israel's glory is gone." She named him this because the Ark of God had been captured and because her father-in-law and husband were dead. <sup>22</sup>Then she said, "The glory has departed from Israel, for the Ark of God has been captured."

**4:21**
Ps 106:20

### The Ark in Philistia

**5** After the Philistines captured the Ark of God, they took it from the battleground at Ebenezer to the town of Ashdod. <sup>2</sup>They carried the Ark of God into the temple of Dagon and placed it beside an idol of Dagon. <sup>3</sup>But when the citizens of Ashdod went to see it the next morning, Dagon had fallen with his face to the ground in front of the Ark of the LORD!

**5:2**
Judg 16:23
Ps 78:61
**5:3**
Isa 19:1; 46:7

---

**4:11** This event fulfills the prophecy in 2:34 stating that Eli's sons, Hophni and Phinehas, would die "on the same day."

**4:12** At this time, the city of Shiloh was Israel's religious center (Joshua 18:1; 1 Samuel 4:3). The Tabernacle was permanently set up there. Because Israel did not have a civil capital—a seat

**THE ARK'S TRAVELS** Eli's sons took the Ark from Shiloh to the battlefield on the lower plains at Ebenezer and Aphek. The Philistines captured the Ark and took it to Ashdod, Gath, and Ekron. Plagues forced the people to send the Ark back to Israel, where it finally was taken by cattle-drawn carts to Beth-shemesh and on to the home of Eleazar in Kiriath-jearim.

of national government—Shiloh was the natural place for a messenger to deliver the sad news from the battle. Many scholars believe that it was during this battle that Shiloh was destroyed (Jeremiah 7:12; 26:2-6; also see the note on 7:1).

**4:18** Eli was Israel's judge and high priest. His death marked the end of the dark period of the judges when most of the nation ignored God. Although Samuel was also a judge, his career saw the transition from Israel's rule by judges to the nation's monarchy. He began the great revival that Israel would experience for the next century. The Bible does not say who became the next high priest (Samuel was not eligible because he was not a direct descendant of Aaron), but Samuel acted as high priest at this time by offering the important sacrifices throughout Israel.

**4:19-22** This incident illustrates the spiritual darkness and decline of Israel. This young boy, Ichabod, was supposed to succeed his father, Phinehas, in the priesthood, but his father had been killed because he was an evil man who desecrated the Tabernacle. The terror of God's leaving his people overshadowed the joy of childbirth. When sin dominates our lives, even God-given joys and pleasures seem empty.

**5:1ff** Dagon was the chief god of the Philistines, whom they believed sent rain and assured a bountiful harvest. But the Philistines, like most of their pagan neighbors, worshiped many gods. The more gods they could have on their side, the more secure they felt. That was why they wanted the Ark, thinking that if it helped the Israelites, it could help them, too. But when the people living nearby began to get sick and die, the Philistines real-

5:4
Ezek 6:6
Mic 1:7

5:6
Exod 9:3
1 Sam 6:4-5

5:8
Judg 16:18

5:9
1 Sam 7:13; 12:15

5:10
Josh 13:3

So they took Dagon and put him in his place again. ⁴But the next morning the same thing happened—Dagon had fallen face down before the Ark of the LORD again. This time his head and hands had broken off and were lying in the doorway. Only the trunk of his body was left intact. ⁵That is why to this day neither the priests of Dagon nor anyone who enters the temple of Dagon in Ashdod will step on its threshold.

⁶Then the LORD's heavy hand struck the people of Ashdod and the nearby villages with a plague of tumors.* ⁷When the people realized what was happening, they cried out, "We can't keep the Ark of the God of Israel here any longer! He is against us! We will all be destroyed along with Dagon, our god." ⁸So they called together the rulers of the Philistine towns and asked, "What should we do with the Ark of the God of Israel?"

The rulers discussed it and replied, "Move it to the town of Gath." So they moved the Ark of the God of Israel to Gath. ⁹But when the Ark arrived at Gath, the LORD's heavy hand fell on its men, young and old; he struck them with a plague of tumors, and there was a great panic.

¹⁰So they sent the Ark of God to the town of Ekron, but when the people of Ekron saw it coming they cried out, "They are bringing the Ark of the God of Israel here to kill us, too!" ¹¹The people summoned the Philistine rulers again and begged them, "Please send the Ark of the God of Israel back to its own country, or it* will kill us all." For the deadly plague from God had already begun, and great fear was sweeping across the town. ¹²Those who didn't die were afflicted with tumors; and the cry from the town rose to heaven.

### The Philistines Return the Ark

6:2
Gen 41:8
Exod 7:11

6:3
Lev 5:15-16

6:4
Josh 13:3
1 Sam 5:6, 11; 6:5

6:6
Exod 8:15, 31-32;
12:31

6:7
Deut 21:3
2 Sam 6:3

6:9
Josh 15:10
1 Sam 6:3

**6** The Ark of the LORD remained in Philistine territory seven months in all. ²Then the Philistines called in their priests and diviners and asked them, "What should we do about the Ark of the LORD? Tell us how to return it to its own country."

³"Send the Ark of the God of Israel back with a gift," they were told. "Send a guilt offering so the plague will stop. Then, if you are healed, you will know it was his hand that caused the plague."

⁴"What sort of guilt offering should we send?" they asked.

And they were told, "Since the plague has struck both you and your five rulers, make five gold tumors and five gold rats, just like those that have ravaged your land. ⁵Make these things to show honor to the God of Israel. Perhaps then he will stop afflicting you, your gods, and your land. ⁶Don't be stubborn and rebellious as Pharaoh and the Egyptians were. By the time God was finished with them, they were eager to let Israel go.

⁷"Now build a new cart, and find two cows that have just given birth to calves. Make sure the cows have never been yoked to a cart. Hitch the cows to the cart, but shut their calves away from them in a pen. ⁸Put the Ark of the LORD on the cart, and beside it place a chest containing the gold rats and gold tumors you are sending as a guilt offering. Then let the cows go wherever they want. ⁹If they cross the border of our land and go to Beth-shemesh, we will know it was the LORD who brought this great disaster upon us. If they don't, we will know it was not his hand that caused the plague. It came simply by chance."

**5:6** Greek version and Latin Vulgate read *tumors; and rats appeared in their land, and death and destruction were throughout the city.* **5:11** Or *he.*

ized that the Ark was not a good omen. It was a source of greater power than they had ever seen—power they could not control.

**5:6, 7** Although the Philistines had just witnessed a great victory by Israel's God over their god, Dagon, they didn't act upon that insight until they were afflicted with tumors (possibly bubonic plague). Similarly, today many people don't respond to biblical truth until they experience pain. Are you willing to listen to God for truth's sake, or do you turn to him only when you are hurting?

**5:8** The Philistines were governed by five rulers. Each ruler lived in a different city—Gath, Ekron, Ashdod, Ashkelon, Gaza. The Ark was taken to three of these capital cities, and each time it brought great trouble and chaos to the citizens.

**6:3** What was this guilt offering supposed to accomplish? This was a normal reaction to trouble in the Canaanite religion. The Philistines thought their problems were the result of their gods being angry. They recognized their guilt in taking the Ark and now were trying everything they could to placate Israel's God. The diviners (6:2) probably helped choose the gift they thought would placate Yahweh. But the offering consisted of images of tumors and rats,

not the kind of guilt offering prescribed in God's laws (Leviticus 5:14–6:7; 7:1-10). How easy it is to design our own methods of acknowledging God rather than serving him in the way he requires.

**6:7-12** The Philistine priests and diviners devised a test to see if God was really the one who had caused all their recent troubles. Two cows who had just given birth were hitched to a cart and sent toward Israel's border carrying the Ark of the Covenant. For a cow to leave her nursing calf, she would have to go against all her motherly instincts. Only God, who has power over the natural order, could cause this to happen. God sent the cows to Israel, not to pass the Philistines' test, but to show them his mighty power.

**6:9** The Philistines acknowledged the existence of the Hebrew God, but only as one of many deities whose favor they sought. Thinking of God in this way made it easy for them to ignore his demand that people worship him alone. Many people "worship" God this way. They see God as just one ingredient in a successful life. But God is far more than an ingredient—he is the source of life itself. Are you a "Philistine," seeing God's favor as only an ingredient of the good life?

10So these instructions were carried out. Two cows were hitched to the cart, and their newborn calves were shut up in a pen. 11Then the Ark of the Lord and the chest containing the gold rats and gold tumors were placed on the cart. 12And sure enough, without veering off in other directions, the cows went straight along the road toward Beth-shemesh, lowing as they went. The Philistine rulers followed them as far as the border of Beth-shemesh.

13The people of Beth-shemesh were harvesting wheat in the valley, and when they saw the Ark, they were overjoyed! 14The cart came into the field of a man named Joshua and stopped beside a large rock. So the people broke up the wood of the cart for a fire and killed the cows and sacrificed them to the Lord as a burnt offering. 15Several men of the tribe of Levi lifted the Ark of the Lord and the chest containing the gold rats and gold tumors from the cart and placed them on the large rock. Many sacrifices and burnt offerings were offered to the Lord that day by the people of Beth-shemesh. 16The five Philistine rulers watched all this and then returned to Ekron that same day.

17The five gold tumors sent by the Philistines as a guilt offering to the Lord were gifts from the rulers of Ashdod, Gaza, Ashkelon, Gath, and Ekron. 18The five gold rats represented the five Philistine towns and their surrounding villages, which were controlled by the five rulers. The large rock at Beth-shemesh, where they set the Ark of the Lord, still stands in the field of Joshua as a witness to what happened there.

### The Ark Moved to Kiriath-Jearim

19But the Lord killed seventy men* from Beth-shemesh because they looked into the Ark of the Lord. And the people mourned greatly because of what the Lord had done. 20"Who is able to stand in the presence of the Lord, this holy God?" they cried out. "Where can we send the Ark from here?"

21So they sent messengers to the people at Kiriath-jearim and told them, "The Philistines have returned the Ark of the Lord. Come here and get it!"

**7** So the men of Kiriath-jearim came to get the Ark of the Lord. They took it to the hillside home of Abinadab and ordained Eleazar, his son, to be in charge of it. 2The Ark remained in Kiriath-jearim for a long time—twenty years in all. During that time all Israel mourned because it seemed the Lord had abandoned them.

### Samuel Leads Israel to Victory

3Then Samuel said to all the people of Israel, "If you are really serious about wanting to return to the Lord, get rid of your foreign gods and your images of Ashtoreth. Determine to obey only the Lord; then he will rescue you from the Philistines." 4So the Israelites got rid of their images of Baal and Ashtoreth and worshiped only the Lord.

**Side references:**
**6:14** 2 Sam 24:22
**6:15** Josh 3:2-4
**6:17** 1 Sam 6:4
**6:18** Deut 3:5
**6:19** 2 Sam 6:7
**6:20** Lev 11:44-45; 2 Sam 6:9; Mal 3:2
**6:21** Josh 15:9, 60
**7:1** 2 Sam 6:3-4
**7:3** Deut 6:13; 13:4; Josh 24:14, 23; Judg 2:12-13; 10:16

**6:19** As in a few Hebrew manuscripts; most Hebrew manuscripts read *70 men, 50,000 men.* Perhaps the text should be understood to read *the Lord killed 70 men and 50 oxen.*

---

**6:19** Why were people killed for looking into the Ark? The Israelites had made an idol of the Ark. They had tried to harness God's power, to use it for their own purposes (victory in battle). But the Lord of the universe cannot be controlled by humans. To protect the Israelites from his power, he had warned them not even to look at the sacred sanctuary objects in the Most Holy Place or they would die (Numbers 4:20). Only Levites were allowed to move the Ark. Because of their disobedience, God carried out his promised judgment.

God could not allow the people to think they could use his power for their own ends. He could not permit them to disregard his warnings and come into his presence lightly. He did not want the cycle of disrespect, disobedience, and defeat to start all over again. God did not kill the men of Beth-shemesh to be cruel. He killed them because overlooking their presumptuous sin would encourage the whole nation of Israel to ignore God.

**7:1** The Ark was taken to Kiriath-jearim, a city near the battlefield, for safekeeping, and Eleazar was given the task of caring for it. Why wasn't it taken back to the Tabernacle at Shiloh? Shiloh had probably been defeated and destroyed by the Philistines in an earlier battle (4:1-18; Jeremiah 26:2-6) because of the evil deeds of its priests (2:12-17). Apparently, the Tabernacle and its furniture were saved because we read that the Tabernacle was set up in Nob during Saul's reign (21:1-6) and in Gibeon during the reigns of David

and Solomon (1 Chronicles 16:39; 21:29, 30; 2 Chronicles 1). Shiloh, however, is never again mentioned in the historical books of the Old Testament. Samuel's new home became Ramah (7:15-17; 8:4), his birthplace (further evidence of Shiloh's destruction).

**7:2, 3** Israel mourned, and sorrow gripped the nation for 20 years. The Ark was put away like an unwanted box in an attic, and it seemed as if the Lord had abandoned his people. Samuel, now a grown man, roused them to action by saying that if they were truly sorry, they should do something about it. How easy it is for us to complain about our problems, even to God, while we refuse to act, change, and do what he requires. We don't even take the advice he has already given us. Do you ever feel as if God has abandoned you? Check to see if there is anything he has already told you to do. You may not receive new guidance from God until you have acted on his previous directions.

**7:3** Samuel urged the Israelites to get rid of their foreign gods. Idols today are much more subtle than gods of wood and stone, but they are just as dangerous. Whatever holds first place in our lives or controls us is our god. Money, success, material goods, pride, or anything else can be an idol if it takes the place of God in our lives. The Lord alone is worthy of our service and worship, and we must let nothing rival him. If we have "foreign gods," we need to ask God to help us dethrone them, making the true God our first priority.

**7:4** Baal was believed to be the son of El, chief deity of the

7:6
Judg 10:10
Neh 9:1
Lam 2:19

7:7
1 Sam 13:6; 17:11

7:8
1 Sam 12:19
Isa 37:4

7:9
Lev 22:26-27
Ps 99:6
Jer 15:1

⁵Then Samuel told them, "Gather all of Israel to Mizpah, and I will pray to the LORD for you." ⁶So they gathered at Mizpah and, in a great ceremony, drew water from a well and poured it out before the LORD. They also went without food all day and confessed that they had sinned against the LORD. (It was at Mizpah that Samuel became Israel's judge.)

⁷When the Philistine rulers heard that Israel had gathered at Mizpah, they mobilized their army and advanced. The Israelites were badly frightened when they learned that the Philistines were approaching. ⁸"Don't stop pleading with the LORD our God to save us from the Philistines!" they begged Samuel. ⁹So Samuel took a young lamb and offered it to the LORD as a whole burnt offering. He pleaded with the LORD to help Israel, and the LORD answered him.

**SAMUEL**

We often wonder about the childhoods of great people. We have little information about the early years of most of the people mentioned in the Bible. One delightful exception is Samuel; he came as a result of God's answer to Hannah's fervent prayer for a child. (In fact, the name *Samuel* comes from the Hebrew expression "heard of God.") God shaped Samuel from the start. Like Moses, Samuel was called to fill many different roles: judge, priest, prophet, counselor, and God's man at a turning point in the history of Israel. God worked through Samuel because Samuel was willing to be one thing: God's servant.

Samuel showed that those whom God finds faithful in small things will be trusted with greater things. He grew up assisting the high priest (Eli) in the Tabernacle until God directed him to other responsibilities. God was able to use Samuel because he was genuinely dedicated to God.

Samuel moved ahead because he was listening to God's directions. Too often we ask God to control our lives without making us give up the goals for which we strive. We ask God to help us get where *we* want to go. The first step in correcting this tendency is to turn over both the control and destination of our lives to him. The second step is to do what we *already know* God requires of us. The third step is to listen for further direction from his Word—God's map for life.

| | |
|---|---|
| **Strengths and accomplishments** | • Used by God to assist Israel's transition from a loosely governed tribal people to a monarchy<br>• Anointed the first two kings of Israel<br>• Was the last and most effective of Israel's judges<br>• Is listed in the Hall of Faith in Hebrews 11 |
| **Weakness and mistake** | • Was unable to lead his sons into a close relationship with God |
| **Lessons from his life** | • The significance of what people accomplish is directly related to their relationship with God<br>• The kind of person we are is more important than anything we might do |
| **Vital statistics** | • Where: Ephraim<br>• Occupations: Judge, prophet, priest<br>• Relatives: Mother: Hannah. Father: Elkanah. Sons: Joel and Abijah.<br>• Contemporaries: Eli, Saul, David |
| **Key verses** | "As Samuel grew up, the LORD was with him, and everything Samuel said proved to be reliable. And all Israel, from Dan in the north to Beersheba in the south, knew that Samuel was confirmed as a prophet of the LORD" (1 Samuel 3:19, 20). |

His story is told in 1 Samuel 1—28. He is also mentioned in Psalm 99:6; Jeremiah 15:1; Acts 3:24; 13:20; Hebrews 11:32.

Canaanites. Baal was regarded as the god of thunder and rain; thus he controlled vegetation and agriculture. Ashtoreth was a goddess of love and war (she was called Ishtar in Babylon and Astarte or Aphrodite in Greece). She represented fertility. The Canaanites believed that by the sexual union of Baal and Ashtoreth, the earth would be magically rejuvenated and made fertile.

**7:5** Mizpah held special significance for the Israelite nation. It was there that the Israelites had gathered to mobilize against the tribe of Benjamin (Judges 20:1); Samuel was appointed to be leader (1 Samuel 7:6); and Saul, Israel's first king, would be identified and presented to the people (10:17ff).

**7:6** Pouring water on the ground "before the LORD" was a sign

of repenting from sin, turning from idols, and determining to obey God alone.

**7:6** Samuel became the last in the long line of Israel's judges (leaders). For a list of these judges, see the chart in Judges 1, p. 355. A judge was both a political and a religious leader. God was Israel's true leader, while the judge was to be God's spokesperson to the people and administrator of justice throughout the land. While some of Israel's judges relied more on their own judgment than on God's, Samuel's obedience and dedication to God made him one of the greatest judges in Israel's history. (For more on Samuel as a judge, see the note on 4:18.)

¹⁰Just as Samuel was sacrificing the burnt offering, the Philistines arrived to attack Israel. But the LORD spoke with a mighty voice of thunder from heaven that day, and the Philistines were thrown into such confusion that the Israelites defeated them. ¹¹The men of Israel chased them from Mizpah to a place below Beth-car, slaughtering them all along the way.

**7:10**
1 Sam 2:10
2 Sam 22:14
Ps 18:14

¹²Samuel then took a large stone and placed it between the towns of Mizpah and Jeshanah.* He named it Ebenezer (which means "the stone of help"), for he said, "Up to this point the LORD has helped us!"

**7:12**
Gen 35:13-15
Josh 4:9; 24:26

¹³So the Philistines were subdued and didn't invade Israel again for some time. And throughout Samuel's lifetime, the LORD's powerful hand was raised against the Philistines. ¹⁴The Israelite villages near Ekron and Gath that the Philistines had captured were restored to Israel, along with the rest of the territory that the Philistines had taken. And there was peace between Israel and the Amorites in those days.

**7:13**
Judg 13:1
1 Sam 13:5

**7:15**
1 Sam 7:6; 12:11

¹⁵Samuel continued as Israel's judge for the rest of his life. ¹⁶Each year he traveled around, setting up his court first at Bethel, then at Gilgal, and then at Mizpah. He judged the people of Israel at each of these places. ¹⁷Then he would return to his home at Ramah, and he would hear cases there, too. And Samuel built an altar to the LORD at Ramah.

**7:16**
Gen 28:19
1 Sam 7:5

**7:17**
1 Sam 1:1, 19;
2:11; 15:34

## B. SAMUEL AND SAUL (8:1—15:35)

Samuel judges Israel well, saves them from the Philistines, and leads them back to God. But when he retires, the nation does not want another judge. Instead, they demand to be given a king in order to be like the nations around them. Although God is unhappy with their request, he tells Samuel to anoint Saul as Israel's first king. Saul is a skillful soldier who successfully leads the nation into many battles against their enemies. But in God's eyes Saul is a failure because he constantly disobeys and does things his own way. God eventually rejects Saul as king. Sometimes we want to go our own way rather than follow the ways of God. This will always end in ruin as it did for Saul.

### 1. Saul becomes king of Israel
*Israel Requests a King*

**8** As Samuel grew old, he appointed his sons to be judges over Israel. ²Joel and Abijah, his oldest sons, held court in Beersheba. ³But they were not like their father, for they were greedy for money. They accepted bribes and perverted justice.

**8:2**
1 Kgs 19:3

**8:3**
Exod 23:6, 8
Deut 16:19

⁴Finally, all the elders of Israel met at Ramah to discuss the matter with Samuel. ⁵"Look," they told him, "you are now old, and your sons are not like you. Give us a king to judge us like all the other nations have."

**8:5**
Deut 17:14-15
1 Sam 12:2

**7:12** As in Greek and Syriac versions; Hebrew reads *Shen*.

---

**7:12** The Israelites had great difficulty with the Philistines, but God rescued them. In response, the people set up a large stone as a memorial of God's great help and deliverance. During tough times, we may need to remember the crucial turning points in our past to help us through the present. Memorials can help us remember God's past victories and gain confidence and strength for the present.

**7:14** In Joshua's time, the Amorites were a powerful tribe scattered throughout the hill country on both sides of the Jordan with a heavy concentration occupying the east side of the Jordan River opposite the Dead Sea. In the context of this verse, however, *Amorites* is another general name for all the inhabitants of Canaan who were not Israelites.

**8:1-3** As an old man, Samuel appointed his sons to be judges over Israel in his place. But they turned out to be corrupt, much like Eli's sons (2:12). We don't know why Samuel's sons went wrong, but we do know that Eli was held responsible for his own sons' corruption (2:29-34).

It is impossible to know if Samuel was a bad parent. His children were old enough to be on their own. We must be careful not to blame ourselves for the sins of our children. On the other hand, parenthood is an awesome responsibility, and nothing is more important than molding and shaping our children's lives.

If your grown children are not following God, realize that you can't control them any longer. Don't blame yourself for something that is no longer your responsibility. But if your children

are still in your care, know that what you do and teach can profoundly affect your children and lasts a lifetime.

**8:4-9** Israel wanted a king for several reasons: (1) Samuel's sons were not fit to lead Israel. (2) The 12 tribes of Israel continually had problems working together because each tribe had its own leader and territory. It was hoped that a king would unite the tribes into one nation and one army. (3) The people wanted to be like the neighboring nations. This is exactly what God didn't want. Having a king would make it easy to forget that God was their real leader. It was not wrong for Israel to want a king; God had mentioned the possibility in Deuteronomy 17:14-20. Yet, in reality, the people were rejecting God as their leader. The Israelites wanted laws, an army, and a human monarch in the place of God. They wanted to run the nation through human strength, even though only God's strength could make them flourish in the hostile land of Canaan.

**8:5, 6** The people clamored for a king, thinking that a new system of government would bring about a change in the nation. But because their basic problem was disobedience to God, their other problems would only continue under the new administration. What they needed was a unified faith, not a uniform rule.

Had the Israelites submitted to God's leadership, they would have thrived beyond their expectations (Deuteronomy 28:1). Our obedience is weak if we ask God to lead our family or personal life but continue to live by the world's standards and values. Faith in God must touch all the practical areas of life.

8:6
1 Sam 12:17; 15:11
8:7
Exod 16:8

8:9
1 Sam 8:11-18

8:11
Deut 17:16
1 Sam 14:52
2 Sam 15:1
1 Kgs 1:5
8:12
1 Sam 22:7
1 Kgs 4:7
8:14
1 Sam 22:7
1 Kgs 21:7
Ezek 46:18

8:18
Job 27:9
Prov 1:25-28
Mic 3:4
8:19
Jer 44:16

8:22
1 Sam 8:7

9:1
1 Chr 8:33; 9:36-39
9:2
1 Sam 10:23-24
2 Sam 14:25

⁶Samuel was displeased with their request and went to the LORD for guidance. ⁷"Do everything they say to you," the LORD replied, "for it is me they are rejecting, not you. They don't want me to be their king any longer. ⁸Ever since I brought them from Egypt they have continually abandoned me and followed other gods. And now they are giving you the same treatment. ⁹Do as they ask, but solemnly warn them about the way a king will reign over them."

### Samuel Warns against a Kingdom

¹⁰So Samuel passed on the LORD's warning to the people who were asking him for a king. ¹¹"This is how a king will reign over you," Samuel said. "The king will draft your sons and assign them to his chariots and his charioteers, making them run before his chariots. ¹²Some will be generals and captains in his army,* some will be forced to plow in his fields and harvest his crops, and some will make his weapons and chariot equipment. ¹³The king will take your daughters from you and force them to cook and bake and make perfumes for him. ¹⁴He will take away the best of your fields and vineyards and olive groves and give them to his own officials. ¹⁵He will take a tenth of your grain and your grape harvest and distribute it among his officers and attendants. ¹⁶He will take your male and female slaves and demand the finest of your cattle* and donkeys for his own use. ¹⁷He will demand a tenth of your flocks, and you will be his slaves. ¹⁸When that day comes, you will beg for relief from this king you are demanding, but then the LORD will not help you."

¹⁹But the people refused to listen to Samuel's warning. "Even so, we still want a king," they said. ²⁰"We want to be like the nations around us. Our king will judge us and lead us into battle."

²¹So Samuel repeated to the LORD what the people had said, ²²and the LORD replied, "Do as they say, and give them a king." Then Samuel agreed and sent the people home.

### Saul Meets Samuel

**9** There was a wealthy, influential man named Kish from the tribe of Benjamin. He was the son of Abiel, son of Zeror, son of Becorath, son of Aphiah, of the tribe of Benjamin. ²His son Saul was the most handsome man in Israel—head and shoulders taller than anyone else in the land.

**8:12** Hebrew *commanders of thousands and commanders of fifties.* **8:16** As in Greek version; Hebrew reads *young men.*

---

**THE PROBLEMS WITH HAVING A KING**

| Problems (warned by Samuel) | Reference Fulfillment |
|---|---|
| Drafting young men into the army | 8:11, 12 . . 14:52—"So whenever Saul observed a young man who was brave and strong, he drafted him into his army." |
| Having the young men "run before his chariots" | 8:11 . . . . . 2 Samuel 15:1—"Absalom bought a chariot and horses, and he hired fifty bodyguards to run ahead of him." |
| Making slave laborers | 8:12, 17 . . 2 Chronicles 2:17, 18—Solomon assigned laborers to build the temple. |
| Taking the best of your fields and vineyards | 8:14 . . . . . 1 Kings 21:5-16—Jezebel stole Naboth's vineyard |
| Using your property for his personal gain | 8:14-16. . . 1 Kings 9:10-14—Solomon gave away 20 towns to Hiram of Tyre. |
| Demanding a tenth of your harvest and flocks | 8:15, 17 . . 1 Kings 12:1-16—Rehoboam was going to demand heavier taxation than Solomon. |

---

**8:19, 20** Samuel carefully explained all the negative consequences of having a king, but the Israelites refused to listen. When you have an important decision to make, weigh the positives and negatives carefully, considering everyone who might be affected by your choice. When you want something badly enough, it is difficult to see the potential problems. But don't discount the negatives. Unless you have a plan to handle each one, they will cause you great difficulty later.

**8:19, 20** Israel was called to be a holy nation, separate from and unique among all others (Leviticus 20:26). The Israelites' motive in asking for a king was to be like the nations around them. This

was in total opposition to God's original plan. It was not their desire for a king that was wrong, but their reasons for wanting a king.

Often we let others' values and actions dictate our attitudes and behavior. Have you ever made a wrong choice because you wanted to be like everyone else? Be careful that the values of your friends or "heroes" don't pull you away from what God says is right. When God's people want to be like unbelievers, they are heading for spiritual disaster.

³One day Kish's donkeys strayed away, and he told Saul, "Take a servant with you, and go look for the donkeys." ⁴So Saul took one of the servants and traveled through the hill country of Ephraim, the land of Shalishah, the Shaalim area, and the entire land of Benjamin, but they couldn't find the donkeys anywhere.

⁵Finally, they entered the region of Zuph, and Saul said to his servant, "Let's go home. By now my father will be more worried about us than about the donkeys!"

⁶But the servant said, "I've just thought of something! There is a man of God who lives here in this town. He is held in high honor by all the people because everything he says comes true. Let's go find him. Perhaps he can tell us which way to go."

⁷"But we don't have anything to offer him," Saul replied. "Even our food is gone, and we don't have a thing to give him."

⁸"Well," the servant said, "I have one small silver piece.* We can at least offer it to the man of God and see what happens!" ⁹(In those days if people wanted a message from God, they would say, "Let's go and ask the seer," for prophets used to be called seers.)

¹⁰"All right," Saul agreed, "let's try it!" So they started into the town where the man of God lived.

¹¹As they were climbing the hill to the town, they met some young women coming out to draw water. So Saul and his servant asked, "Is the seer here today?"

¹²"Yes," they replied. "Stay right on this road. He is at the town gates. He has just arrived to take part in a public sacrifice up at the place of worship. ¹³Hurry and catch him before he goes up there to eat. The guests won't begin eating until he arrives to bless the food."

¹⁴So they entered the town, and as they passed through the gates, Samuel was coming out toward them to go up to the place of worship.

¹⁵Now the LORD had told Samuel the previous day, ¹⁶"About this time tomorrow I will send you a man from the land of Benjamin. Anoint him to be the leader of my people, Israel. He will rescue them from the Philistines, for I have looked down on my people in mercy and have heard their cry."

¹⁷When Samuel saw Saul, the LORD said, "That's the man I told you about! He will rule my people."

¹⁸Just then Saul approached Samuel at the gateway and asked, "Can you please tell me where the seer's house is?"

¹⁹"I am the seer!" Samuel replied. "Go up to the place of worship ahead of me. We will eat there together, and in the morning I'll tell you what you want to know and send you on your way. ²⁰And don't worry about those donkeys that were lost three days ago, for they have been found. And I am here to tell you that you and your family are the focus of all Israel's hopes."

²¹Saul replied, "But I'm only from the tribe of Benjamin, the smallest tribe in Israel, and my family is the least important of all the families of that tribe! Why are you talking like this to me?"

**9:8** Hebrew *1/4 shekel of silver*, about 0.1 ounces or 3 grams in weight.

**9:3** 1 Sam 10:2, 14
**9:5** 1 Sam 1:1
**9:6** Deut 33:1 / 1 Sam 3:19-20 / 2 Kgs 5:8
**9:7** 1 Kgs 14:3 / 2 Kgs 5:15; 8:8-9 / Ezek 13:19
**9:9** 2 Sam 24:11 / 1 Chr 26:28
**9:12** Luke 9:16 / John 6:11
**9:15** 1 Sam 15:1
**9:16** Exod 3:7, 9 / Acts 13:21
**9:17** 1 Sam 16:12
**9:20** 1 Sam 12:13
**9:21** Judg 20:46-48 / 1 Sam 15:17

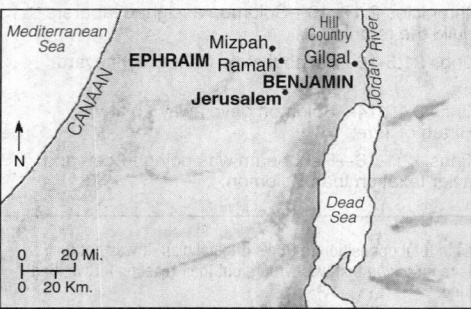

**SAUL CHOSEN AS KING** Saul and a servant searched for their lost donkeys in the hill country of Ephraim and the territory of Benjamin. They went to Ramah, looking for help from Samuel the prophet. While Saul was there, he found himself unexpectedly anointed by Samuel as Israel's first king. Samuel called Israel together at Mizpah to tell them God's choice for their king.

**9:3** Saul was sent by his father on an important mission—to find their stray donkeys. Donkeys were all-purpose animals, the "pickup trucks" of Bible times. Used for transportation, hauling, and farming, they were considered necessities. Even the poorest family owned one. To own many donkeys was a sign of wealth, and to lose them was a disaster. Saul's father was wealthy, and his many donkeys were evidence of that wealth.

**9:3ff** Often we think that events "just happen" to us, but as we learn from this story about Saul, God may use common occurrences to lead us where he wants. It is important to evaluate all situations as potential "divine appointments" designed to shape our lives. Think of all the good and bad circumstances that have affected you lately. Can you see God's purpose in them? Perhaps he is building a certain quality in you or leading you to serve him in a new area.

**9:6** The city where the servant said the prophet lived was probably Ramah, where Samuel moved after the Philistine battle near Shiloh (7:17). Saul's lack of knowledge about Samuel showed his ignorance of spiritual matters. Saul and Samuel even lived in the same territory—Benjamin.

**9:21** "Why are you talking like this to me?" Saul's outburst reveals a problem he would face repeatedly—feeling inferior. Like

22 Then Samuel brought Saul and his servant into the hall and placed them at the head of the table, honoring them above the thirty special guests. 23 Samuel then instructed the cook to bring Saul the finest cut of meat, the piece that had been set aside for the guest of honor. 24 So the cook brought in the meat and placed it before Saul. "Go ahead and eat it," Samuel said. "I was saving it for you even before I invited these others!" So Saul ate with Samuel that day.

25 When they came down from the place of worship and returned to town, Samuel took Saul up to the roof of the house and prepared a bed for him there.* 26 At daybreak the next morning, Samuel called to Saul, "Get up! It's time you were on your way." So Saul got ready, and he and Samuel left the house together. 27 When they reached the edge of town, Samuel told Saul to send his servant on ahead. After the servant was gone, Samuel said, "Stay here, for I have received a special message for you from God."

### Samuel Anoints Saul as King

**10** Then Samuel took a flask of olive oil and poured it over Saul's head. He kissed Saul and said, "I am doing this because the LORD has appointed you to be the ruler over Israel, his special possession.* 2 When you leave me today, you will see two men beside Rachel's tomb at Zelzah, on the border of Benjamin. They will tell you that the donkeys have been found and that your father has stopped worrying about them and is now worried about you. He is asking, 'Have you seen my son?'

**9:25** As in Greek version; Hebrew reads *and talked with him there.* **10:1** Greek version reads *over Israel. And you will rule over the LORD's people and save them from their enemies around them. This will be the sign to you that the LORD has appointed you to be leader over his special possession.*

**9:25**
Deut 22:8
Acts 10:9-10

**10:1**
1 Sam 9:16;
16:13; 26:9
2 Sam 1:14
2 Kgs 9:3, 6

**10:2**
Gen 35:19; 48:7

---

**RELIGIOUS AND POLITICAL CENTERS OF ISRAEL**
During the period of the judges, Israel may have had more than one capital. This may explain why the Scriptures overlap with reference to some cities.

| | |
|---|---|
| Gilgal | Joshua 4:19; Judges 2:1; Hosea 4:15; Micah 6:5 |
| Shiloh | Joshua 18:1-10; 19:51; Judges 18:31; 1 Samuel 1:3; Jeremiah 7:12-14 |
| Shechem | Joshua 24:1 |
| Ramah | 1 Samuel 7:17; 8:4 |
| Mizpah | Judges 11:11; 20:1; 1 Samuel 10:17 |
| Bethel | Judges 20:18, 26; 1 Samuel 10:3 |
| Gibeah (political center only) | 1 Samuel 10:26 |
| Gibeon (religious center only) | 1 Kings 3:4; 2 Chronicles 1:2, 3 |
| Jerusalem | 1 Kings 8:1ff; Psalm 51:16-19 |

Samuel called the Israelites together at Mizpah, where he would anoint Saul as their first king. Up to this point, the political seat of the nation seems to have been the religious center of the nation as well. Above are the cities which probably served as both the religious and political centers of Israel since the days of Joshua. Saul may have been the first Israelite leader to separate the nation's religious center (probably Mizpah at this time) from its political center (Gibeah—1 Samuel 11:4; 26:1). Politically, the nation grew strong for a while. But when Saul and his officials stopped seeking God's will, internal jealousies and strife soon began to decay the nation from within. When David became king, he brought the Ark of the Covenant back to Jerusalem, his capital. King Solomon then completely united the religious and political centers at Jerusalem.

---

a leaf tossed about by the wind, Saul vacillated between his feelings and his convictions. Everything he said and did was selfish because he was worried about himself. For example, Saul said his clan was "the least important" in the smallest tribe in Israel, but 9:1 says his father was "a wealthy, influential man." (The tribe of Benjamin was the smallest because they were nearly wiped out as punishment for their immorality—see Judges 19–21.) Saul didn't want to face the responsibility God had given him. Later, Saul kept some war plunder that he shouldn't have and then tried to blame his soldiers (15:21) while claiming that they really wanted it to sacrifice to God (15:15).

Although Saul had been called by God and had a mission in life, he struggled constantly with jealousy, insecurity, arrogance, impulsiveness, and deceit. He did not decide to be wholeheartedly committed to God. Because Saul would not let God's love give rest to his heart, he never became God's man.

**10:1** When an Israelite king took office, he was not only crowned, he was anointed. The coronation was the political act of establishing the king as ruler; the anointing was the religious act of making the king God's representative to the people. A king was always anointed by a priest or prophet. The special anointing oil was a mixture of olive oil, myrrh, and other expensive spices. It was poured over the king's head to symbolize the presence and power of the Holy Spirit of God in his life. This anointing ceremony was to remind the king of his great responsibility to lead his people by God's wisdom and not his own.

<sup>3</sup>"When you get to the oak of Tabor, you will see three men coming toward you who are on their way to worship God at Bethel. One will be bringing three young goats, another will have three loaves of bread, and the third will be carrying a wineskin full of wine. <sup>4</sup>They will greet you and offer you two of the loaves, which you are to accept.

<sup>5</sup>"When you arrive at Gibeah of God,* where the garrison of the Philistines is located, you will meet a band of prophets coming down from the place of worship. They will be playing a harp, a tambourine, a flute, and a lyre, and they will be prophesying. <sup>6</sup>At that time the Spirit of the LORD will come powerfully upon you, and you will prophesy with them. You will be changed into a different person. <sup>7</sup>After these signs take place, do what must be done, for God is with you. <sup>8</sup>Then go down to Gilgal ahead of me. I will join you there to sacrifice burnt offerings and peace offerings. You must wait for seven days until I arrive and give you further instructions."

### Samuel's Signs Are Fulfilled

<sup>9</sup>As Saul turned and started to leave, God gave him a new heart, and all Samuel's signs were fulfilled that day. <sup>10</sup>When Saul and his servant arrived at Gibeah, they saw a group of prophets coming toward them. Then the Spirit of God came powerfully upon Saul, and he, too, began to prophesy. <sup>11</sup>When those who knew Saul heard about it, they exclaimed, "What? Is even Saul a prophet? How did the son of Kish become a prophet?"

<sup>12</sup>And one of those standing there said, "Can anyone become a prophet, no matter who his father is?"* So that is the origin of the saying "Is even Saul a prophet?"

<sup>13</sup>When Saul had finished prophesying, he went up to the place of worship. <sup>14</sup>"Where have you been?" Saul's uncle asked him and his servant.

"We were looking for the donkeys," Saul replied, "but we couldn't find them. So we went to Samuel to ask him where they were."

<sup>15</sup>"Oh? And what did he say?" his uncle asked.

<sup>16</sup>"He told us that the donkeys had already been found," Saul replied. But Saul didn't tell his uncle what Samuel said about the kingdom.

### Saul Is Acclaimed King

<sup>17</sup>Later Samuel called all the people of Israel to meet before the LORD at Mizpah. <sup>18</sup>And he said, "This is what the LORD, the God of Israel, has declared: I brought you from Egypt and rescued you from the Egyptians and from all of the nations that were oppressing you. <sup>19</sup>But though I have rescued you from your misery and distress, you have rejected your God today and have said, 'No, we want a king instead!' Now, therefore, present yourselves before the LORD by tribes and clans."

<sup>20</sup>So Samuel brought all the tribes of Israel before the LORD, and the tribe of Benjamin was chosen by lot. <sup>21</sup>Then he brought each family of the tribe of Benjamin before the LORD, and the family of the Matrites was chosen. And finally Saul son of Kish was chosen from among them. But when they looked for him, he had disappeared! <sup>22</sup>So they asked the LORD, "Where is he?"

**10:5** Hebrew *Gibeath-elohim.*   **10:12** Hebrew *said, "Who is their father?"*

---

**Cross-references (margin):**

**10:3** Gen 35:1, 3, 7

**10:5** 1 Sam 19:20; 2 Kgs 2:3, 5, 15; 1 Chr 25:1

**10:6** Num 11:25, 29; Judg 3:10; 14:6; 1 Sam 19:23-24

**10:8** 1 Sam 7:16; 11:14-15; 13:8

**10:9** 1 Sam 10:6

**10:10** 1 Sam 10:5

**10:11** 1 Sam 19:24; Amos 7:14-15; Matt 13:54-57

**10:14** 1 Sam 9:3

**10:16** 1 Sam 9:20

**10:17** Judg 20:1; 1 Sam 7:5-6

**10:18** Judg 6:8

**10:19** 1 Sam 8:5-7

---

**10:6** How could Saul be so filled with the Spirit and yet later commit such evil acts? Throughout the Old Testament, God's Spirit "came upon" a person temporarily so that God could use him or her for great acts. This happened frequently to Israel's judges when they were called by God to rescue the nation (Judges 3:8-10). This was not always a permanent, abiding influence, but sometimes a temporary manifestation of the Holy Spirit. Yet, at times in the Old Testament, the Spirit even came upon unbelievers to enable them to do unusual tasks (Numbers 24; 2 Chronicles 36:22, 23). The Holy Spirit gave the person power to do what God asked, but it did not always produce the other fruits of the Spirit, such as self-control. Saul, in his early years as king, was a different person (10:1-10) as a result of the Holy Spirit's work in him. But as Saul's power grew, so did his pride. After a while he refused to seek God; the Spirit left him (16:14), and his good attitude melted away.

**10:10, 11** A prophet is someone who speaks God's words. While God told many prophets to predict certain events, what God wanted most was for them to instruct and inspire people to live in faithfulness to God. When Saul's friends heard inspired words coming from Saul, they exclaimed, "Is even Saul a prophet?" This was an expression of surprise at worldly Saul's becoming religious. It is equivalent to "What? Has he got religion?"

**10:19** Israel's true king was God, but the nation demanded another. Imagine wanting a human being instead of God as guide and leader! Throughout history, men and women have rejected God, and they continue to do it today. Are you rejecting God by pushing him aside and acknowledging someone or something else as your "king" or top priority? Learn from these stories of Israel's kings, and don't push God aside.

**10:20** The Israelites chose their first king by casting lots—perhaps by using the Urim and Thummim, two plates or flat stones carried by the high priest. The fact that Saul was chosen may seem like luck, but it was really the opposite. God had instructed the Israelites to make the Urim and Thummim for the specific purpose of consulting him in times such as this (Exodus 28:30; Numbers 27:12-21). By using the Urim and Thummim, the Israel-

**10:23**
1 Sam 9:2

**10:24**
2 Sam 21:6
1 Kgs 1:25, 34, 39
2 Kgs 11:12

**10:25**
Deut 17:15
1 Sam 8:11-18

And the LORD replied, "He is hiding among the baggage." ²³So they found him and brought him out, and he stood head and shoulders above anyone else.

²⁴Then Samuel said to all the people, "This is the man the LORD has chosen as your king. No one in all Israel is like him!"

And all the people shouted, "Long live the king!"

²⁵Then Samuel told the people what the rights and duties of a king were. He wrote them down on a scroll and placed it before the LORD. Then Samuel sent the people home again.

---

First impressions can be deceiving, especially when the image created by a person's appearance is contradicted by his or her qualities and abilities. Saul presented the ideal visual image of a king, but the tendencies of his character often went contrary to God's commands for a king. Saul was God's chosen leader, but this did not mean he was capable of being king on his own.

During his reign, Saul had his greatest successes when he obeyed God. His greatest failures resulted from acting on his own. Saul had the raw materials to be a good leader—appearance, courage, and action. Even his weaknesses could have been used by God if Saul had recognized them and left them in God's hands. His own choices cut him off from God and eventually alienated him from his own people.

From Saul we learn that while our strengths and abilities make us useful, it is our weaknesses that make us usable. Our skills and talents make us tools, but our failures and shortcomings remind us that we need a Craftsman in control of our lives. Whatever we accomplish on our own is only a hint of what God could do through our lives. Does he control your life?

| | |
|---|---|
| **Strengths and accomplishments** | • First God-appointed king of Israel<br>• Known for his personal courage and generosity<br>• Stood tall, with a striking appearance |
| **Weaknesses and mistakes** | • His leadership abilities did not match the expectations created by his appearance<br>• Impulsive by nature, he tended to overstep his bounds<br>• Allowed jealousy to overcome him so that he tried to kill David<br>• He specifically disobeyed God on several occasions |
| **Lessons from his life** | • God wants obedience from the heart, not mere acts of religious ritual<br>• Obedience always involves sacrifice, but sacrifice is not always obedience<br>• God wants to make use of our strengths and weaknesses<br>• Weaknesses should help us remember our need for God's guidance and help |
| **Vital statistics** | • Where: The land of Benjamin<br>• Occupation: King of Israel<br>• Relatives: Father: Kish. Wife: Ahinoam. Sons: Jonathan, Malkishua, Abinadab, Ishbosheth (and possibly Ishvi). Daughters: Merab, Michal. |
| **Key verses** | "But Samuel replied, 'What is more pleasing to the LORD: your burnt offerings and sacrifices or your obedience to his voice? Listen! Obedience is better than sacrifice, and submission is better than offering the fat of rams. Rebellion is as sinful as witchcraft, and stubbornness as bad as worshiping idols. So because you have rejected the command of the LORD, he has rejected you as king'" (1 Samuel 15:22, 23). |

His story is told in 1 Samuel 9—31. He is also mentioned in Acts 13:21.

---

ites were taking the decision out of their own hands and turning it over to God. Only the high priest could use the Urim and Thummim, which were designed to give only yes or no answers.

**10:22** When the Israelites assembled to choose a king, Saul already knew he was the one (10:1). Instead of coming forward, however, he hid among the baggage. Often we hide from important responsibilities because we are afraid of failure, afraid of what others will think, or perhaps unsure about how to proceed. Prepare now to step up to your future responsibilities. Count on God's provision rather than your feelings of adequacy.

**10:25** The kings of Israel, unlike kings of other nations, had specific regulations outlined for them (Deuteronomy 17:14-20). Pagan kings were considered gods; they made their own laws

and answered to no one. By contrast, Israel's king had to answer to a higher authority—the Lord of heaven and earth. The Israelites now had a king like everyone else, just as they wanted. But Samuel, in his charge to both the king and the people, wanted to make sure that the rule of Israel's king would be different from that of his pagan counterparts. "Placed it before the LORD" means that Samuel put the scroll, as a witness to the agreement, in a special place at Mizpah.

26When Saul returned to his home at Gibeah, a group of men whose hearts God had touched went with him. 27But there were some scoundrels who complained, "How can this man save us?" And they scorned him and refused to bring him gifts. But Saul ignored them.

[Nahash, king of the Ammonites, had been grievously oppressing the people of Gad and Reuben who lived east of the Jordan River. He gouged out the right eye of each of the Israelites living there, and he didn't allow anyone to come and rescue them. In fact, of all the Israelites east of the Jordan, there wasn't a single one whose right eye Nahash had not gouged out. But there were 7,000 men who had escaped from the Ammonites, and they had settled in Jabesh-gilead.]*

10:27
1 Kgs 10:24-25

### Saul Defeats the Ammonites

**11** About a month later,* King Nahash of Ammon led his army against the Israelite town of Jabesh-gilead. But all the citizens of Jabesh asked for peace. "Make a treaty with us, and we will be your servants," they pleaded.

2"All right," Nahash said, "but only on one condition. I will gouge out the right eye of every one of you as a disgrace to all Israel!"

3"Give us seven days to send messengers throughout Israel!" replied the elders of Jabesh. "If no one comes to save us, we will agree to your terms."

4When the messengers came to Gibeah of Saul and told the people about their plight, everyone broke into tears. 5Saul had been plowing a field with his oxen, and when he returned to town, he asked, "What's the matter? Why is everyone crying?" So they told him about the message from Jabesh.

6Then the Spirit of God came powerfully upon Saul, and he became very angry. 7He took two oxen and cut them into pieces and sent the messengers to carry them throughout Israel with this message: "This is what will happen to the oxen of anyone who refuses to follow Saul and Samuel into battle!" And the LORD made the people afraid of Saul's anger, and all of them came out together as one. 8When Saul mobilized them at Bezek, he found that there were 300,000 men from Israel and 30,000* men from Judah.

9So Saul sent the messengers back to Jabesh-gilead to say, "We will rescue you by noontime tomorrow!" There was great joy throughout the town when that message arrived!

11:1
Judg 11:4-6; 21:8
1 Sam 12:12; 31:11

11:2
1 Sam 17:26

11:4
1 Sam 10:26; 30:4
11:5
1 Kgs 19:19

11:6
Judg 3:10; 6:34
1 Sam 10:10
11:7
Judg 19:29; 20:1
11:8
Judg 1:4-6

10:27 This paragraph, which is not included in the Masoretic Text, is found in Dead Sea Scroll 4QSamª.   11:1 As in Greek version; Hebrew lacks *About a month later.*   11:8 Dead Sea Scrolls and Greek version read *70,000.*

---

10:26, 27 Some men became Saul's constant companions, while others despised him. Criticism will always be directed toward those who lead because they are out in front. At this time, Saul took no notice of those who seemed to be against him, although later he would become consumed with jealousy (19:1-3; 26:17-21). As you lead, listen to constructive criticism, but don't spend valuable time and energy worrying about those who may oppose you. Instead, focus your attention on those who are ready and willing to help.

11:1ff At this time, Israel was very susceptible to invasion by marauding tribes such as these Ammonites from east of the Jordan River. Saul's leadership in battle against this warlike tribe helped unify the nation and proved that he was a worthy military ruler. Saul's kingship was solidified when he saved the nation from disgrace and spared the people who had criticized him.

11:3 Why would Nahash give the city of Jabesh-gilead seven days to find an army to help them? Because Israel was still disorganized, Nahash was betting that no one would come to the city's aid. He was hoping to take the city without a fight and avoid a battle. He also may not have been prepared to attack the city because a siege against its walls could last weeks or months.

11:6 Anger is a powerful emotion. Often it may drive people to hurt others with words or physical violence. But anger directed at sin and the mistreatment of others is not wrong. Saul was angered by the Ammonites' threat to humiliate and mistreat his fellow Israelites. The Holy Spirit used Saul's anger to bring justice and freedom. When injustice or sin makes you angry, ask God how you can channel that anger in constructive ways to help bring about a positive change.

11:8 Judah, one of the 12 tribes of Israel, is often mentioned separately from the other 11. There are several reasons for this. Judah was the largest tribe (Numbers 1:20-46), and it was the tribe from which most of Israel's kings would come (Genesis 49:8-12). Later, Judah would be one of the few tribes to return to God after a century of captivity under a hostile foreign power. Judah would also be the tribe through which the Messiah would come (Micah 5:2).

**SAUL DEFEATS THE AMMONITES**
The Ammonites prepared to attack Jabesh-gilead. The people of Jabesh sent messengers to Saul in Gibeah asking for help. Saul mobilized an army at Bezek and then attacked the Ammonites. After the battle, the Israelites returned to Gilgal to crown Saul as king.

**11:10**
1 Sam 11:3
**11:11**
Judg 7:16

¹⁰The men of Jabesh then told their enemies, "Tomorrow we will come out to you, and you can do to us whatever you wish." ¹¹But before dawn the next morning, Saul arrived, having divided his army into three detachments. He launched a surprise attack against the Ammonites and slaughtered them the whole morning. The remnant of their army was so badly scattered that no two of them were left together.

**11:12**
1 Sam 10:27
Luke 19:27
**11:13**
Exod 14:13
1 Sam 19:5
2 Sam 19:22
**11:14**
1 Sam 10:1, 8

¹²Then the people exclaimed to Samuel, "Now where are those men who said, 'Why should Saul rule over us?' Bring them here, and we will kill them!"

¹³But Saul replied, "No one will be executed today, for today the LORD has rescued Israel!"

¹⁴Then Samuel said to the people, "Come, let us all go to Gilgal to renew the kingdom." ¹⁵So they all went to Gilgal, and in a solemn ceremony before the LORD they made Saul king. Then they offered peace offerings to the LORD, and Saul and all the Israelites were filled with joy.

## Samuel's Farewell Address

**12:1**
1 Sam 8:7, 9, 22
**12:2**
1 Sam 3:10, 19-20
**12:3**
Exod 23:8
Num 16:15
Deut 16:19

**12** Then Samuel addressed all Israel: "I have done as you asked and given you a king. ²Your king is now your leader. I stand here before you—an old, gray-haired man—and my sons serve you. I have served as your leader from the time I was a boy to this very day. ³Now testify against me in the presence of the LORD and before his anointed one. Whose ox or donkey have I stolen? Have I ever cheated any of you? Have I ever oppressed you? Have I ever taken a bribe and perverted justice? Tell me and I will make right whatever I have done wrong."

⁴"No," they replied, "you have never cheated or oppressed us, and you have never taken even a single bribe."

**12:5**
Exod 22:4

⁵"The LORD and his anointed one are my witnesses today," Samuel declared, "that my hands are clean."

"Yes, he is a witness," they replied.

**12:6**
Exod 6:26
**12:7**
Mic 6:4
**12:8**
Exod 2:23-25; 3:10;
4:14-16
**12:9**
Deut 32:18
Judg 3:7; 10:7;
13:1
**12:10**
Judg 10:10, 15-16
**12:11**
Judg 4:6; 6:32;
11:1
**12:12**
Judg 8:22-23
**12:13**
1 Sam 8:5; 10:24
Hos 13:11

⁶"It was the LORD who appointed Moses and Aaron," Samuel continued. "He brought your ancestors out of the land of Egypt. ⁷Now stand here quietly before the LORD as I remind you of all the great things the LORD has done for you and your ancestors.

⁸"When the Israelites were* in Egypt and cried out to the LORD, he sent Moses and Aaron to rescue them from Egypt and to bring them into this land. ⁹But the people soon forgot about the LORD their God, so he handed them over to Sisera, the commander of Hazor's army, and also to the Philistines and to the king of Moab, who fought against them.

¹⁰"Then they cried to the LORD again and confessed, 'We have sinned by turning away from the LORD and worshiping the images of Baal and Ashtoreth. But we will worship you and you alone if you will rescue us from our enemies.' ¹¹Then the LORD sent Gideon,* Bedan,* Jephthah, and Samuel* to save you, and you lived in safety.

¹²"But when you were afraid of Nahash, the king of Ammon, you came to me and said that you wanted a king to reign over you, even though the LORD your God was already your king. ¹³All right, here is the king you have chosen. You asked for him, and the LORD has granted your request.

**12:8** Hebrew *When Jacob was.* The names "Jacob" and "Israel" are often interchanged throughout the Old Testament, referring sometimes to the individual patriarch and sometimes to the nation.   **12:11a** Hebrew *Jerub-baal,* another name for Gideon; see Judg 6:32.   **12:11b** Greek and Syriac versions read *Barak.*   **12:11c** Greek and Syriac versions read *Samson.*

---

**11:14** Saul had been anointed by Samuel at Ramah (10:1); then Saul was publicly chosen at Mizpah (10:17-27); his defeat of the Ammonites confirmed his kingship in the people's minds; at this time, all the people confirmed his rule.

**11:15** The Israelites offered peace offerings to God as they made Saul their first king. The instructions for giving these offerings are found in Leviticus 3. The peace offering was an expression of gratitude and thanksgiving to God, symbolizing the peace that comes to those who know him and who live in accordance with his commands. Although God did not want his people to have a human king, the people were demonstrating through their offerings that he was still their true King. Unfortunately, this attitude did not last, just as God had predicted (8:7-19).

**12:1ff** Samuel continued to serve the people as their priest, prophet, and judge, but Saul exercised more and more political and military control over the tribes (see 7:15).

**12:1-3** In his farewell speech, Samuel asked the Israelites to point out any wrongs he had committed during his time as Israel's judge. By doing so, Samuel was reminding them that he could be trusted to tell the truth. He was also reminding them that having a king was their idea, not his. Samuel was setting the stage for the miraculous thunderstorm recorded in 12:16-19, so that the people could not blame him when God punished them for their selfish motives.

**12:10** "The images of Baal and the Ashtoreth" were pagan gods. See the note on 7:4 for more information.

**12:12-15** God granted the nation's request for a king, but his commands and requirements remained the same. God was to be their true King, and both Saul and the people were to be subject to his laws. No person is ever exempt from God's laws. No human action is outside his jurisdiction. God is the true King of every area of life. We must recognize his kingship and pattern our relationships, work life, and home life according to his principles.

<sup>14</sup>"Now if you fear and worship the LORD and listen to his voice, and if you do not rebel against the LORD's commands, then both you and your king will show that you recognize the LORD as your God. <sup>15</sup>But if you rebel against the LORD's commands and refuse to listen to him, then his hand will be as heavy upon you as it was upon your ancestors.

<sup>16</sup>"Now stand here and see the great thing the LORD is about to do. <sup>17</sup>You know that it does not rain at this time of the year during the wheat harvest. I will ask the LORD to send thunder and rain today. Then you will realize how wicked you have been in asking the LORD for a king!"

<sup>18</sup>So Samuel called to the LORD, and the LORD sent thunder and rain that day. And all the people were terrified of the LORD and of Samuel. <sup>19</sup>"Pray to the LORD your God for us, or we will die!" they all said to Samuel. "For now we have added to our sins by asking for a king."

<sup>20</sup>"Don't be afraid," Samuel reassured them. "You have certainly done wrong, but make sure now that you worship the LORD with all your heart, and don't turn your back on him. <sup>21</sup>Don't go back to worshiping worthless idols that cannot help or rescue you—they are totally useless! <sup>22</sup>The LORD will not abandon his people, because that would dishonor his great name. For it has pleased the LORD to make you his very own people.

<sup>23</sup>"As for me, I will certainly not sin against the LORD by ending my prayers for you. And I will continue to teach you what is good and right. <sup>24</sup>But be sure to fear the LORD and faithfully serve him. Think of all the wonderful things he has done for you. <sup>25</sup>But if you continue to sin, you and your king will be swept away."

## 2. God rejects Saul for disobedience
### Continued War with Philistia

**13** Saul was thirty* years old when he became king, and he reigned for forty-two years.* <sup>2</sup>Saul selected 3,000 special troops from the army of Israel and sent the rest of the men home. He took 2,000 of the chosen men with him to Micmash and the hill country of Bethel. The other 1,000 went with Saul's son Jonathan to Gibeah in the land of Benjamin.

<sup>3</sup>Soon after this, Jonathan attacked and defeated the garrison of Philistines at Geba. The news spread quickly among the Philistines. So Saul blew the ram's horn throughout the land, saying, "Hebrews, hear this! Rise up in revolt!" <sup>4</sup>All Israel heard the news that Saul had destroyed the Philistine garrison at Geba and that the Philistines now hated the Israelites more than ever. So the entire Israelite army was summoned to join Saul at Gilgal.

<sup>5</sup>The Philistines mustered a mighty army of 3,000* chariots, 6,000 charioteers, and as many warriors as the grains of sand on the seashore! They camped at Micmash east of Beth-aven. <sup>6</sup>The men of Israel saw what a tight spot they were in; and because they were hard pressed by the enemy, they tried to hide in caves, thickets, rocks, holes, and cisterns. <sup>7</sup>Some of them crossed the Jordan River and escaped into the land of Gad and Gilead.

**13:1a** As in a few Greek manuscripts; the number is missing in the Hebrew.   **13:1b** Hebrew *reigned . . . and two;* the number is incomplete in the Hebrew. Compare Acts 13:21.   **13:5** As in Greek and Syriac versions; Hebrew reads *30,000.*

**12:14**
Josh 24:14, 20

**12:15**
Josh 24:20
Isa 1:2, 20

**12:16**
Exod 14:13, 21, 31

**12:17**
1 Sam 7:10; 8:6-7

**12:20**
Deut 11:16

**12:21**
Deut 11:16
Hab 2:18

**12:22**
Exod 32:12
Num 14:13
Deut 7:6; 31:6

**12:23**
1 Kgs 8:36
Rom 1:9
Col 1:9
1 Thes 3:10

**12:24**
Deut 10:21

**12:25**
Josh 24:20
1 Sam 31:1-5

**13:2**
1 Sam 10:26

**13:3**
Judg 3:27; 6:34
1 Sam 10:5
2 Sam 2:28; 20:1

**13:5**
Josh 11:4

**13:6**
Judg 6:2

**12:17** The wheat harvest came near the end of the dry season during the months of May and June. Because rain rarely fell during this period, a great thunderstorm was considered a miraculous event. It was not a beneficial miracle, however, because rain during the wheat harvest could damage the crops and cause them to rot quickly. This unusual occurrence showed God's displeasure with Israel's demand for a king.

**12:22** Why did God make Israel "his very own people"? God did not choose them because they deserved it (Deuteronomy 7:7, 8), but in order that they might become his channel of blessing to all people through the Messiah (Genesis 12:1-3). Because God chose the people of Israel, he would never abandon them; but because they were his special nation, he would often punish them for their disobedience in order to bring them back to a right relationship with him.

**12:23** Is failing to pray for others a sin? Samuel's words seem to indicate that it is. His actions illustrate two of God's people's responsibilities: (1) They should pray consistently for others (Ephesians 6:18), and (2) they should teach others the right way to God (2 Timothy 2:2). Samuel disagreed with the Israelites' demand for a king, but he assured them that he would continue

to pray for them and teach them. We may disagree with others, but we shouldn't stop praying for them.

**12:24** This is the second time in his farewell speech that Samuel reminded the people to take time to consider what great things God had done for them (see 12:7). Taking time for reflection allows us to focus our attention upon God's goodness and strengthens our faith. Sometimes we are so progress- and future-oriented that we fail to take time to recall all that God has already done. Remember what God has done for you so that you may move ahead with gratitude.

**13:3, 4** Jonathan attacked and destroyed the Philistine outpost, but Saul took all the credit for it. Although this was normal in that culture, it didn't make his action right. Saul's growing pride started out small—taking credit for a battle that was won by his son. Left unchecked, his pride grew into an ugly obsession; thus, it destroyed him, tore his family apart, and threatened the well-being of the nation. Taking credit for the accomplishments of others indicates that pride is controlling your life. When you notice pride taking a foothold, take immediate steps to put it in check by giving credit to those who deserve it.

**13:6** When we forget who is on our side or see only our own resources, we tend to panic at the sight of the opposition. The

## Saul's Disobedience and Samuel's Rebuke

**13:8**
1 Sam 10:8

**13:9**
2 Sam 24:25
1 Kgs 3:4

**13:10**
1 Sam 15:13

Meanwhile, Saul stayed at Gilgal, and his men were trembling with fear. 8Saul waited there seven days for Samuel, as Samuel had instructed him earlier, but Samuel still didn't come. Saul realized that his troops were rapidly slipping away. 9So he demanded, "Bring me the burnt offering and the peace offerings!" And Saul sacrificed the burnt offering himself.

10Just as Saul was finishing with the burnt offering, Samuel arrived. Saul went out to meet and welcome him, 11but Samuel said, "What is this you have done?"

Saul replied, "I saw my men scattering from me, and you didn't arrive when you said you would, and the Philistines are at Micmash ready for battle. 12So I said, 'The Philistines are ready to march against us at Gilgal, and I haven't even asked for the LORD's help!' So I felt compelled to offer the burnt offering myself before you came."

**13:13**
1 Sam 15:23-24, 28
2 Chr 16:9

**13:14**
†Acts 13:22

13"How foolish!" Samuel exclaimed. "You have not kept the command the LORD your God gave you. Had you kept it, the LORD would have established your kingdom over Israel forever. 14But now your kingdom must end, for the LORD has sought out a man after his own heart. The LORD has already appointed him to be the leader of his people, because you have not kept the LORD's command."

## Israel's Military Disadvantage

**13:15**
1 Sam 14:2

**13:16**
Josh 18:24

**13:18**
Neh 11:31-35

15Samuel then left Gilgal and went on his way, but the rest of the troops went with Saul to meet the army. They went up from Gilgal to Gibeah in the land of Benjamin.* When Saul counted the men who were still with him, he found only 600 were left! 16Saul and Jonathan and the troops with them were staying at Geba in the land of Benjamin. The Philistines set up their camp at Micmash. 17Three raiding parties soon left the camp of the Philistines. One went north toward Ophrah in the land of Shual, 18another went west to Beth-horon, and the third moved toward the border above the valley of Zeboim near the wilderness.

**13:15** As in Greek version; Hebrew reads *Samuel then left Gilgal and went to Gibeah in the land of Benjamin.*

---

**GLOOM AND DOOM**
Samuel's messages to Israel

| Reference | Message |
|---|---|
| 3:11-14 | Judgment will come to the house of Eli. |
| 7:1-4 | The nation must turn from idol worship. |
| 8:10-22 | Your kings will bring you nothing but trouble. |
| 12:25 | If you continue in sin, you will be destroyed by God. |
| 13:13, 14 | Saul's kingdom will not continue. |
| 15:17-31 | Saul, you have sinned before God. |

It wasn't easy being a prophet. Most of the messages they had to give were very unpleasant to hear. They preached of repentance, judgment, impending destruction, sin, and, in general, how displeased God was over the behavior of his people. Prophets were not the most popular people in town (unless they were *false* prophets and said just what the people wanted to hear). But popularity was not the bottom line for true prophets of God—it was obedience to God and faithfully proclaiming his word. Samuel is a good example of a faithful prophet.

God has words for us to proclaim as well. And although his messages are loaded with "good news," there is also "bad news" to give. May we, like true prophets, faithfully deliver *all* God's words, regardless of their popularity or lack of it.

---

Israelites became terrified and hid when they saw the mighty Philistine army. They forgot that God was on their side and that he couldn't be defeated. As you face problems and temptations, focus your attention on God and his resources, trusting him to help you (Romans 8:31-37).

**13:9** Rather than waiting for a priest, Saul offered the sacrifice himself. This was against God's laws (Deuteronomy 12:5-14) and against the specific instructions of Samuel (10:8). Under pressure from the approaching Philistines, he took matters into his own hands and disobeyed God. He was doing a good thing (offering a sacrifice to God before a crucial battle), but he did it in the wrong way. Like Saul, our true spiritual character is revealed under pressure. The methods we use to accomplish our goals are as important as the attainment of those goals.

**13:11, 12** It is difficult to trust God when you feel your

resources slipping away. When Saul felt that time was running out, he became impatient with God's timing. In thinking that the ritual was all he needed, he substituted the ritual for faith in God.

When faced with a difficult decision, don't allow impatience to drive you to disobey God. When you know what God wants, follow his plan regardless of the consequences. God often uses delays to test our obedience and patience.

**13:12, 13** Saul had plenty of excuses for his disobedience. But Samuel zeroed in on the real issue: "You have not kept the command the LORD your God gave you." Like Saul, we often gloss over our mistakes and sins, trying to justify our actions because of our "special" circumstances. Our excuses, however, are nothing more than disobedience. God knows our true motives. He forgives, restores, and blesses only when we are honest about our sins. By trying to hide his sins behind excuses, Saul lost his kingship (13:14).

¹⁹There were no blacksmiths in the land of Israel in those days. The Philistines wouldn't allow them for fear they would make swords and spears for the Hebrews. ²⁰So whenever the Israelites needed to sharpen their plowshares, picks, axes, or sickles,* they had to take them to a Philistine blacksmith. ²¹(The charges were as follows: a quarter of an ounce of silver* for sharpening a plowshare or a pick, and an eighth of an ounce* for sharpening an ax, a sickle, or an ox goad.) ²²So on the day of the battle none of the people of Israel had a sword or spear, except for Saul and Jonathan.

²³The pass at Micmash had meanwhile been secured by a contingent of the Philistine army.

**13:19**
Judg 5:8
1 Sam 17:47
2 Kgs 24:14
Jer 24:1

**13:23**
1 Sam 14:4
Isa 10:28

### Jonathan's Daring Plan

**14** One day Jonathan said to his armor bearer, "Come on, let's go over to where the Philistines have their outpost." But Jonathan did not tell his father what he was doing.

²Meanwhile, Saul and his 600 men were camped on the outskirts of Gibeah, around the pomegranate tree* at Migron. ³Among Saul's men was Ahijah the priest, who was wearing the ephod, the priestly vest. Ahijah was the son of Ichabod's brother Ahitub, son of Phinehas, son of Eli, the priest of the LORD who had served at Shiloh.

No one realized that Jonathan had left the Israelite camp. ⁴To reach the Philistine outpost, Jonathan had to go down between two rocky cliffs that were called Bozez and Seneh. ⁵The cliff on the north was in front of Micmash, and the one on the south was in front of Geba. ⁶"Let's go across to the outpost of those pagans," Jonathan said to his armor bearer. "Perhaps the LORD will help us, for nothing can hinder the LORD. He can win a battle whether he has many warriors or only a few!"

⁷"Do what you think is best," the armor bearer replied. "I'm with you completely, whatever you decide."

⁸"All right then," Jonathan told him. "We will cross over and let them see us. ⁹If they say to us, 'Stay where you are or we'll kill you,' then we will stop and not go up to them. ¹⁰But if they say, 'Come on up and fight,' then we will go up. That will be the LORD's sign that he will help us defeat them."

**14:2**
1 Sam 13:15

**14:3**
1 Sam 1:3;
22:11-12

**14:6**
Judg 7:4

**14:10**
Gen 24:14
Judg 6:36

**13:20** As in Greek version; Hebrew reads *or plowshares.* **13:21a** Hebrew *1 pim* [8 grams]. **13:21b** Hebrew *1/3 of a shekel* [4 grams]. **14:2** Or *around the rock of Rimmon;* compare Judg 20:45, 47; 21:13.

---

**13:19-22** Israel was in no position to conquer anyone. The army had no iron weapons, and there were no facilities for turning their tools into weapons. In fact, if an Israelite wanted to sharpen his tools, he had to pay a Philistine blacksmith to do it because the Philistines had a carefully guarded monopoly on iron and blacksmithing. And they charged high prices for sharpening farm implements. The Philistines' tight control over the technology, along with their surprise raids, demoralized the Israelites and kept them in subjection.

Against such superiority, the Israelites were at a serious disadvantage. How could they hope to rout their oppressors? Only with God's help. God wanted to give Israel victory without swords so they would realize their true source of strength.

**14:1ff** In this chapter we read about the miserable job Saul did as leader: he had no communication with Jonathan (14:1, 17); he made a foolish curse (14:24); and he ignored the well-being of his own soldiers (14:31). Saul's poor leadership was not a result of personality traits but of decaying spiritual character. What we do is often a direct result of our spiritual condition. We cannot ignore the importance of spiritual character in effective leadership.

**14:1** Why would Jonathan go alone to attack the Philistines? Jonathan may have been weary of the long, hopeless standoff in the battle; he trusted God to give the victory and wanted to act on that trust. He also knew that the number of Philistines was no problem for God. Perhaps he didn't tell his father about his mission because he thought Saul would not let him go.

**14:6** Jonathan and his armor bearer weren't much of a force to attack the huge Philistine army. But while everyone else was afraid, they trusted God, knowing that the size of the enemy army would not restrict God's ability to help them. God honored the faith and brave action of these two men with a tremendous victory.

Have you ever felt surrounded by the "enemy" or faced overwhelming odds? God is never intimidated by the size of the enemy or the complexity of a problem. With him, there are always enough resources to resist the pressures and win the battle. If God has called you to action, then bravely commit what resources you have to God, and rely upon him to lead you to victory.

**JONATHAN'S BRAVERY** Jonathan, Saul's son, left the camp at Gibeah and crept to the Philistine camp at Micmash. With God's help, Jonathan and his armor bearer surprised the Philistines, who panicked and began killing each other! Saul's army heard the commotion and chased the Philistines as far as Beth-aven and Aijalon.

**14:11**
1 Sam 13:6

**14:12**
2 Sam 5:24

**14:15**
1 Sam 7:10
2 Kgs 7:6

**14:18**
1 Sam 23:9; 30:7

**14:19**
Num 27:21

**14:20**
Judg 7:21-22
2 Chr 20:23

**14:21**
1 Sam 29:4

**14:22**
1 Sam 13:6; 31:7

**14:23**
Exod 14:30
2 Chr 32:22

**14:24**
Josh 6:26

**14:29**
1 Kgs 18:18

**14:31**
Josh 10:12

**14:32**
Gen 9:4
Lev 17:10
1 Sam 15:19
Acts 15:20

¹¹When the Philistines saw them coming, they shouted, "Look! The Hebrews are crawling out of their holes!" ¹²Then the men from the outpost shouted to Jonathan, "Come on up here, and we'll teach you a lesson!"

"Come on, climb right behind me," Jonathan said to his armor bearer, "for the LORD will help us defeat them!"

¹³So they climbed up using both hands and feet, and the Philistines fell before Jonathan, and his armor bearer killed those who came behind them. ¹⁴They killed some twenty men in all, and their bodies were scattered over about half an acre.*

¹⁵Suddenly, panic broke out in the Philistine army, both in the camp and in the field, including even the outposts and raiding parties. And just then an earthquake struck, and everyone was terrified.

### Israel Defeats the Philistines

¹⁶Saul's lookouts in Gibeah of Benjamin saw a strange sight—the vast army of Philistines began to melt away in every direction. ¹⁷"Call the roll and find out who's missing," Saul ordered. And when they checked, they found that Jonathan and his armor bearer were gone.

¹⁸Then Saul shouted to Ahijah, "Bring the ephod here!" For at that time Ahijah was wearing the ephod in front of the Israelites.* ¹⁹But while Saul was talking to the priest, the confusion in the Philistine camp grew louder and louder. So Saul said to the priest, "Never mind; let's get going!"*

²⁰Then Saul and all his men rushed out to the battle and found the Philistines killing each other. There was terrible confusion everywhere. ²¹Even the Hebrews who had previously gone over to the Philistine army revolted and joined in with Saul, Jonathan, and the rest of the Israelites. ²²Likewise, the men of Israel who were hiding in the hill country of Ephraim joined the chase when they saw the Philistines running away. ²³So the LORD saved Israel that day, and the battle continued to rage even beyond Beth-aven.

### Saul's Foolish Oath

²⁴Now the men of Israel were pressed to exhaustion that day, because Saul had placed them under an oath, saying, "Let a curse fall on anyone who eats before evening—before I have full revenge on my enemies." So no one ate anything all day, ²⁵even though they had all found honeycomb on the ground in the forest. ²⁶They didn't dare touch the honey because they all feared the oath they had taken.

²⁷But Jonathan had not heard his father's command, and he dipped the end of his stick into a piece of honeycomb and ate the honey. After he had eaten it, he felt refreshed.* ²⁸But one of the men saw him and said, "Your father made the army take a strict oath that anyone who eats food today will be cursed. That is why everyone is weary and faint."

²⁹"My father has made trouble for us all!" Jonathan exclaimed. "A command like that only hurts us. See how refreshed I am now that I have eaten this little bit of honey. ³⁰If the men had been allowed to eat freely from the food they found among our enemies, think how many more Philistines we could have killed!"

³¹They chased and killed the Philistines all day from Micmash to Aijalon, growing more and more faint. ³²That evening they rushed for the battle plunder and butchered the sheep,

**14:14** Hebrew *half a yoke;* a "yoke" was the amount of land plowed by a pair of yoked oxen in one day. **14:18** As in some Greek manuscripts; Hebrew reads *"Bring the Ark of God."* For at that time the Ark of God was with the Israelites. **14:19** Hebrew *Withdraw your hand.* **14:27** Or *his eyes brightened;* similarly in 14:29.

---

**14:12** Jonathan did not have the authority to lead all the troops into battle, but he could start a small skirmish in one corner of the enemy camp. When he did, panic broke out among the Philistines; the Hebrews who had been drafted into the Philistine army revolted; and the men who were hiding in the hills regained their courage and returned to fight.

When you are facing a difficult situation that is beyond your control, ask yourself, What steps can I take now to work toward a solution? A few small steps may be just what is needed to begin the chain of events leading to eventual victory.

**14:19** "Let's get going" refers to the use of the Urim and Thummim. These small objects were withdrawn from the linen ephod (vest) worn by the priest and used to determine God's will (see the note on 10:20). Saul was rushing the formalities of getting an

answer from God so he could hurry and get into battle to take advantage of the confusion of the Philistines.

**14:24** Saul made an oath without thinking through the implications. The results? (1) His men were too tired to fight; (2) they were so hungry they ate meat that still contained blood, which was against God's law (14:32); (3) Saul almost killed his own son (14:42-45).

Saul's impulsive oath sounded heroic, but it had disastrous side effects. If you are in the middle of a conflict, guard against impulsive statements that you may be forced to honor.

goats, cattle, and calves, but they ate them without draining the blood. 33 Someone reported to Saul, "Look, the men are sinning against the LORD by eating meat that still has blood in it."

"That is very wrong," Saul said. "Find a large stone and roll it over here. 34 Then go out among the troops and tell them, 'Bring the cattle, sheep, and goats here to me. Kill them here, and drain the blood before you eat them. Do not sin against the LORD by eating meat with the blood still in it.'"

So that night all the troops brought their animals and slaughtered them there. 35 Then Saul built an altar to the LORD; it was the first of the altars he built to the LORD.

36 Then Saul said, "Let's chase the Philistines all night and plunder them until sunrise. Let's destroy every last one of them."

His men replied, "We'll do whatever you think is best."

But the priest said, "Let's ask God first."

37 So Saul asked God, "Should we go after the Philistines? Will you help us defeat them?" But God made no reply that day.

38 Then Saul said to the leaders, "Something's wrong! I want all my army commanders to come here. We must find out what sin was committed today. 39 I vow by the name of the LORD who rescued Israel that the sinner will surely die, even if it is my own son Jonathan!" But no one would tell him what the trouble was.

40 Then Saul said, "Jonathan and I will stand over here, and all of you stand over there." And the people responded to Saul, "Whatever you think is best."

41 Then Saul prayed, "O LORD, God of Israel, please show us who is guilty and who is innocent.*" Then they cast sacred lots, and Jonathan and Saul were chosen as the guilty ones, and the people were declared innocent.

42 Then Saul said, "Now cast lots again and choose between me and Jonathan." And Jonathan was shown to be the guilty one.

43 "Tell me what you have done," Saul demanded of Jonathan.

"I tasted a little honey," Jonathan admitted. "It was only a little bit on the end of my stick. Does that deserve death?"

44 "Yes, Jonathan," Saul said, "you must die! May God strike me and even kill me if you do not die for this."

45 But the people broke in and said to Saul, "Jonathan has won this great victory for Israel. Should he die? Far from it! As surely as the LORD lives, not one hair on his head will be touched, for God helped him do a great deed today." So the people rescued Jonathan, and he was not put to death.

46 Then Saul called back the army from chasing the Philistines, and the Philistines returned home.

14:41 Greek version adds *If the fault is with me or my son Jonathan, respond with Urim; but if the men of Israel are at fault, respond with Thummim.*

14:35 1 Sam 7:12, 17
14:37 1 Sam 22:42; 28:5-6; 30:7-8
14:38 Josh 7:10-12
14:39 2 Sam 12:5
14:41 Acts 1:24
14:43 Josh 7:19; 1 Sam 14:27
14:44 Ruth 1:17; 1 Sam 3:17; 14:39; 25:22
14:45 2 Sam 14:11; Luke 21:18; Acts 27:34

**14:32-34** One of the oldest and strongest Hebrew food laws was the prohibition against eating meat containing the animal's blood (Leviticus 7:26, 27). This law began in Noah's day (Genesis 9:4) and was still observed by the early Christians (Acts 15:27-29). It was wrong to eat blood because blood represented life, and life belonged to God. (For a further explanation, see Leviticus 17:10-14.)

**14:35, 36** After being king for several years, Saul finally built his first altar to God, but only as a last resort. Throughout Saul's reign he consistently approached God only after he had tried everything else. This was in sharp contrast to the priest, who suggested that God be consulted *first*. How much better if Saul had gone to God first, building an altar as his first official act as king. God is too great to be an afterthought. When we turn to him first, we will never have to turn to him as a last resort.

**14:39** This is the second of Saul's foolish vows. Saul made the first of his two oaths (14:24-26) because he was overly anxious to defeat the Philistines and wanted to give his soldiers an incentive to finish the battle quickly. In the Bible, God never asked people to make oaths or vows, but if they did, he expected them to keep them (Leviticus 5:4; Numbers 30).

Saul's vow was not something God would have condoned, but still it was an oath. And Jonathan, although he didn't know about

Saul's oath, was nevertheless guilty of breaking it. Like Jephthah (Judges 11), Saul made an oath that risked the life of his own child. Fortunately, the people intervened and spared Jonathan's life.

**14:39** Saul had issued a ridiculous command and had driven his men to sin, but still he wouldn't back down even if he had to kill his son. When we make ridiculous statements, it is difficult to admit we are wrong. Sticking to the story, just to save face, only compounds the problem. It takes more courage to admit a mistake than to hold resolutely to an error.

**14:43** Jonathan's spiritual character was in striking contrast to Saul's. Jonathan admitted what he had done; he did not try to make excuses. Even though he was unaware of Saul's oath, Jonathan was willing to accept the consequences of his actions. When you do wrong, even unintentionally, respond like Jonathan, not like Saul.

**14:44, 45** Saul made another foolish statement, this time because he was more concerned about saving face than being right. To spare Jonathan's life would require him to admit he had acted foolishly, an embarrassment for a king. Saul was really more interested in protecting his image than in enforcing his vow. Fortunately, the people came to Jonathan's rescue. Don't be like Saul. Admit your mistakes, and show that you are more interested in doing what is right than in looking good.

## Saul's Military Successes

**14:48**
1 Sam 15:3, 7
**14:49**
1 Sam 18:17, 20,
27; 19:11-12; 31:2
2 Sam 6:20
1 Chr 8:33; 10:2
**14:50**
2 Sam 2:8
**14:51**
1 Sam 9:1
**14:52**
1 Sam 8:11

⁴⁷Now when Saul had secured his grasp on Israel's throne, he fought against his enemies in every direction—against Moab, Ammon, Edom, the kings of Zobah, and the Philistines. And wherever he turned, he was victorious.* ⁴⁸He performed great deeds and conquered the Amalekites, saving Israel from all those who had plundered them.

⁴⁹Saul's sons included Jonathan, Ishbosheth,* and Malkishua. He also had two daughters: Merab, who was older, and Michal. ⁵⁰Saul's wife was Ahinoam, the daughter of Ahimaaz. The commander of Saul's army was Abner, the son of Saul's uncle Ner. ⁵¹Saul's father, Kish, and Abner's father, Ner, were both sons of Abiel.

⁵²The Israelites fought constantly with the Philistines throughout Saul's lifetime. So whenever Saul observed a young man who was brave and strong, he drafted him into his army.

## Saul Destroys the Amalekites

**15:1**
1 Sam 9:16; 10:1
**15:2**
Exod 17:8-16
Num 24:20
Deut 25:17
**15:3**
Deut 20:16-18
Josh 6:17-18

**15** One day Samuel said to Saul, "It was the Lᴏʀᴅ who told me to anoint you as king of his people, Israel. Now listen to this message from the Lᴏʀᴅ! ²This is what the Lᴏʀᴅ of Heaven's Armies has declared: I have decided to settle accounts with the nation of Amalek for opposing Israel when they came from Egypt. ³Now go and completely destroy* the entire Amalekite nation—men, women, children, babies, cattle, sheep, goats, camels, and donkeys."

**15:6**
Num 24:21-22
Judg 1:16; 4:11
**15:7**
Gen 16:7; 25:18
Exod 15:22
1 Sam 27:8
**15:8**
Num 24:7
**15:9**
1 Sam 15:15, 21

⁴So Saul mobilized his army at Telaim. There were 200,000 soldiers from Israel and 10,000 men from Judah. ⁵Then Saul and his army went to a town of the Amalekites and lay in wait in the valley. ⁶Saul sent this warning to the Kenites: "Move away from where the Amalekites live, or you will die with them. For you showed kindness to all the people of Israel when they came up from Egypt." So the Kenites packed up and left.

⁷Then Saul slaughtered the Amalekites from Havilah all the way to Shur, east of Egypt. ⁸He captured Agag, the Amalekite king, but completely destroyed everyone else. ⁹Saul and his men spared Agag's life and kept the best of the sheep and goats, the cattle, the fat calves, and the lambs—everything, in fact, that appealed to them. They destroyed only what was worthless or of poor quality.

## The Lᴏʀᴅ Rejects Saul

**15:11**
Gen 6:6-7
Exod 32:9, 11, 14
2 Sam 24:16
Luke 6:12

¹⁰Then the Lᴏʀᴅ said to Samuel, ¹¹"I am sorry that I ever made Saul king, for he has not been loyal to me and has refused to obey my command." Samuel was so deeply moved when he heard this that he cried out to the Lᴏʀᴅ all night.

**14:47** As in Greek version; Hebrew reads *he acted wickedly.*   **14:49** Hebrew *Ishvi*, a variant name for Ishbosheth; also known as Esh-baal.   **15:3** The Hebrew term used here refers to the complete consecration of things or people to the Lᴏʀᴅ, either by destroying them or by giving them as an offering; also in 15:8, 9, 15, 18, 20, 21.

---

**14:47** Why was Saul so successful right after he had disobeyed God and been told that his reign would end (13:13, 14)? Sometimes ungodly people win battles. Victory is neither guaranteed nor limited to the righteous. God provides according to his will. God might have given Saul success for the sake of the people, not for Saul. He may have left Saul on the throne for a while to utilize his military talents so that David, Israel's next king, could spend more time focusing on the nation's spiritual battles. Regardless of God's reasons for delaying Saul's demise, his reign ended exactly the way God had foretold. The timing of God's plans and promises is known only to him. Our task is to commit our ways to God and then trust him for the outcome.

**15:2, 3** Why did God command such utter destruction? The Amalekites were a band of guerrilla terrorists. They lived by attacking other nations and carrying off their wealth and their families. They were the first to attack the Israelites as they entered the Promised Land, and they continued to raid Israelite camps at every opportunity. God knew that the Israelites could never live peacefully in the Promised Land as long as the Amalekites existed. He also knew that their corrupt, idolatrous religious practices threatened Israel's relationship with him. The only way to protect the Israelites' bodies and souls was to utterly destroy the people of this warlike nation and all their possessions, including their idols.

**15:9** Saul and his men did not destroy all the plunder from the battle as God commanded (15:3). The law of devoting some-

thing—setting it aside—entirely for destruction was well known to the Israelites. Anything under God's ban was to be completely destroyed (Deuteronomy 20:16-18). This was set up in order to prevent idolatry from taking hold in Israel because many of the valuables were idols. To break this law was punishable by death (Joshua 7). It showed disrespect and disregard for God because it directly violated his command.

When we gloss over sin in order to protect what we have or for material gain, we aren't being shrewd; we are disobeying God's law. Selective obedience is just another form of disobedience.

**15:11** When God said he was sorry that he had made Saul king, was he saying he had made a mistake? God's comment was an expression of sorrow, not an admission of error (Genesis 6:5-7). An omniscient God cannot make a mistake (15:29); therefore, God did not change his mind. He did, however, change his attitude toward Saul when Saul changed. Saul's heart no longer belonged to God but to his own interests.

¹²Early the next morning Samuel went to find Saul. Someone told him, "Saul went to the town of Carmel to set up a monument to himself; then he went on to Gilgal."

15:12
Josh 15:55

¹³When Samuel finally found him, Saul greeted him cheerfully. "May the LORD bless you," he said. "I have carried out the LORD's command!"

¹⁴"Then what is all the bleating of sheep and goats and the lowing of cattle I hear?" Samuel demanded.

¹⁵"It's true that the army spared the best of the sheep, goats, and cattle," Saul admitted. "But they are going to sacrifice them to the LORD your God. We have destroyed everything else."

15:15
Gen 3:12-13
1 Sam 15:9, 21

¹⁶Then Samuel said to Saul, "Stop! Listen to what the LORD told me last night!"

"What did he tell you?" Saul asked.

¹⁷And Samuel told him, "Although you may think little of yourself, are you not the leader of the tribes of Israel? The LORD has anointed you king of Israel. ¹⁸And the LORD sent you on a mission and told you, 'Go and completely destroy the sinners, the Amalekites, until they are all dead.' ¹⁹Why haven't you obeyed the LORD? Why did you rush for the plunder and do what was evil in the LORD's sight?"

15:17
1 Sam 9:21; 10:22

15:19
1 Sam 14:32

²⁰"But I did obey the LORD," Saul insisted. "I carried out the mission he gave me. I brought back King Agag, but I destroyed everyone else. ²¹Then my troops brought in the best of the sheep, goats, cattle, and plunder to sacrifice to the LORD your God in Gilgal."

15:21
1 Sam 15:9, 15

²²But Samuel replied,

15:22
Pss 40:6-8;
51:16-17
Isa 1:11-15
Jer 7:22-23
Hos 6:6
Mic 6:7-8
Mark 12:33

"What is more pleasing to the LORD:
> your burnt offerings and sacrifices
> or your obedience to his voice?
Listen! Obedience is better than sacrifice,
> and submission is better than offering the fat of rams.
²³ Rebellion is as sinful as witchcraft,
> and stubbornness as bad as worshiping idols.
So because you have rejected the command of the LORD,
> he has rejected you as king."

15:23
Deut 18:10
1 Sam 13:14

### Saul Pleads for Forgiveness

²⁴Then Saul admitted to Samuel, "Yes, I have sinned. I have disobeyed your instructions and the LORD's command, for I was afraid of the people and did what they demanded. ²⁵But now, please forgive my sin and come back with me so that I may worship the LORD."

15:24
Num 22:34
2 Sam 12:13
Ps 51:4
Isa 51:12-13

15:25
Exod 10:17

²⁶But Samuel replied, "I will not go back with you! Since you have rejected the LORD's command, he has rejected you as king of Israel."

15:27
1 Kgs 11:30-31

²⁷As Samuel turned to go, Saul tried to hold him back and tore the hem of his robe. ²⁸And Samuel said to him, "The LORD has torn the kingdom of Israel from you today and has given it to someone else—one who is better than you. ²⁹And he who is the Glory of Israel will not lie, nor will he change his mind, for he is not human that he should change his mind!"

15:28
1 Sam 28:17-18

15:29
Num 23:19
Ezek 24:14

---

**15:12** Saul built a monument in honor of himself. What a contrast to Moses and Joshua, who gave all the credit to God.

**15:13, 14** Saul thought he had won a great victory over the Amalekites, but God saw it as a great failure because Saul had disobeyed him and then lied to Samuel about the results of the battle. Saul may have thought his lie wouldn't be detected, or that what he did was not wrong. Saul was deceiving himself.

Dishonest people soon begin to believe the lies they construct around themselves. Then they lose the ability to tell the difference between truth and lies. By believing your own lies, you deceive yourself, you alienate yourself from God, and you lose credibility in all your relationships. In the long run, honesty wins out.

**15:22, 23** This is the first of numerous places in the Bible where the theme "obedience is better than sacrifice" is stated (Psalms 40:6-8; 51:16, 17; Proverbs 21:3; Isaiah 1:11-17; Jeremiah 7:21-23; Hosea 6:6; Micah 6:6-8; Matthew 12:7; Mark 12:33; Hebrews 10:8, 9). Was Samuel saying that sacrifice was unimportant? No, he was urging Saul to look at his reasons for making the sacrifice rather than at the sacrifice itself. A sacrifice was a ritual transaction between a person and God that physically demonstrated a relation-

ship between them. But if the person's heart was not truly repentant or if he did not truly love God, the sacrifice was a hollow ritual. Religious ceremonies or rituals are empty unless they are performed with an attitude of love and obedience. "Being religious" (going to church, serving on a committee, giving to charity) is not enough if we do not act out of devotion and obedience to God.

**15:23** Rebellion and stubbornness are serious sins. They involve far more than being independent and strong-minded. Scripture equates them with witchcraft and idolatry, sins worthy of death (Exodus 22:18; Leviticus 20:6; Deuteronomy 13:12-15; 18:10; Micah 5:10-14).

Saul became both rebellious and stubborn, so it is little wonder that God finally rejected him and took away his kingdom. Rebellion against God is perhaps the most serious sin of all because as long as a person rebels, he or she closes the door to forgiveness and restoration with God.

**15:26** Saul's excuses had come to an end. It was the time of reckoning. God wasn't rejecting Saul as a person; the king could still seek forgiveness and restore his relationship with God, but it was too late to get his kingdom back. If you do not act responsibly

**15:30**
Isa 29:13

<sup>30</sup>Then Saul pleaded again, "I know I have sinned. But please, at least honor me before the elders of my people and before Israel by coming back with me so that I may worship the Lord your God." <sup>31</sup>So Samuel finally agreed and went back with him, and Saul worshiped the Lord.

### Samuel Executes King Agag

<sup>32</sup>Then Samuel said, "Bring King Agag to me." Agag arrived full of hope, for he thought, "Surely the worst is over, and I have been spared!"* <sup>33</sup>But Samuel said, "As your sword has killed the sons of many mothers, now your mother will be childless." And Samuel cut Agag to pieces before the Lord at Gilgal.

**15:33**
Gen 9:5-6
Judg 1:7

**15:34**
1 Sam 7:17; 11:4

**15:35**
1 Sam 16:1; 19:24

<sup>34</sup>Then Samuel went home to Ramah, and Saul returned to his house at Gibeah of Saul. <sup>35</sup>Samuel never went to meet with Saul again, but he mourned constantly for him. And the Lord was sorry he had ever made Saul king of Israel.

### C. SAUL AND DAVID (16:1—31:13)

While Saul is still on the throne, Samuel anoints David as Israel's next king. Young David then bravely conquers Goliath, the Philistine champion, and establishes a lifelong friendship with Jonathan, Saul's son. When Saul realizes that David will become king one day, he grows very jealous and tries to kill David on several occasions. David escapes into Philistine territory until Saul is killed in battle. When treated unjustly, we should not take matters into our own hands. God, who is faithful and just, sees all that is happening and will judge all evil.

### 1. Samuel anoints David

**16:1**
1 Sam 9:16;
13:13-14
2 Kgs 9:1-2

**16** Now the Lord said to Samuel, "You have mourned long enough for Saul. I have rejected him as king of Israel, so fill your flask with olive oil and go to Bethlehem. Find a man named Jesse who lives there, for I have selected one of his sons to be my king."

**16:2**
1 Sam 20:28-29

<sup>2</sup>But Samuel asked, "How can I do that? If Saul hears about it, he will kill me."

"Take a heifer with you," the Lord replied, "and say that you have come to make a sacri-

**16:3**
Deut 17:14-15

fice to the Lord. <sup>3</sup>Invite Jesse to the sacrifice, and I will show you which of his sons to anoint for me."

**16:4**
1 Kgs 2:13
Luke 2:4

<sup>4</sup>So Samuel did as the Lord instructed. When he arrived at Bethlehem, the elders of the town came trembling to meet him. "What's wrong?" they asked. "Do you come in peace?"

**16:5**
Gen 35:2
Exod 19:10

<sup>5</sup>"Yes," Samuel replied. "I have come to sacrifice to the Lord. Purify yourselves and come with me to the sacrifice." Then Samuel performed the purification rite for Jesse and his sons and invited them to the sacrifice, too.

**16:6**
1 Sam 17:13

<sup>6</sup>When they arrived, Samuel took one look at Eliab and thought, "Surely this is the Lord's anointed!"

**16:7**
1 Sam 9:2
1 Kgs 8:39
1 Chr 28:9
Luke 16:15

<sup>7</sup>But the Lord said to Samuel, "Don't judge by his appearance or height, for I have rejected him. The Lord doesn't see things the way you see them. People judge by outward appearance, but the Lord looks at the heart."

**16:8**
1 Sam 17:13

<sup>8</sup>Then Jesse told his son Abinadab to step forward and walk in front of Samuel. But Samuel said, "This is not the one the Lord has chosen." <sup>9</sup>Next Jesse summoned Shimea,* but Samuel said, "Neither is this the one the Lord has chosen." <sup>10</sup>In the same way all seven of Jesse's sons were presented to Samuel. But Samuel said to Jesse, "The Lord has not chosen any of these." <sup>11</sup>Then Samuel asked, "Are these all the sons you have?"

**16:11**
2 Sam 7:8

**15:32** Dead Sea Scrolls and Greek version read *Agag arrived hesitantly, for he thought, "Surely this is the bitterness of death."*　**16:9** Hebrew *Shammah*, a variant spelling of Shimea; compare 1 Chr 2:13; 20:7.

---

with what God has entrusted to you, eventually you will run out of excuses. All of us must one day give an account for our actions (Romans 14:12; Revelation 22:12).

**15:30** Saul was more concerned about what others would think of him than he was about the status of his relationship with God (15:24). He begged Samuel to go with him to worship as a public demonstration that Samuel still supported him. If Samuel had refused, the people probably would have lost all confidence in Saul.

**16:5** Samuel performed the purification rite for Jesse and his sons to prepare them to come before God in worship or to offer a sacrifice. For more on this ceremony, see Genesis 35:2; Exodus 19:10, 14; and the note on Joshua 3:5.

**16:7** Saul was tall and handsome; he was an impressive-looking man. Samuel may have been trying to find someone who looked

like Saul to be Israel's next king, but God warned him against judging by appearance alone. When people judge by outward appearance, they may overlook quality individuals who lack the particular physical qualities society currently admires. Appearance doesn't reveal what people are really like or what their true value is.

Fortunately, God judges by faith and character, not appearances. And because only God can see on the inside, only he can accurately judge people. Most people spend hours each week maintaining their outward appearance; they should do even more to develop their inner character. While everyone can see your face, only you and God know what your heart really looks like. What steps are you taking to improve your heart's attitude?

"There is still the youngest," Jesse replied. "But he's out in the fields watching the sheep and goats."

"Send for him at once," Samuel said. "We will not sit down to eat until he arrives."

12 So Jesse sent for him. He was dark and handsome, with beautiful eyes. And the LORD said, "This is the one; anoint him."

13 So as David stood there among his brothers, Samuel took the flask of olive oil he had brought and anointed David with the oil. And the Spirit of the LORD came powerfully upon David from that day on. Then Samuel returned to Ramah.

### David Serves in Saul's Court

14 Now the Spirit of the LORD had left Saul, and the LORD sent a tormenting spirit* that filled him with depression and fear.

15 Some of Saul's servants said to him, "A tormenting spirit from God is troubling you. 16 Let us find a good musician to play the harp whenever the tormenting spirit troubles you. He will play soothing music, and you will soon be well again."

17 "All right," Saul said. "Find me someone who plays well, and bring him here."

18 One of the servants said to Saul, "One of Jesse's sons from Bethlehem is a talented harp player. Not only that—he is a brave warrior, a man of war, and has good judgment. He is also a fine-looking young man, and the LORD is with him."

19 So Saul sent messengers to Jesse to say, "Send me your son David, the shepherd." 20 Jesse responded by sending David to Saul, along with a young goat, a donkey loaded with bread, and a wineskin full of wine.

21 So David went to Saul and began serving him. Saul loved David very much, and David became his armor bearer.

22 Then Saul sent word to Jesse asking, "Please let David remain in my service, for I am very pleased with him."

23 And whenever the tormenting spirit from God troubled Saul, David would play the harp. Then Saul would feel better, and the tormenting spirit would go away.

### 2. David and Goliath
*Goliath Challenges the Israelites*

**17** The Philistines now mustered their army for battle and camped between Socoh in Judah and Azekah at Ephes-dammim. 2 Saul countered by gathering his Israelite troops near the valley of Elah. 3 So the Philistines and Israelites faced each other on opposite hills, with the valley between them.

4 Then Goliath, a Philistine champion from Gath, came out of the Philistine ranks to face the forces of Israel. He was over nine feet* tall! 5 He wore a bronze helmet, and his bronze

**Margin references:**
16:12 Gen 39:6; Exod 2:1-2; 1 Sam 9:17; Acts 7:20
16:14 Judg 16:20; 1 Sam 11:6; 18:10-12; 19:9; 1 Kgs 22:22
16:18 1 Sam 3:19; 17:32-37
16:21 Gen 41:46
17:1 1 Sam 13:5; 1 Chr 11:13
17:2 1 Sam 21:9
17:4 Josh 11:21-22; 2 Sam 21:19

---

16:14 Or *an evil spirit;* also in 16:15, 16, 23. **17:4** Hebrew *6 cubits and 1 span* [which totals about 9.75 feet or 3 meters]; Dead Sea Scrolls and Greek version read *4 cubits and 1 span* [which totals about 6.75 feet or 2 meters].

---

**16:13** David was anointed king, but it was done in secret; he was not publicly anointed until much later (2 Samuel 2:4; 5:3). Saul was still legally the king, but God was preparing David for his future responsibilities. The anointing oil poured over David's head stood for holiness. It was used to set people or objects apart for God's service. Each king and high priest of Israel was anointed with oil. This commissioned him as God's representative to the nation. Although God rejected Saul's kingship by not allowing any of his descendants to sit on Israel's throne, Saul himself remained in his position until his death.

**16:14** What was this tormenting spirit the Lord sent? Perhaps Saul was simply depressed. Or perhaps the Holy Spirit had left Saul, and God allowed an evil spirit (a demon) to torment him as judgment for his disobedience (this would demonstrate God's power over the spirit world—1 Kings 22:19-23). Either way, Saul was driven to insanity, which led him to attempt to murder David.

**16:15, 16** Harps were popular musical instruments in Saul's day, and their music is still known for its soothing qualities. The simplest harps were merely two pieces of wood fastened at right angles to each other. The strings were stretched across the wood to give the harp a triangular shape. Simple strings could be made of twisted grasses, but better strings were made of dried animal intestine. Harps could have up to 40 strings and were louder than the smaller three- or four-stringed instruments called lyres. David, known for his shepherding skills and bravery, was also an accomplished harpist and musician, who would eventually write many of the psalms found in the Bible.

**16:19-21** When Saul asked David to be in his service, he obviously did not know that David had been secretly anointed king (16:12). Saul's invitation presented an excellent opportunity for the young man and future king to gain firsthand information about leading a nation ("David went back and forth so he could help his father with the sheep in Bethlehem," 17:15).

Sometimes our plans—even the ones we think God has approved—have to be put on hold indefinitely. Like David, we can use this waiting time profitably. We can choose to learn and grow in our present circumstances, whatever they may be.

**17:4-7** When they had first approached the Promise Land, most of the Israelites had been afraid to enter because of the giants living there (Numbers 13:32, 33). King Og of Bashan needed a bed over 13 feet long (Deuteronomy 3:11). Now Goliath, over nine feet tall, taunted Israel's soldiers and appeared invincible to them. Saul, the tallest of the Israelites, may have been especially worried because he was obviously the best match for Goliath. In God's eyes, however, Goliath was no different than anyone else.

coat of mail weighed 125 pounds.* 6He also wore bronze leg armor, and he carried a bronze javelin on his shoulder. 7The shaft of his spear was as heavy and thick as a weaver's beam, tipped with an iron spearhead that weighed 15 pounds.* His armor bearer walked ahead of him carrying a shield.

8Goliath stood and shouted a taunt across to the Israelites. "Why are you all coming out to fight?" he called. "I am the Philistine champion, but you are only the servants of Saul. Choose one man to come down here and fight me! 9If he kills me, then we will be your slaves. But if I kill him, you will be our slaves! 10I defy the armies of Israel today! Send me a man who will fight me!" 11When Saul and the Israelites heard this, they were terrified and deeply shaken.

### Jesse Sends David to Saul's Camp

12Now David was the son of a man named Jesse, an Ephrathite from Bethlehem in the land of Judah. Jesse was an old man at that time, and he had eight sons. 13Jesse's three oldest sons—Eliab, Abinadab, and Shimea*—had already joined Saul's army to fight the Philistines. 14David was the youngest son. David's three oldest brothers stayed with Saul's army, 15but David went back and forth so he could help his father with the sheep in Bethlehem.

16For forty days, every morning and evening, the Philistine champion strutted in front of the Israelite army.

17:9 2 Sam 2:12-16
17:10 1 Sam 17:26, 45
17:12 Gen 35:19 Ruth 4:18-22 1 Chr 2:13
17:13 1 Sam 16:6-9
17:15 1 Sam 16:19

17:5 Hebrew *5,000 shekels* [57 kilograms].    17:7 Hebrew *600 shekels* [6.8 kilograms].    17:13 Hebrew *Shammah*, a variant spelling of Shimea; compare 1 Chr 2:13; 20:7.

---

**GOLIATH**

Goliath was a giant with an attitude. As champion of the Philistines, he immobilized an entire army of Israelites by challenging one of them to duel with him. He made them forget they had an absolute champion in the Lord their God. It took a bold shepherd boy named David to remind them all they were the armies of the living God.

Goliath was a problem to be faced on his terms but not with his weapons. Goliath's strengths were so obvious (size, armor, arrogance) that others missed his vulnerability. For Goliath had a glaring weakness that never occurred to him until David's stone struck him down. When David was given Goliath's kind of weapons, David quickly concluded he couldn't even function—much less fight—with those tools. Goliath's strengths would have been David's handicaps. Armor plating and heavy weapons were of little use to the shepherd boy. David went with the two weapons he knew he could rely on: his trust in God and his shepherd's sling. When others looked at Goliath, they saw an opponent too powerful to defeat; when David looked at Goliath, he saw a target too big to miss!

David had armor to match Goliath's, but it was invisible. He was spiritually equipped. Ephesians 6:10–18 describes in detail the resources that God places at our disposal. How unfortunate that we face our world each day on its terms and too often try to wield its weapons. God's weapons are not as obvious, but they never fail us! How much of your spiritual armor are you wearing today?

| | |
|---|---|
| **Strengths and accomplishments** | • Designated champion of the Philistine army<br>• Held the entire army of Israel at bay by intimidation and derision<br>• Recognized as a giant in his day |
| **Weaknesses and mistakes** | • Defied the armies of the living God<br>• Failed to take David seriously |
| **Lessons from his life** | • Strengths often conceal weaknesses<br>• God will not be mocked<br>• God transforms strength into weakness and weakness into strength<br>• God equips those who trust him with spiritual armor |
| **Vital statistics** | • Where: Gath<br>• Occupation: Soldier<br>• Relatives: At least one brother<br>• Contemporaries: Saul, Jonathan, David |
| **Key verse** | "Who is this pagan Philistine anyway, that he is allowed to defy the armies of the living God?" (1 Samuel 17:26). |

His story is told in 1 Samuel 17.

---

**17:9** An army often avoided the high cost of battle by pitting its strongest warrior against the strongest warrior of the enemy. This avoided great bloodshed because the winner of the fight was considered the winner of the battle. Goliath had the definite advantage against David from a human standpoint. But Goliath didn't realize that in fighting David, he also had to fight God.

**17:16** Why would this go on for 40 days without one side attacking the other? They were camped on opposite sides of a valley with steep walls. Whoever would rush down the valley and up the steep cliffs would be at a disadvantage at the beginning of the battle and probably suffer great casualties. Each side was waiting for the other to attack first.

17One day Jesse said to David, "Take this basket* of roasted grain and these ten loaves of bread, and carry them quickly to your brothers. 18And give these ten cuts of cheese to their captain. See how your brothers are getting along, and bring back a report on how they are doing.*" 19David's brothers were with Saul and the Israelite army at the valley of Elah, fighting against the Philistines.

20So David left the sheep with another shepherd and set out early the next morning with the gifts, as Jesse had directed him. He arrived at the camp just as the Israelite army was leaving for the battlefield with shouts and battle cries. 21Soon the Israelite and Philistine forces stood facing each other, army against army. 22David left his things with the keeper of supplies and hurried out to the ranks to greet his brothers. 23As he was talking with them, Goliath, the Philistine champion from Gath, came out from the Philistine ranks. Then David heard him shout his usual taunt to the army of Israel.

24As soon as the Israelite army saw him, they began to run away in fright. 25"Have you seen the giant?" the men asked. "He comes out each day to defy Israel. The king has offered a huge reward to anyone who kills him. He will give that man one of his daughters for a wife, and the man's entire family will be exempted from paying taxes!"

26David asked the soldiers standing nearby, "What will a man get for killing this Philistine and ending his defiance of Israel? Who is this pagan Philistine anyway, that he is allowed to defy the armies of the living God?"

27And these men gave David the same reply. They said, "Yes, that is the reward for killing him."

28But when David's oldest brother, Eliab, heard David talking to the men, he was angry. "What are you doing around here anyway?" he demanded. "What about those few sheep you're supposed to be taking care of? I know about your pride and deceit. You just want to see the battle!"

29"What have I done now?" David replied. "I was only asking a question!" 30He walked over to some others and asked them the same thing and received the same answer. 31Then David's question was reported to King Saul, and the king sent for him.

### David Kills Goliath

32"Don't worry about this Philistine," David told Saul. "I'll go fight him!"

33"Don't be ridiculous!" Saul replied. "There's no way you can fight this Philistine and possibly win! You're only a boy, and he's been a man of war since his youth."

34But David persisted. "I have been taking care of my father's sheep and goats," he said. "When a lion or a bear comes to steal a lamb from the flock, 35I go after it with a club and rescue the lamb from its mouth. If the animal turns on me, I catch it by the jaw and club it to death. 36I have done this to both lions and bears, and I'll do it to this pagan Philistine, too, for he has defied the armies of the living God! 37The LORD who rescued me from the claws of the lion and the bear will rescue me from this Philistine!"

17:17 Hebrew *ephah* [20 quarts or 22 liters]. 17:18 Hebrew *and take their pledge.*

**Cross-references (margin):**

17:17 1 Sam 25:18
17:18 Gen 37:13-14
17:23 1 Sam 17:8-10
17:25 Josh 15:16; 1 Sam 18:17
17:26 1 Sam 11:2; 14:6; 2 Kgs 19:4
17:28 Gen 37:4, 8
17:32 Deut 20:1
17:35 Amos 3:12
17:37 1 Sam 20:13; 2 Tim 4:17

---

**17:26** What a difference perspective can make. Most of the onlookers saw only a giant. David, however, saw a mortal man defying almighty God. Goliath was a target too big to miss. He knew he would not be alone when he faced Goliath; God would fight with him. He looked at his situation from God's point of view. Who or what are the "giants" you are facing? Viewing impossible situations from God's point of view helps us put giant problems in perspective. Once we see clearly, we can fight more effectively.

**17:28-32** Criticism couldn't stop David. While the rest of the army stood around, he knew the importance of taking action. With God to fight for him, there was no reason to wait. People may try to discourage you with negative comments or mockery, but continue to do what you know is right. By doing what is right, you will be pleasing God, whose opinion matters most.

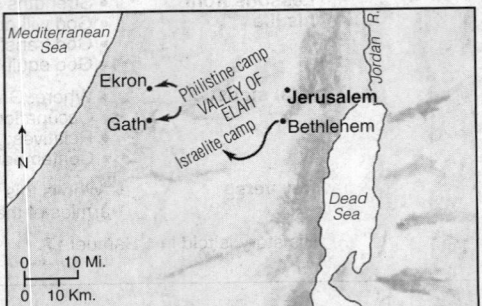

**DAVID AND GOLIATH** The armies of Israel and Philistia faced each other across the valley of Elah. David arrived from Bethlehem and offered to fight the giant Goliath. After David defeated Goliath, the Israelite army chased the Philistines to Ekron and Gath (Goliath's hometown).

Saul finally consented. "All right, go ahead," he said. "And may the LORD be with you!"
[38]Then Saul gave David his own armor—a bronze helmet and a coat of mail. [39]David put it on, strapped the sword over it, and took a step or two to see what it was like, for he had never worn such things before.

"I can't go in these," he protested to Saul. "I'm not used to them." So David took them off again. [40]He picked up five smooth stones from a stream and put them into his shepherd's bag. Then, armed only with his shepherd's staff and sling, he started across the valley to fight the Philistine.

[41]Goliath walked out toward David with his shield bearer ahead of him, [42]sneering in contempt at this ruddy-faced boy. [43]"Am I a dog," he roared at David, "that you come at me with a stick?" And he cursed David by the names of his gods. [44]"Come over here, and I'll give your flesh to the birds and wild animals!" Goliath yelled.

[45]David replied to the Philistine, "You come to me with sword, spear, and javelin, but I come to you in the name of the LORD of Heaven's Armies—the God of the armies of Israel, whom you have defied. [46]Today the LORD will conquer you, and I will kill you and cut off your head. And then I will give the dead bodies of your men to the birds and wild animals,

**17:42**
1 Sam 16:12

**17:43**
1 Sam 24:14
2 Sam 3:8; 9:8
1 Kgs 20:10

**17:45**
2 Chr 32:8
Ps 124:8
Heb 11:32-34

**17:46**
Exod 7:5
Josh 4:24
1 Kgs 18:36
2 Kgs 19:19
Isa 37:20

**DAVID**

When we think of David, we think: shepherd, poet, giant-killer, king, ancestor of Jesus—in short, one of the greatest men in the Old Testament. But alongside that list stands another: betrayer, liar, adulterer, murderer. The first list gives qualities we all might like to have; the second, qualities that might be true of any one of us. The Bible makes no effort to hide David's failures. Yet he is remembered and respected for his heart for God. Knowing how much more we share in David's failures than in his greatness, we should be curious to find out what made God refer to David as "a man after my own heart" (Acts 13:22).

David, more than anything else, had an unchangeable belief in the faithful and forgiving nature of God. He was a man who lived with great zest. He sinned, but he was quick to confess his sins. His confessions were from the heart, and his repentance was genuine. David never took God's forgiveness lightly or his blessing for granted. In return, God never held back from David either his forgiveness or the consequences of his actions. David experienced the joy of forgiveness even when he had to suffer the consequences of his sins.

We tend to get these two reversed. Too often we would rather avoid the consequences than experience forgiveness. Another big difference between us and David is that while he sinned greatly, he did not sin repeatedly. He learned from his mistakes because he accepted the suffering they brought. Often we don't seem to learn from our mistakes or the consequences that result from those mistakes. What changes would it take for God to find this kind of obedience in you?

| | |
|---|---|
| **Strengths and accomplishments** | • Greatest king of Israel<br>• Ancestor of Jesus Christ<br>• Listed in the Hall of Faith in Hebrews 11<br>• A man described by God himself as a man after his own heart |
| **Weaknesses and mistakes** | • Committed adultery with Bathsheba<br>• Arranged the murder of Uriah, Bathsheba's husband<br>• Directly disobeyed God in taking a census of the people<br>• Did not deal decisively with the sins of his children |
| **Lessons from his life** | • Willingness to honestly admit our mistakes is the first step in dealing with them<br>• Forgiveness does not remove the consequences of sin<br>• God greatly desires our complete trust and worship |
| **Vital statistics** | • Where: Bethlehem, Jerusalem<br>• Occupations: Shepherd, musician, poet, soldier, king<br>• Relatives: Father: Jesse. Wives: included Michal, Ahinoam, Bathsheba, Abigail. Sons: included Absalom, Amnon, Solomon, Adonijah. Daughters: included Tamar.<br>• Contemporaries: Saul, Jonathan, Samuel, Nathan |
| **Key verses** | "For you are God, O Sovereign LORD. Your words are truth, and you have promised these good things to your servant. And now, may it please you to bless the house of your servant, so that it may continue forever before you. For you have spoken, and when you grant a blessing to your servant, O Sovereign LORD, it is an eternal blessing!" (2 Samuel 7:28, 29). |

His story is told in 1 Samuel 16—1 Kings 2. He is also mentioned in Amos 6:5; Matthew 1:1, 6; 22:43–45; Luke 1:32; Acts 13:22; Romans 1:3; Hebrews 11:32.

and the whole world will know that there is a God in Israel! 47And everyone assembled here will know that the LORD rescues his people, but not with sword and spear. This is the LORD's battle, and he will give you to us!"

**17:47**
1 Sam 14:6
2 Chr 14:11; 20:15
Ps 44:6
Hos 1:7

48As Goliath moved closer to attack, David quickly ran out to meet him. 49Reaching into his shepherd's bag and taking out a stone, he hurled it with his sling and hit the Philistine in the forehead. The stone sank in, and Goliath stumbled and fell face down on the ground.

50So David triumphed over the Philistine with only a sling and a stone, for he had no sword. 51Then David ran over and pulled Goliath's sword from its sheath. David used it to kill him and cut off his head.

**17:50**
1 Sam 25:29

### Israel Routs the Philistines

When the Philistines saw that their champion was dead, they turned and ran. 52Then the men of Israel and Judah gave a great shout of triumph and rushed after the Philistines, chasing them as far as Gath* and the gates of Ekron. The bodies of the dead and wounded Philistines were strewn all along the road from Shaaraim, as far as Gath and Ekron. 53Then the Israelite army returned and plundered the deserted Philistine camp. 54(David took the Philistine's head to Jerusalem, but he stored the man's armor in his own tent.)

**17:52**
Josh 15:11, 36

55As Saul watched David go out to fight the Philistine, he asked Abner, the commander of his army, "Abner, whose son is this young man?"

"I really don't know," Abner declared.

56"Well, find out who he is!" the king told him.

57As soon as David returned from killing Goliath, Abner brought him to Saul with the Philistine's head still in his hand. 58"Tell me about your father, young man," Saul said.

And David replied, "His name is Jesse, and we live in Bethlehem."

## 3. David and Jonathan become friends

### Saul Becomes Jealous of David

**18** After David had finished talking with Saul, he met Jonathan, the king's son. There was an immediate bond between them, for Jonathan loved David. 2From that day on Saul kept David with him and wouldn't let him return home. 3And Jonathan made a solemn pact with David, because he loved him as he loved himself. 4Jonathan sealed the pact by taking off his robe and giving it to David, together with his tunic, sword, bow, and belt.

**18:1**
Gen 44:30
2 Sam 1:26; 9:1

**18:4**
Gen 41:42
Esth 6:8

5Whatever Saul asked David to do, David did it successfully. So Saul made him a commander over the men of war, an appointment that was welcomed by the people and Saul's officers alike.

6When the victorious Israelite army was returning home after David had killed the Philistine, women from all the towns of Israel came out to meet King Saul. They sang and danced for joy with tambourines and cymbals.* 7This was their song:

**18:6**
Exod 15:20
Judg 11:34
Pss 68:25; 149:3
**18:7**
1 Sam 21:11; 29:5

"Saul has killed his thousands,
   and David his ten thousands!"

**17:52** As in some Greek manuscripts; Hebrew reads *a valley.*   **18:6** The type of instrument represented by the word *cymbals* is uncertain.

---

**17:48-49** David was able to move faster than Goliath because David carried no heavy weapons or armor. David was an expert marksman with a sling, and as he advanced on Goliath, he stayed out of range of Goliath's huge weapons. What made David effective, however, was more than his ability with a sling; it was his courage and his faith in God. To fight like David we need David's kind of fearlessness. David had grown strong in his confidence by trusting God when he had encountered wild animals while guarding his father's sheep (17:34-37). When you face towering problems, recall how God has helped you in the past. Take heart because God gives you strength. Use the skills God has already given you and move forward.

**17:55-58** Although David had played his harp many times in front of Saul, Saul's question to Abner seems to show he didn't know David very well. Perhaps, since David was scheduled to marry Saul's daughter if he was successful (17:25), Saul wanted to know more about his family. Or possibly Saul's unstable mental condition (16:14) may have prevented him from recognizing David.

**18:1-4** When David and Jonathan met, they became close friends at once. Their friendship is one of the deepest and closest recorded in the Bible: (1) They based their friendship on commitment to God, not just each other; (2) they let nothing come between them, not even career or family problems; (3) they drew closer together when their friendship was tested; (4) they remained friends to the end.

Jonathan, the prince of Israel, later realized that David, and not he, would be the next king (23:17). But that did not weaken his love for David. Jonathan would much rather lose the throne of Israel than lose his closest friend.

**18:8**
1 Sam 15:28-29

8This made Saul very angry. "What's this?" he said. "They credit David with ten thousands and me with only thousands. Next they'll be making him their king!" 9So from that time on Saul kept a jealous eye on David.

**18:10**
1 Sam 16:14

**18:11**
1 Sam 19:10

10The very next day a tormenting spirit* from God overwhelmed Saul, and he began to rave in his house like a madman. David was playing the harp, as he did each day. But Saul had a spear in his hand, 11and he suddenly hurled it at David, intending to pin him to the wall. But David escaped him twice.

**18:13**
2 Sam 5:2

12Saul was then afraid of David, for the LORD was with David and had turned away from Saul. 13Finally, Saul sent him away and appointed him commander over 1,000 men, and David faithfully led his troops into battle.

**18:14**
Gen 39:3-4

14David continued to succeed in everything he did, for the LORD was with him. 15When Saul recognized this, he became even more afraid of him. 16But all Israel and Judah loved David because he was so successful at leading his troops into battle.

### David Marries Saul's Daughter

**18:17**
1 Sam 17:25;
25:28

17One day Saul said to David, "I am ready to give you my older daughter, Merab, as your wife. But first you must prove yourself to be a real warrior by fighting the LORD's battles." For Saul thought, "I'll send him out against the Philistines and let them kill him rather than doing it myself."

**18:18**
1 Sam 9:21
2 Sam 7:18

**18:19**
Judg 7:22
2 Sam 21:8

18"Who am I, and what is my family in Israel that I should be the king's son-in-law?" David exclaimed. "My father's family is nothing!" 19So* when the time came for Saul to give his daughter Merab in marriage to David, he gave her instead to Adriel, a man from Meholah.

**18:10** Or an evil spirit.  **18:19** Or But.

---

**GOD USES SIMPLE OBJECTS**

God often uses simple, ordinary objects to accomplish his tasks in the world. It is important only that they be dedicated to him for his use. What do you have that God can use? Anything and everything is a possible "instrument" for him.

| Object | Reference | Who Used It? | How Was It Used? |
|---|---|---|---|
| A staff | Exodus 4:2-4 | Moses | To work miracles before Pharaoh |
| Horns | Joshua 6:3-5 | Joshua | To flatten the walls of Jericho |
| A fleece | Judges 6:36-40 | Gideon | To confirm God's will |
| Horns, jars, and torches | Judges 7:19-22 | Gideon | To defeat the Midianites |
| Jawbone | Judges 15:15 | Samson | To kill 1,000 Philistines |
| Smooth stone | 1 Samuel 17:40 | David | To kill Goliath |
| Olive oil | 2 Kings 4:1-7 | Elisha | To demonstrate God's power to provide |
| A river | 2 Kings 5:9-14 | Elisha | To heal a man of leprosy |
| Linen loincloth | Jeremiah 13:1-11 | Jeremiah | As an object lesson of God's wrath |
| Clay jar | Jeremiah 19:1-13 | Jeremiah | As an object lesson of God's wrath |
| Iron griddle, water, and food | Ezekiel 4:1-17 | Ezekiel | As an object lesson of judgment |
| Five loaves and two fish | Mark 6:30-44 | Jesus | To feed a crowd of over 5,000 people |

---

**18:8** Saul's appreciation for David turned to jealousy as people began to applaud David's exploits. In a jealous rage, Saul attempted to murder David by hurling his spear at him (18:11, 12).

Jealousy may not seem to be a major sin, but in reality, it is one step short of murder. Jealousy starts as you resent a rival; it leads to your wishing he or she were removed; then it manifests itself in your seeking ways to harm that person in word or action. Beware of letting jealousy get a foothold in your life.

**18:10** The note on 16:14 explains what this tormenting spirit might have been.

**18:11, 12** Saul tried to kill David because he was jealous of David's popularity, yet David continued to protect and comfort Saul. Perhaps people have been jealous of you and have even attacked you in some way. They may be intimidated by your strengths, which make them conscious of their own shortcomings. It would be natural to strike back or to avoid them.

A better response is to befriend them (Matthew 5:43, 44) and to ask God for the strength to continue to love them, as David kept on loving Saul.

**18:15-18** While Saul's popularity made him proud and arrogant, David remained humble (18:23), even when the entire nation praised him. Although David succeeded in almost everything he tried and became famous throughout the land, he refused to use his popular support to his advantage against Saul. Don't allow popularity to twist your perception of your own importance. It's comparatively easy to be humble when you're not on center stage, but how will you react to praise and honor?

20In the meantime, Saul's daughter Michal had fallen in love with David, and Saul was delighted when he heard about it. 21"Here's another chance to see him killed by the Philistines!" Saul said to himself. But to David he said, "Today you have a second chance to become my son-in-law!"

22Then Saul told his men to say to David, "The king really likes you, and so do we. Why don't you accept the king's offer and become his son-in-law?"

23When Saul's men said these things to David, he replied, "How can a poor man from a humble family afford the bride price for the daughter of a king?"

24When Saul's men reported this back to the king, 25he told them, "Tell David that all I want for the bride price is 100 Philistine foreskins! Vengeance on my enemies is all I really want." But what Saul had in mind was that David would be killed in the fight.

26David was delighted to accept the offer. Before the time limit expired, 27he and his men went out and killed 200 Philistines. Then David fulfilled the king's requirement by presenting all their foreskins to him. So Saul gave his daughter Michal to David to be his wife.

28When Saul realized that the LORD was with David and how much his daughter Michal loved him, 29Saul became even more afraid of him, and he remained David's enemy for the rest of his life.

30Every time the commanders of the Philistines attacked, David was more successful against them than all the rest of Saul's officers. So David's name became very famous.

### Saul Tries to Kill David

**19** Saul now urged his servants and his son Jonathan to assassinate David. But Jonathan, because of his strong affection for David, 2told him what his father was planning. "Tomorrow morning," he warned him, "you must find a hiding place out in the fields. 3I'll ask my father to go out there with me, and I'll talk to him about you. Then I'll tell you everything I can find out."

4The next morning Jonathan spoke with his father about David, saying many good things about him. "The king must not sin against his servant David," Jonathan said. "He's never done anything to harm you. He has always helped you in any way he could. 5Have you forgotten about the time he risked his life to kill the Philistine giant and how the LORD brought a great victory to all Israel as a result? You were certainly happy about it then. Why should you murder an innocent man like David? There is no reason for it at all!"

6So Saul listened to Jonathan and vowed, "As surely as the LORD lives, David will not be killed."

7Afterward Jonathan called David and told him what had happened. Then he brought David to Saul, and David served in the court as before.

8War broke out again after that, and David led his troops against the Philistines. He attacked them with such fury that they all ran away.

9But one day when Saul was sitting at home, with spear in hand, the tormenting spirit* from the LORD suddenly came upon him again. As David played his harp, 10Saul hurled his spear at David. But David dodged out of the way, and leaving the spear stuck in the wall, he fled and escaped into the night.

### Michal Saves David's Life

11Then Saul sent troops to watch David's house. They were told to kill David when he came out the next morning. But Michal, David's wife, warned him, "If you don't escape tonight, you will be dead by morning." 12So she helped him climb out through a window, and he fled and escaped. 13Then she took an idol* and put it in his bed, covered it with blankets, and put a cushion of goat's hair at its head.

14When the troops came to arrest David, she told them he was sick and couldn't get out of bed.

15But Saul sent the troops back to get David. He ordered, "Bring him to me in his bed so I can kill him!" 16But when they came to carry David out, they discovered that it was only an idol in the bed with a cushion of goat's hair at its head.

**19:9** Or *evil spirit.*   **19:13** Hebrew *teraphim;* also in 19:16.

*Marginal cross-references:*
18:20 / 1 Sam 18:28
18:23 / Gen 29:20; 34:12
18:27 / 2 Sam 3:14
19:1 / 1 Sam 18:1-3
19:3 / 1 Sam 20:9, 12
19:5 / Deut 19:10-13 / 1 Sam 11:13; 17:49-50 / Ps 94:21
19:7 / 1 Sam 16:21
19:9 / 1 Sam 16:14; 18:10-12
19:11 / Judg 16:2 / Ps 59:title, 3-4, 6
19:12 / Josh 2:15 / Acts 9:25
19:13 / Judg 18:14, 17

---

**19:1, 2** Is it ever right to disobey your father, as Jonathan did here? It is clearly a principle of Scripture that when a father instructs a son to break God's laws, the son should obey God rather than man. This principle assumes that the son is old enough to be accountable and to see through any deception. A son's role is to be respectful, helpful, and obedient to his father (Ephesians 6:1-3), but not to follow commands or advice that violate God's laws.

19:18
1 Sam 7:17;
19:22-23

19:20
Num 11:24-25
1 Sam 10:5-6, 10
Joel 2:28

19:23
1 Sam 10:13

19:24
1 Sam 10:10-12
2 Sam 6:20
Mic 1:8

20:1
1 Sam 24:9

20:3
Deut 6:13
2 Kgs 2:6-7

20:5
Num 10:10;
28:11-17
1 Sam 19:2

20:6
1 Sam 16:2; 17:58

20:7
1 Sam 25:17

20:8
1 Sam 18:1-3
2 Sam 1:26; 14:23

20:13
Ruth 1:17
1 Sam 3:17; 14:44;
18:11-12
1 Chr 28:20

20:15
2 Sam 9:1

<sup>17</sup>"Why have you betrayed me like this and let my enemy escape?" Saul demanded of Michal.

"I had to," Michal replied. "He threatened to kill me if I didn't help him."

<sup>18</sup>So David escaped and went to Ramah to see Samuel, and he told him all that Saul had done to him. Then Samuel took David with him to live at Naioth. <sup>19</sup>When the report reached Saul that David was at Naioth in Ramah, <sup>20</sup>he sent troops to capture him. But when they arrived and saw Samuel leading a group of prophets who were prophesying, the Spirit of God came upon Saul's men, and they also began to prophesy. <sup>21</sup>When Saul heard what had happened, he sent other troops, but they, too, prophesied! The same thing happened a third time. <sup>22</sup>Finally, Saul himself went to Ramah and arrived at the great well in Secu. "Where are Samuel and David?" he demanded.

"They are at Naioth in Ramah," someone told him.

<sup>23</sup>But on the way to Naioth in Ramah the Spirit of God came even upon Saul, and he, too, began to prophesy all the way to Naioth! <sup>24</sup>He tore off his clothes and lay naked on the ground all day and all night, prophesying in the presence of Samuel. The people who were watching exclaimed, "What? Is even Saul a prophet?"

## Jonathan Helps David

**20** David now fled from Naioth in Ramah and found Jonathan. "What have I done?" he exclaimed. "What is my crime? How have I offended your father that he is so determined to kill me?"

<sup>2</sup>"That's not true!" Jonathan protested. "You're not going to die. He always tells me everything he's going to do, even the little things. I know my father wouldn't hide something like this from me. It just isn't so!"

<sup>3</sup>Then David took an oath before Jonathan and said, "Your father knows perfectly well about our friendship, so he has said to himself, 'I won't tell Jonathan—why should I hurt him?' But I swear to you that I am only a step away from death! I swear it by the LORD and by your own soul!"

<sup>4</sup>"Tell me what I can do to help you," Jonathan exclaimed.

<sup>5</sup>David replied, "Tomorrow we celebrate the new moon festival. I've always eaten with the king on this occasion, but tomorrow I'll hide in the field and stay there until the evening of the third day. <sup>6</sup>If your father asks where I am, tell him I asked permission to go home to Bethlehem for an annual family sacrifice. <sup>7</sup>If he says, 'Fine!' you will know all is well. But if he is angry and loses his temper, you will know he is determined to kill me. <sup>8</sup>Show me this loyalty as my sworn friend—for we made a solemn pact before the LORD—or kill me yourself if I have sinned against your father. But please don't betray me to him!"

<sup>9</sup>"Never!" Jonathan exclaimed. "You know that if I had the slightest notion my father was planning to kill you, I would tell you at once."

<sup>10</sup>Then David asked, "How will I know whether or not your father is angry?"

<sup>11</sup>"Come out to the field with me," Jonathan replied. And they went out there together. <sup>12</sup>Then Jonathan told David, "I promise by the LORD, the God of Israel, that by this time tomorrow, or the next day at the latest, I will talk to my father and let you know at once how he feels about you. If he speaks favorably about you, I will let you know. <sup>13</sup>But if he is angry and wants you killed, may the LORD strike me and even kill me if I don't warn you so you can escape and live. May the LORD be with you as he used to be with my father. <sup>14</sup>And may you treat me with the faithful love of the LORD as long as I live. But if I die, <sup>15</sup>treat my family with this faithful love, even when the LORD destroys all your enemies from the face of the earth."

---

**19:20-24** This was the second time that Saul surprised everyone by joining a group of prophets and prophesying. This seems to be a group of people in Spirit-filled ecstasy. It was very powerful and contagious to anyone who found them. We do not know if they were speaking messages from God or merely joining in ecstatic expression. The first time this happened to Saul (chapter 10) was right after he was anointed king and did not want to accept the responsibility. This time Saul was consumed with jealousy over David's growing popularity, but the Spirit of God immobilized him so he was unable to harm David. Although Saul was receptive to the Spirit of God and was caught up in prophesying, his heart and mind were far from loving God and thinking God's thoughts.

**20:5** At the beginning of each month, the Israelites gathered to celebrate the new moon festival. While this was mainly a time to be enjoyed, it was also a way to dedicate the next month to God. Other nations had celebrations during the full moon and worshiped the moon itself. The Israelites, however, celebrated their festival at the time of the new moon, when the moon was not visible in the sky. This was an added precaution against false worship. Nothing in the creation is to be worshiped—only the Creator.

**20:15** Jonathan asked David to keep a promise to treat his children kindly in the future. Years later David took great pains to fulfill this promise: He invited Jonathan's son Mephibosheth into his palace to live (2 Samuel 9).

16So Jonathan made a solemn pact with David,* saying, "May the LORD destroy all your enemies!" 17And Jonathan made David reaffirm his vow of friendship again, for Jonathan loved David as he loved himself.

18Then Jonathan said, "Tomorrow we celebrate the new moon festival. You will be missed when your place at the table is empty. 19The day after tomorrow, toward evening, go to the place where you hid before, and wait there by the stone pile.* 20I will come out and shoot three arrows to the side of the stone pile as though I were shooting at a target. 21Then I will send a boy to bring the arrows back. If you hear me tell him, 'They're on this side,' then you will know, as surely as the LORD lives, that all is well, and there is no trouble. 22But if I tell him, 'Go farther—the arrows are still ahead of you,' then it will mean that you must leave immediately, for the LORD is sending you away. 23And may the LORD make us keep our promises to each other, for he has witnessed them."

24So David hid himself in the field, and when the new moon festival began, the king sat down to eat. 25He sat at his usual place against the wall, with Jonathan sitting opposite him* and Abner beside him. But David's place was empty. 26Saul didn't say anything about it that day, for he said to himself, "Something must have made David ceremonially unclean." 27But when David's place was empty again the next day, Saul asked Jonathan, "Why hasn't the son of Jesse been here for the meal either yesterday or today?"

28Jonathan replied, "David earnestly asked me if he could go to Bethlehem. 29He said, 'Please let me go, for we are having a family sacrifice. My brother demanded that I be there. So please let me get away to see my brothers.' That's why he isn't here at the king's table."

30Saul boiled with rage at Jonathan. "You stupid son of a whore!"* he swore at him. "Do you think I don't know that you want him to be king in your place, shaming yourself and your mother? 31As long as that son of Jesse is alive, you'll never be king. Now go and get him so I can kill him!"

32"But why should he be put to death?" Jonathan asked his father. "What has he done?" 33Then Saul hurled his spear at Jonathan, intending to kill him. So at last Jonathan realized that his father was really determined to kill David.

34Jonathan left the table in fierce anger and refused to eat on that second day of the festival, for he was crushed by his father's shameful behavior toward David.

35The next morning, as agreed, Jonathan went out into the field and took a young boy with him to gather his arrows. 36"Start running," he told the boy, "so you can find the arrows as I shoot them." So the boy ran, and Jonathan shot an arrow beyond him. 37When the boy had almost reached the arrow, Jonathan shouted, "The arrow is still ahead of you. 38Hurry, hurry, don't wait." So the boy quickly gathered up the arrows and ran back to his master. 39He, of course, suspected nothing; only Jonathan and David understood the signal. 40Then Jonathan gave his bow and arrows to the boy and told him to take them back to town.

**20:23**
Gen 31:49-50, 53

**20:26**
Lev 7:20-21
1 Sam 16:5

**20:28**
1 Sam 20:6

**20:32**
Matt 27:23
**20:33**
1 Sam 18:11;
19:10-11

**20:36**
1 Sam 20:20-21

20:16 Hebrew *with the house of David.*   20:19 Hebrew *the stone Ezel.* The meaning of the Hebrew is uncertain. 20:25 As in Greek version; Hebrew reads *with Jonathan standing.*   20:30 Hebrew *You son of a perverse and rebellious woman.*

---

**20:26** Because the new moon festival involved making a sacrifice to God (Numbers 28:11-15), those attending the festival had to be ceremonially clean according to God's laws (Exodus 19:10; Leviticus 15; Numbers 19:11-22; also see the note on Joshua 3:5). This cleansing involved washing the body and clothes before approaching God to offer a sacrifice. The outward cleansing was a symbol of the inward desire for a purified heart and right relationship with God. Today our hearts are purified by faith in God through the death of Jesus Christ on our behalf (Hebrews 10:10, 22) and by reading and heeding God's Word (John 17:17).

**20:31, 32** Saul was still trying to secure his throne for future generations even though he had already been told his dynasty would end with him (13:13, 14). Even worse, he was trying to do this by sinful human means because he knew he would get no help from God. Jonathan could have made a move to become the next king by killing his rival, but he bypassed this opportunity because of his love for both God and David (23:16-18).

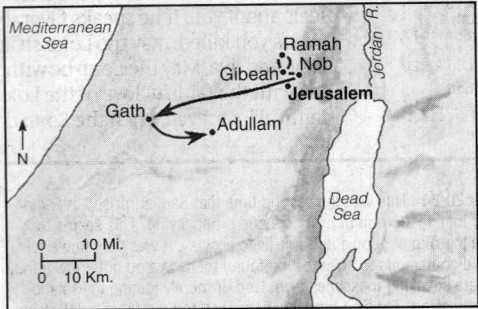

**DAVID'S ESCAPE**   David learned of Saul's plans to kill him and fled to Samuel at Ramah. Returning to Gibeah to say good-bye to Jonathan, he then escaped to Nob, where he received food and a sword from the priest. He then fled to Gath in Philistine territory. When the Philistines became suspicious, he escaped to the cave of Adullam, where many men joined him.

⁴¹As soon as the boy was gone, David came out from where he had been hiding near the stone pile.* Then David bowed three times to Jonathan with his face to the ground. Both of them were in tears as they embraced each other and said good-bye, especially David.

**20:42**
1 Sam 20:14-15

⁴²At last Jonathan said to David, "Go in peace, for we have sworn loyalty to each other in the LORD's name. The LORD is the witness of a bond between us and our children forever." Then David left, and Jonathan returned to the town.*

## 4. Saul pursues David
### David Runs from Saul

**21:1**
1 Sam 16:4; 22:19
Neh 11:32

**21** ¹*David went to the town of Nob to see Ahimelech the priest. Ahimelech trembled when he saw him. "Why are you alone?" he asked. "Why is no one with you?"

²"The king has sent me on a private matter," David said. "He told me not to tell anyone why I am here. I have told my men where to meet me later. ³Now, what is there to eat? Give me five loaves of bread or anything else you have."

**21:4**
Exod 19:14-15
Lev 24:5-9
Matt 12:4

⁴"We don't have any regular bread," the priest replied. "But there is the holy bread, which you can have if your young men have not slept with any women recently."

**20:41** As in Greek version; Hebrew reads *near the south edge.* **20:42** This sentence is numbered 21:1 in Hebrew text. **21:1** Verses 21:1-15 are numbered 21:2-16 in Hebrew text.

Loyalty is one of life's most costly qualities; it is the most selfless part of love. To be loyal, you cannot live only for yourself. Loyal people not only stand by their commitments; they are willing to suffer for them. Jonathan is a shining example of loyalty. Sometimes he was forced to deal with conflicting loyalties: to his father, Saul, and to his friend David. His solution to that conflict teaches us both how to be loyal and what must guide loyalty. In Jonathan, truth always guided loyalty.

Jonathan realized that the source of truth was God, who demanded his ultimate loyalty. It was his relationship with God that gave Jonathan the ability to deal effectively with the complicated situations in his life. He was loyal to Saul because Saul was his father and the king. He was loyal to David because David was his friend. His loyalty to God guided him through the conflicting demands of his human relationships.

The conflicting demands of our relationships challenge us as well. If we attempt to settle these conflicts only at the human level, we will be constantly dealing with a sense of betrayal. But if we communicate to our friends that our ultimate loyalty is to God and his truth, many of our choices will be much clearer. The truth in his Word, the Bible, will bring light to our decisions. Do those closest to you know who has your greatest loyalty?

| | |
|---|---|
| **Strengths and accomplishments** | • Brave, loyal, and a natural leader<br>• The closest friend David ever had<br>• Did not put his personal well-being ahead of those he loved<br>• Depended on God |
| **Lessons from his life** | • Loyalty is one of the strongest parts of courage<br>• An allegiance to God puts all other relationships in perspective<br>• Great friendships are costly |
| **Vital statistics** | • Occupation: Military leader<br>• Relatives: Father: Saul. Mother: Ahinoam. Brothers: Malkishua, Abinadab, Ishbosheth (and possibly Ishvi). Sisters: Merab, Michal. Son: Mephibosheth. |
| **Key verse** | "How I weep for you, my brother Jonathan! Oh, how much I loved you! And your love for me was deep, deeper than the love of women!" (2 Samuel 1:26). |

His story is told in 1 Samuel 13—31. He is also mentioned in 2 Samuel 9.

**JONATHAN**

**21:1ff** This is the first time Ahimelech is mentioned. Either he was the Ahijah mentioned in 14:3, 18, or, more likely, he was Ahijah's successor. In either case, Ahimelech had to go against the law to give the holy bread to David because the bread was supposed to be given only to the priests (Leviticus 24:5-9). But Ahimelech put David's need and life ahead of religious ceremony and fed him the holy food. This upheld a higher law of love (Leviticus 19:18). Centuries later, Jesus would refer to this incident to show that God's laws should be applied with compassion. To do good and to save life is God's greater law (Matthew 12:1-8; Luke 6:1-5).

**21:2** David lied to protect himself from Saul (21:10). Some excuse this lie because a war was going on, and it is the duty of a good soldier to deceive the enemy. But nowhere is David's lie condoned. In fact, the opposite is true because his lie led to the death of 85 priests (22:9-19). David's small lie seemed harmless enough, but it led to tragedy. The Bible makes it very clear that lying is wrong (Leviticus 19:11). Lying, like every other sin, is serious in God's sight and may lead to all sorts of harmful consequences. Don't minimize or categorize sins. All sins must be avoided whether or not we can foresee their potential consequences.

5"Don't worry," David replied. "I never allow my men to be with women when they are on a campaign. And since they stay clean even on ordinary trips, how much more on this one!"

6Since there was no other food available, the priest gave him the holy bread—the Bread of the Presence that was placed before the LORD in the Tabernacle. It had just been replaced that day with fresh bread.

**21:6**
Matt 12:3-4
Mark 2:25-28
Luke 6:3-4

7Now Doeg the Edomite, Saul's chief herdsman, was there that day, having been detained before the LORD.*

**21:7**
1 Sam 22:9, 22
Ps 52:1

8David asked Ahimelech, "Do you have a spear or sword? The king's business was so urgent that I didn't even have time to grab a weapon!"

9"I only have the sword of Goliath the Philistine, whom you killed in the valley of Elah," the priest replied. "It is wrapped in a cloth behind the ephod. Take that if you want it, for there is nothing else here."

**21:9**
1 Sam 17:2, 50-51

"There is nothing like it!" David replied. "Give it to me!"

10So David escaped from Saul and went to King Achish of Gath. 11But the officers of Achish were unhappy about his being there. "Isn't this David, the king of the land?" they asked. "Isn't he the one the people honor with dances, singing,

**21:10**
1 Sam 27:2
**21:11**
1 Sam 18:7; 29:5

'Saul has killed his thousands,
    and David his ten thousands'?"

12David heard these comments and was very afraid of what King Achish of Gath might do to him. 13So he pretended to be insane, scratching on doors and drooling down his beard.

**21:13**
Ps 34:title

14Finally, King Achish said to his men, "Must you bring me a madman? 15We already have enough of them around here! Why should I let someone like this be my guest?"

### David at the Cave of Adullam

**22** So David left Gath and escaped to the cave of Adullam. Soon his brothers and all his other relatives joined him there. 2Then others began coming—men who were in trouble or in debt or who were just discontented—until David was the captain of about 400 men.

**22:1-2**
2 Sam 23:13

3Later David went to Mizpeh in Moab, where he asked the king, "Please allow my father and mother to live here with you until I know what God is going to do for me." 4So David's parents stayed in Moab with the king during the entire time David was living in his stronghold.

**21:7** The meaning of the Hebrew is uncertain.

---

**21:5** The men's bodies were ceremonially clean because they had not had sexual intercourse during this journey. Therefore, the priest allowed them to eat the holy bread.

**21:6** Once a week on the Sabbath, a priest entered the Holy Place in the Tabernacle and placed 12 freshly baked loaves of bread on a small table. This bread, called the Bread of the Presence, symbolized God's presence among his people as well as his loving care that met their physical needs. The bread that was replaced was to be eaten only by the priests on duty.

**21:9** An ephod was a vest worn by the priest (see the note on 2:18 for a more detailed explanation). David didn't know Goliath's sword was there, probably because David was a young man when he killed the giant and he had spent much of his time at home.

**21:10-15** Gath was one of the five major Philistine cities. Why did the Philistines allow their archenemy, David, into their camp? The Philistines may have been initially happy to accept a defector who was a high military leader. Any enemy of Saul would have been a friend of theirs. They could not have known that David had been anointed Israel's next king (16:13). Soon, however, the Philistines became nervous about David's presence. After all, he had slain thousands of their people (18:7). David then protected himself by acting insane because it was the custom not to harm mentally unstable people.

**22:2** Those in trouble, in debt, or discontented joined David, who himself was an outlaw. These people were outcasts themselves and could only improve their lot by helping David become king. David's control over this band of men again shows his resourcefulness and ability to lead and motivate others. It is difficult enough to build an army out of good men, but it takes even greater leadership to build one out of the kind of men that followed David. This group eventually formed the core of his military leadership (2 Samuel 23:8ff).

**DAVID FLEES FROM SAUL**  David and his men attacked the Philistines at Keilah from the forest of Hereth. Saul came from Gibeah to attack David, but David escaped into the wilderness of Ziph. At Horesh he met Jonathan, who encouraged him. Then he fled into the wilderness of Maon and into the strongholds of En-gedi.

**22:5**
2 Sam 24:11
1 Chr 21:9; 29:29
2 Chr 29:25-26

**22:6**
Judg 4:5
1 Sam 14:2

**22:7**
1 Sam 8:12, 14
1 Chr 12:16-18

**22:8**
1 Sam 23:21

**22:9**
1 Sam 21:1, 7

**22:10**
1 Sam 21:6

**22:14**
1 Sam 19:4-5;
20:32

**22:15**
2 Sam 5:19, 23

**22:17**
1 Sam 14:45
2 Kgs 10:25

**22:18**
1 Sam 2:18, 30-33

**22:20**
1 Sam 2:30-33;
23:6; 30:7
1 Kgs 2:26-27

**22:22**
1 Sam 21:7

⁵One day the prophet Gad told David, "Leave the stronghold and return to the land of Judah." So David went to the forest of Hereth.

⁶The news of his arrival in Judah soon reached Saul. At the time, the king was sitting beneath the tamarisk tree on the hill at Gibeah, holding his spear and surrounded by his officers.

⁷"Listen here, you men of Benjamin!" Saul shouted to his officers when he heard the news. "Has that son of Jesse promised every one of you fields and vineyards? Has he promised to make you all generals and captains in his army?* ⁸Is that why you have conspired against me? For not one of you told me when my own son made a solemn pact with the son of Jesse. You're not even sorry for me. Think of it! My own son—encouraging him to kill me, as he is trying to do this very day!"

⁹Then Doeg the Edomite, who was standing there with Saul's men, spoke up. "When I was at Nob," he said, "I saw the son of Jesse talking to the priest, Ahimelech son of Ahitub. ¹⁰Ahimelech consulted the LORD for him. Then he gave him food and the sword of Goliath the Philistine."

### The Slaughter of the Priests

¹¹King Saul immediately sent for Ahimelech and all his family, who served as priests at Nob. ¹²When they arrived, Saul shouted at him, "Listen to me, you son of Ahitub!"

"What is it, my king?" Ahimelech asked.

¹³"Why have you and the son of Jesse conspired against me?" Saul demanded. "Why did you give him food and a sword? Why have you consulted God for him? Why have you encouraged him to kill me, as he is trying to do this very day?"

¹⁴"But sir," Ahimelech replied, "is anyone among all your servants as faithful as David, your son-in-law? Why, he is the captain of your bodyguard and a highly honored member of your household! ¹⁵This was certainly not the first time I had consulted God for him! May the king not accuse me and my family in this matter, for I knew nothing at all of any plot against you."

¹⁶"You will surely die, Ahimelech, along with your entire family!" the king shouted. ¹⁷And he ordered his bodyguards, "Kill these priests of the LORD, for they are allies and conspirators with David! They knew he was running away from me, but they didn't tell me!" But Saul's men refused to kill the LORD's priests.

¹⁸Then the king said to Doeg, "You do it." So Doeg the Edomite turned on them and killed them that day, eighty-five priests in all, still wearing their priestly garments. ¹⁹Then he went to Nob, the town of the priests, and killed the priests' families—men and women, children and babies—and all the cattle, donkeys, sheep, and goats.

²⁰Only Abiathar, one of the sons of Ahimelech, escaped and fled to David. ²¹When he told David that Saul had killed the priests of the LORD, ²²David exclaimed, "I knew it! When I saw Doeg the Edomite there that day, I knew he was sure to tell Saul. Now I have caused the death of all your father's family. ²³Stay here with me, and don't be afraid. I will protect you with my own life, for the same person wants to kill us both."

**22:7** Hebrew *commanders of thousands and commanders of hundreds?*

---

**22:7, 8** Apparently Saul's key officers were from the tribe of Benjamin, just as he was. David was from the neighboring tribe of Judah. Saul was appealing to tribal loyalty to maintain his hold on the throne.

**22:18** Why would Saul have his own priests killed? Saul suspected a conspiracy among Jonathan, David, and the priests. His suspicion came from Doeg's report of seeing David talking to Ahimelech, the high priest, and receiving food and a weapon from him (22:9, 10). Saul's action showed his mental and emotional instability and how far he had strayed from God.

By destroying everything in Nob, Saul was placing the city under the ban (declaring it to be utterly destroyed) described in Deuteronomy 13:12-17, which was supposed to be used only in cases of idolatry and rebellion against God. But it was Saul, not the priests, who had rebelled against God.

**22:18, 19** Why did God allow 85 innocent priests and their families to be killed? Their deaths served to dramatize to the nation how a king could become an evil tyrant. Where were

Saul's advisers? Where were the elders of Israel? Sometimes God allows evil to develop to teach us not to let evil systems flourish. Serving God is not a ticket to wealth, success, or health. God does not promise to protect good people from evil in this world, but he does promise that ultimately all evil will be abolished. Those who have remained faithful through their trials will experience great rewards in the age to come (Matthew 5:11, 12; Revelation 21:1-7; 22:1-21).

**22:20** Abiathar escaped to David with an ephod (23:6), a priestly garment containing the Urim and Thummim, two objects David used to consult God. The ephod was probably the only symbol of the priesthood that survived Saul's raid and made it into David's camp (23:6). Saul destroyed Israel's priesthood, but when David became king, he installed Abiathar as the new high priest. Abiathar remained in that position during David's entire reign.

## David Protects the Town of Keilah

**23** One day news came to David that the Philistines were at Keilah stealing grain from the threshing floors. ²David asked the Lord, "Should I go and attack them?"

"Yes, go and save Keilah," the Lord told him.

³But David's men said, "We're afraid even here in Judah. We certainly don't want to go to Keilah to fight the whole Philistine army!"

⁴So David asked the Lord again, and again the Lord replied, "Go down to Keilah, for I will help you conquer the Philistines."

⁵So David and his men went to Keilah. They slaughtered the Philistines and took all their livestock and rescued the people of Keilah. ⁶Now when Abiathar son of Ahimelech fled to David at Keilah, he brought the ephod with him.

⁷Saul soon learned that David was at Keilah. "Good!" he exclaimed. "We've got him now! God has handed him over to me, for he has trapped himself in a walled town!" ⁸So Saul mobilized his entire army to march to Keilah and besiege David and his men.

⁹But David learned of Saul's plan and told Abiathar the priest to bring the ephod and ask the Lord what he should do. ¹⁰Then David prayed, "O Lord, God of Israel, I have heard that Saul is planning to come and destroy Keilah because I am here. ¹¹Will the leaders of Keilah betray me to him?* And will Saul actually come as I have heard? O Lord, God of Israel, please tell me."

And the Lord said, "He will come."

¹²Again David asked, "Will the leaders of Keilah betray me and my men to Saul?"

And the Lord replied, "Yes, they will betray you."

## David Hides in the Wilderness

¹³So David and his men—about 600 of them now—left Keilah and began roaming the countryside. Word soon reached Saul that David had escaped, so he didn't go to Keilah after all. ¹⁴David now stayed in the strongholds of the wilderness and in the hill country of Ziph. Saul hunted him day after day, but God didn't let Saul find him.

¹⁵One day near Horesh, David received the news that Saul was on the way to Ziph to search for him and kill him. ¹⁶Jonathan went to find David and encouraged him to stay strong in his faith in God. ¹⁷"Don't be afraid," Jonathan reassured him. "My father will never find you! You are going to be the king of Israel, and I will be next to you, as my father, Saul, is well aware." ¹⁸So the two of them renewed their solemn pact before the Lord. Then Jonathan returned home, while David stayed at Horesh.

¹⁹But now the men of Ziph went to Saul in Gibeah and betrayed David to him. "We know where David is hiding," they said. "He is in the strongholds of Horesh on the hill of Hakilah, which is in the southern part of Jeshimon. ²⁰Come down whenever you're ready, O king, and we will catch him and hand him over to you!"

**23:11** Some manuscripts lack the first sentence of 23:11.

---

**23:1**
Josh 15:44
Neh 3:17

**23:2**
1 Sam 23:4, 12; 30:8
2 Sam 5:19, 23

**23:4**
Josh 8:7
Judg 7:7

**23:6**
1 Sam 22:20

**23:9**
1 Sam 22:20; 30:7

**23:13**
1 Sam 22:2; 25:13
2 Sam 15:20

**23:14**
Josh 15:55
2 Chr 11:8

**23:17**
1 Sam 20:31; 24:20

**23:18**
1 Sam 18:3
2 Sam 9:1

**23:19**
1 Sam 26:1

---

**23:1** Threshing floors were open circular areas where the grain kernels were separated from their husks. (In order to separate the grain from the husk, farmers would toss their grain into the air. The wind would blow the husks away, leaving only the grain. This process is called *winnowing*.) By looting the threshing floors, the Philistines were robbing Keilah's citizens of all their food supplies. (For more on threshing, see the note on Ruth 3:2.)

**23:2** Through the Urim and Thummim that Abiathar the priest brought (23:6), David sought the Lord's guidance *before* he took action. He listened to God's directions and then proceeded accordingly. Rather than trying to find God's will *after* the fact or having to ask God to undo the results of our hasty decisions, we should take time to discern God's will beforehand. We can hear him speak through the counsel of others, his Word, and the leading of his Spirit in our heart, as well as through circumstances.

**23:6** An ephod was a sleeveless linen vest worn by priests. The high priest's ephod was brightly colored and had a breastplate with 12 gemstones, each stone representing one of the 12 tribes. The Urim and Thummim were kept in a pouch of the high priest's

ephod. (See the note on 2:18 for a more detailed explanation of the ephod.)

**23:7** When Saul heard that David was trapped in a walled city (one with gates and bars), he thought God was putting David at his mercy. Saul wanted to kill David so badly that he would have interpreted any sign as God's approval to move ahead with his plan. Had Saul known God better, he would have known what God wanted and would not have misread the situation as God's approval for murder.

Not every opportunity is sent from God. We may want something so much that we assume any opportunity to obtain it is of divine origin. As we see from Saul's case, however, this may not be true. An opportunity to do something against God's will can never be from God because God does not tempt us. When opportunities come your way, double-check your motives. Make sure you are following God's desires and not just your own.

**23:16-18** This may have been the last time David and Jonathan were together. As true friends they were more than just companions who enjoyed each other's company. They encouraged each other's faith in God and trusted each other with their deepest thoughts and closest confidences. These are the marks of true friendship.

**23:21**
1 Sam 22:8

²¹"The LORD bless you," Saul said. "At last someone is concerned about me! ²²Go and check again to be sure of where he is staying and who has seen him there, for I know that he is very crafty. ²³Discover his hiding places, and come back when you are sure. Then I'll go with you. And if he is in the area at all, I'll track him down, even if I have to search every hiding place in Judah!" ²⁴So the men of Ziph returned home ahead of Saul.

**23:24**
Josh 15:55

Meanwhile, David and his men had moved into the wilderness of Maon in the Arabah Valley south of Jeshimon. ²⁵When David heard that Saul and his men were searching for him, he went even farther into the wilderness to the great rock, and he remained there in the wilderness of Maon. But Saul kept after him in the wilderness.

**23:26**
Ps 17:9

²⁶Saul and David were now on opposite sides of a mountain. Just as Saul and his men began to close in on David and his men, ²⁷an urgent message reached Saul that the Philistines were raiding Israel again. ²⁸So Saul quit chasing David and returned to fight the Philistines. Ever since that time, the place where David was camped has been called the Rock of Escape.* ²⁹*David then went to live in the strongholds of En-gedi.

**23:29**
Josh 15:62
2 Chr 20:2

### David Spares Saul's Life

**24:2**
1 Sam 26:2

**24** ¹*After Saul returned from fighting the Philistines, he was told that David had gone into the wilderness of En-gedi. ²So Saul chose 3,000 elite troops from all Israel and went to search for David and his men near the rocks of the wild goats.

**24:3**
Judg 3:24

³At the place where the road passes some sheepfolds, Saul went into a cave to relieve himself. But as it happened, David and his men were hiding farther back in that very cave!

**24:4**
1 Sam 26:8, 11

⁴"Now's your opportunity!" David's men whispered to him. "Today the LORD is telling you, 'I will certainly put your enemy into your power, to do with as you wish.'" So David crept forward and cut off a piece of the hem of Saul's robe.

**24:5**
2 Sam 24:10

**24:6**
1 Sam 26:11

⁵But then David's conscience began bothering him because he had cut Saul's robe. ⁶"The

**23:28** Hebrew *Sela-hammahlekoth.*   **23:29** Verse 23:29 is numbered 24:1 in Hebrew text.   **24:1** Verses 24:1-22 are numbered 24:2-23 in Hebrew text.

---

**LIFE OF DAVID VERSUS LIFE OF SAUL**

| Life of David | Life of Saul |
|---|---|
| David was God's kind of king (2 Samuel 7:8-16) | Saul was man's kind of king (1 Samuel 10:23, 24) |
| David was a man after God's heart (Acts 13:22) | Saul was a man after people's praise (1 Samuel 18:6-8) |
| David's kingship was eternal (through Jesus) (2 Samuel 7:29) | Saul's kingship was rejected (1 Samuel 15:23) |
| David was kind and benevolent (2 Samuel 9; 1 Chronicles 19:2) | Saul was cruel (1 Samuel 20:30-34; 22:11-19) |
| David was forgiving (1 Samuel 26) | Saul was unforgiving (1 Samuel 14:44; 18:9) |
| David repented (2 Samuel 12:13; 24:10) | When confronted, Saul lied (1 Samuel 15:10-31) |
| David was courageous (1 Samuel 17; 1 Chronicles 18) | Saul was fearful (1 Samuel 17:11; 18:12) |
| David was at peace with God (Psalms 4:8; 37:11) | Saul was separated from God (1 Samuel 16:14) |

---

**24:3** David and his 600 men found the wilderness of En-gedi a good place to hide because of the many caves in the area. These caves were used by local people for housing and as tombs. For David's men they were places of refuge. These caves can still be seen today. Some are large enough to hold thousands of people.

**24:4** Scripture does not record that God made any such statement to David or his men. The men were probably offering their own interpretation of some previous event such as David's anointing (16:13) or Jonathan's prediction that David would become king (23:17). When David's men saw Saul entering their cave, they wrongly assumed that this was an indication from God that they should act.

**24:5, 6** David had great respect for Saul, in spite of the fact that Saul was trying to kill him. Although Saul was sinning and rebel-

ling against God, David still respected the position he held as God's anointed king. David knew he would one day be king, and he also knew it was not right to strike down the man God had placed on the throne. If he assassinated Saul, he would be setting a precedent for his own opponents to remove him some day.

Romans 13:1-7 teaches that God has placed the government and its leaders in power. We may not know why, but, like David, we are to respect the positions and roles of those to whom God has given authority. There is one exception, however. Because God is our highest authority, we should not allow a leader to pressure us to violate God's law.

LORD knows I shouldn't have done that to my lord the king," he said to his men. "The LORD forbid that I should do this to my lord the king and attack the LORD's anointed one, for the LORD himself has chosen him." 7So David restrained his men and did not let them kill Saul.

After Saul had left the cave and gone on his way, 8David came out and shouted after him, "My lord the king!" And when Saul looked around, David bowed low before him.

9Then he shouted to Saul, "Why do you listen to the people who say I am trying to harm you? 10This very day you can see with your own eyes it isn't true. For the LORD placed you at my mercy back there in the cave. Some of my men told me to kill you, but I spared you. For I said, 'I will never harm the king—he is the LORD's anointed one.' 11Look, my father, at what I have in my hand. It is a piece of the hem of your robe! I cut it off, but I didn't kill you. This proves that I am not trying to harm you and that I have not sinned against you, even though you have been hunting for me to kill me.

12"May the LORD judge between us. Perhaps the LORD will punish you for what you are trying to do to me, but I will never harm you. 13As that old proverb says, 'From evil people come evil deeds.' So you can be sure I will never harm you. 14Who is the king of Israel trying to catch anyway? Should he spend his time chasing one who is as worthless as a dead dog or a single flea? 15May the LORD therefore judge which of us is right and punish the guilty one. He is my advocate, and he will rescue me from your power!"

16When David had finished speaking, Saul called back, "Is that really you, my son David?" Then he began to cry. 17And he said to David, "You are a better man than I am, for you have repaid me good for evil. 18Yes, you have been amazingly kind to me today, for when the LORD put me in a place where you could have killed me, you didn't do it. 19Who else would let his enemy get away when he had him in his power? May the LORD reward you well for the kindness you have shown me today. 20And now I realize that you are surely going to be king, and that the kingdom of Israel will flourish under your rule. 21Now swear to me by the LORD that when that happens you will not kill my family and destroy my line of descendants!"

22So David promised this to Saul with an oath. Then Saul went home, but David and his men went back to their stronghold.

### The Death of Samuel

**25** Now Samuel died, and all Israel gathered for his funeral. They buried him at his house in Ramah.

### Nabal Angers David

Then David moved down to the wilderness of Maon.* 2There was a wealthy man from Maon who owned property near the town of Carmel. He had 3,000 sheep and 1,000 goats, and it was sheep-shearing time. 3This man's name was Nabal, and his wife, Abigail, was a sensible and beautiful woman. But Nabal, a descendant of Caleb, was crude and mean in all his dealings.

4When David heard that Nabal was shearing his sheep, 5he sent ten of his young men to Carmel with this message for Nabal: 6"Peace and prosperity to you, your family, and everything you own! 7I am told that it is sheep-shearing time. While your shepherds stayed among us near Carmel, we never harmed them, and nothing was ever stolen from them. 8Ask your own men, and they will tell you this is true. So would you be kind to us, since we have come at a time of celebration? Please share any provisions you might have on hand with us and with your friend David." 9David's young men gave this message to Nabal in David's name, and they waited for a reply.

25:1 As in Greek version (see also 25:2); Hebrew reads *Paran.*

**Marginal cross-references:**

24:7 1 Kgs 1:31
24:9 1 Sam 26:19
24:11 1 Sam 23:14, 23; 26:20
24:12 Gen 31:53 Judg 11:27
24:13 Matt 7:16-20
24:14 1 Sam 26:20
24:15 Ps 35:1
24:16 1 Sam 26:17
24:17 1 Sam 26:21 Matt 5:44
24:18 1 Sam 26:23
24:19 Ruth 2:12
24:20 1 Sam 13:14; 23:17
24:21 Gen 21:23 1 Sam 20:14-17 2 Sam 21:7
24:22 1 Sam 23:29
25:1 Deut 34:8
25:2 Josh 15:55
25:3 Josh 15:13 1 Sam 30:14
25:6 1 Chr 12:18
25:7 1 Sam 25:15
25:8 Neh 8:10

---

**24:16-19** The means we use to accomplish a goal are just as important as the goal we are trying to accomplish. David's goal was to become king, so his men urged him to kill Saul when he had the chance. David's refusal was not an example of cowardice but of courage—the courage to stand against the group and do what he knew was right. Don't compromise your moral standards by giving in to group pressure or taking the easy way out.

**24:21, 22** David kept his promise—he never took revenge on Saul's family or descendants. Most of Saul's sons were killed later, however, by the Philistines (31:2) and the Gibeonites (2 Samuel 21:1-14). David had promised to be kind to the descendants of Saul's son Jonathan (20:14, 15), and he kept this

promise when he invited Mephibosheth to live in his palace (2 Samuel 9).

**25:1** Saul was king, but Samuel had been the nation's spiritual leader. As a young boy and an older man, Samuel was always careful to listen to (3:10; 9:14-17) and obey (3:21; 10:1, 2) the Lord. With Samuel gone, Israel would be without this spiritual leadership until David became king. (For more on Samuel, read his Profile in chapter 7, p. 419.)

**25:2-11** Nabal rudely refused David's request to feed his 600 men. If we sympathize with Nabal, it is because customs are so different today. First, simple hospitality demanded that travelers—any number of them—be fed. Nabal was very rich and

25:10
Judg 9:28

25:13
1 Sam 23:13

25:15
1 Sam 25:7

25:16
Exod 14:22

25:18
2 Sam 16:1
1 Chr 12:40
25:19
Gen 32:16, 20

25:21
Ps 109:5

25:22
1 Sam 3:17
1 Kgs 14:10

¹⁰"Who is this fellow David?" Nabal sneered to the young men. "Who does this son of Jesse think he is? There are lots of servants these days who run away from their masters. ¹¹Should I take my bread and my water and my meat that I've slaughtered for my shearers and give it to a band of outlaws who come from who knows where?"

¹²So David's young men returned and told him what Nabal had said. ¹³"Get your swords!" was David's reply as he strapped on his own. Then 400 men started off with David, and 200 remained behind to guard their equipment.

¹⁴Meanwhile, one of Nabal's servants went to Abigail and told her, "David sent messengers from the wilderness to greet our master, but he screamed insults at them. ¹⁵These men have been very good to us, and we never suffered any harm from them. Nothing was stolen from us the whole time they were with us. ¹⁶In fact, day and night they were like a wall of protection to us and the sheep. ¹⁷You need to know this and figure out what to do, for there is going to be trouble for our master and his whole family. He's so ill-tempered that no one can even talk to him!"

¹⁸Abigail wasted no time. She quickly gathered 200 loaves of bread, two wineskins full of wine, five sheep that had been slaughtered, nearly a bushel* of roasted grain, 100 clusters of raisins, and 200 fig cakes. She packed them on donkeys ¹⁹and said to her servants, "Go on ahead. I will follow you shortly." But she didn't tell her husband Nabal what she was doing.

²⁰As she was riding her donkey into a mountain ravine, she saw David and his men coming toward her. ²¹David had just been saying, "A lot of good it did to help this fellow. We protected his flocks in the wilderness, and nothing he owned was lost or stolen. But he has repaid me evil for good. ²²May God strike me and kill me* if even one man of his household is still alive tomorrow morning!"

25:18 Hebrew *5 seahs* [30 liters].  25:22 As in Greek version; Hebrew reads *May God strike and kill the enemies of David.*

**ABIGAIL**

Some men don't deserve their wives. Abigail was probably the best woman Nabal could afford, and he got even more than he bargained for when he arranged to marry her. She was beautiful and more suited than he was to manage his wealth. But Nabal took this wife for granted.

In spite of his shortcomings, Nabal's household did what they could to keep him out of trouble. This loyalty must have been inspired by Abigail. Although her culture and her husband placed a low value on her, she made the most of her skills and opportunities. David was impressed with her abilities, and when Nabal died, he married her.

Abigail was an effective counselor to both of the men in her life, working hard to prevent them from making rash moves. By her swift action and skillful negotiation, she kept David from taking vengeance upon Nabal. She saw the big picture and left plenty of room for God to get involved.

Do you, like Abigail, look beyond the present crisis to the big picture? Do you use your skills to promote peace? Are you loyal without being blind? What challenge or responsibility do you face today that needs a person under God's control?

| | |
|---|---|
| **Strengths and accomplishments** | • Sensible and capable<br>• A persuasive speaker, able to see beyond herself |
| **Lessons from her life** | • Life's tough situations can bring out the best in people<br>• One does not need a prestigious title to play a significant role |
| **Vital statistics** | • Where: Carmel<br>• Occupation: Homemaker<br>• Relatives: First husband: Nabal. Second husband: David. Son: Kileab (Daniel).<br>• Contemporaries: Saul, Michal, Ahinoam |
| **Key verses** | "David replied to Abigail, 'Praise the LORD, the God of Israel, who has sent you to meet me today! Thank God for your good sense! Bless you for keeping me from murder and from carrying out vengeance with my own hands'" (1 Samuel 25:32, 33). |

Her story is told in 1 Samuel 25—2 Samuel 2. She is also mentioned in 1 Chronicles 3:1.

could have easily afforded to meet David's request. Second, David wasn't asking for a handout. He and his men had been protecting Nabal's workforce, and part of Nabal's prosperity was due to David's vigilance. We should be generous with those who protect us and help us prosper, even if we are not obligated to do so by law or custom.

## Abigail Intercedes for Nabal

23When Abigail saw David, she quickly got off her donkey and bowed low before him. 24She fell at his feet and said, "I accept all blame in this matter, my lord. Please listen to what I have to say. 25I know Nabal is a wicked and ill-tempered man; please don't pay any attention to him. He is a fool, just as his name suggests.* But I never even saw the young men you sent.

26"Now, my lord, as surely as the LORD lives and you yourself live, since the LORD has kept you from murdering and taking vengeance into your own hands, let all your enemies and those who try to harm you be as cursed as Nabal is. 27And here is a present that I, your servant, have brought to you and your young men. 28Please forgive me if I have offended you in any way. The LORD will surely reward you with a lasting dynasty, for you are fighting the LORD's battles. And you have not done wrong throughout your entire life.

29"Even when you are chased by those who seek to kill you, your life is safe in the care of the LORD your God, secure in his treasure pouch! But the lives of your enemies will disappear like stones shot from a sling! 30When the LORD has done all he promised and has made you leader of Israel, 31don't let this be a blemish on your record. Then your conscience won't have to bear the staggering burden of needless bloodshed and vengeance. And when the LORD has done these great things for you, please remember me, your servant!"

32David replied to Abigail, "Praise the LORD, the God of Israel, who has sent you to meet me today! 33Thank God for your good sense! Bless you for keeping me from murder and from carrying out vengeance with my own hands. 34For I swear by the LORD, the God of Israel, who has kept me from hurting you, that if you had not hurried out to meet me, not one of Nabal's men would still be alive tomorrow morning." 35Then David accepted her present and told her, "Return home in peace. I have heard what you said. We will not kill your husband."

36When Abigail arrived home, she found that Nabal was throwing a big party and was celebrating like a king. He was very drunk, so she didn't tell him anything about her meeting with David until dawn the next day. 37In the morning when Nabal was sober, his wife told him what had happened. As a result he had a stroke,* and he lay paralyzed on his bed like a stone. 38About ten days later, the LORD struck him, and he died.

## David Marries Abigail

39When David heard that Nabal was dead, he said, "Praise the LORD, who has avenged the insult I received from Nabal and has kept me from doing it myself. Nabal has received the punishment for his sin." Then David sent messengers to Abigail to ask her to become his wife.

40When the messengers arrived at Carmel, they told Abigail, "David has sent us to take you back to marry him."

41She bowed low to the ground and responded, "I, your servant, would be happy to marry David. I would even be willing to become a slave, washing the feet of his servants!" 42Quickly getting ready, she took along five of her servant girls as attendants, mounted her donkey, and went with David's messengers. And so she became his wife. 43David also married Ahinoam from Jezreel, making both of them his wives. 44Saul, meanwhile, had given his daughter Michal, David's wife, to a man from Gallim named Palti son of Laish.

## David Spares Saul Again

**26** Now some men from Ziph came to Saul at Gibeah to tell him, "David is hiding on the hill of Hakilah, which overlooks Jeshimon."

2So Saul took 3,000 of Israel's elite troops and went to hunt him down in the wilderness of Ziph. 3Saul camped along the road beside the hill of Hakilah, near Jeshimon, where David was hiding. When David learned that Saul had come after him into the wilderness, 4he sent out spies to verify the report of Saul's arrival.

**25:25** The name *Nabal* means "fool." **25:37** Hebrew *his heart failed him.*

---

**25:24** David was in no mood to listen when he set out for Nabal's property (25:13, 22). Nevertheless, he stopped to hear what Abigail had to say. If he had ignored her, he would have been guilty of taking vengeance into his own hands. No matter how right we think we are, we must always be careful to stop and listen to others. The extra time and effort can save us pain and trouble in the long run.

**25:36** Because Nabal was drunk, Abigail waited until morning to tell him what she had done. Abigail knew that Nabal, in his drunkenness, may not have understood her or may have reacted foolishly. When discussing difficult matters with people, especially family members, timing is everything. Ask God for wisdom to know the best time for confrontation and for bringing up touchy subjects.

**25:44** The story of David and Michal does not end here. (See 2 Samuel 3:12-16 for the next episode.)

---

**Cross-references (margin):**

25:26 — 2 Sam 18:32
25:27 — Gen 33:11; 1 Sam 30:26
25:28 — 1 Sam 18:17; 2 Sam 7:11, 16
25:29 — 1 Sam 20:1; Jer 10:18
25:30 — 1 Sam 13:14
25:32 — Exod 18:10
25:33 — 1 Sam 25:26
25:35 — Gen 19:21
25:42 — Gen 24:61-67
25:43 — 1 Sam 27:2-3; 30:5
25:44 — 1 Sam 18:27; 2 Sam 3:14-15
26:1 — 1 Sam 23:19
26:2 — 1 Sam 13:2; 24:2
26:3 — 1 Sam 23:19

26:5
1 Sam 14:50-51

26:6
1 Chr 2:16

26:9
1 Sam 24:6
2 Sam 1:14, 16
26:10
Deut 31:14
1 Sam 25:38; 31:6
26:12
Gen 2:21; 15:12
Isa 29:10

26:17
1 Sam 24:16
26:19
1 Sam 24:9
2 Sam 16:11

26:20
1 Sam 24:14

⁵David slipped over to Saul's camp one night to look around. Saul and Abner son of Ner, the commander of his army, were sleeping inside a ring formed by the slumbering warriors. ⁶"Who will volunteer to go in there with me?" David asked Ahimelech the Hittite and Abishai son of Zeruiah, Joab's brother.

"I'll go with you," Abishai replied. ⁷So David and Abishai went right into Saul's camp and found him asleep, with his spear stuck in the ground beside his head. Abner and the soldiers were lying asleep around him.

⁸"God has surely handed your enemy over to you this time!" Abishai whispered to David. "Let me pin him to the ground with one thrust of the spear; I won't need to strike twice!"

⁹"No!" David said. "Don't kill him. For who can remain innocent after attacking the LORD's anointed one? ¹⁰Surely the LORD will strike Saul down someday, or he will die of old age or in battle. ¹¹The LORD forbid that I should kill the one he has anointed! But take his spear and that jug of water beside his head, and then let's get out of here!"

¹²So David took the spear and jug of water that were near Saul's head. Then he and Abishai got away without anyone seeing them or even waking up, because the LORD had put Saul's men into a deep sleep.

¹³David climbed the hill opposite the camp until he was at a safe distance. ¹⁴Then he shouted down to the soldiers and to Abner son of Ner, "Wake up, Abner!"

"Who is it?" Abner demanded.

¹⁵"Well, Abner, you're a great man, aren't you?" David taunted. "Where in all Israel is there anyone as mighty? So why haven't you guarded your master the king when someone came to kill him? ¹⁶This isn't good at all! I swear by the LORD that you and your men deserve to die, because you failed to protect your master, the LORD's anointed! Look around! Where are the king's spear and the jug of water that were beside his head?"

¹⁷Saul recognized David's voice and called out, "Is that you, my son David?"

And David replied, "Yes, my lord the king. ¹⁸Why are you chasing me? What have I done? What is my crime? ¹⁹But now let my lord the king listen to his servant. If the LORD has stirred you up against me, then let him accept my offering. But if this is simply a human scheme, then may those involved be cursed by the LORD. For they have driven me from my home, so I can no longer live among the LORD's people, and they have said, 'Go, worship pagan gods.' ²⁰Must I die on foreign soil, far from the presence of the LORD? Why has the king of Israel come out to search for a single flea? Why does he hunt me down like a partridge on the mountains?"

---

**26:5-9** Abishai showed great courage when he volunteered to go into Saul's camp with David. In the heat of emotion, Abishai wanted to kill Saul, but David restrained him. Although Abishai was only trying to protect David, his leader, David could not hurt Saul because of his respect for Saul's authority and position as God's anointed king. Abishai may have disagreed with David, but he also respected the one in authority over him. Eventually he became the greatest warrior in David's army (2 Samuel 23:18, 19).

**26:8ff** The strongest moral decisions are the ones we make before temptation strikes. David was determined to follow God, and this carried over into his decision not to murder God's anointed king, Saul, even when his men and the circumstances seemed to make it a feasible option. Who would you have been like in such a situation—David or David's men? To be like David and follow God, we must realize that we can't do wrong in order to execute justice. Even when our closest friends counsel us to do something that seems right, we must always put God's commands first.

**26:9** Why did David refuse to kill Saul? God had placed Saul in power and had not yet removed him. David did not want to run ahead of God's timing. We are in similar situations when we have leaders in church or government who are unfaithful or incompetent. It may be easy for us to criticize or move against a leader oblivious to God's hidden purposes and timing. Determining not to do wrong, David left Saul's destiny in God's hands. While we should not ignore sin or sit back and allow evil leaders to carry on their wickedness, neither should we take actions that are against God's laws. We should work for righteousness while trusting God.

**26:15, 16** David could have killed Saul and Abner, but he would have disobeyed God and set into motion possible cycles of vengeance and assassination. Instead, he took a spear and water jug, showing that he could have killed the king but had not done it. And he made the point that he had great respect for both God and God's anointed king. When you need to make a point, look for creative, God-honoring ways to do so. It will have a more significant impact.

**SAUL CHASES DAVID** The men of Ziph again betrayed David to Saul, who was in his palace in Gibeah. Saul took 3,000 troops to the area around Horesh in order to find David. David could have killed Saul, but he refused. Saul, feeling foolish at David's kindness, returned to Gibeah, and David went to Gath.

21 Then Saul confessed, "I have sinned. Come back home, my son, and I will no longer try to harm you, for you valued my life today. I have been a fool and very, very wrong."

22 "Here is your spear, O king," David replied. "Let one of your young men come over and get it. 23 The LORD gives his own reward for doing good and for being loyal, and I refused to kill you even when the LORD placed you in my power, for you are the LORD's anointed one. 24 Now may the LORD value my life, even as I have valued yours today. May he rescue me from all my troubles."

25 And Saul said to David, "Blessings on you, my son David. You will do many heroic deeds, and you will surely succeed." Then David went away, and Saul returned home.

## 5. Saul's defeat and death
### David among the Philistines

**27** But David kept thinking to himself, "Someday Saul is going to get me. The best thing I can do is escape to the Philistines. Then Saul will stop hunting for me in Israelite territory, and I will finally be safe."

2 So David took his 600 men and went over and joined Achish son of Maoch, the king of Gath. 3 David and his men and their families settled there with Achish at Gath. David brought his two wives along with him—Ahinoam from Jezreel and Abigail, Nabal's widow from Carmel. 4 Word soon reached Saul that David had fled to Gath, so he stopped hunting for him.

5 One day David said to Achish, "If it is all right with you, we would rather live in one of the country towns instead of here in the royal city."

6 So Achish gave him the town of Ziklag (which still belongs to the kings of Judah to this day), 7 and they lived there among the Philistines for a year and four months.

8 David and his men spent their time raiding the Geshurites, the Girzites, and the Amalekites—people who had lived near Shur, toward the land of Egypt, since ancient times. 9 David did not leave one person alive in the villages he attacked. He took the sheep, goats, cattle, donkeys, camels, and clothing before returning home to see King Achish.

10 "Where did you make your raid today?" Achish would ask.

And David would reply, "Against the south of Judah, the Jerahmeelites, and the Kenites."

11 No one was left alive to come to Gath and tell where he had really been. This happened again and again while he was living among the Philistines. 12 Achish believed David and thought to himself, "By now the people of Israel must hate him bitterly. Now he will have to stay here and serve me forever!"

### Saul Consults a Medium

**28** About that time the Philistines mustered their armies for another war with Israel. King Achish told David, "You and your men will be expected to join me in battle."

2 "Very well!" David agreed. "Now you will see for yourself what we can do."

Then Achish told David, "I will make you my personal bodyguard for life."

---

**26:21** 1 Sam 15:24, 30; 24:17
**26:23** 1 Sam 24:19
**26:24** Ps 54:7
**27:2** 1 Sam 21:10 / 2 Sam 2:2-3 / 1 Kgs 2:39
**27:3** 1 Sam 25:43
**27:6** Josh 15:31; 19:5 / Neh 11:28
**27:7** 1 Sam 29:3
**27:8** Exod 17:8 / Josh 13:2-7, 13 / 1 Sam 15:7-8
**27:9** 1 Sam 15:3
**27:10** Judg 1:16; 4:11 / 1 Sam 30:27-31 / 1 Chr 2:9, 25
**28:1-2** 1 Sam 29:1-2

---

**26:25** Saul had opportunities to kill David, but he never did. Why? First, every time David and Saul were face to face, David did something generous for Saul. The king did not want to respond to David's kindness with cruelty in front of all his men. Second, David had a large following in Israel. By killing him, Saul would risk his hold on the kingdom. Third, God had appointed David to become king of Israel and was protecting him.

**27:4** Saul finally stopped pursuing David. His army was not strong enough to invade Philistine territory just to seek one man. Besides, the immediate threat to Saul's throne was gone while David was out of the country.

**27:5-7** Gath was one of five principal cities in Philistia, and Achish was one of five co-rulers. David may have wanted to move out of this important city to avoid potential skirmishes or attacks upon his family. He may also have wanted to escape the close scrutiny of the Philistine officials. Achish let David move to Ziklag, where he lived until Saul's death (2 Samuel 2:1).

**27:8, 9** David probably conducted these guerrilla-style raids because these three tribes were known for their surprise attacks and cruel treatment of innocent people. These desert tribes were

a danger, not just to the Philistines, but especially to the Israelites, the people David would one day lead.

**27:10-12** Was David wrong in falsely reporting his activities to Achish? No doubt David was lying, but he may have felt his strategy was justified in a time of war against a pagan enemy. David knew he would one day be Israel's king. The Philistines were still his enemies, but this was an excellent place to hide from Saul. When Achish asked David to go into battle against Israel, David agreed, once again pretending loyalty to the Philistines (28:1ff). Whether he would have actually fought Saul's army we can't know, but we can be sure that his ultimate loyalty was to God and not to Achish or Saul.

**28:1, 2** Achish's request put David in a difficult position. To refuse to help Achish fight the Israelites would give away David's loyalty to Israel and endanger the lives of his soldiers and family. But to fight his own people would hurt the very people he loved and would soon lead. David, however, never had to solve his dilemma because God protected him. The other Philistine leaders objected to his presence in battle; thus, he did not have to fight his countrymen.

**28:3**
Lev 19:31
Deut 18:10
1 Sam 15:23; 25:1

**28:4**
1 Sam 31:1, 3
2 Sam 1:6

**28:6**
Exod 28:30

**28:7**
Ps 83:10
Acts 16:16

**28:8**
Isa 8:19

**28:9**
1 Sam 28:3

**28:14**
1 Sam 15:27

**28:15**
1 Sam 16:14

³Meanwhile, Samuel had died, and all Israel had mourned for him. He was buried in Ramah, his hometown. And Saul had banned from the land of Israel all mediums and those who consult the spirits of the dead.

⁴The Philistines set up their camp at Shunem, and Saul gathered all the army of Israel and camped at Gilboa. ⁵When Saul saw the vast Philistine army, he became frantic with fear. ⁶He asked the LORD what he should do, but the LORD refused to answer him, either by dreams or by sacred lots* or by the prophets. ⁷Saul then said to his advisers, "Find a woman who is a medium, so I can go and ask her what to do."

His advisers replied, "There is a medium at Endor."

⁸So Saul disguised himself by wearing ordinary clothing instead of his royal robes. Then he went to the woman's home at night, accompanied by two of his men.

"I have to talk to a man who has died," he said. "Will you call up his spirit for me?"

⁹"Are you trying to get me killed?" the woman demanded. "You know that Saul has outlawed all the mediums and all who consult the spirits of the dead. Why are you setting a trap for me?"

¹⁰But Saul took an oath in the name of the LORD and promised, "As surely as the LORD lives, nothing bad will happen to you for doing this."

¹¹Finally, the woman said, "Well, whose spirit do you want me to call up?"

"Call up Samuel," Saul replied.

¹²When the woman saw Samuel, she screamed, "You've deceived me! You are Saul!"

¹³"Don't be afraid!" the king told her. "What do you see?"

"I see a god* coming up out of the earth," she said.

¹⁴"What does he look like?" Saul asked.

"He is an old man wrapped in a robe," she replied. Saul realized it was Samuel, and he fell to the ground before him.

¹⁵"Why have you disturbed me by calling me back?" Samuel asked Saul.

"Because I am in deep trouble," Saul replied. "The Philistines are at war with me, and God has left me and won't reply by prophets or dreams. So I have called for you to tell me what to do."

**28:6** Hebrew *by Urim.*    **28:13** Or *gods.*

---

**28:3-8** Saul had banned all mediums and those who consult with the spirits of the dead from Israel, but in desperation he turned to one for counsel. Although he had removed the sin of witchcraft from the land, he did not remove it from his heart. We may make a great show of denouncing sin, but if our hearts do not change, the sins will return. Knowing what is right and condemning what is wrong do not take the place of *doing* what is right.

**28:5, 6** Casting sacred lots meant using the Urim and Thummim to determine God's guidance in certain matters. (See the notes on 2:18 and 10:20 for further information on the use of the Urim and Thummim.)

**28:5-7** Saul was overwhelmed at the sight of the Philistine army, and so he turned to the occult. Regard life's difficulties and obstacles as reminders to turn you in God's direction and make you depend upon him. As we see from Saul's story, turning to anything or anyone else leads only to disaster.

**28:7, 8** God had strictly forbidden the Israelites to have anything to do with divination, sorcery, witchcraft, mediums, spiritists, or anyone who consults the dead (Deuteronomy 18:9-14). In fact, sorcerers were to be put to death (Exodus 22:18). Occult practices were carried on in the name of pagan gods, and people turned to the occult for answers that God would not give.

Practitioners of the occult have Satan and demons as the source of their information; God does not reveal his will to them. Instead, he speaks through his own channels: the Bible, his Son Jesus Christ, and the Holy Spirit.

**28:12** Did Samuel really come back from the dead at the medium's call? The medium shrieked at the appearance of Samuel—she knew too well that the spirits she usually contacted were either contrived or satanic. Somehow Samuel's appearance revealed to her that she was dealing with a power far greater than she had known. She did not call up Samuel by trickery or by the power of Satan; God brought Samuel back to give Saul a prediction regarding his fate, a message Saul already knew. This in no way justifies efforts to contact the dead or communicate with persons or spirits from the past. God is against all such practices (Galatians 5:19-21).

**28:15** God did not answer Saul's appeals because Saul had not followed God's previous directions. Sometimes people wonder why their prayers are not answered. But if they don't fulfill the responsibilities God has already given them, they should not be surprised when he does not give further guidance.

**THE BATTLE AT GILBOA**
David pretended loyalty to Achish, but when war broke out with Israel, he was sent to Ziklag from Aphek. The Philistines defeated the Israelites at Mount Gilboa. David returned to Ziklag to find that the Amalekites had destroyed Ziklag. So David and his men pursued the Amalekite raiders and slaughtered them, recovering all that was taken.

¹⁶But Samuel replied, "Why ask me, since the LORD has left you and has become your enemy? ¹⁷The LORD has done just as he said he would. He has torn the kingdom from you and given it to your rival, David. ¹⁸The LORD has done this to you today because you refused to carry out his fierce anger against the Amalekites. ¹⁹What's more, the LORD will hand you and the army of Israel over to the Philistines tomorrow, and you and your sons will be here with me. The LORD will bring down the entire army of Israel in defeat."

²⁰Saul fell full length on the ground, paralyzed with fright because of Samuel's words. He was also faint with hunger, for he had eaten nothing all day and all night.

²¹When the woman saw how distraught he was, she said, "Sir, I obeyed your command at the risk of my life. ²²Now do what I say, and let me give you a little something to eat so you can regain your strength for the trip back."

²³But Saul refused to eat anything. Then his advisers joined the woman in urging him to eat, so he finally yielded and got up from the ground and sat on the couch.

²⁴The woman had been fattening a calf, so she hurried out and killed it. She took some flour, kneaded it into dough and baked unleavened bread. ²⁵She brought the meal to Saul and his advisers, and they ate it. Then they went out into the night.

### The Philistines Reject David

**29** The entire Philistine army now mobilized at Aphek, and the Israelites camped at the spring in Jezreel. ²As the Philistine rulers were leading out their troops in groups of hundreds and thousands, David and his men marched at the rear with King Achish. ³But the Philistine commanders demanded, "What are these Hebrews doing here?"

And Achish told them, "This is David, the servant of King Saul of Israel. He's been with me for years, and I've never found a single fault in him from the day he arrived until today."

⁴But the Philistine commanders were angry. "Send him back to the town you've given him!" they demanded. "He can't go into the battle with us. What if he turns against us in battle and becomes our adversary? Is there any better way for him to reconcile himself with his master than by handing our heads over to him? ⁵Isn't this the same David about whom the women of Israel sing in their dances,

'Saul has killed his thousands,
    and David his ten thousands'?"

⁶So Achish finally summoned David and said to him, "I swear by the LORD that you have been a trustworthy ally. I think you should go with me into battle, for I've never found a single flaw in you from the day you arrived until today. But the other Philistine rulers won't hear of it. ⁷Please don't upset them, but go back quietly."

⁸"What have I done to deserve this treatment?" David demanded. "What have you ever found in your servant, that I can't go and fight the enemies of my lord the king?"

⁹But Achish insisted, "As far as I'm concerned, you're as perfect as an angel of God. But the Philistine commanders are afraid to have you with them in the battle. ¹⁰Now get up early in the morning, and leave with your men as soon as it gets light."

¹¹So David and his men headed back into the land of the Philistines, while the Philistine army went on to Jezreel.

### David Destroys the Amalekites

**30** Three days later, when David and his men arrived home at their town of Ziklag, they found that the Amalekites had made a raid into the Negev and Ziklag; they had crushed Ziklag and burned it to the ground. ²They had carried off the women and children and everyone else but without killing anyone.

³When David and his men saw the ruins and realized what had happened to their families, ⁴they wept until they could weep no more. ⁵David's two wives, Ahinoam from Jezreel and Abigail, the widow of Nabal from Carmel, were among those captured. ⁶David was now in great danger because all his men were very bitter about losing their sons and daughters, and they began to talk of stoning him. But David found strength in the LORD his God.

| | |
|---|---|
| **28:17** | 1 Sam 15:28 |
| **28:19** | 1 Sam 31:2, 6 |
| **28:21** | Judg 12:3 |
| **28:23** | 2 Kgs 5:13 |
| **28:24** | Gen 18:6-7 |
| **29:1** | Josh 12:18; 1 Sam 4:1; 2 Kgs 9:30 |
| **29:2** | 1 Sam 28:2 |
| **29:3** | 1 Sam 27:1-7; 1 Chr 12:19-20 |
| **29:4** | 1 Sam 14:21 |
| **29:5** | 1 Sam 18:7; 21:11 |
| **29:6** | 1 Sam 27:12; 29:3 |
| **29:9** | 2 Sam 14:17, 20; 19:27; 29:4 |
| **30:1** | 1 Sam 15:7; 27:6, 8 |
| **30:5** | 1 Sam 25:39-43; 2 Sam 2:2 |
| **30:6** | Exod 17:4; 1 Sam 23:16; Ps 18:2 |

---

**29:4** The other Philistine commanders knew that David was the one who, as a young man, had killed their champion, Goliath (17:32-54), had killed hundreds of Philistine soldiers (18:27), and was the hero of Israelite victory songs (21:11). They were afraid that, in the heat of battle, David might turn against them. Although David was upset at this at first, God used the commanders' suspicion to keep him from having to fight against Saul and his countrymen.

**30:6** Faced with the tragedy of losing their families, David's soldiers began to turn against him and even talked about killing

**30:7**
1 Sam 23:9
**30:8**
1 Sam 23:2, 4

**30:9**
1 Sam 27:2

**30:12**
Judg 15:19

**30:14**
1 Sam 30:1
2 Sam 1:1;
15:17-18
1 Chr 18:17

**30:15**
Deut 23:15

**30:17**
1 Sam 15:3

**30:21**
1 Sam 30:10-11

**30:24**
Num 31:27
Josh 22:7-8

**30:26**
Gen 33:11
1 Sam 25:27

**30:27**
Josh 15:48

**30:28**
Josh 13:16

**30:29**
1 Sam 27:10

7 Then he said to Abiathar the priest, "Bring me the ephod!" So Abiathar brought it. 8 Then David asked the LORD, "Should I chase after this band of raiders? Will I catch them?"

And the LORD told him, "Yes, go after them. You will surely recover everything that was taken from you!"

9 So David and his 600 men set out, and they came to the brook Besor. 10 But 200 of the men were too exhausted to cross the brook, so David continued the pursuit with 400 men.

11 Along the way they found an Egyptian man in a field and brought him to David. They gave him some bread to eat and water to drink. 12 They also gave him part of a fig cake and two clusters of raisins, for he hadn't had anything to eat or drink for three days and nights. Before long his strength returned.

13 "To whom do you belong, and where do you come from?" David asked him.

"I am an Egyptian—the slave of an Amalekite," he replied. "My master abandoned me three days ago because I was sick. 14 We were on our way back from raiding the Kerethites in the Negev, the territory of Judah, and the land of Caleb, and we had just burned Ziklag."

15 "Will you lead me to this band of raiders?" David asked.

The young man replied, "If you take an oath in God's name that you will not kill me or give me back to my master, then I will guide you to them."

16 So he led David to them, and they found the Amalekites spread out across the fields, eating and drinking and dancing with joy because of the vast amount of plunder they had taken from the Philistines and the land of Judah. 17 David and his men rushed in among them and slaughtered them throughout that night and the entire next day until evening. None of the Amalekites escaped except 400 young men who fled on camels. 18 David got back everything the Amalekites had taken, and he rescued his two wives. 19 Nothing was missing: small or great, son or daughter, nor anything else that had been taken. David brought everything back. 20 He also recovered all the flocks and herds, and his men drove them ahead of the other livestock. "This plunder belongs to David!" they said.

21 Then David returned to the brook Besor and met up with the 200 men who had been left behind because they were too exhausted to go with him. They went out to meet David and his men, and David greeted them joyfully. 22 But some evil troublemakers among David's men said, "They didn't go with us, so they can't have any of the plunder we recovered. Give them their wives and children, and tell them to be gone."

23 But David said, "No, my brothers! Don't be selfish with what the LORD has given us. He has kept us safe and helped us defeat the band of raiders that attacked us. 24 Who will listen when you talk like this? We share and share alike—those who go to battle and those who guard the equipment." 25 From then on David made this a decree and regulation for Israel, and it is still followed today.

26 When he arrived at Ziklag, David sent part of the plunder to the elders of Judah, who were his friends. "Here is a present for you, taken from the LORD's enemies," he said.

27 The gifts were sent to the people of the following towns David had visited: Bethel, Ramoth-negev, Jattir, 28 Aroer, Siphmoth, Eshtemoa, 29 Racal,* the towns of the Jerahmeel-ites, the towns of the Kenites, 30 Hormah, Bor-ashan, Athach, 31 Hebron, and all the other places David and his men had visited.

**30:29** Greek version reads *Carmel.*

---

him. Instead of planning a rescue, they looked for someone to blame. But David found his strength in God and began looking for a solution instead of a scapegoat. When facing problems, remember that it is useless to look for someone to blame or criticize. Instead, consider how you can help find a solution.

**30:7** David couldn't go to the Tabernacle to ask the Lord for guidance because it was in Saul's territory. Therefore, he called for the ephod, the only Tabernacle-related object he possessed. In the presence of the priest and this priestly garment, he asked God for direction. When David called for the ephod, he was really asking the priest to bring him the Urim and Thummim, which were kept in a pouch attached to the ephod. Only the high priest could carry and use the Urim and Thummim. (For more information on the ephod and its contents, see the note on Exodus 39:1-21.)

**30:11-15** The Amalekites cruelly left this slave to die, but God used him to lead David and his men to the Amalekite camp. David and his men treated the young man kindly, and he returned the

kindness by leading them to the enemy. Treat those you meet with respect and dignity no matter how insignificant they may seem. You never know how God will use them to help you or haunt you, depending upon your response to them.

**30:24, 25** David made a law that those who guarded the equipment were to be treated equally with those who fought in battle. Today it takes several people to provide the support services needed for every soldier in battle. In the church and other organizations, we need to treat those who provide support services equally with those on the front lines. Without bookkeepers, secretaries, trainers, and administrators, those with a public ministry would be unable to do their jobs. Are you on the front lines? Don't forget those who are backing you up. Are you in the support group? Realize that your position, although it may be less glamorous or exciting, is vital to the work of the entire group.

## The Death of Saul

**31** Now the Philistines attacked Israel, and the men of Israel fled before them. Many were slaughtered on the slopes of Mount Gilboa. ²The Philistines closed in on Saul and his sons, and they killed three of his sons—Jonathan, Abinadab, and Malkishua. ³The fighting grew very fierce around Saul, and the Philistine archers caught up with him and wounded him severely.

⁴Saul groaned to his armor bearer, "Take your sword and kill me before these pagan Philistines come to run me through and taunt and torture me."

But his armor bearer was afraid and would not do it. So Saul took his own sword and fell on it. ⁵When his armor bearer realized that Saul was dead, he fell on his own sword and died beside the king. ⁶So Saul, his three sons, his armor bearer, and his troops all died together that same day.

⁷When the Israelites on the other side of the Jezreel Valley and beyond the Jordan saw that the Israelite army had fled and that Saul and his sons were dead, they abandoned their towns and fled. So the Philistines moved in and occupied their towns.

⁸The next day, when the Philistines went out to strip the dead, they found the bodies of Saul and his three sons on Mount Gilboa. ⁹So they cut off Saul's head and stripped off his armor. Then they proclaimed the good news of Saul's death in their pagan temple and to the people throughout the land of Philistia. ¹⁰They placed his armor in the temple of the Ashtoreths, and they fastened his body to the wall of the city of Beth-shan.

¹¹But when the people of Jabesh-gilead heard what the Philistines had done to Saul, ¹²all their mighty warriors traveled through the night to Beth-shan and took the bodies of Saul and his sons down from the wall. They brought them to Jabesh, where they burned the bodies. ¹³Then they took their bones and buried them beneath the tamarisk tree at Jabesh, and they fasted for seven days.

**31:1-13**
//2 Sam 1:4-12
//1 Chr 10:1-12

**31:1**
1 Sam 28:4

**31:3**
2 Sam 1:6, 10

**31:4**
Judg 9:54

**31:9**
Judg 16:23-24
2 Sam 1:20

**31:10**
Josh 17:11
Judg 2:12-14
1 Sam 7:3

**31:11-12**
1 Sam 11:1-13
2 Sam 21:12-14

---

**31:3, 4** The Philistines had a well-earned reputation for torturing their captives. Saul no doubt knew about Samson's fate (Judges 16:18-31) and did not want to risk physical mutilation or other abuse. When his armor bearer refused to kill him, he took his own life.

**31:3, 4** Saul was tall, handsome, strong, rich, and powerful, but all of this was not enough to make him someone we should emulate. He was tall physically, but he was small in God's eyes. He was handsome, but his sin made him ugly. He was strong, but his lack of faith made him weak. He was rich, but he was spiritually bankrupt. He could give orders to many, but he couldn't command their respect or allegiance. Saul looked good on the outside, but he was decaying on the inside. A right relationship with God and a strong character are much more valuable than a good-looking exterior.

**31:3, 4** Saul's armor bearer faced a moral dilemma—should he carry out a sinful order from a man he was supposed to obey? He knew he should obey his master, the king, but he also knew murder was wrong. He decided not to kill Saul.

There is a difference between following an order with which you don't agree and following one you know is wrong. It is never right or ethical to carry out a wrong act, no matter who gives the order or what the consequences for disobedience may be. What shapes your choice when you face a moral dilemma? Have the courage to follow God's law above human commands.

**31:4** Saul faced death the same way he faced life. He took matters into his own hands without thinking of God or asking for his guidance. If our lives aren't the way we would like them to be now, we can't assume that change will come more easily

later. When nearing death, we will respond to God the same way we have been responding all along. Coming face to face with death only shows us what we are *really* like. How do you want to face death? Start facing life that way right now.

**31:10** To put Saul's armor in the Philistine temple gave credit to a pagan goddess for victory over Saul. Ashtoreth was a goddess of fertility and sex. Beth-shan was a town on the eastern slopes of Mount Gilboa, overlooking the Jordan Valley.

**31:13** Consider the difference between the last judge of Israel and its first king. Saul, the king, was characterized by inconsistency, disobedience, and self-will. He did not have a heart for God. Samuel, the judge, was characterized by consistency, obedience, and a deep desire for God's will. He had a genuine desire for God.

When God called, Samuel said, "LORD, your servant is listening" (3:9). But when God, through Samuel, called Saul, Saul replied, "Why are you talking like this to me?" (9:21). Saul was dedicated to himself; Samuel was dedicated to God.

**31:13** Saul's death was also the death of an ideal—Israel could no longer believe that having a king like the other nations would solve all their troubles. The real problem was not the form of government but the sinful king. Saul tried to please God by spurts of religiosity, but real spirituality takes a lifetime of consistent obedience.

Heroic spiritual lives are built by stacking days of obedience one on top of the other. Like a brick, each obedient act is small in itself, but in time the acts will pile up, and a huge wall of strong character will be built—a great defense against temptation. We should strive for consistent obedience each day.

# KEY PLACES IN 2 SAMUEL

The broken lines (— ·—·—) indicate modern boundaries.

they did give David sanctuary when he was hiding from Saul (1 Samuel 27). But when Saul died and David became king, the Philistines planned to defeat him. In a battle near Jerusalem, David and his troops routed the Philistines (5:17–25), but they were not completely subdued until David conquered their largest city (8:1).

**4 Moab** During the time of the judges, Moab controlled many cities in Israel and demanded heavy taxes (Judges 3:12–30). David conquered Moab and, in turn, levied tribute from them (8:2).

**5 Edom** Though the Edomites and the Israelites traced their ancestry back to the same man, Isaac (Genesis 25:19–23), they were long-standing enemies. David defeated Edom and forced them to pay tribute also (8:14).

**6 Rabbah** The Ammonites insulted David's delegation and turned a peacemaking mission into angry warfare. The Ammonites called troops from Aram, but David defeated this alliance first at Helam, then at Rabbah, the capital city (10:1—12:31).

**7 Mahanaim** David had victory in the field, but problems at home. His son Absalom incited a rebellion and crowned himself king at Hebron. David and his men fled to Mahanaim. Acting on bad advice, Absalom mobilized his army to fight David (13:1—17:29).

**8 Forest of Ephraim** The armies of Absalom and David fought in the forest of Ephraim. Absalom's hair got caught in a tree, and Joab, David's general, found and killed him. With Absalom's death the rebellion died, and David was welcomed back to Jerusalem (18:1—19:43).

**9 Abel-beth-maacah** A man named Sheba also incited a rebellion against David. He fled to Abel-beth-maacah, but Joab and a small troop besieged the city. The citizens of Abel-beth-maacah killed Sheba themselves (20:1–26). David's victories laid the foundation for the peaceful reign of his son Solomon.

**1 Hebron** After Saul's death, David moved from the Philistine city of Ziklag to Hebron, where the tribe of Judah crowned him king. But the rest of Israel's tribes backed Saul's son Ishbosheth and crowned him king at Mahanaim. As a result, there was war between Judah and the rest of the tribes of Israel until Ishbosheth was assassinated. Then all of Israel pledged loyalty to David as their king (1:1—5:5).

**2 Jerusalem** One of David's first battles as king occurred at the fortress of Zion (Jerusalem). David and his troops took the city by surprise, and it became his capital. It was here that David brought the Ark of the Covenant and made a special covenant with God (5:6—7:29).

**3 Gath** The Philistines were Israel's constant enemy, though

# 2 SAMUEL

Judges
begin
to rule
1375 B.C.
(1220 B.C.)

Saul
becomes
king
1050
(1045)

## VITAL STATISTICS

**PURPOSES:**
(1) to record the history of David's reign;
(2) to demonstrate effective leadership under God;
(3) to reveal that one person can make a difference;
(4) to show the personal qualities that please God;
(5) to depict David as an ideal leader of an imperfect kingdom, and to foreshadow Christ, who will be the ideal leader of a new and perfect kingdom (chapter 7)

**AUTHOR:**
Unknown. Some have suggested that Nathan's son Zabud may have been the author (1 Kings 4:5). The book also includes the writings of Nathan and Gad (1 Chronicles 29:29).

**ORIGINAL AUDIENCE:**
The people of Israel

**DATE WRITTEN:**
930 B.C.; written soon after David's reign, 1010–970 B.C.

**SETTING:**
The land of Israel under David's rule

**KEY VERSE:**
"And David realized that the LORD had confirmed him as king over Israel and had blessed his kingdom for the sake of his people Israel" (5:12).

**KEY PEOPLE:**
David, Joab, Bathsheba, Nathan, Absalom

**SPECIAL FEATURES:**
This book was named after the prophet who anointed David and guided him in living for God.

THE CHILD enters the room with long gown flowing, trailing well behind her high-heeled shoes. The wide-brimmed hat rests precariously atop her head, tilted to the right, and the long necklace swings like a pendulum as she walks. Following close is the "man." His fingertips peek out of the coat sleeves that are already pushed upward six inches. With feet shuffling in the double-sized boots, his unsteady steps belie his confident smile. Children at play, dressing up—they copy Mom and Dad, having watched them dress and walk. Models . . . everyone has them . . . people we emulate, people who are our ideals. Unconsciously, perhaps, we copy their actions and adopt their ideas.

Among all the godly role models mentioned in the Bible, probably no one stands out more than King David. Born halfway between Abraham and Jesus, he became God's leader for all of Israel and the ancestor of the Messiah. David was "a man after [God's] own heart" (1 Samuel 13:14). What are the personal qualities that David possessed that pleased God?

The book of 2 Samuel tells David's story. As you read, you will be filled with excitement as he is crowned king over Judah and then king over all of Israel (5:1–5), praising God as he brings the Ark of the Covenant back to the Tabernacle (6:1–23) and exulting as he leads his armies to victory over all their enemies and completes the conquest of the Promised Land begun by Joshua (8—10). David accomplished much.

But David was human, and during dark times he stumbled and fell into sin. The record of lust, adultery, and murder is not easy to read (11—13) and reveals that even great people who try to follow God are susceptible to temptation and sin.

Godliness does not guarantee an easy and carefree life. David had family problems—his own son incited the entire nation to rebellion and crowned himself king (14:1—18:33). And greatness can cause pride, as we see in David's sinful act of taking a census in order to glory in the strength of his nation (24:1–25). But the story of this fallen hero does not end in tragedy. Through repentance, his fellowship and peace with God were restored, but he had to face the consequences of the sins he committed (12—20). These consequences stayed with him the rest of his life as a reminder of his sinful deeds and his need for God.

As you read 2 Samuel, look for David's godlike characteristics—his faithfulness, patience, courage, generosity, commitment, honesty—as well as other God-honoring characteristics, such as modesty and penitence. Valuable lessons can be learned from his sins and from his repentance. You, like David, can become a person after God's own heart.

| Saul dies; David is king over Judah 1010 | David becomes king over all Israel 1003 | David and Bathsheba sin 997(?) | Solomon born 991 | David's census 980(?) | David dies; Solomon made king 970 | The kingdom is divided 930 |

## THE BLUEPRINT

A. DAVID'S SUCCESSES
(1:1—10:19)
1. David becomes king over Judah
2. David becomes king over Israel
3. David conquers the surrounding nations

David took the fractured kingdom that Saul had left behind and built a strong, united power. Forty years later, David would turn this kingdom over to his son Solomon. David had a heart for God. He was a king who governed God's people by God's principles, and God blessed him greatly. We may not have David's earthly success, but following God is, ultimately, the most successful decision we can make.

B. DAVID'S STRUGGLES
(11:1—24:25)
1. David and Bathsheba
2. Turmoil in David's family
3. National rebellion against David
4. The later years of David's rule

David sinned with Bathsheba and then tried to cover his sin by having her husband killed. Although he was forgiven for his sin, the consequences remained—he experienced trouble and distress, both with his family and with the nation. God is always ready to forgive, but we must live with the consequences of our actions. Covering up our sin will only multiply sin's painful consequences.

## MEGATHEMES

| THEME | EXPLANATION | IMPORTANCE |
|---|---|---|
| Kingdom Growth | Under David's leadership, Israel's kingdom grew rapidly. With the growth came many changes: from tribal independence to centralized government, from the leadership of judges to a monarchy, from decentralized worship to worship at Jerusalem. | No matter how much growth or how many changes we experience, God provides for us if we love him and highly regard his principles. God's work done in God's way never lacks God's supply of wisdom and energy. |
| Personal Greatness | David's popularity and influence increased greatly. He realized that the Lord was behind his success because he wanted to pour out his kindness on Israel. David regarded God's interests as more important than his own. | God graciously pours out his favor on us because of what Christ has done. God does not regard personal greatness as something to be used selfishly, but as an instrument to carry out his work among his people. The greatness we should desire is to love others as God loves us. |
| Justice | King David showed justice, mercy, and fairness to Saul's family, enemies, rebels, allies, and close friends alike. His just rule was grounded in his faith in and knowledge of God. God's perfect moral nature is the standard for justice. | Although David was the most just of all Israel's kings, he was still imperfect. His use of justice offered hope for a heavenly, ideal kingdom. This hope will never be satisfied in our hearts until Christ, the Son of David, comes to rule in perfect justice forever. |
| Consequences of Sin | David abandoned his purpose as leader and king in time of war. His desire for prosperity and ease led him from triumph to trouble. Because David committed adultery with Bathsheba, he experienced consequences of his sin that destroyed both his family and the nation. | Temptation quite often comes when a person's life is aimless. We sometimes think that sinful pleasures and freedom from God's restraint will bring us a feeling of vitality; but sin creates a cycle of suffering that is not worth the fleeting pleasures it offers. |
| Feet of Clay | David not only sinned with Bathsheba, he murdered an innocent man. He neglected to discipline his sons when they got involved in rape and murder. This great hero showed a lack of character in some of his most important personal decisions. The man of iron had feet of clay. | Sin should never be considered as a mere weakness or flaw. Sin is fatal and must be eradicated from our lives. David's life teaches us to have compassion for all people, including those whose sinful nature leads them into sinful acts. It serves as a warning to us not to excuse sin in our own lives, even in times of success. |

## A. DAVID'S SUCCESSES (1:1—10:19)

After years of running from Saul, David was finally crowned king over the tribe of Judah. The rest of Israel, however, followed Ishbosheth, Saul's son. David did not attempt to take the tribes by force but placed the matter in God's hands. After a few years Ishbosheth was assassinated, and the rest of the tribes finally put their support behind David. David moved the capital to Jerusalem, defeated the surrounding nations, and even showed kindness to Saul's family. We may not understand why God seems to move slowly at times, but we must trust him and be faithful with what he has given us.

### 1. David becomes king over Judah

*David Learns of Saul's Death*

**1** After the death of Saul, David returned from his victory over the Amalekites and spent two days in Ziklag. 2On the third day a man arrived from Saul's army camp. He had torn his clothes and put dirt on his head to show that he was in mourning. He fell to the ground before David in deep respect.

3"Where have you come from?" David asked.

"I escaped from the Israelite camp," the man replied.

4"What happened?" David demanded. "Tell me how the battle went."

The man replied, "Our entire army fled from the battle. Many of the men are dead, and Saul and his son Jonathan are also dead."

5"How do you know Saul and Jonathan are dead?" David demanded of the young man.

6The man answered, "I happened to be on Mount Gilboa, and there was Saul leaning on his spear with the enemy chariots and charioteers closing in on him. 7When he turned and saw me, he cried out for me to come to him. 'How can I help?' I asked him.

8"He responded, 'Who are you?'

"'I am an Amalekite,' I told him.

9"Then he begged me, 'Come over here and put me out of my misery, for I am in terrible pain and want to die.'

10"So I killed him," the Amalekite told David, "for I knew he couldn't live. Then I took his crown and his armband, and I have brought them here to you, my lord."

11David and his men tore their clothes in sorrow when they heard the news. 12They mourned and wept and fasted all day for Saul and his son Jonathan, and for the LORD's army and the nation of Israel, because they had died by the sword that day.

13Then David said to the young man who had brought the news, "Where are you from?" And he replied, "I am a foreigner, an Amalekite, who lives in your land."

14"Why were you not afraid to kill the LORD's anointed one?" David asked.

**1:1**
1 Sam 30:1, 17

**1:2**
1 Sam 4:12

**1:4-12**
//1 Sam 31:1-13
//1 Chr 10:1-12

**1:4**
1 Sam 4:16-17

**1:6**
1 Sam 28:4; 31:1-6

**1:8**
1 Sam 15:2-3;
30:1, 13, 17

**1:11**
Gen 37:29, 34

**1:14**
1 Sam 26:9-11

---

**1:1** David had great faith in God. He waited for God to fulfill his promises. The book of 1 Samuel tells of David's struggles as he waited to become king of Israel (Samuel had anointed David as king of Israel many years earlier). King Saul became jealous of David because the people were praising him for his accomplishments. Eventually, Saul's jealousy became so intense that he tried to kill David. As a result, David had to run and hide. For many years David hid from Saul in enemy territory and in the barren wilderness south and east of Jerusalem. David may have wondered when God's promise that he would be king would come true, but his struggles prepared him for the great responsibilities he would later face. The book of 2 Samuel tells how David was finally rewarded for his patience and consistent faith in God.

**1:1** When Saul died, David and his men were still living in Ziklag, a Philistine city. Because Saul had driven him out of Israel, David had pretended to be loyal to Achish, a Philistine ruler (1 Samuel 27). There he was safe from Saul.

**1:11, 12** "They mourned and wept and fasted all day." David and his men were visibly shaken over Saul's death. Their actions showed their genuine sorrow over the loss of their king, their friend Jonathan, and the other soldiers of Israel who died that day. They were not ashamed to grieve. Today, some people consider expressing emotions to be a sign of weakness. Those who wish to appear strong try to hide their feelings. But expressing our grief can help us deal with our intense sorrow when a loved one dies.

**1:13** The man identified himself as an Amalekite from Saul's camp (1:2). He may have been an Amalekite under Israelite jurisdiction, but more likely he was a battlefield scavenger. Obviously the man was lying both about his identity and about what happened on the battlefield. (Compare his story with the account in 1 Samuel 31:3, 4.) Because he had Saul's crown with him, something the Philistines wouldn't have left behind, we can infer that he found Saul dead on the battlefield before the Philistines arrived (1 Samuel 31:8).

A life of deceit leads to disaster. The man lied to gain some personal reward for killing David's rival, but he misread David's character. If David had rewarded him for murdering the king, David would have shared his guilt. Instead, David had the messenger killed. Lying can bring disaster upon the liar, even for something he or she has not done.

**1:13** The Amalekites were a fierce nomadic tribe that frequently conducted surprise raids on Canaanite villages. They had been Israel's enemies since Moses' time. David had just destroyed an Amalekite band of raiders who had burned his city and kidnapped its women and children (1 Samuel 30:1-20). This man was probably unaware of David's recent confrontations with the Amalekites, or he may not have come. Instead, he incurred David's wrath by posing as an enemy of Israel and claiming to have killed God's chosen king.

**1:15**
2 Sam 4:10, 12
**1:16**
1 Sam 26:9
2 Sam 1:10

¹⁵Then David said to one of his men, "Kill him!" So the man thrust his sword into the Amalekite and killed him. ¹⁶"You have condemned yourself," David said, "for you yourself confessed that you killed the LORD's anointed one."

### David's Song for Saul and Jonathan

**1:17**
2 Chr 35:27
**1:18**
Josh 10:13

¹⁷Then David composed a funeral song for Saul and Jonathan, ¹⁸and he commanded that it be taught to the people of Judah. It is known as the Song of the Bow, and it is recorded in *The Book of Jashar.**

**1:19**
2 Sam 3:38
**1:20**
1 Sam 31:8
Mic 1:10

¹⁹ Your pride and joy, O Israel, lies dead on the hills!
   Oh, how the mighty heroes have fallen!
²⁰ Don't announce the news in Gath,
   don't proclaim it in the streets of Ashkelon,
or the daughters of the Philistines will rejoice
   and the pagans will laugh in triumph.

**1:21**
1 Sam 31:1
Ezek 31:15

²¹ O mountains of Gilboa,
   let there be no dew or rain upon you,
   nor fruitful fields producing offerings of grain.*
For there the shield of the mighty heroes was defiled;
   the shield of Saul will no longer be anointed with oil.
²² The bow of Jonathan was powerful,
   and the sword of Saul did its mighty work.
They shed the blood of their enemies
   and pierced the bodies of mighty heroes.

**1:23**
Judg 14:18

²³ How beloved and gracious were Saul and Jonathan!
   They were together in life and in death.
They were swifter than eagles,
   stronger than lions.
²⁴ O women of Israel, weep for Saul,
for he dressed you in luxurious scarlet clothing,
   in garments decorated with gold.

**1:25**
2 Sam 1:19

²⁵ Oh, how the mighty heroes have fallen in battle!
   Jonathan lies dead on the hills.

**1:18** Or *The Book of the Upright.*  **1:21** The meaning of the Hebrew is uncertain.

---

| CHARACTERS IN THE DRAMA OF 2 SAMUEL | Character | Relation | Position | Whose Side? |
|---|---|---|---|---|
| It can be confusing to keep track of all the characters introduced in the first few chapters of 2 Samuel. Here is some help. | Joab | Son of Zeruiah, David's half sister | One of David's military leaders and, later, commander in chief | David's |
| | Abner | Saul's cousin | Saul's commander in chief | Saul and Ishbosheth's, but made overtures to David |
| | Abishai | Joab's brother | High officer in David's army— Commander of "the Thirty" | Joab and David's |
| | Asahel | Joab and Abishai's brother | High officer—one of David's 30 select warriors ("mighty men") | Joab and David's |
| | Ishbosheth | Saul's son | Saul and Abner's selection as king | Saul's |

---

**1:15, 16** Why did David consider it a crime to kill the king, even though Saul was his enemy? David believed that God anointed Saul, and only God could remove him from office. If it became casual or commonplace to assassinate the king, the whole society would become chaotic. It was God's job, not David's, to judge Saul's sins (Leviticus 19:18). We must realize that God has placed rulers in authority over us, and we should respect their positions (Romans 13:1-7).

**1:17, 18** David was a talented musician. He played the harp (1 Samuel 16:23), he brought music into the worship services of the Temple (1 Chronicles 25), and he wrote many of the psalms.

Here we are told that he wrote a funeral song in memory of Saul and his son Jonathan, David's closest friend. Music played an important role in Israel's history. (For other famous songs in the Bible, see the chart in Exodus 15, p. 119.)

**1:17-27** Saul had caused much trouble for David, but when he died, David composed a song in memory of the king and his son. David had every reason to hate Saul, but he chose not to. Instead, he chose to look at the good Saul had done and to ignore the times when Saul had attacked him. It takes courage to lay aside hatred and hurt and to respect the positive side of another person, especially an enemy.

<sup>26</sup> How I weep for you, my brother Jonathan!
  Oh, how much I loved you!
And your love for me was deep,
  deeper than the love of women!

<sup>27</sup> Oh, how the mighty heroes have fallen!
  Stripped of their weapons, they lie dead.

### David Anointed King of Judah

**2** After this, David asked the LORD, "Should I move back to one of the towns of Judah?"
  "Yes," the LORD replied.
  Then David asked, "Which town should I go to?"
  "To Hebron," the LORD answered.
<sup>2</sup>David's two wives were Ahinoam from Jezreel and Abigail, the widow of Nabal from Carmel. So David and his wives <sup>3</sup>and his men and their families all moved to Judah, and they settled in the villages near Hebron. <sup>4</sup>Then the men of Judah came to David and anointed him king over the people of Judah.

When David heard that the men of Jabesh-gilead had buried Saul, <sup>5</sup>he sent them this message: "May the LORD bless you for being so loyal to your master Saul and giving him a decent burial. <sup>6</sup>May the LORD be loyal to you in return and reward you with his unfailing love! And I, too, will reward you for what you have done. <sup>7</sup>Now that Saul is dead, I ask you to be my strong and loyal subjects like the people of Judah, who have anointed me as their new king."

### Ishbosheth Proclaimed King of Israel

<sup>8</sup>But Abner son of Ner, the commander of Saul's army, had already gone to Mahanaim with Saul's son Ishbosheth.* <sup>9</sup>There he proclaimed Ishbosheth king over Gilead, Jezreel, Ephraim, Benjamin, the land of the Ashurites, and all the rest of Israel.

<sup>10</sup>Ishbosheth, Saul's son, was forty years old when he became king, and he ruled from Mahanaim for two years. Meanwhile, the people of Judah remained loyal to David. <sup>11</sup>David made Hebron his capital, and he ruled as king of Judah for seven and a half years.

**2:8** *Ishbosheth* is another name for Esh-baal.

**Marginal cross-references:**

**1:26** 1 Sam 18:1

**2:1** Josh 14:13-14; 1 Sam 23:2, 4, 9-12

**2:2** 1 Sam 25:39, 42-43

**2:4** 1 Sam 16:13; 31:11-13; 2 Sam 5:3-5

**2:5** 1 Sam 23:21; 24:19

**2:6** Exod 34:5-6

**2:8** 1 Sam 14:50; 2 Sam 17:24

---

**1:26** By saying that Jonathan's love was "deeper than the love of women," David was not implying that he had a sexual relationship with Jonathan. Homosexual acts were absolutely forbidden in Israel. Leviticus 18:22 calls homosexuality "detestable," and Leviticus 20:13 decrees the death penalty for those who practice homosexuality. David was simply restating the deep brotherhood and faithful friendship he had with Jonathan. (For more on their friendship, see the note on 1 Samuel 18:1-4.)

**JOAB VERSUS ABNER**
David was crowned king of Judah in Hebron; Ishbosheth was crowned king of Israel in Mahanaim. The opposing armies of Judah and Israel met at Gibeon for battle—Judah under Joab, Israel under Abner.

**2:1** Although David knew he would become king (1 Samuel 16:13; 23:17; 24:20), and although the time seemed right now that Saul was dead, David still asked God if he should move back to Judah, the home territory of his tribe. Before moving ahead with what seems obvious, first bring the matter to God, who alone knows the best timing.

**2:1** God told David to return to Hebron, where he would soon be crowned king of Judah. David made Hebron his capital because (1) it was the largest city in Judah at that time; (2) it was secure against attack; (3) it was located near the center of Judah's territory, an ideal location for a capital city; (4) many key trade routes converged at Hebron, making it difficult for supply lines to be cut off in wartime.

**2:4** The men of Judah publicly anointed David as their king. David had been anointed king by Samuel years earlier (1 Samuel 16:13), but that ceremony had taken place in private. This one was like inaugurating a public official who has already been elected to office. The rest of Israel, however, didn't accept David's kingship for seven and a half years (2:10, 11).

**2:4-7** David sent a message thanking the men of Jabesh-gilead who had risked their lives to bury Saul's body (1 Samuel 31:11-13). Saul had rescued Jabesh-gilead from certain defeat when Nahash the Ammonite had surrounded the city (1 Samuel 11), so these citizens showed their gratitude and kindness. In his message, he also suggested that they follow Judah's lead and acknowledge him as their king. Jabesh-gilead was to the north in the land of Gilead, and David was seeking to gain support among the 10 remaining tribes who had not yet recognized him as king.

**2:10, 11** David ruled over Judah for seven and a half years, while Ishbosheth reigned in Israel for only two years. The five-year gap may be due to Ishbosheth's not assuming the throne immediately after Saul's death. Because of constant danger from

### War between Israel and Judah

**2:12**
Josh 10:12

**2:13**
2 Sam 8:16
1 Chr 2:16; 11:5-6

¹²One day Abner led Ishbosheth's troops from Mahanaim to Gibeon. ¹³About the same time, Joab son of Zeruiah led David's troops out and met them at the pool of Gibeon. The two groups sat down there, facing each other from opposite sides of the pool.

¹⁴Then Abner suggested to Joab, "Let's have a few of our warriors fight hand to hand here in front of us."

"All right," Joab agreed. ¹⁵So twelve men were chosen to fight from each side—twelve men of Benjamin representing Ishbosheth son of Saul, and twelve representing David. ¹⁶Each one grabbed his opponent by the hair and thrust his sword into the other's side so that all of them died. So this place at Gibeon has been known ever since as the Field of Swords.*

**2:16** Hebrew *Helkath-hazzurim.*

---

**ABNER**

The honest compliments of an opponent are often the best measure of someone's greatness. Although Abner and David frequently saw each other across battle lines, the Bible gives a glimpse of the respect they had for each other. As a young man, David had served under Abner. But later, Saul's campaign to kill David was carried out by Abner. After Saul's death, Abner temporarily upheld the power of the king's family. But the struggle between Abner and Saul's heir, Ishbosheth, brought about Abner's decision to support David's claim to the throne. It was during his efforts to unite the kingdom that Abner was murdered by Joab.

Several years earlier, in a battle between Ishbosheth's army under Abner and David's forces under Joab, Abner fled and was pursued by Joab's brother, Asahel. Abner told Asahel twice to stop following him. But the eager young soldier refused, so Abner killed him. Joab was determined to avenge his brother.

Abner realized Saul's family was doomed to defeat and that David would be the next king, so he decided to change sides. He hoped that in exchange for his delivering Saul's kingdom, David would make him commander in chief of his army. David's willingness to accept this proposal was probably another reason for Joab's action.

Abner lived by his wits and his will. To him, God was someone with whom he would cooperate if it suited his plans. Otherwise he did what seemed best for him at the time. We can identify with Abner's tendency to give God conditional cooperation. Obedience is easy when the instructions in God's Word fit in with our plans. But our allegiance to God is tested when his plans are contrary to ours. What action should you take today in obedience to God's Word?

| | |
|---|---|
| **Strengths and accomplishments** | • Commander in chief of Saul's army and a capable military leader<br>• Held Israel together for several years under the weak king Ishbosheth<br>• Recognized and accepted God's plan to make David king over both Israel and Judah |
| **Weaknesses and mistakes** | • He had selfish motives in his effort to reunite Judah and Israel rather than godly conviction<br>• He slept with one of the royal concubines after Saul's death |
| **Lesson from his life** | • God requires more than conditional, halfhearted cooperation |
| **Vital statistics** | • Where: Territory of Benjamin<br>• Occupation: Commander of the armies under Saul and Ishbosheth<br>• Relatives: Father: Ner. Cousin: Saul. Son: Jaasiel.<br>• Contemporaries: David, Asahel, Joab, Abishai |
| **Key verse** | "Then King David said to his officials, 'Don't you realize that a great commander has fallen today in Israel?'" (2 Samuel 3:38). |

Abner's story is told in 1 Samuel 14:50—2 Samuel 4:12. He is also mentioned in 1 Kings 2:5, 32; 1 Chronicles 26:28; 27:16–22.

---

the Philistines in the northern part of Israel, five years may have passed before Ishbosheth could begin his reign. During that time, Abner, commander of his army, probably played a principal role in driving out the Philistines and leading the northern confederacy. Regardless of when Ishbosheth began to rule, his control was weak and limited. The Philistines still dominated the area, and Ishbosheth was intimidated by Abner (3:11).

**2:12ff** With Israel divided, there was constant tension between north and south. David's true rival in the north, however, was not Ishbosheth but Abner. In this incident, Abner suggested hand-to-hand combat between the champions of his army and the champions of David's army, led by Joab. The fact that this confrontation occurred at the pool of Gibeon (located in Saul's

home territory of Benjamin) suggests that Joab's men were pushing northward, gaining more territory. Abner may have suggested this confrontation in hopes of stopping Joab's advance.

Twelve men from each side were supposed to fight each other, and the side with the most survivors would be declared the winner. The confrontation between David and Goliath (1 Samuel 17) was a similar battle strategy—a way to avoid terrible bloodshed from an all-out war. In this case, however, all 24 champions were killed before either side could claim victory. Nothing was accomplished, and the civil war continued.

17A fierce battle followed that day, and Abner and the men of Israel were defeated by the forces of David.

**2:17**
2 Sam 3:1

### The Death of Asahel
18Joab, Abishai, and Asahel—the three sons of Zeruiah—were among David's forces that day. Asahel could run like a gazelle, 19and he began chasing Abner. He pursued him relentlessly, not stopping for anything. 20When Abner looked back and saw him coming, he called out, "Is that you, Asahel?"

**2:18**
1 Chr 2:16; 11:26;
12:8

"Yes, it is," he replied.

21"Go fight someone else!" Abner warned. "Take on one of the younger men, and strip him of his weapons." But Asahel kept right on chasing Abner.

22Again Abner shouted to him, "Get away from here! I don't want to kill you. How could I ever face your brother Joab again?"

**2:22**
2 Sam 3:27

23But Asahel refused to turn back, so Abner thrust the butt end of his spear through Asahel's stomach, and the spear came out through his back. He stumbled to the ground and died there. And everyone who came by that spot stopped and stood still when they saw Asahel lying there.

24When Joab and Abishai found out what had happened, they set out after Abner. The sun was just going down as they arrived at the hill of Ammah near Giah, along the road to the wilderness of Gibeon. 25Abner's troops from the tribe of Benjamin regrouped there at the top of the hill to take a stand.

26Abner shouted down to Joab, "Must we always be killing each other? Don't you realize that bitterness is the only result? When will you call off your men from chasing their Israelite brothers?"

**2:26**
Deut 32:42

27Then Joab said, "God only knows what would have happened if you hadn't spoken, for we would have chased you all night if necessary." 28So Joab blew the ram's horn, and his men stopped chasing the troops of Israel.

29All that night Abner and his men retreated through the Jordan Valley.* They crossed the Jordan River, traveling all through the morning,* and didn't stop until they arrived at Mahanaim.

**2:29**
Deut 3:17

30Meanwhile, Joab and his men also returned home. When Joab counted his casualties, he discovered that only 19 men were missing in addition to Asahel. 31But 360 of Abner's men had been killed, all from the tribe of Benjamin. 32Joab and his men took Asahel's body to Bethlehem and buried him there in his father's tomb. Then they traveled all night and reached Hebron at daybreak.

**2:32**
Gen 49:29

**3** That was the beginning of a long war between those who were loyal to Saul and those loyal to David. As time passed David became stronger and stronger, while Saul's dynasty became weaker and weaker.

**3:1**
1 Kgs 14:30

### David's Sons Born in Hebron
2These are the sons who were born to David in Hebron:

**3:2-5**
//1 Chr 3:1-4

The oldest was Amnon, whose mother was Ahinoam from Jezreel.

**3:2**
1 Sam 25:43
2 Sam 13:1
1 Chr 3:1

**2:29a** Hebrew the *Arabah.*   **2:29b** Or *continued on through the Bithron.* The meaning of the Hebrew is uncertain.

---

**2:21-23** Abner repeatedly warned Asahel to turn back or risk losing his life, but Asahel refused to turn from his self-imposed duty. Persistence is a good trait if it is for a worthy cause. But if the goal is only personal honor or gain, persistence may be no more than stubbornness. Asahel's stubbornness not only cost him his life, but it also spurred unfortunate disunity in David's army for years to come (3:26, 27; 1 Kings 2:28-35). Before you decide to pursue a goal, make sure it is worthy of your devotion.

**2:28** This battle ended with a victory for Joab's troops (2:17), but war in the divided nation continued until David was finally crowned king over all Israel (5:1-5).

**3:1** The events recorded in chapter 2 led to a long war between David's followers and the troops loyal to Abner and Ishbosheth. Civil war rocked the country at great cost to both sides. This war occurred because Israel and Judah had lost sight of God's vision

and purpose: to settle the land (Genesis 12:7), to drive out the Canaanites (Deuteronomy 7:1-4), and to obey God's laws (Deuteronomy 8:1). Instead of uniting to accomplish these goals, they fought each other. When you face conflict, step back from the hostilities and consider whether you and your enemy have common goals that are bigger than your differences. Appeal to those interests as you work for a settlement.

**3:2-5** David suffered much heartache because of his many wives. Polygamy was a socially acceptable practice for kings at this time, although God specifically warned against it (Deuteronomy 17:14-17). Sadly, the numerous sons born to David's wives caused him great trouble. Rape (13:14), murder (13:28), rebellion (15:13), and greed (1 Kings 1:5, 6) all resulted from the jealous rivalries among the half brothers. Solomon, one of David's sons and his successor to the throne, also took many wives who eventually turned him away from God (1 Kings 11:3, 4).

**3:3**
1 Sam 25:42
1 Chr 3:2

**3:4**
1 Chr 3:2-3

**3:5**
1 Chr 3:3

3 The second was Daniel,* whose mother was Abigail, the widow of Nabal from Carmel. The third was Absalom, whose mother was Maacah, the daughter of Talmai, king of Geshur.
4 The fourth was Adonijah, whose mother was Haggith. The fifth was Shephatiah, whose mother was Abital.
5 The sixth was Ithream, whose mother was Eglah, David's wife.

These sons were all born to David in Hebron.

### Abner Joins Forces with David

**3:7**
2 Sam 21:8-11

**3:8**
1 Sam 24:14
2 Sam 9:8; 16:9

**3:9**
1 Sam 15:28

6As the war between the house of Saul and the house of David went on, Abner became a powerful leader among those loyal to Saul. 7One day Ishbosheth,* Saul's son, accused Abner of sleeping with one of his father's concubines, a woman named Rizpah, daughter of Aiah.

8Abner was furious. "Am I some Judean dog to be kicked around like this?" he shouted. "After all I have done for your father, Saul, and his family and friends by not handing you over to David, is this my reward—that you find fault with me about this woman? 9May God strike me and even kill me if I don't do everything I can to help David get what the LORD has promised him! 10I'm going to take Saul's kingdom and give it to David. I will establish the throne of David over Israel as well as Judah, all the way from Dan in the north to Beersheba in the south." 11Ishbosheth didn't dare say another word because he was afraid of what Abner might do.

12Then Abner sent messengers to David, saying, "Doesn't the entire land belong to you? Make a solemn pact with me, and I will help turn over all of Israel to you."

**3:13**
1 Sam 18:20

**3:14**
1 Sam 18:25-27

**3:15**
1 Sam 25:44

**3:16**
2 Sam 16:5

13"All right," David replied, "but I will not negotiate with you unless you bring back my wife Michal, Saul's daughter, when you come."

14David then sent this message to Ishbosheth, Saul's son: "Give me back my wife Michal, for I bought her with the lives* of 100 Philistines."

15So Ishbosheth took Michal away from her husband, Palti* son of Laish. 16Palti followed along behind her as far as Bahurim, weeping as he went. Then Abner told him, "Go back home!" So Palti returned.

**3:18**
1 Sam 9:16; 15:28

**3:19**
1 Sam 10:20-21
1 Chr 12:29

17Meanwhile, Abner had consulted with the elders of Israel. "For some time now," he told them, "you have wanted to make David your king. 18Now is the time! For the LORD has said, 'I have chosen David to save my people Israel from the hands of the Philistines and from all their other enemies.'" 19Abner also spoke with the men of Benjamin. Then he went to Hebron to tell David that all the people of Israel and Benjamin had agreed to support him.

**3:21**
1 Kgs 11:37

20When Abner and twenty of his men came to Hebron, David entertained them with a great feast. 21Then Abner said to David, "Let me go and call an assembly of all Israel to support my lord the king. They will make a covenant with you to make you their king, and you will rule over everything your heart desires." So David sent Abner safely on his way.

**3:3** As in parallel text at 1 Chr 3:1 (see also Greek version, which reads *Daluia*, and Dead Sea Scrolls, which read *Dan[iel]*); Hebrew reads *Kileab*. **3:7** *Ishbosheth* is another name for Esh-baal. **3:14** Hebrew *the foreskins*. **3:15** As in 1 Sam 25:44; Hebrew reads *Paltiel*, a variant spelling of Palti.

---

**3:6, 7** To sleep with any of the king's wives or concubines was to make a claim to the throne, and it was considered treason. Because Ishbosheth was a weak ruler, Abner was running the country; thus, he may have felt justified in sleeping with Saul's concubine. Ishbosheth, however, saw that Abner's power was becoming too great.

**3:7** Ishbosheth may have been right to speak out against Abner's behavior, but he didn't have the moral strength to maintain his authority (3:11). Lack of moral backbone became the root of Israel's troubles over the next four centuries. Only 4 of the next 40 kings of Israel were called "good." It takes courage and strength to stand firm in your convictions and to confront wrongdoing in the face of opposition. When you believe something is wrong, do not let yourself be talked out of your position. Firmly attack the wrong and uphold the right.

**3:8** By saying, "Am I some Judean dog to be kicked around?" Abner meant, "Am I a traitor for Judah?" He may have been refuting the accusation that he was trying to take over the throne, or he may have been angry that Ishbosheth scolded him after Abner had helped put him on the throne in the first place. Prior to this

conversation, Abner realized that he could not keep David from eventually taking over Israel. Because he was angry at Ishbosheth, Abner devised a plan to turn over the kingdom of Israel to David.

**3:13, 14** Michal had been married to David. Saul had arranged the marriage as a reward for David's acts of bravery (1 Samuel 17:25; 18:24-27). Later, however, in one of his jealous fits, Saul took Michal away from David and forced her to marry Palti (1 Samuel 25:44). Now David wanted his wife back before he would begin to negotiate peace with the northern tribes. Perhaps David still loved her (but see 6:20-23 for the tension in their relationship). More likely, he thought that marriage to Saul's daughter would strengthen his claim to rule all Israel and demonstrate that he had no animosity toward Saul's house. Palti was the unfortunate victim caught in the web of Saul's jealousy.

**3:19** Because Saul, Ishbosheth, and Abner were all from the tribe of Benjamin, the support of the elders of that tribe meant that Abner was serious about his offer. There was a strong possibility of overcoming tribal jealousies and uniting the kingdom.

## Joab Murders Abner

22But just after David had sent Abner away in safety, Joab and some of David's troops returned from a raid, bringing much plunder with them. 23When Joab arrived, he was told that Abner had just been there visiting the king and had been sent away in safety.

24Joab rushed to the king and demanded, "What have you done? What do you mean by letting Abner get away? 25You know perfectly well that he came to spy on you and find out everything you're doing!"

26Joab then left David and sent messengers to catch up with Abner, asking him to return. They found him at the well of Sirah and brought him back, though David knew nothing about it. 27When Abner arrived back at Hebron, Joab took him aside at the gateway as if to speak with him privately. But then he stabbed Abner in the stomach and killed him in revenge for killing his brother Asahel.

28When David heard about it, he declared, "I vow by the LORD that I and my kingdom are forever innocent of this crime against Abner son of Ner. 29Joab and his family are the guilty ones. May the family of Joab be cursed in every generation with a man who has open sores or leprosy* or who walks on crutches* or dies by the sword or begs for food!"

30So Joab and his brother Abishai killed Abner because Abner had killed their brother Asahel at the battle of Gibeon.

## David Mourns Abner's Death

31Then David said to Joab and all those who were with him, "Tear your clothes and put on burlap. Mourn for Abner." And King David himself walked behind the procession to the grave. 32They buried Abner in Hebron, and the king and all the people wept at his graveside. 33Then the king sang this funeral song for Abner:

"Should Abner have died as fools die?
34 Your hands were not bound;
    your feet were not chained.
No, you were murdered—
    the victim of a wicked plot."

All the people wept again for Abner. 35David had refused to eat anything on the day of the funeral, and now everyone begged him to eat. But David had made a vow, saying, "May God strike me and even kill me if I eat anything before sundown."

36This pleased the people very much. In fact, everything the king did pleased them! 37So everyone in Judah and all Israel understood that David was not responsible for Abner's murder.

38Then King David said to his officials, "Don't you realize that a great commander has fallen today in Israel? 39And even though I am the anointed king, these two sons of Zeruiah—Joab and Abishai—are too strong for me to control. So may the LORD repay these evil men for their evil deeds."

**Cross-references (margin):**
- 3:22 1 Sam 27:8
- 3:24 1 Sam 29:3
- 3:27 2 Sam 2:22-23; 20:8-10; 1 Kgs 2:5
- 3:29 Lev 13:45-46; Deut 21:7-8; 1 Kgs 2:31-33
- 3:30 2 Sam 2:23
- 3:31 Gen 37:34; Judg 11:35
- 3:32 Prov 24:17
- 3:35 2 Sam 1:12; 12:17
- 3:39 2 Sam 19:5-7

**3:29a** Or *or a contagious skin disease.* The Hebrew word used here can describe various skin diseases.   **3:29b** Or *who is effeminate;* Hebrew reads *who handles a spindle.*

---

**3:26-29** Joab took revenge for the death of his brother instead of leaving justice to God. But that revenge backfired on him (1 Kings 2:31-34). God will repay those who deserve it (Romans 12:19). Refuse to rejoice when your enemies suffer, and don't try to get revenge. Seeking revenge will ruin your own peace of mind and increase the chances of further retaliation.

**3:27** Abner killed Joab's brother Asahel in self-defense. Joab then killed Abner to avenge his brother's death and also to save his position of military leadership. People who killed in self-defense were supposed to be safe in cities of refuge (Numbers 35:22-25). Joab showed his disrespect for God's laws by killing Abner out of revenge in Hebron, a city of refuge (Joshua 20:7).

**3:29** David was saying that Joab's descendants would be unclean, unhealthy, and in want. Why did David say such harsh words about Joab? David was upset over Abner's death for several reasons. (1) He was grieved over the loss of a skilled military officer. (2) He wanted to place the guilt of Abner's murder on Joab, not himself. (3) He was on the verge of becoming king over the entire nation, and utilizing Abner was the key to winning over the northern tribes. Abner's death could have revived the civil war. (4) Joab violated David's agreement to protect Abner. Joab's murderous act ruined David's plans, and David was especially angry that his own commander had committed the crime.

**3:31** By walking behind the procession (that is, behind the casket), David was leading the mourning.

**3:31ff** David ordered Joab to mourn, possibly because few people were aware that Joab had committed the crime and because David did not want any further trouble. If this is true, David was thinking more about strengthening his kingdom than about justice.

**3:39** Joab and Abishai were the two sons of Zeruiah David mentioned. David had an especially hard time controlling Joab because, although he was intensely loyal, he was strong willed, preferring to do things his own way. In exchange for his loyalty, however, David was willing to give him the flexibility he craved.

Joab's murder of Abner is an example of his fierce independence. While David opposed the murder, he allowed it to remain unpunished because (1) to punish Joab could cause the troops to rebel; (2) Joab was David's nephew, and any harsh treatment could

### The Murder of Ishbosheth

**4:1**
2 Sam 3:27
**4:2**
Josh 9:17; 18:25

4 When Ishbosheth,* Saul's son, heard about Abner's death at Hebron, he lost all courage, and all Israel became paralyzed with fear. ²Now there were two brothers, Baanah and Recab, who were captains of Ishbosheth's raiding parties. They were sons of Rimmon, a member of the tribe of Benjamin who lived in Beeroth. The town of Beeroth is now part of Benjamin's territory ³because the original people of Beeroth fled to Gittaim, where they still live as foreigners.

**4:3**
Neh 11:33

**4:4**
1 Sam 31:1-4
2 Sam 9:3, 5-6
1 Chr 8:34; 9:40

⁴(Saul's son Jonathan had a son named Mephibosheth,* who was crippled as a child. He was five years old when the report came from Jezreel that Saul and Jonathan had been killed in battle. When the child's nurse heard the news, she picked him up and fled. But as she hurried away, she dropped him, and he became crippled.)

**4:5**
2 Sam 2:8
**4:6**
2 Sam 2:23

⁵One day Recab and Baanah, the sons of Rimmon from Beeroth, went to Ishbosheth's house around noon as he was taking his midday rest. ⁶The doorkeeper, who had been sifting wheat, became drowsy and fell asleep. So Recab and Baanah slipped past her.* ⁷They went into the house and found Ishbosheth sleeping on his bed. They struck and killed him and cut off his head. Then, taking his head with them, they fled across the Jordan Valley* through the night. ⁸When they arrived at Hebron, they presented Ishbosheth's head to David. "Look!" they exclaimed to the king. "Here is the head of Ishbosheth, the son of your enemy Saul who tried to kill you. Today the LORD has given my lord the king revenge on Saul and his entire family!"

**4:9**
1 Kgs 1:29
**4:10**
2 Sam 1:1-2, 4, 15
**4:11**
Gen 9:5
Ps 9:12

⁹But David said to Recab and Baanah, "The LORD, who saves me from all my enemies, is my witness. ¹⁰Someone once told me, 'Saul is dead,' thinking he was bringing me good news. But I seized him and killed him at Ziklag. That's the reward I gave him for his news! ¹¹How much more should I reward evil men who have killed an innocent man in his own house and on his own bed? Shouldn't I hold you responsible for his blood and rid the earth of you?"

**4:12**
2 Sam 1:15; 3:32

¹²So David ordered his young men to kill them, and they did. They cut off their hands and feet and hung their bodies beside the pool in Hebron. Then they took Ishbosheth's head and buried it in Abner's tomb in Hebron.

### 2. David becomes king over Israel

**5:1-3**
//1 Chr 11:1-3
**5:2**
1 Sam 18:5, 14;
25:30

5 Then all the tribes of Israel went to David at Hebron and told him, "We are your own flesh and blood. ²In the past,* when Saul was our king, you were the one who really led the forces of Israel. And the LORD told you, 'You will be the shepherd of my people Israel. You will be Israel's leader.'"

**4:1** *Ishbosheth* is another name for Esh-baal.   **4:4** *Mephibosheth* is another name for Merib-baal.   **4:6** As in Greek version; Hebrew reads *So they went into the house pretending to fetch wheat, but they stabbed him in the stomach. Then Recab and Baanah escaped.*   **4:7** Hebrew *the Arabah*.   **5:2** Or *For some time.*

---

cause family problems; (3) Joab was from the tribe of Judah, and David didn't want rebellion from his own tribe; (4) to get rid of Joab would mean losing a skilled and competent commander who had been invaluable in strengthening his army.

**4:1**  Ishbosheth was a man who took his courage from another man (Abner) rather than from God. When Abner died, Ishbosheth was left with nothing. In crisis and under pressure, he collapsed in fear. Fear can paralyze us, but faith and trust in God can overcome fear (2 Timothy 1:6-8; Hebrews 13:6). If we trust in God, we will be free to respond boldly to the events around us.

**4:4**  The rest of Mephibosheth's story is told in chapter 9; 16:1-4; and 19:24-30.

**4:11**  David called Ishbosheth an "innocent man." As Saul's son, Ishbosheth had reason to think he was in line for the throne. He was not wicked for wanting to be king; rather, he was simply too weak to stand against injustice. Although David knew Ishbosheth was not the strong leader needed to unite Israel, he had no intention of killing him. God had promised the kingdom to David, and he knew that God would fulfill his promise.

When David learned of Ishbosheth's death, he was angry. He had never harmed Saul, and he thought the assassins' method was cowardly. David wanted to unite Israel, not drive a permanent wedge between him and Ishbosheth's supporters. To show that he had nothing to do with the extermination of Saul's royal line, he

ordered the assassins killed and gave Ishbosheth a proper burial. All the tribes of Israel, recognizing in David the strong leader they needed, pledged their loyalty to him. No doubt the Philistine threat and David's military reputation (1 Samuel 18:7) also helped unify the people.

**DAVID DEFEATS THE PHILISTINES**   The Philistines camped in the valley of Rephaim. David defeated them at Baal-perazim, but they remained in the valley. He attacked again and chased them from Gibeon to Gezer.

³So there at Hebron, King David made a covenant before the LORD with all the elders of Israel. And they anointed him king of Israel.

⁴David was thirty years old when he began to reign, and he reigned forty years in all. ⁵He had reigned over Judah from Hebron for seven years and six months, and from Jerusalem he reigned over all Israel and Judah for thirty-three years.

### David Captures Jerusalem

⁶David then led his men to Jerusalem to fight against the Jebusites, the original inhabitants of the land who were living there. The Jebusites taunted David, saying, "You'll never get in here! Even the blind and lame could keep you out!" For the Jebusites thought they were safe. ⁷But David captured the fortress of Zion, which is now called the City of David.

⁸On the day of the attack, David said to his troops, "I hate those 'lame' and 'blind' Jebusites.* Whoever attacks them should strike by going into the city through the water tunnel.*" That is the origin of the saying, "The blind and the lame may not enter the house."*

⁹So David made the fortress his home, and he called it the City of David. He extended the city, starting at the supporting terraces* and working inward. ¹⁰And David became more and more powerful, because the LORD God of Heaven's Armies was with him.

¹¹Then King Hiram of Tyre sent messengers to David, along with cedar timber and carpenters and stonemasons, and they built David a palace. ¹²And David realized that the LORD had confirmed him as king over Israel and had blessed his kingdom for the sake of his people Israel.

¹³After moving from Hebron to Jerusalem, David married more concubines and wives, and they had more sons and daughters. ¹⁴These are the names of David's sons who were born in Jerusalem: Shammua, Shobab, Nathan, Solomon, ¹⁵Ibhar, Elishua, Nepheg, Japhia, ¹⁶Elishama, Eliada, and Eliphelet.

### David Conquers the Philistines

¹⁷When the Philistines heard that David had been anointed king of Israel, they mobilized all their forces to capture him. But David was told they were coming, so he went into the stronghold. ¹⁸The Philistines arrived and spread out across the valley of Rephaim. ¹⁹So David asked the LORD, "Should I go out to fight the Philistines? Will you hand them over to me?"

5:8a Or *Those 'lame' and 'blind' Jebusites hate me.*   5:8b Or *with scaling hooks.* The meaning of the Hebrew is uncertain.
5:8c The meaning of this saying is uncertain.   5:9 Hebrew *the millo.* The meaning of the Hebrew is uncertain.

**5:3** 1 Sam 16:1, 13; 2 Sam 2:4; 3:21
**5:4** Gen 41:46; 1 Kgs 2:11; Luke 3:23
**5:6-10** //1 Chr 11:4-9
**5:7** 1 Kgs 2:10
**5:9** 1 Kgs 9:15, 24
**5:10** 2 Sam 3:1
**5:11-16** //1 Chr 3:5-9; 14:1-7
**5:11** 1 Kgs 5:10, 18; 1 Chr 14:1
**5:12** Num 24:7
**5:13** Deut 17:17; 1 Chr 3:9
**5:14** 1 Chr 3:5
**5:17-25** //1 Chr 14:8-17
**5:18** Josh 15:8; 18:16
**5:19** 1 Sam 23:2

**5:3-5** This was the third time David was anointed king. First he was privately anointed by Samuel (1 Samuel 16:13). Then he was made king over the tribe of Judah (2:4). Finally he was crowned king over all Israel. David's life as an outlaw had looked bleak, but God's promise to make him king over all Israel was now being fulfilled. Although the kingdom would be divided again in less than 75 years, David's dynasty would reign over Judah, the southern kingdom, for over 400 years.

**5:4, 5** David did not become king over all Israel until he was 37 years old, although he had been promised the kingdom many years earlier (1 Samuel 16:13). During those years, David had to wait patiently for the fulfillment of God's promise. If you feel pressured to achieve instant results and success, remember David's patience. Just as his time of waiting prepared him for his important task, a waiting period may help prepare you by strengthening your character.

**5:6** The fortress of Zion (which became the city of Jerusalem) was located on a high ridge near the center of the united Israelite kingdom. It was considered neutral territory because it stood on the border of the territory of the tribes of Benjamin and Judah, and it was still occupied by the Jebusites, a Canaanite tribe that had never been expelled from the land (Judges 1:21). Because of its strategic advantages, David made Jerusalem his capital.

**5:6, 7** The Jebusites had a clear military advantage, and they boasted of their security behind the impregnable walls of Zion. But they soon discovered that their walls would not protect them. David caught them by surprise by entering the city through the water tunnel.

Only in God are we truly safe and secure. Anything else is false security. Whether you are surrounded by mighty walls of stone, a comfortable home, or a secure job, no one can predict what

tomorrow may bring. Our relationship with God is the only security that cannot be taken away.

**5:12** "David realized that the LORD had confirmed him as king. . . ." Although the pagan kingdoms based their greatness on conquest, power, armies, and wealth, David knew that his greatness came only from God. To be great means keeping a close relationship with God personally and nationally. To do this, David had to keep his ambition under control. Although he was famous, successful, and well liked, he gave God first place in his life and served the people according to God's purposes. Do you seek greatness from God or from people? In the drive for success, remember to keep your ambition under God's control.

**5:17** "The stronghold" is the mountain stronghold in the wilderness of Judah that David used when defending himself against Saul (see 23:14 and 1 Chronicles 12:8).

**5:17** The Philistine oppression of Israel had begun in the days of Samson (Judges 13–16). The Philistines were still Israel's most powerful enemy although David was once considered a friend and ally (1 Samuel 27; 29). Because they occupied much of Israel's northern territory, they apparently did not bother David while he was king of Judah to the south. But when they learned that David was planning to unite all Israel, they tried to stop him.

**5:19** How could David get such a clear message from God? He may have prayed and been urged to action by the Holy Spirit. He may have asked God through a prophet. Most likely, however, he went to the high priest, who consulted God through the Urim and Thummim that God had told the Israelites to use for just such a purpose. (For more on the Urim and Thummim, see the notes on Leviticus 8:8 and 1 Samuel 10:20.)

**5:19-25** David fought his battles the way God instructed him. In each instance he (1) asked if he should fight or not, (2) followed

The LORD replied to David, "Yes, go ahead. I will certainly hand them over to you."
20So David went to Baal-perazim and defeated the Philistines there. "The LORD did it!" David exclaimed. "He burst through my enemies like a raging flood!" So he named that place Baal-perazim (which means "the Lord who bursts through"). 21The Philistines had abandoned their idols there, so David and his men confiscated them.

22But after a while the Philistines returned and again spread out across the valley of Rephaim. 23And again David asked the LORD what to do. "Do not attack them straight on," the LORD replied. "Instead, circle around behind and attack them near the poplar* trees. 24When you hear a sound like marching feet in the tops of the poplar trees, be on the alert! That will be the signal that the LORD is moving ahead of you to strike down the Philistine army." 25So David did what the LORD commanded, and he struck down the Philistines all the way from Gibeon* to Gezer.

### Moving the Ark to Jerusalem

**6** Then David again gathered all the elite troops in Israel, 30,000 in all. 2He led them to Baalah of Judah* to bring back the Ark of God, which bears the name of the LORD of Heaven's Armies,* who is enthroned between the cherubim. 3They placed the Ark of God on a new cart and brought it from Abinadab's house, which was on a hill. Uzzah and Ahio, Abinadab's sons, were guiding the cart as it left the house, 4carrying the Ark of God. Ahio walked in front of the Ark. 5David and all the people of Israel were celebrating before the LORD, singing songs* and playing all kinds of musical instruments—lyres, harps, tambourines, castanets, and cymbals.

**5:20**
1 Chr 14:11

**5:24**
Judg 4:14
**5:25**
Josh 12:12;
21:20-22

**6:1-11**
//1 Chr 13:1-14
**6:2**
Lev 24:16
**6:3**
Num 7:4-9
1 Sam 6:7
**6:5**
1 Chr 13:7-8; 16:5

**5:23** Or *aspen,* or *balsam;* also in 5:24. The exact identification of this tree is uncertain. **5:25** As in Greek version (see also 1 Chr 14:16); Hebrew reads *Geba.* **6:2a** *Baalah of Judah* is another name for Kiriath-jearim; compare 1 Chr 13:6. **6:2b** Or *the Ark of God where the Name is proclaimed—the name of the LORD of Heaven's Armies.* **6:5** As in Dead Sea Scrolls and Greek version (see also 1 Chr 13:8); Masoretic Text reads *before the LORD with all manner of cypress wood.*

---

**CRITICIZING GOD'S LEADERS** It is dangerous to criticize God's leaders. Consider the consequences for these men and women.

| Person/Situation | Result | Reference |
|---|---|---|
| Miriam: Mocked Moses because he had a Cushite wife | Stricken with leprosy | Numbers 12 |
| Korah and followers: Led the people of Israel to rebel against Moses' leadership | Swallowed by the earth | Numbers 16 |
| Michal: Despised David because he danced before the Lord | Remained childless | 2 Samuel 6 |
| Shimei: Cursed and threw stones at David | Executed at Solomon's order | 2 Samuel 16 1 Kings 2 |
| Youths: Mocked Elisha and laughed at his baldness | Killed by bears | 2 Kings 2 |
| Sanballat and Tobiah: Spread rumors and lies to stop the building of Jerusalem's walls | Frightened and humiliated | Nehemiah 2; 4; 6 |
| Hananiah: Contradicted Jeremiah's prophecies with false predictions | Died two months later | Jeremiah 28 |
| Bar-Jesus, a sorcerer: Lied about Paul in an attempt to turn the governor against him | Stricken with blindness | Acts 13 |

---

instructions carefully, and (3) gave God the glory. We can err in our "battles" by ignoring these steps and instead (1) do what we want without considering God's will, (2) do things our way and ignore advice in the Bible or from other wise people, and (3) take the glory ourselves or give it to someone else without acknowledging the help we received from God. All these responses are sinful.

**5:25** After David became king, his first order of business was to subdue his enemies—a task the nation had failed to complete when they first entered the land (Judges 2:1-4). David knew this had to be done in order to (1) protect the nation, (2) unify the kingdom, and (3) prepare for building the Temple (which would unify religion under God and help abolish idolatrous influences).

**6:3** The Ark of God was Israel's national treasure and was ordinarily kept in the Tabernacle. When the Ark was returned to Israel after a brief Philistine captivity (1 Samuel 4:1–7:2), it was kept in Abinadab's home for 20 years. David saw how God blessed Abinadab, and he wanted to bring the Ark to Jerusalem to ensure God's blessing on the entire nation. (See the notes on Exodus 37:1 and Joshua 3:2-4 for more information on the Ark.)

6But when they arrived at the threshing floor of Nacon, the oxen stumbled, and Uzzah reached out his hand and steadied the Ark of God. 7Then the LORD's anger was aroused against Uzzah, and God struck him dead because of this.* So Uzzah died right there beside the Ark of God.

8David was angry because the LORD's anger had burst out against Uzzah. He named that place Perez-uzzah (which means "to burst out against Uzzah"), as it is still called today.

9David was now afraid of the LORD, and he asked, "How can I ever bring the Ark of the LORD back into my care?" 10So David decided not to move the Ark of the LORD into the City of David. Instead, he took it to the house of Obed-edom of Gath. 11The Ark of the LORD remained there in Obed-edom's house for three months, and the LORD blessed Obed-edom and his entire household.

12Then King David was told, "The LORD has blessed Obed-edom's household and everything he has because of the Ark of God." So David went there and brought the Ark of God from the house of Obed-edom to the City of David with a great celebration. 13After the men who were carrying the Ark of the LORD had gone six steps, David sacrificed a bull and a fattened calf. 14And David danced before the LORD with all his might, wearing a priestly garment.* 15So David and all the people of Israel brought up the Ark of the LORD with shouts of joy and the blowing of rams' horns.

### Michal's Contempt for David

16But as the Ark of the LORD entered the City of David, Michal, the daughter of Saul, looked down from her window. When she saw King David leaping and dancing before the LORD, she was filled with contempt for him.

17They brought the Ark of the LORD and set it in its place inside the special tent David had prepared for it. And David sacrificed burnt offerings and peace offerings to the LORD. 18When he had finished his sacrifices, David blessed the people in the name of the LORD of Heaven's Armies. 19Then he gave to every Israelite man and woman in the crowd a loaf of bread, a cake of dates,* and a cake of raisins. Then all the people returned to their homes.

20When David returned home to bless his own family, Michal, the daughter of Saul, came out to meet him. She said in disgust, "How distinguished the king of Israel looked today, shamelessly exposing himself to the servant girls like any vulgar person might do!"

21David retorted to Michal, "I was dancing before the LORD, who chose me above your father and all his family! He appointed me as the leader of Israel, the people of the LORD, so I celebrate before the LORD. 22Yes, and I am willing to look even more foolish than this, even to be humiliated in my own eyes! But those servant girls you mentioned will indeed think I am distinguished!" 23So Michal, the daughter of Saul, remained childless throughout her entire life.

**6:6**
Num 4:15
**6:7**
1 Sam 6:19

**6:10**
1 Chr 26:4-5

**6:12-19**
1 Chr 15:25–16:3
**6:12**
1 Kgs 8:1
**6:13**
1 Kgs 8:5
**6:14**
Exod 15:20
1 Sam 2:18, 28

**6:16**
1 Sam 18:27

**6:17**
1 Kgs 8:62-65
1 Chr 15:1
2 Chr 1:4

**6:21**
1 Sam 13:14

6:7 As in Dead Sea Scrolls; Masoretic Text reads *because of his irreverence.*   6:14 Hebrew *a linen ephod.*
6:19 Or *a portion of meat.* The meaning of the Hebrew is uncertain.

---

**6:6, 7** Uzzah was only trying to protect the Ark, so was God's anger against Uzzah just? According to Numbers 4:5-15, the Ark was to be moved only by the Levites, who were to carry it using the carrying poles—they were *never* to touch the Ark itself. To touch it was a capital offense under Hebrew law (Numbers 4:15). God's action was directed against both David and Uzzah. David placed the Ark on a cart, following the Philistines' example (1 Samuel 6:7, 8) rather than God's commands. Uzzah, though sincere in his desire to protect the Ark, had to face the consequences of the sin of touching it. Also, Uzzah may not have been a Levite. As David sought to bring Israel back into a relationship with God, God had to remind the nation dramatically that enthusiasm must be accompanied by obedience to his laws. The next time David tried to bring the Ark to Jerusalem, he was careful to handle it correctly (1 Chronicles 15:1-15).

**6:8-12** David was angry that a well-meaning man had been killed and that his plans for a joyous return of the Ark had been spoiled (6:8). He undoubtedly knew that the fault was his own for transporting the Ark carelessly. After cooling down, he had the Ark put into temporary storage while he waited to see if the Lord would allow him to bring it to Jerusalem. This also gave David time to consider the right way to transport the Ark. The fact that

God blessed the home of Obed-edom was a sign to David that he could try once again to move the Ark to Jerusalem.

**6:14** David wore a priestly garment, possibly because it was a religious celebration.

**6:16ff** Michal was David's first wife, but here she is called daughter of Saul, possibly to show how similar her attitude was to her father's. Her contempt for David probably did not start with David's grand entrance into the city. Perhaps she thought it was undignified to be so concerned with public worship at a time when it was so unimportant in the kingdom. Or maybe she thought it was not fitting for a king to display such emotion. She may have resented David's taking her from Palti (see the note on 3:13, 14). Whatever the reason, this contempt she felt toward her husband escalated into a difficult confrontation, and Michal ended up childless for life. Feelings of bitterness and resentment that go unchecked will destroy a relationship. Deal with your feelings before they escalate into open warfare.

**6:17** Only a priest could place the sacrifices on the altar. Leviticus 1:2-13 indicates that anyone who was ceremonially clean could assist a priest in offering the sacrifice (see the notes on Joshua 3:5; 1 Samuel 20:26). So David probably offered these sacrifices to God with the aid of a priest. Solomon did the same (1 Kings 8:62-65).

**7:1-17**
//1 Chr 17:1-15

**7:2**
2 Sam 5:11
1 Kgs 1:22
1 Chr 29:29

### The LORD's Covenant Promise to David

**7** When King David was settled in his palace and the LORD had given him rest from all the surrounding enemies, ²the king summoned Nathan the prophet. "Look," David said, "I am living in a beautiful cedar palace,* but the Ark of God is out there in a tent!"

³Nathan replied to the king, "Go ahead and do whatever you have in mind, for the LORD is with you."

⁴But that same night the LORD said to Nathan,

**7:2** Hebrew *a house of cedar.*

**MICHAL**

**S**ometimes love is not enough—especially if that love is little more than the strong emotional attraction that grows between a hero and an admirer. To Michal, Saul's daughter, the courageous young David must have seemed like a dream come true. Her feelings about this hero gradually became obvious to others, and eventually, her father heard about her love for David. He saw this as an opportunity to get rid of his rival for the people's loyalty. He promised Michal's hand in marriage in exchange for David's success in the impossible task of killing 100 Philistines. But David was victorious, and so Saul lost a daughter and saw his rival become even more popular with the people.

Michal's love for David did not have time to be tested by the realities of marriage. Instead, she became involved in saving David's life. Her quick thinking helped him escape, but it resulted in Saul's anger and her separation from David. Her father gave her to another man, Palti, but David eventually took her back.

Unlike her brother Jonathan, Michal did not have the kind of deep relationship with God that would have helped her through the difficulties in her life. Instead, she became bitter. She could not share David's joyful worship of God, so she hated it. As a result, she never bore David any children.

Beyond feeling sorry for her, we need to see Michal as a person mirroring our own tendencies. How quickly and easily we become bitter with life's unexpected turns. But bitterness cannot remove or change the bad things that have happened. Often bitterness only makes a bad situation worse. On the other hand, a willingness to respond to God gives him the opportunity to bring good out of the difficult situations. That willingness has two parts: asking God for his guidance and looking for that guidance in his Word.

| | |
|---|---|
| **Strengths and accomplishments** | • Loved David and became his first wife<br>• Saved David's life<br>• Could think and act quickly when it was needed |
| **Weaknesses and mistakes** | • Lied under pressure<br>• Allowed herself to become bitter over her circumstances<br>• In her unhappiness, she hated David for loving God |
| **Lessons from her life** | • We are not as responsible for what happens to us as we are for how we respond to our circumstances<br>• Disobedience to God almost always harms others as well as harming us |
| **Vital statistics** | • Occupations: Daughter of King Saul, wife of King David<br>• Relatives: Parents: Saul and Ahinoam. Brothers: Jonathan, Malkishua, Abinadab, Ishbosheth (and possibly Ishvi). Sister: Merab. Husbands: David, Palti. |
| **Key verse** | "But as the Ark of the LORD entered the City of David, Michal, the daughter of Saul, looked down from her window. When she saw King David leaping and dancing before the LORD, she was filled with contempt for him" (2 Samuel 6:16). |

Michal's story is told in 1 Samuel 14—2 Samuel 6. She is also mentioned in 1 Chronicles 15:29.

---

**7:1ff** This chapter records the covenant God made with David, promising to carry on David's line forever. This promise would be fully realized in the birth of Jesus Christ. Although the word *covenant* is not specifically stated in the Bible text here, it is used elsewhere to describe this occasion (23:5; Psalm 89:28, 34).

**7:2** This is the first time Nathan the prophet is mentioned. God made certain that a prophet was living during the reign of each of the kings of Israel. The prophet's main tasks were to urge the people to follow God and to communicate God's laws and plans to the king. Most of the kings rejected the prophets God sent. But at least God had given them the opportunity to listen and obey. In earlier years, judges and priests had the role of prophets. Samuel served as judge, priest, and prophet, bridging the gap between the period of the judges and the monarchy.

5"Go and tell my servant David, 'This is what the LORD has declared: Are you the one to build a house for me to live in? 6I have never lived in a house, from the day I brought the Israelites out of Egypt until this very day. I have always moved from one place to another with a tent and a Tabernacle as my dwelling. 7Yet no matter where I have gone with the Israelites, I have never once complained to Israel's tribal leaders, the shepherds of my people Israel. I have never asked them, "Why haven't you built me a beautiful cedar house?"'

8"Now go and say to my servant David, 'This is what the LORD of Heaven's Armies has declared: I took you from tending sheep in the pasture and selected you to be the leader of my people Israel. 9I have been with you wherever you have gone, and I have destroyed all your enemies before your eyes. Now I will make your name as famous as anyone who has ever lived on the earth! 10And I will provide a homeland for my people Israel, planting them in a secure place where they will never be disturbed. Evil nations won't oppress them as they've done in the past, 11starting from the time I appointed judges to rule my people Israel. And I will give you rest from all your enemies.

"'Furthermore, the LORD declares that he will make a house for you—a dynasty of kings! 12For when you die and are buried with your ancestors, I will raise up one of your descendants, your own offspring, and I will make his kingdom strong. 13He is the one who will build a house—a temple—for my name. And I will secure his royal throne forever. 14I will be his father, and he will be my son. If he sins, I will correct and discipline him with the rod, like any father would do. 15But my favor will not be taken from him as I took it from Saul, whom I removed from your sight. 16Your house and your kingdom will continue before me* for all time, and your throne will be secure forever.'"

17So Nathan went back to David and told him everything the LORD had said in this vision.

## David's Prayer of Thanks

18Then King David went in and sat before the LORD and prayed,

"Who am I, O Sovereign LORD, and what is my family, that you have brought me this far? 19And now, Sovereign LORD, in addition to everything else, you speak of giving your servant a lasting dynasty! Do you deal with everyone this way, O Sovereign LORD?*

20"What more can I say to you? You know what your servant is really like, Sovereign LORD. 21Because of your promise and according to your will, you have done all these great things and have made them known to your servant.

22"How great you are, O Sovereign LORD! There is no one like you. We have never even heard of another God like you! 23What other nation on earth is like your people Israel? What other nation, O God, have you redeemed from slavery to be your own people? You made a great name for yourself when you redeemed your people from Egypt. You performed awesome miracles and drove out the nations and gods that stood in their way.* 24You made Israel your very own people forever, and you, O LORD, became their God.

7:16 As in Greek version and some Hebrew manuscripts; Masoretic Text reads before you.   7:19 Or This is your instruction for all humanity, O Sovereign LORD.   7:23 As in Greek version (see also 1 Chr 17:21); Hebrew reads You made a great name for yourself and performed awesome miracles for your land. You did this in the sight of your people, whom you redeemed from Egypt, from nations and their gods.

### Cross-references

7:5 1 Kgs 5:3, 5; 8:17-19
7:6 Exod 40:18, 34 1 Kgs 8:16
7:7 Lev 26:11-12
7:8 1 Sam 16:10-11 Ps 78:70-71 †2 Cor 6:18
7:9 Ps 18:37-42
7:10 Ps 89:22 Isa 60:18
7:11 1 Sam 12:9-11; 25:28
7:12 1 Kgs 2:1 †Acts 2:30
7:13 1 Kgs 6:11-12; 8:19 Isa 9:7
7:14 Ps 89:26-27 Heb 1:5-6
7:15 1 Sam 15:23; 16:14 Ps 89:33
7:16 1 Sam 25:28 Ps 89:36-37
7:18-29 //1 Chr 17:16-27
7:18 Exod 3:11 1 Sam 18:18
7:19 1 Chr 17:17 Isa 55:8-9
7:22 Exod 10:2 Deut 3:24 1 Sam 2:2 Ps 44:1
7:23 Deut 4:32; 9:26; 10:21
7:24 Gen 17:7-8 Exod 6:7 Deut 32:6 Ps 48:14

---

7:5 In this message from Nathan, God is saying that he doesn't want David to build a temple for him. God told David that his job was to unify and lead Israel and to destroy its enemies. This huge task would require David to shed a great deal of blood. In 1 Chronicles 28:3, we learn that God did not want his Temple built by a warrior. Therefore, David made the plans and collected the materials so that his son Solomon could begin work on the Temple as soon as he became king (1 Kings 5–7). David accepted his part in God's plan and did not try to go beyond it. Sometimes God says no to our plans. When he does, we should utilize the other opportunities he gives us.

7:8-16 David's request was good, but God said no. This does not mean that God rejected David. In fact, God was planning to do something even greater in David's life than allowing him the prestige of building the Temple. Although God turned down David's request, he promised to continue the house (or dynasty) of David forever. David's earthly dynasty ended four centuries later, but Jesus Christ, a direct descendant of David, was the ultimate fulfillment of this promise (Acts 2:22-36). Christ will reign for eternity—now in his spiritual kingdom and in heaven, and later, on earth, in the new Jerusalem (Luke 1:30-33; Revelation 21). Have you prayed with good intentions, only to have God say no? This is God's way of directing you to a greater purpose in your life. Accepting God's no requires as great a faith as carrying out his yes.

7:18ff This section records David's prayer expressing his humble acceptance of God's promise to extend his dynasty forever. David realized that these blessings were given to him and his descendants in order that Israel might benefit from them. They would help fulfill God's greater purpose and promises that through the nation the whole world would be blessed (Genesis 12:1-3).

25 "And now, O LORD God, I am your servant; do as you have promised concerning me and my family. Confirm it as a promise that will last forever. 26 And may your name be honored forever so that everyone will say, 'The LORD of Heaven's Armies is God over Israel!' And may the house of your servant David continue before you forever.

27 "O LORD of Heaven's Armies, God of Israel, I have been bold enough to pray this prayer to you because you have revealed all this to your servant, saying, 'I will build a house for you—a dynasty of kings!' 28 For you are God, O Sovereign LORD. Your words are truth, and you have promised these good things to your servant. 29 And now, may it please you to bless the house of your servant, so that it may continue forever before you. For you have spoken, and when you grant a blessing to your servant, O Sovereign LORD, it is an eternal blessing!"

### 3. David conquers the surrounding nations
*David's Military Victories*

**8** After this, David defeated and subdued the Philistines by conquering Gath, their largest town.* 2 David also conquered the land of Moab. He made the people lie down on the ground in a row, and he measured them off in groups with a length of rope. He measured off two groups to be executed for every one group to be spared. The Moabites who were spared became David's subjects and paid him tribute money.

3 David also destroyed the forces of Hadadezer son of Rehob, king of Zobah, when Hadadezer marched out to strengthen his control along the Euphrates River. 4 David captured 1,000 chariots, 7,000 charioteers,* and 20,000 foot soldiers. He crippled all the chariot horses except enough for 100 chariots.

**8:1** Hebrew *by conquering Metheg-ammah*, a name that means "the bridle," possibly referring to the size of the town or the tribute money taken from it. Compare 1 Chr 18:1. **8:4** As in Dead Sea Scrolls and Greek version (see also 1 Chr 18:4); Masoretic Text reads *captured 1,700 charioteers.*

**7:28**
Exod 34:5-6
John 17:17
**7:29**
Num 6:23-27

**8:1-14**
//1 Chr 18:1-13
**8:2**
2 Kgs 3:4; 17:3

**8:3**
1 Sam 14:47
2 Sam 10:16, 19
**8:4**
Josh 11:6, 9

---

**COVENANTS**
A covenant is a legally binding obligation (promise). Throughout history God has made covenants with his people— he would keep his side if they would keep theirs. Here are seven covenants found in the Bible.

| Name and Reference | God's Promise | Sign |
|---|---|---|
| In Eden Genesis 3:15 | Satan and mankind will be enemies. | Pain of childbirth |
| Noah Genesis 9:8-17 | God would never again destroy the earth with a flood. | Rainbow |
| Abraham Genesis 15:12-21; 17:1-14 | Abraham's descendants would become a great nation if they obeyed God. God would be their God forever. | Smoking firepot and flaming torch |
| At Mount Sinai Exodus 19:5, 6 | Israel would be God's special people, a holy nation. But they would have to keep their part of the covenant— obedience. | The Exodus |
| The Priesthood Numbers 25:10-13 | Aaron's descendants would be priests forever. | The Aaronic priesthood |
| David 2 Samuel 7:13; 23:5 | Salvation would come through David's line through the birth of the Messiah. | David's line continued, and the Messiah was born a descendant of David |
| New Covenant Hebrews 8:6-13 | Forgiveness and salvation are available through faith in Christ. | Christ's resurrection |

---

**8:1-5** Part of God's covenant with David included the promise that the Israelites' enemies would be defeated and would no longer oppress them (7:10, 11). God fulfilled this promise by helping David defeat the opposing nations. Several enemies are listed in this chapter: (1) *The Moabites*, descendants of Lot who lived east of the Dead Sea. They posed a constant military and religious threat to Israel (Numbers 25:1-3; Judges 3:12-30; 1 Samuel 14:47). David seemed to have a good relationship with the Moabites at one time; David's great-grandmother Ruth had been from Moab. (2) *King Hadadezer of Zobah*. His defeat at David's hands fulfilled God's promise to Abraham that Israel would control the land as far north as the Euphrates River (Genesis 15:18). (3) *The Edomites*, descendants of Esau (Genesis 36:1) who were also archenemies of Israel (see 2 Kings 8:20; Jeremiah 49:7-22; Ezekiel 25:12-14; and the note on Genesis 36:9).

⁵When Arameans from Damascus arrived to help King Hadadezer, David killed 22,000 of them. ⁶Then he placed several army garrisons in Damascus, the Aramean capital, and the Arameans became David's subjects and paid him tribute money. So the LORD made David victorious wherever he went.

⁷David brought the gold shields of Hadadezer's officers to Jerusalem, ⁸along with a large amount of bronze from Hadadezer's towns of Tebah* and Berothai.

⁹When King Toi of Hamath heard that David had destroyed the entire army of Hadadezer, ¹⁰he sent his son Joram to congratulate King David for his successful campaign. Hadadezer and Toi had been enemies and were often at war. Joram presented David with many gifts of silver, gold, and bronze.

¹¹King David dedicated all these gifts to the LORD, as he did with the silver and gold from the other nations he had defeated—¹²from Edom,* Moab, Ammon, Philistia, and Amalek—and from Hadadezer son of Rehob, king of Zobah.

¹³So David became even more famous when he returned from destroying 18,000 Edomites* in the Valley of Salt. ¹⁴He placed army garrisons throughout Edom, and all the Edomites became David's subjects. In fact, the LORD made David victorious wherever he went.

¹⁵So David reigned over all Israel and did what was just and right for all his people. ¹⁶Joab son of Zeruiah was commander of the army. Jehoshaphat son of Ahilud was the royal historian. ¹⁷Zadok son of Ahitub and Ahimelech son of Abiathar were the priests. Seraiah was the court secretary. ¹⁸Benaiah son of Jehoiada was captain of the king's bodyguard.* And David's sons served as priestly leaders.*

### David's Kindness to Mephibosheth

**9** One day David asked, "Is anyone in Saul's family still alive—anyone to whom I can show kindness for Jonathan's sake?" ²He summoned a man named Ziba, who had been one of Saul's servants. "Are you Ziba?" the king asked.

"Yes sir, I am," Ziba replied.

³The king then asked him, "Is anyone still alive from Saul's family? If so, I want to show God's kindness to them."

Ziba replied, "Yes, one of Jonathan's sons is still alive. He is crippled in both feet."

⁴"Where is he?" the king asked.

"In Lo-debar," Ziba told him, "at the home of Makir son of Ammiel."

**8:5** 1 Kgs 11:23-25
**8:6** 2 Sam 3:18
**8:7** 1 Kgs 10:16
**8:8** Ezek 47:16
**8:11** 1 Kgs 7:51
**8:13** 2 Kgs 14:7; 1 Chr 18:12
**8:14** Gen 27:30, 37-40
**8:15-18** //1 Chr 18:14-17
**8:16** 2 Sam 2:13
**8:18** 2 Sam 20:7, 23; 1 Kgs 1:38, 44; 1 Chr 18:17
**9:1** 1 Sam 20:14-17, 42
**9:2** 2 Sam 16:1-4; 19:17
**9:3** 1 Sam 20:15; 2 Sam 4:4
**9:4** 2 Sam 17:27-29

**8:8** As in some Greek manuscripts (see also 1 Chr 18:8); Hebrew reads *Betah*.   **8:12** As in a few Hebrew manuscripts and Greek and Syriac versions (see also 8:14; 1 Chr 18:11); most Hebrew manuscripts read *Aram*.   **8:13** As in a few Hebrew manuscripts and Greek and Syriac versions (see also 8:14; 1 Chr 18:12); most Hebrew manuscripts read *Arameans*.   **8:18a** Hebrew *of the Kerethites and Pelethites*.   **8:18b** Hebrew *David's sons were priests;* compare parallel text at 1 Chr 18:17.

---

**8:6** The *tribute money* was the tax levied on conquered nations. The tax helped to support Israel's government and demonstrated that the conquered nation was under Israel's control.

**DAVID'S ENEMIES**
David wanted to complete the conquest of Canaan begun by Joshua. He defeated the Jebusites at Jerusalem and the Philistines in the vicinity of Gath. The Ammonites, Arameans, and Moabites became his subjects. He put garrisons in Edom and levied a tax upon them.

**8:15** David pleased the people (3:36), not because he tried to please them, but because he tried to please God. Often those who try the hardest to become popular never make it. But the praise of people is not that important. Don't spend your time devising ways to become accepted in the public eye. Instead, strive to do what is right, and both God and people will respect your convictions.

**8:15** King David's reign was characterized by doing what was "just and right." David was fair in interpreting the law, administering punishment with mercy, respecting people's rights, and recognizing people's duty toward God. Is it any wonder that almost everyone trusted and followed David? Why was it good for David to pursue justice? (1) It was God's command (Deuteronomy 16:18-20) and in keeping with his character (Deuteronomy 32:4). God's laws were meant to establish a just society. (2) It was in the nation's best interest because times would arise when each individual would need justice. Justice should characterize the way you relate to people. Make sure you are fair in the way you treat them.

**9:1ff** Most kings in David's day tried to wipe out the families of their rivals in order to prevent any descendants from seeking the throne. But David showed kindness to Mephibosheth, whose father was Jonathan and whose grandfather was King Saul. David was kind, partly because of his loyalty to God's previously anointed king (see the note on 1 Samuel 24:5, 6); partly for political reasons—to unite Judah and Israel (see the notes on 3:13, 14 and 3:29); and mainly because of his vow to show kindness to all of Jonathan's descendants (1 Samuel 20:14-17).

⁵So David sent for him and brought him from Makir's home. ⁶His name was Mephibosheth*; he was Jonathan's son and Saul's grandson. When he came to David, he bowed low to the ground in deep respect. David said, "Greetings, Mephibosheth."

Mephibosheth replied, "I am your servant."

**9:7**
2 Sam 19:28
2 Kgs 25:29

⁷"Don't be afraid!" David said. "I intend to show kindness to you because of my promise to your father, Jonathan. I will give you all the property that once belonged to your grandfather Saul, and you will eat here with me at the king's table!"

⁸Mephibosheth bowed respectfully and exclaimed, "Who is your servant, that you should show such kindness to a dead dog like me?"

**9:9**
2 Sam 16:4; 19:29
**9:10**
2 Sam 19:28

⁹Then the king summoned Saul's servant Ziba and said, "I have given your master's grandson everything that belonged to Saul and his family. ¹⁰You and your sons and servants are to farm the land for him to produce food for your master's household.* But Mephibosheth, your master's grandson, will eat here at my table." (Ziba had fifteen sons and twenty servants.)

¹¹Ziba replied, "Yes, my lord the king; I am your servant, and I will do all that you have commanded." And from that time on, Mephibosheth ate regularly at David's table,* like one of the king's own sons.

¹²Mephibosheth had a young son named Mica. From then on, all the members of Ziba's household were Mephibosheth's servants. ¹³And Mephibosheth, who was crippled in both feet, lived in Jerusalem and ate regularly at the king's table.

### David Defeats the Ammonites

**10:1-19**
//1 Chr 19:1-19

**10** Some time after this, King Nahash* of the Ammonites died, and his son Hanun became king. ²David said, "I am going to show loyalty to Hanun just as his father, Nahash, was always loyal to me." So David sent ambassadors to express sympathy to Hanun about his father's death.

But when David's ambassadors arrived in the land of Ammon, ³the Ammonite commanders said to Hanun, their master, "Do you really think these men are coming here to honor your father? No! David has sent them to spy out the city so they can come in and conquer it!"

**10:4**
Isa 15:2; 20:4
Jer 41:5

⁴So Hanun seized David's ambassadors and shaved off half of each man's beard, cut off their robes at the buttocks, and sent them back to David in shame.

⁵When David heard what had happened, he sent messengers to tell the men, "Stay at Jericho until your beards grow out, and then come back." For they felt deep shame because of their appearance.

**10:6**
Gen 34:30
2 Kgs 7:6

**9:6** *Mephibosheth* is another name for Merib-baal. **9:10** As in Greek version; Hebrew reads *your master's grandson.* **9:11** As in Greek version; Hebrew reads *my table.* **10:1** As in parallel text at 1 Chr 19:1; Hebrew reads *the king.*

---

**9:3** How Mephibosheth became crippled is recorded in 4:4. Mephibosheth was five years old when Saul and Jonathan died.

**9:5, 6** Mephibosheth was afraid to visit the king, who wanted to treat him like a prince. Although Mephibosheth feared for his life and may have felt unworthy, that didn't mean he should refuse David's gifts. When God graciously offers us forgiveness of sins and a place in heaven, we may feel unworthy, but we will receive these gifts if we accept them. A reception even warmer than the one David gave Mephibosheth waits for all who receive God's gifts through trusting Jesus Christ, not because we deserve it, but because of God's promise (Ephesians 2:8, 9).

**9:7** His treatment of Mephibosheth shows David's integrity as a leader who accepted his obligation to show love and mercy. His generous provision for Jonathan's son goes beyond any political benefit he might have received. Are you able to forgive those who have wronged you? Can you be generous with those less deserving? Each time we show compassion, our character is strengthened.

**10:4, 5** In Israelite culture, all men wore full beards. It was a sign of maturity and authority. Thus when these ambassadors had their beards half shaved, they suffered great indignity. Cutting off their robes also exposed them to ridicule.

**10:6** Because Hanun took the wrong advice, he suspected the motives of the ambassadors and humiliated them. Then he realized that David was angry and immediately marshaled his forces for battle. Hanun should have thought through the advice more carefully; but even if he had not, he should have tried to negotiate

with David. Instead, he refused to admit any fault and got ready for war. Often we respond angrily and defensively rather than admitting our mistakes, apologizing, and trying to defuse the other person's anger. Instead of fighting, we should seek peace.

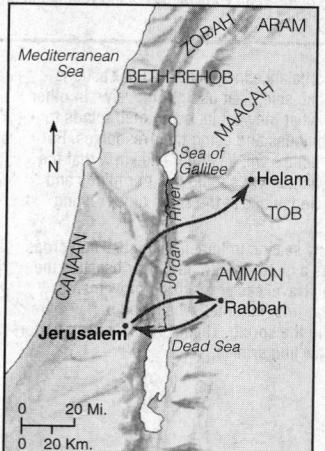

**DAVID AND THE AMMONITES**
Ammon gathered together its troops from the north; Joab brought the Israelite army to attack them near Rabbah. Joab returned to Jerusalem victorious, but the enemy recruited additional forces and regrouped at Helam. David himself led the next victorious attack.

6When the people of Ammon realized how seriously they had angered David, they sent and hired 20,000 Aramean foot soldiers from the lands of Beth-rehob and Zobah, 1,000 from the king of Maacah, and 12,000 from the land of Tob. 7When David heard about this, he sent Joab and all his warriors to fight them. 8The Ammonite troops came out and drew up their battle lines at the entrance of the city gate, while the Arameans from Zobah and Rehob and the men from Tob and Maacah positioned themselves to fight in the open fields.

9When Joab saw that he would have to fight on both the front and the rear, he chose some of Israel's elite troops and placed them under his personal command to fight the Arameans in the fields. 10He left the rest of the army under the command of his brother Abishai, who was to attack the Ammonites. 11"If the Arameans are too strong for me, then come over and help me," Joab told his brother. "And if the Ammonites are too strong for you, I will come and help you. 12Be courageous! Let us fight bravely for our people and the cities of our God. May the LORD's will be done."

**10:12**
Deut 31:6
1 Sam 3:18
1 Cor 16:13

13When Joab and his troops attacked, the Arameans began to run away. 14And when the Ammonites saw the Arameans running, they ran from Abishai and retreated into the city. After the battle was over, Joab returned to Jerusalem.

**10:13**
1 Kgs 20:13-21

15The Arameans now realized that they were no match for Israel. So when they regrouped, 16they were joined by additional Aramean troops summoned by Hadadezer from the other side of the Euphrates River.* These troops arrived at Helam under the command of Shobach, the commander of Hadadezer's forces.

17When David heard what was happening, he mobilized all Israel, crossed the Jordan River, and led the army to Helam. The Arameans positioned themselves in battle formation and fought against David. 18But again the Arameans fled from the Israelites. This time David's forces killed 700 charioteers and 40,000 foot soldiers,* including Shobach, the commander of their army. 19When all the kings allied with Hadadezer saw that they had been defeated by Israel, they surrendered to Israel and became their subjects. After that, the Arameans were afraid to help the Ammonites.

**10:18**
1 Chr 19:17-18

**10:19**
2 Sam 8:6

## B. DAVID'S STRUGGLES (11:1—24:25)
After restoring the nation to peace and great military power, David's personal life becomes entangled in sin. He commits adultery with Bathsheba and then orders her husband killed in an attempted cover-up. David deeply regretted what he had done and sought God's forgiveness, but the child of his sinful act died. We may be forgiven by God for our sins, but we will often experience harsh consequences.

## 1. David and Bathsheba
*David Sins with Bathsheba*

**11** In the spring of the year,* when kings normally go out to war, David sent Joab and the Israelite army to fight the Ammonites. They destroyed the Ammonite army and laid siege to the city of Rabbah. However, David stayed behind in Jerusalem.

**11:1**
2 Sam 12:26-29
1 Chr 20:1
Amos 1:14

**10:16** Hebrew *the river.*   **10:18** As in some Greek manuscripts (see also 1 Chr 19:18); Hebrew reads *charioteers.*
**11:1** Hebrew *At the turn of the year.* The first day of the year in the ancient Hebrew lunar calendar occurred in March or April.

---

**10:12** There must be a balance in life between our actions and our faith in God. Joab said, "Let us fight bravely." In other words, they should do what they could, using their minds to figure out the best techniques and using their resources. But he also said, "May the LORD's will be done." He knew that the outcome was in God's hands. We should use our minds and our resources to obey God, while at the same time trusting God for the outcome.

**11:1** Winter is the rainy season in Israel, the time when crops are planted. Spring was a good time to go to war because the roads were dry, making travel easier for troop movements, supply wagons, and chariots. In Israel, wheat and barley were ready to be harvested in the spring. These crops were an important food source for traveling armies.

**11:1** This successful siege (see 12:26, 27) put an end to the Ammonites' power. From this time on, the Ammonites were subject to Israel.

**11:1ff** In the episode with Bathsheba, David allowed himself to fall deeper and deeper into sin. (1) David abandoned his purpose by staying home from war (11:1). (2) He focused on his own desires (11:2). (3) When temptation came, he looked into it instead of turning away from it (11:3). (4) He sinned deliberately (11:4). (5) He tried to cover up his sin by deceiving others (11:6-15). (6) He committed murder to continue the cover-up (11:15, 17). Eventually David's sin was exposed (12:9) and punished (12:10-14). (7) The consequences of David's sin were far-reaching, affecting many others (11:17; 12:11, 14, 15).

David could have chosen to stop and turn from evil at any stage along the way. But once sin gets started, it is difficult to stop (James 1:14, 15). The deeper the mess, the less we want to admit having caused it. It's much easier to stop sliding down a hill when you are near the top than when you are halfway down. The best solution is to stop sin before it starts.

2 SAMUEL 11

**11:2**
Deut 22:8

**11:3**
2 Sam 23:39
1 Chr 3:5

**11:4**
Lev 15:19;
18:20-28
Ps 51:title

**11:5**
Lev 20:10
Deut 22:22

**11:11**
2 Sam 7:2

²Late one afternoon, after his midday rest, David got out of bed and was walking on the roof of the palace. As he looked out over the city, he noticed a woman of unusual beauty taking a bath. ³He sent someone to find out who she was, and he was told, "She is Bathsheba, the daughter of Eliam and the wife of Uriah the Hittite." ⁴Then David sent messengers to get her; and when she came to the palace, he slept with her. She had just completed the purification rites after having her menstrual period. Then she returned home. ⁵Later, when Bathsheba discovered that she was pregnant, she sent David a message, saying, "I'm pregnant."

⁶Then David sent word to Joab: "Send me Uriah the Hittite." So Joab sent him to David. ⁷When Uriah arrived, David asked him how Joab and the army were getting along and how the war was progressing. ⁸Then he told Uriah, "Go on home and relax.*" David even sent a gift to Uriah after he had left the palace. ⁹But Uriah didn't go home. He slept that night at the palace entrance with the king's palace guard.

¹⁰When David heard that Uriah had not gone home, he summoned him and asked, "What's the matter? Why didn't you go home last night after being away for so long?" ¹¹Uriah replied, "The Ark and the armies of Israel and Judah are living in tents,* and Joab and my master's men are camping in the open fields. How could I go home to wine and dine and sleep with my wife? I swear that I would never do such a thing."

¹²"Well, stay here today," David told him, "and tomorrow you may return to the army." So Uriah stayed in Jerusalem that day and the next. ¹³Then David invited him to dinner and got

**11:8** Hebrew *and wash your feet,* an expression that may also have a connotation of ritualistic washing.
**11:11** Or *at Succoth.*

| DAVID'S FAMILY TROUBLES | Wife | Children | What Happened |
|---|---|---|---|
| | Michal (Saul's daughter) | She was childless | David gave her five nephews to the Gibeonites to be killed because of Saul's sins |
| | Ahinoam (from Jezreel) | Amnon, David's first-born | He raped Tamar, his half sister, and was later murdered by Absalom in revenge |
| | Maacah (daughter of King Talmai of Geshur) | Absalom, third son Tamar, the only daughter mentioned by name | Absalom killed Amnon for raping Tamar and then fled to Geshur. Later he returned, only to rebel against David. He set up a tent on the roof and slept with 10 of his father's concubines there. His pride led to his death. |
| | Haggith | Adonijah, fourth son. He was very handsome, but it is recorded that he was never disciplined | He set himself up as king before David's death. His plot was exposed, and David spared his life, but his half brother Solomon later had him executed |
| | Bathsheba | Unnamed son | Died in fulfillment of God's punishment for David and Bathsheba's adultery |
| | Bathsheba | Solomon | Became the next king of Israel. Ironically Solomon's many wives caused his downfall |

David's many wives caused him much grief. And as a result of David's sin with Bathsheba, God said that murder would be a constant threat in his family, his family would rebel, and someone else would sleep with his wives. All this happened as the prophet Nathan had predicted. The consequences of sin affect not only us but those we know and love. Remember that the next time you are tempted to sin.

**11:3** See 1 Kings 1, p. 511 for Bathsheba's Profile.

**11:3, 4** As David looked from the roof of the palace, he saw a beautiful woman bathing, and he was filled with lust. David should have left the roof and fled the temptation. Instead, he entertained the temptation by inquiring about Bathsheba. The results were devastating.

To flee temptation, (1) ask God in earnest prayer to help you stay away from people, places, and situations that may tempt you. (2) Memorize and meditate on portions of Scripture that combat your specific weaknesses. At the root of most temptation is a real need or desire that God can fill, but we must trust in his timing. (3) Find another believer with whom you can openly share your struggles, and call this person for help when temptation strikes.

**11:4** That Bathsheba had just completed the purification rites following menstruation means that she could not have already been pregnant by her own husband when David slept with her. Leviticus 15:19-30 gives more information on the purification rites Bathsheba had to perform.

him drunk. But even then he couldn't get Uriah to go home to his wife. Again he slept at the palace entrance with the king's palace guard.

### David Arranges for Uriah's Death

14So the next morning David wrote a letter to Joab and gave it to Uriah to deliver. 15The letter instructed Joab, "Station Uriah on the front lines where the battle is fiercest. Then pull back so that he will be killed." 16So Joab assigned Uriah to a spot close to the city wall where he knew the enemy's strongest men were fighting. 17And when the enemy soldiers came out of the city to fight, Uriah the Hittite was killed along with several other Israelite soldiers.

18Then Joab sent a battle report to David. 19He told his messenger, "Report all the news of the battle to the king. 20But he might get angry and ask, 'Why did the troops go so close to the city? Didn't they know there would be shooting from the walls? 21Wasn't Abimelech son of Gideon* killed at Thebez by a woman who threw a millstone down on him from the wall? Why would you get so close to the wall?' Then tell him, 'Uriah the Hittite was killed, too.'"

22So the messenger went to Jerusalem and gave a complete report to David. 23"The enemy came out against us in the open fields," he said. "And as we chased them back to the city gate, 24the archers on the wall shot arrows at us. Some of the king's men were killed, including Uriah the Hittite."

25"Well, tell Joab not to be discouraged," David said. "The sword devours this one today and that one tomorrow! Fight harder next time, and conquer the city!"

26When Uriah's wife heard that her husband was dead, she mourned for him. 27When the period of mourning was over, David sent for her and brought her to the palace, and she became one of his wives. Then she gave birth to a son. But the LORD was displeased with what David had done.

### Nathan Rebukes David

**12** So the LORD sent Nathan the prophet to tell David this story: "There were two men in a certain town. One was rich, and one was poor. 2The rich man owned a great many sheep and cattle. 3The poor man owned nothing but one little lamb he had bought. He raised that little lamb, and it grew up with his children. It ate from the man's own plate and drank from his cup. He cuddled it in his arms like a baby daughter. 4One day a guest arrived at the home of the rich man. But instead of killing an animal from his own flock or herd, he took the poor man's lamb and killed it and prepared it for his guest."

5David was furious. "As surely as the LORD lives," he vowed, "any man who would do such a thing deserves to die! 6He must repay four lambs to the poor man for the one he stole and for having no pity."

7Then Nathan said to David, "You are that man! The LORD, the God of Israel, says: I anointed you king of Israel and saved you from the power of Saul. 8I gave you your master's house and his wives and the kingdoms of Israel and Judah. And if that had not been enough, I would have given you much, much more. 9Why, then, have you despised the word of the LORD and done this horrible deed? For you have murdered Uriah the Hittite with the sword

**11:14**
1 Kgs 21:8-10
**11:15**
2 Sam 12:9

**11:21**
Judg 9:50-54

**11:26**
Deut 34:8
1 Sam 31:13
**11:27**
Ps 51:4-5

**12:1**
2 Sam 7:2, 17
Ps 51:title

**12:5**
1 Kgs 20:40
**12:6**
Exod 22:1
**12:7**
1 Sam 16:13
1 Kgs 20:42
**12:8**
2 Sam 9:7
**12:9**
2 Sam 11:14-17, 27

**11:21** Hebrew *son of Jerub-besheth*. Jerub-besheth is a variation on the name Jerub-baal, which is another name for Gideon; see Judg 6:32.

---

**11:15** David put both Bathsheba and Joab in difficult situations. Bathsheba knew it was wrong to commit adultery, but to refuse a king's request could mean punishment or death. Joab did not know why Uriah had to die, but it was obvious the king wanted him killed. We sometimes face situations with only two apparent choices, and both seem wrong. When that happens, we must not lose sight of what God wants. The answer may be to seek out more choices. By doing this, we are likely to find a choice that honors God.

**11:25** David's response to Uriah's death seems flippant and insensitive. While he grieved deeply for Saul and Abner, his rivals (chapter 1; 3:31-39), he showed no grief for Uriah, a good man with strong spiritual character. Why? David had become callous to his own sin. The only way he could cover up his first sin (adultery) was to sin again, and soon he no longer felt guilty for what he had done. Feelings are not reliable guides for determining right and wrong. Deliberate, repeated sinning had dulled David's sensitivity to God's laws and others' rights. The more you try to cover up a sin, the more insensitive you become toward it. Don't

become hardened to sin, as David did. Confess your wrong actions to God before you forget they are sins.

**12:1ff** As a prophet, Nathan was required to confront sin, even the sin of a king. It took great courage, skill, and tact to speak to David in a way that would make him aware of his wrong actions. When you have to confront someone with unpleasant news, pray for courage, skill, and tact. If you want that person to respond constructively, think through what you are going to say. How you present your message may be as important as what you say. Season your words with wisdom.

**12:5, 6** It was a year later, and by then David had become so insensitive to his own sins that he didn't realize he was the villain in Nathan's story. The qualities we condemn in others are often our own character flaws. Which friends, associates, or family members do you find easy to criticize and hard to accept? Instead of trying to change them, ask God to help you understand their feelings and see your own flaws more clearly. You may discover that in condemning others, you have been condemning yourself.

**12:10**
2 Sam 13:28-29;
18:14
1 Kgs 2:23
**12:11**
2 Sam 16:21-22

of the Ammonites and stolen his wife. 10From this time on, your family will live by the sword because you have despised me by taking Uriah's wife to be your own.

11"This is what the LORD says: Because of what you have done, I will cause your own household to rebel against you. I will give your wives to another man before your very eyes, and he will go to bed with them in public view. 12You did it secretly, but I will make this happen to you openly in the sight of all Israel."

**12:13**
Lev 20:10; 24:17
Prov 28:13
Mic 7:18
Luke 18:13
**12:14**
Isa 52:5
Rom 2:23-24

### David Confesses His Guilt

13Then David confessed to Nathan, "I have sinned against the LORD."

Nathan replied, "Yes, but the LORD has forgiven you, and you won't die for this sin. 14Nevertheless, because you have shown utter contempt for the LORD* by doing this, your child will die."

**12:14** As in Dead Sea Scrolls; Masoretic Text reads *the LORD's enemies.*

**NATHAN**

This prophet lived up to the meaning of his name, "He [God] has given." He was a necessary and helpful gift from God to David. He served as God's spokesman to David and proved himself a fearless friend and counselor, always willing to speak the truth, even when he knew great pain would result.

In confronting David's multiple sin of coveting, theft, adultery, and murder in his affair with Bathsheba, Nathan was able to help David see his own wrongdoing by showing that he would not have tolerated such actions from anyone else. David's repentance allowed Nathan to comfort him with the reality of God's forgiveness and at the same time remind him of the painful consequences his sin would bring.

Nathan's approach helps us judge our actions. How often do we make choices that we would condemn others for making? It is helpful to ask ourselves how God and others see our actions. Unfortunately, we have a huge capacity to lie to ourselves. God still provides two safeguards against self-deception: his Word and true friends. In each case, we get a view beyond ourselves. You are holding God's Word. Let it speak to you about yourself, even if the truth is painful. If you don't have a friend like Nathan, ask God for one. And ask God to use you as a suitable Nathan for someone else.

| | |
|---|---|
| **Strengths and accomplishments** | • A trusted adviser to David<br>• A prophet of God<br>• A fearless but careful confronter<br>• One of God's controls in David's life |
| **Weakness and mistake** | • His eagerness to see David build a temple for God in Jerusalem made him speak without God's instruction |
| **Lessons from his life** | • We should not be afraid to tell the truth to those we care about<br>• A trustworthy companion is one of God's greatest gifts<br>• God cares enough to find a way to communicate to us when we are in the wrong |
| **Vital statistics** | • Occupations: Prophet, royal adviser<br>• Contemporaries: David, Bathsheba, Solomon, Zadok, Adonijah |
| **Key verse** | "So Nathan went back to David and told him everything the LORD had said" (2 Samuel 7:17). |

Nathan's story is told in 2 Samuel 7—1 Kings 1. He is also mentioned in 1 Chronicles 17:15; 2 Chronicles 9:29; 29:25.

**12:10-14** The predictions in these verses came true. Because David murdered Uriah and stole his wife, (1) murder was a constant threat in his family (13:26-30; 18:14, 15; 1 Kings 2:23-25); (2) his household rebelled against him (15:13); (3) his wives were given to another in public view (16:20-23); (4) his first child by Bathsheba died (12:18). If David had known the painful consequences of his sin, he might not have pursued the pleasures of the moment.

**12:13** During this incident, David wrote Psalm 51, giving valuable insight into his character and offering hope for us as well. No matter how miserable guilt makes you feel or how terribly you have sinned, you can pour out your heart to God and seek his forgiveness as David did. There is forgiveness for us when we sin. David also wrote Psalm 32 to express the joy he felt after he was forgiven.

**12:14** David confessed and repented of his sin (12:13), but God's judgment was that his child would die. The consequences of David's sin were irreversible. Sometimes an apology isn't enough.

When God forgives us and restores our relationship with him, he doesn't eliminate all the consequences of our wrongdoing. We may be tempted to say, "If this is wrong, I can always apologize to God," but we must remember that we may set into motion events with irreversible consequences.

**12:14** Why did this child have to die? This was not a judgment on the child for being conceived out of wedlock, but a judgment on David for his sin. David and Bathsheba deserved to die, but God spared their lives and took the child instead. God still had work for David to do in building the kingdom. The child's death was a horrible punishment for David and Bathsheba to bear.

It is also possible that had the child lived, God's name would have been dishonored among Israel's pagan neighbors. What would they have thought of a God who rewards murder and adultery by giving a king a new heir? A baby's death is tragic, but despising God brings death to entire nations. While God readily forgave David's sin, he did not negate all its consequences.

15After Nathan returned to his home, the Lord sent a deadly illness to the child of David and Uriah's wife. 16David begged God to spare the child. He went without food and lay all night on the bare ground. 17The elders of his household pleaded with him to get up and eat with them, but he refused.

18Then on the seventh day the child died. David's advisers were afraid to tell him. "He wouldn't listen to reason while the child was ill," they said. "What drastic thing will he do when we tell him the child is dead?"

19When David saw them whispering, he realized what had happened. "Is the child dead?" he asked.

"Yes," they replied, "he is dead."

20Then David got up from the ground, washed himself, put on lotions,* and changed his clothes. He went to the Tabernacle and worshiped the Lord. After that, he returned to the palace and was served food and ate.

21His advisers were amazed. "We don't understand you," they told him. "While the child was still living, you wept and refused to eat. But now that the child is dead, you have stopped your mourning and are eating again."

22David replied, "I fasted and wept while the child was alive, for I said, 'Perhaps the Lord will be gracious to me and let the child live.' 23But why should I fast when he is dead? Can I bring him back again? I will go to him one day, but he cannot return to me."

24Then David comforted Bathsheba, his wife, and slept with her. She became pregnant and gave birth to a son, and David* named him Solomon. The Lord loved the child 25and sent word through Nathan the prophet that they should name him Jedidiah (which means "beloved of the Lord"), as the Lord had commanded.*

## David Captures Rabbah

26Meanwhile, Joab was fighting against Rabbah, the capital of Ammon, and he captured the royal fortifications.* 27Joab sent messengers to tell David, "I have fought against Rabbah and captured its water supply.* 28Now bring the rest of the army and capture the city. Otherwise, I will capture it and get credit for the victory."

29So David gathered the rest of the army and went to Rabbah, and he fought against it and captured it. 30David removed the crown from the king's head,* and it was placed on his own head. The crown was made of gold and set with gems, and it weighed seventy-five pounds.* David took a vast amount of plunder from the city. 31He also made slaves of the people of Rabbah and forced them to labor with* saws, iron picks, and iron axes, and to work in the brick kilns.* That is how he dealt with the people of all the Ammonite towns. Then David and all the army returned to Jerusalem.

## 2. Turmoil in David's family
### The Rape of Tamar

**13** Now David's son Absalom had a beautiful sister named Tamar. And Amnon, her half brother, fell desperately in love with her. 2Amnon became so obsessed with Tamar that he became ill. She was a virgin, and Amnon thought he could never have her.

3But Amnon had a very crafty friend—his cousin Jonadab. He was the son of David's brother Shimea.* 4One day Jonadab said to Amnon, "What's the trouble? Why should the son of a king look so dejected morning after morning?"

**12:17** 2 Sam 3:35
**12:22** Isa 38:1-5 / Jon 3:9
**12:23** Gen 37:35 / Job 7:9-10
**12:24** 1 Chr 22:9
**12:26** Deut 3:11 / 1 Chr 20:1-3
**12:29-31** //1 Chr 20:1-3
**13:1** 2 Sam 3:2-3 / 1 Chr 3:1, 9
**13:3** 1 Sam 16:9

**12:20** Hebrew *anointed himself.* **12:24** Hebrew *he;* an alternate Hebrew reading and some Hebrew manuscripts read *she.* **12:25** As in Greek version; Hebrew reads *because of the Lord.* **12:26** Or *the royal city.* **12:27** Or *captured the city of water.* **12:30a** Or *from the head of Milcom* (as in Greek version). Milcom, also called Molech, was the god of the Ammonites. **12:30b** Hebrew *1 talent* [34 kilograms]. **12:31a** Or *He also brought out the people of Rabbah and put them under.* **12:31b** Or *and he made them pass through the brick kilns.* **13:3** Hebrew *Shimeah* (also in 13:32), a variant spelling of Shimea; compare 1 Chr 2:13.

**12:20-24** David did not continue to dwell on his sin. He returned to God, and God forgave him, opening the way to begin life anew. Even the name God gave Solomon, *Jedidiah* ("beloved of the Lord"; 12:25) was a reminder of God's grace. When we return to God, accept his forgiveness, and change our ways, he gives us a fresh start. To feel forgiven as David did, admit your sins to God and turn to him. Then move ahead with a new and fresh approach to life.

**12:22, 23** Perhaps the most bitter experience in life is the death of one's child. For comfort in such difficult circumstances, see Psalms 16:9-11; 17:15; 139; Isaiah 40:11.

**12:24** Solomon was the fourth son of David and Bathsheba (1 Chronicles 3:5). Therefore, several years passed between the death of their first child and Solomon's birth. Bathsheba may still have been grieving over the child's death.

**13:3-5** Amnon was encouraged by his cousin Jonadab to commit sexual sin. We may be more vulnerable to the advice of our relatives because we are close to them. However, we must make sure to evaluate every piece of advice by God's standards, even when it comes from relatives.

So Amnon told him, "I am in love with Tamar, my brother Absalom's sister."

⁵"Well," Jonadab said, "I'll tell you what to do. Go back to bed and pretend you are ill. When your father comes to see you, ask him to let Tamar come and prepare some food for you. Tell him you'll feel better if she prepares it as you watch and feeds you with her own hands."

⁶So Amnon lay down and pretended to be sick. And when the king came to see him, Amnon asked him, "Please let my sister Tamar come and cook my favorite dish* as I watch. Then I can eat it from her own hands." ⁷So David agreed and sent Tamar to Amnon's house to prepare some food for him.

⁸When Tamar arrived at Amnon's house, she went to the place where he was lying down so he could watch her mix some dough. Then she baked his favorite dish for him. ⁹But when she set the serving tray before him, he refused to eat. "Everyone get out of here," Amnon told his servants. So they all left.

¹⁰Then he said to Tamar, "Now bring the food into my bedroom and feed it to me here." So Tamar took his favorite dish to him. ¹¹But as she was feeding him, he grabbed her and demanded, "Come to bed with me, my darling sister."

¹²"No, my brother!" she cried. "Don't be foolish! Don't do this to me! Such wicked things aren't done in Israel. ¹³Where could I go in my shame? And you would be called one of the greatest fools in Israel. Please, just speak to the king about it, and he will let you marry me."

**13:9**
Gen 45:1

**13:11**
Gen 39:12

**13:12**
Lev 20:17

13:6 Or *a couple of cakes;* also in 13:8, 10.

---

**AMNON**

Amnon was king David's firstborn son, born and raised during the years between David's rise to fame and his rise to power. He grew into a prince with too much time on his hands and too little control over his thoughts. Amnon set in motion one of the most shameful and destructive series of actions in the royal family. He allowed himself to become obsessed with sexual desire for his half sister Tamar. When his attempt to seduce Tamar failed, he raped her. Then his "desire" for her became loathing and he humiliated her. He even made it look like the incest was his sister's fault. Tamar's full brother Absalom later avenged her shame by killing Amnon.

David was an ineffective father. He failed to train or discipline his children. Although he found out and was furious about Amnon's actions, he did nothing. Amnon, like the rest of his siblings, was a child out of control. He was frustrated when he couldn't have his way, yet was disgusted when he did get his way. Without direction, his actions led to self-destruction. The Bible records not even a hint of remorse for what he had done to Tamar.

Family relationships can be sources of strength or systems of dysfunction. We can think about childhood by counting scars and nightmares or by remembering security and dreams. We may be creating in our own children one or the other of these histories. In what specific ways have you been settling the painful issues of the past in your own life? In what ways are you contributing to a better past for your children?

| | |
|---|---|
| **Weaknesses and mistakes** | • Allowed lustful desires to dominate his life<br>• Listened to his cousin Jonadab's bad advice<br>• Raped and then rejected his half sister, Tamar |
| **Lessons from his life** | • Children who have everything often lack purpose and direction in their lives<br>• Thoughts and impulses turn self-destructive if not controlled or channeled<br>• Parents contribute good or evil by action or inaction in their children's lives<br>• The distance between lust and hatred is very short |
| **Vital statistics** | • Where: Hebron<br>• Occupation: Prince<br>• Relatives: Father: David. Mother: Ahinoam. Many half brothers including Absalom, Adonijah, and Solomon. Half sister: Tamar.<br>• Contemporaries: Nathan, Jonadab, Joab, Ahithophel, Hushai |
| **Key verse** | "Then suddenly Amnon's love turned to hate, and he hated her even more than he had loved her. 'Get out of here!' he snarled at her" (2 Samuel 13:15). |

Amnon's story is told in 2 Samuel 13:1–39. He is also mentioned in 2 Samuel 3:2 and 1 Chronicles 3:1.

¹⁴But Amnon wouldn't listen to her, and since he was stronger than she was, he raped her. ¹⁵Then suddenly Amnon's love turned to hate, and he hated her even more than he had loved her. "Get out of here!" he snarled at her.

¹⁶"No, no!" Tamar cried. "Sending me away now is worse than what you've already done to me."

But Amnon wouldn't listen to her. ¹⁷He shouted for his servant and demanded, "Throw this woman out, and lock the door behind her!"

¹⁸So the servant put her out and locked the door behind her. She was wearing a long, beautiful robe,* as was the custom in those days for the king's virgin daughters. ¹⁹But now Tamar tore her robe and put ashes on her head. And then, with her face in her hands, she went away crying.

²⁰Her brother Absalom saw her and asked, "Is it true that Amnon has been with you? Well, my sister, keep quiet for now, since he's your brother. Don't you worry about it." So Tamar lived as a desolate woman in her brother Absalom's house.

²¹When King David heard what had happened, he was very angry.* ²²And though Absalom never spoke to Amnon about this, he hated Amnon deeply because of what he had done to his sister.

### Absalom's Revenge on Amnon

²³Two years later, when Absalom's sheep were being sheared at Baal-hazor near Ephraim, Absalom invited all the king's sons to come to a feast. ²⁴He went to the king and said, "My sheep-shearers are now at work. Would the king and his servants please come to celebrate the occasion with me?"

²⁵The king replied, "No, my son. If we all came, we would be too much of a burden on you." Absalom pressed him, but the king would not come, though he gave Absalom his blessing.

²⁶"Well, then," Absalom said, "if you can't come, how about sending my brother Amnon with us?"

"Why Amnon?" the king asked. ²⁷But Absalom kept on pressing the king until he finally agreed to let all his sons attend, including Amnon. So Absalom prepared a feast fit for a king.*

²⁸Absalom told his men, "Wait until Amnon gets drunk; then at my signal, kill him! Don't be afraid. I'm the one who has given the command. Take courage and do it!" ²⁹So at Absalom's signal they murdered Amnon. Then the other sons of the king jumped on their mules and fled.

³⁰As they were on the way back to Jerusalem, this report reached David: "Absalom has killed all the king's sons; not one is left alive!" ³¹The king got up, tore his robe, and threw himself on the ground. His advisers also tore their clothes in horror and sorrow.

³²But just then Jonadab, the son of David's brother Shimea, arrived and said, "No, don't believe that all the king's sons have been killed! It was only Amnon! Absalom has been plotting this ever since Amnon raped his sister Tamar. ³³No, my lord the king, your sons aren't all dead! It was only Amnon." ³⁴Meanwhile Absalom escaped.

13:18 Gen 37:23
13:19 Gen 37:29; 2 Sam 1:11; Esth 4:1
13:22 Gen 31:24; Lev 19:17-18; 1 Jn 2:9-11
13:29 2 Sam 18:9
13:31 2 Sam 12:16
13:32 2 Sam 13:3-5
13:34 2 Sam 18:24

13:18 Or *a robe with sleeves*, or *an ornamented robe.* The meaning of the Hebrew is uncertain. 13:21 Dead Sea Scrolls and Greek version add *But he did not punish his son Amnon, because he loved him, for he was his firstborn.* 13:27 As in Greek and Latin versions (compare also Dead Sea Scrolls); the Hebrew text lacks this sentence.

13:14, 15 Love and lust are very different. After Amnon raped his half sister, his "love" turned to hate. Although he had claimed to be in love, he was actually overcome by lust. Love is patient; lust requires immediate satisfaction. Love is kind; lust is harsh. Love does not demand its own way; lust does. You can read about the characteristics of real love in 1 Corinthians 13. Lust may feel like love at first, but when physically expressed, it results in self-disgust and hatred of the other person. If you just can't wait, what you feel is not true love.

13:16 Rape was strictly forbidden by God (Deuteronomy 22:28, 29). Why was sending Tamar away an even greater crime? By throwing her out, Amnon made it look as if Tamar had made a shameful proposition to him, and there were no witnesses on her behalf because he had gotten rid of the servants. His crime destroyed her chances of marriage—because she was no longer a virgin, she could not be given in marriage.

13:20 Absalom tried to comfort Tamar and persuade her not to turn the incident into a public scandal. Secretly, he planned to take revenge against Amnon himself. This he did two years later (13:23-33). Absalom told Tamar the crime was only a family matter. But God's standards for moral conduct are not suspended when we deal with family matters.

13:21-24 David was angry with Amnon for raping Tamar, but David did not punish him. David probably hesitated because (1) he didn't want to cross Amnon, who was his firstborn son (1 Chronicles 3:1) and therefore next in line to be king, and (2) David was guilty of a similar sin himself in his adultery with Bathsheba. While David was unsurpassed as a king and military leader, he lacked skill and sensitivity as a husband and father.

Then the watchman on the Jerusalem wall saw a great crowd coming down the hill on the road from the west. He ran to tell the king, "I see a crowd of people coming from the Horonaim road along the side of the hill."*

35"Look!" Jonadab told the king. "There they are now! The king's sons are coming, just as I said."

36They soon arrived, weeping and sobbing, and the king and all his servants wept bitterly with them. 37And David mourned many days for his son Amnon.

Absalom fled to his grandfather, Talmai son of Ammihud, the king of Geshur. 38He stayed there in Geshur for three years. 39And King David,* now reconciled to Amnon's death, longed to be reunited with his son Absalom.*

### Joab Arranges for Absalom's Return

**14** Joab realized how much the king longed to see Absalom. 2So he sent for a woman from Tekoa who had a reputation for great wisdom. He said to her, "Pretend you are in mourning; wear mourning clothes and don't put on lotions.* Act like a woman who has been mourning for the dead for a long time. 3Then go to the king and tell him the story I am about to tell you." Then Joab told her what to say.

4When the woman from Tekoa approached the king, she bowed with her face to the ground in deep respect and cried out, "O king! Help me!"

5"What's the trouble?" the king asked.

"Alas, I am a widow!" she replied. "My husband is dead. 6My two sons had a fight out in the field. And since no one was there to stop it, one of them was killed. 7Now the rest of the family is demanding, 'Let us have your son. We will execute him for murdering his brother. He doesn't deserve to inherit his family's property.' They want to extinguish the only coal I have left, and my husband's name and family will disappear from the face of the earth."

8"Leave it to me," the king told her. "Go home, and I'll see to it that no one touches him."

9"Oh, thank you, my lord the king," the woman from Tekoa replied. "If you are criticized for helping me, let the blame fall on me and on my father's house, and let the king and his throne be innocent."

10"If anyone objects," the king said, "bring him to me. I can assure you he will never complain again!"

11Then she said, "Please swear to me by the LORD your God that you won't let anyone take vengeance against my son. I want no more bloodshed."

"As surely as the LORD lives," he replied, "not a hair on your son's head will be disturbed!"

12"Please allow me to ask one more thing of my lord the king," she said.

"Go ahead and speak," he responded.

13She replied, "Why don't you do as much for the people of God as you have promised to do for me? You have convicted yourself in making this decision, because you have refused to bring home your own banished son. 14All of us must die eventually. Our lives are like water spilled out on the ground, which cannot be gathered up again. But God does not just sweep life away; instead, he devises ways to bring us back when we have been separated from him.

**13:34** As in Greek version; Hebrew lacks this sentence. **13:39a** Dead Sea Scrolls and Greek version read *And the spirit of the king.* **13:39b** Or *no longer felt a need to go out after Absalom.* **14:2** Hebrew *don't anoint yourself with oil.*

**13:37** 
2 Sam 3:3; 
14:23, 32 
**13:39** 
2 Sam 12:19-23

**14:2** 
2 Chr 11:5-10 
Amos 1:1 
**14:3** 
2 Sam 14:19

**14:7** 
Num 35:19 
Deut 19:12-13

**14:9** 
Gen 43:9 
1 Sam 25:24

**14:11** 
Num 35:12, 19, 21 
Deut 19:4-10 
1 Sam 14:45

**14:13** 
2 Sam 13:37-39 
1 Kgs 20:40-42 
**14:14** 
Job 34:14-15 
Heb 9:27

---

**13:37-39** Absalom fled to Geshur because King Talmai was his grandfather (1 Chronicles 3:2), and he would be welcomed.

**14:1** Why is so much attention given to Absalom in chapters 13–19? His revenge against Amnon and rebellion against David were beginning the final decline of David's kingdom that had been prophesied in 12:10-12. The cycle of lust and murder had begun with David's adultery with Bathsheba. By killing his half brother Amnon, Absalom was getting revenge for the rape of his sister Tamar, as well as getting rid of the firstborn son, the one next in line to be king. Clearly he had his sights set on being Israel's king and he did everything in his power to obtain that goal—killing a half brother and rebelling against his father. Absalom was handsome and popular like his father, but lacked his father's heart for God.

What can we learn from this terrible story? (1) Even the highest-ranking and best-equipped people are sinners and rebels at heart. We must guard our own hearts against sin and rebel-

lion. (2) David failed to teach his children God's ways. Even if our children are raised in church, we must teach and exemplify character and obedience to God. (3) David was preoccupied with government, wives, and concubines; he failed to act decisively to correct the evil in his family. At times, his guilt over his own sin caused him to decline to discipline his sons caught in similar sins. That proved to be his family's undoing. Whenever possible, we must break cycles of lust, hatred, and rebellion. To do so, we must stay involved in guiding our children's lives while they are still under our care.

**14:11** The law provided for a way to avenge murder. Numbers 35:9-21 records how cities of refuge protected people from revenge and how blood avengers were to pursue murderers. This woman was asking for the king's protection against any claim against her.

¹⁵"I have come to plead with my lord the king because people have threatened me. I said to myself, 'Perhaps the king will listen to me ¹⁶and rescue us from those who would cut us off from the inheritance* God has given us. ¹⁷Yes, my lord the king will give us peace of mind again.' I know that you are like an angel of God in discerning good from evil. May the LORD your God be with you."

**14:17**
1 Sam 29:9
2 Sam 19:27

¹⁸"I must know one thing," the king replied, "and tell me the truth."

"Yes, my lord the king," she responded.

¹⁹"Did Joab put you up to this?"

And the woman replied, "My lord the king, how can I deny it? Nobody can hide anything from you. Yes, Joab sent me and told me what to say. ²⁰He did it to place the matter before you in a different light. But you are as wise as an angel of God, and you understand everything that happens among us!"

**14:19**
2 Sam 14:3

²¹So the king sent for Joab and told him, "All right, go and bring back the young man Absalom."

²²Joab bowed with his face to the ground in deep respect and said, "At last I know that I have gained your approval, my lord the king, for you have granted me this request!"

²³Then Joab went to Geshur and brought Absalom back to Jerusalem. ²⁴But the king gave this order: "Absalom may go to his own house, but he must never come into my presence." So Absalom did not see the king.

**14:23**
2 Sam 13:37-39

### Absalom Reconciled to David

²⁵Now Absalom was praised as the most handsome man in all Israel. He was flawless from head to foot. ²⁶He cut his hair only once a year, and then only because it was so heavy. When he weighed it out, it came to five pounds!* ²⁷He had three sons and one daughter. His daughter's name was Tamar, and she was very beautiful.

**14:27**
2 Sam 13:1

²⁸Absalom lived in Jerusalem for two years, but he never got to see the king. ²⁹Then Absalom sent for Joab to ask him to intercede for him, but Joab refused to come. Absalom sent for him a second time, but again Joab refused to come. ³⁰So Absalom said to his servants, "Go and set fire to Joab's barley field, the field next to mine." So they set his field on fire, as Absalom had commanded.

**14:28**
2 Sam 14:24

³¹Then Joab came to Absalom at his house and demanded, "Why did your servants set my field on fire?"

³²And Absalom replied, "Because I wanted you to ask the king why he brought me back from Geshur if he didn't intend to see me. I might as well have stayed there. Let me see the king; if he finds me guilty of anything, then let him kill me."

**14:32**
1 Sam 20:8

³³So Joab told the king what Absalom had said. Then at last David summoned Absalom, who came and bowed low before the king, and the king kissed him.

**14:33**
Gen 33:4
Luke 15:20

**14:16** Or *the property*; or *the people.*  **14:26** Hebrew *200 shekels* [2.3 kilograms] *by the royal standard.*

---

**14:27** By naming his daughter Tamar, Absalom was showing his love and respect for his sister Tamar. This was also a reminder to everyone of the Amnon/Tamar incident.

**14:30** Already we can see the seeds of rebellion in Absalom. As an independent and scheming young man, he took matters into his own hands and killed his brother (13:22-29). Without his father or anyone else to keep him in check, he probably did whatever he wanted, as evidenced by his setting Joab's field on fire to get his attention (14:30). Undoubtedly his good looks also added to his self-centeredness (14:25). Children need discipline, especially those with natural abilities and beauty. Otherwise, like Absalom, they will grow up thinking they can do whatever they want whenever they want to.

**14:33** David only made halfhearted efforts to correct his children. He did not punish Amnon for his sin against Tamar, nor did he deal decisively with Absalom's murder of Amnon. Such indecisiveness became David's undoing. When we ignore sin, we experience greater pain than if we deal with it immediately.

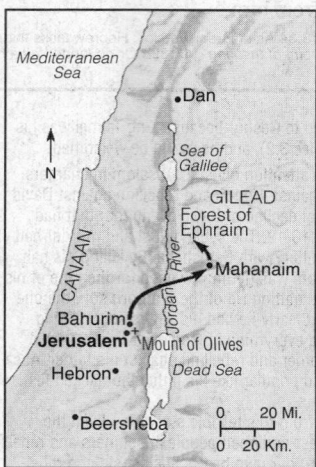

**ABSALOM'S REBELLION**
Absalom crowned himself king in Hebron. David and his men fled from Jerusalem, crossed the Jordan and went to Mahanaim. Absalom and his army followed, only to be defeated in the forest of Ephraim, where Absalom was killed.

### 3. National rebellion against David

*Absalom's Rebellion*

**15:1**
1 Kgs 1:5

**15** After this, Absalom bought a chariot and horses, and he hired fifty bodyguards to run ahead of him. [2]He got up early every morning and went out to the gate of the city. When people brought a case to the king for judgment, Absalom would ask where in Israel they were from, and they would tell him their tribe. [3]Then Absalom would say, "You've really got a strong case here! It's too bad the king doesn't have anyone to hear it. [4]I wish I were the judge. Then everyone could bring their cases to me for judgment, and I would give them justice!"

**15:4**
Judg 9:29

[5]When people tried to bow before him, Absalom wouldn't let them. Instead, he took them by the hand and kissed them. [6]Absalom did this with everyone who came to the king for judgment, and so he stole the hearts of all the people of Israel.

**15:5**
2 Sam 14:33
**15:6**
Rom 16:18

**A** father's mistakes are often reflected in the lives of his children. In Absalom, David saw a bitter replay and amplification of many of his own past sins. God had predicted that David's family would suffer because of his sins against Bathsheba and Uriah. David's heart was broken as he realized that God's predictions were coming true. God forgave David, but he did not cancel the consequences of his sin. David was horrified as he saw his son's strengths run wild without the controls God had built into his own life.

By most casual evaluations, Absalom would have made an excellent king, and the people loved him. But he lacked the inner character and control needed in a good leader. His appearance, skill, and position did not make up for his lack of personal integrity.

David's sins took him away from God, but repentance brought him back. In contrast, Absalom sinned and kept on sinning. Although he relied heavily on the advice of others, he was not wise enough to evaluate the counsel he received.

Can you identify with Absalom? Do you find yourself on a fast track toward self-destruction? Absalom wasn't able to say, "I was wrong. I need forgiveness." God offers forgiveness, but we will not experience that forgiveness until we genuinely admit our sins and confess them to God. Absalom rejected his father's love and ultimately God's love. How often do you miss entering back into God's love through the door of forgiveness?

| | |
|---|---|
| **Strengths and accomplishments** | • Was handsome and charismatic like his father, David<br>• Kindly comforted his sister, Tamar, after she had been raped and allowed her to live with him |
| **Weaknesses and mistakes** | • Avenged the rape of his sister, Tamar, by killing his half brother Amnon<br>• Plotted against his father to take away the throne<br>• Consistently listened to the wrong advice |
| **Lessons from his life** | • The sins of parents are often repeated and amplified in their children<br>• A smart man gets a lot of advice; a wise man evaluates the advice he gets<br>• Actions against God's plans will fail, sooner or later |
| **Vital statistics** | • Where: Hebron<br>• Occupation: Prince<br>• Relatives: Father: David. Mother: Maacah. Half brothers: Amnon, Kileab, Solomon, and others. Sister: Tamar.<br>• Contemporaries: Nathan, Jonadab, Joab, Ahithophel, Hushai |
| **Key verse** | "But while he was there, he sent secret messengers to all the tribes of Israel to stir up a rebellion against the king. 'As soon as you hear the ram's horn,' his message read, 'you are to say, "Absalom has been crowned king in Hebron"'" (2 Samuel 15:10). |

Absalom's story is told in 2 Samuel 3:3; 13—19.

**15:1ff** David wrote several psalms during the days of Absalom's rebellion. Some of them are Psalms 39, 41, 55, 61, and 63.

**15:2** The city gate was like city hall and a shopping center combined. Because Jerusalem was the nation's capital, both local and national leaders met there daily to transact business and conduct government affairs. The city gate was the perfect spot for this because government and business transactions needed witnesses to be legitimate, and anyone entering or leaving the city had to enter through the gate. Merchants set up their tent-shops near the gate for the same reason. Absalom, therefore, went to the city gate to win the hearts of Israel's leaders as well as those of the common people.

**15:5, 6** Absalom's political strategy was to steal the hearts of the people with his good looks, grand entrances, apparent concern for justice, and friendly embraces. Many were fooled and switched their allegiance. Later, however, Absalom proved to be an evil ruler.

We need to evaluate our leaders to make sure their charisma is not a mask covering graft, deception, or hunger for power. Make sure that underneath their style and charm, they are able to make good decisions and handle people wisely.

7After four years,* Absalom said to the king, "Let me go to Hebron to offer a sacrifice to the LORD and fulfill a vow I made to him. 8For while your servant was at Geshur in Aram, I promised to sacrifice to the LORD in Hebron* if he would bring me back to Jerusalem."

**15:8**
Gen 28:20
2 Sam 13:37-39

9"All right," the king told him. "Go and fulfill your vow."

So Absalom went to Hebron. 10But while he was there, he sent secret messengers to all the tribes of Israel to stir up a rebellion against the king. "As soon as you hear the ram's horn," his message read, "you are to say, 'Absalom has been crowned king in Hebron.' " 11He took 200 men from Jerusalem with him as guests, but they knew nothing of his intentions. 12While Absalom was offering the sacrifices, he sent for Ahithophel, one of David's counselors who lived in Giloh. Soon many others also joined Absalom, and the conspiracy gained momentum.

**15:10**
1 Kgs 1:34
2 Kgs 9:13

**15:12**
Josh 15:51
2 Sam 17:14
Ps 3:1

### David Escapes from Jerusalem

13A messenger soon arrived in Jerusalem to tell David, "All Israel has joined Absalom in a conspiracy against you!"

**15:13**
Judg 9:3

14"Then we must flee at once, or it will be too late!" David urged his men. "Hurry! If we get out of the city before Absalom arrives, both we and the city of Jerusalem will be spared from disaster."

**15:14**
2 Sam 12:11
Ps 3:title

15"We are with you," his advisers replied. "Do what you think is best."

16So the king and all his household set out at once. He left no one behind except ten of his concubines to look after the palace. 17The king and all his people set out on foot, pausing at the last house 18to let all the king's men move past to lead the way. There were 600 men from Gath who had come with David, along with the king's bodyguard.*

**15:16**
2 Sam 16:21-22

19Then the king turned and said to Ittai, a leader of the men from Gath, "Why are you coming with us? Go on back to King Absalom, for you are a guest in Israel, a foreigner in exile. 20You arrived only recently, and should I force you today to wander with us? I don't even know where we will go. Go on back and take your kinsmen with you, and may the LORD show you his unfailing love and faithfulness.*"

**15:19**
2 Sam 18:2

21But Ittai said to the king, "I vow by the LORD and by your own life that I will go wherever my lord the king goes, no matter what happens—whether it means life or death."

**15:21**
Ruth 1:16-17

22David replied, "All right, come with us." So Ittai and all his men and their families went along.

23Everyone cried loudly as the king and his followers passed by. They crossed the Kidron Valley and then went out toward the wilderness.

24Zadok and all the Levites also came along, carrying the Ark of the Covenant of God. They set down the Ark of God, and Abiathar offered sacrifices* until everyone had passed out of the city.

**15:24**
Num 4:15
1 Sam 4:4-5
2 Sam 8:17; 20:25

25Then the king instructed Zadok to take the Ark of God back into the city. "If the LORD sees fit," David said, "he will bring me back to see the Ark and the Tabernacle* again. 26But if he is through with me, then let him do what seems best to him."

**15:25**
1 Sam 3:18
Ps 43:3

**15:7** As in Greek and Syriac versions; Hebrew reads *forty years*. **15:8** As in some Greek manuscripts; Hebrew lacks *in Hebron*. **15:18** Hebrew *the Kerethites and Pelethites*. **15:20** As in Greek version; Hebrew reads *and may unfailing love and faithfulness go with you*. **15:24** Or *Abiathar went up*. **15:25** Hebrew *and his dwelling place*.

**15:9** Absalom went to Hebron because it was his hometown (3:2, 3). Hebron was David's first capital as well, and there Absalom could expect to find loyal friends who would be proud of him.

**15:14** Had David not escaped from Jerusalem, the ensuing fight might have killed him as well as many innocent inhabitants of the city. Some fights that we think necessary can be costly and destructive to those around us. In such cases, it may be wise to back down and save the fight for another day—even if doing so hurts our pride. It takes courage to stand and fight, but it also takes courage to back down for the sake of others.

**15:14** Why couldn't David just crush this rebellion? There were several reasons he chose to flee: (1) The rebellion was widespread (15:10-13) and would not have been easily suppressed; (2) David did not want the city of Jerusalem to be destroyed; (3) David still cared for his son and did not want to hurt him. We know that David expected to return to Jerusalem soon because he left 10 of his concubines to take care of the palace (15:16).

**15:17, 18** David had many loyal non-Israelites in his armed forces. The men from the Philistine city of Gath were apparently friends David had acquired while hiding from Saul. "The king's bodyguard" is also translated "the Kerethites and Pelethites"; these men were also from Philistine territory. Although Israel was supposed to destroy wicked enemies, the nation was to welcome foreigners who came on friendly terms (Exodus 23:9; Deuteronomy 10:19) and to try to show them the importance of obeying God.

**15:24, 25** The priests and Levites were also loyal to David.

**15:27**
2 Sam 17:17
**15:28**
2 Sam 17:16

**15:30**
Esth 6:12
Ezek 24:23
**15:31**
2 Sam 15:12;
16:23; 17:14, 23

**15:32**
Josh 16:2
**15:34**
2 Sam 16:19
**15:35**
2 Sam 17:15-16
**15:36**
2 Sam 15:27
**15:37**
1 Chr 27:33

**16:1**
2 Sam 9:1-13

**16:2**
2 Sam 17:27-29

**16:3**
2 Sam 9:9-10;
19:26-27

27 The king also told Zadok the priest, "Look,* here is my plan. You and Abiathar* should return quietly to the city with your son Ahimaaz and Abiathar's son Jonathan. 28 I will stop at the shallows of the Jordan River* and wait there for a report from you." 29 So Zadok and Abiathar took the Ark of God back to the city and stayed there.

30 David walked up the road to the Mount of Olives, weeping as he went. His head was covered and his feet were bare as a sign of mourning. And the people who were with him covered their heads and wept as they climbed the hill. 31 When someone told David that his adviser Ahithophel was now backing Absalom, David prayed, "O LORD, let Ahithophel give Absalom foolish advice!"

32 When David reached the summit of the Mount of Olives where people worshiped God, Hushai the Arkite was waiting there for him. Hushai had torn his clothing and put dirt on his head as a sign of mourning. 33 But David told him, "If you go with me, you will only be a burden. 34 Return to Jerusalem and tell Absalom, 'I will now be your adviser, O king, just as I was your father's adviser in the past.' Then you can frustrate and counter Ahithophel's advice. 35 Zadok and Abiathar, the priests, will be there. Tell them about the plans being made in the king's palace, 36 and they will send their sons Ahimaaz and Jonathan to tell me what is going on."

37 So David's friend Hushai returned to Jerusalem, getting there just as Absalom arrived.

### David and Ziba

**16** When David had gone a little beyond the summit of the Mount of Olives, Ziba, the servant of Mephibosheth,* was waiting there for him. He had two donkeys loaded with 200 loaves of bread, 100 clusters of raisins, 100 bunches of summer fruit, and a wineskin full of wine.

2 "What are these for?" the king asked Ziba.

Ziba replied, "The donkeys are for the king's people to ride on, and the bread and summer fruit are for the young men to eat. The wine is for those who become exhausted in the wilderness."

3 "And where is Mephibosheth, Saul's grandson?" the king asked him.

**15:27a** As in Greek version; Hebrew reads *Are you a seer?* or *Do you see?* compare 15:29. **15:27b** Hebrew lacks *and Abiathar;* compare 15:29. **15:28** Hebrew *at the crossing points of the wilderness.* **16:1** *Mephibosheth* is another name for Merib-baal.

---

**HIGHS AND LOWS OF DAVID'S LIFE**

The Bible calls David a man after God's own heart (1 Samuel 13:14; Acts 13:22), but that didn't mean his life was free of troubles. David's life was full of highs and lows. Some of David's troubles were a result of his sins; some were a result of the sins of others. We can't always control our ups and downs, but we can trust God every day. We can be certain that he will help us through our trials, just as he helped David. In the end, he will reward us for our consistent faith.

Anointed king (1 Samuel 16)
Killed Goliath (1 Samuel 17)
Crowned king over Judah (2 Samuel 12)
Crowned king over all Israel (2 Samuel 15)
God made a special covenant with him; Israel had peace (2 Samuel 7, 8)
Solomon born (2 Samuel 12)
David restored as king (2 Samuel 19)
David planned the Temple (1 Kings 2)

Fled from Saul (1 Samuel 18—31)
Ziklag destroyed (1 Samuel 30)
Committed adultery and murder (2 Samuel 11)
Absalom rebelled (2 Samuel 15—18)
David sinned in taking the census (2 Samuel 24)

---

**15:27-37** David needed spies in Absalom's court to inform him of Absalom's decisions. By sending Hushai to Absalom as a supposed traitor to David, Hushai could offer advice contradictory to Ahithophel's advice. Ahithophel was Absalom's adviser (he was also Bathsheba's grandfather).

**16:3** Saul was Mephibosheth's grandfather. Most likely Ziba was lying, hoping to receive a reward from David. (See 19:24-30 for Mephibosheth's side of the story.) For the story of Mephibosheth, see chapter 9.

"He stayed in Jerusalem," Ziba replied. "He said, 'Today I will get back the kingdom of my grandfather Saul.'"

4"In that case," the king told Ziba, "I give you everything Mephibosheth owns."

"I bow before you," Ziba replied. "May I always be pleasing to you, my lord the king."

## Shimei Curses David

5As King David came to Bahurim, a man came out of the village cursing them. It was Shimei son of Gera, from the same clan as Saul's family. 6He threw stones at the king and the king's officers and all the mighty warriors who surrounded him. 7"Get out of here, you murderer, you scoundrel!" he shouted at David. 8"The LORD is paying you back for all the bloodshed in Saul's clan. You stole his throne, and now the LORD has given it to your son Absalom. At last you will taste some of your own medicine, for you are a murderer!"

9"Why should this dead dog curse my lord the king?" Abishai son of Zeruiah demanded. "Let me go over and cut off his head!"

10"No!" the king said. "Who asked your opinion, you sons of Zeruiah! If the LORD has told him to curse me, who are you to stop him?"

11Then David said to Abishai and to all his servants, "My own son is trying to kill me. Doesn't this relative of Saul* have even more reason to do so? Leave him alone and let him curse, for the LORD has told him to do it. 12And perhaps the LORD will see that I am being wronged and will bless me because of these curses today." 13So David and his men continued down the road, and Shimei kept pace with them on a nearby hillside, cursing as he went and throwing stones at David and tossing dust into the air.

14The king and all who were with him grew weary along the way, so they rested when they reached the Jordan River.*

## Ahithophel Advises Absalom

15Meanwhile, Absalom and all the army of Israel arrived at Jerusalem, accompanied by Ahithophel. 16When David's friend Hushai the Arkite arrived, he went immediately to see Absalom. "Long live the king!" he exclaimed. "Long live the king!"

17"Is this the way you treat your friend David?" Absalom asked him. "Why aren't you with him?"

18"I'm here because I belong to the man who is chosen by the LORD and by all the men of Israel," Hushai replied. 19"And anyway, why shouldn't I serve you? Just as I was your father's adviser, now I will be your adviser!"

20Then Absalom turned to Ahithophel and asked him, "What should I do next?"

21Ahithophel told him, "Go and sleep with your father's concubines, for he has left them here to look after the palace. Then all Israel will know that you have insulted your father beyond hope of reconciliation, and they will throw their support to you." 22So they set up a tent on the palace roof where everyone could see it, and Absalom went in and had sex with his father's concubines.

23Absalom followed Ahithophel's advice, just as David had done. For every word Ahithophel spoke seemed as wise as though it had come directly from the mouth of God.

**17** Now Ahithophel urged Absalom, "Let me choose 12,000 men to start out after David tonight. 2I will catch up with him while he is weary and discouraged. He and his troops will panic, and everyone will run away. Then I will kill only the king, 3and I will bring all the people back to you as a bride returns to her husband. After all, it is only one man's life that you seek.* Then you will be at peace with all the people." 4This plan seemed good to Absalom and to all the elders of Israel.

**16:5**
Exod 22:28
1 Sam 17:43
2 Sam 19:16-23
2 Kgs 2:8
**16:7**
2 Sam 12:9
**16:9**
Exod 22:28
1 Sam 26:8
2 Sam 19:21
**16:10**
2 Sam 3:39; 19:22
John 18:11
Rom 9:20
**16:11**
Gen 45:5
1 Sam 26:19
2 Sam 12:11
**16:12**
Deut 23:5
Rom 8:28
**16:15**
2 Sam 15:12, 37
**16:16**
1 Sam 10:24
2 Sam 15:33-34
2 Kgs 11:12
**16:19**
2 Sam 15:33-34
**16:21**
2 Sam 15:16
**16:22**
2 Sam 12:11; 20:3
**16:23**
2 Sam 15:12; 17:14, 23
**17:2**
2 Sam 16:14
1 Kgs 22:31

**16:11** Hebrew *this Benjaminite.* **16:14** As in Greek version (see also 17:16); Hebrew reads *when they reached their destination.* **17:3** As in Greek version; Hebrew reads *like the return of all is the man whom you seek.*

**16:4** David believed Ziba's charge against Mephibosheth without checking into it or even being skeptical. Don't be hasty to accept someone's condemnation of another, especially when the accuser may profit from the other's downfall. David should have been skeptical of Ziba's comments until he checked them out for himself.

**16:5-14** Shimei kept up a steady tirade against David. Although his curses were unjustified because David had had no part in Saul's death, David and his followers quietly tolerated the abuse. Maintaining your composure in the face of unjustified criticism can be

a trying experience and an emotional drain, but if you can't stop criticism, it is best just to ignore it. Remember that God knows what you are enduring, and he will vindicate you if you are in the right.

**16:21, 22** This incident fulfilled Nathan's prediction that because of David's sin, another man would sleep with his wives (12:11, 12). (See the note on 3:6, 7 for the cultural significance of this act.)

**16:23** Ahithophel was an adviser to Absalom. Most rulers had advisers to help them make decisions about governmental and political matters. They probably arranged the king's marriages as

## Hushai Counters Ahithophel's Advice

17:5
2 Sam 15:32-34

5 But then Absalom said, "Bring in Hushai the Arkite. Let's see what he thinks about this." 6 When Hushai arrived, Absalom told him what Ahithophel had said. Then he asked, "What is your opinion? Should we follow Ahithophel's advice? If not, what do you suggest?"

17:7
2 Sam 16:21
17:8
Hos 13:8

7 "Well," Hushai replied to Absalom, "this time Ahithophel has made a mistake. 8 You know your father and his men; they are mighty warriors. Right now they are as enraged as a mother bear who has been robbed of her cubs. And remember that your father is an experienced man of war. He won't be spending the night among the troops. 9 He has probably already hidden in some pit or cave. And when he comes out and attacks and a few of your men fall, there will be panic among your troops, and the word will spread that Absalom's men are

17:10
Josh 2:9, 11

being slaughtered. 10 Then even the bravest soldiers, though they have the heart of a lion, will be paralyzed with fear. For all Israel knows what a mighty warrior your father is and how courageous his men are.

11 "I recommend that you mobilize the entire army of Israel, bringing them from as far away as Dan in the north and Beersheba in the south. That way you will have an army as numerous as the sand on the seashore. And I advise that you personally lead the troops.

17:13
Mic 1:6

12 When we find David, we'll fall on him like dew that falls on the ground. Then neither he nor any of his men will be left alive. 13 And if David were to escape into some town, you will have all Israel there at your command. Then we can take ropes and drag the walls of the town into the nearest valley until every stone is torn down."

17:14
2 Sam 15:31-34

14 Then Absalom and all the men of Israel said, "Hushai's advice is better than Ahithophel's." For the LORD had determined to defeat the counsel of Ahithophel, which really was the better plan, so that he could bring disaster on Absalom!

## Hushai Warns David to Escape

17:15
2 Sam 15:35-36
17:16
2 Sam 15:28

15 Hushai told Zadok and Abiathar, the priests, what Ahithophel had said to Absalom and the elders of Israel and what he himself had advised instead. 16 "Quick!" he told them. "Find David and urge him not to stay at the shallows of the Jordan River* tonight. He must go across at once into the wilderness beyond. Otherwise he will die and his entire army with him."

17:17
Josh 15:7
2 Sam 15:27,
35-36; 18:19
17:18
2 Sam 3:16; 16:5
17:19
Josh 2:4-6
17:20
Exod 1:19
Lev 19:11
1 Sam 19:12-17

17 Jonathan and Ahimaaz had been staying at En-rogel so as not to be seen entering and leaving the city. Arrangements had been made for a servant girl to bring them the message they were to take to King David. 18 But a boy spotted them at En-rogel, and he told Absalom about it. So they quickly escaped to Bahurim, where a man hid them down inside a well in his courtyard. 19 The man's wife put a cloth over the top of the well and scattered grain on it to dry in the sun; so no one suspected they were there.

20 When Absalom's men arrived, they asked her, "Have you seen Ahimaaz and Jonathan?"

The woman replied, "They were here, but they crossed over the brook." Absalom's men looked for them without success and returned to Jerusalem.

21 Then the two men crawled out of the well and hurried on to King David. "Quick!" they told him, "cross the Jordan tonight!" And they told him how Ahithophel had advised that he be captured and killed. 22 So David and all the people with him went across the Jordan River during the night, and they were all on the other bank before dawn.

17:23
2 Sam 16:23
2 Kgs 20:1
Matt 27:5

23 When Ahithophel realized that his advice had not been followed, he saddled his donkey, went to his hometown, set his affairs in order, and hanged himself. He died there and was buried in the family tomb.

17:24
Gen 32:2
2 Sam 2:8

24 David soon arrived at Mahanaim. By now, Absalom had mobilized the entire army of Israel and was leading his troops across the Jordan River. 25 Absalom had appointed Amasa as

17:25
2 Sam 19:13; 20:12
1 Kgs 2:5
1 Chr 2:16-17

commander of his army, replacing Joab, who had been commander under David. (Amasa was Joab's cousin. His father was Jether,* an Ishmaelite.* His mother, Abigail daughter of Nahash, was the sister of Joab's mother, Zeruiah.) 26 Absalom and the Israelite army set up camp in the land of Gilead.

17:16 Hebrew *at the crossing points of the wilderness.*   17:25a Hebrew *Ithra*, a variant spelling of Jether.
17:25b As in some Greek manuscripts (see also 1 Chr 2:17); Hebrew reads *an Israelite.*

---

well because these were usually politically motivated unions. But God made Ahithophel's advice seem foolish, just as David had prayed (15:31).

**17:11** Hushai appealed to Absalom through flattery, and Absalom's vanity became his own trap. Hushai predicted great glory for Absalom if he personally led the entire army against David.

"Pride goes before destruction" (Proverbs 16:18) is an appropriate comment on Absalom's ambitions.

**17:25** Joab and Amasa were David's nephews and Absalom's cousins. Because Joab had left Jerusalem with David (see 18:5, 10ff), Amasa took his place as commander of Israel's troops.

27 When David arrived at Mahanaim, he was warmly greeted by Shobi son of Nahash, who came from Rabbah of the Ammonites, and by Makir son of Ammiel from Lo-debar, and by Barzillai of Gilead from Rogelim. 28 They brought sleeping mats, cooking pots, serving bowls, wheat and barley, flour and roasted grain, beans, lentils, 29 honey, butter, sheep, goats, and cheese for David and those who were with him. For they said, "You must all be very hungry and tired and thirsty after your long march through the wilderness."

### Absalom's Defeat and Death

**18** David now mustered the men who were with him and appointed generals and captains* to lead them. 2 He sent the troops out in three groups, placing one group under Joab, one under Joab's brother Abishai son of Zeruiah, and one under Ittai, the man from Gath. The king told his troops, "I am going out with you."

3 But his men objected strongly. "You must not go," they urged. "If we have to turn and run—and even if half of us die—it will make no difference to Absalom's troops; they will be looking only for you. You are worth 10,000 of us,* and it is better that you stay here in the town and send help if we need it."

4 "If you think that's the best plan, I'll do it," the king answered. So he stood alongside the gate of the town as all the troops marched out in groups of hundreds and of thousands.

5 And the king gave this command to Joab, Abishai, and Ittai: "For my sake, deal gently with young Absalom." And all the troops heard the king give this order to his commanders.

6 So the battle began in the forest of Ephraim, 7 and the Israelite troops were beaten back by David's men. There was a great slaughter that day, and 20,000 men laid down their lives. 8 The battle raged all across the countryside, and more men died because of the forest than were killed by the sword.

9 During the battle, Absalom happened to come upon some of David's men. He tried to escape on his mule, but as he rode beneath the thick branches of a great tree, his hair* got caught in the tree. His mule kept going and left him dangling in the air. 10 One of David's men saw what had happened and told Joab, "I saw Absalom dangling from a great tree."

11 "What?" Joab demanded. "You saw him there and didn't kill him? I would have rewarded you with ten pieces of silver* and a hero's belt!"

12 "I would not kill the king's son for even a thousand pieces of silver,*" the man replied to Joab. "We all heard the king say to you and Abishai and Ittai, 'For my sake, please spare young Absalom.' 13 And if I had betrayed the king by killing his son—and the king would certainly find out who did it—you yourself would be the first to abandon me."

14 "Enough of this nonsense," Joab said. Then he took three daggers and plunged them into Absalom's heart as he dangled, still alive, in the great tree. 15 Ten of Joab's young armor bearers then surrounded Absalom and killed him.

16 Then Joab blew the ram's horn, and his men returned from chasing the army of Israel. 17 They threw Absalom's body into a deep pit in the forest and piled a great heap of stones over it. And all Israel fled to their homes.

18 During his lifetime, Absalom had built a monument to himself in the King's Valley, for he said, "I have no son to carry on my name." He named the monument after himself, and it is known as Absalom's Monument to this day.

### David Mourns Absalom's Death

19 Then Zadok's son Ahimaaz said, "Let me run to the king with the good news that the LORD has rescued him from his enemies."

20 "No," Joab told him, "it wouldn't be good news to the king that his son is dead. You can be my messenger another time, but not today."

21 Then Joab said to a man from Ethiopia,* "Go tell the king what you have seen." The man bowed and ran off.

**17:27** 2 Sam 9:4; 10:1-2; 12:26, 29 1 Kgs 2:7
**17:29** 2 Sam 16:2
**18:1** Exod 18:25 1 Sam 22:7
**18:2** 1 Sam 11:11 2 Sam 15:19-22
**18:3** 2 Sam 21:17
**18:4** 2 Sam 18:24
**18:6** Josh 17:15
**18:9** 2 Sam 14:26
**18:13** 2 Sam 14:19-20
**18:16** 2 Sam 2:28; 20:22
**18:17** Josh 7:26; 8:29
**18:18** Gen 14:17 1 Sam 15:12 2 Sam 14:27
**18:19** 2 Sam 15:36

**18:1** Hebrew *appointed commanders of thousands and commanders of hundreds.* **18:3** As in two Hebrew manuscripts and some Greek and Latin manuscripts; most Hebrew manuscripts read *Now there are 10,000 like us.* **18:9** Hebrew *his head.* **18:11** Hebrew *10 shekels of silver,* about 4 ounces or 114 grams in weight. **18:12** Hebrew *1,000 shekels,* about 25 pounds or 11.4 kilograms in weight. **18:21** Hebrew *from Cush;* similarly in 18:23, 31, 32.

**18:1** David took command as he had in former days. In recent years, his life had been characterized by indecisiveness and moral paralysis. At this time he began to take charge and do his duty.

**18:12-14** This man had caught Joab in his hypocrisy. He knew Joab would have turned on him for killing the man if the king had found out about it. Joab could not answer, but only dismissed him. Those about to do evil often do not take the time to consider what they are about to do. They don't care whether or not it is right or lawful. Don't rush into action without thinking. Consider whether what you are about to do is right or wrong.

22But Ahimaaz continued to plead with Joab, "Whatever happens, please let me go, too." "Why should you go, my son?" Joab replied. "There will be no reward for your news." 23"Yes, but let me go anyway," he begged.

Joab finally said, "All right, go ahead." So Ahimaaz took the less demanding route by way of the plain and ran to Mahanaim ahead of the Ethiopian.

**18:24**
2 Sam 13:34;
19:8-10
2 Kgs 9:17

24While David was sitting between the inner and outer gates of the town, the watchman climbed to the roof of the gateway by the wall. As he looked, he saw a lone man running toward them. 25He shouted the news down to David, and the king replied, "If he is alone, he has news."

As the messenger came closer, 26the watchman saw another man running toward them. He shouted down, "Here comes another one!"

**18:27**
1 Kgs 1:42

The king replied, "He also will have news."

27"The first man runs like Ahimaaz son of Zadok," the watchman said.

---

**REBELLION**

The Bible records many rebellions. Many were against God's chosen leaders. They were doomed for failure. Others were begun by wicked men against wicked men. While these were sometimes successful, the rebel's life usually came to a violent end. Still other rebellions were made by good people against the wicked or unjust actions of others. This kind of rebellion is sometimes good in freeing the common people from oppression and giving them the freedom to turn back to God.

| Who rebelled? | Whom they rebelled against | What happened | Reference |
|---|---|---|---|
| Adam and Eve | God | Expelled from Eden | Genesis 3 |
| Israelites | God, Moses | Forced to wander in wilderness for 40 years | Numbers 14 |
| Korah | Moses | Swallowed by the earth | Numbers 16 |
| Israelites | God | God took away his special promise of protection | Judges 2 |
| Absalom (David's son) | David | Killed in battle | 2 Samuel 15–18 |
| Sheba | David | Killed in battle | 2 Samuel 20 |
| Adonijah (David's son) | David, Solomon | Killed for treason | 1 Kings 1–2 |
| Joab | David, Solomon | Supported Adonijah's kingship without seeking God's choice. Killed for treason | 1 Kings 1–2 |
| Ten tribes of Israel | Rehoboam | The kingdom was divided. The 10 tribes forgot about God, sinned, and were eventually taken into captivity | 1 Kings 12:16-20 |
| Baasha, king of Israel | Nadab, king of Israel | Overthrew the throne and became king. God destroyed his descendants | 1 Kings 15:27–16:7 |
| Zimri, king of Israel | Elah, king of Israel | Overthrew the throne, but killed himself when his rule was not accepted | 1 Kings 16:9-16 |
| Jehu, king of Israel | Joram, king of Israel Ahaziah, king of Judah | Killed both kings. Later turned from God and his dynasty was wiped out | 2 Kings 9–10 |
| Joash, king of Judah Jehoiada, a priest | Athaliah, queen of Judah | Athaliah, a wicked queen, was overthrown. This was a "good" rebellion | 2 Kings 11 |
| Shallum, king of Israel | Zechariah, king of Israel | Overthrew the throne, but then was assassinated | 2 Kings 15:8-15 |
| Menahem, king of Israel | Shallum, king of Israel | Overthrew the throne, but then was invaded by Assyrian army | 2 Kings 15:16-22 |
| Hoshea, king of Israel | Assyria | The city of Samaria was destroyed, the nation of Israel taken into captivity | 2 Kings 17 |
| Zedekiah, king of Judah | Nebuchadnezzar, king of Babylon | The city of Jerusalem was destroyed, the nation of Judah taken into captivity | 2 Kings 24–25 |

"He is a good man and comes with good news," the king replied.

²⁸Then Ahimaaz cried out to the king, "Everything is all right!" He bowed before the king with his face to the ground and said, "Praise to the LORD your God, who has handed over the rebels who dared to stand against my lord the king."

²⁹"What about young Absalom?" the king demanded. "Is he all right?"

Ahimaaz replied, "When Joab told me to come, there was a lot of commotion. But I didn't know what was happening."

³⁰"Wait here," the king told him. So Ahimaaz stepped aside.

³¹Then the man from Ethiopia arrived and said, "I have good news for my lord the king. Today the LORD has rescued you from all those who rebelled against you."

³²"What about young Absalom?" the king demanded. "Is he all right?"

And the Ethiopian replied, "May all of your enemies, my lord the king, both now and in the future, share the fate of that young man!"

³³*The king was overcome with emotion. He went up to the room over the gateway and burst into tears. And as he went, he cried, "O my son Absalom! My son, my son Absalom! If only I had died instead of you! O Absalom, my son, my son."

### Joab Rebukes the King

**19** ¹*Word soon reached Joab that the king was weeping and mourning for Absalom. ²As all the people heard of the king's deep grief for his son, the joy of that day's victory was turned into deep sadness. ³They crept back into the town that day as though they were ashamed and had deserted in battle. ⁴The king covered his face with his hands and kept on crying, "O my son Absalom! O Absalom, my son, my son!"

⁵Then Joab went to the king's room and said to him, "We saved your life today and the lives of your sons, your daughters, and your wives and concubines. Yet you act like this, making us feel ashamed of ourselves. ⁶You seem to love those who hate you and hate those who love you. You have made it clear today that your commanders and troops mean nothing to you. It seems that if Absalom had lived and all of us had died, you would be pleased. ⁷Now go out there and congratulate your troops, for I swear by the LORD that if you don't go out, not a single one of them will remain here tonight. Then you will be worse off than ever before."

⁸So the king went out and took his seat at the town gate, and as the news spread throughout the town that he was there, everyone went to him.

Meanwhile, the Israelites who had supported Absalom fled to their homes. ⁹And throughout all the tribes of Israel there was much discussion and argument going on. The people were saying, "The king rescued us from our enemies and saved us from the Philistines, but Absalom chased him out of the country. ¹⁰Now Absalom, whom we anointed to rule over us, is dead. Why not ask David to come back and be our king again?"

¹¹Then King David sent Zadok and Abiathar, the priests, to say to the elders of Judah, "Why are you the last ones to welcome back the king into his palace? For I have heard that all Israel is ready. ¹²You are my relatives, my own tribe, my own flesh and blood! So why are you the last ones to welcome back the king?" ¹³And David told them to tell Amasa, "Since you are my own flesh and blood, like Joab, may God strike me and even kill me if I do not appoint you as commander of my army in his place."

**18:28**
1 Sam 17:46; 25:23

**18:32**
1 Sam 25:26

**18:33**
Exod 32:32
2 Sam 19:4
Rom 9:1-3

**19:1**
2 Sam 18:5, 14

**19:4**
2 Sam 15:30; 18:33

**19:8**
2 Sam 8:1; 15:2;
18:24

**19:9**
2 Sam 8:1-14;
15:14

**19:11**
2 Sam 15:24

**19:13**
2 Sam 17:25

**18:33** Verse 18:33 is numbered 19:1 in Hebrew text.    **19:1** Verses 19:1-43 are numbered 19:2-44 in Hebrew text.

---

**18:29** Although he reached the city first, Ahimaaz was afraid to tell the king the truth about the death of his son Absalom.

**18:33** Why was David so upset over the death of his rebel son? (1) David realized that he, in part, was responsible for Absalom's death. Nathan the prophet had said that because David had killed Uriah, his own sons would rebel against him. (2) David was angry at Joab and his officers for killing Absalom against his wishes. (3) David truly loved his son, even though Absalom did nothing to deserve his love. It would have been kinder and more loving to deal with Absalom and his runaway ego when he was younger.

**19:4-7** At times we must reprove those in authority over us. Joab knew he was risking the king's displeasure by confronting him, but he saw what had to be done. Joab told David that there would be dreadful consequences if he didn't commend the troops for their victory. Joab's actions are a helpful example to us when personal confrontation is necessary.

**19:8** David sat at the town gate because that was where business was conducted and judgment rendered. His presence there showed that he was over his mourning and back in control.

**19:8-10** Just a few days before, most of Israel was supporting the rebel ruler Absalom. Now the people wanted David back as their king. Because crowds are often fickle, there must be a higher moral code to follow than the pleasure of the majority. Following the moral principles given in God's Word will help you avoid being swayed by the popular opinions of the crowd.

**19:13** David's appointment of Amasa was a shrewd political move. First, Amasa had been commander of Absalom's army; by making Amasa his commander, David would secure the allegiance of the rebel army. Second, by replacing Joab as commander in chief, David punished him for his previous crimes (3:26-29). Third, Amasa had a great deal of influence over the

¹⁴Then Amasa* convinced all the men of Judah, and they responded unanimously. They sent word to the king, "Return to us, and bring back all who are with you."

### David's Return to Jerusalem

**19:15**
Josh 5:8-9
1 Sam 11:14-15

**19:16**
2 Sam 16:5-13
1 Kgs 2:8

**19:17**
2 Sam 9:2

¹⁵So the king started back to Jerusalem. And when he arrived at the Jordan River, the people of Judah came to Gilgal to meet him and escort him across the river. ¹⁶Shimei son of Gera, the man from Bahurim in Benjamin, hurried across with the men of Judah to welcome King David. ¹⁷A thousand other men from the tribe of Benjamin were with him, including Ziba, the chief servant of the house of Saul, and Ziba's fifteen sons and twenty servants. They rushed down to the Jordan to meet the king. ¹⁸They crossed the shallows of the Jordan to bring the king's household across the river, helping him in every way they could.

### David's Mercy to Shimei

**19:19**
2 Sam 16:6-9

As the king was about to cross the river, Shimei fell down before him. ¹⁹"My lord the king, please forgive me," he pleaded. "Forget the terrible thing your servant did when you left

**19:14** Or *David;* Hebrew reads *he.*

---

**JOAB**

Joab, the great military leader, had two brothers who were also famous soldiers: Abishai and Asahel. Joab proved to be the greatest leader of the three and was the commander of David's army throughout most of David's reign. There is no record that his troops ever lost a battle.

Joab was a fearless fighter like his brothers. Unlike them, he was also a brilliant and ruthless strategist. His plans usually worked, but he was seldom concerned about those hurt or killed by them. He did not hesitate to use treachery or murder to achieve his goals. His career is a story of great accomplishments and shameful acts. He conquered Jerusalem and the surrounding nations, defeated Abner, and reconciled Absalom and David. But he also murdered Abner, Amasa, and Absalom, took part in Uriah's murder, and plotted with Adonijah against Solomon. That plot led to his execution.

Joab set his own standards—he lived by them and died because of them. There is little evidence that Joab ever acknowledged God's standards. On one occasion he confronted David about the danger of taking a census without God's command, but this may have been little more than a move to protect himself. Joab's self-centeredness eventually destroyed him. He was loyal only to himself, even willing to betray his lifelong relationship with David to preserve his power.

Joab's life illustrates the disastrous results of having no source of direction outside oneself. Brilliance and power are self-destructive without God's guidance. Only God can give the direction we need. For that reason, he has made available his Word, the Bible, and he is willing to be personally present in the lives of those who admit their need for him.

| | |
|---|---|
| **Strengths and accomplishments** | • Brilliant planner and strategist<br>• Fearless fighter and resourceful commander<br>• Confident leader who did not hesitate to confront even the king<br>• Helped reconcile David and Absalom<br>• Masterminded the conquest of Jerusalem |
| **Weaknesses and mistakes** | • Was repeatedly ruthless, violent, and vengeful<br>• Carried out David's scheme to have Uriah, Bathsheba's husband, killed<br>• Avenged his brother's murder by murdering Abner<br>• Killed Absalom against David's orders<br>• Plotted with Adonijah against David and Solomon |
| **Lessons from his life** | • Those who live by violence often die by violence<br>• Even brilliant leaders need guidance |
| **Vital statistics** | • Occupation: Commander in chief of David's army<br>• Relatives: Mother: Zeruiah. Brothers: Abishai, Asahel. Uncle: David.<br>• Contemporaries: Saul, Abner, Absalom |
| **Key verse** | "'Do as he said,' the king replied. 'Kill him there beside the altar and bury him. This will remove the guilt of Joab's senseless murders from me and from my father's family'" (1 Kings 2:31). |

Joab's story is told in 2 Samuel 2—1 Kings 2. He is also mentioned in 1 Chronicles 2:16; 11:5–9, 20, 26; 19:8–15; 20:1; 21:2–6; 26:28; and in the title of Psalm 60.

---

leaders of Judah (19:14). All of these moves would help to unite the kingdom.

**19:19, 20** By admitting his wrong and asking David's forgiveness, Shimei was trying to save his own life. His plan worked

for a while. This was a day of celebration, not execution. But we read in 1 Kings 2:8, 9 that David advised Solomon to execute Shimei.

Jerusalem. May the king put it out of his mind. 20I know how much I sinned. That is why I have come here today, the very first person in all Israel* to greet my lord the king."

21Then Abishai son of Zeruiah said, "Shimei should die, for he cursed the LORD's anointed king!"

22"Who asked your opinion, you sons of Zeruiah!" David exclaimed. "Why have you become my adversary* today? This is not a day for execution but for celebration! Today I am once again the king of Israel!" 23Then, turning to Shimei, David vowed, "Your life will be spared."

### David's Kindness to Mephibosheth

24Now Mephibosheth,* Saul's grandson, came down from Jerusalem to meet the king. He had not cared for his feet, trimmed his beard, or washed his clothes since the day the king left Jerusalem. 25"Why didn't you come with me, Mephibosheth?" the king asked him.

26Mephibosheth replied, "My lord the king, my servant Ziba deceived me. I told him, 'Saddle my donkey'* so I can go with the king.' For as you know I am crippled. 27Ziba has slandered me by saying that I refused to come. But I know that my lord the king is like an angel of God, so do what you think is best. 28All my relatives and I could expect only death from you, my lord, but instead you have honored me by allowing me to eat at your own table! What more can I ask?"

29"You've said enough," David replied. "I've decided that you and Ziba will divide your land equally between you."

30"Give him all of it," Mephibosheth said. "I am content just to have you safely back again, my lord the king!"

### David's Kindness to Barzillai

31Barzillai of Gilead had come down from Rogelim to escort the king across the Jordan. 32He was very old, about eighty, and very wealthy. He was the one who had provided food for the king during his stay in Mahanaim. 33"Come across with me and live in Jerusalem," the king said to Barzillai. "I will take care of you there."

34"No," he replied, "I am far too old to go with the king to Jerusalem. 35I am eighty years old today, and I can no longer enjoy anything. Food and wine are no longer tasty, and I cannot hear the singers as they sing. I would only be a burden to my lord the king. 36Just to go across the Jordan River with the king is all the honor I need! 37Then let me return again to die in my own town, where my father and mother are buried. But here is your servant, my son Kimham. Let him go with my lord the king and receive whatever you want to give him."

38"Good," the king agreed. "Kimham will go with me, and I will help him in any way you would like. And I will do for you anything you want." 39So all the people crossed the Jordan with the king. After David had blessed Barzillai and kissed him, Barzillai returned to his own home.

40The king then crossed over to Gilgal, taking Kimham with him. All the troops of Judah and half the troops of Israel escorted the king on his way.

### An Argument over the King

41But all the men of Israel complained to the king, "The men of Judah stole the king and didn't give us the honor of helping take you, your household, and all your men across the Jordan."

42The men of Judah replied, "The king is one of our own kinsmen. Why should this make you angry? We haven't eaten any of the king's food or received any special favors!"

43"But there are ten tribes in Israel," the others replied. "So we have ten times as much right to the king as you do. What right do you have to treat us with such contempt? Weren't we the first to speak of bringing him back to be our king again?" The argument continued back and forth, and the men of Judah spoke even more harshly than the men of Israel.

**19:21**
Exod 22:28
**19:22**
1 Sam 11:13
2 Sam 16:9-10
**19:23**
1 Kgs 2:8
**19:24**
2 Sam 9:5-10
**19:25**
2 Sam 16:17
**19:26**
2 Sam 9:2-3, 13
**19:27**
2 Sam 14:17, 20
**19:28**
2 Sam 9:7
**19:31**
2 Sam 17:27-29
1 Kgs 2:7
**19:35**
Ps 90:10
**19:37**
1 Kgs 2:7
Jer 41:17
**19:39**
Gen 31:55
Ruth 1:14
2 Sam 14:33
**19:43**
2 Sam 5:1

19:20 Hebrew *in the house of Joseph.*   19:22 Or *my prosecutor.*   19:24 *Mephibosheth* is another name for *Merib-baal.*   19:26 As in Greek, Syriac, and Latin versions; Hebrew reads *I will saddle a donkey for myself.*

**19:21ff** David showed tremendous mercy and generosity as he returned to Jerusalem. He spared Shimei, restored Mephibosheth, and rewarded faithful Barzillai. David's fairness sets a standard for government that will be fully realized in Christ's righteous rule in the coming Kingdom.

**19:24-30** David could not be certain if Mephibosheth or Ziba was in the right, and Scripture leaves the question unanswered. (For the whole story on Mephibosheth, see also 9:1-13 and 16:1-4.)

### The Revolt of Sheba

20:1
1 Sam 22:7-8
1 Kgs 12:16
2 Chr 10:16

**20** There happened to be a troublemaker there named Sheba son of Bicri, a man from the tribe of Benjamin. Sheba blew a ram's horn and began to chant:

"Down with the dynasty of David!
  We have no interest in the son of Jesse.
Come on, you men of Israel,
  back to your homes!"

2 So all the men of Israel deserted David and followed Sheba son of Bicri. But the men of Judah stayed with their king and escorted him from the Jordan River to Jerusalem.

20:3
2 Sam 15:16;
16:21-22

3 When David came to his palace in Jerusalem, he took the ten concubines he had left to look after the palace and placed them in seclusion. Their needs were provided for, but he no longer slept with them. So each of them lived like a widow until she died.

20:4
2 Sam 17:25; 19:13

4 Then the king told Amasa, "Mobilize the army of Judah within three days, and report back at that time." 5 So Amasa went out to notify Judah, but it took him longer than the time he had been given.

20:6
2 Sam 21:17

6 Then David said to Abishai, "Sheba son of Bicri is going to hurt us more than Absalom did. Quick, take my troops and chase after him before he gets into a fortified town where we can't reach him."

20:7
2 Sam 8:18;
15:17-18
1 Kgs 1:38
20:8
2 Sam 2:18

7 So Abishai and Joab,* together with the king's bodyguard* and all the mighty warriors, set out from Jerusalem to go after Sheba. 8 As they arrived at the great stone in Gibeon, Amasa met them. Joab was wearing his military tunic with a dagger strapped to his belt. As he stepped forward to greet Amasa, he slipped the dagger from its sheath.*

20:10
1 Kgs 2:5

9 "How are you, my cousin?" Joab said and took him by the beard with his right hand as though to kiss him. 10 Amasa didn't notice the dagger in his left hand, and Joab stabbed him in the stomach with it so that his insides gushed out onto the ground. Joab did not need to strike again, and Amasa soon died. Joab and his brother Abishai left him lying there and continued after Sheba.

11 One of Joab's young men shouted to Amasa's troops, "If you are for Joab and David, come and follow Joab." 12 But Amasa lay in his blood in the middle of the road, and Joab's man saw that everyone was stopping to stare at him. So he pulled him off the road into a field and threw a cloak over him. 13 With Amasa's body out of the way, everyone went on with Joab to capture Sheba son of Bicri.

14 Meanwhile, Sheba traveled through all the tribes of Israel and eventually came to the town of Abel-beth-maacah. All the members of his own clan, the Bicrites,* assembled for battle and followed him into the town. 15 When Joab's forces arrived, they attacked Abel-beth-maacah. They built a siege ramp against the town's fortifications and began battering

20:15
Ezek 4:2

**20:7a** Hebrew *So Joab's men.* **20:7b** Hebrew *the Kerethites and Pelethites;* also in 20:23. **20:8** Hebrew *As he stepped forward, it fell out.* **20:14** As in Greek and Latin versions; Hebrew reads *All the Berites.*

---

**SHEBA'S REBELLION**
After defeating Absalom, David returned to Jerusalem from Mahanaim. But Sheba incited a rebellion against David, so David sent Joab, Abishai, and a small army after him. Joab and his troops besieged Abel-beth-maacah, Sheba's hideout, until the people of Abel-beth-maacah killed Sheba themselves.

Mediterranean Sea
Abel-beth-maacah
N
Sea of Galilee
Jordan River
CANAAN
Mahanaim
Gibeon
Gilgal
Jerusalem
Dead Sea
0   20 Mi.
0   20 Km.

**20:1** Although Israel was a united kingdom, it was still made up of 12 separate tribes. These tribes often had difficulty agreeing on the goals of the nation as a whole. Tribal jealousies had originally kept Israel from completely conquering the Promised Land (read the book of Joshua), and now tribal jealousies were threatening the stability of David's reign by giving Sheba an opportunity to rebel (20:1ff).

**20:7-10** Once again Joab's murderous act went unpunished, just as it did when he killed Abner (3:26, 27). Eventually, however, justice caught up with him (1 Kings 2:28-35). It may seem that sin and treachery often go unpunished, but God's justice is not limited to this life's rewards. Even if Joab had died of old age, he would have had to face the day of judgment.

down the wall. [16]But a wise woman in the town called out to Joab, "Listen to me, Joab. Come over here so I can talk to you." [17]As he approached, the woman asked, "Are you Joab?"

"I am," he replied.

So she said, "Listen carefully to your servant."

"I'm listening," he said.

[18]Then she continued, "There used to be a saying, 'If you want to settle an argument, ask advice at the town of Abel.' [19]I am one who is peace loving and faithful in Israel. But you are destroying an important town in Israel.* Why do you want to devour what belongs to the LORD?"

[20]And Joab replied, "Believe me, I don't want to devour or destroy your town! [21]That's not my purpose. All I want is a man named Sheba son of Bicri from the hill country of Ephraim, who has revolted against King David. If you hand over this one man to me, I will leave the town in peace."

"All right," the woman replied, "we will throw his head over the wall to you." [22]Then the woman went to all the people with her wise advice, and they cut off Sheba's head and threw it out to Joab. So he blew the ram's horn and called his troops back from the attack. They all returned to their homes, and Joab returned to the king at Jerusalem.

[23]Now Joab was the commander of the army of Israel. Benaiah son of Jehoiada was captain of the king's bodyguard. [24]Adoniram* was in charge of the labor force. Jehoshaphat son of Ahilud was the royal historian. [25]Sheva was the court secretary. Zadok and Abiathar were the priests. [26]And Ira, a descendant of Jair, was David's personal priest.

## 4. The later years of David's rule

### David Avenges the Gibeonites

**21** There was a famine during David's reign that lasted for three years, so David asked the LORD about it. And the LORD said, "The famine has come because Saul and his family are guilty of murdering the Gibeonites."

[2]So the king summoned the Gibeonites. They were not part of Israel but were all that was left of the nation of the Amorites. The people of Israel had sworn not to kill them, but Saul, in his zeal for Israel and Judah, had tried to wipe them out. [3]David asked them, "What can I do for you? How can I make amends so that you will bless the LORD's people again?"

[4]"Well, money can't settle this matter between us and the family of Saul," the Gibeonites replied. "Neither can we demand the life of anyone in Israel."

"What can I do then?" David asked. "Just tell me and I will do it for you."

[5]Then they replied, "It was Saul who planned to destroy us, to keep us from having any place at all in the territory of Israel. [6]So let seven of Saul's sons be handed over to us, and we will execute them before the LORD at Gibeon, on the mountain of the LORD.*"

"All right," the king said, "I will do it." [7]The king spared Jonathan's son Mephibosheth,* who was Saul's grandson, because of the oath David and Jonathan had sworn before the LORD. [8]But he gave them Saul's two sons Armoni and Mephibosheth, whose mother was Rizpah daughter of Aiah. He also gave them the five sons of Saul's daughter Merab,*

Cross-references (margin):
- 20:16 — 2 Sam 14:2
- 20:19 — Deut 20:10; 2 Sam 14:15-16
- 20:21 — Josh 24:33; 2 Sam 20:2
- 20:22 — Eccl 9:13
- 20:23 — 2 Sam 8:16-18
- 20:25 — 1 Sam 2:35
- 21:1 — Gen 12:10; 26:1; 42:5
- 21:2 — Josh 9:15-20
- 21:3 — 1 Sam 26:19
- 21:4 — Num 35:33-34
- 21:5 — 2 Sam 21:1
- 21:6 — Num 25:4; 1 Sam 10:24
- 21:7 — 1 Sam 18:1-3; 20:12-17; 23:18; 2 Sam 4:4
- 21:8 — 1 Sam 18:19; 2 Sam 3:7

---

20:19 Hebrew *a town that is a mother in Israel.* 20:24 As in Greek version (see also 1 Kgs 4:6; 5:14); Hebrew reads *Adoram.* 21:6 As in Greek version (see also 21:9); Hebrew reads *at Gibeah of Saul, the chosen of the LORD.* 21:7 *Mephibosheth* is another name for Merib-baal. 21:8 As in a few Hebrew and Greek manuscripts and Syriac version (see also 1 Sam 18:19); most Hebrew manuscripts read *Michal.*

---

**20:16ff** Joab's men were attacking the city, and it looked as if it would be destroyed. Though women in that society were usually quiet in public, this woman spoke out. She stopped Joab's attack, not with weapons, but with wise words and a plan of action. Often the courage to speak a few sensible words can prevent great disaster.

**20:23** Benaiah was the captain of David's bodyguard and a famous member of that special group of mighty men called "the Thirty" (23:24). He remained loyal to David during Absalom's rebellion. Later he helped establish Solomon as king (1 Kings 1:32-40; 2:28-34) and eventually replaced Joab as commander of Israel's army (1 Kings 2:35).

**21:1** Farmers relied heavily on spring and fall rains for their crops. If the rains stopped or came at the wrong time, or if the plants became insect infested, there would be drastic food shortages in the coming year. Agriculture at that time was completely dependent upon natural conditions. There were no irrigation sprinklers, fertilizers, or pesticides. Even moderate variations in rainfall or insect activity could destroy an entire harvest.

**21:1ff** The next four chapters are an appendix to the book. The events described are not presented in chronological order. They tell of David's exploits at various times during his reign.

**21:1-14** Although the Bible does not record Saul's act of vengeance against the Gibeonites, it was apparently a serious crime making him guilty of their blood. Still, why were Saul's sons killed for the murders their father committed? In many Near Eastern cultures, including Israel's, an entire family was held guilty for the crime of the father because the family was considered an indissoluble unit. Saul broke the vow that the Israelites made to the Gibeonites (Joshua 9:16-20). This was a serious offense against God's law (Numbers 30:1, 2). Either David was following the custom of treating the family as a unit, or Saul's sons were guilty of helping Saul kill the Gibeonites.

the wife of Adriel son of Barzillai from Meholah. ⁹The men of Gibeon executed them on the mountain before the LORD. So all seven of them died together at the beginning of the barley harvest.

**21:10**
Deut 21:23
1 Sam 17:44

¹⁰Then Rizpah daughter of Aiah, the mother of two of the men, spread burlap on a rock and stayed there the entire harvest season. She prevented the scavenger birds from tearing at their bodies during the day and stopped wild animals from eating them at night. ¹¹When David learned what Rizpah, Saul's concubine, had done, ¹²he went to the people of Jabesh-gilead and retrieved the bones of Saul and his son Jonathan. (When the Philistines had killed Saul and Jonathan on Mount Gilboa, the people of Jabesh-gilead stole their bodies from the public square of Beth-shan, where the Philistines had hung them.) ¹³So David obtained the bones of Saul and Jonathan, as well as the bones of the men the Gibeonites had executed.

**21:12**
1 Sam 31:11-13

¹⁴Then the king ordered that they bury the bones in the tomb of Kish, Saul's father, at the town of Zela in the land of Benjamin. After that, God ended the famine in the land.

**21:15-22**
//1 Chr 20:4-8
**21:16**
Num 13:28
**21:17**
2 Sam 18:2-3; 20:6

### Battles against Philistine Giants

¹⁵Once again the Philistines were at war with Israel. And when David and his men were in the thick of battle, David became weak and exhausted. ¹⁶Ishbi-benob was a descendant of the giants*; his bronze spearhead weighed more than seven pounds,* and he was armed with a new sword. He had cornered David and was about to kill him. ¹⁷But Abishai son of Zeruiah came to David's rescue and killed the Philistine. Then David's men declared, "You are not going out to battle with us again! Why risk snuffing out the light of Israel?"

**21:16a** Or *a descendant of the Rapha;* also in 21:18, 20, 22.   **21:16b** Hebrew *300 shekels* [3.4 kilograms].

---

Most great leaders struggle with a few followers who try too hard. For David, Abishai was that kind of follower. His fierce loyalty to David had to be kept from becoming destructive—he was too willing to leap to his leader's defense. David never put down Abishai's eager loyalty. Instead, he patiently tried to direct its powerful energy. This approach, while not completely successful, saved David's life on at least one occasion. At three other times, however, Abishai would have killed for the king if David had not stopped him.

Abishai was an excellent soldier, but he was better at taking orders than giving them. When he wasn't carrying out David's orders, Abishai was usually under the command of his younger brother Joab. The two brothers helped each other accomplish great military feats as well as shameful acts of violence—Abishai helped Joab murder Abner and Amasa. When he was effective as a leader, he led mostly by example. But all too often he did not think before he acted.

We should be challenged by Abishai's admirable qualities of fearlessness and loyalty, but we should be warned by his tendency to act without thinking. It is not enough to be strong and effective; we must also have the self-control and wisdom that God can give us. We are to follow and obey with our hearts and our minds.

| | |
|---|---|
| **Strengths and accomplishments** | • Known as one of the heroes among David's fighting men<br>• A fearless and willing volunteer, fiercely loyal to David<br>• Saved David's life |
| **Weaknesses and mistakes** | • Tended to act without thinking<br>• Helped Joab murder Abner and Amasa |
| **Lessons from his life** | • The most effective followers combine careful thought and action<br>• Blind loyalty can cause great evil |
| **Vital statistics** | • Occupation: Soldier<br>• Relatives: Mother: Zeruiah. Brothers: Joab, Asahel. Uncle: David. |
| **Key verses** | "Abishai son of Zeruiah, the brother of Joab, was the leader of the Thirty. He once used his spear to kill 300 enemy warriors in a single battle. It was by such feats that he became as famous as the Three. Abishai was the most famous of the Thirty and was their commander, though he was not one of the Three" (2 Samuel 23:18, 19). |

Abishai's story is told in 2 Samuel 2:18—23:19. He is also mentioned in 1 Samuel 26:1–13; 1 Chronicles 2:16; 11:20; 18:12; 19:11, 15.

---

**21:9, 10** The barley harvest was in late April and early May. Barley was similar to wheat but less suitable for breadmaking. Rizpah guarded the men's bodies during the entire harvest season, which lasted from April to October.

**21:16-18** For more information on giants, see 1 Samuel 17:4-7 and the note on Genesis 6:4.

¹⁸After this, there was another battle against the Philistines at Gob. As they fought, Sibbecai from Hushah killed Saph, another descendant of the giants.

¹⁹During another battle at Gob, Elhanan son of Jair* from Bethlehem killed the brother of Goliath of Gath.* The handle of his spear was as thick as a weaver's beam!

²⁰In another battle with the Philistines at Gath, they encountered a huge man with six fingers on each hand and six toes on each foot, twenty-four in all, who was also a descendant of the giants. ²¹But when he defied and taunted Israel, he was killed by Jonathan, the son of David's brother Shimea.*

²²These four Philistines were descendants of the giants of Gath, but David and his warriors killed them.

## David's Song of Praise

**22** David sang this song to the LORD on the day the LORD rescued him from all his enemies and from Saul. ²He sang:

"The LORD is my rock, my fortress, and my savior;
3   my God is my rock, in whom I find protection.
He is my shield, the power that saves me,
    and my place of safety.
He is my refuge, my savior,
    the one who saves me from violence.
⁴ I called on the LORD, who is worthy of praise,
    and he saved me from my enemies.

⁵ "The waves of death overwhelmed me;
    floods of destruction swept over me.
⁶ The grave* wrapped its ropes around me;
    death laid a trap in my path.
⁷ But in my distress I cried out to the LORD;
    yes, I cried to my God for help.
He heard me from his sanctuary;
    my cry reached his ears.

⁸ "Then the earth quaked and trembled.
    The foundations of the heavens shook;
    they quaked because of his anger.
⁹ Smoke poured from his nostrils;
    fierce flames leaped from his mouth.
    Glowing coals blazed forth from him.
¹⁰ He opened the heavens and came down;
    dark storm clouds were beneath his feet.
¹¹ Mounted on a mighty angelic being,* he flew,
    soaring* on the wings of the wind.
¹² He shrouded himself in darkness,
    veiling his approach with dense rain clouds.
¹³ A great brightness shone around him,
    and burning coals* blazed forth.
¹⁴ The LORD thundered from heaven;
    the voice of the Most High resounded.
¹⁵ He shot arrows and scattered his enemies;
    his lightning flashed, and they were confused.
¹⁶ Then at the command of the LORD,
    at the blast of his breath,

| | |
|---|---|
| **21:18** | 1 Chr 11:29; 20:4-8; 27:11 |
| **21:19** | 1 Sam 17:4-7 |
| **21:22** | 1 Chr 20:8 |
| **22:1-51** | //Ps 18:1-50 |
| **22:1** | Exod 15:1; Ps 18:title |
| **22:2** | 1 Sam 2:2; Pss 31:3; 71:3 |
| **22:3** | Deut 33:29; Ps 3:3; Luke 1:69 |
| **22:4** | Pss 48:1; 96:4 |
| **22:5** | Pss 69:14; 93:4; Jon 2:3 |
| **22:6** | Ps 116:3-4 |
| **22:7** | Pss 116:4; 120:1 |
| **22:8** | Judg 5:4; Job 26:11; Ps 97:4 |
| **22:9** | Deut 32:22; Heb 12:29 |
| **22:10** | Exod 20:21; 1 Kgs 8:12-13; Ps 97:2; Nah 1:3 |
| **22:12** | Ps 104:3 |
| **22:14** | Job 37:2; Ps 29:3 |
| **22:15** | Deut 32:23; Josh 10:10; 1 Sam 7:10 |
| **22:16** | Exod 15:8; Nah 1:4 |

**21:19a** As in parallel text at 1 Chr 20:5; Hebrew reads *son of Jaare-oregim.*   **21:19b** As in parallel text at 1 Chr 20:5; Hebrew reads *killed Goliath of Gath.*   **21:21** As in parallel text at 1 Chr 20:7; Hebrew reads *Shimei,* a variant spelling of Shimea.   **22:6** Hebrew *Sheol.*   **22:11a** Hebrew *a cherub.*   **22:11b** As in some Hebrew manuscripts (see also Ps 18:10); other Hebrew manuscripts read *appearing.*   **22:13** Or *and lightning bolts.*

**22:1ff** David was a skilled musician who played his harp for Saul (1 Samuel 16:23), instituted the music programs in the Temple (1 Chronicles 25), and wrote more of the book of Psalms than anyone else. Writing a song like this was not unusual for David. This royal hymn of thanksgiving is almost identical to Psalm 18. (For other songs in the Bible, see the chart in Exodus 15, p. 119.)

the bottom of the sea could be seen,
and the foundations of the earth were laid bare.

**22:17**
Ps 144:7

17 "He reached down from heaven and rescued me;
he drew me out of deep waters.

**22:18**
Ps 23:4

18 He rescued me from my powerful enemies,
from those who hated me and were too strong for me.

**22:19**
Ps 23:4

19 They attacked me at a moment when I was in distress,
but the LORD supported me.

**22:20**
Pss 31:8; 118:5

20 He led me to a place of safety;
he rescued me because he delights in me.

**22:21**
1 Sam 26:23
Pss 24:4-5; 128:1

21 The LORD rewarded me for doing right;
he restored me because of my innocence.

**22:22**
Gen 18:19
Ps 128:1

22 For I have kept the ways of the LORD;
I have not turned from my God to follow evil.

**22:23**
Deut 6:6-9

23 I have followed all his regulations;
I have never abandoned his decrees.

**22:24**
Gen 6:9-10; 7:1
Eph 1:4

24 I am blameless before God;
I have kept myself from sin.

25 The LORD rewarded me for doing right.
He has seen my innocence.

**22:26**
Matt 5:7

26 "To the faithful you show yourself faithful;
to those with integrity you show integrity.

**22:27**
Lev 26:23-24
Matt 5:8

27 To the pure you show yourself pure,
but to the wicked you show yourself hostile.

**22:28**
Exod 3:7-8
Ps 72:12-13
Isa 2:11-12, 17;
5:15

28 You rescue the humble,
but your eyes watch the proud and humiliate them.

**22:29**
Ps 27:1

29 O LORD, you are my lamp.
The LORD lights up my darkness.

30 In your strength I can crush an army;
with my God I can scale any wall.

**22:31**
Deut 32:4
2 Sam 22:3
Pss 12:6; 119:140
Prov 30:5
Matt 5:48

31 "God's way is perfect.
All the LORD's promises prove true.
He is a shield for all who look to him for protection.

**22:32**
1 Sam 2:2

32 For who is God except the LORD?
Who but our God is a solid rock?

33 God is my strong fortress,
and he makes my way perfect.

34 He makes me as surefooted as a deer,
enabling me to stand on mountain heights.

**22:35**
Ps 144:1

35 He trains my hands for battle;
he strengthens my arm to draw a bronze bow.

---

| DAVID REVEALS TRUTHS ABOUT GOD IN HIS SONG OF PRAISE. | David says, "The LORD is my . . ." | Rock, Fortress, Savior, Protection, Shield, Power that Saves, Place of Safety, Refuge, Lamp |
|---|---|---|
| | David names these characteristics of God. He is . . . | Saving, Worthy of praise, Hearing, Angry (against enemies), Rescuing, Rewarding, Seeing, Faithful, Showing (revealing) himself, Shrewd, Powerful, Strong, Perfect, Pure, Flawless, Shielding (us from enemies), Giving, Gentle, Preserving, Living |

---

**22:22-24** David was not denying that he had ever sinned. Psalm 51 shows his tremendous anguish over his sin against Uriah and Bathsheba. But David understood God's faithfulness and was writing this hymn from God's perspective. He knew that God had made him clean again—"whiter than snow" (Psalm 51:7), with a "clean heart" (Psalm 51:10). Through the death and resurrection of Jesus Christ, we also are made clean and perfect. God replaces our sin with his purity, and he no longer sees our sin.

**22:27** "To the wicked you show yourself hostile" means that to those who sin, God is a judge who will punish them for their sins. God destroys those who are evil.

36 You have given me your shield of victory;
  your help* has made me great.

37 You have made a wide path for my feet
  to keep them from slipping.

38 "I chased my enemies and destroyed them;
  I did not stop until they were conquered.

39 I consumed them;
  I struck them down so they did not get up;
  they fell beneath my feet.

40 You have armed me with strength for the battle;
  you have subdued my enemies under my feet.

41 You placed my foot on their necks.
  I have destroyed all who hated me.

42 They looked for help, but no one came to their rescue.
  They even cried to the LORD, but he refused to answer.

43 I ground them as fine as the dust of the earth;
  I trampled them* in the gutter like dirt.

44 "You gave me victory over my accusers.
  You preserved me as the ruler over nations;
  people I don't even know now serve me.

45 Foreign nations cringe before me;
  as soon as they hear of me, they submit.

46 They all lose their courage
  and come trembling* from their strongholds.

47 "The LORD lives! Praise to my Rock!
  May God, the Rock of my salvation, be exalted!

48 He is the God who pays back those who harm me;
  he brings down the nations under me

49   and delivers me from my enemies.
  You hold me safe beyond the reach of my enemies;
  you save me from violent opponents.

50 For this, O LORD, I will praise you among the nations;
  I will sing praises to your name.

51 You give great victories to your king;
  you show unfailing love to your anointed,
  to David and all his descendants forever."

## David's Last Words

**23** These are the last words of David:

"David, the son of Jesse, speaks—
  David, the man who was raised up so high,
  David, the man anointed by the God of Jacob,
  David, the sweet psalmist of Israel.*

2 "The Spirit of the LORD speaks through me;
  his words are upon my tongue.

**Cross-references (right margin):**

**22:36** Eph 6:16-17

**22:39** Mal 4:3

**22:41** Exod 23:27

**22:42** 1 Sam 28:5-6; Isa 1:15

**22:43** Isa 10:6; Mic 7:10

**22:44** 2 Sam 3:1; 8:1-14; 19:8-10; Isa 55:5

**22:45** Ps 66:3; Isa 55:5; 60:12

**22:46** Mic 7:17

**22:47** 2 Sam 22:2, 32; Ps 89:26

**22:48** 1 Sam 24:12; 25:39; Pss 94:1; 144:2

**22:49** Pss 44:5; 140:1, 4, 11

**22:50** †Rom 15:9

**22:51** 2 Sam 7:12-16; Pss 89:20; 144:9-10

**23:1** 1 Sam 16:12-13; 2 Sam 7:8-9; Pss 78:70-72; 89:20

**23:2** 2 Pet 1:20-21

---

**22:36** As in Dead Sea Scrolls (see also Ps 18:35); Masoretic Text reads *your answering*.   **22:43** As in Dead Sea Scrolls (see also Ps 18:42); Masoretic Text reads *I crushed and trampled them*.   **22:46** As in parallel text at Ps 18:45; Hebrew reads *come girding themselves*.   **23:1** Or *the favorite subject of the songs of Israel*; or *the favorite of the Strong One of Israel*.

---

**22:47** David praises God wholeheartedly. Praise is not just a song *about* God; it is a song *to* God. In this song, David uses many word pictures such as rock, light, and shield to portray God's marvelous attributes. Praising God has several aspects to it. We praise God when we: (1) Say thank you to him for each attribute of his divine nature. As you read the Bible, look for other characteristics of God for which to thank him. (2) Focus our hearts on God. Take one attribute of God, such as his mercy, then concentrate on it for an entire week in your meditation and prayer. (3) Thank God for his many gracious gifts to us. Make a list and count your blessings. (4) Thank God for our relationship with him. Through Christ you have been given the gift of salvation. Tell God afresh how much you appreciate it.

23:3
2 Sam 22:2, 32
2 Chr 19:7, 9
Ps 72:1-3
Isa 11:1-5

3 The God of Israel spoke.
    The Rock of Israel said to me:
  'The one who rules righteously,
      who rules in the fear of God,

23:4
Judg 5:31
Pss 72:6; 110:3

4 is like the light of morning at sunrise,
      like a morning without clouds,
  like the gleaming of the sun
      on new grass after rain.'

23:5
2 Sam 7:12
Ps 89:29
Isa 55:3

5 "Is it not my family God has chosen?
    Yes, he has made an everlasting covenant with me.
  His agreement is arranged and guaranteed in every detail.
    He will ensure my safety and success.

23:6
Matt 13:41-42

6 But the godless are like thorns to be thrown away,
    for they tear the hand that touches them.
7 One must use iron tools to chop them down;
    they will be totally consumed by fire."

### David's Mightiest Warriors

23:8
1 Chr 11:11-47

8These are the names of David's mightiest warriors. The first was Jashobeam the Hacmonite,* who was leader of the Three*—the three mightiest warriors among David's men. He once used his spear to kill 800 enemy warriors in a single battle.*

23:9
1 Chr 27:4

9Next in rank among the Three was Eleazar son of Dodai, a descendant of Ahoah. Once Eleazar and David stood together against the Philistines when the entire Israelite army had fled. 10He killed Philistines until his hand was too tired to lift his sword, and the LORD gave him a great victory that day. The rest of the army did not return until it was time to collect the plunder!

11Next in rank was Shammah son of Agee from Harar. One time the Philistines gathered at Lehi and attacked the Israelites in a field full of lentils. The Israelite army fled, 12but Shammah* held his ground in the middle of the field and beat back the Philistines. So the LORD brought about a great victory.

23:13
1 Sam 22:1
2 Sam 5:18
23:14
1 Sam 22:4-5

13Once during the harvest, when David was at the cave of Adullam, the Philistine army was camped in the valley of Rephaim. The Three (who were among the Thirty—an elite group among David's fighting men) went down to meet him there. 14David was staying in the stronghold at the time, and a Philistine detachment had occupied the town of Bethlehem.

23:16
Gen 35:13-14

23:17
Lev 17:10

15David remarked longingly to his men, "Oh, how I would love some of that good water from the well by the gate in Bethlehem." 16So the Three broke through the Philistine lines, drew some water from the well by the gate in Bethlehem, and brought it back to David. But he refused to drink it. Instead, he poured it out as an offering to the LORD. 17"The LORD forbid that I should drink this!" he exclaimed. "This water is as precious as the blood of these men* who risked their lives to bring it to me." So David did not drink it. These are examples of the exploits of the Three.

23:8a As in parallel text at 1 Chr 11:11; Hebrew reads *Josheb-basshebeth the Tahkemonite.*    23:8b As in Greek and Latin versions (see also 1 Chr 11:11); the meaning of the Hebrew is uncertain.    23:8c As in some Greek manuscripts (see also 1 Chr 11:11); the meaning of the Hebrew is uncertain, though it might be rendered *the Three. It was Adino the Eznite who killed 800 men at one time.*    23:12 Hebrew *he.*    23:17 Hebrew *Shall I drink the blood of these men?*

---

**23:3** In the style of a prophet, David spoke of a righteous ruler. This will be fulfilled in Jesus Christ when he returns to rule in perfect justice and peace. For similar prophecies, see Isaiah 11:1-10; Jeremiah 23:5, 6; 33:15-18; Zechariah 9:9, 10. For the fulfillment of some of these prophecies, see Matthew 4:14-16; Luke 24:25-27, 44-49; John 5:45-47; 8:28, 29.

**23:8-39** These verses tell of some of the exploits that the special corps of David's army carried out. There were two elite groups of men: "the Thirty" and "the Three" (23:18, 23; 1 Chronicles 11:11-25). To become a member of such a group a man had to show unparalleled courage in battle as well as wisdom in leadership. "The Three" was the most elite group. The list of "the Thirty" actually contains 37 names, but it mentions some warriors known to be dead (Uriah, for example,

in 23:39). Apparently, new members were appointed to replace those who had fallen in battle.

**23:16** David poured out the water as an offering to God because he was so moved by the sacrifice it represented. When Hebrews offered sacrifices, they never consumed the blood. It represented life, and they poured it out before God. David would not drink this water that represented the lives of his soldiers. Instead, he offered it to God.

## David's Thirty Mighty Men

[18] Abishai son of Zeruiah, the brother of Joab, was the leader of the Thirty.* He once used his spear to kill 300 enemy warriors in a single battle. It was by such feats that he became as famous as the Three. [19] Abishai was the most famous of the Thirty* and was their commander, though he was not one of the Three.

[20] There was also Benaiah son of Jehoiada, a valiant warrior* from Kabzeel. He did many heroic deeds, which included killing two champions* of Moab. Another time, on a snowy day, he chased a lion down into a pit and killed it. [21] Once, armed only with a club, he killed a great Egyptian warrior who was armed with a spear. Benaiah wrenched the spear from the Egyptian's hand and killed him with it. [22] Deeds like these made Benaiah as famous as the Three mightiest warriors. [23] He was more honored than the other members of the Thirty, though he was not one of the Three. And David made him captain of his bodyguard.

[24] Other members of the Thirty included:

Asahel, Joab's brother;
Elhanan son of Dodo from Bethlehem;
[25] Shammah from Harod;
Elika from Harod;
[26] Helez from Pelon*;
Ira son of Ikkesh from Tekoa;
[27] Abiezer from Anathoth;
Sibbecai* from Hushah;
[28] Zalmon from Ahoah;
Maharai from Netophah;
[29] Heled* son of Baanah from Netophah;
Ithai* son of Ribai from Gibeah (in the land of Benjamin);
[30] Benaiah from Pirathon;
Hurai* from Nahale-gaash*;
[31] Abi-albon from Arabah;
Azmaveth from Bahurim;
[32] Eliahba from Shaalbon;
the sons of Jashen;
Jonathan [33] son of Shagee* from Harar;
Ahiam son of Sharar from Harar;
[34] Eliphelet son of Ahasbai from Maacah;
Eliam son of Ahithophel from Giloh;
[35] Hezro from Carmel;
Paarai from Arba;
[36] Igal son of Nathan from Zobah;
Bani from Gad;
[37] Zelek from Ammon;
Naharai from Beeroth, Joab's armor bearer;
[38] Ira from Jattir;
Gareb from Jattir;
[39] Uriah the Hittite.

There were thirty-seven in all.

## David Takes a Census

**24** Once again the anger of the LORD burned against Israel, and he caused David to harm them by taking a census. "Go and count the people of Israel and Judah," the LORD told him.

**23:18** 2 Sam 10:10, 14; 18:2
1 Chr 11:20-21

**23:20** Josh 15:21
2 Sam 8:18; 20:23

**23:24** 2 Sam 2:18

**23:25** Judg 7:1

**23:27** Josh 21:18

**23:28** 2 Kgs 25:27

**23:30** Josh 24:30

**23:34** 2 Sam 11:3; 15:12

**23:38** 1 Chr 2:53

**23:39** 2 Sam 11:3

**24:1-17** 1 Chr 21:1-17

**24:1** 1 Chr 27:23

**23:18** As in a few Hebrew manuscripts and Syriac version; most Hebrew manuscripts read *the Three*. **23:19** As in Syriac version; Hebrew reads *the Three*. **23:20a** Or *son of Jehoiada, son of Ish-hai*. **23:20b** Hebrew *two of Ariel*. **23:26** As in parallel text at 1 Chr 11:27 (see also 1 Chr 27:10); Hebrew reads *from Palti*. **23:27** As in some Greek manuscripts (see also 1 Chr 11:29); Hebrew reads *Mebunnai*. **23:29a** As in some Hebrew manuscripts (see also 1 Chr 11:30); most Hebrew manuscripts read *Heleb*. **23:29b** As in parallel text at 1 Chr 11:31; Hebrew reads *Ittai*. **23:30a** As in some Greek manuscripts (see also 1 Chr 11:32); Hebrew reads *Hiddai*. **23:30b** Or *from the ravines of Gaash*. **23:33** As in parallel text at 1 Chr 11:34; Hebrew reads *Jonathan, Shammah*; some Greek manuscripts read *Jonathan son of Shammah*.

**24:1** Did God cause David to sin? God does not cause people to sin, but he does allow sinners to reveal the sinfulness of their hearts by their actions. God presented the opportunity to David in order to deal with a disastrous national tendency, and he wanted

**24:2**
Judg 20:1
2 Sam 3:9-10

**24:3**
Deut 1:11

**24:5**
Num 21:32;
32:34-36
Josh 13:9, 16

**24:6**
Josh 19:28

**24:9**
Num 1:20-46
1 Chr 21:5

²So the king said to Joab and the commanders* of the army, "Take a census of all the tribes of Israel—from Dan in the north to Beersheba in the south—so I may know how many people there are."

³But Joab replied to the king, "May the LORD your God let you live to see a hundred times as many people as there are now! But why, my lord the king, do you want to do this?"

⁴But the king insisted that they take the census, so Joab and the commanders of the army went out to count the people of Israel. ⁵First they crossed the Jordan and camped at Aroer, south of the town in the valley, in the direction of Gad. Then they went on to Jazer, ⁶then to Gilead in the land of Tahtim-hodshi* and to Dan-jaan and around to Sidon. ⁷Then they came to the fortress of Tyre, and all the towns of the Hivites and Canaanites. Finally, they went south to Judah* as far as Beersheba.

⁸Having gone through the entire land for nine months and twenty days, they returned to Jerusalem. ⁹Joab reported the number of people to the king. There were 800,000 capable warriors in Israel who could handle a sword, and 500,000 in Judah.

**24:2** As in Greek version (see also 24:4 and 1 Chr 21:2); Hebrew reads *Joab the commander.* **24:6** Greek version reads *to Gilead and to Kadesh in the land of the Hittites.* **24:7** Or *they went to the Negev of Judah.*

## DAVID'S MIGHTY MEN

One way to understand David's success is to notice the kind of men who followed him. During the time he was being hunted by Saul, David gradually built a fighting force of several hundred men. Some were relatives, others were outcasts of society, many were in trouble with the law. They all had at least one trait in common—complete devotion to David. Their achievements made them famous. Among these men were elite military groups like "the Three" and "the Thirty." They were true heroes.

Scripture gives the impression that these men were motivated to greatness by the personal qualities of their leader. David inspired them to achieve beyond their goals and meet their true potential. Likewise, the leaders we follow and the causes to which we commit ourselves will affect our lives. David's effectiveness was clearly connected with his awareness of God's leading. He was a good leader when he was following *his* Leader. Do you know whom the people you respect most are following? Your answer should help you decide whether they deserve your loyalty. Do you also recognize God's leading in your life? No one can lead you to excellence as your Creator can.

| | |
|---|---|
| **Strengths and accomplishments** | • Able soldiers and military leaders<br>• Shared many special skills<br>• Though frequently outnumbered, were consistently victorious<br>• Loyal to David |
| **Weakness and mistake** | • Often had little in common beyond their loyalty to David and their military expertise |
| **Lessons from their lives** | • Greatness is often inspired by the quality and character of the leadership<br>• Even a small force of able and loyal men can accomplish great feats |
| **Vital statistics** | • Where: They came from all over Israel (primarily Judah and Benjamin) and from some of the other surrounding nations as well<br>• Occupations: Various backgrounds—almost all were fugitives |
| **Key verses** | "So David left Gath and escaped to the cave of Adullam. Soon his brothers and all his other relatives joined him there. Then others began coming—men who were in trouble or in debt or who were just discontented—until David was the captain of about 400 men" (1 Samuel 22:1, 2). |

Their stories are told in 1 Samuel 22—2 Samuel 23:39. They are also mentioned in 1 Chronicles 11—12.

this desire to show itself. First Chronicles 21:1 says Satan incited David to do it. Hebrew writers do not always distinguish between primary and secondary causes. So if God allowed Satan to tempt David, to them it is as if God did it.

**24:1-3** What was wrong with taking a census? A census was commanded in Numbers to prepare an army for conquering the Promised Land (Numbers 1:2; 26:2). A census amounted to a draft or conscription for the army. The land was now at peace, so there was no need to enlist troops. Israel had extended its borders and become a recognized power. David's sin was pride

and ambition in counting the people so that he could glory in the size of his army, its power and defenses. By doing this, he put his faith in the size of his army rather than in God's ability to protect them regardless of their number. Even Joab knew a census was wrong, but David did not heed his advice. We sin in a similar way when we place our security in money, possessions, or the might of our nation.

## Judgment for David's Sin

¹⁰But after he had taken the census, David's conscience began to bother him. And he said to the LORD, "I have sinned greatly by taking this census. Please forgive my guilt, LORD, for doing this foolish thing."

24:10
1 Sam 24:5
2 Sam 12:13

¹¹The next morning the word of the LORD came to the prophet Gad, who was David's seer. This was the message: ¹²"Go and say to David, 'This is what the LORD says: I will give you three choices. Choose one of these punishments, and I will inflict it on you.'"

24:11
1 Sam 9:9; 22:5

¹³So Gad came to David and asked him, "Will you choose three* years of famine throughout your land, three months of fleeing from your enemies, or three days of severe plague throughout your land? Think this over and decide what answer I should give the LORD who sent me."

24:13
1 Chr 21:12

¹⁴"I'm in a desperate situation!" David replied to Gad. "But let us fall into the hands of the LORD, for his mercy is great. Do not let me fall into human hands."

24:14
Pss 51:1;
130:3-4, 7-8

¹⁵So the LORD sent a plague upon Israel that morning, and it lasted for three days.* A total of 70,000 people died throughout the nation, from Dan in the north to Beersheba in the south. ¹⁶But as the angel was preparing to destroy Jerusalem, the LORD relented and said to the death angel, "Stop! That is enough!" At that moment the angel of the LORD was by the threshing floor of Araunah the Jebusite.

24:15
1 Chr 21:14; 27:24
24:16
Exod 12:23
2 Kgs 19:35

¹⁷When David saw the angel, he said to the LORD, "I am the one who has sinned and done wrong! But these people are as innocent as sheep—what have they done? Let your anger fall against me and my family."

24:17
Ps 74:1

## David Builds an Altar

¹⁸That day Gad came to David and said to him, "Go up and build an altar to the LORD on the threshing floor of Araunah the Jebusite."

24:18-25
//1 Chr 21:18-26

¹⁹So David went up to do what the LORD had commanded him. ²⁰When Araunah saw the king and his men coming toward him, he came and bowed before the king with his face to the ground. ²¹"Why have you come, my lord the king?" Araunah asked.

24:21
Num 16:44-50

David replied, "I have come to buy your threshing floor and to build an altar to the LORD there, so that he will stop the plague."

²²"Take it, my lord the king, and use it as you wish," Araunah said to David. "Here are oxen for the burnt offering, and you can use the threshing boards and ox yokes for wood to build a fire on the altar. ²³I will give it all to you, Your Majesty, and may the LORD your God accept your sacrifice."

24:22
1 Sam 6:14
1 Kgs 19:21

²⁴But the king replied to Araunah, "No, I insist on buying it, for I will not present burnt offerings to the LORD my God that have cost me nothing." So David paid him fifty pieces of silver* for the threshing floor and the oxen.

24:24
Gen 23:16

²⁵David built an altar there to the LORD and sacrificed burnt offerings and peace offerings. And the LORD answered his prayer for the land, and the plague on Israel was stopped.

24:25
2 Sam 21:14

**24:13** As in Greek version (see also 1 Chr 21:12); Hebrew reads *seven*.   **24:15** Hebrew *for the designated time*.
**24:24** Hebrew *50 shekels of silver*, about 20 ounces or 570 grams in weight.

---

**24:12-14** Both David and the Israelites were guilty of sin (24:1). David's sin was pride, but the Bible does not say why God was angry with the people of Israel. Perhaps it was due to their support of the rebellions of Absalom (chapters 15–18) and Sheba (chapter 20), or perhaps they put their security in military and financial prosperity rather than in God, as David did. God dealt with the whole nation through David, who exemplified the national sin of pride.

God gave David three choices. Each was a form of punishment God had told the people they could expect if they disobeyed his laws (plague—Deuteronomy 28:20-22; famine—28:23, 24; war—28:25, 26). David wisely chose the form of punishment that came most directly from God. He knew how brutal and harsh men in war could be, and he also knew God's great mercy. When you sin greatly, turn back to God. To be punished by him is far better than to take your chances without him.

**24:18** Many believe that this threshing floor where David built the altar is the location where Abraham nearly sacrificed his son

Isaac (Genesis 22:1-18). After David's death, Solomon built the Temple on this spot. Centuries later, Jesus would teach and preach here.

**24:25** The book of 2 Samuel describes David's reign. Since the Israelites first entered the Promised Land under Joshua, they had been struggling to unite the nation and drive out the wicked inhabitants. Now, after more than 400 years, Israel was finally at peace. David had accomplished what no leader before him, judge or king, had done. His administration was run on the principle of dedication to God and to the well-being of the people. Yet David also sinned. Despite his sins, however, the Bible calls David a man after God's own heart (1 Samuel 13:14; Acts 13:22) because when he sinned, he recognized it and confessed his sins to God. David committed his life to God and remained loyal to him throughout his lifetime. Psalms gives an even deeper insight into David's love for God.

# KEY PLACES IN 1 KINGS

The broken lines (— ·— ·—) indicate modern boundaries.

Solomon, David's son, brought Israel into its golden age. His wealth and wisdom were acclaimed worldwide. But he ignored God in his later years (1:1—11:43).

**1 Shechem** After Solomon's death, Israel assembled at Shechem to inaugurate his son Rehoboam. However, Rehoboam foolishly angered the people by threatening even heavier burdens, causing a revolt (12:1–19).

**2 Israel** Jeroboam, leader of the rebels, was made king of Israel, now called the northern kingdom. Jeroboam made Shechem his capital city (12:20, 25).

**3 Judah** Only the tribes of Judah and part of Benjamin remained loyal to Rehoboam. These two tribes became the southern kingdom. Rehoboam returned to Judah from Shechem and prepared to force the rebels into submission, but a prophet's message halted these plans (12:21–24).

**4 Jerusalem** Jerusalem was the capital city of Judah. Its Temple, built by Solomon, was the focal point of Jewish worship. This worried Jeroboam. How could he keep his people loyal if they were constantly going to Rehoboam's capital to worship (12:26, 27)?

**5 Dan** Jeroboam's solution was to set up his own worship centers. Two gold calves were made and proclaimed to be Israel's gods. One was placed in Dan, and the people were told that they could go there instead of to Jerusalem to worship (12:28, 29).

**6 Bethel** The other gold calf was placed in Bethel. The people of the northern kingdom had two convenient locations for worship in their own country, but their sin displeased God. In Jerusalem, meanwhile, Rehoboam was also allowing idolatry to creep in. The two nations were constantly at war (12:29—15:26).

**7 Tirzah** Jeroboam had moved the capital city to Tirzah (14:17). Next, Baasha became king of Israel after assassinating Nadab (15:27—16:22).

**8 Samaria** Israel continued to gain and lose kings through plots, assassinations, and warfare. When Omri became king, he bought a hill on which he built a new capital city, Samaria. Omri's son, Ahab, became the most wicked king of Israel. His wife, Jezebel, worshiped Baal. Ahab erected a temple to Baal in Samaria (16:23–34).

**9 Mount Carmel** Great evil often brings great people who oppose it. Elijah challenged the prophets of Baal and Asherah at Mount Carmel, where he would prove that they were false prophets. There Elijah humiliated these prophets and then executed them (17:1—18:46).

**10 Jezreel** Elijah returned to Jezreel. But Queen Jezebel, furious at the execution of her prophets, vowed to kill Elijah. He ran for his life, but God cared for and encouraged him. During his travels he anointed the future kings of Aram and Israel, as well as Elisha, his own replacement (19:1–21).

**11 Ramoth-gilead** The king of Aram declared war on Israel and was defeated in two battles. But the Arameans occupied Ramoth-gilead. Ahab and Jehoshaphat joined forces to recover the city. In this battle, Ahab was killed. Jehoshaphat later died (20:1—22:53).

# 1 KINGS

## VITAL STATISTICS

**PURPOSE:**
To contrast the lives of those who live for God and those who refuse to do so through the history of the kings of Israel and Judah

**AUTHOR:**
Unknown. Possibly Jeremiah or a group of prophets

**ORIGINAL AUDIENCE:**
The people of Israel

**SETTING:**
The once great nation of Israel turned into a land divided, not only physically, but also spiritually.

**KEY VERSES:**
"As for you, if you will follow me with integrity and godliness, as David your father did, obeying all my commands, decrees, and regulations, then I will establish the throne of your dynasty over Israel forever. For I made this promise to your father, David: 'One of your descendants will always sit on the throne of Israel'" (9:4, 5).

**KEY PEOPLE:**
David, Solomon, Rehoboam, Jeroboam, Elijah, Ahab, Jezebel

**SPECIAL FEATURE:**
The books of 1 and 2 Kings were originally one book.

"I DON'T CARE what anyone says, I'm going to do it!" the boy yells at his mother as he storms out of the house.

This is a familiar scene in our society. The words change, but the essential message is the same: A person is *not* open to advice because his or her mind is closed. Some advice may be sought, but it is heeded only if it reinforces the decision already made or is an easier path to take. It is human nature to reject help and to do things *our* way.

A much wiser approach is to seek, hear, and heed the advice of good counselors. Solomon, the world's wisest man, urges this in Proverbs (see 11:14; 15:22; 24:6). How ironic that his son and successor, Rehoboam, listened instead to foolish advice, with devastating results. At Rehoboam's inauguration, he was petitioned by the people to be a kind and generous ruler. The older men counseled him to "be a servant . . . and give them a favorable answer" (12:7). But Rehoboam agreed to the cruel advice of his peers who urged him to be harsh. As a result, Rehoboam split the kingdom. Learn from Rehoboam's mistake. Commit yourself to seeking and following wise counsel.

The main events of 1 Kings are David's death, Solomon's reign, the division of the kingdom, and Elijah's ministry. As Solomon ascended the throne, David charged him to obey God's laws and to "follow all his ways" (2:3). This Solomon did; and when given the choice of gifts from God, he humbly asked for wisdom (3:9). As a result, Solomon's reign began with great success, including the construction of the Temple—his greatest achievement. Unfortunately, Solomon took many pagan wives and concubines who eventually turned his heart away from the Lord to their false gods (11:1–4).

Rehoboam succeeded Solomon and had the opportunity to be a wise, compassionate, and just king. Instead, he accepted the poor advice of his young friends and attempted to rule with an iron hand. But the people rebelled, and the kingdom split with 10 tribes in the north (Israel) ruled by Jeroboam, and only Judah and Benjamin remaining with Rehoboam. Both kingdoms wove a path through the reigns of corrupt and idolatrous kings with only the clear voice of the prophets continuing to warn and call the nation back to God.

Elijah is surely one of the greatest prophets, and chapters 17 through 22 feature his conflict with wicked Ahab and Jezebel in Israel. In one of the most dramatic confrontations in history, Elijah defeated the prophets of Baal at Mount Carmel. In spite of incredible opposition, Elijah stood for God and proved that *one plus God* is a majority. If God is on our side, no one can stand against us (Romans 8:31).

## THE BLUEPRINT

A. THE UNITED KINGDOM
(1:1—11:43)
1. Solomon becomes king
2. Solomon's wisdom
3. Solomon builds the Temple
4. Solomon's greatness and downfall

Solomon was a botanist, zoologist, architect, poet, and philosopher. He was the wisest king in the history of Israel, but his wives led to the introduction of false gods and false worship in Israel. It is good for us to have wisdom, but that is not enough. The highest goal in life is to obey the Lord. Patient obedience to God should characterize our lives.

B. THE DIVIDED KINGDOM
(12:1—22:53)
1. Revolt of the northern tribes
2. Kings of Israel and Judah
3. Elijah's ministry
4. Kings of Israel and Judah

When the northern kingdom of Israel was being led by wicked kings, God raised up a prophet to proclaim his messages. Elijah single-handedly challenged the priesthood of the state religion and had them removed in one day. Through the dividing of the kingdom and the send-ing of Elijah, God dealt with the people's sin in powerful ways. Sin in our lives is graciously forgiven by God. However, the sin of an unrepentant person will be handled harshly. We must turn from sin and turn to God to be saved from judgment.

## MEGATHEMES

| THEME | EXPLANATION | IMPORTANCE |
|---|---|---|
| The King | Solomon's wisdom, power, and achievements brought honor to the Israelite nation and to God. All the kings of Israel and Judah were told to obey God and to govern according to his laws. But their tendency to abandon God's commands and to worship other gods led them to change the religion and government to meet their personal desires. This neglect of God's law led to their downfall. | Wisdom, power, and achievement do not ultimately come from any human source; they are from God. No matter what we lead or govern, we can't do well when we ignore God's guidelines. Whether or not we are leaders, effectiveness depends upon listening and obeying God's Word. Don't let your personal desires distort God's Word. |
| The Temple | Solomon's Temple was a beautiful place of wor-ship and prayer. This sanctuary was the center of Jewish religion. It was the place of God's special presence and housed the Ark of the Covenant containing the Ten Commandments. | A beautiful house of worship doesn't always guarantee heartfelt worship of God. Providing opportunities for true worship doesn't ensure that it will happen. God wants to live in our hearts, not just meet us in a sanctuary. |
| Other Gods | Although the Israelites had God's law and experienced his presence among them, they became attracted to other gods. When this happened, their hearts became cold to God's law, resulting in the ruin of families and govern-ment, and eventually leading to the destruction of the nation. | Through the years, the people took on the false qualities of the false gods they worshiped. They became cruel, power-hungry, and sexually perverse. We tend to become what we worship. Unless we serve the true God, we will become slaves to whatever takes his place. |
| The Prophet's Message | The prophet's responsibility was to confront and correct any deviation from God's law. Elijah was a bolt of judgment against Israel. His messages and miracles were a warning to the evil and rebellious kings and people. | The Bible, the truth in sermons, and the wise counsel of believers are warnings to us. Anyone who points out how we deviate from obeying God's Word is a blessing to us. Changing our lives in order to obey God and get back on track often takes painful discipline and hard work. |
| Sin and Repentance | Each king had God's commands, a priest or prophet, and the lessons of the past to draw him back to God. All the people had the same resources. Whenever they repented and returned to God, God heard their prayers and forgave them. | God hears and forgives us when we pray—if we are willing to trust him and turn from sin. Our desire to forsake our sin must be heartfelt and sincere. Then he will give us a fresh start and a desire to live for him. |

## A. THE UNITED KINGDOM (1:1—11:43)

When Solomon is anointed king, he eliminates all opposition to the throne, builds the Temple, establishes a strong army, and becomes the richest and wisest king in the history of Israel. But his pagan wives lead him into idolatry, and as a result, he leads the nation into spiritual decline. No matter what position in life we attain, we are always ripe for a downfall and must never let our guard down against sin and temptation.

### 1. Solomon becomes king

*David in His Old Age*

**1** King David was now very old, and no matter how many blankets covered him, he could not keep warm. ²So his advisers told him, "Let us find a young virgin to wait on you and look after you, my lord. She will lie in your arms and keep you warm."

³So they searched throughout the land of Israel for a beautiful girl, and they found Abishag from Shunem and brought her to the king. ⁴The girl was very beautiful, and she looked after the king and took care of him. But the king had no sexual relations with her.

*Adonijah Claims the Throne*

⁵About that time David's son Adonijah, whose mother was Haggith, began boasting, "I will make myself king." So he provided himself with chariots and charioteers and recruited fifty men to run in front of him. ⁶Now his father, King David, had never disciplined him at any time, even by asking, "Why are you doing that?" Adonijah had been born next after Absalom, and he was very handsome.

⁷Adonijah took Joab son of Zeruiah and Abiathar the priest into his confidence, and they agreed to help him become king. ⁸But Zadok the priest, Benaiah son of Jehoiada, Nathan the prophet, Shimei, Rei, and David's personal bodyguard refused to support Adonijah.

**1:3**
Josh 19:18
1 Sam 28:4

**1:5**
2 Sam 3:4

**1:7**
1 Sam 22:20, 23
2 Sam 20:25
1 Kgs 2:22, 28

**1:8**
2 Sam 8:18; 12:1;
20:25; 23:8-39

---

**1:1** Israel was near the end of the golden years of David's reign. The book of 1 Kings begins with a unified kingdom, glorious and God-centered; it ends with a divided kingdom, degraded and idolatrous. The reason for Israel's decline appears simple to us—they failed to obey God. But we are vulnerable to the same forces that brought about Israel's decay—greed, jealousy, lust for power,

weakening of marriage vows, and superficiality in our devotion to God. As we read about these tragic events in Israel's history, we must see ourselves in the mirror of their experiences.

**1:4** David was about 70 years old. His health had deteriorated from years of hardship. Abishag served as his nurse and to help keep him warm. In times when polygamy was accepted and kings had harems, this action was not considered offensive.

**1:5** Adonijah was David's fourth son and the logical choice to succeed him as king. David's first son, Amnon, had been killed by Absalom for having raped his sister (2 Samuel 13:20-33). His second son, Daniel, is mentioned only in the genealogy of 1 Chronicles 3:1 and had probably died by this time. David's third son, Absalom, died in an earlier rebellion (2 Samuel 18:1-18). Although many people expected Adonijah to be the next king (2:13-25), David (and God) had other plans (1:29, 30).

**1:5** Adonijah decided to seize the throne without David's knowledge. He knew that Solomon, not he, was David's first choice to be the next king (1:17). This was why he did not invite Solomon and David's loyal advisers when he declared himself king (1:9, 10). But his deceptive plans to gain the throne were unsuccessful. The proud Adonijah was self-exalted and self-defeated.

**1:6** God-fearing people like David and Samuel were used by God to lead nations; nevertheless they had problems in family relationships. God-fearing leaders cannot take for granted the spiritual well-being of their children. They are used to have others follow their orders, but they cannot expect their children to manufacture faith upon request. Moral and spiritual character takes years to build, and it requires constant attention and patient discipline.

David served God well as a king, but as a parent he often failed both God and his children. Don't let your service to God, even in leadership positions, take up so much of your time and energy that you neglect your other God-given responsibilities.

**1:6** Because David had never interfered by opposing or even questioning his son, Adonijah did not know how to work within limits. The result was that he always wanted his own way, regardless of how it affected others. Adonijah did whatever he wanted and paid no respect to God's wishes. An undisciplined child may look cute to his or her parents, but an undisciplined adult destroys himself and others. As you set limits for your children, you make it possible for them to develop the self-restraint they

**JERUSALEM**
**(modern day)**

Royal
Palace

MISHNEH

OPHEL

CITY
OF
DAVID

°Gihon
Spring

N

0    .1 Mi.

0    .1 Km.

to En-rogel

Tombs of the
house of David

**TWO CORONATIONS**  As David lay on his deathbed, his son Adonijah crowned himself king at En-rogel outside Jerusalem. When the news reached David, he declared that Solomon was to be the next ruler. Solomon was anointed at Gihon. It may have been more than coincidence that Gihon was not only within shouting distance of En-rogel but also closer to the royal palace.

1:10
2 Sam 12:24

[9]Adonijah went to the Stone of Zoheleth* near the spring of En-rogel, where he sacrificed sheep, cattle, and fattened calves. He invited all his brothers—the other sons of King David—and all the royal officials of Judah. [10]But he did not invite Nathan the prophet or Benaiah or the king's bodyguard or his brother Solomon.

[11]Then Nathan went to Bathsheba, Solomon's mother, and asked her, "Haven't you heard that Haggith's son, Adonijah, has made himself king, and our lord David doesn't even know about it? [12]If you want to save your own life and the life of your son Solomon, follow

1:9 Or to the Serpent's Stone; Greek version supports reading Zoheleth as a proper name.

**BATHSHEBA**

Bathsheba was the unlikely link between Israel's two most famous kings—David and Solomon. She was lover and wife to one, mother to the other. Her adultery with David almost brought an end to the family through which God planned to physically enter his world. Out of the ashes of that sin, however, God brought good. Eventually Jesus Christ, the salvation of mankind, was born to a descendant of David and Bathsheba.

David and Bathsheba's story shows that little wrong decisions often lead to big mistakes. It is likely that neither was where he or she should have been. Bathsheba may have been rash in bathing where she might be seen; David should have been at war with his army. Each decision contributed to the beginning of a very sad series of events.

Bathsheba must have been devastated by the chain of events—unfaithfulness to her husband, discovery of pregnancy, death of her husband, death of her child. We are told that David comforted her (2 Samuel 12:24), and she lived to see another son, Solomon, sit on the throne.

From her life we see that the little, day-to-day choices we make are very important. They prepare us to make the right choices when the big decisions come. The wisdom to make right choices in small and large matters is a gift from God. Understanding this should make us more conscious of the decisions we make and more willing to include God in our decision making. Have you asked for his help with today's decisions?

| | |
|---|---|
| **Strengths and accomplishments** | • Became influential in the palace alongside her son Solomon<br>• Was the mother of Israel's wisest king and an ancestor of Jesus Christ |
| **Weakness and mistake** | • Committed adultery |
| **Lessons from her life** | • Although we may feel caught up in a chain of events, we are still responsible for the way we participate in those events<br>• A sin may seem like one small seed, but the harvest of consequences is beyond measure<br>• In the worst possible situations, God is still able to bring about good when people truly turn to him<br>• While we must live with the natural consequences of our sins, God's forgiveness of sin is complete |
| **Vital statistics** | • Where: Jerusalem<br>• Occupations: Queen and queen mother<br>• Relatives: Father: Elim. Husbands: Uriah and David. Son: Solomon.<br>• Contemporaries: Nathan, Joab, Adonijah |
| **Key verses** | "When Uriah's wife heard that her husband was dead, she mourned for him. When the period of mourning was over, David sent for her and brought her to the palace, and she became one of his wives. Then she gave birth to a son. But the LORD was displeased with what David had done" (2 Samuel 11:26, 27). |

Her story is told in 2 Samuel 11—12 and 1 Kings 1—2. A related passage is Psalm 51.

---

will need in order to control themselves later. Discipline your children carefully while they are young, so that they will grow into self-disciplined adults.

**1:7** See Joab's Profile in 2 Samuel 18, p. 495, for a more complete picture of his life. For more information on Abiathar, see the note on 1 Samuel 22:20.

**1:9** When Saul was anointed king, peace offerings were sacrificed as a reminder of the nation's covenant with God given at Mount Sinai. Adonijah wanted sacrifices offered, perhaps hoping to legitimize his takeover. But Adonijah was not God's choice to succeed David. Sealing an action with religious ceremony does not make it God's will.

**1:11** For more on Bathsheba, David's wife, read 2 Samuel 11–12. As wife of the king, Bathsheba was highly influential in the royal palace.

**1:11-14** When Nathan learned of Adonijah's conspiracy, he immediately tried to stop it. He was a man of both faith and action. He knew that Solomon should rightly be king, and he moved quickly when he saw someone else trying to take the throne. We often know what is right but don't act on it. Perhaps we don't want to get involved, or maybe we are fearful or lazy. Don't stop with prayer, good intentions, or angry feelings. Take the action needed to correct the situation.

my advice. ¹³Go at once to King David and say to him, 'My lord the king, didn't you make a
vow and say to me, "Your son Solomon will surely be the next king and will sit on my
throne"? Why then has Adonijah become king?' ¹⁴And while you are still talking with him, I
will come and confirm everything you have said."

¹⁵So Bathsheba went into the king's bedroom. (He was very old now, and Abishag was taking care of him.) ¹⁶Bathsheba bowed down before the king.

"What can I do for you?" he asked her.

¹⁷She replied, "My lord, you made a vow before the LORD your God when you said to me,
'Your son Solomon will surely be the next king and will sit on my throne.' ¹⁸But instead,
Adonijah has made himself king, and my lord the king does not even know about it. ¹⁹He has
sacrificed many cattle, fattened calves, and sheep, and he has invited all the king's sons to
attend the celebration. He also invited Abiathar the priest and Joab, the commander of the
army. But he did not invite your servant Solomon. ²⁰And now, my lord the king, all Israel
is waiting for you to announce who will become king after you. ²¹If you do not act, my son
Solomon and I will be treated as criminals as soon as my lord the king has died."

²²While she was still speaking with the king, Nathan the prophet arrived. ²³The king's
officials told him, "Nathan the prophet is here to see you."

Nathan went in and bowed before the king with his face to the ground. ²⁴Nathan asked,
"My lord the king, have you decided that Adonijah will be the next king and that he will sit on
your throne? ²⁵Today he has sacrificed many cattle, fattened calves, and sheep, and he has
invited all the king's sons to attend the celebration. He also invited the commanders of the
army and Abiathar the priest. They are feasting and drinking with him and shouting, 'Long
live King Adonijah!' ²⁶But he did not invite me or Zadok the priest or Benaiah or your servant
Solomon. ²⁷Has my lord the king really done this without letting any of his officials know
who should be the next king?"

### David Makes Solomon King

²⁸King David responded, "Call Bathsheba!" So she came back in and stood before the king.
²⁹And the king repeated his vow: "As surely as the LORD lives, who has rescued me from every
danger, ³⁰your son Solomon will be the next king and will sit on my throne this very day, just
as I vowed to you before the LORD, the God of Israel."

³¹Then Bathsheba bowed down with her face to the ground before the king and exclaimed, "May my lord King David live forever!"

³²Then King David ordered, "Call Zadok the priest, Nathan the prophet, and Benaiah son
of Jehoiada." When they came into the king's presence, ³³the king said to them, "Take Solomon and my officials down to Gihon Spring. Solomon is to ride on my own mule. ³⁴There
Zadok the priest and Nathan the prophet are to anoint him king over Israel. Blow the ram's
horn and shout, 'Long live King Solomon!' ³⁵Then escort him back here, and he will sit on
my throne. He will succeed me as king, for I have appointed him to be ruler over Israel and
Judah."

³⁶"Amen!" Benaiah son of Jehoiada replied. "May the LORD, the God of my lord the king,
decree that it happen. ³⁷And may the LORD be with Solomon as he has been with you, my
lord the king, and may he make Solomon's reign even greater than yours!"

³⁸So Zadok the priest, Nathan the prophet, Benaiah son of Jehoiada, and the king's bodyguard* took Solomon down to Gihon Spring, with Solomon riding on King David's own mule.
³⁹There Zadok the priest took the flask of olive oil from the sacred tent and anointed Solomon with the oil. Then they sounded the ram's horn and all the people shouted, "Long live
King Solomon!" ⁴⁰And all the people followed Solomon into Jerusalem, playing flutes and
shouting for joy. The celebration was so joyous and noisy that the earth shook with the sound.

1:38 Hebrew the Kerethites and Pelethites; also in 1:44.

### Cross-references (right margin)

**1:13**
1 Chr 22:9-13

**1:19**
1 Kgs 1:9

**1:25**
1 Sam 10:24
1 Kgs 1:9

**1:28-53**
//1 Chr 29:21-25

**1:29**
2 Sam 4:9

**1:34**
1 Sam 10:1;
16:3, 12
2 Sam 15:10

**1:37**
Josh 1:5, 17
1 Sam 20:13
1 Kgs 1:47

**1:39**
1 Kgs 1:34
1 Chr 16:39; 29:22
Ps 89:20

---

**1:13** The Bible does not record David's promise that Solomon
would be Israel's next king, but it is clear that Solomon was the
choice of both David (1:17, 30) and God (1 Chronicles 22:9, 10).

**1:33** We might expect King David to send a great war horse
to bring his son Solomon to the ceremony; instead, Solomon
rode David's mule. In David's time, mules were prized animals,
ridden by the wealthy and powerful. When Jesus entered Jerusalem, he came in not on a horse, but on a donkey (Zechariah
9:9; Matthew 21:7).

**1:39** The olive oil was used to anoint Israel's kings and high
priests, as well as to dedicate certain objects to God. The sacred
tent where the oil was kept was probably the tent David set up
to shelter the Ark of the Covenant (2 Samuel 6:17). It was not
the Tabernacle Moses carried in the wilderness; that Tabernacle
was still at Gibeon (see the note on 1 Samuel 7:1 for more
details). The recipe and uses for the sacred oil are found in
Exodus 30:22-33. For more on anointing, see the notes on
1 Samuel 10:1 and 16:13.

**1:42**
2 Sam 18:26-27

**1:47**
1 Kgs 1:37

**1:48**
2 Sam 7:12
1 Kgs 3:6

**1:49**
1 Kgs 2:28

41Adonijah and his guests heard the celebrating and shouting just as they were finishing their banquet. When Joab heard the sound of the ram's horn, he asked, "What's going on? Why is the city in such an uproar?"

42And while he was still speaking, Jonathan son of Abiathar the priest arrived. "Come in," Adonijah said to him, "for you are a good man. You must have good news."

43"Not at all!" Jonathan replied. "Our lord King David has just declared Solomon king! 44The king sent him down to Gihon Spring with Zadok the priest, Nathan the prophet, and Benaiah son of Jehoiada, protected by the king's bodyguard. They had him ride on the king's own mule, 45and Zadok and Nathan have anointed him at Gihon Spring as the new king. They have just returned, and the whole city is celebrating and rejoicing. That's what all the noise is about. 46What's more, Solomon is now sitting on the royal throne as king. 47And all the royal officials have gone to King David and congratulated him, saying, 'May your God make Solomon's fame even greater than your own, and may Solomon's reign be even greater than yours!' Then the king bowed his head in worship as he lay in his bed, 48and he said, 'Praise the LORD, the God of Israel, who today has chosen a successor to sit on my throne while I am still alive to see it.'"

49Then all of Adonijah's guests jumped up in panic from the banquet table and quickly scattered. 50Adonijah was afraid of Solomon, so he rushed to the sacred tent and grabbed on to the horns of the altar. 51Word soon reached Solomon that Adonijah had seized the horns of the altar in fear, and that he was pleading, "Let King Solomon swear today that he will not kill me!"

---

**WHO JOINED ADONIJAH'S CONSPIRACY AND WHO REMAINED LOYAL TO DAVID?** Contrast the fate of those who rebelled and those who remained loyal to David, God's appointed leader. Adonijah, the leader of the conspiracy, met a violent death (2:25). Those who rebel against God's leaders rebel against God.

*Joined Adonijah*

**Joab (1:7)** Brilliant military general and commander of David's army. He continually demonstrated his belief that cold-blooded murder was as acceptable as a fairly fought battle. Solomon later had him executed.

**Abiathar (1:7)** One of two high priests under David. He was a son of Ahimelech who had helped David, and David promised to protect him. Abiathar repaid David with treachery. Solomon later had him banished, fulfilling the prophecy that Eli's priestly line would end (1 Samuel 2:31).

**Jonathan (1:42)** Abiathar's son. He helped David stop Absalom's rebellion (2 Samuel 17:17-22) but supported this rebellion by another of David's sons.

**Charioteers (1:5)** Hired by Adonijah, apparently more loyal to money than to their king.

**50 Runners (1:5)** Recruited to give Adonijah a "royal" appearance.

*Remained with David*

**Zadok (1:8)** The other high priest under David. His loyalty gave him the privilege of crowning Solomon. He became the sole high priest under King Solomon.

**Benaiah (1:8)** Distinguished himself as a great warrior. Commanded a division of David's army—over 24,000 men. One of the Thirty, he was also placed in charge of David's bodyguard. Solomon later made him chief commander of the army.

**Nathan (1:8)** God's prominent prophet during David's reign. The Bible says he wrote a history of David and Solomon.

**Shimei (1:8)** This man was probably the Shimei who was rewarded by Solomon and appointed district governor in Benjamin (4:18). (He was not the same person who cursed David at Bahurim and brought on his own death under Solomon.)

**Rei (1:8)** Only mentioned here. Possibly he was an army officer. The word means "and his friends."

**David's Bodyguard (1:8, 10)** David's army was highly organized with several different divisions of troops. It is enough to know that many of his leaders remained true to their king.

---

**1:49, 50** Sometimes it takes getting caught before someone is willing to give up his scheme. When Adonijah learned that his plans were doomed to fail, he ran in panic to the altar, the place of God's mercy and forgiveness. He went there, however, *after* his plans for treason were exposed. If Adonijah had first considered what God wanted, he might have avoided trouble. Don't wait until you have made a mess of your life before you run to God. Seek God's guidance *before* you act.

**1:49-51** Adonijah thought he would be safe by clutching the horns (or corner posts) of the sacred altar of burnt offering in the Tabernacle court. By doing this, he hoped to place himself under God's protection. Solomon granted Adonijah a reprieve, hoping that this would end Adonijah's conspiracy. Unfortunately, it did not, and he was later executed (2:25). At the execution of Adonijah, Joab ran and clutched the horns of the altar hoping for safety, but Solomon had Joab killed right at the altar (2:28-34). This punishment was appropriate justice for a cold-blooded murderer such as Joab (Exodus 21:14).

<sup>52</sup>Solomon replied, "If he proves himself to be loyal, not a hair on his head will be touched. But if he makes trouble, he will die." <sup>53</sup>So King Solomon summoned Adonijah, and they brought him down from the altar. He came and bowed respectfully before King Solomon, who dismissed him, saying, "Go on home."

### David's Final Instructions to Solomon

**2** As the time of King David's death approached, he gave this charge to his son Solomon: <sup>2</sup>"I am going where everyone on earth must someday go. Take courage and be a man. <sup>3</sup>Observe the requirements of the LORD your God, and follow all his ways. Keep the decrees, commands, regulations, and laws written in the Law of Moses so that you will be successful in all you do and wherever you go. <sup>4</sup>If you do this, then the LORD will keep the promise he made to me. He told me, 'If your descendants live as they should and follow me faithfully with all their heart and soul, one of them will always sit on the throne of Israel.'

<sup>5</sup>"And there is something else. You know what Joab son of Zeruiah did to me when he murdered my two army commanders, Abner son of Ner and Amasa son of Jether. He pretended that it was an act of war, but it was done in a time of peace,* staining his belt and sandals with innocent blood.* <sup>6</sup>Do with him what you think best, but don't let him grow old and go to his grave in peace.*

<sup>7</sup>"Be kind to the sons of Barzillai of Gilead. Make them permanent guests at your table, for they took care of me when I fled from your brother Absalom.

<sup>8</sup>"And remember Shimei son of Gera, the man from Bahurim in Benjamin. He cursed me with a terrible curse as I was fleeing to Mahanaim. When he came down to meet me at the Jordan River, I swore by the LORD that I would not kill him. <sup>9</sup>But that oath does not make him innocent. You are a wise man, and you will know how to arrange a bloody death for him.*"

<sup>10</sup>Then David died and was buried with his ancestors in the City of David. <sup>11</sup>David had reigned over Israel for forty years, seven of them in Hebron and thirty-three in Jerusalem. <sup>12</sup>Solomon became king and sat on the throne of David his father, and his kingdom was firmly established.

### Solomon Establishes His Rule

<sup>13</sup>One day Adonijah, whose mother was Haggith, came to see Bathsheba, Solomon's mother. "Have you come with peaceful intentions?" she asked him.

"Yes," he said, "I come in peace. <sup>14</sup>In fact, I have a favor to ask of you."

"What is it?" she asked.

<sup>15</sup>He replied, "As you know, the kingdom was rightfully mine; all Israel wanted me to be the next king. But the tables were turned, and the kingdom went to my brother instead; for that is the way the LORD wanted it. <sup>16</sup>So now I have just one favor to ask of you. Please don't turn me down."

**2:2**
Josh 23:14

**2:3**
Deut 18:18-19
Josh 1:6-7; 23:14
1 Chr 22:12

**2:4**
2 Sam 7:12-13, 25
1 Kgs 8:25; 9:5

**2:5**
2 Sam 3:27; 20:10

**2:7**
2 Sam 17:27-29;
19:31-38

**2:8**
2 Sam 16:5-8;
19:18-23

**2:10-12**
//1 Chr 29:26-28

**2:10**
2 Sam 5:7
1 Chr 29:28
Acts 2:29; 13:36

**2:11**
2 Sam 5:4-5

**2:12**
1 Chr 29:23
2 Chr 1:1

**2:5a** Or *He murdered them during a time of peace as revenge for deaths they had caused in time of war.*   **2:5b** As in some Greek and Old Latin manuscripts; Hebrew reads *with the blood of war.*   **2:6** Hebrew *don't let his white head go down to Sheol in peace.*   **2:9** Hebrew *how to bring his white head down to Sheol in blood.*

**1:52, 53** While Adonijah feared for his life and expected the severest punishment, Solomon simply dismissed his brother and sent him home. As a new king, Solomon had the power to kill his rivals, something Adonijah would have done had his conspiracy succeeded. But Solomon acted as if he had nothing to prove, thus demonstrating his authority and power. Sometimes forgiving a personal attack shows more strength than lashing out in revenge. Trying to prove one's power and authority often proves only one's fear and self-doubt. Only after Adonijah made another attempt to secure royal power was Solomon forced to have him executed (2:13-25).

**2:3, 4** David stressed to Solomon the need to make God and his laws the center of personal life and government in order to preserve the kingdom, as God had promised to do (2 Samuel 7). This promise from God had two parts. One part was conditional and depended upon the king's actions. The other part was unconditional.

God's conditional promise was that David and his descendants would remain in office as kings *only* when they honored and obeyed him. When David's descendants failed to do this, they lost the throne (2 Kings 25). God's unconditional promise was that David's line would go on forever. This was fulfilled in the birth of Jesus Christ, a descendant of David who was also the eternal Son

of God (Romans 1:3, 4). David, whose life exemplified obedience, gave well-seasoned advice to his son, the next king. It would be up to Solomon to follow it.

**2:5-7** Joab epitomizes those who are ruthless in accomplishing their goals. To Joab, winning was everything. He wanted to get power for himself and protect it. In contrast, Barzillai stands for those who are loyal to God and live by his standards. When offered glory, for example, he unselfishly asked that it be given to his son. Is your leadership self-serving or God-serving?

**2:5-9** David had some harsh advice for Solomon concerning his enemies. This advice was designed to help the young king establish and secure his throne, and it was directed only toward blatant enemies—those who opposed God by opposing God's appointed king. Legally, David was asking Solomon to give his enemies the punishment they deserved. It was against both civil law and God's laws for Shimei to curse a king (Exodus 22:28).

**2:10** David died at about age 70 (2 Samuel 5:4, 5). See David's Profile in 1 Samuel 17, p. 439, for more on his life.

**2:15-22** This was not a case of thwarted love; Adonijah had more in mind than his supposed love for Abishag. Although she was still a virgin, Abishag was considered part of David's harem.

"What is it?" she asked.

2:17
1 Kgs 1:3

[17]He replied, "Speak to King Solomon on my behalf, for I know he will do anything you request. Ask him to let me marry Abishag, the girl from Shunem."

[18]"All right," Bathsheba replied. "I will speak to the king for you."

2:19
Ps 45:9

[19]So Bathsheba went to King Solomon to speak on Adonijah's behalf. The king rose from his throne to meet her, and he bowed down before her. When he sat down on his throne again, the king ordered that a throne be brought for his mother, and she sat at his right hand.

[20]"I have one small request to make of you," she said. "I hope you won't turn me down."

"What is it, my mother?" he asked. "You know I won't refuse you."

[21]"Then let your brother Adonijah marry Abishag, the girl from Shunem," she replied.

[22]"How can you possibly ask me to give Abishag to Adonijah?" King Solomon demanded. "You might as well ask me to give him the kingdom! You know that he is my older brother, and that he has Abiathar the priest and Joab son of Zeruiah on his side."

2:23
Ruth 1:17

2:25
2 Sam 8:18

2:26
Josh 21:17-18
1 Sam 22:20; 26:16
2 Sam 15:24
Jer 1:1

[23]Then King Solomon made a vow before the LORD: "May God strike me and even kill me if Adonijah has not sealed his fate with this request. [24]The LORD has confirmed me and placed me on the throne of my father, David; he has established my dynasty as he promised. So as surely as the LORD lives, Adonijah will die this very day!" [25]So King Solomon ordered Benaiah son of Jehoiada to execute him, and Adonijah was put to death.

[26]Then the king said to Abiathar the priest, "Go back to your home in Anathoth. You

---

**ABISHAG**

Chosen for her youth and beauty, Abishag found herself one day the live-in nurse of the great but elderly King David. Her job was to keep the ailing king warm. Within months her patient died. We know little about their relationship (although, for those who might wonder, the writer makes it clear that they never had sexual intercourse).

Almost immediately after David's death, Abishag became the bargaining chip in a power struggle between his sons Solomon and Adonijah. Solomon had been chosen for the throne; Adonijah had tried to usurp it. Solomon could have killed his rival, but instead said that if Adonijah proved to be loyal, he would not be harmed (1:52).

Loyalty, however, was not in Adonijah's vocabulary. When he went to Bathsheba asking for Abishag's hand in marriage, he had strong ulterior motives. For Adonijah, Abishag was probably little more than a possible angle to renew his claim to the throne of David. Bathsheba may have been trying to do Abishag a favor as well as to pacify Adonijah. Solomon saw through the ruse, however, and understood that Adonijah was planning to use Abishag (who had technically been a part of King David's harem) to gain leverage in his fight for the throne. Adonijah paid for this request with his life, for he had proven that he would not be loyal to Solomon. These maneuvers revealed one clear fact: no one cared what Abishag thought. She might as well have been listed with the furniture.

Home and work are both settings in which persons are sometimes treated as objects. You may be hurt today by such treatment. Family members may withhold appreciation. Fellow workers may treat you like just another office machine. Resist these invitations to hopelessness by remembering that God knows you intimately and will always treat you as a person.

| | |
|---|---|
| **Strengths and accomplishments** | • Served an apparently thankless role as a king's personal servant with grace and silence<br>• Witnessed David's decision to pass the throne to his son Solomon |
| **Lessons from her life** | • We may go unnoticed and devalued by others, but God never loses track of us<br>• We frequently know only a small part of the significance of events in our lives as they relate to God's larger plan for the world |
| **Vital statistics** | • Where: Shunem, Jerusalem<br>• Occupation: King David's nurse and companion<br>• Contemporaries: Nathan, Bathsheba, Solomon, Adonijah |
| **Key verse** | "The girl was very beautiful, and she looked after the king and took care of him. But the king had no sexual relations with her" (1 Kings 1:4). |

Abishag's story is told in 1 Kings 1:1–4; 2:13–24.

---

Adonijah wanted Abishag because possessing the king's harem was equivalent to claiming the throne. Absalom had done the same thing in his rebellion against David (2 Samuel 16:20-23). Solomon well understood what Adonijah was trying to do.

**2:26, 27** As a young man, Abiathar had been the only one to escape when King Saul massacred all the priests in the city of

Nob (1 Samuel 22:11-23). Abiathar then became the high priest under David and remained loyal to David throughout his reign. When Abiathar supported Adonijah's wrongful claim to the throne after David's death (1:7), Solomon forced him to give up the priesthood, fulfilling the prophecy of 1 Samuel 2:27-36 that Eli's descendants would not continue to serve as priests.

deserve to die, but I will not kill you now, because you carried the Ark of the Sovereign LORD for David my father and you shared all his hardships." 27So Solomon deposed Abiathar from his position as priest of the LORD, thereby fulfilling the prophecy the LORD had given at Shiloh concerning the descendants of Eli.

**2:27**
1 Sam 2:27-36

28Joab had not joined Absalom's earlier rebellion, but he had joined Adonijah's rebellion. So when Joab heard about Adonijah's death, he ran to the sacred tent of the LORD and grabbed on to the horns of the altar. 29When this was reported to King Solomon, he sent Benaiah son of Jehoiada to execute him.

**2:28**
2 Sam 17:25
1 Kgs 1:49-50

30Benaiah went to the sacred tent of the LORD and said to Joab, "The king orders you to come out!"

But Joab answered, "No, I will die here."

So Benaiah returned to the king and told him what Joab had said.

31"Do as he said," the king replied. "Kill him there beside the altar and bury him. This will remove the guilt of Joab's senseless murders from me and from my father's family. 32The LORD will repay him* for the murders of two men who were more righteous and better than he. For my father knew nothing about the deaths of Abner son of Ner, commander of the army of Israel, and of Amasa son of Jether, commander of the army of Judah. 33May their blood be on Joab and his descendants forever, and may the LORD grant peace forever to David, his descendants, his dynasty, and his throne."

**2:31**
Exod 21:14
Num 35:33
Deut 19:13

**2:32**
Gen 9:5-6
Judg 9:24, 56-57
2 Sam 3:27;
20:8-10
2 Chr 21:13

34So Benaiah son of Jehoiada returned to the sacred tent and killed Joab, and he was buried at his home in the wilderness. 35Then the king appointed Benaiah to command the army in place of Joab, and he installed Zadok the priest to take the place of Abiathar.

**2:33**
2 Sam 3:29

**2:35**
1 Chr 29:22

36The king then sent for Shimei and told him, "Build a house here in Jerusalem and live there. But don't step outside the city to go anywhere else. 37On the day you so much as cross the Kidron Valley, you will surely die; and your blood will be on your own head."

**2:36**
2 Sam 16:5
1 Kgs 2:8

**2:37**
2 Sam 15:23

38Shimei replied, "Your sentence is fair; I will do whatever my lord the king commands." So Shimei lived in Jerusalem for a long time.

39But three years later two of Shimei's slaves ran away to King Achish son of Maacah of Gath. When Shimei learned where they were, 40he saddled his donkey and went to Gath to search for them. When he found them, he brought them back to Jerusalem.

**2:39**
1 Sam 27:2

41Solomon heard that Shimei had left Jerusalem and had gone to Gath and returned. 42So the king sent for Shimei and demanded, "Didn't I make you swear by the LORD and warn you not to go anywhere else or you would surely die? And you replied, 'The sentence is fair; I will do as you say.' 43Then why haven't you kept your oath to the LORD and obeyed my command?"

44The king also said to Shimei, "You certainly remember all the wicked things you did to my father, David. May the LORD now bring that evil on your own head. 45But may I, King Solomon, receive the LORD's blessings, and may one of David's descendants always sit on this throne in the presence of the LORD." 46Then, at the king's command, Benaiah son of Jehoiada took Shimei outside and killed him.

**2:44**
1 Sam 25:39
2 Sam 16:5-13

**2:45**
2 Sam 7:13

**2:46**
1 Kgs 2:12
2 Chr 1:1

So the kingdom was now firmly in Solomon's grip.

**2:32** Hebrew *will return his blood on his own head.*

---

**2:31** Joab had spent his life trying to defend his position as David's commander. Twice David tried to replace him, and both times Joab treacherously killed his rivals before they could assume command (2 Samuel 3:17-30; 19:13; 20:4-10). Because Joab was in his service, David was ultimately responsible for these senseless deaths. But for political and military reasons (see the note on 2 Samuel 3:39), David decided not to publicly punish Joab. Instead, he put a curse on Joab and his family (2 Samuel 3:29). Solomon, in punishing Joab, was publicly declaring that David was not part of Joab's crimes, thus removing the guilt from David and placing it on Joab, where it belonged.

**2:35** Abiathar the high priest and Joab the army commander were key men in David's kingdom. But when they conspired against Solomon, they were replaced with Zadok and Benaiah. Zadok, a descendant of Aaron, had been a prominent priest during David's reign, and he was also loyal to Solomon after David's death. He was put in charge of the Ark of the Covenant (2 Samuel 15:24ff). His descendants were in charge of the Temple until its destruction. At one time, Benaiah was one of David's mighty men (2 Samuel 23:20-23) and the captain of David's bodyguard.

**2:46** Solomon ordered the executions of Adonijah, Joab, and Shimei; forced Abiathar out as priest; and then appointed new men to take their places. He took these actions swiftly, securing his grip on the kingdom. By executing justice and tying up loose ends that could affect the future stability of his kingdom, Solomon was promoting peace, not bloodshed. He was a man of peace in two ways: He did not go to war, and he put an end to internal rebellion.

3:1
1 Kgs 7:8; 9:24

3:2
Lev 17:3-5
Deut 12:13-14

3:3
Deut 6:5

3:4-15
//2 Chr 1:2-13

3:4
1 Chr 16:39; 21:29

3:5
1 Kgs 9:2-3

3:6
2 Sam 7:8; 12:7

3:7
1 Chr 22:9-13; 29:1
Jer 1:6-7

3:8
Gen 13:16; 15:5;
22:17
Exod 19:6
Deut 7:6

3:9
2 Sam 14:17
1 Kgs 3:12-13
2 Chr 1:10
Ps 72:1
Prov 2:3-5, 9
Jas 1:5

3:12
1 Kgs 4:29-31
1 Jn 5:14-15

3:13
1 Kgs 3:28;
4:20-24; 10:23

3:14
Ps 91:16
Prov 3:1-2, 16

3:15
1 Kgs 8:63, 65

## 2. Solomon's wisdom

*Solomon Asks for Wisdom*

**3** Solomon made an alliance with Pharaoh, the king of Egypt, and married one of his daughters. He brought her to live in the City of David until he could finish building his palace and the Temple of the LORD and the wall around the city. ²At that time the people of Israel sacrificed their offerings at local places of worship, for a temple honoring the name of the LORD had not yet been built.

³Solomon loved the LORD and followed all the decrees of his father, David, except that Solomon, too, offered sacrifices and burned incense at the local places of worship. ⁴The most important of these places of worship was at Gibeon, so the king went there and sacrificed 1,000 burnt offerings. ⁵That night the LORD appeared to Solomon in a dream, and God said, "What do you want? Ask, and I will give it to you!"

⁶Solomon replied, "You showed faithful love to your servant my father, David, because he was honest and true and faithful to you. And you have continued your faithful love to him today by giving him a son to sit on his throne.

⁷"Now, O LORD my God, you have made me king instead of my father, David, but I am like a little child who doesn't know his way around. ⁸And here I am in the midst of your own chosen people, a nation so great and numerous they cannot be counted! ⁹Give me an understanding heart so that I can govern your people well and know the difference between right and wrong. For who by himself is able to govern this great people of yours?"

¹⁰The Lord was pleased that Solomon had asked for wisdom. ¹¹So God replied, "Because you have asked for wisdom in governing my people with justice and have not asked for a long life or wealth or the death of your enemies—¹²I will give you what you asked for! I will give you a wise and understanding heart such as no one else has had or ever will have! ¹³And I will also give you what you did not ask for—riches and fame! No other king in all the world will be compared to you for the rest of your life! ¹⁴And if you follow me and obey my decrees and my commands as your father, David, did, I will give you a long life."

¹⁵Then Solomon woke up and realized it had been a dream. He returned to Jerusalem and stood before the Ark of the Lord's Covenant, where he sacrificed burnt offerings and peace offerings. Then he invited all his officials to a great banquet.

*Solomon Judges Wisely*

¹⁶Some time later two prostitutes came to the king to have an argument settled. ¹⁷"Please, my lord," one of them began, "this woman and I live in the same house. I gave birth to a baby

---

**3:1** Marriage between royal families was a common practice in the ancient Near East because it secured peace. Although Solomon's marital alliances built friendships with surrounding nations, they were also the beginning of his downfall. These relationships became inroads for pagan ideas and practices. Solomon's foreign wives brought their gods to Jerusalem and eventually lured him into idolatry (11:1-6).

It is easy to minimize religious differences in order to encourage the development of a friendship. What can seem small in a friendship, however, will have an enormous impact upon a marriage. When you're young and in love, you may be idealistic, minimizing religious differences as something you can "work out." The reality is, however, that God gives us standards to follow for all our relationships, including marriage, for our own good. If we follow God's will, we will not be lured away from our true focus.

**3:2, 3** God's laws said that the Israelites could make sacrifices only in specified places (Deuteronomy 12:13, 14). This was to prevent the people from instituting their own methods of worship and allowing pagan practices to creep into their worship. But many Israelites, including Solomon, made sacrifices in the surrounding hills. Solomon loved God, but this act was sin. It took the offerings out of the watchful care of priests and ministers loyal to God and opened the way for false teaching to be tied to these sacrifices. God appeared to Solomon to grant him wisdom, not during the sacrifice, but at night. God honored his prayer but did not condone the sacrifice.

**3:6-9** When given a chance to have anything in the world, Solomon asked for wisdom—"an understanding heart"—in order to lead well and to make right decisions. We can ask God for this

same wisdom (James 1:5). Notice that Solomon asked for understanding to carry out his job; he did not ask God to do the job for him. We should not ask God to do *for* us what he wants to do *through* us. Instead, we should ask God to give us the wisdom to know what to do and the courage to follow through on it.

**3:11-14** Solomon asked for wisdom, not wealth, but God gave him riches and long life as well. While God does not promise riches to those who follow him, he gives us what we need if we put his kingdom, his interests, and his principles first (Matthew 6:31-33). Setting your sights on riches will only leave you dissatisfied because even if you get the riches you crave, you will still want something more. But if you put God and his work first, he will satisfy your deepest needs.

**3:12** Solomon received "a wise and understanding heart" from God, but it was up to Solomon to apply that wisdom to all areas of his life. Solomon was obviously wise in governing the nation, but he was foolish in running his household. Wisdom is both the ability to discern what is best and the strength of character to act upon that knowledge. While Solomon remained wise all his life, he did not always act upon his wisdom (11:6).

**3:16-28** Solomon's settlement of this dispute was a classic example of his wisdom. This wise ruling was verification that God had answered Solomon's prayer and given him an understanding heart. We have God's wisdom available to us as we pray and request it. But, like Solomon, we must put it into action. Applying wisdom to life demonstrates our understanding.

while she was with me in the house. ¹⁸Three days later this woman also had a baby. We were alone; there were only two of us in the house.

¹⁹"But her baby died during the night when she rolled over on it. ²⁰Then she got up in the night and took my son from beside me while I was asleep. She laid her dead child in my arms and took mine to sleep beside her. ²¹And in the morning when I tried to nurse my son, he was dead! But when I looked more closely in the morning light, I saw that it wasn't my son at all."

²²Then the other woman interrupted, "It certainly was your son, and the living child is mine."

"No," the first woman said, "the living child is mine, and the dead one is yours." And so they argued back and forth before the king.

²³Then the king said, "Let's get the facts straight. Both of you claim the living child is yours, and each says that the dead one belongs to the other. ²⁴All right, bring me a sword." So a sword was brought to the king.

²⁵Then he said, "Cut the living child in two, and give half to one woman and half to the other!"

²⁶Then the woman who was the real mother of the living child, and who loved him very much, cried out, "Oh no, my lord! Give her the child—please do not kill him!"

But the other woman said, "All right, he will be neither yours nor mine; divide him between us!"

²⁷Then the king said, "Do not kill the child, but give him to the woman who wants him to live, for she is his mother!"

²⁸When all Israel heard the king's decision, the people were in awe of the king, for they saw the wisdom God had given him for rendering justice.

**3:26** Isa 49:15 Jer 31:20 Hos 11:8

**3:28** 1 Kgs 3:9-12; 4:29

## Solomon's Officials and Governors

**4** King Solomon now ruled over all Israel, ²and these were his high officials:

Azariah son of Zadok was the priest.
³ Elihoreph and Ahijah, the sons of Shisha, were court secretaries.
Jehoshaphat son of Ahilud was the royal historian.
⁴ Benaiah son of Jehoiada was commander of the army.
Zadok and Abiathar were priests.
⁵ Azariah son of Nathan was in charge of the district governors.
Zabud son of Nathan, a priest, was a trusted adviser to the king.
⁶ Ahishar was manager of the palace property.
Adoniram son of Abda was in charge of the labor force.

**4:3** 2 Sam 8:16

⁷Solomon also had twelve district governors who were over all Israel. They were responsible for providing food for the king's household. Each of them arranged provisions for one month of the year. ⁸These are the names of the twelve governors:

**4:1ff** Solomon was well organized, with 11 high officials who had specific responsibilities, 12 district governors, and a governor in charge of the district governors. Each person had a specific responsibility or territory to manage. This organization was essential to maintain the government's effectiveness: It was a wise move by a wise man. It is good stewardship to be well organized. Good organization helps people work together in harmony and ensures that the desired goal will be reached.

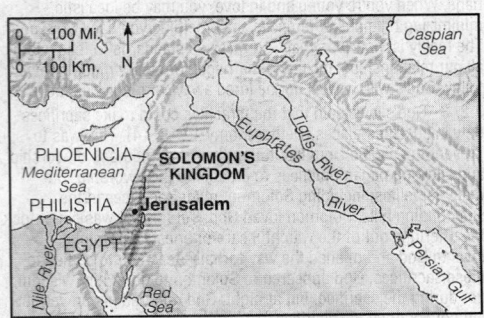

**SOLOMON'S KINGDOM** Solomon's kingdom spread from the Euphrates River in the north to the borders of Egypt. The entire land was at peace under his rule.

Ben-hur, in the hill country of Ephraim.

**4:9**
Judg 1:35

⁹ Ben-deker, in Makaz, Shaalbim, Beth-shemesh, and Elon-bethhanan.

**4:10**
Josh 12:17

¹⁰ Ben-hesed, in Arubboth, including Socoh and all the land of Hepher.

¹¹ Ben-abinadab, in all of Naphoth-dor.* (He was married to Taphath, one of Solomon's daughters.)

**4:12**
Josh 17:11

¹² Baana son of Ahilud, in Taanach and Megiddo, all of Beth-shan* near Zarethan below Jezreel, and all the territory from Beth-shan to Abel-meholah and over to Jokmeam.

**4:13**
Num 32:41
Deut 3:4

¹³ Ben-geber, in Ramoth-gilead, including the Towns of Jair (named for Jair of the tribe of Manasseh*) in Gilead, and in the Argob region of Bashan, including sixty large fortified towns with bronze bars on their gates.

¹⁴ Ahinadab son of Iddo, in Mahanaim.

¹⁵ Ahimaaz, in Naphtali. (He was married to Basemath, another of Solomon's daughters.)

¹⁶ Baana son of Hushai, in Asher and in Aloth.

**4:11** Hebrew *Naphath-dor*, a variant spelling of Naphoth-dor.  **4:12** Hebrew *Beth-shean*, a variant spelling of Beth-shan; also in 4:12b.  **4:13** Hebrew *Jair son of Manasseh*; compare 1 Chr 2:22.

---

**SOLOMON**

Wisdom is only effective when it is put into action. Early in his life, Solomon had the sense to recognize his need for wisdom. But by the time Solomon asked for wisdom to rule his kingdom, he had already started a habit that would make his wisdom ineffective for his own life—he sealed a pact with Egypt by marrying Pharaoh's daughter. She was the first of hundreds of wives married for political reasons. In doing this, Solomon went against not only his father's last words but also against God's direct commands. His action reminds us how easy it is to know what is right and yet not do it.

It is clear that God's gift of wisdom to Solomon did not mean that he couldn't make mistakes. He had been given great possibilities as the king of God's chosen people, but with them came great responsibilities; unfortunately, he tended to pursue the former and neglect the latter. While becoming famous as the builder of the Temple and the palace, he became infamous as a leader who excessively taxed and overworked his people. Visitors from distant lands came to admire this wise king, while his own people were gradually alienated from him.

Little is mentioned in the Bible about the last decade of Solomon's reign. Ecclesiastes probably records his last reflections on life. In that book we find a man proving through bitter experience that finding meaning in life apart from God is a vain pursuit. Security and contentment are found only in a personal relationship with God. The contentment we find in the opportunities and successes of this life is temporary. The more we expect our successes to be permanent, the more quickly they are gone. Be sure to balance your pursuit of life's possibilities with reliable fulfillment of your responsibilities.

| | |
|---|---|
| **Strengths and accomplishments** | • Third king of Israel, David's chosen heir<br>• The wisest man who ever lived<br>• Author of Ecclesiastes and Song of Songs, as well as many of the proverbs and a couple of the psalms<br>• Built God's Temple in Jerusalem<br>• Diplomat, trader, collector, patron of the arts |
| **Weaknesses and mistakes** | • Sealed many foreign agreements by marrying pagan women<br>• Allowed his wives to affect his loyalty to God<br>• Excessively taxed his people and drafted them into labor and military forces |
| **Lessons from his life** | • Effective leadership can be nullified by an ineffective personal life<br>• Solomon failed to obey God, but did not learn the lesson of repentance until late in life<br>• Knowing what actions are required of us means little without the will to do those actions |
| **Vital statistics** | • Where: Jerusalem<br>• Occupation: King of Israel<br>• Relatives: Father: David. Mother: Bathsheba. Brothers: Absalom, Adonijah. Sister: Tamar. Son: Rehoboam. |
| **Key verse** | "'Wasn't this exactly what led King Solomon of Israel into sin?' I demanded. 'There was no king from any nation who could compare to him, and God loved him and made him king over all Israel. But even he was led into sin by his foreign wives'" (Nehemiah 13:26). |

Solomon's story is told in 2 Samuel 12:24—1 Kings 11:43. He is also mentioned in 1 Chronicles 28—29; 2 Chronicles 1—10; Nehemiah 13:26; Psalm 72; and Matthew 6:29; 12:42.

17 Jehoshaphat son of Paruah, in Issachar.
18 Shimei son of Ela, in Benjamin.
19 Geber son of Uri, in the land of Gilead,* including the territories of King Sihon of the Amorites and King Og of Bashan.

There was also one governor over the land of Judah.*

**4:19**
Deut 3:8-10

## Solomon's Prosperity and Wisdom

20The people of Judah and Israel were as numerous as the sand on the seashore. They were very contented, with plenty to eat and drink. 21*Solomon ruled over all the kingdoms from the Euphrates River* in the north to the land of the Philistines and the border of Egypt in the south. The conquered peoples of those lands sent tribute money to Solomon and continued to serve him throughout his lifetime.

**4:20**
Gen 32:12

**4:21**
2 Sam 8:2, 6
2 Chr 9:26
Ps 72:10-11

22The daily food requirements for Solomon's palace were 150 bushels of choice flour and 300 bushels of meal*; 23also 10 oxen from the fattening pens, 20 pasture-fed cattle, 100 sheep or goats, as well as deer, gazelles, roe deer, and choice poultry.*

24Solomon's dominion extended over all the kingdoms west of the Euphrates River, from Tiphsah to Gaza. And there was peace on all his borders. 25During the lifetime of Solomon, all of Judah and Israel lived in peace and safety. And from Dan in the north to Beersheba in the south, each family had its own home and garden.*

**4:24**
1 Chr 22:9

**4:25**
Jer 23:5-6
Mic 4:4
Zech 3:10

26Solomon had 4,000* stalls for his chariot horses, and he had 12,000 horses.*

**4:26**
1 Kgs 10:26
2 Chr 1:14

27The district governors faithfully provided food for King Solomon and his court; each made sure nothing was lacking during the month assigned to him. 28They also brought the necessary barley and straw for the royal horses in the stables.

**4:29**
1 Kgs 3:12

29God gave Solomon very great wisdom and understanding, and knowledge as vast as the sands of the seashore. 30In fact, his wisdom exceeded that of all the wise men of the East and the wise men of Egypt. 31He was wiser than anyone else, including Ethan the Ezrahite and the sons of Mahol—Heman, Calcol, and Darda. His fame spread throughout all the surrounding nations. 32He composed some 3,000 proverbs and wrote 1,005 songs. 33He could speak with authority about all kinds of plants, from the great cedar of Lebanon to the tiny hyssop that grows from cracks in a wall. He could also speak about animals, birds, small creatures, and fish. 34And kings from every nation sent their ambassadors to listen to the wisdom of Solomon.

**4:30**
Isa 19:11
Acts 7:22

**4:31**
1 Kgs 3:12

**4:32**
Prov 1:1
Eccl 12:9
Song 1:1

**4:34**
1 Kgs 10:1
2 Chr 9:23

## 3. Solomon builds the Temple
### Preparations for Building the Temple

**5** 1*King Hiram of Tyre had always been a loyal friend of David. When Hiram learned that David's son Solomon was the new king of Israel, he sent ambassadors to congratulate him. 2Then Solomon sent this message back to Hiram:

**5:1-16**
//2 Chr 2:1-18

**5:1**
2 Sam 5:11
1 Chr 14:1

3"You know that my father, David, was not able to build a Temple to honor the name of the LORD his God because of the many wars waged against him by surrounding nations. He could not build until the LORD gave him victory over all his enemies. 4But now the LORD my God has given me peace on every side; I have no enemies, and all is well. 5So I am planning to build a Temple to honor the name of the LORD my God, just as he had instructed my father, David. For the LORD told him, 'Your son, whom I will place on your throne, will build the Temple to honor my name.'

**5:3**
1 Chr 28:3

**5:4**
1 Kgs 4:24
1 Chr 22:9

**5:5**
2 Sam 7:12-13
1 Chr 17:12

6"Therefore, please command that cedars from Lebanon be cut for me. Let my men work alongside yours, and I will pay your men whatever wages you ask. As you know, there is no one among us who can cut timber like you Sidonians!"

---

**4:19a** Greek version reads *of Gad*; compare 4:13.   **4:19b** As in some manuscripts; Hebrew lacks *of Judah*. The meaning of the Hebrew is uncertain.   **4:21a** Verses 4:21-34 are numbered 5:1-14 in Hebrew text.   **4:21b** Hebrew *the river*; also in 4:24.   **4:22** Hebrew *30 cors* [5.5 kiloliters] *of choice flour and 60 cors* [11 kiloliters] *of meal*. **4:23** Or *and fattened geese*.   **4:25** Hebrew *each family lived under its own grapevine and under its own fig tree*. **4:26a** As in some Greek manuscripts (see also 2 Chr 9:25); Hebrew reads *40,000*.   **4:26b** Or *12,000 charioteers*. **5:1** Verses 5:1-18 are numbered 5:15-32 in Hebrew text.

---

**4:20-25** Throughout most of his reign, Solomon applied his wisdom well because he sought God. The fruits of this wisdom were peace, security, and prosperity for the nation. Solomon's era is often looked upon as the ideal of what any nation can become when united in its trust in and obedience to God.

**4:32** The book of Proverbs records many of these 3,000 wise

proverbs. Other biblical writings of Solomon include Psalms 72 and 127, and the books of Ecclesiastes and Song of Songs. Solomon's wisdom was known throughout the world.

**5:2, 3** When David offered to build a Temple, God said no through the prophet Nathan (2 Samuel 7:1-17). God wanted a peacemaker, not a warrior, to build his house of prayer (1 Chronicles 28:2, 3).

7 When Hiram received Solomon's message, he was very pleased and said, "Praise the LORD today for giving David a wise son to be king of the great nation of Israel." 8 Then he sent this reply to Solomon:

**5:9**
2 Chr 2:16
Ezra 3:7
Ezek 27:17

"I have received your message, and I will supply all the cedar and cypress timber you need. 9 My servants will bring the logs from the Lebanon mountains to the Mediterranean Sea* and make them into rafts and float them along the coast to whatever place you choose. Then we will break the rafts apart so you can carry the logs away. You can pay me by supplying me with food for my household."

10 So Hiram supplied as much cedar and cypress timber as Solomon desired. 11 In return, Solomon sent him an annual payment of 100,000 bushels* of wheat for his household and 110,000 gallons* of pure olive oil. 12 So the LORD gave wisdom to Solomon, just as he had promised. And Hiram and Solomon made a formal alliance of peace.

**5:12**
1 Kgs 3:12
**5:14**
1 Kgs 4:6

13 Then King Solomon conscripted a labor force of 30,000 men from all Israel. 14 He sent them to Lebanon in shifts, 10,000 every month, so that each man would be one month in Lebanon and two months at home. Adoniram was in charge of this labor force. 15 Solomon also had 70,000 common laborers, 80,000 quarry workers in the hill country, 16 and 3,600* foremen to supervise the work. 17 At the king's command, they quarried large blocks of high-quality stone and shaped them to make the foundation of the Temple. 18 Men from the city of Gebal helped Solomon's and Hiram's builders prepare the timber and stone for the Temple.

**5:17**
2 Chr 22:2

### Solomon Builds the Temple

**6** It was in midspring, in the month of Ziv,* during the fourth year of Solomon's reign, that he began to construct the Temple of the LORD. This was 480 years after the people of Israel were rescued from their slavery in the land of Egypt.

**6:1-29**
//2 Chr 3:1-14

2 The Temple that King Solomon built for the LORD was 90 feet long, 30 feet wide, and 45 feet high.* 3 The entry room at the front of the Temple was 30 feet* wide, running across the entire width of the Temple. It projected outward 15 feet* from the front of the Temple. 4 Solomon also made narrow recessed windows throughout the Temple.

**6:4**
Ezek 41:16
**6:5**
Ezek 41:5-6

5 He built a complex of rooms against the outer walls of the Temple, all the way around the sides and rear of the building. 6 The complex was three stories high, the bottom floor being 7½ feet wide, the second floor 9 feet wide, and the top floor 10½ feet wide.* The rooms were connected to the walls of the Temple by beams resting on ledges built out from the wall. So the beams were not inserted into the walls themselves.

**6:7**
Exod 20:25
Deut 27:5-6

7 The stones used in the construction of the Temple were finished at the quarry, so there was no sound of hammer, ax, or any other iron tool at the building site.

8 The entrance to the bottom floor* was on the south side of the Temple. There were winding stairs going up to the second floor, and another flight of stairs between the second and third floors. 9 After completing the Temple structure, Solomon put in a ceiling made of

**6:9**
1 Kgs 6:14, 38

**5:9** Hebrew *the sea.* **5:11a** Hebrew *20,000 cors* [3,640 kiloliters]. **5:11b** As in Greek version, which reads *20,000 baths* [420 kiloliters] (see also 2 Chr 2:10); Hebrew reads *20 cors,* about 800 gallons or 3.6 kiloliters in volume. **5:16** As in some Greek manuscripts (see also 2 Chr 2:2, 18); Hebrew reads *3,300.* **6:1** Hebrew *It was in the month of Ziv, which is the second month.* This month of the ancient Hebrew lunar calendar usually occurs within the months of April and May. **6:2** Hebrew *60 cubits* [27.6 meters] *long, 20 cubits* [9.2 meters] *wide, and 30 cubits* [13.8 meters] *high.* **6:3a** Hebrew *20 cubits* [9.2 meters]; also in 6:16, 20. **6:3b** Hebrew *10 cubits* [4.6 meters]. **6:6** Hebrew *the bottom floor being 5 cubits* [2.3 meters] *wide, the second floor 6 cubits* [2.8 meters] *wide, and the top floor 7 cubits* [3.2 meters] *wide.* **6:8** As in Greek version; Hebrew reads *middle floor.*

---

**5:13, 14** Solomon drafted three times the number of workers needed for the Temple project and then arranged their schedules so they didn't have to be away from home for long periods of time. This showed his concern for the welfare of his workers and the importance he placed on family life. The strength of a nation is in direct proportion to the strength of its families. Solomon wisely recognized that family should always be a top priority. As you structure your own work or arrange the schedules of others, watch for the impact of your plans on families.

**5:18** Gebal, also called Byblos, was located north of what is now Beirut, near the cedar forest. These men were Phoenicians, probably skilled as shipbuilders, but employed for this project.

**6:1ff** For more information on the purpose of the Temple, see the note on 2 Chronicles 5:1ff.

**6:3** The entry room was like a large porch.

**6:4** These narrow, recessed windows were near the tops of the walls to help light the center of the Temple.

**6:7** In honor of God, the Temple in Jerusalem was built without the sound of a hammer or any other tool at the building site. This meant that the stone had to be "prefinished" (cut and shaped) miles away at the quarry. The people's honor and respect for God extended to every aspect of constructing this house of worship. This detail is recorded not to teach us how to build a church but to show us the importance of demonstrating care, concern, honor, and respect for God and his sanctuary.

cedar beams and planks. [10]As already stated, he built a complex of rooms on three sides of the building, attached to the Temple walls by cedar timbers. Each story of the complex was 7½ feet* high.

[11]Then the LORD gave this message to Solomon: [12]"Concerning this Temple you are building, if you keep all my decrees and regulations and obey all my commands, I will fulfill through you the promise I made to your father, David. [13]I will live among the Israelites and will never abandon my people Israel."

### The Temple's Interior

[14]So Solomon finished building the Temple. [15]The entire inside, from floor to ceiling, was paneled with wood. He paneled the walls and ceilings with cedar, and he used planks of cypress for the floors. [16]He partitioned off an inner sanctuary—the Most Holy Place—at the far end of the Temple. It was 30 feet deep and was paneled with cedar from floor to ceiling. [17]The main room of the Temple, outside the Most Holy Place, was 60 feet* long. [18]Cedar paneling completely covered the stone walls throughout the Temple, and the paneling was decorated with carvings of gourds and open flowers.

[19]He prepared the inner sanctuary at the far end of the Temple, where the Ark of the LORD's Covenant would be placed. [20]This inner sanctuary was 30 feet long, 30 feet wide, and 30 feet high. He overlaid the inside with solid gold. He also overlaid the altar made of cedar.* [21]Then Solomon overlaid the rest of the Temple's interior with solid gold, and he made gold chains to protect the entrance* to the Most Holy Place. [22]So he finished overlaying the entire Temple with gold, including the altar that belonged to the Most Holy Place.

[23]He made two cherubim of wild olive* wood, each 15 feet* tall, and placed them in the inner sanctuary. [24]The wingspan of each of the cherubim was 15 feet, each wing being 7½ feet* long. [25]The two cherubim were identical in shape and size; [26]each was 15 feet tall. [27]He placed them side by side in the inner sanctuary of the Temple. Their outspread wings reached from wall to wall, while their inner wings touched at the center of the room. [28]He overlaid the two cherubim with gold.

[29]He decorated all the walls of the inner sanctuary and the main room with carvings of cherubim, palm trees, and open flowers. [30]He overlaid the floor in both rooms with gold.

[31]For the entrance to the inner sanctuary, he made double doors of wild olive wood with five-sided doorposts.* [32]These double doors were decorated with carvings of cherubim, palm trees, and open flowers. The doors, including the decorations of cherubim and palm trees, were overlaid with gold.

[33]Then he made four-sided doorposts of wild olive wood for the entrance to the Temple. [34]There were two folding doors of cypress wood, and each door was hinged to fold back upon itself. [35]These doors were decorated with carvings of cherubim, palm trees, and open flowers—all overlaid evenly with gold.

[36]The walls of the inner courtyard were built so that there was one layer of cedar beams between every three layers of finished stone.

[37]The foundation of the LORD's Temple was laid in midspring, in the month of Ziv,* during the fourth year of Solomon's reign. [38]The entire building was completed in every detail by midautumn, in the month of Bul,* during the eleventh year of his reign. So it took seven years to build the Temple.

**6:12**
2 Sam 7:12-16
1 Kgs 9:4-5

**6:13**
Exod 25:8
Deut 31:6
Josh 1:5

**6:16**
Exod 26:33
Lev 16:1-2
2 Chr 3:8

**6:23**
Exod 25:20; 37:1-9
2 Chr 3:10-12

**6:34**
Ezek 41:23-25

**6:36**
1 Kgs 7:12

**6:10** Hebrew *5 cubits* [2.3 meters].   **6:17** Hebrew *40 cubits* [18.4 meters].   **6:20** Or *overlaid the altar with cedar.* The meaning of the Hebrew is uncertain.   **6:21** Or *to draw curtains across.* The meaning of the Hebrew is uncertain. **6:23a** Or *pine;* Hebrew reads *oil tree;* also in 6:31, 33.   **6:23b** Hebrew *10 cubits* [4.6 meters]; also in 6:24, 25. **6:24** Hebrew *5 cubits* [2.3 meters].   **6:31** The meaning of the Hebrew is uncertain.   **6:37** Hebrew *was laid in the month of Ziv.* This month of the ancient Hebrew lunar calendar usually occurs within the months of April and May. **6:38** Hebrew *by the month of Bul, which is the eighth month.* This month of the ancient Hebrew lunar calendar usually occurs within the months of October and November.

---

**6:13** This verse summarizes the Temple's main purpose. God promised that his eternal presence would never leave the Temple as long as one condition was met: The Israelites had to obey God's law. Knowing how many laws they had to follow, we may think this condition was difficult. But the Israelites' situation was much like ours today: They were not cut off from God for failing to keep some small part of a law. Forgiveness was amply provided for all their sins, no matter how large or small. As you read the history of the kings, you will see that lawbreaking was the result, not the cause, of estrangement from God. The kings abandoned God in their hearts first and *then* failed to keep his laws. When we close our hearts to God, we soon lose his power and presence.

**6:14** The concept of Solomon's Temple was more like a palace for God than a place of worship. As a dwelling place for God, it was fitting for it to be ornate and beautiful. It had small inside dimensions because most worshipers would gather outside.

## Solomon Builds His Palace

**7** Solomon also built a palace for himself, and it took him thirteen years to complete the construction.

7:1
1 Kgs 3:1; 9:10
2 Chr 8:1
7:2
1 Kgs 10:17
2 Chr 9:16

²One of Solomon's buildings was called the Palace of the Forest of Lebanon. It was 150 feet long, 75 feet wide, and 45 feet high.* There were four rows of cedar pillars, and great cedar beams rested on the pillars. ³The hall had a cedar roof. Above the beams on the pillars were forty-five side rooms,* arranged in three tiers of fifteen each. ⁴On each end of the long hall were three rows of windows facing each other. ⁵All the doorways and doorposts* had rectangular frames and were arranged in sets of three, facing each other.

⁶Solomon also built the Hall of Pillars, which was 75 feet long and 45 feet wide.* There was a porch in front, along with a canopy supported by pillars.

7:7
1 Kgs 6:9, 15-16
7:8
1 Kgs 3:1
2 Chr 8:11

⁷Solomon also built the throne room, known as the Hall of Justice, where he sat to hear legal matters. It was paneled with cedar from floor to ceiling.* ⁸Solomon's living quarters surrounded a courtyard behind this hall, and they were constructed the same way. He also built similar living quarters for Pharaoh's daughter, whom he had married.

⁹From foundation to eaves, all these buildings were built from huge blocks of high-quality stone, cut with saws and trimmed to exact measure on all sides. ¹⁰Some of the huge foundation stones were 15 feet long, and some were 12 feet* long. ¹¹The blocks of high-quality stone used in the walls were also cut to measure, and cedar beams were also used.

7:12
1 Kgs 6:36

¹²The walls of the great courtyard were built so that there was one layer of cedar beams between every three layers of finished stone, just like the walls of the inner courtyard of the LORD's Temple with its entry room.

## Furnishings for the Temple

7:13
2 Chr 2:13-14

¹³King Solomon then asked for a man named Huram* to come from Tyre. ¹⁴He was half Israelite, since his mother was a widow from the tribe of Naphtali, and his father had been a craftsman in bronze from Tyre. Huram was extremely skillful and talented in any work in bronze, and he came to do all the metal work for King Solomon.

7:15
2 Kgs 25:17
2 Chr 3:15; 4:12

¹⁵Huram cast two bronze pillars, each 27 feet tall and 18 feet in circumference.* ¹⁶For the tops of the pillars he cast bronze capitals, each 7½ feet* tall. ¹⁷Each capital was decorated with seven sets of latticework and interwoven chains. ¹⁸He also encircled the latticework with two rows of pomegranates to decorate the capitals over the pillars. ¹⁹The capitals on the columns inside the entry room were shaped like water lilies, and they were six feet* tall.

7:20
2 Chr 3:16; 4:13
7:21
2 Chr 3:17

²⁰The capitals on the two pillars had 200 pomegranates in two rows around them, beside the rounded surface next to the latticework. ²¹Huram set the pillars at the entrance of the Temple, one toward the south and one toward the north. He named the one on the south Jakin, and the one on the north Boaz.* ²²The capitals on the pillars were shaped like water lilies. And so the work on the pillars was finished.

7:23-26
//2 Chr 4:2-5
7:23
2 Kgs 25:13

²³Then Huram cast a great round basin, 15 feet across from rim to rim, called the Sea. It was 7½ feet deep and about 45 feet in circumference.* ²⁴It was encircled just below its rim by two rows of decorative gourds. There were about six gourds per foot* all the way around, and they were cast as part of the basin.

²⁵The Sea was placed on a base of twelve bronze oxen,* all facing outward. Three faced north, three faced west, three faced south, and three faced east, and the Sea rested on them. ²⁶The walls of the Sea were about three inches* thick, and its rim flared out like a cup and resembled a water lily blossom. It could hold about 11,000 gallons* of water.

7:2 Hebrew 100 cubits [46 meters] long, 50 cubits [23 meters] wide, and 30 cubits [13.5 meters] high.   7:3 Or 45 rafters, or 45 beams, or 45 pillars. The architectural details in 7:2-6 can be interpreted in many different ways.   7:5 Greek version reads windows.   7:6 Hebrew 50 cubits [23 meters] long and 30 cubits [13.8 meters] wide.   7:7 As in Syriac version and Latin Vulgate; Hebrew reads from floor to floor.   7:10 Hebrew 10 cubits [4.6 meters] . . . 8 cubits [3.7 meters].   7:13 Hebrew Hiram (also in 7:40, 45); compare 2 Chr 2:13. This is not the same person mentioned in 5:1.   7:15 Hebrew 18 cubits [8.3 meters] tall and 12 cubits [5.5 meters] in circumference.   7:16 Hebrew 5 cubits [2.3 meters].   7:19 Hebrew 4 cubits [1.8 meters]; also in 7:38.   7:21 Jakin probably means "he establishes"; Boaz probably means "in him is strength."   7:23 Hebrew 10 cubits [4.6 meters] across. . . . 5 cubits [2.3 meters] deep and 30 cubits [13.8 meters] in circumference.   7:24 Or 20 gourds per meter; Hebrew reads 10 per cubit.   7:25 Hebrew 12 oxen; compare 2 Kgs 16:17, which specifies bronze oxen.   7:26a Hebrew a handbreadth [8 centimeters].   7:26b Hebrew 2,000 baths [42 kiloliters].

**7:1** That Solomon took longer to build his palace than to build the Temple is not a comment on his priorities. His palace project took longer because it was part of a huge civic building project including barracks and housing for his harem.

**7:14** Huram was an expert craftsman. Solomon chose only the best.

**7:23** The "Sea" was an enormous tank. Designed and used for the priests' ceremonial washings, it stood in the Temple court near the altar of burnt offering. There the priests washed themselves before offering sacrifices or entering the Temple (Exodus 30:17-21).

27Huram also made ten bronze water carts, each 6 feet long, 6 feet wide, and 4½ feet tall.* 28They were constructed with side panels braced with crossbars. 29Both the panels and the crossbars were decorated with carved lions, oxen, and cherubim. Above and below the lions and oxen were wreath decorations. 30Each of these carts had four bronze wheels and bronze axles. There were supporting posts for the bronze basins at the corners of the carts; these supports were decorated on each side with carvings of wreaths. 31The top of each cart had a rounded frame for the basin. It projected 1½ feet* above the cart's top like a round pedestal, and its opening was 2¼ feet* across; it was decorated on the outside with carvings of wreaths. The panels of the carts were square, not round. 32Under the panels were four wheels that were connected to axles that had been cast as one unit with the cart. The wheels were 2¼ feet in diameter 33and were similar to chariot wheels. The axles, spokes, rims, and hubs were all cast from molten bronze.

34There were handles at each of the four corners of the carts, and these, too, were cast as one unit with the cart. 35Around the top of each cart was a rim nine inches wide.* The corner supports and side panels were cast as one unit with the cart. 36Carvings of cherubim, lions, and palm trees decorated the panels and corner supports wherever there was room, and there were wreaths all around. 37All ten water carts were the same size and were made alike, for each was cast from the same mold.

38Huram also made ten smaller bronze basins, one for each cart. Each basin was six feet across and could hold 220 gallons* of water. 39He set five water carts on the south side of the Temple and five on the north side. The great bronze basin called the Sea was placed near the southeast corner of the Temple. 40He also made the necessary washbasins, shovels, and bowls.

So at last Huram completed everything King Solomon had assigned him to make for the Temple of the LORD:

41 the two pillars;
   the two bowl-shaped capitals on top of the pillars;
   the two networks of interwoven chains that decorated the capitals;
42 the 400 pomegranates that hung from the chains on the capitals (two rows of pomegranates for each of the chain networks that decorated the capitals on top of the pillars);
43 the ten water carts holding the ten basins;
44 the Sea and the twelve oxen under it;
45 the ash buckets, the shovels, and the bowls.

Huram made all these things of burnished bronze for the Temple of the LORD, just as King Solomon had directed. 46The king had them cast in clay molds in the Jordan Valley between Succoth and Zarethan. 47Solomon did not weigh all these things because there were so many; the weight of the bronze could not be measured.

48Solomon also made all the furnishings of the Temple of the LORD:

   the gold altar;
   the gold table for the Bread of the Presence;
49 the lampstands of solid gold, five on the south and five on the north, in front of the Most Holy Place;
   the flower decorations, lamps, and tongs—all of gold;
50 the small bowls, lamp snuffers, bowls, dishes, and incense burners—all of solid gold; the doors for the entrances to the Most Holy Place and the main room of the Temple, with their fronts overlaid with gold.

51So King Solomon finished all his work on the Temple of the LORD. Then he brought all the gifts his father, David, had dedicated—the silver, the gold, and the various articles—and he stored them in the treasuries of the LORD's Temple.

7:27 Hebrew 4 cubits [1.8 meters] long, 4 cubits wide, and 3 cubits [1.4 meters] high.   7:31a Hebrew a cubit [46 centimeters].   7:31b Hebrew 1½ cubits [69 centimeters]; also in 7:32.   7:35 Hebrew half a cubit wide [23 centimeters].   7:38 Hebrew 40 baths [840 liters].

7:27-39 These 10 "water carts" held basins of water. The basins were used for washing the various parts of the animal sacrifices. The basins were movable so they could be used where needed.
7:40-47 Huram's items of bronze would look strange in today's churches, but we use other articles to enhance worship. Stained-glass windows, crosses, pulpits, hymnbooks, banners, and communion tables serve as aids to worship. While the instruments of worship may change, the purpose of worship should never change—to give honor and praise to God.

## The Ark Brought to the Temple

**8:1-21**
2 Chr 5:2–6:11

**8:1**
Num 7:2
2 Sam 5:7; 6:17

**8:2**
Lev 23:33-34
2 Chr 5:3; 7:8-10

**8** Solomon then summoned to Jerusalem the elders of Israel and all the heads of the tribes—the leaders of the ancestral families of the Israelites. They were to bring the Ark of the Lord's Covenant to the Temple from its location in the City of David, also known as Zion. ²So all the men of Israel assembled before King Solomon at the annual Festival of Shelters, which is held in early autumn in the month of Ethanim.*

**8:2** Hebrew *at the festival in the month Ethanim, which is the seventh month.* The Festival of Shelters began on the fifteenth day of the seventh month of the ancient Hebrew lunar calendar. This day occurred in late September, October, or early November.

**SOLOMON'S TEMPLE 960–586 B.C.**
Solomon's Temple was a beautiful sight. It took over seven years to build and was a magnificent building containing gold, silver, bronze, and cedar. This house for God was without equal. The description is found in 1 Kings 6–7 and 2 Chronicles 2–4.

© Hugh Claycombe 1986

## FURNISHINGS

*Cherubim:* represented heavenly beings, symbolized God's presence and holiness (gold-plated, 15 feet wide)

*Ark of the Covenant:* contained the law written on two tablets, symbolized God's presence with Israel (wood overlaid with gold)

*Curtain:* separated the Holy Place from the Most Holy Place (blue, purple, and scarlet yarn and fine linen, with cherubim worked into it)

*Doors:* between Holy Place and Most Holy Place (wood overlaid with gold)

*Golden tables* (wood overlaid with gold), *gold lampstands* (with seven lamps on each stand), and *altar of incense* (wood overlaid with gold): instruments for priestly functions in the Holy Place

*Bronze pillars:* named Jakin (meaning "he establishes") and Boaz (meaning "in him is strength")—taken together they could mean "God provides the strength"

*Altar:* for burning of sacrifices (bronze)

*Sea:* for priests' washing (had 16,500-gallon capacity)

*Bronze basins:* for washing the sacrifices (water basins on wheeled bases)

*Portico:* the entry room

This reconstruction uses known archaeological parallels to supplement the text, and assumes interior dimensions from 1 Kings 6:17-20.
© Hugh Claycombe

**8:1ff** Solomon gathered the people not just to dedicate the Temple, but to rededicate themselves to God's service. Solomon could well be speaking these words to us today: "And may you be completely faithful to the Lord our God. May you always obey his decrees and commands, just as you are doing today" (8:61).

**8:1ff** What was the difference between the Tabernacle and the Temple, and why did the Israelites change from one to the other?

As a tent, the Tabernacle was a portable place of worship designed for the people as they were traveling toward the Promised Land. The Temple was a permanent place to worship God after the Israelites were at peace in their land. To bring the Ark of the Lord's Covenant to the Temple signified God's actual presence there.

³When all the elders of Israel arrived, the priests picked up the Ark. ⁴The priests and Levites brought up the Ark of the Lord along with the special tent* and all the sacred items that had been in it. ⁵There, before the Ark, King Solomon and the entire community of Israel sacrificed so many sheep, goats, and cattle that no one could keep count!

⁶Then the priests carried the Ark of the Lord's Covenant into the inner sanctuary of the Temple—the Most Holy Place—and placed it beneath the wings of the cherubim. ⁷The cherubim spread their wings over the Ark, forming a canopy over the Ark and its carrying poles. ⁸These poles were so long that their ends could be seen from the Temple's main room—the Holy Place—but not from the outside. They are still there to this day. ⁹Nothing was in the Ark except the two stone tablets that Moses had placed in it at Mount Sinai,* where the Lord made a covenant with the people of Israel when they left the land of Egypt.

¹⁰When the priests came out of the Holy Place, a thick cloud filled the Temple of the Lord. ¹¹The priests could not continue their service because of the cloud, for the glorious presence of the Lord filled the Temple.

### Solomon Praises the Lord

¹²Then Solomon prayed, "O Lord, you have said that you would live in a thick cloud of darkness. ¹³Now I have built a glorious Temple for you, a place where you can live forever!*"

¹⁴Then the king turned around to the entire community of Israel standing before him and gave this blessing: ¹⁵"Praise the Lord, the God of Israel, who has kept the promise he made to my father, David. For he told my father, ¹⁶'From the day I brought my people Israel out of Egypt, I have never chosen a city among any of the tribes of Israel as the place where a Temple should be built to honor my name. But I have chosen David to be king over my people Israel.'"

¹⁷Then Solomon said, "My father, David, wanted to build this Temple to honor the name of the Lord, the God of Israel. ¹⁸But the Lord told him, 'You wanted to build the Temple to honor my name. Your intention is good, ¹⁹but you are not the one to do it. One of your own sons will build the Temple to honor me.'

²⁰"And now the Lord has fulfilled the promise he made, for I have become king in my father's place, and I now sit on the throne of Israel, just as the Lord promised. I have built this Temple to honor the name of the Lord, the God of Israel. ²¹And I have prepared a place there for the Ark, which contains the covenant that the Lord made with our ancestors when he brought them out of Egypt."

### Solomon's Prayer of Dedication

²²Then Solomon stood before the altar of the Lord in front of the entire community of Israel. He lifted his hands toward heaven, ²³and he prayed,

"O Lord, God of Israel, there is no God like you in all of heaven above or on the earth below. You keep your covenant and show unfailing love to all who walk before you in wholehearted devotion. ²⁴You have kept your promise to your servant David, my father. You made that promise with your own mouth, and with your own hands you have fulfilled it today.

²⁵"And now, O Lord, God of Israel, carry out the additional promise you made to your servant David, my father. For you said to him, 'If your descendants guard their behavior and faithfully follow me as you have done, one of them will always sit on the throne of Israel.' ²⁶Now, O God of Israel, fulfill this promise to your servant David, my father.

²⁷"But will God really live on earth? Why, even the highest heavens cannot contain you. How much less this Temple I have built! ²⁸Nevertheless, listen to my prayer and

8:3 Num 7:9 | 8:5 2 Sam 6:13; 2 Chr 1:5-6 | 8:8 Exod 25:13-15; 37:4-5 | 8:9 Exod 24:7; 25:16; Deut 4:13-14; 10:2; Heb 9:4 | 8:10 Exod 40:34-35; 2 Chr 7:1-2 | 8:12 2 Chr 6:1; Ps 97:2 | 8:15 2 Sam 7:12-13; 1 Chr 22:10 | 8:16 Deut 12:4-5, 11; 1 Sam 16:1 | 8:17 2 Sam 7:2-3; 1 Chr 17:1-2 | 8:19 2 Sam 7:12-13; 1 Chr 17:11-12; 22:8-10 | 8:20 1 Chr 28:6 | 8:23 Deut 7:9; Neh 1:5; 9:32 | 8:25 2 Sam 7:25; 1 Kgs 2:4; 1 Chr 17:23 | 8:27 2 Chr 2:6; Ps 139:7-16; Isa 66:1; Jer 23:24; Acts 7:48-49

8:4 Hebrew *the Tent of Meeting;* i.e., the tent mentioned in 2 Sam 6:17 and 1 Chr 16:1.  8:9 Hebrew *at Horeb,* another name for Sinai.  8:13 Some Greek texts add the line *Is this not written in the Book of Jashar?*

8:6 Cherubim are mighty angels.

8:15-21 For 480 years after Israel's escape from Egypt, God did not ask his people to build a temple for him. Instead, he emphasized the importance of his presence among them and their need for spiritual leaders. It is easy to think of a building as the focus of God's presence and power, but God chooses and uses *people* to do his work. Building or enlarging our place of worship may be necessary, but it should never take priority over developing spiritual leaders.

8:24 Solomon was referring to the promise God had made to David in 2 Samuel 7:12-15 that one of David's sons would build the Temple.

8:27 In his prayer of dedication, Solomon declared that even the highest heavens cannot contain God. Isn't it amazing that, though the heavens can't contain God, he is willing to live in the hearts of those who love him? The God of the universe takes up residence in his people.

**8:29**
Deut 12:11
2 Chr 7:12, 15-16
**8:30**
Neh 1:5-7

**8:31**
Exod 22:8-11
Lev 5:1
**8:32**
Deut 25:1

**8:33**
Lev 26:14-17,
40-42
Deut 28:25, 47-48

**8:35**
Lev 26:19
Deut 11:16-17
**8:36**
1 Sam 12:23
Ps 27:11

**8:37**
Lev 26:16, 25-26
Deut 28:21-23

**8:39**
1 Sam 2:3
1 Chr 28:9
Jer 17:10
John 2:24-25

**8:42**
Deut 3:24
**8:43**
1 Sam 17:46

**8:44**
2 Chr 14:11

**8:46**
2 Kgs 17:6, 18;
25:21
Prov 20:9
1 Jn 1:8-10
**8:47**
Lev 26:40-42
Ezra 9:5-7
Neh 1:6-7
Ps 106:6-7
Dan 9:5
**8:48**
Deut 4:29
1 Sam 7:3-4
**8:50**
2 Chr 30:9
Ps 106:46
**8:51**
Exod 32:11-12
Deut 4:20; 9:26-29
Jer 11:4

my plea, O Lord my God. Hear the cry and the prayer that your servant is making to you today. 29May you watch over this Temple night and day, this place where you have said, 'My name will be there.' May you always hear the prayers I make toward this place. 30May you hear the humble and earnest requests from me and your people Israel when we pray toward this place. Yes, hear us from heaven where you live, and when you hear, forgive.

31"If someone wrongs another person and is required to take an oath of innocence in front of your altar in this Temple, 32then hear from heaven and judge between your servants—the accuser and the accused. Punish the guilty as they deserve. Acquit the innocent because of their innocence.

33"If your people Israel are defeated by their enemies because they have sinned against you, and if they turn to you and acknowledge your name and pray to you here in this Temple, 34then hear from heaven and forgive the sin of your people Israel and return them to this land you gave their ancestors.

35"If the skies are shut up and there is no rain because your people have sinned against you, and if they pray toward this Temple and acknowledge your name and turn from their sins because you have punished them, 36then hear from heaven and forgive the sins of your servants, your people Israel. Teach them to follow the right path, and send rain on your land that you have given to your people as their special possession.

37"If there is a famine in the land or a plague or crop disease or attacks of locusts or caterpillars, or if your people's enemies are in the land besieging their towns—whatever disaster or disease there is—38and if your people Israel pray about their troubles, raising their hands toward this Temple, 39then hear from heaven where you live, and forgive. Give your people what their actions deserve, for you alone know each human heart. 40Then they will fear you as long as they live in the land you gave to our ancestors.

41"In the future, foreigners who do not belong to your people Israel will hear of you. They will come from distant lands because of your name, 42for they will hear of your great name and your strong hand and your powerful arm. And when they pray toward this Temple, 43then hear from heaven where you live, and grant what they ask of you. In this way, all the people of the earth will come to know and fear you, just as your own people Israel do. They, too, will know that this Temple I have built honors your name.

44"If your people go out where you send them to fight their enemies, and if they pray to the Lord by turning toward this city you have chosen and toward this Temple I have built to honor your name, 45then hear their prayers from heaven and uphold their cause.

46"If they sin against you—and who has never sinned?—you might become angry with them and let their enemies conquer them and take them captive to their land far away or near. 47But in that land of exile, they might turn to you in repentance and pray, 'We have sinned, done evil, and acted wickedly.' 48If they turn to you with their whole heart and soul in the land of their enemies and pray toward the land you gave to their ancestors—toward this city you have chosen, and toward this Temple I have built to honor your name—49then hear their prayers and their petition from heaven where you live, and uphold their cause. 50Forgive your people who have sinned against you. Forgive all the offenses they have committed against you. Make their captors merciful to them, 51for they are your people—your special possession—whom you brought out of the iron-smelting furnace of Egypt.

---

**8:33, 34** After Solomon's reign, the people continually turned away from God. The rest of the kingdom era is a vivid fulfillment of Solomon's description in these verses. As a result of the people's sin, God let them be overrun by enemies several times. Then, in desperation, they cried out to God for forgiveness, and God restored them.

**8:41-43** God chose Israel to be a blessing to the whole world (Genesis 12:1-3). This blessing found its fulfillment in Jesus—a descendant of Abraham and David (Galatians 3:8, 9)—who became the Messiah for all people, Jews and non-Jews. When the Israelites first entered the Promised Land, they were ordered to clear out several wicked nations; thus, we read in the Old Testa-

ment of many wars. But we should not conclude that war was Israel's first duty. After subduing the evil people, Israel was to become a light to the surrounding nations. Sadly, Israel's own sin and spiritual blindness prevented them from reaching out to the rest of the world with God's love. Reaching out to the world is still the commission of God's people today. Christians need to take every opportunity to spread God's love to the world.

**8:46-53** Solomon, who seemed to have prophetic insight into the future captivities of his people (2 Kings 17; 25), asked God to be merciful to them when they cried out to him, to forgive them, and to return them to their homeland. Reference to their return is made in Ezra 1–2; Nehemiah 1–2.

52"May your eyes be open to my requests and to the requests of your people Israel. May you hear and answer them whenever they cry out to you. 53For when you brought our ancestors out of Egypt, O Sovereign LORD, you told your servant Moses that you had set Israel apart from all the nations of the earth to be your own special possession."

**8:53**
Exod 19:5-6

### The Dedication of the Temple

54When Solomon finished making these prayers and petitions to the LORD, he stood up in front of the altar of the LORD, where he had been kneeling with his hands raised toward heaven. 55He stood and in a loud voice blessed the entire congregation of Israel:

56"Praise the LORD who has given rest to his people Israel, just as he promised. Not one word has failed of all the wonderful promises he gave through his servant Moses. 57May the LORD our God be with us as he was with our ancestors; may he never leave us or abandon us. 58May he give us the desire to do his will in everything and to obey all the commands, decrees, and regulations that he gave our ancestors. 59And may these words that I have prayed in the presence of the LORD be before him constantly, day and night, so that the LORD our God may give justice to me and to his people Israel, according to each day's needs. 60Then people all over the earth will know that the LORD alone is God and there is no other. 61And may you be completely faithful to the LORD our God. May you always obey his decrees and commands, just as you are doing today."

**8:56**
Josh 21:45;
23:14-15
2 Kgs 10:9-10

**8:57**
Josh 1:5
1 Sam 12:22

**8:58**
Ps 119:36
Jer 31:33

**8:60**
Deut 4:35
1 Sam 17:46
1 Kgs 18:39

62Then the king and all Israel with him offered sacrifices to the LORD. 63Solomon offered to the LORD a peace offering of 22,000 cattle and 120,000 sheep and goats. And so the king and all the people of Israel dedicated the Temple of the LORD.

**8:61**
Deut 18:13
1 Kgs 11:4
2 Kgs 20:3

**8:62-66**
2 Chr 7:1-10

64That same day the king consecrated the central area of the courtyard in front of the LORD's Temple. He offered burnt offerings, grain offerings, and the fat of peace offerings there, because the bronze altar in the LORD's presence was too small to hold all the burnt offerings, grain offerings, and the fat of the peace offerings.

**8:64**
2 Chr 4:1

65Then Solomon and all Israel celebrated the Festival of Shelters* in the presence of the LORD our God. A large congregation had gathered from as far away as Lebo-hamath in the north and the Brook of Egypt in the south. The celebration went on for fourteen days in all—seven days for the dedication of the altar and seven days for the Festival of Shelters.* 66After the festival was over,* Solomon sent the people home. They blessed the king and went to their homes joyful and glad because the LORD had been good to his servant David and to his people Israel.

**8:65**
Gen 15:18

## 4. Solomon's greatness and downfall
### The LORD's Response to Solomon

**9** So Solomon finished building the Temple of the LORD, as well as the royal palace. He completed everything he had planned to do. 2Then the LORD appeared to Solomon a second time, as he had done before at Gibeon. 3The LORD said to him,

**9:1-9**
//2 Chr 7:11-22

**9:1**
1 Kgs 7:1-2
2 Chr 8:6

"I have heard your prayer and your petition. I have set this Temple apart to be holy—this place you have built where my name will be honored forever. I will always watch over it, for it is dear to my heart.

**9:3**
2 Kgs 20:5

4"As for you, if you will follow me with integrity and godliness, as David your father did, obeying all my commands, decrees, and regulations, 5then I will establish the throne of your dynasty over Israel forever. For I made this promise to your father, David: 'One of your descendants will always sit on the throne of Israel.'

**9:4**
1 Kgs 3:14; 11:4

**9:5**
2 Sam 7:12

**9:6**
2 Sam 7:14-16
1 Chr 28:9

6"But if you or your descendants abandon me and disobey the commands and decrees I have given you, and if you serve and worship other gods, 7then I will uproot Israel from this land that I have given them. I will reject this Temple that I have made holy to honor my name. I will make Israel an object of mockery and ridicule among the

**9:7**
Lev 18:24-29
Deut 4:26-27
2 Kgs 17:23
Jer 7:4

8:65a Hebrew *the festival;* see note on 8:2.   8:65b Hebrew *seven days and seven days, fourteen days;* compare parallel text at 2 Chr 7:8-10.   8:66 Hebrew *On the eighth day,* probably referring to the day following the seven-day Festival of Shelters; compare parallel text at 2 Chr 7:9-10.

---

**8:56-60** Solomon praised the Lord and prayed for the people. His prayer can be a pattern for our prayers. He had five basic requests: (1) for God's presence (8:57); (2) for the desire to do God's will in everything (8:58); (3) for the desire and ability to obey God's decrees and commands (8:58); (4) for help with each day's needs (8:59); (5) for the spread of God's Kingdom to the entire world (8:60). These prayer requests are just as important today. When you pray for your church or family, you can make these same requests to God.

**9:4-9** God appeared to Solomon a second time; the first had been at Gibeon (3:4-15). For more on the conditions of God's great promise to David and his descendants, see the note on 2:3, 4.

9:8
Deut 29:24-26
2 Chr 7:21
Jer 22:8-9, 28
9:9
Deut 29:25-28

nations. ⁸And though this Temple is impressive now, all who pass by will be appalled and will shake their heads in amazement. They will ask, 'Why did the LORD do such terrible things to this land and to this Temple?'

⁹"And the answer will be, 'Because his people abandoned the LORD their God, who brought their ancestors out of Egypt, and they worshiped other gods instead and bowed down to them. That is why the LORD has brought all these disasters on them.'"

### Solomon's Agreement with Hiram

9:10-28
2 Chr 8:1-18
9:11
1 Kgs 5:1
2 Chr 2:4
9:13
Josh 19:27

¹⁰It took Solomon twenty years to build the LORD's Temple and his own royal palace. At the end of that time, ¹¹he gave twenty towns in the land of Galilee to King Hiram of Tyre. (Hiram had previously provided all the cedar and cypress timber and gold that Solomon had requested.) ¹²But when Hiram came from Tyre to see the towns Solomon had given him, he was not at all pleased with them. ¹³"What kind of towns are these, my brother?" he asked. So Hiram called that area Cabul (which means "worthless"), as it is still known today. ¹⁴Nevertheless, Hiram paid* Solomon 9,000 pounds* of gold.

### Solomon's Many Achievements

9:15
2 Sam 5:9

¹⁵This is the account of the forced labor that King Solomon conscripted to build the LORD's Temple, the royal palace, the supporting terraces,* the wall of Jerusalem, and the cities of Hazor, Megiddo, and Gezer. ¹⁶(Pharaoh, the king of Egypt, had attacked and captured Gezer, killing the Canaanite population and burning it down. He gave the city to his daughter as a wedding gift when she married Solomon. ¹⁷So Solomon rebuilt the city of Gezer.)

9:19
1 Kgs 4:26

He also built up the towns of Lower Beth-horon, ¹⁸Baalath, and Tamar* in the wilderness within his land. ¹⁹He built towns as supply centers and constructed towns where his chariots and horses* could be stationed. He built everything he desired in Jerusalem and Lebanon and throughout his entire realm.

9:21
Josh 15:63
9:22
Lev 25:39

²⁰There were still some people living in the land who were not Israelites, including Amorites, Hittites, Perizzites, Hivites, and Jebusites. ²¹These were descendants of the nations whom the people of Israel had not completely destroyed.* So Solomon conscripted them for his labor force, and they serve in the labor force to this day. ²²But Solomon did not conscript any of the Israelites for forced labor. Instead, he assigned them to serve as fighting men, government officials, officers and captains in his army, commanders of his chariots, and charioteers. ²³Solomon appointed 550 of them to supervise the people working on his various projects.

9:24
1 Kgs 3:1; 7:8;
11:1, 27
2 Chr 32:5

²⁴Solomon moved his wife, Pharaoh's daughter, from the City of David to the new palace he had built for her. Then he constructed the supporting terraces.

9:14a Or For Hiram had paid.   9:14b Hebrew 120 talents [4,000 kilograms].   9:15 Hebrew the millo; also in 9:24. The meaning of the Hebrew is uncertain.   9:18 An alternate reading in the Masoretic Text reads Tadmor. 9:19 Or and charioteers.   9:21 The Hebrew term used here refers to the complete consecration of things or people to the LORD, either by destroying them or by giving them as an offering.

---

**SOLOMON'S BUILDING PROJECTS**
Solomon became known as one of the great builders in Israel's history. He built Hazor, Megiddo, and Gezer as fortress cities at key points during his reign. He also rebuilt the cities of lower Beth-horon, Baalath, and Tadmor.

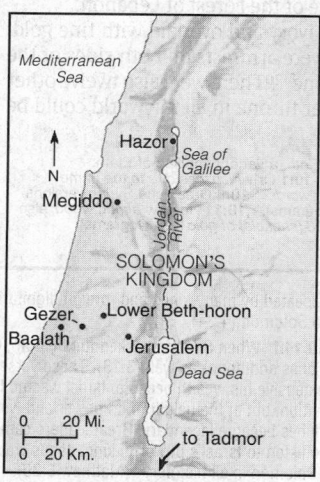

**9:11-14** Was Solomon being unfair to Hiram? It is not clear from these verses whether Solomon gave these towns to Hiram, or they were collateral until he could repay Hiram for the gold he had borrowed. Second Chronicles 8:1, 2 implies that the towns were returned to Solomon. In either case, Hiram probably preferred a piece of land on the coast more suitable for trade (the name he gave these cities, *Cabul*, sounds like the Hebrew word for "worthless"). In the end, Hiram was repaid many times over through his trade partnerships with Solomon (2 Chronicles 9:10, 21). Because Phoenicia was on friendly terms with Israel and dependent on it for grain and oil, Hiram's relationship with Solomon was more important than a feud over some cities.

**9:16** At this time Israel and Egypt were the major powers in the Near East. For many years Egypt had retained control of Gezer, even though it was in Israelite territory. In Solomon's time the Pharaoh gave the city to his daughter, whom Solomon married, putting Gezer under Israelite control. Intermarriage among royal families was common, but it was not endorsed by God (Deuteronomy 17:17).

25Three times each year Solomon presented burnt offerings and peace offerings on the altar he had built for the LORD. He also burned incense to the LORD. And so he finished the work of building the Temple.

26King Solomon also built a fleet of ships at Ezion-geber, a port near Elath* in the land of Edom, along the shore of the Red Sea.* 27Hiram sent experienced crews of sailors to sail the ships with Solomon's men. 28They sailed to Ophir and brought back to Solomon some sixteen tons* of gold.

### Visit of the Queen of Sheba

**10** When the queen of Sheba heard of Solomon's fame, which brought honor to the name of the LORD,* she came to test him with hard questions. 2She arrived in Jerusalem with a large group of attendants and a great caravan of camels loaded with spices, large quantities of gold, and precious jewels. When she met with Solomon, she talked with him about everything she had on her mind. 3Solomon had answers for all her questions; nothing was too hard for the king to explain to her. 4When the queen of Sheba realized how very wise Solomon was, and when she saw the palace he had built, 5she was overwhelmed. She was also amazed at the food on his tables, the organization of his officials and their splendid clothing, the cup-bearers, and the burnt offerings Solomon made at the Temple of the LORD.

6She exclaimed to the king, "Everything I heard in my country about your achievements* and wisdom is true! 7I didn't believe what was said until I arrived here and saw it with my own eyes. In fact, I had not heard the half of it! Your wisdom and prosperity are far beyond what I was told. 8How happy your people* must be! What a privilege for your officials to stand here day after day, listening to your wisdom! 9Praise the LORD your God, who delights in you and has placed you on the throne of Israel. Because of the LORD's eternal love for Israel, he has made you king so you can rule with justice and righteousness."

10Then she gave the king a gift of 9,000 pounds* of gold, great quantities of spices, and precious jewels. Never again were so many spices brought in as those the queen of Sheba gave to King Solomon.

11(In addition, Hiram's ships brought gold from Ophir, and they also brought rich cargoes of red sandalwood* and precious jewels. 12The king used the sandalwood to make railings for the Temple of the LORD and the royal palace, and to construct lyres and harps for the musicians. Never before or since has there been such a supply of sandalwood.)

13King Solomon gave the queen of Sheba whatever she asked for, besides all the customary gifts he had so generously given. Then she and all her attendants returned to their own land.

### Solomon's Wealth and Splendor

14Each year Solomon received about 25 tons* of gold. 15This did not include the additional revenue he received from merchants and traders, all the kings of Arabia, and the governors of the land.

16King Solomon made 200 large shields of hammered gold, each weighing more than fifteen pounds.* 17He also made 300 smaller shields of hammered gold, each weighing nearly four pounds.* The king placed these shields in the Palace of the Forest of Lebanon.

18Then the king made a huge throne, decorated with ivory and overlaid with fine gold. 19The throne had six steps and a rounded back. There were armrests on both sides of the seat, and the figure of a lion stood on each side of the throne. 20There were also twelve other lions, one standing on each end of the six steps. No other throne in all the world could be compared with it!

**9:25**
Exod 23:14-17
Deut 16:16

**9:26**
Num 33:35
1 Kgs 22:48

**9:27**
1 Kgs 10:11

**10:1-13**
//2 Chr 9:1-12

**10:1**
2 Chr 9:1
Ps 72:10, 15
Matt 12:42

**10:8**
Prov 8:34

**10:9**
2 Sam 8:15; 23:3
1 Kgs 5:7
2 Chr 2:11

**10:11**
1 Kgs 9:27

**10:14-29**
//2 Chr 1:14-17;
9:13-28

**10:16**
1 Kgs 14:26-28
2 Chr 12:9-10

**10:17**
1 Kgs 7:2

---

**9:26a** As in Greek version (see also 2 Kgs 14:22; 16:6); Hebrew reads *Eloth,* a variant spelling of Elath.
**9:26b** Hebrew *sea of reeds.* **9:28** Hebrew *420 talents* [14 metric tons]. **10:1** Or *which was due to the name of the LORD.* The meaning of the Hebrew is uncertain. **10:6** Hebrew *your words.* **10:8** Greek and Syriac versions and Latin Vulgate read *your wives.* **10:10** Hebrew *120 talents* [4,000 kilograms]. **10:11** Hebrew *almug wood;* also in 10:12. **10:14** Hebrew *666 talents* [23 metric tons]. **10:16** Hebrew *600 [shekels] of gold* [6.8 kilograms]. **10:17** Hebrew *3 minas* [1.8 kilograms].

---

**10:1-5** The queen of Sheba came to see for herself if everything she had heard about Solomon was true. Contests using riddles or proverbs were often used to test wisdom. The queen may have used some of these as she questioned Solomon (10:1, 3). When she realized the extent of his riches and wisdom, she was overwhelmed and no longer questioned his power or wisdom. No longer a competitor, she became an admirer. Her experience was repeated by many kings and foreign dignitaries who paid honor to Solomon (4:34).

**10:14ff** When Solomon asked for wisdom, God promised him riches and honor as well (3:13). These verses show just how extensive his wealth became. Israel was no longer a second-rate nation, but at the height of its power and wealth. Solomon's riches became legendary. Great leaders came from many nations to listen to Israel's powerful king. Jesus would later refer to "Solomon in all his glory" (Matthew 6:29).

²¹All of King Solomon's drinking cups were solid gold, as were all the utensils in the Palace of the Forest of Lebanon. They were not made of silver, for silver was considered worthless in Solomon's day!

²²The king had a fleet of trading ships* that sailed with Hiram's fleet. Once every three years the ships returned, loaded with gold, silver, ivory, apes, and peacocks.*

**10:23**
1 Kgs 3:12-13; 4:30

²³So King Solomon became richer and wiser than any other king on earth. ²⁴People from every nation came to consult him and to hear the wisdom God had given him. ²⁵Year after year everyone who visited brought him gifts of silver and gold, clothing, weapons, spices, horses, and mules.

²⁶Solomon built up a huge force of chariots and horses.* He had 1,400 chariots and 12,000 horses. He stationed some of them in the chariot cities and some near him in Jeru-

**10:27**
2 Chr 1:14-17;
9:25, 27

salem. ²⁷The king made silver as plentiful in Jerusalem as stone. And valuable cedar timber was as common as the sycamore-fig trees that grow in the foothills of Judah.* ²⁸Solomon's

**10:28**
2 Chr 1:16; 9:28

horses were imported from Egypt* and from Cilicia*; the king's traders acquired them from Cilicia at the standard price. ²⁹At that time chariots from Egypt could be purchased for

**10:29**
2 Kgs 7:6-7

600 pieces of silver,* and horses for 150 pieces of silver.* They were then exported to the kings of the Hittites and the kings of Aram.

**10:22a** Hebrew *fleet of ships of Tarshish.*   **10:22b** Or *and baboons.*   **10:26** Or *charioteers;* also in 10:26b.
**10:27** Hebrew *the Shephelah.*   **10:28a** Possibly *Muzur,* a district near Cilicia; also in 10:29.   **10:28b** Hebrew *Kue,*
probably another name for Cilicia.   **10:29a** Hebrew *600 [shekels] of silver,* about 15 pounds or 6.8 kilograms in
weight.   **10:29b** Hebrew *150 [shekels],* about 3.8 pounds or 1.7 kilograms in weight.

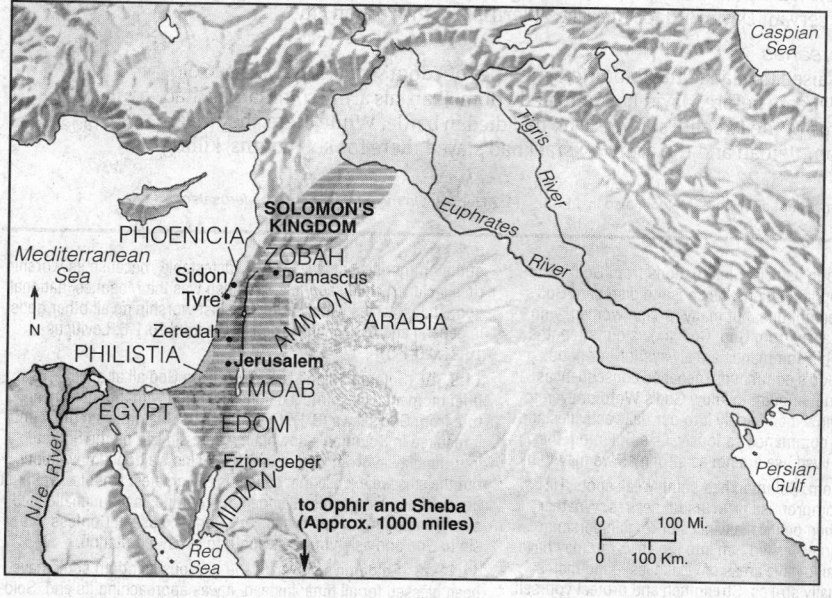

**FRIENDS AND ENEMIES**
Solomon's reputation brought acclaim and riches from many nations, but he disobeyed God, marrying pagan women and worshiping their gods. So God raised up enemies like Hadad from Edom and Rezon from Zobah (modern-day Syria). Jeroboam from Zeredah was another enemy who would eventually divide this mighty kingdom.

**10:23** Why does the Bible place so much emphasis on Solomon's material possessions? In the Old Testament, riches were considered tangible evidence of God's blessing. Prosperity was seen as a proof of right living. In the books of Ecclesiastes and Job this concept is placed in a broader perspective. In ideal conditions, people prosper when God runs their lives, but prosperity is not guaranteed. Wealth does not prove that a person is living right before God, and poverty does not indicate sin.

In fact, a greater evidence that a person is living for God is the presence of suffering and persecution (Mark 10:29-31; 13:13). The most important "treasure" is not earthly but heavenly (Matthew 6:19-21; 19:21; 1 Timothy 6:17-19). The gift of greatest worth has no price tag—it is the gift of salvation freely offered by God.

**10:26–11:3** In accumulating chariots and horses, a huge harem, and incredible wealth, Solomon was violating God's commands for a king (Deuteronomy 17:14-20). God prohibited these actions because he knew how they would hurt the nation both politically and spiritually (1 Samuel 8:11-18). The more luxurious Solomon's court became, the more the people were taxed. Excessive taxation created unrest, and soon conditions became ripe for a revolution. Having everything he wanted, Solomon forgot God and allowed pagan influences to enter his court through his pagan wives, thus accelerating the spiritual corruption of the nation.

## Solomon's Many Wives

**11** Now King Solomon loved many foreign women. Besides Pharaoh's daughter, he married women from Moab, Ammon, Edom, Sidon, and from among the Hittites. ²The LORD had clearly instructed the people of Israel, 'You must not marry them, because they will turn your hearts to their gods.' Yet Solomon insisted on loving them anyway. ³He had 700 wives of royal birth and 300 concubines. And in fact, they did turn his heart away from the LORD.

⁴In Solomon's old age, they turned his heart to worship other gods instead of being completely faithful to the LORD his God, as his father, David, had been. ⁵Solomon worshiped Ashtoreth, the goddess of the Sidonians, and Molech,* the detestable god of the Ammonites. ⁶In this way, Solomon did what was evil in the LORD's sight; he refused to follow the LORD completely, as his father, David, had done.

⁷On the Mount of Olives, east of Jerusalem,* he even built a pagan shrine for Chemosh, the detestable god of Moab, and another for Molech, the detestable god of the Ammonites. ⁸Solomon built such shrines for all his foreign wives to use for burning incense and sacrificing to their gods.

⁹The LORD was very angry with Solomon, for his heart had turned away from the LORD, the God of Israel, who had appeared to him twice. ¹⁰He had warned Solomon specifically about worshiping other gods, but Solomon did not listen to the LORD's command. ¹¹So now the LORD said to him, "Since you have not kept my covenant and have disobeyed my decrees, I will surely tear the kingdom away from you and give it to one of your servants. ¹²But for the sake of your father, David, I will not do this while you are still alive. I will take the kingdom away from your son. ¹³And even so, I will not take away the entire kingdom; I will let him be king of one tribe, for the sake of my servant David and for the sake of Jerusalem, my chosen city."

## Solomon's Adversaries

¹⁴Then the LORD raised up Hadad the Edomite, a member of Edom's royal family, to be Solomon's adversary. ¹⁵Years before, David had defeated Edom. Joab, his army commander, had stayed to bury some of the Israelite soldiers who had died in battle. While there, they killed every male in Edom. ¹⁶Joab and the army of Israel had stayed there for six months, killing them.

**11:1** Neh 13:23-27
**11:2** Exod 23:31-33; 34:12-16 Deut 7:3-4
**11:3** 2 Sam 5:13-16
**11:5** Judg 2:12-14; 10:6 1 Sam 7:3-4
**11:7** Lev 20:2-5 Num 21:27-30 Judg 11:24 2 Kgs 23:10, 13
**11:9** 1 Kgs 3:5; 9:2-3
**11:10** 1 Kgs 6:12; 9:6
**11:11** 1 Sam 2:30 1 Kgs 6:11-12; 11:31
**11:12** 2 Sam 7:15
**11:15** 2 Sam 8:13-14 1 Chr 18:12-13

**11:5** Hebrew *Milcom*, a variant spelling of Molech; also in 11:33.    **11:7** Hebrew *On the mountain east of Jerusalem*.

---

**11:2** Although Solomon had clear instructions from God *not* to marry women from foreign nations, he chose to disregard God's commands. He married not one, but many foreign women, who subsequently led him away from God. God knows our strengths and weaknesses, and his commands are always for our good. When people ignore God's commands, negative consequences inevitably result. It is not enough to know God's Word or even to believe it; we must follow it and apply it to our daily activities and decisions. Take God's commands seriously. Like Solomon, the wisest man who ever lived, we are not as strong as we may think.

**11:3** For all his wisdom, Solomon had some weak spots. He could not say no to compromise or to lustful desires. Whether he married to strengthen political alliances or to gain personal pleasure, these foreign wives led him into idolatry. You may have strong faith, but you also have areas of weakness—and that is where temptation usually strikes. Strengthen and protect yourself where you are weak because a chain is only as strong as its weakest link. If Solomon, the wisest man, could fall, so can you.

**11:4** Solomon handled great pressures in running the government, but he could not handle the pressure from his wives who wanted him to worship their gods. In marriage and close friendships, it is difficult to resist pressure to compromise. Our love leads us to identify with the desires of those we care about.

Faced with such pressure, Solomon at first *resisted* it, maintaining pure faith. Then he *tolerated* a more widespread practice of idolatry. Finally, he became involved in idolatrous worship, *rationalizing* away the potential danger to himself and to the kingdom. Because we want to please and identify with our loved ones, God asks us not to marry those who do not share our commitment to him.

**11:5-8** Ashtoreth was a goddess that symbolized reproductive power—a mistress of the god Baal. Molech was the national god

of the Ammonites and was called "detestable" because its worship rites included child sacrifice. Chemosh was the Moabites' national god. The Israelites were warned against worshiping all other gods in general and Molech in particular (Exodus 20:1-6; Leviticus 18:21; 20:1-5).

**11:9, 10** Solomon didn't turn away from God all at once or in a brief moment. His spiritual coldness started with a minor departure from God's laws (3:1). Over the years, that little sin grew until it resulted in Solomon's downfall. A little sin can be the first step in turning away from God. It is not the sins we don't know about but the sins we excuse that cause us the greatest trouble. We must never let any sin go unchallenged. In your life, is an unchallenged sin spreading like a deadly cancer? Don't excuse it. Confess this sin to God and ask him for strength to resist temptation.

**11:11-13** Solomon's powerful and glorious kingdom could have been blessed for all time; instead, it was approaching its end. Solomon had God's promises, guidance, and answers to prayer, yet he allowed sin to remain all around him. Eventually it corrupted him so much that he was no longer interested in God. Psalm 127:1, written by Solomon, says, "Unless the LORD builds a house, the work of the builders is wasted." Solomon had begun by laying the foundation with God, but he did not follow through in his later years. As a result, he lost everything. It is not enough to get off to a right start in building our marriage, career, or church on God's principles; we must remain faithful to God to the end (Mark 13:13). God must be in control of our lives from start to finish.

**11:14-22** Edom was the kingdom southeast of the Dead Sea. David had added this nation to his empire (2 Samuel 8:13, 14). It was of strategic importance because it controlled the route to the Red Sea. Edom's revolt was disturbing the peace of Solomon's kingdom.

17But Hadad and a few of his father's royal officials escaped and headed for Egypt. (Hadad was just a boy at the time.) 18They set out from Midian and went to Paran, where others joined them. Then they traveled to Egypt and went to Pharaoh, who gave them a home, food, and some land. 19Pharaoh grew very fond of Hadad, and he gave him his wife's sister in marriage—the sister of Queen Tahpenes. 20She bore him a son named Genubath. Tahpenes raised him* in Pharaoh's palace among Pharaoh's own sons.

**11:21**
1 Kgs 2:10, 34

21When the news reached Hadad in Egypt that David and his commander Joab were both dead, he said to Pharaoh, "Let me return to my own country."

22"Why?" Pharaoh asked him. "What do you lack here that makes you want to go home?"

"Nothing," he replied. "But even so, please let me return home."

**11:23**
2 Sam 8:3;
10:15-16
**11:24**
2 Sam 10:7-8, 18

23God also raised up Rezon son of Eliada as Solomon's adversary. Rezon had fled from his master, King Hadadezer of Zobah, 24and had become the leader of a gang of rebels. After David conquered Hadadezer, Rezon and his men fled to Damascus, where he became king. 25Rezon was Israel's bitter adversary for the rest of Solomon's reign, and he made trouble, just as Hadad did. Rezon hated Israel intensely and continued to reign in Aram.

## Jeroboam Rebels against Solomon

**11:26**
2 Chr 13:6

26Another rebel leader was Jeroboam son of Nebat, one of Solomon's own officials. He came from the town of Zeredah in Ephraim, and his mother was Zeruah, a widow.

**11:27**
1 Kgs 9:24

27This is the story behind his rebellion. Solomon was rebuilding the supporting terraces* and repairing the walls of the city of his father, David. 28Jeroboam was a very capable young man, and when Solomon saw how industrious he was, he put him in charge of the labor force from the tribes of Ephraim and Manasseh, the descendants of Joseph.

**11:29**
1 Kgs 12:15; 14:2
**11:30**
1 Sam 15:27-28
**11:31**
1 Kgs 11:11-12

29One day as Jeroboam was leaving Jerusalem, the prophet Ahijah from Shiloh met him along the way. Ahijah was wearing a new cloak. The two of them were alone in a field, 30and Ahijah took hold of the new cloak he was wearing and tore it into twelve pieces. 31Then he said to Jeroboam, "Take ten of these pieces, for this is what the LORD, the God of Israel, says: 'I am about to tear the kingdom from the hand of Solomon, and I will give ten of the tribes to you! 32But I will leave him one tribe for the sake of my servant David and for the sake of Jerusalem, which I have chosen out of all the tribes of Israel. 33For Solomon has* abandoned me and worshiped Ashtoreth, the goddess of the Sidonians; Chemosh, the god of Moab; and Molech, the god of the Ammonites. He has not followed my ways and done what is pleasing in my sight. He has not obeyed my decrees and regulations as David his father did.

**11:33**
1 Kgs 11:5-8

**11:35**
1 Kgs 12:16
**11:36**
1 Kgs 15:4
2 Kgs 8:19
2 Chr 21:7
**11:38**
2 Sam 7:11, 27

34"'But I will not take the entire kingdom from Solomon at this time. For the sake of my servant David, the one whom I chose and who obeyed my commands and decrees, I will keep Solomon as leader for the rest of his life. 35But I will take the kingdom away from his son and give ten of the tribes to you. 36His son will have one tribe so that the descendants of David my servant will continue to reign, shining like a lamp in Jerusalem, the city I have chosen to be the place for my name. 37And I will place you on the throne of Israel, and you will rule over all that your heart desires. 38If you listen to what I tell you and follow my ways and do whatever I consider to be right, and if you obey my decrees and commands, as my servant David did, then I will always be with you. I will establish an enduring dynasty for you as I did for David, and I will give Israel to you. 39Because of Solomon's sin I will punish the descendants of David—though not forever.'"

**11:40**
1 Kgs 14:25
2 Chr 12:2

40Solomon tried to kill Jeroboam, but he fled to King Shishak of Egypt and stayed there until Solomon died.

## Summary of Solomon's Reign

**11:41-43**
//2 Chr 9:29-31

41The rest of the events in Solomon's reign, including all his deeds and his wisdom, are recorded in *The Book of the Acts of Solomon.* 42Solomon ruled in Jerusalem over all Israel for forty years. 43When he died, he was buried in the City of David, named for his father. Then his son Rehoboam became the next king.

**11:20** As in Greek version; Hebrew reads *weaned him.*    **11:27** Hebrew *the millo.* The meaning of the Hebrew is uncertain.    **11:33** As in Greek, Syriac, and Latin Vulgate; Hebrew reads *For they have.*

---

**11:29-39** The prophet Ahijah predicted the division of the kingdom of Israel. After Solomon's death, 10 of Israel's 12 tribes would follow Jeroboam. The other two tribes, Judah and the area of Benjamin around Jerusalem, would remain loyal to David. Judah, the largest tribe, and Benjamin, the smallest, were often mentioned as one tribe because they shared the same border.

Both Jeroboam and Ahijah were from Ephraim, the most prominent of the 10 rebel tribes. (For more on the divided kingdom, see the note on 12:20.)

**11:41** Nothing is known of *The Book of the Acts of Solomon.* See also the note on 14:19.

## B. THE DIVIDED KINGDOM (12:1—22:53)

After Solomon's death, the northern tribes revolt, forming two separate nations. Each nation experiences disastrous consequences from having evil kings. Elijah appears on the scene, confronting these kings for their sin. God deals with sin in powerful ways. Although judgment may appear to be slow, God will judge evil harshly.

### 1. Revolt of the northern tribes

*The Northern Tribes Revolt*

**12** Rehoboam went to Shechem, where all Israel had gathered to make him king. ²When Jeroboam son of Nebat heard of this, he returned from Egypt,* for he had fled to Egypt to escape from King Solomon. ³The leaders of Israel summoned him, and Jeroboam and the whole assembly of Israel went to speak with Rehoboam. ⁴"Your father was a hard master," they said. "Lighten the harsh labor demands and heavy taxes that your father imposed on us. Then we will be your loyal subjects."

⁵Rehoboam replied, "Give me three days to think this over. Then come back for my answer." So the people went away.

⁶Then King Rehoboam discussed the matter with the older men who had counseled his father, Solomon. "What is your advice?" he asked. "How should I answer these people?"

⁷The older counselors replied, "If you are willing to be a servant to these people today and give them a favorable answer, they will always be your loyal subjects."

⁸But Rehoboam rejected the advice of the older men and instead asked the opinion of the young men who had grown up with him and were now his advisers. ⁹"What is your advice?" he asked them. "How should I answer these people who want me to lighten the burdens imposed by my father?"

¹⁰The young men replied, "This is what you should tell those complainers who want a lighter burden: 'My little finger is thicker than my father's waist! ¹¹Yes, my father laid heavy burdens on you, but I'm going to make them even heavier! My father beat you with whips, but I will beat you with scorpions!'"

¹²Three days later Jeroboam and all the people returned to hear Rehoboam's decision, just as the king had ordered. ¹³But Rehoboam spoke harshly to the people, for he rejected the advice of the older counselors ¹⁴and followed the counsel of his younger advisers. He told the people, "My father laid heavy burdens on you, but I'm going to make them even heavier! My father beat you with whips, but I will beat you with scorpions!"

¹⁵So the king paid no attention to the people. This turn of events was the will of the LORD, for it fulfilled the LORD's message to Jeroboam son of Nebat through the prophet Ahijah from Shiloh.

¹⁶When all Israel realized that the king had refused to listen to them, they responded,

**12:1-24**
//2 Chr 10:1—11:4

**12:1**
Judg 9:1, 6
2 Chr 10:1

**12:4**
1 Sam 8:11-18

**12:5**
1 Kgs 12:12

**12:12**
1 Kgs 12:5

**12:15**
Deut 2:30
Judg 14:4
2 Chr 10:15

**12:16**
2 Sam 20:1

**12:2** As in Greek version and Latin Vulgate (see also 2 Chr 10:2); Hebrew reads *he lived in Egypt.*

---

**12:1** Rehoboam was made king at Shechem, about 35 miles north of Jerusalem. It would have been normal to anoint the new king in Jerusalem, the capital city, but Rehoboam saw trouble brewing with Jeroboam and went north to try to maintain good relations with the northern tribes. He probably chose Shechem because it was an ancient location for making covenants (Joshua 24:1). When the kingdom divided, Shechem became the capital of the northern kingdom for a short time (12:25).

**12:6-14** Rehoboam asked for advice, but he didn't carefully evaluate what he was told. If he had, he would have realized that the advice offered by the elders was wiser than that of his peers. To evaluate advice, ask if it is realistic, workable, and consistent with biblical principles. Determine if the results of following the advice will be fair, make improvements, and give a positive solution or direction. Seek counsel from those who are more experienced and wiser. Advice is helpful only if it is consistent with God's standards.

**12:15-19** Both Jeroboam and Rehoboam did what was good for themselves, not what was good for their people. Rehoboam was harsh and did not listen to the people's demands; Jeroboam established new places of worship to keep his people from traveling to Jerusalem, Rehoboam's capital. Both actions backfired. Rehoboam's move divided the nation, and Jeroboam's turned the people from God. Good leaders put the best interests of the "followers" above their own. Making decisions only for yourself

will backfire and cause you to lose more than if you had kept the welfare of others in mind.

**THE KINGDOM DIVIDES**
Rehoboam's threat of heavier burdens caused a rebellion and divided the nation. Rehoboam ruled the southern kingdom; Jeroboam ruled the northern kingdom. Jeroboam set up idols in Dan and Bethel to discourage worship in Jerusalem. At the same time Aram, Ammon, Moab, and Edom claimed independence from the divided nation.

"Down with the dynasty of David!
    We have no interest in the son of Jesse.
Back to your homes, O Israel!
    Look out for your own house, O David!"

So the people of Israel returned home. [17]But Rehoboam continued to rule over the Israelites who lived in the towns of Judah.

**12:17**
1 Kgs 11:13, 36

[18]King Rehoboam sent Adoniram,* who was in charge of the labor force, to restore order, but the people of Israel stoned him to death. When this news reached King Rehoboam, he quickly jumped into his chariot and fled to Jerusalem. [19]And to this day the northern tribes of Israel have refused to be ruled by a descendant of David.

**12:18**
2 Sam 20:24

**12:19**
2 Kgs 17:21

[20]When the people of Israel learned of Jeroboam's return from Egypt, they called an assembly and made him king over all Israel. So only the tribe of Judah remained loyal to the family of David.

**12:20**
1 Kgs 11:13, 32

### Shemaiah's Prophecy

[21]When Rehoboam arrived at Jerusalem, he mobilized the men of Judah and the tribe of Benjamin—180,000 select troops—to fight against the men of Israel and to restore the kingdom to himself.

**12:21**
2 Chr 11:1

[22]But God said to Shemaiah, the man of God, [23]"Say to Rehoboam son of Solomon, king of Judah, and to all the people of Judah and Benjamin, and to the rest of the people, [24]'This is what the LORD says: Do not fight against your relatives, the Israelites. Go back home, for what has happened is my doing!'" So they obeyed the message of the LORD and went home, as the LORD had commanded.

**12:22**
2 Chr 11:2; 12:5-7

### Jeroboam Makes Gold Calves

[25]Jeroboam then built up the city of Shechem in the hill country of Ephraim, and it became his capital. Later he went and built up the town of Peniel.*

**12:25**
Judg 8:8, 17

[26]Jeroboam thought to himself, "Unless I am careful, the kingdom will return to the dynasty of David. [27]When these people go to Jerusalem to offer sacrifices at the Temple of the LORD, they will again give their allegiance to King Rehoboam of Judah. They will kill me and make him their king instead."

**12:27**
Deut 12:4-6, 14

**12:18** As in some Greek manuscripts and Syriac version (see also 4:6; 5:14); Hebrew reads *Adoram.* **12:25** Hebrew *Penuel,* a variant spelling of Peniel.

---

**TRIBAL JEALOUSIES**

Although the kingdom of Israel was "united" under David and Solomon, the tensions between north and south were never resolved. The jealousy and animosity behind this civil war didn't begin with Rehoboam and Jeroboam but had its roots in the days of the judges, when the people were more interested in tribal loyalty than in national unity. Note how easily tension arose between Ephraim, the most prominent tribe in the north, and Judah, the prominent tribe of the south.

- Ephraim claimed the promises in Genesis 48:17-22 and 49:22-26 for its leadership role.
- Joshua, who conquered the Promised Land, was an Ephraimite (Numbers 13:8).
- Samuel, Israel's greatest judge, was from Ephraim (1 Samuel 1:1ff).
- Ephraim allied with Ishbosheth in revolt against David, who was from the tribe of Judah (2 Samuel 2:8-11).
- David, a shepherd from the tribe of Judah, became king over all Israel, including Ephraim, which no longer had a claim to leadership.
- Although David helped to smooth over the bad feelings, the heavy yoke under Solomon and Rehoboam led the northern tribes to the breaking point.

Such tension developed because Ephraim was the key tribe in the north. They resented Judah's role in leadership under David and resented that the nation's capital and center of worship were located in Jerusalem.

---

**12:20** This marks the beginning of the division of the kingdom that lasted for centuries. Ten of Israel's 12 tribes followed Jeroboam and called their new nation Israel (the northern kingdom). The other two tribes remained loyal to Rehoboam and called their nation Judah (the southern kingdom). The kingdom did not split overnight. It was already dividing as early as the days of the judges because of tribal jealousies, especially between Ephraim, the most influential tribe of the north, and Judah, the chief tribe of the south.

Before the days of Saul and David, the religious center of Israel was located, for the most part, in the territory of Ephraim. When Solomon built the Temple, Jerusalem became the religious center of Israel. This eventually brought tribal rivalries to the breaking point. (For more information on tribal jealousies and how they affected Israel, see Judges 12:1ff; 2 Samuel 2:4ff; 19:41-43.)

28So on the advice of his counselors, the king made two gold calves. He said to the people,* "It is too much trouble for you to worship in Jerusalem. Look, Israel, these are the gods who brought you out of Egypt!"

29He placed these calf idols in Bethel and in Dan—at either end of his kingdom. 30But this became a great sin, for the people worshiped the idols, traveling as far north as Dan to worship the one there.

31Jeroboam also erected buildings at the pagan shrines and ordained priests from the common people—those who were not from the priestly tribe of Levi. 32And Jeroboam instituted a religious festival in Bethel, held on the fifteenth day of the eighth month,* in imitation of the annual Festival of Shelters in Judah. There at Bethel he himself offered sacrifices to the calves he had made, and he appointed priests for the pagan shrines he had made. 33So on the fifteenth day of the eighth month, a day that he himself had designated, Jeroboam offered sacrifices on the altar at Bethel. He instituted a religious festival for Israel, and he went up to the altar to burn incense.

**12:28**
Exod 32:4
2 Kgs 10:29
2 Chr 11:15
Hos 8:4-7

**12:29**
Gen 28:19
Judg 18:27-31

**12:30**
2 Kgs 17:21

**12:31**
2 Kgs 17:32
2 Chr 11:13-15

**12:32**
Lev 23:33-34
Num 29:12

## 2. Kings of Israel and Judah
*A Prophet Denounces Jeroboam*

**13** At the LORD's command, a man of God from Judah went to Bethel, arriving there just as Jeroboam was approaching the altar to burn incense. 2Then at the LORD's command, he shouted, "O altar, altar! This is what the LORD says: A child named Josiah will be born into the dynasty of David. On you he will sacrifice the priests from the pagan shrines who come here to burn incense, and human bones will be burned on you." 3That same day the man of God gave a sign to prove his message. He said, "The LORD has promised to give this sign: This altar will split apart, and its ashes will be poured out on the ground."

4When King Jeroboam heard the man of God speaking against the altar at Bethel, he pointed at him and shouted, "Seize that man!" But instantly the king's hand became paralyzed in that position, and he couldn't pull it back. 5At the same time a wide crack appeared in the altar, and the ashes poured out, just as the man of God had predicted in his message from the LORD.

6The king cried out to the man of God, "Please ask the LORD your God to restore my hand again!" So the man of God prayed to the LORD, and the king's hand was restored and he could move it again.

7Then the king said to the man of God, "Come to the palace with me and have something to eat, and I will give you a gift."

**13:1**
2 Kgs 23:17

**13:2**
2 Kgs 23:15-16, 20

**13:6**
Exod 8:8, 28; 9:28
Jer 37:3
Acts 8:24

**13:7**
1 Sam 9:7
2 Kgs 5:15

**12:28** Hebrew *to them.*   **12:32** This day of the ancient Hebrew lunar calendar occurred in late October or early November, exactly one month after the annual Festival of Shelters in Judah (see Lev 23:34).

---

**12:28** All Jewish men were required to travel to the Temple three times each year (Deuteronomy 16:16), but Jeroboam set up his own worship centers and told his people it was too much trouble to travel all the way to Jerusalem. Those who obeyed Jeroboam were disobeying God. Some ideas, though practical, may include suggestions that lead you away from God. Don't let anyone talk you out of doing what is right by telling you that moral actions are not worth the effort. Do what God wants, no matter what the cost in time, energy, reputation, or resources.

**12:28, 29** Calves were used as idols to symbolize fertility and strength. Pagan gods of the Canaanites were often depicted as standing on calves or bulls. Jeroboam shrewdly placed the gold calves in Bethel and Dan, strategic locations. Bethel was just 10 miles north of Jerusalem on the main road, enticing the citizens from the north to stop there instead of traveling the rest of the way to Jerusalem. Dan was the northernmost city in Israel, so people living in the far north from Jerusalem were attracted to its convenient location. As leader of the northern kingdom, Jeroboam wanted to establish his own worship centers; otherwise his people would make regular trips to Jerusalem, and his authority would be undermined. Soon this substitute religion had little in common with true faith in God.

**12:30** Jeroboam and his advisers did not learn from Israel's previous disaster with a gold calf (Exodus 32). Perhaps they were ignorant of Scripture, or maybe they knew about the event and decided to ignore it. Study the Bible to become aware of God's acts in history, and then apply the important lessons to your life. If you learn from the past, you will not face disaster as a result of repeating others' mistakes (Isaiah 42:23; 1 Corinthians 10:11).

**12:32, 33** Early in Israel's history, the city of Bethel was a symbol of commitment to God because there Jacob had rededicated himself to God (Genesis 28:16-22). But Jeroboam turned the city into Israel's chief religious center, intending it to compete with Jerusalem. Bethel's religion, however, centered on an idol, and this led to Israel's eventual downfall. Bethel developed a reputation as a wicked and idolatrous city. The prophets Hosea and Amos recognized the sins of Bethel and condemned the city for its godless ways (Hosea 4:15-17; 10:8; Amos 5:4-6).

**13:2** Three hundred years later, this prophecy was fulfilled in every detail when Josiah killed the pagan priests at their own altars. The story is found in 2 Kings 23:1-20.

**13:7-32** This prophet had been given strict orders from God not to eat or drink anything while on his mission (13:9). He died because he listened to a man who claimed to have a message from God, rather than to God himself. This prophet should have followed God's word instead of hearsay. Trust what God's Word says rather than what someone claims is true. And disregard what others claim are messages from God if their words contradict the Bible.

**13:8**
Num 22:18
**13:9**
Num 22:18; 24:13

⁸But the man of God said to the king, "Even if you gave me half of everything you own, I would not go with you. I would not eat or drink anything in this place. ⁹For the LORD gave me this command: 'You must not eat or drink anything while you are there, and do not return to Judah by the same way you came.'" ¹⁰So he left Bethel and went home another way.

¹¹As it happened, there was an old prophet living in Bethel, and his sons* came home and told him what the man of God had done in Bethel that day. They also told their father what the man had said to the king. ¹²The old prophet asked them, "Which way did he go?" So they showed their father* which road the man of God had taken. ¹³"Quick, saddle the donkey," the old man said. So they saddled the donkey for him, and he mounted it.

¹⁴Then he rode after the man of God and found him sitting under a great tree. The old prophet asked him, "Are you the man of God who came from Judah?"

"Yes, I am," he replied.

13:11 As in Greek version; Hebrew reads *son.*   13:12 As in Greek version; Hebrew reads *They had seen.*

## JEROBOAM

Even clear warnings are hard to obey. The Bible is filled with stories of people who had direction from God and yet chose their own way. Their disobedience was rarely due to ignorance of what God wanted; rather, it grew out of stubborn selfishness. Jeroboam was a consistent example of this all-too-human trait.

During his construction activities, Solomon noticed young Jeroboam's natural leadership skills and made him a special project foreman. Shortly after this, God contacted Jeroboam through the prophet Ahijah. He told Jeroboam that God would punish David's dynasty by tearing the kingdom from Solomon's son and that Jeroboam would rule the 10 northern tribes. And God made it clear that the same fate would destroy the people of Jeroboam's family if they refused to obey God. Apparently Solomon heard about these events and tried to have Jeroboam killed. The future king escaped to Egypt, where he stayed until Solomon died.

When Rehoboam, Solomon's heir, took the throne, Jeroboam returned. He represented the people in demanding that the new king be more lenient than his father. Rehoboam's unwise choice to reject his people's request led to their rejecting him as king. Only Judah and the annexed tribe of Benjamin remained loyal to David's dynasty. The other 10 tribes made Jeroboam king.

Rather than seeing this fulfillment of God's promise as motivation to obey God, Jeroboam decided to do whatever he could to secure his position. He led his kingdom away from the God who had allowed him to reign. God had already warned him of the consequences of this action—his family was eventually wiped out. And Jeroboam set into motion events that would lead to the destruction of the northern kingdom.

Sin's consequences are guaranteed in God's Word, but the timing of those consequences is hard to predict. When we do something directly opposed to God's commands and there isn't immediate disaster, we are often fooled into believing we got away with disobedience. But that is a dangerous assumption. Jeroboam's life should make us recognize our frequent need to admit our disobedience and ask God to forgive us.

| | |
|---|---|
| **Strengths and accomplishments** | • An effective leader and organizer<br>• First king of the 10 tribes of Israel in the divided kingdom<br>• A charismatic leader with much popular support |
| **Weaknesses and mistakes** | • Erected idols in Israel to keep people away from the Temple in Jerusalem<br>• Appointed priests from outside the tribe of Levi<br>• Depended more on his own cunning than on God's promises |
| **Lessons from his life** | • Great opportunities are often destroyed by small decisions<br>• Careless efforts to correct another's errors often lead to the same errors<br>• Mistakes always occur when we attempt to take over God's role in a situation |
| **Vital statistics** | • Where: The northern kingdom of Israel<br>• Occupations: Project foreman, king of Israel<br>• Relatives: Father: Nebat. Mother: Zeruah. Sons: Abijah, Nadab.<br>• Contemporaries: Solomon, Nathan, Ahijah, Rehoboam |
| **Key verses** | "But even after this, Jeroboam did not turn from his evil ways. He continued to choose priests from the common people. He appointed anyone who wanted to become a priest for the pagan shrines. This became a great sin and resulted in the utter destruction of Jeroboam's dynasty from the face of the earth" (1 Kings 13:33, 34). |

Jeroboam's story is told in 1 Kings 11:26—14:20. He is also mentioned in 2 Chronicles 10—13.

15Then he said to the man of God, "Come home with me and eat some food."

16"No, I cannot," he replied. "I am not allowed to eat or drink anything here in this place. 17For the LORD gave me this command: 'You must not eat or drink anything while you are there, and do not return to Judah by the same way you came.'"

18But the old prophet answered, "I am a prophet, too, just as you are. And an angel gave me this command from the LORD: 'Bring him home with you so he can have something to eat and drink.'" But the old man was lying to him. 19So they went back together, and the man of God ate and drank at the prophet's home.

20Then while they were sitting at the table, a command from the LORD came to the old prophet. 21He cried out to the man of God from Judah, "This is what the LORD says: You have defied the word of the LORD and have disobeyed the command the LORD your God gave you. 22You came back to this place and ate and drank where he told you not to eat or drink. Because of this, your body will not be buried in the grave of your ancestors."

23After the man of God had finished eating and drinking, the old prophet saddled his own donkey for him, 24and the man of God started off again. But as he was traveling along, a lion came out and killed him. His body lay there on the road, with the donkey and the lion standing beside it. 25People who passed by saw the body lying in the road and the lion standing beside it, and they went and reported it in Bethel, where the old prophet lived.

26When the prophet heard the report, he said, "It is the man of God who disobeyed the LORD's command. The LORD has fulfilled his word by causing the lion to attack and kill him."

27Then the prophet said to his sons, "Saddle a donkey for me." So they saddled a donkey, 28and he went out and found the body lying in the road. The donkey and lion were still standing there beside it, for the lion had not eaten the body nor attacked the donkey. 29So the prophet laid the body of the man of God on the donkey and took it back to the town to mourn over him and bury him. 30He laid the body in his own grave, crying out in grief, "Oh, my brother!"

31Afterward the prophet said to his sons, "When I die, bury me in the grave where the man of God is buried. Lay my bones beside his bones. 32For the message the LORD told him to proclaim against the altar in Bethel and against the pagan shrines in the towns of Samaria will certainly come true."

33But even after this, Jeroboam did not turn from his evil ways. He continued to choose priests from the common people. He appointed anyone who wanted to become a priest for the pagan shrines. 34This became a great sin and resulted in the utter destruction of Jeroboam's dynasty from the face of the earth.

## Ahijah's Prophecy against Jeroboam

**14** At that time Jeroboam's son Abijah became very sick. 2So Jeroboam told his wife, "Disguise yourself so that no one will recognize you as my wife. Then go to the prophet Ahijah at Shiloh—the man who told me I would become king. 3Take him a gift of ten loaves of bread, some cakes, and a jar of honey, and ask him what will happen to the boy."

4So Jeroboam's wife went to Ahijah's home at Shiloh. He was an old man now and could no longer see. 5But the LORD had told Ahijah, "Jeroboam's wife will come here, pretending to be someone else. She will ask you about her son, for he is very sick. Give her the answer I give you."

6So when Ahijah heard her footsteps at the door, he called out, "Come in, wife of Jeroboam! Why are you pretending to be someone else?" Then he told her, "I have bad news for you. 7Give your husband, Jeroboam, this message from the LORD, the God of Israel: 'I promoted you from the ranks of the common people and made you ruler over my people Israel. 8I ripped the kingdom away from the family of David and gave it to you. But you have not been like my servant David, who obeyed my commands and followed me with all his heart

### Cross-references (margin)

**13:16** 1 Kgs 13:8

**13:21** 1 Sam 13:14

**13:24** 1 Kgs 20:36

**13:31** 2 Kgs 23:17-18

**13:32** 1 Kgs 16:24

**13:33** 1 Kgs 12:31; 2 Chr 13:9

**13:34** 1 Kgs 14:10; 15:29; 2 Kgs 17:21

**14:2** 1 Sam 28:7-8; 2 Sam 14:2-3; 2 Chr 18:29

**14:3** 1 Sam 9:7-8; 2 Kgs 4:42

**14:4** 1 Sam 3:2-3; 4:15

**14:7** 1 Kgs 11:28, 31

**14:8** 1 Kgs 11:33, 38; 15:5

---

**13:24, 25** Lions are mentioned frequently in the Old Testament. They were common enough to be a threat both to people and to their flocks. Samson (Judges 14:5, 6), David (1 Samuel 17:34-37), and Benaiah (2 Samuel 23:20) all faced lions. The fact that the lion and the donkey were standing by the prophet's body showed that this was a divine judgment. Normally, the lion would have attacked the donkey or devoured the man.

**13:33, 34** Under penalty of death, God had forbidden anyone to be a priest who was not from the tribe of Levi (Numbers 3:10). Levites were assured of lifetime support from the tithe, so they did not have to spend time farming, worrying about tribal interests, or fearing for their financial future. Jeroboam's new priests were financed by the king and his fees. They had to mix priestly and secular duties, and they quickly fell into party politics. Because they didn't have job security, these priests were easily corrupted by bribes. Jeroboam's disobedience was the downfall of true religion in the northern kingdom.

**14:9**
Exod 34:17
2 Chr 11:15
Ps 50:17
Ezek 23:35

**14:10**
Deut 32:36
1 Kgs 15:29; 21:22
2 Kgs 9:8-9

**14:11**
1 Kgs 16:4-7; 21:24

**14:12**
1 Kgs 14:17

**14:14**
1 Kgs 15:27, 29

**14:15**
Deut 12:3-4
Ps 52:5

**14:16**
1 Kgs 12:30

**14:17**
1 Kgs 15:21, 33;
16:6-9

**14:19**
1 Kgs 14:29; 15:7,
23, 31; 16:4-7,
14, 20
1 Chr 9:1

**14:21, 25-31**
//2 Chr 12:9-16

**14:21**
1 Kgs 11:32, 36
2 Chr 12:13

**14:22**
Deut 32:21
2 Chr 12:1, 14

**14:23**
Deut 12:2; 16:22
2 Kgs 17:10
Jer 2:20
Ezek 16:24

**14:24**
Deut 23:17-18
2 Kgs 23:7

**14:25**
2 Chr 12:2, 9

**14:26**
1 Kgs 10:16-17;
15:18

and always did whatever I wanted. ⁹You have done more evil than all who lived before you. You have made other gods for yourself and have made me furious with your gold calves. And since you have turned your back on me, ¹⁰I will bring disaster on your dynasty and will destroy every one of your male descendants, slave and free alike, anywhere in Israel. I will burn up your royal dynasty as one burns up trash until it is all gone. ¹¹The members of Jeroboam's family who die in the city will be eaten by dogs, and those who die in the field will be eaten by vultures. I, the LORD, have spoken.'"

¹²Then Ahijah said to Jeroboam's wife, "Go on home, and when you enter the city, the child will die. ¹³All Israel will mourn for him and bury him. He is the only member of your family who will have a proper burial, for this child is the only good thing that the LORD, the God of Israel, sees in the entire family of Jeroboam.

¹⁴"In addition, the LORD will raise up a king over Israel who will destroy the family of Jeroboam. This will happen today, even now! ¹⁵Then the LORD will shake Israel like a reed whipped about in a stream. He will uproot the people of Israel from this good land that he gave their ancestors and will scatter them beyond the Euphrates River,* for they have angered the LORD with the Asherah poles they have set up for worship. ¹⁶He will abandon Israel because Jeroboam sinned and made Israel sin along with him."

¹⁷So Jeroboam's wife returned to Tirzah, and the child died just as she walked through the door of her home. ¹⁸And all Israel buried him and mourned for him, as the LORD had promised through the prophet Ahijah.

¹⁹The rest of the events in Jeroboam's reign, including all his wars and how he ruled, are recorded in *The Book of the History of the Kings of Israel.* ²⁰Jeroboam reigned in Israel twenty-two years. When Jeroboam died, his son Nadab became the next king.

## Rehoboam Rules in Judah

²¹Meanwhile, Rehoboam son of Solomon was king in Judah. He was forty-one years old when he became king, and he reigned seventeen years in Jerusalem, the city the LORD had chosen from among all the tribes of Israel as the place to honor his name. Rehoboam's mother was Naamah, an Ammonite woman.

²²During Rehoboam's reign, the people of Judah did what was evil in the LORD's sight, provoking his anger with their sin, for it was even worse than that of their ancestors. ²³For they also built for themselves pagan shrines and set up sacred pillars and Asherah poles on every high hill and under every green tree. ²⁴There were even male and female shrine prostitutes throughout the land. The people imitated the detestable practices of the pagan nations the LORD had driven from the land ahead of the Israelites.

²⁵In the fifth year of King Rehoboam's reign, King Shishak of Egypt came up and attacked Jerusalem. ²⁶He ransacked the treasuries of the LORD's Temple and the royal palace; he stole everything, including all the gold shields Solomon had made. ²⁷King Rehoboam later replaced them with bronze shields as substitutes, and he entrusted them to the care of the commanders of the guard who protected the entrance to the royal palace. ²⁸Whenever the king went to the Temple of the LORD, the guards would also take the shields and then return them to the guardroom.

**14:15** Hebrew *the river.*

---

**14:10, 11** These disasters were practical applications to Israel of the specific teachings of Deuteronomy (see Deuteronomy 28:15-19, 36-68; 30:15-20). Ahijah was prophesying the downfall of Israel for its flagrant violation of God's commands.

**14:14** Who was this king who would "destroy the family of Jeroboam"? His name was Baasha, and he would kill all of Jeroboam's descendants (15:27-30).

**14:15** "Asherah poles" refers to idol worship. Wooden images were used in the worship of Asherah, a Canaanite mother-goddess.

**14:19** Three non-biblical books are mentioned in 1 and 2 Kings— *The Book of the History of the Kings of Israel* (14:19), *The Book of the History of the Kings of Judah* (14:29), and *The Book of the Acts of Solomon* (11:41). These historical records of Israel and Judah were the main sources of material God directed the author to use to write 1 and 2 Kings. No copies of these books have been found.

**14:23** "Sacred pillars" were pillars of stone placed next to pagan altars. These pillars were supposed to represent deity.

**14:25** When Rehoboam came to power, he inherited a mighty kingdom. Everything he could ever want was given to him. But apparently he did not recognize why he had so much or how it had been obtained. To teach Rehoboam a lesson, God allowed Shishak of Egypt to invade Judah and Israel. Egypt was no longer the world power it had once been, and Shishak, possibly resenting Solomon's enormous success, was determined to change that. Shishak's army was not strong enough to destroy Judah and Israel, but he weakened them so much that they were never the same again.

**14:25, 26** Just five years after Solomon died, the Temple and palace were ransacked by foreign invaders. How quickly the glory, power, and money disappeared! When the people became spiritually corrupt and immoral (14:24), it was just a short time until they lost everything. Wealth, idol worship, and immorality had become more important to them than God. When God is gone from our lives, everything else becomes useless, no matter how valuable it seems.

<sup>29</sup>The rest of the events in Rehoboam's reign and everything he did are recorded in *The Book of the History of the Kings of Judah*. <sup>30</sup>There was constant war between Rehoboam and Jeroboam. <sup>31</sup>When Rehoboam died, he was buried among his ancestors in the City of David. His mother was Naamah, an Ammonite woman. Then his son Abijam* became the next king.

**14:30**
1 Kgs 12:21; 15:6

### Abijam Rules in Judah

**15** Abijam* began to rule over Judah in the eighteenth year of Jeroboam's reign in Israel. <sup>2</sup>He reigned in Jerusalem three years. His mother was Maacah, the daughter of Absalom.*

**15:1-2**
//2 Chr 13:1-2

<sup>3</sup>He committed the same sins as his father before him, and he was not faithful to the LORD his God, as his ancestor David had been. <sup>4</sup>But for David's sake, the LORD his God allowed his descendants to continue ruling, shining like a lamp, and he gave Abijam a son to rule after him in Jerusalem. <sup>5</sup>For David had done what was pleasing in the LORD's sight and had obeyed the LORD's commands throughout his life, except in the affair concerning Uriah the Hittite.

**15:3**
1 Kgs 11:4
**15:4**
2 Chr 21:7
**15:5**
2 Sam 11:2-27
1 Kgs 9:4; 14:8

<sup>6</sup>There was war between Abijam and Jeroboam* throughout Abijam's reign. <sup>7</sup>The rest of the events in Abijam's reign and everything he did are recorded in *The Book of the History of the Kings of Judah*. There was constant war between Abijam and Jeroboam. <sup>8</sup>When Abijam died, he was buried in the City of David. Then his son Asa became the next king.

**15:6-8**
2 Chr 13:22–14:1

### Asa Rules in Judah

<sup>9</sup>Asa began to rule over Judah in the twentieth year of Jeroboam's reign in Israel. <sup>10</sup>He reigned in Jerusalem forty-one years. His grandmother* was Maacah, the daughter of Absalom.

**15:9-22**
//2 Chr 14:2-3;
15:6–16:6

<sup>11</sup>Asa did what was pleasing in the LORD's sight, as his ancestor David had done. <sup>12</sup>He banished the male and female shrine prostitutes from the land and got rid of all the idols* his ancestors had made. <sup>13</sup>He even deposed his grandmother Maacah from her position as queen mother because she had made an obscene Asherah pole. He cut down her obscene pole and burned it in the Kidron Valley. <sup>14</sup>Although the pagan shrines were not removed, Asa's heart remained completely faithful to the LORD throughout his life. <sup>15</sup>He brought into the Temple of the LORD the silver and gold and the various items that he and his father had dedicated.

**15:11**
2 Chr 14:2; 15:17
**15:12**
Deut 23:17-18
1 Kgs 22:46
2 Chr 15:2-5
**15:13**
1 Kgs 14:24
2 Chr 15:16-18
**15:14**
1 Kgs 8:61; 22:43
2 Kgs 12:3

<sup>16</sup>There was constant war between King Asa of Judah and King Baasha of Israel. <sup>17</sup>King Baasha of Israel invaded Judah and fortified Ramah in order to prevent anyone from entering or leaving King Asa's territory in Judah.

**15:17**
Josh 18:25
2 Chr 16:1-6

<sup>18</sup>Asa responded by removing all the silver and gold that was left in the treasuries of the Temple of the LORD and the royal palace. He sent it with some of his officials to Ben-hadad son of Tabrimmon, son of Hezion, the king of Aram, who was ruling in Damascus, along with this message:

**15:18**
1 Kgs 14:26
2 Kgs 12:17-18

<sup>19</sup>"Let there be a treaty* between you and me like the one between your father and my father. See, I am sending you a gift of silver and gold. Break your treaty with King Baasha of Israel so that he will leave me alone."

**15:19**
2 Chr 16:7

<sup>20</sup>Ben-hadad agreed to King Asa's request and sent the commanders of his army to attack the towns of Israel. They conquered the towns of Ijon, Dan, Abel-beth-maacah, and all Kinnereth, and all the land of Naphtali. <sup>21</sup>As soon as Baasha of Israel heard what was happening, he abandoned his project of fortifying Ramah and withdrew to Tirzah. <sup>22</sup>Then King Asa sent an order throughout Judah, requiring that everyone, without exception, help to carry away the building stones and timbers that Baasha had been using to fortify Ramah. Asa used these materials to fortify the town of Geba in Benjamin and the town of Mizpah.

**15:22**
Josh 18:24
2 Chr 16:6

**14:31** Also known as *Abijah*.  **15:1** Also known as *Abijah*.  **15:2** Hebrew *Abishalom* (also in 15:10), a variant spelling of Absalom; compare 2 Chr 11:20.  **15:6** As in a few Hebrew and Greek manuscripts; most Hebrew manuscripts read *between Rehoboam and Jeroboam*.  **15:10** Or *The queen mother*; Hebrew reads *His mother* (also in 15:13); compare 15:2.  **15:12** The Hebrew term (literally *round things*) probably alludes to dung.  **15:19** As in Greek version; Hebrew reads *There is a treaty*.

**15:5** See 2 Samuel 11 for the story of David and Uriah the Hittite.

**15:9** See Asa's Profile in 2 Chronicles 14, p. 685, for more information on this king.

**15:15** These gifts for the Temple were articles dedicated to God as sacred offerings that Abijah had taken in his war with Jeroboam (2 Chronicles 13:16, 17) and that Asa had taken when he defeated the Ethiopians (2 Chronicles 14:12, 13).

**15:16** Baasha seized the throne from Nadab (15:27, 28), who had replaced his father, Jeroboam, as king.

**15:23-24**
//2 Chr 16:11–17:1

²³The rest of the events in Asa's reign—the extent of his power, everything he did, and the names of the cities he built—are recorded in *The Book of the History of the Kings of Judah*. In his old age his feet became diseased. ²⁴When Asa died, he was buried with his ancestors in the City of David.

Then Jehoshaphat, Asa's son, became the next king.

### Nadab Rules in Israel

**15:25**
1 Kgs 14:20
**15:26**
1 Kgs 12:28-33;
13:33; 14:16
**15:27**
Josh 19:44;
21:23-24

²⁵Nadab son of Jeroboam began to rule over Israel in the second year of King Asa's reign in Judah. He reigned in Israel two years. ²⁶But he did what was evil in the LORD's sight and followed the example of his father, continuing the sins that Jeroboam had led Israel to commit.

²⁷Then Baasha son of Ahijah, from the tribe of Issachar, plotted against Nadab and assassinated him while he and the Israelite army were laying siege to the Philistine town of Gibbethon. ²⁸Baasha killed Nadab in the third year of King Asa's reign in Judah, and he became the next king of Israel.

**15:29**
1 Kgs 14:9-16

²⁹He immediately slaughtered all the descendants of King Jeroboam, so that not one of the royal family was left, just as the LORD had promised concerning Jeroboam by the prophet Ahijah from Shiloh. ³⁰This was done because Jeroboam had provoked the anger of the LORD, the God of Israel, by the sins he had committed and the sins he had led Israel to commit.

**15:31**
1 Kgs 14:19

³¹The rest of the events in Nadab's reign and everything he did are recorded in *The Book of the History of the Kings of Israel*.

### Baasha Rules in Israel

**15:32**
2 Chr 15:16

³²There was constant war between King Asa of Judah and King Baasha of Israel. ³³Baasha son of Ahijah began to rule over all Israel in the third year of King Asa's reign in Judah. Baasha reigned in Tirzah twenty-four years. ³⁴But he did what was evil in the LORD's sight and followed the example of Jeroboam, continuing the sins that Jeroboam had led Israel to commit.

---

**THE APPEAL OF IDOLS**
On the surface, the lives of the kings don't make sense. How could they run to idolatry so fast when they had God's word (at least some of it), prophets, and the example of David? Here are some of the reasons for the enticement of idols:

| | The Appeal of Idols | Modern Parallel |
|---|---|---|
| Power | The people wanted freedom from the authority of both God and the priests. They wanted their religion to fit their lifestyle, not their lifestyle to fit their religion. | People do not want to answer to a greater authority. Instead of having power *over* others, God wants us to have the Holy Spirit's power to *help* others. |
| Pleasure | Idol worship exalted sensuality without responsibility or guilt. People acted out the vicious and sensuous personalities of the gods they worshiped, thus gaining approval for their degraded lives. | People deify pleasure, seeking it at the expense of everything else. Instead of seeking pleasure that leads to long-range disaster, God calls us to seek the kind of pleasure that leads to long-range rewards. |
| Passion | Humanity was reduced to little more than animals. The people did not have to be viewed as unique individuals but could be exploited sexually, politically, and economically. | Like animals, people let physical drives and passion rule them. Instead of seeking passion that exploits others, God calls us to redirect our passions to areas that build others up. |
| Praise and Popularity | The high and holy nature of God was replaced by gods who were more a reflection of human nature, thus more culturally suitable to the people. These gods no longer required sacrifice, just a token of appeasement. | Sacrifice is seen as self inflicted punishment, making no sense. Success is to be sought at all costs. Instead of seeking praise for ourselves, God calls us to praise him and those who honor him. |

As societies change, they often throw out norms and values no longer considered necessary or acceptable. Believers must be careful not to follow society's example if it discards God's Word. When society does that, only godlessness and evil remain.

---

**15:29** See 1 Kings 14:12-14 for Ahijah's prediction of this event.
**15:30** All the descendants of Jeroboam were killed because Jeroboam had led Israel into sin. Sin is always judged harshly, but the worst sinners are those who lead others into doing wrong. Jesus said it would be better if such people had millstones tied around their necks and were thrown into the sea (Mark 9:42). If you have taken the responsibility for leading others, remember the consequences of leading them astray. Teaching the truth is a responsibility that goes with the privilege of leadership.

**16** This message from the Lord was delivered to King Baasha by the prophet Jehu son of Hanani: ²"I lifted you out of the dust to make you ruler of my people Israel, but you have followed the evil example of Jeroboam. You have provoked my anger by causing my people Israel to sin. ³So now I will destroy you and your family, just as I destroyed the descendants of Jeroboam son of Nebat. ⁴The members of Baasha's family who die in the city will be eaten by dogs, and those who die in the field will be eaten by vultures."

⁵The rest of the events in Baasha's reign and the extent of his power are recorded in *The Book of the History of the Kings of Israel.* ⁶When Baasha died, he was buried in Tirzah. Then his son Elah became the next king.

⁷The message from the Lord against Baasha and his family came through the prophet Jehu son of Hanani. It was delivered because Baasha had done what was evil in the Lord's sight (just as the family of Jeroboam had done), and also because Baasha had destroyed the family of Jeroboam. The Lord's anger was provoked by Baasha's sins.

### Elah Rules in Israel
⁸Elah son of Baasha began to rule over Israel in the twenty-sixth year of King Asa's reign in Judah. He reigned in the city of Tirzah for two years.

⁹Then Zimri, who commanded half of the royal chariots, made plans to kill him. One day in Tirzah, Elah was getting drunk at the home of Arza, the supervisor of the palace. ¹⁰Zimri walked in and struck him down and killed him. This happened in the twenty-seventh year of King Asa's reign in Judah. Then Zimri became the next king.

¹¹Zimri immediately killed the entire royal family of Baasha, leaving him not even a single male child. He even destroyed distant relatives and friends. ¹²So Zimri destroyed the dynasty of Baasha as the Lord had promised through the prophet Jehu. ¹³This happened because of all the sins Baasha and his son Elah had committed, and because of the sins they led Israel to commit. They provoked the anger of the Lord, the God of Israel, with their worthless idols.

¹⁴The rest of the events in Elah's reign and everything he did are recorded in *The Book of the History of the Kings of Israel.*

### Zimri Rules in Israel
¹⁵Zimri began to rule over Israel in the twenty-seventh year of King Asa's reign in Judah, but his reign in Tirzah lasted only seven days. The army of Israel was then attacking the Philistine town of Gibbethon. ¹⁶When they heard that Zimri had committed treason and had assassinated the king, that very day they chose Omri, commander of the army, as the new king of Israel. ¹⁷So Omri led the entire army of Israel up from Gibbethon to attack Tirzah, Israel's capital. ¹⁸When Zimri saw that the city had been taken, he went into the citadel of the palace and burned it down over himself and died in the flames. ¹⁹For he, too, had done what was evil in the Lord's sight. He followed the example of Jeroboam in all the sins he had committed and led Israel to commit.

²⁰The rest of the events in Zimri's reign and his conspiracy are recorded in *The Book of the History of the Kings of Israel.*

### Omri Rules in Israel
²¹But now the people of Israel were split into two factions. Half the people tried to make Tibni son of Ginath their king, while the other half supported Omri. ²²But Omri's supporters defeated the supporters of Tibni. So Tibni was killed, and Omri became the next king.

²³Omri began to rule over Israel in the thirty-first year of King Asa's reign in Judah. He reigned twelve years in all, six of them in Tirzah. ²⁴Then Omri bought the hill now known as Samaria from its owner, Shemer, for 150 pounds of silver.* He built a city on it and called the city Samaria in honor of Shemer.

**16:24** Hebrew *for 2 talents* [68 kilograms] *of silver.*

### Cross-references
**16:1**
1 Kgs 16:7
2 Chr 19:2; 20:34

**16:2**
1 Sam 2:8
1 Kgs 14:7-9

**16:3**
1 Kgs 14:10; 15:29;
21:21

**16:4**
1 Kgs 14:11

**16:7**
1 Kgs 16:1

**16:9**
2 Kgs 9:30-33

**16:11**
1 Kgs 15:29

**16:13**
Deut 32:21
1 Kgs 15:30

**16:14**
1 Kgs 16:4-7,
20, 28, 30

**16:18**
1 Sam 31:4-5
2 Sam 17:23

**16:19**
1 Kgs 12:28

**16:20**
1 Kgs 16:14, 27

**16:24**
1 Kgs 13:32

---

**16:1-7** God had destroyed Jeroboam's descendants for their flagrant sins, and yet Baasha repeated the same mistakes. He did not learn from the example of those who had gone before him; he did not stop to think that his sin would be punished. Make sure you learn from your past, the experiences of others, and the lives of those whose stories are told in the Bible. Don't repeat mistakes.

**16:21, 22** Omri began his reign as political dissension brewed in Israel. After Zimri killed himself, the Israelite army chose Omri, their commander, as the next ruler. Tibni, Omri's chief rival to the throne, died, and Omri then began his evil reign. During his 12-year rule over Israel, he was a shrewd and capable leader. He organized the building of his new capital city, Samaria, while strengthening the nation politically and militarily. But he did not care about the nation's spiritual condition (Micah 6:16), and he purposely led Israel farther from God in order to put more power in his own hands.

**16:24** Omri's new capital, Samaria, offered some political advantages. The city was his personal property, so he had total control

**16:25**
1 Kgs 14:9
Mic 6:16

**16:26**
1 Kgs 15:30

25 But Omri did what was evil in the LORD's sight, even more than any of the kings before him. 26 He followed the example of Jeroboam son of Nebat in all the sins he had committed and led Israel to commit. The people provoked the anger of the LORD, the God of Israel, with their worthless idols.

**16:28**
2 Chr 18:1

27 The rest of the events in Omri's reign, the extent of his power, and everything he did are recorded in *The Book of the History of the Kings of Israel.* 28 When Omri died, he was buried in Samaria. Then his son Ahab became the next king.

### Ahab Rules in Israel

**16:30**
1 Kgs 14:9

**16:31**
Deut 7:3-4
1 Kgs 11:5
2 Kgs 10:18; 17:16

**16:32**
2 Kgs 10:21, 26-27

**16:33**
1 Kgs 21:19, 25
2 Kgs 13:6

**16:34**
Josh 6:26

29 Ahab son of Omri began to rule over Israel in the thirty-eighth year of King Asa's reign in Judah. He reigned in Samaria twenty-two years. 30 But Ahab son of Omri did what was evil in the LORD's sight, even more than any of the kings before him. 31 And as though it were not enough to follow the example of Jeroboam, he married Jezebel, the daughter of King Ethbaal of the Sidonians, and he began to bow down in worship of Baal. 32 First Ahab built a temple and an altar for Baal in Samaria. 33 Then he set up an Asherah pole. He did more to provoke the anger of the LORD, the God of Israel, than any of the other kings of Israel before him.

34 It was during his reign that Hiel, a man from Bethel, rebuilt Jericho. When he laid its foundations, it cost him the life of his oldest son, Abiram. And when he completed it and set up its gates, it cost him the life of his youngest son, Segub.* This all happened according to the message from the LORD concerning Jericho spoken by Joshua son of Nun.

**16:34** An ancient Hebrew scribal tradition reads *He killed his oldest son when he laid its foundations, and he killed his youngest son when he set up its gates.*

## KINGS TO DATE AND THEIR ENEMIES

**908**
**BAASHA**
Harassed by Asa
(Judah) and Ben-
hadad (Aram)
1 Kgs 15:27—16:7
2 Chr 16:1–6

**930**
**JEROBOAM I**
Defeated by
Abijah (Judah)
1 Kgs 11:26—14:20
2 Chr 10:12—13:20

**909**
**NADAB**
1 Kgs 14:20;
15:25–28

**885**
**ZIMRI**
1 Kgs 16:9–20

**886**
**ELAH**
Philistines
1 Kgs 16:6–14

**885**
**TIBNI**
1 Kgs 16:21, 22

**885**
**OMRI**
Philistines
1 Kgs 16:16–28

**874**
**AHAB**
Twice defeated
Ben-hadad II
(Aram) and was
later killed in battle
against Aram
1 Kgs 16:28—22:40
2 Chr 18:1–34

853

I S R A E L

J U D A H

**930**
**REHOBOAM**
Defeated by
Shishak (Egypt)
1 Kgs 11:43—14:31
2 Chr 9:31—12:16

**913**
**ABIJAH**
Defeated
Jeroboam (Israel)
1 Kgs 14:31—15:8
2 Chr 13:1—14:1

**910**
**ASA**
Defeated Zerah
(the Ethiopian) and
harassed Baasha
1 Kgs 15:8–24
2 Chr 14:1—16:14

869

All dates are B.C.
For all the kings of Israel and Judah, see the chart at the end of 1 Kings.

over it. Samaria also commanded a hilltop position, which made it easy to defend. Omri died before completing the city. So his son, Ahab, completed it, building not only the beautiful ivory palace (1 Kings 22:39; Amos 3:13-15), but also a temple to the god Baal. Samaria served as the capital city for the rest of Israel's dynasties until it fell to the Assyrians in 722 B.C. (2 Kings 17:5).

**16:31** Ahab's evil wife, Jezebel, came from the Phoenician city of Tyre where her father had been a high priest and eventually king. Jezebel worshiped the god Baal. In order to please her, Ahab built a temple and an altar for Baal (16:32), thus promoting idolatry and leading the entire nation into sin. (For more about Baal, see the note on 18:18.)

### 3. Elijah's ministry

*Elijah Fed by Ravens*

**17** Now Elijah, who was from Tishbe in Gilead, told King Ahab, "As surely as the LORD, the God of Israel, lives—the God I serve—there will be no dew or rain during the next few years until I give the word!"

**17:1**
Judg 12:4
1 Kgs 22:14
Luke 4:25
Jas 5:17

²Then the LORD said to Elijah, ³"Go to the east and hide by Kerith Brook, near where it enters the Jordan River. ⁴Drink from the brook and eat what the ravens bring you, for I have commanded them to bring you food."

⁵So Elijah did as the LORD told him and camped beside Kerith Brook, east of the Jordan. ⁶The ravens brought him bread and meat each morning and evening, and he drank from the brook. ⁷But after a while the brook dried up, for there was no rainfall anywhere in the land.

*The Widow at Zarephath*

⁸Then the LORD said to Elijah, ⁹"Go and live in the village of Zarephath, near the city of Sidon. I have instructed a widow there to feed you."

**17:9**
Obad 1:20
Luke 4:26

¹⁰So he went to Zarephath. As he arrived at the gates of the village, he saw a widow gathering sticks, and he asked her, "Would you please bring me a little water in a cup?" ¹¹As she was going to get it, he called to her, "Bring me a bite of bread, too."

**17:10**
Gen 24:17
John 4:7

¹²But she said, "I swear by the LORD your God that I don't have a single piece of bread in the house. And I have only a handful of flour left in the jar and a little cooking oil in the bottom of the jug. I was just gathering a few sticks to cook this last meal, and then my son and I will die."

**17:12**
2 Kgs 4:2-7

¹³But Elijah said to her, "Don't be afraid! Go ahead and do just what you've said, but make a little bread for me first. Then use what's left to prepare a meal for yourself and your son. ¹⁴For this is what the LORD, the God of Israel, says: There will always be flour and olive oil left in your containers until the time when the LORD sends rain and the crops grow again!"

¹⁵So she did as Elijah said, and she and Elijah and her family continued to eat for many days. ¹⁶There was always enough flour and olive oil left in the containers, just as the LORD had promised through Elijah.

¹⁷Some time later the woman's son became sick. He grew worse and worse, and finally he died. ¹⁸Then she said to Elijah, "O man of God, what have you done to me? Have you come here to point out my sins and kill my son?"

---

**17:1** Elijah was the first in a long line of important prophets God sent to Israel and Judah. Israel, the northern kingdom, had no faithful kings throughout its history. Each king was wicked, actually leading the people in worshiping pagan gods. Few priests were left from the tribe of Levi (most had gone to Judah), and the priests appointed by Israel's kings were corrupt and ineffective. With no king or priests to bring God's word to the people, God called prophets to try to rescue Israel from its moral and spiritual decline. For the next 300 years these men and women would play vital roles in both nations, encouraging the people and leaders to turn back to God.

**17:1** Those who worshiped Baal believed he was the god who brought the rains and bountiful harvests. So when Elijah walked into the presence of this Baal-worshiping king and told him there would be no rain for several years, Ahab was shocked. Ahab had built a strong military defense, but it would be no help against drought. He had many priests of Baal, but they could not bring rain. Elijah bravely confronted the man who led his people into evil, and he told of a power far greater than any pagan god—the Lord God of Israel. When rebellion and heresy were at an all-time high in Israel, God responded not only with words but with action.

**17:10ff** In a nation that was required by law to care for its prophets, it is ironic that God turned to ravens (unclean birds) and a widow (a foreigner from Jezebel's home territory) to care for Elijah. God has help where we least expect it. He provides for us in ways that go beyond our narrow definitions or expectations. No matter how bitter our trials or how seemingly hopeless our situation, we should look for God's caring touch. We may find his providence in some strange places!

**17:13-16** When the widow of Zarephath met Elijah, she thought she was preparing her last meal. But a simple act of faith produced a miracle. She trusted Elijah and gave all she had to eat to him. Faith is the step between promise and assurance. Miracles seem so out of reach for our feeble faith. But every miracle, large or small, begins with an act of obedience. We may not see the solution until we take the first step of faith.

**17:17** Even when God has done a miracle in our lives, our troubles may not be over. The famine was a terrible experience, but the worst was yet to come. God's provision is never given in order to let us rest upon it. We need to depend on him as we face each new trial.

**ELIJAH HIDES FROM AHAB**
Elijah prophesied a drought and then hid from King Ahab by the Kerith Brook, where he was fed by ravens. When the brook dried up, God sent him to Zarephath in Phoenicia, where a widow and her son fed him and gave him lodging.

¹⁹But Elijah replied, "Give me your son." And he took the child's body from her arms, carried him up the stairs to the room where he was staying, and laid the body on his bed. ²⁰Then Elijah cried out to the LORD, "O LORD my God, why have you brought tragedy to this widow who has opened her home to me, causing her son to die?"

²¹And he stretched himself out over the child three times and cried out to the LORD, "O LORD my God, please let this child's life return to him." ²²The LORD heard Elijah's prayer, and the life of the child returned, and he revived! ²³Then Elijah brought him down from the upper room and gave him to his mother. "Look!" he said. "Your son is alive!"

²⁴Then the woman told Elijah, "Now I know for sure that you are a man of God, and that the LORD truly speaks through you."

**17:21**
2 Kgs 4:34
Acts 20:10-12

**17:23**
Heb 11:35

**17:24**
John 2:11; 3:1-2;
16:30

**ELIJAH**

Elijah's single-minded commitment to God shocks and challenges us. He was sent to confront—not comfort. And Elijah spoke God's words to a king who often rejected his message just because he brought it. Elijah chose to carry out his ministry for God alone and paid for that decision by experiencing isolation from others who were also faithful to God.

It is interesting to think about the amazing miracles God accomplished through Elijah, but we would do well to focus on the relationship they shared. All that happened in Elijah's life began with the same miracle that is available to us—he responded to the miracle of being able to know God.

For example, after God worked an overwhelming miracle through Elijah in defeating the prophets of Baal, Queen Jezebel retaliated by threatening Elijah's life. And Elijah ran. He felt afraid, depressed, and abandoned. Despite God's provision of food and shelter in the wilderness, Elijah wanted to die. So God presented Elijah with an "audiovisual display" and a message he needed to hear. Elijah witnessed a windstorm, an earthquake, and a fire. But the Lord was not in any of those powerful things. Instead, God displayed his presence in a gentle whisper.

Elijah, like us, struggled with his feelings even after this comforting message from God. So God confronted Elijah's emotions and commanded action. He told Elijah what to do next and informed him that part of his loneliness was based on ignorance: Seven thousand others in Israel were still faithful to God.

Even today, God often speaks through the gentle and obvious rather than the spectacular and unusual. God has work for us to do even when we feel fear and failure. And God always has more resources and people than we know about. Although we might wish to do amazing miracles for God, we should instead focus on developing a relationship with him. The real miracle of Elijah's life was his very personal relationship with God. And that miracle is available to us.

| | |
|---|---|
| **Strengths and accomplishments** | • Was the most famous and dramatic of Israel's prophets<br>• Predicted the beginning and end of a three-year drought<br>• Was used by God to restore a dead child to his mother<br>• Represented God in a showdown with priests of Baal and Asherah<br>• Appeared with Moses and Jesus in the New Testament Transfiguration scene |
| **Weaknesses and mistakes** | • Chose to work alone and paid for it with isolation and loneliness<br>• Fled in fear from Jezebel when she threatened his life |
| **Lessons from his life** | • We are never closer to defeat than in our moments of greatest victory<br>• We are never as alone as we may feel; God is always there<br>• God speaks more frequently in persistent whispers than in shouts |
| **Vital statistics** | • Where: Gilead<br>• Occupation: Prophet<br>• Contemporaries: Ahab, Jezebel, Ahaziah, Obadiah, Jehu, Hazael |
| **Key verses** | "At the usual time for offering the evening sacrifice, Elijah the prophet walked up to the altar and prayed, 'O LORD, God of Abraham, Isaac, and Jacob, prove today that you are God in Israel and that I am your servant. Prove that I have done all this at your command. O LORD, answer me! Answer me so these people will know that you, O LORD, are God and that you have brought them back to yourself.'<br>"Immediately the fire of the LORD flashed down from heaven and burned up the young bull, the wood, the stones, and the dust. It even licked up all the water in the trench!" (1 Kings 18:36–38). |

Elijah's story is told in 1 Kings 17:1—2 Kings 2:11. He is also mentioned in 2 Chronicles 21:12–15; Malachi 4:5, 6; Matthew 11:14; 16:14; 17:3–13; 27:47–49; Luke 1:17; 4:25, 26; John 1:19–25; Romans 11:2–4; James 5:17, 18.

## The Contest on Mount Carmel

**18** Later on, in the third year of the drought, the LORD said to Elijah, "Go and present yourself to King Ahab. Tell him that I will soon send rain!" 2 So Elijah went to appear before Ahab.

Meanwhile, the famine had become very severe in Samaria. 3 So Ahab summoned Obadiah, who was in charge of the palace. (Obadiah was a devoted follower of the LORD. 4 Once when Jezebel had tried to kill all the LORD's prophets, Obadiah had hidden 100 of them in two caves. He put fifty prophets in each cave and supplied them with food and water.) 5 Ahab said to Obadiah, "We must check every spring and valley in the land to see if we can find enough grass to save at least some of my horses and mules." 6 So they divided the land between them. Ahab went one way by himself, and Obadiah went another way by himself.

7 As Obadiah was walking along, he suddenly saw Elijah coming toward him. Obadiah recognized him at once and bowed low to the ground before him. "Is it really you, my lord Elijah?" he asked.

8 "Yes, it is," Elijah replied. "Now go and tell your master, 'Elijah is here.'"

9 "Oh, sir," Obadiah protested, "what harm have I done to you that you are sending me to my death at the hands of Ahab? 10 For I swear by the LORD your God that the king has searched every nation and kingdom on earth from end to end to find you. And each time he was told, 'Elijah isn't here,' King Ahab forced the king of that nation to swear to the truth of his claim. 11 And now you say, 'Go and tell your master, "Elijah is here."' 12 But as soon as I leave you, the Spirit of the LORD will carry you away to who knows where. When Ahab comes and cannot find you, he will kill me. Yet I have been a true servant of the LORD all my life. 13 Has no one told you, my lord, about the time when Jezebel was trying to kill the LORD's prophets? I hid 100 of them in two caves and supplied them with food and water. 14 And now you say, 'Go and tell your master, "Elijah is here."' Sir, if I do that, Ahab will certainly kill me."

15 But Elijah said, "I swear by the LORD Almighty, in whose presence I stand, that I will present myself to Ahab this very day."

16 So Obadiah went to tell Ahab that Elijah had come, and Ahab went out to meet Elijah. 17 When Ahab saw him, he exclaimed, "So, is it really you, you troublemaker of Israel?"

18 "I have made no trouble for Israel," Elijah replied. "You and your family are the troublemakers, for you have refused to obey the commands of the LORD and have worshiped the images of Baal instead. 19 Now summon all Israel to join me at Mount Carmel, along with the 450 prophets of Baal and the 400 prophets of Asherah who are supported by Jezebel.*"

20 So Ahab summoned all the people of Israel and the prophets to Mount Carmel. 21 Then Elijah stood in front of them and said, "How much longer will you waver, hobbling between two opinions? If the LORD is God, follow him! But if Baal is God, then follow him!" But the people were completely silent.

**18:19** Hebrew *who eat at Jezebel's table.*

**18:1**
Jas 5:17-18
**18:2**
1 Kgs 16:24
**18:3**
1 Kgs 18:16

**18:12**
2 Kgs 2:16
Ezek 3:12, 14
Acts 8:39
**18:13**
1 Kgs 18:3-4

**18:17**
Josh 7:25
**18:18**
1 Kgs 9:9; 21:25

**18:19**
Josh 19:26
**18:21**
Josh 24:15
2 Kgs 17:41

---

**THE SHOWDOWN AT CARMEL**
In a showdown with the false prophets of Baal at Mount Carmel, Elijah set out to prove to evil Ahab that only the Lord is God. Elijah then killed the false prophets by the Kishon Valley and fled back to Jezreel.

**18:3, 4** Although Elijah was alone in his confrontation with Ahab and Jezebel, he was not the only one in Israel who believed in God. Obadiah had been faithful in hiding 100 prophets still true to the Lord.

**18:18** Instead of worshiping the true God, Ahab and his wife, Jezebel, worshiped Baal, the most popular Canaanite god. Baal idols were often made in the shape of a bull, representing strength and fertility and reflecting lust for power and sexual pleasure.

**18:19** Ahab brought 850 pagan prophets to Mount Carmel to match wits and power with Elijah. Evil kings hated God's prophets because they spoke against sin and idolatry and undermined their control over the people. With the wicked kings' backing, many pagan prophets sprang up to counter the words of God's prophets. But Elijah showed the people that speaking a prophecy wasn't enough. One needed the power of the living God to fulfill it.

**18:21** Elijah challenged the people to take a stand—to follow whoever was the true God. Why did so many people waver between the two choices? Perhaps some were not sure. Many, however, knew that the Lord was God, but they enjoyed the sinful pleasures and other benefits that came with following Ahab in his

**18:22**
1 Kgs 19:10, 14

**18:24**
1 Sam 7:8
1 Kgs 18:38

**18:26**
Ps 115:4-5
Jer 10:5

**18:28**
Lev 19:28
Deut 14:1

**18:30**
1 Kgs 19:10, 14
**18:31**
2 Kgs 17:34
**18:32**
Col 3:17
**18:33**
Gen 22:9

**18:36**
Exod 3:6; 4:5
Num 16:28-32

22 Then Elijah said to them, "I am the only prophet of the LORD who is left, but Baal has 450 prophets. 23 Now bring two bulls. The prophets of Baal may choose whichever one they wish and cut it into pieces and lay it on the wood of their altar, but without setting fire to it. I will prepare the other bull and lay it on the wood on the altar, but not set fire to it. 24 Then call on the name of your god, and I will call on the name of the LORD. The god who answers by setting fire to the wood is the true God!" And all the people agreed.

25 Then Elijah said to the prophets of Baal, "You go first, for there are many of you. Choose one of the bulls, and prepare it and call on the name of your god. But do not set fire to the wood."

26 So they prepared one of the bulls and placed it on the altar. Then they called on the name of Baal from morning until noontime, shouting, "O Baal, answer us!" But there was no reply of any kind. Then they danced, hobbling around the altar they had made.

27 About noontime Elijah began mocking them. "You'll have to shout louder," he scoffed, "for surely he is a god! Perhaps he is daydreaming, or is relieving himself.* Or maybe he is away on a trip, or is asleep and needs to be wakened!"

28 So they shouted louder, and following their normal custom, they cut themselves with knives and swords until the blood gushed out. 29 They raved all afternoon until the time of the evening sacrifice, but still there was no sound, no reply, no response.

30 Then Elijah called to the people, "Come over here!" They all crowded around him as he repaired the altar of the LORD that had been torn down. 31 He took twelve stones, one to represent each of the tribes of Israel,* 32 and he used the stones to rebuild the altar in the name of the LORD. Then he dug a trench around the altar large enough to hold about three gallons.* 33 He piled wood on the altar, cut the bull into pieces, and laid the pieces on the wood.

Then he said, "Fill four large jars with water, and pour the water over the offering and the wood."

34 After they had done this, he said, "Do the same thing again!" And when they were finished, he said, "Now do it a third time!" So they did as he said, 35 and the water ran around the altar and even filled the trench.

36 At the usual time for offering the evening sacrifice, Elijah the prophet walked up to the altar and prayed, "O LORD, God of Abraham, Isaac, and Jacob,* prove today that you are God in Israel and that I am your servant. Prove that I have done all this at your command. 37 O LORD, answer me! Answer me so these people will know that you, O LORD, are God and that you have brought them back to yourself."

**18:27** Or *is busy somewhere else,* or *is engaged in business.* **18:31** Hebrew *each of the tribes of the sons of Jacob to whom the LORD had said, "Your name will be Israel."* **18:32** Hebrew *2 seahs* [12 liters] *of seed.* **18:36** Hebrew *and Israel.* The names "Jacob" and "Israel" are often interchanged throughout the Old Testament, referring sometimes to the individual patriarch and sometimes to the nation.

---

**PROPHETS— FALSE AND TRUE**

| *False Prophets* | *True Prophets* |
|---|---|
| Worked for political purposes to benefit themselves | Worked for spiritual purposes to serve God and the people |
| Held positions of great wealth | Owned little or nothing |
| Gave false messages | Spoke only true messages |
| Spoke only what the people wanted to hear | Spoke only what God told them to say—no matter how unpopular |

---

idolatrous worship. It is important to take a stand for the Lord. If we just drift along with whatever is pleasant and easy, we will someday discover that we have been worshiping a false god—ourselves.

**18:29** Although the prophets of Baal "raved all afternoon," no one answered them. Their god was silent because it was not real. The gods we may be tempted to follow are not idols of wood or stone, but they are just as false and dangerous because they cause us to depend on something other than God. Power, status, appearance, or material possessions can become our gods if we devote our lives to them. But when we reach times of crisis and desperately call out to these gods, there will only be silence. They can offer no true answers, no guidance, and no wisdom.

**18:31** Using 12 stones to build the altar took courage. This

would have angered some of the people because it was a silent reminder of the split between the tribes. While the 10 tribes of the north called themselves Israel, this name originally was given to all 12 of the tribes together.

**18:36-38** God flashed fire from heaven for Elijah. He will also help us accomplish what he commands us to do. The proof may not be as dramatic in our lives as in Elijah's, but God will make resources available to us in creative ways to accomplish his purposes. He will give us the wisdom to raise a family, the courage to take a stand for truth, or the means to provide help for someone in need. Like Elijah, we can have faith that whatever God commands us to do, he will provide what we need to carry it through.

³⁸Immediately the fire of the LORD flashed down from heaven and burned up the young bull, the wood, the stones, and the dust. It even licked up all the water in the trench! ³⁹And when all the people saw it, they fell face down on the ground and cried out, "The LORD—he is God! Yes, the LORD is God!"

**18:38**
Gen 15:17
Lev 9:24; 10:1
2 Kgs 1:12
Job 1:16

⁴⁰Then Elijah commanded, "Seize all the prophets of Baal. Don't let a single one escape!" So the people seized them all, and Elijah took them down to the Kishon Valley and killed them there.

**18:40**
Deut 13:5; 18:20
2 Kgs 10:24

### Elijah Prays for Rain

⁴¹Then Elijah said to Ahab, "Go get something to eat and drink, for I hear a mighty rainstorm coming!"

⁴²So Ahab went to eat and drink. But Elijah climbed to the top of Mount Carmel and bowed low to the ground and prayed with his face between his knees.

**18:42**
Jas 5:18

⁴³Then he said to his servant, "Go and look out toward the sea."

The servant went and looked, then returned to Elijah and said, "I didn't see anything."

Seven times Elijah told him to go and look. ⁴⁴Finally the seventh time, his servant told him, "I saw a little cloud about the size of a man's hand rising from the sea."

Then Elijah shouted, "Hurry to Ahab and tell him, 'Climb into your chariot and go back home. If you don't hurry, the rain will stop you!'"

⁴⁵And soon the sky was black with clouds. A heavy wind brought a terrific rainstorm, and Ahab left quickly for Jezreel. ⁴⁶Then the LORD gave special strength to Elijah. He tucked his cloak into his belt* and ran ahead of Ahab's chariot all the way to the entrance of Jezreel.

**18:46**
2 Kgs 4:29

### Elijah Flees to Sinai

**19** When Ahab got home, he told Jezebel everything Elijah had done, including the way he had killed all the prophets of Baal. ²So Jezebel sent this message to Elijah: "May the gods strike me and even kill me if by this time tomorrow I have not killed you just as you killed them."

**19:2**
2 Kgs 6:31

³Elijah was afraid and fled for his life. He went to Beersheba, a town in Judah, and he left his servant there. ⁴Then he went on alone into the wilderness, traveling all day. He sat down under a solitary broom tree and prayed that he might die. "I have had enough, LORD," he said. "Take my life, for I am no better than my ancestors who have already died."

**19:3**
Gen 21:31
**19:4**
Num 11:5
Jer 20:14-18
Jon 4:3, 8

⁵Then he lay down and slept under the broom tree. But as he was sleeping, an angel touched him and told him, "Get up and eat!" ⁶He looked around and there beside his head was some bread baked on hot stones and a jar of water! So he ate and drank and lay down again.

**18:46** Hebrew *He bound up his loins.*

---

**ELIJAH FLEES FROM JEZEBEL**
After killing Baal's prophets, Elijah ran from the furious Queen Jezebel. He fled to Beersheba, then into the wilderness, and finally to Mount Sinai. There, like Moses centuries earlier, he talked with God.

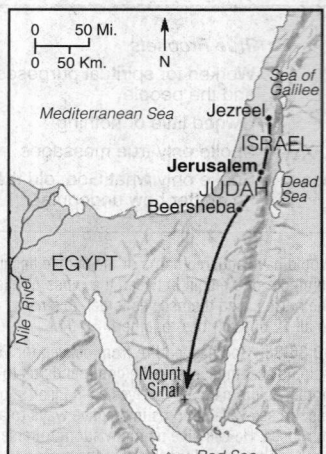

**18:46** Elijah ran the six miles back to the city in order to give Ahab a last chance to turn from his sin before joining Jezebel in Jezreel. His run also ensured that the correct story of what happened would reach Jezreel.

**19:2** Jezebel was enraged about the death of her prophets because they had told her everything *she* wanted to hear, prophesying her future power and glory. Their job was to deify the king and queen and help perpetuate their kingdom. Jezebel was also angry because her supporters had been eliminated and her pride and authority damaged. The money she had invested in these prophets was now lost.

Elijah, who caused the prophets' deaths, was a constant thorn in Jezebel's side because he was always predicting gloom and doom. Since she could not control his actions, Jezebel vowed to kill him. As long as God's prophet was around, she could not carry out all the evil she wanted.

**19:3ff** Elijah experienced the depths of fatigue and discouragement just after his two great spiritual victories: the defeat of the prophets of Baal and the answered prayer for rain. Often discouragement sets in after great spiritual experiences, especially those requiring physical effort or involving great emotion. To lead him out of depression, God first let Elijah rest and eat. Then God confronted him with the need to return to his mission—to speak God's words in Israel. Elijah's battles were not over; he still had work to do. When you feel let down after a great spiritual experience, remember that God's purpose for your life is not yet over.

7 Then the angel of the LORD came again and touched him and said, "Get up and eat some more, or the journey ahead will be too much for you."

8 So he got up and ate and drank, and the food gave him enough strength to travel forty days and forty nights to Mount Sinai,* the mountain of God. 9 There he came to a cave, where he spent the night.

**19:8**
Exod 3:1; 4:27;
24:18; 34:28
Deut 9:9
Matt 4:2

19:8 Hebrew *to Horeb,* another name for Sinai.

**AHAB**

The kings of Israel and Judah, both good and evil, had prophets sent by God to advise, confront, and aid them. King David had a faithful friend in God's prophet Nathan; Ahab could have had an equally faithful friend in Elijah. But while David listened to Nathan and was willing to repent of his sins, Ahab saw Elijah as his enemy. Why? Because Elijah always brought bad news to Ahab, and Ahab refused to acknowledge that it was his own constant disobedience to God and persistent idol worship, not Elijah's prophecies, that brought the evil on his nation. He blamed Elijah for bringing the prophecies of judgment, rather than taking his advice and changing his own evil ways.

Ahab was trapped by his own choices, and he was unwilling to take the right action. As king, he was responsible to God and his prophet Elijah, but he was married to an evil woman who drew him into idol worship. He was a childish man who brooded for days if unable to get his own way. He took his evil wife's advice, listened only to the "prophets" who gave good news, and surrounded himself with people who encouraged him to do whatever he wanted. But the value of advice cannot be judged by the number of people for or against it. Ahab consistently chose to follow the majority opinion of those who surrounded him, and that led to his death.

It may seem nice to have someone encourage us to do whatever we want because advice that goes against our wishes is difficult to accept. However, our decisions must be based on the quality of the advice, not on its attractiveness or the majority opinion of our peers. God encourages us to get advice from wise counselors, but how can we test the advice we receive? Advice that agrees with the principles in God's Word is reliable. We must always separate advice from our own desires, the majority opinion, or whatever seems best in our limited perspective, and weigh it against God's commands. He will never lead us to do what he has forbidden in his Word—even in principle. Unlike Ahab, we should trust godly counselors and have the courage to stand against those who would have us do otherwise.

| | |
|---|---|
| **Strengths and accomplishments** | • Eighth king of Israel<br>• Capable leader and military strategist |
| **Weaknesses and mistakes** | • Was the most evil king of Israel<br>• Married Jezebel, a pagan woman, and allowed her to promote Baal worship<br>• Brooded about not being able to get a piece of land, which prompted his wife to have its owner, Naboth, killed<br>• Was used to getting his own way and got depressed when he didn't |
| **Lessons from his life** | • The choice of a spouse will have a significant effect on life—physically, spiritually, and emotionally<br>• Selfishness, left unchecked, can lead to great evil |
| **Vital statistics** | • Where: Northern kingdom of Israel<br>• Occupation: King<br>• Relatives: Wife: Jezebel. Father: Omri. Sons: Ahaziah, Joram.<br>• Contemporaries: Elijah, Naboth, Jehu, Ben-hadad, Jehoshaphat |
| **Key verses** | "But Ahab son of Omri did what was evil in the LORD's sight, even more than any of the kings before him. And as though it were not enough to follow the example of Jeroboam, he married Jezebel, the daughter of King Ethbaal of the Sidonians, and he began to bow down in worship of Baal. First Ahab built a temple and an altar for Baal in Samaria. Then he set up an Asherah pole. He did more to provoke the anger of the LORD, the God of Israel, than any of the other kings of Israel before him" (1 Kings 16:30–33). |

Ahab's story is told in 1 Kings 16:28—22:40. He is also mentioned in 2 Chronicles 18—22; Micah 6:16.

**19:8** When Elijah fled to Mount Sinai, he was returning to the sacred place where God had met Moses and had given his laws to the people. Obviously, God gave Elijah special strength to travel this great distance—over 200 miles—without additional food. Like Moses before him and Jesus after him, Elijah fasted for 40 days and 40 nights (Deuteronomy 9:9; Matthew 4:1, 2). Centuries later, Moses, Elijah, and Jesus would meet together on a mountaintop (Luke 9:28-36).

### The Lord Speaks to Elijah

But the Lord said to him, "What are you doing here, Elijah?"

[10]Elijah replied, "I have zealously served the Lord God Almighty. But the people of Israel have broken their covenant with you, torn down your altars, and killed every one of your prophets. I am the only one left, and now they are trying to kill me, too."

[11]"Go out and stand before me on the mountain," the Lord told him. And as Elijah stood there, the Lord passed by, and a mighty windstorm hit the mountain. It was such a terrible blast that the rocks were torn loose, but the Lord was not in the wind. After the wind there was an earthquake, but the Lord was not in the earthquake. [12]And after the earthquake there was a fire, but the Lord was not in the fire. And after the fire there was the sound of a gentle whisper. [13]When Elijah heard it, he wrapped his face in his cloak and went out and stood at the entrance of the cave.

And a voice said, "What are you doing here, Elijah?"

[14]He replied again, "I have zealously served the Lord God Almighty. But the people of Israel have broken their covenant with you, torn down your altars, and killed every one of your prophets. I am the only one left, and now they are trying to kill me, too."

[15]The Lord told him, "Go back the same way you came, and travel to the wilderness of Damascus. When you arrive there, anoint Hazael to be king of Aram. [16]Then anoint Jehu grandson of Nimshi* to be king of Israel, and anoint Elisha son of Shaphat from the town of Abel-meholah to replace you as my prophet. [17]Anyone who escapes from Hazael will be killed by Jehu, and those who escape Jehu will be killed by Elisha! [18]Yet I will preserve 7,000 others in Israel who have never bowed down to Baal or kissed him!"

### The Call of Elisha

[19]So Elijah went and found Elisha son of Shaphat plowing a field. There were twelve teams of oxen in the field, and Elisha was plowing with the twelfth team. Elijah went over to him and threw his cloak across his shoulders and then walked away. [20]Elisha left the oxen standing there, ran after Elijah, and said to him, "First let me go and kiss my father and mother good-bye, and then I will go with you!"

Elijah replied, "Go on back, but think about what I have done to you."

[21]So Elisha returned to his oxen and slaughtered them. He used the wood from the plow to build a fire to roast their flesh. He passed around the meat to the townspeople, and they all ate. Then he went with Elijah as his assistant.

### Ben-Hadad Attacks Samaria

**20** About that time King Ben-hadad of Aram mobilized his army, supported by the chariots and horses of thirty-two allied kings. They went to besiege Samaria, the capital of Israel, and launched attacks against it. [2]Ben-hadad sent messengers into the city to

**19:16** Hebrew *descendant of Nimshi;* compare 2 Kgs 9:2, 14.

**19:10** †Rom 11:2-4

**19:11** Exod 19:16, 19-20; 24:12  Ezek 1:4

**19:12** Job 4:16

**19:13** Exod 3:6

**19:15** 2 Kgs 8:7-15

**19:16** 2 Kgs 2:9, 15; 9:1

**19:18** Hos 13:2 †Rom 11:4

**19:19** 2 Kgs 2:8, 13-14

**20:1** 1 Kgs 15:18  2 Kgs 6:24

**20:2** 2 Chr 16:2

---

**19:10** Elijah thought he was the only person left who was still true to God. He had seen both the king's court and the priesthood become corrupt. After experiencing great victory at Mount Carmel, he had to run for his life. Lonely and discouraged, he forgot that others had remained faithful during the nation's wickedness. When you are tempted to think that you are the only one remaining faithful to a task, don't stop to feel sorry for yourself. Self-pity will dilute the good you are doing. Be assured that even if you don't know who they are, others are faithfully obeying God and fulfilling their duties.

**19:11-13** Elijah knew that the sound of a gentle whisper was God's voice. He realized that God doesn't reveal himself only in powerful, miraculous ways. To look for God only in something big (rallies, churches, conferences, highly visible leaders) may be to miss him because he is often found gently whispering in the quietness of a humbled heart. Are you listening for God? Step back from the noise and activity of your busy life and listen humbly and quietly for his guidance. It may come when you least expect it.

**19:15, 16** God asked Elijah to anoint three different people. The first was Hazael, as king of Aram. Elijah was told to anoint an enemy king because God doesn't reveal himself as his instrument to punish Israel for its sin. Aram brought Israel's *external* punishment.

Israel's *internal* punishment came from Jehu, the next man

Elijah was to anoint. As king of Israel, Jehu would destroy those who worshiped the false god Baal (2 Kings 9-10).

The third person Elijah was told to anoint was Elisha, the prophet who would succeed him. Elisha's job was to work in Israel, the northern kingdom, to help point the people back to God. At this time, the southern kingdom was ruled by Jehoshaphat, a king devoted to God.

**19:18** Kissing Baal meant kissing some object representing him to show loyalty to him.

**19:19** The cloak was the most important article of clothing a person could own. It was used as protection against the weather, as bedding, as a place to sit, and as luggage. It could be given as a pledge for a debt or torn into pieces to show grief. Elijah put his cloak on Elisha's shoulders to show that he would become Elijah's successor. Later, when the transfer of authority was complete, Elijah left his cloak for Elisha (2 Kings 2:11-14).

**19:21** By killing his oxen, Elisha made a strong commitment to follow Elijah. Without them, he could not return to his life as a wealthy farmer. This meal was more than a feast among farmers. It was an offering of thanks to the Lord who chose Elisha to be his prophet.

**20:1ff** With two evil and two good kings up to this point, the southern kingdom, Judah, wavered between godly and ungodly living. But the northern kingdom, Israel, had eight evil kings in relay this message to King Ahab of Israel: "This is what Ben-hadad says: ³'Your silver and gold are mine, and so are your wives and the best of your children!'"

⁴"All right, my lord the king," Israel's king replied. "All that I have is yours!"

⁵Soon Ben-hadad's messengers returned again and said, "This is what Ben-hadad says: 'I have already demanded that you give me your silver, gold, wives, and children. ⁶But about this time tomorrow I will send my officials to search your palace and the homes of your people. They will take away everything you consider valuable!'"

**20:7**
2 Kgs 5:7

⁷Then Ahab summoned all the elders of the land and said to them, "Look how this man is stirring up trouble! I already agreed with his demand that I give him my wives and children and silver and gold."

⁸"Don't give in to any more demands," all the elders and the people advised.

⁹So Ahab told the messengers from Ben-hadad, "Say this to my lord the king: 'I will give you everything you asked for the first time, but I cannot accept this last demand of yours.'" So the messengers returned to Ben-hadad with that response.

**20:10**
1 Kgs 19:2
2 Kgs 6:31

¹⁰Then Ben-hadad sent this message to Ahab: "May the gods strike me and even kill me if there remains enough dust from Samaria to provide even a handful for each of my soldiers."

**20:11**
Prov 27:1

¹¹The king of Israel sent back this answer: "A warrior putting on his sword for battle should not boast like a warrior who has already won."

¹²Ahab's reply reached Ben-hadad and the other kings as they were drinking in their tents.* "Prepare to attack!" Ben-hadad commanded his officers. So they prepared to attack the city.

### Ahab's Victory over Ben-Hadad

¹³Then a certain prophet came to see King Ahab of Israel and told him, "This is what the LORD says: Do you see all these enemy forces? Today I will hand them all over to you. Then you will know that I am the LORD."

¹⁴Ahab asked, "How will he do it?"

And the prophet replied, "This is what the LORD says: The troops of the provincial commanders will do it."

"Should we attack first?" Ahab asked.

"Yes," the prophet answered.

**20:16**
1 Kgs 16:9

¹⁵So Ahab mustered the troops of the 232 provincial commanders. Then he called out the rest of the army of Israel, some 7,000 men. ¹⁶About noontime, as Ben-hadad and the thirty-two allied kings were still in their tents drinking themselves into a stupor, ¹⁷the troops of the provincial commanders marched out of the city as the first contingent.

As they approached, Ben-hadad's scouts reported to him, "Some troops are coming from Samaria."

**20:12** Or *in Succoth;* also in 20:16.

---

**GOD DELIVERS AHAB**
Despite Ahab's wickedness, God approached him in love. When Samaria was surrounded by Aramean forces, God miraculously delivered the city. But Ahab refused to give God credit. A year later, the Arameans attacked near Aphek. Again God gave Ahab victory, but again the king refused to acknowledge God's help.

Mediterranean Sea
ARAM
Sea of Galilee
N
Aram's first invasion
Aram's second invasion
Samaria
AHAB'S FORCES
Aphek
ISRAEL (Northern Kingdom)
Jerusalem
Dead Sea
JUDAH (Southern Kingdom)
0    20 Mi.
0    20 Km.

succession. To punish both kingdoms for living their own way instead of following God, God allowed other nations to gain strength and become their enemies. Three main enemies threatened Israel and Judah during the next two centuries—Aram, Assyria, and Babylon. Aram, the first to rise to power, presented an immediate threat to Ahab and Israel.

**20:13** God defeated the Aramean army for Ahab so that Ahab would know that God alone is the Lord. Despite this great victory and the one to follow on the plains (20:28, 29), Ahab continued to live without God. Evidence of God's greatness surrounds us, but, like Ahab, we can choose to ignore it and go our own way. But when we do, as with this evil king of Israel, disaster will strike. Open your eyes to the evidence—the victories that God is winning for you. Then rededicate yourself to him.

¹⁸"Take them alive," Ben-hadad commanded, "whether they have come for peace or for war."

¹⁹But Ahab's provincial commanders and the entire army had now come out to fight. ²⁰Each Israelite soldier killed his Aramean opponent, and suddenly the entire Aramean army panicked and fled. The Israelites chased them, but King Ben-hadad and a few of his charioteers escaped on horses. ²¹However, the king of Israel destroyed the other horses and chariots and slaughtered the Arameans.

²²Afterward the prophet said to King Ahab, "Get ready for another attack. Begin making plans now, for the king of Aram will come back next spring.*"

> **20:22**
> 2 Sam 11:1

### Ben-Hadad's Second Attack

²³After their defeat, Ben-hadad's officers said to him, "The Israelite gods are gods of the hills; that is why they won. But we can beat them easily on the plains. ²⁴Only this time replace the kings with field commanders! ²⁵Recruit another army like the one you lost. Give us the same number of horses, chariots, and men, and we will fight against them on the plains. There's no doubt that we will beat them." So King Ben-hadad did as they suggested.

²⁶The following spring he called up the Aramean army and marched out against Israel, this time at Aphek. ²⁷Israel then mustered its army, set up supply lines, and marched out for battle. But the Israelite army looked like two little flocks of goats in comparison to the vast Aramean forces that filled the countryside!

> **20:26**
> 2 Kgs 13:17
> **20:27**
> Judg 6:3-5
> 1 Sam 13:5-8

²⁸Then the man of God went to the king of Israel and said, "This is what the LORD says: The Arameans have said, 'The LORD is a god of the hills and not of the plains.' So I will defeat this vast army for you. Then you will know that I am the LORD."

²⁹The two armies camped opposite each other for seven days, and on the seventh day the battle began. The Israelites killed 100,000 Aramean foot soldiers in one day. ³⁰The rest fled into the town of Aphek, but the wall fell on them and killed another 27,000. Ben-hadad fled into the town and hid in a secret room.

> **20:30**
> 1 Kgs 22:25
> 2 Chr 18:24

³¹Ben-hadad's officers said to him, "Sir, we have heard that the kings of Israel are merciful. So let's humble ourselves by wearing burlap around our waists and putting ropes on our heads, and surrender to the king of Israel. Then perhaps he will let you live."

> **20:31**
> Gen 37:34

³²So they put on burlap and ropes, and they went to the king of Israel and begged, "Your servant Ben-hadad says, 'Please let me live!'"

The king of Israel responded, "Is he still alive? He is my brother!"

³³The men took this as a good sign and quickly picked up on his words. "Yes," they said, "your brother Ben-hadad!"

"Go and get him," the king of Israel told them. And when Ben-hadad arrived, Ahab invited him up into his chariot.

³⁴Ben-hadad told him, "I will give back the towns my father took from your father, and you may establish places of trade in Damascus, as my father did in Samaria."

> **20:34**
> 1 Kgs 15:20

Then Ahab said, "I will release you under these conditions." So they made a new treaty, and Ben-hadad was set free.

### A Prophet Condemns Ahab

³⁵Meanwhile, the LORD instructed one of the group of prophets to say to another man, "Hit me!" But the man refused to hit the prophet. ³⁶Then the prophet told him, "Because you have not obeyed the voice of the LORD, a lion will kill you as soon as you leave me." And when he had gone, a lion did attack and kill him.

> **20:35**
> 1 Kgs 13:16-18
> **20:36**
> 1 Kgs 13:24

³⁷Then the prophet turned to another man and said, "Hit me!" So he struck the prophet and wounded him.

**20:22** Hebrew *at the turn of the year;* similarly in 20:26. The first day of the year in the ancient Hebrew lunar calendar occurred in March or April.

---

**20:23** Since the days of Joshua, Israel's soldiers had the reputation of being superior fighters in the hills but ineffective in the open plains and valleys because they did not use chariots in battle. Horse-drawn chariots, useless in hilly terrain and dense forests, could easily run down great numbers of foot soldiers on the plains. What Ben-hadad's officers did not understand was that God, not chariots, made the difference in battle.

**20:31** Burlap was coarse cloth usually made of goats' hair and was worn as a symbol of mourning for the dead or for natural disaster. Wearing ropes around the head may have been a symbol of putting oneself at another's disposal. In other words, Ahab could have hung them if he wished. Wearing ropes around the head, therefore, showed submission.

**20:35, 36** The prophet needed a wound so he would look like an injured soldier and could effectively deliver his prophecy to Ahab. The first man was killed by a lion because he refused to obey the Lord's instructions through the prophet.

**20:38**
1 Kgs 14:2
**20:39**
2 Kgs 10:24

³⁸The prophet placed a bandage over his eyes to disguise himself and then waited beside the road for the king. ³⁹As the king passed by, the prophet called out to him, "Sir, I was in the thick of battle, and suddenly a man brought me a prisoner. He said, 'Guard this man; if for any reason he gets away, you will either die or pay a fine of seventy-five pounds* of silver!' ⁴⁰But while I was busy doing something else, the prisoner disappeared!"

"Well, it's your own fault," the king replied. "You have brought the judgment on yourself."

⁴¹Then the prophet quickly pulled the bandage from his eyes, and the king of Israel recognized him as one of the prophets. ⁴²The prophet said to him, "This is what the Lord says: Because you have spared the man I said must be destroyed,* now you must die in his place, and your people will die instead of his people." ⁴³So the king of Israel went home to Samaria angry and sullen.

**20:43**
1 Kgs 21:4

20:39 Hebrew *1 talent* [34 kilograms].   20:42 The Hebrew term used here refers to the complete consecration of things or people to the Lord, either by destroying them or by giving them as an offering.

---

The Bible is as honest about the lives of its heroes as it is about those who rejected God. Some Bible characters found out what God can do with failures when they turned to him. Many, however, neither admitted their failures nor turned to God.

Jezebel ranks as the most evil woman in the Bible. The Bible even uses her name as an example of people who completely reject God (Revelation 2:20, 21). Many pagan women married into Israel without acknowledging the God their husbands worshiped. They brought their religions with them. But no one was as determined as Jezebel to make all Israel worship *her* gods. To the prophet Elijah, she seemed to have succeeded. He felt he was the only one still faithful to God until God told him there were still 7,000 who had not turned from the faith. Jezebel's one outstanding "success" was in contributing to the cause of the eventual downfall of the northern kingdom—idolatry. God punished the northern tribes for their idolatry by having them carried off into captivity.

Jezebel held great power. She not only managed her husband, Ahab, but she also had 850 assorted pagan priests under her control. She was committed to her gods and to getting what she wanted. She believed that the king had the right to possess anything he wanted. When Naboth refused to sell Ahab his vineyard, Jezebel ruthlessly had Naboth killed and took ownership of the land. Jezebel's plan to wipe out worship of God in Israel led to painful consequences. Before she died, Jezebel suffered the loss of her husband in combat and her son at the hand of Jehu, who took the throne by force. She died in the defiant and scornful way she had lived.

When comparing Jezebel and Elijah, we have to admire each one's strength of commitment. The big difference was to *whom* they were committed. Jezebel was committed to herself and her false gods; Elijah was totally committed to the one true God. In the end, God proved Elijah right. To what or to whom are you most committed? How would God evaluate your commitment?

| | |
|---|---|
| **Weaknesses and mistakes** | • Systematically eliminated the representatives of God in Israel<br>• Promoted and funded Baal worship<br>• Threatened to have Elijah killed<br>• Believed kings and queens could rightfully do or have anything they wanted<br>• Used her strong convictions to get her own way |
| **Lessons from her life** | • It is not enough to be committed or sincere. Where our commitment lies makes a great difference<br>• Rejecting God always leads to disaster |
| **Vital statistics** | • Where: Sidon, Samaria<br>• Occupation: Queen of Israel<br>• Relatives: Husband: Ahab. Father: Ethbaal. Sons: Joram, Ahaziah.<br>• Contemporaries: Elijah, Jehu |
| **Key verse** | "No one else so completely sold himself to what was evil in the Lord's sight as Ahab did under the influence of his wife Jezebel" (1 Kings 21:25). |

Jezebel's story is told in 1 Kings 16:31—2 Kings 9:37. Her name is used as a synonym for great evil in Revelation 2:20.

---

**20:41, 42** It is difficult to explain why Ahab let Ben-hadad go, especially after all the trouble the Arameans had caused him. God helped Ahab destroy the Aramean army to prove to Ahab and to Aram that he alone was God. But Ahab failed to destroy the king, his greatest enemy. Ben-hadad was under God's judgment to die, and Ahab had no authority to let him live. For this, God told Ahab that he must now die instead. This prophet's message soon came true when Ahab was killed on the battlefield (22:35).

## Naboth's Vineyard

**21** Now there was a man named Naboth, from Jezreel, who owned a vineyard in Jezreel beside the palace of King Ahab of Samaria. ²One day Ahab said to Naboth, "Since your vineyard is so convenient to my palace, I would like to buy it to use as a vegetable garden. I will give you a better vineyard in exchange, or if you prefer, I will pay you for it."

³But Naboth replied, "The LORD forbid that I should give you the inheritance that was passed down by my ancestors."

⁴So Ahab went home angry and sullen because of Naboth's answer. The king went to bed with his face to the wall and refused to eat!

⁵"What's the matter?" his wife Jezebel asked him. "What's made you so upset that you're not eating?"

⁶"I asked Naboth to sell me his vineyard or trade it, but he refused!" Ahab told her.

⁷"Are you the king of Israel or not?" Jezebel demanded. "Get up and eat something, and don't worry about it. I'll get you Naboth's vineyard!"

⁸So she wrote letters in Ahab's name, sealed them with his seal, and sent them to the elders and other leaders of the town where Naboth lived. ⁹In her letters she commanded: "Call the citizens together for fasting and prayer, and give Naboth a place of honor. ¹⁰And then seat two scoundrels across from him who will accuse him of cursing God and the king. Then take him out and stone him to death."

¹¹So the elders and other town leaders followed the instructions Jezebel had written in the letters. ¹²They called for a fast and put Naboth at a prominent place before the people. ¹³Then the two scoundrels came and sat down across from him. And they accused Naboth before all the people, saying, "He cursed God and the king." So he was dragged outside the town and stoned to death. ¹⁴The town leaders then sent word to Jezebel, "Naboth has been stoned to death."

¹⁵When Jezebel heard the news, she said to Ahab, "You know the vineyard Naboth wouldn't sell you? Well, you can have it now! He's dead!" ¹⁶So Ahab immediately went down to the vineyard of Naboth to claim it.

¹⁷But the LORD said to Elijah,* ¹⁸"Go down to meet King Ahab of Israel, who rules in Samaria. He will be at Naboth's vineyard in Jezreel, claiming it for himself. ¹⁹Give him this message: 'This is what the LORD says: Wasn't it enough that you killed Naboth? Must you rob him, too? Because you have done this, dogs will lick your blood at the very place where they licked the blood of Naboth!'"

²⁰"So, my enemy, you have found me!" Ahab exclaimed to Elijah.

"Yes," Elijah answered, "I have come because you have sold yourself to what is evil in the LORD's sight. ²¹So now the LORD says, 'I will bring disaster on you and consume you. I will destroy every one of your male descendants, slave and free alike, anywhere in Israel! ²²I am going to destroy your family as I did the family of Jeroboam son of Nebat and the family of Baasha son of Ahijah, for you have made me very angry and have led Israel into sin.'

²³"And regarding Jezebel, the LORD says, 'Dogs will eat Jezebel's body at the plot of land in Jezreel.*'

²⁴"The members of Ahab's family who die in the city will be eaten by dogs, and those who die in the field will be eaten by vultures."

²⁵(No one else so completely sold himself to what was evil in the LORD's sight as Ahab did under the influence of his wife Jezebel. ²⁶His worst outrage was worshiping idols* just as the Amorites had done—the people whom the LORD had driven out from the land ahead of the Israelites.

---

**21:1** 2 Kgs 9:21

**21:3** Lev 25:23 Num 36:6-7 Ezek 46:18

**21:7** 1 Sam 8:14

**21:8** 2 Sam 11:14 2 Chr 32:17 Esth 3:12; 8:8

**21:10** Exod 22:28 Lev 24:15-16 Acts 6:11

**21:19** 1 Kgs 22:38 2 Kgs 9:26

**21:20** 1 Kgs 18:17 Rom 7:14

**21:21** 1 Kgs 14:10 2 Kgs 9:8

**21:22** 1 Kgs 14:16; 15:29; 16:3

**21:23** 2 Kgs 9:10, 30-37

**21:24** 1 Kgs 14:11; 16:4-7

**21:26** Gen 15:16 Lev 18:25-30 2 Kgs 21:11

---

**21:17** Hebrew *Elijah the Tishbite;* also in 21:28. **21:23** As in several Hebrew manuscripts, Syriac, and Latin Vulgate (see also 2 Kgs 9:26, 36); most Hebrew manuscripts read *at the city wall.* **21:26** The Hebrew term (literally *round things*) probably alludes to dung.

---

**21:4** After hearing God's judgment (20:42), Ahab went home to pout. Driven by anger and rebellion against God, he had a fit of rage when Naboth refused to sell his vineyard. The same feelings that led him to a career of power grabbing drove him to resent Naboth. Rage turned to hatred and led to murder. Naboth, however, wanted to uphold God's laws: It was considered a duty to keep ancestral land in the family. This incident shows the cruel interplay between Ahab and Jezebel, two of the most wicked leaders in Israel's history.

**21:13** Jezebel devised a scheme that appeared legal to get the land for her husband. Two witnesses were required to establish

guilt, and the punishment for blasphemy was death by stoning. Those who twist the law and legal procedures to get what they want today may be more sophisticated in how they go about it, but they are guilty of the same sin.

**21:19, 23** For the fulfillment of these verses, see 22:38 where dogs licked Ahab's blood, and 2 Kings 9:30–10:28 where Jezebel and the rest of Ahab's family were destroyed.

**21:20** Ahab still refused to admit his sin against God. Instead, he accused Elijah of being his enemy. When we are blinded by envy and hatred, we find it almost impossible to see our own sin.

21:27
Gen 37:34
2 Kgs 6:26-30

21:29
1 Kgs 22:38
2 Kgs 9:25-37
2 Chr 12:7; 34:27

<sup>27</sup>But when Ahab heard this message, he tore his clothing, dressed in burlap, and fasted. He even slept in burlap and went about in deep mourning.

<sup>28</sup>Then another message from the LORD came to Elijah: <sup>29</sup>"Do you see how Ahab has humbled himself before me? Because he has done this, I will not do what I promised during his lifetime. It will happen to his sons; I will destroy his dynasty."

## 4. Kings of Israel and Judah
### Jehoshaphat and Ahab

22:1-28
//2 Chr 18:1-27

22:2
1 Kgs 15:24

22:3
Deut 4:43

22:4
2 Kgs 3:6-8

22:5
2 Kgs 3:11

**22** For three years there was no war between Aram and Israel. <sup>2</sup>Then during the third year, King Jehoshaphat of Judah went to visit King Ahab of Israel. <sup>3</sup>During the visit, the king of Israel said to his officials, "Do you realize that the town of Ramoth-gilead belongs to us? And yet we've done nothing to recapture it from the king of Aram!"

<sup>4</sup>Then he turned to Jehoshaphat and asked, "Will you join me in battle to recover Ramoth-gilead?"

Jehoshaphat replied to the king of Israel, "Why, of course! You and I are as one. My troops are your troops, and my horses are your horses." <sup>5</sup>Then Jehoshaphat added, "But first let's find out what the LORD says."

<sup>6</sup>So the king of Israel summoned the prophets, about 400 of them, and asked them, "Should I go to war against Ramoth-gilead, or should I hold back?"

They all replied, "Yes, go right ahead! The Lord will give the king victory."

## KINGS TO DATE AND THEIR ENEMIES

**874**
**AHAB**
Twice defeated
Ben-hadad II
(Aram) and was
later killed in battle
against Aram
1 Kgs 16:28—22:40
2 Chr 18:1–34

**853**
**AHAZIAH**
1 Kgs 22:40—
2 Kgs 1:18
2 Chr 20:35–37

852

*I S R A E L*

*J U D A H*

869

**872**
**JEHOSHAPHAT**
Defeated by Ben-
hadad II (Aram),
gained miraculous
victory over Moab
and Ammon, and
crushed a rebellion
by Mesha (Moab)
1 Kgs 22:41–50
2 Chr 17:1—21:1
Co-regency
853–848

853  848  841

**JEHORAM**
Lost dominion
over Edom,
assaulted by
Philistines and
Arabs
2 Kgs 8:16–24
2 Chr 21:1–20

**910**
**ASA**
Defeated Zerah
(the Ethiopian) and
harassed Baasha
1 Kgs 15:8–24
2 Chr 14:1—16:14
Co-regency
872–869

All dates are B.C.
Solid section of the timeline indicates co-regency.
For all the kings of Israel and Judah, see the chart
at the end of 1 Kings.

**21:29** Ahab was more wicked than any other king of Israel (16:30; 21:25), but when he repented in deep humility, God took notice and reduced his punishment. The same Lord who was merciful to Ahab wants to be merciful to you. No matter how evil you have been, it is never too late to humble yourself, turn to God, and ask for forgiveness.

**22:6** These 400 prophets may have been the 400 Asherah

priests left alive by Elijah at Carmel, although 450 prophets of Baal were killed (see 18:19-40).

7 But Jehoshaphat asked, "Is there not also a prophet of the LORD here? We should ask him the same question."

8 The king of Israel replied to Jehoshaphat, "There is one more man who could consult the LORD for us, but I hate him. He never prophesies anything but trouble for me! His name is Micaiah son of Imlah."

Jehoshaphat replied, "That's not the way a king should talk! Let's hear what he has to say."

9 So the king of Israel called one of his officials and said, "Quick! Bring Micaiah son of Imlah."

## Micaiah Prophesies against Ahab

10 King Ahab of Israel and King Jehoshaphat of Judah, dressed in their royal robes, were sitting on thrones at the threshing floor near the gate of Samaria. All of Ahab's prophets were prophesying there in front of them. 11 One of them, Zedekiah son of Kenaanah, made some iron horns and proclaimed, "This is what the LORD says: With these horns you will gore the Arameans to death!"

12 All the other prophets agreed. "Yes," they said, "go up to Ramoth-gilead and be victorious, for the LORD will give the king victory!"

13 Meanwhile, the messenger who went to get Micaiah said to him, "Look, all the prophets are promising victory for the king. Be sure that you agree with them and promise success."

14 But Micaiah replied, "As surely as the LORD lives, I will say only what the LORD tells me to say."

15 When Micaiah arrived before the king, Ahab asked him, "Micaiah, should we go to war against Ramoth-gilead, or should we hold back?"

Micaiah replied sarcastically, "Yes, go up and be victorious, for the LORD will give the king victory!"

16 But the king replied sharply, "How many times must I demand that you speak only the truth to me when you speak for the LORD?"

17 Then Micaiah told him, "In a vision I saw all Israel scattered on the mountains, like sheep without a shepherd. And the LORD said, 'Their master has been killed.* Send them home in peace.'"

18 "Didn't I tell you?" the king of Israel exclaimed to Jehoshaphat. "He never prophesies anything but trouble for me."

19 Then Micaiah continued, "Listen to what the LORD says! I saw the LORD sitting on his throne with all the armies of heaven around him, on his right and on his left. 20 And the LORD said, 'Who can entice Ahab to go into battle against Ramoth-gilead so he can be killed?'

"There were many suggestions, 21 and finally a spirit approached the LORD and said, 'I can do it!'

22:7
2 Kgs 3:11

22:11
Deut 33:17
2 Chr 18:10
Zech 1:18-21

22:14
Num 22:18; 24:13
2 Chr 18:13

22:17
Num 27:17
1 Kgs 22:33-37
†Matt 9:36
Mark 6:34

22:19
Isa 6:1
Dan 7:9-10

22:17 Hebrew These people have no master.

---

22:7 Jehoshaphat knew the difference between these pagan prophets and the "prophet of the LORD," so he asked if God's prophet was available. Evidently Jehoshaphat wanted to do what was right, although Ahab didn't. Both kings disregarded God's message, however, and listened only to the pagan prophets.

22:10 Threshing floors were placed in elevated areas to allow the wind to blow away the discarded hulls of grain.

22:15, 16 Why did Micaiah tell Ahab to attack when he had previously vowed to speak only what God had told him? Perhaps he was speaking sarcastically, making fun of the messages from the pagan prophets by showing that they were telling the king only what he wanted to hear. Somehow, Micaiah's tone of voice let everyone know he was mocking the pagan prophets. When confronted, he predicted that the king would die and the battle would be lost. Although Ahab repented temporarily (21:27), he still maintained the system of false prophets. These false prophets would be instrumental in leading him to his own ruin.

22:19-22 The vision Micaiah saw was either a picture of a real incident in heaven or a parable of what was happening on earth, illustrating that the seductive influence of the false prophets would be part of God's judgment upon Ahab (22:23). Whether or not God sent an angel in disguise, he used the system of false prophets to snare Ahab in his sin. The lying spirit (22:22) symbolized the way of life for these prophets, who told the king only what he wanted to hear.

22:20-22 Does God allow angels to entice people to do evil? To understand evil, we must first understand God. (1) God himself is good (Psalm 11:7). (2) God created a good world that fell because of sin (Romans 5:12). (3) Someday God will recreate the world, and it will be good again (Revelation 21:1). (4) God is stronger than evil (Matthew 13:41-43; Revelation 19:11-21). (5) God allows evil, and thus he has control over it. God did not create evil, and he offers help to those who wish to overcome it (Matthew 11:28-30). (6) God uses everything—both good and evil—for his good purposes (Genesis 50:20; Romans 8:28).

The Bible shows us a God who hates all evil and will one day do away with it completely and forever (Revelation 20:10-15). God does not entice anyone to become evil. Those committed to evil, however, may be used by God to sin even more in order to hurry their deserved judgment (Exodus 11:10). We don't need to understand every detail of how God works in order to have perfect confidence in his absolute power over evil and his total goodness toward us.

**22:22**
Judg 9:23
2 Thes 2:11

22 " 'How will you do this?' the Lord asked.

"And the spirit replied, 'I will go out and inspire all of Ahab's prophets to speak lies.'

" 'You will succeed,' said the Lord. 'Go ahead and do it.'

**22:23**
Ezek 14:9

23 "So you see, the Lord has put a lying spirit in the mouths of all your prophets. For the Lord has pronounced your doom."

**22:24**
2 Chr 18:23

24 Then Zedekiah son of Kenaanah walked up to Micaiah and slapped him across the face. "Since when did the Spirit of the Lord leave me to speak to you?" he demanded.

25 And Micaiah replied, "You will find out soon enough when you are trying to hide in some secret room!"

**22:27**
2 Chr 16:10;
18:25-27

26 "Arrest him!" the king of Israel ordered. "Take him back to Amon, the governor of the city, and to my son Joash. 27 Give them this order from the king: 'Put this man in prison, and feed him nothing but bread and water until I return safely from the battle!' "

**22:28**
Deut 18:22

28 But Micaiah replied, "If you return safely, it will mean that the Lord has not spoken through me!" Then he added to those standing around, "Everyone mark my words!"

### The Death of Ahab

**22:29-36**
//2 Chr 18:28-34

**22:30**
2 Chr 35:22

29 So King Ahab of Israel and King Jehoshaphat of Judah led their armies against Ramoth-gilead. 30 The king of Israel said to Jehoshaphat, "As we go into battle, I will disguise myself so no one will recognize me, but you wear your royal robes." So the king of Israel disguised himself, and they went into battle.

**22:31**
2 Chr 18:30

31 Meanwhile, the king of Aram had issued these orders to his thirty-two chariot commanders: "Attack only the king of Israel. Don't bother with anyone else!" 32 So when the Aramean chariot commanders saw Jehoshaphat in his royal robes, they went after him. "There is the king of Israel!" they shouted. But when Jehoshaphat called out, 33 the chariot commanders realized he was not the king of Israel, and they stopped chasing him.

34 An Aramean soldier, however, randomly shot an arrow at the Israelite troops and hit the king of Israel between the joints of his armor. "Turn the horses* and get me out of here!" Ahab groaned to the driver of his chariot. "I'm badly wounded!"

35 The battle raged all that day, and the king remained propped up in his chariot facing the Arameans. The blood from his wound ran down to the floor of his chariot, and as evening arrived he died. 36 Just as the sun was setting, the cry ran through his troops: "We're done for! Run for your lives!"

**22:38**
1 Kgs 21:19

37 So the king died, and his body was taken to Samaria and buried there. 38 Then his chariot was washed beside the pool of Samaria, and dogs came and licked his blood at the place where the prostitutes bathed,* just as the Lord had promised.

**22:39**
Amos 3:15

39 The rest of the events in Ahab's reign and everything he did, including the story of the ivory palace and the towns he built, are recorded in *The Book of the History of the Kings of Israel.* 40 So Ahab died, and his son Ahaziah became the next king.

### Jehoshaphat Rules in Judah

**22:41-50**
//2 Chr 20:31–21:1

41 Jehoshaphat son of Asa began to rule over Judah in the fourth year of King Ahab's reign in Israel. 42 Jehoshaphat was thirty-five years old when he became king, and he reigned in Jerusalem twenty-five years. His mother was Azubah, the daughter of Shilhi.

**22:43**
1 Kgs 15:14
2 Kgs 12:3

43 Jehoshaphat was a good king, following the example of his father, Asa. He did what was pleasing in the Lord's sight. *During his reign, however, he failed to remove all the pagan shrines, and the people still offered sacrifices and burned incense there. 44 Jehoshaphat also made peace with the king of Israel.

**22:34** Hebrew *Turn your hand.*   **22:38** Or *his blood, and the prostitutes bathed [in it];* or *his blood, and they washed his armor.*   **22:43** Verses 22:43b-53 are numbered 22:44-54 in Hebrew text.

---

**22:34** Ahab could not escape God's judgment. The king of Aram sent 32 of his best chariot commanders with the sole purpose of killing Ahab. Thinking he could escape, Ahab tried a disguise, but a random arrow struck him while the chariots chased the wrong king—Jehoshaphat. It was foolish for Ahab to think he could escape by wearing a disguise. Sometimes people try to escape reality by disguising themselves— changing jobs, moving to a new town, even changing spouses. But God sees and evaluates the motives of each person. Any attempted disguise is futile.

**22:35** Just as the prophet had predicted (20:42), Ahab was killed. See Ahab's Profile in chapter 19, p. 549, for more of Ahab's sad story.

**22:41-50** For more details on Jehoshaphat, see the other account of his reign in 2 Chronicles 17–20.

**22:43** Just like his ancestors Solomon and Asa, Jehoshaphat followed God, but he didn't remove the pagan shrines in the hills (2 Chronicles 20:33). It was against God's laws to worship idols in the shrines (Numbers 33:52), and at first Jehoshaphat attempted to remove them (2 Chronicles 17:6). They were so popular, however, that this proved difficult. In spite of Jehoshaphat's many contributions to the spiritual, moral, and material health of his country, he did not succeed in eradicating the hill shrines.

45 The rest of the events in Jehoshaphat's reign, the extent of his power, and the wars he waged are recorded in *The Book of the History of the Kings of Judah*. 46 He banished from the land the rest of the male and female shrine prostitutes, who still continued their practices from the days of his father, Asa.

47 (There was no king in Edom at that time, only a deputy.)

48 Jehoshaphat also built a fleet of trading ships* to sail to Ophir for gold. But the ships never set sail, for they met with disaster in their home port of Ezion-geber. 49 At one time Ahaziah son of Ahab had proposed to Jehoshaphat, "Let my men sail with your men in the ships." But Jehoshaphat refused the request.

50 When Jehoshaphat died, he was buried with his ancestors in the City of David. Then his son Jehoram became the next king.

## Ahaziah Rules in Israel

51 Ahaziah son of Ahab began to rule over Israel in the seventeenth year of King Jehoshaphat's reign in Judah. He reigned in Samaria two years. 52 But he did what was evil in the LORD's sight, following the example of his father and mother and the example of Jeroboam son of Nebat, who had led Israel to sin. 53 He served Baal and worshiped him, provoking the anger of the LORD, the God of Israel, just as his father had done.

22:48 Hebrew *fleet of ships of Tarshish*.

**22:46**
Deut 23:17
1 Kgs 15:12

**22:47**
2 Sam 8:14
2 Kgs 3:9

**22:48**
1 Kgs 9:26-28

**22:50**
2 Chr 21:1

**22:52**
1 Kgs 15:26

---

**22:52, 53** The book of 1 Kings begins with a nation united under David, the most devout king in Israel's history. The book ends with a divided kingdom and the death of Ahab, the most wicked king of all. What happened? The people forgot to acknowledge God as their ultimate leader; they appointed human leaders who ignored God; then they conformed to the life-styles of these evil leaders.

Occasional wrongdoing gradually turned into a way of life. Their blatant wickedness could be met only with judgment from God, who allowed enemy nations to arise and defeat Israel and Judah in battle as punishment for their sins. Failing to acknowledge God as our ultimate leader is the first step toward ruin.

**NAMES OF GOD**

| Name of God | Meaning | Reference | Significance |
|---|---|---|---|
| Elohim | God | Genesis 1:1; Numbers 23:19; Psalm 19:1 | Refers to God's power and might. He is the only supreme and true God. |
| Yahweh | The LORD | Genesis 2:4; Exodus 6:2, 3 | The proper name of the divine person. |
| El Elyon | God Most High | Genesis 14:17-20; Numbers 24:16; Psalm 7:17; Isaiah 14:13, 14 | He is above all gods; nothing in life is more sacred. |
| El Roi | God Who Sees | Genesis 16:13 | God oversees all creation and the affairs of people. |
| El Shaddai | God Almighty | Genesis 17:1; Psalm 91:1 | God is all-powerful. |
| Yahweh Yireh | The LORD Will Provide | Genesis 22:13, 14 | God will provide our real needs. |
| Yahweh Nissi | The LORD Is My Banner | Exodus 17:15 | We should remember God for helping us. |
| Adonai | Lord | Deuteronomy 6:4 | God alone is the head over all. |
| Yahweh Elohe Yisrael | LORD God of Israel | Judges 5:3; Psalm 59:5; Isaiah 17:6; Zephaniah 2:9 | He is the God of the nation. |
| Yahweh Shalom | The LORD Is Peace | Judges 6:24 | God gives us peace so we need not fear. |
| Qedosh Yisrael | Holy One of Israel | Isaiah 1:4 | God is morally perfect. |
| Yahweh Sabaoth | LORD of Hosts (*Hosts* refers to armies but also to all the heavenly powers.) | 1 Samuel 1:3; Isaiah 6:1-3 | God is our savior and protector. |
| El Olam | The Everlasting God | Isaiah 40:28-31 | God is eternal. He will never die. |
| Yahweh Tsidkenu | The LORD Is Our Righteousness | Jeremiah 23:6; 33:16 | God is our standard for right behavior. He alone can make us righteous. |
| Yahweh Shammah | The LORD Is There | Ezekiel 48:35 | God is always present with us. |
| Attiq Yomin | Ancient of Days | Daniel 7:9, 13 | God is the ultimate authority. He will one day judge all nations. |

# A HARMONY OF THE BOOKS OF KINGS AND CHRONICLES

This chart gives a harmony of the history recorded in 1 & 2 Kings and 1 & 2 Chronicles. It provides you with the names of the kings listed chronologically (showing those in the northern kingdom at the top and the southern kingdom at the bottom), a brief overview of each king's reign, and where you can read about each king. The bold lines above and below the chart give you the names and timelines of prophets who prophesied during the reigns of particular kings.

ELIJAH 875–848

AHIJAH 934–909

**930**
**JEROBOAM I**
*(22 years)*
*Fortified a capital city (Shechem), set up two golden calf-idols, led the nation into sin, allowed anyone to be a priest*
*1 Kgs 11:26—14:34*
*2 Chr 10:12—13:20*

**909**
**NADAB**
*(2 years)*
*1 Kgs 15:25–28*

**908**
**BAASHA**
*(24 years)*
*Led people into idol worship*
*1 Kgs 15:27—16:7*
*2 Chr 16:1–6*

**886**
**ELAH**
*(2 years)*
*Continued idol worship*
*1 Kgs 16:6–14*

**885**
**ZIMRI**
*(7 days)*
*1 Kgs 16:9–20*

**885**
**OMRI**
*(12 years)*
*Built the capital city of Samaria, had great military power, but continued to lead Israel into idolatry*
*1 Kgs 16:16–28*

**885**
**TIBNI**
*(4 years)*
*1 Kgs 16:21–22*

**874**
**AHAB**
*(22 years)*
*Married Jezebel (a non-Jew and extremely wicked woman), worshiped Baal, and suffered three years of famine caused by his consistent disobedience to God*
*1 Kgs 16:28—22:40*
*2 Chr 18:1–34*

**CAPITAL: SHECHEM, THEN TIRZAH, THEN SAMARIA**
**THE NORTHERN KINGDOM OF ISRAEL (TEN TRIBES)**

**THE SOUTHERN KINGDOM OF JUDAH (TWO TRIBES)**
**CAPITAL: JERUSALEM**

**930**
**REHOBOAM**
*(17 years)*
*Built many fortified cities, strengthened the economy (despite the tribute paid to Egypt), followed God for three years, but then set up idols and shrines to foreign gods*
*1 Kgs 11:43—14:31*
*2 Chr 9:31—12:16*

**913**
**ABIJAH**
*(3 years)*
*Despite his wickedness, he called for God's help to win the battle against Israel*
*1 Kgs 14:31—15:8*
*2 Chr 13:1—14:1*

**910**
**ASA**
*(41 years)*
*Destroyed pagan altars and rebuilt altar of God, built fortified cities, gained much wealth from plunder of foreign conquest, removed the queen mother for worshiping Asherah, led the people to worship God with their hearts, provided peace on home soil, was greatly loved and given a beautiful funeral*
*1 Kgs 15:8–24*
*2 Chr 14:1—16:14*

**872**
**JEHOSHAPHAT**
*(25 years)*
*Arranged for the marriage of his son to a daughter of Ahab (who made trouble later on), had a strong military (kept troops in cities of Israel his father had conquered), collected tribute from the Philistines, worshiped the Lord and destroyed idols, established education, and appointed judges and courts*
*1 Kgs 15:24; 22:41–50*
*2 Chr 17:1—21:1*

All dates are B.C. The total years of reign sometimes includes years of co-regency.

ELISHA 848–797

JONAH 793–753(?)

**841**
**JEHU**
*(28 years)*
*Was responsible for
the deaths of Joram
(king of Israel),
Ahaziah (king of
Judah), and Jezebel
(wicked mother of
Joram); destroyed the
priests and temples of
Baal but did not con-
sistently follow God
2 Kgs 9:1—10:36
2 Chr 22:7–12*

**798**
**JEHOASH**
*(16 years)*
*Even though he was
evil, he recognized
the authority of Elisha
as a prophet of God
2 Kgs 13:10—14:16
2 Chr 25:17–24*

**853**
**AHAZIAH**
*(2 years)*
*Proposed a joint
trade venture
with Judah
1 Kgs 22:40—
2 Kgs 1:18
2 Chr 20:35–37*

**852**
**JORAM**
*(12 years)*
*Suffered famine
and war during
most of his reign
2 Kgs 3:1—8:25
2 Chr 22:5–7*

**814**
**JEHOAHAZ**
*(17 years)*
*Evil reign included
worship of Asherah,
usually called
"detestable"
2 Kgs 13:1–9*

**793**
**JEROBOAM II**
*(41 years)*
*Very evil but
politically
powerful; his
nation enjoyed
economic
prosperity and
military peace
2 Kgs 14:16–29*

**853**
**JEHORAM**
*(8 years)*
*Married a wicked
daughter of Ahab,
compelled the
people to worship
idols, and killed
all his brothers
2 Kgs 8:16–24
2 Chr 21:1–20*

**841**
**AHAZIAH**
*(1 year)*
*Friend of Joram
of Israel
2 Kgs 8:24—9:29
2 Chr 22:1–10*

**841**
**ATHALIAH
(QUEEN)**
*(6 years)*
*Killed all her
grandchildren
except Joash,
who was hidden
by his nurse for
six years, ravaged
the Temple to
furnish Baal's temple
2 Kgs 11:1–20
2 Chr 22:10—23:21*

**835**
**JOASH**
*(40 years)*
*Was crowned king
at the age of seven
by Jehoiada (the
high priest), pro-
moted peace and
prosperity, repaired
the Temple, and
smashed the altars
to Baal; abandoned
God after Jehoiada
died, and even
had Jehoiada's
son killed
2 Kgs 11:2—12:21
2 Chr 22:11—24:27*

**796**
**AMAZIAH**
*(29 years)*
*Was basically
good but did not
completely wipe
out idol worship;
organized and
mustered the army
2 Kgs 14:1–20
2 Chr 25:1–28*

**792**
**UZZIAH**
*(52 years)*
*Rebuilt a city named
Elath, owned many
farms and vineyards,
constructed water
reservoirs and
fortified towers,
reorganized the
army (so powerful
that his fame
spread to Egypt),
but violated God's
laws for priestly
function—so
God struck him
with leprosy
2 Kgs 15:1–17
2 Chr 26:1–23*

HOSEA 753–715

AMOS 760–750

752
**SHALLUM**
(1 month)
2 Kgs 15:10–15

742
**PEKAHIAH**
(2 years)
Continued idol
worship
2 Kgs 15:22–26

732
**HOSHEA**
(9 years)
Suffered heavy taxa-
tion by Assyria and
eventual conquest—
bringing about
Israelite captivity
and resettlement of
foreigners in Israel
2 Kgs 15:30; 17:1–6

722
END OF THE
NORTHERN
KINGDOM—
Israel taken
to Assyria by
Shalmaneser

753
**ZECHARIAH**
(6 months)
Encouraged idol
worship
2 Kgs 14:29—15:11

752
**MENAHEM**
(10 years)
Imposed heavy
taxes and
oppressed
his people
2 Kgs 15:14–22

740
**PEKAH**
(8 years)
During his reign
many of the
people were taken
captive to Assyria
2 Kgs 15:25–31
2 Chr 28:5–8

ISRAEL

JUDAH

750
**JOTHAM**
(16 years)
Rebuilt the upper
gate of the Temple,
rebuilt walls and
cities, but still per-
mitted idol worship
2 Kgs 15:32–38
2 Chr 27:1–9

735
**AHAZ**
(16 years)
Sacrificed his own
son to pagan gods,
nailed the Temple
doors shut
2 Kgs 16:1–20
2 Chr 28:1–27

715
**HEZEKIAH**
(29 years)
Was a devoted follower of God,
reopened the Temple doors,
purified the Temple, reinstated
priests and their duties, organized an orchestra to aid worship, destroyed idols (including
the bronze serpent of Moses
because people had begun
to worship it), celebrated the
Passover and even invited people
who were living in the north to
participate, constructed large
public waterworks, was given
15 extra years of life, foolishly
showed Babylonian messengers
the wealth in the Temple
2 Kgs 16:20; 18:1—20:21
2 Chr 29:1—32:33

697
**MANASSEH**
(55 years)
Rebuilt all the
pagan shrines,
sacrificed one
of his own sons,
practiced sorcery,
set up an idol
right in the
Temple, murdered
many of his own
people, but
repented during
his Assyrian
captivity
2 Kgs 21:1–18
2 Chr 33:1–20

MICAH 742–687

ISAIAH 740–681

586
*END OF THE SOUTHERN KINGDOM—*
*carried off captive*
*to Babylon by*
*Nebuchadnezzar*

642
**AMON**
(2 years)
2 Kgs 21:18–26
2 Chr 33:20–25

640
**JOSIAH**
(31 years)
Loved God with all his heart, repaired the Temple, found a lost scroll of the law (he promised to obey it, thus God delayed destruction for Judah until after his death), personally oversaw the major project of destroying idol shrines, reinstated the priests of God, celebrated the Passover with greater zeal than had been since Samuel's day, was greatly loved by his people
2 Kgs 21:26—23:30
2 Chr 33:25—35:27

609
**JEHOAHAZ**
(3 months)
Jailed and taken to Egypt, where he died
2 Kgs 23:30–34
2 Chr 36:1–4

609
**JEHOIAKIM**
(11 years)
Burned part of God's Word given to Jeremiah, was a puppet king for Egypt and then Babylon, watched gold and articles taken from the Temple to Babylon, saw first exile (in which Daniel was taken)
2 Kgs 23:34—24:6
2 Chr 36:5–8

598
**JEHOIACHIN**
(3 months)
Saw next exile to Babylon
2 Kgs 24:6–15; 25:27–30
2 Chr 36:8–10

597
**ZEDEKIAH**
(11 years)
Saw the Temple burned and Jerusalem destroyed, was tortured and carried away in the final exile to Babylon
2 Kgs 24:17—25:21
2 Chr 36:10–21

NAHUM 663–654

ZEPHANIAH 640–621

HABAKKUK 612–589

HULDAH 632

JEREMIAH 627–586

OBADIAH 598–580(?)

# 2 KINGS

## VITAL STATISTICS

**PURPOSE:**
To demonstrate the fate that awaits all who refuse to make God their true leader

**AUTHOR:**
Unknown. Possibly Jeremiah or a group of prophets

**ORIGINAL AUDIENCE:**
The people of Israel

**SETTING:**
The once-united nation of Israel has been divided into two kingdoms, Israel and Judah, for over a century.

**KEY VERSES:**
"Again and again the LORD had sent his prophets and seers to warn both Israel and Judah: 'Turn from all your evil ways. Obey my commands and decrees—the entire law that I commanded your ancestors to obey, and that I gave you through my servants the prophets.' But the Israelites would not listen. They were as stubborn as their ancestors who had refused to believe in the LORD their God" (17:13, 14).

**KEY PEOPLE:**
Elijah, Elisha, the woman from Shunem, Naaman, Jezebel, Jehu, Joash, Hezekiah, Sennacherib, Isaiah, Manasseh, Josiah, Jehoiakim, Zedekiah, Nebuchadnezzar

**SPECIAL FEATURES:**
The 17 prophetic books at the end of the Old Testament give great insights into the time period of 2 Kings.

SPARKLING as it crashes against boulders along its banks, the river swiftly cascades toward the sea. The current grabs, pushes, and tugs at leaves and logs, carrying them along for the ride. Here and there a sportsman is spotted in a kayak or a canoe, going with the flow. Gravity pulls the water, and the river pulls the rest . . . downward. Suddenly, a silver missile breaks the surface and darts upstream, and then another. Oblivious to the swirling opposition, the shining salmon swim against the stream. They must go upstream, and nothing will stop them from reaching their destination.

The current of society's river is flowing fast and furious, pulling downward everything in its way. It would be easy to float along with the current. But God calls us to swim against the flow. It will not be easy, and we may be alone, but it will be right.

In the book of 2 Kings, we read of evil rulers, rampant idolatry, and a complacent populace—certainly pulling downward. Despite the pressure to conform, to turn from the Lord and to serve only self, a minority of chosen people moved in the opposite direction, toward God. The Bethel prophets and others, as well as two righteous kings, spoke God's word and stood for him. As you read 2 Kings, watch these courageous individuals. Catch the strength and force of Elijah and Elisha and the commitment of Hezekiah and Josiah, and determine to be one who swims against the current!

Second Kings continues the history of Israel, halfway between the death of David and the death of the nation. Israel had been divided (1 Kings 12), and the two kingdoms had begun to slide into idolatry and corruption toward collapse and captivity. Second Kings relates the sordid stories of the 12 kings of the northern kingdom (called Israel) and the 16 kings of the southern kingdom (called Judah). For 130 years Israel endured the succession of evil rulers until they were conquered by Shalmaneser of Assyria and led into captivity in 722 B.C. (17:6). Of all the kings in both the north and south, only two—Hezekiah and Josiah—were called good. Because of their obedience to God and the spiritual revivals during their reigns, Judah stood for an additional 136 years until falling to Nebuchadnezzar and the Babylonians in 586 B.C.

Throughout this dark period, the Bible mentions 30 prophets who proclaimed God's message to the people and their leaders. Most notable of these fearless people of God are Elijah and Elisha. As Elijah neared the end of his earthly ministry, Elisha asked that he might become Elijah's rightful successor (2:9). Soon after, Elijah was taken to heaven in a whirlwind (2:11), and Elisha became God's spokesman to the northern kingdom. Elisha's life was filled with signs, proclamations, warnings, and miracles. Four of the most memorable are the flowing oil (4:1–7), the healing of the Shunammite woman's son (4:8–37), the healing of Naaman's leprosy (5:1–27), and the floating ax head (6:1–7).

Even in the midst of terrible situations, God will have his faithful minority, his remnant (19:31). He desires courageous men and women to proclaim his truth.

## THE BLUEPRINT

A. THE DIVIDED KINGDOM
   (1:1—17:41)
   1. Elisha's ministry
   2. Kings of Israel and Judah
   3. Israel is exiled to Assyria

Although Israel had the witness and power of Elisha, the nation turned from God and was exiled to Assyria. Assyria filled the northern kingdom with people from other lands. There has been no return from this captivity—it was permanent. Such is the end of all who shut God out of their lives.

B. THE SURVIVING KINGDOM
   (18:1—25:30)
   1. Kings of Judah
   2. Judah is exiled to Babylon

The northern kingdom was destroyed, and prophets were predicting the same fate for Judah. What more could cause the nation to repent? Hezekiah and Josiah were able to stem the tide of evil. They both repaired the Temple and gathered the people for the Passover. Josiah eradicated idolatry from the land, but as soon as these good kings were gone, the people returned again to living their own way instead of God's way. Each individual must believe and live for God in his or her family, church, and nation.

## MEGATHEMES

| THEME | EXPLANATION | IMPORTANCE |
|---|---|---|
| Elisha | The purpose of Elisha's ministry was to restore respect for God and his message, and he stood firmly against the evil kings of Israel. By faith, with courage and prayer, he revealed not only God's judgment on sin but also his mercy, love, and tenderness toward faithful people. | Elisha's mighty miracles showed that God controls not only great armies but also events in everyday life. When we listen to and obey God, he shows us his power to transform any situation. God's care is for all who are willing to follow him. He can perform miracles in our lives. |
| Idolatry | Every evil king in both Israel and Judah encouraged idolatry. These false gods represented war, cruelty, power, and sex. Although they had God's law, priests, and prophets to guide them, these kings sought priests and prophets whom they could manipulate to their own advantage. | An idol is any idea, ability, possession, or person that we regard more highly than God. We condemn Israel and Judah for foolishly worshiping idols, but we also worship other gods—power, money, physical attractiveness. Those who believe in God must resist the lure of these attractive idols. |
| Evil Kings/ Good Kings | Only 20 percent of Israel and Judah's kings followed God. The evil kings were shortsighted. They thought they could control their nations' destinies by importing other religions, forming alliances with pagan nations, and enriching themselves. The good kings had to spend most of their time undoing the evil done by their predecessors. | Although the evil kings led the people into sin, the priests, princes, heads of families, and military leaders all had to cooperate with the evil plans and practices in order for them to be carried out. We cannot discharge our responsibility to obey God by blaming our leaders. We are responsible to know God's Word and obey it. |
| God's Patience | God told his people that if they obeyed him, they would live successfully; if they disobeyed, they would be judged and destroyed. God had been patient with the people for hundreds of years. He sent many prophets to guide them. And he gave ample warning of coming destruction. But even God's patience has limits. | God is patient with us. He gives us many chances to hear his message, to turn from sin, and to believe him. His patience does not mean he is indifferent to how we live, nor does it mean we can ignore his warnings. His patience should make us want to come to him now. |
| Judgment | After King Solomon's reign, Israel lasted 209 years before the Assyrians destroyed it; Judah lasted 345 years before the Babylonians took Jerusalem. After repeated warnings to his people, God used these evil nations as instruments for his justice. | The consequences of rejecting God's commands and purpose for our lives are severe. He will not ignore unbelief or rebellion. We must believe in him and accept Christ's sacrificial death on our behalf, or we will be judged also. |

# KEY PLACES IN 2 KINGS

The broken lines (—·—·—) indicate modern boundaries.

sell. For another family in Shunem, he raised a son from the dead (4:1–37).

**4 Gilgal** Elisha cared for the young prophets in Gilgal—he removed poison from a stew, made a small amount of food feed everyone, and even caused an ax head to float so it could be retrieved. It was to Elisha that Naaman, a commander in the Aramean army, came to be healed of leprosy (4:38—6:7).

**5 Dothan** Although he cured an Aramean commander's leprosy, Elisha was loyal to Israel. He knew the Aramean army's battle plans and kept Israel's king informed. The Aramean king tracked Elisha down in Dothan and surrounded the city, hoping to kill him. But Elisha prayed that the Arameans would be blinded; then he led the blinded army into Samaria, Israel's capital city (6:8–23).

**6 Samaria** But the Arameans didn't learn their lesson. They later besieged Samaria. Ironically, Israel's king thought it was Elisha's fault, but Elisha said food would be available in abundance the next day. True to Elisha's word, the Lord caused panic in the Aramean camp, and the enemy ran, leaving their supplies to Samaria's starving people (6:24—7:20).

**7 Damascus** Despite Elisha's loyalty to Israel, he obeyed God and traveled to Damascus, the capital of Aram. King Ben-hadad was sick, and he sent Hazael to ask Elisha if he would recover. Elisha knew the king would die and told this to Hazael. But Hazael then murdered Ben-hadad, making himself king. Later, Israel and Judah joined forces to fight this new Aramean threat (8:1–29).

**8 Ramoth-gilead** As Israel and Judah warred with Aram, Elisha sent a young prophet to Ramoth-gilead to anoint Jehu as Israel's next king. Jehu set out to destroy the wicked dynasties of Israel and Judah, killing kings Joram and Ahaziah, and wicked Queen Jezebel. He then destroyed King Ahab's family and all the Baal worshipers in Israel (9:1—11:1).

**9 Jerusalem** Power-hungry Athaliah became queen of Judah when her son Ahaziah was killed. She had all her grandsons killed except Joash, who was hidden by his aunt. Joash was crowned king at the age of seven and overthrew Athaliah. Meanwhile in Samaria, the Arameans continued to harass Israel. Israel's new king met with Elisha and was told that he would be victorious over Aram three times (11:2—13:19).

Following Elisha's death came a series of evil kings in Israel. Their idolatry and rejection of God caused their downfall. The Assyrian Empire captured Samaria and took most of the Israelites into captivity (13:20—17:41). Judah had a short reprieve because of a few good kings who destroyed idols and worshiped God. But many strayed from God. So Jerusalem fell to the next world power, Babylon (18:1—25:30).

The history of both Israel and Judah was much affected by the prophet Elisha's ministry. He served Israel for 50 years, fighting the idolatry of its kings and calling its people back to God.

**1 Jericho** Elijah's ministry had come to an end. He touched his cloak to the Jordan River, and he and Elisha crossed on dry ground. Elijah was taken by God in a whirlwind, and Elisha returned alone with the cloak. The prophets in Jericho realized that Elisha was Elijah's replacement (1:1—2:25).

**2 Wilderness of Edom** The king of Moab rebelled against Israel, so the nations of Israel, Judah, and Edom decided to attack from the wilderness of Edom but ran out of water. The kings consulted Elisha, who said God would send both water and victory (3:1–27).

**3 Shunem** Elisha cared for individuals and their needs. He helped a woman clear a debt by giving her a supply of oil to

## A. THE DIVIDED KINGDOM (1:1—17:41)

Elisha begins his ministry to the northern kingdom after Elijah is taken away by a whirlwind. Elisha performs many miracles and calls Israel to return to God, but they persist in their wickedness. Israel is defeated by Assyria, and the people of the northern kingdom are exiled, never to return. Such is the end of all those who ignore God's warnings and demand their own way in their desire to sin.

### Elijah Confronts King Ahaziah

**1** After King Ahab's death, the land of Moab rebelled against Israel.

²One day Israel's new king, Ahaziah, fell through the latticework of an upper room at his palace in Samaria and was seriously injured. So he sent messengers to the temple of Baal-zebub, the god of Ekron, to ask whether he would recover.

³But the angel of the LORD told Elijah, who was from Tishbe, "Go and confront the messengers of the king of Samaria and ask them, 'Is there no God in Israel? Why are you going to Baal-zebub, the god of Ekron, to ask whether the king will recover? ⁴Now, therefore, this is what the LORD says: You will never leave the bed you are lying on; you will surely die.'" So Elijah went to deliver the message.

⁵When the messengers returned to the king, he asked them, "Why have you returned so soon?"

⁶They replied, "A man came up to us and told us to go back to the king and give him this message. 'This is what the LORD says: Is there no God in Israel? Why are you sending men to Baal-zebub, the god of Ekron, to ask whether you will recover? Therefore, because you have done this, you will never leave the bed you are lying on; you will surely die.'"

⁷"What sort of man was he?" the king demanded. "What did he look like?"

⁸They replied, "He was a hairy man,* and he wore a leather belt around his waist."

"Elijah from Tishbe!" the king exclaimed.

⁹Then he sent an army captain with fifty soldiers to arrest him. They found him sitting on top of a hill. The captain said to him, "Man of God, the king has commanded you to come down with us."

¹⁰But Elijah replied to the captain, "If I am a man of God, let fire come down from heaven and destroy you and your fifty men!" Then fire fell from heaven and killed them all.

¹¹So the king sent another captain with fifty men. The captain said to him, "Man of God, the king demands that you come down at once."

¹²Elijah replied, "If I am a man of God, let fire come down from heaven and destroy you and your fifty men!" And again the fire of God fell from heaven and killed them all.

¹³Once more the king sent a third captain with fifty men. But this time the captain went up the hill and fell to his knees before Elijah. He pleaded with him, "O man of God, please spare my life and the lives of these, your fifty servants. ¹⁴See how the fire from heaven came down and destroyed the first two groups. But now please spare my life!"

¹⁵Then the angel of the LORD said to Elijah, "Go down with him, and don't be afraid of him." So Elijah got up and went with him to the king.

**1:8** Or *He was wearing clothing made of hair.*

---

**1:1**
2 Sam 8:2
2 Kgs 3:5

**1:2**
2 Kgs 1:16; 8:7-10
Mark 3:22

**1:3**
1 Kgs 17:1

**1:4**
2 Kgs 1:16-17

**1:8**
Matt 3:4
Mark 1:6

**1:10**
1 Kgs 18:36-38
Job 1:16
Luke 9:54

**1:15**
2 Kgs 1:3
Isa 51:12
Jer 1:17
Ezek 2:6

---

**1:1** Because 1 and 2 Kings were originally one book, 2 Kings continues where 1 Kings ends. The once great nation of Israel was split in two because the people forgot God. The book begins with Elijah, a prophet of God, being carried away to heaven. It ends with the people of Israel and Judah being taken into captivity. In 1 Kings, the beautiful Temple of God was built. In 2 Kings, it is desecrated and destroyed.

Our world is strikingly similar to the world described in 2 Kings. National and local governments do not seek God, and countries are tormented by war. Many people follow the false gods of technology, materialism, and war. True worship of God is rare on the earth.

In our chaotic and corrupt world, we can turn to examples such as David, Elijah, and Elisha, who were devoted to God's high honor and moral law and who brought about renewal and change in their society. More important, we can look to Jesus Christ, the perfect example. For nations to do God's will, they need individuals who will do God's work. If your heart is committed to God, he can work through you to accomplish the work he has called you to do.

**1:2** Baal-zebub was not the same god as Baal, the Canaanite god worshiped by Ahab and Jezebel (1 Kings 16:31-33). Baal-zebub was another popular god whose temple was located in the city of Ekron. Because this god was thought to have the power of prophecy, King Ahaziah sent messengers to Ekron to learn of his fate. Supernatural power and mystery were associated with Baal-zebub. Ahaziah's action showed the king's disrespect for God.

**1:8** For more information on Elijah, see his Profile in 1 Kings 18, p. 545.

**1:13-15** Notice how the third captain went to Elijah. Although the first two captains called Elijah "man of God," they were not being genuine—God was not in their hearts. The third captain also called him "man of God," but he humbly begged for mercy. His attitude showed respect for God and his power and saved the lives of his men. Effective living begins with a right attitude toward God. Before religious words come to your mouth, make sure they are from your heart. Let respect, humility, and servanthood characterize your attitude toward God and others.

¹⁶And Elijah said to the king, "This is what the Lᴏʀᴅ says: Why did you send messengers to Baal-zebub, the god of Ekron, to ask whether you will recover? Is there no God in Israel to answer your question? Therefore, because you have done this, you will never leave the bed you are lying on; you will surely die."

¹⁷So Ahaziah died, just as the Lᴏʀᴅ had promised through Elijah. Since Ahaziah did not have a son to succeed him, his brother Joram* became the next king. This took place in the second year of the reign of Jehoram son of Jehoshaphat, king of Judah.

¹⁸The rest of the events in Ahaziah's reign are recorded in *The Book of the History of the Kings of Israel.*

## 1. Elisha's ministry
*Elijah Taken into Heaven*

**2** When the Lᴏʀᴅ was about to take Elijah up to heaven in a whirlwind, Elijah and Elisha were traveling from Gilgal. ²And Elijah said to Elisha, "Stay here, for the Lᴏʀᴅ has told me to go to Bethel."

But Elisha replied, "As surely as the Lᴏʀᴅ lives and you yourself live, I will never leave you!" So they went down together to Bethel.

³The group of prophets from Bethel came to Elisha and asked him, "Did you know that the Lᴏʀᴅ is going to take your master away from you today?"

"Of course I know," Elisha answered. "But be quiet about it."

⁴Then Elijah said to Elisha, "Stay here, for the Lᴏʀᴅ has told me to go to Jericho."

But Elisha replied again, "As surely as the Lᴏʀᴅ lives and you yourself live, I will never leave you." So they went on together to Jericho.

⁵Then the group of prophets from Jericho came to Elisha and asked him, "Did you know that the Lᴏʀᴅ is going to take your master away from you today?"

"Of course I know," Elisha answered. "But be quiet about it."

⁶Then Elijah said to Elisha, "Stay here, for the Lᴏʀᴅ has told me to go to the Jordan River."

But again Elisha replied, "As surely as the Lᴏʀᴅ lives and you yourself live, I will never leave you." So they went on together.

⁷Fifty men from the group of prophets also went and watched from a distance as Elijah and Elisha stopped beside the Jordan River. ⁸Then Elijah folded his cloak together and struck the water with it. The river divided, and the two of them went across on dry ground!

⁹When they came to the other side, Elijah said to Elisha, "Tell me what I can do for you before I am taken away."

And Elisha replied, "Please let me inherit a double share of your spirit and become your successor."

¹⁰"You have asked a difficult thing," Elijah replied. "If you see me when I am taken from you, then you will get your request. But if not, then you won't."

¹¹As they were walking along and talking, suddenly a chariot of fire appeared, drawn by horses of fire. It drove between the two men, separating them, and Elijah was carried by a whirlwind into heaven. ¹²Elisha saw it and cried out, "My father! My father! I see the chariots and charioteers of Israel!" And as they disappeared from sight, Elisha tore his clothes in distress.

**1:17** Hebrew *Jehoram,* a variant spelling of Joram.

*marginal references:* **1:17** 2 Kgs 3:1; 8:16 · **2:1** Gen 5:23-24; 1 Kgs 19:16-21; Heb 11:5 · **2:6** Ruth 1:16; 2 Kgs 2:1-2 · **2:8** Exod 14:21; 1 Kgs 19:19 · **2:11** 2 Kgs 6:17 · **2:12** 2 Kgs 13:14

**1:18** *The Book of the History of the Kings of Israel* and *The Book of the History of the Kings of Judah* (8:23) were history books. The inspired writer of 2 Kings selected facts from these books to retell the story of Israel and Judah from God's perspective. God directed the writer's thoughts and selection process to make sure that the truth, God's Word, would be written.

**2:3** A "group of prophets from Bethel" was similar to a school, a gathering of disciples around a recognized prophet, such as Elijah or Elisha. These groups of prophets, located throughout the country, helped stem the tide of spiritual and moral decline in the nation begun under Jeroboam. The students at Bethel were eyewitnesses to the succession of the prophetic ministry from Elijah to Elisha.

**2:8** Elijah's cloak was a symbol of his authority as a prophet.

**2:9** Elisha asked to be Elijah's "successor" (that is why he asked for a double share of Elijah's spirit). Deuteronomy 21:17 helps

explain Elisha's request. According to custom, the firstborn son would receive a double portion of the father's inheritance (see the note on Genesis 25:31). Elisha was asking to be Elijah's successor, or heir, the one who would continue Elijah's work as leader of the prophets. But the decision to grant this request was up to God. Elijah only told Elisha how he would know if his request had been granted.

**2:9** God granted Elisha's request because Elisha's motives were pure. His main goal was not to be better or more powerful than Elijah but to accomplish more for God. If our motives are pure, we don't have to be afraid to ask great things from God. When we ask God for great power or ability, we need to examine our desires and get rid of any selfishness we find. To have the Holy Spirit's help, we must be willing to ask.

**2:11** Elijah was taken to heaven without dying. He is the second person mentioned in Scripture to have this honor. Enoch was the

2:14
2 Kgs 2:8

[13]Elisha picked up Elijah's cloak, which had fallen when he was taken up. Then Elisha returned to the bank of the Jordan River. [14]He struck the water with Elijah's cloak and cried out, "Where is the LORD, the God of Elijah?" Then the river divided, and Elisha went across.

[15]When the group of prophets from Jericho saw from a distance what happened, they exclaimed, "Elijah's spirit rests upon Elisha!" And they went to meet him and bowed to the ground before him.

2:16
1 Kgs 18:12
Acts 8:39

[16]"Sir," they said, "just say the word and fifty of our strongest men will search the wilderness for your master. Perhaps the Spirit of the LORD has left him on some mountain or in some valley."

"No," Elisha said, "don't send them." [17]But they kept urging him until they shamed him into agreeing, and he finally said, "All right, send them." So fifty men searched for three days but did not find Elijah. [18]Elisha was still at Jericho when they returned. "Didn't I tell you not to go?" he asked.

### Elisha's First Miracles

[19]One day the leaders of the town of Jericho visited Elisha. "We have a problem, my lord," they told him. "This town is located in pleasant surroundings, as you can see. But the water is bad, and the land is unproductive."

2:21
Exod 15:25-26
2 Kgs 4:41; 6:6

[20]Elisha said, "Bring me a new bowl with salt in it." So they brought it to him. [21]Then he went out to the spring that supplied the town with water and threw the salt into it. And he said, "This is what the LORD says: I have purified this water. It will no longer cause death or infertility.*" [22]And the water has remained pure ever since, just as Elisha said.

**2:21** Or *or make the land unproductive;* Hebrew reads *or barrenness.*

---

## KINGS TO DATE AND THEIR ENEMIES

852
**JORAM**
With Judah, defeated Mesha (Moab), and was miraculously delivered from Ben-hadad II (Aram)
2 Kgs 1:17; 3:1—8:25
2 Chr 22:5–7

853
**AHAZIAH**
1 Kgs 22:40—
2 Kgs 1:18
2 Chr 20:35–37

841

*I S R A E L*

*J U D A H*

872
**JEHOSHAPHAT**
Defeated by Ben-hadad II (Aram), gained miraculous victory over Moab and Ammon, and crushed a rebellion by Mesha (Moab)
2 Kgs 22:41–50
2 Chr 17:1—21:1
Co-regency 853–848

853        848        841
**JEHORAM**
Lost dominion over Edom, assaulted by Philistines and Arabs
2 Kgs 8:16–24
2 Chr 21:1–20

All dates are B.C.
Solid section of the timeline indicates co-regency.
For all the kings of Israel and Judah, see the chart at the end of 1 Kings.

---

first (Genesis 5:21-24). The other prophets may not have seen God take Elijah, or they may have had a difficult time believing what they had seen. In either case, they wanted to search for Elijah (2:16-18). Finding no physical trace of him would confirm what had happened and strengthen their faith. The only other person taken to heaven in bodily form was Jesus after his resurrection from the dead (Acts 1:9).

**2:13-25** These three incidents were testimonies to Elisha's commission as a prophet of God. They are recorded to demonstrate Elisha's new power and authority as Israel's chief prophet under God's ultimate power and authority.

**2:14** Elisha did not strike the water out of disrespect for God or Elijah. He was pleading with God to confirm his appointment as Elijah's successor.

23Elisha left Jericho and went up to Bethel. As he was walking along the road, a group of boys from the town began mocking and making fun of him. "Go away, baldy!" they chanted. "Go away, baldy!" 24Elisha turned around and looked at them, and he cursed them in the name of the LORD. Then two bears came out of the woods and mauled forty-two of them. 25From there Elisha went to Mount Carmel and finally returned to Samaria.

2:25
1 Kgs 18:20

### War between Israel and Moab

**3** Ahab's son Joram* began to rule over Israel in the eighteenth year of King Jehoshaphat's reign in Judah. He reigned in Samaria twelve years. 2He did what was evil in the LORD's sight, but not to the same extent as his father and mother. He at least tore down the sacred pillar of Baal that his father had set up. 3Nevertheless, he continued in the sins that Jeroboam son of Nebat had committed and led the people of Israel to commit.

4King Mesha of Moab was a sheep breeder. He used to pay the king of Israel an annual tribute of 100,000 lambs and the wool of 100,000 rams. 5But after Ahab's death, the king of Moab rebelled against the king of Israel. 6So King Joram promptly mustered the army of Israel and marched from Samaria. 7On the way, he sent this message to King Jehoshaphat of Judah: "The king of Moab has rebelled against me. Will you join me in battle against him?"

And Jehoshaphat replied, "Why, of course! You and I are as one. My troops are your troops, and my horses are your horses." 8Then Jehoshaphat asked, "What route will we take?"

"We will attack from the wilderness of Edom," Joram replied.

9The king of Edom and his troops joined them, and all three armies traveled along a roundabout route through the wilderness for seven days. But there was no water for the men or their animals.

3:1
2 Kgs 1:17; 8:16
3:2
1 Kgs 16:30-32
2 Kgs 10:25-26
3:3
1 Kgs 12:28; 14:16
3:4
2 Sam 8:2
Isa 16:1-2
3:5
2 Kgs 1:1
3:7
1 Kgs 22:4
3:9
1 Kgs 22:47

**3:1** Hebrew *Jehoram*, a variant spelling of Joram; also in 3:6.

---

**2:23, 24** This group of boys was from Bethel, the religious center of idolatry in the northern kingdom, and they probably were warning Elisha not to speak against their immorality as Elijah had done. They were not merely teasing Elisha about his baldness, but showing severe disrespect for Elisha's message and God's power. They may also have jeered because of their disbelief in the chariot of fire that had taken Elijah. When Elisha cursed them, he did not call out the bears himself. God sent them as a judgment for their callous unbelief.

**2:23, 24** These young men mocked God's messenger and paid for it with their lives. Making fun of religious leaders has been a popular sport through the ages. To take a stand for God is to be different from the world and vulnerable to verbal abuse. When we are cynical and sarcastic toward religious leaders, we are in

danger of mocking not just the person but also the spiritual message. While we are not to condone the sin that some leaders commit, we need to pray for them, not laugh at them. True leaders, those who follow God, need to be heard with respect and encouraged in their ministry.

**3:1** Although 1:17 says that Jehoram was king of Judah, 3:1 says that Jehoshaphat was Judah's king. As a king grew older, often his son would rule beside him. Jehoshaphat, nearing the end of his reign, appointed his son Jehoram to rule with him. Jehoram served as co-ruler with Jehoshaphat for five years (853–848 B.C.; he is mentioned again in 8:16-24). Joram, king of Israel, was Ahab's son and Ahaziah's brother (1:17). Both Ahab (1 Kings 16:29–22:40) and Ahaziah (1:2-18) served as kings of Israel before Joram.

**3:3** The sins of Israel's kings are often compared to the sins of Jeroboam, the first ruler of the northern kingdom of Israel. His great sin was to institute idol worship throughout his kingdom, causing people to turn away from God (1 Kings 12:25-33). By ignoring God and allowing idol worship, Joram clung to Jeroboam's sins.

**3:4, 5** Israel and Judah held some of the most fertile land and strategic positions in the ancient Near East. It is no wonder that neighboring nations like Moab envied them and constantly attempted to seize the land. Moab lay just southeast of Israel. The country had been under Israel's control for some time due to Ahab's strong military leadership. When Ahab died, Mesha, the Moabite king, took the opportunity to rebel. While Israel's next king, Ahaziah, did nothing about the revolt, his successor, Joram, decided to take action. He joined forces with Jehoshaphat, king of Judah, and went to fight the Moabites. Together, Israel and Judah brought the Moabites to the brink of surrender. But when they saw the Moabite king sacrifice his own son and successor (3:27), they withdrew even though they had won the battle. Moab fought many other battles with both Israel and Judah. Some of them, in fact, are recorded by Mesha (c. 840 B.C.), who carved his exploits on a plaque called the Moabite Stone (discovered in 1868).

**3:9, 10** Edom was under Judah's control; thus, they marched with them, making three kings.

**WAR AGAINST MOAB**

Moab's king rebelled against Israel. So Joram, Israel's king, and Jehoshaphat, Judah's king, attacked Moab. In the parched and rugged wilderness of Edom, the armies ran out of water, but Elisha promised that both water and victory would soon come.

Mediterranean Sea
0    20 Mi.
0    20 Km.
N
Sea of Galilee
ISRAEL
Samaria
Jordan River
Jerusalem
Dead Sea
JUDAH
MOAB
Kir-hareseth
WILDERNESS OF EDOM

**3:11**
1 Kgs 19:21; 22:7

10 "What should we do?" the king of Israel cried out. "The Lord has brought the three of us here to let the king of Moab defeat us."

11 But King Jehoshaphat of Judah asked, "Is there no prophet of the Lord with us? If there is, we can ask the Lord what to do through him."

One of King Joram's officers replied, "Elisha son of Shaphat is here. He used to be Elijah's personal assistant.*"

12 Jehoshaphat said, "Yes, the Lord speaks through him." So the kings of Israel, Judah, and Edom went to consult with Elisha.

**3:13**
1 Kgs 22:6-11,
22-25

13 "Why are you coming to me?"* Elisha asked the king of Israel. "Go to the pagan prophets of your father and mother!"

But King Joram of Israel said, "No! For it was the Lord who called us three kings here—only to be defeated by the king of Moab!"

**3:15**
1 Sam 16:23

14 Elisha replied, "As surely as the Lord Almighty lives, whom I serve, I wouldn't even bother with you except for my respect for King Jehoshaphat of Judah. 15 Now bring me someone who can play the harp."

While the harp was being played, the power* of the Lord came upon Elisha 16 and he said, "This is what the Lord says: This dry valley will be filled with pools of water! 17 You will see neither wind nor rain, says the Lord, but this valley will be filled with water. You will have plenty for yourselves and your cattle and other animals. 18 But this is only a simple thing for the Lord, for he will make you victorious over the army of Moab! 19 You will conquer the best of their towns, even the fortified ones. You will cut down all their good trees, stop up all their springs, and ruin all their good land with stones."

**3:20**
Exod 29:39-40

20 The next day at about the time when the morning sacrifice was offered, water suddenly appeared! It was flowing from the direction of Edom, and soon there was water everywhere.

**3:11** Hebrew *He used to pour water on the hands of Elijah.* **3:13** Hebrew *What is there in common between you and me?* **3:15** Hebrew *the hand.*

| MIRACLES OF ELIJAH & ELISHA | Miracle | Reference | Factors |
|---|---|---|---|
| Baal, the false god worshiped by many Israelites, was the god of rain, fire, and farm crops. He also demanded child sacrifice. Elijah's and Elisha's miracles repeatedly show the power of the true God over the purported realm of Baal, as well as the value God places on the life of a child. | **ELIJAH** | | |
| | 1. Food brought by ravens | 1 Kings 17:5, 6 | Food |
| | 2. Widow's food multiplied | 1 Kings 17:12-16 | Flour and oil |
| | 3. Widow's son raised to life | 1 Kings 17:17-24 | Life of a child |
| | 4. Altar and sacrifice consumed | 1 Kings 18:16-46 | Fire and water |
| | 5. Ahaziah's soldiers consumed | 2 Kings 1:9-14 | Fire |
| | 6. Jordan River parted | 2 Kings 2:6-8 | Water |
| | 7. Transported to heaven | 2 Kings 2:11, 12 | Fire and wind |
| | **ELISHA** | | |
| | 1. Jordan River parted | 2 Kings 2:13, 14 | Water |
| | 2. Spring purified at Jericho | 2 Kings 2:19-22 | Water |
| | 3. Widow's oil multiplied | 2 Kings 4:1-7 | Oil |
| | 4. Dead boy raised to life | 2 Kings 4:18-37 | Life of a child |
| | 5. Poison in stew purified | 2 Kings 4:38-41 | Flour |
| | 6. Prophets' food multiplied | 2 Kings 4:42-44 | Bread and grain |
| | 7. Naaman healed of leprosy | 2 Kings 5:1-14 | Water |
| | 8. Gehazi became leprous | 2 Kings 5:15-27 | Words alone |
| | 9. Ax head floated | 2 Kings 6:1-7 | Water |
| | 10. Aramean army blinded | 2 Kings 6:8-23 | Elisha's prayer |

**3:11-20** Jehoshaphat's request for a "prophet of the Lord" shows how true worship and religious experience in both Israel and Judah had declined. In David's day, both the high priest and the prophets gave the king advice. But most of the priests had left Israel (see the first note on 1 Kings 17:1), and God's prophets were seen as messengers of doom (1 Kings 22:18). This miracle predicted by Elisha affirmed God's power and authority and validated Elisha's ministry. In 2 Chronicles 18, King Jehoshaphat of Judah and King Ahab of Israel gave the prophet Micaiah a similar request. But they ignored God's advice—with disastrous results.

**3:15** In Old Testament times music often accompanied prophecy (1 Chronicles 25:1).

**3:20** The morning sacrifice was one of two sacrifices that the priests were required to offer each day.

²¹Meanwhile, when the people of Moab heard about the three armies marching against them, they mobilized every man who was old enough to strap on a sword, and they stationed themselves along their border. ²²But when they got up the next morning, the sun was shining across the water, making it appear red to the Moabites—like blood. ²³"It's blood!" the Moabites exclaimed. "The three armies must have attacked and killed each other! Let's go, men of Moab, and collect the plunder!"

²⁴But when the Moabites arrived at the Israelite camp, the army of Israel rushed out and attacked them until they turned and ran. The army of Israel chased them into the land of Moab, destroying everything as they went.* ²⁵They destroyed the towns, covered their good land with stones, stopped up all the springs, and cut down all the good trees. Finally, only Kir-hareseth and its stone walls were left, but men with slings surrounded and attacked it.

²⁶When the king of Moab saw that he was losing the battle, he led 700 of his swordsmen in a desperate attempt to break through the enemy lines near the king of Edom, but they failed. ²⁷Then the king of Moab took his oldest son, who would have been the next king, and sacrificed him as a burnt offering on the wall. So there was great anger against Israel,* and the Israelites withdrew and returned to their own land.

### Elisha Helps a Poor Widow

**4** One day the widow of a member of the group of prophets came to Elisha and cried out, "My husband who served you is dead, and you know how he feared the LORD. But now a creditor has come, threatening to take my two sons as slaves."

²"What can I do to help you?" Elisha asked. "Tell me, what do you have in the house?"
"Nothing at all, except a flask of olive oil," she replied.

³And Elisha said, "Borrow as many empty jars as you can from your friends and neighbors. ⁴Then go into your house with your sons and shut the door behind you. Pour olive oil from your flask into the jars, setting each one aside when it is filled."

⁵So she did as she was told. Her sons kept bringing jars to her, and she filled one after another. ⁶Soon every container was full to the brim!

"Bring me another jar," she said to one of her sons.

"There aren't any more!" he told her. And then the olive oil stopped flowing.

⁷When she told the man of God what had happened, he said to her, "Now sell the olive oil and pay your debts, and you and your sons can live on what is left over."

**3:25**
Isa 16:7
Jer 48:31, 36

**3:27**
Mic 6:7

**4:1**
Lev 25:39-41, 48
Neh 5:2-5

**4:2**
1 Kgs 17:12

**4:7**
1 Kgs 12:22

**3:24** The meaning of the Hebrew is uncertain.   **3:27** Or *So Israel's anger was great.* The meaning of the Hebrew is uncertain.

---

**THE FAMILY IN SHUNEM**
Elisha often stayed with a kind family in Shunem. When the son suddenly died, his mother traveled to Mount Carmel to find Elisha. He returned with her and raised the boy from the dead. Elisha then went to his home in Gilgal.

**4:1** Poor people and debtors were allowed to pay their debts by selling themselves or their children as slaves. God ordered rich people and creditors not to take advantage of these people during their time of extreme need (see Deuteronomy 15:1-18 for an explanation of these practices). This woman's creditor was not acting in the spirit of God's law. Elisha's kind deed demonstrates that God wants us to go beyond simply keeping the law. We must also show compassion.

**4:1ff** This chapter records four of God's miracles through Elisha: providing money for a poverty-stricken widow (4:1-7); raising a dead boy to life (4:32-37); purifying poisonous food (4:38-41); and providing food for 100 men (4:42-44). These miracles show God's tenderness and care for those who are faithful to him.

When reading the Old Testament, it is easy to focus on God's harsh judgment of the rebellious and to minimize his tender care for those who love and serve him. Seeing God at work providing for his followers helps us keep his severe justice toward the unrepentant in proper perspective.

**4:6** The woman and her sons collected jars from their neighbors, pouring olive oil into them from their one flask. The olive oil was used for cooking, for lamps, and for fuel. The oil stopped flowing only when they ran out of containers. The number of jars they gathered was an indication of their faith. God's provision was as large as their faith and willingness to obey. Beware of limiting God's blessings by a lack of faith and obedience. God is able to do immeasurably more than all we ask or imagine (Ephesians 3:20).

### Elisha and the Woman from Shunem

**4:8**
Josh 19:18

⁸One day Elisha went to the town of Shunem. A wealthy woman lived there, and she urged him to come to her home for a meal. After that, whenever he passed that way, he would stop there for something to eat.

**4:10**
Matt 10:41
Rom 12:13

⁹She said to her husband, "I am sure this man who stops in from time to time is a holy man of God. ¹⁰Let's build a small room for him on the roof and furnish it with a bed, a table, a chair, and a lamp. Then he will have a place to stay whenever he comes by."

¹¹One day Elisha returned to Shunem, and he went up to this upper room to rest. ¹²He said to his servant Gehazi, "Tell the woman from Shunem I want to speak to her." When she appeared, ¹³Elisha said to Gehazi, "Tell her, 'We appreciate the kind concern you have shown us. What can we do for you? Can we put in a good word for you to the king or to the commander of the army?'"

"No," she replied, "my family takes good care of me."

¹⁴Later Elisha asked Gehazi, "What can we do for her?"

Gehazi replied, "She doesn't have a son, and her husband is an old man."

**4:15**
Gen 18:14

¹⁵"Call her back again," Elisha told him. When the woman returned, Elisha said to her as she stood in the doorway, ¹⁶"Next year at this time you will be holding a son in your arms!"

"No, my lord!" she cried. "O man of God, don't deceive me and get my hopes up like that."

¹⁷But sure enough, the woman soon became pregnant. And at that time the following year she had a son, just as Elisha had said.

¹⁸One day when her child was older, he went out to help his father, who was working with the harvesters. ¹⁹Suddenly he cried out, "My head hurts! My head hurts!"

His father said to one of the servants, "Carry him home to his mother."

**4:21**
2 Kgs 4:32

²⁰So the servant took him home, and his mother held him on her lap. But around noontime he died. ²¹She carried him up and laid him on the bed of the man of God, then shut the door and left him there. ²²She sent a message to her husband: "Send one of the servants and a donkey so that I can hurry to the man of God and come right back."

²³"Why go today?" he asked. "It is neither a new moon festival nor a Sabbath."

But she said, "It will be all right."

²⁴So she saddled the donkey and said to the servant, "Hurry! Don't slow down unless I tell you to."

²⁵As she approached the man of God at Mount Carmel, Elisha saw her in the distance. He said to Gehazi, "Look, the woman from Shunem is coming. ²⁶Run out to meet her and ask her, 'Is everything all right with you, your husband, and your child?'"

"Yes," the woman told Gehazi, "everything is fine."

²⁷But when she came to the man of God at the mountain, she fell to the ground before him and caught hold of his feet. Gehazi began to push her away, but the man of God said, "Leave her alone. She is deeply troubled, but the LORD has not told me what it is."

²⁸Then she said, "Did I ask you for a son, my lord? And didn't I say, 'Don't deceive me and get my hopes up'?"

**4:29**
Exod 4:17; 7:19;
14:16
1 Kgs 18:46

²⁹Then Elisha said to Gehazi, "Get ready to travel*; take my staff and go! Don't talk to anyone along the way. Go quickly and lay the staff on the child's face."

³⁰But the boy's mother said, "As surely as the LORD lives and you yourself live, I won't go home unless you go with me." So Elisha returned with her.

³¹Gehazi hurried on ahead and laid the staff on the child's face, but nothing happened. There was no sign of life. He returned to meet Elisha and told him, "The child is still dead."

**4:34**
1 Kgs 17:21-23

³²When Elisha arrived, the child was indeed dead, lying there on the prophet's bed. ³³He went in alone and shut the door behind him and prayed to the LORD. ³⁴Then he lay down on the child's body, placing his mouth on the child's mouth, his eyes on the child's eyes, and his

**4:29** Hebrew *Bind up your loins.*

---

**4:9** The woman from Shunem realized that Elisha was a man of God, and so she prepared a room for him to use whenever he was in town. She did this out of kindness and because she sensed a need, not for any selfish motives. Soon, however, her kindness would be rewarded far beyond her wildest dreams. How sensitive are you to those who pass by your home and flow through your life—especially those who teach and preach God's Word? What special needs do they have that you could meet? Look for ways to serve and help.

**4:32-36** Elisha's prayer and method of raising the dead boy show God's personal care for hurting people. We must express genuine concern for others as we carry God's message to them. Only then will we faithfully represent our compassionate Father in heaven.

hands on the child's hands. And as he stretched out on him, the child's body began to grow warm again! 35Elisha got up, walked back and forth across the room once, and then stretched himself out again on the child. This time the boy sneezed seven times and opened his eyes!

36Then Elisha summoned Gehazi. "Call the child's mother!" he said. And when she came in, Elisha said, "Here, take your son!" 37She fell at his feet and bowed before him, overwhelmed with gratitude. Then she took her son in her arms and carried him downstairs.

**4:37**
Heb 11:35

## Miracles during a Famine

38Elisha now returned to Gilgal, and there was a famine in the land. One day as the group of prophets was seated before him, he said to his servant, "Put a large pot on the fire, and make some stew for the rest of the group."

**4:38**
2 Kgs 2:1; 8:1

39One of the young men went out into the field to gather herbs and came back with a pocketful of wild gourds. He shredded them and put them into the pot without realizing they were poisonous. 40Some of the stew was served to the men. But after they had eaten a bite or two they cried out, "Man of God, there's poison in this stew!" So they would not eat it.

41Elisha said, "Bring me some flour." Then he threw it into the pot and said, "Now it's all right; go ahead and eat." And then it did not harm them.

**4:41**
Exod 15:25
2 Kgs 2:21-22

42One day a man from Baal-shalishah brought the man of God a sack of fresh grain and twenty loaves of barley bread made from the first grain of his harvest. Elisha said, "Give it to the people so they can eat."

43"What?" his servant exclaimed. "Feed a hundred people with only this?"

**4:43**
Luke 9:13
John 6:9, 12

But Elisha repeated, "Give it to the people so they can eat, for this is what the LORD says: Everyone will eat, and there will even be some left over!" 44And when they gave it to the people, there was plenty for all and some left over, just as the LORD had promised.

**4:44**
Matt 14:16, 20

## The Healing of Naaman

**5** The king of Aram had great admiration for Naaman, the commander of his army, because through him the LORD had given Aram great victories. But though Naaman was a mighty warrior, he suffered from leprosy.*

**5:1**
Luke 4:27

2At this time Aramean raiders had invaded the land of Israel, and among their captives was a young girl who had been given to Naaman's wife as a maid. 3One day the girl said to her mistress, "I wish my master would go to see the prophet in Samaria. He would heal him of his leprosy."

**5:2**
2 Kgs 6:23

4So Naaman told the king what the young girl from Israel had said. 5"Go and visit the prophet," the king of Aram told him. "I will send a letter of introduction for you to take to the king of Israel." So Naaman started out, carrying as gifts 750 pounds of silver, 150 pounds of gold,* and ten sets of clothing. 6The letter to the king of Israel said: "With this letter I present my servant Naaman. I want you to heal him of his leprosy."

**5:5**
1 Sam 9:7-8

7When the king of Israel read the letter, he tore his clothes in dismay and said, "This man sends me a leper to heal! Am I God, that I can give life and take it away? I can see that he's just trying to pick a fight with me."

**5:7**
Gen 30:2; 37:29
1 Kgs 20:7

**5:1** Or *from a contagious skin disease.* The Hebrew word used here and throughout this passage can describe various skin diseases.   **5:5** Hebrew *10 talents* [340 kilograms] *of silver, 6,000 shekels* [68 kilograms] *of gold.*

---

**5:1** Leprosy, much like AIDS today, was one of the most feared diseases of the time. Some forms were extremely contagious and, in many cases, incurable. In its worst forms, leprosy led to death. Many lepers were forced out of the cities into quarantined camps. Because Naaman still held his post, he probably had a mild form of the disease, or perhaps it was still in the early stages. In either case, his life would have been tragically shortened by his disease. (For more about leprosy in Bible times, see the note on Leviticus 13:1ff.)

**5:2** Aram was Israel's neighbor to the northeast, but the two nations were rarely on friendly terms. Under David, Aram paid tribute to Israel. In Elisha's day, Aram was growing in power and frequently conducted raids on Israel, trying to frustrate the people and bring about political confusion. Israelite captives often would be taken back to Aram after successful raids.

Naaman's servant girl was an Israelite, kidnapped from her home and family. Ironically, Naaman's only hope of being cured came from Israel.

**5:3, 4** The little girl's faith and Naaman's quest contrast with the stubbornness of Israel's king (5:7). A leader in mighty Aram sought the God of Israel; Israel's own king would not. We don't know the little girl's name or much about her, but her brief word to her mistress brought healing and faith in God to a powerful Aramean captain. God had placed her for a purpose, and she was faithful. Where has God put you? No matter how humble or small your position, God can use you to spread his Word. Look for opportunities to tell others what God can do. There's no telling who will hear your message!

**5:5** The name of Israel's king is not mentioned in this story. The events of 2 Kings 1–8 are mainly about Elisha's ministry and are not intended to be chronological. The king was most likely Jehoram (3:1), but we cannot know for sure.

[8]But when Elisha, the man of God, heard that the king of Israel had torn his clothes in dismay, he sent this message to him: "Why are you so upset? Send Naaman to me, and he will learn that there is a true prophet here in Israel."

**5:10**
John 9:7

[9]So Naaman went with his horses and chariots and waited at the door of Elisha's house. [10]But Elisha sent a messenger out to him with this message: "Go and wash yourself seven times in the Jordan River. Then your skin will be restored, and you will be healed of your leprosy."

[11]But Naaman became angry and stalked away. "I thought he would certainly come out to meet me!" he said. "I expected him to wave his hand over the leprosy and call on the name of the LORD his God and heal me! [12]Aren't the rivers of Damascus, the Abana and the Pharpar, better than any of the rivers of Israel? Why shouldn't I wash in them and be healed?" So Naaman turned and went away in a rage.

**5:12**
Prov 14:17; 19:11

**ELISHA**

Few "replacements" in Scripture were as effective as Elisha, who was Elijah's replacement as God's prophet to Israel. But Elisha had a great example to follow in the prophet Elijah. He remained with Elijah until the last moments of his teacher's life on earth. He was willing to follow and learn in order to gain power to do the work to which God had called him.

Both Elijah and Elisha concentrated their efforts on the particular needs of the people around them. The fiery Elijah confronted and exposed idolatry, helping to create an atmosphere where people could freely and publicly worship God. Elisha then moved in to demonstrate God's powerful, yet caring, nature to all who came to him for help. He spent less time in conflict with evil and more in compassionate care of people. The Bible records 18 encounters between Elisha and needy people.

Elisha saw more *in* life than most people because he recognized that with God there was more *to* life. He knew that all we are and have come to us from God. The miracles that occurred during Elisha's ministry put people in touch with the personal and all-powerful God. Elijah would have been proud of his replacement's work.

We, too, have great examples to follow—both people in Scripture and those who have positively influenced our lives. We must resist the tendency to think about the limitations that our family background or environment create for us. Instead, we should ask God to use us for his purposes—perhaps, like Elijah, to take a stand against great wrongs or, like Elisha, to show compassion for the daily needs of those around us. Ask him to use you as only he can.

| | |
|---|---|
| **Strengths and accomplishments** | • Was Elijah's successor as a prophet of God<br>• Had a ministry that lasted over 50 years<br>• Had a major impact on four nations: Israel, Judah, Moab, and Aram<br>• Was a man of integrity who did not try to enrich himself at others' expense<br>• Did many miracles to help those in need |
| **Lessons from his life** | • In God's eyes, one measure of greatness is the willingness to serve the poor as well as the powerful<br>• An effective replacement not only learns from his master but also builds upon his master's achievements |
| **Vital statistics** | • Where: Prophesied to the northern kingdom<br>• Occupations: Farmer, prophet<br>• Relative: Father: Shaphat<br>• Contemporaries: Elijah, Ahab, Jezebel, Jehu |
| **Key verse** | "When they came to the other side, Elijah said to Elisha, 'Tell me what I can do for you before I am taken away.' And Elisha replied, 'Please let me inherit a double share of your spirit and become your successor'" (2 Kings 2:9). |

Elisha's story is told in 1 Kings 19:16—2 Kings 13:20. He is also mentioned in Luke 4:27.

**5:9-15** Naaman, a great hero, was used to getting respect, so he was outraged when Elisha treated him like an ordinary person. A proud man, he expected royal treatment. To wash in a great river would be one thing, but the Jordan was small and dirty. To wash in the Jordan, Naaman thought, was beneath a man of his position. But Naaman had to humble himself and obey Elisha's commands in order to be healed.

Obedience to God begins with humility. We must believe that his way is better than our own. We may not always understand his ways of working, but by humbly obeying, we will receive his blessings. We must remember that (1) God's ways are best; (2) God wants our obedience more than anything else; (3) God can use anything to accomplish his purposes.

**5:12** Naaman left in a rage because the cure for his disease seemed too simple. He was a hero, and he expected a heroic cure. Full of pride and self-will, Naaman could not accept the simple cure of faith. Sometimes people react to God's offer of forgiveness in the same way. Just to *believe* in Jesus Christ somehow doesn't seem significant enough to bring eternal life. To obey God's commands doesn't seem heroic. What Naaman had to do to have his leprosy washed away is similar to what we must do to have our sin washed away—humbly accept God's mercy. Don't let your reaction to the way of faith keep you from the cure you need the most.

¹³But his officers tried to reason with him and said, "Sir,* if the prophet had told you to do something very difficult, wouldn't you have done it? So you should certainly obey him when he says simply, 'Go and wash and be cured!'" ¹⁴So Naaman went down to the Jordan River and dipped himself seven times, as the man of God had instructed him. And his skin became as healthy as the skin of a young child's, and he was healed!

¹⁵Then Naaman and his entire party went back to find the man of God. They stood before him, and Naaman said, "Now I know that there is no God in all the world except in Israel. So please accept a gift from your servant."

¹⁶But Elisha replied, "As surely as the LORD lives, whom I serve, I will not accept any gifts." And though Naaman urged him to take the gift, Elisha refused.

¹⁷Then Naaman said, "All right, but please allow me to load two of my mules with earth from this place, and I will take it back home with me. From now on I will never again offer burnt offerings or sacrifices to any other god except the LORD. ¹⁸However, may the LORD pardon me in this one thing: When my master the king goes into the temple of the god Rimmon to worship there and leans on my arm, may the LORD pardon me when I bow, too."

¹⁹"Go in peace," Elisha said. So Naaman started home again.

### The Greed of Gehazi

²⁰But Gehazi, the servant of Elisha, the man of God, said to himself, "My master should not have let this Aramean get away without accepting any of his gifts. As surely as the LORD lives, I will chase after him and get something from him." ²¹So Gehazi set off after Naaman.

When Naaman saw Gehazi running after him, he climbed down from his chariot and went to meet him. "Is everything all right?" Naaman asked.

²²"Yes," Gehazi said, "but my master has sent me to tell you that two young prophets from the hill country of Ephraim have just arrived. He would like 75 pounds* of silver and two sets of clothing to give to them."

²³"By all means, take twice as much* silver," Naaman insisted. He gave him two sets of clothing, tied up the money in two bags, and sent two of his servants to carry the gifts for Gehazi. ²⁴But when they arrived at the citadel,* Gehazi took the gifts from the servants and sent the men back. Then he went and hid the gifts inside the house.

²⁵When he went in to his master, Elisha asked him, "Where have you been, Gehazi?"

"I haven't been anywhere," he replied.

²⁶But Elisha asked him, "Don't you realize that I was there in spirit when Naaman stepped down from his chariot to meet you? Is this the time to receive money and clothing, olive groves and vineyards, sheep and cattle, and male and female servants? ²⁷Because you have done this, you and your descendants will suffer from Naaman's leprosy forever." When Gehazi left the room, he was covered with leprosy; his skin was white as snow.

### The Floating Ax Head

**6** One day the group of prophets came to Elisha and told him, "As you can see, this place where we meet with you is too small. ²Let's go down to the Jordan River, where there are plenty of logs. There we can build a new place for us to meet."

"All right," he told them, "go ahead."

**Cross-references (right margin):**
5:14 Job 33:23-25 Luke 4:27; 5:13
5:15 1 Sam 17:46-47
5:16 Gen 14:22-23 2 Kgs 3:14
5:17 Exod 20:24
5:18 2 Kgs 7:2
5:20 2 Kgs 4:11-12, 31, 36
5:22 2 Kgs 5:5
5:26 2 Kgs 5:16
5:27 Exod 4:6 Num 12:10
6:1 2 Kgs 2:3, 5, 7

**5:13** Hebrew *My father.*   **5:22** Hebrew *1 talent* [34 kilograms].   **5:23** Hebrew *take 2 talents* [68 kilograms].
**5:24** Hebrew *the Ophel.*

---

**5:16** Elisha refused Naaman's money to show that God's favor cannot be purchased. Our money, like Naaman's, is useless when we face death. No matter how much wealth we accumulate in this life, it will evaporate when we stand before God, our Creator. Our faith in Jesus Christ will save us, not our bank accounts.

**5:18, 19** How could Naaman be forgiven for bowing to a pagan idol? Naaman was not asking for permission to worship the god Rimmon but to do his civil duty, helping the king get down and up as he bowed. Also known as Hadad, Rimmon, the god of Damascus, was believed to be a god of rain and thunder. Unlike most of his contemporaries, Naaman showed a keen awareness of God's power. Instead of adding God to his nation's collection of idols, he acknowledged that there was only one true God. He did not intend to worship other gods. His asking for pardon in this one area shows the marked contrast between Naaman and the Israelites, who were continually worshiping many idols.

**5:20-27** Gehazi saw a perfect opportunity to get rich by selfishly asking for the reward Elisha had refused. Unfortunately, his plan had three problems: (1) He willingly accepted money that had been offered to someone else; (2) he wrongly implied that money could be exchanged for God's free gift of healing and mercy; (3) he lied and tried to cover up his motives for accepting the money. Although Gehazi had been a helpful servant, personal gain had become more important to him than serving God.

This passage is not teaching that money is evil or that ministers should not get paid; instead, it is warning against greed and deceit. True service is motivated by love and devotion to God and seeks no personal gain. As you serve God, check your motives—you can't serve both money and God (Matthew 6:24).

**6:1-7** The incident of the floating ax head is recorded to show God's care and provision for those who trust him, even in the insignificant events of everyday life. God is always present. Placed

3"Please come with us," someone suggested.

"I will," he said. 4So he went with them.

When they arrived at the Jordan, they began cutting down trees. 5But as one of them was cutting a tree, his ax head fell into the river. "Oh, sir!" he cried. "It was a borrowed ax!"

**6:6**
Exod 15:25
2 Kgs 2:21; 4:41

6"Where did it fall?" the man of God asked. When he showed him the place, Elisha cut a stick and threw it into the water at that spot. Then the ax head floated to the surface. 7"Grab it," Elisha said. And the man reached out and grabbed it.

### Elisha Traps the Arameans

8When the king of Aram was at war with Israel, he would confer with his officers and say, "We will mobilize our forces at such and such a place."

**6:9**
1 Kgs 20:13, 28
2 Kgs 6:12

9But immediately Elisha, the man of God, would warn the king of Israel, "Do not go near that place, for the Arameans are planning to mobilize their troops there." 10So the king of Israel would send word to the place indicated by the man of God. Time and again Elisha warned the king, so that he would be on the alert there.

11The king of Aram became very upset over this. He called his officers together and demanded, "Which of you is the traitor? Who has been informing the king of Israel of my plans?"

12"It's not us, my lord the king," one of the officers replied. "Elisha, the prophet in Israel, tells the king of Israel even the words you speak in the privacy of your bedroom!"

**6:13**
Gen 37:17

13"Go and find out where he is," the king commanded, "so I can send troops to seize him."

And the report came back: "Elisha is at Dothan." 14So one night the king of Aram sent a great army with many chariots and horses to surround the city.

15When the servant of the man of God got up early the next morning and went outside, there were troops, horses, and chariots everywhere. "Oh, sir, what will we do now?" the young man cried to Elisha.

**6:16**
Exod 14:13
2 Chr 32:7
Rom 8:31
**6:17**
2 Kgs 2:11-12

16"Don't be afraid!" Elisha told him. "For there are more on our side than on theirs!" 17Then Elisha prayed, "O LORD, open his eyes and let him see!" The LORD opened the young man's eyes, and when he looked up, he saw that the hillside around Elisha was filled with horses and chariots of fire.

**6:18**
Gen 19:11

18As the Aramean army advanced toward him, Elisha prayed, "O LORD, please make them blind." So the LORD struck them with blindness as Elisha had asked.

**6:19**
1 Kgs 20:1
2 Kgs 3:1

19Then Elisha went out and told them, "You have come the wrong way! This isn't the right city! Follow me, and I will take you to the man you are looking for." And he led them to the city of Samaria.

20As soon as they had entered Samaria, Elisha prayed, "O LORD, now open their eyes and let them see." So the LORD opened their eyes, and they discovered that they were in the middle of Samaria.

**6:21**
1 Sam 24:4, 19;
26:8

21When the king of Israel saw them, he shouted to Elisha, "My father, should I kill them? Should I kill them?"

---

**ELISHA AND THE ARAMEANS**
Elisha knew Aram's battle plans and kept Israel's king informed. The Aramean king tracked down Elisha at Dothan, but Elisha prayed that the Aramean army would be blinded. He then led the blind army into Samaria, Israel's capital city!

in the Bible between the healing of an Aramean general and the deliverance of Israel's army, this miracle also shows Elisha's personal contact with the students in the groups of the prophets. Although he had the respect of kings, Elisha never forgot to care for the faithful. Don't let the importance of your work crowd out your concern for human need.

**6:16, 17** Elisha's servant was no longer afraid when he saw God's mighty heavenly army. Faith reveals that God is doing more for his people than we can ever realize through sight alone. When you face difficulties that seem insurmountable, remember that spiritual resources are there even if you can't see them. Look with the eyes of faith, and let God show you his resources. If you don't see God working in your life, the problem may be your spiritual eyesight, not God's power.

22"Of course not!" Elisha replied. "Do we kill prisoners of war? Give them food and drink and send them home again to their master."

23So the king made a great feast for them and then sent them home to their master. After that, the Aramean raiders stayed away from the land of Israel.

*6:22*
Deut 20:11
2 Chr 28:8-15
Rom 12:20

*6:23*
2 Kgs 5:2

### Ben-Hadad Besieges Samaria

24Some time later, however, King Ben-hadad of Aram mustered his entire army and besieged Samaria. 25As a result, there was a great famine in the city. The siege lasted so long that a donkey's head sold for eighty pieces of silver, and a cup of dove's dung sold for five pieces* of silver.

26One day as the king of Israel was walking along the wall of the city, a woman called to him, "Please help me, my lord the king!"

27He answered, "If the LORD doesn't help you, what can I do? I have neither food from the threshing floor nor wine from the press to give you." 28But then the king asked, "What is the matter?"

She replied, "This woman said to me: 'Come on, let's eat your son today, then we will eat my son tomorrow.' 29So we cooked my son and ate him. Then the next day I said to her, 'Kill your son so we can eat him,' but she has hidden her son."

30When the king heard this, he tore his clothes in despair. And as the king walked along the wall, the people could see that he was wearing burlap under his robe next to his skin. 31"May God strike me and even kill me if I don't separate Elisha's head from his shoulders this very day," the king vowed.

32Elisha was sitting in his house with the elders of Israel when the king sent a messenger to summon him. But before the messenger arrived, Elisha said to the elders, "A murderer has sent a man to cut off my head. When he arrives, shut the door and keep him out. We will soon hear his master's steps following him."

33While Elisha was still saying this, the messenger arrived. And the king* said, "All this misery is from the LORD! Why should I wait for the LORD any longer?"

*6:24*
1 Kgs 20:1

*6:28*
Lev 26:29
Deut 28:53-55

*6:29*
Lev 26:29
Deut 28:53

*6:31*
1 Kgs 19:2

*6:32*
1 Kgs 18:3-4, 14
Ezek 8:1; 14:1; 20:1

*6:33*
Isa 8:21

7 Elisha replied, "Listen to this message from the LORD! This is what the LORD says: By this time tomorrow in the markets of Samaria, five quarts of choice flour will cost only one piece of silver,* and ten quarts of barley grain will cost only one piece of silver.*"

2The officer assisting the king said to the man of God, "That couldn't happen even if the LORD opened the windows of heaven!"

But Elisha replied, "You will see it happen with your own eyes, but you won't be able to eat any of it!"

*7:2*
Gen 7:11
2 Kgs 5:18
Mal 3:10

**6:25** Hebrew *sold for 80 shekels* [2 pounds, or 0.9 kilograms] *of silver, and 1/4 of a cab* [0.3 liters] *of dove's dung sold for 5 shekels* [2 ounces, or 57 grams]. *Dove's dung* may be a variety of wild vegetable.    **6:33** Hebrew *he.*
**7:1a** Hebrew *1 seah* [6 liters] *of choice flour will cost 1 shekel* [0.4 ounces, or 11 grams]; also in 7:16, 18.
**7:1b** Hebrew *2 seahs* [12 liters] *of barley grain will cost 1 shekel* [0.4 ounces, or 11 grams]; also in 7:16, 18.

---

**6:21, 22** Elisha told the king not to kill the Arameans. The king was not to take credit for what God alone had done. In setting food and water before them, he was heaping "burning coals" on their heads (Proverbs 25:21, 22).

**6:23** How long the Arameans stayed away from Israel is not known, but a number of years probably passed before the invasion recorded in 6:24 occurred. The Arameans must have forgotten the time their army had been supernaturally blinded and sent home.

**6:24** This was probably Ben-hadad II, whose father had ruled Aram in the days of Baasha (1 Kings 15:18). Elisha constantly frustrated Ben-hadad II in his attempts to take control of Israel.

**6:25** When a city like Samaria faced famine, it was no small matter. Although its farmers grew enough food to feed the people for a specific season, they did not have enough to sustain them in prolonged times of emergency when all supplies were cut off. This famine was so severe that mothers resorted to eating their children (6:26-30). Deuteronomy 28:49-57 predicted that this would happen when the people of Israel rejected God's leadership.

**6:31-33** Why did the king blame Elisha for the famine and troubles of the siege? Here are some possible reasons: (1) Some commentators say that Elisha must have told the king to trust God for deliverance. The king did this and even wore burlap (6:30), but at this point the situation seemed hopeless. Apparently the king thought Elisha had given him bad advice and not even God could help them. (2) For years the kings of Israel and the prophets of God had been in conflict. The prophets often predicted doom because of the kings' evil, so the kings saw them as troublemakers. Thus, Israel's king was striking out in frustration at Elisha. (3) The king may have remembered when Elijah helped bring an end to a famine (1 Kings 18:41-46). Knowing Elisha was a man of God, perhaps the king thought he could do any miracle he wanted and was angry that he had not come to Israel's rescue.

**7:1, 2** When Elisha prophesied God's deliverance, the king's officer said it couldn't happen. The officer's faith and hope were gone, but God's words came true anyway (7:14-16)! Sometimes we become preoccupied with problems when we should be looking for opportunities. Instead of focusing on the negatives, we should develop an attitude of expectancy. To say that God *cannot* rescue someone or that a situation is *impossible* demonstrates a lack of faith.

## Lepers Visit the Enemy Camp

7:3
Lev 13:45-46
Num 5:1-4

7:4
2 Kgs 6:24

3Now there were four men with leprosy* sitting at the entrance of the city gates. "Why should we sit here waiting to die?" they asked each other. 4"We will starve if we stay here, but with the famine in the city, we will starve if we go back there. So we might as well go out and surrender to the Aramean army. If they let us live, so much the better. But if they kill us, we would have died anyway."

7:6
2 Sam 5:24
2 Chr 12:2-3

5So at twilight they set out for the camp of the Arameans. But when they came to the edge of the camp, no one was there! 6For the Lord had caused the Aramean army to hear the clatter of speeding chariots and the galloping of horses and the sounds of a great army approaching. "The king of Israel has hired the Hittites and Egyptians* to attack us!" they

7:7
Ps 48:4-6
Prov 28:1

cried to one another. 7So they panicked and ran into the night, abandoning their tents, horses, donkeys, and everything else, as they fled for their lives.

8When the lepers arrived at the edge of the camp, they went into one tent after another, eating and drinking wine; and they carried off silver and gold and clothing and hid it. 9Finally, they said to each other, "This is not right. This is a day of good news, and we aren't sharing it with anyone! If we wait until morning, some calamity will certainly fall upon us. Come on, let's go back and tell the people at the palace."

10So they went back to the city and told the gatekeepers what had happened. "We went out to the Aramean camp," they said, "and no one was there! The horses and donkeys were tethered and the tents were all in order, but there wasn't a single person around!" 11Then the gatekeepers shouted the news to the people in the palace.

## Israel Plunders the Camp

7:12
Josh 8:6-12
2 Kgs 6:25-29

12The king got out of bed in the middle of the night and told his officers, "I know what has happened. The Arameans know we are starving, so they have left their camp and have hidden in the fields. They are expecting us to leave the city, and then they will take us alive and capture the city."

13One of his officers replied, "We had better send out scouts to check into this. Let them take five of the remaining horses. If something happens to them, it will be no worse than if they stay here and die with the rest of us."

14So two chariots with horses were prepared, and the king sent scouts to see what had happened to the Aramean army. 15They went all the way to the Jordan River, following a trail of clothing and equipment that the Arameans had thrown away in their mad rush to escape.

7:16
2 Kgs 7:1

The scouts returned and told the king about it. 16Then the people of Samaria rushed out and plundered the Aramean camp. So it was true that five quarts of choice flour were sold that day for one piece of silver, and ten quarts of barley grain were sold for one piece of silver, just

7:17
2 Kgs 7:2

as the Lord had promised. 17The king appointed his officer to control the traffic at the gate, but he was knocked down and trampled to death as the people rushed out.

7:3 Or *with a contagious skin disease.* The Hebrew word used here and throughout this passage can describe various skin diseases.   7:6 Possibly *and the people of Muzur,* a district near Cilicia.

---

**PEOPLE RAISED FROM THE DEAD**
God is all-powerful. Nothing in life is beyond his control, not even death.

| | |
|---|---|
| Elijah raised a boy from the dead | 1 Kings 17:22 |
| Elisha raised a boy from the dead | 2 Kings 4:34, 35 |
| Elisha's bones raised a man from the dead | 2 Kings 13:20, 21 |
| Jesus raised a boy from the dead | Luke 7:14, 15 |
| Jesus raised a girl from the dead | Luke 8:52-56 |
| Jesus raised Lazarus from the dead | John 11:38-44 |
| Peter raised a woman from the dead | Acts 9:40, 41 |
| Paul raised a man from the dead | Acts 20:9-20 |

---

**7:3** According to the law, lepers were not allowed in the city but were to depend on charity outside the gate (Leviticus 13:45, 46; Numbers 5:1-4). Because of the famine and the presence of the Aramean army, their situation was desperate.

**7:3-10** The lepers discovered the deserted camp and realized that their lives had been spared. At first they kept the good news to themselves, forgetting their fellow citizens who were starving in the city. The Good News about Jesus Christ must be shared, too,

for no news is more important. We must not forget those who are dying without it. We must not become so preoccupied with our own faith that we neglect sharing it with those around us. Our "good news," like that of the lepers, will not "wait until morning."

So everything happened exactly as the man of God had predicted when the king came to his house. [18]The man of God had said to the king, "By this time tomorrow in the markets of Samaria, five quarts of choice flour will cost one piece of silver, and ten quarts of barley grain will cost one piece of silver."

[19]The king's officer had replied, "That couldn't happen even if the Lord opened the windows of heaven!" And the man of God had said, "You will see it happen with your own eyes, but you won't be able to eat any of it!" [20]And so it was, for the people trampled him to death at the gate!

### The Woman from Shunem Returns Home

**8** Elisha had told the woman whose son he had brought back to life, "Take your family and move to some other place, for the Lord has called for a famine on Israel that will last for seven years." [2]So the woman did as the man of God instructed. She took her family and settled in the land of the Philistines for seven years.

[3]After the famine ended she returned from the land of the Philistines, and she went to see the king about getting back her house and land. [4]As she came in, the king was talking with Gehazi, the servant of the man of God. The king had just said, "Tell me some stories about the great things Elisha has done." [5]And Gehazi was telling the king about the time Elisha had brought a boy back to life. At that very moment, the mother of the boy walked in to make her appeal to the king about her house and land.

"Look, my lord the king!" Gehazi exclaimed. "Here is the woman now, and this is her son—the very one Elisha brought back to life!"

[6]"Is this true?" the king asked her. And she told him the story. So he directed one of his officials to see that everything she had lost was restored to her, including the value of any crops that had been harvested during her absence.

### Hazael Murders Ben-Hadad

[7]Elisha went to Damascus, the capital of Aram, where King Ben-hadad lay sick. When someone told the king that the man of God had come, [8]the king said to Hazael, "Take a gift to the man of God. Then tell him to ask the Lord, 'Will I recover from this illness?'"

[9]So Hazael loaded down forty camels with the finest products of Damascus as a gift for Elisha. He went to him and said, "Your servant Ben-hadad, the king of Aram, has sent me to ask, 'Will I recover from this illness?'"

[10]And Elisha replied, "Go and tell him, 'You will surely recover.' But actually the Lord has shown me that he will surely die!" [11]Elisha stared at Hazael* with a fixed gaze until Hazael became uneasy.* Then the man of God started weeping.

[12]"What's the matter, my lord?" Hazael asked him.

Elisha replied, "I know the terrible things you will do to the people of Israel. You will burn their fortified cities, kill their young men with the sword, dash their little children to the ground, and rip open their pregnant women!"

[13]Hazael responded, "How could a nobody like me* ever accomplish such great things?"

Elisha answered, "The Lord has shown me that you are going to be the king of Aram."

[14]When Hazael left Elisha and went back, the king asked him, "What did Elisha tell you?" And Hazael replied, "He told me that you will surely recover."

[15]But the next day Hazael took a blanket, soaked it in water, and held it over the king's face until he died. Then Hazael became the next king of Aram.

**8:11a** Hebrew *He stared at him.*   **8:11b** The meaning of the Hebrew is uncertain.   **8:13** Hebrew *a dog.*

Cross-references: 7:19 2 Kgs 7:2; 8:1 Gen 41:27, Ps 105:16, Hag 1:11; 8:2 2 Kgs 4:18, 31-35; 8:4 2 Kgs 4:11-12; 5:20-27; 8:5 2 Kgs 4:34-35; 8:7 2 Kgs 6:24; 8:8 1 Kgs 14:3; 19:15; 8:11 Luke 19:41; 8:12 2 Kgs 10:32-33; 12:17; 13:3; 15:16; 8:13 1 Sam 17:43, 2 Sam 9:8, 1 Kgs 19:15

**7:19, 20** God, not worthless idols, provides our daily food. Although our faith may be weak or very small, we must avoid becoming skeptical of God's provision. When our resources are low and our doubts are the strongest, remember God can open the floodgates of heaven.

**8:1-6** This story must have happened before the events recorded in chapter 5 because the seven-year famine would have ended before Gehazi was struck with leprosy. This shows Elisha's long-term concern for this widow and contrasts his miraculous public ministry with his private ministry to this family. Elisha exemplifies the kind of concern we should have for others.

**8:12, 13** When Elisha told Hazael he would sin greatly, Hazael protested that he would never do that sort of thing. He did not acknowledge his personal potential for evil. In our enlightened society, we might think that we are above gross sin and can control our actions. We think that we would never sink so low. Instead, we should take a more biblical and realistic look at ourselves and admit our sinful potential. Then we will ask for God's strength to resist such evil.

**8:12-15** Elisha's words about Hazael's treatment of Israel were partially fulfilled in 10:32, 33. Apparently Hazael had known he would be king because Elijah had anointed him (1 Kings 19:15). But he was impatient and, instead of waiting for God's timing, took matters into his own hands, killing Ben-hadad. God used Hazael as an instrument of judgment against the disobedient Israelites.

## 2. Kings of Israel and Judah
### Jehoram Rules in Judah

8:16-24
//2 Chr 21:5-20
8:17
2 Chr 21:5-10
8:19
2 Sam 7:12-15
1 Kgs 11:36
8:20
1 Kgs 22:47
2 Kgs 3:9, 26
8:22
Gen 27:39-40
Josh 21:13
8:24
2 Chr 21:20; 22:1

16Jehoram son of King Jehoshaphat of Judah began to rule over Judah in the fifth year of the reign of Joram son of Ahab, king of Israel. 17Jehoram was thirty-two years old when he became king, and he reigned in Jerusalem eight years. 18But Jehoram followed the example of the kings of Israel and was as wicked as King Ahab, for he had married one of Ahab's daughters. So Jehoram did what was evil in the LORD's sight. 19But the LORD did not want to destroy Judah, for he had made a covenant with David and promised that his descendants would continue to rule, shining like a lamp forever.

20During Jehoram's reign, the Edomites revolted against Judah and crowned their own king. 21So Jehoram* went with all his chariots to attack the town of Zair.* The Edomites surrounded him and his chariot commanders, but he went out at night and attacked them* under cover of darkness. But Jehoram's army deserted him and fled to their homes. 22So Edom has been independent from Judah to this day. The town of Libnah also revolted about that same time.

23The rest of the events in Jehoram's reign and everything he did are recorded in *The Book of the History of the Kings of Judah.* 24When Jehoram died, he was buried with his ancestors in the City of David. Then his son Ahaziah became the next king.

### Ahaziah Rules in Judah

8:25-29
//2 Chr 22:1-6
8:26
2 Kgs 11:1
8:27
1 Kgs 16:30
8:29
2 Kgs 9:14-15
2 Chr 22:5-6

25Ahaziah son of Jehoram began to rule over Judah in the twelfth year of the reign of Joram son of Ahab, king of Israel.

26Ahaziah was twenty-two years old when he became king, and he reigned in Jerusalem one year. His mother was Athaliah, a granddaughter of King Omri of Israel. 27Ahaziah followed the evil example of King Ahab's family. He did what was evil in the LORD's sight, just as Ahab's family had done, for he was related by marriage to the family of Ahab.

28Ahaziah joined Joram son of Ahab, the king of Israel, in his war against King Hazael of Aram at Ramoth-gilead. When the Arameans wounded King Joram in the battle, 29he returned to Jezreel to recover from the wounds he had received at Ramoth.* Because Joram was wounded, King Ahaziah of Judah went to Jezreel to visit him.

### Jehu Anointed King of Israel

9:1
1 Sam 10:1; 16:1
1 Kgs 1:39
2 Kgs 8:28
9:3
1 Kgs 19:16

**9** Meanwhile, Elisha the prophet had summoned a member of the group of prophets. "Get ready to travel,"* he told him, "and take this flask of olive oil with you. Go to Ramoth-gilead, 2and find Jehu son of Jehoshaphat, son of Nimshi. Call him into a private room away from his friends, 3and pour the oil over his head. Say to him, 'This is what the LORD says: I anoint you to be the king over Israel.' Then open the door and run for your life!"

4So the young prophet did as he was told and went to Ramoth-gilead. 5When he arrived there, he found Jehu sitting around with the other army officers. "I have a message for you, Commander," he said.

8:21a Hebrew *Joram,* a variant spelling of Jehoram; also in 8:23, 24. 8:21b Greek version reads *Seir.* 8:21c Or *he went out and escaped.* The meaning of the Hebrew is uncertain. 8:29 Hebrew *Ramah,* a variant spelling of Ramoth. 9:1 Hebrew *Bind up your loins.*

8:18 King Jehoshaphat arranged the marriage between Jehoram, his son, and Athaliah, the daughter of wicked Ahab and Jezebel. Athaliah followed the idolatrous ways of the northern kingdom, bringing Baal worship into Judah and starting the southern kingdom's decline. When Jehoram died, his son Ahaziah became king. Then, when Ahaziah was killed in battle, Athaliah murdered all her grandsons except Joash and made herself queen (11:1-3). Jehoram's marriage may have been politically advantageous, but spiritually it was deadly.

8:20-22 Although Judah and Edom shared a common border and a common ancestor (Isaac), the two nations fought continually. Edom had been a vassal state of the united kingdom of Israel and then the southern kingdom of Judah since the days of David (2 Samuel 8:13, 14). Here Edom rebelled against Judah and declared independence. Immediately Jehoram marched out to attack Edom, but his ambush failed. Thus, Jehoram lost some of his borderlands as punishment for his failure to honor God.

8:26 Ahaziah was the only remaining son of Jehoram of Judah. Although he was the youngest son, he took the throne because the rest of his brothers had been taken captive in a raid by the Philistines and Arabs (2 Chronicles 21:16, 17).

8:26, 27 Ahaziah's mother was Athaliah, daughter of Ahab and Jezebel, former king and queen of Israel, and granddaughter of Omri, Ahab's father and predecessor. The evil of Ahab and Jezebel spread to Judah through Athaliah.

8:29 Jezreel was the location of the summer palace of the kings of Israel.

9:3 Elijah had prophesied that many people would be killed when Jehu became king (1 Kings 19:16, 17). Thus Elisha advised the young prophet to get out of the area as soon as he delivered his message, before the slaughter began. Jehu's actions seem harsh, as he hunted down relatives and friends of Ahab (2 Chronicles 22:8, 9), but unchecked Baal worship was destroying the nation. If Israel was to survive, the followers of Baal had to be eliminated. Jehu fulfilled the need of the hour—justice.

"For which one of us?" Jehu asked.

"For you, Commander," he replied.

6So Jehu left the others and went into the house. Then the young prophet poured the oil over Jehu's head and said, "This is what the LORD, the God of Israel, says: I anoint you king over the LORD's people, Israel. 7You are to destroy the family of Ahab, your master. In this way, I will avenge the murder of my prophets and all the LORD's servants who were killed by Jezebel. 8The entire family of Ahab must be wiped out. I will destroy every one of his male descendants, slave and free alike, anywhere in Israel. 9I will destroy the family of Ahab as I destroyed the families of Jeroboam son of Nebat and of Baasha son of Ahijah. 10Dogs will eat Ahab's wife Jezebel at the plot of land in Jezreel, and no one will bury her." Then the young prophet opened the door and ran.

11Jehu went back to his fellow officers, and one of them asked him, "What did that madman want? Is everything all right?"

"You know how a man like that babbles on," Jehu replied.

12"You're hiding something," they said. "Tell us."

So Jehu told them, "He said to me, 'This is what the LORD says: I have anointed you to be king over Israel.'"

13Then they quickly spread out their cloaks on the bare steps and blew the ram's horn, shouting, "Jehu is king!"

### Jehu Kills Joram and Ahaziah

14So Jehu son of Jehoshaphat, son of Nimshi, led a conspiracy against King Joram. (Now Joram had been with the army at Ramoth-gilead, defending Israel against the forces of King Hazael of Aram. 15But King Joram* was wounded in the fighting and returned to Jezreel to recover from his wounds.) So Jehu told the men with him, "If you want me to be king, don't let anyone leave town and go to Jezreel to report what we have done."

16Then Jehu got into a chariot and rode to Jezreel to find King Joram, who was lying there wounded. King Ahaziah of Judah was there, too, for he had gone to visit him. 17The watchman on the tower of Jezreel saw Jehu and his company approaching, so he shouted to Joram, "I see a company of troops coming!"

"Send out a rider to ask if they are coming in peace," King Joram ordered.

18So a horseman went out to meet Jehu and said, "The king wants to know if you are coming in peace."

Jehu replied, "What do you know about peace? Fall in behind me!"

The watchman called out to the king, "The messenger has met them, but he's not returning."

19So the king sent out a second horseman. He rode up to them and said, "The king wants to know if you come in peace."

**9:15** Hebrew *Jehoram*, a variant spelling of Joram; also in 9:17, 21, 22, 23, 24.

---

**9:6**
1 Kgs 19:16

**9:7**
Deut 32:35
1 Sam 25:22
1 Kgs 18:3-4; 21:15, 21
2 Kgs 10:17

**9:9**
1 Kgs 14:10; 15:29; 16:3, 11

**9:10**
1 Kgs 21:23
2 Kgs 9:35-36

**9:13**
2 Sam 15:10
1 Kgs 1:34, 39
Matt 21:8

**9:14-15**
2 Kgs 8:28-29

---

**9:7** Elisha's statement fulfilled Elijah's prophecy made 20 years earlier that all of Ahab's family would be killed (1 Kings 21:17-24). Jezebel's death, predicted by Elijah, is described in 9:30-37.

**9:9** Ahab's dynasty would end as had those of Jeroboam and Baasha. Ahijah had prophesied the end of Jeroboam's dynasty (1 Kings 14:1-11), and this was fulfilled by Baasha (1 Kings 15:29). The prophet Jehu—not King Jehu—then foretold the end of Baasha's family (1 Kings 16:1-7), and this, too, was fulfilled (1 Kings 16:11, 12). The end of Ahab's family, therefore, was certain—Elijah had predicted it (1 Kings 21:17-24), and God brought it to pass.

**9:18, 19** The riders met Jehu and asked if he came in peace. But Jehu responded, "What do you know about peace?" Peace, properly understood, comes from God. It is not genuine except when rooted in belief in God and love for him. Jehu knew the men represented a disobedient, wicked king. Don't seek peace and friendship with those who are enemies of the good and the true. Lasting peace can come only from knowing God who gives it to us.

**JEHU TAKES OVER ISRAEL**
Elisha sent a prophet to Ramoth-gilead to anoint Jehu as Israel's new king. Jehu immediately rode to Jezreel to find and kill King Joram of Israel and King Ahaziah of Judah. Jehu killed Joram; Ahaziah fled toward Beth-haggan, where he was wounded. He later died at Megiddo. Back in Jezreel, Jehu had Jezebel killed.

9:20
2 Sam 18:27

9:21-29
1 Kgs 21:1
//2 Chr 22:7-9

9:22
1 Kgs 16:31; 18:19

Again Jehu answered, "What do you know about peace? Fall in behind me!"
20The watchman exclaimed, "The messenger has met them, but he isn't returning either! It must be Jehu son of Nimshi, for he's driving like a madman."
21"Quick! Get my chariot ready!" King Joram commanded.
Then King Joram of Israel and King Ahaziah of Judah rode out in their chariots to meet Jehu. They met him at the plot of land that had belonged to Naboth of Jezreel. 22King Joram demanded, "Do you come in peace, Jehu?"
Jehu replied, "How can there be peace as long as the idolatry and witchcraft of your mother, Jezebel, are all around us?"

9:23
2 Kgs 11:14

9:24
1 Kgs 22:34

9:25
1 Kgs 21:1, 19

9:26
1 Kgs 21:19

23Then King Joram turned the horses around* and fled, shouting to King Ahaziah, "Treason, Ahaziah!" 24But Jehu drew his bow and shot Joram between the shoulders. The arrow pierced his heart, and he sank down dead in his chariot.
25Jehu said to Bidkar, his officer, "Throw him into the plot of land that belonged to Naboth of Jezreel. Do you remember when you and I were riding along behind his father, Ahab? The LORD pronounced this message against him: 26'I solemnly swear that I will repay him here on this plot of land, says the LORD, for the murder of Naboth and his sons that I saw yesterday.' So throw him out on Naboth's property, just as the LORD said."

**9:23** Hebrew *turned his hands.*

**JEHU**

Jehu had the basic qualities that could have made him a great success. From a human perspective, in fact, he was a successful king. His family ruled the northern kingdom longer than any other. He was used by God as an instrument of punishment to Ahab's evil dynasty, and he fiercely attacked Baal worship. He came close to being God's kind of king, but he recklessly went beyond God's commands and failed to follow through on the obedient actions that began his reign. Within sight of victory, he settled for mediocrity.

Jehu was a man of immediate action but without ultimate purpose. His kingdom moved, but its destination was unclear. He eliminated one form of idolatry, Baal worship, only to uphold another by continuing to worship the gold calves Jeroboam had set up. He could have accomplished much for God if he had been obedient to the one who made him king. Even when he was carrying out God's directions, Jehu's style showed he was not fully aware of who was directing him.

As he did with Jehu, God gives each person strengths and abilities that will find their greatest usefulness only under his control. Outside that control, however, they don't accomplish what they could and often become tools for evil. One way to make sure this does not happen is to tell God of your willingness to be under his control. With his presence in your life, your natural strengths and abilities will be used to their greatest potential for the greatest good.

| | |
|---|---|
| **Strengths and accomplishments** | • Took the throne from Ahab's family and destroyed his evil influence<br>• Founded the longest-lived dynasty of the northern kingdom<br>• Was anointed by Elijah and confirmed by Elisha<br>• Destroyed Baal worship |
| **Weaknesses and mistakes** | • Had a reckless outlook on life that made him bold and prone to error<br>• Worshiped Jeroboam's gold calves<br>• Was devoted to God only to the point that obedience served his own interests |
| **Lessons from his life** | • Fierce commitment needs control because it can result in recklessness<br>• Obedience involves both action and direction |
| **Vital statistics** | • Where: The northern kingdom of Israel<br>• Occupations: Commander in the army of Joram, king of Israel<br>• Relatives: Grandfather: Nimshi. Father: Jehoshaphat. Son: Jehoahaz.<br>• Contemporaries: Elijah, Elisha, Ahab, Jezebel, Joram, Ahaziah |
| **Key verse** | "But Jehu did not obey the Law of the LORD, the God of Israel, with all his heart. He refused to turn from the sins that Jeroboam had led Israel to commit" (2 Kings 10:31). |

Jehu's story is told in 1 Kings 19:16—2 Kings 10:36. He is also mentioned in 2 Kings 15:12; 2 Chronicles 22:7–9; Hosea 1:4, 5.

**9:26** Joram of Israel was wicked like his father and mother, Ahab and Jezebel; therefore, his body was thrown into the field that his parents had unlawfully taken. Jezebel had arranged the murder of Naboth, the previous owner, because he would not sell his vineyard—which Ahab wanted for a garden (1 Kings 21:1-24). Little did Ahab know that it would become a burial plot for his evil son.

²⁷When King Ahaziah of Judah saw what was happening, he fled along the road to Beth-haggan. Jehu rode after him, shouting, "Shoot him, too!" So they shot Ahaziah in his chariot at the Ascent of Gur, near Ibleam. He was able to go on as far as Megiddo, but he died there. ²⁸His servants took him by chariot to Jerusalem, where they buried him with his ancestors in the City of David. ²⁹Ahaziah had become king over Judah in the eleventh year of the reign of Joram son of Ahab.

### The Death of Jezebel

³⁰When Jezebel, the queen mother, heard that Jehu had come to Jezreel, she painted her eyelids and fixed her hair and sat at a window. ³¹When Jehu entered the gate of the palace, she shouted at him, "Have you come in peace, you murderer? You're just like Zimri, who murdered his master!"*

³²Jehu looked up and saw her at the window and shouted, "Who is on my side?" And two or three eunuchs looked out at him. ³³"Throw her down!" Jehu yelled. So they threw her out the window, and her blood spattered against the wall and on the horses. And Jehu trampled her body under his horses' hooves.

³⁴Then Jehu went into the palace and ate and drank. Afterward he said, "Someone go and bury this cursed woman, for she is the daughter of a king." ³⁵But when they went out to bury her, they found only her skull, her feet, and her hands.

³⁶When they returned and told Jehu, he stated, "This fulfills the message from the Lord, which he spoke through his servant Elijah from Tishbe: 'At the plot of land in Jezreel, dogs will eat Jezebel's body. ³⁷Her remains will be scattered like dung on the plot of land in Jezreel, so that no one will be able to recognize her.'"

### Jehu Kills Ahab's Family

**10** Ahab had seventy sons living in the city of Samaria. So Jehu wrote letters and sent them to Samaria, to the elders and officials of the city,* and to the guardians of King Ahab's sons. He said, ²"The king's sons are with you, and you have at your disposal chariots, horses, a fortified city, and weapons. As soon as you receive this letter, ³select the best qualified of your master's sons to be your king, and prepare to fight for Ahab's dynasty."

⁴But they were paralyzed with fear and said, "We've seen that two kings couldn't stand against this man! What can we do?"

⁵So the palace and city administrators, together with the elders and the guardians of the king's sons, sent this message to Jehu: "We are your servants and will do anything you tell us. We will not make anyone king; do whatever you think is best."

⁶Jehu responded with a second letter: "If you are on my side and are going to obey me, bring the heads of your master's sons to me at Jezreel by this time tomorrow." Now the seventy sons of the king were being cared for by the leaders of Samaria, where they had been raised since childhood. ⁷When the letter arrived, the leaders killed all seventy of the king's sons. They placed their heads in baskets and presented them to Jehu at Jezreel.

⁸A messenger went to Jehu and said, "They have brought the heads of the king's sons."

So Jehu ordered, "Pile them in two heaps at the entrance of the city gate, and leave them there until morning."

⁹In the morning he went out and spoke to the crowd that had gathered around them. "You are not to blame," he told them. "I am the one who conspired against my master and killed him. But who killed all these? ¹⁰You can be sure that the message of the Lord that was spoken concerning Ahab's family will not fail. The Lord declared through his servant Elijah that this would happen." ¹¹Then Jehu killed all who were left of Ahab's relatives living in Jezreel and all his important officials, his personal friends, and his priests. So Ahab was left without a single survivor.

**9:27**
Josh 17:11
Judg 1:27
2 Chr 22:7, 9

**9:28**
2 Kgs 23:30

**9:29**
2 Kgs 8:25, 28

**9:30**
Jer 4:30
Ezek 23:40

**9:31**
1 Kgs 16:9-20

**9:34**
1 Kgs 16:30-31

**9:36**
1 Kgs 21:23

**9:37**
Jer 8:2

**10:1**
1 Kgs 16:24-29

**10:5**
Josh 9:8, 11

**10:7**
Judg 9:5
2 Kgs 11:1

**10:10**
1 Kgs 21:29
2 Kgs 9:7-10

---

9:31 See 1 Kgs 16:9-10, where Zimri killed his master, King Elah.   10:1 As in some Greek manuscripts and Latin Vulgate (see also 10:6); Hebrew reads *of Jezreel.*

---

9:31 Why did Jezebel refer to Zimri? Zimri was an army commander who, some 40 years earlier, had killed Elah and then had declared himself king of Israel (1 Kings 16:8-10). Jezebel was accusing Jehu of trying the same treachery.

9:35 Jezebel's skull, feet, and hands were all that remained of her evil life—no power, no money, no prestige, no royal finery, no family, no spiritual heritage. In the end, her life of luxury and treachery amounted to nothing. Power, health, and wealth may

make you feel as if you can live forever. But death strips everyone of all external security. The time to set your life's course is now, while you still have time and before your heart becomes hardened. The end will come soon enough.

10:7 This fulfilled Elijah's prophecy that not one of Ahab's male descendants would survive (1 Kings 21:17-24).

10:11 In his zeal, Jehu went far beyond the Lord's command with this bloodbath. The prophet Hosea later announced punishment

**10:13**
2 Kgs 8:24, 29
2 Chr 22:8

<sup>12</sup>Then Jehu set out for Samaria. Along the way, while he was at Beth-eked of the Shepherds, <sup>13</sup>he met some relatives of King Ahaziah of Judah. "Who are you?" he asked them.

And they replied, "We are relatives of King Ahaziah. We are going to visit the sons of King Ahab and the sons of the queen mother."

<sup>14</sup>"Take them alive!" Jehu shouted to his men. And they captured all forty-two of them and killed them at the well of Beth-eked. None of them escaped.

**10:15**
2 Kgs 10:23
Jer 35:6-19

<sup>15</sup>When Jehu left there, he met Jehonadab son of Recab, who was coming to meet him. After they had greeted each other, Jehu said to him, "Are you as loyal to me as I am to you?"

"Yes, I am," Jehonadab replied.

"If you are," Jehu said, "then give me your hand." So Jehonadab put out his hand, and Jehu helped him into the chariot. <sup>16</sup>Then Jehu said, "Now come with me, and see how devoted I am to the Lord." So Jehonadab rode along with him.

**10:17**
2 Kgs 9:8

<sup>17</sup>When Jehu arrived in Samaria, he killed everyone who was left there from Ahab's family, just as the Lord had promised through Elijah.

### Jehu Kills the Priests of Baal

**10:18**
1 Kgs 16:31-32

<sup>18</sup>Then Jehu called a meeting of all the people of the city and said to them, "Ahab's worship of Baal was nothing compared to the way I will worship him! <sup>19</sup>Therefore, summon all the prophets and worshipers of Baal, and call together all his priests. See to it that every one of them comes, for I am going to offer a great sacrifice to Baal. Anyone who fails to come will be put to death." But Jehu's cunning plan was to destroy all the worshipers of Baal.

**10:20**
Exod 32:5

<sup>20</sup>Then Jehu ordered, "Prepare a solemn assembly to worship Baal!" So they did. <sup>21</sup>He sent messengers throughout all Israel summoning those who worshiped Baal. They all came—not a single one remained behind—and they filled the temple of Baal from one end to the other. <sup>22</sup>And Jehu instructed the keeper of the wardrobe, "Be sure that every worshiper of Baal wears one of these robes." So robes were given to them.

<sup>23</sup>Then Jehu went into the temple of Baal with Jehonadab son of Recab. Jehu said to the worshipers of Baal, "Make sure no one who worships the Lord is here—only those who worship Baal." <sup>24</sup>So they were all inside the temple to offer sacrifices and burnt offerings. Now Jehu had stationed eighty of his men outside the building and had warned them, "If you let anyone escape, you will pay for it with your own life."

**10:25**
1 Sam 22:17
1 Kgs 18:40

<sup>25</sup>As soon as Jehu had finished sacrificing the burnt offering, he commanded his guards and officers, "Go in and kill all of them. Don't let a single one escape!" So they killed them all with their swords, and the guards and officers dragged their bodies outside.* Then Jehu's men went into the innermost fortress* of the temple of Baal. <sup>26</sup>They dragged out the sacred

**10:26**
1 Kgs 14:23
2 Kgs 3:2

pillar* used in the worship of Baal and burned it. <sup>27</sup>They smashed the sacred pillar and wrecked the temple of Baal, converting it into a public toilet, as it remains to this day.

**10:29**
1 Kgs 12:28-30;
13:33-34

<sup>28</sup>In this way, Jehu destroyed every trace of Baal worship from Israel. <sup>29</sup>He did not, however, destroy the gold calves at Bethel and Dan, with which Jeroboam son of Nebat had caused Israel to sin.

**10:25a** Or *they left their bodies lying there;* or *they threw them out into the outermost court.*   **10:25b** Hebrew *city.*
**10:26** As in Greek and Syriac versions and Latin Vulgate; Hebrew reads *sacred pillars.*

---

upon Jehu's dynasty for this senseless slaughter (Hosea 1:4, 5). Many times in history, "religious" people have mixed faith with personal ambition, power, or cruelty, without God's consent or blessing. To use God or the Bible to condone oppression is wrong. When people attack Christianity because of atrocities that "Christians" carried out, help them to see that these men and women were using faith for their own political ends and not following Christ.

**10:15** Jehonadab was a man who, like Jehu, was zealous in following God. Jehonadab, however, demonstrated his zeal by separating himself and his family from the materialistic, idol-worshiping culture. He founded a group called the Recabites (named after his father Recab), who strove to keep their lives pure by living apart from society's pressures and temptations. Jeremiah 35 gives us an example of their dedication to God. Because of their dedication, God promised that they would always have descendants who would worship him.

**10:24** Israel was supposed to be intolerant of any religion that did not worship the true God. The religions of surrounding nations were evil and corrupt. They were designed to destroy life, not uphold it. Israel was God's special nation, chosen to be an example

of what was right. But Israel's kings, priests, and elders first tolerated, then incorporated surrounding pagan beliefs and thus became apathetic to God's way. We are to be completely intolerant of sin and remove it from our lives. We should be tolerant of people who hold differing views, but we should not condone beliefs or practices that lead people away from God's standards of living.

**10:28, 29** Why did Jehu destroy the idols of Baal but not the gold calves in Bethel and Dan? Jehu's motives may have been more political than spiritual. (1) If Jehu had destroyed the gold calves, his people would have traveled to the Temple in Jerusalem, in the rival southern kingdom, and worshiped there (which is why Jeroboam set them up in the first place; see 1 Kings 12:25-33). (2) Baal worship was associated with the dynasty of Ahab, so it was politically advantageous to destroy Baal. The gold calves, on the other hand, had a longer history in the northern kingdom and were valued by all political factions. (3) Baal worship was anti-God, but the gold calves were thought by many to be visible representations of God himself, even though God's law stated clearly that such worship was idolatrous (Exodus 20:3-6). Like Jehu, it is easy for us to denounce the sins of others while excusing sin in our own lives.

30Nonetheless the LORD said to Jehu, "You have done well in following my instructions to destroy the family of Ahab. Therefore, your descendants will be kings of Israel down to the fourth generation." 31But Jehu did not obey the Law of the LORD, the God of Israel, with all his heart. He refused to turn from the sins that Jeroboam had led Israel to commit.

### The Death of Jehu
32At about that time the LORD began to cut down the size of Israel's territory. King Hazael conquered several sections of the country 33east of the Jordan River, including all of Gilead, Gad, Reuben, and Manasseh. He conquered the area from the town of Aroer by the Arnon Gorge to as far north as Gilead and Bashan.

34The rest of the events in Jehu's reign—everything he did and all his achievements—are recorded in *The Book of the History of the Kings of Israel.*

35When Jehu died, he was buried in Samaria. Then his son Jehoahaz became the next king. 36In all, Jehu reigned over Israel from Samaria for twenty-eight years.

### Queen Athaliah Rules in Judah
**11** When Athaliah, the mother of King Ahaziah of Judah, learned that her son was dead, she began to destroy the rest of the royal family. 2But Ahaziah's sister Jehosheba, the daughter of King Jehoram,* took Ahaziah's infant son, Joash, and stole him away from among the rest of the king's children, who were about to be killed. She put Joash and his nurse in a bedroom to hide him from Athaliah, so the child was not murdered. 3Joash remained hidden in the Temple of the LORD for six years while Athaliah ruled over the land.

### Revolt against Athaliah
4In the seventh year of Athaliah's reign, Jehoiada the priest summoned the commanders, the Carite mercenaries, and the palace guards to come to the Temple of the LORD. He made a solemn pact with them and made them swear an oath of loyalty there in the LORD's Temple; then he showed them the king's son.

5Jehoiada told them, "This is what you must do. A third of you who are on duty on the Sabbath are to guard the royal palace itself. 6Another third of you are to stand guard at the Sur Gate. And the final third must stand guard behind the palace guard. These three groups will all guard the palace. 7The other two units who are off duty on the Sabbath must stand guard for the king at the LORD's Temple. 8Form a bodyguard around the king and keep your weapons in hand. Kill anyone who tries to break through. Stay with the king wherever he goes."

9So the commanders did everything as Jehoiada the priest ordered. The commanders took charge of the men reporting for duty that Sabbath, as well as those who were going off duty. They brought them all to Jehoiada the priest, 10and he supplied them with the spears and small shields that had once belonged to King David and were stored in the Temple of the LORD. 11The palace guards stationed themselves around the king, with their weapons ready. They formed a line from the south side of the Temple around to the north side and all around the altar.

12Then Jehoiada brought out Joash, the king's son, placed the crown on his head, and presented him with a copy of God's laws.* They anointed him and proclaimed him king, and everyone clapped their hands and shouted, "Long live the king!"

### The Death of Athaliah
13When Athaliah heard all the noise made by the palace guards and the people, she hurried to the LORD's Temple to see what was happening. 14When she arrived, she saw the newly crowned king standing in his place of authority by the pillar, as was the custom at times of coronation. The commanders and trumpeters were surrounding him, and people from all

11:2 Hebrew *Joram,* a variant spelling of Jehoram.   11:12 Or *a copy of the covenant.*

---

**10:30, 31** Jehu did much of what the Lord told him to, but he did not obey him with all his heart. He had become God's *instrument* for carrying out justice, but he had not become God's *servant.* As a result, he gave only lip service to God while permitting the worship of the gold calves. Check the condition of your heart toward God. We can be very active in our work for God and still not give the heartfelt obedience he desires.

**11:1** This story is continued from 9:27, where Ahaziah, Athaliah's son, had been killed by Jehu. Athaliah's attempt to kill all of Aha-

ziah's sons was futile because God had promised that the Messiah would be born through David's descendants (2 Samuel 7).

**11:2, 3** Jehosheba was the wife of Jehoiada, the high priest, so the Temple was a practical and natural place to hide baby Joash. Athaliah, who loved idolatry, would have had no interest in the Temple.

**11:4** The Carites were mercenary troops possibly associated with the Philistines. Some scholars believe they settled in southern Palestine from Crete.

over the land were rejoicing and blowing trumpets. When Athaliah saw all this, she tore her clothes in despair and shouted, "Treason! Treason!"

15Then Jehoiada the priest ordered the commanders who were in charge of the troops, "Take her to the soldiers in front of the Temple,* and kill anyone who tries to rescue her." For the priest had said, "She must not be killed in the Temple of the LORD." 16So they seized her and led her out to the gate where horses enter the palace grounds, and she was killed there.

### Jehoiada's Religious Reforms

17Then Jehoiada made a covenant between the LORD and the king and the people that they would be the LORD's people. He also made a covenant between the king and the people. 18And all the people of the land went over to the temple of Baal and tore it down. They demolished the altars and smashed the idols to pieces, and they killed Mattan the priest of Baal in front of the altars.

Jehoiada the priest stationed guards at the Temple of the LORD. 19Then the commanders, the Carite mercenaries, the palace guards, and all the people of the land escorted the king from the Temple of the LORD. They went through the gate of the guards and into the palace, and the king took his seat on the royal throne. 20So all the people of the land rejoiced, and the city was peaceful because Athaliah had been killed at the king's palace.

21*Joash* was seven years old when he became king.

### Joash Repairs the Temple

**12** 1*Joash* began to rule over Judah in the seventh year of King Jehu's reign in Israel. He reigned in Jerusalem forty years. His mother was Zibiah from Beersheba. 2All his life Joash did what was pleasing in the LORD's sight because Jehoiada the priest instructed him. 3Yet even so, he did not destroy the pagan shrines, and the people still offered sacrifices and burned incense there.

4One day King Joash said to the priests, "Collect all the money brought as a sacred offering to the LORD's Temple, whether it is a regular assessment, a payment of vows, or a voluntary gift. 5Let the priests take some of that money to pay for whatever repairs are needed at the Temple."

6But by the twenty-third year of Joash's reign, the priests still had not repaired the Temple. 7So King Joash called for Jehoiada and the other priests and asked them, "Why haven't you repaired the Temple? Don't use any more money for your own needs. From now on, it must all be spent on Temple repairs." 8So the priests agreed not to accept any more money from the people, and they also agreed to let others take responsibility for repairing the Temple.

**11:17**
Josh 24:25
2 Sam 5:3
2 Chr 15:12-14;
34:31

**11:18**
Deut 12:2-3
1 Kgs 18:40

**11:19**
2 Kgs 11:4

**11:20**
Prov 11:10

**11:21**
2 Chr 24:1-14

**12:1-21**
//2 Chr 24:1-14,
23-27

**12:3**
2 Kgs 14:4;
15:34-35

**12:4**
Exod 35:5-9, 22, 29
2 Kgs 22:3-6
1 Chr 29:3-9

**11:15** Or *Bring her out from between the ranks;* or *Take her out of the Temple precincts.* The meaning of the Hebrew is uncertain.   **11:21a** Verse 11:21 is numbered 12:1 in Hebrew text.   **11:21b** Hebrew *Jehoash,* a variant spelling of Joash.   **12:1a** Verses 12:1-21 are numbered 12:2-22 in Hebrew text.   **12:1b** Hebrew *Jehoash,* a variant spelling of Joash; also in 12:2, 4, 6, 7, 18.

---

**11:17** This covenant was, in fact, a recommitment to a very old covenant—the one set up in the book of Deuteronomy for the righteous rule of the nation. It was meant to function as a constitution for the people. This covenant, however, had been virtually ignored for over 100 years. Unfortunately, after Jehoiada's death, the reforms were discontinued.

**11:21** If Joash became king at only seven years of age, who really ran the country? Although the answer is not spelled out in the Bible, Judah was probably run during the first seven years of Joash's reign by the king's mother, the high priest Jehoiada, and other advisers.

**12:2ff** Joash didn't go far enough in removing sin from the nation, but he did much that was good and right. When we aren't sure if we've gone far enough in correcting our actions, we can ask: (1) Does the Bible expressly prohibit this action? (2) Does this action take me away from loving, worshiping, or serving God? (3) Does it make me its slave? (4) Is it bringing out the best in me, consistent with God's purpose? (5) Does it benefit other believers?

**12:3** The Israelites were supposed to offer sacrifices to God only in designated areas under supervision of the priests, not

just anywhere (Deuteronomy 12:13, 14). Making sacrifices in the shrines copied pagan customs and encouraged other pagan practices to enter into their worship. By blending in these beliefs, people were custom-making their religion, and it led them far away from God. (For more information on these pagan shrines, see the note on 1 Kings 22:43.)

**12:4, 5** The Temple needed repair because it had been damaged and neglected by previous evil leaders, especially Athaliah (2 Chronicles 24:7). The Temple was to be a holy place, set apart for worship of God. Thanks to Joash's fund-raising program, it could be restored. The dirt and filth that had collected inside over the years were cleaned out; joints were remortared; pagan idols and other traces of idol worship were removed; and the gold and bronze were polished. The neglected condition of the Temple reveals how far the people had strayed from God.

⁹Then Jehoiada the priest bored a hole in the lid of a large chest and set it on the right-hand side of the altar at the entrance of the Temple of the LORD. The priests guarding the entrance put all of the people's contributions into the chest. ¹⁰Whenever the chest became full, the court secretary and the high priest counted the money that had been brought to the LORD's Temple and put it into bags. ¹¹Then they gave the money to the construction supervisors, who used it to pay the people working on the LORD's Temple—the carpenters, the builders, ¹²the masons, and the stonecutters. They also used the money to buy the timber and the finished stone needed for repairing the LORD's Temple, and they paid any other expenses related to the Temple's restoration.

¹³The money brought to the Temple was not used for making silver bowls, lamp snuffers, basins, trumpets, or other articles of gold or silver for the Temple of the LORD. ¹⁴It was paid to the workmen, who used it for the Temple repairs. ¹⁵No accounting of this money was required from the construction supervisors, because they were honest and trustworthy men. ¹⁶However, the money that was contributed for guilt offerings and sin offerings was not brought into the LORD's Temple. It was given to the priests for their own use.

### The End of Joash's Reign

¹⁷About this time King Hazael of Aram went to war against Gath and captured it. Then he turned to attack Jerusalem. ¹⁸King Joash collected all the sacred objects that Jehoshaphat, Jehoram, and Ahaziah, the previous kings of Judah, had dedicated, along with what he himself had dedicated. He sent them all to Hazael, along with all the gold in the treasuries of the LORD's Temple and the royal palace. So Hazael called off his attack on Jerusalem.

¹⁹The rest of the events in Joash's reign and everything he did are recorded in *The Book of the History of the Kings of Judah.*

²⁰Joash's officers plotted against him and assassinated him at Beth-millo on the road to Silla. ²¹The assassins were Jozacar* son of Shimeath and Jehozabad son of Shomer—both trusted advisers. Joash was buried with his ancestors in the City of David. Then his son Amaziah became the next king.

### Jehoahaz Rules in Israel

**13** Jehoahaz son of Jehu began to rule over Israel in the twenty-third year of King Joash's reign in Judah. He reigned in Samaria seventeen years. ²But he did what was evil in the LORD's sight. He followed the example of Jeroboam son of Nebat, continuing the sins that Jeroboam had led Israel to commit. ³So the LORD was very angry with Israel, and he allowed King Hazael of Aram and his son Ben-hadad to defeat them repeatedly.

⁴Then Jehoahaz prayed for the LORD's help, and the LORD heard his prayer, for he could see how severely the king of Aram was oppressing Israel. ⁵So the LORD provided someone to rescue the Israelites from the tyranny of the Arameans. Then Israel lived in safety again as they had in former days.

⁶But they continued to sin, following the evil example of Jeroboam. They also allowed the Asherah pole in Samaria to remain standing. ⁷Finally, Jehoahaz's army was reduced to 50 charioteers, 10 chariots, and 10,000 foot soldiers. The king of Aram had killed the others, trampling them like dust under his feet.

12:21 As in Greek and Syriac versions; Hebrew reads *Jozabad.*

**12:9** Mark 12:41; Luke 21:1
**12:13** 1 Kgs 7:48-51
**12:15** 2 Kgs 22:7
**12:17** 2 Kgs 8:12; 10:32-33
**12:18** 1 Kgs 15:18; 2 Kgs 16:8; 18:15-16
**12:20** 2 Sam 5:9; 2 Chr 24:25-27
**13:2** 1 Kgs 12:26-33
**13:3** Judg 2:12-14; 2 Kgs 12:17
**13:4** Exod 3:7-9; Num 21:7-9
**13:5** Judg 2:18; Neh 9:27
**13:6** 1 Kgs 16:33

**12:15** What a contrast between the construction supervisors, who needed no accounting of their use of the money, and the priests, who couldn't be trusted to handle their funds well enough to set some aside for the Temple (12:7, 8). As trained men of God, the Levites should have been responsible and concerned. After all, the Temple was their life's work. Though the priests were not dishonest, they did not have the commitment or energy needed to finish the work. Sometimes God's work is better accomplished by devoted laypeople. Don't let your lack of training or position stop you from contributing to God's Kingdom. Everyone's energy is needed to carry out God's work.

**12:16** To read more about guilt and sin offerings, see Leviticus 4–5; 6:24–7:10.

**12:20** The reasons for the officers' plot against Joash are listed in 2 Chronicles 24:17-26. Joash had begun to worship idols, had killed the prophet Zechariah, and had been conquered by the Arameans. When Joash turned away from God, his life began

to unravel. The officers didn't kill Joash because he turned from God; they killed him because his kingdom was out of control. In the end he became an evil man and was killed by evil people.

**13:4-6** The Lord heard Jehoahaz's prayer for help. God delayed his judgment on Israel when they turned to him, but they did not sustain their dependence on God for long. Although Israel had periodic breaks in their idol worship, they rarely showed genuine faith. It is not enough to say no to sin; we must also say yes to a life of commitment to God. An occasional call for help is not a substitute for a daily life of trust in God.

**13:5** Aram, which lay to the north of Israel, was always Israel's enemy. This was partly because Israel blocked most of Aram's trade from the south, and Aram cut off most of Israel's from the north. If one nation could conquer the other, all its trade routes would be open, and its economy would flourish. Israel and Aram were so busy fighting each other that they didn't notice the rapidly

8The rest of the events in Jehoahaz's reign—everything he did and the extent of his power—are recorded in *The Book of the History of the Kings of Israel.* 9When Jehoahaz died, he was buried in Samaria. Then his son Jehoash* became the next king.

### Jehoash Rules in Israel

10Jehoash son of Jehoahaz began to rule over Israel in the thirty-seventh year of King Joash's reign in Judah. He reigned in Samaria sixteen years. 11But he did what was evil in the LORD's sight. He refused to turn from the sins that Jeroboam son of Nebat had led Israel to commit.

**13:12**
2 Kgs 14:8, 15, 28

12The rest of the events in Jehoash's reign and everything he did, including the extent of his power and his war with King Amaziah of Judah, are recorded in *The Book of the History of the Kings of Israel.* 13When Jehoash died, he was buried in Samaria with the kings of Israel. Then his son Jeroboam II became the next king.

### Elisha's Final Prophecy

**13:14**
2 Kgs 2:12

14When Elisha was in his last illness, King Jehoash of Israel visited him and wept over him. "My father! My father! I see the chariots and charioteers of Israel!" he cried.

15Elisha told him, "Get a bow and some arrows." And the king did as he was told. 16Elisha told him, "Put your hand on the bow," and Elisha laid his own hands on the king's hands.

**13:17**
1 Kgs 20:26

17Then he commanded, "Open that eastern window," and he opened it. Then he said, "Shoot!" So he shot an arrow. Elisha proclaimed, "This is the LORD's arrow, an arrow of victory over Aram, for you will completely conquer the Arameans at Aphek."

18Then he said, "Now pick up the other arrows and strike them against the ground." So the king picked them up and struck the ground three times. 19But the man of God was angry with him. "You should have struck the ground five or six times!" he exclaimed. "Then you would have beaten Aram until it was entirely destroyed. Now you will be victorious only three times."

**13:20**
2 Kgs 3:7; 24:2
**13:21**
Matt 27:52

20Then Elisha died and was buried.

Groups of Moabite raiders used to invade the land each spring. 21Once when some Israelites were burying a man, they spied a band of these raiders. So they hastily threw the corpse into the tomb of Elisha and fled. But as soon as the body touched Elisha's bones, the dead man revived and jumped to his feet!

**13:9** Hebrew *Joash,* a variant spelling of Jehoash; also in 13:10, 12, 13, 14, 25.

---

**GOD OR IDOLS**
Why did people continually turn to idols instead of to God?

*Idols were:*
Tangible
Morally similar—had human characteristics
Comprehensible
Able to be manipulated

*Worshiping idols involved:*
Materialism
Sexual immorality
Doing whatever a person wanted
Focusing on self

*God is:*
Intangible—no physical form
Morally dissimilar—had divine characteristics
Incomprehensible
Not able to be manipulated

*Worshiping God involved:*
Sacrifice
Purity and commitment
Doing what God wants
Focusing on others

---

growing strength of the Assyrians to the far north. Soon both nations would be surprised (16:9; 17:6).

**13:9, 10** Jehoash assumed the throne of Israel in 798 B.C. At that time the king of Judah, Joash, was nearing the end of his reign. In Hebrew, Jehoash and Joash are two forms of the same name. Thus, two kings with the same name, one in the south and one in the north, reigned at approximately the same time. While Joash of Judah began as a good king, Jehoash of Israel was evil.

**13:14** Elisha was highly regarded for his prophetic powers and miracles on Israel's behalf. Jehoash called him "The chariots and charioteers of Israel!" This recalls the title Elisha had given to Elijah (2:12). Jehoash feared Elisha's death because he ascribed the nation's well-being to Elisha rather than to God. Jehoash's fear reveals his lack of spiritual understanding. At least 43 years had passed since Elisha was last mentioned in Scripture (9:1),

when he anointed Jehu king (841 B.C.). Jehoash's reign began in 798 B.C.

**13:15-19** When Jehoash was told to strike the ground with the arrows, he did it only halfheartedly. As a result, Elisha told the king that his victory over Aram would not be complete. Receiving the full benefits of God's plan for our lives requires us to receive and obey God's commands fully. If we don't follow God's complete instructions, we should not be surprised that we don't receive his full benefits and blessings.

**13:20, 21** Elisha was dead, but his good influence remained, even causing miracles. This demonstrated that Elisha was indeed a prophet of God. It also attested to God's power—no pagan idol had ever raised anyone from the dead. This miracle served as one more reminder to Israel that it had rejected God's word as given through Elisha.

²²King Hazael of Aram had oppressed Israel during the entire reign of King Jehoahaz. ²³But the LORD was gracious and merciful to the people of Israel, and they were not totally destroyed. He pitied them because of his covenant with Abraham, Isaac, and Jacob. And to this day he still has not completely destroyed them or banished them from his presence.

²⁴King Hazael of Aram died, and his son Ben-hadad became the next king. ²⁵Then Jehoash son of Jehoahaz recaptured from Ben-hadad son of Hazael the towns that had been taken from Jehoash's father, Jehoahaz. Jehoash defeated Ben-hadad on three occasions, and he recovered the Israelite towns.

**13:22**
2 Kgs 8:12
**13:23**
Gen 13:16; 17:2-5
2 Kgs 14:27
**13:25**
2 Kgs 10:32-33;
14:25

## Amaziah Rules in Judah

**14** Amaziah son of Joash began to rule over Judah in the second year of the reign of King Jehoash* of Israel. ²Amaziah was twenty-five years old when he became king, and he reigned in Jerusalem twenty-nine years. His mother was Jehoaddin from Jerusalem. ³Amaziah did what was pleasing in the LORD's sight, but not like his ancestor David. Instead, he followed the example of his father, Joash. ⁴Amaziah did not destroy the pagan shrines, and the people still offered sacrifices and burned incense there.

**14:1-7**
//2 Chr 25:1-4,
11-12

**14:4**
2 Kgs 12:3

⁵When Amaziah was well established as king, he executed the officials who had assassinated his father. ⁶However, he did not kill the children of the assassins, for he obeyed the command of the LORD as written by Moses in the Book of the Law: "Parents must not be put to death for the sins of their children, nor children for the sins of their parents. Those deserving to die must be put to death for their own crimes."*

**14:5**
2 Kgs 12:2
**14:6**
Deut 24:16
Jer 31:30
Ezek 18:4, 20

⁷Amaziah also killed 10,000 Edomites in the Valley of Salt. He also conquered Sela and changed its name to Joktheel, as it is called to this day.

**14:7**
2 Sam 8:13
1 Chr 18:12
2 Chr 25:11
Isa 16:1

⁸One day Amaziah sent messengers with this challenge to Israel's king Jehoash, the son of Jehoahaz and grandson of Jehu: "Come and meet me in battle!"*

**14:8-22**
2 Chr 25:17–26:2

⁹But King Jehoash of Israel replied to King Amaziah of Judah with this story: "Out in the Lebanon mountains, a thistle sent a message to a mighty cedar tree: 'Give your daughter in marriage to my son.' But just then a wild animal of Lebanon came by and stepped on the thistle, crushing it!

**14:9**
Judg 9:8-15

¹⁰"You have indeed defeated Edom, and you are very proud of it. But be content with your victory and stay at home! Why stir up trouble that will only bring disaster on you and the people of Judah?"

¹¹But Amaziah refused to listen, so King Jehoash of Israel mobilized his army against King Amaziah of Judah. The two armies drew up their battle lines at Beth-shemesh in Judah. ¹²Judah was routed by the army of Israel, and its army scattered and fled for home. ¹³King Jehoash of Israel captured Judah's king, Amaziah son of Joash and grandson of Ahaziah, at Beth-shemesh. Then he marched to Jerusalem, where he demolished 600 feet* of Jerusalem's wall, from the Ephraim Gate to the Corner Gate. ¹⁴He carried off all the gold and silver and all the articles from the Temple of the LORD. He also seized the treasures from the royal palace, along with hostages, and then returned to Samaria.

**14:11**
Josh 19:35-39

**14:13**
2 Chr 25:23
Neh 8:16; 12:39

**14:14**
2 Kgs 12:18

¹⁵The rest of the events in Jehoash's reign and everything he did, including the extent of his power and his war with King Amaziah of Judah, are recorded in *The Book of the History of the Kings of Israel.* ¹⁶When Jehoash died, he was buried in Samaria with the kings of Israel. And his son Jeroboam II became the next king.

**14:15**
2 Kgs 13:12-13

¹⁷King Amaziah of Judah lived for fifteen years after the death of King Jehoash of Israel. ¹⁸The rest of the events in Amaziah's reign are recorded in *The Book of the History of the Kings of Judah.*

**14:17**
2 Chr 25:25-28

¹⁹There was a conspiracy against Amaziah's life in Jerusalem, and he fled to Lachish. But his enemies sent assassins after him, and they killed him there. ²⁰They brought his body back to Jerusalem on a horse, and he was buried with his ancestors in the City of David.

**14:19**
2 Kgs 12:20
**14:20**
2 Kgs 9:28

**14:1** Hebrew *Joash,* a variant spelling of Jehoash; also in 14:13, 23, 27.   **14:6** Deut 24:16.   **14:8** Hebrew *Come, let us look one another in the face.*   **14:13** Hebrew *400 cubits* [180 meters].

---

**14:7** Sela was the ancient stronghold of Petra, a city carved into a rock cliff. It was not only a stronghold for Edom but also a wealthy outpost for trade with India.

**14:9, 10** This parable compares Judah to a small thistle. King Amaziah of Judah had become proud after defeating the Edomites. Here he was trying to pick a fight with Israel because he was sure

his army was stronger. Jehoash tried to warn Amaziah not to attack by comparing his army to a thistle and Israel's army to a cedar tree. Amaziah had overrated his strength; his ambition was greater than his ability. He didn't listen to Jehoash and was soundly defeated.

**14:13** A broken-down city wall disgraced the citizens and left them defenseless against future invasions.

**14:21**
2 Chr 26:23
Hos 1:1
Matt 1:9

²¹All the people of Judah had crowned Amaziah's sixteen-year-old son, Uzziah,* as king in place of his father, Amaziah. ²²After his father's death, Uzziah rebuilt the town of Elath and restored it to Judah.

### Jeroboam II Rules in Israel

**14:23**
2 Kgs 13:13
Amos 1:1

**14:24**
1 Kgs 15:30

**14:25**
Deut 3:17
2 Kgs 13:25
Jon 1:1

**14:26**
Deut 32:36
2 Kgs 13:4

**14:27**
2 Kgs 13:5, 23

²³Jeroboam II, the son of Jehoash, began to rule over Israel in the fifteenth year of King Amaziah's reign in Judah. Jeroboam reigned in Samaria forty-one years. ²⁴He did what was evil in the LORD's sight. He refused to turn from the sins that Jeroboam son of Nebat had led Israel to commit. ²⁵Jeroboam II recovered the territories of Israel between Lebo-hamath and the Dead Sea,* just as the LORD, the God of Israel, had promised through Jonah son of Amittai, the prophet from Gath-hepher.

²⁶For the LORD saw the bitter suffering of everyone in Israel, and that there was no one in Israel, slave or free, to help them. ²⁷And because the LORD had not said he would blot out the name of Israel completely, he used Jeroboam II, the son of Jehoash, to save them.

²⁸The rest of the events in the reign of Jeroboam II and everything he did—including the

**14:21** Hebrew *Azariah*, a variant spelling of Uzziah.   **14:25** Hebrew *the sea of the Arabah.*

## KINGS TO DATE AND THEIR ENEMIES

**841**
**JEHU**
Lost a large portion
of northern Israel to
Hazael (Aram)
2 Kgs 9:1—10:36
2 Chr 22:7—9

**814**
**JEHOAHAZ**
Continually
defeated by
Hazael (Aram)
2 Kgs 10:35;
13:1—9

**798**
**JEHOASH**
2 Kgs 13:10—14:16
2 Chr 25:17—24
Co-regency 793—782

**793**
**JEROBOAM II**
Recaptured Israel's
former territories
from Aram
2 Kgs 14:16—29

782

753

*I S R A E L*

*J U D A H*

**835**
**JOASH**
Averted Hazael's attack
by paying tribute,
and later was defeated
by Aram
2 Kgs 11:2—12:21
2 Chr 22:11—24:27

**796**
**AMAZIAH**
Defeated by
Jehoash and
Jeroboam II (Israel)
2 Kgs 14:1—20
2 Chr 24:27—25:28

**767**

**841**
**AHAZIAH**
Hazael (Aram)
2 Kgs 8:24—9:29
2 Chr 22:1—9

**841**
**ATHALIAH (QUEEN)**
2 Kgs 11:1—20
2 Chr 22:10—23:21

All dates are B.C.
Solid section of the timeline indicates co-regency.
For all the kings of Israel and Judah, see the chart at the end of 1 Kings.

**14:25** During this period of history, many prophets—such as Hosea, Amos, Jonah, Micah, and Isaiah—began collecting their prophecies and writing them under God's direction. They continued to preach about the worldwide significance of God's work as they looked forward to the future spiritual Kingdom. God would use Israel's moral and spiritual decline to prepare the way for the Messiah's coming. Because the kingdom and military power of Israel would be stripped away, many people would be ready to turn to the Good News that Jesus would bring.

**14:25** For more information about the prophet Jonah, see the book of Jonah.

**14:28** Jeroboam II had no devotion to God, yet under his warlike policies and skillful administration, Israel enjoyed more national power and material prosperity than at any time since the days of

Solomon. The prophets Amos and Hosea, however, tell us what was really happening within the kingdom (Hosea 13:4-8; Amos 6:11-14). Jeroboam's administration ignored policies of justice and fairness. As a result, the rich became richer, and the poor, poorer. The people became self-centered, relying more on their power, security, and possessions than on God. The poor were so oppressed that it was hard for them to believe God noticed their plight. Material prosperity is not always an indication of God's blessing. It can also be a result of self-centeredness. If you are experiencing prosperity, remember that God holds us accountable for how we attain success and how we use our wealth. Everything we have really belongs to him. We must use God's gifts with his interests in mind.

extent of his power, his wars, and how he recovered for Israel both Damascus and Hamath, which had belonged to Judah*—are recorded in *The Book of the History of the Kings of Israel.* 29 When Jeroboam II died, he was buried in Samaria* with the kings of Israel. Then his son Zechariah became the next king.

### Uzziah Rules in Judah

**15** Uzziah* son of Amaziah began to rule over Judah in the twenty-seventh year of the reign of King Jeroboam II of Israel. 2 He was sixteen years old when he became king, and he reigned in Jerusalem fifty-two years. His mother was Jecoliah from Jerusalem.

3 He did what was pleasing in the LORD's sight, just as his father, Amaziah, had done. 4 But he did not destroy the pagan shrines, and the people still offered sacrifices and burned incense there. 5 The LORD struck the king with leprosy,* which lasted until the day he died. He lived in isolation in a separate house. The king's son Jotham was put in charge of the royal palace, and he governed the people of the land.

6 The rest of the events in Uzziah's reign and everything he did are recorded in *The Book of the History of the Kings of Judah.* 7 When Uzziah died, he was buried with his ancestors in the City of David. And his son Jotham became the next king.

### Zechariah Rules in Israel

8 Zechariah son of Jeroboam II began to rule over Israel in the thirty-eighth year of King Uzziah's reign in Judah. He reigned in Samaria six months. 9 Zechariah did what was evil in the LORD's sight, as his ancestors had done. He refused to turn from the sins that Jeroboam son of Nebat had led Israel to commit. 10 Then Shallum son of Jabesh conspired against Zechariah, assassinated him in public,* and became the next king.

11 The rest of the events in Zechariah's reign are recorded in *The Book of the History of the Kings of Israel.* 12 So the LORD's message to Jehu came true: "Your descendants will be kings of Israel down to the fourth generation."

### Shallum Rules in Israel

13 Shallum son of Jabesh began to rule over Israel in the thirty-ninth year of King Uzziah's reign in Judah. Shallum reigned in Samaria only one month. 14 Then Menahem son of Gadi went to Samaria from Tirzah and assassinated him, and he became the next king.

15 The rest of the events in Shallum's reign, including his conspiracy, are recorded in *The Book of the History of the Kings of Israel.*

### Menahem Rules in Israel

16 At that time Menahem destroyed the town of Tappuah* and all the surrounding countryside as far as Tirzah, because its citizens refused to surrender the town. He killed the entire population and ripped open the pregnant women.

**15:1**
2 Kgs 14:21;
15:13, 17

**15:5**
Lev 13:46

**15:8**
2 Kgs 14:29

**15:10**
Amos 7:9

**15:12**
2 Kgs 10:30

**15:13**
2 Kgs 15:1, 8

**15:16**
2 Kgs 8:12
Hos 13:16

**14:28** Or *to Yaudi.* The meaning of the Hebrew is uncertain. **14:29** As in some Greek manuscripts; Hebrew lacks *he was buried in Samaria.* **15:1** Hebrew *Azariah,* a variant spelling of Uzziah; also in 15:6, 7, 8, 17, 23, 27. **15:5** Or *with a contagious skin disease.* The Hebrew word used here and throughout this passage can describe various skin diseases. **15:10** Or *at Ibleam.* **15:16** As in some Greek manuscripts; other Greek manuscripts read *at Ibleam.* Hebrew reads *Tiphsah.*

---

**15:1** Uzziah was also known as Azariah. His story is given in greater detail in 2 Chronicles 26. He is mentioned in Isaiah 1:1 and 6:1. Before the beginning of Uzziah's reign, Israel broke down 600 feet of Jerusalem's walls after defeating Judah and carrying off their king, Amaziah (14:13; 2 Chronicles 25:23, 24). But during Uzziah's 52-year reign, Judah rebuilt the wall, refortified the city with anti-siege weapons, and gained independence from Israel. Uzziah's devotion to God helped Judah enjoy peace and prosperity such as it had not experienced since the days of Solomon.

**15:4** Although Uzziah accomplished a great deal, he failed to destroy the pagan shrines in Judah just as his father, Amaziah, and grandfather Joash had failed to do. Uzziah imitated the kings he had heard stories about and had watched while growing up. Although Uzziah's father and grandfather were basically good kings, they were poor models in some important areas. To rise above the influence of poor models, we must seek better ones. Christ provides a perfect model. No matter how you were raised or who has influenced your life, you can move beyond those limitations by taking Christ as your example and consciously trying to live as he did.

**15:5** For 10 years Jotham was the co-ruler with his father,

Uzziah. A father and son would rule together for any of the following reasons: (1) The father was very old and needed help; (2) the father wanted to train his son in leading the nation; (3) the father was sick or exiled. Many co-regents ruled during the period of the kings—Asa/Jehoshaphat; Jehoshaphat/Jehoram; Azariah/Jotham; Jehoash/Jeroboam II; Hezekiah/Manasseh.

**15:8** Zechariah was an evil king because he encouraged Israel to sin by worshiping idols. Sin in our lives is serious. But it is even more serious to encourage others to disobey God. We are responsible for the way we influence others. Beware of double sins: ones that not only hurt us but also hurt others by encouraging them to sin.

**15:10** Zechariah was warned by the prophet Amos of his impending death and the subsequent end of Jeroboam's dynasty (Amos 7:9).

**15:14** Ancient historical documents say that Menahem was the commander in chief of Jeroboam's army (see 14:23-29 for an account of Jeroboam II's reign). After Jeroboam's son was assassinated (15:8-10), Menahem probably saw himself, and not Shallum, as the rightful successor to Israel's throne.

17Menahem son of Gadi began to rule over Israel in the thirty-ninth year of King Uzziah's reign in Judah. He reigned in Samaria ten years. 18But Menahem did what was evil in the Lord's sight. During his entire reign, he refused to turn from the sins that Jeroboam son of Nebat had led Israel to commit.

15:19
1 Chr 5:26

19Then King Tiglath-pileser* of Assyria invaded the land. But Menahem paid him thirty-seven tons* of silver to gain his support in tightening his grip on royal power. 20Menahem extorted the money from the rich of Israel, demanding that each of them pay fifty pieces* of silver to the king of Assyria. So the king of Assyria turned from attacking Israel and did not stay in the land.

21The rest of the events in Menahem's reign and everything he did are recorded in *The Book of the History of the Kings of Israel.* 22When Menahem died, his son Pekahiah became the next king.

### Pekahiah Rules in Israel

23Pekahiah son of Menahem began to rule over Israel in the fiftieth year of King Uzziah's reign in Judah. He reigned in Samaria two years. 24But Pekahiah did what was evil in the Lord's sight. He refused to turn from the sins that Jeroboam son of Nebat had led Israel to commit.

25Then Pekah son of Remaliah, the commander of Pekahiah's army, conspired against him. With fifty men from Gilead, Pekah assassinated the king, along with Argob and Arieh, in the citadel of the palace at Samaria. And Pekah reigned in his place.

26The rest of the events in Pekahiah's reign and everything he did are recorded in *The Book of the History of the Kings of Israel.*

### Pekah Rules in Israel

15:27
2 Kgs 15:32; 16:5
2 Chr 28:6

27Pekah son of Remaliah began to rule over Israel in the fifty-second year of King Uzziah's reign in Judah. He reigned in Samaria twenty years. 28But Pekah did what was evil in the Lord's sight. He refused to turn from the sins that Jeroboam son of Nebat had led Israel to commit.

15:29
2 Kgs 17:6

29During Pekah's reign, King Tiglath-pileser of Assyria attacked Israel again, and he captured the towns of Ijon, Abel-beth-maacah, Janoah, Kedesh, and Hazor. He also conquered the regions of Gilead, Galilee, and all of Naphtali, and he took the people to Assyria as captives. 30Then Hoshea son of Elah conspired against Pekah and assassinated him. He began to rule over Israel in the twentieth year of Jotham son of Uzziah.

15:30
2 Kgs 12:20

31The rest of the events in Pekah's reign and everything he did are recorded in *The Book of the History of the Kings of Israel.*

### Jotham Rules in Judah

15:32
2 Chr 27:1
Matt 1:9

15:33-38
//2 Chr 27:1-4, 7-9

15:34
2 Chr 26:4-5

32Jotham son of Uzziah began to rule over Judah in the second year of King Pekah's reign in Israel. 33He was twenty-five years old when he became king, and he reigned in Jerusalem sixteen years. His mother was Jerusha, the daughter of Zadok.

34Jotham did what was pleasing in the Lord's sight. He did everything his father, Uzziah, had done. 35But he did not destroy the pagan shrines, and the people still offered sacrifices and burned incense there. He rebuilt the upper gate of the Temple of the Lord.

15:19a Hebrew *Pul,* another name for Tiglath-pileser.    15:19b Hebrew *1,000 talents* [34 metric tons].
15:20 Hebrew *50 shekels* [20 ounces, or 570 grams].

---

**15:18** Menahem, like the kings before him, led his people into sin: He "did what was evil in the Lord's sight." What a horrible epitaph for a leader! Leaders profoundly affect the people they serve. They can either encourage or discourage devotion to God both by their example and by the structure they give their organization. Good leaders put up no obstacles to faith in God or to right living.

**15:19, 20** When King Tiglath-pileser took the throne of Assyria, the Assyrian Empire was becoming a world power, and the nations of Aram, Israel, and Judah were in decline. This is the first mention of Assyria in 2 Kings. Tiglath-pileser's invasion occurred in 743 B.C. Assyria made Israel a vassal state, and Menahem was forced to pay tribute to Assyria. This was the first of three Assyrian invasions (15:29 and 17:6 tell of the other ones).

**15:30** Hoshea was Israel's last king.

**15:32** A year after Pekah became king, Uzziah (also called Azariah) of Judah died, and Isaiah the prophet had a vision of God's holiness and Israel's future destruction. See Isaiah 6 for more details on what Isaiah saw.

**15:34, 35** Much good can be said of Jotham and his reign as king of Judah, but he failed in a most important area: He didn't destroy the pagan shrines, and leaving them clearly violated the first commandment (Exodus 20:3). Like Jotham, we may live basically good lives and yet miss doing what is most important. A lifetime of doing good is not enough if we make the crucial mistake of not following God with all our hearts. A true follower of God puts him first in all areas of life.

36The rest of the events in Jotham's reign and everything he did are recorded in *The Book of the History of the Kings of Judah*. 37In those days the LORD began to send King Rezin of Aram and King Pekah of Israel to attack Judah. 38When Jotham died, he was buried with his ancestors in the City of David. And his son Ahaz became the next king.

**15:36**
2 Kgs 15:6; 16:19;
20:20

**15:37**
2 Kgs 16:5
Isa 7:1

## Ahaz Rules in Judah

**16** Ahaz son of Jotham began to rule over Judah in the seventeenth year of King Pekah's reign in Israel. 2Ahaz was twenty years old when he became king, and he reigned in Jerusalem sixteen years. He did not do what was pleasing in the sight of the LORD his God, as his ancestor David had done. 3Instead, he followed the example of the kings of Israel, even sacrificing his own son in the fire.* In this way, he followed the detestable practices of the pagan nations the LORD had driven from the land ahead of the Israelites. 4He offered sacrifices and burned incense at the pagan shrines and on the hills and under every green tree.

**16:1-20**
//2 Chr 28:1-27

**16:2**
2 Kgs 14:3

**16:3**
Lev 18:21
Deut 12:31
2 Kgs 17:17; 21:6

**16:4**
Deut 12:2

5Then King Rezin of Aram and King Pekah of Israel came up to attack Jerusalem. They besieged Ahaz but could not conquer him. 6At that time the king of Edom* recovered the town of Elath for Edom.* He drove out the people of Judah and sent Edomites* to live there, as they do to this day.

**16:5**
2 Kgs 15:37
2 Chr 28:5
Isa 7:1-6

**16:6**
2 Kgs 14:22
2 Chr 26:2

7King Ahaz sent messengers to King Tiglath-pileser of Assyria with this message: "I am your servant and your vassal.* Come up and rescue me from the attacking armies of Aram and Israel." 8Then Ahaz took the silver and gold from the Temple of the LORD and the palace treasury and sent it as a payment to the Assyrian king. 9So the king of Assyria attacked the Aramean capital of Damascus and led its population away as captives, resettling them in Kir. He also killed King Rezin.

**16:7**
2 Kgs 15:29

**16:8**
2 Kgs 12:17-18;
18:15

**16:9**
Amos 1:3-5

10King Ahaz then went to Damascus to meet with King Tiglath-pileser of Assyria. While he was there, he took special note of the altar. Then he sent a model of the altar to Uriah the priest, along with its design in full detail. 11Uriah followed the king's instructions and built an altar just like it, and it was ready before the king returned from Damascus. 12When the king returned, he inspected the altar and made offerings on it. 13He presented a burnt offering and a grain offering, he poured out a liquid offering, and he sprinkled the blood of peace offerings on the altar.

**16:10**
Isa 8:2

**16:12**
2 Chr 26:16, 19

14Then King Ahaz removed the old bronze altar from its place in front of the LORD's Temple, between the entrance and the new altar, and placed it on the north side of the new altar. 15He told Uriah the priest, "Use the new altar* for the morning sacrifices of burnt offering, the evening grain offering, the king's burnt offering and grain offering, and the burnt offerings of all the people, as well as their grain offerings and liquid offerings. Sprinkle the blood from all the burnt offerings and sacrifices on the new altar. The bronze altar will be for my personal use only." 16Uriah the priest did just as King Ahaz commanded him.

**16:14**
Exod 40:6
1 Kgs 8:64

**16:15**
Exod 29:38-41

17Then the king removed the side panels and basins from the portable water carts. He also removed the great bronze basin called the Sea from the backs of the bronze oxen and placed it on the stone pavement. 18In deference to the king of Assyria, he also removed the canopy that had been constructed inside the palace for use on the Sabbath day,* as well as the king's outer entrance to the Temple of the LORD.

**16:17**
1 Kgs 7:23, 25, 27

**16:3** Or *even making his son pass through the fire.*   **16:6a** As in Latin Vulgate; Hebrew reads *Rezin king of Aram.*
**16:6b** As in Latin Vulgate; Hebrew reads *Aram.*   **16:6c** As in Greek version, Latin Vulgate, and an alternate reading of the Masoretic Text; the other alternate reads *Arameans.*   **16:7** Hebrew *your son.*   **16:15** Hebrew *the great altar.*
**16:18** The meaning of the Hebrew is uncertain.

**16:3** Ahaz was so depraved that he sacrificed his own son to the pagan gods. This was a practice of the Canaanites, whom the Israelites were supposed to drive out of the land.

**16:5** Israel and Aram were both under Assyria's control. They joined forces against Judah, hoping to force the southern kingdom to join their revolt against Assyria and strengthen their western alliance. But the plan backfired when King Ahaz of Judah unexpectedly asked Assyria to come to his aid (16:8, 9).

**16:10** Ahaz went to Damascus to express gratitude and loyalty to Tiglath-pileser. Because the Assyrians had captured Damascus, the capital of Aram (732 B.C.), Ahaz was afraid of a southern sweep. But he was relying more on money than on God to keep the powerful king out of his land, and his plan failed. Although Tiglath-pileser did not conquer Judah, he caused much trouble, and Ahaz regretted asking for his help (2 Chronicles 28:20, 21).

**16:10-16** Evil King Ahaz copied pagan religious customs, changed the Temple services, and used the Temple altar for his personal benefit. In so doing, he demonstrated a callous disregard for God's commands. We condemn Ahaz for his action, but we act the same way if we try to mold God's message to fit our personal preferences. We must worship God for who he is, not what we would selfishly like him to be.

**16:14-18** Ahaz replaced the bronze altar (the altar of burnt offering) with a replica of the pagan altar he had seen in Damascus. (The bronze altar was not thrown out, but was kept for use in divination. The sacrifices were washed in the basins. The Sea was a huge reservoir of water for temple use.) This was extremely serious because God had given specific directions on how the altar should look and be used (Exodus 27:1-8). Building this new altar was like installing an idol. But because Judah was

**16:20**
2 Chr 28:27; 29:1

[19]The rest of the events in Ahaz's reign and everything he did are recorded in *The Book of the History of the Kings of Judah*. [20]When Ahaz died, he was buried with his ancestors in the City of David. Then his son Hezekiah became the next king.

### 3. Israel is exiled to Assyria
*Hoshea Rules in Israel*

**17:1**
2 Kgs 15:30

**17** Hoshea son of Elah began to rule over Israel in the twelfth year of King Ahaz's reign in Judah. He reigned in Samaria nine years. [2]He did what was evil in the LORD's sight, but not to the same extent as the kings of Israel who ruled before him.

## KINGS TO DATE AND THEIR ENEMIES

742
**PEKAHIAH**
2 Kgs 15:22–26

740
**PEKAH**
Suffered first
conquest
by Assyria
2 Kgs 15:25–31
2 Chr 28:5–8

752
**MENAHEM**
Paid tribute to
Tiglath-pileser
(Assyria)
2 Kgs 15:14–22

732
**HOSHEA**
Suffered complete
conquest by
Shalmaneser
(Assyria)
2 Kgs 15:30; 17:1–6

752
**SHALLUM**
2 Kgs 15:10–15

753
**ZECHARIAH**
2 Kgs 14:29—15:12

793
**JEROBOAM II**
Recaptured Israel's
former territories
from Aram
2 Kgs 14:16–29

722
Captivity

*I S R A E L*

*J U D A H*

767

750

740

732

715

792
**UZZIAH**
Conquered Gath
in Philistia
2 Kgs 15:1–7
2 Chr 26:1–23
Co-regency 750–740

750
**JOTHAM**
Won battles against
Ammonites and
Arabs, harassed by
Pekah (Israel) and
Rezin (Aram)
2 Kgs 15:32–38
2 Chr 26:23—27:9
Co-regency 735–732

735
**AHAZ**
Harassed by
Pekah (Israel),
paid Assyria for
protection against
Rezin (Aram), also
harassed by Edom
and Philistia
2 Kgs 15:38—16:20
2 Chr 27:9—28:27

796
**AMAZIAH**
Won battles against
Edom and Selah,
defeated by
Jehoash and
Jeroboam II (Israel)
2 Kgs 14:1–20
2 Chr 24:27—25:28
Co-regency
792–767

All dates are B.C.
Solid section of the timeline indicates co-regency.
For all the kings of Israel and Judah, see the chart at the end of 1 Kings.

Assyria's vassal state, Ahaz was eager to please the Assyrian king. Sadly, Ahaz allowed the king of Assyria to replace God as Judah's leader. No one, no matter how attractive or powerful, should replace God's leadership in our lives.

**16:18** Ahaz had become a weak king with a weak and compromising high priest. Judah's religious system was in shambles. It now included pagan customs, and its chief aim was only to

please those in power. If we copy others in order to please them, we risk making them more important than God in our lives.

³King Shalmaneser of Assyria attacked King Hoshea, so Hoshea was forced to pay heavy tribute to Assyria. ⁴But Hoshea stopped paying the annual tribute and conspired against the king of Assyria by asking King So of Egypt* to help him shake free of Assyria's power. When the king of Assyria discovered this treachery, he seized Hoshea and put him in prison.

### Samaria Falls to Assyria

⁵Then the king of Assyria invaded the entire land, and for three years he besieged the city of Samaria. ⁶Finally, in the ninth year of King Hoshea's reign, Samaria fell, and the people of Israel were exiled to Assyria. They were settled in colonies in Halah, along the banks of the Habor River in Gozan, and in the cities of the Medes.

⁷This disaster came upon the people of Israel because they worshiped other gods. They sinned against the LORD their God, who had brought them safely out of Egypt and had rescued them from the power of Pharaoh, the king of Egypt. ⁸They had followed the practices of the pagan nations the LORD had driven from the land ahead of them, as well as the practices the kings of Israel had introduced. ⁹The people of Israel had also secretly done many things that were not pleasing to the LORD their God. They built pagan shrines for themselves in all their towns, from the smallest outpost to the largest walled city. ¹⁰They set up sacred pillars and Asherah poles at the top of every hill and under every green tree. ¹¹They offered sacrifices on all the hilltops, just like the nations the LORD had driven from the land ahead of them. So the people of Israel had done many evil things, arousing the LORD's anger. ¹²Yes, they worshiped idols,* despite the LORD's specific and repeated warnings.

¹³Again and again the LORD had sent his prophets and seers to warn both Israel and Judah: "Turn from all your evil ways. Obey my commands and decrees—the entire law that I commanded your ancestors to obey, and that I gave you through my servants the prophets."

**17:3-7**
//2 Kgs 18:9-12
**17:4**
2 Kgs 18:20-21

**17:6**
Deut 28:64;
29:27-28
2 Kgs 18:11
1 Chr 5:26
Hos 13:16
**17:7**
Josh 23:15-16
**17:8**
Lev 18:3
Deut 18:9
**17:9**
2 Kgs 18:8

**17:12**
Exod 20:4

**17:13**
Neh 9:29-30
Jer 7:5-6; 18:11
Acts 7:51-52

**17:4** Or by asking the king of Egypt at Sais.  **17:12** The Hebrew term (literally round things) probably alludes to dung.

---

**17:3** This was probably Shalmaneser V, who had become king of Assyria after Tiglath-pileser (727–722 B.C.). He continued to demand heavy tribute from Israel. Israel's king Hoshea decided to rebel against Assyria and join forces with King So of Egypt (17:4). This was not only foolish but also against God's commands. To destroy this alliance, Shalmaneser attacked and besieged Samaria for three years. Just before Samaria fell, however, Shalmaneser died. His successor, Sargon II, took credit for capturing the city, destroying the nation of Israel, and carrying away its people.

**17:5, 6** This was Assyria's third and final invasion of Israel. (The first two invasions are recorded in 15:19 and 15:29.) The first wave had been merely a warning to Israel—to avoid further attack, pay money, and not rebel. The people should have learned their lesson and returned to God. When they didn't, God had allowed Assyria to invade again, this time carrying off some captives from the northern border. But the people still did not realize that they had caused their own troubles. Thus, Assyria invaded

for the third and final time, destroying Israel completely, carrying away most of the people, and resettling the land with foreigners.

God was doing what he had said he would do (Deuteronomy 28). He had given Israel ample warning; they knew what would come, but they still ignored God. Israel was now no better than the pagan nations it had destroyed in the days of Joshua. The nation had turned sour and rejected its original purpose—to honor God and be a light to the world.

**17:7-17** The Lord judged the people of Israel because they had copied the evil customs of the surrounding nations, worshiping false gods, accommodating pagan customs, and following their own desires. Those who create their own religion tend to live selfishly. And to live for oneself, as Israel learned, brings serious consequences from God. Sometimes following God is difficult and painful, but consider the alternative. You can live for God or die for yourself. Determine to be God's person and do what he says regardless of the cost. What God thinks of you is infinitely more important than what those around you think. (See Romans 12:1, 2; 1 John 2:15-17.)

**17:9** Ruin came upon Israel for both their public sins and their secret sins. Not only did they condone wickedness and idolatry in public, but they committed even worse sins in private. Secret sins are the ones we don't want others to know about because they are embarrassing or incriminating. Sins done in private are not secret to God, and secret defiance of him is just as damaging as open rebellion.

**17:13-15** The people took on the characteristics of the idols and imitated the godless nations around them. Israel had forgotten the importance and benefits of obeying God's word. The king and the people had become mired in wickedness. Time and again God had sent prophets to warn them about how far they had turned away from him and to call them to turn back.

God's patience and mercy are beyond our ability to understand. He will pursue us until we either respond to him or, by our own choice and hardness of heart, make ourselves unreachable. Then God's judgment is swift and sure. The only safe course is to turn to God before our stubbornness puts us out of his reach.

**ISRAEL TAKEN CAPTIVE**  Finally the sins of Israel's people caught up with them. God allowed Assyria to defeat and disperse the people. They were led into captivity, swallowed up by the mighty, evil Assyrian Empire. Sin always brings discipline, and the consequences of that sin are sometimes irreversible.

**17:14**
Exod 32:9; 33:3

**17:15**
Exod 24:6-8
Deut 12:30-31;
29:25; 32:21

**17:16**
1 Kgs 12:28; 16:31

**17:17**
Lev 19:26
Deut 18:10-12
2 Kgs 3:27; 16:3;
21:6

**17:19**
1 Kgs 14:22-24

**17:21**
1 Kgs 11:11, 31;
12:20

**17:23**
2 Kgs 18:11-12

**17:24**
2 Kgs 18:34
Ezra 4:2, 10

¹⁴But the Israelites would not listen. They were as stubborn as their ancestors who had re-fused to believe in the LORD their God. ¹⁵They rejected his decrees and the covenant he had made with their ancestors, and they despised all his warnings. They worshiped worthless idols, so they became worthless themselves. They followed the example of the nations around them, disobeying the LORD's command not to imitate them.

¹⁶They rejected all the commands of the LORD their God and made two calves from metal. They set up an Asherah pole and worshiped Baal and all the forces of heaven. ¹⁷They even sacrificed their own sons and daughters in the fire.* They consulted fortune-tellers and practiced sorcery and sold themselves to evil, arousing the LORD's anger.

¹⁸Because the LORD was very angry with Israel, he swept them away from his presence. Only the tribe of Judah remained in the land. ¹⁹But even the people of Judah refused to obey the commands of the LORD their God, for they followed the evil practices that Israel had in-troduced. ²⁰The LORD rejected all the descendants of Israel. He punished them by handing them over to their attackers until he had banished Israel from his presence.

²¹For when the LORD* tore Israel away from the kingdom of David, they chose Jeroboam son of Nebat as their king. But Jeroboam drew Israel away from following the LORD and made them commit a great sin. ²²And the people of Israel persisted in all the evil ways of Jer-oboam. They did not turn from these sins ²³until the LORD finally swept them away from his presence, just as all his prophets had warned. So Israel was exiled from their land to Assyria, where they remain to this day.

### Foreigners Settle in Israel

²⁴The king of Assyria transported groups of people from Babylon, Cuthah, Avva, Hamath, and Sepharvaim and resettled them in the towns of Samaria, replacing the people of Israel. They took possession of Samaria and lived in its towns. ²⁵But since these foreign settlers did not worship the LORD when they first arrived, the LORD sent lions among them, which killed some of them.

²⁶So a message was sent to the king of Assyria: "The people you have sent to live in the towns of Samaria do not know the religious customs of the God of the land. He has sent lions among them to destroy them because they have not worshiped him correctly."

²⁷The king of Assyria then commanded, "Send one of the exiled priests back to Samaria. Let him live there and teach the new residents the religious customs of the God of the land." ²⁸So one of the priests who had been exiled from Samaria returned to Bethel and taught the new residents how to worship the LORD.

**17:17** Or *They even made their sons and daughters pass through the fire.*   **17:21** Hebrew *he;* compare 1 Kgs 11:31-32.

---

**17:16** The "forces of heaven" refers to the Canaanite practice of worshiping the sun, moon, and constellations. These were Assyrian gods that were being added to their religion. (See also 21:1-6; 23:4, 5.)

**17:17** Forms of witchcraft, fortune-telling, and black magic were forbidden by God (Deuteronomy 18:9-14). They were wrong because they sought power and guidance totally apart from God, his law, and his word. Isaiah echoed this law and prophesied of the complete destruction these occult practices would bring to those who participated in them (Isaiah 8:19-22).

**17:23** Israel was taken into exile, just as God's prophets had warned. Whatever God predicts will come to pass. This, of course, is good news to those who trust and obey him—they can be confident of his promises; but it is bad news to those who ignore or disobey him. Both the promises and warnings God has given in his Word will surely come true.

**17:24** Moving the Israelites out and moving foreigners in was Assyria's resettlement policy to prevent revolt. Spreading the captives across Assyria prevented their uniting, and repopulating Israel with foreign captives made it difficult for the remaining Isra-elites to unite as well. This mixture of peoples resettled in Israel came to be known as *Samaritans.* They were despised by the Jews, even through the time of Christ (John 4:9).

**ISRAEL RESETTLED BY FOREIGNERS** After the Israelites were deported, foreigners from the Assyrian Empire were sent to resettle the land. This policy helped Assyria keep peace in conquered territories.

# WHO WERE

| Who? | When? (B.C.) | Ministered during the reign of these kings | Main message | Significance |
|------|--------------|--------------------------------------------|--------------|--------------|
| AHIJAH | 934–909 | Jeroboam I of Israel (1 Kings 11:29–39) | Israel would split in two, and God had chosen Jeroboam to lead the 10 tribes. Warned him to remain obedient to God. | We should not take lightly our God-given responsibilities. Jeroboam did and lost his kingdom. |
| ELIJAH | 875–848 | Ahab of Israel (1 Kings 17:1— 2 Kings 2:11) | In fiery style, urged wicked Ahab to turn back to God. Proved on Mount Carmel who the one true God is (1 Kings 18). | Even giants of faith can't force sinners to change. But those who remain faithful to God have a great impact for him. |
| MICAIAH | 865–853 | Ahab of Israel Jehoshaphat of Judah (1 Kings 22:8; 2 Chronicles 18:28) | Ahab would be unsuccessful in fighting the Arameans. | It is foolish to move ahead with plans that are contrary to God's Word. |
| JEHU | 853 | Jehoshaphat of Judah (2 Chronicles 19:1–3) | Jehoshaphat should never have allied himself with wicked Ahab. | Partnerships with immoral people can lead us into trouble. |
| OBADIAH | 855–840 (?) | Jehoram of Judah (The book of Obadiah) | God would judge the Edomites for taking advantage of God's people. | Pride is one of the most dangerous sins because it causes us to take advantage of others. |
| ELISHA | 848–797 | Joram, Jehu, Jehoahaz, and Jehoash, all of Israel (2 Kings 2:1—9:1; 13:10–21) | Expressed by his actions the importance of helping ordinary people in need. | God is concerned about the everyday needs of his people. |
| JOEL | 835–796 (?) | Joash of Judah (The book of Joel) | Because a plague of locusts had come to punish the nation, called the people to turn back to God before an even greater judgment occurred. | While God judges all people for their sins, he gives eternal salvation only to those who have turned to him. |
| JONAH | 793–753 | Jeroboam II of Israel (2 Kings 14:25; the book of Jonah) | Warned Nineveh, the capital of Assyria, to repent of its sins. | God wants all nations to turn to him. His love reaches out to all peoples. |
| AMOS | 760–750 | Jeroboam II of Israel (The book of Amos) | Warned those who exploited or ignored the needy. (In Amos's day, Israel was an affluent and materialistic society.) | Believing in God is more than a personal matter. God calls all believers to work against injustices in society and to aid those less fortunate. |
| HOSEA | 753–715 | The last seven kings of Israel; Uzziah, Jotham, Ahaz, and Hezekiah of Judah (The book of Hosea) | Condemned the people of Israel because they had sinned against God as an adulterous woman sins against her husband. | When we sin, we sever our relationship to God, breaking our commitment to him. While all must answer to God for their sins, those who seek God's forgiveness are spared from eternal judgment. |

"Again and again the LORD had sent his prophets and seers to warn both Israel and Judah: 'Turn from all your evil ways. Obey my commands and decrees . . .'" (2 Kings 17:13). Who were these prophets? Here are some of those who tried to turn people back to God. Predicting the future as revealed by God was just

# THESE PROPHETS?

| Who? | When? (B.C.) | Ministered during the reign of these kings | Main message | Significance |
|------|--------------|--------------------------------------------|--------------|--------------|
| MICAH | 742–687 | Jotham, Ahaz, and Hezekiah of Judah (The book of Micah) | Predicted the fall of both the northern and southern kingdoms. This was God's discipline on the people, actually showing how much he cared for them. | Choosing to live a life apart from God is making a commitment to sin. Sin leads to judgment and death. God alone shows us the way to eternal peace. His discipline often keeps us on the right path. |
| ISAIAH | 740–681 | Uzziah, Jotham, Ahaz, Hezekiah, and Manasseh of Judah (The book of Isaiah) | Called the people back to a special relationship with God—although judgment through other nations was inevitable. | Sometimes we must suffer judgment and discipline before we are restored to God. |
| NAHUM | 663–654 | Manasseh of Judah (The book of Nahum) | The mighty empire of Assyria that oppressed God's people would soon tumble. | Those who do evil and oppress others will one day meet a bitter end. |
| ZEPHANIAH | 640–621 | Josiah of Judah (The book of Zephaniah) | A day would come when God, as Judge, would severely punish all nations; but afterward he would show mercy to his people. | We will all be judged for our disobedience to God, but if we remain faithful to him, he will show us mercy. |
| JEREMIAH | 627–586 | Josiah, Jehoahaz, Jehoiakim, Jehoiachin, Zedekiah of Judah (The book of Jeremiah) | Repentance would postpone Judah's coming judgment at the hands of Babylon. | Repentance is one of the greatest needs in our world of immorality. God's promises to the faithful shine brightly. |
| HABAKKUK | 612–589 | Josiah, Jehoahaz, Jehoiakim, Jehoiachin, Zedekiah of Judah (The book of Habakkuk) | Couldn't understand why God seemed to do nothing about the wickedness in society. Then realized that faith in God alone would one day supply the answer. | Instead of questioning the ways of God, we should realize that he is completely just, and we should have faith that he is in control and that one day evil will be utterly destroyed. |
| DANIEL | 605–536 | Prophesied as an exile in Babylon during the reigns of Nebuchadnezzar, Darius the Mede, and Cyrus of Persia (The book of Daniel) | Described both near and distant future events. Through it all, God is sovereign and triumphant. | We should spend less time wondering when the events will happen and more time learning how we should live now so we won't be victims of those events. |
| EZEKIEL | 593–571 | Prophesied as an exile in Babylon during the reign of Nebuchadnezzar (The book of Ezekiel) | Sent messages back to Jerusalem urging the people to turn back to God before they were all forced to join him in exile. After Jerusalem fell, he urged his fellow exiles to turn back to God so they could eventually return to their homeland. | God disciplines his people to draw them closer to him. |

one part of a prophet's job; his main role was to preach God's word to the people—warning, instructing, and encouraging them to live as they ought. (The prophets Haggai, Zechariah, and Malachi were prophets to the people of Judah after they returned from exile. For more information, see the chart in Ezra 6, p. 731.)

29 But these various groups of foreigners also continued to worship their own gods. In town after town where they lived, they placed their idols at the pagan shrines that the people of Samaria had built. 30 Those from Babylon worshiped idols of their god Succoth-benoth. Those from Cuthah worshiped their god Nergal. And those from Hamath worshiped Ashima. 31 The Avvites worshiped their gods Nibhaz and Tartak. And the people from Sepharvaim even burned their own children as sacrifices to their gods Adrammelech and Anammelech.

17:29
1 Kgs 12:31; 13:32

32 These new residents worshiped the LORD, but they also appointed from among themselves all sorts of people as priests to offer sacrifices at their places of worship. 33 And though they worshiped the LORD, they continued to follow their own gods according to the religious customs of the nations from which they came. 34 And this is still going on today. They continue to follow their former practices instead of truly worshiping the LORD and obeying the decrees, regulations, instructions, and commands he gave the descendants of Jacob, whose name he changed to Israel.

17:31
2 Kgs 17:24; 19:37

17:32
1 Kgs 12:31

17:34
Gen 32:28; 35:10

35 For the LORD had made a covenant with the descendants of Jacob and commanded them: "Do not worship any other gods or bow before them or serve them or offer sacrifices to them. 36 But worship only the LORD, who brought you out of Egypt with great strength and a powerful arm. Bow down to him alone, and offer sacrifices only to him. 37 Be careful at all times to obey the decrees, regulations, instructions, and commands that he wrote for you. You must not worship other gods. 38 Do not forget the covenant I made with you, and do not worship other gods. 39 You must worship only the LORD your God. He is the one who will rescue you from all your enemies."

17:35
Exod 20:5

17:37
Deut 5:32

17:38
Deut 4:23; 6:10-12

40 But the people would not listen and continued to follow their former practices. 41 So while these new residents worshiped the LORD, they also worshiped their idols. And to this day their descendants do the same.

17:41
Zeph 1:5
Matt 6:24

## B. THE SURVIVING KINGDOM (18:1—25:30)

After seeing their brothers and sisters carried away into exile, the people of Judah still lapse into sin. Hezekiah and Josiah begin many reforms, but this is not enough to permanently turn the nation back to God. Judah is defeated by the Babylonians, who exile many of them, but they are not scattered, and the land is not repopulated. Sometimes we do not learn from the examples of sin and foolishness around us.

### 1. Kings of Judah

*Hezekiah Rules in Judah*

**18** Hezekiah son of Ahaz began to rule over Judah in the third year of King Hoshea's reign in Israel. 2 He was twenty-five years old when he became king, and he reigned in Jerusalem twenty-nine years. His mother was Abijah,* the daughter of Zechariah. 3 He did what was pleasing in the LORD's sight, just as his ancestor David had done. 4 He removed the pagan shrines, smashed the sacred pillars, and cut down the Asherah poles. He broke up the bronze serpent that Moses had made, because the people of Israel had been offering sacrifices to it. The bronze serpent was called Nehushtan.*

5 Hezekiah trusted in the LORD, the God of Israel. There was no one like him among all the kings of Judah, either before or after his time. 6 He remained faithful to the LORD in everything, and he carefully obeyed all the commands the LORD had given Moses. 7 So

18:1
2 Chr 28:27

18:2-4
//2 Chr 29:1-2; 31:1

18:4
Num 21:8-9
2 Chr 31:1

18:5-7
//2 Chr 31:20-21

18:5
2 Kgs 19:10; 23:25

18:6
Deut 10:20

18:7
Gen 39:2-3
1 Sam 18:14

**18:2** As in parallel text at 2 Chr 29:1; Hebrew reads *Abi*, a variant spelling of Abijah.    **18:4** *Nehushtan* sounds like the Hebrew terms that mean "snake," "bronze," and "unclean thing."

---

**17:27-29** The new settlers in Israel worshiped God without giving up their pagan customs. They worshiped God to appease him rather than to please him, treating him as a good luck charm or just another idol to add to their collection. A similar attitude is common today. Many people claim to believe in God while refusing to give up attitudes and actions that God denounces. God cannot be added to the values we already have. He must come first, and his Word must shape all our actions and attitudes.

**17:29-31** Israel was conquered because it had lost sight of the only true God and the importance of following him. When conquering the land, the Israelites were told to destroy the pagan influences that could lead them away from God. Their failure to do so brought about their ruin. Here they faced an even greater influx of gods from the many pagan peoples moving into the land.

**18:4** The bronze serpent had been made to cure the Israelites

of the bite of poisonous snakes (Numbers 21:4-9). It had demonstrated God's presence and power and had reminded the people of his mercy and forgiveness. But it had become an object of worship instead of a reminder of *whom* to worship, so Hezekiah was forced to destroy it. We must be careful that aids to our worship don't become objects of worship themselves. Most objects are not made to be idols—they become idols by the way people use them.

**18:5** "There was no one like him among all the kings of Judah. . . ." In dramatic contrast with his father, Ahaz, Hezekiah followed God more closely and sincerely than any other king of Judah or Israel. This statement refers to the kings after the division of the kingdom and so does not include David, considered the king most devoted to God.

**18:7** Judah was sandwiched between two world powers, Egypt and Assyria. Both wanted to control Judah and Israel because

18:8
2 Kgs 17:9
2 Chr 28:18

the Lord was with him, and Hezekiah was successful in everything he did. He revolted against the king of Assyria and refused to pay him tribute. 8He also conquered the Philistines as far distant as Gaza and its territory, from their smallest outpost to their largest walled city.

**HEZEKIAH**

The past is an important part of today's actions and tomorrow's plans. The people and kings of Judah had a rich past, filled with God's action, guidance, and commands. But with each passing generation, they also had a growing list of tragedies that occurred when the people forgot that their God, who had cared for them in the past, also cared about the present and the future—and demanded their continued obedience. Hezekiah was one of the few kings of Judah who was constantly aware of God's acts in the past and his interest in the events of every day. The Bible describes him as a king who had a close relationship with God.

As a reformer, Hezekiah was most concerned with present obedience. Judah was filled with visual reminders of the people's lack of trust in God, and Hezekiah boldly cleaned house. Altars, idols, and pagan temples were destroyed. Even the bronze serpent Moses had made in the wilderness was not spared because it had ceased to point the people to God and had also become an idol. The Temple in Jerusalem, whose doors had been nailed shut by Hezekiah's own father, was cleaned out and reopened. The Passover was reinstituted as a national holiday, and there was revival in Judah.

Although he had a natural inclination to respond to present problems, Hezekiah's life shows little evidence of concern about the future. He took few actions to preserve the effects of his sweeping reforms. His successful efforts made him proud. His unwise display of wealth to the Babylonian delegation got Judah included on Babylon's "Nations to Conquer" list. When Isaiah informed Hezekiah of the foolishness of his act, the king's answer displayed his persistent lack of foresight—he was thankful that any evil consequences would be delayed until after he died. And the lives of three kings who followed him—Manasseh, Amon, and Josiah—were deeply affected by both Hezekiah's accomplishments *and* his weaknesses.

The past affects your decisions and actions today, and these, in turn, affect the future. There are lessons to learn and errors to avoid repeating. Remember that part of the success of your past will be measured by what you do with it now and how well you use it to prepare for the future.

| | |
|---|---|
| **Strengths and accomplishments** | • Was the king of Judah who instigated civil and religious reforms<br>• Had a personal, growing relationship with God<br>• Developed a powerful prayer life<br>• Noted as the patron of several chapters in the book of Proverbs (Proverbs 25:1) |
| **Weaknesses and mistakes** | • Showed little interest or wisdom in planning for the future and protecting for others the spiritual heritage he enjoyed<br>• Rashly showed all his wealth to messengers from Babylon |
| **Lessons from his life** | • Sweeping reforms are short-lived when little action is taken to preserve them for the future<br>• Past obedience to God does not remove the possibility of present disobedience<br>• Complete dependence on God yields amazing results |
| **Vital statistics** | • Where: Jerusalem<br>• Occupation: 13th king of Judah, the southern kingdom<br>• Relatives: Father: Ahaz. Mother: Abijah. Son: Manasseh.<br>• Contemporaries: Isaiah, Hoshea, Micah, Sennacherib |
| **Key verses** | "Hezekiah trusted in the Lord, the God of Israel. There was no one like him among all the kings of Judah, either before or after his time. He remained faithful to the Lord in everything, and he carefully obeyed all the commands the Lord had given Moses" (2 Kings 18:5, 6). |

Hezekiah's story is told in 2 Kings 16:20—20:21; 2 Chronicles 28:27—32:33; Isaiah 36:1—39:8. He is also mentioned in Proverbs 25:1; Isaiah 1:1; Jeremiah 15:4; 26:18, 19; Hosea 1:1; Micah 1:1.

they lay at the vital crossroads of all ancient Near East trade. The nation that controlled Judah would have a military and economic advantage over its rivals. When Hezekiah became king, Assyria controlled Judah. Acting with great courage, Hezekiah rebelled against this mighty empire to whom his father had submitted. He placed his faith in God's strength rather than his own, and he obeyed God's commands in spite of the obstacles and dangers that, from a purely human standpoint, looked overwhelming.

9During the fourth year of Hezekiah's reign, which was the seventh year of King Hoshea's reign in Israel, King Shalmaneser of Assyria attacked the city of Samaria and began a siege against it. 10Three years later, during the sixth year of King Hezekiah's reign and the ninth year of King Hoshea's reign in Israel, Samaria fell. 11At that time the king of Assyria exiled the Israelites to Assyria and placed them in colonies in Halah, along the banks of the Habor River in Gozan, and in the cities of the Medes. 12For they refused to listen to the Lord their God and obey him. Instead, they violated his covenant—all the laws that Moses the Lord's servant had commanded them to obey.

18:9-12<br>//2 Kgs 17:3-7

18:12<br>1 Kgs 9:6<br>Dan 9:6, 10

### Assyria Invades Judah

13In the fourteenth year of King Hezekiah's reign,* King Sennacherib of Assyria came to attack the fortified towns of Judah and conquered them. 14King Hezekiah sent this message to the king of Assyria at Lachish: "I have done wrong. I will pay whatever tribute money you demand if you will only withdraw." The king of Assyria then demanded a settlement of more than eleven tons of silver and one ton of gold.* 15To gather this amount, King Hezekiah used all the silver stored in the Temple of the Lord and in the palace treasury. 16Hezekiah even stripped the gold from the doors of the Lord's Temple and from the doorposts he had overlaid with gold, and he gave it all to the Assyrian king.

18:13<br>2 Chr 32:1<br>Isa 36:1

18:15<br>1 Kgs 15:18-19<br>2 Kgs 12:18

17Nevertheless, the king of Assyria sent his commander in chief, his field commander, and his chief of staff* from Lachish with a huge army to confront King Hezekiah in Jerusalem. The Assyrians took up a position beside the aqueduct that feeds water into the upper pool, near the road leading to the field where cloth is washed.* 18They summoned King Hezekiah, but the king sent these officials to meet with them: Eliakim son of Hilkiah, the palace administrator; Shebna the court secretary; and Joah son of Asaph, the royal historian.

18:17-37<br>//2 Chr 32:9-19<br>//Isa 36:1-22

18:18<br>2 Kgs 19:2<br>Isa 22:15-16, 20

### Sennacherib Threatens Jerusalem

19Then the Assyrian king's chief of staff told them to give this message to Hezekiah:

"This is what the great king of Assyria says: What are you trusting in that makes you so confident? 20Do you think that mere words can substitute for military skill and strength? Who are you counting on, that you have rebelled against me? 21On Egypt? If you lean on Egypt, it will be like a reed that splinters beneath your weight and pierces your hand. Pharaoh, the king of Egypt, is completely unreliable!

22"But perhaps you will say to me, 'We are trusting in the Lord our God!' But isn't he the one who was insulted by Hezekiah? Didn't Hezekiah tear down his shrines and altars and make everyone in Judah and Jerusalem worship only at the altar here in Jerusalem?

23"I'll tell you what! Strike a bargain with my master, the king of Assyria. I will give you 2,000 horses if you can find that many men to ride on them! 24With your tiny army, how can you think of challenging even the weakest contingent of my master's troops, even with the help of Egypt's chariots and charioteers? 25What's more, do you think we have invaded your land without the Lord's direction? The Lord himself told us, 'Attack this land and destroy it!'"

26Then Eliakim son of Hilkiah, Shebna, and Joah said to the Assyrian chief of staff, "Please speak to us in Aramaic, for we understand it well. Don't speak in Hebrew,* for the people on the wall will hear."

18:26<br>Ezra 4:7<br>Dan 2:4

27But Sennacherib's chief of staff replied, "Do you think my master sent this message only to you and your master? He wants all the people to hear it, for when we put this city under siege, they will suffer along with you. They will be so hungry and thirsty that they will eat their own dung and drink their own urine."

18:13 The fourteenth year of Hezekiah's reign was 701 B.C.    18:14 Hebrew *300 talents* [10 metric tons] *of silver and 30 talents* [1 metric ton] *of gold.*    18:17a Or *the rabshakeh;* also in 18:19, 26, 27, 28, 37.    18:17b Or *bleached.*
18:26 Hebrew *in the dialect of Judah;* also in 18:28.

---

18:9-12 These verses flash back to the days just before Israel's destruction. Hezekiah reigned with his father, Ahaz, for 14 years (729–715 B.C.), by himself for 18 years (715–697 B.C.), and with his son Manasseh for 11 years (697–686 B.C.), a total of 43 years. The 29 years listed in 18:2 indicate only those years in which Hezekiah had complete control of the kingdom. While Hezekiah was on the throne, the nation of Israel to the north was

destroyed (722 B.C.). Knowing Israel's fate probably caused Hezekiah to reform his own nation. (For more on Hezekiah, see 2 Chronicles 29–32 and Isaiah 36–39.)

18:13 This event occurred in 701 B.C., four years after Sennacherib had become Assyria's king. Sennacherib was the son of Sargon II, the king who had deported Israel's people into captivity (see the note on 17:3). To keep Assyria from attacking, the south-

<sup>28</sup>Then the chief of staff stood and shouted in Hebrew to the people on the wall, "Listen to this message from the great king of Assyria! <sup>29</sup>This is what the king says: Don't let Hezekiah deceive you. He will never be able to rescue you from my power. <sup>30</sup>Don't let him fool you into trusting in the LORD by saying, 'The LORD will surely rescue us. This city will never fall into the hands of the Assyrian king!'

<sup>31</sup>"Don't listen to Hezekiah! These are the terms the king of Assyria is offering: Make peace with me—open the gates and come out. Then each of you can continue eating from your own grapevine and fig tree and drinking from your own well. <sup>32</sup>Then I will arrange to take you to another land like this one—a land of grain and new wine, bread and vineyards, olive groves and honey. Choose life instead of death!

"Don't listen to Hezekiah when he tries to mislead you by saying, 'The LORD will rescue us!' <sup>33</sup>Have the gods of any other nations ever saved their people from the king of Assyria? <sup>34</sup>What happened to the gods of Hamath and Arpad? And what about the gods of Sepharvaim, Hena, and Ivvah? Did any god rescue Samaria from my power? <sup>35</sup>What god of any nation has ever been able to save its people from my power? So what makes you think that the LORD can rescue Jerusalem from me?"

<sup>36</sup>But the people were silent and did not utter a word because Hezekiah had commanded them, "Do not answer him."

<sup>37</sup>Then Eliakim son of Hilkiah, the palace administrator; Shebna the court secretary; and Joah son of Asaph, the royal historian, went back to Hezekiah. They tore their clothes in despair, and they went in to see the king and told him what the Assyrian chief of staff had said.

### Hezekiah Seeks the LORD's Help

**19** When King Hezekiah heard their report, he tore his clothes and put on burlap and went into the Temple of the LORD. <sup>2</sup>And he sent Eliakim the palace administrator, Shebna the court secretary, and the leading priests, all dressed in burlap, to the prophet Isaiah son of Amoz. <sup>3</sup>They told him, "This is what King Hezekiah says: Today is a day of trouble, insults, and disgrace. It is like when a child is ready to be born, but the mother has no strength to deliver the baby. <sup>4</sup>But perhaps the LORD your God has heard the Assyrian chief of staff,* sent by the king to defy the living God, and will punish him for his words. Oh, pray for those of us who are left!"

<sup>5</sup>After King Hezekiah's officials delivered the king's message to Isaiah, <sup>6</sup>the prophet replied, "Say to your master, 'This is what the LORD says: Do not be disturbed by this blasphemous speech against me from the Assyrian king's messengers. <sup>7</sup>Listen! I myself will move against him,* and the king will receive a message that he is needed at home. So he will return to his land, where I will have him killed with a sword.'"

<sup>8</sup>Meanwhile, the Assyrian chief of staff left Jerusalem and went to consult the king of Assyria, who had left Lachish and was attacking Libnah.

<sup>9</sup>Soon afterward King Sennacherib received word that King Tirhakah of Ethiopia* was leading an army to fight against him. Before leaving to meet the attack, he sent messengers back to Hezekiah in Jerusalem with this message:

**19:4** Or *the rabshakeh;* also in 19:8.   **19:7** Hebrew *I will put a spirit in him.*   **19:9** Hebrew *of Cush.*

---

ern kingdom paid tribute annually. But when Sennacherib became king, Hezekiah stopped paying this money, hoping Assyria would ignore him. When Sennacherib and his army retaliated, Hezekiah realized his mistake and paid the tribute money (18:14), but Sennacherib attacked anyway (18:19ff). Although Sennacherib attacked Judah, he was not as war-hungry as the previous Assyrian kings, preferring to spend most of his time building and beautifying his capital city, Nineveh. With less frequent invasions, Hezekiah was able to institute many reforms and strengthen the nation.

**18:17** Sending the commander in chief, the field commander, and the chief of staff was like sending the vice president, secretary of state, and the head general of the army to speak to the enemy prior to a battle. All of these men were sent in an effort to impress and discourage the Israelites.

**19:1-7** Sennacherib, whose armies had captured all the fortified cities of Judah, sent a message to Hezekiah to surrender. Realizing the situation was hopeless, Hezekiah went to the Temple and prayed. God answered Hezekiah's prayer and delivered Judah by sending an army to attack the Assyrian camp, forcing Sen-

nacherib to leave at once. Prayer should be our first response in any crisis. Don't wait until things are hopeless. Pray daily for his guidance. Our problems are God's opportunities.

**19:2** Isaiah the prophet had been working for God since the days of Uzziah—40 years (Isaiah 6:1). Although Assyria was a world power, it could not conquer Judah as long as Isaiah counseled the kings. Isaiah prophesied during the reigns of Uzziah (Azariah), Jotham, Ahaz, and Hezekiah. Ahaz ignored Isaiah, but Hezekiah listened to his advice. To read his prophecies, see the book of Isaiah.

10 "This message is for King Hezekiah of Judah. Don't let your God, in whom you trust, deceive you with promises that Jerusalem will not be captured by the king of Assyria. 11 You know perfectly well what the kings of Assyria have done wherever they have gone. They have completely destroyed everyone who stood in their way! Why should you be any different? 12 Have the gods of other nations rescued them—such nations as Gozan, Haran, Rezeph, and the people of Eden who were in Tel-assar? My predecessors destroyed them all! 13 What happened to the king of Hamath and the king of Arpad? What happened to the kings of Sepharvaim, Hena, and Ivvah?"

**19:10**
2 Kgs 18:5, 30

**19:12**
2 Kgs 17:6; 18:33
Isa 37:12

**19:13**
2 Kgs 18:34

14 After Hezekiah received the letter from the messengers and read it, he went up to the LORD's Temple and spread it out before the LORD. 15 And Hezekiah prayed this prayer before the LORD: "O LORD, God of Israel, you are enthroned between the mighty cherubim! You alone are God of all the kingdoms of the earth. You alone created the heavens and the earth. 16 Bend down, O LORD, and listen! Open your eyes, O LORD, and see! Listen to Sennacherib's words of defiance against the living God.

**19:14-19**
//Isa 37:14-20

**19:16**
1 Kgs 8:29-30
2 Chr 6:40

17 "It is true, LORD, that the kings of Assyria have destroyed all these nations. 18 And they have thrown the gods of these nations into the fire and burned them. But of course the Assyrians could destroy them! They were not gods at all—only idols of wood and stone shaped by human hands. 19 Now, O LORD our God, rescue us from his power; then all the kingdoms of the earth will know that you alone, O LORD, are God."

**19:18**
Isa 44:9-20
Acts 17:29

**19:19**
1 Kgs 8:42-43

### Isaiah Predicts Judah's Deliverance

20 Then Isaiah son of Amoz sent this message to Hezekiah: "This is what the LORD, the God of Israel, says: I have heard your prayer about King Sennacherib of Assyria. 21 And the LORD has spoken this word against him:

**19:20-37**
//Isa 37:21-38

**19:21**
Lam 2:13

"The virgin daughter of Zion
　despises you and laughs at you.
The daughter of Jerusalem
　shakes her head in derision as you flee.

22 "Whom have you been defying and ridiculing?
　Against whom did you raise your voice?
At whom did you look with such haughty eyes?
　It was the Holy One of Israel!
23 By your messengers you have defied the Lord.
　You have said, 'With my many chariots
I have conquered the highest mountains—
　yes, the remotest peaks of Lebanon.
I have cut down its tallest cedars
　and its finest cypress trees.
I have reached its farthest corners
　and explored its deepest forests.
24 I have dug wells in many foreign lands
　and refreshed myself with their water.
With the sole of my foot
　I stopped up all the rivers of Egypt!'

**19:22**
Exod 5:2
Isa 5:24; 30:10-15

25 "But have you not heard?
　I decided this long ago.
Long ago I planned it,
　and now I am making it happen.
I planned for you to crush fortified cities
　into heaps of rubble.

**19:25**
Isa 10:5-7; 45:5-7

---

**19:15** Cherubim are mighty angels.

**19:15-19** Although Hezekiah came boldly to God, he did not take God for granted or approach him flippantly. Instead, Hezekiah acknowledged God's sovereignty and Judah's total dependence on him. Hezekiah's prayer provides a good model for us. We should not be afraid to approach God with our prayers, but we must come to him with respect for who he is and what he can do.

**19:21-34** God replied to Sennacherib's taunting words (18:19-25), indicting him for arrogance. Sennacherib believed his kingdom had grown because of his own efforts and strength. In reality, said God, he succeeded only because of what God had allowed and caused. It is arrogance to think we are solely responsible for our achievements. God, as Creator, rules over nations and people.

**19:26**
Ps 129:6-7

26 That is why their people have so little power
   and are so frightened and confused.
They are as weak as grass,
   as easily trampled as tender green shoots.
They are like grass sprouting on a housetop,
   scorched before it can grow lush and tall.

**19:27**
Ps 139:1-4

27 "But I know you well—
   where you stay
and when you come and go.
I know the way you have raged against me.

**19:28**
2 Kgs 19:33
Ezek 29:4

28 And because of your raging against me
   and your arrogance, which I have heard for myself,
I will put my hook in your nose
   and my bit in your mouth.
I will make you return
   by the same road on which you came."

**19:29**
Exod 3:12
2 Kgs 20:8-9

29 Then Isaiah said to Hezekiah, "Here is the proof that what I say is true:

"This year you will eat only what grows up by itself,
   and next year you will eat what springs up from that.
But in the third year you will plant crops and harvest them;
   you will tend vineyards and eat their fruit.

**19:30**
2 Chr 32:22-23

30 And you who are left in Judah,
   who have escaped the ravages of the siege,
will put roots down in your own soil
   and will grow up and flourish.

**19:31**
Isa 9:7

31 For a remnant of my people will spread out from Jerusalem,
   a group of survivors from Mount Zion.
The passionate commitment of the LORD of Heaven's Armies*
   will make this happen!

32 "And this is what the LORD says about the king of Assyria:

"His armies will not enter Jerusalem.
   They will not even shoot an arrow at it.
They will not march outside its gates with their shields
   nor build banks of earth against its walls.

**19:33**
2 Kgs 19:28

33 The king will return to his own country
   by the same road on which he came.
He will not enter this city,
   says the LORD.

**19:34**
1 Kgs 11:12-13
2 Kgs 20:6

34 For my own honor and for the sake of my servant David,
   I will defend this city and protect it."

**19:35-37**
//2 Chr 32:20-21

**19:36**
Jon 1:2

35 That night the angel of the LORD went out to the Assyrian camp and killed 185,000 Assyrian soldiers. When the surviving Assyrians* woke up the next morning, they found corpses everywhere. 36 Then King Sennacherib of Assyria broke camp and returned to his own land. He went home to his capital of Nineveh and stayed there.

**19:31** As in Greek and Syriac versions, Latin Vulgate, and an alternate reading of the Masoretic Text (see also Isa 37:32); the other alternate reads *the LORD.*   **19:35** Hebrew *When they.*

---

**19:28** The Assyrians treated captives with cruelty. They tortured prisoners for entertainment by blinding them, cutting them, or pulling off strips of their skin until they died. If the Assyrians wished to make a captive a slave, they would often put a hook in his nose. God was saying that the Assyrians would be treated the way they had treated others.

**19:31** As long as a tiny spark remains, a fire can be rekindled and fanned into a roaring blaze. Similarly, if just a small remnant of true believers retains the spark of faith, God can rebuild it into a strong nation. And if only a glimmer of faith remains in

a heart, God can use it to restore blazing faith in that believer. If you feel that only a spark of faith remains in you, ask God to use it to rekindle a blazing fire of commitment to him.

37 One day while he was worshiping in the temple of his god Nisroch, his sons* Adramme-lech and Sharezer killed him with their swords. They then escaped to the land of Ararat, and another son, Esarhaddon, became the next king of Assyria.

**19:37**
Gen 8:4
Ezra 4:2

## Hezekiah's Sickness and Recovery

**20** About that time Hezekiah became deathly ill, and the prophet Isaiah son of Amoz went to visit him. He gave the king this message: "This is what the LORD says: Set your affairs in order, for you are going to die. You will not recover from this illness."

**20:1-11**
//2 Chr 32:24-26
//Isa 38:1-8

2 When Hezekiah heard this, he turned his face to the wall and prayed to the LORD, 3 "Remember, O LORD, how I have always been faithful to you and have served you single-mindedly, always doing what pleases you." Then he broke down and wept bitterly.

**20:3**
2 Kgs 18:3-6

4 But before Isaiah had left the middle courtyard,* this message came to him from the LORD: 5 "Go back to Hezekiah, the leader of my people. Tell him, 'This is what the LORD, the God of your ancestor David, says: I have heard your prayer and seen your tears. I will heal you, and three days from now you will get out of bed and go to the Temple of the LORD. 6 I will add fifteen years to your life, and I will rescue you and this city from the king of Assyria. I will defend this city for my own honor and for the sake of my servant David.'"

**20:5**
2 Kgs 19:20
Ps 39:12
**20:6**
2 Kgs 19:34

7 Then Isaiah said, "Make an ointment from figs." So Hezekiah's servants spread the ointment over the boil, and Hezekiah recovered!

8 Meanwhile, Hezekiah had said to Isaiah, "What sign will the LORD give to prove that he will heal me and that I will go to the Temple of the LORD three days from now?"

9 Isaiah replied, "This is the sign from the LORD to prove that he will do as he promised. Would you like the shadow on the sundial to go forward ten steps or backward ten steps?*"

**20:9**
Isa 38:7-8

10 "The shadow always moves forward," Hezekiah replied, "so that would be easy. Make it go ten steps backward instead." 11 So Isaiah the prophet asked the LORD to do this, and he caused the shadow to move ten steps backward on the sundial* of Ahaz!

**20:11**
Josh 10:12-14

## Envoys from Babylon

12 Soon after this, Merodach-baladan son of Baladan, king of Babylon, sent Hezekiah his best wishes and a gift, for he had heard that Hezekiah had been very sick. 13 Hezekiah received the Babylonian envoys and showed them everything in his treasure-houses—the silver, the gold, the spices, and the aromatic oils. He also took them to see his armory and showed them everything in his royal treasuries! There was nothing in his palace or kingdom that Hezekiah did not show them.

**20:12-19**
//Isa 39:1-8
**20:13**
2 Chr 32:27

14 Then Isaiah the prophet went to King Hezekiah and asked him, "What did those men want? Where were they from?"

Hezekiah replied, "They came from the distant land of Babylon."

15 "What did they see in your palace?" Isaiah asked.

"They saw everything," Hezekiah replied. "I showed them everything I own—all my royal treasuries."

16 Then Isaiah said to Hezekiah, "Listen to this message from the LORD: 17 The time is coming when everything in your palace—all the treasures stored up by your ancestors until now—will be carried off to Babylon. Nothing will be left, says the LORD. 18 Some of your very own sons will be taken away into exile. They will become eunuchs who will serve in the palace of Babylon's king."

**20:17**
2 Kgs 24:13;
25:13-15
Jer 52:17-23
**20:18**
2 Kgs 24:12, 15
2 Chr 33:11

**19:37** As in Greek version and an alternate reading of the Masoretic Text (see also Isa 37:38); the other alternate reading lacks *his sons*.   **20:4** As in Greek version and an alternate reading in the Masoretic Text; the other alternate reads *the middle of the city*.   **20:9** Or *The shadow on the sundial has gone forward ten steps; do you want it to go backward ten steps?*   **20:11** Hebrew *the steps*.

---

**20:5, 6** Over a 100-year period of Judah's history (732–640 B.C.), Hezekiah was the only faithful king; but what a difference he made! Because of Hezekiah's faith and prayer, God healed him and saved his city from the Assyrians. You can make a difference, too, even if your faith puts you in the minority. Faith and prayer, if they are sincere and directed toward the one true God, can change any situation.

**20:11** Egyptian sundials in this period were sometimes made in the form of miniature staircases so that the shadows moved up and down the steps.

**20:12-19** Hezekiah had been a good and faithful king. But when Isaiah asked him what he had shown the messengers

from Babylon, he replied, "I showed them everything I own—all my royal treasuries." From the account in 2 Chronicles 32:24-31, it appears that Hezekiah's prosperity, success, and deliverance from sickness had made him proud. Rather than giving credit to God for all his blessings, he tried to impress the foreigners. When God helps us, we must not use his blessings to impress others. A testimony of victory can quickly degenerate into vanity and self-congratulations.

**20:14** Babylon, a city that had rebelled against the Assyrian Empire, was destroyed by Sennacherib in 689 B.C. This event probably occurred shortly before that date. When Sennacherib died in 681 B.C., his son, Esarhaddon, foolishly rebuilt the city of Babylon. Assyria, whose rulers at that time were weak, allowed Babylon

<sup>19</sup>Then Hezekiah said to Isaiah, "This message you have given me from the LORD is good." For the king was thinking, "At least there will be peace and security during my lifetime." <sup>20</sup>The rest of the events in Hezekiah's reign, including the extent of his power and how he built a pool and dug a tunnel* to bring water into the city, are recorded in *The Book of the History of the Kings of Judah.* <sup>21</sup>Hezekiah died, and his son Manasseh became the next king.

### Manasseh Rules in Judah

**21** Manasseh was twelve years old when he became king, and he reigned in Jerusalem fifty-five years. His mother was Hephzibah. <sup>2</sup>He did what was evil in the LORD's sight, following the detestable practices of the pagan nations that the LORD had driven from the land ahead of the Israelites. <sup>3</sup>He rebuilt the pagan shrines his father, Hezekiah, had destroyed. He constructed altars for Baal and set up an Asherah pole, just as King Ahab of Israel had done. He also bowed before all the powers of the heavens and worshiped them.

<sup>4</sup>He built pagan altars in the Temple of the LORD, the place where the LORD had said, "My name will remain in Jerusalem forever." <sup>5</sup>He built these altars for all the powers of the heavens in both courtyards of the LORD's Temple. <sup>6</sup>Manasseh also sacrificed his own son in the fire.* He practiced sorcery and divination, and he consulted with mediums and psychics. He did much that was evil in the LORD's sight, arousing his anger.

<sup>7</sup>Manasseh even made a carved image of Asherah and set it up in the Temple, the very place where the LORD had told David and his son Solomon: "My name will be honored forever in this Temple and in Jerusalem—the city I have chosen from among all the tribes of Israel. <sup>8</sup>If the Israelites will be careful to obey my commands—all the laws my servant Moses gave them—I will not send them into exile from this land that I gave their ancestors." <sup>9</sup>But the people refused to listen, and Manasseh led them to do even more evil than the pagan nations that the LORD had destroyed when the people of Israel entered the land.

<sup>10</sup>Then the LORD said through his servants the prophets: <sup>11</sup>"King Manasseh of Judah has done many detestable things. He is even more wicked than the Amorites, who lived in this land before Israel. He has caused the people of Judah to sin with his idols.* <sup>12</sup>So this is what the LORD, the God of Israel, says: I will bring such disaster on Jerusalem and Judah that the ears of those who hear about it will tingle with horror. <sup>13</sup>I will judge Jerusalem by the same standard I used for Samaria and the same measure* I used for the family of Ahab. I will wipe away the people of Jerusalem as one wipes a dish and turns it upside down. <sup>14</sup>Then I will reject even the remnant of my own people who are left, and I will hand them over as plunder for their enemies. <sup>15</sup>For they have done great evil in my sight and have angered me ever since their ancestors came out of Egypt."

<sup>16</sup>Manasseh also murdered many innocent people until Jerusalem was filled from one end to the other with innocent blood. This was in addition to the sin that he caused the people of Judah to commit, leading them to do evil in the LORD's sight.

**20:20** Hebrew *watercourse.*   **21:6** Or *also made his son pass through the fire.*   **21:11** The Hebrew term (literally *round things*) probably alludes to dung; also in 21:21.   **21:13** Hebrew *the same plumb line I used for Samaria and the same plumb bob.*

### Marginal cross-references

**20:20-21** //2 Chr 32:32-33
**20:21** 2 Chr 32:33

**21:1-10** //2 Chr 33:1-10
**21:2** 2 Kgs 16:3
**21:3** Lev 18:25; Deut 12:31; 17:3; 1 Kgs 16:29-33; 2 Kgs 18:4
**21:4** 2 Sam 7:13
**21:6** Lev 18:21; 19:26, 31; Deut 18:10; 2 Kgs 16:3; 17:17
**21:7** Deut 16:21; 1 Kgs 9:3; 2 Kgs 23:6
**21:8** 2 Sam 7:10; 2 Kgs 18:11-12; 2 Chr 15:2
**21:11** Gen 15:16; 1 Kgs 21:26; 2 Kgs 24:3-4
**21:12** Jer 19:3
**21:13** Isa 34:11; Amos 7:7-8
**21:16** 2 Kgs 24:3-4

### Study notes

plenty of opportunity to become strong. As the Assyrian army marched off to conquer and oppress faraway lands, the city of Babylon grew and expanded into a small nation. After some years, Babylon was strong enough to rebel again. It eventually crushed Assyria (612 B.C.) and became the next world power.

**20:19** Hezekiah was saying that it was good that these terrible events foretold by Isaiah wouldn't happen during his lifetime. Hezekiah's statement seems selfish, shortsighted, and proud. He knew that his nation would be punished for its sins, so he may have been acknowledging and thanking God for choosing not to destroy Judah during his lifetime.

**20:20** The pool and the tunnel refer to a 1,777-foot tunnel built from the upper spring of Gihon to the pool of Siloam (see 2 Chronicles 32:30). It was from a water source outside the wall of Jerusalem to a secure reservoir inside the city. This was done so the Assyrian army would not cut off the city's water supply.

**21:1ff** Manasseh followed the example of his grandfather Ahaz more than that of his father. He adopted the wicked practices of the Babylonians and Canaanites, including sacrificing his own son (21:6). Manasseh did not listen to the words of God's

prophets but willfully led his people into sin. (See his Profile in 2 Chronicles 33, p. 713, for more information about his life.)

**21:6** Manasseh was an evil king, and he angered God with his sin. Listed among Manasseh's sins are occult practices—sorcery and divination, and consulting mediums and psychics. These acts are strictly forbidden by God (Leviticus 19:31; Deuteronomy 18:9-13) because they demonstrate a lack of faith in him, involve sinful actions, and open the door to demonic influences. Today, many books, television shows, and games emphasize fortune-telling, séances, and other occult practices. Don't let desire to know the future or the belief that superstition is harmless lead you into condoning occult practices. They are counterfeits of God's power and have as their root a system of beliefs totally opposed to God.

**21:7** Asherah was a Canaanite mother-goddess, a mistress of Baal. Her images were made of wood. In Exodus 34:13 and Deuteronomy 12:3, the Israelites were expressly forbidden to associate with Asherah practices in any way.

**21:16** Tradition says that during Manasseh's massive slaughter, Isaiah was sawed in two when trying to hide in a hollow log (see Hebrews 11:37, 38). Other prophets may have been killed at this time.

17The rest of the events in Manasseh's reign and everything he did, including the sins he committed, are recorded in *The Book of the History of the Kings of Judah.* 18When Manasseh died, he was buried in the palace garden, the garden of Uzza. Then his son Amon became the next king.

21:17-18
//2 Chr 33:18-20
21:18
2 Kgs 21:26

## Amon Rules in Judah

19Amon was twenty-two years old when he became king, and he reigned in Jerusalem two years. His mother was Meshullemeth, the daughter of Haruz from Jotbah. 20He did what was evil in the LORD's sight, just as his father, Manasseh, had done. 21He followed the example of his father, worshiping the same idols his father had worshiped. 22He abandoned the LORD, the God of his ancestors, and he refused to follow the LORD's ways.

21:22
2 Kgs 22:17

23Then Amon's own officials conspired against him and assassinated him in his palace. 24But the people of the land killed all those who had conspired against King Amon, and they made his son Josiah the next king.

21:23
2 Kgs 12:20; 14:19

25The rest of the events in Amon's reign and what he did are recorded in *The Book of the History of the Kings of Judah.* 26He was buried in his tomb in the garden of Uzza. Then his son Josiah became the next king.

21:26
2 Kgs 21:18

## Josiah Rules in Judah

**22** Josiah was eight years old when he became king, and he reigned in Jerusalem thirty-one years. His mother was Jedidah, the daughter of Adaiah from Bozkath. 2He did what was pleasing in the LORD's sight and followed the example of his ancestor David. He did not turn away from doing what was right.

22:1-20
//2 Chr 34:1-2, 8-28
22:1
Josh 15:39

3In the eighteenth year of his reign, King Josiah sent Shaphan son of Azaliah and grandson of Meshullam, the court secretary, to the Temple of the LORD. He told him, 4"Go to Hilkiah the high priest and have him count the money the gatekeepers have collected from the people at the LORD's Temple. 5Entrust this money to the men assigned to supervise the Temple's restoration. Then they can use it to pay workers to repair the Temple of the LORD. 6They will need to hire carpenters, builders, and masons. Also have them buy the timber and the finished stone needed to repair the Temple. 7But don't require the construction supervisors to keep account of the money they receive, for they are honest and trustworthy men."

22:3
2 Chr 34:8-9
22:4
2 Kgs 12:4
22:5
2 Kgs 12:11-14
22:7
2 Kgs 12:15

## Hilkiah Discovers God's Law

8Hilkiah the high priest said to Shaphan the court secretary, "I have found the Book of the Law in the LORD's Temple!" Then Hilkiah gave the scroll to Shaphan, and he read it.

22:8
Deut 31:24-26
2 Chr 34:14-16

9Shaphan went to the king and reported, "Your officials have turned over the money collected at the Temple of the LORD to the workers and supervisors at the Temple." 10Shaphan also told the king, "Hilkiah the priest has given me a scroll." So Shaphan read it to the king.

11When the king heard what was written in the Book of the Law, he tore his clothes in despair. 12Then he gave these orders to Hilkiah the priest, Ahikam son of Shaphan, Acbor son of Micaiah, Shaphan the court secretary, and Asaiah the king's personal adviser: 13"Go to the Temple and speak to the LORD for me and for the people and for all Judah. Inquire about the words written in this scroll that has been found. For the LORD's great anger is burning against us because our ancestors have not obeyed the words in this scroll. We have not been doing everything it says we must do."

22:11
Josh 7:6
22:12
2 Kgs 25:22
2 Chr 34:20
Jer 26:24
22:13
Deut 29:23-28

---

**22:1, 2** In reading the biblical lists of kings, it is rare to find one who obeyed God completely. Josiah was such a person, and he was only eight years old when he began to reign. For 18 years Josiah reigned obediently; then, when he was 26, he began the reforms based on God's laws. Children are the future leaders of our churches and our world. A person's major work for God may have to wait until he or she is an adult, but no one is ever too young to take God seriously and obey him. Josiah's early years laid the base for his later task of reforming Judah. God can use you, regardless of your age.

**22:4** The gatekeepers controlled who entered the Temple and supervised the collection of the money.

**22:8** This book may have been the entire Pentateuch (Genesis—Deuteronomy) or just the book of Deuteronomy. Because of the long line of evil kings, the record of God's laws had been lost. Josiah, who was about 26 years old at this time, wanted religious reform throughout the nation. When God's Word was found, drastic changes had to be made to bring the kingdom in line with God's commands. Today you have God's Word at your fingertips. How much change must you make in order to bring your life into line with it?

**22:11ff** When Josiah heard the law, he tore his clothes in despair. He immediately instituted reforms. With just one reading of God's law, he changed the course of the nation. Today many people own Bibles, but few are affected by the truths found in God's Word. The Word of God should cause us, like Josiah, to take action immediately to reform our lives and bring them into harmony with God's will.

**22:14**
2 Chr 34:22

[14]So Hilkiah the priest, Ahikam, Acbor, Shaphan, and Asaiah went to the New Quarter* of Jerusalem to consult with the prophet Huldah. She was the wife of Shallum son of Tikvah, son of Harhas, the keeper of the Temple wardrobe.

**22:16**
Dan 9:11

[15]She said to them, "The LORD, the God of Israel, has spoken! Go back and tell the man who sent you, [16]'This is what the LORD says: I am going to bring disaster on this city* and its people. All the words written in the scroll that the king of Judah has read will come true. [17]For my people have abandoned me and offered sacrifices to pagan gods, and I am very angry with them for everything they have done. My anger will burn against this place, and it will not be quenched.'

**22:19**
Lev 26:31
Jer 26:6

[18]"But go to the king of Judah who sent you to seek the LORD and tell him: 'This is what the LORD, the God of Israel, says concerning the message you have just heard: [19]You were sorry and humbled yourself before the LORD when you heard what I said against this city and its people—that this land would be cursed and become desolate. You tore your clothing in despair and wept before me in repentance. And I have indeed heard you, says the LORD. [20]So I will not send the promised disaster until after you have died and been buried in peace. You will not see the disaster I am going to bring on this city.'"

So they took her message back to the king.

## Josiah's Religious Reforms

**23:1-3**
//2 Chr 34:29-32
**23:2**
Deut 31:11

**23** Then the king summoned all the elders of Judah and Jerusalem. [2]And the king went up to the Temple of the LORD with all the people of Judah and Jerusalem, along with the priests and the prophets—all the people from the least to the greatest. There the king read to them the entire Book of the Covenant that had been found in the LORD's Temple.

**23:3**
Deut 13:4
2 Kgs 11:14, 17

[3]The king took his place of authority beside the pillar and renewed the covenant in the LORD's presence. He pledged to obey the LORD by keeping all his commands, laws, and decrees with all his heart and soul. In this way, he confirmed all the terms of the covenant that were written in the scroll, and all the people pledged themselves to the covenant.

[4]Then the king instructed Hilkiah the high priest and the priests of the second rank and the Temple gatekeepers to remove from the LORD's Temple all the articles that were used to worship Baal, Asherah, and all the powers of the heavens. The king had all these things burned outside Jerusalem on the terraces of the Kidron Valley, and he carried the ashes away to Bethel. [5]He did away with the idolatrous priests, who had been appointed by the previous kings of Judah, for they had offered sacrifices at the pagan shrines throughout Judah and even in the vicinity of Jerusalem. They had also offered sacrifices to Baal, and to the sun, the moon, the constellations, and to all the powers of the heavens. [6]The king removed the Asherah pole from the LORD's Temple and took it outside Jerusalem to the Kidron Valley, where he burned it. Then he ground the ashes of the pole to dust and threw the dust over the graves of the people. [7]He also tore down the living quarters of the male and female shrine prostitutes that were inside the Temple of the LORD, where the women wove coverings for the Asherah pole.

**23:6**
2 Chr 34:4

**23:7**
1 Kgs 14:24; 15:12;
22:46
Ezek 16:16

**23:8**
1 Kgs 15:22

[8]Josiah brought to Jerusalem all the priests who were living in other towns of Judah. He also defiled the pagan shrines, where they had offered sacrifices—all the way from Geba to Beersheba. He destroyed the shrines at the entrance to the gate of Joshua, the governor of

**22:14** Or *the Second Quarter,* a newer section of Jerusalem. Hebrew reads *the Mishneh.*   **22:16** Hebrew *this place;* also in 22:19, 20.

---

**22:14** Huldah was a prophet, as were Miriam (Exodus 15:20) and Deborah (Judges 4:4). God freely selects his servants to carry out his will—rich or poor, male or female, king or slave (Joel 2:28-30). Huldah was obviously highly regarded by the people of her time.

**22:19** When Josiah realized how corrupt his nation had become, he tore his clothes and wept before God. Then God had mercy on him and the nation. Josiah used the customs of his day to show his repentance. Today, we are unlikely to tear our clothes in sorrow for our sin, but weeping, fasting, and making restitution or apologies (if our sin has involved others) demonstrate our sincerity when we repent. The hardest part of repentance is changing the attitudes that originally produced the sinful behavior.

**23:1, 2** For more about the importance and operation of the Temple, see 1 Kings 5–8 and 2 Chronicles 2–7.

**23:4-8** When Josiah realized the terrible state of Judah's religious life, he did something about it. It is not enough to say we believe what is right; we must respond with action, doing what faith requires. This is what James was emphasizing when he wrote, "Can't you see that faith without good deeds is useless?" (James 2:20). This means acting differently at home, school, work, and church. Simply talking about obedience is not enough.

**23:6** This shameful Asherah pole had been set up in God's Temple by the evil King Manasseh (21:7). Asherah is most often identified as a sea goddess and the mistress of Baal. She was a chief goddess of the Canaanites. Her worship glorified sex and war and was accompanied by male prostitution.

Jerusalem. This gate was located to the left of the city gate as one enters the city. ⁹The priests who had served at the pagan shrines were not allowed* to serve at the LORD's altar in Jerusalem, but they were allowed to eat unleavened bread with the other priests.

**23:9**
Ezek 44:9-14

¹⁰Then the king defiled the altar of Topheth in the valley of Ben-Hinnom, so no one could ever again use it to sacrifice a son or daughter in the fire* as an offering to Molech. ¹¹He removed from the entrance of the LORD's Temple the horse statues that the former kings of Judah had dedicated to the sun. They were near the quarters of Nathan-melech the eunuch, an officer of the court.* The king also burned the chariots dedicated to the sun.

**23:10**
Lev 18:21
1 Kgs 11:7
Jer 7:31-32

¹²Josiah tore down the altars that the kings of Judah had built on the palace roof above the upper room of Ahaz. The king destroyed the altars that Manasseh had built in the two courtyards of the LORD's Temple. He smashed them to bits* and scattered the pieces in the Kidron Valley. ¹³The king also desecrated the pagan shrines east of Jerusalem, to the south of the Mount of Corruption, where King Solomon of Israel had built shrines for Ashtoreth, the detestable goddess of the Sidonians; and for Chemosh, the detestable god of the Moabites; and for Molech,* the vile god of the Ammonites. ¹⁴He smashed the sacred pillars and cut down the Asherah poles. Then he desecrated these places by scattering human bones over them.

**23:12**
2 Kgs 21:3-5
2 Chr 33:4-5
Jer 19:13
Zeph 1:5
**23:13**
1 Kgs 11:7
Jer 48:7

**23:14**
Deut 7:5, 25

¹⁵The king also tore down the altar at Bethel—the pagan shrine that Jeroboam son of Nebat had made when he caused Israel to sin. He burned down the shrine and ground it to dust, and he burned the Asherah pole. ¹⁶Then Josiah turned around and noticed several tombs in the side of the hill. He ordered that the bones be brought out, and he burned them on the altar at Bethel to desecrate it. (This happened just as the LORD had promised through the man of God when Jeroboam stood beside the altar at the festival.)

**23:15**
1 Kgs 12:28-33
**23:16**
1 Kgs 13:2, 32

Then Josiah turned and looked up at the tomb of the man of God* who had predicted these things. ¹⁷"What is that monument over there?" Josiah asked.

And the people of the town told him, "It is the tomb of the man of God who came from Judah and predicted the very things that you have just done to the altar at Bethel!"

**23:17**
1 Kgs 13:1-2,
30-31

¹⁸Josiah replied, "Leave it alone. Don't disturb his bones." So they did not burn his bones or those of the old prophet from Samaria.

**23:18**
1 Kgs 13:11, 31

¹⁹Then Josiah demolished all the buildings at the pagan shrines in the towns of Samaria, just as he had done at Bethel. They had been built by the various kings of Israel and had made the LORD* very angry. ²⁰He executed the priests of the pagan shrines on their own altars, and he burned human bones on the altars to desecrate them. Finally, he returned to Jerusalem.

**23:19**
2 Chr 34:6-7
**23:20**
2 Kgs 11:18

### Josiah Celebrates Passover

²¹King Josiah then issued this order to all the people: "You must celebrate the Passover to the LORD your God, as required in this Book of the Covenant." ²²There had not been a Passover celebration like that since the time when the judges ruled in Israel, nor throughout all the years of the kings of Israel and Judah. ²³This Passover was celebrated to the LORD in Jerusalem in the eighteenth year of King Josiah's reign.

**23:21**
Deut 16:2-8
**23:22**
2 Chr 35:18-19

²⁴Josiah also got rid of the mediums and psychics, the household gods, the idols,* and every other kind of detestable practice, both in Jerusalem and throughout the land of Judah. He did this in obedience to the laws written in the scroll that Hilkiah the priest had found in

**23:24**
Lev 19:31
Deut 18:10-12
2 Kgs 21:6; 22:8

**23:9** Hebrew *did not come up.*   **23:10** Or *to make a son or daughter pass through the fire.*   **23:11** The meaning of the Hebrew is uncertain.   **23:12** Or *He quickly removed them.*   **23:13** Hebrew *Milcom,* a variant spelling of Molech. **23:16** In Greek version; Hebrew lacks *when Jeroboam stood beside the altar at the festival. Then Josiah turned and looked up at the tomb of the man of God.*   **23:19** As in Greek and Syriac versions and Latin Vulgate; Hebrew lacks *the LORD.*   **23:24** The Hebrew term (literally *round things*) probably alludes to dung.

---

**23:13** The Mount of Olives is here called the Mount of Corruption because it had become a favorite spot to build pagan shrines. Solomon built a pagan shrine, and other kings built places of idol worship there, too. But God-fearing kings, such as Hezekiah and Josiah, destroyed these pagan worship centers. In New Testament times, Jesus often sat on the Mount of Olives and taught his disciples about serving only God (Matthew 24:3ff). For more background on Ashtoreth, Chemosh, and Molech, see the note on 1 Kings 11:5-8.

**23:16-18** The prophecies mentioned in this passage appear in 1 Kings 13:21-32.

**23:21-23** When Josiah rediscovered the Passover in the Book of the Covenant, he ordered everyone to observe the ceremonies exactly as prescribed. This Passover celebration was to have been a yearly holiday celebrated in remembrance of the entire nation's deliverance from slavery in Egypt (Exodus 12), but it had not been kept for many years. As a result, "there had not been a Passover celebration like that since the time when the judges ruled in Israel, nor throughout all the years of the kings of Israel and Judah." A common misconception states that God is against celebration, wanting to take all the fun out of life. In reality, God wants to give us life in its fullness (John 10:10), and those who love him have the most to celebrate.

**23:25**
2 Kgs 18:5

**23:26**
2 Kgs 21:11-13;
22:15-16

**23:27**
2 Kgs 21:13-14

**23:28-30**
2 Chr 35:20—36:1

the LORD's Temple. 25Never before had there been a king like Josiah, who turned to the LORD with all his heart and soul and strength, obeying all the laws of Moses. And there has never been a king like him since.

26Even so, the LORD was very angry with Judah because of all the wicked things Manasseh had done to provoke him. 27For the LORD said, "I will also banish Judah from my presence just as I have banished Israel. And I will reject my chosen city of Jerusalem and the Temple where my name was to be honored."

28The rest of the events in Josiah's reign and all his deeds are recorded in *The Book of the History of the Kings of Judah.*

**JOSIAH**

Josiah never knew his great-grandfather Hezekiah, but they were alike in many ways. Both had close, personal relationships with God. Both were passionate reformers, making valiant efforts to lead their people back to God. Both were bright flashes of obedience to God among kings with darkened consciences who seemed bent on outdoing each other in disobedience and evil.

Although Josiah's father and grandfather were exceptionally wicked, his life is an example of God's willingness to provide ongoing guidance to those who set out to be obedient. At a young age, Josiah already understood that there was spiritual sickness in his land. Idols were sprouting in the countryside faster than crops. In a sense, Josiah began his search for God by destroying and cleaning up whatever he recognized as not belonging to the worship of the true God. In the process, God's Word was rediscovered. The king's intentions and the power of God's written revelation were brought together.

As the Book of the Law was read to Josiah, he was shocked, frightened, and humbled. He realized what a great gap existed between his efforts to lead his people to God and God's expectations for his chosen nation. He was overwhelmed by God's holiness and immediately tried to expose his people to that holiness. The people did respond, but the Bible makes it clear that their renewed worship of God was much more out of respect for Josiah than out of personal understanding of their own guilt before God.

How would you describe your relationship with God? Are your feeble efforts at holiness based mostly on a desire to "go along" with a well-liked leader or popular opinion? Or are you, like Josiah, deeply humbled by God's Word, realizing the great gap between your life and the kind of life God expects, and realizing your deep need to be cleansed and renewed by him? Humble obedience pleases God. Good intentions, even reforms, are not enough. You must allow God's Word to truly humble you and change your life.

| | |
|---|---|
| **Strengths and accomplishments** | • Was king of Judah<br>• Sought after God and was open to him<br>• Was a reformer like his great-grandfather Hezekiah<br>• Cleaned out the Temple and revived obedience to God's law |
| **Weakness and mistake** | • Became involved in a military conflict that he had been warned against |
| **Lessons from his life** | • God consistently responds to those with repentant and humble hearts<br>• Even sweeping outward reforms are of little lasting value if there are no changes in people's lives |
| **Vital statistics** | • Where: Jerusalem<br>• Occupation: 16th king of Judah, the southern kingdom<br>• Relatives: Father: Amon. Mother: Jedidah. Son: Jehoahaz.<br>• Contemporaries: Jeremiah, Huldah, Hilkiah, Zephaniah |
| **Key verse** | "Never before had there been a king like Josiah, who turned to the LORD with all his heart and soul and strength, obeying all the laws of Moses. And there has never been a king like him since" (2 Kings 23:25). |

Josiah's story is told in 2 Kings 21:24—23:30; 2 Chronicles 33:25—35:27. He is also mentioned in Jeremiah 1:1–3; 22:11, 18.

**23:25** Josiah is remembered as Judah's most obedient king. His obedience followed this pattern: (1) He recognized sin; (2) he eliminated sinful practices; (3) he attacked the causes of sin. This approach for dealing with sin works. Not only must we remove sinful actions, we must also eliminate causes for sin—those situations, relationships, routines, and patterns of life that lead us to the door of temptation.

**23:25** Both Josiah and Hezekiah (18:5) are praised for their reverence toward God. Hezekiah was said to be greatest in trust-ing God (faith), while Josiah is said to be greatest in following the law of God (obedience). May we follow their example through our trust in God and our obedient actions.

²⁹While Josiah was king, Pharaoh Neco, king of Egypt, went to the Euphrates River to help the king of Assyria. King Josiah and his army marched out to fight him,* but King Neco* killed him when they met at Megiddo. ³⁰Josiah's officers took his body back in a chariot from Megiddo to Jerusalem and buried him in his own tomb. Then the people of the land anointed Josiah's son Jehoahaz and made him the next king.

**23:29**
2 Chr 35:20-24

**23:30**
2 Chr 36:1-4

### Jehoahaz Rules in Judah

³¹Jehoahaz was twenty-three years old when he became king, and he reigned in Jerusalem three months. His mother was Hamutal, the daughter of Jeremiah from Libnah. ³²He did what was evil in the LORD's sight, just as his ancestors had done.

³³Pharaoh Neco put Jehoahaz in prison at Riblah in the land of Hamath to prevent him from ruling* in Jerusalem. He also demanded that Judah pay 7,500 pounds of silver and 75 pounds of gold* as tribute.

**23:31-34**
//2 Chr 36:2-4
**23:31**
2 Kgs 24:18
Jer 22:11
**23:33**
2 Kgs 23:29

### 2. Judah is exiled to Babylon

#### Jehoiakim Rules in Judah

³⁴Pharaoh Neco then installed Eliakim, another of Josiah's sons, to reign in place of his father, and he changed Eliakim's name to Jehoiakim. Jehoahaz was taken to Egypt as a prisoner, where he died.

³⁵In order to get the silver and gold demanded as tribute by Pharaoh Neco, Jehoiakim collected a tax from the people of Judah, requiring them to pay in proportion to their wealth.

³⁶Jehoiakim was twenty-five years old when he became king, and he reigned in Jerusalem eleven years. His mother was Zebidah, the daughter of Pedaiah from Rumah. ³⁷He did what was evil in the LORD's sight, just as his ancestors had done.

**23:34**
1 Chr 3:15
2 Chr 36:4-8
Jer 22:12
Ezek 19:3-4

**23:36–24:6**
//2 Chr 36:5-8
Jer 1:3; 26:21

**24** During Jehoiakim's reign, King Nebuchadnezzar of Babylon invaded the land of Judah. Jehoiakim surrendered and paid him tribute for three years but then rebelled. ²Then the LORD sent bands of Babylonian,* Aramean, Moabite, and Ammonite raiders against Judah to destroy it, just as the LORD had promised through his prophets. ³These disasters happened to Judah because of the LORD's command. He had decided to banish Judah from his presence because of the many sins of Manasseh, ⁴who had filled Jerusalem with innocent blood. The LORD would not forgive this.

**24:1**
2 Chr 36:6
Jer 25:1, 9
**24:2**
2 Kgs 13:20-21;
23:27
**24:3**
2 Kgs 18:25; 23:26
**24:4**
2 Kgs 21:16

23:29a Or *Josiah went out to meet him.*   23:29b Hebrew *he.*   23:33a The meaning of the Hebrew is uncertain.
23:33b Hebrew *100 talents* [3,400 kilograms] *of silver and 1 talent* [34 kilograms] *of gold.*   24:2 Or *Chaldean.*

---

**23:29** Pharaoh Neco of Egypt was marching through Judah to Assyria. Egypt and Assyria had formed an alliance to battle Babylon, which was threatening to become the dominant world power. Josiah may have thought that both nations would turn on him after the battle with Babylon, so he tried to stop Egypt's army from marching through his land. But Josiah was killed, his army was defeated, and the nation of Judah became a vassal state of Egypt (609 B.C.). A more detailed account of this story is found in 2 Chronicles 35:20-25.

**23:31-34** The people appointed Jehoahaz, one of Josiah's sons, to be Judah's next king. But Neco was not happy with their choice, and he exiled Jehoahaz to Egypt, where he died. Neco then installed Eliakim, another of Josiah's sons, king of Judah, changing his name to Jehoiakim. Jehoiakim was little more than a puppet ruler. In 605 B.C., Egypt was defeated by Babylon. Judah then became a vassal state of Babylon (24:1).

**23:36, 37** Josiah followed God, but Jehoiakim, his son, was evil. He killed the prophet Uriah (Jeremiah 26:20-23) and was dishonest, greedy, and unjust with the people (Jeremiah 22:13-19). Jehoiakim also rebelled against Babylon, switching his allegiance to Egypt. This proved to be a crucial mistake. Nebuchadnezzar crushed Jehoiakim's rebellion and took him

to Babylon (2 Chronicles 36:6), but he was eventually allowed to return to Jerusalem, where he died. The Bible does not record the cause of Jehoiakim's death.

**23:37** Many good kings had children who did not follow God. Perhaps it was because of neglect or preoccupation with political and military affairs or because these kings delegated the religious education to others. No doubt many of the children simply rebelled at the way they were raised. Being a strong believer as a parent doesn't guarantee that your children will pick up your beliefs. Children must be taught about faith, and parents dare not leave that task for others to do. Make sure you practice, explain, and teach what you preach.

**24:1** Babylon became the new world power after overthrowing Assyria in 612 B.C. and defeating Egypt at the battle of Carchemish in 605 B.C. After defeating Egypt, the Babylonians invaded Judah and brought it under their control. This was the first of three Babylonian invasions of Judah over the next 20 years. The other two invasions occurred in 597 and 586 B.C. With each invasion, captives were taken back to Babylon. Daniel was one of the captives taken during this first invasion (605 B.C.; Daniel 1:1-6).

**24:1** For more information on Nebuchadnezzar, see his Profile in Daniel 4, p. 1385.

**24:1-4** Nebuchadnezzar took control as king of Babylon in 605 B.C. Earlier that year Nebuchadnezzar had defeated the Egyptians led by Pharaoh Neco at Carchemish. Thus, Babylon had taken control of all Egypt's vassals (including Judah). Later, Nebuchadnezzar invaded the land in order to establish his rule by force.

24:6
Jer 22:19, 24-25
24:7
Jer 37:5, 7; 46:2

⁵The rest of the events in Jehoiakim's reign and all his deeds are recorded in *The Book of the History of the Kings of Judah.* ⁶When Jehoiakim died, his son Jehoiachin became the next king.

⁷The king of Egypt did not venture out of his country after that, for the king of Babylon captured the entire area formerly claimed by Egypt—from the Brook of Egypt to the Euphrates River.

### Jehoiachin Rules in Judah

24:8-17
//2 Chr 36:9-10

⁸Jehoiachin was eighteen years old when he became king, and he reigned in Jerusalem three months. His mother was Nehushta, the daughter of Elnathan from Jerusalem. ⁹Jehoiachin did what was evil in the LORD's sight, just as his father had done.

24:12
2 Chr 36:10
Jer 24:1; 29:1-2

¹⁰During Jehoiachin's reign, the officers of King Nebuchadnezzar of Babylon came up against Jerusalem and besieged it. ¹¹Nebuchadnezzar himself arrived at the city during the siege. ¹²Then King Jehoiachin, along with the queen mother, his advisers, his commanders, and his officials, surrendered to the Babylonians.

24:13
1 Kgs 7:48-50
2 Kgs 20:17;
25:13-15
Isa 39:6

In the eighth year of Nebuchadnezzar's reign, he took Jehoiachin prisoner. ¹³As the LORD had said beforehand, Nebuchadnezzar carried away all the treasures from the LORD's Temple and the royal palace. He stripped away* all the gold objects that King Solomon of Israel

**24:13** Or *He cut apart.*

---

## KINGS TO DATE AND THEIR ENEMIES

722
Captivity in Assyria

I S R A E L

J U D A H

686

586

| 715 **HEZEKIAH** | 697 **MANASSEH** | 642 **AMON** | 609 **JEHOAHAZ** | 598 **JEHOIACHIN** | 597 **ZEDEKIAH** |
|---|---|---|---|---|---|

715
**HEZEKIAH**
Miraculously
delivered from
Sennacherib's
(Assyria) attack,
conquered Gaza
in Philistia
2 Kgs 18:1—20:21
2 Chr 28:27—32:33
Co-regency
697–686

697
**MANASSEH**
Taken captive
by Assyria,
imprisoned in
Babylon and
later released
2 Kgs 21:1—21:18
2 Chr 32:33—33:20

642
**AMON**
2 Kgs 21:18–26
2 Chr 33:20–24

640
**JOSIAH**
Died in battle
against Neco
(Egypt)
2 Kgs 22:1—23:30
2 Chr 33:25—35:27

609
**JEHOAHAZ**
Neco (Egypt)
2 Kgs 23:30–34
2 Chr 36:1–4

609
**JEHOIAKIM**
2 Kgs
23:34—24:6
2 Chr 36:4–8

598
**JEHOIACHIN**
Rebelled against
Babylon and was
taken captive
2 Kgs 24:6–16;
25:27–30
2 Chr 36:8–10

597
**ZEDEKIAH**
Rebelled,
completely
conquered by
Babylon
2 Kgs
24:17—25:21
2 Chr
36:10–20

735
**AHAZ**
Harassed by
Pekah (Israel),
paid Assyria for
protection against
Rezin (Aram),
also harassed by
Edom and Philistia
2 Kgs 15:38—16:20
2 Chr 27:9—28:27

All dates are B.C.
Solid section of the timeline indicates co-regency.
For all the kings of Israel and Judah, see the chart at the end of 1 Kings.

---

**24:10** Babylonian troops were already on the march to crush Jehoiakim's rebellion when he died. After Jehoiakim's death, his son Jehoiachin became king of Judah, only to face the mightiest army on earth just weeks after he was crowned (597 B.C.). During this second of three invasions, the Babylonians looted the Temple and took most of the leaders captive, including the king. Then Nebuchadnezzar placed Zedekiah, another son of Josiah, on the throne.

The Jews, however, didn't recognize him as their true king as long as Jehoiachin was still alive, even though he was a captive in Babylon.

had placed in the Temple. [14]King Nebuchadnezzar took all of Jerusalem captive, including all the commanders and the best of the soldiers, craftsmen, and artisans—10,000 in all. Only the poorest people were left in the land.

    [15]Nebuchadnezzar led King Jehoiachin away as a captive to Babylon, along with the queen mother, his wives and officials, and all Jerusalem's elite. [16]He also exiled 7,000 of the best troops and 1,000 craftsmen and artisans, all of whom were strong and fit for war. [17]Then the king of Babylon installed Mattaniah, Jehoiachin's* uncle, as the next king, and he changed Mattaniah's name to Zedekiah.

### Zedekiah Rules in Judah

[18]Zedekiah was twenty-one years old when he became king, and he reigned in Jerusalem eleven years. His mother was Hamutal, the daughter of Jeremiah from Libnah. [19]But Zedekiah did what was evil in the LORD's sight, just as Jehoiakim had done. [20]These things happened because of the LORD's anger against the people of Jerusalem and Judah, until he finally banished them from his presence and sent them into exile.

### The Fall of Jerusalem

Zedekiah rebelled against the king of Babylon.

**25** So on January 15,* during the ninth year of Zedekiah's reign, King Nebuchadnezzar of Babylon led his entire army against Jerusalem. They surrounded the city and built siege ramps against its walls. [2]Jerusalem was kept under siege until the eleventh year of King Zedekiah's reign.

    [3]By July 18 in the eleventh year of Zedekiah's reign,* the famine in the city had become very severe, and the last of the food was entirely gone. [4]Then a section of the city wall was broken down, and all the soldiers fled. Since the city was surrounded by the Babylonians,* they waited for nightfall. Then they slipped through the gate between the two walls behind the king's garden and headed toward the Jordan Valley.*

    [5]But the Babylonian* troops chased the king and caught him on the plains of Jericho, for his men had all deserted him and scattered. [6]They took him to the king of Babylon at Riblah, where they pronounced judgment upon Zedekiah. [7]They made Zedekiah watch as they slaughtered his sons. Then they gouged out Zedekiah's eyes, bound him in bronze chains, and led him away to Babylon.

### The Temple Destroyed

[8]On August 14 of that year,* which was the nineteenth year of King Nebuchadnezzar's reign, Nebuzaradan, the captain of the guard and an official of the Babylonian king, arrived

**Cross-references (margin):**

24:14 / 2 Kgs 25:12 / Jer 24:1; 52:28

24:17 / 2 Chr 36:10-13 / Jer 37:1

24:18-20 / //2 Chr 36:11-13 / //Jer 52:1-3

24:20 / 2 Chr 36:13 / Jer 27:12; 38:17, 21-22; 39:1

25:1-12 / //Jer 39:1-7

25:1 / 2 Chr 36:17-20 / Ezek 21:22; 24:2

25:3 / 2 Kgs 6:24-25 / Lam 4:9-10

25:6 / Jer 32:4

25:7 / Jer 39:6-7 / Ezek 12:13

25:8 / Jer 52:12

---

24:17 Hebrew *his.*   25:1 Hebrew *on the tenth day of the tenth month,* of the ancient Hebrew lunar calendar. A number of events in 2 Kings can be cross-checked with dates in surviving Babylonian records and related accurately to our modern calendar. This day was January 15, 588 B.C.   25:3 Hebrew *By the ninth day of the [fourth] month* [in the eleventh year of Zedekiah's reign] (compare Jer 52:6 and the note there). This day was July 18, 586 B.C.; also see note on 25:1.   25:4a Or *the Chaldeans;* also in 25:13, 25, 26.   25:4b Hebrew *the Arabah.*   25:5 Or *Chaldean;* also in 25:10, 24.   25:8 Hebrew *On the seventh day of the fifth month,* of the ancient Hebrew lunar calendar. This day was August 14, 586 B.C.; also see note on 25:1.

---

**24:14** The Babylonian policy for taking captives was different from that of the Assyrians who moved most of the people out and resettled the land with foreigners (see the note on 17:24). The Babylonians took only the strong and skilled, leaving the poor and weak to rule the land, thus elevating them to positions of authority and winning their loyalty. The leaders were taken to Babylonian cities, where they were permitted to live together, find jobs, and become an important part of the society. This policy kept the Jews united and faithful to God throughout the captivity and made it possible for their return in the days of Zerubbabel and Ezra as recorded in the book of Ezra.

**25:1** Judah was invaded by the Babylonians three times (24:1; 24:10; 25:1), just as Israel was invaded by the Assyrians three times. Once again, God demonstrated his mercy in the face of deserved judgment by giving the people repeated opportunities to repent.

**JUDAH EXILED** Evil permeated Judah, and God's anger flared against his rebellious people. Babylon conquered Assyria and became the new world power. The Babylonian army marched into Jerusalem, burned the Temple, tore down the city's massive walls, and carried off the people into captivity.

25:9
2 Chr 36:19
Ps 74:3-8
Amos 2:5

25:10
Neh 1:3

25:11
2 Chr 36:20

25:12
2 Kgs 24:14
Jer 40:7; 52:16

25:13
1 Kgs 7:15-22
2 Chr 36:18

25:14
1 Kgs 7:47-50
2 Chr 24:14

25:17
1 Kgs 7:15-22

25:18
1 Chr 6:14
Ezra 7:1
Jer 29:25-26, 29

25:20
2 Kgs 23:33
25:21
Deut 28:64
2 Kgs 23:27

25:22-26
//Jer 40:7-9; 41:1-3,
16-18
25:23
Jer 40:7-9

25:25
Jer 41:1-2

25:26
Jer 43:5-7

in Jerusalem. 9He burned down the Temple of the LORD, the royal palace, and all the houses of Jerusalem. He destroyed all the important buildings* in the city. 10Then he supervised the entire Babylonian army as they tore down the walls of Jerusalem on every side. 11Nebuzaradan, the captain of the guard, then took as exiles the rest of the people who remained in the city, the defectors who had declared their allegiance to the king of Babylon, and the rest of the population. 12But the captain of the guard allowed some of the poorest people to stay behind in Judah to care for the vineyards and fields.

13The Babylonians broke up the bronze pillars in front of the LORD's Temple, the bronze water carts, and the great bronze basin called the Sea, and they carried all the bronze away to Babylon. 14They also took all the ash buckets, shovels, lamp snuffers, dishes, and all the other bronze articles used for making sacrifices at the Temple. 15Nebuzaradan, the captain of the guard, also took the incense burners and basins, and all the other articles made of pure gold or silver.

16The weight of the bronze from the two pillars, the Sea, and the water carts was too great to be measured. These things had been made for the LORD's Temple in the days of King Solomon. 17Each of the pillars was 27 feet* tall. The bronze capital on top of each pillar was 7½ feet* high and was decorated with a network of bronze pomegranates all the way around.

18Nebuzaradan, the captain of the guard, took with him as prisoners Seraiah the high priest, Zephaniah the priest of the second rank, and the three chief gatekeepers. 19And from among the people still hiding in the city, he took an officer who had been in charge of the Judean army; five of the king's personal advisers; the army commander's chief secretary, who was in charge of recruitment; and sixty other citizens. 20Nebuzaradan, the captain of the guard, took them all to the king of Babylon at Riblah. 21And there at Riblah, in the land of Hamath, the king of Babylon had them all put to death. So the people of Judah were sent into exile from their land.

### Gedaliah Governs in Judah

22Then King Nebuchadnezzar appointed Gedaliah son of Ahikam and grandson of Shaphan as governor over the people he had left in Judah. 23When all the army commanders and their men learned that the king of Babylon had appointed Gedaliah as governor, they went to see him at Mizpah. These included Ishmael son of Nethaniah, Johanan son of Kareah, Seraiah son of Tanhumeth the Netophathite, and Jezaniah* son of the Maacathite, and all their men.

24Gedaliah vowed to them that the Babylonian officials meant them no harm. "Don't be afraid of them. Live in the land and serve the king of Babylon, and all will go well for you," he promised.

25But in midautumn of that year,* Ishmael son of Nethaniah and grandson of Elishama, who was of the royal family, went to Mizpah with ten men and killed Gedaliah. He also killed all the Judeans and Babylonians who were with Gedaliah at Mizpah.

26Then all the people of Judah, from the least to the greatest, as well as the army commanders, fled in panic to Egypt, for they were afraid of what the Babylonians would do to them.

25:9 Or *destroyed the houses of all the important people.*   25:17a Hebrew *18 cubits* [8.1 meters].   25:17b As in parallel texts at 1 Kgs 7:16, 2 Chr 3:15, and Jer 52:22, all of which read *5 cubits* [2.3 meters]; Hebrew reads *3 cubits,* which is 4.5 feet or 1.4 meters.   25:23 As in parallel text at Jer 40:8; Hebrew reads *Jaazaniah,* a variant spelling of Jezaniah.   25:25 Hebrew *in the seventh month,* of the ancient Hebrew lunar calendar. This month occurred within the months of October and November 586 B.C.; also see note on 25:1.

---

25:13 The bronze basin called the Sea was used to hold the huge reservoir of water for ritual cleansing for the priests. The bronze was so valuable that it was broken up and carried off to Babylon.

25:21 Judah, like Israel, was unfaithful to God. So God, as he had warned, allowed Judah to be destroyed and taken away (Deuteronomy 28). The book of Lamentations records the prophet Jeremiah's sorrow at seeing Jerusalem destroyed.

25:22 In place of the king (Zedekiah) who was deported to Babylon, Nebuchadnezzar appointed a governor (Gedaliah), who would faithfully administer the Babylonian policies.

25:22-30 This story shows that Israel's last hope of gaining back its land was gone—even the army commanders (now guerrilla rebels) had fled. Judah's earthly kingdom was absolutely demolished. But through prophets like Ezekiel and Daniel, who were also captives, God was able to keep his spiritual Kingdom alive in the hearts of many of the exiles.

## Hope for Israel's Royal Line

27 In the thirty-seventh year of the exile of King Jehoiachin of Judah, Evil-merodach ascended to the Babylonian throne. He was kind to* Jehoiachin and released him from prison on April 2 of that year.* 28 He spoke kindly to Jehoiachin and gave him a higher place than all the other exiled kings in Babylon. 29 He supplied Jehoiachin with new clothes to replace his prison garb and allowed him to dine in the king's presence for the rest of his life. 30 So the Babylonian king gave him a regular food allowance as long as he lived.

25:27
2 Kgs 24:12
Jer 52:31-34

25:27a Hebrew He raised the head of.   25:27b Hebrew on the twenty-seventh day of the twelfth month, of the ancient Hebrew lunar calendar. This day was April 2, 561 B.C.; also see note on 25:1.

---

**25:27** Evil-merodach, the son of Nebuchadnezzar, became king of the Babylonian Empire in 562 B.C., 24 years after the beginning of the general captivity and 37 years after Jehoiachin was removed from Jerusalem. The new king treated Jehoiachin with kindness, even allowing him to eat at his table (25:29). Evil-merodach was later killed in a plot by his brother-in-law, Nergal-sharezer, who succeeded him to the throne.

**25:30** The book of 2 Kings opens with Elijah being carried to heaven—the destination awaiting those who follow God. But the book ends with the people of Judah being carried off to foreign lands as humiliated slaves—the result of failing to follow God.

Second Kings is an illustration of what happens when we make anything more important than God, when we make ruinous alliances, when our consciences become desensitized to right and wrong, and when we are no longer able to discern God's purpose for our lives. We may fail, like the people of Judah and Israel, but God's promises do not. He is always available to help us straighten out our lives and start over. And that is just what would happen in the book of Ezra. When the people acknowledged their sins, God was ready and willing to help them return to their land and start again.

# KEY PLACES IN 1 CHRONICLES

The broken lines (— · — ·) indicate modern boundaries.

1 **Hebron** Although David had been anointed king years earlier, his reign began when the leaders of Israel accepted him as king at Hebron (11:1–3).

2 **Jerusalem** David set out to complete the conquest of the land begun by Joshua. He attacked Jerusalem, captured it, and made it his capital (11:4—12:40).

3 **Kiriath-jearim** The Ark of the Covenant, which had been captured by the Philistines in battle and returned (1 Samuel 4—6), was in safekeeping in Kiriath-jearim. David summoned all Israel to this city to join in bringing the Ark to Jerusalem. Unfortunately, it was not moved according to God's instructions, and as a result, one man died. David left the Ark in the home of Obed-edom until he could discover how to transport it correctly (13:1–14).

4 **Tyre** David did much building in Jerusalem. King Hiram of Tyre sent workers and supplies to help build David's palace. Cedar, abundant in the mountains north of Israel, was a valuable and hardy wood for the beautiful buildings in Jerusalem (14:1—17:27).

5 **Baal-perazim** David was not very popular with the Philistines because he had slain Goliath, one of their greatest warriors (1 Samuel 17). When David began to rule over a united Israel, the Philistines set out to capture him. But as David and his army approached Jerusalem, they attacked the Philistines at Baal-perazim. His army defeated the mighty Philistines twice, causing all the surrounding nations to fear David's power (14:11–17). After these battles, David moved the Ark to Jerusalem (this time in accordance with God's instructions for transporting the Ark). There was great celebration as the Ark was brought into Jerusalem (15:1—17:27). David spent the remainder of his life making preparations for the building of the Temple, a central place for the worship of God (18:1—29:30).

The genealogies of 1 Chronicles present an overview of Israel's history. The first nine chapters are filled with genealogies tracing the lineages of people from the Creation to the exile in Babylon. Saul's death is recorded in chapter 10. Chapter 11 begins the history of David's reign over Israel.

# 1 CHRONICLES

## VITAL STATISTICS

**PURPOSE:**
To unify God's people, to trace the Davidic line, and to teach that genuine worship ought to be the center of individual and national life

**AUTHOR:**
Ezra, according to Jewish tradition

**ORIGINAL AUDIENCE:**
The exiles who returned from captivity

**DATE WRITTEN:**
Approximately 430 B.C., recording events that occurred from about 1000–960 B.C.

**SETTING:**
First Chronicles parallels 2 Samuel and serves as a commentary on it. Written after the Exile from a priestly point of view, 1 Chronicles emphasizes the religious history of Judah and Israel.

**KEY VERSE:**
"And David realized that the LORD had confirmed him as king over Israel and had greatly blessed his kingdom for the sake of his people Israel" (14:2).

**KEY PEOPLE:**
David, Solomon

**KEY PLACES:**
Hebron, Jerusalem, the Temple

IN THE WIDE shade of the ageless oak, a mother watches her toddler discover acorns, leaves, and dandelions. Nearby, her mother, aunt, and uncle spread the checkerboard cloth over park tables and cover it with bowls and platters of fried chicken, potato salad, baked beans, and assorted family recipes. The clanging of Grandpa's and Dad's horseshoes against stakes regularly pierces the air and mixes with the cheers, laughs, and shouts of teenagers playing a game of touch football. A family reunion—a sunny afternoon filled with four generations of miscellaneous kids, parents, and second cousins once removed.

Reunions are important. They are times for touching and connecting with others from branches of the family tree, tracing one's personal history back through time and culture, seeing physical reminders (her eyes, his nose), recalling warm traditions. Knowing one's genetic and relational path gives a sense of identity, heritage, and destiny.

With this same high purpose, the writer of Chronicles begins his unifying work with an extensive genealogy. He traces the roots of the nation in a literary family reunion from Adam onward, recounting its royal line and the loving plan of a personal God. We read 1 Chronicles and gain a glimpse of God at work through his people for generations. If you are a believer, these people are your ancestors, too. As you approach this part of God's Word, read their names with awe and respect, and gain new security and identity in your relationship with God.

The previous book, 2 Kings, ends with both Israel and Judah in captivity, surely a dark age for God's people. Then follows Chronicles (1 and 2 Chronicles were originally one book). Written after the Captivity, it summarizes Israel's history, emphasizing the Jewish people's spiritual heritage in an attempt to unify the nation. The chronicler is selective in his history telling. Instead of writing an exhaustive work, he carefully weaves the narrative, highlighting spiritual lessons and teaching moral truths. In Chronicles the northern kingdom is virtually ignored, David's triumphs—not his sins—are recalled, and the Temple is given great prominence as the vital center of national life.

First Chronicles begins with Adam, and for nine chapters, the writer gives us a "Who's Who" of Israel's history with special emphasis on David's royal line. The rest of the book tells the story of David—the great man of God, Israel's king—who served God and laid out the plans for the construction of and worship in the Temple.

First Chronicles is an invaluable supplement to 2 Samuel and a strong reminder of the necessity for tracing our roots and thus rediscovering our spiritual foundation. As you read 1 Chronicles, trace your own godly heritage, thank God for your spiritual forefathers, and recommit yourself to passing on God's truth to the next generation.

| | | |
|---|---|---|
| David's census 980(?) | Solomon becomes king 970 | The kingdom divides 930 |

## THE BLUEPRINT

**A. THE GENEALOGIES OF ISRAEL**
(1:1—9:44)
1. Ancestry of the nation
2. The tribes of Israel
3. Returnees from exile in Babylon

The long list of names that follows presents a history of God's work in the world from Adam through Zerubbabel. Some of these names remind us of stories of great faith, and others, of tragic failure. About most of the people named, however, we know nothing. But those who died unknown to us are known by God. God will also remember us when we die.

**B. THE REIGN OF DAVID**
(10:1—29:30)
1. David becomes king over all of Israel
2. David brings the Ark to Jerusalem
3. David's military exploits
4. David arranges for the building of the Temple

David loved the Lord and wanted to build a Temple to replace the Tabernacle, but God denied his request. David's greatest contribution to the Temple would not be the construction but the preparation. We may be unable to see the results of our labors for God in our lifetime, but David's example helps us understand that we serve God so *he* will see *his* results, not so we will see ours.

## MEGATHEMES

| THEME | EXPLANATION | IMPORTANCE |
|---|---|---|
| Israel's History | By retelling Israel's history in the genealogies and the stories of the kings, the writer laid down the true spiritual foundation for the nation. God kept his promises, and we are reminded of them in the historical record of his people, leaders, prophets, priests, and kings. | Israel's past formed a reliable basis for reconstructing the nation after the Exile. Because God's promises are revealed in the Bible, we can know God and trust him to keep his word. Like Israel, we should have no higher goal in life than devoted service to God. |
| God's People | By listing the names of people in Israel's past, God established Israel's true heritage. They were all one family in Adam, one nation in Abraham, one priesthood under Levi, and one kingdom under David. The national and spiritual unity of the people was important to the rebuilding of the nation. | God is always faithful to his people. He protects them in every generation and provides leaders to guide them. Because God has been at work throughout the centuries, his people can trust him to work in the present. You can rely on his presence today. |
| David, the King | The story of David's life and his relationship with God showed that he was God's appointed leader. David's devotion to God, the law, the Temple, true worship, the people, and justice sets the standard for what God's chosen king should be like. | Jesus Christ came to earth as a descendant of David. One day he will rule as King over all the earth. His strength and justice will fulfill God's ideal for the king. He is our hope. We can experience God's Kingdom now by giving Christ complete control of our lives. |
| True Worship | David brought the Ark of the Covenant to the Tabernacle at Jerusalem to restore true worship to the people. God gave the plans for building the Temple, and David organized the priests to make worship central to all Israel. | The Temple stood as the throne of God on earth, the place of true worship. God's true throne is in the hearts of his people. When we acknowledge him as the true King over our lives, true worship takes place. |
| The Priests | God ordained the priests and Levites to guide the people in faithful worship according to his law. By leading the people in worship according to God's design, the priests and Levites were an important safeguard to Israel's faith. | For true worship to remain central in our lives, God's people need to take a firm stand for the ways of God recorded in the Bible. Today, all believers are priests for one another, and we should encourage each other to faithful worship. |

## A. THE GENEALOGIES OF ISRAEL (1:1—9:44)
These genealogies are the official family records of the nation of Israel. They give us an over-view of the history of God's work from Creation through the captivity of his people. These records served to teach the exiles returning from Babylon about their spiritual heritage as a nation and to inspire them to renew their faithfulness to God. Although these lists show the racial heritage of the Jews, they contain the spiritual heritage for every believer. We are a part of the community of faith that has existed from generation to generation since the dawn of man.

## 1. Ancestry of the nation
*From Adam to Noah's Sons*

**1** The descendants of Adam were Seth, Enosh, ²Kenan, Mahalalel, Jared, ³Enoch, Methuselah, Lamech, ⁴and Noah.
The sons of Noah were Shem, Ham, and Japheth.

**1:1**
Gen 5:1-32
Luke 3:36-38

*Descendants of Japheth*
⁵The descendants of Japheth were Gomer, Magog, Madai, Javan, Tubal, Meshech, and Tiras.
⁶The descendants of Gomer were Ashkenaz, Riphath,* and Togarmah.
⁷The descendants of Javan were Elishah, Tarshish, Kittim, and Rodanim.

**1:5-7**
//Gen 10:2-5

*Descendants of Ham*
⁸The descendants of Ham were Cush, Mizraim,* Put, and Canaan.
⁹The descendants of Cush were Seba, Havilah, Sabtah, Raamah, and Sabteca. The descendants of Raamah were Sheba and Dedan. ¹⁰Cush was also the ancestor of Nimrod, who was the first heroic warrior on earth.
¹¹Mizraim was the ancestor of the Ludites, Anamites, Lehabites, Naphtuhites, ¹²Pathrusites, Casluhites, and the Caphtorites, from whom the Philistines came.*
¹³Canaan's oldest son was Sidon, the ancestor of the Sidonians. Canaan was also the ancestor of the Hittites,* ¹⁴Jebusites, Amorites, Girgashites, ¹⁵Hivites, Arkites, Sinites, ¹⁶Arvadites, Zemarites, and Hamathites.

**1:8-16**
//Gen 10:6-20

**1:11**
Gen 10:13-18

**1:13**
Gen 15:19-21

*Descendants of Shem*
¹⁷The descendants of Shem were Elam, Asshur, Arphaxad, Lud, and Aram.
The descendants of Aram were* Uz, Hul, Gether, and Mash.*

**1:17-23**
//Gen 10:21-31;
11:10-27
Luke 3:36

**1:4** As in Greek version (see also Gen 5:3-32); Hebrew lacks *The sons of Noah were.*   **1:6** As in some Hebrew manuscripts and Greek version (see also Gen 10:3); most Hebrew manuscripts read *Diphath.*   **1:8** Or *Egypt;* also in 1:11.   **1:12** Hebrew *Casluhites, from whom the Philistines came, Caphtorites.* See Jer 47:4; Amos 9:7.   **1:13** Hebrew *ancestor of Heth.*   **1:17a** As in one Hebrew manuscript and some Greek manuscripts (see also Gen 10:23); most Hebrew manuscripts lack *The descendants of Aram were.*   **1:17b** As in parallel text at Gen 10:23; Hebrew reads *and Meshech.*

---

**1:1** This record of names demonstrates that God is interested not only in nations but also in individuals. Although billions of people have lived since Adam, God knows and remembers the face and name of each person. Each of us is more than a name on a list; we are special persons whom God knows and loves. As we recognize and accept his love, we discover both our unique-ness as individuals and our solidarity with the rest of his family.

**1:1ff** This long list of names was compiled after the people of Judah, the southern kingdom, were taken captive to Babylon. As the exiles looked forward to the day when they would return to their homeland, one of their biggest fears was that the records of their heritage would be lost. The Jews placed great importance upon their heritage because each person wanted to be able to prove that he was a descendant of Abraham, the father of the Jewish people. Only then could he enjoy the benefits of the special blessings God promised to Abraham and his descendants (see the notes on Genesis 12:1-3 and 17:2-8 for what these special bless-ings were).

This list reconstructed the family tree for both Judah, the southern kingdom, and Israel, the northern kingdom, before their captivities and served as proof for those who claimed to

be Abraham's descendants. (For more information about why the Bible includes genealogies, read the notes on Genesis 5:1ff, Matthew 1:1, and Luke 3:23-38.)

**1:1ff** There is more to this long genealogy than meets the eye. It holds importance for us today because it supports the Old Testament promise that Jesus the Messiah would be a descen-dant of Abraham and David. This promise is recorded in Genesis 12:1-3 and 2 Samuel 7:12, 13.

**1:1, 4** Adam's story and Profile are found in Genesis 1–5, p. 9. Noah's story and Profile are found in Genesis 6–9, p. 19.

**1:5-9** A biblical genealogy may skip several generations. These lists were not meant to be exhaustive, but to give adequate infor-mation about the various family lines.

**1:10** Nimrod is also mentioned in Genesis 10:8, 9.

**1:11, 12** The Philistines had been Israel's constant enemy from the days of the judges. King David finally weakened them, and by this time they were no longer a threat. (For more information on the Philistines, see the notes on Judges 13:1 and 1 Samuel 4:1.)

**1:13-16** Canaan was the ancestor of the Canaanites, who inhabited the Promised Land (also called Canaan) before the Israelites entered under Joshua's leadership. God helped the Israelites drive out the Canaanites, a wicked and idolatrous people. The land's name was then changed to Israel. The book of Joshua tells that story.

<sup>18</sup>Arphaxad was the father of Shelah.

Shelah was the father of Eber.

**1:19**
Gen 11:16

<sup>19</sup>Eber had two sons. The first was named Peleg (which means "division"), for during his lifetime the people of the world were divided into different language groups. His brother's name was Joktan.

<sup>20</sup>Joktan was the ancestor of Almodad, Sheleph, Hazarmaveth, Jerah, <sup>21</sup>Hadoram, Uzal, Diklah, <sup>22</sup>Obal,* Abimael, Sheba, <sup>23</sup>Ophir, Havilah, and Jobab. All these were descendants of Joktan.

**1:24**
Gen 11:10-26
Luke 3:34-36

<sup>24</sup>So this is the family line descended from Shem: Arphaxad, Shelah,* <sup>25</sup>Eber, Peleg, Reu, <sup>26</sup>Serug, Nahor, Terah, <sup>27</sup>and Abram, later known as Abraham.

### Descendants of Abraham

**1:29-31**
//Gen 25:12-16

<sup>28</sup>The sons of Abraham were Isaac and Ishmael. <sup>29</sup>These are their genealogical records:

The sons of Ishmael were Nebaioth (the oldest), Kedar, Adbeel, Mibsam, <sup>30</sup>Mishma, Dumah, Massa, Hadad, Tema, <sup>31</sup>Jetur, Naphish, and Kedemah. These were the sons of Ishmael.

**1:32-33**
//Gen 25:1-4

<sup>32</sup>The sons of Keturah, Abraham's concubine, were Zimran, Jokshan, Medan, Midian, Ishbak, and Shuah.

The sons of Jokshan were Sheba and Dedan.

<sup>33</sup>The sons of Midian were Ephah, Epher, Hanoch, Abida, and Eldaah.

All these were descendants of Abraham through his concubine Keturah.

**1:34**
Gen 25:25-26;
32:28
Matt 1:2

### Descendants of Isaac

<sup>34</sup>Abraham was the father of Isaac. The sons of Isaac were Esau and Israel.*

**1:35**
Gen 36:4, 19

### Descendants of Esau

<sup>35</sup>The sons of Esau were Eliphaz, Reuel, Jeush, Jalam, and Korah.

**1:35-37**
//Gen 36:10-14

<sup>36</sup>The descendants of Eliphaz were Teman, Omar, Zepho,* Gatam, Kenaz, and Amalek, who was born to Timna.*

<sup>37</sup>The descendants of Reuel were Nahath, Zerah, Shammah, and Mizzah.

**1:38-42**
//Gen 36:20-28

### Original Peoples of Edom

<sup>38</sup>The descendants of Seir were Lotan, Shobal, Zibeon, Anah, Dishon, Ezer, and Dishan.

<sup>39</sup>The descendants of Lotan were Hori and Hemam.* Lotan's sister was named Timna.

<sup>40</sup>The descendants of Shobal were Alvan,* Manahath, Ebal, Shepho,* and Onam.

The descendants of Zibeon were Aiah and Anah.

<sup>41</sup>The son of Anah was Dishon.

The descendants of Dishon were Hemdan,* Eshban, Ithran, and Keran.

<sup>42</sup>The descendants of Ezer were Bilhan, Zaavan, and Akan.*

The descendants of Dishan* were Uz and Aran.

**1:22** As in some Hebrew manuscripts and Syriac version (see also Gen 10:28); most Hebrew manuscripts read *Ebal.*
**1:24** Some Greek manuscripts read *Arphaxad, Cainan, Shelah.* See notes on Gen 10:24; 11:12-13. **1:34** *Israel* is the name that God gave to Jacob. **1:36a** As in many Hebrew manuscripts and a few Greek manuscripts (see also Gen 36:11); most Hebrew manuscripts read *Zephi.* **1:36b** As in some Greek manuscripts (see also Gen 36:12); Hebrew reads *Kenaz, Timna, and Amalek.* **1:39** As in parallel text at Gen 36:22; Hebrew reads *and Homam.*
**1:40a** As in many Hebrew manuscripts and a few Greek manuscripts (see also Gen 36:23); most Hebrew manuscripts read *Alian.* **1:40b** As in some Hebrew manuscripts (see also Gen 36:23); most Hebrew manuscripts read *Shephi.* **1:41** As in many Hebrew manuscripts and some Greek manuscripts (see also Gen 36:26); most Hebrew manuscripts read *Hamran.* **1:42a** As in many Hebrew and Greek manuscripts (see also Gen 36:27); most Hebrew manuscripts read *Jaakan.* **1:42b** Hebrew *Dishon;* compare 1:38 and parallel text at Gen 36:28.

**1:19** At one time, everyone spoke a single language. But some people became proud of their accomplishments and gathered to build a monument to themselves—the tower of Babel. The building project was brought to an abrupt conclusion when God caused the people to speak different languages. Without the ability to communicate with one another, the people could not be unified. God showed them that their great efforts were useless without him. Pride in our achievements must not lead us to conclude that we no longer need God. This story is told in Genesis 11:1-9.

**1:24-27** Abraham's story and Profile are found in Genesis 11:26–25:10, p. 33.

**1:28-31** Ishmael's story and Profile are found in Genesis 16 and 21, p. 31.

**1:34** Israel is another name for Jacob, given to him by God (Genesis 32:28). It means "someone who struggles with God." Israel's (Jacob's) 12 sons became the nation of Israel. Esau's descendants became the nation of Edom, a constant enemy of Israel. To learn more about the lives of Isaac and his two sons, Jacob and Esau, read their stories in Genesis 21–36, 46–49, and their Profiles on pp. 47, 49.

**1:36** Amalek, Esau's grandson, was the son of his father's concubine (Genesis 36:12). He was the ancestor of the wicked tribe known as the Amalekites, the first people to attack the Israelites on their way to the Promised Land. (For more about the Amalekites, read the note on Exodus 17:8.)

## Rulers of Edom

43 These are the kings who ruled in the land of Edom before any king ruled over the Israelites*:

Bela son of Beor, who ruled from his city of Dinhabah. 44 When Bela died, Jobab son of Zerah from Bozrah became king in his place. 45 When Jobab died, Husham from the land of the Temanites became king in his place. 46 When Husham died, Hadad son of Bedad became king in his place and ruled from the city of Avith. He was the one who destroyed the Midianite army in the land of Moab. 47 When Hadad died, Samlah from the city of Masrekah became king in his place. 48 When Samlah died, Shaul from the city of Rehoboth-on-the-River became king in his place. 49 When Shaul died, Baal-hanan son of Acbor became king in his place. 50 When Baal-hanan died, Hadad became king in his place and ruled from the city of Pau.* His wife was Mehetabel, the daughter of Matred and granddaughter of Me-zahab. 51 Then Hadad died.

The clan leaders of Edom were Timna, Alvah,* Jetheth, 52 Oholibamah, Elah, Pinon, 53 Kenaz, Teman, Mibzar, 54 Magdiel, and Iram. These are the clan leaders of Edom.

## Descendants of Israel

**2** The sons of Israel* were Reuben, Simeon, Levi, Judah, Issachar, Zebulun, 2 Dan, Joseph, Benjamin, Naphtali, Gad, and Asher.

## Descendants of Judah

3 Judah had three sons from Bathshua, a Canaanite woman. Their names were Er, Onan, and Shelah. But the LORD saw that the oldest son, Er, was a wicked man, so he killed him. 4 Later Judah had twin sons from Tamar, his widowed daughter-in-law. Their names were Perez and Zerah. So Judah had five sons in all.

5 The sons of Perez were Hezron and Hamul. 6 The sons of Zerah were Zimri, Ethan, Heman, Calcol, and Darda*—five in all. 7 The son of Carmi (a descendant of Zimri) was Achan,* who brought disaster on Israel by taking plunder that had been set apart for the LORD.* 8 The son of Ethan was Azariah.

## From Judah's Grandson Hezron to David

9 The sons of Hezron were Jerahmeel, Ram, and Caleb.* 10 Ram was the father of Amminadab.
Amminadab was the father of Nahshon, a leader of Judah.
11 Nahshon was the father of Salmon.*
Salmon was the father of Boaz.
12 Boaz was the father of Obed.
Obed was the father of Jesse.

*Cross-references (right margin):*
1:43-54 //Gen 36:31-43
1:45 Job 2:11
2:1-2 //Gen 35:23-26; 46:8-25 Exod 1:1-4 Num 1:2-15 Rev 7:4-8
2:3 Gen 38:2-10
2:4 Gen 38:13-30
2:5-15 //Ruth 4:18-22 Matt 1:3-6
2:7 Josh 7:1
2:10 Num 1:7
2:12 Ruth 4:17 Matt 1:5

**1:43** Or *before an Israelite king ruled over them.* **1:50** As in many Hebrew manuscripts, some Greek manuscripts, Syriac version, and Latin Vulgate (see also Gen 36:39); most Hebrew manuscripts read *Pai.* **1:51** As in parallel text at Gen 36:40; Hebrew reads *Aliah.* **2:1** *Israel* is the name that God gave to Jacob. **2:6** As in many Hebrew manuscripts, some Greek manuscripts, and Syriac version (see also 1 Kgs 4:31); Hebrew reads *Dara.* **2:7a** Hebrew *Achar*; compare Josh 7:1. *Achar* means "disaster." **2:7b** The Hebrew term used here refers to the complete consecration of things or people to the LORD, either by destroying them or by giving them as an offering. **2:9** Hebrew *Kelubai,* a variant spelling of Caleb; compare 2:18. **2:11** As in Greek version (see also Ruth 4:21); Hebrew reads *Salma.*

**1:43-54** Why are we given information in this genealogy about the descendants of Edom, who were Israel's enemies? Esau, ancestor of the Edomites, was Isaac's oldest son and thus a direct descendant of Abraham. As Abraham's first grandson, he deserved a place in the Jewish records. It was through Esau's marriages to pagan women, however, that the nation of Edom began. This genealogy shows the ancestry of enemy nations; they were *not* a part of the direct lineage of King David, and thus of the Messiah. This listing further identified Israel's special identity and role.

**2:1, 2** The story of Israel's (Jacob's) sons is found in Genesis 29:32–50:26. Profiles of Joseph, Reuben, and Judah are found on pp. 71, 73, and 85.

**2:3** This long genealogy not only lists names but gives us insights into some of the people. Here, almost as an epitaph, the genealogy states that Er "was a wicked man," so the Lord killed him. Now, thousands of years later, this is all we know of the man. Each of us is forging a reputation, developing personal qualities by which we will be remembered. How would God summarize your life up to now? Some defiantly claim that how they live is their own business. But Scripture teaches that the way you live today will determine how you will be remembered by others and how you will be judged by God. What you do now *does* matter.

**2:7** The plunder referred to in this verse was taken by Achan in direct disobedience to God's instructions following the destruction of Jericho. His greed led to the defeat of Israel at Ai and the death of Achan and his entire family (see Joshua 7).

**2:12** Boaz was Ruth's husband and an ancestor of both David and Jesus. Boaz's story and Profile are found in the book of Ruth.

**2:13**
1 Sam 16:6
**2:16**
1 Sam 26:6
2 Sam 2:18
**2:17**
2 Sam 17:25

¹³Jesse's first son was Eliab, his second was Abinadab, his third was Shimea, ¹⁴his fourth was Nethanel, his fifth was Raddai, ¹⁵his sixth was Ozem, and his seventh was David.
¹⁶Their sisters were named Zeruiah and Abigail. Zeruiah had three sons named Abishai, Joab, and Asahel. ¹⁷Abigail married a man named Jether, an Ishmaelite, and they had a son named Amasa.

### Other Descendants of Hezron

¹⁸Hezron's son Caleb had sons from his wife Azubah and from Jerioth.* Her sons were named Jesher, Shobab, and Ardon. ¹⁹After Azubah died, Caleb married Ephrathah,* and they had a son named Hur. ²⁰Hur was the father of Uri. Uri was the father of Bezalel.

²¹When Hezron was sixty years old, he married Gilead's sister, the daughter of Makir. They had a son named Segub. ²²Segub was the father of Jair, who ruled twenty-three towns in the land of Gilead. ²³(But Geshur and Aram captured the Towns of Jair* and also took Kenath and its sixty surrounding villages.) All these were descendants of Makir, the father of Gilead.

²⁴Soon after Hezron died in the town of Caleb-ephrathah, his wife Abijah gave birth to a son named Ashhur (the father of* Tekoa).

### Descendants of Hezron's Son Jerahmeel

²⁵The sons of Jerahmeel, the oldest son of Hezron, were Ram (the firstborn), Bunah, Oren, Ozem, and Ahijah. ²⁶Jerahmeel had a second wife named Atarah. She was the mother of Onam.

²⁷The sons of Ram, the oldest son of Jerahmeel, were Maaz, Jamin, and Eker.
²⁸The sons of Onam were Shammai and Jada.
The sons of Shammai were Nadab and Abishur.
²⁹The sons of Abishur and his wife Abihail were Ahban and Molid.
³⁰The sons of Nadab were Seled and Appaim. Seled died without children, ³¹but Appaim had a son named Ishi. The son of Ishi was Sheshan. Sheshan had a descendant named Ahlai.

³²The sons of Jada, Shammai's brother, were Jether and Jonathan. Jether died without children, ³³but Jonathan had two sons named Peleth and Zaza.
These were all descendants of Jerahmeel.

³⁴Sheshan had no sons, though he did have daughters. He also had an Egyptian servant named Jarha. ³⁵Sheshan gave one of his daughters to be the wife of Jarha, and they had a son named Attai.

**2:36**
1 Chr 11:41

³⁶ Attai was the father of Nathan.
Nathan was the father of Zabad.
³⁷ Zabad was the father of Ephlal.
Ephlal was the father of Obed.
³⁸ Obed was the father of Jehu.
Jehu was the father of Azariah.
³⁹ Azariah was the father of Helez.
Helez was the father of Eleasah.
⁴⁰ Eleasah was the father of Sismai.
Sismai was the father of Shallum.
⁴¹ Shallum was the father of Jekamiah.
Jekamiah was the father of Elishama.

**2:18** Or *Caleb had a daughter named Jerioth from his wife, Azubah.* The meaning of the Hebrew is uncertain.
**2:19** Hebrew *Ephrath,* a variant spelling of Ephrathah; compare 2:50 and 4:4. **2:23** Or *captured Havvoth-jair.*
**2:24** Or *the founder of;* also in 2:42, 45, 49.

---

**2:15** David is one of the best-known people of the Bible. He was certainly not perfect, but he exemplified what it means to seek God first in all areas of life. God called David "a man after my own heart" (Acts 13:22) because David's greatest desire was to serve and worship God. We can please God in the same way by making God our first consideration in all our desires and plans. David's story is found in 1 Samuel 16:1— 1 Kings 2:10 and 1 Chronicles 10:14—29:30. David's Profile is found in 1 Samuel 17, p. 439.

**2:16** Joab's story is found in 2 Samuel 2–3; 10–20; 24; 1 Kings 1–2; 1 Chronicles 11:4-9; 19–21. His Profile is found in 2 Samuel 18, p. 495. Abishai's story is found in 1 Samuel 26; 2 Samuel 2–3; 10; 15–21; 23; 1 Chronicles 18:12; 19. Abishai's Profile is found in 2 Samuel 21, p. 499.

**2:18** This is not the Caleb who spied out the Promised Land with Joshua. Caleb the spy is listed in 4:15.

## Descendants of Hezron's Son Caleb

42 The descendants of Caleb, the brother of Jerahmeel, included Mesha (the firstborn), who became the father of Ziph. Caleb's descendants also included the sons of Mareshah, the father of Hebron.*
43 The sons of Hebron were Korah, Tappuah, Rekem, and Shema. 44Shema was the father of Raham. Raham was the father of Jorkeam. Rekem was the father of Shammai.
45 The son of Shammai was Maon. Maon was the father of Beth-zur.
46Caleb's concubine Ephah gave birth to Haran, Moza, and Gazez. Haran was the father of Gazez.
47 The sons of Jahdai were Regem, Jotham, Geshan, Pelet, Ephah, and Shaaph.
48Another of Caleb's concubines, Maacah, gave birth to Sheber and Tirhanah. 49She also gave birth to Shaaph (the father of Madmannah) and Sheva (the father of Macbenah and Gibea). Caleb also had a daughter named Acsah.
50These were all descendants of Caleb.

## Descendants of Caleb's Son Hur

The sons of Hur, the oldest son of Caleb's wife Ephrathah, were Shobal (the founder of Kiriath-jearim), 51Salma (the founder of Bethlehem), and Hareph (the founder of Beth-gader).
52 The descendants of Shobal (the founder of Kiriath-jearim) were Haroeh, half the Manahathites, 53and the families of Kiriath-jearim—the Ithrites, Puthites, Shumathites, and Mishraites, from whom came the people of Zorah and Eshtaol.
54The descendants of Salma were the people of Bethlehem, the Netophathites, Atroth-beth-joab, the other half of the Manahathites, the Zorites, 55and the families of scribes living at Jabez—the Tirathites, Shimeathites, and Sucathites. All these were Kenites who descended from Hammath, the father of the family of Recab.*

## Descendants of David

**3** These are the sons of David who were born in Hebron:

The oldest was Amnon, whose mother was Ahinoam from Jezreel.
The second was Daniel, whose mother was Abigail from Carmel.
2 The third was Absalom, whose mother was Maacah, the daughter of Talmai, king of Geshur.
The fourth was Adonijah, whose mother was Haggith.
3 The fifth was Shephatiah, whose mother was Abital.
The sixth was Ithream, whose mother was Eglah, David's wife.
4These six sons were born to David in Hebron, where he reigned seven and a half years.

Then David reigned another thirty-three years in Jerusalem. 5The sons born to David in Jerusalem included Shammua,* Shobab, Nathan, and Solomon. Their mother was Bathsheba,* the daughter of Ammiel. 6David also had nine other sons: Ibhar, Elishua,* Elpelet,* 7Nogah, Nepheg, Japhia, 8Elishama, Eliada, and Eliphelet.
9 These were the sons of David, not including his sons born to his concubines. Their sister was named Tamar.

## Descendants of Solomon

10The descendants of Solomon were Rehoboam, Abijah, Asa, Jehoshaphat, 11Jehoram,* Ahaziah, Joash, 12Amaziah, Uzziah,* Jotham, 13Ahaz, Hezekiah, Manasseh, 14Amon, and Josiah.

**Side references:**
2:45 Josh 15:55
2:50 1 Chr 4:4
2:55 2 Kgs 10:15
3:1-4 //2 Sam 3:2-5
3:1 1 Sam 25:43
3:2 2 Sam 3:4; 13:20; 14:23
3:4 2 Sam 5:4-5
3:5-8 //2 Sam 5:14-16 //1 Chr 14:4-7
3:9 2 Sam 13:1
3:10 1 Kgs 15:1, 8, 24 2 Chr 13:1; 17:1
3:11 2 Kgs 8:24-25; 11:21 2 Chr 21:1; 22:11

2:42 Or who founded Hebron. The meaning of the Hebrew is uncertain.   2:55 Or the founder of Beth-recab.
3:5a As in Syriac version (see also 14:4; 2 Sam 5:14); Hebrew reads Shimea.   3:5b Hebrew Bathshua, a variant spelling of Bathsheba.   3:6a As in some Hebrew and Greek manuscripts (see also 14:5-7 and 2 Sam 5:15); most Hebrew manuscripts read Elishama.   3:6b Hebrew Eliphelet; compare parallel text at 14:5-7.   3:11 Hebrew Joram, a variant spelling of Jehoram.   3:12 Hebrew Azariah, a variant spelling of Uzziah.

3:1 Abigail's story and Profile are found in 1 Samuel 25, p. 451.
3:2 Absalom's story and Profile are found in 2 Samuel 13–18, p. 487.
3:5 Bathsheba's story is found in 2 Samuel 11–12; 1 Kings 1, and her Profile is in 1 Kings 1, p. 511. The story of her son, Solomon, who became Israel's third king, is found in 1 Kings 1–11 and 2 Chronicles 1–9. Solomon's Profile is in 1 Kings 4, p. 519.

3:9 The tragic story of Tamar, David's daughter, is found in 2 Samuel 13–14.
3:10-14 Many of Solomon's descendants ruled the nation of Judah. For Rehoboam's story and Profile, see 2 Chronicles 10–12, p. 679. For Jehoshaphat's story and Profile, see 2 Chronicles 17–20, p. 687. Uzziah's story and Profile are found in 2 Chronicles 26, p. 701. Hezekiah's story and Profile are in 2 Kings 18–20, p. 601. For Josiah's story, see 2 Kings 22–23. His Profile is in 2 Kings 23, p. 611.

3:15
2 Kgs 23:34

15 The sons of Josiah were Johanan (the oldest), Jehoiakim (the second), Zedekiah (the third), and Jehoahaz* (the fourth).

16 The successors of Jehoiakim were his son Jehoiachin and his brother Zedekiah.*

### Descendants of Jehoiachin

17 The sons of Jehoiachin,* who was taken prisoner by the Babylonians, were Shealtiel, 18 Malkiram, Pedaiah, Shenazzar, Jekamiah, Hoshama, and Nedabiah.

19 The sons of Pedaiah were Zerubbabel and Shimei.

The sons of Zerubbabel were Meshullam and Hananiah. (Their sister was Shelomith.) 20 His five other sons were Hashubah, Ohel, Berekiah, Hasadiah, and Jushab-hesed.

21 The sons of Hananiah were Pelatiah and Jeshaiah. Jeshaiah's son was Rephaiah. Rephaiah's son was Arnan. Arnan's son was Obadiah. Obadiah's son was Shecaniah.

3:22
Ezra 8:2-3

22 The descendants of Shecaniah were Shemaiah and his sons, Hattush, Igal, Bariah, Neariah, and Shaphat—six in all.

23 The sons of Neariah were Elioenai, Hizkiah, and Azrikam—three in all.

24 The sons of Elioenai were Hodaviah, Eliashib, Pelaiah, Akkub, Johanan, Delaiah, and Anani—seven in all.

## 2. The tribes of Israel

### Other Descendants of Judah

4:1
Num 26:21
1 Chr 2:3

4 The descendants of Judah were Perez, Hezron, Carmi, Hur, and Shobal. 2 Shobal's son Reaiah was the father of Jahath. Jahath was the father of Ahumai and Lahad. These were the families of the Zorathites.

3 The descendants of* Etam were Jezreel, Ishma, Idbash, their sister Hazzelelponi, 4 Penuel (the father of* Gedor), and Ezer (the father of Hushah). These were the descendants of Hur (the firstborn of Ephrathah), the ancestor of Bethlehem.

5 Ashhur (the father of Tekoa) had two wives, named Helah and Naarah. 6 Naarah gave birth to Ahuzzam, Hepher, Temeni, and Haahashtari. 7 Helah gave birth to Zereth, Izhar,* Ethnan, 8 and Koz, who became the ancestor of Anub, Zobebah, and all the families of Aharhel son of Harum.

9 There was a man named Jabez who was more honorable than any of his brothers. His mother named him Jabez* because his birth had been so painful. 10 He was the one who prayed to the God of Israel, "Oh, that you would bless me and expand my territory! Please be with me in all that I do, and keep me from all trouble and pain!" And God granted him his request.

11 Kelub (the brother of Shuhah) was the father of Mehir. Mehir was the father of Eshton. 12 Eshton was the father of Beth-rapha, Paseah, and Tehinnah. Tehinnah was the father of Ir-nahash. These were the descendants of Recah.

4:13
Josh 15:17

13 The sons of Kenaz were Othniel and Seraiah. Othniel's sons were Hathath and Meonothai.* 14 Meonothai was the father of Ophrah. Seraiah was the father of Joab, the founder of the Valley of Craftsmen,* so called because they were craftsmen.

15 The sons of Caleb son of Jephunneh were Iru, Elah, and Naam. The son of Elah was Kenaz.

3:15 Hebrew *Shallum,* another name for Jehoahaz. 3:16 Hebrew *The sons of Jehoiakim were his son Jeconiah* [a variant spelling of Jehoiachin] *and his son Zedekiah.* 3:17 Hebrew *Jeconiah,* a variant spelling of Jehoiachin. 4:3 As in Greek version; Hebrew reads *father of.* The meaning of the Hebrew is uncertain. 4:4 Or *the founder of;* also in 4:5, 12, 14, 17, 18, and perhaps other instances where the text reads *the father of.* 4:7 As in an alternate reading in the Masoretic Text (see also Latin Vulgate); the other alternate and the Greek version read *Zohar.* 4:9 *Jabez* sounds like a Hebrew word meaning "distress" or "pain." 4:13 As in some Greek manuscripts and Latin Vulgate; Hebrew lacks *and Meonothai.* 4:14 Or *Joab, the father of Ge-harashim.*

---

**3:15** Jehoiakim's story is found in Jeremiah 22–28; 35; 36. Zedekiah's story is found in Jeremiah 21–39.

**3:19, 20** Zerubbabel was the leader of the first exiles to return from Babylon. His story and Profile are found in the book of Ezra.

**4:9, 10** Jabez is remembered for a prayer request rather than a heroic act. In his prayer, he asked God to (1) bless him, (2) help him in his work ("expand my territory"), (3) be with him in all he did, and (4) keep him from trouble and pain. Jabez acknowledged God as the true center of his life. When we pray for God's blessing, we should also ask him to take his rightful position as Lord over our work, our family time, and our recreation. Obeying him in daily responsibilities *is* heroic living.

**4:10** Jabez prayed specifically to be protected from trouble and pain. We live in a fallen world filled with sin, and it is important

to ask God to keep us safe from the unavoidable evil that comes our way. But we must also avoid evil motives, desires, and actions that begin within us. Therefore, not only must we seek God's protection from evil, but we must also ask God to guard our thoughts and actions. We can begin to utilize his protection by filling our mind with positive thoughts and attitudes.

**4:13** Othniel was Israel's first judge. He reformed the nation and brought peace to the land. His story is found in Judges 1:9-15 and 3:5-11.

**4:15** Caleb was one of the 12 scouts sent into the Promised Land by Moses. He and Joshua were the only two scouts to return with a positive report, believing in God's promise to help the Israelites conquer the land. Caleb's story is told in Numbers 13–14 and Joshua 14–15. His Profile is found in Numbers 14, p. 225.

<sup>16</sup>The sons of Jehallelel were Ziph, Ziphah, Tiria, and Asarel.

<sup>17</sup>The sons of Ezrah were Jether, Mered, Epher, and Jalon. One of Mered's wives became*
the mother of Miriam, Shammai, and Ishbah (the father of Eshtemoa). <sup>18</sup>He married
a woman from Judah, who became the mother of Jered (the father of Gedor), Heber (the
father of Soco), and Jekuthiel (the father of Zanoah). Mered also married Bithia,
a daughter of Pharaoh, and she bore him children.

<sup>19</sup>Hodiah's wife was the sister of Naham. One of her sons was the father of Keilah the
Garmite, and another was the father of Eshtemoa the Maacathite.

<sup>20</sup>The sons of Shimon were Amnon, Rinnah, Ben-hanan, and Tilon.
The descendants of Ishi were Zoheth and Ben-zoheth.

### Descendants of Judah's Son Shelah

<sup>21</sup>Shelah was one of Judah's sons. The descendants of Shelah were Er (the father of Lecah);
Laadah (the father of Mareshah); the families of linen workers at Beth-ashbea; <sup>22</sup>Jokim;
the men of Cozeba; and Joash and Saraph, who ruled over Moab and Jashubi-lehem.
These names all come from ancient records. <sup>23</sup>They were the pottery makers who lived
in Netaim and Gederah. They lived there and worked for the king.

### Descendants of Simeon

<sup>24</sup>The sons of Simeon were Jemuel,* Jamin, Jarib, Zohar,* and Shaul.

<sup>25</sup>The descendants of Shaul were Shallum, Mibsam, and Mishma.

<sup>26</sup>The descendants of Mishma were Hammuel, Zaccur, and Shimei.

<sup>27</sup>Shimei had sixteen sons and six daughters, but none of his brothers had large families.
So Simeon's tribe never grew as large as the tribe of Judah.

<sup>28</sup>They lived in Beersheba, Moladah, Hazar-shual, <sup>29</sup>Bilhah, Ezem, Tolad, <sup>30</sup>Bethuel, Hormah,
Ziklag, <sup>31</sup>Beth-marcaboth, Hazar-susim, Beth-biri, and Shaaraim. These towns were under
their control until the time of King David. <sup>32</sup>Their descendants also lived in Etam, Ain,
Rimmon, Token, and Ashan—five towns <sup>33</sup>and their surrounding villages as far away as
Baalath.* This was their territory, and these names are listed in their genealogical records.

<sup>34</sup>Other descendants of Simeon included Meshobab, Jamlech, Joshah son of Amaziah,
<sup>35</sup>Joel, Jehu son of Joshibiah, son of Seraiah, son of Asiel, <sup>36</sup>Elioenai, Jaakobah,
Jeshohaiah, Asaiah, Adiel, Jesimiel, Benaiah, <sup>37</sup>and Ziza son of Shiphi, son of Allon,
son of Jedaiah, son of Shimri, son of Shemaiah.

<sup>38</sup>These were the names of some of the leaders of Simeon's wealthy clans. Their families
grew, <sup>39</sup>and they traveled to the region of Gerar,* in the east part of the valley, seeking pastureland for their flocks. <sup>40</sup>They found lush pastures there, and the land was quiet and peaceful.
Some of Ham's descendants had been living in that region. <sup>41</sup>But during the reign of King
Hezekiah of Judah, these leaders of Simeon invaded the region and completely destroyed*
the homes of the descendants of Ham and of the Meunites. No trace of them remains today.
They killed everyone who lived there and took the land for themselves, because they wanted
its good pastureland for their flocks. <sup>42</sup>Five hundred of these invaders from the tribe of Simeon went to Mount Seir, led by Pelatiah, Neariah, Rephaiah, and Uzziel—all sons of Ishi. <sup>43</sup>They
destroyed the few Amalekites who had survived, and they have lived there ever since.

### Descendants of Reuben

**5** The oldest son of Israel* was Reuben. But since he dishonored his father by sleeping
with one of his father's concubines, his birthright was given to the sons of his brother
Joseph. For this reason, Reuben is not listed in the genealogical records as the firstborn son.
<sup>2</sup>The descendants of Judah became the most powerful tribe and provided a ruler for the
nation,* but the birthright belonged to Joseph.

---

4:17 Or *Jether's wife became;* Hebrew reads *She became.*   4:24a As in Syriac version (see also Gen 46:10; Exod
6:15); Hebrew reads *Nemuel.*   4:24b As in parallel texts at Gen 46:10 and Exod 6:15; Hebrew reads *Zerah.*   4:33 As
in some Greek manuscripts (see also Josh 19:8); Hebrew reads *Baal.*   4:39 As in Greek version; Hebrew reads
*Gedor.*   4:41 The Hebrew term used here refers to the complete consecration of things or people to the Lord, either
by destroying them or by giving them as an offering.   5:1 *Israel* is the name that God gave to Jacob.   5:2 Or *and
from Judah came a prince.*

---

**4:28-33**
//Josh 19:2-10

**4:40**
Judg 18:7-10

**4:42**
Gen 36:8-9

**4:43**
1 Sam 15:7-8;
30:16-17

**5:1**
Gen 29:32; 35:22;
48:15-22; 49:4
1 Chr 2:1

**5:2**
Gen 49:8-10, 12
Mic 5:2
Matt 2:6

---

**5:1** Reuben's sin of incest was recorded for all future generations to read. The purpose of this epitaph was not to smear
Reuben's name, but to show that painful memories aren't the
only results of sin. The real consequences of sin are ruined lives.
As the oldest son, Reuben was the rightful heir to both a double
portion of his father's estate and the leadership of Abraham's

descendants, who had grown into a large tribe. But his sin
stripped away his rights and privileges and destroyed his family.
Before you give in to temptation, consider the disastrous consequences sin may produce in your life and the lives of others.

**5:2** This ruler from the tribe of Judah refers to David and his
royal line and to Jesus the Messiah, David's greatest descendant.

**5:3**
Gen 46:9
Exod 6:14
Num 26:5
**5:6**
2 Kgs 15:19
**5:7-8**
Num 32:34
Josh 12:2

³The sons of Reuben, the oldest son of Israel, were Hanoch, Pallu, Hezron, and Carmi. ⁴The descendants of Joel were Shemaiah, Gog, Shimei, ⁵Micah, Reaiah, Baal, ⁶and Beerah. Beerah was the leader of the Reubenites when they were taken into captivity by King Tiglath-pileser* of Assyria.

⁷Beerah's* relatives are listed in their genealogical records by their clans: Jeiel (the leader), Zechariah, ⁸and Bela son of Azaz, son of Shema, son of Joel.

**5:6** Hebrew *Tilgath-pilneser*, a variant spelling of Tiglath-pileser; also in 5:26. **5:7** Hebrew *His*.

---

## WHO'S WHO IN THE BIBLE

Here are some of the people mentioned in this genealogy who are also mentioned elsewhere in the Bible. The writer of Chronicles reproduced a thorough history of Israel in one list of people. Many of the people in this list have exciting stories that can be traced through the Bible. Look up some of the names here that intrigue you. You may be surprised at what you discover!

| Name | Key Life Lesson | Reference |
|------|-----------------|-----------|
| Adam (1:1) | Our sins have far greater implications than we realize. | Genesis 2–3 |
| Noah (1:4) | Great rewards come from obeying God. | Genesis 6–9 |
| Abraham (1:27) | Faith alone makes one right in God's eyes. | Genesis 11:26–25:10 |
| Isaac (1:28) | Seeking peace brings true respect. | Genesis 21–35 |
| Esau (1:35) | It is never too late to put away bitterness and forgive. | Genesis 25:20–36:43 |
| Amalek (1:36) | There are evil men and nations who seek to harm God's people. | Exodus 17:8-16 |
| Israel (Jacob) (2:1) | While our sins may haunt us, God will honor our faith. | Genesis 25:20–50:13 |
| Judah (2:3) | God can change the hearts of even the most wicked people. | Genesis 37–50 |
| Tamar (2:4) | God works his purposes even through sinful events. | Genesis 38 |
| Perez (2:5) | Your background does not matter to God. | Genesis 38:27-30 |
| Boaz (2:12) | Those who are kind to others will receive kindness themselves. | The book of Ruth |
| Jesse (2:13) | Never take lightly the impact you may have on your children. | 1 Samuel 16 |
| David (2:15) | True greatness is having a heart for God. | The books of 1 and 2 Samuel |
| Joab (2:16) | Those who seek power die with nothing. | 2 Samuel 2:13 — 1 Kings 2:34 |
| Amnon (3:1) | Giving in to lust leads only to tragedy. | 2 Samuel 13 |
| Absalom (3:2) | Those seeking to oust a God-appointed leader will have a difficult battle. | 2 Samuel 13–18 |
| Adonijah (3:2) | God must determine what is rightfully ours. | 1 Kings 1–2 |
| Bathsheba (3:5) | One wrong act does not disqualify us from accomplishing things for God. | 2 Samuel 11–12; 1 Kings 1–2 |
| Solomon (3:5) | Human wisdom is foolishness without God. | 1 Kings 1–11 |
| Reuben (5:1) | What is gained from a moment of passion is only perceived; what is lost is real and permanent. | Genesis 35:22; 37; 49:3, 4 |
| Aaron (6:3) | Don't expect God's leaders to be perfect, but don't let them get away with sin either. | Exodus 4—Numbers 20 |
| Nadab (6:3) | Pretending to be God's representative is dangerous business. | Leviticus 10 |
| Eleazar (6:3) | Those who are consistent in their faith are the best models to follow. | Numbers 20:25-29; 26–34; Joshua 24:33 |
| Korah (6:22) | Rebelling against God's leaders is rebelling against God and will always be unsuccessful. | Numbers 16 |
| Joshua (7:27) | Real courage comes from God. | The book of Joshua |
| Saul (8:33) | Those who say they follow God but don't live like it waste their God-given potential. | 1 Samuel 8–31 |
| Jonathan (8:33) | True friends always think of the other person, not just themselves. | 1 Samuel 14–31 |

The Reubenites lived in the area that stretches from Aroer to Nebo and Baal-meon. ⁹And since they had so many livestock in the land of Gilead, they spread east toward the edge of the desert that stretches to the Euphrates River. ¹⁰During the reign of Saul, the Reubenites defeated the Hagrites in battle. Then they moved into the Hagrite settlements all along the eastern edge of Gilead.

**5:9**
Josh 22:8-9

**5:10**
1 Chr 5:18-21

### Descendants of Gad

¹¹Next to the Reubenites, the descendants of Gad lived in the land of Bashan as far east as Salecah. ¹²Joel was the leader in the land of Bashan, and Shapham was second-in-command, followed by Janai and Shaphat. ¹³Their relatives, the leaders of seven other clans, were Michael, Meshullam, Sheba, Jorai, Jacan, Zia, and Eber. ¹⁴These were all descendants of Abihail son of Huri, son of Jaroah, son of Gilead, son of Michael, son of Jeshishai, son of Jahdo, son of Buz. ¹⁵Ahi son of Abdiel, son of Guni, was the leader of their clans.

**5:11**
Josh 13:11, 24-28

¹⁶The Gadite lived in the land of Gilead, in Bashan and its villages, and throughout all the pasturelands of Sharon. ¹⁷All of these were listed in the genealogical records during the days of King Jotham of Judah and King Jeroboam of Israel.

**5:16**
1 Chr 27:29

**5:17**
2 Kgs 14:16, 28;
15:5, 32-33

### The Tribes East of the Jordan

¹⁸There were 44,760 capable warriors in the armies of Reuben, Gad, and the half-tribe of Manasseh. They were all skilled in combat and armed with shields, swords, and bows. ¹⁹They waged war against the Hagrites, the Jeturites, the Naphishites, and the Nodabites. ²⁰They cried out to God during the battle, and he answered their prayer because they trusted in him. So the Hagrites and all their allies were defeated. ²¹The plunder taken from the Hagrites included 50,000 camels, 250,000 sheep and goats, 2,000 donkeys, and 100,000 captives. ²²Many of the Hagrites were killed in the battle because God was fighting against them. The people of Reuben, Gad, and Manasseh lived in their land until they were taken into exile.

**5:18**
Num 1:3

**5:19**
Gen 25:15
1 Chr 1:31; 5:10

**5:20**
2 Chr 14:11-13
Ps 9:10

**5:22**
Josh 23:10
2 Kgs 15:29; 17:6
2 Chr 32:8

²³The half-tribe of Manasseh was very large and spread through the land from Bashan to Baal-hermon, Senir, and Mount Hermon. ²⁴These were the leaders of their clans: Epher,* Ishi, Eliel, Azriel, Jeremiah, Hodaviah, and Jahdiel. These men had a great reputation as mighty warriors and leaders of their clans.

**5:23**
Deut 3:9

²⁵But these tribes were unfaithful to the God of their ancestors. They worshiped the gods of the nations that God had destroyed. ²⁶So the God of Israel caused King Pul of Assyria (also known as Tiglath-pileser) to invade the land and take away the people of Reuben, Gad, and the half-tribe of Manasseh as captives. The Assyrians exiled them to Halah, Habor, Hara, and the Gozan River, where they remain to this day.

**5:25**
Exod 34:15
2 Kgs 17:7

**5:26**
2 Kgs 15:19, 29

### The Priestly Line

**6** ¹*The sons of Levi were Gershon, Kohath, and Merari. ²The descendants of Kohath included Amram, Izhar, Hebron, and Uzziel. ³The children of Amram were Aaron, Moses, and Miriam.
The sons of Aaron were Nadab, Abihu, Eleazar, and Ithamar.

**6:1**
Gen 46:11
Exod 6:16-25

**6:3**
Lev 10:1

**5:24** As in Greek version and Latin Vulgate; Hebrew reads *and Epher.*   **6:1** Verses 6:1-15 are numbered 5:27-41 in Hebrew text.

---

**5:18-22** The armies of Reuben, Gad, and Manasseh succeeded in battle because they trusted God. Although they had instinct and skill as soldiers, they prayed and sought God's direction. The natural and developed abilities God gives us are meant to be used for him, but they should never replace our dependence on him. When we trust in our own cleverness, skill, and strength rather than in God, we open the door for pride. When facing difficult situations, seek God's purpose and ask for his guidance and strength. Psalm 20:7 says, "Some nations boast of their chariots and horses, but we boast in the name of the LORD our God."

**5:22** The Exile mentioned here refers to the exile of the 10 northern tribes (the northern kingdom of Israel) to Assyria in 722 B.C. These tribes never returned to their homeland. This story is found in 2 Kings 15:29–17:41.

**5:24, 25** As warriors and leaders, these men had established

excellent reputations for their great skill and leadership qualities. But in God's eyes they failed in the most important quality— being faithful to God. If you try to measure up to society's standards for fame and success, you may neglect your true purpose—to please and obey God. In the end, God alone examines our hearts and determines our final standing. How is your present reputation with God?

**6:1ff** The tribe of Levi was set apart to serve God in the Tabernacle (Numbers 3–4), and later in the Temple (1 Chronicles 23–26). Aaron, Levi's descendant (6:3), became Israel's first high priest. God required all future priests to be descendants of Aaron. The rest of the Levites assisted the priests in various Tabernacle or Temple duties; they taught the people God's Word and encouraged them to obey it.

**6:3** The people listed here played major roles in the drama of the Exodus. Aaron's story is found in the books of Exodus,

<sup>4</sup> Eleazar was the father of Phinehas.
Phinehas was the father of Abishua.
<sup>5</sup> Abishua was the father of Bukki.
Bukki was the father of Uzzi.
<sup>6</sup> Uzzi was the father of Zerahiah.
Zerahiah was the father of Meraioth.
<sup>7</sup> Meraioth was the father of Amariah.
Amariah was the father of Ahitub.

**6:8**
Ezra 7:2

<sup>8</sup> Ahitub was the father of Zadok.
Zadok was the father of Ahimaaz.
<sup>9</sup> Ahimaaz was the father of Azariah.
Azariah was the father of Johanan.
<sup>10</sup> Johanan was the father of Azariah, the high priest at the Temple* built by Solomon
in Jerusalem.
<sup>11</sup> Azariah was the father of Amariah.
Amariah was the father of Ahitub.
<sup>12</sup> Ahitub was the father of Zadok.
Zadok was the father of Shallum.
<sup>13</sup> Shallum was the father of Hilkiah.
Hilkiah was the father of Azariah.

**6:15**
Neh 12:1
Hag 1:1, 14
Zech 6:11

<sup>14</sup> Azariah was the father of Seraiah.
Seraiah was the father of Jehozadak, <sup>15</sup>who went into exile when the LORD sent the
people of Judah and Jerusalem into captivity under Nebuchadnezzar.

### The Levite Clans

<sup>16</sup>*The sons of Levi were Gershon,* Kohath, and Merari.
<sup>17</sup>The descendants of Gershon included Libni and Shimei.

**6:19**
1 Chr 23:21

<sup>18</sup>The descendants of Kohath included Amram, Izhar, Hebron, and Uzziel.
<sup>19</sup>The descendants of Merari included Mahli and Mushi.

The following were the Levite clans, listed according to their ancestral descent:

<sup>20</sup>The descendants of Gershon included Libni, Jahath, Zimmah, <sup>21</sup>Joah, Iddo, Zerah,
and Jeatherai.
<sup>22</sup>The descendants of Kohath included Amminadab, Korah, Assir, <sup>23</sup>Elkanah, Abiasaph,*
Assir, <sup>24</sup>Tahath, Uriel, Uzziah, and Shaul.

**6:27**
1 Sam 1:1, 20
**6:28**
1 Sam 8:2
1 Chr 6:33

<sup>25</sup>The descendants of Elkanah included Amasai, Ahimoth, <sup>26</sup>Elkanah, Zophai, Nahath,
<sup>27</sup>Eliab, Jeroham, Elkanah, and Samuel.*
<sup>28</sup>The sons of Samuel were Joel* (the older) and Abijah (the second).
<sup>29</sup>The descendants of Merari included Mahli, Libni, Shimei, Uzzah, <sup>30</sup>Shimea, Haggiah,
and Asaiah.

**6:10** Hebrew *the house.*   **6:16a** Verses 6:16-81 are numbered 6:1-66 in Hebrew text.   **6:16b** Hebrew *Gershom,*
a variant spelling of Gershon (see 6:1); also in 6:17, 20, 43, 62, 71.   **6:23** Hebrew *Ebiasaph,* a variant spelling of
Abiasaph (also in 6:37); compare parallel text at Exod 6:24.   **6:27** As in some Greek manuscripts (see also 6:33-34);
Hebrew lacks *and Samuel.*   **6:28** As in some Greek manuscripts and the Syriac version (see also 6:33 and 1 Sam
8:2); Hebrew lacks *Joel.*

---

Leviticus, and Numbers. His Profile is found in Exodus 32,
p. 145. Moses was one of the greatest prophets and leaders
in Israel's history. His story is found in the books of Exodus,
Leviticus, Numbers, and Deuteronomy. His Profile is found in
Exodus 14, p. 117. The story of Miriam, Moses and Aaron's
sister, is found in Exodus 2; 15:20, 21; and Numbers 12; 20:1.
Her Profile is found in Numbers 13, p. 221. Nadab and Abihu
were killed for disobeying God (Leviticus 10). Eleazar became
Israel's high priest after Aaron (Numbers 20:24-28), and Ithamar
played an important role in organizing the worship services of
the Tabernacle (Numbers 4:28, 33; 7:8).

**6:28** When Samuel became God's leader and spokesman, Israel
was on the brink of collapse. The last few chapters of the book
of Judges give a vivid picture of the moral decay and the resulting decline of the nation. But with God's help, Samuel almost
single-handedly brought the nation from ruin to revival. He

unified the people by showing them that God was their common
Leader and that any nation that focused on him would find and
fulfill its true purpose. For the rest of Samuel's story, and to see
how he set up rules for governing a nation based on spiritual
principles, read the book of 1 Samuel and his Profile in
1 Samuel 7, p. 419.

## The Temple Musicians

31 David assigned the following men to lead the music at the house of the LORD after the Ark was placed there. 32 They ministered with music at the Tabernacle* until Solomon built the Temple of the LORD in Jerusalem. They carried out their work, following all the regulations handed down to them. 33 These are the men who served, along with their sons:

Heman the musician was from the clan of Kohath. His genealogy was traced back through Joel, Samuel, 34 Elkanah, Jeroham, Eliel, Toah, 35 Zuph, Elkanah, Mahath, Amasai, 36 Elkanah, Joel, Azariah, Zephaniah, 37 Tahath, Assir, Abiasaph, Korah, 38 Izhar, Kohath, Levi, and Israel.*

39 Heman's first assistant was Asaph from the clan of Gershon.* Asaph's genealogy was traced back through Berekiah, Shimea, 40 Michael, Baaseiah, Malkijah, 41 Ethni, Zerah, Adaiah, 42 Ethan, Zimmah, Shimei, 43 Jahath, Gershon, and Levi.

44 Heman's second assistant was Ethan from the clan of Merari. Ethan's genealogy was traced back through Kishi, Abdi, Malluch, 45 Hashabiah, Amaziah, Hilkiah, 46 Amzi, Bani, Shemer, 47 Mahli, Mushi, Merari, and Levi.

48 Their fellow Levites were appointed to various other tasks in the Tabernacle, the house of God.

## Aaron's Descendants

49 Only Aaron and his descendants served as priests. They presented the offerings on the altar of burnt offering and the altar of incense, and they performed all the other duties related to the Most Holy Place. They made atonement for Israel by doing everything that Moses, the servant of God, had commanded them.

50 The descendants of Aaron were Eleazar, Phinehas, Abishua, 51 Bukki, Uzzi, Zerahiah, 52 Meraioth, Amariah, Ahitub, 53 Zadok, and Ahimaaz.

## Territory for the Levites

54 This is a record of the towns and territory assigned by means of sacred lots to the descendants of Aaron, who were from the clan of Kohath. 55 This territory included Hebron and its surrounding pasturelands in Judah, 56 but the fields and outlying areas belonging to the city were given to Caleb son of Jephunneh. 57 So the descendants of Aaron were given the following towns, each with its pasturelands: Hebron (a city of refuge),* Libnah, Jattir, Eshtemoa, 58 Holon,* Debir, 59 Ain,* Juttah,* and Beth-shemesh. 60 And from the territory of Benjamin they were given Gibeon,* Geba, Alemeth, and Anathoth, each with its pasturelands. So thirteen towns were given to the descendants of Aaron. 61 The remaining descendants of Kohath received ten towns from the territory of the half-tribe of Manasseh by means of sacred lots.

**6:31**
2 Sam 6:17
1 Chr 15:16-22, 27;
16:4-6

**6:50**
1 Chr 6:4-8

**6:54**
Josh 21:4, 10
**6:55-56**
Josh 14:13; 15:13

**6:58**
Josh 10:3
**6:61**
Josh 21:5
1 Chr 6:66-70

**6:32** Hebrew *the Tabernacle, the Tent of Meeting.*   **6:38** *Israel* is the name that God gave to Jacob.   **6:39** Hebrew lacks *from the clan of Gershon;* see 6:43.   **6:57** As in parallel text at Josh 21:13; Hebrew reads *were given the cities of refuge: Hebron, and the following towns, each with its pasturelands.*   **6:58** As in parallel text at Josh 21:15; Masoretic Text reads *Hilez;* other manuscripts read *Hilen.*   **6:59a** As in parallel text at Josh 21:16; Hebrew reads *Ashan.*   **6:59b** As in Syriac version (see also Josh 21:16); Hebrew lacks *Juttah.*   **6:60** As in parallel text at Josh 21:17; Hebrew lacks *Gibeon.*

---

**6:31** David did much to bring music into worship. He established song leaders and choirs to perform regularly at the Temple (chapter 25). As a young man, David was hired to play the harp for King Saul (1 Samuel 16:15-23). He also wrote many of the songs found in the book of Psalms.

**6:31ff** The builders and craftsmen had completed the Temple, and the priests and Levites had been given their responsibilities for taking care of it. Then it was time for another group of people—the musicians—to exercise their talents for God. Some of those who served with music are recorded here. You don't have to be an ordained minister to have an important place in the body of believers. Builders, craftsmen, worship assistants, choir members, and song leaders all have significant contributions to make. God has given you a unique combination of talents. Use them to serve and honor him.

**6:49** Aaron and his descendants strictly followed the details of worship commanded by God through Moses. They did not choose only those commands they *wanted* to obey. Note what happened when Uzzah when important details in handling the Ark of the Covenant were neglected (13:6-10). We should not try to obey God selectively, choosing those commands we will obey

and those we will ignore. God's Word has authority over every aspect of our lives, not just selected areas.

**6:49** For more information on priests, see the note on Leviticus 8:1ff.

**6:54** The tribe of Levi was not given a specific area of land as were the other tribes. Instead, the Levites were to live throughout the land in order to aid the people of *every* tribe in their worship of God. Thus, the Levites were given towns or pasturelands within the allotted areas of the other tribes (Joshua 13:14, 33).

**6:57ff** God had told the tribes to designate specific cities to be cities of refuge (Numbers 35). These cities were to provide refuge for a person who accidentally killed someone. This instruction may have seemed unimportant when it was given—the Israelites hadn't even entered the Promised Land. Sometimes God gives us instructions that do not seem relevant to us at the moment. But later we can see the importance of those instructions. Don't discard the lessons of the Bible because certain details seem irrelevant. Obey God now—in the future you will have a clearer understanding of the reasons for his instructions.

**6:61** The Israelites cast lots in order to take the decision-making

**6:63**
Josh 21:7, 34-40

**6:64**
Num 35:1-8
Josh 21:3, 41-42
1 Chr 6:57-60

**6:66**
Josh 21:20-26

62 The descendants of Gershon received by sacred lots thirteen towns from the territories of Issachar, Asher, Naphtali, and from the Bashan area of Manasseh, east of the Jordan.

63 The descendants of Merari received by sacred lots twelve towns from the territories of Reuben, Gad, and Zebulun.

64 So the people of Israel assigned all these towns and pasturelands to the Levites. 65 The towns in the territories of Judah, Simeon, and Benjamin, mentioned above, were assigned to them by means of sacred lots.

66 The descendants of Kohath were given the following towns from the territory of Ephraim, each with its pasturelands: 67 Shechem (a city of refuge in the hill country of Ephraim),* Gezer, 68 Jokmeam, Beth-horon, 69 Aijalon, and Gath-rimmon. 70 The remaining descendants of Kohath were assigned the towns of Aner and Bileam from the territory of the half-tribe of Manasseh, each with its pasturelands.

71 The descendants of Gershon received the towns of Golan (in Bashan) and Ashtaroth from the territory of the half-tribe of Manasseh, each with its pasturelands. 72 From the territory of Issachar, they were given Kedesh, Daberath, 73 Ramoth, and Anem, each with its pasturelands. 74 From the territory of Asher, they received Mashal, Abdon, 75 Hukok, and Rehob, each with its pasturelands. 76 From the territory of Naphtali, they were given Kedesh in Galilee, Hammon, and Kiriathaim, each with its pasturelands.

77 The remaining descendants of Merari received the towns of Jokneam, Kartah,* Rimmon,* and Tabor from the territory of Zebulun, each with its pasturelands. 78 From the territory of Reuben, east of the Jordan River opposite Jericho, they received Bezer (a desert town), Jahaz,* 79 Kedemoth, and Mephaath, each with its pasturelands. 80 And from the territory of Gad, they received Ramoth in Gilead, Mahanaim, 81 Heshbon, and Jazer, each with its pasturelands.

## Descendants of Issachar

**7:1**
Gen 46:13

**7:2**
2 Sam 24:1-9

**7** The four sons of Issachar were Tola, Puah, Jashub, and Shimron. 2 The sons of Tola were Uzzi, Rephaiah, Jeriel, Jahmai, Ibsam, and Shemuel. Each of them was the leader of an ancestral clan. At the time of King David, the total number of mighty warriors listed in the records of these clans was 22,600.

3 The son of Uzzi was Izrahiah. The sons of Izrahiah were Michael, Obadiah, Joel, and Isshiah. These five became the leaders of clans. 4 All of them had many wives and many sons, so the total number of men available for military service among their descendants was 36,000.

5 The total number of mighty warriors from all the clans of the tribe of Issachar was 87,000. All of them were listed in their genealogical records.

## Descendants of Benjamin

**7:6**
1 Chr 8:1-40

6 Three of Benjamin's sons were Bela, Beker, and Jediael. 7 The five sons of Bela were Ezbon, Uzzi, Uzziel, Jerimoth, and Iri. Each of them was the leader of an ancestral clan. The total number of mighty warriors from these clans was 22,034, as listed in their genealogical records.

8 The sons of Beker were Zemirah, Joash, Eliezer, Elioenai, Omri, Jeremoth, Abijah, Anathoth, and Alemeth. 9 Each of them was the leader of an ancestral clan. The total number of mighty warriors and leaders from these clans was 20,200, as listed in their genealogical records.

10 The son of Jediael was Bilhan. The sons of Bilhan were Jeush, Benjamin, Ehud, Kenaanah, Zethan, Tarshish, and Ahishahar. 11 Each of them was the leader of an ancestral clan. From these clans the total number of mighty warriors ready for war was 17,200.

12 The sons of Ir were Shuppim and Huppim. Hushim was the son of Aher.

## Descendants of Naphtali

**7:13**
Gen 30:8

13 The sons of Naphtali were Jahzeel,* Guni, Jezer, and Shillem.* They were all descendants of Jacob's concubine Bilhah.

6:66-67 As in parallel text at Josh 21:21. Hebrew text reads *were given the cities of refuge: Shechem in the hill country of Ephraim, and the following towns, each with its pasturelands.* 6:77a As in Greek version (see also Josh 21:34); Hebrew lacks *Jokneam, Kartah.* 6:77b As in Greek version (see also Josh 19:13); Hebrew reads *Rimmono.* 6:78 Hebrew *Jahzah,* a variant spelling of Jahaz. 7:13a As in parallel text at Gen 46:24; Hebrew reads *Jahziel,* a variant spelling of Jahzeel. 7:13b As in some Hebrew and Greek manuscripts (see also Gen 46:24; Num 26:49); most Hebrew manuscripts read *Shallum.*

## Descendants of Manasseh

[14] The descendants of Manasseh through his Aramean concubine included Asriel. She also bore Makir, the father of Gilead. [15] Makir found wives for* Huppim and Shuppim. Makir had a sister named Maacah. One of his descendants was Zelophehad, who had only daughters.

[16] Makir's wife, Maacah, gave birth to a son whom she named Peresh. His brother's name was Sheresh. The sons of Peresh were Ulam and Rakem. [17] The son of Ulam was Bedan. All these were considered Gileadites, descendants of Makir son of Manasseh.

[18] Makir's sister Hammoleketh gave birth to Ishhod, Abiezer, and Mahlah.

[19] The sons of Shemida were Ahian, Shechem, Likhi, and Aniam.

**7:14**
Gen 50:23
Num 26:29-30

## Descendants of Ephraim

[20] The descendants of Ephraim were Shuthelah, Bered, Tahath, Eleadah, Tahath, [21] Zabad, Shuthelah, Ezer, and Elead. These two were killed trying to steal livestock from the local farmers near Gath. [22] Their father, Ephraim, mourned for them a long time, and his relatives came to comfort him. [23] Afterward Ephraim slept with his wife, and she became pregnant and gave birth to a son. Ephraim named him Beriah* because of the tragedy his family had suffered. [24] He had a daughter named Sheerah. She built the towns of Lower and Upper Beth-horon and Uzzen-sheerah.

[25] The descendants of Ephraim included Rephah, Resheph, Telah, Tahan, [26] Ladan, Ammihud, Elishama, [27] Nun, and Joshua.

[28] The descendants of Ephraim lived in the territory that included Bethel and its surrounding towns to the south, Naaran to the east, Gezer and its villages to the west, and Shechem and its surrounding villages to the north as far as Ayyah and its towns. [29] Along the border of Manasseh were the towns of Beth-shan,* Taanach, Megiddo, Dor, and their surrounding villages. The descendants of Joseph son of Israel* lived in these towns.

**7:20**
Num 26:35-36

**7:24**
Josh 16:3, 5

**7:25-27**
Exod 17:9-14;
24:13

**7:29**
Josh 17:7-11

## Descendants of Asher

[30] The sons of Asher were Imnah, Ishvah, Ishvi, and Beriah. They had a sister named Serah.

[31] The sons of Beriah were Heber and Malkiel (the father of Birzaith).

[32] The sons of Heber were Japhlet, Shomer, and Hotham. They had a sister named Shua.

[33] The sons of Japhlet were Pasach, Bimhal, and Ashvath.

[34] The sons of Shomer were Ahi,* Rohgah, Hubbah, and Aram.

[35] The sons of his brother Helem* were Zophah, Imna, Shelesh, and Amal.

[36] The sons of Zophah were Suah, Harnepher, Shual, Beri, Imrah, [37] Bezer, Hod, Shamma, Shilshah, Ithran,* and Beera.

[38] The sons of Jether were Jephunneh, Pispah, and Ara.

[39] The sons of Ulla were Arah, Hanniel, and Rizia.

[40] Each of these descendants of Asher was the head of an ancestral clan. They were all select men—mighty warriors and outstanding leaders. The total number of men available for military service was 26,000, as listed in their genealogical records.

**7:30**
Gen 46:17
Num 26:44-46

## Descendants of Benjamin

**8** Benjamin's first son was Bela, the second was Ashbel, the third was Aharah, [2] the fourth was Nohah, and the fifth was Rapha.

[3] The sons of Bela were Addar, Gera, Abihud,* [4] Abishua, Naaman, Ahoah, [5] Gera, Shephuphan, and Huram.

[6] The sons of Ehud, leaders of the clans living at Geba, were exiled to Manahath. [7] Ehud's sons were Naaman, Ahijah, and Gera. Gera, who led them into exile, was the father of Uzza and Ahihud.*

[8] After Shaharaim divorced his wives Hushim and Baara, he had children in the land

**8:1**
Gen 46:21
1 Chr 7:6-12

**7:15** Or *Makir took a wife from.* The meaning of the Hebrew is uncertain.   **7:23** *Beriah* sounds like a Hebrew term meaning "tragedy" or "misfortune."   **7:29a** Hebrew *Beth-shean,* a variant spelling of Beth-shan.   **7:29b** *Israel* is the name that God gave to Jacob.   **7:34** Or *The sons of Shomer, his brother, were.*   **7:35** Possibly another name for *Hotham;* compare 7:32.   **7:37** Possibly another name for *Jether;* compare 7:38.   **8:3** Possibly *Gera the father of Ehud;* compare 8:6.   **8:7** Or *Gera, that is Heglam, was the father of Uzza and Ahihud.*

**7:27** Joshua was one of Israel's great leaders, leading the people into the Promised Land. His story is told in the book of Joshua. His Profile is found in Joshua 2, p. 317.

**8:8-10** These verses list Shaharaim's children by Hodesh after he had divorced his first two wives, Hushim and Baara. Divorce and polygamy are sometimes recorded in the Old Testament of Moab. [9]His wife Hodesh gave birth to Jobab, Zibia, Mesha, Malcam, [10]Jeuz, Sakia, and Mirmah. These sons all became the leaders of clans.

8:12
Ezra 2:33
Neh 6:2; 7:37;
11:35

[11]Shaharaim's wife Hushim had already given birth to Abitub and Elpaal. [12]The sons of Elpaal were Eber, Misham, Shemed (who built the towns of Ono and Lod and their nearby villages), [13]Beriah, and Shema. They were the leaders of the clans living in Aijalon, and they drove out the inhabitants of Gath.

8:13
Josh 10:12; 11:22

[14]Ahio, Shashak, Jeremoth, [15]Zebadiah, Arad, Eder, [16]Michael, Ishpah, and Joha were the sons of Beriah.

[17]Zebadiah, Meshullam, Hizki, Heber, [18]Ishmerai, Izliah, and Jobab were the sons of Elpaal.

[19]Jakim, Zicri, Zabdi, [20]Elienai, Zillethai, Eliel, [21]Adaiah, Beraiah, and Shimrath were the sons of Shimei.

[22]Ishpan, Eber, Eliel, [23]Abdon, Zicri, Hanan, [24]Hananiah, Elam, Anthothijah, [25]Iphdeiah, and Penuel were the sons of Shashak.

[26]Shamsherai, Shehariah, Athaliah, [27]Jaareshiah, Elijah, and Zicri were the sons of Jeroham.

[28]These were the leaders of the ancestral clans; they were listed in their genealogical records, and they all lived in Jerusalem.

## The Family of Saul

8:29
Josh 9:3

[29]Jeiel* (the father of* Gibeon) lived in the town of Gibeon. His wife's name was Maacah, [30]and his oldest son was named Abdon. Jeiel's other sons were Zur, Kish, Baal, Ner,* Nadab, [31]Gedor, Ahio, Zechariah,* [32]and Mikloth, who was the father of Shimeam.* All these families lived near each other in Jerusalem.

8:33
1 Sam 9:1;
14:49-50
1 Chr 9:39-44

[33] Ner was the father of Kish.

Kish was the father of Saul.

Saul was the father of Jonathan, Malkishua, Abinadab, and Esh-baal.

8:34
2 Sam 4:4

[34] Jonathan was the father of Merib-baal.

Merib-baal was the father of Micah.

[35] Micah was the father of Pithon, Melech, Tahrea,* and Ahaz.

[36] Ahaz was the father of Jadah.*

Jadah was the father of Alemeth, Azmaveth, and Zimri.

Zimri was the father of Moza.

[37] Moza was the father of Binea.

Binea was the father of Rephaiah.*

Rephaiah was the father of Eleasah.

Eleasah was the father of Azel.

[38]Azel had six sons: Azrikam, Bokeru, Ishmael, Sheariah, Obadiah, and Hanan. These were the sons of Azel.

[39]Azel's brother Eshek had three sons: the first was Ulam, the second was Jeush, and the third was Eliphelet. [40]Ulam's sons were all mighty warriors and expert archers. They had many sons and grandsons—150 in all.

All these were descendants of Benjamin.

**8:29a** As in some Greek manuscripts (see also 9:35); Hebrew lacks *Jeiel*. **8:29b** Or *the founder of.* **8:30** As in some Greek manuscripts (see also 9:36); Hebrew lacks *Ner.* **8:31** As in parallel text at 9:37; Hebrew reads *Zeker,* a variant spelling of Zechariah. **8:32** As in parallel text at 9:38; Hebrew reads *Shimeah,* a variant spelling of Shimeam. **8:35** As in parallel text at 9:41; Hebrew reads *Tarea,* a variant spelling of Tahrea. **8:36** As in parallel text at 9:42; Hebrew reads *Jehoaddah,* a variant spelling of Jadah. **8:37** As in parallel text at 9:43; Hebrew reads *Raphah,* a variant spelling of Rephaiah.

---

without critical comments. This does not mean that God takes divorce lightly. Malachi 2:15, 16 says to "remain loyal to the wife of your youth. 'For I hate divorce!' says the LORD, the God of Israel." Jesus explained that although divorce was allowed, it was not God's will: "Moses permitted divorce only as a concession to your hard hearts, but it was not what God had originally intended" (Matthew 19:8). Don't assume that God approves of an act because it isn't vigorously condemned in every related Bible reference.

**8:33** Saul, Israel's first king, was very inconsistent. His story is found in 1 Samuel 9–31, and his Profile is in 1 Samuel 10,

p. 425. Saul's son Jonathan was the opposite. Although Jonathan was the rightful heir to the throne, he realized that David was God's choice to be Israel's next king. Instead of being jealous, Jonathan was David's friend and even helped him escape from Saul's attempts at murder. Jonathan's story is told in 1 Samuel 14–31. His Profile is found in 1 Samuel 21, p. 445.

# 9

So all Israel was listed in the genealogical records in *The Book of the Kings of Israel.*

## 3. Returnees from exile in Babylon
### *The Returning Exiles*

The people of Judah were exiled to Babylon because they were unfaithful to the LORD. ²The first of the exiles to return to their property in their former towns were priests, Levites, Temple servants, and other Israelites. ³Some of the people from the tribes of Judah, Benjamin, Ephraim, and Manasseh came and settled in Jerusalem.

⁴One family that returned was that of Uthai son of Ammihud, son of Omri, son of Imri, son of Bani, a descendant of Perez son of Judah.
⁵Others returned from the Shilonite clan, including Asaiah (the oldest) and his sons.
⁶From the Zerahite clan, Jeuel returned with his relatives.
In all, 690 families from the tribe of Judah returned.

⁷From the tribe of Benjamin came Sallu son of Meshullam, son of Hodaviah, son of Hassenuah; ⁸Ibneiah son of Jeroham; Elah son of Uzzi, son of Micri; and Meshullam son of Shephatiah, son of Reuel, son of Ibnijah.
⁹These men were all leaders of clans, and they were listed in their genealogical records. In all, 956 families from the tribe of Benjamin returned.

### *The Returning Priests*

¹⁰Among the priests who returned were Jedaiah, Jehoiarib, Jakin, ¹¹Azariah son of Hilkiah, son of Meshullam, son of Zadok, son of Meraioth, son of Ahitub. Azariah was the chief officer of the house of God.
¹²Other returning priests were Adaiah son of Jeroham, son of Pashhur, son of Malkijah, and Maasai son of Adiel, son of Jahzerah, son of Meshullam, son of Meshillemith, son of Immer.
¹³In all, 1,760 priests returned. They were heads of clans and very able men. They were responsible for ministering at the house of God.

### *The Returning Levites*

¹⁴The Levites who returned were Shemaiah son of Hasshub, son of Azrikam, son of Hashabiah, a descendant of Merari; ¹⁵Bakbakkar; Heresh; Galal; Mattaniah son of Mica, son of Zicri, son of Asaph; ¹⁶Obadiah son of Shemaiah, son of Galal, son of Jeduthun; and Berekiah son of Asa, son of Elkanah, who lived in the area of Netophah.
¹⁷The gatekeepers who returned were Shallum, Akkub, Talmon, Ahiman, and their relatives. Shallum was the chief gatekeeper. ¹⁸Prior to this time, they were responsible for the King's Gate on the east side. These men served as gatekeepers for the camps of the Levites. ¹⁹Shallum was the son of Kore, a descendant of Abiasaph,* from the clan of Korah. He and his relatives, the Korahites, were responsible for guarding the entrance to the sanctuary, just as their ancestors had guarded the Tabernacle in the camp of the LORD.
²⁰Phinehas son of Eleazar had been in charge of the gatekeepers in earlier times, and the LORD had been with him. ²¹And later Zechariah son of Meshelemiah was responsible for guarding the entrance to the Tabernacle.*

**9:19** Hebrew *Ebiasaph,* a variant spelling of Abiasaph; compare Exod 6:24.  **9:21** Hebrew *Tent of Meeting.*

**9:1**
1 Chr 5:25
**9:2**
Ezra 2:43, 58, 70;
8:20
Neh 11:3-22
**9:4**
Gen 46:12
**9:9**
Neh 11:8
**9:10**
Neh 11:10-14
**9:14**
Neh 11:15-19
**9:17**
Ezek 46:1-2
**9:20**
Num 25:7-13
**9:21**
1 Chr 26:2, 14

---

**9:1** Although not every person in Judah was unfaithful, the entire nation was carried away into captivity. Everyone was affected by the sin of a few. Even if we don't participate in a certain widespread wrongdoing, we will still be affected by those who do. It is not enough to say, "I didn't do it." We must speak out against the sins of our society.

**9:1ff** Chronologically, this chapter could be placed at the end of 2 Chronicles because it records the names of the exiles who returned from the Babylonian captivity. The writer included it here to show his concern for their need, as a nation, to return to what made them great in the first place—obedience to God.

**9:10, 11** When we think of doing God's work, usually preaching, teaching, singing, and other kinds of up-front leadership come to mind. Azariah, however, was chief officer in charge of

the house of God, and he was singled out for special mention. Whatever role you have in church, it is important to God. He appreciates your service and the attitude you have as you do it.

**9:17, 18** Gatekeepers guarded the four main entrances to the Temple and opened the gates each morning for those who wanted to worship. In addition, they did other day-to-day chores to keep the Temple running smoothly—cleaning, preparing the offerings for sacrifice, and accounting for the gifts designated to the Temple (9:22-32).

Gatekeepers had to be reliable, honest, and trustworthy. The people in our churches who handle the offerings and care for the materials and functions of the building follow in a great tradition, and we should honor them for their reliability and service.

22In all, there were 212 gatekeepers in those days, and they were listed according to the genealogies in their villages. David and Samuel the seer had appointed their ancestors because they were reliable men. 23These gatekeepers and their descendants, by their divisions, were responsible for guarding the entrance to the house of the LORD when that house was a tent. 24The gatekeepers were stationed on all four sides—east, west, north, and south. 25Their relatives in the villages came regularly to share their duties for seven-day periods. 26The four chief gatekeepers, all Levites, were trusted officials, for they were responsible for the rooms and treasuries at the house of God. 27They would spend the night around the house of God, since it was their duty to guard it and to open the gates every morning.

28Some of the gatekeepers were assigned to care for the various articles used in worship. They checked them in and out to avoid any loss. 29Others were responsible for the furnishings, the items in the sanctuary, and the supplies, such as choice flour, wine, olive oil, frankincense, and spices. 30But it was the priests who blended the spices. 31Mattithiah, a Levite and the oldest son of Shallum the Korahite, was entrusted with baking the bread used in the offerings. 32And some members of the clan of Kohath were in charge of preparing the bread to be set on the table each Sabbath day.

33The musicians, all prominent Levites, lived at the Temple. They were exempt from other responsibilities since they were on duty at all hours. 34All these men lived in Jerusalem. They were the heads of Levite families and were listed as prominent leaders in their genealogical records.

## King Saul's Family Tree

35Jeiel (the father of* Gibeon) lived in the town of Gibeon. His wife's name was Maacah, 36and his oldest son was named Abdon. Jeiel's other sons were Zur, Kish, Baal, Ner, Nadab, 37Gedor, Ahio, Zechariah, and Mikloth. 38Mikloth was the father of Shimeam. All these families lived near each other in Jerusalem.

39 Ner was the father of Kish.
Kish was the father of Saul.
Saul was the father of Jonathan, Malkishua, Abinadab, and Esh-baal.
40 Jonathan was the father of Merib-baal.
Merib-baal was the father of Micah.
41 The sons of Micah were Pithon, Melech, Tahrea, and Ahaz.*
42 Ahaz was the father of Jadah.*
Jadah was the father of Alemeth, Azmaveth, and Zimri.
Zimri was the father of Moza.
43 Moza was the father of Binea.
Binea's son was Rephaiah.
Rephaiah's son was Eleasah.
Eleasah's son was Azel.
44Azel had six sons, whose names were Azrikam, Bokeru, Ishmael, Sheariah, Obadiah, and Hanan. These were the sons of Azel.

9:35 Or the founder of.   9:41 As in Syriac version and Latin Vulgate (see also 8:35); Hebrew lacks and Ahaz.
9:42 As in some Hebrew manuscripts and Greek version (see also 8:36); Hebrew reads Jarah.

### Cross-references (margin)
9:25 2 Kgs 11:5, 7; 2 Chr 23:8
9:27 1 Chr 23:30-32
9:29 1 Chr 23:29
9:30 Exod 30:23-25
9:32 Lev 24:5-8
9:33 1 Chr 6:31-47; 25:1-31; Ps 134:1
9:35 1 Chr 8:29-32
9:39 1 Chr 8:33-38
9:41 1 Chr 8:35-37

---

9:22-32 The priests put a great deal of time and care into worship. Not only did they perform rather complicated tasks (described in Leviticus 1–9); they also took care of many pieces of equipment. Everything relating to worship was carefully prepared and maintained so they and all the people could enter worship with their minds and hearts focused on God.

In our busy world, it is easy to rush into our one-hour-a-week worship services without preparing ourselves for worship beforehand. We reflect and worry about the week's problems; we pray about whatever comes into our minds; and we do not meditate on the words we are singing. But God wants our worship to be conducted "properly and in order" (1 Corinthians 14:40). Just as we prepare to meet a business associate or invited guests, we should carefully prepare to meet our King in worship.

9:33, 34 Worship was the primary focus of many Israelites, whose vocation centered on the house of the Lord. Worship

(appreciating God for his nature and worth) should occupy the core of our lives and not just a few minutes once a week. We, too, can worship at any time if we stay aware of God's presence and guidance in all situations and if we maintain an attitude of serving him. Build your life around the worship of God rather than making worship just another activity in a busy schedule.

## B. THE REIGN OF DAVID (10:1—29:30)

David becomes king over all Israel and captures the city of Jerusalem. God promises blessings to him and the nation, but David is not allowed to build the Temple. Instead, he begins to make preparations for its construction. Although stumbling and falling occasionally, David walks step by step with God, sincerely wanting to be obedient. Through David's successes and his failures, we learn the importance of giving our whole heart to God and letting him be the focus of our life, striving each day to be consistent in our obedience to his will.

### 1. David becomes king over all of Israel

*The Death of King Saul*

**10** Now the Philistines attacked Israel, and the men of Israel fled before them. Many were slaughtered on the slopes of Mount Gilboa. ²The Philistines closed in on Saul and his sons, and they killed three of his sons—Jonathan, Abinadab, and Malkishua. ³The fighting grew very fierce around Saul, and the Philistine archers caught up with him and wounded him.

⁴Saul groaned to his armor bearer, "Take your sword and kill me before these pagan Philistines come to taunt and torture me."

But his armor bearer was afraid and would not do it. So Saul took his own sword and fell on it. ⁵When his armor bearer realized that Saul was dead, he fell on his own sword and died. ⁶So Saul and his three sons died there together, bringing his dynasty to an end.

⁷When all the Israelites in the Jezreel Valley saw that their army had fled and that Saul and his sons were dead, they abandoned their towns and fled. So the Philistines moved in and occupied their towns.

⁸The next day, when the Philistines went out to strip the dead, they found the bodies of Saul and his sons on Mount Gilboa. ⁹So they stripped off Saul's armor and cut off his head. Then they proclaimed the good news of Saul's death before their idols and to the people throughout the land of Philistia. ¹⁰They placed his armor in the temple of their gods, and they fastened his head to the temple of Dagon.

¹¹But when everyone in Jabesh-gilead heard about everything the Philistines had done to Saul, ¹²all their mighty warriors brought the bodies of Saul and his sons back to Jabesh. Then they buried their bones beneath the great tree at Jabesh, and they fasted for seven days.

¹³So Saul died because he was unfaithful to the LORD. He failed to obey the LORD's command, and he even consulted a medium ¹⁴instead of asking the LORD for guidance. So the LORD killed him and turned the kingdom over to David son of Jesse.

**10:1**
1 Sam 31:1-13
**10:2**
1 Sam 31:2, 4

**10:9**
1 Sam 31:9

**10:13**
Lev 19:31
1 Sam 13:13-14;
15:23; 28:7
**10:14**
1 Sam 15:28
1 Chr 12:23

---

**10:1** The chronology of chapters 1–9 covers Israelite history from Creation to the exile in Babylon (586 B.C.). At this point, the narrative goes back to the beginning of Israel's kingdom period, picking up with Israel's first king, Saul. First Chronicles 10 begins with Saul's death. To learn about his reign, read 1 Samuel.

**10:10** Dagon, the most important god of the Philistines, was believed to bring rain and provide rich harvests. The Philistines built temples to him when they settled in the grain-producing land of Canaan. In times of drought, people begged Dagon for pity, even to the point of sacrificing their children in his temples. In times of plenty, the temples were used for twisted forms of entertainment, such as the humiliation of captives (see Judges 16:23-30). But Dagon, like the other pagan gods, was powerless against the one true God (1 Samuel 5:1-7).

**10:11, 12** The actions of the valiant warriors who brought back and buried the bodies of King Saul and his sons should encourage us to respect our God-given leaders. David showed respect for Saul's position, even when Saul was chasing him to kill him (1 Samuel 26). How easy it is to be critical of those in authority over us, focusing only on their weaknesses. We cannot excuse sin, but we should respect the positions of those in authority, whether at work, at church, or in government. First Thessalonians 5:12, 13 gives instructions for honoring church leaders. Romans 13:1ff gives instructions for relating to government leaders.

**10:13, 14** Saul's unfaithfulness was both active and passive; he not only did wrong, but he also *failed to do right*. He actively disobeyed by attempting murder, ignoring God's instructions, and seeking guidance from a medium. He passively disobeyed

by neglecting to ask God for guidance as he ran the kingdom. Obedience, too, is both passive and active. It is not enough just to avoid what is wrong; we need to actively pursue what is right.

**10:13, 14** In the account in 1 Samuel 28, Saul asked the Lord for guidance but received no answer; this account implies that he did not ask God for help. The answer to this apparent contradiction lies in understanding Saul's motives and the timing of his request to God. His frantic requests came only when he had tried everything his own way. He never went to God unless there was nowhere else to turn. When he finally asked, God refused to answer. Saul sought God only when it suited him, and God rejected him for his constant stubbornness and rebellion.

**10:14** Throughout much of Saul's reign, David was forced to hide from him (1 Samuel 19–30). During this time David had opportunities to kill Saul (1 Samuel 24; 26) and to assume the throne that God had promised him (1 Samuel 16:1-13). But David trusted in God's promise that he would be king in God's good timing. It was not up to David to decide when Saul's reign would end. During the battle, God ended Saul's reign just as he had promised.

**10:14** Why does this verse say that the Lord killed Saul, when Saul took his own life (1 Samuel 31:3, 4)? God had rejected Saul because of his stubbornness and rebellion (1 Samuel 15:22-26) and had judged him for his sins (1 Samuel 28:16-19). God arranged a defeat in battle so that Saul would die and his kingdom would be taken from his family. If Saul had not taken his own life, the Philistine soldiers would have killed him.

### David Becomes King of All Israel

**11** Then all Israel gathered before David at Hebron and told him, "We are your own flesh and blood. ²In the past,* even when Saul was king, you were the one who really led the forces of Israel. And the LORD your God told you, 'You will be the shepherd of my people Israel. You will be the leader of my people Israel.'"

³So there at Hebron, David made a covenant before the LORD with all the elders of Israel. And they anointed him king of Israel, just as the LORD had promised through Samuel.

### David Captures Jerusalem

⁴Then David and all Israel went to Jerusalem (or Jebus, as it used to be called), where the Jebusites, the original inhabitants of the land, were living. ⁵The people of Jebus taunted David, saying, "You'll never get in here!" But David captured the fortress of Zion, which is now called the City of David.

⁶David had said to his troops, "Whoever is first to attack the Jebusites will become the commander of my armies!" And Joab, the son of David's sister Zeruiah, was first to attack, so he became the commander of David's armies.

⁷David made the fortress his home, and that is why it is called the City of David. ⁸He extended the city from the supporting terraces* to the surrounding area, while Joab rebuilt the rest of Jerusalem. ⁹And David became more and more powerful, because the LORD of Heaven's Armies was with him.

### David's Mightiest Warriors

¹⁰These are the leaders of David's mighty warriors. Together with all Israel, they decided to make David their king, just as the LORD had promised concerning Israel.

¹¹Here is the record of David's mightiest warriors: The first was Jashobeam the Hacmonite, who was leader of the Three—the mightiest warriors among David's men.* He once used his spear to kill 300 enemy warriors in a single battle.

¹²Next in rank among the Three was Eleazar son of Dodai,* a descendant of Ahoah. ¹³He was with David in the battle against the Philistines at Pas-dammim. The battle took place in a field full of barley, and the Israelite army fled. ¹⁴But Eleazar and David* held their ground in the middle of the field and beat back the Philistines. So the LORD saved them by giving them a great victory.

¹⁵Once when David was at the rock near the cave of Adullam, the Philistine army was camped in the valley of Rephaim. The Three (who were among the Thirty—an elite group among David's fighting men) went down to meet him there. ¹⁶David was staying in the stronghold at the time, and a Philistine detachment had occupied the town of Bethlehem.

**Cross-references (left margin):**
11:1-3 //2 Sam 5:1-3
11:2 2 Sam 5:2; 7:7
11:3 1 Sam 16:1-13
11:4-9 //2 Sam 5:6-10
11:4 Josh 15:8, 63; Judg 1:21
11:6 2 Sam 8:16
11:9 2 Sam 3:1
11:10 2 Sam 23:8-39; 1 Chr 11:3
11:11 2 Sam 23:8
11:12 1 Chr 27:4
11:13 2 Sam 23:11-12
11:15 1 Chr 14:9
11:16 1 Sam 10:5

**11:2** Or *For some time.* **11:8** Hebrew *the millo.* The meaning of the Hebrew is uncertain. **11:11** As in some Greek manuscripts (see also 2 Sam 23:8); Hebrew reads *leader of the Thirty,* or *leader of the captains.* **11:12** As in parallel text at 2 Sam 23:9 (see also 1 Chr 27:4); Hebrew reads *Dodo,* a variant spelling of Dodai. **11:14** Hebrew *they.*

---

**11:1, 2** The details of how David came to power are given more completely in 2 Samuel. Chronicles emphasizes that *God* declared David to be the ruler although he used the efforts of many people, even some of Saul's own family. God is still sovereign over history, directing events to accomplish his will. The books of Chronicles demonstrate that no matter what people may do to try to hinder God's work, God still controls all events and works his will in them.

**11:3, 4** David was king over Judah for seven and a half years before he captured Jerusalem. When David was finally anointed king over all Israel, 20 years had passed since Samuel had anointed him (1 Samuel 16:1-13). God's promises are worth waiting for, even when his timetable doesn't match our expectations or desires.

**11:4** David chose Jerusalem as his capital for both political and military reasons. Jerusalem was near the center of the kingdom and, because it rested on a tribal border, was in neutral territory. Thus, its location decreased tribal jealousies. Jerusalem also sat on a high ridge, making it difficult to attack. (For more information on the city of Jerusalem, see the note on 2 Samuel 5:6.)

**11:9** David's power increased as a direct result of his consistent trust in God. In contrast, Saul's power decreased because he wanted all the credit for himself and ignored God (1 Samuel 15:17-26). Those who are concerned about building a name for themselves risk losing the very recognition they crave. Like David, we should be concerned for righteousness, honesty, and excellence and leave the results to God.

**11:12-14** Eleazar's action changed the course of a battle. When everyone around him ran, he held his ground alongside David and was saved by the Lord. In any struggle, fear can keep us from taking a stand for God and from participating in God's victories. Face your fear head-on. Find other believers along the way who are worth standing beside through thick and thin. If you are grounded in God, victory will come when you hold that ground.

**11:15** The Thirty were the most courageous and highest-ranking officers of David's army.

**11:15-19** These three men risked their lives just to serve and please David. David recognized that their loyalty to him was inspired by their devotion to God, so he poured out the water as a drink offering, demonstrating that only God is worthy of such devotion. Just as these men gave of themselves to serve David, we should put aside our own interests to serve other Christians (Romans 12:10). When we serve others, we are also serving God.

¹⁷David remarked longingly to his men, "Oh, how I would love some of that good water from the well by the gate in Bethlehem." ¹⁸So the Three broke through the Philistine lines, drew some water from the well by the gate in Bethlehem, and brought it back to David. But David refused to drink it. Instead, he poured it out as an offering to the LORD. ¹⁹"God forbid that I should drink this!" he exclaimed. "This water is as precious as the blood of these men* who risked their lives to bring it to me." So David did not drink it. These are examples of the exploits of the Three.

### David's Thirty Mighty Men

²⁰Abishai, the brother of Joab, was the leader of the Thirty.* He once used his spear to kill 300 enemy warriors in a single battle. It was by such feats that he became as famous as the Three. ²¹Abishai was the most famous of the Thirty and was their commander, though he was not one of the Three.

²²There was also Benaiah son of Jehoiada, a valiant warrior from Kabzeel. He did many heroic deeds, which included killing two champions* of Moab. Another time, on a snowy day, he chased a lion down into a pit and killed it. ²³Once, armed only with a club, he killed an Egyptian warrior who was 7½ feet* tall and whose spear was as thick as a weaver's beam. Benaiah wrenched the spear from the Egyptian's hand and killed him with it. ²⁴Deeds like these made Benaiah as famous as the three mightiest warriors. ²⁵He was more honored than the other members of the Thirty, though he was not one of the Three. And David made him captain of his bodyguard.

²⁶David's mighty warriors also included:

Asahel, Joab's brother;
Elhanan son of Dodo from Bethlehem;
²⁷ Shammah from Harod;*
Helez from Pelon;
²⁸ Ira son of Ikkesh from Tekoa;
Abiezer from Anathoth;
²⁹ Sibbecai from Hushah;
Zalmon* from Ahoah;
³⁰ Maharai from Netophah;
Heled son of Baanah from Netophah;
³¹ Ithai son of Ribai from Gibeah (in the land of Benjamin);
Benaiah from Pirathon;
³² Hurai from near Nahale-gaash*;
Abi-albon* from Arabah;
³³ Azmaveth from Bahurim*;
Eliahba from Shaalbon;
³⁴ the sons of Jashen* from Gizon;
Jonathan son of Shagee from Harar;
³⁵ Ahiam son of Sharar* from Harar;
Eliphal son of Ur;
³⁶ Hepher from Mekerah;
Ahijah from Pelon;
³⁷ Hezro from Carmel;
Paarai* son of Ezbai;
³⁸ Joel, the brother of Nathan;
Mibhar son of Hagri;
³⁹ Zelek from Ammon;
Naharai from Beeroth, Joab's armor bearer;
⁴⁰ Ira from Jattir;
Gareb from Jattir;
⁴¹ Uriah the Hittite;
Zabad son of Ahlai;

**11:22**
2 Sam 8:18

**11:23**
1 Sam 17:7

**11:19** Hebrew *Shall I drink the lifeblood of these men?*   **11:20** As in Syriac version; Hebrew reads *the Three;* also in 11:21.   **11:22** Or *two sons of Ariel.*   **11:23** Hebrew *5 cubits* [2.3 meters].   **11:27** As in parallel text at 2 Sam 23:25; Hebrew reads *Shammoth from Haror.*   **11:29** As in parallel text at 2 Sam 23:28; Hebrew reads *Ilai.*   **11:32a** Or *from the ravines of Gaash.*   **11:32b** As in parallel text at 2 Sam 23:31; Hebrew reads *Abiel.*   **11:33** As in parallel text at 2 Sam 23:31; Hebrew reads *Baharum.*   **11:34** As in parallel text at 2 Sam 23:32; Hebrew reads *sons of Hashem.* **11:35** As in parallel text at 2 Sam 23:33; Hebrew reads *son of Sacar.*   **11:37** As in parallel text at 2 Sam 23:35; Hebrew reads *Naarai.*

<sup>42</sup> Adina son of Shiza, the Reubenite leader who had thirty men with him;
<sup>43</sup> Hanan son of Maacah;
Joshaphat from Mithna;
<sup>44</sup> Uzzia from Ashtaroth;
Shama and Jeiel, the sons of Hotham, from Aroer;
<sup>45</sup> Jediael son of Shimri;
Joha, his brother, from Tiz;
<sup>46</sup> Eliel from Mahavah;
Jeribai and Joshaviah, the sons of Elnaam;
Ithmah from Moab;
<sup>47</sup> Eliel and Obed;
Jaasiel from Zobah.*

## Warriors Join David's Army

12:1
1 Sam 27:2-6

12:2
Judg 3:15; 20:16

**12** The following men joined David at Ziklag while he was hiding from Saul son of Kish. They were among the warriors who fought beside David in battle. <sup>2</sup>All of them were expert archers, and they could shoot arrows or sling stones with their left hand as well as their right. They were all relatives of Saul from the tribe of Benjamin. <sup>3</sup>Their leader was Ahiezer son of Shemaah from Gibeah; his brother Joash was second-in-command. These were the other warriors:

Jeziel and Pelet, sons of Azmaveth;
Beracah;
Jehu from Anathoth;
<sup>4</sup> Ishmaiah from Gibeon, a famous warrior and leader among the Thirty;
*Jeremiah, Jahaziel, Johanan, and Jozabad from Gederah;
<sup>5</sup> Eluzai, Jerimoth, Bealiah, Shemariah, and Shephatiah from Haruph;
<sup>6</sup> Elkanah, Isshiah, Azarel, Joezer, and Jashobeam, who were Korahites;
<sup>7</sup> Joelah and Zebadiah, sons of Jeroham from Gedor.

12:8
2 Sam 2:18

<sup>8</sup>Some brave and experienced warriors from the tribe of Gad also defected to David while he was at the stronghold in the wilderness. They were expert with both shield and spear, as fierce as lions and as swift as deer on the mountains.

<sup>9</sup> Ezer was their leader.
Obadiah was second.
Eliab was third.
<sup>10</sup> Mishmannah was fourth.
Jeremiah was fifth.
<sup>11</sup> Attai was sixth.
Eliel was seventh.

**11:47** Or *the Mezobaite*.    **12:4** Verses 12:4b-40 are numbered 12:5-41 in Hebrew text.

---

**12:1** Ziklag was a city in Philistia to which David had escaped to hide from Saul. Achish, the Philistine ruler of the area, was happy to have a famous Israelite warrior defect to his land. He did not know, however, that David was only pretending loyalty. Achish gave the city of Ziklag to David, his family, and his army (1 Samuel 27:5-7). David's whereabouts were not a great secret, and many loyal followers joined him there.

**12:1ff** David surrounded himself with great warriors, the best of the Israelite army. What qualities made them worthy to be David's warriors and servants? (1) They had practiced long and hard to perfect their skills (with bow, sling, and spear); (2) they were mentally tough and determined ("fierce as lions," 12:8); (3) they were physically in shape ("as swift as deer," 12:8); (4) they were dedicated to serving God and David. Weak leaders are easily threatened by competent subordinates, but strong leaders surround themselves with the best. They are not intimidated by able and competent followers.

**12:1-7** All the warriors mentioned here were from the tribe of Benjamin. Even members of Saul's own tribe (1 Samuel 9:1, 2) were deserting him to help David become king over all Israel.

It was clear to them that God had chosen David to be Israel's next leader.

**12:2** Archers and slingers had special weapons. The sling was unassuming in appearance but deadly in battle. A shallow leather pouch with a cord of leather or goats' hair attached to each side, the sling was whirled around the head. When one side was released, it sent a stone to its target. The bow and arrow had been in use for thousands of years. Arrowheads were made of stone, wood, or bone because the Philistines still had a monopoly on metalworking (1 Samuel 13:19, 20). Arrow shafts were made of reed or wood, and bowstrings were made of animal gut.

**12:8** While the men of Benjamin were expert archers and slingers, the warriors of Gad were experts with the shield and spear. Israelite spears had wood shafts with spearheads of bone or stone and were often thrown through the air toward their mark. Philistine spears had bronze shafts and iron spearheads, and their shields were made of wood and overlaid with leather. Large shields were often carried by an armor bearer, whose main task was to protect the warrior.

¹²Johanan was eighth.
   Elzabad was ninth.
¹³Jeremiah was tenth.
   Macbannai was eleventh.

¹⁴These warriors from Gad were army commanders. The weakest among them could take on a hundred regular troops, and the strongest could take on a thousand! ¹⁵These were the men who crossed the Jordan River during its seasonal flooding at the beginning of the year and drove out all the people living in the lowlands on both the east and west banks.

¹⁶Others from Benjamin and Judah came to David at the stronghold. ¹⁷David went out to meet them and said, "If you have come in peace to help me, we are friends. But if you have come to betray me to my enemies when I am innocent, then may the God of our ancestors see it and punish you."

¹⁸Then the Spirit came upon Amasai, the leader of the Thirty, and he said,

"We are yours, David!
   We are on your side, son of Jesse.
Peace and prosperity be with you,
   and success to all who help you,
   for your God is the one who helps you."

So David let them join him, and he made them officers over his troops.

¹⁹Some men from Manasseh defected from the Israelite army and joined David when he set out with the Philistines to fight against Saul. But as it turned out, the Philistine rulers refused to let David and his men go with them. After much discussion, they sent them back, for they said, "It will cost us our heads if David switches loyalties to Saul and turns against us."

²⁰Here is a list of the men from Manasseh who defected to David as he was returning to Ziklag: Adnah, Jozabad, Jediael, Michael, Jozabad, Elihu, and Zillethai. Each commanded 1,000 troops from the tribe of Manasseh. ²¹They helped David chase down bands of raiders, for they were all brave and able warriors who became commanders in his army. ²²Day after day more men joined David until he had a great army, like the army of God.

²³These are the numbers of armed warriors who joined David at Hebron. They were all eager to see David become king instead of Saul, just as the Lord had promised.

²⁴From the tribe of Judah, there were 6,800 warriors armed with shields and spears.
²⁵From the tribe of Simeon, there were 7,100 brave warriors.
²⁶From the tribe of Levi, there were 4,600 warriors. ²⁷This included Jehoiada, leader of
   the family of Aaron, who had 3,700 under his command. ²⁸This also included Zadok,
   a brave young warrior, with 22 members of his family who were all officers.
²⁹From the tribe of Benjamin, Saul's relatives, there were 3,000 warriors. Most of the
   men from Benjamin had remained loyal to Saul until this time.
³⁰From the tribe of Ephraim, there were 20,800 brave warriors, each highly respected
   in his own clan.
³¹From the half-tribe of Manasseh west of the Jordan, 18,000 men were designated
   by name to help David become king.

**12:14** Deut 32:30
**12:15** Josh 3:15; 4:18
**12:18** Judg 3:10; 6:34 1 Chr 2:17
**12:19** 1 Sam 29:2-9
**12:21** 1 Sam 30:1
**12:22** Josh 5:13-15
**12:23** 2 Sam 2:3-4 1 Chr 10:14; 11:10
**12:28** 1 Chr 6:8
**12:29** 2 Sam 2:8-9

---

**12:18** How did the Holy Spirit work in Old Testament times? When there was an important job to be done, God chose a person to do it, and the Spirit gave that person the needed power and ability. The Spirit gave Bezalel artistic ability (Exodus 31:1-5), Jephthah military prowess (Judges 11:29), David power to rule (1 Samuel 16:13), and Zechariah an authoritative word of prophecy (2 Chronicles 24:20). Here the Holy Spirit came upon Amasai, one of David's warriors. The Spirit came upon individuals in order to accomplish specific goals. Beginning at Pentecost, however, the Spirit came upon all believers, not only to empower them to do God's will, but also to dwell in them day by day (Acts 2:14-21). If you are a believer in Jesus Christ, you will experience the Holy Spirit's ongoing work in your life as well as special times of filling for God's purposes. Expect God's Spirit to work in and through you.

**12:22** David "had a great army, like the army of God." Men were drawn to David by the reputation of his great warriors, the news of their victories, and their desire to see God's will done in making David king. People are often drawn to a great cause and the brave, determined people who support it. As believers, we have the greatest cause—the salvation of people. If we are brave, determined, and faithful, others will be drawn to work with us.

**12:26-29** In Numbers 1:47-50, God said that the Levites were to be exempt from military service. Why then are they listed as part of David's army? Although they were exempt from the draft, they strongly supported David and volunteered their services to help install him as king.

12:32
Esth 1:13
Ps 12:2

32From the tribe of Issachar, there were 200 leaders of the tribe with their relatives. All these men understood the signs of the times and knew the best course for Israel to take.

33From the tribe of Zebulun, there were 50,000 skilled warriors. They were fully armed and prepared for battle and completely loyal to David.

34From the tribe of Naphtali, there were 1,000 officers and 37,000 warriors armed with shields and spears.

35From the tribe of Dan, there were 28,600 warriors, all prepared for battle.

36From the tribe of Asher, there were 40,000 trained warriors, all prepared for battle.

37From the east side of the Jordan River—where the tribes of Reuben and Gad and the half-tribe of Manasseh lived—there were 120,000 troops armed with every kind of weapon.

12:38
2 Sam 5:1-3
1 Chr 12:33

38All these men came in battle array to Hebron with the single purpose of making David the king over all Israel. In fact, everyone in Israel agreed that David should be their king.

12:40
1 Sam 25:18

39They feasted and drank with David for three days, for preparations had been made by their relatives for their arrival. 40And people from as far away as Issachar, Zebulun, and Naphtali brought food on donkeys, camels, mules, and oxen. Vast supplies of flour, fig cakes, clusters of raisins, wine, olive oil, cattle, sheep, and goats were brought to the celebration. There was great joy throughout the land of Israel.

## 2. David brings the Ark to Jerusalem
### David Attempts to Move the Ark

13:1-4
//2 Sam 6:1-11

**13** David consulted with all his officials, including the generals and captains of his army.* 2Then he addressed the entire assembly of Israel as follows: "If you approve and if it is the will of the LORD our God, let us send messages to all the Israelites throughout the land, including the priests and Levites in their towns and pasturelands. Let us invite them to come and join us. 3It is time to bring back the Ark of our God, for we neglected it during the reign of Saul."

13:3
1 Sam 7:1-2
13:5
1 Sam 6:21; 7:1
2 Sam 6:1
1 Kgs 8:65
1 Chr 15:3
13:6
Josh 15:9
2 Kgs 19:15
13:7
1 Sam 7:1

4The whole assembly agreed to this, for the people could see it was the right thing to do. 5So David summoned all Israel, from the Shihor Brook of Egypt in the south all the way to the town of Lebo-hamath in the north, to join in bringing the Ark of God from Kiriath-jearim. 6Then David and all Israel went to Baalah of Judah (also called Kiriath-jearim) to bring back the Ark of God, which bears the name* of the LORD who is enthroned between the cherubim. 7They placed the Ark of God on a new cart and brought it from Abinadab's

13:1 Hebrew *the commanders of thousands and of hundreds.*   13:6 Or *the Ark of God, where the Name is proclaimed—the name.*

---

**12:32** The 200 leaders from the tribe of Issachar "understood the signs of the times." As a result, their knowledge and judgment provided needed help in making decisions for the nation. For leaders today, it is equally necessary to know what is happening in society in order to plan the best course of action for the church. Knowledge of current events, trends, and needs helps us understand people's thoughts and attitudes. This gives leaders information to help them make wise decisions for the church and make God's message relevant to people's lives.

**12:40** The people were ready for change. They had suffered under Saul's leadership because of his disobedience to God (see 10:13). They were so overjoyed with David's coronation that they contributed lavishly to the celebration. It is right and proper to give generously for celebration and joyous worship. God is the author of joy, and he will join us in our celebrations.

**13:1** David took time to confer with all his officials. As king, he had ultimate authority and could have given orders on his own, but he chose to involve others in leadership. Perhaps this is why there was unanimous support for his decisions (13:1-5). When we are in charge, it is tempting to make unilateral decisions, pushing through our own opinions. But effective leaders listen carefully to others' opinions, and they encourage others to participate in making decisions. Of course, we should always consult God first. We can run into big problems if we don't talk to him (see the note on 13:10).

**13:1ff** The parallel account of moving the Ark (2 Samuel 5–6) shows that David's building projects were completed *before* he brought the Ark to Jerusalem. The writer of Chronicles puts the moving of the Ark first in order to highlight David's spiritual accomplishments and relationship to God.

**13:3** The Ark of our God is also called the Ark of the Covenant. The most sacred object of the Hebrew faith, it was a large box containing the stone tablets on which God had written the Ten Commandments (Exodus 25:10-22). David had already made Jerusalem his political capital (11:4-9). At this time, David brought the Ark there in order to make Jerusalem the nation's center for worship as well.

**13:3** The Ark of God had been in Kiriath-jearim for many years. The neglect of the Ark symbolized Israel's neglect of God. Bringing the Ark back to the center of Israel's life reflected David's desire to remind the nation of its true foundation—God. Neglecting those things that remind us of God—the Bible, the church, and contact with Christians—will cause us also to neglect God. How would an observer know that God is at the center of your life?

**13:6** Cherubim are mighty angels.

house. Uzzah and Ahio were guiding the cart. ⁸David and all Israel were celebrating before God with all their might, singing songs and playing all kinds of musical instruments—lyres, harps, tambourines, cymbals, and trumpets.

13:8
1 Chr 15:13-16

⁹But when they arrived at the threshing floor of Nacon,* the oxen stumbled, and Uzzah reached out his hand to steady the Ark. ¹⁰Then the LORD's anger was aroused against Uzzah, and he struck him dead because he had laid his hand on the Ark. So Uzzah died there in the presence of God.

13:9
2 Sam 6:6

13:10
Lev 10:2
1 Chr 15:13, 15

¹¹David was angry because the LORD's anger had burst out against Uzzah. He named that place Perez-uzzah (which means "to burst out against Uzzah"), as it is still called today.

¹²David was now afraid of God, and he asked, "How can I ever bring the Ark of God back into my care?" ¹³So David did not move the Ark into the City of David. Instead, he took it to the house of Obed-edom of Gath. ¹⁴The Ark of God remained there in Obed-edom's house for three months, and the LORD blessed the household of Obed-edom and everything he owned.

13:13
2 Chr 25:24-25

13:14
1 Chr 26:4-5

## David's Palace and Family

**14** Then King Hiram of Tyre sent messengers to David, along with cedar timber, and stonemasons and carpenters to build him a palace. ²And David realized that the LORD had confirmed him as king over Israel and had greatly blessed his kingdom for the sake of his people Israel.

14:1-7
//2 Sam 5:11-16
//1 Chr 3:5-8

14:1
2 Sam 5:11

³Then David married more wives in Jerusalem, and they had more sons and daughters. ⁴These are the names of David's sons who were born in Jerusalem: Shammua, Shobab, Nathan, Solomon, ⁵Ibhar, Elishua, Elpelet, ⁶Nogah, Nepheg, Japhia, ⁷Elishama, Eliada,* and Eliphelet.

14:4
1 Chr 3:5-9

## David Conquers the Philistines

⁸When the Philistines heard that David had been anointed king over all Israel, they mobilized all their forces to capture him. But David was told they were coming, so he marched out to meet them. ⁹The Philistines arrived and made a raid in the valley of Rephaim. ¹⁰So David asked God, "Should I go out to fight the Philistines? Will you hand them over to me?"

14:8-17
//2 Sam 5:17-25

14:9
1 Chr 11:15; 14:13

**13:9** As in parallel text at 2 Sam 6:6; Hebrew reads *Kidon.*   **14:7** Hebrew *Beeliada,* a variant spelling of Eliada; compare 3:8 and parallel text at 2 Sam 5:16.

---

**13:8** Worship in the Old Testament was more than a sober religious exercise. David's exuberance as he worshiped God with dancing and music is approved in Scripture. Our worship should reflect a healthy balance: Sometimes we should be reflective and serious (see Exodus 19:14ff), and sometimes we should show enthusiasm and jubilation. What do you need—more serious reflection or more joyous celebration?

**13:10** Why did Uzzah die? He touched the Ark, and that offense was punishable by death. God had given specific instructions about how the Ark was to be moved and carried (Numbers 4:5-15), and those instructions had been ignored. The Levites were responsible to move the Ark (there is no record that Uzzah was a Levite), and it was to be carried on their shoulders with poles through its rings (Numbers 7:9). It was *never* to be touched. Bringing the Ark on a cart followed the Philistines' example (1 Samuel 6:1ff). Uzzah, though sincere in his desire to protect the Ark, had to face the consequences of his sin, and David was reminded that his obedience to God's laws was more important than his enthusiasm. Also David had "consulted with all his officials" (13:1), but he neglected to ask God. The advice of our friends and colleagues is no substitute for God's direction.

**13:10-14** Uzzah died instantly for touching the Ark, but God blessed Obed-edom's home where the Ark was stored. This demonstrates the two-edged aspect of God's character: He is perfectly loving and perfectly just. Great blessings come to those who obey his commands, but severe punishment comes to those who disobey him. This punishment may come swiftly or over time, but it will come. Sometimes we focus only on the blessings God gives us, while forgetting that when we sin, "It is a terrible thing to fall into the hands of the living God" (Hebrews 10:31). At other times, however, we concentrate so much on judgment that we miss his blessings. Don't fall into a one-sided view of God.

Along with God's blessings comes the responsibility to live up to his demands for fairness, honesty, and justice.

**13:11** David was angry at both God and himself. David knew that he had done something wrong in transporting the Ark, and he was angry that his plans for the joyous return of the Ark had ended in a man's death. Once David's anger cooled, it was replaced by fear as the king realized the importance God placed on the Ark, the symbol of his presence and covenant with Israel. David left the Ark in Obed-edom's home until he could consider how to get it to Jerusalem. This allowed David to discover God's instructions for transporting the Ark. The next trip would be carried out according to God's commands.

**14:1** King Hiram also sent lumber and craftsmen to help Solomon build the Temple (2 Chronicles 2:1ff).

**14:2** God gave David honor and success, but not simply for David's personal gain. David realized that God had prospered him for a special reason—for the sake of God's people! Often we are tempted to use our position or possessions only for our own good. Instead, we must remember that God has placed us where we are and given us all we have so that we may encourage others and give to those in need.

**14:3** Accumulating wives and concubines in a harem was the custom of the day among Middle Eastern royalty, but it was not God's ideal (Genesis 2:24). David's marriages brought him greater power and influence, but they also caused strife, jealousy, and even murder within his family. (See the chart in 2 Samuel 11, p. 479, for other consequences of polygamy.)

**14:8-16** A map of this battle is in 2 Samuel 5, p. 469.

**14:10** Before David went to battle, he inquired of God first, asking for his presence and guidance. Too often we wait until we are in trouble before turning to God. By then the consequences of our actions are already unfolding. Do you ask for

The LORD replied, "Yes, go ahead. I will hand them over to you."

¹¹So David and his troops went up to Baal-perazim and defeated the Philistines there. "God did it!" David exclaimed. "He used me to burst through my enemies like a raging flood!" So they named that place Baal-perazim (which means "the Lord who bursts through"). ¹²The Philistines had abandoned their gods there, so David gave orders to burn them.

¹³But after a while the Philistines returned and raided the valley again. ¹⁴And once again David asked God what to do. "Do not attack them straight on," God replied. "Instead, circle around behind and attack them near the poplar* trees. ¹⁵When you hear a sound like marching feet in the tops of the poplar trees, go out and attack! That will be the signal that God is moving ahead of you to strike down the Philistine army." ¹⁶So David did what God commanded, and they struck down the Philistine army all the way from Gibeon to Gezer.

¹⁷So David's fame spread everywhere, and the LORD caused all the nations to fear David.

### Preparing to Move the Ark

**15** David now built several buildings for himself in the City of David. He also prepared a place for the Ark of God and set up a special tent for it. ²Then he commanded, "No one except the Levites may carry the Ark of God. The LORD has chosen them to carry the Ark of the LORD and to serve him forever."

³Then David summoned all Israel to Jerusalem to bring the Ark of the LORD to the place he had prepared for it. ⁴This is the number of the descendants of Aaron (the priests) and the Levites who were called together:

⁵From the clan of Kohath, 120, with Uriel as their leader.
⁶From the clan of Merari, 220, with Asaiah as their leader.
⁷From the clan of Gershon,* 130, with Joel as their leader.
⁸From the descendants of Elizaphan, 200, with Shemaiah as their leader.
⁹From the descendants of Hebron, 80, with Eliel as their leader.
¹⁰From the descendants of Uzziel, 112, with Amminadab as their leader.

¹¹Then David summoned the priests, Zadok and Abiathar, and these Levite leaders: Uriel, Asaiah, Joel, Shemaiah, Eliel, and Amminadab. ¹²He said to them, "You are the leaders of the Levite families. You must purify yourselves and all your fellow Levites, so you can bring the Ark of the LORD, the God of Israel, to the place I have prepared for it. ¹³Because you Levites did not carry the Ark the first time, the anger of the LORD our God burst out against us. We failed to ask God how to move it properly." ¹⁴So the priests and the Levites

**14:14** Or *aspen,* or *balsam;* also in 14:15. The exact identification of this tree is uncertain. **15:7** Hebrew *Gershom,* a variant spelling of Gershon.

Margin references: 14:13 / 1 Chr 14:9 | 14:17 / Exod 15:14-16 / Deut 2:25 | 15:1 / 1 Chr 16:1; 17:1-5 | 15:2 / Num 4:15 / Deut 10:8 | 15:3 / 2 Sam 6:12, 17 / 1 Kgs 8:1 / 1 Chr 13:5; 15:1, 12 | 15:4 / 1 Chr 6:16-30; 12:26 | 15:11 / 1 Sam 22:20-23 / 1 Kgs 2:26, 35 / 1 Chr 12:28 | 15:12 / Exod 19:14-15 / 2 Sam 35:6 | 15:13 / 1 Chr 13:7

---

God's help only as a desperate last resort? Instead, go to him first! Like David, you may receive incredible help and avoid serious trouble. Make sure you give God the credit when you see what he does on your behalf.

**14:12** David's quick and decisive action against idols helped unify his kingdom and focus the people on worshiping the one true God. He was obeying the law that said, "You must break down their pagan altars and shatter their sacred pillars. Cut down their Asherah poles and burn their idols" (Deuteronomy 7:5). Most of David's successors failed to destroy idols, and this led to unbelievable moral corruption in Israel.

**14:12** Often the soldiers wanted to keep souvenirs from the battle (and 2 Samuel 5:21 states that some of the men kept some of these idols), but David ordered them to burn the idols. The only proper response to sin is to get rid of it completely. You cannot be a follower of God while continuing to hold on to parts of your life where God is not the center of your thoughts and actions. Eliminate whatever takes God's rightful place in your life, and follow him with complete devotion.

**15:12** The priests purified themselves so they would be prepared to carry the Ark. To *purify* literally means "to separate," to set apart for sacred purposes, to consecrate. The priests symbolically separated themselves from common use. This was done by washing themselves and their clothing in a special ceremony (Numbers 8:5-8). While we are not required to carry out such ceremonies today, we can purify ourselves by reading God's Word, thoughtfully applying it to our lives, and preparing our

hearts to participate in worship through anticipation, self-examination, and meditation. Just as we "set apart" time for worship, we also "set apart" ourselves to be in God's presence.

**15:13** "The first time" refers to the incident recorded in 13:8-11 and 2 Samuel 6:1-11. As the Ark was being brought back to Israel on an oxcart, the oxen stumbled. Uzzah, trying to steady the Ark with his hand, was killed instantly for touching it. The mistake was not in David's desire to move the Ark but in his method for its return. David either ignored or was unaware of the specific instructions in God's law about how the Ark was to be moved. Obviously he had discovered his mistake and was now preparing to correct it. This incident was a divine object lesson to all Israel that God governed the king and not the other way around. If David had been allowed to handle the Ark of God carelessly, what would that have said to the people about their faith?

**15:13-15** When David's first attempt to move the Ark failed (13:8-14), he learned an important lesson: When God gives specific instructions, it is wise to follow them precisely. This time David saw to it that the Levites carried the Ark (Numbers 4:5-15). We may not fully understand the reasons behind God's instructions, but we do know that his wisdom is complete and his judgment infallible. The way to know God's instructions is to know his Word. But just as children do not understand the reasons for all their parents' instructions until they are older, we may not understand all of God's reasons in this life. It is far better to obey God first and then discover the reasons. We are never free to disobey God just because we don't understand.

purified themselves in order to bring the Ark of the LORD, the God of Israel, to Jerusalem. 15Then the Levites carried the Ark of God on their shoulders with its carrying poles, just as the LORD had instructed Moses.

**15:15**
Exod 25:14

16David also ordered the Levite leaders to appoint a choir of Levites who were singers and musicians to sing joyful songs to the accompaniment of harps, lyres, and cymbals. 17So the Levites appointed Heman son of Joel along with his fellow Levites: Asaph son of Berekiah, and Ethan son of Kushaiah from the clan of Merari. 18The following men were chosen as their assistants: Zechariah, Jaaziel,* Shemiramoth, Jehiel, Unni, Eliab, Benaiah, Maaseiah, Mattithiah, Eliphelehu, Mikneiah, and the gatekeepers—Obed-edom and Jeiel.

**15:16**
1 Chr 13:8; 25:1

**15:17**
1 Chr 25:1

19The musicians Heman, Asaph, and Ethan were chosen to sound the bronze cymbals. 20Zechariah, Aziel, Shemiramoth, Jehiel, Unni, Eliab, Maaseiah, and Benaiah were chosen to play the harps.* 21Mattithiah, Eliphelehu, Mikneiah, Obed-edom, Jeiel, and Azaziah were chosen to play the lyres.* 22Kenaniah, the head Levite, was chosen as the choir leader because of his skill.

23Berekiah and Elkanah were chosen to guard* the Ark. 24Shebaniah, Joshaphat, Nethanel, Amasai, Zechariah, Benaiah, and Eliezer—all of whom were priests—were chosen to blow the trumpets as they marched in front of the Ark of God. Obed-edom and Jehiah were chosen to guard the Ark.

**15:24**
1 Chr 16:6

## Moving the Ark to Jerusalem

25Then David and the elders of Israel and the generals of the army* went to the house of Obed-edom to bring the Ark of the LORD's Covenant up to Jerusalem with a great celebration. 26And because God was clearly helping the Levites as they carried the Ark of the LORD's Covenant, they sacrificed seven bulls and seven rams.

**15:25–16:3**
//2 Sam 6:12-19

**15:25**
1 Chr 13:13

**15:26**
Num 23:1-4, 29

27David was dressed in a robe of fine linen, as were all the Levites who carried the Ark, and also the singers, and Kenaniah the choir leader. David was also wearing a priestly garment.* 28So all Israel brought up the Ark of the LORD's Covenant with shouts of joy, the blowing of rams' horns and trumpets, the crashing of cymbals, and loud playing on harps and lyres.

29But as the Ark of the LORD's Covenant entered the City of David, Michal, the daughter of Saul, looked down from her window. When she saw King David skipping about and laughing with joy, she was filled with contempt for him.

**16** They brought the Ark of God and placed it inside the special tent David had prepared for it. And they presented burnt offerings and peace offerings to God. 2When he had finished his sacrifices, David blessed the people in the name of the LORD. 3Then he gave to every man and woman in all Israel a loaf of bread, a cake of dates,* and a cake of raisins.

**16:1**
1 Chr 15:1

4David appointed the following Levites to lead the people in worship before the Ark of the LORD—to invoke his blessings, to give thanks, and to praise the LORD, the God of Israel. 5Asaph, the leader of this group, sounded the cymbals. Second to him was Zechariah, followed by Jeiel, Shemiramoth, Jehiel, Mattithiah, Eliab, Benaiah, Obed-edom, and Jeiel. They played the harps and lyres. 6The priests, Benaiah and Jahaziel, played the trumpets regularly before the Ark of God's Covenant.

**16:4**
1 Chr 15:2

**15:18** As in several Hebrew manuscripts and Greek version (see also parallel lists in 15:20; 16:5); Masoretic Text reads *Zechariah ben Jaaziel.* **15:20** Hebrew adds *according to Alamoth,* which is probably a musical term. The meaning of the Hebrew is uncertain. **15:21** Hebrew adds *according to the Sheminith,* which is probably a musical term. The meaning of the Hebrew is uncertain. **15:23** Hebrew *chosen as gatekeepers for;* also in 15:24. **15:25** Hebrew *the commanders of thousands.* **15:27** Hebrew *a linen ephod.* **16:3** Or *a portion of meat.* The meaning of the Hebrew is uncertain.

---

**15:16-25** The great musical procession was designed as a worthy accompaniment to this great occasion. It heightened the excitement, elevated the people's hearts and minds, and focused their attention on the event. It also helped seal it in their memory for years to come. Beginning any task by praising God can inspire us to give him our best. Develop the practice of giving praise to God, and you will experience greater joy and strength to face anything.

**15:29** David was willing to look foolish in the eyes of some people in order to express his thankfulness to God fully and honestly. In contrast, Michal was so disgusted by his undignified actions that she could not rejoice in the Ark's return to Jerusalem.

Worship had so deteriorated under the reign of her father, Saul, that it had become stilted and ritualistic. Michal could accept David as a military conqueror and as a king, but she could not accept his free and spontaneous expression of praise to God. Some devoted people may look foolish to us in their heartfelt expressions of worship, but we must accept them. In the same way, we should not be afraid to worship God with whatever expressions seem appropriate.

**16:4** Certain Levites were appointed to give continual praise and thanks to God. Praise and thanksgiving should be a regular part of our routine, not reserved only for celebrations. Praise God continually, and you will find that you won't take his blessings for granted.

## David's Song of Praise

7On that day David gave to Asaph and his fellow Levites this song of thanksgiving to the LORD:

**16:8-22**
*//Ps 105:1-15*

**16:8**
*1 Kgs 8:43*
*2 Kgs 19:19*

8 Give thanks to the LORD and proclaim his greatness.
    Let the whole world know what he has done.
9 Sing to him; yes, sing his praises.
    Tell everyone about his wonderful deeds.
10 Exult in his holy name;
    rejoice, you who worship the LORD.

**16:11**
*Ps 24:6*

11 Search for the LORD and for his strength;
    continually seek him.

**16:12**
*Pss 78:43; 103:2*

12 Remember the wonders he has performed,
    his miracles, and the rulings he has given,
13 you children of his servant Israel,
    you descendants of Jacob, his chosen ones.

**16:14**
*Ps 48:10*

14 He is the LORD our God.
    His justice is seen throughout the land.
15 Remember his covenant forever—
    the commitment he made to a thousand generations.

**16:16**
*Gen 17:2;*
*22:16-18; 26:3*

16 This is the covenant he made with Abraham
    and the oath he swore to Isaac.

**16:17**
*Gen 35:9-12*

17 He confirmed it to Jacob as a decree,
    and to the people of Israel as a never-ending covenant:

**16:18**
*Gen 13:14-17*

18 "I will give you the land of Canaan
    as your special possession."

**16:19**
*Gen 34:30*
*Deut 7:7*

19 He said this when you were few in number,
    a tiny group of strangers in Canaan.
20 They wandered from nation to nation,
    from one kingdom to another.

**16:21**
*Gen 12:17; 20:3*
*Exod 7:15-18*

21 Yet he did not let anyone oppress them.
    He warned kings on their behalf:

**16:22**
*Gen 20:7*

22 "Do not touch my chosen people,
    and do not hurt my prophets."

**16:23-33**
*//Ps 96:1-13*

23 Let the whole earth sing to the LORD!
    Each day proclaim the good news that he saves.
24 Publish his glorious deeds among the nations.
    Tell everyone about the amazing things he does.

**16:25**
*Pss 89:7; 144:3-6*

25 Great is the LORD! He is most worthy of praise!
    He is to be feared above all gods.

**16:26**
*Lev 19:4*
*Ps 102:25*

26 The gods of other nations are mere idols,
    but the LORD made the heavens!
27 Honor and majesty surround him;
    strength and joy fill his dwelling.

28 O nations of the world, recognize the LORD,
    recognize that the LORD is glorious and strong.

---

**16:7-36** Four elements of true thanksgiving are found in this song (psalm): (1) *remembering* what God has done, (2) *telling* others about it, (3) *showing* God's glory to others, and (4) *offering* gifts of self, time, and resources. If you are truly thankful, your life will show it.

**16:8ff** Several parts of this psalm are parallel to songs in the book of Psalms: 16:8-22 with Psalm 105:1-15; 16:23-33 with Psalm 96; 16:34-36 with Psalm 106:1, 47, 48.

**16:15-18** This covenant was given to Abraham (Genesis 15:18-21) and then passed on to Isaac (Genesis 26:24, 25) and Jacob (Genesis 28:13-15). God promised to give the land

of Canaan (present-day Israel) to their descendants. He also promised that the Messiah would come from their line.

**16:25** Genuine praise results when we declare God's character and attributes in the presence of others. When we recognize and affirm his goodness, we are holding up his perfect moral nature for all to see. Praise benefits us because it takes our mind off our problems and needs and focuses on God's power, mercy, majesty, and love.

29 Give to the Lord the glory he deserves!
    Bring your offering and come into his presence.
Worship the Lord in all his holy splendor.
30    Let all the earth tremble before him.
    The world stands firm and cannot be shaken.

31 Let the heavens be glad, and the earth rejoice!
    Tell all the nations, "The Lord reigns!"
32 Let the sea and everything in it shout his praise!
    Let the fields and their crops burst out with joy!
33 Let the trees of the forest rustle with praise,
    for the Lord is coming to judge the earth.

34 Give thanks to the Lord, for he is good!
    His faithful love endures forever.
35 Cry out, "Save us, O God of our salvation!
    Gather and rescue us from among the nations,
so we can thank your holy name
    and rejoice and praise you."

36 Praise the Lord, the God of Israel,
    who lives from everlasting to everlasting!

And all the people shouted "Amen!" and praised the Lord.

### Worship at Jerusalem and Gibeon

37David arranged for Asaph and his fellow Levites to serve regularly before the Ark of the Lord's Covenant, doing whatever needed to be done each day. 38This group included Obed-edom (son of Jeduthun), Hosah, and sixty-eight other Levites as gatekeepers.

39Meanwhile, David stationed Zadok the priest and his fellow priests at the Tabernacle of the Lord at the place of worship in Gibeon, where they continued to minister before the Lord. 40They sacrificed the regular burnt offerings to the Lord each morning and evening on the altar set aside for that purpose, obeying everything written in the Law of the Lord, as he had commanded Israel. 41David also appointed Heman, Jeduthun, and the others chosen by name to give thanks to the Lord, for "his faithful love endures forever." 42They used their trumpets, cymbals, and other instruments to accompany their songs of praise to God.* And the sons of Jeduthun were appointed as gatekeepers.

43Then all the people returned to their homes, and David turned and went home to bless his own family.

### The Lord's Covenant Promise to David

**17** When David was settled in his palace, he summoned Nathan the prophet. "Look," David said, "I am living in a beautiful cedar palace,* but the Ark of the Lord's Covenant is out there under a tent!"

2Nathan replied to David, "Do whatever you have in mind, for God is with you."

3But that same night God said to Nathan,

**16:29** Ps 29:2
**16:31** Pss 93:1; 96:10
Isa 44:23; 49:13
**16:32** Ps 98:7
**16:34-36** //Ps 106:1, 47-48
**16:34** Ezra 3:11
Pss 106:1; 136:1
Jer 33:11
**16:35** Ps 106:47-48
**16:36** Deut 27:15
1 Kgs 8:15, 56
Neh 8:6
Ps 72:18-19
**16:37** 2 Chr 8:14
Ezra 3:4
**16:38** 1 Chr 13:13-14; 26:10
**16:39** 1 Kgs 3:4
1 Chr 15:11
**16:40** Exod 29:38-42
Num 28:1-8
**16:41** 1 Chr 6:33; 25:1-6
2 Chr 5:13
**16:42** 1 Chr 25:7
2 Chr 7:6; 29:27
**17:1-15** //2 Sam 7:1-17

**16:42** Or *to accompany the sacred music;* or *to accompany singing to God.*  **17:1** Hebrew *a house of cedar.*

---

**16:29** Genuine praise also involves ascribing glory to God. This means that we give credit where credit is due. Remember this in your worship and give God all the glory.

**16:37** Asaph and his fellow Levites ministered in the Tabernacle, doing each day whatever was needed. To carry out God's work is not merely to engage in religious exercises. It includes other necessary tasks. Even if you don't have the opportunity to teach or preach, God can use you in the ministry. What needs to be done—cleaning, serving, singing, planning, administering? Look for ways to minister each day.

**16:39** David brought the Ark to Jerusalem although the Tabernacle was still at Gibeon. His plan was to reunite the Tabernacle and Ark in a new Temple at Jerusalem that would then become Israel's only worship center. The Temple, however, was not built until Solomon's time. In the meantime, Israel had two worship

centers and two high priests (15:11), one at Gibeon and one at Jerusalem.

**17:1** David felt disturbed that the Ark, the symbol of God's presence, sat in a tent while he lived in a beautiful palace. David's desire was right, but his timing was wrong. God told David *not* to build a Temple (17:3, 4), and David was willing to abide by God's timing. If you live in comparative luxury while God's work, house, or ministers are lacking, perhaps God wants you to change the situation. Like David, take action to correct the imbalance, but be willing to move according to God's timing.

**17:3-14** God did not want a warrior to build his Temple (28:3; 1 Kings 5:3), and David had shed much blood in unifying the nation. So the honor of building the Temple would go to David's son Solomon. David would pass on to Solomon a peaceful and united kingdom, ready to begin work on a beautiful Temple.

**17:4**
1 Chr 28:2-3

**17:5**
Exod 40:2-3
2 Sam 7:6

**17:6**
2 Sam 7:7

⁴"Go and tell my servant David, 'This is what the LORD has declared: You are not the one to build a house for me to live in. ⁵I have never lived in a house, from the day I brought the Israelites out of Egypt until this very day. My home has always been a tent, moving from one place to another in a Tabernacle. ⁶Yet no matter where I have gone with the Israelites, I have never once complained to Israel's leaders,* the shepherds of my people. I have never asked them, "Why haven't you built me a beautiful cedar house?"'

⁷"Now go and say to my servant David, 'This is what the LORD of Heaven's Armies has declared: I took you from tending sheep in the pasture and selected you to be the leader of my people Israel. ⁸I have been with you wherever you have gone, and I have destroyed all your enemies before your eyes. Now I will make your name as famous as anyone who has ever lived on the earth! ⁹And I will provide a homeland for my people Israel, planting them in a secure place where they will never be disturbed. Evil nations won't oppress them as they've done in the past, ¹⁰starting from the time I appointed judges to rule my people Israel. And I will defeat all your enemies.

**17:13**
1 Chr 10:14
Heb 1:5

"'Furthermore, I declare that the LORD will build a house for you—a dynasty of kings! ¹¹For when you die and join your ancestors, I will raise up one of your descendants, one of your sons, and I will make his kingdom strong. ¹²He is the one who will build a house—a temple—for me. And I will secure his throne forever. ¹³I will be his father, and he will be my son. I will never take my favor from him as I took it from the one who ruled before you. ¹⁴I will confirm him as king over my house and my kingdom for all time, and his throne will be secure forever.'"

¹⁵So Nathan went back to David and told him everything the LORD had said in this vision.

### David's Prayer of Thanks

**17:16-27**
//2 Sam 7:18-29

¹⁶Then King David went in and sat before the LORD and prayed,

"Who am I, O LORD God, and what is my family, that you have brought me this far?

**17:17**
2 Sam 7:19

¹⁷And now, O God, in addition to everything else, you speak of giving your servant a lasting dynasty! You speak as though I were someone very great,* O LORD God!

¹⁸"What more can I say to you about the way you have honored me? You know what your servant is really like. ¹⁹For the sake of your servant, O LORD, and according to your will, you have done all these great things and have made them known.

**17:19**
2 Sam 7:21, 25
Isa 37:35

²⁰"O LORD, there is no one like you. We have never even heard of another God like you! ²¹What other nation on earth is like your people Israel? What other nation, O God, have you redeemed from slavery to be your own people? You made a great name for yourself when you redeemed your people from Egypt. You performed awesome miracles and drove out the nations that stood in their way. ²²You chose Israel to be your very own people forever, and you, O LORD, became their God.

**17:22**
Exod 19:5-6

²³"And now, O LORD, I am your servant; do as you have promised concerning me and my family. May it be a promise that will last forever. ²⁴And may your name be established and honored forever so that everyone will say, 'The LORD of Heaven's Armies, the God of Israel, is Israel's God!' And may the house of your servant David continue before you forever.

**17:6** As in Greek version (see also 2 Sam 7:7); Hebrew reads *judges*.　**17:17** The meaning of the Hebrew is uncertain.

---

**17:10** God promised to subdue David's enemies. Chapters 18–20 tell how God kept that promise.

**17:12-14** Why, after this eternal promise, were the Israelites eventually taken from the Promised Land into captivity? The promise to David had two parts. The first part was conditional: As long as David's descendants followed God's laws and honored him, they would continually be on the throne of Israel. The second part was unconditional: A son of David would occupy his throne forever. This was Jesus the Messiah. The first part of the promise was based on the faithful obedience of David's descendants. The second part would come true regardless of the way his descendants acted.

**17:16-20** God told David that Solomon would be given the honor of building the Temple. David responded with deep humility, not resentment. This king who had conquered his enemies and was loved by his people said, "Who am I . . . that you have brought me this far?" David recognized that God was the *true* king. God has done just as much for us, and he plans to do even more! Like David, we should humble ourselves and give glory to God, saying, "O LORD, there is no one like you." When God chooses someone else to implement your ideas, will you respond with such humility?

**17:16-27** David prayed by humbling himself (17:16-18), praising God (17:19, 20), recognizing God's blessings (17:21, 22), and accepting God's decisions, promises, and commands (17:23, 24). Sometimes we are quick to make requests to God and to tell him our troubles, but these other dimensions of prayer can deepen our spiritual life. Take time to praise God, to count his blessings, and to affirm your commitment to do what he has already said to do.

**17:21** David's reference to Israel's exodus from Egypt would have had special significance to the original readers of 1 Chronicles, who were either beginning or had just completed a second great exodus back to Israel from captivity in Babylon. Remembering God's promises, mercy, and protection during the first exodus would have encouraged the exiles returning once again to Israel, just as God had promised.

25"O my God, I have been bold enough to pray to you because you have revealed to your servant that you will build a house for him—a dynasty of kings! 26For you are God, O Lord. And you have promised these good things to your servant. 27And now, it has pleased you to bless the house of your servant, so that it will continue forever before you. For when you grant a blessing, O Lord, it is an eternal blessing!"

## 3. David's military exploits

*David's Military Victories*

**18** After this, David defeated and subdued the Philistines by conquering Gath and its surrounding towns. 2David also conquered the land of Moab, and the Moabites who were spared became David's subjects and paid him tribute money.

3David also destroyed the forces of Hadadezer, king of Zobah, as far as Hamath,* when Hadadezer marched out to strengthen his control along the Euphrates River. 4David captured 1,000 chariots, 7,000 charioteers, and 20,000 foot soldiers. He crippled all the chariot horses except enough for 100 chariots.

5When Arameans from Damascus arrived to help King Hadadezer, David killed 22,000 of them. 6Then he placed several army garrisons* in Damascus, the Aramean capital, and the Arameans became David's subjects and paid him tribute money. So the Lord made David victorious wherever he went.

7David brought the gold shields of Hadadezer's officers to Jerusalem, 8along with a large amount of bronze from Hadadezer's towns of Tebah* and Cun. Later Solomon melted the bronze and molded it into the great bronze basin called the Sea, the pillars, and the various bronze articles used at the Temple.

9When King Toi* of Hamath heard that David had destroyed the entire army of King Hadadezer of Zobah, 10he sent his son Joram* to congratulate King David for his successful campaign. Hadadezer and Toi had been enemies and were often at war. Joram presented David with many gifts of gold, silver, and bronze.

11King David dedicated all these gifts to the Lord, along with the silver and gold he had taken from the other nations—from Edom, Moab, Ammon, Philistia, and Amalek.

12Abishai son of Zeruiah destroyed 18,000 Edomites in the Valley of Salt. 13He placed army garrisons in Edom, and all the Edomites became David's subjects. In fact, the Lord made David victorious wherever he went.

14So David reigned over all Israel and did what was just and right for all his people. 15Joab son of Zeruiah was commander of the army. Jehoshaphat son of Ahilud was the royal

**18:1-13** //2 Sam 8:1-14

**18:11** Num 24:18-20

**18:14-17** //2 Sam 8:15-18

**18:15** 1 Chr 11:6

**18:3** The meaning of the Hebrew is uncertain.  **18:6** As in Greek version and Latin Vulgate (see also 2 Sam 8:6); Hebrew lacks *several army garrisons*.  **18:8** Hebrew reads *Tibhath*, a variant spelling of Tebah; compare parallel text at 2 Sam 8:8.  **18:9** As in parallel text at 2 Sam 8:9; Hebrew reads *Tou;* also in 18:10.  **18:10** As in parallel text at 2 Sam 8:10; Hebrew reads *Hadoram*, a variant spelling of Joram.

**18:2** In 2 Samuel 8:1, 2, it is recorded that David killed two-thirds of the people of Moab. His ancestor Ruth was originally from the land of Moab.

**18:6, 14** David was a victorious and fair ruler. We see in David's glowing success a hint of what Christ's reign will be like—complete victory and justice. If David's glory was great, how much greater will Christ's glory be! The great news for us is that we can be rightly related to Jesus Christ through faith. One day we will share in his glory as we reign with him.

**18:9-11** When David received gifts from King Toi, he dedicated them to God, realizing that they had come from God and were to be used for him. It is easy to think that our financial and material blessings are the result of our own skill and hard work rather than coming from a loving God (James 1:17). What has God given you? Dedicate all your gifts and resources to him, and use them for his service. He will lead you in the method you should use. The first step is to be willing. The second step is to follow up your willingness with action.

**18:13** The list of battles in this chapter shows how God gave David victory after victory. Unbelieving people think that victory comes from their own skill plus a little luck. Just as David

acknowledged God's role in his success, so should we. Don't take credit for the work God does.

**DAVID SUBDUES HIS ENEMIES**
David expanded his kingdom as the Lord continued to give him victory. He subdued the Philistines by taking Gath, conquered Moab, won battles as far north as Zobah and Hamath (conquering Aram when they came to help these enemy nations), and subdued the other surrounding nations of Ammon and Amalek.

historian. 16Zadok son of Ahitub and Ahimelech* son of Abiathar were the priests. Seraiah* was the court secretary. 17Benaiah son of Jehoiada was captain of the king's bodyguard.* And David's sons served as the king's chief assistants.

### David Defeats the Ammonites

**19:1-19**
*//2 Sam 10:1-19*

**19** Some time after this, King Nahash of the Ammonites died, and his son Hanun* became king. 2David said, "I am going to show loyalty to Hanun because his father, Nahash, was always loyal to me." So David sent messengers to express sympathy to Hanun about his father's death.

But when David's ambassadors arrived in the land of Ammon, 3the Ammonite commanders said to Hanun, "Do you really think these men are coming here to honor your father? No! David has sent them to spy out the land so they can come in and conquer it!" 4So Hanun seized David's ambassadors and shaved them, cut off their robes at the buttocks, and sent them back to David in shame.

5When David heard what had happened to the men, he sent messengers to tell them, "Stay at Jericho until your beards grow out, and then come back." For they felt deep shame because of their appearance.

**19:7**
*Num 21:30*
*Josh 13:9, 16*

6When the people of Ammon realized how seriously they had angered David, Hanun and the Ammonites sent 75,000 pounds* of silver to hire chariots and charioteers from Aram-naharaim, Aram-maacah, and Zobah. 7They also hired 32,000 chariots and secured the support of the king of Maacah and his army. These forces camped at Medeba, where they were joined by the Ammonite troops that Hanun had recruited from his own towns. 8When David heard about this, he sent Joab and all his warriors to fight them. 9The Ammonite troops came out and drew up their battle lines at the entrance of the city, while the other kings positioned themselves to fight in the open fields.

10When Joab saw that he would have to fight on both the front and the rear, he chose some of Israel's elite troops and placed them under his personal command to fight the Arameans in the fields. 11He left the rest of the army under the command of his brother Abishai, who was to attack the Ammonites. 12"If the Arameans are too strong for me, then come over and help me," Joab told his brother. "And if the Ammonites are too strong for you, I will help you. 13Be courageous! Let us fight bravely for our people and the cities of our God. May the LORD's will be done."

**19:14**
*2 Sam 10:14*

14When Joab and his troops attacked, the Arameans began to run away. 15And when the Ammonites saw the Arameans running, they also ran from Abishai and retreated into the city. Then Joab returned to Jerusalem.

**19:16**
*2 Sam 10:15-16*

16The Arameans now realized that they were no match for Israel, so they sent messengers and summoned additional Aramean troops from the other side of the Euphrates River.* These troops were under the command of Shobach,* the commander of Hadadezer's forces. 17When David heard what was happening, he mobilized all Israel, crossed the Jordan River, and positioned his troops in battle formation. Then David engaged the Arameans in battle, and they fought against him. 18But again the Arameans fled from the Israelites. This time David's forces killed 7,000 charioteers and 40,000 foot soldiers, including Shobach, the commander of their army. 19When Hadadezer's allies saw that they had been defeated by Israel, they surrendered to David and became his subjects. After that, the Arameans were no longer willing to help the Ammonites.

**18:16a** As in some Hebrew manuscripts, Syriac version, and Latin Vulgate (see also 2 Sam 8:17); most Hebrew manuscripts read *Abimelech.* **18:16b** As in parallel text at 2 Sam 8:17; Hebrew reads *Shavsha.* **18:17** Hebrew *of the Kerethites and Pelethites.* **19:1** As in parallel text at 2 Sam 10:1; Hebrew lacks *Hanun.* **19:6** Hebrew *1,000 talents* [34,000 kilograms]. **19:16a** Hebrew *the river.* **19:16b** As in parallel text at 2 Sam 10:16; Hebrew reads *Shophach;* also in 19:18.

**19:1** The land of Ammon bordered Israel to the east. The nation had a sordid beginning: Its founding ancestor, Ben-ammi, was conceived through incest between Lot and his daughter (Genesis 19:30-38). The Ammonites, who were constant enemies of Israel, reached their greatest strength in the days of the judges. David was the first military leader of Israel to crush them. They were unable to cause further trouble for many years.

**19:2, 3** Hanun misread David's intentions. He was overly suspicious and brought disaster upon himself. Because of past experiences, it is easy to be overly suspicious of others, questioning every move and second-guessing their motives. While we should be cautious and wise as we deal with others, we should not assume their every action is ill-intended.

**19:4, 5** Israelite men always wore beards. To be forcibly shaven was embarrassing enough, but these men were also left half naked. Hanun's actions humiliated these men and insulted Israel.

**19:6** Rather than admit his mistake and seek forgiveness and reconciliation, Hanun spent an enormous amount of money to cover up his error. His cover-up cost him dearly (20:1-3). It often costs more to cover up an error than to admit it honestly. Rather than compound an error through defensiveness, seek forgiveness and reconciliation as soon as you realize your mistake. You will save yourself and others a lot of pain and trouble.

## David Captures Rabbah

**20** In the spring of the year,* when kings normally go out to war, Joab led the Israelite army in successful attacks against the land of the Ammonites. In the process he laid siege to the city of Rabbah. However, David stayed behind in Jerusalem.

²When David arrived at Rabbah, he removed the crown from the king's head,* and it was placed on his own head. The crown was made of gold and set with gems, and he found that it weighed seventy-five pounds.* David took a vast amount of plunder from the city. ³He also made slaves of the people of Rabbah and forced them to labor with saws, iron picks, and iron axes.* That is how David dealt with the people of all the Ammonite towns. Then David and all the army returned to Jerusalem.

**20:1-3**
//2 Sam 11:1;
12:29-31

## Battles against Philistine Giants

⁴After this, war broke out with the Philistines at Gezer. As they fought, Sibbecai from Hushah killed Saph,* a descendant of the giants,* and so the Philistines were subdued.

**20:4-8**
//2 Sam 21:15-22

⁵During another battle with the Philistines, Elhanan son of Jair killed Lahmi, the brother of Goliath of Gath. The handle of Lahmi's spear was as thick as a weaver's beam!

**20:5**
1 Sam 17:4-7
2 Sam 21:19
1 Chr 11:23

⁶In another battle with the Philistines at Gath, they encountered a huge man with six fingers on each hand and six toes on each foot, twenty-four in all, who was also a descendant of the giants. ⁷But when he defied and taunted Israel, he was killed by Jonathan, the son of David's brother Shimea.

⁸These Philistines were descendants of the giants of Gath, but David and his warriors killed them.

## David Takes a Census

**21** Satan rose up against Israel and caused David to take a census of the people of Israel. ²So David said to Joab and the commanders of the army, "Take a census of all the people of Israel—from Beersheba in the south to Dan in the north—and bring me a report so I may know how many there are."

**21:1-26**
//2 Sam 24:1-25
**21:2**
1 Chr 27:23-24

³But Joab replied, "May the LORD increase the number of his people a hundred times over! But why, my lord the king, do you want to do this? Are they not all your servants? Why must you cause Israel to sin?"

**21:3**
Deut 1:11

**20:1** Hebrew *At the turn of the year.* The first day of the year in the ancient Hebrew lunar calendar occurred in March or April.   **20:2a** Or *from the head of Milcom* (as in Greek version and Latin Vulgate). Milcom, also called Molech, was the god of the Ammonites.   **20:2b** Hebrew *1 talent* [34 kilograms].   **20:3** As in parallel text at 2 Sam 12:31; Hebrew reads *and cut them with saws, iron picks, and saws.*   **20:4a** As in parallel text at 2 Sam 21:18; Hebrew reads *Sippai.*   **20:4b** Hebrew *descendant of the Rephaites;* also in 20:6, 8.

---

**20:1** David's adultery occurred at this time while he remained in Jerusalem instead of going to battle (2 Samuel 11–12). This story may have been excluded from 1 Chronicles because the book was written to focus on God's long-term interest in Israel and on the Temple as a symbol of God's presence among them. The story of David and Bathsheba did not fit this purpose. The story of Absalom's rebellion, which occurred between this chapter and the next, was probably omitted for the same reason (2 Samuel 15–18).

**20:1** Kings went out to battle following the spring harvest. At this time, farm work eased off, and the armies could live off the land. During the winter, they plotted and planned future conquests. Then, when fair weather permitted, their armies went to war. But David ignored this opportunity. He stayed home and sent Joab out to lead the army. It was during this time of inactivity that he sinned with Bathsheba. Look for the "springs" in your life, the times when God wants you to respond, take the initiative, and move out to do his will. It is during these critical times that we may be most sensitive to temptation. Resolve to take the action God has prescribed. Don't give temptation a foothold in your inactivity.

**20:1** Rabbah was the capital of the Ammonites and is the site of modern Amman in Jordan.

**21:1** David's census brought disaster because, unlike the census taken in the book of Numbers (Numbers 1–2) that God had ordered, this census was taken so David could take pride in the strength of his army. In determining his military strength, he was beginning to trust more in military power than in God. There is a thin line between feeling confident because you are relying on God's power and becoming proud because you have been used by God for great purposes.

**21:1** The Bible text says Satan *caused* David to take a census. Can Satan force people to do wrong? No, Satan only *tempted* David with the idea, but David *decided to act* on the temptation. Ever since the Garden of Eden, Satan has been tempting people to sin. David's census was not against God's law, but his reason for the census was wrong—pride in his mighty army. He forgot that his real strength came from God. Even Joab, not known for his high moral ideals, recognized the census as sin. From David's example we learn that an action that may not be wrong in itself can be sinful if it is motivated by greed, arrogance, or selfishness. Often our motives, not the action itself, contain the sin. We must constantly weigh our motives before we act.

**21:1-3** David fell to Satan's temptation. God provided a way out in Joab's counsel, but David's curiosity was spurred on by arrogance. His faith was in his own strength rather than in God's. If we feel self-sufficient and put confidence in ourselves apart from God, we soon fall to Satan's schemes. Self-sufficiency pulls us away from God. When you are tempted, examine your inner desires to understand why the external temptation is so appealing. (See 1 Corinthians 10:13 for more about escaping temptation.)

**21:5**
2 Sam 24:9

**21:6**
1 Chr 27:24

<sup>4</sup>But the king insisted that they take the census, so Joab traveled throughout all Israel to count the people. Then he returned to Jerusalem <sup>5</sup>and reported the number of people to David. There were 1,100,000 warriors in all Israel who could handle a sword, and 470,000 in Judah. <sup>6</sup>But Joab did not include the tribes of Levi and Benjamin in the census because he was so distressed at what the king had made him do.

### Judgment for David's Sin

**21:8**
2 Sam 12:13

<sup>7</sup>God was very displeased with the census, and he punished Israel for it. <sup>8</sup>Then David said to God, "I have sinned greatly by taking this census. Please forgive my guilt for doing this foolish thing."

**21:9**
1 Sam 9:9
2 Sam 24:11
1 Chr 29:29

<sup>9</sup>Then the LORD spoke to Gad, David's seer. This was the message: <sup>10</sup>"Go and say to David, 'This is what the LORD says: I will give you three choices. Choose one of these punishments, and I will inflict it on you.'"

**21:12**
2 Sam 24:13

<sup>11</sup>So Gad came to David and said, "These are the choices the LORD has given you. <sup>12</sup>You may choose three years of famine, three months of destruction by the sword of your enemies, or three days of severe plague as the angel of the LORD brings devastation throughout the land of Israel. Decide what answer I should give the LORD who sent me."

**21:13**
Pss 51:1; 130:4, 7

<sup>13</sup>"I'm in a desperate situation!" David replied to Gad. "But let me fall into the hands of the LORD, for his mercy is very great. Do not let me fall into human hands."

**21:14**
1 Chr 27:24

**21:15**
Exod 32:14
1 Sam 15:11
Jon 3:10

<sup>14</sup>So the LORD sent a plague upon Israel, and 70,000 people died as a result. <sup>15</sup>And God sent an angel to destroy Jerusalem. But just as the angel was preparing to destroy it, the LORD relented and said to the death angel, "Stop! That is enough!" At that moment the angel of the LORD was standing by the threshing floor of Araunah* the Jebusite.

**21:16**
1 Kgs 21:27

**21:17**
2 Sam 7:8
Ps 74:1

<sup>16</sup>David looked up and saw the angel of the LORD standing between heaven and earth with his sword drawn, reaching out over Jerusalem. So David and the leaders of Israel put on burlap to show their deep distress and fell face down on the ground. <sup>17</sup>And David said to God, "I am the one who called for the census! I am the one who has sinned and done wrong! But these people are as innocent as sheep—what have they done? O LORD my God, let your anger fall against me and my family, but do not destroy your people."

### David Builds an Altar

**21:18**
2 Chr 3:1

<sup>18</sup>Then the angel of the LORD told Gad to instruct David to go up and build an altar to the LORD on the threshing floor of Araunah the Jebusite. <sup>19</sup>So David went up to do what the LORD had commanded him through Gad. <sup>20</sup>Araunah, who was busy threshing wheat at the time, turned and saw the angel there. His four sons, who were with him, ran away and hid. <sup>21</sup>When Araunah saw David approaching, he left his threshing floor and bowed before David with his face to the ground.

**21:15** As in parallel text at 2 Sam 24:16; Hebrew reads *Ornan*, another name for Araunah; also in 21:18-28.

---

**21:8** When David realized his sin, he took full responsibility, admitted he was wrong, and asked God to forgive him. Many people want to add God and the benefits of Christianity to their lives without acknowledging their personal sin and guilt. But confession and repentance must come before receiving forgiveness. Like David, we must take full responsibility for our actions and confess them to God before we can expect him to forgive us and continue his work in us.

**21:13, 14** Sin has a domino effect; once a sin is committed, a series of consequences follows. God will forgive our sin if we ask him, but the consequences of that sin have already been set in motion. David pleaded for mercy, and God responded by stopping the angel before his mission of death was complete. The consequences of David's sin, however, had already caused severe damage. God will always forgive our sins and will often intervene to make their bitter consequences less severe, but the scars will remain. Thinking through the possible consequences before we act can stop us and thus save us much sorrow and suffering.

**21:14** Why did 70,000 innocent people die for David's sin? Our society places great emphasis upon the individual. In ancient times, however, the family leaders, tribal leaders, and kings represented the people they led, and all expected to share in their successes as well as in their failures and punishments. David

deserved punishment for his sin, but his death could have resulted in political chaos and invasion by enemy armies, leaving hundreds of thousands dead. Instead, God graciously spared David's life. He also put a stop to the plague so that most of the people of Jerusalem were spared.

God made us to work together interdependently. Whether we think it is fair or not, the group usually suffers because of the sins of its leaders. Similarly, our actions always affect other people whether we want them to or not. We cannot fully know the mind of God in this severe judgment. We don't know where the prophets, the tribal leaders, and the other advisers were during this incident and whether or not they chose to go along with the king. We do know that putting confidence in military might alone is idolatry. To allow anything to take God's place is sinful, and it may cause disastrous consequences.

22David said to Araunah, "Let me buy this threshing floor from you at its full price. Then I will build an altar to the LORD there, so that he will stop the plague."

23"Take it, my lord the king, and use it as you wish," Araunah said to David. "I will give the oxen for the burnt offerings, and the threshing boards for wood to build a fire on the altar, and the wheat for the grain offering. I will give it all to you."

24But King David replied to Araunah, "No, I insist on buying it for the full price. I will not take what is yours and give it to the LORD. I will not present burnt offerings that have cost me nothing!" 25So David gave Araunah 600 pieces of gold* in payment for the threshing floor.

26David built an altar there to the LORD and sacrificed burnt offerings and peace offerings. And when David prayed, the LORD answered him by sending fire from heaven to burn up the offering on the altar. 27Then the LORD spoke to the angel, who put the sword back into its sheath.

28When David saw that the LORD had answered his prayer, he offered sacrifices there at Araunah's threshing floor. 29At that time the Tabernacle of the LORD and the altar of burnt offering that Moses had made in the wilderness were located at the place of worship in Gibeon. 30But David was not able to go there to inquire of God, because he was terrified by the drawn sword of the angel of the LORD.

**22** Then David said, "This will be the location for the Temple of the LORD God and the place of the altar for Israel's burnt offerings!"

## 4. David arranges for the building of the Temple
### Preparations for the Temple

2So David gave orders to call together the foreigners living in Israel, and he assigned them the task of preparing finished stone for building the Temple of God. 3David provided large amounts of iron for the nails that would be needed for the doors in the gates and for the clamps, and he gave more bronze than could be weighed. 4He also provided innumerable cedar logs, for the men of Tyre and Sidon had brought vast amounts of cedar to David.

5David said, "My son Solomon is still young and inexperienced. And since the Temple to be built for the LORD must be a magnificent structure, famous and glorious throughout the world, I will begin making preparations for it now." So David collected vast amounts of building materials before his death.

6Then David sent for his son Solomon and instructed him to build a Temple for the LORD, the God of Israel. 7"My son, I wanted to build a Temple to honor the name of the LORD my God," David told him. 8"But the LORD said to me, 'You have killed many men in the battles you have fought. And since you have shed so much blood in my sight, you will not be the one to build a Temple to honor my name. 9But you will have a son who will be a man of peace. I will give him peace with his enemies in all the surrounding lands. His name will be Solomon,* and I will give peace and quiet to Israel during his reign. 10He is the one who will build a Temple to honor my name. He will be my son, and I will be his father. And I will secure the throne of his kingdom over Israel forever.'

**21:26**
Lev 9:24
Judg 6:21

**21:29**
1 Kgs 3:4
1 Chr 16:39

**22:1**
1 Chr 21:18-28
2 Chr 3:1

**22:2**
1 Kgs 5:17-18;
9:20-21
2 Chr 2:17-18

**22:4**
1 Kgs 5:6-10

**22:5**
1 Kgs 3:7
1 Chr 29:1

**22:7**
2 Sam 7:2-3
1 Chr 17:1-2

**22:8**
1 Chr 28:3

**22:9**
2 Sam 12:24-25
1 Kgs 4:20, 25

**22:10**
2 Sam 7:13
1 Chr 17:12

21:25 Hebrew *600 shekels of gold*, about 15 pounds or 6.8 kilograms in weight.     22:9 *Solomon* sounds like and is probably derived from the Hebrew word for "peace."

---

**21:22-24** When David wanted to buy Araunah's land to build an altar, Araunah generously offered it as a gift. But David refused, saying, "I will not take what is yours and give it to the LORD. I will not present burnt offerings that have cost me nothing!" David wanted to offer an offering (or sacrifice) to God. An offering should cost the giver in terms of self, time, or money. To give sacrificially requires more than a token effort or gift. God wants us to give voluntarily, but he wants it to mean something. Giving to God what costs you nothing does not demonstrate commitment.

**21:29–22:1** Gibeon was a Benjaminite city about two hours' journey northwest of Jerusalem. Years before, Saul had moved the Tabernacle there. In this instance, David didn't go there because he was overwhelmed by God's holy wrath, as he had been earlier when one person died moving the Ark toward Jerusalem. Now 70,000 had died as a result of his pride. The fear David felt was the kind of awe that each of us should have when we consider God's character and God's standards. While

we may enjoy God's mercy and acceptance, we dare not take for granted that our God is awesome and holy.

**22:1** Out of David's tragic mistake came the purchase of a plot of land that would become the site of God's Temple, the symbol of God's presence among his people. Every time the people would go to the Temple they would remember that God was their true King and that everyone, including their human king, was fallible and subject to sin. God can use our sins for good purposes if we are sorry for them and seek his forgiveness. When we confess our sins, the way is opened for God to bring good from a bad situation.

**22:7-10** God told David he would not be the one to build the Temple. Instead, the task would be left to his son Solomon. David graciously accepted this no from God. He was not jealous of the fact that his son would have the honor of building God's Temple but instead made preparations for Solomon to carry out his task. Similarly, we should take steps now to prepare the way for our children to find and fulfill God's purpose. Sooner or later our children will have to make their own decisions, but we can

**22:11**
1 Chr 22:16
**22:12**
1 Kgs 3:9-12
2 Chr 1:10
**22:13**
Josh 1:6-9
1 Chr 28:7
**22:14**
1 Chr 22:3; 29:4

**22:16**
1 Chr 22:11
**22:17**
1 Chr 28:1-6
**22:18**
1 Chr 22:9; 23:25
**22:19**
1 Kgs 8:6, 21
1 Chr 28:9
2 Chr 5:7

**23:1**
1 Chr 28:5;
29:22, 28
**23:3**
Num 4:3-49
1 Chr 23:24

[11]"Now, my son, may the Lord be with you and give you success as you follow his directions in building the Temple of the Lord your God. [12]And may the Lord give you wisdom and understanding, that you may obey the Law of the Lord your God as you rule over Israel. [13]For you will be successful if you carefully obey the decrees and regulations that the Lord gave to Israel through Moses. Be strong and courageous; do not be afraid or lose heart!

[14]"I have worked hard to provide materials for building the Temple of the Lord—nearly 4,000 tons of gold, 40,000 tons of silver,* and so much iron and bronze that it cannot be weighed. I have also gathered timber and stone for the walls, though you may need to add more. [15]You have a large number of skilled stonemasons and carpenters and craftsmen of every kind. [16]You have expert goldsmiths and silversmiths and workers of bronze and iron. Now begin the work, and may the Lord be with you!"

[17]Then David ordered all the leaders of Israel to assist Solomon in this project. [18]"The Lord your God is with you," he declared. "He has given you peace with the surrounding nations. He has handed them over to me, and they are now subject to the Lord and his people. [19]Now seek the Lord your God with all your heart and soul. Build the sanctuary of the Lord God so that you can bring the Ark of the Lord's Covenant and the holy vessels of God into the Temple built to honor the Lord's name."

## Duties of the Levites

**23** When David was an old man, he appointed his son Solomon to be king over Israel. [2]David summoned all the leaders of Israel, together with the priests and Levites. [3]All the Levites who were thirty years old or older were counted, and the total came to

**22:14** Hebrew *100,000 talents* [3,400 metric tons] *of gold, 1,000,000 talents* [34,000 metric tons] *of silver.*

---

**DUTIES ASSIGNED IN THE TEMPLE**
King David charged all these people to do their jobs "to honor the Lord's name" (22:17-19). God needs people of every talent—not just prophets and priests—to obey him.

| Duty type | Role | Reference |
|---|---|---|
| Administrative Duties | Supervisors | 1 Chronicles 23:4, 5 |
| | Officials | 1 Chronicles 23:4, 5 |
| | Judges | 1 Chronicles 23:4, 5 |
| | Public administrators | 1 Chronicles 26:29, 30 |
| Ministerial Duties | Priests | 1 Chronicles 24:1 |
| | Prophets | 1 Chronicles 25:1 |
| | Assistants for sacrifices | 1 Chronicles 23:29-31 |
| | Assistants for purification ceremonies | 1 Chronicles 23:28 |
| Service Duties | Bakers of the sacred bread | 1 Chronicles 23:29 |
| | Those who checked the weights and measures | 1 Chronicles 23:29 |
| | Caretakers | 1 Chronicles 23:28 |
| Financial Duties | Those who cared for the treasuries | 1 Chronicles 26:20 |
| | Those who cared for the dedicated gifts | 1 Chronicles 26:26-28 |
| Artistic Duties | Musicians | 1 Chronicles 25:6 |
| | Singers | 1 Chronicles 25:7 |
| Protective Duties | Gatekeepers | 1 Chronicles 26:12-18 |
| Individual Assignments | Chief of the gatekeepers | 1 Chronicles 9:19-21 |
| | Secretary | 1 Chronicles 24:6 |
| | Seer | 1 Chronicles 25:5 |
| | Prophet under the king | 1 Chronicles 25:2 |
| | Chief officer of the treasuries | 1 Chronicles 26:23, 24 |

---

help by supplying them with the proper tools: showing them how to pray and study God's Word, the difference between right and wrong, and the importance of church involvement.

**22:11-16** David made it a point to explain to Solomon exactly why he would be charged with the privilege of building the Temple. His instructions to Solomon, including God's reasons for using David in a limited way, must have been memorable moments for Solomon. The conversations we have with our children deserve our attention, honesty, and vision. Times when we tell our children what we pray God will accomplish in their lives can be some of the best gifts we give them.

**23:1** For more information on Solomon's coronation and the attempts to seize his throne, see 1 Kings 1–2.

**23:1ff** Although David couldn't build the Temple, he could make preparations, and he took that job seriously. He not only gathered funds and materials for God's house but also planned much of the administration and arranged the worship services. The original readers of Chronicles were rebuilding the Temple after it had been destroyed by invading armies, and this information about its procedures was invaluable to them. The next five chapters demonstrate that organization is essential for smooth and effective service.

38,000. [4]Then David said, "From all the Levites, 24,000 will supervise the work at the Temple of the Lord. Another 6,000 will serve as officials and judges. [5]Another 4,000 will work as gatekeepers, and 4,000 will praise the Lord with the musical instruments I have made." [6]Then David divided the Levites into divisions named after the clans descended from the three sons of Levi—Gershon, Kohath, and Merari.

**23:4**
1 Chr 26:29
Ezra 3:8-9
**23:5**
1 Chr 15:16
**23:6**
1 Chr 6:1

### The Gershonites

[7]The Gershonite family units were defined by their lines of descent from Libni* and Shimei, the sons of Gershon. [8]Three of the descendants of Libni were Jehiel (the family leader), Zetham, and Joel. [9]These were the leaders of the family of Libni.
Three of the descendants of Shimei were Shelomoth, Haziel, and Haran. [10]Four other descendants of Shimei were Jahath, Ziza,* Jeush, and Beriah. [11]Jahath was the family leader, and Ziza was next. Jeush and Beriah were counted as a single family because neither had many sons.

### The Kohathites

[12]Four of the descendants of Kohath were Amram, Izhar, Hebron, and Uzziel. [13]The sons of Amram were Aaron and Moses. Aaron and his descendants were set apart to dedicate the most holy things, to offer sacrifices in the Lord's presence, to serve the Lord, and to pronounce blessings in his name forever.

**23:13**
Exod 6:20; 28:1;
30:6-10
**23:14**
Deut 33:1

[14]As for Moses, the man of God, his sons were included with the tribe of Levi. [15]The sons of Moses were Gershom and Eliezer. [16]The descendants of Gershom included Shebuel, the family leader. [17]Eliezer had only one son, Rehabiah, the family leader. Rehabiah had numerous descendants.
[18]The descendants of Izhar included Shelomith, the family leader.
[19]The descendants of Hebron included Jeriah (the family leader), Amariah (the second), Jahaziel (the third), and Jekameam (the fourth).
[20]The descendants of Uzziel included Micah (the family leader) and Isshiah (the second).

### The Merarites

[21]The descendants of Merari included Mahli and Mushi.
The sons of Mahli were Eleazar and Kish. [22]Eleazar died with no sons, only daughters. His daughters married their cousins, the sons of Kish.
[23]Three of the descendants of Mushi were Mahli, Eder, and Jerimoth.

**23:21**
1 Chr 6:19

[24]These were the descendants of Levi by clans, the leaders of their family groups, registered carefully by name. Each had to be twenty years old or older to qualify for service in the house of the Lord. [25]For David said, "The Lord, the God of Israel, has given us peace, and he will always live in Jerusalem. [26]Now the Levites will no longer need to carry the Tabernacle and its furnishings from place to place." [27]In accordance with David's final instructions, all the Levites twenty years old or older were registered for service.

**23:24**
Num 10:17, 21
1 Chr 23:3
**23:25**
1 Chr 22:18
**23:26**
Num 4:5, 15; 7:9
Deut 10:8

[28]The work of the Levites was to assist the priests, the descendants of Aaron, as they served at the house of the Lord. They also took care of the courtyards and side rooms, helped perform the ceremonies of purification, and served in many other ways in the house of God. [29]They were in charge of the sacred bread that was set out on the table, the choice flour for the grain offerings, the wafers made without yeast, the cakes cooked in olive oil, and the other mixed breads. They were also responsible to check all the weights and measures. [30]And each morning and evening they stood before the Lord to sing songs of thanks

**23:29**
Lev 6:20-21;
19:35-36; 24:5-9
1 Chr 9:29, 32

**23:7** Hebrew *Ladan* (also in 23:8, 9), a variant spelling of Libni; compare 6:17.   **23:10** As in Greek version and Latin Vulgate (see also 23:11); Hebrew reads *Zina*.

**23:3** Why was this census acceptable when the other was not (chapter 21)? This census counted only the Levites—those set apart to serve God—and was used to organize the work in the Temple. The census was not based on pride or self-sufficiency, as was the previous census of fighting men.

**23:14** All that is stated here about Moses is that he was "the man of God." What a profound description of a person! A man or woman of God is one whose life reflects God's presence, priorities, and power.

**23:28-32** Priests and Levites had different jobs in and around the Temple. Priests were authorized to perform the sacrifices. Levites were set apart to help the priests. They did the work of elders, deacons, custodians, assistants, musicians, moving men, and repairmen. Both priests and Levites came from the tribe of Levi, but priests also had to be descendants of Aaron, Israel's first high priest (Exodus 28:1-3). Priests and Levites were supported by Israel's tithes and by revenues from certain cities that had been given to them. Worship in the house of the Lord could not have taken place without the combined efforts of the priests and Levites. Their responsibilities were different, but they were equally important to God's plan. No matter what place of service you have in the church, you are important to the healthy functioning of the congregation.

23:31
Lev 23:2-4
Isa 1:13-14

23:32
Num 1:53;
3:6-9, 38

24:1
Exod 6:23
24:2
Lev 10:1-2

24:5
1 Chr 24:31

24:6
1 Chr 18:16

24:7
Neh 12:6

24:10
Neh 12:4
Luke 1:5

and praise to him. 31 They assisted with the burnt offerings that were presented to the LORD on Sabbath days, at new moon celebrations, and at all the appointed festivals. The required number of Levites served in the LORD's presence at all times, following all the procedures they had been given.

32 And so, under the supervision of the priests, the Levites watched over the Tabernacle and the Temple* and faithfully carried out their duties of service at the house of the LORD.

## Duties of the Priests

**24** This is how Aaron's descendants, the priests, were divided into groups for service. The sons of Aaron were Nadab, Abihu, Eleazar, and Ithamar. 2 But Nadab and Abihu died before their father, and they had no sons. So only Eleazar and Ithamar were left to carry on as priests.

3 With the help of Zadok, who was a descendant of Eleazar, and of Ahimelech, who was a descendant of Ithamar, David divided Aaron's descendants into groups according to their various duties. 4 Eleazar's descendants were divided into sixteen groups and Ithamar's into eight, for there were more family leaders among the descendants of Eleazar.

5 All tasks were assigned to the various groups by means of sacred lots so that no preference would be shown, for there were many qualified officials serving God in the sanctuary from among the descendants of both Eleazar and Ithamar. 6 Shemaiah son of Nethanel, a Levite, acted as secretary and wrote down the names and assignments in the presence of the king, the officials, Zadok the priest, Ahimelech son of Abiathar, and the family leaders of the priests and Levites. The descendants of Eleazar and Ithamar took turns casting lots.

> 7 The first lot fell to Jehoiarib.
> The second lot fell to Jedaiah.
> 8 The third lot fell to Harim.
> The fourth lot fell to Seorim.
> 9 The fifth lot fell to Malkijah.
> The sixth lot fell to Mijamin.
> 10 The seventh lot fell to Hakkoz.
> The eighth lot fell to Abijah.
> 11 The ninth lot fell to Jeshua.
> The tenth lot fell to Shecaniah.
> 12 The eleventh lot fell to Eliashib.
> The twelfth lot fell to Jakim.
> 13 The thirteenth lot fell to Huppah.
> The fourteenth lot fell to Jeshebeab.
> 14 The fifteenth lot fell to Bilgah.
> The sixteenth lot fell to Immer.
> 15 The seventeenth lot fell to Hezir.
> The eighteenth lot fell to Happizzez.
> 16 The nineteenth lot fell to Pethahiah.
> The twentieth lot fell to Jehezkel.
> 17 The twenty-first lot fell to Jakin.
> The twenty-second lot fell to Gamul.

**23:32** Hebrew *the Tent of Meeting and the sanctuary.*

---

**24:1ff** The Temple service was highly structured, but this did not hinder the Spirit of God. Rather, it provided an orderly context for worship. (Compare 1 Corinthians 14:40.) Sometimes we feel that planning and structure are unspiritual activities that may hinder spontaneity in worship. But order and structure can free us to respond to God. Order brings glory to God as we experience the joy, freedom, and calm that come when we have wisely planned in advance.

**24:3** This Ahimelech was the son of Abiathar and the grandson of another Ahimelech, one of the priests massacred by Saul (1 Samuel 22:11-18). Abiathar and Zadok were co–high priests under David: One was at Jerusalem where the Ark of God was kept, and one was at Gibeon serving at the Tabernacle. It appears from this verse and 18:16 that Ahimelech began to assume some of Abiathar's duties as his father grew old.

**24:4** Eleazar's descendants were divided into 16 groups (as opposed to Ithamar's 8) for three reasons. (1) Eleazar had received the birthright since his two older brothers, Nadab and Abihu, had been killed (Leviticus 10). The birthright included a double portion of the father's estate. (2) His descendants were greater in number than Ithamar's. (3) His descendants had greater leadership ability. These 24 groups gave order to the functioning of the house of the Lord.

**24:7-18** Each of these 24 groups of priests served two-week shifts each year at the house of the Lord. The rest of the time they served in their hometowns. This system was still in place in Jesus' day (Luke 1:5-9). Zechariah was a member of the Abijah division. During his shift at the Temple, an angel appeared to him and predicted that he would have a son, John.

18 The twenty-third lot fell to Delaiah.
   The twenty-fourth lot fell to Maaziah.

19Each group carried out its appointed duties in the house of the LORD according to the procedures established by their ancestor Aaron in obedience to the commands of the LORD, the God of Israel.

*Family Leaders among the Levites*
20These were the other family leaders descended from Levi:

From the descendants of Amram, the leader was Shebuel.*
From the descendants of Shebuel, the leader was Jehdeiah.
21 From the descendants of Rehabiah, the leader was Isshiah.
22 From the descendants of Izhar, the leader was Shelomith.*
From the descendants of Shelomith, the leader was Jahath.
23 From the descendants of Hebron, Jeriah was the leader,* Amariah was second, Jahaziel was third, and Jekameam was fourth.
24 From the descendants of Uzziel, the leader was Micah.
From the descendants of Micah, the leader was Shamir, 25along with Isshiah, the brother of Micah.
From the descendants of Isshiah, the leader was Zechariah.
26 From the descendants of Merari, the leaders were Mahli and Mushi.
From the descendants of Jaaziah, the leader was Beno.
27 From the descendants of Merari through Jaaziah, the leaders were Beno, Shoham, Zaccur, and Ibri.
28 From the descendants of Mahli, the leader was Eleazar, though he had no sons.
29 From the descendants of Kish, the leader was Jerahmeel.
30 From the descendants of Mushi, the leaders were Mahli, Eder, and Jerimoth.

**24:23**
1 Chr 23:19

These were the descendants of Levi in their various families. 31Like the descendants of Aaron, they were assigned to their duties by means of sacred lots, without regard to age or rank. Lots were drawn in the presence of King David, Zadok, Ahimelech, and the family leaders of the priests and the Levites.

**24:31**
1 Chr 24:5-6

*Duties of the Musicians*

**25** David and the army commanders then appointed men from the families of Asaph, Heman, and Jeduthun to proclaim God's messages to the accompaniment of lyres, harps, and cymbals. Here is a list of their names and their work:

**25:1**
2 Kgs 3:15
1 Chr 6:33, 39;
15:16

2From the sons of Asaph, there were Zaccur, Joseph, Nethaniah, and Asarelah. They worked under the direction of their father, Asaph, who proclaimed God's messages by the king's orders.

3From the sons of Jeduthun, there were Gedaliah, Zeri, Jeshaiah, Shimei,* Hashabiah, and Mattithiah, six in all. They worked under the direction of their father, Jeduthun, who proclaimed God's messages to the accompaniment of the lyre, offering thanks and praise to the LORD.

**25:3**
1 Chr 16:41-42

4From the sons of Heman, there were Bukkiah, Mattaniah, Uzziel, Shubael,* Jerimoth, Hananiah, Hanani, Eliathah, Giddalti, Romamti-ezer, Joshbekashah, Mallothi, Hothir, and Mahazioth. 5All these were the sons of Heman, the king's seer, for God had honored him with fourteen sons and three daughters.

**25:4**
2 Sam 24:11

6All these men were under the direction of their fathers as they made music at the house of the LORD. Their responsibilities included the playing of cymbals, harps, and lyres at the house of God. Asaph, Jeduthun, and Heman reported directly to the king. 7They and their

**25:6**
1 Chr 15:16, 19

**24:20** Hebrew *Shubael* (also in 24:20b), a variant spelling of Shebuel; compare 23:16 and 26:24.   **24:22** Hebrew *Shelomoth* (also in 24:22b), a variant spelling of Shelomith; compare 23:18.   **24:23** Hebrew *From the descendants of Jeriah;* compare 23:19.   **25:3** As in one Hebrew manuscript and some Greek manuscripts (see also 25:17); most Hebrew manuscripts lack *Shimei*.   **25:4** Hebrew *Shebuel,* a variant spelling of Shubael; compare 25:20.

**25:1-7** There were many ways to contribute to the worship in the Tabernacle. Some proclaimed God's messages (25:1), some offered thanks and praise (25:3), and others played instruments (25:6, 7). God wants all his people to participate in worship. You may not be a master musician, a prophet, or a teacher, but God appreciates whatever you have to offer. Develop your special gifts to offer in service to God (Romans 12:3-8; 1 Corinthians 12:29-31).

25:8
1 Chr 26:13

families were all trained in making music before the LORD, and each of them—288 in all—was an accomplished musician. ⁸The musicians were appointed to their term of service by means of sacred lots, without regard to whether they were young or old, teacher or student.

9 The first lot fell to Joseph of the Asaph clan and twelve of his sons and relatives.*
The second lot fell to Gedaliah and twelve of his sons and relatives.
10 The third lot fell to Zaccur and twelve of his sons and relatives.
11 The fourth lot fell to Zeri* and twelve of his sons and relatives.
12 The fifth lot fell to Nethaniah and twelve of his sons and relatives.
13 The sixth lot fell to Bukkiah and twelve of his sons and relatives.
14 The seventh lot fell to Asarelah* and twelve of his sons and relatives.
15 The eighth lot fell to Jeshaiah and twelve of his sons and relatives.
16 The ninth lot fell to Mattaniah and twelve of his sons and relatives.
17 The tenth lot fell to Shimei and twelve of his sons and relatives.
18 The eleventh lot fell to Uzziel* and twelve of his sons and relatives.
19 The twelfth lot fell to Hashabiah and twelve of his sons and relatives.
20 The thirteenth lot fell to Shubael and twelve of his sons and relatives.
21 The fourteenth lot fell to Mattithiah and twelve of his sons and relatives.
22 The fifteenth lot fell to Jerimoth* and twelve of his sons and relatives.
23 The sixteenth lot fell to Hananiah and twelve of his sons and relatives.
24 The seventeenth lot fell to Joshbekashah* and twelve of his sons and relatives.
25 The eighteenth lot fell to Hanani and twelve of his sons and relatives.

**25:9** As in Greek version; Hebrew lacks *and twelve of his sons and relatives.* **25:11** Hebrew *Izri,* a variant spelling of Zeri; compare 25:3. **25:14** Hebrew *Jesarelah,* a variant spelling of Asarelah; compare 25:2. **25:18** Hebrew *Azarel,* a variant spelling of Uzziel; compare 25:4. **25:22** Hebrew *Jeremoth,* a variant spelling of Jerimoth; compare 25:4. **25:24** Hebrew *Joshbekasha,* a variant spelling of Joshbekashah; compare 25:4.

---

**MUSIC IN BIBLE TIMES**

| *Highlights of Musical Use in Scripture* | *Reference* |
| --- | --- |
| Jubal was father of all musicians | Genesis 4:21 |
| Miriam and other women sang and danced to praise God | Exodus 15:1-21 |
| The priest was to have bells on his robes. | Exodus 28:34, 35 |
| Jericho fell to the sound of horns | Joshua 6:4-20 |
| Saul experienced the soothing effect of music | 1 Samuel 16:14-23 |
| The king's coronation was accompanied by music. | 1 Kings 1:39, 40 |
| The Ark was accompanied by trumpeters | 1 Chronicles 16:6 |
| There were musicians for the king's court | Ecclesiastes 2:8 |
| From David's time on, the use of music in worship was much more organized. Music for the Temple became refined | 1 Chronicles 15:16-24 / 1 Chronicles 16:4-7 / 2 Chronicles 5:11-14 |
| Everything was to be used by everyone to praise the Lord | Psalm 150 |

*In the New Testament, worship continued in the synagogues until the Christians became unwelcome there, so there was a rich musical heritage already established. The fact that music is mentioned less often in the New Testament does not mean it was less important.*

| | |
| --- | --- |
| Jesus and the disciples sang a hymn. | Matthew 26:30 |
| Paul and Silas sang in jail. | Acts 16:25 |
| We are to sing to the Lord as a response to what he has done in our lives | Ephesians 5:19, 20 / Colossians 3:16 / James 5:13 |

Paul clearly puts forth the Christian's view that things are not good or bad in and of themselves (see Romans 14 and 1 Corinthians 14:7, 8, 26). The point should always be to worship the Lord or help others by means of the things of this world, including music. Music was created by God and can be returned to him in praise. Does the music you play or listen to have a negative or positive impact upon your relationship with God?

---

**25:9-31** The musicians were divided into 24 groups to match the 24 groups of Levites (24:7-18). This division of labor gave order to the planning of Temple work, promoted excellence by making train-ing easier, gave variety to worship because each group worked a term, and provided opportunities for many to be involved.

26 The nineteenth lot fell to Mallothi and twelve of his sons and relatives.
27 The twentieth lot fell to Eliathah and twelve of his sons and relatives.
28 The twenty-first lot fell to Hothir and twelve of his sons and relatives.
29 The twenty-second lot fell to Giddalti and twelve of his sons and relatives.
30 The twenty-third lot fell to Mahazioth and twelve of his sons and relatives.
31 The twenty-fourth lot fell to Romamti-ezer and twelve of his sons and relatives.

25:31
1 Chr 9:33

### Duties of the Gatekeepers

**26** These are the divisions of the gatekeepers:

From the Korahites, there was Meshelemiah son of Kore, of the family of Abiasaph.* 2 The sons of Meshelemiah were Zechariah (the oldest), Jediael (the second), Zebadiah (the third), Jathniel (the fourth), 3 Elam (the fifth), Jehohanan (the sixth), and Eliehoenai (the seventh).

4 The sons of Obed-edom, also gatekeepers, were Shemaiah (the oldest), Jehozabad (the second), Joah (the third), Sacar (the fourth), Nethanel (the fifth), 5 Ammiel (the sixth), Issachar (the seventh), and Peullethai (the eighth). God had richly blessed Obed-edom.

6 Obed-edom's son Shemaiah had sons with great ability who earned positions of great authority in the clan. 7 Their names were Othni, Rephael, Obed, and Elzabad. Their relatives, Elihu and Semakiah, were also very capable men.

8 All of these descendants of Obed-edom, including their sons and grandsons—sixty-two of them in all—were very capable men, well qualified for their work. 9 Meshelemiah's eighteen sons and relatives were also very capable men.

10 Hosah, of the Merari clan, appointed Shimri as the leader among his sons, though he was not the oldest. 11 His other sons included Hilkiah (the second), Tebaliah (the third), and Zechariah (the fourth). Hosah's sons and relatives, who served as gatekeepers, numbered thirteen in all.

26:10
1 Chr 16:38

12 These divisions of the gatekeepers were named for their family leaders, and like the other Levites, they served at the house of the LORD. 13 They were assigned by families for guard duty at the various gates, without regard to age or training, for it was all decided by means of sacred lots.

26:13
1 Chr 24:5, 31;
25:8

14 The responsibility for the east gate went to Meshelemiah* and his group. The north gate was assigned to his son Zechariah, a man of unusual wisdom. 15 The south gate went to Obed-edom, and his sons were put in charge of the storehouse. 16 Shuppim and Hosah were assigned the west gate and the gateway leading up to the Temple.* Guard duties were divided evenly. 17 Six Levites were assigned each day to the east gate, four to the north gate, four to the south gate, and two pairs at the storehouse. 18 Six were assigned each day to the west gate, four to the gateway leading up to the Temple, and two to the courtyard.*

19 These were the divisions of the gatekeepers from the clans of Korah and Merari.

### Treasurers and Other Officials

20 Other Levites, led by Ahijah, were in charge of the treasuries of the house of God and the treasuries of the gifts dedicated to the LORD. 21 From the family of Libni* in the clan of Gershon, Jehiel* was the leader. 22 The sons of Jehiel, Zetham and his brother Joel, were in charge of the treasuries of the house of the LORD.

26:20
1 Chr 26:22, 24;
28:12

23 These are the leaders that descended from Amram, Izhar, Hebron, and Uzziel:

**26:1** As in Greek version (see also Exod 6:24); Hebrew reads *Asaph.* **26:14** Hebrew *Shelemiah,* a variant spelling of Meshelemiah; compare 26:2. **26:16** Or *the gate of Shalleketh on the upper road* (also in 26:18). The meaning of the Hebrew is uncertain. **26:18** Or *the colonnade.* The meaning of the Hebrew is uncertain. **26:21a** Hebrew *Ladan,* a variant spelling of Libni; compare 6:17. **26:21b** Hebrew *Jehieli* (also in 26:22), a variant spelling of Jehiel; compare 23:8.

**26:1** There were 4,000 gatekeepers (23:5). They were all Levites and did many other jobs as well. Some of their duties included (1) checking out the equipment and utensils used each day and making sure they were returned, (2) storing, ordering, and maintaining the food supplies for the priests and sacrifices, (3) caring for the furniture, (4) mixing the incense that was burned daily, and (5) accounting for the gifts brought. (For more on gatekeepers, see the note on 9:17, 18.)

**26:5** "God had richly blessed Obed-edom." The status of children in society has fluctuated throughout history; sometimes they are highly esteemed, and sometimes abused and cheated. But Scripture shows no such vacillation—children are called a gift from the Lord, and God never views them as a burden (Psalm 127:3-5; Mark 10:13-15).

<sup>24</sup>From the clan of Amram, Shebuel was a descendant of Gershom son of Moses. He was the chief officer of the treasuries. <sup>25</sup>His relatives through Eliezer were Rehabiah, Jeshaiah, Joram, Zicri, and Shelomoth.

26:26
2 Sam 8:11

<sup>26</sup>Shelomoth and his relatives were in charge of the treasuries containing the gifts that King David, the family leaders, and the generals and captains* and other officers of the army had dedicated to the LORD. <sup>27</sup>These men dedicated some of the plunder they had gained in battle to maintain the house of the LORD. <sup>28</sup>Shelomoth* and his relatives also cared for the gifts dedicated to the LORD by Samuel the seer, Saul son of Kish, Abner son of Ner, and Joab son of Zeruiah. All the other dedicated gifts were in their care, too.

26:29
1 Chr 23:4
26:30
1 Chr 27:17

<sup>29</sup>From the clan of Izhar came Kenaniah. He and his sons were given administrative responsibilities* over Israel as officials and judges.

<sup>30</sup>From the clan of Hebron came Hashabiah. He and his relatives—1,700 capable men—were put in charge of the Israelite lands west of the Jordan River. They were responsible for all matters related to the things of the LORD and the service of the king in that area.

26:31
1 Chr 23:19

<sup>31</sup>Also from the clan of Hebron came Jeriah,* who was the leader of the Hebronites according to the genealogical records. (In the fortieth year of David's reign, a search was made in the records, and capable men from the clan of Hebron were found at Jazer in the land of Gilead.) <sup>32</sup>There were 2,700 capable men among the relatives of Jeriah. King David sent them to the east side of the Jordan River and put them in charge of the tribes of Reuben and Gad and the half-tribe of Manasseh. They were responsible for all matters related to God and to the king.

## Military Commanders and Divisions

**27** This is the list of Israelite generals and captains,* and their officers, who served the king by supervising the army divisions that were on duty each month of the year. Each division served for one month and had 24,000 troops.

27:2
2 Sam 23:8
1 Chr 11:11-31

<sup>2</sup>Jashobeam son of Zabdiel was commander of the first division of 24,000 troops, which was on duty during the first month. <sup>3</sup>He was a descendant of Perez and was in charge of all the army officers for the first month.

<sup>4</sup>Dodai, a descendant of Ahoah, was commander of the second division of 24,000 troops, which was on duty during the second month. Mikloth was his chief officer.

<sup>5</sup>Benaiah son of Jehoiada the priest was commander of the third division of 24,000 troops, which was on duty during the third month. <sup>6</sup>This was the Benaiah who commanded David's elite military group known as the Thirty. His son Ammizabad was his chief officer.

<sup>7</sup>Asahel, the brother of Joab, was commander of the fourth division of 24,000 troops, which was on duty during the fourth month. Asahel was succeeded by his son Zebadiah.

<sup>8</sup>Shammah* the Izrahite was commander of the fifth division of 24,000 troops, which was on duty during the fifth month.

<sup>9</sup>Ira son of Ikkesh from Tekoa was commander of the sixth division of 24,000 troops, which was on duty during the sixth month.

<sup>10</sup>Helez, a descendant of Ephraim from Pelon, was commander of the seventh division of 24,000 troops, which was on duty during the seventh month.

<sup>11</sup>Sibbecai, a descendant of Zerah from Hushah, was commander of the eighth division of 24,000 troops, which was on duty during the eighth month.

<sup>12</sup>Abiezer from Anathoth in the territory of Benjamin was commander of the ninth division of 24,000 troops, which was on duty during the ninth month.

<sup>13</sup>Maharai, a descendant of Zerah from Netophah, was commander of the tenth division of 24,000 troops, which was on duty during the tenth month.

**26:26** Hebrew *the commanders of thousands and of hundreds.* **26:28** Hebrew *Shelomith,* a variant spelling of Shelomoth. **26:29** Or *were given outside work;* or *were given work away from the Temple area.* **26:31** Hebrew *Jerijah,* a variant spelling of Jeriah; compare 23:19. **27:1** Hebrew *commanders of thousands and of hundreds.* **27:8** Hebrew *Shamhuth,* a variant spelling of Shammah; compare 11:27 and 2 Sam 23:25.

**26:27** War plunder rightfully belonged to the victorious army. These soldiers, however, gave their portion of all the plunder to the house of the Lord to express their dedication to God. Like these commanders, we should think of what we *can* give, rather than what we are obligated to give. Is your giving a matter of rejoicing rather than duty? Give as a response of joy and love for God.

14Benaiah from Pirathon in Ephraim was commander of the eleventh division of 24,000 troops, which was on duty during the eleventh month. 15Heled,* a descendant of Othniel from Netophah, was commander of the twelfth division of 24,000 troops, which was on duty during the twelfth month.

### Leaders of the Tribes

16The following were the tribes of Israel and their leaders:

| Tribe | Leader | |
|---|---|---|
| Reuben | Eliezer son of Zicri | |
| Simeon | Shephatiah son of Maacah | |
| 17 Levi | Hashabiah son of Kemuel | 27:17 1 Chr 12:28 |
| Aaron (the priests) | Zadok | |
| 18 Judah | Elihu (a brother of David) | |
| Issachar | Omri son of Michael | |
| 19 Zebulun | Ishmaiah son of Obadiah | |
| Naphtali | Jeremoth son of Azriel | |
| 20 Ephraim | Hoshea son of Azaziah | |
| Manasseh (west) | Joel son of Pedaiah | |
| 21 Manasseh in Gilead (east) | Iddo son of Zechariah | |
| Benjamin | Jaasiel son of Abner | |
| 22 Dan | Azarel son of Jeroham | |

These were the leaders of the tribes of Israel.

23When David took his census, he did not count those who were younger than twenty years of age, because the LORD had promised to make the Israelites as numerous as the stars in heaven. 24Joab son of Zeruiah began the census but never finished it because* the anger of God fell on Israel. The total number was never recorded in King David's official records.

27:23 2 Sam 24:1

27:24 2 Sam 24:12-15 1 Chr 21:1-7

### Officials of David's Kingdom

25Azmaveth son of Adiel was in charge of the palace treasuries. Jonathan son of Uzziah was in charge of the regional treasuries throughout the towns, villages, and fortresses of Israel. 26Ezri son of Kelub was in charge of the field workers who farmed the king's lands. 27Shimei from Ramah was in charge of the king's vineyards. Zabdi from Shepham was responsible for the grapes and the supplies of wine. 28Baal-hanan from Geder was in charge of the king's olive groves and sycamore-fig trees in the foothills of Judah.* Joash was responsible for the supplies of olive oil. 29Shitrai from Sharon was in charge of the cattle on the Sharon Plain. Shaphat son of Adlai was responsible for the cattle in the valleys. 30Obil the Ishmaelite was in charge of the camels. Jehdeiah from Meronoth was in charge of the donkeys. 31Jaziz the Hagrite was in charge of the king's flocks of sheep and goats. All these officials were overseers of King David's property.

27:28 1 Kgs 10:27 2 Chr 1:15

27:29 1 Chr 5:16

27:31 1 Chr 5:10

32Jonathan, David's uncle, was a wise counselor to the king, a man of great insight, and a scribe. Jehiel the Hacmonite was responsible for teaching the king's sons. 33Ahithophel was the royal adviser. Hushai the Arkite was the king's friend. 34Ahithophel was succeeded by Jehoiada son of Benaiah and by Abiathar. Joab was commander of the king's army.

27:33 2 Sam 15:12, 32, 37

27:34 1 Kgs 1:7 1 Chr 11:6; 27:5

### David's Instructions to Solomon

**28** David summoned all the officials of Israel to Jerusalem—the leaders of the tribes, the commanders of the army divisions, the other generals and captains,* the overseers of the royal property and livestock, the palace officials, the mighty men, and all

28:1 1 Chr 11:10-47; 23:2; 27:1-31

27:15 Hebrew *Heldai*, a variant spelling of Heled; compare 11:30 and 2 Sam 23:29.   27:24 Or *never finished it, and yet.*   27:28 Hebrew *the Shephelah.*   28:1 Hebrew *the commanders of thousands and commanders of hundreds.*

---

27:24  King David's official records were historical documents kept in the royal archives with other official records. They no longer exist. See 1 Kings 14:19.

27:33, 34  When Absalom rebelled against David, Ahithophel betrayed David and joined the rebellion. Hushai pretended loyalty to Absalom, and his advice caused Absalom's downfall (2 Samuel 15:31–17:23).

28:1  The last two chapters of 1 Chronicles present the transition from David to Solomon as king of Israel. The writer doesn't mention Adonijah's conspiracy or David's frailty (1 Kings 1–2).

**28:2**
1 Chr 17:1-2
Ps 132:7
Isa 66:1

**28:3**
1 Chr 17:4; 22:8

**28:4**
Gen 49:8-10
1 Sam 16:1-6
1 Chr 5:2;
17:23, 27

**28:5**
1 Chr 3:1-9; 14:3-7;
22:9-10

**28:6**
2 Sam 7:13-14

**28:7**
1 Chr 22:13

**28:9**
1 Kgs 8:61
2 Chr 15:2
Jer 29:13

**28:10**
1 Chr 22:13

**28:11**
Exod 25:17-22, 40

**28:12**
1 Chr 26:20, 28

**28:13**
1 Chr 23:6; 24:1

**28:15**
Exod 25:31

the other brave warriors in the kingdom. 2David rose to his feet and said: "My brothers and my people! It was my desire to build a temple where the Ark of the LORD's Covenant, God's footstool, could rest permanently. I made the necessary preparations for building it, 3but God said to me, 'You must not build a temple to honor my name, for you are a warrior and have shed much blood.'

4"Yet the LORD, the God of Israel, has chosen me from among all my father's family to be king over Israel forever. For he has chosen the tribe of Judah to rule, and from among the families of Judah he chose my father's family. And from among my father's sons the LORD was pleased to make me king over all Israel. 5And from among my sons—for the LORD has given me many—he chose Solomon to succeed me on the throne of Israel and to rule over the LORD's kingdom. 6He said to me, 'Your son Solomon will build my Temple and its courtyards, for I have chosen him as my son, and I will be his father. 7And if he continues to obey my commands and regulations as he does now, I will make his kingdom last forever.'

8"So now, with God as our witness, and in the sight of all Israel—the LORD's assembly—I give you this charge. Be careful to obey all the commands of the LORD your God, so that you may continue to possess this good land and leave it to your children as a permanent inheritance.

9"And Solomon, my son, learn to know the God of your ancestors intimately. Worship and serve him with your whole heart and a willing mind. For the LORD sees every heart and knows every plan and thought. If you seek him, you will find him. But if you forsake him, he will reject you forever. 10So take this seriously. The LORD has chosen you to build a Temple as his sanctuary. Be strong, and do the work."

11Then David gave Solomon the plans for the Temple and its surroundings, including the entry room, the storerooms, the upstairs rooms, the inner rooms, and the inner sanctuary—which was the place of atonement. 12David also gave Solomon all the plans he had in mind* for the courtyards of the LORD's Temple, the outside rooms, the treasuries, and the rooms for the gifts dedicated to the LORD. 13The king also gave Solomon the instructions concerning the work of the various divisions of priests and Levites in the Temple of the LORD. And he gave specifications for the items in the Temple that were to be used for worship.

14David gave instructions regarding how much gold and silver should be used to make the items needed for service. 15He told Solomon the amount of gold needed for the gold lampstands and lamps, and the amount of silver for the silver lampstands and lamps, depending on how each would be used. 16He designated the amount of gold for the table on which the Bread of the Presence would be placed and the amount of silver for other tables.

**28:12** Or *the plans of the spirit that was with him.*

---

**PRINCIPLES TO LIVE BY**

King David gave his son Solomon principles to guide him through life (see 1 Chronicles 28:9, 10). These same ideas are ones that any Christian parent would want to present to a child:

1. Get to know God personally.
2. Learn God's commands and discover what he wants you to do.
3. Worship God with wholehearted devotion.
4. Serve God with a willing mind.
5. Be faithful.
6. Don't become discouraged.

---

Instead, he focuses on the positive—God's plans for Israel and his promise to David's descendants.

**28:5** The kingdom of Israel belonged to the Lord, not to David or anyone else. Israel's king, then, was God's deputy, commissioned to carry out God's will for the nation. Thus, God could choose the person he wanted as king without following customary lines of succession. David was not Saul's heir, and Solomon was not David's oldest son, but this did not matter because God appointed them.

**28:8** David told Solomon to be careful to obey every one of God's commands to ensure Israel's prosperity and the continuation of David's descendants upon the throne. It was the king's solemn duty to study and obey God's laws. The teachings of Scripture are the keys to security, happiness, and justice, but you'll never discover them unless you search God's Word. If

we ignore God's will and neglect his teaching, anything we attempt to build, even if it has God's name on it, will be headed for collapse. Get to know God's commands through regular Bible study, and find ways to apply them consistently.

**28:9** "The LORD sees every heart." Nothing can be hidden from God. He sees and understands everything in our hearts. David found this out the hard way when God sent Nathan to expose David's sins of adultery and murder (2 Samuel 12). David told Solomon to be completely open with God and dedicated to him. It makes no sense to try to hide any thoughts or actions from an all-knowing God. This should cause us joy, not fear, because God knows even the worst about us and loves us anyway.

**28:13** Some of the instructions about the work of the priests and Levites are in chapters 23 and 24.

¹⁷David also designated the amount of gold for the solid gold meat hooks used to handle the sacrificial meat and for the basins, pitchers, and dishes, as well as the amount of silver for every dish. ¹⁸He designated the amount of refined gold for the altar of incense. Finally, he gave him a plan for the Lord's "chariot"—the gold cherubim* whose wings were stretched out over the Ark of the Lord's Covenant. ¹⁹"Every part of this plan," David told Solomon, "was given to me in writing from the hand of the Lord.*"

²⁰Then David continued, "Be strong and courageous, and do the work. Don't be afraid or discouraged, for the Lord God, my God, is with you. He will not fail you or forsake you. He will see to it that all the work related to the Temple of the Lord is finished correctly. ²¹The various divisions of priests and Levites will serve in the Temple of God. Others with skills of every kind will volunteer, and the officials and the entire nation are at your command."

### Gifts for Building the Temple

**29** Then King David turned to the entire assembly and said, "My son Solomon, whom God has clearly chosen as the next king of Israel, is still young and inexperienced. The work ahead of him is enormous, for the Temple he will build is not for mere mortals—it is for the Lord God himself! ²Using every resource at my command, I have gathered as much as I could for building the Temple of my God. Now there is enough gold, silver, bronze, iron, and wood, as well as great quantities of onyx, other precious stones, costly jewels, and all kinds of fine stone and marble.

³"And now, because of my devotion to the Temple of my God, I am giving all of my own private treasures of gold and silver to help in the construction. This is in addition to the building materials I have already collected for his holy Temple. ⁴I am donating more than 112 tons of gold* from Ophir and 262 tons of refined silver* to be used for overlaying the walls of the buildings ⁵and for the other gold and silver work to be done by the craftsmen. Now then, who will follow my example and give offerings to the Lord today?"

⁶Then the family leaders, the leaders of the tribes of Israel, the generals and captains of the army,* and the king's administrative officers all gave willingly. ⁷For the construction of the Temple of God, they gave about 188 tons of gold,* 10,000 gold coins,* 375 tons of silver,* 675 tons of bronze,* and 3,750 tons of iron.* ⁸They also contributed numerous precious stones, which were deposited in the treasury of the house of the Lord under the care of Jehiel, a descendant of Gershon. ⁹The people rejoiced over the offerings, for they had given freely and wholeheartedly to the Lord, and King David was filled with joy.

### David's Prayer of Praise

¹⁰Then David praised the Lord in the presence of the whole assembly:

"O Lord, the God of our ancestor Israel,* may you be praised forever and ever! ¹¹Yours, O Lord, is the greatness, the power, the glory, the victory, and the majesty. Everything in the heavens and on earth is yours, O Lord, and this is your kingdom. We adore you as the one who is over all things. ¹²Wealth and honor come from you alone, for you rule over everything. Power and might are in your hand, and at your discretion people are made great and given strength.

**28:18** Hebrew *for the gold cherub chariot.* **28:19** Or *was written under the direction of the Lord.* **29:4a** Hebrew *3,000 talents* [102 metric tons] *of gold.* **29:4b** Hebrew *7,000 talents* [238 metric tons] *of silver.* **29:6** Hebrew *the commanders of thousands and commanders of hundreds.* **29:7a** Hebrew *5,000 talents* [170 metric tons] *of gold.* **29:7b** Hebrew *10,000 darics* [a Persian coin] *of gold,* about 185 pounds or 84 kilograms in weight. **29:7c** Hebrew *10,000 talents* [340 metric tons] *of silver.* **29:7d** Hebrew *18,000 talents* [612 metric tons] *of bronze.* **29:7e** Hebrew *100,000 talents* [3,400 metric tons] *of iron.* **29:10** *Israel* is the name that God gave to Jacob.

**28:18**
Exod 25:18-22;
30:1
**28:19**
1 Chr 28:11-12
**28:20**
Josh 1:5
1 Chr 22:13
Heb 13:5
**28:21**
Exod 35:25-35;
36:1-2
**29:1**
1 Chr 22:5
**29:2**
1 Chr 22:2-5
**29:4**
1 Kgs 9:28
1 Chr 22:14
**29:6**
1 Chr 27:1, 25;
28:1
**29:8**
1 Chr 23:8
**29:9**
1 Kgs 8:61
2 Cor 9:7
**29:11**
Rev 5:12-13
**29:12**
2 Chr 1:12; 20:6

---

**28:20** David advised Solomon not to be frightened about the size of his task as king and builder of the Temple. Fear can immobilize us. The size of a job, its risks, or the pressure of the situation can cause us to freeze and do nothing. One remedy for fear is found here: Don't focus on the fear; instead, get to work. Getting started is often the most difficult and frightening part of a job.

**29:1** Solomon became king in 970 B.C.

**29:1** It is possible to be obsessed with a church building to the neglect of the real church—the people of God. But the opposite response, neglecting the church building, is also wrong. David makes this point when he says that the Temple is "for the Lord God himself!" Although we should avoid wasteful extravagance, we must remember that every church building can be a visible witness for God. How can your church building be better used to tell the world about God?

**29:3-5** David gave from his personal fortune to the Temple. He encouraged others to follow his example, and they willingly did. Both the Tabernacle (Exodus 35:5–36:7) and the Temple were built from the voluntary gifts of the people. Like David, we can acknowledge that all we have comes from God (29:14-16). We may not have David's wealth, but we can develop his willingness to give. It is not what we have that counts with God, but our willingness to give it.

**29:6-9** These leaders displayed a right attitude toward their money by giving willingly to God's work. This attitude is described by Paul in 2 Corinthians 9:7: "You must each decide in your heart how much to give. And don't give reluctantly or

<sup>13</sup>"O our God, we thank you and praise your glorious name! <sup>14</sup>But who am I, and who are my people, that we could give anything to you? Everything we have has come from you, and we give you only what you first gave us! <sup>15</sup>We are here for only a moment, visitors and strangers in the land as our ancestors were before us. Our days on earth are like a passing shadow, gone so soon without a trace.

<sup>16</sup>"O LORD our God, even this material we have gathered to build a Temple to honor your holy name comes from you! It all belongs to you! <sup>17</sup>I know, my God, that you examine our hearts and rejoice when you find integrity there. You know I have done all this with good motives, and I have watched your people offer their gifts willingly and joyously.

<sup>18</sup>"O LORD, the God of our ancestors Abraham, Isaac, and Israel, make your people always want to obey you. See to it that their love for you never changes. <sup>19</sup>Give my son Solomon the wholehearted desire to obey all your commands, laws, and decrees, and to do everything necessary to build this Temple, for which I have made these preparations."

<sup>20</sup>Then David said to the whole assembly, "Give praise to the LORD your God!" And the entire assembly praised the LORD, the God of their ancestors, and they bowed low and knelt before the LORD and the king.

### Solomon Named as King

<sup>21</sup>The next day they brought 1,000 bulls, 1,000 rams, and 1,000 male lambs as burnt offerings to the LORD. They also brought liquid offerings and many other sacrifices on behalf of all Israel. <sup>22</sup>They feasted and drank in the LORD's presence with great joy that day.

And again they crowned David's son Solomon as their new king. They anointed him before the LORD as their leader, and they anointed Zadok as priest. <sup>23</sup>So Solomon took the throne of the LORD in place of his father, David, and he succeeded in everything, and all Israel obeyed him. <sup>24</sup>All the officials, the warriors, and the sons of King David pledged their loyalty to King Solomon. <sup>25</sup>And the LORD exalted Solomon in the sight of all Israel, and he gave Solomon greater royal splendor than any king in Israel before him.

### Summary of David's Reign

<sup>26</sup>So David son of Jesse reigned over all Israel. <sup>27</sup>He reigned over Israel for forty years, seven of them in Hebron and thirty-three in Jerusalem. <sup>28</sup>He died at a ripe old age, having enjoyed long life, wealth, and honor. Then his son Solomon ruled in his place.

<sup>29</sup>All the events of King David's reign, from beginning to end, are written in *The Record of Samuel the Seer, The Record of Nathan the Prophet,* and *The Record of Gad the Seer.* <sup>30</sup>These accounts include the mighty deeds of his reign and everything that happened to him and to Israel and to all the surrounding kingdoms.

---

**29:15** Lev 25:23 / Job 14:2, 10-12

**29:17** 1 Chr 28:9

**29:19** 1 Chr 28:9 / Ps 72:1

**29:20** Josh 22:33

**29:21** 1 Kgs 8:62-63

**29:22** 1 Kgs 1:33-34 / 1 Chr 29:1

**29:25** 2 Chr 1:1, 12

**29:26-28** //1 Kgs 2:10-12

**29:26** 1 Chr 18:14

**29:27** 2 Sam 5:4-5

**29:28** 1 Chr 23:1 / Acts 13:36

---

in response to pressure. 'For God loves a person who gives cheerfully.'" When we are generous because we are thankful, our attitude can inspire others. Give generously to God's work.

**29:15** David contrasts God's everlasting nature with the fleeting lives of his people. Nothing lasts unless it is rooted in God's unchanging character. If our most impressive deeds fade to dust before God, where should we place our confidence? Only in a relationship with God can we find anything permanent. His love never fades, and nothing can take it away.

**29:19** "Wholehearted desire to obey" means to be entirely dedicated to God. This is what David prayed for Solomon—that he would desire, above all else, to serve God. Do you find it hard to do what God wants, or find it harder to *want* to do it? God can give you wholehearted devotion. If you believe in Jesus Christ, this is already happening in you. Paul wrote: "For God is working in you, giving you the desire and the power to do what pleases him" (Philippians 2:13). Consider yourself blessed if someone in your life is praying this way for you.

**29:21** Liquid offerings of wine were poured out as sacrifices to God to acknowledge his role in providing for his people.

**29:25** Solomon surpassed his father's wealth and splendor. David's legacy resulted from his vital relationship with the Lord,

and he passed his spiritual values on to Solomon. Any money or power we leave to our children is far less valuable than the spiritual legacy we pass on. What spiritual inheritance will your children receive? In what specific ways are you passing on that legacy today?

**29:29** A seer was someone who received messages from God for the nation in visions or dreams.

**29:30** First Chronicles vividly illustrates the importance of maintaining a relationship with God. The genealogies in chapters 1–9 emphasize the importance of a spiritual heritage. The second part of the book details the life of David. Few men or women in the Bible were as close to God as David was. His daily contact with God increased his capacity to worship and strengthened his desire to build God's Temple. David's life shows us the importance of staying close to God—through studying and obeying his Word and communicating with him daily. Second Chronicles, on the other hand, reveals how quickly our lives can deteriorate (spiritually, mentally, and socially) when we fail to stay well grounded in God.

## VITAL STATISTICS

**PURPOSE:**
To unify the nation around true worship of God by showing his standard for judging kings. The righteous kings of Judah and the religious revivals under their rule are highlighted, and the sins of the evil kings are exposed.

**AUTHOR:**
Ezra, according to Jewish tradition

**ORIGINAL AUDIENCE:**
The exiles who returned from captivity

**DATE WRITTEN:**
Approximately 430 B.C., recording events from the beginning of Solomon's reign (970 B.C.) to the beginning of the Babylonian captivity (586 B.C.)

**SETTING:**
Second Chronicles parallels 1 and 2 Kings and serves as their commentary. Originally 1 and 2 Chronicles were one book. It was written after the Exile from a priestly perspective, highlighting the importance of the Temple and the religious revivals in Judah. The northern kingdom, Israel, is virtually ignored in this history.

**KEY VERSE:**
"Then if my people who are called by my name will humble themselves and pray and seek my face and turn from their wicked ways, I will hear from heaven and will forgive their sins and restore their land" (7:14).

**KEY PEOPLE:**
Solomon, the queen of Sheba, Rehoboam, Asa, Jehoshaphat, Jehoram, Joash, Uzziah, Ahaz, Hezekiah, Manasseh, Josiah

**KEY PLACES:**
Jerusalem, the Temple

**SPECIAL FEATURES:**
Includes a detailed record of the Temple's construction

THE SLIDE clicks, and our eyes focus on the image flashed onto the screen in the darkened sanctuary. "This idol," explains the missionary, "is made of stone and is worshiped daily. The natives believe that this will guarantee good crops and healthy children." With condescending smiles, we wonder at their ignorance. How could anyone worship an object? Idols are for the naive and the superstitious! But after the presentation, we return home to *our* idols of wealth, prestige, or self-fulfillment. Whatever we put in God's place we worship, despite what we profess.

Our experience parallels Israel's. They were chosen by God to represent him on earth. But too often they forgot the truth and their calling, stumbling blindly after idols as the neighboring nations did. Then prophets, priests, and judgment would push them abruptly back to the one true God. Second Chronicles relates this sordid history of Judah's corrupt and idolatrous kings. Here and there a good king would arise in Judah, and for a time revival would follow, but the downward spiral would continue—ending in chaos, destruction, and captivity.

The chronicler writes this volume to bring the people of Israel back to God by reminding them of their past. Only by following God would they prosper! As you read 2 Chronicles, you will catch a vivid glimpse of Judah's history (the history of Israel, the northern kingdom, is virtually ignored), and you will see the tragic results of idolatry. Learn the lessons of the past: Determine to get rid of any idols in your life and to worship God alone.

Second Chronicles continues the history of 1 Chronicles. David's son Solomon was inaugurated as king. Solomon built the magnificent Temple in Jerusalem, thus fulfilling his father's wish and last request (chapters 2—5). Solomon enjoyed a peaceful and prosperous reign of 40 years that made him world famous. After Solomon died, his son Rehoboam assumed the throne, and his immaturity divided the kingdom.

In Judah there were a few good kings and many evil ones. The writer of Chronicles faithfully records their achievements and failures, noting how each king measured up to God's standard for success. Clearly a good king obeyed God's laws, eliminated the places of idol worship, and made no alliances with other nations. Judah's good kings include Asa, Jehoshaphat, Uzziah, Hezekiah, and Josiah. Of its many evil ones, Ahaz and Manasseh were perhaps the worst. Eventually the nation was conquered and taken captive, and the Temple was destroyed.

The writer's purpose was to reunite the nation around the true worship of God after the Captivity. In these pages, he reminds the people of their past. He clearly broadcasts his message through one of the best-known verses in Scripture, "Then if my people who are called by my name will humble themselves and pray and seek my face and turn from their wicked ways, I will hear from heaven and will forgive their sins and restore their land" (7:14). As you read 2 Chronicles, listen to God's voice and obey him; and receive his redemptive, healing touch.

## THE BLUEPRINT

A. THE REIGN OF SOLOMON
(1:1—9:31)
1. Solomon asks for wisdom
2. Solomon builds the Temple
3. Solomon dedicates the Temple
4. Solomon's riches and wisdom

Solomon achieved much in business and government, but most important, he was the man God used to build the glorious Temple. This beautiful building was the religious center of the nation. It symbolized the unity of all the tribes, the presence of God among them, and the nation's high calling. We may achieve great things in life, but we must not neglect any effort that will help nurture God's people or bring others into God's Kingdom. It is easy for us to get the wrong perspective on what's really important in life.

B. THE KINGDOM OF JUDAH
(10:1—36:23)
1. The northern tribes revolt
2. History of apostasy and reform
3. Judah is exiled to Babylon

Throughout the reigns of 20 kings, the nation of Judah wavered between obedience to God and apostasy. The reigning king's response to God determined the spiritual climate of the nation and whether or not God would send judgment upon his people. Our personal history is shaped by our response to God. Just as Judah's failure to repent brought them captivity in Babylon, so the abuse of our high calling by sinful living will ultimately bring us catastrophe and destruction.

## MEGATHEMES

| THEME | EXPLANATION | IMPORTANCE |
|---|---|---|
| Temple | The Temple was the symbol of God's presence and the place set aside for worship and prayer. Built by Solomon from the plans God gave to David, the Temple was the spiritual center of the nation. | As Christians meet together to worship God, they experience the presence of God in a way that no individual believer can, for the dwelling place of God is the people of God. The body of Christ is God's temple. |
| Peace | As Solomon and his descendants were faithful to God, they experienced victory in battle, success in government, and peace with other nations. Peace was the result of the people being unified and loyal to God and his law. | Only God can bring true peace. God is greater than any enemy, army, or nation. Just as Israel's faithful response was key to her peace and survival as a nation, so our obedience to God as individuals and nations is vital to peace today. |
| Prayer | After Solomon died, David's kingdom was divided. When a king led the Israelites into idolatry, the nation suffered. When the king and his people prayed to God for deliverance and they turned from their sinful ways, God delivered them. | God still answers prayer today. We have God's promise that if we humble ourselves, seek him, turn from our sin, and pray, God will hear, restore, and forgive us. If we are alert, we can pray for God's guidance before we get into trouble. |
| Reform | Although idolatry and injustice were common, some kings turned to God and led the people in spiritual revival—renewing their commitment to God and reforming their society. Revival included the destruction of idols, obedience to the law, and the restoration of the priesthood. | We must constantly commit ourselves to obeying God. We are never secure in what others have done before us. Believers in each generation must dedicate themselves to the task of carrying out God's will in their own lives as well as in society. |
| National Collapse | In 586 B.C. the Babylonians completely destroyed Solomon's beautiful Temple. The formal worship of God was ended. The Israelites had abandoned God. As a result, God brought judgment upon his people, and they were carried off into captivity. | Although our disobedience may not be as blatant as Israel's, quite often our commitment to God is insincere and casual. When we forget that all our power, wisdom, and wealth come from God and not ourselves, we are in danger of the same spiritual and moral collapse that Israel experienced. |

# KEY PLACES IN 2 CHRONICLES

LEBANON

SYRIA

Mediterranean
Sea

Sea of
Galilee

ISRAEL

I S R A E L

Ramoth-gilead

Hill Country
of Ephraim · Samaria

Shechem·

Gibeon·
Jerusalem·

JORDAN

Dead
Sea

J U D A H

0        20 Mi.

0        20 Km.

The broken lines (— · —·) indicate modern boundaries.

Everyone but the tribes of Judah and Benjamin deserted Rehoboam and set up their own kingdom to the north called Israel. Rehoboam returned to Jerusalem as ruler over the southern kingdom called Judah (10:1—12:16). The remainder of 2 Chronicles records the history of Judah.

4 **Hill Country of Ephraim**   Abijah became the next king of Judah, and soon war broke out between Israel and Judah. When the armies of the two nations arrived for battle in the hill country of Ephraim, Israel had twice as many troops as Judah. It looked like Judah's defeat was certain. But they cried out to God, and God gave them victory over Israel. In their history as separate nations, Judah had a few godly kings, who instituted reforms and brought the people back to God. Israel, however, had a succession of only evil kings (13:1–22).

5 **Aram (Syria)**   Asa, a godly king, removed every trace of pagan worship from Judah and renewed the people's covenant with God in Jerusalem. But King Baasha of Israel built a fortress to control traffic into Judah. Instead of looking to God for guidance, Asa took the silver and gold from the Temple and sent it to the king of Aram, requesting his help against King Baasha. As a result, God became angry with Judah (14:1—16:14).

6 **Samaria**   Although Jehoshaphat was a godly king, he allied himself with Israel's most evil king, Ahab. Ahab's capital was Samaria. Ahab wanted help fighting against Ramoth-gilead. Jehoshaphat wanted advice, but rather than listening to God's prophet who had promised defeat, he joined Ahab in battle (17:1—18:27).

7 **Ramoth-gilead**   The alliance with Israel against Ramoth-gilead ended in defeat and Ahab's death. Shaken by his defeat, Jehoshaphat returned to Jerusalem and to God. But his son Jehoram was a wicked king, as was his son Ahaziah, and history repeated itself. Ahaziah formed an alliance with Israel's king Joram to do battle with the Arameans at Ramoth-gilead. This led to the death of both kings (18:28—22:9).

8 **Jerusalem**   The rest of Judah's history recorded in 2 Chronicles centers on Jerusalem. Some kings caused Judah to sin by bringing idol worship into their midst. Others cleaned up the idol worship, reopened and restored the Temple, and in the case of Josiah, tried to follow God's laws as they were written by Moses. In spite of the few good influences, a series of evil kings sent Judah into a downward spiral that ended with the Babylonian Empire overrunning the country. The Temple was burned, the walls of the city were broken down, and the people were deported to Babylon.

1 **Gibeon**   David's son Solomon became king over Israel. He summoned the nation's leaders to a ceremony in Gibeon. Here God told Solomon to ask for whatever he desired. Solomon asked for wisdom and knowledge to rule Israel (1:1–12).

2 **Jerusalem**   After the ceremony in Gibeon, Solomon returned to the capital city, Jerusalem. His reign began a golden age for Israel. Solomon implemented the plans for the Temple, which had been drawn up by his father, David. It was a magnificent construction. It symbolized Solomon's wealth and wisdom, which became known worldwide (1:13—9:31).

3 **Shechem**   After Solomon's death, his son Rehoboam was ready to be crowned in Shechem. However, his promise of higher taxes and harder work for the people led to rebellion.

## A. THE REIGN OF SOLOMON (1:1—9:31)

In response to Solomon's request, God gives to Solomon great wisdom. Solomon launches great building programs, including the Temple, his greatest achievement. In the midst of the celebration dedicating the Temple, fire flashes down from heaven, and God's glory fills the Temple, God wants to live among his people and to be central in their lives. Today, our bodies are God's temple, the place where God, through his Holy Spirit, lives and reigns.

### 1. Solomon asks for wisdom

**1:1** 1 Kgs 2:12, 46; 1 Chr 29:25

1 Solomon son of David took firm control of his kingdom, for the LORD his God was with him and made him very powerful.

**1:2** 1 Chr 28:1

2 Solomon called together all the leaders of Israel—the generals and captains of the army,* the judges, and all the political and clan leaders. 3 Then he led the entire assembly

**1:3** Exod 40:18; 1 Kgs 3:4

to the place of worship in Gibeon, for God's Tabernacle* was located there. (This was the Tabernacle that Moses, the LORD's servant, had made in the wilderness.)

**1:4** 1 Chr 15:25-28

4 David had already moved the Ark of God from Kiriath-jearim to the tent he had pre-

**1:5** Exod 31:2; 38:1-7

pared for it in Jerusalem. 5 But the bronze altar made by Bezalel son of Uri and grandson of Hur was there* at Gibeon in front of the Tabernacle of the LORD. So Solomon and the

**1:6** 1 Kgs 3:4

people gathered in front of it to consult the LORD.* 6 There in front of the Tabernacle, Solomon went up to the bronze altar in the LORD's presence and sacrificed 1,000 burnt offerings on it.

**1:7** 1 Kgs 3:5-14

7 That night God appeared to Solomon and said, "What do you want? Ask, and I will give it to you!"

**1:8** 1 Chr 28:5

8 Solomon replied to God, "You showed faithful love to David, my father, and now you

**1:9** Gen 13:16; 22:17; 2 Sam 7:12-16

have made me king in his place. 9 O LORD God, please continue to keep your promise to David my father, for you have made me king over a people as numerous as the dust of the earth! 10 Give me the wisdom and knowledge to lead them properly,* for who could pos-

**1:10** 2 Sam 5:2; 1 Kgs 3:9

sibly govern this great people of yours?"

**1:11** 1 Kgs 3:11

11 God said to Solomon, "Because your greatest desire is to help your people, and you did not ask for wealth, riches, fame, or even the death of your enemies or a long life, but rather you asked for wisdom and knowledge to properly govern my people— 12 I will certainly give

**1:12** 1 Chr 29:25; 2 Chr 9:22

you the wisdom and knowledge you requested. But I will also give you wealth, riches, and fame such as no other king has had before you or will ever have in the future!"

**1:13** 2 Chr 1:3

13 Then Solomon returned to Jerusalem from the Tabernacle at the place of worship in Gibeon, and he reigned over Israel.

**1:2** Hebrew *the commanders of thousands and of hundreds.* **1:3** Hebrew *Tent of Meeting;* also in 1:6, 13. **1:5a** As in Greek version and Latin Vulgate, and some Hebrew manuscripts. Masoretic Text reads *he placed.* **1:5b** Hebrew *to consult him.* **1:10** Hebrew *to go out and come in before this people.*

---

**1:1** While the book of 1 Chronicles focuses mainly on David's life, 2 Chronicles focuses on the lives of the rest of the kings of Judah, the southern kingdom. Very little is mentioned about Israel, the northern kingdom, because (1) Chronicles was written for Judeans who had returned from captivity in Babylon, and (2) Judah represented David's family, from which the Messiah would come. Israel was in a state of constant turmoil, anarchy, and rebellion against God, but Judah, at least, made sporadic efforts to follow God.

**1:1** More details about Solomon's rise to the throne can be read in 1 Kings 1–2. Solomon's Profile is found in 1 Kings 3, p. 519.

**1:2-5** The Tabernacle that Moses had built centuries earlier (Exodus 35–40) was still in operation although it had been moved several times. When Solomon became king, the Tabernacle was located at Gibeon, a town about six miles northwest of Jerusalem. All the Tabernacle furniture was kept at Gibeon except the Ark of God, which David had moved to Jerusalem (1 Chronicles 13; 15–16). David wanted the Ark, the symbol of God's presence, to reside in the city where he ruled the people. The Tabernacle at Gibeon, however, was still considered Israel's main religious center until Solomon built the Temple in Jerusalem.

**1:10** Wisdom is the ability to make good decisions based on proper discernment and judgment. Knowledge, in this verse, refers to the practical know-how necessary for handling everyday matters. Wisdom applies knowledge. Solomon used his wisdom and knowledge not only to build the Temple from his father's plans but also to put the nation on firm economic footing.

**1:10** God's offer to Solomon stretches the imagination: "Ask, and I will give it to you!" (1:7). But Solomon put the needs of his people first and asked for wisdom rather than riches. He realized that wisdom would be the most valuable asset he could have as king. Later he wrote, "Wisdom is more precious than rubies; nothing you desire can compare with her" (Proverbs 3:15). The same wisdom that was given to Solomon is available to us; the same God offers it. How can we acquire wisdom? First, we must ask God, who "will not rebuke you for asking" (James 1:5). Second, we must devote ourselves wholeheartedly to studying and applying God's Word, the source of divine wisdom, to our lives. (For more on Solomon's wisdom, read the notes on 1 Kings 3:6-9 and 3:12.)

**1:11, 12** Solomon could have had anything, but he asked for wisdom to rule the nation. Because God approved of the way Solomon ordered his priorities, he gave Solomon wealth, riches, and honor as well. Jesus also spoke about priorities. He said that when we put God first, everything we really need will be given to us as well (Matthew 6:33). This does not guarantee that we will be wealthy and famous like Solomon, but it means that when we put God first, the wisdom he gives will enable us to have richly rewarding lives. When we have a purpose for living and learn to be content with what we have, we have greater wealth than we could ever imagine.

¹⁴Solomon built up a huge force of chariots and horses.* He had 1,400 chariots and 12,000 horses. He stationed some of them in the chariot cities and some near him in Jerusalem. ¹⁵The king made silver and gold as plentiful in Jerusalem as stone. And valuable cedar timber was as common as the sycamore-fig trees that grow in the foothills of Judah.* ¹⁶Solomon's horses were imported from Egypt* and from Cilicia*; the king's traders acquired them from Cilicia at the standard price. ¹⁷At that time chariots from Egypt could be purchased for 600 pieces of silver,* and horses for 150 pieces of silver.* They were then exported to the kings of the Hittites and the kings of Aram.

**1:14**
1 Kgs 4:26; 9:19;
10:26-29

**1:15**
1 Kgs 10:27

## 2. Solomon builds the Temple
*Preparations for Building the Temple*

**2** ¹*Solomon decided to build a Temple to honor the name of the LORD, and also a royal palace for himself. ²*He enlisted a force of 70,000 laborers, 80,000 men to quarry stone in the hill country, and 3,600 foremen.

³Solomon also sent this message to King Hiram* at Tyre:

"Send me cedar logs as you did for my father, David, when he was building his palace. ⁴I am about to build a Temple to honor the name of the LORD my God. It will be a place set apart to burn fragrant incense before him, to display the special sacrificial bread, and to sacrifice burnt offerings each morning and evening, on the Sabbaths, at new moon celebrations, and at the other appointed festivals of the LORD our God. He has commanded Israel to do these things forever.

⁵"This must be a magnificent Temple because our God is greater than all other gods. ⁶But who can really build him a worthy home? Not even the highest heavens can contain him! So who am I to consider building a Temple for him, except as a place to burn sacrifices to him?

⁷"So send me a master craftsman who can work with gold, silver, bronze, and iron, as well as with purple, scarlet, and blue cloth. He must be a skilled engraver who can work with the craftsmen of Judah and Jerusalem who were selected by my father, David.

**2:1**
1 Kgs 5:5

**2:2**
1 Kgs 5:15-16
2 Chr 2:18

**2:3**
1 Kgs 5:2-11
1 Chr 14:1

**2:4**
Exod 25:30;
29:38-42; 30:7
Num 28:9-10

**2:5**
Exod 15:11
1 Chr 16:25

**2:6**
1 Kgs 8:27
2 Chr 6:18

**2:7**
Exod 31:3-5
1 Chr 22:15
2 Chr 2:13-15

**1:14** Or *charioteers;* also in 1:14b.   **1:15** Hebrew *the Shephelah.*   **1:16a** Possibly *Muzur,* a district near Cilicia; also in 1:17.   **1:16b** Hebrew *Kue,* probably another name for Cilicia.   **1:17a** Hebrew *600 [shekels] of silver,* about 15 pounds or 6.8 kilograms in weight.   **1:17b** Hebrew *150 [shekels],* about 3.8 pounds or 1.7 kilograms in weight.   **2:1** Verse 2:1 is numbered 1:18 in Hebrew text.   **2:2** Verses 2:2-18 are numbered 2:1-17 in Hebrew text.   **2:3** Hebrew *Huram,* a variant spelling of Hiram; also in 2:11.

---

**2:1** David had wanted to build a Temple for God (2 Samuel 7). God denied his request because David had been a warrior, but

**SHIPPING RESOURCES FOR THE TEMPLE** Solomon asked King Hiram of Tyre to provide supplies and skilled workmen to help build God's Temple in Jerusalem. The plan was to cut the cedar logs in the mountains of Lebanon, float them by sea to Joppa, then bring them inland to Jerusalem by the shortest and easiest route.

God said that David's son Solomon would build the Temple. God allowed David to make the plans and preparations for the Temple (1 Chronicles 23–26; 28:11-19). David bought the land (2 Samuel 24:18-25; 1 Chronicles 22:1), gathered most of the construction materials (1 Chronicles 22:14-16), and received the plans from God (1 Chronicles 28:11, 12, 19). It was Solomon's responsibility to make the plans a reality. His job was made easier by his father's exhaustive preparations. God's work can be moved forward when the older generation paves the way for the younger.

**2:3-12** Although Hiram was one of David's and Solomon's friendly allies, he was the ruler of a nation that worshiped many different gods. Hiram was happy to send materials for the Temple, and both David and Solomon used this occasion to testify about the one true God.

**2:5, 6** We should try our best to build beautiful, accessible, and welcoming places of worship to be a testimony and credit to God. In so doing, however, we must remember that God cannot be contained in our building or lovely setting. He is far greater than any structure, so we must focus our praise on him and not merely on the place of worship.

**2:7** Why use foreign craftsmen? The Israelites had great knowledge of agriculture but knew little about metalworking. So they found people who were experts in this area. It is not a sin to obtain secular expertise as we go about God's work. He distributes talents as he chooses, and he often decides to give skill to non-Christians. When we hire secular contractors to build or repair our church buildings, we are recognizing that God gives gifts liberally. We may also be gaining an opportunity to tell the workers about God.

**2:8**
2 Chr 9:10-11

**2:10**
1 Kgs 5:11

**2:11**
1 Kgs 10:9
2 Chr 9:8

**2:12**
2 Chr 2:1
Pss 33:6; 102:25

**2:14**
1 Kgs 7:14

**2:15**
2 Chr 2:10

**2:16**
1 Kgs 5:8-9

**2:17**
1 Chr 22:2

**2:18**
2 Chr 2:2

**3:1-14**
1 Kgs 6:1-29

**3:1**
1 Chr 21:18

**3:4**
1 Kgs 6:3

**3:5**
1 Kgs 6:17

**3:7**
1 Kgs 6:20-22,
29-35

⁸"Also send me cedar, cypress, and red sandalwood* logs from Lebanon, for I know that your men are without equal at cutting timber in Lebanon. I will send my men to help them. ⁹An immense amount of timber will be needed, for the Temple I am going to build will be very large and magnificent. ¹⁰In payment for your woodcutters, I will send 100,000 bushels of crushed wheat, 100,000 bushels of barley,* 110,000 gallons of wine, and 110,000 gallons of olive oil.*"

¹¹King Hiram sent this letter of reply to Solomon:

"It is because the LORD loves his people that he has made you their king! ¹²Praise the LORD, the God of Israel, who made the heavens and the earth! He has given King David a wise son, gifted with skill and understanding, who will build a Temple for the LORD and a royal palace for himself.

¹³"I am sending you a master craftsman named Huram-abi, who is extremely talented. ¹⁴His mother is from the tribe of Dan in Israel, and his father is from Tyre. He is skillful at making things from gold, silver, bronze, and iron, and he also works with stone and wood. He can work with purple, blue, and scarlet cloth and fine linen. He is also an engraver and can follow any design given to him. He will work with your craftsmen and those appointed by my lord David, your father.

¹⁵"Send along the wheat, barley, olive oil, and wine that my lord has mentioned. ¹⁶We will cut whatever timber you need from the Lebanon mountains and will float the logs in rafts down the coast of the Mediterranean Sea* to Joppa. From there you can transport the logs up to Jerusalem."

¹⁷Solomon took a census of all foreigners in the land of Israel, like the census his father had taken, and he counted 153,600. ¹⁸He assigned 70,000 of them as common laborers, 80,000 as quarry workers in the hill country, and 3,600 as foremen.

### Solomon Builds the Temple

**3** So Solomon began to build the Temple of the LORD in Jerusalem on Mount Moriah, where the LORD had appeared to David, his father. The Temple was built on the threshing floor of Araunah* the Jebusite, the site that David had selected. ²The construction began in midspring,* during the fourth year of Solomon's reign.

³These are the dimensions Solomon used for the foundation of the Temple of God (using the old standard of measurement).* It was 90 feet long and 30 feet wide.* ⁴The entry room at the front of the Temple was 30 feet* wide, running across the entire width of the Temple, and 30 feet* high. He overlaid the inside with pure gold.

⁵He paneled the main room of the Temple with cypress wood, overlaid it with fine gold, and decorated it with carvings of palm trees and chains. ⁶He decorated the walls of the Temple with beautiful jewels and with gold from the land of Parvaim. ⁷He overlaid the beams, thresholds, walls, and doors throughout the Temple with gold, and he carved figures of cherubim on the walls.

**2:8** Or *juniper;* Hebrew reads *algum,* perhaps a variant spelling of *almug;* compare 9:10-11 and parallel text at 1 Kgs 10:11-12. **2:10a** Hebrew *20,000 cors* [3,640 kiloliters] *of crushed wheat, 20,000 cors of barley.* **2:10b** Hebrew *20,000 baths* [420 kiloliters] *of wine, and 20,000 baths of olive oil.* **2:16** Hebrew *the sea.* **3:1** Hebrew reads *Ornan,* a variant spelling of Araunah; compare 2 Sam 24:16. **3:2** Hebrew *on the second day of the second month.* This day of the ancient Hebrew lunar calendar occurred in April or May. **3:3a** The "old standard of measurement" was a cubit equal to 18 inches [46 centimeters]. The new standard was a cubit of approximately 21 inches [53 centimeters]. **3:3b** Hebrew *60 cubits* [27.6 meters] *long and 20 cubits* [9.2 meters] *wide.* **3:4a** Hebrew *20 cubits* [9.2 meters]; also in 3:8, 11, 13. **3:4b** As in some Greek and Syriac manuscripts, which read *20 cubits* [9.2 meters]; Hebrew reads *120* [cubits], which is 180 feet or 55 meters.

**2:8, 9** Israel did not have much wood, but Lebanon, a small nation on the seacoast, had some of the finest cedar forests in the ancient Near East. Lebanon also imported a great deal of food from Israel. Thus, the two kings made a trade agreement that was beneficial to both nations.

**2:17, 18** Why would Solomon force foreigners living in Israel to do the work of slaves? These foreigners were descendants of the pagan nations that had not been driven out of the land in Joshua's day (Joshua 9:23-27; Judges 1:21-33; 1 Kings 9:20, 21). Scripture has specific laws about treating slaves fairly (Leviticus 25:39-55), so Solomon would not have treated them harshly as other nations might. Solomon's action was probably only in force during the construction of the Temple.

**3:1** Solomon built a permanent Temple on Mount Moriah to replace the movable Tabernacle (now at Gibeon) that had accompanied Israel in the wilderness. Mount Moriah was also the place where God had stopped Abraham from sacrificing Isaac (Genesis 22:1-18). David purchased the land when it was a threshing floor (see 2 Samuel 24:15-25 and the note on 1 Chronicles 21:22-24).

**3:1ff** Why was the Temple decorated so ornately? Although no one can build God a worthy home (2:6), this Temple was going to be the best that humans could design. The care and craftsmanship were acts of worship in themselves. Although a simple chapel is an adequate place to pray and meet God, it is not wrong to want to make a beautiful place of worship.

⁸He made the Most Holy Place 30 feet wide, corresponding to the width of the Temple, and 30 feet deep. He overlaid its interior with 23 tons* of fine gold. ⁹The gold nails that were used weighed 20 ounces* each. He also overlaid the walls of the upper rooms with gold.

**3:8**
Exod 26:33
1 Kgs 6:16

**3:9**
1 Chr 28:11

¹⁰He made two figures shaped like cherubim, overlaid them with gold, and placed them in the Most Holy Place. ¹¹The total wingspan of the two cherubim standing side by side was 30 feet. One wing of the first figure was 7½ feet* long, and it touched the Temple wall. The other wing, also 7½ feet long, touched one of the wings of the second figure. ¹²In the same way, the second figure had one wing 7½ feet long that touched the opposite wall. The other wing, also 7½ feet long, touched the wing of the first figure. ¹³So the wingspan of the two cherubim side by side was 30 feet. They stood on their feet and faced out toward the main room of the Temple.

**3:10**
1 Kgs 6:23-28

¹⁴Across the entrance of the Most Holy Place he hung a curtain made of fine linen, decorated with blue, purple, and scarlet thread and embroidered with figures of cherubim.

**3:14**
Exod 26:31

¹⁵For the front of the Temple, he made two pillars that were 27 feet* tall, each topped by a capital extending upward another 7½ feet. ¹⁶He made a network of interwoven chains and used them to decorate the tops of the pillars. He also made 100 decorative pomegranates and attached them to the chains. ¹⁷Then he set up the two pillars at the entrance of the Temple, one to the south of the entrance and the other to the north. He named the one on the south Jakin, and the one on the north Boaz.*

**3:15**
1 Kgs 7:15-20

**3:17**
1 Kgs 7:21

### Furnishings for the Temple

**4** Solomon* also made a bronze altar 30 feet long, 30 feet wide, and 15 feet high.* ²Then he cast a great round basin, 15 feet across from rim to rim, called the Sea. It was 7½ feet deep and about 45 feet in circumference.* ³It was encircled just below its rim by two rows of figures that resembled oxen. There were about six oxen per foot* all the way around, and they were cast as part of the basin.

**4:1**
Exod 27:1-2
2 Kgs 16:14

**4:2**
1 Kgs 7:23-26

⁴The Sea was placed on a base of twelve bronze oxen, all facing outward. Three faced north, three faced west, three faced south, and three faced east, and the Sea rested on them.

⁵The walls of the Sea were about three inches* thick, and its rim flared out like a cup and resembled a water lily blossom. It could hold about 16,500 gallons* of water.

**4:5**
1 Kgs 7:26

⁶He also made ten smaller basins for washing the utensils for the burnt offerings. He set five on the south side and five on the north. But the priests washed themselves in the Sea.

**4:6**
1 Kgs 7:38, 40

⁷He then cast ten gold lampstands according to the specifications that had been given, and he put them in the Temple. Five were placed against the south wall, and five were placed against the north wall.

**4:7**
Exod 25:31-40
1 Kgs 7:49

⁸He also built ten tables and placed them in the Temple, five along the south wall and five along the north wall. Then he molded 100 gold basins.

**4:8**
1 Kgs 7:48

⁹He then built a courtyard for the priests, and also the large outer courtyard. He made doors for the courtyard entrances and overlaid them with bronze. ¹⁰The great bronze basin called the Sea was placed near the southeast corner of the Temple.

**4:9**
1 Kgs 6:36

**4:10**
1 Kgs 7:39

¹¹Huram-abi also made the necessary washbasins, shovels, and bowls.

So at last Huram-abi completed everything King Solomon had assigned him to make for the Temple of God:

**4:11**
1 Kgs 7:14, 40

¹² the two pillars;

the two bowl-shaped capitals on top of the pillars;

the two networks of interwoven chains that decorated the capitals;

**4:12**
1 Kgs 20:27-43
2 Chr 2:13

**3:8** Hebrew *600 talents* [20.4 metric tons]. **3:9** Hebrew *50 shekels* [570 grams]. **3:11** Hebrew *5 cubits* [2.3 meters]; also in 3:11b, 12, 15. **3:15** As in Syriac version (see also 1 Kgs 7:15; 2 Kgs 25:17; Jer 52:21), which reads *18 cubits* [8.3 meters]; Hebrew reads *35 cubits*, which is 52.5 feet or 16.5 meters. **3:17** *Jakin* probably means "he establishes"; *Boaz* probably means "in him is strength." **4:1a** Or *Huram-abi*; Hebrew reads *He*. **4:1b** Hebrew *20 cubits* [9.2 meters] *long, 20 cubits wide, and 10 cubits* [4.6 meters] *high*. **4:2** Hebrew *10 cubits* [4.6 meters] *across . . . 5 cubits* [2.3 meters] *deep and 30 cubits* [13.8 meters] *in circumference.* **4:3** Or *20 oxen per meter*; Hebrew reads *10 per cubit.* **4:5a** Hebrew *a handbreadth* [8 centimeters]. **4:5b** Hebrew *3,000 baths* [63 kiloliters].

---

**3:10** Cherubim are angels.

**4:6** Why was everything in the Temple built on such a grand scale? The great size and numbers were necessary to accommodate the huge crowds that would visit for the festivals, such as the Passover (30:13). The numerous daily sacrifices required many priests and much equipment.

**4:7** The craftsmen followed God's specifications carefully— with spectacular results. When God gives specific instructions,

they must be followed to the letter. There is a time to be creative and to put forth our own ideas, but not when the ideas add to, alter, or contradict any specific directions God has already given to us in the Bible. For best results in your spiritual life, carefully seek and follow God's instructions.

**4:11-16** Washbasins, shovels, and bowls—these are implements of worship unfamiliar to us. Although the articles we use to aid our worship have changed, the purpose of worship remains the

**4:13**
1 Kgs 7:20

13 the 400 pomegranates that hung from the chains on the capitals (two rows of pomegranates for each of the chain networks that decorated the capitals on top of the pillars);

**4:14**
1 Kgs 7:27

14 the water carts holding the basins;

**4:16**
1 Kgs 7:14

15 the Sea and the twelve oxen under it;

16 the ash buckets, the shovels, the meat hooks, and all the related articles.

**4:17-18**
1 Kgs 7:47

Huram-abi made all these things of burnished bronze for the Temple of the LORD, just as King Solomon had directed. 17 The king had them cast in clay molds in the Jordan Valley between Succoth and Zarethan.* 18 Solomon used such great quantities of bronze that its weight could not be determined.

19 Solomon also made all the furnishings for the Temple of God:

the gold altar;

the tables for the Bread of the Presence;

**4:20**
Exod 25:31-37

20 the lampstands and their lamps of solid gold, to burn in front of the Most Holy Place as prescribed;

21 the flower decorations, lamps, and tongs—all of the purest gold;

22 the lamp snuffers, bowls, dishes, and incense burners—all of solid gold;

the doors for the entrances to the Most Holy Place and the main room of the Temple, overlaid with gold.

**5:1**
1 Kgs 7:51

**5** So Solomon finished all his work on the Temple of the LORD. Then he brought all the gifts his father, David, had dedicated—the silver, the gold, and the various articles—and he stored them in the treasuries of the Temple of God.

**4:17** As in parallel text at 1 Kgs 7:46; Hebrew reads *Zeredah*.

---

**CAREFUL OBEDIENCE**
Solomon and his workers carefully followed God's instructions. As a result, the Temple work was blessed by God and completed in every detail. Here are a few examples of people in the Bible who did not carefully follow one of God's instructions, and the resulting consequences. It is *not* enough to obey God half-heartedly.

| Who? | God's Instruction | Disobedience | Result |
|---|---|---|---|
| Adam and Eve | Don't eat fruit from the tree of the knowledge of good and evil (Genesis 2:16, 17) | Satan tempted them, and they ate (Genesis 3:1-6) | They were banished from the Garden of Eden, pain and death were inflicted on all people (Genesis 3:24; Romans 5:12) |
| Nadab and Abihu | Fire for the sacrifice must come from the proper source (Leviticus 6:12, 13) | They used the wrong kind of fire for their sacrifice (Leviticus 10:1) | They were struck dead (Leviticus 10:2) |
| Moses | "Speak to the rock . . . it will pour out its water" (Numbers 20:8) | He spoke to the rock, but also struck it with his staff (Numbers 20:11) | He was not allowed to enter the Promised Land (Numbers 20:12) |
| Saul | Completely destroy the evil Amalekites (1 Samuel 15:3) | He spared the king and kept some of the plunder (1 Samuel 15:8, 9) | God promised to end his reign (1 Samuel 15:16-26) |
| Uzzah | Only a priest can touch the sacred utensils and objects (Numbers 4:15) | He touched the Ark of the Covenant (2 Samuel 6:6) | He died instantly (2 Samuel 6:7) |
| Uzziah | Only the priests can offer incense in the Temple or Tabernacle sanctuary (Numbers 16:39, 40; 18:7) | He entered the Holy Place in the Temple where only priests were allowed to go (2 Chronicles 26:16-18) | He became a leper (2 Chronicles 26:19) |

---

same—to give honor and praise to God. We must never let our worship of God be overshadowed by things we use to help us worship him.

**4:22** All these details about the Temple demonstrated the care Israel gave to acts of worship (see the note on 3:1ff). The instructions also served as a manual to the original readers of 2 Chronicles, those who would rebuild a new Temple on its original site

(Ezra 3:8–6:15) after Solomon's Temple was destroyed by the Babylonians (2 Kings 25).

**5:1ff** Why is there so much emphasis on the Temple in the Old Testament?
(1) *It was a symbol of religious authority.* The Temple was God's way of centralizing worship at Jerusalem in order to ensure that correct belief would be kept intact through many generations.

## 3. Solomon dedicates the Temple

*The Ark Brought to the Temple*

2 Solomon then summoned to Jerusalem the elders of Israel and all the heads of tribes—the leaders of the ancestral families of Israel. They were to bring the Ark of the LORD's Covenant to the Temple from its location in the City of David, also known as Zion. 3 So all the men of Israel assembled before the king at the annual Festival of Shelters, which is held in early autumn.*

4 When all the elders of Israel arrived, the Levites picked up the Ark. 5 The priests and Levites brought up the Ark along with the special tent* and all the sacred items that had been in it. 6 There, before the Ark, King Solomon and the entire community of Israel sacrificed so many sheep, goats, and cattle that no one could keep count!

7 Then the priests carried the Ark of the LORD's Covenant into the inner sanctuary of the Temple—the Most Holy Place—and placed it beneath the wings of the cherubim. 8 The cherubim spread their wings over the Ark, forming a canopy over the Ark and its carrying poles. 9 These poles were so long that their ends could be seen from the Temple's main room—the Holy Place*—but not from the outside. They are still there to this day. 10 Nothing was in the Ark except the two stone tablets that Moses had placed in it at Mount Sinai,* where the LORD made a covenant with the people of Israel when they left Egypt.

11 Then the priests left the Holy Place. All the priests who were present had purified themselves, whether or not they were on duty that day. 12 And the Levites who were musicians—Asaph, Heman, Jeduthun, and all their sons and brothers—were dressed in fine linen robes and stood at the east side of the altar playing cymbals, lyres, and harps. They were joined by 120 priests who were playing trumpets. 13 The trumpeters and singers performed together in unison to praise and give thanks to the LORD. Accompanied by trumpets, cymbals, and other instruments, they raised their voices and praised the LORD with these words:

**5:2–6:11**
//1 Kgs 8:1-21

**5:2**
2 Sam 6:12
2 Chr 1:4

**5:4**
2 Chr 5:7

**5:9**
1 Kgs 8:8-9

**5:10**
Deut 10:2-5
Heb 9:4

**5:11**
1 Chr 24:1-5

**5:12**
1 Chr 25:1-4
2 Chr 7:6

**5:13**
1 Chr 16:34, 42
2 Chr 7:3

5:3 Hebrew *at the festival that is in the seventh month.* The Festival of Shelters began on the fifteenth day of the seventh month of the ancient Hebrew lunar calendar. This day occurred in late September, October, or early November.   5:5 Hebrew *the Tent of Meeting;* i.e., the tent mentioned in 2 Sam 6:17 and 1 Chr 16:1.   5:9 As in some Hebrew manuscripts and Greek version (see also 1 Kgs 8:8); Masoretic Text reads *from the Ark in front of the Most Holy Place.*   5:10 Hebrew *Horeb,* another name for Sinai.

(2) *It was a symbol of God's holiness.* The Temple's beautiful atmosphere inspired respect and awe for God; it was the setting for many of the great visions of the prophets.

(3) *It was a symbol of God's covenant with Israel.* The Temple kept the people focused upon God's law (the tablets of the Ten Commandments were kept in the Temple) rather than on the kings' exploits. It was a place where God was especially present with his people.

(4) *It was a symbol of forgiveness.* The Temple's design, furniture, and customs were great object lessons for all the people, reminding them of the seriousness of sin, the penalty that sin incurred, and their need of forgiveness.

(5) *It prepared the people for the Messiah.* In the New Testament, Christ said he came to fulfill the law, not destroy it. Hebrews 8:1, 2 and 9:11, 12 use Temple customs to explain what Christ did when he died for us.

(6) *It was a testimony to human effort and creativity.* Inspired by the beauty of God's character, people devoted themselves to high achievements in engineering, science, and art in order to praise him.

(7) *It was a place of prayer.* In the Temple, people could spend time in prayer to God.

**5:1-3** The Temple took seven years to build. First Kings 6:38 says that the Temple was completed in the eighth month (November) of Solomon's eleventh year as king (959 B.C.). Because 5:3 states that the dedication ceremonies were held in early autumn, they must have occurred either one month before or eleven months after the Temple's completion.

**5:3** The Festival of Shelters celebrated God's protection of Israel as they wandered in the wilderness before entering the Promised Land. The purpose of this annual festival was to renew Israel's commitment to God and their trust in his guidance and protection. The festival beautifully coincided with the dedication of the Temple. As the people remembered the wanderings in the wilderness when their ancestors had lived in tents, they were even more thankful for the permanence of this glorious Temple.

**5:7-12** The priests came out of the Holy Place after having placed the Ark in the Most Holy Place of the Temple. The Holy Place is the outer room, where the Bread of the Presence, altar of incense, and lampstand were kept. Ordinarily the Most Holy Place could be entered only once a year by the high priest on the Day of Atonement. On this unique occasion, however, several priests had to enter the Most Holy Place to carry the Ark to its new resting place. The Levites praised God when these priests emerged from the Holy Place because they then knew God had accepted this new home for the Ark (5:13).

**5:9** Under God's inspiration, some books of the Bible were compiled and edited from other sources. Because 1 and 2 Chronicles cover many centuries, they were compiled from several sources by a single person. The phrase "they are still there to this day" (see also 1 Kings 8:8) was taken from material written before Judah's exile in 586 B.C. Although 1 and 2 Chronicles were compiled after the Exile and after Solomon's Temple was destroyed, the writer thought it best to leave this phrase in the narrative.

**5:13** The first service at the Temple began with honoring God and acknowledging his presence and goodness. In the same way, our worship should begin by acknowledging God's love. Praise God first; then you will be prepared to present your needs to him. Recalling God's love and mercy will inspire you to worship him daily. Psalm 107 is an example of how the psalmist recalled God's enduring love.

"He is good!
His faithful love endures forever!"

5:14
1 Kgs 8:11

At that moment a thick cloud filled the Temple of the LORD. 14The priests could not continue their service because of the cloud, for the glorious presence of the LORD filled the Temple of God.

## Solomon Praises the LORD

6:1
1 Kgs 8:12-50

**6** Then Solomon prayed, "O LORD, you have said that you would live in a thick cloud of darkness. 2Now I have built a glorious Temple for you, a place where you can live forever!"

3Then the king turned around to the entire community of Israel standing before him and gave this blessing: 4"Praise the LORD, the God of Israel, who has kept the promise he made to my father, David. For he told my father, 5'From the day I brought my people out of the land of Egypt, I have never chosen a city among any of the tribes of Israel as the place where a Temple should be built to honor my name. Nor have I chosen a king to lead my people Israel.

6:6
1 Chr 28:4
2 Chr 12:13
6:7
1 Chr 28:2
6:8
1 Kgs 5:3

6But now I have chosen Jerusalem as the place for my name to be honored, and I have chosen David to be king over my people Israel.'"

7Then Solomon said, "My father, David, wanted to build this Temple to honor the name of the LORD, the God of Israel. 8But the LORD told him, 'You wanted to build the Temple to honor my name. Your intention is good, 9but you are not the one to do it. One of your own sons will build the Temple to honor me.'

6:11
2 Chr 5:7, 10

10"And now the LORD has fulfilled the promise he made, for I have become king in my father's place, and now I sit on the throne of Israel, just as the LORD promised. I have built this Temple to honor the name of the LORD, the God of Israel. 11There I have placed the Ark, which contains the covenant that the LORD made with the people of Israel."

## Solomon's Prayer of Dedication

6:12-40
//1 Kgs 8:22-53
6:12
Neh 8:4
6:14
Exod 15:11
Deut 3:24; 7:9

12Then Solomon stood before the altar of the LORD in front of the entire community of Israel, and he lifted his hands in prayer. 13Now Solomon had made a bronze platform 7½ feet long, 7½ feet wide, and 4½ feet high* and had placed it at the center of the Temple's outer courtyard. He stood on the platform, and then he knelt in front of the entire community of Israel and lifted his hands toward heaven. 14He prayed,

"O LORD, God of Israel, there is no God like you in all of heaven and earth. You keep your covenant and show unfailing love to all who walk before you in wholehearted devotion. 15You have kept your promise to your servant David, my father. You made that promise with your own mouth, and with your own hands you have fulfilled it today.

6:15
1 Chr 22:9-10

6:16
1 Kgs 2:4
2 Chr 7:18

16"And now, O LORD, God of Israel, carry out the additional promise you made to your servant David, my father. For you said to him, 'If your descendants guard their behavior and faithfully follow my Law as you have done, one of them will always sit on the throne of Israel.' 17Now, O LORD, God of Israel, fulfill this promise to your servant David.

6:18
2 Chr 2:6

18"But will God really live on earth among people? Why, even the highest heavens

6:13 Hebrew *5 cubits* [2.3 meters] *long, 5 cubits wide, and 3 cubits* [1.4 meters] *high.*

---

**6:3** As the people received Solomon's blessing, they stood; as Solomon prayed, he knelt (6:13). Both standing and kneeling are acts of reverence. Acts of reverence make us feel more worshipful, and they let others see that we are honoring God. When you stand or kneel in church or at prayer, make these actions more than mere forms prescribed by tradition. Let them indicate your love for God.

**6:12, 13** It was unusual for a king to kneel before someone else in front of his own people because kneeling meant submitting to a higher authority. Solomon demonstrated his great love and respect for God by kneeling before him. His action showed that he acknowledged God as the ultimate king and authority, and it encouraged the people to do the same.

**6:18** Solomon marveled that God would be willing to live on earth among sinful people. We marvel that God, through his Son, Jesus, lived among us in human form to reveal his eternal

purposes to us. In doing so, God was reaching out to us in love. God wants us to reach out to him in return in order to know him and to love him with all our heart. Don't simply marvel at his power; take time to get to know him.

cannot contain you. How much less this Temple I have built! 19Nevertheless, listen to my prayer and my plea, O LORD my God. Hear the cry and the prayer that your servant is making to you. 20May you watch over this Temple day and night, this place where you have said you would put your name. May you always hear the prayers I make toward this place. 21May you hear the humble and earnest requests from me and your people Israel when we pray toward this place. Yes, hear us from heaven where you live, and when you hear, forgive.

**6:21**
Mic 7:18

22"If someone wrongs another person and is required to take an oath of innocence in front of your altar at this Temple, 23then hear from heaven and judge between your servants—the accuser and the accused. Pay back the guilty as they deserve. Acquit the innocent because of their innocence.

24"If your people Israel are defeated by their enemies because they have sinned against you, and if they turn back and acknowledge your name and pray to you here in this Temple, 25then hear from heaven and forgive the sin of your people Israel and return them to this land you gave to them and to their ancestors.

26"If the skies are shut up and there is no rain because your people have sinned against you, and if they pray toward this Temple and acknowledge your name and turn from their sins because you have punished them, 27then hear from heaven and forgive the sins of your servants, your people Israel. Teach them to follow the right path, and send rain on your land that you have given to your people as their special possession.

**6:26**
1 Kgs 17:1

28"If there is a famine in the land or a plague or crop disease or attacks of locusts or caterpillars, or if your people's enemies are in the land besieging their towns—whatever disaster or disease there is—29and if your people Israel pray about their troubles or sorrow, raising their hands toward this Temple, 30then hear from heaven where you live, and forgive. Give your people what their actions deserve, for you alone know each human heart. 31Then they will fear you and walk in your ways as long as they live in the land you gave to our ancestors.

**6:28**
2 Chr 20:9

**6:30**
1 Sam 16:7
1 Chr 28:9

32"In the future, foreigners who do not belong to your people Israel will hear of you. They will come from distant lands when they hear of your great name and your strong hand and your powerful arm. And when they pray toward this Temple, 33then hear from heaven where you live, and grant what they ask of you. In this way, all the people of the earth will come to know and fear you, just as your own people Israel do. They, too, will know that this Temple I have built honors your name.

**6:33**
2 Chr 7:14

34"If your people go out where you send them to fight their enemies, and if they pray to you by turning toward this city you have chosen and toward this Temple I have built to honor your name, 35then hear their prayers from heaven and uphold their cause.

36"If they sin against you—and who has never sinned?—you might become angry with them and let their enemies conquer them and take them captive to a foreign land far away or near. 37But in that land of exile, they might turn to you in repentance and pray, 'We have sinned, done evil, and acted wickedly.' 38If they turn to you with their whole heart and soul in the land of their captivity and pray toward the land you gave to their ancestors—toward this city you have chosen, and toward this Temple I have built to honor your name—39then hear their prayers and their petitions from heaven where you live, and uphold their cause. Forgive your people who have sinned against you.

**6:36**
Job 15:14-16
1 Jn 1:8-10

---

**6:19-42** As Solomon led the people in prayer, he asked God to hear their prayers concerning a variety of situations: (1) crime (6:22, 23); (2) enemy attacks (6:24, 25); (3) drought (6:26, 27); (4) famine (6:28-31); (5) the influx of foreigners (6:32, 33); (6) war (6:34, 35); (7) sin (6:36-39). God is concerned with whatever we face, even the difficult consequences we bring upon ourselves. He wants us to turn to him in prayer. When you pray, remember that God hears you. Don't let the extremity of your situation cause you to doubt his care for you.

**6:26** Why would Solomon assume that drought would come as a result of sin? Sin is not necessarily the direct cause of natural disasters today, but this was a special case. God had made a specific covenant with the Israelites that drought could be a consequence of their sins (Deuteronomy 28:20-24).

**6:30** Have you ever felt far from God, separated by feelings of failure and personal problems? In his prayer, Solomon underscored the fact that God stands ready to hear his people, to forgive their sins, and to restore their relationship with him. God is waiting and listening for our confessions of guilt and our recommitment to obey him. He hears us when we pour out our needs and problems to him and is ready to forgive us and restore us to fellowship with him. Don't wait to experience his loving forgiveness.

**6:36** "Who has never sinned?" The Bible makes it clear that no one is exempt from sin, not even God's appointed kings. Sin is a condition we all share, and we all should acknowledge it as Solomon did. When we realize we have sinned, we should quickly ask God for forgiveness and restoration. Knowing we have a tendency to sin should keep us close to God, seeking his guidance and strength. This truth is also mentioned in Psalm 14:3, Ecclesiastes 7:20, and Romans 3:23.

6:40
2 Chr 7:15
Neh 1:6, 11
Ps 17:1

6:41-42
//Ps 132:8-10

7:1-10
1 Kgs 8:62-66
7:1
1 Kgs 8:54;
18:24, 38
7:3
2 Chr 5:13; 20:21

7:4
1 Kgs 8:62-63

7:6
1 Chr 15:16-21
2 Chr 5:12

7:7
1 Kgs 8:64-66

7:8
1 Kgs 8:65
7:9
Lev 23:26

7:11-22
//1 Kgs 9:1-9

7:13
2 Chr 6:26-28
7:14
2 Chr 6:37-39

⁴⁰"O my God, may your eyes be open and your ears attentive to all the prayers made to you in this place.

⁴¹ "And now arise, O Lord God, and enter your resting place,
     along with the Ark, the symbol of your power.
   May your priests, O Lord God, be clothed with salvation;
     may your loyal servants rejoice in your goodness.
   ⁴² O Lord God, do not reject the king you have anointed.
     Remember your unfailing love for your servant David."

## The Dedication of the Temple

**7** When Solomon finished praying, fire flashed down from heaven and burned up the burnt offerings and sacrifices, and the glorious presence of the Lord filled the Temple. ²The priests could not enter the Temple of the Lord because the glorious presence of the Lord filled it. ³When all the people of Israel saw the fire coming down and the glorious presence of the Lord filling the Temple, they fell face down on the ground and worshiped and praised the Lord, saying,

   "He is good!
     His faithful love endures forever!"

⁴Then the king and all the people offered sacrifices to the Lord. ⁵King Solomon offered a sacrifice of 22,000 cattle and 120,000 sheep and goats. And so the king and all the people dedicated the Temple of God. ⁶The priests took their assigned positions, and so did the Levites who were singing, "His faithful love endures forever!" They accompanied the singing with music from the instruments King David had made for praising the Lord. Across from the Levites, the priests blew the trumpets, while all Israel stood.

⁷Solomon then consecrated the central area of the courtyard in front of the Lord's Temple. He offered burnt offerings and the fat of peace offerings there, because the bronze altar he had built could not hold all the burnt offerings, grain offerings, and sacrificial fat.

⁸For the next seven days Solomon and all Israel celebrated the Festival of Shelters.* A large congregation had gathered from as far away as Lebo-hamath in the north and the Brook of Egypt in the south. ⁹On the eighth day they had a closing ceremony, for they had celebrated the dedication of the altar for seven days and the Festival of Shelters for seven days. ¹⁰Then at the end of the celebration,* Solomon sent the people home. They were all joyful and glad because the Lord had been so good to David and to Solomon and to his people Israel.

## The Lord's Response to Solomon

¹¹So Solomon finished the Temple of the Lord, as well as the royal palace. He completed everything he had planned to do in the construction of the Temple and the palace. ¹²Then one night the Lord appeared to Solomon and said,

   "I have heard your prayer and have chosen this Temple as the place for making sacrifices. ¹³At times I might shut up the heavens so that no rain falls, or command grasshoppers to devour your crops, or send plagues among you. ¹⁴Then if my people

**7:8** Hebrew *the festival* (also in 7:9); see note on 5:3.   **7:10** Hebrew *Then on the twenty-third day of the seventh month.* This day of the ancient Hebrew lunar calendar occurred in October or early November.

---

**7:1, 2** God sent fire from heaven to consume the offering and to begin the fire that was to burn continuously under the altar of burnt offering (see Leviticus 6:8-13). This perpetual fire symbolized God's presence. God also sent fire when inaugurating the Tabernacle (Leviticus 9:22-24). This was the real dedication of the Temple because only God's purifying power can make something holy.

**7:4, 5** The Temple was dedicated to God, and Solomon and the people prepared to worship him. Dedication means setting apart a place, an object, or a person for an exclusive purpose. The purpose of this dedication was to set apart the Temple as a place to worship God. Today, our bodies are God's temple (2 Corinthians 6:16). Solomon's dedication of the Temple shows us that we should dedicate ourselves to carry out God's special purpose (Ephesians 1:11, 12).

**7:12** Months, maybe years, had passed since Solomon's prayer

of dedication (chapter 6). Several other building projects had been completed after the Temple (7:11; 8:1). Then after all this time, God told Solomon that he had heard Solomon's prayer. How often do we look for immediate answers to our prayers and, when nothing happens, wonder if God has heard us? God does hear, and he will provide for us. We must trust that God will answer at the proper time.

**7:14** In chapter 6, Solomon asked God to make provisions for the people when they sinned. God answered with four conditions for forgiveness: (1) Humble yourself by admitting your sins, (2) pray to God, asking for forgiveness, (3) seek God continually, and (4) turn from sinful behavior. True repentance is more than talk—it is changed behavior. Whether we sin individually, as a group, or as a nation, following these steps will lead to forgiveness. God will answer our earnest prayers.

who are called by my name will humble themselves and pray and seek my face and turn from their wicked ways, I will hear from heaven and will forgive their sins and restore their land. 15My eyes will be open and my ears attentive to every prayer made in this place. 16For I have chosen this Temple and set it apart to be holy—a place where my name will be honored forever. I will always watch over it, for it is dear to my heart.

17"As for you, if you faithfully follow me as David your father did, obeying all my commands, decrees, and regulations, 18then I will establish the throne of your dynasty. For I made this covenant with your father, David, when I said, 'One of your descendants will always rule over Israel.'

19"But if you or your descendants abandon me and disobey the decrees and commands I have given you, and if you serve and worship other gods, 20then I will uproot the people from this land that I have given them. I will reject this Temple that I have made holy to honor my name. I will make it an object of mockery and ridicule among the nations. 21And though this Temple is impressive now, all who pass by will be appalled. They will ask, 'Why did the LORD do such terrible things to this land and to this Temple?'

22"And the answer will be, 'Because his people abandoned the LORD, the God of their ancestors, who brought them out of Egypt, and they worshiped other gods instead and bowed down to them. That is why he has brought all these disasters on them.'"

## 4. Solomon's riches and wisdom

### Solomon's Many Achievements

**8** It took Solomon twenty years to build the LORD's Temple and his own royal palace. At the end of that time, 2Solomon turned his attention to rebuilding the towns that King Hiram* had given him, and he settled Israelites in them.

3Solomon also fought against the town of Hamath-zobah and conquered it. 4He rebuilt Tadmor in the wilderness and built towns in the region of Hamath as supply centers. 5He fortified the towns of Upper Beth-horon and Lower Beth-horon, rebuilding their walls and installing barred gates. 6He also rebuilt Baalath and other supply centers and constructed towns where his chariots and horses* could be stationed. He built everything he desired in Jerusalem and Lebanon and throughout his entire realm.

7There were still some people living in the land who were not Israelites, including the Hittites, Amorites, Perizzites, Hivites, and Jebusites. 8These were descendants of the nations whom the people of Israel had not destroyed. So Solomon conscripted them for his labor force, and they serve in the labor force to this day. 9But Solomon did not conscript any of the Israelites for his labor force. Instead, he assigned them to serve as fighting men, officers in his army, commanders of his chariots, and charioteers. 10King Solomon appointed 250 of them to supervise the people.

11Solomon moved his wife, Pharaoh's daughter, from the City of David to the new palace he had built for her. He said, "My wife must not live in King David's palace, for the Ark of the LORD has been there, and it is holy ground."

12Then Solomon presented burnt offerings to the LORD on the altar he had built for him in front of the entry room of the Temple. 13He offered the sacrifices for the Sabbaths, the new moon festivals, and the three annual festivals—the Passover celebration, the Festival of Harvest,* and the Festival of Shelters—as Moses had commanded.

**7:15**
2 Chr 6:20, 40
**7:16**
2 Chr 7:12
**7:18**
2 Chr 6:16
**7:19**
Lev 26:14, 33
Deut 28:15
**7:20**
Deut 28:37; 29:28
1 Kgs 14:15
**7:21**
Deut 29:24-27

**8:1-18**
//1 Kgs 9:10-28
**8:5**
1 Chr 7:24
2 Chr 14:7
**8:8**
1 Kgs 4:6; 9:21
**8:11**
1 Kgs 3:1; 7:8
**8:12**
2 Chr 4:1
**8:13**
Exod 23:14-17;
29:38-42
Num 28:3

**8:2** Hebrew *Huram*, a variant spelling of Hiram; also in 8:18.    **8:6** Or *and charioteers*.    **8:13** Or *Festival of Weeks*.

---

**7:17-22** God plainly set forth certain conditions for Solomon to meet if he wanted the kingdom to continue. If Solomon followed God, he and his descendants would prosper; if Solomon did not, he and the nation would be destroyed. In Deuteronomy 27 and 28, these conditions were outlined before all the people.

But sin is deceptively attractive, and Solomon eventually turned from God. As a result, his son and heir lost most of the kingdom. Following God brings benefits and rewards (not necessarily material). Turning away from God brings suffering, punishment, and ultimately destruction. Today, God's conditions are just as clear as they were in Solomon's day. Choose to obey God no matter what happens, knowing that God will eventually bless your efforts.

**7:21, 22** Soon after Solomon's reign, the Temple was ransacked (12:9). It is difficult for us to imagine that such a great and wise

king could become corrupted by idols—symbols of power, prosperity, and sexuality. But even today these idols lure us into their traps. When we allow any desire to rival God's proper place, we have taken the first step toward moral and spiritual decay.

**8:11** Solomon married Pharaoh's daughter to secure a military alliance with Egypt. He did not let the woman live in David's palace, however, where the Ark of God had once been kept. This implies that Solomon knew his pagan marriage would not please God. Solomon married many other foreign women, and this was contrary to God's law (Deuteronomy 7:3, 4). These women worshiped false gods and were certain to contaminate Israel with their beliefs and practices. Eventually Solomon's pagan wives caused his downfall (1 Kings 11:1-11).

**8:14**
1 Chr 24:1; 25:1;
26:1
Neh 12:24, 36

¹⁴In assigning the priests to their duties, Solomon followed the regulations of his father, David. He also assigned the Levites to lead the people in praise and to assist the priests in their daily duties. And he assigned the gatekeepers to their gates by their divisions, following the commands of David, the man of God. ¹⁵Solomon did not deviate in any way from David's commands concerning the priests and Levites and the treasuries.

¹⁶So Solomon made sure that all the work related to building the Temple of the Lord was carried out, from the day its foundation was laid to the day of its completion.

**8:17**
1 Kgs 9:26
2 Kgs 14:22
**8:18**
2 Chr 9:10, 13

¹⁷Later Solomon went to Ezion-geber and Elath,* ports along the shore of the Red Sea* in the land of Edom. ¹⁸Hiram sent him ships commanded by his own officers and manned by experienced crews of sailors. These ships sailed to Ophir with Solomon's men and brought back to Solomon almost seventeen tons* of gold.

### Visit of the Queen of Sheba

**9:1**
1 Kgs 10:1-13
Matt 12:42
Luke 11:31

**9** When the queen of Sheba heard of Solomon's fame, she came to Jerusalem to test him with hard questions. She arrived with a large group of attendants and a great caravan of camels loaded with spices, large quantities of gold, and precious jewels. When she met with Solomon, she talked with him about everything she had on her mind. ²Solomon had answers for all her questions; nothing was too hard for him to explain to her. ³When the queen of Sheba realized how wise Solomon was, and when she saw the palace he had built, ⁴she was overwhelmed. She was also amazed at the food on his tables, the organization of his officials and their splendid clothing, the cup-bearers and their robes, and the burnt offerings Solomon made at the Temple of the Lord.

⁵She exclaimed to the king, "Everything I heard in my country about your achievements* and wisdom is true! ⁶I didn't believe what was said until I arrived here and saw it with my own eyes. In fact, I had not heard the half of your great wisdom! It is far beyond what I was told. ⁷How happy your people must be! What a privilege for your officials to stand here day after day, listening to your wisdom! ⁸Praise the Lord your God, who delights in you and has placed you on the throne as king to rule for him. Because God loves Israel and desires this kingdom to last forever, he has made you king over them so you can rule with justice and righteousness."

**9:8**
Deut 7:8
1 Chr 28:5; 29:23
2 Chr 2:11

⁹Then she gave the king a gift of 9,000 pounds* of gold, great quantities of spices, and precious jewels. Never before had there been spices as fine as those the queen of Sheba gave to King Solomon.

**9:10**
2 Chr 8:18

¹⁰(In addition, the crews of Hiram and Solomon brought gold from Ophir, and they also brought red sandalwood* and precious jewels. ¹¹The king used the sandalwood to make steps* for the Temple of the Lord and the royal palace, and to construct lyres and harps for the musicians. Never before had such beautiful things been seen in Judah.)

¹²King Solomon gave the queen of Sheba whatever she asked for—gifts of greater value than the gifts she had given him. Then she and all her attendants returned to their own land.

### Solomon's Wealth and Splendor

**9:13-28**
//1 Kgs 10:14-28
//2 Chr 1:14-17

¹³Each year Solomon received about 25 tons* of gold. ¹⁴This did not include the additional revenue he received from merchants and traders. All the kings of Arabia and the governors of the provinces also brought gold and silver to Solomon.

**8:17a** As in Greek version (see also 2 Kgs 14:22; 16:6); Hebrew reads *Eloth,* a variant spelling of Elath.   **8:17b** As in parallel text at 1 Kgs 9:26; Hebrew reads *the sea.*   **8:18** Hebrew *450 talents* [15.3 metric tons].   **9:5** Hebrew *your words.*   **9:9** Hebrew *120 talents* [4,000 kilograms].   **9:10** Hebrew *algum wood* (also in 9:11); perhaps a variant spelling of *almug.* Compare parallel text at 1 Kgs 10:11-12.   **9:11** Or *gateways.* The meaning of the Hebrew is uncertain.   **9:13** Hebrew *666 talents* [23 metric tons].

---

**8:15** Although Solomon carefully followed God's instructions for building the Temple and offering sacrifices (8:13), he paid no attention to what God said about marrying pagan women. His sin in marrying a foreign wife (8:11) began his slide away from God. No matter how good or spiritual we are in most areas of life, one unsurrendered area can begin a downfall. Guard carefully *every* area of your life, especially your relationships. Don't give sin any foothold.

**9:1-8** The queen of Sheba had heard about Solomon's wisdom, but she was overwhelmed when she saw for herself the fruits of that wisdom. Although Solomon had married Pharaoh's daughter, he still sincerely tried to follow God at this stage in his life. When people get to know you and ask hard questions, will your responses reflect God? Your life can be a powerful witness; let others see God at work in you.

**9:8** The queen of Sheba marveled at Solomon, claiming that God must love his people greatly to give them such a king. Israel greatly prospered during Solomon's reign, witnessing to God's power and love for his people. The good times show God's love and faithfulness, but hard times come to believers, too. Our perseverance and steadfast hope during those times will demonstrate our love and faithfulness to God.

**9:11** Sandalwood was a smooth, red-colored wood that accepts a high polish. This beautiful wood was extremely expensive.

<sup>15</sup>King Solomon made 200 large shields of hammered gold, each weighing more than 15 pounds.* <sup>16</sup>He also made 300 smaller shields of hammered gold, each weighing more than 7½ pounds.* The king placed these shields in the Palace of the Forest of Lebanon.

<sup>17</sup>Then the king made a huge throne, decorated with ivory and overlaid with pure gold. <sup>18</sup>The throne had six steps, with a footstool of gold. There were armrests on both sides of the seat, and the figure of a lion stood on each side of the throne. <sup>19</sup>There were also twelve other lions, one standing on each end of the six steps. No other throne in all the world could be compared with it!

<sup>20</sup>All of King Solomon's drinking cups were solid gold, as were all the utensils in the Palace of the Forest of Lebanon. They were not made of silver, for silver was considered worthless in Solomon's day!

<sup>21</sup>The king had a fleet of trading ships* manned by the sailors sent by Hiram.* Once every three years the ships returned, loaded with gold, silver, ivory, apes, and peacocks.*

<sup>22</sup>So King Solomon became richer and wiser than any other king on earth. <sup>23</sup>Kings from every nation came to consult him and to hear the wisdom God had given him. <sup>24</sup>Year after year everyone who visited brought him gifts of silver and gold, clothing, weapons, spices, horses, and mules.

<sup>25</sup>Solomon had 4,000 stalls for his horses and chariots, and he had 12,000 horses.* He stationed some of them in the chariot cities, and some near him in Jerusalem. <sup>26</sup>He ruled over all the kings from the Euphrates River* in the north to the land of the Philistines and the border of Egypt in the south. <sup>27</sup>The king made silver as plentiful in Jerusalem as stone. And valuable cedar timber was as common as the sycamore-fig trees that grow in the foothills of Judah.* <sup>28</sup>Solomon's horses were imported from Egypt* and many other countries.

### Summary of Solomon's Reign

<sup>29</sup>The rest of the events of Solomon's reign, from beginning to end, are recorded in *The Record of Nathan the Prophet,* and *The Prophecy of Ahijah from Shiloh,* and also in *The Visions of Iddo the Seer,* concerning Jeroboam son of Nebat. <sup>30</sup>Solomon ruled in Jerusalem over all Israel for forty years. <sup>31</sup>When he died, he was buried in the City of David, named for his father. Then his son Rehoboam became the next king.

## B. THE KINGDOM OF JUDAH (10:1—36:23)

After Solomon's death, the northern tribes revolt, and we read little more about them in 2 Chronicles. The remainder of 2 Chronicles recounts the alternating periods of apostasy and reform in Judah. In the end, Judah would not turn from its sin, and the tragic result was a 70-year captivity in Babylon. Sin in our lives will also lead to judgment and devastation. Although God's judgment may seem slow, it is nevertheless certain.

### 1. The northern tribes revolt

**10** Rehoboam went to Shechem, where all Israel had gathered to make him king. <sup>2</sup>When Jeroboam son of Nebat heard of this, he returned from Egypt, for he had fled to Egypt to escape from King Solomon. <sup>3</sup>The leaders of Israel summoned him, and Jeroboam and all Israel went to speak with Rehoboam. <sup>4</sup>"Your father was a hard master," they said. "Lighten the harsh labor demands and heavy taxes that your father imposed on us. Then we will be your loyal subjects."

<sup>5</sup>Rehoboam replied, "Come back in three days for my answer." So the people went away.

**9:15** Hebrew *600 [shekels] of hammered gold* [6.8 kilograms].   **9:16** Hebrew *300 [shekels] of gold* [3.4 kilograms].   **9:21a** Hebrew *fleet of ships that could sail to Tarshish.*   **9:21b** Hebrew *Huram,* a variant spelling of Hiram.   **9:21c** Or *and baboons.*   **9:25** Or *12,000 charioteers.*   **9:26** Hebrew *the river.*   **9:27** Hebrew *the Shephelah.*   **9:28** Possibly Muzur, a district near Cilicia.

**9:22**
1 Kgs 3:13
2 Chr 1:12

**9:25**
Deut 17:16
1 Kgs 4:26; 10:26
2 Chr 1:14

**9:26**
1 Kgs 4:21, 24

**9:27**
2 Chr 1:15-17

**9:28**
2 Chr 1:16

**9:29-31**
//1 Kgs 11:41-43

**9:30**
1 Kgs 11:42-43

**9:31**
1 Kgs 2:10

**10:1**
1 Kgs 12:1-20

**10:2**
1 Kgs 11:40

---

**9:29** For the rest of Solomon's story, see 1 Kings 10:26—11:43. In his later years, Solomon turned away from God and led the nation into worshiping idols.

**10:1** The crowning of an Israelite king would normally have taken place in Jerusalem, the capital city. But Rehoboam saw that there was the possibility of trouble in the north; so to maintain his hold on the country, he chose Shechem, a city about 35 miles north of Jerusalem. Shechem was an ancient site for making covenants (Joshua 24:1).

**10:1-15** Following bad advice can cause disaster. Rehoboam lost the chance to rule a peaceful, united kingdom because he rejected the advice of Solomon's older counselors, preferring the counsel of his peers. Rehoboam made two errors in seeking

advice: (1) He did not give extra consideration to the suggestions of those who knew the situation better than he, and (2) he did not ask God for wisdom to discern which was the better option.

It is easy to follow the advice of our peers because they often feel as we do. But their view may be limited. It is important to listen carefully to those who have more experience than we do—they can see the bigger picture.

**10:2, 3** Why was Jeroboam in Egypt? Ahijah the prophet had predicted that Israel would split in two and that Jeroboam would become king of the northern section. When Solomon learned of this prophecy, he tried to kill Jeroboam, and Jeroboam was forced to flee to Egypt (1 Kings 11:26-40).

⁶Then King Rehoboam discussed the matter with the older men who had counseled his father, Solomon. "What is your advice?" he asked. "How should I answer these people?"

⁷The older counselors replied, "If you are good to these people and do your best to please them and give them a favorable answer, they will always be your loyal subjects."

⁸But Rehoboam rejected the advice of the older men and instead asked the opinion of the young men who had grown up with him and were now his advisers. ⁹"What is your advice?" he asked them. "How should I answer these people who want me to lighten the burdens imposed by my father?"

¹⁰The young men replied, "This is what you should tell those complainers who want a lighter burden: 'My little finger is thicker than my father's waist! ¹¹Yes, my father laid heavy burdens on you, but I'm going to make them even heavier! My father beat you with whips, but I will beat you with scorpions!'"

¹²Three days later Jeroboam and all the people returned to hear Rehoboam's decision, just as the king had ordered. ¹³But Rehoboam spoke harshly to them, for he rejected the advice of the older counselors ¹⁴and followed the counsel of his younger advisers. He told

**REHOBOAM**

Settling for cheap imitations in exchange for the real thing is a poor way to live. In every area of his life, Rehoboam consistently traded away what was real for what was counterfeit. Given wise and unwise counsel by his advisers at his coronation, he chose to grab for power and control rather than being patient and taking the counsel of those older and wiser than he to treat his people with kindness. Although his position came from God, he chose to abandon God. These unwise decisions made him weaker rather than stronger. As a result, he was invaded by the Egyptians and stripped of the riches he had inherited from David and Solomon. To replace them, he had cheap bronze copies made.

Throughout the early part of his reign, Rehoboam fluctuated between obeying God and going his own way. Outward appearances were kept up, but his inward attitudes were evil. Following in the tradition of David gave Rehoboam many opportunities for real greatness. Instead, he ended up with a divided and broken kingdom.

How much of real living have we traded away for the things that do not last? We trade healthy bodies for momentary excitement, personal integrity for fast-fading wealth, honesty for lies, God's wise guidance for our selfish ways. We sin when we willingly give little value to "the real thing" God has already given us.

Our counterfeit lives may fool some people, but they never fool God. Yet in spite of what he sees in us, God offers mercy. Are you a self-managed enterprise, counterfeit at best? Or have you placed yourself in God's care? Do the decisions you must make today need a second consideration in light of Rehoboam's example?

| | |
|---|---|
| **Strengths and accomplishments** | • Fourth and last king of the united nation of Israel, but only for a short time<br>• Fortified his kingdom and achieved a measure of popularity |
| **Weaknesses and mistakes** | • Followed unwise advice and divided his kingdom<br>• Married foreign women, as his father, Solomon, had done<br>• Abandoned the worship of God and allowed idolatry to flourish |
| **Lessons from his life** | • Thoughtless decisions often lead to exchanging what is most valuable for something of far less value<br>• Every choice we make has real and long-lasting consequences |
| **Vital statistics** | • Where: Jerusalem<br>• Occupation: King of the united kingdom of Israel and later of the southern kingdom of Judah<br>• Relatives: Father: Solomon. Mother: Naamah. Wife: Maacah. Son: Abijah.<br>• Contemporaries: Jeroboam, Shishak, Shemaiah |
| **Key verse** | "But when Rehoboam was firmly established and strong, he abandoned the Law of the LORD, and all Israel followed him in this sin" (2 Chronicles 12:1). |

Rehoboam's story is told in 1 Kings 11:43—14:31 and 2 Chronicles 9:31—13:7. He is also mentioned in Matthew 1:7.

**10:14** Rehoboam must have gotten an unbalanced picture of leadership from his father, Solomon. Apparently Rehoboam saw only the difficulty of leading the nation, not the opportunities. He mentioned only the harsher aspects of Solomon's rule, and he himself decided to be very harsh toward the people. As you discuss your responsibilities with your children, be sure that you temper words of complaint with words of joy. Otherwise you may sour their attitudes toward the work you do and those you serve.

the people, "My father laid* heavy burdens on you, but I'm going to make them even heavier! My father beat you with whips, but I will beat you with scorpions!"

¹⁵So the king paid no attention to the people. This turn of events was the will of God, for it fulfilled the Lord's message to Jeroboam son of Nebat through the prophet Ahijah from Shiloh.

**10:15**
1 Kgs 11:29-39

¹⁶When all Israel realized* that the king had refused to listen to them, they responded,

**10:16**
2 Sam 20:1
2 Chr 10:19

"Down with the dynasty of David!
    We have no interest in the son of Jesse.
Back to your homes, O Israel!
    Look out for your own house, O David!"

So all the people of Israel returned home. ¹⁷But Rehoboam continued to rule over the Israelites who lived in the towns of Judah.

¹⁸King Rehoboam sent Adoniram,* who was in charge of the labor force, to restore order, but the people of Israel stoned him to death. When this news reached King Rehoboam, he quickly jumped into his chariot and fled to Jerusalem. ¹⁹And to this day the northern tribes of Israel have refused to be ruled by a descendant of David.

**10:18**
1 Kgs 4:6; 5:14
**10:19**
1 Kgs 12:19

## Shemaiah's Prophecy

**11** When Rehoboam arrived at Jerusalem, he mobilized the men of Judah and Benjamin—180,000 select troops—to fight against Israel and to restore the kingdom to himself.

**11:1**
1 Kgs 12:21-24

²But the Lord said to Shemaiah, the man of God, ³"Say to Rehoboam son of Solomon, king of Judah, and to all the Israelites in Judah and Benjamin: ⁴'This is what the Lord says: Do not fight against your relatives. Go back home, for what has happened is my doing!'" So they obeyed the message of the Lord and did not fight against Jeroboam.

**11:2**
2 Chr 12:5-7, 15
**11:4**
2 Chr 10:15;
28:8-11

## Rehoboam Fortifies Judah

⁵Rehoboam remained in Jerusalem and fortified various towns for the defense of Judah. ⁶He built up Bethlehem, Etam, Tekoa, ⁷Beth-zur, Soco, Adullam, ⁸Gath, Mareshah, Ziph, ⁹Adoraim, Lachish, Azekah, ¹⁰Zorah, Aijalon, and Hebron. These became the fortified towns of Judah and Benjamin. ¹¹Rehoboam strengthened their defenses and stationed commanders in them, and he stored supplies of food, olive oil, and wine. ¹²He also put shields and spears in these towns as a further safety measure. So only Judah and Benjamin remained under his control.

**11:5**
2 Chr 8:2-6; 11:23

¹³But all the priests and Levites living among the northern tribes of Israel sided with Rehoboam. ¹⁴The Levites even abandoned their pasturelands and property and moved to Judah and Jerusalem, because Jeroboam and his sons would not allow them to serve the Lord as priests. ¹⁵Jeroboam appointed his own priests to serve at the pagan shrines, where they worshiped the goat and calf idols he had made. ¹⁶From all the tribes of Israel, those who sincerely wanted to worship the Lord, the God of Israel, followed the Levites to Jerusalem, where they could offer sacrifices to the Lord, the God of their ancestors. ¹⁷This strengthened the kingdom of Judah, and for three years they supported Rehoboam son of Solomon, for during those years they faithfully followed in the footsteps of David and Solomon.

**11:14**
Num 35:2-5

**11:15**
1 Kgs 12:31; 13:33
**11:16**
2 Chr 15:9
**11:17**
2 Chr 12:1

---

**10:14** As in Greek version and many Hebrew manuscripts (see also 1 Kgs 12:14); Masoretic Text reads *I will lay.*
**10:16** As in Syriac version, Latin Vulgate, and many Hebrew manuscripts (see also 1 Kgs 12:16); Masoretic Text lacks *realized.*   **10:18** Hebrew *Hadoram,* a variant spelling of Adoniram; compare 1 Kgs 4:6; 5:14; 12:18.

---

**10:16-19** In trying to have it all, Rehoboam lost almost everything. Motivated by greed and power, he pressed too hard and divided his kingdom. He didn't need more money or power because he had inherited the richest kingdom in the world. He didn't need more control because he was the king. His demands were based on selfishness rather than reason or spiritual discernment. Those who insist on having it all often wind up with little or nothing.

**10:16-19** This is the beginning of the divided kingdom. The peaceful united kingdom under Solomon divided into two parts. Ten of the tribes followed Jeroboam and called their nation Israel, or the northern kingdom. The other two tribes, Judah and Benjamin, remained loyal to David's line and accepted Rehoboam's rule. They called their nation Judah, or the southern kingdom.

**11:1** Rehoboam's foolishness divided his kingdom, and he tried to reunite it by force. True unity, however, cannot be forced—

it must be the free response of willing hearts. If you want the loyalty of employees, children, or anyone else in your charge, win their respect through love instead of trying to gain their submission through force.

**11:4** Why would God support this rebellion? It was part of the nation's punishment for turning away from God (1 Kings 11:11). It may also have been God's way of saving Rehoboam's smaller kingdom from defeat. In doing so, God preserved David's line and kept intact his plan for the Messiah to be a descendant of David (see 2 Samuel 7:16). When we see division, especially in a church that splits, we wonder what God would have us do. God desires unity, but while we should always work toward reconciliation, we must recognize that only God knows the future. He may allow a division in order to fulfill his greater purposes.

**11:13, 14** Before the nation split, the center of worship was in Jerusalem, and people flocked there for the three great annual

## 2. History of apostasy and reform

### Rehoboam's Family

**11:18**
1 Sam 16:6

18Rehoboam married his cousin Mahalath, the daughter of David's son Jerimoth and of Abihail, the daughter of Eliab son of Jesse. 19Mahalath had three sons—Jeush, Shemariah, and Zaham.

20Later Rehoboam married another cousin, Maacah, the daughter of Absalom. Maacah

**11:21**
Deut 17:17

gave birth to Abijah, Attai, Ziza, and Shelomith. 21Rehoboam loved Maacah more than any of his other wives and concubines. In all, he had eighteen wives and sixty concubines, and they gave birth to twenty-eight sons and sixty daughters.

**11:22**
Deut 21:15-17

22Rehoboam appointed Maacah's son Abijah as leader among the princes, making it clear that he would be the next king. 23Rehoboam also wisely gave responsibilities to his other sons and stationed some of them in the fortified towns throughout the land of Judah and Benjamin. He provided them with generous provisions, and he found many wives for them.

### Egypt Invades Judah

**12:1**
2 Chr 11:17

**12** But when Rehoboam was firmly established and strong, he abandoned the Law of the LORD, and all Israel followed him in this sin. 2Because they were unfaithful to the LORD, King Shishak of Egypt came up and attacked Jerusalem in the fifth year of King Reho-

**12:3**
2 Chr 16:8
Nah 3:9

boam's reign. 3He came with 1,200 chariots, 60,000 horses,* and a countless army of foot soldiers, including Libyans, Sukkites, and Ethiopians.* 4Shishak conquered Judah's forti-

**12:4**
2 Chr 11:5-12

fied towns and then advanced to attack Jerusalem.

**12:5**
Deut 28:15
2 Chr 11:2; 15:2

5The prophet Shemaiah then met with Rehoboam and Judah's leaders, who had all fled to Jerusalem because of Shishak. Shemaiah told them, "This is what the LORD says: You have abandoned me, so I am abandoning you to Shishak."

**12:6**
Exod 9:27
Dan 9:14

6Then the leaders of Israel and the king humbled themselves and said, "The LORD is right in doing this to us!"

**12:7**
1 Kgs 21:29
2 Chr 34:25-27
Ps 78:38

7When the LORD saw their change of heart, he gave this message to Shemaiah: "Since the people have humbled themselves, I will not completely destroy them and will soon give them some relief. I will not use Shishak to pour out my anger on Jerusalem. 8But they will

**12:8**
Deut 28:47-48

become his subjects, so they will know the difference between serving me and serving earthly rulers."

**12:3a** Or *charioteers,* or *horsemen.*   **12:3b** Hebrew *and Cushites.*

---

religious festivals. During the rest of the year, other worship services and rituals were conducted in the tribal territories by priests and Levites who lived throughout the land. They offered sacrifices, taught God's laws, and encouraged the people to continue to follow God and avoid pagan influences.

After the nation split, Jeroboam, the new king of Israel, saw these priests and Levites as threats to his new government because they retained loyalty to Jerusalem, now the capital of Judah. So he appointed his own priests, effectively banning the Levites from their duties and forcing them to move to the southern kingdom. Jeroboam's pagan priests encouraged idol worship. With the absence of spiritual leaders, the new northern kingdom was in danger of abandoning God.

**11:16** These people obeyed God rather than Jeroboam. By their actions, they preserved their integrity and strengthened the southern kingdom. In the future, most of the people in the northern kingdom would go along with the evil designs of the kings, hoping to benefit by cooperating. Don't follow their example and rationalize away God's teachings in order to gain earthly reward.

**12:1, 2** Here "Israel" refers to Judah, the southern kingdom. During his first three years on the throne, Rehoboam made an attempt to obey God, and as a result, Judah prospered. But then, at his peak of popularity and power, he abandoned God. The result was destruction because God allowed Judah to be conquered by Egypt. How could this happen? Often it is more difficult to be a believer in good times than in bad. Tough times push us toward God; but easy times can make us feel self-sufficient and self-satisfied. When everything is going right, guard your faith closely.

**12:2** A record of this invasion has been found on an Egyptian stone that says Shishak's army penetrated as far north as the Sea of Galilee, in the northern kingdom. Egypt was not the world power it had once been, and Shishak wanted to restore his nation to its former greatness. He was not strong enough to conquer both Israel and Judah, but he managed to destroy key cities in Judah in an effort to regain control of the trade routes and strike terror among the people.

**12:6-8** God lessened his judgment when Israel's leaders confessed their sins, humbled themselves, and recognized God's justice in punishing them. It's never too late to repent, even in the midst of punishment. Regardless of what we have done, God is willing to receive us back into fellowship. Are you struggling and alone because sin has broken your fellowship with God? Confession and humility will open the door to receiving God's mercy.

**12:8** Subjection to other kings was the price Judah had to pay for disobeying God. The nation's leaders thought they could succeed in their own strength, but they were wrong. When we rebel against God, we always pay for it. When we leave God out of our lives, we lose more spiritually than we ever gain financially.

⁹So King Shishak of Egypt came up and attacked Jerusalem. He ransacked the treasuries of the LORD's Temple and the royal palace; he stole everything, including all the gold shields Solomon had made. ¹⁰King Rehoboam later replaced them with bronze shields as substitutes, and he entrusted them to the care of the commanders of the guard who protected the entrance to the royal palace. ¹¹Whenever the king went to the Temple of the LORD, the guards would also take the shields and then return them to the guardroom. ¹²Because Rehoboam humbled himself, the LORD's anger was turned away, and he did not destroy him completely. There were still some good things in the land of Judah.

**12:9-16**
//1 Kgs 14:25-31
2 Chr 9:15-16

**12:12**
2 Chr 12:6-7; 19:3

## Summary of Rehoboam's Reign

¹³King Rehoboam firmly established himself in Jerusalem and continued to rule. He was forty-one years old when he became king, and he reigned seventeen years in Jerusalem, the city the LORD had chosen from among all the tribes of Israel as the place to honor his name. Rehoboam's mother was Naamah, a woman from Ammon. ¹⁴But he was an evil king, for he did not seek the LORD with all his heart.

**12:13**
1 Kgs 14:21

**12:14**
2 Chr 19:3

¹⁵The rest of the events of Rehoboam's reign, from beginning to end, are recorded in *The Record of Shemaiah the Prophet* and *The Record of Iddo the Seer,* which are part of the genealogical record. Rehoboam and Jeroboam were continually at war with each other. ¹⁶When Rehoboam died, he was buried in the City of David. Then his son Abijah became the next king.

**12:15**
1 Kgs 14:29
2 Chr 9:29; 12:5

**12:16**
2 Chr 11:20

## Abijah's War with Jeroboam

**13** Abijah began to rule over Judah in the eighteenth year of Jeroboam's reign in Israel. ²He reigned in Jerusalem three years. His mother was Maacah,* the daughter of Uriel from Gibeah.

Then war broke out between Abijah and Jeroboam. ³Judah, led by King Abijah, fielded 400,000 select warriors, while Jeroboam mustered 800,000 select troops from Israel.

⁴When the army of Judah arrived in the hill country of Ephraim, Abijah stood on Mount Zemaraim and shouted to Jeroboam and all Israel: "Listen to me! ⁵Don't you realize that the LORD, the God of Israel, made a lasting covenant* with David, giving him and his descendants the throne of Israel forever? ⁶Yet Jeroboam son of Nebat, a mere servant of David's son Solomon, rebelled against his master. ⁷Then a whole gang of scoundrels joined him, defying Solomon's son Rehoboam when he was young and inexperienced and could not stand up to them.

⁸"Do you really think you can stand against the kingdom of the LORD that is led by the descendants of David? You may have a vast army, and you have those gold calves that Jeroboam made as your gods. ⁹But you have chased away the priests of the LORD (the descendants of Aaron) and the Levites, and you have appointed your own priests, just like the pagan nations. You let anyone become a priest these days! Whoever comes to be dedicated with a young bull and seven rams can become a priest of these so-called gods of yours!

**13:1-2**
//1 Kgs 15:1-2
2 Chr 11:20

**13:2**
1 Kgs 15:6

**13:4**
Josh 18:22

**13:5**
Num 18:19
2 Sam 7:12-16

**13:6**
1 Kgs 11:26

**13:7**
2 Chr 12:13

**13:8**
1 Kgs 12:28
2 Chr 11:15

**13:9**
Exod 29:29-33
2 Chr 11:14-15
Jer 2:11; 5:7

**13:2** As in most Greek manuscripts and Syriac version (see also 2 Chr 11:20-21; 1 Kgs 15:2); Hebrew reads *Micaiah,* a variant spelling of Maacah.   **13:5** Hebrew *a covenant of salt.*

---

**12:10, 11** How ironic that the treasures in Solomon's Temple were removed and the missing royal shields were replaced by cheaper bronze. Rehoboam tried to maintain the trappings and appearance of former glory, but he couldn't measure up. When God is no longer central in our lives, maintaining the appearance of a Christian life becomes superficial. Outer beauty must come from inner strength.

**12:14** Rehoboam's story is tragic because he "did not seek the LORD with all his heart." How tragic a description of the grandson of David, who had been called a man after God's own heart (1 Samuel 13:14). It is dangerous to put off responding to God. God asks us for a firm commitment, and unless we respond by trusting him completely, we will find ourselves alienated from him.

**13:1ff** First Kings 15:3 says Abijah committed many sins, but the Chronicles account has only positive comments about him. For

the most part, Abijah was, no doubt, a wicked king. The writer of Chronicles chose to highlight the little good he did in order to show that he was still under God's covenant promise to David. Because of Abijah's fiery speech to Jeroboam (13:4-12), he was spared the immediate consequences of his sin.

**13:8** Jeroboam's army was cursed because of the gold calves they carried with them. It was as though they had put sin into a physical form so they could haul it around. Consider carefully the things you cherish. If you value anything more than God, it becomes your gold calf and will one day drag you down. Let go of anything that interferes with your relationship with God.

**13:9** Abijah criticized Jeroboam's low standards in appointing priests. Anyone is qualified to represent a god that is worthless. To represent the Lord God Almighty, however, a person must live by God's standards. Those appointed to positions of responsibility in your church should not be selected merely because they volunteer, are influential, or are highly educated. Instead, they should demonstrate sound doctrine, dedication to God, and strong spiritual character (see 1 Timothy 3).

¹⁰"But as for us, the LORD is our God, and we have not abandoned him. Only the descendants of Aaron serve the LORD as priests, and the Levites alone may help them in their work. ¹¹They present burnt offerings and fragrant incense to the LORD every morning and evening. They place the Bread of the Presence on the holy table, and they light the gold lampstand every evening. We are following the instructions of the LORD our God, but you have abandoned him. ¹²So you see, God is with us. He is our leader. His priests blow their trumpets and lead us into battle against you. O people of Israel, do not fight against the LORD, the God of your ancestors, for you will not succeed!"

¹³Meanwhile, Jeroboam had secretly sent part of his army around behind the men of Judah to ambush them. ¹⁴When Judah realized that they were being attacked from the front and the rear, they cried out to the LORD for help. Then the priests blew the trumpets, ¹⁵and the men of Judah began to shout. At the sound of their battle cry, God defeated Jeroboam and all Israel and routed them before Abijah and the army of Judah.

¹⁶The Israelite army fled from Judah, and God handed them over to Judah in defeat. ¹⁷Abijah and his army inflicted heavy losses on them; 500,000 of Israel's select troops were killed that day. ¹⁸So Judah defeated Israel on that occasion because they trusted in the LORD, the God of their ancestors. ¹⁹Abijah and his army pursued Jeroboam's troops and captured some of his towns, including Bethel, Jeshanah, and Ephron, along with their surrounding villages.

²⁰So Jeroboam of Israel never regained his power during Abijah's lifetime, and finally the LORD struck him down and he died. ²¹Meanwhile, Abijah of Judah grew more and more powerful. He married fourteen wives and had twenty-two sons and sixteen daughters.

²²The rest of the events of Abijah's reign, including his words and deeds, are recorded in *The Commentary of Iddo the Prophet.*

### Early Years of Asa's Reign

**14** ¹*When Abijah died, he was buried in the City of David. Then his son Asa became the next king. There was peace in the land for ten years. ²*Asa did what was pleasing and good in the sight of the LORD his God. ³He removed the foreign altars and the pagan shrines. He smashed the sacred pillars and cut down the Asherah poles. ⁴He commanded the people of Judah to seek the LORD, the God of their ancestors, and to obey his law and his commands. ⁵Asa also removed the pagan shrines, as well as the incense altars from every one of Judah's towns. So Asa's kingdom enjoyed a period of peace. ⁶During those peaceful years, he was able to build up the fortified towns throughout Judah. No one tried to make war against him at this time, for the LORD was giving him rest from his enemies.

**14:1** Verse 14:1 is numbered 13:23 in the Hebrew text.   **14:2** Verses 14:2-15 are numbered 14:1-14 in Hebrew text.

---

**13:18, 19** Although outnumbered by Israel, Judah won this conflict by depending on God's help. Some kings in Judah's history focused on God, but not one Israelite king consistently followed God—all followed Jeroboam's idolatry or served Baal. As a result, Israel experienced God's punishment many years before Judah did.

Judah had an advantage: The Temple, with its sacrifices and the loyal priests and prophets, was in the southern kingdom. Many of Judah's kings were good, at least for parts of their reigns. Whenever an idolatrous king reigned, his rule was later followed by that of a God-honoring king who reformed religious life. Also, the idolatrous kings usually served for a much shorter time than the good ones. The result was that true faith in God ran stronger and deeper in Judah than in Israel, but it was still not up to God's standards.

**14:1-6** Asa's reign was marked by peace because he "did what was pleasing and good in the sight of the LORD his God." This refrain is often repeated in Chronicles—*obedience* to God leads to *peace* with God and others. In the case of Judah's kings, obedience to God led to national peace, just as God had promised centuries earlier. In our case, obedience may not always bring peace with our enemies, but it will bring peace with God and complete peace in his future Kingdom. Obeying God is the first step on the path to peace.

**14:3-5** Simply attending worship services is not enough to secure God's peace. Like Asa, we must also actively remove anything that is offensive to God. Becoming more active in church

attendance or doing good deeds will still leave us in turmoil if we have failed to eliminate sinful practices from our lives. We should continually ask God to help us remove any source of temptation from our lives.

**ASA'S BATTLES**
A huge army from Ethiopia under Zerah advanced toward Mareshah, greatly outnumbering King Asa's army. Asa sent his troops to meet them, and the battle took place in the valley north of Mareshah. Asa prayed to God, and the Ethiopians were defeated and chased as far as Gerar.

⁷Asa told the people of Judah, "Let us build towns and fortify them with walls, towers, gates, and bars. The land is still ours because we sought the LORD our God, and he has given us peace on every side." So they went ahead with these projects and brought them to completion.

⁸King Asa had an army of 300,000 warriors from the tribe of Judah, armed with large shields and spears. He also had an army of 280,000 warriors from the tribe of Benjamin, armed with small shields and bows. Both armies were composed of well-trained fighting men.

⁹Once an Ethiopian* named Zerah attacked Judah with an army of 1,000,000 men* and 300 chariots. They advanced to the town of Mareshah, ¹⁰so Asa deployed his armies for battle in the valley north of Mareshah.* ¹¹Then Asa cried out to the LORD his God, "O LORD, no one but you can help the powerless against the mighty! Help us, O LORD our God, for we trust in you alone. It is in your name that we have come against this vast horde. O LORD, you are our God; do not let mere men prevail against you!"

¹²So the LORD defeated the Ethiopians* in the presence of Asa and the army of Judah, and the enemy fled. ¹³Asa and his army pursued them as far as Gerar, and so many Ethiopians fell that they were unable to rally. They were destroyed by the LORD and his army, and the army of Judah carried off a vast amount of plunder.

¹⁴While they were at Gerar, they attacked all the towns in that area, and terror from the LORD came upon the people there. As a result, a vast amount of plunder was taken from these towns, too. ¹⁵They also attacked the camps of herdsmen and captured many sheep, goats, and camels before finally returning to Jerusalem.

## Asa's Religious Reforms

**15** Then the Spirit of God came upon Azariah son of Oded, ²and he went out to meet King Asa as he was returning from the battle. "Listen to me, Asa!" he shouted. "Listen, all you people of Judah and Benjamin! The LORD will stay with you as long as you stay with him! Whenever you seek him, you will find him. But if you abandon him, he will abandon you. ³For a long time Israel was without the true God, without a priest to teach them, and without the Law to instruct them. ⁴But whenever they were in trouble and turned to the LORD, the God of Israel, and sought him out, they found him.

⁵"During those dark times, it was not safe to travel. Problems troubled the people of every land. ⁶Nation fought against nation, and city against city, for God was troubling them with every kind of problem. ⁷But as for you, be strong and courageous, for your work will be rewarded."

⁸When Asa heard this message from Azariah the prophet,* he took courage and removed all the detestable idols from the land of Judah and Benjamin and in the towns he had captured in the hill country of Ephraim. And he repaired the altar of the LORD, which stood in front of the entry room of the LORD's Temple.

**14:9a** Hebrew *a Cushite.* **14:9b** Or *an army of thousands and thousands;* Hebrew reads *an army of a thousand thousands.* **14:10** Or *in the Zephathah Valley near Mareshah.* **14:12** Hebrew *Cushites;* also in 14:13. **15:8** As in Syriac version and Latin Vulgate (see also 15:1); Hebrew reads *from Oded the prophet.*

---

**14:7** Judah had peace with all her neighbors. Times of peace are not just for resting. They allow us to prepare for times of trouble. King Asa recognized the period of peace as the right time to build his defenses—the moment of attack would be too late. It is also difficult to withstand spiritual attack unless defenses are prepared beforehand. Decisions about how to face temptation must be made with cool heads long before we feel the heat of temptation. Build your defenses now before temptation strikes.

**14:11** If you are facing battles you feel you can't possibly win, don't give up. In the face of a vast horde of enemy soldiers, Asa prayed for God's help, recognizing his powerlessness against such a mighty army. The secret of victory is first to admit the futility of unaided human effort and then to trust God to save. His power works best through those who recognize their limitations (2 Corinthians 12:9). It is those who think they can do it all on their own who are in the greatest danger.

**15:1, 2** Asa wisely welcomed people who had a close relationship with God, and he listened to their messages. Azariah gave the armies an important warning and encouraged them to stay close to God. Keep in contact with people who are filled with God's Spirit, and you will learn God's counsel. Spend regular time in discussion and prayer with those who can help explain and apply God's message.

**15:3** Azariah said that Israel, the northern kingdom, was "without the true God." Eight kings reigned in Israel during the 41-year rule of Asa in Judah, and all eight were evil. Jeroboam, the first ruler of Israel, began this wicked trend by setting up idols and expelling God's priests (11:13-15). Azariah used Israel's problems as an example of the evil that would come to the people of Judah if they turned away from God as their northern brothers and sisters had.

**15:7** Azariah encouraged the men of Judah to keep up the good work, "for your work will be rewarded." This is an inspiration for us, too. Recognition and reward are great motivators that have two dimensions: (1) *The temporal dimension.* Living by God's standards may result in acclaim here on earth. (2) *The eternal dimension.* Permanent recognition and reward will be given in the next life. Don't be discouraged if you feel your faith in God is going unrewarded here on earth. The best rewards are not in this life but in the life to come.

*Cross-references: 14:7 2 Chr 8:5; 14:8 2 Chr 13:3; 14:9 2 Chr 11:8; 12:2-3; 16:8; 14:11 2 Chr 13:14, 18; 14:12 2 Chr 13:15; 14:13 Gen 10:19; 14:14 2 Chr 17:10; 15:1 2 Chr 20:14; 24:20; 15:2 2 Chr 15:4, 15; 15:3 Lev 10:8-11; 1 Kgs 12:28-33; 2 Chr 17:9; 15:4 Deut 4:29; 15:5 Judg 5:6; 15:6 Matt 24:7; 15:7 Josh 1:7, 9; 15:8 2 Chr 4:1; 8:12*

15:9
2 Chr 11:16

⁹Then Asa called together all the people of Judah and Benjamin, along with the people of Ephraim, Manasseh, and Simeon who had settled among them. For many from Israel had moved to Judah during Asa's reign when they saw that the LORD his God was with him. ¹⁰The people gathered at Jerusalem in late spring,* during the fifteenth year of Asa's reign.

15:11
2 Chr 14:13-15

15:12
2 Chr 23:16

15:13
Exod 22:20
Deut 13:6-9, 15

15:15
2 Chr 14:7

¹¹On that day they sacrificed to the LORD 700 cattle and 7,000 sheep and goats from the plunder they had taken in the battle. ¹²Then they entered into a covenant to seek the LORD, the God of their ancestors, with all their heart and soul. ¹³They agreed that anyone who refused to seek the LORD, the God of Israel, would be put to death—whether young or old, man or woman. ¹⁴They shouted out their oath of loyalty to the LORD with trumpets blaring and rams' horns sounding. ¹⁵All in Judah were happy about this covenant, for they had entered into it with all their heart. They earnestly sought after God, and they found him. And the LORD gave them rest from their enemies on every side.

**15:10** Hebrew *in the third month.* This month of the ancient Hebrew lunar calendar usually occurs within the months of May and June.

**ASA**

God does not condone the idea that "the end justifies the means." He is just and perfect in all his ways. People, on the other hand, are far from perfect. That a bond can exist between a loving and merciful Creator and his rebellious creation is as great a miracle as creation itself! As a king, Asa came very close to being good. He traveled a long way with God before getting off track. His sin was not so much deliberate disobedience as choosing the *easy* way rather than the *right* way.

When the odds seemed impossible in the battle with the Ethiopians, Asa recognized his need to depend on God. Following that victory, God's promise of peace based on obedience spurred the king and people to many years of right living. But Asa was to face a tougher test.

Years of animosity between Asa and Israel's king Baasha took an ugly turn. Baasha, king of the rival northern kingdom, was building a fort that threatened both the peace and the economy of Judah. Asa thought he saw a way out—he bribed King Ben-hadad of Aram to break his alliance with King Baasha. The plan worked brilliantly, but it wasn't God's way. When Asa was confronted by God's prophet Hanani, he flew into a rage, jailed Hanani, and took out his anger on his people. Asa rejected correction and refused to admit his error to God. His greatest failure was missing what God could have done with his life if he had been willing to be humble. His pride ruined the health of his reign. He stubbornly held on to his failure until his death.

Does this attitude sound familiar? Can you identify failures in your life that you have continued to rationalize rather than admit to God and accept his forgiveness for? The end does not justify the means. Such a belief leads to sin and failure. The stubborn refusal to admit a failure due to sin can become a big problem because it makes you spend time rationalizing rather than learning from your mistakes and moving on.

| | |
|---|---|
| **Strengths and accomplishments** | • Obeyed God during the first 10 years of his reign<br>• Carried out a partially successful effort to abolish idolatry<br>• Deposed his idolatrous grandmother, Maacah<br>• Defeated Ethiopia's mighty army |
| **Weaknesses and mistakes** | • Responded with rage when confronted about his sin<br>• Made alliances with foreign nations and evil people |
| **Lessons from his life** | • God not only reinforces good, he confronts evil<br>• Efforts to follow God's plans and rules yield positive results<br>• How well a plan works is no measure of its rightness or approval by God |
| **Vital statistics** | • Where: Jerusalem<br>• Occupation: King of Judah<br>• Relatives: Grandmother: Maacah. Father: Abijah. Son: Jehoshaphat.<br>• Contemporaries: Hanani, Ben-hadad, Zerah, Azariah, Baasha |
| **Key verse** | "The eyes of the LORD search the whole earth in order to strengthen those whose hearts are fully committed to him. What a fool you have been! From now on you will be at war" (2 Chronicles 16:9). |

Asa's story is told in 1 Kings 15:8-24 and 2 Chronicles 14—16. He is also mentioned in Jeremiah 41:9; Matthew 1:7.

**15:14, 15** Many people find it difficult to commit themselves to anything. They are tentative, indecisive, and afraid of responsibility. Asa and his people were different—they had clearly declared themselves for God. Their oath of allegiance was punctuated with shouts and trumpet blasts! This decisive and wholehearted commitment pleased God and resulted in peace for the nation. If you want peace, check to see if there is some area where you lack total commitment to God. Peace comes as a by-product of giving your life wholeheartedly to God.

16King Asa even deposed his grandmother* Maacah from her position as queen mother because she had made an obscene Asherah pole. He cut down her obscene pole, broke it up, and burned it in the Kidron Valley. 17Although the pagan shrines were not removed from Israel, Asa's heart remained completely faithful throughout his life. 18He brought into the Temple of God the silver and gold and the various items that he and his father had dedicated.

19So there was no more war until the thirty-fifth year of Asa's reign.

### Final Years of Asa's Reign

**16** In the thirty-sixth year of Asa's reign, King Baasha of Israel invaded Judah and fortified Ramah in order to prevent anyone from entering or leaving King Asa's territory in Judah.

2Asa responded by removing the silver and gold from the treasuries of the Temple of the Lord and the royal palace. He sent it to King Ben-hadad of Aram, who was ruling in Damascus, along with this message:

3"Let there be a treaty* between you and me like the one between your father and my father. See, I am sending you silver and gold. Break your treaty with King Baasha of Israel so that he will leave me alone."

4Ben-hadad agreed to King Asa's request and sent the commanders of his army to attack the towns of Israel. They conquered the towns of Ijon, Dan, Abel-beth-maacah,* and all the store cities in Naphtali. 5As soon as Baasha of Israel heard what was happening, he abandoned his project of fortifying Ramah and stopped all work on it. 6Then King Asa called out all the men of Judah to carry away the building stones and timbers that Baasha had been using to fortify Ramah. Asa used these materials to fortify the towns of Geba and Mizpah.

7At that time Hanani the seer came to King Asa and told him, "Because you have put your trust in the king of Aram instead of in the Lord your God, you missed your chance to destroy the army of the king of Aram. 8Don't you remember what happened to the Ethiopians* and Libyans and their vast army, with all of their chariots and charioteers?* At that time you relied on the Lord, and he handed them over to you. 9The eyes of the Lord search the whole earth in order to strengthen those whose hearts are fully committed to him. What a fool you have been! From now on you will be at war."

10Asa became so angry with Hanani for saying this that he threw him into prison and put him in stocks. At that time Asa also began to oppress some of his people.

### Summary of Asa's Reign

11The rest of the events of Asa's reign, from beginning to end, are recorded in *The Book of the Kings of Judah and Israel.* 12In the thirty-ninth year of his reign, Asa developed a serious foot disease. Yet even with the severity of his disease, he did not seek the Lord's help but turned only to his physicians. 13So he died in the forty-first year of his reign. 14He was buried in the tomb he had carved out for himself in the City of David. He was laid on a bed perfumed with sweet spices and fragrant ointments, and the people built a huge funeral fire in his honor.

**15:16-19**
//1 Kgs 15:13-15
2 Chr 14:2-5

**16:1-6**
//1 Kgs 15:17-22

**16:4**
Exod 1:11

**16:7**
1 Kgs 16:1
2 Chr 14:11; 19:2;
32:7-8
**16:8**
2 Chr 12:3; 13:16,
18; 14:9
**16:9**
2 Chr 15:17
Prov 15:3
Zech 4:10

**16:11–17:1**
//1 Kgs 15:23-24
**16:12**
Jer 17:5
**16:14**
Gen 50:2
2 Chr 21:19
John 19:39-40

**15:16** Hebrew *his mother.* **16:3** As in Greek version; Hebrew reads *There is a treaty.* **16:4** As in parallel text at 1 Kgs 15:20; Hebrew reads *Abel-maim,* another name for Abel-beth-maacah. **16:8a** Hebrew *Cushites.* **16:8b** Or *and horsemen?*

---

**15:16** The Ten Commandments tell us to honor our fathers and mothers, and yet Asa removed his grandmother from the throne. While honoring parents is God's command, maintaining loyalty to God is an even higher priority. Jesus warned that respect for parents should never keep us from following him (Luke 14:26). If you have unbelieving parents, you must respect and honor them, but you must make devotion to God an even higher priority.

**16:7-10** Both Judah and Israel suffered from faithless forgetfulness! Although God had delivered them even when they were outnumbered (13:3ff; 14:9ff), they repeatedly sought help from pagan nations rather than from God. That Asa sought help from Aram was evidence of national spiritual decline. With help from God alone, Asa had defeated the Ethiopians in open battle. But his confidence in God had slipped, and now he sought only a

human solution to his problem. When confronted by the prophet Hanani, Asa threw him in prison, revealing the true condition of his heart. It is not sin to use human means to solve our problems, but it is sin to trust them more than God, to think they are better than God's ways, or to leave God completely out of the problem-solving process.

**16:12** The criticism of Asa's visit to the physicians was not a general indictment of medicine. Asa's problem was that he completely ignored God's help. The medicine practiced at this time was a mixture of superstition and folk remedies. We should certainly avoid any medicinal treatments derived from occult sources. Asa's experience should encourage us to follow the New Testament practice of receiving prayer for our sickness (James 5:14) as we seek responsible medical help.

**17:1**
1 Kgs 15:24

**17:2**
2 Chr 11:5; 15:8

**17:4**
1 Kgs 12:28

**17:5**
2 Chr 18:1

**17:6**
2 Chr 15:17

**17:7**
2 Chr 15:3; 19:8;
35:3

### Jehoshaphat Rules in Judah

**17** Then Jehoshaphat, Asa's son, became the next king. He strengthened Judah to stand against any attack from Israel. ²He stationed troops in all the fortified towns of Judah, and he assigned additional garrisons to the land of Judah and to the towns of Ephraim that his father, Asa, had captured.

³The LORD was with Jehoshaphat because he followed the example of his father's early years* and did not worship the images of Baal. ⁴He sought his father's God and obeyed his commands instead of following the evil practices of the kingdom of Israel. ⁵So the LORD established Jehoshaphat's control over the kingdom of Judah. All the people of Judah brought gifts to Jehoshaphat, so he became very wealthy and highly esteemed. ⁶He was deeply committed to* the ways of the LORD. He removed the pagan shrines and Asherah poles from Judah.

⁷In the third year of his reign Jehoshaphat sent his officials to teach in all the towns of

**17:3** Some Hebrew manuscripts read *the example of his father, David.*   **17:6** Hebrew *His heart was courageous in.*

---

**JEHOSHAPHAT**

**A**re children more likely to learn from their parents' mistakes or to simply repeat them? In the lives of the people in the Bible, we find that the effects of parental examples are powerful and long lasting. For much of his life, Jehoshaphat seems to have been a son who learned from his father Asa's mistakes and followed his positive actions. But on several occasions, his decisions reveal the negative aspects of his father's example.

When the challenges were obvious, like the need for religious education of the people or the threat of war with a vast army, Jehoshaphat turned to God for guidance and made the right choices. His dependence on God was consistent when the odds were clearly against him. It was in depending on God for the day-to-day plans and actions that Jehoshaphat was weak. He allowed his son to marry Athaliah, the daughter of the wicked Ahab and Jezebel of Israel, who did her best to be as evil as her parents. Jehoshaphat was almost killed when, without asking God, he made an alliance with Ahab. Later, he got involved in an unwise ship-building venture with Ahab's son, Ahaziah—a venture that was shipwrecked by God.

God's faithfulness when the issues are clear and the enemy overwhelming is more than enough reason to seek his guidance when the issues are unclear and the enemy unseen. Jehoshaphat knew this, yet he made little use of that knowledge.

We repeat Jehoshaphat's error when we relegate God to the background in the "easy" decisions of life. Then, when things get out of hand, we want him to get us out of the mess we got ourselves into. God wants us to give him not only the major decisions but also our daily lives—the things we are most often fooled into believing we can control. Perhaps there is nothing major facing you today. Have you paused long enough to give your day to God anyway?

| | |
|---|---|
| **Strengths and accomplishments** | • A bold follower of God, he reminded the people of the early years of his father, Asa<br>• Carried out a national program of religious education<br>• Had many military victories<br>• Developed an extensive legal structure throughout the kingdom |
| **Weaknesses and mistakes** | • Failed to recognize the long-term results of his decisions<br>• Did not completely destroy idolatry in the land<br>• Became entangled with evil King Ahab through alliances<br>• Allowed his son Jehoram to marry Athaliah, Ahab's daughter<br>• Became Ahaziah's business partner in an ill-fated shipping venture |
| **Vital statistics** | • Where: Jerusalem<br>• Occupation: King of Judah<br>• Relatives: Father: Asa. Mother: Azubah. Son: Jehoram. Daughter-in-law: Athaliah.<br>• Contemporaries: Ahab, Jezebel, Micaiah, Ahaziah, Jehu |
| **Key verses** | "Jehoshaphat was a good king, following the ways of his father, Asa. He did what was pleasing in the LORD's sight. During his reign, however, he failed to remove all the pagan shrines, and the people never fully committed themselves to follow the God of their ancestors" (2 Chronicles 20:32, 33). |

Jehoshaphat's story is told in 1 Kings 15:24—22:50 and 2 Chronicles 17:1—21:1. He is also mentioned in 2 Kings 3:1–14 and Joel 3:2, 12.

---

**17:7-9** The people of Judah were biblically illiterate. They had never taken time to listen to and discuss God's law and understand how it could change them. Jehoshaphat realized that knowing God's commands was the first step to getting people to live as they should, so he initiated a nationwide religious education program. He reversed the religious decline that had occurred at the end of Asa's reign by putting God first in the people's minds and instilling in them a sense of commitment and mission. Because of this action, the nation began to follow God. Churches and Christian schools today need solid Christian education programs. Exposure to good Bible teaching through Sunday school, church, Bible study, and personal and family devotions is essential for living as God intended.

Judah. These officials included Ben-hail, Obadiah, Zechariah, Nethanel, and Micaiah. ⁸He sent Levites along with them, including Shemaiah, Nethaniah, Zebadiah, Asahel, Shemiramoth, Jehonathan, Adonijah, Tobijah, and Tob-adonijah. He also sent out the priests Elishama and Jehoram. ⁹They took copies of the Book of the Law of the LORD and traveled around through all the towns of Judah, teaching the people.

**17:8**
2 Chr 19:8

**17:9**
Deut 6:4-9

¹⁰Then the fear of the LORD fell over all the surrounding kingdoms so that none of them wanted to declare war on Jehoshaphat. ¹¹Some of the Philistines brought him gifts and silver as tribute, and the Arabs brought 7,700 rams and 7,700 male goats.

**17:10**
2 Chr 14:14
**17:11**
2 Chr 9:14; 26:8

¹²So Jehoshaphat became more and more powerful and built fortresses and storage cities throughout Judah. ¹³He stored numerous supplies in Judah's towns and stationed an army of seasoned troops at Jerusalem. ¹⁴His army was enrolled according to ancestral clans.

From Judah there were 300,000 troops organized in units of 1,000, under the command of Adnah. ¹⁵Next in command was Jehohanan, who commanded 280,000 troops. ¹⁶Next was Amasiah son of Zicri, who volunteered for the LORD's service, with 200,000 troops under his command.

**17:16**
Judg 5:2, 9
1 Chr 29:9

¹⁷From Benjamin there were 200,000 troops equipped with bows and shields. They were under the command of Eliada, a veteran soldier. ¹⁸Next in command was Jehozabad, who commanded 180,000 armed men.

¹⁹These were the troops stationed in Jerusalem to serve the king, besides those Jehoshaphat stationed in the fortified towns throughout Judah.

**17:19**
2 Chr 17:2

### Jehoshaphat and Ahab

**18** Jehoshaphat enjoyed great riches and high esteem, and he made an alliance with Ahab of Israel by having his son marry Ahab's daughter. ²A few years later he went to Samaria to visit Ahab, who prepared a great banquet for him and his officials. They butchered great numbers of sheep, goats, and cattle for the feast. Then Ahab enticed Jehoshaphat to join forces with him to recover Ramoth-gilead.

**18:1-27**
//1 Kgs 22:1-28
**18:1**
2 Chr 17:5
**18:2**
1 Kgs 22:2-35

³"Will you go with me to Ramoth-gilead?" King Ahab of Israel asked King Jehoshaphat of Judah.

Jehoshaphat replied, "Why, of course! You and I are as one, and my troops are your troops. We will certainly join you in battle." ⁴Then Jehoshaphat added, "But first let's find out what the LORD says."

⁵So the king of Israel summoned the prophets, 400 of them, and asked them, "Should we go to war against Ramoth-gilead, or should I hold back?"

---

**18:1ff** Although Jehoshaphat was deeply committed to God, he arranged for his son to marry Athaliah, the daughter of wicked King Ahab of Israel, and then made a military alliance with him. Jehoshaphat's popularity and power made him attractive to the cunning and opportunistic Ahab. This alliance had three devas-

tating consequences: (1) Jehoshaphat incurred God's anger (19:2); (2) when Jehoshaphat's grandson died, Athaliah seized the throne and almost destroyed all of David's descendants (22:10-12); (3) Athaliah brought the evil practices of Israel into Judah, which eventually led to the nation's downfall.

When believers in leadership positions become allied with unbelievers, values can be compromised and spiritual awareness dulled. The Bible often warns against teaming up with unbelievers (2 Corinthians 6:14). (See the note on 20:37 for more on alliances.)

**BATTLE WITH ARAM**

King Jehoshaphat made an alliance with evil King Ahab of Israel. Together they decided to attack Ramoth-gilead and rout the Arameans who had occupied the city. But Jehoshaphat first wanted to seek the advice of a prophet. Ahab's prophets predicted victory, but Micaiah predicted defeat. The two kings were defeated, and Ahab was killed.

**18:3-8** Evil kings did not like God's prophets bringing messages of doom (18:17; Jeremiah 5:13). Many, therefore, hired prophets who told them only what they wanted to hear (Isaiah 30:10, 11; Jeremiah 14:13-16; 23:16, 21, 30-36). These men were false prophets because they extolled the greatness of the king and predicted victory regardless of the real situation.

**18:3-8** Wicked Ahab asked Jehoshaphat to join forces with him in battle (18:2, 3). Before making that commitment, Jehoshaphat rightly sought God's advice. However, when God gave his answer through the prophet Micaiah (18:16), Jehoshaphat ignored it (18:28). It does us no good to seek God's advice if we ignore it when it is given. Real love for God is shown, not by merely asking for direction, but by following that direction once it is given.

**18:5-16** When you want to please or impress someone, it is tempting to lie to make yourself look good. Ahab's 400 prophets did just that, telling Ahab only what he wanted to hear. They were then rewarded for making Ahab happy. Micaiah, however, told

They all replied, "Yes, go right ahead! God will give the king victory."

⁶But Jehoshaphat asked, "Is there not also a prophet of the Lᴏʀᴅ here? We should ask him the same question."

⁷The king of Israel replied to Jehoshaphat, "There is one more man who could consult the Lᴏʀᴅ for us, but I hate him. He never prophesies anything but trouble for me! His name is Micaiah son of Imlah."

Jehoshaphat replied, "That's not the way a king should talk! Let's hear what he has to say."

⁸So the king of Israel called one of his officials and said, "Quick! Bring Micaiah son of Imlah."

### Micaiah Prophesies against Ahab

⁹King Ahab of Israel and King Jehoshaphat of Judah, dressed in their royal robes, were sitting on thrones at the threshing floor near the gate of Samaria. All of Ahab's prophets were prophesying there in front of them. ¹⁰One of them, Zedekiah son of Kenaanah, made some iron horns and proclaimed, "This is what the Lᴏʀᴅ says: With these horns you will gore the Arameans to death!"

¹¹All the other prophets agreed. "Yes," they said, "go up to Ramoth-gilead and be victorious, for the Lᴏʀᴅ will give the king victory!"

¹²Meanwhile, the messenger who went to get Micaiah said to him, "Look, all the prophets are promising victory for the king. Be sure that you agree with them and promise success."

**18:13**
Num 22:18-20, 35

¹³But Micaiah replied, "As surely as the Lᴏʀᴅ lives, I will say only what my God says."

¹⁴When Micaiah arrived before the king, Ahab asked him, "Micaiah, should we go to war against Ramoth-gilead, or should I hold back?"

Micaiah replied sarcastically, "Yes, go up and be victorious, for you will have victory over them!"

¹⁵But the king replied sharply, "How many times must I demand that you speak only the truth to me when you speak for the Lᴏʀᴅ?"

**18:16**
Num 27:17
Ezek 34:4-8
Matt 9:36
†Mark 6:34

¹⁶Then Micaiah told him, "In a vision I saw all Israel scattered on the mountains, like sheep without a shepherd. And the Lᴏʀᴅ said, 'Their master has been killed.* Send them home in peace.'"

¹⁷"Didn't I tell you?" the king of Israel exclaimed to Jehoshaphat. "He never prophesies anything but trouble for me."

**18:18**
Isa 6:1-5
Dan 7:9-10

¹⁸Then Micaiah continued, "Listen to what the Lᴏʀᴅ says! I saw the Lᴏʀᴅ sitting on his throne with all the armies of heaven around him, on his right and on his left. ¹⁹And the Lᴏʀᴅ said, 'Who can entice King Ahab of Israel to go into battle against Ramoth-gilead so he can be killed?'

**18:20**
Job 1:6

"There were many suggestions, ²⁰and finally a spirit approached the Lᴏʀᴅ and said, 'I can do it!'

"'How will you do this?' the Lᴏʀᴅ asked.

²¹"And the spirit replied, 'I will go out and inspire all of Ahab's prophets to speak lies.'

"'You will succeed,' said the Lᴏʀᴅ. 'Go ahead and do it.'

**18:22**
Ezek 14:9

²²"So you see, the Lᴏʀᴅ has put a lying spirit in the mouths of your prophets. For the Lᴏʀᴅ has pronounced your doom."

**18:23**
Jer 20:2
Mark 14:65
Acts 23:2

²³Then Zedekiah son of Kenaanah walked up to Micaiah and slapped him across the face. "Since when did the Spirit of the Lᴏʀᴅ leave me to speak to you?" he demanded.

²⁴And Micaiah replied, "You will find out soon enough when you are trying to hide in some secret room!"

**18:16** Hebrew *These people have no master.*

---

the truth and got arrested (18:25, 26). Obeying God doesn't always protect us from evil consequences. Obedience may, in fact, provoke them. But it is better to suffer from people's displeasure than from God's wrath (Matthew 10:28). If you are ridiculed for being honest, remember that this can be a sign that you are indeed doing what is right in God's eyes (Matthew 5:10-12; Romans 8:17, 35-39).

**18:22** God used the seductive influence of false prophets to judge Ahab. They were determined to tell Ahab what he wanted to hear. God confirmed their plans to lie as a means to remove Ahab from the throne. These prophets, supported by Ahab, snared him in his sin. Because he listened to them instead of God, he was killed in battle. The lying spirit is a picture of the prophets' entire way of life—telling the king only what he wanted to hear, not what he needed to hear. Leaders will only find trouble if they surround themselves with advisers whose only thought is to please them.

25"Arrest him!" the king of Israel ordered. "Take him back to Amon, the governor of the city, and to my son Joash. 26Give them this order from the king: 'Put this man in prison, and feed him nothing but bread and water until I return safely from the battle!'"

27But Micaiah replied, "If you return safely, it will mean that the LORD has not spoken through me!" Then he added to those standing around, "Everyone mark my words!"

**18:25**
2 Chr 18:8
**18:26**
2 Chr 16:10

### The Death of Ahab

28So King Ahab of Israel and King Jehoshaphat of Judah led their armies against Ramoth-gilead. 29The king of Israel said to Jehoshaphat, "As we go into battle, I will disguise myself so no one will recognize me, but you wear your royal robes." So the king of Israel disguised himself, and they went into battle.

**18:28-34**
//1 Kgs 22:29-36

**BIBLE**

| The Persecuted | The Persecutors | Why the Persecution | Result | Reference |
|---|---|---|---|---|
| Isaac | The Philistines | God was blessing Isaac, and they envied him | The Philistines could not subdue Isaac, so they made peace with him | Genesis 26:12-33 |
| Moses | Israelites | The Israelites wanted water | God provided water, in answer to Moses' prayer | Exodus 17:1-7 |
| David | Saul and others | David was becoming a powerful leader, threatening Saul's position as king | David endured the persecution and became king | 1 Samuel 20—27 Psalms 31:13; 59:1-4 |
| Priests of Nob | Saul and Doeg | Saul and Doeg thought the priests helped David escape | 85 priests were killed | 1 Samuel 22 |
| Prophets | Jezebel | Jezebel didn't like to have her evil ways pointed out | Many prophets were killed | 1 Kings 18:3, 4 |
| Elijah | Ahab and Jezebel | Elijah confronted their sins | Elijah had to flee for his life | 1 Kings 18:10–19:2 |
| Micaiah | Ahab | Ahab thought Micaiah was stirring up trouble rather than prophesying from God | Micaiah was thrown into prison | 2 Chronicles 18:12-26 |
| Elisha | A king of Israel (Probably Joram) | The king thought Elisha had caused the famine | Elisha ignored the threatened persecution and prophesied the famine's end | 2 Kings 6:31 |
| Hanani | Asa | Hanani criticized Asa for trusting in Aram's help more than in God's help | Hanani was thrown in prison | 2 Chronicles 16:7-10 |
| Zechariah | Joash | Zechariah confronted the people of Judah for disregarding God's commands | Zechariah was executed | 2 Chronicles 24:20-22 |
| Uriah | Jehoiakim | Uriah confronted Jehoiakim about his evil ways | Uriah was killed with a sword | Jeremiah 26:20-23 |
| Jeremiah | Zedekiah | Zedekiah thought Jeremiah was a traitor for prophesying Jerusalem's fall | Jeremiah was thrown in prison, then into a muddy cistern | Jeremiah 37:1–38:13 |
| Shadrach, Meshach, Abednego | Nebuchadnezzar | The three men refused to bow down to anyone but God | They were thrown into a blazing furnace, but God miraculously saved them | Daniel 3 |

**18:31** Jehoshaphat's troubles began when he joined forces with the evil King Ahab. Almost at once he found himself the target for soldiers who mistakenly identified him as Ahab. He could have accepted this fate because he deserved it, but instead he cried out to God, who miraculously saved him.

When we sin and the inevitable consequences follow, we may be tempted to give up. "I chose to sin," we may think, "it's my fault, and I must accept the consequences." While we may deserve what comes to us, that is no reason to avoid calling on God for urgent help. Had Jehoshaphat given up, he might

**18:31**
2 Chr 13:14-15

³⁰Meanwhile, the king of Aram had issued these orders to his chariot commanders: "Attack only the king of Israel! Don't bother with anyone else." ³¹So when the Aramean chariot commanders saw Jehoshaphat in his royal robes, they went after him. "There is the king of Israel!" they shouted. But Jehoshaphat called out, and the LORD saved him. God helped him by turning the attackers away from him. ³²As soon as the chariot commanders realized he was not the king of Israel, they stopped chasing him.

³³An Aramean soldier, however, randomly shot an arrow at the Israelite troops and hit the king of Israel between the joints of his armor. "Turn the horses* and get me out of here!" Ahab groaned to the driver of the chariot. "I'm badly wounded!"

18:33 Hebrew *Turn your hand.*

# PERSECUTIONS

| The Persecuted | The Persecutors | Why the Persecution | Result | Reference |
|---|---|---|---|---|
| Daniel | National leaders | Daniel was praying | Daniel was thrown into a den of lions, but God miraculously saved him | Daniel 6 |
| Job | Satan | Satan wanted to prove that pain and suffering would make a person abandon God | Job remained faithful to God and was restored | Job 1:8-12; 2:3-7 |
| John the Baptist | Herod and Herodias | John confronted King Herod's adultery | John was beheaded | Matthew 14:3-13 |
| Jesus | Religious leaders | Jesus exposed their sinful motives | Jesus was crucified, but rose again from the dead to show his authority over all evil | Mark 7:1-16; Luke 22:63–24:7 |
| Peter and John | Religious leaders | Peter and John preached that Jesus was God's Son and the only way to salvation | They were thrown into prison, but later released | Acts 4:1-31 |
| Stephen | Religious leaders | Stephen exposed their guilt in crucifying Jesus | Stephen was stoned to death | Acts 6–7 |
| The church | Paul and others | The Christians preached Jesus as the Messiah | Believers faced death, prison, torture, exile | Acts 8:1-3; 9:1-9 |
| James | Herod Agrippa I | To please the Jewish leaders | James was executed | Acts 12:1, 2 |
| Peter | Herod Agrippa I | To please the Jewish leaders | Peter was thrown into prison | Acts 12:3-17 |
| Paul | Jews, city officials | Paul preached about Jesus and confronted those who made money by manipulating others | Paul was stoned; thrown into prison | Acts 14:19; 16:16-24 |
| Timothy | Unknown | Unknown | Timothy was thrown into prison | Hebrews 13:23 |
| John | Probably the Romans | John told others about Jesus | John was sent into exile on a remote island | Revelation 1:9 |

Micaiah, like thousands of believers before and after him, was persecuted for his faith. The chart shows that persecution comes from a variety of people and is given in a variety of ways. Sometimes God protects us from it; sometimes he doesn't. But as long as we remain faithful to God *alone*, we must expect persecution (see also Luke 6:22; 2 Corinthians 6:4-10; 2 Timothy 2:9-12; Revelation 2:10). God also seems to have a special reward for those who endure such persecution (Revelation 6:9-11; 20:4).

have died. No matter how greatly you have sinned, you can still call upon God.

**18:33** Micaiah prophesied death for Ahab (18:16, 27), so Ahab disguised himself to fool the enemy. Apparently the disguise worked, but that didn't change the prophecy. A random Aramean arrow found a crack in his armor and killed him. God fulfills his will despite the defenses people try to erect. God can use anything, even an error, to bring his will to pass. This is good news for God's followers because we can trust him to work out his plans and keep his promises no matter how desperate our circumstances are.

³⁴The battle raged all that day, and the king of Israel propped himself up in his chariot facing the Arameans. In the evening, just as the sun was setting, he died.

## Jehoshaphat Appoints Judges

**19** When King Jehoshaphat of Judah arrived safely home in Jerusalem, ²Jehu son of Hanani the seer went out to meet him. "Why should you help the wicked and love those who hate the LORD?" he asked the king. "Because of what you have done, the LORD is very angry with you. ³Even so, there is some good in you, for you have removed the Asherah poles throughout the land, and you have committed yourself to seeking God."

⁴Jehoshaphat lived in Jerusalem, but he went out among the people, traveling from Beer-sheba to the hill country of Ephraim, encouraging the people to return to the LORD, the God of their ancestors. ⁵He appointed judges throughout the nation in all the fortified towns, ⁶and he said to them, "Always think carefully before pronouncing judgment. Remember that you do not judge to please people but to please the LORD. He will be with you when you render the verdict in each case. ⁷Fear the LORD and judge with integrity, for the LORD our God does not tolerate perverted justice, partiality, or the taking of bribes."

⁸In Jerusalem, Jehoshaphat appointed some of the Levites and priests and clan leaders in Israel to serve as judges for cases involving the LORD's regulations and for civil disputes. ⁹These were his instructions to them: "You must always act in the fear of the LORD, with faithfulness and an undivided heart. ¹⁰Whenever a case comes to you from fellow citizens in an outlying town, whether a murder case or some other violation of God's laws, commands, decrees, or regulations, you must warn them not to sin against the LORD, so that he will not be angry with you and them. Do this and you will not be guilty.

¹¹"Amariah the high priest will have final say in all cases involving the LORD. Zebadiah son of Ishmael, a leader from the tribe of Judah, will have final say in all civil cases. The Levites will assist you in making sure that justice is served. Take courage as you fulfill your duties, and may the LORD be with those who do what is right."

## War with Surrounding Nations

**20** After this, the armies of the Moabites, Ammonites, and some of the Meunites* declared war on Jehoshaphat. ²Messengers came and told Jehoshaphat, "A vast army from Edom* is marching against you from beyond the Dead Sea.* They are already at Hazazon-tamar." (This was another name for En-gedi.)

³Jehoshaphat was terrified by this news and begged the LORD for guidance. He also ordered everyone in Judah to begin fasting. ⁴So people from all the towns of Judah came to Jerusalem to seek the LORD's help.

⁵Jehoshaphat stood before the community of Judah and Jerusalem in front of the new courtyard at the Temple of the LORD. ⁶He prayed, "O LORD, God of our ancestors, you alone are the God who is in heaven. You are ruler of all the kingdoms of the earth. You are powerful and mighty; no one can stand against you! ⁷O our God, did you not drive out those who lived in this land when your people Israel arrived? And did you not give this land forever to

---

**19:2**
1 Kgs 16:1
2 Chr 18:1, 3;
20:34; 24:18

**19:3**
2 Chr 12:12; 17:6

**19:4**
Deut 16:18-20
2 Chr 15:8-13

**19:6**
Lev 19:15
Deut 1:17

**19:7**
Gen 18:25
Deut 10:17-18;
32:4

**19:8**
2 Chr 17:8-9

**19:10**
Deut 17:8
2 Chr 19:2

**19:11**
1 Chr 28:20
2 Chr 19:8

**20:2**
Gen 14:7

**20:3**
1 Sam 7:6
2 Chr 19:3
Ezra 8:21

**20:6**
Deut 4:39
1 Chr 29:11

**20:7**
Isa 41:8

---

**20:1** As in some Greek manuscripts (see also 26:7); Hebrew repeats *Ammonites.*    **20:2a** As in one Hebrew manuscript; most Hebrew manuscripts and ancient versions read *Aram.*    **20:2b** Hebrew *the sea.*

---

**19:5-10** Jehoshaphat delegated some of the responsibilities for ruling and judging the people, but he warned his appointees that they were accountable to God for the standards they used to judge others. Jehoshaphat's advice is helpful for all leaders: (1) Realize that you are judging for God (19:6); (2) be impartial and honest (19:7); (3) be faithful (19:9); (4) act only out of fear of God, not people (19:9). God holds us accountable for the authority we exercise.

**19:8** Jehoshaphat appointed priests and Levites to help in administering civil laws. Many years earlier, Moses had chosen men who were capable, faithful, and honest to help him judge disputes among the people (Exodus 18:21, 22). Obviously the best kind of leader is one who always acts with reverence for God. Effective leaders get the job done; faithful leaders make sure the job is done in God's way and in God's time. They are careful to instill God's wisdom in future leaders and God's values in the entire community.

**20:3** When the nation was faced with disaster, Jehoshaphat called upon the people to get serious with God by going without food (fasting) for a designated time. By separating themselves from the daily routine of food preparation and eating, they could devote that extra time to considering their sin and praying to God for help. Hunger pangs would reinforce their penitence and remind them of their weakness and their dependence upon God. Fasting still can be helpful today as we seek God's will in special situations.

**20:6ff** Jehoshaphat's prayer had several essential ingredients. (1) He committed the situation to God, acknowledging that only God could save the nation. (2) He sought God's favor because his people were God's people. (3) He acknowledged God's sovereignty over the current situation. (4) He praised God's glory and took comfort in his promises. (5) He professed complete dependence on God, not himself, for deliverance. To be God's kind of leader today, follow Jehoshaphat's example: Focus entirely on God's power rather than your own.

**20:9**
2 Chr 6:20, 28-30

**20:10**
Num 20:17-21
2 Chr 20:1, 22

**20:11**
Ps 83:12

**20:12**
Judg 11:27
Pss 25:15; 121:1-2

**20:14**
2 Chr 15:1; 24:20

**20:15**
Exod 14:13
1 Sam 17:47
2 Chr 32:7-8

**20:17**
Exod 14:13
2 Chr 15:2

**20:20**
Isa 7:9

**20:21**
1 Chr 16:29, 34, 41
Ps 29:2

**20:22**
2 Chr 13:13; 20:10

**20:23**
Judg 7:22
1 Sam 14:20

**20:27**
Neh 12:43

**20:30**
2 Chr 14:6-7, 14;
15:15; 17:10

the descendants of your friend Abraham? ⁸Your people settled here and built this Temple to honor your name. ⁹They said, 'Whenever we are faced with any calamity such as war,* plague, or famine, we can come to stand in your presence before this Temple where your name is honored. We can cry out to you to save us, and you will hear us and rescue us.'

¹⁰"And now see what the armies of Ammon, Moab, and Mount Seir are doing. You would not let our ancestors invade those nations when Israel left Egypt, so they went around them and did not destroy them. ¹¹Now see how they reward us! For they have come to throw us out of your land, which you gave us as an inheritance. ¹²O our God, won't you stop them? We are powerless against this mighty army that is about to attack us. We do not know what to do, but we are looking to you for help."

¹³As all the men of Judah stood before the LORD with their little ones, wives, and children, ¹⁴the Spirit of the LORD came upon one of the men standing there. His name was Jahaziel son of Zechariah, son of Benaiah, son of Jeiel, son of Mattaniah, a Levite who was a descendant of Asaph.

¹⁵He said, "Listen, all you people of Judah and Jerusalem! Listen, King Jehoshaphat! This is what the LORD says: Do not be afraid! Don't be discouraged by this mighty army, for the battle is not yours, but God's. ¹⁶Tomorrow, march out against them. You will find them coming up through the ascent of Ziz at the end of the valley that opens into the wilderness of Jeruel. ¹⁷But you will not even need to fight. Take your positions; then stand still and watch the LORD's victory. He is with you, O people of Judah and Jerusalem. Do not be afraid or discouraged. Go out against them tomorrow, for the LORD is with you!"

¹⁸Then King Jehoshaphat bowed low with his face to the ground. And all the people of Judah and Jerusalem did the same, worshiping the LORD. ¹⁹Then the Levites from the clans of Kohath and Korah stood to praise the LORD, the God of Israel, with a very loud shout.

²⁰Early the next morning the army of Judah went out into the wilderness of Tekoa. On the way Jehoshaphat stopped and said, "Listen to me, all you people of Judah and Jerusalem! Believe in the LORD your God, and you will be able to stand firm. Believe in his prophets, and you will succeed."

²¹After consulting the people, the king appointed singers to walk ahead of the army, singing to the LORD and praising him for his holy splendor. This is what they sang:

"Give thanks to the LORD;
    his faithful love endures forever!"

²²At the very moment they began to sing and give praise, the LORD caused the armies of Ammon, Moab, and Mount Seir to start fighting among themselves. ²³The armies of Moab and Ammon turned against their allies from Mount Seir and killed every one of them. After they had destroyed the army of Seir, they began attacking each other. ²⁴So when the army of Judah arrived at the lookout point in the wilderness, all they saw were dead bodies lying on the ground as far as they could see. Not a single one of the enemy had escaped.

²⁵King Jehoshaphat and his men went out to gather the plunder. They found vast amounts of equipment, clothing,* and other valuables—more than they could carry. There was so much plunder that it took them three days just to collect it all! ²⁶On the fourth day they gathered in the Valley of Blessing,* which got its name that day because the people praised and thanked the LORD there. It is still called the Valley of Blessing today.

²⁷Then all the men returned to Jerusalem, with Jehoshaphat leading them, overjoyed that the LORD had given them victory over their enemies. ²⁸They marched into Jerusalem to the music of harps, lyres, and trumpets, and they proceeded to the Temple of the LORD.

²⁹When all the surrounding kingdoms heard that the LORD himself had fought against the enemies of Israel, the fear of God came over them. ³⁰So Jehoshaphat's kingdom was at peace, for his God had given him rest on every side.

**20:9** Or *sword of judgment;* or *sword, judgment.*  **20:25** As in some Hebrew manuscripts and Latin Vulgate; most Hebrew manuscripts read *corpses.*  **20:26** Hebrew *valley of Beracah.*

---

**20:15** As the enemy bore down on Judah, God spoke through Jahaziel: "Do not be afraid! . . . for the battle is not yours, but God's." We may not fight an enemy army, but every day we battle temptation, pressure, and "rulers . . . of the unseen world" (Ephesians 6:12) who want us to rebel against God. Remember, as believers, we have God's Spirit in us. If we ask for God's help when we face struggles, God will fight for us. And God always triumphs.

How do we let God fight for us? (1) Realize that the battle is not ours, but God's; (2) recognize human limitations and allow God's strength to work through our fears and weaknesses; (3) make sure we are pursuing God's interests and not just our own selfish desires; (4) ask God for help in our daily battles.

## Summary of Jehoshaphat's Reign

31 So Jehoshaphat ruled over the land of Judah. He was thirty-five years old when he became king, and he reigned in Jerusalem twenty-five years. His mother was Azubah, the daughter of Shilhi.

20:31–21:1
//1 Kgs 22:41-50
2 Chr 17:6

32 Jehoshaphat was a good king, following the ways of his father, Asa. He did what was pleasing in the Lord's sight. 33 During his reign, however, he failed to remove all the pagan shrines, and the people never fully committed themselves to follow the God of their ancestors.

20:33
2 Chr 17:6; 19:3

34 The rest of the events of Jehoshaphat's reign, from beginning to end, are recorded in *The Record of Jehu Son of Hanani,* which is included in *The Book of the Kings of Israel.*

20:34
1 Kgs 16:1, 7

35 Some time later King Jehoshaphat of Judah made an alliance with King Ahaziah of Israel, who was very wicked.* 36 Together they built a fleet of trading ships* at the port of Eziongeber. 37 Then Eliezer son of Dodavahu from Mareshah prophesied against Jehoshaphat. He said, "Because you have allied yourself with King Ahaziah, the Lord will destroy your work." So the ships met with disaster and never put out to sea.*

20:35
1 Kgs 22:48-49

20:36
2 Chr 9:21

## Jehoram Rules in Judah

**21** When Jehoshaphat died, he was buried with his ancestors in the City of David. Then his son Jehoram became the next king.

21:1
1 Kgs 22:50

2 Jehoram's brothers—the other sons of Jehoshaphat—were Azariah, Jehiel, Zechariah, Azariahu, Michael, and Shephatiah; all these were the sons of Jehoshaphat king of Judah.* 3 Their father had given each of them valuable gifts of silver, gold, and costly items, and also some of Judah's fortified towns. However, he designated Jehoram as the next king because he was the oldest. 4 But when Jehoram had become solidly established as king, he killed all his brothers and some of the other leaders of Judah.

21:3
2 Chr 11:5

5 Jehoram was thirty-two years old when he became king, and he reigned in Jerusalem eight years. 6 But Jehoram followed the example of the kings of Israel and was as wicked as King Ahab, for he had married one of Ahab's daughters. So Jehoram did what was evil in the Lord's sight. 7 But the Lord did not want to destroy David's dynasty, for he had made a covenant with David and promised that his descendants would continue to rule, shining like a lamp forever.

21:5-10
//2 Kgs 8:16-24

21:6
1 Kgs 12:28-30
2 Chr 18:1

21:7
2 Sam 7:12-17
1 Kgs 11:13

8 During Jehoram's reign, the Edomites revolted against Judah and crowned their own king. 9 So Jehoram went out with his full army and all his chariots. The Edomites surrounded him and his chariot commanders, but he went out at night and attacked them* under cover of darkness. 10 Even so, Edom has been independent from Judah to this day. The town of Libnah also revolted about that same time. All this happened because Jehoram had abandoned the Lord, the God of his ancestors. 11 He had built pagan shrines in the hill country of Judah and had led the people of Jerusalem and Judah to give themselves to pagan gods and to go astray.

21:8
2 Chr 20:22-23;
21:10

21:11
Lev 20:5
1 Kgs 11:7

20:35 Or *who made him do what was wicked.*   20:36 Hebrew *fleet of ships that could go to Tarshish.*   20:37 Hebrew *never set sail for Tarshish.*   21:2 Masoretic Text reads *of Israel;* also in 21:4. The author of Chronicles sees Judah as representative of the true Israel. (Some Hebrew manuscripts, Greek and Syriac versions, and Latin Vulgate read *of Judah.*)   21:9 Or *he went out and escaped.* The meaning of the Hebrew is uncertain.

---

**20:33** This summary says that Jehoshaphat did not remove the pagan shrines, while 17:6 and 19:3 say he did remove them. Jehoshaphat destroyed most of the Baal and Asherah idols, but since he did not succeed in wiping out the corrupt religions practiced at the shrines, they were probably rebuilt each time he had them removed.

**20:37** Jehoshaphat met disaster when he joined forces with wicked King Ahaziah. He did not learn from his disastrous alliance with Ahab (18:28-34) or from his father's alliance with Aram (16:2-9). The partnership stood on unequal footing because one man served the Lord and the other worshiped idols. We court disaster when we enter into partnership with unbelievers because our very foundations differ (2 Corinthians 6:14-18). While one serves the Lord, the other does not recognize God's authority. Inevitably, the one who serves God is faced with the temptation to compromise values. When that happens, spiritual disaster results.

Before entering into partnerships, ask: (1) What are my motives? (2) What problems am I avoiding by seeking this partnership? (3) Is this partnership the best solution, or is it only a quick solution to my problem? (4) Have I prayed or asked others to pray for guidance? (5) Are my partner and I really working

toward the same goals? (6) Am I willing to settle for less financial gain in order to do what God wants?

**21:6** Jehoram, the new king of Judah, married Athaliah, one of the daughters of King Ahab of Israel. She became the mother of Judah's next king, Ahaziah (22:2). Athaliah's mother was Jezebel, the most wicked woman Israel had ever known. Jehoram's marriage to Athaliah was Judah's downfall, for Athaliah brought her mother's wicked influence into Judah, causing the nation to forget God and turn to Baal worship (22:3).

**21:7** God promised that a descendant of David would always sit on the throne (2 Samuel 7:8-16). What happened to this promise when the nation was destroyed and carried away? There were two parts to God's promise. (1) In the physical sense, as long as there was an actual throne in Judah, a descendant of David would sit upon it. But this part of the promise depended on the obedience of these kings. When they disobeyed, God was not bound to continue David's temporal line. (2) In the spiritual sense, this promise was completely fulfilled in the coming of Jesus the Messiah, a descendant of David, who would sit on the throne of David forever.

**21:8-11** Jehoram's reign was marked by sin and cruelty. He married a woman who worshiped idols; he killed his six brothers;

21:12
2 Chr 14:2-5;
17:3-4

¹²Then Elijah the prophet wrote Jehoram this letter:

"This is what the LORD, the God of your ancestor David, says: You have not followed the good example of your father, Jehoshaphat, or your grandfather King Asa of Judah.

21:13
1 Kgs 16:31-33
2 Chr 21:4, 6, 11

¹³Instead, you have been as evil as the kings of Israel. You have led the people of Jerusalem and Judah to worship idols, just as King Ahab did in Israel. And you have even killed your own brothers, men who were better than you. ¹⁴So now the LORD is about to strike you, your people, your children, your wives, and all that is yours with a

21:15
2 Chr 21:18-19

heavy blow. ¹⁵You yourself will suffer with a severe intestinal disease that will get worse each day until your bowels come out."

21:16
2 Chr 17:11; 22:1;
33:11

¹⁶Then the LORD stirred up the Philistines and the Arabs, who lived near the Ethiopians,* to attack Jehoram. ¹⁷They marched against Judah, broke down its defenses, and carried

21:17
2 Chr 25:23

away everything of value in the royal palace, including the king's sons and his wives. Only his youngest son, Ahaziah,* was spared.

21:18
2 Chr 21:15

¹⁸After all this, the LORD struck Jehoram with the severe intestinal disease. ¹⁹The disease grew worse and worse, and at the end of two years it caused his bowels to come out, and he

21:19
2 Chr 16:14

died in agony. His people did not build a great funeral fire to honor him as they had done for his ancestors.

21:20
2 Chr 24:25; 28:27
Jer 22:18, 28

²⁰Jehoram was thirty-two years old when he became king, and he reigned in Jerusalem eight years. No one was sorry when he died. They buried him in the City of David, but not in the royal cemetery.

### Ahaziah Rules in Judah

22:1-6
//2 Kgs 8:25-29
22:1
2 Chr 21:16-17

**22** Then the people of Jerusalem made Ahaziah, Jehoram's youngest son, their next king, since the marauding bands who came with the Arabs* had killed all the older sons. So Ahaziah son of Jehoram reigned as king of Judah.

22:3
2 Chr 21:6-7

²Ahaziah was twenty-two* years old when he became king, and he reigned in Jerusalem one year. His mother was Athaliah, a granddaughter of King Omri. ³Ahaziah also followed the evil example of King Ahab's family, for his mother encouraged him in doing wrong. ⁴He did what was evil in the LORD's sight, just as Ahab's family had done. They even became his advisers after the death of his father, and they led him to ruin.

22:5
2 Kgs 8:28

⁵Following their evil advice, Ahaziah joined King Joram,* the son of King Ahab of Israel, in his war against King Hazael of Aram at Ramoth-gilead. When the Arameans wounded Joram in the battle, ⁶he returned to Jezreel to recover from the wounds he had received at Ramoth.* Because Joram was wounded, King Ahaziah* of Judah went to Jezreel to visit him.

22:7-9
//2 Kgs 9:21-29

⁷But God had decided that this visit would be Ahaziah's downfall. While he was there, Ahaziah went out with Joram to meet Jehu grandson of Nimshi,* whom the LORD had appointed to destroy the dynasty of Ahab.

22:8
2 Kgs 10:13-14
22:9
2 Kgs 9:27-28
2 Chr 17:4

⁸While Jehu was executing judgment against the family of Ahab, he happened to meet some of Judah's officials and Ahaziah's relatives* who were traveling with Ahaziah. So Jehu killed them all. ⁹Then Jehu's men searched for Ahaziah, and they found him hiding in the city of Samaria. They brought him to Jehu, who killed him. Ahaziah was given a decent burial because the people said, "He was the grandson of Jehoshaphat—a man who sought the LORD with all his heart." But none of the surviving members of Ahaziah's family was capable of ruling the kingdom.

**21:16** Hebrew *the Cushites.*   **21:17** Hebrew *Jehoahaz,* a variant spelling of Ahaziah; compare 22:1.   **22:1** Or *marauding bands of Arabs.*   **22:2** As in some Greek manuscripts and Syriac version (see also 2 Kgs 8:26); Hebrew reads *forty-two.*   **22:5** Hebrew *Jehoram,* a variant spelling of Joram; also in 22:6, 7.   **22:6a** Hebrew *Ramah,* a variant spelling of Ramoth.   **22:6b** As in some Hebrew manuscripts, Greek and Syriac versions, and Latin Vulgate (see also 2 Kgs 8:29); most Hebrew manuscripts read *Azariah.*   **22:7** Hebrew *descendant of Nimshi;* compare 2 Kgs 9:2, 14.   **22:8** As in Greek version (see also 2 Kgs 10:13); Hebrew reads *and sons of the brothers of Ahaziah.*

---

he allowed and even promoted idol worship. Yet he was not killed in battle or by treachery—he died by a lingering and painful disease (21:18, 19). Punishment for sin is not always immediate or dramatic. But if we ignore God's laws, we will eventually suffer the consequences of our sin.

**21:12** Chronicles mentions Elijah only here. Much more about this great prophet can be found in 1 Kings 17:1—2 Kings 2:11. Elijah's Profile is found in 1 Kings 17, p. 545.

**22:4, 5** Although it is wise to seek advice, we must also carefully weigh the advice we receive. Ahaziah had advisers, but they

were wicked and led him to ruin. When you seek advice, listen carefully and use God's Word to "test everything. . . . Hold on to what is good" (1 Thessalonians 5:21).

**22:7** Jehu's Profile and a more complete story of his reign are found in 2 Kings 9:1—10:36, p. 583.

### Queen Athaliah Rules in Judah

¹⁰When Athaliah, the mother of King Ahaziah of Judah, learned that her son was dead, she began to destroy the rest of Judah's royal family. ¹¹But Ahaziah's sister Jehosheba,* the daughter of King Jehoram, took Ahaziah's infant son, Joash, and stole him away from among the rest of the king's children, who were about to be killed. She put Joash and his nurse in a bedroom. In this way, Jehosheba, wife of Jehoiada the priest and sister of Ahaziah, hid the child so that Athaliah could not murder him. ¹²Joash remained hidden in the Temple of God for six years while Athaliah ruled over the land.

22:10–23:21
2 Kgs 11:1-21

### Revolt against Athaliah

**23** In the seventh year of Athaliah's reign, Jehoiada the priest decided to act. He summoned his courage and made a pact with five army commanders: Azariah son of Jeroham, Ishmael son of Jehohanan, Azariah son of Obed, Maaseiah son of Adaiah, and Elishaphat son of Zicri. ²These men traveled secretly throughout Judah and summoned the Levites and clan leaders in all the towns to come to Jerusalem. ³They all gathered at the Temple of God, where they made a solemn pact with Joash, the young king.

23:1
2 Kgs 11:4-20

23:3
2 Sam 7:12
2 Chr 21:7

Jehoiada said to them, "Here is the king's son! The time has come for him to reign! The LORD has promised that a descendant of David will be our king. ⁴This is what you must do. When you priests and Levites come on duty on the Sabbath, a third of you will serve as gatekeepers. ⁵Another third will go over to the royal palace, and the final third will be at the Foundation Gate. Everyone else should stay in the courtyards of the LORD's Temple. ⁶Remember, only the priests and Levites on duty may enter the Temple of the LORD, for they are set apart as holy. The rest of the people must obey the LORD's instructions and stay outside. ⁷You Levites, form a bodyguard around the king and keep your weapons in hand. Kill anyone who tries to enter the Temple. Stay with the king wherever he goes."

23:4
1 Chr 9:26

23:6
1 Sam 10:24
1 Chr 23:28-32

⁸So the Levites and all the people of Judah did everything as Jehoiada the priest ordered. The commanders took charge of the men reporting for duty that Sabbath, as well as those who were going off duty. Jehoiada the priest did not let anyone go home after their shift ended. ⁹Then Jehoiada supplied the commanders with the spears and the large and small shields that had once belonged to King David and were stored in the Temple of God. ¹⁰He stationed all the people around the king, with their weapons ready. They formed a line from the south side of the Temple around to the north side and all around the altar.

23:8
1 Chr 24:1

¹¹Then Jehoiada and his sons brought out Joash, the king's son, placed the crown on his head, and presented him with a copy of God's laws.* They anointed him and proclaimed him king, and everyone shouted, "Long live the king!"

### The Death of Athaliah

¹²When Athaliah heard the noise of the people running and the shouts of praise to the king, she hurried to the LORD's Temple to see what was happening. ¹³When she arrived, she saw the newly crowned king standing in his place of authority by the pillar at the Temple entrance. The commanders and trumpeters were surrounding him, and people from all over the land were rejoicing and blowing trumpets. Singers with musical instruments were leading the people in a great celebration. When Athaliah saw all this, she tore her clothes in despair and shouted, "Treason! Treason!"

¹⁴Then Jehoiada the priest ordered the commanders who were in charge of the troops, "Take her to the soldiers in front of the Temple,* and kill anyone who tries to rescue her." For the priest had said, "She must not be killed in the Temple of the LORD." ¹⁵So they seized her and led her out to the entrance of the Horse Gate on the palace grounds, and they killed her there.

23:15
Neh 3:28

---

22:11 As in parallel text at 2 Kgs 11:2; Hebrew lacks *Ahaziah's sister* and reads *Jehoshabeath* [a variant spelling of Jehosheba]. 23:11 Or *a copy of the covenant.* 23:14 Or *Bring her out from between the ranks;* or *Take her out of the Temple precincts.* The meaning of the Hebrew is uncertain.

---

**23:1** After seven years of rule by Athaliah, the queen mother, Jehoiada the priest finally got up his courage and took action to get rid of the idolatrous ruler. To confront the king (or queen) with the demands of God's law was supposed to be the role of every priest in every generation. Tragically, many priests shied away from this duty, and thus only a few made a difference in the nation.

**23:1** Although it could have cost him his life, this priest did what was right, restoring the Temple worship and anointing the new king. There are times when we must correct a wrong or speak out

for what is right. When such a situation arises, gather up your courage and act.

**23:12-15** Athaliah thought she had it made. After assuming the throne, she killed all potential heirs to it—so she thought. But even the best plans for evil go sour. When the truth was revealed, she was overthrown immediately. It is much safer to live according to the truth, even if it means not obtaining everything you want.

**23:15-17** Athaliah's life ended as her mother Jezebel's had—by execution. Her life of idolatry and treachery was cut short by God's

## Jehoiada's Religious Reforms

23:17
Deut 13:9

16Then Jehoiada made a covenant between himself and the king and the people that they would be the LORD's people. 17And all the people went over to the temple of Baal and tore it down. They demolished the altars and smashed the idols, and they killed Mattan the priest of Baal in front of the altars.

23:18
1 Chr 23:6, 25-31
2 Chr 5:5

18Jehoiada now put the priests and Levites in charge of the Temple of the LORD, following all the directions given by David. He also commanded them to present burnt offerings to the LORD, as prescribed by the Law of Moses, and to sing and rejoice as David had instructed.

23:19
1 Chr 9:22
23:20
2 Kgs 11:19

19He also stationed gatekeepers at the gates of the LORD's Temple to keep out those who for any reason were ceremonially unclean.

20Then the commanders, nobles, rulers, and all the people of the land escorted the king from the Temple of the LORD. They went through the upper gate and into the palace, and they seated the king on the royal throne. 21So all the people of the land rejoiced, and the city was peaceful because Athaliah had been killed.

## Joash Repairs the Temple

24:1-14
//2 Kgs 12:1-16
24:1
2 Kgs 11:21

**24** Joash was seven years old when he became king, and he reigned in Jerusalem forty years. His mother was Zibiah from Beersheba. 2Joash did what was pleasing in the LORD's sight throughout the lifetime of Jehoiada the priest. 3Jehoiada chose two wives for Joash, and he had sons and daughters.

24:4
2 Chr 24:7

4At one point Joash decided to repair and restore the Temple of the LORD. 5He summoned the priests and Levites and gave them these instructions: "Go to all the towns of Judah and collect the required annual offerings, so that we can repair the Temple of your God. Do not delay!" But the Levites did not act immediately.

24:6
Exod 30:12-16

6So the king called for Jehoiada the high priest and asked him, "Why haven't you demanded that the Levites go out and collect the Temple taxes from the towns of Judah and from Jerusalem? Moses, the servant of the LORD, levied this tax on the community of Israel in order to maintain the Tabernacle of the Covenant.*"

24:7
2 Chr 21:17

7Over the years the followers of wicked Athaliah had broken into the Temple of God, and they had used all the dedicated things from the Temple of the LORD to worship the images of Baal.

24:9
2 Chr 24:6; 36:22

8So now the king ordered a chest to be made and set outside the gate leading to the Temple of the LORD. 9Then a proclamation was sent throughout Judah and Jerusalem, telling the people to bring to the LORD the tax that Moses, the servant of God, had required of the Israelites in the wilderness. 10This pleased all the leaders and the people, and they gladly brought their money and filled the chest with it.

24:11
2 Kgs 12:10

11Whenever the chest became full, the Levites would carry it to the king's officials. Then the court secretary and an officer of the high priest would come and empty the chest and take it back to the Temple again. This went on day after day, and a large amount of money was collected. 12The king and Jehoiada gave the money to the construction supervisors, who hired masons and carpenters to restore the Temple of the LORD. They also hired metalworkers, who made articles of iron and bronze for the LORD's Temple.

13The men in charge of the renovation worked hard and made steady progress. They restored the Temple of God according to its original design and strengthened it. 14When all the repairs were finished, they brought the remaining money to the king and Jehoiada. It was used to make various articles for the Temple of the LORD—articles for worship services and for burnt offerings, including ladles and other articles made of gold and silver. And the burnt offerings were sacrificed continually in the Temple of the LORD during the lifetime of Jehoiada the priest.

**24:6** Hebrew *Tent of the Testimony.*

---

judgment of her sin. By this time Judah had slipped so far away from God that Baal was worshiped in Jerusalem.

**23:18** Jehoiada restored the Temple procedures and its worship services according to David's original plans, recorded in 1 Chronicles 24–25.

**24:5** The Levites took their time carrying out the king's order, even though he told them not to delay. Offerings for keeping the Temple in order were not just the king's wish, but God's command (Exodus 30:11-16). The Levites, therefore, were not only disregarding the king but disregarding God. When it comes to following God's commands, a slow response may be little better than disobedience. Obey God willingly and immediately.

**24:10** Evidently the Levites weren't convinced that the people would want to contribute to the rebuilding of the Temple (24:5), but the people were glad to give of what they had for this project. Don't underestimate people's desire to be faithful to God. When challenged to do God's work, they will often respond willingly and generously.

¹⁵Jehoiada lived to a very old age, finally dying at 130. ¹⁶He was buried among the kings in the City of David, because he had done so much good in Israel for God and his Temple.

### Jehoiada's Reforms Reversed

¹⁷But after Jehoiada's death, the leaders of Judah came and bowed before King Joash and persuaded him to listen to their advice. ¹⁸They decided to abandon the Temple of the LORD, the God of their ancestors, and they worshiped Asherah poles and idols instead! Because of this sin, divine anger fell on Judah and Jerusalem. ¹⁹Yet the LORD sent prophets to bring them back to him. The prophets warned them, but still the people would not listen.

²⁰Then the Spirit of God came upon Zechariah son of Jehoiada the priest. He stood before the people and said, "This is what God says: Why do you disobey the LORD's commands and keep yourselves from prospering? You have abandoned the LORD, and now he has abandoned you!"

²¹Then the leaders plotted to kill Zechariah, and King Joash ordered that they stone him to death in the courtyard of the LORD's Temple. ²²That was how King Joash repaid Jehoiada for his loyalty—by killing his son. Zechariah's last words as he died were, "May the LORD see what they are doing and avenge my death!"

### The End of Joash's Reign

²³In the spring of the year* the Aramean army marched against Joash. They invaded Judah and Jerusalem and killed all the leaders of the nation. Then they sent all the plunder back to their king in Damascus. ²⁴Although the Arameans attacked with only a small army, the LORD helped them conquer the much larger army of Judah. The people of Judah had abandoned the LORD, the God of their ancestors, so judgment was carried out against Joash.

²⁵The Arameans withdrew, leaving Joash severely wounded. But his own officials plotted to kill him for murdering the son* of Jehoiada the priest. They assassinated him as he lay in bed. Then he was buried in the City of David, but not in the royal cemetery. ²⁶The assassins were Jozacar,* the son of an Ammonite woman named Shimeath, and Jehozabad, the son of a Moabite woman named Shomer.*

²⁷The account of the sons of Joash, the prophecies about him, and the record of his restoration of the Temple of God are written in *The Commentary on the Book of the Kings*. His son Amaziah became the next king.

### Amaziah Rules in Judah

**25** Amaziah was twenty-five years old when he became king, and he reigned in Jerusalem twenty-nine years. His mother was Jehoaddin* from Jerusalem. ²Amaziah did what was pleasing in the LORD's sight, but not wholeheartedly.

³When Amaziah was well established as king, he executed the officials who had assassinated his father. ⁴However, he did not kill the children of the assassins, for he obeyed the command of the LORD as written by Moses in the Book of the Law: "Parents must not be put to death for the sins of their children, nor children for the sins of their parents. Those deserving to die must be put to death for their own crimes."*

**24:18**
Exod 34:12-14
Josh 24:20

**24:19**
Jer 7:25

**24:20**
Num 14:41
2 Chr 15:2; 20:14

**24:21**
Neh 9:26
Matt 23:35

**24:22**
Gen 9:5

**24:23-27**
//2 Kgs 12:17-21

**24:24**
2 Chr 16:7-8

**24:25**
2 Kgs 12:20-21

**24:27**
2 Chr 13:22; 24:12

**25:1-4**
//2 Kgs 14:1-6

**25:2**
2 Chr 24:2

**25:4**
Deut 24:16

---

**24:23** Hebrew *At the turn of the year.* The first day of the year in the ancient Hebrew lunar calendar occurred in March or April.   **24:25** As in Greek version and Latin Vulgate; Hebrew reads *sons.*   **24:26a** As in parallel text at 2 Kgs 12:21; Hebrew reads *Zabad.*   **24:26b** As in parallel text at 2 Kgs 12:21; Hebrew reads *Shimrith,* a variant spelling of Shomer.   **25:1** As in parallel text at 2 Kgs 14:2; Hebrew reads *Jehoaddan,* a variant spelling of Jehoaddin.
**25:4** Deut 24:16.

---

**24:18** If everything went so well in Judah when the people worshiped God, why did they turn away from him? Prosperity can be both a blessing and a curse. While it can be a sign of God's blessing to those who follow him, it carries with it the potential for moral and spiritual decline. Prosperous people are tempted to become self-sufficient and proud—to take God for granted. In our prosperity, we must not forget that God is the source of our blessings. See Deuteronomy 6:10-12; 8:11-14.

**24:18-20** When King Joash and the nation of Judah abandoned God, God sent Zechariah to call them to repentance. Before dispensing judgment and punishment, God gave them another chance. In the same way, God does not abandon us or lash out in revenge when we sin. Instead, he aggressively pursues us through his Word, his Spirit in us, the words of others, and sometimes discipline. He does not intend to destroy us but to urge us to return to him. When you are moving away from God,

remember that he is pursuing you. Stop and listen. Allow him to point out your sin so you can repent and follow him again.

**24:19** God sent many prophets to Joash and the people to warn them that they were headed for destruction. Joel may have been one of these prophets. Read the book of Joel for more information about the political and spiritual climate of the times.

**24:22** Zechariah asked God to call the people to account for their sins. He was not seeking revenge but pleading for justice. When we feel like despairing over the wickedness around us, we can rest assured that in the end, God will bring complete justice to the earth.

**25:2** Amaziah did what was right on the outside, but inside he often resented what he had to do. His obedience was at best half-hearted. When the prophet promised God's deliverance, Amaziah first complained about the money that had been lost (25:9). And he valued military success more than God's will. We must search

**25:5**
Num 1:3
2 Chr 26:13

⁵Then Amaziah organized the army, assigning generals and captains* for all Judah and Benjamin. He took a census and found that he had an army of 300,000 select troops, twenty years old and older, all trained in the use of spear and shield. ⁶He also paid about 7,500 pounds* of silver to hire 100,000 experienced fighting men from Israel.

**25:8**
2 Chr 14:11; 20:6

⁷But a man of God came to him and said, "Your Majesty, do not hire troops from Israel, for the LORD is not with Israel. He will not help those people of Ephraim! ⁸If you let them go with your troops into battle, you will be defeated by the enemy no matter how well you fight. God will overthrow you, for he has the power to help you or to trip you up."

25:5 Hebrew *commanders of thousands and commanders of hundreds.*    25:6 Hebrew *100 talents* [3,400 kilograms].

---

**JOASH**

All parents want their children to make the right decisions. But to do this, children must first learn to make *their own* decisions. Making bad ones helps them learn to make good ones. If parents make all the decisions for their children, they leave their children without the skills for wise decision making when they are on their own. This problem seriously affected Joash. He had great advice, but he never grew up. He became so dependent on what he was told that his effectiveness was limited to the quality of his advisers.

When Joash was one year old, his grandmother Athaliah decided to slaughter all her descendants in a desperate bid for power. Joash, the only survivor, was rescued and hidden by his aunt and uncle, Jehosheba and Jehoiada. Jehoiada's work as a priest made it possible to keep Joash hidden in the Temple for six years. At that point, Jehoiada arranged for the overthrow of Athaliah and the crowning of Joash. For many years following, Jehoiada made most of the kingdom's decisions for Joash. When the old priest died, he was buried in the royal cemetery as a tribute to his role.

But after Jehoiada's death, Joash didn't know what to do. He listened to counsel that led him into evil. Within a short time he even ordered the death of Jehoiada's son Zechariah. After a few months, Joash's army had been soundly defeated by the Arameans. Jerusalem was saved only because Joash stripped the Temple of its treasures as a bribe. Finally, the king's own officials assassinated him. In contrast to Jehoiada, Joash was not buried among the kings; he is not even listed in Jesus' genealogy in the New Testament.

As dependent as Joash was on Jehoiada, there is little evidence that he ever established a real dependence on the God Jehoiada obeyed. Like many children, Joash's knowledge of God was secondhand. It was a start, but the king needed his own relationship with God that would outlast and overrule the changes in the advice he received.

It would be easy to criticize Joash's failure were it not for the fact that we often fall into the same traps. How often have we acted on poor advice without considering God's Word?

| | |
|---|---|
| **Strengths and accomplishments** | • Carried out extensive repairs on the Temple<br>• Was faithful to God as long as Jehoiada lived |
| **Weaknesses and mistakes** | • Allowed idolatry to continue among his people<br>• Used the Temple treasures to bribe King Hazael of Aram<br>• Killed Jehoiada's son Zechariah<br>• Allowed his advisers to lead the people away from God |
| **Lessons from his life** | • A good and hopeful start can be ruined by an evil end<br>• Even the best counsel is ineffective if it does not help us make wise decisions<br>• As helpful or hurtful as others may be, we are individually responsible for what we do |
| **Vital statistics** | • Where: Jerusalem<br>• Occupation: King of Judah<br>• Relatives: Father: Ahaziah. Mother: Zibiah. Grandmother: Athaliah. Aunt: Jehosheba. Uncle: Jehoiada. Son: Amaziah. Cousin: Zechariah.<br>• Contemporaries: Jehu, Hazael |
| **Key verses** | "But after Jehoiada's death, the leaders of Judah came and bowed before King Joash and persuaded him to listen to their advice. They decided to abandon the Temple of the LORD, the God of their ancestors, and they worshiped Asherah poles and idols instead! Because of this sin, divine anger fell on Judah and Jerusalem" (2 Chronicles 24:17, 18). |

Joash's story is told in 2 Kings 11:1—12:21 and 2 Chronicles 22:11—24:27.

---

our own hearts and root out any resistance to obeying God. Grudging compliance is not true obedience.

9Amaziah asked the man of God, "But what about all that silver I paid to hire the army of Israel?"

The man of God replied, "The LORD is able to give you much more than this!" 10So Amaziah discharged the hired troops and sent them back to Ephraim. This made them very angry with Judah, and they returned home in a great rage.

11Then Amaziah summoned his courage and led his army to the Valley of Salt, where they killed 10,000 Edomite troops from Seir. 12They captured another 10,000 and took them to the top of a cliff and threw them off, dashing them to pieces on the rocks below.

25:11-12
//2 Kgs 14:7

13Meanwhile, the hired troops that Amaziah had sent home raided several of the towns of Judah between Samaria and Beth-horon. They killed 3,000 people and carried off great quantities of plunder.

14When King Amaziah returned from slaughtering the Edomites, he brought with him idols taken from the people of Seir. He set them up as his own gods, bowed down in front of them, and offered sacrifices to them! 15This made the LORD very angry, and he sent a prophet to ask, "Why do you turn to gods who could not even save their own people from you?"

25:14
2 Chr 28:23

25:15
2 Chr 25:11-12

16But the king interrupted him and said, "Since when have I made you the king's counselor? Be quiet now before I have you killed!"

So the prophet stopped with this warning: "I know that God has determined to destroy you because you have done this and have refused to accept my counsel."

17After consulting with his advisers, King Amaziah of Judah sent this challenge to Israel's king Jehoash,* the son of Jehoahaz and grandson of Jehu: "Come and meet me in battle!"*

25:17-28
//2 Kgs 14:8-20

18But King Jehoash of Israel replied to King Amaziah of Judah with this story: "Out in the Lebanon mountains, a thistle sent a message to a mighty cedar tree: 'Give your daughter in marriage to my son.' But just then a wild animal of Lebanon came by and stepped on the thistle, crushing it!

25:18
Judg 9:8-15

19"You are saying, 'I have defeated Edom,' and you are very proud of it. But my advice is to stay at home. Why stir up trouble that will only bring disaster on you and the people of Judah?"

25:19
2 Chr 26:16; 32:25

20But Amaziah refused to listen, for God was determined to destroy him for turning to the gods of Edom. 21So King Jehoash of Israel mobilized his army against King Amaziah of Judah. The two armies drew up their battle lines at Beth-shemesh in Judah. 22Judah was routed by the army of Israel, and its army scattered and fled for home. 23King Jehoash of Israel captured Judah's king, Amaziah son of Joash and grandson of Ahaziah, at Beth-shemesh. Then he brought him to Jerusalem, where he demolished 600 feet* of Jerusalem's wall, from the Ephraim Gate to the Corner Gate. 24He carried off all the gold and silver and all the articles from the Temple of God that had been in the care of Obed-edom. He also seized the treasures of the royal palace, along with hostages, and then returned to Samaria.

25:23
2 Chr 21:17

25:24
1 Chr 26:15

25King Amaziah of Judah lived on for fifteen years after the death of King Jehoash of Israel. 26The rest of the events in Amaziah's reign, from beginning to end, are recorded in *The Book of the Kings of Judah and Israel.*

25:25
2 Kgs 14:17-22

27After Amaziah turned away from the LORD, there was a conspiracy against his life in Jerusalem, and he fled to Lachish. But his enemies sent assassins after him, and they killed him there. 28They brought his body back on a horse, and he was buried with his ancestors in the City of David.*

25:17a Hebrew *Joash*, a variant spelling of Jehoash; also in 25:18, 21, 23, 25.    25:17b Hebrew *Come, let us look one another in the face.*    25:23 Hebrew *400 cubits* [180 meters].    25:28 As in some Hebrew manuscripts and other ancient versions (see also 2 Kgs 14:20); most Hebrew manuscripts read *the city of Judah.*

---

25:9, 10 Amaziah made a financial agreement with Israelite soldiers, offering to pay them to fight for him (25:6). But before they could go to battle, Amaziah sent them home with their pay because of the prophet's warning. Although it cost him plenty, he wisely realized that the money was not worth the ruin the alliance could cause. How would you have reacted? Money must never stand in the way of making right decisions. The Lord's favor is priceless, worth more than any amount of money.

25:14 After the victory, Amaziah returned and sacrificed to idols. We are very susceptible to sin after great victories. It is then that we feel confident, relaxed, and ready to celebrate. If, in that excitement, we let our defenses down, Satan can attack

with all sorts of temptations. When you win, watch out. After the mountain peaks come the valleys.

25:15 Amaziah made a foolish mistake by worshiping the gods of the nation he had just conquered. Impressed by the accomplishments of the Edomites, Amaziah worshiped their idols! How foolish to serve the gods of a defeated enemy. We make the same mistake as Amaziah when we run after money, power, or recognition. By recognizing the emptiness of these worldly pursuits, we can free ourselves from the desire to follow them.

25:18 In this parable, Judah is the thistle and Israel's army is the cedar. Amaziah was proud after defeating Edom. He wanted

## Uzziah Rules in Judah

**26** All the people of Judah had crowned Amaziah's sixteen-year-old son, Uzziah, as king in place of his father. ²After his father's death, Uzziah rebuilt the town of Elath* and restored it to Judah.

³Uzziah was sixteen years old when he became king, and he reigned in Jerusalem fifty-two years. His mother was Jecoliah from Jerusalem. ⁴He did what was pleasing in the LORD's sight, just as his father, Amaziah, had done. ⁵Uzziah sought God during the days of Zechariah, who taught him to fear God.* And as long as the king sought guidance from the LORD, God gave him success.

⁶Uzziah declared war on the Philistines and broke down the walls of Gath, Jabneh, and Ashdod. Then he built new towns in the Ashdod area and in other parts of Philistia. ⁷God helped him in his wars against the Philistines, his battles with the Arabs of Gur,* and his wars with the Meunites. ⁸The Meunites* paid annual tribute to him, and his fame spread even to Egypt, for he had become very powerful.

⁹Uzziah built fortified towers in Jerusalem at the Corner Gate, at the Valley Gate, and at the angle in the wall. ¹⁰He also constructed forts in the wilderness and dug many water cisterns,

**26:1-4**
//2 Kgs 14:21-22;
15:1-3

**26:5**
2 Chr 15:2; 24:2
Dan 1:17

**26:6**
Isa 14:29

**26:7**
2 Chr 21:16

**26:8**
2 Chr 17:11

**26:9**
2 Chr 25:23
Neh 3:13

**26:10**
Gen 26:18-21

**26:2** As in Greek version (see also 2 Kgs 14:22; 16:6); Hebrew reads *Eloth,* a variant spelling of Elath.   **26:5** As in Syriac and Greek versions; Hebrew reads *who instructed him in divine visions.*   **26:7** As in Greek version; Hebrew reads *Gur-baal.*   **26:8** As in Greek version; Hebrew reads *Ammonites.* Compare 26:7.

We are never closer to failure than during our greatest successes. If we fail to recognize God's part in our achievements, they are no better than failures. Uzziah was a remarkably successful king. His achievements brought him fame. He was successful in war and peace, in planning and execution, in building and planting.

Uzziah overestimated his own importance in bringing about the great achievements he experienced. He did so many things well that a consuming pride gradually invaded his life like the leprous disease that finally destroyed his body. In trying to act like a priest, he took on a role that God did not mean for him to have. He had forgotten not only how much God had given him but also that God had certain roles for others that he needed to respect.

Uzziah's pride was rooted in his lack of thankfulness. We have no accounts of this king's ever showing appreciation to God for the marvelous gifts he received. Our accomplishments may not compare with Uzziah's, but we still owe a debt of thanksgiving to God for our very lives. If God is not getting the credit for your successes, shouldn't you start looking at your life differently?

| | |
|---|---|
| **Strengths and accomplishments** | • Pleased God during his early years as king<br>• Successful warrior and city builder<br>• Skillful in organizing and delegating<br>• Reigned for 52 years |
| **Weaknesses and mistakes** | • Developed a prideful attitude due to his great success<br>• Tried to perform the priests' duties, in direct disobedience to God<br>• Failed to remove many of the symbols of idolatry in the land |
| **Lessons from his life** | • Lack of thankfulness to God can lead to pride<br>• Even successful people must acknowledge the role God has for others in their lives |
| **Vital statistics** | • Where: Jerusalem<br>• Occupation: King of Judah<br>• Relatives: Father: Amaziah. Mother: Jecoliah. Son: Jotham.<br>• Contemporaries: Isaiah, Amos, Hosea, Jeroboam, Zechariah, Azariah |
| **Key verses** | "And he built structures on the walls of Jerusalem, designed by experts to protect those who shot arrows and hurled large stones from the towers and the corners of the wall. His fame spread far and wide, for the LORD gave him marvelous help, and he became very powerful.<br>But when he had become powerful, he also became proud, which led to his downfall. He sinned against the LORD his God by entering the sanctuary of the LORD's Temple and personally burning incense on the incense altar." (2 Chronicles 26:15, 16). |

Uzziah's story is told in 2 Kings 15:1–7 and in 2 Chronicles 26:1–23. He is also mentioned in Isaiah 1:1; 6:1; 7:1; Hosea 1:1; Amos 1:1; Zechariah 14:5.

to defeat Israel, but Jehoash warned him not to attack. Amaziah had more ambition than ability, and he paid for it when he was soundly defeated. Don't let ambition and pride into your life, for they will cause you to forget God.

because he kept great herds of livestock in the foothills of Judah* and on the plains. He was also a man who loved the soil. He had many workers who cared for his farms and vineyards, both on the hillsides and in the fertile valleys.

<sup>11</sup>Uzziah had an army of well-trained warriors, ready to march into battle, unit by unit. This army had been mustered and organized by Jeiel, the secretary of the army, and his assistant, Maaseiah. They were under the direction of Hananiah, one of the king's officials. <sup>12</sup>These regiments of mighty warriors were commanded by 2,600 clan leaders. <sup>13</sup>The army consisted of 307,500 men, all elite troops. They were prepared to assist the king against any enemy.

**26:13**
2 Chr 25:5

<sup>14</sup>Uzziah provided the entire army with shields, spears, helmets, coats of mail, bows, and sling stones. <sup>15</sup>And he built structures on the walls of Jerusalem, designed by experts to protect those who shot arrows and hurled large stones* from the towers and the corners of the wall. His fame spread far and wide, for the LORD gave him marvelous help, and he became very powerful.

### Uzziah's Sin and Punishment

<sup>16</sup>But when he had become powerful, he also became proud, which led to his downfall. He sinned against the LORD his God by entering the sanctuary of the LORD's Temple and personally burning incense on the incense altar. <sup>17</sup>Azariah the high priest went in after him with eighty other priests of the LORD, all brave men. <sup>18</sup>They confronted King Uzziah and said, "It is not for you, Uzziah, to burn incense to the LORD. That is the work of the priests alone, the descendants of Aaron who are set apart for this work. Get out of the sanctuary, for you have sinned. The LORD God will not honor you for this!"

**26:16**
Deut 32:15
1 Kgs 13:1-4
2 Chr 25:19
**26:17**
1 Chr 6:10
**26:18**
Exod 30:7-8
Num 16:39-40

<sup>19</sup>Uzziah, who was holding an incense burner, became furious. But as he was standing there raging at the priests before the incense altar in the LORD's Temple, leprosy* suddenly broke out on his forehead. <sup>20</sup>When Azariah the high priest and all the other priests saw the leprosy, they rushed him out. And the king himself was eager to get out because the LORD had struck him. <sup>21</sup>So King Uzziah had leprosy until the day he died. He lived in isolation in a separate house, for he was excluded from the Temple of the LORD. His son Jotham was put in charge of the royal palace, and he governed the people of the land.

**26:19**
2 Kgs 5:25-27
**26:21-23**
//2 Kgs 15:5-7

<sup>22</sup>The rest of the events of Uzziah's reign, from beginning to end, are recorded by the prophet Isaiah son of Amoz. <sup>23</sup>When Uzziah died, he was buried with his ancestors; his grave was in a nearby burial field belonging to the kings, for the people said, "He had leprosy." And his son Jotham became the next king.

**26:22**
Isa 1:1
**26:23**
2 Chr 21:20; 28:27
Isa 6:1

### Jotham Rules in Judah

**27** Jotham was twenty-five years old when he became king, and he reigned in Jerusalem sixteen years. His mother was Jerusha, the daughter of Zadok. <sup>2</sup>Jotham did what was pleasing in the LORD's sight. He did everything his father, Uzziah, had done, except that Jotham did not sin by entering the Temple of the LORD. But the people continued in their corrupt ways.

**27:1-9**
//2 Kgs 15:33-38
**27:2**
2 Chr 26:16

26:10 Hebrew *the Shephelah.*   26:15 Or *to shoot arrows and hurl large stones.*   26:19 Or *a contagious skin disease.* The Hebrew word used here and throughout this passage can describe various skin diseases.

---

**26:15** These machines were similar to the catapults later used by the Romans and were capable of slinging stones or arrows a great distance.

**26:16** After God gave Uzziah great prosperity and power, he became proud and corrupt. It is true that "pride goes before destruction" (Proverbs 16:18). If God has given you wealth, influence, popularity, and power, be thankful, but be careful. God hates pride. While it is normal to feel elation when we accomplish something, it is wrong to be disdainful of God or to look down on others. Check your attitudes and remember to give God the credit for what you have. Use your gifts in ways that please him.

**26:17-21** When people have power, they often think they can live above the law. But even rulers are subject to God, as Uzziah discovered. No matter what your position in society, God expects you to honor, worship, and obey him.

**26:21** For much of his life, Uzziah "did what was pleasing in the LORD's sight" (26:4). But Uzziah turned away from God, and he was struck with leprosy and remained leprous until his death. He is remembered more for his arrogant act and subsequent punishment than for his great reforms. God requires lifelong obedience. Spurts of obedience are not enough. Only "the one who endures to the end" will be rewarded (Mark 13:13). Practice being consistent in your faith every day; that way you will build a lifetime of obedience. Otherwise you, too, may become more famous for your downfall than for your success.

**26:23** This was the year that God called Isaiah to be a prophet (Isaiah 6:1).

**27:2** Jotham was generally a good king (27:6), but his people remained corrupt as they had during his father Uzziah's reign. Those you lead will not always follow your example, but that should not affect the way you live for God. This sinfulness of Jotham's kingdom is vividly portrayed in Isaiah 1–5.

27:3
2 Chr 33:14
Neh 3:26

27:4
2 Chr 11:5

27:6
2 Chr 26:5

27:7
2 Kgs 15:36

27:8
2 Chr 27:1

28:1-27
//2 Kgs 16:1-20

28:2
Exod 34:17
2 Chr 22:3

28:3
Lev 18:21
Josh 15:8
2 Chr 33:2, 6

³Jotham rebuilt the upper gate of the Temple of the LORD. He also did extensive rebuilding on the wall at the hill of Ophel. ⁴He built towns in the hill country of Judah and constructed fortresses and towers in the wooded areas. ⁵Jotham went to war against the Ammonites and conquered them. Over the next three years he received from them an annual tribute of 7,500 pounds* of silver, 50,000 bushels of wheat, and 50,000 bushels of barley.*

⁶King Jotham became powerful because he was careful to live in obedience to the LORD his God.

⁷The rest of the events of Jotham's reign, including all his wars and other activities, are recorded in *The Book of the Kings of Israel and Judah*. ⁸He was twenty-five years old when he became king, and he reigned in Jerusalem sixteen years. ⁹When Jotham died, he was buried in the City of David. And his son Ahaz became the next king.

### Ahaz Rules in Judah

**28** Ahaz was twenty years old when he became king, and he reigned in Jerusalem sixteen years. He did not do what was pleasing in the sight of the LORD, as his ancestor David had done. ²Instead, he followed the example of the kings of Israel. He cast metal images for the worship of Baal. ³He offered sacrifices in the valley of Ben-Hinnom, even sacrificing his own sons in the fire.* In this way, he followed the detestable practices of the pagan

**27:5a** Hebrew *100 talents* [3,400 kilograms].   **27:5b** Hebrew *10,000 cors* [1,820 kiloliters] *of wheat, and 10,000 cors of barley.*   **28:3** Or *even making his sons pass through the fire.*

---

O ur heritage influences, but doesn't necessarily determine, our life decisions. King Ahaz of Judah illustrates this truth in two ways: he turned away from the good examples of his father Jotham and his grandfather Uzziah, but his poor example seems to have had little effect on his own son Hezekiah, who proved to be a great and godly king.

The circumstances in the life of King Ahaz fall into the general categories of bad and worse. When Judah suffered a debilitating attack from rivals Israel and Aram, the king ignored an opportunity to seek God's help and turned instead to Assyria for assistance. Ahaz's cowardly leadership forced Judah into virtual slavery to the Assyrians.

Soon every evidence that Judah had once been a God-fearing nation was smashed, defaced, or tucked out of sight. Ahaz imported idolatry. He even presented some of his children as offerings to the gods he hoped would rescue him and his nation from their disastrous situation.

We share Ahaz's sin when, from beneath a load of failures and trials, we turn away from good examples and from God. Instead of repenting of any known sin and calling upon God for relief, we, like Ahaz, may appeal to every other source of aid but God—our own abilities, money, or harmful habits. The results only serve to increase our tragic circumstances.

Difficulties and mistakes will either devastate our faith or they will stimulate growth and maturity. The positive differences come when we humbly seek God's help, whatever the situation. Trials that tempt us to turn away from God should, instead, spur us to turn toward God.

| | |
|---|---|
| **Weaknesses and mistakes** | • Failed to trust God<br>• Asked Assyria for help and submitted Judah to crushing domination<br>• Adopted Assyrian religious practices that undermined his people's faith<br>• Sacrificed some of his own children in Baal worship |
| **Lessons from his life** | • Fear is never a good excuse for failing to trust God<br>• Some people or things that seem like obvious sources of help or relief may turn out to be controlling and enslaving instead<br>• Good examples in our lives can't prevent us from making the wrong choices |
| **Vital statistics** | • Where: Jerusalem<br>• Occupation: King of Judah<br>• Relatives: Father: Jotham. Son: Hezekiah. |
| **Key verse** | "Even during this time of trouble, King Ahaz continued to reject the LORD" (2 Chronicles 28:22). |

Ahaz's story is told in 2 Kings 16 and 2 Chronicles 28. Isaiah 7–10 records several amazing prophecies given during his reign.

---

**28:3** Imagine the monstrous evil of a religion that offers young children as sacrifices. God allowed the nation to be conquered in response to Ahaz's evil practices. Even today the practice hasn't abated. The sacrifice of children to the harsh gods of convenience, economy, and whim continues in sterile medical facilities in numbers that would astound the wicked Ahaz. If we are to allow children to come to Christ (Matthew 19:14), we must first allow them to come into the world.

nations the LORD had driven from the land ahead of the Israelites. 4He offered sacrifices and burned incense at the pagan shrines and on the hills and under every green tree.

5Because of all this, the LORD his God allowed the king of Aram to defeat Ahaz and to exile large numbers of his people to Damascus. The armies of the king of Israel also defeated Ahaz and inflicted many casualties on his army. 6In a single day Pekah son of Remaliah, Israel's king, killed 120,000 of Judah's troops, all of them experienced warriors, because they had abandoned the LORD, the God of their ancestors. 7Then Zicri, a warrior from Ephraim, killed Maaseiah, the king's son; Azrikam, the king's palace commander; and Elkanah, the king's second-in-command. 8The armies of Israel captured 200,000 women and children from Judah and seized tremendous amounts of plunder, which they took back to Samaria.

9But a prophet of the LORD named Oded was there in Samaria when the army of Israel returned home. He went out to meet them and said, "The LORD, the God of your ancestors, was angry with Judah and let you defeat them. But you have gone too far, killing them without mercy, and all heaven is disturbed. 10And now you are planning to make slaves of these people from Judah and Jerusalem. What about your own sins against the LORD your God? 11Listen to me and return these prisoners you have taken, for they are your own relatives. Watch out, because now the LORD's fierce anger has been turned against you!"

12Then some of the leaders of Israel*—Azariah son of Jehohanan, Berekiah son of Meshillemoth, Jehizkiah son of Shallum, and Amasa son of Hadlai—agreed with this and confronted the men returning from battle. 13"You must not bring the prisoners here!" they declared. "We cannot afford to add to our sins and guilt. Our guilt is already great, and the LORD's fierce anger is already turned against Israel."

14So the warriors released the prisoners and handed over the plunder in the sight of the leaders and all the people. 15Then the four men just mentioned by name came forward and distributed clothes from the plunder to the prisoners who were naked. They provided clothing and sandals to wear, gave them enough food and drink, and dressed their wounds with olive oil. They put those who were weak on donkeys and took all the prisoners back to their own people in Jericho, the city of palms. Then they returned to Samaria.

### Ahaz Closes the Temple

16At that time King Ahaz of Judah asked the king of Assyria for help. 17The armies of Edom had again invaded Judah and taken captives. 18And the Philistines had raided towns located in the foothills of Judah* and in the Negev of Judah. They had already captured and occupied Beth-shemesh, Aijalon, Gederoth, Soco with its villages, Timnah with its villages, and Gimzo with its villages. 19The LORD was humbling Judah because of King Ahaz of Judah,* for he had encouraged his people to sin and had been utterly unfaithful to the LORD.

20So when King Tiglath-pileser* of Assyria arrived, he attacked Ahaz instead of helping him. 21Ahaz took valuable items from the LORD's Temple, the royal palace, and from the homes of his officials and gave them to the king of Assyria as tribute. But this did not help him.

22Even during this time of trouble, King Ahaz continued to reject the LORD. 23He offered sacrifices to the gods of Damascus who had defeated him, for he said, "Since these gods helped the kings of Aram, they will help me, too, if I sacrifice to them." But instead, they led to his ruin and the ruin of all Judah.

24The king took the various articles from the Temple of God and broke them into pieces. He shut the doors of the LORD's Temple so that no one could worship there, and he set up altars to pagan gods in every corner of Jerusalem. 25He made pagan shrines in all the towns of Judah for offering sacrifices to other gods. In this way, he aroused the anger of the LORD, the God of his ancestors.

26The rest of the events of Ahaz's reign and everything he did, from beginning to end, are recorded in *The Book of the Kings of Judah and Israel.* 27When Ahaz died, he was buried in Jerusalem but not in the royal cemetery of the kings of Judah. Then his son Hezekiah became the next king.

**28:4**
2 Chr 28:25

**28:5**
2 Kgs 16:5
2 Chr 24:24
Isa 7:1

**28:6**
2 Kgs 16:5

**28:8**
Deut 28:25, 41
2 Chr 11:4

**28:9**
2 Chr 25:15
Ezra 9:6
Isa 47:6
Rev 18:5

**28:10**
Lev 25:39

**28:11**
2 Chr 28:8

**28:15**
Deut 34:3
2 Kgs 6:22
2 Chr 28:12
Prov 25:21-22

**28:16**
2 Kgs 16:7

**28:18**
Ezek 16:57

**28:19**
2 Chr 21:2

**28:20**
1 Chr 5:26

**28:21**
2 Kgs 16:8-9

**28:23**
2 Chr 25:14
Jer 44:17-18

**28:24**
2 Kgs 16:17
2 Chr 29:7; 30:14;
33:3-5

**28:26**
2 Kgs 16:19-20

**28:27**
2 Chr 24:25

**28:12** Hebrew *Ephraim,* referring to the northern kingdom of Israel.   **28:18** Hebrew *the Shephelah.*   **28:19** Masoretic Text reads *of Israel;* also in 28:23, 27. The author of Chronicles sees Judah as representative of the true Israel. (Some Hebrew manuscripts and Greek version read *of Judah.*)   **28:20** Hebrew *Tilgath-pilneser,* a variant spelling of Tiglath-pileser.

**28:22** Difficulties and struggles can devastate people, or they can stimulate growth and maturity. For Ahaz, deep troubles led to spiritual collapse. We do not need to respond like Ahaz. When facing problems or tragedy, we must remember that rough times

29:1-2
//2 Kgs 18:1-3
29:2
2 Chr 34:2

29:3
2 Chr 28:24; 29:7
29:5
2 Chr 29:15, 34;
35:6
29:6
Ezek 8:16

29:8
Deut 28:25
2 Chr 24:18; 28:5
Jer 25:9, 18
29:9
2 Chr 28:5-8, 17
29:10
2 Chr 23:16
29:11
Num 3:6; 8:6, 14
29:12
Num 3:19-20
2 Chr 31:13

### Hezekiah Rules in Judah

**29** Hezekiah was twenty-five years old when he became the king of Judah, and he reigned in Jerusalem twenty-nine years. His mother was Abijah, the daughter of Zechariah. [2]He did what was pleasing in the LORD's sight, just as his ancestor David had done.

### Hezekiah Reopens the Temple

[3]In the very first month of the first year of his reign, Hezekiah reopened the doors of the Temple of the LORD and repaired them. [4]He summoned the priests and Levites to meet him at the courtyard east of the Temple. [5]He said to them, "Listen to me, you Levites! Purify yourselves, and purify the Temple of the LORD, the God of your ancestors. Remove all the defiled things from the sanctuary. [6]Our ancestors were unfaithful and did what was evil in the sight of the LORD our God. They abandoned the LORD and his dwelling place; they turned their backs on him. [7]They also shut the doors to the Temple's entry room, and they snuffed out the lamps. They stopped burning incense and presenting burnt offerings at the sanctuary of the God of Israel.

[8]"That is why the LORD's anger has fallen upon Judah and Jerusalem. He has made them an object of dread, horror, and ridicule, as you can see with your own eyes. [9]Because of this, our fathers have been killed in battle, and our sons and daughters and wives have been captured. [10]But now I will make a covenant with the LORD, the God of Israel, so that his fierce anger will turn away from us. [11]My sons, do not neglect your duties any longer! The LORD has chosen you to stand in his presence, to minister to him, and to lead the people in worship and present offerings to him."

[12]Then these Levites got right to work:

From the clan of Kohath: Mahath son of Amasai and Joel son of Azariah.
From the clan of Merari: Kish son of Abdi and Azariah son of Jehallelel.
From the clan of Gershon: Joah son of Zimmah and Eden son of Joah.
[13]From the family of Elizaphan: Shimri and Jeiel.
From the family of Asaph: Zechariah and Mattaniah.
[14]From the family of Heman: Jehiel and Shimei.
From the family of Jeduthun: Shemaiah and Uzziel.

---

**GREAT REVIVALS IN THE BIBLE**
The Bible records several great revivals where people in great numbers turned to God and gave up their sinful ways of living. Each revival was characterized by a *leader* who recognized his nation's spiritual dryness. And in each case, the leader *took action* and was not afraid to make his desires known to the people.

| Leader | Reference | How the People Responded |
|---|---|---|
| Moses | Exodus 32–33 | Accepted God's laws and built the Tabernacle |
| Samuel | 1 Samuel 7:2-13 | Promised to make God first in their lives by destroying their idols |
| David | 2 Samuel 6 | Brought the Ark of the Covenant to Jerusalem; praised God with singing and musical instruments |
| Jehoshaphat | 2 Chronicles 20 | Decided to trust in God alone to help them, and their discouragement turned to joy |
| Hezekiah | 2 Chronicles 29–31 | Purified the Temple; got rid of idols; brought tithes to God's house |
| Josiah | 2 Chronicles 34–35 | Made a commitment to obey God's commands and remove sinful influences from their lives |
| Ezra | Ezra 9–10 Haggai 1 | Stopped associating with those who caused them to compromise their faith; renewed their commitment to God's commands; began rebuilding the Temple |
| Nehemiah (with Ezra) | Nehemiah 8–10 | Fasted, confessed their sins, read God's Word publicly, and promised in writing to again serve God wholeheartedly |

---

give us a chance to grow (James 1:2-4). When you are facing trials, don't turn away from God; turn *to* him. See these times as opportunities for you to claim God's help.

**29:1** Hezekiah's Profile is found in 2 Kings 18, p. 601.

**29:11** The Levites, chosen by God to serve in the Temple, had been kept from their duties by Ahaz's wickedness (28:24). But Hezekiah called them back into service, reminding them that the Lord had chosen them to minister.

We may not have to face a wicked king, but pressures or responsibilities can render us inactive and ineffective. When you have been given the responsibility to minister, don't neglect your duty. If you have become inactive in Christian service, either by choice or by circumstance, look for opportunities to minister (and listen to the "Hezekiahs") God will send your way. Then, like the Levites, be ready for action (29:12-15).

<sup>15</sup>These men called together their fellow Levites, and they all purified themselves. Then they began to cleanse the Temple of the Lord, just as the king had commanded. They were careful to follow all the Lord's instructions in their work. <sup>16</sup>The priests went into the sanctuary of the Temple of the Lord to cleanse it, and they took out to the Temple courtyard all the defiled things they found. From there the Levites carted it all out to the Kidron Valley.

<sup>17</sup>They began the work in early spring, on the first day of the new year,* and in eight days they had reached the entry room of the Lord's Temple. Then they purified the Temple of the Lord itself, which took another eight days. So the entire task was completed in sixteen days.

### The Temple Rededication

<sup>18</sup>Then the Levites went to King Hezekiah and gave him this report: "We have cleansed the entire Temple of the Lord, the altar of burnt offering with all its utensils, and the table of the Bread of the Presence with all its utensils. <sup>19</sup>We have also recovered all the items discarded by King Ahaz when he was unfaithful and closed the Temple. They are now in front of the altar of the Lord, purified and ready for use."

<sup>20</sup>Early the next morning King Hezekiah gathered the city officials and went to the Temple of the Lord. <sup>21</sup>They brought seven bulls, seven rams, and seven male lambs as a burnt offering, together with seven male goats as a sin offering for the kingdom, for the Temple, and for Judah. The king commanded the priests, who were descendants of Aaron, to sacrifice the animals on the altar of the Lord.

<sup>22</sup>So they killed the bulls, and the priests took the blood and sprinkled it on the altar. Next they killed the rams and sprinkled their blood on the altar. And finally, they did the same with the male lambs. <sup>23</sup>The male goats for the sin offering were then brought before the king and the assembly of people, who laid their hands on them. <sup>24</sup>The priests then killed the goats as a sin offering and sprinkled their blood on the altar to make atonement for the sins of all Israel. The king had specifically commanded that this burnt offering and sin offering should be made for all Israel.

<sup>25</sup>King Hezekiah then stationed the Levites at the Temple of the Lord with cymbals, lyres, and harps. He obeyed all the commands that the Lord had given to King David through Gad, the king's seer, and the prophet Nathan. <sup>26</sup>The Levites then took their positions around the Temple with the instruments of David, and the priests took their positions with the trumpets.

<sup>27</sup>Then Hezekiah ordered that the burnt offering be placed on the altar. As the burnt offering was presented, songs of praise to the Lord were begun, accompanied by the trumpets and other instruments of David, the former king of Israel. <sup>28</sup>The entire assembly worshiped the Lord as the singers sang and the trumpets blew, until all the burnt offerings were finished. <sup>29</sup>Then the king and everyone with him bowed down in worship. <sup>30</sup>King Hezekiah and the officials ordered the Levites to praise the Lord with the psalms written by David and by Asaph the seer. So they offered joyous praise and bowed down in worship.

<sup>31</sup>Then Hezekiah declared, "Now that you have consecrated yourselves to the Lord, bring your sacrifices and thanksgiving offerings to the Temple of the Lord." So the people brought their sacrifices and thanksgiving offerings, and all whose hearts were willing brought burnt offerings, too. <sup>32</sup>The people brought to the Lord 70 bulls, 100 rams, and 200 male lambs for burnt offerings. <sup>33</sup>They also brought 600 cattle and 3,000 sheep and goats as sacred offerings.

<sup>34</sup>But there were too few priests to prepare all the burnt offerings. So their relatives the Levites helped them until the work was finished and more priests had been purified, for the Levites had been more conscientious about purifying themselves than the priests had been. <sup>35</sup>There was an abundance of burnt offerings, along with the usual liquid offerings, and a great deal of fat from the many peace offerings.

**29:17** Hebrew *on the first day of the first month.* This day in the ancient Hebrew lunar calendar occurred in March or early April, 715 B.C.

---

**Cross-references (right margin):**

29:15
1 Chr 23:28
2 Chr 29:5; 30:12

29:16
2 Chr 15:16

29:17
2 Chr 29:3

29:19
2 Chr 28:24

29:21
Lev 4:3-14

29:22
Lev 4:18

29:23
Lev 4:15

29:24
Lev 4:26

29:25
2 Sam 7:2; 24:11
1 Chr 25:6
2 Chr 8:14

29:26
1 Chr 23:5
2 Chr 5:12

29:27
2 Chr 23:18

29:29
2 Chr 20:18

29:31
Exod 35:5, 22

29:34
2 Chr 30:3; 35:11

29:35
Lev 3:16
Num 15:5-10
2 Chr 29:32

---

**29:21** Throughout the Old Testament, the sacrifice was God's appointed way of approaching him and restoring a right relationship with him. The sin offering made by Hezekiah was a sacrifice given to God for forgiveness for unintentional sins. (For more information on why God required sacrifices and how they were carried out, see the notes in Leviticus 1.)

**29:22** The blood sprinkled on the altar represented the innocence of the sacrificed animal taking the place of the person making the

offering. The animal died so the sinner could live. This ritual looked forward to the day when Jesus Christ, God's perfect Son, would sacrifice his innocent life on the cross in order that the sinful and guilty human race might be spared the punishment it deserves (Hebrews 10:1-14).

**29:30** A seer was someone who received messages from God for the nation through visions or dreams.

**29:31** A thanksgiving offering, one type of peace offering (see Leviticus 7:12-15), was given as an expression of gratitude to

So the Temple of the LORD was restored to service. [36] And Hezekiah and all the people rejoiced because of what God had done for the people, for everything had been accomplished so quickly.

## Preparations for Passover

**30** King Hezekiah now sent word to all Israel and Judah, and he wrote letters of invitation to the people of Ephraim and Manasseh. He asked everyone to come to the Temple of the LORD at Jerusalem to celebrate the Passover of the LORD, the God of Israel. [2] The king, his officials, and all the community of Jerusalem decided to celebrate Passover a month later than usual.* [3] They were unable to celebrate it at the prescribed time because not enough priests could be purified by then, and the people had not yet assembled at Jerusalem.

[4] This plan for keeping the Passover seemed right to the king and all the people. [5] So they sent a proclamation throughout all Israel, from Beersheba in the south to Dan in the north, inviting everyone to come to Jerusalem to celebrate the Passover of the LORD, the God of Israel. The people had not been celebrating it in great numbers as required in the Law.

[6] At the king's command, runners were sent throughout Israel and Judah. They carried letters that said:

"O people of Israel, return to the LORD, the God of Abraham, Isaac, and Israel,* so that he will return to the few of us who have survived the conquest of the Assyrian kings. [7] Do not be like your ancestors and relatives who abandoned the LORD, the God of their ancestors, and became an object of derision, as you yourselves can see. [8] Do not be stubborn, as they were, but submit yourselves to the LORD. Come to his Temple, which he has set apart as holy forever. Worship the LORD your God so that his fierce anger will turn away from you.

[9] "For if you return to the LORD, your relatives and your children will be treated mercifully by their captors, and they will be able to return to this land. For the LORD your God is gracious and merciful. If you return to him, he will not continue to turn his face from you."

## Celebration of Passover

[10] The runners went from town to town throughout Ephraim and Manasseh and as far as the territory of Zebulun. But most of the people just laughed at the runners and made fun of them. [11] However, some people from Asher, Manasseh, and Zebulun humbled themselves and went to Jerusalem.

[12] At the same time, God's hand was on the people in the land of Judah, giving them all one heart to obey the orders of the king and his officials, who were following the word of the LORD. [13] So a huge crowd assembled at Jerusalem in midspring* to celebrate the Festival of

---

**30:2** Hebrew *in the second month.* Passover was normally observed in the first month (of the ancient Hebrew lunar calendar).  **30:6** *Israel* is the name that God gave to Jacob.  **30:13** Hebrew *in the second month.* The second month of the ancient Hebrew lunar calendar usually occurs within the months of April and May.

---

God. As a peace offering, it symbolized restored peace and fellowship with God.

**30:1** The Passover celebration commemorated the time when God spared the lives of Israel's firstborn sons in Egypt. God had promised to send a plague to kill all the firstborn sons except in those homes where the blood of a slain lamb had been painted on the doorposts. The Israelites obeyed, and when the destroyer saw the blood, he "passed over" the house and did not harm anyone in it (Exodus 12:23). After this plague, Pharaoh freed the Israelites from slavery. This celebration was to be a yearly reminder of how God delivered his people. The careful preparations, both in the Temple and for the festival, show that this was not a temporary or impulsive revival, but a deep-seated change of heart and life.

**30:2, 3** God's law had a provision that, under certain circumstances, the Passover could be celebrated one month later (Numbers 9:10, 11).

**30:6-9** Hezekiah was a king dedicated to God and to the spiritual progress of the nation. He sent letters throughout Judah and Israel urging everyone to return to God. He told them not to be stubborn but submit to the Lord. To submit means to obey him

first, yielding our bodies, minds, wills, and emotions to him. His Holy Spirit must guide and renew every part of us. Only then will we be able to temper our stubborn selfishness.

**30:10** The northern kingdom of Israel had recently been conquered by Assyria, and most of the people had been carried away to foreign lands. Hezekiah sent a proclamation to the few people who remained, inviting them to come to the Passover (30:1), but most responded with scorn and ridicule. People may mock you when you try to promote spiritual renewal and growth. Are you prepared to be ridiculed for your faith? When it comes your way, do not waver. Stand strong in your faith, as Hezekiah did, and God will honor you.

**30:11** These people invited to the Passover scorned Hezekiah's messengers, but some accepted the invitation. Our efforts to tell others about God often meet with similar reactions. Many people will laugh at an invitation to accept Christ. But this must not stop us from reaching out. If you know and understand that rejecting the gospel is common, you can guard against feelings of personal rejection. Remember that the Holy Spirit convicts and convinces. Our task is to invite others to consider God's actions, his claims, and his promises.

---

**30:2**
Num 9:10-11
2 Chr 30:13, 15
**30:3**
2 Chr 29:34

**30:5**
Judg 20:1

**30:6**
2 Chr 28:20
Esth 8:14
Jer 51:31

**30:7**
2 Chr 29:8
Ezek 20:13, 18
**30:8**
Exod 3:9
2 Chr 29:10

**30:9**
Exod 34:6-7
Deut 30:2
Mic 7:18

**30:10**
2 Chr 36:16
**30:11**
2 Chr 30:18, 21

**30:13**
2 Chr 30:2

Unleavened Bread. [14]They set to work and removed the pagan altars from Jerusalem. They took away all the incense altars and threw them into the Kidron Valley.

[15]On the fourteenth day of the second month, one month later than usual,* the people slaughtered the Passover lamb. This shamed the priests and Levites, so they purified themselves and brought burnt offerings to the Temple of the LORD. [16]Then they took their places at the Temple as prescribed in the Law of Moses, the man of God. The Levites brought the sacrificial blood to the priests, who then sprinkled it on the altar.

[17]Since many of the people had not purified themselves, the Levites had to slaughter their Passover lamb for them, to set them apart for the LORD. [18]Most of those who came from Ephraim, Manasseh, Issachar, and Zebulun had not purified themselves. But King Hezekiah prayed for them, and they were allowed to eat the Passover meal anyway, even though this was contrary to the requirements of the Law. For Hezekiah said, "May the LORD, who is good, pardon those [19]who decide to follow the LORD, the God of their ancestors, even though they are not properly cleansed for the ceremony." [20]And the LORD listened to Hezekiah's prayer and healed the people.

[21]So the people of Israel who were present in Jerusalem joyously celebrated the Festival of Unleavened Bread for seven days. Each day the Levites and priests sang to the LORD, accompanied by loud instruments.* [22]Hezekiah encouraged all the Levites regarding the skill they displayed as they served the LORD. The celebration continued for seven days. Peace offerings were sacrificed, and the people gave thanks to the LORD, the God of their ancestors.

[23]The entire assembly then decided to continue the festival another seven days, so they celebrated joyfully for another week. [24]King Hezekiah gave the people 1,000 bulls and 7,000 sheep and goats for offerings, and the officials donated 1,000 bulls and 10,000 sheep and goats. Meanwhile, many more priests purified themselves.

[25]The entire assembly of Judah rejoiced, including the priests, the Levites, all who came from the land of Israel, the foreigners who came to the festival, and all those who lived in Judah. [26]There was great joy in the city, for Jerusalem had not seen a celebration like this one since the days of Solomon, King David's son. [27]Then the priests and Levites stood and blessed the people, and God heard their prayer from his holy dwelling in heaven.

### Hezekiah's Religious Reforms

**31** When the festival ended, the Israelites who attended went to all the towns of Judah, Benjamin, Ephraim, and Manasseh, and they smashed all the sacred pillars, cut down the Asherah poles, and removed the pagan shrines and altars. After this, the Israelites returned to their own towns and homes.

[2]Hezekiah then organized the priests and Levites into divisions to offer the burnt offerings and peace offerings, and to worship and give thanks and praise to the LORD at the gates of the Temple. [3]The king also made a personal contribution of animals for the daily morning and evening burnt offerings, the weekly Sabbath festivals, the monthly new moon festivals,

**30:14** 2 Chr 28:24; 29:16

**30:15** 2 Chr 29:34; 30:2-3

**30:16** 2 Chr 35:10, 15

**30:18** Exod 12:43-49 Num 9:6-10

**30:21** Exod 12:15; 13:6
**30:22** 2 Chr 32:6 Ezra 10:11
**30:23** 1 Kgs 8:65
**30:24** 2 Chr 29:34; 30:3; 35:7-8
**30:25** 2 Chr 30:11, 18
**30:26** 2 Chr 7:8-10
**30:27** Num 6:23 Deut 26:15 2 Chr 23:18 Ps 68:5

**31:1** 2 Kgs 18:4

**31:2** 1 Chr 23:28-31; 24:1

**31:3** Num 28:1-29, 40 2 Chr 35:7

---

**30:15** Hebrew *On the fourteenth day of the second month.* Passover normally began on the fourteenth day of the first month (see Lev 23:5).    **30:21** Or *sang to the LORD with all their strength.*

---

**30:14** Just as the priests had purified the Temple (29:4, 5), so the people cleared the city of pagan idols and then purified themselves to prepare for worship (30:17-19). Even the good kings of Judah found it difficult to get rid of the idols and altars in the pagan shrines (2 Kings 14:4; 2 Chronicles 20:33). Finally, Hezekiah, with the help of his people, completed this task.

**30:15** The people were so zealous to celebrate the Passover and bring offerings to the Temple that the priests and Levites were ashamed they did not share the same enthusiasm. The zeal of common people's faith motivated the ministers to take action. Devout laypeople today can motivate professional church staff to rekindle their enthusiasm for God's work. Laypeople should never be shut out of church government or decision making. The church needs their good examples of faith.

**30:22** One important purpose of the peace offering was to express gratitude to God for health or for safety in times of crisis.

**30:26** It had been more than 200 years since there had been such a celebration in Jerusalem.

**31:1ff** Why was idol worship so bad? The Israelites had access to the one true God, but they constantly fell into worshiping lifeless idols made of wood or stone. They put aside worshiping the Creator in order to worship the creation. We are just as guilty when God no longer holds first place in our lives. When we think more about wealth, pleasure, prestige, or material possessions than about God, we are actually worshiping them as gods. Because of idol worship, the people of Judah were eventually sent into captivity in foreign lands (36:14-17). We may not be sent into captivity, but discipline awaits all those who continually put earthly desires above spiritual priorities.

**31:2-21** The priests had not been supported by the government during the evil kings' reigns. Now that the Temple was repaired, Hezekiah organized the priests and resumed the work of the Temple according to the plan originally set up by David (1 Chronicles 23:6-24; 24:3-19).

31:4
Num 18:8

31:5
Neh 13:12

31:6
Lev 27:30
Deut 14:28

31:10
1 Chr 6:8-9
Mal 3:10

31:11
1 Kgs 6:5, 8

31:15
Josh 21:9-19
2 Chr 29:12

31:17
1 Chr 23:24

and the annual festivals as prescribed in the Law of the LORD. ⁴In addition, he required the people in Jerusalem to bring a portion of their goods to the priests and Levites, so they could devote themselves fully to the Law of the LORD.

⁵When the people of Israel heard these requirements, they responded generously by bringing the first share of their grain, new wine, olive oil, honey, and all the produce of their fields. They brought a large quantity—a tithe of all they produced. ⁶The people who had moved to Judah from Israel, and the people of Judah themselves, brought in the tithes of their cattle, sheep, and goats and a tithe of the things that had been dedicated to the LORD their God, and they piled them up in great heaps. ⁷They began piling them up in late spring, and the heaps continued to grow until early autumn.* ⁸When Hezekiah and his officials came and saw these huge piles, they thanked the LORD and his people Israel!

⁹"Where did all this come from?" Hezekiah asked the priests and Levites.

¹⁰And Azariah the high priest, from the family of Zadok, replied, "Since the people began bringing their gifts to the LORD's Temple, we have had enough to eat and plenty to spare. The LORD has blessed his people, and all this is left over."

¹¹Hezekiah ordered that storerooms be prepared in the Temple of the LORD. When this was done, ¹²the people faithfully brought all the tithes and gifts to the Temple. Conaniah the Levite was put in charge, assisted by his brother Shimei. ¹³The supervisors under them were Jehiel, Azaziah, Nahath, Asahel, Jerimoth, Jozabad, Eliel, Ismakiah, Mahath, and Benaiah. These appointments were made by King Hezekiah and Azariah, the chief official in the Temple of God.

¹⁴Kore son of Imnah the Levite, who was the gatekeeper at the East Gate, was put in charge of distributing the voluntary offerings given to God, the gifts, and the things that had been dedicated to the LORD. ¹⁵His faithful assistants were Eden, Miniamin, Jeshua, Shemaiah, Amariah, and Shecaniah. They distributed the gifts among the families of priests in their towns by their divisions, dividing the gifts fairly among old and young alike. ¹⁶They distributed the gifts to all males three years old or older, regardless of their place in the genealogical records. The distribution went to all who would come to the LORD's Temple to perform their daily duties according to their divisions. ¹⁷They distributed gifts to the priests who were listed by their families in the genealogical records, and to the Levites twenty years old or older who were listed according to their jobs and their divisions. ¹⁸Food

31:7 Hebrew *in the third month . . . until the seventh month.* The third month of the ancient Hebrew lunar calendar usually occurs within the months of May and June; the seventh month usually occurs within September and October.

---

**DAVID'S DYNASTY**

| | |
|---|---|
| David (40 years, 1 Chr. 10–29) | Uzziah (52 years, 2 Chr. 26) |
| Solomon (40 years, 2 Chr. 1–9) | Jotham (16 years, 2 Chr. 27) |
| Rehoboam (17 years, 2 Chr. 10–12) | Ahaz (16 years, 2 Chr. 27) |
| Abijah (3 years, 2 Chr. 13) | Hezekiah (29 years, 2 Chr. 29–32) |
| Asa (41 years, 2 Chr. 14–16) | Manasseh (55 years, 2 Chr. 33:1-20) |
| Jehoshaphat (25 years, 2 Chr. 17–20) | Amon (2 years, 2 Chr. 33:21-25) |
| Jehoram (8 years, 2 Chr. 21) | Josiah (31 years, 2 Chr. 34–35) |
| Ahaziah (1 year, 2 Chr. 22:1-9) | Jehoahaz (3 months, 2 Chr. 36:1-4) |
| Athaliah (6 years, 2 Chr. 22:10–23:21) | Jehoiakim (11 years, 2 Chr. 36:5-8) |
| Joash (40 years, 2 Chr. 24) | Jehoiachin (3 months, 2 Chr. 36:9-10) |
| Amaziah (29 years, 2 Chr. 25) | Zedekiah (11 years, 2 Chr. 36:11-16) |

The Lord promised David that his kingdom would endure and his throne would be established forever (2 Samuel 7:16). As a partial fulfillment of this promise, David and his descendants ruled Judah for over 400 years. Jesus Christ was a direct descendant of David and was the ultimate fulfillment of this promise (Acts 2:22-36).

---

**31:4-8** Hezekiah reinstated the practice of tithing—giving a tenth of one's income to the priests and Levites so they could be free to serve God and minister to the people. The people responded immediately and generously. God's work needs the support of God's people. Does God receive a regular percentage of your income? Generosity makes our giving delightful to us and to God (2 Corinthians 8–9). How different the church would be today if all believers consistently followed this pattern.

allotments were also given to the families of all those listed in the genealogical records, including their little babies, wives, sons, and daughters. For they had all been faithful in purifying themselves.

¹⁹As for the priests, the descendants of Aaron, who were living in the open villages around the towns, men were appointed by name to distribute portions to every male among the priests and to all the Levites listed in the genealogical records.

²⁰In this way, King Hezekiah handled the distribution throughout all Judah, doing what was pleasing and good in the sight of the LORD his God. ²¹In all that he did in the service of the Temple of God and in his efforts to follow God's laws and commands, Hezekiah sought his God wholeheartedly. As a result, he was very successful.

31:19
Lev 25:34
Num 35:2
2 Chr 31:12-15

31:20-21
//2 Kgs 18:5-7

## Assyria Invades Judah

**32** After Hezekiah had faithfully carried out this work, King Sennacherib of Assyria invaded Judah. He laid siege to the fortified towns, giving orders for his army to break through their walls. ²When Hezekiah realized that Sennacherib also intended to attack Jerusalem, ³he consulted with his officials and military advisers, and they decided to stop the flow of the springs outside the city. ⁴They organized a huge work crew to stop the flow of the springs, cutting off the brook that ran through the fields. For they said, "Why should the kings of Assyria come here and find plenty of water?"

⁵Then Hezekiah worked hard at repairing all the broken sections of the wall, erecting towers, and constructing a second wall outside the first. He also reinforced the supporting terraces* in the City of David and manufactured large numbers of weapons and shields. ⁶He appointed military officers over the people and assembled them before him in the square at the city gate. Then Hezekiah encouraged them by saying: ⁷"Be strong and courageous! Don't be afraid or discouraged because of the king of Assyria or his mighty army, for there is a power far greater on our side! ⁸He may have a great army, but they are merely men. We have the LORD our God to help us and to fight our battles for us!" Hezekiah's words greatly encouraged the people.

32:1
Isa 36:1–37:37

32:4
2 Kgs 20:20
2 Chr 32:30

32:5
1 Kgs 9:24
2 Kgs 25:4
2 Chr 25:23

32:6
2 Chr 30:22

32:7
2 Kgs 6:16
1 Chr 22:13

32:8
2 Chr 20:17
Jer 17:5

32:5 Hebrew *the millo*. The meaning of the Hebrew is uncertain.

---

**31:20, 21** Because Hezekiah did "what was pleasing and good in the sight of the LORD his God," he led the people of Judah in spiritual renewal. His actions serve as a model of renewal for us: (1) He remembered God's compassion (30:9); (2) he kept going despite ridicule (30:10); (3) he aggressively removed evil influences from his life (30:14; 31:1); (4) he interceded for the people, asking for the Lord's pardon (30:15-20); (5) he was open to spontaneity in worship (30:23); (6) he contributed generously to God's work (31:3). If any of these are lacking in your life, consider how they might apply, and renew your commitment to God.

**32:1** Assyria was a great empire by Hezekiah's time, controlling most of the Middle East. From a small strip of land located in present-day Iran and Iraq, it began to establish its power under Ashurnasirpal II (883–859 B.C.) and his son Shalmaneser III (859–824). Under Tiglath-pileser III (745–727), Assyria's boundaries extended to the borders of Israel, making it one of the largest empires in ancient history. Shalmaneser V destroyed the northern kingdom in 722, and his grandson Sennacherib (705–681) tried to bring Judah, the southern kingdom, under his control. Less than a century later, Assyria would lie in ruins (612).

**32:1** Sennacherib wanted to conquer these cities so he could force them to pay tribute. Forcing captured cities to pay tribute was a way for kings to build their income base. Often Assyria would require an oath of allegiance from a country, including the promise to pay taxes in the form of livestock, wine, battle equipment (horses, chariots, weapons), gold, silver, and anything else that pleased the invading king. Tribute was more important to Assyria than captives because captives cost money. Thus, captives were taken only in cases of extreme rebellion or to repopulate cities that had been destroyed.

**32:1ff** When Hezekiah was confronted with the frightening prospect of an Assyrian invasion, he made two important decisions. He did everything he could to deal with the situation, and he trusted God for the outcome. That is exactly what we must do when faced with difficult or frightening situations. Take all the steps you possibly can to solve the problem or improve the situation. But also commit the situation to God in prayer, trusting him for the solution.

**32:3, 4** Cities had to be built near reliable water sources. Natural springs were some of Jerusalem's major sources of water. In a brilliant military move, Hezekiah plugged the springs outside the city and channeled the water through an underground tunnel (32:30); therefore, Jerusalem would have water even through a long siege. Hezekiah's tunnel has been discovered along with an inscription describing how it was built: Two groups of workers started digging underground, one in Jerusalem and one at the Gihon Spring, and they met in the middle.

**THE ASSYRIAN EMPIRE** The mighty Assyrian Empire extended from the Persian Gulf, across the Fertile Crescent, and south to Egypt. Shalmaneser III extended the empire toward the Mediterranean Sea by conquering cities as far west as Qarqar. Tiglath-pileser extended the empire south into Aram, Israel, Judah, and Philistia. It was Shalmaneser V who destroyed Samaria, Israel's capital.

## Sennacherib Threatens Jerusalem

32:9-19
//2 Kgs 18:17-35
//Isa 36:2-20
9While King Sennacherib of Assyria was still besieging the town of Lachish, he sent his officers to Jerusalem with this message for Hezekiah and all the people in the city:

10"This is what King Sennacherib of Assyria says: What are you trusting in that makes you think you can survive my siege of Jerusalem? 11Hezekiah has said, 'The LORD our God will rescue us from the king of Assyria.' Surely Hezekiah is misleading you, sentencing you to death by famine and thirst! 12Don't you realize that Hezekiah is the very person who destroyed all the LORD's shrines and altars? He commanded Judah and Jerusalem to worship only at the altar at the Temple and to offer sacrifices on it alone.

32:12
2 Chr 31:1

32:13
2 Kgs 18:33-35

32:14
Isa 10:9-11
13"Surely you must realize what I and the other kings of Assyria before me have done to all the people of the earth! Were any of the gods of those nations able to rescue their people from my power? 14Which of their gods was able to rescue its people from the destructive power of my predecessors? What makes you think your God can rescue you from me? 15Don't let Hezekiah deceive you! Don't let him fool you like this! I say it again—no god of any nation or kingdom has ever yet been able to rescue his people from me or my ancestors. How much less will your God rescue you from my power!"

32:17
2 Chr 32:14
16And Sennacherib's officers further mocked the LORD God and his servant Hezekiah, heaping insult upon insult. 17The king also sent letters scorning the LORD, the God of Israel. He wrote, "Just as the gods of all the other nations failed to rescue their people from my power, so the God of Hezekiah will also fail." 18The Assyrian officials who brought the letters shouted this in Hebrew* to the people gathered on the walls of the city, trying to terrify them so it would be easier to capture the city. 19These officers talked about the God of Jerusalem as though he were one of the pagan gods, made by human hands.

32:20-21
//2 Kgs 19:35-37
//Isa 37:36-38
20Then King Hezekiah and the prophet Isaiah son of Amoz cried out in prayer to God in heaven. 21And the LORD sent an angel who destroyed the Assyrian army with all its commanders and officers. So Sennacherib was forced to return home in disgrace to his own land. And when he entered the temple of his god, some of his own sons killed him there with a sword.

32:23
2 Sam 8:10
22That is how the LORD rescued Hezekiah and the people of Jerusalem from King Sennacherib of Assyria and from all the others who threatened them. So there was peace throughout the land. 23From then on King Hezekiah became highly respected among all the surrounding nations, and many gifts for the LORD arrived at Jerusalem, with valuable presents for King Hezekiah, too.

## Hezekiah's Sickness and Recovery

32:24-33
//2 Kgs 20:1-21
//Isa 37:21-38;
38:1-8
24About that time Hezekiah became deathly ill. He prayed to the LORD, who healed him and gave him a miraculous sign. 25But Hezekiah did not respond appropriately to the kindness shown him, and he became proud. So the LORD's anger came against him and against Judah and Jerusalem. 26Then Hezekiah humbled himself and repented of his pride, as did the people of Jerusalem. So the LORD's anger did not fall on them during Hezekiah's lifetime.

32:25
2 Chr 24:18; 26:16

32:26
Jer 26:18-19

32:29
1 Chr 29:12
27Hezekiah was very wealthy and highly honored. He built special treasury buildings for his silver, gold, precious stones, and spices, and for his shields and other valuable items. 28He also constructed many storehouses for his grain, new wine, and olive oil; and he made many stalls for his cattle and pens for his flocks of sheep and goats. 29He built many towns and acquired vast flocks and herds, for God had given him great wealth. 30He blocked up the upper spring of Gihon and brought the water down through a tunnel to the west side of the City of David. And so he succeeded in everything he did.

32:30
1 Kgs 1:33
2 Kgs 20:20

32:31
Deut 8:16
2 Kgs 20:12
2 Chr 32:24
Isa 38:7-8; 39:1
31However, when ambassadors arrived from Babylon to ask about the remarkable events

32:18 Hebrew *in the dialect of Judah.*

---

**32:7, 8** Hezekiah could see with eyes of faith. The number of his opponents meant nothing as long as he was on the Lord's side. Victory is "not by force nor by strength, but by my Spirit, says the LORD of Heaven's Armies" (Zechariah 4:6). Hezekiah could confidently encourage his men because he had no doubt about where he stood with God. Are you on the Lord's side? You may never face an enemy army, but the battles you face every day can be won with God's strength.

**32:31** A test can bring out a person's true character. God tested Hezekiah to see what he was really like and to show him his own

shortcomings and the attitude of his heart. God did not totally abandon Hezekiah, nor did he tempt him to sin or trick him. The test was meant to strengthen Hezekiah, develop his character, and prepare him for the tasks ahead. In times of success, most of us can live good lives. But pressure, trouble, or pain will quickly remove our thin veneer of goodness unless our strength comes from God. What are you like under pressure or when everything is going wrong? Do you give in or turn to God? Those who are consistently in touch with God don't have to worry about what pressure may reveal about them.

that had taken place in the land, God withdrew from Hezekiah in order to test him and to see what was really in his heart.

## Summary of Hezekiah's Reign

32 The rest of the events in Hezekiah's reign and his acts of devotion are recorded in *The Vision of the Prophet Isaiah Son of Amoz,* which is included in *The Book of the Kings of Judah and Israel.* 33 When Hezekiah died, he was buried in the upper area of the royal cemetery, and all Judah and Jerusalem honored him at his death. And his son Manasseh became the next king.

## Manasseh Rules in Judah

**33** Manasseh was twelve years old when he became king, and he reigned in Jerusalem fifty-five years. 2 He did what was evil in the LORD's sight, following the detestable practices of the pagan nations that the LORD had driven from the land ahead of the Israelites. 3 He rebuilt the pagan shrines his father, Hezekiah, had broken down. He constructed altars for the images of Baal and set up Asherah poles. He also bowed before all the powers of the heavens and worshiped them.

4 He built pagan altars in the Temple of the LORD, the place where the LORD had said, "My name will remain in Jerusalem forever." 5 He built these altars for all the powers of the heavens in both courtyards of the LORD's Temple. 6 Manasseh also sacrificed his own sons in the fire* in the valley of Ben-Hinnom. He practiced sorcery, divination, and witchcraft, and he consulted with mediums and psychics. He did much that was evil in the LORD's sight, arousing his anger.

7 Manasseh even took a carved idol he had made and set it up in God's Temple, the very place where God had told David and his son Solomon: "My name will be honored forever in this Temple and in Jerusalem—the city I have chosen from among all the tribes of Israel. 8 If the Israelites will be careful to obey my commands—all the laws, decrees, and regulations given through Moses—I will not send them into exile from this land that I set aside for your ancestors." 9 But Manasseh led the people of Judah and Jerusalem to do even more evil than the pagan nations that the LORD had destroyed when the people of Israel entered the land.

10 The LORD spoke to Manasseh and his people, but they ignored all his warnings. 11 So the LORD sent the commanders of the Assyrian armies, and they took Manasseh prisoner. They put a ring through his nose, bound him in bronze chains, and led him away to Babylon. 12 But while in deep distress, Manasseh sought the LORD his God and sincerely humbled himself before the God of his ancestors. 13 And when he prayed, the LORD listened to him and was moved by his request. So the LORD brought Manasseh back to Jerusalem and to his kingdom. Then Manasseh finally realized that the LORD alone is God!

14 After this Manasseh rebuilt the outer wall of the City of David, from west of the Gihon Spring in the Kidron Valley to the Fish Gate, and continuing around the hill of Ophel. He built the wall very high. And he stationed his military officers in all of the fortified towns of Judah. 15 Manasseh also removed the foreign gods and the idol from the LORD's Temple. He tore down all the altars he had built on the hill where the Temple stood and all the altars that

**33:1-10**
//2 Kgs 21:1-10
**33:2**
2 Chr 28:3
**33:3**
Deut 16:21
2 Kgs 23:5-6
2 Chr 31:1
**33:4**
2 Chr 7:16; 28:24
**33:5**
2 Chr 4:9
**33:6**
Lev 19:31; 20:27
2 Chr 28:3
**33:8**
2 Sam 7:10
**33:11**
Deut 28:36
2 Chr 36:6
**33:12**
2 Chr 32:26
**33:13**
Ezra 8:23
Dan 4:25, 32
**33:14**
1 Kgs 1:33
2 Chr 27:3
Neh 3:3
**33:15**
2 Chr 33:3-7

**33:6** Or *also made his sons pass through the fire.*

---

**32:31** Babylon was slowly and quietly rising to become a world power. At the same time, the Assyrian Empire was slowly declining due to internal strife and a succession of weak kings. When Assyria was finally crushed in 612 B.C., Babylon, under Nebuchadnezzar, moved into its place of prominence. (For more information on Babylon, see the note on 2 Kings 20:14.)

**32:31** Why did God withdraw from Hezekiah? After Hezekiah was healed of his sickness, he became proud. When ambassadors came to inquire about his miraculous healing, God stepped back to see how Hezekiah would respond. Unfortunately, Hezekiah's actions revealed his runaway pride. He pointed to his own accomplishments rather than to God (see 2 Kings 20:12-19). Pride is any attitude that elevates our effort or abilities above God's or treats with disdain his work in us. It causes us to congratulate ourselves for our successes and to look down on other people. God does not object to self-confidence, healthy self-esteem, or good feelings about our accomplishments. He

objects to the foolish attitude of taking full credit for what he has done or for setting ourselves up as superior to others.

**33:6** Sorcery is using power gained from evil spirits. Divination is predicting the future through omens.

**33:11** Between 652 and 648 B.C., the city of Babylon rebelled against Assyria. The rebellion was crushed, but Assyria may have suspected that Manasseh supported it. That may explain why Manasseh was taken to Babylon for trial rather than to the Assyrian capital of Nineveh.

**33:12, 13** In a list of corrupt kings, Manasseh would rank near the top. His life was a catalog of evil deeds including idol worship, sacrificing his own children, and Temple desecration. Eventually, however, he realized his sins and cried out to God for forgiveness. And God listened. If God can forgive Manasseh, surely he can forgive anyone. Are you burdened by overpowering guilt? Do you doubt that anyone could forgive what you have done? Take heart—until death, no one is beyond the reach of God's forgiveness.

were in Jerusalem, and he dumped them outside the city. ¹⁶Then he restored the altar of the LORD and sacrificed peace offerings and thanksgiving offerings on it. He also encouraged the people of Judah to worship the LORD, the God of Israel. ¹⁷However, the people still sacrificed at the pagan shrines, though only to the LORD their God.

**33:17**
2 Chr 32:12

¹⁸The rest of the events of Manasseh's reign, his prayer to God, and the words the seers spoke to him in the name of the LORD, the God of Israel, are recorded in *The Book of the Kings of Israel.* ¹⁹Manasseh's prayer, the account of the way God answered him, and an account of all his sins and unfaithfulness are recorded in *The Record of the Seers.*\* It includes a list of the locations where he built pagan shrines and set up Asherah poles and idols before he humbled himself and repented. ²⁰When Manasseh died, he was buried in his palace. Then his son Amon became the next king.

**33:18-20**
//2 Kgs 21:17-18

**33:19**
2 Chr 33:3, 13

### Amon Rules in Judah

**33:21-25**
//2 Kgs 21:19-24

**33:23**
2 Chr 33:12, 19

**33:24**
2 Chr 25:27

²¹Amon was twenty-two years old when he became king, and he reigned in Jerusalem two years. ²²He did what was evil in the LORD's sight, just as his father, Manasseh, had done. He worshiped and sacrificed to all the idols his father had made. ²³But unlike his father, he did not humble himself before the LORD. Instead, Amon sinned even more.

²⁴Then Amon's own officials conspired against him and assassinated him in his palace. ²⁵But the people of the land killed all those who had conspired against King Amon, and they made his son Josiah the next king.

**33:19** Or *The Record of Hozai.*

Even a brief outline of King Manasseh's evil sickens us, and we wonder how God could ever forgive him. Not only did he intentionally offend God by desecrating Solomon's Temple with idols, but he also worshiped pagan gods and even sacrificed his children to them! Child sacrifice is a vile act of pagan idolatry, an act against both God and people. Such blatant sins require severe correction.

God showed justice to Manasseh in warning and punishing him. He showed mercy in responding to Manasseh's heartfelt repentance by forgiving and restoring him. Given the nature of Manasseh's rebellion, we are not surprised by God's punishment—defeat and exile at the hands of the Assyrians. But Manasseh's repentance and God's forgiveness are unexpected. Manasseh's life was changed. He was given a new start.

How far has God gone to get your attention? Have you ever, like Manasseh, come to your senses and cried out to God for help? Only your repentance and a prayer for a new attitude stand between you and God's complete forgiveness.

**MANASSEH**

| | |
|---|---|
| **Strengths and accomplishments** | • Despite the bitter consequences of his sins, he learned from them<br>• Humbly repented of his sins before God |
| **Weaknesses and mistakes** | • Challenged God's authority and was defeated<br>• Reversed many of the positive effects of his father Hezekiah's rule<br>• Sacrificed his children to idols |
| **Lessons from his life** | • God will go a long way to get someone's attention<br>• Forgiveness is limited, not by the amount of sin, but by our willingness to repent |
| **Vital statistics** | • Where: Jerusalem<br>• Occupation: King of Judah<br>• Relatives: Father: Hezekiah. Mother: Hephzibah. Son: Amon. |
| **Key verses** | "But while in deep distress, Manasseh sought the LORD his God and sincerely humbled himself before the God of his ancestors. And when he prayed, the LORD listened to him and was moved by his request. So the LORD brought Manasseh back to Jerusalem and to his kingdom. Then Manasseh finally realized that the LORD alone is God!" (2 Chronicles 33:12–13). |

Manasseh's story is told in 2 Kings 21:1–18 and 2 Chronicles 32:33—33:20. He is also mentioned in Jeremiah 15:4.

**33:17** Although the people worshiped God alone, they worshiped him in the wrong way. God had told them to make their sacrifices only in certain places (Deuteronomy 12:13, 14). This kept them from changing their way of worship and protected them against the dangerous influence of pagan religious practices. Unfortunately, the people continued to use these places of worship, not realizing that (1) they were adopting practices God opposed, and (2) these places were against God's law. They were mixing pagan beliefs with worship of God. Blending religious ideas leads to confusion about who God really is. We must take care that subtle secular influences do not distort our worship practices.

## Josiah Rules in Judah

**34** Josiah was eight years old when he became king, and he reigned in Jerusalem thirty-one years. ²He did what was pleasing in the LORD's sight and followed the example of his ancestor David. He did not turn away from doing what was right.

³During the eighth year of his reign, while he was still young, Josiah began to seek the God of his ancestor David. Then in the twelfth year he began to purify Judah and Jerusalem, destroying all the pagan shrines, the Asherah poles, and the carved idols and cast images. ⁴He ordered that the altars of Baal be demolished and that the incense altars which stood above them be broken down. He also made sure that the Asherah poles, the carved idols, and the cast images were smashed and scattered over the graves of those who had sacrificed to them. ⁵He burned the bones of the pagan priests on their own altars, and so he purified Judah and Jerusalem.

⁶He did the same thing in the towns of Manasseh, Ephraim, and Simeon, even as far as Naphtali, and in the regions* all around them. ⁷He destroyed the pagan altars and the Asherah poles, and he crushed the idols into dust. He cut down all the incense altars throughout the land of Israel. Finally, he returned to Jerusalem.

⁸In the eighteenth year of his reign, after he had purified the land and the Temple, Josiah appointed Shaphan son of Azaliah, Maaseiah the governor of Jerusalem, and Joah son of Joahaz, the royal historian, to repair the Temple of the LORD his God. ⁹They gave Hilkiah the high priest the money that had been collected by the Levites who served as gatekeepers at the Temple of God. The gifts were brought by people from Manasseh, Ephraim, and from all the remnant of Israel, as well as from all Judah, Benjamin, and the people of Jerusalem.

¹⁰He entrusted the money to the men assigned to supervise the restoration of the LORD's Temple. Then they paid the workers who did the repairs and renovation of the Temple. ¹¹They hired carpenters and builders, who purchased finished stone for the walls and timber for the rafters and beams. They restored what earlier kings of Judah had allowed to fall into ruin.

¹²The workers served faithfully under the leadership of Jahath and Obadiah, Levites of the Merarite clan, and Zechariah and Meshullam, Levites of the Kohathite clan. Other Levites, all of whom were skilled musicians, ¹³were put in charge of the laborers of the various trades. Still others assisted as secretaries, officials, and gatekeepers.

## Hilkiah Discovers God's Law

¹⁴While they were bringing out the money collected at the LORD's Temple, Hilkiah the priest found the Book of the Law of the LORD that was written by Moses. ¹⁵Hilkiah said to Shaphan the court secretary, "I have found the Book of the Law in the LORD's Temple!" Then Hilkiah gave the scroll to Shaphan.

¹⁶Shaphan took the scroll to the king and reported, "Your officials are doing everything they were assigned to do. ¹⁷The money that was collected at the Temple of the LORD has been turned over to the supervisors and workmen." ¹⁸Shaphan also told the king, "Hilkiah the priest has given me a scroll." So Shaphan read it to the king.

¹⁹When the king heard what was written in the Law, he tore his clothes in despair. ²⁰Then he gave these orders to Hilkiah, Ahikam son of Shaphan, Acbor son of Micaiah,* Shaphan the court secretary, and Asaiah the king's personal adviser: ²¹"Go to the Temple and speak to the LORD for me and for all the remnant of Israel and Judah. Inquire about the words written in the scroll that has been found. For the LORD's great anger has been poured out on us because our ancestors have not obeyed the word of the LORD. We have not been doing everything this scroll says we must do."

**34:1-2**
//2 Kgs 22:1-2
**34:2**
2 Chr 29:2
**34:3**
1 Kgs 13:2
2 Chr 15:2;
33:17, 22
**34:4**
Exod 32:20
2 Kgs 23:4-5, 11
**34:5**
1 Kgs 13:2
2 Kgs 23:20
**34:6**
2 Kgs 23:15, 19
**34:7**
2 Chr 31:1
**34:8-13**
//2 Kgs 22:3-7
**34:9**
2 Chr 30:10, 18;
35:8
**34:11**
2 Chr 33:4-7
**34:12**
1 Chr 25:1
**34:13**
Neh 4:10
**34:14-28**
//2 Kgs 22:8-20
**34:14**
2 Chr 34:9
**34:19**
Josh 7:6
**34:21**
2 Chr 29:8

---

**34:6** As in Syriac version. Hebrew reads *in their temples,* or *in their ruins.* The meaning of the Hebrew is uncertain.
**34:20** As in parallel text at 2 Kgs 22:12; Hebrew reads *Abdon son of Micah.*

---

**34:1** Josiah's Profile is found in 2 Kings 23, p. 611.

**34:3** In Josiah's day, boys were considered men at age 12. By 16, Josiah understood the responsibility of his office. Even at this young age, he showed greater wisdom than many of the older kings who came before him because he had decided to seek the Lord God and his wisdom. Don't let your age hinder you from serving God.

**34:14, 15** The Book of the Law of the Lord that Hilkiah found was probably the book of Deuteronomy that had been lost during the reigns of the evil kings. Now that it was found, Josiah realized

that drastic changes had to be made in order to bring the nation back in line with God's commands. This account is also recorded in 2 Kings 22:8-13.

**34:19** It is human nature to treat sin lightly—to make excuses, blame somebody else, or minimize the harm done. Not so with Josiah. He was so appalled at the people's neglect of the law that he tore his clothing to express his grief. True understanding of our sins should lead to "sorrow" that "leads us away from sin" (2 Corinthians 7:10). Are you always excusing your sin, blaming others, and pretending that it's not so bad? God does not take

²²So Hilkiah and the other men went to the New Quarter* of Jerusalem to consult with the prophet Huldah. She was the wife of Shallum son of Tikvah, son of Harhas,* the keeper of the Temple wardrobe.

²³She said to them, "The LORD, the God of Israel, has spoken! Go back and tell the man who sent you, ²⁴'This is what the LORD says: I am going to bring disaster on this city* and its people. All the curses written in the scroll that was read to the king of Judah will come true. ²⁵For my people have abandoned me and offered sacrifices to pagan gods, and I am very angry with them for everything they have done. My anger will be poured out on this place, and it will not be quenched.'

²⁶"But go to the king of Judah who sent you to seek the LORD and tell him: 'This is what the LORD, the God of Israel, says concerning the message you have just heard: ²⁷You were sorry and humbled yourself before God when you heard his words against this city and its people. You humbled yourself and tore your clothing in despair and wept before me in repentance. And I have indeed heard you, says the LORD. ²⁸So I will not send the promised disaster until after you have died and been buried in peace. You yourself will not see the disaster I am going to bring on this city and its people.'"

So they took her message back to the king.

### Josiah's Religious Reforms

²⁹Then the king summoned all the elders of Judah and Jerusalem. ³⁰And the king went up to the Temple of the LORD with all the people of Judah and Jerusalem, along with the priests and the Levites—all the people from the greatest to the least. There the king read to them the entire Book of the Covenant that had been found in the LORD's Temple. ³¹The king took his place of authority beside the pillar and renewed the covenant in the LORD's presence. He pledged to obey the LORD by keeping all his commands, laws, and decrees with all his heart and soul. He promised to obey all the terms of the covenant that were written in the scroll. ³²And he required everyone in Jerusalem and the people of Benjamin to make a similar pledge. The people of Jerusalem did so, renewing their covenant with God, the God of their ancestors.

³³So Josiah removed all detestable idols from the entire land of Israel and required everyone to worship the LORD their God. And throughout the rest of his lifetime, they did not turn away from the LORD, the God of their ancestors.

### Josiah Celebrates Passover

**35** Then Josiah announced that the Passover of the LORD would be celebrated in Jerusalem, and so the Passover lamb was slaughtered on the fourteenth day of the first month.* ²Josiah also assigned the priests to their duties and encouraged them in their work at the Temple of the LORD. ³He issued this order to the Levites, who were to teach all Israel and who had been set apart to serve the LORD: "Put the holy Ark in the Temple that was built by Solomon son of David, the king of Israel. You no longer need to carry it back and forth on your shoulders. Now spend your time serving the LORD your God and his people Israel. ⁴Report for duty according to the family divisions of your ancestors, following the directions of King David of Israel and the directions of his son Solomon.

⁵"Then stand in the sanctuary at the place appointed for your family division and help the families assigned to you as they bring their offerings to the Temple. ⁶Slaughter the Passover lambs, purify yourselves, and prepare to help those who come. Follow all the directions that the LORD gave through Moses."

**34:24**
Deut 28:15-68
2 Chr 36:14-20

**34:25**
2 Chr 33:3

**34:27**
2 Chr 12:7; 32:26

**34:29-32**
//2 Kgs 23:1-3

**34:30**
Neh 8:1-3

**34:31**
2 Chr 23:16; 29:10

**34:33**
2 Kgs 23:3
2 Chr 34:3-7

**35:1**
Exod 12:6
Num 9:3
2 Kgs 23:21-22

**35:2**
2 Chr 29:11

**35:3**
1 Chr 23:26
2 Chr 17:8-9
Neh 8:7

**35:4**
1 Chr 9:10-13
2 Chr 8:14

**35:6**
2 Chr 29:5, 15;
35:1

---

**34:22a** Or *the Second Quarter,* a newer section of Jerusalem. Hebrew reads *the Mishneh.* **34:22b** As in parallel text at 2 Kgs 22:14; Hebrew reads *son of Tokhath, son of Hasrah.* **34:24** Hebrew *this place;* also in 34:27, 28. **35:1** This day in the ancient Hebrew lunar calendar was April 5, 622 B.C.

---

sin lightly, and he wants us to respond with true remorse as Josiah did.

**34:31** When Josiah read the book that Hilkiah discovered (34:14), he responded with repentance and humility and promised to follow God's commands as written in the book. The Bible is God's word to us, "alive and powerful" (Hebrews 4:12), but we cannot know what God wants us to do if we do not read it. And even reading God's Word is not enough; we must be willing to do what it says. There is not much difference between the book hidden in the Temple and the Bible hidden on the bookshelf. An unread Bible is as useless as a lost one.

**35:3** In Moses' day, one of the duties of the Levites was to carry the Ark of the Covenant whenever Israel traveled. The Ark was now permanently housed in the Temple and would no longer be carried about in procession as it was in the wilderness. Josiah was telling the Levites that they were now free to take on other responsibilities (1 Chronicles 24).

7 Then Josiah provided 30,000 lambs and young goats for the people's Passover offerings, along with 3,000 cattle, all from the king's own flocks and herds. 8 The king's officials also made willing contributions to the people, priests, and Levites. Hilkiah, Zechariah, and Jehiel, the administrators of God's Temple, gave the priests 2,600 lambs and young goats and 300 cattle as Passover offerings. 9 The Levite leaders—Conaniah and his brothers Shemaiah and Nethanel, as well as Hashabiah, Jeiel, and Jozabad—gave 5,000 lambs and young goats and 500 cattle to the Levites for their Passover offerings.

10 When everything was ready for the Passover celebration, the priests and the Levites took their places, organized by their divisions, as the king had commanded. 11 The Levites then slaughtered the Passover lambs and presented the blood to the priests, who sprinkled the blood on the altar while the Levites prepared the animals. 12 They divided the burnt offerings among the people by their family groups, so they could offer them to the Lord as prescribed in the Book of Moses. They did the same with the cattle. 13 Then they roasted the Passover lambs as prescribed; and they boiled the holy offerings in pots, kettles, and pans, and brought them out quickly so the people could eat them.

14 Afterward the Levites prepared Passover offerings for themselves and for the priests—the descendants of Aaron—because the priests had been busy from morning till night offering the burnt offerings and the fat portions. The Levites took responsibility for all these preparations.

15 The musicians, descendants of Asaph, were in their assigned places, following the commands that had been given by David, Asaph, Heman, and Jeduthun, the king's seer. The gatekeepers guarded the gates and did not need to leave their posts of duty, for their Passover offerings were prepared for them by their fellow Levites.

16 The entire ceremony for the Lord's Passover was completed that day. All the burnt offerings were sacrificed on the altar of the Lord, as King Josiah had commanded. 17 All the Israelites present in Jerusalem celebrated Passover and the Festival of Unleavened Bread for seven days. 18 Never since the time of the prophet Samuel had there been such a Passover. None of the kings of Israel had ever kept a Passover as Josiah did, involving all the priests and Levites, all the people of Jerusalem, and people from all over Judah and Israel. 19 This Passover celebration took place in the eighteenth year of Josiah's reign.

### Josiah Dies in Battle

20 After Josiah had finished restoring the Temple, King Neco of Egypt led his army up from Egypt to do battle at Carchemish on the Euphrates River, and Josiah and his army marched out to fight him.* 21 But King Neco sent messengers to Josiah with this message:

**35:20** Or *Josiah went out to meet him.*

**Cross-references (right margin):**
- 35:8 — 2 Chr 31:13
- 35:9 — 2 Chr 31:12
- 35:10 — 2 Chr 35:5
- 35:11 — 2 Chr 29:22, 34; 35:1, 6
- 35:13 — Exod 12:8-9; Lev 6:25
- 35:15 — 1 Chr 25:1; 26:12-19
- 35:17 — Exod 12:15; 2 Chr 30:21
- 35:18-19 — //2 Kgs 23:21-23
- 35:20—36:1 — //2 Kgs 23:28-30

---

**35:15** The Temple gatekeepers, who were all Levites, guarded the four main entrances to the Temple and opened the gates each morning. They also did other day-to-day chores, such as cleaning and preparing the offerings for sacrifice and accounting for the gifts given to the Temple. (For more on gatekeepers, see 1 Chronicles 26:1ff.)

**35:17** The Festival of Unleavened Bread was a seven-day celebration beginning the day after Passover. Like Passover, it commemorated the Exodus from Egypt. For seven days the people ate bread without yeast, just as their ancestors did while leaving Egypt, because it could be made quickly in preparation for their swift departure (Exodus 12:14-20). This festival reminded the people that they had left slavery behind and had come to the land God promised them.

**35:20** This event occurred in 609 B.C. Nineveh, the Assyrian capital, had been destroyed three years earlier by the Babylonians. The defeated Assyrians regrouped at Haran and Carchemish, but Babylon sent its army to destroy them once and for all. Pharaoh Neco, who wanted to make Egypt a world power, was worried about Babylon's growing strength, so he marched his army north through Judah to help the Assyrians at Carchemish. But King Josiah of Judah tried to prevent Neco from passing through his land on his way to Carchemish. Josiah was killed, and Judah became subject to Egypt. (2 Kings 23:25-30 helps explain the tragedy. Even though Josiah followed the Lord, God did not turn from his judgment on Judah because of Manasseh's sin and Judah's superficial repentance.) Neco went on to Carchemish and held off the Babylonians for four years, but in 605 he was soundly defeated, and Babylon moved into the spotlight as the dominant world power.

**35:21-24** Josiah ignored Neco's message because of who Neco

**THE BATTLE AT CARCHEMISH** A world war was brewing in 609 B.C. when Pharaoh Neco of Egypt set out for the city of Carchemish to join the Assyrians in an attempt to defeat the Babylonians, who were rising to great power. Neco marched his armies through Judah, where King Josiah tried to stop him at Megiddo, but was killed. The battle began at Carchemish in 605 B.C., and the Egyptians and Assyrians were soundly defeated, chased to Hamath, and defeated again. Babylon was now the new world power.

"What do you want with me, king of Judah? I have no quarrel with you today! I am on my way to fight another nation, and God has told me to hurry! Do not interfere with God, who is with me, or he will destroy you."

**35:22**
Judg 5:19
2 Chr 18:29; 35:21

22But Josiah refused to listen to Neco, to whom God had indeed spoken, and he would not turn back. Instead, he disguised himself and led his army into battle on the plain of Megiddo. 23But the enemy archers hit King Josiah with their arrows and wounded him. He cried out to his men, "Take me from the battle, for I am badly wounded!"

**35:25**
Jer 22:10-13
Lam 4:20
Zech 12:11

24So they lifted Josiah out of his chariot and placed him in another chariot. Then they brought him back to Jerusalem, where he died. He was buried there in the royal cemetery. And all Judah and Jerusalem mourned for him. 25The prophet Jeremiah composed funeral songs for Josiah, and to this day choirs still sing these sad songs about his death. These songs of sorrow have become a tradition and are recorded in *The Book of Laments*.

26The rest of the events of Josiah's reign and his acts of devotion (carried out according to what was written in the Law of the LORD), 27from beginning to end—all are recorded in *The Book of the Kings of Israel and Judah*.

### 3. Judah is exiled to Babylon
*Jehoahaz Rules in Judah*

**36:1**
Jer 22:11

**36** Then the people of the land took Josiah's son Jehoahaz and made him the next king in Jerusalem.

**36:2-4**
//2 Kgs 23:31-34

2Jehoahaz* was twenty-three years old when he became king, and he reigned in Jerusalem three months.

3Then he was deposed by the king of Egypt, who demanded that Judah pay 7,500 pounds of silver and 75 pounds of gold* as tribute.

*Jehoiakim Rules in Judah*

**36:4**
Jer 22:10, 12

4The king of Egypt then installed Eliakim, the brother of Jehoahaz, as the next king of Judah and Jerusalem, and he changed Eliakim's name to Jehoiakim. Then Neco took Jehoahaz to Egypt as a prisoner.

**36:5-8**
//2 Kgs 23:36—24:6
**36:5**
Jer 22:13-19
**36:6**
2 Chr 33:11
Jer 22:19-20
**36:7**
2 Kgs 24:13

5Jehoiakim was twenty-five years old when he became king, and he reigned in Jerusalem eleven years. He did what was evil in the sight of the LORD his God.

6Then King Nebuchadnezzar of Babylon came to Jerusalem and captured it, and he bound Jehoiakim in bronze chains and led him away to Babylon. 7Nebuchadnezzar also took some of the treasures from the Temple of the LORD, and he placed them in his palace* in Babylon.

8The rest of the events in Jehoiakim's reign, including all the evil things he did and everything found against him, are recorded in *The Book of the Kings of Israel and Judah*. Then his son Jehoiachin became the next king.

**36:9-10**
//2 Kgs 24:8-17

*Jehoiachin Rules in Judah*

9Jehoiachin was eighteen* years old when he became king, and he reigned in Jerusalem three months and ten days. Jehoiachin did what was evil in the LORD's sight.

**36:10**
Jer 37:1

10In the spring of the year* King Nebuchadnezzar took Jehoiachin to Babylon. Many treasures from the Temple of the LORD were also taken to Babylon at that time. And Nebuchadnezzar installed Jehoiachin's uncle,* Zedekiah, as the next king in Judah and Jerusalem.

**36:11-16**
//2 Kgs 24:18-20
//Jer 52:1-3
**36:12**
2 Chr 33:23
Jer 21:3-7

*Zedekiah Rules in Judah*

11Zedekiah was twenty-one years old when he became king, and he reigned in Jerusalem eleven years. 12He did what was evil in the sight of the LORD his God, and he refused to

**36:2** Hebrew *Joahaz*, a variant spelling of Jehoahaz; also in 36:4. **36:3** Hebrew *100 talents* [3,400 kilograms] *of silver and 1 talent* [34 kilograms] *of gold.* **36:7** Or *temple.* **36:9** As in one Hebrew manuscript, some Greek manuscripts, and Syriac version (see also 2 Kgs 24:8); most Hebrew manuscripts read *eight.* **36:10a** Hebrew *At the turn of the year.* The first day of this year in the ancient Hebrew lunar calendar was April 13, 597 B.C. **36:10b** As in parallel text at 2 Kgs 24:17; Hebrew reads *brother*, or *relative.*

was—king of a pagan nation. The mistaken assumption that Neco could not be part of God's larger plan cost Josiah his life. While not everyone who claims to have a message from God really does, God's messages may come in unexpected ways. God had spoken to pagan kings in the past (Genesis 12:17-20; 20:3-7; see also Daniel 4:1-3). Don't let prejudice or false assumptions blind you to God's message.

**35:25** Though Jeremiah recorded these laments for the death of Josiah, they are not the same as the book of Lamentations.

**36:6** Nebuchadnezzar was the son of the founder of the new Babylonian Empire. In 605 B.C., the year he became king, Nebuchadnezzar won the battle of Carchemish. That loss crushed Assyria (see the note on 35:20). (For more information about Nebuchadnezzar, read his Profile in Daniel 4, p. 1385.)

**36:9, 10** In 2 Kings 24:8, Jehoiachin is listed as 18 years old. Many Hebrew manuscripts list him as 8 years old. The age given in 2 Kings 24:8 is most likely accurate because he had wives at that time (see 2 Kings 24:15).

humble himself when the prophet Jeremiah spoke to him directly from the LORD. ¹³He also rebelled against King Nebuchadnezzar, even though he had taken an oath of loyalty in God's name. Zedekiah was a hard and stubborn man, refusing to turn to the LORD, the God of Israel.

¹⁴Likewise, all the leaders of the priests and the people became more and more unfaithful. They followed all the pagan practices of the surrounding nations, desecrating the Temple of the LORD that had been consecrated in Jerusalem.

¹⁵The LORD, the God of their ancestors, repeatedly sent his prophets to warn them, for he had compassion on his people and his Temple. ¹⁶But the people mocked these messengers of God and despised their words. They scoffed at the prophets until the LORD's anger could no longer be restrained and nothing could be done.

### The Fall of Jerusalem

¹⁷So the LORD brought the king of Babylon against them. The Babylonians* killed Judah's young men, even chasing after them into the Temple. They had no pity on the people, killing both young men and young women, the old and the infirm. God handed all of them over to Nebuchadnezzar. ¹⁸The king took home to Babylon all the articles, large and small, used in the Temple of God, and the treasures from both the LORD's Temple and from the palace of the king and his officials. ¹⁹Then his army burned the Temple of God, tore down the walls of Jerusalem, burned all the palaces, and completely destroyed everything of value.* ²⁰The few who survived were taken as exiles to Babylon, and they became servants to the king and his sons until the kingdom of Persia came to power.

²¹So the message of the LORD spoken through Jeremiah was fulfilled. The land finally enjoyed its Sabbath rest, lying desolate until the seventy years were fulfilled, just as the prophet had said.

### Cyrus Allows the Exiles to Return

²²In the first year of King Cyrus of Persia,* the LORD fulfilled the prophecy he had given through Jeremiah.* He stirred the heart of Cyrus to put this proclamation in writing and to send it throughout his kingdom:

²³"This is what King Cyrus of Persia says:

"The LORD, the God of heaven, has given me all the kingdoms of the earth. He has appointed me to build him a Temple at Jerusalem, which is in Judah. Any of you who are the LORD's people may go there for this task. And may the LORD your God be with you!"

**36:17** Or *Chaldeans.*   **36:19** Or *destroyed all the valuable articles from the Temple.*   **36:22a** The first year of Cyrus's reign over Babylon was 538 B.C.   **36:22b** See Jer 25:11-12; 29:10.

| | |
|---|---|
| **36:13** | 2 Chr 30:8 / Jer 52:3 / Ezek 17:15 |
| **36:15** | Jer 7:13; 25:3-4 |
| **36:16** | 2 Chr 30:10 / Ezra 5:12 / Prov 1:24-32 / Jer 5:12-13 |
| **36:17-20** | //2 Kgs 25:1-21 / //Jer 52:4-27 |
| **36:18** | 2 Chr 36:7, 10 |
| **36:19** | 2 Kgs 25:9 / Jer 52:13 |
| **36:20** | 2 Kgs 25:11 / Jer 27:7 |
| **36:21** | Lev 25:4; 26:33-34 / Jer 29:10 |
| **36:22-23** | //Ezra 1:1-3 |
| **36:22** | Isa 44:28 / Jer 29:10 |

---

**36:16** God warned Judah about its sin and continually restored the people to his favor, only to have them turn away. Eventually the situation was beyond remedy. Beware of harboring sin in your heart. The day will come when remedy is no longer possible and God's judgment replaces his mercy. Sin often repeated, but never repented of, invites disaster.

**36:21** Leviticus 26:27-45 strikingly predicts the captivity, telling how God's people would be torn from their land for disobeying him. One of the laws they had ignored stated that one year in every seven the land should lie fallow, resting from producing crops (Exodus 23:10, 11). The 70-year captivity allowed the land to rest, making up for all the years the Israelites had not observed this law. We know that God keeps all his promises—not only his promises of blessing, but also his promises of judgment.

**36:22, 23** Cyrus made this proclamation 48 years after the Temple was destroyed (36:18, 19), in the year after he conquered Babylon. The book of Ezra tells the story of this proclamation and the return of the exiles to Judah.

**36:22, 23** Second Chronicles focuses on the proper and improper worship of God as symbolized by the Jerusalem Temple. David planned the Temple; Solomon built it and then put on the greatest dedication service the world has ever seen. Worship in the Temple was superbly organized.

But several evil kings defiled the Temple and degraded worship so that the people revered idols more highly than God. Finally, King Nebuchadnezzar of Babylon destroyed the Temple (36:19). The

kings were gone, the Temple was destroyed, and the people were removed. The nation was stripped to its very foundation. But fortunately there was a greater foundation—God himself. When everything in life seems stripped away from us, we, too, still have God—his Word, his presence, and his promises.

**EXILE TO BABYLON** Despite Judah's few good kings and timely reforms, the people never truly changed. Their evil continued, and finally God used the Babylonian Empire, under Nebuchadnezzar, to conquer Judah, destroy Jerusalem, and take the people captive to Babylon.

# EZRA

NAME the truly great men and women of your lifetime. Celebrities, including politicians, war heroes, sports figures, and maybe your parents and special friends come to mind. You remember them because of certain acts or character qualities. Now, name some biblical heroes—figures etched in your mind through countless sermons and church school lessons. This list undoubtedly includes many who served God faithfully and courageously. Does your list include Ezra? Far from being well known, this unheralded man of God deserves to be mentioned in any discussion of greatness.

Ezra was a priest, a scribe, and a great leader. His name means "help," and his whole life was dedicated to serving God and God's people. Tradition says that Ezra wrote most of 1 and 2 Chronicles, Ezra, Nehemiah, and Psalm 119 and that he led the council of 120 men who compiled the Old Testament canon. The narrative of the book of Ezra is centered on God and his promise that the Jews would return to their land, as prophesied by Jeremiah (see the third note on 1:1). This message formed the core of Ezra's life. The last half of the book gives a very personal glimpse of Ezra. His knowledge of Scripture and his God-given wisdom were so obvious to the king that he appointed Ezra to lead the second emigration to Jerusalem, to teach the people God's Word, and to administer national life (7:14–26).

Ezra not only knew God's Word, he believed and obeyed it. Upon learning of the Israelites' sins of intermarriage and idolatry, Ezra fell in humility before God and prayed for the nation (9:1–15). Their disobedience touched him deeply (10:1). His response helped lead the people back to God.

Second Chronicles ends with Cyrus, king of Persia, asking for volunteers to return to Jerusalem to build a house for God. Ezra continues this account (1:1–3 is almost identical to 2 Chronicles 36:22, 23) as two caravans of God's people were returning to Jerusalem. Zerubbabel, the leader of the first trip, was joined by 42,360 pilgrims who journeyed homeward (chapter 2). After arriving, they began to build the altar and the Temple foundations (chapter 3). But opposition arose from the local inhabitants, and a campaign of accusations and rumors temporarily halted the project (chapter 4). During this time, the prophets Haggai and Zechariah encouraged the people (chapter 5). Finally, Darius decreed that the work should proceed unhindered (chapter 6).

After a 58-year gap, Ezra led a group of Jews from Persia. Armed with decrees and authority from Artaxerxes I, Ezra's task was to administer the affairs of the land (chapters 7—8). Upon arriving, he learned of intermarriage between God's people and their pagan neighbors. He wept and prayed for the nation (chapter 9). Ezra's example of humble confession led to national revival (chapter 10). Ezra, a man of God and a true hero, was a model for Israel, and he is a fitting model for us.

Read Ezra, the book, and remember Ezra, the man—a humble, obedient helper. Commit yourself to serving God as he did, with your whole life.

## VITAL STATISTICS

**PURPOSE:**
To show God's faithfulness and the way he kept his promise to restore his people to their land

**AUTHOR:**
Not stated, but probably Ezra

**ORIGINAL AUDIENCE:**
The exiles who returned from captivity

**DATE WRITTEN:**
Around 450 B.C., recording events from about 538–450 B.C. (omitting 516–458 B.C.); possibly begun earlier in Babylon and finished in Jerusalem

**SETTING:**
Ezra follows 2 Chronicles as a history of the Jewish people, recording their return to the land after the Captivity.

**KEY VERSES:**
"The Passover meal was eaten by the people of Israel who had returned from exile and by the others in the land who had turned from their immoral customs to worship the LORD, the God of Israel. Then they celebrated the Festival of Unleavened Bread for seven days. There was great joy throughout the land because the LORD had caused the king of Assyria to be favorable to them, so that he helped them to rebuild the Temple of God, the God of Israel" (6:21, 22).

**KEY PEOPLE:**
Cyrus, Zerubbabel, Haggai, Zechariah, Darius I, Artaxerxes I, Ezra

**KEY PLACES:**
Babylon, Jerusalem

**SPECIAL FEATURES:**
Ezra and Nehemiah were one book in the Hebrew Bible, and, with Esther, they comprise the post-captivity historical books. The post-captivity prophetic books are Haggai, Zechariah, and Malachi. Haggai and Zechariah should be studied with Ezra because they prophesied during the period of the reconstruction.

## THE BLUEPRINT

A. THE RETURN LED BY ZERUBBABEL
(1:1—6:22)
1. The first group of exiles returns
to the land
2. The people rebuild the Temple

B. THE RETURN LED BY EZRA (7:1—10:44)
1. The second group of exiles returns
to the land
2. Ezra opposes intermarriage

Finally given the chance to return to their homeland, the people started to rebuild the Temple, only to be stopped by opposition from their enemies. God's work in the world is not without opposition. We must not get discouraged and quit, as the returning people did at first, but continue on boldly in the face of difficulties, as they did later with encouragement from the prophets.

Ezra returned to Jerusalem almost 80 years after Zerubbabel, only to discover that the people had married pagan or foreign spouses. This polluted the religious purity of the people and endangered the future of the nation. Believers today must be careful not to threaten their walk with God by taking on the practices of unbelievers.

## MEGATHEMES

| THEME | EXPLANATION | IMPORTANCE |
|---|---|---|
| The Jews Return | By returning to the land of Israel from Babylon, the Jews showed their faith in God's promise to restore them as a people. They returned not only to their homeland but also to the place where their forefathers had promised to follow God. | God shows his mercy to every generation. He compassionately restores his people. No matter how difficult our present "captivity," we are never far from his love and mercy. He restores us when we return to him. |
| Rededication | In 536 B.C., Zerubbabel led the people in rebuilding the altar and laying the Temple foundation. They reinstated daily sacrifices and annual festivals, and rededicated themselves to a new spiritual worship of God. | In rededicating the altar, the people were recommitting themselves to God and his service. To grow spiritually, our commitment must be reviewed and renewed often. As we rededicate ourselves to God, our lives become altars to him. |
| Opposition | Opposition came soon after the altar was built and the Temple foundation laid. Enemies of the Jews used deceit to hinder the building for over six years. Finally, there was a decree to stop the building altogether. This opposition severely tested their wavering faith. | There will always be adversaries who oppose God's work. The life of faith is never easy. But God can overrule all opposition to his service. When we face opposition, we must not falter or withdraw, but keep active and patient. |
| God's Word | When the people returned to the land, they were also returning to the influence of God's Word. The prophets Haggai and Zechariah helped encourage them, while Ezra's preaching of Scripture built them up. God's Word gave them what they needed to do God's work. | We also need the encouragement and direction of God's Word. We must make it the basis for our faith and actions to finish God's work and fulfill our obligations. We must never waver in our commitment to hear and obey his Word. |
| Faith and Action | The urging of Israel's leaders motivated the people to complete the Temple. Over the years they had intermarried with idol worshipers and adopted their pagan practices. Their faith, tested and revived, also led them to remove these sins from their lives. | Faith led them to complete the Temple and to remove sin from their society. As we trust God with our hearts and minds, we must also act by completing our daily responsibilities. It is not enough to say we believe; we must make the changes God requires. |

## A. THE RETURN LED BY ZERUBBABEL (1:1—6:22)

After 70 years in exile, the captives from Judah were allowed to return to their homeland. Nearly 50,000 people made this journey. Upon arrival they began to rebuild the Temple, but became discouraged by opposition. After encouragement from Haggai and Zechariah, they returned to the task and completed the Temple. The message of the prophets still speaks to us today, encouraging us to continue building up God's church.

### 1. The first group of exiles returns to the land
*Cyrus Allows the Exiles to Return*

**1** In the first year of King Cyrus of Persia,* the LORD fulfilled the prophecy he had given through Jeremiah.* He stirred the heart of Cyrus to put this proclamation in writing and to send it throughout his kingdom:

1:1-3
//2 Chr 36:22-23
1:1
Jer 25:11-12;
29:10-14

**1:1a** The first year of Cyrus's reign over Babylon was 538 B.C.   **1:1b** See Jer 25:11-12; 29:10.

**1:1** The book of Ezra opens in 538 B.C., 48 years after Nebuchadnezzar destroyed Jerusalem, defeated the southern

kingdom of Judah, and carried the Jews away to Babylon as captives (2 Kings 25; 2 Chronicles 36). Nebuchadnezzar died

**1:2**
Isa 44:28; 45:1-13

**1:3**
Dan 6:26

²"This is what King Cyrus of Persia says:

"The LORD, the God of heaven, has given me all the kingdoms of the earth. He has appointed me to build him a Temple at Jerusalem, which is in Judah. ³Any of you who are his people may go to Jerusalem in Judah to rebuild this Temple of the LORD, the God of Israel, who lives in Jerusalem. And may your God be with you! ⁴Wherever this Jewish remnant is found, let their neighbors contribute toward their expenses by giving them silver and gold, supplies for the journey, and livestock, as well as a voluntary offering for the Temple of God in Jerusalem."

---

## PROPHECIES FULFILLED BY THE RETURN OF ISRAEL FROM EXILE

| Reference | Prophecy | Approximate Date | Fulfillment Date | Significance |
|---|---|---|---|---|
| Isaiah 44:28 | Cyrus would be used by God to guarantee the return of a remnant. Jerusalem would be rebuilt and the Temple restored. | 688 B.C. | 538 B.C. | As God named Cyrus even before he was born, God knows what will happen—he is in control. |
| Jeremiah 25:12 | Babylon would be punished for destroying Jerusalem and exiling God's people. | 605 B.C. | 539 B.C. | Babylon was conquered by Cyrus the Great. God may seem to allow evil to go unpunished, but consequences for wrongdoing are inevitable. God will punish evil. |
| Jeremiah 29:10 | The people would spend 70 years in Babylon; then God would bring them back to their homeland. | 594 B.C. | 538 B.C. | The 70 years of captivity passed (see the third note on 1:1), and God provided the opportunity for Zerubbabel to lead the first group of captives home. God's plans may allow for hardship, but his desire is for our good. |
| Daniel 5:17-30 | God had judged the Babylonian Empire. It would be given to the Medes and the Persians, forming a new world power. | 539 B.C. | 539 B.C. | Belshazzar was killed and Babylon was conquered the same night. God's judgment is accurate and swift. God knows the point of no return in each of our lives. Until then, he allows the freedom for us to repent and seek his forgiveness. |

God, through his faithful prophets, said that the people of Judah would be taken into captivity because of their sinfulness. But he also promised that they would return to Jerusalem and rebuild the city, the Temple, and the nation.

---

in 562, and because his successors were not strong, Babylon was overthrown by Persia in 539, just prior to the events recorded in this book. Both the Babylonians and the Persians had a relaxed policy toward their captives, allowing them to own land and homes and to take ordinary jobs. Many Jews such as Daniel, Mordecai, and Esther rose to prominent positions within the nation. King Cyrus of Persia went a step further: He allowed many groups of exiles, including the Jews, to return to their homelands. By doing this, he hoped to win their loyalty and thus provide buffer zones around the borders of his empire. For the Jews this was a day of hope, a new beginning.

**1:1** Cyrus, king of Persia (539–530 B.C.), had already begun his rise to power in the Near East by unifying the Medes and Persians into a strong empire. As he conquered cities, he treated the inhabitants with mercy. Although not a servant of Yahweh, Cyrus was used by God to return the Jews to their homeland. Cyrus may have been shown the prophecy of Isaiah 44:28–45:6, written over a century earlier, which predicted that Cyrus himself would help the Jews return to Jerusalem. Daniel, a prominent government official (Daniel 5:29; 6:28), would have been familiar with the prophecy. The book of Daniel has more to say about Cyrus.

**1:1** Jeremiah prophesied that the Jews would remain in captivity for 70 years (Jeremiah 25:11; 29:10). The 70-year period

has been calculated two different ways: (1) from the first captivity in 605 B.C. (2 Kings 24:1) until the altar was rebuilt by the returned exiles in 537 (Ezra 3:1-6), or (2) from the destruction of the Temple in 586 until the exiles finished rebuilding it in 515. Many scholars prefer the second approach because the Temple was the focus and heartbeat of the nation. Without the Temple, the Jews did not consider themselves reestablished as a nation.

**1:2** Cyrus was not a Jew, but God worked through him to return the exiled Jews to their homeland. Cyrus gave the proclamation allowing their return, and he gave them protection, money, and the Temple articles taken by Nebuchadnezzar. When you face difficult situations and feel surrounded, outnumbered, overpowered, or outclassed, remember that God's power is not limited to your resources. He is able to use anyone to carry out his plans.

**1:2-4** This proclamation permitted the Jews to work together to accomplish the huge task of rebuilding the Temple. Some did the actual building, while others operated the supply lines. Significant ventures require teamwork, with certain people serving in the forefront and others providing support. Each function is vital to accomplishing the task. When you're asked to serve, do so faithfully as a team member, no matter who gets the credit.

⁵Then God stirred the hearts of the priests and Levites and the leaders of the tribes of Judah and Benjamin to go to Jerusalem to rebuild the Temple of the LORD. ⁶And all their neighbors assisted by giving them articles of silver and gold, supplies for the journey, and livestock. They gave them many valuable gifts in addition to all the voluntary offerings.

⁷King Cyrus himself brought out the articles that King Nebuchadnezzar had taken from the LORD's Temple in Jerusalem and had placed in the temple of his own gods. ⁸Cyrus directed Mithredath, the treasurer of Persia, to count these items and present them to Sheshbazzar, the leader of the exiles returning to Judah.* ⁹This is a list of the items that were returned:

| | |
|---|---:|
| gold basins | 30 |
| silver basins | 1,000 |
| silver incense burners* | 29 |
| ¹⁰ gold bowls | 30 |
| silver bowls | 410 |
| other items | 1,000 |

¹¹In all, there were 5,400 articles of gold and silver. Sheshbazzar brought all of these along when the exiles went from Babylon to Jerusalem.

### Exiles Who Returned with Zerubbabel

**2** Here is the list of the Jewish exiles of the provinces who returned from their captivity. King Nebuchadnezzar had deported them to Babylon, but now they returned to Jerusalem and the other towns in Judah where they originally lived. ²Their leaders were Zerubbabel, Jeshua, Nehemiah, Seraiah, Reelaiah, Mordecai, Bilshan, Mispar, Bigvai, Rehum, and Baanah.

**1:8** Hebrew *Sheshbazzar, the prince of Judah.*   **1:9** The meaning of this Hebrew word is uncertain.

*Marginal cross-references:*
1:5 2 Chr 36:22
1:7 2 Kgs 24:13; 25:13-16; 2 Chr 36:7-18; Ezra 6:5
1:8 Ezra 5:14-16
2:1-70 //Neh 7:6-73
2:1 2 Kgs 24:14-16; 25:11; 2 Chr 36:20
2:2 Neh 7:7

---

**1:5** Cyrus was king over the entire region that had once been Assyria and Babylon. Assyria had deported the Israelites from the northern kingdom (Israel) in 722 B.C. Babylon, the next world power, had taken Israelites captive from the southern kingdom (Judah) in 586 B.C. Therefore, when the Medo-Persian Empire came to power, King Cyrus's proclamation of freedom went to all the original 12 tribes, but only Judah and Benjamin responded and returned to rebuild God's Temple. The 10 tribes of the northern kingdom had been so fractured and dispersed by Assyria, and so much time had elapsed since their captivity, that many may have been unsure of their real heritage. Thus, they were unwilling to share in the vision of rebuilding the Temple.

**1:5** God moved the hearts of the leaders, family heads, priests, and Levites and gave them a great desire to return to Jerusalem to rebuild the Temple. Major changes begin on the inside as God works on our attitudes, beliefs, and desires. These inner changes lead to faithful actions. After 48 years of captivity, the arrogant Jewish nation had been humbled. When the people's attitudes and desires changed, God ended their punishment and gave them another opportunity to go home and try again. In the New Testament, Paul reminds us that "God is working in you, giving you the desire and the power to do what pleases him" (Philippians 2:13). Doing God's will begins with your desires. Are you willing to be humble, to be open to his opportunities, and to move at his direction? Ask God to give you the desire to follow him more closely.

**1:5, 6** Many Jews chose to go to Jerusalem, but many more chose to remain in Babylon rather than return to their homeland. The journey back to Jerusalem was difficult, dangerous, and expensive, lasting over four months. Travel conditions were poor; Jerusalem and the surrounding countryside were in ruins; and the people living in the area were hostile.

Persian records indicate that many Jews in captivity had accumulated great wealth. Returning to Jerusalem would have meant giving up everything they had and starting over. Many people couldn't bring themselves to do that; they preferred wealth and security to the sacrifice that God's work would require. Their priorities were upside down (Mark 4:18, 19). We must not let our comfort, security, or material possessions prevent us from doing what God wants.

**1:7** When King Nebuchadnezzar ransacked the Temple, he took many of the valuable furnishings with him. What he did not take, he burned (2 Chronicles 36:18, 19). Most of the captured items were made of solid gold (1 Kings 7:48-50), and Cyrus kindly returned them to the Jews for the Temple they would soon rebuild.

**1:8** Either Sheshbazzar was the Babylonian name for Zerubbabel, one of the Jewish leaders during the first return (2:2; 3:8; 4:3), or he was a government official with responsibility for the returning party. The reasons Sheshbazzar may be identified with Zerubbabel are as follows: (1) Both were called governors (5:14; Haggai 1:1); (2) both laid the Temple foundation (3:8; 5:16); (3) Jews in exile were often given Babylonian names (see Daniel 1:7 where Daniel and his companions were given new names).

**1:9-11** Every article of gold and silver was a witness to God's protection and care. Although many years had passed, God delivered these Temple articles back to his people. We may be discouraged by events in life, but we must never give up our hope in God's promises to us. The turning point may be just ahead.

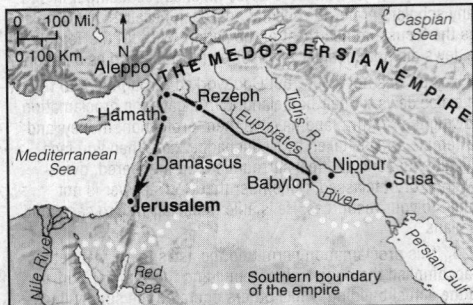

**THE JOURNEY HOME** The vast Medo-Persian Empire included all the area on this map and more. A group of exiles began the long trip back to their homeland. Many exiles, however, preferred the comfort and security they had in Babylon to the dangerous trip back to Jerusalem, and so they decided to stay in Babylon.

This is the number of the men of Israel who returned from exile:

2:5-6
Neh 7:10-11

| | |
|---|---|
| ³ The family of Parosh | 2,172 |
| ⁴ The family of Shephatiah | 372 |
| ⁵ The family of Arah | 775 |
| ⁶ The family of Pahath-moab (descendants of Jeshua and Joab) | 2,812 |
| ⁷ The family of Elam | 1,254 |
| ⁸ The family of Zattu | 945 |
| ⁹ The family of Zaccai | 760 |
| ¹⁰ The family of Bani | 642 |
| ¹¹ The family of Bebai | 623 |
| ¹² The family of Azgad | 1,222 |
| ¹³ The family of Adonikam | 666 |
| ¹⁴ The family of Bigvai | 2,056 |
| ¹⁵ The family of Adin | 454 |
| ¹⁶ The family of Ater (descendants of Hezekiah) | 98 |
| ¹⁷ The family of Bezai | 323 |
| ¹⁸ The family of Jorah | 112 |
| ¹⁹ The family of Hashum | 223 |
| ²⁰ The family of Gibbar | 95 |
| ²¹ The people of Bethlehem | 123 |
| ²² The people of Netophah | 56 |
| ²³ The people of Anathoth | 128 |
| ²⁴ The people of Beth-azmaveth* | 42 |
| ²⁵ The people of Kiriath-jearim,* Kephirah, and Beeroth | 743 |
| ²⁶ The people of Ramah and Geba | 621 |
| ²⁷ The people of Micmash | 122 |
| ²⁸ The people of Bethel and Ai | 223 |
| ²⁹ The citizens of Nebo | 52 |
| ³⁰ The citizens of Magbish | 156 |
| ³¹ The citizens of West Elam* | 1,254 |

**2:24** As in parallel text at Neh 7:28; Hebrew reads *Azmaveth.* **2:25** As in some Hebrew manuscripts and Greek version (see also Neh 7:29); Hebrew reads *Kiriath-arim.* **2:31** Or *of the other Elam.*

| THE RETURN FROM EXILE | Year | Number of People Returned | Persian King | Jewish Leader | Main Accomplishment |
|---|---|---|---|---|---|
| | 538 B.C. | 50,000 | Cyrus | Zerubbabel | They rebuilt the Temple, but only after a 20-year struggle. The work was halted for several years but was finally finished. |
| | 458 B.C. | 2,000 men and their families | Artaxerxes | Ezra | Ezra confronted the spiritual disobedience of the people, and they repented and established worship at the Temple. But the wall of Jerusalem remained in ruins. |
| | 445 B.C. | Small group | Artaxerxes | Nehemiah | The city was rebuilt, and a spiritual awakening followed. But the people still struggled with ongoing disobedience. |

Babylon, the once-mighty nation that had destroyed Jerusalem and carried the people of Judah into captivity, had itself become a defeated nation. Persia was the new world power, and under its new foreign policy, captured peoples were allowed to return to their homelands. The people of Judah and Israel returned to their land in three successive waves.

**2:2** The Nehemiah listed here is a different person from the one who rebuilt Jerusalem's walls 80 years later, and the Mordecai listed here is not the one who appears in the book of Esther.
**2:2** This first list is made up of men who were leaders. The same list occurs in Nehemiah 7:7.

**2:2-35** These people were from the tribes of Judah and Benjamin (1:5).
**2:3-35** This list is the major group of those returning, divided by families (2:3-20) or by cities (2:21-35). Verse 36 begins listing priests, Levites, and other Temple servants.

32 The citizens of Harim.................................................. 320
33 The citizens of Lod, Hadid, and Ono............................... 725
34 The citizens of Jericho ............................................... 345
35 The citizens of Senaah ............................................. 3,630

36 These are the priests who returned from exile:
   The family of Jedaiah (through the line of Jeshua) ................. 973
37 The family of Immer ................................................ 1,052
38 The family of Pashhur............................................... 1,247
39 The family of Harim ................................................ 1,017

40 These are the Levites who returned from exile:
   The families of Jeshua and Kadmiel (descendants of Hodaviah).......... 74
41 The singers of the family of Asaph ................................. 128
42 The gatekeepers of the families of Shallum, Ater, Talmon,
    Akkub, Hatita, and Shobai ........................................ 139

43 The descendants of the following Temple servants returned from exile:
   Ziha, Hasupha, Tabbaoth,
44 Keros, Siaha, Padon,
45 Lebanah, Hagabah, Akkub,
46 Hagab, Shalmai,* Hanan,
47 Giddel, Gahar, Reaiah,
48 Rezin, Nekoda, Gazzam,
49 Uzza, Paseah, Besai,
50 Asnah, Meunim, Nephusim,
51 Bakbuk, Hakupha, Harhur,
52 Bazluth, Mehida, Harsha,
53 Barkos, Sisera, Temah,
54 Neziah, and Hatipha.

55 The descendants of these servants of King Solomon returned from exile:
   Sotai, Hassophereth, Peruda,
56 Jaalah, Darkon, Giddel,
57 Shephatiah, Hattil, Pokereth-hazzebaim, and Ami.

58 In all, the Temple servants and the descendants of Solomon's servants numbered 392.

59 Another group returned at this time from the towns of Tel-melah, Tel-harsha, Kerub, Addan, and Immer. However, they could not prove that they or their families were descendants of Israel. 60 This group included the families of Delaiah, Tobiah, and Nekoda—a total of 652 people.

61 Three families of priests—Hobaiah, Hakkoz, and Barzillai—also returned. (This Barzillai had married a woman who was a descendant of Barzillai of Gilead, and he had taken her family name.) 62 They searched for their names in the genealogical records, but they were not found, so they were disqualified from serving as priests. 63 The governor told them not to eat the priests' share of food from the sacrifices until a priest could consult the LORD about the matter by using the Urim and Thummim—the sacred lots.

64 So a total of 42,360 people returned to Judah, 65 in addition to 7,337 servants and 200 singers, both men and women. 66 They took with them 736 horses, 245 mules, 67 435 camels, and 6,720 donkeys.

68 When they arrived at the Temple of the LORD in Jerusalem, some of the family leaders

**2:36**
1 Chr 24:7-18

**2:38**
1 Chr 9:12

**2:39**
1 Chr 24:8

**2:40**
Neh 12:24

**2:43**
1 Chr 9:2

**2:55-57**
Neh 7:57-60

**2:61**
2 Sam 17:27

**2:62**
Num 3:10;
16:39-40
Ezra 2:59

**2:63**
Exod 28:30
Lev 2:3, 10

**2:64**
Neh 7:66-67

**2:46** As in an alternate reading of the Masoretic Text (see also Neh 7:48); the other alternate reads *Shamlai.*

---

**2:59-63** Genealogies were very important credentials to the Hebrew people. If they could not prove they had descended from Abraham, they were not considered true Jews and were excluded from full participation in Jewish community life. In addition, some privileges were restricted to members of certain tribes. For example, only descendants of Levi (Abraham's great-grandson) could serve in the Temple.

**2:63** The governor mentioned here was probably Zerubbabel.

The sacred lots were probably the Urim and Thummim, two objects originally carried in the garment worn by the high priest. They were used to determine God's will in important matters. (For more on the Urim and Thummim, see the note on Leviticus 8:8.) The priests' share of food was their allotted portion of meat that was sacrificed on the altar.

**2:68, 69** As the Temple reconstruction progressed, everyone contributed freewill offerings according to his or her ability. Some

2:69
Ezra 8:25-34

2:70
Neh 7:73

made voluntary offerings toward the rebuilding of God's Temple on its original site, 69and each leader gave as much as he could. The total of their gifts came to 61,000 gold coins,* 6,250 pounds* of silver, and 100 robes for the priests.

70So the priests, the Levites, the singers, the gatekeepers, the Temple servants, and some of the common people settled in villages near Jerusalem. The rest of the people returned to their own towns throughout Israel.

## 2. The people rebuild the Temple
### The Altar Is Rebuilt

3:1
Neh 7:73; 8:1

3:2
Lev 1:1-17; 6:8-13
1 Chr 3:17-20
Ezra 2:2
Neh 12:1, 8
Hag 1:1
Zech 6:11

3:3
Num 28:1-8

3:4
Exod 23:16
Num 29:12
Neh 8:14

3:5
Exod 29:38, 42
Num 28:11-14

**3** In early autumn,* when the Israelites had settled in their towns, all the people assembled in Jerusalem with a unified purpose. 2Then Jeshua son of Jehozadak* joined his fellow priests and Zerubbabel son of Shealtiel with his family in rebuilding the altar of the God of Israel. They wanted to sacrifice burnt offerings on it, as instructed in the Law of Moses, the man of God. 3Even though the people were afraid of the local residents, they rebuilt the altar at its old site. Then they began to sacrifice burnt offerings on the altar to the LORD each morning and evening.

4They celebrated the Festival of Shelters as prescribed in the Law, sacrificing the number of burnt offerings specified for each day of the festival. 5They also offered the regular burnt offerings and the offerings required for the new moon celebrations and the annual festivals as prescribed by the LORD. The people also gave voluntary offerings to the LORD. 6Fifteen days before the Festival of Shelters began,* the priests had begun to sacrifice burnt offerings to the LORD. This was even before they had started to lay the foundation of the LORD's Temple.

### The People Begin to Rebuild the Temple

3:7
1 Kgs 5:9-11
2 Chr 2:10-16
Ezra 1:2; 6:3

7Then the people hired masons and carpenters and bought cedar logs from the people of Tyre and Sidon, paying them with food, wine, and olive oil. The logs were brought down from the Lebanon mountains and floated along the coast of the Mediterranean Sea* to Joppa, for King Cyrus had given permission for this.

**2:69a** Hebrew *61,000 darics of gold,* about 1,100 pounds or 500 kilograms in weight. **2:69b** Hebrew *5,000 minas* [3,000 kilograms]. **3:1** Hebrew *in the seventh month.* The year is not specified, so it may have been during Cyrus's first year (538 B.C.) or second year (537 B.C.). The seventh month of the ancient Hebrew lunar calendar occurred within the months of September/October 538 B.C. and October/November 537 B.C. **3:2** Hebrew *Jozadak,* a variant spelling of Jehozadak; also in 3:8. **3:6** Hebrew *On the first day of the seventh month.* This day in the ancient Hebrew lunar calendar occurred in September or October. The Festival of Shelters began on the fifteenth day of the seventh month. **3:7** Hebrew *the sea.*

---

were able to give huge gifts and did so generously. Everyone's effort and cooperation were required, and the people gave as much as they could. Often we limit our giving to 10 percent of our income. The Bible, however, emphasizes that we should give from the heart *all* that we are able (2 Corinthians 8:12; 9:6). Let your gift be decided by God's call to give generously, not by the amount you have left over.

**2:69** The money given was enough to start rebuilding the Temple. The people put what resources they had to their best use. They were enthusiastic and sincere, but this Temple would never match the splendor of Solomon's. The amount of money David gathered to start the building of Solomon's Temple was a thousand times more (1 Chronicles 22:14). Some people wept as they remembered the glorious Temple that had been destroyed (3:12).

**3:2, 3** The Jews built the altar as one of their first official acts. It symbolized God's presence and protection. It also demonstrated their purpose as a nation and their commitment to serve God alone. Zerubbabel sacrificed burnt offerings as the law of Moses instructed (Leviticus 1–7). The sacrifices were essential because they demonstrated that the people were seeking God's guidance, rededicating themselves to living as he commanded, and daily asking him to forgive their sins.

**3:3** The Jews were afraid they were going to be attacked by the surrounding people—a mixed group whose ancestors had been conquered by the Assyrians. Foreigners had been forced to resettle in the northern kingdom of Israel after Israel was defeated and her people taken captive in 722 B.C. (4:1, 2). This resettlement procedure was a common tactic of the Assyrians to prevent strong nationalistic uprisings by conquered peoples. Some of the resettled people in Israel had migrated south near

Jerusalem, and they may have thought the returning exiles threatened their claim on the land.

**3:4** The Festival of Shelters lasted seven days. During this time the people lived in temporary dwellings (tents, booths, lean-tos) as their ancestors had done years before as they journeyed through the wilderness on their way to the Promised Land. The festival reminded the people of God's past protection and guidance in the wilderness and of his continued love for them. The Festival of Shelters is described in detail in Leviticus 23:33-36.

**3:5** Almost immediately after arriving in the new land, the returning exiles built an altar. The people began worshiping God through sacrifices even before the Temple foundation was laid. After many years in captivity, they had learned their lesson—they knew that God does not offer special protection to people who ignore him. They had been carried off by the Babylonians when they were relatively strong; here they were few, weak, and surrounded by enemies. If ever they needed to rely on God's power, it was at this time. They realized the importance of obeying God from the heart, and not merely out of habit. If we want God's help when we undertake large tasks, we must make staying close to him our top priority.

**3:5** These sacrifices were originally set up under the law of Moses in Leviticus 1 and 6:8-13. The festivals are described in Leviticus 23. At the beginning of every month, they held a special observance (Numbers 10:10).

**3:7** When Solomon built the first Temple (2 Chronicles 2), he also exchanged food and olive oil—plentiful resources in Israel—for wood, a resource Israel lacked. The wood came from Tyre and Sidon that time, too.

⁸The construction of the Temple of God began in midspring,* during the second year after they arrived in Jerusalem. The work force was made up of everyone who had returned from exile, including Zerubbabel son of Shealtiel, Jeshua son of Jehozadak and his fellow priests, and all the Levites. The Levites who were twenty years old or older were put in charge of rebuilding the LORD's Temple. ⁹The workers at the Temple of God were supervised by Jeshua with his sons and relatives, and Kadmiel and his sons, all descendants of Hodaviah.* They were helped in this task by the Levites of the family of Henadad.

¹⁰When the builders completed the foundation of the LORD's Temple, the priests put on their robes and took their places to blow their trumpets. And the Levites, descendants of Asaph, clashed their cymbals to praise the LORD, just as King David had prescribed. ¹¹With praise and thanks, they sang this song to the LORD:

> "He is so good!
> His faithful love for Israel endures forever!"

Then all the people gave a great shout, praising the LORD because the foundation of the LORD's Temple had been laid. ¹²But many of the older priests, Levites, and other leaders who had seen the first Temple wept aloud when they saw the new Temple's foundation. The others, however, were shouting for joy. ¹³The joyful shouting and weeping mingled together in a loud noise that could be heard far in the distance.

### Enemies Oppose the Rebuilding

**4** The enemies of Judah and Benjamin heard that the exiles were rebuilding a Temple to the LORD, the God of Israel. ²So they approached Zerubbabel and the other leaders and said, "Let us build with you, for we worship your God just as you do. We have sacrificed to him ever since King Esarhaddon of Assyria brought us here."

| | |
|---|---|
| **3:8** | Num 4:3<br>1 Chr 23:24-32<br>Ezra 3:2; 4:2 |
| **3:9** | Ezra 2:40 |
| **3:10** | 1 Chr 6:31; 25:1 |
| **3:11** | 1 Chr 16:34, 41<br>2 Chr 7:3<br>Neh 12:24, 40<br>Ps 106:1 |
| **3:12** | Hag 2:3 |
| **4:1** | Ezra 4:7-10 |
| **4:2** | 2 Kgs 17:32; 19:37 |

**3:8** Hebrew *in the second month.* This month in the ancient Hebrew lunar calendar occurred within the months of April and May 536 B.C. **3:9** Hebrew *sons of Judah* (i.e., *bene Yehudah*). *Bene* might also be read here as the proper name Binnui; *Yehudah* is probably another name for Hodaviah. Compare 2:40; Neh 7:43; 1 Esdras 5:58.

---

**3:8** Why was the Lord's Temple begun first, even before the city wall? The Temple was used for spiritual purposes; the wall, for military and political purposes. God had always been the nation's protector, and the Jews knew that the strongest stone wall would not protect them if God was not with them. They knew that putting their spiritual lives in order was a far higher priority than assuring the national defense.

**3:8** It took from September (3:1; September was the seventh month because the year began in March) to April just to *prepare* to build the Temple. The exiles took time to make plans because the project was important to them. Preparation may not feel heroic or spiritual, but it is vital to any project meant to be done well.

**3:10, 11** David had given clear instructions concerning the use of music in worship services in the Temple (1 Chronicles 16; 25).

**3:10, 11** Completing the foundation for the Temple required great effort on the part of all involved. But no one tried to get praise for himself and his own hard work. Instead, everyone praised God for what had been done. All good gifts come from God—talents, abilities, strength, and leadership. We should thank God for what has been done in and through us!

**3:11** The Bible records many songs and musical events. For a list of such events, see the chart in Exodus 15, p. 119.

**3:12** Fifty years after its destruction, the Temple was being rebuilt (536 B.C.). Some of the older people remembered Solomon's Temple, and they wept because the new Temple would not be as glorious as the first one. But the beauty of the building was not nearly as important to God as were the attitudes of the builders and worshipers. God cares more about who we are than what we accomplish. Our world is always changing, and once-magnificent accomplishments decay and disappear. Seek to serve God wholeheartedly. Then you won't need to compare your work with anyone else's.

**3:12** Because the new Temple was built on the foundation of Solomon's Temple, the two structures were not that different in size. But the old Temple was far more ornate and was surrounded by many buildings and a vast courtyard. Both Temples were constructed of imported cedarwood, but Solomon's was decorated with vast amounts of gold and precious stones. Solomon's Temple took over seven years to build; Zerubbabel's took about four years. Solomon's Temple was at the hub of a thriving city; Zerubbabel's was surrounded by ruins. No wonder the people wept.

**3:13** The celebration after laying the Temple foundation was marked by contrasts of emotion—shouts of joy and sounds of weeping. Both were appropriate. The Holy Spirit can stimulate us both to rejoice over the goodness of his grace and to grieve over the sins that required him to correct us. When we come into the presence of almighty God, we may feel full of joy and thanksgiving, yet at the same time be sobered by our shortcomings.

**4:1-3** The enemies of Judah and Benjamin were people who had been relocated in the northern kingdom when Assyria conquered Israel (see 2 Kings 17 and the note on 3:3). In an attempt to infiltrate and disrupt the project, these people offered to help in the rebuilding project. They wanted to keep a close eye on what the Jews were doing. They were hoping to keep Jerusalem from becoming strong again. The Jews, however, saw through their ploy. Such a partnership with unbelievers would have led God's people to compromise their faith.

**4:1-6** Believers can expect opposition when they do God's work (2 Timothy 3:12). Unbelievers and evil spiritual forces are always working against God and his people. The opposition may offer compromising alliances (4:2), attempt to discourage and intimidate us (4:4, 5), or accuse us unjustly (4:6). If you expect these tactics, you won't be hindered by them. Move ahead with the work God has planned for you, and trust him to show you how to overcome the obstacles.

**4:2** These enemies claimed to worship the same God as Zerubbabel and the rest of the Jews. In one sense, this was true; they worshiped God, but they also worshiped many other gods (see 2 Kings 17:27-29, 32-34, 41). In God's eyes, this was not

**4:3**
Ezra 1:1-4; 6:3-5
Neh 2:20

³But Zerubbabel, Jeshua, and the other leaders of Israel replied, "You may have no part in this work. We alone will build the Temple for the LORD, the God of Israel, just as King Cyrus of Persia commanded us."

## ZERUBBABEL

Sometimes God's ownership of a project is recognized only *after* our best efforts have failed. It is dangerous to think that God is responsible for only insignificant details of a project while we take charge of the larger aspects. Instead, it is God who is in control and we only play a part in his overall plan. When God gives us important jobs to do, it isn't because he needs our help. Zerubbabel learned this lesson.

God's people had been exiled in Babylon for many years. Many had settled into comfortable lifestyles there and wanted to stay. There were, however, almost 60,000 who had not forgotten Judah. When Babylon was defeated in 539 B.C., the Persian ruler, Cyrus, allowed the Jews to return to Jerusalem and rebuild their Temple. Zerubbabel led the first and largest group back to the Promised Land.

Zerubbabel's leadership was by right and recognition. Not only was he a descendant of David, he also had personal leadership qualities. When the people arrived in Judah, they were given time to establish living quarters and then were called to begin the work. They began not by laying the city walls or constructing government buildings, but by rebuilding the altar, worshiping God together, and celebrating a feast. Under Zerubbabel's leadership, they established a spiritual foundation for their building efforts.

The Temple foundation was then quickly completed, and another round of celebration followed. But soon two problems arose. A few old men remembered Solomon's glorious Temple and were saddened at how much smaller and less glorious this one was. Also, some enemies of the Jews tried to infiltrate the workforce and stop the building with political pressure. Fear caused the work to grind to a halt. The people went to their homes, and 16 years passed.

We do not know what Zerubbabel did during this time. His discouragement, following those first months of excitement and accomplishment, must have been deep. Those feelings eventually hardened into hopelessness. So God sent the prophets Haggai and Zechariah to be Zerubbabel's encouraging companions. They confronted the people's reluctance and comforted their fears. The work began once again with renewed energy and was completed in four years.

Zerubbabel, like many of us, knew how to start well but found it hard to keep going. His successes depended on the quality of encouragement he received. Zerubbabel let discouragement get the better of him. But when he let God take control, the work was finished. God is always in control. We must not let circumstances or lack of encouragement slow us from doing the tasks God has given us.

| | |
|---|---|
| **Strengths and accomplishments** | • Led the first group of Jewish exiles back to Jerusalem from Babylon<br>• Completed the rebuilding of God's Temple<br>• Demonstrated wisdom in the help he accepted and refused<br>• Started his building project with worship as the focal point |
| **Weaknesses and mistakes** | • Needed constant encouragement<br>• Allowed problems and resistance to stop the rebuilding work |
| **Lessons from his life** | • A leader needs to provide not only the initial motivation for a project but the continued encouragement necessary to keep the project going<br>• A leader must find his/her own dependable source of encouragement<br>• God's faithfulness is shown in the way he preserved David's line |
| **Vital statistics** | • Where: Babylon, Jerusalem<br>• Occupation: Recognized leader of the exiles<br>• Relatives: Father: Shealtiel. Grandfather: Jehoiachin.<br>• Contemporaries: Cyrus, Darius, Zechariah, Haggai |
| **Key verses** | "Then he said to me, 'This is what the LORD says to Zerubbabel: It is not by force nor by strength, but by my Spirit, says the LORD of Heaven's Armies. Nothing, not even a mighty mountain, will stand in Zerubbabel's way; it will become a level plain before him! And when Zerubbabel sets the final stone of the Temple in place, the people will shout: "May God bless it! May God bless it!"'" (Zechariah 4:6, 7). |

Zerubbabel's story is told in Ezra 2:2—5:2. He is also mentioned in 1 Chronicles 3:19; Nehemiah 7:7; 12:1, 47; Haggai 1:1, 12, 14; 2:4, 21, 23; Zechariah 4:6–10; Matthew 1:12, 13; Luke 3:27.

worship—it was sin and rebellion. True worship involves devotion to God alone (Exodus 20:3-5). To these foreigners, God was just another "idol" to be added to their collection. Their real motive was to disrupt the Temple project. Believers today must beware of those who claim to be Christians but whose actions clearly reveal they are using Christianity to serve their own interests.

⁴Then the local residents tried to discourage and frighten the people of Judah to keep them from their work. ⁵They bribed agents to work against them and to frustrate their plans. This went on during the entire reign of King Cyrus of Persia and lasted until King Darius of Persia took the throne.*

**4:4**
Ezra 3:3

### Later Opposition under Xerxes and Artaxerxes

⁶Years later when Xerxes* began his reign, the enemies of Judah wrote a letter of accusation against the people of Judah and Jerusalem.

**4:6**
Esth 1:1
Dan 9:1

⁷Even later, during the reign of King Artaxerxes of Persia,* the enemies of Judah, led by Bishlam, Mithredath, and Tabeel, sent a letter to Artaxerxes in the Aramaic language, and it was translated for the king.

**4:7**
2 Kgs 18:26
Isa 36:11
Dan 2:4

⁸*Rehum the governor and Shimshai the court secretary wrote the letter, telling King Artaxerxes about the situation in Jerusalem. ⁹They greeted the king for all their colleagues— the judges and local leaders, the people of Tarpel, the Persians, the Babylonians, and the people of Erech and Susa (that is, Elam). ¹⁰They also sent greetings from the rest of the people whom the great and noble Ashurbanipal* had deported and relocated in Samaria and throughout the neighboring lands of the province west of the Euphrates River.* ¹¹This is a copy of their letter:

**4:8**
Ezra 5:6

"To King Artaxerxes, from your loyal subjects in the province west of the Euphrates River.

¹²"The king should know that the Jews who came here to Jerusalem from Babylon are rebuilding this rebellious and evil city. They have already laid the foundation and will soon finish its walls. ¹³And the king should know that if this city is rebuilt and its walls are completed, it will be much to your disadvantage, for the Jews will then refuse to pay their tribute, customs, and tolls to you.

**4:12**
Ezra 5:3, 9

**4:13**
Ezra 7:24
Neh 5:4

¹⁴"Since we are your loyal subjects* and do not want to see the king dishonored in this way, we have sent the king this information. ¹⁵We suggest that a search be made in your ancestors' records, where you will discover what a rebellious city this has been in the past. In fact, it was destroyed because of its long and troublesome history of revolt against the kings and countries who controlled it. ¹⁶We declare to the king that if this city is rebuilt and its walls are completed, the province west of the Euphrates River will be lost to you."

¹⁷Then King Artaxerxes sent this reply:

"To Rehum the governor, Shimshai the court secretary, and their colleagues living in Samaria and throughout the province west of the Euphrates River. Greetings.

¹⁸"The letter you sent has been translated and read to me. ¹⁹I ordered a search of the records and have found that Jerusalem has indeed been a hotbed of insurrection against many kings. In fact, rebellion and revolt are normal there! ²⁰Powerful kings have ruled over Jerusalem and the entire province west of the Euphrates River, receiving tribute, customs, and tolls. ²¹Therefore, issue orders to have these men stop their work. That city must not be rebuilt except at my express command. ²²Be diligent, and don't neglect this matter, for we must not permit the situation to harm the king's interests."

**4:18**
Neh 8:8

**4:20**
1 Kgs 4:21, 24
1 Chr 18:3
Ezra 4:13

**4:5** Darius reigned 521–486 B.C.  **4:6** Hebrew *Ahasuerus,* another name for Xerxes. He reigned 486–465 B.C.
**4:7** Artaxerxes reigned 465–424 B.C.  **4:8** The original text of 4:8–6:18 is in Aramaic.  **4:10a** Aramaic *Osnappar,*
another name for Ashurbanipal.  **4:10b** Aramaic *the province beyond the river;* also in 4:11, 16, 17, 20.
**4:14** Aramaic *Since we eat the salt of the palace.*

---

**4:4, 5** Discouragement and fear are two of the greatest obstacles to completing God's work. Most often they come when you least expect them. Discouragement eats away at our motivation, and fear paralyzes us so we don't act at all. Recognize these common barriers. Remember that God's people in every age have faced these problems and with God's help have overcome them. By standing together with other believers, you can overcome fear and discouragement and fulfill God's purposes for your life.

**4:6-23** In these verses, Ezra summarizes the entire story of the opposition to building the Temple, the walls, and other important buildings in Jerusalem. Chronologically, 4:6 fits between chapters 6 and 7; 4:7-23 refers to the events between Ezra 7 and

Nehemiah 1. Ezra grouped them here to highlight the persistent opposition to God's people over the years and God's ability to overcome it.

**4:7** This letter sent to King Artaxerxes may have been inscribed on a clay tablet, a fragment of pottery, or sheets of parchment.

**4:10** Ashurbanipal (669–627 B.C.) was the Assyrian king who completed the relocation of Israelite captives. He was the last of the strong Assyrian kings. After his death the nation quickly declined. Assyria was conquered by Babylon in 612.

**4:19, 20** Artaxerxes said that Jerusalem had been "a hotbed of insurrection against many kings." By reading the historical records, he learned that mighty kings had come from Jerusalem,

23When this letter from King Artaxerxes was read to Rehum, Shimshai, and their colleagues, they hurried to Jerusalem. Then, with a show of strength, they forced the Jews to stop building.

## The Rebuilding Resumes

**4:24**
Hag 1:1, 15
Zech 1:1

24So the work on the Temple of God in Jerusalem had stopped, and it remained at a standstill until the second year of the reign of King Darius of Persia.*

**5:1**
Ezra 6:14
Hag 1:1
Zech 1:1
**5:2**
Ezra 3:2
**5:3**
Ezra 1:3; 5:6, 9, 17;
6:6, 13
**5:4**
Ezra 5:10
**5:5**
Ezra 7:6, 28
Ps 33:18

**5** At that time the prophets Haggai and Zechariah son of Iddo prophesied to the Jews in Judah and Jerusalem. They prophesied in the name of the God of Israel who was over them. 2Zerubbabel son of Shealtiel and Jeshua son of Jehozadak* responded by starting again to rebuild the Temple of God in Jerusalem. And the prophets of God were with them and helped them.

3But Tattenai, governor of the province west of the Euphrates River,* and Shethar-bozenai and their colleagues soon arrived in Jerusalem and asked, "Who gave you permission to rebuild this Temple and restore this structure?" 4They also asked for the names of all the men working on the Temple. 5But because their God was watching over them, the leaders of the Jews were not prevented from building until a report was sent to Darius and he returned his decision.

**4:24** The second year of Darius's reign was 520 B.C. The narrative started in 4:1-5 is resumed at verse 24.
**5:2** Aramaic *Jozadak*, a variant spelling of Jehozadak. **5:3** Aramaic *the province beyond the river;* also in 5:6.

---

| THE PERSIAN KINGS OF EZRA'S DAY | Name | Date of Reign | Relationship to Israel |
|---|---|---|---|
| | Cyrus | 559–530 B.C. | Conquered Babylon. Established a policy of returning exiles to their homelands. Sent Zerubbabel to Jerusalem, financed his project, and returned the gold and silver articles that Nebuchadnezzar had taken from the Temple. He probably knew Daniel. |
| | Darius | 522–486 B.C. | Supported construction of the Temple in Jerusalem. |
| | Xerxes (Ahasuerus) | 486–465 B.C. | Was Esther's husband. Allowed the Jews to protect themselves against Haman's attempt to eliminate their people. |
| | Artaxerxes I | 465–424 B.C. | Had Nehemiah as his cup-bearer. Allowed both Ezra and Nehemiah to return to Jerusalem. |

---

and he may have feared that another would arise if the city were rebuilt. Solomon had ruled a huge empire (1 Kings 4:21), and Jerusalem's kings had rebelled against mighty powers. For example, Zedekiah rebelled against Nebuchadnezzar despite his oath of loyalty (2 Chronicles 36:13). Artaxerxes did not want to aid the rebuilding of a rebellious city and nation.

**4:23** Setbacks and standstills are painful and discouraging to God's workers. These exiles had received a double dose (see 4:1-5 and 4:6-22). Leaders should do everything to keep work from grinding to a halt; yet circumstances sometimes really are beyond our control. When you have been brought to a standstill, remember to still stand strong in the Lord.

**4:24** Ezra resumes his chronological account here. It may have been 10 years since the Israelites had worked on the Temple. It did not begin again until 520 B.C., the second year of Darius's reign (5:1ff).

**5:1** More details about the work and messages of Haggai and Zechariah are found in the books of the Bible that bear their names.

**5:1, 2** "The prophets of God were with them and helped them." God sometimes sends prophets to encourage and strengthen his people. To accomplish this, Haggai and Zechariah not only preached but also got involved in the labor. In the church today

God appoints prophetic voices to help us with our work (Ephesians 4:11-13). Their ministry should have the same effect upon us as Haggai's and Zechariah's had on Israel. "One who prophesies strengthens others, encourages them, and comforts them" (1 Corinthians 14:3). In turn, we should encourage those who bring God's words to us.

**5:3-5** The non-Jews who lived nearby attempted to hinder the construction of the Temple. But while the legal debate went on and the decision was under appeal, the Jews continued to rebuild. When we are doing God's work, others may try to delay, confuse, or frustrate us, but we can proceed confidently. God will accomplish his purposes in our world, no matter who attempts to block them. Just as he watched over the Jewish elders, he watches over you. Concentrate on God's purpose, and don't be sidetracked by intrigues or slander.

## Tattenai's Letter to King Darius

6This is a copy of the letter that Tattenai the governor, Shethar-bozenai, and the other officials of the province west of the Euphrates River sent to King Darius:

7"To King Darius. Greetings.

8"The king should know that we went to the construction site of the Temple of the great God in the province of Judah. It is being rebuilt with specially prepared stones, and timber is being laid in its walls. The work is going forward with great energy and success.

9"We asked the leaders, 'Who gave you permission to rebuild this Temple and restore this structure?' 10And we demanded their names so that we could tell you who the leaders were.

11"This was their answer: 'We are the servants of the God of heaven and earth, and we are rebuilding the Temple that was built here many years ago by a great king of Israel. 12But because our ancestors angered the God of heaven, he abandoned them to King Nebuchadnezzar of Babylon,* who destroyed this Temple and exiled the people to Babylonia. 13However, King Cyrus of Babylon,* during the first year of his reign, issued a decree that the Temple of God should be rebuilt. 14King Cyrus returned the

**5:11**
1 Kgs 6:1-38
2 Chr 3:1-2

**5:12**
2 Kgs 24:2, 10;
25:1, 8-11
2 Chr 36:6-20

**5:13**
Ezra 1:1-8

**5:14**
Ezra 1:7-8, 11;
5:16; 6:3-5
Dan 5:2

5:12 Aramaic *Nebuchadnezzar the Chaldean.*     5:13 King Cyrus of Persia is here identified as the king of Babylon because Persia had conquered the Babylonian Empire.

**THE MEDO-PERSIAN EMPIRE**
The Medo-Persian Empire included the lands of Media and Persia, much of the area shown on this map and more. The Jewish exiles were concentrated in the area around Nippur in the Babylonian province. The decree by King Cyrus that allowed the Israelites to return to their homeland and rebuild the Temple was discovered in the palace at Ecbatana.

Persian royal road
Southern boundary of the empire

**5:6-17** This letter, in comparison with the previous one (4:11-16), at least stated the facts correctly and asked a fair question. The earlier letter accused the Jews of preparing the foundation for the entire city, rather than reporting that they were doing only what they had been permitted by Cyrus to do. Perhaps the opposition simply thought that sending this letter to Babylon would create enough concern to stop the Jews from rebuilding the Temple. God had other plans, however. We can't predict how God will get his purposes accomplished, but we can certainly trust he will succeed!

**5:11** While rebuilding the Temple, the workers were confronted by the Persia-appointed governor, demanding to know who gave permission for their construction project (5:3). This could have been intimidating, but, as we learn from the letter, they boldly replied, "We are the servants of the God of heaven and earth."

It is not always easy to speak up for our faith in an unbelieving world, but we must. The way to deal with pressure and intimidation is to recognize that we are workers for God. Our allegiance is to him first, people second. When we contemplate the reactions and criticisms of hostile people, we can become paralyzed with fear. If we try to offend no one or to please everyone, we won't be effective. God is our leader, and his rewards are most important. So don't be intimidated. Let others know by your words and actions whom you really serve.

**5:13-17** Cyrus is called king of Persia in 1:1 and king of Babylon in 5:13. Because Persia had just conquered Babylon, Cyrus was king of both nations. Babylon is more important to this story because it was the location of the Hebrews' 70-year captivity. The Babylon in 5:17 may refer to the city of Babylon, which was the capital of the nation of Babylon.

gold and silver cups that Nebuchadnezzar had taken from the Temple of God in Jerusalem and had placed in the temple of Babylon. These cups were taken from that temple and presented to a man named Sheshbazzar, whom King Cyrus appointed as governor of Judah. 15The king instructed him to return the cups to their place in Jerusalem and to rebuild the Temple of God there on its original site. 16So this Sheshbazzar came and laid the foundations of the Temple of God in Jerusalem. The people have been working on it ever since, though it is not yet completed.'

**5:17**
Ezra 6:1-2

17"Therefore, if it pleases the king, we request that a search be made in the royal archives of Babylon to discover whether King Cyrus ever issued a decree to rebuild God's Temple in Jerusalem. And then let the king send us his decision in this matter."

### Darius Approves the Rebuilding

**6:1**
Ezra 5:17

**6** So King Darius issued orders that a search be made in the Babylonian archives, which were stored in the treasury. 2But it was at the fortress at Ecbatana in the province of Media that a scroll was found. This is what it said:

"Memorandum:

**6:3**
Ezra 3:10

3"In the first year of King Cyrus's reign, a decree was sent out concerning the Temple of God at Jerusalem.

"Let the Temple be rebuilt on the site where Jews used to offer their sacrifices, using the original foundations. Its height will be ninety feet, and its width will be ninety feet.*

**6:4**
1 Kgs 6:36

4Every three layers of specially prepared stones will be topped by a layer of timber. All expenses will be paid by the royal treasury. 5Furthermore, the gold and silver cups, which were taken to Babylon by Nebuchadnezzar from the Temple of God in Jerusalem, must be returned to Jerusalem and put back where they belong. Let them be taken back to the Temple of God."

**6:3** Aramaic *Its height will be 60 cubits* [27.6 meters]*, and its width will be 60 cubits.* It is commonly held that this verse should be emended to read: "Its height will be 30 cubits [45 feet, or 13.8 meters], its length will be 60 cubits [90 feet, or 27.6 meters], and its width will be 20 cubits [30 feet, or 9.2 meters]"; compare 1 Kgs 6:2. The emendation regarding the width is supported by the Syriac version.

## THE POSTEXILIC PROPHETS

God used these men to confront and comfort his people after their return to their homeland from exile in Babylon.

| Who? | When? | Ministered to These Contemporary Leaders | Main Message | Significance |
|---|---|---|---|---|
| Haggai | 520 B.C. | Zerubbabel Joshua | • Encouraged the leaders and the people to continue rebuilding the Temple, which God would bless<br>• Challenged the people's careless worship, which God would not bless | Disobedience and careless obedience of God's commands lead to judgment. |
| Zechariah | 520 B.C. | Zerubbabel Joshua | • Emphasized God's command to rebuild his Temple<br>• Gave the people another look at God's plan to bless the world through Israel and its coming King—the Messiah (9:9, 10) | Encouragement for today's effort sometimes requires that we remember God has a plan and purpose for tomorrow. Meanwhile the challenge is to live for him today. |
| Malachi | 430 B.C. | The priests are the only leaders mentioned | • Confronted the people and priests with God's promises of judgment on those who reject him and God's blessing on those who live as he desires | God expects our obedience to him to affect our attitude toward him and our treatment of one another. |

**6:1, 2** Many clay and papyrus documents recording business transactions and historical data have been discovered in this area (near present-day Syria). A great library and archives with thousands of such records have been discovered at Ebla in Syria.

6So King Darius sent this message:

6:6
Ezra 5:3; 6:13

"Now therefore, Tattenai, governor of the province west of the Euphrates River,* and Shethar-bozenai, and your colleagues and other officials west of the Euphrates River—stay away from there! 7Do not disturb the construction of the Temple of God. Let it be rebuilt on its original site, and do not hinder the governor of Judah and the elders of the Jews in their work.

8"Moreover, I hereby decree that you are to help these elders of the Jews as they rebuild this Temple of God. You must pay the full construction costs, without delay, from my taxes collected in the province west of the Euphrates River so that the work will not be interrupted.

9"Give the priests in Jerusalem whatever is needed in the way of young bulls, rams, and male lambs for the burnt offerings presented to the God of heaven. And without fail, provide them with as much wheat, salt, wine, and olive oil as they need each day. 10Then they will be able to offer acceptable sacrifices to the God of heaven and pray for the welfare of the king and his sons.

6:10
Ezra 7:23

11"Those who violate this decree in any way will have a beam pulled from their house. Then they will be tied to it and flogged, and their house will be reduced to a pile of rubble.* 12May the God who has chosen the city of Jerusalem as the place to honor his name destroy any king or nation that violates this command and destroys this Temple.

6:11
Ezra 7:26
Dan 2:5; 3:29
6:12
Deut 12:4-5, 11
1 Kgs 9:2-3

"I, Darius, have issued this decree. Let it be obeyed with all diligence."

### The Temple's Dedication

13Tattenai, governor of the province west of the Euphrates River, and Shethar-bozenai and their colleagues complied at once with the command of King Darius. 14So the Jewish elders continued their work, and they were greatly encouraged by the preaching of the prophets Haggai and Zechariah son of Iddo. The Temple was finally finished, as had been commanded by the God of Israel and decreed by Cyrus, Darius, and Artaxerxes, the kings of Persia. 15The Temple was completed on March 12,* during the sixth year of King Darius's reign.

6:13
Ezra 6:6
6:14
Ezra 5:1-2; 6:12;
7:1, 7-9, 11
Zech 4:9

16The Temple of God was then dedicated with great joy by the people of Israel, the priests, the Levites, and the rest of the people who had returned from exile. 17During the dedication ceremony for the Temple of God, 100 young bulls, 200 rams, and 400 male lambs were sacrificed. And 12 male goats were presented as a sin offering for the twelve tribes of Israel. 18Then the priests and Levites were divided into their various divisions to serve at the Temple of God in Jerusalem, as prescribed in the Book of Moses.

6:16
1 Kgs 8:63
2 Chr 7:5
6:17
Ezra 8:35
6:18
Num 3:6
1 Chr 23:6
2 Chr 35:4-5

### Celebration of Passover

19On April 21* the returned exiles celebrated Passover. 20The priests and Levites had purified themselves and were ceremonially clean. So they slaughtered the Passover lamb for all the returned exiles, for their fellow priests, and for themselves. 21The Passover meal was eaten by the people of Israel who had returned from exile and by the others in the land who had turned from their immoral customs to worship the LORD, the God of Israel. 22Then they

6:19
Exod 12:6
6:21
Num 9:6-7, 10-14
Ezra 9:1-15
Neh 9:2; 10:28
6:22
Exod 12:15
Ezra 1:1; 7:27

6:6 Aramaic *the province beyond the river;* also in 6:6b, 8, 13.   6:11 Aramaic *a dunghill.*   6:15 Aramaic *on the third day of the month Adar,* of the ancient Hebrew lunar calendar. A number of events in Ezra can be cross-checked with dates in surviving Persian records and related accurately to our modern calendar. This day was March 12, 515 B.C.   6:19 Hebrew *On the fourteenth day of the first month,* of the ancient Hebrew lunar calendar. This day was April 21, 515 B.C.; also see note on 6:15.

6:14 Ezra carefully pointed out that rebuilding the Temple was commanded first by God and then by the kings, who were his instruments. How ironic and wonderful that God's work was carried on by the discovery of a lost paragraph in a pagan library. All the opposition of powerful forces was stopped by a clause in a legal document. God's will is supreme over all rulers, all historical events, and all hostile forces. He can deliver us in ways we can't imagine. If we trust in his power and love, no opposition can stop us.

6:15 The Temple was completed in 515 B.C.

6:16-22 Feasting and celebration were in order at the great Temple dedication. This celebration was similar to the one that Solomon had when he dedicated the Temple in 1 Kings 8:63, although Solomon offered more than 200 times as many cattle and sheep. This Book of Moses was probably Leviticus. The

priests and Levites were organized into groups in order to "serve at the Temple of God . . . as prescribed in the Book of Moses." There is a time to celebrate, but there is also a time to work. Both are proper and necessary when worshiping God, and both are pleasing to him.

6:19 The Passover was an annual celebration commemorating Israel's deliverance from Egypt. After a series of plagues failed to convince Pharaoh to free the Israelites, God said that he would send the death angel to kill the firstborn in every household. But the angel would pass over every home that had the blood of a specified type of lamb on the sides and top of the doorframe. See Exodus 12:1-30 for the story of this event and the establishment of the Passover celebration.

6:22 There are many ways to pray for God's help. Have you ever considered that God would change the attitude of a celebrated the Festival of Unleavened Bread for seven days. There was great joy throughout the land because the LORD had caused the king of Assyria* to be favorable to them, so that he helped them to rebuild the Temple of God, the God of Israel.

## B. THE RETURN LED BY EZRA (7:1—10:44)

Ezra returned to the land with a second group of exiles, 80 years after Zerubbabel. Ezra found the Temple rebuilt, but the lives of the people in shambles. Intermarriage with foreigners opposed to God threatened the spiritual future of the nation. So Ezra prayed for guidance and then followed through with action. Christians today must also strive to keep their lives pure, refusing to let the sinful allurements of the world around them compromise their lifestyle.

**6:22** King Darius of Persia is here identified as the king of Assyria because Persia had conquered the Babylonian Empire, which included the earlier Assyrian Empire.

**EZRA**

It is not personal achievement but personal commitment to live for God that is important. Achievements are simply examples of what God can do through someone's life. The most effective leaders spoken of in the Bible had little awareness of the impact their lives had on others. They were too busy obeying God to keep track of their successes. Ezra fits that description.

About 80 years after the rebuilding of the Temple under Zerubbabel, Ezra returned to Judah with about 2,000 men and their families. He was given a letter from Artaxerxes instructing him to carry out a program of religious education. Along with the letter came significant power. But long before Ezra's mission began, God had shaped him in three important ways so that he would use the power well. First, as a scribe, Ezra dedicated himself to carefully studying God's Word. Second, he intended to apply and obey personally the commands he discovered in God's Word. Third, he was committed to teaching others God's Word and its application to life.

Knowing Ezra's priorities, it is not surprising to note his actions when he arrived in Jerusalem. The people had disobeyed God's command not to marry women of foreign nations. On a cold and rainy day, Ezra addressed the people and made it clear that they had sinned. Because of the sins of many, all were under God's condemnation. Confession, repentance, and action were needed. The people admitted their sin and devised a plan to deal with the problem.

This initial effort on Ezra's part set the stage for what Nehemiah would later accomplish. Ezra continued his ministry under Nehemiah, and the two were used by God to start a spiritual movement that swept the nation following the rebuilding of Jerusalem.

Ezra achieved great things and made a significant impact because he had the right starting place for his actions and his life: God's Word. He studied it seriously and applied it faithfully. He taught others what he learned. He is, therefore, a great model for anyone who wants to live for God.

| | |
|---|---|
| **Strengths and accomplishments** | • Committed to study, follow, and teach God's Word<br>• Led the second group of exiles from Babylon to Jerusalem<br>• May have written 1 and 2 Chronicles<br>• Concerned about keeping the details of God's commands<br>• Sent by King Artaxerxes to Jerusalem to evaluate the situation, set up a religious education system, and return with a firsthand report<br>• Worked alongside Nehemiah during the last spiritual awakening recorded in the Old Testament |
| **Lessons from his life** | • A person's willingness to know and practice God's Word will have a direct effect on how God uses his or her life<br>• The starting place for serving God is a personal commitment to serve him today, even before knowing what that service will be |
| **Vital statistics** | • Where: Babylon, Jerusalem<br>• Occupations: Scribe among the exiles in Babylon, king's envoy, teacher<br>• Relative: Father: Seraiah<br>• Contemporaries: Nehemiah, Artaxerxes |
| **Key verse** | "Ezra had determined to study and obey the Law of the LORD and to teach those decrees and regulations to the people of Israel" (Ezra 7:10). |

Ezra's story is told in Ezra 7:1—10:16 and Nehemiah 8:1—12:36.

person or group of people? God is infinitely powerful; his insight and wisdom transcend the laws of human nature.

While you must always change your attitude as a first step, remember that he can change the attitude of others.

## 1. The second group of exiles returns to the land
*Ezra Arrives in Jerusalem*

**7** Many years later, during the reign of King Artaxerxes of Persia,* there was a man named Ezra. He was the son* of Seraiah, son of Azariah, son of Hilkiah, ²son of Shallum, son of Zadok, son of Ahitub, ³son of Amariah, son of Azariah, son* of Meraioth, ⁴son of Zerahiah, son of Uzzi, son of Bukki, ⁵son of Abishua, son of Phinehas, son of Eleazar, son of Aaron the high priest.* ⁶This Ezra was a scribe who was well versed in the Law of Moses, which the LORD, the God of Israel, had given to the people of Israel. He came up to Jerusalem from Babylon, and the king gave him everything he asked for, because the gracious hand of the LORD his God was on him. ⁷Some of the people of Israel, as well as some of the priests, Levites, singers, gatekeepers, and Temple servants, traveled up to Jerusalem with him in the seventh year of King Artaxerxes' reign.

⁸Ezra arrived in Jerusalem in August* of that year. ⁹He had arranged to leave Babylon on April 8, the first day of the new year,* and he arrived at Jerusalem on August 4,* for the gracious hand of his God was on him. ¹⁰This was because Ezra had determined to study and obey the Law of the LORD and to teach those decrees and regulations to the people of Israel.

*Artaxerxes' Letter to Ezra*
¹¹King Artaxerxes had given a copy of the following letter to Ezra, the priest and scribe who studied and taught the commands and decrees of the LORD to Israel:

¹²*"From Artaxerxes, the king of kings, to Ezra the priest, the teacher of the law of the God of heaven. Greetings.

¹³"I decree that any of the people of Israel in my kingdom, including the priests and Levites, may volunteer to return to Jerusalem with you. ¹⁴I and my council of seven hereby instruct you to conduct an inquiry into the situation in Judah and Jerusalem, based on your God's law, which is in your hand. ¹⁵We also commission you to take with you silver and gold, which we are freely presenting as an offering to the God of Israel who lives in Jerusalem.

¹⁶"Furthermore, you are to take any silver and gold that you may obtain from the province of Babylon, as well as the voluntary offerings of the people and the priests that are presented for the Temple of their God in Jerusalem. ¹⁷These donations are to be used specifically for the purchase of bulls, rams, male lambs, and the appropriate grain offerings and liquid offerings, all of which will be offered on the altar of the Temple of your God in Jerusalem. ¹⁸Any silver and gold that is left over may be used in whatever way you and your colleagues feel is the will of your God.

¹⁹"But as for the cups we are entrusting to you for the service of the Temple of your God, deliver them all to the God of Jerusalem. ²⁰If you need anything else for your God's Temple or for any similar needs, you may take it from the royal treasury.

| Ref | |
|---|---|
| **7:1** | 1 Chr 6:9-14<br>Ezra 7:12, 21;<br>8:1–10:44<br>Neh 8:1-18 |
| **7:6** | Ezra 7:10-11,<br>21-29<br>Neh 8:9, 13 |
| **7:7** | Ezra 8:1-20 |
| **7:9** | Ezra 7:6 |
| **7:10** | Neh 8:1 |
| **7:12** | Ezek 26:7<br>Dan 2:37, 47 |
| **7:14** | Ezra 7:15, 28 |
| **7:16** | 1 Chr 29:6<br>Ezra 8:25 |
| **7:17** | Num 15:4-13<br>Deut 12:4-11 |
| **7:20** | Ezra 6:4 |

**7:1a** Artaxerxes reigned 465–424 B.C. **7:1b** Or *descendant;* see 1 Chr 6:14. **7:3** Or *descendant;* see 1 Chr 6:6-10. **7:5** Or *the first priest.* **7:8** Hebrew *in the fifth month.* This month in the ancient Hebrew lunar calendar occurred within the months of August and September 458 B.C. **7:9a** Hebrew *on the first day of the first month,* of the ancient Hebrew lunar calendar. This day was April 8, 458 B.C.; also see note on 6:15. **7:9b** Hebrew *on the first day of the fifth month,* of the ancient Hebrew lunar calendar. This day was August 4, 458 B.C.; also see note on 6:15. **7:12** The original text of 7:12-26 is in Aramaic.

---

**7:1** There is a gap of almost 60 years between the events of chapters 6 and 7. The story in the book of Esther occurred during this time, in the reign of Xerxes, who ruled from 486–465 B.C. Artaxerxes, his son, became king in 465, and Ezra returned to Jerusalem in 458.

**7:6** Eighty years after the first exiles returned to Jerusalem (2:1), Ezra himself returned. This was his first trip, and it took four months. The Temple had been standing for about 58 years. Up to this point in the narrative, Ezra had remained in Babylon, probably compiling a record of the events that had taken place.

Why did he have to ask the king if he could return? Ezra wanted to lead many Jews back to Jerusalem, and he needed a decree from the king stating that any Jew who wanted to return could do so. This decree would be like a passport in case they ran into opposition along the way. The king's generous decree showed that God was blessing Ezra (7:6, 28). It also indicated that

Ezra was probably a prominent man in Artaxerxes' kingdom. He was willing to give up this position in order to return to his homeland and teach the Israelites God's laws.

**7:6-10** Ezra demonstrates how a gifted Bible teacher can move God's people forward. He was effective because he was a well-versed student of the law of the Lord and because he was determined to obey those laws. He taught through both his speaking and his example. Like Ezra, we should determine both to study and to obey God's Word.

**7:14** The council of seven was Artaxerxes' supreme court (see Esther 1:14).

**7:14** When Nebuchadnezzar destroyed the Temple, he took a vast amount of plunder that may have included a copy of the Book of the Law (2 Chronicles 36:18). It is also possible that this book was brought by the Jews into exile and was confiscated and read by their conquerors. Foreign leaders who worshiped many gods liked to have records of the gods of other nations for military and political reasons.

7:21
Ezra 7:6

<sup>21</sup>"I, Artaxerxes the king, hereby send this decree to all the treasurers in the province west of the Euphrates River*: 'You are to give Ezra, the priest and teacher of the law of the God of heaven, whatever he requests of you. <sup>22</sup>You are to give him up to 7,500 pounds* of silver, 500 bushels* of wheat, 550 gallons of wine, 550 gallons of olive oil,* and an unlimited supply of salt. <sup>23</sup>Be careful to provide whatever the God of heaven demands for his Temple, for why should we risk bringing God's anger against the realm of the king and his sons? <sup>24</sup>I also decree that no priest, Levite, singer, gatekeeper, Temple servant, or other worker in this Temple of God will be required to pay tribute, customs, or tolls of any kind.'

7:25
Exod 18:21-25
Deut 16:18
Ezra 7:6, 10
7:26
Ezra 6:11-12

<sup>25</sup>"And you, Ezra, are to use the wisdom your God has given you to appoint magistrates and judges who know your God's laws to govern all the people in the province west of the Euphrates River. Teach the law to anyone who does not know it. <sup>26</sup>Anyone who refuses to obey the law of your God and the law of the king will be punished immediately, either by death, banishment, confiscation of goods, or imprisonment."

### Ezra Praises the LORD

7:27
Ezra 6:22
7:28
Ezra 9:9

<sup>27</sup>Praise the LORD, the God of our ancestors, who made the king want to beautify the Temple of the LORD in Jerusalem! <sup>28</sup>And praise him for demonstrating such unfailing love to me by honoring me before the king, his council, and all his mighty nobles! I felt encouraged because the gracious hand of the LORD my God was on me. And I gathered some of the leaders of Israel to return with me to Jerusalem.

### Exiles Who Returned with Ezra

8:1
Ezra 7:7

**8** Here is a list of the family leaders and the genealogies of those who came with me from Babylon during the reign of King Artaxerxes:

<sup>2</sup> From the family of Phinehas: Gershom.
From the family of Ithamar: Daniel.

8:3
Ezra 2:3

From the family of David: Hattush, <sup>3a</sup> a descendant of Shecaniah.
From the family of Parosh: Zechariah and 150 other men were registered.
<sup>4</sup> From the family of Pahath-moab: Eliehoenai son of Zerahiah and 200 other men.
<sup>5</sup> From the family of Zattu*: Shecaniah son of Jahaziel and 300 other men.
<sup>6</sup> From the family of Adin: Ebed son of Jonathan and 50 other men.
<sup>7</sup> From the family of Elam: Jeshaiah son of Athaliah and 70 other men.
<sup>8</sup> From the family of Shephatiah: Zebadiah son of Michael and 80 other men.
<sup>9</sup> From the family of Joab: Obadiah son of Jehiel and 218 other men.
<sup>10</sup> From the family of Bani*: Shelomith son of Josiphiah and 160 other men.

7:21 Aramaic *the province beyond the river;* also in 7:25.   7:22a Aramaic *100 talents* [3,400 kilograms].
7:22b Aramaic *100 cors* [18.2 kiloliters].   7:22c Aramaic *100 baths* [2.1 kiloliters] *of wine, 100 baths of olive oil.*
8:5 As in some Greek manuscripts (see also 1 Esdras 8:32); Hebrew lacks *Zattu.*   8:10 As in some Greek manuscripts (see also 1 Esdras 8:36); Hebrew lacks *Bani.*

---

**7:24** Why did Artaxerxes exempt Temple workers from paying taxes? He recognized that the priests and Levites filled an important role in society as spiritual leaders, so he freed them of tax burdens. While the Bible does not teach tax exemption for religious employees, Artaxerxes, a pagan king, recognized and supported the principle. Today, churches have the responsibility to keep worldly burdens off the shoulders of spiritual workers.

**7:27** In Ezra's doxology, he acknowledges that God "made the king want to beautify the Temple." God can change a king's heart (see Proverbs 21:1). When we face life's challenges, we often must work diligently and with extraordinary effort, realizing that God oversees all our work. Recognize his hand in your success, and remember to praise him for his help and protection.

**7:27, 28** Ezra praised God for all that God had done for him and through him. Ezra had honored God throughout his life, and God chose to honor him. Ezra could have assumed that his own greatness and charisma had won over the king and his princes, but he gave the credit to God. We, too, should be grateful to God for our success and not think that we did it in our own power.

**7:28** The speaker here is Ezra. He writes in the first person for the remainder of the book.

**EZRA'S JOURNEY** Ezra led a second group of exiles back to Judah and Jerusalem about 80 years after the first group. He traveled the dangerous route without military escort (8:22), but the people prayed and, under Ezra's godly leadership, arrived safely in Jerusalem after several months.

11 From the family of Bebai: Zechariah son of Bebai and 28 other men.
12 From the family of Azgad: Johanan son of Hakkatan and 110 other men.
13 From the family of Adonikam, who came later*: Eliphelet, Jeuel, Shemaiah, and
       60 other men.
14 From the family of Bigvai: Uthai, Zaccur,* and 70 other men.

### Ezra's Journey to Jerusalem

15I assembled the exiles at the Ahava Canal, and we camped there for three days while I went over the lists of the people and the priests who had arrived. I found that not one Levite had volunteered to come along. 16So I sent for Eliezer, Ariel, Shemaiah, Elnathan, Jarib, Elnathan, Nathan, Zechariah, and Meshullam, who were leaders of the people. I also sent for Joiarib and Elnathan, who were men of discernment. 17I sent them to Iddo, the leader of the Levites at Casiphia, to ask him and his relatives and the Temple servants to send us ministers for the Temple of God at Jerusalem.

18Since the gracious hand of our God was on us, they sent us a man named Sherebiah, along with eighteen of his sons and brothers. He was a very astute man and a descendant of Mahli, who was a descendant of Levi son of Israel.* 19They also sent Hashabiah, together with Jeshaiah from the descendants of Merari, and twenty of his sons and brothers, 20and 220 Temple servants. The Temple servants were assistants to the Levites—a group of Temple workers first instituted by King David and his officials. They were all listed by name.

21And there by the Ahava Canal, I gave orders for all of us to fast and humble ourselves before our God. We prayed that he would give us a safe journey and protect us, our children, and our goods as we traveled. 22For I was ashamed to ask the king for soldiers and horsemen* to accompany us and protect us from enemies along the way. After all, we had told the king, "Our God's hand of protection is on all who worship him, but his fierce anger rages against those who abandon him." 23So we fasted and earnestly prayed that our God would take care of us, and he heard our prayer.

24I appointed twelve leaders of the priests—Sherebiah, Hashabiah, and ten other priests—25to be in charge of transporting the silver, the gold, the gold bowls, and the other items that the king, his council, his officials, and all the people of Israel had presented for the Temple of God. 26I weighed the treasure as I gave it to them and found the totals to be as follows:

       24 tons* of silver,
       7,500 pounds* of silver articles,
       7,500 pounds of gold,
27 20 gold bowls, equal in value to 1,000 gold coins,*
       2 fine articles of polished bronze, as precious as gold.

**8:15** Ezra 7:7; 8:21, 31
**8:17** Ezra 2:43-54
**8:18** Ezra 7:6
**8:20** Ezra 2:43
**8:21** 2 Chr 20:3 Ezra 8:15, 31 Ps 27:11 Isa 58:3, 5
**8:22** 2 Chr 15:2 Ezra 7:6, 9, 28
**8:23** 2 Chr 33:13
**8:25** Ezra 7:15-16

**8:13** Or *who were the last of his family.*   **8:14** As in Greek and Syriac versions and an alternate reading of the Masoretic Text; the other alternate reads *Zabbud.*   **8:18** *Israel* is the name that God gave to Jacob.   **8:22** Or *charioteers.*   **8:26a** Hebrew *650 talents* [22 metric tons].   **8:26b** Hebrew *100 talents* [3,400 kilograms]; also in 8:26c.   **8:27** Hebrew *1,000 darics*, about 19 pounds or 8.6 kilograms in weight.

---

**8:15** Ezra's progress back to Jerusalem was halted while he waited to recruit Levites. God had called these men to a special service, and yet few were willing to volunteer when their services were needed. God has gifted each of us with abilities so we can make a contribution to his kingdom work (Romans 12:4-8). Don't wait to be recruited, but look for opportunities to volunteer. Don't hinder God's work by holding back. "God has given each of you a gift from his great variety of spiritual gifts. Use them well to serve one another" (1 Peter 4:10).

**8:21** Ezra and the people traveled approximately 900 miles on foot. The trip took them through dangerous and difficult territory and lasted about four months. They prayed that God would give them a safe journey. Our journeys today may not be as difficult and dangerous as Ezra's, but we should recognize our need to ask God for guidance and protection.

**8:21-23** Before making all the physical preparations for the journey, Ezra made spiritual preparations. Their prayers and fasting prepared them spiritually and showed their dependence on God for protection, their faith that God was in control, and their affirmation that they were not strong enough to make the trip without him. When we take time to put God first in any endeavor, we are preparing well for whatever lies ahead.

**8:23** Ezra knew God's promises to protect his people, but he didn't take them for granted. He also knew that God's blessings are appropriated through prayer, so Ezra and the people humbled themselves by fasting and praying. And their prayers were answered. Fasting humbled them because going without food was a reminder of their complete dependence on God. Fasting also gave them more time to pray and meditate on God.

Too often we pray glibly and superficially. Serious prayer, by contrast, requires concentration. It puts us in touch with God's will and can really change us. Without serious prayer, we reduce God to a quick-service pharmacist with painkillers for our every ailment.

**8:26** This was a large amount of treasure to transport, with or without a detachment of soldiers for protection.

**8:28**
Lev 21:6-8; 22:2-3
Isa 52:11

**8:29**
Ezra 8:33-34

**8:31**
Ezra 7:9

**8:32**
Neh 2:11

**8:33**
Ezra 8:30

**8:35**
Ezra 2:1; 6:17

**8:36**
Ezra 7:21

**9:1**
Exod 23:28
Lev 18:24-30
Deut 20:17

**9:2**
Exod 34:16

**9:3**
Neh 1:4

**9:4**
Exod 29:38-39

**9:5**
Exod 9:29, 33

**9:6**
2 Chr 28:9
Rev 18:5

²⁸And I said to these priests, "You and these treasures have been set apart as holy to the LORD. This silver and gold is a voluntary offering to the LORD, the God of our ancestors. ²⁹Guard these treasures well until you present them to the leading priests, the Levites, and the leaders of Israel, who will weigh them at the storerooms of the LORD's Temple in Jerusalem." ³⁰So the priests and the Levites accepted the task of transporting these treasures of silver and gold to the Temple of our God in Jerusalem.

³¹We broke camp at the Ahava Canal on April 19* and started off to Jerusalem. And the gracious hand of our God protected us and saved us from enemies and bandits along the way. ³²So we arrived safely in Jerusalem, where we rested for three days.

³³On the fourth day after our arrival, the silver, gold, and other valuables were weighed at the Temple of our God and entrusted to Meremoth son of Uriah the priest and to Eleazar son of Phinehas, along with Jozabad son of Jeshua and Noadiah son of Binnui—both of whom were Levites. ³⁴Everything was accounted for by number and weight, and the total weight was officially recorded.

³⁵Then the exiles who had come out of captivity sacrificed burnt offerings to the God of Israel. They presented twelve bulls for all the people of Israel, as well as ninety-six rams and seventy-seven male lambs. They also offered twelve male goats as a sin offering. All this was given as a burnt offering to the LORD. ³⁶The king's decrees were delivered to his highest officers and the governors of the province west of the Euphrates River,* who then cooperated by supporting the people and the Temple of God.

## 2. Ezra opposes intermarriage

### Ezra's Prayer concerning Intermarriage

**9** When these things had been done, the Jewish leaders came to me and said, "Many of the people of Israel, and even some of the priests and Levites, have not kept themselves separate from the other peoples living in the land. They have taken up the detestable practices of the Canaanites, Hittites, Perizzites, Jebusites, Ammonites, Moabites, Egyptians, and Amorites. ²For the men of Israel have married women from these people and have taken them as wives for their sons. So the holy race has become polluted by these mixed marriages. Worse yet, the leaders and officials have led the way in this outrage."

³When I heard this, I tore my cloak and my shirt, pulled hair from my head and beard, and sat down utterly shocked. ⁴Then all who trembled at the words of the God of Israel came and sat with me because of this outrage committed by the returned exiles. And I sat there utterly appalled until the time of the evening sacrifice.

⁵At the time of the sacrifice, I stood up from where I had sat in mourning with my clothes torn. I fell to my knees and lifted my hands to the LORD my God. ⁶I prayed,

**8:31** Hebrew *on the twelfth day of the first month,* of the ancient Hebrew lunar calendar. This day was April 19, 458 B.C.; also see note on 6:15.   **8:36** Hebrew *the province beyond the river.*

---

**8:28, 29** Every object used in Temple service was dedicated to God; each was considered a holy treasure to be guarded carefully and set apart for his special use. *Stewardship* means taking special care of whatever God has entrusted to you. This means considering what God has given to you as being *from* him and *for* his use. What has God entrusted to your care?

**9:1, 2** Since the time of the judges, Israelite men had married pagan women and then adopted their religious practices (Judges 3:5-7). Even Israel's great king Solomon was guilty of this sin (1 Kings 11:1-8). Although this practice was forbidden in God's law (Exodus 34:11-16; Deuteronomy 7:1-4), it happened in Ezra's day and again only a generation after him (Nehemiah 13:23-27). Opposition to mixed marriage was not racial prejudice because Jews and non-Jews of this area were of the same Semitic background. The reasons were strictly spiritual. A person who married a pagan was inclined to adopt that person's pagan beliefs and practices. If the Israelites were insensitive enough to disobey God in something as important as marriage, they wouldn't be strong enough to stand firm against their spouses' idolatry. Until the Israelites finally stopped this practice, idolatry remained a constant problem.

**9:2** Some Israelites had married pagan spouses and lost track of God's purpose for them. The New Testament says that believers should not "team up with those who are unbelievers" (2 Corinthians 6:14). Such marriages cannot have unity in the most important issue in life—commitment and obedience to God. Because

marriage involves two people becoming one, faith may become an issue, and one spouse may have to compromise beliefs for the sake of unity. Many people discount this problem only to regret it later. Don't allow emotion or passion to blind you to the importance of marrying someone with whom you can be united spiritually.

**9:3-5** Tearing one's clothes and pulling hair from one's head or beard were signs of self-abasement or humility. They expressed sorrow for sin.

**9:5-15** After learning about the sins of the people, Ezra fell to his knees in prayer. His heartfelt prayer provides a good perspective on sin. He recognized (1) that sin is serious (9:6); (2) that no one sins without affecting others (9:7); (3) that he was not sinless, although he didn't have a pagan wife (9:10ff); and (4) that God's love and mercy had spared the nation when they did nothing to deserve it (9:8, 9, 15). It is easy to view sin lightly in a world that sees sin as inconsequential, but we should view sin as seriously as Ezra did.

**9:5-15** Ezra confessed the sins of his people. Although he had not sinned in the way his people had, he identified with their sins. With weeping, he expressed shame for sin, fear of the consequences, and desire that the people would come to their senses and repent. His prayer moved the people to tears (10:1). Ezra demonstrated the need for a holy community around the rebuilt Temple. We need a holy community in our local churches, too. Even when we sin in the worst imaginable way, we can turn to God with prayers of repentance.

"O my God, I am utterly ashamed; I blush to lift up my face to you. For our sins are piled higher than our heads, and our guilt has reached to the heavens. 7 From the days of our ancestors until now, we have been steeped in sin. That is why we and our kings and our priests have been at the mercy of the pagan kings of the land. We have been killed, captured, robbed, and disgraced, just as we are today.

8 "But now we have been given a brief moment of grace, for the LORD our God has allowed a few of us to survive as a remnant. He has given us security in this holy place. Our God has brightened our eyes and granted us some relief from our slavery. 9 For we were slaves, but in his unfailing love our God did not abandon us in our slavery. Instead, he caused the kings of Persia to treat us favorably. He revived us so we could rebuild the Temple of our God and repair its ruins. He has given us a protective wall in Judah and Jerusalem.

10 "And now, O our God, what can we say after all of this? For once again we have abandoned your commands! 11 Your servants the prophets warned us when they said, 'The land you are entering to possess is totally defiled by the detestable practices of the people living there. From one end to the other, the land is filled with corruption. 12 Don't let your daughters marry their sons! Don't take their daughters as wives for your sons. Don't ever promote the peace and prosperity of those nations. If you follow these instructions, you will be strong and will enjoy the good things the land produces, and you will leave this prosperity to your children forever.'

13 "Now we are being punished because of our wickedness and our great guilt. But we have actually been punished far less than we deserve, for you, our God, have allowed some of us to survive as a remnant. 14 But even so, we are again breaking your commands and intermarrying with people who do these detestable things. Won't your anger be enough to destroy us, so that even this little remnant no longer survives? 15 O LORD, God of Israel, you are just. We come before you in our guilt as nothing but an escaped remnant, though in such a condition none of us can stand in your presence."

## The People Confess Their Sin

**10** While Ezra prayed and made this confession, weeping and lying face down on the ground in front of the Temple of God, a very large crowd of people from Israel—men, women, and children—gathered and wept bitterly with him. 2 Then Shecaniah son of Jehiel, a descendant of Elam, said to Ezra, "We have been unfaithful to our God, for we have married these pagan women of the land. But in spite of this there is hope for Israel. 3 Let us now make a covenant with our God to divorce our pagan wives and to send them away with their children. We will follow the advice given by you and by the others who respect the commands of our God. Let it be done according to the Law of God. 4 Get up, for it is your duty to tell us how to proceed in setting things straight. We are behind you, so be strong and take action."

5 So Ezra stood up and demanded that the leaders of the priests and the Levites and all the people of Israel swear that they would do as Shecaniah had said. And they all swore a solemn oath. 6 Then Ezra left the front of the Temple of God and went to the room of Jehohanan son of Eliashib. He spent the night* there without eating or drinking anything. He was still in mourning because of the unfaithfulness of the returned exiles.

10:6 As in parallel text at 1 Esdras 9:2; Hebrew reads *He went.*

**9:9**
Exod 1:11-14
Neh 9:36-37
Ps 106:45-46

**9:12**
Deut 7:3

**9:14**
Deut 9:7-8, 13-14
**9:15**
Neh 9:33-34
Ps 130:3
Dan 9:7-11

**10:1**
2 Chr 20:9
Dan 9:4, 20
**10:2**
Ezra 9:2; 10:11
Neh 13:27
**10:3**
Deut 7:2-3

**10:5**
Neh 5:12; 13:25
**10:6**
Deut 9:18

---

**9:9** Building a wall was not only a matter of civic pride or architectural beauty; it was essential for security and defense against robbers and marauders (see 9:7). God in his kindness had given them new life and protection.

**9:15** Ezra recognized that if God gave the people the justice they deserved, they would not be able to stand before him. Often we cry out for justice when we feel abused and unfairly treated. In those moments, we forget the reality of our own sin and the righteous judgment we deserve. How fortunate we are that God gives us mercy and grace rather than only justice. The next time you ask God for fair treatment, pause to think what would happen if God gave you what you really deserve. Plead instead for his mercy.

**10:1** Ezra set the standard of repentance by his own behavior. His weeping brought others to the point of sorrow. Some may respond when we tell them what to do, but more will follow if we show them what to do and participate ourselves. In this case, Ezra's actions actually motivated a leader to make a significant

stand. We can never predict who will follow or benefit from our example.

**10:3** Why were the men commanded to send away their wives and children? Although the measure was extreme, intermarriage to pagans was strictly forbidden (Deuteronomy 7:3, 4). Even the priests and Levites had intermarried, which could be compared today to a Christian marrying a devil worshiper. Although a severe solution, it only involved 113 of the approximately 29,000 families.

Ezra's strong act, though very difficult for some, was necessary to preserve Israel as a nation committed to God. Some of the exiles of the northern kingdom of Israel had lost both their spiritual and physical identity through intermarriage. Their pagan spouses had caused the people to worship idols. Ezra did not want this to happen to the exiles of the southern kingdom of Judah.

**10:3, 4, 11** Following Ezra's earnest prayer, the people confessed their sin to God. Then they asked for direction in restoring their relationship with God. True repentance does not end with

10:9
1 Sam 12:17-18
Ezra 9:4

10:11
Lev 26:40
Ezra 10:3

10:14
2 Chr 29:10; 30:8

10:19
Lev 5:15

7 Then a proclamation was made throughout Judah and Jerusalem that all the exiles should come to Jerusalem. 8 Those who failed to come within three days would, if the leaders and elders so decided, forfeit all their property and be expelled from the assembly of the exiles. 9 Within three days, all the people of Judah and Benjamin had gathered in Jerusalem. This took place on December 19,* and all the people were sitting in the square before the Temple of God. They were trembling both because of the seriousness of the matter and because it was raining. 10 Then Ezra the priest stood and said to them: "You have committed a terrible sin. By marrying pagan women, you have increased Israel's guilt. 11 So now confess your sin to the Lord, the God of your ancestors, and do what he demands. Separate yourselves from the people of the land and from these pagan women."

12 Then the whole assembly raised their voices and answered, "Yes, you are right; we must do as you say!" 13 Then they added, "This isn't something that can be done in a day or two, for many of us are involved in this extremely sinful affair. And this is the rainy season, so we cannot stay out here much longer. 14 Let our leaders act on behalf of us all. Let everyone who has a pagan wife come at a scheduled time, accompanied by the leaders and judges of his city, so that the fierce anger of our God concerning this affair may be turned away from us."

15 Only Jonathan son of Asahel and Jahzeiah son of Tikvah opposed this course of action, and they were supported by Meshullam and Shabbethai the Levite.

16 So this was the plan they followed. Ezra selected leaders to represent their families, designating each of the representatives by name. On December 29,* the leaders sat down to investigate the matter. 17 By March 27, the first day of the new year,* they had finished dealing with all the men who had married pagan wives.

## Those Guilty of Intermarriage

18 These are the priests who had married pagan wives:

From the family of Jeshua son of Jehozadak* and his brothers: Maaseiah, Eliezer, Jarib, and Gedaliah. 19 They vowed to divorce their wives, and they each acknowledged their guilt by offering a ram as a guilt offering.

20 From the family of Immer: Hanani and Zebadiah.

21 From the family of Harim: Maaseiah, Elijah, Shemaiah, Jehiel, and Uzziah.

22 From the family of Pashhur: Elioenai, Maaseiah, Ishmael, Nethanel, Jozabad, and Elasah.

23 These are the Levites who were guilty: Jozabad, Shimei, Kelaiah (also called Kelita), Pethahiah, Judah, and Eliezer.

24 This is the singer who was guilty: Eliashib.

These are the gatekeepers who were guilty: Shallum, Telem, and Uri.

25 These are the other people of Israel who were guilty:

From the family of Parosh: Ramiah, Izziah, Malkijah, Mijamin, Eleazar, Hashabiah,* and Benaiah.

26 From the family of Elam: Mattaniah, Zechariah, Jehiel, Abdi, Jeremoth, and Elijah.

27 From the family of Zattu: Elioenai, Eliashib, Mattaniah, Jeremoth, Zabad, and Aziza.

28 From the family of Bebai: Jehohanan, Hananiah, Zabbai, and Athlai.

29 From the family of Bani: Meshullam, Malluch, Adaiah, Jashub, Sheal, and Jeremoth.

10:9 Hebrew *on the twentieth day of the ninth month,* of the ancient Hebrew lunar calendar. This day was December 19, 458 B.C.; also see note on 6:15.   10:16 Hebrew *On the first day of the tenth month,* of the ancient Hebrew lunar calendar. This day was December 29, 458 B.C.; also see note on 6:15.   10:17 Hebrew *By the first day of the first month,* of the ancient Hebrew lunar calendar. This day was March 27, 457 B.C.; also see note on 6:15.   10:18 Hebrew *Jozadak,* a variant spelling of Jehozadak.   10:25 As in parallel text at 1 Esdras 9:26; Hebrew reads *Malkijah.*

words of confession—that would be mere lip service. It must lead to changed attitudes and behavior. When you sin and are truly sorry, confess this to God, ask his forgiveness, and accept his grace and mercy. Then, as an act of thankfulness for your forgiveness, make the needed corrections.

**10:8** To forfeit one's property meant to be disinherited, to lose one's legal right to own land. This was to ensure that no pagan children would inherit Israel's land. In addition, the person who refused to come to Jerusalem would be expelled from the assembly of the exiles and not be allowed to worship in the Temple. The Jews considered this a horrible punishment.

**10:11** As believers in Christ, all our sins are forgiven. His death cleansed us from all sin. Why do we then still confess our sins? Confession is more than appropriating Christ's forgiveness for what we have done wrong. Confession is agreeing with God that our thoughts, words, and actions are wrong and contrary to his will. It is recommitting ourselves to do his will and renouncing any acts of disobedience. We do not have to confess sins that were previously confessed. Confession involves turning away from all known sin and asking God for fresh power to live for him.

30From the family of Pahath-moab: Adna, Kelal, Benaiah, Maaseiah, Mattaniah, Bezalel, Binnui, and Manasseh.

31From the family of Harim: Eliezer, Ishijah, Malkijah, Shemaiah, Shimeon, 32Benjamin, Malluch, and Shemariah.

33From the family of Hashum: Mattenai, Mattattah, Zabad, Eliphelet, Jeremai, Manasseh, and Shimei.

34From the family of Bani: Maadai, Amram, Uel, 35Benaiah, Bedeiah, Keluhi, 36Vaniah, Meremoth, Eliashib, 37Mattaniah, Mattenai, and Jaasu.

38From the family of Binnui*: Shimei, 39Shelemiah, Nathan, Adaiah, 40Macnadebai, Shashai, Sharai, 41Azarel, Shelemiah, Shemariah, 42Shallum, Amariah, and Joseph.

43From the family of Nebo: Jeiel, Mattithiah, Zabad, Zebina, Jaddai, Joel, and Benaiah.

44Each of these men had a pagan wife, and some even had children by these wives.*

**10:44**
Ezra 10:3

10:37-38 As in Greek version; Hebrew reads *Jaasu*, 38*Bani, Binnui*.   10:44 Or *and they sent them away with their children*. The meaning of the Hebrew is uncertain.

---

**10:44** The book of Ezra opens with God's Temple in ruins and the people of Judah captive in Babylon. Ezra tells of the return of God's people, the rebuilding of the Temple, and the restoration of the sacrificial worship system. Similarly, God is able to restore and rebuild the lives of people today. No one is so far away from God that he or she cannot be restored. Repentance is all that is required. No matter how far we have strayed or how long it has been since we have worshiped God, he is able to restore our relationship to him and rebuild our lives.

# NEHEMIAH

| Jerusalem destroyed; exiles go to Babylon 586 B.C. | First exiles return to Jerusalem 538 | Temple completed 515 | Xerxes becomes king of Persia 486 | Artaxerxes I becomes king of Persia 465 | Ezra comes to Jerusalem 458 | Nehemiah comes to Jerusalem; wall completed 445 | Nehemiah returns to Babylon 433 | Nehemiah goes back to Jerusalem 432 | Malachi begins his ministry 430(?) |
|---|---|---|---|---|---|---|---|---|---|

"WHAT this church needs is . . . !" "I can't believe our government officials. If I were there I would . . . !" "Our schools are really in bad shape. Someone ought to do something!"

Gripers, complainers, self-proclaimed prophets, and "armchair quarterbacks" abound. It is easy to analyze, scrutinize, and *talk* about all the problems in the world. But what we really need are people who will not just discuss a situation but who will *do* something about it!

Nehemiah saw a problem and was distressed. Instead of complaining or wallowing in self-pity and grief, he took action. Nehemiah knew that God wanted him to motivate the Jews to rebuild Jerusalem's walls, so he left a responsible position in the Persian government to do what God wanted. Nehemiah knew God could use his talents to get the job done. From the moment he arrived in Jerusalem, everyone knew who was in charge. He organized, managed, supervised, encouraged, met opposition, confronted injustice, and kept going until the walls were built. Nehemiah was a man of action.

The story begins with Nehemiah talking with fellow Jews who reported that the walls and gates of Jerusalem were in disrepair. This was disturbing news, and rebuilding those walls became Nehemiah's burden. At the appropriate time, Nehemiah asked King Artaxerxes for permission to go to Jerusalem to rebuild its fallen walls. The king approved.

Armed with royal letters, Nehemiah traveled to Jerusalem. He organized the people into groups and assigned them to specific sections of the wall (chapter 3). The construction project was not without opposition, however. Sanballat, Tobiah, and others tried to halt the work with insults, ridicule, threats, and sabotage. Some of the workers became fearful; others became weary. In each case, Nehemiah employed a strategy to frustrate the enemies—prayer, encouragement, guard duty, consolidation (chapter 4). But a different problem arose—an internal one. Rich Jews were profiteering off the plight of their working countrymen. Hearing of their oppression and greed, Nehemiah confronted the extortioners face to face (chapter 5). Then, with the walls almost complete, Sanballat, Tobiah, and company tried one last time to stop Nehemiah. But Nehemiah stood firm, and the wall was finished in just 52 days. What a tremendous monument to God's love and faithfulness. Enemies and friends alike knew that God had helped (chapter 6).

After building the walls, Nehemiah continued to organize the people, taking a registration and appointing gatekeepers, Levites, and other officials (chapter 7). Ezra led the city in worship and Bible instruction (chapters 8—9). This led to a reaffirmation of faith and religious revival as the people promised to serve God faithfully (chapters 10—11).

Nehemiah closes with the listing of the clans and their leaders, the dedication of the new wall of Jerusalem, and the purging of sin from the land (chapters 12—13). As you read this book, watch Nehemiah in action—and determine to be a person on whom God can depend to *act* for him in the world.

## VITAL STATISTICS

**PURPOSE:**
Nehemiah is the last of the Old Testament historical books. It records the history of the third return to Jerusalem after captivity, telling how the walls were rebuilt and the people were renewed in their faith.

**AUTHOR:**
Much of the book is written in the first person, suggesting Nehemiah as the author. Nehemiah probably wrote the book with Ezra serving as editor.

**ORIGINAL AUDIENCE:**
The exiles who returned from captivity

**DATE WRITTEN:**
Approximately 445–432 B.C.

**SETTING:**
Zerubbabel led the first return to Jerusalem in 538 B.C. In 458, Ezra led the second return. Finally, in 445, Nehemiah returned with the third group of exiles to rebuild the city walls.

**KEY VERSES:**
"So on October 2 the wall was finished—just fifty-two days after we had begun. When our enemies and the surrounding nations heard about it, they were frightened and humiliated. They realized this work had been done with the help of our God" (6:15, 16).

**KEY PEOPLE:**
Nehemiah, Ezra, Sanballat, Tobiah

**KEY PLACE:**
Jerusalem

**SPECIAL FEATURES:**
The book shows the fulfillment of the prophecies of Zechariah and Daniel concerning the rebuilding of Jerusalem's walls.

## THE BLUEPRINT

A. REBUILDING THE WALL
   (1:1—7:73)
   1. Nehemiah returns to Jerusalem
   2. Nehemiah leads the people

Nehemiah's life is an example of leadership and organization. Giving up a comfortable and wealthy position in Persia, he returned to the fractured homeland of his ancestors and rallied the people to rebuild Jerusalem's wall. In the face of opposition, he used wise defense measures to care for the people and to keep the project moving. To accomplish more for the sake of God's Kingdom, we must pray, persevere, and sacrifice, as did Nehemiah.

B. REFORMING THE PEOPLE
   (7:73—13:31)
   1. Ezra renews the covenant
   2. Nehemiah establishes policies

After the wall was rebuilt, Ezra read the law to the people, bringing about national repentance. Nehemiah and Ezra were very different people, yet God used them both to lead the nation. Remember, there is a place for you in God's work even if you're different from most other people. God uses each person in a unique way to accomplish his purposes.

## MEGATHEMES

| THEME | EXPLANATION | IMPORTANCE |
|---|---|---|
| Vision | Although the Jews completed the Temple in 515 B.C., the city walls remained in shambles for the next 70 years. These walls represented power, protection, and beauty to the city of Jerusalem. They were also desperately needed to protect the Temple from attack and to ensure the continuity of worship. God put the desire to rebuild the walls in Nehemiah's heart, giving him a vision for the work. | Does God have a vision for us? Are there "walls" that need to be built today? God still wants his people to be united and trained to do his work. As we recognize deep needs in our world, God can give us the vision and desire to "build." With that vision, we can mobilize others to pray and put together a plan of action. |
| Prayer | Both Nehemiah and Ezra responded to problems with prayer. When Nehemiah began his work, he recognized the problem, immediately prayed, and then acted on the problem. | Prayer is still God's mighty force in solving problems today. Prayer and action go hand in hand. Through prayer, God guides our preparation, teamwork, and diligent efforts to carry out his will. |
| Leadership | Nehemiah demonstrated excellent leadership. He was spiritually ready to heed God's call. He used careful planning, teamwork, problem solving, and courage to get the work done. Although he had tremendous faith, he never avoided the extra work necessary for good leadership. | Being God's leader is not just gaining recognition, holding a position, or being the boss. It requires planning, hard work, courage, and perseverance. Positive expectations are never a substitute for doing the difficult work. And in order to lead others, you need to listen for God's direction in your own life. |
| Problems | After the work began, Nehemiah faced scorn, slander, and threats from enemies, as well as fear, conflict, and discouragement from his own workers. Although these problems were difficult, they did not stop Nehemiah from finishing the work. | When difficulties come, there is a tendency for conflict and discouragement to set in. We must recognize that there are no triumphs without troubles. When problems arise, we must face them squarely and press on to complete God's work. |
| Repentance/ Revival | Although God had enabled them to build the wall, the work wasn't complete until the people rebuilt their lives spiritually. Ezra instructed the people in God's Word. As they listened, they recognized the sin in their lives, admitted it, and took steps to remove it. | Recognizing and admitting sin are not enough; revival must result in reform, or it is merely the expression of enthusiasm. God does not want halfhearted measures. We must not only remove sin from our lives but also ask God to move into the center of all we do. |

## A. REBUILDING THE WALL (1:1—7:73)

Despite the fact that the returned exiles had been in Jerusalem for many years, the walls of the city remained unrepaired, leaving its people defenseless and vulnerable. Upon hearing this news, Nehemiah seeks permission from the Persian king to go to Jerusalem. Arriving in Jerusalem, he mobilizes the people to begin rebuilding the wall. Faced with opposition, both from without and from within, Nehemiah perseveres until the project is complete and the city resettled. Seemingly impossible tasks can be accomplished when God is helping those who honor him and when their efforts are united.

### 1. Nehemiah returns to Jerusalem

**1** These are the memoirs of Nehemiah son of Hacaliah.

*Nehemiah's Concern for Jerusalem*

In late autumn, in the month of Kislev, in the twentieth year of King Artaxerxes' reign,* I was at the fortress of Susa. ²Hanani, one of my brothers, came to visit me with some other men

**1:1**
Neh 2:1; 10:1
Esth 1:2
Dan 8:2
Zech 7:1

**1:2**
Neh 7:2

**1:1** Hebrew *In the month of Kislev of the twentieth year.* A number of dates in the book of Nehemiah can be cross-checked with dates in surviving Persian records and related accurately to our modern calendar. This month of the ancient Hebrew lunar calendar occurred within the months of November and December 446 B.C. The *twentieth year* probably refers to the reign of King Artaxerxes I; compare 2:1; 5:14.

who had just arrived from Judah. I asked them about the Jews who had returned there from captivity and about how things were going in Jerusalem.

**1:3**
Neh 2:3, 17; 7:6

3 They said to me, "Things are not going well for those who returned to the province of Judah. They are in great trouble and disgrace. The wall of Jerusalem has been torn down, and the gates have been destroyed by fire."

---

## HOW NEHEMIAH USED PRAYER

| Reference | Occasion | Summary of His Prayer | What Prayer Accomplished | Our Prayers |
|---|---|---|---|---|
| 1:4-11 | After receiving the bad news about the state of Jerusalem's walls | Recognized God's holiness. Asked for a hearing. Confessed sin. Asked for specific help in approaching the king | Included God in Nehemiah's plans and concerns. Prepared Nehemiah's heart and gave God room to work | How often do you pour out your heart to God? How often do you give him a specific request to answer? |
| 2:4 | During his conversation with the king | "Here's where you can help, God!" | Put the expected results in God's hands | Giving God credit for what happens before it happens keeps us from taking more credit than we should. |
| 4:4, 5 | After being taunted and ridiculed by Tobiah and Sanballat | "They're mocking you, God. You decide what to do with them." | Expressed anger to God, but Nehemiah did not take matters into his own hands | We are prone to do exactly the opposite— take matters into our hands and not tell God how we feel. |
| 4:9 | After threats of attack by enemies | "We are in your hands, God. We'll keep our weapons handy in case you want us to use them." | Showed trust in God even while taking necessary precautions | Trusting God does not mean we do nothing. Action does not mean we do not trust. |
| 6:9 | Responding to threats | "O Lord God, please strengthen me!" | Showed Nehemiah's reliance on God for emotional and mental stability | How often do you ask God for help when under pressure? |
| 13:29 | Reflecting on the actions of his enemies | Asked God to deal with the enemies and their evil plans | Took away the compulsion to get revenge, and entrusted justice to God | When did you last settle a desire for revenge by turning the matter over to God? |
| 5:19; 13:14, 22, 31 | Reflecting on his own efforts to serve God | "Remember me, God." | Kept clear in Nehemiah's mind his own motives for action | How many of your actions today will be done with the purpose of pleasing God? |

---

**1:1** Nehemiah wasn't the first of the exiles to return to Jerusalem. Zerubbabel had led the first group back in 538 B.C., more than 90 years earlier (Ezra 1–2). Ezra followed with a second group in 458 B.C. (Ezra 7), and here Nehemiah was ready to lead the third major return to Jerusalem (445 B.C.). When he arrived after a three-month journey, he saw the completed Temple and became acquainted with others who had returned to their homeland.

But Nehemiah also found a disorganized group of people and a defenseless city with no walls to protect it. Before the Exile, Israel had its own language, king, army, and identity. At this time it had none of these. What the Jews lacked most was leadership; there was no one to show them where to start and what direction to take as they tried to rebuild their city. As soon as Nehemiah arrived, he began a back-to-the-basics program. He helped care for the people's physical needs by setting up a fair system of government and rebuilding Jerusalem's walls. He also cared for their spiritual needs by rebuilding broken lives. Nehemiah is a model of committed,

God-honoring leadership, and his book contains many useful lessons for today.

**1:2-4** Nehemiah was concerned about Jerusalem because it was the Jews' holy city. As Judah's capital city, it represented Jewish national identity, and it was blessed with God's special presence in the Temple. Jewish history centered around the city from the time of Abraham's gifts to Melchizedek, king of Salem (Genesis 14:17-20), to the days when Solomon built the glorious Temple (1 Kings 7:51), and throughout the history of the kings. Nehemiah loved his homeland even though he had lived his whole life in Babylon. He wanted to return to Jerusalem to reunite the Jews and to remove the shame of Jerusalem's broken-down walls. This would bring glory to God and restore the reality and power of God's presence among his people.

⁴When I heard this, I sat down and wept. In fact, for days I mourned, fasted, and prayed to the God of heaven. ⁵Then I said,

"O LORD, God of heaven, the great and awesome God who keeps his covenant of unfailing love with those who love him and obey his commands, ⁶listen to my prayer! Look down and see me praying night and day for your people Israel. I confess that we have sinned against you. Yes, even my own family and I have sinned! ⁷We have sinned terribly by not obeying the commands, decrees, and regulations that you gave us through your servant Moses.

⁸"Please remember what you told your servant Moses: 'If you are unfaithful to me, I will scatter you among the nations. ⁹But if you return to me and obey my commands and live by them, then even if you are exiled to the ends of the earth, I will bring you back to the place I have chosen for my name to be honored.'

¹⁰"The people you rescued by your great power and strong hand are your servants. ¹¹O Lord, please hear my prayer! Listen to the prayers of those of us who delight in honoring you. Please grant me success today by making the king favorable to me.* Put it into his heart to be kind to me."

In those days I was the king's cup-bearer.

### Nehemiah Goes to Jerusalem

**2** Early the following spring, in the month of Nisan,* during the twentieth year of King Artaxerxes' reign, I was serving the king his wine. I had never before appeared sad in his presence. ²So the king asked me, "Why are you looking so sad? You don't look sick to me. You must be deeply troubled."

**1:4** Ezra 9:3; 10:1
**1:5** Exod 20:6; Neh 4:14; 9:32
**1:6** 2 Chr 29:6; Ezra 10:1; Dan 9:20
**1:7** Deut 28:14; Dan 9:5
**1:8** Lev 26:33
**1:9** Deut 12:5; 30:2-4
**1:10** Exod 32:11; Deut 9:29
**1:11** Gen 40:21; Neh 1:6; 2:1
**2:1** Ezra 7:1; Neh 1:1, 11
**2:2** Prov 15:13

**1:11** Hebrew *today in the sight of this man.*   **2:1** Hebrew *In the month of Nisan.* This month of the ancient Hebrew lunar calendar occurred within the months of April and May 445 B.C.

---

**1:4** Nehemiah broke down and wept when he heard that Jerusalem's walls still had not been rebuilt. Why did this upset him? Walls mean little in most present-day cities, but in Nehemiah's day they were as essential as we would consider electrical power or a police force. They offered safety from raids and symbolized strength and peace. Nehemiah also mourned for his people, the Jews, who had been stifled by a previous edict that had kept them from rebuilding their walls (Ezra 4:6-23).

**1:4** Nehemiah was deeply grieved about the condition of Jerusalem, but he didn't just brood about it. After his initial grief, he prayed, pouring his heart out to God (1:5-11), and he looked for ways to improve the situation. Nehemiah put all his resources of knowledge, experience, and organization into determining what should be done. When tragic news comes to you, first pray. Then seek ways to move beyond grief to specific action that helps those who need it.

**1:5** God's "covenant of unfailing love" refers to God's promise to love the descendants of Abraham. It is also mentioned in Deuteronomy 7:7-9.

**1:5ff** Nehemiah fasted and prayed for several days, expressing his sorrow for Israel's sin and his desire that Jerusalem would again come alive with the worship of the one true God. Nehemiah demonstrated the elements of effective prayer: (1) praise, (2) thanksgiving, (3) repentance, (4) specific requests, and (5) commitment.

Heartfelt prayers like Nehemiah's can help clarify (1) any problem you may be facing, (2) God's great power to help you, and (3) the job you have to do. By the end of his prayer time, Nehemiah knew what action he had to take (1:11). When God's people pray, difficult decisions fall into proper perspective, and appropriate actions follow.

**1:11** Nehemiah was in a unique position to speak to the king. He was the trusted cup-bearer, who ensured the safety and quality of the king's food and drink. Nehemiah was concerned, prayerful, and prepared as he looked for the right opportunity to tell the king about God's people. Each of us is unique and capable of serving no matter what our position. Just as Nehemiah used his place as the king's trusted servant to intercede for his people, we can use our present positions to serve God.

**1:11** Nehemiah prayed for success in this venture, not just for the strength to cope with his problems (see also 2:20). Yet the success he prayed for was not for personal advantage, position, or acclaim. He requested success for God's work. When God's purposes are at work, don't hesitate to ask for success.

**2:2** The king noticed Nehemiah's sad appearance. It surprised Nehemiah to be singled out for attention and it frightened him because it was dangerous to show sorrow before the king, who could execute anyone who displeased him. In fact, anyone wearing mourning clothes was barred from the palace (Esther 4:2).

**2:2, 3** Nehemiah wasn't ashamed to admit his fear, but he refused to allow fear to stop him from doing what God had called him to do. He acknowledged the king's position and clearly stated the reasons for his own sorrow. When we allow fear to rule us, we make fear more powerful than God. Is there a task God wants you to do, but fear is holding you back? God is greater than all

**NEHEMIAH GOES TO JERUSALEM** Nehemiah worked in Susa as a cup-bearer for the king of the vast Medo-Persian Empire. When he heard that the rebuilding projects in Jerusalem were progressing slowly, he asked the king if he could go there to help his people complete the task of rebuilding their city's walls. The king agreed to let him go; so he left as soon as possible, traveling along much the same route Ezra had taken.

2:3
Neh 1:3
Dan 2:4

2:4
Neh 1:4

2:6
Neh 13:6

2:7
Ezra 7:21; 8:36
Neh 2:9

2:8
Eccl 2:5-6

2:9
Ezra 8:22
Neh 2:7

2:10
Neh 2:19; 4:1-3

2:13
Neh 1:3; 3:13

Then I was terrified, ³but I replied, "Long live the king! How can I not be sad? For the city where my ancestors are buried is in ruins, and the gates have been destroyed by fire." ⁴The king asked, "Well, how can I help you?"

With a prayer to the God of heaven, ⁵I replied, "If it please the king, and if you are pleased with me, your servant, send me to Judah to rebuild the city where my ancestors are buried."

⁶The king, with the queen sitting beside him, asked, "How long will you be gone? When will you return?" After I told him how long I would be gone, the king agreed to my request.

⁷I also said to the king, "If it please the king, let me have letters addressed to the governors of the province west of the Euphrates River,* instructing them to let me travel safely through their territories on my way to Judah. ⁸And please give me a letter addressed to Asaph, the manager of the king's forest, instructing him to give me timber. I will need it to make beams for the gates of the Temple fortress, for the city walls, and for a house for myself." And the king granted these requests, because the gracious hand of God was on me.

⁹When I came to the governors of the province west of the Euphrates River, I delivered the king's letters to them. The king, I should add, had sent along army officers and horsemen* to protect me. ¹⁰But when Sanballat the Horonite and Tobiah the Ammonite official heard of my arrival, they were very displeased that someone had come to help the people of Israel.

## 2. Nehemiah leads the people
### Nehemiah Inspects Jerusalem's Wall
¹¹So I arrived in Jerusalem. Three days later, ¹²I slipped out during the night, taking only a few others with me. I had not told anyone about the plans God had put in my heart for Jerusalem. We took no pack animals with us except the donkey I was riding. ¹³After dark I went out through the Valley Gate, past the Jackal's Well,* and over to the Dung Gate to inspect the

**2:7** Hebrew *the province beyond the river;* also in 2:9.   **2:9** Or *charioteers.*   **2:13** Or *Serpent's Well.*

your fears. Recognizing why you are afraid is the first step in committing your fear to God. Realize that if God has called you to a task, he will help you accomplish it.

**2:4** With little time to think, Nehemiah immediately prayed. Eight times in this book we read that he prayed spontaneously (2:4; 4:4, 5, 9; 5:19; 6:14; 13:14, 22, 29). Nehemiah prayed at any time, even while talking with others. He knew that God is always in charge, is always present, and hears and answers every prayer. Nehemiah could confidently pray throughout the day because he had established an intimate relationship with God during times of extended prayer (1:4-7). If we want to reach God with our emergency prayers, we need to take time to cultivate a strong relationship with God through times of in-depth prayer.

**2:6** The king asked Nehemiah how long he would be gone. The Bible does not record Nehemiah's immediate answer, but he ended up staying in Jerusalem for 12 years (5:14; 13:6).

**2:7, 8** After his prayer, Nehemiah asked the king for permission to go to Judah. As soon as he got a positive answer, he began asking for additional help. Sometimes when we have needs, we hesitate to ask the right people for help because we are afraid to approach them. Not Nehemiah! He went directly to the person who could help him the most. Don't be reluctant to ask those who are most able to help. They may be more interested and approachable than you think. God's answers to prayer may come as a result of our asking others.

**2:8** Nehemiah had position, power, and many good organizational skills, but he acknowledged that God's gracious hand was upon him. He knew that without God's strength, his efforts would be in vain. Do you acknowledge God as your power source and the giver of your gifts?

**2:9, 10, 19** When Nehemiah arrived in Judah, opposition greeted him. Opposition to the rebuilding of Jerusalem had been going on for 90 years by those who settled in the area when the Jews were taken captive. In every generation there are those who hate God's people and try to block God's purpose. When you attempt to do God's work, some will oppose you; some will

even hope you fail. If you expect opposition, you will be prepared rather than surprised (1 John 3:13). Knowing that God is behind your task is the best incentive to move ahead in the face of opposition.

**2:10** Sanballat was governor of Samaria, and Tobiah was probably governor of Transjordan under the Persians. Why were these government officials so concerned about the arrival of Nehemiah and his small band of exiles? There are several possible reasons. (1) When Zerubbabel first returned with his group (Ezra 1–2), his refusal to accept help from the Samaritans had caused bad relations. (2) Nehemiah was no ordinary exile; he was the king's personal adviser and cup-bearer, arriving in Jerusalem with the king's approval to build and fortify the city. If anyone could rebuild Jerusalem, he could. A rebuilt Jerusalem was a threat to the authority of the Samaritan officials who had been in charge of the land since Judah's exile. (3) This was the third group to return from exile. The increasing number of people in Jerusalem made Sanballat and Tobiah angry. They did not want returning exiles taking control of the land and threatening their secure position.

**2:11-17** Nehemiah arrived quietly in Jerusalem and spent several days carefully observing and assessing the damage to the walls. Following this time of thoughtful consideration, he confidently presented his plan. Nehemiah demonstrated an excellent approach to problem solving. He got firsthand information and carefully considered the situation. Then he presented a realistic strategy. Before jumping into a project, follow Nehemiah's example and plan ahead. Check your information to make sure your ideas will work—be realistic. Then you will be able to present your plan with confidence.

**2:12, 16** Nehemiah kept his mission a secret and surveyed the walls by moonlight to avoid unhealthy gossip about his arrival and to prevent enemies from being alerted to his plans. Only after planning carefully would he be ready to go public with his mission from God. A premature announcement could have caused rivalry among the Jews as to the best way to begin. In this case, Nehemiah didn't need tedious planning sessions; he needed one plan that would bring quick action.

broken walls and burned gates. [14]Then I went to the Fountain Gate and to the King's Pool, but my donkey couldn't get through the rubble. [15]So, though it was still dark, I went up the Kidron Valley* instead, inspecting the wall before I turned back and entered again at the Valley Gate.

[16]The city officials did not know I had been out there or what I was doing, for I had not yet said anything to anyone about my plans. I had not yet spoken to the Jewish leaders—the priests, the nobles, the officials, or anyone else in the administration. [17]But now I said to them, "You know very well what trouble we are in. Jerusalem lies in ruins, and its gates have been destroyed by fire. Let us rebuild the wall of Jerusalem and end this disgrace!" [18]Then I told them about how the gracious hand of God had been on me, and about my conversation with the king.

They replied at once, "Yes, let's rebuild the wall!" So they began the good work.

[19]But when Sanballat, Tobiah, and Geshem the Arab heard of our plan, they scoffed contemptuously. "What are you doing? Are you rebelling against the king?" they asked.

[20]I replied, "The God of heaven will help us succeed. We, his servants, will start rebuilding this wall. But you have no share, legal right, or historic claim in Jerusalem."

### Rebuilding the Wall of Jerusalem

**3** Then Eliashib the high priest and the other priests started to rebuild at the Sheep Gate. They dedicated it and set up its doors, building the wall as far as the Tower of the Hundred, which they dedicated, and the Tower of Hananel. [2]People from the town of Jericho worked next to them, and beyond them was Zaccur son of Imri.

**2:14**
2 Kgs 20:20
Neh 3:15

**2:17**
Neh 1:3

**2:19**
Neh 6:6

**2:20**
Ezra 4:3
Neh 2:4

**3:1**
Neh 3:20, 32; 6:1;
7:1; 12:39; 13:28
Jer 31:38

**3:2**
Neh 7:36

2:15 Hebrew *the valley.*

**THE RESTORATION OF THE CITY WALLS** Nehemiah takes us on a counterclockwise tour around Jerusalem (beginning with the Sheep Gate). He describes for us each section, gate, and tower on the wall and who worked to rebuild it.

**2:17, 18** Spiritual renewal often begins with one person's vision. Nehemiah had a vision, and he shared it with enthusiasm, inspiring Jerusalem's leaders to rebuild the walls.

We frequently underestimate people and don't challenge them with our dreams for God's work in the world. When God plants an idea in your mind to accomplish something for him, share it with others and trust the Holy Spirit to impress them with similar thoughts. Don't regard yourself as the only one through whom God is working. Often God uses one person to express the vision and others to turn it into reality. When you encourage and inspire others, you put teamwork into action to accomplish God's goals.

**2:19** Sanballat and Tobiah labeled the rebuilding of Jerusalem's walls as rebellion against the king, probably threatening to report the builders as traitors. These enemies also ridiculed Nehemiah, saying that the walls could never be rebuilt because the damage was too extensive. Nehemiah did not tell them he already had permission from the king to rebuild. Instead, he simply said he had God's approval—that was enough.

**3:1** The high priest is the first person mentioned who pitched in and helped with the work. Spiritual leaders must lead not only by word but also by action. The Sheep Gate was the gate used to bring sheep into the city to the Temple for sacrifices. Nehemiah had the priests repair this gate and section of the wall, respecting the priests' area of interest and at the same time emphasizing the priority of worship.

**3:1ff** All the citizens of Jerusalem did their part on the huge job of rebuilding the city wall. Similarly, the work of the church requires every member's effort in order for the body of Christ to function effectively (1 Corinthians 12:12-27). The body needs you! Are you doing your part? Find a place to serve God, and start contributing whatever time, talent, and money are needed.

**3:1ff** Jerusalem was a large city, and because many roads converged there, it required many gates. The wall on each side of these heavy wooden gates was taller and thicker so soldiers could stand guard to defend the gates against attack. Sometimes two stone towers guarded the gate. In times of peace, the city gates were hubs of activity—city council was held there, and shopkeepers set up their wares at the entrance. Building the city walls and gates was not only a military priority but also a boost for trade and commerce.

**3:3**
Neh 12:39

**3:6**
Neh 12:39

**3:8**
Neh 3:31-32; 12:38

**3:9**
Neh 3:12, 17

**3:11**
Neh 12:38

**3:12**
Neh 3:9

**3:13**
Neh 2:13

**3:14**
Neh 2:13

**3:15**
2 Kgs 25:4-5
Neh 2:14; 12:37

**3:16**
2 Kgs 20:20
Neh 2:14; 3:9,
12, 17

**3:19**
2 Chr 26:9
Neh 3:15-16

**3:20**
Neh 3:1

**3:22**
Neh 12:28

**3:24**
Neh 3:19

**3:25**
Jer 32:2

³The Fish Gate was built by the sons of Hassenaah. They laid the beams, set up its doors, and installed its bolts and bars. ⁴Meremoth son of Uriah and grandson of Hakkoz repaired the next section of wall. Beside him were Meshullam son of Berekiah and grandson of Meshezabel, and then Zadok son of Baana. ⁵Next were the people from Tekoa, though their leaders refused to work with the construction supervisors.

⁶The Old City Gate* was repaired by Joiada son of Paseha and Meshullam son of Besodeiah. They laid the beams, set up its doors, and installed its bolts and bars. ⁷Next to them were Melatiah from Gibeon, Jadon from Meronoth, people from Gibeon, and people from Mizpah, the headquarters of the governor of the province west of the Euphrates River.* ⁸Next was Uzziel son of Harhaiah, a goldsmith by trade, who also worked on the wall. Beyond him was Hananiah, a manufacturer of perfumes. They left out a section of Jerusalem as they built the Broad Wall.*

⁹Rephaiah son of Hur, the leader of half the district of Jerusalem, was next to them on the wall. ¹⁰Next Jedaiah son of Harumaph repaired the wall across from his own house, and next to him was Hattush son of Hashabneiah. ¹¹Then came Malkijah son of Harim and Hasshub son of Pahath-moab, who repaired another section of the wall and the Tower of the Ovens. ¹²Shallum son of Hallohesh and his daughters repaired the next section. He was the leader of the other half of the district of Jerusalem.

¹³The Valley Gate was repaired by the people from Zanoah, led by Hanun. They set up its doors and installed its bolts and bars. They also repaired the 1,500 feet* of wall to the Dung Gate.

¹⁴The Dung Gate was repaired by Malkijah son of Recab, the leader of the Beth-hakkerem district. He rebuilt it, set up its doors, and installed its bolts and bars.

¹⁵The Fountain Gate was repaired by Shallum* son of Col-hozeh, the leader of the Mizpah district. He rebuilt it, roofed it, set up its doors, and installed its bolts and bars. Then he repaired the wall of the pool of Siloam* near the king's garden, and he rebuilt the wall as far as the stairs that descend from the City of David. ¹⁶Next to him was Nehemiah son of Azbuk, the leader of half the district of Beth-zur. He rebuilt the wall from a place across from the tombs of David's family as far as the water reservoir and the House of the Warriors.

¹⁷Next to him, repairs were made by a group of Levites working under the supervision of Rehum son of Bani. Then came Hashabiah, the leader of half the district of Keilah, who supervised the building of the wall on behalf of his own district. ¹⁸Next down the line were his countrymen led by Binnui* son of Henadad, the leader of the other half of the district of Keilah.

¹⁹Next to them, Ezer son of Jeshua, the leader of Mizpah, repaired another section of wall across from the ascent to the armory near the angle in the wall. ²⁰Next to him was Baruch son of Zabbai, who zealously repaired an additional section from the angle to the door of the house of Eliashib the high priest. ²¹Meremoth son of Uriah and grandson of Hakkoz rebuilt another section of the wall extending from the door of Eliashib's house to the end of the house.

²²The next repairs were made by the priests from the surrounding region. ²³After them, Benjamin and Hasshub repaired the section across from their house, and Azariah son of Maaseiah and grandson of Ananiah repaired the section across from his house. ²⁴Next was Binnui son of Henadad, who rebuilt another section of the wall from Azariah's house to the angle and the corner. ²⁵Palal son of Uzai carried on the work from a point opposite the angle

**3:6** Or *The Mishneh Gate,* or *The Jeshanah Gate.*   **3:7** Hebrew *the province beyond the river.*   **3:8** Or *They fortified Jerusalem up to the Broad Wall.*   **3:13** Hebrew *1,000 cubits* [450 meters].   **3:15a** As in Syriac version; Hebrew reads *Shallun.*   **3:15b** Hebrew *pool of Shelah,* another name for the pool of Siloam.   **3:18** As in a few Hebrew manuscripts, some Greek manuscripts, and Syriac version (see also 3:24; 10:9); most Hebrew manuscripts read *Bavvai.*

---

**3:3** One of the main roads through Jerusalem entered the city through the Fish Gate (2 Chronicles 33:14). The fish market was near the gate, and merchants from Tyre, the Sea of Galilee, and other fishing areas entered this gate to sell their goods.

**3:5** The leaders from Tekoa were lazy and wouldn't help. These men were the only ones who did not support the building project in Jerusalem. Every group, even churches, will have those who think they are too wise or important to work hard. Gentle encouragement doesn't seem to help. Sometimes the best policy is to ignore them. They may think they are getting away with something, but their inactivity will be remembered by all who worked hard.

**3:12** Shallum's daughters helped with the difficult work of repairing the city walls. Rebuilding Jerusalem's walls was a matter of national emergency for the Jews, not just a civic beautification project. Nearly everyone was dedicated to the task and willing to work at it.

**3:14** The Dung Gate was the gate through which the people carried their garbage to be burned in the Valley of Hinnom.

and the tower that projects up from the king's upper house beside the court of the guard. Next to him were Pedaiah son of Parosh, 26with the Temple servants living on the hill of Ophel, who repaired the wall as far as a point across from the Water Gate to the east and the projecting tower. 27Then came the people of Tekoa, who repaired another section across from the great projecting tower and over to the wall of Ophel.

3:26
Neh 7:46; 8:1, 3;
11:21

3:27
Neh 3:5, 26

28Above the Horse Gate, the priests repaired the wall. Each one repaired the section immediately across from his own house. 29Next Zadok son of Immer also rebuilt the wall across from his own house, and beyond him was Shemaiah son of Shecaniah, the gatekeeper of the East Gate. 30Next Hananiah son of Shelemiah and Hanun, the sixth son of Zalaph, repaired another section, while Meshullam son of Berekiah rebuilt the wall across from where he lived. 31Malkijah, one of the goldsmiths, repaired the wall as far as the housing for the Temple servants and merchants, across from the Inspection Gate. Then he continued as far as the upper room at the corner. 32The other goldsmiths and merchants repaired the wall from that corner to the Sheep Gate.

3:28
2 Kgs 11:16
2 Chr 23:15
Jer 31:40

3:31
Neh 3:1, 8, 32

3:32
Neh 3:1; 12:39

## Enemies Oppose the Rebuilding

**4** 1*Sanballat was very angry when he learned that we were rebuilding the wall. He flew into a rage and mocked the Jews, 2saying in front of his friends and the Samarian army officers, "What does this bunch of poor, feeble Jews think they're doing? Do they think they can build the wall in a single day by just offering a few sacrifices?* Do they actually think they can make something of stones from a rubbish heap—and charred ones at that?"

4:1
Neh 2:10, 19

3Tobiah the Ammonite, who was standing beside him, remarked, "That stone wall would collapse if even a fox walked along the top of it!"

4:3
Neh 2:10

4Then I prayed, "Hear us, our God, for we are being mocked. May their scoffing fall back on their own heads, and may they themselves become captives in a foreign land! 5Do not ignore their guilt. Do not blot out their sins, for they have provoked you to anger here in front of* the builders."

4:4
Pss 79:12; 123:3-4

4:5
Ps 69:27-28
Jer 18:23

6At last the wall was completed to half its height around the entire city, for the people had worked with enthusiasm.

7*But when Sanballat and Tobiah and the Arabs, Ammonites, and Ashdodites heard that the work was going ahead and that the gaps in the wall of Jerusalem were being repaired,

4:1 Verses 4:1-6 are numbered 3:33-38 in Hebrew text.   4:2 The meaning of the Hebrew is uncertain.   4:5 Or *for they have thrown insults in the face of.*   4:7 Verses 4:7-23 are numbered 4:1-17 in Hebrew text.

---

**3:28** The Horse Gate was at the far eastern point of the wall, facing the Kidron Valley.

**3:28** Each priest also repaired the wall in front of his own house, in addition to other sections. If each person was responsible for the part of the wall closest to his own house, (1) he would be more motivated to build it quickly and properly, (2) he wouldn't waste time traveling to more distant parts of the wall, (3) he would defend his own home if the wall were attacked, and (4) he would be able to make the building a family effort. Nehemiah blended self-interest with the group's objectives, helping everyone to feel that the wall project was his own. If you are part of a group working on a large project, make sure each person sees the importance and meaning of the job that he or she has to do. This will ensure high-quality work and personal satisfaction.

**3:31** The Inspection Gate was in the northern part of the eastern wall.

**4:1** Sanballat was governor of Samaria, the region just north of Judea, where Jerusalem was located. Sanballat may have hoped to become governor of Judea as well, but Nehemiah's arrival spoiled his plans. (For his other reasons for opposing Nehemiah, see the note on 2:10.) Sanballat tried to scare Nehemiah away or at least discourage him by scorn (4:2; 6:6), threats (4:8), and bluffs (6:7).

**4:1, 2** Almost 300 years before Nehemiah's time, the northern kingdom of Israel was conquered, and most of the people were carried away captive (722 B.C.). Sargon of Assyria repopulated Israel with captives from other lands. These captives eventually intermarried with the few Israelites who remained in the land to form a mixed race of people who became known as Samaritans. The Jews who returned to Jerusalem and the southern region of Judea during the days of Ezra and Nehemiah would have nothing to do with Samaritans, whom they considered to be racially impure. Relations between both groups grew progressively worse—400 years later, the Jews and Samaritans hated each other (John 4:9).

**4:1-5** Ridicule can cut deeply, causing discouragement and despair. Sanballat and Tobiah used ridicule to try to dissuade the Jews from building the wall. Instead of trading insults, however, Nehemiah prayed, and the work continued. When you are mocked for your faith or criticized for doing what you know is right, refuse to respond in the same way or to become discouraged. Tell God how you feel and remember his promise to be with you. This will give you encouragement and strength to carry on.

**4:4, 5** Nehemiah is not praying for revenge but for God's justice to be carried out. His prayer is similar to many of David's (see the note on Psalm 7:1-6 and the chart "How Nehemiah Used Prayer," p. 743).

**4:6** The work of rebuilding the wall progressed well because the people had set their hearts and minds on accomplishing the task. They did not lose faith or give up, but they persevered in the work. If God has called you to a task, determine to complete it, even if you face opposition or discouragement. The rewards of work well done will be worth the effort.

**4:9**
Neh 4:11

they were furious. [8]They all made plans to come and fight against Jerusalem and throw us into confusion. [9]But we prayed to our God and guarded the city day and night to protect ourselves.

[10]Then the people of Judah began to complain, "The workers are getting tired, and there is so much rubble to be moved. We will never be able to build the wall by ourselves."

God is in the business of working through his people to accomplish seemingly impossible tasks. God often shapes people with personality characteristics, experiences, and training that prepare them for his purpose, and usually the people have no idea what God has in store for them. God prepared and positioned Nehemiah to accomplish one of the Bible's "impossible" tasks.

Nehemiah was a common man in a unique position. He was secure and successful as cup-bearer to the Persian king, Artaxerxes. Nehemiah had little power, but he had great influence. He was trusted by the king. He was also a man of God, concerned about the fate of Jerusalem.

Seventy years earlier, Zerubbabel had managed to rebuild God's Temple. Thirteen years had passed since Ezra had returned to Jerusalem and helped the people with their spiritual needs. Now Nehemiah was needed. Jerusalem's wall was still in ruins, and the news broke his heart. As he talked to God, a plan began to take form in Nehemiah's mind about his own role in the rebuilding of the city walls. He willingly left the security of his home and job in Persia to follow God on an "impossible" mission. And the rest is history.

From beginning to end, Nehemiah prayed for God's help. He never hesitated to ask God to remember him, closing his autobiography with these words: "Remember this in my favor, O my God" (13:31). Throughout the "impossible" task, Nehemiah displayed unusual leadership. The wall around Jerusalem was rebuilt in record time, despite resistance. Even Israel's enemies grudgingly and fearfully admitted that God was with these builders. Not only that, but God worked through Nehemiah to bring about a spiritual awakening among the people of Judah.

You may not have Nehemiah's unique abilities or feel that you are in a position where you can do anything great for God, but there are two ways you can become useful to God. First, be a person who *talks* to God. Welcome him into your thoughts and share yourself with him—your concerns, feelings, and dreams. Second, be a person who *walks* with God. Put what you learn from his Word into action. God may have an "impossible" mission that he wants to do through you.

| | |
|---|---|
| **Strengths and accomplishments** | • A man of character, persistence, and prayer<br>• Brilliant planner, organizer, and motivator<br>• Under his leadership, the wall around Jerusalem was rebuilt in 52 days<br>• As political leader, led the nation to religious reform and spiritual awakening<br>• Was calm in the face of opposition<br>• Was capable of being bluntly honest with his people when they were sinning |
| **Lessons from his life** | • The first step in any venture is to pray<br>• People under God's direction can accomplish "impossible" tasks<br>• There are two parts to real service for God: talking with him and walking with him |
| **Vital statistics** | • Where: Persia, Jerusalem<br>• Occupations: King's cup-bearer, city builder, governor of Judah<br>• Relative: Father: Hacaliah<br>• Contemporaries: Ezra, Artaxerxes, Tobiah, Sanballat |
| **Key verse** | "Then I told them about how the gracious hand of God had been on me, and about my conversation with the king. They replied at once, 'Yes, let's rebuild the wall!' So they began the good work" (Nehemiah 2:18). |

Nehemiah's story is told in the book of Nehemiah.

**4:9** Nehemiah constantly combined prayer with preparation and planning. His people trusted God and at the same time kept vigilant watch over what had been entrusted to them. Too often we pray without looking for what God wants us to do. We show God we are serious when we combine prayer with thought, preparation, and effort.

**4:10-14** Accomplishing any large task is tiring. There are always pressures that foster discouragement—the task seems impossi-

ble, it can never be finished, or too many factors are working against us. The only cure for fatigue and discouragement is focusing on God's purposes. Nehemiah reminded the workers of their calling, their goal, and God's protection. If you are overwhelmed by an assignment, tired and discouraged, remember God's purpose for your life and his special purpose for the project.

**4:10-15** The people working on the walls faced the continual threat of terrorist attacks from those who didn't want to see

11Meanwhile, our enemies were saying, "Before they know what's happening, we will swoop down on them and kill them and end their work."

12The Jews who lived near the enemy came and told us again and again, "They will come from all directions and attack us!"* 13So I placed armed guards behind the lowest parts of the wall in the exposed areas. I stationed the people to stand guard by families, armed with swords, spears, and bows.

14Then as I looked over the situation, I called together the nobles and the rest of the people and said to them, "Don't be afraid of the enemy! Remember the Lord, who is great and glorious, and fight for your brothers, your sons, your daughters, your wives, and your homes!"

15When our enemies heard that we knew of their plans and that God had frustrated them, we all returned to our work on the wall. 16But from then on, only half my men worked while the other half stood guard with spears, shields, bows, and coats of mail. The leaders stationed themselves behind the people of Judah 17who were building the wall. The laborers carried on their work with one hand supporting their load and one hand holding a weapon. 18All the builders had a sword belted to their side. The trumpeter stayed with me to sound the alarm.

19Then I explained to the nobles and officials and all the people, "The work is very spread out, and we are widely separated from each other along the wall. 20When you hear the blast of the trumpet, rush to wherever it is sounding. Then our God will fight for us!"

21We worked early and late, from sunrise to sunset. And half the men were always on guard. 22I also told everyone living outside the walls to stay in Jerusalem. That way they and their servants could help with guard duty at night and work during the day. 23During this time, none of us—not I, nor my relatives, nor my servants, nor the guards who were with me—ever took off our clothes. We carried our weapons with us at all times, even when we went for water.*

## Nehemiah Defends the Oppressed

**5** About this time some of the men and their wives raised a cry of protest against their fellow Jews. 2They were saying, "We have such large families. We need more food to survive."

3Others said, "We have mortgaged our fields, vineyards, and homes to get food during the famine."

4And others said, "We have had to borrow money on our fields and vineyards to pay our taxes. 5We belong to the same family as those who are wealthy, and our children are just like theirs. Yet we must sell our children into slavery just to get enough money to live. We have already sold some of our daughters, and we are helpless to do anything about it, for our fields and vineyards are already mortgaged to others."

4:13 Neh 4:9, 17-18
4:14 Num 14:9; Deut 1:29-30; 2 Sam 10:12
4:15 2 Sam 17:14
4:20 Exod 14:14; Deut 1:30
5:1-2 Lev 25:35; Deut 15:7
5:4 Ezra 4:13; 7:24
5:5 Gen 37:27; Lev 25:39

4:12 The meaning of the Hebrew is uncertain. 4:23 Or *Each carried his weapon in his right hand.* Hebrew reads *Each his weapon the water.* The meaning of the Hebrew is uncertain.

Jerusalem rebuilt. Threats demoralize. The tension created by the possibility of sudden assaults adds to fatigue. Nehemiah took wise, practical steps to counter the threats: (1) he stationed guards at obvious weak points; (2) he reminded the workers to keep weapons close at hand and to fight for God, their families, and the nation if an attack came; (3) he established duty rotations so that some stood guard while others worked. The preparations for defense and the continuation of the work reversed the effects of terrorism and demoralized the enemies. Obstacles and foes can make us work smarter and live wiser or make us give up our purpose and our way of living. If they accomplish the latter, they have won even if they haven't actually attacked us. But if we adjust our way of living wisely while continuing resolutely to live under God's instructions, the opposition will fail.

**4:16** The workers were spread out along the wall, so Nehemiah devised a plan of defense that would unite and protect his people—half the men worked while the other half stood guard. Christians need to help one another in the same way because we can become so afraid of possible dangers that we can't get anything done. By looking out for each other, we will be free to put forth our best efforts, confident that others are ready to offer help when needed. Don't cut yourself off from others; instead, join together for mutual benefit. You need them as much as they need you.

**4:18-20** To further relieve the anxieties of the people, Nehemiah set up a communication system. The man who sounded the trumpet stayed with Nehemiah, and the people knew what to do if they heard it. We have no record that the trumpet was ever used, but simply knowing it would issue a warning when needed was reassuring. The system also put doubt into the minds of those trying to terrorize the workforce since the people on the wall were no longer passive targets. The promise of open, immediate communication helped the group counter the enemy threats and accomplish the reconstruction of the wall in record time.

**4:23** Although the exact meaning of the Hebrew phrase "even when we went for water" is unclear (it has been translated, "in his right hand" or "at his right hand at night"), the point is that each man always had his weapon close at hand. The guards were prepared and took their responsibilities seriously.

**5:1-5** Who were these bitterly resented Jews? They were either (1) Jews who had become wealthy in exile and brought this wealth with them to Jerusalem, or (2) descendants of Jews who had arrived almost a century earlier during the first return under Zerubbabel (Ezra 1–2) and had established lucrative businesses.

5:7
Exod 22:25
Lev 25:36

⁶When I heard their complaints, I was very angry. ⁷After thinking it over, I spoke out against these nobles and officials. I told them, "You are hurting your own relatives by charging interest when they borrow money!" Then I called a public meeting to deal with the problem.

5:8
Lev 25:48

⁸At the meeting I said to them, "We are doing all we can to redeem our Jewish relatives who have had to sell themselves to pagan foreigners, but you are selling them back into slavery again. How often must we redeem them?" And they had nothing to say in their defense.

⁹Then I pressed further, "What you are doing is not right! Should you not walk in the fear of our God in order to avoid being mocked by enemy nations? ¹⁰I myself, as well as my brothers and my workers, have been lending the people money and grain, but now let us stop this business of charging interest. ¹¹You must restore their fields, vineyards, olive groves, and homes to them this very day. And repay the interest you charged when you lent them money, grain, new wine, and olive oil."

5:12
Ezra 10:5
Neh 10:31

¹²They replied, "We will give back everything and demand nothing more from the people. We will do as you say." Then I called the priests and made the nobles and officials swear to do what they had promised.

5:13
Neh 8:6
Acts 18:6

¹³I shook out the folds of my robe and said, "If you fail to keep your promise, may God shake you like this from your homes and from your property!"

The whole assembly responded, "Amen," and they praised the LORD. And the people did as they had promised.

5:14
Neh 1:1; 13:6

5:15
Neh 5:9

¹⁴For the entire twelve years that I was governor of Judah—from the twentieth year to the thirty-second year of the reign of King Artaxerxes*—neither I nor my officials drew on our official food allowance. ¹⁵The former governors, in contrast, had laid heavy burdens on the people, demanding a daily ration of food and wine, besides forty pieces* of silver. Even their assistants took advantage of the people. But because I feared God, I did not act that way.

5:17
1 Kgs 18:19

5:18
1 Kgs 4:22-23
2 Thes 3:8

¹⁶I also devoted myself to working on the wall and refused to acquire any land. And I required all my servants to spend time working on the wall. ¹⁷I asked for nothing, even though I regularly fed 150 Jewish officials at my table, besides all the visitors from other lands! ¹⁸The provisions I paid for each day included one ox, six choice sheep or goats, and a large number of poultry. And every ten days we needed a large supply of all kinds of wine. Yet I refused to claim the governor's food allowance because the people already carried a heavy burden.

5:19
Neh 13:14, 22, 31

¹⁹Remember, O my God, all that I have done for these people, and bless me for it.

5:14 That is, 445–433 B.C.   5:15 Hebrew 40 shekels [1 pound, or 456 grams].

5:7-9 Many of the returned exiles were suffering at the hands of some of their rich countrymen. These people would lend large sums of money; then, when the debtors missed a payment, they would take over their fields. Left with no means of income, the debtors were forced to sell their children into slavery, a common practice of this time. Nehemiah was angry with these Jews, who were taking advantage of their own people in order to enrich themselves. These practices violated the law set forth in Exodus 22:25.

5:9-11 God's concern for the poor is revealed in almost every book of the Bible. Here, Nehemiah insisted that fairness to the poor and oppressed was central to following God. The books of Moses clearly spelled out the Israelites' responsibility to care for the poor (Exodus 22:22-27; Leviticus 25:35-37; Deuteronomy 14:28, 29; 15:7-11). The way we help those in need ought to mirror God's love and concern.

5:10 Nehemiah told the rich Jews to stop charging interest on their loans to their needy brothers. God never intended people to profit from others' misfortune. In contrast to the values of this world, God says that caring for one another is more important than personal gain. When a Christian brother or sister suffers, we all suffer (1 Corinthians 12:26). We should help needy believers, not exploit them. The Jerusalem church was praised for working together to eliminate poverty (Acts 4:34, 35). Remember, "Whoever gives to the poor will lack noth-

ing" (Proverbs 28:27). Make it a practice to help those in need around you.

5:13 This symbolic act was a curse. Nehemiah shook out the folds of his robe and pronounced that anyone who did not keep his promise would likewise be "shaken out and emptied," losing all he had.

5:14, 15 This comment by Nehemiah is a parenthetical statement, comparing his 12 years as governor with the unjust proceedings in the land before he arrived. The governor was appointed by the Persian king, not elected by the people.

5:16 Nehemiah led the entire construction project, but he also worked on the wall alongside the others. He was not a bureaucrat in a well-guarded office but a leader who got involved in the day-to-day work. He did not use his position to lord it over his people. A good leader keeps in touch with the work to be done. Those who lead best lead by what they do as well as by what they say.

## Continued Opposition to Rebuilding

**6** Sanballat, Tobiah, Geshem the Arab, and the rest of our enemies found out that I had finished rebuilding the wall and that no gaps remained—though we had not yet set up the doors in the gates. ²So Sanballat and Geshem sent a message asking me to meet them at one of the villages* in the plain of Ono.

But I realized they were plotting to harm me, ³so I replied by sending this message to them: "I am engaged in a great work, so I can't come. Why should I stop working to come and meet with you?"

⁴Four times they sent the same message, and each time I gave the same reply. ⁵The fifth time, Sanballat's servant came with an open letter in his hand, ⁶and this is what it said:

"There is a rumor among the surrounding nations, and Geshem* tells me it is true, that you and the Jews are planning to rebel and that is why you are building the wall. According to his reports, you plan to be their king. ⁷He also reports that you have appointed prophets in Jerusalem to proclaim about you, 'Look! There is a king in Judah!'

"You can be very sure that this report will get back to the king, so I suggest that you come and talk it over with me."

⁸I replied, "There is no truth in any part of your story. You are making up the whole thing."

⁹They were just trying to intimidate us, imagining that they could discourage us and stop the work. So I continued the work with even greater determination.*

¹⁰Later I went to visit Shemaiah son of Delaiah and grandson of Mehetabel, who was confined to his home. He said, "Let us meet together inside the Temple of God and bolt the doors shut. Your enemies are coming to kill you tonight."

¹¹But I replied, "Should someone in my position run from danger? Should someone in my position enter the Temple to save his life? No, I won't do it!" ¹²I realized that God had not spoken to him, but that he had uttered this prophecy against me because Tobiah and Sanballat had hired him. ¹³They were hoping to intimidate me and make me sin. Then they would be able to accuse and discredit me.

¹⁴Remember, O my God, all the evil things that Tobiah and Sanballat have done. And remember Noadiah the prophet and all the prophets like her who have tried to intimidate me.

| | |
|---|---|
| **6:1** | Neh 3:1, 3 |
| **6:2** | 1 Chr 8:12 |
| **6:6** | Neh 2:19 |
| **6:10** | Jer 36:5 |
| **6:13** | Neh 6:6 |
| **6:14** | Neh 13:29 / Ezek 13:17 |

**6:2** As in Greek version; Hebrew reads *at Kephirim*. **6:6** Hebrew *Gashmu*, a variant spelling of Geshem. **6:9** As in Greek version; Hebrew reads *But now to strengthen my hands*.

---

**6:1ff** Sanballat and Tobiah were desperate. The wall was almost complete, and their efforts to stop its construction were failing. So they tried a new approach, centering their attacks on Nehemiah's character. They attacked him personally with rumors (6:6), deceit (6:10-13), and false reports (6:17). Personal attacks hurt, and when the criticism is unjustified, it is easy to despair. When you are doing God's work, you may receive attacks on your character. Follow Nehemiah's example by trusting God to accomplish the task and by overlooking unjustified insults.

**6:2** The plain of Ono was about 20 miles northwest of Jerusalem. If Sanballat and Geshem could get Nehemiah to agree to meet them there, they could ambush him on the way.

**6:7** During these days, prophets such as Malachi proclaimed the coming of the Messiah (Malachi 3:1-3). Sanballat, with his usual flair for stirring up trouble, tried to turn Nehemiah's people against him by saying that Nehemiah was trying to set himself up as the king. Sanballat also tried to turn the local officials against Nehemiah by threatening to report to the king of Persia that Nehemiah was starting a revolt. The fact that Sanballat had an open, or unsealed, letter delivered to Nehemiah shows that he wanted to make sure the letter's contents were made public.

But Sanballat's accusations were untrue and did not divert Nehemiah from his task.

**6:9** When opposition builds up against you or God's work, it is tempting to pray, "God, get me out of this situation." But Nehemiah prayed for strength. He showed tremendous determination and character to remain steadfast in his responsibility. When we pray for strength, God always answers.

**6:10** Shemaiah warned Nehemiah of danger and told him to hide in the Temple. Nehemiah wisely tested the message, exposing it as another trick of the enemy. People may misuse God's name by saying they know God's will when they have other motives. Examine self-proclaimed messengers from God to see if they stand up to the test of being consistent with what is revealed in God's Word.

**6:10-13** Nehemiah did not have the full support of the people. Shemaiah (6:10), Noadiah (6:14), and many of the officials (6:17) were working against him. When Nehemiah was attacked personally, he refused to give in to fear and flee to the Temple. According to God's law, it would have been wrong for Nehemiah to go into the Temple to hide because he wasn't a priest (Numbers 18:22). If he had run for his life, he would have undermined the courage he was trying to instill in the people. Leaders are targets for attacks. Make it a practice to pray for those in authority (1 Timothy 2:1, 2). Request God to give them strength to stand against personal attacks and temptation. They need God-given courage to overcome fear.

## The Builders Complete the Wall

**6:15**
Neh 4:1-2
**6:16**
Neh 2:10; 4:1, 7

15So on October 2* the wall was finished—just fifty-two days after we had begun. 16When our enemies and the surrounding nations heard about it, they were frightened and humiliated. They realized this work had been done with the help of our God.

17During those fifty-two days, many letters went back and forth between Tobiah and the nobles of Judah. 18For many in Judah had sworn allegiance to him because his father-in-law was Shecaniah son of Arah, and his son Jehohanan was married to the daughter of Meshullam son of Berekiah. 19They kept telling me about Tobiah's good deeds, and then they told him everything I said. And Tobiah kept sending threatening letters to intimidate me.

**7:1**
Neh 6:1, 15
**7:2**
Neh 1:2; 10:23

**7** After the wall was finished and I had set up the doors in the gates, the gatekeepers, singers, and Levites were appointed. 2I gave the responsibility of governing Jerusalem to my brother Hanani, along with Hananiah, the commander of the fortress, for he was a faithful man who feared God more than most. 3I said to them, "Do not leave the gates open during the hottest part of the day.* And even while the gatekeepers are on duty, have them shut and bar the doors. Appoint the residents of Jerusalem to act as guards, everyone on a regular watch. Some will serve at sentry posts and some in front of their own homes."

## Nehemiah Registers the People

4At that time the city was large and spacious, but the population was small, and none of the houses had been rebuilt. 5So my God gave me the idea to call together all the nobles and leaders of the city, along with the ordinary citizens, for registration. I had found the genealogical record of those who had first returned to Judah. This is what was written there:

**7:6-73**
//Ezra 2:1-70
**7:7**
Ezra 2:2

6Here is the list of the Jewish exiles of the provinces who returned from their captivity. King Nebuchadnezzar had deported them to Babylon, but now they returned to Jerusalem and the other towns in Judah where they originally lived. 7Their leaders were Zerubbabel, Jeshua, Nehemiah, Seraiah,* Reelaiah,* Nahamani, Mordecai, Bilshan, Mispar,* Bigvai, Rehum,* and Baanah.

This is the number of the men of Israel who returned from exile:
8 The family of Parosh . . . . . . . . . . . . . . . . . . . . . . . . . . . . . . . . . 2,172
9 The family of Shephatiah . . . . . . . . . . . . . . . . . . . . . . . . . . . . . . . 372
10 The family of Arah . . . . . . . . . . . . . . . . . . . . . . . . . . . . . . . . . . . 652
11 The family of Pahath-moab (descendants of Jeshua and Joab) . . . . . . . . . . 2,818
12 The family of Elam . . . . . . . . . . . . . . . . . . . . . . . . . . . . . . . . . . 1,254
13 The family of Zattu . . . . . . . . . . . . . . . . . . . . . . . . . . . . . . . . . . . 845
14 The family of Zaccai . . . . . . . . . . . . . . . . . . . . . . . . . . . . . . . . . . 760
15 The family of Bani* . . . . . . . . . . . . . . . . . . . . . . . . . . . . . . . . . . . 648

**6:15** Hebrew *on the twenty-fifth day of the month Elul,* of the ancient Hebrew lunar calendar. This day was October 2, 445 B.C.; also see note on 1:1.   **7:3** Or *Keep the gates of Jerusalem closed until the sun is hot.*   **7:7a** As in parallel text at Ezra 2:2; Hebrew reads *Azariah.*   **7:7b** As in parallel text at Ezra 2:2; Hebrew reads *Raamiah.*   **7:7c** As in parallel text at Ezra 2:2; Hebrew reads *Mispereth.*   **7:7d** As in parallel text at Ezra 2:2; Hebrew reads *Nehum.*   **7:15** As in parallel text at Ezra 2:10; Hebrew reads *Binnui.*

---

**6:15** Daniel, who was among the first group of captives taken from Jerusalem to Babylon (605 B.C.), predicted the rebuilding of the city (Daniel 9:25). Here his prophecy comes true. He, like Nehemiah, was a Jew who held a prominent position in the kingdom where he had been exiled (Daniel 5:29–6:3).

**6:15** They said it couldn't be done. The job was too big and the problems were too great. But God's men and women, joined together for special tasks, can solve huge problems and accomplish great goals. The vision that Nehemiah saw through humble tears in Persia became a reality with God's help every step of the way. Don't let the size of a task or the length of time needed to accomplish it keep you from doing it. With God's help, it can be done.

**7:2** Faithfulness and fear of God were the key character traits that qualified these men to govern Jerusalem. Faithful people can be trusted to carry out their work; God-fearing people can be expected to do so in line with God's priorities. These men had both qualities. If you are in a position of selecting leaders, look for faithfulness and reverence as two of the most important qual-

ifications. Although other qualities may seem more impressive, faithfulness and reverence pass the test of time.

**7:3** City gates were usually opened at sunrise, enabling merchants to enter and set up their tent-stores. Nehemiah didn't want Jerusalem to be caught unprepared by an enemy attack, so he ordered the gates closed until well after sunrise when the people were sure to be awake and alert.

**7:3** The wall was complete, but the work was not finished. Nehemiah assigned each family the task of protecting the section of wall next to their home. It is tempting to relax our guard and rest on past accomplishments after we have completed a large task. But we must continue to serve and to take care of all that God has entrusted to us. Following through after a project is completed is as vital as doing the project itself.

**7:5ff** Nehemiah found the genealogical record. Because this genealogy is almost identical to Ezra's (Ezra 2), most likely Ezra's list was stored in the Temple archives and was the one Nehemiah found.

16 The family of Bebai. . . . . . . . . . . . . . . . . . . . . . . . . . . . . . . . . 628
17 The family of Azgad . . . . . . . . . . . . . . . . . . . . . . . . . . . . . . . 2,322
18 The family of Adonikam . . . . . . . . . . . . . . . . . . . . . . . . . . . . 667
19 The family of Bigvai . . . . . . . . . . . . . . . . . . . . . . . . . . . . . . . 2,067
20 The family of Adin . . . . . . . . . . . . . . . . . . . . . . . . . . . . . . . . . 655
21 The family of Ater (descendants of Hezekiah) . . . . . . . . . . . . . . 98
22 The family of Hashum. . . . . . . . . . . . . . . . . . . . . . . . . . . . . . 328
23 The family of Bezai. . . . . . . . . . . . . . . . . . . . . . . . . . . . . . . . 324
24 The family of Jorah* . . . . . . . . . . . . . . . . . . . . . . . . . . . . . . . 112
25 The family of Gibbar* . . . . . . . . . . . . . . . . . . . . . . . . . . . . . . . 95
26 The people of Bethlehem and Netophah . . . . . . . . . . . . . . . . . 188
27 The people of Anathoth . . . . . . . . . . . . . . . . . . . . . . . . . . . . 128
28 The people of Beth-azmaveth . . . . . . . . . . . . . . . . . . . . . . . . . 42
29 The people of Kiriath-jearim, Kephirah, and Beeroth . . . . . . . . . . 743
30 The people of Ramah and Geba . . . . . . . . . . . . . . . . . . . . . . . 621
31 The people of Micmash . . . . . . . . . . . . . . . . . . . . . . . . . . . . . 122
32 The people of Bethel and Ai . . . . . . . . . . . . . . . . . . . . . . . . . . 123
33 The people of West Nebo* . . . . . . . . . . . . . . . . . . . . . . . . . . . . 52
34 The citizens of West Elam* . . . . . . . . . . . . . . . . . . . . . . . . . 1,254
35 The citizens of Harim . . . . . . . . . . . . . . . . . . . . . . . . . . . . . 320
36 The citizens of Jericho. . . . . . . . . . . . . . . . . . . . . . . . . . . . . 345
37 The citizens of Lod, Hadid, and Ono . . . . . . . . . . . . . . . . . . . . 721
38 The citizens of Senaah . . . . . . . . . . . . . . . . . . . . . . . . . . . . 3,930

39 These are the priests who returned from exile:

    The family of Jedaiah (through the line of Jeshua) . . . . . . . . . . . . 973    **7:39** Ezra 2:36-39

40 The family of Immer. . . . . . . . . . . . . . . . . . . . . . . . . . . . . . 1,052
41 The family of Pashhur. . . . . . . . . . . . . . . . . . . . . . . . . . . . . 1,247
42 The family of Harim . . . . . . . . . . . . . . . . . . . . . . . . . . . . . . 1,017

43 These are the Levites who returned from exile:

    The families of Jeshua and Kadmiel (descendants of Hodaviah*) . . . . . . . . . . 74    **7:43** Ezra 2:40-42

44 The singers of the family of Asaph . . . . . . . . . . . . . . . . . . . . . 148
45 The gatekeepers of the families of Shallum, Ater, Talmon, Akkub,

    Hatita, and Shobai. . . . . . . . . . . . . . . . . . . . . . . . . . . . . . 138

46 The descendants of the following Temple servants returned from exile:    **7:46** Ezra 2:43-54

    Ziha, Hasupha, Tabbaoth,

47 Keros, Siaha,* Padon,
48 Lebanah, Hagabah, Shalmai,
49 Hanan, Giddel, Gahar,
50 Reaiah, Rezin, Nekoda,
51 Gazzam, Uzza, Paseah,
52 Besai, Meunim, Nephusim,*
53 Bakbuk, Hakupha, Harhur,
54 Bazluth,* Mehida, Harsha,
55 Barkos, Sisera, Temah,
56 Neziah, and Hatipha.

57 The descendants of these servants of King Solomon returned from exile:    **7:57** Ezra 2:55-57

    Sotai, Hassophereth, Peruda,*

58 Jaalah,* Darkon, Giddel,
59 Shephatiah, Hattil, Pokereth-hazzebaim, and Ami.*

60 In all, the Temple servants and the descendants of Solomon's servants numbered 392.

61 Another group returned at this time from the towns of Tel-melah, Tel-harsha, Kerub, Addan,* and Immer. However, they could not prove that they or their families

**7:24** As in parallel text at Ezra 2:18; Hebrew reads *Hariph.* **7:25** As in parallel text at Ezra 2:20; Hebrew reads *Gibeon.* **7:33** Or *of the other Nebo.* **7:34** Or *of the other Elam.* **7:43** As in parallel text at Ezra 2:40; Hebrew reads *Hodevah.* **7:47** As in parallel text at Ezra 2:44; Hebrew reads *Sia.* **7:52** As in parallel text at Ezra 2:50; Hebrew reads *Nephushesim.* **7:54** As in parallel text at Ezra 2:52; Hebrew reads *Bazlith.* **7:57** As in parallel text at Ezra 2:55; Hebrew reads *Sotai, Sophereth, Perida.* **7:58** As in parallel text at Ezra 2:56; Hebrew reads *Jaala.* **7:59** As in parallel text at Ezra 2:57; Hebrew reads *Amon.* **7:61** As in parallel text at Ezra 2:59; Hebrew reads *Addon.*

7:63
Ezra 2:61

were descendants of Israel. 62 This group included the families of Delaiah, Tobiah, and Nekoda—a total of 642 people.

63 Three families of priests—Hobaiah, Hakkoz, and Barzillai—also returned. (This Barzillai had married a woman who was a descendant of Barzillai of Gilead, and he had taken her family name.) 64 They searched for their names in the genealogical records, but they were not found, so they were disqualified from serving as priests. 65 The governor told them not to eat the priests' share of food from the sacrifices until a priest could consult the LORD about the matter by using the Urim and Thummim—the sacred lots.

66 So a total of 42,360 people returned to Judah, 67 in addition to 7,337 servants and 245 singers, both men and women. 68 They took with them 736 horses, 245 mules,* 69 435 camels, and 6,720 donkeys.

7:70
Neh 8:9

70 Some of the family leaders gave gifts for the work. The governor gave to the treasury 1,000 gold coins,* 50 gold basins, and 530 robes for the priests. 71 The other leaders gave to the treasury a total of 20,000 gold coins* and some 2,750 pounds* of silver for the work. 72 The rest of the people gave 20,000 gold coins, about 2,500 pounds* of silver, and 67 robes for the priests.

7:73
Ezra 3:1

73 So the priests, the Levites, the gatekeepers, the singers, the Temple servants, and some of the common people settled near Jerusalem. The rest of the people returned to their own towns throughout Israel.

## B. REFORMING THE PEOPLE (7:73—13:31)

When Nehemiah arrived in Jerusalem he found more than just broken walls; he found broken lives. In response, Nehemiah gathers the people together to hear Ezra read God's law. The people repent and promise to change their lives by obeying God's words. No matter where we live, backsliding is an ever-present danger. We must constantly check our behavior against God's standards in the Bible so that we do not slide back into sinful ways of living.

### 1. Ezra renews the covenant
*Ezra Reads the Law*

8:1
2 Chr 34:15
Ezra 7:6
Neh 3:26

**8** In October,* when the Israelites had settled in their towns, 8:1 all the people assembled with a unified purpose at the square just inside the Water Gate. They asked Ezra the scribe to bring out the Book of the Law of Moses, which the LORD had given for Israel to obey.

8:2
Lev 23:24
Deut 31:9-12

2 So on October 8* Ezra the priest brought the Book of the Law before the assembly, which included the men and women and all the children old enough to understand. 3 He faced the square just inside the Water Gate from early morning until noon and read aloud to everyone who could understand. All the people listened closely to the Book of the Law.

**7:68** As in some Hebrew manuscripts (see also Ezra 2:66); most Hebrew manuscripts lack this verse. Verses 7:69-73 are numbered 7:68-72 in Hebrew text.    **7:70** Hebrew *1,000 darics of gold,* about 19 pounds or 8.6 kilograms in weight.    **7:71a** Hebrew *20,000 darics of gold,* about 375 pounds or 170 kilograms in weight; also in 7:72.    **7:71b** Hebrew *2,200 minas* [1,300 kilograms].    **7:72** Hebrew *2,000 minas* [1,200 kilograms].    **7:73** Hebrew *in the seventh month.* This month of the ancient Hebrew lunar calendar occurred within the months of October and November 445 B.C.    **8:2** Hebrew *on the first day of the seventh month,* of the ancient Hebrew lunar calendar. This day was October 8, 445 B.C.; also see note on 1:1.

**7:61** Genealogies were greatly valued because it was vitally important for a Jew to be able to prove that he or she was a descendant of Abraham and was, therefore, part of God's people (Genesis 12:1-3; 15; Exodus 19:5, 6; Deuteronomy 11:22-28). A lost genealogy put one's status as a Jew at risk.

**7:64, 65** "Sacred lots" referred to the Urim and Thummim, a means of learning God's will (Exodus 28:30). If someone's name wasn't in the genealogies, he could still be admitted as a priest if the Urim and Thummim proved him to be a Jew and a Levite. It is not clear whether the Urim and Thummim were the originals that had survived the destruction of Jerusalem or if they were new. The "priests' share of food" was meat dedicated to God as part of the sacrifice. Only true priests could eat it.

**8:1-5** The Book of the Law of Moses was probably the Pentateuch, the first five books of the Bible. The people rose to their feet in respect and anticipation. They listened attentively to Ezra as he read God's Word, and their lives were changed. Because we hear the Bible so often, we can become dulled to its words and immune to its teachings. Instead, we should *listen carefully* to every verse and ask the Holy Spirit to help us answer the question, How does this apply to *my* life?

**8:1** This is the first mention of Ezra in this book. He had arrived in Jerusalem from Babylon 13 years before Nehemiah (458 B.C., see Ezra 7:6-9). Given the fact that the first seven chapters are taken with the account of Nehemiah's trip to Jerusalem and the three-month monumental construction task, Ezra's appearance at this point in the book emphasizes that the special role he had all along now came to the forefront. Nehemiah led the rebuilding of the wall; Ezra led the spiritual revival of the nation.

**8:1** Ezra and Nehemiah were contemporaries (8:9), although Ezra was probably much older. Nehemiah, as governor, was the political leader; and Ezra, as priest and scribe, was the religious leader. A scribe in these days was a combination lawyer, notary public, scholar, and consultant. Scribes were among the most educated people, so they were teachers. No doubt the Jews would have liked to set up the kingdom again as in the days of David, but this would have signaled rebellion against the king of Persia to whom they were subject. The best alternative was to divide the leadership between Nehemiah and Ezra.

[4]Ezra the scribe stood on a high wooden platform that had been made for the occasion. To his right stood Mattithiah, Shema, Anaiah, Uriah, Hilkiah, and Maaseiah. To his left stood Pedaiah, Mishael, Malkijah, Hashum, Hashbaddanah, Zechariah, and Meshullam. [5]Ezra stood on the platform in full view of all the people. When they saw him open the book, they all rose to their feet.

[6]Then Ezra praised the LORD, the great God, and all the people chanted, "Amen! Amen!" as they lifted their hands. Then they bowed down and worshiped the LORD with their faces to the ground.

[7]The Levites—Jeshua, Bani, Sherebiah, Jamin, Akkub, Shabbethai, Hodiah, Maaseiah, Kelita, Azariah, Jozabad, Hanan, and Pelaiah—then instructed the people in the Law while everyone remained in their places. [8]They read from the Book of the Law of God and clearly explained the meaning of what was being read, helping the people understand each passage.

[9]Then Nehemiah the governor, Ezra the priest and scribe, and the Levites who were interpreting for the people said to them, "Don't mourn or weep on such a day as this! For today is a sacred day before the LORD your God." For the people had all been weeping as they listened to the words of the Law.

[10]And Nehemiah* continued, "Go and celebrate with a feast of rich foods and sweet drinks, and share gifts of food with people who have nothing prepared. This is a sacred day before our Lord. Don't be dejected and sad, for the joy of the LORD is your strength!"

[11]And the Levites, too, quieted the people, telling them, "Hush! Don't weep! For this is a sacred day." [12]So the people went away to eat and drink at a festive meal, to share gifts of food, and to celebrate with great joy because they had heard God's words and understood them.

### The Festival of Shelters

[13]On October 9* the family leaders of all the people, together with the priests and Levites, met with Ezra the scribe to go over the Law in greater detail. [14]As they studied the Law, they discovered that the LORD had commanded through Moses that the Israelites should live in shelters during the festival to be held that month.* [15]He had said that a proclamation should be made throughout their towns and in Jerusalem, telling the people to go to the hills to get branches from olive, wild olive,* myrtle, palm, and other leafy trees. They were to use these branches to make shelters in which they would live during the festival, as prescribed in the Law.

[16]So the people went out and cut branches and used them to build shelters on the roofs of their houses, in their courtyards, in the courtyards of God's Temple, or in the squares just inside the Water Gate and the Ephraim Gate. [17]So everyone who had returned from captivity lived in these shelters during the festival, and they were all filled with great joy! The Israelites had not celebrated like this since the days of Joshua* son of Nun.

[18]Ezra read from the Book of the Law of God on each of the seven days of the festival. Then on the eighth day they held a solemn assembly, as was required by law.

**8:6**
Exod 4:31
Neh 5:13
1 Tim 2:8

**8:7**
Lev 10:11
Deut 33:10

**8:9**
Deut 12:7, 12
Neh 8:2

**8:10**
Deut 26:11-13
Esth 9:22

**8:12**
Neh 8:7-8, 10

**8:14**
Lev 23:34, 40, 42

**8:16**
2 Kgs 14:13
Neh 8:1; 12:39
Jer 32:29

**8:17**
2 Chr 7:8; 8:13;
30:21

**8:18**
Lev 23:36
Num 29:35
Deut 31:11

**8:10** Hebrew *he.*   **8:13** Hebrew *On the second day,* of the seventh month of the ancient Hebrew lunar calendar. This day was October 9, 445 B.C.; also see notes on 1:1 and 8:2.   **8:14** Hebrew *in the seventh month.* This month of the ancient Hebrew lunar calendar usually occurs within the months of September and October. See Lev 23:39-43. **8:15** Or *pine;* Hebrew reads *oil tree.*   **8:17** Hebrew *Jeshua,* a variant spelling of Joshua.

**8:9** Ezra, not Nehemiah, was the official religious leader. It is significant that Nehemiah was a layman, not a member of the religious establishment or a prophet. He was motivated by his relationship with God, and he devoted his life to doing God's will in a secular world. Such people are crucial to God's work in all aspects of life. No matter what your work or role in life, view it as God's special calling to serve him. God can accomplish his purposes through you, beginning right where you are.

**8:9, 10** The people wept openly when they heard God's laws and realized how far they were from obeying them. But Ezra told them they should be filled with joy because the day was sacred. It was time to celebrate and to give gifts to those in need.

Celebration is not to be self-centered. Ezra connected celebration with giving. This gave those in need an opportunity to celebrate as well. Often when we celebrate and give to others (even when we don't feel like it), we are strengthened spiritually and

filled with joy. Enter into celebrations that honor God, and allow him to fill you with his joy.

**8:13ff** After Ezra read God's laws to the people, they studied them further and then acted upon them. A careful reading of Scripture always calls for a response to these questions: What should we *do* with this knowledge? How should our lives change? We must *do* something about what we have learned if it is to have real significance for our lives.

**8:14-17** During the seven-day Festival of Shelters, the people lived in shelters made of branches. This practice was instituted as a reminder of their rescue from Egypt and the time spent in shelters in the wilderness (Leviticus 23:43). They were to think about God's protection and guidance during their years of wandering and the fact that God would still protect and guide them if they obeyed him. This was a time to remember their origins. It is helpful to remember our beginnings in order to appreciate where we are today. Think back on your life to see where God has led you. Then thank God for his continuing work to protect you and provide for your needs.

## The People Confess Their Sins

9:1
1 Sam 4:12
Ezra 8:23
Neh 8:2
Job 2:12

9:2
Ezra 10:11
Neh 13:3

9:3
Neh 8:4

9:4
Neh 8:7

**9** On October 31* the people assembled again, and this time they fasted and dressed in burlap and sprinkled dust on their heads. ²Those of Israelite descent separated themselves from all foreigners as they confessed their own sins and the sins of their ancestors. ³They remained standing in place for three hours* while the Book of the Law of the LORD their God was read aloud to them. Then for three more hours they confessed their sins and worshiped the LORD their God. ⁴The Levites—Jeshua, Bani, Kadmiel, Shebaniah, Bunni, Sherebiah, Bani, and Kenani—stood on the stairway of the Levites and cried out to the LORD their God with loud voices.

⁵Then the leaders of the Levites—Jeshua, Kadmiel, Bani, Hashabneiah, Sherebiah, Hodiah, Shebaniah, and Pethahiah—called out to the people: "Stand up and praise the LORD your God, for he lives from everlasting to everlasting!" Then they prayed:

"May your glorious name be praised! May it be exalted above all blessing and praise!

9:6
Gen 1:1
Deut 6:4
2 Kgs 19:15
Ps 103:20
Col 1:16-17

9:7
Gen 11:31; 12:1;
15:7; 17:5

9:8
Gen 15:6, 18-21
Josh 21:43-45

9:9
Exod 14:10-14

9:10
Exod 3:7; 5:2; 9:16

9:11
Exod 14:21;
15:1, 5, 10

9:12
Exod 13:21-22

9:13
Exod 19:11, 18-20
Ps 19:7-9

9:14
Exod 16:23; 20:8

9:15
Exod 16:4, 14-15;
17:6
Num 20:7-13
Deut 1:8, 21
Josh 1:2-4

9:16
Deut 31:27
Neh 9:10, 29

9:17
Exod 34:6-7
Num 14:4
Ps 78:11

9:18
Exod 32:4-8, 31

⁶"You alone are the LORD. You made the skies and the heavens and all the stars. You made the earth and the seas and everything in them. You preserve them all, and the angels of heaven worship you.

⁷"You are the LORD God, who chose Abram and brought him from Ur of the Chaldeans and renamed him Abraham. ⁸When he had proved himself faithful, you made a covenant with him to give him and his descendants the land of the Canaanites, Hittites, Amorites, Perizzites, Jebusites, and Girgashites. And you have done what you promised, for you are always true to your word.

⁹"You saw the misery of our ancestors in Egypt, and you heard their cries from beside the Red Sea.* ¹⁰You displayed miraculous signs and wonders against Pharaoh, his officials, and all his people, for you knew how arrogantly they were treating our ancestors. You have a glorious reputation that has never been forgotten. ¹¹You divided the sea for your people so they could walk through on dry land! And then you hurled their enemies into the depths of the sea. They sank like stones beneath the mighty waters. ¹²You led our ancestors by a pillar of cloud during the day and a pillar of fire at night so that they could find their way.

¹³"You came down at Mount Sinai and spoke to them from heaven. You gave them regulations and instructions that were just, and decrees and commands that were good. ¹⁴You instructed them concerning your holy Sabbath. And you commanded them, through Moses your servant, to obey all your commands, decrees, and instructions.

¹⁵"You gave them bread from heaven when they were hungry and water from the rock when they were thirsty. You commanded them to go and take possession of the land you had sworn to give them.

¹⁶"But our ancestors were proud and stubborn, and they paid no attention to your commands. ¹⁷They refused to obey and did not remember the miracles you had done for them. Instead, they became stubborn and appointed a leader to take them back to their slavery in Egypt! But you are a God of forgiveness, gracious and merciful, slow to become angry, and rich in unfailing love. You did not abandon them, ¹⁸even when they made an idol shaped like a calf and said, 'This is your god who brought you out of Egypt!' They committed terrible blasphemies.

9:1 Hebrew *On the twenty-fourth day of that same month*, the seventh month of the ancient Hebrew lunar calendar. This day was October 31, 445 B.C.; also see notes on 1:1 and 8:2. 9:3 Hebrew *for a quarter of a day.* 9:9 Hebrew *sea of reeds.*

---

9:1 Fasting, wearing burlap, and sprinkling dust on the head were public signs of sorrow and repentance.

9:2, 3 The Hebrews practiced open confession, admitting their sins to one another. Reading and studying God's Word should precede confession (see 8:18) because God can show us where we are sinning. Honest confession should precede worship, because we cannot have a right relationship with God if we hold on to certain sins.

9:7-38 Many prayers and speeches in the Bible include a long summary of Israel's history because individuals did not have their own copies of the Bible as we do today. This summary of God's past works reminded the people of their great heritage and God's promises.

Remembering our personal history can certainly help us to avoid repeating our mistakes so that we can serve God better. Reviewing our past helps us understand how to improve our behavior. It shows us the pattern to our spiritual growth. Learn from your past so that you will become the kind of person God wants you to be.

9:16-21 Seeing how God continued to be with his people shows that his patience is amazing! In spite of our repeated failings, pride, and stubbornness, he is always ready to forgive (9:17), and his Spirit is always ready to instruct (9:20). Realizing the extent of God's forgiveness helps us forgive those who fail us, even "seventy times seven" if necessary (Matthew 18:21, 22).

¹⁹"But in your great mercy you did not abandon them to die in the wilderness. The pillar of cloud still led them forward by day, and the pillar of fire showed them the way through the night. ²⁰You sent your good Spirit to instruct them, and you did not stop giving them manna from heaven or water for their thirst. ²¹For forty years you sustained them in the wilderness, and they lacked nothing. Their clothes did not wear out, and their feet did not swell!

²²"Then you helped our ancestors conquer kingdoms and nations, and you placed your people in every corner of the land.* They took over the land of King Sihon of Heshbon and the land of King Og of Bashan. ²³You made their descendants as numerous as the stars in the sky and brought them into the land you had promised to their ancestors.

²⁴"They went in and took possession of the land. You subdued whole nations before them. Even the Canaanites, who inhabited the land, were powerless! Your people could deal with these nations and their kings as they pleased. ²⁵Our ancestors captured fortified cities and fertile land. They took over houses full of good things, with cisterns already dug and vineyards and olive groves and fruit trees in abundance. So they ate until they were full and grew fat and enjoyed themselves in all your blessings.

²⁶"But despite all this, they were disobedient and rebelled against you. They turned their backs on your Law, they killed your prophets who warned them to return to you, and they committed terrible blasphemies. ²⁷So you handed them over to their enemies, who made them suffer. But in their time of trouble they cried to you, and you heard them from heaven. In your great mercy, you sent them liberators who rescued them from their enemies.

²⁸"But as soon as they were at peace, your people again committed evil in your sight, and once more you let their enemies conquer them. Yet whenever your people turned and cried to you again for help, you listened once more from heaven. In your wonderful mercy, you rescued them many times!

²⁹"You warned them to return to your Law, but they became proud and obstinate and disobeyed your commands. They did not follow your regulations, by which people will find life if only they obey. They stubbornly turned their backs on you and refused to listen. ³⁰In your love, you were patient with them for many years. You sent your Spirit, who warned them through the prophets. But still they wouldn't listen! So once again you allowed the peoples of the land to conquer them. ³¹But in your great mercy, you did not destroy them completely or abandon them forever. What a gracious and merciful God you are!

³²"And now, our God, the great and mighty and awesome God, who keeps his covenant of unfailing love, do not let all the hardships we have suffered seem insignificant to you. Great trouble has come upon us and upon our kings and leaders and priests and prophets and ancestors—all of your people—from the days when the kings of Assyria first triumphed over us until now. ³³Every time you punished us you were being just. We have sinned greatly, and you gave us only what we deserved. ³⁴Our kings, leaders, priests, and ancestors did not obey your Law or listen to the warnings in your commands and laws. ³⁵Even while they had their own kingdom, they did not serve you, though you showered your goodness on them. You gave them a large, fertile land, but they refused to turn from their wickedness.

³⁶"So now today we are slaves in the land of plenty that you gave our ancestors for their enjoyment! We are slaves here in this good land. ³⁷The lush produce of this land

9:19
Neh 9:12, 27, 31

9:20
Num 11:17
Neh 9:15, 30
Isa 63:11-14

9:21
Deut 2:7

9:22
Num 21:21-35
Deut 2:26–3:11

9:23
Gen 15:5

9:24
Josh 18:1; 21:43

9:25
Num 13:27
Deut 3:5; 6:11;
32:15
1 Kgs 8:66

9:26
Judg 2:11
1 Kgs 14:9
2 Chr 36:16

9:27
Judg 2:14, 16, 18

9:28
Judg 3:11
Ps 106:43

9:29
Lev 18:5
Zech 7:11

9:30
2 Kgs 17:13
Neh 9:20

9:31
Neh 9:17
Jer 4:27

9:32
2 Kgs 15:19, 29;
17:3-6

9:33
Gen 18:25
Jer 12:1

9:35
Deut 28:45-47

9:36
Deut 28:48

9:37
Deut 28:33

9:22 The meaning of the Hebrew is uncertain.

9:28-31 Israel was devastated by times of intense rebellion and sin. Yet when the people repented and returned to God, he delivered them. God puts no limit on the number of times we can come to him to obtain mercy, but we must *come* in order to obtain it, recognizing our need and asking him for help. This miracle of grace should inspire us to say, "What a gracious and merciful God you are!" If there is a recurring problem or difficulty in your life, continue to ask God for help, and be willing and ready to make changes in your attitude and behavior that will correct that situation.

9:35 Sometimes the way we take for granted the very blessings

God has showered on us leads us to forget him (9:28). We are often tempted to rely on wealth for security rather than on God who makes it possible. As you see what happened to the Israelites, look at your own life. Do your blessings make you thankful to God and draw you closer to him, or do they make you feel self-sufficient and forgetful of God?

9:36 The Israelites were in the strange position of being slaves in their own land, having to turn over a part of their resources each year to a foreign king. How ironic, since God had given the land to them. This was certainly a bitter reminder of the lasting consequences of sin.

piles up in the hands of the kings whom you have set over us because of our sins. They have power over us and our livestock. We serve them at their pleasure, and we are in great misery."

### The People Agree to Obey

38*The people responded, "In view of all this,* we are making a solemn promise and putting it in writing. On this sealed document are the names of our leaders and Levites and priests."

# 10

1*The document was ratified and sealed with the following names:

The governor:

Nehemiah son of Hacaliah, and also Zedekiah.

2 The following priests:

Seraiah, Azariah, Jeremiah, 3Pashhur, Amariah, Malkijah, 4Hattush, Shebaniah, Malluch, 5Harim, Meremoth, Obadiah, 6Daniel, Ginnethon, Baruch, 7Meshullam, Abijah, Mijamin, 8Maaziah, Bilgai, and Shemaiah. These were the priests.

9 The following Levites:

Jeshua son of Azaniah, Binnui from the family of Henadad, Kadmiel, 10and their fellow Levites: Shebaniah, Hodiah, Kelita, Pelaiah, Hanan, 11Mica, Rehob, Hashabiah, 12Zaccur, Sherebiah, Shebaniah, 13Hodiah, Bani, and Beninu.

14 The following leaders:

Parosh, Pahath-moab, Elam, Zattu, Bani, 15Bunni, Azgad, Bebai, 16Adonijah, Bigvai, Adin, 17Ater, Hezekiah, Azzur, 18Hodiah, Hashum, Bezai, 19Hariph, Anathoth, Nebai, 20Magpiash, Meshullam, Hezir, 21Meshezabel, Zadok, Jaddua, 22Pelatiah, Hanan, Anaiah, 23Hoshea, Hananiah, Hasshub, 24Hallohesh, Pilha, Shobek, 25Rehum, Hashabnah, Maaseiah, 26Ahiah, Hanan, Anan, 27Malluch, Harim, and Baanah.

### The Vow of the People

28Then the rest of the people—the priests, Levites, gatekeepers, singers, Temple servants, and all who had separated themselves from the pagan people of the land in order to obey the Law of God, together with their wives, sons, daughters, and all who were old enough to

**10:8-9**
Neh 12:1

**10:28**
Ezra 2:36-58
Neh 9:2
**10:29**
Neh 5:12

9:38a Verse 9:38 is numbered 10:1 in Hebrew text.   9:38b Or *In spite of all this.*   10:1 Verses 10:1-39 are numbered 10:2-40 in Hebrew text.

---

**GOING HOME: TWO GREAT JOURNEYS OF ISRAEL**

| What about the Journeys? | The Exodus | The Return from Exile |
|---|---|---|
| Where were they? | Egypt (430 years) | Babylon (70 years) |
| How many? | About 1 million | 60,000 |
| How long did the journey take them? | 40 years and 2 attempts | 100 years and 3 journeys |
| Who led them? | Moses/Aaron/Joshua | Zerubbabel/Ezra/Nehemiah |
| What was their purpose? | To reclaim the Promised Land | To rebuild the Temple and city of Jerusalem |
| What obstacles did they face? | Red Sea/Wilderness/Enemies | Ruins/Limited Resources/Enemies |
| What failures did they experience? | Complaining/Disobedience/Retreat—all of which turned a journey of a few weeks into a 40-year ordeal | Fear/Discouragement/Apathy—all of which turned a project of a few months into one that required a century to complete |
| What successes did they have? | Eventually entered the Promised Land | Eventually rebuilt Jerusalem's Temple and wall |
| What lessons did they learn? | God will build his nation. God is both faithful and just. God will accomplish great acts to make his promises come true. | God will preserve his nation. God will continue to have a chosen people, a home for them, and a plan to offer himself to them. |

---

**9:38** This "solemn promise" between the people and God had six provisions. They agreed to (1) not marry non-Jewish neighbors (10:30), (2) observe the Sabbath (10:31), (3) observe every seventh year as a Sabbath year (10:31), (4) pay a Temple tax (10:32, 33), (5) supply wood for the burnt offerings in the Temple (10:34), and (6) give dues to the Temple (10:35-38). After years of decadence and exile, the people once again took seriously their responsibility to follow God and keep his laws wholeheartedly.

understand—29joined their leaders and bound themselves with an oath. They swore a curse on themselves if they failed to obey the Law of God as issued by his servant Moses. They solemnly promised to carefully follow all the commands, regulations, and decrees of the LORD our Lord:

30"We promise not to let our daughters marry the pagan people of the land, and not to let our sons marry their daughters.

31"We also promise that if the people of the land should bring any merchandise or grain to be sold on the Sabbath or on any other holy day, we will refuse to buy it. Every seventh year we will let our land rest, and we will cancel all debts owed to us.

32"In addition, we promise to obey the command to pay the annual Temple tax of one-eighth of an ounce of silver* for the care of the Temple of our God. 33This will provide for the Bread of the Presence; for the regular grain offerings and burnt offerings; for the offerings on the Sabbaths, the new moon celebrations, and the annual festivals; for the holy offerings; and for the sin offerings to make atonement for Israel. It will provide for everything necessary for the work of the Temple of our God.

34"We have cast sacred lots to determine when—at regular times each year—the families of the priests, Levites, and the common people should bring wood to God's Temple to be burned on the altar of the LORD our God, as is written in the Law.

35"We promise to bring the first part of every harvest to the LORD's Temple year after year—whether it be a crop from the soil or from our fruit trees. 36We agree to give God our oldest sons and the firstborn of all our herds and flocks, as prescribed in the Law. We will present them to the priests who minister in the Temple of our God. 37We will store the produce in the storerooms of the Temple of our God. We will bring the best of our flour and other grain offerings, the best of our fruit, and the best of our new wine and olive oil. And we promise to bring to the Levites a tenth of everything our land produces, for it is the Levites who collect the tithes in all our rural towns.

38"A priest—a descendant of Aaron—will be with the Levites as they receive these tithes. And a tenth of all that is collected as tithes will be delivered by the Levites to the Temple of our God and placed in the storerooms. 39The people and the Levites must bring these offerings of grain, new wine, and olive oil to the storerooms and place them in the sacred containers near the ministering priests, the gatekeepers, and the singers.

"We promise together not to neglect the Temple of our God."

10:32 Hebrew *tax of 1/3 of a shekel* [4 grams].

| Reference |
| --- |
| **10:30** Exod 34:16; Deut 7:3 |
| **10:31** Exod 23:10-11; Lev 25:1-7; Deut 15:1-2; Neh 13:15-22 |
| **10:32** Exod 30:11-16; Matt 17:24 |
| **10:33** Lev 23:1-44; 24:5-7 |
| **10:34** Neh 11:1; 13:31 |
| **10:35** Exod 23:19; Deut 26:2 |
| **10:36** Exod 13:2 |
| **10:37** Lev 23:17; 27:30; Neh 13:5, 9 |
| **10:38** Num 18:26; Neh 13:12-13 |
| **10:39** Deut 12:6; Neh 13:10-11 |

**10:28ff** The wall was completed, and the covenant God had made with his people in the days of Moses was restored (Deuteronomy 8). This promise has principles that are important for us today. Our relationship with God must go far beyond church attendance and regular devotions. It should affect our relationships (10:30), our time (10:31), and our material resources (10:32-39). When you chose to follow God, you promised to serve him in this way. The Israelites had fallen away from their original commitment. We must keep our promise to God in times of adversity or prosperity.

**10:30** If God's chosen people were going to witness for him in a pagan world, they needed united, God-fearing families. They also needed to avoid any enticements to worship the idols of the people who lived around them. This was why God prohibited marriage between Israelites and the pagan inhabitants of the land (Deuteronomy 7:3, 4). But Israelites and pagans often intermarried anyway, and the results were disastrous for the families and for the nation. Time after time, marrying foreigners led God's people into idolatry (1 Kings 11:1-11). Whenever the nation turned its back on God, it also lost its prosperity and influence for good.

**10:31** The promise to forgive trade inside the city on the Sabbath was an application of the fourth commandment. The people recognized that the lure of money would conflict with the need for a day of rest, keeping the Sabbath holy. By deciding to honor God first, the Israelites would be refusing to make money their god. Our culture often makes us choose between convenience and profit on the one hand, and putting God first on the other. Look at your work and worship habits: Is God really first?

**10:31** Canceling all debts every seventh year was a part of the law (see Exodus 23:10, 11 and Deuteronomy 15:1, 2). The people were reciting and promising to obey God's law and keep the covenant.

**10:32** The Temple had been rebuilt under Ezra's leadership about 70 years earlier (Ezra 6:14, 15). So the Temple tax, offerings, and festivals had been restored.

**10:35** This practice was instituted at the time of the Exodus from Egypt (see the note on Exodus 13:12-14). The people needed to relearn the importance of dedicating the first part of their yield to God. Nehemiah was simply reinstating this practice from the early days of the nation (Exodus 13:1, 2; Numbers 3:40-51). Although this principle was not carried over to New Testament times, the concept of giving God the first portion of our time, treasure, and talent still remains. Do you give God your first and best or merely what is left over?

**10:37-39** According to God's law, the people were to give a tenth of their produce to the Temple for the support of the Levites (those who cared for the Temple and the religious observances). A tenth of what the Levites received or produced went to the priests for their support. The principle at work was to ensure the support of the house of God and his workers. We must not overlook our responsibility to God's workers today.

## 2. Nehemiah establishes policies
### The People Occupy Jerusalem

11:1
Neh 7:4; 10:34;
11:18
Isa 48:2

**11** The leaders of the people were living in Jerusalem, the holy city. A tenth of the people from the other towns of Judah and Benjamin were chosen by sacred lots to live there, too, while the rest stayed where they were. ²And the people commended everyone who volunteered to resettle in Jerusalem.

11:3-19
//1 Chr 9:1-17
Ezra 2:43-57
Neh 7:57-59; 11:20

³Here is a list of the names of the provincial officials who came to live in Jerusalem. (Most of the people, priests, Levites, Temple servants, and descendants of Solomon's servants continued to live in their own homes in the various towns of Judah, ⁴but some of the people from Judah and Benjamin resettled in Jerusalem.)

From the tribe of Judah:

Athaiah son of Uzziah, son of Zechariah, son of Amariah, son of Shephatiah, son of Mahalalel, of the family of Perez. ⁵Also Maaseiah son of Baruch, son of Col-hozeh, son of Hazaiah, son of Adaiah, son of Joiarib, son of Zechariah, of the family of Shelah.* ⁶There were 468 descendants of Perez who lived in Jerusalem—all outstanding men. ⁷From the tribe of Benjamin:

Sallu son of Meshullam, son of Joed, son of Pedaiah, son of Kolaiah, son of Maaseiah, son of Ithiel, son of Jeshaiah. ⁸After him were Gabbai and Sallai and a total of 928 relatives. ⁹Their chief officer was Joel son of Zicri, who was assisted by Judah son of Hassenuah, second-in-command over the city.

¹⁰From the priests:

Jedaiah son of Joiarib; Jakin; ¹¹and Seraiah son of Hilkiah, son of Meshullam, son of Zadok, son of Meraioth, son of Ahitub, the supervisor of the Temple of God. ¹²Also 822 of their associates, who worked at the Temple. Also Adaiah son of Jeroham, son of Pelaliah, son of Amzi, son of Zechariah, son of Pashhur, son of Malkijah, ¹³along with 242 of his associates, who were heads of their families. Also Amashsai son of Azarel, son of Ahzai, son of Meshillemoth, son of Immer, ¹⁴and 128 of his* outstanding associates. Their chief officer was Zabdiel son of Haggedolim.

¹⁵From the Levites:

Shemaiah son of Hasshub, son of Azrikam, son of Hashabiah, son of Bunni. ¹⁶Also Shabbethai and Jozabad, who were in charge of the work outside the Temple of God. ¹⁷Also Mattaniah son of Mica, son of Zabdi, a descendant of Asaph, who led in thanksgiving and prayer. Also Bakbukiah, who was Mattaniah's assistant, and Abda son of Shammua, son of Galal, son of Jeduthun. ¹⁸In all, there were 284 Levites in the holy city. ¹⁹From the gatekeepers:

11:18
Neh 11:1, 3

Akkub, Talmon, and 172 of their associates, who guarded the gates.

11:21
Neh 3:26

²⁰The other priests, Levites, and the rest of the Israelites lived wherever their family inheritance was located in any of the towns of Judah. ²¹The Temple servants, however, whose leaders were Ziha and Gishpa, all lived on the hill of Ophel.

11:22
Neh 11:9, 14,
17, 23

²²The chief officer of the Levites in Jerusalem was Uzzi son of Bani, son of Hashabiah, son of Mattaniah, son of Mica, a descendant of Asaph, whose family served as singers at God's Temple. ²³Their daily responsibilities were carried out according to the terms of a royal command.

²⁴Pethahiah son of Meshezabel, a descendant of Zerah son of Judah, was the royal adviser in all matters of public administration.

11:25
Josh 13:9, 17;
14:15

²⁵As for the surrounding villages with their open fields, some of the people of Judah lived in Kiriath-arba with its settlements, Dibon with its settlements, and Jekabzeel with its villages. ²⁶They also lived in Jeshua, Moladah, Beth-pelet, ²⁷Hazar-shual, Beersheba with its

**11:5** Hebrew *son of the Shilonite.*   **11:14** As in Greek version; Hebrew reads *their.*

---

**11:1ff** The exiles who returned were few in number compared to Jerusalem's population in the days of the kings. And because the walls had been rebuilt on their original foundations, the city seemed sparsely populated. Nehemiah asked one-tenth of the people from the outlying areas to move inside the city walls to keep large areas of the city from being vacant. Apparently these people did not want to move into the city. Only a few people volunteered (11:1, 2), and Nehemiah determined by sacred lot who among the remaining people would have to move.

Many of them may not have wanted to live in the city because (1) non-Jews attached a stigma to Jerusalem residents, often excluding them from trade because of their religious beliefs; (2) moving into the city meant rebuilding their homes and reestablishing their businesses, a major investment of time and money; (3) living in Jerusalem required stricter obedience to God's Word because of greater social pressure and proximity to the Temple.

settlements, [28]Ziklag, and Meconah with its settlements. [29]They also lived in En-rimmon, Zorah, Jarmuth, [30]Zanoah, and Adullam with their surrounding villages. They also lived in Lachish with its nearby fields and Azekah with its surrounding villages. So the people of Judah were living all the way from Beersheba in the south to the valley of Hinnom.

[31]Some of the people of Benjamin lived at Geba, Micmash, Aija, and Bethel with its settlements. [32]They also lived in Anathoth, Nob, Ananiah, [33]Hazor, Ramah, Gittaim, [34]Hadid, Zeboim, Neballat, [35]Lod, Ono, and the Valley of Craftsmen.* [36]Some of the Levites who lived in Judah were sent to live with the tribe of Benjamin.

## A History of the Priests and Levites

**12** Here is the list of the priests and Levites who returned with Zerubbabel son of Shealtiel and Jeshua the high priest:

*12:1*
*Ezra 2:1-2*

Seraiah, Jeremiah, Ezra,
[2] Amariah, Malluch, Hattush,
[3] Shecaniah, Harim,* Meremoth,
[4] Iddo, Ginnethon,* Abijah,
[5] Miniamin, Moadiah,* Bilgah,
[6] Shemaiah, Joiarib, Jedaiah,
[7] Sallu, Amok, Hilkiah, and Jedaiah.
These were the leaders of the priests and their associates in the days of Jeshua.

[8]The Levites who returned with them were Jeshua, Binnui, Kadmiel, Sherebiah, Judah, and Mattaniah, who with his associates was in charge of the songs of thanksgiving. [9]Their associates, Bakbukiah and Unni, stood opposite them during the service.

*12:8*
*Ezra 2:2*
*Neh 11:17*

[10] Jeshua the high priest was the father of Joiakim.
Joiakim was the father of Eliashib.
Eliashib was the father of Joiada.
[11] Joiada was the father of Johanan.*
Johanan was the father of Jaddua.

[12]Now when Joiakim was high priest, the family leaders of the priests were as follows:

Meraiah was leader of the family of Seraiah.
Hananiah was leader of the family of Jeremiah.
[13] Meshullam was leader of the family of Ezra.
Jehohanan was leader of the family of Amariah.
[14] Jonathan was leader of the family of Malluch.*
Joseph was leader of the family of Shecaniah.*
[15] Adna was leader of the family of Harim.
Helkai was leader of the family of Meremoth.*
[16] Zechariah was leader of the family of Iddo.
Meshullam was leader of the family of Ginnethon.
[17] Zicri was leader of the family of Abijah.
There was also a* leader of the family of Miniamin.
Piltai was leader of the family of Moadiah.
[18] Shammua was leader of the family of Bilgah.
Jehonathan was leader of the family of Shemaiah.
[19] Mattenai was leader of the family of Joiarib.
Uzzi was leader of the family of Jedaiah.
[20] Kallai was leader of the family of Sallu.*
Eber was leader of the family of Amok.
[21] Hashabiah was leader of the family of Hilkiah.
Nethanel was leader of the family of Jedaiah.

[22]A record of the Levite families was kept during the years when Eliashib, Joiada, Johanan, and Jaddua served as high priest. Another record of the priests was kept during the

**11:35** Or *and Ge-harashim.*   **12:3** Hebrew *Rehum;* compare 7:42; 12:15; Ezra 2:39.   **12:4** As in some Hebrew manuscripts and Latin Vulgate (see also 12:16); most Hebrew manuscripts read *Ginnethoi.*   **12:5** Hebrew *Mijamin, Maadiah;* compare 12:17.   **12:11** Hebrew *Jonathan;* compare 12:22.   **12:14a** As in Greek version (see also 10:4; 12:2); Hebrew reads *Malluchi.*   **12:14b** As in many Hebrew manuscripts, some Greek manuscripts, and Syriac version (see also 12:3); most Hebrew manuscripts read *Shebaniah.*   **12:15** As in some Greek manuscripts (see also 12:3); Hebrew reads *Meraioth.*   **12:17** Hebrew lacks the name of this family leader.   **12:20** Hebrew *Sallai;* compare 12:7.

reign of Darius the Persian.* [23]A record of the heads of the Levite families was kept in *The Book of History* down to the days of Johanan, the grandson* of Eliashib.

12:24
Neh 11:17

[24]These were the family leaders of the Levites: Hashabiah, Sherebiah, Jeshua, Binnui,* Kadmiel, and other associates, who stood opposite them during the ceremonies of praise and thanksgiving, one section responding to the other, as commanded by David, the man of God. [25]This included Mattaniah, Bakbukiah, and Obadiah.

12:25
1 Chr 26:15
12:26
Neh 8:9

Meshullam, Talmon, and Akkub were the gatekeepers in charge of the storerooms at the gates. [26]These all served in the days of Joiakim son of Jeshua, son of Jehozadak,* and in the days of Nehemiah the governor and of Ezra the priest and scribe.

### Dedication of Jerusalem's Wall

12:27
1 Chr 15:16, 28

[27]For the dedication of the new wall of Jerusalem, the Levites throughout the land were asked to come to Jerusalem to assist in the ceremonies. They were to take part in the joyous occasion with their songs of thanksgiving and with the music of cymbals, harps, and lyres.

12:28
1 Chr 9:16

[28]The singers were brought together from the region around Jerusalem and from the villages of the Netophathites. [29]They also came from Beth-gilgal and the rural areas near Geba and Azmaveth, for the singers had built their own settlements around Jerusalem. [30]The priests and Levites first purified themselves; then they purified the people, the gates, and the wall.

12:30
Neh 13:22, 30

12:31
Neh 2:13; 3:13-14

[31]I led the leaders of Judah to the top of the wall and organized two large choirs to give thanks. One of the choirs proceeded southward* along the top of the wall to the Dung Gate. [32]Hoshaiah and half the leaders of Judah followed them, [33]along with Azariah, Ezra, Meshullam, [34]Judah, Benjamin, Shemaiah, and Jeremiah. [35]Then came some priests who played trumpets, including Zechariah son of Jonathan, son of Shemaiah, son of Mattaniah, son of Micaiah, son of Zaccur, a descendant of Asaph. [36]And Zechariah's colleagues were Shemaiah, Azarel, Milalai, Gilalai, Maai, Nethanel, Judah, and Hanani. They used the musical instruments prescribed by David, the man of God. Ezra the scribe led this procession.

12:37
Neh 2:14; 3:15, 26

[37]At the Fountain Gate they went straight up the steps on the ascent of the city wall toward the City of David. They passed the house of David and then proceeded to the Water Gate on the east.

12:38
Neh 3:8, 11

[38]The second choir giving thanks went northward* around the other way to meet them. I followed them, together with the other half of the people, along the top of the wall past the Tower of the Ovens to the Broad Wall, [39]then past the Ephraim Gate to the Old City Gate,* past the Fish Gate and the Tower of Hananel, and on to the Tower of the Hundred. Then we continued on to the Sheep Gate and stopped at the Guard Gate.

12:39
Neh 3:1, 3, 6, 25,
31-32; 8:16
Jer 31:38

[40]The two choirs that were giving thanks then proceeded to the Temple of God, where they took their places. So did I, together with the group of leaders who were with me. [41]We went together with the trumpet-playing priests—Eliakim, Maaseiah, Miniamin, Micaiah, Elioenai, Zechariah, and Hananiah—[42]and the singers—Maaseiah, Shemaiah, Eleazar, Uzzi, Jehohanan, Malkijah, Elam, and Ezer. They played and sang loudly under the direction of Jezrahiah the choir director.

[43]Many sacrifices were offered on that joyous day, for God had given the people cause for great joy. The women and children also participated in the celebration, and the joy of the people of Jerusalem could be heard far away.

**12:22** *Darius the Persian* is probably Darius II, who reigned 423–404 B.C., or possibly Darius III, who reigned 336–331 B.C. **12:23** Hebrew *descendant;* compare 12:10-11. **12:24** Hebrew *son of* (i.e., *ben*), which should probably be read here as the proper name Binnui; compare Ezra 3:9 and the note there. **12:26** Hebrew *Jozadak,* a variant spelling of Jehozadak. **12:31** Hebrew *to the right.* **12:38** Hebrew *to the left.* **12:39** Or *the Mishneh Gate,* or *the Jeshanah Gate.*

---

**12:35, 36** How could the priests have used musical instruments? David had instituted music as a part of worship in the Temple, and so his instruments had probably been stored there. Although Nebuchadnezzar destroyed the Temple, he took many Temple items back to Babylon with him (2 Chronicles 36:18). These were most likely preserved in Babylon and given back to the Israelites by Cyrus when they returned to their land (Ezra 1:7-11).

**12:35, 36** The trumpet that earlier was a tool to rally the workers against a potential threat (4:18) now became one of the instruments used to celebrate the completion of a task, the rededication of the people, and praise to God. Not only had he written powerful psalms, King David also had instituted

music as part of worship in the Temple. Although Nebuchadnezzar had destroyed the Temple, he couldn't destroy worship or the music that served that purpose so well. The reconstruction of the Temple and the walls signaled the worship band to start playing again with gusto!

## Provisions for Temple Worship

44On that day men were appointed to be in charge of the storerooms for the offerings, the first part of the harvest, and the tithes. They were responsible to collect from the fields outside the towns the portions required by the Law for the priests and Levites. For all the people of Judah took joy in the priests and Levites and their work. 45They performed the service of their God and the service of purification, as commanded by David and his son Solomon, and so did the singers and the gatekeepers. 46The custom of having choir directors to lead the choirs in hymns of praise and thanksgiving to God began long ago in the days of David and Asaph. 47So now, in the days of Zerubbabel and of Nehemiah, all Israel brought a daily supply of food for the singers, the gatekeepers, and the Levites. The Levites, in turn, gave a portion of what they received to the priests, the descendants of Aaron.

## Nehemiah's Various Reforms

**13** On that same day, as the Book of Moses was being read to the people, the passage was found that said no Ammonite or Moabite should ever be permitted to enter the assembly of God.* 2For they had not provided the Israelites with food and water in the wilderness. Instead, they hired Balaam to curse them, though our God turned the curse into a blessing. 3When this passage of the Law was read, all those of foreign descent were immediately excluded from the assembly.

4Before this had happened, Eliashib the priest, who had been appointed as supervisor of the storerooms of the Temple of our God and who was also a relative of Tobiah, 5had converted a large storage room and placed it at Tobiah's disposal. The room had previously been used for storing the grain offerings, the frankincense, various articles for the Temple, and the tithes of grain, new wine, and olive oil (which were prescribed for the Levites, the singers, and the gatekeepers), as well as the offerings for the priests.

6I was not in Jerusalem at that time, for I had returned to King Artaxerxes of Babylon in the thirty-second year of his reign,* though I later asked his permission to return. 7When I arrived back in Jerusalem, I learned about Eliashib's evil deed in providing Tobiah with a room in the courtyards of the Temple of God. 8I became very upset and threw all of Tobiah's belongings out of the room. 9Then I demanded that the rooms be purified, and I brought back the articles for God's Temple, the grain offerings, and the frankincense.

10I also discovered that the Levites had not been given their prescribed portions of food, so they and the singers who were to conduct the worship services had all returned to work their fields. 11I immediately confronted the leaders and demanded, "Why has the Temple of God been neglected?" Then I called all the Levites back again and restored them to their proper duties. 12And once more all the people of Judah began bringing their tithes of grain, new wine, and olive oil to the Temple storerooms.

**12:44** Neh 13:4-5, 12-13

**12:45** 1 Chr 25:1-8; 26:1-32

**12:46** 2 Chr 29:30

**12:47** Num 18:21-29

**13:1** Deut 23:3-5 Neh 13:23

**13:2** Num 22:3-11

**13:3** Neh 9:2; 10:28

**13:4** Neh 6:17-19; 12:44

**13:5** Num 18:21

**13:6** Neh 5:14

**13:7** Neh 13:5

**13:9** 2 Chr 29:5, 15-19

**13:10** Neh 10:37; 12:28-29

**13:12** Neh 10:37-39; 12:44

**13:1** See Deut 23:3-6.  **13:6** King Artaxerxes of Persia is here identified as the king of Babylon because Persia had conquered the Babylonian Empire. The thirty-second year of Artaxerxes was 433 B.C.

---

**12:44** Further arrangements were made for supporting those who served at the Temple. The storerooms were administered by men who made sure the tithes and contributions were collected and distributed appropriately. These storerooms had to be large to hold all the grain presented by the people. This storeroom administration was an important responsibility.

**12:44-47** The dedication of the city wall was characterized by joy, praise, and singing (12:24, 27-29, 35, 36, 40-43). Nehemiah repeatedly mentioned David, who began the custom of using choirs in worship. In David's day, Israel was a vigorous, God-fearing nation. These exiles who had returned wanted their rebuilt Jerusalem to be the hub of a renewed nation, strengthened by God; therefore, they dedicated themselves and their city to God.

**13:3** "Those of foreign descent" refers to the Ammonites and Moabites, two nations who were bitter enemies of Israel (13:1). God's law clearly stated that these two peoples should never be allowed in the Temple (Deuteronomy 23:3-5). This had nothing to do with racial prejudice because God clearly loved all people, including foreigners (Deuteronomy 10:18). He allowed foreigners to make sacrifices (Numbers 15:15, 16), and he desires all nations to know and love him (Isaiah 42:6). But while God

wants all to come to him, he warns believers to stay away from those bent on evil (Proverbs 24:1). The relationships established between Jews and pagans had caused their captivity in the first place. In their celebration and rededication, they had to show they were serious about following God's law.

**13:6, 7** Nehemiah had to return to Babylon in 433 B.C., 12 years after he had arrived in Jerusalem. Either he was recalled by Artaxerxes, or he was fulfilling an agreement to return. It is not known exactly how long he remained in Babylon, but when he returned to Jerusalem (13:7), he found that one of his major opponents in rebuilding the wall, Tobiah, had been given his own room at the Temple. He was an Ammonite (4:3) and thus forbidden to enter the Temple. Eliashib the priest had married Tobiah's daughter, so Tobiah used his influence with his son-in-law to get this special room. Chapters 2, 4, and 6 tell about Tobiah's opposition to Nehemiah and Nehemiah's appropriate action.

**13:10** Because the Levites were no longer supported, they had returned to their farms to support themselves, neglecting their Temple duties and the spiritual welfare of the people. Spiritual workers deserve their pay, and their support ought to be enough to care for their needs. They shouldn't have to suffer (or leave) because believers don't adequately assess and meet their needs.

**13:13**
Neh 7:2

¹³I assigned supervisors for the storerooms: Shelemiah the priest, Zadok the scribe, and Pedaiah, one of the Levites. And I appointed Hanan son of Zaccur and grandson of Mattaniah as their assistant. These men had an excellent reputation, and it was their job to make honest distributions to their fellow Levites.

**13:14**
Neh 5:19;
13:22, 31

¹⁴Remember this good deed, O my God, and do not forget all that I have faithfully done for the Temple of my God and its services.

**13:15**
Exod 20:8-11;
34:21
Neh 13:21

¹⁵In those days I saw men of Judah treading out their winepresses on the Sabbath. They were also bringing in grain, loading it on donkeys, and bringing their wine, grapes, figs, and all sorts of produce to Jerusalem to sell on the Sabbath. So I rebuked them for selling their produce on that day. ¹⁶Some men from Tyre, who lived in Jerusalem, were bringing in fish and all kinds of merchandise. They were selling it on the Sabbath to the people of Judah—and in Jerusalem at that!

**13:17**
Neh 13:11, 15
**13:18**
Jer 17:21

¹⁷So I confronted the nobles of Judah. "Why are you profaning the Sabbath in this evil way?" I asked. ¹⁸"Wasn't it just this sort of thing that your ancestors did that caused our God to bring all this trouble upon us and our city? Now you are bringing even more wrath upon Israel by permitting the Sabbath to be desecrated in this way!"

**13:19**
Lev 23:32

¹⁹Then I commanded that the gates of Jerusalem should be shut as darkness fell every Friday evening,* not to be opened until the Sabbath ended. I sent some of my own servants to guard the gates so that no merchandise could be brought in on the Sabbath day. ²⁰The merchants and tradesmen with a variety of wares camped outside Jerusalem once or twice.

**13:21**
Neh 13:15

²¹But I spoke sharply to them and said, "What are you doing out here, camping around the wall? If you do this again, I will arrest you!" And that was the last time they came on the Sabbath. ²²Then I commanded the Levites to purify themselves and to guard the gates in order to preserve the holiness of the Sabbath.

**13:22**
Neh 13:14, 31

Remember this good deed also, O my God! Have compassion on me according to your great and unfailing love.

**13:23**
Ezra 9:2
Neh 10:30
**13:25**
Deut 25:2
Neh 10:29-30;
13:11, 17

²³About the same time I realized that some of the men of Judah had married women from Ashdod, Ammon, and Moab. ²⁴Furthermore, half their children spoke the language of Ashdod or of some other people and could not speak the language of Judah at all. ²⁵So I confronted them and called down curses on them. I beat some of them and pulled out their hair. I made them swear in the name of God that they would not let their children intermarry with the pagan people of the land.

**13:26**
1 Kgs 3:13; 11:1-8
2 Chr 1:12
**13:27**
Ezra 10:2
Neh 13:23

²⁶"Wasn't this exactly what led King Solomon of Israel into sin?" I demanded. "There was no king from any nation who could compare to him, and God loved him and made him king over all Israel. But even he was led into sin by his foreign wives. ²⁷How could you even think of committing this sinful deed and acting unfaithfully toward God by marrying foreign women?"

**13:19** Hebrew *on the day before the Sabbath.*

---

**13:16** Tyre was a large Phoenician city and port on the Mediterranean Sea.

**13:17** God had commanded Israel not to work on the Sabbath, but to rest in remembrance of Creation and the Exodus (Exodus 20:8-11; Deuteronomy 5:12-15). The Sabbath rest, lasting from sunset Friday to sunset Saturday, was to be honored and observed by all Jews, servants, visiting foreigners, and even farm animals. Jerusalem's busy Sabbath trade directly violated God's law, so Nehemiah commanded that the city gates be shut and traders be sent home every Friday afternoon as the Sabbath hours approached.

**13:24** Ashdod was on the Mediterranean coast, in the region controlled by the Philistines. Ammon and Moab were across the Jordan to the east. These nations were abhorrent to those who knew Israel's history.

**13:25** Nehemiah was filled with righteous indignation at the blatant way the Jews were breaking God's laws and disregarding the covenant they had previously reaffirmed (10:30). The people had promised not to allow their children to marry pagans. But during Nehemiah's absence, the people had been intermarrying,

breaking their solemn promise with God. Nehemiah's severe treatment of these people shows the contrast between his great faithfulness to God and the people's neglect, disobedience, and disloyalty (see also Ezra 10:3).

**13:26** Nehemiah used the example of Solomon's mistakes to teach his people. If one of the greatest kings of Israel fell because of the influence of unbelievers, others could too. Nehemiah saw this principle in Solomon's example: Your gifts and strengths won't be of much benefit if you fail to deal with your weaknesses. Although Solomon was a great king, his marriages to foreign women brought tragedy to the whole kingdom. A tendency to sin must be recognized and dealt with swiftly; otherwise, it may overpower you and bring you down. One of the strongest reasons for reading the Bible is to learn from the mistakes of God's people.

28One of the sons of Joiada son of Eliashib the high priest had married a daughter of Sanballat the Horonite, so I banished him from my presence.

13:28
Neh 2:10, 19

29Remember them, O my God, for they have defiled the priesthood and the solemn vows of the priests and Levites.

13:29
Num 25:13
Neh 6:14

30So I purged out everything foreign and assigned tasks to the priests and Levites, making certain that each knew his work. 31I also made sure that the supply of wood for the altar and the first portions of the harvest were brought at the proper times.

13:30
Neh 10:30
13:31
Neh 10:34;
13:14, 22

Remember this in my favor, O my God.

---

**13:31** "Remember this in my favor" means "look favorably upon me for all that I have done."

**13:31** Nehemiah's life story provides many principles of effective leadership that are still valid today: (1) *Have a clear purpose and keep evaluating it in light of God's will.* Nothing prevented Nehemiah from staying on track. (2) *Be straightforward and honest.* Everyone knew exactly what Nehemiah needed, and he spoke the truth even when it made his goal harder to achieve. (3) *Live above reproach.* The accusations against Nehemiah were empty and false. (4) *Be a person of constant prayer,* deriving power and wisdom from your contact with God. Everything Nehemiah did glorified God.

Leadership appears glamorous at times, but it is often lonely, thankless, and filled with pressures to compromise values and standards. Nehemiah was able to accomplish a huge task against incredible odds because he learned that there is no success without risk of failure, no reward without hard work, no opportunity without criticism, and no true leadership without trust in God. This book is about rebuilding the wall of a great city, but it is also about spiritual renewal, rebuilding a people's dependence on God. When we take our eyes off God, our lives begin to crumble.

# ESTHER

| Jerusalem destroyed; exiles go to Babylon 586 B.C. | First exiles return to Jerusalem 538 | Temple completed 515 | Xerxes becomes king of Persia 486 | Esther becomes queen 479 | Haman's decree to destroy the Jews 474 | First Festival of Purim 473 |
| --- | --- | --- | --- | --- | --- | --- |

DRAMA, power, romance, intrigue—this is the stuff of which best-selling novels are made. But far from a modern piece of fiction, those words describe a true story, lived and written centuries ago. More than entertaining reading, it is a story of the profound interplay of God's sovereignty and human will. God prepared the place and the opportunity, and his people, Esther and Mordecai, chose to act.

The book of Esther begins with Queen Vashti refusing to obey an order from her husband, King Xerxes. She was subsequently banished, and the search began for a new queen. The king sent out a decree to gather together all the beautiful young women in the empire and bring them into the royal harem. Esther, a young Jewish woman, was one of those chosen. King Xerxes was so pleased with Esther that he made her his queen.

Meanwhile, Mordecai, Esther's older cousin, became a government official and during his tenure foiled an assassination plot. But the ambitious and self-serving Haman was appointed second-in-command in the empire. When Mordecai refused to bow in reverence to him, Haman became furious and determined to destroy Mordecai and all the Jews along with him.

To accomplish his vengeful deed, Haman deceived the king and persuaded him to issue an edict condemning the Jews to death. Mordecai told Queen Esther about this edict, and she decided to risk her life to save her people. Esther asked King Xerxes and Haman to be her guests at a banquet. During the feast, the king asked Esther what she really wanted, and he promised to give her anything. Esther simply invited both men to another banquet the next day.

That night, unable to sleep, the king was flipping through some records in the royal archives when he read of the assassination plot that Mordecai had thwarted. Surprised to learn that Mordecai had never been rewarded for this deed, the king asked Haman what should be done to properly thank a hero. Haman thought the king must be talking about him, and so he described a lavish reward. The king agreed, but to Haman's shock and utter humiliation, he learned that Mordecai was the person to be so honored.

During the second banquet, the king again asked Esther what she desired. She replied that someone had plotted to destroy her and her people, and she named Haman as the culprit. Immediately the king sentenced Haman to die on the impaling pole that he had set up for Mordecai.

In the final act of this true-life drama, Mordecai was appointed to Haman's position, and the Jews were guaranteed protection throughout the land. To celebrate this historic occasion, the Festival of Purim was established.

Because of Queen Esther's courageous act, a whole nation was saved. Seeing her God-given opportunity, she seized it! Her life made a difference. Read Esther and watch for God at work in *your* life. Perhaps he has prepared you to act in "such a time as this" (4:14).

## VITAL STATISTICS

**PURPOSE:**
To demonstrate God's sovereignty and his loving care for his people

**AUTHOR:**
Unknown. Possibly Mordecai (9:29). Some have suggested Ezra or Nehemiah because of the similarity of the writing style.

**ORIGINAL AUDIENCE:**
The people of Israel

**DATE WRITTEN:**
Approximately 470 B.C. (Esther became queen in 479.)

**SETTING:**
Although Esther follows Nehemiah in the Bible, its events are about 30 years prior to those recorded in Nehemiah. The story is set in the Persian Empire, and most of the action takes place in the king's palace in Susa, the Persian capital.

**KEY VERSE:**
"If you keep quiet at a time like this, deliverance and relief for the Jews will arise from some other place, but you and your relatives will die. Who knows if perhaps you were made queen for just such a time as this?" (4:14)

**KEY PEOPLE:**
Esther, Mordecai, King Xerxes I, Haman

**KEY PLACE:**
The king's palace in Susa, Persia

**SPECIAL FEATURES:**
Esther is one of only two books named for women (Ruth is the other). The book is unusual in that in the original version no name, title, or pronoun for God appears (see the note on 4:14). This caused some church fathers to question the book's inclusion in Scripture. But God's presence is clear throughout the book.

## THE BLUEPRINT

1. Esther becomes queen (1:1—2:23)
2. The Jews are threatened (3:1—4:17)
3. Esther intercedes for the Jews (5:1—8:17)
4. The Jews are delivered (9:1—10:3)

The book of Esther is an example of God's divine guidance and care over our lives. God's sovereignty and power are seen throughout this book. Although we may question certain circumstances in our lives, we must have faith that God is in control, working through both the pleasant and difficult times so that we can serve him effectively.

## MEGATHEMES

| THEME | EXPLANATION | IMPORTANCE |
|---|---|---|
| God's Sovereignty | The book of Esther tells of the circumstances that were essential to the survival of God's people in Persia. These "circumstances" were not the result of chance but of God's grand design. God is sovereign over every area of life. | With God in charge, we can take courage. He can guide us through the circumstances we face in our lives. We should expect God to display his power in carrying out his will. As we unite our life's purposes to God's purpose, we benefit from his sovereign care. |
| Racial Hatred | The Jews in Persia had been a minority since their deportation from Judah 100 years earlier. Haman was a descendant of King Agag, an enemy of the Jews. Lust for power and pride drove Haman to hate Mordecai, Esther's cousin. Haman convinced the king to kill all the Jews. | Racial hatred is always sinful. We must never condone it in any form. Every person on earth has intrinsic worth because God created people in his own image. Therefore, God's people must stand against racism whenever and wherever it occurs. |
| Deliverance | In February or March, the Jews celebrate the Festival of Purim, which symbolizes God's deliverance. *Purim* means "lots," such as those used by Haman to set the date for the extermination of all Jews from Persia. But God overruled, using Queen Esther to intercede on behalf of the Jews. | Because God is in control of history, he is never frustrated by any turn of events or human action. He is able to save us from the evil of this world and deliver us from sin and death. Because we trust God, we are not to fear what people may do to us; instead, we are to be confident in God's control. |
| Action | Faced with death, Esther and Mordecai set aside their own fear and took action. Esther risked her life by asking King Xerxes to save the Jews. | When outnumbered and powerless, it is natural for us to feel helpless. Esther and Mordecai resisted this temptation and acted with courage. It is not enough to know that God is in control; we must act with self-sacrifice and courage to follow God's guidance. |
| Wisdom | The Jews were a minority in a world hostile to them. It took great wisdom for Mordecai to survive. Serving as a faithful official of the king, Mordecai took steps to understand and work within the Persian law. Yet he did not compromise his integrity. | It takes great wisdom to survive in a non-believing world. In a setting which is for the most part hostile to Christianity, we can demonstrate wisdom by giving respect to what is true and good and by humbly standing against what is wrong. |

## 1. Esther becomes queen

### The King's Banquet

**1** These events happened in the days of King Xerxes,* who reigned over 127 provinces stretching from India to Ethiopia.* ²At that time Xerxes ruled his empire from his royal throne at the fortress of Susa. ³In the third year of his reign, he gave a banquet for all his nobles and officials. He invited all the military officers of Persia and Media as well as the princes and nobles of the provinces. ⁴The celebration lasted 180 days—a tremendous display of the opulent wealth of his empire and the pomp and splendor of his majesty.

**1:1**
Ezra 4:6
Esth 8:9-10
Dan 8:2
**1:2**
Neh 1:1
**1:3**
Esth 2:18

**1:1a** Hebrew *Ahasuerus,* another name for Xerxes; also throughout the book of Esther. Xerxes reigned 486–465 B.C.
**1:1b** Hebrew *to Cush.*

**1:1** Esther's story begins in 483 B.C., 103 years after Nebuchadnezzar had taken the Jews into captivity (2 Kings 25), 54 years after Zerubbabel led the first group of exiles back to Jerusalem (Ezra 1–2), and 25 years before Ezra led the second group to Jerusalem (Ezra 7). Esther lived in the kingdom of Persia, the dominant kingdom in the Middle East after Babylon's fall in 539 B.C. Esther's parents must have been among those exiles who chose not to return to Jerusalem, even though Cyrus, the Persian king, had issued a decree allowing them to do so. The Jewish exiles had great freedom in Persia, and many remained because they had established themselves there or were fearful of the dangerous journey back to their homeland.

**1:1** Xerxes the Great was Persia's fifth king (486–465 B.C.). He was proud and impulsive, as we see from the events in chapter 1. His winter palace was in Susa, where he held the banquet described in 1:3-7. Persian kings often held great banquets before going to war. In 481, Xerxes launched an attack against Greece. After his fleet won a great victory at Thermopylae, he

**1:5**
Esth 7:7-8

**1:6**
Ezek 23:41
Amos 6:4

**1:7**
Esth 2:18

**1:10**
Judg 16:25
Dan 5:1-4

⁵When it was all over, the king gave a banquet for all the people, from the greatest to the least, who were in the fortress of Susa. It lasted for seven days and was held in the courtyard of the palace garden. ⁶The courtyard was beautifully decorated with white cotton curtains and blue hangings, which were fastened with white linen cords and purple ribbons to silver rings embedded in marble pillars. Gold and silver couches stood on a mosaic pavement of porphyry, marble, mother-of-pearl, and other costly stones.

⁷Drinks were served in gold goblets of many designs, and there was an abundance of royal wine, reflecting the king's generosity. ⁸By edict of the king, no limits were placed on the drinking, for the king had instructed all his palace officials to serve each man as much as he wanted.

⁹At the same time, Queen Vashti gave a banquet for the women in the royal palace of King Xerxes.

## Queen Vashti Deposed

¹⁰On the seventh day of the feast, when King Xerxes was in high spirits because of the wine, he told the seven eunuchs who attended him—Mehuman, Biztha, Harbona, Bigtha, Abagtha, Zethar, and Carcas—¹¹to bring Queen Vashti to him with the royal crown on her head. He wanted the nobles and all the other men to gaze on her beauty, for she was a very beautiful

**THE WORLD OF ESTHER'S DAY**
Esther lived in the capital of the vast Medo-Persian Empire, which incorporated the provinces of Media and Persia, as well as the previous empires of Assyria and Babylon. Esther, a Jew, was chosen by King Xerxes to be his queen. The story of how she saved her people takes place in the palace in Susa.

was defeated at Salamis in 480 and had to return to Persia. Esther became queen in 479.

**1:2** In this context, "fortress" means "palace."

**1:4** The celebration lasted 180 days (about six months) because its real purpose was to plan the battle strategy for invading Greece and to demonstrate that the king had sufficient wealth to carry it out. Waging war was not only for survival; it was a means of acquiring more wealth, territory, and power.

**1:5-7** Persia was a world power, and the king, as the center of that power, was one of the wealthiest people in the world. Persian kings loved to flaunt their wealth, even wearing precious gemstones in their beards. Jewelry was a sign of rank for Persian men. Even soldiers wore great amounts of gold jewelry into battle.

**1:9** Ancient Greek documents call Xerxes' wife Amestris, probably a Greek form of *Vashti*. Vashti was deposed in 483/482 B.C., but she is mentioned again in ancient records as the queen mother

during the reign of her son, Artaxerxes, who succeeded Xerxes. Toward the end of Xerxes' reign, either Esther died or Vashti was able through her son to regain the influence she had lost.

**1:10** Some advisers and government officials were castrated in order to prevent them from having children and then rebelling and trying to establish a dynasty of their own. A castrated official was called a eunuch.

**1:10, 11** Xerxes made a rash, half-drunk decision, based purely on feelings. His self-restraint and practical wisdom were weakened by too much wine. Poor decisions are made when people don't think clearly. Base your decisions on careful thinking, not on the emotions of the moment. Impulsive decision-making leads to severe complications.

woman. 12But when they conveyed the king's order to Queen Vashti, she refused to come. This made the king furious, and he burned with anger.

13He immediately consulted with his wise advisers, who knew all the Persian laws and customs, for he always asked their advice. 14The names of these men were Carshena, Shethar, Admatha, Tarshish, Meres, Marsena, and Memucan—seven nobles of Persia and Media. They met with the king regularly and held the highest positions in the empire.

1:13
1 Chr 12:32

15"What must be done to Queen Vashti?" the king demanded. "What penalty does the law provide for a queen who refuses to obey the king's orders, properly sent through his eunuchs?"

16Memucan answered the king and his nobles, "Queen Vashti has wronged not only the king but also every noble and citizen throughout your empire. 17Women everywhere will begin to despise their husbands when they learn that Queen Vashti has refused to appear before the king. 18Before this day is out, the wives of all the king's nobles throughout Persia and Media will hear what the queen did and will start treating their husbands the same way. There will be no end to their contempt and anger.

19"So if it please the king, we suggest that you issue a written decree, a law of the Persians and Medes that cannot be revoked. It should order that Queen Vashti be forever banished from the presence of King Xerxes, and that the king should choose another queen more worthy than she. 20When this decree is published throughout the king's vast empire, husbands everywhere, whatever their rank, will receive proper respect from their wives!"

1:19
Esth 8:8
Dan 6:8, 15

21The king and his nobles thought this made good sense, so he followed Memucan's counsel. 22He sent letters to all parts of the empire, to each province in its own script and language, proclaiming that every man should be the ruler of his own home and should say whatever he pleases.*

1:22
Esth 3:12; 8:9-10

## Esther Becomes Queen

**2** But after Xerxes' anger had subsided, he began thinking about Vashti and what she had done and the decree he had made. 2So his personal attendants suggested, "Let us search the empire to find beautiful young virgins for the king. 3Let the king appoint agents in each province to bring these beautiful young women into the royal harem at the fortress of Susa. Hegai, the king's eunuch in charge of the harem, will see that they are all given beauty treatments. 4After that, the young woman who most pleases the king will be made queen instead of Vashti." This advice was very appealing to the king, so he put the plan into effect.

2:1
Esth 1:19-20; 7:10

2:3
Esth 2:8-9, 15

1:22 Or *and should speak in the language of his own people.*

---

**1:12** Queen Vashti refused to parade before the king's all-male party, possibly because it was against Persian custom for a woman to appear before a public gathering of men. This conflict between Persian custom and the king's command put her in a difficult situation, and she chose to refuse her half-drunk husband, hoping he would come to his senses later. Some have suggested that Vashti was pregnant with Artaxerxes, who was born in 483 B.C., and that she did not want to be seen in public in that state.

Whatever the reason, her action was a breach of protocol that also placed Xerxes in a difficult situation. Once he made the command, as a Persian king he could not reverse it (see the note on 1:19). While preparing to invade Greece, Xerxes had invited important officials from all over his land to see his power, wealth, and authority. If it was perceived that he had no authority over his own wife, his military credibility would be damaged—the greatest criterion of success for an ancient king. In addition, King Xerxes was accustomed to getting what he wanted.

**1:13-15** Xerxes, like most leaders past and present, kept a handful of advisers whom he consulted on almost all matters. Often a king's success rose or fell on the wisdom of these men. Daniel was such an adviser under Darius and Cyrus (Daniel 6:28).

**1:15** Middle Eastern kings often did not have close personal relationships with their wives. Xerxes demonstrates this because (1) he had a harem (2:3); (2) he showed no respect for Vashti's personhood (1:10-12); (3) Esther, when she became queen, did not see him for long periods of time (4:11).

**1:16-21** Perhaps the men's thinking had been clouded by drinking. Obviously this law would not cause the women of the country to respect their husbands. Respect between men and women comes from mutual regard and appreciation for each other as those created in God's image, not from legal pronouncements and orders. Forced obedience is a poor substitute for the love and respect wives and husbands should have for each other.

**1:19** A Persian king was thought to be a god by many of his people; therefore, when he issued a law or command, it stood forever (see the notes on 8:8 and Daniel 6:8). The law could never be canceled, even if it was ill-advised; but if necessary, a new law could be issued to neutralize the effects of the old law.

**2:1** The phrase "he began thinking about Vashti" may mean that the king began to miss his queen and what she had done for him. But he also remembered that in his anger he had banished her from his presence with a decree that couldn't be rescinded.

**2:3, 14-17** Persian kings collected not only vast amounts of jewelry but also great numbers of women. These young virgins were taken from their homes and were required to live in a separate building near the palace called a harem. Their sole purpose was to serve the king and to await his call for sexual pleasure. They rarely saw the king, and their lives were restricted and boring. If rejected, Esther would be one of many girls the king had seen once and forgotten. But Esther's presence and beauty pleased the king enough that he crowned her queen in place of Vashti. The queen held a more influential position than a concubine, and she was given more freedom and authority than others in the harem. But even as queen, Esther had few rights—especially because she had been chosen to replace a woman who had become too assertive.

**2:5**
Esth 3:2-6

**2:6**
2 Kgs 24:14-15

**2:7-8**
Esth 2:15

⁵At that time there was a Jewish man in the fortress of Susa whose name was Mordecai son of Jair. He was from the tribe of Benjamin and was a descendant of Kish and Shimei. ⁶His family* had been among those who, with King Jehoiachin* of Judah, had been exiled from Jerusalem to Babylon by King Nebuchadnezzar. ⁷This man had a very beautiful and lovely young cousin, Hadassah, who was also called Esther. When her father and mother died, Mordecai adopted her into his family and raised her as his own daughter.

⁸As a result of the king's decree, Esther, along with many other young women, was brought

**2:6a** Hebrew *He.*  **2:6b** Hebrew *Jeconiah,* a variant spelling of Jehoiachin.

**MORDECAI**

Following Jerusalem's last stand against Nebuchadnezzar, Mordecai's family was deported to Babylonia. He was probably born in Susa, a city that became one of Persia's capitals after Cyrus conquered Babylon. Mordecai then inherited an official position among the Jewish captives that kept him around the palace even after the Babylonians were driven out. At one time, when Mordecai overheard plans to assassinate King Xerxes, he reported the plot and saved the king's life.

Mordecai's life was filled with challenges that he turned into opportunities. When his aunt and uncle died, he adopted Esther, their daughter and his young cousin, probably because his own parents were dead and he felt responsible for her. Later, when she was drafted into Xerxes' harem and chosen to be queen, Mordecai continued to advise her. Shortly after this, he found himself in conflict with Xerxes' recently appointed second-in-command, Haman. Although willing to serve the king, Mordecai refused to worship the king's representative. Haman was furious with Mordecai. So he planned to have Mordecai and all the Jews killed. His plan became a law of the Medes and Persians, and it looked as though the Jews were doomed.

Mordecai, willing to be God's servant wherever he was, responded by contacting Esther and telling her that one reason God had allowed her to be queen might well be to save her people from this threat. But God had also placed *him* in the right place years earlier. God revealed to the king through his nighttime reading of historical documents that Mordecai had once saved his life, and the king realized he had never thanked Mordecai. The great honor then given to Mordecai ruined Haman's plan to impale him on the specially built pole he had set up. God had woven an effective counterstrategy against which Haman's plan could not stand.

Later, Mordecai instituted the Jewish Festival of Purim. He had a lengthy career of service to the king on behalf of the Jews. In Mordecai's life, God blended both character and circumstances to accomplish great things. God has not changed the way he works. He is using the situations you face each day to weave a pattern of godliness into your character. Pause and ask God to help you respond appropriately to the situations you find yourself in today.

| | |
|---|---|
| **Strengths and accomplishments** | • Exposed an assassination plot against the king<br>• Cared enough to adopt his cousin<br>• Refused to bow to anyone except God<br>• Took Haman's place as second-in-command under Xerxes |
| **Lessons from his life** | • The opportunities we have are more important than the ones we wish we had<br>• We can trust God to weave together the events of life for our best, even though we may not be able to see the overall pattern<br>• The rewards for doing right are sometimes delayed, but they are guaranteed by God himself |
| **Vital statistics** | • Where: Susa, one of several capital cities in Persia<br>• Occupation: Jewish official who became second in rank to Xerxes<br>• Relatives: Adopted daughter: Esther. Father: Jair.<br>• Contemporaries: Xerxes, Haman |
| **Key verse** | "Mordecai the Jew became the prime minister, with authority next to that of King Xerxes himself. He was very great among the Jews, who held him in high esteem, because he continued to work for the good of his people and to speak up for the welfare of all their descendants" (Esther 10:3). |

Mordecai's story is told in the book of Esther.

**2:5, 6** Mordecai was a Jew. The Jewish population had increased since their exile over 100 years earlier. They had been given great freedom and were allowed to run their own businesses and hold positions in government (2:19; Daniel 6:3).
**2:6** The Bible says that Mordecai's family had been carried into exile from Jerusalem by Nebuchadnezzar. If this referred to

Mordecai himself, he would have been over 100 years old at the time of this story. Most likely this means that Mordecai's great-grandparents had been carried into captivity, rather than Mordecai himself.

to the king's harem at the fortress of Susa and placed in Hegai's care. ⁹Hegai was very impressed with Esther and treated her kindly. He quickly ordered a special menu for her and provided her with beauty treatments. He also assigned her seven maids specially chosen from the king's palace, and he moved her and her maids into the best place in the harem.

²:9
Esth 2:3, 12

¹⁰Esther had not told anyone of her nationality and family background, because Mordecai had directed her not to do so. ¹¹Every day Mordecai would take a walk near the courtyard of the harem to find out about Esther and what was happening to her.

2:10
Esth 2:20

¹²Before each young woman was taken to the king's bed, she was given the prescribed twelve months of beauty treatments—six months with oil of myrrh, followed by six months with special perfumes and ointments. ¹³When it was time for her to go to the king's palace, she was given her choice of whatever clothing or jewelry she wanted to take from the harem. ¹⁴That evening she was taken to the king's private rooms, and the next morning she was brought to the second harem,* where the king's wives lived. There she would be under the care of Shaashgaz, the king's eunuch in charge of the concubines. She would never go to the king again unless he had especially enjoyed her and requested her by name.

¹⁵Esther was the daughter of Abihail, who was Mordecai's uncle. (Mordecai had adopted his younger cousin Esther.) When it was Esther's turn to go to the king, she accepted the advice of Hegai, the eunuch in charge of the harem. She asked for nothing except what he suggested, and she was admired by everyone who saw her.

2:15
Esth 9:29

¹⁶Esther was taken to King Xerxes at the royal palace in early winter* of the seventh year of his reign. ¹⁷And the king loved Esther more than any of the other young women. He was so delighted with her that he set the royal crown on her head and declared her queen instead of Vashti. ¹⁸To celebrate the occasion, he gave a great banquet in Esther's honor for all his nobles and officials, declaring a public holiday for the provinces and giving generous gifts to everyone.

2:17
Esth 1:11
2:18
Esth 1:3-8

¹⁹Even after all the young women had been transferred to the second harem* and Mordecai had become a palace official,* ²⁰Esther continued to keep her family background and nationality a secret. She was still following Mordecai's directions, just as she did when she lived in his home.

2:20
Esth 2:10

### Mordecai's Loyalty to the King

²¹One day as Mordecai was on duty at the king's gate, two of the king's eunuchs, Bigthana* and Teresh—who were guards at the door of the king's private quarters—became angry at King Xerxes and plotted to assassinate him. ²²But Mordecai heard about the plot and gave the information to Queen Esther. She then told the king about it and gave Mordecai credit for the report. ²³When an investigation was made and Mordecai's story was found to be true, the two men were impaled on a sharpened pole. This was all recorded in *The Book of the History of King Xerxes' Reign.*

2:21
Esth 1:10; 6:2
2:22
Esth 6:1-2
2:23
Esth 10:2

### 2. The Jews are threatened
### Haman's Plot against the Jews

**3** Some time later King Xerxes promoted Haman son of Hammedatha the Agagite over all the other nobles, making him the most powerful official in the empire. ²All the king's officials would bow down before Haman to show him respect whenever he passed by, for so the king had commanded. But Mordecai refused to bow down or show him respect.

3:1
Esth 3:10; 5:11
3:2
Esth 5:9

**2:14** Or *to another part of the harem.*  **2:16** Hebrew *in the tenth month, the month of Tebeth.* A number of dates in the book of Esther can be cross-checked with dates in surviving Persian records and related accurately to our modern calendar. This month of the ancient Hebrew lunar calendar occurred within the months of December 479 B.C. and January 478 B.C.  **2:19a** The meaning of the Hebrew is uncertain.  **2:19b** Hebrew *and Mordecai was sitting in the gate of the king.*  **2:21** Hebrew *Bigthan;* compare 6:2.

**2:10** With virtually no rights and little access to the king, it was better for Esther not to reveal her identity. While boldness in stating our identity as God's people is our responsibility, at times a good strategy is to keep quiet until we have won the right to be heard. This is especially true when dealing with those in authority over us. But we can always let them see the difference God makes in our lives.

**2:17** God placed Esther on the throne even before the Jews faced the possibility of complete destruction (3:5ff), so that when trouble came, a person would already be in the position to help. No human effort could thwart God's plan to send the Messiah to earth as a Jew. If you are changing jobs, position, or location and

can't see God's purpose in your situation, understand that God is in control. He may be placing you in a position so you can help when the need arises.

**3:2** Mordecai's determination came from his faith in God. He did not take a poll first to determine the safest or most popular course of action; he had the courage to stand alone. Doing what is right will not always make you popular. Those who do right will be in the minority, but to obey God is more important than to obey people (Acts 5:29).

**3:2-4** Mordecai refused to kneel down before Haman. Jews did bow down to government authorities, at times, as a sign of respect (Genesis 23:7; 1 Samuel 24:8), but Haman's ancestors

**3:3**
Esth 3:2

**3:5**
Esth 5:9

**3:6**
Ps 83:4

**3:7**
Esth 9:24-26

**3:8**
Ezra 4:12-15
Acts 16:20-21

³Then the palace officials at the king's gate asked Mordecai, "Why are you disobeying the king's command?" ⁴They spoke to him day after day, but still he refused to comply with the order. So they spoke to Haman about this to see if he would tolerate Mordecai's conduct, since Mordecai had told them he was a Jew.

⁵When Haman saw that Mordecai would not bow down or show him respect, he was filled with rage. ⁶He had learned of Mordecai's nationality, so he decided it was not enough to lay hands on Mordecai alone. Instead, he looked for a way to destroy all the Jews throughout the entire empire of Xerxes.

⁷So in the month of April,* during the twelfth year of King Xerxes' reign, lots were cast in Haman's presence (the lots were called *purim*) to determine the best day and month to take action. And the day selected was March 7, nearly a year later.*

⁸Then Haman approached King Xerxes and said, "There is a certain race of people scattered through all the provinces of your empire who keep themselves separate from everyone else. Their laws are different from those of any other people, and they refuse to obey the laws of the king. So it is not in the king's interest to let them live. ⁹If it please the king, issue a decree that they be destroyed, and I will give 10,000 large sacks* of silver to the government administrators to be deposited in the royal treasury."

**3:7a** Hebrew *in the first month, the month of Nisan.* This month of the ancient Hebrew lunar calendar occurred within the months of April and May 474 B.C.; also see note on 2:16.   **3:7b** As in 3:13, which reads *the thirteenth day of the twelfth month, the month of Adar;* Hebrew reads *in the twelfth month,* of the ancient Hebrew lunar calendar. The date selected was March 7, 473 B.C.; also see note on 2:16.   **3:9** Hebrew *10,000 talents,* about 375 tons or 340 metric tons in weight.

---

**GOD BEHIND THE SCENES IN ESTHER**
Although God's name is not mentioned in the Hebrew text of Esther, he makes himself known in these ways:

| | |
|---|---|
| *Indirect References* . . . . . . 2:17. . . . | Esther, who worshiped God, became queen. |
| 4:14. . . . | God's existence and his power over the affairs of people are assumed. |
| 4:16. . . . | Fasting was a distinct spiritual activity usually connected with prayer. |
| *Divine Incidents* . . . . . . 2:21, 23. . . . | Mordecai overhears a death plot and saves the king's life. |
| 6:1. . . . | Xerxes can't sleep and decides to read a history book. |
| 6:2. . . . | Xerxes reads the exact page needed for the moment, reminding him of an unpaid reward to Mordecai. |
| 7:9, 10. . . . | Haman's plan is exactly reversed—the intended victims are the victors. |

*The book of Esther is filled with divine interventions*

Why was God's name hidden in the book of Esther? There were many gods in the Middle East and Persian Empire. Usually, their names were mentioned in official documents in order to control the peoples who worshiped those particular gods. The Jews were unique in being the people of one God. A story about them was naturally a story about God, for even the name "Jew" carried with it the connotation of one who worshiped Yahweh.

---

were ancient enemies of the Jews. Israel had been commanded by God to "destroy the Amalekites and erase their memory from under heaven" (Deuteronomy 25:17-19; see also Exodus 17:16). Mordecai was not about to kneel before wicked Haman and, by his act, acknowledge Haman as a god. Daniel's three friends had the same convictions (Daniel 3). We must worship God alone. We should never let any person, institution, or government take God's place. When people demand loyalties or duties from you that do not honor God, don't give in. It may be time to take a stand.

**3:5, 6** Why did Haman want to destroy all Jews just because of one man's action? (1) Haman was an Agagite (3:1), a descendant of Agag, king of the Amalekites (1 Samuel 15:20). The Amalekites were ancient enemies of the Israelites (see Exodus 17:16; Deuteronomy 25:17-19). Haman's hatred was directed not just at Mordecai but at all the Jews. (2) As second-in-command in the Persian Empire (3:1), Haman loved his power and authority and the reverence shown him. The Jews, however, looked to God as their final authority, not to any man. Haman realized that the only way to fulfill his self-centered desires was to kill all those who disregarded his authority. His quest for personal power and his hatred of the Jewish race consumed him.

**3:5, 6** Haman enjoyed the power and prestige of his position, and he was enraged when Mordecai did not respond with the expected reverential bow. Haman's anger was not directed just toward Mordecai, but toward what Mordecai stood for—the Jews' dedication to God as the only authority worthy of reverence. Haman's attitude was prejudiced: He hated a group of people because of a difference in belief or culture. Prejudice grows out of personal pride—considering oneself better than others. In the end, Haman was punished for his arrogant attitude (7:9, 10). God will harshly judge those who are prejudiced or whose pride causes them to look down on others.

**3:7** Haman cast lots to determine the best day to carry out his decree. Little did he know that he was playing into the hands of God, for the day of death was set for almost a year away, giving Esther time to make her plea to the king. The Persian word for "lots" was *purim,* which became the name for the holiday celebrated by the Jews when they were delivered, not killed, on the day appointed by Haman.

**3:9** Haman must have hoped to acquire this tremendous sum of money by plundering the homes and businesses of the Jews who would be killed through his decree.

¹⁰The king agreed, confirming his decision by removing his signet ring from his finger and giving it to Haman son of Hammedatha the Agagite, the enemy of the Jews. ¹¹The king said, "The money and the people are both yours to do with as you see fit."

¹²So on April 17* the king's secretaries were summoned, and a decree was written exactly as Haman dictated. It was sent to the king's highest officers, the governors of the respective provinces, and the nobles of each province in their own scripts and languages. The decree was written in the name of King Xerxes and sealed with the king's signet ring. ¹³Dispatches were sent by swift messengers into all the provinces of the empire, giving the order that all Jews—young and old, including women and children—must be killed, slaughtered, and annihilated on a single day. This was scheduled to happen on March 7 of the next year.* The property of the Jews would be given to those who killed them.

¹⁴A copy of this decree was to be issued as law in every province and proclaimed to all peoples, so that they would be ready to do their duty on the appointed day. ¹⁵At the king's command, the decree went out by swift messengers, and it was also proclaimed in the fortress of Susa. Then the king and Haman sat down to drink, but the city of Susa fell into confusion.

## Mordecai Requests Esther's Help

**4** When Mordecai learned about all that had been done, he tore his clothes, put on burlap and ashes, and went out into the city, crying with a loud and bitter wail. ²He went as far as the gate of the palace, for no one was allowed to enter the palace gate while wearing clothes of mourning. ³And as news of the king's decree reached all the provinces, there was great mourning among the Jews. They fasted, wept, and wailed, and many people lay in burlap and ashes.

⁴When Queen Esther's maids and eunuchs came and told her about Mordecai, she was deeply distressed. She sent clothing to him to replace the burlap, but he refused it. ⁵Then Esther sent for Hathach, one of the king's eunuchs who had been appointed as her attendant. She ordered him to go to Mordecai and find out what was troubling him and why he was in mourning. ⁶So Hathach went out to Mordecai in the square in front of the palace gate.

⁷Mordecai told him the whole story, including the exact amount of money Haman had promised to pay into the royal treasury for the destruction of the Jews. ⁸Mordecai gave Hathach a copy of the decree issued in Susa that called for the death of all Jews. He asked Hathach to show it to Esther and explain the situation to her. He also asked Hathach to direct her to go to the king to beg for mercy and plead for her people. ⁹So Hathach returned to Esther with Mordecai's message.

¹⁰Then Esther told Hathach to go back and relay this message to Mordecai: ¹¹"All the king's officials and even the people in the provinces know that anyone who appears before the king in his inner court without being invited is doomed to die unless the king holds out his gold scepter. And the king has not called for me to come to him for thirty days." ¹²So Hathach* gave Esther's message to Mordecai.

**3:10** Gen 41:42; Esth 8:2
**3:12** 1 Kgs 21:8; Esth 8:8-10
**3:13** Esth 8:9-14; 9:2, 7-10, 17
**3:14** Esth 4:8; 8:13-14
**3:15** Esth 8:15
**4:1** 2 Sam 1:11; Esth 3:8-10; Ezek 27:30; Jon 3:4-9
**4:7** Esth 3:9
**4:8** Esth 3:14-15
**4:11** Esth 5:1-2; 6:4; 8:4; Dan 2:9

**3:12** Hebrew *On the thirteenth day of the first month,* of the ancient Hebrew lunar calendar. This day was April 17, 474 B.C.; also see note on 2:16.   **3:13** Hebrew *on the thirteenth day of the twelfth month, the month of Adar,* of the ancient Hebrew lunar calendar. The date selected was March 7, 473 B.C.; also see note on 2:16.   **4:12** As in Greek version; Hebrew reads *they.*

**3:10-12** Officials in the ancient world used signet rings as personal signatures. The ring's surface had a raised imprint made of metal, wood, or bone; Xerxes' was probably made of silver or gold. Each individual had his own imprint. Letters were sealed by pressing the ring into soft wax, and official documents were certified by using the royal signet. By giving Haman his signet ring, Xerxes gave him his personal signature and with it the authority to do whatever he wished. Little did the king realize that his own ring would sign the death warrant for his queen, Esther.

**3:13** Haman's death decree was against all Jews in the Persian Empire; thus, it would have included the land of Israel. If his decree had been carried out, all of God's chosen people could have been exterminated, and God's plan to send his Son to earth as a Jew could have been ruined. But God's plans cannot be stopped. Haman was doomed to fail.

**4:11–5:2** Esther risked her life by coming before the king. Her courageous act gives us a model to follow in approaching a difficult or dangerous task. Like Esther, we can: (1) *Calculate the cost.* Esther realized her life was at stake. (2) *Set priorities.* She believed that the safety of the Jewish race was more important than her life. (3) *Prepare.* She gathered support and fasted. (4) *Determine a course of action and move ahead boldly.* She didn't think too long about it, allowing the interlude to lessen her commitment to what she had to do.

Do you have to face a hostile audience, confront a friend on a delicate subject, or talk to your family about changes to be made? Rather than dreading difficult situations or putting them off, take action with confidence by following Esther's inspiring example.

¹³Mordecai sent this reply to Esther: "Don't think for a moment that because you're in the palace you will escape when all other Jews are killed. ¹⁴If you keep quiet at a time like this, deliverance and relief for the Jews will arise from some other place, but you and your relatives will die. Who knows if perhaps you were made queen for just such a time as this?"

¹⁵Then Esther sent this reply to Mordecai: ¹⁶"Go and gather together all the Jews of Susa

We treasure security, even though we know that security in this life carries no guarantees—possessions can be destroyed, beauty fades, relationships can be broken, death is inevitable. Real security, then, must be found beyond this life. Only when our security rests on God and his unchanging nature can we face the challenges that life is sure to bring our way.

Esther's beauty and character won Xerxes' heart, and he made her his queen. Even in her favored position, however, she would risk her life by attempting to see the king when he had not requested her presence. There was no guarantee that the king would even see her. Although she was queen, she was still not secure. But, cautiously and courageously, Esther decided to risk her life by approaching the king on behalf of her people.

She made her plans carefully. The Jews were asked to fast and pray with her before she went to the king. Then on the chosen day she went before him, and he *did* ask her to come forward and speak. But instead of issuing her request directly, she invited him and Haman to a banquet. He was astute enough to realize she had something on her mind; yet she conveyed the importance of the matter by insisting on a second banquet.

In the meantime, God was working behind the scenes. He caused Xerxes to read the historical records of the kingdom late one night, and the king discovered that Mordecai had once saved his life. Xerxes lost no time in honoring Mordecai for that act. During the second banquet, Esther told the king of Haman's plot against the Jews, and Haman was doomed. There is grim justice in Haman's death on the impaling pole he had set up for Mordecai, and it seems fitting that the day on which the Jews were to be slaughtered became the day their enemies died. Esther's risk confirmed that God was the source of her security.

How much of your security lies in your possessions, position, or reputation? God has not placed you in your present position for your own benefit. He put you there *to serve him.* As in Esther's case, this may involve risking your security. Are you willing to let God be your ultimate security?

| | |
|---|---|
| **Strengths and accomplishments** | • Her beauty and character won the heart of Persia's king<br>• She combined courage with careful planning<br>• She was open to advice and willing to act<br>• She was more concerned for others than for her own security |
| **Lessons from her life** | • Serving God often demands that we risk our own security<br>• God has a purpose for the situations in which he places us<br>• Courage, while often vital, does not replace careful planning |
| **Vital statistics** | • Where: Persian Empire<br>• Occupation: Xerxes' wife, queen of Persia<br>• Relatives: Cousin: Mordecai. Husband: Xerxes. Father: Abihail. |
| **Key verse** | "Go and gather together all the Jews of Susa and fast for me. Do not eat or drink for three days, night or day. My maids and I will do the same. And then, though it is against the law, I will go in to see the king. If I must die, I must die" (Esther 4:16). |

Esther's story is told in the book of Esther.

**4:13** Although Esther was the queen and shared some of the king's power and wealth, she still needed God's protection and wisdom. No one is secure in his or her own strength in any political system. It is foolish to believe that wealth or position can make us impervious to danger. Deliverance and safety come only from God.

**4:13, 14** After the decree to kill the Jews was given, Mordecai and Esther could have despaired, decided to save only themselves, or just waited for God's intervention. Instead, they saw that God had placed them in their positions for a purpose, so they seized the moment and acted. When it is within our reach to save others, we must do so. In a life-threatening situation, don't withdraw, behave selfishly, wallow in despair, or wait for God to fix everything. Instead, ask God for his direction, and *act!* God may have placed you where you are "for just such a time as this."

**4:14** God is not specifically mentioned in the book of Esther, but it is obvious that Mordecai expected a divine deliverance. While the book of Esther does not mention God by name or title, his presence fills the pages. Esther and Mordecai believed in God's care, and because they acted at the right time, God used them to save his people.

When you face challenges in life, seek to know what God wants you to do, and then do it, confident that he will do his part. You don't know ahead of time how he will accomplish his will. Trust God and prepare to be surprised by the ways he demonstrates his trustworthiness.

and fast for me. Do not eat or drink for three days, night or day. My maids and I will do the same. And then, though it is against the law, I will go in to see the king. If I must die, I must die." 17So Mordecai went away and did everything as Esther had ordered him.

## 3. Esther intercedes for the Jews
### Esther's Request to the King

**5** On the third day of the fast, Esther put on her royal robes and entered the inner court of the palace, just across from the king's hall. The king was sitting on his royal throne, facing the entrance. 2When he saw Queen Esther standing there in the inner court, he welcomed her and held out the gold scepter to her. So Esther approached and touched the end of the scepter.

3Then the king asked her, "What do you want, Queen Esther? What is your request? I will give it to you, even if it is half the kingdom!"

4And Esther replied, "If it please the king, let the king and Haman come today to a banquet I have prepared for the king."

5The king turned to his attendants and said, "Tell Haman to come quickly to a banquet, as Esther has requested." So the king and Haman went to Esther's banquet.

6And while they were drinking wine, the king said to Esther, "Now tell me what you really want. What is your request? I will give it to you, even if it is half the kingdom!"

7Esther replied, "This is my request and deepest wish. 8If I have found favor with the king, and if it pleases the king to grant my request and do what I ask, please come with Haman tomorrow to the banquet I will prepare for you. Then I will explain what this is all about."

### Haman's Plan to Kill Mordecai

9Haman was a happy man as he left the banquet! But when he saw Mordecai sitting at the palace gate, not standing up or trembling nervously before him, Haman became furious. 10However, he restrained himself and went on home.

Then Haman gathered together his friends and Zeresh, his wife, 11and boasted to them about his great wealth and his many children. He bragged about the honors the king had given him and how he had been promoted over all the other nobles and officials.

12Then Haman added, "And that's not all! Queen Esther invited only me and the king himself to the banquet she prepared for us. And she has invited me to dine with her and the king again tomorrow!" 13Then he added, "But this is all worth nothing as long as I see Mordecai the Jew just sitting there at the palace gate."

14So Haman's wife, Zeresh, and all his friends suggested, "Set up a sharpened pole that stands seventy-five feet* tall, and in the morning ask the king to impale Mordecai on it. When this is done, you can go on your merry way to the banquet with the king." This pleased Haman, and he ordered the pole set up.

5:14 Hebrew *50 cubits* [22.5 meters].

**Cross-references (right margin):**
- 4:16 — 2 Chr 20:3
- 5:1 — Esth 4:11, 16; 6:4
- 5:2 — Esth 4:11; 8:4
- 5:3 — Esth 5:6; 7:2; Mark 6:23; Luke 18:41
- 5:5 — Esth 6:14
- 5:6 — Esth 5:3; 7:2
- 5:8 — Esth 6:14; 7:3; 8:5
- 5:9 — Esth 3:2, 5
- 5:10 — Esth 6:13
- 5:14 — Esth 5:10; 6:4; 7:9-10

---

**4:16** By calling for a fast, Esther was asking the Jews to pray for God's help on her dangerous mission. In the Old Testament, prayer always accompanied fasting (see Exodus 34:28; Deuteronomy 9:9; Ezra 8:21-23). An important function of a community of believers is mutual support in difficult times. When you are experiencing struggles, turn to fellow believers for support by sharing your trials with them and gaining strength from the bond that unites you. Ask them to pray for you. And when others need your support, give it willingly.

**4:16** "Save your own skin" and "Watch out for number one" are mottoes that reflect our world's selfish outlook on life. Esther's attitude stands in bold contrast to this. She knew what she had to do, and she knew it could cost her her life. And yet she responded, "If I must die, I must die." We should have the same commitment to do what is right despite the possible consequences. Do you try to save yourself by remaining silent rather than standing up for what is right? Decide to do what God wants, and trust him for the outcome.

**4:17–5:1** God was in control, yet Mordecai and Esther had to act. We cannot understand how both can be true at the same time, and yet they are. God chooses to work through those *willing* to act for him. We should pray as if all depended on God and

act as if all depended on us. We should avoid two extremes: doing nothing, and feeling that we must do everything.

**5:9** Hatred and bitterness are like weeds with long roots that grow in the heart and corrupt all of life. Haman was so consumed with hatred toward Mordecai that he could not even enjoy the honor of being invited to Esther's party. Hebrews 12:15 warns us to "watch out that no poisonous root of bitterness grows up to trouble you, corrupting many." Don't let hatred and its resulting bitterness build in your heart. Like Haman, you will find it backfiring against you (see 6:13; 7:9, 10). If the mere mention of someone's name provokes you to anger, confess your bitterness as sin. Ignoring bitterness, hiding it from others, or making superficial changes in behavior is not enough. If bitterness isn't completely removed, it will grow back, making matters worse.

**5:14** Haman's family and friends, who were as arrogant as he, suggested that the sharpened pole be 75 feet high, probably built on the city wall or some prominent building. They wanted to make sure that all the people of the city saw Mordecai's death and would be reminded of the consequences of disobeying Haman. Ironically, this impaling pole later allowed everyone to see Haman's death.

## The King Honors Mordecai

**6:1**
Esth 2:21-23; 10:2
Dan 6:18

**6:2**
Esth 2:21-22

**6** That night the king had trouble sleeping, so he ordered an attendant to bring the book of the history of his reign so it could be read to him. [2]In those records he discovered an account of how Mordecai had exposed the plot of Bigthana and Teresh, two of the eunuchs who guarded the door to the king's private quarters. They had plotted to assassinate King Xerxes.

[3]"What reward or recognition did we ever give Mordecai for this?" the king asked.

His attendants replied, "Nothing has been done for him."

**6:4**
Esth 4:11; 5:14

[4]"Who is that in the outer court?" the king inquired. As it happened, Haman had just arrived in the outer court of the palace to ask the king to impale Mordecai on the pole he had prepared.

[5]So the attendants replied to the king, "Haman is out in the court."

**6:6**
Esth 6:7, 9, 11

"Bring him in," the king ordered. [6]So Haman came in, and the king said, "What should I do to honor a man who truly pleases me?"

---

**HAMAN**

The most arrogant people are often those who must measure their self-worth by the power or influence they think they have over others. Haman was an extremely arrogant leader. He recognized the king as his superior but could not accept anyone as an equal. When one man, Mordecai, refused to bow in submission to him, Haman wanted to destroy him. He became consumed with hatred for Mordecai. He was already filled with racial hatred for all the Jewish people because of the long-standing hatred between the Jews and Haman's ancestors, the Amalekites. Mordecai's dedication to God and his refusal to give homage to any human person challenged Haman's self-centered religion. Haman saw the Jews as a threat to his power, and he decided to kill them all.

God was preparing Haman's downfall and the protection of his people long before Haman came to power under Xerxes. Esther, a Jew, became queen, and Mordecai's role in exposing an assassination plot indebted the king to him. Not only was Haman prevented from killing Mordecai; he also had to suffer the humiliation of publicly honoring him. Within hours, Haman died on the pole he had built to impale Mordecai, and his plan to wipe out the Jews was thwarted. In contrast to Esther, who risked everything for God and won, Haman risked everything for an evil purpose and lost.

Our initial response to the story about Haman is to say that he got what he deserved. But the Bible leads us to ask deeper questions: How much of Haman is in me? Do I desire to control others? Am I threatened when others don't appreciate me as I think they should? Do I want revenge when my pride is attacked? Confess these attitudes to God, and ask him to replace them with an attitude of forgiveness. Otherwise, God's justice will settle the matter.

| | |
|---|---|
| **Strength and accomplishment** | • Achieved great power, second in rank to Persia's king Xerxes |
| **Weaknesses and mistakes** | • The desire to control others and receive honor was his highest goal<br>• Was blinded by arrogance and self-importance<br>• Planned to murder Mordecai and built an impaling pole for him<br>• Orchestrated the plan to slaughter God's people throughout the empire |
| **Lessons from his life** | • Hatred will be punished<br>• God has an amazing record for making evil plans backfire on the planners<br>• Pride and self-importance will be punished<br>• An insatiable thirst for power and prestige is self-destructive |
| **Vital statistics** | • Where: Susa, the capital of Persia<br>• Occupation: Second in rank in the empire<br>• Relative: Wife: Zeresh<br>• Contemporaries: Xerxes, Mordecai, Esther |
| **Key verses** | "When Haman saw that Mordecai would not bow down or show him respect, he was filled with rage. He learned of Mordecai's nationality, so he decided it was not enough to lay hands on Mordecai alone. Instead, he looked for a way to destroy all the Jews throughout the entire empire of Xerxes" (Esther 3:5–6). |

Haman's story is told in the book of Esther.

---

**6:1, 2** Unable to sleep, the king decided to review the history of his reign, and his servants read to him about Mordecai's good deed. This seems coincidental, but God is *always* at work. God has been working quietly and patiently throughout your life as well. The events that have come together for good are not mere coincidence; they are the result of God's sovereign control over the course of people's lives (Romans 8:28).

Haman thought to himself, "Whom would the king wish to honor more than me?" [7]So he replied, "If the king wishes to honor someone, [8]he should bring out one of the king's own royal robes, as well as a horse that the king himself has ridden—one with a royal emblem on its head. [9]Let the robes and the horse be handed over to one of the king's most noble officials. And let him see that the man whom the king wishes to honor is dressed in the king's robes and led through the city square on the king's horse. Have the official shout as they go, 'This is what the king does for someone he wishes to honor!'"

[10]"Excellent!" the king said to Haman. "Quick! Take the robes and my horse, and do just as you have said for Mordecai the Jew, who sits at the gate of the palace. Leave out nothing you have suggested!"

[11]So Haman took the robes and put them on Mordecai, placed him on the king's own horse, and led him through the city square, shouting, "This is what the king does for someone he wishes to honor!" [12]Afterward Mordecai returned to the palace gate, but Haman hurried home dejected and completely humiliated.

[13]When Haman told his wife, Zeresh, and all his friends what had happened, his wise advisers and his wife said, "Since Mordecai—this man who has humiliated you—is of Jewish birth, you will never succeed in your plans against him. It will be fatal to continue opposing him."

[14]While they were still talking, the king's eunuchs arrived and quickly took Haman to the banquet Esther had prepared.

## The King Executes Haman

**7** So the king and Haman went to Queen Esther's banquet. [2]On this second occasion, while they were drinking wine, the king again said to Esther, "Tell me what you want, Queen Esther. What is your request? I will give it to you, even if it is half the kingdom!"

[3]Queen Esther replied, "If I have found favor with the king, and if it pleases the king to grant my request, I ask that my life and the lives of my people will be spared. [4]For my people and I have been sold to those who would kill, slaughter, and annihilate us. If we had merely been sold as slaves, I could remain quiet, for that would be too trivial a matter to warrant disturbing the king."

[5]"Who would do such a thing?" King Xerxes demanded. "Who would be so presumptuous as to touch you?"

[6]Esther replied, "This wicked Haman is our adversary and our enemy." Haman grew pale with fright before the king and queen. [7]Then the king jumped to his feet in a rage and went out into the palace garden.

Haman, however, stayed behind to plead for his life with Queen Esther, for he knew that the king intended to kill him. [8]In despair he fell on the couch where Queen Esther was reclining, just as the king was returning from the palace garden.

The king exclaimed, "Will he even assault the queen right here in the palace, before my very eyes?" And as soon as the king spoke, his attendants covered Haman's face, signaling his doom.

[9]Then Harbona, one of the king's eunuchs, said, "Haman has set up a sharpened pole that stands seventy-five feet* tall in his own courtyard. He intended to use it to impale Mordecai, the man who saved the king from assassination."

"Then impale Haman on it!" the king ordered. [10]So they impaled Haman on the pole he had set up for Mordecai, and the king's anger subsided.

**7:9** Hebrew *50 cubits* [22.5 meters].

*Cross references (right margin):*
**6:8** 1 Kgs 1:33
**6:9** Gen 41:43
**6:12** 2 Sam 15:30; Esth 7:8; Jer 14:3
**6:13** Esth 5:10, 14
**6:14** Esth 5:5-8
**7:2** Esth 5:3, 6
**7:3** Esth 5:7-8; 8:5
**7:4** Esth 3:9; 4:7
**7:6** Esth 3:10
**7:8** Esth 1:6
**7:9** Esth 5:14
**7:10** Esth 9:25; Pss 7:16; 94:23

---

**6:7-9** Haman had wealth, but he craved something even his money couldn't buy—respect. He could buy the trappings of success and power, but his lust for popularity had become an obsession. Don't let your desire for approval, applause, and popularity drive you to immoral actions.

**6:10-13** Mordecai had exposed a plot to assassinate Xerxes—thus, he had saved the king's life (2:21-23). Although his good deed was recorded in the history books, Mordecai had gone unrewarded. But God was saving Mordecai's reward for the right time. Just as Haman was about to impale Mordecai unjustly, the king was ready to give the reward. Although God promises to reward our good deeds, we sometimes feel our "payoff" is too far away. Be patient. God steps in when it will do the most good.

**7:6-10** Haman's hatred and evil plotting turned against him when the king discovered his true intentions. He was impaled on the pole he had set up for someone else. Proverbs 26:27 teaches that if you set a trap for others, you will get caught in it yourself. What happened to Haman shows the often violent results of setting any kind of trap for others.

**7:8** A veil was placed over the face of someone condemned to death because Persian kings refused to look upon the face of a condemned person.

### A Decree to Help the Jews

**8:1**
Esth 2:7; 7:6
**8:2**
Esth 3:10

**8** On that same day King Xerxes gave the property of Haman, the enemy of the Jews, to Queen Esther. Then Mordecai was brought before the king, for Esther had told the king how they were related. [2] The king took off his signet ring—which he had taken back from Haman—and gave it to Mordecai. And Esther appointed Mordecai to be in charge of Haman's property.

**8:4**
Esth 4:11; 5:2

[3] Then Esther went again before the king, falling down at his feet and begging him with tears to stop the evil plot devised by Haman the Agagite against the Jews. [4] Again the king held out the gold scepter to Esther. So she rose and stood before him.

**8:5**
Esth 3:13; 5:7-8;
7:3

[5] Esther said, "If it please the king, and if I have found favor with him, and if he thinks it is right, and if I am pleasing to him, let there be a decree that reverses the orders of Haman son of Hammedatha the Agagite, who ordered that Jews throughout all the king's provinces should be destroyed. [6] For how can I endure to see my people and my family slaughtered and destroyed?"

**8:6**
Esth 3:13; 7:4; 9:1

**8:7**
Esth 7:10

[7] Then King Xerxes said to Queen Esther and Mordecai the Jew, "I have given Esther the property of Haman, and he has been impaled on a pole because he tried to destroy the Jews.

---

**HOW GOD WORKS IN THE WORLD**

| | | | |
|---|---|---|---|
| *God's Will* | *What God wants done—he works through . . .* | | |
| *God's Action* | ☛*Natural Order* | ☛*Miracles* | ☛*Providence* |
| | ☛God set into action through Creation a normal working of his universe. He also revealed his expectations of people through his Word and people's consciences. | ☛God breaks into the natural order to respond to the expressed needs of people. | ☛God overrules the natural order to accomplish an act that people may or may not have requested. |
| *Examples from Esther* | ☛God gave Esther natural beauty. | ☛God allowed Esther to speak to the king. | ☛God allowed Mordecai to over-hear a plot. |
| | ☛Esther planned a way to save her people. | ☛The people prayed and fasted. | ☛Mordecai trusted God to accomplish what was impossible in human terms. |
| *People's Will* | *What people want done—we either . . .* | | |
| *Action We Can Take* | ☛Plan | ☛Pray | ☛Trust and Obey |
| | ☛Can make plans based on the order and dependability of God's creation. Know and obey his words. | ☛Can ask God to intervene in certain affairs while realizing that our knowledge and perspective are limited. | ☛Can trust that God is in control even when circumstances seem to indicate that he is not. |
| | *or . . .* | | |
| *Mistakes We Can Make* | ☛Disobey | ☛Demand | ☛Despair |
| | ☛Can violate the natural order, disobey God's commands. | ☛Can assume that we understand what is needed and expect God to agree and answer our prayers that way. | ☛Can assume God doesn't answer prayer or respond to our needs and live as though there is nothing but the natural order. |

---

**8:1-7** While we should not expect earthly rewards for being faithful to God, they often come—and in unexpected ways. Esther and Mordecai were faithful, even to the point of risking their lives to save others. They were willing to give up everything, and God rewarded in proportion to their all-out commitment in ways they could not have foreseen.

⁸Now go ahead and send a message to the Jews in the king's name, telling them whatever you want, and seal it with the king's signet ring. But remember that whatever has already been written in the king's name and sealed with his signet ring can never be revoked."

⁹So on June 25* the king's secretaries were summoned, and a decree was written exactly as Mordecai dictated. It was sent to the Jews and to the highest officers, the governors, and the nobles of all the 127 provinces stretching from India to Ethiopia.* The decree was written in the scripts and languages of all the peoples of the empire, including that of the Jews. ¹⁰The decree was written in the name of King Xerxes and sealed with the king's signet ring. Mordecai sent the dispatches by swift messengers, who rode fast horses especially bred for the king's service.

¹¹The king's decree gave the Jews in every city authority to unite to defend their lives. They were allowed to kill, slaughter, and annihilate anyone of any nationality or province who might attack them or their children and wives, and to take the property of their enemies. ¹²The day chosen for this event throughout all the provinces of King Xerxes was March 7 of the next year.*

¹³A copy of this decree was to be issued as law in every province and proclaimed to all peoples, so that the Jews would be ready to take revenge on their enemies on the appointed day. ¹⁴So urged on by the king's command, the messengers rode out swiftly on fast horses bred for the king's service. The same decree was also proclaimed in the fortress of Susa.

¹⁵Then Mordecai left the king's presence, wearing the royal robe of blue and white, the great crown of gold, and an outer cloak of fine linen and purple. And the people of Susa celebrated the new decree. ¹⁶The Jews were filled with joy and gladness and were honored everywhere. ¹⁷In every province and city, wherever the king's decree arrived, the Jews rejoiced and had a great celebration and declared a public festival and holiday. And many of the people of the land became Jews themselves, for they feared what the Jews might do to them.

## 4. The Jews are delivered
### The Victory of the Jews

**9** So on March 7* the two decrees of the king were put into effect. On that day, the enemies of the Jews had hoped to overpower them, but quite the opposite happened. It was the Jews who overpowered their enemies. ²The Jews gathered in their cities throughout all the king's provinces to attack anyone who tried to harm them. But no one could make a stand against them, for everyone was afraid of them. ³And all the nobles of the provinces, the highest officers, the governors, and the royal officials helped the Jews for fear of Mordecai. ⁴For Mordecai had been promoted in the king's palace, and his fame spread throughout all the provinces as he became more and more powerful.

⁵So the Jews went ahead on the appointed day and struck down their enemies with the sword. They killed and annihilated their enemies and did as they pleased with those who hated them. ⁶In the fortress of Susa itself, the Jews killed 500 men. ⁷They also killed Parshandatha, Dalphon, Aspatha, ⁸Poratha, Adalia, Aridatha, ⁹Parmashta, Arisai, Aridai, and Vaizatha—¹⁰the ten sons of Haman son of Hammedatha, the enemy of the Jews. But they did not take any plunder.

**8:8**
Esth 1:19; 3:12;
8:2, 9-10, 14
Dan 6:15

**8:9**
Esth 1:1-2, 22; 3:12

**8:11**
Esth 3:13; 9:2, 10

**8:12**
Esth 3:13; 9:1

**8:13**
Esth 3:14

**9:1**
Esth 3:13; 8:11-12;
9:17

**9:2**
Esth 8:11, 17;
9:15-18

**9:3**
Esth 8:17

**9:5**
Esth 3:13

**9:10**
Esth 5:11; 8:11

**8:9a** Hebrew *on the twenty-third day of the third month, the month of Sivan,* of the ancient Hebrew lunar calendar. This day was June 25, 474 B.C.; also see note on 2:16.   **8:9b** Hebrew *to Cush.*   **8:12** Hebrew *the thirteenth day of the twelfth month, the month of Adar,* of the ancient Hebrew lunar calendar. The date selected was March 7, 473 B.C.; also see note on 2:16.   **9:1** Hebrew *on the thirteenth day of the twelfth month, the month of Adar,* of the ancient Hebrew lunar calendar. This day was March 7, 473 B.C.; also see note on 2:16.

**8:8** Haman's message had been sealed with the king's signet ring and could not be reversed, even by the king. It was part of the famed "law of the Medes and Persians." Now the king gave permission for whatever other decree Mordecai could devise that would offset the first, without actually canceling it.

**8:12** This was the day set by Haman for the extermination of the Jews (3:13).

**8:15-17** Everyone wants to be a hero and receive praise, honor, and wealth. But few are willing to pay the price. Mordecai served the government faithfully for years, bore Haman's hatred and oppression, and risked his life for his people. He was faithful in obscurity. The price to be paid by God's heroes is long-term

commitment, whether or not they receive recognition. Are you ready and willing to pay the price?

**9:5-16** Haman had decreed that on March 7 anyone could kill the Jews and take their property. Mordecai's decree could not reverse Haman's because no law signed by the king could be repealed. Instead, Mordecai had the king sign a new law giving Jews the right to fight back. When the dreaded day arrived, there was much fighting, but the Jews killed only those who wanted to kill them, and they did not take their enemies' possessions, even though they could have (8:11; 9:10, 16). There were no additional riots after the two-day slaughter, so obviously selfish gain or revenge was not a primary motive of the Jews. They simply wanted to defend themselves and their families from those who hated them.

9:12
Esth 7:2

9:13
Esth 8:11

9:15
Esth 9:10

9:16
Esth 9:2

9:17-18
Esth 9:1-2, 21

9:19
Neh 8:10
Esth 9:20-31

9:24
Esth 3:1, 6-7

9:25
Esth 3:6-15; 7:4-10
Ps 7:16

9:26
Esth 3:7; 9:20

9:27
Esth 8:17; 9:20-21

9:29
Esth 2:15; 9:20-21

9:30
Esth 1:1

9:31
Esth 4:3

11 That very day, when the king was informed of the number of people killed in the fortress of Susa, 12he called for Queen Esther. He said, "The Jews have killed 500 men in the fortress of Susa alone, as well as Haman's ten sons. If they have done that here, what has happened in the rest of the provinces? But now, what more do you want? It will be granted to you; tell me and I will do it."

13Esther responded, "If it please the king, give the Jews in Susa permission to do again tomorrow as they have done today, and let the bodies of Haman's ten sons be impaled on a pole."

14So the king agreed, and the decree was announced in Susa. And they impaled the bodies of Haman's ten sons. 15Then the Jews at Susa gathered together on March 8* and killed 300 more men, and again they took no plunder.

16Meanwhile, the other Jews throughout the king's provinces had gathered together to defend their lives. They gained relief from all their enemies, killing 75,000 of those who hated them. But they did not take any plunder. 17This was done throughout the provinces on March 7, and on March 8 they rested,* celebrating their victory with a day of feasting and gladness. 18(The Jews at Susa killed their enemies on March 7 and again on March 8, then rested on March 9,* making that their day of feasting and gladness.) 19So to this day, rural Jews living in remote villages celebrate an annual festival and holiday on the appointed day in late winter,* when they rejoice and send gifts of food to each other.

### The Festival of Purim

20Mordecai recorded these events and sent letters to the Jews near and far, throughout all the provinces of King Xerxes, 21calling on them to celebrate an annual festival on these two days.* 22He told them to celebrate these days with feasting and gladness and by giving gifts of food to each other and presents to the poor. This would commemorate a time when the Jews gained relief from their enemies, when their sorrow was turned into gladness and their mourning into joy.

23So the Jews accepted Mordecai's proposal and adopted this annual custom. 24Haman son of Hammedatha the Agagite, the enemy of the Jews, had plotted to crush and destroy them on the date determined by casting lots (the lots were called *purim*). 25But when Esther came before the king, he issued a decree causing Haman's evil plot to backfire, and Haman and his sons were impaled on a sharpened pole. 26That is why this celebration is called Purim, because it is the ancient word for casting lots.

So because of Mordecai's letter and because of what they had experienced, 27the Jews throughout the realm agreed to inaugurate this tradition and to pass it on to their descendants and to all who became Jews. They declared they would never fail to celebrate these two prescribed days at the appointed time each year. 28These days would be remembered and kept from generation to generation and celebrated by every family throughout the provinces and cities of the empire. This Festival of Purim would never cease to be celebrated among the Jews, nor would the memory of what happened ever die out among their descendants.

29Then Queen Esther, the daughter of Abihail, along with Mordecai the Jew, wrote another letter putting the queen's full authority behind Mordecai's letter to establish the Festival of Purim. 30Letters wishing peace and security were sent to the Jews throughout the 127 provinces of the empire of Xerxes. 31These letters established the Festival of Purim—

9:15 Hebrew *the fourteenth day of the month of Adar*, of the Hebrew lunar calendar. This day was March 8, 473 B.C.; also see note on 2:16. 9:17 Hebrew *on the thirteenth day of the month of Adar, and on the fourteenth day they rested*. These days were March 7 and 8, 473 B.C.; also see note on 2:16. 9:18 Hebrew *killed their enemies on the thirteenth day and the fourteenth day, and then rested on the fifteenth day*, of the Hebrew month of Adar. 9:19 Hebrew *on the fourteenth day of the month of Adar*. This day of the Hebrew lunar calendar occurs in February or March. 9:21 Hebrew *on the fourteenth and fifteenth days of Adar*, of the Hebrew lunar calendar.

---

**9:11** Here the word *fortress* seems to refer to the fortified city of Susa. The king appears to be more concerned about Esther's wishes than the slaughter of his subjects.

**9:19-22** People tend to have short memories when it comes to God's faithfulness. To help counter this, Mordecai wrote down these events and encouraged an annual holiday to commemorate the historic days of Purim. Jews still celebrate Purim today. Celebrations of feasting, gladness, and gift-giving are important ways to remember God's specific acts. Today the festivities of Christmas and Easter help us remember the birth and resurrection of

Jesus Christ. Don't let the celebration or the exchanging of gifts hide the meaning of these great events.

**9:29-31** Among Jews, women were expected to be quiet, to serve in the home, and to stay on the fringe of religious and political life. But Esther was a Jewish woman who broke through the cultural norms, stepping outside her expected role to risk her life to help God's people. Whatever your place in life, God can use you. Be open, available, and ready because God may use you to do what others are afraid to even consider.

an annual celebration of these days at the appointed time, decreed by both Mordecai the Jew and Queen Esther. (The people decided to observe this festival, just as they had decided for themselves and their descendants to establish the times of fasting and mourning.) 32 So the command of Esther confirmed the practices of Purim, and it was all written down in the records.

### The Greatness of Xerxes and Mordecai

**10** King Xerxes imposed a tribute throughout his empire, even to the distant coastlands. 2His great achievements and the full account of the greatness of Mordecai, whom the king had promoted, are recorded in *The Book of the History of the Kings of Media and Persia.* 3Mordecai the Jew became the prime minister, with authority next to that of King Xerxes himself. He was very great among the Jews, who held him in high esteem, because he continued to work for the good of his people and to speak up for the welfare of all their descendants.

**10:1**
Isa 24:15
**10:2**
Esth 2:23; 8:15; 9:4
**10:3**
Gen 41:43-44
Neh 2:10

---

**10:3** Mordecai enjoyed a good reputation among the Jews because he was still their friend when he rose to a place of power. Corruption and abuse of authority often characterize those in power. But power used to lift the fallen and ease the burden of the oppressed is power used well. People placed by God in positions of power or political influence must not turn their backs on those in need.

**10:3** No archaeological records of Mordecai's being prime minister and second-in-command have been discovered, but during this time there is a strange gap in ancient Persian records. The records indicate that another man held that position in 465 B.C., about seven years after Mordecai was first appointed. One tablet has been discovered naming Mardukaya as an official in the early years of Xerxes' reign; some believe this was Mordecai.

**10:3** In the book of Esther, we clearly see God at work in the lives of individuals and in the affairs of a nation. Even when it looks as if the world is in the hands of evil people, God is still in control, protecting those who are his. Although we may not understand everything happening around us, we must trust in God's protection and retain our integrity by doing what we know is right. Esther, who risked her life by appearing before the king, became a heroine. Mordecai, who was effectively condemned to death, rose to become the second highest ranking official in the nation. No matter how hopeless our condition, or how much we would like to give up, we need not despair. God is in control of our world.

TREES snap like toothpicks or fly upward, wrenched from the earth. Whole rooftops sail, cars tumble like toys, houses collapse, and a wall of water obliterates the shore and inundates the land. A hurricane cuts and tears, and only solid foundations survive its unbridled fury. But those foundations can be used for rebuilding after the storm.

For any building, the foundation is critical. It must be deep enough and solid enough to withstand the weight of the building and other stresses. Lives are like buildings, and the quality of each one's foundation will determine the quality of the whole. Too often inferior materials are used, and when tests come, lives crumble.

Job was tested. With a life filled with prestige, possessions, and people, he was suddenly assaulted on every side, devastated, stripped down to his foundation. But his life had been built on God, and he endured.

Job, the book, tells the story of Job, the man of God. It is a gripping drama of riches-to-rags-to-riches, a theological treatise about suffering and divine sovereignty, and a picture of faith that endures. As you read Job, analyze your life and check your foundation. May you be able to say that when all is gone but God, he is enough.

Job was a prosperous farmer living in the land of Uz. He had thousands of sheep, camels, and other livestock, a large family, and many servants. Suddenly, Satan the Accuser came before God claiming that Job was trusting God only because he was wealthy and everything was going well for him. And thus the testing of Job's faith began.

Satan was allowed to destroy Job's children, servants, livestock, herdsmen, and home; but Job continued to trust in God. Next Satan attacked Job physically, covering him with painful sores. Job's wife told him to curse God and die (2:9), but Job suffered in silence.

Three of Job's friends, Eliphaz, Bildad, and Zophar, came to visit him. At first they silently grieved with Job. But when they began to talk about the reasons for Job's tragedies, they told him that sin had caused his suffering. They told him to confess his sins and turn back to God. But Job maintained his innocence.

Unable to convince Job of his sin, the three men fell silent (32:1). At this point, another voice—the young Elihu—entered the debate. Although his argument also failed to convince Job, it prepared the way for God to speak.

Finally, God spoke out of a mighty storm. Confronted with the great power and majesty of God, Job fell in humble reverence before him—speechless. God rebuked Job's friends (and Job), and the drama ended with Job restored to happiness and wealth.

It is easy to think that we have all the answers. In reality, only God knows exactly why events unfold as they do, and we must submit to him as our Sovereign. As you read this book, emulate Job and decide to trust God no matter what happens.

## VITAL STATISTICS

**PURPOSE:**
To demonstrate God's sovereignty and the meaning of true faith. It addresses the question, "Why do the righteous suffer?"

**AUTHOR:**
Unknown, possibly Job. Some have suggested Moses, Solomon, or Elihu.

**DATE WRITTEN:**
Unknown. Records events that probably occurred during the time of the patriarchs, approximately 2000–1800 B.C.

**SETTING:**
The land of Uz, probably located northeast of Palestine, near desert land between Damascus and the Euphrates River

**KEY VERSE:**
"Then the LORD asked Satan, 'Have you noticed my servant Job? He is the finest man in all the earth. He is blameless—a man of complete integrity. He fears God and stays away from evil. And he has maintained his integrity, even though you urged me to harm him without cause'" (2:3).

**KEY PEOPLE:**
Job, Eliphaz the Temanite, Bildad the Shuhite, Zophar the Naamathite, Elihu the Buzite

**SPECIAL FEATURES:**
Job is the first of the poetic books in the Hebrew Bible. Some believe this was the first book of the Bible to be written. The book gives us insights into the work of Satan. Ezekiel 14:14, 20 and James 5:11 mention Job as a historical character.

## THE BLUEPRINT

**A. JOB IS TESTED**
(1:1—2:13)

Job, a wealthy and upright man, lost his possessions, his children, and his health. Job did not understand why he was suffering. Why does God allow his children to suffer? Although there is an explanation, we may not know it while we are here on earth. In the meantime, we must always be ready for testing in our lives.

**B. THREE FRIENDS ANSWER JOB**
(3:1—31:40)
1. First round of discussion
2. Second round of discussion
3. Third round of discussion

Job's friends wrongly assumed that suffering always came as a result of sin. With this in mind, they tried to persuade Job to repent of his sin. But the three friends were wrong. Suffering is not always a direct result of personal sin. When we experience severe suffering, it may not be our fault, so we don't have to add to our pain by feeling guilty that some hidden sin is causing our trouble.

**C. A YOUNG MAN ANSWERS JOB**
(32:1—37:24)

A young man named Elihu, who had been listening to the entire conversation, criticized the three friends for being unable to answer Job. He said that although Job was a good man, he had allowed himself to become proud, and God was punishing him in order to humble him. This answer was partially true because suffering does purify our faith. But God is beyond our comprehension, and we cannot know why he allows each instance of suffering to come into our lives. Our part is simply to remain faithful.

**D. GOD ANSWERS JOB**
(38:1—41:34)

God himself finally answered Job. God is in control of the world, and only he understands why the good are allowed to suffer. This only becomes clear to us when we see God for who he is. We must courageously accept what God allows to happen in our lives and remain firmly committed to him.

**E. JOB IS RESTORED**
(42:1—17)

Job finally learned that when nothing else was left, he had God, and that was enough. Through suffering, we learn that God is enough for our lives and our future. We must love God regardless of whether he allows blessing or suffering to come to us. Testing is difficult, but the result is often a deeper relationship with God. Those who endure the testing of their faith will experience God's great rewards in the end.

## MEGATHEMES

| THEME | EXPLANATION | IMPORTANCE |
|---|---|---|
| Suffering | Through no fault of his own, Job lost his wealth, children, and health. Even his friends were convinced that Job had brought this suffering upon himself. For Job, the greatest trial was not the pain or the loss; it was not being able to understand why God allowed him to suffer. | Suffering can be, but is not always, a penalty for sin. In the same way, prosperity is not always a reward for being good. Those who love God are not exempt from trouble. Although we may not be able to understand fully the pain we experience, it can lead us to rediscover God. |
| Satan's Attacks | Satan attempted to drive a wedge between Job and God by getting Job to believe that God's governing of the world was not just and good. Satan had to ask God for permission to take Job's wealth, children, and health away. Satan was limited to what God allowed. | We must learn to recognize but not fear Satan's attacks because Satan cannot exceed the limits that God sets. Don't let any experience drive a wedge between you and God. Although you can't control how Satan may attack, you can always choose how you will respond when it happens. |
| God's Goodness | God is all-wise and all-powerful. His will is perfect, yet he doesn't always act in ways that we understand. Job's suffering didn't make sense because everyone believed good people were supposed to prosper. When Job was at the point of despair, God spoke to him, showing him his great power and wisdom. | Although God is present everywhere, at times he may seem far away. This may cause us to feel alone and to doubt his care for us. We should serve God for who he is, not what we feel. He is never insensitive to our suffering. Because God is sufficient, we must hold on to him. |
| Pride | Job's friends were certain that they were correct in their judgment of him. God rebuked them for their pride and arrogance. Human wisdom is always partial and temporary, so undue pride in our own conclusions is sin. | We must be careful not to judge others who are suffering. We may be demonstrating the sin of pride. We must be cautious in maintaining the certainty of our own conclusions about how God treats us. When we congratulate ourselves for being right, we become proud. |

*Trusting*

God alone knew the purpose behind Job's suffering, and yet he never explained it to Job. In spite of this, Job never gave up on God—even in the midst of suffering. He never placed his hope in his experience, his wisdom, his friends, or his wealth. Job focused on God.

Job showed the kind of trust we are to have. When everything is stripped away, we are to recognize that God is all we ever really had. We should not demand that God explain everything. God gives us himself, but not all the details of his plans. We must remember that this life, with all its pain, is not our final destiny.

## A. JOB IS TESTED (1:1—2:13)

Job is portrayed as a wealthy man of upright character who loves God. Yet God allows Satan to destroy his flocks, his possessions, his children, and his health. Job refuses to give up on God, even though he does not understand why this is happening to him. We, too, must trust God when we do not understand the difficulties we face.

*Prologue*

**1:1**
Gen 6:9; 17:1
Exod 18:21
Job 28:28; 29:25
Jer 25:20
Lam 4:21
Ezek 14:14
Jas 5:11

**1:2**
Job 42:13

**1:3**
Job 42:12

**1:5**
Gen 8:20
1 Kgs 21:10-11
Job 8:4; 42:8

**1** There once was a man named Job who lived in the land of Uz. He was blameless—a man of complete integrity. He feared God and stayed away from evil. ²He had seven sons and three daughters. ³He owned 7,000 sheep, 3,000 camels, 500 teams of oxen, and 500 female donkeys. He also had many servants. He was, in fact, the richest person in that entire area.

⁴Job's sons would take turns preparing feasts in their homes, and they would also invite their three sisters to celebrate with them. ⁵When these celebrations ended—sometimes after several days—Job would purify his children. He would get up early in the morning and offer a burnt offering for each of them. For Job said to himself, "Perhaps my children have sinned and have cursed God in their hearts." This was Job's regular practice.

---

**1:1** As we read the book of Job, we have information that the characters of the story do not. Job, the main character of the book, lost all he had through no fault of his own. As he struggled to understand why all this was happening to him, it became clear that he was not meant to know the reasons. He would have to face life with the answers and explanations held back. Only then would his faith fully develop.

We must experience life as Job did—one day at a time and without complete answers to all of life's questions. Will we, like Job, trust God no matter what? Or will we give in to the temptation to say that God doesn't really care?

**1:1** The location of the land of Uz is uncertain. We only know that Uz had plentiful pastures and crops (1:3), was located near a wilderness area (1:19), and was close enough to the Sabeans and Chaldeans to be raided (1:14-17). Uz is also mentioned in Jeremiah 25:19, 20. Most scholars believe Uz was located east of the Jordan River near Canaan (Israel), where the Jews (those to whom God first revealed himself) lived.

**1:1ff** As we see calamity and suffering in the book of Job, we must remember that we live in a fallen world where good behavior is not always rewarded and bad behavior is not always punished. When we see a notorious criminal prospering or an innocent child in pain, we say, "That's wrong." And it is. Sin has twisted justice and made our world unpredictable and ugly.

The book of Job shows a good man suffering for no apparent fault of his own. Sadly, our world is like that. But Job's story does not end in despair. Through Job's life we can see that faith in God is justified even when our situations look hopeless. Faith based on rewards or prosperity is hollow. To be unshakable, faith must be built on the confidence that God's ultimate purpose will come to pass.

**1:5** It is not known for sure, but Job probably lived during the days of the patriarchs (Abraham, Isaac, Jacob) before God gave his written law or appointed priests to be religious leaders. During Job's day, the father was the family's religious leader. Because there were no priests to instruct him in God's laws, Job acted as the priest and offered sacrifices to God to ask for forgiveness for sins he and his family had committed.

This demonstrated that Job did not consider himself sinless. Job did this out of conviction and love for God, not just because it was his role as head of the house. Do you carry out your spiritual duties because they are expected or spontaneously from a heart of devotion?

**1:5** Job showed deep concern for the spiritual welfare of his children. Fearful that they might have sinned unknowingly, he offered sacrifices for them. Parents today can show the same concern by praying for their children. This means "sacrificing" some time each day to ask God to forgive them, to help them grow, to protect them, and to help them please him.

## Job's First Test

⁶One day the members of the heavenly court* came to present themselves before the LORD, and the Accuser, Satan,* came with them. ⁷"Where have you come from?" the LORD asked Satan.

Satan answered the LORD, "I have been patrolling the earth, watching everything that's going on."

⁸Then the LORD asked Satan, "Have you noticed my servant Job? He is the finest man in all the earth. He is blameless—a man of complete integrity. He fears God and stays away from evil."

⁹Satan replied to the LORD, "Yes, but Job has good reason to fear God. ¹⁰You have always put a wall of protection around him and his home and his property. You have made him prosper in everything he does. Look how rich he is! ¹¹But reach out and take away everything he has, and he will surely curse you to your face!"

¹²"All right, you may test him," the LORD said to Satan. "Do whatever you want with everything he possesses, but don't harm him physically." So Satan left the LORD's presence.

¹³One day when Job's sons and daughters were feasting at the oldest brother's house, ¹⁴a messenger arrived at Job's home with this news: "Your oxen were plowing, with the donkeys feeding beside them, ¹⁵when the Sabeans raided us. They stole all the animals and killed all the farmhands. I am the only one who escaped to tell you."

¹⁶While he was still speaking, another messenger arrived with this news: "The fire of God has fallen from heaven and burned up your sheep and all the shepherds. I am the only one who escaped to tell you."

¹⁷While he was still speaking, a third messenger arrived with this news: "Three bands of Chaldean raiders have stolen your camels and killed your servants. I am the only one who escaped to tell you."

**1:6** Job 38:7
**1:7** 1 Pet 5:8
**1:8** Num 12:7; Josh 1:2, 7; Job 1:1; 7:8; 42:7-8
**1:10** Job 29:2-6; 31:25
**1:11** Job 2:5; 19:21
**1:15** Job 6:19
**1:16** Gen 19:24; Lev 10:2; Num 11:1-3
**1:17** Gen 11:28, 31

**1:6a** Hebrew *the sons of God.* **1:6b** Hebrew *and the satan;* similarly throughout this chapter.

---

**1:6** The Bible speaks of other heavenly councils where God and the angels plan their activities on earth and where angels are required to give account of themselves (i.e., 1 Kings 22:19-23). Because God is Creator of all angels—both of those who serve him and of those who rebelled—he has complete power and authority over them.

**1:6, 7** Satan, originally an angel of God, had become corrupt through his own pride. He has been evil since his rebellion against God (1 John 3:8). Satan considers God as his enemy. He tries to hinder God's work in people, but he is limited by God's power and can do only what he is permitted (Luke 22:31, 32; 1 Timothy 1:19, 20; 2 Timothy 2:23-26). Satan is our enemy because he actively looks for people to attack with temptation (1 Peter 5:8, 9) and because he wants to make people hate God. He does this through lies and deception (Genesis 3:1-6). Job, a blameless and upright man who had been greatly blessed, was a perfect target for Satan. Any person who is committed to God should expect Satan's attacks. Satan, who hates God, also hates God's people.

**1:6-12** From this conversation, we learn a great deal about Satan. (1) He is accountable to God. All angelic beings, good and evil, are compelled to present themselves before God (1:6). God knew that Satan was intent on attacking Job. (2) Satan can be at only one place at a time (1:6, 7). His demons aid him in his work; but as a created being, he is limited. (3) Satan cannot see into our minds or foretell the future (1:9-11). If he could, he would have known that Job would not break under pressure. (4) Because Satan can do nothing without God's permission (1:12), God's people can overcome his attacks through God's power. (5) God puts limitations on what Satan can do (1:12; 2:6). Satan's response to the Lord's question (1:7) tells us that Satan is real and active on earth. Knowing this about Satan should cause us to remain close to the one who is greater than Satan—God himself.

**1:7ff** Some people suggest that this dialogue was made up by the author of this book. Could this conversation between God and Satan really have happened? Other Bible passages tell us that Satan does indeed have access to God (see Revelation 12:10). He even went into God's presence to make accusations against

Joshua the high priest (Zechariah 3:1, 2). If this conversation didn't take place, then the reasons for Job's suffering become meaningless, and the book of Job is reduced to fiction rather than fact.

**1:8, 12** Job was a model of trust and obedience to God, yet God permitted Satan to attack him in an especially harsh manner. Although God loves us, believing and obeying him do not shelter us from life's calamities. Setbacks, tragedies, and sorrows strike Christians and non-Christians alike. But in our tests and trials, God expects us to express our faith to the world. How do you respond to your troubles? Do you ask God, "Why me?" or do you say, "Use me!"?

**1:9** Satan attacked Job's motives, saying that Job was blameless and had integrity only because he had no reason to turn against God. Ever since he had started following God, everything had gone well for Job. Satan wanted to prove that Job worshiped God, not out of love, but because God had given him so much.

Satan accurately analyzed why many people trust God. They are fair-weather believers, following God only when everything is going well or for what they can get. Adversity destroys this superficial faith. But adversity strengthens real faith by causing believers to dig their roots deeper into God in order to withstand the storms. How deep does your faith go? Put the roots of your faith down deep into God so that you can withstand any storm you may face.

**1:12** This conversation between God and Satan teaches us an important fact about God—he is fully aware of every attempt by Satan to bring suffering and difficulty upon us. While God may allow us to suffer for a reason beyond our understanding, he is never caught by surprise by our troubles and is always compassionate.

**1:15-17** The Sabeans were from southwest Arabia, while the Chaldeans were from the region north of the Persian Gulf.

**1:16** "The fire of God" was a poetic way to describe lightning (1 Kings 18:38; 2 Kings 1:10-14). In this case, it had to be unusually powerful to kill 7,000 sheep.

¹⁸While he was still speaking, another messenger arrived with this news: "Your sons and daughters were feasting in their oldest brother's home. ¹⁹Suddenly, a powerful wind swept in from the wilderness and hit the house on all sides. The house collapsed, and all your children are dead. I am the only one who escaped to tell you."

²⁰Job stood up and tore his robe in grief. Then he shaved his head and fell to the ground to worship. ²¹He said,

"I came naked from my mother's womb,
	and I will be naked when I leave.
The Lord gave me what I had,
	and the Lord has taken it away.
Praise the name of the Lord!"

²²In all of this, Job did not sin by blaming God.

### Job's Second Test

**2** One day the members of the heavenly court* came again to present themselves before the Lord, and the Accuser, Satan,* came with them. ²"Where have you come from?" the Lord asked Satan.

Satan answered the Lord, "I have been patrolling the earth, watching everything that's going on."

³Then the Lord asked Satan, "Have you noticed my servant Job? He is the finest man in all the earth. He is blameless—a man of complete integrity. He fears God and stays away from evil. And he has maintained his integrity, even though you urged me to harm him without cause."

⁴Satan replied to the Lord, "Skin for skin! A man will give up everything he has to save his life. ⁵But reach out and take away his health, and he will surely curse you to your face!"

2:1a Hebrew *the sons of God.* 2:1b Hebrew *and the satan*; similarly throughout this chapter.

**Marginal references:**
1:20 Gen 37:29, 34
1:21 1 Sam 2:7-8; Job 2:10; Eccl 5:15; 1 Tim 6:7
1:22 Job 2:10
2:1 Job 1:6-8
2:3 Job 27:5-6
2:5 Job 1:11

| THE SOURCES OF SUFFERING | Sources | Who Is Responsible | Who Is Affected | Needed Response |
|---|---|---|---|---|
| | My sin | I am | Myself and others | Repentance and confession to God |
| | Others' sin | Person who sinned and others who allowed the sin | Probably many people, including those who sinned | Active resistance to the sinful behavior, while accepting the sinner |
| | Avoidable physical (or natural) disaster | Persons who ignore the facts or refuse to take precautions | Most of those exposed to the cause | Prevent them if possible; be prepared if they can't be prevented |
| | Unavoidable physical (or natural) disaster | God, Satan | Most of those present | Ongoing trust in God's faithfulness |

When suffering or troubles happen, do they always come from Satan? In Job's story, his series of tragedies did come from Satan, but this is not always the case. The chart above demonstrates the four main causes of suffering. Any one of these or a combination of them may create suffering. If knowing why we are suffering will teach us to avoid the cause, then the causes are worth knowing. However, it is most important to know how to respond during suffering.

**1:20-22** Job did not hide his overwhelming grief. He had not lost his faith in God; instead, his emotions showed that he was human and that he loved his family. God created our emotions, and it is not sinful or inappropriate to express them as Job did. If you have experienced a deep loss, a disappointment, or a heartbreak, admit your feelings to yourself and others, and grieve.

**1:20-22** Job had lost his possessions and family in this first of Satan's tests, but he reacted rightly toward God by acknowledging God's sovereign authority over everything God had given him. Satan lost this first round. Job passed the test and proved that people can love God for who he is, not for what he gives.

**2:3-6** Can Satan persuade God to change his plans? At first God said he did not want Job harmed physically, but then he decided to allow it. Satan is unable to persuade God to go against his character: God is completely and eternally good. But God was willing to go along with Satan's plan because God knew the eventual outcome of Job's story. God cannot be fooled by Satan. Job's suffering was a test for Job, Satan, and us—not God.

**2:4, 5** "Skin for skin" was Satan's comment concerning Job's response to the loss of his family. Satan still held to his opinion that Job was faithful only because of God's blessings. Satan believed that Job was willing to accept the loss of family and property as long as his own skin was safe. Satan's next step was to inflict physical suffering upon Job to prove his original accusation (1:9).

⁶"All right, do with him as you please," the LORD said to Satan. "But spare his life." ⁷So Satan left the LORD's presence, and he struck Job with terrible boils from head to foot.

⁸Job scraped his skin with a piece of broken pottery as he sat among the ashes. ⁹His wife said to him, "Are you still trying to maintain your integrity? Curse God and die."

¹⁰But Job replied, "You talk like a foolish woman. Should we accept only good things from the hand of God and never anything bad?" So in all this, Job said nothing wrong.

### Job's Three Friends Share His Anguish

¹¹When three of Job's friends heard of the tragedy he had suffered, they got together and traveled from their homes to comfort and console him. Their names were Eliphaz the Temanite, Bildad the Shuhite, and Zophar the Naamathite. ¹²When they saw Job from a distance, they scarcely recognized him. Wailing loudly, they tore their robes and threw dust into the air over their heads to show their grief. ¹³Then they sat on the ground with him for seven days and nights. No one said a word to Job, for they saw that his suffering was too great for words.

## B. THREE FRIENDS ANSWER JOB (3:1—31:40)

Job agonizes over his situation. His three friends explain that he must be suffering because of some terrible sin he committed. They try to persuade Job to repent of his sin. When Job argues that he has not sinned enough to deserve such suffering, his friends respond with even harsher accusations. While there are elements of truth in the speeches of Job's three friends, they are based on wrong assumptions. We must be careful what we assume to be true in the lives of others. We cannot assume that suffering is their own fault or a result of their sin.

## 1. First round of discussion

### Job's First Speech

**3** At last Job spoke, and he cursed the day of his birth. ²He said:

³ "Let the day of my birth be erased,
   and the night I was conceived.
⁴ Let that day be turned to darkness.
   Let it be lost even to God on high,
   and let no light shine on it.
⁵ Let the darkness and utter gloom claim that day for its own.
   Let a black cloud overshadow it,
   and let the darkness terrify it.
⁶ Let that night be blotted off the calendar,
   never again to be counted among the days of the year,
   never again to appear among the months.

**2:7**
Deut 28:35
Job 7:5; 13:28

**2:8**
Job 42:6
Jer 6:26
Ezek 27:30
Jon 3:6
Matt 11:21

**2:10**
Job 1:21-22
Ps 39:1

**2:12**
Josh 7:6
Job 1:20
Lam 2:10
Ezek 27:30

**2:13**
Gen 50:10
Ezek 3:15

**3:3**
Jer 20:14

---

**2:6** Again Satan had to seek permission from God to inflict pain upon Job. God limits Satan, and in this case he did not allow Satan to destroy Job.

**2:9** Why was Job's wife spared when the rest of his family was killed? It is possible that her very presence caused Job even more suffering through either her chiding or her sorrow over all they had lost.

**2:10** Many people think that believing in God protects them from trouble, so when calamity comes, they question God's goodness and justice. But the message of Job is that you should not give up on God because he allows you to have bad experiences. Faith in God does not guarantee personal prosperity, and lack of faith does not guarantee troubles in this life. If this were so, people would believe in God simply to get rich. God is capable of rescuing us from suffering, but he may also allow suffering to come for reasons we cannot understand. It is Satan's strategy to get us to doubt God at exactly this moment. Here Job shows a perspective broader than seeking his own personal comfort. If we always knew why we were suffering, our faith would have no room to grow.

**2:11** Eliphaz, Bildad, and Zophar were not only Job's friends, they were also known for their wisdom. In the end, however, their wisdom was shown to be narrow-minded and incomplete.

**2:11** Upon learning of Job's difficulties, three of his friends came to sympathize with him and comfort him. Later we learn that their

words of comfort were not helpful—but at least they came. While God rebuked them for what they said (42:7), he did not rebuke them for what they did—making the effort to come to someone who was in need. Unfortunately, when they came, they did a poor job of comforting Job because they were proud of their own advice and insensitive to Job's needs. When someone is in need, go to that person, but be sensitive about how you comfort him or her.

**2:13** Why did the friends arrive and then just sit quietly? According to Jewish tradition, people who come to comfort someone in mourning should not speak until the mourner speaks. Often the best response to another person's suffering is silence. Job's friends realized that his pain was too deep to be healed with mere words, so they said nothing. (If only they had continued to sit quietly!) Often, we feel we must say something spiritual and insightful to a hurting friend. Perhaps what he or she needs most is just our presence, showing that we care. Pat answers and trite quotations say much less than empathetic silence and loving companionship.

**3:1ff** Job's response to his second test—physical affliction—contrasts greatly to his attitude after the first test (1:20-22). Job still did not curse God, but he cursed the day of his birth. He felt it would be better never to be born than to be forsaken by God. Job was struggling emotionally, physically, and spiritually; his

**3:8**
Job 41:1, 10, 25

⁷ Let that night be childless.
  Let it have no joy.
⁸ Let those who are experts at cursing—
  whose cursing could rouse Leviathan*—
  curse that day.

**3:8** The identification of Leviathan is disputed, ranging from an earthly creature to a mythical sea monster in ancient literature.

---

Children never tire of asking why. Yet the question produces a bitter taste the older we get. Children wonder about everything; adults wonder about suffering. We notice that the world seems to run by a system of cause and effect, yet there are some effects for which we can't find a clear cause, and some causes that don't lead to the expected effects. We would expect Job's wealth and family to give him a very happy life and, for a while, they did. But the loss and pain he experienced shock us. The first two chapters of his story are more than we can bear. To those so quick to ask why at the smallest misfortune, Job's faithfulness seems incredible. But even Job had something to learn. We can learn with him.

Our age of "instant" everything has caused us to lose the ability to wait. We expect to learn patience instantly, and in our hurry, we miss the contradiction. Of all that we want now, relief from pain is at the top of our list. We want an instant cure for everything from toothaches to heartbreaks.

Although some pains have been cured, we still live in a world where many people suffer. Job was not expecting instant answers for the intense emotional and physical pain he endured. But in the end, what broke Job's patience was not the suffering, but not knowing *why* he suffered.

When Job expressed his frustration, his friends were ready with their answers. They believed that the law of cause and effect applied to all people's experiences. Their view of life boiled down to this: Good things happen to good people, and bad things happen to bad people. Because of this, they felt their role was to help Job admit to whatever sin was causing his suffering.

Job actually looked at life almost the same way as his friends. What he couldn't understand was why he was suffering so much when he was sure he had done nothing to deserve such punishment. The last friend, Elihu, did offer another explanation for the pain by pointing out that God might be allowing it to purify Job. But this was only partly helpful. When God finally spoke, he didn't offer Job an answer. Instead, he drove home the point that it is better to know God than to know answers.

Often we suffer consequences for bad decisions and actions. Job's willingness to repent and confess known wrongs is a good guideline for us. Sometimes suffering shapes us for special service to others. Sometimes suffering is an attack by Satan on our lives. And sometimes we don't know why we suffer. At those times, are we willing to trust God in spite of unanswered questions?

| | |
|---|---|
| **Strengths and accomplishments** | • A man of faith, patience, and endurance<br>• Known as a generous and caring person<br>• Very wealthy |
| **Weakness and mistake** | • Allowed his desire to understand why he was suffering to overwhelm him and make him question God |
| **Lessons from his life** | • Knowing God is better than knowing answers<br>• God is not arbitrary or uncaring<br>• Pain is not always punishment |
| **Vital statistics** | • Where: Uz<br>• Occupation: Wealthy landowner and livestock owner<br>• Relatives: Wife and first 10 children not named. Daughters from the second set of children: Jemimah, Keziah, Keren-happuch.<br>• Contemporaries: Eliphaz, Bildad, Zophar, Elihu |
| **Key verses** | "For examples of patience in suffering, dear brothers and sisters, look at the prophets who spoke in the name of the Lord. We give great honor to those who endure under suffering. For instance, you know about Job, a man of great endurance. You can see how the Lord was kind to him at the end, for the Lord is full of tenderness and mercy" (James 5:10, 11). |

Job's story is told in the book of Job. He is also referred to in Ezekiel 14:14, 20 and James 5:11.

---

misery was pervasive and deep. Never underestimate how vulnerable we are during times of suffering and pain. We must hold on to our faith even if there is no relief.

**3:8** In Job's day, people were hired to pronounce curses. Job desires that the experts at cursing would call up the sea monster, Leviathan, to swallow up the day of Job's birth.

9 Let its morning stars remain dark.
   Let it hope for light, but in vain;
      may it never see the morning light.
10 Curse that day for failing to shut my mother's womb,
      for letting me be born to see all this trouble.

11 "Why wasn't I born dead?
      Why didn't I die as I came from the womb?
12 Why was I laid on my mother's lap?
      Why did she nurse me at her breasts?
13 Had I died at birth, I would now be at peace.
      I would be asleep and at rest.
14 I would rest with the world's kings and prime ministers,
      whose great buildings now lie in ruins.
15 I would rest with princes, rich in gold,
      whose palaces were filled with silver.
16 Why wasn't I buried like a stillborn child,
      like a baby who never lives to see the light?
17 For in death the wicked cause no trouble,
      and the weary are at rest.
18 Even captives are at ease in death,
      with no guards to curse them.
19 Rich and poor are both there,
      and the slave is free from his master.

20 "Oh, why give light to those in misery,
      and life to those who are bitter?
21 They long for death, and it won't come.
      They search for death more eagerly than for hidden treasure.
22 They're filled with joy when they finally die,
      and rejoice when they find the grave.
23 Why is life given to those with no future,
      those God has surrounded with difficulties?
24 I cannot eat for sighing;
      my groans pour out like water.
25 What I always feared has happened to me.
      What I dreaded has come true.
26 I have no peace, no quietness.
      I have no rest; only trouble comes."

## Eliphaz's First Response to Job

**4** Then Eliphaz the Temanite replied to Job:

2 "Will you be patient and let me say a word?
      For who could keep from speaking out?

**3:9**
Job 41:18

**3:11**
Job 10:18-19

**3:13**
Job 14:10-15;
19:25-27

**3:21**
Rev 9:6

**3:23**
Job 19:6, 8, 12
Ps 88:8
Lam 3:7

**3:24**
Job 6:7; 33:20
Ps 42:3-4

**3:26**
Job 7:13-14

---

**3:11** Job was experiencing extreme physical pain as well as grief over the loss of his family and possessions. He can't be blamed for wishing he were dead. Job's grief placed him at the crossroads of his faith, shattering many misconceptions about God (e.g., he makes you rich, always keeps you from trouble and pain, or protects your loved ones). Job was driven back to the basics of his faith in God. He had only two choices: (1) He could curse God and give up, or (2) he could trust God and draw strength from him to continue.

**3:23-26** Job had been careful not to worship material possessions but to worship God alone. Here he was overwhelmed by calamities that mocked his caution, and he complained about trials that came despite his right living. All the principles by which he had lived were crumbling, and Job began to lose his perspective. Trials and grief, whether temporary or enduring, do not destroy the real purpose of life. Life is not given merely for happiness and personal fulfillment but for us to serve and honor God. The worth

and meaning of life is not based on what we feel but on the one reality no one can take away—God's love for us. Don't assume that because God truly loves you, he will always prevent suffering. The opposite may be true. God's love cannot be measured or limited by how great or how little we may suffer. Romans 8:38, 39 teaches us that nothing can separate us from God's love.

**4:1ff** Eliphaz claimed to have been given secret knowledge through a special revelation from God (4:12-16), and that he had learned much from personal experience (4:8). He argued that suffering is a direct result of sin, so if Job would only confess his sin, his suffering would end. Eliphaz saw suffering as God's punishment, which should be welcomed in order to bring a person back to God. In some cases, of course, this may be true (Galatians 6:7, 8), but it was not true with Job. Although Eliphaz had many good and true comments, he made three wrong assumptions: (1) A good and innocent person never suffers; (2) those who suffer are being punished for their past sins; and

**4:3**
Job 29:21, 25

3 "In the past you have encouraged many people;
　　you have strengthened those who were weak.
4 Your words have supported those who were falling;
　　you encouraged those with shaky knees.
5 But now when trouble strikes, you lose heart.
　　You are terrified when it touches you.

**4:6**
Job 1:1
Prov 3:26

6 Doesn't your reverence for God give you confidence?
　　Doesn't your life of integrity give you hope?

**4:7-8**
Ps 37:25
Prov 22:8
Gal 6:7-8

7 "Stop and think! Do the innocent die?
　　When have the upright been destroyed?
8 My experience shows that those who plant trouble
　　and cultivate evil will harvest the same.

**4:9**
Isa 30:33
2 Thes 2:8

9 A breath from God destroys them.
　　They vanish in a blast of his anger.
10 The lion roars and the wildcat snarls,
　　but the teeth of strong lions will be broken.

**4:11**
Job 5:4
Ps 34:10

11 The fierce lion will starve for lack of prey,
　　and the cubs of the lioness will be scattered.

---

**ADVICE FROM JOB'S FRIENDS**　　Overwhelmed by suffering, Job was not comforted but condemned by his friends. Each of their views represents a well-known way to understand suffering. God proves that each explanation given by Job's friends has less than the whole answer.

| Who They Were | Reference | How They Helped | Their Reasoning | Their Advice | Job's Response | God's Response |
|---|---|---|---|---|---|---|
| Eliphaz the Temanite | Job 4–5; 15; 22 | They sat in silence with Job for seven days. (2:11-13) | Job is suffering because he has sinned. | Go to God and present your case to him. (5:8) | Stop assuming my guilt. (6:29) | God rebukes Job's friends. (42:7) |
| Bildad the Shuhite | Job 8; 18; 25 | | Job won't admit he sinned, so he's still suffering. | How long will you go on like this? (8:2) | I will say to God, . . . Tell me the charge you are bringing against me. (10:2) | |
| Zophar the Naamathite | Job 11; 20 | | Job's sin deserves even more suffering than he's experienced. | Get rid of your sins. (11:13, 14) | I will be proved innocent. (13:18) | |
| Elihu the Buzite | Job 32–37 | Confronted Job with the need to be content even though he didn't know why he was suffering | God is using suffering to mold and train Job. | Keep silent and I will teach you wisdom. (33:33) | No response | God does not directly address Elihu. |
| God | Job 38–41 | | Did not explain the reason for the pain | Do you still want to argue with the Almighty? (40:2) | I was talking about things I did not understand. (42:3-5) | |

---

(3) Job, because he was suffering, had done something wrong in God's eyes. (For more about Eliphaz, see his Profile, chapter 8, p. 797 and the chart in chapter 28, p. 819. Teman was a trading city in Edom, noted as a place of wisdom; see Jeremiah 49:7.)

**4:7, 8** Part of what Eliphaz said is true, and part is false. It is true that those who promote sin and trouble eventually will be punished; it is false that anyone who is good and innocent will never suffer.

All the material recorded and quoted in the Bible is here by God's choice. Some is a record of what people said and did but is not an example to follow. The sins, the defeats, the evil thoughts, and misconceptions about God are all recorded in God's divinely inspired Word, but we should not follow those wrong examples just because they are in the Bible. The Bible gives us teachings and examples of what we *should* do as well as what we *should not* do. Eliphaz's comments are an example of what we should try to avoid—making false assumptions about others based on our own experiences.

12 "This truth was given to me in secret,
    as though whispered in my ear.
13 It came to me in a disturbing vision at night,
    when people are in a deep sleep.
14 Fear gripped me,
    and my bones trembled.
15 A spirit* swept past my face,
    and my hair stood on end.*
16 The spirit stopped, but I couldn't see its shape.
    There was a form before my eyes.
    In the silence I heard a voice say,
17 'Can a mortal be innocent before God?
    Can anyone be pure before the Creator?'

18 "If God does not trust his own angels
    and has charged his messengers with foolishness,
19 how much less will he trust people made of clay!
    They are made of dust, crushed as easily as a moth.
20 They are alive in the morning but dead by evening,
    gone forever without a trace.
21 Their tent-cords are pulled and the tent collapses,
    and they die in ignorance.

### Eliphaz's Response Continues

**5** 1 "Cry for help, but will anyone answer you?
    Which of the angels* will help you?
2 Surely resentment destroys the fool,
    and jealousy kills the simple.
3 I have seen that fools may be successful for the moment,
    but then comes sudden disaster.
4 Their children are abandoned far from help;
    they are crushed in court with no one to defend them.
5 The hungry devour their harvest,
    even when it is guarded by brambles.*
    The thirsty pant after their wealth.
6 But evil does not spring from the soil,
    and trouble does not sprout from the earth.
7 People are born for trouble
    as readily as sparks fly up from a fire.

8 "If I were you, I would go to God
    and present my case to him.
9 He does great things too marvelous to understand.
    He performs countless miracles.
10 He gives rain for the earth
    and water for the fields.

**4:12**
Job 26:14;
33:15-18

**4:17**
Job 9:2; 35:10

**4:19**
Gen 2:7; 3:19
Job 10:9; 15:15;
22:16
**4:20**
Job 14:2, 20; 20:7
**4:21**
Job 8:22

**5:2**
Prov 12:16; 27:3

**5:3**
Job 24:18

**5:5**
Job 18:8-10

**5:9**
Job 9:10; 37:14,
16; 42:3
**5:10**
Job 36:27-29;
37:6-11
Ps 65:9

**4:15a** Or *wind;* also in 4:16.   **4:15b** Or *its wind sent shivers up my spine.*   **5:1** Hebrew *the holy ones.*
**5:5** The meaning of the Hebrew for this phrase is uncertain.

---

**4:12, 13** Although Eliphaz claimed that his vision was divinely inspired, it is doubtful that it came from God because later God criticized Eliphaz for misrepresenting him (42:7). Whatever the vision's source, it is summarized in 4:17. On the surface, this statement is completely true—a mere mortal cannot compare to God and should not try to question God's motives and actions. Eliphaz, however, took this thought and expounded on it later, expressing his own opinions. His conclusion (5:8) reveals a very shallow understanding of Job and his suffering. It is easy for teachers, counselors, and well-meaning friends to begin with a portion of God's truth but then go off on a tangent. Don't limit God to your perspective and finite understanding of life.

**4:18, 19** Do angels really make errors? Remember that Eliphaz was speaking, not God, so we must be careful about building our

knowledge of the spiritual world from Eliphaz's opinions. In addition, the word translated "foolishness" is used only here, and its meaning is unclear. We could save Eliphaz's credibility by saying he meant fallen angels, but this passage is not meant to teach about angels. Eliphaz was saying that sinful human beings are far beneath God and the angels. Eliphaz was right about God's greatness, but he did not understand God's greater purposes concerning suffering.

**5:8** All three of Job's friends made the mistake of assuming that Job had committed some great sin that had caused his suffering. Neither they nor Job knew of Satan's conversation with God (1:6–2:6). It is human nature to blame people for their own troubles, but Job's story makes it clear that blame cannot always be attached to those whom trouble strikes.

**5:11**
Job 22:29; 36:7

11 He gives prosperity to the poor
    and protects those who suffer.
12 He frustrates the plans of schemers
    so the work of their hands will not succeed.

**5:13**
1 Cor 3:19

13 He traps the wise in their own cleverness
    so their cunning schemes are thwarted.

**5:14**
Deut 28:29

14 They find it is dark in the daytime,
    and they grope at noon as if it were night.
15 He rescues the poor from the cutting words of the strong,
    and rescues them from the clutches of the powerful.

**5:16**
Ps 107:42

16 And so at last the poor have hope,
    and the snapping jaws of the wicked are shut.

**5:17**
Ps 94:12
Heb 12:5-11

17 "But consider the joy of those corrected by God!
    Do not despise the discipline of the Almighty when you sin.

**5:18**
Deut 32:39
Isa 30:26
Hos 6:1

18 For though he wounds, he also bandages.
    He strikes, but his hands also heal.
19 From six disasters he will rescue you;
    even in the seventh, he will keep you from evil.

**5:20**
Pss 33:19; 144:10

20 He will save you from death in time of famine,
    from the power of the sword in time of war.
21 You will be safe from slander
    and have no fear when destruction comes.
22 You will laugh at destruction and famine;
    wild animals will not terrify you.

**5:23**
Isa 11:6-9; 65:25

23 You will be at peace with the stones of the field,
    and its wild animals will be at peace with you.

**5:24**
Job 8:6

24 You will know that your home is safe.
    When you survey your possessions, nothing will be missing.
25 You will have many children;
    your descendants will be as plentiful as grass!

**5:26**
Gen 15:15
Job 42:17
Prov 9:11

26 You will go to the grave at a ripe old age,
    like a sheaf of grain harvested at the proper time!

27 "We have studied life and found all this to be true.
    Listen to my counsel, and apply it to yourself."

### Job's Second Speech: A Response to Eliphaz

**6** Then Job spoke again:

**6:2**
Job 31:6

2 "If my misery could be weighed
    and my troubles be put on the scales,

**6:3**
Job 23:2

3 they would outweigh all the sands of the sea.
    That is why I spoke impulsively.

**6:4**
Job 16:13; 21:20;
30:15
Ps 38:2

4 For the Almighty has struck me down with his arrows.
    Their poison infects my spirit.
    God's terrors are lined up against me.

---

**5:13** Paul later quoted part of this verse (1 Corinthians 3:19)—the only time Job is clearly quoted in the New Testament. Although God rebuked Eliphaz for being wrong in his advice to Job (42:7), not all he said was in error. The part Paul quoted was correct—people are often caught in their own traps. This illustrates how Scripture must be used to explain and comment on itself. We must be familiar with the entire scope of God's Word to properly understand the difficult portions of it.

**5:17** Eliphaz was correct—it is a joy to be disciplined by God when we do wrong. Eliphaz's advice, however, did not apply to Job. As we know from the beginning of the book, Job's suffering was not a result of some great sin. We sometimes give people excellent advice only to learn that it does not apply to them and is therefore not very helpful. All who offer counsel from God's Word

should take care to thoroughly understand a person's situation *before* giving advice.

**5:17-26** Eliphaz's words in 5:17, 18 show a view of discipline that has been almost forgotten: Pain can help us grow. These are good words to remember when we face hardship and loss. Because Job did not understand why he suffered, his faith in God had a chance to grow. On the other hand, we must not make Eliphaz's mistake. God does not eliminate all hardship when we are following him closely, and good behavior is not always rewarded by prosperity. Rewards for good and punishment for evil are in God's hands and given out according to his timetable. Satan's ploy is to get us to doubt God's love and faithfulness toward us.

5 Don't I have a right to complain?
   Don't wild donkeys bray when they find no grass,
   and oxen bellow when they have no food?
6 Don't people complain about unsalted food?
   Does anyone want the tasteless white of an egg?*
7 My appetite disappears when I look at it;
   I gag at the thought of eating it!

8 "Oh, that I might have my request,
   that God would grant my desire.
9 I wish he would crush me.
   I wish he would reach out his hand and kill me.
10 At least I can take comfort in this:
   Despite the pain,
   I have not denied the words of the Holy One.
11 But I don't have the strength to endure.
   I have nothing to live for.
12 Do I have the strength of a stone?
   Is my body made of bronze?
13 No, I am utterly helpless,
   without any chance of success.

14 "One should be kind to a fainting friend,
   but you accuse me without any fear of the Almighty.*
15 My brothers, you have proved as unreliable as a seasonal brook
   that overflows its banks in the spring
16    when it is swollen with ice and melting snow.
17 But when the hot weather arrives, the water disappears.
   The brook vanishes in the heat.
18 The caravans turn aside to be refreshed,
   but there is nothing to drink, so they die.
19 The caravans from Tema search for this water;
   the travelers from Sheba hope to find it.
20 They count on it but are disappointed.
   When they arrive, their hopes are dashed.
21 You, too, have given no help.
   You have seen my calamity, and you are afraid.
22 But why? Have I ever asked you for a gift?
   Have I begged for anything of yours for myself?
23 Have I asked you to rescue me from my enemies,
   or to save me from ruthless people?
24 Teach me, and I will keep quiet.
   Show me what I have done wrong.
25 Honest words can be painful,
   but what do your criticisms amount to?
26 Do you think your words are convincing
   when you disregard my cry of desperation?
27 You would even send an orphan into slavery*
   or sell a friend.
28 Look at me!
   Would I lie to your face?

**6:6** Or the tasteless juice of the mallow plant?   **6:14** Or friend, / or he might lose his fear of the Almighty.
**6:27** Hebrew even gamble over an orphan.

---

**6:5** Job 39:5-8

**6:9** 1 Kgs 19:4

**6:10** Job 23:11-12

**6:11** Job 21:4

**6:13** Job 26:2-3

**6:14** Job 1:5; 4:5

**6:15** Jer 15:18

**6:17** Job 24:19

**6:19** Gen 25:15
Job 1:15
Isa 21:14

**6:20** Jer 14:3

**6:26** Job 8:2

**6:27** Joel 3:3
Nah 3:10
2 Pet 2:3

---

**6:6, 7** Job said that Eliphaz's advice was like eating the taste-less white of an egg. When people are going through severe trials, ill-advised counsel is distasteful. They may listen politely, but inside they are upset. Be slow to give advice to those who are hurting. They often need compassion more than they need advice.

**6:8, 9** In his grief, Job wanted to give in, to be freed from his discomfort, and to die. But God did not grant Job's request. He had a greater plan for him. Our tendency, like Job's, is to want to give up and get out when the going gets rough. To trust God in the good times is commendable, but to trust him during the difficult times tests us to our limits and exercises our faith. In your struggles, large or small, trust that God is in control and that he will take care of you (Romans 8:28).

**6:30**
Job 12:11

29 Stop assuming my guilt,
    for I have done no wrong.
30 Do you think I am lying?
    Don't I know the difference between right and wrong?

**7:1**
Lev 25:50
Job 14:6, 14

**7** ¹ "Is not all human life a struggle?
    Our lives are like that of a hired hand,
² like a worker who longs for the shade,
    like a servant waiting to be paid.
³ I, too, have been assigned months of futility,
    long and weary nights of misery.

**7:4**
Deut 28:67
Job 7:13-14

⁴ Lying in bed, I think, 'When will it be morning?'
    But the night drags on, and I toss till dawn.
⁵ My body is covered with maggots and scabs.
    My skin breaks open, oozing with pus.

### Job Cries Out to God

⁶ "My days fly faster than a weaver's shuttle.
    They end without hope.

**7:7**
Job 7:16; 9:25
Ps 78:39

⁷ O God, remember that my life is but a breath,
    and I will never again feel happiness.

**7:8**
Job 7:21; 20:9

⁸ You see me now, but not for long.
    You will look for me, but I will be gone.
⁹ Just as a cloud dissipates and vanishes,
    those who die* will not come back.

**7:10**
Ps 103:16

10 They are gone forever from their home—
    never to be seen again.

11 "I cannot keep from speaking.
    I must express my anguish.
    My bitter soul must complain.
12 Am I a sea monster or a dragon
    that you must place me under guard?

**7:13**
Job 7:4
Ps 6:6

13 I think, 'My bed will comfort me,
    and sleep will ease my misery,'
14 but then you shatter me with dreams
    and terrify me with visions.
15 I would rather be strangled—
    rather die than suffer like this.
16 I hate my life and don't want to go on living.
    Oh, leave me alone for my few remaining days.

**7:17**
Job 22:2
Heb 2:6

17 "What are people, that you should make so much of us,
    that you should think of us so often?
18 For you examine us every morning
    and test us every moment.

**7:9** Hebrew *who go down to Sheol.*

---

**6:29, 30** Job referred to his own righteousness, not because he was sinless, but because he had a right relationship with God. He was not guilty of the sins his friends accused him of (see chapter 31 for his summary of the life he had led). When Job says, "I have done no wrong," he is not claiming sinlessness. No one but Jesus Christ has ever been sinless—free from all wrong thoughts and actions. Even Job needed to make some changes in his attitude toward God, as we will see by the end of the book. Nevertheless Job was blameless (1:8). He carefully obeyed God to the best of his ability in all aspects of his life.

**7:11** Job felt deep anguish and bitterness, and he spoke honestly to God about his feelings to let out his frustrations. If we express our feelings to God, we can deal with them without exploding in harsh words and actions, possibly hurting ourselves and others. The next time strong emotions threaten to overwhelm you, express them openly to God in prayer. This will help you gain an eternal perspective on the situation and give you greater ability to deal with it constructively.

**7:12** Job stopped talking to Eliphaz and spoke directly to God. Although Job had lived a blameless life, he was beginning to doubt the value of living in such a way. By doing this, he was coming dangerously close to suggesting that God didn't care about him and was not being fair. Later God reproved Job for this attitude (38:2). Satan always exploits these thoughts to get us to forsake God. Our suffering, like Job's, may not be the result of our sin, but we must be careful not to sin as a result of our suffering.

19 Why won't you leave me alone,
   at least long enough for me to swallow!
20 If I have sinned, what have I done to you,
   O watcher of all humanity?
   Why make me your target?
   Am I a burden to you?
21 Why not just forgive my sin
   and take away my guilt?
   For soon I will lie down in the dust and die.
   When you look for me, I will be gone."

*Bildad's First Response to Job*

**8** Then Bildad the Shuhite replied to Job:

2 "How long will you go on like this?
   You sound like a blustering wind.
3 Does God twist justice?
   Does the Almighty twist what is right?
4 Your children must have sinned against him,
   so their punishment was well deserved.
5 But if you pray to God
   and seek the favor of the Almighty,
6 and if you are pure and live with integrity,
   he will surely rise up and restore your happy home.
7 And though you started with little,
   you will end with much.

8 "Just ask the previous generation.
   Pay attention to the experience of our ancestors.
9 For we were born but yesterday and know nothing.
   Our days on earth are as fleeting as a shadow.
10 But those who came before us will teach you.
   They will teach you the wisdom of old.

11 "Can papyrus reeds grow tall without a marsh?
   Can marsh grass flourish without water?
12 While they are still flowering, not ready to be cut,
   they begin to wither more quickly than grass.
13 The same happens to all who forget God.
   The hopes of the godless evaporate.
14 Their confidence hangs by a thread.
   They are leaning on a spider's web.
15 They cling to their home for security, but it won't last.
   They try to hold it tight, but it will not endure.
16 The godless seem like a lush plant growing in the sunshine,
   its branches spreading across the garden.
17 Its roots grow down through a pile of stones;
   it takes hold on a bed of rocks.

**7:20**
Job 35:3, 6

**7:21**
Job 10:9, 14

**8:3**
Gen 18:25
Deut 32:4
2 Chr 19:7
Job 34:10, 12
Rom 3:5

**8:6**
Job 22:27
Ps 7:6

**8:7**
Job 42:12

**8:8**
Deut 4:32; 32:7
Job 15:18

**8:13**
Ps 9:17

**8:15**
Job 27:18
Ps 49:11

**8:16**
Pss 37:35; 80:11

---

**7:20** Job referred to God as a watcher or observer of humanity. He was expressing his feeling that God seemed like an enemy to him—someone who mercilessly watched him squirm in his misery. We know that God does watch over everything that happens to us. We must never forget that he sees us with compassion, not merely with critical scrutiny. His eyes are eyes of love.

**8:1ff** Bildad was upset that Job still claimed innocence while questioning God's justice. The basis of Bildad's argument (the justice of God) was correct, but his idea of God's justice was not. Bildad's argument went like this: God could not be unjust, and God would not punish a just man; therefore, Job must be unjust. Bildad felt there were no exceptions to his theory. Like Eliphaz,

Bildad wrongly assumed that people suffer only as a result of their sins. Bildad was even less sensitive and compassionate, saying that Job's children died because of *their* wickedness. (For more information about Bildad, see his Profile, chapter 8, p. 797 and the chart in chapter 28, p. 819.)

**8:14, 15** Bildad wrongly assumed that Job was trusting in something other than God for security, so he pointed out that such supports will collapse. One of people's basic needs is security, and many will do almost anything to feel secure. Eventually, however, our money, possessions, knowledge, and relationships will fail or be gone. Only God can give lasting security. What have you trusted for your security? How lasting is it? If you have a secure foundation with God, feelings of insecurity will not undermine you.

8:19
Job 20:5

8:21
Pss 126:1-2;
132:16

8:22
Job 8:15
Ps 132:18

¹⁸ But when it is uprooted,
    it's as though it never existed!
¹⁹ That's the end of its life,
    and others spring up from the earth to replace it.

²⁰ "But look, God will not reject a person of integrity,
    nor will he lend a hand to the wicked.
²¹ He will once again fill your mouth with laughter
    and your lips with shouts of joy.
²² Those who hate you will be clothed with shame,
    and the home of the wicked will be destroyed."

## ELIPHAZ, BILDAD, ZOPHAR

Few people in history have experienced the kind of tragedy that crushed Job. He lost everything. His children were killed, his possessions and wealth were taken, his wife turned her back on him, and his health was broken—all in a matter of days.

Upon learning of Job's difficulties, some of his friends came to help. Eliphaz, Bildad, and Zophar were shocked when they found Job. They wept for him. They tore their clothes and put dust on their heads in acts of sorrow. Then they sat in silence with Job for seven days.

Why did his friends remain silent for so long? One ancient Jewish tradition teaches that people who come to comfort someone in mourning should not speak until the mourner speaks. That is a wise tradition, for often the best response to another person's suffering is to say nothing.

If Job's losses were his first test and his painful boils his second, then his friends provided a third and perhaps most frustrating test. When Job finally vented his grief, each of the friends took turns attempting to explain Job's agony. They heard Job's questions as arrogant claims of not deserving such suffering rather than expressions of deep grief and misunderstanding. They offered answers that only served to make Job's pain go deeper. Eliphaz appealed to personal experience; Bildad pointed to universal wisdom; and Zophar declared what he felt was common sense. They all agreed that Job's problems were his own doing and that questioning God simply made matters worse.

The harder Eliphaz, Bildad, and Zophar tried to explain Job's suffering, the less they helped. Consolation turned to condemnation as the grief-stricken Job rejected their reasoning and demanded a hearing with God. When God finally did speak, he never answered Job's questions. He simply challenged Job to trust, even beyond understanding.

Friendship in grief requires patience. Friends in need don't have to have all their questions answered as much as they need to have someone listen. Some questions are so deep that their best response is silence. Make it a point to be with those in pain, but let your physical presence be your strongest statement of support. Pray for patience. When in doubt about a question, wait. Sit quietly and be the best friend you can be during difficult times.

| | |
|---|---|
| **Strengths and accomplishments** | • Understood the importance of personal contact in sharing grief<br>• Approached Job with silence rather than immediate conversation<br>• Demonstrated a fine understanding of God's justice, but gross ignorance about God's grace |
| **Weaknesses and mistakes** | • Assumed that tragedy and suffering inevitably represent some kind of punishment for sin<br>• Decided to try to explain Job's suffering rather than help him endure it<br>• Heard Job's questions as challenges rather than expressions of grief<br>• Took offense and became abusive when Job did not agree with their assessments or answers |
| **Lessons from their lives** | • Those who wish to comfort people in sorrow should consider silence before speech, empathy before explanations, and patience with their pain<br>• Even the hardest questions that come out of grief do not require instant answers<br>• Genuine friendship includes attentive, compassionate presence in times of sorrow and loss |
| **Vital statistics** | • Where: Uz<br>• Contemporaries: Job, Elihu |
| **Key verse** | "When three of Job's friends heard of the tragedy he had suffered, they got together and traveled from their homes to comfort and console him. Their names were Eliphaz the Temanite, Bildad the Shuhite, and Zophar the Naamathite" (Job 2:11). |

Job's interaction with his three friends is found in the Old Testament book of Job.

*Job's Third Speech: A Response to Bildad*

**9** Then Job spoke again:

2 "Yes, I know all this is true in principle.
But how can a person be declared innocent in God's sight?

3 If someone wanted to take God to court,*
would it be possible to answer him even once in a thousand times?

4 For God is so wise and so mighty.
Who has ever challenged him successfully?

5 "Without warning, he moves the mountains,
overturning them in his anger.

6 He shakes the earth from its place,
and its foundations tremble.

7 If he commands it, the sun won't rise
and the stars won't shine.

8 He alone has spread out the heavens
and marches on the waves of the sea.

9 He made all the stars—the Bear and Orion,
the Pleiades and the constellations of the southern sky.

10 He does great things too marvelous to understand.
He performs countless miracles.

11 "Yet when he comes near, I cannot see him.
When he moves by, I do not see him go.

12 If he snatches someone in death, who can stop him?
Who dares to ask, 'What are you doing?'

13 And God does not restrain his anger.
Even the monsters of the sea* are crushed beneath his feet.

14 "So who am I, that I should try to answer God
or even reason with him?

15 Even if I were right, I would have no defense.
I could only plead for mercy.

16 And even if I summoned him and he responded,
I'm not sure he would listen to me.

17 For he attacks me with a storm
and repeatedly wounds me without cause.

18 He will not let me catch my breath,
but fills me instead with bitter sorrows.

19 If it's a question of strength, he's the strong one.
If it's a matter of justice, who dares to summon him to court?

20 Though I am innocent, my own mouth would pronounce me guilty.
Though I am blameless, it* would prove me wicked.

21 "I am innocent,
but it makes no difference to me—
I despise my life.

22 Innocent or wicked, it is all the same to God.
That's why I say, 'He destroys both the blameless and the wicked.'

| | |
|---|---|
| | **9:2**<br>Job 4:17; 25:4 |
| | **9:5**<br>Job 26:6-14 |
| | **9:6**<br>Isa 2:19, 21; 13:13<br>Hag 2:6<br>Heb 12:26 |
| | **9:7**<br>Isa 13:10 |
| | **9:8**<br>Gen 1:1 |
| | **9:9**<br>Pss 77:19; 104:2<br>Isa 40:22 |
| | **9:11**<br>Job 23:8-9 |
| | **9:12**<br>Job 10:7; 11:10<br>Isa 45:9 |
| | **9:13**<br>Job 26:12<br>Ps 89:10 |
| | **9:15**<br>Job 8:5; 10:15 |
| | **9:17**<br>Job 16:12, 14 |
| | **9:18**<br>Job 27:2 |
| | **9:20**<br>Job 9:15, 29 |
| | **9:22**<br>Eccl 9:2-3 |

**9:3** Or *If God wanted to take someone to court.*    **9:13** Hebrew *the helpers of Rahab,* the name of a mythical sea monster that represents chaos in ancient literature.    **9:20** Or *he.*

---

**9:1ff** Bildad said nothing new to Job. Job knew that the wicked ultimately perish, but his situation confused him. Why, then, was *he* perishing? Job didn't think his life warranted such suffering, so he wanted his case presented before God (9:32-35). He recognized, however, that arguing with God would be futile and unproductive (9:4). Job didn't claim to be perfect (7:20, 21; 9:20), but he did claim to be good and faithful (6:29, 30). While Job showed impatience toward God, he did not reject or curse God.

**9:9** The Bear, Orion, and Pleiades are constellations of stars.

**9:20, 21** "Though I am innocent, my own mouth would pronounce me guilty." Job was saying, "In spite of my good life, God is determined to condemn me." As his suffering continued, he became more impatient. Although Job remained loyal to God, he made statements he would later regret. In times of extended sickness or prolonged pain, it is natural for people to doubt, to despair, or to become impatient. During those times, people need someone to listen to them, to help them work through their feelings and frustrations. Your patience with their impatience will help them.

<sup>23</sup> When a plague* sweeps through,
    he laughs at the death of the innocent.

**9:24**
Job 12:6, 17; 16:11

<sup>24</sup> The whole earth is in the hands of the wicked,
    and God blinds the eyes of the judges.
    If he's not the one who does it, who is?

**9:25**
Job 7:6-7

<sup>25</sup> "My life passes more swiftly than a runner.
    It flees away without a glimpse of happiness.

**9:26**
Hab 1:8

<sup>26</sup> It disappears like a swift papyrus boat,
    like an eagle swooping down on its prey.
<sup>27</sup> If I decided to forget my complaints,
    to put away my sad face and be cheerful,

**9:28**
Job 3:25; 7:21;
10:14

<sup>28</sup> I would still dread all the pain,
    for I know you will not find me innocent, O God.

**9:29**
Ps 37:33

<sup>29</sup> Whatever happens, I will be found guilty.
    So what's the use of trying?

**9:30**
Job 31:7
Jer 2:22

<sup>30</sup> Even if I were to wash myself with soap
    and clean my hands with lye,
<sup>31</sup> you would plunge me into a muddy ditch,
    and my own filthy clothing would hate me.

**9:32**
1 Sam 2:25
Rom 9:20

<sup>32</sup> "God is not a mortal like me,
    so I cannot argue with him or take him to trial.

**9:33**
1 Sam 2:25

<sup>33</sup> If only there were a mediator between us,
    someone who could bring us together.

**9:34**
Ps 39:10

<sup>34</sup> The mediator could make God stop beating me,
    and I would no longer live in terror of his punishment.
<sup>35</sup> Then I could speak to him without fear,
    but I cannot do that in my own strength.

## Job Frames His Plea to God

**10:1**
1 Kgs 19:4
Job 7:11, 16

**10** <sup>1</sup> "I am disgusted with my life.
    Let me complain freely.
    My bitter soul must complain.

**10:2**
Job 9:29

<sup>2</sup> I will say to God, 'Don't simply condemn me—
    tell me the charge you are bringing against me.

**10:3**
Job 9:22-24; 10:8;
19:6; 21:16; 22:18

<sup>3</sup> What do you gain by oppressing me?
    Why do you reject me, the work of your own hands,
    while smiling on the schemes of the wicked?

**10:4**
1 Sam 16:7
Job 9:12; 36:26

<sup>4</sup> Are your eyes like those of a human?
    Do you see things only as people see them?
<sup>5</sup> Is your lifetime only as long as ours?
    Is your life so short
<sup>6</sup> that you must quickly probe for my guilt
    and search for my sin?
<sup>7</sup> Although you know I am not guilty,
    no one can rescue me from your hands.

**10:8**
Job 9:22
Ps 119:73

<sup>8</sup> "'You formed me with your hands; you made me,
    yet now you completely destroy me.

**10:9**
Job 4:19; 7:21;
33:6

<sup>9</sup> Remember that you made me from dust—
    will you turn me back to dust so soon?
<sup>10</sup> You guided my conception
    and formed me in the womb.*

**9:23** Or *disaster.* **10:10** Hebrew *You poured me out like milk / and curdled me like cheese.*

---

**10:1** Job began to wallow in self-pity. When we face baffling affliction, our pain lures us toward feeling sorry for ourselves. At this point we are only one step from self-righteousness, where we keep track of life's injustices and say, "Look what happened to me; how unfair it is!" We may feel like blaming God. Remember that life's trials, whether allowed by God or sent by God, can be the means for development and refinement. When facing trials, ask, "What can I learn and how can I grow?" rather than "Who did this to me and how can I get out of it?"

11 You clothed me with skin and flesh,
   and you knit my bones and sinews together.
12 You gave me life and showed me your unfailing love.
   My life was preserved by your care.

13 "'Yet your real motive—
   your true intent—
14 was to watch me, and if I sinned,
   you would not forgive my guilt.
15 If I am guilty, too bad for me;
   and even if I'm innocent, I can't hold my head high,
   because I am filled with shame and misery.
16 And if I hold my head high, you hunt me like a lion
   and display your awesome power against me.
17 Again and again you witness against me.
   You pour out your growing anger on me
   and bring fresh armies against me.

18 "'Why, then, did you deliver me from my mother's womb?
   Why didn't you let me die at birth?
19 It would be as though I had never existed,
   going directly from the womb to the grave.
20 I have only a few days left, so leave me alone,
   that I may have a moment of comfort
21 before I leave—never to return—
   for the land of darkness and utter gloom.
22 It is a land as dark as midnight,
   a land of gloom and confusion,
   where even the light is dark as midnight.'"

### Zophar's First Response to Job

**11** Then Zophar the Naamathite replied to Job:

2 "Shouldn't someone answer this torrent of words?
   Is a person proved innocent just by a lot of talking?
3 Should I remain silent while you babble on?
   When you mock God, shouldn't someone make you ashamed?
4 You claim, 'My beliefs are pure,'
   and 'I am clean in the sight of God.'
5 If only God would speak;
   if only he would tell you what he thinks!
6 If only he would tell you the secrets of wisdom,
   for true wisdom is not a simple matter.
   Listen! God is doubtless punishing you
   far less than you deserve!

7 "Can you solve the mysteries of God?
   Can you discover everything about the Almighty?
8 Such knowledge is higher than the heavens—
   and who are you?

| | |
|---|---|
| 10:12 | Job 33:4 |
| 10:13 | Job 23:13 |
| 10:14 | Job 9:28 |
| 10:15 | Job 6:29 |
| | Isa 3:11 |
| 10:16 | Job 5:9 |
| 10:17 | Job 16:8 |
| 10:18 | Job 3:11-13 |
| 10:20 | Job 7:19; 14:1 |
| 10:21 | Ps 23:4; 88:12 |
| 11:3 | Job 17:2; 21:3 |
| 11:4 | Job 6:10; 10:7 |
| 11:6 | Job 22:5 |
| 11:7 | Job 33:12-13; 36:26; 37:5 |
| 11:8 | Job 22:12; 38:17 |

---

**10:13, 14** In frustration, Job jumped to the false conclusion that God was out to get him. Wrong assumptions lead to wrong conclusions. We dare not take our limited experiences and jump to conclusions about life in general. If you find yourself doubting God, remember that you don't have all the facts. God wants only the very best for your life. Many people endure great pain, but ultimately they find some greater good came from it. When you're struggling, don't assume the worst.

**10:20-22** Job was expressing the view of death common in Old Testament times, that the dead went to a joyless, dark place.

There was no punishment or reward there, and no escape from it. (See the note on 19:25-27 for a broader picture of Job's view of death.)

**11:1ff** Zophar is the third of Job's friends to speak, and the least courteous. Full of anger, he lashed out at Job, saying that Job deserved more punishment, not less. Zophar took the same position as Eliphaz (chapters 4–5) and Bildad (chapter 8)—that Job was suffering because of sin—but his speech was by far the most arrogant. Zophar was the kind of person who has an answer for everything; he was totally insensitive to Job's unique situation. (For more on Zophar, see his Profile, chapter 8, p. 797 and the chart in chapter 28, p. 819.)

It is deeper than the underworld*—
    what do you know?
⁹ It is broader than the earth
    and wider than the sea.
¹⁰ If God comes and puts a person in prison
    or calls the court to order, who can stop him?
¹¹ For he knows those who are false,
    and he takes note of all their sins.
¹² An empty-headed person won't become wise
    any more than a wild donkey can bear a human child.*

**11:13**
Pss 78:8; 88:9

¹³ "If only you would prepare your heart
    and lift up your hands to him in prayer!
¹⁴ Get rid of your sins,
    and leave all iniquity behind you.

**11:15**
Pss 27:3; 46:2

¹⁵ Then your face will brighten with innocence.
    You will be strong and free of fear.

**11:16**
Job 22:11
Isa 65:16

¹⁶ You will forget your misery;
    it will be like water flowing away.

**11:17**
Ps 37:6

¹⁷ Your life will be brighter than the noonday.
    Even darkness will be as bright as morning.
¹⁸ Having hope will give you courage.
    You will be protected and will rest in safety.

**11:19**
Lev 26:6
Zeph 3:13

¹⁹ You will lie down unafraid,
    and many will look to you for help.

**11:20**
Deut 28:65
Job 6:9; 34:22

²⁰ But the wicked will be blinded.
    They will have no escape.
    Their only hope is death."

## Job's Fourth Speech: A Response to Zophar

**12** Then Job spoke again:

**12:2**
Job 17:10

² "You people really know everything, don't you?
    And when you die, wisdom will die with you!
³ Well, I know a few things myself—
    and you're no better than I am.
    Who doesn't know these things you've been saying?

**12:4**
Job 6:29; 17:6;
30:1, 9-10

⁴ Yet my friends laugh at me,
    for I call on God and expect an answer.
    I am a just and blameless man,
        yet they laugh at me.
⁵ People who are at ease mock those in trouble.
    They give a push to people who are stumbling.

**12:6**
Job 9:24; 21:7-9

⁶ But robbers are left in peace,
    and those who provoke God live in safety—
    though God keeps them in his power.

⁷ "Just ask the animals, and they will teach you.
    Ask the birds of the sky, and they will tell you.
⁸ Speak to the earth, and it will instruct you.
    Let the fish in the sea speak to you.

**11:8** Hebrew *than Sheol.*    **11:12** Or *than a wild male donkey can bear a tame colt.*

---

**11:11** By calling Job "false," Zophar was accusing Job of hiding secret faults and sins. Although Zophar's assumption was wrong, he explained quite accurately that God knows and sees everything. We are often tempted by the thought "No one will ever know!" Perhaps we can hide some sin from others, but we can do *nothing* without God knowing about it. Because our very thoughts are known to God, of course he will notice our sins. Job understood this as well as Zophar did, but it didn't apply to his current dilemma.

**12:1ff** Job answered Zophar's argument with great sarcasm: "Wisdom will die with you!" He went on to say that his three friends didn't need to explain God to him—they were saying nothing he didn't already know (12:7-9; 13:1, 2). Job continued to maintain that his friends had completely misunderstood the reason for his suffering. Job did not know it either, but he was certain that his friends' reasons were both narrow-minded and incorrect. Once again Job appealed to God to give him an answer (13:3).

9 For they all know
　　that my disaster* has come from the hand of the LORD.
10 For the life of every living thing is in his hand,
　　and the breath of every human being.
11 The ear tests the words it hears
　　just as the mouth distinguishes between foods.
12 Wisdom belongs to the aged,
　　and understanding to the old.

13 "But true wisdom and power are found in God;
　　counsel and understanding are his.
14 What he destroys cannot be rebuilt.
　　When he puts someone in prison, there is no escape.
15 If he holds back the rain, the earth becomes a desert.
　　If he releases the waters, they flood the earth.
16 Yes, strength and wisdom are his;
　　deceivers and deceived are both in his power.
17 He leads counselors away, stripped of good judgment;
　　wise judges become fools.
18 He removes the royal robe of kings.
　　They are led away with ropes around their waist.
19 He leads priests away, stripped of status;
　　he overthrows those with long years in power.
20 He silences the trusted adviser
　　and removes the insight of the elders.
21 He pours disgrace upon princes
　　and disarms the strong.

22 "He uncovers mysteries hidden in darkness;
　　he brings light to the deepest gloom.
23 He builds up nations, and he destroys them.
　　He expands nations, and he abandons them.
24 He strips kings of understanding
　　and leaves them wandering in a pathless wasteland.
25 They grope in the darkness without a light.
　　He makes them stagger like drunkards.

## Job Wants to Argue His Case with God

**13** ¹ "Look, I have seen all this with my own eyes
　　and heard it with my own ears, and now I understand.
2 I know as much as you do.
　　You are no better than I am.
3 As for me, I would speak directly to the Almighty.
　　I want to argue my case with God himself.
4 As for you, you smear me with lies.
　　As physicians, you are worthless quacks.
5 If only you could be silent!
　　That's the wisest thing you could do.
6 Listen to my charge;
　　pay attention to my arguments.

12:9 Hebrew *that this.*

12:9
Isa 41:20

12:10
Job 33:4; 34:3

12:12
Job 32:7

12:13
Job 9:4; 11:6

12:14
Job 19:10
Isa 25:2

12:15
Gen 7:11-24
Deut 11:17
1 Kgs 8:35

12:16
Job 13:7, 9; 37:7

12:18
Ps 116:16

12:21
Job 12:18; 34:19
Ps 107:40

12:22
Dan 2:22
1 Cor 4:5

12:23
Isa 9:3

12:24
Job 12:20

13:3
Job 13:22; 23:4

13:4
Ps 119:69
Jer 23:32

13:5
Prov 17:28

---

**12:24, 25** Job affirmed that no leader has any real wisdom apart from God. No research or report can outweigh God's opinion. No scientific discovery or medical advance takes him by surprise. When we look for guidance for our decisions, we must recognize that God's wisdom is superior to any the world has to offer. Don't let earthly advisers dampen your desire to know God better.

**13:4** Job compared his three friends to physicians who did not know what they were doing. They were like eye surgeons trying to perform open-heart surgery. Many of their ideas about God were true, but they did not apply to Job's situation. They were right to say that God is just. They were right to say God punishes sin. But they were wrong to assume that Job's suffering was a just punishment for his sin. They took a true principle and applied it wrongly, ignoring the vast differences in human circumstances. We must be careful and compassionate in how we apply biblical condemnations to others; we must be slow to judge.

13:7
Job 27:4

7 "Are you defending God with lies?
Do you make your dishonest arguments for his sake?
8 Will you slant your testimony in his favor?
Will you argue God's case for him?
9 What will happen when he finds out what you are doing?
Can you fool him as easily as you fool people?

13:10
Job 32:21

10 No, you will be in trouble with him
if you secretly slant your testimony in his favor.
11 Doesn't his majesty terrify you?
Doesn't your fear of him overwhelm you?

13:12
Job 15:3

12 Your platitudes are as valuable as ashes.
Your defense is as fragile as a clay pot.

13:13
Job 13:5

13 "Be silent now and leave me alone.
Let me speak, and I will face the consequences.
14 Yes, I will take my life in my hands
and say what I really think.

13:15
Job 7:6; 27:5;
34:21-23

15 God might kill me, but I have no other hope.*
I am going to argue my case with him.
16 But this is what will save me—I am not godless.
If I were, I could not stand before him.

17 "Listen closely to what I am about to say.
Hear me out.

13:18
Job 9:21; 23:4

18 I have prepared my case;
I will be proved innocent.

13:19
Isa 50:8

19 Who can argue with me over this?
And if you prove me wrong, I will remain silent and die.

### Job Asks How He Has Sinned

20 "O God, grant me these two things,
and then I will be able to face you.

13:21
Job 9:34
Ps 39:10

21 Remove your heavy hand from me,
and don't terrify me with your awesome presence.
22 Now summon me, and I will answer!
Or let me speak to you, and you reply.
23 Tell me, what have I done wrong?
Show me my rebellion and my sin.

13:24
Job 19:11; 33:10
Ps 13:1

24 Why do you turn away from me?
Why do you treat me as your enemy?

13:25
Lev 26:36

25 Would you terrify a leaf blown by the wind?
Would you chase dry straw?

13:26
Ps 25:7

26 "You write bitter accusations against me
and bring up all the sins of my youth.
27 You put my feet in stocks.
You examine all my paths.
You trace all my footprints.
28 I waste away like rotting wood,
like a moth-eaten coat.

14:1
Job 5:7
Eccl 2:23

## 14

1 "How frail is humanity!
How short is life, how full of trouble!
2 We blossom like a flower and then wither.
Like a passing shadow, we quickly disappear.

13:15 An alternate reading in the Masoretic Text reads *God might kill me, but I hope in him.*

---

**14:1ff** Life is short and full of trouble, Job laments in his closing remarks to this first round of conversation. Sickness, loneliness, disappointment, and death cause Job to say that life is not fair. Some understand verses 14 and 15 to mean that, even in his gloom, Job hoped for the resurrection of the dead. If this is true, then Job understood the one truth that could put his suffering in perspective. God's solution to believers who live in an unfair world is to guarantee life with him forever. No matter how unfair your present world seems, God offers the hope of being in his presence eternally. Have you accepted this offer?

3 Must you keep an eye on such a frail creature
     and demand an accounting from me?
4 Who can bring purity out of an impure person?
     No one!
5 You have decided the length of our lives.
     You know how many months we will live,
     and we are not given a minute longer.
6 So leave us alone and let us rest!
     We are like hired hands, so let us finish our work in peace.

7 "Even a tree has more hope!
     If it is cut down, it will sprout again
     and grow new branches.
8 Though its roots have grown old in the earth
     and its stump decays,
9 at the scent of water it will bud
     and sprout again like a new seedling.

10 "But when people die, their strength is gone.
     They breathe their last, and then where are they?
11 As water evaporates from a lake
     and a river disappears in drought,
12 people are laid to rest and do not rise again.
     Until the heavens are no more, they will not wake up
     nor be roused from their sleep.

13 "I wish you would hide me in the grave*
     and forget me there until your anger has passed.
     But mark your calendar to think of me again!
14 Can the dead live again?
     If so, this would give me hope through all my years of struggle,
     and I would eagerly await the release of death.
15 You would call and I would answer,
     and you would yearn for me, your handiwork.
16 For then you would guard my steps,
     instead of watching for my sins.
17 My sins would be sealed in a pouch,
     and you would cover my guilt.

18 "But instead, as mountains fall and crumble
     and as rocks fall from a cliff,
19 as water wears away the stones
     and floods wash away the soil,
     so you destroy people's hope.
20 You always overpower them, and they pass from the scene.
     You disfigure them in death and send them away.
21 They never know if their children grow up in honor
     or sink to insignificance.
22 They suffer painfully;
     their life is full of trouble."

**14:13** Hebrew *in Sheol.*

| | |
|---|---|
| **14:4** | Job 15:14; 25:4 |
| **14:5** | Job 21:21 |
| **14:10** | Job 13:19 |
| **14:11** | Isa 19:5 |
| **14:13** | Isa 26:20 |
| **14:16** | Job 10:6; 31:4; 34:21 Prov 5:21 |
| **14:17** | Deut 32:32-34 |
| **14:19** | Job 7:6 |
| **14:20** | Job 20:7; 34:20 |
| **14:21** | Eccl 9:5 |

---

**14:7-22** The Old Testament does not say much about the resurrection of the dead. This is not surprising because Jesus had not yet conquered death. Job's pessimism about death is understandable. What is remarkable is his budding hope (14:14). If only God would hide him with the dead and then bring him out again! If only he could die and live again! When we must endure suffering, we have an advantage over Job. We *know* that the dead will rise. Christ arose, and we have hope based on Christ's promise in John 14:19.

**14:22** Job's profound speech in this chapter illustrates a great truth: To have a right set of doctrines is not enough. To know what to believe is not all that is required to please God. Truth untested by life's experiences may become static and stagnant. Suffering can bring a dynamic quality to life. Just as drought drives the roots of a tree deeper to find water, so suffering can drive us beyond superficial acceptance of truth to dependence on God for hope and life.

## 2. Second round of discussion
*Eliphaz's Second Response to Job*

**15** Then Eliphaz the Temanite replied:

2 "A wise man wouldn't answer with such empty talk!
You are nothing but a windbag.

3 The wise don't engage in empty chatter.
What good are such words?

4 Have you no fear of God,
no reverence for him?

5 Your sins are telling your mouth what to say.
Your words are based on clever deception.

6 Your own mouth condemns you, not I.
Your own lips testify against you.

7 "Were you the first person ever born?
Were you born before the hills were made?

8 Were you listening at God's secret council?
Do you have a monopoly on wisdom?

9 What do you know that we don't?
What do you understand that we do not?

10 On our side are aged, gray-haired men
much older than your father!

11 "Is God's comfort too little for you?
Is his gentle word not enough?

12 What has taken away your reason?
What has weakened your vision,*

13 that you turn against God
and say all these evil things?

14 Can any mortal be pure?
Can anyone born of a woman be just?

**15:7** Job 38:4, 21
Prov 8:25

**15:8** Rom 11:34

**15:11** Job 6:10

**15:12** Job 36:13

**15:14** Prov 20:9
Eccl 7:20

**15:12** Or *Why do your eyes flash with anger;* Hebrew reads *Why do your eyes blink.*

---

**BIBLE "WAITERS"**
In the Bible we find many people who had to "wait on the Lord," just as believers today must patiently wait for Christ's return. We can learn a lesson in patience from these Bible waiters.

| | |
|---|---|
| Noah waited for God's timing before leaving the ark | Genesis 8:10, 12 |
| Moses waited on God on the mountain | Exodus 24:12 |
| Job waited for God's answers | Job 14:14 |
| Isaiah waited for God to work in Israel | Isaiah 8:17; 25:9; 26:8; 30:18; 33:2; 40:31; 49:23; 59:9, 11; 64:4 |
| Jeremiah understood the need to wait quietly for God's salvation | Lamentations 3:25 |
| Hosea warned the people to return to God and wait for him to work | Hosea 12:6 |
| Micah waited for the God of his salvation | Micah 7:7 |
| Habakkuk warned the people to hold on to their hope and to wait because it would surely come | Habakkuk 2:3 |
| Zephaniah explained that the Lord wanted his people to wait for him | Zephaniah 3:8 |
| Joseph of Arimathea was waiting for God's Kingdom | Luke 23:51 |
| The disciples were ordered by Jesus to wait in Jerusalem for the coming of the Holy Spirit | Acts 1:4 |
| Believers are called to wait for heaven, for the promise is sure | Romans 8:23, 25; Galatians 5:5; 1 Thessalonians 1:10; Titus 2:13; 2 Peter 3:12-14 |

---

**15:1ff** With the first round of talks concluded, each friend, in the same order, pressed the argument further. Again Job answered each argument (chapters 15–31). This time Eliphaz was more rude, more intense, and more threatening, but he said nothing new. (See his first speech in chapters 4–5.) He began by saying that Job's words were empty and useless; then he restated his opinion that Job must be a great sinner. According to Eliphaz, the experience and wisdom of their ancestors were more valuable than Job's individual thoughts. Eliphaz assumed that his words were as true as God's. It is easy to spot his arrogance.

<sup>15</sup> Look, God does not even trust the angels.*
    Even the heavens are not absolutely pure in his sight.
<sup>16</sup> How much less pure is a corrupt and sinful person
    with a thirst for wickedness!

<sup>17</sup> "If you will listen, I will show you.
    I will answer you from my own experience.
<sup>18</sup> And it is confirmed by the reports of wise men
    who have heard the same thing from their fathers—
<sup>19</sup> from those to whom the land was given
    long before any foreigners arrived.

<sup>20</sup> "The wicked writhe in pain throughout their lives.
    Years of trouble are stored up for the ruthless.
<sup>21</sup> The sound of terror rings in their ears,
    and even on good days they fear the attack of the destroyer.
<sup>22</sup> They dare not go out into the darkness
    for fear they will be murdered.
<sup>23</sup> They wander around, saying, 'Where can I find bread?'*
    They know their day of destruction is near.
<sup>24</sup> That dark day terrifies them.
    They live in distress and anguish,
    like a king preparing for battle.
<sup>25</sup> For they shake their fists at God,
    defying the Almighty.
<sup>26</sup> Holding their strong shields,
    they defiantly charge against him.

<sup>27</sup> "These wicked people are heavy and prosperous;
    their waists bulge with fat.
<sup>28</sup> But their cities will be ruined.
    They will live in abandoned houses
    that are ready to tumble down.
<sup>29</sup> Their riches will not last,
    and their wealth will not endure.
    Their possessions will no longer spread across the horizon.

<sup>30</sup> "They will not escape the darkness.
    The burning sun will wither their shoots,
    and the breath of God will destroy them.
<sup>31</sup> Let them no longer fool themselves by trusting in empty riches,
    for emptiness will be their only reward.
<sup>32</sup> Like trees, they will be cut down in the prime of life;
    their branches will never again be green.
<sup>33</sup> They will be like a vine whose grapes are harvested too early,
    like an olive tree that loses its blossoms before the fruit can form.
<sup>34</sup> For the godless are barren.
    Their homes, enriched through bribery, will burn.
<sup>35</sup> They conceive trouble and give birth to evil.
    Their womb produces deceit."

*Job's Fifth Speech: A Response to Eliphaz*

**16** Then Job spoke again:

<sup>2</sup> "I have heard all this before.
    What miserable comforters you are!

---

**Cross-references (right margin):**

15:15 Job 4:18; 25:5

15:16 Job 34:7; Ps 14:1, 3

15:18 Job 8:8

15:21 Job 18:11; 20:21, 25

15:22 Job 15:30; 19:29; 27:14

15:25 Job 36:9

15:27 Pss 73:7; 119:70

15:29 Job 27:16-17

15:30 Job 4:9; 5:14; 22:20

15:31 Isa 59:4

15:32 Job 18:16; 22:16

15:34 Job 8:22

15:35 Ps 7:14; Isa 59:4

16:2 Job 13:4; 21:34

---

15:15 Hebrew *the holy ones.*   15:23 Greek version reads *He is appointed to be food for a vulture.*

---

15:15, 16 "Even the heavens are not absolutely pure in his sight." Eliphaz was repeating his argument that anything created, whether angels or people, is not a sufficient basis for trust and hope. Only in God can we be sure. (See the note on 4:18, 19.)

16:1ff Job's friends were supposed to be comforting him in his grief. Instead, they condemned him for causing his own suffering. Job began his reply to Eliphaz by calling him and his friends "miserable comforters." Job's words reveal several ways to

16:4
Pss 22:7; 109:25

3 Won't you ever stop blowing hot air?
  What makes you keep on talking?
4 I could say the same things if you were in my place.
  I could spout off criticism and shake my head at you.
5 But if it were me, I would encourage you.
  I would try to take away your grief.

16:6
Job 9:27-28

6 Instead, I suffer if I defend myself,
  and I suffer no less if I refuse to speak.

16:7
Job 7:3; 16:20;
19:13-15

7 "O God, you have ground me down
  and devastated my family.

16:8
Job 10:17; 19:20

8 As if to prove I have sinned, you've reduced me to skin and bones.
  My gaunt flesh testifies against me.

16:9
Job 13:24; 33:10

9 God hates me and angrily tears me apart.
  He snaps his teeth at me
  and pierces me with his eyes.
10 People jeer and laugh at me.
  They slap my cheek in contempt.
  A mob gathers against me.
11 God has handed me over to sinners.
  He has tossed me into the hands of the wicked.

16:12
Job 7:20; 9:17

12 "I was living quietly until he shattered me.
  He took me by the neck and broke me in pieces.
  Then he set me up as his target,

16:13
Job 6:4; 19:12

13    and now his archers surround me.
  His arrows pierce me without mercy.
  The ground is wet with my blood.*

16:14
Job 9:17
Joel 2:7

14 Again and again he smashes against me,
  charging at me like a warrior.

16:15
Gen 37:34
Job 30:19
Ps 69:11
Jon 3:8

15 I wear burlap to show my grief.
  My pride lies in the dust.
16 My eyes are red with weeping;
  dark shadows circle my eyes.

16:16
Job 16:20; 24:17

17 Yet I have done no wrong,
  and my prayer is pure.

16:17
Job 27:4

18 "O earth, do not conceal my blood.
  Let it cry out on my behalf.

16:19
Job 19:25-27; 31:2

19 Even now my witness is in heaven.
  My advocate is there on high.
20 My friends scorn me,
  but I pour out my tears to God.
21 I need someone to mediate between God and me,
  as a person mediates between friends.
22 For soon I must go down that road
  from which I will never return.

## Job Continues to Defend His Innocence

17:1
Ps 88:3-4

**17** 1"My spirit is crushed,
     and my life is nearly snuffed out.
  The grave is ready to receive me.

**16:13** Hebrew *my gall.*

become a better comforter to those in pain: (1) Don't talk just for the sake of talking; (2) don't sermonize by giving pat answers; (3) don't accuse or criticize; (4) put yourself in the other person's place; and (5) offer help and encouragement. Try Job's suggestions, knowing that they are given by a person who needed great comfort. The best comforters are those who know something about personal suffering.

**16:19** Job was afraid that God had abandoned him. Yet he appealed directly to God (his witness and advocate) and to God's knowledge of his innocence. A *witness* is someone who has seen what has happened, and an *advocate* is like a lawyer who speaks on behalf of the plaintiff. By using these terms, Job showed he had cast all his hope for any fair defense upon God in heaven because he would probably die before it happened on earth. In the New Testament we learn that Jesus Christ intercedes on our behalf (Hebrews 7:25; 1 John 2:1); therefore, we have nothing to fear.

2 I am surrounded by mockers.
  I watch how bitterly they taunt me.

3 "You must defend my innocence, O God,
  since no one else will stand up for me.
4 You have closed their minds to understanding,
  but do not let them triumph.
5 They betray their friends for their own advantage,
  so let their children faint with hunger.

6 "God has made a mockery of me among the people;
  they spit in my face.
7 My eyes are swollen with weeping,
  and I am but a shadow of my former self.
8 The virtuous are horrified when they see me.
  The innocent rise up against the ungodly.
9 The righteous keep moving forward,
  and those with clean hands become stronger and stronger.

10 "As for all of you, come back with a better argument,
  though I still won't find a wise man among you.
11 My days are over.
  My hopes have disappeared.
  My heart's desires are broken.
12 These men say that night is day;
  they claim that the darkness is light.
13 What if I go to the grave*
  and make my bed in darkness?
14 What if I call the grave my father,
  and the maggot my mother or my sister?
15 Where then is my hope?
  Can anyone find it?
16 No, my hope will go down with me to the grave.
  We will rest together in the dust!"

### Bildad's Second Response to Job

**18** Then Bildad the Shuhite replied:

2 "How long before you stop talking?
  Speak sense if you want us to answer!
3 Do you think we are mere animals?
  Do you think we are stupid?
4 You may tear out your hair in anger,
  but will that destroy the earth?
  Will it make the rocks tremble?

5 "Surely the light of the wicked will be snuffed out.
  The sparks of their fire will not glow.

17:13 Hebrew *to Sheol;* also in 17:16.

**17:3**
Ps 119:122

**17:6**
Job 30:9-10

**17:9**
Job 22:30

**17:10**
Job 12:2

**17:11**
Job 7:6

**17:13**
Job 3:13

**17:14**
Job 21:26

**17:15**
Job 7:6

**17:16**
Job 3:17; 21:33

**18:3**
Ps 73:22

**18:5**
Job 21:17

---

**17:10** Job's three friends had a reputation for being wise, but Job could not find wisdom in any of them. God backed up Job's claim in 42:7, when he condemned these men for their false portrayal of him. Obviously these men had a faulty view of wisdom. They assumed that because they were prosperous and successful, God must be pleased with the way they were living and thinking. Job, however, told his friends that they were starting with the wrong idea because earthly success and prosperity are not a reward for faith in God. Likewise, trouble and affliction do not prove faithlessness. The truly wise man knows that wisdom comes from God alone, not from human successes or failures. And the truly wise man never forsakes God. God's wisdom proved superior to Job and to all his friends.

**17:15** Job was giving up hope of any future restoration of wealth and family and wrapping himself in thoughts of death and the rest from grief and pain it promised. The rewards that Job's friends described were all related to this present life. They were silent about the possibility of life after death. We must not evaluate life only in terms of this present world, because God promises a never-ending, wonderful future to those who are faithful to him.

**18:1ff** Bildad thought he knew how the universe should be run, and he saw Job as an illustration of the consequences of sin. Bildad rejected Job's side of the story because it did not fit in with his outlook on life. It is easy to condemn Bildad because his errors are obvious; unfortunately, however, we often act the same way when our ideas are threatened.

⁶ The light in their tent will grow dark.
  The lamp hanging above them will be quenched.
⁷ The confident stride of the wicked will be shortened.
  Their own schemes will be their downfall.
⁸ The wicked walk into a net.
  They fall into a pit.
⁹ A trap grabs them by the heel.
  A snare holds them tight.
¹⁰ A noose lies hidden on the ground.
   A rope is stretched across their path.

¹¹ "Terrors surround the wicked
   and trouble them at every step.
¹² Hunger depletes their strength,
   and calamity waits for them to stumble.
¹³ Disease eats their skin;
   death devours their limbs.
¹⁴ They are torn from the security of their homes
   and are brought down to the king of terrors.
¹⁵ The homes of the wicked will burn down;
   burning sulfur rains on their houses.
¹⁶ Their roots will dry up,
   and their branches will wither.
¹⁷ All memory of their existence will fade from the earth;
   no one will remember their names.
¹⁸ They will be thrust from light into darkness,
   driven from the world.
¹⁹ They will have neither children nor grandchildren,
   nor any survivor in the place where they lived.
²⁰ People in the west are appalled at their fate;
   people in the east are horrified.
²¹ They will say, 'This was the home of a wicked person,
   the place of one who rejected God.'"

### Job's Sixth Speech: A Response to Bildad

**19** Then Job spoke again:

² "How long will you torture me?
   How long will you try to crush me with your words?
³ You have already insulted me ten times.
   You should be ashamed of treating me so badly.
⁴ Even if I have sinned,
   that is my concern, not yours.
⁵ You think you're better than I am,
   using my humiliation as evidence of my sin.
⁶ But it is God who has wronged me,
   capturing me in his net.*

**19:6** Or *for I am like a city under siege.*

**Cross-references (left margin):**

18:8
Job 22:10

18:11
Job 15:21; 18:18

18:14
Job 8:22; 15:21

18:16
Isa 5:24
Hos 9:1-16
Amos 2:9

18:17
Job 24:20
Ps 34:16
Prov 10:7

18:18
Job 5:14; 27:21-23

18:19
Job 27:14-15
Isa 14:22
Jer 22:30

18:20
Jer 50:27
Obad 1:12

19:5
Pss 35:26; 38:16

19:6
Job 18:8-10; 27:2
Ps 66:11

---

**18:14** The "king of terrors" is a figure of speech referring to death. Bildad viewed death as a great devourer (18:13), but the Bible teaches that God has the power to devour even death (Psalm 49:15; Isaiah 25:8; 1 Corinthians 15:54-56).

**19:3-5** It is easy to point out someone else's faults or sins. Job's friends accused him of sin to make him feel guilty, not to encourage or correct him. If we feel we must admonish someone, we should be sure we are confronting that person because we love him, not because we are annoyed, inconvenienced, or seeking to blame him.

**19:6** Job felt that God was treating him as an enemy when, in fact, God was his friend and thought highly of him (1:8; 2:3).

In his difficulty, Job pointed at the wrong person. It was Satan, not God, who was Job's enemy. Because they stressed ultimate causes, most Israelites believed that both good and evil came from God; they also thought people were responsible for their own destinies. But the evil power loose in this world accounts for much of the suffering we experience. In verse 7, Job continued to cry out to be heard by God.

7 "I cry out, 'Help!' but no one answers me.
  I protest, but there is no justice.
8 God has blocked my way so I cannot move.
  He has plunged my path into darkness.
9 He has stripped me of my honor
  and removed the crown from my head.
10 He has demolished me on every side, and I am finished.
  He has uprooted my hope like a fallen tree.
11 His fury burns against me;
  he counts me as an enemy.
12 His troops advance.
  They build up roads to attack me.
  They camp all around my tent.

13 "My relatives stay far away,
  and my friends have turned against me.
14 My family is gone,
  and my close friends have forgotten me.
15 My servants and maids consider me a stranger.
  I am like a foreigner to them.
16 When I call my servant, he doesn't come;
  I have to plead with him!
17 My breath is repulsive to my wife.
  I am rejected by my own family.
18 Even young children despise me.
  When I stand to speak, they turn their backs on me.
19 My close friends detest me.
  Those I loved have turned against me.
20 I have been reduced to skin and bones
  and have escaped death by the skin of my teeth.

21 "Have mercy on me, my friends, have mercy,
  for the hand of God has struck me.
22 Must you also persecute me, like God does?
  Haven't you chewed me up enough?

23 "Oh, that my words could be recorded.
  Oh, that they could be inscribed on a monument,
24 carved with an iron chisel and filled with lead,
  engraved forever in the rock.

25 "But as for me, I know that my Redeemer lives,
  and he will stand upon the earth at last.
26 And after my body has decayed,
  yet in my body I will see God*!
27 I will see him for myself.
  Yes, I will see him with my own eyes.
  I am overwhelmed at the thought!

28 "How dare you go on persecuting me,
  saying, 'It's his own fault'?

19:7
Hab 1:2

19:8
Lam 3:7, 9

19:9
Ps 89:39, 44
Lam 5:16

19:13
Pss 69:8; 88:8, 18

19:19
Pss 38:11;
55:12-13

19:20
Ps 102:5
Lam 4:8

19:22
Ps 69:26

19:23
Isa 30:8
Jer 36:2

19:25
Ps 78:35
Isa 43:14
Jer 50:34

19:26
Matt 5:8
1 Cor 13:12
1 Jn 3:2

19:26 Or *without my body I will see God.* The meaning of the Hebrew is uncertain.

19:25-27 At the heart of the book of Job comes his ringing affirmation of confidence: "I know that my Redeemer lives." In ancient Israel a *redeemer* was a family member who bought a slave's way to freedom or who took care of a widow (see the note on Ruth 3:1). What tremendous faith Job had, especially in light of the fact that he was unaware of the conference between God and Satan. Job thought that God had brought all these disasters upon him! Faced with death and decay, Job still expected to see God—and he expected to do so in his body. When the book of Job was written, Israel did not have a well-developed doctrine of the resurrection. Although Job struggled with the idea that God was presently against him, he firmly believed that in the end God would be on his side. This belief was so strong that Job became one of the first to talk about the resurrection of the body (see also Psalm 16:10; Isaiah 26:19; Daniel 12:2, 13).

19:26 Job said: "In my body I will see God." In Job's situation, it seemed unlikely to him that he would, in his body, see God. And that's just the point of Job's faith! He was confident that God's justice would triumph, even if it would take a miracle like resurrection to accomplish this.

29 You should fear punishment yourselves,
  for your attitude deserves punishment.
  Then you will know that there is indeed a judgment."

## Zophar's Second Response to Job

**20** Then Zophar the Naamathite replied:

2 "I must reply
  because I am greatly disturbed.

3 I've had to endure your insults,
  but now my spirit prompts me to reply.

4 "Don't you realize that from the beginning of time,
  ever since people were first placed on the earth,

5 the triumph of the wicked has been short lived
  and the joy of the godless has been only temporary?

6 Though the pride of the godless reaches to the heavens
  and their heads touch the clouds,
7 yet they will vanish forever,
  thrown away like their own dung.
  Those who knew them will ask,
  'Where are they?'

8 They will fade like a dream and not be found.
  They will vanish like a vision in the night.
9 Those who once saw them will see them no more.
  Their families will never see them again.

10 Their children will beg from the poor,
  for they must give back their stolen riches.
11 Though they are young,
  their bones will lie in the dust.

12 "They enjoyed the sweet taste of wickedness,
  letting it melt under their tongue.
13 They savored it,
  holding it long in their mouths.
14 But suddenly the food in their bellies turns sour,
  a poisonous venom in their stomach.
15 They will vomit the wealth they swallowed.
  God won't let them keep it down.

16 They will suck the poison of cobras.
  The viper will kill them.

17 They will never again enjoy streams of olive oil
  or rivers of milk and honey.
18 They will give back everything they worked for.
  Their wealth will bring them no joy.
19 For they oppressed the poor and left them destitute.
  They foreclosed on their homes.

20 They were always greedy and never satisfied.
  Nothing remains of all the things they dreamed about.

21 Nothing is left after they finish gorging themselves.
  Therefore, their prosperity will not endure.

---

**20:1ff** Zophar's speech again revealed his false assumption because he based his arguments purely on the idea that Job was an evil hypocrite. Zophar said that although Job had it good for a while, he didn't live righteously, so God took his wealth from him. According to Zophar, Job's calamities *proved* his wickedness.

**20:6, 7** Although Zophar was wrong in directing this tirade against Job, he was correct in talking about the final end of evil people. At first, sin seems enjoyable and attractive. Lying, stealing, or oppressing others often brings temporary gain to those who practice these sins. Some live a long time with ill-gotten gain. But in the end, God's justice will prevail. What Zophar missed is that judgment for these sins may not come in the lifetime of the sinner. Punishment may be deferred until the last judgment, when sinners will be eternally cut off from God. We should not be impressed with the success and power of evil people. God's judgment on them is certain.

22 "In the midst of plenty, they will run into trouble
    and be overcome by misery.
23 May God give them a bellyful of trouble.
    May God rain down his anger upon them.
24 When they try to escape an iron weapon,
    a bronze-tipped arrow will pierce them.
25 The arrow is pulled from their back,
    and the arrowhead glistens with blood.*
    The terrors of death are upon them.
26   Their treasures will be thrown into deepest darkness.
  A wildfire will devour their goods,
    consuming all they have left.
27 The heavens will reveal their guilt,
    and the earth will testify against them.
28 A flood will sweep away their house.
    God's anger will descend on them in torrents.
29 This is the reward that God gives the wicked.
    It is the inheritance decreed by God."

## Job's Seventh Speech: A Response to Zophar

**21** Then Job spoke again:

2 "Listen closely to what I am saying.
    That's one consolation you can give me.
3 Bear with me, and let me speak.
    After I have spoken, you may resume mocking me.

4 "My complaint is with God, not with people.
    I have good reason to be so impatient.
5 Look at me and be stunned.
    Put your hand over your mouth in shock.
6 When I think about what I am saying, I shudder.
    My body trembles.

7 "Why do the wicked prosper,
    growing old and powerful?
8 They live to see their children grow up and settle down,
    and they enjoy their grandchildren.
9 Their homes are safe from every fear,
    and God does not punish them.
10 Their bulls never fail to breed.
    Their cows bear calves and never miscarry.
11 They let their children frisk about like lambs.
    Their little ones skip and dance.
12 They sing with tambourine and harp.
    They celebrate to the sound of the flute.
13 They spend their days in prosperity,
    then go down to the grave* in peace.
14 And yet they say to God, 'Go away.
    We want no part of you and your ways.
15 Who is the Almighty, and why should we obey him?
    What good will it do us to pray?'
16 (They think their prosperity is of their own doing,
    but I will have nothing to do with that kind of thinking.)

**20:23**
Num 11:18-20, 33
Ps 78:30-31

**20:24**
Isa 24:18
Amos 5:19

**20:25**
Job 16:13; 18:11

**20:26**
Job 15:30; 18:18
Ps 21:9

**20:27**
Deut 31:28

**20:28**
Deut 28:31

**20:29**
Job 27:13; 31:2-3

**21:4**
Job 6:11; 7:11

**21:5**
Judg 18:19
Job 29:9; 40:4

**21:6**
Ps 55:5

**21:7**
Ps 73:3
Jer 12:1

**21:8**
Ps 17:14

**21:9**
Ps 73:5

**21:13**
Job 36:11

**20:25** Hebrew *with gall.*  **21:13** Hebrew *to Sheol.*

---

**21:1ff** Job refuted Zophar's idea that evil people never experience wealth and happiness, pointing out that in the real world the wicked do indeed prosper. See Psalm 73 for more on the apparent prosperity of evil people. God does as he wills to individuals (21:22-25), and people cannot use their circumstances to measure their own goodness or God's—they are sometimes (but not always) related. Success to Job's friends was based on outward performance; success to God, however, is based on a person's heart.

17 "Yet the light of the wicked never seems to be extinguished.
   Do they ever have trouble?
   Does God distribute sorrows to them in anger?

21:18
Pss 1:4; 35:5;
83:13
Isa 17:13

18 Are they driven before the wind like straw?
   Are they carried away by the storm like chaff?
   Not at all!

21:19
Exod 20:5
Ezek 18:4

19 "'Well,' you say, 'at least God will punish their children!'
   But I say he should punish the ones who sin,
   so that they understand his judgment.

21:20
Isa 51:17
Jer 25:15
Rev 14:10

20 Let them see their destruction with their own eyes.
   Let them drink deeply of the anger of the Almighty.
21 For they will not care what happens to their family
   after they are dead.

21:22
Job 36:22
Ps 82:1
Isa 40:13-14
Rom 11:34

22 "But who can teach a lesson to God,
   since he judges even the most powerful?
23 One person dies in prosperity,
   completely comfortable and secure,
24 the picture of good health,
   vigorous and fit.
25 Another person dies in bitter poverty,
   never having tasted the good life.

21:26
Job 3:13; 24:20

26 But both are buried in the same dust,
   both eaten by the same maggots.

27 "Look, I know what you're thinking.
   I know the schemes you plot against me.

21:28
Job 1:3

28 You will tell me of rich and wicked people
   whose houses have vanished because of their sins.
29 But ask those who have been around,
   and they will tell you the truth.

21:30
Job 20:29
Prov 16:4
Rom 2:5
2 Pet 2:9

30 Evil people are spared in times of calamity
   and are allowed to escape disaster.
31 No one criticizes them openly
   or pays them back for what they have done.
32 When they are carried to the grave,
   an honor guard keeps watch at their tomb.

21:33
Job 3:19, 22;
17:16; 24:24

33 A great funeral procession goes to the cemetery.
   Many pay their respects as the body is laid to rest,
   and the earth gives sweet repose.

21:34
Job 16:2

34 "How can your empty clichés comfort me?
   All your explanations are lies!"

### 3. Third round of discussion
*Eliphaz's Third Response to Job*

**22** Then Eliphaz the Temanite replied:

22:2
Job 35:7
Luke 17:10

2 "Can a person do anything to help God?
   Can even a wise person be helpful to him?

---

**21:22** Although baffled by the reasons for his suffering, Job affirmed God's superior understanding by asking, "Who can teach a lesson to God?" The way you respond to your personal struggles shows your attitude toward God. Rather than becoming angry with God, continue to trust him, no matter what your circumstances may be. Although it is sometimes difficult to see, God *is* in control. We must commit ourselves to him so we will not resent his timing.

**21:29-33** If wicked people become wealthy despite their sin, why should we try to be good? The wicked may *seem* to get away with sin, but there is a higher Judge and a future judgment (Revelation 20:11-15). The final settlement of justice will come, not in this life,

but in the next. What is important is how a person views God in prosperity or poverty, not the prosperity or poverty itself.

**22:1ff** This is Eliphaz's third and final speech to Job. When he first spoke to Job (chapters 4–5), he commended Job's good deeds and gently suggested that Job might need to repent of some sin. While he said nothing new in this speech, he did get more specific. He couldn't shake his belief that suffering is God's punishment for evil deeds, so he suggested several possible sins that Job might have committed. Eliphaz wasn't trying to destroy Job; at the end of his speech he promised that Job would receive peace and restoration if he would only admit his sin and repent.

3 Is it any advantage to the Almighty if you are righteous?
  Would it be any gain to him if you were perfect?
4 Is it because you're so pious that he accuses you
  and brings judgment against you?
5 No, it's because of your wickedness!
  There's no limit to your sins.

6 "For example, you must have lent money to your friend
  and demanded clothing as security.
  Yes, you stripped him to the bone.
7 You must have refused water for the thirsty
  and food for the hungry.
8 You probably think the land belongs to the powerful
  and only the privileged have a right to it!
9 You must have sent widows away empty-handed
  and crushed the hopes of orphans.
10 That is why you are surrounded by traps
   and tremble from sudden fears.
11 That is why you cannot see in the darkness,
   and waves of water cover you.

12 "God is so great—higher than the heavens,
   higher than the farthest stars.
13 But you reply, 'That's why God can't see what I am doing!
   How can he judge through the thick darkness?
14 For thick clouds swirl about him, and he cannot see us.
   He is way up there, walking on the vault of heaven.'

15 "Will you continue on the old paths
   where evil people have walked?
16 They were snatched away in the prime of life,
   the foundations of their lives washed away.
17 For they said to God, 'Leave us alone!
   What can the Almighty do to us?'
18 Yet he was the one who filled their homes with good things,
   so I will have nothing to do with that kind of thinking.

19 "The righteous will be happy to see the wicked destroyed,
   and the innocent will laugh in contempt.
20 They will say, 'See how our enemies have been destroyed.
   The last of them have been consumed in the fire.'

21 "Submit to God, and you will have peace;
   then things will go well for you.
22 Listen to his instructions,
   and store them in your heart.
23 If you return to the Almighty, you will be restored—
   so clean up your life.
24 If you give up your lust for money
   and throw your precious gold into the river,
25 the Almighty himself will be your treasure.
   He will be your precious silver!

26 "Then you will take delight in the Almighty
   and look up to God.

**22:6**
Exod 22:26
Deut 24:6, 17
Ezek 18:16
**22:7**
Job 31:31
Matt 10:42
**22:8**
Job 9:24; 12:19
**22:9**
Job 6:27; 24:3, 21

**22:13**
Pss 10:11; 64:5;
94:7
Isa 29:15

**22:16**
Job 14:14; 15:32
Matt 7:26-27
**22:17**
Job 21:14-15
**22:18**
Job 12:6; 21:16
**22:19**
Pss 58:10; 107:42
**22:20**
Job 15:30

**22:22**
Job 6:10; 23:12
Prov 2:6
**22:23**
Job 8:5; 11:14
Isa 19:22
Zech 1:3
**22:24**
Job 31:24-25

**22:26**
Ps 37:4

---

**22:12-14** Eliphaz declared that Job's view of God was too small, and he criticized Job for thinking that God was too far removed from earth to care about him. If Job knew of God's intense, personal interest in him, Eliphaz said, he wouldn't dare take his sins so lightly. Eliphaz had a point—some people do take sin lightly because they think God is far away and doesn't notice all we do. But his point did not apply to Job.

**22:21-30** Several times Job's friends showed a partial knowledge of God's truth and character, but they had trouble accurately applying this truth to life. Such was the case with Eliphaz, who gave a beautiful summary of repentance. He was correct in saying that we must ask for God's forgiveness when we sin, but his statement did not apply to Job, who had already sought God's forgiveness (7:20, 21; 9:20; 13:23) and had lived closely in touch with God all along.

22:27
Isa 58:9

27 You will pray to him, and he will hear you,
   and you will fulfill your vows to him.
28 You will succeed in whatever you choose to do,
   and light will shine on the road ahead of you.

22:29
Matt 23:12
1 Pet 5:5

29 If people are in trouble and you say, 'Help them,'
   God will save them.
30 Even sinners will be rescued;
   they will be rescued because your hands are pure."

## Job's Eighth Speech: A Response to Eliphaz

# 23

Then Job spoke again:

23:2
Job 6:2-3; 7:11

2 "My complaint today is still a bitter one,
   and I try hard not to groan aloud.
3 If only I knew where to find God,
   I would go to his court.

23:4
Job 13:18

4 I would lay out my case
   and present my arguments.
5 Then I would listen to his reply
   and understand what he says to me.

23:6
Job 9:4
23:7
Job 13:3, 16

6 Would he use his great power to argue with me?
   No, he would give me a fair hearing.
7 Honest people can reason with him,
   so I would be forever acquitted by my judge.

23:8
Job 9:11

8 I go east, but he is not there.
   I go west, but I cannot find him.
9 I do not see him in the north, for he is hidden.
   I look to the south, but he is concealed.

23:10
Job 7:18
Pss 7:9; 11:5

10 "But he knows where I am going.
   And when he tests me, I will come out as pure as gold.

23:11
Job 31:7
Pss 17:5; 44:18

11 For I have stayed on God's paths;
   I have followed his ways and not turned aside.

23:12
Job 6:10

12 I have not departed from his commands,
   but have treasured his words more than daily food.
13 But once he has made his decision, who can change his mind?
   Whatever he wants to do, he does.
14 So he will do to me whatever he has planned.
   He controls my destiny.
15 No wonder I am so terrified in his presence.
   When I think of it, terror grips me.

23:16
Deut 20:3
Jer 51:46

16 God has made me sick at heart;
   the Almighty has terrified me.

23:17
Job 10:18-19; 19:8

17 Darkness is all around me;
   thick, impenetrable darkness is everywhere.

---

**23:1–24:25** Job continued his questioning, saying that his suffering would be more bearable if only he knew why it was happening. If there was sin for which he could repent, he would! He knew about the wicked and the fact that they would be punished; he knew God could vindicate him if he so chose. In all his examples of the wicked in the world, his overriding desire was for God to clear his name, prove his righteousness, and explain why he was chosen to receive all this calamity. Job tried to make his friends see that questions about God, life, and justice are not as simple as they assumed.

**23:10** In chapter 22, Eliphaz had tried to condemn Job by identifying some secret sin that he may have committed. Here Job declares his confidence in his integrity and God's justice. We are always likely to have hidden sin in our lives, sin we don't even know about because God's standards are so high and our performance is so imperfect. If we are true believers, however, all our sins are forgiven because of what Christ did

on the cross in our behalf (Romans 5:1; 8:1). The Bible also teaches that even if we feel guilty, God is greater than our feelings (1 John 3:20). His forgiveness and cleansing are sufficient; they overrule our nagging doubts. The Holy Spirit in us is our proof that we are forgiven in God's eyes even though we may *feel* guilty. If we, like Job, are truly seeking God, we can stand up to others' accusations as well as our own nagging doubts. If God has forgiven and accepted us, we are forgiven indeed.

## Job Asks Why the Wicked Are Not Punished

**24** 1 "Why doesn't the Almighty bring the wicked to judgment?
  Why must the godly wait for him in vain?

2 Evil people steal land by moving the boundary markers.
  They steal livestock and put them in their own pastures.

3 They take the orphan's donkey
  and demand the widow's ox as security for a loan.

4 The poor are pushed off the path;
  the needy must hide together for safety.

5 Like wild donkeys in the wilderness,
  the poor must spend all their time looking for food,
  searching even in the desert for food for their children.

6 They harvest a field they do not own,
  and they glean in the vineyards of the wicked.

7 All night they lie naked in the cold,
  without clothing or covering.

8 They are soaked by mountain showers,
  and they huddle against the rocks for want of a home.

9 "The wicked snatch a widow's child from her breast,
  taking the baby as security for a loan.

10 The poor must go about naked, without any clothing.
  They harvest food for others while they themselves are starving.

11 They press out olive oil without being allowed to taste it,
  and they tread in the winepress as they suffer from thirst.

12 The groans of the dying rise from the city,
  and the wounded cry for help,
  yet God ignores their moaning.

13 "Wicked people rebel against the light.
  They refuse to acknowledge its ways
  or stay in its paths.

14 The murderer rises in the early dawn
  to kill the poor and needy;
  at night he is a thief.

15 The adulterer waits for the twilight,
  saying, 'No one will see me then.'
  He hides his face so no one will know him.

16 Thieves break into houses at night
  and sleep in the daytime.
  They are not acquainted with the light.

17 The black night is their morning.
  They ally themselves with the terrors of the darkness.

18 "But they disappear like foam down a river.
  Everything they own is cursed,
  and they are afraid to enter their own vineyards.

19 The grave* consumes sinners
  just as drought and heat consume snow.

20 Their own mothers will forget them.
  Maggots will find them sweet to eat.
  No one will remember them.
  Wicked people are broken like a tree in the storm.

21 They cheat the woman who has no son to help her.
  They refuse to help the needy widow.

**24:19** Hebrew *Sheol*.

Cross references:
- **24:1** Isa 2:12; Jer 46:10
- **24:2** Deut 19:14; 27:17
- **24:3** Exod 22:26; Deut 24:17
- **24:4** Job 29:16; 30:25; Prov 14:31; Amos 8:4
- **24:5** Job 39:5-8; Ps 104:23
- **24:7** Exod 22:26
- **24:8** Lam 4:5
- **24:14** Ps 10:8; Mic 2:1
- **24:15** Prov 7:9
- **24:16** Exod 22:2; Matt 6:19
- **24:17** Ps 91:5
- **24:19** Job 6:16-17; 21:13
- **24:20** Prov 10:7; Isa 49:15; Dan 4:14

**24:18-21** Job suddenly seemed to be arguing on his friends' side. For this reason, some commentators think one of Job's friends said these words. But we shouldn't expect Job to present a unified argument. He was confused. He was not arguing that, in every case, God rewards the wicked and punishes the righteous; he was simply asserting that in his case, a righteous man was suffering.

22 "God, in his power, drags away the rich.
They may rise high, but they have no assurance of life.
23 They may be allowed to live in security,
but God is always watching them.
24 And though they are great now,
in a moment they will be gone like all others,
cut off like heads of grain.
25 Can anyone claim otherwise?
Who can prove me wrong?"

### Bildad's Third Response to Job

**25** Then Bildad the Shuhite replied:

2 "God is powerful and dreadful.
He enforces peace in the heavens.
3 Who is able to count his heavenly army?
Doesn't his light shine on all the earth?
4 How can a mortal be innocent before God?
Can anyone born of a woman be pure?
5 God is more glorious than the moon;
he shines brighter than the stars.
6 In comparison, people are maggots;
we mortals are mere worms."

### Job's Ninth Speech: A Response to Bildad

**26** Then Job spoke again:

2 "How you have helped the powerless!
How you have saved the weak!
3 How you have enlightened my stupidity!
What wise advice you have offered!
4 Where have you gotten all these wise sayings?
Whose spirit speaks through you?

5 "The dead tremble—
those who live beneath the waters.
6 The underworld* is naked in God's presence.
The place of destruction* is uncovered.
7 God stretches the northern sky over empty space
and hangs the earth on nothing.
8 He wraps the rain in his thick clouds,
and the clouds don't burst with the weight.
9 He covers the face of the moon,*
shrouding it with his clouds.
10 He created the horizon when he separated the waters;
he set the boundary between day and night.

**26:6a** Hebrew *Sheol*.  **26:6b** Hebrew *Abaddon*.  **26:9** Or *covers his throne*.

Cross-references:
24:23 Job 11:11; 12:6
24:24 Job 14:21; Ps 37:10
24:25 Job 6:28; 27:4
25:2 Job 9:4; 16:19; 31:2; 36:5; 37:23
25:4 Job 4:17; 9:2
25:5 Job 15:15; 31:26
25:6 Job 7:17
26:2 Ps 71:9
26:5 Job 3:13; Ps 88:10
26:8 Job 37:11; Prov 30:4
26:9 Job 22:14; Pss 97:2; 105:39
26:10 Job 38:1-11, 19-20, 24; Prov 8:29

---

**25:1ff** Bildad's final reply was weak. It ignored Job's examples of the prosperity of the wicked. Instead of attempting to refute Job, Bildad accused Job of pride because he was claiming that his suffering was not the result of sin. Job never claimed to be without sin, but only that his sin could not have caused his present trouble.

**25:6** It is important to understand that Bildad, not God, was calling people worms. Human beings are created in God's image (Genesis 1:26, 27). Psalm 8:5 says that people are "a little lower than God." Bildad may have simply been using a poetic description to contrast our worth to the worth and power of God. To come to God, we need not crawl like worms. We can approach him boldly in faith (Hebrews 4:16).

**26:1ff** Job has the distinction of giving the longest speech in the book—six chapters—weaving together pictures of God's mystery and power in a beautiful poem of trust. Beginning by brushing off Bildad's latest reply as irrelevant (chapter 25), Job then told Bildad and his friends that they could not possibly know everything about God. Wisdom does not originate from this life or from the human mind—it comes from God (28:27, 28). Job then defended his upright and honest life. He had effectively sought to follow God's way of living. While admitting that he was not perfect, Job maintained that his motives were right.

**26:2-4** With great sarcasm, Job attacked Bildad's comments. Job's friends' theological explanations failed to bring any relief because they were unable to turn their knowledge into helpful counsel. When dealing with people, it is more important to love and understand them than to analyze them or give advice. Compassion produces greater results than criticism or blame.

11 The foundations of heaven tremble;
    they shudder at his rebuke.
12 By his power the sea grew calm.
    By his skill he crushed the great sea monster.*
13 His Spirit made the heavens beautiful,
    and his power pierced the gliding serpent.
14 These are just the beginning of all that he does,
    merely a whisper of his power.
    Who, then, can comprehend the thunder of his power?"

**26:13**
Job 9:8
Isa 27:1

### Job's Final Speech

**27** Job continued speaking:

2 "I vow by the living God, who has taken away my rights,
    by the Almighty who has embittered my soul—
3 As long as I live,
    while I have breath from God,
4 my lips will speak no evil,
    and my tongue will speak no lies.
5 I will never concede that you are right;
    I will defend my integrity until I die.
6 I will maintain my innocence without wavering.
    My conscience is clear for as long as I live.

7 "May my enemy be punished like the wicked,
    my adversary like those who do evil.
8 For what hope do the godless have when God cuts them off
    and takes away their life?
9 Will God listen to their cry
    when trouble comes upon them?
10 Can they take delight in the Almighty?
    Can they call to God at any time?
11 I will teach you about God's power.
    I will not conceal anything concerning the Almighty.
12 But you have seen all this,
    yet you say all these useless things to me.

13 "This is what the wicked will receive from God;
    this is their inheritance from the Almighty.
14 They may have many children,
    but the children will die in war or starve to death.
15 Those who survive will die of a plague,
    and not even their widows will mourn them.

16 "Evil people may have piles of money
    and may store away mounds of clothing.
17 But the righteous will wear that clothing,
    and the innocent will divide that money.
18 The wicked build houses as fragile as a spider's web,*
    as flimsy as a shelter made of branches.
19 The wicked go to bed rich
    but wake to find that all their wealth is gone.

**27:2**
Job 9:18; 16:11

**27:4**
Job 6:28; 33:3

**27:6**
Job 2:3; 13:18

**27:8**
Job 8:13; 11:20

**27:9**
Prov 1:27-28
Isa 1:15

**27:13**
Job 15:20; 20:29

**27:14**
Job 20:18-21

**27:15**
Ps 78:64

**27:18**
Job 8:15

**27:19**
Job 7:8, 21

**26:12** Hebrew *Rahab*, the name of a mythical sea monster that represents chaos in ancient literature.  **27:18** As in Greek and Syriac versions (see also 8:14); Hebrew reads *a moth.*

**27:6** In the midst of all the accusations, Job was able to declare that his conscience was clear. Only God's forgiveness and the determination to live right before God can bring a clear conscience. How important Job's record became as he was being accused. Like Job, we can't claim sinless lives, but we *can* claim forgiven lives. When we confess our sins to God, he forgives us. Then we can live with clear consciences (1 John 1:9).

**27:13-23** Job agreed with his friends that the end of the wicked will be disaster, but he did not agree that *he* was wicked and deserving of punishment. Most of the punishments Job listed never happened to him. So he wasn't including himself as one of the wicked. On the contrary, he continually pleaded for God to vindicate him.

27:20
Job 15:21; 20:8

27:21
Job 7:10; 18:18;
20:8; 21:18

27:22
Jer 13:14
Ezek 5:11; 24:14

20 Terror overwhelms them like a flood,
 and they are blown away in the storms of the night.
21 The east wind carries them away, and they are gone.
 It sweeps them away.
22 It whirls down on them without mercy.
 They struggle to flee from its power.
23 But everyone jeers at them
 and mocks them.

## Job Speaks of Wisdom and Understanding

**28** 1 "People know where to mine silver
 and how to refine gold.
2 They know where to dig iron from the earth
 and how to smelt copper from rock.
3 They know how to shine light in the darkness
 and explore the farthest regions of the earth
 as they search in the dark for ore.
4 They sink a mine shaft into the earth
 far from where anyone lives.
 They descend on ropes, swinging back and forth.

28:5
Ps 104:14

5 Food is grown on the earth above,
 but down below, the earth is melted as by fire.
6 Here the rocks contain precious lapis lazuli,
 and the dust contains gold.
7 These are treasures no bird of prey can see,
 no falcon's eye observe.
8 No wild animal has walked upon these treasures;
 no lion has ever set his paw there.

28:9
Deut 8:15; 32:13

9 People know how to tear apart flinty rocks
 and overturn the roots of mountains.
10 They cut tunnels in the rocks
 and uncover precious stones.
11 They dam up the trickling streams
 and bring to light the hidden treasures.

28:12
Job 28:23, 28

12 "But do people know where to find wisdom?
 Where can they find understanding?
13 No one knows where to find it,
 for it is not found among the living.

---

| WHERE CAN WISDOM BE FOUND? Job and his friends differed in their ideas of how people become wise. | Person | His Source of Wisdom | Attitude toward God |
|---|---|---|---|
| | Eliphaz . . . | Wisdom is learned by observing and experiencing life. He based his advice to Job on his confident, firsthand knowledge (4:7, 8; 5:3, 27). | "I have personally observed how God works and have figured him out." |
| | Bildad . . . . | Wisdom is inherited from the past. Trustworthy knowledge is secondhand. He based his advice to Job on traditional proverbs and sayings that he frequently quoted (8:8, 9; 18:5-21). | "Those who have gone before us figured God out, and all we have to do is use that knowledge." |
| | Zophar . . . | Wisdom belongs to the wise. He based his advice on his wisdom that had no other source than himself (11:6; 20:1-29). | "The wise know what God is like, but there aren't many of us around." |
| | Job . . . . . . | God is the source of wisdom, and the first step toward wisdom is to fear God (28:20-28). | "God reveals his wisdom to those who humbly trust him." |

---

**28:13** Job stated that wisdom cannot be found among the living. It is natural for people who do not understand the importance of God's Word to seek wisdom here on earth. They look to philosophers and other leaders to give them direction for living. Yet Job said that wisdom is not found there. No leader or group of leaders can produce enough knowledge or insight to explain the totality of human experience. The ultimate interpretation of life, of who we are and where we are going, must come from outside and above our mortal life. When looking for guidance, seek God's wisdom as revealed in the Bible. To be lifted above and beyond the boundaries of life, we must know and trust the Lord of life.

14 'It is not here,' says the ocean.
　　'Nor is it here,' says the sea.
15 It cannot be bought with gold.
　　It cannot be purchased with silver.
16 It's worth more than all the gold of Ophir,
　　greater than precious onyx or lapis lazuli.
17 Wisdom is more valuable than gold and crystal.
　　It cannot be purchased with jewels mounted in fine gold.
18 Coral and jasper are worthless in trying to get it.
　　The price of wisdom is far above rubies.
19 Precious peridot from Ethiopia* cannot be exchanged for it.
　　It's worth more than the purest gold.

20 "But do people know where to find wisdom?
　　Where can they find understanding?
21 It is hidden from the eyes of all humanity.
　　Even the sharp-eyed birds in the sky cannot discover it.
22 Destruction* and Death say,
　　'We've heard only rumors of where wisdom can be found.'

23 "God alone understands the way to wisdom;
　　he knows where it can be found,
24 for he looks throughout the whole earth
　　and sees everything under the heavens.
25 He decided how hard the winds should blow
　　and how much rain should fall.
26 He made the laws for the rain
　　and laid out a path for the lightning.
27 Then he saw wisdom and evaluated it.
　　He set it in place and examined it thoroughly.
28 And this is what he says to all humanity:
　　'The fear of the Lord is true wisdom;
　　to forsake evil is real understanding.'"

## Job Speaks of His Former Blessings

**29** Job continued speaking:

2 "I long for the years gone by
　　when God took care of me,
3 when he lit up the way before me
　　and I walked safely through the darkness.
4 When I was in my prime,
　　God's friendship was felt in my home.
5 The Almighty was still with me,
　　and my children were around me.
6 My cows produced milk in abundance,
　　and my groves poured out streams of olive oil.

7 "Those were the days when I went to the city gate
　　and took my place among the honored leaders.

28:19 Hebrew *from Cush.*  28:22 Hebrew *Abaddon.*

**28:17** Prov 8:10; 16:16
**28:18** Prov 8:11
**28:19** Prov 8:19
**28:23** Prov 8:22-36
**28:24** Ps 33:13-14 Prov 15:3
**28:25** Job 12:15; 38:8-11 Ps 135:7
**28:26** Job 37:3, 6, 11-12
**28:28** Ps 111:10 Prov 1:7; 9:10
**29:1** Job 27:1
**29:2** Jer 31:28
**29:3** Job 11:17
**29:6** Deut 32:13 Ps 81:16

---

**28:16** Gold of Ophir was considered the finest gold available. Ophir may have been located in Africa, along the Arabian coast or in India. Wherever it was, it was a good distance from Israel, for it took Solomon's ships three years to make the voyage (1 Kings 9:28; 10:22).

**28:28** "The fear of the Lord" is a key theme in the wisdom literature of the Bible (Job through Song of Songs). It means to have respect and reverence for God and to be in awe of his majesty and power. This is the starting point to finding real wisdom (see Proverbs 1:7-9).

**29:6** Milk and olive oil were symbols of material prosperity in an agricultural society. Job's flocks and olive trees were so plentiful that everything seemed to overflow.

**29:7ff** Job was walking a fine line between bragging about past accomplishments and recalling good deeds in order to answer the charges against him. Job's one weakness throughout his conversations is that he came dangerously close to pride. Pride is especially deceptive when we are doing right. But it separates us from God by making us think we're better than we really are. Then comes the tendency to trust our own opinions, which leads to

<sup>8</sup> The young stepped aside when they saw me,
  and even the aged rose in respect at my coming.
<sup>9</sup> The princes stood in silence
  and put their hands over their mouths.

29:9
Job 21:5; 29:21

<sup>10</sup> The highest officials of the city stood quietly,
  holding their tongues in respect.

29:11
Job 4:3-4

<sup>11</sup> "All who heard me praised me.
  All who saw me spoke well of me.

29:12
Job 24:4, 9;
31:16-17, 21; 34:28

<sup>12</sup> For I assisted the poor in their need
  and the orphans who required help.

29:13
Job 31:19-20

<sup>13</sup> I helped those without hope, and they blessed me.
  And I caused the widows' hearts to sing for joy.

29:14
Ps 132:9
Isa 59:17; 61:10
Eph 6:14

<sup>14</sup> Everything I did was honest.
  Righteousness covered me like a robe,
  and I wore justice like a turban.
<sup>15</sup> I served as eyes for the blind
  and feet for the lame.

29:16
Prov 29:7

<sup>16</sup> I was a father to the poor
  and assisted strangers who needed help.

29:17
Ps 3:7

<sup>17</sup> I broke the jaws of godless oppressors
  and plucked their victims from their teeth.

<sup>18</sup> "I thought, 'Surely I will die surrounded by my family
  after a long, good life.*

29:19
Jer 17:8
Hos 14:5

<sup>19</sup> For I am like a tree whose roots reach the water,
  whose branches are refreshed with the dew.

29:20
Gen 49:24
Ps 18:34

<sup>20</sup> New honors are constantly bestowed on me,
  and my strength is continually renewed.'

<sup>21</sup> "Everyone listened to my advice.
  They were silent as they waited for me to speak.
<sup>22</sup> And after I spoke, they had nothing to add,
  for my counsel satisfied them.
<sup>23</sup> They longed for me to speak as people long for rain.
  They drank my words like a refreshing spring rain.
<sup>24</sup> When they were discouraged, I smiled at them.
  My look of approval was precious to them.

29:25
Job 1:3; 4:4; 16:5

<sup>25</sup> Like a chief, I told them what to do.
  I lived like a king among his troops
  and comforted those who mourned.

### Job Speaks of His Anguish

30:1
Job 12:4

# 30

<sup>1</sup> "But now I am mocked by people younger than I,
  by young men whose fathers are not worthy to run with my sheepdogs.
<sup>2</sup> A lot of good they are to me—
  those worn-out wretches!
<sup>3</sup> They are gaunt with hunger
  and flee to the deserts,
  to desolate and gloomy wastelands.

29:18 Hebrew *after I have counted my days like sand.*

---

other kinds of sin. While it is not wrong to recount past deeds, it is far better to recount God's blessings to us. This will help keep us from inadvertently falling into pride.

**29:7-17** Because of this description of Job's work, many commentators believe that Job was a judge. In Job's day, a judge served as both a city councilman and a magistrate, helping to manage the community and settle disputes. In most cases, this was not a full-time position but a part-time post held on the basis of one's respect and standing in the area.

**30:1ff** To suffer extreme loss, as Job did, was humiliating. But to face abuse at the hands of young upstarts added insult to injury. Job had lost his family, possessions, health, position, and good name. He was not even respected for suffering bravely. Unfortunately, young people sometimes mock and take advantage of older people and those who are limited in some way. Instead, they should realize that their own physical abilities and attributes are short-lived and that God loves all people equally.

4 They pluck wild greens from among the bushes
  and eat from the roots of broom trees.
5 They are driven from human society,
  and people shout at them as if they were thieves.
6 So now they live in frightening ravines,
  in caves and among the rocks.
7 They sound like animals howling among the bushes,
  huddled together beneath the nettles.
8 They are nameless fools,
  outcasts from society.

9 "And now they mock me with vulgar songs!
   They taunt me!
10 They despise me and won't come near me,
   except to spit in my face.
11 For God has cut my bowstring.
   He has humbled me,
   so they have thrown off all restraint.
12 These outcasts oppose me to my face.
   They send me sprawling
   and lay traps in my path.
13 They block my road
   and do everything they can to destroy me.
   They know I have no one to help me.
14    They come at me from all directions.
   They jump on me when I am down.
15    I live in terror now.
   My honor has blown away in the wind,
   and my prosperity has vanished like a cloud.

16 "And now my life seeps away.
   Depression haunts my days.
17 At night my bones are filled with pain,
   which gnaws at me relentlessly.
18 With a strong hand, God grabs my shirt.
   He grips me by the collar of my coat.
19 He has thrown me into the mud.
   I'm nothing more than dust and ashes.

20 "I cry to you, O God, but you don't answer.
   I stand before you, but you don't even look.
21 You have become cruel toward me.
   You use your power to persecute me.
22 You throw me into the whirlwind
   and destroy me in the storm.
23 And I know you are sending me to my death—
   the destination of all who live.

24 "Surely no one would turn against the needy
   when they cry for help in their trouble.
25 Did I not weep for those in trouble?
   Was I not deeply grieved for the needy?
26 So I looked for good, but evil came instead.
   I waited for the light, but darkness fell.
27 My heart is troubled and restless.
   Days of suffering torment me.
28 I walk in gloom, without sunlight.
   I stand in the public square and cry for help.
29 Instead, I am considered a brother to jackals
   and a companion to owls.
30 My skin has turned dark,
   and my bones burn with fever.

30:9
Job 12:4; 17:6
Ps 69:11-12

30:10
Num 12:14
Deut 25:9
Isa 50:6
Matt 26:67

30:11
Ruth 1:21
Ps 88:7

30:12
Ps 140:4-5
Isa 3:5

30:15
Ps 55:3-5
Hos 13:3

30:16
Pss 22:14; 42:4

30:19
Ps 69:2, 14

30:20
Job 19:7

30:21
Job 16:9, 14

30:22
Job 9:17; 10:3

30:23
Job 3:19; 9:22;
10:8

30:26
Job 3:25-26; 19:8
Jer 8:15

30:28
Pss 38:6; 42:9;
43:2

30:29
Mic 1:8

30:30
Ps 102:3

31 My harp plays sad music,
and my flute accompanies those who weep.

### Job's Final Protest of Innocence

# 31

1 "I made a covenant with my eyes
not to look with lust at a young woman.
2 For what has God above chosen for us?
What is our inheritance from the Almighty on high?

3 Isn't it calamity for the wicked
and misfortune for those who do evil?

4 Doesn't he see everything I do
and every step I take?

5 "Have I lied to anyone
or deceived anyone?

6 Let God weigh me on the scales of justice,
for he knows my integrity.

7 If I have strayed from his pathway,
or if my heart has lusted for what my eyes have seen,
or if I am guilty of any other sin,

8 then let someone else eat the crops I have planted.
Let all that I have planted be uprooted.

9 "If my heart has been seduced by a woman,
or if I have lusted for my neighbor's wife,

10 then let my wife belong to* another man;
let other men sleep with her.

11 For lust is a shameful sin,
a crime that should be punished.
12 It is a fire that burns all the way to hell.*
It would wipe out everything I own.

13 "If I have been unfair to my male or female servants
when they brought their complaints to me,
14 how could I face God?
What could I say when he questioned me?
15 For God created both me and my servants.
He created us both in the womb.

16 "Have I refused to help the poor,
or crushed the hopes of widows?

17 Have I been stingy with my food
and refused to share it with orphans?
18 No, from childhood I have cared for orphans like a father,
and all my life I have cared for widows.

19 Whenever I saw the homeless without clothes
and the needy with nothing to wear,
20 did they not praise me
for providing wool clothing to keep them warm?

21 "If I raised my hand against an orphan,
knowing the judges would take my side,

22 then let my shoulder be wrenched out of place!
Let my arm be torn from its socket!

23 That would be better than facing God's judgment.
For if the majesty of God opposes me, what hope is there?

**31:10** Hebrew *grind for.*   **31:12** Hebrew *to Abaddon.*

---

**31:1-4** Job had not only avoided committing the great sin of adultery; he had not even taken the first step toward that sin by looking at a woman with lust. Job said he was innocent of both outward and inward sins. In chapter 29, Job reviewed his good deeds. Here in chapter 31 he listed sins he had not committed—in his heart (31:1-12), against his neighbors (31:13-23), or against God (31:24-34).

24 "Have I put my trust in money
    or felt secure because of my gold?
25 Have I gloated about my wealth
    and all that I own?

26 "Have I looked at the sun shining in the skies,
    or the moon walking down its silver pathway,
27 and been secretly enticed in my heart
    to throw kisses at them in worship?
28 If so, I should be punished by the judges,
    for it would mean I had denied the God of heaven.

29 "Have I ever rejoiced when disaster struck my enemies,
    or become excited when harm came their way?
30 No, I have never sinned by cursing anyone
    or by asking for revenge.

31 "My servants have never said,
    'He let others go hungry.'
32 I have never turned away a stranger
    but have opened my doors to everyone.

33 "Have I tried to hide my sins like other people do,
    concealing my guilt in my heart?
34 Have I feared the crowd
    or the contempt of the masses,
    so that I kept quiet and stayed indoors?

35 "If only someone would listen to me!
    Look, I will sign my name to my defense.
Let the Almighty answer me.
    Let my accuser write out the charges against me.
36 I would face the accusation proudly.
    I would wear it like a crown.
37 For I would tell him exactly what I have done.
    I would come before him like a prince.

38 "If my land accuses me
    and all its furrows cry out together,
39 or if I have stolen its crops
    or murdered its owners,
40 then let thistles grow on that land instead of wheat,
    and weeds instead of barley."

Job's words are ended.

## C. A YOUNG MAN ANSWERS JOB (32:1—37:24)

Young Elihu rebukes the three friends for being unable to give Job a reasonable answer for why he was suffering. But he only gives a partial answer to Job's question by saying that people cannot understand all that God allows but must trust him. This was the best answer that a human could give, yet it was incomplete. Often the best human answers are incomplete because we do not have all the facts.

### Elihu Responds to Job's Friends

**32** Job's three friends refused to reply further to him because he kept insisting on his innocence.

#### Cross references (right margin)

**31:24** Job 22:23-25; Mark 10:23
**31:25** Ps 62:10
**31:30** Job 5:3
**31:31** Job 22:7
**31:34** Prov 29:25
**31:35** Job 19:7; 27:7; 30:20, 24, 28; 35:14; Ps 26:1
**31:37** Job 1:3; 29:25; 31:4
**31:38** Job 24:2, 6, 10-12
**31:40** Isa 5:6
**32:1** Job 10:7; 13:18; 31:6; 33:9

#### Study notes (bottom)

**31:24-28** Job affirmed that depending on wealth for happiness is idolatry and denies the God of heaven. We excuse our society's obsession with money and possessions as a necessary evil or "the way it works" in the modern world. But every society in every age has valued the power and prestige that money brings. True believers must purge themselves of the deep-seated desire for more power, prestige, and possessions. They must also not withhold their resources from neighbors near and far who have desperate physical needs.

**31:33, 34** Job declared that he did not try to hide his sin as people often do. The fear that our sins will be discovered leads us to patterns of deception. We cover up with lies so that we will appear good to others. But we cannot hide from God. Do you try to keep people from seeing the real you? When you acknowledge your sins, you free yourself to receive forgiveness and a new life.

**32:1** If Job was really a good man, his three friends would have to drop their theory that suffering is always God's punishment for evil actions. Instead of considering another viewpoint, however, they

32:2
Gen 22:21

2 Then Elihu son of Barakel the Buzite, of the clan of Ram, became angry. He was angry because Job refused to admit that he had sinned and that God was right in punishing him. 3 He was also angry with Job's three friends, for they made God* appear to be wrong by their inability to answer Job's arguments. 4 Elihu had waited for the others to speak to Job because they were older than he. 5 But when he saw that they had no further reply, he spoke out angrily. 6 Elihu son of Barakel the Buzite said,

32:6
Job 15:10

"I am young and you are old,
　so I held back from telling you what I think.
7 I thought, 'Those who are older should speak,
　for wisdom comes with age.'

32:8
Job 33:4; 38:36
Prov 2:6
1 Cor 2:11

8 But there is a spirit* within people,
　the breath of the Almighty within them,
　that makes them intelligent.
9 Sometimes the elders are not wise.
　Sometimes the aged do not understand justice.
10 So listen to me,
　and let me tell you what I think.

32:11
Prov 18:17

11 "I have waited all this time,
　listening very carefully to your arguments,
　listening to you grope for words.
12 I have listened,
　but not one of you has refuted Job
　or answered his arguments.

32:13
Jer 9:23

13 And don't tell me, 'He is too wise for us.
　Only God can convince him.'
14 If Job had been arguing with me,
　I would not answer with your kind of logic!
15 You sit there baffled,
　with nothing more to say.
16 Should I continue to wait, now that you are silent?
　Must I also remain silent?
17 No, I will say my piece.
　I will speak my mind.
18 For I am full of pent-up words,
　and the spirit within me urges me on.
19 I am like a cask of wine without a vent,
　like a new wineskin ready to burst!
20 I must speak to find relief,
　so let me give my answers.

32:21
Lev 19:15
Job 13:8, 10; 34:19

21 I won't play favorites
　or try to flatter anyone.

32:3 As in ancient Hebrew scribal tradition; the Masoretic Text reads *Job*. 32:8 Or *Spirit;* also in 32:18.

cut off the discussion. They were convinced that Job had some hidden fault or sin, so there was no point in talking if Job would not confess it. But Job knew he had lived uprightly before God and others (chapter 29) and had avoided wrong thoughts and actions (chapter 31). He wasn't about to invent a sin to satisfy his friends!

**32:2ff** When Eliphaz, Bildad, and Zophar had nothing more to say, Elihu became the fourth person to speak to Job. This was the first and only time he spoke. Apparently he was a bystander and much younger than the others (32:6, 7), but he introduced a new viewpoint. While Job's three friends said he was suffering from some past sins, Elihu said Job's suffering would not go away until he realized his *present* sin. He maintained that Job wasn't suffering because of sin; he was sinning because of suffering. Elihu pointed out that Job's attitude had become arrogant as he tried to defend his innocence. Elihu also said that suffering is not meant to punish us as much as it is meant to correct and restore us, to keep us on the right path.

There is much truth in Elihu's speech. He was urging Job to look at his suffering from a different perspective and with a greater purpose in mind. While his speech is on a higher spiritual plateau than the others, Elihu still wrongly assumed that a correct response to suffering always brings healing and restoration (33:23-30) and that suffering is always in some way connected to sin (34:11).

**32:7-9** "The breath of the Almighty within them, that makes them intelligent." It is not enough to recognize a great truth; it must be lived out each day. Elihu recognized the truth that God was the only source of real wisdom, but he did not use God's wisdom to help Job. While he recognized where wisdom came from, he did not seek to acquire it. Becoming wise is an ongoing, lifelong pursuit. Don't be content just to know about wisdom; make it part of your life.

22 For if I tried flattery,
    my Creator would soon destroy me.

*Elihu Presents His Case against Job*

# 33

¹ "Listen to my words, Job;
    pay attention to what I have to say.
² Now that I have begun to speak,
    let me continue.
³ I speak with all sincerity;
    I speak the truth.
⁴ For the Spirit of God has made me,
    and the breath of the Almighty gives me life.
⁵ Answer me, if you can;
    make your case and take your stand.
⁶ Look, you and I both belong to God.
    I, too, was formed from clay.
⁷ So you don't need to be afraid of me.
    I won't come down hard on you.

⁸ "You have spoken in my hearing,
    and I have heard your very words.
⁹ You said, 'I am pure; I am without sin;
    I am innocent; I have no guilt.
¹⁰ God is picking a quarrel with me,
    and he considers me his enemy.
¹¹ He puts my feet in the stocks
    and watches my every move.'

¹² "But you are wrong, and I will show you why.
    For God is greater than any human being.
¹³ So why are you bringing a charge against him?
    Why say he does not respond to people's complaints?
¹⁴ For God speaks again and again,
    though people do not recognize it.
¹⁵ He speaks in dreams, in visions of the night,
    when deep sleep falls on people
    as they lie in their beds.
¹⁶ He whispers in their ears
    and terrifies them with warnings.
¹⁷ He makes them turn from doing wrong;
    he keeps them from pride.
¹⁸ He protects them from the grave,
    from crossing over the river of death.

¹⁹ "Or God disciplines people with pain on their sickbeds,
    with ceaseless aching in their bones.
²⁰ They lose their appetite
    for even the most delicious food.
²¹ Their flesh wastes away,
    and their bones stick out.

**33:3**
Job 6:28; 27:4;
36:4
**33:4**
Job 10:3; 27:3;
32:8
**33:5**
Job 33:32
**33:7**
Job 13:22
**33:10**
Job 13:23-24
**33:11**
Job 13:27
**33:13**
Job 40:2
Isa 45:9
**33:14**
Job 40:5
Ps 62:11
**33:16**
Job 36:10, 15
**33:18**
Job 33:24, 28, 30
**33:20**
Job 3:24; 6:7
Ps 107:18
**33:21**
Job 16:8; 19:20
Ps 22:17

---

**33:13** Being informed brings a sense of security. It's natural to want to know what's happening in our lives. Job wanted to know what was going on, why he was suffering. In previous chapters, we sense his frustration. Elihu claimed to have the answer for Job's biggest question, "Why doesn't God tell me what is happening?" Elihu told Job that God was trying to answer him, but he was not listening. Elihu misjudged God on this point. If God were to answer all our questions, we would not be adequately tested. What if God had said, "Job, Satan's going to test you and afflict you, but in the end you'll be healed and get everything back"? Job's greatest test was not the pain but that he did not know *why* he was suffering. Our greatest test may be that we must trust God's goodness even though we don't understand why our lives are going a certain way. We must learn to trust in *God*, who is good, and not in the goodness of life.

**33:14-24** Elihu's point was that God had spoken again and again. He spoke in dreams and visions (33:15-18), through suffering (33:19-22), and by mediating angels (33:23, 24). Job already knew that. Elihu accused Job of not listening to God, which was not true.

22 They are at death's door;
the angels of death wait for them.

23 "But if an angel from heaven appears—
a special messenger to intercede for a person
and declare that he is upright—

**33:24**
Isa 38:17

24 he will be gracious and say,
'Rescue him from the grave,
for I have found a ransom for his life.'

25 Then his body will become as healthy as a child's,
firm and youthful again.

26 When he prays to God,
he will be accepted.
And God will receive him with joy
and restore him to good standing.

**33:27**
2 Sam 12:13
Luke 15:21
Rom 6:21

27 He will declare to his friends,
'I sinned and twisted the truth,
but it was not worth it.*

**33:28**
Job 22:28

28 God rescued me from the grave,
and now my life is filled with light.'

**33:29**
Eph 1:11
Phil 2:13

29 "Yes, God does these things
again and again for people.

30 He rescues them from the grave
so they may enjoy the light of life.

31 Mark this well, Job. Listen to me,
for I have more to say.

32 But if you have anything to say, go ahead.
Speak, for I am anxious to see you justified.

**33:33**
Ps 34:11

33 But if not, then listen to me.
Keep silent and I will teach you wisdom!"

### Elihu Accuses Job of Arrogance

**34** Then Elihu said:

2 "Listen to me, you wise men.
Pay attention, you who have knowledge.

**34:3**
Job 12:11

3 Job said, 'The ear tests the words it hears
just as the mouth distinguishes between foods.'

4 So let us discern for ourselves what is right;
let us learn together what is good.

**34:5**
Job 27:2; 33:9

5 For Job also said, 'I am innocent,
but God has taken away my rights.

**33:27** Greek version reads *but he [God] did not punish me as my sin deserved.*

---

**HOW SUFFERING AFFECTS US**

*Suffering is helpful when:*

We turn to God for understanding, endurance, and deliverance

We ask important questions we might not take time to think about in our normal routine

We are prepared by it to identify with and comfort others who suffer

We are open to being helped by others who are obeying God

We are ready to learn from a trustworthy God

We realize we can identify with what Christ suffered on the cross for us

We are sensitized to the amount of suffering in the world

*Suffering is harmful when:*

We become hardened and reject God

We refuse to ask any questions and miss any lessons that might be good for us

We allow it to make us self-centered and selfish

We withdraw from the help others can give

We reject the fact that God can bring good out of calamity

We accuse God of being unjust and perhaps lead others to reject him

We refuse to be open to any changes in our lives

6 I am innocent, but they call me a liar.
My suffering is incurable, though I have not sinned.'

7 "Tell me, has there ever been a man like Job,
with his thirst for irreverent talk?
8 He chooses evil people as companions.
He spends his time with wicked men.
9 He has even said, 'Why waste time
trying to please God?'

**34:7**
Job 15:16

**34:9**
Job 21:15; 35:3

10 "Listen to me, you who have understanding.
Everyone knows that God doesn't sin!
The Almighty can do no wrong.
11 He repays people according to their deeds.
He treats people as they deserve.
12 Truly, God will not do wrong.
The Almighty will not twist justice.
13 Did someone else put the world in his care?
Who set the whole world in place?
14 If God were to take back his spirit
and withdraw his breath,
15 all life would cease,
and humanity would turn again to dust.

**34:11**
Ps 62:12
Prov 24:12
Matt 16:27
Rom 2:6
2 Cor 5:10
Rev 22:12

**34:15**
Gen 3:19; 7:21
Job 9:22; 10:9

16 "Now listen to me if you are wise.
Pay attention to what I say.
17 Could God govern if he hated justice?
Are you going to condemn the almighty judge?
18 For he says to kings, 'You are wicked,'
and to nobles, 'You are unjust.'
19 He doesn't care how great a person may be,
and he pays no more attention to the rich than to the poor.
He made them all.
20 In a moment they die.
In the middle of the night they pass away;
the mighty are removed without human hand.

**34:19**
Deut 10:17
Acts 10:34
Rom 2:11
Gal 2:6
Eph 6:9
1 Pet 1:17

**34:20**
Exod 12:29

21 "For God watches how people live;
he sees everything they do.
22 No darkness is thick enough
to hide the wicked from his eyes.
23 We don't set the time
when we will come before God in judgment.
24 He brings the mighty to ruin without asking anyone,
and he sets up others in their place.
25 He knows what they do,
and in the night he overturns and destroys them.
26 He strikes them down because they are wicked,
doing it openly for all to see.
27 For they turned away from following him.
They have no respect for any of his ways.
28 They cause the poor to cry out, catching God's attention.
He hears the cries of the needy.
29 But if he chooses to remain quiet,
who can criticize him?

**34:21**
Prov 5:21; 15:3

**34:22**
Ps 139:11-12
Amos 9:2-3

**34:27**
1 Sam 15:11

**34:28**
Exod 22:23

**34:29**
Job 5:15

---

**34:10-15** God doesn't sin and is never unjust, Elihu claimed. Throughout this book, Eliphaz, Bildad, Zophar, and Elihu all have elements of truth in their speeches. Unfortunately, the nuggets of truth are buried under layers of false assumptions and conclusions. Although we might have a wealth of Bible knowledge and life experiences, we must make sure our conclusions are consistent with all of God's Word, not just parts of it.

When he hides his face, no one can find him,
whether an individual or a nation.

**34:30**
Job 34:17

30 He prevents the godless from ruling
so they cannot be a snare to the people.

31 "Why don't people say to God, 'I have sinned,
but I will sin no more'?

32 Or 'I don't know what evil I have done—tell me.
If I have done wrong, I will stop at once'?

33 "Must God tailor his justice to your demands?
But you have rejected him!
The choice is yours, not mine.
Go ahead, share your wisdom with us.

34 After all, bright people will tell me,
and wise people will hear me say,

**34:35**
Job 35:16

35 'Job speaks out of ignorance;
his words lack insight.'

**34:36**
Pss 17:3; 26:2

36 Job, you deserve the maximum penalty
for the wicked way you have talked.

37 For you have added rebellion to your sin;
you show no respect,
and you speak many angry words against God."

## Elihu Reminds Job of God's Justice

**35** Then Elihu said:

2 "Do you think it is right for you to claim,
'I am righteous before God'?

3 For you also ask, 'What's in it for me?
What's the use of living a righteous life?'

4 "I will answer you
and all your friends, too.

5 Look up into the sky,
and see the clouds high above you.

**35:6**
Prov 8:36
Jer 7:19

6 If you sin, how does that affect God?
Even if you sin again and again,
what effect will it have on him?

**35:7**
Prov 9:12
Luke 17:10
Rom 11:35

7 If you are good, is this some great gift to him?
What could you possibly give him?

8 No, your sins affect only people like yourself,
and your good deeds also affect only humans.

**35:9**
Exod 2:23

9 "People cry out when they are oppressed.
They groan beneath the power of the mighty.

**35:10**
Pss 42:8; 149:5
Acts 16:25

10 Yet they don't ask, 'Where is God my Creator,
the one who gives songs in the night?

**35:11**
Ps 94:12
Jer 32:33

11 Where is the one who makes us smarter than the animals
and wiser than the birds of the sky?'

**35:12**
Prov 1:28

12 And when they cry out, God does not answer
because of their pride.

**35:13**
Isa 1:15
Jas 4:3

13 But it is wrong to say God doesn't listen,
to say the Almighty isn't concerned.

**35:14**
Ps 37:5-6

14 You say you can't see him,
but he will bring justice if you will only wait.*

**35:13-14** These verses can also be translated as follows: ¹³Indeed, God doesn't listen to their empty plea; / the
Almighty is not concerned. / ¹⁴How much less will he listen when you say you don't see him, / and that your case
is before him and you're waiting for justice.

---

**35:1ff** Sometimes we wonder if being faithful to our convictions really does any good at all. Elihu spoke to this very point. His conclusion was that God is still concerned even though he doesn't intervene immediately in every situation. In the broad scope of time, God executes justice. We have his promise on that. Don't lose hope. Wait upon God. He notices your right living and your faith.

15 You say he does not respond to sinners with anger
   and is not greatly concerned about wickedness.*
16 But you are talking nonsense, Job.
   You have spoken like a fool."

# 36 Elihu continued speaking:

2 "Let me go on, and I will show you the truth.
   For I have not finished defending God!
3 I will present profound arguments
   for the righteousness of my Creator.
4 I am telling you nothing but the truth,
   for I am a man of great knowledge.

5 "God is mighty, but he does not despise anyone!
   He is mighty in both power and understanding.
6 He does not let the wicked live
   but gives justice to the afflicted.
7 He never takes his eyes off the innocent,
   but he sets them on thrones with kings
   and exalts them forever.
8 If they are bound in chains
   and caught up in a web of trouble,
9 he shows them the reason.
   He shows them their sins of pride.
10 He gets their attention
   and commands that they turn from evil.

11 "If they listen and obey God,
   they will be blessed with prosperity throughout their lives.
   All their years will be pleasant.
12 But if they refuse to listen to him,
   they will be killed by the sword*
   and die from lack of understanding.
13 For the godless are full of resentment.
   Even when he punishes them,
   they refuse to cry out to him for help.
14 They die when they are young,
   after wasting their lives in immoral living.
15 But by means of their suffering, he rescues those who suffer.
   For he gets their attention through adversity.

16 "God is leading you away from danger, Job,
   to a place free from distress.
   He is setting your table with the best food.
17 But you are obsessed with whether the godless will be judged.
   Don't worry, judgment and justice will be upheld.
18 But watch out, or you may be seduced by wealth.*
   Don't let yourself be bribed into sin.
19 Could all your wealth*
   or all your mighty efforts
   keep you from distress?
20 Do not long for the cover of night,
   for that is when people will be destroyed.*
21 Be on guard! Turn back from evil,
   for God sent this suffering
   to keep you from a life of evil.

*Elihu Reminds Job of God's Power*
22 "Look, God is all-powerful.
   Who is a teacher like him?

36:3
Job 8:3; 37:23

36:5
Pss 22:24; 69:33;
102:17

36:6
Job 5:15; 8:22;
34:26

36:7
Pss 33:18; 34:15;
113:8

36:9
Job 15:25

36:10
2 Kgs 17:13
Job 33:16; 36:21
Jon 3:8

36:12
Job 4:21; 15:22

36:15
Job 36:10

36:17
Job 22:5, 10-11;
33:24; 34:33
Jon 4:4, 9

36:20
Job 34:20, 25

36:21
Ps 66:18

35:15 As in Greek and Latin versions; the meaning of this Hebrew word is uncertain.   36:12 Or *they will cross the river* [of death].   36:18 Or *But don't let your anger lead you to mockery.*   36:19 Or *Could all your cries for help.*
36:16-20 The meaning of the Hebrew in this passage is uncertain.

23 No one can tell him what to do,
   or say to him, 'You have done wrong.'
24 Instead, glorify his mighty works,
   singing songs of praise.
25 Everyone has seen these things,
   though only from a distance.

**36:26**
Pss 90:2;
102:24, 27
**36:27**
Job 5:10; 37:6, 11
Ps 147:8

26 "Look, God is greater than we can understand.
   His years cannot be counted.
27 He draws up the water vapor
   and then distills it into rain.
28 The rain pours down from the clouds,
   and everyone benefits.

**36:29**
Job 26:14; 37:11

29 Who can understand the spreading of the clouds
   and the thunder that rolls forth from heaven?
30 See how he spreads the lightning around him
   and how it lights up the depths of the sea.

**36:31**
Job 37:13
Acts 14:17
**36:32**
Job 37:11-12, 15

31 By these mighty acts he nourishes* the people,
   giving them food in abundance.
32 He fills his hands with lightning bolts
   and hurls each at its target.
33 The thunder announces his presence;
   the storm announces his indignant anger.*

**37** 1 "My heart pounds as I think of this.
        It trembles within me.
2 Listen carefully to the thunder of God's voice
   as it rolls from his mouth.

36:31 Or *he governs.*   36:33 Or *even the cattle know when a storm is coming.* The meaning of the Hebrew is uncertain.

---

| **GOD SPEAKS** | *Whom He Spoke To* | *What He Said* | *Reference* |
|---|---|---|---|
| On various occasions in the Old Testament, God chose to communicate audibly with individuals. God will always find a way to make contact with those who want to know him. Some of those occasions are listed here. | Adam and Eve | Confronted them about sin | Genesis 3:8-13 |
| | Noah | Gave him directions about building the boat | Genesis 6:13-22; 7:1; 8:15-17 |
| | Abraham | Commanded him to follow God's leading and promised to bless him | Genesis 12:1-9 |
| | | Tested his obedience by commanding him to sacrifice his son | Genesis 22:1-14 |
| | Jacob | Permitted him to go to Egypt | Genesis 46:1-4 |
| | Moses | Sent him to lead the people out of Egypt | Exodus 3:1-10 |
| | | Gave him the Ten Commandments | Exodus 19:1–20:20 |
| | Moses, Aaron, Miriam | Pronounced judgment on a family conflict | Numbers 12:1-15 |
| | Joshua | Promised to be with him as he was with Moses | Joshua 1:1-9 |
| | Samuel | Chose him to be his spokesman | 1 Samuel 3:1-18 |
| | Isaiah | Sent him to the people with his message | Isaiah 6:1-13 |
| | Jeremiah | Encouraged him to be his prophet | Jeremiah 1:4-10 |
| | Ezekiel | Sent him to Israel to warn them of coming judgment | Ezekiel 2:1-8 |

---

**36:26** One theme in the poetic literature of the Bible is that God is incomprehensible; we cannot know him completely. We can have some knowledge about him, for the Bible is full of details about who God is, how we can know him, and how we can have an eternal relationship with him. But we can never know enough to answer all of life's questions (Ecclesiastes 3:11), to predict our own future, or to manipulate God for our own ends. Life always creates more questions than we have answers, and we must constantly go to God for fresh insights into life's dilemmas. (See 37:19-24.)

**37:2** Nothing can compare to God. His power and presence are awesome, and when he speaks, we must listen. Too often we presume to speak for God (as did Job's friends), to put words in his mouth, to take him for granted, or to interpret his silence to mean that he is absent or unconcerned. But God cares. He is in control, and he will speak. Be ready to hear his message—in the Bible, in your life through the Holy Spirit, and through circumstances and relationships.

3 It rolls across the heavens,
    and his lightning flashes in every direction.
4 Then comes the roaring of the thunder—
    the tremendous voice of his majesty.
    He does not restrain it when he speaks.
5 God's voice is glorious in the thunder.
    We can't even imagine the greatness of his power.

**37:5**
Job 5:9; 26:14
Rom 11:33

6 "He directs the snow to fall on the earth
    and tells the rain to pour down.
7 Then everyone stops working
    so they can watch his power.
8 The wild animals take cover
    and stay inside their dens.
9 The stormy wind comes from its chamber,
    and the driving winds bring the cold.
10 God's breath sends the ice,
    freezing wide expanses of water.
11 He loads the clouds with moisture,
    and they flash with his lightning.
12 The clouds churn about at his direction.
    They do whatever he commands throughout the earth.
13 He makes these things happen either to punish people
    or to show his unfailing love.

**37:6**
Job 36:27; 38:22

**37:8**
Job 38:40
Ps 104:21-22

**37:9**
Job 9:9

**37:10**
Job 38:29
Ps 147:17

**37:11**
Job 36:27, 29;
37:15

**37:12**
Ps 148:8

**37:13**
Exod 9:18-19
1 Kgs 18:45

14 "Pay attention to this, Job.
    Stop and consider the wonderful miracles of God!
15 Do you know how God controls the storm
    and causes the lightning to flash from his clouds?
16 Do you understand how he moves the clouds
    with wonderful perfection and skill?
17 When you are sweltering in your clothes
    and the south wind dies down and everything is still,
18 he makes the skies reflect the heat like a bronze mirror.
    Can you do that?

**37:18**
Ps 104:2
Isa 44:24; 45:12
Jer 10:12

19 "So teach the rest of us what to say to God.
    We are too ignorant to make our own arguments.
20 Should God be notified that I want to speak?
    Can people even speak when they are confused?*
21 We cannot look at the sun,
    for it shines brightly in the sky
    when the wind clears away the clouds.
22 So also, golden splendor comes from the mountain of God.*
    He is clothed in dazzling splendor.
23 We cannot imagine the power of the Almighty;
    but even though he is just and righteous,
    he does not destroy us.
24 No wonder people everywhere fear him.
    All who are wise show him reverence."

**37:23**
Isa 63:9

**37:24**
Job 5:13
Matt 10:28; 11:25
1 Cor 1:26

**37:20** Or *speak without being swallowed up?*   **37:22** Or *from the north; or from the abode.*

---

**37:21-24** Elihu concluded his speech with the tremendous truth that faith in God is far more important than Job's desire for an explanation for his suffering. He came so close to helping Job but then went down the wrong path. Significantly, it is here that God himself breaks into the discussion to draw the right conclusions from this important truth (38:1ff).

**37:23** Elihu stressed God's sovereignty over all of nature as a reminder of his sovereignty over our lives. God is in control—he directs, preserves, and maintains his created order. Although we can't see it, God is divinely governing the moral and political affairs of people as well. By spending time observing the majestic and intricate parts of God's creation, we can be reminded of his power in every aspect of our lives.

## D. GOD ANSWERS JOB (38:1—41:34)

Instead of answering Job's question directly, God asks Job a series of questions which no human could possibly answer. Job responds by recognizing that God's ways are best. During difficult times, we, too, must humbly remember our position before the eternal, holy, incomprehensible God.

### The LORD Challenges Job

**38** Then the LORD answered Job from the whirlwind:

2 "Who is this that questions my wisdom
    with such ignorant words?
3 Brace yourself like a man,
    because I have some questions for you,
    and you must answer them.

4 "Where were you when I laid the foundations of the earth?
    Tell me, if you know so much.
5 Who determined its dimensions
    and stretched out the surveying line?
6 What supports its foundations,
    and who laid its cornerstone
7 as the morning stars sang together
    and all the angels* shouted for joy?

8 "Who kept the sea inside its boundaries
    as it burst from the womb,
9 and as I clothed it with clouds
    and wrapped it in thick darkness?
10 For I locked it behind barred gates,
    limiting its shores.
11 I said, 'This far and no farther will you come.
    Here your proud waves must stop!'

12 "Have you ever commanded the morning to appear
    and caused the dawn to rise in the east?
13 Have you made daylight spread to the ends of the earth,
    to bring an end to the night's wickedness?
14 As the light approaches,
    the earth takes shape like clay pressed beneath a seal;
    it is robed in brilliant colors.*

**38:7** Hebrew *the sons of God.*   **38:14** Or *its features stand out like folds in a robe.*

**38:2**
Job 35:16; 42:3

**38:3**
Job 40:7; 42:4

**38:4**
Job 15:7
Ps 104:5
Prov 8:29; 30:4

**38:7**
Job 1:6

**38:8**
Gen 1:9

**38:10**
Gen 1:9
Ps 33:7
Prov 8:29
Jer 5:22

---

**GOD'S JUSTICE**

| Wrong View | Correct View |
| --- | --- |
| LAW OF FAIRNESS | GOD |
| GOD | JUSTICE |

There is a law of fairness or justice that is higher and more absolute than God. It is binding even for God. God must act in response to that law in order to be fair. Our response is to appeal to that law.

God himself is the standard of justice. He uses his power according to his own moral perfection. Thus, whatever he does is fair, even if we don't understand it. Our response is to appeal directly to him.

---

**38:1ff** Out of a whirlwind, God spoke. Surprisingly, he didn't answer any of Job's questions; Job's questions were not at the heart of the issue. Instead, God used Job's ignorance of the earth's natural order to reveal his ignorance of God's moral order. If Job did not understand the workings of God's physical creation, how could he possibly understand God's mind and character? There is no standard or criterion higher than God himself by which to judge. God himself is the standard. Our only option is to submit to his authority and rest in his care.

15 The light disturbs the wicked
   and stops the arm that is raised in violence.

16 "Have you explored the springs from which the seas come?
   Have you explored their depths?
17 Do you know where the gates of death are located?
   Have you seen the gates of utter gloom?
18 Do you realize the extent of the earth?
   Tell me about it if you know!

19 "Where does light come from,
   and where does darkness go?
20 Can you take each to its home?
   Do you know how to get there?
21 But of course you know all this!
   For you were born before it was all created,
   and you are so very experienced!

22 "Have you visited the storehouses of the snow
   or seen the storehouses of hail?
23 (I have reserved them as weapons for the time of trouble,
   for the day of battle and war.)
24 Where is the path to the source of light?
   Where is the home of the east wind?

25 "Who created a channel for the torrents of rain?
   Who laid out the path for the lightning?
26 Who makes the rain fall on barren land,
   in a desert where no one lives?
27 Who sends rain to satisfy the parched ground
   and make the tender grass spring up?

28 "Does the rain have a father?
   Who gives birth to the dew?
29 Who is the mother of the ice?
   Who gives birth to the frost from the heavens?
30 For the water turns to ice as hard as rock,
   and the surface of the water freezes.

31 "Can you direct the movement of the stars—
   binding the cluster of the Pleiades
   or loosening the cords of Orion?
32 Can you direct the sequence of the seasons
   or guide the Bear with her cubs across the heavens?
33 Do you know the laws of the universe?
   Can you use them to regulate the earth?

34 "Can you shout to the clouds
   and make it rain?
35 Can you make lightning appear
   and cause it to strike as you direct?
36 Who gives intuition to the heart
   and instinct to the mind?

**38:15** Pss 10:15; 37:17
**38:16** Gen 7:11; 8:2 Prov 8:24, 28
**38:17** Job 28:24; 34:33 Ps 9:13
**38:20** Job 26:10
**38:21** Job 15:7
**38:22** Exod 9:18 Isa 30:30 Ezek 13:11, 13 Rev 16:21
**38:24** Job 26:10
**38:26** Job 36:27
**38:27** Ps 104:13-14
**38:29** Job 37:10 Pss 104:13-14; 147:16-17
**38:31** Job 9:9
**38:36** Job 32:8 Ps 51:6 Eccl 2:26

**38:22, 23** God said he was reserving the storehouses of the snow and hail for times of trouble. God used hail to help Joshua and the Israelites win a battle (Joshua 10:11). Just as armies keep weapons in the armory, God has all the forces of nature in his control. Sometimes he uses them to confound those opposed to him or his people. Job couldn't even begin to know all of God's resources.

**38:22-35** God stated that he has all the forces of nature at his command and that he can unleash or restrain them at will. No one completely understands such common occurrences as rain or snow, and no one can command them—only God who created them has that power. God's point was that if Job could not explain such common events in nature, how could he possibly explain or question God? And if nature is beyond our grasp, God's moral purposes may not be what we imagine either.

**38:31, 32** These are star constellations, and they are all under God's control.

37 Who is wise enough to count all the clouds?
   Who can tilt the water jars of heaven
38 when the parched ground is dry
   and the soil has hardened into clods?

38:39
Ps 104:21

39 "Can you stalk prey for a lioness
   and satisfy the young lions' appetites
40 as they lie in their dens
   or crouch in the thicket?

38:41
Ps 147:9
Luke 12:24

41 Who provides food for the ravens
   when their young cry out to God
   and wander about in hunger?

### The LORD's Challenge Continues

39:1
Deut 14:5
Ps 29:9

**39** 1 "Do you know when the wild goats give birth?
   Have you watched as deer are born in the wild?
2 Do you know how many months they carry their young?
   Are you aware of the time of their delivery?
3 They crouch down to give birth to their young
   and deliver their offspring.
4 Their young grow up in the open fields,
   then leave home and never return.

39:5
Job 6:5; 11:12;
24:5

5 "Who gives the wild donkey its freedom?
   Who untied its ropes?

39:6
Job 24:5
Jer 2:24

6 I have placed it in the wilderness;
   its home is the wasteland.
7 It hates the noise of the city
   and has no driver to shout at it.
8 The mountains are its pastureland,
   where it searches for every blade of grass.

39:9
Num 23:22
Deut 33:17
Ps 92:10

9 "Will the wild ox consent to being tamed?
   Will it spend the night in your stall?
10 Can you hitch a wild ox to a plow?
   Will it plow a field for you?
11 Given its strength, can you trust it?
   Can you leave and trust the ox to do your work?
12 Can you rely on it to bring home your grain
   and deliver it to your threshing floor?

13 "The ostrich flaps her wings grandly,
   but they are no match for the feathers of the stork.
14 She lays her eggs on top of the earth,
   letting them be warmed in the dust.
15 She doesn't worry that a foot might crush them
   or a wild animal might destroy them.

---

**FOUR VIEWS OF SUFFERING**

| | |
|---|---|
| Satan's view . . . . . . . . . . . . . . . . . . | People believe in God only when they are prospering and not suffering. This is wrong. |
| The view of Job's three friends . . . . . | Suffering is God's judgment for sin. This is not always true. |
| Elihu's view . . . . . . . . . . . . . . . . . . . | Suffering is God's way to teach, discipline, and refine. This is true, but an incomplete explanation. |
| God's view . . . . . . . . . . . . . . . . . . . . | Suffering causes us to trust God for who he is, not what he does. |

---

**39:1ff** God asked Job several questions about the animal kingdom in order to demonstrate how limited Job's knowledge really was. God was not seeking answers from Job. Instead, he was getting Job to recognize and submit to God's power and sovereignty. Only then could he hear what God was really saying to him.

¹⁶ She is harsh toward her young,
    as if they were not her own.
    She doesn't care if they die.
¹⁷ For God has deprived her of wisdom.
    He has given her no understanding.
¹⁸ But whenever she jumps up to run,
    she passes the swiftest horse with its rider.

¹⁹ "Have you given the horse its strength
    or clothed its neck with a flowing mane?
²⁰ Did you give it the ability to leap like a locust?
    Its majestic snorting is terrifying!
²¹ It paws the earth and rejoices in its strength
    when it charges out to battle.
²² It laughs at fear and is unafraid.
    It does not run from the sword.
²³ The arrows rattle against it,
    and the spear and javelin flash.
²⁴ It paws the ground fiercely
    and rushes forward into battle when the ram's horn blows.
²⁵ It snorts at the sound of the horn.
    It senses the battle in the distance.
    It quivers at the captain's commands and the noise of battle.

²⁶ "Is it your wisdom that makes the hawk soar
    and spread its wings toward the south?
²⁷ Is it at your command that the eagle rises
    to the heights to make its nest?
²⁸ It lives on the cliffs,
    making its home on a distant, rocky crag.
²⁹ From there it hunts its prey,
    keeping watch with piercing eyes.
³⁰ Its young gulp down blood.
    Where there's a carcass, there you'll find it."

**40** Then the LORD said to Job,

²"Do you still want to argue with the Almighty?
You are God's critic, but do you have the answers?"

### Job Responds to the LORD
³ Then Job replied to the LORD,

⁴ "I am nothing—how could I ever find the answers?
    I will cover my mouth with my hand.
⁵ I have said too much already.
    I have nothing more to say."

### The LORD Challenges Job Again
⁶Then the LORD answered Job from the whirlwind:

⁷ "Brace yourself like a man,
    because I have some questions for you,
    and you must answer them.

**Margin references:**
39:16 Lam 4:3
39:20 Jer 8:16; Joel 2:5
39:21 Jer 8:6
39:27 Jer 49:16; Obad 1:4
39:29 Job 9:26
39:30 Matt 24:28; Luke 17:37
40:2 Job 9:3; 10:2; 13:3; 23:4; 31:35; 33:13
40:4 Job 21:5; 29:9
40:5 Job 9:3, 15
40:6 Job 38:1
40:7 Job 38:3; 42:4

---

**40:2-5** How do you argue or criticize almighty God? Do you demand answers when things don't go your way, you lose a job, someone close to you is ill or dies, finances are tight, you fail, or unexpected changes occur? The next time you are tempted to complain to God, consider how much he loves you. And remember Job's reaction when he had his chance to speak. Are you worse off than Job or more righteous than he? Give God a chance to reveal his greater purposes for you, but remember that they may unfold over the course of your life and not at the moment you desire.

**40:4** Throughout his time of suffering, Job longed to have an opportunity to plead his innocence before God. Here God appeared to Job and gave him that opportunity. But Job decided to remain quiet because it was no longer necessary for him to speak. God had shown Job that, as a limited human being, he had neither the ability to judge the God who created the universe nor the right to ask why. God's actions do not depend on ours. He will do what he knows is best, regardless of what we think is fair. It is important to note, however, that God came to Job, demonstrating his love and care for him.

**40:8**
Job 10:3, 7; 13:18;
27:2, 6
Rom 3:4
**40:9**
Job 37:5
**40:10**
Pss 93:1; 104:1
**40:11**
Isa 2:12; 42:25
Dan 4:37
Nah 1:6, 8
**40:12**
Isa 13:11; 63:3
**40:13**
Isa 2:10-12

8 "Will you discredit my justice
    and condemn me just to prove you are right?
9 Are you as strong as God?
    Can you thunder with a voice like his?
10 All right, put on your glory and splendor,
    your honor and majesty.
11 Give vent to your anger.
    Let it overflow against the proud.
12 Humiliate the proud with a glance;
    walk on the wicked where they stand.
13 Bury them in the dust.
    Imprison them in the world of the dead.
14 Then even I would praise you,
    for your own strength would save you.

**40:15**
Job 40:19

15 "Take a look at Behemoth,*
    which I made, just as I made you.
    It eats grass like an ox.
16 See its powerful loins
    and the muscles of its belly.
17 Its tail is as strong as a cedar.
    The sinews of its thighs are knit tightly together.
18 Its bones are tubes of bronze.
    Its limbs are bars of iron.

**40:19**
Job 40:15; 41:33

19 It is a prime example of God's handiwork,
    and only its Creator can threaten it.
20 The mountains offer it their best food,
    where all the wild animals play.
21 It lies under the lotus plants,*
    hidden by the reeds in the marsh.
22 The lotus plants give it shade
    among the willows beside the stream.
23 It is not disturbed by the raging river,
    not concerned when the swelling Jordan rushes around it.
24 No one can catch it off guard
    or put a ring in its nose and lead it away.

### The LORD's Challenge Continues

**41:1**
Job 3:8
Pss 74:14; 104:26
Isa 27:1
**41:2**
2 Kgs 19:28
Isa 37:29

**41** 1*"Can you catch Leviathan* with a hook
    or put a noose around its jaw?
2 Can you tie it with a rope through the nose
    or pierce its jaw with a spike?
3 Will it beg you for mercy
    or implore you for pity?
4 Will it agree to work for you,
    to be your slave for life?

**40:15** The identification of Behemoth is disputed, ranging from an earthly creature to a mythical sea monster in ancient literature. **40:21** Or *bramble bushes;* also in 40:22. **41:1a** Verses 41:1-8 are numbered 40:25-32 in Hebrew text. **41:1b** The identification of Leviathan is disputed, ranging from an earthly creature to a mythical sea monster in ancient literature.

---

**JOB AND JESUS**
The book of Job is intimately tied to the New Testament because Job's questions and problems are answered perfectly in Jesus Christ.

| Subject/Reference in Job | How Jesus Is the Answer |
|---|---|
| Someone must help us approach God (9:32, 33) | 1 Timothy 2:5 |
| Is there life after death? (14:14) | John 11:25 |
| There is one in heaven working on our behalf (16:19) | Hebrews 9:24 |
| There is one who can save us from judgment (19:25) | Hebrews 7:24, 25 |
| What is important in life? (21:7-15) | Matthew 16:26; John 3:16 |
| Where do we find God? (23:3-5) | John 14:9 |

5 Can you make it a pet like a bird,
    or give it to your little girls to play with?
6 Will merchants try to buy it
    to sell it in their shops?
7 Will its hide be hurt by spears
    or its head by a harpoon?
8 If you lay a hand on it,
    you will certainly remember the battle that follows.
    You won't try that again!
9*No, it is useless to try to capture it.
    The hunter who attempts it will be knocked down.
10 And since no one dares to disturb it,
    who then can stand up to me?
11 Who has given me anything that I need to pay back?
    Everything under heaven is mine.

12 "I want to emphasize Leviathan's limbs
    and its enormous strength and graceful form.
13 Who can strip off its hide,
    and who can penetrate its double layer of armor?*
14 Who could pry open its jaws?
    For its teeth are terrible!
15 Its scales are like rows of shields
    tightly sealed together.
16 They are so close together
    that no air can get between them.
17 Each scale sticks tight to the next.
    They interlock and cannot be penetrated.

18 "When it sneezes, it flashes light!
    Its eyes are like the red of dawn.
19 Lightning leaps from its mouth;
    flames of fire flash out.
20 Smoke streams from its nostrils
    like steam from a pot heated over burning rushes.
21 Its breath would kindle coals,
    for flames shoot from its mouth.

22 "The tremendous strength in Leviathan's neck
    strikes terror wherever it goes.
23 Its flesh is hard and firm
    and cannot be penetrated.
24 Its heart is hard as rock,
    hard as a millstone.
25 When it rises, the mighty are afraid,
    gripped by terror.
26 No sword can stop it,
    no spear, dart, or javelin.
27 Iron is nothing but straw to that creature,
    and bronze is like rotten wood.
28 Arrows cannot make it flee.
    Stones shot from a sling are like bits of grass.
29 Clubs are like a blade of grass,
    and it laughs at the swish of javelins.
30 Its belly is covered with scales as sharp as glass.
    It plows up the ground as it drags through the mud.

**41:9** Verses 41:9-34 are numbered 41:1-26 in Hebrew text.    **41:13** As in Greek version; Hebrew reads *its bridle?*

**41:10**
Job 3:8

**41:11**
Exod 19:5
Deut 10:14
Pss 24:1; 50:12
Rom 11:35
1 Cor 10:26

**41:18**
Job 3:9

**41:9-11** It is foolish for people to think they can stand up against God when they are afraid to confront even a crocodile. How much more powerful is God!

³¹ "Leviathan makes the water boil with its commotion.
    It stirs the depths like a pot of ointment.
³² The water glistens in its wake,
    making the sea look white.
³³ Nothing on earth is its equal,
    no other creature so fearless.
³⁴ Of all the creatures, it is the proudest.
    It is the king of beasts."

**41:33**
Job 40:19
**41:34**
Job 28:8

## E. JOB IS RESTORED (42:1-17)

In response to God's speech, Job humbles himself. God rebukes his three friends for adding to Job's suffering by their false assumptions and critical attitudes. Job's material possessions and family are restored, and he receives even greater blessings than he had before. Those who persist in trusting God will be rewarded.

### Job Responds to the LORD

**42** Then Job replied to the LORD:

² "I know that you can do anything,
    and no one can stop you.
³ You asked, 'Who is this that questions my wisdom with such ignorance?'
    It is I—and I was talking about things I knew nothing about,
    things far too wonderful for me.
⁴ You said, 'Listen and I will speak!
    I have some questions for you,
    and you must answer them.'
⁵ I had only heard about you before,
    but now I have seen you with my own eyes.
⁶ I take back everything I said,
    and I sit in dust and ashes to show my repentance."

**42:2**
Gen 18:14
Matt 19:26
**42:3**
Job 38:2
Pss 40:5; 131:1;
139:6
**42:4**
Job 38:3; 40:7

**42:5**
Job 26:14
Isa 6:5

---

**WHEN WE SUFFER**
Here are six questions to ask ourselves when we suffer, and what to do if the answer is yes.

| *Questions* | *Our Response* |
|---|---|
| Am I being punished by God for sin? | Confess known sin. |
| Is Satan attacking me as I try to survive as a Christian? | Call on God for strength. |
| Am I being prepared for a special service, learning to be compassionate to those who suffer? | Resist self-pity. Ask God to open up doors of opportunity and help you discover others who suffer as you do. |
| Am I specifically selected for testing, like Job? | Accept help from the body of believers. Trust God to work his purpose through you. |
| Is my suffering a result of natural consequences for which I am not directly responsible? | Recognize that in a sinful world, both good and evil people will suffer. But the good person has a promise from God that his or her suffering will one day come to an end. |
| Is my suffering due to some unknown reason? | Don't draw inward from the pain. Proclaim your faith in God, know that he cares, and wait patiently for his aid. |

---

**42:1ff** Throughout the book, Job's friends had asked him to admit his sin and ask for forgiveness, and eventually Job did indeed repent. Ironically, Job's repentance was not the kind called for by his friends. He asked for forgiveness, not for committing secret sins, but for questioning God's sovereignty and justice. Job repented of his attitude and acknowledged God's great power and perfect justice. We sin when we angrily ask, "If God is in control, how could he let this happen?" Because we are locked into time, unable to see beyond today, we cannot know the reasons for everything that happens. Thus, we must often choose between doubt and trust. Will you trust God with your unanswered questions?

**42:2-4** Job was quoting the Lord's earlier questions to him (38:2, 3). He openly and honestly faced God and admitted that he was the one who had been foolish. Are you using what you can't understand as an excuse for your lack of trust? Admit to God that you don't even have enough faith to trust him. True faith begins in such humility.

## Conclusion: The LORD Blesses Job

7After the LORD had finished speaking to Job, he said to Eliphaz the Temanite: "I am angry with you and your two friends, for you have not spoken accurately about me, as my servant Job has. 8So take seven bulls and seven rams and go to my servant Job and offer a burnt offering for yourselves. My servant Job will pray for you, and I will accept his prayer on your behalf. I will not treat you as you deserve, for you have not spoken accurately about me, as my servant Job has." 9So Eliphaz the Temanite, Bildad the Shuhite, and Zophar the Naamathite did as the LORD commanded them, and the LORD accepted Job's prayer.

10When Job prayed for his friends, the LORD restored his fortunes. In fact, the LORD gave him twice as much as before! 11Then all his brothers, sisters, and former friends came and feasted with him in his home. And they consoled him and comforted him because of all the trials the LORD had brought against him. And each of them brought him a gift of money* and a gold ring.

12So the LORD blessed Job in the second half of his life even more than in the beginning. For now he had 14,000 sheep, 6,000 camels, 1,000 teams of oxen, and 1,000 female donkeys. 13He also gave Job seven more sons and three more daughters. 14He named his first daughter Jemimah, the second Keziah, and the third Keren-happuch. 15In all the land no women were as lovely as the daughters of Job. And their father put them into his will along with their brothers.

16Job lived 140 years after that, living to see four generations of his children and grandchildren. 17Then he died, an old man who had lived a long, full life.

42:11 Hebrew a kesitah; the value or weight of the kesitah is no longer known.

**42:7**
Job 40:3-5; 42:1-6
**42:8**
Job 1:5; 22:30
Jas 5:16
**42:10**
Pss 14:7; 85:1-3;
126:1-6
**42:11**
Job 2:11; 19:13
**42:12**
Job 1:3, 10; 8:7
1 Tim 6:17
**42:17**
Gen 15:15; 25:8

---

**42:7, 8** God made it clear that Job's friends were wrong. The fact that God did not mention any specific sins shows that God confirmed Job's claim to have led a devout and obedient life. Job's friends had made the error of assuming that Job's suffering was caused by some great sin. They were judging Job without knowing what God was doing. We must be careful to avoid making judgments about a person because God may be working in ways we know nothing about.

**42:8-10** After receiving much criticism, Job was still able to pray for his three friends. It is difficult to forgive someone who has accused us of wrongdoing, but Job did. Are you praying for those who have hurt you? Can you forgive them? Follow the actions of Job and pray for those who have wronged you.

**42:10, 11** Would the message of the book of Job change if God had not restored to Job his former blessings? No. God is still sovereign. Jesus said that anyone who gives up something for the Kingdom of God will be repaid (Luke 18:29, 30). Our restoration may or may not be the same kind as Job's, which was both spiritual and material. Our complete restoration may not be in this life—but it will happen. God loves us, and he is just. He not only will restore whatever we have lost unjustly, but he also will give us more than we can imagine as we live with him in eternity. Cling tightly to your faith through all your trials, and you, too, will be rewarded by God—if not now, in the life to come.

**42:17** The main question in the book of Job is timely: Why do believers experience troubles and suffering? Through a long

debate, Job's supposedly wise friends were unable to answer this question. Job's friends made a serious error for which God rebuked them. They assumed that trouble comes only because people sin. People make the same mistake today when they assert that sickness or lack of material blessing is a sign of unconfessed sin or lack of faith. Though normally (but not always) following God leads to a happier life, and rebelling against God normally (but not always) leads to an unhappy life, God is in control. In our world invaded by sin, calamity and suffering come to good and bad alike.

This does not mean that God is indifferent, uncaring, unjust, or powerless to protect us. Bad things happen because we live in a fallen world, where both believers and unbelievers are hit with the tragic consequences of sin. God allows evil for a time although he turns it around for our good (Romans 8:28). We may have no answers as to why God allows evil, but we can be sure he is all-powerful and knows what he is doing. The next time you face trials and dilemmas, see them as opportunities to turn to God for strength. You will find a God who only desires to show his love and compassion to you. If you can trust him in pain, confusion, and loneliness, you will win the victory and eliminate doubt, one of Satan's greatest footholds in your life. Make God your foundation. You can never be separated from his love.

# PSALMS

"HI, how are you?" "Fine." Not exactly an "in-depth" discussion, this brief interchange is normal as friends and acquaintances pass and briefly touch each other with a cliché or two. Actually, clichés are a way of life, saturating sentences and permeating paragraphs. But if this is the essence of our communication, our relationships will stall on a superficial plateau. Facts and opinions also fill our verbiage. These words go deeper, but the true person still lies hidden beneath them. In reality, only when honest feelings and emotions are shared can real people be known, loved, and helped.

Often, patterns of superficial communication spill over into our talks with God. We easily slide through well-worn lines recited for decades, or we quickly toss a cliché or two at God and call it prayer. Certainly God hears and understands these feeble attempts, but by limiting the depth of our communication, we become shallow in our relationship with him. But God knows us, and he wants to have genuine communication with us.

At the center of the Bible is the book of Psalms. This great collection of songs and prayers expresses the heart and soul of humanity. In them we find the whole range of human experiences expressed. This book holds no clichés. Instead, David and the other writers honestly poured out their true feelings, reflecting a dynamic, powerful, and life-changing friendship with God. The psalmists confess their sins, express their doubts and fears, ask God for help in times of trouble, and praise and worship him.

As you read the book of Psalms, you will hear believers crying out to God from the depths of despair, and you will hear them singing to him in the heights of celebration. But whether the psalm writers are despairing or rejoicing, you will always hear them sharing honest feelings with their God. Because of the honesty expressed by these writers, men and women throughout history have come, again and again, to the book of Psalms for comfort during times of struggle and distress. And through the psalms, they have risen from the depths of despair to new heights of joy and praise as they also discovered the power of God's everlasting love and forgiveness. Let the honesty of the psalms guide you into a deep and genuine relationship with God.

## VITAL STATISTICS

**PURPOSE:**
To provide poetry for the expression of praise, worship, and confession to God

**AUTHORS:**
David wrote 73 psalms; Asaph wrote 12; the sons of Korah wrote 9; Solomon wrote 2; Heman (with the sons of Korah), Ethan, and Moses each wrote one; 51 psalms are anonymous. The New Testament ascribes two of the anonymous psalms (Psalms 2 and 95) to David (see Acts 4:25; Hebrews 4:7).

**ORIGINAL AUDIENCE:**
The people of Israel

**DATE WRITTEN:**
Between the time of Moses (approximately 1440 B.C.) and the Babylonian captivity (586 B.C.)

**SETTING:**
For the most part, the psalms were not intended to be narrations of historical events. However, they often parallel events in history, such as David's flight from Saul and his sin with Bathsheba.

**KEY VERSE:**
"Let everything that breathes sing praises to the LORD! Praise the LORD!" (150:6)

**KEY PERSON:**
David

**KEY PLACE:**
God's holy Temple

---

## THE BLUEPRINT

**BOOK ONE**
**PSALMS 1:1—41:13**

While the psalms are not organized by topic, it is helpful to compare the dominant themes in each section of the Psalms to the five books of Moses. This first collection of psalms, mainly written by David, is similar to the book of Genesis. Just as Genesis tells how mankind was created, fell into sin, and was then promised redemption, many of these psalms discuss humans as blessed, fallen, and redeemed by God.

**BOOK TWO**
**PSALMS 42:1—72:20**

This collection of psalms, mainly written by David and the sons of Korah, is similar to the book of Exodus. Just as Exodus describes the nation of Israel, many of these psalms describe the nation as ruined and then recovered. As God rescued the nation of Israel, he also rescues us. We do not have to work out solutions first, but we can go to God with our problems and ask him to help.

**BOOK THREE**
**PSALMS 73:1—89:52**

This collection of psalms, mainly written by Asaph or Asaph's descendants, is similar to the book of Leviticus. Just as Leviticus discusses the Tabernacle and God's holiness, many of these psalms discuss the Temple and God's enthronement. Because God is almighty, we can turn to him for deliverance. These psalms praise God because he is holy, and his perfect holiness deserves our worship and reverence.

| | |
|---|---|
| BOOK FOUR<br>PSALMS 90:1—106:48 | This collection of psalms, mainly written by unknown authors, is similar to the book of Numbers. Just as Numbers discusses the relationship of the nation of Israel to surrounding nations, these psalms often mention the relationship of God's overruling Kingdom to the other nations. Because we are citizens of the Kingdom of God, we can keep the events and troubles of earth in their proper perspective. |
| BOOK FIVE<br>PSALMS 107:1—150:6 | This collection of psalms, mainly written by David, is similar to the book of Deuteronomy. Just as Deuteronomy was concerned with God and his Word, these psalms are anthems of praise and thanksgiving for God and his Word. Most of the psalms were originally set to music and used in worship. We can use these psalms today as they were used in the past, as a hymnbook of praise and worship. This is a book that ought to make our hearts sing. |

## MEGATHEMES

| THEME | EXPLANATION | IMPORTANCE |
|---|---|---|
| *Praise* | Psalms are songs of praise to God as our Creator, Sustainer, and Redeemer. Praise is recognizing, appreciating, and expressing God's greatness. | Focusing our thoughts on God moves us to praise him. The more we know him, the more we can appreciate what he has done for us. |
| *God's power* | God is all-powerful; and he always acts at the right time. He is sovereign over every situation. God's power is shown by the ways he reveals himself in creation, history, and his Word. | When we feel powerless, God can help us. His strength can overcome the despair of any pain or trial. We can always pray that he will deliver, protect, and sustain us. |
| *Forgiveness* | Many psalms are intense prayers asking God for forgiveness. God forgives us when we confess our sin and turn from it. | Because God forgives us, we can pray to him honestly and directly. When we receive his forgiveness, we move from alienation to intimacy, from guilt to love. |
| *Thankfulness* | We are grateful to God for his personal concern, help, and mercy. Not only does he protect, guide, and forgive us, but his creation provides everything we need. | When we realize how we benefit from knowing God, we can fully express our thanks to him. By thanking him often, we develop spontaneity in our prayer life. |
| *Trust* | God is faithful and just. When we put our trust in him, he quiets our hearts. Because he has been faithful throughout history, we can trust him in times of trouble. | People can be unfair and friends may desert us. But we can trust God. Knowing God intimately drives away doubt, fear, and loneliness. |

## BOOK ONE   Psalms 1:1—41:13

In this book, the psalm writers praise God for his justice, express confidence in God's compassion, recount the depravity of humanity, plead for vindication, ask God to deliver them from their enemies, speak of the blessedness of the forgiven sinner, and portray God as a shepherd. We should worship God with the same sense of adoration found in these psalms.

**Theme:** Life's two roads. The life of the faithful person is contrasted with the life of the faithless person.
**Author:** Anonymous

**1** ¹ Oh, the joys of those who do not
    follow the advice of the wicked,
or stand around with sinners,
    or join in with mockers.

1:1
Pss 17:4; 26:5
Prov 4:14
Jer 15:17

**1:1** The writer begins this psalm extolling the joys of obeying God and refusing to listen to those who discredit or ridicule him. Our friends and associates can have a profound influence on us, often in very subtle ways. If we insist on friendships with those who mock what God considers important, we might sin by becoming indifferent to God's will. This attitude is the same as mocking. Do your friends build up your faith, or do they tear it down? True friends should help you to draw closer to God, not hinder your relationship with him.

**1:1ff** God doesn't judge people on the basis of race, sex, or national origin. He judges them on the basis of their faith in him and their response to his revealed will. Those who diligently try to obey God's will are blessed. They are like healthy, fruit-bearing trees planted along a riverbank with strong roots (Jeremiah 17:7, 8), and God promises to watch over them. God's wisdom guides their lives. In contrast, those who don't trust and obey God have meaningless lives that blow away like dust.

Only two paths of life lay before us—God's way of obedience or the way of rebellion and destruction. Be sure to choose God's path because the path you choose determines how you will spend eternity.

**1:2**
Pss 25:5; 63:5-6;
119:13-16

**1:3**
Gen 39:3
Jer 17:7-8
Ezek 47:12

**1:4**
Job 21:18
Ps 35:5
Isa 17:13

**1:5**
Pss 5:5; 9:7-8;
89:5, 7

**1:6**
Neh 1:7
Pss 9:5-6; 11:6
John 10:14
2 Tim 2:19

2 But they delight in the law of the LORD,
meditating on it day and night.
3 They are like trees planted along the riverbank,
bearing fruit each season.
Their leaves never wither,
and they prosper in all they do.

4 But not the wicked!
They are like worthless chaff, scattered by the wind.
5 They will be condemned at the time of judgment.
Sinners will have no place among the godly.
6 For the LORD watches over the path of the godly,
but the path of the wicked leads to destruction.

**Theme:** God's ultimate rule. A psalm written to celebrate the coronation of an Israelite king, but also written for the coronation of Christ, the eternal King.
**Author:** David (see Acts 4:25, 26)

# 2

1 Why are the nations so angry?
Why do they waste their time with futile plans?
2 The kings of the earth prepare for battle;
the rulers plot together
against the LORD
and against his anointed one.

**2:1**
Pss 21:11; 46:6
Acts 4:25-26

**2:2**
Pss 48:4-6;
74:18, 23
Jer 5:5
John 1:41

**REASONS TO READ PSALMS**

| When you want . . . | Read . . . |
| --- | --- |
| to find comfort | Psalm 23 |
| to meet God intimately | Psalm 103 |
| to learn a new prayer | Psalm 136 |
| to learn a new song | Psalm 92 |
| to learn more about God | Psalm 24 |
| to understand yourself more clearly | Psalm 8 |
| to know how to come to God each day | Psalm 5 |
| to be forgiven for your sins | Psalm 51 |
| to feel worthwhile | Psalm 139 |
| to understand why you should read the Bible | Psalm 119 |
| to give praise to God | Psalm 145 |
| to know that God is in control | Psalm 146 |
| to give thanks to God | Psalm 136 |
| to please God | Psalm 15 |
| to know why you should worship God | Psalm 104 |

God's Word was written to be studied, understood, and applied, and the book of Psalms lends itself most directly to application. We understand the psalms best when we "stand under" them and allow them to flow over us like a rain shower. We may turn to Psalms looking for something, but sooner or later we will meet Someone. As we read and memorize the psalms, we will gradually discover how much they are already part of us. They put into words our deepest hurts, longings, thoughts, and prayers. They gently push us toward being what God designed us to be—people loving and living for him.

**1:2** You can learn how to follow God by meditating on his Word. This means spending time reading and thinking about what you have read. It means asking yourself how you should change so you will live as God wants. Knowing and thinking about God's Word are the first steps toward applying it to your everyday life. If you want to follow God more closely, you must know what he says.

**1:2** This "law" means all of Scripture: the first five books of Moses, the Prophets, and the other writings. The more we know of the whole scope of God's Word, the more resources we will have to guide us in our daily decisions.

**1:2, 3** These two verses hold simple wisdom: The more we delight in obeying God, the more fruitful we are. On the other hand, the more we allow those who ridicule God to affect our thoughts and attitudes, the more we separate ourselves from our source of nourishment. We must have contact with unbelievers if we are to witness to them, but we must not join in or imitate their sinful behavior. If you want despair, spend time with mocking sinners; but if you want God's blessing, make friends with those who love God and his Word.

3 "Let us break their chains," they cry,
   "and free ourselves from slavery to God."

4 But the one who rules in heaven laughs.
   The Lord scoffs at them.
5 Then in anger he rebukes them,
   terrifying them with his fierce fury.
6 For the Lord declares, "I have placed my chosen king on the throne
   in Jerusalem,* on my holy mountain."

7 The king proclaims the LORD's decree:
   "The LORD said to me, 'You are my son.*
   Today I have become your Father.*
8 Only ask, and I will give you the nations as your inheritance,
   the whole earth as your possession.
9 You will break* them with an iron rod
   and smash them like clay pots.'"

10 Now then, you kings, act wisely!
   Be warned, you rulers of the earth!
11 Serve the LORD with reverent fear,
   and rejoice with trembling.
12 Submit to God's royal son,* or he will become angry,
   and you will be destroyed in the midst of all your activities—
for his anger flares up in an instant.
   But what joy for all who take refuge in him!

**2:4**
Pss 37:12-13; 59:8

**2:5**
Pss 76:7; 78:49-50

**2:6**
Pss 3:4; 45:6;
48:1-2

**2:7**
†Acts 13:32-33
†Heb 1:5-6; 5:5

**2:8**
Pss 21:1-2; 22:27

**2:9**
Pss 28:5; 110:5-6
Rev 2:26-27; 12:5;
19:15

**2:10**
Prov 8:14-15

**2:11**
Pss 5:7;
119:119-120
Heb 12:28

**2:12**
Pss 5:11; 34:8, 22
John 5:23
Rom 9:33
Rev 6:16

**2:6** Hebrew on Zion.   **2:7a** Or Son; also in 2:12.   **2:7b** Or Today I reveal you as my son.   **2:9** Greek version reads rule. Compare Rev 2:27.   **2:12** The meaning of the Hebrew is uncertain.

**1:3** The phrase, "they prosper in all they do," does not mean immunity to failure or difficulties. Nor does it guarantee health, wealth, and happiness. What the Bible means by prosperity is this: When we apply God's wisdom, the fruit (results or by-products) we bear will be good and will receive God's approval. Just as a tree soaks up water and bears luscious fruit, we also are to soak up God's Word, producing actions and attitudes that honor God. To achieve anything worthwhile, we must have God's Word in our hearts.

**1:4** Chaff is the outer shell (or husk) that must be removed to get at the valuable kernels of grain inside. Chaff was removed by a process called threshing and winnowing. After the plants were cut, they were crushed, and then the pieces were thrown into the air. Chaff is very light and is carried away by even the slightest wind, while the good grain falls back to the earth. Chaff is a symbol of a faithless life that drifts along without direction. Good grain is a symbol of a faithful life that can be used by God. Unlike grain, however, we can choose the direction we will take.

**2:1ff** Several psalms are called "messianic" because of their prophetic descriptions of Jesus the Messiah (Christ)—his life, death, resurrection, and future reign. David, who may have written this psalm, was a shepherd, soldier, and king. Clearly he was also a prophet (Acts 2:29, 30) because this psalm describes the rebellion of the nations and the coming of Christ to establish his eternal reign. This psalm is often mentioned in the New Testament

(see Acts 4:25, 26; 13:33; Hebrews 1:5, 6; 5:5; Revelation 2:26, 27; 12:5; 19:15).

**2:1ff** David may have written these words during a conspiracy against Israel by some of the surrounding pagan nations. Chosen and anointed by God, David knew that God would fulfill his promise to bring the Messiah into the world through his bloodline (2 Samuel 7:16; 1 Chronicles 17:11, 12).

**2:3** People often think they will be free if they can get away from God. Yet, inevitably, everyone serves somebody or something, whether a human king, an organization, or even one's own selfish desires. Just as a fish is not free when it leaves the water and a tree is not free when it leaves the soil, we are not free when we leave the Lord. We can find the one sure route to freedom by wholeheartedly serving God the Creator. God can set you free to be the person he created you to be.

**2:4** God laughs, not at the nations, but at their confused thoughts about power. It is the laughter of a father when his three-year-old boasts that he or she can outrun him or beat him in a wrestling match. The father knows the limited strength of his little child, and God knows the boundaries of power of the nations. Every nation is limited, but God is omnipotent. If you have to choose between confidence in God and confidence in any nation, choose God!

**2:4** God is all-powerful. He created the world and knew about the empires of the earth long before they came into being (Daniel 2:26-45). But pride and power cause nations and leaders to rebel against God and try to break free of him. Many world leaders boast of their power, rant and rave against God and his people, and promise to take over and form their own empires. But God laughs because any power they have comes from him, and he can also take it from them. We need not fear the boasts of tyrants—they are in God's hands and will be judged by him.

**2:11, 12** We must surrender fully and submit to the Son. Christ is not only God's chosen King, he is also the rightful King of our hearts and lives. To be ready for Christ's return, we must submit to his leadership every day.

**Theme:** Confidently trusting God for protection and peace.
**Author:** David

**3** *A psalm of David, regarding the time David fled from his son Absalom.*

**3:1**
2 Sam 15:12
Ps 69:4

**3:2**
Pss 22:7-8; 71:11

**3:3**
Pss 5:12; 27:5-6;
28:7; 62:7

**3:4**
Pss 4:3; 34:4; 99:9

[1] O Lord, I have so many enemies;
    so many are against me.
[2] So many are saying,
    "God will never rescue him!"                                              *Interlude**

[3] But you, O Lord, are a shield around me;
    you are my glory, the one who holds my head high.
[4] I cried out to the Lord,
    and he answered me from his holy mountain.                          *Interlude*

**3:2** Hebrew *Selah*. The meaning of this word is uncertain, though it is probably a musical or literary term. It is rendered *Interlude* throughout the Psalms.

---

**PSALMS FROM DAVID'S LIFE**
Of the more than 70 psalms attributed to David, at least 14 of them are connected with specific events in his life. From them we see an outline of a growing relationship with God. They are listed here, roughly in chronological order.

| Event in David's Life | Reference | Psalm | What David Learned about God |
|---|---|---|---|
| When Saul sent men to David's home to kill him | 1 Samuel 19 | 59 | God is my refuge. |
| While running from Saul | 1 Samuel 21 | 34 | I will praise the Lord at all times. |
| While running from Saul | 1 Samuel 21 | 56 | When I am afraid, I put my trust in God. |
| While hiding in the cave of Adullam | 1 Samuel 22 | 142 | God is my refuge. |
| After learning that Doeg had murdered 85 priests and their families | 1 Samuel 22 | 52 | God will strike down evil people. |
| When the Ziphites tried to betray him | 1 Samuel 23 | 54 | God is my helper. |
| While hiding in a cave | 1 Samuel 24 | 57 | I will hide in the shadow of God's wings until the danger has passed. |
| While hiding in the wilderness of En-gedi | 1 Samuel 24 | 63 | My soul thirsts for God; his right hand holds me securely. |
| When Saul's pursuit was over | 2 Samuel 22 | 18 | To the faithful, God shows himself faithful. |
| After being confronted about his adultery with Bathsheba | 2 Samuel 12 | 51 | The sacrifices God desires are a broken spirit; a broken and repentant heart he will not reject. |
| During Absalom's rebellion | 2 Samuel 15 | 3 | Victory comes from the Lord. |
| During Absalom's rebellion | 2 Samuel 15 | 7 | He is a righteous God who searches minds and hearts and can bring to an end the violence of the wicked and make the righteous secure. |

---

**3:1, 2** David felt like he was in the minority. As many as 10,000 soldiers may have been surrounding him at this time (3:6). Not only did David's enemies view life differently, they actively sought to harm him. As king, David could have trusted his army to defeat Absalom. Instead, he depended upon God's mercy (3:4); therefore, he was at peace with whatever outcome occurred, knowing that God's great purposes would prevail. We can overcome fear by trusting God for his protection in our darkest hour.

**3:1-3** David was not sitting on his throne in a place of power; he was running for his life from his rebellious son, Absalom, and a host of traitors. When circumstances go against us, we may be tempted to think that God also is against us. But David reminds us that the opposite is true. When everything seems to go wrong, God is still for us. If a circumstance has turned against you, don't blame God—seek him!

**3:2** The word *Interlude* is a translation of the Hebrew word *Selah* which occurs 71 times in Psalms and three times in Habakkuk

(3:3, 9, 13). Though its precise use is unknown, the word was most likely a musical sign. Three suggestions for its meaning include: (1) It was a musical direction to the singers and orchestra to play *forte* or *crescendo*. (2) It was a signal to lift up the hands or voice in worship, or to the priest to give a benediction. (3) It was a phrase like "Amen" meaning "So be it," or "Hallelujah" meaning "Praise the Lord."

**3:4** God's holy mountain was Mount Moriah in Jerusalem, the place where David's son Solomon would build the Temple (2 Chronicles 3:1). David knew that God could not be confined to any space, but he wrote poetically, expressing confidence that God would hear him when he prayed. God responds to us when we earnestly pray to him.

5 I lay down and slept,
  yet I woke up in safety,
  for the LORD was watching over me.
6 I am not afraid of ten thousand enemies
  who surround me on every side.

7 Arise, O LORD!
  Rescue me, my God!
  Slap all my enemies in the face!
  Shatter the teeth of the wicked!
8 Victory comes from you, O LORD.
  May you bless your people.                                    *Interlude*

**3:5**
Lev 26:6
Pss 4:8; 139:17-18
Prov 3:24-26

**3:6**
Pss 23:4; 27:3;
118:10-13

**3:8**
Pss 28:8; 29:11
Isa 43:11
Jer 3:23

**Theme:** Rejoicing in God's protection and peace. We can place our confidence in God
because he will listen when we call on him.
**Author:** David

**4** *For the choir director: A psalm of David, to be accompanied by stringed instruments.*

1 Answer me when I call to you,
  O God who declares me innocent.
  Free me from my troubles.
  Have mercy on me and hear my prayer.

2 How long will you people ruin my reputation?
  How long will you make groundless accusations?
  How long will you continue your lies?                         *Interlude*

3 You can be sure of this:
  The LORD set apart the godly for himself.
  The LORD will answer when I call to him.

4 Don't sin by letting anger control you.
  Think about it overnight and remain silent.                   *Interlude*

5 Offer sacrifices in the right spirit,
  and trust the LORD.

6 Many people say, "Who will show us better times?"
  Let your face smile on us, LORD.

7 You have given me greater joy
  than those who have abundant harvests of grain and new wine.

**4:1**
Pss 3:4; 17:6; 18:6,
18-19; 25:16

**4:2**
Pss 31:6, 18;
69:7-10, 19-20

**4:3**
Pss 17:6; 50:5;
135:4

**4:4**
Pss 37:8; 77:6
Eph 4:26

**4:5**
Pss 37:3, 5; 50:14;
51:19

**4:6**
Num 6:26
Job 7:7; 9:25
Ps 80:3, 7, 19

**4:7**
Ps 97:11-12
Acts 14:17

**3:5** Sleep does not come easily during a crisis. David could have had sleepless nights when his son Absalom rebelled and gathered an army to kill him. But he slept peacefully, even during the rebellion. What made the difference? David cried out to the Lord, and the Lord heard him. The assurance of answered prayer brings peace. It is easier to sleep well when we have full assurance that God is in control of circumstances. If you are lying awake at night worrying about what you can't change, pour out your heart to God, and thank him that he is in control. Then sleep will come.

**3:7** David's call for God to act reveals his desire for justice against his persecutors. David himself had been slapped and insulted, and here he simply asks for equal treatment for his enemies. He did this, not out of personal revenge, but for the sake of God's justice. Verse 8 shows the humility behind David's words—he realized that faith in God's timing was the answer to his question about the success the wicked had unfairly achieved.

**4:1ff** This psalm may have been written as David was asking his enemies to reconsider their support of Absalom. Others see this psalm as a prayer for relief from a calamity such as a drought (see 4:7). It was probably written shortly after Psalm 3.

**4:3** The godly are those who are faithful and devoted to God. David knew that God would hear him when he called and would answer him. We, too, can be confident that God listens to our

prayers and answers when we call on him. Sometimes we think that God will not hear us because we have fallen short of his high standards for holy living. But if we have trusted Christ for salvation, God has forgiven us and he will listen to us. When you feel as though your prayers are bouncing off the ceiling, remember that as a believer you have been set apart by God and that he loves you. He hears and answers although his answers may not be what you expect. Look at your problems in the light of God's power instead of looking at God in the shadow of your problems.

**4:5** Worship in David's day included animal sacrifices by the priests in the Tabernacle. The animal's blood covered the sins of the one who offered the animal. Specific rules had been given for offering sacrifices, but more important to God than ceremony was the offerer's attitude of submission and obedience (1 Samuel 15:22, 23). Today, a sacrifice offered in the right spirit is still pleasing to God. He wants our obedience and our praise before our gifts (Hebrews 13:15). Offer God your sacrifice of total obedience and heartfelt praise.

**4:7** Two kinds of joy are contrasted here—inward joy that comes from knowing and trusting God and happiness that comes as a result of pleasant circumstances. Inward joy is steady as long as we trust God; happiness is unpredictable. Inward joy defeats discouragement; happiness covers it up. Inward joy is lasting; happiness is temporary.

4:8
Lev 25:18
Deut 12:10
Job 11:19
Pss 3:5; 16:9

8 In peace I will lie down and sleep,
  for you alone, O LORD, will keep me safe.

**Theme:** The lies of enemies. God is able to defend us from lies spoken against us.
**Author:** David

# 5

*For the choir director: A psalm of David, to be accompanied by the flute.*

5:1
Ps 54:2
5:2
Ps 84:3

1 O LORD, hear me as I pray;
  pay attention to my groaning.
2 Listen to my cry for help, my King and my God,
  for I pray to no one but you.

5:3
Pss 88:13; 130:5

3 Listen to my voice in the morning, LORD.
  Each morning I bring my requests to you and wait expectantly.

5:4
Pss 11:5; 34:16;
92:15

4 O God, you take no pleasure in wickedness;
  you cannot tolerate the sins of the wicked.

5:5
Pss 1:5; 11:5; 45:7;
75:4

5 Therefore, the proud may not stand in your presence,
  for you hate all who do evil.

5:6
Pss 52:4-5; 55:23

6 You will destroy those who tell lies.
  The LORD detests murderers and deceivers.

5:7
Pss 69:13;
115:11, 13

7 Because of your unfailing love, I can enter your house;
  I will worship at your Temple with deepest awe.

5:8
Pss 27:11; 31:1, 3

8 Lead me in the right path, O LORD,
  or my enemies will conquer me.
  Make your way plain for me to follow.

5:9
†Rom 3:13
Luke 11:44

9 My enemies cannot speak a truthful word.
  Their deepest desire is to destroy others.
  Their talk is foul, like the stench from an open grave.
  Their tongues are filled with flattery.*

5:10
Pss 9:16; 36:12;
107:10-11

10 O God, declare them guilty.
  Let them be caught in their own traps.
  Drive them away because of their many sins,
  for they have rebelled against you.

5:11
Pss 2:12; 12:7;
33:1; 64:10
Isa 65:13

11 But let all who take refuge in you rejoice;
  let them sing joyful praises forever.
  Spread your protection over them,
  that all who love your name may be filled with joy.

5:12
Pss 29:11; 32:7, 10

12 For you bless the godly, O LORD;
  you surround them with your shield of love.

**Theme:** Deliverance in trouble. God is able to rescue us.
**Author:** David

# 6

*For the choir director: A psalm of David, to be accompanied by an eight-stringed instrument.*

6:1
Pss 2:5; 38:1

1 O LORD, don't rebuke me in your anger
  or discipline me in your rage.

**5:9** Greek version reads *with lies.* Compare Rom 3:13.   **6:TITLE** Hebrew *with stringed instruments; according to the sheminith.*

---

**5:1-3** The secret of a close relationship with God is to pray to him earnestly *each morning.* In the morning, our minds are more free from problems, and then we can commit the whole day to God. Regular communication helps any friendship and is certainly necessary for a strong relationship with God. We need to communicate with him daily. Do you have a regular time to pray and read God's Word?

**5:5** God cannot condone or excuse even the smallest sin; therefore, we cannot excuse ourselves for sinning only a little bit. As we grow spiritually, our sensitivity to sin increases. What is your reaction to sin in your life? Are you insensitive, unconcerned, disappointed, or comfortable? As God makes us aware of sin, we must be intolerant toward it and be willing to change. All believers should strive to be more tolerant of people but less tolerant of the sin in themselves and others.

**6:1ff** This is the first of seven "penitential" psalms, in which the writer humbly realizes his predicament (usually the result of sin), expresses sorrow over it, and demonstrates a fresh commitment to remain close to God. We don't know the cause of David's pain, but whatever the cause, he sought God for the remedy.

2 Have compassion on me, LORD, for I am weak.
Heal me, LORD, for my bones are in agony.
3 I am sick at heart.
How long, O LORD, until you restore me?

4 Return, O LORD, and rescue me.
Save me because of your unfailing love.
5 For the dead do not remember you.
Who can praise you from the grave?*

6 I am worn out from sobbing.
All night I flood my bed with weeping,
drenching it with my tears.
7 My vision is blurred by grief;
my eyes are worn out because of all my enemies.

8 Go away, all you who do evil,
for the LORD has heard my weeping.
9 The LORD has heard my plea;
the LORD will answer my prayer.
10 May all my enemies be disgraced and terrified.
May they suddenly turn back in shame.

**6:2**
Ps 22:14

**6:3**
Pss 88:3; 90:13
John 12:27

**6:4**
Ps 17:13
**6:5**
Ps 30:9
Isa 38:18

**6:6**
Pss 42:3; 69:3

**6:7**
Ps 31:9

**6:10**
Pss 71:24; 73:19

**Theme:** A request for justice against those who make slanderous comments. God is the perfect judge and will punish those who persecute the innocent.
**Author:** David

**7** *A psalm of David, which he sang to the* LORD *concerning Cush of the tribe of Benjamin.*

1 I come to you for protection, O LORD my God.
Save me from my persecutors—rescue me!
2 If you don't, they will maul me like a lion,
tearing me to pieces with no one to rescue me.
3 O LORD my God, if I have done wrong
or am guilty of injustice,
4 if I have betrayed a friend
or plundered my enemy without cause,
5 then let my enemies capture me.
Let them trample me into the ground
and drag my honor in the dust.

6 Arise, O LORD, in anger!
Stand up against the fury of my enemies!
Wake up, my God, and bring justice!
7 Gather the nations before you.
Rule over them from on high.

*Interlude*

**7:1**
Pss 11:1;
31:1, 14-15
**7:2**
Pss 17:12; 57:4

**7:3**
1 Sam 24:11

**7:4**
1 Sam 24:7; 26:9

**7:6**
Pss 3:7; 35:23;
94:2; 138:7

**6:5** Hebrew *from Sheol?*

**6:1-3** David accepted God's punishment, but he begged God not to discipline him in anger. Jeremiah also asked God to correct him gently and not in anger (Jeremiah 10:24). David recognized that if God treated him with justice alone and not with mercy, he would be wiped out by God's wrath. Often we want God to show mercy to us and justice to everyone else. God in his kindness forgives us instead of giving us what we deserve.

**6:6** Pouring out his heart with tears, David was completely honest with God. We can be honest with God even when we are filled with anger or despair because God knows us thoroughly and

wants the very best for us. Anger may result in rash outward acts or turning inward in depression. But because we trust in our all-powerful God, we don't have to be victims of circumstance or be weighed down by the guilt of sin. Be honest with God, and he will help you turn your attention from yourself to him and his mercy.

**7:1-6** Have you ever been falsely accused or so badly hurt that you wanted revenge? David wrote this psalm in response to the slanderous accusations of those who claimed he was trying to kill Saul and seize the throne (1 Samuel 24:9-11). Instead of taking matters into his own hands and striking back, David cried out to God for justice. The proper response to slander is prayer, not revenge, because God says, "I will take revenge; I will pay them back" (Romans 12:19; see also Deuteronomy 32:35, 36; Hebrews 10:30). Instead of striking back, ask God to take your case, bring justice, and restore your reputation.

**7:8**
Pss 18:20; 35:24;
96:13

**7:9**
1 Chr 28:9
Pss 11:4-5; 34:21;
94:23
Jer 11:20
Rev 2:23

**7:10**
Pss 18:2, 30;
97:10-11; 125:4

**7:11**
Pss 50:6; 90:9

**7:12**
Deut 32:41
Ps 64:7
Ezek 33:9

**7:13**
Pss 18:14; 45:5;
64:7

**7:14**
Job 15:35
Isa 59:4
Jas 1:15

**7:15**
Job 4:7-8
Ps 57:6

**7:16**
Esth 9:24-25
Ps 140:9, 11

**7:17**
Pss 9:2; 66:1-2, 4;
71:15-16

8 The LORD judges the nations.
Declare me righteous, O LORD,
for I am innocent, O Most High!
9 End the evil of those who are wicked,
and defend the righteous.
For you look deep within the mind and heart,
O righteous God.
10 God is my shield,
saving those whose hearts are true and right.
11 God is an honest judge.
He is angry with the wicked every day.
12 If a person does not repent,
God* will sharpen his sword;
he will bend and string his bow.
13 He will prepare his deadly weapons
and shoot his flaming arrows.
14 The wicked conceive evil;
they are pregnant with trouble
and give birth to lies.
15 They dig a deep pit to trap others,
then fall into it themselves.
16 The trouble they make for others backfires on them.
The violence they plan falls on their own heads.
17 I will thank the LORD because he is just;
I will sing praise to the name of the LORD Most High.

**Theme:** The greatness of God assures the worth of mankind. God, the all-powerful Creator, cares for his most valuable creation—people.
**Author:** David

**8** *For the choir director: A psalm of David, to be accompanied by a stringed instrument.**

**8:1**
Pss 57:5, 11; 66:2;
113:4; 148:13

**8:2**
Matt 21:16

1 O LORD, our Lord, your majestic name fills the earth!
Your glory is higher than the heavens.
2 You have taught children and infants
to tell of your strength,*
silencing your enemies
and all who oppose you.

**7:12** Hebrew *he.*    **8:TITLE** Hebrew *according to the gittith.*    **8:2** Greek version reads *to give you praise.* Compare Matt 21:16.

**7:9** God looks "deep within the mind and heart." Nothing is hidden from God—this can be either terrifying or comforting. Our thoughts are an open book to him. Because God knows even our motives, we have no place to hide, no way to pretend we can get away with sin. But that very knowledge also gives us great comfort. We don't have to impress God or put up a false front. Instead, we can trust God to help us work through our weaknesses in order to serve him as he has planned. When we truly follow God, he rewards our efforts.

**7:14-16** When allowed to run its course, evil destroys itself. Violent people become victims of violence, and liars become victims of others' deceit (9:15, 16). In the process, however, innocent people are hurt. Sometimes God intervenes and stops evildoers in their tracks in order to protect his followers. At other times, for reasons known only to him, God allows evil to continue even though innocent people are hurt. It is during these times that we must ask God to protect us. Remember that God will execute final justice, although it may not be during our lifetime.

**7:17** During a time of great evil and injustice, David was grateful that God was just and fair (see also 7:11). When we wonder if anyone is honest or fair, we can be assured that God will continue to bring justice and fairness when we involve him in our activities. If you ever feel that you are being treated unfairly, ask the one who is always fair and just to be with you. Then thank him for his presence (see Isaiah 42:1-6).

**8:1ff** Portions of this psalm are quoted in the New Testament and applied to Christ (1 Corinthians 15:27; Hebrews 2:6-8). God became human—lower than God—in the person of Jesus (8:5), and he will raise all who belong to him when he comes to reign over the new heaven and new earth. Jesus is the only person who perfectly reflects God's image (Galatians 2:20; Colossians 1:15).

**8:2** Children are able to trust and praise God without doubts or reservations. As we get older, many of us find this more and more difficult to do. Ask God to give you childlike faith, removing any barriers to having a closer walk with him.

3 When I look at the night sky and see the work of your fingers—
    the moon and the stars you set in place—
4 what are mere mortals that you should think about them,
    human beings that you should care for them?*
5 Yet you made them only a little lower than God*
    and crowned them* with glory and honor.
6 You gave them charge of everything you made,
    putting all things under their authority—
7 the flocks and the herds
    and all the wild animals,
8 the birds in the sky, the fish in the sea,
    and everything that swims the ocean currents.

9 O Lord, our Lord, your majestic name fills the earth!

**8:3**
Pss 89:11; 136:9

**8:4**
Job 7:17
Ps 144:3
Heb 2:6-8

**8:5**
Pss 21:5; 82:6;
103:4

**8:6**
Gen 1:26, 28
†1 Cor 15:27

**Theme:** God never ignores our cries for help.
**Author:** David, probably written after a victory over the Philistines

# 9

*For the choir director: A psalm of David, to be sung to the tune "Death of the Son."*

1 I will praise you, Lord, with all my heart;
    I will tell of all the marvelous things you have done.
2 I will be filled with joy because of you.
    I will sing praises to your name, O Most High.

3 My enemies retreated;
    they staggered and died when you appeared.
4 For you have judged in my favor;
    from your throne you have judged with fairness.
5 You have rebuked the nations and destroyed the wicked;
    you have erased their names forever.
6 The enemy is finished, in endless ruins;
    the cities you uprooted are now forgotten.

7 But the Lord reigns forever,
    executing judgment from his throne.
8 He will judge the world with justice
    and rule the nations with fairness.
9 The Lord is a shelter for the oppressed,
    a refuge in times of trouble.

**9:1**
Pss 26:7; 86:12

**9:2**
Pss 66:2, 4; 92:1;
104:34

**9:3**
Pss 27:2; 56:9

**9:4**
Pss 47:8; 140:12
1 Pet 2:23

**9:5**
Pss 69:28; 119:21

**9:6**
Pss 34:16; 40:15

**9:7**
Pss 10:16;
89:14-15

**9:8**
Ps 96:13

**9:9**
Pss 18:2; 37:39;
59:9, 16-17

**8:4** Hebrew *what is man that you should think of him, / the son of man that you should care for him?* **8:5a** Or *Yet you made them only a little lower than the angels;* Hebrew reads *Yet you made him* [i.e., man] *a little lower than Elohim.* **8:5b** Hebrew *him* [i.e., man]; similarly in 8:6.

---

**8:3, 4** To respect God's majesty, we must compare ourselves to his greatness. When we look at creation, we often feel small by comparison. This is a healthy way to get back to reality, but God does not want us to dwell on our smallness. Humility means proper respect for God, not self-depreciation.

**8:3-5** When we look at the vast expanse of creation, we wonder how God could be concerned for people who constantly disappoint him. Yet God created us only a little lower than himself and the angels! The next time you question your worth as a person, remember that God considers you highly valuable. We have great worth because we bear the stamp of the Creator. (See Genesis 1:26, 27 for the extent of worth God places on all people.) Because God has already declared how valuable we are to him, we can be set free from feelings of worthlessness.

**8:6** God gave human beings tremendous authority—to be in charge of the whole earth. But with great authority comes great responsibility. If we own a pet, we have the legal authority to do with it as we wish, but we also have the responsibility to feed and

care for it. How do you treat God's creation? Use your resources wisely because God holds you accountable as his steward.

**9:1ff** Praise is expressing to God our appreciation and understanding of his worth. It is saying thank you for each aspect of his divine nature. Our inward attitude becomes outward expression. When we praise God, we help ourselves by expanding our awareness of who he is. In each psalm you read, look for an attribute or characteristic of God for which you can thank him.

**9:4** God upholds our just cause; he is our vindicator (one who clears us from criticism and justifies us before others). In this life, we may face many injustices: (1) we may be falsely accused and misunderstood by friends and enemies; (2) we may not be truly appreciated by others for the love we show; (3) the true value of our work and service may not be duly rewarded; (4) our ideas may be ignored. But God is to be praised, for he sees and remembers all the good we do, and it is up to him to decide the timing and the appropriateness of our rewards. If we do not trust him to vindicate us, then we will be susceptible to hatred and self-pity. If we do trust him, we can experience God's peace and be free from the worry of how others perceive us and treat us.

**9:10**
Pss 37:28; 91:14;
94:14

10 Those who know your name trust in you,
    for you, O LORD, do not abandon those who search for you.

**9:11**
Pss 76:2; 105:1

11 Sing praises to the LORD who reigns in Jerusalem.*
    Tell the world about his unforgettable deeds.

**9:12**
Gen 9:5-6
Ps 72:14

12 For he who avenges murder cares for the helpless.
    He does not ignore the cries of those who suffer.

**9:13**
Pss 30:3; 38:19;
86:13

13 LORD, have mercy on me.
    See how my enemies torment me.
    Snatch me back from the jaws of death.

**9:14**
Pss 13:5; 20:5;
35:9; 51:12; 106:2

14 Save me so I can praise you publicly at Jerusalem's gates,
    so I can rejoice that you have rescued me.

**9:15**
Pss 7:15; 35:8

15 The nations have fallen into the pit they dug for others.
    Their own feet have been caught in the trap they set.
16 The LORD is known for his justice.
    The wicked are trapped by their own deeds.

*Quiet Interlude**

**9:17**
Pss 49:14; 50:22
**9:18**
Pss 9:12; 62:5;
71:5

17 The wicked will go down to the grave.*
    This is the fate of all the nations who ignore God.
18 But the needy will not be ignored forever;
    the hopes of the poor will not always be crushed.

**9:19**
Num 10:35
2 Chr 14:11

19 Arise, O LORD!
    Do not let mere mortals defy you!
    Judge the nations!

**9:20**
Ps 62:9

20 Make them tremble in fear, O LORD.
    Let the nations know they are merely human.

*Interlude*

**Theme:** Why do the wicked succeed? Although God may seem to be hidden at times, we can be assured that he is aware of every injustice.
**Author:** Anonymous, but probably David. Many ancient manuscripts combine Psalms 9 and 10, and Psalm 9 was written by David.

**10:1**
Pss 13:1; 22:1;
55:1

**10** 1 O LORD, why do you stand so far away?
        Why do you hide when I am in trouble?

**10:2**
Pss 7:15; 9:16;
73:6, 8

2 The wicked arrogantly hunt down the poor.
    Let them be caught in the evil they plan for others.

**10:3**
Pss 49:6; 94:3-4

3 For they brag about their evil desires;
    they praise the greedy and curse the LORD.

**9:11** Hebrew *Zion;* also in 9:14.   **9:16** Hebrew *Higgaion Selah.* The meaning of this phrase is uncertain.
**9:17** Hebrew *to Sheol.*

---

**9:10** God will never abandon those who seek him. God's promise does not mean that if we trust in him we will escape loss or suffering; it means that God himself will never leave us no matter what we face.

**9:11** God does not live only in Jerusalem (or Zion, another name for Mount Moriah, the hill on which the Temple was built); he is everywhere all the time. The focal point of Israelite worship, however, came to be Jerusalem and its beautiful Temple. God was present in the Tabernacle (Exodus 25:8, 9) and in the Temple built by Solomon (2 Chronicles 7:16). From this central place of worship, the Jews were to tell the world about the one true God.

**9:13, 14** All of us want God to help us when we are in trouble, but often for different reasons. Some want God's help so that they will be successful and other people will like them. Others want God's help so that they will be comfortable and feel good about themselves. David, however, wanted help from God so that justice would be restored to Israel and so that he could show others God's power. When you call to God for help, consider your motive. Is it to save yourself pain and embarrassment or to bring God glory and honor?

**9:18** The world may ignore the plight of the needy, crushing any earthly hope they may have. But God, the champion of the weak, promises that this will not be the case forever. Wicked nations, which forget the Lord and refuse to help their people, will be judged by God. He knows our needs, he knows our tendency to despair, and he has promised to care for us (see also 9:9, 12). Even when others forget us, he will remember.

**10:1** "Why do you hide when I am in trouble?" To the psalm writer, God seemed far away. But even though the writer had honest doubts, he did not stop praying or conclude that God no longer cared. He was not complaining but simply asking God to hurry to his aid. It is during those times when we feel most alone or oppressed that we need to keep praying, telling God about our troubles.

<sup>4</sup> The wicked are too proud to seek God.
    They seem to think that God is dead.

<sup>5</sup> Yet they succeed in everything they do.
    They do not see your punishment awaiting them.
    They sneer at all their enemies.

<sup>6</sup> They think, "Nothing bad will ever happen to us!
    We will be free of trouble forever!"

<sup>7</sup> Their mouths are full of cursing, lies, and threats.*
    Trouble and evil are on the tips of their tongues.

<sup>8</sup> They lurk in ambush in the villages,
    waiting to murder innocent people.
    They are always searching for helpless victims.

<sup>9</sup> Like lions crouched in hiding,
    they wait to pounce on the helpless.
Like hunters they capture the helpless
    and drag them away in nets.

<sup>10</sup> Their helpless victims are crushed;
    they fall beneath the strength of the wicked.

<sup>11</sup> The wicked think, "God isn't watching us!
    He has closed his eyes and won't even see what we do!"

<sup>12</sup> Arise, O LORD!
    Punish the wicked, O God!
    Do not ignore the helpless!

<sup>13</sup> Why do the wicked get away with despising God?
    They think, "God will never call us to account."

<sup>14</sup> But you see the trouble and grief they cause.
    You take note of it and punish them.
The helpless put their trust in you.
    You defend the orphans.

<sup>15</sup> Break the arms of these wicked, evil people!
    Go after them until the last one is destroyed.

<sup>16</sup> The LORD is king forever and ever!
    The godless nations will vanish from the land.

<sup>17</sup> LORD, you know the hopes of the helpless.
    Surely you will hear their cries and comfort them.

<sup>18</sup> You will bring justice to the orphans and the oppressed,
    so mere people can no longer terrify them.

| | |
|---|---|
| | **10:4** Pss 14:1; 36:1-2 |
| | **10:5** Pss 28:5; 52:7 |
| | **10:6** Pss 30:6-7; 49:11 |
| | **10:7** Pss 59:12; 73:8; 140:3 †Rom 3:14 |
| | **10:8** Pss 11:2; 94:6-7 |
| | **10:9** Pss 10:2; 17:12; 59:3; 140:5 |
| | **10:11** Ps 10:4 |
| | **10:12** Pss 9:12; 17:7 |
| | **10:14** Pss 9:12; 22:9-11; 37:5 |
| | **10:15** Pss 37:17; 140:11 |
| | **10:16** Deut 8:20 Ps 29:10 |
| | **10:17** Pss 9:18; 34:15; 145:19 |
| | **10:18** Pss 9:9; 74:21; 146:9 Isa 29:20 |

**Theme:** God's rule provides stability in the midst of panic. Because we can trust him, we can face our problems.
**Author:** David

# 11 *For the choir director: A psalm of David.*

<sup>1</sup> I trust in the LORD for protection.
    So why do you say to me,
    "Fly like a bird to the mountains for safety!

**11:1** Ps 121:1-2

**10:7** Greek version reads *cursing and bitterness.* Compare Rom 3:14.

---

**10:4-6** Some people succeed in everything they do, and they brag that no one, not even God, can keep them down. We may wonder why God allows these people to amass great wealth while they despise him as they do. But why are we upset when the wicked prosper? Are we angry about the damage they are doing or just jealous of their success? To answer these questions, we must gain the right perspective on wickedness and wealth. The wicked will surely be punished because God hates their evil deeds. Wealth is only temporary. It is not necessarily a sign of God's approval on a person's life; nor is lack of it a sign of God's disapproval. Don't let wealth become your obsession. See Proverbs 30:7, 8 for a prayer you can pray about money.

**10:11** There is an incompatibility between blind arrogance and the presence of God in our hearts. Proud people depend on themselves rather than on God. This causes God's guiding influences to leave their lives. When God's presence is welcome, there is no room for pride because he makes us aware of our true selves.

**10:14** God sees and takes note of each evil deed, encourages us, and listens to our cries (10:17). He is always with us. We can face the wicked because we do not face them alone. God is by our side.

**11:1-4** David was forced to flee for safety several times. Being God's anointed king did not make him immune to injustice and hatred from others. He may have written this psalm when he was

**11:2**
Pss 7:12; 64:3-4

2 The wicked are stringing their bows
    and fitting their arrows on the bowstrings.
They shoot from the shadows
    at those whose hearts are right.

**11:3**
Ps 82:5

3 The foundations of law and order have collapsed.
    What can the righteous do?"

**11:4**
Pss 34:15-16;
103:19

4 But the LORD is in his holy Temple;
    the LORD still rules from heaven.
He watches everyone closely,
    examining every person on earth.

**11:5**
Gen 22:1
Ps 5:5

5 The LORD examines both the righteous and the wicked.
    He hates those who love violence.

**11:6**
Jer 4:11-12
Ezek 38:22

6 He will rain down blazing coals and burning sulfur on the wicked,
    punishing them with scorching winds.

**11:7**
Pss 7:9-11; 17:15;
33:5

7 For the righteous LORD loves justice.
    The virtuous will see his face.

**Theme:** The proud and lying words of people versus the true and pure words of God. A call for protection against those who try to manipulate us.
**Author:** David

# 12

*For the choir director: A psalm of David, to be accompanied by an eight-stringed instrument.**

**12:1**
Mic 7:1-2

1 Help, O LORD, for the godly are fast disappearing!
    The faithful have vanished from the earth!

**12:2**
Pss 28:3; 41:6
Jer 9:8
Rom 16:18

2 Neighbors lie to each other,
    speaking with flattering lips and deceitful hearts.

**12:3**
Pss 55:21; 73:8-9

3 May the LORD cut off their flattering lips
    and silence their boastful tongues.
4 They say, "We will lie to our hearts' content.
    Our lips are our own—who can stop us?"

**12:5**
Pss 3:7; 34:6;
35:10

5 The LORD replies, "I have seen violence done to the helpless,
    and I have heard the groans of the poor.
Now I will rise up to rescue them,
    as they have longed for me to do."

**12:TITLE** Hebrew *according to the sheminith.*

---

being hunted by Saul (1 Samuel 18–31) or during the days of Absalom's rebellion (2 Samuel 15–18). In both instances, David fled, but not as if all was lost. He knew God was in control. While David wisely avoided trouble, he did not fearfully run away from his troubles.

**11:1-4** David seems to be speaking to those who are advising him to run from his enemies. David's faith contrasts dramatically with the fear of the advisers who tell him to flee. Faith in God keeps us from losing hope and helps us resist fear. David's advisers were afraid because they saw only frightening circumstances and crumbling foundations. David was comforted and optimistic because he knew God was greater than anything his enemies could bring against him (7:10; 16:1; 31:2, 3).

**11:4** When the foundations are shaking and you wish you could hide, remember that God is still in control. His power is not diminished by any turn of events. Nothing happens without his knowledge and permission. When you feel like running away—run to God. He will restore justice and goodness on the earth in his good time.

**11:5** God does not shield believers from difficult circumstances, but he examines (or tests) both the righteous and the wicked. For some, God's tests become a refining fire, while for others they become an incinerator for destruction. Don't ignore or defy the tests and challenges that come your way. Use them as opportunities for you to grow.

**12:1** Living for God in a deceitful world can be difficult and lonely. At one time the great prophet Elijah felt so lonely he wanted to die. But God told him that there were 7,000 other faithful servants (1 Kings 19:4, 14, 18). We are never alone in our battle against evil. When you feel alone, seek out other believers for strength and support.

**12:2-4** We may be tempted to believe that some lies are relatively harmless, even useful at times. But God does not overlook lies, flattery, deception, or boasting. Each of these sins originates from a bad attitude that is eventually expressed in our speech. The tongue can be our greatest enemy because, though small, it can do great damage (James 3:5, 6). Be careful how you use yours.

**12:5** God cares for the helpless and the poor. Here he promises to protect the downtrodden and confront their oppressors. We should identify with God's attitude. His work is not done until we care for the needs of the poor.

6 The LORD's promises are pure,
    like silver refined in a furnace,
    purified seven times over.
7 Therefore, LORD, we know you will protect the oppressed,
    preserving them forever from this lying generation,
8 even though the wicked strut about,
    and evil is praised throughout the land.

**Theme:** Praying for relief from despair. We must continue to trust God even when
he doesn't answer us immediately.
**Author:** David

# 13 *For the choir director: A psalm of David.*

1 O LORD, how long will you forget me? Forever?
    How long will you look the other way?
2 How long must I struggle with anguish in my soul,
    with sorrow in my heart every day?
    How long will my enemy have the upper hand?

3 Turn and answer me, O LORD my God!
    Restore the sparkle to my eyes, or I will die.
4 Don't let my enemies gloat, saying, "We have defeated him!"
    Don't let them rejoice at my downfall.

5 But I trust in your unfailing love.
    I will rejoice because you have rescued me.
6 I will sing to the LORD
    because he is good to me.

**Theme:** Only the fool denies God. How foolish it must seem to God when people
say there is no God.
**Author:** David

# 14 *For the choir director: A psalm of David.*

1 Only fools say in their hearts,
    "There is no God."
  They are corrupt, and their actions are evil;
    not one of them does good!

2 The LORD looks down from heaven
    on the entire human race;
  he looks to see if anyone is truly wise,
    if anyone seeks God.

**12:6**
Pss 19:8-10;
119:140
Prov 30:5

**12:7**
Pss 37:28; 97:10

**12:8**
Ps 55:10-11

**13:1**
Job 13:24
Pss 44:24; 89:46

**13:2**
Ps 42:4-5, 9

**13:3**
Ezra 9:8
Job 33:29-30
Ps 5:1

**13:4**
Pss 25:2; 38:16

**13:5**
Pss 9:14; 52:8

**13:6**
Ps 116:7

**14:1-7**
//Ps 53:1-6

**14:1**
Pss 10:4; 53:1
†Rom 3:10-12

**14:2**
Pss 33:13-15;
102:19

---

**12:6** Sincerity and truth are extremely valuable because they
are so rare. Many people are deceivers, liars, flatterers; they think
they will get what they want by deception. As a king, David certainly faced his share of such people, who hoped to win his favor
and gain advancement through flattery. When we feel as though
sincerity and truth have nearly gone out of existence, we have one
hope—the Word of God. God's Word is as pure and flawless as
refined silver. So listen carefully when he speaks to you through
his Word.

**13:1** Sometimes all we need to do is talk over a problem with
a friend to help put it in perspective. In this psalm, the phrase
"how long" occurs four times in the first two verses, indicating
the depth of David's distress. David expressed his feelings to
God and found strength. By the end of his prayer, he was able
to profess hope and trust in God. Through prayer we can express
our feelings and talk our problems out with God. He helps us
regain the right perspective, and this gives us peace (Habakkuk
3:17-19).

**13:1-5** David frequently claimed that God was slow to act on his
behalf. We often feel this same impatience. It seems that evil and
suffering go unchecked, and we wonder when God is going to
stop them. David affirmed that he would continue to trust God
no matter how long he had to wait for God's justice to be realized.
When you feel impatient, remember David's steadfast faith in
God's unfailing love.

**13:5, 6** David was faithful to God and trusted wholeheartedly in
him, but he felt the pressure of his problems as much as anyone.
Instead of giving up or giving in, however, David held on to his
faith. In times of despair, it is much harder to hold on than to
give up. But if you give up on God, you give in to a life of despair.

**14:1-3** The true atheist is either foolish or wicked—foolish
because he ignores the evidence that God exists or wicked because
he refuses to live by God's truths. We become atheists in practice
when we rely more on ourselves than on God. The fools mentioned
here are aggressively perverse in their actions. To speak in direct
defiance of God is utterly foolish according to the Bible.

**14:3**
Pss 58:3; 143:2

³ But no, all have turned away;
  all have become corrupt.*
No one does good,
  not a single one!

**14:4**
Isa 64:7

⁴ Will those who do evil never learn?
  They eat up my people like bread
  and wouldn't think of praying to the LORD.
⁵ Terror will grip them,
  for God is with those who obey him.

**14:6**
Pss 9:9; 40:17

⁶ The wicked frustrate the plans of the oppressed,
  but the LORD will protect his people.

**14:7**
Job 42:10
Pss 53:6; 85:1-2

⁷ Who will come from Mount Zion to rescue Israel?
  When the LORD restores his people,
  Jacob will shout with joy, and Israel will rejoice.

**Theme:** Guidelines for living a blameless life.
**Author:** David

# 15 *A psalm of David.*

**15:1**
Pss 24:3; 27:5-6

¹ Who may worship in your sanctuary, LORD?
  Who may enter your presence on your holy hill?

**14:3** Greek version reads *have become useless.* Compare Rom 3:12.

---

**TROUBLES AND COMPLAINTS IN PSALMS**

We can relate to the psalms because they express our feelings. We all face troubles, as did the psalm writers hundreds of years ago, and we often respond as they did. In Psalm 3, David told God how he felt about the odds against him. But within three verses, the king realized that God's presence and care made the odds meaningless. This experience is repeated in many of the psalms. Usually, the hope and confidence in God outweigh the fear and suffering; sometimes they do not. Still, the psalm writers consistently poured out their thoughts and emotions to God. When they felt abandoned by God, they told him so. When they were impatient with how slowly God seemed to be answering their prayers, they also told him so. Because they recognized the difference between themselves and God, they were free to be human and to be honest with their Creator. That is why so many of the dark psalms end in the light. The psalm writers started by expressing their feelings and ended up remembering to whom they were speaking!

Although we have much in common with these writers, we may differ in two ways: We might not tell God what we are really thinking and feeling; therefore, we also might not recognize, even faintly, who is listening to our prayers!

Notice this pattern as you read Psalms, and put the writers' insights to the test. You may well find that your awareness and appreciation of God will grow as you are honest with him. (See Psalms 3; 6; 13; 31; 37; 64; 77; 102; 121; 142.)

---

**14:3** No one but God is perfect; all of us stand guilty before him (see Romans 3:23) and need his forgiveness. No matter how well we perform or how much we achieve compared to others, none of us can boast of his or her goodness when compared to God's standard. God not only expects us to obey his laws, but he wants us to love him with all our heart. No one except Jesus Christ has done that perfectly. Because we all fall short, we must turn to Christ to save us (Romans 10:9-11). Have you asked him to save you?

**14:3, 4** David applies these observations to his enemies when he says the evildoers "eat up my people like bread" (14:4). "All have turned away; all have become corrupt. No one does good, not a single one!" (14:3). By contrast, David said, "You have scrutinized me and found nothing wrong" (17:3).

There is a clear distinction between those who worship God and those who refuse to worship him. David worshiped God, and under his leadership Israel obeyed God and prospered. Several hundred years later, however, Israel forgot God, and it became difficult to distinguish between God's followers and those who worshiped idols. When Isaiah called Israel to repentance, he, like David, spoke of people who had gone astray (Isaiah 53:6). But Isaiah was talking about the Israelites themselves. Paul quoted

Psalm 14 in Romans 3:10-12. He made the image of straying sheep even more general, referring to all people. The whole human race—Jew and Gentile alike—has turned away from God.

**14:5** If "God is with those who obey him," then those who attack God's followers may be attacking God. To attack God is utterly futile (see 2:4, 5, 10-12). Thus, while we may feel we are losing the battle, we can be absolutely sure that our ultimate victory is in God.

**15:1** *Sanctuary* and *holy hill* are interchangeable words describing the focal point of Israelite worship—the dwelling place of God. In Hebrew poetry the repeating pattern is found more in the thought than in the sound or rhythm.

**15:1ff** God calls his people to be morally upright, and, in this psalm, he gives us 10 standards to determine how we are doing. We live among evil people whose standards and morals are eroding. Our standards for living should not come from our evil society but from God. For other references where righteous conduct is summarized, see Isaiah 33:15; 56:1; Micah 6:8; Habakkuk 2:4; and Mark 12:29-31.

2 Those who lead blameless lives and do what is right,
  speaking the truth from sincere hearts.
3 Those who refuse to gossip
  or harm their neighbors
  or speak evil of their friends.
4 Those who despise flagrant sinners,
  and honor the faithful followers of the LORD,
  and keep their promises even when it hurts.
5 Those who lend money without charging interest,
  and who cannot be bribed to lie about the innocent.
  Such people will stand firm forever.

**Theme:** The joys and benefits of a life lived in companionship with God. We enjoy
these benefits now and eternally.
**Author:** David

# 16 *A psalm\* of David.*

1 Keep me safe, O God,
  for I have come to you for refuge.
2 I said to the LORD, "You are my Master!
  Every good thing I have comes from you."
3 The godly people in the land
  are my true heroes!
  I take pleasure in them!
4 Troubles multiply for those who chase after other gods.
  I will not take part in their sacrifices of blood
  or even speak the names of their gods.
5 LORD, you alone are my inheritance, my cup of blessing.
  You guard all that is mine.
6 The land you have given me is a pleasant land.
  What a wonderful inheritance!
7 I will bless the LORD who guides me;
  even at night my heart instructs me.
8 I know the LORD is always with me.
  I will not be shaken, for he is right beside me.
9 No wonder my heart is glad, and I rejoice.\*
  My body rests in safety.

**16:TITLE** Hebrew *miktam*. This may be a literary or musical term.  **16:9** Greek version reads *and my tongue shouts his praises.* Compare Acts 2:26.

| Reference | |
|---|---|
| **15:2** | Ps 24:4 / Eph 4:25 |
| **15:3** | Exod 23:1 / Ps 28:3 |
| **15:4** | Judg 11:35 / Acts 28:10 |
| **15:5** | Exod 22:25; 23:8 / Deut 16:19 |
| **16:1** | Pss 7:1; 17:8 |
| **16:2** | Ps 73:25 |
| **16:3** | Pss 101:6; 119:63 |
| **16:4** | Exod 23:13 / Josh 23:7 / Pss 32:10; 106:37-38 |
| **16:6** | Ps 78:55 / Jer 3:19 |
| **16:7** | Pss 73:24; 77:6 |
| **16:8** | Pss 27:8; 73:23; 110:5; 123:1-2 |

**15:2-5** As we grow in our relationship with our Redeemer, we develop a desire to live by his standards. The depth of our eternal relationship with him can often be measured by the way we reflect his standards in our daily activities.

**15:3, 4** Words are powerful, and how you use them reflects on your relationship with God. Perhaps nothing so identifies Christians as their ability to control their speech—speaking the truth, refusing to slander, and keeping oaths (promises). Watch what you say. (See James 3:1-12 for more on the importance of controlling your tongue.)

**15:5** God was against the Jews' charging interest or making a profit on loans to needy, fellow Jews (see also Exodus 22:25; Leviticus 25:35-37), although charging interest on loans to foreigners was allowed (Deuteronomy 23:20). Interest was also permitted for business purposes, as long as it wasn't exorbitant (Proverbs 28:8).

**15:5** Some people are so obsessed with money that they will change their God-given standards and life-style to get it. If money is a controlling force in your life, it must be curbed, or it will harm others and destroy your relationship with God.

**16:7, 8** It is human nature to make our own plans and *then* ask God to bless them. Instead, we should seek God's will first. By constantly thinking about the Lord and his way of living, we will gain insights that will help us make right decisions and live the way God desires. Communicating with God allows him to counsel us and give us wisdom.

**16:8** By saying that he "will not be shaken," David was talking about the unique sense of security felt by believers. God does not exempt believers from the day-to-day circumstances of life. Believers and unbelievers alike experience pain, trouble, and failure at times (Matthew 5:45). Unbelievers have a sense of hopelessness about life and confusion over their true purpose on earth. Those who seek God, however, can move ahead, confident in knowing what is right in God's eyes. They know that God will keep them from straying off his chosen path.

**16:8-11** This psalm is often called a messianic psalm because it is quoted in the New Testament as referring to the resurrection of Jesus Christ. Both Peter and Paul quoted from this psalm when speaking of Christ's bodily resurrection (see Acts 2:25-28, 31; 13:35-37).

**16:9** David's heart was glad—he had found the secret to joy. True joy is far deeper than happiness; we can feel joy in spite of

**16:10**
Pss 49:15; 86:13
†Acts 2:25-28;
13:35

¹⁰ For you will not leave my soul among the dead*
    or allow your holy one* to rot in the grave.

**16:11**
Ps 36:7-8

¹¹ You will show me the way of life,
    granting me the joy of your presence
    and the pleasures of living with you forever.*

**Theme:** A plea for justice in the face of false accusations and persecution. David urges us to realize the true goal of life—to know God—and the true reward of life—to see God one day.
**Author:** David, written while he was being persecuted by Saul.

# 17 *A prayer of David.*

**17:1**
Pss 61:1; 88:2;
142:6

¹ O LORD, hear my plea for justice.
    Listen to my cry for help.
Pay attention to my prayer,
    for it comes from honest lips.

**17:2**
Pss 98:8-9; 99:4;
103:6

² Declare me innocent,
    for you see those who do right.

**17:3**
Job 23:10
Pss 26:1-2; 39:1;
66:10
Jer 50:20

³ You have tested my thoughts and examined my heart in the night.
    You have scrutinized me and found nothing wrong.
    I am determined not to sin in what I say.

**17:4**
Pss 10:5-11;
119:9, 101

⁴ I have followed your commands,
    which keep me from following cruel and evil people.

**17:5**
Pss 18:36;
37:30-31; 44:18

⁵ My steps have stayed on your path;
    I have not wavered from following you.

⁶ I am praying to you because I know you will answer, O God.
    Bend down and listen as I pray.
⁷ Show me your unfailing love in wonderful ways.
    By your mighty power you rescue
    those who seek refuge from their enemies.

**17:8**
Deut 32:10
Ruth 2:12
Pss 36:7; 91:1, 4

⁸ Guard me as you would guard your own eyes.*
    Hide me in the shadow of your wings.
⁹ Protect me from wicked people who attack me,
    from murderous enemies who surround me.

**17:10**
1 Sam 2:3
Pss 31:18; 73:7-8

¹⁰ They are without pity.
    Listen to their boasting!

**17:11**
Pss 37:14; 88:17

¹¹ They track me down and surround me,
    watching for the chance to throw me to the ground.

**17:12**
Pss 7:2; 10:9

¹² They are like hungry lions, eager to tear me apart—
    like young lions hiding in ambush.

**16:10a** Hebrew *in Sheol.* **16:10b** Or *your Holy One.* **16:11** Greek version reads *You have shown me the way of life, / and you will fill me with the joy of your presence.* Compare Acts 2:28. **17:8** Hebrew *as the pupil of your eye.*

---

our deepest troubles. Happiness is temporary because it is based on external circumstances, but joy is lasting because it is based on God's presence within us. As we contemplate his daily presence, we will find contentment. As we understand the future he has for us, we will experience joy. Don't base your life on circumstances, but on God.

**16:10** David stated confidently that God would not leave him in the grave. Many people fear death because they can neither control nor understand it. As believers, we can be assured that God will not forget us when we die. He will bring us to life again to live with him forever. This provides *real* security. For other passages about resurrection, see Job 19:25, 26; Isaiah 26:19; Daniel 12:2, 13; Mark 13:27; 1 Corinthians 15:12-58; 1 Thessalonians 4:13-18; Revelation 20:11–21:4.

**17:3** Was David saying he was sinless? Far from a proud assumption of purity, David's claim was an understanding of his

relationship with God. In Psalms 32 and 51, David freely acknowledged his own sins. Nevertheless his relationship with God was one of close fellowship and constant repentance and forgiveness. His claim to goodness, therefore, was based on his continual seeking after God.

**17:8** Just as we protect our eyes, so God will protect us. We must not conclude, however, that we have somehow missed God's protection if we experience troubles. God's protection has far greater purposes than helping us avoid pain; it is to make us better servants for him. God also protects us by guiding us through painful circumstances, not only by helping us escape them.

**17:8** The "shadow of your wings" is a figure of speech symbolizing God's protection. He guards us just as a mother bird protects her young by covering them with her wings. Moses used a similar metaphor in Deuteronomy 32:11.

13 Arise, O LORD!
   Stand against them, and bring them to their knees!
   Rescue me from the wicked with your sword!
14 By the power of your hand, O LORD,
   destroy those who look to this world for their reward.
   But satisfy the hunger of your treasured ones.
   May their children have plenty,
   leaving an inheritance for their descendants.
15 Because I am righteous, I will see you.
   When I awake, I will see you face to face and be satisfied.

**17:13**
Ps 22:20

**17:14**
Ps 73:3-7

**17:15**
Pss 4:6-7; 16:11;
140:13

**Theme:** Gratitude for deliverance and victory. The only sure way to be delivered from
surrounding evil is to call upon God for help and strength.
**Author:** David

**18** *For the choir director: A psalm of David, the servant of the LORD. He sang this song to the LORD
on the day the LORD rescued him from all his enemies and from Saul. He sang:*

**18:TITLE**
//2 Sam 22:1-51

1 I love you, LORD;
   you are my strength.
2 The LORD is my rock, my fortress, and my savior;
   my God is my rock, in whom I find protection.
   He is my shield, the power that saves me,
   and my place of safety.
3 I called on the LORD, who is worthy of praise,
   and he saved me from my enemies.

**18:1**
Ps 59:17

**18:2**
1 Sam 2:2
Pss 19:14; 28:1;
59:9, 11; 71:3;
75:10; 144:2

**18:3**
Num 10:9
Pss 34:6; 96:4

4 The ropes of death entangled me;
   floods of destruction swept over me.
5 The grave* wrapped its ropes around me;
   death laid a trap in my path.
6 But in my distress I cried out to the LORD;
   yes, I prayed to my God for help.
   He heard me from his sanctuary;
   my cry to him reached his ears.

**18:4**
Pss 69:1-2; 116:3;
124:2-5

**18:5**
Ps 116:3

**18:6**
Pss 3:4; 34:15

7 Then the earth quaked and trembled.
   The foundations of the mountains shook;
   they quaked because of his anger.
8 Smoke poured from his nostrils;
   fierce flames leaped from his mouth.
   Glowing coals blazed forth from him.
9 He opened the heavens and came down;
   dark storm clouds were beneath his feet.
10 Mounted on a mighty angelic being,* he flew,
   soaring on the wings of the wind.

**18:7**
Ps 114:4, 6-7

**18:9**
Exod 20:21
Pss 97:2; 144:5

**18:10**
Pss 80:1; 99:1

**18:5** Hebrew *Sheol.*   **18:10** Hebrew *a cherub.*

---

**17:13-15** We deceive ourselves when we measure our happiness
or contentment in life by the amount of wealth we possess. When
we put riches at the top of our value system, we let power, pleasure, and financial security overshadow the eternal value of our
relationship with God. We think we will be happy or content when
we get riches, only to discover that they don't really satisfy, and
the pleasures fade away. The true measurement of happiness or
contentment is found in God's love and in doing his will. You will
find true happiness if you put your relationship with God above
earthly riches.

**17:15** The word *awake* shows that David believed in life after
death. Although belief in resurrection was not widespread in Old
Testament times, several verses show that it was partially understood. Some of these are Job 19:25-27; Psalms 16:10; 49:15;
139:17, 18; Isaiah 26:19; and Daniel 12:2, 13.

**18:1ff** This psalm is almost a duplicate of 2 Samuel 22. It may
have been written toward the end of David's life when there was
peace. God is praised for his glorious works and blessings
through the years.

**18:2, 3** God's protection of his people is limitless and can take
many forms. David characterized God's care with five military symbols. God is like (1) a *rock* that can't be moved by any who would
harm us, (2) a *fortress* or place of safety where the enemy can't
follow, (3) a *shield* that comes between us and harm, (4) *power that
saves*, a symbol of might that can save us, (5) a *place of safety* high
above our enemies. If you need protection, look to God.

**18:10** One of the functions of this "mighty angelic being" was
to serve as a guardian. Angels guarded the entrances to both
the tree of life (Genesis 3:24) and the Most Holy Place (Exodus
26:31-33). Two angels of hammered gold were part of the Ark of

11 He shrouded himself in darkness,
    veiling his approach with dark rain clouds.

**18:12**
Pss 97:2; 104:1-2

12 Thick clouds shielded the brightness around him
    and rained down hail and burning coals.*

**18:13**
Pss 29:3; 104:7-8

13 The LORD thundered from heaven;
    the voice of the Most High resounded
    amid the hail and burning coals.

**18:14**
Ps 144:6

14 He shot his arrows and scattered his enemies;
    his lightning flashed, and they were greatly confused.

**18:15**
Exod 15:8
Ps 106:9

15 Then at your command, O LORD,
    at the blast of your breath,
    the bottom of the sea could be seen,
    and the foundations of the earth were laid bare.

**18:16**
Ps 144:7

16 He reached down from heaven and rescued me;
    he drew me out of deep waters.

**18:17**
Ps 35:10

17 He rescued me from my powerful enemies,
    from those who hated me and were too strong for me.

**18:18**
Pss 16:8; 59:16

18 They attacked me at a moment when I was in distress,
    but the LORD supported me.

**18:19**
Pss 31:8; 37:23;
41:1, 11; 118:5

19 He led me to a place of safety;
    he rescued me because he delights in me.

**18:20**
Pss 7:8; 24:4

20 The LORD rewarded me for doing right;
    he restored me because of my innocence.

**18:21**
2 Chr 34:33
Pss 37:34; 119:33,
102-103

21 For I have kept the ways of the LORD;
    I have not turned from my God to follow evil.

22 I have followed all his regulations;
    I have never abandoned his decrees.

23 I am blameless before God;
    I have kept myself from sin.

24 The LORD rewarded me for doing right.
    He has seen my innocence.

**18:25**
Ps 62:12
Matt 5:7

25 To the faithful you show yourself faithful;
    to those with integrity you show integrity.

26 To the pure you show yourself pure,
    but to the wicked you show yourself hostile.

**18:27**
Pss 72:12; 101:5
Prov 6:16-19

27 You rescue the humble,
    but you humiliate the proud.

**18:28**
Job 18:6
Ps 27:1

28 You light a lamp for me.
    The LORD, my God, lights up my darkness.

**18:29**
Ps 118:10-12
2 Cor 12:9

29 In your strength I can crush an army;
    with my God I can scale any wall.

**18:30**
Pss 12:6; 19:7

30 God's way is perfect.
    All the LORD's promises prove true.
    He is a shield for all who look to him for protection.

**18:12** Or *and lightning bolts;* also in 18:13.

---

the Covenant (Exodus 25:18-22). The living beings carrying God's throne in Ezekiel 1 may have been these mighty angels.

**18:13** The "Most High" was an important designation for David to make. Pagan idol worship was deeply rooted in the land, and each region had its own deity. But these images of wood and stone were powerless. David was placing the Lord alone in a superior category: He is by far the Most High.

**18:16** Do your troubles, like "deep waters," threaten to drown you? David, helpless and weak, knew that God alone had rescued him from his enemies when he was defenseless. When you wish that God would quickly rescue you from your troubles, remember that he can either deliver you or be your support as you go through them (18:18). Either way, his protection is best for you. When

you feel as though you're drowning in troubles, ask God to help you, hold you steady, and protect you. In his care, you are never helpless.

**18:30** Some people think that belief in God is a crutch for weak people who cannot make it on their own. God is indeed a shield to protect us when we are too weak to face certain trials by ourselves, but he does not want us to remain weak. He strengthens, protects, and guides us in order to send us back into an evil world to fight for him. Then he continues to work with us because the strongest person on earth is infinitely weaker than God and needs his help. David was not a coward; he was a mighty warrior who, even with all his armies and weapons, knew that only God could ultimately protect and save him.

31 For who is God except the LORD?
   Who but our God is a solid rock?

**18:31**
Deut 32:31, 39
Pss 62:2; 86:8-10

32 God arms me with strength,
   and he makes my way perfect.

**18:32**
Isa 45:5

33 He makes me as surefooted as a deer,
   enabling me to stand on mountain heights.

**18:33**
Deut 32:13
Hab 3:19

34 He trains my hands for battle;
   he strengthens my arm to draw a bronze bow.

35 You have given me your shield of victory.
   Your right hand supports me;
   your help has made me great.

**18:35**
Pss 33:20; 63:8;
119:117

36 You have made a wide path for my feet
   to keep them from slipping.

**18:36**
Pss 31:8; 66:9

37 I chased my enemies and caught them;
   I did not stop until they were conquered.

**18:37**
Ps 44:5

38 I struck them down so they could not get up;
   they fell beneath my feet.

**18:38**
Pss 36:12; 47:3

39 You have armed me with strength for the battle;
   you have subdued my enemies under my feet.

40 You placed my foot on their necks.
   I have destroyed all who hated me.

**18:40**
Pss 21:12; 94:23

41 They called for help, but no one came to their rescue.
   They even cried to the LORD, but he refused to answer.

**18:41**
Ps 50:22

42 I ground them as fine as dust in the wind.
   I swept them into the gutter like dirt.

**18:42**
Ps 83:13

43 You gave me victory over my accusers.
   You appointed me ruler over nations;
   people I don't even know now serve me.

**18:43**
2 Sam 3:1
Ps 89:27
Isa 55:5

44 As soon as they hear of me, they submit;
   foreign nations cringe before me.

**18:44**
Ps 66:3

45 They all lose their courage
   and come trembling from their strongholds.

46 The LORD lives! Praise to my Rock!
   May the God of my salvation be exalted!

47 He is the God who pays back those who harm me;
   he subdues the nations under me

**18:47**
Pss 47:3; 94:1-2;
144:2

48    and rescues me from my enemies.
   You hold me safe beyond the reach of my enemies;
   you save me from violent opponents.

**18:48**
Pss 3:7; 27:5-6

49 For this, O LORD, I will praise you among the nations;
   I will sing praises to your name.

**18:49**
Ps 108:1
†Rom 15:9

50 You give great victories to your king;
   you show unfailing love to your anointed,
   to David and all his descendants forever.

**18:50**
Pss 21:1; 28:8;
89:4

---

**18:32-34** God doesn't promise to eliminate challenges; instead, he promises to give us strength to meet those challenges. If he gave us no rough roads to walk, no mountains to climb, and no battles to fight, we would not grow. He does not leave us alone with our challenges, however. Instead, he stands beside us, teaches us, and strengthens us to face them.

**18:40-42** David was a merciful man. He spared the lives of Saul (1 Samuel 24:1-8), Nabal (1 Samuel 25:21-35), and Shimei (2 Samuel 16:5-12) and showed great kindness to Mephibosheth (2 Samuel 9). In asking God to destroy his enemies, David was simply asking him to give the wicked the punishment they deserved.

**18:43-45** David's great power had become legendary. God had given him victory in every battle. The book of 2 Samuel records victories over the Jebusites (5:6-10), the Philistines (5:17-25; 8:1), Hadadezer of Zobah (8:3, 4), the Arameans (8:5, 6; 10), the Edomites (8:13, 14), and the Ammonites (12:26-31). In addition, the king of Tyre had sent supplies and workmen to help David build his palace (5:11). But David did not attribute his victories to himself. He fully realized that the purpose of his position was to bless God's people (1 Chronicles 14:2).

**Theme:** Both God's creation and his word reveal his greatness.
**Author:** David

# 19
*For the choir director: A psalm of David.*

**19:1**
Gen 1:6-8
Rom 1:19-20

1 The heavens proclaim the glory of God.
　　The skies display his craftsmanship.

**19:2**
Ps 74:16

2 Day after day they continue to speak;
　　night after night they make him known.

3 They speak without a sound or word;
　　their voice is never heard.*

**19:4**
†Rom 10:18

4 Yet their message has gone throughout the earth,
　　and their words to all the world.

God has made a home in the heavens for the sun.

5 It bursts forth like a radiant bridegroom after his wedding.
　　It rejoices like a great athlete eager to run the race.

**19:6**
Ps 113:3

6 The sun rises at one end of the heavens
　　and follows its course to the other end.
　　Nothing can hide from its heat.

**19:7**
Pss 23:3; 36:9;
111:7; 119:14,
98-100, 160

7 The instructions of the LORD are perfect,
　　reviving the soul.
The decrees of the LORD are trustworthy,
　　making wise the simple.

**19:8**
Pss 12:6; 119:128

8 The commandments of the LORD are right,
　　bringing joy to the heart.
The commands of the LORD are clear,
　　giving insight for living.

**19:9**
Ps 119:138, 142

9 Reverence for the LORD is pure,
　　lasting forever.
The laws of the LORD are true;
　　each one is fair.

**19:10**
Ps 119:127

10 They are more desirable than gold,
　　even the finest gold.
They are sweeter than honey,
　　even honey dripping from the comb.

**19:11**
Ps 17:4
Prov 29:18-19

11 They are a warning to your servant,
　　a great reward for those who obey them.

**19:12**
Pss 51:1-2; 90:8;
139:23-24

12 How can I know all the sins lurking in my heart?
　　Cleanse me from these hidden faults.

**19:3** Or *There is no speech or language where their voice is not heard.*

---

**19:1ff** In this psalm, David meditates on God's creation, God's Word, his own sinfulness, and God's forgiveness. As God reveals himself through nature (19:1-6), we learn about his power and our finiteness. As God reveals himself through Scripture (19:7-11), we learn about his holiness and our sinfulness. As God reveals himself through daily experiences (19:12-14), we learn about his gracious forgiveness that frees us from guilt.

**19:1-6** We are surrounded by fantastic displays of God's craftsmanship—the heavens give dramatic evidence of his existence, his power, his love, his care. To say that the universe happened by chance is absurd. Its design, intricacy, and orderliness point to a personally involved Creator. As you look at God's handiwork in nature and the heavens, thank him for such magnificent beauty and the truth it reveals about the Creator.

**19:3, 4** The apostle Paul referred to this psalm when he explained that everyone knows about God because nature proclaims God's existence and power (Romans 1:19, 20). This does not cancel the need for missions because the message of God's salvation found in his Word, the Bible, must still be told to the ends of the earth. While nature points to the existence of God, the Bible tells us about

God's plan of salvation. God's people must explain to others how they can have a relationship with God. Although most people believe in a Creator because of the evidence of nature around them, they need to know about his love, mercy, and grace. What are you doing to take God's message to the world?

**19:7-11** When we think of instructions, decrees, and commandments, we often think of rules that keep us from having fun. But here we see the opposite: God's laws revive us, make us wise, bring joy to the heart, give insight, warn us, and reward us. God's laws are guidelines and lights for our path, rather than chains on our hands and feet. They point at danger to warn us, and then point at success to guide us.

**19:12, 13** Many Christians are plagued by guilt. They worry that they may have committed a sin unknowingly, done something good with selfish intentions, failed to put their whole heart into a task, or neglected what they should have done. Guilt can play an important role in bringing us to Christ and in helping us behave properly, but it should not cripple us or make us fearful. God fully and completely forgives us—even for those sins we do unknowingly.

13 Keep your servant from deliberate sins!
   Don't let them control me.
Then I will be free of guilt
   and innocent of great sin.

14 May the words of my mouth
   and the meditation of my heart
be pleasing to you,
   O LORD, my rock and my redeemer.

19:13
Pss 25:11; 32:2

19:14
Pss 18:2; 104:34

**Theme:** A prayer for victory in battle. Such a prayer can help us prepare for any great challenge. David knew that trust should be placed in the Lord more than in human power.
**Author:** David. The events in 2 Samuel 10 may have prompted this prayer.

# 20 *For the choir director: A psalm of David.*

1 In times of trouble, may the LORD answer your cry.
   May the name of the God of Jacob keep you safe from all harm.
2 May he send you help from his sanctuary
   and strengthen you from Jerusalem.*
3 May he remember all your gifts
   and look favorably on your burnt offerings.        *Interlude*

4 May he grant your heart's desires
   and make all your plans succeed.
5 May we shout for joy when we hear of your victory
   and raise a victory banner in the name of our God.
   May the LORD answer all your prayers.

6 Now I know that the LORD rescues his anointed king.
   He will answer him from his holy heaven
   and rescue him by his great power.
7 Some nations boast of their chariots and horses,
   but we boast in the name of the LORD our God.
8 Those nations will fall down and collapse,
   but we will rise up and stand firm.

9 Give victory to our king, O LORD!
   Answer our cry for help.

20:1
Ps 46:7, 11

20:2
Pss 3:4; 110:2;
119:28

20:3
Ps 51:19
Acts 10:4

20:4
Pss 21:2; 145:19

20:5
1 Sam 1:17
Pss 9:14; 60:4

20:6
Pss 28:8; 41:11
Isa 58:9

20:7
2 Chr 32:8
Ps 33:16-17

20:9
Ps 17:6

**Theme:** Praising God after victory in battle. When God answers our prayers for victory, we must quickly and openly thank him for his help.
**Author:** David

# 21 *For the choir director: A psalm of David.*

1 How the king rejoices in your strength, O LORD!
   He shouts with joy because you give him victory.
2 For you have given him his heart's desire;
   you have withheld nothing he requested.               *Interlude*

21:1
Ps 59:16-17

21:2
Ps 37:4

**20:2** Hebrew *Zion.*

**19:14** Would you change the way you live if you knew that every word and thought would be examined by God first? David asks that God approve his words and reflections as though they were offerings brought to the altar. As you begin each day, determine that God's love will guide what you say and how you think.

**20:6-8** As long as there have been armies and weapons, nations have boasted of their power, but such power does not last. Throughout history, empires and kingdoms have risen to great power only to vanish in the dust. David, however, knew that the true might of his nation was not in weaponry but in worship, not in firepower but in God's power. Because God alone can preserve a nation or an individual, be sure your confidence is in God, who gives eternal victory. Whom do you trust?

**21:1-6** David described all that he had as gifts from God: his heart's desire, success and prosperity, a crown of finest gold, long life, splendor and majesty, eternal blessings, joy. We, too, should look upon all we have—position, family, wealth, talent—as gifts from God. Only then will we use them to give glory back to him.

**21:3**
Ps 59:10

3 You welcomed him back with success and prosperity.
  You placed a crown of finest gold on his head.

**21:4**
Pss 61:6; 91:16;
133:3

4 He asked you to preserve his life,
  and you granted his request.
  The days of his life stretch on forever.

**21:5**
Pss 8:5; 96:6

5 Your victory brings him great honor,
  and you have clothed him with splendor and majesty.

6 You have endowed him with eternal blessings
  and given him the joy of your presence.

**21:7**
Pss 112:6; 125:1

7 For the king trusts in the LORD.
  The unfailing love of the Most High will keep him from stumbling.

**21:8**
Isa 10:10

8 You will capture all your enemies.
  Your strong right hand will seize all who hate you.

**21:9**
Lam 2:2
Mal 4:1

9 You will throw them in a flaming furnace
  when you appear.
  The LORD will consume them in his anger;
  fire will devour them.

10 You will wipe their children from the face of the earth;
   they will never have descendants.

**21:11**
Ps 2:1-3

11 Although they plot against you,
   their evil schemes will never succeed.

**21:12**
Pss 7:12-13; 18:40

12 For they will turn and run
   when they see your arrows aimed at them.

**21:13**
Pss 59:16; 81:1

13 Rise up, O LORD, in all your power.
   With music and singing we celebrate your mighty acts.

**Theme:** A prayer that carries us from great suffering to great joy. Despite apparent rejection by his friends and God, David believed that God would lead him out of despair. He looked forward to that future day when God would rule over the entire earth.
**Author:** David

# 22
*For the choir director: A psalm of David, to be sung to the tune "Doe of the Dawn."*

**22:1**
†Matt 27:46
†Mark 15:34

1 My God, my God, why have you abandoned me?
  Why are you so far away when I groan for help?

**22:2**
Pss 42:3; 88:1

2 Every day I call to you, my God, but you do not answer.
  Every night you hear my voice, but I find no relief.

**22:3**
Pss 99:9; 148:14

3 Yet you are holy,
  enthroned on the praises of Israel.

4 Our ancestors trusted in you,
  and you rescued them.

5 They cried out to you and were saved.
  They trusted in you and were never disgraced.

**22:6**
Job 25:6
Ps 31:11
Isa 41:14; 49:7

6 But I am a worm and not a man.
  I am scorned and despised by all!

---

**21:7** A good leader trusts the Lord and depends upon his unfailing love. Too often leaders trust in their own cleverness, popular support, or military power. But God is above all these "gods." If you aspire to leadership, keep the Lord God at the center of your life and depend on him. His love will keep you from stumbling.

**21:7** Because David trusted in God, God would not let him stumble (be removed from the throne). When we trust in God, we have permanence and stability. We may lose a great deal—families, jobs, material possessions—but we cannot be shaken from God's favor. He will be our foundation of solid rock. He will never leave or desert us.

**21:11** When you see evil schemes unfold, remember that they will not succeed forever. The power of evildoers is only temporary, and God's very presence can send them scattering in a moment. God, according to his plan and purpose, will intervene for his

people and give the wicked the judgment they deserve. We should not be dismayed when we see the temporary advantage God's enemies seem to have.

**22:1** David gave an amazingly accurate description of the suffering the Messiah would endure hundreds of years later. David was obviously enduring some great trial, but through his suffering, he, like the Messiah to come, gained victory. Jesus, the Messiah, quoted this verse while hanging on the cross carrying our burden of sin (Matthew 27:46). It was not a cry of doubt, but an urgent appeal to God.

**22:6** When others despise us and heap scorn upon us, they treat us as less than human. After much degradation, we, like David, may begin to feel like worms. When we feel the sting of rejection, we must keep in mind the hope and victory that God promises us (22:22ff).

7 Everyone who sees me mocks me.
    They sneer and shake their heads, saying,
8 "Is this the one who relies on the LORD?
    Then let the LORD save him!
If the LORD loves him so much,
    let the LORD rescue him!"

**22:7**
Isa 53:3
Matt 27:39
Mark 15:29-30
**22:8**
Matt 27:43

9 Yet you brought me safely from my mother's womb
    and led me to trust you at my mother's breast.
10 I was thrust into your arms at my birth.
    You have been my God from the moment I was born.

**22:9**
Ps 71:5-6
**22:10**
Isa 46:3

11 Do not stay so far from me,
    for trouble is near,
    and no one else can help me.
12 My enemies surround me like a herd of bulls;
    fierce bulls of Bashan have hemmed me in!
13 Like lions they open their jaws against me,
    roaring and tearing into their prey.
14 My life is poured out like water,
    and all my bones are out of joint.
My heart is like wax,
    melting within me.
15 My strength has dried up like sunbaked clay.
    My tongue sticks to the roof of my mouth.
You have laid me in the dust and left me for dead.
16 My enemies surround me like a pack of dogs;
    an evil gang closes in on me.
They have pierced my hands and feet.
17 I can count all my bones.
    My enemies stare at me and gloat.
18 They divide my garments among themselves
    and throw dice* for my clothing.

**22:11**
Ps 72:12

**22:13**
Ps 17:12

**22:14**
Job 30:16
Ps 31:9-10

**22:15**
Pss 38:10; 104:29
†John 19:28

**22:16**
Ps 59:6-7
Matt 27:35
John 20:25

**22:18**
†Matt 27:35
†Mark 15:24
Luke 23:34
John 19:23-24

19 O LORD, do not stay far away!
    You are my strength; come quickly to my aid!
20 Save me from the sword;
    spare my precious life from these dogs.
21 Snatch me from the lion's jaws
    and from the horns of these wild oxen.

**22:19**
Pss 22:11; 70:5
**22:20**
Pss 35:17; 37:14
**22:21**
Pss 34:4; 118:5;
120:1

22 I will proclaim your name to my brothers and sisters.*
    I will praise you among your assembled people.
23 Praise the LORD, all you who fear him!
    Honor him, all you descendants of Jacob!
Show him reverence, all you descendants of Israel!
24 For he has not ignored or belittled the suffering of the needy.
    He has not turned his back on them,
    but has listened to their cries for help.

**22:22**
†Heb 2:12
**22:23**
Pss 33:8; 86:12;
135:19-20

**22:24**
Pss 27:9; 31:22
Heb 5:7

25 I will praise you in the great assembly.
    I will fulfill my vows in the presence of those who worship you.

**22:25**
Pss 35:18; 40:9-10

**22:18** Hebrew *cast lots.*   **22:22** Hebrew *my brothers.*

---

**22:9-11** God's loving concern does not begin on the day we are born and conclude on the day we die. It reaches back to those days before we were born and reaches ahead along the unending path of eternity. Our only sure help comes from a God whose concern for us reaches beyond our earthly existence. How can anyone reject such love?

**22:12** The land of Bashan, located east of the Sea of Galilee, was known for its strong and well-fed cattle (Amos 4:1). Because of its grain fields, it was often called the breadbasket of Palestine.

**22:22** David would praise God among the people because his private deliverance deserved a public testimony. God may wonderfully deliver us in the quiet moments when we are hurting, and we must be prepared to offer public praise for his care.

**22:26**
Pss 40:16; 69:32;
107:9

26 The poor will eat and be satisfied.
   All who seek the LORD will praise him.
   Their hearts will rejoice with everlasting joy.
27 The whole earth will acknowledge the LORD and return to him.
   All the families of the nations will bow down before him.

**22:28**
Ps 47:6-8

28 For royal power belongs to the LORD.
   He rules all the nations.

29 Let the rich of the earth feast and worship.
   Bow before him, all who are mortal,
   all whose lives will end as dust.

**22:30**
Ps 102:18, 28

30 Our children will also serve him.
   Future generations will hear about the wonders of the Lord.
31 His righteous acts will be told to those not yet born.
   They will hear about everything he has done.

---

**CHRIST IN
THE PSALMS**

Both the Jewish and Christian faiths have long believed that many psalms referred as much to the promised Messiah as they did to events at the time. Because the Messiah was to be a descendant of David, it was expected that many of the royal psalms would apply to him. Christians noted how many of the passages seemed to describe in detail events from Christ's life and death. Jesus himself frequently quoted from Psalms. Almost everything that happened at the Crucifixion and most of Jesus' words during his final hours were prophesied in Psalms.

The following is a list of the main references in Psalms pertaining to Christ.

| Reference in Psalms | Reference to Christ | Fulfillment in the New Testament |
| --- | --- | --- |
| 2:7 | The Messiah will be God's Son | Hebrews 1:5, 6 |
| 16:8-10 | He will rise from the dead | Luke 24:5-7 |
| 22:1-21 | He will experience agony on the cross | Matthew 26; 27 |
| 22:15 | He will thirst while on the cross | John 19:28 |
| 22:18 | Evil men will throw dice for his clothing | Matthew 27:35; John 19:23, 24 |
| 22:22 | He will declare God's name | Hebrews 2:12 |
| 34:20 | His bones will not be broken | John 19:36, 37 |
| 40:6-8 | He will come to do God's will | Hebrews 10:5-7 |
| 41:9 | His close friend will betray him | Luke 22:48 |
| 45:6, 7 | His throne will last forever | Hebrews 1:8, 9 |
| 68:18 | He will ascend into heaven | Ephesians 4:8-10 |
| 69:9 | He will be zealous for God | John 2:17 |
| 69:21 | He will be offered vinegar for his thirst on the cross | Matthew 27:48 |
| 89:3, 4, 35, 36 | He will be a descendant of David | Luke 1:31-33 |
| 96:13 | He will return to judge the world | 1 Thessalonians 1:10 |
| 110:1 | He is David's son and David's Lord | Matthew 22:44 |
| 110:4 | He is the eternal priest-king | Hebrews 6:20 |
| 118:22 | He is rejected by many but accepted by God | 1 Peter 2:7, 8 |

---

**22:30, 31** Unborn generations are depending on our faithfulness today. As we teach our children about the Lord, so they will teach their children and their children's children. If we fail to tell our children about the Lord, we may well be breaking the chain of God's influence in generations to come. We must view our children and all the young people we meet as God's future leaders. If we are faithful in opportunities today, we may well be affecting the future.

**22:30, 31** If we want our children to serve the Lord, they must hear about him from us. It is not enough to rely on the church or those with more knowledge to provide all their Christian education. We must reinforce the lessons of the Bible in our homes.

**Theme:** God is seen as a caring shepherd and a dependable guide. We must follow
God and obey his commands. He is our only hope for eternal life and security.
**Author:** David

# 23 *A psalm of David.*

¹ The LORD is my shepherd;
  I have all that I need.
² He lets me rest in green meadows;
  he leads me beside peaceful streams.
³    He renews my strength.
  He guides me along right paths,
  bringing honor to his name.
⁴ Even when I walk
    through the darkest valley,*
  I will not be afraid,
    for you are close beside me.
  Your rod and your staff
    protect and comfort me.
⁵ You prepare a feast for me
    in the presence of my enemies.
  You honor me by anointing my head with oil.
    My cup overflows with blessings.
⁶ Surely your goodness and unfailing love will pursue me
    all the days of my life,
  and I will live in the house of the LORD
    forever.

**23:1**
John 10:11
1 Pet 2:25

**23:2**
Pss 5:8; 46:4
Ezek 34:14
Rev 7:17

**23:3**
Pss 5:8; 19:7;
85:13

**23:4**
Pss 27:1; 107:14

**23:5**
Pss 16:5; 78:19;
92:10

**23:6**
Pss 25:6-7, 10;
27:4-6

**Theme:** Everything belongs to God—the glorious eternal King. Let us worship him
and welcome his glorious reign.
**Author:** David

# 24 *A psalm of David.*

¹ The earth is the LORD's, and everything in it.
  The world and all its people belong to him.

**24:1**
Ps 89:11
†1 Cor 10:26

**23:4** Or *the dark valley of death.*

---

**23:1** In describing the Lord as a shepherd, David wrote out of
his own experience because he had spent his early years caring
for sheep (1 Samuel 16:10, 11). Sheep are completely dependent
on the shepherd for provision, guidance, and protection. The
New Testament calls Jesus the good shepherd (John 10:11),
the great Shepherd (Hebrews 13:20), and the Great Shepherd
(1 Peter 5:4). As the Lord is the good shepherd, so we are his
sheep—not frightened, passive animals, but obedient followers,
wise enough to follow one who will lead us in the right places
and in right ways. This psalm does not focus on the animal-like
qualities of sheep but on the discipleship qualities of those who
follow. When you recognize the good shepherd, follow him!

**23:2, 3** When we allow God, our shepherd, to guide us, we
have contentment. When we choose to sin and go our own way,
however, we cannot blame God for the environment we create for
ourselves. Our shepherd knows the "green meadows" and
"peaceful streams" that will restore us. We will reach these
places only by following him obediently. Rebelling against the
shepherd's leading is actually rebelling against our own best
interests. We must remember this the next time we are tempted
to go our own way rather than the shepherd's way.

**23:4** Death casts a frightening shadow over us because we
are entirely helpless in its presence. We can struggle with other
enemies—pain, suffering, disease, injury—but strength and courage cannot overcome death. It has the final word. Only one person
can walk with us through death's dark valley and bring us safely
to the other side—the God of life, our shepherd. Because life is
uncertain, we should follow this shepherd who offers us eternal
comfort.

**23:5, 6** In ancient Near Eastern culture, at a feast it was customary to anoint a person with fragrant oil. Hosts were also expected
to protect their guests at all costs. God offers the protection of a
host even when enemies surround us. In the final scene of this
psalm, we see that believers will dwell with the Lord. God, the perfect shepherd and host, promises to guide and protect us throughout our life and to bring us into his house forever.

**24:1** Because "the earth is the LORD's," all of us are stewards, or
caretakers. We should be committed to the proper management
of this world and its resources. We are not to become devoted to
anything created or act as sole proprietors, however, because this
world will pass away (1 John 2:17).

**24:1ff** This psalm may have been written to celebrate moving
the Ark of the Covenant from Obed-edom's house to Jerusalem
(2 Samuel 6:10-12). Tradition says that this psalm was sung on
the first day of each week in the Temple services. Verses 1-6 tell
who is worthy to join in such a celebration of worship.

² For he laid the earth's foundation on the seas
    and built it on the ocean depths.

**24:3**
Pss 15:1; 65:4

³ Who may climb the mountain of the Lord?
    Who may stand in his holy place?

**24:4**
Job 17:9
Pss 51:10; 73:1
Matt 5:8

⁴ Only those whose hands and hearts are pure,
    who do not worship idols
    and never tell lies.

**24:5**
Deut 11:26-27

⁵ They will receive the Lord's blessing
    and have a right relationship with God their savior.

**24:6**
Ps 27:8

⁶ Such people may seek you
    and worship in your presence, O God of Jacob.     *Interlude*

⁷ Open up, ancient gates!
    Open up, ancient doors,
    and let the King of glory enter.

**24:8**
Exod 15:3, 6
Ps 76:3-6

⁸ Who is the King of glory?
    The Lord, strong and mighty;
    the Lord, invincible in battle.

**24:9**
Zech 9:9
Matt 21:5

⁹ Open up, ancient gates!
    Open up, ancient doors,
    and let the King of glory enter.

¹⁰ Who is the King of glory?
    The Lord of Heaven's Armies—
    he is the King of glory.     *Interlude*

---

**PSALMS TO LEARN AND LOVE**

Almost everyone, whether religious or not, has heard Psalm 23 because it is quoted so frequently. Many other psalms are also familiar because they are quoted in music, in literature, or in the words of the worship service.

The psalms we know and love are the ones that come into our minds when we need them. They inspire us, comfort us, or correct us just when we need a word from the Lord. If you want to begin memorizing psalms, start with some of these favorites. Memorize the whole psalm or just the verses that speak most directly to you. Or read the psalm aloud several times a day until it is part of you.

Psalms to bring us into God's presence . . . . . . . . . . 29; 95:1-7a; 96; 100
Psalms about goodness . . . . . . . . . . . . . . . . . . . . . 1; 19; 24; 133; 136; 139
Psalms of praise . . . . . . . . . . . . . . . . . . . . . . . . . . 8; 97; 103; 107; 113; 145; 150
Psalms of repentance and forgiveness . . . . . . . . . . . 32:1-5; 51; 103
Psalms for times of trouble . . . . . . . . . . . . . . . . . . . 3; 14; 22; 37:1-11; 42; 46; 53; 116:1-7
Psalms of confidence and trust . . . . . . . . . . . . . . . . 23; 40:1-4; 91; 119:11; 121; 127

---

**24:4** This refers to all lies, especially those told under oath. How greatly God values honesty! Dishonesty comes easily, especially when complete truthfulness could cost us something, make us uncomfortable, or put us in an unfavorable light. Dishonest communication hinders relationships. Without honesty, a relationship with God is impossible. If we lie to others, we will begin to deceive ourselves. God cannot hear us or speak to us if we are building a wall of self-deception.

**24:7-10** Who is this King of glory? The King of glory, identified here also as the Lord of Heaven's Armies, is the Messiah himself, eternal, holy, and mighty. This psalm is not only a battle cry for the church, but it also looks forward to Christ's future entry into the new Jerusalem to reign forever (Revelation 19:11-21).

**24:7-10** This psalm, often set to music, was probably used in corporate worship. It may have been reenacted many times at the Temple. The people outside would call out to the Temple gates to open up and let the King of glory in. From inside, the priests or another group would ask, "Who is the King of glory?" Outside, the people would respond in unison, "The Lord, strong and mighty, the Lord, invincible in battle," proclaiming his great power and strength. The exchange then would be repeated (24:9, 10), and the Temple gates would swing open, symbolizing the people's desire to have God's presence among them. This would have been an important lesson for children who were participating.

**Theme:** A prayer for defense, guidance, and pardon. As we trust in God, he grants these same requests for us.
**Author:** David

# 25 *
*A psalm of David.*

¹ O LORD, I give my life to you.
² I trust in you, my God!
Do not let me be disgraced,
or let my enemies rejoice in my defeat.
³ No one who trusts in you will ever be disgraced,
but disgrace comes to those who try to deceive others.

⁴ Show me the right path, O LORD;
point out the road for me to follow.
⁵ Lead me by your truth and teach me,
for you are the God who saves me.
All day long I put my hope in you.
⁶ Remember, O LORD, your compassion and unfailing love,
which you have shown from long ages past.
⁷ Do not remember the rebellious sins of my youth.
Remember me in the light of your unfailing love,
for you are merciful, O LORD.

⁸ The LORD is good and does what is right;
he shows the proper path to those who go astray.
⁹ He leads the humble in doing right,
teaching them his way.
¹⁰ The LORD leads with unfailing love and faithfulness
all who keep his covenant and obey his demands.

¹¹ For the honor of your name, O LORD,
forgive my many, many sins.
¹² Who are those who fear the LORD?
He will show them the path they should choose.
¹³ They will live in prosperity,
and their children will inherit the land.
¹⁴ The LORD is a friend to those who fear him.
He teaches them his covenant.
¹⁵ My eyes are always on the LORD,
for he rescues me from the traps of my enemies.

¹⁶ Turn to me and have mercy,
for I am alone and in deep distress.

| | |
|---|---|
| **25:3** | Pss 37:9; 40:1 Isa 49:23 |
| **25:4** | Pss 5:8; 86:11 |
| **25:5** | Pss 24:5; 40:1 |
| **25:6** | Ps 103:17 |
| **25:7** | Job 13:26 Ps 51:1 |
| **25:8** | Ps 86:5 |
| **25:9** | Pss 23:3; 32:8 |
| **25:10** | Pss 40:11; 103:17-18 |
| **25:11** | Ps 79:9 |
| **25:13** | Pss 37:11; 69:36 |
| **25:14** | Prov 3:32 John 7:17 |
| **25:15** | Pss 31:4; 123:2; 141:8 |
| **25:16** | Ps 69:16 |

**25** This psalm is a Hebrew acrostic poem; each verse begins with a successive letter of the Hebrew alphabet.

---

**25:2** Seventy-two psalms—almost half the book—speak about enemies. Enemies are those who oppose not only us, but also God's way of living. We can view temptations—money, success, prestige, lust—as our enemies. And our greatest enemy is Satan. David asked God to keep his enemies from overcoming him because they opposed what God stood for. If his enemies succeeded, David feared that many would think that living for God was futile. David did not question his own faith—he knew that God would triumph. But he didn't want his enemies' success to be an obstacle to the faith of others.

**25:4** David expressed his desire for guidance. How do we receive God's guidance? The first step is to *want* to be guided and to realize that God's primary guidance system is in his Word, the Bible. Psalm 119 tells of the endless knowledge found in God's Word. By reading the Bible and constantly learning from it, we will gain the wisdom to perceive God's direction for our lives. We may be tempted to demand answers from God, but David asked for direc-

tion. When we are willing to seek God, learn from his Word, and obey his commands, then we will receive his specific guidance.

**25:12** To fear the Lord is to recognize God's attributes: He is holy, almighty, righteous, pure, all-knowing, all-powerful, and all-wise. When we regard God correctly, we gain a clearer picture of ourselves: sinful, weak, frail, and needy. When we recognize who God is and who we are, we will fall at his feet in humble respect. Only then will he show us how to choose his way.

**25:14** "The LORD is a friend to those who fear him." God offers intimate and lasting friendship to those who revere him, who hold him in highest honor. What relationship could ever compare with having the Lord of all creation for a friend? Your everlasting friendship with God will grow as you respect and honor him.

**25:16, 17** Do life's problems always seem to go from bad to worse? God is the only one who can reverse this downward spiral. He can take our problems and turn them into glorious victories. The first and most important step is that we, like David,

**25:17**
Pss 40:12; 107:6

**25:18**
Pss 31:7; 103:3

**25:19**
Pss 3:1; 9:13

**25:20**
Pss 25:2; 86:2

**25:21**
Pss 25:3; 41:12

17 My problems go from bad to worse.
    Oh, save me from them all!
18 Feel my pain and see my trouble.
    Forgive all my sins.
19 See how many enemies I have
    and how viciously they hate me!
20 Protect me! Rescue my life from them!
    Do not let me be disgraced, for in you I take refuge.
21 May integrity and honesty protect me,
    for I put my hope in you.

22 O God, ransom Israel
    from all its troubles.

**Theme:** Declaring loyalty to God. If we are genuinely committed to God, we can stand up to opposition and examination.
**Author:** David, possibly written during the days of Absalom's rebellion

# 26 *A psalm of David.*

**26:1**
Pss 7:8; 13:5
Heb 10:23

**26:2**
Pss 7:9; 139:23

**26:3**
Pss 1:2; 48:9

**26:4**
Ps 1:1

**26:5**
Pss 1:1; 31:6;
139:21

**26:6**
Ps 43:3-4

**26:7**
Ps 9:1

**26:8**
Ps 27:4

**26:9**
Ps 28:3

**26:11**
Pss 26:1; 44:26;
69:18

**26:12**
Pss 22:22; 27:11;
40:2

1 Declare me innocent, O LORD,
    for I have acted with integrity;
    I have trusted in the LORD without wavering.
2 Put me on trial, LORD, and cross-examine me.
    Test my motives and my heart.
3 For I am always aware of your unfailing love,
    and I have lived according to your truth.
4 I do not spend time with liars
    or go along with hypocrites.
5 I hate the gatherings of those who do evil,
    and I refuse to join in with the wicked.
6 I wash my hands to declare my innocence.
    I come to your altar, O LORD,
7 singing a song of thanksgiving
    and telling of all your wonders.
8 I love your sanctuary, LORD,
    the place where your glorious presence dwells.

9 Don't let me suffer the fate of sinners.
    Don't condemn me along with murderers.
10 Their hands are dirty with evil schemes,
    and they constantly take bribes.
11 But I am not like that; I live with integrity.
    So redeem me and show me mercy.
12 Now I stand on solid ground,
    and I will publicly praise the LORD.

---

must cry out, "Turn to me and have mercy." When we are willing to do that, God will do his work in us and in our situation. The next step is yours—God has already made his offer.

**25:21** We need integrity and honesty to preserve us along life's way. The psalm writer asks for these to protect him step by step. Honesty says, "This is the Shepherd's way," and integrity says, "I will walk consistently in it."

**26:1-3** In asking God to declare him "innocent," David was not claiming to be sinless—that is impossible for any human being to achieve. Instead, he was pleading with God to clear his name of the false charges made against him by his enemies. We also can ask God to examine us, trusting him to forgive our sins and clear our record according to his mercy.

**26:4, 5** Should we stay away from unbelievers? No. Although Christians should avoid some places, Jesus demonstrated that

we must go among unbelievers to help them. There is a difference, however, between being *with* unbelievers and being *one of* them. Acting like unbelievers harms our witness for God. Ask yourself about the people you enjoy: If you are with them often, will you become less obedient to God in outlook or action? If the answer is yes, carefully monitor how you spend your time with these people and their effect on you.

**26:8** God's sanctuary in this verse refers to either the Tabernacle in Gibeon (the one constructed in the days of Moses; see Exodus 40:35) or the temporary dwelling David built to house the Ark of the Covenant (2 Samuel 6:17). David exclaimed how he loved to worship God at this place. Do you love to worship?

**26:12** Too often we complain about our problems to anyone who will listen and we praise God only in private. Instead, we ought to complain privately and praise God publicly.

**Theme:** God offers help for today and hope for the future. Unwavering confidence in God is our antidote for fear and loneliness.
**Author:** David

# 27 *A psalm of David.*

1 The Lord is my light and my salvation—
  so why should I be afraid?
 The Lord is my fortress, protecting me from danger,
  so why should I tremble?
2 When evil people come to devour me,
  when my enemies and foes attack me,
  they will stumble and fall.
3 Though a mighty army surrounds me,
  my heart will not be afraid.
 Even if I am attacked,
  I will remain confident.

4 The one thing I ask of the Lord—
  the thing I seek most—
 is to live in the house of the Lord all the days of my life,
  delighting in the Lord's perfections
  and meditating in his Temple.
5 For he will conceal me there when troubles come;
  he will hide me in his sanctuary.
 He will place me out of reach on a high rock.
6 Then I will hold my head high
  above my enemies who surround me.
 At his sanctuary I will offer sacrifices with shouts of joy,
  singing and praising the Lord with music.

7 Hear me as I pray, O Lord.
  Be merciful and answer me!
8 My heart has heard you say, "Come and talk with me."
  And my heart responds, "Lord, I am coming."
9 Do not turn your back on me.
  Do not reject your servant in anger.
  You have always been my helper.
 Don't leave me now; don't abandon me,
  O God of my salvation!
10 Even if my father and mother abandon me,
  the Lord will hold me close.

11 Teach me how to live, O Lord.
  Lead me along the right path,
  for my enemies are waiting for me.

Cross-refs: 27:1 Pss 18:28; 118:6, 14 — 27:3 Pss 3:6-7; 14:4 — 27:4 Pss 23:6; 26:8 — 27:5 Pss 17:8; 31:20 — 27:6 Pss 13:6; 107:22 — 27:7 Ps 13:3 — 27:8 Ps 105:4 — 27:9 Pss 6:1; 40:17; 69:17; 94:14 — 27:10 Isa 40:11; 49:15 — 27:11 Pss 5:8; 25:4; 86:11

**27:1** Fear is a dark shadow that envelops us and ultimately imprisons us within ourselves. Everyone has been a prisoner of fear at one time or another—fear of rejection, misunderstanding, uncertainty, sickness, or even death. But we can conquer fear by trusting in the Lord, who brings salvation. If we want to dispel the darkness of fear, let us remember with the psalm writer that "the Lord is my light and my salvation."

**27:4** By the "house of the Lord" and "his Temple," David could be referring to the Tabernacle in Gibeon, to the sanctuary he had built to house the Ark of the Covenant, or to the Temple that his son Solomon was to build. David probably had the Temple in mind because he made many of the plans for it (1 Chronicles 22). David may also have used the word *Temple* to refer to the presence of the Lord. David's greatest desire was to live in God's presence each day of his life. Sadly, this is not the greatest desire of many

who claim to be believers. What do you most desire? Do you look forward to being in the presence of the Lord?

**27:7** We often run to God when we experience difficulties. But David sought God's guiding presence *every day*. When troubles came his way, he was *already* in God's presence and prepared to handle any test. Believers can call to God for help at any time, but how shortsighted to call on God only when troubles come. Many of our problems could be avoided or handled far more easily by seeking God's help and direction beforehand.

**27:10** Many have had the sad experience of being abandoned by father or mother. Broken homes, differences of belief, addiction to drugs or alcohol, even psychological isolation can leave children crippled by this loss. Even as adults, the pain may linger. God can take that place in our life, fill that void, and heal that hurt. He can direct us to those who may take the role of father or mother for us. His love is sufficient for all our needs.

**27:12**
Ps 35:11
Matt 26:60
Acts 9:1

12 Do not let me fall into their hands.
For they accuse me of things I've never done;
with every breath they threaten me with violence.

**27:13**
Pss 116:9; 142:5
Isa 38:11

13 Yet I am confident I will see the LORD's goodness
while I am here in the land of the living.

**27:14**
Pss 31:24; 37:34

14 Wait patiently for the LORD.
Be brave and courageous.
Yes, wait patiently for the LORD.

**Theme:** Prayer when surrounded by trouble or wickedness. God is our only real source of safety. Prayer is our best help when trials come our way because it keeps us in communion with God.
**Author:** David

# 28 *A psalm of David.*

**28:1**
Pss 18:2; 35:22;
83:1; 88:4

1 I pray to you, O LORD, my rock.
Do not turn a deaf ear to me.
For if you are silent,
I might as well give up and die.

**28:2**
Ps 141:2
Lam 2:19
1 Tim 2:8

2 Listen to my prayer for mercy
as I cry out to you for help,
as I lift my hands toward your holy sanctuary.

**28:3**
Pss 26:9-10;
55:21; 62:4
Jer 9:8

3 Do not drag me away with the wicked—
with those who do evil—
those who speak friendly words to their neighbors
while planning evil in their hearts.

**28:4**
Ps 62:12
2 Tim 4:14
Rev 18:6

4 Give them the punishment they so richly deserve!
Measure it out in proportion to their wickedness.
Pay them back for all their evil deeds!
Give them a taste of what they have done to others.

**28:5**
Isa 5:12

5 They care nothing for what the LORD has done
or for what his hands have made.
So he will tear them down,
and they will never be rebuilt!

**28:6**
Ps 116:1
**28:7**
Pss 13:5-6; 16:9;
40:3; 59:17

6 Praise the LORD!
For he has heard my cry for mercy.
7 The LORD is my strength and shield.
I trust him with all my heart.
He helps me, and my heart is filled with joy.
I burst out in songs of thanksgiving.

**28:8**
Ps 20:6

8 The LORD gives his people strength.
He is a safe fortress for his anointed king.

---

**27:13** The "land of the living" simply means "this life" or "while I am living." David was obviously going through a trial, but he was confident that in this present life, God would see him through it.

**27:14** David knew from experience what it meant to wait for the Lord. He had been anointed king at age 16 but didn't become king until he was 30. During the interim, he had been chased through the wilderness by jealous King Saul. David had to wait on God for the fulfillment of his promise to reign. Later, after becoming king, he was chased by his rebellious son, Absalom.
Waiting for God is not easy. Often it seems that he isn't answering our prayers or doesn't understand the urgency of our situation. That kind of thinking implies that God is not in control or is not fair. But God is worth waiting for. Lamentations 3:24-26 calls us to hope in and wait for the Lord because often God uses times of waiting to refresh, renew, and teach us. Make good use

of your waiting times by discovering what God may be trying to teach you in them.

**28:3-5** It's easy to pretend friendship. Wicked people often put on a show of kindness or friendship in order to gain their own ends. David, in his royal position, may have met many who pretended friendship only to meet their own needs. David knew that God would punish these people eventually, but he prayed that their punishment would come swiftly. True believers should be straightforward and sincere in all their relationships.

9 Save your people!
　　Bless Israel, your special possession.*
　Lead them like a shepherd,
　　and carry them in your arms forever.

28:9
Deut 9:29; 32:9
Pss 33:12; 80:1
Isa 40:11

**Theme:** God reveals his great power in nature. We can trust God to give us both the peace and the strength to weather the storms of life.
**Author:** David

# 29 *A psalm of David.*

1 Honor the LORD, you heavenly beings*;
　　honor the LORD for his glory and strength.
2 Honor the LORD for the glory of his name.
　　Worship the LORD in the splendor of his holiness.

29:1
1 Chr 16:28-29
Ps 96:7-9

3 The voice of the LORD echoes above the sea.
　　The God of glory thunders.
　　The LORD thunders over the mighty sea.
4 The voice of the LORD is powerful;
　　the voice of the LORD is majestic.

29:4
Ps 68:33

5 The voice of the LORD splits the mighty cedars;
　　the LORD shatters the cedars of Lebanon.

29:5
Ps 104:16
Isa 2:13

6 He makes Lebanon's mountains skip like a calf;
　　he makes Mount Hermon* leap like a young wild ox.

29:6
Deut 3:9
Ps 114:4

7 The voice of the LORD strikes
　　with bolts of lightning.
8 The voice of the LORD makes the barren wilderness quake;
　　the LORD shakes the wilderness of Kadesh.

29:8
Num 13:26

9 The voice of the LORD twists mighty oaks*
　　and strips the forests bare.
　In his Temple everyone shouts, "Glory!"

29:9
Ps 26:8

10 The LORD rules over the floodwaters.
　　The LORD reigns as king forever.

29:10
Gen 6:17
Ps 10:16

11 The LORD gives his people strength.
　　The LORD blesses them with peace.

29:11
Pss 28:8; 37:11;
68:35
Isa 40:29

**Theme:** A celebration of God's deliverance. Earthly security is uncertain, but God is always faithful.
**Author:** David

# 30 *A psalm of David. A song for the dedication of the Temple.*

1 I will exalt you, LORD, for you rescued me.
　　You refused to let my enemies triumph over me.
2 O LORD my God, I cried to you for help,
　　and you restored my health.

30:1
Pss 25:2; 35:19,
24; 118:28; 145:1

30:2
Pss 6:2; 88:13

**28:9** Hebrew *Bless your inheritance.*　**29:1** Hebrew *you sons of God.*　**29:6** Hebrew *Sirion*, another name for Mount Hermon.　**29:9** Or *causes the deer to writhe in labor.*

---

**29:5, 6** The cedars of Lebanon were giant trees that could grow to 120 feet in height and 30 feet in circumference. A voice that could split the cedars of Lebanon would be a truly powerful voice—the voice of God. All that was impressive to people was under God's complete control.

**29:10, 11** Throughout history, God has revealed his power through mighty miracles over nature, such as the great Flood (Genesis 6–9). He promises to continue to reveal his power. Paul urged us to understand how great God's power is (Ephesians

1:18-23). The same power that raised Christ from the dead is available to help us with our daily problems. When you feel weak and limited, don't despair. Remember that God can give you strength. The same power that controls creation and raises the dead is available to you.

**30:1ff** David may have written this psalm when he dedicated Araunah's threshing floor (which became the future site of the Temple), after God stopped the great plague he had used to discipline David (1 Chronicles 21:1–22:6). The serious illness mentioned in 30:2, 3 may refer to an illness David experienced or to the plague itself.

30:3
Pss 28:1; 86:13

3 You brought me up from the grave,* O Lord.
    You kept me from falling into the pit of death.

30:4
Pss 97:12; 149:1

4 Sing to the Lord, all you godly ones!
    Praise his holy name.

30:5
Pss 103:9; 118:1

5 For his anger lasts only a moment,
    but his favor lasts a lifetime!
Weeping may last through the night,
    but joy comes with the morning.

30:6
Ps 10:6

6 When I was prosperous, I said,
    "Nothing can stop me now!"

30:7
Ps 104:29

7 Your favor, O Lord, made me as secure as a mountain.
    Then you turned away from me, and I was shattered.

8 I cried out to you, O Lord.
    I begged the Lord for mercy, saying,

30:9
Ps 6:5

9 "What will you gain if I die,
    if I sink into the grave?
Can my dust praise you?
    Can it tell of your faithfulness?

30:10
Pss 4:1; 27:7, 9

10 Hear me, Lord, and have mercy on me.
    Help me, O Lord."

30:11
Ps 6:8
Jer 31:4, 13

11 You have turned my mourning into joyful dancing.
    You have taken away my clothes of mourning and clothed me with joy,

30:12
Pss 44:8; 57:8;
108:1

12 that I might sing praises to you and not be silent.
    O Lord my God, I will give you thanks forever!

**Theme:** In times of stress, depending upon God requires complete commitment.
**Author:** David, although some say Jeremiah

# 31 *For the choir director: A psalm of David.*

31:1-4
//Ps 71:1-3

1 O Lord, I have come to you for protection;
    don't let me be disgraced.
    Save me, for you do what is right.

31:1
Pss 25:2; 143:1

31:2
Pss 71:3; 86:1;
102:2

2 Turn your ear to listen to me;
    rescue me quickly.
Be my rock of protection,
    a fortress where I will be safe.

31:3
Pss 18:2; 23:2-3

3 You are my rock and my fortress.
    For the honor of your name, lead me out of this danger.

31:4
Ps 25:15

4 Pull me from the trap my enemies set for me,
    for I find protection in you alone.

31:5
Luke 23:46
Acts 7:59

5 I entrust my spirit into your hand.
    Rescue me, Lord, for you are a faithful God.

30:3 Hebrew *from Sheol.*

---

**30:5** Like a shot given by a doctor, the discomfort of God's anger lasts only a moment, but the good effects go on for a long time. Let God's anger be a sharp pain that warns you to turn from sin.

**30:6, 7** Security had made David feel invincible. Although he knew that his riches and power had come from God, they had gone to his head, making him proud. Wealth, power, and fame can be intoxicating, making us feel self-reliant, self-secure, and independent of God. But this false security can be easily shattered. Don't be trapped by the false security of prosperity. Depend on God for your security, and you won't be shaken when worldly possessions disappear.

**31:1** David called on the Lord to deliver him. He wanted God to stop those who were unjustly causing trouble. Therefore, David

made his request based upon what he knew of God's name, or character. Because God is righteous and loving, he desires to deliver his people.

**31:1-6** We say we have faith in God, but do we really trust him? David's words, "I entrust my spirit into your hand," convey his complete trust in God. Jesus used these words as he was dying on the cross—showing his absolute dependence on God the Father (Luke 23:46). Stephen repeated these words as he was being stoned to death (Acts 7:59), confident that in death he was simply passing from God's earthly care to God's eternal care. We should commit our possessions, our families, and our vocations to God. But first and foremost, we should commit *ourselves* completely to him.

6 I hate those who worship worthless idols.
  I trust in the LORD.

31:6
Jon 2:8-9

7 I will be glad and rejoice in your unfailing love,
    for you have seen my troubles,
    and you care about the anguish of my soul.

31:7
Pss 10:14; 90:14

8 You have not handed me over to my enemies
    but have set me in a safe place.

31:8
Deut 32:30

9 Have mercy on me, LORD, for I am in distress.
    Tears blur my eyes.
    My body and soul are withering away.

31:9
Pss 6:7; 32:3;
38:3-4; 39:11; 63:1;
69:17; 102:1, 3-4

10 I am dying from grief;
     my years are shortened by sadness.
   Sin has drained my strength;
     I am wasting away from within.

31:10
Ps 13:2

11 I am scorned by all my enemies
     and despised by my neighbors—
     even my friends are afraid to come near me.
   When they see me on the street,
     they run the other way.

31:11
Pss 38:11; 88:8, 18
Isa 53:3

12 I am ignored as if I were dead,
     as if I were a broken pot.

31:12
Ps 88:5

13 I have heard the many rumors about me,
     and I am surrounded by terror.
   My enemies conspire against me,
     plotting to take my life.

31:13
Ps 41:7
Jer 20:10
Matt 27:1

14 But I am trusting you, O LORD,
     saying, "You are my God!"

31:14
Pss 140:6; 143:9

15 My future is in your hands.
   Rescue me from those who hunt me down relentlessly.

31:15
Job 24:1
Ps 143:9

16 Let your favor shine on your servant.
   In your unfailing love, rescue me.

31:16
Num 6:24-26
Ps 6:4

17 Don't let me be disgraced, O LORD,
     for I call out to you for help.
   Let the wicked be disgraced;
     let them lie silent in the grave.*

31:17
1 Sam 2:9
Ps 25:2-3, 20

18 Silence their lying lips—
     those proud and arrogant lips that accuse the godly.

31:18
1 Sam 2:3
Pss 94:4; 120:2

19 How great is the goodness
     you have stored up for those who fear you.
   You lavish it on those who come to you for protection,
     blessing them before the watching world.

31:19
Ps 5:11
Rom 11:22

20 You hide them in the shelter of your presence,
     safe from those who conspire against them.
   You shelter them in your presence,
     far from accusing tongues.

31:20
Job 5:21
Pss 27:5; 31:13

31:17 Hebrew in Sheol.

---

31:6 Why did David suddenly bring up the subject of idol worship? He wanted to contrast his total devotion to God with the diluted worship offered by many Israelites. Pagan religious rituals were never completely banished from Israel and Judah, despite the efforts of David and a few other kings. Obviously a person who clung to idols could not commit his spirit into God's hands. When we put today's idols (wealth, material possessions, success) first in our lives, we cannot expect God's Spirit to guide us. God is our highest authority and requires our first allegiance.

31:9-13 In describing his feelings, David wrote of the helplessness and hopelessness everyone feels when hated or rejected.

But adversity is easier to accept when we recognize our true relationship with the sovereign God (31:14-18). Although our enemies may seem to have the upper hand, they are ultimately the helpless and hopeless ones. Those who know God will be victorious in the end (31:23). We can have courage today because God will preserve us.

31:14, 15 In saying, "My future is in your hands," David was expressing his belief that all of life's circumstances are under God's control. Knowing that God loves and cares for us enables us to keep steady in our faith regardless of our circumstances. It keeps us from sinning foolishly by taking matters into our own hands or resenting God's timetable.

**31:21**
Ps 17:7

²¹ Praise the Lᴏʀᴅ,
for he has shown me the wonders of his unfailing love.
He kept me safe when my city was under attack.

**31:22**
Pss 66:19;
116:11-12; 145:19
Lam 3:54-56

²² In panic I cried out,
"I am cut off from the Lᴏʀᴅ!"
But you heard my cry for mercy
and answered my call for help.

**31:23**
Deut 32:40-41
Ps 37:28

²³ Love the Lᴏʀᴅ, all you godly ones!
For the Lᴏʀᴅ protects those who are loyal to him,
but he harshly punishes the arrogant.

**31:24**
Ps 27:14

²⁴ So be strong and courageous,
all you who put your hope in the Lᴏʀᴅ!

**Theme:** Forgiveness brings true joy. Only when we ask God to forgive our sins will
he give us real happiness and relief from guilt.
**Author:** David

# 32 *A psalm\* of David.*

¹ Oh, what joy for those
whose disobedience is forgiven,
whose sin is put out of sight!

**32:2**
Ps 85:2
†Rom 4:7-8

² Yes, what joy for those
whose record the Lᴏʀᴅ has cleared of guilt,\*
whose lives are lived in complete honesty!

**32:3**
Pss 31:10; 39:2

³ When I refused to confess my sin,
my body wasted away,
and I groaned all day long.

**32:4**
Pss 22:15; 39:10

⁴ Day and night your hand of discipline was heavy on me.
My strength evaporated like water in the summer heat.          *Interlude*

**32:5**
Lev 26:40
Job 31:33
Ps 38:18
1 Jn 1:9

⁵ Finally, I confessed all my sins to you
and stopped trying to hide my guilt.
I said to myself, "I will confess my rebellion to the Lᴏʀᴅ."
And you forgave me! All my guilt is gone.          *Interlude*

**32:TITLE** Hebrew *maskil.* This may be a literary or musical term.  **32:2** Greek version reads *of sin.* Compare Rom 4:7.

---

**CONFESSION, REPENTANCE, AND FORGIVENESS IN THE PSALMS**

Over the centuries, many believers, overcome by an awareness of their own sins, have found
in the words of the penitential (repentance) psalms a ray of hope. The psalm writers shared
with God the depth of their sorrow and repentance, as well as the height of joy at being forgiven. They rejoiced in the knowledge that God would respond to confession and repentance
with complete forgiveness. We who live on the other side of the cross of Christ can rejoice
even more because we understand more. God has shown us that he is willing to forgive
because his judgment on sin was satisfied by Christ's death on the cross.

As you read these psalms, note the pattern followed by the psalm writers in responding
to God: (1) They recognized their sinfulness and tendency to do wrong; (2) they realized that
sin was rebellion against God himself; (3) they admitted their sins to God; (4) they trusted in
God's willingness to forgive; and (5) they accepted his forgiveness. Use these psalms as a
reminder of how easy it is to drift away from God and fall into sin, and what is needed to
reestablish that fellowship.

Selected psalms that emphasize these themes are 6; 14; 31; 32; 38; 41; 51; 102; 130; 143.

---

**32:1ff** Read this psalm in conjunction with Psalm 51—both are
penitential psalms. Here David expressed the joy of forgiveness.
God had forgiven him for the sins he had committed against
Bathsheba and Uriah (2 Samuel 11–12). This is another of the
penitential (repentance) psalms where the writer confesses his sin
to God.

**32:1, 2** God *wants* to forgive sinners. Forgiveness has always
been part of his loving nature. He announced this to Moses
(Exodus 34:6, 7); he revealed it to David; he dramatically showed
it to the world through Jesus Christ. These verses convey several

aspects of God's forgiveness: He forgives disobedience, puts
sin out of sight, and clears our record of guilt. Paul quoted these
verses in Romans 4:7, 8 and showed that we can have this joyous
experience of forgiveness through faith in Christ.

**32:5** What is confession? To confess our sin is to agree with
God, acknowledging that he is right to declare what we have
done as sinful and that we are wrong to desire or to do it. It
means affirming our intention of forsaking that sin in order to
follow God more faithfully.

6 Therefore, let all the godly pray to you while there is still time,
   that they may not drown in the floodwaters of judgment.
7 For you are my hiding place;
   you protect me from trouble.
   You surround me with songs of victory.                          *Interlude*

8 The LORD says, "I will guide you along the best pathway for your life.
   I will advise you and watch over you.
9 Do not be like a senseless horse or mule
   that needs a bit and bridle to keep it under control."

10 Many sorrows come to the wicked,
   but unfailing love surrounds those who trust the LORD.
11 So rejoice in the LORD and be glad, all you who obey him!
   Shout for joy, all you whose hearts are pure!

**Theme:** Because God is Creator, Lord, Savior, and Deliverer, he is worthy of our trust and praise. Because he is faithful and his word is dependable, we can rejoice and sing, giving thanks and praise.
**Author:** Anonymous

# 33

1 Let the godly sing for joy to the LORD;
   it is fitting for the pure to praise him.
2 Praise the LORD with melodies on the lyre;
   make music for him on the ten-stringed harp.
3 Sing a new song of praise to him;
   play skillfully on the harp, and sing with joy.
4 For the word of the LORD holds true,
   and we can trust everything he does.
5 He loves whatever is just and good;
   the unfailing love of the LORD fills the earth.

6 The LORD merely spoke,
   and the heavens were created.
He breathed the word,
   and all the stars were born.
7 He assigned the sea its boundaries
   and locked the oceans in vast reservoirs.
8 Let the whole world fear the LORD,
   and let everyone stand in awe of him.
9 For when he spoke, the world began!
   It appeared at his command.

10 The LORD frustrates the plans of the nations
   and thwarts all their schemes.
11 But the LORD's plans stand firm forever;
   his intentions can never be shaken.

**32:6**
Ps 69:13
Isa 43:2

**32:7**
Exod 15:1
Pss 31:20; 40:3;
121:7

**32:8**
Pss 25:8; 33:18-19

**32:10**
Ps 16:4
Prov 16:20
Rom 2:9-10

**33:1**
Pss 32:11; 147:1

**33:2**
Ps 92:3

**33:3**
Pss 96:1; 98:1
Rev 5:9

**33:4**
Ps 19:8

**33:5**
Pss 11:7; 119:64

**33:6**
Gen 1:6-7
Ps 148:5
Heb 11:3

**33:7**
Exod 15:8

**33:8**
Pss 67:7; 96:9

**33:9**
Gen 1:3
Ps 148:5

**33:10**
Isa 8:9-10; 19:3

---

**32:8, 9** God describes some people as being like horses or mules that have to be controlled by bits and bridles. Rather than letting God guide them step by step, they stubbornly leave God only one option. If God wants to keep them useful for him, he must use discipline and punishment. God longs to guide us with love and wisdom rather than punishment. He offers to teach us the *best* way to go. Accept the advice written in God's Word and don't let your stubbornness keep you from obeying God.

**33:2, 3** David, who some believe wrote this psalm, was an accomplished harpist (1 Samuel 16:15-23). His psalms frequently refer to musical instruments. He undoubtedly composed music for many of the psalms, and he commissioned musicians for Temple worship (1 Chronicles 25).

**33:4** All God's words are true and trustworthy. The Bible is reliable because, unlike people, God does not lie, forget, change his words, or leave his promises unfulfilled. We can trust the Bible because it contains the words of a holy, trustworthy, and unchangeable God.

**33:6-9** This is a poetic summary of the first chapter of Genesis. God is not just the coordinator of natural forces; he is the Lord of creation, the almighty God. Because he is all-powerful, we should revere him in all we do.

**33:11** "The LORD's plans stand firm forever." Are you frustrated by inconsistencies you see in others or even in yourself? God is completely trustworthy—his intentions never change. The Bible promises that whatever is good and perfect comes to us from the Creator who never changes (James 1:17). When you wonder if there is anyone whom you can trust, remember that God is completely consistent. Let him counsel you.

**33:12**
Exod 19:5
Ps 144:15

¹² What joy for the nation whose God is the Lord,
　　whose people he has chosen as his inheritance.

¹³ The Lord looks down from heaven
　　and sees the whole human race.
¹⁴ From his throne he observes
　　all who live on the earth.
¹⁵ He made their hearts,
　　so he understands everything they do.

**33:16**
Pss 44:6; 147:10
**33:17**
Ps 20:7
Prov 21:31

¹⁶ The best-equipped army cannot save a king,
　　nor is great strength enough to save a warrior.
¹⁷ Don't count on your warhorse to give you victory—
　　for all its strength, it cannot save you.

**33:18**
Ps 34:15
**33:19**
Ps 37:19

¹⁸ But the Lord watches over those who fear him,
　　those who rely on his unfailing love.
¹⁹ He rescues them from death
　　and keeps them alive in times of famine.

**33:20**
Ps 115:9
Isa 8:17

²⁰ We put our hope in the Lord.
　　He is our help and our shield.
²¹ In him our hearts rejoice,
　　for we trust in his holy name.
²² Let your unfailing love surround us, Lord,
　　for our hope is in you alone.

**Theme:** God pays attention to those who call on him. Whether God offers escape from trouble or help in times of trouble, we can be certain that he always hears and acts on behalf of those who love him.
**Author:** David, after pretending to be insane in order to escape from King Achish (1 Samuel 21:10-15)

# 34 *  *A psalm of David, regarding the time he pretended to be insane in front of Abimelech, who sent him away.*

**34:1**
Ps 71:6
Eph 5:20

¹ I will praise the Lord at all times.
　　I will constantly speak his praises.

**34:2**
Jer 9:24

² I will boast only in the Lord;
　　let all who are helpless take heart.

**34:3**
Luke 1:46

³ Come, let us tell of the Lord's greatness;
　　let us exalt his name together.

⁴ I prayed to the Lord, and he answered me.
　　He freed me from all my fears.

**34:5**
Ps 36:9

⁵ Those who look to him for help will be radiant with joy;
　　no shadow of shame will darken their faces.
⁶ In my desperation I prayed, and the Lord listened;
　　he saved me from all my troubles.

**34:7**
Dan 6:22

⁷ For the angel of the Lord is a guard;
　　he surrounds and defends all who fear him.

**34** This psalm is a Hebrew acrostic poem; each verse begins with a successive letter of the Hebrew alphabet.

---

**33:16, 17** *Warhorse* refers to military strength. Because God rules and overrules every nation, leaders should never put their trust in their physical power. Military might is not the basis for our hope. Our hope is in God and in his gracious offer to save us if we will trust in him.

**33:18, 19** This is not an ironclad guarantee that all believers will be delivered from death and starvation. Thousands of Christian saints have been beaten to death, whipped, fed to lions, or executed (Romans 8:35, 36; Hebrews 11:32-40). God can (and often does) miraculously deliver his followers from pain and death; although sometimes, for purposes known only to him, he chooses not to. When faced with these harsh realities, we must focus on

the wise judgments of God. The writer was pleading for God's watchful care and protection. In times of crisis, we can place our hope in God.

**34:1ff** God promises great blessings to his people, but many of these blessings require active participation. He will set us free from our fears (34:4, 6), guard and defend us (34:7), show us goodness (34:8), supply our needs (34:9), listen when we call to him (34:15), and redeem us (34:22), but we must do our part. We can appropriate his blessings when we trust him (34:4, 10); cry out to him (34:6, 17); take refuge in him (34:8); fear him (34:9); refrain from lying (34:13); turn from evil, do good, and search for peace (34:14); are brokenhearted (34:18); and serve him (34:22).

8 Taste and see that the LORD is good.
  Oh, the joys of those who take refuge in him!

9 Fear the LORD, you his godly people,
  for those who fear him will have all they need.

10 Even strong young lions sometimes go hungry,
   but those who trust in the LORD will lack no good thing.

11 Come, my children, and listen to me,
   and I will teach you to fear the LORD.

12 Does anyone want to live a life
   that is long and prosperous?

13 Then keep your tongue from speaking evil
   and your lips from telling lies!

14 Turn away from evil and do good.
   Search for peace, and work to maintain it.

15 The eyes of the LORD watch over those who do right;
   his ears are open to their cries for help.

16 But the LORD turns his face against those who do evil;
   he will erase their memory from the earth.

17 The LORD hears his people when they call to him for help.
   He rescues them from all their troubles.

18 The LORD is close to the brokenhearted;
   he rescues those whose spirits are crushed.

19 The righteous person faces many troubles,
   but the LORD comes to the rescue each time.

20 For the LORD protects the bones of the righteous;
   not one of them is broken!

21 Calamity will surely overtake the wicked,
   and those who hate the righteous will be punished.

22 But the LORD will redeem those who serve him.
   No one who takes refuge in him will be condemned.

**34:8**
1 Pet 2:3

**34:9**
Pss 23:1; 31:23

**34:10**
Ps 84:11

**34:11**
Ps 111:10

**34:12**
1 Pet 3:10-12

**34:13**
Jas 1:26
1 Pet 2:22

**34:14**
Ps 37:27
Rom 14:18-19
Heb 12:14

**34:15**
Job 36:7
Ps 33:18-19

**34:16**
Pss 9:6; 109:15

**34:18**
Pss 51:17; 145:18
Isa 57:15

**34:19**
Ps 71:20
Prov 24:16

**34:21**
Ps 94:23

**34:22**
Ps 71:23

---

**34:8** "Taste and see" does not mean, "Check out God's credentials." Instead, it is a warm invitation: "Try this; I know you'll like it." When we take that first step of obedience in following God, we will discover that he is good and kind. When we begin the Christian life, our knowledge of God is partial and incomplete. As we trust him daily, we experience how good he is.

**34:9** You say you belong to the Lord, but do you fear him? To fear the Lord means to show him deep respect, reverence, and honor. We demonstrate this attitude by humility and genuine worship. Abraham (Genesis 17:2-4), Moses (Exodus 3:5, 6), and the Israelites (Exodus 19:16-24) showed this kind of fear of the Lord.

**34:9, 10** At first we may question David's statement because we seem to lack many good things. This is not a blanket promise that all Christians will have everything they want. Instead, this is David's praise for God's goodness—all those who call upon God in their need will be answered, sometimes in unexpected ways.

Remember, God knows what we need, and our deepest needs are spiritual. Even though many Christians face unbearable poverty and hardship, they still have enough spiritual nourishment to live for God. David was saying that if you have God, you have all you really need. God is enough.

If you feel you don't have everything you need, ask: (1) Is this really a need? (2) Is this really good for me? (3) Is this the best time for me to have what I desire? Even if you answer yes to all three questions, God may allow you to go without

to help you grow more dependent on him. He may want you to learn that you need *him* more than having your immediate desires met.

**34:11-14** The Bible often connects the fear of the Lord (love and reverence for him) with obedience. "Fear God and obey his commands" (Ecclesiastes 12:13); "All those who love me will do what I say" (John 14:23). David said that a person who fears the Lord doesn't lie, turns from evil, does good, and promotes peace. Reverence is much more than sitting quietly in church. It includes obeying God in the way we speak and the way we treat others.

**34:14** Some may think that peace should come with no effort. But David explained that we are to work hard at peace. Paul echoed this thought in Romans 12:18. A person who wants peace cannot be argumentative and contentious. Because peaceful relationships come from our efforts at peacemaking, work hard at living in peace with others each day.

**34:18, 19** We often wish we could escape troubles—the pain of grief, loss, sorrow, and failure, or even the small daily frustrations that constantly wear us down. God promises to be "close to the brokenhearted" and to be our source of power, courage, and wisdom, helping us through our problems. Sometimes he chooses to deliver us from those problems. When trouble strikes, don't get frustrated with God. Instead, admit that you need God's help and thank him for being by your side.

**34:20** This is a prophecy about Christ when he was crucified. Although it was the Roman custom to break the legs of the victim to speed death, not one of Jesus' bones was broken (John 19:32-37). In addition to the prophetic meaning, David was pleading for God's protection in times of crisis.

**Theme:** A prayer to God for help against those who try to inflict injury for no reason. When our enemies are unjust and lie about us, even when we do good to them, we can appeal to God who is always just.
**Author:** David, possibly written when he was being hunted by Saul (1 Samuel 24)

# 35 *A psalm of David.*

**35:1**
Ps 56:1-2
Isa 49:25

1 O LORD, oppose those who oppose me.
    Fight those who fight against me.

**35:2**
Ps 91:4

2 Put on your armor, and take up your shield.
    Prepare for battle, and come to my aid.

**35:3**
Ps 62:2

3 Lift up your spear and javelin
    against those who pursue me.
  Let me hear you say,
    "I will give you victory!"

**35:4**
Pss 40:14; 70:2-3

4 Bring shame and disgrace on those trying to kill me;
    turn them back and humiliate those who want to harm me.

**35:5**
Job 21:18
Pss 1:4; 83:13
Isa 29:5

5 Blow them away like chaff in the wind—
    a wind sent by the angel of the LORD.

**35:6**
Ps 73:18
Jer 23:12

6 Make their path dark and slippery,
    with the angel of the LORD pursuing them.

**35:7**
Pss 69:4; 109:3

7 I did them no wrong, but they laid a trap for me.
    I did them no wrong, but they dug a pit to catch me.

**35:8**
Ps 9:15
Isa 47:11
1 Thes 5:3

8 So let sudden ruin come upon them!
    Let them be caught in the trap they set for me!
    Let them be destroyed in the pit they dug for me.

**35:9**
Isa 61:10
Luke 1:47

9 Then I will rejoice in the LORD.
    I will be glad because he rescues me.

**35:10**
Exod 15:11-12
Pss 18:17; 37:14

10 With every bone in my body I will praise him:
    "LORD, who can compare with you?
  Who else rescues the helpless from the strong?
  Who else protects the helpless and poor from those who rob them?"

**35:11**
Ps 27:12

11 Malicious witnesses testify against me.
    They accuse me of crimes I know nothing about.

**35:12**
Ps 38:20
John 10:32

12 They repay me evil for good.
    I am sick with despair.

**35:13**
Job 30:25
Ps 69:10

13 Yet when they were ill, I grieved for them.
    I denied myself by fasting for them,
    but my prayers returned unanswered.

14 I was sad, as though they were my friends or family,
    as if I were grieving for my own mother.

15 But they are glad now that I am in trouble;
    they gleefully join together against me.
  I am attacked by people I don't even know;
    they slander me constantly.

**35:16**
Lam 2:16

16 They mock me and call me names;
    they snarl at me.

---

**35:1ff** This is one of the "imprecatory" (cursing) psalms that call upon God to deal with enemies. These psalms sound extremely harsh, but we must remember the following: (1) David could not understand why he was forced to flee from men who were unjustly seeking to kill him. He was God's anointed king over a nation called to annihilate the evil people of the land. (2) David's call for justice was sincere; it was not a cover for his own personal vengeance. He truly wanted God's perfect ideal for his nation. (3) David did not say that *he* would take revenge, but he gave the matter to God. These are merely his suggestions. (4) These psalms use hyperbole (or overstatement). They were meant to motivate others to take a strong stand against sin and evil.

Cruelty may be far removed from some people's experience, but it is a daily reality to others. God promises to help the persecuted and to bring judgment on unrepentant sinners. When we pray for justice to be done, we are praying as David did. When Christ returns, the wicked will be punished.

**35:13** David was sad when his prayers seemed "unanswered." When our deliverance is delayed, we may assume that God hasn't answered our prayers. God hears every prayer, but he answers according to his wisdom. Don't let the absence of an immediate answer cause you to doubt or resent God. Instead, let it be an occasion to deepen your faith.

17 How long, O Lord, will you look on and do nothing?
  Rescue me from their fierce attacks.
  Protect my life from these lions!
18 Then I will thank you in front of the great assembly.
  I will praise you before all the people.
19 Don't let my treacherous enemies rejoice over my defeat.
  Don't let those who hate me without cause gloat over my sorrow.
20 They don't talk of peace;
  they plot against innocent people who mind their own business.
21 They shout, "Aha! Aha!
  With our own eyes we saw him do it!"

22 O Lord, you know all about this.
  Do not stay silent.
  Do not abandon me now, O Lord.
23 Wake up! Rise to my defense!
  Take up my case, my God and my Lord.
24 Declare me not guilty, O Lord my God, for you give justice.
  Don't let my enemies laugh about me in my troubles.
25 Don't let them say, "Look, we got what we wanted!
  Now we will eat him alive!"

26 May those who rejoice at my troubles
  be humiliated and disgraced.
  May those who triumph over me
  be covered with shame and dishonor.
27 But give great joy to those who came to my defense.
  Let them continually say, "Great is the Lord,
  who delights in blessing his servant with peace!"
28 Then I will proclaim your justice,
  and I will praise you all day long.

**Theme:** God's faithfulness, justice, and love are contrasted with the sinful hearts of men and women. In spite of our fallen condition, God pours out his love on those who know him.
**Author:** David

# 36 *For the choir director: A psalm of David, the servant of the Lord.*

1 Sin whispers to the wicked, deep within their hearts.
  They have no fear of God at all.
2 In their blind conceit,
  they cannot see how wicked they really are.
3 Everything they say is crooked and deceitful.
  They refuse to act wisely or do good.
4 They lie awake at night, hatching sinful plots.
  Their actions are never good.
  They make no attempt to turn from evil.

5 Your unfailing love, O Lord, is as vast as the heavens;
  your faithfulness reaches beyond the clouds.

**Marginal cross-references:**

35:17 Pss 13:1; 22:20-21 Hab 1:13
35:18 Ps 22:23, 25
35:19 Pss 13:4; 38:16, 19; 69:4 †John 15:25
35:21 Pss 22:13; 40:15
35:22 Exod 3:7 Ps 10:14
35:24 Pss 9:4; 43:1
35:25 Ps 56:1 Lam 2:16
35:26 Pss 38:16; 40:14
35:27 Pss 40:16; 70:4; 149:4-5
35:28 Ps 51:14-15
36:1 †Rom 3:18
36:3 Ps 10:7 Jer 4:22
36:4 Prov 4:16 Isa 65:2 Mic 2:1
36:5 Pss 57:10; 103:11; 108:4

**35:21-23** David cried out to God to defend him when people wrongly accused him. If you are unjustly accused, your natural reaction may be to lash out in revenge or to give a detailed defense of your every move. Instead, ask God to fight the battle for you. He will clear your name in the eyes of those who really matter.

**36:1** Because the wicked have no fear of God, nothing restrains them from sinning. They plunge ahead as if nothing will happen to them. But God is just and is only delaying their punishment. This

knowledge should hold us back from sinning. Let the fear of God do its work in you to keep you from sin. In your gratitude for God's love and mercy, don't ignore his justice.

**36:5-8** In contrast to evil people and their wicked plots that end in failure, God will triumph. He is faithful, righteous, and just. His love is as vast as the heavens; his faithfulness reaches beyond the clouds; his righteousness is as solid as mighty mountains; his judgments are as full of wisdom as the oceans are with water. We need not fear evil people because we know God loves us, judges evil, and will care for us throughout eternity.

**36:6**
Job 11:8
Pss 104:14-15;
145:16-17
Rom 11:33

6 Your righteousness is like the mighty mountains,
   your justice like the ocean depths.
You care for people and animals alike, O LORD.

**36:7**
Ruth 2:12
Pss 91:4;
139:17-18

7   How precious is your unfailing love, O God!
All humanity finds shelter
   in the shadow of your wings.

**36:8**
Isa 25:6
Rev 22:1

8 You feed them from the abundance of your own house,
   letting them drink from your river of delights.

**36:9**
1 Pet 2:9

9 For you are the fountain of life,
   the light by which we see.

10 Pour out your unfailing love on those who love you;
    give justice to those with honest hearts.

11 Don't let the proud trample me
    or the wicked push me around.

**36:12**
Ps 140:10

12 Look! Those who do evil have fallen!
    They are thrown down, never to rise again.

**Theme:** Trust in the Lord and wait patiently for him to act. This psalm vividly contrasts the wicked person with the righteous.
**Author:** David

# 37 *A psalm of David.

**37:1**
Ps 73:3
Prov 3:31

1 Don't worry about the wicked
   or envy those who do wrong.

**37:2**
Job 14:2
Ps 90:5-6

2 For like grass, they soon fade away.
   Like spring flowers, they soon wither.

**37:3**
Deut 30:20
Ps 62:8
Isa 40:11

3 Trust in the LORD and do good.
   Then you will live safely in the land and prosper.

**37:4**
Ps 145:19
Isa 58:14

4 Take delight in the LORD,
   and he will give you your heart's desires.

**37:5**
Ps 55:22
Prov 16:3
1 Pet 5:7

5 Commit everything you do to the LORD.
   Trust him, and he will help you.

**37:6**
Isa 58:8, 10
Mic 7:9

6 He will make your innocence radiate like the dawn,
   and the justice of your cause will shine like the noonday sun.

**37:7**
Pss 40:1; 62:5
Jer 12:1

7 Be still in the presence of the LORD,
   and wait patiently for him to act.
Don't worry about evil people who prosper
   or fret about their wicked schemes.

**37:8**
Eph 4:31
Col 3:8

8 Stop being angry!
   Turn from your rage!

37 This psalm is a Hebrew acrostic poem; each stanza begins with a successive letter of the Hebrew alphabet.

---

**36:9** "Fountain of life" is a vivid image of fresh, cleansing water that gives life to the spiritually thirsty. This same picture is used in Jeremiah 2:13, where God is called the "fountain of living water." Jesus spoke of himself as living water that could quench thirst forever and give eternal life (John 4:14).

**37:1** We should never envy evil people, even though some may be extremely popular or excessively rich. No matter how much they have, it will fade and vanish like grass that withers and dies. Those who follow God live differently from the wicked and, in the end, will have treasures in heaven. What an unbeliever gets on earth may last a lifetime, but what you get from following God lasts forever.

**37:4, 5** David calls us to take delight in the Lord and to commit everything we have and do to him. But how do we do this? To *delight* in someone means to experience great pleasure and joy in his or her presence. This happens only when we know that person

well. Thus, to delight in the Lord, we must know him better. Knowledge of God's great love for us will indeed give us delight.

To *commit* ourselves to the Lord means entrusting everything—our lives, families, jobs, possessions—to his control and guidance. To commit ourselves to the Lord means to trust in him (37:5), believing that he can care for us better than we can ourselves. We should be willing to wait patiently (37:7) for him to work out what is best for us.

**37:8, 9** Anger, rage, and losing our temper are very destructive emotions. They reveal a lack of faith that God loves us and is in control. We should not worry; instead, we should trust in God, giving ourselves to him for his use and safekeeping. When you dwell on your problems, you will become anxious and angry. But if you concentrate on God and his goodness, you will find peace. Where do you focus your attention?

Do not lose your temper—
it only leads to harm.
9 For the wicked will be destroyed,
but those who trust in the LORD will possess the land.

10 Soon the wicked will disappear.
Though you look for them, they will be gone.
11 The lowly will possess the land
and will live in peace and prosperity.

12 The wicked plot against the godly;
they snarl at them in defiance.
13 But the Lord just laughs,
for he sees their day of judgment coming.

14 The wicked draw their swords
and string their bows
to kill the poor and the oppressed,
to slaughter those who do right.
15 But their swords will stab their own hearts,
and their bows will be broken.

16 It is better to be godly and have little
than to be evil and rich.
17 For the strength of the wicked will be shattered,
but the LORD takes care of the godly.

18 Day by day the LORD takes care of the innocent,
and they will receive an inheritance that lasts forever.
19 They will not be disgraced in hard times;
even in famine they will have more than enough.

20 But the wicked will die.
The LORD's enemies are like flowers in a field—
they will disappear like smoke.

21 The wicked borrow and never repay,
but the godly are generous givers.
22 Those the LORD blesses will possess the land,
but those he curses will die.

23 The LORD directs the steps of the godly.
He delights in every detail of their lives.
24 Though they stumble, they will never fall,
for the LORD holds them by the hand.

25 Once I was young, and now I am old.
Yet I have never seen the godly abandoned
or their children begging for bread.

**37:9** Ps 25:13 Isa 60:21
**37:10** Job 24:24
**37:11** Matt 5:3, 5
**37:12** Ps 35:16
**37:13** Ps 2:4
**37:14** Pss 11:2; 35:10
**37:15** Pss 9:16; 46:9
**37:16** Prov 15:16; 16:8
**37:17** Job 38:15 Ps 10:15
**37:19** Job 5:20 Ps 33:18-19
**37:20** Pss 68:2; 73:27; 102:3
**37:22** Job 5:3 Prov 3:33
**37:23** 1 Sam 2:9 Pss 40:2; 147:11
**37:24** Pss 145:14; 147:6 Prov 24:15-16
**37:25** Isa 41:17 Heb 13:5

**37:11** Being lowly hardly seems the proper demeanor to deal with enemies. God's warfare, however, must be carried out with calm faith, humility before God, and hope in his deliverance. Jesus also promises a sure reward for those with humble attitudes (Matthew 5:5).

**37:21** You can tell a lot about a person's character by the way he or she handles money. The wicked person steals under the guise of borrowing. The righteous person gives generously to the needy. Wicked people, therefore, focus on themselves, while righteous people look to the welfare of others.

**37:23, 24** The person in whom God delights is one who follows God, trusts him, and tries to do his will. God watches over and makes firm every step that person takes. If you would like to have God direct your way, then seek his advice before you step out.

**37:25** Because children starve today, as they did in David's time, what did David mean by these words? The children of the righteous need not go hungry because other believers should help them in their time of need. In David's day, Israel obeyed God's laws, which ensured that the poor were treated fairly and mercifully. As long as Israel was obedient, food would be available for everyone. When Israel forgot God, the rich took care of themselves only, and the poor suffered (Amos 2:6, 7).

When we see a Christian brother or sister suffering today, we can respond in one of three ways: (1) We can say, as Job's friends did, that the afflicted person brought this on himself. (2) We can

**37:26**
Ps 37:21

**37:27**
Ps 34:14

**37:28**
Pss 11:7; 21:10

**37:29**
Ps 37:9, 18

**37:31**
Pss 37:23; 40:8
Isa 51:7

**37:32**
Pss 10:8; 37:14
**37:33**
2 Pet 2:9

**37:34**
Pss 27:14; 37:9

**37:35**
Job 5:3

**37:38**
Pss 1:1; 73:19

**37:39**
Pss 3:8; 9:9

**38:1**
Ps 6:1

26 The godly always give generous loans to others,
    and their children are a blessing.

27 Turn from evil and do good,
    and you will live in the land forever.
28 For the LORD loves justice,
    and he will never abandon the godly.

He will keep them safe forever,
    but the children of the wicked will die.
29 The godly will possess the land
    and will live there forever.

30 The godly offer good counsel;
    they teach right from wrong.
31 They have made God's law their own,
    so they will never slip from his path.

32 The wicked wait in ambush for the godly,
    looking for an excuse to kill them.
33 But the LORD will not let the wicked succeed
    or let the godly be condemned when they are put on trial.

34 Put your hope in the LORD.
    Travel steadily along his path.
He will honor you by giving you the land.
    You will see the wicked destroyed.

35 I have seen wicked and ruthless people
    flourishing like a tree in its native soil.
36 But when I looked again, they were gone!
    Though I searched for them, I could not find them!

37 Look at those who are honest and good,
    for a wonderful future awaits those who love peace.
38 But the rebellious will be destroyed;
    they have no future.

39 The LORD rescues the godly;
    he is their fortress in times of trouble.
40 The LORD helps them,
    rescuing them from the wicked.
He saves them,
    and they find shelter in him.

**Theme:** Sorrow for sin brings hope. God alone is the true source of healing and protection for those who confess their sins to him.
**Author:** David

# 38 *A psalm of David, asking God to remember him.*

1 O LORD, don't rebuke me in your anger
    or discipline me in your rage!

---

say that this is a test to help the person develop more patience and trust in God. (3) We can help the person in need. David would approve of only the last option. Although many governments today have their own programs for helping those in need, this is no excuse for ignoring the poor and needy within our reach.

**38:1** As a child might cry to his father, so David cried to God. David was not saying, "Don't punish me," but, "Don't punish me while you are angry." He acknowledged that he deserved to be punished, but he asked that God temper his discipline with mercy. Like children, we are free to ask for mercy, but we should not deny that we deserve punishment.

**38:1ff** This is called a penitential psalm because David expressed sorrow for his sin (38:18). He stated that his sin led to health problems (38:1-8) and separated him from God and others, causing extreme loneliness (38:9-14). He then confessed his sin and repented (38:15-22).

2 Your arrows have struck deep,
   and your blows are crushing me.
3 Because of your anger, my whole body is sick;
   my health is broken because of my sins.
4 My guilt overwhelms me—
   it is a burden too heavy to bear.
5 My wounds fester and stink
   because of my foolish sins.
6 I am bent over and racked with pain.
   All day long I walk around filled with grief.
7 A raging fever burns within me,
   and my health is broken.
8 I am exhausted and completely crushed.
   My groans come from an anguished heart.

9 You know what I long for, Lord;
   you hear my every sigh.
10 My heart beats wildly, my strength fails,
   and I am going blind.
11 My loved ones and friends stay away, fearing my disease.
   Even my own family stands at a distance.
12 Meanwhile, my enemies lay traps to kill me.
   Those who wish me harm make plans to ruin me.
   All day long they plan their treachery.

13 But I am deaf to all their threats.
   I am silent before them as one who cannot speak.
14 I choose to hear nothing,
   and I make no reply.
15 For I am waiting for you, O Lord.
   You must answer for me, O Lord my God.
16 I prayed, "Don't let my enemies gloat over me
   or rejoice at my downfall."

17 I am on the verge of collapse,
   facing constant pain.
18 But I confess my sins;
   I am deeply sorry for what I have done.
19 I have many aggressive enemies;
   they hate me without reason.
20 They repay me evil for good
   and oppose me for pursuing good.
21 Do not abandon me, O Lord.
   Do not stand at a distance, my God.
22 Come quickly to help me,
   O Lord my savior.

**Theme:** Apart from God, life is fleeting and empty. This is an appeal for God's mercy because life is so brief.
**Author:** David

# 39 *For Jeduthun, the choir director: A psalm of David.*

1 I said to myself, "I will watch what I do
   and not sin in what I say.

**Cross-references:**
38:2 Job 6:4; Ps 32:4
38:3 Pss 6:2; 31:9-10; Isa 1:5-6
38:4 Ezra 9:6
38:5 Ps 69:5
38:6 Pss 35:14; 42:9
38:7 Ps 102:3-4
38:8 Job 3:24; Ps 22:1
38:9 Pss 6:6; 10:17
38:10 Pss 6:7; 31:10
38:12 Pss 35:20; 54:3; 140:5
38:15 Ps 17:6
38:16 Pss 13:4; 35:26
38:17 Ps 13:2
38:18 2 Cor 7:9-10
38:19 Pss 18:17; 35:19
38:20 Ps 35:12; 1 Jn 3:12
38:21 Pss 22:19; 35:22
38:22 Pss 27:1; 40:13, 17
39:1 Pss 34:13; 141:3; Jas 3:2, 5-12

**38:2-4** David saw his anguish as judgment from God for his sins. Although God does not always send physical illness to punish us for sin, this verse and others in Scripture (Acts 12:21-23; 1 Corinthians 11:30-32) indicate that he does in certain circumstances. Our sin can have physical or mental side effects that can cause great suffering. Sometimes God has to punish his children in order to bring them back to himself (Hebrews 12:5-11). When we repent of our sin, God promises to forgive us. He delivers us from sin's eternal consequences, although he does not promise to undo all of sin's earthly consequences.

**38:13, 14** Being silent can be extremely difficult when others tear us down because we want to protect our reputation. We find it

I will hold my tongue
  when the ungodly are around me."
2 But as I stood there in silence—
  not even speaking of good things—
  the turmoil within me grew worse.
3 The more I thought about it,
  the hotter I got,
  igniting a fire of words:
4 "LORD, remind me how brief my time on earth will be.
  Remind me that my days are numbered—
  how fleeting my life is.
5 You have made my life no longer than the width of my hand.
  My entire lifetime is just a moment to you;
  at best, each of us is but a breath."

*Interlude*

6 We are merely moving shadows,
  and all our busy rushing ends in nothing.
We heap up wealth,
  not knowing who will spend it.
7 And so, Lord, where do I put my hope?
  My only hope is in you.
8 Rescue me from my rebellion.
  Do not let fools mock me.
9 I am silent before you; I won't say a word,
  for my punishment is from you.
10 But please stop striking me!
  I am exhausted by the blows from your hand.
11 When you discipline us for our sins,
  you consume like a moth what is precious to us.
  Each of us is but a breath.

*Interlude*

12 Hear my prayer, O LORD!
  Listen to my cries for help!
  Don't ignore my tears.
For I am your guest—
  a traveler passing through,
  as my ancestors were before me.
13 Leave me alone so I can smile again
  before I am gone and exist no more.

**Cross-references:**

39:4 Pss 78:39; 90:12; 103:14-15

39:5 Job 14:2 Pss 62:9; 89:47; 144:4

39:6 Ps 127:2 Luke 12:20 1 Pet 1:24

39:8 Pss 51:9; 79:4, 9

39:9 Job 2:10

39:10 Job 9:34 Ps 32:4

39:11 Job 13:27-28 Ps 90:7 2 Pet 2:16

39:12 Ps 102:1 Heb 11:13 1 Pet 2:11

39:13 Job 10:20; 14:6

---

difficult to do nothing while they assault something so precious to us. But we don't need to lash out in revenge or justify our position; we can trust God to protect our reputation. Jesus was silent before his accusers (Luke 23:9, 10); he left his case in God's hands (1 Peter 2:21-24). That is a good place to leave our case, too!

**39:1-3** David resolved to keep his tongue from sin; that is, he decided not to complain to other people about God's treatment of him. David certainly had reason to complain. He was the anointed king of Israel, but he had to wait many years before taking the throne. Then one of his sons tried to kill him and become king instead. But when David could not keep still any longer, he took his complaints directly to God. We all have complaints about our job, money, or situation, but complaining to others may make them think that God cannot take care of us. It may also look as if we blame God for our troubles. Instead, like David, we should take our complaints directly to God. He can take it.

**39:4** Life is short no matter how long we live. If we have something important we want to do, we must not put it off for a better day. Ask yourself, If I had only six months to live, what would I do? Tell someone that you love him or her? Deal with an undisciplined area in your life? Tell someone about Jesus? Because life is short, don't neglect what is truly important.

**39:5, 6** The brevity of life is a theme throughout the books of Psalms, Proverbs, and Ecclesiastes. Jesus also spoke about it (Luke 12:20). Ironically, people spend so much time securing their lives on earth but take little or no thought about where they will spend eternity. David realized that amassing riches and busily accomplishing worldly tasks would make no difference in eternity. Few people understand that their only hope is in the Lord. (For other verses on the brevity of life, see Ecclesiastes 2:18 and James 4:14.)

**39:10** What did David mean when he asked God to stop punishing him with "blows" from his hand? It may be a picture of the difficulties David was facing that caused him to feel as if he were being struck. Evidently David thought God was disciplining him, punishing him for his sins. David was expressing his feelings to God, yet David also submitted himself to his powerful and loving heavenly Father.

**Theme:** Doing God's will sometimes means waiting patiently. While we wait, we can love God, serve others, and tell others about him.
**Author:** David

**40** *For the choir director: A psalm of David.*

1 I waited patiently for the Lord to help me,
   and he turned to me and heard my cry.

2 He lifted me out of the pit of despair,
   out of the mud and the mire.
   He set my feet on solid ground
   and steadied me as I walked along.

3 He has given me a new song to sing,
   a hymn of praise to our God.
   Many will see what he has done and be amazed.
   They will put their trust in the Lord.

4 Oh, the joys of those who trust the Lord,
   who have no confidence in the proud
   or in those who worship idols.

5 O Lord my God, you have performed many wonders for us.
   Your plans for us are too numerous to list.
   You have no equal.
   If I tried to recite all your wonderful deeds,
   I would never come to the end of them.

6 You take no delight in sacrifices or offerings.
   Now that you have made me listen, I finally understand*—
   you don't require burnt offerings or sin offerings.

7 Then I said, "Look, I have come.
   As is written about me in the Scriptures:

8 I take joy in doing your will, my God,
   for your instructions are written on my heart."

9 I have told all your people about your justice.
   I have not been afraid to speak out,
   as you, O Lord, well know.

10 I have not kept the good news of your justice hidden in my heart;
    I have talked about your faithfulness and saving power.
    I have told everyone in the great assembly
    of your unfailing love and faithfulness.

11 Lord, don't hold back your tender mercies from me.
    Let your unfailing love and faithfulness always protect me.

40:1 Pss 27:14; 34:15
40:2 Pss 27:5; 69:1-2 / Jer 38:6
40:3 Pss 32:7; 33:3; 64:9
40:4 Ps 84:12
40:5 Job 5:9 / Pss 136:4; 139:17-18 / Isa 55:8
40:6-8 1 Sam 15:22 / Jer 7:22-23 / Mic 6:6-8 / †Heb 10:5-7
40:8 Ps 37:31 / 2 Cor 3:3 / John 4:34 / Rom 7:22
40:9 Pss 22:25; 119:13
40:10 Ps 89:1 / Acts 20:20, 27
40:11 Ps 61:7

40:6 Greek text reads *You have given me a body.* Compare Heb 10:5.

**40:1-3** Waiting for God to help us is not easy, but David received four benefits from waiting: (1) God lifted him out of his despair, (2) God set his feet on solid ground, (3) God steadied him as he walked, and (4) God put a new song of praise in his mouth. Often blessings cannot be received unless we go through the trial of waiting.

**40:6** The religious ritual of David's day involved sacrificing animals in the Tabernacle. David said these acts were meaningless unless done for the right reasons. Today we often make rituals of going to church, taking Communion, or paying tithes. These activities are also empty if our reasons for doing them are selfish. God doesn't want these sacrifices and offerings without an attitude of devotion to him. The prophet Samuel told Saul, "Obedience is better than sacrifice" (1 Samuel 15:22). Make sure that you give God the obedience and lifelong service he desires from you.

**40:7, 8** "I take joy in doing your will, my God." Jesus portrayed this attitude of obeying and serving God (John 4:34; 5:30). He came as the prophets foretold, proclaiming the Good News of God's righteousness and forgiveness of sins. In Hebrews 10:5-10, verses 6-8 are applied to Jesus.

**40:9, 10** David said he would speak of God's faithfulness and salvation to those around him. When we realize the impact of God's righteousness on our lives, we cannot keep it hidden. We want to tell other people what God has done for us. If God's faithfulness has changed your life, don't be timid. It is natural to share a good bargain with others or recommend a skillful doctor, so it should also be natural to share what God has done for us.

**40:10** When we think of faithfulness, a friend or a spouse may come to mind. Friends who are faithful accept and love us, even when we are unlovable. Faithful people keep their promises, whether of support or made in marriage vows. God's faithfulness is like human faithfulness, only perfect. His love is absolute, and his promises are irrevocable. He loves us in spite of our constant bent toward sin, and he keeps all the promises he has made to us, even when we break our promises to him.

**40:12**
Pss 18:5; 38:4;
73:26; 116:3

12 For troubles surround me—
  too many to count!
My sins pile up so high
  I can't see my way out.
They outnumber the hairs on my head.
  I have lost all courage.

**40:13-17**
//Ps 70:1-5

13 Please, LORD, rescue me!
  Come quickly, LORD, and help me.

**40:14**
Pss 35:4, 26;
70:2-3

14 May those who try to destroy me
  be humiliated and put to shame.
May those who take delight in my trouble
  be turned back in disgrace.
15 Let them be horrified by their shame,
  for they said, "Aha! We've got him now!"

**40:16**
Pss 35:27; 70:4

16 But may all who search for you
  be filled with joy and gladness in you.
May those who love your salvation
  repeatedly shout, "The LORD is great!"

**40:17**
Ps 70:5

17 As for me, since I am poor and needy,
  let the Lord keep me in his thoughts.
You are my helper and my savior.
  O my God, do not delay.

**Theme:** A prayer for God's mercy when feeling sick or abandoned. When we're sick or when everyone deserts us, God remains at our side.
**Author:** David

# 41
*For the choir director: A psalm of David.*

**41:1**
Pss 37:19; 82:3-4
Prov 14:21

1 Oh, the joys of those who are kind to the poor!
  The LORD rescues them when they are in trouble.

**41:2**
Ps 37:22, 28

2 The LORD protects them
  and keeps them alive.
He gives them prosperity in the land
  and rescues them from their enemies.
3 The LORD nurses them when they are sick
  and restores them to health.

**41:4**
Pss 6:2; 51:4;
103:3

4 "O LORD," I prayed, "have mercy on me.
  Heal me, for I have sinned against you."

**41:5**
Ps 38:12

5 But my enemies say nothing but evil about me.
  "How soon will he die and be forgotten?" they ask.

**41:6**
Ps 12:2

6 They visit me as if they were my friends,
  but all the while they gather gossip,
  and when they leave, they spread it everywhere.

**41:7**
Ps 56:5

7 All who hate me whisper about me,
  imagining the worst.

**41:9**
Job 19:19
Ps 55:12-13, 20
Jer 20:10
†Mark 14:18
†John 13:18

8 "He has some fatal disease," they say.
  "He will never get out of that bed!"
9 Even my best friend, the one I trusted completely,
  the one who shared my food, has turned against me.

**41:10**
Ps 3:3

10 LORD, have mercy on me.
  Make me well again, so I can pay them back!

---

**41:1** The Bible often speaks of God's care for the weak, poor, and needy, and of his blessing those who share this concern. God wants our generosity to reflect his own free giving. As he has blessed us, we should bless others.

**41:9** This verse, a prophecy of Christ's betrayal, is referred to in John 13:18. Judas, one of Jesus' 12 disciples, had spent three years learning from Jesus, traveling and eating with him (Mark 3:14-19), and handling the finances for the group. Eventually this "best friend" betrayed Jesus (Matthew 26:14-16, 20-25).

<sup>11</sup> I know you are pleased with me,
>    for you have not let my enemies triumph over me.
<sup>12</sup> You have preserved my life because I am innocent;
>    you have brought me into your presence forever.

<sup>13</sup> Praise the LORD, the God of Israel,
>    who lives from everlasting to everlasting.
>    Amen and amen!

### BOOK TWO    Psalms 42:1—72:20

These psalms include a prayer for rescue, a call to worship, a confession of sin, an encouragement to trust God, a psalm for those hurt by friends, a prayer for those who have been slandered, and a missionary psalm. These psalms can help us retain a sense of wonder in our worship.

**Theme:** A thirst for God. When you feel lonely or depressed, meditate on God's kindness and love.

**Author:** The sons of Korah, who were Temple musicians and assistants

# 42 For the choir director: A psalm* of the descendants of Korah.

<sup>1</sup> As the deer longs for streams of water,
>    so I long for you, O God.
<sup>2</sup> I thirst for God, the living God.
>    When can I go and stand before him?
<sup>3</sup> Day and night I have only tears for food,
>    while my enemies continually taunt me, saying,
>    "Where is this God of yours?"

<sup>4</sup> My heart is breaking
>    as I remember how it used to be:
> I walked among the crowds of worshipers,
>    leading a great procession to the house of God,
> singing for joy and giving thanks
>    amid the sound of a great celebration!

<sup>5</sup> Why am I discouraged?
>    Why is my heart so sad?
> I will put my hope in God!
>    I will praise him again—
>    my Savior and <sup>6</sup>my God!

> Now I am deeply discouraged,
>    but I will remember you—
> even from distant Mount Hermon, the source of the Jordan,
>    from the land of Mount Mizar.
<sup>7</sup> I hear the tumult of the raging seas
>    as your waves and surging tides sweep over me.

**42:TITLE** Hebrew *maskil*. This may be a literary or musical term.

**Cross-references (right margin):**

41:11 Pss 25:2; 37:23-24; 147:11
41:12 Job 36:7; Pss 21:6; 37:17
41:13 Pss 72:18-19; 106:48
42:1 Ps 63:1
42:2 Pss 43:4; 84:2; 143:6; Jer 10:10; Rom 9:26
42:3 Pss 79:10; 80:5; Joel 2:17
42:4 Job 30:16; Ps 100:4; Isa 30:29
42:5 Pss 38:6; 44:3; 77:3; Lam 3:24
42:6 Ps 61:2; †Mark 14:34
42:7 Ps 88:7; Jon 2:3

---

**41:13** Psalms is divided into five books, and each one ends with a doxology or an expression of praise to God. The first book of the psalms, chapters 1 through 41, takes us on a journey through suffering, sorrow, and great joy. It teaches us about God's eternal love and care for us and how we should trust him even in the day-to-day experiences of life.

**42:1ff** Psalms 42–49 were written by the descendants of Korah. Korah was a Levite who led a rebellion against Moses (Numbers 16:1-35). He was killed, but his descendants remained faithful to God and continued to serve God in the Temple. David appointed men from the clan of Korah to serve as choir leaders (1 Chronicles 6:31-38), and they continued to be Temple musicians for hundreds of years (2 Chronicles 20:18, 19).

**42:1, 2** As the life of a deer depends upon water, so our lives depend upon God. Those who seek him and long to understand him find eternal life. Feeling separated from God, this psalmist wouldn't rest until he restored his relationship with God because he knew that his very life depended on it. Do you thirst for God?

**42:4, 5** The writer of this psalm was discouraged because he was exiled to a place far from Jerusalem and could not worship in the Temple. During these God-given holidays, the nation was to remember all that God had done for them. Many of these festivals are explained in the chart in Leviticus 22, p. 189.

**42:5, 6** Depression is one of the most common emotional ailments. One antidote for depression is to meditate on the record of God's goodness to his people. This will take your mind off the present situation as you focus your thoughts on God's ability to help you rather than on your inability to help yourself. When you feel depressed, take advantage of this psalm's antidepressant: Read the Bible's accounts of God's goodness, and meditate on them.

42:8
Job 35:10
Pss 16:7; 57:3;
77:6; 149:4-5

8 But each day the LORD pours his unfailing love upon me,
    and through each night I sing his songs,
    praying to God who gives me life.

42:9
Pss 17:9; 38:6

9 "O God my rock," I cry,
    "Why have you forgotten me?
Why must I wander around in grief,
    oppressed by my enemies?"
10 Their taunts break my bones.
    They scoff, "Where is this God of yours?"

11 Why am I discouraged?
    Why is my heart so sad?
I will put my hope in God!
    I will praise him again—
    my Savior and my God!

**Theme:** Hope in a time of discouragement. In the face of discouragement, our only hope is in God.
**Author:** The sons of Korah (Temple assistants). Psalms 42 and 43 are one psalm in many Hebrew manuscripts.

43:1
1 Sam 24:15
Pss 26:1; 35:24

# 43

1 Declare me innocent, O God!
    Defend me against these ungodly people.
Rescue me from these unjust liars.

43:2
Pss 42:9; 44:9

2 For you are God, my only safe haven.
    Why have you tossed me aside?
Why must I wander around in grief,
    oppressed by my enemies?

43:3
Pss 36:9; 84:1

3 Send out your light and your truth;
    let them guide me.
Let them lead me to your holy mountain,
    to the place where you live.

43:4
Pss 26:6; 33:2

4 There I will go to the altar of God,
    to God—the source of all my joy.
I will praise you with my harp,
    O God, my God!

5 Why am I discouraged?
    Why is my heart so sad?
I will put my hope in God!
    I will praise him again—
    my Savior and my God!

**Theme:** A plea for victory by the battle-weary and defeated. When it seems that God has let you down, don't despair. Instead, remember God's past deliverance and be confident that he will restore you.
**Author:** The sons of Korah (Temple assistants)

44:1
Exod 12:26-27

# 44
*For the choir director: A psalm\* of the descendants of Korah.*

1 O God, we have heard it with our own ears—
    our ancestors have told us

**44:TITLE** Hebrew *maskil.* This may be a literary or musical term.

---

**43:3** The "holy mountain" is Mount Zion, in Jerusalem, the city that David named as Israel's capital. The Temple was built there as the place for the people to meet God in worship and prayer.

**43:3, 4** The psalm writer asked God to send his light and truth to guide him to the holy mountain, the Temple, where he would meet God. God's truth (see 1 John 2:27) provides the right path to follow, and God's light (see 1 John 1:5) provides the clear vision to follow it. If you feel surrounded by darkness and uncertainty, follow God's light and truth. He will guide you.

**44:1ff** This psalm may have been sung at an occasion like the one in

2 Chronicles 20:18, 19, where the faithful Jehoshaphat was surrounded by enemies and the Levites sang to the Lord before the battle.

**44:1-3** "You drove out the pagan nations" refers to the conquest of Canaan (the Promised Land) described in the book of Joshua. God gave the land to the Israelites; they were supposed to enter and drive out anyone who was wicked and opposed to God. Israel was told to settle the land and to be a witness to the world of God's power and love. Surrounded by enemies, the psalm writer remembered what God had done for his people and took heart. We can have this same confidence in God when we feel attacked.

of all you did in their day,
in days long ago:
2 You drove out the pagan nations by your power
and gave all the land to our ancestors.
You crushed their enemies
and set our ancestors free.
3 They did not conquer the land with their swords;
it was not their own strong arm that gave them victory.
It was your right hand and strong arm
and the blinding light from your face that helped them,
for you loved them.

4 You are my King and my God.
You command victories for Israel.*
5 Only by your power can we push back our enemies;
only in your name can we trample our foes.
6 I do not trust in my bow;
I do not count on my sword to save me.
7 You are the one who gives us victory over our enemies;
you disgrace those who hate us.
8 O God, we give glory to you all day long
and constantly praise your name. *Interlude*

9 But now you have tossed us aside in dishonor.
You no longer lead our armies to battle.
10 You make us retreat from our enemies
and allow those who hate us to plunder our land.
11 You have butchered us like sheep
and scattered us among the nations.
12 You sold your precious people for a pittance,
making nothing on the sale.
13 You let our neighbors mock us.
We are an object of scorn and derision to those around us.
14 You have made us the butt of their jokes;
they shake their heads at us in scorn.
15 We can't escape the constant humiliation;
shame is written across our faces.
16 All we hear are the taunts of our mockers.
All we see are our vengeful enemies.

17 All this has happened though we have not forgotten you.
We have not violated your covenant.
18 Our hearts have not deserted you.
We have not strayed from your path.
19 Yet you have crushed us in the jackal's desert home.
You have covered us with darkness and death.
20 If we had forgotten the name of our God
or spread our hands in prayer to foreign gods,
21 God would surely have known it,
for he knows the secrets of every heart.
22 But for your sake we are killed every day;
we are being slaughtered like sheep.

| | |
|---|---|
| | **44:2**<br>Pss 78:55; 80:8 |
| | **44:3**<br>Deut 4:37<br>Josh 24:12<br>Ps 77:15 |
| | **44:4**<br>Ps 74:12 |
| | **44:5**<br>Ps 60:12 |
| | **44:7**<br>Pss 53:5; 136:24 |
| | **44:8**<br>Pss 30:12; 34:2 |
| | **44:9**<br>Pss 43:2; 60:10;<br>74:1 |
| | **44:10**<br>Josh 7:8, 12<br>Ps 89:41 |
| | **44:11**<br>Deut 4:27; 28:64<br>Ps 106:27<br>Ezek 20:23-24 |
| | **44:12**<br>Isa 52:3-4 |
| | **44:13**<br>Pss 79:4; 80:6 |
| | **44:14**<br>Ps 109:25<br>Jer 24:9 |
| | **44:17**<br>Pss 119:61, 83,<br>109, 141, 153, 176 |
| | **44:18**<br>Job 23:11<br>Ps 119:51, 157 |
| | **44:19**<br>Job 3:5<br>Ps 51:8 |
| | **44:20**<br>Ps 81:9 |
| | **44:22**<br>Isa 53:7<br>†Rom 8:36 |

**44:4** Hebrew *for Jacob.* The names "Jacob" and "Israel" are often interchanged throughout the Old Testament, referring sometimes to the individual patriarch and sometimes to the nation.

---

**44:6, 7** In whom or in what do you trust? Only God is trustworthy. He will never let you down.

**44:9-22** Israel had been defeated despite their faith (44:17) and obedience (44:18) to God. The psalm writer could not understand why God allowed this to happen, but he did not give up hope of discovering the answer (44:17-22). Although he felt his suffering was undeserved, he revealed the real reason for it: He suffered because he was *committed to the Lord.* Paul quoted the psalm writer's complaint (Romans 8:36) to show that we must always be ready to face death for the cause of Christ. Thus, our suffering may not be a punishment but a battle scar that demonstrates our loyalty.

**44:22-26** The writer cried out to God to save his people because

**44:23**
Pss 7:6; 77:7;
78:65
**44:24**
Job 13:24
Pss 42:9; 88:14
**44:25**
Ps 119:25

23 Wake up, O Lord! Why do you sleep?
　　Get up! Do not reject us forever.
24 Why do you look the other way?
　　Why do you ignore our suffering and oppression?
25 We collapse in the dust,
　　lying face down in the dirt.
26 Rise up! Help us!
　　Ransom us because of your unfailing love.

**Theme:** A poem to the king (possibly Solomon) on the occasion of his wedding. While this psalm was written for a historic occasion, it is also seen as a prophecy about Christ and his bride, the church, who will praise him throughout all generations.
**Author:** The sons of Korah (Temple assistants)

## 45 *For the choir director: A love song to be sung to the tune "Lilies." A psalm\* of the descendants of Korah.*

1 Beautiful words stir my heart.
　　I will recite a lovely poem about the king,
　　for my tongue is like the pen of a skillful poet.

**45:2**
Ps 21:6
Luke 4:22

2 You are the most handsome of all.
　　Gracious words stream from your lips.
　　God himself has blessed you forever.
3 Put on your sword, O mighty warrior!
　　You are so glorious, so majestic!

**45:4**
Rev 6:2

4 In your majesty, ride out to victory,
　　defending truth, humility, and justice.
　　Go forth to perform awe-inspiring deeds!

**45:5**
Ps 120:4
Isa 5:28

5 Your arrows are sharp, piercing your enemies' hearts.
　　The nations fall beneath your feet.

**45:6**
Pss 93:2; 98:8-9
†Heb 1:8-9
**45:7**
Pss 11:7; 21:6;
33:5

6 Your throne, O God,\* endures forever and ever.
　　You rule with a scepter of justice.
7 You love justice and hate evil.
　　Therefore God, your God, has anointed you,
　　pouring out the oil of joy on you more than on anyone else.

**45:8**
Song 1:3; 4:13-14

8 Myrrh, aloes, and cassia perfume your robes.
　　In ivory palaces the music of strings entertains you.

**45:9**
1 Kgs 2:19; 9:28
Song 6:8
Isa 13:12

9 Kings' daughters are among your noble women.
　　At your right side stands the queen,
　　wearing jewelry of finest gold from Ophir!

**45:10**
Deut 21:13

10 Listen to me, O royal daughter; take to heart what I say.
　　Forget your people and your family far away.
11 For your royal husband delights in your beauty;
　　honor him, for he is your lord.

**45:TITLE** Hebrew *maskil*. This may be a literary or musical term.　　**45:6** Or *Your divine throne.*

---

of his unfailing love. Nothing can separate us from God's love, not even death (Romans 8:36-39). When you fear for your life, ask God for deliverance, and remember that even death cannot separate you from him.

**44:23-25** The writer's words suggest that he did not believe God had left him. God was still in control, but he seemed to be asleep, and the writer wondered why. In the New Testament, the disciples wondered why Jesus was asleep when they needed his help during a storm (Mark 4:35-41). In both cases, of course, God was ready to help, but he wanted first to build faith in his followers.

**45:1ff** This is called a messianic psalm because it prophetically describes the Messiah's future relationship to the church, his body of believers. Verse 2 expresses God's abundant blessing

on his Messiah; verses 6-8 find their ultimate fulfillment in Christ (Hebrews 1:8, 9). The church is described as the bride of Christ in Revelation 19:7, 8; 21:9; 22:17.

**45:8, 9** Myrrh is a fragrant gum of an Arabian tree, generally used in perfumes. Aloes, a spice, may have come from sandalwood, a close-grained and fragrant wood often used for storage boxes or chests (see also Proverbs 7:14-17; Song of Songs 4:13, 14). Cassia was probably made from flowers of the cinnamon tree. These expensive fragrances were appropriate for a king's wedding. The location of Ophir is unknown but believed to be in either Arabia or Africa. It was famous as a source of gold.

12 The princess of Tyre* will shower you with gifts.
   The wealthy will beg your favor.
13 The bride, a princess, looks glorious
   in her golden gown.
14 In her beautiful robes, she is led to the king,
   accompanied by her bridesmaids.
15 What a joyful and enthusiastic procession
   as they enter the king's palace!

16 Your sons will become kings like their father.
   You will make them rulers over many lands.
17 I will bring honor to your name in every generation.
   Therefore, the nations will praise you forever and ever.

**Theme:** God is always there to help, providing refuge, security, and peace. God's power is complete and his ultimate victory is certain. He will not fail to rescue those who love him.

**Author:** The sons of Korah (Temple assistants)

# 46

*For the choir director: A song of the descendants of Korah, to be sung by soprano voices.* *

1 God is our refuge and strength,
   always ready to help in times of trouble.
2 So we will not fear when earthquakes come
   and the mountains crumble into the sea.
3 Let the oceans roar and foam.
   Let the mountains tremble as the waters surge!                    *Interlude*

4 A river brings joy to the city of our God,
   the sacred home of the Most High.
5 God dwells in that city; it cannot be destroyed.
   From the very break of day, God will protect it.
6 The nations are in chaos,
   and their kingdoms crumble!
   God's voice thunders,
   and the earth melts!

7 The LORD of Heaven's Armies is here among us;
   the God of Israel* is our fortress.                              *Interlude*

8 Come, see the glorious works of the LORD:
   See how he brings destruction upon the world.
9 He causes wars to end throughout the earth.
   He breaks the bow and snaps the spear;
   he burns the shields with fire.

10 "Be still, and know that I am God!
   I will be honored by every nation.
   I will be honored throughout the world."

45:12 Hebrew *The daughter of Tyre.*   46:TITLE Hebrew *according to alamoth.*   46:7 Hebrew *of Jacob;* also in 46:11.
See note on 44:4.

**Cross-references:**
45:12 Ps 72:10-11
45:13 Isa 61:10
45:14 Song 1:4; Ezek 16:9-13
45:17 Ps 138:4; Mal 1:11
46:1 Deut 4:7; Pss 9:9; 14:6; 62:7-8; 145:18
46:2 Pss 18:7; 23:4; 82:5
46:4 Ps 87:3; Rev 3:12; 22:1
46:5 Isa 12:6; 41:14; Ezek 43:7; Luke 1:54
46:6 Ps 2:1; Mic 1:4
46:7 Num 14:9; 2 Chr 13:12; Ps 9:9
46:8 Ps 66:5; Isa 61:4; Jer 51:43
46:9 Isa 2:4; 9:5; Mic 4:3
46:10 Ps 100:3; Isa 2:11, 17

**45:13-17** This beautiful section of poetry pictures Christ's bride, the church, with the richest blessings as she unites forever with him (see Revelation 19:6-8; 21:2).

**46–48** Psalms 46–48 are hymns of praise, celebrating deliverance from some great foe. Psalm 46 may have been written when the Assyrian army invaded the land and surrounded Jerusalem (2 Kings 18:13–19:37).

**46:1-3** The fear of mountains or cities suddenly crumbling into the sea as the result of an earthquake or a nuclear blast haunts many people today. But the psalm writer says that even if the world were to end, we need not fear. In the face of utter destruction, the writer expressed a quiet confidence in God's ability to save him. It seems impossible to consider the end of the world without becoming consumed by fear, but the Bible is clear—God is our refuge even in the midst of total destruction. He is not merely a temporary retreat; he is our eternal refuge and can provide strength in any circumstance.

**46:4, 5** Many great cities have rivers flowing through them, sustaining people's lives by making agriculture possible and facilitating trade with other cities. Jerusalem had no river, but it had God, who, like a river, sustained the people's lives. As long as God lived among the people, the city was invincible. But when the people abandoned him, God no longer protected them, and Jerusalem fell to the Babylonian army.

**46:10** War and destruction are inevitable, but so is God's final victory. At that time, all will stand quietly before the all-powerful

11 The LORD of Heaven's Armies is here among us;
   the God of Israel is our fortress. *Interlude*

**Theme:** God is still King of the world. All nations of the earth will eventually recognize his lordship.
**Author:** The sons of Korah (Temple assistants)

# 47 *For the choir director: A psalm of the descendants of Korah.*

**47:1**
Pss 98:8-9; 106:47

1 Come, everyone! Clap your hands!
   Shout to God with joyful praise!

**47:2**
Deut 7:21

2 For the LORD Most High is awesome.
   He is the great King of all the earth.

**47:3**
Ps 18:47

3 He subdues the nations before us,
   putting our enemies beneath our feet.

**47:4**
1 Pet 1:4

4 He chose the Promised Land as our inheritance,
   the proud possession of Jacob's descendants, whom he loves. *Interlude*

**47:5**
Pss 68:18, 25, 33;
98:6

5 God has ascended with a mighty shout.
   The LORD has ascended with trumpets blaring.

**47:6**
Ps 68:4

6 Sing praises to God, sing praises;
   sing praises to our King, sing praises!

7 For God is the King over all the earth.
   Praise him with a psalm.*

**47:8**
1 Chr 16:31

8 God reigns above the nations,
   sitting on his holy throne.

**47:9**
Pss 72:11; 89:18;
97:9
Isa 49:7, 23
Rom 4:11-12

9 The rulers of the world have gathered together
   with the people of the God of Abraham.
For all the kings of the earth belong to God.
   He is highly honored everywhere.

**47:7** Hebrew *maskil.* This may be a literary or musical term.

---

**PSALMS THAT HAVE INSPIRED HYMNS**

---

Lord. How proper, then, for us to be still now, reverently honoring him and his power and majesty. Take time each day to be still and to honor God.

**47:1ff** This psalm may have been written about the same event as Psalm 46—the Assyrian invasion of Judah by Sennacherib (2 Kings 18:13–19:37).

**47:2** The Lord Most High is awesome beyond words, but this didn't keep Bible writers from trying to describe him. And it shouldn't keep us from talking about him either. We can't describe God completely, but we can tell others what he has done for us. Don't let the indescribable aspects of God's greatness prevent you from telling others what you know about him.

**47:9** Abraham was the father of the Israelite nation. The one true God was sometimes called the "God of Abraham" (Exodus

3:6; 1 Kings 18:36). In a spiritual sense, God's promises to Abraham apply to all who believe in God, Jew or Gentile (Romans 4:11, 12; Galatians 3:7-9). Thus, the God of Abraham is our God, too.

**Theme:** God's presence is our joy, security, and salvation. God is praised as the defender of Jerusalem, the holy city of the Jews. He is also our defender and guide forever.
**Author:** The sons of Korah (Temple assistants)

# 48 *A song. A psalm of the descendants of Korah.*

1 How great is the LORD,
    how deserving of praise,
in the city of our God,
    which sits on his holy mountain!

2 It is high and magnificent;
    the whole earth rejoices to see it!
Mount Zion, the holy mountain,*
    is the city of the great King!

3 God himself is in Jerusalem's towers,
    revealing himself as its defender.

4 The kings of the earth joined forces
    and advanced against the city.

5 But when they saw it, they were stunned;
    they were terrified and ran away.

6 They were gripped with terror
    and writhed in pain like a woman in labor.

7 You destroyed them like the mighty ships of Tarshish
    shattered by a powerful east wind.

8 We had heard of the city's glory,
    but now we have seen it ourselves—
    the city of the LORD of Heaven's Armies.
It is the city of our God;
    he will make it safe forever.                              *Interlude*

9 O God, we meditate on your unfailing love
    as we worship in your Temple.

10 As your name deserves, O God,
    you will be praised to the ends of the earth.
    Your strong right hand is filled with victory.

11 Let the people on Mount Zion rejoice.
    Let all the towns of Judah be glad
    because of your justice.

12 Go, inspect the city of Jerusalem.*
    Walk around and count the many towers.

13 Take note of the fortified walls,
    and tour all the citadels,
that you may describe them
    to future generations.

| |
|---|
| **48:1**<br>1 Chr 16:25<br>Pss 87:1; 96:4;<br>145:3<br>Zech 8:3 |
| **48:2**<br>Ps 50:2<br>Lam 2:15<br>Matt 5:35 |
| **48:3**<br>Ps 46:7 |
| **48:4**<br>2 Sam 10:6-19 |
| **48:5**<br>Exod 15:15 |
| **48:6**<br>Isa 13:8 |
| **48:8**<br>Ps 87:5 |
| **48:9**<br>Pss 26:3; 40:10 |
| **48:10**<br>Josh 7:9<br>Isa 41:10<br>Mal 1:11 |
| **48:11**<br>Ps 97:8 |
| **48:13**<br>Ps 78:5-7 |

**48:2** Or *Mount Zion, in the far north;* Hebrew reads *Mount Zion, the heights of Zaphon.*   **48:12** Hebrew *Zion.*

---

**48:2** Why is Mount Zion—Jerusalem—"the city of the great King"? Because the Temple was located in Jerusalem, the city was seen as the center of God's presence in the world. The Bible pictures Jerusalem as the place where believers will gather in the last days (Isaiah 2:2ff) and as the spiritual home of all believers, where God will live among them (Revelation 21:2, 3).

**48:8** Because Jerusalem has been destroyed several times since this psalm was written, the phrase God "will make it safe forever" may refer prophetically to the new Jerusalem, where God will judge all nations and live with all believers (Revelation 21).

**48:11** The people of Judah were from Israel's largest tribe, which settled in the southern part of Canaan, where Jerusalem was located (Joshua 15:1-12). David was from Judah, and he

made Jerusalem his capital and the center of the nation's worship. Jesus was also a member of the tribe of Judah. The psalm writer was saying that the day would come when God would bring justice to the land and God's people would get the respect they deserved.

**48:12, 13** After an enemy army had unsuccessfully besieged Jerusalem, the people had to make a tour of the city, inspecting its defenses and praising God for the protection he had given. In times of great joy or after God has brought us through some great trial, we ought to inspect our defenses to make sure that the foundations—faith in God, knowledge of his Word, and the fellowship and prayers of the body of believers—remain strong (Ephesians 2:20-22). Then we should praise God for his protection!

**48:14**
Ps 23:4
Isa 58:11

14 For that is what God is like.
   He is our God forever and ever,
   and he will guide us until we die.

**Theme:** Trusting in worldly possessions is futile. You cannot take possessions with you when you die, and they cannot buy forgiveness from sin.
**Author:** The sons of Korah (Temple assistants)

# 49 *For the choir director: A psalm of the descendants of Korah.*

**49:1**
Pss 33:8; 78:1

1 Listen to this, all you people!
   Pay attention, everyone in the world!
2 High and low,
   rich and poor—listen!

**49:3**
Pss 37:30; 119:130

3 For my words are wise,
   and my thoughts are filled with insight.

**49:4**
Num 12:8
2 Kgs 3:15
Ps 78:2

4 I listen carefully to many proverbs
   and solve riddles with inspiration from a harp.

**49:5**
Pss 23:4; 27:1

5 Why should I fear when trouble comes,
   when enemies surround me?

**49:6**
Ps 52:7
Mark 10:24-25

6 They trust in their wealth
   and boast of great riches.

**49:7**
Job 36:18

7 Yet they cannot redeem themselves from death*
   by paying a ransom to God.

**49:8**
Matt 16:26

8 Redemption does not come so easily,
   for no one can ever pay enough

**49:9**
Pss 22:29; 89:48

9 to live forever
   and never see the grave.

**49:10**
Ps 39:6
Luke 12:20-21

10 Those who are wise must finally die,
   just like the foolish and senseless,
   leaving all their wealth behind.

**49:11**
Deut 3:14
Ps 10:6

11 The grave is their eternal home,
   where they will stay forever.
   They may name their estates after themselves,
12   but their fame will not last.
   They will die, just like animals.

**49:13**
Jer 17:11

13 This is the fate of fools,
   though they are remembered as being wise.*

**49:14**
Ps 9:17
Dan 7:18
Mal 4:3
1 Cor 6:2
Rev 2:26

                                                                    *Interlude*

14 Like sheep, they are led to the grave,*
   where death will be their shepherd.

**49:7** Or *no one can redeem the life of another.*   **49:13** The meaning of the Hebrew is uncertain.   **49:14** Hebrew *Sheol*; also in 49:14b, 15.

---

**48:14** We often pray for God's guidance as we struggle with decisions. What we need is both a map that gives us directions and a constant companion who has an intimate knowledge of the way and will make sure we interpret the map correctly. The Bible is such a map, and the Holy Spirit is our constant companion and guide. As you make your way through life, use both the map and your Guide.

**49:1ff** The futility of worldliness—riches, pride, fame—resounds from this psalm. Comparable in form to the book of Ecclesiastes, this psalm is one of the few written more to instruct than to praise God.

**49:7, 8, 15** In the slave market of the ancient world, a slave had to be redeemed (someone had to pay the price) in order to go free. In Mark 10:45, Ephesians 1:7, and Hebrews 9:12, we learn that Jesus paid such a price so that we could be set free from slavery to sin in order to begin a new life with him.
   There is no way for a person to buy eternal life with God.

Only God can redeem a soul. Don't count on wealth and physical comforts to keep you happy because you will never have enough wealth to keep from dying.

**49:10-14** The rich and poor have one similarity: When they die, they leave all they own here on earth. At the moment of death (and all of us will face that moment), both rich and poor are naked and empty-handed before God. The only riches we have at that time are those we have already invested in our eternal heritage. At the time of death, each of us will wish we had invested less on earth, where we must leave it, and more in heaven, where we will retain it forever. To have treasure in heaven, we must place our faith in God, pledge ourselves to obey him, and utilize our resources for the good of his Kingdom. This is a good time to check up on your investments and see where you have invested the most. Then do whatever it takes to place your investments where they really count.

In the morning the godly will rule over them.
    Their bodies will rot in the grave,
      far from their grand estates.
15 But as for me, God will redeem my life.
    He will snatch me from the power of the grave. *Interlude*

49:15
Ps 16:10-11

16 So don't be dismayed when the wicked grow rich
    and their homes become ever more splendid.

49:16
Ps 37:7

17 For when they die, they take nothing with them.
    Their wealth will not follow them into the grave.

49:17
Ps 17:14
1 Tim 6:7

18 In this life they consider themselves fortunate
    and are applauded for their success.

49:18
Ps 10:3
Luke 12:19

19 But they will die like all before them
    and never again see the light of day.

49:19
Job 33:29-30

20 People who boast of their wealth don't understand;
    they will die, just like animals.

49:20
Ps 49:12

**Theme:** The contrast between true and false faith. God desires sincere thanks, trust, and praise.
**Author:** Asaph, one of David's chief musicians

# 50 *A psalm of Asaph.*

1 The LORD, the Mighty One, is God,
    and he has spoken;
he has summoned all humanity
    from where the sun rises to where it sets.

50:1
Josh 22:22
Ps 113:3

2 From Mount Zion, the perfection of beauty,
    God shines in glorious radiance.

50:2
Deut 33:2
Pss 48:2; 80:1

3 Our God approaches,
    and he is not silent.
Fire devours everything in his way,
    and a great storm rages around him.

50:3
Ps 18:12-13
Dan 7:10

4 He calls on the heavens above and earth below
    to witness the judgment of his people.

50:4
Deut 4:26; 32:1
Isa 1:2

5 "Bring my faithful people to me—
    those who made a covenant with me by giving sacrifices."

50:5
Exod 24:7

6 Then let the heavens proclaim his justice,
    for God himself will be the judge. *Interlude*

50:6
Pss 75:7; 96:13;
97:6

7 "O my people, listen as I speak.
    Here are my charges against you, O Israel:
    I am God, your God!

8 I have no complaint about your sacrifices
    or the burnt offerings you constantly offer.

50:8
Ps 40:6

9 But I do not need the bulls from your barns
    or the goats from your pens.

50:9
Ps 69:31

10 For all the animals of the forest are mine,
    and I own the cattle on a thousand hills.

50:10
Ps 104:24

---

**50:1ff** God judges people for treating him lightly. First, he speaks to the superficially religious people who bring their sacrifices but are only going through the motions (50:1-15). They do not honor God with true praise and thankfulness. Second, he chides wicked, hard-hearted people for their evil words and immoral lives (50:16-22). He asks the superficially religious for genuine thanksgiving and trust, and he warns the evil people to consider their deeds, lest he destroy them in his anger.

**50:1-4** Asaph begins his psalm by describing God's final judgment of people on earth. Surprisingly, we read that God's great fury is leveled against his own people (or at least those who claim

to be his). God's judgment must first begin with his own children (1 Peter 4:17).

**50:5-9** God's perfect moral nature demands that the penalty for sin be death; however, people could offer an animal to God as a substitute for their own lives, symbolizing their faith in the merciful, forgiving God. But the people were offering sacrifices and forgetting their significance! The very act of sacrifice showed that they had once agreed to follow God wholeheartedly. But at this time their hearts were not in it. We may fall into the same pattern when we participate in religious activities, tithe, or attend church out of habit or conformity rather than out of heartfelt love and obedience. God wants righteousness, not empty ritual. (See the note on 40:6.)

¹¹ I know every bird on the mountains,
  and all the animals of the field are mine.

**50:12**
Exod 19:5

¹² If I were hungry, I would not tell you,
  for all the world is mine and everything in it.

**50:13**
Hos 6:6

¹³ Do I eat the meat of bulls?
  Do I drink the blood of goats?

**50:14**
Deut 23:21
Hos 14:2
Rom 12:1
Heb 13:15

¹⁴ Make thankfulness your sacrifice to God,
  and keep the vows you made to the Most High.
¹⁵ Then call on me when you are in trouble,
  and I will rescue you,
  and you will give me glory."

**50:16**
Isa 29:13

¹⁶ But God says to the wicked:
  "Why bother reciting my decrees
  and pretending to obey my covenant?

**50:17**
Neh 9:26
Rom 2:21-22

¹⁷ For you refuse my discipline
  and treat my words like trash.

**50:18**
Rom 1:32
1 Tim 5:22

¹⁸ When you see thieves, you approve of them,
  and you spend your time with adulterers.

**50:19**
Pss 10:7; 36:3

¹⁹ Your mouth is filled with wickedness,
  and your tongue is full of lies.

**50:20**
Matt 10:21

²⁰ You sit around and slander your brother—
  your own mother's son.

**50:21**
Ps 90:8
Eccl 8:11
Isa 42:14

²¹ While you did all this, I remained silent,
  and you thought I didn't care.
  But now I will rebuke you,
  listing all my charges against you.

**50:22**
Job 8:13
Ps 9:17

²² Repent, all of you who forget me,
  or I will tear you apart,
  and no one will help you.

**50:23**
Pss 50:14; 85:13;
91:16

²³ But giving thanks is a sacrifice that truly honors me.
  If you keep to my path,
  I will reveal to you the salvation of God."

**Theme:** David's plea for mercy, forgiveness, and cleansing. God wants our hearts to be right with him.
**Author:** David

## 51

*For the choir director: A psalm of David, regarding the time Nathan the prophet came to him after David had committed adultery with Bathsheba.*

**51:1**
Ps 4:1
Acts 3:19

¹ Have mercy on me, O God,
  because of your unfailing love.
  Because of your great compassion,
  blot out the stain of my sins.

---

**50:16-22** Some people glibly recite God's laws but are filled with deceit and evil. They claim his promises but refuse to obey him. This is sin, and God will judge people for it. We, too, are hypocrites when we are not what we claim to be. To let this inconsistency remain shows that we are not true followers of God.

**50:21** Just because God is silent does not mean he is condoning sin or is indifferent to it. Instead, he is withholding deserved punishment, giving time for people to repent (2 Peter 3:9). God takes no pleasure in the death of the wicked and wants them to turn from evil (Ezekiel 33:11). But his silence does not last forever—a time of punishment will surely come.

**51:1ff** This psalm expresses one of the clearest examples of repentance in all of Scripture. Countless broken sinners have found in these words an exquisite expression of their deeply felt need for God's mercy and forgiveness. David's confession has helped people examine excuses, half-hearted repentance, and lack of sorrow over sin that can keep them from experiencing pardon.

David's words also demonstrate the place of hope within confession. Use this psalm as a starting point when dealing with a sense of distance or with guilt that is affecting your relationship with God. It will help you identify and rectify sin in your life through confession and repentance.

**51:1-7** David was truly sorry for his adultery with Bathsheba and for murdering her husband to cover it up. He knew that his actions had hurt many people. But because David repented of those sins, God mercifully forgave him. No sin is too great to be forgiven! Do you feel that you could never come close to God because you have done something terrible? God can and will forgive you of any sin. While God forgives us, however, he does not always erase the natural consequences of our sin. David's life and family were never the same as a result of what he had done (see 2 Samuel 12:1-23).

² Wash me clean from my guilt.
  Purify me from my sin.
³ For I recognize my rebellion;
  it haunts me day and night.
⁴ Against you, and you alone, have I sinned;
  I have done what is evil in your sight.
  You will be proved right in what you say,
  and your judgment against me is just.*
⁵ For I was born a sinner—
  yes, from the moment my mother conceived me.
⁶ But you desire honesty from the womb,*
  teaching me wisdom even there.

⁷ Purify me from my sins,* and I will be clean;
  wash me, and I will be whiter than snow.
⁸ Oh, give me back my joy again;
  you have broken me—
  now let me rejoice.
⁹ Don't keep looking at my sins.
  Remove the stain of my guilt.
¹⁰ Create in me a clean heart, O God.
  Renew a loyal spirit within me.
¹¹ Do not banish me from your presence,
  and don't take your Holy Spirit* from me.

¹² Restore to me the joy of your salvation,
  and make me willing to obey you.
¹³ Then I will teach your ways to rebels,
  and they will return to you.
¹⁴ Forgive me for shedding blood, O God who saves;
  then I will joyfully sing of your forgiveness.
¹⁵ Unseal my lips, O Lord,
  that my mouth may praise you.

¹⁶ You do not desire a sacrifice, or I would offer one.
  You do not want a burnt offering.
¹⁷ The sacrifice you desire is a broken spirit.
  You will not reject a broken and repentant heart, O God.
¹⁸ Look with favor on Zion and help her;
  rebuild the walls of Jerusalem.
¹⁹ Then you will be pleased with sacrifices offered in the right spirit—
  with burnt offerings and whole burnt offerings.
  Then bulls will again be sacrificed on your altar.

**51:2**
Jer 33:8
Acts 22:16
Heb 9:13-14
1 Jn 1:7, 9
**51:3**
Isa 59:12
**51:4**
Gen 20:6
Luke 15:21
†Rom 3:4
**51:5**
Ps 58:3
Job 14:4
Eph 2:3
**51:7**
Exod 12:22
Isa 1:18
**51:8**
Ps 35:10
**51:9**
Jer 16:17
**51:10**
Ps 78:37
Matt 5:8
Acts 15:9
Eph 2:10
**51:11**
Eph 4:30
**51:13**
Ps 22:27
**51:14**
2 Sam 12:9
Pss 9:14; 25:5;
71:15
**51:16**
1 Sam 15:22
Ps 40:6
**51:17**
Ps 34:18
**51:18**
Isa 51:3
**51:19**
Pss 4:5; 66:13, 15

**51:4** Greek version reads *and you will win your case in court.* Compare Rom 3:4.   **51:6** Or *from the heart;* Hebrew reads *in the inward parts.*   **51:7** Hebrew *Purify me with the hyssop branch.*   **51:11** Or *your spirit of holiness.*

**51:4** Although David had sinned with Bathsheba, David said that he had sinned against God. When someone steals, murders, or slanders, it is against someone else—a victim. According to the world's standards, extramarital sex between two consenting adults is acceptable if nobody gets hurt. But people *do* get hurt—in David's case, a man was murdered, and a baby died. All sin hurts us and others, but ultimately it offends God because sin in any form is rebellion against God's way of living. When you are tempted to do wrong, remember that you will be sinning against God. That may help you avoid the danger.

**51:10** Because we are born sinners (51:5), our natural inclination is to please ourselves rather than God. David followed that inclination when he took another man's wife. Like David, we must ask God to cleanse us from within (51:7), filling our hearts and spirits with new thoughts and desires. Right conduct can come only from a clean heart and spirit. Ask God to create a pure heart and spirit in you.

**51:12** Do you ever feel stagnant in your faith, as though you are

just going through the motions? Has sin ever driven a wedge between you and God, making him seem distant? David felt this way. He had sinned with Bathsheba and had just been confronted by Nathan the prophet. In his prayer he cried, "Restore to me the joy of your salvation." God wants us to be close to him and to experience his full and complete life. But sin that remains unconfessed makes such intimacy impossible. Confess your sin to God. You may still have to face some earthly consequences, as David did, but God will give back the joy of your relationship with him.

**51:13** When God forgives our sin and restores our fellowship with him, we want to reach out to others who need this forgiveness and reconciliation. The more you have felt God's forgiveness, the more you will desire to tell others about it.

**51:17** God wants a broken spirit and a broken and repentant heart. You can never please God by outward actions—no matter how good—if your heart attitude is not right. Are you sorry for your sin? Do you genuinely intend to stop? God is pleased by this kind of repentance.

**Theme:** God will judge the evildoer. Our anger must not block our confidence in God's ability to defeat evil.
**Author:** David

# 52
*For the choir director: A psalm\* of David, regarding the time Doeg the Edomite said to Saul, "David has gone to see Ahimelech."*

**52:1**
Ps 94:4

<sup></sup>1 Why do you boast about your crimes, great warrior?
  Don't you realize God's justice continues forever?

**52:2**
Pss 5:9; 57:4; 59:7

2 All day long you plot destruction.
  Your tongue cuts like a sharp razor;
  you're an expert at telling lies.

**52:3**
Pss 36:4; 58:3
Jer 9:4-5

3 You love evil more than good
  and lies more than truth.                                          *Interlude*

**52:4**
Ps 120:3

4 You love to destroy others with your words,
  you liar!

**52:5**
Prov 2:22
Isa 22:18-19

5 But God will strike you down once and for all.
  He will pull you from your home
  and uproot you from the land of the living.                        *Interlude*

**52:6**
Job 22:19
Ps 40:3

6 The righteous will see it and be amazed.
  They will laugh and say,
7 "Look what happens to mighty warriors
  who do not trust in God.
  They trust their wealth instead
  and grow more and more bold in their wickedness."

**52:8**
Pss 13:5; 128:3
Jer 11:16

8 But I am like an olive tree, thriving in the house of God.
  I will always trust in God's unfailing love.

**52:9**
Pss 30:12; 54:6

9 I will praise you forever, O God,
  for what you have done.
  I will trust in your good name
  in the presence of your faithful people.

**Theme:** All have sinned. Because of sin, no person can find God on his own. Only God can save us.
**Author:** David

# 53
*For the choir director: A meditation; a psalm\* of David.*

**53:1-6**
//Ps 14:1-7

<sup></sup>1 Only fools say in their hearts,
  "There is no God."
  They are corrupt, and their actions are evil;
  not one of them does good!

**53:2**
Ps 33:13-15

2 God looks down from heaven
  on the entire human race;
  he looks to see if anyone is truly wise,
  if anyone seeks God.

**52:TITLE** Hebrew *maskil.* This may be a literary or musical term.     **53:TITLE** Hebrew *According to mahalath; a maskil.* These may be literary or musical terms.

---

**52:1** This psalm was written about Doeg the Edomite, who had betrayed Ahimelech and David and then killed God's priests (see 1 Samuel 21:7; 22:9-23). Doeg thought he was a great warrior—even boasting about his deed. In reality, his deed was evil, an offense to God. It is easy to mistake "accomplishment" for goodness. Just because something is done well or thoroughly doesn't mean it is good (for example, someone may be a great gambler or a skillful liar). Measure all you do by the rule of God's Word, not by how proficiently you do it.

**52:8** With God by his side, David compared himself to an olive tree, thriving in the house of God. Not only is an olive tree a thriv-ing tree, it is one of the longest-living trees. David was contrasting God's eternal protection of his faithful servants with the sudden destruction of the wicked (52:5-7).

**53:1** Echoing the message of Psalm 14, this psalm proclaims the foolishness of atheism (see also Romans 3:10). People may say there is no God in order to cover up their sin, to have an excuse to continue in sin, and/or to ignore the Judge in order to avoid the judgment. "Fools" do not necessarily lack intelligence; many atheists and unbelievers are highly educated. Fools are people who reject God, the only one who can save them.

3 But no, all have turned away;
     all have become corrupt.*
No one does good,
     not a single one!

4 Will those who do evil never learn?
     They eat up my people like bread
     and wouldn't think of praying to God.

5 Terror will grip them,
     terror like they have never known before.
God will scatter the bones of your enemies.
     You will put them to shame, for God has rejected them.

6 Who will come from Mount Zion to rescue Israel?
     When God restores his people,
     Jacob will shout with joy, and Israel will rejoice.

**53:3**
Rom 3:10, 12

**53:5**
Lev 26:17, 36
Ps 44:7
Jer 6:30; 8:1-2
Ezek 6:5

**53:6**
Ps 14:7

**Theme:** A call for God to overcome enemies. God is our helper, even in times of hurt and betrayal.
**Author:** David

**54** *For the choir director: A psalm\* of David, regarding the time the Ziphites came and said to Saul, "We know where David is hiding." To be accompanied by stringed instruments.*

1 Come with great power, O God, and rescue me!
     Defend me with your might.
2 Listen to my prayer, O God.
     Pay attention to my plea.
3 For strangers are attacking me;
     violent people are trying to kill me.
     They care nothing for God.                          *Interlude*

4 But God is my helper.
     The Lord keeps me alive!
5 May the evil plans of my enemies be turned against them.
     Do as you promised and put an end to them.

6 I will sacrifice a voluntary offering to you;
     I will praise your name, O LORD,
     for it is good.
7 For you have rescued me from my troubles
     and helped me to triumph over my enemies.

**54:1**
2 Chr 20:6
Ps 20:1

**54:3**
1 Sam 20:1
Pss 36:1; 40:14;
86:14; 140:1, 4

**54:4**
Ps 37:17, 24, 40

**54:6**
Ps 50:14

**54:7**
Pss 34:6; 59:10

**Theme:** Expressing deep dismay over the treachery of a close friend. When friends hurt us, the burden is too difficult to carry alone.
**Author:** David

**55** *For the choir director: A psalm\* of David, to be accompanied by stringed instruments.*

1 Listen to my prayer, O God.
     Do not ignore my cry for help!

**55:1**
Pss 27:9; 61:1

**53:3** Greek version reads *have become useless.* Compare Rom 3:12.    **54:TITLE** Hebrew *maskil.* This may be a literary or musical term.    **55:TITLE** Hebrew *maskil.* This may be a literary or musical term.

---

**53:4, 5** While God is not affected by what we think of him, we are definitely and eternally affected by what God thinks of us. This psalm begins with the bold claim that there is no God, but by this verse, the true reason for rejecting God has become clear. The reason people reject God has nothing to do with God's existence and everything to do with people's sinfulness. In our desire to do wrong, we treat God as if he doesn't exist. When God passes judgment, it will be too late to apologize and admit we were wrong. Rejection of God will turn into terror of God.

**54:3, 4** Many of David's psalms follow the pattern found in these two verses—a transition from prayer to praise. David was not afraid to come to God and express his true feelings and needs. Thus, his spirit was lifted, and he praised God, his helper, protector, and friend.

**54:5** David asked God to repay evil to his enemies. He simply stated his confidence in God's promise. Proverbs 26:27 warns that those who cause trouble will reap trouble. What we have intended for others may blow up in our own face. To be honest and straightforward before God and others is simpler, easier, and safer in the long run.

**55:1ff** This psalm was most likely written during the time of Absalom's rebellion and Ahithophel's betrayal (2 Samuel 15–17).

**55:2**
1 Sam 1:16
Pss 77:3; 86:6-7
Isa 38:14

**55:3**
2 Sam 16:7-8
Pss 17:9; 71:11

**55:4**
Ps 116:3

**55:5**
Job 21:6

**55:6**
Job 3:13

**55:8**
Isa 4:6

**55:9**
Jer 6:7

**55:11**
Pss 5:9; 10:7

**55:12-13**
Ps 41:9

**55:14**
Ps 42:4

**55:15**
Num 16:30, 33
Ps 64:7

**55:16**
Ps 57:2-3

**55:17**
Pss 5:3; 88:13;
141:2
Dan 6:10
Acts 3:1

**55:18**
Ps 103:4

**55:19**
Pss 36:1; 93:2

2 Please listen and answer me,
    for I am overwhelmed by my troubles.
3 My enemies shout at me,
    making loud and wicked threats.
    They bring trouble on me
    and angrily hunt me down.

4 My heart pounds in my chest.
    The terror of death assaults me.
5 Fear and trembling overwhelm me,
    and I can't stop shaking.
6 Oh, that I had wings like a dove;
    then I would fly away and rest!
7 I would fly far away
    to the quiet of the wilderness.
8 How quickly I would escape—
    far from this wild storm of hatred.                    *Interlude*

9 Confuse them, Lord, and frustrate their plans,
    for I see violence and conflict in the city.
10 Its walls are patrolled day and night against invaders,
    but the real danger is wickedness within the city.
11 Everything is falling apart;
    threats and cheating are rampant in the streets.

12 It is not an enemy who taunts me—
    I could bear that.
    It is not my foes who so arrogantly insult me—
    I could have hidden from them.
13 Instead, it is you—my equal,
    my companion and close friend.
14 What good fellowship we once enjoyed
    as we walked together to the house of God.

15 Let death stalk my enemies;
    let the grave* swallow them alive,
    for evil makes its home within them.

16 But I will call on God,
    and the LORD will rescue me.
17 Morning, noon, and night
    I cry out in my distress,
    and the LORD hears my voice.
18 He ransoms me and keeps me safe
    from the battle waged against me,
    though many still oppose me.
19 God, who has ruled forever,
    will hear me and humble them.                          *Interlude*

**55:15** Hebrew *let Sheol.*

---

Some say verses 12-14 are messianic because they also describe Judas's betrayal of Christ (Matthew 26:14-16, 20-25).

**55:6-8** Even those who are especially close to God, as David was, have moments when they want to escape from their problems and pressures.

**55:9-11** The city that was supposed to be holy was plagued by internal problems: violence, conflict, wickedness, threats, and cheating. External enemies, though a constant threat, were not nearly as dangerous as the corruption inside. Even today, churches often look to defend themselves against troubles from the sinful world while failing to see that their own sins are causing their troubles.

**55:12-14** Nothing hurts more than a wound from a friend. At times friends may need to lovingly confront you in order to help you, but betrayal truly hurts. Betrayal by a friend has caused David great anguish. Real friends stick by you in times of trouble and bring healing, love, acceptance, and understanding. What kind of friend are you? Don't betray those you love.

**55:17** Praying morning, noon, and night is certainly an excellent way to maintain correct priorities throughout every day. Daniel followed this pattern (Daniel 6:10), as did Peter (Acts 10:9, 10). The prayers of God's people are effective against the overwhelming evil in the world.

For my enemies refuse to change their ways;
    they do not fear God.

20 As for my companion, he betrayed his friends;
    he broke his promises.
21 His words are as smooth as butter,
    but in his heart is war.
His words are as soothing as lotion,
    but underneath are daggers!

22 Give your burdens to the LORD,
    and he will take care of you.
He will not permit the godly to slip and fall.

23 But you, O God, will send the wicked
    down to the pit of destruction.
Murderers and liars will die young,
    but I am trusting you to save me.

**55:20**
Num 30:2
Pss 7:3-4; 89:34

**55:21**
Pss 12:2; 28:3
Prov 5:3-4

**55:22**
Pss 37:5; 112:6
1 Pet 5:7

**55:23**
Pss 5:6; 56:3-4;
73:18

**Theme:** Trusting in God's care in the midst of fear. When all seems dark, one truth still shines bright: When God is for us, those against us will never succeed.
**Author:** David

# 56

*For the choir director: A psalm\* of David, regarding the time the Philistines seized him in Gath. To be sung to the tune "Dove on Distant Oaks."*

1 O God, have mercy on me,
    for people are hounding me.
My foes attack me all day long.
2 I am constantly hounded by those who slander me,
    and many are boldly attacking me.
3 But when I am afraid,
    I will put my trust in you.
4 I praise God for what he has promised.
    I trust in God, so why should I be afraid?
What can mere mortals do to me?

5 They are always twisting what I say;
    they spend their days plotting to harm me.
6 They come together to spy on me—
    watching my every step, eager to kill me.
7 Don't let them get away with their wickedness;
    in your anger, O God, bring them down.

8 You keep track of all my sorrows.\*
    You have collected all my tears in your bottle.
    You have recorded each one in your book.

9 My enemies will retreat when I call to you for help.
    This I know: God is on my side!
10 I praise God for what he has promised;
    yes, I praise the LORD for what he has promised.

**56:1**
Pss 17:9; 35:1, 25

**56:3**
Pss 11:1; 56:10-11

**56:4**
Ps 118:6
Heb 13:6

**56:5**
Ps 41:7
2 Pet 3:15-16

**56:6**
Pss 17:11; 59:3

**56:7**
Pss 36:12; 55:23

**56:8**
Pss 39:12; 139:3
Mal 3:16

**56:9**
Pss 41:11; 118:6
Rom 8:31

**56:TITLE** Hebrew *miktam*. This may be a literary or musical term.    **56:8** Or *my wanderings*.

---

**55:22** God wants us to give our burdens to him, but often we continue to bear them ourselves even when we say we are trusting in him. Trust the same strength that sustains you to carry your cares also.

**56:1ff** This was probably written on the same occasion as Psalm 34, when David fled from Saul to Philistine territory. He had to pretend insanity before Achish when some servants grew suspicious of him (1 Samuel 21:10-15).

**56:3, 4** David stated, "What can mere mortals do to me?" How much harm can people do to us? They can inflict pain, suffering, and death. But no person can rob us of our souls or our future

beyond this life. How much harm can we do to ourselves? The worst thing we can do is to reject God and lose our eternal life. Jesus said, "Don't be afraid of those who want to kill your body; they cannot touch your soul" (Matthew 10:28). Instead, we should fear God, who controls this life and the next.

**56:8** Even in our deepest sorrow, God cares! Jesus reminded us further of how much God understands us—even the hairs on our head are all numbered (Matthew 10:30). Often we waver between faith and fear. When you feel so discouraged that you are sure no one understands, remember that God knows every problem and sees every tear.

<sup>11</sup> I trust in God, so why should I be afraid?
  What can mere mortals do to me?

**56:12**
Ps 50:14-15

<sup>12</sup> I will fulfill my vows to you, O God,
  and will offer a sacrifice of thanks for your help.

**56:13**
Job 33:30
Pss 33:19; 86:13;
116:8-9

<sup>13</sup> For you have rescued me from death;
  you have kept my feet from slipping.
So now I can walk in your presence, O God,
  in your life-giving light.

**Theme:** God's faithful help and love in times of trouble. When we face trials, God will quiet our hearts and give us confidence.
**Author:** David

**57** *For the choir director: A psalm\* of David, regarding the time he fled from Saul and went into the cave. To be sung to the tune "Do Not Destroy!"*

**57:1**
Ruth 2:12
Pss 36:7; 91:4
Isa 26:20

<sup>1</sup> Have mercy on me, O God, have mercy!
    I look to you for protection.
  I will hide beneath the shadow of your wings
    until the danger passes by.

**57:2**
Ps 138:8

<sup>2</sup> I cry out to God Most High,\*
    to God who will fulfill his purpose for me.

**57:3**
Pss 18:16; 25:10;
56:2; 144:5, 7

<sup>3</sup> He will send help from heaven to rescue me,
    disgracing those who hound me.                              *Interlude*
  My God will send forth his unfailing love and faithfulness.

**57:4**
Pss 58:6; 64:3
Prov 30:13-14

<sup>4</sup> I am surrounded by fierce lions
    who greedily devour human prey—
  whose teeth pierce like spears and arrows,
    and whose tongues cut like swords.

**57:5**
Ps 108:5

<sup>5</sup> Be exalted, O God, above the highest heavens!
    May your glory shine over all the earth.

**57:6**
Pss 10:9; 35:7;
140:5
Prov 26:27

<sup>6</sup> My enemies have set a trap for me.
    I am weary from distress.
  They have dug a deep pit in my path,
    but they themselves have fallen into it.                    *Interlude*

**57:7-11**
//Ps 108:1-5

<sup>7</sup> My heart is confident in you, O God;
    my heart is confident.
  No wonder I can sing your praises!

**57:8**
Pss 16:9; 30:12;
150:3

<sup>8</sup> Wake up, my heart!
    Wake up, O lyre and harp!
  I will wake the dawn with my song.
<sup>9</sup> I will thank you, Lord, among all the people.
    I will sing your praises among the nations.

**57:10**
Ps 36:5

<sup>10</sup> For your unfailing love is as high as the heavens.
    Your faithfulness reaches to the clouds.

<sup>11</sup> Be exalted, O God, above the highest heavens.
    May your glory shine over all the earth.

**57:TITLE** Hebrew *miktam*. This may be a literary or musical term.   **57:2** Hebrew *Elohim-Elyon*.

---

**57:1ff** This psalm was probably written about David's reflections when he was hiding in a cave from Saul (see 1 Samuel 22–24).

**57:4** At times we may be surrounded by people who gossip about us or criticize us. Verbal cruelty can damage us as badly as physical abuse. Rather than answering with hateful words, we, like David, can talk with God about the problem.

**57:7** David's firm faith in God contrasted sharply with his enemies' loud lying and boasting. When confronted with verbal attacks, the best defense is simply to be quiet and praise God, realizing that our confidence is in his love and faithfulness

(57:10). In times of suffering, don't turn inward to self-pity or outward to revenge, but turn upward to God.

**57:8** David calls out to his soul and his instruments to prepare for praise. Before a new day begins, he wants to "wake the dawn" with his song honoring God's faithfulness. Instead of spending a sleepless night worrying about what he cannot change, he uses those wakeful hours to meditate on an expression suitable for the world. David's example shows us how to turn times of stress into times of blessing by considering God's faithfulness in comparison with our fleeting problems. Why worry when you can invest that time in praise?

**Theme:** A prayer for God's justice. When no justice can be found, rejoice in knowing that justice will triumph because there is a God who will judge with complete fairness.
**Author:** David, at a time when men in authority were twisting justice

# 58 *For the choir director: A psalm\* of David, to be sung to the tune "Do Not Destroy!"*

1 Justice—do you rulers\* know the meaning of the word?
　　Do you judge the people fairly?
2 No! You plot injustice in your hearts.
　　You spread violence throughout the land.
3 These wicked people are born sinners;
　　even from birth they have lied and gone their own way.
4 They spit venom like deadly snakes;
　　they are like cobras that refuse to listen,
5 ignoring the tunes of the snake charmers,
　　no matter how skillfully they play.

6 Break off their fangs, O God!
　　Smash the jaws of these lions, O LORD!
7 May they disappear like water into thirsty ground.
　　Make their weapons useless in their hands.\*
8 May they be like snails that dissolve into slime,
　　like a stillborn child who will never see the sun.
9 God will sweep them away, both young and old,
　　faster than a pot heats over burning thorns.

10 The godly will rejoice when they see injustice avenged.
　　They will wash their feet in the blood of the wicked.
11 Then at last everyone will say,
　　"There truly is a reward for those who live for God;
　　surely there is a God who judges justly here on earth."

**58:1**
Ps 82:2

**58:2**
Ps 94:20
Mal 3:15

**58:3**
Ps 53:3
Isa 48:8

**58:4**
Deut 32:33
Pss 81:11; 140:3

**58:6**
Job 4:10
Ps 3:7

**58:7**
Josh 7:5
Pss 64:3; 112:10

**58:8**
Job 3:16

**58:9**
Job 27:21
Ps 118:12
Prov 10:25

**58:10**
Pss 32:11; 64:10;
68:22-23; 91:8

**58:11**
Pss 9:8; 18:20
Luke 6:23, 35

**Theme:** Prayer and praise for God's saving help. God's constant love is our place of safety in a wicked world.
**Author:** David

# 59 *For the choir director: A psalm\* of David, regarding the time Saul sent soldiers to watch David's house in order to kill him. To be sung to the tune "Do Not Destroy!"*

1 Rescue me from my enemies, O God.
　　Protect me from those who have come to destroy me.
2 Rescue me from these criminals;
　　save me from these murderers.
3 They have set an ambush for me.
　　Fierce enemies are out there waiting, LORD,
　　though I have not sinned or offended them.

**59:1**
Pss 20:1; 143:9

**59:2**
Pss 14:4; 28:3;
94:16; 139:19

**59:3**
Pss 7:3-4; 56:6;
69:4

**58:TITLE** Hebrew *miktam*. This may be a literary or musical term.　**58:1** Or *you gods*.　**58:7** Or *Let them be trodden down and wither like grass*. The meaning of the Hebrew is uncertain.　**59:TITLE** Hebrew *miktam*. This may be a literary or musical term.

---

**58:1ff** This is called an imprecatory psalm (see the note on 35:1ff). It is a cry for justice so intense that it seems, at first glance, to be a call for revenge.

**58:1ff** The Old Testament is filled with references to justice—it is a key topic in the psalms. Unfortunately, many judges and rulers in ancient times took justice into their own hands. They had complete authority with no accountability and the power to make their own laws. When earth's judges are corrupt, there is little hope of justice in this life. But God loves justice, and those who obey him will experience perfect justice in eternity.

**58:6-10** Shifting from prayer to prediction, David fervently calls for justice that veers into grisly judgment. Broken fangs and smashed jaws give way to the godly wading in the blood of the wicked. The words convey ugly pictures of the gruesome results of sin. Even uglier pictures of the darkness are often revealed by

our own demands for justice and more. This is certainly not the only time David's forceful sense of justice turned back on him (see 2 Samuel 12:1-15). Ironically, David himself would eventually occupy the throne and be subject to the very imprecation he called down on others. We can be grateful that God hears our prayers, but we can also be grateful that God doesn't have to abide by our requests.

**58:11** Of all people, our national leaders should be just and fair. When they are unjust and unfair, people suffer as politicians wrest power from the people, national morality deteriorates, and God is ignored. When right triumphs at last, "the godly will rejoice" (58:10). Be assured that there will be a day of accountability and that God judges fairly. Be careful never to side with injustice lest you find yourself standing before an angry Judge.

**59:4**
Ps 35:19, 23

4 I have done nothing wrong,
    yet they prepare to attack me.
  Wake up! See what is happening and help me!

**59:5**
Pss 9:5; 84:8
Jer 18:23

5 O Lord God of Heaven's Armies, the God of Israel,
    wake up and punish those hostile nations.
  Show no mercy to wicked traitors.                    *Interlude*

6 They come out at night,
    snarling like vicious dogs
    as they prowl the streets.

**59:7**
Job 22:13
Pss 10:11; 73:11;
94:4-7

7 Listen to the filth that comes from their mouths;
    their words cut like swords.
  "After all, who can hear us?" they sneer.

**59:8**
Pss 2:4; 37:13

8 But Lord, you laugh at them.
    You scoff at all the hostile nations.

**59:9**
Ps 9:9

9 You are my strength; I wait for you to rescue me,
    for you, O God, are my fortress.

**59:10**
Ps 54:7

10 In his unfailing love, my God will stand with me.
    He will let me look down in triumph on all my enemies.

**59:11**
Deut 4:9
Pss 106:27; 144:6

11 Don't kill them, for my people soon forget such lessons;
    stagger them with your power, and bring them to their knees,
    O Lord our shield.

**59:12**
Ps 10:7
Prov 12:13
Zeph 3:11

12 Because of the sinful things they say,
    because of the evil that is on their lips,
  let them be captured by their pride,
    their curses, and their lies.

**59:13**
Pss 83:18; 104:35

13 Destroy them in your anger!
    Wipe them out completely!
  Then the whole world will know
    that God reigns in Israel.*            *Interlude*

**59:14**
Ps 59:6

14 My enemies come out at night,
    snarling like vicious dogs
    as they prowl the streets.

15 They scavenge for food
    but go to sleep unsatisfied.*

**59:16**
Pss 21:13; 46:1;
101:1

16 But as for me, I will sing about your power.
    Each morning I will sing with joy about your unfailing love.
  For you have been my refuge,
    a place of safety when I am in distress.

**59:17**
Ps 59:9-10

17 O my Strength, to you I sing praises,
    for you, O God, are my refuge,
    the God who shows me unfailing love.

**59:13** Hebrew *in Jacob.* See note on 44:4.    **59:15** Or *and growl if they don't get enough.*

---

**59:7, 8** Vile men curse God as if he cannot hear or will not respond. But God scoffs at them. Evil people live as if God cannot see them or will not punish them. But God watches patiently until that day when their deeds will rise up to accuse them. As believers we must be careful not to follow the same foolish practices as evil people. We must remember that God hears and sees all we do.

**59:10** David was hunted by those whose love had turned to jealousy, and this was driving them to try to murder him. Trusted friends and even his mentor, the king, had turned against him. What changeable love! But David knew that God's love for him was *changeless.* "His unfailing love continues forever" (100:5). God's mercy to all who trust him is just as permanent as his mercy to David. When the love of others fails or disappoints us, we can rest in God's unfailing love.

**59:16** Throughout this psalm, David describes in grim detail the behavior of his enemies. He conveys his own feelings of dread with the desperation and despair that he sees in the lives of those who want to harm him. What a delight, then, in these final verses to read about God's role in David's life as refuge, a place of safety, and a source of unfailing love. David had learned to turn negative circumstances into reminders of God's faithful presence. What stresses in your life might be transformed today if you made them a starting point for praising God?

**Theme:** Real help comes from God alone. When a situation seems out of control, we can trust God to do mighty things.
**Author:** David, when Israel was away at war with Aram in the north, and Edom invaded Judah from the south (2 Samuel 8)

# 60

*For the choir director: A psalm\* of David useful for teaching, regarding the time David fought Aram-naharaim and Aram-zobah, and Joab returned and killed 12,000 Edomites in the Valley of Salt. To be sung to the tune "Lily of the Testimony."*

1 You have rejected us, O God, and broken our defenses.
   You have been angry with us; now restore us to your favor.
2 You have shaken our land and split it open.
   Seal the cracks, for the land trembles.
3 You have been very hard on us,
   making us drink wine that sent us reeling.
4 But you have raised a banner for those who fear you—
   a rallying point in the face of attack.                                          *Interlude*

5 Now rescue your beloved people.
   Answer and save us by your power.
6 God has promised this by his holiness\*:
   "I will divide up Shechem with joy.
   I will measure out the valley of Succoth.
7 Gilead is mine,
   and Manasseh, too.
   Ephraim, my helmet, will produce my warriors,
   and Judah, my scepter, will produce my kings.
8 But Moab, my washbasin, will become my servant,
   and I will wipe my feet on Edom
   and shout in triumph over Philistia."

9 Who will bring me into the fortified city?
   Who will bring me victory over Edom?
10 Have you rejected us, O God?
   Will you no longer march with our armies?
11 Oh, please help us against our enemies,
   for all human help is useless.
12 With God's help we will do mighty things,
   for he will trample down our foes.

**60:1**
Pss 44:9; 79:5; 80:3

**60:2**
2 Chr 7:14
Ps 18:7

**60:3**
Ps 66:12

**60:5-12**
//Ps 108:6-13

**60:6**
Gen 33:17
Josh 17:7
Ps 89:35

**60:7**
Gen 49:10
Deut 33:17
Josh 13:31

**60:8**
2 Sam 8:1-2, 14

**60:9**
Ps 44:9

**60:10**
Ps 60:1

**60:11**
Ps 146:3

**60:12**
Num 24:15-19
Pss 44:5; 118:16

**Theme:** Prayer for security and assurance. Wherever we are, we can trust that God will be there to answer our cries for help.
**Author:** David, written when he was forced to escape during the days of Absalom's rebellion (2 Samuel 15—18), or after he had narrowly escaped one of Saul's efforts to kill him while hiding in the wilderness

# 61

*For the choir director: A psalm of David, to be accompanied by stringed instruments.*

1 O God, listen to my cry!
   Hear my prayer!

**61:1**
Pss 64:1; 86:6

**60:TITLE** Hebrew *miktam*. This may be a literary or musical term.  **60:6** Or *in his sanctuary.*

---

**60:1ff** This psalm gives us information about David's reign not found in the books of 1 and 2 Samuel or 1 and 2 Chronicles. Although the setting of the psalm is found in 2 Samuel 8, that passage makes no reference to the fact that David's forces had met stiff resistance (60:1-3) and apparently even a temporary defeat (60:9, 10). The closer we get to God, the more our enemies will attack us because we threaten their evil and selfish way of living.

**60:3** Instead of the wine of blessing, God had given them the cup of his judgment. God's rejection was intended to bring them back to himself.

**60:6-10** God said the cities and territories of Israel were his, and he knew the future of each of the nations. When the world seems

out of control, we must remind ourselves that God owns the cities and knows the future of every nation. God is in control. With God's help, we will gain the victory.

**60:8** David mentioned the enemy nations that surrounded Israel: Moab lay directly to the east, Edom to the south, and Philistia to the west. At the time this psalm was written, David was fighting Aram to the north. Although he was surrounded by enemies, David remembered that God had promised triumph over those nations. He knew that Israel's future was closely tied to God's reputation of keeping his promises.

**61:1, 2** David must have been far from home when he wrote this psalm. Fortunately, God is not limited to any geographic location.

2 From the ends of the earth,
    I cry to you for help
    when my heart is overwhelmed.
  Lead me to the towering rock of safety,

3   for you are my safe refuge,
    a fortress where my enemies cannot reach me.

4 Let me live forever in your sanctuary,
    safe beneath the shelter of your wings!

5 For you have heard my vows, O God.
    You have given me an inheritance reserved for those who fear your name.
6 Add many years to the life of the king!
    May his years span the generations!

7 May he reign under God's protection forever.
    May your unfailing love and faithfulness watch over him.

8 Then I will sing praises to your name forever
    as I fulfill my vows each day.

*Interlude*

**Theme:** Placing all hope in God. Knowing that God is in control allows us to wait patiently for him to rescue us. True relief does not come when the problem is resolved because more problems are on the way! True relief comes from an enduring hope in God's ultimate salvation. Only then will all trials be resolved.
**Author:** David, written during the days of Absalom's rebellion (2 Samuel 15—18)

# 62  *For Jeduthun, the choir director: A psalm of David.*

1 I wait quietly before God,
    for my victory comes from him.

2 He alone is my rock and my salvation,
    my fortress where I will never be shaken.

3 So many enemies against one man—
    all of them trying to kill me.
  To them I'm just a broken-down wall
    or a tottering fence.

4 They plan to topple me from my high position.
    They delight in telling lies about me.
  They praise me to my face
    but curse me in their hearts.

*Interlude*

5 Let all that I am wait quietly before God,
    for my hope is in him.
6 He alone is my rock and my salvation,
    my fortress where I will not be shaken.

7 My victory and honor come from God alone.
    He is my refuge, a rock where no enemy can reach me.

8 O my people, trust in him at all times.
    Pour out your heart to him,
    for God is our refuge.

*Interlude*

9 Common people are as worthless as a puff of wind,
    and the powerful are not what they appear to be.

---

Even when we are among strange people and surroundings, God never abandons us. His all-surpassing strength is always with us.
**61:8** David made a vow to praise God each day. David continually praised God through both the good and difficult times of his life. Do you find something to praise God for each day? As you do, you will find your heart elevated from daily distractions to lasting confidence.
**62:3-6** David expressed his feelings to God and then reaffirmed his faith. Prayer can release our tensions in times of emotional stress. Trusting God to be our rock, salvation, and fortress (62:2)

will change our entire outlook on life. No longer must we be held captive by resentment toward others when they hurt us. When we are resting in God's strength, nothing can shake us.

**62:9-12** It is tempting to use honor, power, wealth, or prestige to measure people. We may even think that such people are really getting ahead in life. But on God's scales, these people are "lighter than a breath of air." What, then, can tilt the scales when God weighs us? Trusting God and working for him (62:12). Wealth, honor, power, or prestige add nothing to our value in God's eyes; only the faithful work we do for him has eternal value.

If you weigh them on the scales,
   together they are lighter than a breath of air.

10 Don't make your living by extortion
   or put your hope in stealing.
And if your wealth increases,
   don't make it the center of your life.

11 God has spoken plainly,
   and I have heard it many times:
Power, O God, belongs to you;
12   unfailing love, O Lord, is yours.
Surely you repay all people
   according to what they have done.

**62:10**
Ps 49:6
Isa 30:12-13; 61:8
Mark 10:25
Luke 12:15
1 Tim 6:10

**62:12**
Job 34:11
Matt 16:27
†Rom 2:6

**Theme:** A desire for God's presence, provision, and protection. No matter where we are, our desire should be for God because only he satisfies fully.
**Author:** David

# 63 *A psalm of David, regarding a time when David was in the wilderness of Judah.*

1 O God, you are my God;
   I earnestly search for you.
My soul thirsts for you;
   my whole body longs for you
in this parched and weary land
   where there is no water.
2 I have seen you in your sanctuary
   and gazed upon your power and glory.
3 Your unfailing love is better than life itself;
   how I praise you!
4 I will praise you as long as I live,
   lifting up my hands to you in prayer.
5 You satisfy me more than the richest feast.
   I will praise you with songs of joy.

6 I lie awake thinking of you,
   meditating on you through the night.
7 Because you are my helper,
   I sing for joy in the shadow of your wings.
8 I cling to you;
   your strong right hand holds me securely.

9 But those plotting to destroy me will come to ruin.
   They will go down into the depths of the earth.
10 They will die by the sword
   and become the food of jackals.
11 But the king will rejoice in God.
   All who trust in him will praise him,
   while liars will be silenced.

**63:1**
Pss 42:2; 84:2

**63:2**
Ps 27:4

**63:3**
Ps 69:16

**63:4**
Pss 28:2; 104:33

**63:5**
Pss 36:8; 71:23

**63:6**
Pss 4:4; 16:7; 42:8

**63:8**
Ps 18:35

**63:9**
Pss 40:14; 55:15

**63:11**
Deut 6:13
Isa 45:23

**63:1ff** Psalms 61, 62, and 63 were probably written when David was seeking refuge during Absalom's rebellion (2 Samuel 15–18). David had already lived a full life. David's quiet confidence as stated in these psalms can be seen in the account in 2 Samuel of the events that shook his life. His actions closely paralleled his beliefs during those turbulent days.

**63:1-5** Hiding from his enemies in the barren wilderness of Judah, David was intensely lonely. He longed for a friend he could trust to ease his loneliness. No wonder he cried out, "O God, . . . My soul thirsts for you . . . in this parched and weary land." If you are lonely or thirsty for something lasting in your life, remember David's prayer. God alone can satisfy our deepest longings!

**63:6** During sleepless, uncomfortable nights, David thought about God. Instead of counting sheep, he meditated on his Shepherd. He reviewed all the ways God had already helped him, and he greeted the next day with songs of praise. In quiet moments or wakeful nights, make it a point to count examples of God's faithfulness to you. Doing so is far more likely to give you rest than any other items you might count!

**Theme:** A complaint against conspiracy. When others conspire against us, we can ask God for protection because he knows everything.
**Author:** David

# 64 *For the choir director: A psalm of David.*

<sup>1</sup> O God, listen to my complaint.
 Protect my life from my enemies' threats.
<sup>2</sup> Hide me from the plots of this evil mob,
 from this gang of wrongdoers.
<sup>3</sup> They sharpen their tongues like swords
 and aim their bitter words like arrows.
<sup>4</sup> They shoot from ambush at the innocent,
 attacking suddenly and fearlessly.
<sup>5</sup> They encourage each other to do evil
 and plan how to set their traps in secret.
 "Who will ever notice?" they ask.
<sup>6</sup> As they plot their crimes, they say,
 "We have devised the perfect plan!"
 Yes, the human heart and mind are cunning.
<sup>7</sup> But God himself will shoot them with his arrows,
 suddenly striking them down.
<sup>8</sup> Their own tongues will ruin them,
 and all who see them will shake their heads in scorn.
<sup>9</sup> Then everyone will be afraid;
 they will proclaim the mighty acts of God
 and realize all the amazing things he does.
<sup>10</sup> The godly will rejoice in the LORD
 and find shelter in him.
 And those who do what is right
 will praise him.

**64:2** Pss 56:6; 59:2
**64:3** Ps 140:3
**64:4** Pss 10:8; 11:2
**64:5** Ps 140:5
**64:7** Ps 7:12-13
**64:8** Ps 9:3; Prov 18:6-7
**64:10** Pss 11:1; 25:20; 32:11

**Theme:** God provides abundantly. We can be thankful to God for his many blessings.
**Author:** David

# 65 *For the choir director: A song. A psalm of David.*

<sup>1</sup> What mighty praise, O God,
 belongs to you in Zion.
 We will fulfill our vows to you,
<sup>2</sup> for you answer our prayers.
 All of us must come to you.
<sup>3</sup> Though we are overwhelmed by our sins,
 you forgive them all.

**65:1** Pss 86:9; 116:18
**65:2** Isa 66:23
**65:3** Pss 38:4; 40:12; Heb 9:14

---

**64:1ff** Evil can come in the form of a conspiracy or an ambush because Satan wants to catch us unprepared. He tempts us in our weakest areas when we least expect it. But God himself will strike down our enemies (64:7), whether they are physical or spiritual. Wickedness is widespread and affects us in many ways, but the final victory already belongs to God and to those who trust and believe in him.

**64:1, 2** We may believe that God hears only certain requests from us. While it is true that we should offer praise, confession, and respectful petitions, it is true also that God is willing to listen to *anything* we want to tell him. David expressed himself honestly knowing that God would hear his voice. God will always listen to us, and he fully understands us.

**64:3-10** Words spoken against us are among the most painful attacks we may have to face. If we trust in God, however, these attacks need not cause any lasting damage.

**65:1, 2** In Old Testament times, vows were taken seriously and fulfilled completely. No one had to make a vow, but once made, it was binding (Deuteronomy 23:21-23). The vows mentioned here involved promises to praise God for his answers to prayer.

**65:3** Although we may feel overwhelmed by the multitude of our sins, God will forgive them all if we ask sincerely. Do you feel as though God could never forgive you, that your sins are too many, or that some of them are too great? The good news is that God can and will forgive them all. Nobody is beyond redemption, and nobody is so full of sin that he or she cannot be forgiven.

4 What joy for those you choose to bring near,
　those who live in your holy courts.
What festivities await us
　inside your holy Temple.

65:4
Pss 4:3; 33:12;
36:8

5 You faithfully answer our prayers with awesome deeds,
　O God our savior.
You are the hope of everyone on earth,
　even those who sail on distant seas.

65:5
Pss 45:4; 48:10

6 You formed the mountains by your power
　and armed yourself with mighty strength.

65:6
Pss 93:1; 95:4

7 You quieted the raging oceans
　with their pounding waves
　and silenced the shouting of the nations.

65:7
Ps 89:9
Isa 17:12-13
Matt 8:26

8 Those who live at the ends of the earth
　stand in awe of your wonders.
From where the sun rises to where it sets,
　you inspire shouts of joy.

65:8
Ps 139:9-10

9 You take care of the earth and water it,
　making it rich and fertile.
The river of God has plenty of water;
　it provides a bountiful harvest of grain,
　for you have ordered it so.

65:9
Pss 46:4;
104:13-14, 24

10 You drench the plowed ground with rain,
　melting the clods and leveling the ridges.
You soften the earth with showers
　and bless its abundant crops.

11 You crown the year with a bountiful harvest;
　even the hard pathways overflow with abundance.

12 The grasslands of the wilderness become a lush pasture,
　and the hillsides blossom with joy.

65:12
Job 38:26-27

13 The meadows are clothed with flocks of sheep,
　and the valleys are carpeted with grain.
They all shout and sing for joy!

65:13
Pss 98:8; 144:13
Isa 30:23; 55:12

**Theme:** God answers prayer. Individually and as a body of believers, we should praise
and worship God.
**Author:** Anonymous, written after a great victory in battle

# 66 *For the choir director: A song. A psalm.*

1 Shout joyful praises to God, all the earth!
2 　Sing about the glory of his name!
　Tell the world how glorious he is.
3 Say to God, "How awesome are your deeds!
　Your enemies cringe before your mighty power.

66:3
Pss 18:44; 47:2

4 Everything on earth will worship you;
　they will sing your praises,
　shouting your name in glorious songs."

66:4
Pss 22:27; 67:4

*Interlude*

5 Come and see what our God has done,
　what awesome miracles he performs for people!

66:5
Ps 46:8

---

**65:4** Access to God, the joy of living in the Temple courts, was
a great honor. God had chosen a special group of Israelites from
the tribe of Levi to serve as priests in the Tabernacle (Numbers
3:5-51). They were the only ones who could enter the sacred
rooms where God's presence resided. Because of Jesus' death on
the cross, believers today have access to God's presence in every
place and at any time.

**65:6-13** This harvest psalm glorifies God the Creator as reflected

in the beauty of nature. Nature helps us understand something of
God's character. The Jews believed that God's care of nature was a
sign of his love and provision for them. Nature shows God's generosity—giving us more than we need or deserve. God's abundant
generosity should make us grateful to him and generous to others.

**66:5-7** The writer was remembering God's rescue of the Israelites by parting the Red Sea during the Exodus. God saved the
Israelites then, and he continues to save his people today.

**66:6**
Exod 14:21
Ps 105:43

6 He made a dry path through the Red Sea,*
  and his people went across on foot.
  There we rejoiced in him.

**66:7**
Pss 11:4; 140:8;
145:13

7 For by his great power he rules forever.
  He watches every movement of the nations;
  let no rebel rise in defiance.                                                          *Interlude*

8 Let the whole world bless our God
  and loudly sing his praises.

**66:9**
Ps 30:3

9 Our lives are in his hands,
  and he keeps our feet from stumbling.

**66:10**
Ps 17:3
Zech 13:9
1 Pet 1:6-7

10 You have tested us, O God;
   you have purified us like silver.

**66:11**
Lam 1:13

11 You captured us in your net
   and laid the burden of slavery on our backs.

**66:12**
Ps 18:19
Isa 43:2; 51:23

12 Then you put a leader over us.*
   We went through fire and flood,
   but you brought us to a place of great abundance.

**66:13**
Ps 22:25
Eccl 5:4

13 Now I come to your Temple with burnt offerings
   to fulfill the vows I made to you—

**66:14**
Ps 18:6

14 yes, the sacred vows that I made
   when I was in deep trouble.

**66:15**
Num 6:14
Ps 51:19

15 That is why I am sacrificing burnt offerings to you—
   the best of my rams as a pleasing aroma,
   and a sacrifice of bulls and male goats.                                               *Interlude*

**66:16**
Pss 34:11;
71:15, 24

16 Come and listen, all you who fear God,
   and I will tell you what he did for me.

17 For I cried out to him for help,
   praising him as I spoke.

**66:18**
Job 36:21
Ps 18:41
Isa 1:15
Jas 4:3

18 If I had not confessed the sin in my heart,
   the Lord would not have listened.

19 But God did listen!
   He paid attention to my prayer.

**66:19**
Ps 116:1-2

20 Praise God, who did not ignore my prayer
   or withdraw his unfailing love from me.

**66:20**
Ps 22:24

**Theme:** Joy comes from spreading the news about God around the world.
**Author:** Anonymous, possibly written for one of the harvest festivals

# 67
*For the choir director: A song. A psalm, to be accompanied by stringed instruments.*

**67:1**
Num 6:25
Pss 4:6; 80:3, 7, 19

1 May God be merciful and bless us.
  May his face smile with favor on us.                                                    *Interlude*

**66:6** Hebrew *the sea.*   **66:12** Or *You made people ride over our heads.*

---

**66:10-12** Just as fire purifies silver in the smelting process, trials refine our character. They bring us a new and deeper wisdom, helping us discern truth from falsehood and giving us the discipline to do what we know is right. Above all, these trials help us realize that life is a gift from God to be cherished, not a right to be taken for granted.

**66:13-15** People sometimes make bargains with God, saying, "If you heal me [or get me out of this mess], I'll obey you for the rest of my life." However, soon after they recover, the vow is forgotten and the old lifestyle is resumed. This writer made a promise to God, but he remembered the promise and was prepared to carry it out. God always keeps his promises and wants us to follow his example. Be careful to follow through on whatever you promise to do.

**66:18** Our confession of sin must be continual because we continue to do wrong. But true confession requires us to listen to God and to want to stop doing what is wrong. David confessed his sin and prayed, "Cleanse me from these hidden faults. Keep your servant from deliberate sins" (19:12, 13). When we *refuse* to repent or when we harbor and cherish certain sins, we place a wall between us and God. We may not be able to remember *every* sin we have ever committed, but our attitude should be one of confession and obedience.

2 May your ways be known throughout the earth,
   your saving power among people everywhere.
3 May the nations praise you, O God.
   Yes, may all the nations praise you.
4 Let the whole world sing for joy,
   because you govern the nations with justice
   and guide the people of the whole world.                    *Interlude*

5 May the nations praise you, O God.
   Yes, may all the nations praise you.
6 Then the earth will yield its harvests,
   and God, our God, will richly bless us.
7 Yes, God will bless us,
   and people all over the world will fear him.

**67:2**
Acts 18:25
Titus 2:11

**67:3**
Ps 66:4

**67:4**
Ps 96:10, 13

**67:5**
Ps 22:27

**67:6**
Lev 26:4
Ezek 34:27

**67:7**
Ps 33:8

**Theme:** Remembering God's glory and power. Times and cultures change, but God is always majestically present as defender and provider.
**Author:** David

# 68 *For the choir director: A song. A psalm of David.*

1 Rise up, O God, and scatter your enemies.
   Let those who hate God run for their lives.
2 Blow them away like smoke.
   Melt them like wax in a fire.
   Let the wicked perish in the presence of God.
3 But let the godly rejoice.
   Let them be glad in God's presence.
   Let them be filled with joy.
4 Sing praises to God and to his name!
   Sing loud praises to him who rides the clouds.
   His name is the LORD—
   rejoice in his presence!

5 Father to the fatherless, defender of widows—
   this is God, whose dwelling is holy.
6 God places the lonely in families;
   he sets the prisoners free and gives them joy.
   But he makes the rebellious live in a sun-scorched land.

7 O God, when you led your people out from Egypt,
   when you marched through the dry wasteland,                  *Interlude*
8 the earth trembled, and the heavens poured down rain
   before you, the God of Sinai,
   before God, the God of Israel.

**68:1**
Num 10:35

**68:2**
Ps 37:20
Isa 9:18
Hos 13:3
Mic 1:4

**68:4**
Pss 40:3; 68:33

**68:5**
Deut 10:18; 26:15

**68:7**
Exod 13:21

**68:8**
Exod 19:18
Judg 5:4-5

---

**67:2** Could the psalm writer have looked across the years to see the gospel go throughout the earth? This psalm surely speaks of the fulfillment of the great commission (Matthew 28:18-20), when Jesus commanded that the gospel be taken to all nations. Count yourself among that great crowd of believers worldwide who know the Savior; praise him for his Good News; and share that gospel so that the harvest will be abundant.

**67:7** Every verse in this psalm mentions God's relationship with the entire globe. The intended audience of this message spans the world. God repeatedly spoke to and through his people about his love for all nations. Read this psalm with the realization that it was written for and about you!

**68:1ff** This psalm begins just like Moses' cry in Numbers 10:35 as the Israelites followed the Ark of the Covenant. It undoubtedly brought to mind the time when David led a joyous procession and brought the Ark from the house of Obed-edom to Jerusalem (2 Samuel 6:11-15).

**68:3-6** With shouts of praise and the sound of trumpets, David and his people took the holy Ark toward Mount Zion (2 Samuel 6:15). It was a time to sing praises to the Lord, whose presence brings great joy. Only in God is there hope for orphans, widows, prisoners, and all other lonely people. If you are lonely or disadvantaged, join David in praise, and discover great joy from loving and praising God.

**68:4-6** David praised God for his protection and provision. When we see God's true majesty, our response should be to praise him. This was a song of faith because many of these benefits had not yet come true in David's time. It should also be our song of faith. We must continue to trust God because, in time, he will fulfill all his promises.

**68:8** Mount Sinai had a prominent role in Israelite history. It was at Mount Sinai that God met Moses and commissioned him to lead Israel out of Egypt (Exodus 3:1-10). It was to Mount Sinai that the nation of Israel returned to receive God's laws (Exodus

**68:9**
Deut 11:11

⁹ You sent abundant rain, O God,
  to refresh the weary land.
¹⁰ There your people finally settled,
  and with a bountiful harvest, O God,
  you provided for your needy people.

**68:11**
Exod 15:20

¹¹ The Lord gives the word,
  and a great army* brings the good news.
¹² Enemy kings and their armies flee,
  while the women of Israel divide the plunder.

**68:13**
Gen 49:14

¹³ Even those who lived among the sheepfolds found treasures—
  doves with wings of silver
  and feathers of gold.

**68:14**
Josh 10:10

¹⁴ The Almighty scattered the enemy kings
  like a blowing snowstorm on Mount Zalmon.

**68:15**
Ps 36:6

¹⁵ The mountains of Bashan are majestic,
  with many peaks stretching high into the sky.
¹⁶ Why do you look with envy, O rugged mountains,
  at Mount Zion, where God has chosen to live,
  where the Lᴏʀᴅ himself will live forever?

**68:17**
Deut 33:2
Dan 7:10

¹⁷ Surrounded by unnumbered thousands of chariots,
  the Lord came from Mount Sinai into his sanctuary.

**68:18**
†Eph 4:8

¹⁸ When you ascended to the heights,
  you led a crowd of captives.
You received gifts from the people,
  even from those who rebelled against you.
  Now the Lᴏʀᴅ God will live among us there.

**68:19**
Pss 55:22; 65:5
Isa 46:4

¹⁹ Praise the Lord; praise God our savior!
  For each day he carries us in his arms.

**68:20**
Ps 56:13

²⁰ Our God is a God who saves!
  The Sovereign Lᴏʀᴅ rescues us from death.

*Interlude*

**68:21**
Ps 110:6
Hab 3:13

²¹ But God will smash the heads of his enemies,
  crushing the skulls of those who love their guilty ways.

**68:22**
Amos 9:1-3

²² The Lord says, "I will bring my enemies down from Bashan;
  I will bring them up from the depths of the sea.

**68:23**
1 Kgs 21:19
Ps 58:10
Jer 15:3

²³ You, my people, will wash your feet in their blood,
  and even your dogs will get their share!"

**68:24**
Ps 63:2

²⁴ Your procession has come into view, O God—
  the procession of my God and King as he goes into the sanctuary.

**68:25**
Exod 15:20
Judg 11:34
1 Chr 13:8

²⁵ Singers are in front, musicians behind;
  between them are young women playing tambourines.

**68:26**
Deut 33:28
Pss 22:22-23;
26:12

²⁶ Praise God, all you people of Israel;
  praise the Lᴏʀᴅ, the source of Israel's life.

**68:11** Or *a host of women.*

---

19:1-3), and God's presence made the entire mountain tremble (Exodus 19:18). This sacred mountain was a constant reminder of God's words and promises.

**68:13** The dove is a symbol of God's beloved Israel, who is so protected and blessed that it has taken silver and gold from its enemies, even though it stayed in camp.

**68:15, 16** Bashan, the land northeast of Israel, was the home of mighty mountains, including Mount Hermon, the tallest and most awesome mountain in the region. God's choice of Mount Zion, a foothill by comparison, for the site of the Temple led the psalm writer to poetically describe the envy of the mountains of Bashan.

**68:17** This psalm celebrates the final stages of a journey that began at Mount Sinai with the construction of the Ark of the Cov-

enant and finally ended at Mount Zion (site of the sanctuary), the chosen dwelling place of God among his people. It may describe the moving of the Ark of the Covenant into Jerusalem.

**68:18** This verse, quoted in Ephesians 4:8, is applied to the ministry of the ascended Christ. It celebrates his victory over evil. It assures all of us who believe in Christ that by trusting him, we can overcome evil.

**68:19-21** God sets his people free and crushes his enemies. Salvation is freedom from sin and death. Those who refuse to turn to God will be crushed by sin and death. They will be trapped by the sin they loved and destroyed by the death they feared. How much better it will be for those who love God and fear the consequences of sin.

27 Look, the little tribe of Benjamin leads the way.
  Then comes a great throng of rulers from Judah
  and all the rulers of Zebulun and Naphtali.

28 Summon your might, O God.
  Display your power, O God, as you have in the past.

29 The kings of the earth are bringing tribute
  to your Temple in Jerusalem.

30 Rebuke these enemy nations—
  these wild animals lurking in the reeds,
  this herd of bulls among the weaker calves.
  Make them bring bars of silver in humble tribute.
  Scatter the nations that delight in war.

31 Let Egypt come with gifts of precious metals*;
  let Ethiopia* bow in submission to God.

32 Sing to God, you kingdoms of the earth.
  Sing praises to the Lord.                                              *Interlude*

33 Sing to the one who rides across the ancient heavens,
  his mighty voice thundering from the sky.

34 Tell everyone about God's power.
  His majesty shines down on Israel;
  his strength is mighty in the heavens.

35 God is awesome in his sanctuary.
  The God of Israel gives power and strength to his people.

  Praise be to God!

**68:28**
Pss 29:11; 44:4

**68:29**
Ps 72:10

**68:30**
Ps 89:10

**68:31**
Isa 19:19-21; 45:14

**68:32**
Ps 102:21-22

**68:33**
Deut 10:14
Pss 18:10; 29:4

**68:35**
Deut 10:17
Pss 29:11; 47:2

**Theme:** A cry of distress in a sea of trouble. We may have to suffer severely for our devotion to God, but that should cause us to look forward with joy to the day when evil and injustice will be gone forever.
**Author:** David

# 69 *For the choir director: A psalm of David, to be sung to the tune "Lilies."*

1 Save me, O God,
  for the floodwaters are up to my neck.

2 Deeper and deeper I sink into the mire;
  I can't find a foothold.
  I am in deep water,
  and the floods overwhelm me.

3 I am exhausted from crying for help;
  my throat is parched.
  My eyes are swollen with weeping,
  waiting for my God to help me.

4 Those who hate me without cause
  outnumber the hairs on my head.
  Many enemies try to destroy me with lies,
  demanding that I give back what I didn't steal.

**69:2**
Jon 2:3

**69:3**
Pss 6:6; 119:82,
123
Isa 38:14

**69:4**
Pss 35:11; 59:3
†John 15:25

**68:31a** Or *of rich cloth.*   **68:31b** Hebrew *Cush.*

**68:34, 35** When we consider all God has done for us, we should feel an overwhelming sense of awe as we kneel before the Lord in his sanctuary. Nature surrounds us with countless signs of God's wonderful power. His unlimited power and unspeakable majesty leave us breathless in his presence. How fortunate we are that God cares for us.

**69:1ff** This is one of the most quoted psalms in the New Testament, and it is often applied to the ministry and suffering of Jesus. Verse 4, like John 15:25, speaks of Jesus' many enemies. The experience of being scorned by his brothers (69:8) is expressed in John 7:5. Verse 9 portrays David's zeal for God; Christ showed

great zeal when he threw the money changers out of the Temple (John 2:14-17). Paul quoted part of 69:9 in Romans 15:3. Christ's great suffering is portrayed in 69:20, 21 (Matthew 27:48; Mark 15:23; Luke 23:36; John 19:28-30). Verses 22 through 28 are quoted in Romans 11:9, 10; and Peter applied 69:25 to Judas (Acts 1:20).

**69:3** David cried out until he was physically exhausted, with a parched throat and eyes swollen from weeping. Yet he still trusted God to save him. When devastated by death or tragedy, we need not collapse or despair because we can turn to God and ask him to save us and help us. The tears will still come, but we will not be crying in vain.

**69:5**
Ps 44:21

5 O God, you know how foolish I am;
my sins cannot be hidden from you.

**69:6**
2 Sam 12:14

6 Don't let those who trust in you be ashamed because of me,
O Sovereign LORD of Heaven's Armies.
Don't let me cause them to be humiliated,
O God of Israel.

7 For I endure insults for your sake;
humiliation is written all over my face.

**69:8**
Pss 31:11; 38:11

8 Even my own brothers pretend they don't know me;
they treat me like a stranger.

**69:9**
†John 2:17
†Rom 15:3

9 Passion for your house has consumed me,
and the insults of those who insult you have fallen on me.

10 When I weep and fast,
they scoff at me.

11 When I dress in burlap to show sorrow,
they make fun of me.

**69:12**
Job 30:9

12 I am the favorite topic of town gossip,
and all the drunks sing about me.

**69:13**
Ps 32:6
Isa 49:8
2 Cor 6:2

13 But I keep praying to you, LORD,
hoping this time you will show me favor.
In your unfailing love, O God,
answer my prayer with your sure salvation.

**69:14**
Ps 144:7

14 Rescue me from the mud;
don't let me sink any deeper!
Save me from those who hate me,
and pull me from these deep waters.

**69:15**
Num 16:33
Ps 124:4-5

15 Don't let the floods overwhelm me,
or the deep waters swallow me,
or the pit of death devour me.

**69:16**
Pss 25:16; 51:1;
63:3

16 Answer my prayers, O LORD,
for your unfailing love is wonderful.
Take care of me,
for your mercy is so plentiful.

17 Don't hide from your servant;
answer me quickly, for I am in deep trouble!

**69:18**
Pss 49:15; 119:134

18 Come and redeem me;
free me from my enemies.

**69:19**
Ps 22:6-7
Isa 53:3

19 You know of my shame, scorn, and disgrace.
You see all that my enemies are doing.

20 Their insults have broken my heart,
and I am in despair.
If only one person would show some pity;
if only one would turn and comfort me.

**69:21**
†Matt 27:48
†John 19:29

21 But instead, they give me poison* for food;
they offer me sour wine for my thirst.

22 Let the bountiful table set before them become a snare
and their prosperity become a trap.*

**69:23**
†Rom 11:9-10

23 Let their eyes go blind so they cannot see,
and make their bodies shake continually.*

**69:21** Or *gall.*   **69:22** Greek version reads *Let their bountiful table set before them become a snare, / a trap that makes them think all is well. / Let their blessings cause them to stumble, / and let them get what they deserve.* Compare Rom 11:9.   **69:23** Greek version reads *and let their backs be bent forever.* Compare Rom 11:10.

**69:13** What problems David faced! He was scoffed at, mocked, insulted, humiliated, and made the object of citywide gossip. But still he prayed. When we are completely beaten down, we are tempted to turn from God, give up, and quit trusting him. When your situation seems hopeless, determine that no matter how bad things become you will continue to pray. God will hear your prayer, and he will rescue you. When others reject us, we need God most. Don't turn from your most faithful friend.

24 Pour out your fury on them;
    consume them with your burning anger.
25 Let their homes become desolate
    and their tents be deserted.
26 To the one you have punished, they add insult to injury;
    they add to the pain of those you have hurt.
27 Pile their sins up high,
    and don't let them go free.
28 Erase their names from the Book of Life;
    don't let them be counted among the righteous.

29 I am suffering and in pain.
    Rescue me, O God, by your saving power.

30 Then I will praise God's name with singing,
    and I will honor him with thanksgiving.
31 For this will please the LORD more than sacrificing cattle,
    more than presenting a bull with its horns and hooves.
32 The humble will see their God at work and be glad.
    Let all who seek God's help be encouraged.
33 For the LORD hears the cries of the needy;
    he does not despise his imprisoned people.

34 Praise him, O heaven and earth,
    the seas and all that move in them.
35 For God will save Jerusalem*
    and rebuild the towns of Judah.
His people will live there
    and settle in their own land.
36 The descendants of those who obey him will inherit the land,
    and those who love him will live there in safety.

| | |
|---|---|
| | **69:25** |
| | Matt 23:38 |
| | Luke 13:35 |
| | †Acts 1:20 |
| | **69:26** |
| | 2 Chr 28:9 |
| | Isa 53:4 |
| | **69:28** |
| | Exod 32:32-33 |
| | Luke 10:20 |
| | Rev 3:5; 13:8; |
| | 20:15 |
| | **69:30** |
| | Pss 28:7; 50:14-15 |
| | **69:31** |
| | Ps 50:13-14 |
| | **69:32** |
| | Pss 22:26; 34:2 |
| | **69:34** |
| | Ps 148:1-13 |
| | **69:35** |
| | Ps 147:2 |
| | Isa 44:26 |
| | **69:36** |
| | Ps 25:13 |

**Theme:** An urgent prayer for help. It can be your prayer when you're short on time and long on need.
**Author:** David

# 70
*For the choir director: A psalm of David, asking God to remember him.*

1 Please, God, rescue me!
    Come quickly, LORD, and help me.
2 May those who try to kill me
    be humiliated and put to shame.
May those who take delight in my trouble
    be turned back in disgrace.
3 Let them be horrified by their shame,
    for they said, "Aha! We've got him now!"
4 But may all who search for you
    be filled with joy and gladness in you.
May those who love your salvation
    repeatedly shout, "God is great!"

| | |
|---|---|
| | **70:1-5** |
| | //Ps 40:13-17 |
| | **70:2** |
| | Ps 35:4, 26 |

**69:35** Hebrew *Zion.*

---

**69:28** The "Book of Life" is God's list of those who are in right relationship to him and who remain faithful (1:3; 7:9; 11:7; 34:12; 37:17, 29; 55:22; 75:10; 92:12-14; 140:13). This term in the New Testament refers to those who will receive eternal life (see Philippians 4:3; Revelation 3:5; 13:8; 20:15).

**70:1-5** When others disappoint and threaten us, we feel empty, as though a vital part of ourselves has been stolen. When others break the trust we have placed in them, they also break our spirits. At those empty, broken moments, we must join the writer in begging God to rush to our aid. He alone can fill our lives with

his joy (70:4). With the psalm writer we should cry out, "O LORD, do not delay."

**70:4** This short psalm (similar in content to 40:13-17) was David's plea for God to come quickly with his help. Yet even in his moment of panic, he did not forget praise. Praise is important because it helps us remember who God is. Often our prayers are filled with requests for ourselves and others, and we forget to thank God for what he has done and to worship him for who he is. Don't take God for granted and treat him as a vending machine. Even when David was afraid, he praised God.

5 But as for me, I am poor and needy;
  please hurry to my aid, O God.
  You are my helper and my savior;
  O LORD, do not delay.

**Theme:** God's constant help—from childhood to old age. Our lives are a testimony of what God has done for us.
**Author:** Anonymous

# 71

71:1
Pss 25:2-3; 31:1-3

¹ O LORD, I have come to you for protection;
  don't let me be disgraced.

71:2
Pss 17:6; 31:1

² Save me and rescue me,
  for you do what is right.
  Turn your ear to listen to me,
  and set me free.

71:3
Deut 33:27
Ps 18:2

³ Be my rock of safety
  where I can always hide.
  Give the order to save me,
  for you are my rock and my fortress.
⁴ My God, rescue me from the power of the wicked,
  from the clutches of cruel oppressors.

71:5
Ps 22:9-11
Jer 17:7, 17

⁵ O Lord, you alone are my hope.
  I've trusted you, O LORD, from childhood.

71:6
Pss 22:9-10; 34:1
Isa 46:3

⁶ Yes, you have been with me from birth;
  from my mother's womb you have cared for me.
  No wonder I am always praising you!

71:7
Ps 61:3

⁷ My life is an example to many,
  because you have been my strength and protection.
⁸ That is why I can never stop praising you;
  I declare your glory all day long.

71:9
Ps 92:14

⁹ And now, in my old age, don't set me aside.
  Don't abandon me when my strength is failing.

71:10
Matt 27:1

¹⁰ For my enemies are whispering against me.
  They are plotting together to kill me.

71:11
Pss 3:2; 7:2

¹¹ They say, "God has abandoned him.
  Let's go and get him,
  for no one will help him now."

71:12
Ps 22:9-11

¹² O God, don't stay away.
  My God, please hurry to help me.

71:13
Ps 35:4, 26

¹³ Bring disgrace and destruction on my accusers.
  Humiliate and shame those who want to harm me.
¹⁴ But I will keep on hoping for your help;
  I will praise you more and more.

71:15
Pss 35:28; 40:5

¹⁵ I will tell everyone about your righteousness.
  All day long I will proclaim your saving power,
  though I am not skilled with words.*

71:16
Ps 106:2

¹⁶ I will praise your mighty deeds, O Sovereign LORD.
  I will tell everyone that you alone are just.

¹⁷ O God, you have taught me from my earliest childhood,
  and I constantly tell others about the wonderful things you do.

**71:15** Or *though I cannot count it.*

---

**71:1ff** The writer was old and saw his life as an "example," a solemn sign or testimony to others of all God had done for him (71:7, 18). Remembering our lifetime of blessings will help us to see the consistency of God's grace throughout the years, trust him for the future, and share with others the benefits of following him.

**71:14** As we face the sunset years, we recognize that God has been our constant help in the past. As physical powers wane, we need God even more, and we realize he is still our constant help. We must never despair, but keep on expecting his help no matter how severe our limitations. Hope in him helps us to keep going, to keep serving him.

¹⁸ Now that I am old and gray,
　　do not abandon me, O God.
　Let me proclaim your power to this new generation,
　　your mighty miracles to all who come after me.

**71:18**
Pss 22:31; 78:4, 6

¹⁹ Your righteousness, O God, reaches to the highest heavens.
　　You have done such wonderful things.
　　Who can compare with you, O God?

**71:19**
Deut 3:24
Pss 35:10; 57:10
Luke 1:49

²⁰ You have allowed me to suffer much hardship,
　　but you will restore me to life again
　　and lift me up from the depths of the earth.

**71:20**
Pss 23:4; 60:3-4;
119:25
Hos 6:2

²¹ You will restore me to even greater honor
　　and comfort me once again.

²² Then I will praise you with music on the harp,
　　because you are faithful to your promises, O my God.
　I will sing praises to you with a lyre,
　　O Holy One of Israel.

**71:22**
Pss 33:2; 89:18;
147:7

²³ I will shout for joy and sing your praises,
　　for you have ransomed me.

**71:23**
Pss 5:11; 103:4

²⁴ I will tell about your righteous deeds
　　all day long,
　for everyone who tried to hurt me
　　has been shamed and humiliated.

**71:24**
Pss 35:28; 71:13

**Theme:** The perfect king. In this psalm, a king asks God to help his son rule the nation justly and wisely. It looks forward to the endless reign of the Messiah, who alone can rule with perfect justice and whose citizens will enjoy perfect peace.
**Author:** Solomon

# 72 *A psalm of Solomon.*

¹ Give your love of justice to the king, O God,
　　and righteousness to the king's son.

**72:1**
1 Kgs 3:9

² Help him judge your people in the right way;
　　let the poor always be treated fairly.

**72:2**
Ps 82:3
Isa 9:7; 11:2-5

³ May the mountains yield prosperity for all,
　　and may the hills be fruitful.

**72:3**
Isa 9:5-6
Mic 4:3-4
Zech 9:10

⁴ Help him to defend the poor,
　　to rescue the children of the needy,
　　and to crush their oppressors.

**72:4**
Isa 11:4

⁵ May they fear you* as long as the sun shines,
　　as long as the moon remains in the sky.
　　Yes, forever!

**72:5**
Ps 89:36-37

⁶ May the king's rule be refreshing like spring rain on freshly cut grass,
　　like the showers that water the earth.

**72:6**
Deut 32:2
Ps 65:10
Hos 6:3

⁷ May all the godly flourish during his reign.
　　May there be abundant prosperity until the moon is no more.

**72:7**
Ps 92:12

⁸ May he reign from sea to sea,
　　and from the Euphrates River* to the ends of the earth.

**72:8**
Exod 23:31
Zech 9:10

⁹ Desert nomads will bow before him;
　　his enemies will fall before him in the dust.

**72:9**
Isa 49:23
Mic 7:17

**72:5** Greek version reads *May they endure.*　**72:8** Hebrew *the river.*

---

**71:18** A person is never too old to serve God, never too old to pray. Though age may stop us from certain physical activities, it need not stifle our desire or limit our opportunities to tell others (especially children) about all we have seen God do in our many years of life.

**72:1, 2** What qualities do we want most in our leaders? God desires all who rule under him to be just and righteous. Think how the world would change if world leaders would commit themselves to these two qualities. Pray for leaders as you hear about them in the news. Ask God to help them see their need for him; ask God to help them lead with justice and righteousness (see 1 Timothy 2:1, 2).

**72:10**
Pss 45:12; 68:29
Isa 42:4, 10; 60:6

10 The western kings of Tarshish and other distant lands
    will bring him tribute.
The eastern kings of Sheba and Seba
    will bring him gifts.

**72:11**
Pss 86:9; 138:4
Isa 49:23

11 All kings will bow before him,
    and all nations will serve him.

**72:12**
Job 29:12

12 He will rescue the poor when they cry to him;
    he will help the oppressed, who have no one to defend them.
13 He feels pity for the weak and the needy,
    and he will rescue them.

**72:14**
Ps 116:15

14 He will redeem them from oppression and violence,
    for their lives are precious to him.

**72:15**
Isa 60:6

15 Long live the king!
    May the gold of Sheba be given to him.
May the people always pray for him
    and bless him all day long.

**72:16**
Job 5:25

16 May there be abundant grain throughout the land,
    flourishing even on the hilltops.
May the fruit trees flourish like the trees of Lebanon,
    and may the people thrive like grass in a field.

**72:17**
Gen 12:3; 22:18
Ps 89:36

17 May the king's name endure forever;
    may it continue as long as the sun shines.
May all nations be blessed through him
    and bring him praise.

**72:18**
Exod 15:11
Pss 41:13; 77:14

18 Praise the LORD God, the God of Israel,
    who alone does such wonderful things.

**72:19**
Num 14:20-21
Neh 9:5

19 Praise his glorious name forever!
    Let the whole earth be filled with his glory.
Amen and amen!

20 (This ends the prayers of David son of Jesse.)

## BOOK THREE   Psalms 73:1—89:52

These psalms celebrate the sovereignty of God, God's hand in history, God's faithfulness, and God's covenant with David. These psalms remind us that our worship should be continual.

**Theme:** The temporary prosperity of the wicked and the lasting rewards of the righteous. We should live holy lives and trust God for our future rewards.
**Author:** Asaph, a leader of one of the Temple choirs (see 1 Chronicles 25:1)

# 73 *A psalm of Asaph.*

**73:1**
Pss 24:3-4; 51:10
Matt 5:8

1 Truly God is good to Israel,
    to those whose hearts are pure.

---

**72:12-14** God cares for the poor, oppressed, weak, and needy because they are precious to him. If God feels so strongly about these needy ones and loves them so deeply, how can we ignore their plight? Examine what you are doing to reach out with God's love. Are you ignoring their plight or are you helping to meet their needs?

**72:17** Solomon, David's son, reigned in Israel's golden age. He built the magnificent Temple, and the land rested in peace. This psalm, though written by Solomon, looks beyond Solomon's reign to that of Jesus the Messiah, whose kingdom extends "to the ends of the earth" (72:8) and is greater than any human empire. This will be fulfilled when Christ returns to reign forever (Revelation 11:15). When we anticipate his worldwide rule, it fills our hearts with hope.

**72:19, 20** Book Two ends with "Amen and amen," as did Psalm 41, which closed Book One. This last verse does not mean that David wrote this psalm but that he wrote most of the psalms in Book Two.

**73:1ff** Asaph was the leader of one of David's levitical choirs. He collected Psalms 73–83 but may not have written all of them. In this psalm, Asaph explains that until he entered God's sanctuary, he could not understand the justice in allowing the wicked to thrive while the righteous endured hardship. But when he saw that one day justice would be done, he acknowledged God's wisdom.

**73:1-20** Two strong themes wind their way through these verses: (1) The wicked prosper, leaving godly people wondering why they bother to be good, and (2) the wealth of the wicked looks so inviting that faithful people may wish they could trade places. But these two themes come to unexpected ends, for the wealth of the wicked suddenly loses its power at death, and the rewards for the godly suddenly take on eternal value. What seemed like wealth is now waste, and what seemed worthless now lasts forever. Don't wish you could trade places with evil people to get their wealth. One day they will wish they could trade places with you and have your eternal wealth.

2 But as for me, I almost lost my footing.
My feet were slipping, and I was almost gone.
3 For I envied the proud
when I saw them prosper despite their wickedness.
4 They seem to live such painless lives;
their bodies are so healthy and strong.
5 They don't have troubles like other people;
they're not plagued with problems like everyone else.
6 They wear pride like a jeweled necklace
and clothe themselves with cruelty.
7 These fat cats have everything
their hearts could ever wish for!
8 They scoff and speak only evil;
in their pride they seek to crush others.
9 They boast against the very heavens,
and their words strut throughout the earth.
10 And so the people are dismayed and confused,
drinking in all their words.
11 "What does God know?" they ask.
"Does the Most High even know what's happening?"
12 Look at these wicked people—
enjoying a life of ease while their riches multiply.

13 Did I keep my heart pure for nothing?
Did I keep myself innocent for no reason?
14 I get nothing but trouble all day long;
every morning brings me pain.

15 If I had really spoken this way to others,
I would have been a traitor to your people.
16 So I tried to understand why the wicked prosper.
But what a difficult task it is!
17 Then I went into your sanctuary, O God,
and I finally understood the destiny of the wicked.
18 Truly, you put them on a slippery path
and send them sliding over the cliff to destruction.
19 In an instant they are destroyed,
completely swept away by terrors.
20 When you arise, O Lord,
you will laugh at their silly ideas
as a person laughs at dreams in the morning.

21 Then I realized that my heart was bitter,
and I was all torn up inside.
22 I was so foolish and ignorant—
I must have seemed like a senseless animal to you.
23 Yet I still belong to you;
you hold my right hand.
24 You guide me with your counsel,
leading me to a glorious destiny.
25 Whom have I in heaven but you?
I desire you more than anything on earth.

**73:2**
Ps 94:18
**73:3**
Ps 37:1, 7
Jer 12:1
**73:5**
Job 21:9-10
**73:6**
Ps 109:18
**73:7**
Job 15:27-28
Ps 17:10
**73:8**
Pss 1:1; 17:10
Jude 1:16
**73:11**
Job 22:13
**73:12**
Ps 49:6
**73:13**
Job 21:15; 34:9
Ps 26:6
**73:14**
Pss 38:5-6; 118:18
**73:16**
Eccl 8:16-17
**73:17**
Ps 27:4
**73:19**
Num 16:21
Isa 47:11
**73:22**
Eccl 3:18
**73:24**
Pss 32:8; 48:14

---

**73:20** Asaph realized that the rich who put their hope, joy, and confidence in their wealth live in a dream world. A dream exists only in the mind of the dreamer. Don't let your life's goals be so unreal that you awaken too late and miss the reality of God's truth. Happiness and hope can be a reality, but only when they are based on God, not on riches. Because reality is in God, we should get as close to him as we can in order to be realistic about life.

**73:23, 24** Asaph declares his confidence in God's presence and guidance. From birth to death, we are continually in God's grip. But far more, we have the hope of the resurrection. Though our courage and strength may fail, we know that one day we will be raised to life to serve him forever. He is our security, and we must cling to him.

**73:26**
Pss 16:5; 38:10

26 My health may fail, and my spirit may grow weak,
   but God remains the strength of my heart;
   he is mine forever.

**73:27**
Ps 37:20

27 Those who desert him will perish,
   for you destroy those who abandon you.

**73:28**
Pss 40:5; 71:7
Heb 10:22

28 But as for me, how good it is to be near God!
   I have made the Sovereign LORD my shelter,
   and I will tell everyone about the wonderful things you do.

**Theme:** A plea for God to help his people defend his cause and remember his promises. When we feel devastated or forgotten, we can ask God for help, knowing that he hears.
**Author:** Asaph (or one of his descendants, since many believe this to have been written after Jerusalem's fall in 586 B.C.)

# 74 *A psalm\* of Asaph.*

**74:1**
Deut 29:20
Pss 44:9; 89:46

1 O God, why have you rejected us so long?
   Why is your anger so intense against the sheep of your own pasture?

**74:2**
Deut 32:6, 9
Ps 68:16

2 Remember that we are the people you chose long ago,
   the tribe you redeemed as your own special possession!
   And remember Jerusalem,\* your home here on earth.

**74:3**
Ps 79:1
Isa 61:4

3 Walk through the awful ruins of the city;
   see how the enemy has destroyed your sanctuary.

4 There your enemies shouted their victorious battle cries;
   there they set up their battle standards.

**74:5**
Jer 46:22

5 They swung their axes
   like woodcutters in a forest.

6 With axes and picks,
   they smashed the carved paneling.

**74:7**
2 Kgs 25:9

7 They burned your sanctuary to the ground.
   They defiled the place that bears your name.

**74:8**
Ps 83:4

8 Then they thought, "Let's destroy everything!"
   So they burned down all the places where God was worshiped.

**74:9**
Lev 24:16
Ps 78:43

9 We no longer see your miraculous signs.
   All the prophets are gone,
   and no one can tell us when it will end.

**74:10**
Ps 44:16

10 How long, O God, will you allow our enemies to insult you?
   Will you let them dishonor your name forever?

**74:11**
Ps 59:13

11 Why do you hold back your strong right hand?
   Unleash your powerful fist and destroy them.

**74:12**
Ps 44:4

12 You, O God, are my king from ages past,
   bringing salvation to the earth.

**74:13**
Exod 14:21

13 You split the sea by your strength
   and smashed the heads of the sea monsters.

74:TITLE Hebrew *maskil.* This may be a literary or musical term.   74:2 Hebrew *Mount Zion.*

---

**74:1, 2** God's anger against Israel had grown hot during the many years of their sin and idolatry. His patience endured for generations, but at last it was set aside for judgment. If you fall into sin but quickly seek God's forgiveness, his mercy may come quickly and his anger may leave quickly. If you persist in sinning against him, don't be surprised when his patience runs out.

**74:8** When enemy armies defeated Israel, they sacked and burned Jerusalem, trying to wipe out every trace of God. This has often been the response of people who hate God. Today many are trying to eliminate God from our public life and particularly from our schools. Do what you can to maintain a Christian influence, but don't become discouraged when others appear to make great strides in removing all traces of God. They cannot eliminate his presence among believers.

**74:10-18** From our perspective, God sometimes seems slow to intervene on our behalf. But what might appear slow to us is good timing from God's perspective. It's easy to become impatient while waiting for God to act, but we must never give up on him. When God is silent and you are in deep anguish, follow the method in this psalm. Review the great acts of God throughout biblical history; then review what he has done for you. This will remind you that God is at work, not only in history, but also in your life today.

**74:13, 14** "The sea monster" recalls the Lord's words to Egypt (Ezekiel 32:2ff). "Leviathan" refers to the Canaanite seven-headed serpent, Lotan. In their legends, Baal defeated these creatures. This psalm praised God for doing in reality what the Canaanite gods could only do in legends.

14 You crushed the heads of Leviathan*
    and let the desert animals eat him.
15 You caused the springs and streams to gush forth,
    and you dried up rivers that never run dry.
16 Both day and night belong to you;
    you made the starlight* and the sun.
17 You set the boundaries of the earth,
    and you made both summer and winter.

18 See how these enemies insult you, LORD.
    A foolish nation has dishonored your name.
19 Don't let these wild beasts destroy your turtledoves.
    Don't forget your suffering people forever.

20 Remember your covenant promises,
    for the land is full of darkness and violence!
21 Don't let the downtrodden be humiliated again.
    Instead, let the poor and needy praise your name.

22 Arise, O God, and defend your cause.
    Remember how these fools insult you all day long.
23 Don't overlook what your enemies have said
    or their growing uproar.

**74:15**
Exod 14:21-22;
17:5-6

**74:16**
Gen 1:14-18
Ps 136:7-8

**74:17**
Gen 8:22
Acts 17:26

**74:18**
Deut 32:6
Pss 39:8; 74:10

**74:20**
Gen 17:7
Ps 106:45

**74:21**
Ps 35:10
Isa 41:17

**74:22**
Ps 43:1

**74:23**
Ps 65:7

**Theme:** Because God is the final judge, the tables will be turned upon the wicked. When arrogant people threaten our security, we can be confident that God will ultimately overrule and destroy them.
**Author:** Asaph

# 75 *For the choir director: A psalm of Asaph. A song to be sung to the tune "Do Not Destroy!"*

1 We thank you, O God!
    We give thanks because you are near.
    People everywhere tell of your wonderful deeds.

2 God says, "At the time I have planned,
    I will bring justice against the wicked.
3 When the earth quakes and its people live in turmoil,
    I am the one who keeps its foundations firm.       *Interlude*

4 "I warned the proud, 'Stop your boasting!'
    I told the wicked, 'Don't raise your fists!
5 Don't raise your fists in defiance at the heavens
    or speak with such arrogance.'"
6 For no one on earth—from east or west,
    or even from the wilderness—
    should raise a defiant fist.*
7 It is God alone who judges;
    he decides who will rise and who will fall.

**75:1**
Pss 44:1; 71:17

**75:3**
1 Sam 2:8
Ps 46:6

**75:5**
Ps 94:4

**75:7**
1 Sam 2:7

**74:14** The identification of Leviathan is disputed, ranging from an earthly creature to a mythical sea monster in ancient literature.   **74:16** Or *moon;* Hebrew reads *light.*   **75:6** Hebrew *should lift.*

**75:2** God will act when he is ready. Children have difficulty grasping the concept of time. "It's not time yet" is not a reason they easily understand because they only comprehend the present. As limited human beings, we can't understand God's perspective about time. We want everything now, unaware that God's timing is better. When God is ready, he will do what needs to be done, not what we would like him to do. We may be as impatient as children, but we must not doubt the wisdom of God's timing. Wait for God to reveal his plan. Don't take matters into your own hands.

**75:8** The cup of wine represents God's judgment that is coming against the wicked. God will pour out his fury on his enemies, and they will be forced to drink it. Drinking the cup of God's judgment is a picture used frequently in Scripture (Isaiah 51:17, 22; Jeremiah 25:15; 49:12; Habakkuk 2:16; Revelation 14:10; 16:19; 18:6). It gives the impression of taking a dose of one's own medicine. To drink it down "to the dregs" means to be punished completely.

8 For the LORD holds a cup in his hand
    that is full of foaming wine mixed with spices.
He pours out the wine in judgment,
    and all the wicked must drink it,
        draining it to the dregs.

**75:9**
Ps 40:10

9 But as for me, I will always proclaim what God has done;
    I will sing praises to the God of Jacob.

**75:10**
Pss 89:17; 148:14

10 For God says, "I will break the strength of the wicked,
    but I will increase the power of the godly."

**Theme:** A call for God to punish evildoers. Even people's angry revolts will be used by God to bring glory to himself.
**Author:** Asaph

## 76 *For the choir director: A psalm of Asaph. A song to be accompanied by stringed instruments.*

1 God is honored in Judah;
    his name is great in Israel.

**76:2**
Pss 48:2-3; 132:13;
135:21

2 Jerusalem* is where he lives;
    Mount Zion is his home.

**76:3**
Ps 46:9

3 There he has broken the fiery arrows of the enemy,
    the shields and swords and weapons of war.

*Interlude*

4 You are glorious and more majestic
    than the everlasting mountains.*

**76:5**
Isa 10:12

5 Our boldest enemies have been plundered.
    They lie before us in the sleep of death.
    No warrior could lift a hand against us.

**76:6**
Exod 15:1, 21
Ps 78:53

6 At the blast of your breath, O God of Jacob,
    their horses and chariots lay still.

**76:7**
Ps 89:7
Nah 1:6
Rev 6:17

7 No wonder you are greatly feared!
    Who can stand before you when your anger explodes?

**76:8**
1 Chr 16:30

8 From heaven you sentenced your enemies;
    the earth trembled and stood silent before you.

**76:9**
Pss 9:7-9; 72:4

9 You stand up to judge those who do evil, O God,
    and to rescue the oppressed of the earth.

*Interlude*

**76:10**
Exod 9:16
Rom 9:17

10 Human defiance only enhances your glory,
    for you use it as a weapon.*

11 Make vows to the LORD your God, and keep them.
    Let everyone bring tribute to the Awesome One.
12 For he breaks the pride of princes,
    and the kings of the earth fear him.

**76:2** Hebrew *Salem,* another name for Jerusalem.   **76:4** As in Greek version; Hebrew reads *than mountains filled with beasts of prey.*   **76:10** The meaning of the Hebrew is uncertain.

---

**75:10** God will have the last word. He will decide the final outcome, settling all matters that concern both the wicked and the godly. The former will eventually experience his judgment; the latter will experience his faithful love. No matter how dark the days you face, make it your continual practice to acknowledge God's sovereignty over your world. Tell him regularly how grateful you are that he has the final word.

**76:1ff** This psalm praises God for his awesome power. It was most likely written to celebrate the defeat of Sennacherib's army after it invaded Judah (see 2 Kings 18:13-19, 37).

**76:10** How can defiance bring glory to God? Hostility to God and his people gives God the opportunity to do great deeds. For example, the pharaoh of Egypt refused to free the Hebrew slaves (Exodus 5:1, 2) and thus allowed God to work mighty miracles for his people (Exodus 11:9). God turns the tables on

evildoers and brings glory to himself from the foolishness of those who deny him or revolt against him. God's wrath expressed in judgment brings praise from those who have been delivered.

**76:11, 12** This psalm closes with an invitation to the reader or listener. Having stated the futility of resisting God, the writer shifts to the alternatives. These verses speak of more than surrender to God; they encourage us to actively move toward God, making commitments (vows) to him and carrying them out. What was the last promise you made to God? How much progress have you made in fulfilling it?

**Theme:** We are comforted through the hard times by remembering God's help in the past. Recalling God's miracles and previous works can give us courage to continue.
**Author:** Asaph

# 77 *For Jeduthun, the choir director: A psalm of Asaph.*

1 I cry out to God; yes, I shout.
    Oh, that God would listen to me!
2 When I was in deep trouble,
    I searched for the Lord.
All night long I prayed, with hands lifted toward heaven,
    but my soul was not comforted.

**77:2**
Job 11:13
Pss 50:15; 88:9
Isa 26:9, 16

3 I think of God, and I moan,
    overwhelmed with longing for his help.    *Interlude*

**77:3**
Pss 43:5; 61:2;
142:2-3

4 You don't let me sleep.
    I am too distressed even to pray!
5 I think of the good old days,
    long since ended,

**77:5**
Ps 143:5

6 when my nights were filled with joyful songs.
    I search my soul and ponder the difference now.

**77:6**
Ps 42:8

7 Has the Lord rejected me forever?
    Will he never again be kind to me?
8 Is his unfailing love gone forever?
    Have his promises permanently failed?

**77:8**
Ps 89:49

9 Has God forgotten to be gracious?
    Has he slammed the door on his compassion?    *Interlude*

**77:9**
Ps 25:6

10 And I said, "This is my fate;
    the Most High has turned his hand against me."
11 But then I recall all you have done, O LORD;
    I remember your wonderful deeds of long ago.

**77:11**
Exod 15:11
Ps 86:8

12 They are constantly in my thoughts.
    I cannot stop thinking about your mighty works.
13 O God, your ways are holy.
    Is there any god as mighty as you?

**77:13**
Exod 15:11
Ps 86:8

14 You are the God of great wonders!
    You demonstrate your awesome power among the nations.
15 By your strong arm, you redeemed your people,
    the descendants of Jacob and Joseph.    *Interlude*

**77:15**
Exod 6:6
Deut 9:29

16 When the Red Sea* saw you, O God,
    its waters looked and trembled!
    The sea quaked to its very depths.

**77:16**
Exod 14:21

17 The clouds poured down rain;
    the thunder rumbled in the sky.
    Your arrows of lightning flashed.

**77:17**
Ps 68:33

18 Your thunder roared from the whirlwind;
    the lightning lit up the world!
    The earth trembled and shook.

**77:18**
Judg 5:4

**77:16** Hebrew *the waters.*

---

**77:1ff** Asaph cried out to God for courage during a time of deep distress. The source of Asaph's distress (77:4) was his doubt (77:7-9). He said, "I cry out to God." But in 77:13-20, the *I* is gone. As Asaph expressed his requests to God, his focus changed from thinking of himself to worshiping God: "You are the God of great wonders!" (77:14). Only after he put aside his doubts about God's holiness and care for him (77:13, 14) did he eliminate his distress (77:20). As we pray to God, he shifts our focus from ourselves to him.

**77:11, 12** Memories of God's miracles and faithfulness sustained Israel through their difficulties. They knew that God was capable and trustworthy. When you meet new trials, review how good God has been to you, and this will strengthen your faith.

**77:16-20** These verses refer to the miraculous parting of the Red Sea. This great event is mentioned many times in the Old Testament (Exodus 14:21, 22; Joshua 24:6; Nehemiah 9:9; Psalm 74:13; 106:9; 136:13-15). The story of this incredible miracle was handed down from generation to generation, continually reminding the Israelites of God's power, protection, and love.

**77:19**
Hab 3:15

19 Your road led through the sea,
  your pathway through the mighty waters—
  a pathway no one knew was there!

**77:20**
Exod 6:26; 13:21
Ps 78:52
Isa 63:11-13

20 You led your people along that road like a flock of sheep,
  with Moses and Aaron as their shepherds.

**Theme:** Lessons from history. Asaph retells the history of the Jewish nation from the time of slavery in Egypt to David's reign. It was told over and over to each generation so they would not forget God and make the same mistakes as their ancestors.
**Author:** Asaph

# 78 *A psalm\* of Asaph.*

1 O my people, listen to my instructions.
  Open your ears to what I am saying,

**78:2**
†Matt 13:34-35

2 for I will speak to you in a parable.
  I will teach you hidden lessons from our past—

**78:3**
Ps 44:1

3 stories we have heard and known,
  stories our ancestors handed down to us.

**78:4**
Deut 11:19
Ps 22:30

4 We will not hide these truths from our children;
  we will tell the next generation
  about the glorious deeds of the LORD,
  about his power and his mighty wonders.

**78:5**
Deut 6:4-9

5 For he issued his laws to Jacob;
  he gave his instructions to Israel.
  He commanded our ancestors
  to teach them to their children,

**78:6**
Deut 11:19
Ps 102:18

6 so the next generation might know them—
  even the children not yet born—
  and they in turn will teach their own children.

**78:7**
Deut 4:2, 9
Josh 22:5

7 So each generation should set its hope anew on God,
  not forgetting his glorious miracles
  and obeying his commands.

**78:8**
Exod 32:9
Ezek 20:18

8 Then they will not be like their ancestors—
  stubborn, rebellious, and unfaithful,
  refusing to give their hearts to God.

9 The warriors of Ephraim, though armed with bows,
  turned their backs and fled on the day of battle.

**78:10**
2 Kgs 18:12

10 They did not keep God's covenant
  and refused to live by his instructions.

**78:11**
Ps 106:13

11 They forgot what he had done—
  the great wonders he had shown them,

**78:12**
Num 13:22
Isa 19:11

12 the miracles he did for their ancestors
  on the plain of Zoan in the land of Egypt.

**78:TITLE** Hebrew *maskil*. This may be a literary or musical term.

---

**78:1ff** The people of Israel rebelled and were not faithful to God (78:8). They forgot about the miracles God had done (78:11, 12) and put God to the test by making demands of him (78:19). They lied to him, tried to flatter him (78:36), and continued to turn away from him even after he did great works on their behalf (78:42-56). God recorded these painful and shameful truths in his Word so that we can avoid the same errors. In 1 Corinthians 10:5-12, Paul used this classic story of Israel's unfaithfulness to warn the early Christians to be faithful.

**78:5** God commanded that the stories of his mighty acts in Israel's history and his laws be passed on from parents to children. This shows the purpose and importance of religious education: to help each generation obey God and set its hope on him. It is important to keep children from repeating the same mistakes as their ancestors. What are you doing to pass on the history of God's work to the next generation?

**78:9, 10** Ephraim was the most prominent tribe of Israel from the days of Moses to Saul's time. The Tabernacle was set up in its territory. There is no biblical record of Ephraim's soldiers turning back from battle, so this is probably a metaphor referring to Ephraim's failure to provide strong leadership during those years. When David became king, the tribe of Judah gained prominence. Because of David's faith and obedience, God chose Jerusalem in Judah to be the place for the new Temple and rejected Ephraim (78:67). This caused tension between the two tribes. This psalm may have been written because of that tension in order to demonstrate once again why God chose Judah. God works through those who are faithful to him.

13 For he divided the sea and led them through,
　making the water stand up like walls!
14 In the daytime he led them by a cloud,
　and all night by a pillar of fire.
15 He split open the rocks in the wilderness
　to give them water, as from a gushing spring.
16 He made streams pour from the rock,
　making the waters flow down like a river!

17 Yet they kept on sinning against him,
　rebelling against the Most High in the desert.
18 They stubbornly tested God in their hearts,
　demanding the foods they craved.
19 They even spoke against God himself, saying,
　"God can't give us food in the wilderness.
20 Yes, he can strike a rock so water gushes out,
　but he can't give his people bread and meat."
21 When the LORD heard them, he was furious.
　The fire of his wrath burned against Jacob.
　Yes, his anger rose against Israel,
22 for they did not believe God
　or trust him to care for them.
23 But he commanded the skies to open;
　he opened the doors of heaven.
24 He rained down manna for them to eat;
　he gave them bread from heaven.
25 They ate the food of angels!
　God gave them all they could hold.
26 He released the east wind in the heavens
　and guided the south wind by his mighty power.
27 He rained down meat as thick as dust—
　birds as plentiful as the sand on the seashore!
28 He caused the birds to fall within their camp
　and all around their tents.
29 The people ate their fill.
　He gave them what they craved.
30 But before they satisfied their craving,
　while the meat was yet in their mouths,
31 the anger of God rose against them,
　and he killed their strongest men.
　He struck down the finest of Israel's young men.

32 But in spite of this, the people kept sinning.
　Despite his wonders, they refused to trust him.
33 So he ended their lives in failure,
　their years in terror.
34 When God began killing them,
　they finally sought him.
　They repented and took God seriously.
35 Then they remembered that God was their rock,
　that God Most High* was their redeemer.
36 But all they gave him was lip service;
　they lied to him with their tongues.
37 Their hearts were not loyal to him.
　They did not keep his covenant.

**78:35** Hebrew *El-Elyon.*

Cross references:
78:13 Exod 14:21; 15:18
78:14 Exod 13:21
78:15 Exod 17:5-6 †1 Cor 10:4
78:16 Num 20:8, 10-11
78:17 Heb 3:16
78:18 Num 11:4-5 †1 Cor 10:9-10
78:19 Exod 16:3 Num 21:5
78:20 Num 20:11
78:21 Num 11:1
78:22-23 Heb 3:18
78:23 Mal 3:10
78:24 Exod 16:4 †John 6:30-31
78:26 Num 11:31
78:27 Exod 16:13 Ps 105:40
78:29 Num 11:19-20
78:31 Num 11:33-34
78:32 Num 14:10-11
78:33 Num 14:29, 34-35
78:34 Hos 5:15
78:35 Deut 9:26; 32:4
78:36 Exod 32:7-8 Ezek 33:31

**78:36, 37** Over and over the children of Israel claimed that they would follow God, but then they turned away from him. The problem was that they made commitments to God with their mouths and not with their hearts; thus, their repentance was empty. Talk is cheap. God wants our conduct to back up our spiritual claims and promises.

**78:38**
Exod 34:5-6
Num 14:18-20

38 Yet he was merciful and forgave their sins
   and did not destroy them all.
   Many times he held back his anger
   and did not unleash his fury!

**78:39**
Job 7:7, 16
Jas 4:14

39 For he remembered that they were merely mortal,
   gone like a breath of wind that never returns.

40 Oh, how often they rebelled against him in the wilderness
   and grieved his heart in that dry wasteland.

**78:41**
2 Kgs 19:22

41 Again and again they tested God's patience
   and provoked the Holy One of Israel.

**78:42**
Judg 8:34

42 They did not remember his power
   and how he rescued them from their enemies.

**78:43**
Exod 7:3

43 They did not remember his miraculous signs in Egypt,
   his wonders on the plain of Zoan.

**78:44**
Exod 7:20
Ps 105:29

44 For he turned their rivers into blood,
   so no one could drink from the streams.

**78:45**
Exod 8:6, 24
Ps 105:30-31

45 He sent vast swarms of flies to consume them
   and hordes of frogs to ruin them.

**78:46**
Exod 10:14

46 He gave their crops to caterpillars;
   their harvest was consumed by locusts.

**78:47**
Exod 9:23-25
Ps 105:32

47 He destroyed their grapevines with hail
   and shattered their sycamore-figs with sleet.

**78:48**
Exod 9:19

48 He abandoned their cattle to the hail,
   their livestock to bolts of lightning.

**78:49**
Exod 15:7

49 He loosed on them his fierce anger—
   all his fury, rage, and hostility.
   He dispatched against them
   a band of destroying angels.

50 He turned his anger against them;
   he did not spare the Egyptians' lives
   but ravaged them with the plague.

**78:51**
Exod 12:29-30
Ps 105:36

51 He killed the oldest son in each Egyptian family,
   the flower of youth throughout the land of Egypt.*

**78:52**
Ps 77:20

52 But he led his own people like a flock of sheep,
   guiding them safely through the wilderness.

**78:53**
Exod 14:19-20,
27-28

53 He kept them safe so they were not afraid;
   but the sea covered their enemies.

**78:54**
Exod 15:17

54 He brought them to the border of his holy land,
   to this land of hills he had won for them.

**78:55**
Josh 23:4-5
Pss 44:1-2;
105:10-11

55 He drove out the nations before them;
   he gave them their inheritance by lot.
   He settled the tribes of Israel into their homes.

56 But they kept testing and rebelling against God Most High.
   They did not obey his laws.

57 They turned back and were as faithless as their parents.
   They were as undependable as a crooked bow.

**78:58**
Lev 26:1
Deut 32:16, 21

58 They angered God by building shrines to other gods;
   they made him jealous with their idols.

**78:59**
Lev 26:30
Deut 32:19

59 When God heard them, he was very angry,
   and he completely rejected Israel.

**78:60**
1 Sam 4:11

60 Then he abandoned his dwelling at Shiloh,
   the Tabernacle where he had lived among the people.

**78:51** Hebrew *in the tents of Ham.*

---

**78:58** Can God be jealous? According to Scripture, yes (see Deuteronomy 4:24; 5:9, Nahum 1:2). Like everything else about God, his jealousy is perfect. In this case, the offense caused by the ungratefulness and unfaithfulness of his people provoked a just and holy response from God. The shock conveyed in these verses comes not from God's jealousy but from the fact that God, though justified in passing absolute judgment, persistently seasons his responses with grace and patience. God's jealousy over you represents an honor worthy of your deepest gratitude.

61 He allowed the Ark of his might to be captured;
  he surrendered his glory into enemy hands.
62 He gave his people over to be butchered by the sword,
  because he was so angry with his own people—his special possession.
63 Their young men were killed by fire;
  their young women died before singing their wedding songs.
64 Their priests were slaughtered,
  and their widows could not mourn their deaths.

65 Then the Lord rose up as though waking from sleep,
  like a warrior aroused from a drunken stupor.
66 He routed his enemies
  and sent them to eternal shame.
67 But he rejected Joseph's descendants;
  he did not choose the tribe of Ephraim.
68 He chose instead the tribe of Judah,
  and Mount Zion, which he loved.
69 There he built his sanctuary as high as the heavens,
  as solid and enduring as the earth.
70 He chose his servant David,
  calling him from the sheep pens.
71 He took David from tending the ewes and lambs
  and made him the shepherd of Jacob's descendants—
  God's own people, Israel.
72 He cared for them with a true heart
  and led them with skillful hands.

| | |
|---|---|
| | 78:61 1 Sam 4:17 |
| | 78:62 Judg 20:21 1 Sam 4:10 |
| | 78:63 Num 11:1 Jer 7:34; 16:9 |
| | 78:64 1 Sam 22:18 |
| | 78:65 Isa 42:13 |
| | 78:66 1 Sam 5:6 |
| | 78:68 Ps 87:1-2 |
| | 78:69 1 Kgs 6:1-38 |
| | 78:70 1 Sam 16:10-12 |
| | 78:71 2 Sam 5:2; 7:8 1 Chr 11:2 |
| | 78:72 1 Kgs 9:4 |

**Theme:** When outraged by injustice, cry out to God, not against him. In times of disaster, our mood may be anger, but our trust must remain in God.
**Author:** Asaph (or one of his descendants), probably written after the Babylonians had leveled Jerusalem (see 2 Kings 25)

# 79 *A psalm of Asaph.*

1 O God, pagan nations have conquered your land,
  your special possession.
They have defiled your holy Temple
  and made Jerusalem a heap of ruins.
2 They have left the bodies of your servants
  as food for the birds of heaven.
The flesh of your godly ones
  has become food for the wild animals.
3 Blood has flowed like water all around Jerusalem;
  no one is left to bury the dead.
4 We are mocked by our neighbors,
  an object of scorn and derision to those around us.

5 O Lord, how long will you be angry with us? Forever?
  How long will your jealousy burn like fire?
6 Pour out your wrath on the nations that refuse to acknowledge you—
  on kingdoms that do not call upon your name.

| | |
|---|---|
| | 79:1 Ps 74:2-7 Jer 26:18 Lam 1:10 |
| | 79:2 Deut 28:26 Jer 7:33; 16:4 |
| | 79:3 Jer 14:16 |
| | 79:4 Ps 44:13 |
| | 79:5 Ps 74:1, 9-10 Zeph 3:8 |
| | 79:6 Jer 10:25 2 Thes 1:8 |

---

**78:71, 72** Although David was occupying the throne of Israel when this psalm was written, he is called a shepherd and not a king. Shepherding, a common profession in biblical times, was a highly responsible job. The flocks were completely dependent upon shepherds for guidance, provision, and protection. David had spent his early years as a shepherd (1 Samuel 16:10, 11). This was a training ground for the future responsibilities God had in store for him. When he was ready, God took him from caring for sheep to caring for Israel, God's people. Don't treat your pres-

ent situation lightly or irresponsibly; it may be God's training ground for your future.

**79:6** According to the Old Testament, God's wrath and judgment often fell on entire nations because of the sins of people within those nations. Here Asaph pleaded for judgment on kingdoms that refused to acknowledge God's authority. Ironically, Asaph's own nation of Judah was being judged by God for refusing to do this very thing (2 Chronicles 36:14-20). These were people who had sworn allegiance to God but were now rejecting him. This made their judgment even worse.

79:7
Ps 53:4

79:8
Pss 106:6; 142:6
Isa 26:5; 64:9

79:9
2 Chr 14:11
Jer 14:7

79:10
Ps 115:2

79:12
Gen 4:15
Ps 74:10, 18, 22

79:13
Pss 74:1; 95:7;
100:3
Isa 43:21

7 For they have devoured your people Israel,*
    making the land a desolate wilderness.
8 Do not hold us guilty for the sins of our ancestors!
    Let your compassion quickly meet our needs,
    for we are on the brink of despair.
9 Help us, O God of our salvation!
    Help us for the glory of your name.
    Save us and forgive our sins
    for the honor of your name.
10 Why should pagan nations be allowed to scoff,
    asking, "Where is their God?"
    Show us your vengeance against the nations,
    for they have spilled the blood of your servants.
11 Listen to the moaning of the prisoners.
    Demonstrate your great power by saving those condemned to die.
12 O Lord, pay back our neighbors seven times
    for the scorn they have hurled at you.
13 Then we your people, the sheep of your pasture,
    will thank you forever and ever,
    praising your greatness from generation to generation.

**Theme:** A prayer for revival and restoration after experiencing destruction. God is our only hope for salvation.
**Author:** Asaph (or one of his descendants), probably written after the northern kingdom of Israel was defeated and its people deported to Assyria.

# 80

*For the choir director: A psalm of Asaph, to be sung to the tune "Lilies of the Covenant."*

80:1
Exod 25:22
Pss 23:1; 77:20

1 Please listen, O Shepherd of Israel,
    you who lead Joseph's descendants like a flock.

**79:7** Hebrew *devoured Jacob.* See note on 44:4.

---

**PRAYER IN THE BOOK OF PSALMS**

Prayer is human communication with God. Psalms could be described as a collection of song-prayers. Probably the most striking feature of these prayers is their unedited honesty. The words often express our own feelings—feelings that we would prefer no one, much less God, ever knew. Making these psalms our prayers can teach us a great deal about how God wants us to communicate with him. Too often we give God a watered-down version of our feelings, hoping we won't offend him or make him curious about our motives. As we use the psalms to express our feelings, we learn that honesty, openness, and sincerity are valuable to God.

Following are several types of prayers with examples from Psalms. Note that the psalm writers communicated with God in a variety of ways for a variety of reasons. Each of us is invited to communicate with God. Using the psalms will enrich your personal prayer life.

| Prayers of: | Psalms: |
| --- | --- |
| Praise to God | 100; 113; 117 |
| Thanksgiving by a community | 67; 75; 136 |
| Thanksgiving by an individual | 18; 30; 32 |
| Request by the community | 79; 80; 123 |
| Request by an individual | 3; 55; 86 |
| Sorrow by the community | 44; 74; 137 |
| Sorrow by an individual | 5; 6; 120 |
| Anger | 35; 109; 140 |
| Confession | 6; 32; 51 |
| Faith | 11; 16; 23 |

---

**79:10** In the end, God's glory will be evident to all people, but in the meantime, we must endure suffering with patience and allow God to strengthen our character through it. For reasons that we do not know, God sometimes allows pagan people to scoff at believers. We should be prepared for criticism, jokes, and unkind remarks because God does not place us beyond the attacks of scoffers.

**80:1** Cherubim are mighty angels. That God is "enthroned above the cherubim" is a reminder of his presence on the Ark of the Covenant (Exodus 25:17-22).

O God, enthroned above the cherubim,
    display your radiant glory
2    to Ephraim, Benjamin, and Manasseh.
Show us your mighty power.
    Come to rescue us!

3 Turn us again to yourself, O God.
    Make your face shine down upon us.
    Only then will we be saved.
4 O LORD God of Heaven's Armies,
    how long will you be angry with our prayers?
5 You have fed us with sorrow
    and made us drink tears by the bucketful.
6 You have made us the scorn* of neighboring nations.
    Our enemies treat us as a joke.

7 Turn us again to yourself, O God of Heaven's Armies.
    Make your face shine down upon us.
    Only then will we be saved.
8 You brought us from Egypt like a grapevine;
    you drove away the pagan nations and transplanted us into your land.
9 You cleared the ground for us,
    and we took root and filled the land.
10 Our shade covered the mountains;
    our branches covered the mighty cedars.
11 We spread our branches west to the Mediterranean Sea;
    our shoots spread east to the Euphrates River.*
12 But now, why have you broken down our walls
    so that all who pass by may steal our fruit?
13 The wild boar from the forest devours it,
    and the wild animals feed on it.

14 Come back, we beg you, O God of Heaven's Armies.
    Look down from heaven and see our plight.
Take care of this grapevine
15    that you yourself have planted,
    this son you have raised for yourself.
16 For we are chopped up and burned by our enemies.
    May they perish at the sight of your frown.
17 Strengthen the man you love,
    the son of your choice.
18 Then we will never abandon you again.
    Revive us so we can call on your name once more.

19 Turn us again to yourself, O LORD God of Heaven's Armies.
    Make your face shine down upon us.
    Only then will we be saved.

80:6 As in Syriac version; Hebrew reads *the strife.*   80:11 Hebrew *west to the sea, . . . east to the river.*

**Cross-references (right margin):**

80:2 Ps 35:23

80:3 Num 6:24-26; Pss 31:16; 60:1; Lam 5:21

80:4 Pss 79:5; 84:8

80:5 Pss 42:3; 102:9

80:6 Pss 44:13; 79:4

80:8 2 Chr 20:7; Ps 44:2; Isa 5:2, 7; Jer 2:21; 11:17; Ezek 17:6, 23; Amos 9:15

80:9 Exod 23:28; Isa 5:2; Hos 14:5

80:11 Ps 72:8

80:12 Ps 89:40; Isa 5:5

80:13 Jer 5:6

80:16 2 Chr 36:19; Ps 39:11; Jer 52:13

80:17 Ps 89:21

80:18 Ps 71:20; Isa 50:5

---

**80:3, 7** Twice the writer calls on God to "turn us again to yourself." Before God can turn us to himself, we must turn away from sin. Repentance involves humbling ourselves and turning to God to receive his forgiveness. As we turn to God, he helps us see ourselves, including our sin, more clearly. Then, as we see our sin, we must repeat the process of repentance. Only then can we constantly be restored to fellowship with God.

**80:17** "The son of your choice" is probably not the Messiah but Israel, whom God calls elsewhere his "firstborn son" (Exodus 4:22). The psalm writer is making a plea that God would restore his mercy to Israel, the people he chose to bring his message into the world.

**Theme:** A holiday hymn. This hymn celebrates the Exodus from Egypt—God's goodness versus Israel's waywardness. God is our deliverer in spite of our wanderings.
**Author:** Asaph, probably written to be used during the Festival of Shelters

# 81   *For the choir director: A psalm of Asaph, to be accompanied by a stringed instrument.**

**81:1**
Pss 46:1; 59:16;
66:1; 95:1-2

1 Sing praises to God, our strength.
   Sing to the God of Jacob.

**81:2**
Pss 108:2; 144:9;
149:3

2 Sing! Beat the tambourine.
   Play the sweet lyre and the harp.

**81:3**
Lev 23:24
Num 10:10

3 Blow the ram's horn at new moon,
   and again at full moon to call a festival!

4 For this is required by the decrees of Israel;
   it is a regulation of the God of Jacob.

**81:5**
Exod 11:4

5 He made it a law for Israel*
   when he attacked Egypt to set us free.

   I heard an unknown voice say,

**81:6**
Isa 9:4; 10:27

6 "Now I will take the load from your shoulders;
   I will free your hands from their heavy tasks.

**81:7**
Exod 2:23; 17:5-7;
19:19
Pss 50:15; 95:8

7 You cried to me in trouble, and I saved you;
   I answered out of the thundercloud
   and tested your faith when there was no water at Meribah.   *Interlude*

**81:8**
Ps 50:7

8 "Listen to me, O my people, while I give you stern warnings.
   O Israel, if you would only listen to me!

**81:9**
Exod 20:3
Isa 43:12

9 You must never have a foreign god;
   you must not bow down before a false god.

**81:10**
Exod 20:2
Pss 78:25; 103:5

10 For it was I, the LORD your God,
   who rescued you from the land of Egypt.
   Open your mouth wide, and I will fill it with good things.

**81:11**
Exod 32:1

11 "But no, my people wouldn't listen.
   Israel did not want me around.

**81:12**
Acts 7:42
Rom 1:24, 26

12 So I let them follow their own stubborn desires,
   living according to their own ideas.

**81:13**
Deut 5:29
Isa 48:18
Jer 7:23

13 Oh, that my people would listen to me!
   Oh, that Israel would follow me, walking in my paths!

**81:14**
Ps 47:3
Amos 1:8

14 How quickly I would then subdue their enemies!
   How soon my hands would be upon their foes!

15 Those who hate the LORD would cringe before him;
   they would be doomed forever.

**81:16**
Deut 32:13-14

16 But I would feed you with the finest wheat.
   I would satisfy you with wild honey from the rock."

**81:TITLE** Hebrew *according to the gittith.*   **81:5** Hebrew *for Joseph.*

---

**81:1-5** Israel's holidays reminded the nation of God's great miracles. They were times of rejoicing and times to renew one's strength for life's daily struggles. At Christmas, do your thoughts revolve mostly around presents? Is Easter only a warm anticipation of spring and Thanksgiving only a good meal? Remember the spiritual origins of these special days, and use them as opportunities to worship God for his goodness to you, your family, and your nation.

**81:2-4** David instituted music for the Temple worship services (1 Chronicles 25). Music and worship go hand in hand. Worship involves the whole person, and music helps lift a person's thoughts and emotions to God. Through music we can reflect upon our needs and shortcomings as well as celebrate God's greatness.

**81:11, 12** God let the Israelites go on blindly, stubbornly, and selfishly, when they should have been obeying and following God's desires. God sometimes lets us continue in our stubbornness to bring us to our senses. He does not keep us from rebelling

because he wants us to learn the consequences of sin. He uses these experiences to turn people away from greater sin to faith in him.

**81:13-16** God had provided in his covenant that he would restore his people if they would listen to him and return to him (Exodus 23:22-27; Leviticus 26:3-13; Deuteronomy 7:12-26; 28:1-14). God remains faithful in our relationship with him (2 Timothy 2:11-13), patiently waiting for our response so he can pour out his blessings. Conduct an inventory of your spiritual life right now. In what ways are you allowing God to affect your daily decisions?

**Theme:** A fair judge. God will judge the wicked who have unfairly treated others.
**Author:** Asaph

# 82 *A psalm of Asaph.*

1 God presides over heaven's court;
    he pronounces judgment on the heavenly beings:

2 "How long will you hand down unjust decisions
    by favoring the wicked?                                                    *Interlude*

3 "Give justice to the poor and the orphan;
    uphold the rights of the oppressed and the destitute.

4 Rescue the poor and helpless;
    deliver them from the grasp of evil people.

5 But these oppressors know nothing;
    they are so ignorant!
  They wander about in darkness,
    while the whole world is shaken to the core.

6 I say, 'You are gods;
    you are all children of the Most High.

7 But you will die like mere mortals
    and fall like every other ruler.'"

8 Rise up, O God, and judge the earth,
    for all the nations belong to you.

| | |
|---|---|
| | **82:1**<br>Ps 58:11<br>Isa 3:13 |
| | **82:2**<br>Deut 1:17<br>Ps 58:1-2<br>Prov 18:5 |
| | **82:3**<br>Deut 24:17 |
| | **82:4**<br>Job 29:12 |
| | **82:6**<br>†John 10:34 |
| | **82:7**<br>Pss 49:12; 83:11 |
| | **82:8**<br>Pss 2:8; 12:5<br>Rev 11:15 |

**Theme:** Combating God's enemies. This psalm is a prayer for God to do whatever
it takes to convince the world that he is indeed God. Someday all will recognize and
admit that God is in charge.
**Author:** Asaph (or one of his descendants)

# 83 *A song. A psalm of Asaph.*

1 O God, do not be silent!
  Do not be deaf.
  Do not be quiet, O God.

2 Don't you hear the uproar of your enemies?
    Don't you see that your arrogant enemies are rising up?

3 They devise crafty schemes against your people;
    they conspire against your precious ones.

4 "Come," they say, "let us wipe out Israel as a nation.
    We will destroy the very memory of its existence."

5 Yes, this was their unanimous decision.
    They signed a treaty as allies against you—

6 these Edomites and Ishmaelites;
    Moabites and Hagrites;

7 Gebalites, Ammonites, and Amalekites;
    and people from Philistia and Tyre.

| | |
|---|---|
| | **83:1**<br>Pss 28:1; 109:1 |
| | **83:2**<br>Pss 2:1; 81:15<br>Isa 17:12 |
| | **83:3**<br>Ps 31:20 |
| | **83:4**<br>Esth 3:5-6 |
| | **83:5**<br>Ps 2:2 |
| | **83:6**<br>Gen 25:12-16<br>2 Chr 20:1, 10<br>Ps 137:7 |
| | **83:7**<br>1 Sam 4:1; 15:2<br>2 Chr 20:10<br>Ezek 27:2-3, 9 |

---

**82:1ff**  God judges human judges. The integrity of the justice
system in a nation provides a clear indication of the health of
that society. As is the case with all leadership, judges derive
their authority ultimately from God and will give an account
to God for their verdicts. Believers are commanded to pray for
"kings and all who are in authority so we can live peaceful and
quiet lives marked by godliness and dignity" (1 Timothy 2:2).
This psalm reminds us to include judges of every kind in our
prayers because we directly benefit from their integrity.

**82:6**  This psalm calls the rulers and judges of Israel "gods"
and "children of the Most High." They were called gods because
they represented God in executing judgment. John 10:34-36
records Jesus using this passage to defend his claims to be God.

His argument was as follows: If God would call mere people
"gods," why was it blasphemous for him, the true Son of God,
to declare himself equal with God?

**83:5-8**  This alliance against God may refer to the gathering
of certain kings to fight against Jehoshaphat and the people
of Judah (2 Chronicles 20). The psalm's author is called Asaph,
but it could be Asaph or one of his descendants. A descendant
of Asaph named Jahaziel prophesied victory for Judah in the battle
against Jehoshaphat (2 Chronicles 20:13-17) and exclaimed,
"The battle is not yours, but God's" (2 Chronicles 20:15). God
is "the Most High, supreme over all the earth" (83:18), and the
enemies of Israel were considered God's enemies.

**83:6**  The Hagrites may have been the descendants of Hagar
(Genesis 21:8-21).

8 Assyria has joined them, too,
    and is allied with the descendants of Lot.

*Interlude*

**83:9**
Judg 4:22-23

9 Do to them as you did to the Midianites
    and as you did to Sisera and Jabin at the Kishon River.
10 They were destroyed at Endor,
    and their decaying corpses fertilized the soil.

**83:11**
Judg 7:25; 8:21

11 Let their mighty nobles die as Oreb and Zeeb did.
    Let all their princes die like Zebah and Zalmunna,

**83:12**
2 Chr 20:11

12 for they said, "Let us seize for our own use
    these pasturelands of God!"
13 O my God, scatter them like tumbleweed,
    like chaff before the wind!

**83:14**
Deut 32:22
Isa 9:18

**83:15**
Job 9:17
Ps 58:9

14 As a fire burns a forest
    and as a flame sets mountains ablaze,
15 chase them with your fierce storm;
    terrify them with your tempest.

**83:16**
Ps 109:29

16 Utterly disgrace them
    until they submit to your name, O LORD.
17 Let them be ashamed and terrified forever.
    Let them die in disgrace.

**83:18**
Ps 59:13
Isa 45:21

18 Then they will learn that you alone are called the LORD,
    that you alone are the Most High,
    supreme over all the earth.

**Theme:** God's living presence is our greatest joy. His radiant presence helps us grow in strength, grace, and glory.
**Author:** The sons of Korah (Temple assistants)

**84** *For the choir director: A psalm of the descendants of Korah, to be accompanied by a stringed instrument.\**

**84:1**
Ps 27:4

1 How lovely is your dwelling place,
    O LORD of Heaven's Armies.

**84:2**
Pss 42:1-2; 63:1

2 I long, yes, I faint with longing
    to enter the courts of the LORD.
With my whole being, body and soul,
    I will shout joyfully to the living God.

**84:3**
Ps 43:4

3 Even the sparrow finds a home,
    and the swallow builds her nest and raises her young
at a place near your altar,
    O LORD of Heaven's Armies, my King and my God!

**84:4**
Ps 65:4

4 What joy for those who can live in your house,
    always singing your praises.

*Interlude*

**84:TITLE** Hebrew *according to the gittith.*

---

**83:8-11** The "descendants of Lot" refers to the Moabites and Ammonites (Genesis 19:36-38). Sisera was the commander of the army of the oppressive Canaanite king Jabin. He was killed by a woman (see Judges 4 for the complete story). (For the story of Oreb and Zeeb, see Judges 7:25; for Zebah and Zalmunna, see Judges 8:21.)

**83:13-18** Surrounding Judah were pagan nations that sought Judah's downfall. The writer prayed that God would blow these nations away like tumbleweed until they recognized that the Lord is supreme over all rulers of the earth. Sometimes we must be humbled by adversity before we will look up and see the Lord; we must be defeated before we can have the ultimate victory. Wouldn't it be better to seek the Lord in times of prosperity than to wait until his judgment is upon us?

**84:1, 4** The writer longed to get away from the bustling world to meet God inside his dwelling place, his holy Temple. We can

meet God anywhere, at any time. But we know that going into a church building can help us step aside from the busy mainstream of life so we can quietly meditate and pray. We find joy and strength not only in the prayers, music, lessons, and sermons but also in fellowshiping with other believers in a special place.

5 What joy for those whose strength comes from the LORD,
  who have set their minds on a pilgrimage to Jerusalem.
6 When they walk through the Valley of Weeping,*
  it will become a place of refreshing springs.
  The autumn rains will clothe it with blessings.
7 They will continue to grow stronger,
  and each of them will appear before God in Jerusalem.*

8 O LORD God of Heaven's Armies, hear my prayer.
  Listen, O God of Jacob.                                    *Interlude*

9 O God, look with favor upon the king, our shield!
  Show favor to the one you have anointed.

10 A single day in your courts
   is better than a thousand anywhere else!
   I would rather be a gatekeeper in the house of my God
   than live the good life in the homes of the wicked.

11 For the LORD God is our sun and our shield.
   He gives us grace and glory.
   The LORD will withhold no good thing
   from those who do what is right.

12 O LORD of Heaven's Armies,
   what joy for those who trust in you.

**Theme:** From reverence to restoration. Reverence leads to forgiveness, restoring our love and joy for God.
**Author:** The sons of Korah (Temple assistants)

# 85 *For the choir director: A psalm of the descendants of Korah.*

1 LORD, you poured out blessings on your land!
  You restored the fortunes of Israel.*
2 You forgave the guilt of your people—
  yes, you covered all their sins.                          *Interlude*
3 You held back your fury.
  You kept back your blazing anger.

4 Now restore us again, O God of our salvation.
  Put aside your anger against us once more.
5 Will you be angry with us always?
  Will you prolong your wrath to all generations?
6 Won't you revive us again,
  so your people can rejoice in you?
7 Show us your unfailing love, O LORD,
  and grant us your salvation.

8 I listen carefully to what God the LORD is saying,
  for he speaks peace to his faithful people.
  But let them not return to their foolish ways.

84:6 Or *Valley of Poplars;* Hebrew reads *valley of Baca.*   84:7 Hebrew *Zion.*   85:1 Hebrew *of Jacob.* See note on 44:4.

84:5
Ps 81:1

84:6
Ps 107:35

84:7
Deut 16:16
Isa 40:31

84:9
Gen 15:1
2 Sam 19:21
Ps 115:9-11

84:10
1 Chr 23:5
Ps 27:4

84:11
Ps 2:12

84:12
Ps 2:12

85:1
Jer 30:18
Joel 3:1

85:2
Num 14:19
Ps 32:1
Jer 31:34

85:3
Exod 32:12
Deut 13:17
Ps 78:38

85:4
Ps 80:3, 7

85:5
Pss 74:1; 79:5;
80:4

85:6
Ps 149:2

85:8
Pss 29:11; 78:57

**84:5-7** The pilgrimage to the Temple passed through the barren Valley of Weeping. No specific valley has been identified. The "weeping" may have been a symbolic reference to the times of struggles and tears through which people must pass on their way to meet God. Growing strong in God's presence is often preceded by a journey through barren places in our lives. The person who loves to spend time with God will see his or her adversity as an opportunity to experience God's faithfulness even more deeply. If you are walking through your own Valley of Weeping today, be sure your pilgrimage leads toward God, not away from him.

**84:11** God does not promise to give us everything *we* think is good, but he will not withhold what is permanently good. He will give us the means to walk along his paths, but we must do the walking. When we obey him, he will not hold anything back that will help us serve him.

**85:6, 7** The writer was asking God to revive his people, bringing them back to spiritual life. God is capable of reviving both churches and individuals. He can pour out his love on us, renewing our love for him. If you need revival in your church, family, or personal spiritual life, ask God to give you a fresh touch of his love.

85:9
Ps 84:11
Isa 46:13
John 1:14

85:10
Ps 72:3
Prov 3:3
Isa 32:17

85:11
Isa 45:8

85:12
Ps 84:11
Jas 1:17

9 Surely his salvation is near to those who fear him,
  so our land will be filled with his glory.
10 Unfailing love and truth have met together.
   Righteousness and peace have kissed!
11 Truth springs up from the earth,
   and righteousness smiles down from heaven.
12 Yes, the LORD pours down his blessings.
   Our land will yield its bountiful harvest.
13 Righteousness goes as a herald before him,
   preparing the way for his steps.

**Theme:** Devoted trust in times of deep trouble.
**Author:** David

# 86 *A prayer of David.*

86:1
Pss 17:6; 40:17

1 Bend down, O LORD, and hear my prayer;
  answer me, for I need your help.

86:2
Pss 4:3; 25:20

2 Protect me, for I am devoted to you.
  Save me, for I serve you and trust you.
  You are my God.
3 Be merciful to me, O Lord,
  for I am calling on you constantly.
4 Give me happiness, O Lord,
  for I give myself to you.

86:5
Pss 103:8; 130:4

5 O Lord, you are so good, so ready to forgive,
  so full of unfailing love for all who ask for your help.

86:6
Ps 55:1

6 Listen closely to my prayer, O LORD;
  hear my urgent cry.

86:7
Ps 50:14-15

7 I will call to you whenever I'm in trouble,
  and you will answer me.

86:8
Exod 15:11
Deut 3:24

8 No pagan god is like you, O Lord.
  None can do what you do!

86:9
Isa 66:23
Rev 15:3-4

9 All the nations you made
  will come and bow before you, Lord;
  they will praise your holy name.

86:10
Deut 32:39
Isa 44:6, 8
Mark 12:29
1 Cor 8:4

10 For you are great and perform wonderful deeds.
   You alone are God.

86:11
Ps 25:5
Jer 32:39

11 Teach me your ways, O LORD,
   that I may live according to your truth!
   Grant me purity of heart,
   so that I may honor you.

86:12
Ps 111:1

12 With all my heart I will praise you, O Lord my God.
   I will give glory to your name forever,

---

**85:9-13** As the psalmist cries out for God's intervention, he can almost see, taste, and hear God's response. These five verses describe what God can do for those who welcome his herald—righteousness (9:13). This psalm illustrates that the greater the presence of righteousness (obedience to God), the clearer the examples of God's blessings. This principle works equally in the life of a nation or an individual. The more we first seek God's righteousness and his kingdom, as Jesus pointed out, the more we will see everything else taken care of by God (see Matthew 6:25-33).

**86:7** Sometimes our trouble or pain is so great that all we can do is cry out to God for protection (86:2). And often, when there is no relief in sight, all we can do is acknowledge the greatness of God and wait for better days ahead. The conviction that God answers prayer will sustain us in such difficult times.

**86:8-10** "No pagan god is like you." The God of the Bible is unique! He is alive and able to do mighty deeds for those who love

him. All human-created deities are powerless because they are merely inventions of the mind, not living beings. The Lord alone is "worthy . . . to receive glory and honor and power" (Revelation 4:11). Although people believe in many gods, you need never fear that God is only one among many or that you may be worshiping the wrong God. The Lord alone is God.

**86:11-14** This prayer within a prayer captures a glimpse of vibrant spiritual vitality. Two requests are made: "teach me your ways" and "grant me purity of heart." Each request has a God-centered purpose: that the person praying would "live according to your truth" and "honor you." No matter how well we know and follow God, we can always ask him to increase our awareness and improve our obedience. Jesus echoed one of these requests in the sixth beatitude, "God blesses those whose hearts are pure, for they will see God" (Matthew 5:8). Commit this prayer to memory and use it often.

13 for your love for me is very great.
 You have rescued me from the depths of death.*

86:13
Ps 30:3

14 O God, insolent people rise up against me;
 a violent gang is trying to kill me.
 You mean nothing to them.

86:14
Ps 54:3

15 But you, O Lord,
 are a God of compassion and mercy,
 slow to get angry
 and filled with unfailing love and faithfulness.

16 Look down and have mercy on me.
 Give your strength to your servant;
 save me, the son of your servant.

86:16
Ps 68:35

17 Send me a sign of your favor.
 Then those who hate me will be put to shame,
 for you, O Lord, help and comfort me.

86:17
Pss 112:10;
118:13; 119:122

**Theme:** The city of God, where all believers will one day gather.
**Author:** The sons of Korah (Temple assistants)

# 87 *A song. A psalm of the descendants of Korah.*

1 On the holy mountain
 stands the city founded by the LORD.

87:1
Ps 78:68-69
Isa 28:16

2 He loves the city of Jerusalem
 more than any other city in Israel.*

87:2
Ps 78:67-68

3 O city of God,
 what glorious things are said of you! *Interlude*

87:3
Pss 46:4; 48:8
Isa 60:1

4 I will count Egypt* and Babylon among those who know me—
 also Philistia and Tyre, and even distant Ethiopia.*
 They have all become citizens of Jerusalem!

87:4
Pss 45:12; 68:31
Isa 19:23-25

5 Regarding Jerusalem* it will be said,
 "Everyone enjoys the rights of citizenship there."
 And the Most High will personally bless this city.

87:5
Ps 48:8

6 When the LORD registers the nations, he will say,
 "They have all become citizens of Jerusalem." *Interlude*

87:6
Isa 4:2-4

7 The people will play flutes* and sing,
 "The source of my life springs from Jerusalem!"

87:7
Ps 36:9

**Theme:** When there is no relief in sight. God understands even our deepest misery.
**Author:** Heman, one of the sons of Korah (possibly the same man mentioned in
1 Chronicles 15:19; 16:41; 25:4-5 as a musician and the king's seer)

# 88 *For the choir director: A psalm of the descendants of Korah. A song to be sung to the tune "The Suffering of Affliction." A psalm\* of Heman the Ezrahite.*

1 O LORD, God of my salvation,
 I cry out to you by day.
 I come to you at night.

88:1
Ps 22:2
Luke 18:7

---

86:13 Hebrew *of Sheol.*   87:2 Hebrew *He loves the gates of Zion more than all the dwellings of Jacob.* See note
on 44:4.   87:4a Hebrew *Rahab,* the name of a mythical sea monster that represents chaos in ancient literature.
The name is used here as a poetic name for Egypt.   87:4b Hebrew *Cush.*   87:5 Hebrew *Zion.*   87:7 Or *will dance.*
88:TITLE Hebrew *maskil.* This may be a literary or musical term.

---

86:17 It is right to pray for a sign of God's favor. As David found, it may be just what we need. But let us not overlook the signs he has already given: the support of family and friends, the fellowship of other Christians, the light of each new day. And we can be confident that he knows our situation no matter how desperate it becomes, and he cares.

87:1ff Jerusalem (the holy mountain, Zion) and its Temple here represent the future community of all believers. This psalm looks ahead to the Holy City of God described in Revelation 21:10-27. The honor of living there will be granted to all whose names are recorded in the Lamb's Book of Life (Revelation 21:27). It is God's grace that forms and sustains this wonderful community. How could anyone refuse God's offer to be part of this celebration?

88:1ff Have you ever felt as though you have hit bottom? The

**88:2**
Pss 18:6; 86:1
2 Now hear my prayer;
  listen to my cry.

**88:3**
Pss 107:18; 116:3
3 For my life is full of troubles,
  and death* draws near.

**88:4**
Ps 28:1
4 I am as good as dead,
  like a strong man with no strength left.

**88:5**
Ps 31:12
Isa 53:8
5 They have left me among the dead,
  and I lie like a corpse in a grave.
I am forgotten,
  cut off from your care.

**88:6**
Pss 32:4; 69:15;
143:3
Lam 3:55
6 You have thrown me into the lowest pit,
  into the darkest depths.

**88:7**
Ps 42:7
7 Your anger weighs me down;
  with wave after wave you have engulfed me.

*Interlude*

**88:8**
Job 19:19; 30:10
Ps 31:11
8 You have driven my friends away
  by making me repulsive to them.
I am in a trap with no way of escape.

**88:9**
Job 11:13
Pss 6:7; 22:2
9 My eyes are blinded by my tears.
Each day I beg for your help, O Lord;
  I lift my hands to you for mercy.

**88:10**
Ps 6:5
10 Are your wonderful deeds of any use to the dead?
  Do the dead rise up and praise you?

*Interlude*

11 Can those in the grave declare your unfailing love?
  Can they proclaim your faithfulness in the place of destruction?*

**88:12**
Job 10:20-21
12 Can the darkness speak of your wonderful deeds?
  Can anyone in the land of forgetfulness talk about your righteousness?

**88:13**
Pss 5:3; 119:147
13 O Lord, I cry out to you.
  I will keep on pleading day by day.

**88:14**
Job 13:24
Ps 13:1
14 O Lord, why do you reject me?
  Why do you turn your face from me?

**88:15**
Job 6:4
15 I have been sick and close to death since my youth.
  I stand helpless and desperate before your terrors.
16 Your fierce anger has overwhelmed me.
  Your terrors have paralyzed me.

**88:17**
Ps 22:12, 16
17 They swirl around me like floodwaters all day long.
  They have engulfed me completely.

**88:18**
Job 19:13
Pss 31:11; 38:11
18 You have taken away my companions and loved ones.
  Darkness is my closest friend.

**88:3** Hebrew *Sheol*.   **88:11** Hebrew *in Abaddon?*

writer is so low that he even despairs of life itself. Although everything is bad and getting worse, he is able to tell it all to God. This is one of the few psalms that gives no answer or expression of hope. Don't think that you must always be cheerful and positive. Grief and depression take time to heal. No matter how low we feel, we can always take our problems to God and express our anguish to him.

**88:5** Our feelings may be as obvious and painful as those expressed by the psalm writer, but they are never the complete picture. In fact, our feelings are usually very unstable. When we bring our unedited feelings to God, we allow him to point out where they are incomplete. We are in trouble whenever we give our feelings divine authority or assume that God can't handle what we feel. Praying the psalms teaches us to bring God everything about us and trains us to experience his presence even when our feelings tell us otherwise.

**88:13, 14** The writer of this psalm was close to death, perhaps debilitated by disease, and forsaken by friends. But he could still pray. Perhaps you are not so afflicted, but you know someone who is. Consider being a prayer companion for that person. This psalm can be a prayer you can lift to God on his or her behalf.

**Theme:** God's promise to preserve David's descendants. God's promise is fulfilled in Jesus Christ, who will reign for eternity. The love and kindness promised to David is ours in Christ.
**Author:** Ethan (a Levite leader and possibly one of the head musicians in the Temple, 1 Chronicles 15:17, 19), or one of his descendants

# 89 *A psalm\* of Ethan the Ezrahite.*

1 I will sing of the LORD's unfailing love forever!
   Young and old will hear of your faithfulness.

2 Your unfailing love will last forever.
   Your faithfulness is as enduring as the heavens.

3 The LORD said, "I have made a covenant with David, my chosen servant.
   I have sworn this oath to him:

4 'I will establish your descendants as kings forever;
   they will sit on your throne from now until eternity.'"          *Interlude*

5 All heaven will praise your great wonders, LORD;
   myriads of angels will praise you for your faithfulness.

6 For who in all of heaven can compare with the LORD?
   What mightiest angel is anything like the LORD?

7 The highest angelic powers stand in awe of God.
   He is far more awesome than all who surround his throne.

8 O LORD God of Heaven's Armies!
   Where is there anyone as mighty as you, O LORD?
   You are entirely faithful.

9 You rule the oceans.
   You subdue their storm-tossed waves.

10 You crushed the great sea monster.\*
   You scattered your enemies with your mighty arm.

11 The heavens are yours, and the earth is yours;
   everything in the world is yours—you created it all.

12 You created north and south.
   Mount Tabor and Mount Hermon praise your name.

13 Powerful is your arm!
   Strong is your hand!
   Your right hand is lifted high in glorious strength.

14 Righteousness and justice are the foundation of your throne.
   Unfailing love and truth walk before you as attendants.

15 Happy are those who hear the joyful call to worship,
   for they will walk in the light of your presence, LORD.

16 They rejoice all day long in your wonderful reputation.
   They exult in your righteousness.

17 You are their glorious strength.
   It pleases you to make us strong.

**89:1**
Pss 40:10; 59:16

**89:2**
Ps 36:5

**89:3**
2 Sam 7:16
Ps 132:11
Isa 9:7
Luke 1:31-33

**89:4**
2 Sam 7:16
Isa 9:7
Luke 1:33

**89:6**
Pss 29:1; 96:4

**89:7**
Pss 47:2; 96:4

**89:8**
Pss 35:10; 71:19

**89:9**
Pss 65:7; 107:29

**89:10**
Ps 18:14

**89:11**
Gen 1:1
1 Chr 29:11
Ps 24:1

**89:12**
Josh 12:1; 19:22

**89:13**
Ps 118:16

**89:14**
Ps 97:2

**89:15**
Num 10:10

**89:17**
Pss 44:3; 75:10;
148:14

**89:TITLE** Hebrew *maskil*. This may be a literary or musical term.   **89:10** Hebrew *Rahab*, the name of a mythical sea monster that represents chaos in ancient literature.

**89:1ff** This psalm was written to describe the glorious reign of David. God had promised to make David the mightiest king on earth and to keep his descendants on the throne forever (2 Samuel 7:8-16). But Jerusalem was destroyed, and kings no longer reign there. So these verses can only look forward, prophetically, to the future reign of Jesus Christ, David's descendant. Verse 27 is a prophecy concerning David's never-ending dynasty, which will reach its fulfillment and highest expression in Christ's future reign over the world (see Revelation 22:5).

**89:5** In the courts of heaven, a host of angels praise the Lord. This scene is one of majesty and grandeur to show that God is beyond compare. His power and purity place him high above

nature and angels. See Deuteronomy 33:2, Luke 2:13, and Hebrews 12:22 for more about angels.

**89:12** Mount Tabor, though low in elevation (1,900 feet), was the scene of Deborah's victory in Judges 4. Mount Hermon (9,000 feet) was tall and majestic.

**89:14, 15** Righteousness, justice, love, and truth are the foundation of God's throne; they are central characteristics of the way God rules. They summarize his character. As God's ambassadors, we should exhibit the same traits when we deal with people. Make sure your actions flow out of righteousness, justice, love, and faithfulness, because any unfair, unloving, or dishonest action cannot come from God.

**89:17, 24** David is promised to have God's power to accomplish

**89:18**
Ps 47:9

18 Yes, our protection comes from the LORD,
  and he, the Holy One of Israel, has given us our king.

**89:19**
2 Sam 17:10
1 Kgs 11:34

19 Long ago you spoke in a vision to your faithful people.
  You said, "I have raised up a warrior.
  I have selected him from the common people to be king.

**89:20**
1 Sam 16:13
†Acts 13:22

20 I have found my servant David.
  I have anointed him with my holy oil.
21 I will steady him with my hand;
  with my powerful arm I will make him strong.

**89:22**
2 Sam 7:10-11

22 His enemies will not defeat him,
  nor will the wicked overpower him.

**89:23**
2 Sam 7:9

23 I will beat down his adversaries before him
  and destroy those who hate him.
24 My faithfulness and unfailing love will be with him,
  and by my authority he will grow in power.
25 I will extend his rule over the sea,
  his dominion over the rivers.

**89:26**
2 Sam 7:14
1 Chr 22:10

26 And he will call out to me, 'You are my Father,
  my God, and the Rock of my salvation.'

**89:27**
Pss 2:7; 72:11
Rev 19:16

27 I will make him my firstborn son,
  the mightiest king on earth.
28 I will love him and be kind to him forever;
  my covenant with him will never end.

**89:29**
1 Kgs 2:4
Isa 9:7
Jer 33:17

29 I will preserve an heir for him;
  his throne will be as endless as the days of heaven.

**89:30**
2 Sam 7:14

30 But if his descendants forsake my instructions
  and fail to obey my regulations,
31 if they do not obey my decrees
  and fail to keep my commands,
32 then I will punish their sin with the rod,
  and their disobedience with beating.

**89:33**
2 Sam 7:15

33 But I will never stop loving him
  nor fail to keep my promise to him.

**89:34**
Num 23:19
Jer 33:20-21

34 No, I will not break my covenant;
  I will not take back a single word I said.
35 I have sworn an oath to David,
  and in my holiness I cannot lie:

**89:36**
Ps 72:5

36 His dynasty will go on forever;
  his kingdom will endure as the sun.
37 It will be as eternal as the moon,
  my faithful witness in the sky!"                        *Interlude*

**89:38**
1 Chr 28:9

38 But now you have rejected him and cast him off.
  You are angry with your anointed king.

**89:39**
Ps 78:59
Lam 2:7; 5:16

39 You have renounced your covenant with him;
  you have thrown his crown in the dust.

**89:40**
Ps 80:12
Lam 2:2, 5

40 You have broken down the walls protecting him
  and ruined every fort defending him.
41 Everyone who comes along has robbed him,
  and he has become a joke to his neighbors.

---

God's will. Without God's help, we are weak and powerless, inadequate for even the simplest spiritual tasks. But when we are filled with God's Spirit, his power flows through us and our accomplishments will exceed our expectations.

**89:34-37** In light of Israel's continual disobedience throughout history, this is an amazing promise. God promised that David's descendants would always sit on the throne (89:29), but that if the people disobeyed, they would be punished (89:30-32). Yet, even through their disobedience and punish-

ment, God would never break faith with them (89:33). Israel *did* disobey, evil ran rampant, the nation was divided, exile came—but through it all, a remnant of God's people remained faithful. Centuries later, the Messiah arrived, the eternal King from David's line, just as God had promised. All that God promises, he fulfills. He will not take back even one word of what he says. God can also be trusted to save us as he promised he would (Hebrews 6:13-18). God is completely reliable.

42 You have strengthened his enemies
    and made them all rejoice.
43 You have made his sword useless
    and refused to help him in battle.
44 You have ended his splendor
    and overturned his throne.
45 You have made him old before his time
    and publicly disgraced him.

46 O LORD, how long will this go on?
    Will you hide yourself forever?
    How long will your anger burn like fire?
47 Remember how short my life is,
    how empty and futile this human existence!
48 No one can live forever; all will die.
    No one can escape the power of the grave.*

49 Lord, where is your unfailing love?
    You promised it to David with a faithful pledge.
50 Consider, Lord, how your servants are disgraced!
    I carry in my heart the insults of so many people.
51 Your enemies have mocked me, O LORD;
    they mock your anointed king wherever he goes.

52 Praise the LORD forever!
    Amen and amen!

*Interlude* (near v.45)

*Interlude* (near v.48)

| Reference marks |
|---|
| **89:42** Pss 13:2; 80:6 |
| **89:43** Ps 44:10 |
| **89:44** Ezek 28:7 |
| **89:45** Ps 44:15-16 |
| **89:46** Pss 13:1; 79:5 |
| **89:47** Job 7:7; 14:1 / Ps 39:5-6 / Eccl 1:2; 2:11 |
| **89:48** Ps 22:29 / Heb 11:5 |
| **89:49** 2 Sam 7:15 |
| **89:51** Ps 74:9-10, 18, 22 |
| **89:52** Pss 41:13; 106:48 |

## BOOK FOUR    Psalms 90:1—106:48

These psalms include a prayer of Moses, a psalm about oppressors, and a psalm praising God as our King. These psalms remind us that we should remember our place and be submissive before our mighty God.

**Theme:** God's eternal nature is contrasted with people's frailty. Our time on earth is limited and we are to use it wisely, not living for the moment, but with our eternal home in mind.

**Author:** Moses, making this the oldest of the psalms

# 90  *A prayer of Moses, the man of God.*

1 Lord, through all the generations
    you have been our home!
2 Before the mountains were born,
    before you gave birth to the earth and the world,
    from beginning to end, you are God.

3 You turn people back to dust, saying,
    "Return to dust, you mortals!"
4 For you, a thousand years are as a passing day,
    as brief as a few night hours.
5 You sweep people away like dreams that disappear.
    They are like grass that springs up in the morning.
6 In the morning it blooms and flourishes,
    but by evening it is dry and withered.
7 We wither beneath your anger;
    we are overwhelmed by your fury.
8 You spread out our sins before you—
    our secret sins—and you see them all.

**90:1** Deut 33:27 / Ezek 11:16 / Rev 21:3

**90:2** Gen 1:1 / Ps 102:24-25, 27 / Prov 8:22-26

**90:3** Job 34:14-15

**90:4** Ps 39:5 / 2 Pet 3:8

**90:5** Job 14:2; 20:8 / Isa 40:6 / Matt 6:30

**90:6** Ps 92:7

**89:48** Hebrew *of Sheol.*

---

**90:4** Moses reminds us that a thousand years are like a day to the Lord. God is not limited by time. It's easy to get discouraged when years pass and the world doesn't get better. We sometimes wonder if God is able to see the future. But don't assume that God has our limitations. God is completely unrestricted by time. Because he is eternal, we can depend on him.

**90:8** God knows all our sins as if they were spread out before him, even the secret ones. We don't need to cover up our sins

**90:9**
Ps 78:33

9 We live our lives beneath your wrath,
　　ending our years with a groan.

**90:10**
Ps 78:39
Eccl 12:2-7

10 Seventy years are given to us!
　　Some even live to eighty.
　But even the best years are filled with pain and trouble;
　　soon they disappear, and we fly away.

**90:11**
Ps 76:7

11 Who can comprehend the power of your anger?
　　Your wrath is as awesome as the fear you deserve.

**90:12**
Ps 39:4

12 Teach us to realize the brevity of life,
　　so that we may grow in wisdom.

**90:13**
Deut 32:36

13 O LORD, come back to us!
　　How long will you delay?
　　Take pity on your servants!

**90:14**
Pss 36:8; 103:5
Jer 31:14

14 Satisfy us each morning with your unfailing love,
　　so we may sing for joy to the end of our lives.

**90:15**
Pss 31:10; 86:4

15 Give us gladness in proportion to our former misery!
　　Replace the evil years with good.

**90:16**
Ps 44:1

16 Let us, your servants, see you work again;
　　let our children see your glory.

**90:17**
Ps 27:4
Isa 26:12

17 And may the Lord our God show us his approval
　　and make our efforts successful.
　　Yes, make our efforts successful!

**Theme:** God's protection in the midst of danger. God doesn't promise a world free from danger, but he does promise his help whenever we face danger.
**Author:** Anonymous

**91:1**
Isa 25:4; 32:2

# 91

1 Those who live in the shelter of the Most High
　　will find rest in the shadow of the Almighty.

**91:2**
Pss 18:2; 142:5
Jer 16:19

2 This I declare about the LORD:
　He alone is my refuge, my place of safety;
　　he is my God, and I trust him.

**91:3**
2 Chr 20:9
Ps 124:7

3 For he will rescue you from every trap
　　and protect you from deadly disease.

**91:4**
Pss 35:2; 57:1;
63:7

4 He will cover you with his feathers.
　　He will shelter you with his wings.
　　His faithful promises are your armor and protection.

**91:5**
Job 5:19-23
Ps 23:4

5 Do not be afraid of the terrors of the night,
　　nor the arrow that flies in the day.

**91:6**
Job 5:22

6 Do not dread the disease that stalks in darkness,
　　nor the disaster that strikes at midday.

7 Though a thousand fall at your side,
　　though ten thousand are dying around you,
　　these evils will not touch you.

**91:8**
Ps 37:34

8 Just open your eyes,
　　and see how the wicked are punished.

---

before him because we can talk openly and honestly with him. But while he knows all that terrible information about us, God still loves us and wants to forgive us. This should encourage us to come to him rather than frighten us into covering up our sin.

**90:12** Realizing that life is short helps us use the little time we have more wisely and for eternal good. Take time to number your days by asking, What do I want to see happen in my life before I die? What small step could I take toward that purpose today?

**90:17** Because our days are numbered, we want our work to count, to be effective and productive. We desire to see God's eternal plan revealed now and for our work to reflect his permanence.

If we feel dissatisfied with this life and all its imperfections, we must remember our desire to see our work established is placed there by God (see the note on Ecclesiastes 3:11). But our desire can only be satisfied in eternity. Until then we must apply ourselves to loving and serving God.

**91:1-6** God is a shelter, a refuge when we are afraid. The writer's faith in God as protector would carry him through all the dangers and fears of life. This should be a picture of our trust—trading all our fears for faith in him, no matter how intense our fears. To do this we must "live" and "rest" with him (91:1). By entrusting ourselves to his protection and pledging our daily devotion to him, we will be kept safe.

9 If you make the LORD your refuge,
    if you make the Most High your shelter,
10 no evil will conquer you;
    no plague will come near your home.
11 For he will order his angels
    to protect you wherever you go.
12 They will hold you up with their hands
    so you won't even hurt your foot on a stone.
13 You will trample upon lions and cobras;
    you will crush fierce lions and serpents under your feet!

14 The LORD says, "I will rescue those who love me.
    I will protect those who trust in my name.
15 When they call on me, I will answer;
    I will be with them in trouble.
    I will rescue and honor them.
16 I will reward them with a long life
    and give them my salvation."

**91:10**
Prov 12:21

**91:11**
Ps 34:7
†Matt 4:6
†Luke 4:9-11

**91:13**
Judg 14:6
Luke 10:19

**91:15**
1 Sam 2:30
Ps 50:15
John 12:26

**Theme:** Be thankful and faithful every day. This psalm was used in Temple services on the Sabbath.
**Author:** Anonymous

# 92 *A psalm. A song to be sung on the Sabbath Day.*

1 It is good to give thanks to the LORD,
    to sing praises to the Most High.
2 It is good to proclaim your unfailing love in the morning,
    your faithfulness in the evening,
3 accompanied by the ten-stringed harp
    and the melody of the lyre.

4 You thrill me, LORD, with all you have done for me!
    I sing for joy because of what you have done.
5 O LORD, what great works you do!
    And how deep are your thoughts.
6 Only a simpleton would not know,
    and only a fool would not understand this:
7 Though the wicked sprout like weeds
    and evildoers flourish,
    they will be destroyed forever.

8 But you, O LORD, will be exalted forever.
9 Your enemies, LORD, will surely perish;
    all evildoers will be scattered.
10 But you have made me as strong as a wild ox.
    You have anointed me with the finest oil.
11 My eyes have seen the downfall of my enemies;
    my ears have heard the defeat of my wicked opponents.
12 But the godly will flourish like palm trees
    and grow strong like the cedars of Lebanon.

**92:3**
1 Sam 10:5
1 Chr 13:8
Neh 12:27

**92:5**
Pss 40:5; 139:17
Rom 11:33
**92:6**
Ps 73:22
**92:7**
Ps 37:38

**92:9**
Pss 37:20; 68:1

**92:10**
Pss 23:5; 75:10

**92:11**
Ps 54:7

**91:11** One of the functions of angels is to watch over believers (Hebrews 1:14). There are examples of guardian angels in Scripture (1 Kings 19:5; Daniel 6:22; Matthew 18:10; Luke 16:22; Acts 12:7), although there is no indication that one angel is assigned to each believer. Angels can also be God's messengers (Matthew 2:13; Acts 27:23, 24). Angels are not visible, except on special occasions (Numbers 22:31; Luke 2:9). Verses 11 and 12 were quoted by Satan when he tempted Jesus (Matthew 4:6; Luke 4:10, 11). It is comforting to know that God watches over us even in times of great stress and fear.

**92:1, 2** During the Thanksgiving holiday, we focus on our blessings and express our gratitude to God for them. But thanks should be on our lips every day. We can never say thank you enough to parents, friends, leaders, and especially to God. When thanksgiving becomes an integral part of your life, you will find that your attitude toward life will change. You will become more positive, gracious, loving, and humble.

**92:12, 13** Palm trees are known for their long life. To flourish like palm trees means to stand tall and to live long. The cedars of Lebanon grew to 120 feet in height and up to 30 feet in circum-

¹³ For they are transplanted to the LORD's own house.
They flourish in the courts of our God.
¹⁴ Even in old age they will still produce fruit;
they will remain vital and green.
¹⁵ They will declare, "The LORD is just!
He is my rock!
There is no evil in him!"

**92:14**
Isa 37:31
John 15:2
**92:15**
Rom 9:14

**Theme:** God's unchanging and almighty nature. His creation reminds us of his great power.
**Author:** Anonymous

**93:1**
Pss 65:6; 96:10;
97:1; 99:1; 104:1
Isa 51:9

## 93

¹ The LORD is king! He is robed in majesty.
Indeed, the LORD is robed in majesty and armed with strength.
The world stands firm
and cannot be shaken.

**93:2**
Lam 5:19

² Your throne, O LORD, has stood from time immemorial.
You yourself are from the everlasting past.

**93:3**
Ps 98:7-8

³ The floods have risen up, O LORD.
The floods have roared like thunder;
the floods have lifted their pounding waves.

**93:4**
Ps 65:7

⁴ But mightier than the violent raging of the seas,
mightier than the breakers on the shore—
the LORD above is mightier than these!

**93:5**
Ps 19:7
1 Cor 3:17

⁵ Your royal laws cannot be changed.
Your reign, O LORD, is holy forever and ever.

**Theme:** God will keep his people from the severe punishment awaiting the wicked. Since God is holy and just, we can be certain that the wicked will not prevail.
**Author:** Anonymous

**94:1**
Deut 32:35
Isa 35:4
Nah 1:2
Rom 12:19

## 94

¹ O LORD, the God of vengeance,
O God of vengeance, let your glorious justice shine forth!
² Arise, O judge of the earth.
Give the proud what they deserve.
³ How long, O LORD?
How long will the wicked be allowed to gloat?

**94:4**
Pss 31:18; 52:1

⁴ How long will they speak with arrogance?
How long will these evil people boast?
⁵ They crush your people, LORD,
hurting those you claim as your own.

**94:6**
Isa 10:2

⁶ They kill widows and foreigners
and murder orphans.
⁷ "The LORD isn't looking," they say,
"and besides, the God of Israel* doesn't care."

⁸ Think again, you fools!
When will you finally catch on?

**94:7** Hebrew *of Jacob.* See note on 44:4.

---

ference; thus, they were solid, strong, and immovable. The writer saw believers as upright, strong, and unmoved by the winds of circumstance. Those who place their faith firmly in God can have this strength and vitality.

**92:14** Honoring God is not restricted to young people who seem to have unlimited strength and energy. Even in old age, devout believers can produce spiritual fruit. There are many faithful older people who continue to have a fresh outlook and can teach us from a lifetime of experience of serving God. Seek out an elderly friend or relative who can tell you about his or her experiences with the Lord and challenge you to new heights of spiritual growth.

**93:1ff** Jewish tradition claims that the next seven psalms (93–99) anticipated some of the works of the Messiah. Psalm 93

is said to have been used in post-captivity Temple services and may have been written during Sennacherib's invasion (2 Kings 18:13–19:37).

**93:5** The atmosphere of God's eternal reign is holiness. Holiness will be the oxygen of heaven. Meanwhile, God's perfect moral character highlights his glory and can be seen everywhere. God will never do anything that is not morally perfect. This reassures us that we can trust him, yet it places a demand on us. Our desire to be holy (dedicated to God and morally clean) is our only suitable response. We must never use unholy means to reach a holy goal because God says, "You must be holy because I, the LORD your God, am holy" (Leviticus 19:2).

⁹ Is he deaf—the one who made your ears?
   Is he blind—the one who formed your eyes?
¹⁰ He punishes the nations—won't he also punish you?
   He knows everything—doesn't he also know what you are doing?
¹¹ The LORD knows people's thoughts;
   he knows they are worthless!

¹² Joyful are those you discipline, LORD,
   those you teach with your instructions.
¹³ You give them relief from troubled times
   until a pit is dug to capture the wicked.
¹⁴ The LORD will not reject his people;
   he will not abandon his special possession.
¹⁵ Judgment will again be founded on justice,
   and those with virtuous hearts will pursue it.

¹⁶ Who will protect me from the wicked?
   Who will stand up for me against evildoers?
¹⁷ Unless the LORD had helped me,
   I would soon have settled in the silence of the grave.
¹⁸ I cried out, "I am slipping!"
   but your unfailing love, O LORD, supported me.
¹⁹ When doubts filled my mind,
   your comfort gave me renewed hope and cheer.

²⁰ Can unjust leaders claim that God is on their side—
   leaders whose decrees permit injustice?
²¹ They gang up against the righteous
   and condemn the innocent to death.
²² But the LORD is my fortress;
   my God is the mighty rock where I hide.
²³ God will turn the sins of evil people back on them.
   He will destroy them for their sins.
   The LORD our God will destroy them.

**Theme:** An invitation to worship God.
**Author:** Anonymous

# 95

¹ Come, let us sing to the LORD!
   Let us shout joyfully to the Rock of our salvation.
² Let us come to him with thanksgiving.
   Let us sing psalms of praise to him.
³ For the LORD is a great God,
   a great King above all gods.
⁴ He holds in his hands the depths of the earth
   and the mightiest mountains.
⁵ The sea belongs to him, for he made it.
   His hands formed the dry land, too.

⁶ Come, let us worship and bow down.
   Let us kneel before the LORD our maker,
⁷   for he is our God.
   We are the people he watches over,
   the flock under his care.

**Cross-references (right margin):**

94:9
Exod 4:11
Prov 20:12

94:10
Ps 44:2

94:11
†1 Cor 3:20

94:12
Deut 8:5
Heb 12:5-6

94:14
1 Sam 12:22
Rom 11:2

94:15
Isa 42:3
Mic 7:9

94:16
Num 10:35
Isa 33:10

94:17
Ps 124:1-2

94:19
Isa 57:18; 66:13

94:20
Ps 58:2

94:21
Exod 23:7
Matt 27:4

94:22
Pss 59:9; 71:7

94:23
Pss 7:16; 140:9, 11

95:2
Mic 6:6-8

95:4
Ps 135:5-6

95:5
Gen 1:9-10

95:7-11
†Heb 3:7-11, 15;
4:7

---

**94:12, 13** At times, God must discipline us to help us. This is similar to a loving parent disciplining his child. The discipline is not very enjoyable to the child, but it is essential to teach him or her right from wrong. The Bible says that "no discipline is enjoyable while it is happening—it's painful! But afterward there will be a peaceful harvest of right living for those who are trained in this way" (Hebrews 12:11). When you feel God's hand of correction,

accept it as proof of his love. Realize that God is urging you to follow his paths instead of stubbornly going your own way.

**95:1-4** Songs, shouts, gratitude, and praise erupted from those gathered to worship the Lord. While there are certainly many examples of stillness and silence in God's presence taught and illustrated in Scripture, there are equally as many examples of raucous worship. Both peaceful silence and enthusiastic praise are appropriate expressions of worship to our great God.

95:8
Num 20:13
Deut 6:16

95:9
Num 14:22

95:10
Acts 7:36; 13:18
Heb 3:10, 17

95:11
Deut 1:35
†Heb 4:3, 5

If only you would listen to his voice today!
⁸ The LORD says, "Don't harden your hearts as Israel did at Meribah,
    as they did at Massah in the wilderness.
⁹ For there your ancestors tested and tried my patience,
    even though they saw everything I did.
¹⁰ For forty years I was angry with them, and I said,
    'They are a people whose hearts turn away from me.
    They refuse to do what I tell them.'
¹¹ So in my anger I took an oath:
    'They will never enter my place of rest.'"

**Theme:** How to praise God. We can sing about him, tell others about him, give him glory, bring offerings to him, and live holy lives.
**Author:** Possibly David because this psalm closely resembles David's hymn of praise in 1 Chronicles 16:23-36

96:1-13
//1 Chr 16:23-33

96:2
Ps 71:15

96:3
Ps 145:12

96:5
1 Chr 16:26
Isa 42:5

96:6
Ps 104:1

96:8
Ps 115:1

**96** ¹ Sing a new song to the LORD!
    Let the whole earth sing to the LORD!
² Sing to the LORD; praise his name.
    Each day proclaim the good news that he saves.
³ Publish his glorious deeds among the nations.
    Tell everyone about the amazing things he does.
⁴ Great is the LORD! He is most worthy of praise!
    He is to be feared above all gods.
⁵ The gods of other nations are mere idols,
    but the LORD made the heavens!
⁶ Honor and majesty surround him;
    strength and beauty fill his sanctuary.

⁷ O nations of the world, recognize the LORD;
    recognize that the LORD is glorious and strong.
⁸ Give to the LORD the glory he deserves!
    Bring your offering and come into his courts.

**JUSTICE IN THE BOOK OF PSALMS**

Justice is a major theme in Psalms. The psalm writers praise God because he is just; they plead for him to intervene and bring justice where there is oppression and wickedness; they condemn the wicked who trust in their wealth; they extol the righteous who are just toward their neighbors.

Justice in Psalms is more than honesty. It is active intervention on behalf of the helpless, especially the poor. The psalm writers do not merely wish the poor could be given what they need, but they plead with God to destroy those nations that are subverting justice and oppressing God's people.

Here are some examples of psalms that speak about justice. As you read them, ask yourself, Who is my neighbor? Does my lifestyle—my work, my play, my buying habits, my giving—help or hurt people who have less than I do? What one thing could I do this week to help a helpless person?

Selected psalms that emphasize this theme are 7; 9; 15; 37; 50; 72; 75; 82; 94; 145.

**95:8** A hardened heart is as useless as a hardened lump of clay or a hardened loaf of bread. Nothing can restore it and make it useful. The writer warns against hardening our hearts as Israel did in the wilderness by continuing to resist God's will (Exodus 17:7). The Israelites had been so convinced that God couldn't deliver them that they simply lost their faith in him. When people become so stubbornly set in their ways that their hearts are hardened, they find it impossible to turn to God. This does not happen all at once; it is the result of a series of choices to disregard God's will. If you resist God long enough, God may toss you aside like hardened bread, useless and worthless.

**95:8** *Meribah* means "arguing," and *Massah* means "testing." These refer to the incident at Rephidim (Exodus 17:1-7) when the Israelites complained to Moses because they had no water (see also Numbers 20:1-13).

**95:11** What keeps us from God's ultimate blessings (entering his "place of rest")? Ungrateful hearts (95:2), not worshiping or submitting to him (95:6), hardening our hearts (95:8), trying God's patience because of stubborn doubts (95:9). In Hebrews 4:5-11, we are warned not to harden our hearts, but to reject the glamour of sin and anything else that would lead us away from God.

**96:1-4** The psalm writer sings out his praises to God, overwhelmed by all that God has done. As we reflect on God's majesty and his goodness to us, we cannot help telling others about him. Witnessing comes naturally when our hearts are full of appreciation for what he has done. God has chosen to use us to "publish his glorious deeds among the nations." Praise for our great God overflows from his creation and should overflow from our lips. How well are you doing at telling others about God's greatness?

9 Worship the LORD in all his holy splendor.
  Let all the earth tremble before him.
10 Tell all the nations, "The LORD reigns!"
  The world stands firm and cannot be shaken.
  He will judge all peoples fairly.

11 Let the heavens be glad, and the earth rejoice!
  Let the sea and everything in it shout his praise!
12 Let the fields and their crops burst out with joy!
  Let the trees of the forest rustle with praise
13 before the LORD, for he is coming!
  He is coming to judge the earth.
  He will judge the world with justice,
    and the nations with his truth.

**96:9**
1 Chr 16:29
2 Chr 20:21

**96:10**
Pss 58:11; 67:4;
93:1

**96:11**
Pss 97:1; 98:7
Isa 49:13

**96:12**
Isa 35:1; 44:23;
55:12-13

**Theme:** God, our awesome conqueror, is righteous and just.
**Author:** Anonymous

# 97

1 The LORD is king!
    Let the earth rejoice!
  Let the farthest coastlands be glad.
2 Dark clouds surround him.
  Righteousness and justice are the foundation of his throne.
3 Fire spreads ahead of him
  and burns up all his foes.
4 His lightning flashes out across the world.
  The earth sees and trembles.
5 The mountains melt like wax before the LORD,
  before the Lord of all the earth.
6 The heavens proclaim his righteousness;
  every nation sees his glory.
7 Those who worship idols are disgraced—
  all who brag about their worthless gods—
  for every god must bow to him.
8 Jerusalem* has heard and rejoiced,
  and all the towns of Judah are glad
  because of your justice, O LORD!
9 For you, O LORD, are supreme over all the earth;
  you are exalted far above all gods.

10 You who love the LORD, hate evil!
  He protects the lives of his godly people
  and rescues them from the power of the wicked.
11 Light shines on the godly,
  and joy on those whose hearts are right.
12 May all who are godly rejoice in the LORD
  and praise his holy name!

**97:1**
Ps 96:10-11

**97:2**
Exod 19:9
Deut 4:11
1 Kgs 8:12
Pss 18:11; 89:14

**97:3**
Heb 12:29

**97:5**
Josh 3:11
Amos 9:5

**97:6**
Ps 50:6

**97:7**
Jer 10:14
†Heb 1:6

**97:8**
Zeph 3:14

**97:9**
Pss 83:18; 95:3

**97:10**
Dan 3:28
Rom 12:9

**97:11**
Job 22:28

**97:12**
Ps 32:11

**97:8** Hebrew *Zion.*

**97:2** The dark clouds that surround God symbolize his unapproachable holiness and the inability of people to find him on their own. If he were uncovered, no one could stand before his blazing holiness and glory.

**97:7** People worship all kinds of images and idols. Although God reveals himself and his love through nature and the Bible, there are many who decide to ignore or reject him and pursue goals they believe are more important. The Bible makes it clear that these people are idol worshipers because they give their highest loyalty to something other than God. One day we will

stand before God in all his glory and power. Then we will see all our goals and accomplishments for what they really are. How foolish our earthly pursuits will seem then!

**97:10** A sincere purpose to please God will result in an alignment of your desires with God's desires. You will love what God loves and hate what God hates. If you love the Lord, you will hate evil. If you do not despise the actions of people who take advantage of others, if you admire people who only look out for themselves, or if you envy those who get ahead using any means to accomplish their ends, then your primary desire in life is not to please God. Learn to love God's ways and hate evil in every form—not only the obvious sins but also the socially acceptable ones.

**Theme:** A song of joy and victory. Because God is victorious over evil, all those who follow him will be victorious with him when he judges the earth.
**Author:** Anonymous

# 98 *A psalm.*

98:1
Exod 15:6
Isa 52:10

¹ Sing a new song to the LORD,
for he has done wonderful deeds.
His right hand has won a mighty victory;
his holy arm has shown his saving power!
² The LORD has announced his victory
and has revealed his righteousness to every nation!

98:3
Luke 1:54, 72

³ He has remembered his promise to love and be faithful to Israel.
The ends of the earth have seen the victory of our God.

98:4
Ps 100:1

⁴ Shout to the LORD, all the earth;
break out in praise and sing for joy!
⁵ Sing your praise to the LORD with the harp,
with the harp and melodious song,

98:6
Num 10:10
2 Chr 15:14

⁶ with trumpets and the sound of the ram's horn.
Make a joyful symphony before the LORD, the King!

98:7
Pss 24:1; 96:11

⁷ Let the sea and everything in it shout his praise!
Let the earth and all living things join in.
⁸ Let the rivers clap their hands in glee!
Let the hills sing out their songs of joy

98:9
Ps 96:10, 13

⁹ before the LORD.
For the LORD is coming to judge the earth.
He will judge the world with justice,
and the nations with fairness.

**Theme:** Praise for God's fairness and holiness. Because God is perfectly just and fair, we can trust him completely.
**Author:** Anonymous

# 99

99:1
Exod 25:22
1 Sam 4:4

¹ The LORD is king!
Let the nations tremble!
He sits on his throne between the cherubim.
Let the whole earth quake!
² The LORD sits in majesty in Jerusalem,*
exalted above all the nations.

99:3
Deut 28:58
Josh 24:19
1 Sam 2:2

³ Let them praise your great and awesome name.
Your name is holy!

99:4
Ps 17:2

⁴ Mighty King, lover of justice,
you have established fairness.
You have acted with justice
and righteousness throughout Israel.*
⁵ Exalt the LORD our God!
Bow low before his feet, for he is holy!

**99:2** Hebrew *Zion.*   **99:4** Hebrew *Jacob.* See note on 44:4.

---

**98:1ff** This is a psalm of praise anticipating the coming of God to rule his people. Jesus fulfilled this anticipation when he came to save all people from their sins (98:2, 3), and he will come again to judge the world (98:8, 9). God is both perfectly loving and perfectly just. He is merciful when he punishes, and he overlooks no sin when he loves. Praise him for his promise to save you and to return again.

**99:1** Cherubim are mighty angels that comprise one of several ranks of angels. (For more on angels, see the note on 91:11.)

**99:3** Everyone should praise God's great and awesome name because his name points to his divine nature, his personage, and his reputation. But the name of God is often used so carelessly in conversation that we have lost sight of its holiness. How easy it is to treat God lightly in everyday life. If you claim him as your Father, live worthy of the family name. Respect God's name and give him praise by both your *words* and your *life.*

**99:5** God's holiness is terribly frightening for sinners, but a wonderful comfort for believers. God is morally perfect and is set apart from people and sin. He has no weaknesses or shortcomings. For sinners, this is frightening because all their inadequacies and evil are exposed by the light of God's holiness. God cannot tolerate, ignore, or excuse sin. For believers, God's holiness gives comfort because, as we worship him, we are lifted from the mire of sin. As we believe in him and humble ourselves before him, we are made holy.

6 Moses and Aaron were among his priests;
   Samuel also called on his name.
They cried to the LORD for help,
   and he answered them.
7 He spoke to Israel from the pillar of cloud,
   and they followed the laws and decrees he gave them.
8 O LORD our God, you answered them.
   You were a forgiving God to them,
   but you punished them when they went wrong.

9 Exalt the LORD our God,
   and worship at his holy mountain in Jerusalem,
   for the LORD our God is holy!

**99:6**
Exod 15:25
1 Sam 7:9

**99:7**
Exod 33:9
Num 12:5

**99:8**
Num 14:20

**Theme:** An invitation to enter joyfully into God's presence. His faithfulness extends to our generation and beyond.
**Author:** Anonymous

# 100 *A psalm of thanksgiving.*

1 Shout with joy to the LORD, all the earth!
2    Worship the LORD with gladness.
   Come before him, singing with joy.
3 Acknowledge that the LORD is God!
   He made us, and we are his.*
   We are his people, the sheep of his pasture.
4 Enter his gates with thanksgiving;
   go into his courts with praise.
   Give thanks to him and praise his name.
5 For the LORD is good.
   His unfailing love continues forever,
   and his faithfulness continues to each generation.

**100:1**
Ps 98:4

**100:2**
Deut 28:47

**100:3**
1 Kgs 18:39
Ezek 34:30-31
Mark 14:27
John 10:11

**100:4**
Pss 95:2; 96:2

**100:5**
Pss 25:8; 119:90

**Theme:** A prayer for help to walk a blameless path. To live with integrity, both our efforts and God's help are necessary.
**Author:** David

# 101 *A psalm of David.*

1 I will sing of your love and justice, LORD.
   I will praise you with songs.
2 I will be careful to live a blameless life—
   when will you come to help me?
I will lead a life of integrity
   in my own home.

**101:1**
Pss 89:1; 145:7

**100:3** As in an alternate reading in the Masoretic Text; the other alternate and some ancient versions read *and not we ourselves.*

---

**99:6** The Bible records several instances where Moses, Aaron, and Samuel cried out to God for help (Exodus 15:25; 17:4; Numbers 11:11-15; 12:13; 14:13ff; 16:44-48; 1 Samuel 7:5, 9; 15:11).

**100:3** David tells us to acknowledge that the Lord is God! How can we do that? We acknowledge him when we shout our praises, appreciate his status as our Creator, accept his authority in every detail of life, enthusiastically agree with the guidance he gives us, and express our thanks for his unfailing love.

**100:3** God is our Creator; we did not create ourselves. Many people live as though they are the creator and center of their own little world. This mind-set leads to pride, greed, idolatry, and if everything should be taken away, a loss of hope itself. But when we realize that God created us and gives us all we have, we will

want to give to others as God gave to us (2 Corinthians 9:8). Then, even if all is lost, we still have God and all he gives us.

**100:4** God alone is worthy of being worshiped. What is your attitude toward worship? Do you willingly and joyfully come into God's presence, or are you just going through the motions, reluctantly going to church? This psalm tells us to remember God's goodness and dependability, and then to worship with thanksgiving and praise!

**101:1ff** David may have written this psalm early in his reign as king as he set down the standards he wanted to follow. David knew that to lead a blameless life he would need God's help (101:2). We can lead blameless lives if we avoid (1) looking at wickedness ("I will refuse to look at anything vile and vulgar," 101:3), (2) evil thoughts ("perverse ideas," 101:4), (3) slander (101:5), and (4) pride (101:5). While avoiding these wrongs, we must also let God's Word show us the standards by which to live.

<sup>3</sup> I will refuse to look at
    anything vile and vulgar.
I hate all who deal crookedly;
    I will have nothing to do with them.

**101:4**
Prov 11:20

<sup>4</sup> I will reject perverse ideas
    and stay away from every evil.

**101:5**
Ps 50:20
Prov 6:16-19

<sup>5</sup> I will not tolerate people who slander their neighbors.
    I will not endure conceit and pride.

**101:6**
Ps 119:1

<sup>6</sup> I will search for faithful people
    to be my companions.
Only those who are above reproach
    will be allowed to serve me.
<sup>7</sup> I will not allow deceivers to serve in my house,
    and liars will not stay in my presence.

**101:8**
Pss 46:4; 75:10;
118:10-12

<sup>8</sup> My daily task will be to ferret out the wicked
    and free the city of the LORD from their grip.

**Theme:** The cure for distress. Because God is living, eternal, and unchanging, we can trust him to help his people in this generation just as he helped his people in past generations.
**Author:** Anonymous

# 102 *A prayer of one overwhelmed with trouble, pouring out problems before the LORD.*

**102:1**
Exod 2:23
1 Sam 9:16

<sup>1</sup> LORD, hear my prayer!
    Listen to my plea!

**102:2**
Ps 69:17

<sup>2</sup> Don't turn away from me
    in my time of distress.
Bend down to listen,
    and answer me quickly when I call to you.

**102:3**
Job 30:30
Jas 4:14

<sup>3</sup> For my days disappear like smoke,
    and my bones burn like red-hot coals.
<sup>4</sup> My heart is sick, withered like grass,
    and I have lost my appetite.

**102:5**
Lam 4:8

<sup>5</sup> Because of my groaning,
    I am reduced to skin and bones.
<sup>6</sup> I am like an owl in the desert,
    like a little owl in a far-off wilderness.

**102:7**
Ps 77:4

<sup>7</sup> I lie awake,
    lonely as a solitary bird on the roof.

**102:8**
2 Sam 16:5
Isa 65:15
Luke 23:11
Acts 26:11

<sup>8</sup> My enemies taunt me day after day.
    They mock and curse me.
<sup>9</sup> I eat ashes for food.
    My tears run down into my drink
<sup>10</sup> because of your anger and wrath.
    For you have picked me up and thrown me out.
<sup>11</sup> My life passes as swiftly as the evening shadows.
    I am withering away like grass.

**102:12**
Exod 3:15
Lam 5:19

<sup>12</sup> But you, O LORD, will sit on your throne forever.
    Your fame will endure to every generation.

---

**101:6** David said that he would "search for faithful people" to be his companions. He would choose as models and as friends those who were godly and truthful. Our friends and associates can have a profound influence on us. Make sure to choose as your closest companions those who are faithful to God and his Word.

**102:3, 4** The writer felt so bad that he lost his appetite. When we face sickness and despair, our days pass blindly, and we don't care about even our basic needs. In these times, God alone is our comfort and strength. Even when we are too weak to fight, we can lean on him. It is often when we recognize our weaknesses that God's greatest strength becomes available.

**102:6, 7** These birds are pictures of loneliness and desolation. At times we may need to be alone, and solitude may comfort us. But we must be careful not to spurn those who reach out to us. Don't reject help and conversation. Suffering silently is neither Christian nor particularly healthy. Instead, accept graciously the support and help from family and friends.

13 You will arise and have mercy on Jerusalem*—
      and now is the time to pity her,
      now is the time you promised to help.
14 For your people love every stone in her walls
      and cherish even the dust in her streets.
15 Then the nations will tremble before the LORD.
      The kings of the earth will tremble before his glory.
16 For the LORD will rebuild Jerusalem.
      He will appear in his glory.
17 He will listen to the prayers of the destitute.
      He will not reject their pleas.

18 Let this be recorded for future generations,
      so that a people not yet born will praise the LORD.
19 Tell them the LORD looked down
      from his heavenly sanctuary.
   He looked down to earth from heaven
20    to hear the groans of the prisoners,
      to release those condemned to die.
21 And so the LORD's fame will be celebrated in Zion,
      his praises in Jerusalem,
22 when multitudes gather together
      and kingdoms come to worship the LORD.

23 He broke my strength in midlife,
      cutting short my days.
24 But I cried to him, "O my God, who lives forever,
      don't take my life while I am so young!
25 Long ago you laid the foundation of the earth
      and made the heavens with your hands.
26 They will perish, but you remain forever;
      they will wear out like old clothing.
   You will change them like a garment
      and discard them.
27 But you are always the same;
      you will live forever.
28 The children of your people
      will live in security.
   Their children's children
      will thrive in your presence."

| Reference |
|---|
| **102:13** Isa 60:10; Zech 1:12 |
| **102:15** 1 Kgs 8:41-42 |
| **102:16** Isa 60:1-2 |
| **102:17** Neh 1:6 |
| **102:18** Deut 31:19; 1 Cor 10:11 |
| **102:19** Deut 26:15 |
| **102:21** Zech 8:20-23 |
| **102:22** Ps 86:9 |
| **102:24** Isa 38:10 |
| **102:25-27** Gen 1:1; †Heb 1:10-12 |
| **102:26** Matt 24:35; 2 Pet 3:10; Rev 20:11 |
| **102:27** Mal 3:6; Jas 1:17 |

**Theme:** God's great love for us. What God does for us tells us what he is really like.
**Author:** David

# 103 *A psalm of David.*

1 Let all that I am praise the LORD;
      with my whole heart, I will praise his holy name.

**103:1** Pss 33:21; 104:1

**102:13** Hebrew *Zion;* also in 102:16.

**102:16-22** Christ's future reign on earth will encompass two events mentioned in these verses. Jerusalem (Zion) will be restored, and the entire world will worship God (Revelation 11:15; 21:1-27).
**102:25-27** The writer of this psalm felt rejected and tossed aside because of his great troubles (102:9, 10). Problems and heartaches can overwhelm us and cause us to feel that God has rejected us. But God our Creator is eternally with us and will keep all his promises, even though we may feel alone. The world will perish, but God will remain. Hebrews 1:10-12 quotes these verses to show that Jesus Christ, God's Son, was also present and active at the creation of the world.
**103:1ff** David's praise focused on the good things God was doing for him. It is easy to complain about life, but David's list gives us plenty for which to praise God: He forgives our sins, heals our diseases, redeems us from death, crowns us with love and compassion, satisfies our desires, and gives righteousness and justice. We receive all of these without deserving any of them. No matter how difficult your life's journey, you can always count your blessings—past, present, and future. When you feel as though you have nothing for which to praise God, read David's list.

<sup>2</sup> Let all that I am praise the LORD;
 may I never forget the good things he does for me.

**103:3**
Exod 34:7
Jer 30:17

<sup>3</sup> He forgives all my sins
 and heals all my diseases.

**103:4**
Ps 49:15

<sup>4</sup> He redeems me from death
 and crowns me with love and tender mercies.

**103:5**
Isa 40:31

<sup>5</sup> He fills my life with good things.
 My youth is renewed like the eagle's!

<sup>6</sup> The LORD gives righteousness
 and justice to all who are treated unfairly.

**103:7**
Exod 33:13

<sup>7</sup> He revealed his character to Moses
 and his deeds to the people of Israel.

**103:8**
Num 14:18
Neh 9:17
Joel 2:13
Jon 4:2
Nah 1:3

<sup>8</sup> The LORD is compassionate and merciful,
 slow to get angry and filled with unfailing love.
<sup>9</sup> He will not constantly accuse us,
 nor remain angry forever.

**103:9**
Ps 30:5
Isa 57:16
Jer 3:5

<sup>10</sup> He does not punish us for all our sins;
 he does not deal harshly with us, as we deserve.

**103:10**
Lam 3:22

<sup>11</sup> For his unfailing love toward those who fear him
 is as great as the height of the heavens above the earth.

**103:11**
Ps 36:5

<sup>12</sup> He has removed our sins as far from us
 as the east is from the west.

**103:12**
Isa 38:17
Heb 9:26

<sup>13</sup> The LORD is like a father to his children,
 tender and compassionate to those who fear him.

**103:13**
Mal 3:17

<sup>14</sup> For he knows how weak we are;
 he remembers we are only dust.

**103:14**
Gen 3:19
Eccl 12:7
Isa 29:16

<sup>15</sup> Our days on earth are like grass;
 like wildflowers, we bloom and die.

**103:15**
Jas 1:10-11
1 Pet 1:24

<sup>16</sup> The wind blows, and we are gone—
 as though we had never been here.

<sup>17</sup> But the love of the LORD remains forever
 with those who fear him.
His salvation extends to the children's children

**103:18**
Deut 7:9

<sup>18</sup> of those who are faithful to his covenant,
 of those who obey his commandments!

<sup>19</sup> The LORD has made the heavens his throne;
 from there he rules over everything.

**103:20**
Matt 6:10
Heb 1:14

<sup>20</sup> Praise the LORD, you angels,
 you mighty ones who carry out his plans,
 listening for each of his commands.

---

**103:7** God's law was given first to Moses and the people of Israel. God's law presents a clear picture of God's character and his will for his people. It was God's training manual to prepare his people to serve him and to follow his ways. Review the Ten Commandments (Exodus 20) and the history of how they were given, asking God to show you his will and his ways through them.

**103:12** East and west can never meet. This is a symbolic portrait of God's forgiveness: When he forgives our sin, he separates it from us and doesn't even remember it. We need never wallow in the past, for God forgives and forgets. We tend to dredge up the ugly past, but God has wiped our record clean. If we are to follow God, we must model his forgiveness. When we forgive another, we must also forget the sin. Otherwise we have not truly forgiven.

**103:13** God is like a father—tender and compassionate. Not every child has a tender and compassionate father, however. Too often, sadly, the cycles of abuse and dysfunction rob children of loving fathers. If that is your situation, God offers himself to you

to be the Father you never had or perhaps felt you never needed. Of course, you can't "go fishing" with God or be held physically by him, but you can receive his love in your heart by means of his Holy Spirit (Romans 5:5). God can tenderly heal your deep loss.

**103:13, 14** We are fragile, but God's care is eternal. Too often we focus on God as judge and lawgiver, ignoring his compassion and concern for us. When God examines our lives, he remembers our human condition. Our weakness should never be used as a justification for sin. His mercy takes everything into account. God will deal with you compassionately. Trust him.

**103:20-22** Everything everywhere is to praise the Lord: all his angels and all his works! Praising God means remembering all he has done for us (103:2), fearing him and obeying his commands (103:17, 18), and doing his will (103:21). Does your life praise the Lord?

21 Yes, praise the LORD, you armies of angels
    who serve him and do his will!
22 Praise the LORD, everything he has created,
    everything in all his kingdom.

Let all that I am praise the LORD.

**Theme:** Appreciating God through his creation. He not only creates, but maintains his creation. The Lord's care is the source of our joy.
**Author:** Anonymous

# 104

1 Let all that I am praise the LORD.

    O LORD my God, how great you are!
    You are robed with honor and majesty.
2    You are dressed in a robe of light.
    You stretch out the starry curtain of the heavens;
3    you lay out the rafters of your home in the rain clouds.
    You make the clouds your chariot;
    you ride upon the wings of the wind.
4 The winds are your messengers;
    flames of fire are your servants.*

5 You placed the world on its foundation
    so it would never be moved.
6 You clothed the earth with floods of water,
    water that covered even the mountains.
7 At your command, the water fled;
    at the sound of your thunder, it hurried away.
8 Mountains rose and valleys sank
    to the levels you decreed.
9 Then you set a firm boundary for the seas,
    so they would never again cover the earth.

10 You make springs pour water into the ravines,
    so streams gush down from the mountains.
11 They provide water for all the animals,
    and the wild donkeys quench their thirst.
12 The birds nest beside the streams
    and sing among the branches of the trees.
13 You send rain on the mountains from your heavenly home,
    and you fill the earth with the fruit of your labor.
14 You cause grass to grow for the livestock
    and plants for people to use.
    You allow them to produce food from the earth—
15    wine to make them glad,
    olive oil to soothe their skin,
    and bread to give them strength.
16 The trees of the LORD are well cared for—
    the cedars of Lebanon that he planted.

**104:2**
Dan 7:9

**104:3**
Ps 18:10
Amos 9:6

**104:4**
2 Kgs 2:11; 6:17
†Heb 1:7

**104:5**
Job 38:4

**104:6**
Gen 1:2

**104:7**
Pss 18:15; 29:3

**104:9**
Job 38:10-11
Jer 5:22

**104:10**
Isa 41:18

**104:12**
Matt 8:20

**104:14**
Gen 1:29
Job 28:5

**104:15**
Judg 9:13; 19:5, 8
Prov 31:6
Eccl 10:19
Luke 7:46

**100:** Greek version reads *He sends his angels like the winds, / his servants like flames of fire.* Compare Heb 1:7.

**104:1ff** This psalm is a poetic summary of God's creation of the world as found in the first chapter of Genesis. What God created each day is mentioned by the writer as a reason to praise God. On day one, God created light (104:1, 2; Genesis 1:3); day two, the heavens and the waters (104:2, 3; Genesis 1:6); day three, land and vegetation (104:6-18; Genesis 1:9-13); day four, the sun,

moon, and stars (104:19-23; Genesis 1:14-16); day five, fish and birds (104:25, 26; Genesis 1:20-23); and on day six, animals, people, and food to sustain them (104:21-24, 27-30; Genesis 1:24-31). God's act of creation deserves the praise of all people.

**104:5** The earth is built on God's foundations, and he guarantees its permanence. "It would never be moved" by anyone other than God. Even though one day the heavens and the earth will be destroyed (2 Peter 3:10), he will create a new heaven and a new earth that will last forever (Isaiah 65:17; Revelation 21:1). The same power that undergirds the world also provides a firm foundation for believers.

| 104:17<br>Lev 11:19 | 17 There the birds make their nests,<br>and the storks make their homes in the cypresses. |

18 High in the mountains live the wild goats,
and the rocks form a refuge for the hyraxes.*

**104:17** Lev 11:19

**104:18** Lev 11:5 / Prov 30:26

**104:19** Gen 1:14
19 You made the moon to mark the seasons,
and the sun knows when to set.

**104:20** Isa 45:7; 56:9
20 You send the darkness, and it becomes night,
when all the forest animals prowl about.
21 Then the young lions roar for their prey,
stalking the food provided by God.

**104:22** Job 37:8
22 At dawn they slink back
into their dens to rest.

**104:23** Gen 3:19
23 Then people go off to their work,
where they labor until evening.

**104:24** Pss 40:5; 65:9 / Jer 10:12; 51:15
24 O Lord, what a variety of things you have made!
In wisdom you have made them all.
The earth is full of your creatures.
25 Here is the ocean, vast and wide,
teeming with life of every kind,
both large and small.

**104:26** Job 41:1
26 See the ships sailing along,
and Leviathan,* which you made to play in the sea.

**104:27** Ps 136:25
27 They all depend on you
to give them food as they need it.
28 When you supply it, they gather it.
You open your hand to feed them,
and they are richly satisfied.

**104:18** Or *coneys*, or *rock badgers*.   **104:26** The identification of Leviathan is disputed, ranging from an earthly creature to a mythical sea monster in ancient literature.

---

**HOW GOD IS DESCRIBED IN PSALMS**

Most of the psalms speak to God or about God. Because they were composed in a variety of situations, various facets of God's character are mentioned. Here is a sample of God's characteristics as understood and experienced by the psalm writers. As you read these psalms, ask yourself if this is the God you know.

| God is . . . | Reference |
|---|---|
| All-knowing and ever present | Psalm 139 |
| Beautiful and desirable | Psalms 27; 36; 45 |
| Creator | Psalms 8; 104; 148 |
| Good and generous | Psalms 34; 81; 107 |
| Great and sovereign | Psalms 33; 89; 96 |
| Holy | Psalms 66; 99; 145 |
| Loving and faithful | Psalms 23; 42; 51 |
| Merciful and forgiving | Psalms 32; 111; 130 |
| Powerful | Psalms 76: 89; 93 |
| Willing to reveal his will, law, and direction | Psalms 1: 19; 119 |
| Righteous and just | Psalms 71; 97; 113 |
| Spirit | Psalms 104; 139; 143 |

---

**104:24** Creation is filled with stunning variety, revealing the rich creativity, goodness, and wisdom of our loving God. As you observe your natural surroundings, thank God for his creativity. Take a fresh look at people, seeing each one as God's unique creation, with his or her own special talents, abilities, and gifts.

**104:26** Here "Leviathan" almost certainly refers to a large and active sea creature.

**104:28-30** Psalm 105 expresses God's sovereignty in history;

this psalm tells of his sovereignty over all creation. God has supreme, unlimited power over the entire universe. He creates; he preserves; he governs. As we understand God's power, we realize that he is sufficient to handle our lives.

29 But if you turn away from them, they panic.
  When you take away their breath,
  they die and turn again to dust.
30 When you give them your breath,* life is created,
  and you renew the face of the earth.

31 May the glory of the LORD continue forever!
  The LORD takes pleasure in all he has made!
32 The earth trembles at his glance;
  the mountains smoke at his touch.

33 I will sing to the LORD as long as I live.
  I will praise my God to my last breath!
34 May all my thoughts be pleasing to him,
  for I rejoice in the LORD.
35 Let all sinners vanish from the face of the earth;
  let the wicked disappear forever.

  Let all that I am praise the LORD.

  Praise the LORD!

**Theme:** God's mighty deeds in bringing Israel to the Promised Land. Remembering his miracles encourages us to keep living close to him.
**Author:** David

# 105
1 Give thanks to the LORD and proclaim his greatness.
  Let the whole world know what he has done.
2 Sing to him; yes, sing his praises.
  Tell everyone about his wonderful deeds.
3 Exult in his holy name;
  rejoice, you who worship the LORD.
4 Search for the LORD and for his strength;
  continually seek him.
5 Remember the wonders he has performed,
  his miracles, and the rulings he has given,
6 you children of his servant Abraham,
  you descendants of Jacob, his chosen ones.

7 He is the LORD our God.
  His justice is seen throughout the land.
8 He always stands by his covenant—
  the commitment he made to a thousand generations.
9 This is the covenant he made with Abraham
  and the oath he swore to Isaac.
10 He confirmed it to Jacob as a decree,
  and to the people of Israel as a never-ending covenant:
11 "I will give you the land of Canaan
  as your special possession."

**104:30** Or *When you send your Spirit.*

| Reference | |
|---|---|
| 104:29 | Gen 3:19 |
| 104:30 | Ezek 37:9 |
| 104:31 | Gen 1:31 |
| 104:32 | Exod 19:18 |
| | Judg 5:5 |
| 104:35 | Pss 37:10; 59:13 |
| 105:1-15 | //1 Chr 16:8-22 |
| 105:2 | Ps 98:5 |
| 105:3 | Ps 33:21 |
| 105:4 | Ps 27:8 |
| 105:7 | Isa 26:9 |
| 105:8 | Gen 22:16-18 |
| | Deut 7:9 |
| | Luke 1:72 |
| 105:10 | Gen 28:13-15 |
| | Josh 23:4 |
| 105:11 | Gen 13:15; 15:18 |

**104:29** Today many people are arrogant enough to think they don't need God. But our every breath depends on the life he has breathed into us (Genesis 2:7; 3:19; Job 33:4; 34:14, 15; Daniel 5:23). Not only do we depend on God for life, but he wants the best for us. We should also desire to learn more of his plans for us each day.

**105:1ff** The first 15 verses of this psalm are also found in 1 Chronicles 16:8-22, where they are sung as part of the celebration of David's bringing the Ark of the Covenant to Jerusalem. Three other psalms are also hymns recounting Israel's history: 78, 106, and 136.

**105:4, 5** If God seems far away, persist in your search for him. God rewards those who sincerely look for him (Hebrews 11:6).

Jesus promised, "Everyone who seeks, finds" (Matthew 7:8). The writer suggested a valuable way to find God—become familiar with the way he has helped his people in the past. The Bible records the history of God's people. In searching its pages we will discover a loving God who is waiting for us to find him.

**105:6-11** The nation Israel, the people through whom God revealed his laws to everyone, is descended from Abraham. God chose Abraham and promised that his descendants would live in the land of Canaan (now called Israel) and that they would be too numerous to count (Genesis 17:6-8). Abraham's son was Isaac; Isaac's son was Jacob. These three men are considered the patriarchs or founders of Israel. God blessed them because of their faith (see Hebrews 11:8-21).

105:12
Gen 34:30
Heb 11:9

12 He said this when they were few in number,
  a tiny group of strangers in Canaan.
13 They wandered from nation to nation,
  from one kingdom to another.

105:14
Gen 12:17; 35:5

14 Yet he did not let anyone oppress them.
  He warned kings on their behalf:
15 "Do not touch my chosen people,
  and do not hurt my prophets."

105:16
Lev 26:26
Isa 3:1
Ezek 4:16

16 He called for a famine on the land of Canaan,
  cutting off its food supply.

105:17
Gen 37:28, 36
Acts 7:9

17 Then he sent someone to Egypt ahead of them—
  Joseph, who was sold as a slave.
18 They bruised his feet with fetters
  and placed his neck in an iron collar.

105:19
Ps 66:10

19 Until the time came to fulfill his dreams,*
  the Lord tested Joseph's character.

105:20
Gen 41:14

20 Then Pharaoh sent for him and set him free;
  the ruler of the nation opened his prison door.
21 Joseph was put in charge of all the king's household;
  he became ruler over all the king's possessions.
22 He could instruct the king's aides as he pleased
  and teach the king's advisers.

23 Then Israel arrived in Egypt;
  Jacob lived as a foreigner in the land of Ham.

105:24
Exod 1:7, 9

24 And the Lord multiplied the people of Israel
  until they became too mighty for their enemies.

105:25
Exod 1:8
Acts 7:19

25 Then he turned the Egyptians against the Israelites,
  and they plotted against the Lord's servants.

105:26
Exod 3:10
Num 16:5

26 But the Lord sent his servant Moses,
  along with Aaron, whom he had chosen.

105:27
Ps 78:43-51

27 They performed miraculous signs among the Egyptians,
  and wonders in the land of Ham.

105:28
Exod 10:22

28 The Lord blanketed Egypt in darkness,
  for they had defied his commands to let his people go.

105:29
Exod 7:20

29 He turned their water into blood,
  poisoning all the fish.

105:30
Exod 8:6

30 Then frogs overran the land
  and even invaded the king's bedrooms.

105:31
Exod 8:16, 21

31 When the Lord spoke, flies descended on the Egyptians,
  and gnats swarmed across Egypt.

105:19 Hebrew *his word.*

---

**HISTORY IN
THE BOOK
OF PSALMS**

For the original hearers, the historical psalms were vivid reminders of God's past acts on behalf of Israel. These history songs were written for passing on important lessons to succeeding generations. They celebrated the many promises God had made and faithfully kept; they also recounted the faithlessness of the people.

We cannot read this ancient history without reflecting on how consistently God's people failed to learn from the past. They repeatedly turned from fresh examples of God's faithfulness and forgiveness only to plunge back into sin. God can use these psalms to remind us how often we do exactly the same thing: Having every reason to live for God, we choose instead to live for everything but God. If we paid more attention to "his story," we wouldn't make so many mistakes in our own stories.

Selected historical psalms include: 68; 78; 95; 105; 106; 111; 114; 135; 136; 149.

---

**105:23-25** Did God cause the Egyptians to hate the Israelites? God is not the author of evil, but the Bible writers don't always distinguish between God's ultimate action and the intermediate steps. Thus, by God blessing the Israelites, the Egyptians came to hate them (Exodus 1:8-22). Because God caused the Israelites' blessing, he is also said to have caused the Egyptians' hatred. God used their animosity as a means to lead the Israelites out of Egypt.

32 He sent them hail instead of rain,
  and lightning flashed over the land.
33 He ruined their grapevines and fig trees
  and shattered all the trees.
34 He spoke, and hordes of locusts came—
  young locusts beyond number.
35 They ate up everything green in the land,
  destroying all the crops in their fields.
36 Then he killed the oldest son in each Egyptian home,
  the pride and joy of each family.

37 The LORD brought his people out of Egypt, loaded with silver and gold;
  and not one among the tribes of Israel even stumbled.
38 Egypt was glad when they were gone,
  for they feared them greatly.
39 The LORD spread a cloud above them as a covering
  and gave them a great fire to light the darkness.
40 They asked for meat, and he sent them quail;
  he satisfied their hunger with manna—bread from heaven.
41 He split open a rock, and water gushed out
  to form a river through the dry wasteland.
42 For he remembered his sacred promise
  to his servant Abraham.
43 So he brought his people out of Egypt with joy,
  his chosen ones with rejoicing.
44 He gave his people the lands of pagan nations,
  and they harvested crops that others had planted.
45 All this happened so they would follow his decrees
  and obey his instructions.

  Praise the LORD!

**Theme:** A song of national repentance as the people return from captivity. God patiently delivers us, in spite of our forgetfulness and self-willed rebellion.
**Author:** Anonymous

# 106
1 Praise the LORD!
  Give thanks to the LORD, for he is good!
His faithful love endures forever.
2 Who can list the glorious miracles of the LORD?
  Who can ever praise him enough?
3 There is joy for those who deal justly with others
  and always do what is right.
4 Remember me, LORD, when you show favor to your people;
  come near and rescue me.
5 Let me share in the prosperity of your chosen ones.
  Let me rejoice in the joy of your people;
  let me praise you with those who are your heritage.
6 Like our ancestors, we have sinned.
  We have done wrong! We have acted wickedly!

Cross references:
105:32 Exod 9:23
105:36 Exod 12:29-30
105:37 Exod 12:33
105:39 Neh 9:12; Isa 4:5
105:40 Num 11:31; John 6:31
105:41 Exod 17:6; Ps 78:15; 1 Cor 10:4
105:43 Exod 15:1
105:44 Josh 13:7
105:45 Deut 4:40
106:1 1 Chr 16:34, 41; Pss 100:4-5; 105:1
106:3 Ps 15:2
106:4 Ps 44:3
106:5 Pss 1:3; 105:3; 118:15
106:6 2 Chr 30:7; Ezra 9:7; Neh 1:7; Zech 1:4

---

**105:45** God's purpose for saving the Israelites was that they would "follow his decrees and obey his instructions." Too often we use our lives and freedom to please ourselves, but we should honor God. That is God's purpose for our lives and why he gave us his Word.

**106:1ff** While Psalm 105 is a summary of God's faithfulness, Psalm 106 is a summary of humanity's sinfulness. Psalm 105 covers events up to the exodus from Egypt (Exodus 5–14), and

Psalm 106 covers events from the Exodus up to what appears to be the Babylonian captivity (2 Kings 25).

**106:2** If we ever stopped to list all the mighty acts or miracles in the Bible, we would be astounded. They cover every aspect of life. The more we think about what God has done, the more we can appreciate the miracles he has done for us individually—birth, personal development, salvation, specific guidance, healing, loving friends and family—the list goes on and on. If you think you have never seen a miracle, look closer. You will see God's power and loving intervention on your behalf. God still performs great miracles!

**106:7**
Judg 3:7

7 Our ancestors in Egypt
were not impressed by the LORD's miraculous deeds.
They soon forgot his many acts of kindness to them.
Instead, they rebelled against him at the Red Sea.*

**106:8**
Ezek 20:9

8 Even so, he saved them—
to defend the honor of his name
and to demonstrate his mighty power.

**106:9**
Exod 14:21
Isa 63:11-13

9 He commanded the Red Sea* to dry up.
He led Israel across the sea as if it were a desert.
10 So he rescued them from their enemies
and redeemed them from their foes.

**106:11**
Exod 15:5

11 Then the water returned and covered their enemies;
not one of them survived.
12 Then his people believed his promises.
Then they sang his praise.

13 Yet how quickly they forgot what he had done!
They wouldn't wait for his counsel!

**106:14**
Num 11:4

14 In the wilderness their desires ran wild,
testing God's patience in that dry wasteland.

**106:15**
Ps 78:29-31

15 So he gave them what they asked for,
but he sent a plague along with it.

**106:16**
Num 16:1-3

16 The people in the camp were jealous of Moses
and envious of Aaron, the LORD's holy priest.

**106:17**
Deut 11:6

17 Because of this, the earth opened up;
it swallowed Dathan
and buried Abiram and the other rebels.

**106:18**
Num 16:35

18 Fire fell upon their followers;
a flame consumed the wicked.

**106:19**
Acts 7:41

19 The people made a calf at Mount Sinai*;
they bowed before an image made of gold.

**106:20**
Jer 2:11
Rom 1:23

20 They traded their glorious God
for a statue of a grass-eating bull.

**106:21**
Deut 10:21

21 They forgot God, their savior,
who had done such great things in Egypt—

**106:22**
Ps 105:27

22 such wonderful things in the land of Ham,
such awesome deeds at the Red Sea.

**106:23**
Exod 32:10-14

23 So he declared he would destroy them.
But Moses, his chosen one, stepped between the LORD and the people.
He begged him to turn from his anger and not destroy them.

**106:24**
Jer 3:19

24 The people refused to enter the pleasant land,
for they wouldn't believe his promise to care for them.
25 Instead, they grumbled in their tents
and refused to obey the LORD.

**106:26**
Heb 3:11

26 Therefore, he solemnly swore
that he would kill them in the wilderness,
27 that he would scatter their descendants among the nations,
exiling them to distant lands.

**106:7** Hebrew *at the sea, the sea of reeds.*   **106:9** Hebrew *sea of reeds;* also in 106:22.   **106:19** Hebrew *at Horeb,* another name for Sinai.

---

**106:13-15** In the wilderness, the Israelites were so intent on getting the food and water *they* wanted that they became blind to what God wanted. They were more concerned about immediate physical gratification than lasting spiritual satisfaction. They did not want what was best for them, and they refused to trust in God's care and provision (Numbers 11:18-33). If you complain enough, God may give you what you ask for, even if it is not the best for you. If you're not getting what you want, perhaps

God knows it is not in your best interest. Trust in his care and provision.

**106:23** Moses served as the people's intercessor. This refers to the time when the Lord wanted to destroy the people for worshiping the gold calf (Exodus 32:7-14).

28 Then our ancestors joined in the worship of Baal at Peor;
    they even ate sacrifices offered to the dead!

106:28
Hos 9:10

29 They angered the LORD with all these things,
    so a plague broke out among them.

30 But Phinehas had the courage to intervene,
    and the plague was stopped.

106:30
Num 25:7-13

31 So he has been regarded as a righteous man
    ever since that time.

32 At Meribah, too, they angered the LORD,
    causing Moses serious trouble.

106:32
Ps 78:40

33 They made Moses angry,*
    and he spoke foolishly.

34 Israel failed to destroy the nations in the land,
    as the LORD had commanded them.

106:34
Judg 1:21, 27-36

35 Instead, they mingled among the pagans
    and adopted their evil customs.

36 They worshiped their idols,
    which led to their downfall.

37 They even sacrificed their sons
    and their daughters to the demons.

106:37
2 Kgs 17:17

38 They shed innocent blood,
    the blood of their sons and daughters.
  By sacrificing them to the idols of Canaan,
    they polluted the land with murder.

39 They defiled themselves by their evil deeds,
    and their love of idols was adultery in the LORD's sight.

106:39
Hos 4:12

40 That is why the LORD's anger burned against his people,
    and he abhorred his own special possession.

106:40
Judg 2:12-14

41 He handed them over to pagan nations,
    and they were ruled by those who hated them.

106:41
Neh 9:27

42 Their enemies crushed them
    and brought them under their cruel power.

43 Again and again he rescued them,
    but they chose to rebel against him,
    and they were finally destroyed by their sin.

106:43
Judg 6:6
Ps 81:12

44 Even so, he pitied them in their distress
    and listened to their cries.

45 He remembered his covenant with them
    and relented because of his unfailing love.

106:45
Lev 26:42

46 He even caused their captors
    to treat them with kindness.

106:46
2 Chr 30:9
Ezra 9:9

47 Save us, O LORD our God!
    Gather us back from among the nations,
  so we can thank your holy name
    and rejoice and praise you.

106:47-48
//1 Chr 16:34-36

**106:33** Hebrew *They embittered his spirit.*

---

**106:34-39** Israel constantly turned away from God. How could they turn from God and worship the idols of the land after the great miracles they saw? We also have seen God's great miracles but sometimes find ourselves enticed by the world's gods: power, money, convenience, fame, sex, and pleasure. As Israel forgot God, so we are susceptible to forgetting him and giving in to the pressures of an evil world. Remember all that God has done for you so that you won't be drawn away from him by the world's pleasures.

**106:40-42** God allowed trouble to come to the Israelites in order to help them. Our troubles can be helpful because they (1) humble

us, (2) wean us from the allurements of the world and drive us back to God, (3) vitalize our prayers, (4) allow us to experience more of God's faithfulness, (5) make us more dependent upon God, (6) encourage us to submit to God's purpose for our lives, and (7) make us more compassionate toward others in trouble.

**106:44-46** This is a beautiful picture of God's great love for his people who deserved only judgment. Fortunately, God's compassion and mercy toward us are not limited by our faithfulness to him. God was merciful to us in sending his Son to die for our sins. If he did this while we were captive to sin, how much more merciful will he be now that we are his children?

48 Praise the Lord, the God of Israel,
    who lives from everlasting to everlasting!
Let all the people say, "Amen!"

Praise the Lord!

## BOOK FIVE    Psalms 107:1—150:6

These psalms praise God's works, recount the blessing of righteous living, thank God for deliverance, and praise God for his wonderful word. These psalms remind us that the best sacrifice we can offer to God is a faithful and obedient life.

**Theme:** Thankfulness to God should constantly be on the lips of those whom he has saved. This psalm was written to celebrate the Jews' return from their exile in Babylon.
**Author:** Anonymous

**107:1**
Ps 106:1

**107:2**
Isa 35:9-10

**107:3**
Neh 1:9
Ps 106:47
Ezek 20:34

**107:4**
Josh 5:6

**107:7**
Jer 31:9

**107:9**
Matt 5:6
Luke 1:53

**107:10**
Mic 7:8
Luke 1:79

**107:11**
Num 15:31

**107:14**
Ps 116:16
Acts 12:7

# 107

1 Give thanks to the Lord, for he is good!
    His faithful love endures forever.
2 Has the Lord redeemed you? Then speak out!
    Tell others he has redeemed you from your enemies.
3 For he has gathered the exiles from many lands,
    from east and west,
    from north and south.

4 Some wandered in the wilderness,
    lost and homeless.
5 Hungry and thirsty,
    they nearly died.
6 "Lord, help!" they cried in their trouble,
    and he rescued them from their distress.
7 He led them straight to safety,
    to a city where they could live.
8 Let them praise the Lord for his great love
    and for the wonderful things he has done for them.
9 For he satisfies the thirsty
    and fills the hungry with good things.

10 Some sat in darkness and deepest gloom,
    imprisoned in iron chains of misery.
11 They rebelled against the words of God,
    scorning the counsel of the Most High.
12 That is why he broke them with hard labor;
    they fell, and no one was there to help them.
13 "Lord, help!" they cried in their trouble,
    and he saved them from their distress.
14 He led them from the darkness and deepest gloom;
    he snapped their chains.
15 Let them praise the Lord for his great love
    and for the wonderful things he has done for them.

**107:1ff** This psalm speaks of four different types of people in distress and how God rescues them: wanderers (107:4-9), prisoners (107:10-16), the distressed (107:17-20), and the storm-tossed (107:23-30). No matter how extreme our calamity, God is able to help us. He is loving and kind to those who are distressed.

**107:1, 2** "Has the Lord redeemed you? Then speak out!" God has done so much for us, and we have so much for which to thank him (see Psalm 103). He wants us to tell everyone all that he has done. These verses are not so much a mandate to witness as a declaration that when we live in God's presence, we will not be able to keep this glorious experience to ourselves (see also Acts 1:8; 2 Corinthians 5:18-20). What has God done for you? Is there someone you can tell?

**107:4-9** Lost, hungry, thirsty, and exhausted, these wanderers typify the Israelites in exile. But they also typify anyone who has not

found the satisfaction that comes from knowing God. Anyone who recognizes his or her own lostness can receive the offer of Jesus to satisfy these needs. Jesus is the way (John 14:6), the bread from heaven (John 6:33, 35), the living water (John 4:10-14), and the giver of rest (Matthew 11:28-30). Have you received his life-giving offer?

**107:10-16** Do you know anyone who is in prison? Most people think that those in prison deserve whatever misery they experience as punishment for their crimes. But God loves all men and women no matter how far they have fallen. He wants to reach them with his love and dispel the gloom they face (Matthew 25:34-46). Throughout the world, people are imprisoned for their faith; others suffer as victims of injustice. Can you reach out to them? Pray for those in prison. Pray for ministries and Christian chaplains who take God's message of love and forgiveness to prisoners. What can you do to support these efforts?

16 For he broke down their prison gates of bronze;
    he cut apart their bars of iron.

17 Some were fools; they rebelled
    and suffered for their sins.
18 They couldn't stand the thought of food,
    and they were knocking on death's door.
19 "LORD, help!" they cried in their trouble,
    and he saved them from their distress.
20 He sent out his word and healed them,
    snatching them from the door of death.
21 Let them praise the LORD for his great love
    and for the wonderful things he has done for them.
22 Let them offer sacrifices of thanksgiving
    and sing joyfully about his glorious acts.

23 Some went off to sea in ships,
    plying the trade routes of the world.
24 They, too, observed the LORD's power in action,
    his impressive works on the deepest seas.
25 He spoke, and the winds rose,
    stirring up the waves.
26 Their ships were tossed to the heavens
    and plunged again to the depths;
    the sailors cringed in terror.
27 They reeled and staggered like drunkards
    and were at their wits' end.
28 "LORD, help!" they cried in their trouble,
    and he saved them from their distress.
29 He calmed the storm to a whisper
    and stilled the waves.
30 What a blessing was that stillness
    as he brought them safely into harbor!
31 Let them praise the LORD for his great love
    and for the wonderful things he has done for them.
32 Let them exalt him publicly before the congregation
    and before the leaders of the nation.

33 He changes rivers into deserts,
    and springs of water into dry, thirsty land.
34 He turns the fruitful land into salty wastelands,
    because of the wickedness of those who live there.
35 But he also turns deserts into pools of water,
    the dry land into springs of water.
36 He brings the hungry to settle there
    and to build their cities.
37 They sow their fields, plant their vineyards,
    and harvest their bumper crops.
38 How he blesses them!
    They raise large families there,
    and their herds of livestock increase.

**Cross-references:**

107:16 Isa 45:1-2

107:17 Isa 65:6-7; Ezek 24:23

107:18 Job 33:19-22; Pss 9:13; 88:3

107:20 2 Kgs 20:5; Matt 8:8

107:22 Lev 7:12; Pss 9:11; 50:14; 73:28; 118:17

107:25 Ps 93:3-4

107:29 Matt 8:26; Luke 8:24

107:32 Ps 22:22, 25; Isa 25:1

107:34 Gen 19:24-25

107:35 Isa 35:6-7; 41:18

107:37 2 Kgs 19:29; Amos 9:14

107:38 Gen 12:2; Exod 1:7

---

**107:17-20** Fools and rebels surely bring trouble upon themselves. This psalm offers hope for those who have made a mess of their lives. By receiving God's free gift of forgiveness (Micah 7:18-20; 1 John 1:9), anyone can begin a new life and break with the past (see Romans 3:23-26; 2 Corinthians 5:17). By faith in Christ, we can break addictions, heal memories, and restore broken relationships. If we ask Christ to take control of our lives, he will answer us. His love reaches even those who have rebelled against him.

**107:32** Those who have never truly suffered may not appreciate God as much as those who have matured under hardship. Those who have seen God work in times of distress have a deeper insight into his loving-kindness. If you have experienced great trials, you have the potential for great praise.

39 When they decrease in number and become impoverished
  through oppression, trouble, and sorrow,
40 the LORD pours contempt on their princes,
  causing them to wander in trackless wastelands.

107:42
Job 22:19
Ps 52:6
Rom 3:19

41 But he rescues the poor from trouble
  and increases their families like flocks of sheep.
42 The godly will see these things and be glad,
  while the wicked are struck silent.

107:43
Ps 64:9
Jer 9:12
Hos 14:9

43 Those who are wise will take all this to heart;
  they will see in our history the faithful love of the LORD.

**Theme:** Victory in God's strength. With God's help, we can do more than we think.
**Author:** David

# 108 *A song. A psalm of David.*

108:1-5
//Ps 57:7-11

1 My heart is confident in you, O God;
  no wonder I can sing your praises with all my heart!
2 Wake up, lyre and harp!
  I will wake the dawn with my song.
3 I will thank you, LORD, among all the people.
  I will sing your praises among the nations.

108:4
Ps 113:4

4 For your unfailing love is higher than the heavens.
  Your faithfulness reaches to the clouds.
5 Be exalted, O God, above the highest heavens.
  May your glory shine over all the earth.

108:6-13
//Ps 60:5-12

6 Now rescue your beloved people.
  Answer and save us by your power.
7 God has promised this by his holiness*:
  "I will divide up Shechem with joy.
  I will measure out the valley of Succoth.
8 Gilead is mine,
  and Manasseh, too.
  Ephraim, my helmet, will produce my warriors,
  and Judah, my scepter, will produce my kings.
9 But Moab, my washbasin, will become my servant,
  and I will wipe my feet on Edom
  and shout in triumph over Philistia."

10 Who will bring me into the fortified city?
  Who will bring me victory over Edom?

108:11
Ps 44:9

11 Have you rejected us, O God?
  Will you no longer march with our armies?
12 Oh, please help us against our enemies,
  for all human help is useless.
13 With God's help we will do mighty things,
  for he will trample down our foes.

**108:7** Or *in his sanctuary.*

---

**108:1ff** The conclusions from two previous psalms have been put together to make this psalm. The first five verses are quoted from Psalm 57:7-11, and the next eight verses (108:6-13) are from Psalm 60:5-12.

**108:9** Moab, Edom, and Philistia were Israel's enemies to the east, south, and west, respectively. They despised the Israelites and Israel's God.

**108:13** Do our prayers end with requests for help to make it through stressful situations? David prayed not merely for rescue, but for victory. With God's help we can claim more than mere survival, we can claim victory! Look for ways God can use your distress as an opportunity to show his mighty power.

**Theme:** Righteous indignation against liars and slanderers. We can tell God our true feelings and desires.
**Author:** David

# 109
*For the choir director: A psalm of David.*

1 O God, whom I praise,
    don't stand silent and aloof
2 while the wicked slander me
    and tell lies about me.
3 They surround me with hateful words
    and fight against me for no reason.
4 I love them, but they try to destroy me with accusations
    even as I am praying for them!
5 They repay evil for good,
    and hatred for my love.

6 They say,* "Get an evil person to turn against him.
    Send an accuser to bring him to trial.
7 When his case comes up for judgment,
    let him be pronounced guilty.
    Count his prayers as sins.
8 Let his years be few;
    let someone else take his position.
9 May his children become fatherless,
    and his wife a widow.
10 May his children wander as beggars
    and be driven from their ruined homes.
11 May creditors seize his entire estate,
    and strangers take all he has earned.
12 Let no one be kind to him;
    let no one pity his fatherless children.
13 May all his offspring die.
    May his family name be blotted out in a single generation.
14 May the LORD never forget the sins of his fathers;
    may his mother's sins never be erased from the record.
15 May the LORD always remember these sins,
    and may his name disappear from human memory.
16 For he refused all kindness to others;
    he persecuted the poor and needy,
    and he hounded the brokenhearted to death.
17 He loved to curse others;
    now you curse him.
    He never blessed others;
    now don't you bless him.
18 Cursing is as natural to him as his clothing,
    or the water he drinks,
    or the rich food he eats.
19 Now may his curses return and cling to him like clothing;
    may they be tied around him like a belt."

**109:1** Ps 83:1
**109:2** Pss 52:4; 120:2
**109:3** Ps 69:4
**109:4** Ps 38:20
**109:5** John 7:7
**109:6** Zech 3:1
**109:7** Prov 28:9
**109:8** †Acts 1:20
**109:9** Exod 22:24
**109:11** Isa 1:7
**109:12** Isa 9:17
**109:14** Neh 4:5; Isa 65:6-7
**109:15** Jer 16:17
**109:16** Ps 37:32
**109:17** Matt 7:2
**109:18** Ps 73:6
**109:19** Ezek 7:27

**109:6** Hebrew lacks *They say.*

**109:1ff** David endured many false accusations (1 Samuel 22:7-13; 2 Samuel 15:3, 4), as did Christ centuries later (Matthew 26:59-61; 27:39-44). Verse 8 is quoted in Acts 1:20 as being fulfilled in Judas's death.

**109:4** David was angry at being attacked by evil people who slandered him and lied. Yet David remained a friend and a man of prayer. While we must hate evil and work to overcome it, we must love everyone, including those who do evil, because God loves them. We are called to hate the sin, but love the person. Only through God's strength will we be able to follow David's example.

**109:6-20** This is another of the imprecatory psalms, a call for God to judge the wicked. (For an explanation of imprecatory psalms, see the note on 35:1ff.) David was not taking vengeance into his own hands; he was asking that God be swift in his promised judgment of evil people. David's words depict the eventual doom of all God's enemies.

**109:20**
Isa 3:11
2 Tim 4:14

20 May those curses become the LORD's punishment
    for my accusers who speak evil of me.

**109:21**
Ps 25:11
Ezek 36:22

21 But deal well with me, O Sovereign LORD,
    for the sake of your own reputation!
Rescue me
    because you are so faithful and good.

**109:22**
Ps 40:17
Prov 18:14

22 For I am poor and needy,
    and my heart is full of pain.

23 I am fading like a shadow at dusk;
    I am brushed off like a locust.

**109:24**
Heb 12:12

24 My knees are weak from fasting,
    and I am skin and bones.

25 I am a joke to people everywhere;
    when they see me, they shake their heads in scorn.

**109:26**
Ps 119:86

26 Help me, O LORD my God!
    Save me because of your unfailing love.

27 Let them see that this is your doing,
    that you yourself have done it, LORD.

**109:28**
2 Sam 16:11-12

28 Then let them curse me if they like,
    but you will bless me!
When they attack me, they will be disgraced!
    But I, your servant, will go right on rejoicing!

**109:29**
Job 8:22
Ps 35:26

29 May my accusers be clothed with disgrace;
    may their humiliation cover them like a cloak.

**109:30**
Ps 35:18

30 But I will give repeated thanks to the LORD,
    praising him to everyone.

**109:31**
Pss 16:8; 37:33

31 For he stands beside the needy,
    ready to save them from those who condemn them.

**Theme:** The credentials for the Messiah. Jesus is the Messiah.
**Author:** David

# 110 *A psalm of David.*

**110:1**
†Matt 22:44
†Mark 12:36; 14:62
†Luke 20:42
†Acts 2:34
†Heb 1:13

1 The LORD said to my Lord,
    "Sit in the place of honor at my right hand
until I humble your enemies,
    making them a footstool under your feet."

**110:2**
Ps 45:6
Dan 7:13-14

2 The LORD will extend your powerful kingdom from Jerusalem*;
    you will rule over your enemies.

**110:3**
Judg 5:2
Ps 96:9

3 When you go to war,
    your people will serve you willingly.
You are arrayed in holy garments,
    and your strength will be renewed each day like the morning dew.

**110:4**
†Heb 5:6; 7:21, 17

4 The LORD has taken an oath and will not break his vow:
    "You are a priest forever in the order of Melchizedek."

**110:2** Hebrew *Zion.*

---

**110:1ff** This is one of the most-quoted psalms in the New Testament because of its clear references to the Messiah. In Matthew 22:41-45, Jesus recited the words of this verse and applied them to himself. Verses 1 and 6 look forward to Christ's final and total destruction of the wicked (Revelation 6—9); 110:2 prophesies Christ's reign on the earth (Revelation 20:1-7); 110:3, 4 tell of Christ's priestly work for his people (Hebrews 5—8); and 110:5, 6 look forward to the final battle on earth when Christ will overcome the forces of evil (Revelation 19:11-21).

**110:1-7** Many people have a vague belief in God but refuse to accept Jesus as anything more than a great human teacher. But the Bible does not allow that option. Both the Old and New

Testaments proclaim the deity of the one who came to save and to reign. Jesus explained that this psalm spoke of the Messiah as greater than David, Israel's greatest king (Mark 12:35-37). Peter used this psalm to show that Jesus, the Messiah, sits at God's right hand and is Lord over all (Acts 2:32-35). You can't straddle the fence, calling Jesus "just a good teacher," because the Bible clearly calls him Lord.

**110:4** For more about Melchizedek, see his Profile in Genesis 15, p. 29. As a priest like Melchizedek, Christ will never abuse his divine position, and his reign will be forever. Jesus is more fully described as our High Priest in Hebrews 5.

5 The Lord stands at your right hand to protect you.
  He will strike down many kings when his anger erupts.
6 He will punish the nations
  and fill their lands with corpses;
  he will shatter heads over the whole earth.
7 But he himself will be refreshed from brooks along the way.
  He will be victorious.

**Theme:** All that God does is good. Reverence for God is the beginning of wisdom.
**Author:** Anonymous

# 111
\* 1 Praise the LORD!

  I will thank the LORD with all my heart
  as I meet with his godly people.
2 How amazing are the deeds of the LORD!
  All who delight in him should ponder them.
3 Everything he does reveals his glory and majesty.
  His righteousness never fails.
4 He causes us to remember his wonderful works.
  How gracious and merciful is our LORD!
5 He gives food to those who fear him;
  he always remembers his covenant.
6 He has shown his great power to his people
  by giving them the lands of other nations.
7 All he does is just and good,
  and all his commandments are trustworthy.
8 They are forever true,
  to be obeyed faithfully and with integrity.
9 He has paid a full ransom for his people.
  He has guaranteed his covenant with them forever.
  What a holy, awe-inspiring name he has!
10 Fear of the LORD is the foundation of true wisdom.
  All who obey his commandments will grow in wisdom.

  Praise him forever!

**Theme:** The advantages of having faith in God. God guards the minds and actions
of those who follow his commands.
**Author:** Anonymous

# 112
\* 1 Praise the LORD!

  How joyful are those who fear the LORD
  and delight in obeying his commands.
2 Their children will be successful everywhere;
  an entire generation of godly people will be blessed.
3 They themselves will be wealthy,
  and their good deeds will last forever.

| |
|---|
| **110:5** |
| Pss 2:5, 12; 16:8 |
| Rom 2:5 |
| Rev 6:17 |
| **111:1** |
| Ps 138:1 |
| **111:2** |
| Ps 92:5 |
| **111:3** |
| Pss 96:6; 145:5 |
| **111:4** |
| Pss 86:15; 103:8 |
| **111:5** |
| Matt 6:31-33 |
| **111:7** |
| Ps 19:7-9 |
| Rev 15:3-4 |
| **111:8** |
| Isa 40:8 |
| Matt 5:18 |
| **111:9** |
| Ps 99:3 |
| Luke 1:68 |
| **111:10** |
| Prov 1:7, 9; 3:4-5; 9:10 |
| **112:1** |
| Ps 119:16 |
| **112:2** |
| Ps 25:13 |
| **112:3** |
| Prov 3:16-17; 8:18 |

111 This psalm is a Hebrew acrostic poem; after the introductory note of praise, each line begins with a successive letter of the Hebrew alphabet.   112 This psalm is a Hebrew acrostic poem; after the introductory note of praise, each line begins with a successive letter of the Hebrew alphabet.

**111–118** Psalms 111–118 are called hallelujah psalms. *Hallelu-jah* means "praise the LORD" and expresses the uplifting and optimistic tone of these songs.

**111:9** The ransom here pictures the rescue by God of the Israelites from Egypt and the future return from captivity in Babylon (see Deuteronomy 7:8; Jeremiah 31:11). *Ransom* means "to free from captivity by paying a price." All people were being held in slavery by sin until Jesus paid the price to free us—giving his life as a perfect sacrifice. Before Jesus offered himself as a sacrifice for sin, people were not permitted into God's presence (the Most

Holy Place); now, all believers can freely approach God's throne through prayer and have God in their lives through the Holy Spirit.

**111:10** The only way to become truly wise is to fear (revere) God. This same thought is expressed in Proverbs 1:7-9. Too often people want to skip this step, thinking they can become wise by life experience and academic knowledge alone. But if we do not acknowledge God as the source of wisdom, then our foundation for making wise decisions is shaky and we are prone to mistakes and foolish choices.

**112:1** Many blessings are available to us—honor, prosperity, security, freedom from fear (112:2-9)—if we *fear* the Lord and

112:4
Job 11:17
Ps 97:11

112:5
Ps 37:21, 26

112:6
Pss 15:5; 55:22

112:7
Ps 56:4

112:8
Ps 56:10-11

112:9
Ps 148:14
†2 Cor 9:9

112:10
Matt 8:12
Luke 13:28

⁴ Light shines in the darkness for the godly.
　　They are generous, compassionate, and righteous.
⁵ Good comes to those who lend money generously
　　and conduct their business fairly.
⁶ Such people will not be overcome by evil.
　　Those who are righteous will be long remembered.
⁷ They do not fear bad news;
　　they confidently trust the LORD to care for them.
⁸ They are confident and fearless
　　and can face their foes triumphantly.
⁹ They share freely and give generously to those in need.
　　Their good deeds will be remembered forever.
　　They will have influence and honor.
¹⁰ The wicked will see this and be infuriated.
　　They will grind their teeth in anger;
　　they will slink away, their hopes thwarted.

**Theme:** The scope of God's care. God's great mercy is demonstrated by his concern for the poor and the oppressed.
**Author:** Anonymous

113:1
Ps 135:1

# 113

¹ Praise the LORD!
　　Yes, give praise, O servants of the LORD.
　　Praise the name of the LORD!

113:2
Dan 2:20

113:3
Ps 50:1

113:4
Pss 8:1; 97:9; 99:2

113:5
Pss 89:6; 103:19

113:6
Ps 11:4
Isa 57:15

113:7
1 Sam 2:8

113:8
Job 36:7

113:9
1 Sam 2:5
Ps 68:6
Isa 54:1

² Blessed be the name of the LORD
　　now and forever.
³ Everywhere—from east to west—
　　praise the name of the LORD.
⁴ For the LORD is high above the nations;
　　his glory is higher than the heavens.

⁵ Who can be compared with the LORD our God,
　　who is enthroned on high?
⁶ He stoops to look down
　　on heaven and on earth.
⁷ He lifts the poor from the dust
　　and the needy from the garbage dump.
⁸ He sets them among princes,
　　even the princes of his own people!
⁹ He gives the childless woman a family,
　　making her a happy mother.

　　Praise the LORD!

**Theme:** The mighty God who delivered Israel from Egypt. We can celebrate God's great work in our life.
**Author:** Anonymous

114:1
Exod 13:3

# 114

¹ When the Israelites escaped from Egypt—
　　when the family of Jacob left that foreign land—

---

*delight* in obeying his commands. If you expect God's blessings, you must revere him and gladly obey him.

**112:5** Generosity can cure two problems that having money can create. The rich person may abuse others in the desire to accumulate wealth. Generosity will eliminate that abuse. Also, the fear of losing money can be a snare. Generosity shows that we have placed our trust in God, not in our money, for justice and security.

**112:7, 8** We all want to live without fear; our heroes are fearless people who take on all dangers and overcome them. The writer teaches us that *fear* of God can lead to a *fearless* life. To fear God means to respect and revere him as the almighty Lord. When we

trust God completely to take care of us, we will find that our other fears—even of death itself—will subside.

**113:5-9** In God's eyes, a person's value has no relationship to his or her wealth or position on the social ladder. Many people who have excelled in God's work began in poverty or humble beginnings. God supersedes the social orders of this world, often choosing his future leaders and ambassadors from among social outcasts. Do you treat the unwanted in society as though they have value? Demonstrate by your actions that all people are valuable and useful in God's eyes.

2 the land of Judah became God's sanctuary,
    and Israel became his kingdom.

3 The Red Sea* saw them coming and hurried out of their way!
    The water of the Jordan River turned away.

4 The mountains skipped like rams,
    the hills like lambs!

5 What's wrong, Red Sea, that made you hurry out of their way?
    What happened, Jordan River, that you turned away?

6 Why, mountains, did you skip like rams?
    Why, hills, like lambs?

7 Tremble, O earth, at the presence of the Lord,
    at the presence of the God of Jacob.

8 He turned the rock into a pool of water;
    yes, a spring of water flowed from solid rock.

**Theme:** God is alive. He is thinking about us and caring for us, and we should put him first in our life.
**Author:** Anonymous

# 115

1 Not to us, O LORD, not to us,
    but to your name goes all the glory
for your unfailing love and faithfulness.

2 Why let the nations say,
    "Where is their God?"

3 Our God is in the heavens,
    and he does as he wishes.

4 Their idols are merely things of silver and gold,
    shaped by human hands.

5 They have mouths but cannot speak,
    and eyes but cannot see.

6 They have ears but cannot hear,
    and noses but cannot smell.

7 They have hands but cannot feel,
    and feet but cannot walk,
    and throats but cannot make a sound.

8 And those who make idols are just like them,
    as are all who trust in them.

9 O Israel, trust the LORD!
    He is your helper and your shield.

10 O priests, descendants of Aaron, trust the LORD!
    He is your helper and your shield.

11 All you who fear the LORD, trust the LORD!
    He is your helper and your shield.

114:3 Hebrew *the sea*; also in 114:5.

**Cross-references (right margin):**

114:2 Exod 19:6; 29:45-46; Ps 78:68-69
114:3 Exod 14:21; Josh 3:13-14, 16
114:4 Ps 29:5-6; Hab 3:6
114:5 Hab 3:8
114:7 Ps 96:9
114:8 Exod 17:5-6; Deut 8:15
115:1 Ps 29:2; Isa 48:11; Ezek 36:22, 32
115:2 Pss 42:3; 79:10
115:3 Pss 103:19; 135:6; Dan 4:35
115:4-11 //Ps 135:15-20
115:5 Jer 10:5
115:8 Ps 135:18
115:9 Pss 33:20; 62:8
115:11 Pss 103:11; 135:20

---

**114:7** When God gave the law at Mount Sinai, the mountain trembled in God's presence. Even with our great technology, the seas, rivers, and mountains still present us with formidable challenges. But to God, who controls nature, they are as nothing. When observing the power of an ocean wave or the majesty of a mountain peak, think of God's greatness and glory, which are far more awesome than the natural wonders you can see. To tremble at God's presence means to recognize God's complete power and authority and our frailty by comparison.

**115–118** Psalms 115–118 were traditionally sung at the Passover meal, commemorating Israel's escape from slavery in Egypt (Exodus 11–12).

**115:1** The writer asked that God's name, not the nation's, be glorified. Too often we ask God to glorify his name *with* ours. For example, we may pray for help to do a good job so that our work will be noticed. Or we may ask that a presentation go well so we will get applause. There is nothing wrong with looking good or impressing others; the problem comes when we want to look good no matter what happens to God's reputation in the process. Before you pray, ask yourself, Who will get the credit if God answers my prayer?

**115:4-8** When the psalms were written, many people worshiped idols—statues of wood, stone, or metal. They took pride in what they could see and had contempt for what they couldn't see. Today, we still may value tangible objects (home, clothing, possessions) rather than intangible realities (spiritual growth, salvation, giving to those in need, spending time with loved ones). Those who spend their time obtaining tangible objects are as foolish and empty as the idols themselves. (For more on the foolishness of idols, see Isaiah 44:9-20.)

**115:12**
Ps 98:3

12 The LORD remembers us and will bless us.
   He will bless the people of Israel
      and bless the priests, the descendants of Aaron.

**115:13**
Ps 128:1, 4

13 He will bless those who fear the LORD,
      both great and lowly.

**115:14**
Deut 1:11

14 May the LORD richly bless
      both you and your children.

**115:15**
Gen 1:1; 14:19

15 May you be blessed by the LORD,
      who made heaven and earth.

**115:16**
Pss 8:6; 89:11

16 The heavens belong to the LORD,
      but he has given the earth to all humanity.

**115:17**
Pss 6:5; 31:17

17 The dead cannot sing praises to the LORD,
      for they have gone into the silence of the grave.

**115:18**
Ps 113:2

18 But we can praise the LORD
      both now and forever!

   Praise the LORD!

**Theme:** Praise for being saved from certain death. Worship is a thankful response and not a repayment for what God has done.
**Author:** Anonymous

**116:1**
Pss 18:1; 66:19

# 116

1 I love the LORD because he hears my voice
      and my prayer for mercy.

**116:2**
Pss 17:6; 31:2

2 Because he bends down to listen,
      I will pray as long as I have breath!

**116:3**
Ps 18:4-6

3 Death wrapped its ropes around me;
      the terrors of the grave* overtook me.
   I saw only trouble and sorrow.

**116:4**
Pss 22:20; 118:5

4 Then I called on the name of the LORD:
      "Please, LORD, save me!"

**116:5**
Exod 34:6

5 How kind the LORD is! How good he is!
      So merciful, this God of ours!

**116:6**
Ps 142:6

6 The LORD protects those of childlike faith;
      I was facing death, and he saved me.

**116:7**
Ps 13:6
Matt 11:29

7 Let my soul be at rest again,
      for the LORD has been good to me.

**116:8**
Pss 49:15; 56:13

8 He has saved me from death,
      my eyes from tears,
      my feet from stumbling.

9 And so I walk in the LORD's presence
      as I live here on earth!

**116:10**
†2 Cor 4:13

10 I believed in you, so I said,
      "I am deeply troubled, LORD."

11 In my anxiety I cried out to you,
      "These people are all liars!"

**116:12**
2 Chr 32:25
1 Thes 3:9

12 What can I offer the LORD
      for all he has done for me?

13 I will lift up the cup of salvation
      and praise the LORD's name for saving me.

**116:14**
Pss 22:25; 50:14

14 I will keep my promises to the LORD
      in the presence of all his people.

**116:3** Hebrew *of Sheol.*

---

**115:12** "The LORD remembers us," says the psalm writer. What a fantastic truth! There are many times when we feel isolated, alone, and abandoned, even by God. In reality, he sees, understands, and thinks about us. When depressed by problems or struggling with self-worth, be encouraged that God keeps you in his thoughts. If he thinks about you, surely his help is near.

**116:1, 2** God is so responsive that you can always reach him. He bends down and listens to your voice. This writer's love for the Lord had grown because he had experienced answers to his prayers. If you are discouraged, remember that God is near, listening carefully to every prayer and answering each one in order to give you his best.

15 The LORD cares deeply
   when his loved ones die.
16 O LORD, I am your servant;
   yes, I am your servant, born into your household;
   you have freed me from my chains.
17 I will offer you a sacrifice of thanksgiving
   and call on the name of the LORD.
18 I will fulfill my vows to the LORD
   in the presence of all his people—
19 in the house of the LORD
   in the heart of Jerusalem.

   Praise the LORD!

**Theme:** Another reason for praise—God's love for the whole world. We should praise God for his unlimited love.
**Author:** Anonymous

# 117

1 Praise the LORD, all you nations.
   Praise him, all you people of the earth.
2 For he loves us with unfailing love;
   the LORD's faithfulness endures forever.

   Praise the LORD!

**Theme:** Confidence in God's eternal love. God's love is unchanging in the midst of changing situations. This gives us security.
**Author:** Anonymous

# 118

1 Give thanks to the LORD, for he is good!
   His faithful love endures forever.

2 Let all Israel repeat:
   "His faithful love endures forever."
3 Let Aaron's descendants, the priests, repeat:
   "His faithful love endures forever."
4 Let all who fear the LORD repeat:
   "His faithful love endures forever."

5 In my distress I prayed to the LORD,
   and the LORD answered me and set me free.
6 The LORD is for me, so I will have no fear.
   What can mere people do to me?
7 Yes, the LORD is for me; he will help me.
   I will look in triumph at those who hate me.
8 It is better to take refuge in the LORD
   than to trust in people.
9 It is better to take refuge in the LORD
   than to trust in princes.

10 Though hostile nations surrounded me,
   I destroyed them all with the authority of the LORD.

**116:15**
Ps 72:14

**117:1**
†Rom 15:11

**117:2**
Ps 100:5

**118:1**
Ps 136:1-26

**118:2**
Ps 115:9

**118:5**
Pss 18:19; 120:1

**118:6**
Job 19:27
†Heb 13:6

**118:7**
Ps 54:7

**118:8**
2 Chr 32:7-8
Isa 57:13

**118:10**
Ps 18:40

---

**116:15** God stays close to us even in death. When someone we love is nearing death, we may become angry and feel abandoned. But believers (the Lord's loved ones) are precious to God, and he carefully chooses the time when they will be called into his presence. Let this truth provide comfort when you've lost a loved one. God sees, and each life is valuable to him (see Jesus' statement in Matthew 10:29).

**117:1, 2** Not only is Psalm 117 the shortest chapter in the Bible, it is also the middle chapter. Paul quotes from this psalm in Romans 15:11 to show that God's salvation is for *all* people, not just the Jews.

**117:1, 2** Have you ever said, "I can't think of anything God has done for me. How can I praise him?" This psalm gives two reasons for praising God: his unfailing love toward us and his faithfulness that endures forever. If he did nothing else for us, he would still be worthy of our highest praise.

**118:8** Pilots put confidence in their planes. Commuters place confidence in trains, cars, or buses. Each day we must put our confidence in something or someone. If you are willing to trust a plane or car to get you to your destination, are you willing to trust God to guide you here on earth and to your eternal destination? Do you trust him more than any human being? How futile it is to trust anything or anyone more than God.

**118:12**
Deut 1:44

11 Yes, they surrounded and attacked me,
   but I destroyed them all with the authority of the LORD.
12 They swarmed around me like bees;
   they blazed against me like a crackling fire.
   But I destroyed them all with the authority of the LORD.
13 My enemies did their best to kill me,
   but the LORD rescued me.

**118:14**
Exod 15:2
Isa 12:2

14 The LORD is my strength and my song;
   he has given me victory.

**118:15**
Ps 89:13
Luke 1:51

15 Songs of joy and victory are sung in the camp of the godly.
   The strong right arm of the LORD has done glorious things!
16 The strong right arm of the LORD is raised in triumph.
   The strong right arm of the LORD has done glorious things!
17 I will not die; instead, I will live
   to tell what the LORD has done.

**118:18**
Jer 31:18
1 Cor 11:32
2 Cor 6:9

18 The LORD has punished me severely,
   but he did not let me die.

**118:19**
Isa 26:2

19 Open for me the gates where the righteous enter,
   and I will go in and thank the LORD.
20 These gates lead to the presence of the LORD,
   and the godly enter there.
21 I thank you for answering my prayer
   and giving me victory!

**118:22**
Matt 21:42
Mark 12:10-11
†Luke 20:17
†Acts 4:11
†1 Pet 2:7

22 The stone that the builders rejected
   has now become the cornerstone.
23 This is the LORD's doing,
   and it is wonderful to see.

**118:23**
†Matt 21:42
†Mark 12:11

24 This is the day the LORD has made.
   We will rejoice and be glad in it.
25 Please, LORD, please save us.
   Please, LORD, please give us success.

**118:26**
†Matt 21:9
†Mark 11:9
†Luke 13:35; 19:38
†John 12:13

26 Bless the one who comes in the name of the LORD.
   We bless you from the house of the LORD.
27 The LORD is God, shining upon us.
   Take the sacrifice and bind it with cords on the altar.

**118:27**
1 Pet 2:9

**118:28**
Exod 15:2
Isa 25:1

28 You are my God, and I will praise you!
   You are my God, and I will exalt you!
29 Give thanks to the LORD, for he is good!
   His faithful love endures forever.

---

**Theme:** God's word is true and wonderful. Stay true to God and his word no matter how bad the world becomes. Obedience to God's laws is the only way to achieve real happiness.

**Author:** Anonymous, some suggest Ezra the priest

# 119* *Aleph*

**119:1**
Prov 11:20; 13:6

1 Joyful are people of integrity,
   who follow the instructions of the LORD.

**119** This psalm is a Hebrew acrostic poem; there are twenty-two stanzas, one for each successive letter of the Hebrew alphabet. Each of the eight verses within each stanza begins with the Hebrew letter named in its heading.

---

**118:22, 23** Jesus referred to this verse when he spoke of being rejected by his own people (Matthew 21:42; Mark 12:10, 11; Luke 20:17). Although he was rejected, Jesus is now the "cornerstone," the most important part of the church (Acts 4:11; Ephesians 2:20; 1 Peter 2:6, 7). The cornerstone is the foundation stone, holding the structure together.

**118:24** There are days when the last thing we want to do is rejoice. Our mood is down, our situation is out of hand, and our sorrow or guilt is overwhelming. We can relate to the writers of

the psalms who often felt this way. But no matter how low the writers felt, they were always honest with God. And as they talked to God, their prayers ended in praise. When you don't feel like rejoicing, tell God how you truly feel. You will find that God will give you a reason to rejoice. God has given you this day to live and to serve him—be glad!

**119:1ff** This is both the longest psalm and the longest chapter in the Bible. It may have been written by Ezra after the Temple was rebuilt (Ezra 6:14, 15) as a repetitive meditation on the

² Joyful are those who obey his laws
　　and search for him with all their hearts.
³ They do not compromise with evil,
　　and they walk only in his paths.
⁴ You have charged us
　　to keep your commandments carefully.
⁵ Oh, that my actions would consistently
　　reflect your decrees!
⁶ Then I will not be ashamed
　　when I compare my life with your commands.
⁷ As I learn your righteous regulations,
　　I will thank you by living as I should!
⁸ I will obey your decrees.
　　Please don't give up on me!

*Beth*

⁹ How can a young person stay pure?
　　By obeying your word.
¹⁰ I have tried hard to find you—
　　don't let me wander from your commands.
¹¹ I have hidden your word in my heart,
　　that I might not sin against you.
¹² I praise you, O Lord;
　　teach me your decrees.
¹³ I have recited aloud
　　all the regulations you have given us.
¹⁴ I have rejoiced in your laws
　　as much as in riches.
¹⁵ I will study your commandments
　　and reflect on your ways.
¹⁶ I will delight in your decrees
　　and not forget your word.

*Gimel*

¹⁷ Be good to your servant,
　　that I may live and obey your word.
¹⁸ Open my eyes to see
　　the wonderful truths in your instructions.
¹⁹ I am only a foreigner in the land.
　　Don't hide your commands from me!

**119:2**
Deut 4:29; 10:12;
11:13; 30:2

**119:4**
Deut 4:13

**119:5**
2 Chr 7:17
Prov 4:26

**119:8**
Ps 71:9, 18

**119:9**
1 Kgs 8:25
2 Chr 6:16

**119:11**
Luke 2:19, 51

**119:13**
Ps 40:9

**119:15**
Isa 58:2

**119:19**
1 Chr 29:15
Heb 11:13

---

beauty of God's Word and how it helps us stay pure and grow in faith. Psalm 119 has 22 carefully constructed sections, each corresponding to a different letter in the Hebrew alphabet and each verse beginning with the letter of its section. Almost every verse mentions God's Word. Such repetition was common in the Hebrew culture. People did not have personal copies of the Scriptures to read as we do, so God's people memorized his Word and passed it along orally. The structure of this psalm allowed for easy memorization. Remember, God's Word, the Bible, is the only sure guide for living a pure life.

**119:9**  We are drowning in a sea of sexual images and sinful attractions. Everywhere we look we find temptation to fill our minds with thoughts of sexual relationships that God wouldn't approve. The writer asked a question that troubles us all: How do we stay pure in a contaminating environment? We cannot do this on our own but must have counsel and strength more dynamic than the tempting influences around us. Where can we find that strength and wisdom? By reading God's Word and doing what it says.

**119:11**  Hiding (keeping) God's Word in our hearts is a deterrent to sin. This alone should inspire us to memorize Scripture. But memorization alone will not keep us from sin; we must also put God's Word to work in our lives, making it a vital guide for everything we do.

**119:12-24**  Most of us chafe under rules, for we think they restrict us from doing what we want. At first glance, then, it may seem strange to hear the writer talk of rejoicing in following God's laws as much as in having great riches. But God's laws were given to us to be all he wants us to be. They restrict us from doing what might cripple us and keep us from being our best. God's guidelines help us follow his path and avoid paths that lead to destruction.

**119:19**  The writer said that he is a "foreigner in the land," and so he needed guidance. Almost any long trip requires a map or guide. As we travel through life, the Bible should be our road map, pointing out safe routes, obstacles to avoid, and our final destination. We must recognize ourselves as pilgrims, travelers here on earth who need to study God's map to learn the way. If we ignore the map, we will wander aimlessly through life and risk missing our real destination.

**119:20**
Ps 42:1-2

²⁰ I am always overwhelmed
  with a desire for your regulations.

**119:21**
Deut 27:26
Ps 37:22

²¹ You rebuke the arrogant;
  those who wander from your commands are cursed.
²² Don't let them scorn and insult me,
  for I have obeyed your laws.
²³ Even princes sit and speak against me,
  but I will meditate on your decrees.
²⁴ Your laws please me;
  they give me wise advice.

### Daleth

**119:25**
Ps 44:25

²⁵ I lie in the dust;
  revive me by your word.
²⁶ I told you my plans, and you answered.
  Now teach me your decrees.
²⁷ Help me understand the meaning of your commandments,
  and I will meditate on your wonderful deeds.

**119:28**
Ps 22:14
1 Pet 5:10

²⁸ I weep with sorrow;
  encourage me by your word.
²⁹ Keep me from lying to myself;
  give me the privilege of knowing your instructions.
³⁰ I have chosen to be faithful;
  I have determined to live by your regulations.

**119:31**
Deut 11:22

³¹ I cling to your laws.
  LORD, don't let me be put to shame!
³² I will pursue your commands,
  for you expand my understanding.

### He

**119:33**
1 Chr 22:12
Ezek 44:24

³³ Teach me your decrees, O LORD;
  I will keep them to the end.
³⁴ Give me understanding and I will obey your instructions;
  I will put them into practice with all my heart.

**119:35**
Pss 25:4; 112:1

³⁵ Make me walk along the path of your commands,
  for that is where my happiness is found.

**119:36**
Luke 12:15
Heb 13:5

³⁶ Give me an eagerness for your laws
  rather than a love for money!

**119:37**
Ps 71:20
Isa 33:15

³⁷ Turn my eyes from worthless things,
  and give me life through your word.*

**119:38**
2 Sam 7:25

³⁸ Reassure me of your promise,
  made to those who fear you.
³⁹ Help me abandon my shameful ways;
  for your regulations are good.
⁴⁰ I long to obey your commandments!
  Renew my life with your goodness.

### Waw

⁴¹ LORD, give me your unfailing love,
  the salvation that you promised me.

**119:37** Some manuscripts read *in your ways.*

---

**119:27, 28** Our lives are cluttered with rule books, but the authors never come with us to help us follow them. But God does. That is the uniqueness of our Bible. God not only provides the rules and guidelines but comes with us personally each day to strengthen us so that we can live according to those rules. All we must do is invite him and respond to his direction.

**119:36** In today's world, people most often covet financial gain. Money represents power, influence, and success. For many people, money is a god. They think about little else. True, money can buy certain comforts and offer some security. But far more valuable than wealth is obedience to God because it is a heavenly treasure rather than an earthly one (Luke 12:33). We should do what God wants, regardless of the financial implications. Make the writer's prayer your own, asking God to turn your heart toward his laws and not toward making money; it's in your own best interest in the long run.

42 Then I can answer those who taunt me,
    for I trust in your word.
43 Do not snatch your word of truth from me,
    for your regulations are my only hope.
44 I will keep on obeying your instructions
    forever and ever.                                                            **119:44**
                                                                                 Acts 26:1-2
45 I will walk in freedom,
    for I have devoted myself to your commandments.
46 I will speak to kings about your laws,                                        **119:46**
    and I will not be ashamed.                                                   Matt 10:18
                                                                                 Acts 26:1-2
47 How I delight in your commands!
    How I love them!
48 I honor and love your commands.
    I meditate on your decrees.

*Zayin*

49 Remember your promise to me;
    it is my only hope.
50 Your promise revives me;                                                      **119:50**
    it comforts me in all my troubles.                                           Rom 15:14
51 The proud hold me in utter contempt,                                          **119:51**
    but I do not turn away from your instructions.                               Job 23:11
                                                                                 Jer 20:7
52 I meditate on your age-old regulations;                                       **119:52**
    O LORD, they comfort me.                                                     Ps 103:18
53 I become furious with the wicked,                                             **119:53**
    because they reject your instructions.                                       Exod 32:19
                                                                                 Neh 13:25
54 Your decrees have been the theme of my songs
    wherever I have lived.
55 I reflect at night on who you are, O LORD;                                    **119:55**
    therefore, I obey your instructions.                                         Pss 42:8; 63:6;
                                                                                 92:2
                                                                                 Acts 16:25
56 This is how I spend my life:
    obeying your commandments.

*Heth*

57 LORD, you are mine!                                                           **119:57**
    I promise to obey your words!                                               Deut 33:9
                                                                                 Ps 16:5
58 With all my heart I want your blessings.                                      **119:58**
    Be merciful as you promised.                                                Ps 41:4
59 I pondered the direction of my life,                                          **119:59**
    and I turned to follow your laws.                                           Mark 14:72
                                                                                 Luke 15:17
60 I will hurry, without delay,
    to obey your commands.
61 Evil people try to drag me into sin,                                          **119:61**
    but I am firmly anchored to your instructions.                              Ps 140:5
62 I rise at midnight to thank you
    for your just regulations.
63 I am a friend to anyone who fears you—                                        **119:63**
    anyone who obeys your commandments.                                          Ps 101:6
64 O LORD, your unfailing love fills the earth;                                  **119:64**
    teach me your decrees.                                                       Ps 33:5

*Teth*

65 You have done many good things for me, LORD,
    just as you promised.
66 I believe in your commands;                                                   **119:66**
    now teach me good judgment and knowledge.                                    Phil 1:9

---

**119:44-46** The writer talks about keeping the laws and yet being free. Contrary to what we often expect, obeying God's laws does not inhibit or restrain us. Instead, it frees us to be what God designed us to be. By seeking God's salvation and forgiveness, we have freedom from sin and the resulting oppressive guilt. By living God's way, we have freedom to fulfill God's plan for our lives.

**119:67**
Jer 31:18-19
Heb 12:5-11

67 I used to wander off until you disciplined me;
  but now I closely follow your word.

**119:68**
Pss 86:5; 125:4

68 You are good and do only good;
  teach me your decrees.

69 Arrogant people smear me with lies,
  but in truth I obey your commandments with all my heart.

**119:70**
Ps 17:10
Isa 6:10
Jer 5:28

70 Their hearts are dull and stupid,
  but I delight in your instructions.

71 My suffering was good for me,
  for it taught me to pay attention to your decrees.

**119:72**
Prov 8:10-11, 19

72 Your instructions are more valuable to me
  than millions in gold and silver.

### Yodh

**119:73**
Job 31:15
Ps 139:15-16

73 You made me; you created me.
  Now give me the sense to follow your commands.

**119:74**
Ps 35:27

74 May all who fear you find in me a cause for joy,
  for I have put my hope in your word.

**119:75**
Heb 12:10

75 I know, O LORD, that your regulations are fair;
  you disciplined me because I needed it.

76 Now let your unfailing love comfort me,
  just as you promised me, your servant.

77 Surround me with your tender mercies so I may live,
  for your instructions are my delight.

**119:78**
Jer 50:32

78 Bring disgrace upon the arrogant people who lied about me;
  meanwhile, I will concentrate on your commandments.

79 Let me be united with all who fear you,
  with those who know your laws.

80 May I be blameless in keeping your decrees;
  then I will never be ashamed.

### Kaph

81 I am worn out waiting for your rescue,
  but I have put my hope in your word.

**119:82**
Isa 38:14
Lam 2:11

82 My eyes are straining to see your promises come true.
  When will you comfort me?

83 I am shriveled like a wineskin in the smoke,
  but I have not forgotten to obey your decrees.

**119:84**
Rev 6:10

84 How long must I wait?
  When will you punish those who persecute me?

**119:85**
Pss 35:19; 57:6
Jer 18:22

85 These arrogant people who hate your instructions
  have dug deep pits to trap me.

86 All your commands are trustworthy.
  Protect me from those who hunt me down without cause.

87 They almost finished me off,
  but I refused to abandon your commandments.

88 In your unfailing love, spare my life;
  then I can continue to obey your laws.

### Lamedh

**119:89**
Isa 40:8
Matt 24:35
1 Pet 1:25

89 Your eternal word, O LORD,
  stands firm in heaven.

**119:90**
Pss 89:1-2; 148:6

90 Your faithfulness extends to every generation,
  as enduring as the earth you created.

**119:91**
Jer 31:35

91 Your regulations remain true to this day,
  for everything serves your plans.

92 If your instructions hadn't sustained me with joy,
  I would have died in my misery.

93 I will never forget your commandments,
  for by them you give me life.

94 I am yours; rescue me!
 For I have worked hard at obeying your commandments.
95 Though the wicked hide along the way to kill me,
 I will quietly keep my mind on your laws.
96 Even perfection has its limits,
 but your commands have no limit.

*Mem*

97 Oh, how I love your instructions!
 I think about them all day long.
98 Your commands make me wiser than my enemies,
 for they are my constant guide.
99 Yes, I have more insight than my teachers,
 for I am always thinking of your laws.
100 I am even wiser than my elders,
 for I have kept your commandments.
101 I have refused to walk on any evil path,
 so that I may remain obedient to your word.
102 I haven't turned away from your regulations,
 for you have taught me well.
103 How sweet your words taste to me;
 they are sweeter than honey.
104 Your commandments give me understanding;
 no wonder I hate every false way of life.

*Nun*

105 Your word is a lamp to guide my feet
 and a light for my path.
106 I've promised it once, and I'll promise it again:
 I will obey your righteous regulations.
107 I have suffered much, O LORD;
 restore my life again as you promised.
108 LORD, accept my offering of praise,
 and teach me your regulations.
109 My life constantly hangs in the balance,
 but I will not stop obeying your instructions.
110 The wicked have set their traps for me,
 but I will not turn from your commandments.
111 Your laws are my treasure;
 they are my heart's delight.
112 I am determined to keep your decrees
 to the very end.

*Samekh*

113 I hate those with divided loyalties,
 but I love your instructions.
114 You are my refuge and my shield;
 your word is my source of hope.
115 Get out of my life, you evil-minded people,
 for I intend to obey the commands of my God.

**119:95**
Ps 40:14
Isa 32:7

**119:98**
Deut 4:6

**119:100**
Job 32:7-9

**119:102**
Deut 17:20
Josh 23:6

**119:103**
Ps 19:10

**119:108**
Hos 14:2
Heb 13:15

**119:110**
Pss 91:3; 140:5

**119:111**
Deut 33:4

**119:113**
1 Kgs 18:21
Jas 1:8; 4:8

**119:114**
Pss 31:20; 61:4

**119:115**
Pss 6:8; 139:19
Matt 7:23

---

**119:97-104** God's Word makes us wise—wiser than our enemies and wiser than any teachers who ignore it. True wisdom goes beyond amassing knowledge; it is *applying* knowledge in a life-changing way. Intelligent or experienced people are not necessarily wise. Wisdom comes from allowing God's teachings to guide us.

**119:105** To walk safely in the woods at night we need a light so we don't trip over tree roots or fall into holes. In this life, we walk through a dark forest of evil. But the Bible can be our light to show us the way ahead so we won't stumble as we walk. It reveals the entangling roots of false values and philosophies. Study the Bible so you will be able to see your way clear enough to stay on the right path.

**119:113** Undecided people cannot make up their minds between good and evil. But when it comes to obeying God, there is no middle ground; you must take a stand. Either you are obeying him or you are not. Either you are doing what he wants or you are undecided. Choose to obey God, and say with the writer, "I love your instructions."

119:116
Pss 25:2, 20;
31:1, 17
Rom 5:5; 9:33
Phil 1:20

116 LORD, sustain me as you promised, that I may live!
　　Do not let my hope be crushed.

119:117
Ps 12:5
Prov 29:25

117 Sustain me, and I will be rescued;
　　then I will meditate continually on your decrees.

118 But you have rejected all who stray from your decrees.
　　They are only fooling themselves.

119:119
Isa 1:22, 25
Ezek 22:18-19

119 You skim off the wicked of the earth like scum;
　　no wonder I love to obey your laws!

119:120
Job 4:14
Hab 3:16

120 I tremble in fear of you;
　　I stand in awe of your regulations.

### Ayin

119:121
2 Sam 8:15
Job 29:14

121 Don't leave me to the mercy of my enemies,
　　for I have done what is just and right.

122 Please guarantee a blessing for me.
　　Don't let the arrogant oppress me!

123 My eyes strain to see your rescue,
　　to see the truth of your promise fulfilled.

119:124
Pss 51:1; 106:45;
109:26

124 I am your servant; deal with me in unfailing love,
　　and teach me your decrees.

125 Give discernment to me, your servant;
　　then I will understand your laws.

119:126
Jer 18:23
Ezek 31:11

126 LORD, it is time for you to act,
　　for these evil people have violated your instructions.

127 Truly, I love your commands
　　more than gold, even the finest gold.

119:128
Ps 19:8

128 Each of your commandments is right.
　　That is why I hate every false way.

### Pe

129 Your laws are wonderful.
　　No wonder I obey them!

119:130
Prov 6:23

130 The teaching of your word gives light,
　　so even the simple can understand.

131 I pant with expectation,
　　longing for your commands.

132 Come and show me your mercy,
　　as you do for all who love your name.

119:133
Ps 19:13

133 Guide my steps by your word,
　　so I will not be overcome by evil.

119:134
Ps 142:6

134 Ransom me from the oppression of evil people;
　　then I can obey your commandments.

119:135
Num 6:25
Ps 67:1

135 Look upon me with love;
　　teach me your decrees.

119:136
Jer 9:1, 18; 14:17
Lam 3:48

136 Rivers of tears gush from my eyes
　　because people disobey your instructions.

### Tsadhe

119:137
Ezra 9:15
Jer 12:1
Dan 9:7, 14

137 O LORD, you are righteous,
　　and your regulations are fair.

138 Your laws are perfect
　　and completely trustworthy.

119:139
Ps 69:9

139 I am overwhelmed with indignation,
　　for my enemies have disregarded your words.

---

**119:125** The writer asked God for discernment. Faith comes alive when we apply Scripture to our daily tasks and concerns. We need discernment so we can understand, and we need the desire to apply Scripture where we need help. The Bible is like medicine: It goes to work only when we apply it to the affected areas. As you read the Bible, be alert for lessons, commands, or examples that you can put into practice.

140 Your promises have been thoroughly tested;
    that is why I love them so much.
141 I am insignificant and despised,
    but I don't forget your commandments.
142 Your justice is eternal,
    and your instructions are perfectly true.
143 As pressure and stress bear down on me,
    I find joy in your commands.
144 Your laws are always right;
    help me to understand them so I may live.

    *Qoph*

145 I pray with all my heart; answer me, LORD!
    I will obey your decrees.
146 I cry out to you; rescue me,
    that I may obey your laws.
147 I rise early, before the sun is up;
    I cry out for help and put my hope in your words.
148 I stay awake through the night,
    thinking about your promise.
149 In your faithful love, O LORD, hear my cry;
    let me be revived by following your regulations.
150 Lawless people are coming to attack me;
    they live far from your instructions.
151 But you are near, O LORD,
    and all your commands are true.
152 I have known from my earliest days
    that your laws will last forever.

    *Resh*

153 Look upon my suffering and rescue me,
    for I have not forgotten your instructions.
154 Argue my case; take my side!
    Protect my life as you promised.
155 The wicked are far from rescue,
    for they do not bother with your decrees.
156 LORD, how great is your mercy;
    let me be revived by following your regulations.
157 Many persecute and trouble me,
    yet I have not swerved from your laws.
158 Seeing these traitors makes me sick at heart,
    because they care nothing for your word.
159 See how I love your commandments, LORD.
    Give back my life because of your unfailing love.
160 The very essence of your words is truth;
    all your just regulations will stand forever.

    *Shin*

161 Powerful people harass me without cause,
    but my heart trembles only at your word.
162 I rejoice in your word
    like one who discovers a great treasure.
163 I hate and abhor all falsehood,
    but I love your instructions.
164 I will praise you seven times a day
    because all your regulations are just.

119:140
Ps 12:6

119:141
Ps 22:6

119:144
Ps 19:9

119:146
Ps 3:7

119:147
Ps 108:2

119:151
Ps 34:18
Isa 50:8

119:152
Luke 21:33

119:154
Ps 35:1
Mic 7:9

119:156
2 Sam 24:14

119:158
Ps 139:21

119:162
1 Sam 30:16
Isa 9:3

119:163
Ps 31:6
Prov 13:5

---

**119:160** One of God's characteristics is truthfulness. He embodies perfect truth; therefore, his Word cannot lie. It is true and dependable for guidance and help (see John 17:14-17). The Bible is completely true and trustworthy.

119:165
Prov 3:23
1 Jn 2:10

165 Those who love your instructions have great peace
and do not stumble.

119:166
Gen 49:18

166 I long for your rescue, LORD,
so I have obeyed your commands.
167 I have obeyed your laws,
for I love them very much.

119:168
Ps 139:3
Prov 5:21

168 Yes, I obey your commandments and laws
because you know everything I do.

*Taw*

119:169
Ps 18:6

169 O LORD, listen to my cry;
give me the discerning mind you promised.

119:170
Pss 22:20; 31:2;
140:6

170 Listen to my prayer;
rescue me as you promised.

119:171
Isa 2:3
Mic 4:2

171 Let praise flow from my lips,
for you have taught me your decrees.

119:172
Ps 51:14

172 Let my tongue sing about your word,
for all your commands are right.

119:173
Josh 24:22
Ps 37:24

173 Give me a helping hand,
for I have chosen to follow your commandments.
174 O LORD, I have longed for your rescue,
and your instructions are my delight.

119:175
Isa 55:3

175 Let me live so I can praise you,
and may your regulations help me.

119:176
Isa 53:6
Luke 15:4

176 I have wandered away like a lost sheep;
come and find me,
for I have not forgotten your commands.

**Theme:** A prayer for deliverance from false accusers. All believers must live with the tension of being in the world but not belonging to it.
**Author:** Anonymous, some suggest Hezekiah

# 120 *A song for pilgrims ascending to Jerusalem.*

120:1
Pss 18:6; 102:2

1 I took my troubles to the LORD;
I cried out to him, and he answered my prayer.

120:2
Ps 52:4
Prov 12:22

2 Rescue me, O LORD, from liars
and from all deceitful people.
3 O deceptive tongue, what will God do to you?
How will he increase your punishment?

120:4
Ps 140:10

4 You will be pierced with sharp arrows
and burned with glowing coals.

120:5
Gen 10:2; 25:13
Jer 2:10; 49:28

5 How I suffer in far-off Meshech.
It pains me to live in distant Kedar.
6 I am tired of living
among people who hate peace.

120:7
Pss 55:21; 109:4

7 I search for peace;
but when I speak of peace, they want war!

**119:165** Modern society longs for peace of mind. Here is clear-cut instruction on how to attain this: If we love God and obey his laws, we will have "great peace." Trust in God, who alone stands above the pressures of daily life and gives us full assurance.

**120–134** Psalms 120–134 are called "pilgrim psalms" or "songs of ascent." They were sung by those who journeyed ("ascended") to the Temple for the annual festivals. Each psalm is a "step" along the journey. Psalm 120 begins the journey in a distant land in hostile surroundings; Psalm 122 pictures the pilgrims arriving in Jerusalem; and the rest of the psalms move toward the Temple, mentioning various characteristics of God.

**120:5, 6** Meshech was a nation far to the north of Israel; Kedar a nation to the southeast. Both were known for being warlike and barbarian. Because the writer couldn't have been in two places at one time, he was lamenting that he felt far from home and surrounded by pagan people.

**120:7** Peacemaking is not always popular. Some people prefer to fight for what they believe in. The glory of battle is in the hope of winning, but someone must be a loser. The glory of peacemaking is that it may actually produce two winners. Peacemaking is God's way, so we should carefully and prayerfully attempt to be peacemakers.

**Theme:** We can depend upon God for help. Pilgrims must travel through lonely country to their destination; they are protected, not by anything created, but by the Creator of everything.
**Author:** Anonymous, some suggest Hezekiah

# 121 *A song for pilgrims ascending to Jerusalem.*

1 I look up to the mountains—
   does my help come from there?
2 My help comes from the LORD,
   who made heaven and earth!

3 He will not let you stumble;
   the one who watches over you will not slumber.
4 Indeed, he who watches over Israel
   never slumbers or sleeps.

5 The LORD himself watches over you!
   The LORD stands beside you as your protective shade.
6 The sun will not harm you by day,
   nor the moon at night.

7 The LORD keeps you from all harm
   and watches over your life.
8 The LORD keeps watch over you as you come and go,
   both now and forever.

**121:2**
Pss 115:15; 124:8

**121:3**
Pss 66:9; 127:1

**121:5**
Ps 91:4

**121:6**
Isa 49:10
Rev 7:16

**121:7**
Ps 91:10-12

---

**Theme:** Stepping into the presence of God. What Jerusalem was for the Israelites, the church is to the believer.
**Author:** David

# 122 *A song for pilgrims ascending to Jerusalem. A psalm of David.*

1 I was glad when they said to me,
   "Let us go to the house of the LORD."
2 And now here we are,
   standing inside your gates, O Jerusalem.
3 Jerusalem is a well-built city;
   its seamless walls cannot be breached.
4 All the tribes of Israel—the LORD's people—
   make their pilgrimage here.
   They come to give thanks to the name of the LORD,
   as the law requires of Israel.
5 Here stand the thrones where judgment is given,
   the thrones of the dynasty of David.

**122:1**
Isa 2:3
Zech 8:21

**122:3**
Ps 48:13

**122:4**
Deut 16:16

**122:5**
Deut 17:8
2 Chr 19:8

---

**121:1ff** This song expresses assurance and hope in God's protection day and night. He not only made the hills but heaven and earth as well. We should never trust a lesser power than God himself. But not only is he all-powerful, he also watches over us. Nothing diverts or deters him. We are safe. We never outgrow our need for God's untiring watch over our life.

**122:1** Going to God's house can be a chore or a delight. For the writer, it was a delight. As a pilgrim attending one of the three great religious festivals, he rejoiced to worship with God's people in God's house. We may find worship a chore if we have unconfessed sin or if our love for God has cooled. But if we are close to God and enjoy his presence, we will be eager to worship and praise him. Our attitude toward God will determine our view of worship.

**122:5** The "thrones where judgment is given" are the courts of justice by the town gate. In Bible times, the elders in a town sat to hear cases and administer justice at the gate (Ruth 4:1, 2). Sometimes the king himself would sit at the gate to meet his subjects and make legal decisions (2 Samuel 19:8). Speeches and prophecies were also made at the city gate (Nehemiah 8:1; Jeremiah 17:19, 20).

122:6
Ps 102:14

122:7
Isa 62:6

122:8
Ps 133:1

6 Pray for peace in Jerusalem.
    May all who love this city prosper.
7 O Jerusalem, may there be peace within your walls
    and prosperity in your palaces.
8 For the sake of my family and friends, I will say,
    "May you have peace."
9 For the sake of the house of the LORD our God,
    I will seek what is best for you, O Jerusalem.

**Theme:** Look to God for mercy. We are encouraged to be attentive to God's leading.
**Author:** Anonymous, some suggest Hezekiah

# 123 *A song for pilgrims ascending to Jerusalem.*

123:1
Pss 11:4; 141:8

123:2
Mal 1:6

123:3
Neh 4:4
Pss 4:1; 51:1; 79:4;
119:22

123:4
Ps 79:4

1 I lift my eyes to you,
    O God, enthroned in heaven.
2 We keep looking to the LORD our God for his mercy,
    just as servants keep their eyes on their master,
    as a slave girl watches her mistress for the slightest signal.
3 Have mercy on us, LORD, have mercy,
    for we have had our fill of contempt.
4 We have had more than our fill of the scoffing of the proud
    and the contempt of the arrogant.

**Theme:** God delivers us from those who seek to destroy us. God is on the side of those who seek him.
**Author:** David, probably written after his defeat of the Philistines (2 Samuel 5:17-25)

# 124 *A song for pilgrims ascending to Jerusalem. A psalm of David.*

124:1
Pss 94:17; 129:1

124:3
Pss 56:1; 57:3

124:4
Pss 18:16; 69:2

124:7
Pss 91:3; 141:10
Prov 6:5

124:8
Gen 1:1
Ps 121:2

1 What if the LORD had not been on our side?
    Let all Israel repeat:
2 What if the LORD had not been on our side
    when people attacked us?
3 They would have swallowed us alive
    in their burning anger.
4 The waters would have engulfed us;
    a torrent would have overwhelmed us.
5 Yes, the raging waters of their fury
    would have overwhelmed our very lives.

6 Praise the LORD,
    who did not let their teeth tear us apart!
7 We escaped like a bird from a hunter's trap.
    The trap is broken, and we are free!
8 Our help is from the LORD,
    who made heaven and earth.

---

**122:6-9** The writer was not praying for his own peace and prosperity but for that of his family and friends in Jerusalem. This is intercessory prayer, prayer on behalf of others. Too often we are quick to pray for our own needs and desires but neglect interceding for others. Will you intercede for someone in need today?

**122:6-9** The peace sought in these verses is much more than the mere absence of conflict. It suggests completeness, health, justice, prosperity, and protection. The world cannot provide this peace. Real peace comes from faith in God, because he alone embodies all the characteristics of peace. To find peace of mind and peace with others, you must find peace with God.

**123:1ff** The writer lifted his eyes to God, waiting and watching for God to send his mercy. The more he waited, the more he cried out to God because he knew that the evil and proud offered no help—they had only contempt for God.

**124:7, 8** Do you ever feel trapped by overwhelming odds? With God, there is always a way out because he is the Creator of all that exists. No problem is beyond his ability to solve; no circumstance is too difficult for him. We can turn to the Creator for help in our time of need, for he is on our side. God will provide a way out; we need only trust him and look for it. David compared this to a bird escaping the hunter's trap.

**Theme:** God is our Protector. The mountains around Jerusalem symbolize God's protection for his people.
**Author:** Anonymous, some suggest Hezekiah

**125** *A song for pilgrims ascending to Jerusalem.*

1 Those who trust in the LORD are as secure as Mount Zion;
   they will not be defeated but will endure forever.
2 Just as the mountains surround Jerusalem,
   so the LORD surrounds his people, both now and forever.
3 The wicked will not rule the land of the godly,
   for then the godly might be tempted to do wrong.
4 O LORD, do good to those who are good,
   whose hearts are in tune with you.
5 But banish those who turn to crooked ways, O LORD.
   Take them away with those who do evil.

   May Israel have peace!

125:1 Ps 46:5
125:2 Ps 121:8 Zech 2:5
125:3 1 Sam 24:10 Prov 22:8 Isa 14:5
125:4 Pss 7:10; 94:15; 119:68
125:5 Gal 6:16

**Theme:** God does great things. His power not only releases us from sin's captive hold but brings us back to him.
**Author:** Anonymous, possibly written to celebrate the exiles' return from captivity (Ezra 1)

**126** *A song for pilgrims ascending to Jerusalem.*

1 When the LORD brought back his exiles to Jerusalem,*
   it was like a dream!
2 We were filled with laughter,
   and we sang for joy.
   And the other nations said,
   "What amazing things the LORD has done for them."
3 Yes, the LORD has done amazing things for us!
   What joy!
4 Restore our fortunes, LORD,
   as streams renew the desert.
5 Those who plant in tears
   will harvest with shouts of joy.
6 They weep as they go to plant their seed,
   but they sing as they return with the harvest.

126:1 Jer 29:14
126:2 Job 8:21 Ps 51:14
126:3 Isa 25:9
126:4 Isa 35:6; 43:19
126:5 Ps 80:5 Gal 6:9

**Theme:** Life without God is senseless. All of life's work—building a home, establishing a career, and raising a family—must have God as the foundation.
**Author:** Solomon

**127** *A song for pilgrims ascending to Jerusalem. A psalm of Solomon.*

1 Unless the LORD builds a house,
   the work of the builders is wasted.

127:1 Ps 78:69

126:1 Hebrew *Zion.*

125:1 Have you ever known people who were drawn to every new fad or idea? Such people are unstable and therefore unreliable. The secret to stability is to trust in God, because he never changes. He cannot be shaken by the changes in our world, and he endures forever. The fads and ideas of our world, and our world itself, will not.

125:3 Although the writer said, "The wicked will not rule the land of the godly," often Israel had to put up with evil rulers. The writer was expressing what will ultimately happen when God executes his final judgment. Human sinfulness often ruins God's ideal on earth, but that doesn't mean God has lost control. Evil prevails only as long as God allows.

126:5, 6 God's ability to restore life is beyond our understanding. Forests burn down and are able to grow back. Broken bones heal. Even grief is not a permanent condition. Our tears can be seeds that will grow into a harvest of joy because God is able to bring good out of tragedy. When burdened by sorrow, know that your times of grief will end and that you will again find joy. We must be patient as we wait. God's great harvest of joy is coming!

127:1 Families establish homes and sentries guard cities, but both these activities are futile unless God is in them. A family

Unless the LORD protects a city,
        guarding it with sentries will do no good.
2 It is useless for you to work so hard
        from early morning until late at night,
anxiously working for food to eat;
        for God gives rest to his loved ones.

**127:2**
Gen 3:17
Job 11:18-19
Eccl 5:12

3 Children are a gift from the LORD;
        they are a reward from him.
4 Children born to a young man
        are like arrows in a warrior's hands.
5 How joyful is the man whose quiver is full of them!
        He will not be put to shame when he confronts his accusers at the city gates.

**127:3**
Deut 28:4

**Theme:** God, the true head of the home. (This is called the marriage prayer because it was often sung at Israelite marriages.) God will reward your devotion to him with inner peace.
**Author:** Anonymous, some suggest Hezekiah

# 128 *A song for pilgrims ascending to Jerusalem.*

1 How joyful are those who fear the LORD—
        all who follow his ways!
2 You will enjoy the fruit of your labor.
        How joyful and prosperous you will be!
3 Your wife will be like a fruitful grapevine,
        flourishing within your home.
Your children will be like vigorous young olive trees
        as they sit around your table.
4 That is the LORD's blessing
        for those who fear him.

**128:1**
Pss 112:1; 119:3

**128:2**
Eccl 8:12
**128:3**
Ps 52:8

5 May the LORD continually bless you from Zion.
        May you see Jerusalem prosper as long as you live.
6 May you live to enjoy your grandchildren.
        May Israel have peace!

**128:5**
Pss 122:9; 134:3

**128:6**
Gen 48:11

**Theme:** Confidence in times of persecution. God will bring us through the tough times.
**Author:** Anonymous, some suggest Hezekiah

# 129 *A song for pilgrims ascending to Jerusalem.*

1 From my earliest youth my enemies have persecuted me.
        Let all Israel repeat this:
2 From my earliest youth my enemies have persecuted me,
        but they have never defeated me.

**129:1**
Exod 1:11

**129:2**
Jer 15:20
Matt 16:18

---

without God can never experience the spiritual bond God brings to relationships. A city without God will crumble from evil and corruption on the inside. Don't make the mistake of leaving God out of your life. If you do, all your accomplishments will be futile. Make God your highest priority, and let him do the building.

**127:2** God is not against human effort. Hard work honors God (Proverbs 31:10-29). But working to the exclusion of rest or to the neglect of family may be a cover-up for an inability to trust God to provide for our needs. We all need adequate rest and times of spiritual refreshment. On the other hand, this verse is not an excuse to be lazy (Proverbs 18:9). Be careful to maintain a balance: Work while trusting God, and also rest while trusting him.

**127:3-5** Too often children are seen as liabilities rather than assets. But the Bible calls children "a gift from the LORD," a reward. We can learn valuable lessons from their inquisitive minds and trusting spirits. Those who view children as a distraction or nuisance should instead see them as an opportunity to

shape the future. We dare not treat children as an inconvenience when God values them so highly.

**128:1ff** A good family life is a reward for following God. The values outlined in God's Word include love, service, honesty, integrity, and prayer. These help all relationships, and they are especially vital to home life. Is your home life heavenly or hectic? Reading and obeying God's Word is a good place to start to make your family all that it should be.

**129:2** The people of Israel were persecuted from their earliest days but never destroyed completely. The same is true of the church. Christians have faced times of severe persecution, but the church has never been destroyed. As Jesus said to Peter, "Now I say to you that you are Peter (which means 'rock'), and upon this rock I will build my church, and all the powers of hell will not conquer it" (Matthew 16:18). When you face persecution and discrimination, take courage—the church will never be destroyed.

3 My back is covered with cuts,
  as if a farmer had plowed long furrows.
4 But the LORD is good;
  he has cut me free from the ropes of the ungodly.

5 May all who hate Jerusalem*
  be turned back in shameful defeat.
6 May they be as useless as grass on a rooftop,
  turning yellow when only half grown,
7 ignored by the harvester,
  despised by the binder.
8 And may those who pass by
  refuse to give them this blessing:
  "The LORD bless you;
  we bless you in the LORD's name."

**129:5**
Ps 71:13
Mic 4:11

**129:6**
2 Kgs 19:26
Ps 37:2

**129:8**
Ruth 2:4
Ps 118:26

**Theme:** Assurance of the Lord's forgiveness. God will surely forgive us if we confess our sins to him.
**Author:** Anonymous, some suggest Hezekiah

# 130 *A song for pilgrims ascending to Jerusalem.*

1 From the depths of despair, O LORD,
  I call for your help.
2 Hear my cry, O Lord.
  Pay attention to my prayer.

3 LORD, if you kept a record of our sins,
  who, O Lord, could ever survive?
4 But you offer forgiveness,
  that we might learn to fear you.

5 I am counting on the LORD;
  yes, I am counting on him.
  I have put my hope in his word.
6 I long for the Lord
  more than sentries long for the dawn,
  yes, more than sentries long for the dawn.

7 O Israel, hope in the LORD;
  for with the LORD there is unfailing love.
  His redemption overflows.
8 He himself will redeem Israel
  from every kind of sin.

**130:1**
Pss 42:7; 69:2

**130:2**
2 Chr 6:40
Pss 28:2; 64:1

**130:3**
Pss 76:7; 86:5

**130:4**
Exod 34:7

**130:5**
Ps 40:1
Isa 8:17

**130:6**
Ps 63:6

**130:7**
Pss 103:4; 131:3

**130:8**
Luke 1:68

**129:5** Hebrew *Zion.*

**129:3** This verse foreshadowed Jesus' unjust punishment before his death. He endured horrible lashes from the whip of his tormentors, which indeed made "furrows" on his back (John 19:1).
**130:1, 2** In the depths of despair, the writer cried out to God. Despair makes us feel isolated and distant from God, but this is precisely when we need God most. Despair over sin should not lead to self-pity, causing us to think more about ourselves than God. Instead, it should lead to confession and then to God's mercy, forgiveness, and redemption. When we feel overwhelmed by a problem, feeling sorry for ourselves will only increase feelings of hopelessness; but crying out to God will turn our attention to the only one who can really help.

**130:3, 4** Keeping a record of sins (or holding a grudge) is like building a wall between you and another person, and it is nearly impossible to talk openly while the wall is there. God doesn't keep a record of our sins; when he forgives, he forgives completely, tearing down any wall between us and him. Therefore, we fear (revere) God, yet we can talk to him about anything. When you pray, realize that God is holding nothing against you. His lines of communication are completely open.

**Theme:** Trust and contentment. Quiet trust in God is the basis for our contentment.
**Author:** David

# 131 *A song for pilgrims ascending to Jerusalem. A psalm of David.*

131:1
Rom 12:16

¹ LORD, my heart is not proud;
    my eyes are not haughty.
I don't concern myself with matters too great
    or too awesome for me to grasp.

131:2
Ps 62:1

² Instead, I have calmed and quieted myself,
    like a weaned child who no longer cries for its mother's milk.
    Yes, like a weaned child is my soul within me.

131:3
Ps 130:7

³ O Israel, put your hope in the LORD—
    now and always.

**Theme:** Honor God and he will honor you. The psalmist reflects upon that great day when the Ark of the Covenant was brought to Jerusalem and praises God for his promise to perpetuate David's line.
**Author:** Anonymous

# 132 *A song for pilgrims ascending to Jerusalem.*

¹ LORD, remember David
    and all that he suffered.

132:2
Gen 49:24
Isa 49:26

² He made a solemn promise to the LORD.
    He vowed to the Mighty One of Israel,*
³ "I will not go home;
    I will not let myself rest.

132:4
Prov 6:4

⁴ I will not let my eyes sleep
    nor close my eyelids in slumber

132:5
Acts 7:46

⁵ until I find a place to build a house for the LORD,
    a sanctuary for the Mighty One of Israel."

132:6
Gen 35:19
1 Sam 7:1; 17:12

⁶ We heard that the Ark was in Ephrathah;
    then we found it in the distant countryside of Jaar.

132:7
1 Chr 28:2
Pss 5:7; 99:5

⁷ Let us go to the sanctuary of the LORD;
    let us worship at the footstool of his throne.

132:8-10
//2 Chr 6:41-42

⁸ Arise, O LORD, and enter your resting place,
    along with the Ark, the symbol of your power.

132:8
Num 10:35
Ps 78:61

⁹ May your priests be clothed in godliness;
    may your loyal servants sing for joy.

132:9
Ps 149:5

¹⁰ For the sake of your servant David,
    do not reject the king you have anointed.

132:11
2 Sam 7:12-16
2 Chr 6:16
†Acts 2:30

¹¹ The LORD swore an oath to David
    with a promise he will never take back:

132:2 Hebrew *of Jacob;* also in 132:5. See note on 44:4.

---

**131:1, 2** Pride results from overvaluing ourselves above others. It leads to restlessness because it makes us dissatisfied with what we have and concerned about what everyone else is doing. It keeps us always hungering for more attention and adoration. By contrast, humility puts others first and allows us to be content with God's leading in our lives. Such contentment gives us security so that we no longer have to prove ourselves to others. Let humility and trust affect your perspective and give you the strength and freedom to serve God and others.

**132:2-5** This refers to David's desire to build the Temple. When David became king, he built a beautiful palace, but he was troubled that the Ark of the Covenant, the symbol of God's presence among his people (Exodus 25:10-22), remained in a tent (2 Samuel 6:17; 7:1-17). This so bothered David that he couldn't sleep until he

corrected the situation. He began to lay the plans for the Temple to house the Ark. (Eventually the Temple was built by his son Solomon.) We must live so close to God that we become restless until God's will is accomplished through us.

**132:11, 12** The promise that David's sons would sit on Israel's throne forever is found in 2 Samuel 7:8-29. This promise had two parts: (1) David's descendants would perpetually rule over Israel as long as they followed God, and (2) David's royal line would never end. The first part was conditional: As long as the kings obeyed God ("obey the terms of my covenant"), their dynasty continued. The second part of the promise was unconditional: It was fulfilled in Jesus Christ, a descendant of David, who reigns forever.

"I will place one of your descendants
　　on your throne.
12 If your descendants obey the terms of my covenant
　　and the laws that I teach them,
　then your royal line
　　will continue forever and ever."

132:12<br>Luke 1:32

13 For the LORD has chosen Jerusalem*;
　　he has desired it for his home.
14 "This is my resting place forever," he said.
　　"I will live here, for this is the home I desired.

132:13<br>Ps 78:68

132:14<br>Matt 23:21

15 I will bless this city and make it prosperous;
　　I will satisfy its poor with food.

132:15<br>Ps 107:9

16 I will clothe its priests with godliness;
　　its faithful servants will sing for joy.
17 Here I will increase the power of David;
　　my anointed one will be a light for my people.
18 I will clothe his enemies with shame,
　　but he will be a glorious king."

**Theme:** The joy of harmonious relationships.
**Author:** David

# 133 *A song for pilgrims ascending to Jerusalem. A psalm of David.*

1 How wonderful and pleasant it is
　　when brothers live together in harmony!
2 For harmony is as precious as the anointing oil
　　that was poured over Aaron's head,
　　that ran down his beard
　　and onto the border of his robe.

133:2<br>Exod 30:25, 30<br>Lev 8:12

3 Harmony is as refreshing as the dew from Mount Hermon
　　that falls on the mountains of Zion.
　And there the LORD has pronounced his blessing,
　　even life everlasting.

133:3<br>Deut 4:48

**Theme:** Worship God and experience the joy of his blessings.
**Author:** Anonymous, some suggest Hezekiah

# 134 *A song for pilgrims ascending to Jerusalem.*

1 Oh, praise the LORD, all you servants of the LORD,
　　you who serve at night in the house of the LORD.

134:1<br>Deut 10:8<br>1 Chr 9:33<br>2 Chr 29:11

**132:13** Hebrew *Zion.*

---

**132:17, 18** The "increase" of David's power refers to one of his mighty descendants. David's son Solomon was indeed a glorious king (1 Kings 3:10-14); but these verses look ahead even further to another descendant of David, Jesus the Messiah (Matthew 1:17). The power, might, and glory of the Messiah will last forever.

**133:1-3** David stated that harmony is pleasant and precious. Unfortunately, harmony is not always found in the church, as it should be. People disagree and cause division over unimportant issues. Some delight in causing tension by discrediting others. Harmony is important because (1) it makes the church a positive example to the world and helps draw others to the Lord; (2) it helps us cooperate as a body of believers as God meant us to, giving us a foretaste of heaven; (3) it renews and revitalizes ministry because there is less tension to sap our energy.

Living in harmony does not mean that we will agree on everything; there will be many opinions just as there are many notes in a musical chord. But we must agree on our purpose in life—to work together for God. Our outward expression of harmony will reflect our inward harmony of purpose.

**133:2** Expensive oil was used by Moses to anoint Aaron as the first high priest of Israel (Exodus 29:7) and to dedicate all the priests to God's service. Brotherly harmony, like the anointing oil, shows that we are dedicated to serving God wholeheartedly.

**133:3** Mount Hermon is the tallest mountain in Palestine, located northeast of the Sea of Galilee.

**134:1-3** This psalm is about a very small group—the Levites who served as Temple watchmen. Singing this psalm, the last of the "songs of ascent" (Psalms 120–134), the worshipers would ascend the hill where the Temple sat and see the watchmen who protected it day and night. They saw the watchmen's work as an act of praise to God, done reverently and responsibly. Make your job or your responsibility in the church an act of praise by doing it with reverence to God. Honor him by the quality of your work and the attitude of service you bring to it.

**134:2**
Ps 28:2
1 Tim 2:8

2 Lift up holy hands in prayer,
and praise the LORD.

**134:3**
Pss 124:8; 128:5

3 May the LORD, who made heaven and earth,
bless you from Jerusalem.*

**Theme:** A hymn of praise. This psalm contrasts the greatness of God with the powerlessness of idols. Pagans worship idols while God's people worship the living God.
**Author:** Anonymous

# 135

1 Praise the LORD!

Praise the name of the LORD!
Praise him, you who serve the LORD,

**135:2**
Ps 116:19

2 you who serve in the house of the LORD,
in the courts of the house of our God.

**135:3**
Pss 68:4; 100:5

3 Praise the LORD, for the LORD is good;
celebrate his lovely name with music.

**135:4**
Exod 19:5
Deut 7:6; 10:15
1 Pet 2:9

4 For the LORD has chosen Jacob for himself,
Israel for his own special treasure.

**135:5**
Pss 48:1; 97:9

5 I know the greatness of the LORD—
that our Lord is greater than any other god.

**135:6**
Ps 115:3

6 The LORD does whatever pleases him
throughout all heaven and earth,
and on the seas and in their depths.

**135:7**
Job 38:25-26
Jer 51:16
Zech 10:1

7 He causes the clouds to rise over the whole earth.
He sends the lightning with the rain
and releases the wind from his storehouses.

**135:8**
Ps 78:51

8 He destroyed the firstborn in each Egyptian home,
both people and animals.

**135:9**
Deut 6:22

9 He performed miraculous signs and wonders in Egypt
against Pharaoh and all his people.

**135:10**
Ps 136:17-21

10 He struck down great nations
and slaughtered mighty kings—

**135:11**
Num 21:33-35
Josh 12:7-24

11 Sihon king of the Amorites,
Og king of Bashan,
and all the kings of Canaan.

**135:12**
Ps 78:55

12 He gave their land as an inheritance,
a special possession to his people Israel.

**135:13**
Exod 3:15
Ps 102:12

13 Your name, O LORD, endures forever;
your fame, O LORD, is known to every generation.

**135:14**
Deut 32:36
Ps 106:45

14 For the LORD will give justice to his people
and have compassion on his servants.

**135:15-20**
//Ps 115:4-11

15 The idols of the nations are merely things of silver and gold,
shaped by human hands.

16 They have mouths but cannot speak,
and eyes but cannot see.

**134:3** Hebrew *Zion*.

**135:4** That the descendants of Jacob (Israel) were a chosen people reflects God's commission to the nation in Deuteronomy 7:6-8 and in Peter's sermon to the church in 1 Peter 2:9. God treasures us. He gives love and mercy to all those who believe in him.

**135:15-18** Those who worshiped idols were as blind and insensitive as the idols themselves. They couldn't see or hear what God had to say. In subtle, imperceptible ways we become like the idols we worship. If the true God is your God, you will become more like him as you worship him. What are your goals? What takes priority in your life? Choose carefully because you will take on the characteristics of whatever you worship.

17 They have ears but cannot hear,
   and noses but cannot smell.
18 And those who make idols are just like them,
   as are all who trust in them.

19 O Israel, praise the LORD!
   O priests—descendants of Aaron—praise the LORD!
20 O Levites, praise the LORD!
   All you who fear the LORD, praise the LORD!
21 The LORD be praised from Zion,
   for he lives here in Jerusalem.

Praise the LORD!

**135:20**
Ps 118:4

**Theme:** The never-ending story of God's love. God deserves our praise because his endless love never fails.
**Author:** Anonymous

# 136
1 Give thanks to the LORD, for he is good!
  *His faithful love endures forever.*
2 Give thanks to the God of gods.
  *His faithful love endures forever.*
3 Give thanks to the Lord of lords.
  *His faithful love endures forever.*

4 Give thanks to him who alone does mighty miracles.
  *His faithful love endures forever.*
5 Give thanks to him who made the heavens so skillfully.
  *His faithful love endures forever.*
6 Give thanks to him who placed the earth among the waters.
  *His faithful love endures forever.*
7 Give thanks to him who made the heavenly lights—
  *His faithful love endures forever.*
8 the sun to rule the day,
  *His faithful love endures forever.*
9 and the moon and stars to rule the night.
  *His faithful love endures forever.*

10 Give thanks to him who killed the firstborn of Egypt.
   *His faithful love endures forever.*
11 He brought Israel out of Egypt.
   *His faithful love endures forever.*
12 He acted with a strong hand and powerful arm.
   *His faithful love endures forever.*
13 Give thanks to him who parted the Red Sea.*
   *His faithful love endures forever.*
14 He led Israel safely through,
   *His faithful love endures forever.*
15 but he hurled Pharaoh and his army into the Red Sea.
   *His faithful love endures forever.*
16 Give thanks to him who led his people through the wilderness.
   *His faithful love endures forever.*

17 Give thanks to him who struck down mighty kings.
   *His faithful love endures forever.*

**136:1**
1 Chr 16:41
2 Chr 20:21
Ps 107:1
**136:2**
Deut 10:17

**136:4**
Ps 72:18

**136:5**
Prov 3:19
**136:6**
Ps 24:2

**136:7**
Ps 74:16

**136:8**
Gen 1:16

**136:10**
Exod 12:29
Ps 78:51
**136:11**
Exod 12:51; 13:3
Deut 9:29
**136:12**
Deut 4:34
Ps 44:3
**136:13**
Exod 14:21
Ps 78:13
**136:14**
Ps 106:9

**136:16**
Exod 13:18
Deut 8:15

**136:17**
Ps 135:10-12

**136:13** Hebrew *sea of reeds;* also in 136:15.

**136:1ff** Repeated throughout this psalm is the phrase "His faithful love endures forever." This psalm may have been a responsive reading, with the congregation saying these words in unison after each sentence. The repetition made this important lesson sink in. God's love includes aspects of love, kindness, mercy, and faithfulness. We never have to worry that God will run out of love because it flows from a well that will never run dry.

<sup>18</sup> He killed powerful kings—
    *His faithful love endures forever.*
<sup>19</sup> Sihon king of the Amorites,
    *His faithful love endures forever.*
<sup>20</sup> and Og king of Bashan.
    *His faithful love endures forever.*

**136:21**
Josh 12:1

<sup>21</sup> God gave the land of these kings as an inheritance—
    *His faithful love endures forever.*

**136:22**
Ps 105:6
Isa 41:8; 45:4

<sup>22</sup> a special possession to his servant Israel.
    *His faithful love endures forever.*

**136:23**
Pss 9:12; 106:45

<sup>23</sup> He remembered us in our weakness.
    *His faithful love endures forever.*

**136:24**
Judg 6:9

<sup>24</sup> He saved us from our enemies.
    *His faithful love endures forever.*

**136:25**
Pss 104:27; 145:15

<sup>25</sup> He gives food to every living thing.
    *His faithful love endures forever.*

**136:26**
2 Chr 36:23
Ezra 3:11

<sup>26</sup> Give thanks to the God of heaven.
    *His faithful love endures forever.*

**Theme:** A person in exile weeps over the bitterness of captivity. Our sorrow can make it difficult to imagine singing joyful songs again.
**Author:** Anonymous

**137:1**
Neh 1:4
Ezek 1:1, 3

# 137

<sup>1</sup> Beside the rivers of Babylon, we sat and wept
    as we thought of Jerusalem.*

**137:2**
Ezek 26:13

<sup>2</sup> We put away our harps,
    hanging them on the branches of poplar trees.

**137:3**
2 Chr 29:27
Neh 12:46

<sup>3</sup> For our captors demanded a song from us.
    Our tormentors insisted on a joyful hymn:
    "Sing us one of those songs of Jerusalem!"
<sup>4</sup> But how can we sing the songs of the LORD
    while in a pagan land?

<sup>5</sup> If I forget you, O Jerusalem,
    let my right hand forget how to play the harp.

**137:6**
Ezek 3:26

<sup>6</sup> May my tongue stick to the roof of my mouth
    if I fail to remember you,
    if I don't make Jerusalem my greatest joy.

**137:7**
Jer 49:7-22
Ezek 25:12-14
Obad 1:10-14

<sup>7</sup> O LORD, remember what the Edomites did
    on the day the armies of Babylon captured Jerusalem.
    "Destroy it!" they yelled.
    "Level it to the ground!"

**137:8**
Isa 13:1-22;
47:1-15
Jer 50:1-46;
51:1-64

<sup>8</sup> O Babylon, you will be destroyed.
    Happy is the one who pays you back
    for what you have done to us.
<sup>9</sup> Happy is the one who takes your babies
    and smashes them against the rocks!

**137:1** Hebrew *Zion;* also in 137:3.

---

**137:7** The Edomites were related to the Israelites, both nations having descended from Isaac and his father, Abraham. Although Israel shared its southern border with Edom, there was bitter hatred between the two nations. The Edomites did not come to help when the city of Jerusalem was besieged by the Babylonian army. In fact, they rejoiced when the city was destroyed (Jeremiah 49:7-22; Joel 3:19; Obadiah 1:1-21).

**137:8, 9** God destroyed Babylon and its offspring for their proud assault against God and his Kingdom. The Medes and Persians destroyed Babylon in 539 B.C. Many of those who were oppressed lived to see the victory. The phrase about the babies is harsh because the writer is crying out for judgment: "Treat the Babylonians the way they treated us."

**Theme:** Thanksgiving for answered prayer. God works out his plans for our lives and will bring us through the difficulties we face.
**Author:** David

# 138 *A psalm of David.*

1 I give you thanks, O LORD, with all my heart;
  I will sing your praises before the gods.
2 I bow before your holy Temple as I worship.
  I praise your name for your unfailing love and faithfulness;
  for your promises are backed
  by all the honor of your name.
3 As soon as I pray, you answer me;
  you encourage me by giving me strength.
4 Every king in all the earth will thank you, LORD,
  for all of them will hear your words.
5 Yes, they will sing about the LORD's ways,
  for the glory of the LORD is very great.
6 Though the LORD is great, he cares for the humble,
  but he keeps his distance from the proud.
7 Though I am surrounded by troubles,
  you will protect me from the anger of my enemies.
  You reach out your hand,
  and the power of your right hand saves me.
8 The LORD will work out his plans for my life—
  for your faithful love, O LORD, endures forever.
  Don't abandon me, for you made me.

**138:1**
Pss 95:3; 96:4;
111:1
**138:2**
Ps 5:7

**138:3**
Pss 28:7; 46:1;
118:5

**138:4**
Ps 102:15

**138:6**
Pss 101:5; 113:4-7
Prov 3:34
Jas 4:6
**138:7**
Exod 15:12
Ezra 9:8-9
Pss 20:6; 23:4;
71:20

**138:8**
Job 10:3
Pss 27:9; 71:9
Phil 1:6

**Theme:** God is all-seeing, all-knowing, all-powerful, and everywhere present. God knows us, God is with us, and his greatest gift is to allow us to know him.
**Author:** David

# 139 *For the choir director: A psalm of David.*

1 O LORD, you have examined my heart
  and know everything about me.
2 You know when I sit down or stand up.
  You know my thoughts even when I'm far away.
3 You see me when I travel
  and when I rest at home.
  You know everything I do.
4 You know what I am going to say
  even before I say it, LORD.
5 You go before me and follow me.
  You place your hand of blessing on my head.
6 Such knowledge is too wonderful for me,
  too great for me to understand!

**139:1**
Ps 44:21
**139:2**
Ps 94:11

**139:3**
Job 14:16

**139:4**
Heb 4:13

**139:5**
Ps 34:7
**139:6**
Job 42:3
Rom 11:33

**138:1** "Before the gods" may mean in the presence of subordinate heavenly beings (angels), or, more likely, it may be a statement ridiculing the kings or gods of the pagan nations. God is supreme in the whole earth.

**138:1-3** Thanksgiving should be an integral part of our praise to God. This theme is woven throughout the Psalms. As we praise and thank God for material and spiritual blessings, we should also thank him for answered prayer. Remember when you asked God for protection, strength, comfort, patience, love, or other special needs, and he supplied them. Beware of taking God's provision and answered prayer for granted.

**138:8** Every person dreams and makes plans for the future. Then they work hard to see those dreams and plans come true. But to make the most of life, we must include God's plan in our plans. He alone knows what is best for us; he alone can fulfill his purpose for us. As you make plans and dream dreams, talk with God about them.

**139:1-5** Sometimes we don't let people get to know us completely because we are afraid they will discover something about us that they won't like. But God already knows everything about us, even the number of hairs on our heads (Matthew 10:30), and still he accepts and loves us. God is with us through every situation, in every trial—protecting, loving, guiding. He knows and loves us completely.

**139:7**
Jer 23:24

7 I can never escape from your Spirit!
  I can never get away from your presence!

**139:8**
Prov 15:11
Amos 9:2-4

8 If I go up to heaven, you are there;
  if I go down to the grave,* you are there.

9 If I ride the wings of the morning,
  if I dwell by the farthest oceans,

**139:10**
Ps 23:2-3

10 even there your hand will guide me,
   and your strength will support me.

**139:11**
Job 22:13

11 I could ask the darkness to hide me
   and the light around me to become night—

**139:12**
Job 34:22
Dan 2:22
1 Jn 1:5

12    but even in darkness I cannot hide from you.
   To you the night shines as bright as day.
   Darkness and light are the same to you.

**139:13**
Ps 119:73

13 You made all the delicate, inner parts of my body
   and knit me together in my mother's womb.

14 Thank you for making me so wonderfully complex!
   Your workmanship is marvelous—how well I know it.

**139:15**
Job 10:8-10
Eccl 11:5

15 You watched me as I was being formed in utter seclusion,
   as I was woven together in the dark of the womb.

**139:16**
Job 14:5
Ps 56:8

16 You saw me before I was born.
   Every day of my life was recorded in your book.
   Every moment was laid out
      before a single day had passed.

**139:17**
Ps 40:5

17 How precious are your thoughts about me,* O God.
   They cannot be numbered!

**139:8** Hebrew *to Sheol.*   **139:17** Or *How precious to me are your thoughts.*

---

**ANGER AND
VENGEANCE
IN THE BOOK
OF PSALMS**

Several psalms shock those familiar with New Testament teachings. The psalm writers didn't hesitate to demand God's justice and make vivid suggestions on how he might carry it out. Apparently, no subject was unsuitable for discussion with God, but our tendency is to avoid the subjects of anger and vengeance in the book of Psalms.

To understand the words of anger and vengeance, we need to understand several things:

(1) The judgments asked for are to be carried out by God and are written out of intense personal and national suffering. The people are unable or unwilling to take revenge themselves and are asking God to intervene. Because few of us have suffered intense cruelty on a personal or national level, we find it difficult to grasp these outbursts.

(2) These writers were intimately aware of God's justice. Some of their words are efforts to vividly imagine what God might allow to happen to those who had harmed his people.

(3) If we dared to write down our thoughts while being unjustly attacked or suffering cruelty, we might be shocked at our own bold desire for vengeance. We would be surprised at how much we have in common with these ancient writers. They did not have Jesus' command to pray for one's enemies, but they did point to the right place to start. We are challenged to pay back good for evil, but until we respond to this challenge, we will not know how much we need God's help in order to forgive others.

(4) There is a helpful parallel between the psalms of anger and the psalms of vengeance. The "angry" psalms are intense and graphic, but they are directed at God. He is boldly told how disappointing it is when he turns his back on his people or acts too slowly. But while these thoughts and feelings were sincerely expressed, we know from the psalms themselves that these passing feelings were followed by renewed confidence in God's faithfulness. It is reasonable to expect the same of the "vengeance" psalms. We read, for example, David's angry outburst against Saul's pursuit in Psalm 59, yet we know that David never took personal revenge on Saul. The psalm writers freely spoke their minds to God, having confidence that he could sort out what was meant and what was felt. Pray with that same confidence—God can be trusted with your heart.

Selected psalms that emphasize these themes are 10; 23; 28; 35; 59; 69; 109; 137; 139; 140.

---

**139:7** God is omnipresent—he is present everywhere. Because this is so, you can never escape from his Spirit. This is good news to those who know and love God, because no matter what we do or where we go, we can never be far from God's comforting presence (see Romans 8:35-39).

**139:13-15** God's character goes into the creation of every person. When you feel worthless or even begin to hate yourself, remember that God's Spirit is ready and willing to work within you. We should have as much respect for ourselves as our Maker has for us.

18 I can't even count them;
    they outnumber the grains of sand!
    And when I wake up,
        you are still with me!

19 O God, if only you would destroy the wicked!
    Get out of my life, you murderers!
20 They blaspheme you;
    your enemies misuse your name.
21 O Lord, shouldn't I hate those who hate you?
    Shouldn't I despise those who oppose you?
22 Yes, I hate them with total hatred,
    for your enemies are my enemies.

23 Search me, O God, and know my heart;
    test me and know my anxious thoughts.
24 Point out anything in me that offends you,
    and lead me along the path of everlasting life.

**139:19**
Isa 11:4

**139:20**
Exod 20:7
Deut 5:11

**139:23**
Ps 26:2
**139:24**
Pss 5:8; 16:11;
143:10

**Theme:** Prayer for protection against those who slander or threaten you. Deliverance begins with concentrating on our future life with God.
**Author:** David

# 140 *For the choir director: A psalm of David.*

1 O Lord, rescue me from evil people.
    Protect me from those who are violent,
2 those who plot evil in their hearts
    and stir up trouble all day long.
3 Their tongues sting like a snake;
    the venom of a viper drips from their lips.       *Interlude*
4 O Lord, keep me out of the hands of the wicked.
    Protect me from those who are violent,
    for they are plotting against me.
5 The proud have set a trap to catch me;
    they have stretched out a net;
    they have placed traps all along the way.       *Interlude*

6 I said to the Lord, "You are my God!"
    Listen, O Lord, to my cries for mercy!
7 O Sovereign Lord, the strong one who rescued me,
    you protected me on the day of battle.
8 Lord, do not let evil people have their way.
    Do not let their evil schemes succeed,
    or they will become proud.       *Interlude*

9 Let my enemies be destroyed
    by the very evil they have planned for me.
10 Let burning coals fall down on their heads.
    Let them be thrown into the fire
    or into watery pits from which they can't escape.

**140:1**
Ps 17:13

**140:2**
Ps 56:6
Prov 6:14
Isa 59:4
**140:3**
Rom 3:13
Jas 3:8
**140:4**
Ps 71:4

**140:5**
Job 18:9
Pss 35:7; 57:6

**140:6**
Esth 9:25
Ps 112:10
**140:7**
Pss 28:8; 144:10
**140:8**
Ps 112:10

**140:9**
Ps 7:16
**140:10**
Pss 11:6; 21:9
Matt 3:10

**139:21-24** David's hatred for his enemies came from his zeal for God. David regarded his enemies as God's enemies, so his hatred was a desire for God's righteous justice and not for personal vengeance. Is it all right to be angry at people who hate God? Yes, but we must remember that it is God who will deal with them, not us. If we truly love God, then we will be deeply hurt if someone hates him. David asked God to search his heart and mind and point out any wrong motives that may have been behind his strong words. But while we seek justice against evil, we must also pray that God's enemies will turn to him before he judges them (see Matthew 5:44).

**139:23, 24** David asked God to search for sin and point it out, even to the level of testing his thoughts. This is exploratory surgery for sin. How are we to recognize sin unless God points it out? Then, when God shows us, we can repent and be forgiven. Make this verse your prayer. If you ask the Lord to search your heart and your thoughts and to reveal your sin, you will be continuing on "the path of everlasting life."

**140:11**
Ps 34:21

11 Don't let liars prosper here in our land.
  Cause great disasters to fall on the violent.

**140:12**
Pss 9:4; 35:10

12 But I know the Lord will help those they persecute;
  he will give justice to the poor.

**140:13**
Pss 16:11; 17:15;
97:12

13 Surely righteous people are praising your name;
  the godly will live in your presence.

**Theme:** A prayer for help when facing temptation. David asks God to protect him and to give him wisdom in accepting criticism. Be open to honest criticism—God may be speaking to you through others.
**Author:** David

# 141 *A psalm of David.*

**141:1**
Ps 70:5

**141:2**
Exod 29:41; 30:8
Rev 5:8; 8:3-4

1 O Lord, I am calling to you. Please hurry!
  Listen when I cry to you for help!
2 Accept my prayer as incense offered to you,
  and my upraised hands as an evening offering.

**141:3**
Ps 39:1
Prov 13:3; 21:23

**141:4**
Ps 119:36
Prov 23:6
Mal 3:15

3 Take control of what I say, O Lord,
  and guard my lips.
4 Don't let me drift toward evil
  or take part in acts of wickedness.
  Don't let me share in the delicacies
  of those who do wrong.

**141:5**
Ps 23:5
Prov 9:8; 19:25;
27:6
Gal 6:1

5 Let the godly strike me!
  It will be a kindness!
  If they correct me, it is soothing medicine.
  Don't let me refuse it.

  But I pray constantly
  against the wicked and their deeds.
6 When their leaders are thrown down from a cliff,
  the wicked will listen to my words and find them true.

**141:7**
Ps 53:5

7 Like rocks brought up by a plow,
  the bones of the wicked will lie scattered without burial.*

**141:8**
Ps 11:1

8 I look to you for help, O Sovereign Lord.
  You are my refuge; don't let them kill me.

**141:9**
Ps 91:3

**141:10**
Ps 35:8

9 Keep me from the traps they have set for me,
  from the snares of those who do wrong.
10 Let the wicked fall into their own nets,
  but let me escape.

**141:7** Hebrew *scattered at the mouth of Sheol.*

---

**140:12** To whom can the poor turn when they are persecuted? They lack the money to get professional help and so are usually unable to defend themselves. But there is always someone on their side—the Lord will stand by them and ultimately bring about justice. This should be a comfort for us all. No matter what our situation may be, the Lord is with us. But this truth should also call us to live responsibly with others. As God's people, we are required to defend the rights of the powerless.

**141:3** James wrote that "the tongue is a flame of fire. It is a whole world of wickedness, corrupting your entire body" (James 3:6). On the average, a person opens his or her mouth approximately 700 times a day to speak. David wisely asked God to keep him from speaking evil—even as he underwent persecution. Jesus himself was silent before his accusers (Matthew 26:63). Knowing the power of the tongue, we would do well to ask God to guard what we say so that our words will bring honor to his name.

**141:4** Evil acts begin with evil desires. It isn't enough to ask God to keep you away from temptation, make you stronger, or change your circumstances. You must ask him to change you on the inside—at the level of your desires.

**141:5** David says that being rebuked by a godly person is a kindness. Nobody really likes criticism, but everybody can benefit from it when it is given wisely and taken humbly. David suggested how to accept criticism: (1) Don't refuse it, (2) consider it a kindness, and (3) keep quiet (don't fight back). Putting these suggestions into practice will help you control how you react to criticism, making it productive rather than destructive, no matter how it was originally intended.

**Theme:** A prayer when overwhelmed and desperate. When we feel cornered by our enemies, only God can keep us safe.
**Author:** David

# 142 *A psalm\* of David, regarding his experience in the cave. A prayer.*

1 I cry out to the LORD;
   I plead for the LORD's mercy.
2 I pour out my complaints before him
   and tell him all my troubles.
3 When I am overwhelmed,
   you alone know the way I should turn.
   Wherever I go,
   my enemies have set traps for me.
4 I look for someone to come and help me,
   but no one gives me a passing thought!
   No one will help me;
   no one cares a bit what happens to me.
5 Then I pray to you, O LORD.
   I say, "You are my place of refuge.
   You are all I really want in life.
6 Hear my cry,
   for I am very low.
   Rescue me from my persecutors,
   for they are too strong for me.
7 Bring me out of prison
   so I can thank you.
   The godly will crowd around me,
   for you are good to me."

142:1 Pss 30:8; 77:1
142:3 Ps 140:5
142:4 Ps 88:8; Jer 30:17
142:5 Ps 91:2, 9
142:6 Pss 18:17; 79:8
142:7 Ps 13:6

**Theme:** A prayer in the midst of hopelessness and depression. Our prayers should fit into what we know is consistent with God's character and plans.
**Author:** David

# 143 *A psalm of David.*

1 Hear my prayer, O LORD;
   listen to my plea!
   Answer me because you are faithful and righteous.
2 Don't put your servant on trial,
   for no one is innocent before you.
3 My enemy has chased me.
   He has knocked me to the ground
   and forces me to live in darkness like those in the grave.
4 I am losing all hope;
   I am paralyzed with fear.
5 I remember the days of old.
   I ponder all your great works
   and think about what you have done.
6 I lift my hands to you in prayer.
   I thirst for you as parched land thirsts for rain.                *Interlude*

143:1 Ps 140:6
143:2 Job 14:3; 22:4
143:3 Lam 3:6
143:4 Lam 3:11
143:5 Ps 77:5, 10-11
143:6 Ps 63:1

142:TITLE Hebrew *maskil*. This may be a literary or musical term.

---

**142:6** Have you ever felt that no one cared what happened to you? David had good reason to feel that way, and he wrote, "Hear my cry, for I am very low." Through prayer we can pull out of our tailspin and be reminded that God cares for us deeply.
**142:7** This psalm was written when David was hiding from Saul in caves like the ones at Adullam (1 Samuel 22) or En-gedi

(1 Samuel 24). These may have seemed like prisons to him because of the confinement.

**143:7** David was losing hope, caught in paralyzing fear and deep depression. At times we feel caught in deepening depression, and we are unable to pull ourselves out. At those times we can come to the Lord and, like David, express our true feelings. Then we will find help as we remember his works (143:5), reach out to him in prayer (143:6), trust him (143:8), and seek to do his will (143:10).

**143:7**
Pss 69:17; 88:4

7 Come quickly, LORD, and answer me,
  for my depression deepens.
Don't turn away from me,
  or I will die.

**143:8**
Ps 32:8

8 Let me hear of your unfailing love each morning,
  for I am trusting you.
Show me where to walk,
  for I give myself to you.

**143:9**
Ps 59:1

9 Rescue me from my enemies, LORD;
  I run to you to hide me.

**143:10**
Neh 9:20
Pss 23:3; 119:12

10 Teach me to do your will,
  for you are my God.
May your gracious Spirit lead me forward
  on a firm footing.

11 For the glory of your name, O LORD, preserve my life.
  Because of your faithfulness, bring me out of this distress.

**143:12**
Pss 52:5; 116:16

12 In your unfailing love, silence all my enemies
  and destroy all my foes,
  for I am your servant.

**Theme:** Rejoicing in God's care. Whether in times of prosperity or adversity, blessed are those whose God is the Lord.
**Author:** David

# 144 *A psalm of David.*

**144:1**
Ps 18:2

1 Praise the LORD, who is my rock.
  He trains my hands for war
  and gives my fingers skill for battle.
2 He is my loving ally and my fortress,
  my tower of safety, my rescuer.
He is my shield, and I take refuge in him.
  He makes the nations* submit to me.

**144:3**
Ps 8:4

3 O LORD, what are human beings that you should notice them,
  mere mortals that you should think about them?

**144:4**
Job 8:9; 14:2
Pss 39:11; 109:23

4 For they are like a breath of air;
  their days are like a passing shadow.

**144:5**
Ps 18:9
Isa 64:1

5 Open the heavens, LORD, and come down.
  Touch the mountains so they billow smoke.

**144:6**
Hab 3:11
Zech 9:14

6 Hurl your lightning bolts and scatter your enemies!
  Shoot your arrows and confuse them!

**144:7**
Pss 18:44; 69:1, 14

7 Reach down from heaven and rescue me;
  rescue me from deep waters,
  from the power of my enemies.

**144:8**
Deut 32:40
Pss 12:2; 41:6
Isa 44:20

8 Their mouths are full of lies;
  they swear to tell the truth, but they lie instead.

**144:9**
Ps 40:3

9 I will sing a new song to you, O God!
  I will sing your praises with a ten-stringed harp.

**144:10**
2 Sam 18:7
Ps 140:7

10 For you grant victory to kings!
  You rescued your servant David from the fatal sword.

**144:2** Some manuscripts read *my people.*

**143:10** David's prayer was to be taught to do God's will, not his own. A prayer for guidance is self-centered if it doesn't recognize God's power to redirect our lives. Asking God to restructure our priorities awakens our minds and stirs our will.

**144:3, 4** Life is short. David reminds us that it is "like a breath" and that our "days are like a passing shadow." James says that our life is "like the morning fog—it's here a little while, then it's gone" (James 4:14). Because life is short, live for God while you have the time. Don't waste your life by selecting an inferior purpose that has no lasting value. Only God can make your life worthwhile, purposeful, and meaningful.

<sup>11</sup> Save me!
>> Rescue me from the power of my enemies.
>> Their mouths are full of lies;
>>> they swear to tell the truth, but they lie instead.

<sup>12</sup> May our sons flourish in their youth
>> like well-nurtured plants.
>> May our daughters be like graceful pillars,
>>> carved to beautify a palace.

<sup>13</sup> May our barns be filled
>> with crops of every kind.
>> May the flocks in our fields multiply by the thousands,
>>> even tens of thousands,

<sup>14</sup>   and may our oxen be loaded down with produce.
>> May there be no enemy breaking through our walls,
>>> no going into captivity,
>>> no cries of alarm in our town squares.

<sup>15</sup> Yes, joyful are those who live like this!
>> Joyful indeed are those whose God is the LORD.

**Theme:** A time will come when all people will join together in recognizing and worshiping God. Because God is full of love, he satisfies all who trust in him.
**Author:** David

# 145 *

*A psalm of praise of David.*

<sup>1</sup> I will exalt you, my God and King,
>> and praise your name forever and ever.

<sup>2</sup> I will praise you every day;
>> yes, I will praise you forever.

<sup>3</sup> Great is the LORD! He is most worthy of praise!
>> No one can measure his greatness.

<sup>4</sup> Let each generation tell its children of your mighty acts;
>> let them proclaim your power.

<sup>5</sup> I will meditate* on your majestic, glorious splendor
>> and your wonderful miracles.

<sup>6</sup> Your awe-inspiring deeds will be on every tongue;
>> I will proclaim your greatness.

<sup>7</sup> Everyone will share the story of your wonderful goodness;
>> they will sing with joy about your righteousness.

<sup>8</sup> The LORD is merciful and compassionate,
>> slow to get angry and filled with unfailing love.

<sup>9</sup> The LORD is good to everyone.
>> He showers compassion on all his creation.

<sup>10</sup> All of your works will thank you, LORD,
>> and your faithful followers will praise you.

<sup>11</sup> They will speak of the glory of your kingdom;
>> they will give examples of your power.

<sup>12</sup> They will tell about your mighty deeds
>> and about the majesty and glory of your reign.

**145** This psalm is a Hebrew acrostic poem; each verse (including 13b) begins with a successive letter of the Hebrew alphabet.    **145:5** Some manuscripts read *They will speak.*

**145:3**
Rom 11:33

**145:4**
Isa 38:19

**145:5**
Ps 119:27

**145:6**
Deut 10:21; 32:3

**145:7**
Ps 51:14
Isa 63:7

**145:8**
Exod 34:6

**145:9**
Ps 100:5
Nah 1:7
Matt 19:17
Mark 10:18

**145:10**
Pss 19:1; 68:26

**145:12**
Ps 105:1
Isa 2:10, 19, 21

**144:11**
Ps 12:2
Isa 44:20

**144:12**
Ps 92:12-14
Prov 3:9-10
Song 4:4; 7:4

**144:14**
2 Kgs 25:11
Isa 24:11
Jer 14:2

**145:14** Sometimes our burdens seem more than we can bear, and we wonder how we can go on. David stands at this bleak intersection of life's road and meditates on the Lord, the great burden bearer. God is able to lift us up because (1) his greatness is beyond discovery (145:3); (2) he does mighty acts for each generation (145:4); (3) he is full of majestic, glorious splendor (145:5); (4) he does awe-inspiring deeds (145:5, 6); (5) he is righteous (145:7); (6) he is kind, merciful, patient, loving, and compassionate (145:8, 9); (7) he rules over an everlasting kingdom (145:13); (8) he is our source of all our daily needs (145:15, 16); (9) he is righteous and kind in all his dealings (145:17); (10) he remains close to those who call on him (145:18); (11) he hears our cries and rescues us (145:19, 20). If you are bending under a burden and feel that you are about to fall, turn to God for help. He is ready to lift you up and bear your burden.

**145:13**
2 Pet 1:11

13 For your kingdom is an everlasting kingdom.
 You rule throughout all generations.

 The LORD always keeps his promises;
  he is gracious in all he does.*
14 The LORD helps the fallen
  and lifts those bent beneath their loads.

**145:15**
Ps 104:27

15 The eyes of all look to you in hope;
  you give them their food as they need it.
16 When you open your hand,
  you satisfy the hunger and thirst of every living thing.
17 The LORD is righteous in everything he does;
  he is filled with kindness.

**145:18**
Deut 4:7
John 4:24

18 The LORD is close to all who call on him,
  yes, to all who call on him in truth.

**145:19**
Ps 10:17
Prov 15:29

19 He grants the desires of those who fear him;
  he hears their cries for help and rescues them.

**145:20**
Pss 31:23; 37:38

20 The LORD protects all those who love him,
  but he destroys the wicked.

**145:21**
Pss 71:8; 150:6

21 I will praise the LORD,
  and may everyone on earth bless his holy name
  forever and ever.

**Theme:** The help of people versus the help of God. Help from people is temporal and unstable, but help from God is lasting and complete.
**Author:** Anonymous

**146:1**
Ps 103:1

# 146

1 Praise the LORD!

 Let all that I am praise the LORD.

**146:2**
Pss 63:4; 104:33

2 I will praise the LORD as long as I live.
 I will sing praises to my God with my dying breath.

**146:3**
Ps 60:11

3 Don't put your confidence in powerful people;
  there is no help for you there.

**146:4**
Pss 33:10; 104:29
Eccl 12:7

4 When they breathe their last, they return to the earth,
  and all their plans die with them.

**146:5**
Ps 71:5

5 But joyful are those who have the God of Israel* as their helper,
  whose hope is in the LORD their God.

**146:6**
Acts 14:15

6 He made heaven and earth,
  the sea, and everything in them.
 He keeps every promise forever.

**146:7**
Ps 68:6

7 He gives justice to the oppressed
  and food to the hungry.
 The LORD frees the prisoners.

**146:8**
Matt 9:30
John 9:7

8  The LORD opens the eyes of the blind.
 The LORD lifts up those who are weighed down.
 The LORD loves the godly.

**145:13** The last two lines of 145:13 are not found in many of the ancient manuscripts. See note on 44:4.  **146:5** Hebrew *of Jacob.*

**146–150** These last five psalms overflow with praise. Each begins and ends with "Praise the LORD." They show us where, why, and how to praise God. What does praise do? (1) Praise takes our mind off our problems and shortcomings and helps us focus on God. (2) Praise leads us from individual meditation to corporate worship. (3) Praise causes us to consider and appreciate God's character. (4) Praise lifts our perspective from the earthly to the heavenly. (5) Praise prepares our hearts to receive God's love and the power of his Holy Spirit.

**146:3-8** The writer portrays powerful people as inadequate saviors, making false promises they cannot deliver (146:3). God

is the hope and the help of the needy. Jesus affirms his concern for the poor and afflicted in Luke 4:18-21; 7:21-23. He does not separate the physical needs from spiritual needs but attends to both. While God, not the government, is the hope of the needy, *we* are his instruments to help here on earth.

9 The LORD protects the foreigners among us.
He cares for the orphans and widows,
but he frustrates the plans of the wicked.

10 The LORD will reign forever.
He will be your God, O Jerusalem,* throughout the generations.

Praise the LORD!

**Theme:** What gives God joy? Although God created everything, his greatest joy comes
from our genuine worship and trust.
**Author:** Anonymous, written when the exiles returned to Jerusalem

# 147

1 Praise the LORD!

How good to sing praises to our God!
How delightful and how fitting!

2 The LORD is rebuilding Jerusalem
and bringing the exiles back to Israel.

3 He heals the brokenhearted
and bandages their wounds.

4 He counts the stars
and calls them all by name.

5 How great is our Lord! His power is absolute!
His understanding is beyond comprehension!

6 The LORD supports the humble,
but he brings the wicked down into the dust.

7 Sing out your thanks to the LORD;
sing praises to our God with a harp.

8 He covers the heavens with clouds,
provides rain for the earth,
and makes the grass grow in mountain pastures.

9 He gives food to the wild animals
and feeds the young ravens when they cry.

10 He takes no pleasure in the strength of a horse
or in human might.

11 No, the LORD's delight is in those who fear him,
those who put their hope in his unfailing love.

12 Glorify the LORD, O Jerusalem!
Praise your God, O Zion!

13 For he has strengthened the bars of your gates
and blessed your children within your walls.

14 He sends peace across your nation
and satisfies your hunger with the finest wheat.

15 He sends his orders to the world—
how swiftly his word flies!

16 He sends the snow like white wool;
he scatters frost upon the ground like ashes.

**146:10** Hebrew *Zion.*

---

**146:9** Exod 22:21; Lev 19:34; Deut 10:18
**146:10** Ps 10:16
**147:1** Pss 33:1; 135:3
**147:2** Isa 11:12; 56:8; Ezek 39:28
**147:4** Gen 15:5; Isa 40:26
**147:5** Ps 98:1; Isa 40:28
**147:8** Job 5:10; 26:8; 38:26
**147:9** Job 38:41; Ps 104:27
**147:10** 1 Sam 16:7; Ps 33:17
**147:13** Neh 3:3; 7:3
**147:14** Deut 32:14; Isa 54:13; 60:17-18
**147:15** Job 37:12; Ps 104:4

---

**146:9** God's plans frustrate the "plans of the wicked" because his values are the opposite of society's. Jesus turned society's values upside down when he proclaimed that "many who seem to be the greatest now will be the least important then, and those who are considered least important now will be the greatest then" (Matthew 19:30). "If you try to hang onto your life, you will lose it. But if you give up your life for my sake, you will save it" (Matthew 16:25). Don't be surprised when others don't understand your Christian values; but don't give in to theirs.

**147:5** Sometimes we feel as if we don't understand ourselves—what we want, how we feel, what's wrong with us, or what we should do about it. But God's understanding has no limit, and therefore he understands us fully. If you feel troubled and don't understand yourself, remember that God understands you perfectly. Take your mind off yourself and focus on God. Seek to become more and more like him. The more you learn about God and his ways, the better you will understand yourself.

**147:10, 11** We may spend a lot of effort trying to sharpen our skills or become physically fit. There is nothing wrong with doing so, and, in fact, our gifts can be used to glorify God. But when we use our gifts with no regard for God, they are indeed worth little. It is our honor and trust that God desires. When he has those, then he will use our gifts and strengths in ways far greater than we can imagine.

¹⁷ He hurls the hail like stones.*
   Who can stand against his freezing cold?
¹⁸ Then, at his command, it all melts.
   He sends his winds, and the ice thaws.
¹⁹ He has revealed his words to Jacob,
   his decrees and regulations to Israel.
²⁰ He has not done this for any other nation;
   they do not know his regulations.

Praise the LORD!

**147:19**
Deut 33:3-4
Mal 4:4
**147:20**
Deut 4:7-8
Ps 79:6

**Theme:** Let all creation praise and worship the Lord.
**Author:** Anonymous

**148:1**
Ps 102:19
†Matt 21:9
†Luke 19:38

# 148

¹ Praise the LORD!

   Praise the LORD from the heavens!
Praise him from the skies!

**148:2**
Ps 103:20-21

² Praise him, all his angels!
   Praise him, all the armies of heaven!
³ Praise him, sun and moon!
   Praise him, all you twinkling stars!

**148:4**
Gen 1:7
Deut 10:14

⁴ Praise him, skies above!
   Praise him, vapors high above the clouds!

**148:5**
Gen 1:1

⁵ Let every created thing give praise to the LORD,
   for he issued his command, and they came into being.

**148:6**
Job 38:33

⁶ He set them in place forever and ever.
   His decree will never be revoked.

**148:7**
Gen 1:21
Ps 74:13
Hab 3:10

⁷ Praise the LORD from the earth,
   you creatures of the ocean depths,
⁸ fire and hail, snow and clouds,*
   wind and weather that obey him,

**148:9**
Isa 44:23; 49:13;
55:12

⁹ mountains and all hills,
   fruit trees and all cedars,
¹⁰ wild animals and all livestock,
   small scurrying animals and birds,
¹¹ kings of the earth and all people,
   rulers and judges of the earth,

**147:17** Hebrew *like bread crumbs.*   **148:8** Or *mist,* or *smoke.*

---

**PRAISE IN THE BOOK OF PSALMS**

Most of the psalms are prayers, and most of the prayers include praise to God. Praise expresses admiration, appreciation, and thanks. Praise in the book of Psalms is often directed to God, and just as often the praise is shared with others. Considering all that God has done and does for us, what could be more natural than outbursts of heartfelt praise?

As you read Psalms, note the praise given to God, not only for what he does—his creation, his blessings, his forgiveness—but also for who he is—loving, just, faithful, forgiving, patient. Note also those times when the praise of God is shared with others and they, too, are encouraged to praise him. In what ways have you recently praised God or told others all that he has done for you?

Selected psalms that emphasize this theme are 8; 19; 30; 65; 84; 96; 100; 136; 145; 150.

---

**147:19, 20** The nation of Israel (the descendants of Jacob) was special to God because to its people God brought his laws, and through its people he sent his Son, Jesus Christ. Now any individual who follows God is just as special to him. In fact, the Bible says that the real nation of Israel is not a specific people or geographic place but the community of all who believe in and obey God (see Galatians 3:28, 29).

**148:5-14** All creation is like a majestic symphony or a great choir composed of many harmonious parts that together offer up songs of praise to the Lord. Each part (independent, yet part

of the whole) is caught up and carried along in swelling tides of praise. This is a picture of how we as believers should praise God—individually, yet as part of the great choir of believers worldwide. Are you singing your part well in the worldwide choir of praise?

12 young men and young women,
   old men and children.

13 Let them all praise the name of the LORD.
   For his name is very great;
   his glory towers over the earth and heaven!

14 He has made his people strong,
   honoring his faithful ones—
   the people of Israel who are close to him.

Praise the LORD!

| | |
|---|---|
| | **148:13** Pss 8:1; 113:4 Rev 5:12 |
| | **148:14** Deut 10:21 1 Sam 2:1 Eph 2:17 |

**Theme:** A victory celebration. We have the assurance that God truly enjoys his people.
**Author:** Anonymous

# 149

1 Praise the LORD!

   Sing to the LORD a new song.
   Sing his praises in the assembly of the faithful.

2 O Israel, rejoice in your Maker.
   O people of Jerusalem,* exult in your King.

3 Praise his name with dancing,
   accompanied by tambourine and harp.

4 For the LORD delights in his people;
   he crowns the humble with victory.

5 Let the faithful rejoice that he honors them.
   Let them sing for joy as they lie on their beds.

6 Let the praises of God be in their mouths,
   and a sharp sword in their hands—

7 to execute vengeance on the nations
   and punishment on the peoples,

8 to bind their kings with shackles
   and their leaders with iron chains,

9 to execute the judgment written against them.
   This is the glorious privilege of his faithful ones.

Praise the LORD!

| | |
|---|---|
| | **149:1** Pss 33:3; 89:5 |
| | **149:2** Judg 8:23 Ps 47:6 |
| | **149:3** Exod 15:20 |
| | **149:4** Ps 35:27 |
| | **149:5** Job 35:10 |
| | **149:6** Ps 66:17 |
| | **149:8** Nah 3:10 |
| | **149:9** Ps 148:14 Ezek 28:26 |

**Theme:** A closing hymn of praise. God's creation praises him everywhere in every way. We should join this rejoicing song of praise.
**Author:** Anonymous

# 150

1 Praise the LORD!

   Praise God in his sanctuary;
   praise him in his mighty heaven!

2 Praise him for his mighty works;
   praise his unequaled greatness!

3 Praise him with a blast of the ram's horn;
   praise him with the lyre and harp!

| | |
|---|---|
| | **150:1** Pss 19:1; 73:17; 102:19 |
| | **150:2** Deut 3:24 |
| | **150:3** Ps 98:6 |

**149:2** Hebrew *Zion*.

---

**149:3-5** Although the Bible invites us to praise God, we often aren't sure how to go about it. Here, several ways are suggested: by singing, dancing, or playing musical instruments. God enjoys his people, and we should enjoy praising him.

**149:6, 7** The sharp sword symbolizes the completeness of judgment that will be executed by the Messiah when he returns to punish all evildoers (Revelation 1:16).

**150:3-5** Music and song were an integral part of Old Testament worship. David introduced music into the Tabernacle and Temple services (1 Chronicles 16:4-7). The music must have been loud and joyous as evidenced by the list of instruments and the presence of choirs and song leaders. Music was also important in New Testament worship (Ephesians 5:19; Colossians 3:16).

**150:4**
Isa 38:20

**150:5**
1 Chr 13:8; 15:16

**150:6**
Ps 145:21

4 Praise him with the tambourine and dancing;
  praise him with strings and flutes!
5 Praise him with a clash of cymbals;
  praise him with loud clanging cymbals.
6 Let everything that breathes sing praises to the LORD!

Praise the LORD!

---

**WHERE TO GET HELP IN THE BOOK OF PSALMS**

**When you feel . . .**

Afraid: 3; 4; 27; 46; 49; 56; 91; 118
Alone: 9; 10; 12; 13; 27; 40; 43
"Burned out": 6; 63
Cheated: 41
Confused: 10; 12; 73
Depressed: 27; 34; 42; 43; 88; 143
Distressed: 13; 25; 31; 40; 107
Elated: 19; 96
Guilty: 19; 32; 38; 51
Hateful: 11
Impatient: 13; 27; 37; 40
Insecure: 3; 5; 12; 91
Insulted: 41; 70
Jealous: 37
Like quitting: 29; 43; 145
Lost: 23; 139
Overwhelmed: 25; 69; 142
Penitent/Sorry: 32; 51; 66
Proud: 14; 30; 49
Purposeless: 14; 25; 39; 49; 90
Sad: 13
Self-confident: 24
Tense: 4
Thankful: 118; 136; 138
Threatened: 3; 11; 17
Tired/Weak: 6; 13; 18; 28; 49; 40; 86
Trapped: 7; 17; 42; 88; 142
Unimportant: 8; 90; 139
Vengeful: 3; 7; 109
Worried: 37
Worshipful: 8; 19; 27; 29; 150

**When you're facing . . .**

Atheists: 10; 14; 19; 52; 53; 115
Competition: 133
Criticism: 35; 56; 120
Danger: 11
Death: 6; 71; 90
Decisions: 1; 119
Discrimination: 54
Doubts: 34; 37; 94
Evil people: 10; 35; 36; 49; 52; 109; 140
Enemies: 3; 25; 35; 41; 56; 59
Heresy: 14
Hypocrisy: 26; 28; 40; 50
Illness: 6; 139
Lies: 5; 12; 120
Old age: 71; 92
Persecution: 1; 3; 7; 56
Poverty: 9; 10; 12
Punishment: 6; 38; 39
Slander/Insults: 7; 15; 35; 43; 120
Slaughter: 6; 46; 83
Sorrow: 23; 34
Success: 18; 112; 127; 128
Temptation: 38; 141
Troubles: 34; 55; 86; 102; 142; 145
Verbal cruelty: 35; 120

**When you want . . .**

Acceptance: 139
Answers: 4; 17
Confidence: 46; 71
Courage: 11; 42
Fellowship with God: 5; 16; 25; 27; 37; 133
Forgiveness: 32; 38; 40; 51; 69; 86; 103; 130
Friendship: 16
Godliness: 15; 25
Guidance: 1; 5; 15; 19; 25; 32; 48
Healing: 6; 41
Hope: 16; 17; 18; 23; 27
Humility: 19; 147
Illumination: 19
Integrity: 24; 25
Joy: 9; 16; 28; 126
Justice: 2; 7; 14; 26; 37; 49; 58; 82
Knowledge: 2; 8; 18; 19; 25; 29; 97; 103
Leadership: 72
Miracles: 60; 111
Money: 15; 16; 17; 49
Peace: 3; 4
Perspective: 2; 11
Prayer: 5; 17; 27; 61
Protection: 3; 4; 7; 16; 17; 18; 23; 27; 31; 91; 121; 125
Provision: 23
Rest: 23; 27
Salvation: 26; 37; 49; 126
Stability: 11; 33; 46
Vindication: 9; 14; 28; 35; 109
Wisdom: 1; 16; 19; 64; 111a

---

**150:6** How could the message be more clear? The writer was telling the individual listeners to praise God. What a fitting way to end this book of praise—with direct encouragement for *you* to praise God, too. Remember to praise him every day!

**150:6** In a way, the book of Psalms parallels our spiritual journey through life. It begins by presenting us with two roads: the way to life and the way to death. If we choose God's way to life, we still face both blessings and troubles, joy and grief, successes and obstacles. Through it all, God is at our side, guiding, encouraging, comforting, and caring. As the wise and faithful person's life draws to an end, it becomes clear that God's road is the right road. Knowing this will cause us to praise God for leading us in the right direction and for assuring us of a place in the perfect world he has in store for those who have faithfully followed him.

## VITAL STATISTICS

**PURPOSE:**
To teach people how to attain wisdom, discipline, and a prudent life, and how to do what is right, just, and fair (see 1:2, 3)—in short, to apply divine wisdom to daily life and to provide moral instruction

**AUTHOR:**
Solomon wrote most of this book, with Agur and Lemuel contributing some of the later sections.

**ORIGINAL AUDIENCE:**
The people of Israel

**DATE WRITTEN:**
Solomon wrote and compiled most of these proverbs early in his reign.

**SETTING:**
This is a book of wise sayings, a textbook for teaching people how to live godly lives through the repetition of wise thoughts.

**KEY VERSE:**
"Fear of the LORD is the foundation of true knowledge, but fools despise wisdom and discipline" (1:7).

**SPECIAL FEATURES:**
The book uses varied literary forms: poems, brief parables, pointed questions, and couplets. Other literary devices include antithesis, comparison, and personification.

ALPHABET letters, vowels, and consonants formed into words, sentences, paragraphs, and books—spoken, signed, whispered, written, and printed. From friendly advice to impassioned speeches and from dusty volumes to daily tabloids, messages are sent and received, with each sender trying to impart knowledge . . . and wisdom.

Woven into human fabric is the desire to learn and understand. Our mind sets us apart from animals, and we analyze, conceptualize, theorize, discuss, and debate everything from science to the supernatural. We build schools, institutes, and universities, where learned professors can teach us about the world and about life.

Knowledge is good, but a vast difference stands between "knowledge" (having the facts) and "wisdom" (applying those facts to life). We may amass knowledge, but without wisdom our knowledge is useless. We must learn how to *live out* what we know.

The wisest man who ever lived, Solomon, left us a legacy of written wisdom in three volumes—Proverbs, Ecclesiastes, and Song of Songs. In these books, under the inspiration of the Holy Spirit, he gives practical insights and guidelines for life.

In the first of these three volumes, Solomon passes on his practical advice in the form of proverbs. A proverb is a short, concise sentence that conveys moral truth. The book of Proverbs is a collection of these wise statements. The main theme of Proverbs, as we might expect, is the nature of true wisdom. Solomon writes, "Fear of the LORD is the foundation of true knowledge, but fools despise wisdom and discipline" (1:7). He then proceeds to give hundreds of practical examples of how to live according to godly wisdom.

Proverbs covers a wide range of topics, including youth and discipline, family life, self-control and resisting temptation, business matters, words and the tongue, knowing God, marriage, seeking the truth, wealth and poverty, immorality, and, of course, wisdom. These proverbs are short poems (usually in couplet form), containing a holy mixture of common sense and timely warnings. Although they are not meant to teach doctrine, a person who follows their advice will walk closely with God. The word *proverb* comes from a Hebrew word that means "to rule or to govern," and these sayings, reminders, and admonitions provide profound advice for governing our lives.

As you read Proverbs, understand that knowing God is the key to wisdom. Listen to the thoughts and lessons from the world's wisest man, and apply these truths to your life. Don't just read these proverbs; act on them!

## THE BLUEPRINT

A. **WISDOM FOR YOUNG PEOPLE**
   **(1:1—9:18)**

   Solomon instructed the young people of his day like a father giving advice to his child. While many of these proverbs are directed toward young people, the principles supporting them are helpful to all believers, male and female, young and old. Anyone beginning his or her journey to discover more of wisdom will benefit greatly from these wise sayings.

B. **WISDOM FOR ALL PEOPLE**
   **(10:1—24:34)**

   Solomon wanted to impart wisdom to all people, regardless of their age, sex, or position in society. These short, wise sayings give us practical wisdom for daily living. We should study them diligently and integrate them into our lives.

C. WISDOM FOR THE LEADERS
(25:1—31:31)

In addition to the proverbs that Solomon collected, the advisers of Hezekiah collected many proverbs that Solomon and others wrote. While most of these are general in nature, many are directed specifically to the king and those who dealt with the king. These are particularly useful for leaders or those who aspire to be leaders.

## MEGATHEMES

| THEME | EXPLANATION | IMPORTANCE |
|---|---|---|
| Wisdom | God wants his people to be wise. Two kinds of people portray two contrasting paths of life. The fool is the wicked, stubborn person who hates or ignores God. The wise person seeks to know and love God. | When we choose God's way, he grants us wisdom. His Word, the Bible, leads us to live right, have right relationships, and make right decisions. |
| Relationships | Proverbs gives us advice for developing our personal relationships with friends, family members, and coworkers. In every relationship, we must show love, dedication, and high moral standards. | To relate to people, we need consistency, tact, and discipline to use the wisdom God gives us. If we don't treat others according to the wisdom God gives, our relationships will suffer. |
| Speech | What we say shows our real attitude toward others. How we talk reveals what we're really like. Our speech is a test of how wise we have become. | To be wise in our speech we need to use self-control. Our words should be honest and well chosen. |
| Work | God controls the final outcome of all we do. We are accountable to carry out our work with diligence and discipline, not laziness. | Because God evaluates how we live, we should work purposefully. We must never be lax or self-satisfied in using our skills. |
| Success | Although people work very hard for money and fame, God views success as having a good reputation, moral character, and the spiritual devotion to obey him. | A successful relationship with God counts for eternity. Everything else is perishable. All our resources, time, and talents come from God. We should strive to use them wisely. |

## A. WISDOM FOR YOUNG PEOPLE (1:1—9:18)

Proverbs begins with a clear statement of its purpose—to impart wisdom for godly living. The first few chapters are Solomon's fatherly advice to young people. Although most of the material in this section is directed toward young people, all who seek wisdom will greatly benefit from these wise words. This is where one can discover the source of wisdom, the value of wisdom, and the benefits of wisdom.

### The Purpose of Proverbs

**1:1**
1 Kgs 4:32
Prov 25:1
Eccl 1:1; 12:9

**1** These are the proverbs of Solomon, David's son, king of Israel.

**1:3**
Prov 2:9; 19:20

2 Their purpose is to teach people wisdom and discipline,
   to help them understand the insights of the wise.

**1:4**
Prov 2:10-11;
8:5, 12

3 Their purpose is to teach people to live disciplined and successful lives,
   to help them do what is right, just, and fair.

**1:5**
Prov 9:9; 14:6
Eccl 9:1

4 These proverbs will give insight to the simple,
   knowledge and discernment to the young.

5 Let the wise listen to these proverbs and become even wiser.
   Let those with understanding receive guidance

---

**1:1** What the book of Psalms is to prayer and devotional life, the book of Proverbs is to everyday life. Proverbs gives practical suggestions for effective living. This book is not just a collection of interesting tidbits; it contains deep spiritual insights drawn from experience. A *proverb* is a short, wise, easy-to-remember saying that calls a person to action. It doesn't argue about basic spiritual and moral beliefs; it assumes we already hold them. The book of Proverbs focuses on God—his character, works, and blessings—and it tells how we can live in close relationship to him.

**1:1** Solomon, the third king of Israel, son of the great king David, reigned during Israel's golden age. When God said he would give him whatever he wanted, he asked for an understanding mind (1 Kings 3:5-14). God was pleased with this request. He not only made Solomon wise but also gave him great riches and power and an era of peace. Solomon built the glorious Temple in Jerusalem (1 Kings 6) and wrote most of the book of Proverbs. His Profile is found in 1 Kings 3, p. 519.

6 by exploring the meaning in these proverbs and parables,
   the words of the wise and their riddles.

7 Fear of the LORD is the foundation of true knowledge,
   but fools despise wisdom and discipline.

*A Father's Exhortation: Acquire Wisdom*
8 My child,* listen when your father corrects you.
   Don't neglect your mother's instruction.
9 What you learn from them will crown you with grace
   and be a chain of honor around your neck.

10 My child, if sinners entice you,
    turn your back on them!
11 They may say, "Come and join us.
    Let's hide and kill someone!
    Just for fun, let's ambush the innocent!
12 Let's swallow them alive, like the grave*;
    let's swallow them whole, like those who go down to the pit of death.
13 Think of the great things we'll get!
    We'll fill our houses with all the stuff we take.
14 Come, throw in your lot with us;
    we'll all share the loot."

15 My child, don't go along with them!
    Stay far away from their paths.
16 They rush to commit evil deeds.
    They hurry to commit murder.
17 If a bird sees a trap being set,
    it knows to stay away.
18 But these people set an ambush for themselves;
    they are trying to get themselves killed.
19 Such is the fate of all who are greedy for money;
    it robs them of life.

*Wisdom Shouts in the Streets*
20 Wisdom shouts in the streets.
    She cries out in the public square.

1:8 Hebrew *My son;* also in 1:10, 15.   1:12 Hebrew *like Sheol.*

**1:7** Prov 9:10; 15:33 Eccl 12:13
**1:8-9** Prov 6:20
**1:10** Ps 1:1 Prov 7:21; 13:20
**1:11** Prov 1:18
**1:15** Pss 1:1; 119:101 Prov 4:14
**1:16** Isa 59:7 †Rom 3:15-17
**1:19** Prov 15:27

**1:6** Riddles were thought-provoking questions.

**1:7** One of the most annoying types of people is a know-it-all, a person who has a dogmatic opinion about everything, is closed to anything new, resents discipline, and refuses to learn. Solomon calls this kind of person a fool. Don't be a know-it-all. Instead, be open to the advice of others, especially those who know you well and can give valuable insight and counsel. Learn how to learn from others. Remember, only God knows it all.

**1:7-9** In this age of information, knowledge is plentiful, but wisdom is scarce. Wisdom means far more than simply knowing a lot. It is a basic attitude that affects every aspect of life. The foundation of knowledge is to fear the Lord—to honor and respect God, to live in awe of his power, and to obey his Word. Faith in God should be the controlling principle for your understanding of the world, your attitudes, and your actions. Trust in God—he will make you truly wise.

**1:8** Our actions speak louder than our words. This is especially true in the home. Children learn values, morals, and priorities by observing how their parents act and react every day. If parents exhibit a deep reverence for and dependence on God, the children will catch these attitudes. Let them see your reverence for God. Teach them right living by giving worship an important place in your family life and by reading the Bible together.

**1:10-19** Sin is enticing because it offers a quick route to prosperity or pleasure and makes us feel like one of the crowd. But when we go along with others and refuse to listen to the truth, our own appetites become our masters, and we'll do anything to satisfy them. Sin, even when attractive, is deadly. We must learn to make choices, not on the basis of flashy appeal or short-range pleasure, but in view of the long-range effects. Sometimes this means steering clear of people who want to entice us into activities that we know are wrong. We can't be friendly with sin and expect our lives to remain unaffected.

**1:19** Being "greedy for money" is one of Satan's surest traps. It begins when he plants the suggestion that we can't live without some possession or more money. Then that desire fans its own fire until it becomes an all-consuming obsession. Ask God for wisdom to recognize any greedy desire before it destroys you. God will help you overcome it.

**1:20** The picture of Wisdom shouting in the streets is a personification—a literary device to make wisdom come alive for us. Wisdom is not a living being; it is the mind of God revealed. By reading about Jesus Christ's earthly ministry, we can see Wisdom in action. In order to understand how to become wise, we need to heed Wisdom calling and instructing us in the book of Proverbs (see the chart in chapter 14, p. 1025). For a New Testament call to wisdom, see James 1:5. Make sure you don't reject God's offer of wisdom to you.

21 She calls to the crowds along the main street,
    to those gathered in front of the city gate:
22 "How long, you simpletons,
        will you insist on being simpleminded?
    How long will you mockers relish your mocking?
        How long will you fools hate knowledge?

**1:23**
Joel 2:28
23 Come and listen to my counsel.
    I'll share my heart with you
        and make you wise.

**1:24**
Isa 65:12; 66:4
24 "I called you so often, but you wouldn't come.
    I reached out to you, but you paid no attention.

**1:25**
2 Chr 36:16
Ps 107:11
25 You ignored my advice
        and rejected the correction I offered.
26 So I will laugh when you are in trouble!
    I will mock you when disaster overtakes you—
27 when calamity overtakes you like a storm,
    when disaster engulfs you like a cyclone,
        and anguish and distress overwhelm you.

**1:28**
Job 27:9
Ps 18:41
Ezek 8:18
Zech 7:13
28 "When they cry for help, I will not answer.
    Though they anxiously search for me, they will not find me.
29 For they hated knowledge
        and chose not to fear the LORD.

**1:29**
Job 21:14
30 They rejected my advice
        and paid no attention when I corrected them.

**1:31**
Job 4:8
31 Therefore, they must eat the bitter fruit of living their own way,
        choking on their own schemes.

**1:32**
Jer 2:19
32 For simpletons turn away from me—to death.
    Fools are destroyed by their own complacency.

**1:33**
Pss 23:4; 25:13
33 But all who listen to me will live in peace,
        untroubled by fear of harm."

### The Benefits of Wisdom

**2:1**
Prov 3:1; 4:10
**2** 1 My child,* listen to what I say,
        and treasure my commands.
2 Tune your ears to wisdom,
        and concentrate on understanding.

**2:1** Hebrew *My son.*

---

| UNDER-STANDING PROVERBS | Type | Description | Key Word(s) | Examples |
|---|---|---|---|---|
| Most often, proverbs are written in the form of couplets. These are constructed in three ways: | Contrasting | Meaning and application come from the differences or contrast between the two statements of the proverb. | "but" | 10:3; 14:11, 18 |
| | Comparing | Meaning and application come from the similarities or comparison between the two statements of the proverb. | "as/so" "better/than" "like" | 15:16, 17; 22:7; 25:25 |
| | Complementing | Meaning and application come from the way the second statement complements the first. | "and" | 14:10, 17; 23:22 |

---

**1:22** In the book of Proverbs, a "simpleton" or a fool is not someone with a *mental* deficiency but someone with a *character* deficiency (such as rebellion, laziness, or anger). The fool is not stupid, but he or she is unable to tell right from wrong or good from bad.

**1:23-28** God is more than willing to pour out his heart and make known his thoughts to us. To receive his advice, we must be willing to listen, refusing to let pride stand in our way. Pride is thinking more highly of our own wisdom and desires than of God's. If

we think we know better than God or feel we have no need of God's direction, we have fallen into foolish and disastrous pride.

**1:31, 32** Many proverbs point out that the "bitter fruit of living their own way" will be the consequence people will experience in this life. Faced with either choosing God's wisdom or persisting in rebellious independence, many decide to go it alone. The problems such people create for themselves will destroy them. Don't ignore God's advice even if it is painful for the present. It will keep you from greater pain in the future.

3 Cry out for insight,
   and ask for understanding.
4 Search for them as you would for silver;
   seek them like hidden treasures.
5 Then you will understand what it means to fear the LORD,
   and you will gain knowledge of God.
6 For the LORD grants wisdom!
   From his mouth come knowledge and understanding.
7 He grants a treasure of common sense to the honest.
   He is a shield to those who walk with integrity.
8 He guards the paths of the just
   and protects those who are faithful to him.

9 Then you will understand what is right, just, and fair,
   and you will find the right way to go.
10 For wisdom will enter your heart,
   and knowledge will fill you with joy.
11 Wise choices will watch over you.
   Understanding will keep you safe.

12 Wisdom will save you from evil people,
   from those whose words are twisted.
13 These men turn from the right way
   to walk down dark paths.
14 They take pleasure in doing wrong,
   and they enjoy the twisted ways of evil.
15 Their actions are crooked,
   and their ways are wrong.

16 Wisdom will save you from the immoral woman,
   from the seductive words of the promiscuous woman.
17 She has abandoned her husband
   and ignores the covenant she made before God.
18 Entering her house leads to death;
   it is the road to the grave.*
19 The man who visits her is doomed.
   He will never reach the paths of life.

20 Follow the steps of good men instead,
   and stay on the paths of the righteous.
21 For only the godly will live in the land,
   and those with integrity will remain in it.
22 But the wicked will be removed from the land,
   and the treacherous will be uprooted.

**2:18** Hebrew *to the spirits of the dead.*

| | |
|---|---|
| **2:4** | Prov 3:14 / Matt 13:44 |
| **2:6** | Job 32:8 / Jas 1:5 |
| **2:8** | 1 Sam 2:9 |
| **2:9** | Prov 8:20 |
| **2:10** | Prov 14:33; 22:18 |
| **2:11** | Ps 82:5 / Prov 6:22 |
| **2:14** | Prov 10:23 / Hab 1:15 |
| **2:16** | Prov 6:24; 23:27 |
| **2:17** | Mal 2:14-15 |
| **2:18** | Prov 7:27 |
| **2:21** | Ps 37:9, 29 / Prov 10:30 |
| **2:22** | Deut 28:63 / Ps 37:38 |

**2:3-6** Wisdom comes in two ways: It is a God-given gift and also the result of an energetic search. Wisdom's starting point is God and his revealed Word, the source of "knowledge and understanding" (2:6). In that sense, wisdom is God's gift to us. But he gives it only to those who earnestly seek it. But because God's wisdom is hidden from the rebellious and foolish, it takes effort to find it and use it. The pathway to wisdom is strenuous. When we are on the path, we discover that true wisdom is God's and that he will guide us and reward our sincere and persistent search.

**2:6, 7** God gives wisdom and victory to the godly but not to those drifting through life or acting irresponsibly with his gifts and resources. If we are faithful to him and keep our purpose in life clearly in mind, he will keep us from pride and greed.

**2:9, 10** We gain wisdom through a constant process of growing. First, we must trust and honor God. Second, we must realize that the Bible reveals God's wisdom to us. Third, we must make a lifelong series of right choices and avoid moral pitfalls. Fourth, when we make sinful choices or mistakes, we must learn from our errors and recover. People don't develop all aspects of wisdom at once. For example, some people have more insight than discretion; others have more knowledge than common sense. But we can pray for all aspects of wisdom and take the steps to develop them.

**2:16, 17** An *immoral* or *promiscuous* woman is seductive or a prostitute. Two of the most difficult sins to resist are pride and sexual immorality. Both are seductive. Pride says, "I deserve it"; sexual desire says, "I need it." In combination, their appeal is deadly. In fact, says Solomon, only by relying on God's strength can we overcome them. Pride appeals to the empty head; sexual enticement to the empty heart. By looking to God, we can fill our heads with his wisdom and our hearts with his love. Don't be fooled—remember what God says about who you are and what you were meant to be. Ask him for strength to resist these temptations.

### Trusting in the LORD

3:1
Exod 20:6
Deut 30:16

**3** [1] My child,* never forget the things I have taught you.
Store my commands in your heart.
[2] If you do this, you will live many years,
and your life will be satisfying.

3:3
Prov 6:21; 7:3
2 Cor 3:3

[3] Never let loyalty and kindness leave you!
Tie them around your neck as a reminder.
Write them deep within your heart.

3:4
1 Sam 2:26
Jer 9:23-24
Luke 2:52

[4] Then you will find favor with both God and people,
and you will earn a good reputation.

[5] Trust in the LORD with all your heart;
do not depend on your own understanding.

**3:1** Hebrew *My son;* also in 3:11, 21.

---

| PEOPLE CALLED "WISE" IN THE BIBLE | The Person | Their Role | Reference | How They Practiced Wisdom |
|---|---|---|---|---|
| The special description "wise" is used for 12 significant people in the Bible. They can be helpful models in our own pursuit of wisdom. | Joseph | Wise leader | Acts 7:10 | Prepared for a major famine; helped rule Egypt |
| | Moses | Wise leader | Acts 7:20-22 | Learned all the Egyptian wisdom, then graduated to God's lessons in wisdom to lead Israel out of Egypt |
| | Bezalel | Wise artist | Exodus 31:1-5 | Designed and supervised the construction of the Tabernacle and its utensils in the wilderness |
| | Joshua | Wise leader | Deuteronomy 34:9 | Learned by observing Moses, obeyed God, led the people into the Promised Land |
| | David | Wise leader | 2 Samuel 14:20 | Never let his failures keep him from the source of wisdom—reverence for God |
| | Abigail | Wise wife | 1 Samuel 25:3 | Managed her household sensibly in spite of a mean and dishonest husband |
| | Solomon | Wise leader | 1 Kings 3:5-14; 4:29-34 | Knew what to do even though he often failed to put his own wisdom into action |
| | Daniel | Wise counselor | Daniel 5:11, 12 | Known as a man in touch with God; a solver of complex problems with God's help |
| | Astrologers | Wise learners | Matthew 2:1-12 | Not only received special knowledge of God's visit to earth but checked it out personally |
| | Stephen | Wise leader | Acts 6:8-10 | Organized the distribution of food to the Grecian widows; preached the gospel to the Jews |
| | Paul | Wise messenger | 2 Peter 3:15, 16 | Spent his life communicating God's love to all who would listen |
| | Christ | Wise youth Wise Savior Wisdom of God | Luke 2:40, 52; 1 Corinthians 1:20-25 | Not only lived a perfect life but died on the cross to save us and make God's wise plan of eternal life available to us |

---

**3:3** Loyalty and kindness are important character qualities. Both involve actions as well as attitudes. A loyal person acts responsibly. A kind person works for justice for others. Thoughts and words are not enough—our life reveals whether we are truly loyal and kind. Do your actions measure up to your attitudes?

**3:5, 6** When we have an important decision to make, we sometimes feel that we can't trust anyone—not even God. But God knows what is best for us. He is a better judge of what we want than we are! We must trust him completely in every choice we make. We should not omit careful thinking or belittle our God-given ability to reason; but we should not trust our own ideas to the exclusion of all others. We must not be wise in our own eyes but be willing to listen to and be corrected by God's Word and wise counselors. Bring your decisions to God in prayer; use the Bible as your guide; and then follow God's leading. He will direct your paths by both guiding and protecting you.

6 Seek his will in all you do,
   and he will show you which path to take.

7 Don't be impressed with your own wisdom.
   Instead, fear the Lord and turn away from evil.
8 Then you will have healing for your body
   and strength for your bones.

9 Honor the Lord with your wealth
   and with the best part of everything you produce.
10 Then he will fill your barns with grain,
   and your vats will overflow with good wine.

11 My child, don't reject the Lord's discipline,
   and don't be upset when he corrects you.
12 For the Lord corrects those he loves,
   just as a father corrects a child in whom he delights.*

13 Joyful is the person who finds wisdom,
   the one who gains understanding.
14 For wisdom is more profitable than silver,
   and her wages are better than gold.
15 Wisdom is more precious than rubies;
   nothing you desire can compare with her.
16 She offers you long life in her right hand,
   and riches and honor in her left.
17 She will guide you down delightful paths;
   all her ways are satisfying.
18 Wisdom is a tree of life to those who embrace her;
   happy are those who hold her tightly.
19 By wisdom the Lord founded the earth;
   by understanding he created the heavens.
20 By his knowledge the deep fountains of the earth burst forth,
   and the dew settles beneath the night sky.
21 My child, don't lose sight of common sense and discernment.
   Hang on to them,

**3:6**
1 Chr 28:9
Prov 16:3

**3:9**
Exod 23:19
Isa 43:23
Mal 3:10

**3:11**
Job 5:17
†Heb 12:5-6

**3:13**
Job 28:17

**3:14**
Prov 8:10, 19

**3:16**
Ps 21:4
Prov 3:2; 8:18;
16:7; 22:4

**3:18**
Gen 2:9
Prov 11:30
Rev 2:7

**3:20**
Gen 7:11

**3:21**
Prov 4:21

3:12 Greek version reads *And he punishes those he accepts as his children.* Compare Heb 12:6.

---

**3:6** To receive God's guidance, said Solomon, we must seek God's will in all we do. This means turning every area of life over to him. About a thousand years later, Jesus emphasized this same truth (Matthew 6:33). Examine your values and priorities. What is important to you? In what areas have you not acknowledged him? You may already acknowledge God in many areas of your life, but the areas where you attempt to restrict or ignore him will cause you grief. Make him a vital part of everything you do; then he will guide you because you will be working to accomplish his purposes.

**3:9, 10** This refers to the practice of giving to God the first and best portion of the harvest (Deuteronomy 26:9-11). Many people give God their leftovers. If they can afford to donate anything after the bills are paid, they do so. These people may be sincere and contribute willingly, but they are not obeying what God says. God wants the first part of our income. This demonstrates that God, not possessions, has first place in our life and that our resources belong to him (we are only managers). Giving to God helps us conquer greed, helps us properly manage God's resources, and opens us up to receive God's special blessings.

**3:11, 12** *Discipline* means "to teach and to train." *Discipline* sounds negative to many people because some disciplinarians

are not loving. God, however, is the source of all love. He doesn't punish us because he enjoys inflicting pain but because he is deeply concerned about our development. He knows that in order to become morally strong and good, we must learn the difference between right and wrong. His loving discipline enables us to do that.

**3:11, 12** It's difficult to know when God has been disciplining us until we look back on the situation later. Not every calamity comes directly from God, of course. But if we rebel against God and refuse to repent when God has identified some sin in our lives, he may use guilt, crises, or bad experiences to bring us back to him. Sometimes, however, difficult times come even when we have no flagrant sin. Then our response should be patience, integrity, and confidence that God will show us what to do.

**3:16, 17** Proverbs contains many strong statements about the benefits of wisdom, including long life, wealth, honor, and peace. If you aren't experiencing them, does this mean you are short on wisdom? Not necessarily. Instead of guarantees, these statements are general principles. In a perfect world, wise behavior would always lead to these benefits. Even in our troubled world, living wisely usually results in obvious blessings—but not always. Sometimes sin intervenes, and some blessings must be delayed until Jesus returns to establish his eternal Kingdom. That is why we must "live by believing and not by seeing" (2 Corinthians 5:7). We can be sure that wisdom ultimately leads to blessing.

<table>
</table>

| 3:22 Deut 32:47 | 22 for they will refresh your soul. |

22 for they will refresh your soul.
They are like jewels on a necklace.
23 They keep you safe on your way,
and your feet will not stumble.

**3:24**
Job 5:21; 11:19
Ps 3:5
Prov 1:33; 6:22

24 You can go to bed without fear;
you will lie down and sleep soundly.
25 You need not be afraid of sudden disaster
or the destruction that comes upon the wicked,
26 for the LORD is your security.
He will keep your foot from being caught in a trap.

**3:27**
Deut 24:15
Rom 13:8

27 Do not withhold good from those who deserve it
when it's in your power to help them.
28 If you can help your neighbor now, don't say,
"Come back tomorrow, and then I'll help you."

29 Don't plot harm against your neighbor,
for those who live nearby trust you.

**3:30**
Rom 12:18

30 Don't pick a fight without reason,
when no one has done you harm.

**3:31**
Ps 37:1

31 Don't envy violent people
or copy their ways.
32 Such wicked people are detestable to the LORD,
but he offers his friendship to the godly.

**3:33**
Deut 11:28
Mal 2:2

33 The LORD curses the house of the wicked,
but he blesses the home of the upright.

**3:34**
Jas 4:6
†1 Pet 5:5

34 The LORD mocks the mockers
but is gracious to the humble.*

35 The wise inherit honor,
but fools are put to shame!

### A Father's Wise Advice

**4:1**
Prov 1:8

**4** 1 My children,* listen when your father corrects you.
Pay attention and learn good judgment,
2 for I am giving you good guidance.
Don't turn away from my instructions.

**3:34** Greek version reads *The LORD opposes the proud / but favors the humble.* Compare Jas 4:6; 1 Pet 5:5.
**4:1** Hebrew *My sons.*

---

**WISDOM: APPLIED TRUTH**
The book of Proverbs tells us about people who have wisdom and enjoy its benefits.

| Reference | The Person Who Has Wisdom | Benefits of Wisdom |
|---|---|---|
| Proverbs 3–4 A father's instructions | Is kind Is loyal Trusts in the Lord Puts God first Turns away from evil Knows right from wrong Listens and learns Does what is right | Long, satisfying life Favor with God and people Reputation for good judgment Success Health, vitality Riches, honor, pleasure, peace Protection |
| Proverbs 8–9 Wisdom speaks | Discovers knowledge and discernment Hates pride, arrogance, and corruption Respects and fears God Gives good advice and has common sense Loves correction and is teachable Knows God | Riches, honor Justice Righteousness Life God's approval Constant learning Understanding |

---

**3:27, 28** Withholding good is inconsiderate and unfair, whether it is repaying a loan, returning a tool, or fulfilling a promise. Withholding destroys trust and creates a great inconvenience for the other person. Be as eager to do good as you are to have good done to you.

3 For I, too, was once my father's son,
   tenderly loved as my mother's only child.

4 My father taught me,
   "Take my words to heart.
   Follow my commands, and you will live.
5 Get wisdom; develop good judgment.
   Don't forget my words or turn away from them.
6 Don't turn your back on wisdom, for she will protect you.
   Love her, and she will guard you.
7 Getting wisdom is the wisest thing you can do!
   And whatever else you do, develop good judgment.
8 If you prize wisdom, she will make you great.
   Embrace her, and she will honor you.
9 She will place a lovely wreath on your head;
   she will present you with a beautiful crown."

10 My child,* listen to me and do as I say,
   and you will have a long, good life.
11 I will teach you wisdom's ways
   and lead you in straight paths.
12 When you walk, you won't be held back;
   when you run, you won't stumble.
13 Take hold of my instructions; don't let them go.
   Guard them, for they are the key to life.

14 Don't do as the wicked do,
   and don't follow the path of evildoers.
15 Don't even think about it; don't go that way.
   Turn away and keep moving.
16 For evil people can't sleep until they've done their evil deed for the day.
   They can't rest until they've caused someone to stumble.
17 They eat the food of wickedness
   and drink the wine of violence!

18 The way of the righteous is like the first gleam of dawn,
   which shines ever brighter until the full light of day.
19 But the way of the wicked is like total darkness.
   They have no idea what they are stumbling over.

20 My child, pay attention to what I say.
   Listen carefully to my words.
21 Don't lose sight of them.
   Let them penetrate deep into your heart,

4:10 Hebrew *My son;* also in 4:20.

4:6
Prov 2:11
2 Thes 2:10

4:7
Prov 23:23

4:8
Prov 3:18

4:10
Prov 2:1; 9:11;
10:27; 22:4

4:13
Prov 3:18, 22

4:14
Ps 1:1
Prov 1:15

4:16
Ps 36:4
Mic 2:1

4:18
2 Sam 23:4
Dan 12:3

4:19
Job 18:5
Isa 59:9-10

---

**4:3, 4** One of the greatest responsibilities of parents is to encourage their children to become wise. Here Solomon tells how his father, David, encouraged him to seek wisdom when he was young (see 1 Kings 2:1-9 and 1 Chronicles 28–29 for David's charge to his son). This encouragement may have prompted Solomon to ask God for an understanding mind above everything else (1 Kings 3:9). Wisdom can be passed on from parents to children, from generation to generation. Ultimately, of course, all wisdom comes from God; parents can only urge their children to turn to him. If your parents never taught you in this way, you can learn from the Scriptures and then create a legacy of wisdom as you teach your own children.

**4:5-7** If you want wisdom, you must decide to go after it. This will take resolve—a determination not to abandon the search once you begin, no matter how difficult the road may become. This is not a once-in-a-lifetime step but a daily process of choosing between two paths—the wicked (4:14-17, 19) and the righteous (4:18). Nothing is more important or more valuable.

**4:7** David taught Solomon as a young boy that seeking God's wisdom was the most important choice he could make. Solomon learned the lesson well. When God appeared to Solomon to fulfill any request, the new king chose wisdom above all else. We should also make God's wisdom our first choice. We don't have to wait for God to appear to us. We can boldly ask him for wisdom today through prayer. James 1:5 assures us that God will grant our request.

**4:13-17** Even friends can make you fall. It is difficult for people to accept the fact that friends and acquaintances may lure them to do wrong. Young people who want to be accepted would never confront or criticize a friend for wrong plans or actions. Many other people can't see how their friends' actions could lead to trouble. While we should be accepting of others, we need a healthy skepticism about human behavior. When you feel yourself being heavily influenced, proceed with caution. Don't let your friends cause you to fall into sin.

**4:22**
Prov 3:8, 22

22 for they bring life to those who find them,
   and healing to their whole body.

**4:23**
Luke 6:45

23 Guard your heart above all else,
   for it determines the course of your life.

24 Avoid all perverse talk;
   stay away from corrupt speech.

25 Look straight ahead,
   and fix your eyes on what lies before you.

**4:26**
†Heb 12:13

26 Mark out a straight path for your feet;
   stay on the safe path.

**4:27**
Deut 5:32; 28:14

27 Don't get sidetracked;
   keep your feet from following evil.

*Avoid Immoral Women*

**5:1**
Prov 4:20

**5** 1 My son, pay attention to my wisdom;
   listen carefully to my wise counsel.

2 Then you will show discernment,
   and your lips will express what you've learned.

**5:3**
Ps 55:21
Prov 5:20; 7:5

3 For the lips of an immoral woman are as sweet as honey,
   and her mouth is smoother than oil.

**5:4**
Ps 57:4
Eccl 7:26

4 But in the end she is as bitter as poison,
   as dangerous as a double-edged sword.

**5:5**
Prov 2:18; 7:27

5 Her feet go down to death;
   her steps lead straight to the grave.*

**5:6**
2 Pet 2:14

6 For she cares nothing about the path to life.
   She staggers down a crooked trail and doesn't realize it.

7 So now, my sons, listen to me.
   Never stray from what I am about to say:

**5:8**
Prov 7:25; 9:14

8 Stay away from her!
   Don't go near the door of her house!

9 If you do, you will lose your honor
   and will lose to merciless people all you have achieved.

10 Strangers will consume your wealth,
   and someone else will enjoy the fruit of your labor.

11 In the end you will groan in anguish
   when disease consumes your body.

**5:5** Hebrew *to Sheol.*

---

**STRATEGY FOR EFFECTIVE LIVING**

| | | |
|---|---|---|
| Begins with . . . God's wisdom . . . . . . . . | Respecting and appreciating who God is; reverence and awe toward God |
| Requires . . . . . Moral application . . . . . . | Trusting in God and his Word; allowing his Word to speak to us personally; being willing to obey |
| Requires . . . . . Practical application. . . . | Acting on God's direction daily |
| Results in . . . . Effective living . . . . . . . | Experiencing what God does with our obedience |

---

**4:23-27** Our heart—our feelings of love and desire—dictates to a great extent how we live because we always find time to do what we enjoy. Solomon tells us to guard our hearts above all else, making sure we concentrate on those desires that will keep us on the right path. Make sure your affections lead you in the right direction. Put boundaries on your desires: Don't go after everything you see. Look straight ahead, keep your eyes fixed on your goal, and don't get sidetracked on detours that lead to sin.

**5:3** This "immoral woman" is a prostitute. Proverbs includes many warnings against illicit sex for several reasons. First, a prostitute's charm is used as an example of any temptation to do wrong or to leave the pursuit of wisdom. Second, sexual immorality of any kind was and still is extremely dangerous because it destroys family life, erodes a person's ability to love, degrades human beings and turns them into objects, can lead to disease, and can result in unwanted children. Third, sexual immorality is against God's law.

**5:3-8** Any person should be on guard against those who use flattery and smooth talk (lips that "are as sweet as honey") that would lead him or her into sin. The best advice is to take a detour and even avoid conversation with such people.

**5:11-13** At the end of your life, it will be too late to ask for advice. When desire is fully activated, people don't want advice—they want satisfaction. The best time to learn the dangers and foolishness of going after forbidden sex (or anything else that is harmful) is long before the temptation comes. Resistance is easier if the decision has already been made. Don't wait to see what happens. Prepare for temptation by deciding *now* how you will act when you face it.

12 You will say, "How I hated discipline!
  If only I had not ignored all the warnings!
13 Oh, why didn't I listen to my teachers?
  Why didn't I pay attention to my instructors?
14 I have come to the brink of utter ruin,
  and now I must face public disgrace."

15 Drink water from your own well—
  share your love only with your wife.*
16 Why spill the water of your springs in the streets,
  having sex with just anyone?*
17 You should reserve it for yourselves.
  Never share it with strangers.

18 Let your wife be a fountain of blessing for you.
  Rejoice in the wife of your youth.
19 She is a loving deer, a graceful doe.
  Let her breasts satisfy you always.
  May you always be captivated by her love.
20 Why be captivated, my son, by an immoral woman,
  or fondle the breasts of a promiscuous woman?

21 For the LORD sees clearly what a man does,
  examining every path he takes.
22 An evil man is held captive by his own sins;
  they are ropes that catch and hold him.
23 He will die for lack of self-control;
  he will be lost because of his great foolishness.

## Lessons for Daily Life

**6** ¹ My child,* if you have put up security for a friend's debt
    or agreed to guarantee the debt of a stranger—
2 if you have trapped yourself by your agreement
  and are caught by what you said—
3 follow my advice and save yourself,
  for you have placed yourself at your friend's mercy.
  Now swallow your pride;
  go and beg to have your name erased.
4 Don't put it off; do it now!
  Don't rest until you do.
5 Save yourself like a gazelle escaping from a hunter,
  like a bird fleeing from a net.

**5:12**
Prov 1:22, 25

**5:16**
Prov 5:18

**5:18**
Eccl 9:9
Mal 2:14
**5:19**
Song 4:5; 7:3

**5:20**
Prov 2:16; 5:3

**5:21**
Job 14:16
Ps 119:168
**5:22**
Num 32:23
**5:23**
Job 4:21; 36:12

**6:1**
Prov 11:15; 17:18;
20:16; 22:26; 27:13

**6:5**
Pss 91:3; 124:7

**5:15** Hebrew *Drink water from your own cistern, / flowing water from your own well.*  **5:16** Hebrew *Why spill your springs in the streets, / your streams in the city squares?*  **6:1** Hebrew *My son.*

**5:15** "Drink water from your own well" is a picture of faithfulness in marriage. It means to enjoy the spouse God has given you. In desert lands, water is precious, and a well is a family's most important possession. In Old Testament times, it was considered a crime to steal water from someone else's well, just as it was a crime to have intercourse with another person's spouse. In both cases, the offender endangers the health and security of family.

**5:15-21** In contrast to much of what we read, see, and hear today, this passage urges couples to look to each other for lifelong satisfaction and companionship. Many temptations entice husbands and wives to leave when marriage becomes dull in order to find excitement and pleasures elsewhere. But God designed marriage and sanctified it, and only within this covenant relationship can we find real love and fulfillment. Don't let God's best for you be wasted on the illusion of greener pastures somewhere else. Instead, rejoice with your spouse as you give yourselves to God and to each other.

**5:18-20** God never intended marriage to become boring, lifeless, and dull. Sex is a gift God gives to married people for their mutual enjoyment. Real happiness comes when we decide to find pleasure in the spouse God has given us and to commit ourselves to meeting his or her needs. The real danger is in doubting that God knows and cares for us. We then may resent his timing and carelessly pursue sexual pleasure without his blessing.

**5:19** See Song of Songs, chapter 4, for parallels to this frank expression of the joys of sexual pleasure in marriage.

**6:1-5** These verses are not a plea against generosity, but against overextending one's financial resources and acting in irresponsible ways that could lead to poverty. It is important to maintain a balance between generosity and good stewardship. God wants us to help our friends and the needy, but he does not promise to cover the costs of every unwise commitment we make. We should also act responsibly so that our families do not suffer.

**6:6**
Prov 10:26; 13:4;
30:24-25

⁶ Take a lesson from the ants, you lazybones.
　　Learn from their ways and become wise!
⁷ Though they have no prince
　　or governor or ruler to make them work,
⁸ they labor hard all summer,
　　gathering food for the winter.
⁹ But you, lazybones, how long will you sleep?
　　When will you wake up?

**6:10**
Prov 24:33

¹⁰ A little extra sleep, a little more slumber,
　　a little folding of the hands to rest—
¹¹ then poverty will pounce on you like a bandit;
　　scarcity will attack you like an armed robber.

¹² What are worthless and wicked people like?
　　They are constant liars,

**6:13**
Ps 35:19
Prov 10:10

¹³ signaling their deceit with a wink of the eye,
　　a nudge of the foot, or the wiggle of fingers.

**6:14**
Prov 6:19
Mic 2:1

¹⁴ Their perverted hearts plot evil,
　　and they constantly stir up trouble.

**6:15**
2 Chr 36:16
Prov 24:22
Jer 19:11

¹⁵ But they will be destroyed suddenly,
　　broken in an instant beyond all hope of healing.

¹⁶ There are six things the LORD hates—
　　no, seven things he detests:

**6:16-19**
Gen 6:5
Prov 1:16; 6:14;
19:5, 9; 21:4; 24:2;
28:17
Isa 1:15

¹⁷ haughty eyes,
　　a lying tongue,
　　hands that kill the innocent,
¹⁸ a heart that plots evil,
　　feet that race to do wrong,
¹⁹ a false witness who pours out lies,
　　a person who sows discord in a family.

²⁰ My son, obey your father's commands,
　　and don't neglect your mother's instruction.

**6:21**
Prov 3:3

²¹ Keep their words always in your heart.
　　Tie them around your neck.

**6:22**
Prov 3:23

²² When you walk, their counsel will lead you.
　　When you sleep, they will protect you.
　　When you wake up, they will advise you.

---

**THINGS GOD HATES**

The book of Proverbs notes 14 types of people and actions that God hates. Let these be guidelines of what we are *not* to be and do!

| | |
|---|---|
| Violent people . . . . . . . . . . . . . . . . . . . . . . . . . . . . . . . . . . . . . . . . . . . . . . . . . . | Proverbs 3:31, 32 |
| Haughtiness, lying, murdering, scheming, eagerness to do wrong, a false witness, stirring up discord . . . . . . . . . . . . . . . . . . . . . . . . . . . . . | Proverbs 6:16-19 |
| Those who are untruthful . . . . . . . . . . . . . . . . . . . . . . . . . . . . . . . . . . . . | Proverbs 12:22 |
| The sacrifice of the wicked . . . . . . . . . . . . . . . . . . . . . . . . . . . . . . . . . . | Proverbs 15:8 |
| The way of the wicked . . . . . . . . . . . . . . . . . . . . . . . . . . . . . . . . . . . . . . | Proverbs 15:9 |
| Evil plans . . . . . . . . . . . . . . . . . . . . . . . . . . . . . . . . . . . . . . . . . . . . . . . . . . | Proverbs 15:26 |
| Those who are proud . . . . . . . . . . . . . . . . . . . . . . . . . . . . . . . . . . . . . . . | Proverbs 16:5 |
| Those who judge unjustly . . . . . . . . . . . . . . . . . . . . . . . . . . . . . . . . . . . | Proverbs 17:15 |

---

**6:6-11** Those last few moments of sleep are delicious; we savor them as we resist beginning another workday. But Proverbs warns against giving in to the temptation of laziness, of sleeping instead of working. This does not mean we should never rest: God gave the Jews the Sabbath, a weekly day of rest and restoration. But we should not rest when we should be working. The ant is used as an example because it utilizes its energy and resources economically. If laziness turns us from our responsibilities, poverty may soon bar us from the legitimate rest we should enjoy. (See also the chart in chapter 28, p. 1053.)

**6:20-23** It is natural and good for children, as they grow toward adulthood, to become increasingly independent of their parents. Young adults, however, should take care not to turn a deaf ear to their parents—to reject their advice just when it is needed most. If you are struggling with a decision or looking for insight, check with your parents or other older adults who know you well. Their years of experience may have given them the wisdom you seek.

23 For their command is a lamp
and their instruction a light;
their corrective discipline
is the way to life.

24 It will keep you from the immoral woman,
from the smooth tongue of a promiscuous woman.

25 Don't lust for her beauty.
Don't let her coy glances seduce you.

26 For a prostitute will bring you to poverty,*
but sleeping with another man's wife will cost you your life.

27 Can a man scoop a flame into his lap
and not have his clothes catch on fire?

28 Can he walk on hot coals
and not blister his feet?

29 So it is with the man who sleeps with another man's wife.
He who embraces her will not go unpunished.

30 Excuses might be found for a thief
who steals because he is starving.

31 But if he is caught, he must pay back seven times what he stole,
even if he has to sell everything in his house.

32 But the man who commits adultery is an utter fool,
for he destroys himself.

33 He will be wounded and disgraced.
His shame will never be erased.

34 For the woman's jealous husband will be furious,
and he will show no mercy when he takes revenge.

35 He will accept no compensation,
nor be satisfied with a payoff of any size.

### Another Warning about Immoral Women

**7** 1 Follow my advice, my son;
always treasure my commands.

2 Obey my commands and live!
Guard my instructions as you guard your own eyes.*

3 Tie them on your fingers as a reminder.
Write them deep within your heart.

4 Love wisdom like a sister;
make insight a beloved member of your family.

5 Let them protect you from an affair with an immoral woman,
from listening to the flattery of a promiscuous woman.

6 While I was at the window of my house,
looking through the curtain,

7 I saw some naive young men,
and one in particular who lacked common sense.

**6:26** Hebrew *to a loaf of bread.*   **7:2** Hebrew *as the pupil of your eye.*

| | |
|---|---|
| **6:23** | Ps 119:105 |
| | Prov 13:9 |
| **6:24** | Prov 2:16; 5:3 |
| **6:25** | 2 Kgs 9:30 |
| | Matt 5:28 |
| **6:26** | Prov 5:9-10; 29:3 |
| **6:29** | Ezek 18:6 |
| **6:31** | Ezek 22:1-4 |
| **6:32** | Prov 7:7, 22-23; |
| | 9:15-18 |
| **6:34** | Prov 11:4; 27:4 |
| | Song 8:6 |
| **7:1** | Prov 2:1; 4:1 |
| **7:2** | Deut 32:10 |
| | Prov 4:4; 9:11 |
| **7:3** | Deut 6:8 |
| | Prov 3:3; 6:21 |
| **7:5** | Prov 6:24 |
| **7:7** | Prov 1:22; 6:32 |

**6:25** Regard lust as a warning sign of danger ahead. When you notice that you are attracted to a person of the opposite sex or preoccupied with thoughts of him or her, your desires may lead you to sin. Ask God to help you change your desires before you are drawn into sin.

**6:25-35** Some people argue that it is all right to break God's law against sexual sin if nobody gets hurt. In truth, somebody always gets hurt. In the case of adultery, spouses are devastated and children are scarred. Even if the partners escape disease and unwanted pregnancy, they may lose their ability to fulfill commitments, to feel sexual desire, to trust, and to be entirely open with another person. God's laws are not arbitrary. They do not forbid

good, clean fun; rather, they warn us against destroying ourselves through unwise actions or running ahead of God's timetable.

**7:6-23** Although this advice is directed toward young men, young women should heed it as well. The person who has no purpose in life is naive (7:7). Without aim or direction, an empty life is unstable, vulnerable to many temptations. Even though the young man in this passage doesn't know where he is going, the immoral woman knows where she wants him. Notice her strategies: She is dressed to allure men (7:10); her approach is bold (7:13); she invites him over to her place (7:16-18); she cunningly answers his every objection (7:19, 20); she persuades him with smooth talk (7:21); she traps him (7:23). To combat temptation, make sure your life is full of God's Word and wisdom (7:4).

**7:8**
Prov 7:12

8 He was crossing the street near the house of an immoral woman,
    strolling down the path by her house.

**7:9**
Job 24:15

9 It was at twilight, in the evening,
    as deep darkness fell.

**7:10**
Gen 38:14-15

10 The woman approached him,
    seductively dressed and sly of heart.

**7:11**
Prov 9:13

11 She was the brash, rebellious type,
    never content to stay at home.

**7:12**
Prov 23:28

12 She is often in the streets and markets,
    soliciting at every corner.

13 She threw her arms around him and kissed him,
    and with a brazen look she said,

14 "I've just made my peace offerings
    and fulfilled my vows.

15 You're the one I was looking for!
    I came out to find you, and here you are!

**7:16**
Prov 31:22
Ezek 27:7

16 My bed is spread with beautiful blankets,
    with colored sheets of Egyptian linen.

17 I've perfumed my bed
    with myrrh, aloes, and cinnamon.

18 Come, let's drink our fill of love until morning.
    Let's enjoy each other's caresses,

19 for my husband is not home.
    He's away on a long trip.

20 He has taken a wallet full of money with him
    and won't return until later this month.*"

**7:21**
Prov 5:3; 6:24

21 So she seduced him with her pretty speech
    and enticed him with her flattery.

22 He followed her at once,
    like an ox going to the slaughter.
    He was like a stag caught in a trap,

**7:23**
Eccl 9:12

23     awaiting the arrow that would pierce its heart.
    He was like a bird flying into a snare,
    little knowing it would cost him his life.

**7:24**
Prov 4:1

24 So listen to me, my sons,
    and pay attention to my words.

**7:25**
Prov 5:8

25 Don't let your hearts stray away toward her.
    Don't wander down her wayward path.

26 For she has been the ruin of many;
    many men have been her victims.

**7:27**
Prov 2:18; 9:18

27 Her house is the road to the grave.*
    Her bedroom is the den of death.

## Wisdom Calls for a Hearing

**8:1**
Prov 1:20-21

**8** ¹ Listen as Wisdom calls out!
    Hear as understanding raises her voice!

² On the hilltop along the road,
    she takes her stand at the crossroads.

**7:20** Hebrew *until the moon is full.*    **7:27** Hebrew *to Sheol.*

---

Recognize the strategies of temptation, and run away from them—fast.

**7:25-27** You can take definite steps to avoid sexual sins. First, guard your mind. Don't read books, look at pictures, or encourage fantasies that stimulate the wrong desires. Second, keep away from settings and friends that tempt you to sin. Third, don't think only of the moment—focus on the future. Today's thrill may lead to tomorrow's ruin.

**8:1ff** Wisdom's call is contrasted to the call of the immoral woman in chapter 7. Wisdom is portrayed as a woman who guides us (8:1-13) and makes us succeed (8:14-21). Wisdom was present at the Creation and works with the Creator (8:22-31). God approves of those who listen to Wisdom's counsel (8:32-35). Those who hate wisdom love death (8:36). Wisdom should affect every aspect of one's life, from beginning to end. Be sure to open all corners of your life to God's direction and guidance.

3 By the gates at the entrance to the town,
    on the road leading in, she cries aloud,
4 "I call to you, to all of you!
    I raise my voice to all people.
5 You simple people, use good judgment.
    You foolish people, show some understanding.
6 Listen to me! For I have important things to tell you.
    Everything I say is right,
7 for I speak the truth
    and detest every kind of deception.
8 My advice is wholesome.
    There is nothing devious or crooked in it.
9 My words are plain to anyone with understanding,
    clear to those with knowledge.
10 Choose my instruction rather than silver,
    and knowledge rather than pure gold.
11 For wisdom is far more valuable than rubies.
    Nothing you desire can compare with it.

12 "I, Wisdom, live together with good judgment.
    I know where to discover knowledge and discernment.
13 All who fear the LORD will hate evil.
    Therefore, I hate pride and arrogance,
    corruption and perverse speech.
14 Common sense and success belong to me.
    Insight and strength are mine.
15 Because of me, kings reign,
    and rulers make just decrees.
16 Rulers lead with my help,
    and nobles make righteous judgments.*

17 "I love all who love me.
    Those who search will surely find me.
18 I have riches and honor,
    as well as enduring wealth and justice.
19 My gifts are better than gold, even the purest gold,
    my wages better than sterling silver!
20 I walk in righteousness,
    in paths of justice.
21 Those who love me inherit wealth.
    I will fill their treasuries.

22 "The LORD formed me from the beginning,
    before he created anything else.
23 I was appointed in ages past,
    at the very first, before the earth began.
24 I was born before the oceans were created,
    before the springs bubbled forth their waters.
25 Before the mountains were formed,
    before the hills, I was born—
26 before he had made the earth and fields
    and the first handfuls of soil.
27 I was there when he established the heavens,
    when he drew the horizon on the oceans.

**8:9**
Prov 3:13; 14:6

**8:11**
Prov 3:14-15;
16:16; 20:15

**8:13**
Prov 3:7; 6:12; 15:9

**8:17**
1 Sam 2:30
Ps 91:14
Prov 2:4-5; 4:6
John 14:21

**8:18**
Ps 112:3
Prov 3:16; 22:4
Matt 6:33
Jas 2:5

**8:20**
Pss 23:3; 25:4

**8:21**
Prov 3:19

**8:22**
Job 28:27

**8:23**
John 17:5, 24

**8:24**
Job 38:16

**8:25**
Ps 90:2

**8:27**
Job 26:10
Prov 3:19

**8:16** Some Hebrew manuscripts and Greek version read *and nobles are judges over the earth.*

---

**8:13** The more a person fears and respects God, the more he or she will hate evil. Love for God and love for sin cannot coexist. Harboring secret sins means that you are tolerating evil within yourself. Make a clean break with sin and commit yourself completely to God.

**8:22-31** God says that wisdom is primary and fundamental. It is the foundation on which all life is built. Paul and John may have alluded to some of Solomon's statements about wisdom to describe Christ's presence at the creation of the world (Colossians 1:15-17; 2:2, 3; Revelation 3:14).

**8:29**
Job 38:6, 10
Ps 104:9

**8:34**
Ps 27:4
Jas 1:22

**8:35**
John 17:3

**9:1**
Eph 2:20-22
1 Pet 2:5

**9:3**
Prov 1:20; 8:1-2
Matt 22:3

**9:5**
Song 5:1
Isa 55:1
John 6:27

**9:7**
Prov 23:9

28 I was there when he set the clouds above,
   when he established springs deep in the earth.
29 I was there when he set the limits of the seas,
   so they would not spread beyond their boundaries.
   And when he marked off the earth's foundations,
30   I was the architect at his side.
   I was his constant delight,
     rejoicing always in his presence.
31 And how happy I was with the world he created;
   how I rejoiced with the human family!

32 "And so, my children,* listen to me,
   for all who follow my ways are joyful.
33 Listen to my instruction and be wise.
   Don't ignore it.
34 Joyful are those who listen to me,
   watching for me daily at my gates,
     waiting for me outside my home!
35 For whoever finds me finds life
   and receives favor from the LORD.
36 But those who miss me injure themselves.
   All who hate me love death."

# 9

1 Wisdom has built her house;
   she has carved its seven columns.
2 She has prepared a great banquet,
   mixed the wines, and set the table.
3 She has sent her servants to invite everyone to come.
   She calls out from the heights overlooking the city.
4 "Come in with me," she urges the simple.
   To those who lack good judgment, she says,
5 "Come, eat my food,
   and drink the wine I have mixed.
6 Leave your simple ways behind, and begin to live;
   learn to use good judgment."

7 Anyone who rebukes a mocker will get an insult in return.
   Anyone who corrects the wicked will get hurt.
8 So don't bother correcting mockers;
   they will only hate you.
   But correct the wise,
     and they will love you.
9 Instruct the wise,
   and they will be even wiser.
   Teach the righteous,
     and they will learn even more.

8:32 Hebrew *my sons.*

---

**9:1** The seven columns are figurative; they do not represent seven principles of wisdom. In the Bible, the number seven represents completeness and perfection. This verse poetically states that wisdom lacks nothing—it is complete and perfect.

**9:1ff** Wisdom and Folly (foolishness) are portrayed in this chapter as rival young women, each preparing a feast and inviting people to it. But Wisdom is a responsible woman of character, while Folly is a prostitute serving stolen food. Wisdom appeals to the mind; Folly to the senses. It is easier to excite the senses, but the pleasures of Folly are temporary. By contrast, the satisfaction that Wisdom brings lasts forever.

**9:1-5** The banquet described in this chapter has some interesting parallels to the banquet Jesus described in one of his parables

(Luke 14:15-24). Many may intend to go, but they never make it because they get sidetracked by other activities that seem more important at the time. Don't let anything become more important than your search for God's wisdom.

**9:7-10** Are you a mocker or a wise person? You can tell by the way you respond to criticism. Instead of replying with a quick put-down or clever retort when rebuked, listen to what is being said. Learn from your critics; this is the path to wisdom. Wisdom begins with knowing God. He gives insight into living because he created life. To know God you must not just know the facts about him; you must have a personal relationship with him. Do you really want to be wise? Get to know God better and better. (See James 1:5 and 2 Peter 1:2-4 for more on how to become wise.)

10 Fear of the LORD is the foundation of wisdom.
  Knowledge of the Holy One results in good judgment.

11 Wisdom will multiply your days
  and add years to your life.

12 If you become wise, you will be the one to benefit.
  If you scorn wisdom, you will be the one to suffer.

### Folly Calls for a Hearing

13 The woman named Folly is brash.
  She is ignorant and doesn't know it.

14 She sits in her doorway
  on the heights overlooking the city.

15 She calls out to men going by
  who are minding their own business.

16 "Come in with me," she urges the simple.
  To those who lack good judgment, she says,

17 "Stolen water is refreshing;
  food eaten in secret tastes the best!"

18 But little do they know that the dead are there.
  Her guests are in the depths of the grave.*

**9:10**
Job 28:28
Ps 111:10
Prov 1:7

**9:11**
Prov 3:2, 16; 9:6;
10:27

**9:13**
Prov 5:6; 7:11

**9:16**
Prov 9:4

**9:17**
Prov 20:17

**9:18**
Prov 7:27

## B. WISDOM FOR ALL PEOPLE (10:1—24:34)

These short couplets are what we commonly recognize as proverbs. They cover a wide range of topics. The first section was written by Solomon. The next two sections were written by others but collected by Solomon. These sayings give people practical wisdom for godly living at every stage of life.

### The Proverbs of Solomon

**10** The proverbs of Solomon:

  A wise child* brings joy to a father;
  a foolish child brings grief to a mother.

2 Tainted wealth has no lasting value,
  but right living can save your life.

3 The LORD will not let the godly go hungry,
  but he refuses to satisfy the craving of the wicked.

4 Lazy people are soon poor;
  hard workers get rich.

5 A wise youth harvests in the summer,
  but one who sleeps during harvest is a disgrace.

**10:2**
Ps 49:6-7
Eccl 2:4

**10:3**
Pss 34:9-10; 37:25
Matt 6:33

**10:4**
Prov 13:4

**9:18** Hebrew *in Sheol.* **10:1** Hebrew *son;* also in 10:1b.

---

**9:14-17** Something is hypnotic and intoxicating about wickedness. One sin leads to another; sinful behavior seems more exciting than the Christian life. That is why many people put aside all thought of Wisdom's sumptuous banquet (9:1-5) in order to eat the stolen food of Folly. Don't be deceived—sin is dangerous. Before reaching for forbidden fruit, take a long look at what happens to those who eat it. (See the chart in chapters 21–22, pp. 1040–1041.)

**10:2** Some people bring unhappiness on themselves by choosing tainted wealth, ill-gotten gain. For example, craving satisfaction, they may do something that destroys their chances of ever achieving happiness. God's principles for right living bring lasting happiness, because they guide us into long-term right behavior in spite of our ever-changing feelings.

**10:3** Proverbs is filled with verses that contrast the godly (righteous) person with the wicked. These statements are not intended to apply universally to all people in every situation. For example, some good people do go hungry. Rather, they are intended to communicate the general truth that the life of the person who

seeks God is better in the long run than the life of the wicked person—a life that leads to ruin. These statements are not iron-clad promises but general truths. In addition, a proverb like this assumes a just government that cares for the poor and needy—the kind of government Israel was intended to have (see Deuteronomy 24:17-22). A corrupt government often thwarts the plans of godly men and women.

**10:3** Proverbs often describes God's care for "the godly." Being "godly" does not mean being "like God" in the sense of being perfect. Obviously that is impossible for human beings. Godly people are those who love the Lord and are seeking to follow him (Psalm 4:3). As Christians, we have been given the power of the Holy Spirit to help us live godly lives (2 Peter 1:3).

**10:4, 5** Every day has 24 hours filled with opportunities to grow, serve, and be productive. Yet it is so easy to waste time, letting life slip from our grasp. Refuse to be a lazy person, sleeping or frittering away the hours meant for productive work. See time as God's gift, and seize your opportunities to live diligently for him.

⁶ The godly are showered with blessings;
  the words of the wicked conceal violent intentions.

**10:7**
Ps 9:5-6

⁷ We have happy memories of the godly,
  but the name of a wicked person rots away.

**10:8**
Prov 9:8
Matt 7:24

⁸ The wise are glad to be instructed,
  but babbling fools fall flat on their faces.

**10:9**
Ps 23:4
Isa 33:15-16
Matt 10:26

⁹ People with integrity walk safely,
  but those who follow crooked paths will slip and fall.

¹⁰ People who wink at wrong cause trouble,
   but a bold reproof promotes peace.*

**10:11**
Ps 37:30
Prov 13:14; 18:4

¹¹ The words of the godly are a life-giving fountain;
   the words of the wicked conceal violent intentions.

**10:12**
1 Cor 13:4-7
†1 Pet 4:8

¹² Hatred stirs up quarrels,
   but love makes up for all offenses.

**10:13**
Prov 10:31; 26:3

¹³ Wise words come from the lips of people with understanding,
   but those lacking sense will be beaten with a rod.

**10:14**
Prov 9:9; 13:3
Jas 3:2, 5

¹⁴ Wise people treasure knowledge,
   but the babbling of a fool invites disaster.

**10:15**
Ps 52:7
Prov 18:11; 19:7

¹⁵ The wealth of the rich is their fortress;
   the poverty of the poor is their destruction.

¹⁶ The earnings of the godly enhance their lives,
   but evil people squander their money on sin.

**10:17**
Prov 6:23

¹⁷ People who accept discipline are on the pathway to life,
   but those who ignore correction will go astray.

¹⁸ Hiding hatred makes you a liar;
   slandering others makes you a fool.

**10:19**
Job 11:2
Eccl 5:3
Jas 3:2

¹⁹ Too much talk leads to sin.
   Be sensible and keep your mouth shut.

²⁰ The words of the godly are like sterling silver;
   the heart of a fool is worthless.

²¹ The words of the godly encourage many,
   but fools are destroyed by their lack of common sense.

**10:22**
Gen 24:35; 26:12
Deut 8:18
Prov 8:21

²² The blessing of the LORD makes a person rich,
   and he adds no sorrow with it.

²³ Doing wrong is fun for a fool,
   but living wisely brings pleasure to the sensible.

**10:24**
Ps 145:19
Prov 1:27; 15:8
Matt 5:6

²⁴ The fears of the wicked will be fulfilled;
   the hopes of the godly will be granted.

**10:10** As in Greek version; Hebrew reads *but babbling fools fall flat on their faces.*

---

**10:18** By hating another person you may become a liar or a fool. If you try to conceal your hatred, you end up lying. If you slander the other person and are proven wrong, you are a fool. The only way out is to admit your hateful feelings to God. Ask him to change your heart, to help you love instead of hate.

**10:20** Words from a good person are valuable ("sterling silver"). A lot of poor advice is worth less than a little good advice. It is easy to get opinions from people who will tell us only what they think will please us, but such advice is not helpful. Instead, we should look for those who will speak the truth, even when it hurts. Think about the people to whom you go for advice. What do you expect to hear from them?

**10:22** God supplies most people with the personal and financial abilities to respond to the needs of others. If we all realized how God has blessed us, and if we all used our resources to do God's will, hunger and poverty would be wiped out. Wealth is a blessing only if we use it in the way God intended.

**10:24** The wicked person dreads death. Those who do not believe in God usually fear death, and with good reason. By contrast, believers desire eternal life and God's salvation—their hopes will be rewarded. This verse offers a choice: You can have either your fears or your hopes come true. You make that choice by rejecting God and living your own way or by accepting God and following him.

25 When the storms of life come, the wicked are whirled away,
      but the godly have a lasting foundation.

26 Lazy people irritate their employers,
      like vinegar to the teeth or smoke in the eyes.

27 Fear of the LORD lengthens one's life,
      but the years of the wicked are cut short.

28 The hopes of the godly result in happiness,
      but the expectations of the wicked come to nothing.

29 The way of the LORD is a stronghold to those with integrity,
      but it destroys the wicked.

30 The godly will never be disturbed,
      but the wicked will be removed from the land.

31 The mouth of the godly person gives wise advice,
      but the tongue that deceives will be cut off.

32 The lips of the godly speak helpful words,
      but the mouth of the wicked speaks perverse words.

**11** ¹ The LORD detests the use of dishonest scales,
          but he delights in accurate weights.

2 Pride leads to disgrace,
      but with humility comes wisdom.

3 Honesty guides good people;
      dishonesty destroys treacherous people.

4 Riches won't help on the day of judgment,
      but right living can save you from death.

5 The godly are directed by honesty;
      the wicked fall beneath their load of sin.

6 The godliness of good people rescues them;
      the ambition of treacherous people traps them.

7 When the wicked die, their hopes die with them,
      for they rely on their own feeble strength.

8 The godly are rescued from trouble,
      and it falls on the wicked instead.

9 With their words, the godless destroy their friends,
      but knowledge will rescue the righteous.

10 The whole city celebrates when the godly succeed;
      they shout for joy when the wicked die.

11 Upright citizens are good for a city and make it prosper,
      but the talk of the wicked tears it apart.

12 It is foolish to belittle one's neighbor;
      a sensible person keeps quiet.

**Cross-references:**
10:25 Ps 15:1-5; Matt 7:24-25
10:27 Ps 55:23; Prov 3:2; 9:11
10:28 Job 11:20
10:30 Ps 37:29
10:32 Prov 6:12; Eccl 12:10
11:1 Deut 25:13-16; Prov 16:11
11:2 Prov 16:18; 18:12; 29:23
11:4 Prov 10:2; Ezek 7:19
11:5 Prov 3:6; 5:22
11:7 Prov 10:28
11:10 Prov 28:12

---

**11:4** "The day of judgment" refers to when we die or to the time when God settles accounts with all people. On judgment day, each person will stand alone, accountable for all of his or her deeds. At that time, no amount of riches will buy reconciliation with God. Only our love for God and obedience to him will count.

**11:7, 8** These verses, like 10:3, contrast two paths in life but are not intended to apply universally to all people in all circumstances. God's people are not excluded from problems or struggles. If a person follows God's wisdom, however, God can rescue him or her from trouble. But a wicked person will fall into his or her own traps. Even if good people suffer, they can be sure they will ultimately be rescued from eternal death.

**11:9** The mouth can be used either as a weapon or a tool, hurting relationships or building them up. Sadly, it is often easier to destroy than to build, and most people have received more destructive comments than those that build up. Every person you meet today is either a demolition site or a construction opportunity. Your words will make a difference. Will they be weapons for destruction or tools for construction?

| | |
|---|---|
| **11:13**<br>Lev 19:16<br>Prov 19:11; 20:19<br>1 Tim 5:13 | <sup>13</sup> A gossip goes around telling secrets,<br>   but those who are trustworthy can keep a confidence. |
| **11:14**<br>Prov 15:22; 20:18;<br>24:6 | <sup>14</sup> Without wise leadership, a nation falls;<br>   there is safety in having many advisers. |
| **11:15**<br>Prov 6:1; 27:13 | <sup>15</sup> There's danger in putting up security for a stranger's debt;<br>   it's safer not to guarantee another person's debt. |
| **11:16**<br>Prov 31:28, 30 | <sup>16</sup> A gracious woman gains respect,<br>   but ruthless men gain only wealth. |
| **11:17**<br>Matt 5:7; 25:34-36 | <sup>17</sup> Your kindness will reward you,<br>   but your cruelty will destroy you. |
| **11:18**<br>Hos 10:12<br>Gal 6:8-9 | <sup>18</sup> Evil people get rich for the moment,<br>   but the reward of the godly will last. |
| **11:19**<br>Prov 10:16; 19:23;<br>21:16<br>Rom 6:23<br>Jas 1:15 | <sup>19</sup> Godly people find life;<br>   evil people find death. |
| **11:20**<br>Prov 13:6 | <sup>20</sup> The LORD detests people with crooked hearts,<br>   but he delights in those with integrity. |
| **11:21**<br>Prov 16:5 | <sup>21</sup> Evil people will surely be punished,<br>   but the children of the godly will go free. |
| | <sup>22</sup> A beautiful woman who lacks discretion<br>   is like a gold ring in a pig's snout. |
| **11:23**<br>Prov 10:28<br>Rom 2:8-9 | <sup>23</sup> The godly can look forward to a reward,<br>   while the wicked can expect only judgment. |
| | <sup>24</sup> Give freely and become more wealthy;<br>   be stingy and lose everything. |

---

**GOD'S ADVICE ABOUT MONEY**

Proverbs gives some practical instruction on the use of money, although sometimes it is advice we would rather not hear. It's more comfortable to continue in our habits than to learn how to use money more wisely. The advice includes

Other verses to study include 11:15; 20:16; 25:14; 27:13.

---

**11:14** A good leader needs and uses wise advisers. One person's perspective and understanding is severely limited; he or she may not have all the facts or may be blinded by bias, emotions, or wrong impressions. To be a wise leader at home, at church, or at work, seek the counsel of others and be open to their advice. Then, after considering all the facts, make your decision. (See the chart in chapter 29, p. 1055.)

**11:19** "Godly people find life" because they live life more fully each day. They also find life because people usually live longer when they live right, with proper diet, exercise, and rest. In addition, they need not fear death because eternal life is God's gift to them (John 11:25). By contrast, evil people not only find eternal death but also miss out on real life on earth.

**11:22** Physical attractiveness without discretion is soon discovered to be quite ugly indeed. We are to seek those character strengths that help us make wise decisions, not just those that make us look good. Not everyone who looks good is pleasant

to live or work with. While taking good care of our body and appearance is not wrong, we also need to develop our ability to think and make wise decisions.

**11:24, 25** These two verses present a paradox: We become richer by being generous. The world says to hold on to as much as possible, but God blesses those who give freely of their possessions, time, and energy. When we give, God supplies us with more so that we can give more. In addition, giving helps us gain a right perspective on our possessions. We realize they were never really ours to begin with, but they were given to us by God to be used to help others. What then do we gain by giving? Freedom from enslavement to our possessions, the joy of helping others, and God's approval.

25 The generous will prosper;
    those who refresh others will themselves be refreshed.

**11:25**
Matt 5:7
2 Cor 9:6-7

26 People curse those who hoard their grain,
    but they bless the one who sells in time of need.

**11:26**
Job 29:13

27 If you search for good, you will find favor;
    but if you search for evil, it will find you!

**11:27**
Ps 7:15

28 Trust in your money and down you go!
    But the godly flourish like leaves in spring.

**11:28**
Pss 1:2-3; 92:12
Jer 17:7-8
Mark 10:24-25
1 Tim 6:17

29 Those who bring trouble on their families inherit the wind.
    The fool will be a servant to the wise.

**11:29**
Prov 14:19; 15:27

30 The seeds of good deeds become a tree of life;
    a wise person wins friends.*

**11:30**
Jas 5:20

31 If the righteous are rewarded here on earth,
    what will happen to wicked sinners?*

**11:31**
†1 Pet 4:18

**12** ¹ To learn, you must love discipline;
    it is stupid to hate correction.

**12:1**
Prov 1:5; 9:9; 25:12

2 The LORD approves of those who are good,
    but he condemns those who plan wickedness.

3 Wickedness never brings stability,
    but the godly have deep roots.

**12:3**
Ps 15:1-5
Prov 10:25; 11:5

4 A worthy wife is a crown for her husband,
    but a disgraceful woman is like cancer in his bones.

**12:4**
Prov 14:1; 31:10
1 Cor 11:7

5 The plans of the godly are just;
    the advice of the wicked is treacherous.

**12:5**
Prov 16:23
Matt 12:34; 15:18

6 The words of the wicked are like a murderous ambush,
    but the words of the godly save lives.

7 The wicked die and disappear,
    but the family of the godly stands firm.

**12:7**
Isa 3:10-11
Matt 7:24-27

8 A sensible person wins admiration,
    but a warped mind is despised.

**12:8**
Eccl 8:1

9 Better to be an ordinary person with a servant
    than to be self-important but have no food.

**12:9**
Luke 14:11

**11:30** Or *and those who win souls are wise.*     **11:31** Greek version reads *If the righteous are barely saved, / what will happen to godless sinners?* Compare 1 Pet 4:18.

---

**11:29** One of the greatest resources God gives us is the family. Families provide acceptance, encouragement, guidance, and counsel. Bringing trouble on your family—whether through anger or through an exaggerated desire for independence—is foolish because you cut yourself off from all they provide. In your family, strive for healing, communication, and understanding.

**11:30** A wise person is a model of a meaningful life. Like a tree attracts people to its shade, a wise person's sense of purpose attracts others who want to know how they, too, can find meaning. Gaining wisdom yourself can be the first step in leading people to God.

**11:31** Contrary to popular opinion, no one sins and gets away with it. The righteous are rewarded for their faith; the wicked are punished for their sins. Don't think for a moment that "it won't matter" or "nobody will know" or "we won't get caught" (see also 1 Peter 4:18).

**12:1** If you don't want to learn, years of schooling will teach you very little. But if you want to be taught, there is no end to what

you can learn. This includes being willing to accept discipline and correction and to learn from the wisdom of others. A person who refuses constructive criticism has a problem with pride. Such a person is unlikely to learn very much.

**12:3** To have deep roots and to be stable means to be successful. Real stability and success come only to those who do what is right. Their efforts stand the test of time. Yet sometimes it seems that wickedness does indeed bring success. We may know people who cheated to pass the course or to get a larger tax refund—is this not success? And what about the person who ignores his family commitments and mistreats his workers but gets ahead in business? These apparent successes are only temporary. They are bought at the expense of character. Cheaters grow more and more dishonest, and those who hurt others become callous and cruel. In the long run, evil behavior does not lead to success; it leads only to more evil. Real success maintains personal integrity. If you are not a success by God's standards, you have not achieved true success. (See the chart in chapter 19, p. 1035.)

<sup></sup>
**12:10**
Gen 33:13

<sup>10</sup> The godly care for their animals,
　　but the wicked are always cruel.

**12:11**
Prov 9:6; 14:24

<sup>11</sup> A hard worker has plenty of food,
　　but a person who chases fantasies has no sense.

<sup>12</sup> Thieves are jealous of each other's loot,
　　but the godly are well rooted and bear their own fruit.

<sup>13</sup> The wicked are trapped by their own words,
　　but the godly escape such trouble.

**12:14**
Isa 3:10

<sup>14</sup> Wise words bring many benefits,
　　and hard work brings rewards.

**12:15**
Prov 14:12; 16:2

<sup>15</sup> Fools think their own way is right,
　　but the wise listen to others.

<sup>16</sup> A fool is quick-tempered,
　　but a wise person stays calm when insulted.

<sup>17</sup> An honest witness tells the truth;
　　a false witness tells lies.

<sup>18</sup> Some people make cutting remarks,
　　but the words of the wise bring healing.

**12:19**
Job 20:5

<sup>19</sup> Truthful words stand the test of time,
　　but lies are soon exposed.

<sup>20</sup> Deceit fills hearts that are plotting evil;
　　joy fills hearts that are planning peace!

**12:21**
Ps 121:7
Prov 1:33
1 Pet 3:13

<sup>21</sup> No harm comes to the godly,
　　but the wicked have their fill of trouble.

---

**TEACHING AND LEARNING**

Good teaching comes from good learning—and Proverbs has more to say to students than to teachers. Proverbs is concerned with the learning of wisdom. The book makes it clear that there are no good alternatives to learning wisdom. We are either becoming wise learners or refusing to learn and becoming foolish failures. Proverbs encourages us to make the right choice.

| Wise Learners | Proverb(s) | Foolish Failures |
|---|---|---|
| Gladly accept instruction | 10:8; 23:12 | Ignore instruction |
| Love discipline | 12:1 | Hate correction |
| Listen to advice | 12:15; 21:11; 24:6 | Think they need no advice |
| Accept parents' discipline | 13:1 | Mock parents |
| Are on the pathway to life | 10:17 | Will go astray |
| Will be honored | 13:18 | End in proverty and disgrace |
| Profit from constructive criticism | 15:31, 32; 29:1 | Harm themselves by refusing criticism |

*Advice to Teachers:*
Help people avoid traps (13:14), use pleasant words (16:21), and speak wise words at the right time (15:23; 18:20).

---

**12:13** Evil people twist the facts to support their claims. Those who do this will eventually be trapped by their own lies. But for those who always tell the truth, the facts—plain and unvarnished—give an unshakable defense. If you find that you always have to defend yourself to others, maybe you are not being honest. (See the chart in chapter 20, p. 1037.)

**12:16** When someone annoys or insults you, it is natural to retaliate. But this solves nothing and only encourages trouble. Instead, stay calm and answer slowly and quietly. Your positive response will achieve positive results. Proverbs 15:1 says, "A gentle answer deflects anger."

**12:19** Truth is always timely; it applies today and in the future.

Because it is connected with God's changeless character, it is also changeless. Think for a moment about the centuries that have passed since these proverbs were written. Consider the countless hours that have been spent carefully studying every sentence of Scripture. The Bible has withstood the test of time. Because God is truth, you can trust his Word to guide you.

**12:21** This is a general, but not universal, truth. Although harm does befall the godly, they are able to see opportunities in their problems and move ahead. The wicked, without God's wisdom, are ill-equipped to handle their problems. (See the notes on 3:16, 17; 10:3; 11:7, 8 for more about general truths that are not intended as universal statements.)

22 The LORD detests lying lips,
   but he delights in those who tell the truth.

23 The wise don't make a show of their knowledge,
   but fools broadcast their foolishness.

24 Work hard and become a leader;
   be lazy and become a slave.

25 Worry weighs a person down;
   an encouraging word cheers a person up.

26 The godly give good advice to their friends;*
   the wicked lead them astray.

27 Lazy people don't even cook the game they catch,
   but the diligent make use of everything they find.

28 The way of the godly leads to life;
   that path does not lead to death.

# 13

1 A wise child accepts a parent's discipline;*
  a mocker refuses to listen to correction.

2 Wise words will win you a good meal,
  but treacherous people have an appetite for violence.

3 Those who control their tongue will have a long life;
  opening your mouth can ruin everything.

4 Lazy people want much but get little,
  but those who work hard will prosper.

5 The godly hate lies;
  the wicked cause shame and disgrace.

6 Godliness guards the path of the blameless,
  but the evil are misled by sin.

7 Some who are poor pretend to be rich;
  others who are rich pretend to be poor.

8 The rich can pay a ransom for their lives,
  but the poor won't even get threatened.

9 The life of the godly is full of light and joy,
  but the light of the wicked will be snuffed out.

**12:22**
Eccl 5:2
Isa 19:21

**12:25**
Prov 15:13; 17:22
18:15

**12:27**
Prov 10:4; 13:4

**12:28**
Ezek 18:9, 20
Rom 5:21

**13:1**
Prov 10:1; 15:12

**13:3**
Prov 18:7, 21;
20:19; 21:23
Jas 3:2

**13:5**
Prov 3:35

**13:7**
Prov 11:24
Luke 12:20-21
2 Cor 6:10
Jas 2:5

**13:9**
Job 18:5; 29:3
Prov 4:18; 24:20

**12:26** Or *The godly are cautious in friendship;* or *The godly are freed from evil.* The meaning of the Hebrew is uncertain.   **13:1** Hebrew *A wise son accepts his father's discipline.*

---

**12:23** Wise people have a quiet confidence. Unstable people (fools) feel the need to prove themselves, but wise people don't have to prove anything. They know they are capable, so they can get on with their work. Beware of showing off. If you are modest, people may not notice you at first, but they will respect you later.

**12:27** The diligent make wise use of their possessions and resources; the lazy waste them. Waste has become a way of life for many who live in a land of plenty. Waste is poor stewardship. Make good use of everything God has given you, and prize it.

**12:28** For many, death is a darkened door at the end of life, a passageway to an unknown and feared destiny. But for God's people, death is a bright pathway to a new and better life. So why do we fear death? Is it fear of the pain we expect, the separation from loved ones, or the unknown? God can help us deal with those fears. He has shown us that death is not final but

just another step in the eternal life we received when we followed him.

**13:3** You have not mastered self-control if you do not control what you say. Words can cut and destroy. James recognized this truth when he stated, "The tongue is a flame of fire. It is a whole world of wickedness" (James 3:6). If you want to be self-controlled, begin with your tongue. Stop and think before you react or speak. If you can control this small but powerful member, you can control the rest of your body. (See the chart in chapter 26, p. 1049.)

**13:6** Blameless living safeguards your life. Every choice for good sets into motion other opportunities for good. Evil choices follow the same pattern, but in the opposite direction. Each decision you make to obey God's Word will bring a greater sense of order to your life, while each decision to disobey will bring confusion and destruction. The right choices you make reflect your integrity. Obedience brings the greatest safeguard and security.

<sup>10</sup> Pride leads to conflict;
   those who take advice are wise.

<sup>11</sup> Wealth from get-rich-quick schemes quickly disappears;
   wealth from hard work grows over time.

<sup>12</sup> Hope deferred makes the heart sick,
   but a dream fulfilled is a tree of life.

**13:13**
2 Chr 36:16

<sup>13</sup> People who despise advice are asking for trouble;
   those who respect a command will succeed.

**13:14**
Ps 18:5
Prov 10:11

<sup>14</sup> The instruction of the wise is like a life-giving fountain;
   those who accept it avoid the snares of death.

**13:15**
Ps 111:10
Prov 3:4

<sup>15</sup> A person with good sense is respected;
   a treacherous person is headed for destruction.*

**13:16**
Prov 12:23

<sup>16</sup> Wise people think before they act;
   fools don't—and even brag about their foolishness.

**13:17**
Prov 25:13

<sup>17</sup> An unreliable messenger stumbles into trouble,
   but a reliable messenger brings healing.

**13:18**
Prov 15:5, 32

<sup>18</sup> If you ignore criticism, you will end in poverty and disgrace;
   if you accept correction, you will be honored.

<sup>19</sup> It is pleasant to see dreams come true,
   but fools refuse to turn from evil to attain them.

**13:20**
Prov 2:20

<sup>20</sup> Walk with the wise and become wise;
   associate with fools and get in trouble.

**13:21**
Ps 32:10
Prov 11:31
Isa 3:10

<sup>21</sup> Trouble chases sinners,
   while blessings reward the righteous.

**13:22**
Ezra 9:12
Ps 37:25
Prov 28:8

<sup>22</sup> Good people leave an inheritance to their grandchildren,
   but the sinner's wealth passes to the godly.

<sup>23</sup> A poor person's farm may produce much food,
   but injustice sweeps it all away.

**13:15** As in Greek version; Hebrew reads *the way of the treacherous is lasting.*

---

**13:10** "I was wrong" or "I need advice" are difficult phrases to utter because they require humility. Pride is an ingredient in every quarrel. It stirs up conflict and divides people. Humility, by contrast, heals. Guard against pride. If you find yourself constantly arguing, examine your life for pride. Be open to the advice of others, ask for help when you need it, and be willing to admit your mistakes.

**13:13** God created us, knows us, and loves us. It only makes sense, then, to listen to his instructions and do what he says. The Bible is his unfailing word to us. It is like an owner's manual for a car. If you obey God's instructions, you will "run right" and find his kind of power to live. If you ignore them, you will have breakdowns, accidents, and failures.

**13:17** In Solomon's day, a king had to rely on messengers for information about his country. These messengers had to be trustworthy. Inaccurate information could lead to bloodshed. Reliable communication is still vital. If the message received is different from the message sent, marriages, businesses, and diplomatic relations can all break down. It is important to choose your words well and to avoid reacting until you clearly understand what the other person means.

**13:19** Whether a "dream come true" is good or bad depends on the nature of the dream or desire. It is pleasant to achieve worthwhile goals, but not all goals are worth pursuing. When you set your heart on something, you may lose your ability to assess it objectively. With your desire blinding your judgment, you may

proceed with an unwise relationship, a wasteful purchase, or a poorly conceived plan. Faithfulness is a virtue, but stubbornness is not.

**13:20** The old saying "A rotten apple spoils the barrel" is often applied to friendships, and with good reason. Our friends and associates affect us, sometimes profoundly. Be careful whom you choose as your closest friends. Spend time with people you want to be like because you and your friends will surely grow to resemble each other.

**13:20** When most people need advice, they go to their friends first because friends accept them and usually agree with them. But that is why they may not be able to help them with difficult problems. Our friends are so much like us that they may not have any answers we haven't already heard. Instead, we should seek out older and wiser people to advise us. Wise people have experienced a lot in life—and have succeeded. They are not afraid to tell the truth. Who are the wise, godly people who can warn you of the pitfalls ahead?

**13:23** The poor are often victims of an unjust society. A poor man's soil may be good, but unjust laws may rob him of his own produce. This proverb does not take poverty lightly or wink at injustice; it simply describes what often occurs. We should do what we can to fight injustice of every sort. Our efforts may seem inadequate; but it is comforting to know that in the end God's justice will prevail.

24 Those who spare the rod of discipline hate their children.
   Those who love their children care enough to discipline them.
**13:24**
Prov 19:18; 22:15;
23:13

25 The godly eat to their hearts' content,
   but the belly of the wicked goes hungry.
**13:25**
Ps 34:10
Prov 10:3

# 14
1 A wise woman builds her home,
   but a foolish woman tears it down with her own hands.
**14:1**
Prov 31:10-27

2 Those who follow the right path fear the LORD;
   those who take the wrong path despise him.

3 A fool's proud talk becomes a rod that beats him,
   but the words of the wise keep them safe.
**14:3**
Prov 12:6

4 Without oxen a stable stays clean,
   but you need a strong ox for a large harvest.

5 An honest witness does not lie;
   a false witness breathes lies.
**14:5**
Prov 6:19; 12:17
Rev 3:14

6 A mocker seeks wisdom and never finds it,
   but knowledge comes easily to those with understanding.

7 Stay away from fools,
   for you won't find knowledge on their lips.
**14:7**
Prov 23:9

8 The prudent understand where they are going,
   but fools deceive themselves.
**14:8**
Prov 15:28

9 Fools make fun of guilt,
   but the godly acknowledge it and seek reconciliation.

10 Each heart knows its own bitterness,
    and no one else can fully share its joy.

11 The house of the wicked will be destroyed,
    but the tent of the godly will flourish.
**14:11**
Prov 12:7

12 There is a path before each person that seems right,
    but it ends in death.
**14:12**
Prov 16:25
Rom 6:21

13 Laughter can conceal a heavy heart,
    but when the laughter ends, the grief remains.
**14:13**
Eccl 2:1-2

14 Backsliders get what they deserve;
    good people receive their reward.
**14:14**
Prov 1:31;
12:14, 21

15 Only simpletons believe everything they're told!
    The prudent carefully consider their steps.

**13:24** It is not easy for a loving parent to discipline a child, but it is necessary. The greatest responsibility that God gives parents is the nurture and guidance of their children. Lack of discipline puts parents' love in question because it shows a lack of concern for the character development of their children. Disciplining children averts long-range disaster. Without correction, children grow up with no clear understanding of right and wrong and with little direction to their lives. Don't be afraid to discipline your children. It is an act of love. Remember, however, that your efforts cannot make your children wise; they can only encourage your children to seek God's wisdom above all else!

**14:4** When a farmer has no oxen, the stable will be clean but he will be unable to make a living. The only way to keep your life free of people problems is to keep it free of people. But if your life is empty of people, it is useless; and if you live only for yourself, your life loses its meaning. Instead of avoiding people, we should serve others, share our faith, and work for justice. Is your life clean but empty? Or does it give evidence of your serving God wholeheartedly?

**14:6** We all know mockers, people who scoff at every word of instruction or advice. They never find wisdom because they don't seek it seriously. Wisdom comes to those who apply God's Word to their lives and seek out godly counselors. If the wisdom you need does not come easily to you, perhaps your attitude is the barrier.

**14:12** The "path . . . that seems right" may offer many options and require few sacrifices. Easy choices, however, should make us take a second look. Is this solution attractive because it allows me to be lazy? because it doesn't ask me to change my lifestyle? because it requires no moral restraints? The right choice often requires hard work and self-sacrifice. Don't be enticed by apparent shortcuts that seem right but end in death.

16 The wise are cautious* and avoid danger;
   fools plunge ahead with reckless confidence.

17 Short-tempered people do foolish things,
   and schemers are hated.

18 Simpletons are clothed with foolishness,*
   but the prudent are crowned with knowledge.

19 Evil people will bow before good people;
   the wicked will bow at the gates of the godly.

20 The poor are despised even by their neighbors,
   while the rich have many "friends."

21 It is a sin to belittle one's neighbor;
   blessed are those who help the poor.

22 If you plan to do evil, you will be lost;
   if you plan to do good, you will receive unfailing love and faithfulness.

23 Work brings profit,
   but mere talk leads to poverty!

**14:16** Hebrew *The wise fear.*   **14:18** Or *inherit foolishness.*

---

**WISDOM AND FOOLISHNESS**
The wise and the foolish are often contrasted in Proverbs. The characteristics, reputation, and results of each are worth knowing if wisdom is our goal.

| | | The Wise | The Foolish | |
|---|---|---|---|---|
| Characteristics | | Give encouragement | Lack common sense | 10:21 |
| | | Enjoy living wisely | Enjoy foolishness | 10:23 |
| | | Consider their steps | Gullible | 14:15 |
| | | | Avoid the wise | 15:12 |
| | | Hungry for knowledge | Feed on the trash of foolishness | 15:14 |
| | | Value wisdom above riches | | 16:16 |
| | | Respond to correction | Do not respond to punishment | 17:10 |
| | | Pursue wisdom | Pursue illusive dreams | 17:24 |
| | | | Blame failure on God | 19:3 |
| | | Profit from correction | An example to others | 19:25 |
| | | | Proud and arrogant | 21:24 |
| | | | Despise wise advice | 23:9 |
| | | | Make truth useless | 26:7 |
| | | | Repeat their folly | 26:11 |
| | | Trust in wisdom | Trust in themselves | 28:26 |
| | | Control their anger | Unleash their anger | 29:11 |
| Reputation | | Crowned with knowledge | Clothed with foolishness | 14:18 |
| | | | Cause quarrels | 22:10 |
| | | | Receive no honor | 26:1 |
| | | Calm anger | Stir up anger | 29:8 |
| Results | | Stay on right paths | Enjoy the wrong paths | 15:21 |
| | | | Lash out when discovered in folly | 17:12 |
| | | | Endangered by their words | 18:6, 7 |
| | | Their wisdom conquers others' strength | | 21:22 |
| | | Avoid wicked paths | Walk a treacherous road | 22:5 |
| | | Grow stronger | | 24:5 |
| | | | Will never be chosen as leaders | 24:7 |
| | | | Must be guided by hardship | 26:3 |
| | | | Persist in foolishness | 27:22 |

24 Wealth is a crown for the wise;
  the effort of fools yields only foolishness.

25 A truthful witness saves lives,
  but a false witness is a traitor.

26 Those who fear the LORD are secure;
  he will be a refuge for their children.

27 Fear of the LORD is a life-giving fountain;
  it offers escape from the snares of death.

28 A growing population is a king's glory;
  a prince without subjects has nothing.

29 People with understanding control their anger;
  a hot temper shows great foolishness.

30 A peaceful heart leads to a healthy body;
  jealousy is like cancer in the bones.

31 Those who oppress the poor insult their Maker,
  but helping the poor honors him.

32 The wicked are crushed by disaster,
  but the godly have a refuge when they die.

33 Wisdom is enshrined in an understanding heart;
  wisdom is not* found among fools.

34 Godliness makes a nation great,
  but sin is a disgrace to any people.

35 A king rejoices in wise servants
  but is angry with those who disgrace him.

## 15

1 A gentle answer deflects anger,
  but harsh words make tempers flare.

2 The tongue of the wise makes knowledge appealing,
  but the mouth of a fool belches out foolishness.

3 The LORD is watching everywhere,
  keeping his eye on both the evil and the good.

4 Gentle words are a tree of life;
  a deceitful tongue crushes the spirit.

5 Only a fool despises a parent's* discipline;
  whoever learns from correction is wise.

14:33 As in Greek and Syriac versions; Hebrew lacks *not*.    15:5 Hebrew *father's*.

**14:25** Prov 14:5

**14:26** Prov 19:23

**14:27** Prov 13:14

**14:29** Prov 16:32; 19:11 Jas 1:19

**14:31** Ps 12:5 Prov 14:21; 17:5; 22:2, 16

**14:32** 2 Cor 1:9

**14:35** Matt 24:45

**15:1** Judg 8:1-3 1 Sam 25:10-13 Prov 15:18; 25:10

**15:2** Prov 12:23; 13:16 Eccl 12:10

**15:3** Job 31:4; 34:21 Heb 4:13

---

**14:29** A nasty and quick temper can be like a fire out of control, burning us and everyone in its path. Anger divides people. It pushes us into hasty decisions that only cause bitterness and guilt. Yet anger, in itself, is not wrong. Anger can be a legitimate reaction to injustice and sin. When you feel yourself getting angry, look for the cause. Are you reacting to an evil situation that you are going to set right? Or are you responding selfishly to a personal insult? Pray that God will help you control a quick temper, channeling your feelings into effective action and conquering selfish anger through humility and repentance.

**14:31** God has a special concern for the poor. He insists that people who have material goods should be generous with those who are needy. Providing for the poor is not just a suggestion in the Bible; it is a command that may require a change of attitude

(see Leviticus 23:22; Deuteronomy 15:7, 8; Psalms 113:5-9; 146:5-9; Isaiah 58:7; 2 Corinthians 9:9; James 2:1-9).

**15:1** Have you ever tried to argue in a whisper? It is equally hard to argue with someone who insists on answering gently. On the other hand, a rising voice and harsh words almost always trigger an angry response. To turn away wrath and seek peace, choose gentle words.

**15:3** At times it seems that God has let evil run rampant in the world and we wonder if he even notices it. But God sees everything clearly—both the evil actions and the evil intentions lying behind them (15:11). He is not an indifferent observer. He cares and is active in our world. Right now, his work may be unseen and unfelt, but don't give up. One day he will wipe out evil and punish the evildoers, just as he will establish the good and reward those who do his will.

15:6
Prov 8:21

⁶ There is treasure in the house of the godly,
   but the earnings of the wicked bring trouble.

⁷ The lips of the wise give good advice;
   the heart of a fool has none to give.

15:8
Isa 1:11

⁸ The LORD detests the sacrifice of the wicked,
   but he delights in the prayers of the upright.

⁹ The LORD detests the way of the wicked,
   but he loves those who pursue godliness.

¹⁰ Whoever abandons the right path will be severely disciplined;
   whoever hates correction will die.

15:11
1 Sam 16:7
2 Chr 6:30
Job 26:6
Acts 1:24

¹¹ Even Death and Destruction* hold no secrets from the LORD.
   How much more does he know the human heart!

15:12
Prov 9:7; 13:1;
19:25; 24:9

¹² Mockers hate to be corrected,
   so they stay away from the wise.

15:13
Prov 17:22
Eccl 8:1

¹³ A glad heart makes a happy face;
   a broken heart crushes the spirit.

15:14
Prov 18:15

¹⁴ A wise person is hungry for knowledge,
   while the fool feeds on trash.

¹⁵ For the despondent, every day brings trouble;
   for the happy heart, life is a continual feast.

15:16
Ps 37:16
Prov 16:8
1 Tim 6:6

¹⁶ Better to have little, with fear for the LORD,
   than to have great treasure and inner turmoil.

15:17
Prov 17:1

¹⁷ A bowl of vegetables with someone you love
   is better than steak with someone you hate.

15:18
Prov 14:29; 16:28;
26:21
Eccl 10:4

¹⁸ A hot-tempered person starts fights;
   a cool-tempered person stops them.

¹⁹ A lazy person's way is blocked with briers,
   but the path of the upright is an open highway.

15:20
Prov 10:1; 29:3;
30:17

²⁰ Sensible children bring joy to their father;
   foolish children despise their mother.

15:21
Eph 5:15

²¹ Foolishness brings joy to those with no sense;
   a sensible person stays on the right path.

²² Plans go wrong for lack of advice;
   many advisers bring success.

²³ Everyone enjoys a fitting reply;
   it is wonderful to say the right thing at the right time!

15:11 Hebrew *Sheol and Abaddon.*

---

**15:14** What we feed our minds is just as important as what we feed our bodies. The kinds of books we read, the people we talk with, the music we listen to, and the films we watch are all part of our mental diet. Be discerning because what you feed your mind influences your total health and well-being. Thus, a strong desire to discover knowledge is a mark of wisdom.

**15:15** Our attitudes color our whole personality. We cannot always choose what happens to us, but we can choose our attitude toward each situation. The secret to a happy heart is filling our mind with thoughts that are true, pure, and lovely, with thoughts that dwell on the good things in life (Philippians 4:8). This was Paul's secret as he faced imprisonment, and it can be ours as we face the struggles of daily living. Look at your attitudes and then examine what you allow to enter your mind and what you choose to dwell on. You may need to make some changes.

**15:17-19** The "path of the upright" doesn't always seem easy (15:19), but look at the alternatives. Hatred (15:17), dissension (15:18), and laziness (15:19) cause problems that the upright person does not have to face. By comparison, his or her life is a smooth, level road because it is built on a solid foundation of love for God.

**15:22** People with tunnel vision—those who are locked into one way of thinking—are likely to miss the right road because they have closed their minds to any new options. We need the help of those who can enlarge our vision and broaden our perspective. Seek out the advice of those who know you and have a wealth of experience. Build a network of advisers. Then be open to new ideas, and be willing to weigh their suggestions carefully. Your plans will be stronger and more likely to succeed.

24 The path of life leads upward for the wise;
   they leave the grave* behind.

25 The LORD tears down the house of the proud,
   but he protects the property of widows.

15:25
Pss 68:5; 146:9
Prov 14:11

26 The LORD detests evil plans,
   but he delights in pure words.

27 Greed brings grief to the whole family,
   but those who hate bribes will live.

15:27
Exod 23:8
Deut 16:19
Prov 28:25

28 The heart of the godly thinks carefully before speaking;
   the mouth of the wicked overflows with evil words.

15:28
Prov 10:19, 32
1 Pet 3:15

29 The LORD is far from the wicked,
   but he hears the prayers of the righteous.

15:29
Ps 145:18-19

30 A cheerful look brings joy to the heart;
   good news makes for good health.

31 If you listen to constructive criticism,
   you will be at home among the wise.

15:31
Prov 15:5

32 If you reject discipline, you only harm yourself;
   but if you listen to correction, you grow in understanding.

33 Fear of the LORD teaches wisdom;
   humility precedes honor.

15:33
Prov 1:7

# 16

1 We can make our own plans,
   but the LORD gives the right answer.

2 People may be pure in their own eyes,
   but the LORD examines their motives.

16:2
Prov 21:2

3 Commit your actions to the LORD,
   and your plans will succeed.

16:3
Pss 37:5; 55:22
Prov 3:6

4 The LORD has made everything for his own purposes,
   even the wicked for a day of disaster.

16:4
Job 38:23
Eccl 3:11
Isa 43:7

5 The LORD detests the proud;
   they will surely be punished.

16:5
Prov 6:16-17; 8:13;
11:21

15:24 Hebrew *Sheol.*

---

**15:28** The godly weigh their answers; the wicked don't think before speaking because they don't care about the effects of their words. It is important to have something to say, but it is equally important to think about it first. Do you carefully plan your words, or do you pour out your thoughts without concern for their impact?

**16:1** This verse can be understood to mean that the final outcome of the plans we make is in God's hands. If this is so, why make plans? In doing God's will, there must be partnership between our efforts and God's control. He wants us to use our minds, to seek the advice of others, and to plan. Nevertheless, the results are up to him. Planning, then, helps us act God's way. As you live for him, ask for guidance as you plan, and then act on your plan as you trust in him.

**16:2** People can rationalize anything if they have no standards for judging right and wrong. We can always prove that we are right. Before putting any plan into action, ask yourself these three questions: (1) Is this plan in harmony with God's truth? (2) Will it work under real-life conditions? (3) Is my attitude pleasing to God?

**16:3** There are different ways to fail to commit whatever we do to the Lord. Some people commit their work only superficially. They say the project is being done for the Lord, but in reality they are doing it for themselves. Others give God temporary control of

their interests, only to take control back the moment things stop going the way they expect. Still others commit a task fully to the Lord but put forth no effort themselves, and then they wonder why they do not succeed. We must maintain a delicate balance: trusting God as if everything depended on him, while working as if everything depended on us. Think of a specific effort in which you are involved right now. Have you committed it to the Lord?

**16:4** This verse doesn't mean that God created some people to be wicked, but rather that God uses even the activities of wicked people for his good purposes (see Genesis 50:20). God is infinite and we are finite. No matter how great our intellects, we will never be able to understand him completely. But we can accept by faith that he is all-powerful, all-loving, and perfectly good. We can believe that he is not the cause of evil (James 1:13, 17); and we can trust that there are no loose ends in his system of judgment. Evil is a temporary condition in the universe. One day God will destroy it.

**16:5** Pride is the inner voice that whispers, "My way is best." It is resisting God's leadership and believing that we are able to live without his help. Whenever you find yourself wanting to do it your way or looking down on other people, you are being controlled by pride. Only when you eliminate pride can God help you become all he meant you to be. (See the chart in chapter 18, p. 1033.)

6 Unfailing love and faithfulness make atonement for sin.
  By fearing the LORD, people avoid evil.

7 When people's lives please the LORD,
  even their enemies are at peace with them.

8 Better to have little, with godliness,
  than to be rich and dishonest.

**16:9**
Ps 37:23
Prov 16:1; 19:21;
20:24
Jer 10:23

9 We can make our plans,
  but the LORD determines our steps.

**16:10**
1 Kgs 3:28

10 The king speaks with divine wisdom;
   he must never judge unfairly.

**16:11**
Prov 11:1

11 The LORD demands accurate scales and balances;
   he sets the standards for fairness.

12 A king detests wrongdoing,
   for his rule is built on justice.

**16:13**
Prov 14:35

13 The king is pleased with words from righteous lips;
   he loves those who speak honestly.

14 The anger of the king is a deadly threat;
   the wise will try to appease it.

15 When the king smiles, there is life;
   his favor refreshes like a spring rain.

**16:16**
Prov 8:10, 19

16 How much better to get wisdom than gold,
   and good judgment than silver!

---

| HOW GOD IS DESCRIBED IN PROVERBS | | |
|---|---|---|
| | *God . . .* | is aware of all that happens (15:3) |
| | | knows the hearts of all people (15:11; 16:2; 21:2) |
| | | controls all things (16:33; 21:30) |
| | | is a place of safety (18:10) |
| | | rescues good people from danger (11:8, 21) |
| | | condemns the wicked (11:31) |
| | | hears and delights in our prayers (15:8, 29) |
| | | loves those who obey him (15:9) |
| | | cares for the poor and needy (15:25; 22:22, 23) |
| | | tests and purifies hearts (17:3) |
| | | detests evil (21:27; 28:9) |
| | *Our response should be . . .* | to fear and revere God (10:27; 14:26, 27; 15:16; 16:6; 19:23; 28:14) |
| | | to obey God's Word (13:13; 19:16) |
| | | to please God by doing what is right and just (21:3) |
| | | to trust in God (22:17-19; 29:25) |

Proverbs is a book about wise living. It often focuses on a person's response and attitude toward God, who is the source of wisdom. And a number of proverbs point out aspects of God's character. Knowing God helps us on the way to wisdom.

**16:7** We want other people to like us, and sometimes we will do almost anything to win their approval. But God tells us to put our energy into pleasing him instead. Our effort to be peacemakers will usually make us more attractive to those around us, even our enemies. But even if it doesn't, we haven't lost anything. We are still pleasing God, the only one who truly matters.

**16:11** Whether we buy or sell, make a product or offer a service, we know what is fair and honest and what is unfair and dishonest. Sometimes we feel pressure to be dishonest in order to advance ourselves or gain more profit. But if we want to obey God, there is no middle ground: God demands honesty in every business transaction. No amount of rationalizing can justify a dishonest business practice. Honesty and fairness are not always easy, but they are what God demands. Ask him for discernment and courage to be consistently honest and fair.

17 The path of the virtuous leads away from evil;
   whoever follows that path is safe.

18 Pride goes before destruction,
   and haughtiness before a fall.

16:18
Jer 49:16

19 Better to live humbly with the poor
   than to share plunder with the proud.

16:19
Isa 57:15

20 Those who listen to instruction will prosper;
   those who trust the LORD will be joyful.

16:20
Pss 2:12; 34:8
Jer 17:7

21 The wise are known for their understanding,
   and pleasant words are persuasive.

16:21
Prov 16:23

22 Discretion is a life-giving fountain to those who possess it,
   but discipline is wasted on fools.

23 From a wise mind comes wise speech;
   the words of the wise are persuasive.

16:23
Ps 37:30
Prov 15:18, 28

24 Kind words are like honey—
   sweet to the soul and healthy for the body.

16:24
Prov 4:22; 15:26;
17:22; 24:13

25 There is a path before each person that seems right,
   but it ends in death.

16:25
Prov 14:12

26 It is good for workers to have an appetite;
   an empty stomach drives them on.

27 Scoundrels create trouble;
   their words are a destructive blaze.

16:27
Prov 6:14, 18
Jas 3:6

28 A troublemaker plants seeds of strife;
   gossip separates the best of friends.

29 Violent people mislead their companions,
   leading them down a harmful path.

16:29
Prov 1:10

30 With narrowed eyes, people plot evil;
   with a smirk, they plan their mischief.

31 Gray hair is a crown of glory;
   it is gained by living a godly life.

16:31
Prov 20:29

32 Better to be patient than powerful;
   better to have self-control than to conquer a city.

16:32
Prov 19:11

33 We may throw the dice,*
   but the LORD determines how they fall.

**16:33** Hebrew *We may cast lots.*

16:18 Proud people take little account of their weaknesses and do not anticipate stumbling blocks. They think they are above the frailties of common people. In this state of mind they are easily tripped up. Ironically, proud people seldom realize that pride is their problem, although everyone around them is well aware of it. Ask someone you trust whether self-satisfaction has blinded you to warning signs. He or she may help you avoid a fall.

16:22 For centuries people sought a fountain of youth, a spring that promised to give eternal life and vitality. It was never found. But God's wisdom gives us discretion that proves to be a life-giving fountain that can make us happy, healthy, and alive forever. How? When we live by God's Word, he washes away the deadly effects of sin (see Titus 3:4-8), and the hope of eternal

life with him gives us a joyful perspective on our present life. The fountain of youth was only a dream, but the life-giving fountain is reality. The choice is yours. You can be enlightened by God's wisdom, or you can be dragged down by the weight of your own foolishness.

16:31 The Hebrews believed that a long life was a sign of God's blessing; therefore, gray hair and old age were good. While young people glory in their strength, old people can rejoice in their years of experience and practical wisdom. Gray hair is not a sign of disgrace to be covered over; it is a crown of splendor. As you deal with older people, treat them with respect.

16:32 Self-control is superior to conquest. Success in business, school, or home life can be ruined by a person who loses control of his or her temper. So it is a great personal victory to control your temper. When you feel yourself ready to explode, remember that losing control may cause you to forfeit what you want the most.

17:1
Prov 15:17

# 17

¹ Better a dry crust eaten in peace
  than a house filled with feasting—and conflict.

² A wise servant will rule over the master's disgraceful son
  and will share the inheritance of the master's children.

17:3
1 Chr 29:17
Ps 26:2

³ Fire tests the purity of silver and gold,
  but the LORD tests the heart.

⁴ Wrongdoers eagerly listen to gossip;
  liars pay close attention to slander.

17:5
Job 31:29
Prov 14:31; 24:17

⁵ Those who mock the poor insult their Maker;
  those who rejoice at the misfortune of others will be punished.

17:6
Gen 48:11
Prov 13:22

⁶ Grandchildren are the crowning glory of the aged;
  parents* are the pride of their children.

⁷ Eloquent words are not fitting for a fool;
  even less are lies fitting for a ruler.

17:8
Prov 21:14
Isa 1:23
Amos 5:12

⁸ A bribe is like a lucky charm;
  whoever gives one will prosper!

17:9
Prov 10:12
Jas 5:20

⁹ Love prospers when a fault is forgiven,
  but dwelling on it separates close friends.

¹⁰ A single rebuke does more for a person of understanding
  than a hundred lashes on the back of a fool.

¹¹ Evil people are eager for rebellion,
  but they will be severely punished.

17:12
Prov 29:9
Hos 13:8

¹² It is safer to meet a bear robbed of her cubs
  than to confront a fool caught in foolishness.

17:13
Ps 109:5
Jer 18:20

¹³ If you repay good with evil,
  evil will never leave your house.

¹⁴ Starting a quarrel is like opening a floodgate,
  so stop before a dispute breaks out.

17:15
Exod 23:7
Isa 5:23

¹⁵ Acquitting the guilty and condemning the innocent—
  both are detestable to the LORD.

¹⁶ It is senseless to pay tuition to educate a fool,
  since he has no heart for learning.

17:6 Hebrew *fathers.*

---

17:3 It takes intense heat to purify gold and silver. Similarly, it often takes the heat of trials for the Christian to be purified. Through trials, God shows us what is in us and clears out anything that gets in the way of complete trust in him. Peter says, "These trials will show that your faith is genuine. It is being tested as fire tests and purifies gold—though your faith is far more precious than mere gold" (1 Peter 1:7). So when tough times come your way, realize that God wants to use them to refine your faith and purify your heart.

17:5 Few acts are as cruel as making fun of the less fortunate, but many people do this because it makes them feel good to be better off or more successful than someone else. Mocking the poor is mocking the God who made them. We also ridicule God when we mock the weak, those who are different, or anyone else. When you catch yourself putting others down just for fun, stop and think about who created them.

17:8 Solomon is not condoning bribery (see 17:15, 23), but he is making an observation about the way the world operates.

Bribes may get people what they want, but the Bible clearly condemns using them (Exodus 23:8; Matthew 28:11-15).

17:9 This proverb is saying that we should be willing to disregard the faults of others. Forgiving faults is necessary to any relationship. It is tempting, especially in an argument, to bring up all the mistakes the other person has ever made. Love, however, keeps its mouth shut—difficult though that may be. Try never to bring anything into an argument that is unrelated to the topic being discussed. As we grow to be like Christ, we will acquire God's ability to forget the confessed sins of the past.

17 A friend is always loyal,
  and a brother is born to help in time of need.

18 It's poor judgment to guarantee another person's debt
  or put up security for a friend.

19 Anyone who loves to quarrel loves sin;
  anyone who trusts in high walls invites disaster.

20 The crooked heart will not prosper;
  the lying tongue tumbles into trouble.

21 It is painful to be the parent of a fool;
  there is no joy for the father of a rebel.

22 A cheerful heart is good medicine,
  but a broken spirit saps a person's strength.

23 The wicked take secret bribes
  to pervert the course of justice.

24 Sensible people keep their eyes glued on wisdom,
  but a fool's eyes wander to the ends of the earth.

25 Foolish children* bring grief to their father
  and bitterness to the one who gave them birth.

26 It is wrong to punish the godly for being good
  or to flog leaders for being honest.

27 A truly wise person uses few words;
  a person with understanding is even-tempered.

28 Even fools are thought wise when they keep silent;
  with their mouths shut, they seem intelligent.

# 18

1 Unfriendly people care only about themselves;
  they lash out at common sense.

2 Fools have no interest in understanding;
  they only want to air their own opinions.

3 Doing wrong leads to disgrace,
  and scandalous behavior brings contempt.

4 Wise words are like deep waters;
  wisdom flows from the wise like a bubbling brook.

5 It is not right to acquit the guilty
  or deny justice to the innocent.

6 Fools' words get them into constant quarrels;
  they are asking for a beating.

17:25 Hebrew *A foolish son.*

---

**17:17** Ruth 1:16
Prov 18:24

**17:18** Prov 6:1; 11:15;
22:26

**17:19** Prov 13:2; 16:18;
29:22-23

**17:20** Jas 3:8

**17:21** Prov 10:1; 17:25

**17:22** Prov 15:13

**17:23** Exod 23:8

**17:24** Eccl 2:14

**17:25** Prov 10:1

**17:27** Prov 10:19
Jas 1:19

**18:2** Prov 12:23

**18:4** Prov 20:5

**18:6** Prov 10:14; 13:3

---

**17:17** What kind of friend are you? There is a vast difference between knowing someone well and being a true friend. The greatest evidence of genuine friendship is loyalty (see 1 Corinthians 13:7)—being available to help in times of distress or personal struggle. Too many people are fair-weather friends. They stick around when the friendship helps them and leave when they're not getting anything out of the relationship. Think of your friends and assess your loyalty to them. Be the kind of true friend the Bible encourages.

**17:22** To be cheerful is to be ready to greet others with a welcome, a word of encouragement, an enthusiasm for the task at hand, and a positive outlook on the future. Such people are as welcome as pain-relieving medicine.

**17:24** While there is something to be said for having big dreams, this proverb points out the folly of chasing fantasies (having eyes that "wander to the ends of the earth," see 12:11). How much better to align your goals with God's, being the kind of person he wants you to be! Such goals (wisdom, honesty, patience, love) may not seem exciting, but they will determine your eternal future. Take time to think about your dreams and goals, and make sure they cover the really important areas of life.

**17:27, 28** This proverb highlights several benefits of keeping quiet: (1) It is the best policy if you have nothing worthwhile to say; (2) it allows you the opportunity to listen and learn; (3) it gives you something in common with those who are wiser. Make sure you pause to think and to listen so that when you do speak, you will have something important to say.

7 The mouths of fools are their ruin;
  they trap themselves with their lips.

8 Rumors are dainty morsels
  that sink deep into one's heart.

9 A lazy person is as bad as
  someone who destroys things.

**18:10**
2 Sam 22:2
Pss 18:2; 61:3;
91:2

10 The name of the LORD is a strong fortress;
   the godly run to him and are safe.

**18:11**
Prov 10:15

11 The rich think of their wealth as a strong defense;
   they imagine it to be a high wall of safety.

**18:12**
Prov 11:2; 16:18;
29:23

12 Haughtiness goes before destruction;
   humility precedes honor.

**18:13**
Prov 20:25
John 7:51

13 Spouting off before listening to the facts
   is both shameful and foolish.

14 The human spirit can endure a sick body,
   but who can bear a crushed spirit?

**18:15**
Prov 15:14

15 Intelligent people are always ready to learn.
   Their ears are open for knowledge.

**18:16**
Gen 32:20
1 Sam 25:27

16 Giving a gift can open doors;
   it gives access to important people!

17 The first to speak in court sounds right—
   until the cross-examination begins.

**18:18**
Prov 16:33

18 Flipping a coin* can end arguments;
   it settles disputes between powerful opponents.

19 An offended friend is harder to win back than a fortified city.
   Arguments separate friends like a gate locked with bars.

**18:20**
Prov 12:14

20 Wise words satisfy like a good meal;
   the right words bring satisfaction.

**18:18** Hebrew *Casting lots.*

---

| **HUMILITY AND PRIDE** | Results of . . . | Humility | Pride | |
|---|---|---|---|---|
| | | Leads to wisdom . . . . . . . . . . . | Leads to disgrace . . . . . . . . . . . . . . | 11:2 |
| | | Takes advice . . . . . . . . . . . . . . | Leads to conflict . . . . . . . . . . . . . | 13:10 |
| | | Leads to honor . . . . . . . . . . . . . . . . . . . . . . . . . . . . . . . . . . . . . . . . . . . . . | | 15:33 |
| | | | Leads to punishment . . . . . . . . . . . | 16:5 |
| | | | Leads to destruction . . . . . . . . . . . | 16:18 |
| | | Ends in honor . . . . . . . . . . . . | Ends in downfall . . . . . . . . . . . . . | 18:12 |
| | | Brings honor . . . . . . . . . . . . . | Brings humiliation . . . . . . . . . . . . . | 29:23 |

Proverbs is direct and forceful in rejecting pride. The proud attitude heads the list of seven things God hates (6:16, 17). The harmful results of pride are constantly contrasted with humility and its benefits.

---

**18:8** It is as hard to refuse to listen to rumors and gossip as it is to turn down a delicious dessert. Taking just one morsel of either one creates a taste for more. You can resist rumors the same way a determined dieter resists candy—never even open the box. If you don't nibble on the first bite of gossip, you can't take the second and the third.

**18:11** In imagining that their wealth is their strongest defense, rich people are sadly mistaken. Money cannot provide safety—there are too many ways for it to lose its power. The government may cease to back it; thieves may steal it; inflation may rob it of

all value. But God never loses his power. He is always dependable. Where do you look for security and safety—uncertain wealth or God who is always faithful?

**18:13, 15, 17** These concise statements give three basic principles for making sound decisions: (1) Get the facts before answering; (2) be open to new ideas; (3) make sure you hear both sides of a story before judging. All three principles center around seeking additional information. This is difficult work, but the only alternative is prejudice—judging before getting the facts.

21 The tongue can bring death or life;
   those who love to talk will reap the consequences.

18:21
Prov 13:3
Matt 12:37

22 The man who finds a wife finds a treasure,
   and he receives favor from the Lord.

18:22
Prov 12:4; 19:14;
31:10-31

23 The poor plead for mercy;
   the rich answer with insults.

18:23
2 Chr 10:13
Prov 19:7
Jas 2:3

24 There are "friends" who destroy each other,
   but a real friend sticks closer than a brother.

# 19
1 Better to be poor and honest
   than to be dishonest and a fool.

19:1
Prov 20:7; 28:6

2 Enthusiasm without knowledge is no good;
   haste makes mistakes.

3 People ruin their lives by their own foolishness
   and then are angry at the Lord.

19:3
Isa 8:21

4 Wealth makes many "friends";
   poverty drives them all away.

5 A false witness will not go unpunished,
   nor will a liar escape.

19:5
Exod 23:1
Deut 19:16-19

6 Many seek favors from a ruler;
   everyone is the friend of a person who gives gifts!

7 The relatives of the poor despise them;
   how much more will their friends avoid them!
   Though the poor plead with them,
      their friends are gone.

19:7
Ps 38:11
Prov 18:23

8 To acquire wisdom is to love oneself;
   people who cherish understanding will prosper.

19:8
Prov 16:20

9 A false witness will not go unpunished,
   and a liar will be destroyed.

10 It isn't right for a fool to live in luxury
   or for a slave to rule over princes!

19:10
Eccl 10:6-7

---

**18:22** This verse is stating that marriage should be enjoyed and viewed as a great gift from God. God created marriage for our enjoyment, and he pronounced it good. Married people need to see their marriages as great treasures—guarding and protecting them as such. This is one of many passages in the Bible that show marriage as a joyful and good creation of God (Genesis 2:21-25; Proverbs 5:15-19; John 2:1-11).

**18:23** This verse does not condone insulting the poor; it is simply recording an unfortunate fact of life. It is wrong for rich people to treat the less fortunate with contempt and arrogance, and God will judge such actions severely (see 14:31).

**18:24** Loneliness is everywhere—many people feel cut off and alienated from others. Being in a crowd just makes people more aware of their isolation. We all need friends who will stick close, listen, care, and offer help when it is needed—in good times and bad. It is better to have one such friend than dozens of superficial acquaintances. Instead of wishing you could find a true friend, seek to become one. If you look around, you'll find people who need your friendship. Ask God to reveal them to you, and then take on the challenge of being a true friend.

**19:1** A blameless life is far more valuable than wealth, but most people don't act as if they believe this. Afraid of not getting everything they want, they will pay any price to increase their wealth—cheating on their taxes, stealing from stores or employers, withholding tithes, refusing to give. But when we know and love God, we realize that a lower standard of living—or even poverty—is a small price to pay for personal integrity. Do your actions show that you sacrifice your integrity to increase your wealth? What changes do you need to make in order to get your priorities straight?

**19:2** We often move hastily through life, rushing headlong into the unknown. Some people marry without really getting to know the other person. Others try illicit sex or drugs without considering the consequences. Some plunge into jobs without evaluating whether or not they are suitable to that line of work. Enthusiasm is no good without knowledge, and it will not make a bad situation better. Don't rush into the unknown. Be sure you understand what you're getting into and where you want to go before you take the first step. Obviously you cannot tell all that the future will hold, but do your homework, ask the right questions, and be sure you are following God.

**19:8** Is it good to love yourself? Yes, when your soul is at stake! This proverb does not condone the self-centered person who loves and protects his or her selfish interests and will do anything to serve them. Instead, it encourages those who really care about themselves to seek wisdom.

**19:11**
Prov 14:29; 16:32

11 Sensible people control their temper;
    they earn respect by overlooking wrongs.

**19:12**
Gen 27:28
Prov 16:14-15

12 The king's anger is like a lion's roar,
    but his favor is like dew on the grass.

**19:13**
Prov 17:25; 21:9

13 A foolish child* is a calamity to a father;
    a quarrelsome wife is as annoying as constant dripping.

**19:14**
2 Cor 12:14

14 Fathers can give their sons an inheritance of houses and wealth,
    but only the LORD can give an understanding wife.

**19:15**
Prov 6:9; 16:26

15 Lazy people sleep soundly,
    but idleness leaves them hungry.

**19:16**
Luke 10:28; 11:28

16 Keep the commandments and keep your life;
    despising them leads to death.

**19:17**
Deut 15:7
Prov 14:31; 28:27
Luke 6:38

17 If you help the poor, you are lending to the LORD—
    and he will repay you!

**19:18**
Prov 13:24

18 Discipline your children while there is hope.
    Otherwise you will ruin their lives.

19 Hot-tempered people must pay the penalty.
    If you rescue them once, you will have to do it again.

20 Get all the advice and instruction you can,
    so you will be wise the rest of your life.

**19:21**
Ps 33:10-11
Prov 16:1, 9

21 You can make many plans,
    but the LORD's purpose will prevail.

22 Loyalty makes a person attractive.
    It is better to be poor than dishonest.

**19:13** Hebrew *son;* also in 19:27.

---

**HOW TO SUCCEED IN GOD'S EYES**
Proverbs notes two significant by-products of wise living: success and good reputation. Several verses also point out what causes failure and poor reputation.

*Qualities that promote success and a good reputation*

| | |
|---|---|
| Godliness (righteousness) | 10:7; 12:3; 28:12 |
| Hating what is false | 13:5 |
| Committing all work to the Lord | 16:3 |
| Using words with restraint; being even-tempered | 17:27, 28 |
| Acquiring wisdom and cherishing understanding | 19:8 |
| Humility and fear of the Lord | 22:4 |
| Willingness to confess and forsake sin | 28:13 |

*Qualities that prevent success and cause a bad reputation*

| | |
|---|---|
| Wickedness | 10:7; 12:3; 28:12 |
| Seeking honors | 25:27 |
| Hatred, especially when masked as kindness | 26:24-26 |
| Praising oneself | 27:2 |
| Concealing sin | 28:13 |

Other verses dealing with one's reputation are 11:10, 16; 14:3; 19:10; 22:1; 23:17, 18; 24:13, 14.

---

**19:16** The commandments we are told to obey are those found in God's Word, such as the Ten Commandments (Exodus 20) and other passages of instruction. To obey what God teaches in the Bible is self-preserving. To disobey is self-destructive.

**19:17** Here God identifies with the poor as Jesus does in Matthew 25:31-46. As our Creator, God values all of us, whether we are poor or rich. When we help the poor, we honor both the Creator and his creation. God accepts our help as if we had offered it directly to him.

23 Fear of the LORD leads to life,
   bringing security and protection from harm.

24 Lazy people take food in their hand
   but don't even lift it to their mouth.

25 If you punish a mocker, the simpleminded will learn a lesson;
   if you correct the wise, they will be all the wiser.

**19:25**
Prov 9:7-8; 21:11

26 Children who mistreat their father or chase away their mother
   are an embarrassment and a public disgrace.

**19:26**
Prov 20:20; 28:24

27 If you stop listening to instruction, my child,
   you will turn your back on knowledge.

28 A corrupt witness makes a mockery of justice;
   the mouth of the wicked gulps down evil.

**19:28**
Job 15:16

29 Punishment is made for mockers,
   and the backs of fools are made to be beaten.

**19:29**
Prov 9:12; 10:13;
26:3

**20** ¹ Wine produces mockers; alcohol leads to brawls.
   Those led astray by drink cannot be wise.

**20:1**
Prov 31:4
Isa 5:22; 56:12

2 The king's fury is like a lion's roar;
   to rouse his anger is to risk your life.

3 Avoiding a fight is a mark of honor;
   only fools insist on quarreling.

**20:3**
Prov 14:29; 16:32;
19:11

4 Those too lazy to plow in the right season
   will have no food at the harvest.

5 Though good advice lies deep within the heart,
   a person with understanding will draw it out.

6 Many will say they are loyal friends,
   but who can find one who is truly reliable?

7 The godly walk with integrity;
   blessed are their children who follow them.

**20:7**
Pss 37:26; 112:2

8 When a king sits in judgment, he weighs all the evidence,
   distinguishing the bad from the good.

9 Who can say, "I have cleansed my heart;
   I am pure and free from sin"?

**20:9**
2 Chr 6:36
Job 14:4

10 False weights and unequal measures*—
   the LORD detests double standards of every kind.

**20:10**
Prov 11:1; 20:23

**20:10** Hebrew *A stone and a stone, an ephah and an ephah.*

---

**19:23** Those who fear the Lord receive "protection from harm" because of their healthy habits, their beneficial lifestyle, and sometimes through God's direct intervention. Nevertheless the fear of the Lord does not always protect us from trouble in this life: Evil things still happen to people who love God. This verse is not a universal promise but a general guideline. It describes what would happen if this world were sinless, and what will happen in the new earth, when faithful believers will be under God's protection forever. (See the note on 3:16, 17 for more about this concept.)

**19:25** A great difference exists between the person who learns from criticism and the person who refuses to accept correction. How we respond to criticism determines whether or not we grow in wisdom. The next time someone criticizes you, listen carefully to all that is said. You might learn something.

**20:3** A person who is truly confident of his or her strength does not need to parade it. A truly brave person does not look

for chances to prove it. A resourceful person can find a way out of a fight and avoid retaliating. Foolish people find it impossible to avoid strife. Men and women of character can. What kind of person are you?

**20:4** You've heard similar warnings: If you don't study, you'll fail the test; if you don't save, you won't have money when you need it. God wants us to anticipate future needs and prepare for them. We can't expect him to come to our rescue when we cause our own problems through lack of planning and action. He provides for us, but he also expects us to be responsible.

**20:9** No one is without sin. As soon as we confess our sin and repent, sinful thoughts and actions begin to creep back into our minds and hearts. We all need ongoing cleansing, moment by moment. Thank God he provides forgiveness by his mercy when we ask for it. Make confession and repentance a regular part of your talks with God. Rely on him moment by moment for the cleansing you need.

**20:11**
Matt 7:16

<sup>11</sup> Even children are known by the way they act,
   whether their conduct is pure, and whether it is right.

**20:12**
Exod 4:11

<sup>12</sup> Ears to hear and eyes to see—
   both are gifts from the Lord.

**20:13**
Prov 6:9-10; 19:15;
24:32-33

<sup>13</sup> If you love sleep, you will end in poverty.
   Keep your eyes open, and there will be plenty to eat!

<sup>14</sup> The buyer haggles over the price, saying, "It's worthless,"
   then brags about getting a bargain!

<sup>15</sup> Wise words are more valuable
   than much gold and many rubies.

<sup>16</sup> Get security from someone who guarantees a stranger's debt.
   Get a deposit if he does it for foreigners.*

<sup>17</sup> Stolen bread tastes sweet,
   but it turns to gravel in the mouth.

**20:18**
Prov 15:22; 24:6
Luke 14:31

<sup>18</sup> Plans succeed through good counsel;
   don't go to war without wise advice.

**20:19**
Prov 11:13

<sup>19</sup> A gossip goes around telling secrets,
   so don't hang around with chatterers.

**20:20**
Exod 21:17
Lev 20:9
Matt 15:4

<sup>20</sup> If you insult your father or mother,
   your light will be snuffed out in total darkness.

<sup>21</sup> An inheritance obtained too early in life
   is not a blessing in the end.

**20:22**
Ps 27:14
Prov 24:28-29
Matt 5:39
Rom 12:17

<sup>22</sup> Don't say, "I will get even for this wrong."
   Wait for the Lord to handle the matter.

**20:16** An alternate reading in the Masoretic Text is *for a promiscuous woman.*

---

## HONESTY AND DISHONESTY

Proverbs tells us plainly that God despises all forms of dishonesty. Not only does God hate dishonesty, but we are told that it works against us—others no longer trust us, and we cannot even enjoy our dishonest gains. It is wiser to be honest because "the godly escape such trouble" (12:13).

*Others' Opinions*

*Quality of Life*

*Short-Term Results*

*Long-Term Results*

*God's Opinion*

23 The LORD detests double standards;
    he is not pleased by dishonest scales.

20:23
Prov 11:1; 20:10

24 The LORD directs our steps,
    so why try to understand everything along the way?

25 Don't trap yourself by making a rash promise to God
    and only later counting the cost.

20:25
Eccl 5:4-5

26 A wise king scatters the wicked like wheat,
    then runs his threshing wheel over them.

20:26
Prov 20:8

27 The LORD's light penetrates the human spirit,*
    exposing every hidden motive.

20:27
1 Cor 2:11

28 Unfailing love and faithfulness protect the king;
    his throne is made secure through love.

20:28
Prov 29:14

29 The glory of the young is their strength;
    the gray hair of experience is the splendor of the old.

20:29
Prov 16:31

30 Physical punishment cleanses away evil;*
    such discipline purifies the heart.

**21** ¹ The king's heart is like a stream of water directed by the LORD;
    he guides it wherever he pleases.

21:1
Ezra 6:21-22

2 People may be right in their own eyes,
    but the LORD examines their heart.

21:2
Prov 16:2;
24:11-12
Luke 16:15

3 The LORD is more pleased when we do what is right and just
    than when we offer him sacrifices.

21:3
Prov 15:8
Isa 1:11
Mic 6:6-8

4 Haughty eyes, a proud heart,
    and evil actions are all sin.

21:4
Prov 6:17; 30:13
Luke 11:34

5 Good planning and hard work lead to prosperity,
    but hasty shortcuts lead to poverty.

21:5
Prov 10:4; 28:22

**20:27** Or *The human spirit is the LORD's light.*   **20:30** The meaning of the Hebrew is uncertain.

---

**20:23** "Dishonest scales" refers to the loaded scales a merchant might use in order to cheat customers. Dishonesty is a difficult sin to avoid. It is easy to cheat if we think no one is looking. But dishonesty affects the very core of a person. It makes him untrustworthy and untrusting. It eventually makes him unable to know himself or relate to others. Don't take dishonesty lightly. Even the smallest portion of dishonesty contains enough of the poison of deceit to kill your spiritual life. If there is any dishonesty in your life, tell God about it now.

**20:24** We are often confused by the events around us. Some things we will never understand until years later when we look back and see how God was working. This proverb counsels us to not worry if we don't understand everything as it happens. Instead, we should trust that God knows what he's doing, even if his timing or design is not clear to us. See Psalm 37:23 for a reassuring promise of God's direction in your life.

**20:25** This proverb points out the danger of making a promise rashly and then reconsidering it. God takes promises seriously and requires that they be carried out (Deuteronomy 23:21-23). We often have good intentions when making a promise because we want to show God that we are determined to please him. Jesus, however, says it is better not to make promises to God because he knows how difficult they are to keep (Matthew 5:33-37). If you still feel it is important to make a promise, make sure that you weigh the consequences of breaking it. (In Judges 11, Jephthah made a rash promise to sacrifice the first thing he saw on his return home.

As it happened, he saw his daughter first.) It is better not to make promises than to make them and then later not keep them. It is best to count the cost beforehand and then to fulfill them. (For a list of other Bible people who made rash promises, see the chart in Judges 11, p. 377.)

**21:1** In Solomon's day, kings possessed absolute authority and were often considered to be like gods. This proverb shows that God has ultimate authority over world rulers. Although they may not have realized it, the earth's most powerful kings have always been under God's control. (See Isaiah 10:5-8 for an example of a pagan king who was used for God's purposes.)

**21:2** People may mistakenly think they are doing right, but God sees the motives of their hearts. We often have to make choices in areas where the right action is difficult to discern. We can help ourselves make such decisions by trying to identify our motives first and then asking, Would God be pleased with my real reasons for doing this? God is not pleased when we do good deeds only to receive something in return.

**21:3** Sacrifices are not bribes to make God overlook our character faults. We can't exchange good behavior in one area for bad behavior in another. If our personal and business dealings are not characterized by justice, no amount of generosity when the offering plate is passed will make up for it.

**21:5** Faithful completion of one's work is a great accomplishment. Being a diligent worker does not come naturally to some people; it is a result of strong character. Don't look for shortcuts that result in inefficiency. Work hard as if in the service of God.

**21:6**
Prov 10:2; 13:11

⁶ Wealth created by a lying tongue
   is a vanishing mist and a deadly trap.*

⁷ The violence of the wicked sweeps them away,
   because they refuse to do what is just.

⁸ The guilty walk a crooked path;
   the innocent travel a straight road.

⁹ It's better to live alone in the corner of an attic
   than with a quarrelsome wife in a lovely home.

**21:10**
Prov 2:14

¹⁰ Evil people desire evil;
    their neighbors get no mercy from them.

**21:11**
Prov 19:25

¹¹ If you punish a mocker, the simpleminded become wise;
    if you instruct the wise, they will be all the wiser.

¹² The Righteous One* knows what is going on in the homes of the wicked;
    he will bring disaster on them.

**21:13**
Matt 18:30-34
Luke 16:19-31
Jas 2:13
1 Jn 3:17

¹³ Those who shut their ears to the cries of the poor
    will be ignored in their own time of need.

¹⁴ A secret gift calms anger;
    a bribe under the table pacifies fury.

¹⁵ Justice is a joy to the godly,
    but it terrifies evildoers.

**21:16**
Ps 49:14

¹⁶ The person who strays from common sense
    will end up in the company of the dead.

**21:17**
Prov 23:19-21

¹⁷ Those who love pleasure become poor;
    those who love wine and luxury will never be rich.

**21:18**
Prov 11:8
Isa 43:3-4

¹⁸ The wicked are punished in place of the godly,
    and traitors in place of the honest.

¹⁹ It's better to live alone in the desert
    than with a quarrelsome, complaining wife.

**21:20**
Job 20:15, 18
Prov 8:21

²⁰ The wise have wealth and luxury,
    but fools spend whatever they get.

**21:21**
Matt 5:6

²¹ Whoever pursues righteousness and unfailing love
    will find life, righteousness, and honor.

**21:22**
2 Sam 5:6-9
Eccl 9:15-16

²² The wise conquer the city of the strong
    and level the fortress in which they trust.

**21:23**
Prov 12:13; 13:3
Jas 3:2

²³ Watch your tongue and keep your mouth shut,
    and you will stay out of trouble.

²⁴ Mockers are proud and haughty;
    they act with boundless arrogance.

**21:6** As in Greek version; Hebrew reads *mist for those who seek death.*   **21:12** Or *The righteous man.*

---

**21:11, 12** It is usually better to learn from the mistakes of others than from our own. We can do this by observing other people's lives and listening to their advice. Take counsel from others instead of plunging ahead and learning the hard way.

**21:13** We should work to meet the needs of the poor and protect their rights, for it is always possible that someday we may find ourselves in their place.

**21:20** This proverb is about saving for the future. Easy credit has many people living on the edge of bankruptcy. The desire to keep up appearances and to accumulate more drives them to spend every penny they earn, and they stretch their credit to the limit. But anyone who spends all he has is spending more than he can afford. A wise person puts money aside for hard times. God approves of foresight and restraint. God's people need to examine their life-styles to see whether their spending is God-pleasing or merely self-pleasing.

25 Despite their desires, the lazy will come to ruin,
   for their hands refuse to work.

21:25
Prov 13:4

26 Some people are always greedy for more,
   but the godly love to give!

27 The sacrifice of an evil person is detestable,
   especially when it is offered with wrong motives.

21:27
Prov 15:8

28 A false witness will be cut off,
   but a credible witness will be allowed to speak.

29 The wicked bluff their way through,
   but the virtuous think before they act.

30 No human wisdom or understanding or plan
   can stand against the LORD.

21:30
Isa 8:9; 14:27
Acts 5:38-39

31 The horse is prepared for the day of battle,
   but the victory belongs to the LORD.

21:31
Ps 20:7
Isa 31:1-3
1 Cor 15:57

## RIGHTEOUSNESS

Proverbs often compares the lifestyles of the wicked and the righteous, and makes a strong case for living by God's pattern. The advantages of righteous living and the disadvantages of wicked living are pointed out. The kind of person we decide to be will affect every area of our lives.

| | | Righteous | Wicked | Reference |
|---|---|---|---|---|
| Outlook on life | | Hopeful | Fearful | 10:24 |
| | | Concerned about the welfare of God's creation | Even their kindness is cruel | 12:10 |
| | | Understand justice | Don't understand justice | 28:5 |
| Response to life | | Showered with blessings | Covered with violence | 10:6 |
| | | | Plot evil | 16:30 |
| | | Proceed with care | Put up a bold front | 21:29 |
| | | Persevere against evil | Brought down by calamity | 24:15, 16 |
| | | Seek out the honest | Hate the honest | 29:10 |
| How they are seen by others | | Are respected | Headed for destruction | 13:15 |
| | | | Lead others into sin | 16:29 |
| | | Walk a straight road | Walk a crooked road | 21:8 |
| | | Are not to desire the company of godless people | Plot violence | 24:1, 2 |
| | | Others are glad when they succeed | Others hide when they rise to power | 28:12 |
| | | Care for the poor | Unconcerned about the poor | 29:7 |
| | | Despise the unjust | Despise the godly | 29:27 |
| Quality of life | | Stand firm | Swept away | 10:25 |
| | | Rescued by godliness | Trapped by evil ambitions | 11:6 |

**21:27** The kind of worship ("sacrifice") described in this proverb is no better than a bribe. How do people try to bribe God? They may go to church, tithe, or volunteer, not because of their love and devotion to God, but because they hope God will bless them in return. But God has made it very clear that he desires obedience and love more than religious ritual (see 21:3; 1 Samuel 15:22). God does not want our sacrifices of time, energy, and money alone; he wants our heart—our complete love and devotion. We may be able to bribe people (21:14), but we cannot bribe God.

**21:31** This proverb refers to preparing for battle. All our preparation for any task is useless without God. But even with God's help we still must do our part and prepare. His control of the outcome does not negate our responsibilities. God may want you to produce a great book, but you must learn to write. God may want to use you in foreign missions, but you must learn the language. God will accomplish his purposes, and he will be able to use you if you have done your part by being well prepared.

**22:4** The general observation that fear of the Lord leads to riches, honor, and long life would have been especially applicable to an obedient Israelite living in Solomon's God-fearing kingdom. Nevertheless some have been martyrs at a young age, and some have given away all their wealth for the sake of God's Kingdom.

**22** ¹ Choose a good reputation over great riches;
         being held in high esteem is better than silver or gold.

**22:2**
Job 31:15
Prov 14:31

² The rich and poor have this in common:
   The LORD made them both.

**22:3**
Prov 14:16; 27:12

³ A prudent person foresees danger and takes precautions.
   The simpleton goes blindly on and suffers the consequences.

**22:4**
Prov 3:16; 4:4

⁴ True humility and fear of the LORD
   lead to riches, honor, and long life.

⁵ Corrupt people walk a thorny, treacherous road;
   whoever values life will avoid it.

**22:6**
Eph 6:4

⁶ Direct your children onto the right path,
   and when they are older, they will not leave it.

**22:7**
Jas 2:6

⁷ Just as the rich rule the poor,
   so the borrower is servant to the lender.

---

## AND WICKEDNESS

| Quality of life (cont.) | Righteous | Wicked | Reference |
|---|---|---|---|
| | No real harm befalls them | Constant trouble befalls them | 12:21 |
| | Income results in treasure | Income results in trouble | 15:6 |
| | Avoid evil | | 16:17 |
| | | Will not prosper | 17:20 |
| | Are bold as lions | Are fearful constantly | 28:1 |
| | Will be rescued | Will be suddenly destroyed | 28:18 |
| Short-term results | Walk safely | Will slip and fall | 10:9 |
| | Chased by blessings | Chased by trouble | 13:21 |
| Long-term results | God protects them | God destroys them | 10:29 |
| | Evil people will bow to them | Will bow to the righteous | 14:19 |
| | | Will be punished for rebellion | 17:11 |
| Eternal expectations | Never disturbed | Removed from the land | 10:30 |
| | Reward will last | Reward will not last | 11:18 |
| | Find life | Find death | 11:19 |
| | Look forward to reward | Look forward to judgment | 11:23 |
| | Will stand firm | Will die and disappear | 12:7 |
| | Have a refuge when they die | Crushed by their sins | 14:32 |
| God's opinion of them | Delights in those with integrity | Detests those with crooked hearts | 11:20 |

---

The book of Proverbs describes life the way it should be. It does not dwell on the exceptions. (For more on this concept, see the note on 3:16, 17.)

**22:6** In the process of helping our children choose the right path, we must discern differing paths for each child. It is natural to want to bring up all our children alike or train them the same way. This verse implies that parents should discern the individuality and special strengths that God has given each one. While we should not condone or excuse self-will, each child has natural inclinations that parents can develop. By talking to teachers, other parents, and grandparents, we can better discern and develop the individual capabilities of each child.

**22:6** Many parents want to make all the choices for their child, but this hurts him or her in the long run. When parents teach a child how to make decisions, they don't have to watch every step he or she takes. They know their children will remain on the right path because they have made the choice themselves. Train your children to choose the right way.

**22:7** Does this mean we should never borrow? No, but it warns us never to take on a loan without carefully examining our ability to repay it. A loan we can handle is enabling; a loan we can't handle is enslaving. The borrower must realize that until the loan is repaid, he is a servant to the individual or institution that made it.

8 Those who plant injustice will harvest disaster,
   and their reign of terror will come to an end.*

*22:8*
Job 4:8

9 Blessed are those who are generous,
   because they feed the poor.

*22:9*
Prov 19:17
Luke 14:13
2 Cor 9:6

10 Throw out the mocker, and fighting goes, too.
   Quarrels and insults will disappear.

11 Whoever loves a pure heart and gracious speech
   will have the king as a friend.

*22:11*
Ps 24:4
Prov 14:35
Matt 5:8

12 The LORD preserves those with knowledge,
   but he ruins the plans of the treacherous.

13 The lazy person claims, "There's a lion out there!
   If I go outside, I might be killed!"

*22:13*
Rom 12:11

14 The mouth of an immoral woman is a dangerous trap;
   those who make the LORD angry will fall into it.

*22:14*
Eccl 7:26

15 A youngster's heart is filled with foolishness,
   but physical discipline will drive it far away.

*22:15*
Prov 13:24; 23:14

16 A person who gets ahead by oppressing the poor
   or by showering gifts on the rich will end in poverty.

*22:16*
Prov 14:31; 28:3

*Sayings of the Wise*
17 Listen to the words of the wise;
   apply your heart to my instruction.

*22:17*
Prov 5:1

18 For it is good to keep these sayings in your heart
   and always ready on your lips.
19 I am teaching you today—yes, you—
   so you will trust in the LORD.
20 I have written thirty sayings* for you,
   filled with advice and knowledge.
21 In this way, you may know the truth
   and take an accurate report to those who sent you.

22 Don't rob the poor just because you can,
   or exploit the needy in court.

*22:22*
Zech 7:10
Mal 3:5

23 For the LORD is their defender.
   He will ruin anyone who ruins them.

24 Don't befriend angry people
   or associate with hot-tempered people,

*22:24*
Prov 29:22

25 or you will learn to be like them
   and endanger your soul.

---

**22:8** The Greek version includes an additional proverb: *God blesses a man who gives cheerfully, / but his worthless deeds will come to an end.* Compare 2 Cor 9:7.    **22:20** Or *excellent sayings;* the meaning of the Hebrew is uncertain.

---

**22:12** "Knowledge" refers to those who have knowledge, those who live right and speak the truth. It takes discipline, determination, and hard work to live God's way, but God protects and rewards those who make the commitment to follow him. The unfaithful may seem to have an easier time of it, but in the long run their plans fail and their lives amount to nothing. Don't resist God and expect lasting success.

**22:13** This proverb refers to an excuse a lazy person might use to avoid going to work. The excuse sounds silly to us, but that's often how our excuses sound to others. Don't rationalize laziness. Take your responsibilities seriously and get to work.

**22:15** Young children often do foolish and dangerous things simply because they don't understand the consequences. Wisdom and common sense are not transferred by a parent's good example alone. Just as God trains and corrects us to make us better, so parents must discipline their children to help them

learn the difference between right and wrong. To see how God corrects us, read 3:11, 12.

**22:22, 23** This proverb is a message of hope to people who must live and work under unjust authoritarian leaders. It is also a warning to those who enjoy ruling with an iron hand. Sometimes God intervenes and directly destroys tyrants. More often, he uses other rulers to overthrow them or their own oppressed people to rebel against them. If you are in a position of authority at church, work, or home, remember what happens to tyrants. Leadership through kindness is more effective and longer lasting than leadership by force.

**22:24, 25** People tend to become like those with whom they spend a lot of time. Even the negative characteristics and habits can rub off. The Bible exhorts us to be cautious in our choice of companions. Choose people with qualities you would like to develop in your own life.

**22:26**
Prov 6:1-5

26 Don't agree to guarantee another person's debt
    or put up security for someone else.
27 If you can't pay it,
    even your bed will be snatched from under you.

**22:28**
Deut 19:14; 27:17

28 Don't cheat your neighbor by moving the ancient boundary markers
    set up by previous generations.

**22:29**
1 Kgs 10:8; 11:28

29 Do you see any truly competent workers?
    They will serve kings
    rather than working for ordinary people.

# 23

1 While dining with a ruler,
    pay attention to what is put before you.

**23:2**
Prov 23:20

2 If you are a big eater,
    put a knife to your throat;
3 don't desire all the delicacies,
    for he might be trying to trick you.

**23:4**
Prov 15:27; 28:20
Matt 6:19
1 Tim 6:9

4 Don't wear yourself out trying to get rich.
    Be wise enough to know when to quit.
5 In the blink of an eye wealth disappears,
    for it will sprout wings
    and fly away like an eagle.

**23:6**
Ps 141:4
Prov 1:15; 4:14;
23:1

6 Don't eat with people who are stingy;
    don't desire their delicacies.
7 They are always thinking about how much it costs.*
    "Eat and drink," they say, but they don't mean it.
8 You will throw up what little you've eaten,
    and your compliments will be wasted.

9 Don't waste your breath on fools,
    for they will despise the wisest advice.

**23:10**
Deut 19:14
Prov 22:28
Jer 22:3
Zech 7:10

10 Don't cheat your neighbor by moving the ancient boundary markers;
    don't take the land of defenseless orphans.
11 For their Redeemer* is strong;
    he himself will bring their charges against you.

**23:12**
Prov 22:17

12 Commit yourself to instruction;
    listen carefully to words of knowledge.

**23:7** The meaning of the Hebrew is uncertain.   **23:11** Or *redeemer.*

---

**22:28** In Joshua 13–21, the land was divided, and the boundaries were marked out for each tribe. Moses had already warned the people that when they reached the Promised Land they shouldn't cheat their neighbors by moving any of the boundary markers to give themselves more land and their neighbors less (Deuteronomy 19:14; 27:17).

**23:1-3** The point of this proverb is to be careful when eating with an important or influential person because he or she may try to influence or bribe you. Unwary meetings over meals can lead to undermined convictions. No good will come from such meals.

**23:4, 5** We have all heard of people who have won millions of dollars and then lost everything. Even the average person can spend an inheritance—or a paycheck—with lightning speed and have little to show for it. Don't spend your time chasing fleeting earthly treasures. Instead, store up treasures in heaven, for such treasures will never be lost. (See Luke 12:33, 34 for Jesus' teaching.)

**23:6-8** In graphic language, the writer warns us not to envy the lifestyles of those who have become rich by being stingy and miserly, and not to gain their favor by fawning over them. Their "friendship" is phony—they will just use you for their own gain.

**23:10, 11** The word *redeemer* referred to someone who bought back a family member who had fallen into slavery or who accepted the obligation to marry the widow of a family member (Ruth 4:3-10). God is also called a Redeemer (Exodus 6:6; Job 19:25). (For an explanation of ancient boundary markers, see the note on 22:28.)

**23:12** The people most likely to gain knowledge are those who are willing to listen. It is a sign of strength, not weakness, to pay attention to what others have to say. People who are eager to listen continue to learn and grow throughout their lives. If we refuse to become set in our ways, we can always expand the limits of our knowledge.

¹³ Don't fail to discipline your children.
　　They won't die if you spank them.
¹⁴ Physical discipline
　　may well save them from death.*

23:13
Prov 13:24; 19:18
1 Cor 5:5

¹⁵ My child,* if your heart is wise,
　　my own heart will rejoice!
¹⁶ Everything in me will celebrate
　　when you speak what is right.

23:15
Prov 15:20; 27:11;
29:3

¹⁷ Don't envy sinners,
　　but always continue to fear the LORD.
¹⁸ You will be rewarded for this;
　　your hope will not be disappointed.

23:17
Pss 37:1; 73:3
Prov 24:1, 14, 19

¹⁹ My child, listen and be wise:
　　Keep your heart on the right course.
²⁰ Do not carouse with drunkards
　　or feast with gluttons,
²¹ for they are on their way to poverty,
　　and too much sleep clothes them in rags.

23:19
Prov 23:29

23:21
Prov 21:17

²² Listen to your father, who gave you life,
　　and don't despise your mother when she is old.

23:22
Prov 1:8; 30:17

²³ Get the truth and never sell it;
　　also get wisdom, discipline, and good judgment.

23:23
Prov 4:7; 18:15

²⁴ The father of godly children has cause for joy.
　　What a pleasure to have children who are wise.*
²⁵ So give your father and mother joy!
　　May she who gave you birth be happy.

23:24
Prov 10:1

²⁶ O my son, give me your heart.
　　May your eyes take delight in following my ways.

23:26
Prov 3:1; 4:4

²⁷ A prostitute is a dangerous trap;
　　a promiscuous woman is as dangerous as falling into a narrow well.
²⁸ She hides and waits like a robber,
　　eager to make more men unfaithful.

²⁹ Who has anguish? Who has sorrow?
　　Who is always fighting? Who is always complaining?
　　Who has unnecessary bruises? Who has bloodshot eyes?
³⁰ It is the one who spends long hours in the taverns,
　　trying out new drinks.
³¹ Don't gaze at the wine, seeing how red it is,
　　how it sparkles in the cup, how smoothly it goes down.
³² For in the end it bites like a poisonous snake;
　　it stings like a viper.
³³ You will see hallucinations,
　　and you will say crazy things.

23:29
Isa 5:11, 22

23:14 Hebrew from Sheol.　23:15 Hebrew My son; also in 23:19.　23:24 Hebrew to have a wise son.

---

**23:13, 14** The stern tone of discipline here is offset by the affection expressed in verse 15. However, many parents are reluctant to discipline their children at all. Some fear that they will forfeit their relationship, their children will resent them, or they will stifle their children's development. But correction won't kill children, and it may prevent them from foolish moves that will.

**23:17, 18** How easy it is to envy those who get ahead, unhampered by responsibility to God's laws. For a time they do seem to prosper without paying any attention to what God wants, but they have no future. To those who follow him, God promises a hope and a wonderful future, even if they don't achieve it in this life.

**23:29, 30** The soothing comfort of alcohol is only temporary. Real relief comes from dealing with the cause of the anguish and sorrow and turning to God for peace. Don't lose yourself in alcohol; find yourself in God.

**23:29-35** Israel was a wine-producing country. In the Old Testament, winepresses bursting with new wine were considered a sign of blessing (3:10). Wisdom is even said to have set her table with wine (9:2, 5). But the Old Testament writers were alert to the dangers of wine. It dulls the senses; it limits clear judgment (31:1-9); it lowers the capacity for control (4:17); it destroys a person's efficiency (21:17). To make wine an end in itself, a means of self-indulgence, or as an escape from life is to misuse it and invite the consequences of the drunkard.

<sup>34</sup> You will stagger like a sailor tossed at sea,
    clinging to a swaying mast.

**23:35**
Isa 56:12

<sup>35</sup> And you will say, "They hit me, but I didn't feel it.
    I didn't even know it when they beat me up.
    When will I wake up
      so I can look for another drink?"

**24:1**
Pss 1:1; 37:1
Prov 1:15; 23:17

**24:2**
Ps 10:7
Jer 22:17

# 24
<sup>1</sup> Don't envy evil people
    or desire their company.
<sup>2</sup> For their hearts plot violence,
    and their words always stir up trouble.

<sup>3</sup> A house is built by wisdom
    and becomes strong through good sense.
<sup>4</sup> Through knowledge its rooms are filled
    with all sorts of precious riches and valuables.

**24:5**
Prov 21:22

<sup>5</sup> The wise are mightier than the strong,*
    and those with knowledge grow stronger and stronger.

**24:6**
Prov 11:14; 20:18

<sup>6</sup> So don't go to war without wise guidance;
    victory depends on having many advisers.

**24:7**
Prov 14:6; 17:16

<sup>7</sup> Wisdom is too lofty for fools.
    Among leaders at the city gate, they have nothing to say.

**24:8**
Prov 6:14; 14:22
Rom 1:30

<sup>8</sup> A person who plans evil
    will get a reputation as a troublemaker.
<sup>9</sup> The schemes of a fool are sinful;
    everyone detests a mocker.

**24:10**
Job 4:5
Heb 12:3

<sup>10</sup> If you fail under pressure,
    your strength is too small.

**24:11**
Ps 82:4
Isa 58:6-7

<sup>11</sup> Rescue those who are unjustly sentenced to die;
    save them as they stagger to their death.

**24:12**
†Rom 2:6

<sup>12</sup> Don't excuse yourself by saying, "Look, we didn't know."
    For God understands all hearts, and he sees you.
  He who guards your soul knows you knew.
  He will repay all people as their actions deserve.

**24:13**
Ps 19:10
Prov 25:16

<sup>13</sup> My child,* eat honey, for it is good,
    and the honeycomb is sweet to the taste.

**24:14**
Prov 2:10

<sup>14</sup> In the same way, wisdom is sweet to your soul.
    If you find it, you will have a bright future,
    and your hopes will not be cut short.

<sup>15</sup> Don't wait in ambush at the home of the godly,
    and don't raid the house where the godly live.

**24:5** As in Greek version; Hebrew reads *A wise man is strength.*   **24:13** Hebrew *My son;* also in 24:21.

---

**24:5** The athlete who has wisdom—who assesses the situation and plans strategies—has an advantage over a physically stronger but unwise opponent. We exercise regularly and eat well to build our strength, but do we take equal pains to develop wisdom and knowledge? Because wisdom is a vital part of strength, it pays to attain it.

**24:6** In any major decision we make concerning college, marriage, career, children, etc., it is not a sign of weakness to ask for advice. Instead, it is foolish not to ask for it. Find good advisers before making any big decision. They can help you expand your alternatives and evaluate your choices.

**24:8** Planning to do evil can be as wrong as doing it because what you think determines what you will do. Left unchecked, wrong desires will lead us to sin. God wants pure hearts, free

from sin, and planning evil brings sinful thoughts into our mind. Should you say, "Then I might as well go ahead and do it because I've already planned it"? No. You have sinned in your attitude, but you have not yet harmed other people. Stop in your tracks and ask God to forgive you and put you on a different path.

**24:10** Times of trouble can be useful. They can show you who you really are—what kind of character you have developed. In addition, they can help you grow stronger. When Jeremiah questioned God because of the trouble he faced, God asked how he ever expected to face big challenges if the little ones tired him out (Jeremiah 12:5). Don't complain about your problems. The trouble you face today is training you to be strong for the more difficult situations you will face in the future.

16 The godly may trip seven times, but they will get up again.
   But one disaster is enough to overthrow the wicked.

17 Don't rejoice when your enemies fall;
   don't be happy when they stumble.

18 For the LORD will be displeased with you
   and will turn his anger away from them.

24:17
Ps 35:15
Rom 11:18-21

19 Don't fret because of evildoers;
   don't envy the wicked.

20 For evil people have no future;
   the light of the wicked will be snuffed out.

24:19
Job 15:31
Prov 13:9; 24:1

21 My child, fear the LORD and the king.
   Don't associate with rebels,

22    for disaster will hit them suddenly.
   Who knows what punishment will come
   from the LORD and the king?

24:21
Rom 13:4
1 Pet 2:17

*More Sayings of the Wise*
23 Here are some further sayings of the wise:

   It is wrong to show favoritism when passing judgment.

24 A judge who says to the wicked, "You are innocent,"
   will be cursed by many people and denounced by the nations.

24:24
Prov 17:15

25 But it will go well for those who convict the guilty;
   rich blessings will be showered on them.

26 An honest answer
   is like a kiss of friendship.

27 Do your planning and prepare your fields
   before building your house.

28 Don't testify against your neighbors without cause;
   don't lie about them.

24:28
Prov 25:18

29 And don't say, "Now I can pay them back for what they've done to me!
   I'll get even with them!"

24:29
Prov 20:22
Matt 5:39

30 I walked by the field of a lazy person,
   the vineyard of one with no common sense.

24:30
Prov 6:6-11

31 I saw that it was overgrown with nettles.
   It was covered with weeds,
   and its walls were broken down.

24:31
Prov 6:10; 12:24;
23:21

32 Then, as I looked and thought about it,
   I learned this lesson:

33 A little extra sleep, a little more slumber,
   a little folding of the hands to rest—

34 then poverty will pounce on you like a bandit;
   scarcity will attack you like an armed robber.

---

**24:17, 18** David, Solomon's father, refused to gloat over the death of his lifelong enemy, Saul (see 2 Samuel 1). On the other hand, the nation of Edom rejoiced over Israel's defeat and was punished by God for their attitude (Obadiah 1:12). To gloat over others' misfortune is to make yourself the avenger and to put yourself in the place of God, who alone is the real Judge of all the earth (see Deuteronomy 32:35).

**24:26** People often think that they should bend the truth to avoid hurting a friend. But one who gives an honest, straightforward answer is a true friend. To be entrusted with the truth even at the risk of offense, says this proverb, represents a gesture of high honor.

**24:27** We should carry out our work in its proper order. If a farmer builds his house in the spring, he will miss the planting season and go a year without food. If a businessman invests his money in a house while his business is struggling to grow, he may lose both. It is possible to work hard and still lose everything if the timing is wrong or the resources to carry it out are not in place.

**24:29** Here is a reverse version of the Golden Rule (see Luke 6:31). Revenge is the way the world operates, but it is not God's way.

## C. WISDOM FOR THE LEADERS (25:1—31:31)

These proverbs were collected by Hezekiah's advisers. The first section was written by Solomon, and the next two sections were written by others. While we all can learn from these proverbs, many were originally directed toward the king or those who dealt with the king. These are particularly helpful for those who are leaders or aspire to become leaders. The book ends with a description of a truly good wife, who is an example of godly wisdom.

### More Proverbs of Solomon

**25** These are more proverbs of Solomon, collected by the advisers of King Hezekiah of Judah.

2 It is God's privilege to conceal things
    and the king's privilege to discover them.

3 No one can comprehend the height of heaven, the depth of the earth,
    or all that goes on in the king's mind!

4 Remove the impurities from silver,
    and the sterling will be ready for the silversmith.
5 Remove the wicked from the king's court,
    and his reign will be made secure by justice.

6 Don't demand an audience with the king
    or push for a place among the great.
7 It's better to wait for an invitation to the head table
    than to be sent away in public disgrace.

Just because you've seen something,
8     don't be in a hurry to go to court.
For what will you do in the end
    if your neighbor deals you a shameful defeat?

9 When arguing with your neighbor,
    don't betray another person's secret.
10 Others may accuse you of gossip,
    and you will never regain your good reputation.

11 Timely advice is lovely,
    like golden apples in a silver basket.

12 To one who listens, valid criticism
    is like a gold earring or other gold jewelry.

13 Trustworthy messengers refresh like snow in summer.
    They revive the spirit of their employer.

14 A person who promises a gift but doesn't give it
    is like clouds and wind that bring no rain.

### Cross-references

**25:1** Prov 1:1

**25:2** Deut 29:29; Ezra 6:1; Rom 11:33

**25:4** Ezek 22:18; Mal 3:2-3

**25:8** Prov 17:14

**25:11** Prov 15:23

**25:12** Prov 15:31; 20:12

**25:13** Prov 13:17

---

**25:1** Hezekiah's story is told in 2 Kings 18–20; 2 Chronicles 29–32; and Isaiah 36–39. He was one of the few kings of Judah who honored the Lord. By contrast, his father, Ahaz, actually nailed the Temple door shut. Hezekiah restored the Temple, destroyed idol worship centers, and earned the respect of surrounding nations, many of whom brought gifts to God because of him. It is not surprising that Hezekiah had these proverbs copied and read, for "in all that he did in the service of the Temple of God and in his efforts to follow God's laws and commands, Hezekiah sought his God wholeheartedly. As a result, he was very successful" (2 Chronicles 31:21).

**25:2-6** These four proverbs all focus on the king. Verse 2 indicates the importance of a king's efforts to discover the truth. This is followed by a parable on the value of a king keeping his own counsel and making up his own mind. Then, because a wise king seeks good advisers, he must be aware of the danger of those who are wicked in places of influence. Last, a warning is issued to those within the court that anyone who makes demands on the king's time treads on dangerous

ground. Hezekiah began his collection of wisdom with words for himself.

**25:6, 7** Jesus made this proverb into a parable (see Luke 14:7-11). We should not seek honors for ourselves. It is better to quietly and faithfully accomplish the work God has given us to do. As others notice the quality of our life, then they will draw attention to us.

**25:13** It is often difficult to find people you can really trust. Faithful employees ("trustworthy messengers") are punctual, responsible, honest, and hardworking. Such people are invaluable as they help take some of the pressure off their employer. Find out what your employer needs from you to make his or her job easier, and do it.

**25:14** Most churches, missions organizations, and Christian groups depend on the gifts of people to keep their ministries going. But many who promise to give fail to follow through. The Bible is very clear about the effect this has on those involved in the ministry. If you make a pledge, keep your promise.

15 Patience can persuade a prince,
and soft speech can break bones.

25:15
Prov 15:1
Eccl 10:4

16 Do you like honey?
Don't eat too much, or it will make you sick!

25:16
Prov 25:27

17 Don't visit your neighbors too often,
or you will wear out your welcome.

18 Telling lies about others
is as harmful as hitting them with an ax,
wounding them with a sword,
or shooting them with a sharp arrow.

25:18
Ps 57:4
Prov 12:18; 24:28
Jer 9:8

19 Putting confidence in an unreliable person in times of trouble
is like chewing with a broken tooth or walking on a lame foot.

25:19
Job 6:15

20 Singing cheerful songs to a person with a heavy heart
is like taking someone's coat in cold weather
or pouring vinegar in a wound.*

21 If your enemies are hungry, give them food to eat.
If they are thirsty, give them water to drink.

22 You will heap burning coals of shame on their heads,
and the LORD will reward you.

25:21
Exod 23:4-5
2 Kgs 6:22
2 Chr 28:15
Matt 5:44
Rom 12:20

23 As surely as a north wind brings rain,
so a gossiping tongue causes anger!

25:23
Prov 13:3; 26:20

24 It's better to live alone in the corner of an attic
than with a quarrelsome wife in a lovely home.

25:24
Prov 21:9

25 Good news from far away
is like cold water to the thirsty.

25:25
Prov 15:30

26 If the godly give in to the wicked,
it's like polluting a fountain or muddying a spring.

25:26
Ezek 32:2; 34:18

27 It's not good to eat too much honey,
and it's not good to seek honors for yourself.

25:27
Prov 25:16; 27:2

28 A person without self-control
is like a city with broken-down walls.

25:28
2 Chr 32:5
Prov 16:32

**26** 1 Honor is no more associated with fools
than snow with summer or rain with harvest.

26:1
1 Sam 12:17

2 Like a fluttering sparrow or a darting swallow,
an undeserved curse will not land on its intended victim.

26:2
Num 23:8
2 Sam 16:12

3 Guide a horse with a whip, a donkey with a bridle,
and a fool with a rod to his back!

26:3
Ps 32:9
Prov 10:13

25:20 As in Greek version; Hebrew reads *pouring vinegar on soda.*

---

**25:18** Lying about someone is as vicious as an act of physical violence. Its effects can be as permanent as those of a wound. The next time you are tempted to pass on a bit of gossip, imagine yourself wounding the victim of your remarks with a sword. This image may shock you into silence.

**25:21, 22** God's form of retaliation is most effective and yet difficult to do. Paul quotes this proverb in Romans 12:19-21. In Matthew 5:44, Jesus encourages us to pray for those who hurt us. By returning good for evil, we are acknowledging God as the balancer of all accounts and trusting him to be the judge.

**25:26** To compromise with the wicked means setting aside your standards of right and wrong. No one is helped by someone who compromises with the wicked.

**25:27** Dwelling on the honors you deserve can only be harmful. It can make you bitter, discouraged, or angry, and it will not bring you the rewards that you think should be yours. Pining for what you should have received may make you miss the satisfaction of knowing you did your best.

**25:28** Even though city walls restricted the inhabitants' movements, people were happy to have them. Without walls, they would have been vulnerable to attack by any passing group of marauders. Self-control limits us, to be sure, but it is necessary. An out-of-control life is open to all sorts of attacks by the enemy. Think of self-control as a wall for defense and protection.

**26:2** "An undeserved curse will not land" means that it has no effect.

**26:4**
Prov 23:9; 29:9

⁴ Don't answer the foolish arguments of fools,
    or you will become as foolish as they are.

⁵ Be sure to answer the foolish arguments of fools,
    or they will become wise in their own estimation.

⁶ Trusting a fool to convey a message
    is like cutting off one's feet or drinking poison!

⁷ A proverb in the mouth of a fool
    is as useless as a paralyzed leg.

⁸ Honoring a fool
    is as foolish as tying a stone to a slingshot.

⁹ A proverb in the mouth of a fool
    is like a thorny branch brandished by a drunk.

¹⁰ An employer who hires a fool or a bystander
    is like an archer who shoots at random.

**26:11**
Exod 8:15
†2 Pet 2:22

¹¹ As a dog returns to its vomit,
    so a fool repeats his foolishness.

**26:12**
Prov 3:7; 29:20

¹² There is more hope for fools
    than for people who think they are wise.

**26:13**
Prov 22:13

¹³ The lazy person claims, "There's a lion on the road!
    Yes, I'm sure there's a lion out there!"

---

**THE FOUR TONGUES**
Other verses about our speech include 10:11, 20, 31; 12:6, 17-19; 13:2; 14:3; 19:5, 28; 25:11; 27:2, 5, 14, 17; 29:9.

| | | |
|---|---|---|
| *The Controlled Tongue* | Those with this speech pattern think before speaking, know when silence is best, and give wise advice. | 10:19; 11:12, 13; 12:16; 13:3; 15:1, 4, 28; 16:23; 17:14, 27, 28; 21:23; 24:26 |
| *The Caring Tongue* | Those with this speech pattern speak truthfully while seeking to encourage. | 10:32; 12:18, 25; 15:23; 16:24; 25:15; 27:9 |
| *The Conniving Tongue* | Those with this speech pattern are filled with wrong motives, gossip, slander, and a desire to twist truth. | 6:12-14; 8:13; 16:28; 18:8; 25:18; 26:20-28 |
| *The Careless Tongue* | Those with this speech pattern are filled with lies, curses, quick-tempered words—which can lead to rebellion and destruction. | 10:18, 32; 11:9; 12:16, 18; 15:4; 17:9, 14, 19; 20:19; 25:23 |

What we say probably affects more people than any other action we take. It is not surprising, then, to find that Proverbs gives special attention to words and how they are used. Four common speech patterns are described in Proverbs. The first two should be copied; the last two should be avoided.

---

**26:4, 5** These two verses seem to contradict, but they actually are purposely demonstrating the contradiction between reason and folly. A fool remains a fool whether he is answered or not. The wise person has a choice to make depending on what he or she sees is the greatest need of the fool. Some fools don't deserve an answer because they are clearly not in a mood to listen, and those who try to answer them will simply stoop to their level. There are other situations where common sense says to answer the fool in order to expose his or her pride and folly.

**26:7** Some people are so dulled that they won't sense the wisdom even if they memorize these proverbs. A mindlessly quoted proverb proves as useless as a paralyzed body part. Only those who want to be wise have the receptive attitude needed to make the most of these wise words. If we want to learn from God, he will respond and pour out his heart to us (1:23).

**26:8** Sometimes when someone in a group causes discord or dissension, the leader tries to make that person loyal and productive by giving him or her a place of privilege or responsibility. This usually doesn't work. In fact, it is like tying a stone to the sling of a slingshot—it won't go anywhere and will swing back and hurt

you. The dissenter's new power may be just what he or she needs to manipulate the group.

**26:9** Normally the first prick of a thorn alerts us, so we remove the thorn before it damages us. A drunk person, however, may not feel the thorn, and so it will work its way into his flesh. Similarly, a fool may not feel the sting of a proverb because he does not see how it applies to his life. Instead of taking its point to heart, a fool will apply it to his church, his employer, his spouse, or whomever he is rebelling against. The next time you find yourself saying, "So-and-so should really pay attention to that," stop and ask yourself, Is there a message in it for me?

**26:13-16** If a person is not willing to work, he or she can find endless excuses to avoid it. But laziness is more dangerous than a prowling lion. The less you do, the less you want to do, and the more useless you become. To overcome laziness, take a few small steps toward change. Set a concrete, realistic goal. Figure out the steps needed to reach it, and follow those steps. Pray for strength and persistence. To keep your excuses from making you useless, stop making useless excuses.

¹⁴ As a door swings back and forth on its hinges,
  so the lazy person turns over in bed.

26:14
Prov 6:9

¹⁵ Lazy people take food in their hand
  but don't even lift it to their mouth.

¹⁶ Lazy people consider themselves smarter
  than seven wise counselors.

¹⁷ Interfering in someone else's argument
  is as foolish as yanking a dog's ears.

26:17
Prov 3:30; 20:3

¹⁸ Just as damaging
  as a madman shooting a deadly weapon
¹⁹ is someone who lies to a friend
  and then says, "I was only joking."

26:18
Prov 24:12, 28
Isa 50:11

²⁰ Fire goes out without wood,
  and quarrels disappear when gossip stops.

26:20
Prov 16:28; 22:10;
24:28

²¹ A quarrelsome person starts fights
  as easily as hot embers light charcoal or fire lights wood.

26:21
Prov 15:18; 29:22

²² Rumors are dainty morsels
  that sink deep into one's heart.

26:22
Prov 18:8

²³ Smooth* words may hide a wicked heart,
  just as a pretty glaze covers a clay pot.

26:23
Luke 11:39

²⁴ People may cover their hatred with pleasant words,
  but they're deceiving you.

26:24
Ps 41:6
Prov 12:20

²⁵ They pretend to be kind, but don't believe them.
  Their hearts are full of many evils.*
²⁶ While their hatred may be concealed by trickery,
  their wrongdoing will be exposed in public.

²⁷ If you set a trap for others,
  you will get caught in it yourself.
  If you roll a boulder down on others,
  it will crush you instead.

26:27
Ps 7:15

²⁸ A lying tongue hates its victims,
  and flattering words cause ruin.

26:28
Prov 28:23

# 27

¹ Don't brag about tomorrow,
  since you don't know what the day will bring.

27:1
Luke 12:19-20
Jas 4:13-16

² Let someone else praise you, not your own mouth—
  a stranger, not your own lips.

27:2
Prov 25:27
2 Cor 10:12, 18

³ A stone is heavy and sand is weighty,
  but the resentment caused by a fool is even heavier.

⁴ Anger is cruel, and wrath is like a flood,
  but jealousy is even more dangerous.

27:4
Prov 6:34

⁵ An open rebuke
  is better than hidden love!

27:5
Prov 25:12

26:23 As in Greek version; Hebrew reads Burning.   26:25 Hebrew seven evils.

---

26:17 Yanking the ears of a dog is a good way to get bitten, and interfering in arguments is a good way to get hurt. Many times both arguers will turn on the person who interferes. It is best simply to keep out of arguments that are none of your business. If you must become involved, try to wait until the arguers have stopped fighting and cooled off a bit. Then maybe you can help them mend their differences and their relationship.

26:20 Talking about every little irritation and piece of gossip only keeps the fires of anger going. Refusing to discuss them cuts the fuel line and makes the fires die out. Does someone continually irritate you? Decide not to complain about the person, and see if your irritation dies from lack of fuel.

27:6
Ps 141:5
Matt 26:49
6 Wounds from a sincere friend
   are better than many kisses from an enemy.

7 A person who is full refuses honey,
   but even bitter food tastes sweet to the hungry.

8 A person who strays from home
   is like a bird that strays from its nest.

9 The heartfelt counsel of a friend
   is as sweet as perfume and incense.

27:10
1 Kgs 12:6
2 Chr 10:6-8
Prov 17:17; 18:24
10 Never abandon a friend—
    either yours or your father's.
   When disaster strikes, you won't have to ask your brother for assistance.
   It's better to go to a neighbor than to a brother who lives far away.

27:11
Prov 10:1; 23:15
11 Be wise, my child,* and make my heart glad.
    Then I will be able to answer my critics.

27:12
Prov 22:3
12 A prudent person foresees danger and takes precautions.
    The simpleton goes blindly on and suffers the consequences.

27:13
Prov 20:16
13 Get security from someone who guarantees a stranger's debt.
    Get a deposit if he does it for foreigners.*

14 A loud and cheerful greeting early in the morning
    will be taken as a curse!

27:15
Prov 19:13
15 A quarrelsome wife is as annoying
    as constant dripping on a rainy day.
16 Stopping her complaints is like trying to stop the wind
    or trying to hold something with greased hands.

17 As iron sharpens iron,
    so a friend sharpens a friend.

27:18
Luke 12:42-44
1 Cor 9:7
2 Tim 2:6
18 As workers who tend a fig tree are allowed to eat the fruit,
    so workers who protect their employer's interests will be rewarded.

19 As a face is reflected in water,
    so the heart reflects the real person.

27:20
Prov 30:15
Eccl 1:8-11
Hab 2:5
20 Just as Death and Destruction* are never satisfied,
    so human desire is never satisfied.

27:21
Prov 17:3
Zech 13:9
Luke 6:26
21 Fire tests the purity of silver and gold,
    but a person is tested by being praised.*

27:11 Hebrew *my son.* 27:13 As in Greek and Latin versions (see also 20:16); Hebrew reads *for a promiscuous woman.* 27:20 Hebrew *Sheol and Abaddon.* 27:21 Or *by flattery.*

---

**27:6** Who would prefer a friend's wounds to an enemy's kisses? Anyone who considers the source. A friend who has your best interests at heart may have to give you unpleasant advice at times, but you know it is for your own good. An enemy, by contrast, may whisper sweet words and happily send you on your way to ruin. We tend to hear what we want to hear, even if an enemy is the only one who will say it. A friend's advice, no matter how painful, is much more valuable.

**27:15, 16** Quarrelsome nagging, a steady stream of unwanted advice, is a form of torture. People nag because they think they're not getting through, but nagging hinders communication more than it helps. When tempted to engage in this destructive habit, stop and examine your motives. Are you more concerned about yourself—getting your way, being right—than about the person you are pretending to help? If you are truly concerned about other people, think of a more effective way to get through to them. Surprise them with words of patience and love, and see what happens.

**27:17** Mental sharpness comes from being around good people. And a meeting of minds can help people see their ideas with new

clarity, refine them, and shape them into brilliant insights. This requires partners who can challenge one another and stimulate thought—people who focus on the idea without involving their egos in the discussion; people who know how to attack the thought and not the thinker. Two friends who bring their ideas together can help each other become sharper.

**27:18** With all the problems and concerns a leader has, it can be easy to overlook the very people who most deserve attention—faithful employees or volunteers (those who "tend a fig tree"). The people who stand behind you, who work hard and help you get the job done, deserve to share in your success. Be sure that in all your planning, organizing, and working, you don't forget the people who are helping you the most.

**27:21** Praise tests a person, just as high temperatures test metal. How does praise affect you? Do you work to get it? Do you work harder after you've gotten it? Your attitude toward praise tells a lot about your character. People of high integrity are not swayed by praise. They are attuned to their inner convictions, and they do what they should whether or not they are praised for it.

<sup>22</sup> You cannot separate fools from their foolishness,
    even though you grind them like grain with mortar and pestle.

<sup>23</sup> Know the state of your flocks,
    and put your heart into caring for your herds,
<sup>24</sup> for riches don't last forever,
    and the crown might not be passed to the next generation.
<sup>25</sup> After the hay is harvested and the new crop appears
    and the mountain grasses are gathered in,
<sup>26</sup> your sheep will provide wool for clothing,
    and your goats will provide the price of a field.
<sup>27</sup> And you will have enough goats' milk for yourself,
    your family, and your servant girls.

# 28

<sup>1</sup> The wicked run away when no one is chasing them,
    but the godly are as bold as lions.

<sup>2</sup> When there is moral rot within a nation, its government topples easily.
    But wise and knowledgeable leaders bring stability.

<sup>3</sup> A poor person who oppresses the poor
    is like a pounding rain that destroys the crops.

<sup>4</sup> To reject the law is to praise the wicked;
    to obey the law is to fight them.

<sup>5</sup> Evil people don't understand justice,
    but those who follow the LORD understand completely.

<sup>6</sup> Better to be poor and honest
    than to be dishonest and rich.

<sup>7</sup> Young people who obey the law are wise;
    those with wild friends bring shame to their parents.*

<sup>8</sup> Income from charging high interest rates
    will end up in the pocket of someone who is kind to the poor.

<sup>9</sup> God detests the prayers
    of a person who ignores the law.

<sup>10</sup> Those who lead good people along an evil path
    will fall into their own trap,
    but the honest will inherit good things.

<sup>11</sup> Rich people may think they are wise,
    but a poor person with discernment can see right through them.

**28:7** Hebrew *their father.*

| Reference | |
|---|---|
| **27:22** | Prov 23:35; 26:11 |
| | Jer 5:3 |
| **27:23** | Ezek 34:12 |
| | John 10:3 |
| **28:1** | Lev 26:17, 36 |
| **28:2** | 1 Kgs 16:8-28 |
| | 2 Kgs 15:8-15 |
| **28:3** | Matt 18:28 |
| **28:4** | Rom 1:32 |
| | Eph 5:11 |
| **28:5** | Ps 92:6-7 |
| **28:6** | Prov 19:1 |
| **28:7** | Prov 23:20 |
| **28:8** | Exod 22:25 |
| | Deut 23:19-20 |
| **28:9** | Pss 66:18; 109:7 |
| **28:10** | Prov 26:27 |
| | Heb 6:12 |

---

**27:23-27** Because life is uncertain, we should be all the more diligent in preparing for the future. We should act with foresight, giving responsible attention to our home, our family, and our career. We should be responsible stewards, like a farmer with his lands and herds. Thinking ahead is a duty, not an option, for God's people.

**28:2** For a government or a society to endure, it needs wise, informed leaders—and these are hard to find. Each person's selfishness quickly affects others. A selfish employee who steals from his company ruins its productivity. A selfish driver who drinks before taking the wheel makes the state highways unsafe. A selfish spouse who has an adulterous affair often breaks up several families. When people live for themselves with little concern for how their actions affect others, the resulting moral rot contaminates the entire nation. Are you part of the problem or the solution?

**28:5** Because justice is part of God's character, a person who follows God treats others justly. Justice begins with concern for

what is happening to others. A Christian cannot be indifferent to human suffering because God isn't. And we certainly must not contribute to human suffering through selfish business practices or unfair government policies. Be sure you are more concerned for justice than merely your own interests. You can't claim to follow God and ignore your neighbor.

**28:9** God does not listen to our prayers if we intend to go back to our sin as soon as we get off our knees. When we forsake our sin and follow him, however, he willingly listens—no matter how bad our sin has been. What closes his ears is not the depth of our sin but our secret intention to do it again. God hears our intentions as clearly as he hears our words.

**28:11** Rich people often think they are wonderful; depending on no one, they take credit for all they do. But that's a hollow self-esteem. Through dependence on God in their struggles, the poor may develop a richness of spirit that no amount of wealth can provide. The rich person can lose all his material wealth, while no

**28:12**
Eccl 10:5-6

**28:13**
Ps 32:1-11
1 Jn 1:6-9

**28:14**
Rom 2:5

**28:15**
Prov 19:12
Matt 2:16
1 Pet 5:8

**28:16**
Eccl 10:16
Isa 3:12

**28:17**
Gen 9:6
Exod 21:14

**28:19**
Prov 12:11

12 When the godly succeed, everyone is glad.
   When the wicked take charge, people go into hiding.

13 People who conceal their sins will not prosper,
   but if they confess and turn from them, they will receive mercy.

14 Blessed are those who fear to do wrong,*
   but the stubborn are headed for serious trouble.

15 A wicked ruler is as dangerous to the poor
   as a roaring lion or an attacking bear.

16 A ruler with no understanding will oppress his people,
   but one who hates corruption will have a long life.

17 A murderer's tormented conscience will drive him into the grave.
   Don't protect him!

18 The blameless will be rescued from harm,
   but the crooked will be suddenly destroyed.

19 A hard worker has plenty of food,
   but a person who chases fantasies ends up in poverty.

**28:14** Or *those who fear the LORD;* Hebrew reads *those who fear.*

---

**DILIGENCE AND LAZINESS**

Proverbs makes it clear that diligence—being willing to work hard and do one's best at any job given to him or her—is a vital part of wise living. We work hard, not to become rich, famous, or admired (although those may be by-products), but to serve God with our very best during our lives.

| The Diligent | The Lazy | Reference |
|---|---|---|
| Become rich | Are soon poor | 10:4 |
| Gather their crops | Sleep during harvest | 10:5 |
| | Are an annoyance | 10:26 |
| Have plenty of food | Have no sense | 12:11 |
| Gain many rewards | | 12:14 |
| Will become leaders | Will become slaves | 12:24 |
| Make good use of resources | Waste good resources | 12:27 |
| Will prosper | Want much but get little | 13:4 |
| Bring profit | Experience poverty | 14:23 |
| Path is open | Path is blocked | 15:19 |
| | Are like those who destroy | 18:9 |
| | Go hungry | 19:15 |
| | Won't feed themselves | 19:24 |
| | Won't plow in season | 20:4 |
| Stay awake and have food to spare | Love sleep and grow poor | 20:13 |
| Make careful plans | Make hasty shortcuts | 21:5 |
| Love to give | Desire things but refuse to work for them | 21:25, 26 |
| | Are full of excuses for not working | 22:13 |
| Will serve before kings | | 22:29 |
| | Sleep too much, which leads to poverty | 24:30-34 |
| Reap abundance through hard work | Experience poverty because of laziness | 28:19 |

---

one can take away the poor person's character. Don't be jealous of the rich; money may be all they will ever have.

**28:13** It is human nature to hide our sins or overlook our mistakes. But it is hard to learn from a mistake you don't acknowledge making. And what good is a mistake if it doesn't teach you something? To learn from an error you need to admit it, confess it, analyze it, and make adjustments so that it doesn't happen again. Everybody makes mistakes, but only fools repeat them.

**28:13** Something in each of us strongly resists admitting we are wrong. That is why we admire people who openly and graciously admit their mistakes and sins. These people have a strong self-image. They do not always have to be right to feel good about

themselves. Be willing to reconsider—to admit you are wrong and to change your plans when necessary. And remember, the first step toward forgiveness is confession.

**28:17, 18** A sinner's conscience will drive him into either guilt, resulting in repentance, or to death itself because of a refusal to repent. It is no act of kindness to try to make him feel better; the more guilt he feels, the more likely he is to turn to God and repent. If we interfere with the natural consequences of his act, we may make it easier for him to continue in sin.

20 The trustworthy person will get a rich reward,
　　but a person who wants quick riches will get into trouble.

**28:20**
Matt 25:21

21 Showing partiality is never good,
　　yet some will do wrong for a mere piece of bread.

**28:21**
Ezek 13:19

22 Greedy people try to get rich quick
　　but don't realize they're headed for poverty.

23 In the end, people appreciate honest criticism
　　far more than flattery.

24 Anyone who steals from his father and mother
　　and says, "What's wrong with that?"
　　is no better than a murderer.

**28:24**
Prov 19:26; 20:20

25 Greed causes fighting;
　　trusting the LORD leads to prosperity.

26 Those who trust their own insight are foolish,
　　but anyone who walks in wisdom is safe.

**28:26**
Prov 3:5

27 Whoever gives to the poor will lack nothing,
　　but those who close their eyes to poverty will be cursed.

**28:27**
Prov 11:24; 19:17

28 When the wicked take charge, people go into hiding.
　　When the wicked meet disaster, the godly flourish.

# 29

1 Whoever stubbornly refuses to accept criticism
　　will suddenly be destroyed beyond recovery.

**29:1**
1 Sam 2:25
2 Chr 36:16

2 When the godly are in authority, the people rejoice.
　　But when the wicked are in power, they groan.

**29:2**
Esth 8:15-16
Prov 11:10; 28:12

3 The man who loves wisdom brings joy to his father,
　　but if he hangs around with prostitutes, his wealth is wasted.

**29:3**
Prov 6:26; 10:1
Luke 15:13

4 A just king gives stability to his nation,
　　but one who demands bribes destroys it.

5 To flatter friends
　　is to lay a trap for their feet.

**29:5**
Ps 5:9

6 Evil people are trapped by sin,
　　but the righteous escape, shouting for joy.

7 The godly care about the rights of the poor;
　　the wicked don't care at all.

**29:7**
Ps 41:1
Prov 31:8-9

8 Mockers can get a whole town agitated,
　　but the wise will calm anger.

**29:8**
Prov 11:11; 16:14

9 If a wise person takes a fool to court,
　　there will be ranting and ridicule but no satisfaction.

---

**28:26** For many people, the rugged individualist is a hero. We admire the bold, self-directed men and women who know what they want and fight for it. They are self-reliant, neither giving nor asking advice. What a contrast to God's way. A person can't know the future or predict the consequences of his or her choices with certainty. And so the totally self-reliant person is doomed to failure. The wise person depends on God.

**28:27** God wants us to identify with the needy, not ignore them. The second part of this proverb could be restated positively:

"Those who open their eyes to poor people will be blessed." If we help others when they are in trouble, they will do whatever they can to return the favor (see 11:24, 25). Paul promises that God will supply all our needs (Philippians 4:19); he usually does this through other people. What can you do today to help God supply someone's need?

**29:1** Warnings rarely come with countdowns. We can't tell when we've had our last chance to change. When we, like the person in this proverb, refuse to consider valid criticism, we leave ourselves open to sudden disaster. The moment we realize that a change is necessary is the best moment to take action. What significant adjustments have been on hold in your life for too long?

<sup>10</sup> The bloodthirsty hate blameless people,
but the upright seek to help them.*

<sup>11</sup> Fools vent their anger,
but the wise quietly hold it back.

<sup>12</sup> If a ruler pays attention to liars,
all his advisers will be wicked.

<sup>13</sup> The poor and the oppressor have this in common—
the LORD gives sight to the eyes of both.

<sup>14</sup> If a king judges the poor fairly,
his throne will last forever.

<sup>15</sup> To discipline a child produces wisdom,
but a mother is disgraced by an undisciplined child.

<sup>16</sup> When the wicked are in authority, sin flourishes,
but the godly will live to see their downfall.

<sup>17</sup> Discipline your children, and they will give you peace of mind
and will make your heart glad.

<sup>18</sup> When people do not accept divine guidance, they run wild.
But whoever obeys the law is joyful.

<sup>19</sup> Words alone will not discipline a servant;
the words may be understood, but they are not heeded.

<sup>20</sup> There is more hope for a fool
than for someone who speaks without thinking.

**29:10** Or *The bloodthirsty hate blameless people, / and they seek to kill the upright;* Hebrew reads *The bloodthirsty hate blameless people; / as for the upright, they seek their life.*

---

**LEADERSHIP**
Since many
of the proverbs
came from King
Solomon, it is
natural to expect
some of his
interest to be
directed toward
leadership.
Other verses
to study: 24:27;
25:13; 27:18.

| Qualities of a good leader | Reference |
| --- | --- |
| Works hard | 12:24 |
| Doesn't penalize people for honesty | 17:26 |
| Listens before answering | 18:13 |
| Open to new ideas | 18:15 |
| Listens to both sides of the story | 18:17 |
| Stands up under pressure | 24:10 |
| Stands up under praise | 27:21 |

| *What happens without good leadership* | |
| --- | --- |
| Fools are honored | 26:8 |
| A wicked ruler is dangerous | 28:15 |
| People groan | 29:2 |
| A wicked ruler has wicked advisers | 29:12 |

---

**29:13** "The LORD gives sight to the eyes of both" means that everyone depends on God for sight. Both the oppressor and the poor have the gift of sight from the same God. God sees and judges both, and his judgment falls on those whose greed or power drives them to oppress the poor.

**29:15** Parents of young children often weary of disciplining them. They feel like all they do is nag, scold, and punish. When you're tempted to give up and let your children do what they want, or when you wonder if you've ruined every chance for a loving relationship with them, remember that kind, firm correction helps them learn, and learning makes them wise. Consistent, loving discipline will ultimately teach them to discipline themselves.

**29:16** When the wicked are in leadership, sin prevails. In any organization—whether a church, a business, a family, or a govern-

ment—the climate comes from the top. The people become like their leaders. What kind of climate are you setting for the people you lead?

**29:18** "Divine guidance" refers to words from God received by prophets. Where there is ignorance or rejection of God, crime and sin run rampant. Public morality depends on the knowledge of God, but it also depends on keeping God's laws. In order for nations and individuals to function well, people must know God's ways and keep his rules. Having God's Word means little if we are not obeying it.

²¹ A servant pampered from childhood
　　will become a rebel.

²² An angry person starts fights;
　　a hot-tempered person commits all kinds of sin.

²³ Pride ends in humiliation,
　　while humility brings honor.

²⁴ If you assist a thief, you only hurt yourself.
　　You are sworn to tell the truth, but you dare not testify.

²⁵ Fearing people is a dangerous trap,
　　but trusting the LORD means safety.

²⁶ Many seek the ruler's favor,
　　but justice comes from the LORD.

²⁷ The righteous despise the unjust;
　　the wicked despise the godly.

### The Sayings of Agur

**30** The sayings of Agur son of Jakeh contain this message.*

　　I am weary, O God;
　　I am weary and worn out, O God.*

² I am too stupid to be human,
　　and I lack common sense.
³ I have not mastered human wisdom,
　　nor do I know the Holy One.

⁴ Who but God goes up to heaven and comes back down?
　　Who holds the wind in his fists?
　　Who wraps up the oceans in his cloak?
　　Who has created the whole wide world?
　　What is his name—and his son's name?
　　Tell me if you know!

⁵ Every word of God proves true.
　　He is a shield to all who come to him for protection.
⁶ Do not add to his words,
　　or he may rebuke you and expose you as a liar.

⁷ O God, I beg two favors from you;
　　let me have them before I die.
⁸ First, help me never to tell a lie.
　　Second, give me neither poverty nor riches!
　　Give me just enough to satisfy my needs.

**30:1a** Or *son of Jakeh from Massa;* or *son of Jakeh, an oracle.*  **30:1b** The Hebrew can also be translated *The man declares this to Ithiel, / to Ithiel and to Ucal.*

**29:23**
Prov 15:33; 22:4
Dan 4:30
Matt 23:12
Jas 4:6

**29:24**
Lev 5:1

**29:25**
Gen 12:11-13
Luke 12:4

**29:26**
Isa 49:4

**29:27**
Pss 69:4;
139:21-22
Matt 10:22; 24:9

**30:2**
Job 42:3-6

**30:4**
Exod 15:10
Job 26:8; 38:8-9
Isa 45:18
Rev 19:12

**30:5**
Pss 3:3; 12:6;
18:30; 84:11

**30:6**
Deut 4:2; 12:32
Rev 22:18

**30:8**
Matt 6:11

---

**29:24** This proverb is saying that a thief's accomplice may not tell the truth when under oath. Thus, by his participation in the crime and his perjury in the courtroom, he will hurt himself. Further, a witness who refuses to report a crime becomes an accomplice.

**29:25** Fear of people can hamper everything you try to do. In extreme forms, it can make you afraid to leave your home. By contrast, fear of God—respect, reverence, and trust—is liberating. Why fear people who can do no eternal harm? Instead, trust God who can turn the harm intended by others into good for those who trust him.

**30:1** The origin of these sayings is not clear. Nothing is known about Agur except that he was a wise teacher who may have come from Lemuel's kingdom (see the note on 31:1).

**30:2-4** Because God is infinite, certain aspects of his nature will always remain a mystery. Compare these questions with the questions God asked Job (Job 38–41). Use these questions to probe your own humility and awe before your Creator.

**30:4** Some scholars feel that the son referred to is the Son of God, the pre-incarnate being of the Messiah who, before the foundation of the earth, participated in the Creation. Colossians 1:16, 17 teaches that through Christ the world was created.

**30:7-9** Having too much money can be dangerous, but so can having too little. Being poor can, in fact, be hazardous to spiritual as well as physical health. On the other hand, being rich is not the answer. As Jesus pointed out, rich people have trouble getting into God's Kingdom (Matthew 19:23, 24). Like Paul, we can learn how to live whether we have little or plenty (Philippians 4:12), but our lives are more likely to be effective if we have "neither poverty nor riches."

**30:9**
Deut 8:12; 31:20
Neh 9:25
Hos 13:6

⁹ For if I grow rich, I may deny you and say, "Who is the Lᴏʀᴅ?"
  And if I am too poor, I may steal and thus insult God's holy name.

**30:10**
Eccl 7:21

¹⁰ Never slander a worker to the employer,
  or the person will curse you, and you will pay for it.

**30:11**
Exod 21:17

¹¹ Some people curse their father
  and do not thank their mother.
¹² They are pure in their own eyes,
  but they are filthy and unwashed.
¹³ They look proudly around,
  casting disdainful glances.

**30:14**
Job 29:17
Ps 14:4

¹⁴ They have teeth like swords
  and fangs like knives.
 They devour the poor from the earth
  and the needy from among humanity.

**30:15**
Prov 27:20

¹⁵ The leech has two suckers
  that cry out, "More, more!"*

There are three things that are never satisfied—
  no, four that never say, "Enough!":
¹⁶ the grave,*
   the barren womb,
   the thirsty desert,
   the blazing fire.

**30:17**
Gen 9:22

¹⁷ The eye that mocks a father
   and despises a mother's instructions
 will be plucked out by ravens of the valley
  and eaten by vultures.

¹⁸ There are three things that amaze me—
  no, four things that I don't understand:
¹⁹ how an eagle glides through the sky,
   how a snake slithers on a rock,
   how a ship navigates the ocean,
   how a man loves a woman.

**30:20**
Prov 5:6

²⁰ An adulterous woman consumes a man,
  then wipes her mouth and says, "What's wrong with that?"

²¹ There are three things that make the earth tremble—
  no, four it cannot endure:
²² a slave who becomes a king,
   an overbearing fool who prospers,
²³ a bitter woman who finally gets a husband,
   a servant girl who supplants her mistress.

²⁴ There are four things on earth that are small but unusually wise:

**30:25**
Prov 6:6

²⁵ Ants—they aren't strong,
   but they store up food all summer.
²⁶ Hyraxes*—they aren't powerful,
   but they make their homes among the rocks.

**30:15** Hebrew *two daughters who cry out, "Give, give!"*   **30:16** Hebrew *Sheol.*   **30:26** Or *Coneys,* or *Rock badgers.*

---

**30:11-14** This sequence of proverbs contains a fourfold description of arrogance. Notice that a life of pride and abuse of others often begins with a lack of appreciation for one's parents. The command to honor one's father and mother does create negative consequences when rejected.

**30:15ff** "Three things . . . no, four" is a poetic way of saying the list is not complete. The writer of these proverbs is observing the world with delighted interest. Verses 15-31 are an invitation to look at nature from the perspective of a keen observer.

**30:24-28** Ants can teach us about preparation; badgers about wise building; locusts about cooperation and order; and lizards about fearlessness. Compare this to Jesus' teaching in Matthew 6:25-34 that an effective way to resist worry involves a careful observation of the birds and the lilies.

²⁷ Locusts—they have no king,
  but they march in formation.
²⁸ Lizards—they are easy to catch,
  but they are found even in kings' palaces.

²⁹ There are three things that walk with stately stride—
  no, four that strut about:
³⁰ the lion, king of animals, who won't turn aside for anything,
³¹   the strutting rooster,
  the male goat,
  a king as he leads his army.

³² If you have been a fool by being proud or plotting evil,
  cover your mouth in shame.

³³ As the beating of cream yields butter
  and striking the nose causes bleeding,
  so stirring up anger causes quarrels.

### The Sayings of King Lemuel

# 31

The sayings of King Lemuel contain this message,* which his mother taught him.

² O my son, O son of my womb,
  O son of my vows,
³ do not waste your strength on women,
  on those who ruin kings.

⁴ It is not for kings, O Lemuel, to guzzle wine.
  Rulers should not crave alcohol.
⁵ For if they drink, they may forget the law
  and not give justice to the oppressed.
⁶ Alcohol is for the dying,
  and wine for those in bitter distress.
⁷ Let them drink to forget their poverty
  and remember their troubles no more.

⁸ Speak up for those who cannot speak for themselves;
  ensure justice for those being crushed.
⁹ Yes, speak up for the poor and helpless,
  and see that they get justice.

### A Wife of Noble Character

¹⁰*Who can find a virtuous and capable wife?
  She is more precious than rubies.
¹¹ Her husband can trust her,
  and she will greatly enrich his life.

**30:32**
Job 21:5; 40:4
Mic 7:16

**30:33**
Prov 10:12; 29:22

**31:2**
1 Sam 1:11
Isa 49:15

**31:3**
Deut 17:17
1 Kgs 11:1
Prov 5:9

**31:4**
Prov 20:1
Eccl 10:16-17
Isa 5:22-23
Hos 4:11

**31:5**
Deut 16:19
Prov 17:15

**31:8**
Job 29:12-17
Ps 82:3-5
Isa 58:9-10

**31:9**
Lev 19:15
Isa 1:17

**31:10**
Ruth 3:11
Prov 12:4; 19:14

**31:1** Or of Lemuel, king of Massa; or of King Lemuel, an oracle.   **31:10** Verses 10-31 comprise a Hebrew acrostic poem; each verse begins with a successive letter of the Hebrew alphabet.

**31:1** Little is known about Lemuel except that he was a king who received wise teachings from his mother. His name means "devoted to God." Some believe that Lemuel and Agur were both from the kingdom of Massa in northern Arabia.

**31:4-7** Drunkenness might be understandable among dying people in great pain, but it is inexcusable for national leaders. Alcohol clouds the mind and can lead to injustice and poor decisions. People in leadership who anesthetize themselves with alcohol will eventually compromise their principles.

**31:10-31** Proverbs has a lot to say about women. How fitting that the book ends with a picture of a woman of strong character, great wisdom, many skills, and great compassion.

Some people have the mistaken idea that the ideal woman in the Bible is retiring, servile, and entirely domestic. Not so!

This woman is an excellent wife and mother. She is also a manufacturer, importer, manager, realtor, farmer, seamstress, upholsterer, and merchant. Her strength and dignity do not come from her amazing achievements, however. They are a result of her reverence for God. In our society, where physical appearance counts for so much, it may surprise us to realize that her appearance is never mentioned. Her attractiveness comes entirely from her character.

The woman described in this chapter has outstanding abilities. Her family's social position is high. In fact, she may not be one woman at all—she may be a composite portrait of ideal womanhood. Do not see her as a model to imitate in every detail; your days are not long enough to do everything she does! See her instead as an inspiration to be all you can be. We can't be just like her, but we can learn from her industry, integrity, and resourcefulness.

<sup>12</sup> She brings him good, not harm,
all the days of her life.

**31:13**
1 Tim 2:9-10

<sup>13</sup> She finds wool and flax
and busily spins it.

<sup>14</sup> She is like a merchant's ship,
bringing her food from afar.

**31:15**
Rom 12:11

<sup>15</sup> She gets up before dawn to prepare breakfast for her household
and plan the day's work for her servant girls.

<sup>16</sup> She goes to inspect a field and buys it;
with her earnings she plants a vineyard.

<sup>17</sup> She is energetic and strong,
a hard worker.

<sup>18</sup> She makes sure her dealings are profitable;
her lamp burns late into the night.

<sup>19</sup> Her hands are busy spinning thread,
her fingers twisting fiber.

**31:20**
Eph 4:28

<sup>20</sup> She extends a helping hand to the poor
and opens her arms to the needy.

<sup>21</sup> She has no fear of winter for her household,
for everyone has warm* clothes.

<sup>22</sup> She makes her own bedspreads.
She dresses in fine linen and purple gowns.

<sup>23</sup> Her husband is well known at the city gates,
where he sits with the other civic leaders.

<sup>24</sup> She makes belted linen garments
and sashes to sell to the merchants.

<sup>25</sup> She is clothed with strength and dignity,
and she laughs without fear of the future.

**31:26**
Prov 10:31

<sup>26</sup> When she speaks, her words are wise,
and she gives instructions with kindness.

**31:27**
Prov 19:15

<sup>27</sup> She carefully watches everything in her household
and suffers nothing from laziness.

<sup>28</sup> Her children stand and bless her.
Her husband praises her:

<sup>29</sup> "There are many virtuous and capable women in the world,
but you surpass them all!"

**31:30**
Prov 22:4

<sup>30</sup> Charm is deceptive, and beauty does not last;
but a woman who fears the LORD will be greatly praised.

<sup>31</sup> Reward her for all she has done.
Let her deeds publicly declare her praise.

**31:21** As in Greek and Latin versions; Hebrew reads *scarlet.*

---

**31:31** The book of Proverbs begins with the command to fear the Lord (1:7) and ends with the picture of a woman who fulfills this command. Her qualities are mentioned throughout the book: hard work, fear of God, respect for spouse, foresight, encouragement, care for others, concern for the poor, wisdom in handling money. These qualities, when coupled with fear of God, lead to enjoyment, success, honor, and worth. Proverbs is practical for us because it shows how to become wise, make good decisions, and live according to God's ideal.

# ECCLESIASTES

## VITAL STATISTICS

**PURPOSE:**
To spare future generations the bitterness of learning through their own experience that life is meaningless apart from God

**AUTHOR:**
Solomon

**ORIGINAL AUDIENCE:**
Solomon's subjects in particular, and all people in general

**DATE WRITTEN:**
Probably around 935 B.C., late in Solomon's life

**SETTING:**
Solomon was looking back on his life, much of which was lived apart from God.

**KEY VERSE:**
"That's the whole story. Here now is my final conclusion: Fear God and obey his commands, for this is everyone's duty" (12:13).

THE CHOCOLATE bunny lies in the basket, surrounded by green paper "grass." With Easter morning eyes wide with anticipation, the little boy carefully lifts the candy figure and bites into one of the long ears. But the sweet taste fades quickly, and the child looks again at the candy in his hand. It's hollow!

Empty, futile, hollow, nothing—the words have a ring of disappointment and disillusionment. Yet this is the life experience of many. Grasping the sweet things—possessions, experience, power, and pleasure—they find nothing inside. Life is empty, meaningless—and they sink into despair.

Almost 3,000 years ago, Solomon spoke of this human dilemma; but the insights and applications of his message are relevant to our time. Ecclesiastes, Solomon's written sermon, is an analysis of life's experiences and a critical essay about life's true meaning. In this profound book, Solomon takes us on a reflective journey through his life, explaining how everything he had tried, tested, or tasted had been "meaningless"—useless, irrational, pointless, foolish, and empty—an exercise in futility. And remember, these words are from one who "had it all"—tremendous intellect, power, and wealth. After this biographical tour, Solomon made his triumphant conclusion: "Fear God and obey his commands, for this is everyone's duty. God will judge us for everything we do, including every secret thing, whether good or bad" (12:13, 14).

When Solomon became king, he asked God for wisdom (2 Chronicles 1:7–12), and he became the wisest man in the world (1 Kings 4:29–34). Solomon studied, taught, judged, and wrote. Kings and leaders from other nations came to Jerusalem to learn from him. But with all of his practical insight on life, Solomon failed to heed his own advice, and he began a downward spiral. Near the end of his life, Solomon looked back with an attitude of humility and repentance. He took stock of his life, hoping to spare his readers the bitterness of learning through personal experience that everything apart from God is empty, hollow, and meaningless.

Although the tone of Ecclesiastes is negative and pessimistic, we must not conclude that the only chapter worth reading and applying is the last one, where he draws his conclusions. In reality, the entire book is filled with practical wisdom (how to accomplish things in the world and stay out of trouble) and spiritual wisdom (how to find and know eternal values).

Solomon had a very honest approach. All of his remarks relating to the futility of life are there for a purpose: to lead us to seek fulfillment and happiness in God alone. He was not trying to destroy all hope, but to direct our hopes to the only one who can truly fulfill them and give our life meaning. Solomon affirms the value of knowledge, relationships, work, and pleasure, but only *in their proper place*. Everything temporal must be seen in light of the eternal.

Read Ecclesiastes and learn about life. Hear the stern warnings and dire predictions, and commit yourself to remember your Creator now (12:1).

## THE BLUEPRINT

1. Solomon's personal experience
   (1:1—2:26)
2. Solomon's general observations
   (3:1—5:20)
3. Solomon's practical counsel
   (6:1—8:17)
4. Solomon's final conclusion
   (9:1—12:14)

Ecclesiastes shows that certain paths in life lead to emptiness. This profound book also helps us discover true purpose in life. Such wisdom can spare us from the emptiness that results from a life without God. Solomon teaches that people will not find meaning in life through knowledge, money, pleasure, work, or popularity. True satisfaction comes from knowing that what we are doing is part of God's purpose for our life. This is a book that can help free us from our scramble for power, approval, and money, and draw us closer to God.

## MEGATHEMES

| THEME | EXPLANATION | IMPORTANCE |
|-------|-------------|------------|
| Searching | Solomon searched for satisfaction almost as though he was conducting a scientific experiment. Through this process, he discovered that life without God is a long and fruitless search for enjoyment, meaning, and fulfillment. True happiness is not in our power to attain because we always want more than we can have. In addition, there are circumstances beyond our control that can snatch away our possessions or attainments. | People are still searching. Yet the more they try to get, the more they realize how little they really have. No pleasure or happiness is possible without God. Without him, satisfaction is a lost search. Above everything we should strive to know and love God. He gives wisdom, knowledge, and joy. |
| Emptiness | Solomon shows how empty it is to pursue the pleasures that this life has to offer rather than seek to have a relationship with the eternal God. The search for pleasure, wealth, and success is ultimately disappointing. Nothing in the world can fill the emptiness and satisfy the deep longings in our restless hearts. | The cure for emptiness is to center on God. His love also can fill the emptiness of human experience. Fear God throughout your life, and fill your life with serving God and others rather than with selfish pleasures. |
| Work | Solomon tried to shake people's confidence in their own efforts, abilities, and wisdom and to direct them to faith in God as the only sound basis for living. Without God, there is no lasting reward or benefit in hard work. | Work done with the wrong attitude will leave us empty. But work accepted as an assignment from God can be seen as a gift. Examine what you expect from your efforts. God gives you abilities and opportunities to work so that you can use your time well. |
| Death | The certainty of death makes all human achievements futile. God has a plan for each one of us that goes beyond life and death. The reality of aging and dying reminds each individual of the end to come when God will judge each person's life. | Because life is short, we need wisdom that is greater than this world can offer. We need the words of God so we can live right. If we listen to him, his wisdom spares us the bitterness of futile human experience and gives us a hope that goes beyond death. |
| Wisdom | Human wisdom doesn't contain all the answers. Knowledge and education have their limits. To understand life and make right choices, we need the wisdom that can be found only in God's Word—the Bible. | When we realize that God will evaluate all that we do, we should learn to live wisely, remembering that he is present each day, and learn to obey his guidelines for living. But in order to have God's wisdom, we must first get to know and honor him. |

## 1. Solomon's personal experience

**1** These are the words of the Teacher,* King David's son, who ruled in Jerusalem.

*Everything Is Meaningless*

2 "Everything is meaningless," says the Teacher, "completely meaningless!"

3 What do people get for all their hard work under the sun? 4 Generations come and generations go, but the earth never changes. 5 The sun rises and the sun sets, then hurries around to rise again. 6 The wind blows south, and then turns north. Around and around it goes, blowing in circles. 7 Rivers run into the sea, but the sea is never full. Then the water returns again to the rivers and flows out again to the sea. 8 Everything is wearisome beyond description. No matter how much we see, we are never satisfied. No matter how much we hear, we are not content.

9 History merely repeats itself. It has all been done before. Nothing under the sun is truly new. 10 Sometimes people say, "Here is something new!" But actually it is old; nothing is ever truly new. 11 We don't remember what happened in the past, and in future generations, no one will remember what we are doing now.

*The Teacher Speaks: The Futility of Wisdom*

12 I, the Teacher, was king of Israel, and I lived in Jerusalem. 13 I devoted myself to search for understanding and to explore by wisdom everything being done under heaven. I soon discovered that God has dealt a tragic existence to the human race. 14 I observed everything going on under the sun, and really, it is all meaningless—like chasing the wind.

15 What is wrong cannot be made right.
　　What is missing cannot be recovered.

16 I said to myself, "Look, I am wiser than any of the kings who ruled in Jerusalem before me. I have greater wisdom and knowledge than any of them." 17 So I set out to learn everything from wisdom to madness and folly. But I learned firsthand that pursuing all this is like chasing the wind.

18 The greater my wisdom, the greater my grief.
　　To increase knowledge only increases sorrow.

1:1 Hebrew *Qoheleth;* this term is rendered "the Teacher" throughout this book.

| | |
|---|---|
| **1:1** Eccl 1:12; 7:27; 12:8-10 | |
| **1:2** Pss 39:5-6; 62:9; 144:4; Rom 8:20 | |
| **1:3** Eccl 2:11; 3:9; 5:16 | |
| **1:4** Pss 104:5; 119:90 | |
| **1:6** John 3:8 | |
| **1:8** Prov 27:20; Eccl 4:8 | |
| **1:9** Eccl 2:12; 3:15 | |
| **1:11** Eccl 2:16; 9:5 | |
| **1:12** Eccl 1:1; 7:27; 12:8-10 | |
| **1:13** Eccl 7:25; 8:17 | |
| **1:14** Eccl 2:11; 4:4; 6:9 | |
| **1:16** 1 Kgs 3:12; 4:30; 10:23 | |
| **1:17** Eccl 2:12; 7:25 | |
| **1:18** Eccl 12:12 | |

**1:1** The author, Solomon (the "king of Israel," see 1:12), referred to himself as the Teacher, or leader of the assembly. He was both assembling people to hear a message and gathering wise sayings (proverbs). Solomon, one person in the Bible who had everything (wisdom, power, riches, honor, reputation, God's favor), is the one who discussed the ultimate emptiness of all that this world has to offer. His purpose in this book is to make people realize that their confidence in their own efforts, abilities, and righteousness was meaningless. Instead, their commitment to God is the only reason for living.

**1:1-11** Solomon had a purpose for writing skeptically and pessimistically. Near the end of his life, looking back on everything he had done, he saw that most of it seemed meaningless. A common belief was that good people prospered and the wicked suffered, but that hadn't proven true in Solomon's experience. Solomon wrote this book after he had tried everything and achieved much, only to find that nothing apart from God made him happy. He wanted his readers to avoid these same senseless pursuits. If we try to find meaning in our accomplishments rather than in God, we will never be satisfied, and everything we pursue will become meaningless.

**1:2** Solomon's kingdom, Israel, was in its golden age, but Solomon wanted the people to understand that success and prosperity don't last long (Psalm 103:14-16; Isaiah 40:6-8; James 4:14). All human accomplishments will one day disappear; we must keep this in mind in order to live wisely. If we don't, we will become either proud and self-sufficient when we succeed or sorely disappointed when we fail. Solomon's goal was to show that earthly possessions and accomplishments are ultimately meaningless. Only the pursuit of God brings real satisfaction. We should honor God in all we say, think, and do.

**1:8-11** Many people feel restless and dissatisfied. They wonder: (1) If I am in God's will, why am I so tired and unfulfilled? (2) What is the meaning of life? (3) When I look back on it all, will I be happy with my accomplishments? (4) Why do I feel burned out, disillusioned, dry? (5) What is to become of me? Solomon tests our faith, challenging us to find true and lasting meaning in God alone. As you take a hard look at your life, as Solomon did his, you will see how important serving God is over all other options. Perhaps God is asking you to rethink your purpose and direction in life, just as Solomon did in Ecclesiastes.

**1:12-15** "What is wrong cannot be made right. What is missing cannot be recovered" refers to the ultimate perplexity and confusion that come to us because of all the unanswered questions in life. Solomon, writing about his own life, discovered that neither his accomplishments nor his wisdom could make him truly happy. True wisdom is found in God, and true happiness comes from pleasing him.

**1:16-18** The more you understand, the greater your pain and difficulty. For example, the more you know, the more imperfection you see around you; and the more you observe, the more evil becomes evident. As you set out with Solomon to find the meaning of life, you must be ready to feel more, think more, question more, hurt more, and do more. Are you ready to pay the price for wisdom?

**1:16-18** Solomon highlights two kinds of wisdom in the book of Ecclesiastes: (1) human knowledge, reasoning, or philosophy, and (2) the wisdom that comes from God. In these verses Solomon is talking about human knowledge. When human knowledge ignores God, it only highlights our problems because it can't provide answers without God's eternal perspective and solution.

### The Futility of Pleasure

**2** I said to myself, "Come on, let's try pleasure. Let's look for the 'good things' in life." But I found that this, too, was meaningless. [2] So I said, "Laughter is silly. What good does it do to seek pleasure?" [3] After much thought, I decided to cheer myself with wine. And while still seeking wisdom, I clutched at foolishness. In this way, I tried to experience the only happiness most people find during their brief life in this world.

[4] I also tried to find meaning by building huge homes for myself and by planting beautiful vineyards. [5] I made gardens and parks, filling them with all kinds of fruit trees. [6] I built reservoirs to collect the water to irrigate my many flourishing groves. [7] I bought slaves, both men and women, and others were born into my household. I also owned large herds and flocks, more than any of the kings who had lived in Jerusalem before me. [8] I collected great sums of silver and gold, the treasure of many kings and provinces. I hired wonderful singers, both men and women, and had many beautiful concubines. I had everything a man could desire!

[9] So I became greater than all who had lived in Jerusalem before me, and my wisdom never failed me. [10] Anything I wanted, I would take. I denied myself no pleasure. I even found great pleasure in hard work, a reward for all my labors. [11] But as I looked at everything I had worked so hard to accomplish, it was all so meaningless—like chasing the wind. There was nothing really worthwhile anywhere.

### The Wise and the Foolish

[12] So I decided to compare wisdom with foolishness and madness (for who can do this better than I, the king?*). [13] I thought, "Wisdom is better than foolishness, just as light is better than darkness. [14] For the wise can see where they are going, but fools walk in the dark." Yet I saw that the wise and the foolish share the same fate. [15] Both will die. So I said to myself, "Since I will end up the same as the fool, what's the value of all my wisdom? This is all so meaningless!" [16] For the wise and the foolish both die. The wise will not be remembered any longer than the fool. In the days to come, both will be forgotten.

[17] So I came to hate life because everything done here under the sun is so troubling. Everything is meaningless—like chasing the wind.

**2:12** The meaning of the Hebrew is uncertain.

---

**2:1ff** Solomon conducted his search for life's meaning as an experiment. He first tried pursuing pleasure. He undertook great projects, bought slaves and herds and flocks, amassed wealth, acquired singers, added many concubines to his harem, and became the greatest person in Jerusalem. But none of these gave him satisfaction: "But as I looked at everything I had worked so hard to accomplish, it was all so meaningless—like chasing the wind. There was nothing really worthwhile anywhere" (2:11). Some of the pleasures Solomon sought were wrong, and some were worthy; but even the worthy pursuits were futile when he pursued them as an end in themselves. We must look beyond our activities to the reasons we do them and the purpose they fulfill. Is your goal in life to search for meaning or to pursue God, who gives meaning?

**2:4-6** Solomon had built houses, the Temple, a kingdom, and a family (see 1 Kings 3–11). In the course of history, they all would be ruined. In Psalm 127:1, Solomon wrote, "Unless the LORD builds a house, the work of the builders is wasted. Unless the LORD protects a city, guarding it with sentries will do no good." This book is part of Solomon's testimony as to what happens to a kingdom or family that forgets God. As you examine your projects or goals, what is your starting point, your motivation? Without God as your foundation, all you are living for is meaningless.

**2:11** Solomon summarized his many attempts at finding life's meaning as "chasing the wind." We feel the wind as it passes, but we can't catch hold of it or keep it. In all our accomplishments, even the big ones, our good feelings are only temporary. Security and self-worth are found, not in these accomplishments, but far beyond them in the love of God. Think about what you consider worthwhile—where you place your time, energy, and money. Will you one day look back and decide that you, too, were "chasing the wind"?

**2:16** Solomon realized that wisdom alone cannot guarantee eternal life. Wisdom, riches, and personal achievement matter very little after death—and everyone must die. We must not build our life on perishable pursuits, but on the solid foundation of God. Then even if everything we have is taken away, we still will have God, who is all we really need anyway. This is the point of the book of Job (see the introduction to Job).

**2:16** Is death the ultimate equalizer of all people, no matter what they attained in life? While this appears to be true from an earthly perspective, God makes it clear (as Solomon later points out in 12:14) that what we do here has a great impact upon our eternal reward.

**2:17** As king, Solomon had everything a person could want, but here he says that he "came to hate life." What happened? His marvelous accomplishments left him sour because he pursued them as a means to personal satisfaction. Personal satisfaction, by itself, is empty because we are alone in the enjoyment we receive. What is your attitude about what you do? If your goals are to satisfy only yourself, you will find yourself empty, seeking one thing after another, as Solomon did. If your goal is to serve God and others, then you will experience a full life, one that won't leave you sour.

## The Futility of Work

18I came to hate all my hard work here on earth, for I must leave to others everything I have earned. 19And who can tell whether my successors will be wise or foolish? Yet they will control everything I have gained by my skill and hard work under the sun. How meaningless! 20So I gave up in despair, questioning the value of all my hard work in this world.

21Some people work wisely with knowledge and skill, then must leave the fruit of their efforts to someone who hasn't worked for it. This, too, is meaningless, a great tragedy. 22So what do people get in this life for all their hard work and anxiety? 23Their days of labor are filled with pain and grief; even at night their minds cannot rest. It is all meaningless.

24So I decided there is nothing better than to enjoy food and drink and to find satisfaction in work. Then I realized that these pleasures are from the hand of God. 25For who can eat or enjoy anything apart from him?* 26God gives wisdom, knowledge, and joy to those who please him. But if a sinner becomes wealthy, God takes the wealth away and gives it to those who please him. This, too, is meaningless—like chasing the wind.

## 2. Solomon's general observations

### A Time for Everything

**3** 1 For everything there is a season,
　　a time for every activity under heaven.
2 A time to be born and a time to die.
　　A time to plant and a time to harvest.
3 A time to kill and a time to heal.
　　A time to tear down and a time to build up.
4 A time to cry and a time to laugh.
　　A time to grieve and a time to dance.
5 A time to scatter stones and a time to gather stones.
　　A time to embrace and a time to turn away.
6 A time to search and a time to quit searching.
　　A time to keep and a time to throw away.
7 A time to tear and a time to mend.
　　A time to be quiet and a time to speak.
8 A time to love and a time to hate.
　　A time for war and a time for peace.

9What do people really get for all their hard work? 10I have seen the burden God has placed on us all. 11Yet God has made everything beautiful for its own time. He has planted eternity in the human heart, but even so, people cannot see the whole scope of God's work from beginning to end. 12So I concluded there is nothing better than to be happy and enjoy

**2:18**
Pss 39:6; 49:10
Eccl 2:11
**2:21**
Eccl 2:18; 4:4
**2:22**
Eccl 1:3
**2:23**
Job 5:7; 14:1
Ps 127:2
Eccl 1:18
**2:24**
Eccl 2:3; 3:12, 22;
5:18; 6:12; 8:15;
9:7
**2:26**
Job 27:16-17; 32:8
Eccl 1:14

**3:1**
Eccl 3:17; 8:6
**3:2**
Heb 9:27
**3:4**
Exod 15:20
Ps 126:2
Rom 12:15
**3:7**
Amos 5:13
**3:8**
Ps 101:3
**3:9**
Eccl 1:3; 2:11; 5:16
**3:10**
Eccl 1:13; 2:26
**3:11**
Gen 1:31
Job 5:9
Eccl 8:17
Rom 11:33
**3:12**
Eccl 2:24

**2:25** As in Greek and Syriac versions; Hebrew reads *apart from me?*

---

**2:18-23** Solomon continued to show that hard work bears no lasting fruit for those who work solely to earn money and gain possessions. Not only will everything be left behind at death, but it may be left to those who have done nothing to earn it. In addition, it may not be well cared for, and all that was gained may be lost. In fact, Solomon's son, who inherited his throne, immediately made a foolish decision which split the kingdom—see 1 Kings 12. Hard work done with proper motives (caring for your family, serving God) is not wrong. We must work to survive, and, more important, we are responsible for the physical and spiritual well-being of those under our care. But the fruit of hard work done to glorify only ourselves will be passed on to those who may later lose or spoil it all. Such toil often leads to grief, while serving God leads to everlasting joy. Do you know the real reason you are working so hard?

**2:24-26** Is Solomon recommending we make life a big, irresponsible party? No, he is encouraging us to take pleasure in what we're doing now and to enjoy life because it comes from God's hand. True enjoyment in life comes only as we follow God's guidelines for living. Without him, satisfaction is a lost search. Those who really know how to enjoy life are the ones who take life each day as a gift from God, thanking him for it and serving him in it. Those without God will have no relief from toil and no direction to guide them through life's complications.

**3:1–5:20** Solomon's point in this section is that God has a plan for all people. Thus, he provides cycles of life, each with its work for us to do. Although we may face many problems that seem to contradict God's plan, these should not be barriers to believing in him, but rather opportunities to discover that, without God, life's problems have no lasting solutions!

**3:1-8** Timing is important. All the experiences listed in these verses are appropriate at certain times. The secret to peace with God is to discover, accept, and appreciate God's perfect timing. The danger is to doubt or resent God's timing. This can lead to despair, rebellion, or moving ahead without his advice.

**3:8** When is the time for hating? We shouldn't hate evil people, but we should hate what they do. We should also hate it when people are mistreated, when children are starving, and when God is being dishonored. In addition, we must hate the sin in our life—this is God's attitude (see Psalm 5:5).

**3:9-13** Your ability to find satisfaction in your work depends to a large extent upon your attitude. You will become dissatisfied if you lose the sense of purpose God intended for your work. We can enjoy our work if we (1) remember that God has given us work to do (3:10), and (2) realize that the fruit of our labor is a gift from him (3:13). See your work as a way to serve God.

**3:13**
Eccl 5:19

ourselves as long as we can. ¹³And people should eat and drink and enjoy the fruits of their labor, for these are gifts from God.

**3:14**
Eccl 5:7; 7:18;
8:12-13; 12:13

**3:15**
Eccl 1:9; 6:10

¹⁴And I know that whatever God does is final. Nothing can be added to it or taken from it. God's purpose is that people should fear him. ¹⁵What is happening now has happened before, and what will happen in the future has happened before, because God makes the same things happen over and over again.

**3:17**
Gen 18:25
Pss 96:13; 98:9
Matt 16:27
Rom 2:6-10
2 Thes 1:6-9

### The Injustices of Life

¹⁶I also noticed that under the sun there is evil in the courtroom. Yes, even the courts of law are corrupt! ¹⁷I said to myself, "In due season God will judge everyone, both good and bad, for all their deeds."

**3:18**
Pss 49:12, 20;
73:22

**3:20**
Gen 3:19
Ps 103:14
Eccl 12:7

**3:22**
Eccl 2:18, 24; 6:12;
8:7; 10:14

¹⁸I also thought about the human condition—how God proves to people that they are like animals. ¹⁹For people and animals share the same fate—both breathe* and both must die. So people have no real advantage over the animals. How meaningless! ²⁰Both go to the same place—they came from dust and they return to dust. ²¹For who can prove that the human spirit goes up and the spirit of animals goes down into the earth? ²²So I saw that there is nothing better for people than to be happy in their work. That is why we are here! No one will bring us back from death to enjoy life after we die.

**4:1**
Isa 5:7
Lam 1:9

**4:2**
Job 3:11-26
Eccl 2:17

**4** Again, I observed all the oppression that takes place under the sun. I saw the tears of the oppressed, with no one to comfort them. The oppressors have great power, and their victims are helpless. ²So I concluded that the dead are better off than the living. ³But most fortunate of all are those who are not yet born. For they have not seen all the evil that is done under the sun.

**4:4**
Eccl 1:14; 2:21

⁴Then I observed that most people are motivated to success because they envy their neighbors. But this, too, is meaningless—like chasing the wind.

**4:5**
Prov 6:10; 24:33
Isa 9:20

⁵ "Fools fold their idle hands,
    leading them to ruin."

**3:19** Or *both have the same spirit.*

---

**3:11** God has "planted eternity in the human heart." This means that we can never be completely satisfied with earthly pleasures and pursuits. Because we are created in God's image, (1) we have a spiritual thirst, (2) we have eternal value, and (3) nothing but the eternal God can truly satisfy us. God has built in us a restless yearning for the kind of perfect world that can only be found in his perfect rule. He has given us a glimpse of the perfection of his creation. But it is only a glimpse; we cannot see into the future or comprehend everything. So we must trust God now and do his work on earth.

**3:12** To be happy and do good are worthy goals for life, but we can pursue them in the wrong way. God wants us to enjoy life. When we have the proper view of God, we discover that real pleasure is found in enjoying whatever we have as gifts from God, not in what we accumulate.

**3:14** What is the purpose of life? It is that we should fear the all-powerful God. To *fear* God means to respect and stand in awe of him because of who he is. Purpose in life starts with *whom* we know, not what we know or how good we are. It is impossible to fulfill your God-given purpose unless you revere God and give him first place in your life.

**3:16** Evil and corruption sit in the place where justice should be, thus affecting the legal system. Solomon asked how God's plan can be perfect when so much injustice and oppression exist in the world (4:1). He concluded that God does not ignore injustice but will bring it to an end at his appointed time (12:13, 14).

**3:16ff** Solomon reflects on several apparent contradictions in God's control of the world: (1) There is evil and corruption where there should be justice (3:16, 17); (2) people created in God's image die just like the animals (3:18-21); (3) no one comforts the oppressed (4:1-3); (4) many people are motivated by envy (4:4-6); (5) people are lonely (4:7-12); (6) recognition

for accomplishments is temporary (4:13-16). It is easy to use such contradictions as excuses to not believe in God. But Solomon used them to show how we can honestly look at life's problems and still keep our faith. This life is not all there is, yet even in this life we should not pass judgment on God because we don't know everything. God's plan is for us to live forever with him. So live with eternal values in view, realizing that all contradictions will one day be cleared up by the Creator himself (12:14).

**3:19-22** Our bodies can't live forever in their present state. In that sense, humans and animals are alike. But Solomon acknowledged that God has given people the hope of eternity (see the note on 3:11), and that we will undergo judgment in the next life (3:17; 12:7, 14)—making us different from animals. Because we have eternity planted in our hearts, we have a unique purpose in God's overall plan. Yet we cannot discover God's purpose for our lives by our own efforts—only through building a relationship with him and seeking his guidance. Are you now living as God wants? Do you see life as a gift from him?

**4:4-6** Some people are lazy while others are workaholics. Lazy people, seeing the futility of dashing about for success, idle away their time and hurt both themselves and those who depend on them. Workaholics are often driven by envy, greed, and a constant desire to stay ahead of everyone else. Both extremes are foolish and irresponsible. The answer is to work hard but with moderation. Take time to enjoy the other gifts God has given, and realize that it is God who gives out the assignments and the rewards, not us.

6And yet,

"Better to have one handful with quietness
  than two handfuls with hard work
  and chasing the wind."

## The Advantages of Companionship

7I observed yet another example of something meaningless under the sun. 8This is the case of a man who is all alone, without a child or a brother, yet who works hard to gain as much wealth as he can. But then he asks himself, "Who am I working for? Why am I giving up so much pleasure now?" It is all so meaningless and depressing.

9Two people are better off than one, for they can help each other succeed. 10If one person falls, the other can reach out and help. But someone who falls alone is in real trouble. 11Likewise, two people lying close together can keep each other warm. But how can one be warm alone? 12A person standing alone can be attacked and defeated, but two can stand back-to-back and conquer. Three are even better, for a triple-braided cord is not easily broken.

## The Futility of Political Power

13It is better to be a poor but wise youth than an old and foolish king who refuses all advice. 14Such a youth could rise from poverty and succeed. He might even become king, though he has been in prison. 15But then everyone rushes to the side of yet another youth* who replaces him. 16Endless crowds stand around him,* but then another generation grows up and rejects him, too. So it is all meaningless—like chasing the wind.

## Approaching God with Care

**5** 1*As you enter the house of God, keep your ears open and your mouth shut. It is evil to make mindless offerings to God. 2*Don't make rash promises, and don't be hasty in bringing matters before God. After all, God is in heaven, and you are here on earth. So let your words be few.

3 Too much activity gives you restless dreams; too many words make you a fool.

4When you make a promise to God, don't delay in following through, for God takes no pleasure in fools. Keep all the promises you make to him. 5It is better to say nothing than to make a promise and not keep it. 6Don't let your mouth make you sin. And don't defend yourself by telling the Temple messenger that the promise you made was a mistake. That would make God angry, and he might wipe out everything you have achieved.

7 Talk is cheap, like daydreams and other useless activities. Fear God instead.

## The Futility of Wealth

8Don't be surprised if you see a poor person being oppressed by the powerful and if justice is being miscarried throughout the land. For every official is under orders from higher up, and matters of justice get lost in red tape and bureaucracy. 9Even the king milks the land for his own profit!*

10Those who love money will never have enough. How meaningless to think that wealth brings true happiness! 11The more you have, the more people come to help you spend it. So what good is wealth—except perhaps to watch it slip through your fingers!

**4:6**
Prov 15:16-17; 16:8

**4:8**
Prov 27:20
Eccl 1:8; 2:21

**4:11**
1 Kgs 1:1-4

**4:13**
Eccl 7:19; 9:15

**4:14**
Gen 41:14, 41-43

**4:16**
Eccl 1:14

**5:1**
Exod 3:5; 30:18-20
1 Sam 15:22
Prov 15:8; 21:27

**5:2**
Prov 10:19; 20:25
Matt 6:7

**5:4**
Num 30:2
Pss 50:14;
66:13-14; 76:11

**5:5**
Prov 20:25
Acts 5:4

**5:6**
Lev 4:2, 22
Num 15:25

**5:7**
Eccl 3:14; 12:13

**5:8**
Ps 12:5
Eccl 4:1
Ezek 18:18
1 Pet 4:12

**5:10**
Eccl 2:10-11

**5:11**
Eccl 2:9

---

**4:15** Hebrew *the second youth.*    **4:16** Hebrew *There is no end to all the people, to all those who are before them.*
**5:1** Verse 5:1 is numbered 4:17 in Hebrew text.    **5:2** Verses 5:2-20 are numbered 5:1-19 in Hebrew text.    **5:9** The meaning of the Hebrew in verses 8 and 9 is uncertain.

---

**4:9-12** Cooperating with others has advantages. Life is designed for companionship, not isolation, for intimacy, not loneliness. Some people prefer isolation, thinking they cannot trust anyone. We are not here on earth to serve ourselves, however, but to serve God and others. Don't isolate yourself and try to go it alone. Seek companions; be a team member.

**4:13-16** Advancement or getting to the top is meaningless. Position, popularity, and prestige are poor goals for a life's work. Although many pursue them, they are shadows without substance. Many people seek recognition for their accomplishments; but people are fickle, changing quickly and easily. How much better to seek God's approval. His love never changes.

**5:1** When we enter the house of God, we should have the attitude of being open and ready to listen to God, not to dictate to him what we think he should do.

**5:4, 5** Solomon warns his readers about making foolish promises to God. In Israelite culture, making vows was a serious matter. Vows were voluntary, but once made, they were unbreakable (Deuteronomy 23:21-23). It is foolish to make a vow you cannot keep or to play games with God by only partially fulfilling your vow (Proverbs 20:25). It's better not to vow than to make a vow to God and break it. If you make a vow, keep it. (See the note on Matthew 5:33ff.)

**5:10, 11** We always want more than we have. Solomon observed that those who spend their lives obsessively seeking after money never find the happiness it promises. Wealth attracts freeloaders and thieves, causes sleeplessness and fear, and ultimately ends in loss because it must be left behind (Mark 10:23-25; Luke 12:16-21). No matter how much you earn, if you try to create happiness by accumulating wealth, you will never have enough. Money in itself

5:12
Prov 3:24

5:13
Eccl 6:2

5:15
Job 1:21
Ps 49:17
1 Tim 6:7

5:16
Prov 11:29
Eccl 1:3; 2:11; 3:9

5:17
Eccl 2:23

5:18
Eccl 2:10, 24

5:19
2 Chr 1:12
Eccl 3:13; 6:2

[12]People who work hard sleep well, whether they eat little or much. But the rich seldom get a good night's sleep.

[13]There is another serious problem I have seen under the sun. Hoarding riches harms the saver. [14]Money is put into risky investments that turn sour, and everything is lost. In the end, there is nothing left to pass on to one's children. [15]We all come to the end of our lives as naked and empty-handed as on the day we were born. We can't take our riches with us.

[16]And this, too, is a very serious problem. People leave this world no better off than when they came. All their hard work is for nothing—like working for the wind. [17]Throughout their lives, they live under a cloud—frustrated, discouraged, and angry.

[18]Even so, I have noticed one thing, at least, that is good. It is good for people to eat, drink, and enjoy their work under the sun during the short life God has given them, and to accept their lot in life. [19]And it is a good thing to receive wealth from God and the good health to enjoy it. To enjoy your work and accept your lot in life—this is indeed a gift from God. [20]God keeps such people so busy enjoying life that they take no time to brood over the past.

### 3. Solomon's practical counsel

6:1
Eccl 5:13

6:2
1 Kgs 3:13
Pss 17:14; 73:7

**6** There is another serious tragedy I have seen under the sun, and it weighs heavily on humanity. [2]God gives some people great wealth and honor and everything they could ever want, but then he doesn't give them the chance to enjoy these things. They die, and someone else, even a stranger, ends up enjoying their wealth! This is meaningless—a sickening tragedy.

6:3
Job 3:16
Eccl 4:3
Isa 14:20
Matt 26:24

6:6
Eccl 2:14

[3]A man might have a hundred children and live to be very old. But if he finds no satisfaction in life and doesn't even get a decent burial, it would have been better for him to be born dead. [4]His birth would have been meaningless, and he would have ended in darkness. He wouldn't even have had a name, [5]and he would never have seen the sun or known of its existence. Yet he would have had more peace than in growing up to be an unhappy man. [6]He might live a thousand years twice over but still not find contentment. And since he must die like everyone else—well, what's the use?

6:7
Prov 16:26

6:8
Eccl 2:15

6:9
Eccl 1:14; 11:9

[7]All people spend their lives scratching for food, but they never seem to have enough. [8]So are wise people really better off than fools? Do poor people gain anything by being wise and knowing how to act in front of others?

[9]Enjoy what you have rather than desiring what you don't have. Just dreaming about nice things is meaningless—like chasing the wind.

*The Future—Determined and Unknown*

6:10
Gen 3:17-19
Job 9:32; 40:2
Eccl 1:9; 3:15
Isa 45:9

6:11
Hos 12:1

[10]Everything has already been decided. It was known long ago what each person would be. So there's no use arguing with God about your destiny.

[11]The more words you speak, the less they mean. So what good are they?

[12]In the few days of our meaningless lives, who knows how our days can best be spent? Our lives are like a shadow. Who can tell what will happen on this earth after we are gone?

---

is not wrong, but loving money leads to all sorts of sin. Whatever your financial situation, don't depend on money to make you happy. Instead, use what you have for the Lord.

**5:19, 20** God wants us to view what we have (whether it is much or little) with the right perspective—our possessions are a gift from God. Although they are not the source of joy, they are a reason to rejoice because every good thing comes from God. We should focus more on the Giver than the gift. We can be content with what we have when we realize that in God we have everything we need.

**6:1–8:15** In this section, Solomon shows that having the right attitude about God can help us deal with present injustices. Prosperity is not always good, and adversity is not always bad. But God is always good; if we live as he wants us to, we will be content.

**6:1-6** This person has died without being able to enjoy his wealth and honor. Everyone dies, and both rich and poor end up in the grave. Many people work hard to prolong life and improve their physical condition. Yet people spend little time or effort on their spiritual health. How shortsighted it is to work hard to extend this life and not take the time to prepare for eternity.

**6:10** God knows and directs everything that happens, and he is in complete control over our lives, even though at times it may not seem that way. How foolish it is for us to contend with our Creator, who knows us completely and can see the future. (See also Jeremiah 18:6; Romans 9:19-24.)

**6:12** Solomon is stating the profound truth that we cannot predict what the future holds. The only One who knows what will happen after we're gone is God. No human knows the future, so each day must be lived for its own value. Solomon is arguing against the notion that human beings can take charge of their own destiny. In all our plans we should look up to God, not just ahead to the future.

## Wisdom for Life

**7** ¹ A good reputation is more valuable than costly perfume.
  And the day you die is better than the day you are born.
² Better to spend your time at funerals than at parties.
  After all, everyone dies—
  so the living should take this to heart.
³ Sorrow is better than laughter,
  for sadness has a refining influence on us.
⁴ A wise person thinks a lot about death,
  while a fool thinks only about having a good time.

⁵ Better to be criticized by a wise person
  than to be praised by a fool.
⁶ A fool's laughter is quickly gone,
  like thorns crackling in a fire.
  This also is meaningless.

⁷ Extortion turns wise people into fools,
  and bribes corrupt the heart.

⁸ Finishing is better than starting.
  Patience is better than pride.

⁹ Control your temper,
  for anger labels you a fool.

¹⁰ Don't long for "the good old days."
  This is not wise.

¹¹ Wisdom is even better when you have money.
  Both are a benefit as you go through life.
¹² Wisdom and money can get you almost anything,
  but only wisdom can save your life.

¹³ Accept the way God does things,
  for who can straighten what he has made crooked?
¹⁴ Enjoy prosperity while you can,
  but when hard times strike, realize that both come from God.
  Remember that nothing is certain in this life.

## The Limits of Human Wisdom

¹⁵I have seen everything in this meaningless life, including the death of good young people and the long life of wicked people. ¹⁶So don't be too good or too wise! Why destroy yourself?

| | |
|---|---|
| | **7:1** Prov 22:1 |
| | **7:2** Ps 90:12 |
| | **7:3** 2 Cor 7:10 |
| | **7:5** Ps 141:5 Prov 6:23; 13:18; 15:31-32; 25:12 |
| | **7:7** Exod 23:8 Deut 16:19 Prov 17:23 |
| | **7:8** Prov 14:29; 16:32 Gal 5:22 Eph 4:2 |
| | **7:9** Prov 14:17 Jas 1:19 |
| | **7:12** Prov 3:18; 8:35 |
| | **7:13** Eccl 1:15; 3:11; 8:17 |
| | **7:14** Deut 8:5; 26:11 Eccl 3:22; 9:7; 11:9 |
| | **7:15** Eccl 6:12; 8:12-14; 9:9 |

**7:1-4** This seems to contradict Solomon's previous advice to eat, drink, and find satisfaction in one's work—to enjoy what God has given. We are to enjoy what we have while we can but realize that adversity also strikes. Adversity reminds us that life is short, teaches us to live wisely, and refines our character. Christianity and Judaism see value in suffering and sorrow. The Greeks and Romans despised it; Eastern religions seek to live above it; but Christians and Jews see it as a refining fire. Most would agree that we learn more about God from difficult times than from happy times. Do you try to avoid sorrow and suffering at all cost? See your struggles as great opportunities to learn from God.

**7:2, 4** Many people avoid thinking about death, refuse to face it, and are reluctant to attend funerals. Solomon is not encouraging us to think morbidly, but he knows that it is helpful to think clearly about death. It reminds us that we still have time to change, time to examine the direction of our lives, and time to confess our sins and find forgiveness from God. Because everyone will eventually die, it makes sense to plan ahead to experience God's mercy rather than his justice.

**7:7** Money talks, and it can confuse those who would otherwise judge fairly. We hear about bribes given to judges, police officers, and witnesses. Bribes are given to hurt those who tell the truth

and help those who oppose it. People who are involved in extortion or take bribes are indeed fools, no matter how wise they thought they were beforehand. It is said that everyone has a price, but those who are truly wise cannot be bought at any price.

**7:8** To finish what we start takes hard work, wisdom, self-discipline, and patience. Anyone with vision can start a big project. But vision without wisdom will result in unfinished projects and goals.

**7:14** God allows both good times and bad times to come to everyone. He blends them in our lives in such a way that we can't predict the future or count on human wisdom and power. We usually give ourselves the credit for the good times. Then in bad times, we tend to blame God without thanking him for the good that comes out of it. When life appears certain and controllable, don't let self-satisfaction or complacency make you too comfortable, or God may allow bad times to drive you back to him. When life seems uncertain and uncontrollable, don't despair—God is in control and will bring good results out of your struggles.

**7:16-18** How can a person be too good or too wise? This is a warning against pride—legalism or false righteousness. Solomon was saying that some people become so good or wise *in their own eyes* that they become deluded by their own religious acts. They are so rigid or narrow in their views that they lose their

**7:18**
Eccl 3:14; 5:7;
8:12-13

**7:20**
1 Kgs 8:46
2 Chr 6:36
Ps 143:2
Prov 20:9
Rom 3:23

**7:24**
Deut 30:11-14
Job 11:7; 37:23
Rom 11:33

**7:25**
Eccl 1:17

**7:26**
Prov 5:4; 6:23-24;
7:23; 22:14

**7:28**
1 Kgs 11:3

**7:29**
Gen 1:27

**8:1**
Exod 34:29-30

**8:2**
Exod 22:11
2 Sam 21:7
Ezek 17:18

**8:4**
Dan 4:35

**8:5**
Exod 1:17-21
Prov 12:21

**8:6**
Eccl 3:1, 17, 22

**8:8**
Deut 20:5-8
Ps 49:7-9

**8:9**
Eccl 4:1, 16; 5:8

**8:11**
Exod 34:6
Ps 86:15
Rom 2:4-5
2 Pet 3:9

[17]On the other hand, don't be too wicked either. Don't be a fool! Why die before your time? [18]Pay attention to these instructions, for anyone who fears God will avoid both extremes.*

[19]One wise person is stronger than ten leading citizens of a town!

[20]Not a single person on earth is always good and never sins.

[21]Don't eavesdrop on others—you may hear your servant curse you. [22]For you know how often you yourself have cursed others.

[23]I have always tried my best to let wisdom guide my thoughts and actions. I said to myself, "I am determined to be wise." But it didn't work. [24]Wisdom is always distant and difficult to find. [25]I searched everywhere, determined to find wisdom and to understand the reason for things. I was determined to prove to myself that wickedness is stupid and that foolishness is madness.

[26]I discovered that a seductive woman* is a trap more bitter than death. Her passion is a snare, and her soft hands are chains. Those who are pleasing to God will escape her, but sinners will be caught in her snare.

[27]"This is my conclusion," says the Teacher. "I discovered this after looking at the matter from every possible angle. [28]Though I have searched repeatedly, I have not found what I was looking for. Only one out of a thousand men is virtuous, but not one woman! [29]But I did find this: God created people to be virtuous, but they have each turned to follow their own downward path."

# 8

[1]How wonderful to be wise,
to analyze and interpret things.
Wisdom lights up a person's face,
softening its harshness.

## Obedience to the King

[2]Obey the king since you vowed to God that you would. [3]Don't try to avoid doing your duty, and don't stand with those who plot evil, for the king can do whatever he wants. [4]His command is backed by great power. No one can resist or question it. [5]Those who obey him will not be punished. Those who are wise will find a time and a way to do what is right, [6]for there is a time and a way for everything, even when a person is in trouble.

[7]Indeed, how can people avoid what they don't know is going to happen? [8]None of us can hold back our spirit from departing. None of us has the power to prevent the day of our death. There is no escaping that obligation, that dark battle. And in the face of death, wickedness will certainly not rescue the wicked.

## The Wicked and the Righteous

[9]I have thought deeply about all that goes on here under the sun, where people have the power to hurt each other. [10]I have seen wicked people buried with honor. Yet they were the very ones who frequented the Temple and are now praised* in the same city where they committed their crimes! This, too, is meaningless. [11]When a crime is not punished quickly,

**7:18** Or *will follow them both.*   **7:26** Hebrew *a woman.*   **8:10** As in some Hebrew manuscripts and Greek version; many Hebrew manuscripts read *and are forgotten.*

---

sensitivity to the true reason for being good—to honor God. Balance is important. God created us to be whole people who seek his righteousness and goodness. Thus, we should avoid both extremes of legalism and immorality.

**7:23-25** Solomon, the wisest man in the world, confesses how difficult it has been to act and think wisely. He emphasizes that no matter how much we know, some mysteries we will never understand. So thinking you have wisdom is a sure sign that you don't.

**7:27, 28** Did Solomon think women were not capable of being virtuous (wise and good)? No, because in the book of Proverbs he personified wisdom as a responsible woman. The point of Solomon's statement is not that women are unwise, but that hardly anyone, man or woman, is upright before God. In his search, Solomon found that goodness and wisdom were almost as scarce among men as among women, even though men were given a religious education program in his culture and women were not. In effect, the verse is saying, "I have found only one in a thousand people who is wise in God's eyes. No, I have found even fewer than that!"

**8:1** Wisdom is the ability to see life from God's perspective and then to know the best course of action to take. Most people would agree that wisdom is a valuable asset, but how can we acquire it? Proverbs 9:10 teaches that the fear of the Lord (respect and honor) is the beginning of wisdom. Wisdom comes from knowing and trusting God; it is not merely the way to find God. Knowing God will lead to understanding and then to sharing this knowledge with others.

**8:10** This verse probably refers to how we quickly forget the evil done by some people after they have died. Returning from the cemetery, we praise them in the very city where they did their evil deeds.

**8:11** If God doesn't punish us immediately for sin, we must not assume that he doesn't care or that sin has no consequences. When a young child does something wrong and is not punished, that child will be much more likely to repeat the act. Remember, God knows every wrong we commit, and one day we will have to answer for all that we have done (12:14).

people feel it is safe to do wrong. ¹²But even though a person sins a hundred times and still lives a long time, I know that those who fear God will be better off. ¹³The wicked will not prosper, for they do not fear God. Their days will never grow long like the evening shadows.

¹⁴And this is not all that is meaningless in our world. In this life, good people are often treated as though they were wicked, and wicked people are often treated as though they were good. This is so meaningless!

¹⁵So I recommend having fun, because there is nothing better for people in this world than to eat, drink, and enjoy life. That way they will experience some happiness along with all the hard work God gives them under the sun.

¹⁶In my search for wisdom and in my observation of people's burdens here on earth, I discovered that there is ceaseless activity, day and night. ¹⁷I realized that no one can discover everything God is doing under the sun. Not even the wisest people discover everything, no matter what they claim.

## 4. Solomon's final conclusion
### Death Comes to All

**9** This, too, I carefully explored: Even though the actions of godly and wise people are in God's hands, no one knows whether God will show them favor. ²The same destiny ultimately awaits everyone, whether righteous or wicked, good or bad,* ceremonially clean or unclean, religious or irreligious. Good people receive the same treatment as sinners, and people who make promises to God are treated like people who don't.

³It seems so tragic that everyone under the sun suffers the same fate. That is why people are not more careful to be good. Instead, they choose their own mad course, for they have no hope. There is nothing ahead but death anyway. ⁴There is hope only for the living. As they say, "It's better to be a live dog than a dead lion!"

⁵The living at least know they will die, but the dead know nothing. They have no further reward, nor are they remembered. ⁶Whatever they did in their lifetime—loving, hating, envying—is all long gone. They no longer play a part in anything here on earth. ⁷So go ahead. Eat your food with joy, and drink your wine with a happy heart, for God approves of this! ⁸Wear fine clothes, with a splash of cologne!

⁹Live happily with the woman you love through all the meaningless days of life that God has given you under the sun. The wife God gives you is your reward for all your earthly toil. ¹⁰Whatever you do, do well. For when you go to the grave,* there will be no work or planning or knowledge or wisdom.

¹¹I have observed something else under the sun. The fastest runner doesn't always win the race, and the strongest warrior doesn't always win the battle. The wise sometimes go hungry, and the skillful are not necessarily wealthy. And those who are educated don't always lead successful lives. It is all decided by chance, by being in the right place at the right time.

**9:2** As in Greek and Syriac versions and Latin Vulgate; Hebrew lacks *or bad.*   **9:10** Hebrew *to Sheol.*

### Cross references

**8:12** Deut 4:40; Ps 37:11; Prov 1:33; Isa 3:10

**8:13** Isa 3:11

**8:14** Job 21:7; Ps 73:3, 12; Jer 12:1; Mal 3:15

**8:16** Eccl 1:13-14

**9:1** Deut 33:3; Eccl 9:6; 10:14

**9:2** Job 9:22; Eccl 2:14; 3:19; 6:6; 7:2

**9:3** Eccl 1:17; 8:11; 9:2

**9:5** Job 14:21; Ps 88:12; Isa 26:14

**9:7** Eccl 2:24

**9:8** Ps 23:5; Rev 3:4

**9:9** Eccl 6:12; 7:15

**9:10** Gen 37:35; Job 21:13; Rom 12:11; Col 3:23

**9:11** Deut 8:17-18; 1 Sam 6:9; 2 Chr 20:15; Ps 76:5; Amos 2:14-15; Zech 4:6

---

**8:15** Solomon recommends the remedy for life's unanswered questions: joy and contentment. We must accept each day with its measure of work, food, and pleasure. Let us learn to enjoy what God has given us to refresh and strengthen us so we may continue his work.

**8:16, 17** Even if he had access to all the world's wisdom, the wisest man would know very little. No one can fully comprehend God and all that he has done, and there are always more questions than answers. But the unknown should not cast a shadow over our joy, faith, or work because we know that someone greater is in control and that we can put our trust in him. Don't let what you don't know about the future destroy the joy God wants to give you today.

**9:2** "The same destiny ultimately awaits everyone" means that all will eventually die.

**9:5, 10** When Solomon says the dead know nothing and that there is no work, planning, knowledge, or wisdom after death, he is not contrasting life with afterlife, but life with death. After you die, you can't change what you have done. Resurrection to a new life after death was a vague concept for Old Testament believers. It was only made clear after Jesus rose from the dead.

**9:7-10** Considering the uncertainties of the future and the certainty of death, Solomon recommends enjoying life as God's gift. He may have been criticizing those who put off all present pleasures in order to accumulate wealth, much like those who get caught up in today's rat race. Solomon asks, "What is your wealth really worth, anyway?" Because the future is so uncertain, we should enjoy God's gifts while we are able.

**9:9** Solomon also wrote a proverb about marriage. "The man who finds a wife finds a treasure, and he receives favor from the LORD" (Proverbs 18:22). How sad it would be to be married and not appreciate or enjoy the companion God has given you.

**9:10, 11** It isn't difficult to think of cases where the fastest and the strongest don't win, the wise are poor, and the skillful are unrewarded with wealth or honor. Some people see such examples and call life unfair, and they are right. The world is finite, and sin has twisted life, making it what God did not intend. Solomon is trying to reduce our expectations. The book of Proverbs emphasizes how life would go if everyone acted fairly; Ecclesiastes explains what usually happens in our sinful and imperfect world. We must keep our perspective. Don't let the inequities of life keep you from earnest, dedicated work. We serve God, not people (see Colossians 3:23).

**9:12**
Isa 24:18
Hos 9:8
Luke 21:34-35

[12]People can never predict when hard times might come. Like fish in a net or birds in a trap, people are caught by sudden tragedy.

### Thoughts on Wisdom and Folly

[13]Here is another bit of wisdom that has impressed me as I have watched the way our world works. [14]There was a small town with only a few people, and a great king came with his army and besieged it. [15]A poor, wise man knew how to save the town, and so it was rescued. But afterward no one thought to thank him. [16]So even though wisdom is better than strength, those who are wise will be despised if they are poor. What they say will not be appreciated for long.

**9:15**
2 Sam 20:22
**9:16**
Prov 21:22

**9:17**
Eccl 7:5; 10:12
**9:18**
Josh 7:1-26
2 Kgs 21:2-17

[17] Better to hear the quiet words of a wise person
    than the shouts of a foolish king.
[18] Better to have wisdom than weapons of war,
    but one sinner can destroy much that is good.

**10:1**
Exod 30:25

**10** [1] As dead flies cause even a bottle of perfume to stink,
        so a little foolishness spoils great wisdom and honor.

[2] A wise person chooses the right road;
    a fool takes the wrong one.

**10:3**
Prov 13:16; 18:2
**10:4**
1 Sam 25:24-33
Prov 25:15
Eccl 8:3

[3] You can identify fools
    just by the way they walk down the street!

[4] If your boss is angry at you, don't quit!
    A quiet spirit can overcome even great mistakes.

### The Ironies of Life

[5]There is another evil I have seen under the sun. Kings and rulers make a grave mistake [6]when they give great authority to foolish people and low positions to people of proven worth. [7]I have even seen servants riding horseback like princes—and princes walking like servants!

**10:6**
Esth 3:1
Prov 28:12; 29:2
**10:7**
Esth 6:8
Prov 19:10
**10:8**
Ps 7:15
Prov 26:27
Amos 5:19

[8] When you dig a well,
    you might fall in.
    When you demolish an old wall,
    you could be bitten by a snake.
[9] When you work in a quarry,
    stones might fall and crush you.
    When you chop wood,
    there is danger with each stroke of your ax.

[10] Using a dull ax requires great strength,
    so sharpen the blade.
    That's the value of wisdom;
    it helps you succeed.

**10:11**
Ps 58:45
Jer 8:17

[11] If a snake bites before you charm it,
    what's the use of being a snake charmer?

---

**9:13-18** Our society honors wealth, attractiveness, and success above wisdom. Yet wisdom is a greater asset than strength, although it is often overlooked. Even though it is more effective, wisdom from people who are poor often goes unheeded. From this parable we can learn to appreciate wisdom, no matter whom it comes from.

**10:4** This proverb has implications for employer/employee relationships. Employees should ride out the temper tantrums of their employer. If we quietly do our work and don't get upset, the employer will probably get over his or her anger and calm down.

**10:5-7** By describing these circumstances that aren't fair or don't make sense, Solomon is saying that wealth alone can't bring justice. Solomon continues to build to his conclusion that every-

thing we have (from wisdom to riches) is nothing without God. But when God uses what little we have, it becomes all we could ever want or need.

**10:10** Trying to do anything without the necessary skills or tools is like chopping wood with a dull ax. If your tool is dull, you should sharpen it to do a better job. Similarly, if you lack skills, you should sharpen them through training and practice. "Sharpening the blade" means recognizing where a problem exists, acquiring or honing the skills (or tools) to do the job better, and then going out and doing it. Find the areas of your life where your "ax" is dull, and sharpen your skills so you can be more effective for God's work.

12 Wise words bring approval,
   but fools are destroyed by their own words.

13 Fools base their thoughts on foolish assumptions,
   so their conclusions will be wicked madness;
14    they chatter on and on.

No one really knows what is going to happen;
   no one can predict the future.

15 Fools are so exhausted by a little work
   that they can't even find their way home.

16 What sorrow for the land ruled by a servant,*
   the land whose leaders feast in the morning.

17 Happy is the land whose king is a noble leader
   and whose leaders feast at the proper time
   to gain strength for their work, not to get drunk.

18 Laziness leads to a sagging roof;
   idleness leads to a leaky house.

19 A party gives laughter,
   wine gives happiness,
   and money gives everything!

20 Never make light of the king, even in your thoughts.
   And don't make fun of the powerful, even in your own bedroom.
   For a little bird might deliver your message
   and tell them what you said.

## The Uncertainties of Life

**11** ¹ Send your grain across the seas,
   and in time, profits will flow back to you.*
² But divide your investments among many places,*
   for you do not know what risks might lie ahead.

³ When clouds are heavy, the rains come down.
   Whether a tree falls north or south, it stays where it falls.

⁴ Farmers who wait for perfect weather never plant.
   If they watch every cloud, they never harvest.

⁵Just as you cannot understand the path of the wind or the mystery of a tiny baby growing in its mother's womb,* so you cannot understand the activity of God, who does all things.

⁶Plant your seed in the morning and keep busy all afternoon, for you don't know if profit will come from one activity or another—or maybe both.

**10:16** Or a child. **11:1** Or Give generously, / for your gifts will return to you later. Hebrew reads Throw your bread on the waters, / for after many days you will find it again. **11:2** Hebrew among seven or even eight. **11:5** Some manuscripts read Just as you cannot understand how breath comes to a tiny baby in its mother's womb.

Cross references (right margin):
**10:12** Prov 10:14, 32; 22:11
**10:14** Prov 15:2; Eccl 3:22; 5:3; 6:12; 7:14; 8:7
**10:16** Isa 3:4-5, 12; 5:11
**10:18** Prov 24:30-34
**10:19** Judg 9:13; Ps 104:15; Eccl 2:3; 7:12
**10:20** Exod 22:28; 2 Kgs 6:12; Luke 12:3; Acts 23:5
**11:1** Deut 15:7-11; Prov 19:17; Isa 32:20; Matt 10:42; 2 Cor 9:8; Gal 6:9; Heb 6:10
**11:5** Ps 139:13-16; Eccl 1:15; 3:10; John 3:8

**10:16-18** When the Israelites had immature and irresponsible leaders, their nation fell. The books of 1 and 2 Kings describe the decline of the kingdoms when the leaders were concerned only about themselves. These verses pinpoint the basic problems of these leaders—selfishness and laziness.

**10:19** Government leaders, businesses, families, even churches get trapped into thinking money can meet all their needs. We throw money at our problems. But just as the thrill of wine is only temporary, the soothing effect of the last purchase soon wears off, and we have to buy more. Scripture recognizes that money is necessary for survival, but it warns against the love of money (see Matthew 6:24; 1 Timothy 6:10; Hebrews 13:5). Money is dangerous because it deceives us into thinking that wealth is the easiest way to get everything we want. The love of money is sinful because we trust money rather than God to solve our problems. Those who pursue its empty promises will one day discover that they have nothing because they are spiritually bankrupt.

**11:1-5** In these verses Solomon summarizes that life involves both risk and opportunity. Because life has no guarantees, we must be prepared. Solomon does not support a stingy, despairing attitude. Just because life is uncertain does not mean we should do nothing. We need a spirit of trust and adventure, facing life's risks and opportunities with God-directed enthusiasm and faith.

**11:4** Waiting for perfect conditions will mean inactivity. This practical insight is especially applicable to our spiritual lives. If we wait for the perfect time and place for personal Bible reading, we will never begin. If we wait for a perfect church, we will never join. If we wait for the perfect ministry, we will never serve. Take steps now to grow spiritually. Don't wait for conditions that may never exist.

## Advice for Young and Old

[7]Light is sweet; how pleasant to see a new day dawning.

[8]When people live to be very old, let them rejoice in every day of life. But let them also remember there will be many dark days. Everything still to come is meaningless.

[9]Young people,* it's wonderful to be young! Enjoy every minute of it. Do everything you want to do; take it all in. But remember that you must give an account to God for everything you do. [10]So refuse to worry, and keep your body healthy. But remember that youth, with a whole life before you, is meaningless.

**12** Don't let the excitement of youth cause you to forget your Creator. Honor him in your youth before you grow old and say, "Life is not pleasant anymore." [2]Remember him before the light of the sun, moon, and stars is dim to your old eyes, and rain clouds continually darken your sky. [3]Remember him before your legs—the guards of your house—start to tremble; and before your shoulders—the strong men—stoop. Remember him before your teeth—your few remaining servants—stop grinding; and before your eyes—the women looking through the windows—see dimly.

[4]Remember him before the door to life's opportunities is closed and the sound of work fades. Now you rise at the first chirping of the birds, but then all their sounds will grow faint.

[5]Remember him before you become fearful of falling and worry about danger in the streets; before your hair turns white like an almond tree in bloom, and you drag along without energy like a dying grasshopper, and the caperberry no longer inspires sexual desire. Remember him before you near the grave, your everlasting home, when the mourners will weep at your funeral.

[6]Yes, remember your Creator now while you are young, before the silver cord of life snaps and the golden bowl is broken. Don't wait until the water jar is smashed at the spring and the pulley is broken at the well. [7]For then the dust will return to the earth, and the spirit will return to God who gave it.

## Concluding Thoughts about the Teacher

[8]"Everything is meaningless," says the Teacher, "completely meaningless."

[9]Keep this in mind: The Teacher was considered wise, and he taught the people everything he knew. He listened carefully to many proverbs, studying and classifying them. [10]The Teacher sought to find just the right words to express truths clearly.*

[11]The words of the wise are like cattle prods—painful but helpful. Their collected sayings are like a nail-studded stick with which a shepherd* drives the sheep.

**11:9** Hebrew *Young man.*   **12:10** Or *sought to write what was upright and true.*   **12:11** Or *one shepherd.*

### Cross-references

**11:9**
Num 15:39
Ps 81:12
Acts 21:25
Rom 14:10

**11:10**
2 Cor 7:1
2 Tim 2:22

**12:1**
Deut 8:18
2 Sam 19:35
Neh 4:14
Pss 63:6; 119:55
Eccl 11:8

**12:2**
Isa 13:10
Ezek 32:7-8
Joel 3:15
Matt 24:29

**12:3**
Ps 35:14

**12:7**
Gen 3:19
Job 34:14
Ps 104:29
Eccl 3:20-21
Isa 57:16
Zech 12:1
Luke 23:46
Acts 7:59

**12:8**
Eccl 1:2

**12:9**
1 Kgs 4:32

**12:11**
Ezra 9:8
Isa 22:23
Acts 2:37

---

**11:7, 8** Solomon is no dreary pessimist in 11:7–12:14. He encourages us to rejoice in every day but to remember that eternity is far longer than a person's life span. Psalm 90:12 says, "Teach us to realize the brevity of life, so that we may grow in wisdom." The wise person does not just think about the moment and its impact; he or she takes the long-range view toward eternity. Approach your decisions with God's perspective—consider their impact 10 years from now and into eternity. Live with the attitude that although our life is short, we will live with God forever.

**11:9, 10** People often say, "It doesn't matter." But many of a person's choices will be irreversible—they will affect that person for a lifetime. What you do when you're young *does* matter. Enjoy life now, but don't do anything physically, morally, or spiritually that will prevent you from enjoying life when you are old.

**12:1** A life without God can produce bitterness, loneliness, and hopelessness in old age. A life centered around God is fulfilling and can be richer and more bearable when we are faced with disabilities, sickness, or handicaps. Being young is exciting. But the excitement of youth can become a barrier to closeness with God if it makes young people focus on passing pleasures instead of eternal values. Make your strength available to God when it is still yours—during your youthful years. Don't waste it on evil or meaningless activities that become bad habits and make you callous. Seek God now.

**12:6-8** The silver cord, golden bowl, water jar, and pulley symbolize life's fragility. How easily death comes to us; how swiftly and unexpectedly we may return to the dust from which we came. Therefore, we should recognize life as a precious resource to be used wisely and not squandered frivolously.

**12:7, 8** Stripped of the life-giving spirit breathed into us by God, our bodies return to dust. Stripped of God's purpose, our work is in vain. Stripped of God's love, our service is futile. We must put God first over all we do and in all we do because without him we have nothing. Knowing that life is futile without God motivates the wise person to seek God first.

¹²But, my child,* let me give you some further advice: Be careful, for writing books is endless, and much study wears you out.

¹³That's the whole story. Here now is my final conclusion: Fear God and obey his commands, for this is everyone's duty. ¹⁴God will judge us for everything we do, including every secret thing, whether good or bad.

**12:12** Hebrew *my son.*

**12:13**
Deut 4:2; 6:2; 10:12
Eccl 3:14; 8:5
Mic 6:8

**12:14**
Matt 10:26
Rom 2:16
1 Cor 4:5

---

**12:12** Opinions about life and philosophies about how we should live could be read and studied forever. It is not wrong to study these opinions, but because our life on earth is so short, we should make the best use of time by learning the important truths in God's Word. They affect this life and eternity. Wise students of the Bible will understand and do what it says.

**12:13, 14** In his conclusion, Solomon presents his antidotes for the two main ailments presented in this book. Those who lack purpose and direction in life should fear God and obey his commands. Those who think life is unfair should remember that God will review every person's life to determine how he or she has responded to him, and he will bring every deed into judgment. Have you committed your life to God? Does your life measure up to his standards?

**12:13, 14** The book of Ecclesiastes cannot be interpreted correctly without reading these final verses. No matter what the mysteries and apparent contradictions of life are, we must work toward the single purpose of knowing God.

In Ecclesiastes, Solomon shows us that we should enjoy life, but this does not exempt us from obeying God's commands. We should search for purpose and meaning in life, but they cannot be found in human endeavors. We should acknowledge the evil, foolishness, and injustice in life yet maintain a positive attitude and strong faith in God.

All people will have to stand before God and be judged for what they have done in this life. We will not be able to use the inequities of life as an excuse for failing to live properly. We need to: (1) recognize that human effort apart from God is futile, (2) put God first—now, (3) receive everything good as a gift from God, and (4) realize that God will judge every person's life, whether good or evil. How strange that people spend their lives striving for the joy that God gives freely.

SATURATED with stories of sexual escapades, secret rendezvous, and extramarital affairs, today's media teach that immorality means freedom, perversion is natural, and commitment is old-fashioned. Sex, created by God and pronounced good in Eden, has been twisted, exploited, and turned into an urgent, illicit, casual, and self-gratifying activity. Love has turned into lust, giving into getting, and lasting commitment into "no strings attached."

In reality, sexual intercourse, the physical and emotional union of male and female, should be a holy means of celebrating love, producing children, and experiencing pleasure, protected by the commitment of marriage.

God thinks sex is important, and Scripture contains numerous guidelines for its use and warnings about its misuse. And sex is always mentioned in the context of a loving relationship between husband and wife. Perhaps the highlight of this is Song of Songs, the intimate story of a man and a woman, their love, courtship, and marriage. Solomon probably wrote this "song" in his youth, before being overtaken by his own obsession with women, sex, and pleasure.

A moving story, drama, and poem, Song of Songs features the love dialogue between a simple Jewish maiden (the young woman) and her lover (Solomon, the king). They describe in intimate detail their feelings for each other and their longings to be together. Throughout the dialogue, sex and marriage are put in their proper, God-given perspective.

Much debate has raged over the meaning of this song. Some say it is an allegory of God's love for Israel or for the church. Others say it is a literal story about married love. In reality, it is both—a historical story with two layers of meaning. On one level, we learn about love, marriage, and sex; and on the other level, we see God's overwhelming love for his people. As you read Song of Songs, remember that you are loved by God, and commit yourself to seeing life, sex, and marriage from his point of view.

## VITAL STATISTICS

**PURPOSE:**
To tell of the love between a bridegroom (King Solomon) and his bride, to affirm the sanctity of marriage, and to picture God's love for his people

**AUTHOR:**
Solomon

**DATE WRITTEN:**
Probably early in Solomon's reign

**SETTING:**
Israel—the Shulammite woman's garden and the king's palace

**KEY VERSE:**
"I am my lover's, and my lover is mine. He browses among the lilies" (6:3).

**KEY PEOPLE:**
King Solomon, the young woman of Shulam, and friends

## THE BLUEPRINT

1. The wedding day (1:1—2:7)
2. Memories of courtship (2:8—3:5)
3. Memories of engagement (3:6—5:1)
4. A troubling dream (5:2—6:3)
5. Praising the bride's beauty (6:4—7:9)
6. The bride's tender appeal (7:10—8:4)
7. The power of love (8:5—14)

Song of Songs is a wedding song honoring marriage. The most explicit statements on sex in the Bible can be found in this book. It has often been criticized down through the centuries because of its sensuous language. The purity and sacredness of love represented here, however, are greatly needed in our day in which distorted attitudes about love and marriage are commonplace. God created sex and intimacy, and they are holy and good when enjoyed within marriage. A husband and wife honor God when they love and enjoy each other.

## MEGATHEMES

| THEME | EXPLANATION | IMPORTANCE |
|---|---|---|
| Sex | Sex is God's gift to his creatures. He endorses sex but restricts its expression to a man and a woman who are committed to each other in marriage. | God wants sex to be motivated by love and commitment, not lust. It is for mutual pleasure, not selfish enjoyment. |

| | | |
|---|---|---|
| Love | As the relationship developed, the beauty and wonder of a romance unfolded between Solomon and his bride. The intense power of love affected the hearts, minds, and bodies of the two lovers. | Because love is such a powerful expression of feeling and commitment between a man and a woman, it is not to be regarded casually. We are not to manipulate others into loving us, and love should not be prematurely encouraged in a relationship. |
| Commitment | The power of love requires more than the language of feeling to protect it. Sexual expression is such an integral part of our selfhood that we need the boundary of marriage to safeguard our love. Marriage is the celebration of daily commitment between a husband and wife. | While romance keeps a marriage interesting, commitment keeps romance from dwindling away. The decision to commit yourself to your spouse alone *begins* at the marriage altar. It must be maintained day by day. |
| Beauty | The two lovers praise the beauty they see in each other. The language they use shows the spontaneity and mystery of love. Praise should not be limited to physical beauty; beautiful personality and moral purity should also be praised. | Our love for someone makes him or her appear beautiful to us. As you consider marriage, don't just look for physical attractiveness in a person. Look for the inner qualities that don't fade with time—spiritual commitment, integrity, sensitivity, and sincerity. |
| Problems | Over time, feelings of loneliness, indifference, and isolation came between Solomon and his bride. During those times, love grew cold, and barriers were raised. | Through careful communication, lovers can be reconciled, commitment can be renewed, and romance refreshed. Don't let walls come between you and your spouse. Take care of problems while they are still small. |

## 1. The wedding day

**1** This is Solomon's song of songs, more wonderful than any other.

1:1
1 Kgs 4:32

*Young Woman**

2 Kiss me and kiss me again,
for your love is sweeter than wine.

1:2
Song 1:4; 4:10

3 How fragrant your cologne;
your name is like its spreading fragrance.
No wonder all the young women love you!

1:3
Eccl 7:1
Song 4:10
John 12:3

4 Take me with you; come, let's run!
The king has brought me into his bedroom.

1:4
Ps 45:14-15

*Young Women of Jerusalem*

How happy we are for you, O king.
We praise your love even more than wine.

1:1 The headings identifying the speakers are not in the original text, though the Hebrew usually gives clues by means of the gender of the person speaking.

---

**1:1** Solomon, a son of King David, became king and was chosen by God to build the Temple in Jerusalem. God gave him extraordinary wisdom. Much of Solomon's reign was characterized by wisdom and reverence for God although, toward the end of his life, he became proud and turned from God. Read about Solomon in 1 Kings 1—11 and 1 Chronicles 28—2 Chronicles 9. Solomon wrote and collected more than 3,000 proverbs (see the book of Proverbs) and over 1,000 songs, one of which is this book, Song of Songs. His Profile is found in 1 Kings 4, p. 519.

**1:1ff** Solomon frequently visited the various parts of his kingdom. One day, as he was visiting some royal vineyards in the north, his royal entourage came by surprise upon a beautiful peasant woman tending the vines. Embarrassed, she ran from them. But Solomon could not forget her. Later, disguised as a shepherd, he returned to the vineyards and won her love. Then he revealed his true identity and asked her to return to Jerusalem

with him. Solomon and his beloved are being married in the palace as this book begins.

The Song of Songs is a series of seven poems, not necessarily in chronological order, describing the first meeting of Solomon and the peasant woman, their engagement, their wedding, their wedding night, and the growth of their marriage after the wedding.

**1:1ff** This book features three characters or groups of characters: the girl (the "young woman"), Solomon (the "young man"), and "young women of Jerusalem." The girl who caught Solomon's attention may have been from Shunem, a farming community about 60 miles north of Jerusalem. Her tanned skin indicates that she probably worked outside in the vineyards (1:6); thus, she may not have been from the upper class. The young women of Jerusalem include either members of Solomon's harem or workers in the palace.

**1:1-4** This vivid description of a love relationship begins with a picture of love itself. Love is "sweeter than wine"; it makes the lovers rejoice. Acts 10:9-16 teaches that what God has created and cleansed we should not misuse or call common. We can enjoy love. God created it as a gift to us and a delight for all our senses.

**Young Woman**

How right they are to adore you.

5 I am dark but beautiful,
   O women of Jerusalem—
   dark as the tents of Kedar,
      dark as the curtains of Solomon's tents.

1:6
Ps 69:8
Song 8:11

6 Don't stare at me because I am dark—
      the sun has darkened my skin.
   My brothers were angry with me;
      they forced me to care for their vineyards,
      so I couldn't care for myself—my own vineyard.

1:7
Song 2:16; 3:1-4;
8:13

7 Tell me, my love, where are you leading your flock today?
   Where will you rest your sheep at noon?
   For why should I wander like a prostitute*
      among your friends and their flocks?

**Young Man**

1:8
Song 5:9; 6:1

8 If you don't know, O most beautiful woman,
      follow the trail of my flock,
      and graze your young goats by the shepherds' tents.

1:9
2 Chr 1:16-17

9 You are as exciting, my darling,
      as a mare among Pharaoh's stallions.

1:10
Gen 24:53
Song 5:13

10 How lovely are your cheeks;
      your earrings set them afire!
   How lovely is your neck,
      enhanced by a string of jewels.

11 We will make for you earrings of gold
      and beads of silver.

**Young Woman**

1:12
Song 4:13-14
Mark 14:3

12 The king is lying on his couch,
      enchanted by the fragrance of my perfume.

1:13
Ps 45:8
John 19:39

13 My lover is like a sachet of myrrh
      lying between my breasts.

1:14
1 Sam 23:29
Song 4:13

14 He is like a bouquet of sweet henna blossoms
      from the vineyards of En-gedi.

**Young Man**

1:15
Song 1:16;
2:10, 13; 4:1

15 How beautiful you are, my darling,
      how beautiful!
   Your eyes are like doves.

**Young Woman**

16 You are so handsome, my love,
      pleasing beyond words!
   The soft grass is our bed;

1:7 Hebrew *like a veiled woman.*

---

**1:5** Kedar was a nomadic community in northern Arabia. It was known for its tents that were woven from black goats' hair.

**1:6** The vineyard mentioned here was apparently owned by Solomon (because he came to visit it) and leased to the girl's brothers, who made her take care of the vineyards in the hot sun. Thus, she could not take care of her own skin. When she was brought to Jerusalem, the young girl was embarrassed about her tanned complexion because the girls in the city had fair, delicate skin that was considered much more beautiful. But Solomon loved her dark skin.

**1:7** The girl felt insecure at being different from the women of Jerusalem (1:6) and at being alone while her lover was away (1:7). She longed for the security of his presence. The basis of true love is commitment; so in a relationship built on genuine love, there is never any fear of deceit, manipulation, or exploitation.

**1:14** En-gedi was an oasis hidden at the base of rugged limestone cliffs west of the Dead Sea. It was known for its fruitful palm trees and fragrant balsam oil. The terrain surrounding En-gedi was some of the most desolate in Palestine and had an extremely hot desert climate. The henna blossoms in En-gedi would have appeared all the more beautiful because of their stark surroundings; thus, the girl was complimenting Solomon's looks, saying that he stood out among all the men.

**1:16, 17** The lover and his beloved describe their woodland surroundings as a wedding bedroom.

17   fragrant cedar branches are the beams of our house,
     and pleasant smelling firs are the rafters.

1:17
1 Kgs 6:9-10
2 Chr 3:5
Jer 22:14
Ezek 41:16

**2** *Young Woman*
1 I am the spring crocus blooming on the Sharon Plain,*
  the lily of the valley.

*Young Man*
2 Like a lily among thistles
  is my darling among young women.

*Young Woman*
3 Like the finest apple tree in the orchard
  is my lover among other young men.
I sit in his delightful shade
  and taste his delicious fruit.

2:3
Song 8:5

4 He escorts me to the banquet hall;
  it's obvious how much he loves me.

2:4
Ps 63:2-5
Song 1:4

5 Strengthen me with raisin cakes,
  refresh me with apples,
  for I am weak with love.

6 His left arm is under my head,
  and his right arm embraces me.

2:6
Prov 4:8
Song 8:3

7 Promise me, O women of Jerusalem,
  by the gazelles and wild deer,
  not to awaken love until the time is right.*

2:7
Gen 49:21
Song 3:5; 5:8; 8:14
Hab 3:19

## 2. Memories of courtship

8 Ah, I hear my lover coming!
  He is leaping over the mountains,
  bounding over the hills.

2:8
Song 2:17
Isa 52:7

9 My lover is like a swift gazelle
  or a young stag.
Look, there he is behind the wall,
  looking through the window,
  peering into the room.

2:9
Judg 5:28
Prov 6:5
Song 2:17; 3:5;
8:14

10 My lover said to me,
  "Rise up, my darling!
  Come away with me, my fair one!
11 Look, the winter is past,
  and the rains are over and gone.
12 The flowers are springing up,
  the season of singing birds* has come,
  and the cooing of turtledoves fills the air.

2:12
Gen 15:9
Ps 74:19

2:1 Traditionally rendered *I am the rose of Sharon.* Sharon Plain is a region in the coastal plain of Palestine.
2:7 Or *not to awaken love until it is ready.*   2:12 Or *the season of pruning vines.*

---

**2:1** The rose of Sharon and lily of the valley were flowers commonly found in Israel. Perhaps the girl was saying, "I'm not so special; I'm just an ordinary flower," to which Solomon replied, "Oh no, you are extraordinary—a lily among thorns." Solomon used the language of love. Nothing is more vital than encouraging and appreciating the person you love. Be sure to tell your spouse, "I love you" every day, and show that love by your actions.

**2:7** Feelings of love can create emotions that overpower reason. Young people are too often in a hurry to develop an intimate relationship based on their strong feelings. But feelings aren't enough to support a lasting relationship. This verse encourages us not to force romance lest the feelings of love grow faster than the commitment needed to make love last. Patiently wait for feelings of love and commitment to develop together.

**2:8–3:5** In this section Solomon's beloved reflects on her courtship with Solomon, remembering the first day they met and recalling one of her dreams about their being together.

**2:12, 13** The lovers celebrated their joy in the creation and in their love. God created the world, the beauty of nature, and the gift of love and sex, and he gave us senses to enjoy them. Never let problems, conflicts, or the ravages of time ruin your ability to enjoy God's gifts. Take time to enjoy the world God has created.

**2:13**
Matt 24:32

13 The fig trees are forming young fruit,
    and the fragrant grapevines are blossoming.
Rise up, my darling!
    Come away with me, my fair one!"

*Young Man*

**2:14**
Song 5:2; 6:9
Jer 48:28

14 My dove is hiding behind the rocks,
    behind an outcrop on the cliff.
Let me see your face;
    let me hear your voice.
For your voice is pleasant,
    and your face is lovely.

*Young Women of Jerusalem*

15 Catch all the foxes,
    those little foxes,
before they ruin the vineyard of love,
    for the grapevines are blossoming!

*Young Woman*

**2:16**
Song 4:5; 6:2-3;
7:10

16 My lover is mine, and I am his.
    He browses among the lilies.

**2:17**
Song 2:8-9; 4:6

17 Before the dawn breezes blow
    and the night shadows flee,
return to me, my love, like a gazelle
    or a young stag on the rugged mountains.*

*Young Woman*

**3:1**
Song 1:7; 5:6

**3** 1 One night as I lay in bed, I yearned for my lover.
    I yearned for him, but he did not come.

**3:2**
Jer 5:1

2 So I said to myself, "I will get up and roam the city,
    searching in all its streets and squares.
I will search for the one I love."
    So I searched everywhere but did not find him.

**3:3**
Song 5:7

3 The watchmen stopped me as they made their rounds,
    and I asked, "Have you seen the one I love?"

**3:4**
Song 8:2

4 Then scarcely had I left them
    when I found my love!
I caught and held him tightly,
    then I brought him to my mother's house,
    into my mother's bed, where I had been conceived.

**3:5**
Song 2:7; 8:2

5 Promise me, O women of Jerusalem,
    by the gazelles and wild deer,
not to awaken love until the time is right.*

### 3. Memories of engagement

*Young Women of Jerusalem*

**3:6**
Exod 13:21-22
Song 1:13; 4:12-14
Rev 5:8; 18:13

6 Who is this sweeping in from the wilderness
    like a cloud of smoke?

**2:17** Or *on the hills of Bether.* **3:5** Or *not to awaken love until it is ready.*

---

**2:15** The "little foxes" are an example of the kinds of problems that can disturb or destroy a relationship. The lovers wanted anything that could potentially cause problems between them to be removed. Often the "little foxes" cause the biggest problems in marriage. These irritations must not be minimized or ignored but identified so that, together, the couple can deal with them.

**3:1-4** Many scholars agree that in these verses the girl is recalling a dream that caused her to become so concerned about her lover's whereabouts that she arose in the middle of the night to search for him. When you love someone, you will do all you can to ensure the safety of that person and care for his or her needs,

even at a cost to your personal comfort. This is demonstrated most often in small actions—getting your spouse a glass of water, leaving work early to attend some function your child is involved in, or sacrificing your personal comfort to tend to the needs of a friend.

**3:6—5:1** Here the scene changes. Some believe that the wedding procession is described in 3:6-11, the wedding night in 4:1–5:1, and the consummation of the marriage in 4:16–5:1. Another possible explanation is that the period of Solomon's engagement to the girl is being remembered. In the previous section (2:8–3:5), Solomon and the girl fell in love. In this section, Solomon returns

Who is it, fragrant with myrrh and frankincense
 and every kind of spice?
7 Look, it is Solomon's carriage,
 surrounded by sixty heroic men,
 the best of Israel's soldiers.
8 They are all skilled swordsmen,
 experienced warriors.
 Each wears a sword on his thigh,
 ready to defend the king against an attack in the night.
9 King Solomon's carriage is built
 of wood imported from Lebanon.
10 Its posts are silver,
 its canopy gold;
 its cushions are purple.
 It was decorated with love
 by the young women of Jerusalem.

**Young Woman**
11 Come out to see King Solomon,
 young women of Jerusalem.*
 He wears the crown his mother gave him on his wedding day,
 his most joyous day.

**4** **Young Man**
¹ You are beautiful, my darling,
 beautiful beyond words.
 Your eyes are like doves
 behind your veil.
 Your hair falls in waves,
 like a flock of goats winding down the slopes of Gilead.
2 Your teeth are as white as sheep,
 recently shorn and freshly washed.
 Your smile is flawless,
 each tooth matched with its twin.*
3 Your lips are like scarlet ribbon;
 your mouth is inviting.
 Your cheeks are like rosy pomegranates
 behind your veil.
4 Your neck is as beautiful as the tower of David,
 jeweled with the shields of a thousand heroes.
5 Your breasts are like two fawns,
 twin fawns of a gazelle grazing among the lilies.
6 Before the dawn breezes blow
 and the night shadows flee,
 I will hurry to the mountain of myrrh
 and to the hill of frankincense.
7 You are altogether beautiful, my darling,
 beautiful in every way.

8 Come with me from Lebanon, my bride,
 come with me from Lebanon.

**3:8**
Pss 45:3; 91:5
Jer 50:9

**3:11**
Isa 62:5

**4:1**
Song 1:15; 5:12;
6:5, 7

**4:3**
Song 5:13, 16; 6:7

**4:4**
Neh 3:19
Song 7:4

**4:5**
Song 2:16; 6:2-3;
7:3

**4:8**
Deut 3:9
1 Kgs 4:33
1 Chr 5:23
Isa 62:5

---

3:11 Hebrew *of Zion*.   4:2 Hebrew *Not one is missing; each has a twin.*

---

to the girl in all his royal splendor (3:6-11), expresses his great love for her (4:1-5), and then proposes (4:7-15). The girl accepts (4:16), and Solomon responds to her acceptance (5:1).

**3:7, 9** Solomon's carriage was probably a covered and curtained couch for a single passenger that was carried on the shoulders of men.

**4:1-7** We feel like awkward onlookers when we read this intensely private and intimate exchange. In the ecstasy of their love, the lovers praise each other using beautiful imagery. Their words may seem strange to readers from a different culture, but their intense feelings of love and admiration are universal. Communicating love and expressing admiration in both words and actions can enhance every marriage.

Come down* from Mount Amana,
  from the peaks of Senir and Hermon,
where the lions have their dens
  and leopards live among the hills.

**4:9**
Ezek 16:11

9 You have captured my heart,
  my treasure,* my bride.
You hold it hostage with one glance of your eyes,
  with a single jewel of your necklace.
10 Your love delights me,
  my treasure, my bride.
Your love is better than wine,
  your perfume more fragrant than spices.

**4:11**
Gen 27:27
Prov 24:13-14
Hos 14:6

11 Your lips are as sweet as nectar, my bride.
  Honey and milk are under your tongue.
Your clothes are scented
  like the cedars of Lebanon.

**4:12**
Gen 29:3
Prov 5:15-18

12 You are my private garden, my treasure, my bride,
  a secluded spring, a hidden fountain.
13 Your thighs shelter a paradise of pomegranates
  with rare spices—
henna with nard,

**4:14**
Exod 30:23
John 19:39

14    nard and saffron,
  fragrant calamus and cinnamon,
with all the trees of frankincense, myrrh, and aloes,
  and every other lovely spice.

**4:15**
Zech 14:8
John 4:10, 14; 7:38

15 You are a garden fountain,
  a well of fresh water
  streaming down from Lebanon's mountains.

*Young Woman*

**4:16**
Song 1:13; 2:3;
5:1; 6:2

16 Awake, north wind!
  Rise up, south wind!
Blow on my garden
  and spread its fragrance all around.
Come into your garden, my love;
  taste its finest fruits.

*Young Man*

**5:1**
Prov 9:5
Song 1:13; 4:9; 6:2
Isa 55:1
John 3:29

**5** 1 I have entered my garden, my treasure,* my bride!
  I gather myrrh with my spices
and eat honeycomb with my honey.
  I drink wine with my milk.

**4:8** Or *Look down.* **4:9** Hebrew *my sister;* also in 4:10, 12. **5:1** Hebrew *my sister;* also in 5:2.

---

**4:12** In comparing his bride to a private garden, Solomon is praising her virginity. Virginity, considered old-fashioned by many in today's culture, has always been God's plan for unmarried people—and with good reason. Sex without marriage is cheap. It cannot compare with the joy of giving yourself completely to the one who is totally committed to you in marriage.

**4:15** Solomon's bride was as refreshing to him as a garden spring. Could your spouse say the same about you? Sometimes the familiarity that comes with marriage causes us to forget the overwhelming feelings of love and bliss we shared at the beginning. Many marriages could use a course in "refreshing." Do you refresh your spouse, or are you a burden of complaints, sorrows, and problems? Partners in marriage should continually work at refreshing each other by an encouraging word, an unexpected gift, a change of pace, a surprise call or note, or even the withholding of a discussion of some problem until the proper time. Your spouse needs you to be a haven of refreshment because the rest of the world usually isn't.

*Young Women of Jerusalem*
> Oh, lover and beloved, eat and drink!
> > Yes, drink deeply of your love!

## 4. A troubling dream
*Young Woman*
2 I slept, but my heart was awake,
> when I heard my lover knocking and calling:
"Open to me, my treasure, my darling,
> my dove, my perfect one.
My head is drenched with dew,
> my hair with the dampness of the night."

5:2
Song 2:14; 4:9; 6:9

3 But I responded,
"I have taken off my robe.
> Should I get dressed again?
I have washed my feet.
> Should I get them soiled?"

5:3
Gen 19:2
Luke 11:7

4 My lover tried to unlatch the door,
> and my heart thrilled within me.
5 I jumped up to open the door for my love,
> and my hands dripped with perfume.
My fingers dripped with lovely myrrh
> as I pulled back the bolt.

5:5
Song 5:13

6 I opened to my lover,
> but he was gone!
My heart sank.
I searched for him
> but could not find him anywhere.
I called to him,
> but there was no reply.

5:6
Prov 1:28
Song 3:1; 5:2; 6:1

7 The night watchmen found me
> as they made their rounds.
They beat and bruised me
> and stripped off my veil,
> those watchmen on the walls.

5:7
Song 3:3

8 Make this promise, O women of Jerusalem—
> If you find my lover,
> tell him I am weak with love.

5:8
Song 2:5, 7; 3:5

*Young Women of Jerusalem*
9 Why is your lover better than all others,
> O woman of rare beauty?
What makes your lover so special
> that we must promise this?

5:9
Song 1:8; 6:1

---

**5:2ff** This new section tells how the couple's marriage grew and matured in spite of problems. Some time had passed since the wedding, and the girl felt as though some indifference had developed in their relationship. She had become cool to her husband's advances, and by the time she changed her mind and responded to him, he had left. Her self-centeredness and impatience, though brief, caused separation. But she quickly moved to correct the problem by searching for her husband (5:6-8).

**5:2-8** Inevitably, with the passing of time and the growth of familiarity, a marriage will start to lose its initial sparkle. Glances and touches no longer produce the same emotional response. Conflicts and pressures may creep in, causing you to lose your tenderness toward your spouse. The world is not a haven for lovers; in fact, external stress often works against the marriage relationship. But you and your spouse can learn to be a haven for each other. If intimacy and passion decline, remember that they can be renewed and regenerated. Take time to remember the commitment you made, those first thrills, the excitement of sex, and your spouse's strengths. When you focus on the positives, reconciliation and renewal can result.

**5:7** The girl was alone outside during the night. In Old Testament times, she would have been looked upon as a criminal or a prostitute and treated as such. This image symbolizes the pain she felt at being separated from her lover.

**Young Woman**

5:10
1 Sam 16:12
Ps 45:2

10 My lover is dark and dazzling,
     better than ten thousand others!
11 His head is finest gold,
     his wavy hair is black as a raven.

5:12
Song 1:15; 4:1

12 His eyes sparkle like doves
     beside springs of water;
   they are set like jewels
     washed in milk.

5:13
Song 2:1; 5:5; 6:2

13 His cheeks are like gardens of spices
     giving off fragrance.
   His lips are like lilies,
     perfumed with myrrh.

5:14
Exod 24:10; 28:18
Job 28:16
Isa 54:11
Ezek 1:16

14 His arms are like rounded bars of gold,
     set with beryl.
   His body is like bright ivory,
     glowing with lapis lazuli.

5:15
1 Kgs 4:33
Song 7:4

15 His legs are like marble pillars
     set in sockets of finest gold.
   His posture is stately,
     like the noble cedars of Lebanon.

5:16
2 Sam 1:23
Song 7:9

16 His mouth is sweetness itself;
     he is desirable in every way.
   Such, O women of Jerusalem,
     is my lover, my friend.

**6** **Young Women of Jerusalem**
1 Where has your lover gone,
   O woman of rare beauty?
 Which way did he turn
   so we can help you find him?

**Young Woman**

6:2
Song 1:7; 2:1; 4:16;
5:1, 13

2 My lover has gone down to his garden,
   to his spice beds,
 to browse in the gardens
   and gather the lilies.

6:3
Song 2:16; 4:5;
7:10

3 I am my lover's, and my lover is mine.
   He browses among the lilies.

**5. Praising the bride's beauty**
**Young Man**

6:4
1 Kgs 14:17
Pss 48:2; 50:2

4 You are beautiful, my darling,
   like the lovely city of Tirzah.
 Yes, as beautiful as Jerusalem,
   as majestic as an army with billowing banners.

6:5
Song 4:1

5 Turn your eyes away,
   for they overpower me.
 Your hair falls in waves,
   like a flock of goats winding down the slopes of Gilead.

---

**5:16** The girl calls Solomon her "friend." In a healthy marriage, lovers are also good friends. Too often people are driven into marriage by the exciting feelings of love and passion before they take the time to develop a deep friendship. This involves listening, sharing, and showing understanding for the other's likes and dislikes. Friendship takes time, but it makes a love relationship much deeper and far more satisfying.

**6:3** The girl said that she and her lover belonged to each other—they had given themselves to each other unreservedly. No matter how close we may be to our parents or our best friends, only in marriage can we realize complete union of mind, heart, and body.

**6:4** Tirzah was a city about 35 miles northeast of Jerusalem. Its name means "pleasure" or "beauty." Jeroboam made Tirzah the first capital of the divided northern kingdom (1 Kings 14:17). "Majestic as an army with billowing banners" means that his beloved must have had awe-inspiring beauty, like a mighty army readying for battle.

6 Your teeth are as white as sheep
    that are freshly washed.
Your smile is flawless,
    each tooth matched with its twin.*
7 Your cheeks are like rosy pomegranates
    behind your veil.

8 Even among sixty queens
    and eighty concubines
    and countless young women,
9 I would still choose my dove, my perfect one—
    the favorite of her mother,
    dearly loved by the one who bore her.
The young women see her and praise her;
    even queens and royal concubines sing her praises:
10 "Who is this, arising like the dawn,
    as fair as the moon,
    as bright as the sun,
    as majestic as an army with billowing banners?"

*Young Woman*
11 I went down to the grove of walnut trees
    and out to the valley to see the new spring growth,
to see whether the grapevines had budded
    or the pomegranates were in bloom.
12 Before I realized it,
    my strong desires had taken me to the chariot of a noble man.*

*Young Women of Jerusalem*
13* Return, return to us, O maid of Shulam.
    Come back, come back, that we may see you again.

*Young Man*
    Why do you stare at this young woman of Shulam,
    as she moves so gracefully between two lines of dancers?*

**7** 1* How beautiful are your sandaled feet,
    O queenly maiden.
Your rounded thighs are like jewels,
    the work of a skilled craftsman.
2 Your navel is perfectly formed
    like a goblet filled with mixed wine.
Between your thighs lies a mound of wheat
    bordered with lilies.
3 Your breasts are like two fawns,
    twin fawns of a gazelle.
4 Your neck is as beautiful as an ivory tower.
Your eyes are like the sparkling pools in Heshbon
    by the gate of Bath-rabbim.
Your nose is as fine as the tower of Lebanon
    overlooking Damascus.

| | |
|---|---|
| 6:8 | 1 Kgs 11:3 |
| 6:9 | Gen 30:13 |
| | Song 2:14; 5:2 |
| 6:10 | Job 31:26 |
| | Song 6:4 |
| | Matt 17:2 |
| | Rev 1:16 |
| 6:11 | Song 4:13; 7:12 |
| 6:13 | Gen 32:2 |
| | Judg 21:21 |
| | 2 Sam 17:24 |
| 7:1ff | Ps 45:13 |
| 7:3 | Song 4:5 |
| 7:4 | Num 21:26 |
| | Song 4:4 |

6:6 Hebrew *Not one is missing; each has a twin.*   6:12 Or *to the royal chariots of my people,* or *to the chariots of Amminadab.* The meaning of the Hebrew is uncertain.   6:13a Verse 6:13 is numbered 7:1 in Hebrew text.
6:13b Or *as you would at the movements of two armies?* or *as you would at the dance of Mahanaim?* The meaning of the Hebrew is uncertain.   7:1 Verses 7:1-13 are numbered 7:2-14 in Hebrew text.

**6:8, 9** Solomon did indeed have many queens (wives) and concubines (1 Kings 11:3). Polygamy, though not condoned, was common in Old Testament days. Solomon said that his love for this woman had not diminished since their wedding night, even though many other women were available to him.

**7:4, 5** Heshbon was the ancient capital of the Amorites. Bathrabbim may have been a gate of Heshbon. The "tower of Lebanon" may have been a watchtower (evidently a prominent one and seen as very beautiful). Some suggest that this refers to the Lebanon mountain range. Mount Carmel overlooks the Mediterranean Sea and Palestine.

**7:5**
Isa 35:2

⁵ Your head is as majestic as Mount Carmel,
and the sheen of your hair radiates royalty.
The king is held captive by its tresses.

**7:6**
Song 1:15-16

⁶ Oh, how beautiful you are!
How pleasing, my love, how full of delights!
⁷ You are slender like a palm tree,
and your breasts are like its clusters of fruit.

**7:8**
Song 2:5

⁸ I said, "I will climb the palm tree
and take hold of its fruit."
May your breasts be like grape clusters,
and the fragrance of your breath like apples.

**7:9**
Prov 23:31
Song 5:16

⁹ May your kisses be as exciting as the best wine,
flowing gently over lips and teeth.*

## 6. The bride's tender appeal

*Young Woman*

**7:10**
Ps 45:11
Song 2:16; 6:3

¹⁰ I am my lover's,
and he claims me as his own.
¹¹ Come, my love, let us go out to the fields
and spend the night among the wildflowers.*

**7:12**
Song 6:11

¹² Let us get up early and go to the vineyards
to see if the grapevines have budded,
if the blossoms have opened,
and if the pomegranates have bloomed.
There I will give you my love.

**7:13**
Gen 30:14
Song 2:3; 4:13, 16

¹³ There the mandrakes give off their fragrance,
and the finest fruits are at our door,
new delights as well as old,
which I have saved for you, my lover.

**8** *Young Woman*

¹ Oh, I wish you were my brother,
who nursed at my mother's breasts.
Then I could kiss you no matter who was watching,
and no one would criticize me.

**8:2**
Song 3:4

² I would bring you to my childhood home,
and there you would teach me.*
I would give you spiced wine to drink,
my sweet pomegranate wine.

**8:3**
Song 2:6

³ Your left arm would be under my head,
and your right arm would embrace me.

**8:4**
Song 2:7; 3:5

⁴ Promise me, O women of Jerusalem,
not to awaken love until the time is right.*

## 7. The power of love

*Young Women of Jerusalem*

**8:5**
Song 2:3; 3:6

⁵ Who is this sweeping in from the desert,
leaning on her lover?

**7:9** As in Greek and Syriac versions and Latin Vulgate; Hebrew reads *over lips of sleepers.*   **7:11** Or *in the villages.*
**8:2** Or *there she will teach me;* or *there she bore me.*   **8:4** Or *not to awaken love until it is ready.*

**7:10-13** As a marriage matures, love and freedom between marriage partners should increase. Here the girl takes the initiative in lovemaking. Many cultures have stereotypes of the roles men and women play in lovemaking, but the security of true love gives both marriage partners the freedom to initiate acts of love and express their true feelings.

**7:13** Mandrakes were a somewhat rare plant often thought to increase fertility. Mandrakes are also mentioned in Genesis 30:14-17.

**8:1** In the ancient Near East, it was improper to show public affection except between family members. The girl is wishing that she could freely show affection to her lover, even in public.

*Young Woman*

I aroused you under the apple tree,
> where your mother gave you birth,
> where in great pain she delivered you.

6 Place me like a seal over your heart,
> like a seal on your arm.
For love is as strong as death,
> its jealousy* as enduring as the grave.*
Love flashes like fire,
> the brightest kind of flame.

7 Many waters cannot quench love,
> nor can rivers drown it.
If a man tried to buy love
> with all his wealth,
> his offer would be utterly scorned.

*The Young Woman's Brothers*

8 We have a little sister
> too young to have breasts.
What will we do for our sister
> if someone asks to marry her?

9 If she is a virgin, like a wall,
> we will protect her with a silver tower.
But if she is promiscuous, like a swinging door,
> we will block her door with a cedar bar.

*Young Woman*

10 I was a virgin, like a wall;
> now my breasts are like towers.
When my lover looks at me,
> he is delighted with what he sees.

11 Solomon has a vineyard at Baal-hamon,
> which he leases out to tenant farmers.
Each of them pays a thousand pieces of silver*
> for harvesting its fruit.

12 But my vineyard is mine to give,
> and Solomon need not pay a thousand pieces of silver.
But I will give two hundred pieces
> to those who care for its vines.

**8:6**
Prov 6:34
Isa 49:16
Jer 22:24
Hag 2:23

**8:8**
Ezek 16:7

**8:9**
1 Kgs 6:15

**8:11**
Eccl 2:4
Song 1:6; 2:3; 8:12
Isa 7:23
Matt 21:33

**8:6a** Or *its passion.*   **8:6b** Hebrew *as Sheol.*   **8:11** Hebrew *1,000 shekels of silver.*

---

**8:6, 7** In this final description of their love, the girl includes some of its significant characteristics (see also 1 Corinthians 13). Love is as strong as death; it cannot be killed by time or disaster and cannot be bought for any price because it is freely given. Love is priceless, and even the richest king cannot buy it. Love must be accepted as a gift from God and then shared within the guidelines God provides. Accept the love of your spouse as God's gift, and strive to make your love a reflection of the perfect love that comes from God himself.

**8:8, 9** The girl is reflecting on the days when she was younger and under the care of her brothers, who wondered how to help her prepare for marriage. They decided that if she remained a virgin before marriage, standing firm like a wall against sexual temptation, they would praise her. But if she was promiscuous and given over to immorality, they would take steps to guard her from doing something foolish. In 8:10, she testifies that she has been persistent in her morality and thus has found favor in Solomon's eyes.

**8:11, 12** Solomon could demand rent from the tenants for his vineyard, but the girl had her own vineyard, and it was her right to assign it. But she willingly gave Solomon its fruit. In a good marriage, there is no private property, for everything is shared between the partners. This is the only time Baal-hamon is mentioned in the Bible, and its location is unknown.

**8:13**
Song 1:7; 2:14

*Young Man*

13 O my darling, lingering in the gardens,
　　your companions are fortunate to hear your voice.
　　Let me hear it, too!

**8:14**
Song 2:7, 9, 17; 4:6

*Young Woman*

14 Come away, my love! Be like a gazelle
　　or a young stag on the mountains of spices.

---

**8:14** The love between Solomon and his bride did not diminish in intensity after their wedding night. The lovers relied on each other and kept no secrets from each other. Devotion and commitment were the keys to their relationship, just as they are in our relationships to our spouses and to God. The faithfulness of our marital love should reflect God's perfect faithfulness to us.

Paul shows how marriage represents Christ's relationship to his church (Ephesians 5:22-33), and John pictures the Second Coming as a great marriage feast for Christ and his bride, his faithful followers (Revelation 19:7, 8; 21:1, 2). Many theologians have thought that Song of Songs is an allegory showing Christ's love for his church. It might be even better to say that it is a love poem about a real human love relationship, and that all loving, committed marriages are reflections of God's love.

# ISAIAH

## VITAL STATISTICS

**PURPOSE:**
To call the nation of Judah back to God and to tell of God's salvation through the Messiah

**AUTHOR:**
The prophet Isaiah son of Amoz

**DATE WRITTEN:**
The events of chapters 1—39 occurred during Isaiah's ministry, so they were probably written about 700 B.C. Chapters 40—66, however, may have been written near the end of his life, about 681 B.C.

**SETTING:**
Isaiah is speaking and writing mainly in Jerusalem

**KEY VERSE:**
"But he was pierced for our rebellion, crushed for our sins. He was beaten so we could be whole. He was whipped so we could be healed" (53:5).

**KEY PEOPLE:**
Isaiah; his two sons, Shear-jashub and Maher-shalal-hash-baz

**SPECIAL FEATURES:**
The book of Isaiah contains both prose and poetry and uses personification (attributing personal qualities to divine beings or inanimate objects). Also, many of the prophecies in Isaiah contain predictions that foretell a soon-to-occur event and a distant future event at the same time.

SLOWLY he rose, and the crowd fell silent. Those at the back leaned forward, straining to hear. The atmosphere was electric. He spoke, and his carefully chosen words flew like swift arrows and found their mark. The great man, a spokesman for God, was warning—and condemning. The crowd became restless—shifting positions, clenching fists, and murmuring. Some agreed with his message, nodding their heads and weeping softly. But most were angry, and they began to shout back insults and threats.

Such was the life of a prophet.

The "office" of prophet was instituted during the days of Samuel, the last of the judges. Prophets stood with the priests as God's special representatives. The prophet's role was to speak for God, confronting the people and their leaders with God's commands and promises. Because of this confrontational stance and the continuing tendency of people to disobey God, true prophets usually were not very popular. But though their message often went unheeded, they faithfully and forcefully proclaimed the truth.

The book of Isaiah is the first of the writings of the prophets in the Bible, and Isaiah, the author, is generally considered to be the greatest prophet. He was probably reared in an aristocratic home and was married to a prophet. In the beginning of his ministry he was well liked. But, like most prophets, he soon became unpopular because his messages were so difficult to hear. He called the people to turn from their lives of sin and warned them of God's judgment and punishment. Isaiah had an active ministry for 60 years before he was executed during Manasseh's reign (according to tradition). As God's special messenger to Judah, Isaiah prophesied during the reigns of several of its rulers. Many of those messages are recorded in his book: Uzziah and Jotham, chapters 1—6; Ahaz, chapters 7—14; and Hezekiah, chapters 15—39.

The first half of the book of Isaiah (chapters 1—39) contains scathing denunciations and pronouncements as he calls Judah, Israel, and the surrounding nations to repent of their sins. The last 27 chapters (40—66), however, are filled with consolation and hope as Isaiah unfolds God's promise of future blessings through his Messiah.

As you read Isaiah, imagine this strong and courageous man of God, fearlessly proclaiming God's word, and listen to his message in relation to your own life—*return, repent, and be renewed.* Then trust in God's *redemption* through Christ and *rejoice.* Your Savior has come, and he's coming again!

## THE BLUEPRINT

### A. WORDS OF JUDGMENT
### (1:1—39:8)
1. The sins of Israel and Judah
2. Judgment against heathen nations
3. God's purpose in judgment
4. Jerusalem's true and false hopes
5. Events during the reign of Hezekiah

The 39 chapters in the first half of Isaiah generally carry the message of judgment for sin. Isaiah brings the message of judgment to Judah, Israel, and the surrounding pagan nations. The people of Judah had a form of godliness, but in their hearts they were corrupt. Isaiah's warnings were intended to purify the people by helping them understand God's true nature and message. However, they ignored the repeated warnings that Isaiah brought. We need to heed the prophetic voice and not repeat their error.

### B. WORDS OF COMFORT
### (40:1—66:24)
1. Israel's release from captivity
2. The future Redeemer
3. The future Kingdom

The 27 chapters in the second half of Isaiah generally bring a message of forgiveness, comfort, and hope. This message of hope looks forward to the coming of the Messiah. Isaiah speaks more about the Messiah than does any other Old Testament prophet. He describes the Messiah as both a suffering Servant and a sovereign Lord. The fact that the Messiah was to be both a suffering Servant and a sovereign Lord could not be understood clearly until New Testament times. Based on what Jesus Christ has done, God freely offers forgiveness to all who turn to him in faith. This is God's message of comfort to us because those who heed it find eternal peace and fellowship with him.

## MEGATHEMES

| THEME | EXPLANATION | IMPORTANCE |
|---|---|---|
| Holiness | God is highly exalted above all his creatures. His moral perfection stands in contrast to evil people and nations. God is perfect and sinless in all his motives and actions, so he is in perfect control of his power, judgment, love, and mercy. His holy nature is our standard for morality. | Because God is without sin, he alone can help us with our sin. It is only right that we regard him as supreme in power and moral perfection. We must never treat God as common or ordinary. He alone deserves our devotion and praise. He is always truthful, fair, and just. |
| Punishment | Because God is holy, he requires his people to treat others justly. He promised to punish Israel, Judah, and other nations for faithless immorality and idolatry. True faith had degenerated into national pride and empty religious rituals. | We must trust in God alone and fulfill his commands. We cannot forsake justice nor give in to selfishness. If we harden our hearts against his message, punishment will surely come to us. |
| Salvation | Because God's judgment is coming, we need a Savior. No person or nation can be saved without God's help. Christ's perfect sacrifice for our sins is foretold and portrayed in Isaiah. All who trust God can be freed from their sin and restored to him. | Christ died to save us from our sin. We cannot save ourselves. He is willing to save all those who turn from their sin and come to him. Salvation is from God alone. No amount of good works can earn it. |
| Messiah | God will send the Messiah to save his people. He will set up his own Kingdom as the faithful Prince of Peace, who rules with righteousness. He will come as sovereign Lord, but he will do so as a servant who will die to take away sins. | Our trust must be in the Messiah, not in ourselves or in any nation or power. There is no hope unless we believe in him. Trust Christ fully and let him rule in your life as your sovereign Lord. |
| Hope | God promises comfort, deliverance, and restoration in his future Kingdom. The Messiah will rule over his faithful followers in the age to come. Hope is possible because Christ is coming. | We can be refreshed because there is compassion for those who repent. No matter how bleak our situation or how evil the world is, we must continue to be God's faithful people who hope for his return. |

## A. WORDS OF JUDGMENT (1:1—39:8)

Isaiah begins by bringing a message of divine judgment for both Israel and Judah. Although the advance of the Assyrians poses a problem for Judah, God foretells the destruction of Assyria and other evil surrounding nations through the prophet Isaiah. The section ends with the Assyrian invasion being held off, demonstrating the clear unfolding of God's plan and promises for the nation at this time.

### 1. The sins of Israel and Judah

**1** These are the visions that Isaiah son of Amoz saw concerning Judah and Jerusalem. He saw these visions during the years when Uzziah, Jotham, Ahaz, and Hezekiah were kings of Judah.*

**1:1**
2 Kgs 15:1, 13;
16:1; 18:1

#### A Message for Rebellious Judah

2 Listen, O heavens! Pay attention, earth!
    This is what the LORD says:
"The children I raised and cared for
    have rebelled against me.

**1:2**
Deut 32:1
Isa 65:2
Jer 3:22
Mic 1:2

3 Even an ox knows its owner,
    and a donkey recognizes its master's care—
but Israel doesn't know its master.
    My people don't recognize my care for them."

**1:3**
Jer 8:7; 9:3, 6

4 Oh, what a sinful nation they are—
    loaded down with a burden of guilt.
They are evil people,
    corrupt children who have rejected the LORD.
They have despised the Holy One of Israel
    and turned their backs on him.

**1:4**
Isa 1:28; 5:24;
14:20

5 Why do you continue to invite punishment?
    Must you rebel forever?
Your head is injured,
    and your heart is sick.

**1:5**
Isa 31:6; 33:24

6 You are battered from head to foot—
    covered with bruises, welts, and infected wounds—
    without any soothing ointments or bandages.

7 Your country lies in ruins,
    and your towns are burned.
Foreigners plunder your fields before your eyes
    and destroy everything they see.

**1:7**
Lev 26:33
Jer 44:6

8 Beautiful Jerusalem* stands abandoned
    like a watchman's shelter in a vineyard,
like a lean-to in a cucumber field after the harvest,
    like a helpless city under siege.

**1:1** These kings reigned from 792 to 686 B.C.    **1:8** Hebrew *The daughter of Zion.*

**1:1** Isaiah was a prophet during the time when the original nation of Israel had been divided into two kingdoms—Israel in the north and Judah in the south. The northern kingdom had sinned greatly against God, and the southern kingdom was headed in the same direction—perverting justice, oppressing the poor, turning from God to idols, and looking for military aid from pagan nations rather than help from God. Isaiah came primarily as a prophet to Judah, but his message was also for the northern kingdom. Sometimes "Israel" refers to both kingdoms. Isaiah lived to see the destruction and captivity of the northern kingdom in 722 B.C. Thus, his ministry began with warning the northern kingdom.

**1:2-4** Here "Israel" means the southern kingdom, Judah. The people of Judah were sinning greatly and had turned against God. God brought charges against them through Isaiah because they had rebelled and had forsaken the Lord. By these acts, they had broken their moral and spiritual covenant with God (see Deuteronomy 28). By breaking their agreement, they were bring-

ing God's punishment upon themselves. First God gave them prosperity, but they didn't serve him. Then God sent them warnings, but they refused to listen. Finally, he would bring the fire of his judgment (see 1:7).

**1:4-9** As long as the people of Judah continued to sin, they cut themselves off from God's help and isolated themselves. When you feel lonely and separated from God, remember that God does not abandon you. Our sins cut us off from him. The only sure cure for this kind of loneliness is to restore a meaningful relationship with God by confessing your sins, obeying his instructions, and communicating regularly with him (see Psalm 140:13; Isaiah 1:16-19; 1 John 1:9).

**1:7** Was this destruction taking place at that time? Judah was attacked many times during Isaiah's lifetime. To be plundered by foreigners was the worst kind of judgment. This verse could be a picture of the results of these invasions or a prediction of the coming invasion of Israel by Assyria. But most likely it pointed to Babylon's future invasion of Judah and the fall of Jerusalem in 586 B.C. as well.

**1:9**
Isa 10:20-22;
11:11, 16
†Rom 9:29

⁹ If the LORD of Heaven's Armies
    had not spared a few of us,*
we would have been wiped out like Sodom,
    destroyed like Gomorrah.

**1:10**
Ezek 16:46
Rev 11:8

¹⁰ Listen to the LORD, you leaders of "Sodom."
    Listen to the law of our God, people of "Gomorrah."

**1:11**
Jer 6:20
Mal 1:10

¹¹ "What makes you think I want all your sacrifices?"
    says the LORD.
"I am sick of your burnt offerings of rams
    and the fat of fattened cattle.
I get no pleasure from the blood
    of bulls and lambs and goats.
¹² When you come to worship me,
    who asked you to parade through my courts with all your ceremony?

**1:13**
1 Chr 23:31

¹³ Stop bringing me your meaningless gifts;
    the incense of your offerings disgusts me!
As for your celebrations of the new moon and the Sabbath
    and your special days for fasting—
they are all sinful and false.
    I want no more of your pious meetings.

**1:14**
Isa 43:24

¹⁴ I hate your new moon celebrations and your annual festivals.
    They are a burden to me. I cannot stand them!

**1:15**
Isa 59:2
Mic 3:4

¹⁵ When you lift up your hands in prayer, I will not look.
    Though you offer many prayers, I will not listen,
for your hands are covered with the blood of innocent victims.

**1:16**
Ps 26:6
Isa 52:11
Jer 25:5

¹⁶ Wash yourselves and be clean!
    Get your sins out of my sight.
    Give up your evil ways.

**1:17**
Jer 22:3

¹⁷ Learn to do good.
    Seek justice.

**1:9** Greek version reads *a few of our children.* Compare Rom 9:29.

---

**ISAIAH**
served as
a prophet
to Judah from
740–681 B.C.

| | |
|---|---|
| Climate of the times . . . . . . | Society was in a great upheaval. Under King Ahaz and King Manasseh, the people reverted to idolatry, and there was even child sacrifice. |
| Main message. . . . . . . . . . | Although judgment from other nations was inevitable, the people could still have a special relationship with God. |
| Importance of message . . . | Sometimes we must suffer judgment and discipline before we are restored to God. |
| Contemporary prophets . . . | Hosea (753–715 B.C.), Micah (742–687 B.C.) |

---

**1:9** Sodom and Gomorrah were two cities that God completely destroyed for their great wickedness (Genesis 19:1-25). They are mentioned elsewhere in the Bible as examples of God's judgment against sin (Jeremiah 50:40; Ezekiel 16:46-63; Matthew 11:23, 24; Jude 1:7). Some survivors from Judah were spared by God because they were faithful.

**1:10** Isaiah compared the rulers and people of Judah to the rulers and people of Sodom and Gomorrah. To hear what God wanted to say, the people had to listen and be willing to obey. When we can't hear God's message, perhaps we are not listening carefully, or we are not truly willing to do what he says.

**1:10-14** God was unhappy with their sacrifices, but he was not revoking the system of sacrifices he had initiated with Moses. Instead, God was calling for sincere faith and devotion. The leaders were carefully making the traditional sacrifices and offerings at holy celebrations, but they were still unfaithful to God in their hearts. Sacrifices were to be an outward sign of their faith in God, but the outward signs became empty because no faith existed. Why, then, did they continue to offer sacrifices? Like many

people today, they had come to place more faith in the rituals of their religion than in the God they worshiped. Examine your own worship experience: Is it just entertainment as you enjoy the music and go along with what others do? Or is it genuine heartfelt praise to God? God does not take pleasure in our outward expressions if our inward faith is missing (see Deuteronomy 10:12-16; 1 Samuel 15:22, 23; Psalm 51:16-19; Hosea 6:6).

**1:13** New moon celebrations and Sabbaths refer to monthly offerings (Numbers 28:11-14) and weekly and special annual Sabbaths on the Day of Atonement and Festival of Shelters (Leviticus 16:23-34). For all the festivals, see the chart in Leviticus 22, p. 189. Although the people did not feel sorry for their sins, they continued to offer sacrifices for forgiveness. Gifts and sacrifices mean nothing to God when they come from someone with a corrupt heart. God wants us to love him, trust him, and turn from our sin; after that, he will be pleased with our "sacrifices" of time, money, or service.

Help the oppressed.
　Defend the cause of orphans.
　Fight for the rights of widows.

18 "Come now, let's settle this,"
　says the LORD.
"Though your sins are like scarlet,
　I will make them as white as snow.
Though they are red like crimson,
　I will make them as white as wool.
19 If you will only obey me,
　you will have plenty to eat.
20 But if you turn away and refuse to listen,
　you will be devoured by the sword of your enemies.
　I, the LORD, have spoken!"

*Unfaithful Jerusalem*
21 See how Jerusalem, once so faithful,
　has become a prostitute.
Once the home of justice and righteousness,
　she is now filled with murderers.
22 Once like pure silver,
　you have become like worthless slag.
Once so pure,
　you are now like watered-down wine.
23 Your leaders are rebels,
　the companions of thieves.
All of them love bribes
　and demand payoffs,
but they refuse to defend the cause of orphans
　or fight for the rights of widows.

24 Therefore, the Lord, the LORD of Heaven's Armies,
　the Mighty One of Israel, says,
"I will take revenge on my enemies
　and pay back my foes!
25 I will raise my fist against you.
　I will melt you down and skim off your slag.
　I will remove all your impurities.
26 Then I will give you good judges again
　and wise counselors like you used to have.
Then Jerusalem will again be called the Home of Justice
　and the Faithful City."

27 Zion will be restored by justice;
　those who repent will be revived by righteousness.

1:18 Ps 51:7; Isa 43:26; 44:22; Rev 7:14
1:19 Deut 30:15-16
1:21 Jer 2:20
1:23 Exod 23:8; Jer 5:28; Ezek 22:7; Mic 7:3
1:24 Isa 35:4; 49:26
1:25 Ezek 22:19-22; Mal 3:3
1:26 Isa 33:5; Zech 8:3

**1:18** Crimson was the color of a deep-red permanent dye, and its deep stain was virtually impossible to remove from clothing. The bloodstained hands of the murderers are probably in view here (see 1:15, 21). The stain of sin seems equally permanent, but God can remove sin's stain from our life as he promised to do for the Israelites. We don't have to go through life permanently soiled. God's Word assures us that if we are willing and obedient, Christ will forgive and remove our most indelible stains (Psalm 51:1-7). Will you ask him to make you clean?

**1:21, 22** Jerusalem here represents all of Judah. God compares the actions of his people to a prostitute. The people had turned from the worship of the true God to worshiping idols. Their faith was worthless, impure, and diluted. Idolatry, outward or inward,

is spiritual adultery, breaking our commitment to God in order to love something else. Jesus described the people of his day as adulterous, even though they were religiously strict. As the church, we are the "bride" of Christ (Revelation 19:7), and, by faith, we can be clothed in his righteousness. Has your faith become impure or watered down? Ask God to restore you. Keep your devotion to him strong and pure.

**1:25** God promised to refine his people similar to the way that metal is purged with lye in a smelting pot. This process involves melting the metal and skimming off the impure slag until the worker can see his own image in the liquid metal. We must be willing to submit to God, allowing him to remove our sin so that we might reflect his image.

**1:26** Isaiah often speaks with both the near present and far future in mind. His prophecies do not necessarily apply to one event, but may apply to a series of present and future events.

**1:28**
Ps 9:5
2 Thes 1:8-9

28 But rebels and sinners will be completely destroyed,
and those who desert the LORD will be consumed.

**1:29**
Isa 57:15; 65:3

29 You will be ashamed of your idol worship
in groves of sacred oaks.
You will blush because you worshiped
in gardens dedicated to idols.
30 You will be like a great tree with withered leaves,
like a garden without water.

**1:31**
Isa 5:24; 33:11-14;
66:24
Matt 3:12

31 The strongest among you will disappear like straw;
their evil deeds will be the spark that sets it on fire.
They and their evil works will burn up together,
and no one will be able to put out the fire.

*The LORD's Future Reign*

**2:1-4**
//Mic 4:1-3

## 2

This is a vision that Isaiah son of Amoz saw concerning Judah and Jerusalem:

2 In the last days, the mountain of the LORD's house
will be the highest of all—
the most important place on earth.
It will be raised above the other hills,
and people from all over the world will stream there to worship.

**2:3**
Isa 51:4-5
Luke 24:47

3 People from many nations will come and say,
"Come, let us go up to the mountain of the LORD,
to the house of Jacob's God.
There he will teach us his ways,
and we will walk in his paths."
For the LORD's teaching will go out from Zion;
his word will go out from Jerusalem.

**2:4**
Isa 32:17-18
Hos 2:18

4 The LORD will mediate between nations
and will settle international disputes.
They will hammer their swords into plowshares
and their spears into pruning hooks.
Nation will no longer fight against nation,
nor train for war anymore.

*A Warning of Judgment*

**2:5**
Isa 58:1; 60:1-2
1 Jn 1:5, 7

5 Come, descendants of Jacob,
let us walk in the light of the LORD!

**2:6**
Deut 31:17
2 Kgs 1:2; 16:7-8

6 For the LORD has rejected his people,
the descendants of Jacob,

---

**1:29, 30** Throughout history, the oak tree has been a symbol of strength, but the people were worshiping "sacred oaks." Ezekiel mentions that oak trees were used as places for idol worship (Ezekiel 6:13). Are you devoted to symbols of strength and power that rival God's place in your life? Does your commitment to any of your interests border on worship? Make God your first loyalty; everything else will fade in time and burn away under his scrutiny.

**1:31** A spark set to tinder ignites a quick, devouring fire. God compares the evil deeds of powerful people to a roaring fire that will devour them. Our life can be destroyed quickly by a small but deadly spark of evil. What potential "fire hazards" do you need to remove?

**2:2** The Temple was built on the mountain of the Lord, Mount Moriah, highly visible to all the people of Jerusalem. For more on the significance of the Temple, see the note on 2 Chronicles 5:1ff. In the last days the Temple will attract the nations, not because of its architecture and prominence, but because of God's presence and influence.

**2:2-4** God gave Isaiah the gift of seeing into the future. At this time, God showed Isaiah what would eventually happen to Jerusalem. Revelation 21 depicts the glorious fulfillment of this prophecy in the new Jerusalem, where only those whose names are written in the Lamb's Book of Life will be allowed to enter. God made a covenant (promise) with his people and will never break it. God's faithfulness gives us hope for the future. Ask God to help you spread his word.

**2:4, 5** This describes a wonderful future of peace when instruments of war will be converted to instruments of farming, and we will be taught God's laws and obey them. Although we know that eventually God will remove all sin, which leads to war, conflicts, and other problems, we should not wait for him to act before we begin to obey him. We should walk in his light now, just as Judah was told to do. Though our eternal reward awaits us, we already can enjoy many benefits of obedience now as we apply God's Word to our life.

because they have filled their land with practices from the East
　　and with sorcerers, as the Philistines do.
　　They have made alliances with pagans.
7 Israel is full of silver and gold;
　　there is no end to its treasures.
　Their land is full of warhorses;
　　there is no end to its chariots.
8 Their land is full of idols;
　　the people worship things they have made
　　　with their own hands.
9 So now they will be humbled,
　　and all will be brought low—
　　do not forgive them.

**2:7**
Deut 17:16

10 Crawl into caves in the rocks.
　　Hide in the dust
　from the terror of the LORD
　　and the glory of his majesty.
11 Human pride will be brought down,
　　and human arrogance will be humbled.
　Only the LORD will be exalted
　　on that day of judgment.

**2:10**
2 Thes 1:9
Rev 6:15-16

12 For the LORD of Heaven's Armies
　　has a day of reckoning.
　He will punish the proud and mighty
　　and bring down everything that is exalted.
13 He will cut down the tall cedars of Lebanon
　　and all the mighty oaks of Bashan.
14 He will level all the high mountains
　　and all the lofty hills.
15 He will break down every high tower
　　and every fortified wall.
16 He will destroy all the great trading ships*
　　and every magnificent vessel.
17 Human pride will be humbled,
　　and human arrogance will be brought down.
　Only the LORD will be exalted
　　on that day of judgment.
18 Idols will completely disappear.
19 When the LORD rises to shake the earth,
　　his enemies will crawl into holes in the ground.

**2:12**
Job 40:11-12
Mal 4:1

**2:13**
Isa 10:33-34
Zech 11:2

**2:16**
1 Kgs 10:22
Isa 23:1, 14

**2:18**
Isa 21:9
Mic 1:7
Heb 12:26

**2:19**
Ps 18:7
Hag 2:6-7

**2:16** Hebrew *every ship of Tarshish.*

**2:6** The people were following practices of the Assyrian Empire. Filling their land with magicians and sorcerers meant that they were claiming to know and control the future by the power of demons or by interpreting omens. These practices were forbidden by God (see Leviticus 19:26; Deuteronomy 18:10, 14). The Philistines worshiped Dagon, Ashtoreth, and Baal-zebub. During the more sinful periods of their history, the people of Israel worshiped these pagan gods along with Yahweh and even gave them Hebrew names.

**2:8, 9** Under the reign of evil kings, idol worship flourished in both Israel and Judah. A few good kings in Judah stopped it during their reigns. Although very few people worship carved or molded images today, worshiping people or objects that symbolize power continues. We pay homage to cars, homes, sports stars, celebrities, money, etc. Idol worship is evil because: (1) it insults God when we worship something he created rather than worshiping him; (2) it keeps us from knowing and serving God when we put our confidence in anything other than him; (3) it causes us to rely on our own efforts rather than on God. (See also Deuteronomy 27:15.)

**2:12** The Lord's "day of reckoning" is the day of judgment, the time when God will judge both evil and good. That day will come, and we will want a proper relationship with God when it does. Pride, however, will cripple us. God alone must be exalted (2:11, 17) as the first step toward developing that relationship with him.

**2:15-17** High towers were part of a city or nation's defenses. This phrase refers to security based on military fortresses. "Great trading ships" picture economic prosperity; and "every magnificent vessel" reveals pleasure and enjoyment. Nothing can compare with or rival the place God must have in our hearts and minds. To place our hope elsewhere is nothing but false pride. Place your confidence in God alone.

**2:19** See Revelation 6:15-17 for a description of the dread in God's enemies on the day of his wrath. The Bible talks of two

They will hide in caves in the rocks
   from the terror of the LORD
   and the glory of his majesty.

**2:20**
Isa 30:22

20 On that day of judgment they will abandon the gold and silver idols
   they made for themselves to worship.
They will leave their gods to the rodents and bats,
21   while they crawl away into caverns
   and hide among the jagged rocks in the cliffs.
They will try to escape the terror of the LORD
   and the glory of his majesty
   as he rises to shake the earth.

**2:22**
Pss 8:4; 144:3-4
Jer 17:5
Jas 4:14

22 Don't put your trust in mere humans.
   They are as frail as breath.
   What good are they?

## Judgment against Judah

**3:1**
Ezek 4:16

**3** ¹ The Lord, the LORD of Heaven's Armies,
   will take away from Jerusalem and Judah
everything they depend on:
   every bit of bread
   and every drop of water,

**3:2**
Lev 26:26
Isa 9:14-15

² all their heroes and soldiers,
   judges and prophets,
   fortune-tellers and elders,
³ army officers and high officials,
   advisers, skilled craftsmen, and astrologers.

**3:4**
Eccl 10:16

⁴ I will make boys their leaders,
   and toddlers their rulers.

**3:5**
Isa 9:19
Jer 9:3-8
Mic 7:3-6

⁵ People will oppress each other—
   man against man,
   neighbor against neighbor.
Young people will insult their elders,
   and vulgar people will sneer at the honorable.

⁶ In those days a man will say to his brother,
"Since you have a coat, you be our leader!
   Take charge of this heap of ruins!"

**3:7**
Ezek 34:4

⁷ But he will reply,
"No! I can't help.
I don't have any extra food or clothes.
   Don't put me in charge!"

**3:8**
Isa 1:7; 6:11; 9:17;
65:3, 5

⁸ For Jerusalem will stumble,
   and Judah will fall,
because they speak out against the LORD and refuse to obey him.
   They provoke him to his face.

---

kinds of fear. In this verse, fear is the panic and peril unbelievers feel at the judgment of God. The right kind of fear means to revere and stand in awe of God. Proverbs 1:7 says, "Fear of the LORD is the foundation of true knowledge." Those who honor and respect God need not fear God's wrath.

**2:22** "As frail as breath" refers to our mortality. People are very limited when compared to God. They can be unreliable, selfish, and shortsighted. Yet we entrust our life and future more readily to mortal human beings than to the all-knowing God. Beware of people who want you to trust them instead of God. Remember that only God is completely reliable. He is perfect, and we can rely on his unfailing love (Psalm 100:5).

**3:1-3** Jerusalem besieged, her leaders destroyed—this unhappy picture would soon become a reality. Disobedience would bring

serious affliction and great destruction, as God had warned (Deuteronomy 28).

**3:2** Isaiah was not condoning fortune-tellers and astrologers by including them in this list. He was showing how far the nation had sunk. See the note on 2:6.

**3:4-9** This section describes what happens when a nation loses its leadership.

9 The very look on their faces gives them away.
　　They display their sin like the people of Sodom
　　　and don't even try to hide it.
　They are doomed!
　　They have brought destruction upon themselves.

10 Tell the godly that all will be well for them.
　　They will enjoy the rich reward they have earned!
11 But the wicked are doomed,
　　for they will get exactly what they deserve.

12 Childish leaders oppress my people,
　　and women rule over them.
　O my people, your leaders mislead you;
　　they send you down the wrong road.

13 The LORD takes his place in court
　　and presents his case against his people!
14 The LORD comes forward to pronounce judgment
　　on the elders and rulers of his people:
　"You have ruined Israel, my vineyard.
　　Your houses are filled with things stolen from the poor.
15 How dare you crush my people,
　　grinding the faces of the poor into the dust?"
　　demands the Lord, the LORD of Heaven's Armies.

## A Warning to Jerusalem

16 The LORD says, "Beautiful Zion* is haughty:
　craning her elegant neck,
　　flirting with her eyes,
　walking with dainty steps,
　　tinkling her ankle bracelets.
17 So the Lord will send scabs on her head;
　　the LORD will make beautiful Zion bald."

18 On that day of judgment
　　the Lord will strip away everything that makes her beautiful:
　ornaments, headbands, crescent necklaces,
19 　earrings, bracelets, and veils;

3:16 Or *The women of Zion* (with corresponding changes to plural forms through verse 24); Hebrew reads *The daughters of Zion;* also in 3:17.

**3:9**
Gen 13:13
Prov 8:36

**3:10**
Deut 28:1-14

**3:11**
Deut 28:15-68

**3:12**
Isa 9:16

**3:13**
Isa 66:16
Hos 4:1
Mic 6:2

**3:14**
Pss 10:9; 14:4
Ezek 18:12;
20:35-36

**3:16**
Isa 4:4

**3:18**
Judg 8:21

---

**3:9-11** The people would be proud of their sins, parading them out in the open. But sin is self-destructive. In today's world, sinful living often appears glamorous, exciting, and clever. But sin is wrong, regardless of how society perceives it, and, in the long run, sin will make us miserable and destroy us. God tries to protect us by warning us about the harm we will cause ourselves by sinning. Those who are proud of their sins will receive the punishment from God they deserve. Having rejected God's path to life (see Psalm 1), they had only one alternative—the path to destruction.

**3:10, 11** In the middle of this gloomy message, God gives hope: Eventually the righteous will receive God's reward, and the wicked will receive their punishment. It is disheartening to see the wicked prosper, while we struggle to obey God and follow his plan. But let us keep holding on to God's truth and take heart! God will bring about justice in the end, and he will reward those who have been faithful.

**3:14** The elders and rulers were responsible to help people, but instead they stole from the poor. Because they were unjust, Isaiah said the leaders would be the first to receive God's judgment. Leaders will be held accountable for how they lead. If you are in a position of leadership, you must lead according to God's just commands. Put the needs of others before your own. Fulfill the

purpose God intended. Don't seek your own advantage. Corruption will bring God's wrath, especially if others follow your example.

**3:14** Why is justice so important in the Bible? (1) Justice is part of God's nature; it is the way he runs the universe. (2) It is a natural desire in every person. Even as sinners, we all want justice for ourselves. (3) When government and church leaders are unjust, the poor and powerless suffer. Thus, they are hindered from worshiping God. (4) God holds the poor in high regard. They are the ones most likely to turn to him for help and comfort. Injustice, then, attacks God's children. When we do nothing to help the oppressed, we are, in fact, joining with the oppressor. Because we follow a just God, we must uphold justice.

**3:16-26** The women of Judah had placed their emphasis on clothing and jewelry rather than on God. They dressed to be noticed, to gain approval, and to be fashionable. Yet they ignored the real purpose for their lives. Instead of being concerned about the oppression around them (3:14, 15), they were self-serving and self-centered. People who abuse their possessions will end up with nothing. These verses are not an indictment against clothing and jewelry, but a judgment on those who use them lavishly while remaining blind to the needs of others. When God blesses you with money or position, don't flaunt it. Use what you have to help others, not impress them.

20 scarves, ankle bracelets, sashes,
   perfumes, and charms;
21 rings, jewels,
22   party clothes, gowns, capes, and purses;
23 mirrors, fine linen garments,
   head ornaments, and shawls.

**3:24**
Esth 2:12
Isa 15:3; 22:12
1 Pet 3:3

24 Instead of smelling of sweet perfume, she will stink.
   She will wear a rope for a sash,
   and her elegant hair will fall out.
   She will wear rough burlap instead of rich robes.
   Shame will replace her beauty.*

**3:25**
Isa 1:20; 65:12

25 The men of the city will be killed with the sword,
   and her warriors will die in battle.

**3:26**
Jer 14:2
Lam 2:10

26 The gates of Zion will weep and mourn.
   The city will be like a ravaged woman,
   huddled on the ground.

**4:1**
Isa 13:12; 54:4

4 In that day so few men will be left that seven women will fight for each man, saying, "Let us all marry you! We will provide our own food and clothing. Only let us take your name so we won't be mocked as old maids."

### A Promise of Restoration

**4:2**
Isa 11:1-5; 52:13;
53:2
Jer 23:5-6
Zech 3:8; 6:12

2 But in that day, the branch* of the LORD
   will be beautiful and glorious;
   the fruit of the land will be the pride and glory
   of all who survive in Israel.

**4:3**
Isa 28:5; 52:1
Luke 10:20

3 All who remain in Zion
   will be a holy people—
   those who survive the destruction of Jerusalem
   and are recorded among the living.

4 The Lord will wash the filth from beautiful Zion*
   and cleanse Jerusalem of its bloodstains
   with the hot breath of fiery judgment.

**4:5**
Num 9:15-23

5 Then the LORD will provide shade for Mount Zion
   and all who assemble there.
   He will provide a canopy of cloud during the day
   and smoke and flaming fire at night,
   covering the glorious land.

**4:6**
Ps 27:5
Isa 25:4; 32:1-2

6 It will be a shelter from daytime heat
   and a hiding place from storms and rain.

**5:1**
Ps 80:8-9
Jer 12:10
Matt 21:33
Mark 12:1
Luke 20:9

### A Song about the LORD's Vineyard

5 1 Now I will sing for the one I love
   a song about his vineyard:
   My beloved had a vineyard
   on a rich and fertile hill.

**5:2**
Jer 2:21
Matt 21:19
Mark 11:13
Luke 13:6

2 He plowed the land, cleared its stones,
   and planted it with the best vines.

**3:24** As in Dead Sea Scrolls; Masoretic Text reads *robes / because instead of beauty.* **4:2** Or *the Branch.*
**4:4** Or *from the women of Zion;* Hebrew reads *from the daughters of Zion.*

**4:2-4** The "branch of the LORD" probably refers to the Messiah, although some believe it refers to Judah. The point is that during the distress predicted by Isaiah, some people will be protected by God's loving grace. Those protected will be set apart to serve God when Messiah rules the earth (Jeremiah 23:5, 6; Zechariah 6:12, 13). Their distinctive mark will be their holiness, not wealth or prestige. This holiness comes from a sincere desire to obey God's moral standards and from their wholehearted devotion to him. Evil will not always continue as it does now. The time will come when

God will put an end to all evil, and his faithful followers will share in his glorious reign.

**5:1-7** The lesson of the song of the vineyard shows that God's chosen nation was to bear fruit—to carry out his work, to uphold justice. It did bear fruit, but the fruit was bad. Jesus said, "Just as you can identify a tree by its fruit, so you can identify people by their actions" (Matthew 7:20). Have you examined your own "fruit" lately? Is it good or bad—useful or wild?

In the middle he built a watchtower
    and carved a winepress in the nearby rocks.
Then he waited for a harvest of sweet grapes,
    but the grapes that grew were bitter.

3 Now, you people of Jerusalem and Judah,
    you judge between me and my vineyard.
4 What more could I have done for my vineyard
    that I have not already done?
When I expected sweet grapes,
    why did my vineyard give me bitter grapes?

**5:4**
Jer 7:25-26
Matt 23:37

5 Now let me tell you
    what I will do to my vineyard:
I will tear down its hedges
    and let it be destroyed.
I will break down its walls
    and let the animals trample it.

**5:5**
Ps 80:12
Lam 1:15
Luke 21:24
Rev 11:2

6 I will make it a wild place
    where the vines are not pruned and the ground is not hoed,
    a place overgrown with briers and thorns.
I will command the clouds
    to drop no rain on it.

**5:6**
Isa 24:13
Jer 14:1-22; 25:11

7 The nation of Israel is the vineyard of the LORD of Heaven's Armies.
    The people of Judah are his pleasant garden.
He expected a crop of justice,
    but instead he found oppression.
He expected to find righteousness,
    but instead he heard cries of violence.

### Judah's Guilt and Judgment

8 What sorrow for you who buy up house after house and field after field,
    until everyone is evicted and you live alone in the land.
9 But I have heard the LORD of Heaven's Armies
    swear a solemn oath:
"Many houses will stand deserted;
    even beautiful mansions will be empty.

**5:8**
Jer 22:13-17
Mic 2:2

**5:9**
Isa 6:11-12
Matt 23:38

10 Ten acres* of vineyard will not produce even six gallons* of wine.
    Ten baskets of seed will yield only one basket* of grain."

**5:10**
Hag 1:6; 2:16

11 What sorrow for those who get up early in the morning
    looking for a drink of alcohol
and spend long evenings drinking wine
    to make themselves flaming drunk.

**5:11**
Prov 23:29-30
Isa 28:1, 3, 7-8

12 They furnish wine and lovely music at their grand parties—
    lyre and harp, tambourine and flute—
but they never think about the LORD
    or notice what he is doing.

**5:12**
Ps 28:5

13 So my people will go into exile far away
    because they do not know me.

**5:13**
Isa 1:3; 3:3
Hos 4:6

5:10a Hebrew *A ten yoke,* that is, the area of land plowed by ten teams of oxen in one day.   5:10b Hebrew *a bath* [21 liters].   5:10c Hebrew *A homer* [5 bushels or 182 liters] *of seed will yield only an ephah* [20 quarts or 22 liters].

---

**5:8-25** In this section, God condemns six sins: (1) exploiting others (5:8-10); (2) drunkenness (5:11, 12); (3) taking pride in sin (5:18, 19); (4) confusing moral standards (5:20); (5) being conceited (5:21); (6) perverting justice (5:22-24). Because of these sins, God punished Israel with destruction by Assyria (5:25-30). A similar fate was awaiting Judah if they didn't turn from these sins.

**5:11-13** These people spent many hours drinking and partying,

but Isaiah predicted that eventually many would die of hunger and thirst. Ironically, our pleasures—if they do not have God's blessing—may destroy us. Leaving God out of our lives allows sin to come in. Pursuing our own pleasure while ignoring or exploiting the needs of others leaves us empty and under God's anger. God wants us to enjoy life (1 Timothy 6:17) but to avoid those activities that could lead us away from him.

**5:13** The nation's heroes—the "great and honored"—would

Those who are great and honored will starve,
and the common people will die of thirst.

**5:14**
Prov 30:16

14 The grave* is licking its lips in anticipation,
opening its mouth wide.
The great and the lowly
and all the drunken mob will be swallowed up.

**5:15**
Isa 2:11

15 Humanity will be destroyed, and people brought down;
even the arrogant will lower their eyes in humiliation.

**5:16**
Isa 33:5, 10

16 But the LORD of Heaven's Armies will be exalted by his justice.
The holiness of God will be displayed by his righteousness.

**5:17**
Isa 29:23
Zeph 2:6

17 In that day lambs will find good pastures,
and fattened sheep and young goats* will feed among the ruins.

**5:18**
Jer 23:10-14

18 What sorrow for those who drag their sins behind them
with ropes made of lies,
who drag wickedness behind them like a cart!

**5:19**
2 Pet 3:3-4

19 They even mock God and say,
"Hurry up and do something!
We want to see what you can do.
Let the Holy One of Israel carry out his plan,
for we want to know what it is."

**5:20**
Prov 17:15
Matt 6:22-23
Luke 11:34-35

20 What sorrow for those who say
that evil is good and good is evil,
that dark is light and light is dark,
that bitter is sweet and sweet is bitter.

**5:21**
Prov 3:7
Rom 12:16
1 Cor 3:18-20

21 What sorrow for those who are wise in their own eyes
and think themselves so clever.

**5:22**
Isa 5:11; 56:12
Hab 2:15

22 What sorrow for those who are heroes at drinking wine
and boast about all the alcohol they can hold.

**5:23**
Ps 94:21
Mic 3:11
Jas 5:6

23 They take bribes to let the wicked go free,
and they punish the innocent.

24 Therefore, just as fire licks up stubble
and dry grass shrivels in the flame,
so their roots will rot
and their flowers wither.
For they have rejected the law of the LORD of Heaven's Armies;
they have despised the word of the Holy One of Israel.

**5:25**
2 Kgs 22:13, 17
Isa 9:12, 17, 21;
10:4; 66:15

25 That is why the LORD's anger burns against his people,
and why he has raised his fist to crush them.
The mountains tremble,
and the corpses of his people litter the streets like garbage.
But even then the LORD's anger is not satisfied.
His fist is still poised to strike!

**5:14** Hebrew *Sheol*.  **5:17** As in Greek version; Hebrew reads *and strangers*.

---

suffer the same humiliation as the common people. Why? Because they lived by their own values rather than God's. Many of today's media, business, and sports heroes are idolized because of their ability to live as they please. Are your heroes those who defy God or those who defy the world in order to serve God?

**5:18, 19** Some people drag their sins around with them. Some do so arrogantly, but for others, their sins have become a burden that wears them out. Are you dragging around a cartload of sins that you refuse to give up? Before you find yourself worn out and useless, turn to the one who promises to take away your burden of sin and replace it with a purpose for living that is a joy to fulfill (see Matthew 11:28-30).

**5:20** When people see no distinction between good and evil, destruction soon follows. It is easy for people to say, "No one can

decide for anyone else what is really right or wrong." They may think getting drunk can't hurt them, extramarital sex isn't really wrong, or money doesn't control them. But when they make excuses for their actions, they break down the distinction between right and wrong. If people do not take God's Word, the Bible, as their standard, soon all moral choices become fuzzy. Without God, they are headed for a breakdown and much suffering.

**5:24** The people suffered because they rejected God's law. It is sad to see so many people today searching for meaning in life while spurning God's Word. We can avoid the error of Israel and Judah by making not only reading the Bible, but also understanding and obeying it, a high priority in our lives.

26 He will send a signal to distant nations far away
  and whistle to those at the ends of the earth.
  They will come racing toward Jerusalem.
27 They will not get tired or stumble.
  They will not stop for rest or sleep.
  Not a belt will be loose,
  not a sandal strap broken.
28 Their arrows will be sharp
  and their bows ready for battle.
  Sparks will fly from their horses' hooves,
  and the wheels of their chariots will spin like a whirlwind.
29 They will roar like lions,
  like the strongest of lions.
  Growling, they will pounce on their victims and carry them off,
  and no one will be there to rescue them.
30 They will roar over their victims on that day of destruction
  like the roaring of the sea.
  If someone looks across the land,
  only darkness and distress will be seen;
  even the light will be darkened by clouds.

### Isaiah's Cleansing and Call

**6** It was in the year King Uzziah died* that I saw the Lord. He was sitting on a lofty throne, and the train of his robe filled the Temple. 2 Attending him were mighty seraphim, each having six wings. With two wings they covered their faces, with two they covered their feet, and with two they flew. 3 They were calling out to each other,

"Holy, holy, holy is the LORD of Heaven's Armies!
  The whole earth is filled with his glory!"

4 Their voices shook the Temple to its foundations, and the entire building was filled with smoke.

5 Then I said, "It's all over! I am doomed, for I am a sinful man. I have filthy lips, and I live among a people with filthy lips. Yet I have seen the King, the LORD of Heaven's Armies."

6 Then one of the seraphim flew to me with a burning coal he had taken from the altar with a pair of tongs. 7 He touched my lips with it and said, "See, this coal has touched your lips. Now your guilt is removed, and your sins are forgiven."

**6:1** King Uzziah died in 740 B.C.

---

**Marginal references:**

**5:26** Isa 13:2-3
**5:27** Joel 2:7-8
**5:28** Ps 7:12-13; Jer 4:13
**5:29** Isa 42:22; Zeph 3:3
**5:30** Isa 8:22; 17:12; Jer 4:23-28; 6:23; Joel 2:10
**6:1** 2 Kgs 15:7; Isa 1:1; John 12:41
**6:2** Rev 4:8
**6:3** Ps 72:19; Rev 4:8
**6:5** Jer 9:3-8; 51:57; Luke 5:8
**6:7** Isa 40:2; Jer 1:9; 1 Jn 1:7

---

**5:26-30** This passage describes what God would do if the people disobeyed him (Deuteronomy 28). Assyria began to torment Israel during the reign of Ahaz (735–715 B.C.). This powerful aggressor destroyed the northern kingdom in 722 B.C. and scattered the people throughout its own empire. Sin has consequences. Although this judgment was not immediate, eventually Israel was punished.

**6:1** The year that King Uzziah died was approximately 740 B.C. He remained leprous until he died because he tried to take over the high priest's duties (2 Chronicles 26:18-21). Although Uzziah was generally a good king with a long and prosperous reign, many of his people turned away from God.

**6:1ff** Isaiah's vision was his commission to be God's messenger to his people. Isaiah was given a difficult mission. He had to tell people who believed they were blessed by God that God was going to destroy them because of their disobedience.

**6:1ff** Isaiah's lofty view of God in 6:1-4 gives us a sense of God's greatness, mystery, and power. Isaiah's example of recognizing his sinfulness before God encourages us to confess our sin. His picture of forgiveness reminds us that we, too, are forgiven. When we recognize how great our God is, how sinful we are, and the extent of God's forgiveness, we receive power to do his work. How does your concept of the greatness of God measure up to Isaiah's?

**6:1-3** The throne, the attending seraphim (angels), and the threefold *holy* all stressed God's holiness. Seraphim were a type of angel whose name is derived from the word for "burn," perhaps indicating their purity as God's ministers. In a time when moral and spiritual decay had peaked, it was important for Isaiah to see God in his holiness. *Holiness* means "morally perfect, pure, and set apart from all sin." We also need to discover God's holiness. Our daily frustrations, society's pressures, and our shortcomings narrow our view of God. We need the Bible's view of God as high and lifted up to empower us to deal with our problems and concerns. God's moral perfection, properly seen, will purify us from sin, cleanse our mind of our problems, and enable us to worship and to serve.

**6:5-8** Seeing the Lord and listening to the praise of the angels, Isaiah realized that he was sinful before God, with no hope of measuring up to God's standard of holiness. When Isaiah's lips were touched with a live burning coal, however, he was told that his sins were forgiven. It wasn't the coal that cleansed him, but God. In response, Isaiah submitted himself entirely to God's service. No matter how difficult his task would be, he said, "Here I am. Send me." The painful cleansing process was necessary before Isaiah could fulfill the task to which God was calling him. Before we accept God's call to speak for him to those around us, we must be cleansed as Isaiah was, confessing our sins and

8Then I heard the Lord asking, "Whom should I send as a messenger to this people? Who will go for us?"

I said, "Here I am. Send me."

**6:9**
†Matt 13:15
†Luke 8:10
Acts 26:19
Rom 11:8
**6:10**
Jer 5:21
†Mark 4:12
†John 12:40
†Acts 28:26-27

9And he said, "Yes, go, and say to this people,

'Listen carefully, but do not understand.
 Watch closely, but learn nothing.'
10 Harden the hearts of these people.
 Plug their ears and shut their eyes.
That way, they will not see with their eyes,
 nor hear with their ears,

---

Trees and prophets share at least one important characteristic—both are planted for the future. Yet seedlings are often overlooked and prophets often ignored. Isaiah is one of the best examples of this. The people of his time could have been rescued by his words. Instead, they refused to believe him. With the passing of centuries, however, Isaiah's words have cast a shadow on all of history.

Isaiah was active as a prophet during the reigns of five kings, but he did not set out to be a prophet. By the time King Uzziah died, Isaiah may have been established as a scribe in the royal palace in Jerusalem. It was a respectable career, but God had other plans for his servant. Isaiah's account of God's call leaves little doubt about what motivated the prophet for the next half century. His vision of God was unforgettable.

His encounter with God permanently affected Isaiah's character. He reflected the God he represented. Isaiah's messages—some comforting, some confronting—are so dissimilar that some have guessed they came from different authors. Isaiah's testimony is that the messages came from the only one capable of being perfect in justice as well as in mercy—God himself.

When he called Isaiah as a prophet, God did not encourage him with predictions of great success. God told Isaiah that the people would not listen. But he was to speak and write his messages anyway because eventually some *would* listen. God compared his people to a tree that would have to be cut down so that a new tree could grow from the old stump (Isaiah 6:13).

We who are part of that future can see that many of the promises God gave through Isaiah have been fulfilled in Jesus Christ. We also gain the hope of knowing that God is active in all of history, including our own.

**ISAIAH**

| | |
|---|---|
| **Strengths and accomplishments** | • Considered the greatest Old Testament prophet<br>• Quoted at least 50 times in the New Testament<br>• Brought powerful messages of both judgment and hope<br>• Carried out a consistent ministry even though there was little positive response from his listeners<br>• His ministry spanned the reigns of five kings of Judah |
| **Lessons from his life** | • God's help is needed in order to comfort people while effectively confronting sin<br>• One result of experiencing forgiveness is the desire to share that forgiveness with others<br>• God is purely and perfectly holy, just, and loving |
| **Vital statistics** | • Where: Jerusalem<br>• Occupations: Scribe, prophet<br>• Relatives: Father: Amoz. Sons: Shear-jashub, Maher-shalal-hash-baz.<br>• Contemporaries: Uzziah, Jotham, Ahaz, Hezekiah, Manasseh, Micah |
| **Key verse** | "Then I heard the Lord asking, 'Whom should I send as a messenger to this people? Who will go for us?' I said, 'Here I am. Send me'" (Isaiah 6:8). |

Isaiah's story is told in 2 Kings 19:2—20:19. He is also mentioned in 2 Chronicles 26:22; 32:20, 32; Matthew 3:3; 8:17; 12:17–21; John 12:38–41; Romans 10:16, 20, 21.

---

submitting to God's control. Letting God purify us may be painful, but we must be purified so that we can truly represent God, who is pure and holy.

**6:8** The more clearly Isaiah saw God (6:5), the more aware Isaiah became of his own powerlessness and inadequacy to do anything of lasting value without God. But he was willing to be God's spokesman. When God calls, will you also say, "Send me"?

**6:9-13** God told Isaiah that the people would listen but not learn from his message because their hearts had become hardened

beyond repentance. God's patience with their chronic rebellion was finally exhausted. His judgment was to abandon them to their rebellion and hardness of heart. Why did God send Isaiah if he knew the people wouldn't listen? Although the nation itself would not repent and would reap judgment, some individuals would listen. In 6:13 God explains his plan for a remnant (holy seed) of faithful followers. God is merciful even when he judges. We can gain encouragement from God's promise to preserve his people. If we are faithful to him, we can be sure of his mercy.

nor understand with their hearts
    and turn to me for healing."*

11 Then I said, "Lord, how long will this go on?"
And he replied,

"Until their towns are empty,
    their houses are deserted,
    and the whole country is a wasteland;
12 until the LORD has sent everyone away,
    and the entire land of Israel lies deserted.
13 If even a tenth—a remnant—survive,
    it will be invaded again and burned.
But as a terebinth or oak tree leaves a stump when it is cut down,
    so Israel's stump will be a holy seed."

*6:11* Lev 26:31; Mic 3:12
*6:12* Jer 4:29
*6:13* Ezra 9:2; Job 14:7

## A Message for Ahaz

**7** When Ahaz, son of Jotham and grandson of Uzziah, was king of Judah, King Rezin of Syria* and Pekah son of Remaliah, the king of Israel, set out to attack Jerusalem. However, they were unable to carry out their plan. 2 The news had come to the royal court of Judah: "Syria is allied with Israel* against us!" So the hearts of the king and his people trembled with fear, like trees shaking in a storm.

3 Then the LORD said to Isaiah, "Take your son Shear-jashub* and go out to meet King Ahaz. You will find him at the end of the aqueduct that feeds water into the upper pool, near the road leading to the field where cloth is washed.* 4 Tell him to stop worrying. Tell him he doesn't need to fear the fierce anger of those two burned-out embers, King Rezin of Syria and Pekah son of Remaliah. 5 Yes, the kings of Syria and Israel are plotting against him, saying, 6 'We will attack Judah and capture it for ourselves. Then we will install the son of Tabeel as Judah's king.' 7 But this is what the Sovereign LORD says:

"This invasion will never happen;
    it will never take place;
8 for Syria is no stronger than its capital, Damascus,
    and Damascus is no stronger than its king, Rezin.
As for Israel, within sixty-five years
    it will be crushed and completely destroyed.
9 Israel is no stronger than its capital, Samaria,
    and Samaria is no stronger than its king, Pekah son of Remaliah.
Unless your faith is firm,
    I cannot make you stand firm."

*7:1* 2 Kgs 15:25, 37; 16:1
*7:2* Isa 7:13; 8:12
*7:4* Exod 14:13; Isa 10:24; 30:15; 35:4; Lam 3:26
*7:7* Isa 8:10
*7:8* Isa 17:1-3
*7:9* 2 Chr 20:20; Isa 30:12-14

**6:9-10** Greek version reads *And he said, "Go and say to this people, / 'When you hear what I say, you will not understand. / When you see what I do, you will not comprehend.' / For the hearts of these people are hardened, / and their ears cannot hear, and they have closed their eyes— / so their eyes cannot see, / and their ears cannot hear, / and their hearts cannot understand, / and they cannot turn to me and let me heal them."* Compare Matt 13:14-15; Mark 4:12; Luke 8:10; Acts 28:26-27. **7:1** Hebrew *Aram;* also in 7:2, 4, 5, 8. **7:2** Hebrew *Ephraim,* referring to the northern kingdom of Israel; also in 7:5, 8, 9, 17. **7:3a** *Shear-jashub* means "A remnant will return." **7:3b** Or *bleached.*

**6:11-13** When would the people listen? Only after they had come to the end and had nowhere to turn but to God. This would happen when the land was destroyed by invading armies and the people taken into captivity. The "tenth" refers either to those who remained in the land after the captivity or to those who returned from Babylon to rebuild the land. Each group was about a tenth of the total population. When will we listen to God? Must we, like Judah, go through calamities before we will listen to God's words? Consider what God may be telling you, and obey him before time runs out.

**7:1** The year was 734 B.C. Ahaz, king of Judah in Jerusalem, was about to be attacked by an alliance of the northern kingdom of Israel and Aram. He was frightened by the prospect of the possible end of his reign and by the invading armies that killed many people or took them as captives (2 Chronicles 28:5-21). But, as Isaiah predicted, the kingdom of Judah did not come to an end at this time. The sign of Immanuel would be a sign of deliverance.

**7:3** *Shear-jashub* means "a remnant will return." God told Isaiah to give his son this name as a reminder of his plan for mercy. From

the beginning of God's judgment he planned to restore a remnant of his people. Shear-jashub was a reminder to the people of God's faithfulness to them.

**7:3** The "aqueduct" may have been the site of the Gihon Spring, located east of Jerusalem. The Gihon Spring was the main source of water for the holy city and was also the spring that emptied into Hezekiah's famous water tunnel (2 Chronicles 32:30). The field where the cloth is washed was a well-known place where clothing or newly woven cloth was laid in the sun to dry and whiten (see 36:2).

**7:4–8:15** Isaiah predicted the breakup of Israel's alliance with Aram (7:4-9). Because of this alliance, Israel would be destroyed; Assyria would be the instrument God would use to destroy them (7:8-25) and to punish Judah. But God would not let Assyria destroy Judah (8:1-15). They would be spared because God's gracious plans cannot be thwarted.

**7:8** Ahaz, one of Judah's worst kings, refused God's help, and instead, he tried to buy aid from the Assyrians with silver and gold from the Temple (2 Kings 16:8). When the Assyrians came,

## The Sign of Immanuel

7:11
2 Kgs 19:29
Isa 37:30; 38:7-8

[10]Later, the LORD sent this message to King Ahaz: [11]"Ask the LORD your God for a sign of confirmation, Ahaz. Make it as difficult as you want—as high as heaven or as deep as the place of the dead.*"

[12]But the king refused. "No," he said, "I will not test the LORD like that."

7:14
Isa 8:8, 10
†Matt 1:23

7:15
Isa 8:4; 17:3

[13]Then Isaiah said, "Listen well, you royal family of David! Isn't it enough to exhaust human patience? Must you exhaust the patience of my God as well? [14]All right then, the Lord himself will give you the sign. Look! The virgin* will conceive a child! She will give birth to a son and will call him Immanuel (which means 'God is with us'). [15]By the time this child is old enough to choose what is right and reject what is wrong, he will be eating yogurt* and honey. [16]For before the child is that old, the lands of the two kings you fear so much will both be deserted.

7:17
1 Kgs 12:16-17
Isa 10:5-6

7:18
Isa 5:26

7:19
Jer 16:16

7:20
Isa 8:7; 10:5, 15;
24:1
Ezek 5:1-4

7:21
Jer 39:10

[17]"Then the LORD will bring things on you, your nation, and your family unlike anything since Israel broke away from Judah. He will bring the king of Assyria upon you!"

[18]In that day the LORD will whistle for the army of southern Egypt and for the army of Assyria. They will swarm around you like flies and bees. [19]They will come in vast hordes and settle in the fertile areas and also in the desolate valleys, caves, and thorny places. [20]In that day the Lord will hire a "razor" from beyond the Euphrates River*—the king of Assyria—and use it to shave off everything: your land, your crops, and your people.*

[21]In that day a farmer will be fortunate to have a cow and two sheep or goats left. [22]Nevertheless, there will be enough milk for everyone because so few people will be left in the land. They will eat their fill of yogurt and honey. [23]In that day the lush vineyards, now worth 1,000 pieces of silver,* will become patches of briers and thorns. [24]The entire land will become a vast expanse of briers and thorns, a hunting ground overrun by wildlife. [25]No one will go to the fertile hillsides where the gardens once grew, for briers and thorns will cover them. Cattle, sheep, and goats will graze there.

## The Coming Assyrian Invasion

8:1
Isa 30:8
Hab 2:2

8:2
2 Kgs 16:10-11,
15-16

**8** Then the LORD said to me, "Make a large signboard and clearly write this name on it: Maher-shalal-hash-baz.*" [2]I asked Uriah the priest and Zechariah son of Jeberekiah, both known as honest men, to witness my doing this.

7:11 Hebrew as deep as Sheol.   7:14 Or young woman.   7:15 Or curds; also in 7:22.   7:20a Hebrew the river.   7:20b Hebrew shave off the head, the hair of the legs, and the beard.   7:23 Hebrew 1,000 shekels of silver, about 25 pounds or 11.4 kilograms in weight.   8:1 Maher-shalal-hash-baz means "Swift to plunder and quick to carry away."

---

they brought further trouble instead of help. In 722 B.C., Samaria, the capital of Israel, the northern kingdom, fell to the Assyrian armies, thus ending the northern kingdom.

**7:12** Ahaz appeared righteous by saying he would not test God with a sign ("I will not test the LORD like that"). In fact, God had told him to ask, but Ahaz didn't really want to know what God would say. Often we use some excuse—such as not wanting to bother God or blaming some theological question that concerns us—to keep us from communicating with him. Don't let anything keep you from hearing and obeying God.

**7:14-16** "Virgin" is translated from a Hebrew word used for an unmarried woman who is old enough to be married, one who is sexually mature (see Genesis 24:43; Exodus 2:8; Psalm 68:25; Proverbs 30:19; Song of Songs 1:3; 6:8). Some have compared this young woman to Isaiah's young wife and newborn son (8:1-4). This is not likely because she had a child, Shear-jashub, and her second child was not named Immanuel. Some believe that Isaiah's first wife may have died, and so this is his second wife. It is more likely that this prophecy had a double fulfillment. (1) A young woman from the house of Ahaz who was not married would marry and have a son. Before three years passed (one year for pregnancy and two for the child to be old enough to talk), the two invading kings would be destroyed. (2) Matthew 1:23 quotes Isaiah 7:14 to show a further fulfillment of this prophecy in that a virgin named Mary conceived and bore a son, Immanuel, the Christ.

**7:18** Flies and bees are symbols of God's judgment (see Exodus 23:28). Egypt and Assyria did not at this time devastate Judah. Hezekiah followed Ahaz as king, and he honored God; therefore,

God held back his hand of judgment. Two more evil kings reigned before Josiah, of whom it was said that no other king turned so completely to the Lord (2 Kings 23:25). However, Judah's doom had been sealed by the extreme evil of Josiah's father, Amon. During Josiah's reign, Egypt marched against the Assyrians. Josiah then declared war on Egypt, although God told him not to. After Josiah was killed (2 Chronicles 35:20-27), only weak kings reigned in Judah. The Egyptians carried off Josiah's son, Jehoahaz, after three months. The next king, Jehoiakim, was taken by Nebuchadnezzar to Babylon. Egypt and Assyria had dealt death blows to Judah.

**7:20** Hiring Assyria to save them would be Judah's downfall (2 Kings 16:7, 8). To "shave" Judah's hair was symbolic of total humiliation. Numbers 6:9 explains that after being defiled, a person who had been set apart for the Lord had to shave his head as part of the cleansing process. Shaving bodily hair was an embarrassment—an exposure of nakedness. For a Hebrew man to have his beard shaved was humiliating (2 Samuel 10:4, 5).

**7:21-25** Judah's rich farmland would be trampled until it became pastureland, fit only for grazing. No longer would it be a place of agricultural abundance, "a land flowing with milk and honey" (Exodus 3:8), but a land with only briers and thorns.

**8:1-4** These verses predict the fall of Israel and Aram. Aram fell to Assyria in 732 B.C., and Israel followed in 722 B.C. Isaiah put his message on a large scroll in a public place. God was warning all his people. The name of the child means "swift to plunder and quick to spoil."

³Then I slept with my wife, and she became pregnant and gave birth to a son. And the LORD said, "Call him Maher-shalal-hash-baz. ⁴For before this child is old enough to say 'Papa' or 'Mama,' the king of Assyria will carry away both the abundance of Damascus and the riches of Samaria."

⁵Then the LORD spoke to me again and said, ⁶"My care for the people of Judah is like the gently flowing waters of Shiloah, but they have rejected it. They are rejoicing over what will happen to* King Rezin and King Pekah.* ⁷Therefore, the Lord will overwhelm them with a mighty flood from the Euphrates River*—the king of Assyria and all his glory. This flood will overflow all its channels ⁸and sweep into Judah until it is chin deep. It will spread its wings, submerging your land from one end to the other, O Immanuel.

⁹ "Huddle together, you nations, and be terrified.
    Listen, all you distant lands.
Prepare for battle, but you will be crushed!
    Yes, prepare for battle, but you will be crushed!
¹⁰ Call your councils of war, but they will be worthless.
    Develop your strategies, but they will not succeed.
    For God is with us!*"

## A Call to Trust the LORD

¹¹The LORD has given me a strong warning not to think like everyone else does. He said,

¹² "Don't call everything a conspiracy, like they do,
    and don't live in dread of what frightens them.
¹³ Make the LORD of Heaven's Armies holy in your life.
    He is the one you should fear.
    He is the one who should make you tremble.
¹⁴    He will keep you safe.
    But to Israel and Judah
        he will be a stone that makes people stumble,
        a rock that makes them fall.
    And for the people of Jerusalem
        he will be a trap and a snare.
¹⁵ Many will stumble and fall,
        never to rise again.
    They will be snared and captured."

¹⁶ Preserve the teaching of God;
    entrust his instructions to those who follow me.
¹⁷ I will wait for the LORD,

8:6a Or *They are rejoicing because of.*   8:6b Hebrew *and the son of Remaliah.*   8:7 Hebrew *the river.*
8:10 Hebrew *Immanuel!*

| | |
|---|---|
| **8:4** | Isa 7:8-9, 16 |
| **8:6** | Isa 7:1; 30:12 |
| **8:7** | Isa 17:12-13<br>Amos 8:8; 9:5 |
| **8:8** | Isa 7:14; 10:6;<br>30:28 |
| **8:9** | Dan 2:34-35 |
| **8:12** | Isa 7:2<br>†1 Pet 3:13-15 |
| **8:13** | Num 20:12<br>Isa 5:16; 29:23 |
| **8:14** | Ezek 11:16<br>Luke 2:34<br>†Rom 9:33<br>†1 Pet 2:8 |
| **8:15** | Luke 20:18<br>Rom 9:32 |
| **8:17** | Deut 31:17<br>Isa 30:18; 54:8<br>Hab 2:3 |

**8:6-8** Because the people of Judah rejected God's kindness, choosing instead to seek help from other nations, God would punish them. We see two distinct attributes of God—his love and his wrath. To ignore his love and guidance results in sin and invites his wrath. We must recognize the consequences of our choices. God wants to protect us from bad choices, but he still gives us the freedom to make them.

**8:7, 8** The heart of the Assyrian Empire was located between the Tigris and Euphrates Rivers. This flood was a poetic way of describing the overwhelming force of the Assyrian army.

**8:9** To "be crushed" means to lose courage by the pressure of sudden fear.

**8:11** Isaiah, along with most of the prophets, was viewed as a traitor because he did not support Judah's national policies. He called the people to commit themselves first to God and then to the king. He even predicted the overthrow of the government.

**8:11-15** For the people of Judah, fear of invasion was a constant threat. They had powerful enemies on their doorstep. Yet Isaiah said, "The LORD of Heaven's Armies . . . is the one you should

fear . . . He will keep you safe." Fear is a powerful enemy of our faith and a strong deterrent to the believer's peace of mind. Fear of war, terrorist attacks, disease, and pollution can rob us of our trust in God. God is our shelter and hiding place (4:6). Ask him to drive inappropriate fear from your heart and to help you fear only him.

**8:16** Because some people faithfully preserved the teaching of God and passed on these words from generation to generation, we have the book of Isaiah today. Each of us needs to accept the responsibility to pass on God's Word to our children and grandchildren, encouraging them to love the Bible, read it, and learn from it. Then they will faithfully pass it on to their children and grandchildren.

**8:17** Isaiah decided to wait for the Lord, though God had "turned away from" the people of Israel. For some believers, patient waiting becomes the most difficult testing they must face: waiting for illness to pass, for a child to return to God and the church, or for God to make matters right in a particular situation. Many of the prophecies God gave through the prophets would not come true for 700 years; others still haven't been fulfilled in our lifetime. Are you willing to accept the Lord's timing, not yours?

who has turned away from the descendants of Jacob.
I will put my hope in him.

8:18
†Heb 2:13

8:19
Lev 20:6
1 Sam 28:8
2 Kgs 21:6
Isa 19:3; 30:2

8:20
Mic 3:6
Luke 16:29

8:22
Isa 5:30
Jer 13:16
Amos 5:18, 20
Zeph 1:14-15

[18]I and the children the LORD has given me serve as signs and warnings to Israel from the LORD of Heaven's Armies who dwells in his Temple on Mount Zion.

[19]Someone may say to you, "Let's ask the mediums and those who consult the spirits of the dead. With their whisperings and mutterings, they will tell us what to do." But shouldn't people ask God for guidance? Should the living seek guidance from the dead?

[20]Look to God's instructions and teachings! People who contradict his word are completely in the dark. [21]They will go from one place to another, weary and hungry. And because they are hungry, they will rage and curse their king and their God. They will look up to heaven [22]and down at the earth, but wherever they look, there will be trouble and anguish and dark despair. They will be thrown out into the darkness.

### Hope in the Messiah

9:1
2 Kgs 15:29
2 Chr 16:4

**9** [1]*Nevertheless, that time of darkness and despair will not go on forever. The land of Zebulun and Naphtali will be humbled, but there will be a time in the future when Galilee of the Gentiles, which lies along the road that runs between the Jordan and the sea, will be filled with glory.

9:2
†Matt 4:15-16

[2]* The people who walk in darkness
    will see a great light.
For those who live in a land of deep darkness,*
    a light will shine.

9:3
Isa 26:15; 35:10;
66:10

[3] You will enlarge the nation of Israel,
    and its people will rejoice.
They will rejoice before you
    as people rejoice at the harvest
    and like warriors dividing the plunder.

9:4
Isa 49:26

[4] For you will break the yoke of their slavery
    and lift the heavy burden from their shoulders.
You will break the oppressor's rod,
    just as you did when you destroyed the army of Midian.

**9:1** Verse 9:1 is numbered 8:23 in Hebrew text.   **9:2a** Verses 9:2-21 are numbered 9:1-20 in Hebrew text.
**9:2b** Greek version reads *a land where death casts its shadow.* Compare Matt 4:16.

---

**NAMES FOR MESSIAH**

*Wonderful Counselor* . . . . . He is exceptional, distinguished, and without peer, the one who gives the right advice.

*Mighty God* . . . . . . . . . . . . He is God himself.

*Everlasting Father* . . . . . . . He is timeless; he is God our Father.

*Prince of Peace* . . . . . . . . . His government is one of justice and peace.

Isaiah uses four names in 9:6 to describe the Messiah. These names have special meaning to us.

---

**8:19** The people would consult mediums and psychics, seeking answers from dead people instead of consulting the living God. God alone knows the future, and only he is eternal. We can trust God to guide us.

**8:21** After rejecting God's plan for them, the people of Judah would blame God for their trials. People continually blame God for their self-induced problems. How do you respond to the unpleasant results of your own choices? Where do you fix the blame? Instead of blaming God, look for ways to grow through your bad choices and failures.

**9:1** In our gloom and despair, we fear that our sorrows and troubles will never end. But we can take comfort in this certainty: Although the Lord may not always spare us from troubles, if we follow him wholeheartedly, he will lead us safely through them.

**9:1-7** This child, who would become their deliverer, is the Messiah, Jesus. Matthew quotes these verses in describing

Christ's ministry (Matthew 4:15, 16). The territories of Zebulun and Naphtali represent the northern kingdom as a whole. These were also the territories where Jesus grew up and often ministered; this is why they would see "a great light."

**9:2** The apostle John also referred to Jesus as the "true light" (John 1:9). Jesus referred to himself as "the light of the world" (John 8:12). Whenever we see the lights of Christmas, let them remind us that they recall Christ, our true Light.

**9:2-6** In a time of great darkness, God promised to send a light who would shine on everyone living in the shadow of death. He is both "Wonderful Counselor" and "Mighty God." This message of hope was fulfilled in the birth of Christ and the establishment of his eternal Kingdom. He came to deliver all people from their slavery to sin.

⁵ The boots of the warrior
  and the uniforms bloodstained by war
will all be burned.
  They will be fuel for the fire.

⁶ For a child is born to us,
  a son is given to us.
The government will rest on his shoulders.
  And he will be called:
Wonderful Counselor,* Mighty God,
  Everlasting Father, Prince of Peace.
⁷ His government and its peace
  will never end.
He will rule with fairness and justice from the throne of his ancestor David
  for all eternity.
The passionate commitment of the LORD of Heaven's Armies
  will make this happen!

**9:6**
Deut 10:17
Neh 9:32
Isa 7:14; 26:3, 12
Matt 28:18
1 Cor 15:25

**9:7**
Dan 2:44
Luke 1:32-33

### The LORD's Anger against Israel

⁸ The Lord has spoken out against Jacob;
  his judgment has fallen upon Israel.
⁹ And the people of Israel* and Samaria,
  who spoke with such pride and arrogance,
  will soon know it.

**9:9**
Isa 7:8-9

¹⁰ They said, "We will replace the broken bricks of our ruins with finished stone,
  and replant the felled sycamore-fig trees with cedars."

¹¹ But the LORD will bring Rezin's enemies against Israel
  and stir up all their foes.
¹² The Syrians* from the east and the Philistines from the west
  will bare their fangs and devour Israel.
But even then the LORD's anger will not be satisfied.
  His fist is still poised to strike.

**9:12**
Ps 79:7

¹³ For after all this punishment, the people will still not repent.
  They will not seek the LORD of Heaven's Armies.
¹⁴ Therefore, in a single day the LORD will destroy both the head and the tail,
  the noble palm branch and the lowly reed.
¹⁵ The leaders of Israel are the head,
  and the lying prophets are the tail.
¹⁶ For the leaders of the people have misled them.
  They have led them down the path of destruction.
¹⁷ That is why the Lord takes no pleasure in the young men
  and shows no mercy even to the widows and orphans.
For they are all wicked hypocrites,
  and they all speak foolishness.
But even then the LORD's anger will not be satisfied.
  His fist is still poised to strike.

**9:13**
Jer 5:3
Hos 7:10

**9:14**
Isa 19:15
Rev 18:8

**9:16**
Matt 15:14

**9:17**
Amos 8:13
Matt 12:34

¹⁸ This wickedness is like a brushfire.
  It burns not only briers and thorns
but also sets the forests ablaze.
  Its burning sends up clouds of smoke.
¹⁹ The land will be blackened
  by the fury of the LORD of Heaven's Armies.

**9:18**
Mal 4:1

**9:19**
Joel 2:3
Mic 7:2, 6

**9:6** Or *Wonderful, Counselor.*  **9:9** Hebrew *of Ephraim,* referring to the northern kingdom of Israel.  **9:12** Hebrew *Arameans.*

**9:8-10** Pride made Israel think it would recover and rebuild in its own strength. Even though God made the people of Israel a nation and gave them the land they occupied, they put their trust in themselves rather than in him. Too often we take pride in our accomplishments, forgetting that it is God who has given us our resources and abilities. We may even become proud of our unique status as Christians. God is not pleased with *any* pride or trust in ourselves because it cuts off our contact with him.

The people will be fuel for the fire,
and no one will spare even his own brother.

**9:20**
Isa 8:21-22; 49:26

20 They will attack their neighbor on the right
but will still be hungry.
They will devour their neighbor on the left
but will not be satisfied.
In the end they will even eat their own children.*

**9:21**
Isa 5:25; 11:13

21 Manasseh will feed on Ephraim,
Ephraim will feed on Manasseh,
and both will devour Judah.
But even then the LORD's anger will not be satisfied.
His fist is still poised to strike.

**10:1**
Ps 94:20

**10:2**
Isa 1:23; 5:23

**10** ¹ What sorrow awaits the unjust judges
and those who issue unfair laws.
² They deprive the poor of justice
and deny the rights of the needy among my people.
They prey on widows
and take advantage of orphans.
³ What will you do when I punish you,
when I send disaster upon you from a distant land?
To whom will you turn for help?
Where will your treasures be safe?

**10:4**
Isa 34:3; 66:16

⁴ You will stumble along as prisoners
or lie among the dead.
But even then the LORD's anger will not be satisfied.
His fist is still poised to strike.

### Judgment against Assyria

**10:5**
Jer 51:20

⁵ "What sorrow awaits Assyria, the rod of my anger.
I use it as a club to express my anger.
⁶ I am sending Assyria against a godless nation,
against a people with whom I am angry.
Assyria will plunder them,
trampling them like dirt beneath its feet.

**10:7**
Gen 50:20
Mic 4:11-12
Acts 2:23-24

⁷ But the king of Assyria will not understand that he is my tool;
his mind does not work that way.
His plan is simply to destroy,
to cut down nation after nation.
⁸ He will say,
'Each of my princes will soon be a king.

**10:9**
2 Kgs 16:9
2 Chr 35:20
Amos 6:2

⁹ We destroyed Calno just as we did Carchemish.
Hamath fell before us as Arpad did.
And we destroyed Samaria just as we did Damascus.

**10:10**
2 Kgs 19:17-18

¹⁰ Yes, we have finished off many a kingdom
whose gods were greater than those in Jerusalem and Samaria.

**9:20** Or *eat their own arms.*

---

**9:21** Ephraim and Manasseh were tribes in the northern kingdom descended from Joseph's two sons. They fought a civil war because of their selfishness and wickedness (see Judges 12:4).

**10:1** God will judge unjust judges and those who make unfair laws. Those who oppress others will be oppressed themselves. It is not enough to live in a land founded on justice; each individual must deal justly with the poor and the powerless. Don't pass your responsibility off onto your nation or even your church. You are accountable to God for what you do for the poor.

**10:7** Although Assyria did not know it was part of God's plan, God used this nation to judge his people. God accomplishes his plans in history despite people or nations who reject him. He did not merely set the world in motion and let it go! Because our all-

powerful, sovereign God is still in control today, we have security even in a rapidly changing world.

**10:9** Calno, Carchemish, Hamath, Arpad, Samaria, and Damascus were cities conquered by Assyria. Assured of great victories that would enlarge their empire, the king of Assyria gave an arrogant speech. Already Assyria had conquered several cities and thought Judah would be defeated along with the others. Little did he know that they were under the mightier hand of God.

**10:10** Samaria and Jerusalem were filled with idols that were powerless against the Assyrian military machine. Only the God of the universe could and would overthrow Assyria, but not until he had used the Assyrians for his purposes.

<sup>11</sup> So we will defeat Jerusalem and her gods,
   just as we destroyed Samaria with hers.'"

<sup>12</sup>After the Lord has used the king of Assyria to accomplish his purposes on Mount Zion
and in Jerusalem, he will turn against the king of Assyria and punish him—for he is proud
and arrogant. <sup>13</sup>He boasts,

**10:12**
2 Kgs 19:31
Jer 50:18

**10:13**
2 Kgs 19:22-24
Isa 37:24-27
Ezek 28:4
Dan 4:30

"By my own powerful arm I have done this.
   With my own shrewd wisdom I planned it.
I have broken down the defenses of nations
   and carried off their treasures.
I have knocked down their kings like a bull.
<sup>14</sup> I have robbed their nests of riches
   and gathered up kingdoms as a farmer gathers eggs.
No one can even flap a wing against me
   or utter a peep of protest."

<sup>15</sup> But can the ax boast greater power than the person who uses it?
   Is the saw greater than the person who saws?
Can a rod strike unless a hand moves it?
   Can a wooden cane walk by itself?

**10:15**
Isa 10:5; 29:16
Jer 51:20
Rom 9:20-21

<sup>16</sup> Therefore, the Lord, the LORD of Heaven's Armies,
   will send a plague among Assyria's proud troops,
   and a flaming fire will consume its glory.
<sup>17</sup> The LORD, the Light of Israel, will be a fire;
   the Holy One will be a flame.
He will devour the thorns and briers with fire,
   burning up the enemy in a single night.
<sup>18</sup> The LORD will consume Assyria's glory
   like a fire consumes a forest in a fruitful land;
   it will waste away like sick people in a plague.
<sup>19</sup> Of all that glorious forest, only a few trees will survive—
   so few that a child could count them!

**10:17**
Isa 27:4; 30:33;
31:9; 33:12; 37:23
Jer 4:4

**10:19**
Isa 21:17

*Hope for the LORD's People*
<sup>20</sup> In that day the remnant left in Israel,
   the survivors in the house of Jacob,
will no longer depend on allies
   who seek to destroy them.
But they will faithfully trust the LORD,
   the Holy One of Israel.
<sup>21</sup> A remnant will return;*
   yes, the remnant of Jacob will return to the Mighty God.

**10:20**
Isa 17:7-8

**10:21** Hebrew *Shear-jashub*; see 7:3; 8:18.

---

**10:12** The predicted punishment of the Assyrians took place in
701 B.C., when 185,000 Assyrian soldiers were slain by the angel
of the Lord (37:36, 37). Later, the Assyrian Empire fell to Babylon,
never to rise again as a world power.

**10:12** The Assyrians were arrogant. Proud of the victories God
permitted, they thought they had accomplished everything in their
own power. Our perspective can also become distorted by pride
in our accomplishments. If we do not acknowledge God to be
in control of our lives, working out his purposes, we are bound
to fail.

**10:15** No instrument or tool accomplishes its purposes without
a greater power. The Assyrians were a tool in God's hands, but
they failed to recognize it. When a tool boasts of greater power
than the one who uses it, it is in danger of being discarded. We
are useful only to the extent that we allow God to use us. If God
has given us resources and special talents, we must not regard
them as our own creation or special privilege.

**10:17** Assyria's downfall came in 612 B.C. when Nineveh, the
capital city, was destroyed. Assyria had been God's instrument
of judgment against Israel, but it, too, would be judged for its
wickedness. No one escapes God's judgment against sin, not even
the most powerful of nations (Psalm 2).

**10:20, 21** Once Assyria's army was destroyed, a small group
of God's people would stop relying on Assyria and start trusting
God. This remnant would be but a fraction of Israel's former
population: see Ezra 2:64, 65 for the small number who returned
to Judah (see also 11:10-16).

**10:20, 21** Those who remained faithful to God despite the
horrors of the invasion are called the remnant. The key to being
a part of the remnant was *faith*. Being a descendant of Abraham,
living in the Promised Land, having trusted God at one time—
none of these were good enough. Are you relying on your Christian heritage, your participation in church, or a past experience
to qualify you for belonging to God's family? The key to being
a true Christian is faith in the mighty God.

10:22
Isa 28:22
†Rom 9:27-28

22 But though the people of Israel are as numerous
    as the sand of the seashore,
only a remnant of them will return.
The LORD has rightly decided to destroy his people.
23 Yes, the Lord, the LORD of Heaven's Armies,
has already decided to destroy the entire land.*

10:24
Exod 5:14-16

10:25
Isa 17:14

10:26
Exod 14:16, 27
Judg 7:25
Isa 37:36-38

24So this is what the Lord, the LORD of Heaven's Armies, says: "O my people in Zion, do not be afraid of the Assyrians when they oppress you with rod and club as the Egyptians did long ago. 25In a little while my anger against you will end, and then my anger will rise up to destroy them." 26The LORD of Heaven's Armies will lash them with his whip, as he did when Gideon triumphed over the Midianites at the rock of Oreb, or when the LORD's staff was raised to drown the Egyptian army in the sea.

10:27
Isa 14:25

27 In that day the LORD will end the bondage of his people.
He will break the yoke of slavery
    and lift it from their shoulders.*

10:28
1 Sam 13:2, 5; 14:2

28 Look, the Assyrians are now at Aiath.
    They are passing through Migron
    and are storing their equipment at Micmash.

10:29
Josh 18:25; 21:17
1 Sam 10:26

29 They are crossing the pass
    and are camping at Geba.
Fear strikes the town of Ramah.
    All the people of Gibeah, the hometown of Saul,
    are running for their lives.

10:30
Josh 21:18
1 Sam 25:44

30 Scream in terror,
    you people of Gallim!
Shout out a warning to Laishah.
    Oh, poor Anathoth!
31 There go the people of Madmenah, all fleeing.
    The citizens of Gebim are trying to hide.

10:32
Isa 19:16
Zech 2:9

32 The enemy stops at Nob for the rest of that day.
    He shakes his fist at beautiful Mount Zion, the mountain of Jerusalem.

10:33
Ezek 31:2-3
Amos 2:9

33 But look! The Lord, the LORD of Heaven's Armies,
    will chop down the mighty tree of Assyria with great power!
He will cut down the proud.
    That lofty tree will be brought down.
34 He will cut down the forest trees with an ax.
    Lebanon will fall to the Mighty One.*

### A Branch from David's Line

11:1
Jer 23:5
Rev 5:5

11:2
Isa 61:1
Matt 3:16
John 1:32
Eph 1:17

**11** ¹ Out of the stump of David's family* will grow a shoot—
    yes, a new Branch bearing fruit from the old root.
² And the Spirit of the LORD will rest on him—
    the Spirit of wisdom and understanding,
the Spirit of counsel and might,
    the Spirit of knowledge and the fear of the LORD.

**10:22-23** Greek version reads *only a remnant of them will be saved. / For he will carry out his sentence quickly and with finality and righteousness; / for God will carry out his sentence upon all the world with finality.* Compare Rom 9:27-28. **10:27** As in Greek version; Hebrew reads *The yoke will be broken, / for you have grown so fat.* **10:34** Or *with an ax / as even the mighty trees of Lebanon fall.* **11:1** Hebrew *the stump of the line of Jesse.* Jesse was King David's father.

---

**10:28-34** The way these cities are listed approximates the route the Assyrians would take in their invasion of Judah in 701 B.C. They would go from Aiath (probably Ai) at the northern border to Nob (only two miles from Jerusalem).

**11:1-9** Assyria would be like a tree cut down at the height of its power (10:33, 34), never to rise again. Judah (the royal line of David) would be like a tree chopped down to a stump. But from that stump a new shoot would grow—the Messiah. He would be greater than the original tree and would bear much fruit. The Messiah is the fulfillment of God's promise that a descendant of David would rule forever (2 Samuel 7:16).

3 He will delight in obeying the Lord.
   He will not judge by appearance
   nor make a decision based on hearsay.

4 He will give justice to the poor
   and make fair decisions for the exploited.
The earth will shake at the force of his word,
   and one breath from his mouth will destroy the wicked.

5 He will wear righteousness like a belt
   and truth like an undergarment.

6 In that day the wolf and the lamb will live together;
   the leopard will lie down with the baby goat.
The calf and the yearling will be safe with the lion,
   and a little child will lead them all.

7 The cow will graze near the bear.
   The cub and the calf will lie down together.
   The lion will eat hay like a cow.

8 The baby will play safely near the hole of a cobra.
   Yes, a little child will put its hand in a nest of deadly snakes without harm.

9 Nothing will hurt or destroy in all my holy mountain,
   for as the waters fill the sea,
   so the earth will be filled with people who know the Lord.

10 In that day the heir to David's throne*
   will be a banner of salvation to all the world.
The nations will rally to him,
   and the land where he lives will be a glorious place.*

11 In that day the Lord will reach out his hand a second time
   to bring back the remnant of his people—
those who remain in Assyria and northern Egypt;
   in southern Egypt, Ethiopia,* and Elam;
   in Babylonia,* Hamath, and all the distant coastlands.

12 He will raise a flag among the nations
   and assemble the exiles of Israel.
He will gather the scattered people of Judah
   from the ends of the earth.

13 Then at last the jealousy between Israel* and Judah will end.
   They will not be rivals anymore.

14 They will join forces to swoop down on Philistia to the west.
   Together they will attack and plunder the nations to the east.

**11:3**
John 2:24-25

**11:4**
Isa 30:28
2 Thes 2:8

**11:6**
Isa 65:25

**11:9**
Job 5:23
Ezek 34:25
Hos 2:18
Hab 2:14

**11:10**
Luke 2:32
John 3:14-15
†Rom 15:12

**11:11**
Isa 60:9; 66:19-20
Zech 10:10

**11:12**
Isa 11:10
Zeph 3:10

**11:13**
Jer 3:18
Ezek 37:16-17, 22

**11:10a** Hebrew *the root of Jesse.*   **11:10b** Greek version reads *In that day the heir to David's throne* [literally *the root of Jesse*] *will come, / and he will rule over the Gentiles. / They will place their hopes on him.* Compare Rom 15:12.
**11:11a** Hebrew *in Pathros, Cush.*   **11:11b** Hebrew *in Shinar.*   **11:13** Hebrew *Ephraim,* referring to the northern kingdom of Israel.

---

**11:3-5** God will judge with righteousness. How we long for fair treatment from others, but do we give it? We hate those who base their judgments on appearance, false evidence, or hearsay, but are we quick to judge others using those standards? Only Christ can be the perfectly fair judge. Only as he governs our hearts can we learn to be as fair in our treatment of others as we expect others to be toward us.

**11:4, 5** Judah had become corrupt and was surrounded by hostile, foreign powers. The nation desperately needed a revival of righteousness, justice, and faithfulness. They needed to turn from selfishness and give justice to the poor and the oppressed. The righteousness that God values is more than refraining from sin. It is actively turning toward others and offering them the help they need.

**11:6-10** A golden age is yet to come, a time of peace when children will play safely with formerly dangerous animals. Not all of this was fulfilled at Christ's first coming. For example, nature has not returned to its intended balance and harmony (see Romans 8:9-22). Such perfect tranquility will be possible only when Christ reigns over the earth.

**11:11** When will this remnant of God's people be returned to their land? Old Testament prophecy is often applied both to the near future and the distant future. Judah would soon be exiled to Babylon, and a remnant would return to Jerusalem in 538 B.C. at Cyrus's decree. In the ages to come, however, God's people would be dispersed throughout the world. These locations represent the four corners of the known world—Hamath in the north, Egypt in the south, Assyria and Babylonia in the east, the distant coastlands in the west. Ultimately God's people will be regathered when Christ comes to reign over the earth.

**11:14** Edom, Moab, and Ammon were three countries bordering Judah (along with Philistia). They were the nations who, when Judah was defeated, rejoiced and took their land.

They will occupy the lands of Edom and Moab,
and Ammon will obey them.

**11:15**
Isa 51:10

15 The LORD will make a dry path through the gulf of the Red Sea.*
He will wave his hand over the Euphrates River,*
sending a mighty wind to divide it into seven streams
so it can easily be crossed on foot.

**11:16**
Exod 14:26-29
Isa 19:23

16 He will make a highway for the remnant of his people,
the remnant coming from Assyria,
just as he did for Israel long ago
when they returned from Egypt.

## Songs of Praise for Salvation

**12:1**
Isa 40:1

**12** 1 In that day you will sing:
"I will praise you, O LORD!
You were angry with me, but not any more.
Now you comfort me.

**12:2**
Ps 118:14
Isa 26:4

2 See, God has come to save me.
I will trust in him and not be afraid.
The LORD GOD is my strength and my song;
he has given me victory."

**12:3**
Jer 2:13
John 4:10; 7:37-38
**12:4**
Ps 145:4

3 With joy you will drink deeply
from the fountain of salvation!
4 In that wonderful day you will sing:
"Thank the LORD! Praise his name!
Tell the nations what he has done.
Let them know how mighty he is!

**12:5**
Ps 98:1
Isa 44:23
**12:6**
Isa 54:1
Zeph 3:14, 15-17

5 Sing to the LORD, for he has done wonderful things.
Make known his praise around the world.
6 Let all the people of Jerusalem* shout his praise with joy!
For great is the Holy One of Israel who lives among you."

## 2. Judgment against pagan nations
### A Message about Babylon

**13:1**
Jer 50:1-51
**13:2**
Isa 45:1-3

**13** Isaiah son of Amoz received this message concerning the destruction of Babylon:
2 "Raise a signal flag on a bare hilltop.
Call up an army against Babylon.
Wave your hand to encourage them
as they march into the palaces of the high and mighty.

**13:3**
Joel 3:11

3 I, the LORD, have dedicated these soldiers for this task.
Yes, I have called mighty warriors to express my anger,
and they will rejoice when I am exalted."

4 Hear the noise on the mountains!
Listen, as the vast armies march!
It is the noise and shouting of many nations.
The LORD of Heaven's Armies has called this army together.

**11:15a** Hebrew *will destroy the tongue of the sea of Egypt.*    **11:15b** Hebrew *the river.*    **12:6** Hebrew *Zion.*

**11:15, 16** Isaiah is talking about a new or second Exodus when God will bring his scattered people back to Judah, and the Messiah will come to rule the world. The Lord dried up the Red Sea so the Israelites could walk through it on their way to the Promised Land (Exodus 14). He dried up the Jordan River so the nation could cross into the land (Joshua 3). God will again provide the way of return for his people.

**12:1ff** This chapter is a hymn of praise—another graphic description of the people's joy when Jesus Christ comes to reign over the earth. Even now we need to express our gratitude to God, thanking him, praising him, and telling others about him. From the depths of our gratitude, we must praise him. And we should share the Good News with others.

**13:1ff** Chapters 1–12 speak of judgment against the southern kingdom and, to a lesser extent, against the northern kingdom. Chapters 13–23 are about the judgment on other nations. Chapter 13 is an oracle or message from God concerning Babylon. Long before Babylon became a world power and threatened Judah, Isaiah spoke of its destruction. Babylon was the rallying point of rebellion against God after the Flood (Genesis 11). Revelation 17 and 18 use Babylon as a symbol of God's enemies. At the time of this oracle, Babylon was still part of the Assyrian Empire. Isaiah communicated a message of challenge and hope to God's people, telling them not to rely on other nations but to rely on God alone. And he let them know that their greatest enemies would receive from God the punishment they deserved.

5 They come from distant countries,
  from beyond the farthest horizons.
They are the LORD's weapons to carry out his anger.
  With them he will destroy the whole land.

6 Scream in terror, for the day of the LORD has arrived—
  the time for the Almighty to destroy.
7 Every arm is paralyzed with fear.
  Every heart melts,
8   and people are terrified.
Pangs of anguish grip them,
  like those of a woman in labor.
They look helplessly at one another,
  their faces aflame with fear.

9 For see, the day of the LORD is coming—
  the terrible day of his fury and fierce anger.
The land will be made desolate,
  and all the sinners destroyed with it.
10 The heavens will be black above them;
  the stars will give no light.
The sun will be dark when it rises,
  and the moon will provide no light.

11 "I, the LORD, will punish the world for its evil
  and the wicked for their sin.
I will crush the arrogance of the proud
  and humble the pride of the mighty.
12 I will make people scarcer than gold—
  more rare than the fine gold of Ophir.
13 For I will shake the heavens.
  The earth will move from its place
when the LORD of Heaven's Armies displays his wrath
  in the day of his fierce anger."

14 Everyone in Babylon will run about like a hunted gazelle,
  like sheep without a shepherd.
They will try to find their own people
  and flee to their own land.
15 Anyone who is captured will be cut down—
  run through with a sword.
16 Their little children will be dashed to death before their eyes.
  Their homes will be sacked, and their wives will be raped.

17 "Look, I will stir up the Medes against Babylon.
  They cannot be tempted by silver
  or bribed with gold.
18 The attacking armies will shoot down the young men with arrows.
  They will have no mercy on helpless babies
  and will show no compassion for children."

19 Babylon, the most glorious of kingdoms,
  the flower of Chaldean pride,
will be devastated like Sodom and Gomorrah
  when God destroyed them.
20 Babylon will never be inhabited again.
  It will remain empty for generation after generation.

**13:5** Isa 5:26

**13:6** Isa 34:2, 8; Ezek 30:3; Amos 5:18

**13:7** Ezek 21:7

**13:8** Isa 21:3; 26:17

**13:9** Isa 66:15-16

**13:10** Matt 24:29; †Mark 13:24-25

**13:11** Dan 5:22-23

**13:12** Isa 6:11-12

**13:13** Hag 2:6

**13:14** 1 Kgs 22:17; Matt 9:36

**13:15** Jer 51:3-4

**13:16** Ps 137:8-9; Hos 10:14

**13:17** Jer 51:11

**13:18** 2 Chr 36:17

**13:19** Gen 19:24; Rev 18:16-17, 19

**13:20** Jer 51:37-43

---

**13:12** Ophir was known for its rare and valuable gold. It is thought to have been located on the southwestern coast of Arabia.

**13:20** Even before Babylon became a world power, Isaiah prophesied that, though it would shine for a while, Babylon's destruction would be so complete that the land would never again be inhabited. Babylon, in present-day Iraq, still lies in utter ruin, buried under mounds of dirt and sand.

Nomads will refuse to camp there,
and shepherds will not bed down their sheep.
21 Desert animals will move into the ruined city,
and the houses will be haunted by howling creatures.
Owls will live among the ruins,
and wild goats will go there to dance.
22 Hyenas will howl in its fortresses,
and jackals will make dens in its luxurious palaces.
Babylon's days are numbered;
its time of destruction will soon arrive.

### A Taunt for Babylon's King

**14** But the LORD will have mercy on the descendants of Jacob. He will choose Israel as his special people once again. He will bring them back to settle once again in their own land. And people from many different nations will come and join them there and unite with the people of Israel.* 2 The nations of the world will help the LORD's people to return, and those who come to live in their land will serve them. Those who captured Israel will themselves be captured, and Israel will rule over its enemies.

3 In that wonderful day when the LORD gives his people rest from sorrow and fear, from slavery and chains, 4 you will taunt the king of Babylon. You will say,

"The mighty man has been destroyed.
Yes, your insolence* is ended.
5 For the LORD has crushed your wicked power
and broken your evil rule.
6 You struck the people with endless blows of rage
and held the nations in your angry grip
with unrelenting tyranny.
7 But finally the earth is at rest and quiet.
Now it can sing again!
8 Even the trees of the forest—
the cypress trees and the cedars of Lebanon—
sing out this joyous song:
'Since you have been cut down,
no one will come now to cut us down!'

9 "In the place of the dead* there is excitement
over your arrival.
The spirits of world leaders and mighty kings long dead
stand up to see you.
10 With one voice they all cry out,
'Now you are as weak as we are!
11 Your might and power were buried with you.*
The sound of the harp in your palace has ceased.
Now maggots are your sheet,
and worms your blanket.'

**Cross-references (left margin):**

13:21
Isa 34:11-15
Zeph 2:14

14:1
Ps 102:13
Isa 41:8-9;
49:13, 15
Zech 2:11-12

14:2
Isa 45:14
Dan 7:18, 27

14:3
Ezra 9:8-9
Jer 30:10

14:4
Hab 2:6

14:6
Isa 47:6

14:7
Ps 98:1-9

14:8
Isa 55:12

14:10
Ezek 32:21

14:11
Isa 5:14

14:1 Hebrew *the house of Jacob*. The names "Jacob" and "Israel" are often interchanged throughout the Old Testament, referring sometimes to the individual patriarch and sometimes to the nation. 14:4 As in Dead Sea Scrolls; the meaning of the Masoretic Text is uncertain. 14:9 Hebrew *Sheol*; also in 14:15. 14:11 Hebrew *were brought down to Sheol*.

**14:1** A prominent theme in Isaiah is that non-Israelites would join the returning Israelites (56:6, 7; 60:10; 61:5). God's intention was that through his faithful people all the world would be blessed (Genesis 12:3). Through the family of David, the whole world could be saved by Christ. God's Word must be available to all people groups in their own languages. We must not limit God's love to our own people. God loves the whole world. We must support and help those missions that are reaching out to people who haven't heard the Good News of salvation.

**14:4-11** These verses could have both present and future significance in reference to Babylon. The historical city and empire would be permanently destroyed. Babylon has also been used as a picture of all those who oppose God. Thus, in the end times, all who oppose God will be destroyed, and all evil will be removed from the earth forever.

**14:5, 6** Power fades quickly. God permitted Babylon to have temporary power for a purpose—to punish his wayward people. When the purpose ended, so did the power. Beware of placing confidence in human power because one day it will fade, no matter how strong it appears now.

<sup>12</sup> "How you are fallen from heaven,
    O shining star, son of the morning!
You have been thrown down to the earth,
    you who destroyed the nations of the world.

<sup>13</sup> For you said to yourself,
    'I will ascend to heaven and set my throne above God's stars.
I will preside on the mountain of the gods
    far away in the north.*

<sup>14</sup> I will climb to the highest heavens
    and be like the Most High.'

<sup>15</sup> Instead, you will be brought down to the place of the dead,
    down to its lowest depths.

<sup>16</sup> Everyone there will stare at you and ask,
    'Can this be the one who shook the earth
    and made the kingdoms of the world tremble?

<sup>17</sup> Is this the one who destroyed the world
    and made it into a wasteland?
Is this the king who demolished the world's greatest cities
    and had no mercy on his prisoners?'

<sup>18</sup> "The kings of the nations lie in stately glory,
    each in his own tomb,

<sup>19</sup> but you will be thrown out of your grave
    like a worthless branch.
Like a corpse trampled underfoot,
    you will be dumped into a mass grave
    with those killed in battle.
You will descend to the pit.

<sup>20</sup>     You will not be given a proper burial,
for you have destroyed your nation
    and slaughtered your people.
The descendants of such an evil person
    will never again receive honor.

<sup>21</sup> Kill this man's children!
    Let them die because of their father's sins!
They must not rise and conquer the earth,
    filling the world with their cities."

<sup>22</sup> This is what the LORD of Heaven's Armies says:
    "I, myself, have risen against Babylon!
I will destroy its children and its children's children,"
    says the LORD.

<sup>23</sup> "I will make Babylon a desolate place of owls,
    filled with swamps and marshes.
I will sweep the land with the broom of destruction.
    I, the LORD of Heaven's Armies, have spoken!"

### A Message about Assyria

<sup>24</sup>The LORD of Heaven's Armies has sworn this oath:

    "It will all happen as I have planned.
    It will be as I have decided.

**14:13** Or *on the heights of Zaphon.*

---

| Ref | Cross-references |
|---|---|
| **14:12** | Luke 10:18<br>Rev 9:1 |
| **14:13** | Ezek 28:2<br>Matt 11:23<br>Luke 10:15 |
| **14:14** | 2 Thes 2:4 |
| **14:15** | Matt 11:23<br>Luke 10:15 |
| **14:19** | Isa 5:25 |
| **14:20** | Job 18:19<br>Ps 21:10 |
| **14:21** | Exod 20:5<br>Isa 13:16 |
| **14:23** | Isa 13:6; 34:11 |
| **14:24** | Job 23:13<br>Isa 46:11 |

---

**14:12** "Shining star, son of the morning" could be names used to worship the kings of Assyria and Babylon. More likely, it means that they will fade like the morning star when the sun rises.

**14:12-14** There are several interpretations for the fallen one in these verses. (1) He is Satan, because the person here is too powerful to be any human king. Although Satan may fit verses 12-14, he does not fit well with the rest of the chapter. (2) This could be Sennacherib or Nebuchadnezzar, kings with supreme power. Their people looked upon them as gods. These kings wanted to rule the world. (3) This could refer to both Satan and a great human king, possibly Nebuchadnezzar, because Babylon is pictured as the seat of evil in Revelation 17–18. Pride was Satan's sin as well as Babylon's. Common to all three viewpoints is the truth that pride willfully opposes God and will result in judgment. Israel made the mistake of being too proud to depend on God, and we are vulnerable to that same mistake.

**14:24-27** This prophecy came true as Isaiah predicted (see 2 Kings 19 and Isaiah 37:21-38).

25 I will break the Assyrians when they are in Israel;
  I will trample them on my mountains.
My people will no longer be their slaves
  nor bow down under their heavy loads.

**14:26**
Isa 23:9

26 I have a plan for the whole earth,
  a hand of judgment upon all the nations.

**14:27**
Exod 15:12
Isa 43:13
Dan 4:31, 35

27 The LORD of Heaven's Armies has spoken—
  who can change his plans?
When his hand is raised,
  who can stop him?"

## A Message about Philistia

**14:28**
2 Kgs 16:20

28 This message came to me the year King Ahaz died:*

29 Do not rejoice, you Philistines,
  that the rod that struck you is broken—
  that the king who attacked you is dead.
For from that snake a more poisonous snake will be born,
  a fiery serpent to destroy you!

30 I will feed the poor in my pasture;
  the needy will lie down in peace.
But as for you, I will wipe you out with famine
  and destroy the few who remain.

**14:31**
Jer 1:14

31 Wail at the gates! Weep in the cities!
  Melt with fear, you Philistines!
A powerful army comes like smoke from the north.
  Each soldier rushes forward eager to fight.

**14:32**
Ps 87:1, 5
Isa 25:4

32 What should we tell the Philistine messengers? Tell them,

"The LORD has built Jerusalem*;
  its walls will give refuge to his oppressed people."

## A Message about Moab

**15:1**
Jer 48:1
Ezek 25:8-11

**15** This message came to me concerning Moab:

In one night the town of Ar will be leveled,
  and the city of Kir will be destroyed.

**15:2**
Jer 48:37

2 Your people will go to their temple in Dibon to mourn.
  They will go to their sacred shrines to weep.
They will wail for the fate of Nebo and Medeba,
  shaving their heads in sorrow and cutting off their beards.

**15:3**
Jer 48:38

3 They will wear burlap as they wander the streets.
  From every home and public square will come the sound of wailing.
4 The people of Heshbon and Elealeh will cry out;
  their voices will be heard as far away as Jahaz!
The bravest warriors of Moab will cry out in utter terror.
  They will be helpless with fear.

**15:5**
Jer 48:5

5 My heart weeps for Moab.
  Its people flee to Zoar and Eglath-shelishiyah.
Weeping, they climb the road to Luhith.
  Their cries of distress can be heard all along the road to Horonaim.

**14:28** King Ahaz died in 715 B.C. **14:32** Hebrew *Zion*.

---

**14:28-31** Isaiah received this message from the Lord in 715 B.C., the year that King Ahaz of Judah died. "The king who attacked you" (14:29) was not Ahaz but Shalmaneser V or Sargon of Assyria. The "powerful army" from the north (14:31) refers to the soldiers of Sargon of Assyria.

**15:1** Moab was east of the Dead Sea. The Moabites were descendants of Lot through his incestuous relationship with his older daughter (Genesis 19:31-37). Moab had always been Israel's enemy. They oppressed Israel and invaded their land (Judges 3:12-14), fought against Saul (1 Samuel 14:47) and against David (2 Samuel 8:2, 11, 12). Moab would be punished for treating Israel harshly.

6 Even the waters of Nimrim are dried up!
  The grassy banks are scorched.
The tender plants are gone;
  nothing green remains.
7 The people grab their possessions
  and carry them across the Ravine of Willows.
8 A cry of distress echoes through the land of Moab
  from one end to the other—
  from Eglaim to Beer-elim.
9 The stream near Dibon* runs red with blood,
  but I am still not finished with Dibon!
Lions will hunt down the survivors—
  both those who try to escape
  and those who remain behind.

**16** 1 Send lambs from Sela as tribute
        to the ruler of the land.
Send them through the desert
  to the mountain of beautiful Zion.
2 The women of Moab are left like homeless birds
  at the shallow crossings of the Arnon River.
3 "Help us," they cry.
  "Defend us against our enemies.
Protect us from their relentless attack.
  Do not betray us now that we have escaped.
4 Let our refugees stay among you.
  Hide them from our enemies until the terror is past."

When oppression and destruction have ended
  and enemy raiders have disappeared,
5 then God will establish one of David's descendants as king.
  He will rule with mercy and truth.
He will always do what is just
  and be eager to do what is right.

6 We have heard about proud Moab—
  about its pride and arrogance and rage.
  But all that boasting has disappeared.
7 The entire land of Moab weeps.
  Yes, everyone in Moab mourns
for the cakes of raisins from Kir-hareseth.
  They are all gone now.
8 The farms of Heshbon are abandoned;
  the vineyards at Sibmah are deserted.
The rulers of the nations have broken down Moab—
  that beautiful grapevine.
Its tendrils spread north as far as the town of Jazer
  and trailed eastward into the wilderness.
Its shoots reached so far west
  that they crossed over the Dead Sea.*

9 So now I weep for Jazer and the vineyards of Sibmah;
  my tears will flow for Heshbon and Elealeh.
There are no more shouts of joy
  over your summer fruits and harvest.

**15:9** As in Dead Sea Scrolls, some Greek manuscripts, and Latin Vulgate; Masoretic Text reads *Dimon;* also in 15:9b.
**16:8** Hebrew *the sea.*

**16:1ff** Attacked by the Assyrians, Moabite refugees would flee to Sela, which lay in the country of Edom to the south. Desperate Moabites, seeking Judah's protection, would send a tribute of lambs to Jerusalem. Jerusalem would be a safe refuge for a while. Isaiah advised Judah to accept these refugees as a sign of compassion during the enemy's time of devastation.

**15:6**
Jer 48:34
Joel 1:10-12

**15:9**
2 Kgs 17:25
Jer 50:17

**16:1**
2 Kgs 3:4; 14:7
Isa 42:11

**16:2**
Num 21:13-14

**16:4**
Isa 9:4; 54:14

**16:6**
Jer 48:29
Zeph 2:8, 10

**16:7**
2 Kgs 3:25
Jer 48:31

**16:8**
Num 32:38
Isa 15:4
Jer 48:32

**16:9**
Jer 48:32

**16:10**
Job 24:11
Isa 24:7-8
Jer 48:33
Amos 5:17

¹⁰ Gone now is the gladness,
    gone the joy of harvest.
There will be no singing in the vineyards,
    no more happy shouts,
no treading of grapes in the winepresses.
    I have ended all their harvest joys.

**16:11**
Isa 15:5; 63:15

¹¹ My heart's cry for Moab is like a lament on a harp.
    I am filled with anguish for Kir-hareseth.*

**16:12**
1 Kgs 18:26-29
Jer 48:35

¹² The people of Moab will worship at their pagan shrines,
    but it will do them no good.
They will cry to the gods in their temples,
    but no one will be able to save them.

¹³ The LORD has already said these things about Moab in the past. ¹⁴ But now the LORD says, "Within three years, counting each day,* the glory of Moab will be ended. From its great population, only a few of its people will be left alive."

## A Message about Damascus and Israel

**17:1**
Isa 10:9; 25:2

**17** This message came to me concerning Damascus:

"Look, the city of Damascus will disappear!
    It will become a heap of ruins.

**17:2**
Zeph 2:6

² The towns of Aroer will be deserted.
    Flocks will graze in the streets and lie down undisturbed,
    with no one to chase them away.

**17:3**
Isa 8:4
Hos 9:11

³ The fortified towns of Israel* will also be destroyed,
    and the royal power of Damascus will end.
All that remains of Syria*
    will share the fate of Israel's departed glory,"
    declares the LORD of Heaven's Armies.

**17:4**
Isa 10:3, 16

⁴ "In that day Israel's* glory will grow dim;
    its robust body will waste away.

**17:5**
Jer 51:33

⁵ The whole land will look like a grainfield
    after the harvesters have gathered the grain.
It will be desolate,
    like the fields in the valley of Rephaim after the harvest.

**17:6**
Deut 4:27
Isa 24:13; 27:12

⁶ Only a few of its people will be left,
    like stray olives left on a tree after the harvest.
Only two or three remain in the highest branches,
    four or five scattered here and there on the limbs,"
    declares the LORD, the God of Israel.

**17:7**
Isa 10:20
Hos 6:1

⁷ Then at last the people will look to their Creator
    and turn their eyes to the Holy One of Israel.

**16:11** Hebrew *Kir-heres*, a variant spelling of Kir-hareseth.   **16:14** Hebrew *Within three years, as a servant bound by contract would count them.*   **17:3a** Hebrew *of Ephraim*, referring to the northern kingdom of Israel.   **17:3b** Hebrew *Aram.*   **17:4** Hebrew *Jacob's.* See note on 14:1.

---

**16:10** The treading out of grapes (squeezing the juice from grapes by mashing them with bare feet) was the climax of the harvest season, a time of great joy in the vineyards. But the joy of harvest would soon be ended because the people in their pride ignored God and rebelled against him.

**16:12** When the people of Moab experienced God's wrath, they sought their own idols and gods. Nothing happened, however, because there was no one there to save them. We may seek our own ways of escaping daily troubles—work, friends, pleasure, or even some human-made religious idea. But our only hope lies in God, the only one who can hear and help us.

**16:13, 14** Tiglath-pileser III invaded Moab in 732 B.C.; Sennacherib invaded Moab the same year that he invaded Judah, 701 B.C. The earlier event occurred three years after Isaiah's prediction, marking Isaiah as a true prophet. In these events, the people of Israel saw prophecy fulfilled before their very eyes.

**17:1ff** The northern kingdom and Aram made an alliance to fight against Assyria. But Tiglath-pileser III captured Damascus, the capital of Aram, in 732 B.C., and annexed the northern kingdom to the Assyrian Empire. Ahaz, king of Judah, paid tribute to Tiglath-pileser III (2 Kings 16:1-14).

**17:7-11** God's message to Damascus was that it would be completely destroyed. The Arameans had turned from the God who could save them, depending instead on their idols and their own strength. No matter how successful they were, God's judgment was sure. Often we depend on the trappings of success (expensive cars, pastimes, clothes, homes) to give us fulfillment. But God says we will reap grief and pain if we have depended on temporal things to give us eternal security. If we don't want the same treatment Damascus received, we must turn from these false allurements and trust in God.

8 They will no longer look to their idols for help
　　or worship what their own hands have made.
They will never again bow down to their Asherah poles
　　or worship at the pagan shrines they have built.
9 Their largest cities will be like a deserted forest,
　　like the land the Hivites and Amorites abandoned*
when the Israelites came here so long ago.
　　It will be utterly desolate.
10 Why? Because you have turned from the God who can save you.
　　You have forgotten the Rock who can hide you.
So you may plant the finest grapevines
　　and import the most expensive seedlings.
11 They may sprout on the day you set them out;
　　yes, they may blossom on the very morning you plant them,
but you will never pick any grapes from them.
　　Your only harvest will be a load of grief and unrelieved pain.

12 Listen! The armies of many nations
　　roar like the roaring of the sea.
Hear the thunder of the mighty forces
　　as they rush forward like thundering waves.
13 But though they thunder like breakers on a beach,
　　God will silence them, and they will run away.
They will flee like chaff scattered by the wind,
　　like a tumbleweed whirling before a storm.
14 In the evening Israel waits in terror,
　　but by dawn its enemies are dead.
This is the just reward of those who plunder us,
　　a fitting end for those who destroy us.

## A Message about Ethiopia

**18** 1 Listen, Ethiopia*—land of fluttering sails*
　　that lies at the headwaters of the Nile,
2 that sends ambassadors
　　in swift boats down the river.

Go, swift messengers!
Take a message to a tall, smooth-skinned people,
　　who are feared far and wide
for their conquests and destruction,
　　and whose land is divided by rivers.

3 All you people of the world,
　　everyone who lives on the earth—
when I raise my battle flag on the mountain, look!
　　When I blow the ram's horn, listen!

**17:8**
Exod 34:13
Isa 27:9; 30:22

**17:10**
Deut 32:4, 18
Isa 30:29; 62:11

**17:11**
Hos 10:13

**17:12**
Jer 6:23

**17:13**
Ps 1:4
Isa 29:5

**17:14**
2 Kgs 19:35
Isa 41:11-12

**18:1**
Ezek 30:4, 6, 9
Zeph 2:12

**18:2**
2 Chr 12:2-4

**18:3**
Ps 49:1
Mic 1:2

**17:9** As in Greek version; Hebrew reads *like places of the wood and the highest bough.*　**18:1a** Hebrew *Cush.*
**18:1b** Or *land of many locusts;* Hebrew reads *land of whirring wings.*

**17:8** The Asherah poles were images of Asherah, a Canaanite goddess who was the female consort of Baal. Queen Jezebel may have brought the worship of Asherah into the northern kingdom. The cult encouraged immoral sexual practices and attracted many people. The Bible warns against worshiping Asherah poles (Deuteronomy 12:3; 16:21), and Manasseh was condemned for putting up an Asherah pole in the Temple (2 Kings 21:7).

Asherah poles are no problem in our world, but a religion based on sexuality is. Pornography has become an addiction for many people. Media and entertainment industries feed our society's obsession with sex. The runaway desire for stimulation and gratification often comes from an empty, lonely heart. God offers real joy and lasting love. Be on the alert for how sexual images divert us from God.

**18:1ff** This prophecy was probably given in the days of Hezekiah (2 Kings 19–20). The king of Ethiopia had heard that Assyria's great army was marching south toward them. He sent messengers up the Nile asking the surrounding nations to form an alliance. Judah was also asked to join, but Isaiah told the messengers to return home because Judah needed only God's help to repel the Assyrians. Isaiah prophesied that Assyria would be destroyed at the proper time (37:21-38).

**18:3** This is a signal of the doom of Ethiopia and Assyria's victory over Ethiopia (see 20:1-6).

4 For the LORD has told me this:
"I will watch quietly from my dwelling place—
    as quietly as the heat rises on a summer day,
    or as the morning dew forms during the harvest."

**18:5**
Isa 26:21
Ezek 17:6-10

5 Even before you begin your attack,
    while your plans are ripening like grapes,
the LORD will cut off your new growth with pruning shears.
    He will snip off and discard your spreading branches.

**18:6**
Isa 56:9
Ezek 39:17-20

6 Your mighty army will be left dead in the fields
    for the mountain vultures and wild animals.
The vultures will tear at the corpses all summer.
    The wild animals will gnaw at the bones all winter.

**18:7**
Zech 14:16-17

7 At that time the LORD of Heaven's Armies will receive gifts
    from this land divided by rivers,
from this tall, smooth-skinned people,
    who are feared far and wide for their conquests and destruction.
They will bring the gifts to Jerusalem,*
    where the LORD of Heaven's Armies dwells.

## A Message about Egypt

**19:1**
Josh 2:11
Ps 104:3
Jer 43:12
Matt 26:64

**19** This message came to me concerning Egypt:

Look! The LORD is advancing against Egypt,
    riding on a swift cloud.
The idols of Egypt tremble.
    The hearts of the Egyptians melt with fear.

**19:2**
Judg 7:22
Matt 10:21, 36

2 "I will make Egyptian fight against Egyptian—
    brother against brother,
neighbor against neighbor,
    city against city,
    province against province.

**19:3**
Isa 8:19

3 The Egyptians will lose heart,
    and I will confuse their plans.
They will plead with their idols for wisdom
    and call on spirits, mediums, and those who consult the spirits of the dead.

**19:4**
Isa 20:4
Ezek 29:19

4 I will hand Egypt over
    to a hard, cruel master.
A fierce king will rule them,"
    says the Lord, the LORD of Heaven's Armies.

**18:7** Hebrew *to Mount Zion.*

---

**ALLIANCES TODAY**

Government . . . . . . . . We rely on government legislation to protect the moral decisions we want made, but legislation cannot change people's hearts.

Science . . . . . . . . . . . . We enjoy the benefits of science and technology. We look to scientific predictions and analysis before we look to the Bible.

Education . . . . . . . . . . We act as though education and degrees can guarantee our future and success without considering what God plans for our future.

Medical care . . . . . . . . We regard medicine as the way to prolong life and preserve its quality—quite apart from faith and moral living.

Financial systems . . . . . We place our faith in financial "security"—making as much money as we can for ourselves—forgetting that, while being wise with our money, we must trust God for our needs.

Isaiah warned Judah not to ally with Egypt (20:5; 30:1, 2; 31:1). He knew that trust in any nation or any military might was futile. Judah's only hope was to trust in God. Although we don't consciously put our hope for deliverance in political alliances in quite the same way, we often put our hope in other places.

---

**19:1** Egypt, the nation where God's people were enslaved for about 400 years (Exodus 1), was hated by the people of Israel. Yet Judah was considering an alliance with Egypt against Assyria (2 Kings 18:17ff). But Isaiah warned against this alliance because God would destroy Assyria in his time.

5 The waters of the Nile will fail to rise and flood the fields.
    The riverbed will be parched and dry.

**19:5**
Ezek 30:12

6 The canals of the Nile will dry up,
    and the streams of Egypt will stink
        with rotting reeds and rushes.

**19:6**
Exod 7:18

7 All the greenery along the riverbank
    and all the crops along the river
        will dry up and blow away.

8 The fishermen will lament for lack of work.
    Those who cast hooks into the Nile will groan,
        and those who use nets will lose heart.

9 There will be no flax for the harvesters,
    no thread for the weavers.

**19:9**
Prov 7:16

10 They will be in despair,
    and all the workers will be sick at heart.

11 What fools are the officials of Zoan!
    Their best counsel to the king of Egypt is stupid and wrong.
        Will they still boast to Pharaoh of their wisdom?
        Will they dare brag about all their wise ancestors?

**19:11**
Gen 41:38-39
1 Kgs 4:30
Acts 7:22

12 Where are your wise counselors, Pharaoh?
    Let them tell you what God plans,
        what the LORD of Heaven's Armies is going to do to Egypt.

**19:12**
Rom 9:17

13 The officials of Zoan are fools,
    and the officials of Memphis* are deluded.
        The leaders of the people
        have led Egypt astray.

**19:13**
Jer 2:16

14 The LORD has sent a spirit of foolishness on them,
    so all their suggestions are wrong.
        They cause Egypt to stagger
        like a drunk in his vomit.

**19:14**
Isa 3:12

15 There is nothing Egypt can do.
    All are helpless—
the head and the tail,
    the noble palm branch and the lowly reed.

16In that day the Egyptians will be as weak as women. They will cower in fear beneath the upraised fist of the LORD of Heaven's Armies. 17Just to speak the name of Israel will terrorize them, for the LORD of Heaven's Armies has laid out his plans against them.

**19:16**
Jer 51:30
Heb 10:31

**19:17**
Dan 4:35

18In that day five of Egypt's cities will follow the LORD of Heaven's Armies. They will even begin to speak Hebrew, the language of Canaan. One of these cities will be Heliopolis, the City of the Sun.*

**19:18**
Isa 45:23; 65:16

19In that day there will be an altar to the LORD in the heart of Egypt, and there will be a monument to the LORD at its border. 20It will be a sign and a witness that the LORD of Heaven's Armies is worshiped in the land of Egypt. When the people cry to the LORD for help against those who oppress them, he will send them a savior who will rescue them. 21The LORD will make himself known to the Egyptians. Yes, they will know the LORD and will give their sacrifices and offerings to him. They will make a vow to the LORD and will keep it. 22The LORD will strike Egypt, and then he will bring healing. For the Egyptians will turn to the LORD, and he will listen to their pleas and heal them.

**19:19**
Gen 28:18
Josh 22:10, 26-27

**19:20**
Isa 43:3, 11;
45:15, 21; 49:25

**19:21**
Isa 56:7

**19:22**
Deut 32:39
Isa 27:13; 45:14
Heb 12:11

**19:13** Hebrew *Noph.*    **19:18** Or *will be the City of Destruction.*

---

**19:11-15** Egypt was noted for its wisdom, but here its wise men and counselors were deceived and foolish. True wisdom can come only from God. We must ask him for wisdom to guide our decisions, or we will also be uncertain and misdirected. Are you confused about something in your life now? Ask God for wisdom to deal with it.

**19:19, 23** After Egypt's chastening, it would turn from idols and worship the one true God. Even more amazing is Isaiah's prophecy that the two chief oppressors of Israel, Egypt and Assyria, would unite in worship. This prophecy will come true "in that day," the future day when Christ comes to reign.

**19:20** When Egypt calls to God for help, he will send a savior to deliver them. Our Savior, Jesus Christ, is available to all who call upon him. We, too, can pray and receive his saving power (John 1:12).

**19:23**
Isa 11:16

**19:25**
Hos 2:23

**20:1**
1 Sam 5:1
2 Kgs 18:17

**20:2**
1 Sam 19:24
Mic 1:8

**20:3**
Isa 8:18; 43:3

**20:4**
Isa 19:4; 47:2-3

**20:5**
Jer 9:23-24

**20:6**
Isa 10:3; 30:3-5, 7

**21:1**
Isa 13:20-22
Zech 9:14

**21:2**
Isa 33:1
Jer 49:34

**21:3**
Ps 48:6
1 Thes 5:3

**21:4**
Deut 28:67

**21:5**
Jer 51:39, 57

23In that day Egypt and Assyria will be connected by a highway. The Egyptians and Assyrians will move freely between their lands, and they will both worship God. 24And Israel will be their ally. The three will be together, and Israel will be a blessing to them. 25For the LORD of Heaven's Armies will say, "Blessed be Egypt, my people. Blessed be Assyria, the land I have made. Blessed be Israel, my special possession!"

## A Message about Egypt and Ethiopia

**20** In the year when King Sargon of Assyria sent his commander in chief to capture the Philistine city of Ashdod,* 2the LORD told Isaiah son of Amoz, "Take off the burlap you have been wearing, and remove your sandals." Isaiah did as he was told and walked around naked and barefoot.

3Then the LORD said, "My servant Isaiah has been walking around naked and barefoot for the last three years. This is a sign—a symbol of the terrible troubles I will bring upon Egypt and Ethiopia.* 4For the king of Assyria will take away the Egyptians and Ethiopians* as prisoners. He will make them walk naked and barefoot, both young and old, their buttocks bared, to the shame of Egypt. 5Then the Philistines will be thrown into panic, for they counted on the power of Ethiopia and boasted of their allies in Egypt! 6They will say, 'If this can happen to Egypt, what chance do we have? We were counting on Egypt to protect us from the king of Assyria.'"

## A Message about Babylon

**21** This message came to me concerning Babylon—the desert by the sea*:

Disaster is roaring down on you from the desert,
　like a whirlwind sweeping in from the Negev.
2 I see a terrifying vision:
　I see the betrayer betraying,
　　the destroyer destroying.
Go ahead, you Elamites and Medes,
　attack and lay siege.
I will make an end
　to all the groaning Babylon caused.

3 My stomach aches and burns with pain.
　Sharp pangs of anguish are upon me,
　　like those of a woman in labor.
I grow faint when I hear what God is planning;
　I am too afraid to look.
4 My mind reels and my heart races.
　I longed for evening to come,
　　but now I am terrified of the dark.

5 Look! They are preparing a great feast.
　They are spreading rugs for people to sit on.
　Everyone is eating and drinking.
But quick! Grab your shields and prepare for battle.
　You are being attacked!

**20:1** Ashdod was captured by Assyria in 711 B.C. **20:3** Hebrew *Cush;* also in 20:5. **20:4** Hebrew *Cushites.*
**21:1** Hebrew *concerning the desert by the sea.*

---

**19:23-25** In Jesus Christ, former enemies may unite in love. In Christ, people and nations that are poles apart politically will bow at his feet as brothers and sisters. Christ breaks down every barrier that threatens relationships (see Ephesians 2:13-19).

**20:1ff** Sargon II was king of Assyria from 722–705 B.C., and this event happened in 711 B.C. Isaiah graphically reminds Judah that they should not count on foreign alliances to protect them.

**20:2** God's command to Isaiah to walk about naked for three years was a humiliating experience. God was using Isaiah to demonstrate the humiliation that Egypt and Ethiopia would experience at the hands of Assyria. But the message was really for Judah: Don't put your trust in foreign governments, or you will experience this kind of shame from your captors. Human governments and institutions can never take God's place.

**20:2** God asked Isaiah to do something that seemed shameful and illogical. At times, God may ask us to take steps we don't understand. We must obey God in complete faith, for he will never ask us to do something wrong.

**21:1ff** Some scholars say this prophecy was fulfilled at Babylon's fall in 539 B.C. (see Daniel 5). But others say this was a prophecy of Babylon's revolt against Assyria around 700 B.C.

**21:5** If the prophecy refers to the fall of Babylon in 539 B.C., this may picture the feast in Daniel 5.

6 Meanwhile, the Lord said to me,
  "Put a watchman on the city wall.
    Let him shout out what he sees.
7 He should look for chariots
    drawn by pairs of horses,
  and for riders on donkeys and camels.
    Let the watchman be fully alert."          21:7
                                                Isa 21:9

8 Then the watchman* called out,               21:8
  "Day after day I have stood on the watchtower, my lord.   Hab 2:1
    Night after night I have remained at my post.
9 Now at last—look!                            21:9
  Here comes a man in a chariot                 Isa 46:1
    with a pair of horses!"                     Jer 50:2
  Then the watchman said,                       Rev 14:8
    "Babylon is fallen, fallen!
  All the idols of Babylon
    lie broken on the ground!"
10 O my people, threshed and winnowed,         21:10
    I have told you everything the LORD of Heaven's Armies has said,   Jer 51:33
    everything the God of Israel has told me.

## A Message about Edom
11 This message came to me concerning Edom*:   21:11
                                                Gen 32:3
  Someone from Edom* keeps calling to me,
  "Watchman, how much longer until morning?
    When will the night be over?"
12 The watchman replies,
  "Morning is coming, but night will soon return.
    If you wish to ask again, then come back and ask."

## A Message about Arabia
13 This message came to me concerning Arabia:  21:13
                                                Jer 49:28
  O caravans from Dedan,
    hide in the deserts of Arabia.
14 O people of Tema,                            21:14
    bring water to these thirsty people,        Gen 25:15
    food to these weary refugees.
15 They have fled from the sword,
    from the drawn sword,
  from the bent bow
    and the terrors of battle.

21:8 As in Dead Sea Scrolls and Syriac version; Masoretic Text reads *a lion*.   21:11a Hebrew *Dumah*, which means
"silence" or "stillness." It is a wordplay on the word *Edom*.   21:11b Hebrew *Seir*, another name for Edom.

---

21:6, 7 Watchmen on the city walls often appear in prophetic visions of destruction. They are the first to see trouble coming. The prophet Habakkuk was a watchman (Habakkuk 2:1). The vision of the riders on horses could represent the Medes and Persians attacking Babylon in 539 B.C.

21:8, 9 Babylon was not only a great and powerful city, it was also filled with horrible sin (idolatry, witchcraft, and temple prostitution). Babylon was, and remains, a symbol of all that stands against God. Despite all its glory and power, Babylon would be destroyed, along with all its idols. They would give no help in time of trouble.

21:10 Threshing and winnowing were two steps in ancient Israel's farming process. The heads of wheat (often used to symbolize Israel) were first trampled to break open the seeds and expose the valued grain inside (threshing). The seeds were then thrown into the air, and the worthless chaff blew away while the grain fell back to the ground (winnowing). Israel would experience this same kind of process: The sinful, rebellious people (worthless chaff) would be taken away, but God would keep the good "grain" to replenish Israel.

21:11 Edom had been a constant enemy of God's people. It rejoiced when Israel fell to the Assyrians, and this sealed Edom's doom (34:8ff; 63:4). Seir was another name for Edom because the hill country of Seir was given to Esau and his descendants (see Joshua 24:4). Obadiah foretells, in great detail, the destruction of Edom.

21:13ff The places listed here are all in Arabia. They are border cities that controlled the trade routes throughout the land. This is Isaiah's prediction of disaster.

21:16
Ps 120:5
Isa 16:14

[16] The Lord said to me, "Within a year, counting each day,* all the glory of Kedar will come to an end. [17] Only a few of its courageous archers will survive. I, the LORD, the God of Israel, have spoken!"

## A Message about Jerusalem

22:1
Jer 21:13
Joel 3:12, 14

**22** This message came to me concerning Jerusalem—the Valley of Vision*:

What is happening?
    Why is everyone running to the rooftops?

22:2
Isa 23:7
Jer 14:18
Lam 2:20

[2] The whole city is in a terrible uproar.
    What do I see in this reveling city?
Bodies are lying everywhere,
    killed not in battle but by famine and disease.

22:3
Isa 21:15

[3] All your leaders have fled.
    They surrendered without resistance.
The people tried to slip away,
    but they were captured, too.

22:4
Jer 9:1

[4] That's why I said, "Leave me alone to weep;
    do not try to comfort me.
Let me cry for my people
    as I watch them being destroyed."

22:5
Isa 37:3
Lam 2:2

[5] Oh, what a day of crushing defeat!
    What a day of confusion and terror
brought by the Lord, the LORD of Heaven's Armies,
    upon the Valley of Vision!
The walls of Jerusalem have been broken,
    and cries of death echo from the mountainsides.

22:6
Isa 21:2

[6] Elamites are the archers,
    with their chariots and charioteers.
The men of Kir hold up the shields.
[7] Chariots fill your beautiful valleys,
    and charioteers storm your gates.

22:8
1 Kgs 7:2; 10:17

[8] Judah's defenses have been stripped away.
    You run to the armory* for your weapons.
[9] You inspect the breaks in the walls of Jerusalem.*
    You store up water in the lower pool.
[10] You survey the houses and tear some down
    for stone to strengthen the walls.

22:11
2 Kgs 20:20; 25:4

[11] Between the city walls, you build a reservoir
    for water from the old pool.
But you never ask for help from the One who did all this.
    You never considered the One who planned this long ago.

22:12
Isa 32:11
Joel 1:13
Mic 1:16

[12] At that time the Lord, the LORD of Heaven's Armies,
    called you to weep and mourn.

21:16 *Within a year, as a servant bound by contract would count it.* Some ancient manuscripts read *Within three years,* as in 16:14.    22:1 Hebrew *concerning the Valley of Vision.*    22:8 Hebrew *to the House of the Forest;* see 1 Kgs 7:2-5.    22:9 Hebrew *the city of David.*

---

**22:1-13** "The Valley of Vision" refers to the city of Jerusalem, where God revealed himself. Jerusalem would be attacked unless God's people returned to him. Instead, they used every means of protection possible except asking God for help. They wanted to trust in their ingenuity, their weapons, and even their pagan neighbors (see 2 Chronicles 32 for the description of a siege of Jerusalem).

**22:4** Isaiah had warned his people, but they did not repent; thus, they experienced God's judgment. Because of his care for them, Isaiah was hurt by their punishment and mourned for them. Sometimes people we care for ignore our attempts to help, so they suffer the very grief we wanted to spare them. At times like that we grieve because of our concern. God expects

us to be involved with others, and this may sometimes require us to suffer with them.

**22:6, 7** Elam and Kir were under Assyrian rule. The entire Assyrian army, including its vassals, joined in the attack against Jerusalem.

**22:8-11** The leaders of Judah did what they could to prepare for war: They got weapons, inspected the walls, and stored up water in a reservoir. But all their work was pointless because they never asked God for help. Too often we take steps that, although good in themselves, really won't give us the help we need. We must get the weapons and inspect the walls, but God must guide the work.

He told you to shave your heads in sorrow for your sins
and to wear clothes of burlap to show your remorse.
13 But instead, you dance and play;
you slaughter cattle and kill sheep.
You feast on meat and drink wine.
You say, "Let's feast and drink,
for tomorrow we die!"

**22:13**
Isa 5:11, 22; 56:12
†1 Cor 15:32

14 The LORD of Heaven's Armies has revealed this to me: "Till the day you die, you will never be forgiven for this sin." That is the judgment of the Lord, the LORD of Heaven's Armies.

**22:14**
Isa 65:7, 20

### A Message for Shebna

15 This is what the Lord, the LORD of Heaven's Armies, said to me: "Confront Shebna, the palace administrator, and give him this message:

16 "Who do you think you are,
and what are you doing here,
building a beautiful tomb for yourself—
a monument high up in the rock?

**22:16**
2 Chr 16:14
Matt 27:60

17 For the LORD is about to hurl you away, mighty man.
He is going to grab you,
18 crumple you into a ball,
and toss you away into a distant, barren land.
There you will die,
and your glorious chariots will be broken and useless.
You are a disgrace to your master!

**22:18**
Job 18:18

19 "Yes, I will drive you out of office," says the LORD. "I will pull you down from your high position. 20 And then I will call my servant Eliakim son of Hilkiah to replace you. 21 I will dress him in your royal robes and will give him your title and your authority. And he will be a father to the people of Jerusalem and Judah. 22 I will give him the key to the house of David—the highest position in the royal court. When he opens doors, no one will be able to close them; when he closes doors, no one will be able to open them. 23 He will bring honor to his family name, for I will drive him firmly in place like a nail in the wall. 24 They will give him great responsibility, and he will bring honor to even the lowliest members of his family.*"

**22:19**
Ezek 17:24
**22:20**
Isa 36:3
**22:21**
Gen 45:8
**22:23**
Job 36:7
Zech 10:4

25 But the LORD of Heaven's Armies also says: "The time will come when I will pull out the nail that seemed so firm. It will come out and fall to the ground. Everything it supports will fall with it. I, the LORD, have spoken!"

**22:25**
Esth 9:24-25
Isa 46:11

### A Message about Tyre

**23** This message came to me concerning Tyre:

Weep, O ships of Tarshish,
for the harbor and houses of Tyre are gone!
The rumors you heard in Cyprus*
are all true.

**23:1**
Josh 19:29
Ezek 26:1–28:19

2 Mourn in silence, you people of the coast
and you merchants of Sidon.

**23:2**
Isa 47:5

**22:24** Hebrew *They will hang on him all the glory of his father's house; its offspring and offshoots, all its lesser vessels, from the bowls to all the jars.* **23:1** Hebrew *Kittim*; also in 23:12.

---

**22:13, 14** The people said, "Let's feast and drink," because they had given up hope. Attacked on every side (22:7), they should have repented (22:12), but they chose to feast instead. The root problem was that Judah did not trust God's power or his promises (see 56:12; 1 Corinthians 15:32). Today we still see people living without hope. There are two common responses to hopelessness: despair and self-indulgence. But we need not act as if we had no hope. As we face difficulties, our proper response should be to trust God and his promises.

**22:15-25** Shebna, the palace administrator, was just as materialistic as the rest of the people in Jerusalem (22:13). He may have been in the group favoring an alliance with foreigners, thus ignor-

ing Isaiah's advice. The Lord revealed that Shebna would lose his position and be replaced by Eliakim (22:20). Eliakim would be the "nail in the wall" driven firmly in place (22:23). Unfortunately, Eliakim too would fall (22:25).

**23:1ff** Isaiah's prophecies against other nations began in the east with Babylon (chapter 13) and ended in the west with Tyre in Phoenicia. Tyre was one of the most famous cities of the ancient world. A major trading center with a large seaport, Tyre was very wealthy and very evil. Tyre was rebuked by Jeremiah (Jeremiah 25:22, 27; 47:4), Ezekiel (Ezekiel 26–28), Joel (Joel 3:4-8), Amos (Amos 1:9, 10), and Zechariah (Zechariah 9:3, 4). This is another warning against political alliances with unstable neighbors.

**23:3**
Ezek 27:3-23

Your traders crossed the sea,
3    sailing over deep waters.
They brought you grain from Egypt*
   and harvests from along the Nile.
You were the marketplace of the world.

**23:4**
Gen 10:15, 19
Jer 47:4

4 But now you are put to shame, city of Sidon,
   for Tyre, the fortress of the sea, says,
"Now I am childless;
   I have no sons or daughters."
5 When Egypt hears the news about Tyre,
   there will be great sorrow.
6 Send word now to Tarshish!
   Wail, you people who live in distant lands!

**23:7**
Isa 32:13

7 Is this silent ruin all that is left of your once joyous city?
   What a long history was yours!
   Think of all the colonists you sent to distant places.

8 Who has brought this disaster on Tyre,
   that great creator of kingdoms?
Her traders were all princes,
   her merchants were nobles.

**23:9**
Isa 5:13
Dan 4:37

9 The Lord of Heaven's Armies has done it
   to destroy your pride
   and bring low all earth's nobility.
10 Come, people of Tarshish,
   sweep over the land like the flooding Nile,
   for Tyre is defenseless.*

**23:11**
Isa 50:2
Zech 9:3-4

11 The Lord held out his hand over the sea
   and shook the kingdoms of the earth.
He has spoken out against Phoenicia,*
   ordering that her fortresses be destroyed.

**23:12**
Rev 18:22

12 He says, "Never again will you rejoice,
   O daughter of Sidon, for you have been crushed.
Even if you flee to Cyprus,
   you will find no rest."

**23:13**
Isa 13:21

13 Look at the land of Babylonia*—
   the people of that land are gone!
The Assyrians have handed Babylon over
   to the wild animals of the desert.
They have built siege ramps against its walls,
   torn down its palaces,
   and turned it to a heap of rubble.

14 Wail, O ships of Tarshish,
   for your harbor is destroyed!

**23:15**
Jer 25:11

15For seventy years, the length of a king's life, Tyre will be forgotten. But then the city will come back to life as in the song about the prostitute:

23:3 Hebrew *from Shihor*, a branch of the Nile River.    23:10 The meaning of the Hebrew in this verse is uncertain.
23:11 Hebrew *Canaan*.    23:13 Or *Chaldea*.

---

**23:5** Why would Egypt experience "great sorrow" when Tyre fell? Egypt depended on Tyre's shipping expertise to promote and carry their products around the world. Egypt would lose an important trading partner with the fall of Tyre.

**23:9** God would destroy Tyre because he hated its people's pride. Pride separates people from God, and he will not tolerate it. As we examine our life, we must remember that all true accomplishment comes as a result of our Creator's help. We have no reason to take pride in ourselves.

**23:15, 16** Some scholars believe this is a literal 70 years; some say it is symbolic of a long period of time. If it is literal, this may have occurred between 700 and 630 B.C. during the Assyrian captivity of Israel, or it may have been during the 70-year captivity of the Jews in Babylon (605–536 B.C.). During the 70 years, the Jews would forget about Tyre. But when they returned from captivity, they would once again trade with Tyre.

16 Take a harp and walk the streets,
      you forgotten harlot.
   Make sweet melody and sing your songs
      so you will be remembered again.

17 Yes, after seventy years the LORD will revive Tyre. But she will be no different than she was before. She will again be a prostitute to all kingdoms around the world. 18 But in the end her profits will be given to the LORD. Her wealth will not be hoarded but will provide good food and fine clothing for the LORD's priests.

**23:18**
Isa 60:5-9
Zech 14:20

## 3. God's purpose in judgment
### Destruction of the Earth

**24** 1 Look! The LORD is about to destroy the earth
      and make it a vast wasteland.
   He devastates the surface of the earth
      and scatters the people.
2 Priests and laypeople,
      servants and masters,
      maids and mistresses,
      buyers and sellers,
      lenders and borrowers,
      bankers and debtors—none will be spared.
3 The earth will be completely emptied and looted.
      The LORD has spoken!

4 The earth mourns and dries up,
      and the crops waste away and wither.
   Even the greatest people on earth waste away.
5 The earth suffers for the sins of its people,
      for they have twisted God's instructions,
   violated his laws,
      and broken his everlasting covenant.
6 Therefore, a curse consumes the earth.
      Its people must pay the price for their sin.
   They are destroyed by fire,
      and only a few are left alive.
7 The grapevines waste away,
      and there is no new wine.
   All the merrymakers sigh and mourn.
8 The cheerful sound of tambourines is stilled;
      the happy cries of celebration are heard no more.
   The melodious chords of the harp are silent.
9 Gone are the joys of wine and song;
      alcoholic drink turns bitter in the mouth.
10 The city writhes in chaos;
      every home is locked to keep out intruders.
11 Mobs gather in the streets, crying out for wine.
      Joy has turned to gloom.
      Gladness has been banished from the land.
12 The city is left in ruins,
      its gates battered down.

**24:5**
Gen 3:17
Num 35:33

**24:6**
Isa 34:5
Zech 5:3-4

**24:7**
Joel 1:10, 12

**24:8**
Jer 16:9

**24:9**
Isa 5:11, 22

**24:11**
Isa 32:13

---

**24–27** These four chapters are often called "Isaiah's Apocalypse." They discuss God's judgment on the entire world for its sin. Isaiah's prophecies were first directed to Judah, then to Israel, then to the surrounding nations, and finally to the whole world. These chapters describe the last days when God will judge the whole world. At that time he will finally and permanently remove evil.

**24:4, 5** Not only the people suffered from their sins; even the land suffered the effects of evil and lawbreaking. Today we see the results of sin in our own land: pollution, crime, addiction, poverty. Sin affects every aspect of society so extensively that even those faithful to God suffer. We cannot blame God for these conditions because sin has brought them about. The more we who are believers renounce sin, speak against immoral practices, and share God's Word with others, the more we slow our society's deterioration. We must not give up: Sin is rampant, but we can make a difference.

24:13
Isa 17:6

13 Throughout the earth the story is the same—
    only a remnant is left,
like the stray olives left on the tree
    or the few grapes left on the vine after harvest.

24:14
Isa 12:6; 52:8

14 But all who are left shout and sing for joy.
    Those in the west praise the LORD's majesty.

24:15
Isa 42:4, 10, 12

15 In eastern lands, give glory to the LORD.
    In the lands beyond the sea, praise the name of the LORD, the God of Israel.

24:16
Isa 11:12; 28:5

16 We hear songs of praise from the ends of the earth,
    songs that give glory to the Righteous One!

But my heart is heavy with grief.
    Weep for me, for I wither away.
Deceit still prevails,
    and treachery is everywhere.

17 Terror and traps and snares will be your lot,
    you people of the earth.

24:18
Gen 7:10-12
Ps 46:2

18 Those who flee in terror will fall into a trap,
    and those who escape the trap will be caught in a snare.

Destruction falls like rain from the heavens;
    the foundations of the earth shake.

24:19
Num 16:31-32

19 The earth has broken up.
    It has utterly collapsed;
    it is violently shaken.

24:20
Isa 19:14; 43:27;
66:24

20 The earth staggers like a drunk.
    It trembles like a tent in a storm.
It falls and will not rise again,
    for the guilt of its rebellion is very heavy.

24:21
Ps 76:12

21 In that day the LORD will punish the gods in the heavens
    and the proud rulers of the nations on earth.
22 They will be rounded up and put in prison.
    They will be shut up in prison
    and will finally be punished.

24:23
Mic 4:7
Heb 12:22
Rev 21:23

23 Then the glory of the moon will wane,
    and the brightness of the sun will fade,
for the LORD of Heaven's Armies will rule on Mount Zion.
He will rule in great glory in Jerusalem,
    in the sight of all the leaders of his people.

*Praise for Judgment and Salvation*

25:1
Exod 15:2
Ps 40:5
Eph 1:11

**25** ¹ O LORD, I will honor and praise your name,
    for you are my God.
You do such wonderful things!
    You planned them long ago,
    and now you have accomplished them.

25:2
Isa 17:1

2 You turn mighty cities into heaps of ruins.
    Cities with strong walls are turned to rubble.
Beautiful palaces in distant lands disappear
    and will never be rebuilt.

---

**24:14-16** The believers who are left behind after God judges Judah will sing to the glory of God's righteousness. Isaiah grieved because of his world's condition. We, too, can become depressed by the evil all around us. At those times we need to hold on to God's promises for the future and look forward to singing praises to him when he restores heaven and earth.

**24:21** "The gods in the heavens" refer to spiritual forces opposed to God. Nobody, not even the so-called gods, will escape due punishment.

**25:1** Isaiah honored and praised God because he realized that God completes his plans as promised. God also fulfills his promises to you. Think of the prayers he has answered, and praise him for his goodness and faithfulness.

³ Therefore, strong nations will declare your glory;
　　ruthless nations will fear you.

⁴ But you are a tower of refuge to the poor, O Lᴏʀᴅ,
　　a tower of refuge to the needy in distress.
You are a refuge from the storm
　　and a shelter from the heat.
For the oppressive acts of ruthless people
　　are like a storm beating against a wall,
⁵　　or like the relentless heat of the desert.
But you silence the roar of foreign nations.
　　As the shade of a cloud cools relentless heat,
　　so the boastful songs of ruthless people are stilled.

⁶ In Jerusalem,* the Lᴏʀᴅ of Heaven's Armies
　　will spread a wonderful feast
　　for all the people of the world.
It will be a delicious banquet
　　with clear, well-aged wine and choice meat.
⁷ There he will remove the cloud of gloom,
　　the shadow of death that hangs over the earth.
⁸ He will swallow up death forever!*
　　The Sovereign Lᴏʀᴅ will wipe away all tears.
He will remove forever all insults and mockery
　　against his land and people.
　　The Lᴏʀᴅ has spoken!

⁹ In that day the people will proclaim,
　"This is our God!
　　We trusted in him, and he saved us!
This is the Lᴏʀᴅ, in whom we trusted.
　　Let us rejoice in the salvation he brings!"
¹⁰ For the Lᴏʀᴅ's hand of blessing will rest on Jerusalem.
　　But Moab will be crushed.
　　It will be like straw trampled down and left to rot.
¹¹ God will push down Moab's people
　　as a swimmer pushes down water with his hands.
He will end their pride
　　and all their evil works.
¹² The high walls of Moab will be demolished.
　　They will be brought down to the ground,
　　down into the dust.

25:4
Isa 32:2

25:5
Jer 51:54-56

25:6
Isa 2:2-4

25:8
Ps 69:9
Isa 65:19
†1 Cor 15:54-55
1 Pet 4:14
Rev 21:4

25:9
Isa 30:18;
35:1-2, 10; 40:9

25:11
Isa 16:6

25:12
Isa 26:5

25:6 Hebrew *On this mountain;* also in 25:10.　25:8 Greek version reads *Death is swallowed up in victory.* Compare
1 Cor 15:54.

---

**25:4** The poor suffered because ruthless people oppressed
them. But God is concerned for the poor and is a refuge for
them. When we are disadvantaged or oppressed, we can turn
to God for comfort and help. Jesus states that the Kingdom of
God belongs to the poor (Luke 6:20).

**25:6** Here is a marvelous prophecy of "all the people of the
world"—Gentiles and Jews together—at God's messianic feast,
celebrating the overthrow of evil and the joy of eternity with God.
It shows that God intended his saving message to go out to the
whole world, not just to the Jews. During the feast, God will end
death forever (25:7, 8). The people who participate in this great
feast will be those who have been living by faith. That is why they

say, "This is our God. We trusted in him, and he saved us"
(25:9). See also chapter 55 for another presentation of this
great feast.

**25:8** When the Lord speaks, he does what he says. It is comforting to know that God's plans and activities are closely tied
to his word. When we pray according to God's will (as expressed
in the Bible) and claim his promises (as recorded in the Bible),
he hears us and answers our requests.

**25:8** Part of this verse is quoted in 1 Corinthians 15:54 to
describe Christ's victory over death. God's ultimate victory is
seen when death, our ultimate enemy, is defeated (see also
Hosea 13:14). Another part of this verse is quoted in Revelation
21:4, which describes the glorious scene of God's presence with
his people.

**25:10** Moab was a symbol of all who oppose God and are
rebellious to the end. Moab was Israel's enemy for years (see
the note on 15:1).

*A Song of Praise to the LORD*

**26:1**
Isa 12:1; 60:18

**26** In that day, everyone in the land of Judah will sing this song:

Our city is strong!
We are surrounded by the walls of God's salvation.

**26:2**
Isa 45:25

2 Open the gates to all who are righteous;
allow the faithful to enter.

**26:3**
Isa 57:19

3 You will keep in perfect peace
all who trust in you,
all whose thoughts are fixed on you!

**26:4**
Isa 50:10

4 Trust in the LORD always,
for the LORD God is the eternal Rock.

5 He humbles the proud
and brings down the arrogant city.
He brings it down to the dust.

**26:6**
Isa 29:19

6 The poor and oppressed trample it underfoot,
and the needy walk all over it.

**26:7**
Ps 25:4-5
Isa 42:16

7 But for those who are righteous,
the way is not steep and rough.
You are a God who does what is right,
and you smooth out the path ahead of them.

**26:8**
Isa 12:4

8 LORD, we show our trust in you by obeying your laws;
our heart's desire is to glorify your name.

**26:9**
Pss 63:1; 77:2
Hos 5:15

9 All night long I search for you;
in the morning I earnestly seek for God.
For only when you come to judge the earth
will people learn what is right.

**26:10**
Isa 22:12-13
John 5:37-38

10 Your kindness to the wicked
does not make them do good.
Although others do right, the wicked keep doing wrong
and take no notice of the LORD's majesty.

**26:11**
Isa 10:17;
66:15, 24

11 O LORD, they pay no attention to your upraised fist.
Show them your eagerness to defend your people.
Then they will be ashamed.
Let your fire consume your enemies.

12 LORD, you will grant us peace;
all we have accomplished is really from you.

**26:13**
Isa 2:8

13 O LORD our God, others have ruled us,
but you alone are the one we worship.

14 Those we served before are dead and gone.
Their departed spirits will never return!
You attacked them and destroyed them,
and they are long forgotten.

**26:15**
Isa 54:2

15 O LORD, you have made our nation great;
yes, you have made us great.

---

**26:1ff** People will praise God on the day of the Lord when Christ establishes his Kingdom (see chapter 12). Chapter 26 is a psalm of trust, praise, and meditation. Once more, God revealed the future to Isaiah.

**26:3** We can never avoid strife in the world around us, but when we fix our thoughts on God, we can know perfect peace even in turmoil. As we focus our mind on God and his Word, we become steady and stable. Supported by God's unchanging love and mighty power, we are not shaken by the surrounding chaos (see Philippians 4:7). Do you want peace? Keep your thoughts on God and your trust in him.

**26:7, 8** At times the "path" of the righteous doesn't seem smooth, and it isn't easy to do God's will, but we are never alone when we face tough times. God is there to help us, to comfort us, and to lead us. God does this by giving us a purpose (keeping our mind centered on him, 26:3) and giving us provisions as we travel. God provides us with relationships of family, friends, and mentors. God gives us wisdom to make decisions and faith to trust him. Don't despair; stay on God's path.

**26:10** Even wicked people receive God's benefits, but that doesn't teach them to do what is right. Sometimes God's judgment teaches us more than God's good gifts. If you have been enriched by God's goodness and grace, respond to him with your grateful devotion.

You have extended our borders,
  and we give you the glory!

<sup>16</sup> LORD, in distress we searched for you.
  We prayed beneath the burden of your discipline.
<sup>17</sup> Just as a pregnant woman
  writhes and cries out in pain as she gives birth,
  so were we in your presence, LORD.
<sup>18</sup> We, too, writhe in agony,
  but nothing comes of our suffering.
  We have not given salvation to the earth,
  nor brought life into the world.
<sup>19</sup> But those who die in the LORD will live;
  their bodies will rise again!
  Those who sleep in the earth
  will rise up and sing for joy!
  For your life-giving light will fall like dew
  on your people in the place of the dead!

### Restoration for Israel
<sup>20</sup> Go home, my people,
  and lock your doors!
  Hide yourselves for a little while
  until the LORD's anger has passed.
<sup>21</sup> Look! The LORD is coming from heaven
  to punish the people of the earth for their sins.
  The earth will no longer hide those who have been killed.
  They will be brought out for all to see.

**27** In that day the LORD will take his terrible, swift sword and punish Leviathan,* the swiftly moving serpent, the coiling, writhing serpent. He will kill the dragon of the sea.

<sup>2</sup> "In that day,
  sing about the fruitful vineyard.
<sup>3</sup> I, the LORD, will watch over it,
  watering it carefully.
  Day and night I will watch so no one can harm it.
<sup>4</sup>   My anger will be gone.
  If I find briers and thorns growing,
  I will attack them;
  I will burn them up—
<sup>5</sup>   unless they turn to me for help.
  Let them make peace with me;
  yes, let them make peace with me."

---

**27:1** The identification of Leviathan is disputed, ranging from an earthly creature to a mythical sea monster in ancient literature.

**Cross-references (right margin):**

26:16 Hos 5:15

26:17 John 16:21

26:18 Isa 33:11

26:19 Ezek 37:1-14 Dan 12:2 Eph 5:14

26:21 Job 16:18 Mic 1:3 Jude 1:14

27:1 Job 3:8 Ps 74:14

27:2 Ps 80:8

27:3 John 10:28

27:4 2 Sam 23:6 Isa 33:12

27:5 Job 22:21 Isa 25:4

---

**26:16-19** The people realized the pain of being away from God's presence, and yet they were assured that they would live again. God turned his back on his people when they disobeyed, but a small number never lost hope and continued to seek him. No matter how difficult times may be, we have hope when we keep our trust in him. Can you wait patiently for God to act?

**26:19** Some people say there is no life after death. Others believe that there is, but it is not physical life. But Isaiah tells us that our bodies shall rise again. According to 1 Corinthians 15:50-53, all the dead believers will arise with new imperishable bodies—bodies like the one Jesus had when he was resurrected (see Philippians 3:21). Isaiah 26:19 is not the only Old Testament verse to speak about the resurrection; see also Job 19:26; Psalm 16:10; Daniel 12:2, 13.

**26:20, 21** When God comes to judge the earth, the guilty will find no place to hide. Jesus said that the hidden will be made

known because his truth, like a light shining in a dark corner, will reveal it (Matthew 10:26). Instead of trying to hide your shameful thoughts and actions from God, confess them to him and receive his forgiveness.

**27:1** "That day" is a reference to the end of the evil world as we know it. In ancient Aramean (Ugaritic) literature, Leviathan was a seven-headed monster, the enemy of God's created order. Thus, Isaiah is comparing God's slaughter of the wicked to the conquering of a great enemy. Although evil is a powerful foe, God will crush it and abolish it from the earth forever.

**27:2-6** The trampled vineyard of chapter 5 will be restored in God's new earth. God will protect and care for the vineyard, his people. It will no longer produce worthless fruit but will produce enough good fruit for the whole world. Gentiles will come to know God through Israel.

**27:6**
Isa 35:1-2; 37:31

6 The time is coming when Jacob's descendants will take root.
Israel will bud and blossom
and fill the whole earth with fruit!

**27:7**
Isa 10:12, 17

7 Has the Lord struck Israel
as he struck her enemies?
Has he punished her
as he punished them?
8 No, but he exiled Israel to call her to account.
She was exiled from her land
as though blown away in a storm from the east.

**27:9**
Isa 17:8
Dan 11:35

9 The Lord did this to purge Israel's* wickedness,
to take away all her sin.
As a result, all the pagan altars will be crushed to dust.
No Asherah pole or pagan shrine will be left standing.
10 The fortified towns will be silent and empty,
the houses abandoned, the streets overgrown with weeds.
Calves will graze there,
chewing on twigs and branches.

**27:11**
Deut 32:18, 28
Isa 43:1, 7

11 The people are like the dead branches of a tree,
broken off and used for kindling beneath the cooking pots.
Israel is a foolish and stupid nation,
for its people have turned away from God.
Therefore, the one who made them
will show them no pity or mercy.

**27:12**
Deut 30:3-4
Isa 11:11

**27:13**
Zech 14:16
Matt 24:31
Rev 11:15

12 Yet the time will come when the Lord will gather them together like handpicked grain. One by one he will gather them—from the Euphrates River* in the east to the Brook of Egypt in the west. 13 In that day the great trumpet will sound. Many who were dying in exile in Assyria and Egypt will return to Jerusalem to worship the Lord on his holy mountain.

## 4. Jerusalem's true and false hopes
### A Message about Samaria

**28** 1 What sorrow awaits the proud city of Samaria—
the glorious crown of the drunks of Israel.*
It sits at the head of a fertile valley,
but its glorious beauty will fade like a flower.
It is the pride of a people
brought down by wine.

**28:2**
Isa 8:7; 30:28
Nah 1:8

2 For the Lord will send a mighty army against it.
Like a mighty hailstorm and a torrential rain,
they will burst upon it like a surging flood
and smash it to the ground.
3 The proud city of Samaria—
the glorious crown of the drunks of Israel*—
will be trampled beneath its enemies' feet.

**27:9** Hebrew *Jacob's.* See note on 14:1.   **27:12** Hebrew *the river.*   **28:1** Hebrew *What sorrow awaits the crowning glory of the drunks of Ephraim,* referring to Samaria, capital of the northern kingdom of Israel.   **28:3** Hebrew *The crowning glory of the drunks of Ephraim;* see note on 28:1.

---

**27:9** Only God can take away sin, but to be driven out of the land was considered the penalty that would purify God's people. Deuteronomy 28:49-52, 64 explains God's warning about these consequences.

**27:11** Isaiah compares the state of Israel's spiritual life with dead branches of a tree that are broken off and used to make fires. Trees in Scripture often represent spiritual life. The trunk is the channel of strength from God; the branches are the people who serve him. Tree branches sometimes waver and blow in the wind. Like Israel, they may dry up from internal rottenness and become useless for anything except building a fire. What kind of branch are you? If you are withering spiritually, check to see if you are firmly attached to God.

**28:1** Samaria, the capital city of the northern kingdom of Israel, represents the entire kingdom, ruled by a line of evil kings. When Israel split into two kingdoms after Solomon's reign, Jerusalem ended up in the southern kingdom. Leaders in the northern kingdom, wishing to stay entirely separate from their relatives to the south, set up idols to keep the people from going to the Temple in Jerusalem to worship (see 1 Kings 12). Thus, the people in the northern kingdom were led into idolatry. Isaiah gave this message to Israel to warn them that destruction was certain. It was also meant to encourage Judah to repent before being punished, as the northern kingdom would be only a few years later.

4 It sits at the head of a fertile valley,
    but its glorious beauty will fade like a flower.
Whoever sees it will snatch it up,
    as an early fig is quickly picked and eaten.

28:4
Hos 9:10
Nah 3:12

5 Then at last the LORD of Heaven's Armies
    will himself be Israel's glorious crown.
He will be the pride and joy
    of the remnant of his people.

28:5
Isa 41:16; 62:3

6 He will give a longing for justice
    to their judges.
He will give great courage
    to their warriors who stand at the gates.

28:6
2 Chr 32:6-8
Isa 11:2; 25:4;
32:16

7 Now, however, Israel is led by drunks
    who reel with wine and stagger with alcohol.
The priests and prophets stagger with alcohol
    and lose themselves in wine.
They reel when they see visions
    and stagger as they render decisions.

28:7
Hab 2:15-16

8 Their tables are covered with vomit;
    filth is everywhere.

28:8
Jer 48:26

9 "Who does the LORD think we are?" they ask.
    "Why does he speak to us like this?
Are we little children,
    just recently weaned?

28:9
Heb 5:12-13

10 He tells us everything over and over—
    one line at a time,
        one line at a time,
    a little here,
        and a little there!"

28:10
Neh 9:30

11 So now God will have to speak to his people
    through foreign oppressors who speak a strange language!

28:11
Isa 33:19
†1 Cor 14:21

12 God has told his people,
    "Here is a place of rest;
        let the weary rest here.
This is a place of quiet rest."
    But they would not listen.

28:12
Jer 6:16
Matt 11:28-29

13 So the LORD will spell out his message for them again,
    one line at a time,
        one line at a time,
    a little here,
        and a little there,
so that they will stumble and fall.
    They will be injured, trapped, and captured.

28:13
Matt 21:44

14 Therefore, listen to this message from the LORD,
    you scoffing rulers in Jerusalem.

28:14
Isa 28:22

15 You boast, "We have struck a bargain to cheat death
    and have made a deal to dodge the grave.*

28:15
Isa 28:18

28:15 Hebrew *Sheol*; also in 28:18.

---

28:9-14 These verses characterize the people's reaction to Isaiah. In effect, they were saying, "He's speaking to us like a school-teacher speaks to small children. We don't need to be taught. We'll make up our own minds." For this attitude, Isaiah prophesied that the Assyrians would teach them in a way they would like even less.

28:15 Judah was afraid of the Assyrians. Instead of trusting God, the Judeans turned to other sources for security. God accused them of making a deal with the grave, referring to the state of being dead. This passage may refer to Hezekiah's alliance with Pharaoh Tirhakah against Assyria (2 Kings 19:9; Isaiah 37:9). God would cancel this agreement—Egypt would be of no help when Assyria attacked. Is it worth selling out what you believe in for temporary protection against an enemy? If you want lasting protection, turn to the only one able to deliver you from *eternal* death—God.

The coming destruction can never touch us,
for we have built a strong refuge made of lies and deception."

**28:16**
Ps 118:22
Matt 21:42
Acts 4:11
†Rom 9:33; 10:11
Eph 2:20
†1 Pet 2:6

16 Therefore, this is what the Sovereign LORD says:
"Look! I am placing a foundation stone in Jerusalem,*
a firm and tested stone.
It is a precious cornerstone that is safe to build on.
Whoever believes need never be shaken.*

**28:17**
Isa 61:8
Amos 7:7-9

17 I will test you with the measuring line of justice
and the plumb line of righteousness.
Since your refuge is made of lies,
a hailstorm will knock it down.
Since it is made of deception,
a flood will sweep it away.

**28:18**
Isa 28:15

18 I will cancel the bargain you made to cheat death,
and I will overturn your deal to dodge the grave.
When the terrible enemy sweeps through,
you will be trampled into the ground.

**28:19**
Ps 88:15

19 Again and again that flood will come,
morning after morning,
day and night,
until you are carried away."

This message will bring terror to your people.
20 The bed you have made is too short to lie on.
The blankets are too narrow to cover you.

**28:21**
2 Sam 5:20
Luke 19:41-44

21 The LORD will come as he did against the Philistines at Mount Perazim
and against the Amorites at Gibeon.
He will come to do a strange thing;
he will come to do an unusual deed:

**28:22**
Isa 10:22-23; 28:14

22 For the Lord, the LORD of Heaven's Armies,
has plainly said that he is determined to crush the whole land.
So scoff no more,
or your punishment will be even greater.

23 Listen to me;
listen, and pay close attention.
24 Does a farmer always plow and never sow?
Is he forever cultivating the soil and never planting?
25 Does he not finally plant his seeds—
black cumin, cumin, wheat, barley, and emmer wheat—
each in its proper way,
and each in its proper place?
26 The farmer knows just what to do,
for God has given him understanding.

**28:27**
Amos 1:3

27 A heavy sledge is never used to thresh black cumin;
rather, it is beaten with a light stick.
A threshing wheel is never rolled on cumin;
instead, it is beaten lightly with a flail.

**28:16a** Hebrew *in Zion.* **28:16b** Greek version reads *Look! I am placing a stone in the foundation of Jerusalem* [literally *Zion*], / *a precious cornerstone for its foundation, chosen for great honor. / Anyone who trusts in him will never be disgraced.* Compare Rom 9:33; 1 Pet 2:6.

---

**28:16** If you're building anything, you need a firm base. Isaiah speaks of a foundation stone, a precious cornerstone, that will be laid in Zion. This cornerstone is the Messiah, the foundation on whom we build our lives. Is your life built on the flimsy base of your own successes or dreams? Or is it set on a firm foundation (see Psalm 118:22; 1 Peter 2:8)?

**28:21** God fought on Joshua's side at the battle of Gibeon (Joshua 10:1-14) and on David's side at Mount Perazim (2 Samuel 5:20). But here he would fight *against* Israel, his own people, in these same places.

**28:23-29** The farmer uses special tools to plant and harvest tender herbs so he will not destroy them. He takes into account how fragile they are. In the same way God takes all our individual circumstances and weaknesses into account. He deals with each of us sensitively. We should follow his example when we deal with others. Different people require different treatment. Be sensitive to the needs of those around you and the special treatment they may need.

28 Grain for bread is easily crushed,
    so he doesn't keep on pounding it.
He threshes it under the wheels of a cart,
    but he doesn't pulverize it.
29 The LORD of Heaven's Armies is a wonderful teacher,
    and he gives the farmer great wisdom.

*A Message about Jerusalem*

## 29
1 "What sorrow awaits Ariel,* the City of David.
    Year after year you celebrate your feasts.
2 Yet I will bring disaster upon you,
    and there will be much weeping and sorrow.
For Jerusalem will become what her name Ariel means—
    an altar covered with blood.
3 I will be your enemy,
    surrounding Jerusalem and attacking its walls.
I will build siege towers
    and destroy it.
4 Then deep from the earth you will speak;
    from low in the dust your words will come.
Your voice will whisper from the ground
    like a ghost conjured up from the grave.

5 "But suddenly, your ruthless enemies will be crushed
    like the finest of dust.
Your many attackers will be driven away
    like chaff before the wind.
Suddenly, in an instant,
6   I, the LORD of Heaven's Armies, will act for you
with thunder and earthquake and great noise,
    with whirlwind and storm and consuming fire.
7 All the nations fighting against Jerusalem*
    will vanish like a dream!
Those who are attacking her walls
    will vanish like a vision in the night.
8 A hungry person dreams of eating
    but wakes up still hungry.
A thirsty person dreams of drinking
    but is still faint from thirst when morning comes.
So it will be with your enemies,
    with those who attack Mount Zion."

9 Are you amazed and incredulous?
    Don't you believe it?
Then go ahead and be blind.
    You are stupid, but not from wine!
    You stagger, but not from liquor!
10 For the LORD has poured out on you a spirit of deep sleep.
    He has closed the eyes of your prophets and visionaries.

11 All the future events in this vision are like a sealed book to them. When you give it to those who can read, they will say, "We can't read it because it is sealed." 12 When you give it to those who cannot read, they will say, "We don't know how to read."

13 And so the Lord says,
    "These people say they are mine.

29:1 *Ariel* sounds like a Hebrew term that means "hearth" or "altar."  29:7 Hebrew *Ariel.*

**Cross-references:**
28:29 Rom 11:33
29:1 2 Sam 5:9
29:2 Lam 2:5
29:3 Luke 19:43-44
29:4 Isa 8:19
29:5 Isa 17:13-14; 41:15-16; 1 Thes 5:3
29:6 Matt 24:7; Mark 13:8; Luke 21:11; Rev 11:13, 19; 16:18
29:7 Zech 12:9
29:8 Isa 54:17
29:9 Isa 51:17
29:10 †Rom 11:8; 2 Thes 2:9-12
29:11 Dan 12:4; Matt 13:11
29:13 Ezek 33:31; Mark 7:6-7

---

**29:1** *Ariel* is a special name for Jerusalem, David's city. It may mean "lion of God" (Jerusalem is strong as a lion) or "altar hearth" (Jerusalem is the place of the altar in the Temple; see 29:2; Ezekiel 43:15, 16).

**29:13, 14** The people claimed to be close to God, but they were disobedient and merely went through the motions; therefore, God would bring judgment upon them. Religion had become routine instead of real. Jesus quoted Isaiah's condemnation of

They honor me with their lips,
  but their hearts are far from me.
And their worship of me
  is nothing but man-made rules learned by rote.*

**29:14**
Isa 44:25
†1 Cor 1:19

14 Because of this, I will once again astound these hypocrites
  with amazing wonders.
The wisdom of the wise will pass away,
  and the intelligence of the intelligent will disappear."

**29:15**
Ps 10:11, 13
Isa 47:10

15 What sorrow awaits those who try to hide their plans from the LORD,
  who do their evil deeds in the dark!
"The LORD can't see us," they say.
  "He doesn't know what's going on!"

**29:16**
Isa 45:9
Rom 9:20-21

16 How foolish can you be?
  He is the Potter, and he is certainly greater than you, the clay!
Should the created thing say of the one who made it,
  "He didn't make me"?
Does a jar ever say,
  "The potter who made me is stupid"?

17 Soon—and it will not be very long—
  the forests of Lebanon will become a fertile field,
  and the fertile field will yield bountiful crops.

**29:18**
Isa 32:3

18 In that day the deaf will hear words read from a book,
  and the blind will see through the gloom and darkness.

**29:19**
Isa 14:30, 32
Matt 5:5
Jas 2:5

19 The humble will be filled with fresh joy from the LORD.
  The poor will rejoice in the Holy One of Israel.
20 The scoffer will be gone,
  the arrogant will disappear,
  and those who plot evil will be killed.

**29:21**
Amos 5:10, 12

21 Those who convict the innocent
  by their false testimony will disappear.
A similar fate awaits those who use trickery to pervert justice
  and who tell lies to destroy the innocent.

**29:22**
Isa 41:8

22 That is why the LORD, who redeemed Abraham, says to the people of Israel,*

"My people will no longer be ashamed
  or turn pale with fear.
23 For when they see their many children
  and all the blessings I have given them,
they will recognize the holiness of the Holy One of Israel.
  They will stand in awe of the God of Jacob.

**29:24**
Isa 30:21; 41:20

24 Then the wayward will gain understanding,
  and complainers will accept instruction.

29:13 Greek version reads *Their worship is a farce, / for they teach man-made ideas as commands from God.*
Compare Mark 7:7.   **29:22** Hebrew *of Jacob.* See note on 14:1.

---

Israel's hypocrisy when he spoke to the Pharisees, the religious leaders of his day (Matthew 15:7-9; Mark 7:6, 7). We are all capable of hypocrisy. Often we slip into routine patterns when we worship, and we neglect to give God our love and devotion. If we want to be called God's people, we must be obedient and worship him honestly and sincerely.

**29:15** Thinking God couldn't see them and didn't know what was happening, the people of Jerusalem tried to hide their plans from him. How strange that so many people think they can hide from God. In Psalm 139 we learn that God has examined us and knows everything about us. Would you be embarrassed if your best friends knew your personal thoughts? Remember that God knows all of them.

**29:17-24** The world described here, under Christ's rule, will be far different from the one we live in today. There will be no more violence or gloom. This new world will be characterized by joy, understanding, justice, and praise to God.

## Judah's Worthless Treaty with Egypt

**30** ¹ "What sorrow awaits my rebellious children,"
        says the LORD.
"You make plans that are contrary to mine.
    You make alliances not directed by my Spirit,
    thus piling up your sins.
² For without consulting me,
    you have gone down to Egypt for help.
You have put your trust in Pharaoh's protection.
    You have tried to hide in his shade.
³ But by trusting Pharaoh, you will be humiliated,
    and by depending on him, you will be disgraced.
⁴ For though his power extends to Zoan
    and his officials have arrived in Hanes,
⁵ all who trust in him will be ashamed.
    He will not help you.
    Instead, he will disgrace you."

⁶This message came to me concerning the animals in the Negev:

The caravan moves slowly
    across the terrible desert to Egypt—
donkeys weighed down with riches
    and camels loaded with treasure—
    all to pay for Egypt's protection.
They travel through the wilderness,
    a place of lionesses and lions,
    a place where vipers and poisonous snakes live.
All this, and Egypt will give you nothing in return.
⁷    Egypt's promises are worthless!
Therefore, I call her Rahab—
    the Harmless Dragon.*

## A Warning for Rebellious Judah

⁸ Now go and write down these words.
    Write them in a book.
They will stand until the end of time
    as a witness
⁹ that these people are stubborn rebels
    who refuse to pay attention to the LORD's instructions.
¹⁰ They tell the seers,
    "Stop seeing visions!"
They tell the prophets,
    "Don't tell us what is right.
Tell us nice things.
    Tell us lies.

| | |
|---|---|
| | **30:1** Isa 8:11-12 |
| | **30:2** Isa 8:19; 31:1 |
| | **30:3** Isa 36:6 Jer 42:18, 22 |
| | **30:5** Isa 31:3 Jer 2:36 |
| | **30:6** Deut 8:15 |
| | **30:7** Isa 51:9 |
| | **30:8** Isa 8:1 |
| | **30:9** Isa 24:5; 28:15; 30:1 |
| | **30:10** 1 Kgs 22:8, 13 Jer 6:14 Ezek 13:7 Amos 2:12 2 Tim 4:3-4 |

**30:7** Hebrew *Rahab who sits still.* Rahab is the name of a mythical sea monster that represents chaos in ancient literature. The name is used here as a poetic name for Egypt.

---

**30:1** The rebellious children are the people of Judah (see 1:2), those who have rebelled against God. The negotiations for an alliance were underway, and Isaiah condemned their twisted plans. The people of Judah sought advice from everyone but God. When we are driven by fear, we tend to search everywhere for comfort, advice, and relief, hoping to find an easy way out of our troubles. Instead, we should consult God. Although he gives emergency help in a crisis, he prefers to be our guide throughout our life. By reading his Word and actively seeking to do his will, we can maintain our bond with him who provides stability no matter what the crisis.

**30:2ff** Hezekiah had been seeking a defensive alliance with Egypt against Sennacherib of Assyria (see 2 Kings 18:21).

**30:6** This message is directed to those who carried bribes to Egypt through the desert in the Negev region.

**30:7** This Harmless Dragon (also called Rahab) was a mythological female sea monster associated with Leviathan (see the note on 27:1; also Job 9:13; 26:12). It was a name associated with Egypt, where hippopotamuses, perhaps a likeness to Rahab, sat on the Nile River and did nothing.

**30:10, 11** Some people in Judah may have sought refuge in Egypt. In their desire to find security, they wanted to hear only good news. They did not welcome the truth from God's prophets. Often the truth makes us uncomfortable. We prefer lies and illusions when they make us feel more secure. It is much better to face reality than to live a lie. Don't settle for something that makes you feel comfortable but is not true.

30:11
Job 21:14

11 Forget all this gloom.
        Get off your narrow path.
    Stop telling us about your
        'Holy One of Israel.'"

30:12
Isa 5:24; 59:13

12 This is the reply of the Holy One of Israel:

    "Because you despise what I tell you
        and trust instead in oppression and lies,

30:13
Isa 26:21; 29:5

13 calamity will come upon you suddenly—
        like a bulging wall that bursts and falls.
    In an instant it will collapse
        and come crashing down.

30:14
Ps 2:9
Jer 19:10-11

14 You will be smashed like a piece of pottery—
        shattered so completely that
    there won't be a piece big enough
        to carry coals from a fireplace
        or a little water from the well."

30:15
Isa 7:28; 28:12;
32:17

15 This is what the Sovereign LORD,
        the Holy One of Israel, says:
    "Only in returning to me
        and resting in me will you be saved.
    In quietness and confidence is your strength.
        But you would have none of it.

30:16
Isa 31:1, 3

16 You said, 'No, we will get our help from Egypt.
        They will give us swift horses for riding into battle.'
    But the only swiftness you are going to see
        is the swiftness of your enemies chasing you!

30:17
Deut 28:25; 32:30

17 One of them will chase a thousand of you.
        Five of them will make all of you flee.
    You will be left like a lonely flagpole on a hill
        or a tattered banner on a distant mountaintop."

### Blessings for the LORD's People

30:18
Isa 25:9
2 Pet 3:9, 15

18 So the LORD must wait for you to come to him
        so he can show you his love and compassion.
    For the LORD is a faithful God.
        Blessed are those who wait for his help.

30:19
Isa 25:8; 65:24

19 O people of Zion, who live in Jerusalem,
        you will weep no more.
    He will be gracious if you ask for help.
        He will surely respond to the sound of your cries.

30:20
Ps 80:5

20 Though the Lord gave you adversity for food
        and suffering for drink,
    he will still be with you to teach you.
        You will see your teacher with your own eyes.

30:21
Isa 35:8-9

21 Your own ears will hear him.
        Right behind you a voice will say,
    "This is the way you should go,"
        whether to the right or to the left.

---

**30:15** God warned Judah that turning to Egypt and other nations for military might could not save them. Only God could do that. They must wait for him "in quietness and confidence." No amount of fast talking or hasty activity could speed up God's grand design. We have nothing to say to God but thank you. Salvation comes from God alone. Because he has saved us, we can trust him and be peacefully confident that he will give us strength to face our difficulties. We should lay aside our well-laid plans and allow him to act.

**30:20** The Lord gave his people adversity for food and suffering for drink, but he promised to be with them, teach them, and guide them during hard times. God expects a lot from us, and many times following him can be painful; but he always acts out of his love for us. Next time you go through a difficult time, try to appreciate the experience and grow from it, learning what God wants to teach you. God may be showing you his love by patiently walking with you through adversity.

**30:21** When the people of Jerusalem left God's path, he would correct them. He will do the same for us. But when we hear his voice of correction, we must be willing to follow it!

22 Then you will destroy all your silver idols
    and your precious gold images.
You will throw them out like filthy rags,
    saying to them, "Good riddance!"

23 Then the Lord will bless you with rain at planting time. There will be wonderful
harvests and plenty of pastureland for your livestock. 24 The oxen and donkeys that till the
ground will eat good grain, its chaff blown away by the wind. 25 In that day, when your
enemies are slaughtered and the towers fall, there will be streams of water flowing down
every mountain and hill. 26 The moon will be as bright as the sun, and the sun will be seven
times brighter—like the light of seven days in one! So it will be when the Lord begins to heal
his people and cure the wounds he gave them.

27 Look! The Lord is coming from far away,
    burning with anger,
    surrounded by thick, rising smoke.
His lips are filled with fury;
    his words consume like fire.
28 His hot breath pours out like a flood
    up to the neck of his enemies.
He will sift out the proud nations for destruction.
    He will bridle them and lead them away to ruin.

29 But the people of God will sing a song of joy,
    like the songs at the holy festivals.
You will be filled with joy,
    as when a flutist leads a group of pilgrims
to Jerusalem, the mountain of the Lord—
    to the Rock of Israel.
30 And the Lord will make his majestic voice heard.
    He will display the strength of his mighty arm.
It will descend with devouring flames,
    with cloudbursts, thunderstorms, and huge hailstones.
31 At the Lord's command, the Assyrians will be shattered.
    He will strike them down with his royal scepter.
32 And as the Lord strikes them with his rod of punishment,
    his people will celebrate with tambourines and harps.
    Lifting his mighty arm, he will fight the Assyrians.
33 Topheth—the place of burning—
    has long been ready for the Assyrian king;
    the pyre is piled high with wood.
The breath of the Lord, like fire from a volcano,
    will set it ablaze.

## The Futility of Relying on Egypt

**31** ¹ What sorrow awaits those who look to Egypt for help,
        trusting their horses, chariots, and charioteers
    and depending on the strength of human armies
        instead of looking to the Lord,
        the Holy One of Israel.

**Cross references (right column):**

**30:22**
Exod 32:2, 4

**30:23**
Ps 65:9-13

**30:24**
Matt 3:12

**30:25**
Isa 41:18

**30:26**
Isa 33:24
Hos 6:1-2
Rev 21:23; 22:5

**30:27**
Isa 66:15

**30:28**
2 Kgs 19:28
Isa 8:7-8
2 Thes 2:8

**30:31**
Isa 31:8

**30:32**
1 Sam 18:6
Jer 31:4

**30:33**
Gen 19:24
Isa 34:9

**31:1**
Ps 20:7
Isa 10:17
Hos 11:9
Hab 1:12

---

**30:27** The judgment of God will be accompanied by thick,
rising smoke and words that consume like fire (see 33:14;
Luke 12:49; Hebrews 12:29). People who were brought up in
a church but dropped out often complain about the preaching
of the wrath of God. Yet his wrath and anger are very real and
are designed for the rebellious and for those who hate God,
not for those who are humble and love him. Are you one of
God's people? Help others discover God's love so that his
wrath will never be an issue for them.

**31:1** It was wrong for Judah to look to other nations for military
help. (1) They were trusting in human beings instead of God.
Judah sought protection from those who were powerless when
compared to God. Both Egypt and Judah would fall as a result
of their arrogance. (2) They were serving their own interests
instead of God's, and thus they did not even consult him. They
violated God's stipulation in Deuteronomy 17:16. (3) They did
not want to pay the price of looking to God and repenting of
their sinful ways. When we have problems, it is good to seek
help, but we must never bypass God or his previous directions
to us.

31:2
Num 23:19
Jer 44:29
Rom 16:27

2 In his wisdom, the LORD will send great disaster;
    he will not change his mind.
He will rise against the wicked
    and against their helpers.

31:3
Jer 15:6
Ezek 28:9

3 For these Egyptians are mere humans, not God!
    Their horses are puny flesh, not mighty spirits!
When the LORD raises his fist against them,
    those who help will stumble,
    and those being helped will fall.
    They will all fall down and die together.

31:4
Isa 42:13

4 But this is what the LORD has told me:

"When a strong young lion
    stands growling over a sheep it has killed,
it is not frightened by the shouts and noise
    of a whole crowd of shepherds.
In the same way, the LORD of Heaven's Armies
    will come down and fight on Mount Zion.

31:5
Deut 32:11
Ps 91:4

5 The LORD of Heaven's Armies will hover over Jerusalem
    and protect it like a bird protecting its nest.
He will defend and save the city;
    he will pass over it and rescue it."

31:6
Isa 55:7
Jer 3:10, 14, 22
31:7
Isa 2:20
31:8
Isa 10:12; 14:2

6 Though you are such wicked rebels, my people, come and return to the LORD. 7 I know the glorious day will come when each of you will throw away the gold idols and silver images your sinful hands have made.

8 "The Assyrians will be destroyed,
    but not by the swords of men.
The sword of God will strike them,
    and they will panic and flee.
The strong young Assyrians
    will be taken away as captives.

31:9
Isa 13:2

9 Even the strongest will quake with terror,
    and princes will flee when they see your battle flags,"
says the LORD, whose fire burns in Zion,
    whose flame blazes from Jerusalem.

## Israel's Ultimate Deliverance

32:1
Jer 23:5
Ezek 37:24
Zech 9:9
32:2
Isa 25:4; 35:6

**32** 1 Look, a righteous king is coming!
        And honest princes will rule under him.
2 Each one will be like a shelter from the wind
    and a refuge from the storm,
like streams of water in the desert
    and the shadow of a great rock in a parched land.

3 Then everyone who has eyes will be able to see the truth,
    and everyone who has ears will be able to hear it.

32:4
Isa 29:24

4 Even the hotheads will be full of sense and understanding.
    Those who stammer will speak out plainly.

---

**31:7** Someday these people would throw their idols away, recognizing that they were nothing but human-made objects. Idols such as money, fame, or success are seductive. Instead of contributing to our spiritual development, they rob us of our time, energy, and devotion that ought to be directed toward God. At first our idols seem exciting and promise to take us places, but in the end we will find that we have become their slaves. We need to recognize their worthlessness now, before they rob us of our freedom.

**32:1** Having suffered much injustice from evil rulers, many in Judah were hungry for a strong king who would rule with justice. This "righteous king" will be Christ. Judah would be destroyed and taken into captivity. But one day, God's Son, a King unlike any other king, will reign in righteousness and rule with justice.

<sup>5</sup> In that day ungodly fools will not be heroes.
    Scoundrels will not be respected.
<sup>6</sup> For fools speak foolishness
    and make evil plans.
  They practice ungodliness
    and spread false teachings about the LORD.
  They deprive the hungry of food
    and give no water to the thirsty.
<sup>7</sup> The smooth tricks of scoundrels are evil.
    They plot crooked schemes.
  They lie to convict the poor,
    even when the cause of the poor is just.
<sup>8</sup> But generous people plan to do what is generous,
    and they stand firm in their generosity.

<sup>9</sup> Listen, you women who lie around in ease.
    Listen to me, you who are so smug.
<sup>10</sup> In a short time—just a little more than a year—
    you careless ones will suddenly begin to care.
  For your fruit crops will fail,
    and the harvest will never take place.
<sup>11</sup> Tremble, you women of ease;
    throw off your complacency.
  Strip off your pretty clothes,
    and put on burlap to show your grief.
<sup>12</sup> Beat your breasts in sorrow for your bountiful farms
    and your fruitful grapevines.
<sup>13</sup> For your land will be overgrown with thorns and briers.
    Your joyful homes and happy towns will be gone.
<sup>14</sup> The palace and the city will be deserted,
    and busy towns will be empty.
  Wild donkeys will frolic and flocks will graze
    in the empty forts* and watchtowers
<sup>15</sup> until at last the Spirit is poured out
    on us from heaven.
  Then the wilderness will become a fertile field,
    and the fertile field will yield bountiful crops.

<sup>16</sup> Justice will rule in the wilderness
    and righteousness in the fertile field.
<sup>17</sup> And this righteousness will bring peace.
    Yes, it will bring quietness and confidence forever.
<sup>18</sup> My people will live in safety, quietly at home.
    They will be at rest.
<sup>19</sup> Even if the forest should be destroyed
    and the city torn down,
<sup>20</sup> the LORD will greatly bless his people.
  Wherever they plant seed, bountiful crops will spring up.
    Their cattle and donkeys will graze freely.

**32:14** Hebrew *the Ophel.*

**Cross-references:**
32:5 1 Sam 25:25
32:6 Isa 10:2; 59:7, 13
32:7 Jer 5:26-28; Mic 7:3
32:8 2 Cor 9:6-11
32:9 Isa 28:23; 47:8
32:10 Isa 5:5-6
32:11 Isa 22:12; 47:2
32:13 Isa 5:5-6, 10, 17
32:15 Ps 107:35; Isa 11:2; Joel 2:28
32:17 Isa 2:4; Rom 14:17; Jas 3:18
32:18 Hos 2:18-23
32:20 Isa 30:23

**32:5, 6** When the righteous king comes, people's motives will become transparent. Fools will not be regarded as heroes. Those who have opposed God's standards of living will be unable to maintain their deception. In the blazing light of the holy Savior, sin cannot disguise itself and appear good. Christ's revealing light shines into the darkest corners of our hearts, showing sin clearly for what it is. When King Jesus reigns in your heart, there is no place for sin, no matter how well hidden you may think it is.

**32:9-13** The people turned their backs on God and concentrated on their own pleasures. This warning is not just to the women of Jerusalem (see 3:16–4:1) but to all who sit back in their thoughtless complacency, enjoying crops, clothes, land, and cities while an enemy approaches. Wealth and luxury bring false security, lulling us into thinking all is well when disaster is around the corner. By abandoning God's purpose for our life, we also abandon his help.

**32:15-17** God acts from above to change people's condition here on earth. Only when God's Spirit is among us can we achieve true peace and fruitfulness (Ezekiel 36:22-38; Galatians 5:22, 23). This will happen in the end times. We can also have

## A Message about Assyria

**33** ¹ What sorrow awaits you Assyrians, who have destroyed others*
    but have never been destroyed yourselves.
You betray others,
    but you have never been betrayed.
When you are done destroying,
    you will be destroyed.
When you are done betraying,
    you will be betrayed.

² But Lord, be merciful to us,
    for we have waited for you.
Be our strong arm each day
    and our salvation in times of trouble.

³ The enemy runs at the sound of your voice.
    When you stand up, the nations flee!
⁴ Just as caterpillars and locusts strip the fields and vines,
    so the fallen army of Assyria will be stripped!

⁵ Though the Lord is very great and lives in heaven,
    he will make Jerusalem* his home of justice and righteousness.
⁶ In that day he will be your sure foundation,
    providing a rich store of salvation, wisdom, and knowledge.
    The fear of the Lord will be your treasure.

⁷ But now your brave warriors weep in public.
    Your ambassadors of peace cry in bitter disappointment.
⁸ Your roads are deserted;
    no one travels them anymore.
The Assyrians have broken their peace treaty
    and care nothing for the promises they made before witnesses.*
    They have no respect for anyone.
⁹ The land of Israel wilts in mourning.
    Lebanon withers with shame.
The plain of Sharon is now a wilderness.
    Bashan and Carmel have been plundered.

¹⁰ But the Lord says: "Now I will stand up.
    Now I will show my power and might.
¹¹ You Assyrians produce nothing but dry grass and stubble.
    Your own breath will turn to fire and consume you.
¹² Your people will be burned up completely,
    like thornbushes cut down and tossed in a fire.
¹³ Listen to what I have done, you nations far away!
    And you that are near, acknowledge my might!"

**33:1** Hebrew *What sorrow awaits you, O destroyer.* The Hebrew text does not specifically name Assyria as the object of the prophecy in this chapter.   **33:5** Hebrew *Zion;* also in 33:14.   **33:8** As in Dead Sea Scrolls; Masoretic Text reads *care nothing for the cities.*

### Cross-references

**33:1** Jer 25:12-14; Hab 2:8
**33:2** Isa 25:9; 40:10
**33:3** Jer 25:30-31
**33:5** Ps 97:9
**33:6** Ps 112:1-3; Isa 51:6
**33:7** 2 Kgs 18:18, 37
**33:9** Isa 10:34; 24:4; 35:2
**33:10** Ps 12:5; Isa 2:19
**33:12** 2 Sam 23:6-7; Isa 10:17
**33:13** Isa 49:1

---

God's Spirit with us now, for he is available to all believers through Christ (John 15:26). But the outpouring mentioned here happens when the worldwide Kingdom of God is established for all eternity (see Joel 2:28, 29).

**33:1** Assyria continually broke its promises but demanded that others keep theirs. It is easy to put ourselves in the same selfish position, demanding our rights while ignoring the rights of others. Broken promises shatter trust and destroy relationships. Determine to keep your promises; at the same time, ask forgiveness for past promises you have broken. Treat others with the same fairness that you demand for yourself.

**33:2** These are the words of the righteous remnant who were waiting for God to deliver them from their oppression.

**33:4** See 2 Kings 19:20-37 and Isaiah 37:21-38 for a description of the victory over Assyria described here.

**33:5** When Christ's Kingdom is established, Jerusalem will be the home of justice and righteousness because the Messiah will reign there. As a light to the world, the new Jerusalem will be the holy city (Revelation 21:2).

**33:9** These fruitful, productive areas would become deserts. Lebanon was known for its huge cedars. Sharon was very fertile. Bashan was very productive in grain and cattle. Carmel was thickly forested.

14 The sinners in Jerusalem shake with fear.
　　Terror seizes the godless.
　"Who can live with this devouring fire?" they cry.
　"Who can survive this all-consuming fire?"

> 33:14
> Isa 1:28; 30:27
> Heb 12:29

15 Those who are honest and fair,
　　who refuse to profit by fraud,
　　who stay far away from bribes,
　who refuse to listen to those who plot murder,
　　who shut their eyes to all enticement to do wrong—

> 33:15
> Ps 24:3-4
> Isa 58:6-11

16 these are the ones who will dwell on high.
　　The rocks of the mountains will be their fortress.
　Food will be supplied to them,
　　and they will have water in abundance.

> 33:16
> Isa 25:4; 49:10

17 Your eyes will see the king in all his splendor,
　　and you will see a land that stretches into the distance.

> 33:17
> Isa 6:5

18 You will think back to this time of terror, asking,
　"Where are the Assyrian officers
　　who counted our towers?
　Where are the bookkeepers
　　who recorded the plunder taken from our fallen city?"

> 33:18
> 1 Cor 1:20

19 You will no longer see these fierce, violent people
　　with their strange, unknown language.

> 33:19
> Deut 28:49-50

20 Instead, you will see Zion as a place of holy festivals.
　　You will see Jerusalem, a city quiet and secure.
　It will be like a tent whose ropes are taut
　　and whose stakes are firmly fixed.

> 33:20
> Ps 46:5

21 The Lord will be our Mighty One.
　　He will be like a wide river of protection
　that no enemy can cross,
　　that no enemy ship can sail upon.

> 33:21
> Isa 48:18

22 For the Lord is our judge,
　　our lawgiver, and our king.
　He will care for us and save us.

> 33:22
> Isa 49:25-26
> Zech 9:9
> Jas 4:12

23 The enemies' sails hang loose
　　on broken masts with useless tackle.
　Their treasure will be divided by the people of God.
　　Even the lame will take their share!

24 The people of Israel will no longer say,
　　"We are sick and helpless,"
　for the Lord will forgive their sins.

> 33:24
> Mic 7:18-19
> 1 Jn 1:7-9

## A Message for the Nations

**34** ¹ Come here and listen, O nations of the earth.
　　Let the world and everything in it hear my words.

> 34:1
> Deut 32:1

2 For the Lord is enraged against the nations.
　　His fury is against all their armies.
　He will completely destroy* them,
　　dooming them to slaughter.

> 34:2
> Isa 26:20-21

3 Their dead will be left unburied,
　　and the stench of rotting bodies will fill the land.
　The mountains will flow with their blood.

**34:2** The Hebrew term used here refers to the complete consecration of things or people to the Lord, either by destroying them or by giving them as an offering; similarly in 34:5.

---

**33:14-16** These sinners realized that they could not live in the presence of the holy God, for he is like a fire that devours evil. Only those who walk uprightly and speak what is right can live with God. Isaiah gives examples of how to demonstrate our righ-

teousness and uprightness: We can reject gain from extortion and bribes, refuse to listen to plots of wrong actions, and shut our eyes to evil. If we are fair and honest in our relationships, we will dwell with God, and he will supply our needs.

<table>
<tr><td>

**34:4**
Joel 2:31
†Matt 24:29
†Mark 13:24-25
2 Pet 3:10
Rev 6:12-14

</td><td>

4 The heavens above will melt away
    and disappear like a rolled-up scroll.
The stars will fall from the sky
    like withered leaves from a grapevine,
    or shriveled figs from a fig tree.

5 And when my sword has finished its work in the heavens,
    it will fall upon Edom,
    the nation I have marked for destruction.

</td></tr>
</table>

**34:6**
Isa 63:1

6 The sword of the Lord is drenched with blood
    and covered with fat—
with the blood of lambs and goats,
    with the fat of rams prepared for sacrifice.
Yes, the Lord will offer a sacrifice in the city of Bozrah.
    He will make a mighty slaughter in Edom.

**34:7**
Ps 68:30

7 Even men as strong as wild oxen will die—
    the young men alongside the veterans.
The land will be soaked with blood
    and the soil enriched with fat.

**34:8**
Isa 13:6; 63:4

**34:9**
Deut 29:23

8 For it is the day of the Lord's revenge,
    the year when Edom will be paid back for all it did to Israel.*
9 The streams of Edom will be filled with burning pitch,
    and the ground will be covered with fire.

**34:10**
Isa 1:31
Ezek 29:11
Mal 1:3-4
Rev 14:11; 19:3

10 This judgment on Edom will never end;
    the smoke of its burning will rise forever.
The land will lie deserted from generation to generation.
    No one will live there anymore.

**34:11**
Lam 2:8

11 It will be haunted by the desert owl and the screech owl,
    the great owl and the raven.*
For God will measure that land carefully;
    he will measure it for chaos and destruction.
12 It will be called the Land of Nothing,
    and all its nobles will soon be gone.*

**34:13**
Jer 9:11; 10:22

13 Thorns will overrun its palaces;
    nettles and thistles will grow in its forts.
The ruins will become a haunt for jackals
    and a home for owls.

**34:14**
Isa 13:21

14 Desert animals will mingle there with hyenas,
    their howls filling the night.
Wild goats will bleat at one another among the ruins,
    and night creatures* will come there to rest.
15 There the owl will make her nest and lay her eggs.
    She will hatch her young and cover them with her wings.
And the buzzards will come,
    each one with its mate.

**34:16**
Isa 40:5

16 Search the book of the Lord,
    and see what he will do.
Not one of these birds and animals will be missing,
    and none will lack a mate,

34:8 Hebrew *to Zion.*   34:11 The identification of some of these birds is uncertain.   34:12 The meaning of the Hebrew is uncertain.   34:14 Hebrew *Lilith,* possibly a reference to a mythical demon of the night.

---

**34:5** The Edomites shared a common ancestry with Israel. The Israelites were descended from Jacob; the Edomites from Jacob's twin brother, Esau. Edom was always Israel's bitter enemy. The destruction of Edom mentioned here is a picture of the ultimate end of all who oppose God and his people.

**34:16** Isaiah referred to the prophecies that God commanded him to write down as the "book of the Lord." Whoever lived to see the time of Edom's destruction would have only to look up these prophecies to find agreement between what happened and what was predicted. Prophecy predicts and history reveals what has been in God's mind for all time.

for the LORD has promised this.
    His Spirit will make it all come true.
17 He has surveyed and divided the land
    and deeded it over to those creatures.
They will possess it forever,
    from generation to generation.

**34:17**
Jer 13:25

## Hope for Restoration

# 35

1 Even the wilderness and desert will be glad in those days.
    The wasteland will rejoice and blossom with spring crocuses.

**35:1**
Isa 41:18-19; 51:3;
55:12-13

2 Yes, there will be an abundance of flowers
    and singing and joy!
The deserts will become as green as the mountains of Lebanon,
    as lovely as Mount Carmel or the plain of Sharon.
There the LORD will display his glory,
    the splendor of our God.

**35:2**
Isa 25:9; 60:13;
66:10, 14

3 With this news, strengthen those who have tired hands,
    and encourage those who have weak knees.

**35:3**
Job 4:3-4
Heb 12:12

4 Say to those with fearful hearts,
    "Be strong, and do not fear,
for your God is coming to destroy your enemies.
    He is coming to save you."

**35:4**
Ps 145:19

5 And when he comes, he will open the eyes of the blind
    and unplug the ears of the deaf.

**35:5**
John 9:6-7

6 The lame will leap like a deer,
    and those who cannot speak will sing for joy!
Springs will gush forth in the wilderness,
    and streams will water the wasteland.

**35:6**
Luke 11:14
John 7:38
Acts 3:7-8

7 The parched ground will become a pool,
    and springs of water will satisfy the thirsty land.
Marsh grass and reeds and rushes will flourish
    where desert jackals once lived.

8 And a great road will go through that once deserted land.
    It will be named the Highway of Holiness.
Evil-minded people will never travel on it.
    It will be only for those who walk in God's ways;
    fools will never walk there.

**35:8**
Matt 7:13-14

9 Lions will not lurk along its course,
    nor any other ferocious beasts.
There will be no other dangers.
    Only the redeemed will walk on it.

**35:9**
Isa 51:10

10 Those who have been ransomed by the LORD will return.
    They will enter Jerusalem* singing,
    crowned with everlasting joy.
Sorrow and mourning will disappear,
    and they will be filled with joy and gladness.

**35:10**
Rev 21:4

**35:10** Hebrew *Zion*.

---

**35:1ff** In chapters 1–34, Isaiah has delivered a message of judgment on all nations, including Israel and Judah, for rejecting God. Although there have been glimpses of relief and restoration for the remnant of faithful believers, the climate of wrath, fury, judgment, and destruction has prevailed. Now Isaiah breaks through with a vision of beauty and encouragement. God is just as thorough in his mercy as he is severe in his judgment. God's complete moral perfection is revealed by his hatred of all sin, and this leads to judgment. This same moral perfection is revealed in his love for all he has created. This leads to mercy for those who have sinned but who have sincerely loved Jesus and put their trust in him.

**35:1ff** This chapter is a beautiful picture of the final Kingdom in

which God will establish his justice and destroy all evil. This is the world the redeemed can anticipate after the judgment when creation itself will rejoice in God. Chapter 34 spoke of great distress when God will judge all people for their actions. Chapter 35 pictures the days when life will be peaceful at last and everything will be made right. Carmel and Sharon were regions of thick vegetation and fertile soil. They were symbols of productivity and plenty.

**35:8-10** This "Highway of Holiness" is the way that righteous pilgrims will take from the desert of suffering to Zion (Jerusalem). It is found only by following God. Only the redeemed will travel God's highway; they will be protected from wicked travelers and harmful animals. God is preparing a way for his people (those who

## 5. Events during the reign of Hezekiah

### Assyria Invades Judah

36:1-22
//2 Kgs 18:13-37
//2 Chr 32:9-19

**36** In the fourteenth year of King Hezekiah's reign,* King Sennacherib of Assyria came to attack the fortified towns of Judah and conquered them. 2 Then the king of Assyria sent his chief of staff* from Lachish with a huge army to confront King Hezekiah in Jerusalem. The Assyrians took up a position beside the aqueduct that feeds water into the upper pool, near the road leading to the field where cloth is washed.*

36:3
Isa 22:15, 20

3 These are the officials who went out to meet with them: Eliakim son of Hilkiah, the palace administrator; Shebna the court secretary; and Joah son of Asaph, the royal historian.

### Sennacherib Threatens Jerusalem

36:4
2 Kgs 18:19

4 Then the Assyrian king's chief of staff told them to give this message to Hezekiah:

36:5
2 Kgs 18:7

36:6
Ps 146:3
Ezek 29:6-7

36:7
Deut 12:2-5
2 Kgs 18:4-5

"This is what the great king of Assyria says: What are you trusting in that makes you so confident? 5 Do you think that mere words can substitute for military skill and strength? Who are you counting on, that you have rebelled against me? 6 On Egypt? If you lean on Egypt, it will be like a reed that splinters beneath your weight and pierces your hand. Pharaoh, the king of Egypt, is completely unreliable!

7 "But perhaps you will say to me, 'We are trusting in the LORD our God!' But isn't he

36:1 The fourteenth year of Hezekiah's reign was 701 B.C.   36:2a Or *the rabshakeh;* also in 36:4, 11, 12, 22.
36:2b Or *bleached.*

**ASSYRIA ADVANCES**
As Sennacherib beautified his capital city, Nineveh, Hezekiah withheld tribute and prepared for battle. The Assyrians advanced toward their rebellious western border, attacking swiftly down the Mediterranean coast. From Lachish, Sennacherib threatened to take Jerusalem, but Isaiah knew his threats would die with him on his return to Nineveh.

walk in his ways) to travel to his home, and he will walk with us. God doesn't simply point the way; he is always beside us as we go.

**36:4-6** Chapter 19 describes Isaiah's prophecy of judgment upon Egypt, while chapters 30 and 31 pronounce woe on those from Judah who would ally themselves with Egypt in the face of Assyria's impending attack. Sennacherib of Assyria was taunting Judah for trusting in Egypt. Even the Assyrians knew that Egypt could not help Judah.

**36:5** Hezekiah put great trust in Pharaoh's promise to help Israel against the Assyrians, but promises are only as good as the credibility of the person making them. It was Pharaoh's word against God's. How quickly we seek human advice when dealing with our problems while we neglect God's eternal promises. When choosing between God's Word and someone else's, whose will you believe?

**36:7** The Assyrian king's chief of staff claimed that Hezekiah had insulted God by tearing down his altars and making the people worship only in Jerusalem. But Hezekiah's reform sought to eliminate idol worship (which occurred mainly on high hills) so that the people worshiped only the true God. Either the Assyrians didn't know about the religion of the true God, or they wanted to deceive the people into thinking they had angered a powerful god.

In the same way, Satan tries to confuse or deceive us. People don't necessarily need to be sinful to be ineffective for God; they need only be confused about what God wants. To avoid Satan's deceit, study God's Word carefully and regularly. When you know what God says, you will not fall for Satan's lies.

the one who was insulted by Hezekiah? Didn't Hezekiah tear down his shrines and altars and make everyone in Judah and Jerusalem worship only at the altar here in Jerusalem?

8 "I'll tell you what! Strike a bargain with my master, the king of Assyria. I will give you 2,000 horses if you can find that many men to ride on them! 9 With your tiny army, how can you think of challenging even the weakest contingent of my master's troops, even with the help of Egypt's chariots and charioteers? 10 What's more, do you think we have invaded your land without the LORD's direction? The LORD himself told us, 'Attack this land and destroy it!'"

**36:9**
Isa 20:5
**36:10**
1 Kgs 13:18

11 Then Eliakim, Shebna, and Joah said to the Assyrian chief of staff, "Please speak to us in Aramaic, for we understand it well. Don't speak in Hebrew,* for the people on the wall will hear."

**36:11**
Ezra 4:7
Dan 2:4

12 But Sennacherib's chief of staff replied, "Do you think my master sent this message only to you and your master? He wants all the people to hear it, for when we put this city under siege, they will suffer along with you. They will be so hungry and thirsty that they will eat their own dung and drink their own urine."

13 Then the chief of staff stood and shouted in Hebrew to the people on the wall, "Listen to this message from the great king of Assyria! 14 This is what the king says: Don't let Hezekiah deceive you. He will never be able to rescue you. 15 Don't let him fool you into trusting in the LORD by saying, 'The LORD will surely rescue us. This city will never fall into the hands of the Assyrian king!'

**36:13**
2 Chr 32:18
**36:14**
Isa 37:10

16 "Don't listen to Hezekiah! These are the terms the king of Assyria is offering: Make peace with me—open the gates and come out. Then each of you can continue eating from your own grapevine and fig tree and drinking from your own well. 17 Then I will arrange to take you to another land like this one—a land of grain and new wine, bread and vineyards.

**36:16**
Zech 3:10

18 "Don't let Hezekiah mislead you by saying, 'The LORD will rescue us!' Have the gods of any other nations ever saved their people from the king of Assyria? 19 What happened to the gods of Hamath and Arpad? And what about the gods of Sepharvaim? Did any god rescue Samaria from my power? 20 What god of any nation has ever been able to save its people from my power? So what makes you think that the LORD can rescue Jerusalem from me?"

**36:19**
2 Kgs 17:6
Isa 10:9-11;
37:11-13
Jer 49:23
**36:20**
1 Kgs 20:23, 28

21 But the people were silent and did not utter a word because Hezekiah had commanded them, "Do not answer him."

22 Then Eliakim son of Hilkiah, the palace administrator; Shebna the court secretary; and Joah son of Asaph, the royal historian, went back to Hezekiah. They tore their clothes in despair, and they went in to see the king and told him what the Assyrian chief of staff had said.

### Hezekiah Seeks the LORD's Help

**37** When King Hezekiah heard their report, he tore his clothes and put on burlap and went into the Temple of the LORD. 2 And he sent Eliakim the palace administrator, Shebna the court secretary, and the leading priests, all dressed in burlap, to the prophet Isaiah son of Amoz. 3 They told him, "This is what King Hezekiah says: Today is a day of trouble, insults, and disgrace. It is like when a child is ready to be born, but the mother has no

**37:1-13**
//2 Kgs 19:1-13
**37:3**
Isa 22:5; 26:17-18

**36:11** Hebrew *in the dialect of Judah;* also in 36:13.

---

**36:10** Sennacherib continued his demoralization campaign by sending his chief of staff to try to convince the people of Judah that God had turned against them. The Assyrians hoped to convince the people of Judah to surrender without fighting. But Isaiah had already said that the Assyrians *would not* destroy Jerusalem, so the people did not need to be afraid of them (10:24-27; 29:5-8).

**36:11** Aramaic was an international language at this time. See also 22:15-25 for Isaiah's prophecies concerning Eliakim and Shebna.

**36:17** Sennacherib's representative tried yet another ploy to demoralize the people. He appealed to the starving city under siege by offering to take them to a land with plenty of food if they surrendered. The Assyrian policy for dealing with conquered nations was to resettle the inhabitants and then to move other conquered peoples into the recently conquered area. This pro-

vided manpower for their armies and prevented revolts in conquered territories.

**36:19, 20** The king's representative said that the gods of the other cities he had conquered had not been able to save their people, so how could the God of Jerusalem save them? The Lord was supposedly the God of Samaria (the northern kingdom), and it fell. But the Lord was the God of Samaria in name only because the people were not worshiping him. That is why prophets foretold the fall of Samaria. But for the Lord's own sake and for the sake of David, the Lord would rescue Jerusalem from the Assyrian army (37:35).

**37:3** Judah is compared to a woman who is trying to give birth to a child but is too weak to deliver. When the situation seemed hopeless, Hezekiah didn't give up. Instead, he asked the prophet Isaiah to pray that God would help his people. No matter how bad your circumstances seem, don't despair. Turn to God.

**37:4**
Isa 1:9; 10:20-22

strength to deliver the baby. 4But perhaps the LORD your God has heard the Assyrian chief of staff,* sent by the king to defy the living God, and will punish him for his words. Oh, pray for those of us who are left!"

**37:6**
Isa 7:4; 35:4

5After King Hezekiah's officials delivered the king's message to Isaiah, 6the prophet replied, "Say to your master, 'This is what the LORD says: Do not be disturbed by this blasphemous speech against me from the Assyrian king's messengers. 7Listen! I myself will move against him,* and the king will receive a message that he is needed at home. So he will return to his land, where I will have him killed with a sword.'"

8Meanwhile, the Assyrian chief of staff left Jerusalem and went to consult the king of Assyria, who had left Lachish and was attacking Libnah.

9Soon afterward King Sennacherib received word that King Tirhakah of Ethiopia* was leading an army to fight against him. Before leaving to meet the attack, he sent messengers back to Hezekiah in Jerusalem with this message:

**37:11**
Isa 10:9-11

**37:12**
Gen 11:31
2 Kgs 17:6
Acts 7:2

10"This message is for King Hezekiah of Judah. Don't let your God, in whom you trust, deceive you with promises that Jerusalem will not be captured by the king of Assyria. 11You know perfectly well what the kings of Assyria have done wherever they have gone. They have completely destroyed everyone who stood in their way! Why should you be any different? 12Have the gods of other nations rescued them—such nations as Gozan, Haran, Rezeph, and the people of Eden who were in Tel-assar? My predecessors destroyed them all! 13What happened to the king of Hamath and the king of Arpad? What happened to the kings of Sepharvaim, Hena, and Ivvah?"

**37:14-20**
//2 Kgs 19:14-19

**37:16**
Exod 25:22
Pss 80:1; 86:10
Jer 10:12

**37:18**
2 Kgs 15:29
1 Chr 5:26

**37:19**
Isa 17:8

**37:20**
1 Kgs 18:36-37
Isa 33:22
Ezek 36:23

14After Hezekiah received the letter from the messengers and read it, he went up to the LORD's Temple and spread it out before the LORD. 15And Hezekiah prayed this prayer before the LORD: 16"O LORD of Heaven's Armies, God of Israel, you are enthroned between the mighty cherubim! You alone are God of all the kingdoms of the earth. You alone created the heavens and the earth. 17Bend down, O LORD, and listen! Open your eyes, O LORD, and see! Listen to Sennacherib's words of defiance against the living God.

18"It is true, LORD, that the kings of Assyria have destroyed all these nations. 19And they have thrown the gods of these nations into the fire and burned them. But of course the Assyrians could destroy them! They were not gods at all—only idols of wood and stone shaped by human hands. 20Now, O LORD our God, rescue us from his power; then all the kingdoms of the earth will know that you alone, O LORD, are God.*"

### Isaiah Predicts Judah's Deliverance

**37:22**
Lam 2:13
Zeph 3:14

21Then Isaiah son of Amoz sent this message to Hezekiah: "This is what the LORD, the God of Israel, says: Because you prayed about King Sennacherib of Assyria, 22the LORD has spoken this word against him:

"The virgin daughter of Zion
    despises you and laughs at you.
The daughter of Jerusalem
    shakes her head in derision as you flee.

**37:23**
Isa 5:15, 21
Ezek 39:7
Hab 1:12

23 "Whom have you been defying and ridiculing?
    Against whom did you raise your voice?
At whom did you look with such haughty eyes?
    It was the Holy One of Israel!

**37:24**
Isa 14:8

24 By your messengers you have defied the Lord.
    You have said, 'With my many chariots

**37:4** Or *the rabshakeh;* also in 37:8.  **37:7** Hebrew *I will put a spirit in him.*  **37:9** Hebrew *of Cush.*  **37:20** As in Dead Sea Scrolls (see also 2 Kgs 19:19); Masoretic Text reads *you alone are the LORD.*

---

**37:4** Hezekiah did exactly what Isaiah had been calling the people to do (chapters 1–35). He turned to God and watched him come to Judah's aid. Turning to God means believing that God is there and that he is able to help you.

**37:8-10** Although the answer to Hezekiah's prayer was already in motion because Tirhakah was poised to attack, Hezekiah did not know it. He persisted in prayer and faith even though he could not see the answer coming. When we pray, we must have faith that

God has already prepared the best answer. Our task is to ask in faith and wait in humility.

**37:16** Cherubim are mighty angels. The phrase "enthroned between the mighty cherubim" refers to the atonement cover on the Ark of the Covenant, which symbolized God's holiness, power, and sovereignty.

I have conquered the highest mountains—
    yes, the remotest peaks of Lebanon.
I have cut down its tallest cedars
    and its finest cypress trees.
I have reached its farthest heights
    and explored its deepest forests.
25 I have dug wells in many foreign lands*
    and refreshed myself with their water.
With the sole of my foot,
    I stopped up all the rivers of Egypt!'

26 "But have you not heard?
    I decided this long ago.
Long ago I planned it,
    and now I am making it happen.
I planned for you to crush fortified cities
    into heaps of rubble.
27 That is why their people have so little power
    and are so frightened and confused.
They are as weak as grass,
    as easily trampled as tender green shoots.
They are like grass sprouting on a housetop,
    scorched* before it can grow lush and tall.

28 "But I know you well—
    where you stay
and when you come and go.
    I know the way you have raged against me.
29 And because of your raging against me
    and your arrogance, which I have heard for myself,
I will put my hook in your nose
    and my bit in your mouth.
I will make you return
    by the same road on which you came."

30 Then Isaiah said to Hezekiah, "Here is the proof that what I say is true:

"This year you will eat only what grows up by itself,
    and next year you will eat what springs up from that.
But in the third year you will plant crops and harvest them;
    you will tend vineyards and eat their fruit.
31 And you who are left in Judah,
    who have escaped the ravages of the siege,
will put roots down in your own soil
    and grow up and flourish.
32 For a remnant of my people will spread out from Jerusalem,
    a group of survivors from Mount Zion.
The passionate commitment of the LORD of Heaven's Armies
    will make this happen!

33 "And this is what the LORD says about the king of Assyria:

"'His armies will not enter Jerusalem.
    They will not even shoot an arrow at it.
They will not march outside its gates with their shields
    nor build banks of earth against its walls.
34 The king will return to his own country
    by the same road on which he came.

**Cross-references:**

37:26 Isa 25:2; Acts 2:23; 4:27-28

37:27 Ps 129:6; Isa 40:7

37:28 Ps 139:1

37:29 Isa 30:28; Ezek 38:4

37:30 Lev 25:5, 11

37:31 Isa 10:20; 27:6

37:32 2 Kgs 19:31

**37:25** As in Dead Sea Scrolls (see also 2 Kgs 19:24); Masoretic Text lacks *in many foreign lands*. **37:27** As in Dead Sea Scrolls and some Greek manuscripts (see also 2 Kgs 19:26); most Hebrew manuscripts read *like a terraced field*.

**37:29** This was a common torture the Assyrians used on their captives. They were often led away with hooks in their noses or bits in their mouths to humiliate them. The Lord was threatening to do to the Assyrians what they had done to others.

He will not enter this city,'
    says the LORD.

**37:35**
2 Kgs 20:6
Isa 48:9, 11

35 'For my own honor and for the sake of my servant David,
    I will defend this city and protect it.'"

**37:36**
2 Kgs 19:35
Isa 10:12, 33-34

36 That night the angel of the LORD went out to the Assyrian camp and killed 185,000 Assyrian soldiers. When the surviving Assyrians* woke up the next morning, they found corpses everywhere. 37 Then King Sennacherib of Assyria broke camp and returned to his own land. He went home to his capital of Nineveh and stayed there.

**37:37**
Gen 10:11
Jon 3:3
Zeph 2:13

38 One day while he was worshiping in the temple of his god Nisroch, his sons Adrammelech and Sharezer killed him with their swords. They then escaped to the land of Ararat, and another son, Esarhaddon, became the next king of Assyria.

**37:38**
Gen 8:4

### Hezekiah's Sickness and Recovery

**38:1-8**
//2 Kgs 20:1-11
2 Chr 32:24-26

**38** About that time Hezekiah became deathly ill, and the prophet Isaiah son of Amoz went to visit him. He gave the king this message: "This is what the LORD says: 'Set your affairs in order, for you are going to die. You will not recover from this illness.'"

**38:3**
2 Kgs 18:5-6
Neh 13:14
Ps 6:6-8

2 When Hezekiah heard this, he turned his face to the wall and prayed to the LORD, 3 "Remember, O LORD, how I have always been faithful to you and have served you single-mindedly, always doing what pleases you." Then he broke down and wept bitterly.

**38:5**
2 Kgs 18:2, 13

4 Then this message came to Isaiah from the LORD: 5 "Go back to Hezekiah and tell him, 'This is what the LORD, the God of your ancestor David, says: I have heard your prayer and seen your tears. I will add fifteen years to your life, 6 and I will rescue you and this city from the king of Assyria. Yes, I will defend this city.

**38:6**
Isa 31:5

**38:7**
Isa 7:11, 14

7 "And this is the sign from the LORD to prove that he will do as he promised: 8 I will cause the sun's shadow to move ten steps backward on the sundial* of Ahaz!'" So the shadow on the sundial moved backward ten steps.

**38:8**
2 Kgs 20:9-11

### Hezekiah's Poem of Praise

9 When King Hezekiah was well again, he wrote this poem:

**38:10**
Pss 102:24; 107:18

10 I said, "In the prime of my life,
    must I now enter the place of the dead?*
    Am I to be robbed of the rest of my years?"

**38:11**
Ps 27:13

11 I said, "Never again will I see the LORD GOD
    while still in the land of the living.
Never again will I see my friends
    or be with those who live in this world.

**38:12**
Job 4:20
2 Cor 5:1

12 My life has been blown away
    like a shepherd's tent in a storm.
It has been cut short,
    as when a weaver cuts cloth from a loom.
Suddenly, my life was over.

**38:13**
Job 10:16

13 I waited patiently all night,
    but I was torn apart as though by lions.
Suddenly, my life was over.

**38:14**
Job 7:11
Ps 119:123
Ezek 7:16

14 Delirious, I chattered like a swallow or a crane,
    and then I moaned like a mourning dove.
My eyes grew tired of looking to heaven for help.
I am in trouble, Lord. Help me!"

**37:36** Hebrew *When they.*    **38:8** Hebrew *the steps.*    **38:10** Hebrew *enter the gates of Sheol?*

---

**37:35** God would defend Jerusalem for the sake of his own honor and for David's sake in remembrance of his promise to David. The Assyrians had insulted God. They would not be his instrument to punish Jerusalem. What Jerusalem could not possibly do, God would do for it. God is prepared to do the impossible if we trust him enough to ask.

**37:38** The death of Sennacherib was prophesied by Isaiah in 10:12, 33, 34 and in 37:7. His death is also recorded in 2 Kings 19.

**38:1ff** The events of chapters 38 and 39 happened before those of chapters 36 and 37.

**38:1-5** When Isaiah went to Hezekiah, who was extremely ill, and told him of his impending death, Hezekiah immediately turned to God. God responded to his prayer, allowing Hezekiah to live another 15 years. If you have a desperate need in your life, bring it to the Lord. In response to fervent prayer, God may change the course of your life, too.

**38:1-6** According to 2 Chronicles 32:24-26, Hezekiah had a problem with pride even after this double miracle of healing and deliverance. Eventually he and his subjects humbled themselves, so God's judgment was put off for several more generations.

¹⁵ But what could I say?
  For he himself sent this sickness.
  Now I will walk humbly throughout my years
    because of this anguish I have felt.
¹⁶ Lord, your discipline is good,
    for it leads to life and health.
  You restore my health
    and allow me to live!
¹⁷ Yes, this anguish was good for me,
    for you have rescued me from death
    and forgiven all my sins.
¹⁸ For the dead* cannot praise you;
    they cannot raise their voices in praise.
  Those who go down to the grave
    can no longer hope in your faithfulness.
¹⁹ Only the living can praise you as I do today.
    Each generation tells of your faithfulness to the next.
²⁰ Think of it—the Lord is ready to heal me!
  I will sing his praises with instruments
  every day of my life
    in the Temple of the Lord.

²¹Isaiah had said to Hezekiah's servants, "Make an ointment from figs and spread it over the boil, and Hezekiah will recover."

²²And Hezekiah had asked, "What sign will prove that I will go to the Temple of the Lord?"

### Envoys from Babylon

**39** Soon after this, Merodach-baladan son of Baladan, king of Babylon, sent Hezekiah his best wishes and a gift. He had heard that Hezekiah had been very sick and that he had recovered. ²Hezekiah was delighted with the Babylonian envoys and showed them everything in his treasure-houses—the silver, the gold, the spices, and the aromatic oils. He also took them to see his armory and showed them everything in his royal treasuries! There was nothing in his palace or kingdom that Hezekiah did not show them.

³Then Isaiah the prophet went to King Hezekiah and asked him, "What did those men want? Where were they from?"

Hezekiah replied, "They came from the distant land of Babylon."

⁴"What did they see in your palace?" asked Isaiah.

"They saw everything," Hezekiah replied. "I showed them everything I own—all my royal treasuries."

⁵Then Isaiah said to Hezekiah, "Listen to this message from the Lord of Heaven's Armies: ⁶'The time is coming when everything in your palace—all the treasures stored up by your ancestors until now—will be carried off to Babylon. Nothing will be left,' says the Lord. ⁷'Some of your very own sons will be taken away into exile. They will become eunuchs who will serve in the palace of Babylon's king.'"

⁸Then Hezekiah said to Isaiah, "This message you have given me from the Lord is good." For the king was thinking, "At least there will be peace and security during my lifetime."

**38:18** Hebrew *Sheol.*

38:16 Pss 39:13; 119:71, 75
38:17 Isa 43:25; Jer 31:34; Jon 2:6
38:18 Ps 6:5
38:19 Pss 78:5-7; 119:175
38:20 Pss 33:1-3; 116:17-19; 146:2
38:21 2 Kgs 20:7-8
39:1-8 //2 Kgs 20:12-19
39:2 2 Kgs 18:15-16; 2 Chr 32:25, 31
39:3 Jer 5:15
39:5 1 Sam 15:16
39:6 2 Kgs 24:13; Jer 20:5
39:7 Dan 1:2-7
39:8 2 Chr 34:28

**38:16-18** Hezekiah realized that his prayer brought deliverance and forgiveness. His words "the dead cannot praise you" may reveal that he was unaware of the blessedness of the future life for those who trust in God (57:1, 2), or he may have meant that dead bodies cannot praise God. In either case, Hezekiah knew that God had spared his life, so in his poem Hezekiah praises God. Hezekiah recognized the good that came from his bitter experience. The next time you have difficult struggles, pray for God's help to gain something beneficial from them.

**38:19** Hezekiah spoke of the significance of passing the joy of the Lord from generation to generation. The heritage of our faith has come to us because of faithful men and women who have

carried God's message to us across the centuries. Do you share with your children or other young people the excitement of your relationship with God?

**39:1ff** Merodach-baladan, a Babylonian prince, was planning a revolt against Assyria and was forming an alliance. He probably hoped to convince Hezekiah to join this alliance against Assyria. Hezekiah, feeling honored by this attention and perhaps feeling some sympathy for their proposal, showed the Babylonian envoys his treasures. But Isaiah warned the king not to trust Babylon. Someday they would turn on Judah and devour Jerusalem's wealth.

**39:4-7** What was so wrong about showing these Babylonians around? Hezekiah failed to see that the Babylonians would become

## B. WORDS OF COMFORT (40:1—66:24)

Isaiah now speaks of events that will occur after the Captivity. This includes the decree by Cyrus to release the remnant captives and allow them to return to Jerusalem after he conquered Babylon. But Isaiah also foretells the coming of the suffering Servant, Jesus Christ, and describes his life and death with incredible detail. Isaiah also speaks about the coming of the new heavens and earth, when God's people will be completely restored. Because all believers will participate in this new world to come, we can have confident hope in the future.

### 1. Israel's release from captivity

*Comfort for God's People*

**40:1**
2 Cor 1:4

**40:2**
Zech 9:12

**40** ¹ "Comfort, comfort my people,"
says your God.
² "Speak tenderly to Jerusalem.
Tell her that her sad days are gone
and her sins are pardoned.
Yes, the LORD has punished her twice over
for all her sins."

**40:3**
Mal 3:1
†Matt 3:3
†Mark 1:3
†Luke 3:4
†John 1:23

³ Listen! It's the voice of someone shouting,
"Clear the way through the wilderness
for the LORD!
Make a straight highway through the wasteland
for our God!

**40:4**
Ezek 17:24
†Luke 3:5

⁴ Fill in the valleys,
and level the mountains and hills.
Straighten the curves,
and smooth out the rough places.

**40:5**
Hab 2:14
†Luke 3:6

⁵ Then the glory of the LORD will be revealed,
and all people will see it together.
The LORD has spoken!"*

⁶ A voice said, "Shout!"
I asked, "What should I shout?"

"Shout that people are like the grass.
Their beauty fades as quickly
as the flowers in a field.

40:3-5 Greek version reads *He is a voice shouting in the wilderness, / "Prepare the way for the LORD's coming! / Clear a road for our God! / Fill in the valleys, / and level the mountains and hills. / And then the glory of the LORD will be revealed, / and all people will see the salvation sent from God. / The LORD has spoken!"* Compare Matt 3:3; Mark 1:3; Luke 3:4-6.

---

his next threat and that they, not the Assyrians, would conquer his city. When Isaiah told him that Babylon would someday carry it all away, this was an amazing prophecy because Babylon was struggling for independence under Assyria. Hezekiah's prideful display of his earthly treasures brought its own consequences (2 Kings 25; Daniel 1:1, 2). His response (39:8) may seem a bit shortsighted, but he simply was expressing gratitude for the blessing from God that peace would reign during his lifetime and that God's judgment would not be more severe.

**39:8** Hezekiah, one of Judah's most faithful kings, worked hard throughout his reign to stamp out idol worship and to purify the worship of the true God at the Jerusalem Temple. Nevertheless he knew his kingdom was not pure. Powerful undercurrents of evil invited destruction, and only God's miraculous interventions preserved Judah from its enemies. Here Hezekiah was grateful that God would preserve peace during his reign. As soon as Hezekiah died, the nation rushed back to its sinful ways under the leadership of Manasseh, Hezekiah's son. He actually rebuilt the centers of idolatry his father had destroyed.

**40:1ff** The book of Isaiah makes a dramatic shift at this point. The following chapters discuss the majesty of God, who is coming to rule the earth and judge all people. God will reunite Israel and Judah and restore them to glory. Instead of warning the people of impending judgment, Isaiah here comforts them. Chapter 40 refers to the restoration after the Exile. Cyrus is the instrument of

their deliverance from Babylon. Isaiah also foretells a time when "Babylon"—the future evil world system—will be destroyed and the persecution of God's people will end.

**40:1, 2** Judah still had 100 years of trouble before Jerusalem would fall, then 70 years of exile. So God tells Isaiah to speak tenderly and to comfort Jerusalem.

The seeds of comfort may take root in the soil of adversity. When your life seems to be falling apart, ask God to comfort you. You may not escape adversity, but you may find God's comfort as you face it. Sometimes, however, the only comfort we have is in the knowledge that someday we will be with God. Appreciate the comfort and encouragement found in his Word, his presence, and his people.

**40:3-5** Preparing a straight highway means removing obstacles and rolling out the red carpet for the coming of the Lord. The wasteland is a picture of life's trials and sufferings. We are not immune to these, but our faith need not be hindered by them. Isaiah told people to prepare to see God work. John the Baptist used these words as he challenged the people to prepare for the coming Messiah (Matthew 3:3).

**40:6-8** People are compared here to grass and flowers that wither away. We are mortal, but God's Word is eternal and unfailing. Public opinion changes and is unreliable, but God's Word is constant. Only in God's eternal Word will we find lasting solutions to our problems and needs.

7 The grass withers and the flowers fade
  beneath the breath of the Lord.
  And so it is with people.

40:7
Jas 1:10-11
1 Pet 1:24

8 The grass withers and the flowers fade,
  but the word of our God stands forever."

40:8
Matt 5:18
†1 Pet 1:25

9 O Zion, messenger of good news,
  shout from the mountaintops!
  Shout it louder, O Jerusalem.*
  Shout, and do not be afraid.
  Tell the towns of Judah,
  "Your God is coming!"

10 Yes, the Sovereign Lord is coming in power.
   He will rule with a powerful arm.
   See, he brings his reward with him as he comes.

40:10
Isa 59:16
Rev 22:12

11 He will feed his flock like a shepherd.
   He will carry the lambs in his arms,
   holding them close to his heart.
   He will gently lead the mother sheep with their young.

40:11
Ezek 34:12-14, 23
John 10:11, 14-16

### The Lord Has No Equal

12 Who else has held the oceans in his hand?
   Who has measured off the heavens with his fingers?
   Who else knows the weight of the earth
   or has weighed the mountains and hills on a scale?

40:12
Isa 48:13

13 Who is able to advise the Spirit of the Lord?*
   Who knows enough to give him advice or teach him?

40:13
†Rom 11:34
†1 Cor 2:16

14 Has the Lord ever needed anyone's advice?
   Does he need instruction about what is good?
   Did someone teach him what is right
   or show him the path of justice?

40:14
Col 2:3

15 No, for all the nations of the world
   are but a drop in the bucket.
   They are nothing more
   than dust on the scales.
   He picks up the whole earth
   as though it were a grain of sand.

40:15
Isa 17:13

16 All the wood in Lebanon's forests
   and all Lebanon's animals would not be enough
   to make a burnt offering worthy of our God.

17 The nations of the world are worth nothing to him.
   In his eyes they count for less than nothing—
   mere emptiness and froth.

18 To whom can you compare God?
   What image can you find to resemble him?

40:18
Exod 8:10
Isa 46:5
Mic 7:18

19 Can he be compared to an idol formed in a mold,
   overlaid with gold, and decorated with silver chains?

40:19
Ps 115:4-8
Hab 2:18-19

20 Or if people are too poor for that,
   they might at least choose wood that won't decay

40:20
Isa 46:7

40:9 Or O messenger of good news, shout to Zion from the mountaintops! Shout it louder to Jerusalem.
40:13 Greek version reads Who can know the Lord's thoughts? Compare Rom 11:34; 1 Cor 2:16.

---

40:11 God is often pictured as a shepherd, gently caring for and guiding his flock. He is powerful (40:10), yet careful and gentle. He is called a shepherd (Psalm 23); the good shepherd (John 10:11, 14); the great Shepherd (Hebrews 13:20); and the Great Shepherd (1 Peter 5:4). Note that the shepherd is caring for the most defenseless members of his society: children and those caring for them. This reinforces the prophetic theme that the truly powerful nation is not the one with a strong military, but rather the one that relies on God's caring strength.

40:12-31 Isaiah describes God's power to create, his provision to sustain, and his presence to help. God is almighty and all-powerful; but even so, he cares for each of us personally. No person or thing can be compared to God (40:25). We describe God as best we can with our limited knowledge and language, but we only limit our understanding of him and his power when we compare him to what we experience on earth. What is your concept of God, especially as revealed in his Son, Jesus Christ? Don't limit his work in your life by underestimating him.

and a skilled craftsman
　　to carve an image that won't fall down!

**40:21**
Isa 51:13
Rom 1:19

21 Haven't you heard? Don't you understand?
　　Are you deaf to the words of God—
the words he gave before the world began?
　　Are you so ignorant?

**40:22**
Ps 104:2

22 God sits above the circle of the earth.
　　The people below seem like grasshoppers to him!
He spreads out the heavens like a curtain
　　and makes his tent from them.

**40:23**
Ps 107:40
Jer 25:18-27

23 He judges the great people of the world
　　and brings them all to nothing.

**40:24**
Isa 17:13

24 They hardly get started, barely taking root,
　　when he blows on them and they wither.
The wind carries them off like chaff.

25 "To whom will you compare me?
　　Who is my equal?" asks the Holy One.

**40:26**
Ps 147:4
Isa 42:5

26 Look up into the heavens.
　　Who created all the stars?
He brings them out like an army, one after another,
　　calling each by its name.
Because of his great power and incomparable strength,
　　not a single one is missing.

**40:27**
Job 34:5-6
Isa 54:8

27 O Jacob, how can you say the LORD does not see your troubles?
　　O Israel, how can you say God ignores your rights?

**40:28**
Pss 90:2; 147:5
Rom 11:33

28 Have you never heard?
　　Have you never understood?
The LORD is the everlasting God,
　　the Creator of all the earth.
He never grows weak or weary.
　　No one can measure the depths of his understanding.

**40:29**
Jer 31:25

29 He gives power to the weak
　　and strength to the powerless.

**40:30**
Jer 9:21

30 Even youths will become weak and tired,
　　and young men will fall in exhaustion.

**40:31**
2 Cor 4:8-10, 16
Heb 12:3

31 But those who trust in the LORD will find new strength.
　　They will soar high on wings like eagles.
They will run and not grow weary.
　　They will walk and not faint.

### God's Help for Israel

**41:1**
Hab 2:20
Zech 2:13

**41** 1 "Listen in silence before me, you lands beyond the sea.
　　　　Bring your strongest arguments.
Come now and speak.
　　The court is ready for your case.

**41:2**
2 Chr 36:23
Isa 46:11

2 "Who has stirred up this king from the east,
　　rightly calling him to God's service?

---

**40:29-31** Even the strongest people get tired at times, but God's power and strength never diminish. He is never too tired or too busy to help and listen. His strength is our source of strength. When you feel all of life crushing you and you cannot go another step, remember that you can call upon God to renew your strength.

**40:31** Trusting in the Lord is the patient expectation that God will fulfill his promises in his Word and strengthen us to rise above life's difficulties. Do you believe God loves you and wants the best for you? Can you relax, confident that his purposes are right? Are you convinced that he has the power to control all of life—and your life as well? Though your faith may be struggling or weak, accept his provisions and care for you.

**41:1ff** The "king from the east" is Cyrus II of Persia, who would be king within a century and a half (he is also mentioned by name in 44:28). He conquered Babylon in 539 B.C. and was responsible for the decree releasing the exiled Jews to return to Jerusalem. God could even use a pagan ruler to protect and care for Israel, because God is in control of all world empires and politics.

Who gives this man victory over many nations
    and permits him to trample their kings underfoot?
With his sword, he reduces armies to dust.
    With his bow, he scatters them like chaff before the wind.
3 He chases them away and goes on safely,
    though he is walking over unfamiliar ground.
4 Who has done such mighty deeds,
    summoning each new generation from the beginning of time?
It is I, the LORD, the First and the Last.
    I alone am he."

**41:4**
Isa 44:7; 48:12
Rev 1:8, 17-18;
22:13

5 The lands beyond the sea watch in fear.
    Remote lands tremble and mobilize for war.
6 The idol makers encourage one another,
    saying to each other, "Be strong!"
7 The carver encourages the goldsmith,
    and the molder helps at the anvil.
"Good," they say. "It's coming along fine."
Carefully they join the parts together,
    then fasten the thing in place so it won't fall over.

**41:5**
Josh 5:1
Ezek 26:15-16
**41:6**
Joel 3:9-11

8 "But as for you, Israel my servant,
    Jacob my chosen one,
    descended from Abraham my friend,
9 I have called you back from the ends of the earth,
    saying, 'You are my servant.'
For I have chosen you
    and will not throw you away.
10 Don't be afraid, for I am with you.
    Don't be discouraged, for I am your God.
I will strengthen you and help you.
    I will hold you up with my victorious right hand.

**41:8**
Isa 51:2
Jas 2:23
**41:9**
Deut 7:6
Isa 11:11
**41:10**
Deut 31:6
Ps 89:13
Rom 8:31

11 "See, all your angry enemies lie there,
    confused and humiliated.
Anyone who opposes you will die
    and come to nothing.
12 You will look in vain
    for those who tried to conquer you.
Those who attack you
    will come to nothing.
13 For I hold you by your right hand—
    I, the LORD your God.
And I say to you,
    'Don't be afraid. I am here to help you.
14 Though you are a lowly worm, O Jacob,
    don't be afraid, people of Israel, for I will help you.
I am the LORD, your Redeemer.
    I am the Holy One of Israel.'

**41:11**
Isa 29:5, 7-8
**41:12**
Job 20:7-9
**41:13**
Isa 45:1
**41:14**
Isa 43:14

**41:4** Each generation gets caught up in its own problems, but God's plan embraces all generations. When your great-grandparents lived, God worked personally in the lives of his people. When your great-grandchildren live, God will still work personally in the lives of his people. He is the only one who sees 100 years from now as clearly as 100 years ago. When you are concerned about the future, talk with God, who knows the generations of the future as well as he knows the generations of the past.

**41:8-10** God chose Israel through Abraham because he wanted to, not because the people deserved it (Deuteronomy 7:6-8; 9:4-6). Although God chose the Israelites to represent him to the world, they failed to do this; so God punished them and sent them into captivity. Now all believers are God's chosen people, and all share the responsibility of representing him to the world. One day God will bring all his faithful people together. We need not fear because (1) God is with us ("I am with you"), (2) God has established a relationship with us ("I am your God"), and (3) God gives us assurance of his strength, help, and victory over sin and death. Are you aware of all the ways God has helped you?

**41:15**
Mic 4:13

15 You will be a new threshing instrument
    with many sharp teeth.
You will tear your enemies apart,
    making chaff of mountains.

**41:16**
Isa 35:10

16 You will toss them into the air,
    and the wind will blow them all away;
    a whirlwind will scatter them.
Then you will rejoice in the LORD.
    You will glory in the Holy One of Israel.

**41:17**
Isa 30:19; 42:16;
44:3

17 "When the poor and needy search for water and there is none,
    and their tongues are parched from thirst,
then I, the LORD, will answer them.
    I, the God of Israel, will never abandon them.

**41:18**
Ps 107:35
Isa 30:25

18 I will open up rivers for them on the high plateaus.
    I will give them fountains of water in the valleys.
I will fill the desert with pools of water.
    Rivers fed by springs will flow across the parched ground.

**41:19**
Isa 55:13

19 I will plant trees in the barren desert—
    cedar, acacia, myrtle, olive, cypress, fir, and pine.

**41:20**
Job 12:7-9

20 I am doing this so all who see this miracle
    will understand what it means—
that it is the LORD who has done this,
    the Holy One of Israel who created it.

21 "Present the case for your idols,"
    says the LORD.
"Let them show what they can do,"
    says the King of Israel.*

**41:22**
Isa 43:9; 45:21

22 "Let them try to tell us what happened long ago
    so that we may consider the evidence.
Or let them tell us what the future holds,
    so we can know what's going to happen.

**41:23**
Jer 10:5
John 13:19

23 Yes, tell us what will occur in the days ahead.
    Then we will know you are gods.
In fact, do anything—good or bad!
    Do something that will amaze and frighten us.

**41:24**
1 Cor 8:4

24 But no! You are less than nothing and can do nothing at all.
    Those who choose you pollute themselves.

**41:25**
Jer 50:3
Mic 7:10

25 "But I have stirred up a leader who will come from the north.
    I have called him by name from the east.
I will give him victory over kings and princes.
    He will trample them as a potter treads on clay.

**41:26**
Isa 44:7

26 "Who told you from the beginning
    that this would happen?
Who predicted this,
    making you admit that he was right?
No one said a word!

**41:27**
Isa 40:9

27 I was the first to tell Zion,
    'Look! Help is on the way!'*
I will send Jerusalem a messenger with good news.

**41:21** Hebrew *the King of Jacob.* See note on 14:1.   **41:27** Or *'Look! They are coming home.'*

---

**41:21-24** Israel was surrounded by many nations whose gods supposedly had special powers, such as helping crops grow and providing victory in war. These gods, however, failed to deliver. A god with limited or no power at all is not really a god. When we are tempted to put our trust in something other than the living God—money, career, family, or even military power—we should stop and ask some serious questions. Will it come through? Will it unfailingly provide what I am looking for? God delivers. When he makes a promise, he keeps it. He is completely trustworthy.

²⁸ Not one of your idols told you this.
  Not one gave any answer when I asked.
²⁹ See, they are all foolish, worthless things.
  All your idols are as empty as the wind.

### The LORD's Chosen Servant

**42** ¹ "Look at my servant, whom I strengthen.
    He is my chosen one, who pleases me.
  I have put my Spirit upon him.
    He will bring justice to the nations.
² He will not shout
    or raise his voice in public.
³ He will not crush the weakest reed
    or put out a flickering candle.
  He will bring justice to all who have been wronged.
⁴ He will not falter or lose heart
    until justice prevails throughout the earth.
  Even distant lands beyond the sea will wait for his instruction.*"

⁵ God, the LORD, created the heavens and stretched them out.
    He created the earth and everything in it.
  He gives breath to everyone,
    life to everyone who walks the earth.
  And it is he who says,
⁶ "I, the LORD, have called you to demonstrate my righteousness.
    I will take you by the hand and guard you,
  and I will give you to my people, Israel,
    as a symbol of my covenant with them.
  And you will be a light to guide the nations.
⁷    You will open the eyes of the blind.
  You will free the captives from prison,
    releasing those who sit in dark dungeons.

⁸ "I am the LORD; that is my name!
    I will not give my glory to anyone else,
    nor share my praise with carved idols.
⁹ Everything I prophesied has come true,
    and now I will prophesy again.
  I will tell you the future before it happens."

### A Song of Praise to the LORD
¹⁰ Sing a new song to the LORD!
    Sing his praises from the ends of the earth!
  Sing, all you who sail the seas,
    all you who live in distant coastlands.

**41:29**
Jer 5:13
Hab 2:18-19

**42:1-4**
†Matt 12:18-21
**42:1**
Isa 11:2; 53:11
Matt 3:17; 12:18

**42:3**
Ps 72:2, 4

**42:4**
Isa 24:15; 66:19

**42:5**
Job 33:4
Ps 104:2
Isa 45:18
Acts 17:25

**42:6**
Jer 23:5-6
Luke 2:32

**42:7**
Isa 35:5; 61:1

**42:8**
Exod 3:15; 20:3-5

**42:10**
Ps 33:3

**42:4** Greek version reads *And his name will be the hope of all the world.* Compare Matt 12:21.

---

**42:1-4** These verses are quoted in Matthew 12:18-21 with reference to Christ. The chosen servant reveals a character of gentleness, encouragement, justice, and truth. When you feel broken and bruised or burned out in your spiritual life, God won't step on you or toss you aside as useless but will gently pick you up. God's loving attributes are desperately needed in the world today. Through God's Spirit, we can show such sensitivity to people around us, reflecting God's goodness and honesty to them.

**42:1-9** Sometimes called the Servant Song, these verses are about the Servant-Messiah, not the servant Cyrus (described in chapter 41). Israel and the Messiah are both often called *servant*. Israel, as God's servant, was to help bring the world to a knowl-

edge of God. The Messiah, Jesus, would fulfill this task and show God himself to the world.

**42:6, 7** Part of Christ's mission on earth was to demonstrate God's righteousness and to be a light for the Gentiles (to all nations). Through Christ, all people have the opportunity to share in his mission. God calls us to be servants of his Son, demonstrating God's righteousness and bringing his light. What a rare privilege it is to help the Messiah fulfill his mission! But we must seek his righteousness (Matthew 6:33) before we demonstrate it to others and let his light shine in us before we can be lights ourselves (Matthew 5:16; 2 Corinthians 4:6).

**42:10** Look at all the Lord will do for us and through us (42:6-9)! Majestic works prompt majestic responses. Do you really appreciate the good things that God does for you and through you? If so, let your praise to him reflect how you really feel.

11 Join in the chorus, you desert towns;
    let the villages of Kedar rejoice!
Let the people of Sela sing for joy;
    shout praises from the mountaintops!
12 Let the whole world glorify the LORD;
    let it sing his praise.

**42:13**
Isa 59:17; 66:14-16

13 The LORD will march forth like a mighty hero;
    he will come out like a warrior, full of fury.
He will shout his battle cry
    and crush all his enemies.

14 He will say, "I have long been silent;
    yes, I have restrained myself.
But now, like a woman in labor,
    I will cry and groan and pant.

**42:15**
Ezek 38:19-20

15 I will level the mountains and hills
    and blight all their greenery.
I will turn the rivers into dry land
    and will dry up all the pools.

**42:16**
Ps 94:14
Isa 40:4
Luke 1:78-79
Eph 5:8

16 I will lead blind Israel down a new path,
    guiding them along an unfamiliar way.
I will brighten the darkness before them
    and smooth out the road ahead of them.
Yes, I will indeed do these things;
    I will not forsake them.

**42:17**
Ps 97:7
Isa 44:9, 11

17 But those who trust in idols,
    who say, 'You are our gods,'
    will be turned away in shame.

### Israel's Failure to Listen and See

**42:18**
Isa 35:5

18 "Listen, you who are deaf!
    Look and see, you blind!
19 Who is as blind as my own people, my servant?
    Who is as deaf as my messenger?
Who is as blind as my chosen people,
    the servant of the LORD?

**42:20**
Jer 6:10

20 You see and recognize what is right
    but refuse to act on it.
You hear with your ears,
    but you don't really listen."

21 Because he is righteous,
    the LORD has exalted his glorious law.

**42:22**
Isa 24:18

22 But his own people have been robbed and plundered,
    enslaved, imprisoned, and trapped.
They are fair game for anyone
    and have no one to protect them,
    no one to take them back home.

---

**THE SERVANT IN ISAIAH**

The nation Israel is called the servant: . . . . . . . . . 41:8; 42:19; 43:10; 44:1, 2, 21; 45:4; 48:20
The Messiah is called the Servant: . . . . . . . . . . . 42:1-17; 49:5-7; 50:10; 52:13; 53:11

The nation was given a mission to serve God, to be custodian of his word, and to be a light to the Gentile nations. Because of sin and rebellion, they failed. God sent his Son, Christ, as Messiah to fulfill that mission on earth.

---

**42:19, 20** How could Israel and Judah be God's servants and yet be so blind? How could they be so close to God and see so little? Jesus condemned the religious leaders of his day for the same disregard of God (John 9:39-41). Yet do we not fail in the same way? Sometimes partial blindness—seeing but not understanding, or knowing what is right but not doing it—can be worse than not seeing at all.

23 Who will hear these lessons from the past
   and see the ruin that awaits you in the future?
24 Who allowed Israel to be robbed and hurt?
   It was the Lord, against whom we sinned,
   for the people would not walk in his path,
   nor would they obey his law.
25 Therefore, he poured out his fury on them
   and destroyed them in battle.
   They were enveloped in flames,
   but they still refused to understand.
   They were consumed by fire,
   but they did not learn their lesson.

### The Savior of Israel

**43** ¹ But now, O Jacob, listen to the Lord who created you.
   O Israel, the one who formed you says,
   "Do not be afraid, for I have ransomed you.
   I have called you by name; you are mine.
² When you go through deep waters,
   I will be with you.
   When you go through rivers of difficulty,
   you will not drown.
   When you walk through the fire of oppression,
   you will not be burned up;
   the flames will not consume you.
³ For I am the Lord, your God,
   the Holy One of Israel, your Savior.
   I gave Egypt as a ransom for your freedom;
   I gave Ethiopia* and Seba in your place.
⁴ Others were given in exchange for you.
   I traded their lives for yours
   because you are precious to me.
   You are honored, and I love you.
⁵ "Do not be afraid, for I am with you.
   I will gather you and your children from east and west.
⁶ I will say to the north and south,
   'Bring my sons and daughters back to Israel
   from the distant corners of the earth.
⁷ Bring all who claim me as their God,
   for I have made them for my glory.
   It was I who created them.'"
⁸ Bring out the people who have eyes but are blind,
   who have ears but are deaf.
⁹ Gather the nations together!
   Assemble the peoples of the world!

**43:3** Hebrew *Cush*.

Marginal references:
- **42:24** Isa 48:18
- **42:25** Isa 5:25; Hos 7:9
- **43:2** Deut 31:6, 8; Dan 3:25, 27
- **43:3** Exod 20:2; Isa 43:11
- **43:4** Isa 63:9
- **43:5** Isa 49:12; Jer 30:10-11
- **43:6** Ps 107:3; 2 Cor 6:17-18
- **43:7** Ps 100:3; Isa 46:13; Eph 2:10
- **43:8** Ezek 12:2
- **43:9** Isa 41:22, 26

---

**42:23** We may condemn our predecessors for their failures, but we are twice as guilty if we repeat the same mistakes that we recognize as failures. We may be so ready to direct God's message at others that we can't see how it touches our own life. Make sure you are willing to take your own advice as you teach or lead.

**43:1ff** Chapter 42 ends with God's sorrow over the spiritual decay of his people. In chapter 43, God says that despite the people's spiritual failure, he will show them mercy, bring them back from captivity, and restore them. He would give them an outpouring of love, not wrath. Then the world would know that God alone had done this.

**43:1-4** God created the people of Israel, and they were special to him. God redeemed them and called them by name to be those who belong to him. God protected Israel in times of trouble. We are important to God, too. If we claim to belong to God, we must never do anything that would bring shame to him.

**43:2** Going through rivers of difficulty will either cause you to drown or force you to grow stronger. If you go in your own strength, you are more likely to drown. If you invite the Lord to go with you, he will protect you.

**43:3** God gave other nations to Persia in exchange for returning the Jews to their homeland. Egypt, Ethiopia, and parts of Arabia (Seba) had attacked Persia, and the Persians defeated them.

**43:5, 6** Isaiah was speaking primarily of Israel's return from Babylon. But there is a broader meaning: All God's people will be regathered when Christ comes to rule in peace over the earth.

Which of their idols has ever foretold such things?
　　Which can predict what will happen tomorrow?
Where are the witnesses of such predictions?
　　Who can verify that they spoke the truth?

10 "But you are my witnesses, O Israel!" says the LORD.
　　"You are my servant.
You have been chosen to know me, believe in me,
　　and understand that I alone am God.
There is no other God—
　　there never has been, and there never will be.

**43:11**
Hos 13:4
11 I, yes I, am the LORD,
　　and there is no other Savior.

**43:12**
Ps 81:9
12 First I predicted your rescue,
　　then I saved you and proclaimed it to the world.
No foreign god has ever done this.
　　You are witnesses that I am the only God,"
　　says the LORD.

**43:13**
Job 9:12
Ps 90:2
13 "From eternity to eternity I am God.
　　No one can snatch anyone out of my hand.
　　No one can undo what I have done."

*The LORD's Promise of Victory*

**43:14**
Isa 41:14
14 This is what the LORD says—your Redeemer, the Holy One of Israel:

"For your sakes I will send an army against Babylon,
　　forcing the Babylonians* to flee in those ships they are so proud of.
15 I am the LORD, your Holy One,
　　Israel's Creator and King.

**43:16**
Exod 14:21-22
Josh 3:15-16
Ps 77:19
16 I am the LORD, who opened a way through the waters,
　　making a dry path through the sea.

**43:17**
Ps 76:5-6
17 I called forth the mighty army of Egypt
　　with all its chariots and horses.
I drew them beneath the waves, and they drowned,
　　their lives snuffed out like a smoldering candlewick.

**43:18**
Jer 16:14
18 "But forget all that—
　　it is nothing compared to what I am going to do.

**43:19**
Deut 8:15
2 Cor 5:17
Rev 21:5
19 For I am about to do something new.
　　See, I have already begun! Do you not see it?
I will make a pathway through the wilderness.
　　I will create rivers in the dry wasteland.

**43:20**
Isa 41:17-18
2 Pet 2:9
20 The wild animals in the fields will thank me,
　　the jackals and owls, too,
　　for giving them water in the desert.
Yes, I will make rivers in the dry wasteland
　　so my chosen people can be refreshed.
21 I have made Israel for myself,
　　and they will someday honor me before the whole world.

**43:22**
Mic 6:3
22 "But, dear family of Jacob, you refuse to ask for my help.
　　You have grown tired of me, O Israel!

**43:14** Or *Chaldeans.*

---

**43:10, 11** Israel's task was to be a witness (44:8), telling the world who God is and what he had done. Believers today share the responsibility of being God's witnesses. Do people know what God is like through your words and example? They cannot see God directly, but they can see him reflected in you.

**43:15-21** This section pictures a new Exodus for a people once again oppressed, as the Israelites had been as slaves in Egypt before the Exodus. They would cry to God, and again he would hear and deliver them. A new Exodus would take place through a new wilderness. The past miracles were nothing compared to what God would do for his people in the future.

**43:22-24** A sacrifice required both giving up a valuable animal and pleading with God for forgiveness. But the people presented God with sins instead of sacrifices. Can you imagine bringing the best of your sins to God's altar? This ironic picture shows the depths to which Israel had sunk. What do you present to God— your sins or a plea for his forgiveness?

<sup>23</sup> You have not brought me sheep or goats for burnt offerings.
 You have not honored me with sacrifices,
though I have not burdened and wearied you
 with requests for grain offerings and frankincense.

43:23
Exod 30:34
Mal 1:6-8

<sup>24</sup> You have not brought me fragrant calamus
 or pleased me with the fat from sacrifices.
Instead, you have burdened me with your sins
 and wearied me with your faults.

43:24
Jer 6:20
Mal 2:17

<sup>25</sup> "I—yes, I alone—will blot out your sins for my own sake
 and will never think of them again.
<sup>26</sup> Let us review the situation together,
 and you can present your case to prove your innocence.
<sup>27</sup> From the very beginning, your first ancestor sinned against me;
 all your leaders broke my laws.
<sup>28</sup> That is why I have disgraced your priests;
 I have decreed complete destruction* for Jacob
 and shame for Israel.

43:25
Isa 55:7
Jer 31:34
Ezek 36:22

43:28
Ezek 5:15

# 44

<sup>1</sup> "But now, listen to me, Jacob my servant,
 Israel my chosen one.
<sup>2</sup> The Lord who made you and helps you says:
Do not be afraid, O Jacob, my servant,
 O dear Israel,* my chosen one.

44:1
Jer 30:10

44:2
Deut 32:15

<sup>3</sup> For I will pour out water to quench your thirst
 and to irrigate your parched fields.
And I will pour out my Spirit on your descendants,
 and my blessing on your children.
<sup>4</sup> They will thrive like watered grass,
 like willows on a riverbank.
<sup>5</sup> Some will proudly claim, 'I belong to the Lord.'
 Others will say, 'I am a descendant of Jacob.'
Some will write the Lord's name on their hands
 and will take the name of Israel as their own."

44:3
Isa 61:9
Joel 2:28

## The Foolishness of Idols

<sup>6</sup>This is what the Lord says—Israel's King and Redeemer, the Lord of Heaven's Armies:

 "I am the First and the Last;
 there is no other God.
<sup>7</sup> Who is like me?
 Let him step forward and prove to you his power.
Let him do as I have done since ancient times
 when I established a people and explained its future.
<sup>8</sup> Do not tremble; do not be afraid.
 Did I not proclaim my purposes for you long ago?
You are my witnesses—is there any other God?
 No! There is no other Rock—not one!"

44:6
Isa 41:21;
45:5-6, 21
Rev 1:8, 17

44:7
Isa 41:22

44:8
Deut 4:35, 39
Isa 30:29

<sup>9</sup> How foolish are those who manufacture idols.
 These prized objects are really worthless.

44:9
Ps 97:7

43:28 The Hebrew term used here refers to the complete consecration of things or people to the Lord, either by destroying them or by giving them as an offering.   44:2 Hebrew *Jeshurun*, a term of endearment for Israel.

**43:25** How tempting it is to remind someone of a past offense! But when God forgives our sins, he totally forgets them. We never have to fear that he will remind us of them later. Because God forgives our sins, we need to forgive others.

**44:5** The time will come when Israel will be proud of belonging to God. If we are truly God's, we should be unashamed and delighted to let everyone know about our relationship with him (44:8).

**44:8, 9** The manufactured idols were guilty of false advertising. They made big promises, but they were worthless and helpless.

In contrast, God fulfills his claims and delivers on all his promises. God challenges us to be his witnesses. When we share our faith with those who can find no meaning in life or have no hope of eternal life, we are not proclaiming anything shoddy or unreliable. God is real and life with him is best. Pray for boldness in your life to share your faith in Christ with friends, relatives, and neighbors.

**44:9-20** Here Isaiah describes how people make their own gods. How absurd to make a god from the same tree that gives

The people who worship idols don't know this,
    so they are all put to shame.

**44:10**
Jer 10:5
Hab 2:18
Acts 19:26

10 Who but a fool would make his own god—
    an idol that cannot help him one bit?
11 All who worship idols will be disgraced
    along with all these craftsmen—mere humans—
    who claim they can make a god.
They may all stand together,
    but they will stand in terror and shame.

**44:12**
Isa 40:19; 41:7

12 The blacksmith stands at his forge to make a sharp tool,
    pounding and shaping it with all his might.
His work makes him hungry and weak.
    It makes him thirsty and faint.

**44:13**
Ps 115:5-7
Isa 41:7

13 Then the wood-carver measures a block of wood
    and draws a pattern on it.
He works with chisel and plane
    and carves it into a human figure.
He gives it human beauty
    and puts it in a little shrine.
14 He cuts down cedars;
    he selects the cypress and the oak;
he plants the pine in the forest
    to be nourished by the rain.

**44:15**
2 Chr 25:14

15 Then he uses part of the wood to make a fire.
    With it he warms himself and bakes his bread.
Then—yes, it's true—he takes the rest of it
    and makes himself a god to worship!
He makes an idol
    and bows down in front of it!
16 He burns part of the tree to roast his meat
    and to keep himself warm.
He says, "Ah, that fire feels good."

**44:17**
1 Kgs 18:26, 28
Isa 45:20

17 Then he takes what's left
    and makes his god: a carved idol!
He falls down in front of it,
    worshiping and praying to it.
"Rescue me!" he says.
    "You are my god!"

**44:18**
Ps 81:12
Isa 6:9-10; 29:10
Jer 10:8, 14

18 Such stupidity and ignorance!
    Their eyes are closed, and they cannot see.
    Their minds are shut, and they cannot think.

**44:19**
Deut 27:15

19 The person who made the idol never stops to reflect,
    "Why, it's just a block of wood!
I burned half of it for heat
    and used it to bake my bread and roast my meat.
How can the rest of it be a god?
    Should I bow down to worship a piece of wood?"

---

**TODAY'S IDOLATRY**

Isaiah tells us, "Who but a fool would make his own god—an idol that cannot help him one bit?" (44:10). We think of idols as statues of wood or stone, but in reality an idol is anything natural that is given sacred value and power. If your answer to any of the following questions is anything or anyone other than God, you may need to check out who or what you are worshiping.

- Who created me?
- Whom do I ultimately trust?
- Whom do I look to for ultimate truth?
- Whom do I look to for security and happiness?
- Who is in charge of my future?

firewood. What are the gods we make—money, fame, or power?
We deceive ourselves if we expect them to empower our life.

20 The poor, deluded fool feeds on ashes.
    He trusts something that can't help him at all.
Yet he cannot bring himself to ask,
    "Is this idol that I'm holding in my hand a lie?"

## Restoration for Jerusalem

21 "Pay attention, O Jacob,
    for you are my servant, O Israel.
I, the LORD, made you,
    and I will not forget you.
22 I have swept away your sins like a cloud.
    I have scattered your offenses like the morning mist.
Oh, return to me,
    for I have paid the price to set you free."

23 Sing, O heavens, for the LORD has done this wondrous thing.
    Shout for joy, O depths of the earth!
Break into song,
    O mountains and forests and every tree!
For the LORD has redeemed Jacob
    and is glorified in Israel.

24 This is what the LORD says—
    your Redeemer and Creator:
"I am the LORD, who made all things.
    I alone stretched out the heavens.
Who was with me
    when I made the earth?
25 I expose the false prophets as liars
    and make fools of fortune-tellers.
I cause the wise to give bad advice,
    thus proving them to be fools.
26 But I carry out the predictions of my prophets!
    By them I say to Jerusalem, 'People will live here again,'
and to the towns of Judah, 'You will be rebuilt;
    I will restore all your ruins!'
27 When I speak to the rivers and say, 'Dry up!'
    they will be dry.
28 When I say of Cyrus, 'He is my shepherd,'
    he will certainly do as I say.
He will command, 'Rebuild Jerusalem';
    he will say, 'Restore the Temple.'"

## Cyrus, the LORD's Chosen One

**45** ¹ This is what the LORD says to Cyrus, his anointed one,
        whose right hand he will empower.
Before him, mighty kings will be paralyzed with fear.
    Their fortress gates will be opened,
    never to shut again.

**44:20**
Ps 102:9
Hos 4:12

**44:21**
Isa 44:1-2; 46:8

**44:22**
Ps 51:1, 9
Isa 55:7
Acts 3:19
1 Pet 1:18-19

**44:23**
Pss 69:34; 98:7-8

**44:24**
Isa 40:22

**44:25**
1 Cor 1:20, 27

**44:26**
Jer 32:15, 44

**44:27**
Isa 50:2
**44:28**
2 Chr 36:22-23
Isa 14:32

**45:1**
Ps 73:23
Jer 51:11, 20, 24

---

**44:21** God said that we should serve our Creator (17:7; 40:28; 43:15; 45:9). Idolaters do the opposite—serving or worshiping what they have made rather than the one who made them. Our Creator paid the price to set us free from our sins against him. By contrast, no idol ever created anybody, and no idol can redeem us from our sins.

**44:25, 26** False prophets were people who claimed to bring messages from the gods. Because God is truth, he is the standard for all teachings. We can always trust his Word as absolute truth. His Word is completely accurate, and against it we can measure all other teachings. If you are unsure about a teaching, test it against God's Word. God condemned the false prophets because they gave advice opposite to his.

**44:28** Isaiah, who prophesied from about 740–681 B.C., called Cyrus by name almost 150 years before he ruled (559–530 B.C.)! Later historians said that Cyrus read this prophecy and was so moved that he carried it out. Isaiah also predicted that Jerusalem would fall more than 100 years before it happened (586 B.C.) and that the Temple would be rebuilt about 200 years before it happened. It is clear these prophecies came from God, who knows the future.

**45:1-8** This is the only place in the Bible where a Gentile ruler is said to be "anointed." God is the power over all rulers, and he anoints whom he chooses for his special tasks. Cyrus's king-

**45:2**
Ps 107:16
Isa 40:4
Jer 51:30

2 This is what the LORD says:

"I will go before you, Cyrus,
and level the mountains.*
I will smash down gates of bronze
and cut through bars of iron.

**45:3**
Isa 49:1
Jer 41:8

3 And I will give you treasures hidden in the darkness—
secret riches.
I will do this so you may know that I am the LORD,
the God of Israel, the one who calls you by name.

**45:4**
Isa 43:1
Acts 17:23

4 "And why have I called you for this work?
Why did I call you by name when you did not know me?
It is for the sake of Jacob my servant,
Israel my chosen one.

**45:5**
Ps 18:39
Isa 44:8

5 I am the LORD;
there is no other God.
I have equipped you for battle,
though you don't even know me,

**45:6**
Mal 1:11

6 so all the world from east to west
will know there is no other God.
I am the LORD, and there is no other.

**45:7**
Ps 104:20
Amos 3:6

7 I create the light and make the darkness.
I send good times and bad times.
I, the LORD, am the one who does these things.

**45:8**
Pss 72:6; 85:11
Isa 61:11

8 "Open up, O heavens,
and pour out your righteousness.
Let the earth open wide
so salvation and righteousness can sprout up together.
I, the LORD, created them.

**45:9**
Rom 9:20-21

9 "What sorrow awaits those who argue with their Creator.
Does a clay pot argue with its maker?
Does the clay dispute with the one who shapes it, saying,
'Stop, you're doing it wrong!'
Does the pot exclaim,
'How clumsy can you be?'

10 How terrible it would be if a newborn baby said to its father,
'Why was I born?'
or if it said to its mother,
'Why did you make me this way?'"

11 This is what the LORD says—
the Holy One of Israel and your Creator:
"Do you question what I do for my children?
Do you give me orders about the work of my hands?

**45:12**
Neh 9:6
Jer 27:5

12 I am the one who made the earth
and created people to live on it.
With my hands I stretched out the heavens.
All the stars are at my command.

**45:13**
2 Chr 36:22-23
Isa 52:3

13 I will raise up Cyrus to fulfill my righteous purpose,
and I will guide his actions.

45:2 As in Dead Sea Scrolls and Greek version; Masoretic Text reads the swellings.

---

dom spread across 2,000 miles (the largest of any empire then known), including the territories of both the Assyrian and the Babylonian Empires. Why did God anoint Cyrus? Because God had a special task for him to do for Israel. Cyrus would allow God's city, Jerusalem, to be rebuilt, and he would set the exiles free without expecting anything in return. Few kings of Israel or Judah had done as much for God's people as Cyrus would.

**45:7** God is ruler over light and darkness, over good times and bad times. Our lives are sprinkled with both types of experiences, and both are needed for us to grow spiritually. When good times come, thank God and use your prosperity for him. When bad times come, don't resent them, but ask what you can learn from this refining experience to make you a better servant of God.

He will restore my city and free my captive people—
    without seeking a reward!
I, the LORD of Heaven's Armies, have spoken!"

## Future Conversion of Gentiles

14 This is what the LORD says:

"You will rule the Egyptians,
    the Ethiopians,* and the Sabeans.
They will come to you with all their merchandise,
    and it will all be yours.
They will follow you as prisoners in chains.
    They will fall to their knees in front of you and say,
    'God is with you, and he is the only God.
    There is no other.'"

15 Truly, O God of Israel, our Savior,
    you work in mysterious ways.
16 All craftsmen who make idols will be humiliated.
    They will all be disgraced together.
17 But the LORD will save the people of Israel
    with eternal salvation.
Throughout everlasting ages,
    they will never again be humiliated and disgraced.

18 For the LORD is God,
    and he created the heavens and earth
    and put everything in place.
He made the world to be lived in,
    not to be a place of empty chaos.
"I am the LORD," he says,
    "and there is no other.

19 I publicly proclaim bold promises.
    I do not whisper obscurities in some dark corner.
I would not have told the people of Israel* to seek me
    if I could not be found.
I, the LORD, speak only what is true
    and declare only what is right.

20 "Gather together and come,
    you fugitives from surrounding nations.
What fools they are who carry around their wooden idols
    and pray to gods that cannot save!
21 Consult together, argue your case.
    Get together and decide what to say.
Who made these things known so long ago?
    What idol ever told you they would happen?
Was it not I, the LORD?
    For there is no other God but me,
a righteous God and Savior.
    There is none but me.
22 Let all the world look to me for salvation!
    For I am God; there is no other.

45:14 Hebrew *Cushites*.   45:19 Hebrew *of Jacob*. See note on 14:1.

---

**Cross references:**

45:14 Isa 14:1-2; 49:23; 1 Cor 14:25

45:16 Isa 44:11

45:17 Isa 51:6; Rom 11:26

45:18 Gen 1:2, 26; Ps 115:16; Isa 42:5

45:19 2 Chr 15:2; Isa 43:12; Jer 29:13-14

45:20 Isa 44:18-19; 46:6-7; Jer 10:5

45:21 Isa 43:3, 11; 44:7; Mark 12:32

45:22 Num 21:8-9; Isa 52:10; Mic 7:7

---

**45:14** The Sabeans were people from Seba in southern Arabia.

**45:17** Until this time, Israel had anticipated temporal salvation— God would save them from their enemies. Here Isaiah tells of eternal salvation with God.

**45:18, 19** God's promises are public, and their fulfillment is sure. So why do we ever doubt him? We never have to be uncertain when we have a God of truth and righteousness.

**45:22** Salvation is for all nations, not just the Israelites. Many times it seems as though Israel had an inside track on salvation. But God makes it clear that his people include *all* those who follow him. Israel was to be the means through which the whole world would come to know God. Jesus, the Messiah, fulfilled Israel's role and gave all people the opportunity to follow God. (See also Romans 11:11; Galatians 3:28; Ephesians 3:6; Philippians 2:10.)

**45:23**
†Rom 14:11
Phil 2:10-11

23 I have sworn by my own name;
    I have spoken the truth,
    and I will never go back on my word:
Every knee will bend to me,
    and every tongue will confess allegiance to me.*"
24 The people will declare,
    "The LORD is the source of all my righteousness and strength."
And all who were angry with him
    will come to him and be ashamed.

**45:25**
Isa 53:11

25 In the LORD all the generations of Israel will be justified,
    and in him they will boast.

### Babylon's False Gods

**46:1**
Isa 21:9
Jer 50:2; 51:44

**46** 1 Bel and Nebo, the gods of Babylon,
    bow as they are lowered to the ground.
They are being hauled away on ox carts.
    The poor beasts stagger under the weight.

**46:2**
Jer 43:12-13

2 Both the idols and their owners are bowed down.
    The gods cannot protect the people,
and the people cannot protect the gods.
    They go off into captivity together.

**46:3**
Isa 10:21-22

3 "Listen to me, descendants of Jacob,
    all you who remain in Israel.
I have cared for you since you were born.
    Yes, I carried you before you were born.

**46:4**
Ps 71:18

4 I will be your God throughout your lifetime—
    until your hair is white with age.
I made you, and I will care for you.
    I will carry you along and save you.

**46:5**
Isa 40:18, 25

5 "To whom will you compare me?
    Who is my equal?

**46:6**
Isa 44:12-17

6 Some people pour out their silver and gold
    and hire a craftsman to make a god from it.
Then they bow down and worship it!

**46:7**
Isa 40:20
Jer 10:5

7 They carry it around on their shoulders,
    and when they set it down, it stays there.
It can't even move!
And when someone prays to it, there is no answer.
    It can't rescue anyone from trouble.

**45:23** Hebrew *will confess;* Greek version reads *will confess and give praise to God.* Compare Rom 14:11.

---

| MAJOR IDOLS MENTIONED IN THE BIBLE | Name | Where they were worshiped | What they stood for | What the worship included |
|---|---|---|---|---|
| | Bel (Marduk) | Babylon | Weather, war, sun god | Prostitution, child sacrifice |
| | Nebo (son of Marduk) | Babylon | Learning, astronomy, science | Prostitution |
| | Ashtoreth (Asherah) | Canaan | Goddess of love, childbirth, and fertility | Child sacrifice |
| | Chemosh | Moab | National god | Child sacrifice |
| | Molech | Ammon | National god | Child sacrifice |
| | Baal | Canaan | Rain, harvest, symbolized strength and fertility | Prostitution |
| | Dagon | Philistia | Harvest, grain, success in farming | Child sacrifice |

---

**46:1-4** Cyrus would carry out God's judgment against Babylon. Bel was the chief deity of the Babylonians; Nebo was the god of science and learning. These gods, however, needed animals and people to carry them around and could not even save themselves from being taken into captivity. They had no power at all. In contrast, our God created us and cares for us. His love is so enduring that he will care for us throughout our lifetime and even through death.

8 "Do not forget this! Keep it in mind!
    Remember this, you guilty ones.
9 Remember the things I have done in the past.
    For I alone am God!
    I am God, and there is none like me.
10 Only I can tell you the future
    before it even happens.
    Everything I plan will come to pass,
    for I do whatever I wish.
11 I will call a swift bird of prey from the east—
    a leader from a distant land to come and do my bidding.
    I have said what I would do,
    and I will do it.

12 "Listen to me, you stubborn people
    who are so far from doing right.
13 For I am ready to set things right,
    not in the distant future, but right now!
    I am ready to save Jerusalem*
    and show my glory to Israel.

*Prediction of Babylon's Fall*

**47** 1 "Come down, virgin daughter of Babylon, and sit in the dust.
    For your days of sitting on a throne have ended.
O daughter of Babylonia,* never again will you be
    the lovely princess, tender and delicate.
2 Take heavy millstones and grind flour.
    Remove your veil, and strip off your robe.
    Expose yourself to public view.
3 You will be naked and burdened with shame.
    I will take vengeance against you without pity."

4 Our Redeemer, whose name is the LORD of Heaven's Armies,
    is the Holy One of Israel.

5 "O beautiful Babylon, sit now in darkness and silence.
    Never again will you be known as the queen of kingdoms.
6 For I was angry with my chosen people
    and punished them by letting them fall into your hands.
    But you, Babylon, showed them no mercy.
    You oppressed even the elderly.
7 You said, 'I will reign forever as queen of the world!'
    You did not reflect on your actions
    or think about their consequences.

8 "Listen to this, you pleasure-loving kingdom,
    living at ease and feeling secure.
    You say, 'I am the only one, and there is no other.
    I will never be a widow or lose my children.'

46:13 Hebrew *Zion.*   47:1 Or *Chaldea;* also in 47:5.

**Cross-references (right column):**

46:10 Isa 41:26-27; 42:9 / Acts 5:39
46:11 Num 23:19
46:12 Zech 7:11-12
46:13 Isa 51:5; 61:3
47:1 Jer 48:18
47:2 Gen 24:65 / 1 Cor 11:5
47:3 Isa 63:4
47:5 Lam 2:10 / Dan 2:37
47:6 Deut 28:50 / Zech 1:15
47:7 Rev 18:7
47:8 Isa 22:13; 32:9, 11 / Rev 18:7

---

**46:8-11** Israel was tempted to waver between the Lord God and pagan gods. Isaiah affirms the sole lordship of God. God is unique in his knowledge and in his control of the future. His consistent purpose is to carry out what he has planned. When we are tempted to pursue anything that promises pleasure, comfort, peace, or security apart from God, we must remember our commitment to God.

**46:13** Much of the book of Isaiah speaks of a future deliverance when we will all live with God in perfect peace. God offers not only this future hope but also hope for our present needs. His righteousness is near us, and we do not have to wait for his salvation.

**47:1ff** Here Isaiah predicted the fall of Babylon more than

150 years before it happened. At this time, Babylon had not yet emerged as the mightiest force on earth, the proud empire that would destroy Judah and Jerusalem. But the Babylonians, Judah's captors, would become captives themselves in 539 B.C. God, not Babylon, has the ultimate power. He used Babylon to punish his sinful people; he would use Medo-Persia to destroy Babylon and free his people.

**47:8, 9** Caught up in the pursuit of power and pleasure, Babylon believed in its own greatness and claimed to be the *only* power on earth. Babylon felt completely secure, and Nebuchadnezzar, its king, exalted himself as a "god." But the true God taught Nebuchadnezzar a powerful lesson by taking everything away from him

**47:9**
Isa 13:16
1 Thes 5:2-3
Rev 18:8, 10, 23

9 Well, both these things will come upon you in a moment:
    widowhood and the loss of your children.
Yes, these calamities will come upon you,
    despite all your witchcraft and magic.

**47:10**
Ps 52:7
Isa 5:21
Ezek 8:12

10 "You felt secure in your wickedness.
    'No one sees me,' you said.
But your 'wisdom' and 'knowledge' have led you astray,
    and you said, 'I am the only one, and there is no other.'

**47:11**
Jer 51:8, 43

11 So disaster will overtake you,
    and you won't be able to charm it away.
Calamity will fall upon you,
    and you won't be able to buy your way out.
A catastrophe will strike you suddenly,
    one for which you are not prepared.

12 "Now use your magical charms!
    Use the spells you have worked at all these years!
Maybe they will do you some good.
    Maybe they can make someone afraid of you.

**47:13**
Isa 8:19

13 All the advice you receive has made you tired.
    Where are all your astrologers,
those stargazers who make predictions each month?
    Let them stand up and save you from what the future holds.

**47:14**
Jer 51:30, 32, 58
Nah 1:10

14 But they are like straw burning in a fire;
    they cannot save themselves from the flame.
You will get no help from them at all;
    their hearth is no place to sit for warmth.

**47:15**
Rev 18:11

15 And all your friends,
    those with whom you've done business since childhood,
will go their own ways,
    turning a deaf ear to your cries.

## God's Stubborn People

**48:1**
Isa 45:23

**48** 1 "Listen to me, O family of Jacob,
    you who are called by the name of Israel
and born into the family of Judah.
Listen, you who take oaths in the name of the LORD
    and call on the God of Israel.
You don't keep your promises,

**48:2**
Rom 2:17

2     even though you call yourself the holy city
and talk about depending on the God of Israel,
    whose name is the LORD of Heaven's Armies.

**48:3**
Josh 21:45
Isa 42:9

3 Long ago I told you what was going to happen.
    Then suddenly I took action,
and all my predictions came true.

**48:4**
Ezek 2:4

4 For I know how stubborn and obstinate you are.
    Your necks are as unbending as iron.
    Your heads are as hard as bronze.

**48:5**
Jer 44:15-18

5 That is why I told you what would happen;
    I told you beforehand what I was going to do.

---

(Daniel 4:28-37). Our society is addicted to pleasure and power, but these can quickly vanish. Look at your own life and ask yourself how you can be more responsible with the talents and possessions God has given you. How can you use your life for God's honor rather than your own?

**47:12-15** The people of Babylon sought advice and help from astrologers and stargazers. But like the idols of wood or gold, astrologers could not even deliver themselves from what was to come from the hand of God. Why rely on those who are powerless? The helpless cannot help us. Alternatives to God

are destined to fail. If you want help, find it in God, who has proven his power in creation and in history.

**48:1** The people of Judah felt confident because they lived in Jerusalem, the city with God's Temple. They depended on their heritage, their city, and their Temple—but this was false security because they did not depend on God. Do you feel secure because you go to church or live in a Christian country? Heritage, buildings, or nations cannot give us a relationship with God; we must truly depend on him personally, with all our hearts and minds.

Then you could never say, 'My idols did it.
My wooden image and metal god commanded it to happen!'
6 You have heard my predictions and seen them fulfilled,
but you refuse to admit it.
Now I will tell you new things,
secrets you have not yet heard.
7 They are brand new, not things from the past.
So you cannot say, 'We knew that all the time!'

8 "Yes, I will tell you of things that are entirely new,
things you never heard of before.
For I know so well what traitors you are.
You have been rebels from birth.
9 Yet for my own sake and for the honor of my name,
I will hold back my anger and not wipe you out.
10 I have refined you, but not as silver is refined.
Rather, I have refined you in the furnace of suffering.
11 I will rescue you for my sake—
yes, for my own sake!
I will not let my reputation be tarnished,
and I will not share my glory with idols!

## Freedom from Babylon

12 "Listen to me, O family of Jacob,
Israel my chosen one!
I alone am God,
the First and the Last.
13 It was my hand that laid the foundations of the earth,
my right hand that spread out the heavens above.
When I call out the stars,
they all appear in order."

14 Have any of your idols ever told you this?
Come, all of you, and listen:
The LORD has chosen Cyrus as his ally.
He will use him to put an end to the empire of Babylon
and to destroy the Babylonian* armies.
15 "I have said it: I am calling Cyrus!
I will send him on this errand and will help him succeed.
16 Come closer, and listen to this.
From the beginning I have told you plainly what would happen."

And now the Sovereign LORD and his Spirit
have sent me with this message.
17 This is what the LORD says—
your Redeemer, the Holy One of Israel:

**48:14** Or *Chaldean.*

| | |
|---|---|
| **48:6** | Isa 43:19 |
| **48:8** | Deut 9:7, 24 / Ps 58:3 |
| **48:9** | Ps 103:8-10 |
| **48:10** | 1 Kgs 8:51 / Ezek 22:18-22 |
| **48:11** | Deut 32:26-27 / Ps 106:8 / Isa 42:8 |
| **48:12** | Rev 1:17 |
| **48:13** | Ps 102:25 |
| **48:14** | Jer 50:21-29 |
| **48:15** | Isa 41:2; 45:1-2 |
| **48:16** | Isa 45:19 |
| **48:17** | Ps 32:8 / Isa 41:14 |

---

**48:9-11** There was nothing in the people's actions, attitudes, or accomplishments to compel God to love and to save them. But for his own sake, to show who he is and what he can do, he saved them. God does not save us because we are good but because he loves us and because of his forgiving nature.

**48:10** Do you find it easy to complain when your life becomes complicated or difficult? Why would a loving God allow all kinds of unpleasant experiences to come to his children? This verse shows us plainly that God tests us in the "furnace of suffering." Rather than complain, our response should be to turn to God in faith for the strength to endure and rejoice in our sufferings (see Romans 5:3; James 1:2-4). For without the testing, we would never know what we are capable of doing, nor would we grow. And without the refining, we will not become more pure and more

like Christ. If you are facing adversity or suffering, seek God and his refining work in your life.

**48:14, 15** That the Lord would choose Cyrus as his "ally" must have shocked his audience. How could the Lord choose a pagan king, an enemy? But it was Cyrus whom God would use to free his people from their captivity in Babylon. Cyrus's mission was to set Israel free by conquering Babylon, then to decree that all Jews could return to their homeland. Who but a prophet of God could predict such an inconceivable but true story almost 200 years before it happened?

**48:17, 18** Like a loving parent, God teaches and guides us. We should listen to him because peace and righteousness come to us as we obey his Word. Refusing to pay attention to God's commands invites punishment and threatens that peace and righteousness.

"I am the LORD your God,
who teaches you what is good for you
and leads you along the paths you should follow.

18 Oh, that you had listened to my commands!
Then you would have had peace flowing like a gentle river
and righteousness rolling over you like waves in the sea.

19 Your descendants would have been like the sands along the seashore—
too many to count!
There would have been no need for your destruction,
or for cutting off your family name."

20 Yet even now, be free from your captivity!
Leave Babylon and the Babylonians.*
Sing out this message!
Shout it to the ends of the earth!
The LORD has redeemed his servants,
the people of Israel.*

21 They were not thirsty
when he led them through the desert.
He divided the rock,
and water gushed out for them to drink.

22 "But there is no peace for the wicked,"
says the LORD.

## 2. The future Redeemer

### The LORD's Servant Commissioned

**49** 1 Listen to me, all you in distant lands!
Pay attention, you who are far away!
The LORD called me before my birth;
from within the womb he called me by name.

2 He made my words of judgment as sharp as a sword.
He has hidden me in the shadow of his hand.
I am like a sharp arrow in his quiver.

3 He said to me, "You are my servant, Israel,
and you will bring me glory."

4 I replied, "But my work seems so useless!
I have spent my strength for nothing and to no purpose.
Yet I leave it all in the LORD's hand;
I will trust God for my reward."

5 And now the LORD speaks—
the one who formed me in my mother's womb to be his servant,
who commissioned me to bring Israel back to him.
The LORD has honored me,
and my God has given me strength.

6 He says, "You will do more than restore the people of Israel to me.
I will make you a light to the Gentiles,
and you will bring my salvation to the ends of the earth."

48:20a Or the Chaldeans.   48:20b Hebrew his servant, Jacob. See note on 14:1.

Cross-references:
48:18 Deut 5:29; 32:29; Ps 119:165; Amos 5:24
48:19 Gen 22:17
48:20 Isa 52:9; Jer 31:10
48:21 Ps 78:15-16
49:2 Isa 51:16; Heb 4:12; Rev 1:16
49:5 Isa 12:2
49:6 Ps 37:28; Acts 13:47; 26:23

48:20 Do you see the captives leaving Babylon many years later? No wonder they are shouting with joy, as their ancestors shouted joyfully after they crossed the Red Sea, free from slavery at last! What is holding you captive? Be free! The Lord has redeemed his servants from slavery to sin. When you let him free you from your captivity, you will feel like shouting with joy.

48:22 Many people cry out for comfort, security, and relief, but they haven't taken the first steps to turn away from sin and open the channels to God. They have not repented and trusted in him. If you want true peace, seek God first. Then he will give you his peace.

49:1-7 Before the Servant, the Messiah, was born, God had chosen him to bring the light of the gospel (the message of salvation) to the world (see Acts 13:47). Christ offered salvation to all nations, and his apostles began the missionary movement to take this gospel to the ends of the earth. Missionary work today continues Jesus' great commission (Matthew 28:18-20), taking the light of the gospel to all nations. Do you support evangelism and missionary efforts with your money? Do you have talent or other resources to help spread the message of Christ? God wants you to be involved. How can you help?

7 The LORD, the Redeemer
    and Holy One of Israel,
says to the one who is despised and rejected by the nations,
    to the one who is the servant of rulers:
"Kings will stand at attention when you pass by.
    Princes will also bow low
because of the LORD, the faithful one,
    the Holy One of Israel, who has chosen you."

**49:7**
Ps 22:6-8
Isa 53:3

## Promises of Israel's Restoration

8 This is what the LORD says:

"At just the right time, I will respond to you.*
    On the day of salvation I will help you.
I will protect you and give you to the people
    as my covenant with them.
Through you I will reestablish the land of Israel
    and assign it to its own people again.

**49:8**
Ps 69:13
Isa 26:3; 44:26
2 Cor 6:2

9 I will say to the prisoners, 'Come out in freedom,'
    and to those in darkness, 'Come into the light.'
They will be my sheep, grazing in green pastures
    and on hills that were previously bare.

**49:9**
Isa 42:7
Luke 4:18

10 They will neither hunger nor thirst.
    The searing sun will not reach them anymore.
For the LORD in his mercy will lead them;
    he will lead them beside cool waters.

**49:10**
Ps 23:2
Rev 7:16

11 And I will make my mountains into level paths for them.
    The highways will be raised above the valleys.

**49:11**
Isa 40:4

12 See, my people will return from far away,
    from lands to the north and west,
    and from as far south as Egypt.*"

**49:12**
Isa 43:5-6

13 Sing for joy, O heavens!
    Rejoice, O earth!
    Burst into song, O mountains!
For the LORD has comforted his people
    and will have compassion on them in their suffering.

**49:13**
Isa 54:7-8, 10
Rev 12:12

14 Yet Jerusalem* says, "The LORD has deserted us;
    the Lord has forgotten us."

15 "Never! Can a mother forget her nursing child?
    Can she feel no love for the child she has borne?
But even if that were possible,
    I would not forget you!

16 See, I have written your name on the palms of my hands.
    Always in my mind is a picture of Jerusalem's walls in ruins.

**49:16**
Song 8:6
Isa 62:6

17 Soon your descendants will come back,
    and all who are trying to destroy you will go away.

18 Look around you and see,
    for all your children will come back to you.
As surely as I live," says the LORD,
    "they will be like jewels or bridal ornaments for you to display.

**49:18**
Isa 45:23

19 "Even the most desolate parts of your abandoned land
    will soon be crowded with your people.

**49:19**
Isa 1:7
Zech 10:10

**49:8** Greek version reads *I heard you*. Compare 2 Cor 6:2.  **49:12** As in Dead Sea Scrolls, which read *from the region of Aswan*, which is in southern Egypt. Masoretic Text reads *from the region of Sinim*.  **49:14** Hebrew *Zion*.

**49:14, 15** The people of Israel felt that God had forgotten them in Babylon; but Isaiah pointed out that God would never forget them, as a loving mother would not forget her little child. When we feel that God has forsaken us, we must ask if we have forsaken and forgotten God (see Deuteronomy 31:6).

Your enemies who enslaved you
will be far away.

**49:20**
Isa 54:1-3

20 The generations born in exile will return and say,
'We need more room! It's crowded here!'

**49:21**
Lam 1:1

21 Then you will think to yourself,
'Who has given me all these descendants?
For most of my children were killed,
and the rest were carried away into exile.
I was left here all alone.
Where did all these people come from?
Who bore these children?
Who raised them for me?'"

**49:22**
Isa 11:10, 12; 14:2

22 This is what the Sovereign LORD says:
"See, I will give a signal to the godless nations.
They will carry your little sons back to you in their arms;
they will bring your daughters on their shoulders.

**49:23**
Pss 25:3; 72:9
Isa 60:14, 16

23 Kings and queens will serve you
and care for all your needs.
They will bow to the earth before you
and lick the dust from your feet.
Then you will know that I am the LORD.
Those who trust in me will never be put to shame."

24 Who can snatch the plunder of war from the hands of a warrior?
Who can demand that a tyrant* let his captives go?

**49:25**
Jer 50:33-34

25 But the LORD says,
"The captives of warriors will be released,
and the plunder of tyrants will be retrieved.
For I will fight those who fight you,
and I will save your children.

**49:26**
Isa 14:4
Ezek 39:7

26 I will feed your enemies with their own flesh.
They will be drunk with rivers of their own blood.
All the world will know that I, the LORD,
am your Savior and your Redeemer,
the Mighty One of Israel.*"

**50:1**
Deut 32:30
Isa 59:2
Jer 3:8

# 50

This is what the LORD says:
"Was your mother sent away because I divorced her?
Did I sell you as slaves to my creditors?
No, you were sold because of your sins.
And your mother, too, was taken because of your sins.

**50:2**
Gen 18:14
Exod 14:21
Josh 3:16

2 Why was no one there when I came?
Why didn't anyone answer when I called?
Is it because I have no power to rescue?
No, that is not the reason!
For I can speak to the sea and make it dry up!
I can turn rivers into deserts covered with dying fish.

**50:3**
Rev 6:12

3 I dress the skies in darkness,
covering them with clothes of mourning."

**49:24** As in Dead Sea Scrolls, Syriac version, and Latin Vulgate (also see 49:25); Masoretic Text reads *a righteous person.*   **49:26** Hebrew *of Jacob.* See note on 14:1.

**49:24, 25** God would prove to the world that he is God by doing the impossible—causing warriors to set their captives free; and these warriors would even return the plunder they had taken from the captives! God had done this before at the Exodus and would do it again when the exiles returned to Israel. Never should we doubt that God will fulfill his promises. He will even do the impossible to make them come true.

**50:1, 2** God promised to fight for Israel, but Israel sold itself into sin. Israel had caused its own problems. The people of Israel forgot God and trusted in other countries to help them. God had not rejected Israel, but Israel had rejected God.

### The LORD's Obedient Servant

4 The Sovereign LORD has given me his words of wisdom,
    so that I know how to comfort the weary.
Morning by morning he wakens me
    and opens my understanding to his will.
5 The Sovereign LORD has spoken to me,
    and I have listened.
I have not rebelled or turned away.
6 I offered my back to those who beat me
    and my cheeks to those who pulled out my beard.
I did not hide my face
    from mockery and spitting.

7 Because the Sovereign LORD helps me,
    I will not be disgraced.
Therefore, I have set my face like a stone,
    determined to do his will.
And I know that I will not be put to shame.
8 He who gives me justice is near.
    Who will dare to bring charges against me now?
Where are my accusers?
    Let them appear!
9 See, the Sovereign LORD is on my side!
    Who will declare me guilty?
All my enemies will be destroyed
    like old clothes that have been eaten by moths!

10 Who among you fears the LORD
    and obeys his servant?
If you are walking in darkness,
    without a ray of light,
trust in the LORD
    and rely on your God.
11 But watch out, you who live in your own light
    and warm yourselves by your own fires.
This is the reward you will receive from me:
    You will soon fall down in great torment.

### A Call to Trust the LORD

**51** 1 "Listen to me, all who hope for deliverance—
    all who seek the LORD!
Consider the rock from which you were cut,
    the quarry from which you were mined.
2 Yes, think about Abraham, your ancestor,
    and Sarah, who gave birth to your nation.
Abraham was only one man when I called him.
    But when I blessed him, he became a great nation."

3 The LORD will comfort Israel* again
    and have pity on her ruins.
Her desert will blossom like Eden,
    her barren wilderness like the garden of the LORD.
Joy and gladness will be found there.
    Songs of thanksgiving will fill the air.

**Cross-references (margin):**

50:4 Ps 5:3; Jer 31:25
50:5 Matt 26:39; John 8:29; 14:31; Acts 26:19
50:6 Matt 26:67; Mark 15:19; Luke 22:63
50:7 Ezek 3:8-9
50:8 Rom 8:33-34
50:10 Eph 5:8
51:1 Gen 17:15-17
51:2 Gen 12:1; Heb 11:11
51:3 Gen 2:8; Isa 41:19

**51:3** Hebrew *Zion;* also in 51:16.

---

**50:10, 11** If we walk by our own light and reject God's, we become self-sufficient, and the result of self-sufficiency is torment. When we place confidence in our own intelligence, appearance, or accomplishments instead of in God, we risk torment later when these strengths fade.
**51:1, 2** The faithful remnant may have felt alone because they were few. But God reminded them of their ancestors, the source of their spiritual heritage—Abraham and Sarah. Abraham was only one person, but much came from his faithfulness. If the faithful few would remain faithful, even more could come from them. If we Christians, even a faithful few, remain faithful, think what God can do through us!

**51:4**
Ps 78:1
Isa 42:4

4 "Listen to me, my people.
　Hear me, Israel,
for my law will be proclaimed,
　and my justice will become a light to the nations.

**51:5**
Isa 46:13

5 My mercy and justice are coming soon.
　My salvation is on the way.
　My strong arm will bring justice to the nations.
All distant lands will look to me
　and wait in hope for my powerful arm.

**51:6**
Ps 102:25-26
Matt 24:35
2 Pet 3:10

6 Look up to the skies above,
　and gaze down on the earth below.
For the skies will disappear like smoke,
　and the earth will wear out like a piece of clothing.
The people of the earth will die like flies,
　but my salvation lasts forever.
　My righteous rule will never end!

**51:7**
Ps 37:30-31
Matt 5:11
Acts 5:40-41

7 "Listen to me, you who know right from wrong,
　you who cherish my law in your hearts.
Do not be afraid of people's scorn,
　nor fear their insults.

**51:8**
Isa 14:11

8 For the moth will devour them as it devours clothing.
　The worm will eat at them as it eats wool.
But my righteousness will last forever.
　My salvation will continue from generation to generation."

**51:9**
Deut 4:34

9 Wake up, wake up, O LORD! Clothe yourself with strength!
　Flex your mighty right arm!
Rouse yourself as in the days of old
　when you slew Egypt, the dragon of the Nile.*

**51:10**
Exod 14:21-22
Isa 63:11-12

10 Are you not the same today,
　the one who dried up the sea,
making a path of escape through the depths
　so that your people could cross over?

**51:11**
Isa 61:7
Rev 7:17; 21:4;
22:3

11 Those who have been ransomed by the LORD will return.
　They will enter Jerusalem* singing,
　crowned with everlasting joy.
Sorrow and mourning will disappear,
　and they will be filled with joy and gladness.

**51:12**
Ps 118:6
1 Pet 1:24

12 "I, yes I, am the one who comforts you.
　So why are you afraid of mere humans,
　who wither like the grass and disappear?

**51:13**
Deut 8:11
Job 9:8

13 Yet you have forgotten the LORD, your Creator,
　the one who stretched out the sky like a canopy
　and laid the foundations of the earth.
Will you remain in constant dread of human oppressors?
　Will you continue to fear the anger of your enemies?

**51:9** Hebrew *You slew Rahab; you pierced the dragon.* Rahab is the name of a mythical sea monster that represents chaos in ancient literature. The name is used here as a poetic name for Egypt. **51:11** Hebrew *Zion.*

---

**51:7** Isaiah encouraged those who follow God's laws. He gave them hope when they faced people's reproach or insults because of their faith. We need not fear when people insult us for our faith because God is with us and truth will prevail. If people make fun of you or dislike you because you believe in God, remember that they are not against you personally but against God. God will deal with them; you should concentrate on loving and obeying him.

**51:9, 10** God had performed many powerful miracles in founding Israel, perhaps none more exciting than making a dry path through the middle of the Red Sea (see Exodus 14). Our God is the same God who made that road through the sea. His methods may change, but his love and care do not.

**51:12-16** God's people feared Babylon but not God. They had reason to fear Babylon for the harm it wanted to do, but they should also have realized that God's power is much greater than Babylon's. Babylon was interested in making the people captives; God was interested in setting them free. The people had misplaced their fear and their love. Jerusalem should have feared God's power and loved his mercy.

Where is their fury and anger now?
It is gone!
14 Soon all you captives will be released!
Imprisonment, starvation, and death will not be your fate!
15 For I am the LORD your God,
who stirs up the sea, causing its waves to roar.
My name is the LORD of Heaven's Armies.
16 And I have put my words in your mouth
and hidden you safely in my hand.
I stretched out* the sky like a canopy
and laid the foundations of the earth.
I am the one who says to Israel,
'You are my people!'"

17 Wake up, wake up, O Jerusalem!
You have drunk the cup of the LORD's fury.
You have drunk the cup of terror,
tipping out its last drops.
18 Not one of your children is left alive
to take your hand and guide you.
19 These two calamities have fallen on you:
desolation and destruction, famine and war.
And who is left to sympathize with you?
Who is left to comfort you?*
20 For your children have fainted and lie in the streets,
helpless as antelopes caught in a net.
The LORD has poured out his fury;
God has rebuked them.

21 But now listen to this, you afflicted ones
who sit in a drunken stupor,
though not from drinking wine.
22 This is what the Sovereign LORD,
your God and Defender, says:
"See, I have taken the terrible cup from your hands.
You will drink no more of my fury.
23 Instead, I will hand that cup to your tormentors,
those who said, 'We will trample you into the dust
and walk on your backs.'"

### Deliverance for Jerusalem

**52** 1 Wake up, wake up, O Zion!
Clothe yourself with strength.
Put on your beautiful clothes, O holy city of Jerusalem,
for unclean and godless people will enter your gates no longer.
2 Rise from the dust, O Jerusalem.
Sit in a place of honor.
Remove the chains of slavery from your neck,
O captive daughter of Zion.
3 For this is what the LORD says:
"When I sold you into exile,
I received no payment.
Now I can redeem you
without having to pay for you."

Cross-references: 51:14 Isa 49:10; 51:15 Ps 107:25; 51:16 Exod 33:22, Deut 18:18; 51:17 Jer 25:15; 51:18 Ps 142:4; 51:20 Isa 66:15, Jer 14:16; 51:21 Isa 29:9; 51:22 Jer 50:34; 51:23 Jer 25:15-17, 26, 28; 52:1 Exod 28:2, 40, Neh 11:1, Isa 48:2; 61:10, Rev 21:2, 27; 52:3 Ps 44:12, Isa 63:4

51:16 As in Syriac version (see also 51:13); Hebrew reads *planted.* 51:19 As in Dead Sea Scrolls and Greek, Latin, and Syriac versions; Masoretic Text reads *How can I comfort you?*

51:17–52:10 Jerusalem was God's holy city, the city with God's Temple. But the people of Judah experienced ruin instead of prosperity, destruction instead of liberty. Because of their sins, the people suffered. But God promised to restore Jerusalem as a holy city where sinners cannot enter. God reigns. Put your entire faith and confidence in his ability to control the course of history—and your life.

**52:5**
Ezek 36:20, 23
†Rom 2:24

4This is what the Sovereign LORD says: "Long ago my people chose to live in Egypt. Now they are oppressed by Assyria. 5What is this?" asks the LORD. "Why are my people enslaved again? Those who rule them shout in exultation. My name is blasphemed all day long.* 6But I will reveal my name to my people, and they will come to know its power. Then at last they will recognize that I am the one who speaks to them."

**52:7**
Ps 93:1
†Rom 10:15

7 How beautiful on the mountains
　　are the feet of the messenger who brings good news,
　　the good news of peace and salvation,
　　　the news that the God of Israel* reigns!

**52:8**
Isa 62:6

8 The watchmen shout and sing with joy,
　　for before their very eyes
　　　they see the LORD returning to Jerusalem.*

**52:9**
Ps 98:4
Isa 61:4

9 Let the ruins of Jerusalem break into joyful song,
　　for the LORD has comforted his people.
　　He has redeemed Jerusalem.

**52:10**
Ps 98:1-3
Luke 3:6

10 The LORD has demonstrated his holy power
　　before the eyes of all the nations.
　　All the ends of the earth will see
　　　the victory of our God.

**52:11**
Isa 1:16
†2 Cor 6:17
2 Tim 2:19

11 Get out! Get out and leave your captivity,
　　where everything you touch is unclean.
　　Get out of there and purify yourselves,
　　　you who carry home the sacred objects of the LORD.

**52:12**
Exod 12:11, 33;
14:19-20
Isa 26:7

12 You will not leave in a hurry,
　　running for your lives.
　　For the LORD will go ahead of you;
　　　yes, the God of Israel will protect you from behind.

### The LORD's Suffering Servant

**52:13**
Phil 2:9

13 See, my servant will prosper;
　　he will be highly exalted.

**52:14**
Ps 22:6-7

14 But many were amazed when they saw him.*
　　His face was so disfigured he seemed hardly human,
　　and from his appearance, one would scarcely know he was a man.

**52:15**
†Rom 15:21

15 And he will startle* many nations.
　　Kings will stand speechless in his presence.
　　For they will see what they had not been told;
　　　they will understand what they had not heard about.*

**53:1**
†Rom 10:16

# 53
1 Who has believed our message?
　　To whom has the LORD revealed his powerful arm?
2 My servant grew up in the LORD's presence like a tender green shoot,
　　like a root in dry ground.

**52:5** Greek version reads *The Gentiles continually blaspheme my name because of you.* Compare Rom 2:24.
**52:7** Hebrew *of Zion.* **52:8** Hebrew *to Zion.* **52:14** As in Syriac version; Hebrew reads *you.* **52:15a** Or *cleanse.*
**52:15b** Greek version reads *Those who have never been told about him will see, / and those who have never heard of him will understand.* Compare Rom 15:21.

---

**52:7** God says that the feet of those who bring good news are "beautiful." It is a wonderful privilege to be able to share God's Good News with others, his news of redemption, salvation, and peace. To whom do you need to give the Good News?

**52:12** The people did not have to leave in fearful haste because Cyrus, God's anointed (45:1), decreed that the Jewish exiles could return safely to Jerusalem (Ezra 1:1-4). They had the king's approval, his guaranteed protection. More important, the Lord would go ahead to point the way and be behind to protect them.

**52:13** The *servant*, as the term is used here, is the Messiah, our Lord Jesus. He would be highly exalted because of his sacrifice, described in chapter 53.

**52:14, 15** This servant, Christ, would be "disfigured"; but

through his suffering, he would cleanse the nations (Hebrews 10:14; 1 Peter 1:2).

**53:1ff** This chapter continues to speak of the Messiah, Jesus, who would suffer for the sins of all people. Such a prophecy is astounding! Who would believe that God would choose to save the world through a humble, suffering servant rather than a glorious king? The idea is contrary to human pride and worldly thinking. But God often works in ways we don't expect. The Messiah's strength is shown by humility, suffering, and mercy.

**53:2** There was nothing beautiful or majestic in the physical appearance of this servant. Israel would miscalculate the servant's importance—they would consider him an ordinary man. But even though Jesus would not attract a large following based on his

There was nothing beautiful or majestic about his appearance,
　　nothing to attract us to him.
³ He was despised and rejected—
　　a man of sorrows, acquainted with deepest grief.
　We turned our backs on him and looked the other way.
　　He was despised, and we did not care.

⁴ Yet it was our weaknesses he carried;
　　it was our sorrows* that weighed him down.
　And we thought his troubles were a punishment from God,
　　a punishment for his own sins!

⁵ But he was pierced for our rebellion,
　　crushed for our sins.
　He was beaten so we could be whole.
　　He was whipped so we could be healed.
⁶ All of us, like sheep, have strayed away.
　　We have left God's paths to follow our own.
　Yet the LORD laid on him
　　the sins of us all.

⁷ He was oppressed and treated harshly,
　　yet he never said a word.
　He was led like a lamb to the slaughter.
　　And as a sheep is silent before the shearers,
　　he did not open his mouth.

⁸ Unjustly condemned,
　　he was led away.*
　No one cared that he died without descendants,
　　that his life was cut short in midstream.*
　But he was struck down
　　for the rebellion of my people.

⁹ He had done no wrong
　　and had never deceived anyone.
　But he was buried like a criminal;
　　he was put in a rich man's grave.

¹⁰ But it was the LORD's good plan to crush him
　　and cause him grief.
　Yet when his life is made an offering for sin,
　　he will have many descendants.
　He will enjoy a long life,
　　and the LORD's good plan will prosper in his hands.
¹¹ When he sees all that is accomplished by his anguish,
　　he will be satisfied.

**53:3**
Luke 18:31-33
John 1:10-11

**53:4**
†Matt 8:17
1 Pet 2:24

**53:5**
Rom 4:25
1 Cor 15:3
Heb 5:8; 9:28
1 Pet 2:24-25

**53:7**
Matt 27:12-14
Luke 23:9

**53:8**
†Acts 8:32-33

**53:9**
Matt 27:57-60
†1 Pet 2:22
Rev 14:5

**53:10**
John 1:29

**53:11**
John 10:14-18
Rom 5:18-19

**53:4** Or *Yet it was our sicknesses he carried; / it was our diseases.*  **53:8a** Greek version reads *He was humiliated and received no justice.* Compare Acts 8:33.  **53:8b** Or *As for his contemporaries, / who cared that his life was cut short in midstream?* Greek version reads *Who can speak of his descendants? / For his life was taken from the earth.* Compare Acts 8:33.

---

physical appearance, he would bring salvation and healing. Many people miscalculate the importance of Jesus' life and work, and they need faithful Christians to point out his extraordinary nature.

**53:4, 5** How could an Old Testament person understand the idea of Christ dying for our sins—actually bearing the punishment that we deserved? The sacrifices suggested this idea, but it is one thing to kill a lamb, and something quite different to think of God's chosen servant as that Lamb. But God was pulling aside the curtain of time to let the people of Isaiah's day look ahead to the suffering of the future Messiah and the resulting forgiveness made available to all people.

**53:6** Isaiah speaks of Israel straying from God and compares them to wandering sheep. Yet God would send the Messiah to bring them back into the fold. We have the hindsight to see and

know the identity of the promised Messiah, who has come and died for our sins. But if we know all that Jesus did and still reject him, our sin is much greater than that of the ancient Israelites, who could not see what we have seen. Have you given your life to Jesus Christ, the "good shepherd" (John 10:11-16), or are you still going your own way like a wandering sheep?

**53:7-12** In the Old Testament, people offered animals as sacrifices for their sins. Here, the sinless servant of the Lord offers himself for our sins. He is the Lamb (53:7) offered for the sins of all people (John 1:29; Revelation 5:6-14). The Messiah suffered for our sake, bearing our sins to make us acceptable to God. What can we say to such love? How will we respond to him?

**53:11** This verse tells of the enormous family of believers who will become right with God, not by their own works, but by the

And because of his experience,
   my righteous servant will make it possible
for many to be counted righteous,
   for he will bear all their sins.
<sup></sup>12 I will give him the honors of a victorious soldier,
   because he exposed himself to death.
He was counted among the rebels.
   He bore the sins of many and interceded for rebels.

**53:12**
Matt 26:38-39, 42
†Mark 15:27
†Luke 22:37
2 Cor 5:21
Phil 2:9-11
1 Pet 2:24

### Future Glory for Jerusalem

## 54

**54:1**
Isa 62:4
†Gal 4:27

1 "Sing, O childless woman,
   you who have never given birth!
Break into loud and joyful song, O Jerusalem,
   you who have never been in labor.
For the desolate woman now has more children
   than the woman who lives with her husband,"
says the LORD.
2 "Enlarge your house; build an addition.
   Spread out your home, and spare no expense!

**54:3**
Gen 28:14
Isa 14:1-2

3 For you will soon be bursting at the seams.
   Your descendants will occupy other nations
   and resettle the ruined cities.

4 "Fear not; you will no longer live in shame.
   Don't be afraid; there is no more disgrace for you.
You will no longer remember the shame of your youth
   and the sorrows of widowhood.

**54:5**
Hos 2:19

5 For your Creator will be your husband;
   the LORD of Heaven's Armies is his name!
He is your Redeemer, the Holy One of Israel,
   the God of all the earth.

**54:6**
Isa 62:4

6 For the LORD has called you back from your grief—
   as though you were a young wife abandoned by her husband,"
says your God.

**54:7**
Isa 11:12
**54:8**
Isa 49:10, 13;
60:10

7 "For a brief moment I abandoned you,
   but with great compassion I will take you back.
8 In a burst of anger I turned my face away for a little while.
   But with everlasting love I will have compassion on you,"
says the LORD, your Redeemer.

**54:9**
Gen 9:9-11
Ezek 39:29

9 "Just as I swore in the time of Noah
   that I would never again let a flood cover the earth,
so now I swear
   that I will never again be angry and punish you.

**54:10**
2 Sam 23:5
Pss 89:34;
102:25-26

10 For the mountains may move
   and the hills disappear,
but even then my faithful love for you will remain.
   My covenant of blessing will never be broken,"
says the LORD, who has mercy on you.

---

Messiah's great work on the cross. They are justified because they have claimed Christ, the righteous servant, as their Savior and Lord (see Romans 10:9; 2 Corinthians 5:21). Their life of sin is stripped away, and they are clothed with Christ's goodness (Ephesians 4:22-24).

**54:1** To be childless at that time was a woman's great shame, a disgrace. Families depended on children for survival, especially when the parents became elderly. Israel (Jerusalem) was unfruitful, like a childless woman, but God would permit her to have many children and change her mourning into singing.

**54:6-8** God said that he had abandoned Israel for a brief moment, so the nation was like a young wife rejected by her husband. But

God still called Israel his own. The God we serve is holy, and he cannot tolerate sin. When his people blatantly sinned, God in his anger chose to punish them. Sin separates us from God and brings us pain and suffering. But if we confess our sin and repent, then God will forgive us. Have you ever been separated from a loved one and then experienced joy when that person returned? That is like the joy God experiences when you repent and return to him.

**54:9-13** God made a covenant with Noah that he has never broken (Genesis 9:8-17). Likewise, God made a covenant of peace with the people of Israel that the time would come when he would stop pouring out his anger on them; he would teach their citizens and give them prosperity.

11 "O storm-battered city,
    troubled and desolate!
I will rebuild you with precious jewels
    and make your foundations from lapis lazuli.
12 I will make your towers of sparkling rubies,
    your gates of shining gems,
    and your walls of precious stones.
13 I will teach all your children,
    and they will enjoy great peace.
14 You will be secure under a government that is just and fair.
    Your enemies will stay far away.
You will live in peace,
    and terror will not come near.
15 If any nation comes to fight you,
    it is not because I sent them.
Whoever attacks you will go down in defeat.

16 "I have created the blacksmith
    who fans the coals beneath the forge
and makes the weapons of destruction.
    And I have created the armies that destroy.
17 But in that coming day
    no weapon turned against you will succeed.
You will silence every voice
    raised up to accuse you.
These benefits are enjoyed by the servants of the LORD;
    their vindication will come from me.
    I, the LORD, have spoken!

### Invitation to the LORD's Salvation

**55** 1 "Is anyone thirsty?
    Come and drink—
even if you have no money!
Come, take your choice of wine or milk—
    it's all free!
2 Why spend your money on food that does not give you strength?
    Why pay for food that does you no good?
Listen to me, and you will eat what is good.
    You will enjoy the finest food.

3 "Come to me with your ears wide open.
    Listen, and you will find life.
I will make an everlasting covenant with you.
    I will give you all the unfailing love I promised to David.
4 See how I used him to display my power among the peoples.
    I made him a leader among the nations.
5 You also will command nations you do not know,
    and peoples unknown to you will come running to obey,
because I, the LORD your God,
    the Holy One of Israel, have made you glorious."

6 Seek the LORD while you can find him.
    Call on him now while he is near.

**54:11**
Isa 28:16

**54:13**
Isa 66:12
Jer 31:34
†John 6:45
**54:14**
Isa 9:4, 7

**54:15**
Isa 41:11-16

**54:17**
Isa 29:8

**55:1**
Lam 5:4
Matt 10:8
John 4:14; 7:37
Rev 3:18; 21:6

**55:2**
Ps 22:26
Eccl 6:2

**55:3**
†Acts 13:34

**55:5**
Zech 8:22

**55:6**
Ps 32:6
2 Cor 6:1-2

---

**55:1-6** Food costs money, lasts only a short time, and meets only physical needs. But God offers us *free* nourishment that feeds our soul. How do we get it? We are to come (55:1), listen (55:2), seek, and call on God (55:6). God's salvation is freely offered, but to nourish our souls we must eagerly receive it. We will starve spiritually without this food as surely as we will starve physically without our daily bread.

**55:3** God's covenant with David promised a permanent homeland for the Israelites, no threat from pagan nations, and no wars (2 Samuel 7:10, 11). But Israel did not fulfill its part of the covenant to obey God and stay away from idols. Even so, God was ready to renew his covenant again. He is a forgiving God!

**55:6** Isaiah tells us to call on the Lord while he is near. God is not planning to move away from us, but we often move far

**55:7**
Isa 1:16; 44:22

7 Let the wicked change their ways
   and banish the very thought of doing wrong.
Let them turn to the LORD that he may have mercy on them.
   Yes, turn to our God, for he will forgive generously.

**55:8**
Isa 65:2

8 "My thoughts are nothing like your thoughts," says the LORD.
   "And my ways are far beyond anything you could imagine.

**55:9**
Ps 103:11

9 For just as the heavens are higher than the earth,
   so my ways are higher than your ways
   and my thoughts higher than your thoughts.

**55:10**
2 Cor 9:10

10 "The rain and snow come down from the heavens
   and stay on the ground to water the earth.
They cause the grain to grow,
   producing seed for the farmer
   and bread for the hungry.

**55:11**
Isa 46:10

11 It is the same with my word.
   I send it out, and it always produces fruit.
It will accomplish all I want it to,
   and it will prosper everywhere I send it.

**55:12**
1 Chr 16:33
Jer 29:11

12 You will live in joy and peace.
   The mountains and hills will burst into song,
   and the trees of the field will clap their hands!

**55:13**
Jer 33:9

13 Where once there were thorns, cypress trees will grow.
   Where nettles grew, myrtles will sprout up.
These events will bring great honor to the LORD's name;
   they will be an everlasting sign of his power and love."

### Blessings for All Nations

**56:1**
Ps 85:9
Isa 1:17

**56** This is what the LORD says:
   "Be just and fair to all.
Do what is right and good,
   for I am coming soon to rescue you
   and to display my righteousness among you.

**56:2**
Exod 31:13-17
Ps 119:1-2
Ezek 20:12, 20

2 Blessed are all those
   who are careful to do this.
Blessed are those who honor my Sabbath days of rest
   and keep themselves from doing wrong.

**56:3**
Acts 8:27, 37

3 "Don't let foreigners who commit themselves to the LORD say,
   'The LORD will never let me be part of his people.'
And don't let the eunuchs say,
   'I'm a dried-up tree with no children and no future.'
4 For this is what the LORD says:
   I will bless those eunuchs
   who keep my Sabbath days holy
   and who choose to do what pleases me
   and commit their lives to me.

---

from him or erect barriers of sin between us. Don't wait until you have drifted far away from God to seek him. Turning to him may be far more difficult later in life. Or God may come to judge the earth before you decide to turn to him. Seek God now, while you can, before it is too late.

**55:8, 9** The people of Israel were foolish to act as if they knew what God was thinking and planning. His knowledge and wisdom are far greater than any human's. We are foolish to try to fit God into our mold—to make his plans and purposes conform to ours. Instead, we must strive to fit into *his* plans.

**56:2** God commanded his people to rest and honor him on the Sabbath (Exodus 20:8-11). He wants us to serve him every day, but he wants us to make one day special when we rest and focus

our thoughts on him. For the Israelites, this special day was the Sabbath (Saturday). Some Christians set Saturday aside as this special day, but many accept Sunday (the day of the week that Jesus rose from the dead) as the "Lord's Day," a day of rest and honor to God. Do you make Sunday special?

**56:3** Isaiah clearly proclaims the radical message that God's blessings are for *all* people, even Gentiles and eunuchs, who were often excluded from worship and not even considered citizens in Israel. Whatever your race, social position, work, or financial situation, God's blessings are as much for you as for anyone else. No one must exclude in any way those God chooses to bless.

5 I will give them—within the walls of my house—
   a memorial and a name
   far greater than sons and daughters could give.
For the name I give them is an everlasting one.
   It will never disappear!

56:5
Isa 2:2-3;
26:1; 62:2

6 "I will also bless the foreigners who commit themselves to the LORD,
   who serve him and love his name,
who worship him and do not desecrate the Sabbath day of rest,
   and who hold fast to my covenant.

56:6
Isa 60:10; 61:5

7 I will bring them to my holy mountain of Jerusalem
   and will fill them with joy in my house of prayer.
I will accept their burnt offerings and sacrifices,
   because my Temple will be called a house of prayer for all nations.
8 For the Sovereign LORD,
   who brings back the outcasts of Israel, says:
I will bring others, too,
   besides my people Israel."

56:7
Isa 65:25
Mic 4:1-2
†Matt 21:13
†Mark 11:17
†Luke 19:46
Rom 12:1
Heb 13:15
56:8
John 10:16

## Sinful Leaders Condemned

9 Come, wild animals of the field!
   Come, wild animals of the forest!
   Come and devour my people!

56:9
Jer 12:9

10 For the leaders of my people—
    the LORD's watchmen, his shepherds—
    are blind and ignorant.
They are like silent watchdogs
   that give no warning when danger comes.
They love to lie around, sleeping and dreaming.

56:10
Jer 14:13-14
Ezek 3:17

11    Like greedy dogs, they are never satisfied.
They are ignorant shepherds,
   all following their own path
   and intent on personal gain.

56:11
Jer 22:17
Mic 3:5, 11

12 "Come," they say, "let's get some wine and have a party.
   Let's all get drunk.
Then tomorrow we'll do it again
   and have an even bigger party!"

56:12
Luke 12:19-20

# 57

1 Good people pass away;
   the godly often die before their time.
But no one seems to care or wonder why.
No one seems to understand
   that God is protecting them from the evil to come.
2 For those who follow godly paths
   will rest in peace when they die.

57:1
2 Kgs 22:19-20
Ps 12:1

## Idolatrous Worship Condemned

3 "But you—come here, you witches' children,
   you offspring of adulterers and prostitutes!
4 Whom do you mock,
   making faces and sticking out your tongues?
   You children of sinners and liars!
5 You worship your idols with great passion
   beneath the oaks and under every green tree.

57:3
Matt 16:4

57:5
Ps 106:37-38
Jer 2:20; 7:31

---

56:7 Jesus quoted from this verse when he threw the money changers out of the Temple (Mark 11:17). See the note on Mark 11:15-17.

56:9-11 The "watchmen" were the nation's leaders. The leaders of Israel were blind to every danger and thus did not warn when dan-

ger was coming. Apathetic about their people's needs, they were more concerned about satisfying their own greed. Leadership's special privileges can cause leaders to either sacrifice for the good of their people or to sacrifice their people for their own greed. If you are in a leadership position, use it for the good of your people.

You sacrifice your children down in the valleys,
among the jagged rocks in the cliffs.

**57:6**
Jer 7:18
Hab 2:19

6 Your gods are the smooth stones in the valleys.
You worship them with liquid offerings and grain offerings.
They, not I, are your inheritance.
Do you think all this makes me happy?

**57:7**
Ezek 16:16, 28

7 You have committed adultery on every high mountain.
There you have worshiped idols
and have been unfaithful to me.

**57:8**
Ezek 23:18

8 You have put pagan symbols
on your doorposts and behind your doors.
You have left me
and climbed into bed with these detestable gods.
You have committed yourselves to them.
You love to look at their naked bodies.

**57:9**
Ezek 23:16, 40

9 You have given olive oil to Molech*
with many gifts of perfume.
You have traveled far,
even into the world of the dead,*
to find new gods to love.

**57:10**
Jer 2:25

10 You grew weary in your search,
but you never gave up.
Desire gave you renewed strength,
and you did not grow weary.

**57:11**
Ps 50:21
Prov 29:25
Jer 2:32

11 "Are you afraid of these idols?
Do they terrify you?
Is that why you have lied to me
and forgotten me and my words?
Is it because of my long silence
that you no longer fear me?

**57:12**
Mic 3:1-4

12 Now I will expose your so-called good deeds.
None of them will help you.

**57:13**
Ps 37:3, 9
Jer 30:14

13 Let's see if your idols can save you
when you cry to them for help.
Why, a puff of wind can knock them down!
If you just breathe on them, they fall over!
But whoever trusts in me will inherit the land
and possess my holy mountain."

### God Forgives the Repentant

**57:14**
Isa 62:10

14 God says, "Rebuild the road!
Clear away the rocks and stones
so my people can return from captivity."

**57:15**
Deut 33:27
Ps 34:18

15 The high and lofty one who lives in eternity,
the Holy One, says this:
"I live in the high and holy place
with those whose spirits are contrite and humble.

**57:9a** Or *to the king.*   **57:9b** Hebrew *into Sheol.*

---

**57:7, 8** Marriage is an exclusive relationship in which a man and a woman become one. Adultery breaks this beautiful bond of unity. When the people turned from God and gave their love to idols, God said they were committing spiritual adultery—breaking their exclusive commitment to God. How could people give their love to worthless wood and stone idols instead of to the God who made them and loved them so very much?

**57:9** Molech was an Ammonite god whose worship included child sacrifice.

**57:12** God says that he will expose their good deeds for what they really were—mere pretensions of doing good. Isaiah warned

these people that their good deeds would not save them any more than their weak, worthless idols. We cannot gain our salvation through good works because our best works are not good enough to outweigh our sins. Salvation is a gift from God, received only through faith in Christ, not good works (Ephesians 2:8, 9).

**57:14-21** Verses 1-13 speak of pride and lust; verses 14-21 tell how God relates to those who are humble and repentant ("contrite"). The high and holy God came down to our level to save us because it is impossible for us to go up to his level to save ourselves (see 2 Chronicles 6:18; Psalm 51:1-7; Philippians 2).

I restore the crushed spirit of the humble
    and revive the courage of those with repentant hearts.
16 For I will not fight against you forever;
    I will not always be angry.
If I were, all people would pass away—
    all the souls I have made.
17 I was angry,
    so I punished these greedy people.
I withdrew from them,
    but they kept going on their own stubborn way.
18 I have seen what they do,
    but I will heal them anyway!
I will lead them.
I will comfort those who mourn,
19     bringing words of praise to their lips.
May they have abundant peace, both near and far,"
    says the LORD, who heals them.
20 "But those who still reject me are like the restless sea,
    which is never still
    but continually churns up mud and dirt.
21 There is no peace for the wicked,"
    says my God.

### True and False Worship

**58** ¹ "Shout with the voice of a trumpet blast.
    Shout aloud! Don't be timid.
Tell my people Israel* of their sins!
2     Yet they act so pious!
They come to the Temple every day
    and seem delighted to learn all about me.
They act like a righteous nation
    that would never abandon the laws of its God.
They ask me to take action on their behalf,
    pretending they want to be near me.
3 'We have fasted before you!' they say.
    'Why aren't you impressed?
We have been very hard on ourselves,
    and you don't even notice it!'

"I will tell you why!" I respond.
    "It's because you are fasting to please yourselves.
Even while you fast,
    you keep oppressing your workers.
4 What good is fasting
    when you keep on fighting and quarreling?
This kind of fasting
    will never get you anywhere with me.
5 You humble yourselves
    by going through the motions of penance,
bowing your heads
    like reeds bending in the wind.
You dress in burlap
    and cover yourselves with ashes.
Is this what you call fasting?
    Do you really think this will please the LORD?

**58:1** Hebrew *Jacob*. See note on 14:1.

**Cross-references (right margin):**

57:16
Mic 7:18

57:19
Acts 2:39
Eph 2:17
Heb 13:15
57:20
Job 18:5-14

57:21
Isa 48:22

58:2
Isa 29:13
Jer 7:9-10
Titus 1:16

58:3
Zech 7:5-6
Luke 18:12

58:4
1 Kgs 21:9-10

**58:1ff** True worship was more than religious ritual, going to the Temple every day, fasting, and listening to Scripture readings. These people missed the point of a living, vital relationship with God. He doesn't want us to act pious when we have unforgiven

58:6
Neh 5:10-12

6 "No, this is the kind of fasting I want:
Free those who are wrongly imprisoned;
lighten the burden of those who work for you.
Let the oppressed go free,
and remove the chains that bind people.

58:7
Deut 22:1-4
Ezek 18:7, 16
Matt 25:35
Luke 3:11
Heb 13:2

7 Share your food with the hungry,
and give shelter to the homeless.
Give clothes to those who need them,
and do not hide from relatives who need your help.

58:8
Ps 85:13
Jer 30:17

8 "Then your salvation will come like the dawn,
and your wounds will quickly heal.
Your godliness will lead you forward,
and the glory of the LORD will protect you from behind.
9 Then when you call, the LORD will answer.
'Yes, I am here,' he will quickly reply.

"Remove the heavy yoke of oppression.
Stop pointing your finger and spreading vicious rumors!

58:10
Deut 15:7

10 Feed the hungry,
and help those in trouble.
Then your light will shine out from the darkness,
and the darkness around you will be as bright as noon.

58:11
Ps 107:9
Song 4:15
John 4:14; 7:37-38

11 The LORD will guide you continually,
giving you water when you are dry
and restoring your strength.
You will be like a well-watered garden,
like an ever-flowing spring.

58:12
Ezek 36:10
Amos 9:11

12 Some of you will rebuild the deserted ruins of your cities.
Then you will be known as a rebuilder of walls
and a restorer of homes.

58:13
Ps 84:2, 10
Jer 17:21-27

13 "Keep the Sabbath day holy.
Don't pursue your own interests on that day,
but enjoy the Sabbath
and speak of it with delight as the LORD's holy day.
Honor the Sabbath in everything you do on that day,
and don't follow your own desires or talk idly.

58:14
Deut 32:13

14 Then the LORD will be your delight.
I will give you great honor
and satisfy you with the inheritance I promised to your ancestor Jacob.
I, the LORD, have spoken!"

59:1
Jer 32:17

59:2
Isa 1:15
Ezek 8:18

## Warnings against Sin

**59** 1 Listen! The LORD's arm is not too weak to save you,
nor is his ear too deaf to hear you call.
2 It's your sins that have cut you off from God.

---

sin in our heart and continue our sinful lifestyle. More important even than correct worship and doctrine is genuine compassion for the oppressed, the poor, and the helpless.

**58:6-12** We cannot be saved without faith in Christ, but our faith lacks sincerity if it doesn't reach out to others. Fasting can be beneficial spiritually and physically, but at its best fasting helps only the person doing it. God says he wants our fasting to go beyond our own personal growth to acts of kindness, charity, justice, and generosity. This truly is pleasing to God.

**58:13, 14** The day of rest should be observed and regarded not only because Sabbath-keeping is a commandment but also because it is best for us and it honors God. Keeping the Sabbath shows proper respect to God, our Creator, who also rested on the seventh day (Genesis 2:3). It also unifies our family and sets prior-

ities for them. Our day of rest refreshes us spiritually and physically—providing time when we can gather together for worship and reflect on God without the stress of our everyday activities.

**59:1-14** Sin offends our holy God and separates us from him. Because God is holy, he cannot ignore, excuse, or tolerate sin as though it didn't matter. Sin cuts people off from him, forming a wall to isolate God from the people he loves. No wonder this long list of wretched sins makes God angry and forces him to look the other way. People who die with their life of sin unforgiven separate themselves eternally from God. God wants them to live with him forever, but he cannot take them into his holy presence unless their sin is removed. Have you confessed your sin to God, allowing him to remove it? The Lord can save you if you turn to him.

Because of your sins, he has turned away
and will not listen anymore.

3 Your hands are the hands of murderers,
and your fingers are filthy with sin.
Your lips are full of lies,
and your mouth spews corruption.

4 No one cares about being fair and honest.
The people's lawsuits are based on lies.
They conceive evil deeds
and then give birth to sin.

5 They hatch deadly snakes
and weave spiders' webs.
Whoever falls into their webs will die,
and there's danger even in getting near them.

6 Their webs can't be made into clothing,
and nothing they do is productive.
All their activity is filled with sin,
and violence is their trademark.

7 Their feet run to do evil,
and they rush to commit murder.
They think only about sinning.
Misery and destruction always follow them.

8 They don't know where to find peace
or what it means to be just and good.
They have mapped out crooked roads,
and no one who follows them knows a moment's peace.

9 So there is no justice among us,
and we know nothing about right living.
We look for light but find only darkness.
We look for bright skies but walk in gloom.

10 We grope like the blind along a wall,
feeling our way like people without eyes.
Even at brightest noontime,
we stumble as though it were dark.
Among the living,
we are like the dead.

11 We growl like hungry bears;
we moan like mournful doves.
We look for justice, but it never comes.
We look for rescue, but it is far away from us.

12 For our sins are piled up before God
and testify against us.
Yes, we know what sinners we are.

13 We know we have rebelled and have denied the LORD.
We have turned our backs on our God.
We know how unfair and oppressive we have been,
carefully planning our deceitful lies.

14 Our courts oppose the righteous,
and justice is nowhere to be found.
Truth stumbles in the streets,
and honesty has been outlawed.

15 Yes, truth is gone,
and anyone who renounces evil is attacked.

The LORD looked and was displeased
to find there was no justice.

| | |
|---|---|
| | **59:3** Jer 2:30, 34 Hos 4:2 |
| | **59:4** Ps 7:14 |
| | **59:5** Job 8:14 |
| | **59:6** Jer 6:7 |
| | **59:7-8** Mark 7:21-22 †Rom 3:15-17 |
| | **59:9** Isa 5:30 |
| | **59:10** Deut 28:29 Lam 3:6 |
| | **59:11** Ezek 7:16 |
| | **59:12** Ezra 9:6 Hos 5:5 |
| | **59:13** Matt 10:33 Titus 1:16 |
| | **59:14** Hab 1:4 |
| | **59:15** Isa 1:21-23; 5:23 |

---

**59:15** Because of Israel's willful, persistent rebellion (chapters 56–59), the nation became unable to take action against its sins. Sin fills the vacuum left when God's truth no longer fills our life. Only God can defeat sin.

59:16
Ezek 22:30

16 He was amazed to see that no one intervened
  to help the oppressed.
So he himself stepped in to save them with his strong arm,
  and his justice sustained him.

59:17
Eph 6:14

17 He put on righteousness as his body armor
  and placed the helmet of salvation on his head.
He clothed himself with a robe of vengeance
  and wrapped himself in a cloak of divine passion.
18 He will repay his enemies for their evil deeds.
  His fury will fall on his foes.
  He will pay them back even to the ends of the earth.

59:19
Isa 30:28

19 In the west, people will respect the name of the LORD;
  in the east, they will glorify him.
For he will come like a raging flood tide
  driven by the breath of the LORD.*

59:20
Ezek 18:30-31
Acts 2:38-39
†Rom 11:26-27

20 "The Redeemer will come to Jerusalem
  to buy back those in Israel
who have turned from their sins,"*
  says the LORD.

59:21
Isa 44:3
Jer 31:31-34

21"And this is my covenant with them," says the LORD. "My Spirit will not leave them, and neither will these words I have given you. They will be on your lips and on the lips of your children and your children's children forever. I, the LORD, have spoken!

## 3. The future kingdom
### *Future Glory for Jerusalem*

60:1
Eph 5:14
60:2
Col 1:13

# 60
1 "Arise, Jerusalem! Let your light shine for all to see.
  For the glory of the LORD rises to shine on you.
2 Darkness as black as night covers all the nations of the earth,
  but the glory of the LORD rises and appears over you.

60:3
Isa 2:3

3 All nations will come to your light;
  mighty kings will come to see your radiance.

4 "Look and see, for everyone is coming home!
  Your sons are coming from distant lands;
  your little daughters will be carried home.

60:5
Ps 34:5
Isa 61:6

5 Your eyes will shine,
  and your heart will thrill with joy,
for merchants from around the world will come to you.
  They will bring you the wealth of many lands.
6 Vast caravans of camels will converge on you,
  the camels of Midian and Ephah.
The people of Sheba will bring gold and frankincense
  and will come worshiping the LORD.

59:19 Or *When the enemy comes like a raging flood tide, / the Spirit of the LORD will drive him back.* **59:20** Hebrew *The Redeemer will come to Zion / to buy back those in Jacob / who have turned from their sins.* Greek version reads *The one who rescues will come on behalf of Zion, / and he will turn Jacob away from ungodliness.* Compare Rom 11:26.

---

**59:16, 17** God would, in fact, act to rescue the nation from enemy armies (Assyria and Babylon) and to punish wicked Israelites as well. He would also rescue his people from sin. Because redemption is an impossible task for any human, God himself, as the Messiah, would personally step in to help (Romans 11:26, 27). Whether we sin once or many times, out of rebellion or out of ignorance, our sin separates us from God and will continue to separate us until God forgives us and removes it.

**59:21** When the Holy Spirit dwells within his people, they change. Their former desires no longer entice them; now their chief aim is to please God. We who are Christians today are the heirs of this prophecy; we are able to respond to God's will and distinguish between good and evil because the Holy Spirit dwells within us (John 14:26; Philippians 2:13; Hebrews 5:14).

**60:1ff** As we read these promises, we long for their fulfillment. But we must patiently wait for God's timing. He is in control of history, and he weaves together all our lives into his plan.

**60:6, 7** The places mentioned belonged to obscure tribes in the Arabian desert hundreds of miles from Israel. All people would come to Jerusalem because God would be living there, and they would be attracted to his light. Don't be discouraged when you look around and see so few people turning to God; one day people throughout the earth will recognize him as the one true God.

7 The flocks of Kedar will be given to you,
   and the rams of Nebaioth will be brought for my altars.
I will accept their offerings,
   and I will make my Temple glorious.

8 "And what do I see flying like clouds to Israel,
   like doves to their nests?
9 They are ships from the ends of the earth,
   from lands that trust in me,
   led by the great ships of Tarshish.
They are bringing the people of Israel home from far away,
   carrying their silver and gold.
They will honor the LORD your God,
   the Holy One of Israel,
   for he has filled you with splendor.

60:9-10
Ps 72:10
Isa 49:22-23

10 "Foreigners will come to rebuild your towns,
   and their kings will serve you.
For though I have destroyed you in my anger,
   I will now have mercy on you through my grace.
11 Your gates will stay open day and night
   to receive the wealth of many lands.
The kings of the world will be led as captives
   in a victory procession.
12 For the nations that refuse to serve you
   will be destroyed.

60:11
Isa 26:2

60:12
Zech 14:17

13 "The glory of Lebanon will be yours—
   the forests of cypress, fir, and pine—
to beautify my sanctuary.
   My Temple will be glorious!
14 The descendants of your tormentors
   will come and bow before you.
Those who despised you
   will kiss your feet.
They will call you the City of the LORD,
   and Zion of the Holy One of Israel.

60:13
Ps 132:7

60:14
Isa 1:26; 14:1-2
Rev 3:9

15 "Though you were once despised and hated,
   with no one traveling through you,
I will make you beautiful forever,
   a joy to all generations.
16 Powerful kings and mighty nations
   will satisfy your every need,
as though you were a child
   nursing at the breast of a queen.
You will know at last that I, the LORD,
   am your Savior and your Redeemer,
   the Mighty One of Israel.*
17 I will exchange your bronze for gold,
   your iron for silver,
your wood for bronze,
   and your stones for iron.
I will make peace your leader
   and righteousness your ruler.
18 Violence will disappear from your land;
   the desolation and destruction of war will end.
Salvation will surround you like city walls,
   and praise will be on the lips of all who enter there.

19 "No longer will you need the sun to shine by day,
   nor the moon to give its light by night,

60:15
Isa 65:18
Jer 30:17-19

60:16
Isa 43:3, 11; 63:16

60:18
Isa 26:1

60:19
Isa 9:2
Zech 2:5
Rev 21:23; 22:5

60:16 Hebrew *of Jacob*. See note on 14:1.

for the Lord your God will be your everlasting light,
　and your God will be your glory.
20 Your sun will never set;
　your moon will not go down.
For the Lord will be your everlasting light,
　Your days of mourning will come to an end.

21 All your people will be righteous.
　They will possess their land forever,
for I will plant them there with my own hands
　in order to bring myself glory.
22 The smallest family will become a thousand people,
　and the tiniest group will become a mighty nation.
At the right time, I, the Lord, will make it happen."

## Good News for the Oppressed

**61** 1 The Spirit of the Sovereign Lord is upon me,
　　for the Lord has anointed me
to bring good news to the poor.
He has sent me to comfort the brokenhearted
　and to proclaim that captives will be released
　and prisoners will be freed.*
2 He has sent me to tell those who mourn
　that the time of the Lord's favor has come,*
　and with it, the day of God's anger against their enemies.
3 To all who mourn in Israel,*
　he will give a crown of beauty for ashes,
a joyous blessing instead of mourning,
　festive praise instead of despair.
In their righteousness, they will be like great oaks
　that the Lord has planted for his own glory.

4 They will rebuild the ancient ruins,
　repairing cities destroyed long ago.
They will revive them,
　though they have been deserted for many generations.
5 Foreigners will be your servants.
　They will feed your flocks
and plow your fields
　and tend your vineyards.
6 You will be called priests of the Lord,
　ministers of our God.
You will feed on the treasures of the nations
　and boast in their riches.
7 Instead of shame and dishonor,
　you will enjoy a double share of honor.
You will possess a double portion of prosperity in your land,
　and everlasting joy will be yours.

61:1 Greek version reads *and the blind will see.* Compare Luke 4:18.　**61:2** Or *to proclaim the acceptable year of the Lord.*　**61:3** Hebrew *in Zion.*

### Cross-references

60:20　Rev 21:4

60:21　Ps 37:22　Isa 45:24-25

60:22　Isa 51:2

61:1-2　Isa 49:8-9　†Luke 4:18-19

61:3　Ps 23:5　Jer 17:7-8

61:4　Ezek 36:33　Amos 9:14

61:5　Isa 14:2

61:6　Isa 66:21

61:7　Zech 9:12

---

**60:19, 20** See Revelation 21:23, 24 and 22:5, where this beautiful reality is also promised.

**61:1, 2** Jesus quoted these words in Luke 4:18, 19. As he read to the people in the synagogue, he stopped in the middle of 61:2 after the words, "the time of the Lord's favor has come." Rolling up the scroll, he said, "The Scripture you've just heard has been fulfilled this very day!" (Luke 4:21). The next phrase in 61:2, "and with it, the day of God's anger against their enemies," will come true when Jesus returns to earth again. We are now under God's favor; his wrath is yet to come.

**61:6** Under the old covenant, God ordained the priests of Israel to stand between him and his people. They brought God's word

to the people and the people's needs and sins to God. Under the new covenant, all believers are priests of the Lord (1 Peter 2:5), reading God's Word and seeking to understand it, confessing their sins directly to God, and ministering to others.

8 "For I, the LORD, love justice.
    I hate robbery and wrongdoing.
  I will faithfully reward my people for their suffering
    and make an everlasting covenant with them.
9 Their descendants will be recognized
    and honored among the nations.
  Everyone will realize that they are a people
    the LORD has blessed."

10 I am overwhelmed with joy in the LORD my God!
    For he has dressed me with the clothing of salvation
      and draped me in a robe of righteousness.
  I am like a bridegroom in his wedding suit
    or a bride with her jewels.
11 The Sovereign LORD will show his justice to the nations of the world.
    Everyone will praise him!
  His righteousness will be like a garden in early spring,
    with plants springing up everywhere.

## Isaiah's Prayer for Jerusalem

**62** ¹ Because I love Zion,
        I will not keep still.
  Because my heart yearns for Jerusalem,
    I cannot remain silent.
  I will not stop praying for her
    until her righteousness shines like the dawn,
    and her salvation blazes like a burning torch.
2 The nations will see your righteousness.
    World leaders will be blinded by your glory.
  And you will be given a new name
    by the LORD's own mouth.
3 The LORD will hold you in his hand for all to see—
    a splendid crown in the hand of God.
4 Never again will you be called "The Forsaken City"*
    or "The Desolate Land."*
  Your new name will be "The City of God's Delight"*
    and "The Bride of God,"*
  for the LORD delights in you
    and will claim you as his bride.
5 Your children will commit themselves to you, O Jerusalem,
    just as a young man commits himself to his bride.
  Then God will rejoice over you
    as a bridegroom rejoices over his bride.
6 O Jerusalem, I have posted watchmen on your walls;
    they will pray day and night, continually.
  Take no rest, all you who pray to the LORD.

**62:8**
Gen 17:7
Isa 5:16

**61:9**
Isa 44:3

**61:10**
Isa 51:3; 52:1

**62:1**
Isa 46:13

**62:2**
Isa 56:5

**62:3**
Zech 9:16
1 Thes 2:19

**62:4**
Isa 54:6-7
Jer 32:41
Zeph 3:17-18

**62:5**
Isa 65:19

**62:6**
Jer 14:21
Ezek 33:7

**62:4a** Hebrew *Azubah*, which means "forsaken." **62:4b** Hebrew *Shemamah*, which means "desolate."
**62:4c** Hebrew *Hephzibah*, which means "my delight is in her." **62:4d** Hebrew *Beulah*, which means "married."

**61:8** We suffer for many reasons—our own mistakes, someone else's mistakes, injustice. When we suffer for our own mistakes, we get what we deserve. When we suffer because of others or because of injustice, God is angry. God in his mercy says that his people have suffered enough. God will reward those who suffer because of injustice. He will settle all accounts.

**61:10** "Me" could refer to the Messiah, the person appointed by the Spirit of the Lord (61:1), or to Zion (62:1), which symbolizes God's people. The imagery of the bridegroom is often used in Scripture to depict the Messiah (see Matthew 9:15), while the imagery of the bride is used to depict God's people (see Revelation 19:6-8). We, too, can put on our new clothes—right relationship with God—by putting our trust in Christ (2 Corinthians 5:21).

**62:1-7** Many commentators believe Isaiah is speaking in verse 1. If so, Isaiah's zeal for his people and his desire to see the work of salvation completed caused him to pray without resting, hoping that Israel would be saved. We should have Isaiah's zeal to see God's will done. This is what we mean when we pray, "May your Kingdom come soon. May your will be done on earth, as it is in heaven" (Matthew 6:10). It is good to keep praying persistently for others.

**62:7**
Luke 18:1-8

7 Give the LORD no rest until he completes his work,
    until he makes Jerusalem the pride of the earth.
8 The LORD has sworn to Jerusalem by his own strength:
    "I will never again hand you over to your enemies.
Never again will foreign warriors come
    and take away your grain and new wine.

**62:9**
Isa 65:13, 21-23

9 You raised the grain, and you will eat it,
    praising the LORD.
Within the courtyards of the Temple,
    you yourselves will drink the wine you have pressed."

**62:10**
Isa 11:10

10 Go out through the gates!
    Prepare the highway for my people to return!
Smooth out the road; pull out the boulders;
    raise a flag for all the nations to see.

**62:11**
Isa 49:6
Zech 9:9
†Matt 21:5
Rev 22:12

11 The LORD has sent this message to every land:
    "Tell the people of Israel,*
'Look, your Savior is coming.
    See, he brings his reward with him as he comes.'"

**62:12**
Deut 7:6
1 Pet 2:9

12 They will be called "The Holy People"
    and "The People Redeemed by the LORD."
And Jerusalem will be known as "The Desirable Place"
    and "The City No Longer Forsaken."

## Judgment against the LORD's Enemies

**63:1**
Jer 49:13
Amos 1:12
Zeph 3:17

**63** 1 Who is this who comes from Edom,
    from the city of Bozrah,
    with his clothing stained red?
Who is this in royal robes,
    marching in his great strength?

"It is I, the LORD, announcing your salvation!
    It is I, the LORD, who has the power to save!"

**63:2**
Rev 19:13, 15

2 Why are your clothes so red,
    as if you have been treading out grapes?

**63:3**
Isa 22:5
Mic 7:10

3 "I have been treading the winepress alone;
    no one was there to help me.
In my anger I have trampled my enemies
    as if they were grapes.
In my fury I have trampled my foes.
    Their blood has stained my clothes.

**63:4**
Jer 51:6
**63:5**
Isa 52:10; 59:16

4 For the time has come for me to avenge my people,
    to ransom them from their oppressors.
5 I was amazed to see that no one intervened
    to help the oppressed.
So I myself stepped in to save them with my strong arm,
    and my wrath sustained me.
6 I crushed the nations in my anger
    and made them stagger and fall to the ground,
    spilling their blood upon the earth."

**62:11** Hebrew *Tell the daughter of Zion.*

---

**62:12** The people of Jerusalem (Zion) will have new names: "The Holy People" and "The People Redeemed by the LORD." Believers today also have new names—Christians. In 1 Peter 2:5, we are called God's "holy priests."

**63:1-4** Edom was a constant enemy of Israel despite its common ancestry in Isaac (Genesis 25:23). Edom rejoiced at any trouble Israel faced. The imagery in this passage is of a watchman on the wall of Jerusalem, seeing Edom approaching and fearing that the Edomite king in his red garment is leading an attack. But it turns out to be the Lord, in bloodstained clothes, who has trampled and destroyed Edom. Bozrah is a city in Edom. (For other prophecies against Edom, see Amos 1:11, 12; Obadiah 1:10, 11; Malachi 1:2-4.)

## Praise for Deliverance

7 I will tell of the LORD's unfailing love.
  I will praise the LORD for all he has done.
  I will rejoice in his great goodness to Israel,
  which he has granted according to his mercy and love.

8 He said, "They are my very own people.
  Surely they will not betray me again."
  And he became their Savior.

9 In all their suffering he also suffered,
  and he personally* rescued them.
In his love and mercy he redeemed them.
  He lifted them up and carried them
  through all the years.

10 But they rebelled against him
  and grieved his Holy Spirit.
So he became their enemy
  and fought against them.

11 Then they remembered those days of old
  when Moses led his people out of Egypt.
They cried out, "Where is the one who brought Israel through the sea,
  with Moses as their shepherd?
Where is the one who sent his Holy Spirit
  to be among his people?

12 Where is the one whose power was displayed
  when Moses lifted up his hand—
the one who divided the sea before them,
  making himself famous forever?

13 Where is the one who led them through the bottom of the sea?
  They were like fine stallions
  racing through the desert, never stumbling.

14 As with cattle going down into a peaceful valley,
  the Spirit of the LORD gave them rest.
You led your people, LORD,
  and gained a magnificent reputation."

## Prayer for Mercy and Pardon

15 LORD, look down from heaven;
  look from your holy, glorious home, and see us.
Where is the passion and the might
  you used to show on our behalf?
Where are your mercy and compassion now?

16 Surely you are still our Father!
  Even if Abraham and Jacob* would disown us,
LORD, you would still be our Father.
  You are our Redeemer from ages past.

17 LORD, why have you allowed us to turn from your path?
  Why have you given us stubborn hearts so we no longer fear you?
Return and help us, for we are your servants,
  the tribes that are your special possession.

18 How briefly your holy people possessed your holy place,
  and now our enemies have destroyed it.

19 Sometimes it seems as though we never belonged to you,
  as though we had never been known as your people.

**63:7**
1 Kgs 8:66
Pss 25:6-7; 86:5
Eph 2:4

**63:8**
Exod 6:7

**63:9**
Exod 23:20-23
Judg 10:16

**63:10**
Ps 78:40
Acts 7:51
Eph 4:30

**63:11**
Num 11:17, 25, 29
Isa 51:9-10

**63:12**
Exod 6:6; 14:21-22

**63:13**
Jer 31:9

**63:14**
Josh 21:44

**63:15**
Ps 80:14

**63:16**
Isa 41:8
Jer 31:20

**63:17**
Num 10:36
Isa 29:13-14

**63:18**
Ps 74:3-7

**63:19**
Lam 3:43-45

**63:9** Hebrew *and the angel of his presence.*   **63:16** Hebrew *Israel.* See note on 14:1.

---

**63:10** Grieving the Holy Spirit is willfully thwarting his leading by disobedience or rebellion. Isaiah mentions the work of the Holy Spirit more than any other Old Testament writer. See the note on Ephesians 4:28-32 for more on grieving the Holy Spirit.

**63:15—64:7** On behalf of the faithful remnant, Isaiah asks God for two favors: to show mercy and compassion to them and to punish their enemies. Before making these requests, Isaiah recited the Lord's past favors, reminding him of his compassion in former days (63:7-14).

**64:1**
Exod 19:18
Judg 5:5
Nah 1:5

**64:2**
Ps 99:1

# 64

¹*Oh, that you would burst from the heavens and come down!
How the mountains would quake in your presence!
²* As fire causes wood to burn
and water to boil,
your coming would make the nations tremble.
Then your enemies would learn the reason for your fame!

**64:3**
Pss 65:5; 66:5

³ When you came down long ago,
you did awesome deeds beyond our highest expectations.
And oh, how the mountains quaked!

**64:4**
Isa 40:31
†1 Cor 2:9

⁴ For since the world began,
no ear has heard
and no eye has seen a God like you,
who works for those who wait for him!

⁵ You welcome those who gladly do good,
who follow godly ways.
But you have been very angry with us,
for we are not godly.
We are constant sinners;
how can people like us be saved?

**64:6**
Ps 90:5-6
Isa 1:30; 48:1

⁶ We are all infected and impure with sin.
When we display our righteous deeds,
they are nothing but filthy rags.
Like autumn leaves, we wither and fall,
and our sins sweep us away like the wind.

**64:7**
Deut 31:18
Isa 1:15

⁷ Yet no one calls on your name
or pleads with you for mercy.
Therefore, you have turned away from us
and turned us over* to our sins.

**64:8**
Ps 100:3
Isa 45:9

⁸ And yet, O LORD, you are our Father.
We are the clay, and you are the potter.
We all are formed by your hand.

**64:1** In the Hebrew text this verse is included in 63:19.   **64:2** Verses 64:2-12 are numbered 64:1-11 in Hebrew text.
**64:7** As in Greek, Syriac, and Aramaic versions; Hebrew reads *melted us*.

---

**THE SPIRIT
IN ISAIAH**

| Reference | Main Teaching |
|---|---|
| 11:2 . . . . . . . . . . . | The Spirit of the Lord brings wisdom, understanding, knowledge, and the fear of the Lord. |
| 32:15 . . . . . . . . . . | The Spirit of the Lord brings abundance. |
| 34:16 . . . . . . . . . | The Spirit of the Lord carries out God's word. |
| 40:13 . . . . . . . . . | The Spirit of the Lord is the Master Counselor. |
| 42:1 . . . . . . . . . . . | The Messiah, God's Servant, will be given the Spirit. |
| 44:3-5 . . . . . . . . . | Through the Spirit, God's true children will thrive. |
| 48:16 . . . . . . . . . . | The Spirit of the Lord sent Isaiah to prophesy. |
| 61:1 . . . . . . . . . . | God's servants (Isaiah and then Jesus) were appointed by the Spirit to proclaim the Good News. |
| 63:10, 11 . . . . . . . | The Spirit of the Lord was grieved because of God's people. |
| 63:14 . . . . . . . . . . | The Spirit of the Lord gives rest. |

---

**64:1-6** God's appearance is so intense that it is like a consuming fire that burns everything in its path. If we are so impure, how can we be saved? Only by God's mercy. The Israelites had experienced God's presence at Mount Sinai (Exodus 19:16-19). When God met with Moses, there was a thunderstorm, smoke, and an earthquake. If God were to meet us today, his glory would overwhelm us, especially when we look at our "filthy rags" (64:6).

**64:6** Sin makes us unclean so that we cannot approach God (6:5; Romans 3:23) any more than a beggar in filthy rags could dine at a king's table. Our best efforts are still infected with sin. Our only

hope, therefore, is faith in Jesus Christ, who can cleanse us and bring us into God's presence (read Romans 3).

This passage can easily be misunderstood. It doesn't mean that God will reject us if we come to him in faith, nor that he despises our efforts to please him. It means that if we come to him demanding acceptance on the basis of our "good" conduct, God will point out that our righteousness is but filthy rags compared to his infinite righteousness. This message is primarily for the unrepentant person, not the true follower of God.

9 Don't be so angry with us, LORD.
 Please don't remember our sins forever.
Look at us, we pray,
 and see that we are all your people.
10 Your holy cities are destroyed.
 Zion is a wilderness;
 yes, Jerusalem is a desolate ruin.
11 The holy and beautiful Temple
 where our ancestors praised you
has been burned down,
 and all the things of beauty are destroyed.
12 After all this, LORD, must you still refuse to help us?
 Will you continue to be silent and punish us?

64:9
Mic 7:18

64:11
Ps 74:3-7

64:12
Ps 83:1

### Judgment and Final Salvation

**65** The LORD says,

"I was ready to respond, but no one asked for help.
 I was ready to be found, but no one was looking for me.
I said, 'Here I am, here I am!'
 to a nation that did not call on my name.*
2 All day long I opened my arms to a rebellious people.*
 But they follow their own evil paths
 and their own crooked schemes.
3 All day long they insult me to my face
 by worshiping idols in their sacred gardens.
 They burn incense on pagan altars.
4 At night they go out among the graves,
 worshiping the dead.
They eat the flesh of pigs
 and make stews with other forbidden foods.
5 Yet they say to each other,
 'Don't come too close or you will defile me!
 I am holier than you!'
These people are a stench in my nostrils,
 an acrid smell that never goes away.

6 "Look, my decree is written out* in front of me:
 I will not stand silent;
I will repay them in full!
 Yes, I will repay them—
7 both for their own sins
 and for those of their ancestors,"
 says the LORD.
"For they also burned incense on the mountains
 and insulted me on the hills.
 I will pay them back in full!

65:1-2
†Rom 10:20-21

65:3
Job 2:5

65:4
Lev 11:7

65:5
Matt 9:11
Luke 18:9-12

65:6
Ps 50:3, 21
Isa 42:14

65:7
Jer 13:25
Ezek 20:27-28
Hos 2:13

65:1 Or *to a nation that did not bear my name.* 65:1-2 Greek version reads *I was found by people who were not looking for me. / I showed myself to those who were not asking for me. / All day long I opened my arms to them, / but they were disobedient and rebellious.* Compare Rom 10:20-21. 65:6 Or *their sins are written out;* Hebrew reads *it stands written.*

---

65:1 Israel considered itself to be the only people of God, but the time would come when other nations would seek him. Paul mentions Isaiah's statement in Romans 10:20 and points out that these other nations were the Gentiles. God's people today are those who accept Jesus as Savior and Lord, whether they are Jews or Gentiles. The gospel is for every person. Do not ignore or reject anyone when you share the gospel. You may be surprised at how many are sincerely searching for God.

65:3-5 God said these people directly disobeyed his laws when they worshiped and sacrificed to idols (Exodus 20:1-6), consulted the dead and evil spirits (Leviticus 19:31), and ate forbidden foods (Leviticus 11). But they were so perverse that they still thought they were spiritually superior to others. Jesus called such people hypocrites (Matthew 23:13-36).

65:6 God said he would pay back the people for their sins. Judgment is not our job but God's because he alone is just. Who else knows our heart and mind? Who else knows what is a completely fair reward or punishment? Leave judgment of others up to God. If he gave *us* what we deserve, he might wipe us out. Instead, pray for his mercy.

8 "But I will not destroy them all,"
  says the LORD.
"For just as good grapes are found among a cluster of bad ones
  (and someone will say, 'Don't throw them all away—
  some of those grapes are good!'),
so I will not destroy all Israel.
  For I still have true servants there.

**65:9**
Amos 9:11-15

9 I will preserve a remnant of the people of Israel*
  and of Judah to possess my land.
Those I choose will inherit it,
  and my servants will live there.

**65:10**
Josh 7:24
Isa 33:9

10 The plain of Sharon will again be filled with flocks
  for my people who have searched for me,
  and the valley of Achor will be a place to pasture herds.

**65:11**
Isa 1:4, 28

11 "But because the rest of you have forsaken the LORD
  and have forgotten his Temple,
and because you have prepared feasts to honor the god of Fate
  and have offered mixed wine to the god of Destiny,

**65:12**
2 Chr 36:15-16
Prov 1:24

12 now I will 'destine' you for the sword.
  All of you will bow down before the executioner.
For when I called, you did not answer.
  When I spoke, you did not listen.
You deliberately sinned—before my very eyes—
  and chose to do what you know I despise."

**65:13**
Isa 5:13

13 Therefore, this is what the Sovereign LORD says:
"My servants will eat,
  but you will starve.
My servants will drink,
  but you will be thirsty.
My servants will rejoice,
  but you will be sad and ashamed.

**65:14**
Matt 8:12
Luke 13:28

14 My servants will sing for joy,
  but you will cry in sorrow and despair.

**65:15**
Jer 24:9

15 Your name will be a curse word among my people,
  for the Sovereign LORD will destroy you
  and will call his true servants by another name.

**65:16**
Isa 45:23

16 All who invoke a blessing or take an oath
  will do so by the God of truth.
For I will put aside my anger
  and forget the evil of earlier days.

**65:17**
2 Cor 5:17
2 Pet 3:13

17 "Look! I am creating new heavens and a new earth,
  and no one will even think about the old ones anymore.

**65:18**
Ps 98:1-9
Isa 35:10

18 Be glad; rejoice forever in my creation!
  And look! I will create Jerusalem as a place of happiness.
  Her people will be a source of joy.

**65:19**
Jer 32:41
Rev 7:17

19 I will rejoice over Jerusalem
  and delight in my people.

**65:9** Hebrew *remnant of Jacob*. See note on 14:1.

**65:8, 9** God will always preserve a faithful remnant of his people. No matter how bad the world is, there are always a few who remain loyal to him. Jesus made this point in Matthew 13:36-43.

**65:10** Sharon is a plain in the western part of Israel. The valley of Achor is in the east, near Jericho. The valley of Achor was also called the Valley of Trouble because Achan was executed there for hiding the devoted goods of battle (Joshua 7:10-26). Even

in this valley there will be peace: The coming restoration will be complete.

**65:17-25** In 65:17-19 we have a pictorial description of the new heavens and the new earth. They are eternal, and in them safety, peace, and plenty will be available to all (see also 66:22, 23; 2 Peter 3:13; Revelation 21:1). Verses 20-25 may refer to the reign of Christ on earth because sin and death have not yet been finally destroyed.

And the sound of weeping and crying
    will be heard in it no more.

20 "No longer will babies die when only a few days old.
    No longer will adults die before they have lived a full life.
No longer will people be considered old at one hundred!
    Only the cursed will die that young!
21 In those days people will live in the houses they build
    and eat the fruit of their own vineyards.
22 Unlike the past, invaders will not take their houses
    and confiscate their vineyards.
For my people will live as long as trees,
    and my chosen ones will have time to enjoy their hard-won gains.
23 They will not work in vain,
    and their children will not be doomed to misfortune.
For they are people blessed by the LORD,
    and their children, too, will be blessed.
24 I will answer them before they even call to me.
    While they are still talking about their needs,
    I will go ahead and answer their prayers!
25 The wolf and the lamb will feed together.
    The lion will eat hay like a cow.
    But the snakes will eat dust.
In those days no one will be hurt or destroyed on my holy mountain.
    I, the LORD, have spoken!"

**66** This is what the LORD says:

"Heaven is my throne,
    and the earth is my footstool.
Could you build me a temple as good as that?
    Could you build me such a resting place?
2 My hands have made both heaven and earth;
    they and everything in them are mine.*
    I, the LORD, have spoken!

"I will bless those who have humble and contrite hearts,
    who tremble at my word.
3 But those who choose their own ways—
    delighting in their detestable sins—
    will not have their offerings accepted.
When such people sacrifice a bull,
    it is no more acceptable than a human sacrifice.
When they sacrifice a lamb,
    it's as though they had sacrificed a dog!
When they bring an offering of grain,
    they might as well offer the blood of a pig.
When they burn frankincense,
    it's as if they had blessed an idol.

**65:20**
Eccl 8:12-13

**65:21**
Amos 9:14

**65:23**
Isa 61:9

**65:24**
Ps 91:15
Dan 10:12

**65:25**
Gen 3:14
Isa 11:6-7, 9

**66:1**
Ps 11:4
Matt 5:34-35
John 4:20-21
†Acts 7:49-50

**66:2**
Ps 34:18
Matt 5:3-4
Luke 18:13-14

66:2 As in Greek, Latin, and Syriac versions; Hebrew reads *these things are.*

---

**66:1** Even the beautiful Temple in Jerusalem was woefully inadequate for a God who is present everywhere. God cannot be confined to any human structure (see 2 Chronicles 6:18; Acts 7:49, 50). This chapter is a fitting climax to the book. God will lift up the humble, judge all people, destroy the wicked, bring all believers together, and establish the new heavens and the new earth. Let this hope encourage you each day.

**66:2, 3** These key verses summarize Isaiah's message. He contrasted humble persons, who have a profound reverence for God's messages and their application to life, with those who choose their own ways. The sacrifices of the arrogant were only external compliance. In their hearts they were murderers, perverts, and idolaters. God shows mercy to the humble, but he curses the proud and self-sufficient (see Luke 1:51-53). Our society urges us to be assertive and to affirm ourselves. Don't let your freedom and right to choose lead you away from God's pathway to eternal life.

**66:4**
Prov 1:31-32; 10:24
Jer 7:13, 30

4 I will send them great trouble—
  all the things they feared.
For when I called, they did not answer.
  When I spoke, they did not listen.
They deliberately sinned before my very eyes
  and chose to do what they know I despise."

**66:5**
Ps 38:20
Matt 5:10-12
Luke 13:17
John 9:34

5 Hear this message from the LORD,
  all you who tremble at his words:
"Your own people hate you
  and throw you out for being loyal to my name.
'Let the LORD be honored!' they scoff.
  'Be joyful in him!'
  But they will be put to shame.

**66:6**
Joel 3:7

6 What is all the commotion in the city?
  What is that terrible noise from the Temple?
It is the voice of the LORD
  taking vengeance against his enemies.

7 "Before the birth pains even begin,
  Jerusalem gives birth to a son.
8 Who has ever seen anything as strange as this?
  Who ever heard of such a thing?
Has a nation ever been born in a single day?
  Has a country ever come forth in a mere moment?
But by the time Jerusalem's* birth pains begin,
  her children will be born.

**66:9**
Isa 37:3

9 Would I ever bring this nation to the point of birth
  and then not deliver it?" asks the LORD.
"No! I would never keep this nation from being born,"
  says your God.

**66:10**
Ps 122:6
Rom 15:10

10 "Rejoice with Jerusalem!
  Be glad with her, all you who love her
  and all you who mourn for her.
11 Drink deeply of her glory
  even as an infant drinks at its mother's comforting breasts."

**66:12**
Isa 48:18; 60:5

12 This is what the LORD says:
"I will give Jerusalem a river of peace and prosperity.
  The wealth of the nations will flow to her.
Her children will be nursed at her breasts,
  carried in her arms, and held on her lap.

**66:13**
2 Cor 1:4

13 I will comfort you there in Jerusalem
  as a mother comforts her child."

**66:14**
Prov 3:8
Zech 10:7

14 When you see these things, your heart will rejoice.
  You will flourish like the grass!
Everyone will see the LORD's hand of blessing on his servants—
  and his anger against his enemies.
15 See, the LORD is coming with fire,
  and his swift chariots roar like a whirlwind.
He will bring punishment with the fury of his anger
  and the flaming fire of his hot rebuke.

**66:16**
Ezek 38:22

16 The LORD will punish the world by fire
  and by his sword.

**66:8** Hebrew *Zion's.*

**66:7-9** God will not leave his work of national restoration unfinished. In this image of birth, God shows that he will accomplish what he has promised. It is as unstoppable as the birth of a baby. When all the pain is over, the joy begins.

**66:15-17** This is a vivid picture of the great judgment that will occur at Christ's second coming (2 Thessalonians 1:7-9).

He will judge the earth,
  and many will be killed by him.

17"Those who 'consecrate' and 'purify' themselves in a sacred garden with its idol in the center—feasting on pork and rats and other detestable meats—will come to a terrible end," says the Lord.

18"I can see what they are doing, and I know what they are thinking. So I will gather all nations and peoples together, and they will see my glory. 19I will perform a sign among them. And I will send those who survive to be messengers to the nations—to Tarshish, to the Libyans* and Lydians* (who are famous as archers), to Tubal and Greece,* and to all the lands beyond the sea that have not heard of my fame or seen my glory. There they will declare my glory to the nations. 20They will bring the remnant of your people back from every nation. They will bring them to my holy mountain in Jerusalem as an offering to the Lord. They will ride on horses, in chariots and wagons, and on mules and camels," says the Lord. 21"And I will appoint some of them to be my priests and Levites. I, the Lord, have spoken!

22 "As surely as my new heavens and earth will remain,
  so will you always be my people,
with a name that will never disappear,"
  says the Lord.
23 "All humanity will come to worship me
  from week to week
  and from month to month.
24 And as they go out, they will see
  the dead bodies of those who have rebelled against me.
For the worms that devour them will never die,
  and the fire that burns them will never go out.
All who pass by
  will view them with utter horror."

66:19a As in some Greek manuscripts, which read *Put* [that is, *Libya*]; Hebrew reads *Pul*.
66:19b Hebrew *Lud*.    66:19c Hebrew *Javan*.

**Cross-references (right margin):**

66:17
Lev 11:7

66:19
1 Chr 16:24
Isa 42:12

66:20
Isa 2:2; 43:5-6;
49:22; 52:11; 60:4
66:21
Isa 61:6
1 Pet 2:5, 9

66:22
John 10:27-29
2 Pet 3:13
Rev 21:1

66:23
Isa 27:13

66:24
Isa 1:31
Dan 12:2
†Mark 9:48

---

**66:19** God's people will go out as missionaries to all parts of the earth—to Tarshish (Spain), to the Libyans in northern Africa, to the Lydians in western Asia Minor, to northeastern Asia Minor (Tubal), and to Greece.

**66:22-24** Isaiah brings his book to a close with great drama. For the faithless there is a sobering portrayal of judgment. For the faithful, there is a glorious picture of rich reward: "So will you always be my people, with a name that will never disappear." The contrast is so striking that it would seem that everyone would want to be God's follower. But we are often just as rebellious, foolish, and reluctant to change as the Israelites. We are just as negligent in feeding the hungry, working for justice, obeying God's Word, and taking up his causes. Make sure you are among those who will be richly blessed.

# JEREMIAH

WHAT is success? Most definitions include references to achieving goals and acquiring wealth, prestige, favor, and power. "Successful" people enjoy the good life—being financially and emotionally secure, being surrounded by admirers, and enjoying the fruits of their labors. They are leaders, opinion makers, and trend-setters. Their example is emulated; their accomplishments are noticed. They know who they are and where they are going, and they stride confidently to meet their goals.

By these standards, Jeremiah was a miserable failure. For 40 years he served as God's spokesman to Judah, but when Jeremiah spoke, nobody listened. Consistently and passionately he urged them to act, but nobody moved. And he certainly did not attain material success. He was poor and underwent severe deprivation to deliver his prophecies. He was thrown into prison (chapter 37) and into a cistern (chapter 38), and he was taken to Egypt against his will (chapter 43). He was rejected by his neighbors (11:19–21), his family (12:6), the false priests and prophets (20:1, 2; 28:1–17), friends (20:10), his audience (26:8), and the kings (36:23). Throughout his life, Jeremiah stood alone, declaring God's messages of doom, announcing the new covenant, and weeping over the fate of his beloved country. In the eyes of the world, Jeremiah was not a success.

But in God's eyes, Jeremiah was one of the most successful people in all of history. Success, as measured by God, involves obedience and faithfulness. Regardless of opposition and personal cost, Jeremiah courageously and faithfully proclaimed the word of God. He was obedient to his calling. Jeremiah's book begins with his call to be a prophet. The next 38 chapters are prophecies about Israel (the nation united) and Judah (the southern kingdom). Chapters 2—20 are general and undated, and chapters 21—39 are particular and dated. The basic theme of Jeremiah's message is simple: "Repent and turn to God, or he will punish." Because the people rejected this warning, Jeremiah then began predicting the destruction of Jerusalem. This terrible event is described in chapter 39. Chapters 40—45 describe events following Jerusalem's fall. The book concludes with prophecies concerning a variety of nations (chapters 46—52).

As you read Jeremiah, feel with him as he agonizes over the message he must deliver, pray with him for those who refuse to respond to the truth, and watch his example of faith and courage. Then commit yourself to being successful in God's eyes.

## VITAL STATISTICS

**PURPOSE:**
To urge God's people to turn from their sins and back to God

**AUTHOR:**
Jeremiah

**ORIGINAL AUDIENCE:**
Judah (the southern kingdom) and its capital city, Jerusalem

**DATE WRITTEN:**
During Jeremiah's ministry, approximately 627–586 B.C.

**SETTING:**
Jeremiah ministered under Judah's last five kings—Josiah, Jehoahaz, Jehoiakim, Jehoiachin, and Zedekiah. The nation was sliding quickly toward destruction and was eventually conquered by Babylon in 586 B.C. (see 2 Kings 21—25). The prophet Zephaniah preceded Jeremiah, and Habakkuk was Jeremiah's contemporary.

**KEY VERSE:**
"Your wickedness will bring its own punishment. Your turning from me will shame you. You will see what an evil, bitter thing it is to abandon the LORD your God and not to fear him. I, the Lord, the LORD of Heaven's Armies, have spoken!" (2:19)

**KEY PEOPLE:**
Judah's kings (listed above), Baruch, Ebed-melech, King Nebuchadnezzar, the Recabites

**KEY PLACES:**
Anathoth, Jerusalem, Ramah, Egypt

**SPECIAL FEATURES:**
This book is a combination of history, poetry, and biography. Jeremiah often used symbolism to communicate his message.

## THE BLUEPRINT

A. GOD'S JUDGMENT ON JUDAH (1:1—45:5)
1. The call of Jeremiah
2. Jeremiah condemns Judah for its sins
3. Jeremiah prophesies destruction
4. Jeremiah accuses Judah's leaders
5. Restoration is promised
6. God's promised judgment arrives

Jeremiah confronts many people with their sins: kings, false prophets, those at the temples, and those at the gates. A lack of response made Jeremiah wonder if he was doing any good at all. He often felt discouraged and sometimes bitter. To bring such gloomy messages to these people was a hard task. We, too, have a responsibility to bring this news to a fallen world: Those who continue in their sinful ways are eternally doomed. Although we may feel discouraged at the lack of response, we must press on to tell others about the consequences of sin and the hope that God offers. Those who tell people only what they want to hear are being unfaithful to God's message.

B.  GOD'S JUDGMENT ON THE NATIONS
(46:1—52:34)
1. Prophecies about foreign nations
2. The fall of Jerusalem

Jeremiah lived to see many of his prophecies come true—most notably the fall of Jerusalem. The fulfillment of this and other prophecies against the foreign nations came as a result of sin. Those who refuse to confess their sin bring judgment upon themselves.

## MEGATHEMES

| THEME | EXPLANATION | IMPORTANCE |
|---|---|---|
| Sin | King Josiah's reformation failed because the people's repentance was shallow. They continued in their selfishness and worship of idols. All the leaders rejected God's law and will for the people. Jeremiah lists all their sins, predicts God's judgment, and begs for repentance. | Judah's deterioration and disaster came from a callous disregard and disobedience of God. When we ignore sin and refuse to listen to God's warning, we invite disaster. Don't settle for half measures in removing sin. |
| Punishment | Because of sin, Jerusalem was destroyed, the Temple was ruined, and the people were captured and carried off to Babylon. The people were responsible for their destruction and captivity because they refused to listen to God's message. | Unconfessed sin brings God's full punishment. It is useless to blame anyone else for our sin; we are accountable to God before anyone else. We must answer to him for how we live. |
| God Is Lord of All | God is the righteous Creator. He is accountable to no one but himself. He wisely and lovingly directs all creation to fulfill his plans, and he brings events to pass according to his timetable. He is Lord over all the world. | Because of God's majestic power and love, our only duty is to submit to his authority. By following his plans, not our own, we can have a loving relationship with him and serve him with our whole heart. |
| New Hearts | Jeremiah predicted that after the destruction of the nation, God would send a new shepherd, the Messiah. He would lead them into a new future, a new covenant, and a new day of hope. He would accomplish this by changing their sinful hearts into hearts of love for God. | God still transforms people by changing their hearts. His love can eliminate the problems created by sin. We can have assurance of a new heart by loving God, trusting Christ to save us, and repenting of our sin. |
| Faithful Service | Jeremiah served God faithfully for 40 years. During that time the people ignored, rejected, and persecuted him. Jeremiah's preaching was unsuccessful by human standards, yet he did not fail in his task. He remained faithful to God. | People's acceptance or rejection of us is not the measure of our success. God's approval alone should be our standard for service. We must bring God's message to others even when we are rejected. We must do God's work even if it means suffering for it. |

## A. GOD'S JUDGMENT ON JUDAH (1:1—45:5)

Jeremiah was called by God to be a prophet to Judah (the southern kingdom). He faithfully confronted the leaders and the people with their sin, prophesied both their 70-year captivity in Babylon and their eventual return from exile. After surviving the fall of Jerusalem, Jeremiah was forcefully taken to Egypt. Yet Jeremiah remained faithful in spite of Jerusalem's destruction. Years of obedience had made him strong and courageous. May we be able to stand through difficult times as did Jeremiah.

### 1. The call of Jeremiah

**1** These are the words of Jeremiah son of Hilkiah, one of the priests from the town of Anathoth in the land of Benjamin. ²The LORD first gave messages to Jeremiah during the thirteenth year of the reign of Josiah son of Amon, king of Judah.* ³The LORD's messages continued throughout the reign of King Jehoiakim, Josiah's son, until the eleventh year of the reign of King Zedekiah, another of Josiah's sons. In August* of that eleventh year the people of Jerusalem were taken away as captives.

1:1
2 Chr 36:12, 21
1:2
1 Kgs 13:2
2 Kgs 21:24
1:3
2 Kgs 23:34
Jer 25:1; 39:2

**1:2** The thirteenth year of Josiah's reign was 627 B.C.   **1:3** Hebrew *In the fifth month*, of the ancient Hebrew lunar calendar. A number of events in Jeremiah can be cross-checked with dates in surviving Babylonian records and related accurately to our modern calendar. The fifth month in the eleventh year of Zedekiah's reign occurred within the months of August and September 586 B.C. Also see 52:12 and the note there.

**1:1, 2** After King Solomon's death, the united kingdom of Israel had split into rival northern and southern kingdoms. The northern kingdom was called Israel; the southern, Judah. Jeremiah was from Anathoth, four miles north of Jerusalem in the southern kingdom. He lived and prophesied during the reigns of the last five kings of Judah. This was a chaotic time politically, morally, and spiritually. As Babylon, Egypt, and Assyria battled for world supremacy, Judah found itself caught in the middle of the triangle. Although Jeremiah prophesied for 40 years, he never saw his people heed his words and turn from their sins.

## Jeremiah's Call and First Visions

⁴The LORD gave me this message:

**1:5**
Ps 139:15-16
Isa 49:1, 5
Jer 25:15-26

⁵ "I knew you before I formed you in your mother's womb.
    Before you were born I set you apart
      and appointed you as my prophet to the nations."

**1:6**
Exod 4:10

⁶"O Sovereign LORD," I said, "I can't speak for you! I'm too young!"

**1:7**
Ezek 2:3-4

⁷The LORD replied, "Don't say, 'I'm too young,' for you must go wherever I send you and say whatever I tell you.

**1:8**
Jer 15:20
Ezek 2:6

⁸And don't be afraid of the people, for I will be with you and will protect you. I, the LORD, have spoken!" ⁹Then the LORD reached out and touched my mouth and said,

**1:9**
Exod 4:11-16
Deut 18:18

"Look, I have put my words in your mouth!
¹⁰ Today I appoint you to stand up
    against nations and kingdoms.

**1:10**
Isa 44:26-28
Jer 24:6; 31:28
2 Cor 10:4

Some you must uproot and tear down,
    destroy and overthrow.
Others you must build up
    and plant."

**1:11**
Jer 24:3
Amos 7:8

¹¹Then the LORD said to me, "Look, Jeremiah! What do you see?"
And I replied, "I see a branch from an almond tree."

**1:12**
Deut 32:35

¹²And the LORD said, "That's right, and it means that I am watching,* and I will certainly carry out all my plans."

**1:13**
Ezek 11:3, 7
Zech 4:2

¹³Then the LORD spoke to me again and asked, "What do you see now?"
And I replied, "I see a pot of boiling water, spilling from the north."

**1:12** The Hebrew word for "watching" *(shoqed)* sounds like the word for "almond tree" *(shaqed).*

---

**JEREMIAH** served as a prophet to Judah from 627 B.C. until the exile in 586 B.C.

| | |
|---|---|
| *Climate of the times* . . . . . . | Society was deteriorating economically, politically, spiritually. Wars and captivity dominated the world scene. God's word was deemed offensive. |
| *Main message* . . . . . . . . . | Repentance from sin would postpone Judah's coming judgment at the hands of Babylon. |
| *Importance of message* . . . . | Repentance is one of the greatest needs in our immoral world. God's promises to the faithful shine brightly by bringing hope for tomorrow and strength for today. |
| *Contemporary prophets* . . . | Habakkuk (612–589 B.C.), Zephaniah (640–621 B.C.). |

---

**1:5** God knew you, as he knew Jeremiah, long before you were born or even conceived. He thought about you and planned for you. When you feel discouraged or inadequate, remember that God has always thought of you as valuable and that he has a purpose in mind for you.

**1:5** Jeremiah was "appointed" by God as his "prophet to the nations." God has a purpose for each Christian, but some people are appointed by God for specific kinds of work. Samson (Judges 13:3-5), David (1 Samuel 16:12, 13), John the Baptist (Luke 1:13-17), and Paul (Galatians 1:15, 16) were also called to do particular jobs for God. Whatever work you do should be done for the glory of God (Philippians 1:11). If God gives you a specific task, accept it cheerfully and do it with diligence. If God has not given you a specific call or assignment, then seek to fulfill the mission common to all believers—to love, obey, and serve God—until his guidance becomes more clear.

**1:6-8** Often people struggle with new challenges because they lack self-confidence, feeling that they have inadequate ability, training, or experience. Jeremiah thought he was "too young" and inexperienced to be God's prophet to the nations. But God promised to be with him. We should not allow feelings of inadequacy to keep us from obeying God. He will *always* be with us. If God gives you a job to do, he will provide all you need to do it.

**1:8** God promised to be with Jeremiah and take care of him, but not to keep trouble from coming. God did not insulate him from imprisonment, deportation, or insults. God does not keep us from encountering life's storms, but he will see us through them. In fact, God walks through these storms with us and rescues us.

**1:10** God appointed Jeremiah to bring his word to "nations and kingdoms." Jeremiah's work was to warn not only the Jews but all the nations of the world about God's judgment for sin. Don't forget in reading the Old Testament that, while God was consistently working through the people of Judah and Israel, his plan was to communicate to every nation and person. We are included in Jeremiah's message of judgment and hope, and as believers we are to share God's desire to reach the whole world for him.

**1:11-14** The vision of the branch from an almond tree revealed the beginning of God's judgment because the almond tree is among the first to blossom in the spring. God saw the sins of Judah and the nations, and he would carry out swift and certain judgment. The pot of boiling water tipping from the north and spilling over Judah pictured Babylon delivering God's scalding judgment against Jeremiah's people.

¹⁴"Yes," the LORD said, "for terror from the north will boil out on the people of this land. ¹⁵Listen! I am calling the armies of the kingdoms of the north to come to Jerusalem. I, the LORD, have spoken!

"They will set their thrones
at the gates of the city.
They will attack its walls
and all the other towns of Judah.
¹⁶ I will pronounce judgment
on my people for all their evil—
for deserting me and burning incense to other gods.
Yes, they worship idols made with their own hands!

¹⁷ "Get up and prepare for action.
Go out and tell them everything I tell you to say.
Do not be afraid of them,
or I will make you look foolish in front of them.
¹⁸ For see, today I have made you strong
like a fortified city that cannot be captured,
like an iron pillar or a bronze wall.
You will stand against the whole land—
the kings, officials, priests, and people of Judah.
¹⁹ They will fight you, but they will fail.
For I am with you, and I will take care of you.
I, the LORD, have spoken!"

## 2. Jeremiah condemns Judah for its sins
*The LORD's Case against His People*

**2** The LORD gave me another message. He said, ²"Go and shout this message to Jerusalem. This is what the LORD says:

"I remember how eager you were to please me
as a young bride long ago,
how you loved me and followed me
even through the barren wilderness.
³ In those days Israel was holy to the LORD,
the first of his children.*
All who harmed his people were declared guilty,
and disaster fell on them.
I, the LORD, have spoken!"

**2:3** Hebrew *the firstfruits of his harvest.*

### Cross-references
**1:14** Isa 41:25
**1:15** Isa 22:7; Jer 9:11; 25:9
**1:16** Isa 2:8; 37:19; Jer 7:9; 10:3-5; 19:4
**1:17** Ezek 2:6; 3:16-18
**1:19** Jer 1:8; 20:11
**2:2** Isa 58:1; Jer 11:6; Ezek 16:8
**2:3** Exod 19:5-6; Deut 7:6; 14:2; Isa 41:11; Jer 30:16

---

**1:14-19** The problems we face may not seem as ominous as Jeremiah's, but they are critical to us and may overwhelm us! God's promise to Jeremiah and to us is that nothing will defeat us completely; he will help us through the most agonizing problems. Face each day with the assurance that God will be with you and see you through.

**1:16** The people of Judah sinned greatly by continuing to worship other gods. God had commanded them specifically against this (Exodus 20:3-6) because idolatry places trust in created things rather than the Creator. Although these people belonged to God, they chose to follow false gods. Many "gods" entice us to turn away from God. Material possessions, dreams for the future, approval of others, and vocational goals compete for our total commitment. Striving after these at the expense of our commitment to God puts our heart where Judah's was—and God severely punished Judah.

**2:1–3:5** In this section, the marriage analogy sharply contrasts God's love for his people with their love for other gods and reveals Judah's faithlessness. Jeremiah condemned Judah (he sometimes called Judah "Jerusalem," the name of its capital city) for seeking security in worthless, changeable things rather than the unchangeable God. We may be tempted to seek security from possessions, people, or our own abilities, but these will fail us. There is no lasting security apart from the eternal God.

**2:2** We appreciate a friend who remains true to his or her commitment, and we are disappointed with someone who fails to keep a promise. God was pleased when his people obeyed initially, but he became angry with them when they refused to keep their commitment. Temptations distract us from God. Think about your original commitment to obey God, and ask yourself if you are remaining truly devoted.

**2:3** The phrase, "first of his children," is a comparison with the firstfruits (the first part) of the harvest. Both were to be set apart for God (Deuteronomy 26:1-11). That's how God's people had declared their allegiance to him in years gone by. Israel had been as eager to please God as if she were his young bride, a holy, devoted people. This contrasted greatly with the situation in Jeremiah's time.

2:5
2 Kgs 17:15
Jer 8:19
Mic 6:3

⁴Listen to the word of the LORD, people of Jacob—all you families of Israel! ⁵This is what the LORD says:

"What did your ancestors find wrong with me
    that led them to stray so far from me?
They worshiped worthless idols,
    only to become worthless themselves.

2:6
Deut 8:15; 32:10

⁶ They did not ask, 'Where is the LORD
    who brought us safely out of Egypt
and led us through the barren wilderness—
    a land of deserts and pits,
a land of drought and death,
    where no one lives or even travels?'

JEREMIAH

Endurance is not a common quality. Many people lack the long-term commitment, caring, and willingness that are vital to sticking with a task against all odds. But Jeremiah was a prophet who endured.

Jeremiah's call by God teaches how intimately God knows us. He valued us before anyone else knew we would exist. He cared for us while we were in our mother's womb. He planned our life while our body was still being formed. He values us more highly than we value ourselves.

Jeremiah had to depend on God's love as he developed endurance. His audiences were usually antagonistic or apathetic to his messages. He was ignored; his life was often threatened. He saw both the excitement of a spiritual awakening and the sorrow of a national return to idolatry. With the exception of the good king Josiah, Jeremiah watched king after king ignore his warnings and lead the people away from God. He saw fellow prophets murdered. He himself was severely persecuted. Finally, he watched Judah's defeat at the hands of the Babylonians.

Jeremiah responded to all this with God's message and human tears. He felt firsthand God's love for his people and the people's rejection of that love. But even when he was angry with God and tempted to give up, Jeremiah knew he had to keep going. God had called him to endure. He expressed intense feelings but saw beyond the feelings to the God who was soon to execute justice but who afterward would show mercy.

It may be easy for us to identify with Jeremiah's frustrations and discouragement, but we need to realize that this prophet's life is also an encouragement to faithfulness.

| | |
|---|---|
| **Strengths and accomplishments** | • Wrote two Old Testament books, Jeremiah and Lamentations<br>• Ministered during the reigns of the last five kings of Judah<br>• Was a catalyst for the great spiritual reformation under King Josiah<br>• Acted as God's faithful messenger in spite of many attempts on his life<br>• Was so deeply sorrowful for the fallen condition of Judah that he earned the title "Weeping Prophet" |
| **Lessons from his life** | • The majority opinion is not necessarily God's will<br>• Although punishment for sin is severe, there is hope in God's mercy<br>• God will not accept empty or insincere worship<br>• Serving God does not guarantee earthly security |
| **Vital statistics** | • Where: Anathoth<br>• Occupation: Prophet<br>• Relative: Father: Hilkiah<br>• Contemporaries: Josiah, Jehoahaz, Jehoiakim, Jehoiachin, Zedekiah, Baruch |
| **Key verses** | "'O Sovereign LORD,' I said, 'I can't speak for you! I'm too young!' The LORD replied, 'Don't say, "I'm too young," for you must go wherever I send you and say whatever I tell you. And don't be afraid of the people, for I will be with you and will protect you. I, the LORD, have spoken!'" (Jeremiah 1:6–8). |

Jeremiah's story is told in the book of Jeremiah. He is also mentioned in Ezra 1:1; Daniel 9:2; Matthew 2:17; 16:14; 27:9. See also 2 Chronicles 34—35 for the story of the spiritual revival under Josiah.

---

**2:4-8** The united nation of Israel included both the "families of Israel" and the "people of Jacob" (Judah). Jeremiah knew Israel's history well. The prophets recited history to the people for several reasons: (1) to remind them of God's faithfulness; (2) to make sure the people wouldn't forget (they didn't have Bibles to read); (3) to emphasize God's love for them; (4) to remind the people that there was a time when they *were* close to God. We should learn from history so we can build on the successes and avoid repeating the failures of others.

7 "And when I brought you into a fruitful land
    to enjoy its bounty and goodness,
you defiled my land and
    corrupted the possession I had promised you.
8 The priests did not ask,
    'Where is the LORD?'
Those who taught my word ignored me,
    the rulers turned against me,
and the prophets spoke in the name of Baal,
    wasting their time on worthless idols!
9 Therefore, I will bring my case against you,"
    says the LORD.
"I will even bring charges against your children's children
    in the years to come.

10 "Go west and look in the land of Cyprus*;
    go east and search through the land of Kedar.
Has anyone ever heard of anything
    as strange as this?
11 Has any nation ever traded its gods for new ones,
    even though they are not gods at all?
Yet my people have exchanged their glorious God*
    for worthless idols!
12 The heavens are shocked at such a thing
    and shrink back in horror and dismay,"
    says the LORD.
13 "For my people have done two evil things:
They have abandoned me—
    the fountain of living water.
And they have dug for themselves cracked cisterns
    that can hold no water at all!

### The Results of Israel's Sin

14 "Why has Israel become a slave?
    Why has he been carried away as plunder?
15 Strong lions have roared against him,
    and the land has been destroyed.
The towns are now in ruins,
    and no one lives in them anymore.
16 Egyptians, marching from their cities of Memphis* and Tahpanhes,
    have destroyed Israel's glory and power.
17 And you have brought this upon yourselves
    by rebelling against the LORD your God,
    even though he was leading you on the way!

**2:7**
Deut 8:7-9;
11:10-12
Jer 3:2; 16:18

**2:8**
Jer 10:21; 23:13
Hab 2:18
Mal 2:6-7

**2:9**
Ezek 20:35-36

**2:10**
Ps 120:5
Isa 23:12; 37:19
Jer 49:28

**2:11**
Ps 106:20

**2:13**
Ps 36:9
Jer 17:13
John 4:14

**2:16**
Jer 44:1
Hos 9:6

**2:17**
Deut 32:10

**2:10** Hebrew *Kittim.*   **2:11** Hebrew *their glory.*   **2:16** Hebrew *Noph.*

---

**2:8** Baal was the chief male god of the Canaanite religion. Baal was the god of fertility. Worship of Baal included animal sacrifice and sacred prostitution (male and female) in the high places. Jezebel, the wife of King Ahab, introduced Baal worship into the northern kingdom, and eventually it spread to Judah. The sexual orientation of this worship was a constant temptation to the Israelites, who were called to be holy.

**2:10** God was saying that even pagan nations like Cyprus (in the west) and Kedar (the home of Arab tribes living in the desert east of Palestine) remained loyal to their national gods. But Israel had abandoned the one and only God for a completely worthless object of worship.

**2:13** Who would set aside a fountain of living water for a cracked cistern, a pit that collected rainwater but could not hold it? God told the Israelites they were doing that very thing when

they turned from him, the fountain of living water, to the worship of idols. Not only that, but the cisterns they chose were broken and empty. The people had built religious systems in which to store truth, but those systems were worthless. Why should we cling to the broken promises of unstable "cisterns" (money, power, religious systems, or whatever transitory thing we are putting in place of God) when God promises to constantly refresh us with living water (John 4:10)?

**2:16, 17** Memphis was near modern Cairo's present location in lower Egypt, and Tahpanhes was in northeastern Egypt. Jeremiah could be speaking of Pharaoh Shishak's previous invasion of Judah in 926 B.C. (1 Kings 14:25), or he may have been predicting Pharaoh Neco's invasion in 609 B.C. when King Josiah of Judah would be killed (2 Kings 23:29, 30). Jeremiah's point is that the people brought this on themselves by rebelling against God.

2:18
Josh 13:3
Isa 30:2

18 "What have you gained by your alliances with Egypt
     and your covenants with Assyria?
What good to you are the streams of the Nile*
     or the waters of the Euphrates River?*

2:19
Ps 36:1
Isa 3:9
Jer 3:8; 5:24
Hos 11:7
Amos 8:10

19 Your wickedness will bring its own punishment.
     Your turning from me will shame you.
You will see what an evil, bitter thing it is
     to abandon the LORD your God and not to fear him.
     I, the Lord, the LORD of Heaven's Armies, have spoken!

2:20
Lev 26:13
Deut 12:2
Isa 57:5
Jer 3:2, 6; 17:2

20 "Long ago I broke the yoke that oppressed you
     and tore away the chains of your slavery,
but still you said,
     'I will not serve you.'
On every hill and under every green tree,
     you have prostituted yourselves by bowing down to idols.

2:21
Exod 15:17
Ps 80:8
Isa 5:2, 4

21 But I was the one who planted you,
     choosing a vine of the purest stock—the very best.
How did you grow into this corrupt wild vine?

2:22
Jer 4:14

22 No amount of soap or lye can make you clean.
     I still see the stain of your guilt.
     I, the Sovereign LORD, have spoken!

### Israel, an Unfaithful Wife

2:23
Prov 30:12
Jer 7:31; 9:14

23 "You say, 'That's not true!
     I haven't worshiped the images of Baal!'
But how can you say that?
     Go and look in any valley in the land!
Face the awful sins you have done.
     You are like a restless female camel
     desperately searching for a mate.
24 You are like a wild donkey,
     sniffing the wind at mating time.
Who can restrain her lust?
     Those who desire her don't need to search,
     for she goes running to them!

2:18a Hebrew of Shihor, a branch of the Nile River. 2:18b Hebrew the river?

| THE KINGS OF JEREMIAH'S LIFETIME | King | Story of his reign | Dates of his reign | Character of reign | Jeremiah's message to the king |
|---|---|---|---|---|---|
| | Josiah | 2 Kings 22:1–23:30 | 640–609 B.C. | Mostly good | 3:6-25 |
| | Jehoahaz | 2 Kings 23:31-33 | 609 B.C. | Evil | 22:11-17 |
| | Jehoiakim | 2 Kings 23:34–24:7 | 609–598 B.C. | Evil | 22:18-23; 25:1-38; 26:1-24; 27:1-11; 35:1-19; 36:1-32 |
| | Jehoiachin | 2 Kings 24:8-17 | 598–597 B.C. | Evil | 13:18-27; 22:24-30 |
| | Zedekiah | 2 Kings 24:18–25:26 | 597–586 B.C. | Evil | 21:1-14; 24:8-10; 27:12-22; 32:1-5; 34:1-22; 37:1-21; 38:1-28; 51:59-64 |

2:22 The stain of sin is more than skin-deep. Israel had stains that could not be washed out, even with the strongest cleansers. Spiritual cleansing must reach deep into the heart—and this is a job that God alone can do. We cannot ignore the effects of sin and hope they will go away. Your sin has caused a deep stain that only God can remove if you are willing to let him cleanse you (Isaiah 1:18; Ezekiel 36:25).

2:23-27 The people are compared to animals who search for mates in mating season. Unrestrained, they rush for power,

money, alliances with foreign powers, and other gods. The idols did not seek the people; the people sought the idols and ran wildly after them. Then they became so comfortable in their sin that they could not think of giving it up. Their only shame was in getting caught. If we desire something so much that we'll do anything to get it, it is a sign that we are addicted to it and out of tune with God.

25 When will you stop running?
  When will you stop panting after other gods?
But you say, 'Save your breath.
  I'm in love with these foreign gods,
  and I can't stop loving them now!'

2:25
Deut 32:16
Jer 14:10; 18:12

26 "Israel is like a thief
  who feels shame only when he gets caught.
They, their kings, officials, priests, and prophets—
  all are alike in this.

2:26
Jer 48:27

27 To an image carved from a piece of wood they say,
  'You are my father.'
To an idol chiseled from a block of stone they say,
  'You are my mother.'
They turn their backs on me,
  but in times of trouble they cry out to me,
  'Come and save us!'

2:27
Isa 26:16
Jer 18:17

28 But why not call on these gods you have made?
  When trouble comes, let them save you if they can!
For you have as many gods
  as there are towns in Judah.

2:28
Deut 32:37
2 Kgs 17:30-31
Isa 45:20
Jer 11:12-13

29 Why do you accuse me of doing wrong?
  You are the ones who have rebelled,"
says the LORD.

2:29
Dan 9:11

30 "I have punished your children,
  but they did not respond to my discipline.
You yourselves have killed your prophets
  as a lion kills its prey.

2:30
Neh 9:26
Isa 1:5

31 "O my people, listen to the words of the LORD!
  Have I been like a desert to Israel?
  Have I been to them a land of darkness?
Why then do my people say, 'At last we are free from God!
  We don't need him anymore!'

2:31
Deut 32:15
Isa 45:19

32 Does a young woman forget her jewelry?
  Does a bride hide her wedding dress?
Yet for years on end
  my people have forgotten me.

2:32
Isa 17:10
Jer 3:21
Hos 8:14

33 "How you plot and scheme to win your lovers.
  Even an experienced prostitute could learn from you!
34 Your clothing is stained with the blood of the innocent and the poor,
  though you didn't catch them breaking into your houses!

2:34
2 Kgs 21:16
Jer 7:6; 19:4

35 And yet you say,
  'I have done nothing wrong.
  Surely God isn't angry with me!'
But now I will punish you severely
  because you claim you have not sinned.

2:35
Jer 25:31
1 Jn 1:8, 10

36 First here, then there—
  you flit from one ally to another asking for help.

2:36
2 Chr 28:16, 20-21
Hos 12:1
1 Jn 1:8, 10

---

**2:30** Being a prophet in Jeremiah's day was risky business. Prophets had to criticize the policies of evil kings, and this made them appear to be traitors. The kings hated the prophets for standing against their policies, and the people often hated the prophets for preaching against their idolatrous lifestyles (see Acts 7:52).

**2:31, 32** Forgetting can be dangerous, whether it is intentional or an oversight. Israel deliberately ignored God by focusing its affections on the allurements of the world. The more we focus on the passing pleasures of this life, the easier it becomes to forget God's care, his love, his dependability, his guidance, and most

of all, God himself. What pleases you most? Have you been forgetting God lately?

**2:36** God is not against alliances or working partnerships, but he is against people trusting others for the help that should come from him. This was the problem in Jeremiah's time. After the days of David and Solomon, Israel fell apart because the leaders turned to other nations and gods instead of the true God. They played power politics, thinking that their strong neighbors could protect them. But Judah would soon learn that its alliance with Egypt would be just as disappointing as its former alliance with Assyria (2 Kings 16:8, 9; Isaiah 7:13-25).

But your new friends in Egypt will let you down,
  just as Assyria did before.
37 In despair, you will be led into exile
  with your hands on your heads,
for the LORD has rejected the nations you trust.
  They will not help you at all.

**2:37**
Jer 37:7-10

**3:1**
Deut 24:4
Jer 4:1
Ezek 16:26, 28-29
Zech 1:3

**3** 1 "If a man divorces a woman
  and she goes and marries someone else,
he will not take her back again,
  for that would surely corrupt the land.
But you have prostituted yourself with many lovers,
  so why are you trying to come back to me?"
  says the LORD.

**3:2**
Deut 12:2
Jer 2:7, 20
Ezek 16:25

2 "Look at the shrines on every hilltop.
  Is there any place you have not been defiled
  by your adultery with other gods?
You sit like a prostitute beside the road waiting for a customer.
  You sit alone like a nomad in the desert.
You have polluted the land with your prostitution
  and your wickedness.

**3:3**
Lev 26:19
Jer 6:15; 14:3-6
**3:4**
Ps 71:17

3 That's why even the spring rains have failed.
  For you are a brazen prostitute and completely shameless.
4 Yet you say to me,
  'Father, you have been my guide since my youth.
5 Surely you won't be angry forever!
  Surely you can forget about it!'
So you talk,
  but you keep on doing all the evil you can."

**3:6**
Jer 17:2
Ezek 23:4-10
**3:7**
Ezek 16:47
**3:8**
Isa 50:1
Ezek 16:46-47;
23:11
**3:9**
Isa 57:6
Jer 2:7, 27
**3:10**
Jer 12:2

### Judah Follows Israel's Example

6During the reign of King Josiah, the LORD said to me, "Have you seen what fickle Israel has done? Like a wife who commits adultery, Israel has worshiped other gods on every hill and under every green tree. 7I thought, 'After she has done all this, she will return to me.' But she did not return, and her faithless sister Judah saw this. 8She saw that I divorced faithless Israel because of her adultery. But that treacherous sister Judah had no fear, and now she, too, has left me and given herself to prostitution. 9Israel treated it all so lightly—she thought nothing of committing adultery by worshiping idols made of wood and stone. So now the land has been polluted. 10But despite all this, her faithless sister Judah has never sincerely returned to me. She has only pretended to be sorry. I, the LORD, have spoken!"

---

**3:1** This law, found in Deuteronomy 24:1-4, says that a divorced woman who remarries can never be reunited with her first husband. Judah "divorced" God and "married" other gods. God had every right to permanently disown his wayward people, but in his mercy he was willing to take them back again.

**3:2** "Like a nomad in the desert" means that Judah anticipated idolatry as a thief might hide in the wilderness to plunder a passing caravan.

**3:4, 5** In spite of their great sin, the people of Israel continued to talk like they were God's children. The only way they could do this was to minimize their sin. When we know we've done something wrong, we want to downplay the error and relieve some of the guilt we feel. As we minimize our sinfulness, we naturally shy away from making changes, and so we keep on sinning. But if we view every wrong attitude and action as a serious offense against God, we will begin to understand what living for God is all about. Is there any sin in your life that you've written off as too small to worry about? God says that we must confess and turn away from *every* sin.

**3:6–6:30** The northern kingdom, Israel, had fallen to Assyria, and its people had been taken into captivity. The tragic lesson of their fall should have caused the southern kingdom, Judah, to return to God, but Judah paid no attention. Jeremiah urged Judah to return to God to avoid certain disaster. This message came between 627 and 621 B.C., during Josiah's reign. Although Josiah obeyed God's commands, his example apparently did not penetrate the hearts of the people. If the people refused to repent, God said he would destroy the nation because of the evils of Josiah's grandfather, King Manasseh (2 Kings 23:25-27).

## Hope for Wayward Israel

11 Then the LORD said to me, "Even faithless Israel is less guilty than treacherous Judah! 12 Therefore, go and give this message to Israel.* This is what the LORD says:

> "O Israel, my faithless people,
> come home to me again,
> for I am merciful.
> I will not be angry with you forever.

3:12
Ps 86:15
Jer 31:20; 33:26

13 Only acknowledge your guilt.
> Admit that you rebelled against the LORD your God
> and committed adultery against him
> by worshiping idols under every green tree.
> Confess that you refused to listen to my voice.
> I, the LORD, have spoken!

3:13
Deut 12:2; 30:1-3
Jer 14:20

14 "Return home, you wayward children,"
> says the LORD,
> "for I am your master.
> I will bring you back to the land of Israel*—
> one from this town and two from that family—
> from wherever you are scattered.

3:14
Jer 50:4-5
Hos 2:19

15 And I will give you shepherds after my own heart,
> who will guide you with knowledge and understanding.

3:15
Jer 23:4
Acts 20:28

16 "And when your land is once more filled with people," says the LORD, "you will no longer wish for 'the good old days' when you possessed the Ark of the LORD's Covenant. You will not miss those days or even remember them, and there will be no need to rebuild the Ark. 17 In that day Jerusalem will be known as 'The Throne of the LORD.' All nations will come there to honor the LORD. They will no longer stubbornly follow their own evil desires. 18 In those days the people of Judah and Israel will return together from exile in the north. They will return to the land I gave their ancestors as an inheritance forever.

3:16
Isa 65:17

3:17
Jer 12:15-16;
16:19; 17:12
Ezek 43:7

3:18
Isa 11:13; 60:9
Jer 16:14-15;
31:8; 50:4-5
Hos 1:11
Amos 9:15

19 "I thought to myself,
> 'I would love to treat you as my own children!'
> I wanted nothing more than to give you this beautiful land—
> the finest possession in the world.
> I looked forward to your calling me 'Father,'
> and I wanted you never to turn from me.

3:19
Ps 16:6
Isa 63:16

20 But you have been unfaithful to me, you people of Israel!
> You have been like a faithless wife who leaves her husband.
> I, the LORD, have spoken."

3:20
Isa 48:8

21 Voices are heard high on the windswept mountains,
> the weeping and pleading of Israel's people.
> For they have chosen crooked paths
> and have forgotten the LORD their God.

3:21
Isa 15:2
Jer 2:32

3:12 Hebrew toward the north.   3:14 Hebrew to Zion.

---

3:11-13 Israel was not even trying to look as if it were obeying God, but Judah maintained the appearance of faith without a true heart. Believing the right doctrines without heartfelt commitment is like offering sacrifices without true repentance. Judah's false repentance brought Jeremiah's words of condemnation. To live without faith is hopeless; to express sorrow without change is hypocritical. Being sorry for sin is not enough. Repentance demands a change of mind and heart that results in changed behavior.

3:12-18 The northern kingdom, Israel, was in captivity, being punished for its sins. The people of Judah undoubtedly looked down on these northern neighbors for their blatant heresy and degraded morals. Even so, Jeremiah promised the remnant of Israel God's blessings if they would turn to him. Judah, still secure in its own mind, should have turned to God after seeing the destruction of Israel. But the people of Judah refused, so

Jeremiah startled them by reaffirming God's promise to Israel's remnant if they would repent.

3:15 God promised to give his people leaders (shepherds) who would follow him, filled with knowledge (wisdom) and understanding. God saw Israel's lack of direction, so he promised to provide the right kind of leadership. We look to and trust our leaders for guidance and direction. But if they do not follow God, they will lead us astray. Pray for God-honoring leaders in our nations, communities, and churches—those who will be good examples and bring us God's wisdom.

3:16, 17 In the days of David and Solomon's reign over a united Israel, the people had a beautiful Temple, where they worshiped God. The Temple housed the Ark of the Covenant, the symbol of God's presence with the people. The Ark held the tablets of the Ten Commandments (see Exodus 25:10-22). Those days with the Ark wouldn't be missed in the future Kingdom because God's

3:22
Hos 6:1; 14:4

22 "My wayward children," says the LORD,
   "come back to me, and I will heal your wayward hearts."

"Yes, we're coming," the people reply,
   "for you are the LORD our God.

3:23
Pss 3:8; 121:1-2
Jer 17:14

23 Our worship of idols on the hills
   and our religious orgies on the mountains
   are a delusion.
Only in the LORD our God
   will Israel ever find salvation.
24 From childhood we have watched
   as everything our ancestors worked for—
   their flocks and herds, their sons and daughters—
   was squandered on a delusion.

3:25
Ezra 9:7
Jer 22:21

25 Let us now lie down in shame
   and cover ourselves with dishonor,
for we and our ancestors have sinned
   against the LORD our God.
From our childhood to this day
   we have never obeyed him."

4:1
Joel 2:12

4 1 "O Israel," says the LORD,
   "if you wanted to return to me, you could.
You could throw away your detestable idols
   and stray away no more.

4:2
Gen 22:18
Deut 10:20
Gal 3:8

2 Then when you swear by my name, saying,
   'As surely as the LORD lives,'
you could do so
   with truth, justice, and righteousness.
Then you would be a blessing to the nations of the world,
   and all people would come and praise my name."

*Coming Judgment against Judah*

4:3
Hos 10:12
Matt 13:7, 22

3 This is what the LORD says to the people of Judah and Jerusalem:

"Plow up the hard ground of your hearts!
   Do not waste your good seed among thorns.

4:4
Deut 10:16
Isa 30:27
Jer 9:25-26; 21:12
Mark 9:43, 48
Rom 2:28-29

4 O people of Judah and Jerusalem,
   surrender your pride and power.
Change your hearts before the LORD,*
   or my anger will burn like an unquenchable fire
   because of all your sins.

4:5
Josh 10:20
Hos 8:1

5 "Shout to Judah, and broadcast to Jerusalem!
   Tell them to sound the alarm throughout the land:
'Run for your lives!
   Flee to the fortified cities!'

4:4 Hebrew *Circumcise yourselves to the LORD, and take away the foreskins of your heart.*

---

presence by the Holy Spirit would be there personally among his people.

**3:22-25** Jeremiah predicted a day when the nation would be reunited, true worship would be reinstated, and sin would be seen for what it is. Our world glorifies the thrill that comes from wealth, winning, and sexual pleasure, and it ignores the sin that is so often associated with these thrills. It is sad that so few see sin as it really is—a deception. Most people can't see this until they are destroyed by the sin they pursue. The advantage of believing God's Word is that we don't have to learn by hard experience the destructive results of sin.

**4:1, 2** Throughout the Old Testament, God consistently revealed his intentions to bless the nations of the world. His global vision included a central role for the people of Israel as the channel

through which God would pour out his blessings on all nations. But their privilege as the chosen people was in jeopardy as long as they insisted on disobedience and idolatry.

**4:3** Jeremiah told the people to plow up the hardness of their hearts as a plow breaks up unplowed ground—soil that has not been tilled for a season. Good kings like Josiah had tried to turn the people back to God, but the people had continued to worship their idols in secret. Their hearts had become hardened to God's will. Unless their hearts were broken and cleaned up, the good seed of God's commands could not take root. Old habits and hidden sins had to be uprooted and rejected. Likewise we must remove our heart-hardening sin if we expect God's Word to take root and grow in our life.

6 Raise a signal flag as a warning for Jerusalem*:
   'Flee now! Do not delay!'
For I am bringing terrible destruction upon you
   from the north."

7 A lion stalks from its den,
   a destroyer of nations.
It has left its lair and is headed your way.
   It's going to devastate your land!
Your towns will lie in ruins,
   with no one living in them anymore.

**4:7**
Isa 1:7; 6:11
Jer 2:15; 5:6;
25:9, 38

8 So put on clothes of mourning
   and weep with broken hearts,
for the fierce anger of the LORD
   is still upon us.

**4:8**
Isa 5:25; 10:4
Jer 30:24

9 "In that day," says the LORD,
   "the king and the officials will tremble in fear.
The priests will be struck with horror,
   and the prophets will be appalled."

10 Then I said, "O Sovereign LORD,
   the people have been deceived by what you said,
for you promised peace for Jerusalem.
   But the sword is held at their throats!"

**4:10**
2 Thes 2:11; 14:13

11 The time is coming when the LORD will say
   to the people of Jerusalem,
"My dear people, a burning wind is blowing in from the desert,
   and it's not a gentle breeze useful for winnowing grain.

**4:11**
Jer 51:1
Ezek 17:10
Hos 13:15

12 It is a roaring blast sent by me!
   Now I will pronounce your destruction!"

13 Our enemy rushes down on us like storm clouds!
   His chariots are like whirlwinds.
His horses are swifter than eagles.
   How terrible it will be, for we are doomed!

**4:13**
Deut 28:49
Isa 66:15
Lam 4:19

14 O Jerusalem, cleanse your heart
   that you may be saved.
How long will you harbor
   your evil thoughts?

**4:14**
Isa 1:16
Jer 13:27
Jas 4:8

15 Your destruction has been announced
   from Dan and the hill country of Ephraim.

**4:15**
Jer 6:19

16 "Warn the surrounding nations
   and announce this to Jerusalem:
The enemy is coming from a distant land,
   raising a battle cry against the towns of Judah.

**4:16**
Jer 5:15
Ezek 21:22

17 They surround Jerusalem like watchmen around a field,
   for my people have rebelled against me,"
   says the LORD.

**4:17**
2 Kgs 25:1
Jer 5:23

18 "Your own actions have brought this upon you.
   This punishment is bitter, piercing you to the heart!"

**4:6** Hebrew *Zion*.

---

**4:6, 7** The destruction from the north came from Babylon when Nabopolassar and his son, Nebuchadnezzar II, attacked (see 2 Chronicles 36).

**4:10** Jeremiah, deeply moved by God's words, expressed his sorrow and confusion to God. Jeremiah was intercessor for the people. These people had false expectations because of the past promises of blessings, their blindness to their

own sin, and the false prophets who kept telling them that all was well.

**4:15** Destruction was announced first from Dan and then on to the hill country of Ephraim because Dan was located at the northern border of Israel. Thus, the Danites would be the first to see the approaching armies as they invaded from the north. No one would be able to stop the armies because they would be coming as punishment for the people's sin.

## Jeremiah Weeps for His People

**4:19**
Isa 21:3; 22:4
Hab 3:16

19 My heart, my heart—I writhe in pain!
My heart pounds within me! I cannot be still.
For I have heard the blast of enemy trumpets
and the roar of their battle cries.

**4:20**
Jer 10:20
Ezek 7:26

20 Waves of destruction roll over the land,
until it lies in complete desolation.
Suddenly my tents are destroyed;
in a moment my shelters are crushed.

21 How long must I see the battle flags
and hear the trumpets of war?

**4:22**
Jer 5:21; 10:8;
13:23
Rom 16:19

22 "My people are foolish
and do not know me," says the LORD.
"They are stupid children
who have no understanding.
They are clever enough at doing wrong,
but they have no idea how to do right!"

## Jeremiah's Vision of Coming Disaster

**4:23**
Isa 24:19

23 I looked at the earth, and it was empty and formless.
I looked at the heavens, and there was no light.

**4:24**
Isa 5:25
Ezek 38:20

24 I looked at the mountains and hills,
and they trembled and shook.

**4:25**
Jer 9:10; 12:4
Zeph 1:3

25 I looked, and all the people were gone.
All the birds of the sky had flown away.

26 I looked, and the fertile fields had become a wilderness.
The towns lay in ruins,
crushed by the LORD's fierce anger.

27 This is what the LORD says:
"The whole land will be ruined,
but I will not destroy it completely.

**4:28**
Num 23:19
Isa 5:30; 50:3
Jer 23:20; 30:24
Hos 4:3
Joel 2:30-31

28 The earth will mourn
and the heavens will be draped in black
because of my decree against my people.
I have made up my mind and will not change it."

29 At the noise of charioteers and archers,
the people flee in terror.
They hide in the bushes
and run for the mountains.
All the towns have been abandoned—
not a person remains!

**4:30**
2 Kgs 9:30
Jer 22:20, 22
Ezek 23:9-10, 22

30 What are you doing,
you who have been plundered?
Why do you dress up in beautiful clothing
and put on gold jewelry?
Why do you brighten your eyes with mascara?
Your primping will do you no good!
The allies who were your lovers
despise you and seek to kill you.

---

**4:19-31** Jeremiah was anguished by the sure devastation of the coming judgment. This judgment would continue until the people turned from their sin and listened to God. Although this prophecy refers to the future destruction by Babylon, it could also describe the judgment of all sinners at the end of the world. These verses also speak to those in an age of terrorism about overwhelming feelings of dread and the importance of recognizing God's ultimate control over the events of history.

**4:22** Judah was clever at doing wrong but did not know how to do what was right. Right living is more than simply avoiding sin. It requires decision and discipline. We must develop skills in right living because our behavior attracts attention to our God. We should pursue excellence in Christian living with as much effort as we pursue excellence at work.

**4:27** God warned that destruction was certain, but he promised that the faithful remnant would be spared. God is committed to preserving those who are faithful to him.

³¹ I hear a cry, like that of a woman in labor,
    the groans of a woman giving birth to her first child.
It is beautiful Jerusalem*
    gasping for breath and crying out,
    "Help! I'm being murdered!"

4:31
Isa 1:15; 42:14
Jer 13:21
Lam 1:17

### The Sins of Judah

**5** ¹ "Run up and down every street in Jerusalem," says the LORD.
    "Look high and low; search throughout the city!
If you can find even one just and honest person,
    I will not destroy the city.

5:1
Gen 18:26, 32
2 Chr 16:9

² But even when they are under oath,
    saying, 'As surely as the LORD lives,'
    they are still telling lies!"

5:2
Titus 1:16

³ LORD, you are searching for honesty.
You struck your people,
    but they paid no attention.
You crushed them,
    but they refused to be corrected.
They are determined, with faces set like stone;
    they have refused to repent.

5:3
Jer 7:26, 28; 8:5;
19:15
Ezek 3:8
Zeph 3:2

⁴ Then I said, "But what can we expect from the poor?
    They are ignorant.
They don't know the ways of the LORD.
    They don't understand God's laws.

5:4
Isa 27:11
Jer 4:22
Hos 4:6

⁵ So I will go and speak to their leaders.
    Surely they know the ways of the LORD
    and understand God's laws."
But the leaders, too, as one man,
    had thrown off God's yoke
    and broken his chains.

5:5
Jer 2:20
Mic 3:1

⁶ So now a lion from the forest will attack them;
    a wolf from the desert will pounce on them.
A leopard will lurk near their towns,
    tearing apart any who dare to venture out.
For their rebellion is great,
    and their sins are many.

5:6
Jer 30:14-15
Hos 13:7
Hab 1:8

⁷ "How can I pardon you?
    For even your children have turned from me.
They have sworn by gods that are not gods at all!
    I fed my people until they were full.
But they thanked me by committing adultery
    and lining up at the brothels.

5:7
Deut 32:21
Josh 23:7
Jer 2:11
Zeph 1:5
Gal 4:8

⁸ They are well-fed, lusty stallions,
    each neighing for his neighbor's wife.

5:8
Jer 13:27; 29:23
Ezek 22:11

**4:31** Hebrew *the daughter of Zion.*

---

**5:1** Jerusalem was the capital city and center of worship for Judah. God was willing to spare the city if only one person who was just and honest could be found (he made a similar statement about Sodom; see Genesis 18:32). Think how significant your testimony may be in your city or community. You may represent the only witness for God to many people. Are you faithful to that opportunity?

**5:3** Nothing but honesty is acceptable to God. When we pray, sing, speak, or serve, nothing closes the door of God's acceptance more than hypocrisy, lying, or pretense. God sees through us and refuses to listen. To be close to God, be honest with him.

**5:4, 5** Even the leaders who knew God's laws and understood his words of judgment had rejected him. They were supposed to teach and guide the people, but instead they led them into sin. Jeremiah observed the poor and ignorant—those who were uninformed of God's ways—and realized they were not learning God's laws from their leaders. Thus, God's search in Jerusalem was complete. There were no true followers in any level of society.

**5:7** God held these people responsible for the sins of their children because the children had followed their parents' example. The sin of leading others, especially our children, astray by our example is one for which God will hold us accountable.

9 Should I not punish them for this?" says the LORD.
 "Should I not avenge myself against such a nation?

**5:10**
Jer 4:27

10 "Go down the rows of the vineyards and destroy the grapevines,
 leaving a scattered few alive.
Strip the branches from the vines,
 for these people do not belong to the LORD.
11 The people of Israel and Judah
 are full of treachery against me,"
says the LORD.

**5:12**
2 Chr 36:16
Jer 43:1-4

12 "They have lied about the LORD
 and said, 'He won't bother us!
No disasters will come upon us.
 There will be no war or famine.

**5:13**
Jer 14:13, 15

13 God's prophets are all windbags
 who don't really speak for him.
Let their predictions of disaster fall on themselves!'"

14 Therefore, this is what the LORD God of Heaven's Armies says:

"Because the people are talking like this,
 my messages will flame out of your mouth
 and burn the people like kindling wood.

**5:15**
Deut 28:49
Isa 5:26; 28:11

15 O Israel, I will bring a distant nation against you,"
 says the LORD.
"It is a mighty nation,
 an ancient nation,
a people whose language you do not know,
 whose speech you cannot understand.
16 Their weapons are deadly;
 their warriors are mighty.

**5:17**
Lev 26:16
Deut 28:31, 33
Jer 8:16
Hos 8:14

17 They will devour the food of your harvest;
 they will devour your sons and daughters.
They will devour your flocks and herds;
 they will devour your grapes and figs.
And they will destroy your fortified towns,
 which you think are so safe.

**5:19**
Deut 28:48;
29:24-26
1 Kgs 9:8-9
Jer 16:10-13

18 "Yet even in those days I will not blot you out completely," says the LORD. 19 "And when your people ask, 'Why did the LORD our God do all this to us?' you must reply, 'You rejected him and gave yourselves to foreign gods in your own land. Now you will serve foreigners in a land that is not your own.'

### A Warning for God's People

20 "Make this announcement to Israel,*
 and say this to Judah:

**5:21**
Matt 13:14
†Mark 8:18

21 Listen, you foolish and senseless people,
 with eyes that do not see
 and ears that do not hear.

**5:20** Hebrew *to the house of Jacob.* The names "Jacob" and "Israel" are often interchanged throughout the Old Testament, referring sometimes to the individual patriarch and sometimes to the nation.

---

**5:15** Babylon was indeed an ancient nation. The old Babylonian Empire had lasted from about 1900 to 1550 B.C., and earlier kingdoms had been on her soil as early as 3000 B.C. Babylon in Jeremiah's day would shortly rebel against Assyrian domination, form its own army, conquer Assyria, and become the next dominant world power.

**5:21** Have you ever spoken to someone, only to realize that the person didn't hear a word you were saying? Jeremiah told the people that their eyes and ears did them no good because they refused to see or hear God's message. The people of Judah and Israel were foolishly deaf when God promised blessings for

obedience and destruction for disobedience. When God speaks through his Word or his messengers, we harm ourselves if we fail to listen. God's message will never change us unless we heed it.

22 Have you no respect for me?
    Why don't you tremble in my presence?
I, the LORD, define the ocean's sandy shoreline
    as an everlasting boundary that the waters cannot cross.
The waves may toss and roar,
    but they can never pass the boundaries I set.
23 But my people have stubborn and rebellious hearts.
    They have turned away and abandoned me.
24 They do not say from the heart,
    'Let us live in awe of the LORD our God,
for he gives us rain each spring and fall,
    assuring us of a harvest when the time is right.'
25 Your wickedness has deprived you of these wonderful blessings.
    Your sin has robbed you of all these good things.

26 "Among my people are wicked men
    who lie in wait for victims like a hunter hiding in a blind.
They continually set traps
    to catch people.
27 Like a cage filled with birds,
    their homes are filled with evil plots.
And now they are great and rich.
28 They are fat and sleek,
    and there is no limit to their wicked deeds.
They refuse to provide justice to orphans
    and deny the rights of the poor.
29 Should I not punish them for this?" says the LORD.
    "Should I not avenge myself against such a nation?
30 A horrible and shocking thing
    has happened in this land—
31 the prophets give false prophecies,
    and the priests rule with an iron hand.
Worse yet, my people like it that way!
    But what will you do when the end comes?

### Jerusalem's Last Warning

**6** 1 "Run for your lives, you people of Benjamin!
    Get out of Jerusalem!
Sound the alarm in Tekoa!
    Send up a signal at Beth-hakkerem!
A powerful army is coming from the north,
    coming with disaster and destruction.
2 O Jerusalem,* you are my beautiful and delicate daughter—
    but I will destroy you!
3 Enemies will surround you, like shepherds camped around the city.
    Each chooses a place for his troops to devour.

6:2 Hebrew *Daughter of Zion.*

**5:22**
Deut 28:58
Job 38:8-11

**5:24**
Gen 8:22
Ps 147:8
Joel 2:23
Matt 5:45

**5:26**
Ps 10:9
Hab 1:15

**5:28**
Deut 32:15
Isa 1:23
Zech 7:10

**5:30**
Jer 23:14
Hos 6:10
**5:31**
Jer 14:14
Ezek 13:6
Mic 2:11

**6:1**
Neh 3:14
Jer 1:14; 4:6

**6:2**
Deut 28:56
**6:3**
2 Kgs 25:1
Jer 4:17; 12:10
Luke 19:43

---

**5:22-24** What is your attitude when you come into God's presence? We should come with respect and trembling because God sets the boundaries of the roaring ocean and sends the rain, assuring us of plentiful harvests. God had to strip away all the benefits that Judah and Israel had grown to expect from him and give the people another opportunity to turn back to him. God still sometimes uses the same method of blessing or withholding blessing to get our attention. Don't wait until God removes your cherished resources before committing yourself to him as you should.

**5:28, 29** People and nations who please God treat the fatherless (orphans) justly and care for the poor. Wicked men in Israel treated the defenseless unjustly, which displeased God greatly. Some defenseless people—orphans, the poor, the homeless, and the lonely—are within your reach. What action can you take to help at least one of them?

**6:1** The Lord warned Jeremiah's own tribe of Benjamin to flee, not to the security of the great walled city of Jerusalem because it would be under siege, but toward Tekoa, a town about 12 miles south of Jerusalem. The warning smoke signal was lit at Beth-hakkerem, halfway between Jerusalem and Bethlehem.

**6:3** The shepherds were the leaders of Babylon's armies.

4 They shout, 'Prepare for battle!
   Attack at noon!'
'No, it's too late; the day is fading,
   and the evening shadows are falling.'

**6:5**
Isa 32:14

5 'Well then, let's attack at night
   and destroy her palaces!'"

**6:6**
Deut 20:19-20
Jer 22:17; 32:24

6 This is what the LORD of Heaven's Armies says:
"Cut down the trees for battering rams.
   Build siege ramps against the walls of Jerusalem.
This is the city to be punished,
   for she is wicked through and through.

**6:7**
Jer 20:8; 30:12-13
Ezek 7:11, 23
Jas 3:10-12

7 She spouts evil like a fountain.
   Her streets echo with the sounds of violence and destruction.
   I always see her sickness and sores.
8 Listen to this warning, Jerusalem,
   or I will turn from you in disgust.
Listen, or I will turn you into a heap of ruins,
   a land where no one lives."

**6:9**
Jer 8:3; 16:16; 49:9
Obad 1:5-6

9 This is what the LORD of Heaven's Armies says:
"Even the few who remain in Israel
   will be picked over again,
as when a harvester checks each vine a second time
   to pick the grapes that were missed."

### Israel's Constant Rebellion

**6:10**
Jer 7:26; 20:8
Acts 7:51

10 To whom can I give warning?
   Who will listen when I speak?
Their ears are closed,
   and they cannot hear.
They scorn the word of the LORD.
   They don't want to listen at all.

**6:11**
Job 32:18-19

11 So now I am filled with the LORD's fury.
   Yes, I am tired of holding it in!

"I will pour out my fury on children playing in the streets
   and on gatherings of young men,
on husbands and wives
   and on those who are old and gray.

**6:12**
Deut 28:30
Jer 8:10; 15:6

12 Their homes will be turned over to their enemies,
   as will their fields and their wives.
For I will raise my powerful fist
   against the people of this land,"
   says the LORD.

**6:13**
Isa 56:11; 57:17
Jer 22:17
Mic 3:5, 11

13 "From the least to the greatest,
   their lives are ruled by greed.
From prophets to priests,
   they are all frauds.

**6:14**
Jer 8:11-12
Ezek 13:10

14 They offer superficial treatments
   for my people's mortal wound.

---

**6:9** The "few who remain in Israel" is not to be confused with the righteous remnant. This remnant refers to those left after the first wave of destruction. Like a grape gatherer, Babylon wouldn't be satisfied until every person was taken. Babylonians invaded Judah three times until they destroyed the nation and its Temple completely (2 Kings 24–25).

**6:10** The people became angry and closed their ears. They wanted no part of God's commands because living for God did not appear very exciting. As in Jeremiah's day, people today dislike God's demand for disciplined living. As unsettling as people's responses might be, we must continue to share God's Word. Our responsibility is to present God's Word; their responsibility is to accept it. We must not let what people want to hear determine what we say.

**6:14** "Ignore it and maybe it will go away!" Sound familiar? This was Israel's response to Jeremiah's warnings. They kept listening to predictions of peace because they did not like Jeremiah's condemnation of their sin. But denying the truth never changes it; what God says always happens. Sin is never removed by denying its existence. We must confess to God that we have sinned and ask him to forgive us.

They give assurances of peace
   when there is no peace.
15 Are they ashamed of their disgusting actions?
   Not at all—they don't even know how to blush!
Therefore, they will lie among the slaughtered.
   They will be brought down when I punish them,"
   says the LORD.

**6:15**
Jer 3:3; 8:12

## Israel Rejects the LORD's Way

16 This is what the LORD says:
   "Stop at the crossroads and look around.
     Ask for the old, godly way, and walk in it.
Travel its path, and you will find rest for your souls.
   But you reply, 'No, that's not the road we want!'
17 I posted watchmen over you who said,
   'Listen for the sound of the alarm.'
But you replied,
   'No! We won't pay attention!'

**6:16**
Jer 18:15; 31:21
Mal 4:4
†Matt 11:29

**6:17**
Isa 21:11; 58:1
Jer 25:4
Ezek 3:17

18 "Therefore, listen to this, all you nations.
   Take note of my people's situation.
19 Listen, all the earth!
   I will bring disaster on my people.
It is the fruit of their own schemes,
   because they refuse to listen to me.
   They have rejected my word.
20 There's no use offering me sweet frankincense from Sheba.
   Keep your fragrant calamus imported from distant lands!
I will not accept your burnt offerings.
   Your sacrifices have no pleasing aroma for me."

**6:20**
Pss 40:6; 50:7-9
Isa 1:11; 60:6; 66:3
Amos 5:21

21 Therefore, this is what the LORD says:
   "I will put obstacles in my people's path.
Fathers and sons will both fall over them.
   Neighbors and friends will die together."

**6:21**
Isa 8:14; 9:14-17
Jer 9:21-22; 13:16

## An Invasion from the North

22 This is what the LORD says:
   "Look! A great army coming from the north!
   A great nation is rising against you from far-off lands.
23 They are armed with bows and spears.
   They are cruel and show no mercy.
They sound like a roaring sea
   as they ride forward on horses.
They are coming in battle formation,
   planning to destroy you, beautiful Jerusalem.*"

**6:22**
Jer 1:15; 10:22;
50:41-43

**6:23**
Isa 5:30
Jer 4:29; 50:42

24 We have heard reports about the enemy,
   and we wring our hands in fright.
Pangs of anguish have gripped us,
   like those of a woman in labor.
25 Don't go out to the fields!
   Don't travel on the roads!
The enemy's sword is everywhere
   and terrorizes us at every turn!

**6:24**
Isa 28:19
Jer 4:19-21

6:23 Hebrew *daughter of Zion.*

---

**6:16** The right path for living is "the old, godly way" and has been marked out by God. But the people refused to take God's path, going their own way instead. We face the same decision today—going God's old but true way, or following a new path of our own choosing. Don't be misled. The only way to find peace and "rest for your souls" is to walk on God's path.

**6:20** Sheba, located in southwest Arabia, was a center of trade in incense and spices used in pagan religious rituals.

**6:25** Ominous travel warnings, increased threat levels, and tight security were as much a part of life in ancient Israel as they are in the world today. Terrorism, in one form or another, has been a tactic throughout history. The question raised about such real

6:26
Jer 4:8; 25:34
Amos 8:10
Mic 1:10
Zech 12:10

26 Oh, my people, dress yourselves in burlap
 and sit among the ashes.
Mourn and weep bitterly, as for the loss of an only son.
 For suddenly the destroying armies will be upon you!

6:27
Jer 1:18; 15:20
6:28
Ezek 22:18

27 "Jeremiah, I have made you a tester of metals,*
 that you may determine the quality of my people.
28 They are the worst kind of rebel,
 full of slander.
They are as hard as bronze and iron,
 and they lead others into corruption.
29 The bellows fiercely fan the flames
 to burn out the corruption.
But it does not purify them,
 for the wickedness remains.

6:30
Ps 119:119
Isa 1:22

30 I will label them 'Rejected Silver,'
 for I, the LORD, am discarding them."

## Jeremiah Speaks at the Temple

7:2
Jer 17:19
7:3
Jer 4:1; 18:11;
26:13
7:4
Mic 3:11
7:5
Isa 1:19
Jer 21:12; 22:3
7:6
Exod 22:21-24
Deut 6:14-15; 8:19
7:7
Deut 4:40
7:9
Exod 20:3
Jer 11:13, 17; 19:4
7:10
Ezek 23:39
7:11
Matt 21:13
†Mark 11:17
†Luke 19:46

**7** The LORD gave another message to Jeremiah. He said, 2 "Go to the entrance of the LORD's Temple, and give this message to the people: 'O Judah, listen to this message from the LORD! Listen to it, all of you who worship here! 3 This is what the LORD of Heaven's Armies, the God of Israel, says:

"'Even now, if you quit your evil ways, I will let you stay in your own land. 4 But don't be fooled by those who promise you safety simply because the LORD's Temple is here. They chant, "The LORD's Temple is here! The LORD's Temple is here!" 5 But I will be merciful only if you stop your evil thoughts and deeds and start treating each other with justice; 6 only if you stop exploiting foreigners, orphans, and widows; only if you stop your murdering; and only if you stop harming yourselves by worshiping idols. 7 Then I will let you stay in this land that I gave to your ancestors to keep forever.

8 "'Don't be fooled into thinking that you will never suffer because the Temple is here. It's a lie! 9 Do you really think you can steal, murder, commit adultery, lie, and burn incense to Baal and all those other new gods of yours, 10 and then come here and stand before me in my Temple and chant, "We are safe!"—only to go right back to all those evils again? 11 Don't you yourselves admit that this Temple, which bears my name, has become a den of thieves? Surely I see all the evil going on there. I, the LORD, have spoken!

6:27 As in Greek version; Hebrew reads *a tester of my people a fortress.*

---

or potential dangers forces us to examine our sense of ultimate security. Whether the outlook is bleak or hopeful, do we actually trust in God? Or does our trust last only as long as the threat seems distant?

**6:29, 30** Metal is purified by fire. As it is heated, impurities are burned away and only the pure metal remains. As God tested the people of Judah, however, he could find no purity in their lives. They continued in their sinful ways. Do you see impurities in your life that should be burned away? Confess these to God and allow him to purify you as he sees fit. Take time right now to reflect on the areas of your life that he has already refined; then thank him for what he is doing.

**7:1–10:25** As this section opens, God sends Jeremiah to the Temple gates to refute the false belief that God would not let harm come to the Temple or to those who lived near it. Jeremiah rebukes the people for their false and worthless religion, their idolatry, and the shameless behavior of the people and their leaders. Judah, he says, is ripe for judgment and exile. This happened during the reign of Jehoiakim, a puppet of Egypt. The nation, in shock over the death of Josiah, was going through a spiritual reversal that removed much of the good Josiah had done. The themes of this section are false religion, idolatry, and hypocrisy. Jeremiah was almost put to death for this sermon, but he was saved by the officials of Judah (see chapter 26).

**7:2, 3** The people followed a worship ritual but maintained a sinful lifestyle. It was religion without personal commitment to God. Attending church, taking communion, teaching church school, singing in the choir—all are empty exercises unless we are truly doing them for God. It is good to do these activities, not because we ought to do them for the church, but because we want to do them for God.

**7:9-11** There are several parallels between how the people of Judah viewed their Temple and how many today view their churches. (1) *They didn't make the Temple part of their daily living.* We may go to beautiful churches well-prepared for worship, but often we don't take the presence of God with us through the week. (2) *The image of the Temple became more important than the substance of faith.* Going to church and belonging to a group can become more important than a life changed for God. (3) *The people used their Temple as a sanctuary.* Many use religious affiliation as a hideout, thinking it will protect them from evil and problems.

**7:11, 12** Jesus used these words from 7:11 in clearing the Temple (Mark 11:17; Luke 19:46). This passage applied to the evil in the Temple in Jesus' day as well as in Jeremiah's. God's Tabernacle had been at Shiloh, but Shiloh had been abandoned (Psalm 78:60; Jeremiah 26:6). If God did not preserve Shiloh because the Tabernacle was there, why would he preserve Jerusalem because of the Temple?

12 "'Go now to the place at Shiloh where I once put the Tabernacle that bore my name. See what I did there because of all the wickedness of my people, the Israelites. 13 While you were doing these wicked things, says the LORD, I spoke to you about it repeatedly, but you would not listen. I called out to you, but you refused to answer. 14 So just as I destroyed Shiloh, I will now destroy this Temple that bears my name, this Temple that you trust in for help, this place that I gave to you and your ancestors. 15 And I will send you out of my sight into exile, just as I did your relatives, the people of Israel.*'

*7:12*
Josh 18:1, 10
Jer 26:6

*7:14*
1 Kgs 9:7
Jer 7:4, 12

*7:15*
2 Kgs 17:23

### Judah's Persistent Idolatry

16 "Pray no more for these people, Jeremiah. Do not weep or pray for them, and don't beg me to help them, for I will not listen to you. 17 Don't you see what they are doing throughout the towns of Judah and in the streets of Jerusalem? 18 No wonder I am so angry! Watch how the children gather wood and the fathers build sacrificial fires. See how the women knead dough and make cakes to offer to the Queen of Heaven. And they pour out liquid offerings to their other idol gods! 19 Am I the one they are hurting?" asks the LORD. "Most of all, they hurt themselves, to their own shame."

*7:16*
Jer 11:14; 15:1

*7:18*
Deut 32:16

*7:19*
Job 35:6
Jer 9:19

20 So this is what the Sovereign LORD says: "I will pour out my terrible fury on this place. Its people, animals, trees, and crops will be consumed by the unquenchable fire of my anger."

*7:21*
Hos 8:13
Amos 5:21

21 This is what the LORD of Heaven's Armies, the God of Israel, says: "Take your burnt offerings and your other sacrifices and eat them yourselves! 22 When I led your ancestors out of Egypt, it was not burnt offerings and sacrifices I wanted from them. 23 This is what I told them: 'Obey me, and I will be your God, and you will be my people. Do everything as I say, and all will be well!'

*7:22*
1 Sam 15:22
Ps 51:16
Hos 6:6

*7:23*
Exod 15:26; 19:5-6
Lev 26:12
Deut 6:3

24 "But my people would not listen to me. They kept doing whatever they wanted, following the stubborn desires of their evil hearts. They went backward instead of forward. 25 From the day your ancestors left Egypt until now, I have continued to send my servants, the prophets—day in and day out. 26 But my people have not listened to me or even tried to hear. They have been stubborn and sinful—even worse than their ancestors.

*7:24*
Ps 81:11
Jer 11:8
Ezek 20:8, 13, 16, 21

*7:26*
Jer 16:12; 17:23
Matt 23:32

27 "Tell them all this, but do not expect them to listen. Shout out your warnings, but do not expect them to respond. 28 Say to them, 'This is the nation whose people will not obey the LORD their God and who refuse to be taught. Truth has vanished from among them; it is no longer heard on their lips. 29 Shave your head in mourning, and weep alone on the mountains. For the LORD has rejected and forsaken this generation that has provoked his fury.'

*7:27*
Isa 65:12
Jer 26:2
Ezek 2:7

*7:29*
Isa 15:2; 22:12
Mic 1:16

### The Valley of Slaughter

30 "The people of Judah have sinned before my very eyes," says the LORD. "They have set up their abominable idols right in the Temple that bears my name, defiling it. 31 They have built pagan shrines at Topheth, the garbage dump in the valley of Ben-Hinnom, and there they burn their sons and daughters in the fire. I have never commanded such a horrible deed; it

*7:30*
2 Kgs 21:4
2 Chr 33:4-5, 7
Jer 32:34

*7:31*
2 Kgs 23:10

**7:15** Hebrew *of Ephraim*, referring to the northern kingdom of Israel.

---

**7:15** Israel, the northern kingdom, had been taken into captivity by Assyria in 722 B.C.

**7:18** The Queen of Heaven was a name for Ishtar, the Mesopotamian goddess of love and fertility. After the fall of Jerusalem, the refugees from Judah who fled to Egypt continued to worship her (44:17). A papyrus dating from the 5th century B.C., found at Hermopolis in Egypt, mentions the Queen of Heaven among the gods honored by the Jewish community living there.

**7:19** This verse answers the question, Who gets hurt when we turn away from God? We do! Separating ourselves from God is like keeping a green plant away from sunlight or water. God is our only source of spiritual strength. Cut yourself off from him, and you cut off life itself.

**7:21-23** God had set up a system of sacrifices to encourage the people to joyfully obey him (see the book of Leviticus). He required the people to make these sacrifices, not because the sacrifices themselves pleased him, but because they caused the people to recognize their sin and refocus on living for God. They faithfully made the sacrifices but forgot the reason they were offering them, and thus they disobeyed God. Jeremiah reminded the people that unless they were prepared to obey God in all areas

of life, acting out religious rituals was meaningless. (See the chart in Hosea 7, p. 1413.)

**7:25** From the time of Moses to the end of the Old Testament period, God sent many prophets to Israel and Judah. No matter how bad the circumstances were, God always raised up a prophet to speak against their stubborn spiritual attitudes.

**7:27** Why did God instruct Jeremiah to prophesy and proclaim if the effort would be fruitless? God demonstrates his consistent faithfulness even in the face of human resistance. God was also "going on record" for those beyond Jeremiah's generation. See 1 Corinthians 10:1-11 for an explanation of God's detailed recording of the past failures of his people. The stories are intended to guide us and prevent us from making the same mistakes.

**7:31, 32** The shrines of Topheth (meaning "fireplace") were set up in the valley of Ben-Hinnom, where debris and rubbish from the city were thrown away. This altar was used to worship Molech—a god who required child sacrifice (2 Kings 23:10). Their valley of sacrifice would become their Valley of Slaughter by the Babylonians. At the place where the people had killed their children in sinful idol worship, they themselves would be slaughtered.

7:32
Jer 19:6-7

7:33
Deut 28:26
Jer 12:9

7:34
Isa 1:7; 24:7
Jer 4:27; 16:9
Ezek 26:13
Hos 2:11

8:1
Ezek 6:5

8:2
2 Kgs 23:5
Jer 22:19; 36:30
Zeph 1:5
Acts 7:42

8:3
Deut 30:1, 4

8:4
Prov 24:16
Mic 7:8

8:6
Job 39:21-25
Ps 14:2
Ezek 22:30
Mal 3:16

8:7
Prov 6:6-8
Song 2:12

8:8
Jer 4:22
Rom 1:22; 2:17

8:9
1 Cor 1:27

8:10
Deut 28:30
Isa 56:11

never even crossed my mind to command such a thing! 32 So beware, for the time is coming," says the LORD, "when that garbage dump will no longer be called Topheth or the valley of Ben-Hinnom, but the Valley of Slaughter. They will bury the bodies in Topheth until there is no more room for them. 33 The bodies of my people will be food for the vultures and wild animals, and no one will be left to scare them away. 34 I will put an end to the happy singing and laughter in the streets of Jerusalem. The joyful voices of bridegrooms and brides will no longer be heard in the towns of Judah. The land will lie in complete desolation.

**8** "In that day," says the LORD, "the enemy will break open the graves of the kings and officials of Judah, and the graves of the priests, prophets, and common people of Jerusalem. 2 They will spread out their bones on the ground before the sun, moon, and stars—the gods my people have loved, served, and worshiped. Their bones will not be gathered up again or buried but will be scattered on the ground like manure. 3 And the people of this evil nation who survive will wish to die rather than live where I will send them. I, the LORD of Heaven's Armies, have spoken!

### Deception by False Prophets

4 "Jeremiah, say to the people, 'This is what the LORD says:

"'When people fall down, don't they get up again?
    When they discover they're on the wrong road, don't they turn back?
5 Then why do these people stay on their self-destructive path?
    Why do the people of Jerusalem refuse to turn back?
They cling tightly to their lies
    and will not turn around.
6 I listen to their conversations
    and don't hear a word of truth.
Is anyone sorry for doing wrong?
    Does anyone say, "What a terrible thing I have done"?
No! All are running down the path of sin
    as swiftly as a horse galloping into battle!
7 Even the stork that flies across the sky
    knows the time of her migration,
as do the turtledove, the swallow, and the crane.*
    They all return at the proper time each year.
But not my people!
    They do not know the LORD's laws.

8 "'How can you say, "We are wise because we have the word of the LORD,"
    when your teachers have twisted it by writing lies?
9 These wise teachers will fall
    into the trap of their own foolishness,
for they have rejected the word of the LORD.
    Are they so wise after all?
10 I will give their wives to others
    and their farms to strangers.
From the least to the greatest,
    their lives are ruled by greed.
Yes, even my prophets and priests are like that.
    They are all frauds.

8:7 The identification of some of these birds is uncertain.

---

**8:1, 2** The threat that the graves of Judah's people would be opened was horrible to a people who highly honored the dead and believed that it was the highest desecration to open graves. This would be an ironic punishment for idol worshipers—their bones would be laid out before the sun, moon, and stars—the gods they thought could save them.

**8:4-6** When people fall down or realize that they are headed in the wrong direction, it only makes sense for them to get up or change directions. But as God watched the nation, he saw people

living sinful lives by choice, deceiving themselves that there would be no consequences. They had lost perspective concerning God's will for their lives and were trying to minimize their sin. Are there some indicators that you have fallen down or are heading the wrong way? What are you doing to get back on the right path?

11 They offer superficial treatments
    for my people's mortal wound.
They give assurances of peace
    when there is no peace.

**8:11**
Jer 6:14; 14:13-14
Lam 2:14
Ezek 13:10

12 Are they ashamed of these disgusting actions?
    Not at all—they don't even know how to blush!
Therefore, they will lie among the slaughtered.
    They will be brought down when I punish them,
    says the LORD.

**8:12**
Deut 32:35
Isa 3:9; 9:14
Zeph 3:5

13 I will surely consume them.
    There will be no more harvests of figs and grapes.
Their fruit trees will all die.
    Whatever I gave them will soon be gone.
    I, the LORD, have spoken!'

**8:13**
Matt 21:19

14 "Then the people will say,
    'Why should we wait here to die?
Come, let's go to the fortified towns and die there.
    For the LORD our God has decreed our destruction
and has given us a cup of poison to drink
    because we sinned against the LORD.

**8:14**
Deut 29:18
Ps 69:21
Jer 3:25; 4:5; 9:15;
14:20
Matt 27:34

15 We hoped for peace, but no peace came.
    We hoped for a time of healing, but found only terror.'

16 "The snorting of the enemies' warhorses can be heard
    all the way from the land of Dan in the north!
The neighing of their stallions makes the whole land tremble.
    They are coming to devour the land and everything in it—
    cities and people alike.

**8:16**
Judg 5:22

17 I will send these enemy troops among you
    like poisonous snakes you cannot charm.
They will bite you, and you will die.
    I, the Lord, have spoken!"

**8:17**
Num 21:6
Deut 32:24
Ps 58:4-5

### Jeremiah Weeps for Sinful Judah

18 My grief is beyond healing;
    my heart is broken.

19 Listen to the weeping of my people;
    it can be heard all across the land.
"Has the LORD abandoned Jerusalem?*" the people ask.
    "Is her King no longer there?"

"Oh, why have they provoked my anger with their carved idols
    and their worthless foreign gods?" says the LORD.

**8:19**
Deut 32:21
Ps 31:6

20 "The harvest is finished,
    and the summer is gone," the people cry,
    "yet we are not saved!"

21 I hurt with the hurt of my people.
    I mourn and am overcome with grief.

**8:21**
Joel 2:6
Nah 2:10

22 Is there no medicine in Gilead?
    Is there no physician there?
Why is there no healing
    for the wounds of my people?

**8:22**
Gen 37:25
Jer 14:19; 30:13;
46:11

**8:19** Hebrew *Zion?*

---

**8:16** Dan was the northernmost tribe in Israel.
**8:18, 19** Jeremiah was pleading with God to save his people.
**8:20-22** These words vividly portray Jeremiah's emotion as he watched his people reject God. He responded with anguish to a world dying in sin. We watch that same world still dying in sin, still rejecting God. But how often is our heart broken for our lost

friends and neighbors, our lost world? Only when we have Jeremiah's kind of passionate concern will we be moved to help. We must begin by asking God to break our heart for the world he loves.

**8:22** Gilead was famous for its healing medicine. This is a rhetorical question. The obvious answer is, "Yes—God," but Israel was not applying the "medicine"; they were not obeying

9:1
Jer 8:18; 13:17

**9** ¹*If only my head were a pool of water
and my eyes a fountain of tears,
I would weep day and night
for all my people who have been slaughtered.

9:2
Pss 55:6-7; 120:5-6

²*Oh, that I could go away and forget my people
and live in a travelers' shack in the desert.
For they are all adulterers—
a pack of treacherous liars.

### Judgment for Disobedience

³ "My people bend their tongues like bows
to shoot out lies.
They refuse to stand up for the truth.
They only go from bad to worse.
They do not know me,"
says the LORD.

9:4
Gen 27:35
Prov 10:18

⁴ "Beware of your neighbor!
Don't even trust your brother!
For brother takes advantage of brother,
and friend slanders friend.

9:5
Mic 6:12

⁵ They all fool and defraud each other;
no one tells the truth.
With practiced tongues they tell lies;
they wear themselves out with all their sinning.

9:6
John 3:19-20

⁶ They pile lie upon lie
and utterly refuse to acknowledge me,"
says the LORD.

**9:1** Verse 9:1 is numbered 8:23 in Hebrew text.   **9:2** Verses 9:2-26 are numbered 9:1-25 in Hebrew text.

---

**OLD TESTAMENT TESTS FOR FALSE PROPHETS**
In the Old Testament, various signs or works pointed to a true or false prophet. Many of these can be applied today.

*1. Does the prophet use fortune-telling?*
Divination was expressly forbidden by God (Deuteronomy 18:9-14). No true teacher or prophet would use fortune-telling or have any dealings with spirits of the dead (Jeremiah 14:14; Ezekiel 12:24; Micah 3:7).

*2. Have the prophet's short-term prophecies been fulfilled?*
Deuteronomy 18:22 used this as a test. Do predictions come to pass?

*3. Is the prophet marked by a desire to say only what pleases people?*
Many false prophets told people what they wanted to hear. A true prophet serves God, not people (Jeremiah 8:11; 14:13; 23:17; Ezekiel 13:10; Micah 3:5).

*4. Does the prophet draw people away from God?*
Many teachers draw people to themselves or to the system or organization they have built (Deuteronomy 13:1-3).

*5. Does the prophet's prophecy confirm the Bible's main teaching?*
If a prophecy is inconsistent with or contradictory to Scripture, it is not to be believed.

*6. What is the prophet's moral character?*
False prophets were charged with lying (Jeremiah 8:10; 14:14), drunkenness (Isaiah 28:7), and immorality (Jeremiah 23:14).

*7. Do other Spirit-led people discern authenticity in this prophet?*
Discernment by others who are led of the Spirit is a key test (1 Kings 22:7). The New Testament speaks of this a great deal (John 10:4-15; 1 Corinthians 2:14; 14:29, 32; 1 John 4:1).

---

the Lord. Although the people's spiritual sickness was very deep it could be healed. But the people refused the medicine. God could heal their self-inflicted wounds, but he would not force his healing on them.

**9:1-6** Jeremiah felt conflicting emotions concerning his people. Lying, deceit, treachery, adultery, and idolatry had become common sins. He was angered by their sin, but he had compassion, too. He was set apart from them by his mission for God,

but he was also one of them. Jesus had similar feelings when he stood before Jerusalem, the city that would reject him (Matthew 23:37).

7 Therefore, this is what the LORD of Heaven's Armies says:
  "See, I will melt them down in a crucible
     and test them like metal.
  What else can I do with my people?*
8     For their tongues shoot lies like poisoned arrows.
  They speak friendly words to their neighbors
     while scheming in their heart to kill them.
9 Should I not punish them for this?" says the LORD.
  "Should I not avenge myself against such a nation?"

10 I will weep for the mountains
     and wail for the wilderness pastures.
  For they are desolate and empty of life;
     the lowing of cattle is heard no more;
     the birds and wild animals have all fled.

11 "I will make Jerusalem into a heap of ruins," says the LORD.
     "It will be a place haunted by jackals.
  The towns of Judah will be ghost towns,
     with no one living in them."

12 Who is wise enough to understand all this? Who has been instructed by the LORD and can explain it to others? Why has the land been so ruined that no one dares to travel through it?

13 The LORD replies, "This has happened because my people have abandoned my instructions; they have refused to obey what I said. 14Instead, they have stubbornly followed their own desires and worshiped the images of Baal, as their ancestors taught them. 15So now, this is what the LORD of Heaven's Armies, the God of Israel, says: Look! I will feed them with bitterness and give them poison to drink. 16I will scatter them around the world, in places they and their ancestors never heard of, and even there I will chase them with the sword until I have destroyed them completely."

*Weeping in Jerusalem*

17 This is what the LORD of Heaven's Armies says:
  "Consider all this, and call for the mourners.
     Send for the women who mourn at funerals.
18 Quick! Begin your weeping!
     Let the tears flow from your eyes.
19 Hear the people of Jerusalem* crying in despair,
     'We are ruined! We are completely humiliated!
  We must leave our land,
     because our homes have been torn down.'"

20 Listen, you women, to the words of the LORD;
     open your ears to what he has to say.
  Teach your daughters to wail;
     teach one another how to lament.
21 For death has crept in through our windows
     and has entered our mansions.
  It has killed off the flower of our youth:
     Children no longer play in the streets,
     and young men no longer gather in the squares.

22 This is what the LORD says:
  "Bodies will be scattered across the fields like clumps of manure,
     like bundles of grain after the harvest.
     No one will be left to bury them."

23 This is what the LORD says:
  "Don't let the wise boast in their wisdom,
     or the powerful boast in their power,
     or the rich boast in their riches.

**9:7**
Isa 1:25
Jer 6:27
Mal 3:3

**9:10**
Jer 4:24-25; 12:4
Ezek 14:15; 29:11;
33:28
Hos 4:3

**9:12**
Ps 107:43
Jer 23:10, 16
Hos 14:9

**9:13**
2 Chr 7:19-20
Ps 89:30
Jer 5:19; 22:9

**9:14**
Rom 1:21-24
1 Pet 1:18

**9:15**
Deut 29:18
Jer 8:14; 23:15

**9:16**
Lev 26:33
Deut 28:64
Ezek 5:2, 12

**9:17**
Amos 5:16

**9:19**
Deut 28:29
2 Chr 35:25

**9:21**
2 Chr 36:17
Jer 6:11; 18:21

**9:23**
1 Kgs 20:10-11
Ps 49:6-9
Eccl 9:11
Ezek 28:3-7

9:7 Hebrew *with the daughter of my people?* Greek version reads *with the evil daughter of my people?*
9:19 Hebrew *Zion.*

**9:24**
Exod 34:6-7
Pss 36:5, 7; 44:8
Isa 10:8-12; 61:8
Mic 7:18
†1 Cor 1:31
2 Cor 10:17
Gal 6:14

24 But those who wish to boast
　　should boast in this alone:
that they truly know me and understand that I am the LORD
　　who demonstrates unfailing love
　　and who brings justice and righteousness to the earth,
and that I delight in these things.
　　I, the LORD, have spoken!

**9:26**
Lev 26:41
Ezek 44:7
Rom 2:28

25 "A time is coming," says the LORD, "when I will punish all those who are circumcised in body but not in spirit—26 the Egyptians, Edomites, Ammonites, Moabites, the people who live in the desert in remote places,* and yes, even the people of Judah. And like all these pagan nations, the people of Israel also have uncircumcised hearts."

## Idolatry Brings Destruction

**10:2**
Lev 18:3
Isa 47:12-14

**10** Hear the word that the LORD speaks to you, O Israel! 2 This is what the LORD says:

　　"Do not act like the other nations,
　　　　who try to read their future in the stars.
　　Do not be afraid of their predictions,
　　　　even though other nations are terrified by them.
3 Their ways are futile and foolish.
　　　　They cut down a tree, and a craftsman carves an idol.
4 They decorate it with gold and silver
　　　　and then fasten it securely with hammer and nails
　　　　so it won't fall over.

**10:5**
Ps 115:5

5 Their gods are like
　　　　helpless scarecrows in a cucumber field!
They cannot speak,
　　　　and they need not be carried because they cannot walk.
Do not be afraid of such gods,
　　　　for they can neither harm you nor do you any good."

**10:6**
Deut 33:26
Pss 48:1; 96:4
Isa 12:6
Jer 10:16

6 LORD, there is no one like you!
　　　　For you are great, and your name is full of power.
7 Who would not fear you, O King of nations?
　　　　That title belongs to you alone!
Among all the wise people of the earth
　　　　and in all the kingdoms of the world,
　　　　there is no one like you.

**10:7**
Ps 22:28
Dan 2:27-28
1 Cor 1:19-20

**10:8**
Jer 4:22

8 People who worship idols are stupid and foolish.
　　　　The things they worship are made of wood!

**9:26** Or *in the desert and clip the corners of their hair.*

---

**9:23, 24** People tend to admire three things about others: wisdom, power, and riches. But God puts a higher priority on knowing him personally and living a life that reflects his justice, righteousness, and love. What do you want people to admire most about you?

**9:25, 26** Circumcision went back to the time of Abraham. For the people of Israel, it was a symbol of their covenant relationship to God (Genesis 17:9-14). Circumcision was also practiced by pagan nations, but not as the sign of a covenant with God. By Jeremiah's time, the Israelites had forgotten the spiritual significance of circumcision even though they continued to do the physical ritual.

**10:2, 3** Most people would like to know the future. Decisions would be easier, failures would be avoided, and successes would be assured. The people of Judah wanted to know the future, too, and they tried to discern it through reading the signs in the sky. God made the earth and the heavens, including stars that people consult and worship (10:12). No one will discover the future in man-made charts of God's stars. But God, who promises to guide you, knows your future and will be with you all the

way. He will not reveal your future to you, but he will walk with you as the future unfolds. Don't trust the stars; trust the one who made the stars.

**10:8** Those who put their trust in a chunk of wood, even though it is carved well and looks beautiful, are foolish. The simplest person who worships God is wiser than the wisest person who worships a worthless substitute because this person has discerned who God really is. In what or whom do you place your trust?

9 They bring beaten sheets of silver from Tarshish
  and gold from Uphaz,
and they give these materials to skillful craftsmen
  who make their idols.
Then they dress these gods in royal blue and purple robes
  made by expert tailors.
10 But the LORD is the only true God.
  He is the living God and the everlasting King!
The whole earth trembles at his anger.
  The nations cannot stand up to his wrath.

11 Say this to those who worship other gods: "Your so-called gods, who did not make the heavens and earth, will vanish from the earth and from under the heavens."*

12 But God made the earth by his power,
  and he preserves it by his wisdom.
With his own understanding
  he stretched out the heavens.
13 When he speaks in the thunder,
  the heavens roar with rain.
He causes the clouds to rise over the earth.
  He sends the lightning with the rain
  and releases the wind from his storehouses.
14 The whole human race is foolish and has no knowledge!
  The craftsmen are disgraced by the idols they make,
for their carefully shaped works are a fraud.
  These idols have no breath or power.
15 Idols are worthless; they are ridiculous lies!
  On the day of reckoning they will all be destroyed.
16 But the God of Israel* is no idol!
  He is the Creator of everything that exists,
including Israel, his own special possession.
  The LORD of Heaven's Armies is his name!

### The Coming Destruction
17 Pack your bags and prepare to leave;
  the siege is about to begin.
18 For this is what the LORD says:
"Suddenly, I will fling out
  all you who live in this land.
I will pour great troubles upon you,
  and at last you will feel my anger."

19 My wound is severe,
  and my grief is great.
My sickness is incurable,
  but I must bear it.
20 My home is gone,
  and no one is left to help me rebuild it.
My children have been taken away,
  and I will never see them again.

**10:9** Pss 72:10; 115:4
Isa 40:19
Dan 10:5

**10:10** Pss 10:16; 29:10; 76:7
Isa 65:16
Jer 50:46

**10:11** Ps 96:5
Isa 2:18
Zeph 2:11

**10:12** Job 9:8; 38:4-7
Pss 78:69; 148:4-5
Isa 40:22; 45:18
Jer 51:15

**10:13** Job 36:27-29
Pss 29:3-9; 135:7

**10:14** Jer 51:17

**10:15** Isa 41:24
Jer 8:12; 14:22

**10:16** Deut 32:9
Isa 45:7
Jer 10:12; 31:35; 32:18; 51:19

**10:17** Ezek 12:3-12

**10:18** 1 Sam 25:29
Jer 14:17

**10:19** Jer 4:31
Mic 7:9

**10:20** Isa 51:18
Jer 4:20; 31:15
Lam 1:5; 2:4

**10:11** The original text of this verse is in Aramaic.   **10:16** Hebrew *the Portion of Jacob.* See note on 5:20.

---

**10:9** Tarshish was located at the westward limit of the ancient world, perhaps in what is now Spain (see Jonah 1:3). It was a source of silver, tin, lead, and iron for Tyre (Ezekiel 27:12). The location of Uphaz is unknown. Instead, it may be a metal-lurgical term for "refined gold." No matter how well made or how beautiful idols are, they can never have the power and life of the true and living God.

**10:19-21** In this section, Jeremiah uses the picture of nomads wandering in the wilderness trying to pitch their tents. The shepherds of the nation are the evil leaders responsible for the distress. "Flocks" are the people of Judah. Instead of guiding the people to God, the leaders were leading them astray.

10:21
Jer 23:2

21 The shepherds of my people have lost their senses.
  They no longer seek wisdom from the LORD.
Therefore, they fail completely,
  and their flocks are scattered.
22 Listen! Hear the terrifying roar of great armies
  as they roll down from the north.
The towns of Judah will be destroyed
  and become a haunt for jackals.

## Jeremiah's Prayer

10:23
Prov 20:24
Isa 26:7

23 I know, LORD, that our lives are not our own.
  We are not able to plan our own course.
24 So correct me, LORD, but please be gentle.
  Do not correct me in anger, for I would die.

10:25
Ps 79:6
Jer 8:16; 50:7
Zeph 1:6; 3:8

25 Pour out your wrath on the nations that refuse to acknowledge you—
  on the peoples that do not call upon your name.
For they have devoured your people Israel*;
  they have devoured and consumed them,
  making the land a desolate wilderness.

## 3. Jeremiah prophesies destruction
### Judah's Broken Covenant

11:3
Deut 27:26
Gal 3:10

**11** The LORD gave another message to Jeremiah. He said, 2 "Remind the people of Judah and Jerusalem about the terms of my covenant with them. 3 Say to them, 'This is what the LORD, the God of Israel, says: Cursed is anyone who does not obey the terms of my covenant! 4 For I said to your ancestors when I brought them out of the iron-smelting furnace of Egypt, "If you obey me and do whatever I command you, then you will be my people, and I will be your God." 5 I said this so I could keep my promise to your ancestors to give you a land flowing with milk and honey—the land you live in today.'"

11:4
Exod 19:5; 24:3, 7
Deut 4:20
1 Kgs 8:51
Jer 31:32
Zech 8:8

11:5
Exod 13:5
Deut 7:12
Jer 32:22

Then I replied, "Amen, LORD! May it be so."

11:7
Exod 15:26
2 Chr 36:15
Jer 7:25; 11:4

6 Then the LORD said, "Broadcast this message in the streets of Jerusalem. Go from town to town throughout the land and say, 'Remember the ancient covenant, and do everything it requires. 7 For I solemnly warned your ancestors when I brought them out of Egypt, "Obey me!" I have repeated this warning over and over to this day, 8 but your ancestors did not listen or even pay attention. Instead, they stubbornly followed their own evil desires. And because they refused to obey, I brought upon them all the curses described in this covenant.'"

11:8
Lev 26:14-43
Ezek 20:8

11:9
Ezek 22:25

9 Again the LORD spoke to me and said, "I have discovered a conspiracy against me among the people of Judah and Jerusalem. 10 They have returned to the sins of their forefathers. They have refused to listen to me and are worshiping other gods. Israel and Judah have both broken the covenant I made with their ancestors. 11 Therefore, this is what the LORD says: I am going to bring calamity upon them, and they will not escape. Though they beg for mercy, I will not listen to their cries. 12 Then the people of Judah and Jerusalem will pray to their idols and burn incense before them. But the idols will not save them when disaster strikes! 13 Look now, people of Judah; you have as many gods as you have towns. You have as many altars of shame—altars for burning incense to your god Baal—as there are streets in Jerusalem.

11:10
Deut 9:7
Judg 2:11-13
Jer 3:6-9; 13:10
Ezek 16:59

11:11
Jer 6:19; 25:35

11:12
Deut 32:37
Jer 44:17

11:13
Jer 2:28; 7:9-10

14 "Pray no more for these people, Jeremiah. Do not weep or pray for them, for I will not listen to them when they cry out to me in distress.

11:14
Ps 66:18
Jer 7:16; 14:11
Hos 5:6

**10:25** Hebrew *devoured Jacob.* See note on 5:20.

---

**10:23, 24** God's ability to direct our lives is far superior to our ability. Sometimes we are afraid of God's power and plans because we know his power would easily crush us if he used it against us. Don't be afraid to let God correct your plans. He will give you wisdom if you are willing.

**11:1–13:27** This section concerns the broken covenant, and a rebuke for those who returned to idols after Josiah's reform. Jeremiah's rebuke prompted a threat against his life by his own countrymen. As Jeremiah suffered, he pondered the prosperity of the wicked. As he brought these words to a close, he used a rotten linen loincloth and filled jars of wine as object lessons of God's coming judgment (see the note on 13:1-11).

**11:14** At first glance this command is shocking: God tells Jeremiah not to pray for the people and says he won't listen to the people if they pray. A time comes when God must dispense justice. Sin brings its own bitter reward. If the people were unrepentant and continued in their sin, neither their prayers nor Jeremiah's would prevent God's judgment. Their only hope was repentance—sorrow for sin, turning from it, and turning to God. How can we keep praying for God's help if we haven't committed our lives to him? God's blessings come when we are committed to him, not when we selfishly hang on to our sinful ways.

15 "What right do my beloved people have to come to my Temple,
    when they have done so many immoral things?
Can their vows and sacrifices prevent their destruction?
    They actually rejoice in doing evil!
16 I, the LORD, once called them a thriving olive tree,
    beautiful to see and full of good fruit.
But now I have sent the fury of their enemies
    to burn them with fire,
    leaving them charred and broken.

11:15
Jer 13:27

11:16
Pss 52:8; 83:2
Isa 27:11
Jer 21:14

17 "I, the LORD of Heaven's Armies, who planted this olive tree, have ordered it destroyed. For the people of Israel and Judah have done evil, arousing my anger by burning incense to Baal."

11:17
Jer 2:21; 32:29

### A Plot against Jeremiah

18 Then the LORD told me about the plots my enemies were making against me. 19 I was like a lamb being led to the slaughter. I had no idea that they were planning to kill me! "Let's destroy this man and all his words," they said. "Let's cut him down, so his name will be forgotten forever."

11:18
1 Sam 23:11-12
2 Kgs 6:9-10
Ezek 8:6

20 O LORD of Heaven's Armies,
    you make righteous judgments,
    and you examine the deepest thoughts and secrets.
Let me see your vengeance against them,
    for I have committed my cause to you.

11:20
Ps 7:9
Jer 17:10; 20:12

21 This is what the LORD says about the men of Anathoth who wanted me dead. They had said, "We will kill you if you do not stop prophesying in the LORD's name." 22 So this is what the LORD of Heaven's Armies says about them: "I will punish them! Their young men will die in battle, and their boys and girls will starve to death. 23 Not one of these plotters from Anathoth will survive, for I will bring disaster upon them when their time of punishment comes."

11:21
Jer 1:1; 12:5-6;
20:10; 26:8; 38:4

11:22
Jer 18:21; 21:14

11:23
Jer 6:9; 23:12
Hos 9:7
Mic 7:4

### Jeremiah Questions the LORD's Justice

**12** 1 LORD, you always give me justice
        when I bring a case before you.
So let me bring you this complaint:
Why are the wicked so prosperous?
    Why are evil people so happy?
2 You have planted them,
    and they have taken root and prospered.
Your name is on their lips,
    but you are far from their hearts.
3 But as for me, LORD, you know my heart.
    You see me and test my thoughts.
Drag these people away like sheep to be butchered!
    Set them aside to be slaughtered!

12:1
Ezra 9:15
Job 13:3
Jer 5:27-28; 11:20
Hab 1:4

12:2
Isa 29:13
Ezek 17:5-10;
33:31
Titus 1:16

4 How long must this land mourn?
    Even the grass in the fields has withered.

12:4
Jer 5:31
Hos 4:3
Joel 1:10-17

---

**11:18-23** To Jeremiah's surprise, the people of Anathoth, his hometown, were plotting to kill him. They wanted to silence Jeremiah's message for several reasons: (1) economic—his condemnation of idol worship would hurt the business of the idol makers; (2) religious—the message of doom and gloom made the people feel depressed and guilty; (3) political—he openly rebuked their hypocritical politics; and (4) personal—the people hated him for showing them that they were wrong. Jeremiah had two options: run and hide, or call on God. Jeremiah called, and God answered. Like Jeremiah, we can either run and hide when we face opposition because of our faithfulness to God, or we can call on God for

help. Hiding compromises our message; calling on God lets him reinforce it.

**12:1-6** Many people have asked, "Why are the wicked so prosperous?" (See, for example, Job 21:4-21 and Habakkuk 1:1-4.) Jeremiah knew that God's justice would ultimately come, but he was impatient because he wanted justice to come quickly. God didn't give a doctrinal answer; instead, he gave a challenge: If Jeremiah couldn't handle this, how would he handle the injustices ahead? It is natural for us to demand fair play and cry for justice against those who take advantage of others. But when we call for justice, we must realize that we ourselves would be in big trouble if God gave each of us what we truly deserve.

The wild animals and birds have disappeared
    because of the evil in the land.
For the people have said,
    "The LORD doesn't see what's ahead for us!"

### The LORD's Reply to Jeremiah

**12:5**
Jer 50:44

5 "If racing against mere men makes you tired,
    how will you race against horses?
If you stumble and fall on open ground,
    what will you do in the thickets near the Jordan?
6 Even your brothers, members of your own family,
    have turned against you.
They plot and raise complaints against you.
Do not trust them,
    no matter how pleasantly they speak.

**12:7**
Jer 7:29; 11:15
Hos 11:1-4

7 "I have abandoned my people, my special possession.
    I have surrendered my dearest ones to their enemies.
8 My chosen people have roared at me like a lion of the forest,
    so I have treated them with contempt.

**12:9**
2 Kgs 24:2
Isa 56:9
Jer 7:33; 15:3;
34:20

9 My chosen people act like speckled vultures,*
    but they themselves are surrounded by vultures.
Bring on the wild animals to pick their corpses clean!

**12:10**
Ps 80:8-16
Isa 5:1-7
Lam 1:10

10 "Many rulers have ravaged my vineyard,
    trampling down the vines
    and turning all its beauty into a barren wilderness.
11 They have made it an empty wasteland;
    I hear its mournful cry.
The whole land is desolate,
    and no one even cares.

**12:12**
Isa 34:6
Jer 47:6
Amos 9:4

12 On all the bare hilltops,
    destroying armies can be seen.
The sword of the LORD devours people
    from one end of the nation to the other.
    No one will escape!

**12:13**
Lev 26:16
Deut 28:38
Isa 55:2
Jer 4:26; 17:10;
25:37-38

13 My people have planted wheat
    but are harvesting thorns.
They have worn themselves out,
    but it has done them no good.
They will harvest a crop of shame
    because of the fierce anger of the LORD."

### A Message for Israel's Neighbors

**12:14**
Isa 11:11-16
Jer 2:3; 49:1
Zeph 2:8-10
Zech 2:8

**12:16**
Josh 23:7
Isa 49:6

14 Now this is what the LORD says: "I will uproot from their land all the evil nations reaching out for the possession I gave my people Israel. And I will uproot Judah from among them. 15 But afterward I will return and have compassion on all of them. I will bring them home to their own lands again, each nation to its own possession. 16 And if these nations truly learn the ways of my people, and if they learn to swear by my name, saying, 'As surely as the LORD lives' (just as they taught my people to swear by the name of Baal), then they will be given a place among my people. 17 But any nation who refuses to obey me will be uprooted and destroyed. I, the LORD, have spoken!"

**12:17**
Ps 2:8-12
Isa 60:12

**12:9** Or *speckled hyenas*.

---

**12:5, 6** Life was extremely difficult for Jeremiah despite his love for and obedience to God. When he called to God for relief, God's reply in effect was, "If you think this is bad, how are you going to cope when it gets really tough?" God's answers to prayer are not always nice or easy to handle. Any Christian who has experienced war, bereavement, or a serious illness knows this. We are to be committed to God even when the going gets tough and when our prayers for relief are not immediately answered.

**12:14-17** God chose a people through whom to demonstrate his care for the world. The nation of Israel was given much; thus, much was required of her. But she repeatedly failed. The fate of other nations depended on their willingness to demonstrate faith in God whether or not God's chosen people accomplished their task of witness. God's love extends to reach every square inch of the globe.

## Jeremiah's Linen Loincloth

**13** This is what the LORD said to me: "Go and buy a linen loincloth and put it on, but do not wash it." [2] So I bought the loincloth as the LORD directed me, and I put it on.

[3] Then the LORD gave me another message: [4] "Take the linen loincloth you are wearing, and go to the Euphrates River.* Hide it there in a hole in the rocks." [5] So I went and hid it by the Euphrates as the LORD had instructed me.

[6] A long time afterward the LORD said to me, "Go back to the Euphrates and get the loincloth I told you to hide there." [7] So I went to the Euphrates and dug it out of the hole where I had hidden it. But now it was rotting and falling apart. The loincloth was good for nothing.

[8] Then I received this message from the LORD: [9] "This is what the LORD says: This shows how I will rot away the pride of Judah and Jerusalem. [10] These wicked people refuse to listen to me. They stubbornly follow their own desires and worship other gods. Therefore, they will become like this loincloth—good for nothing! [11] As a loincloth clings to a man's waist, so I created Judah and Israel to cling to me, says the LORD. They were to be my people, my pride, my glory—an honor to my name. But they would not listen to me.

[12] "So tell them, 'This is what the LORD, the God of Israel, says: May all your jars be filled with wine.' And they will reply, 'Of course! Jars are made to be filled with wine!'

[13] "Then tell them, 'No, this is what the LORD means: I will fill everyone in this land with drunkenness—from the king sitting on David's throne to the priests and the prophets, right down to the common people of Jerusalem. [14] I will smash them against each other, even parents against children, says the LORD. I will not let my pity or mercy or compassion keep me from destroying them.'"

## A Warning against Pride

[15] Listen and pay attention!
    Do not be arrogant, for the LORD has spoken.
[16] Give glory to the LORD your God
    before it is too late.
Acknowledge him before he brings darkness upon you,
    causing you to stumble and fall on the darkening mountains.
For then, when you look for light,
    you will find only terrible darkness and gloom.
[17] And if you still refuse to listen,
    I will weep alone because of your pride.
My eyes will overflow with tears,
    because the LORD's flock will be led away into exile.

[18] Say to the king and his mother,
"Come down from your thrones
    and sit in the dust,
for your glorious crowns
    will soon be snatched from your heads."
[19] The towns of the Negev will close their gates,
    and no one will be able to open them.
The people of Judah will be taken away as captives.
    All will be carried into exile.

**13:4** Hebrew *Perath*; also in 13:5, 6, 7.

### Cross-references

**13:1** Jer 13:11
**13:2** Isa 20:2
**13:4** Jer 51:63
**13:5** Exod 39:42-43; 40:16
**13:9** Lev 26:19
**13:10** Jer 13:15-17
**13:11** Exod 19:5-6 Deut 32:10-11 Ps 81:11 Isa 43:21 Jer 7:24; 33:9
**13:13** Pss 60:3; 75:8 Jer 25:27
**13:14** Isa 27:11 Jer 6:21; 16:5; 19:9-11
**13:15** Prov 16:5
**13:16** Ps 96:8 Isa 5:30; 59:9 Amos 5:18
**13:17** Jer 9:1; 23:1-2 Mal 2:2 Luke 19:41-42
**13:18** 2 Kgs 24:12, 15 2 Chr 33:12, 19

---

**13:1** A linen loincloth was one of the more intimate pieces of clothing, clinging close to the body. It was like underwear. Jeremiah's action showed how God would ruin Judah just as Jeremiah had ruined the linen loincloth.

**13:1-11** Actions speak louder than words. Jeremiah often used vivid object lessons to arouse the people's curiosity and get his point across. This lesson of the linen loincloth illustrated Judah's destiny. Although the people had once been close to God, their pride had made them useless. Proud people may look important, but God says their pride makes them good for nothing, completely useless. Pride rots our hearts until we lose our usefulness to God.

**13:15** While it is good to respect our country and our church, our loyalties always carry a hidden danger—arrogance. When is pride harmful? When it causes us to: (1) look down on others;

(2) be selfish with our resources; (3) force our solutions on others' problems; (4) think God is blessing us because of our own merits; (5) be content with our plans rather than seeking God's plans.

**13:18** The king was Jehoiachin, and the his mother was Nehushta. The king's father, Jehoiakim, had surrendered to Nebuchadnezzar but later rebelled. During Jehoiachin's reign, Nebuchadnezzar's armies besieged Jerusalem, and both Jehoiachin and Nehushta surrendered. Jehoiachin was sent to Babylon and imprisoned (2 Kings 24:1-15). Jeremiah's prophecy came true.

**13:19** The Negev region is the dry wasteland stretching south from Beersheba. The towns in this area would be closed to any refugees fleeing the invading army.

**13:20**
Jer 1:15; 6:22;
13:17; 23:2

20 Open up your eyes and see
the armies marching down from the north!
Where is your flock—
your beautiful flock—
that he gave you to care for?

**13:21**
Isa 13:8
Jer 4:31; 38:22

21 What will you say when the LORD takes the allies you have cultivated
and appoints them as your rulers?
Pangs of anguish will grip you,
like those of a woman in labor!

**13:22**
Jer 2:17-19; 9:2-9

22 You may ask yourself,
"Why is all this happening to me?"
It is because of your many sins!
That is why you have been stripped
and raped by invading armies.

**13:23**
Prov 27:22
Jer 4:22

23 Can an Ethiopian* change the color of his skin?
Can a leopard take away its spots?
Neither can you start doing good,
for you have always done evil.

**13:24**
Lev 26:33
Ezek 5:2, 12

24 "I will scatter you like chaff
that is blown away by the desert winds.
25 This is your allotment,
the portion I have assigned to you,"
says the LORD,
"for you have forgotten me,
putting your trust in false gods.

**13:26**
Lam 1:8
Hos 2:10

26 I myself will strip you
and expose you to shame.

**13:27**
Prov 1:22

27 I have seen your adultery and lust,
and your disgusting idol worship out in the fields and on the hills.
What sorrow awaits you, Jerusalem!
How long before you are pure?"

## Judah's Terrible Drought

**14** This message came to Jeremiah from the LORD, explaining why he was holding back the rain:

**14:2**
Isa 3:26
Jer 11:11
Zech 7:13

2 "Judah wilts;
commerce at the city gates grinds to a halt.
All the people sit on the ground in mourning,
and a great cry rises from Jerusalem.

**14:3**
2 Sam 15:30
1 Kgs 18:5
2 Kgs 18:31

3 The nobles send servants to get water,
but all the wells are dry.
The servants return with empty pitchers,
confused and desperate,
covering their heads in grief.
4 The ground is parched
and cracked for lack of rain.
The farmers are deeply troubled;
they, too, cover their heads.

**13:23** Hebrew *a Cushite.*

**13:23** Not even the threat of captivity could move the people to repent. The people had become so accustomed to doing evil that they had lost their ability to change. God never rejects those who sincerely turn to him. God was warning them to repent before it became impossible to change. We must never put off until tomorrow those changes God wants us to make. Our attitudes and patterns for living can become so set that we will lose all desire to change and will no longer fear the consequences.

**14:1–15:21** This section opens with God sending a drought on Judah and refusing to answer their prayers for rain. It continues with Jeremiah's description of judgment to come.

**14:1ff** Drought was a judgment with devastating consequences. As usual, when their backs were to the wall, the people cried out to God. But God rejected their plea because they did not repent; they merely wanted his rescue. Not even Jeremiah's prayers on their behalf would help. Their only hope was to turn to God.

5 Even the doe abandons her newborn fawn
  because there is no grass in the field.
6 The wild donkeys stand on the bare hills
  panting like thirsty jackals.
  They strain their eyes looking for grass,
  but there is none to be found."

14:6
Joel 1:18

7 The people say, "Our wickedness has caught up with us, LORD,
  but help us for the sake of your own reputation.
  We have turned away from you
  and sinned against you again and again.

14:7
Hos 5:5

8 O Hope of Israel, our Savior in times of trouble,
  why are you like a stranger to us?
  Why are you like a traveler passing through the land,
  stopping only for the night?

14:8
Ps 9:9
Isa 43:3; 63:8
Jer 17:13

9 Are you also confused?
  Is our champion helpless to save us?
  You are right here among us, LORD.
  We are known as your people.
  Please don't abandon us now!"

14:9
Num 11:23
Ps 46:5
Isa 50:2; 63:19
Jer 8:19; 15:16

10 So this is what the LORD says to his people:
  "You love to wander far from me
  and do not restrain yourselves.
  Therefore, I will no longer accept you as my people.
  Now I will remember all your wickedness
  and will punish you for your sins."

14:10
Ps 119:101
Jer 2:25; 6:20;
44:21-23
Hos 8:13

### The LORD Forbids Jeremiah to Intercede

11 Then the LORD said to me, "Do not pray for these people anymore. 12 When they fast, I will pay no attention. When they present their burnt offerings and grain offerings to me, I will not accept them. Instead, I will devour them with war, famine, and disease."

14:11
Jer 7:16; 11:14
14:12
Isa 1:15
Jer 8:13

13 Then I said, "O Sovereign LORD, their prophets are telling them, 'All is well—no war or famine will come. The LORD will surely send you peace.'"

14:13
Jer 5:12; 6:14;
8:11; 23:17

14 Then the LORD said, "These prophets are telling lies in my name. I did not send them or tell them to speak. I did not give them any messages. They prophesy of visions and revelations they have never seen or heard. They speak foolishness made up in their own lying hearts. 15 Therefore, this is what the LORD says: I will punish these lying prophets, for they have spoken in my name even though I never sent them. They say that no war or famine will come, but they themselves will die by war and famine! 16 As for the people to whom they prophesy—their bodies will be thrown out into the streets of Jerusalem, victims of famine and war. There will be no one left to bury them. Husbands, wives, sons, and daughters—all will be gone. For I will pour out their own wickedness on them. 17 Now, Jeremiah, say this to them:

14:14
Jer 5:31; 23:16,
25-26; 27:9-10
14:15
Ezek 14:10
14:16
Ps 79:2-3
Prov 1:31
Jer 7:33; 8:1-2;
13:22-25; 15:2-3
14:17
Jer 8:21; 9:1
Lam 2:13

"Night and day my eyes overflow with tears.
  I cannot stop weeping,
for my virgin daughter—my precious people—
  has been struck down
  and lies mortally wounded.
18 If I go out into the fields,
  I see the bodies of people slaughtered by the enemy.
If I walk the city streets,
  I see people who have died of starvation.
The prophets and priests continue with their work,
  but they don't know what they're doing."

14:18
Jer 6:25
Lam 1:20
Ezek 7:15

---

14:14 What made the people listen to the false prophets? These "prophets" said what the people wanted to hear. False teachers earn fame and money by telling people what they want to hear, but they lead people away from God. If we encourage false teachers, we are as guilty as they are.

## A Prayer for Healing

**14:19**
Job 30:26
Jer 8:15; 30:13
1 Thes 5:3

19 LORD, have you completely rejected Judah?
　　Do you really hate Jerusalem?*
Why have you wounded us past all hope of healing?
　　We hoped for peace, but no peace came.
　　We hoped for a time of healing, but found only terror.

**14:20**
Ps 32:5

20 LORD, we confess our wickedness
　　and that of our ancestors, too.
　　We all have sinned against you.

**14:21**
Jer 3:17; 14:7;
17:12

21 For the sake of your reputation, LORD, do not abandon us.
　　Do not disgrace your own glorious throne.
　　Please remember us,
　　and do not break your covenant with us.

**14:22**
1 Kgs 17:1
Isa 41:29
Jer 5:24; 10:3
Lam 3:26

22 Can any of the worthless foreign gods send us rain?
　　Does it fall from the sky by itself?
No, you are the one, O LORD our God!
　　Only you can do such things.
　　So we will wait for you to help us.

## Judah's Inevitable Doom

**15:1**
Exod 32:11-14
1 Sam 7:9
Pss 99:6; 106:23
Jer 10:18; 52:3
Ezek 14:14, 20

**15:2**
Ezek 5:2, 12

**15** Then the LORD said to me, "Even if Moses and Samuel stood before me pleading for these people, I wouldn't help them. Away with them! Get them out of my sight! 2 And if they say to you, 'But where can we go?' tell them, 'This is what the LORD says:

"'Those who are destined for death, to death;
　　those who are destined for war, to war;
those who are destined for famine, to famine;
　　those who are destined for captivity, to captivity.'

**15:3**
Lev 26:16, 22, 25
Deut 28:26
Isa 18:6
Ezek 14:21

**15:4**
2 Kgs 23:26-27;
24:3-4
Jer 24:9; 29:18

3 "I will send four kinds of destroyers against them," says the LORD. "I will send the sword to kill, the dogs to drag away, the vultures to devour, and the wild animals to finish up what is left. 4 Because of the wicked things Manasseh son of Hezekiah, king of Judah, did in Jerusalem, I will make my people an object of horror to all the kingdoms of the earth.

**15:5**
Ps 69:20
Jer 13:14

**15:6**
Zeph 1:4

5 "Who will feel sorry for you, Jerusalem?
　　Who will weep for you?
　　Who will even bother to ask how you are?
6 You have abandoned me
　　and turned your back on me,"
　　says the LORD.
"Therefore, I will raise my fist to destroy you.
　　I am tired of always giving you another chance.

**15:7**
Jer 18:21; 51:2
Hos 9:12-16

7 I will winnow you like grain at the gates of your cities
　　and take away the children you hold dear.
I will destroy my own people,
　　because they refuse to change their evil ways.

**14:19** Hebrew *Zion*?

---

**14:19-22** Interceding for the people, Jeremiah asked God if Judah's repentance would bring his help. But God refused to come to their aid (15:1) because the people were insincere, wicked, and stubborn. They knew he wanted to bless them, and they knew what they needed to do to receive that blessing. They wanted God to do his part, but they did not want to do theirs. It's easy to express sorrow for wrong actions, especially when we want something, but we must be willing to stop doing what is wrong. God will forgive those who are truly repentant, but hypocrites will be severely punished.

**15:1** Moses and Samuel were two of God's greatest prophets. Like Jeremiah, both interceded for the people before God (Exodus 32:11; Numbers 14:11-20; 1 Samuel 7:9; 12:17; Psalm 99:6). Intercession is often effective. In this case, however, the

people were so wicked and stubborn that God knew they would not turn to him.

**15:3, 4** The goal of these destroyers would be to destroy the living and devour the dead. Because of Manasseh's evil reign and the people's sin (2 Kings 21:1-16; 23:26; 24:3), the destruction would be complete. The people may have argued that they should not be held responsible for Manasseh's sins, but they were continuing what Manasseh began. If we follow corrupt leaders knowingly, we can't excuse ourselves by blaming their bad example.

8 There will be more widows
  than the grains of sand on the seashore.
At noontime I will bring a destroyer
  against the mothers of young men.
I will cause anguish and terror
  to come upon them suddenly.
9 The mother of seven grows faint and gasps for breath;
  her sun has gone down while it is still day.
She sits childless now,
  disgraced and humiliated.
And I will hand over those who are left
  to be killed by the enemy.
  I, the LORD, have spoken!"

**15:8**
Isa 3:25-26; 4:1

**15:9**
1 Sam 2:5
Isa 47:9
Amos 8:9

### Jeremiah's Complaint

10 Then I said,

  "What sorrow is mine, my mother.
    Oh, that I had died at birth!
    I am hated everywhere I go.
  I am neither a lender who threatens to foreclose
    nor a borrower who refuses to pay—
    yet they all curse me."

**15:10**
Deut 23:19
Job 3:3
Jer 1:18-19;
20:7-8, 14

11 The LORD replied,

  "I will take care of you, Jeremiah.
    Your enemies will ask you to plead on their behalf
    in times of trouble and distress.
12 Can a man break a bar of iron from the north,
    or a bar of bronze?
13 At no cost to them,
    I will hand over your wealth and treasures
  as plunder to your enemies,
    for sin runs rampant in your land.
14 I will tell your enemies to take you
    as captives to a foreign land.
  For my anger blazes like a fire
    that will burn forever.*"

**15:11**
Isa 41:10

**15:13**
Jer 17:3

**15:14**
Deut 28:64

15 Then I said,

  "LORD, you know what's happening to me.
    Please step in and help me. Punish my persecutors!
  Please give me time; don't let me die young.
    It's for your sake that I am suffering.
16 When I discovered your words, I devoured them.
    They are my joy and my heart's delight,
  for I bear your name,
    O LORD God of Heaven's Armies.

**15:16**
Job 23:12
Ps 119:103

17 I never joined the people in their merry feasts.
    I sat alone because your hand was on me.
    I was filled with indignation at their sins.
18 Why then does my suffering continue?
    Why is my wound so incurable?

**15:17**
Ps 102:7
2 Cor 6:17

**15:18**
Jer 30:15

**15:14** As in some Hebrew manuscripts (see also 17:4); most Hebrew manuscripts read *will burn against you.*

---

**15:17-21** Jeremiah accused God of not helping him when he really needed it. Jeremiah had taken his eyes off God's purposes and was feeling sorry for himself. He was angry, hurt, and afraid. In response, God didn't get angry at Jeremiah; he answered by rearranging Jeremiah's priorities. As God's mouthpiece, he was to influence the people, not let them influence him. There are three important lessons in this passage: (1) In prayer we can reveal our deepest thoughts to God; (2) God expects us to trust him, no matter what; (3) we are here to influence others for God.

Your help seems as uncertain as a seasonal brook,
     like a spring that has gone dry."

<sup>19</sup>This is how the LORD responds:

"If you return to me, I will restore you
     so you can continue to serve me.
If you speak good words rather than worthless ones,
     you will be my spokesman.
You must influence them;
     do not let them influence you!
<sup>20</sup> They will fight against you like an attacking army,
     but I will make you as secure as a fortified wall of bronze.
They will not conquer you,
     for I am with you to protect and rescue you.
I, the LORD, have spoken!
<sup>21</sup> Yes, I will certainly keep you safe from these wicked men.
     I will rescue you from their cruel hands."

### Jeremiah Forbidden to Marry

**16** The LORD gave me another message. He said, <sup>2</sup>"Do not get married or have children in this place. <sup>3</sup>For this is what the LORD says about the children born here in this city and about their mothers and fathers: <sup>4</sup>They will die from terrible diseases. No one will mourn for them or bury them, and they will lie scattered on the ground like manure. They will die from war and famine, and their bodies will be food for the vultures and wild animals."

### Judah's Coming Punishment

<sup>5</sup>This is what the LORD says: "Do not go to funerals to mourn and show sympathy for these people, for I have removed my protection and peace from them. I have taken away my unfailing love and my mercy. <sup>6</sup>Both the great and the lowly will die in this land. No one will bury them or mourn for them. Their friends will not cut themselves in sorrow or shave their heads in sadness. <sup>7</sup>No one will offer a meal to comfort those who mourn for the dead—not even at the death of a mother or father. No one will send a cup of wine to console them.

<sup>8</sup>"And do not go to their feasts and parties. Do not eat and drink with them at all. <sup>9</sup>For this is what the LORD of Heaven's Armies, the God of Israel, says: In your own lifetime, before your very eyes, I will put an end to the happy singing and laughter in this land. The joyful voices of bridegrooms and brides will no longer be heard.

<sup>10</sup>"When you tell the people all these things, they will ask, 'Why has the LORD decreed such terrible things against us? What have we done to deserve such treatment? What is our sin against the LORD our God?'

<sup>11</sup>"Then you will give them the LORD's reply: 'It is because your ancestors were unfaithful to me. They worshiped other gods and served them. They abandoned me and did not obey my word. <sup>12</sup>And you are even worse than your ancestors! You stubbornly follow your own evil desires and refuse to listen to me. <sup>13</sup>So I will throw you out of this land and send you into a foreign land where you and your ancestors have never been. There you can worship idols day and night—and I will grant you no favors!'

**15:19** Ezek 44:23
**15:20** Ps 46:7; Isa 41:10; Jer 1:8, 18-19; Ezek 3:9
**15:21** Ps 37:40; Isa 49:26; Jer 39:11-12
**16:3** Jer 15:8
**16:4** Pss 79:2; 83:10; Isa 18:6; Jer 15:2-3; 34:20
**16:5** Isa 27:11; Ezek 24:16-23
**16:6** Deut 14:1; Ezek 9:6
**16:8** Eccl 7:2-4; Isa 22:12-14; Jer 15:17
**16:9** Jer 7:34; 25:10; Hos 2:11
**16:10** Deut 29:24-25; 1 Kgs 9:8-9
**16:11** 1 Pet 4:3
**16:12** Mark 7:21
**16:13** Deut 4:26-27; 28:36; Jer 5:19; 15:14

---

**16:1–17:18** This section portrays the coming day of disaster. It begins by showing Jeremiah's loneliness. He is a social outcast because of his harsh messages and his celibate lifestyle. He must not marry, have children, or take part in funerals or festivals. The section concludes with another appeal to avoid judgment by turning to God. The people did not heed Jeremiah's words, however, and the first wave of destruction came almost immediately, in 605 B.C. (2 Kings 24:8-12). The second wave came in 597 B.C., and Judah was completely destroyed in 586 B.C.

**16:5-7** In Jeremiah's culture, it was unthinkable not to show grief publicly. The absence of mourning showed the people how complete their devastation would be. So many people would die that it would be impossible to carry out customary mourning rituals for all of them.

**16:8-13** Jeremiah was also told not to participate in parties or other joyful events to show how seriously God took the nation's sins. In both cases (no public grief or joy), Jeremiah's life was to be an attention getter and an illustration of God's truth. Sometimes we think that the only way to communicate is through speaking or teaching, but God can use a wide variety of means to bring his message. Use your creativity.

### Hope despite the Disaster

14"But the time is coming," says the LORD, "when people who are taking an oath will no longer say, 'As surely as the LORD lives, who rescued the people of Israel from the land of Egypt.' 15Instead, they will say, 'As surely as the LORD lives, who brought the people of Israel back to their own land from the land of the north and from all the countries to which he had exiled them.' For I will bring them back to this land that I gave their ancestors.

16 "But now I am sending for many fishermen who will catch them," says the LORD. "I am sending for hunters who will hunt them down in the mountains, hills, and caves. 17I am watching them closely, and I see every sin. They cannot hope to hide from me. 18I will double their punishment for all their sins, because they have defiled my land with lifeless images of their detestable gods and have filled my territory with their evil deeds."

### Jeremiah's Prayer of Confidence

19 LORD, you are my strength and fortress,
　　my refuge in the day of trouble!
Nations from around the world
　　will come to you and say,
"Our ancestors left us a foolish heritage,
　　for they worshiped worthless idols.
20 Can people make their own gods?
　　These are not real gods at all!"

21 The LORD says,
"Now I will show them my power;
　　now I will show them my might.
At last they will know and understand
　　that I am the LORD.

### Judah's Sin and Punishment

**17** 1"The sin of Judah
　　　is inscribed with an iron chisel—
engraved with a diamond point on their stony hearts
　　and on the corners of their altars.
2 Even their children go to worship
　　at their pagan altars and Asherah poles,
beneath every green tree
　　and on every high hill.
3 So I will hand over my holy mountain—
　　along with all your wealth and treasures
　　and your pagan shrines—
as plunder to your enemies,
　　for sin runs rampant in your land.
4 The wonderful possession I have reserved for you
　　will slip from your hands.
I will tell your enemies to take you
　　as captives to a foreign land.
For my anger blazes like a fire
　　that will burn forever."

---

**16:14**
Deut 15:15
Isa 43:18-19

**16:15**
Isa 11:11-16

**16:16**
Isa 2:21
Amos 4:2; 9:1-3
Hab 1:14-15

**16:17**
Ps 90:8
Jer 23:24; 32:19
Luke 12:2
1 Cor 4:5
Heb 4:13

**16:18**
Num 35:34
Jer 2:7; 3:9
Rev 18:6

**16:19**
Ps 18:1-2
Isa 25:4
Nah 1:7

**16:21**
Ps 83:18
Isa 43:3
Amos 5:8

**17:1**
Job 19:24
Prov 3:3; 7:3
2 Cor 3:3

**17:2**
Exod 34:13

**17:4**
Deut 28:48
Isa 5:25
Jer 7:20; 12:7

---

**16:14, 15** The book of Exodus records God's miraculous rescue of his people from Egyptian slavery (Exodus 1–15). The people's return from exile would be so momentous that it would overshadow even the exodus from Egypt. Even though his people had been so stubborn, God would once again show his great mercy.

**16:17** Small children think that if they can't see you, then you can't see them. The people of Israel may have wished that hiding from God were as simple as closing their eyes. Although they closed their eyes to their sinful ways, their sins certainly weren't hidden from God. He who sees everything cannot be deceived. Do you have a sinful attitude or activity that you hope God won't notice? He knows about it. The first step of repentance is to acknowledge that God knows about your sins.

**16:19** In this prayer, Jeremiah approached God with three descriptive names: strength, fortress, and refuge. Each name gives a slightly different glimpse of how Jeremiah experienced God's presence, and each is a picture of security and protection. Let God be your strength when you feel weak, your fortress when enemies come against you, and your refuge when you need to retreat from life's pressures.

**17:1** God's people continued to sin even though they had the law, the prophets of God, and history replete with God's miracles. How could they do that? Why do we continue in sin even though we understand the eternal consequences? Jeremiah says the heart is deceitful (17:9), and their sin is "engraved with a diamond point on their stony hearts." The Hebrews symbolized

### Wisdom from the LORD

17:5
2 Chr 32:8
Isa 30:1; 31:3
Ezek 29:6-7

5 This is what the LORD says:

"Cursed are those who put their trust in mere humans,
   who rely on human strength
   and turn their hearts away from the LORD.
6 They are like stunted shrubs in the desert,
   with no hope for the future.
They will live in the barren wilderness,
   in an uninhabited salty land.

17:7
Pss 34:8; 40:4;
84:12

17:8
Pss 1:3; 92:12-14

7 "But blessed are those who trust in the LORD
   and have made the LORD their hope and confidence.
8 They are like trees planted along a riverbank,
   with roots that reach deep into the water.
Such trees are not bothered by the heat
   or worried by long months of drought.
Their leaves stay green,
   and they never stop producing fruit.

17:9
Matt 13:15
Mark 2:17; 7:21-22
Rom 1:21; 7:11

17:10
Rom 8:27

9 "The human heart is the most deceitful of all things,
   and desperately wicked.
   Who really knows how bad it is?
10 But I, the LORD, search all hearts
   and examine secret motives.
I give all people their due rewards,
   according to what their actions deserve."

### Jeremiah's Trust in the LORD

11 Like a partridge that hatches eggs she has not laid,
   so are those who get their wealth by unjust means.
At midlife they will lose their riches;
   in the end, they will become poor old fools.

17:12
Jer 14:21

12 But we worship at your throne—
   eternal, high, and glorious!

17:13
Jer 14:8

13 O LORD, the hope of Israel,
   all who turn away from you will be disgraced.
They will be buried in the dust of the earth,
   for they have abandoned the LORD, the fountain of living water.

17:14
Deut 10:21
Ps 54:1
Jer 33:6

17:15
Isa 5:19
Amos 5:18

14 O LORD, if you heal me, I will be truly healed;
   if you save me, I will be truly saved.
   My praises are for you alone!
15 People scoff at me and say,
   "What is this 'message from the LORD' you talk about?
   Why don't your predictions come true?"

17:16
Jer 12:3

16 LORD, I have not abandoned my job
   as a shepherd for your people.

---

the various aspects of a person by locating them in certain physical organs. The heart was the organ of reason, intelligence, and will. So deep is our tendency to sin that only God's redemption can deliver us.

**17:5-8** Two kinds of people are contrasted here: those who trust in human beings and those who trust in the Lord. The people of Judah were trusting in false gods and military alliances instead of God, and thus they were barren and unfruitful. In contrast, those who trust in the Lord flourish like trees planted along a riverbank (see Psalm 1). In times of trouble, those who trust in human beings will be impoverished and spiritually weak, so they will have no strength to draw on. But those who trust in the Lord will have abundant strength, not only for their own needs, but even for the needs of others. Are you satisfied with being unfruitful, or do you,

like a well-watered tree, have strength for times of crisis and even some to share as you bear fruit for the Lord?

**17:9, 10** God makes it clear why we sin—it's a matter of the heart. Our heart is inclined toward sin from the time we are born. It is easy to fall into the routine of forgetting and forsaking God. But we can still choose whether or not to continue in sin. We can yield to a specific temptation, or we can ask God to help us resist temptation when it comes.

**17:11** There is a right way and a wrong way to do any task. Jeremiah says that the person who becomes rich by unjust means will end up foolish and poor. Whether at work, school, or play, we should strive to be honest in all our dealings. Getting a promotion, passing an exam, or gaining prestige by dishonest means will never bring God's blessing or lasting happiness.

I have not urged you to send disaster.
  You have heard everything I've said.
¹⁷ LORD, don't terrorize me!
  You alone are my hope in the day of disaster.
¹⁸ Bring shame and dismay on all who persecute me,
    but don't let me experience shame and dismay.
  Bring a day of terror on them.
    Yes, bring double destruction upon them!

### Observing the Sabbath

¹⁹This is what the LORD said to me: "Go and stand in the gates of Jerusalem, first in the gate where the king goes in and out, and then in each of the other gates. ²⁰Say to all the people, 'Listen to this message from the LORD, you kings of Judah and all you people of Judah and everyone living in Jerusalem. ²¹This is what the LORD says: Listen to my warning! Stop carrying on your trade at Jerusalem's gates on the Sabbath day. ²²Do not do your work on the Sabbath, but make it a holy day. I gave this command to your ancestors, ²³but they did not listen or obey. They stubbornly refused to pay attention or accept my discipline.

²⁴"But if you obey me, says the LORD, and do not carry on your trade at the gates or work on the Sabbath day, and if you keep it holy, ²⁵then kings and their officials will go in and out of these gates forever. There will always be a descendant of David sitting on the throne here in Jerusalem. Kings and their officials will always ride in and out among the people of Judah in chariots and on horses, and this city will remain forever. ²⁶And from all around Jerusalem, from the towns of Judah and Benjamin, from the western foothills* and the hill country and the Negev, the people will come with their burnt offerings and sacrifices. They will bring their grain offerings, frankincense, and thanksgiving offerings to the LORD's Temple.

²⁷"But if you do not listen to me and refuse to keep the Sabbath holy, and if on the Sabbath day you bring loads of merchandise through the gates of Jerusalem just as on other days, then I will set fire to these gates. The fire will spread to the palaces, and no one will be able to put out the roaring flames.'"

### The Potter and the Clay

**18** The LORD gave another message to Jeremiah. He said, ²"Go down to the potter's shop, and I will speak to you there." ³So I did as he told me and found the potter working at his wheel. ⁴But the jar he was making did not turn out as he had hoped, so he crushed it into a lump of clay again and started over.

⁵Then the LORD gave me this message: ⁶"O Israel, can I not do to you as this potter has done to his clay? As the clay is in the potter's hand, so are you in my hand. ⁷If I announce that a certain nation or kingdom is to be uprooted, torn down, and destroyed, ⁸but then that nation renounces its evil ways, I will not destroy it as I had planned. ⁹And if I announce that I will plant and build up a certain nation or kingdom, ¹⁰but then that nation turns to evil and refuses to obey me, I will not bless it as I said I would.

¹¹"Therefore, Jeremiah, go and warn all Judah and Jerusalem. Say to them, 'This is what the LORD says: I am planning disaster for you instead of good. So turn from your evil ways, each of you, and do what is right.'"

¹²But the people replied, "Don't waste your breath. We will continue to live as we want to, stubbornly following our own evil desires."

**17:26** Hebrew *the Shephelah.*

**17:17**
Jer 16:19
Nah 1:7

**17:18**
Ps 35:4, 26
Jer 20:11

**17:20**
Jer 19:3-4

**17:21**
Num 15:32-36
Neh 13:15-21
Mark 4:24
John 5:9-12

**17:22**
Exod 20:8; 31:13
Ezek 20:12

**17:23**
Jer 7:26; 19:15

**17:24**
Exod 15:26;
20:8-11
Deut 11:13
Ezek 20:20

**17:25**
2 Sam 7:16
Ps 132:13-14
Jer 22:4
Luke 1:32
Heb 12:2

**17:26**
Ps 107:22
Jer 33:11

**17:27**
Jer 39:8
Ezek 20:47
Amos 2:5

**18:2**
Jer 19:1-2

**18:6**
Isa 45:9; 64:8
Matt 20:15
Rom 9:20-21

**18:8**
Jer 7:3-7
Ezek 18:21
Jon 3:10

**18:9**
Jer 31:28
Amos 9:11-15

**18:10**
1 Sam 2:30
Jer 7:24-28
Ezek 33:18

**18:11**
2 Kgs 17:13
Isa 1:16-19
Jer 4:6; 11:11
Acts 26:20

**18:12**
Deut 29:19
Jer 2:25; 16:12

---

**17:19-27** The people were working on the Sabbath, their day of rest (Exodus 20:8-11). Instead of entering the gates of the city on their way to worship, they continued the hustle and bustle of business like any other day. They considered making money more important than keeping God's law. If they would repent and put God first in their lives, God promised them honor among the nations. Over a century later, when Nehemiah led the exiles on their return to Jerusalem, one of his most important reforms was to reinstitute Sabbath observance (Nehemiah 13:15-22).

**18:1-19:15** The parables in these chapters, probably written during the early years of Jehoiakim's reign, illustrate God's sovereignty over the nation. God has power over the clay (Judah), and he continues to work with it to make it a useful vessel. But Judah

must soon repent, or the clay will harden the wrong way. Then it will be worth nothing and will be broken and destroyed.

**18:6** As the potter molded or shaped a clay pot on the potter's wheel, defects often appeared. The potter had power over the clay, to permit the defects to remain or to reshape the pot. Likewise, God had power to reshape the nation to conform to his purposes. Our strategy should not be to become mindless and passive—one aspect of clay—but to be willing and receptive to God's impact on us. As we yield to God, he begins reshaping us into valuable vessels.

**18:12** Our society admires assertiveness, independence, and defiance of authority. In a relationship with God these qualities become stubbornness, self-importance, and refusal to listen or

18:13
Jer 2:10-11; 23:14
Hos 6:10
13 So this is what the LORD says:

"Has anyone ever heard of such a thing,
      even among the pagan nations?
My virgin daughter Israel
      has done something terrible!
14 Does the snow ever disappear from the mountaintops of Lebanon?
      Do the cold streams flowing from those distant mountains ever run dry?

18:15
Isa 62:10; 65:7
15 But my people are not so reliable, for they have deserted me;
      they burn incense to worthless idols.
They have stumbled off the ancient highways
      and walk in muddy paths.

18:16
Jer 25:9; 48:27;
50:13
Ezek 33:28-29
16 Therefore, their land will become desolate,
      a monument to their stupidity.
All who pass by will be astonished
      and will shake their heads in amazement.

18:17
Jer 13:24
17 I will scatter my people before their enemies
      as the east wind scatters dust.
And in all their trouble I will turn my back on them
      and refuse to notice their distress."

### A Plot against Jeremiah

18:18
Ps 52:2
Mal 2:7
18 Then the people said, "Come on, let's plot a way to stop Jeremiah. We have plenty of priests and wise men and prophets. We don't need him to teach the word and give us advice and prophecies. Let's spread rumors about him and ignore what he says."

19 LORD, hear me and help me!
      Listen to what my enemies are saying.
18:20
Pss 35:7; 57:6;
106:23
20 Should they repay evil for good?
      They have dug a pit to kill me,
though I pleaded for them
      and tried to protect them from your anger.

---

| GOD'S OBJECT LESSONS IN JEREMIAH | Reference | Object Lesson | Significance |
|---|---|---|---|
| | 1:11, 12 | Branch from an almond tree | God will carry out his threats of punishment. |
| | 1:13 | Pot of boiling water, spilling southward | God will punish Judah. |
| | 13:1-11 | A rotten linen loincloth | Because the people refused to listen to God, they had become useless, good for nothing, like a useless linen loincloth. |
| | 18:1-17 | Potter's clay | God could destroy his sinful people if he so desired. This is a warning to them to repent before he is forced to bring judgment. |
| | 19:1-12 | Shattered clay jars | God would smash Judah just as Jeremiah smashed the clay jars. |
| | 24:1-10 | Two baskets of figs | Good figs represent God's remnant. Bad figs are the people left behind. |
| | 27:2-11 | Yoke | Any nation who refused to submit to Babylon's yoke of control would be punished. |
| | 43:8-13 | Large rocks | The rocks marked the place where Nebuchadnezzar would set his throne when God allowed him to conquer Egypt. |
| | 51:59-64 | Scroll sunk in the river | Babylon would sink to rise no more. |

---

change. Left unchecked, stubbornness becomes a way of life hostile to God.

**18:18** Jeremiah's words and actions challenged the people's social and moral behavior. He had openly spoken against the king, the officials, the priests and prophets, the teachers, and the wise (4:9; 8:8, 9). He wasn't afraid to give unpopular criticism.

The people could either obey him or silence him. They chose the latter. They did not think they needed Jeremiah; their false prophets told them what they wanted to hear. How do you respond to criticism? Listen carefully—God may be trying to tell you something.

21 So let their children starve!
  Let them die by the sword!
Let their wives become childless widows.
  Let their old men die in a plague,
  and let their young men be killed in battle!
22 Let screaming be heard from their homes
  as warriors come suddenly upon them.
For they have dug a pit for me
  and have hidden traps along my path.
23 LORD, you know all about their murderous plots against me.
  Don't forgive their crimes and blot out their sins.
Let them die before you.
  Deal with them in your anger.

18:21
Ps 109:9-20
Jer 9:21; 11:22;
14:16

18:22
Ps 140:5
Jer 6:26

18:23
Jer 6:15, 21; 7:20;
17:4

### Jeremiah's Shattered Jar

**19** This is what the LORD said to me: "Go and buy a clay jar. Then ask some of the leaders of the people and of the priests to follow you. 2 Go out through the Gate of Broken Pots to the garbage dump in the valley of Ben-Hinnom, and give them this message. 3 Say to them, 'Listen to this message from the LORD, you kings of Judah and citizens of Jerusalem! This is what the LORD of Heaven's Armies, the God of Israel, says: I will bring a terrible disaster on this place, and the ears of those who hear about it will ring!

4 "'For Israel has forsaken me and turned this valley into a place of wickedness. The people burn incense to foreign gods—idols never before acknowledged by this generation, by their ancestors, or by the kings of Judah. And they have filled this place with the blood of innocent children. 5 They have built pagan shrines to Baal, and there they burn their sons as sacrifices to Baal. I have never commanded such a horrible deed; it never even crossed my mind to command such a thing! 6 So beware, for the time is coming, says the LORD, when this garbage dump will no longer be called Topheth or the valley of Ben-Hinnom, but the Valley of Slaughter.

7 "'For I will upset the careful plans of Judah and Jerusalem. I will allow the people to be slaughtered by invading armies, and I will leave their dead bodies as food for the vultures and wild animals. 8 I will reduce Jerusalem to ruins, making it a monument to their stupidity. All who pass by will be astonished and will gasp at the destruction they see there. 9 I will see to it that your enemies lay siege to the city until all the food is gone. Then those trapped inside will eat their own sons and daughters and friends. They will be driven to utter despair.'

10 "As these men watch you, Jeremiah, smash the jar you brought. 11 Then say to them, 'This is what the LORD of Heaven's Armies says: As this jar lies shattered, so I will shatter the people of Judah and Jerusalem beyond all hope of repair. They will bury the bodies here in Topheth, the garbage dump, until there is no more room for them. 12 This is what I will do to this place and its people, says the LORD. I will cause this city to become defiled like Topheth. 13 Yes, all the houses in Jerusalem, including the palace of Judah's kings, will become like Topheth—all the houses where you burned incense on the rooftops to your star gods, and where liquid offerings were poured out to your idols.'"

14 Then Jeremiah returned from Topheth, the garbage dump where he had delivered this message, and he stopped in front of the Temple of the LORD. He said to the people there, 15 "This is what the LORD of Heaven's Armies, the God of Israel, says: 'I will bring disaster upon this city and its surrounding towns as I promised, because you have stubbornly refused to listen to me.'"

19:2
Jer 7:31

19:3
1 Sam 3:11

19:4
Deut 28:20
2 Kgs 21:6, 16
Isa 65:11
Jer 2:34; 7:6, 9;
11:13; 17:13
Dan 11:31

19:5
Lev 18:21
2 Kgs 17:17
Ps 106:37-38
Jer 32:35

19:6
Jer 7:32

19:7
Ps 33:10-11
Isa 28:17-18
Jer 16:4

19:8
1 Kgs 9:8
2 Chr 7:21
Jer 18:16

19:9
Deut 28:53, 55
Ezek 5:10
Lam 4:10

19:10
Jer 19:1

19:11
Ps 2:9
Isa 30:14
Jer 7:32
Rev 2:27

19:13
Deut 4:19
2 Kgs 17:16
Jer 7:18; 8:2;
32:29; 52:13
Ezek 20:28
Zeph 1:5

19:15
Neh 9:17, 29
Ps 58:4
Jer 7:26; 17:23

---

**19:6** The valley of Ben-Hinnom was the garbage dump of Jerusalem and the place where children were sacrificed to the god Molech. It is also mentioned in 7:31, 32. Topheth was located in the valley and means "fireplace." God declared that the place of sacrifice would become a place of slaughter. The killers of the innocent would be judged by losing their own lives.

**19:7-13** The horrible carnage that Jeremiah predicted happened twice: in 586 B.C. during the Babylonian invasion under Nebuchadnezzar and in A.D. 70 when Titus destroyed Jerusalem. During the Babylonian siege, food became so scarce that people became cannibals, even eating their own children. (See Leviticus 26:29 and Deuteronomy 28:53-57 for prophecies concerning this; and see 2 Kings 6:28, 29; Lamentations 2:20; 4:10 for accounts of actual occurrences.)

## Jeremiah and Pashhur

20:1
1 Chr 24:14
Ezra 2:37-38

20:2
1 Kgs 22:27
2 Chr 16:10; 24:21
Job 13:27
Zech 14:10

20:4
Jer 29:21; 39:6-7
Ezek 26:21

20:5
2 Kgs 20:17
2 Chr 36:10
Jer 15:13; 17:3

20:6
Jer 14:14-15
Lam 2:14

**20** Now Pashhur son of Immer, the priest in charge of the Temple of the Lord, heard what Jeremiah was prophesying. ²So he arrested Jeremiah the prophet and had him whipped and put in stocks at the Benjamin Gate of the Lord's Temple.

³The next day, when Pashhur finally released him, Jeremiah said, "Pashhur, the Lord has changed your name. From now on you are to be called 'The Man Who Lives in Terror.'* ⁴For this is what the Lord says: 'I will send terror upon you and all your friends, and you will watch as they are slaughtered by the swords of the enemy. I will hand the people of Judah over to the king of Babylon. He will take them captive to Babylon or run them through with the sword. ⁵And I will let your enemies plunder Jerusalem. All the famed treasures of the city—the precious jewels and gold and silver of your kings—will be carried off to Babylon. ⁶As for you, Pashhur, you and all your household will go as captives to Babylon. There you will die and be buried, you and all your friends to whom you prophesied that everything would be all right.'"

## Jeremiah's Complaint

20:7
Lam 3:14
Ezek 3:14
Mic 3:8

⁷ O Lord, you misled me,
    and I allowed myself to be misled.
You are stronger than I am,
    and you overpowered me.
Now I am mocked every day;
    everyone laughs at me.

20:8
2 Chr 36:16
Jer 6:10

⁸ When I speak, the words burst out.
    "Violence and destruction!" I shout.
So these messages from the Lord
    have made me a household joke.

20:9
Job 32:18-20
Ps 39:3
Jer 4:19
Acts 4:20

⁹ But if I say I'll never mention the Lord
    or speak in his name,
his word burns in my heart like a fire.
    It's like a fire in my bones!
I am worn out trying to hold it in!
    I can't do it!

20:10
1 Kgs 19:2
Neh 6:6-13
Pss 31:13; 41:9

¹⁰ I have heard the many rumors about me.
    They call me "The Man Who Lives in Terror."
They threaten, "If you say anything, we will report it."
    Even my old friends are watching me,
    waiting for a fatal slip.
"He will trap himself," they say,
    "and then we will get our revenge on him."

¹¹ But the Lord stands beside me like a great warrior.
    Before him my persecutors will stumble.
    They cannot defeat me.
They will fail and be thoroughly humiliated.
    Their dishonor will never be forgotten.

20:3 Hebrew *Magor-missabib*, which means "surrounded by terror"; also in 20:10.

---

**20:1ff** This event took place during the reign of Jehoiakim of Judah. Jeremiah preached at the valley of Ben-Hinnom, the center of idolatry in the city. He also preached in the Temple, which should have been the center of true worship. Both places attracted many people; both were places of false worship.

**20:1-3** Pashhur was the official in charge of maintaining order in the Temple (see 29:26 for a description of the responsibility). He was also a priest and had pretended to be a prophet. After hearing Jeremiah's words, Pashhur had him whipped and put in the stocks (locked up) instead of taking his message to heart and acting on it. The truth sometimes stings, but our reaction to the truth shows what we are made of. We can deny the charges and destroy evidence of our misdeeds, or we can take the truth humbly to heart and let it change us. Pashhur may have thought he was a strong leader, but he was really a coward.

**20:4-6** This prophecy of destruction came true in three waves of invasion by Babylon. The first wave happened within the year (605 B.C.). Pashhur was probably exiled to Babylon during the second wave in 597 B.C. when Jehoiachin was taken captive. The third invasion occurred in 586 B.C.

**20:7-18** Jeremiah cried out in despair mixed with praise, unburdening his heart to God. He had faithfully proclaimed God's word and had received nothing in return but persecution and sorrow. Yet when he withheld God's word for a while, it became fire in his bones until he could hold it back no longer. When God's living message of forgiveness and love becomes fire in your bones, you also will feel compelled to share it with others, regardless of the results.

12 O Lord of Heaven's Armies,
   you test those who are righteous,
      and you examine the deepest thoughts and secrets.
   Let me see your vengeance against them,
      for I have committed my cause to you.

13 Sing to the Lord!
   Praise the Lord!
   For though I was poor and needy,
      he rescued me from my oppressors.

14 Yet I curse the day I was born!
   May no one celebrate the day of my birth.
15 I curse the messenger who told my father,
   "Good news—you have a son!"
16 Let him be destroyed like the cities of old
      that the Lord overthrew without mercy.
   Terrify him all day long with battle shouts,
17    because he did not kill me at birth.
   Oh, that I had died in my mother's womb,
      that her body had been my grave!
18 Why was I ever born?
   My entire life has been filled
      with trouble, sorrow, and shame.

## 4. Jeremiah accuses Judah's leaders
### No Deliverance from Babylon

**21** The Lord spoke through Jeremiah when King Zedekiah sent Pashhur son of Malki-jah and Zephaniah son of Maaseiah, the priest, to speak with him. They begged Jeremiah, 2"Please speak to the Lord for us and ask him to help us. King Nebuchadnezzar* of Babylon is attacking Judah. Perhaps the Lord will be gracious and do a mighty miracle as he has done in the past. Perhaps he will force Nebuchadnezzar to withdraw his armies."

3Jeremiah replied, "Go back to King Zedekiah and tell him, 4'This is what the Lord, the God of Israel, says: I will make your weapons useless against the king of Babylon and the Babylonians* who are outside your walls attacking you. In fact, I will bring your enemies right into the heart of this city. 5I myself will fight against you with a strong hand and a powerful arm, for I am very angry. You have made me furious! 6I will send a terrible plague upon this city, and both people and animals will die. 7And after all that, says the Lord, I will hand over King Zedekiah, his staff, and everyone else in the city who survives the disease, war, and famine. I will hand them over to King Nebuchadnezzar of Babylon and to their other enemies. He will slaughter them and show them no mercy, pity, or compassion.'

8"Tell all the people, 'This is what the Lord says: Take your choice of life or death! 9Everyone who stays in Jerusalem will die from war, famine, or disease, but those who go out and surrender to the Babylonians will live. Their reward will be life! 10For I have decided to bring disaster and not good upon this city, says the Lord. It will be handed over to the king of Babylon, and he will reduce it to ashes.'

**21:2** Hebrew *Nebuchadrezzar*, a variant spelling of Nebuchadnezzar; also in 21:7.   **21:4** Or *Chaldeans*; also in 21:9.

**20:12**
Pss 7:9; 17:3;
59:10; 62:8; 139:23
Jer 11:20; 17:10

**20:13**
Pss 34:6; 69:33

**20:14**
Job 3:3-6

**20:15**
Gen 21:6-7

**20:17**
Job 3:10-11, 16;
10:18-19

**20:18**
Job 3:20; 14:1
1 Cor 4:9-13

**21:1**
2 Kgs 25:18-21
1 Chr 9:12
Jer 29:25, 29; 37:3

**21:2**
2 Kgs 25:1-2
Ps 44:1-4

**21:4**
Zech 14:2

**21:5**
Isa 5:25; 63:10
Jer 6:12

**21:6**
Jer 14:12; 32:24

**21:7**
2 Chr 36:17
Jer 13:14
Ezek 7:9
Hab 1:6-10

**21:8**
Deut 30:15, 19

**21:10**
2 Chr 36:19
Jer 32:28-29; 39:8;
44:11, 27; 52:13

---

**20:14-18** Probably as troubling as the self-loathing that oozes from these verses is the stark contrast between the exuberant confidence of the previous paragraph and the sudden inward turn of revulsion. In Jeremiah's honestly recorded moments of despair, however, we can find hope. If someone with such intimate awareness of God's presence struggled with insecurity, we ought not to be surprised over our own failures and weaknesses. Jeremiah doesn't give us an excuse, but an example. No matter how we may feel about ourselves at any moment, God remains unchanged, loving, and present in our lives.

**21:1** Chapters 21–28 are Jeremiah's messages concerning Nebuchadnezzar's attacks on Jerusalem between 588 and 586 B.C. (see also 2 Kings 25). King Zedekiah decided to rebel against Nebuchadnezzar (2 Kings 24:20), and the nobles advised allying

with Egypt. Jeremiah pronounced judgment on the kings (21:1–23:8) and false prophets (23:9-40) for leading the people astray.

**21:1, 2** King Zedekiah probably was referring to God's deliverance of Jerusalem from Sennacherib, king of Assyria, in the days of Hezekiah (Isaiah 36–37). But Zedekiah's hopes were dashed. He was Judah's last ruler during the time of the exile in 586 B.C.

**21:1, 2** Pashhur came to the prophet for help. (This is not the same Pashhur as in 20:1.) God still had work for Jeremiah to do. In living out our faith, we may find that rejection, disappointment, or hard work has brought us to the point of despondency. But we are still needed. God has important work for us as well.

**21:1-14** Jeremiah had foretold Jerusalem's destruction. The city's leaders had denied his word and mocked his pronouncements. In desperation, King Zedekiah turned to God for help, but

## Judgment on Judah's Kings

21:12
Isa 1:17
Nah 1:6
Zech 7:9-10

11"Say to the royal family of Judah, 'Listen to this message from the LORD! 12 This is what the LORD says to the dynasty of David:

> "'Give justice each morning to the people you judge!
> Help those who have been robbed;
> rescue them from their oppressors.
> Otherwise, my anger will burn like an unquenchable fire
> because of all your sins.

21:13
2 Sam 5:6-7
Jer 49:4
Lam 4:12
Ezek 13:8
Obad 1:3-4

> 13 I will personally fight against the people in Jerusalem,
> that mighty fortress—
> the people who boast, "No one can touch us here.
> No one can break in here."

21:14
2 Chr 36:19

> 14 And I myself will punish you for your sinfulness,
> says the LORD.
> I will light a fire in your forests
> that will burn up everything around you.'"

## A Message for Judah's Kings

22:2
Isa 9:7
Jer 17:25; 22:4
Luke 1:32

**22** This is what the LORD said to me: "Go over and speak directly to the king of Judah. Say to him, 2'Listen to this message from the LORD, you king of Judah, sitting on David's throne. Let your attendants and your people listen, too. 3 This is what the LORD says: Be fair-minded and just. Do what is right! Help those who have been robbed; rescue them from their oppressors. Quit your evil deeds! Do not mistreat foreigners, orphans, and widows. Stop murdering the innocent! 4If you obey me, there will always be a descendant of David sitting on the throne here in Jerusalem. The king will ride through the palace gates in chariots and on horses, with his parade of attendants and subjects. 5 But if you refuse to pay attention to this warning, I swear by my own name, says the LORD, that this palace will become a pile of rubble.'"

22:3
Exod 22:21-24
Ps 72:4
Jer 7:6; 19:4;
21:12; 22:17

22:5
Amos 6:8
Heb 6:13

## A Message about the Palace

22:6
Isa 6:11
Jer 7:34

6Now this is what the LORD says concerning Judah's royal palace:

> "I love you as much as fruitful Gilead
> and the green forests of Lebanon.
> But I will turn you into a desert,
> with no one living within your walls.
> 7 I will call for wreckers,
> who will bring out their tools to dismantle you.
> They will tear out all your fine cedar beams
> and throw them on the fire.

22:8
Deut 29:24-26
1 Kgs 9:8-9
2 Chr 7:20, 22
Jer 16:10

22:9
2 Chr 34:25
Jer 11:3

8"People from many nations will pass by the ruins of this city and say to one another, 'Why did the LORD destroy such a great city?' 9And the answer will be, 'Because they violated their covenant with the LORD their God by worshiping other gods.'"

## A Message about Jehoahaz

22:10
Jer 16:7; 44:14

10 Do not weep for the dead king or mourn his loss.
> Instead, weep for the captive king being led away!
> For he will never return to see his native land again.

---

without acknowledging God's warnings or admitting his sin. Too often we expect God to help us in our time of trouble even though we have ignored him in our time of prosperity. But God wants a lasting relationship. Are you trying to build a lasting friendship with God, or are you merely using him occasionally to escape trouble? What would you think of your family or friends if they thought of you only as a temporary resource?

**21:13** Jerusalem was built on a plateau with valleys on three sides. Because of its strategic location, the inhabitants thought they were safe.

**22:1ff** Chapters 22–25 may not be in chronological order. In 21:8-10 God implied that it was too late for repentance. In 22:4, however, God said that there was still time to change.

The events to which this chapter refer occurred before those of chapter 21.

**22:3** God gave the king the basis for rebuilding the nation— turn from evil and do right. Doing what is right is more than simply believing all the right doctrines about God. It means living in obedience to God. Good deeds do not save us, but they display our faith (James 2:17-26).

**22:10-12** Good King Josiah had died at the battle of Megiddo (2 Kings 23:29); his son Jehoahaz reigned for only three months in 609 B.C. before being taken away to Egypt by Pharaoh Neco. He would be the first ruler to die in exile. The people were told not to waste their tears on the death of Josiah but to cry for the king who was taken into exile and would never return.

¹¹For this is what the LORD says about Jehoahaz,* who succeeded his father, King Josiah, and was taken away as a captive: "He will never return. ¹²He will die in a distant land and will never again see his own country."

22:11
2 Kgs 23:30-34
22:12
2 Kgs 23:34

### A Message about Jehoiakim

¹³ And the LORD says, "What sorrow awaits Jehoiakim,*
　　who builds his palace with forced labor.*
　He builds injustice into its walls,
　　for he makes his neighbors work for nothing.
　　He does not pay them for their labor.

22:13
Jer 17:11
Hab 2:9
Jas 5:4

¹⁴ He says, 'I will build a magnificent palace
　　with huge rooms and many windows.
　I will panel it throughout with fragrant cedar
　　and paint it a lovely red.'

22:14
Isa 5:8-9
Hab 1:4

¹⁵ But a beautiful cedar palace does not make a great king!
　　Your father, Josiah, also had plenty to eat and drink.
　But he was just and right in all his dealings.
　　That is why God blessed him.

22:15
2 Kgs 23:25
Jer 21:12; 42:6

¹⁶ He gave justice and help to the poor and needy,
　　and everything went well for him.
　Isn't that what it means to know me?"
　　says the LORD.

22:16
Ps 72:1-4, 12-13
Jer 9:24

¹⁷ "But you! You have eyes only for greed and dishonesty!
　　You murder the innocent,
　　oppress the poor, and reign ruthlessly."

22:17
Jer 6:13; 8:10
Luke 12:15-20

¹⁸Therefore, this is what the LORD says about Jehoiakim, son of King Josiah:

　"The people will not mourn for him, crying to one another,
　　'Alas, my brother! Alas, my sister!'
　His subjects will not mourn for him, crying,
　　'Alas, our master is dead! Alas, his splendor is gone!'

22:18
1 Kgs 13:30

¹⁹ He will be buried like a dead donkey—
　　dragged out of Jerusalem and dumped outside the gates!

22:19
Jer 36:30

²⁰ Weep for your allies in Lebanon.
　　Shout for them in Bashan.
　Search for them in the regions east of the river.*
　　See, they are all destroyed.
　　Not one is left to help you.

22:20
Deut 32:49

²¹ I warned you when you were prosperous,
　　but you replied, 'Don't bother me.'
　You have been that way since childhood—
　　you simply will not obey me!

22:21
Jer 3:24-25; 13:10;
19:15; 32:30

²² And now the wind will blow away your allies.
　　All your friends will be taken away as captives.
　Surely then you will see your wickedness and be ashamed.

22:22
Jer 20:11; 30:14

²³ It may be nice to live in a beautiful palace
　　paneled with wood from the cedars of Lebanon,
　but soon you will groan with pangs of anguish—
　　anguish like that of a woman in labor.

22:23
Jer 4:31

22:11 Hebrew *Shallum,* another name for Jehoahaz.　22:13a The brother and successor of the exiled Jehoahaz. See 22:18.　22:13b Hebrew *by unrighteousness.*　22:20 Or *in Abarim.*

---

**22:15, 16** God passed judgment on King Jehoiakim. His father, Josiah, had been one of Judah's great kings, but Jehoiakim was evil. Josiah had been faithful to his responsibility to be a model of right living, but Jehoiakim had been unfaithful to his responsibility to imitate his father. God's judgment was on unfaithful Jehoiakim. He could not claim his father's blessings when he had not followed his father's God. We may inherit our parents' money, but we cannot inherit their faith. A godly heritage, a good education, or a beautiful home doesn't guarantee moral character. We must have our own relationship with God.

**22:21** Jehoiakim had been hardheaded and hard-hearted since childhood. God warned him, but he refused to listen. His prosperity always took a higher priority than his relationship with God. If you ever find yourself so comfortable that you don't have time for God, stop and ask which is more important—the comforts of this life or a close relationship with God.

## A Message for Jehoiachin

**22:24**
Hag 2:23
**22:25**
2 Kgs 24:15-16
Jer 34:20

24"As surely as I live," says the LORD, "I will abandon you, Jehoiachin* son of Jehoiakim, king of Judah. Even if you were the signet ring on my right hand, I would pull you off. 25 I will hand you over to those who seek to kill you, those you so desperately fear—to King Nebuchadnezzar* of Babylon and the mighty Babylonian* army. 26I will expel you and your mother from this land, and you will die in a foreign country, not in your native land. 27 You will never again return to the land you yearn for.

**22:28**
Hos 8:8

28 "Why is this man Jehoiachin like a discarded, broken jar?
    Why are he and his children to be exiled to a foreign land?

**22:29**
Jer 6:19
Mic 1:2

29 O earth, earth, earth!
    Listen to this message from the LORD!

**22:30**
Matt 1:12

30 This is what the LORD says:
    'Let the record show that this man Jehoiachin was childless.
    He is a failure,
    for none of his children will succeed him on the throne of David
        to rule over Judah.'

## The Righteous Descendant

**23:1**
Isa 56:9-12
Jer 10:21; 50:6
Ezek 13:3; 34:1-2
Zech 11:17

**23** "What sorrow awaits the leaders of my people—the shepherds of my sheep—for they have destroyed and scattered the very ones they were expected to care for," says the LORD.

**23:2**
Exod 32:34
Jer 44:22

2 Therefore, this is what the LORD, the God of Israel, says to these shepherds: "Instead of caring for my flock and leading them to safety, you have deserted them and driven them to destruction. Now I will pour out judgment on you for the evil you have done to them. 3But I

**23:3**
Isa 11:11-16
Jer 31:7-8; 32:37

will gather together the remnant of my flock from the countries where I have driven them. I will bring them back to their own sheepfold, and they will be fruitful and increase in number. 4Then I will appoint responsible shepherds who will care for them, and they will never

**23:4**
Jer 3:15; 31:10
John 6:39; 10:28
1 Pet 1:5

be afraid again. Not a single one will be lost or missing. I, the LORD, have spoken!

**23:5**
Isa 9:6-7; 11:1-5;
53:2
Jer 33:15-16
Zech 3:8; 6:12-13

5 "For the time is coming,"
        says the LORD,
    "when I will raise up a righteous descendant*
        from King David's line.
    He will be a King who rules with wisdom.
        He will do what is just and right throughout the land.

**23:6**
Matt 1:21-23
Rom 3:21-22
1 Cor 1:30

6 And this will be his name:
        'The LORD Is Our Righteousness.'*
    In that day Judah will be saved,
        and Israel will live in safety.

**23:7**
Isa 43:18-19
Jer 16:14-15

7"In that day," says the LORD, "when people are taking an oath, they will no longer say, 'As surely as the LORD lives, who rescued the people of Israel from the land of Egypt.' 8Instead, they will say, 'As surely as the LORD lives, who brought the people of Israel back to their own land from the land of the north and from all the countries to which he had exiled them.' Then they will live in their own land."

**22:24** Hebrew *Coniah*, a variant spelling of Jehoiachin; also 22:28.   **22:25a** Hebrew *Nebuchadrezzar*, a variant spelling of Nebuchadnezzar.   **22:25b** Or *Chaldean*.   **23:5** Hebrew *a righteous branch*.   **23:6** Hebrew *Yahweh Tsidqenu*.

---

**22:24, 25** A signet ring was extremely valuable because a king used it to authenticate important documents. Jehoiachin's sins spoiled his usefulness to God. Even if he were God's own signet ring, God would depose him because of his sins (see 24:1).

**22:30** Zedekiah reigned after Jehoiachin but died before him (52:10, 11). Jehoiachin was the last king of David's line to sit on the throne in Judah (1 Chronicles 3:15-20). He had seven sons, but not one served as king. Jehoiachin's grandson Zerubbabel ruled after the return from exile (Ezra 2:2). He was only a governor, not a king.

**23:1-4** Those responsible to lead Israel in God's path were the very ones responsible for Israel's present plight, and so God had

decreed harsh judgment against them. Leaders are held responsible for those entrusted to their care. Whom has God placed in your care? Remember that you are accountable to God for those you influence and lead.

**23:5, 6** Jeremiah contrasted the present corrupt leaders with the coming Messiah, the perfect King, who would come from David's line to reign over Israel.

## Judgment on False Prophets

9 My heart is broken because of the false prophets,
  and my bones tremble.
I stagger like a drunkard,
  like someone overcome by wine,
because of the holy words
  the LORD has spoken against them.

23:9
Hab 3:16

10 For the land is full of adultery,
  and it lies under a curse.
The land itself is in mourning—
  its wilderness pastures are dried up.
For they all do evil
  and abuse what power they have.

23:10
Ps 107:34
Jer 5:7-8; 9:10;
12:4
Hos 4:2-3

11 "Even the priests and prophets
  are ungodly, wicked men.
I have seen their despicable acts
  right here in my own Temple,"
says the LORD.

12 "Therefore, the paths they take
  will become slippery.
They will be chased through the dark,
  and there they will fall.
For I will bring disaster upon them
  at the time fixed for their punishment.
I, the LORD, have spoken!

23:12
Isa 8:22
John 12:35

13 "I saw that the prophets of Samaria were terribly evil,
  for they prophesied in the name of Baal
  and led my people of Israel into sin.

23:13
1 Kgs 18:18-21

14 But now I see that the prophets of Jerusalem are even worse!
  They commit adultery and love dishonesty.
They encourage those who are doing evil
  so that no one turns away from their sins.
These prophets are as wicked
  as the people of Sodom and Gomorrah once were."

23:14
Isa 1:9-10
Jer 5:30-31; 29:23
Ezek 13:22-23
Matt 11:24

15 Therefore, this is what the LORD of Heaven's Armies says concerning the prophets:

"I will feed them with bitterness
  and give them poison to drink.
For it is because of Jerusalem's prophets
  that wickedness has filled this land."

23:15
Deut 29:18
Jer 8:14; 9:15

16 This is what the LORD of Heaven's Armies says to his people:

"Do not listen to these prophets when they prophesy to you,
  filling you with futile hopes.
They are making up everything they say.
  They do not speak for the LORD!

23:16
Jer 14:14
Ezek 13:2-3, 6
Matt 7:15
2 Cor 11:13-15
Gal 1:8-9
1 Jn 4:1

17 They keep saying to those who despise my word,
  'Don't worry! The LORD says you will have peace!'
And to those who stubbornly follow their own desires,
  they say, 'No harm will come your way!'

23:17
Jer 5:12; 8:11
Amos 9:10
Mic 2:11; 3:11

---

**23:9-14** How did the nation become so corrupt? A major factor was false prophecy. The false prophets had a large, enthusiastic audience and were very popular because they made the people believe that all was well. By contrast, Jeremiah's message from God was unpopular because it showed the people how bad they were.

There are four warning signs of false prophets—characteristics we need to watch for even today: (1) They may appear to speak God's message, but they do not live according to God's Word. (2) They water down God's message in order to make it more palatable. (3) They encourage their listeners, often subtly, to disobey God. (4) They tend to be arrogant and self-serving, appealing to the desires of their audience instead of being true to God's Word.

**23:14** Sodom and Gomorrah were sinful cities destroyed by God (Genesis 19:23, 24). In the Bible they typify the ultimate in depraved, sinful behavior and rebellion against God.

**23:18**
Job 15:8; 33:11

18 "Have any of these prophets been in the LORD's presence
    to hear what he is really saying?
    Has even one of them cared enough to listen?

**23:19**
Jer 30:23
Amos 1:14

19 Look! The LORD's anger bursts out like a storm,
    a whirlwind that swirls down on the heads of the wicked.

**23:20**
Isa 55:11
Jer 30:24
Zech 1:5-6

20 The anger of the LORD will not diminish
    until it has finished all he has planned.
    In the days to come
    you will understand all this very clearly.

21 "I have not sent these prophets,
    yet they run around claiming to speak for me.
    I have given them no message,
    yet they go on prophesying.

**23:22**
Zech 1:4
1 Thes 1:9-10

22 If they had stood before me and listened to me,
    they would have spoken my words,
    and they would have turned my people
    from their evil ways and deeds.

**23:23**
Ps 139:1-10

23 Am I a God who is only close at hand?" says the LORD.
    "No, I am far away at the same time.

**23:24**
Job 22:13-14
Ps 139:7-12
Isa 29:15-16

24 Can anyone hide from me in a secret place?
    Am I not everywhere in all the heavens and earth?"
    says the LORD.

**23:25**
Jer 8:6; 29:8

**23:26**
1 Tim 4:1-2

**23:27**
Deut 13:1-3
Judg 3:7; 8:33-34

25 "I have heard these prophets say, 'Listen to the dream I had from God last night.' And then they proceed to tell lies in my name. 26How long will this go on? If they are prophets, they are prophets of deceit, inventing everything they say. 27By telling these false dreams, they are trying to get my people to forget me, just as their ancestors did by worshiping the idols of Baal.

**23:28**
1 Cor 3:12-13

28 "Let these false prophets tell their dreams,
    but let my true messengers faithfully proclaim my every word.
    There is a difference between straw and grain!

**23:29**
2 Cor 10:4-5

29 Does not my word burn like fire?"
    says the LORD.
    "Is it not like a mighty hammer
    that smashes a rock to pieces?

**23:30**
Ezek 13:8

30 "Therefore," says the LORD, "I am against these prophets who steal messages from each other and claim they are from me. 31I am against these smooth-tongued prophets who say, 'This prophecy is from the LORD!' 32I am against these false prophets. Their imaginary dreams are flagrant lies that lead my people into sin. I did not send or appoint them, and they have no message at all for my people. I, the LORD, have spoken!

---

**23:20** "In the days to come, you will understand all this very clearly" means that the people would see the truth of this prophecy when Jerusalem fell.

**23:21-24** In Jeremiah's time, those who claimed to speak for God were often guilty of representing a deity they thought of as limited and localized—a neighborhood god. Their gods frequently had limited interests and shortsighted awareness. God declares his omnipresence with a question: "Am I not everywhere in all the heavens and earth?" We make the same mistake those would-be prophets made when we assume God doesn't know or care about the situations in our lives or when we question his ability to handle things beyond our control. How big is the God you worship?

**23:28** True prophets and false prophets are as different as straw and wheat. Straw is useless for food and cannot compare to nourishing wheat. To share the gospel is a great responsibility because the way we present it and live it will encourage people either to accept it or reject it. Whether we speak from a pulpit, teach in a class, or share with friends, we must accurately

communicate and live out God's Word. As you share God's Word with friends and neighbors, they will look for its effectiveness in your life. Unless it has changed you, why should they let it change them? If you preach it, make sure you live it!

## False Prophecies and False Prophets

33"Suppose one of the people or one of the prophets or priests asks you, 'What prophecy has the LORD burdened you with now?' You must reply, 'You are the burden!* The LORD says he will abandon you!'

34"If any prophet, priest, or anyone else says, 'I have a prophecy from the LORD,' I will punish that person along with his entire family. 35You should keep asking each other, 'What is the LORD's answer?' or 'What is the LORD saying?' 36But stop using this phrase, 'prophecy from the LORD.' For people are using it to give authority to their own ideas, turning upside down the words of our God, the living God, the LORD of Heaven's Armies.

37"This is what you should say to the prophets: 'What is the LORD's answer?' or 'What is the LORD saying?' 38But suppose they respond, 'This is a prophecy from the LORD!' Then you should say, 'This is what the LORD says: Because you have used this phrase, "prophecy from the LORD," even though I warned you not to use it, 39I will forget you completely.* I will expel you from my presence, along with this city that I gave to you and your ancestors. 40And I will make you an object of ridicule, and your name will be infamous throughout the ages.'"

## Good and Bad Figs

**24** After King Nebuchadnezzar* of Babylon exiled Jehoiachin* son of Jehoiakim, king of Judah, to Babylon along with the officials of Judah and all the craftsmen and artisans, the LORD gave me this vision. I saw two baskets of figs placed in front of the LORD's Temple in Jerusalem. 2One basket was filled with fresh, ripe figs, while the other was filled with bad figs that were too rotten to eat.

3Then the LORD said to me, "What do you see, Jeremiah?"

I replied, "Figs, some very good and some very bad, too rotten to eat."

4Then the LORD gave me this message: 5"This is what the LORD, the God of Israel, says: The good figs represent the exiles I sent from Judah to the land of the Babylonians.* 6I will watch over and care for them, and I will bring them back here again. I will build them up and not tear them down. I will plant them and not uproot them. 7I will give them hearts that recognize me as the LORD. They will be my people, and I will be their God, for they will return to me wholeheartedly.

8"But the bad figs," the LORD said, "represent King Zedekiah of Judah, his officials, all the people left in Jerusalem, and those who live in Egypt. I will treat them like bad figs, too rotten to eat. 9I will make them an object of horror and a symbol of evil to every nation on earth. They will be disgraced and mocked, taunted and cursed, wherever I scatter them. 10And I will send war, famine, and disease until they have vanished from the land of Israel, which I gave to them and their ancestors."

## Seventy Years of Captivity

**25** This message for all the people of Judah came to Jeremiah from the LORD during the fourth year of Jehoiakim's reign over Judah.* This was the year when King Nebuchadnezzar* of Babylon began his reign.

*Cross-references (right margin):*

23:34 Lam 2:14; Zech 13:3
23:35 Jer 33:3; 42:4
23:36 Jer 10:10; 2 Pet 3:16
23:39 Jer 7:14-15; Ezek 8:18
23:40 Jer 20:11; Ezek 5:14-15
24:1 2 Kgs 24:10-16; 2 Chr 36:10
24:2 Jer 29:17
24:5 Zech 13:9
24:6 Jer 29:10; 31:4; 32:37, 41; 33:7; Ezek 11:17
24:7 Jer 29:13; 31:33; 32:40; Zech 8:8; Heb 8:10
24:9 1 Kgs 9:7; Ps 44:13-14; Isa 65:15; Jer 15:4; 29:18; 34:17
24:10 Isa 51:19; Jer 21:9; 27:8; Ezek 5:12-17

**23:33** As in Greek version and Latin Vulgate; Hebrew reads *What burden?* **23:39** Some Hebrew manuscripts and Greek version read *I will surely lift you up.* **24:1a** Hebrew *Nebuchadrezzar*, a variant spelling of Nebuchadnezzar. **24:1b** Hebrew *Jeconiah*, a variant spelling of Jehoiachin. **24:5** Or *Chaldeans.* **25:1a** The fourth year of Jehoiakim's reign and the accession year of Nebuchadnezzar's reign was 605 B.C. **25:1b** Hebrew *Nebuchadrezzar*, a variant spelling of Nebuchadnezzar; also in 25:9.

---

**23:33-40** People mocked Jeremiah by saying sarcastically, "What prophecy has the LORD burdened you with now?" It seemed that Jeremiah brought nothing but God's sad news of condemnation. But this sad news was the truth. If they had accepted it, they would have had to repent and turn to God. Because they did not want to do this, they rejected Jeremiah's message. Have you ever rejected a message or made fun of it because it would require you to change your ways? Before dismissing someone who brings sad news, look carefully at your motives.

**24:1** In 597 B.C. Jehoiachin was taken to Babylon, and Zedekiah became king. Often royal officials were exiled to keep them from exerting power and starting a rebellion. Skilled craftsmen and artisans were taken because they were valuable for Babylon's building program. Jeremiah foretold this event in 22:24-28.

**24:2-10** The fresh, ripe figs represented the exiles to Babylon, not because they themselves were good, but because their hearts would respond to God. He would preserve them and bring them

back to the land. The bad, rotten figs represented those who remained in Judah or ran away to Egypt. Those people may have arrogantly believed they would be blessed if they remained in the land or escaped to Egypt, but the opposite was true because God would use the captivity to refine the exiles. We may assume we are blessed when life goes well and cursed when it does not. But trouble is a blessing when it makes us stronger, and prosperity is a curse if it entices us away from God. If you are facing trouble, ask God to help you grow stronger for him. If things are going your way, ask God to help you use your prosperity for him.

**24:6** The exiles in Babylon were cared for by the Lord. Although they were moved to a foreign land, their captivity was not enslavement. The people could function in business and own homes. Some, like Daniel, even held high positions in the government (see Daniel 2:48).

**25:1ff** Jeremiah gave this message in 605 B.C., the year Nebuchadnezzar came to power. From verse 3 we learn that the begin-

25:2
Jer 1:2; 7:25-26;
11:7-8; 26:5; 36:2-3

25:3
2 Kgs 24:1-2
Jer 36:1; 46:2

25:5
Gen 17:8-10
Isa 55:6-7
Jer 4:1; 7:7; 35:15

25:6
Deut 6:14; 8:19
2 Kgs 17:35

25:7
2 Kgs 17:17; 21:15
Jer 7:19; 32:30-33

25:10
Eccl 12:3-4
Isa 24:8-11
Jer 16:9
Ezek 26:13

25:11
Dan 9:2
Zech 7:5

25:12
Ezra 1:1
Isa 13:14
Jer 29:10;
50:1—51:64

25:13
Jer 36:4, 29, 32

25:14
Jer 27:7; 50:9

25:15
Jer 51:7

25:17
Jer 1:10

25:18
Isa 51:17

25:19
Jer 46:2-28

25:20
Job 1:1
Jer 47:1-7

25:21
Jer 48:1-47;
49:1-22

25:22
Jer 47:4
Zech 9:2-4

25:23
Jer 49:7-8

25:25
Jer 49:34

25:26
Jer 50:9; 51:41

25:27
Ezek 21:4-5
Hab 2:17

25:29
Prov 11:31
1 Pet 4:17

²Jeremiah the prophet said to all the people in Judah and Jerusalem, ³"For the past twenty-three years—from the thirteenth year of the reign of Josiah son of Amon,* king of Judah, until now—the LORD has been giving me his messages. I have faithfully passed them on to you, but you have not listened.

⁴"Again and again the LORD has sent you his servants, the prophets, but you have not listened or even paid attention. ⁵Each time the message was this: 'Turn from the evil road you are traveling and from the evil things you are doing. Only then will I let you live in this land that the LORD gave to you and your ancestors forever. ⁶Do not provoke my anger by worshiping idols you made with your own hands. Then I will not harm you.'

⁷"But you would not listen to me," says the LORD. "You made me furious by worshiping idols you made with your own hands, bringing on yourselves all the disasters you now suffer. ⁸And now the LORD of Heaven's Armies says: Because you have not listened to me, ⁹I will gather together all the armies of the north under King Nebuchadnezzar of Babylon, whom I have appointed as my deputy. I will bring them all against this land and its people and against the surrounding nations. I will completely destroy* you and make you an object of horror and contempt and a ruin forever. ¹⁰I will take away your happy singing and laughter. The joyful voices of bridegrooms and brides will no longer be heard. Your millstones will fall silent, and the lights in your homes will go out. ¹¹This entire land will become a desolate wasteland. Israel and her neighboring lands will serve the king of Babylon for seventy years.

¹²"Then, after the seventy years of captivity are over, I will punish the king of Babylon and his people for their sins," says the LORD. "I will make the country of the Babylonians* a wasteland forever. ¹³I will bring upon them all the terrors I have promised in this book—all the penalties announced by Jeremiah against the nations. ¹⁴Many nations and great kings will enslave the Babylonians, just as they enslaved my people. I will punish them in proportion to the suffering they cause my people."

### The Cup of the LORD's Anger

¹⁵This is what the LORD, the God of Israel, said to me: "Take from my hand this cup filled to the brim with my anger, and make all the nations to whom I send you drink from it. ¹⁶When they drink from it, they will stagger, crazed by the warfare I will send against them."

¹⁷So I took the cup of anger from the LORD and made all the nations drink from it—every nation to which the LORD sent me. ¹⁸I went to Jerusalem and the other towns of Judah, and their kings and officials drank from the cup. From that day until this, they have been a desolate ruin, an object of horror, contempt, and cursing. ¹⁹I gave the cup to Pharaoh, king of Egypt, his attendants, his officials, and all his people, ²⁰along with all the foreigners living in that land. I also gave it to all the kings of the land of Uz and the kings of the Philistine cities of Ashkelon, Gaza, Ekron, and what remains of Ashdod. ²¹Then I gave the cup to the nations of Edom, Moab, and Ammon, ²²and the kings of Tyre and Sidon, and the kings of the regions across the sea. ²³I gave it to Dedan, Tema, and Buz, and to the people who live in distant places.* ²⁴I gave it to the kings of Arabia, the kings of the nomadic tribes of the desert, ²⁵and to the kings of Zimri, Elam, and Media. ²⁶And I gave it to the kings of the northern countries, far and near, one after the other—all the kingdoms of the world. And finally, the king of Babylon* himself drank from the cup of the LORD's anger.

²⁷Then the LORD said to me, "Now tell them, 'This is what the LORD of Heaven's Armies, the God of Israel, says: Drink from this cup of my anger. Get drunk and vomit; fall to rise no more, for I am sending terrible wars against you.' ²⁸And if they refuse to accept the cup, tell them, 'The LORD of Heaven's Armies says: You have no choice but to drink from it. ²⁹I have

25:3 The thirteenth year of Josiah's reign was 627 B.C. 25:9 The Hebrew term used here refers to the complete consecration of things or people to the LORD, either by destroying them or by giving them as an offering. 25:12 Or *Chaldeans.* 25:23 Or *who clip the corners of their hair.* 25:26 Hebrew *of Sheshach,* a code name for Babylon.

---

ning of Jeremiah's ministry was in 627 B.C. He predicted the 70 years of captivity a full 20 years before they began.

**25:2-6** Imagine preaching the same message for 23 years and continually being rejected! Jeremiah faced this; but because he had committed his life to God, he continued to proclaim the message: "Turn from the evil road you are traveling and from the evil things you are doing." Regardless of the people's response, Jeremiah did not give up. God never stops loving us, even when we reject him. We can thank God that he won't give up on us, and, like Jeremiah, we can commit ourselves to never forsaking him.

No matter how people respond when you tell them about God, remain faithful to God's high call and continue to witness for him.

**25:12** This event is further described in Daniel 5. The troops of Cyrus the Great entered Babylon in 539 B.C. and killed Belshazzar, the last Babylonian ruler.

**25:15-38** Judah would not be the only nation to drink the cup of God's anger. Here Jeremiah listed other wicked nations that would experience God's wrath at the hands of Babylon. Finally, Babylon itself would be destroyed because of its sin.

begun to punish Jerusalem, the city that bears my name. Now should I let you go unpunished? No, you will not escape disaster. I will call for war against all the nations of the earth. I, the LORD of Heaven's Armies, have spoken!'

30"Now prophesy all these things, and say to them,

"'The LORD will roar against his own land
 from his holy dwelling in heaven.
He will shout like those who tread grapes;
 he will shout against everyone on earth.
31 His cry of judgment will reach the ends of the earth,
 for the LORD will bring his case against all the nations.
He will judge all the people of the earth,
 slaughtering the wicked with the sword.
 I, the LORD, have spoken!'"

32 This is what the LORD of Heaven's Armies says:
 "Look! Disaster will fall upon nation after nation!
A great whirlwind of fury is rising
 from the most distant corners of the earth!"

33In that day those the LORD has slaughtered will fill the earth from one end to the other. No one will mourn for them or gather up their bodies to bury them. They will be scattered on the ground like manure.

34 Weep and moan, you evil shepherds!
 Roll in the dust, you leaders of the flock!
The time of your slaughter has arrived;
 you will fall and shatter like a fragile vase.
35 You will find no place to hide;
 there will be no way to escape.
36 Listen to the frantic cries of the shepherds.
 The leaders of the flock are wailing in despair,
 for the LORD is ruining their pastures.
37 Peaceful meadows will be turned into a wasteland
 by the LORD's fierce anger.
38 He has left his den like a strong lion seeking its prey,
 and their land will be made desolate
by the sword of the enemy
 and the LORD's fierce anger.

## Jeremiah's Escape from Death

**26** This message came to Jeremiah from the LORD early in the reign of Jehoiakim son of Josiah,* king of Judah. 2"This is what the LORD says: Stand in the courtyard in front of the Temple of the LORD, and make an announcement to the people who have come there to worship from all over Judah. Give them my entire message; include every word. 3Perhaps they will listen and turn from their evil ways. Then I will change my mind about the disaster I am ready to pour out on them because of their sins.

**26:1** The first year of Jehoiakim's reign was 608 B.C.

### Cross-references

25:30 Joel 2:11; 3:13; Amos 1:2

25:31 Isa 66:16; Hos 4:1

25:32 Isa 30:30; 34:2-3

25:33 Isa 5:25; Jer 16:4; Ezek 39:4, 7

25:34 Isa 34:7; Jer 50:27

25:35 Jer 11:11

25:37 Isa 27:11

25:38 Jer 4:7; 5:6; Hos 5:14; 13:7-8

26:2 Deut 4:2; Jer 7:2; 19:14; 42:4; Acts 20:20, 27

26:3 Isa 1:16-19; Jer 36:3-7

---

**26:1ff** The events described in this chapter took place in 609–608 B.C., before the events described in chapter 25. Jehoiakim was a materialistic and self-centered king who persecuted and murdered innocent people (36:22-32; 2 Kings 23:36–24:6). Chapter 26 describes how and why Jeremiah was on trial for his life.

**26:2** God reminded Jeremiah that he wanted his entire message given—"include every word." Jeremiah may have been tempted to leave out the parts that would turn his audience against him, sound too harsh, or make him sound like a traitor. But by God's command, he was not to delete parts of God's message to suit himself, his audience, or the circumstances in which he found

himself. Like Jeremiah, we must never ignore or exclude important parts of God's Word to please someone.

**26:2-9** Shiloh was where the Tabernacle had been set up after the conquest of Canaan (Joshua 18:1). It was destroyed in 1050 B.C. by the Philistines. God said he would destroy the Temple as Shiloh had been destroyed. When Jeremiah said that Jerusalem, the city of God, would become an object of cursing and the Temple would be destroyed (26:6), the priests and false prophets were infuriated. The Temple was important to them because the people's reverence for it brought them power. By saying that the Temple would be destroyed, Jeremiah undermined their authority. Jesus also infuriated the religious leaders of his time by foretelling the destruction of Jerusalem and the Temple (Matthew 24:2).

26:4
Lev 26:14
1 Kgs 9:6
Isa 1:20
Jer 17:27; 22:5;
44:10, 23
26:5
Ezra 9:11
Jer 25:4
26:6
Ps 78:60-61
Jer 7:12, 14
26:7
Jer 5:31
Mic 3:11

26:10
Acts 21:31-32
26:11
Jer 18:23; 38:4
Matt 26:66
Acts 6:11-14

26:13
Jer 7:3, 5; 18:11

26:15
Num 35:33
Prov 6:16-17

26:16
Jer 36:19, 25;
38:7, 13
Acts 5:34-39; 23:9,
29; 25:25; 26:31
26:18
Mic 1:1; 3:12

26:19
2 Chr 29:6-11;
32:26
Isa 37:1, 15-20
26:20
Josh 9:17
1 Sam 6:21
26:21
1 Kgs 19:2-4
2 Chr 16:10
Jer 36:26
Matt 10:23, 28
26:22
Jer 36:12
26:23
Jer 2:30
26:24
2 Kgs 22:12-14
Jer 1:18-19; 39:14;
40:5-6

4"Say to them, 'This is what the LORD says: If you will not listen to me and obey my word I have given you, 5and if you will not listen to my servants, the prophets—for I sent them again and again to warn you, but you would not listen to them—6then I will destroy this Temple as I destroyed Shiloh, the place where the Tabernacle was located. And I will make Jerusalem an object of cursing in every nation on earth.'"

7The priests, the prophets, and all the people listened to Jeremiah as he spoke in front of the LORD's Temple. 8But when Jeremiah had finished his message, saying everything the LORD had told him to say, the priests and prophets and all the people at the Temple mobbed him. "Kill him!" they shouted. 9"What right do you have to prophesy in the LORD's name that this Temple will be destroyed like Shiloh? What do you mean, saying that Jerusalem will be destroyed and left with no inhabitants?" And all the people threatened him as he stood in front of the Temple.

10When the officials of Judah heard what was happening, they rushed over from the palace and sat down at the New Gate of the Temple to hold court. 11The priests and prophets presented their accusations to the officials and the people. "This man should die!" they said. "You have heard with your own ears what a traitor he is, for he has prophesied against this city."

12Then Jeremiah spoke to the officials and the people in his own defense. "The LORD sent me to prophesy against this Temple and this city," he said. "The LORD gave me every word that I have spoken. 13But if you stop your sinning and begin to obey the LORD your God, he will change his mind about this disaster that he has announced against you. 14As for me, I am in your hands—do with me as you think best. 15But if you kill me, rest assured that you will be killing an innocent man! The responsibility for such a deed will lie on you, on this city, and on every person living in it. For it is absolutely true that the LORD sent me to speak every word you have heard."

16Then the officials and the people said to the priests and prophets, "This man does not deserve the death sentence, for he has spoken to us in the name of the LORD our God."

17Then some of the wise old men stood and spoke to all the people assembled there. 18They said, "Remember when Micah of Moresheth prophesied during the reign of King Hezekiah of Judah. He told the people of Judah,

'This is what the LORD of Heaven's Armies says:
Mount Zion will be plowed like an open field;
    Jerusalem will be reduced to ruins!
A thicket will grow on the heights
    where the Temple now stands.'*

19But did King Hezekiah and the people kill him for saying this? No, they turned from their sins and worshiped the LORD. They begged him for mercy. Then the LORD changed his mind about the terrible disaster he had pronounced against them. So we are about to do ourselves great harm."

20At this time Uriah son of Shemaiah from Kiriath-jearim was also prophesying for the LORD. And he predicted the same terrible disaster against the city and nation as Jeremiah did. 21When King Jehoiakim and the army officers and officials heard what he was saying, the king sent someone to kill him. But Uriah heard about the plan and escaped in fear to Egypt. 22Then King Jehoiakim sent Elnathan son of Acbor to Egypt along with several other men to capture Uriah. 23They took him prisoner and brought him back to King Jehoiakim. The king then killed Uriah with a sword and had him buried in an unmarked grave.

24Nevertheless, Ahikam son of Shaphan stood up for Jeremiah and persuaded the court not to turn him over to the mob to be killed.

26:18 Mic 3:12.

---

**26:11** Jeremiah was branded a traitor because he prophesied the destruction of the city and the Temple. But the "courageous" people advocated a foreign alliance to fight Babylon and retain their independence. The accusations they leveled at Jeremiah were actually true of themselves—they were the traitors because they had turned away from God.

**26:17-19** The wise old men remembered the words of the prophet Micah (Micah 3:12), which were similar to the words Jeremiah spoke. When Micah called the people to repent, they

turned from their wickedness. Although these people did not kill Jeremiah, they missed the main point—that the application of the story was for them. They spared Jeremiah, but they did not spare themselves by repenting of their sins. As you recall a great story of the Bible, ask how it can be applied to *your* life.

**26:20-23** Uriah is an otherwise unknown prophet who was executed for faithfully proclaiming God's words. This shows us that God has had other prophets whose words are not included in the Bible.

## Jeremiah Wears an Ox Yoke

**27** This message came to Jeremiah from the Lord early in the reign of Zedekiah* son of Josiah, king of Judah.

2 This is what the Lord said to me: "Make a yoke, and fasten it on your neck with leather straps. 3 Then send messages to the kings of Edom, Moab, Ammon, Tyre, and Sidon through their ambassadors who have come to see King Zedekiah in Jerusalem. 4 Give them this message for their masters: 'This is what the Lord of Heaven's Armies, the God of Israel, says: 5 With my great strength and powerful arm I made the earth and all its people and every animal. I can give these things of mine to anyone I choose. 6 Now I will give your countries to King Nebuchadnezzar of Babylon, who is my servant. I have put everything, even the wild animals, under his control. 7 All the nations will serve him, his son, and his grandson until his time is up. Then many nations and great kings will conquer and rule over Babylon. 8 So you must submit to Babylon's king and serve him; put your neck under Babylon's yoke! I will punish any nation that refuses to be his slave, says the Lord. I will send war, famine, and disease upon that nation until Babylon has conquered it.

9 "'Do not listen to your false prophets, fortune-tellers, interpreters of dreams, mediums, and sorcerers who say, "The king of Babylon will not conquer you." 10 They are all liars, and their lies will lead to your being driven out of your land. I will drive you out and send you far away to die. 11 But the people of any nation that submits to the king of Babylon will be allowed to stay in their own country to farm the land as usual. I, the Lord, have spoken!'"

12 Then I repeated this same message to King Zedekiah of Judah. "If you want to live, submit to the yoke of the king of Babylon and his people. 13 Why do you insist on dying—you and your people? Why should you choose war, famine, and disease, which the Lord will bring against every nation that refuses to submit to Babylon's king? 14 Do not listen to the false prophets who keep telling you, 'The king of Babylon will not conquer you.' They are liars. 15 This is what the Lord says: 'I have not sent these prophets! They are telling you lies in my name, so I will drive you from this land. You will all die—you and all these prophets, too.'"

16 Then I spoke to the priests and the people and said, "This is what the Lord says: 'Do not listen to your prophets who claim that soon the gold articles taken from my Temple will be returned from Babylon. It is all a lie! 17 Do not listen to them. Surrender to the king of Babylon, and you will live. Why should this whole city be destroyed? 18 If they really are prophets and speak the Lord's messages, let them pray to the Lord of Heaven's Armies. Let them pray that the articles remaining in the Lord's Temple and in the king's palace and in the palaces of Jerusalem will not be carried away to Babylon!'

19 "For the Lord of Heaven's Armies has spoken about the pillars in front of the Temple, the great bronze basin called the Sea, the water carts, and all the other ceremonial articles. 20 King Nebuchadnezzar of Babylon left them here when he exiled Jehoiachin* son of Jehoiakim, king of Judah, to Babylon, along with all the other nobles of Judah and Jerusalem. 21 Yes, this is what the Lord of Heaven's Armies, the God of Israel, says about the precious things still in the Temple and in the palace of Judah's king: 22 'They will all be carried away to Babylon and will stay there until I send for them,' says the Lord. 'Then I will bring them back to Jerusalem again.'"

27:1 As in some Hebrew manuscripts and Syriac version (see also 27:3, 12); most Hebrew manuscripts read *Jehoiakim.*   27:20 Hebrew *Jeconiah,* a variant spelling of Jehoiachin.

27:2
Jer 28:10, 13; 30:8
27:3
Jer 25:21-22
27:5
Deut 9:29
Pss 115:15-16;
146:5-6
Jer 10:12; 32:17;
51:15
Acts 17:26
27:6
Jer 21:7; 22:25;
28:14; 43:10
Ezek 29:18-20
27:7
Isa 14:4-6
Jer 25:12; 44:30
27:8
Jer 24:10; 29:17;
42:15-16
Ezek 14:21;
17:19-21
27:9
Exod 22:18
Deut 18:10
Isa 8:19
Mal 3:5
27:10
Jer 23:25
27:11
Jer 21:9; 38:2;
40:9-12; 42:10-11
27:13
Jer 38:23
Ezek 18:31
27:14
Ezek 13:22
27:15
2 Chr 25:16
Jer 23:21, 25; 29:9
27:16
2 Kgs 24:13
2 Chr 36:7, 10
Dan 1:2
27:18
1 Sam 7:8;
12:19, 23
1 Kgs 18:24
27:19
1 Kgs 7:15
2 Kgs 25:13, 17
Jer 52:17-23
27:20
2 Kgs 24:14-16
27:22
Ezra 5:13-15; 7:9
Jer 29:10; 32:5;
34:2-3

**27:1ff** The year was 593 B.C., and Nebuchadnezzar had already invaded Judah once and had taken many captives. Jeremiah wore an ox yoke (a wooden frame used to fasten a team of animals to a plow) as a symbol of bondage. This was an object lesson, telling the people they must put themselves under Babylon's yoke or be destroyed.

**27:5, 6** God punished the people of Judah in an unusual way, by appointing a foreign ruler to be his "servant." Nebuchadnezzar was not appointed to proclaim God's message, but to fulfill God's promise of judgment on sin. Because God is in control of all events, he uses whomever he wants. God may use unlikely people or circumstances to correct you. Be ready to accept God's guidance, even if it comes from unexpected sources.

**27:12-18** Zedekiah was in a tough spot. Jeremiah called on him to surrender to Nebuchadnezzar at a time when many of the other leaders wanted him to form an alliance and fight. It would be disgraceful for a king to surrender, and he would look like a coward. This was a great opportunity for the false prophets, who kept saying that the Babylonians would not defeat the great city of Jerusalem and that God would never allow the magnificent, holy Temple to be destroyed.

**27:19-22** When Nebuchadnezzar invaded Judah, first in 605 and then in 597 B.C., he took away many important people living in Jerusalem—including Daniel and Ezekiel. Although these men were captives, they had a profound impact on the exiles and leaders in Babylon. Jeremiah predicted that more people, and even the precious objects in the Temple, would be taken. This happened in 586 B.C. during Babylon's third and last invasion.

28:1
Jer 27:12

28:3
2 Chr 36:10
Jer 27:16
Dan 1:2

28:4
2 Kgs 25:27
Jer 22:10; 27:8

28:7
1 Kgs 22:28

28:8
1 Kgs 14:15;
17:1; 22:17

28:9
Deut 18:22

28:10
Jer 27:2

28:11
Jer 14:14-15;
27:10

28:12
Jer 1:2

28:13
Ps 107:16

28:14
Deut 28:48
Jer 25:11; 27:6, 8

28:15
Jer 29:31
Lam 2:14
Ezek 13:2-3, 22;
22:28

28:16
Deut 6:15; 13:5
1 Kgs 13:34
Jer 20:6; 29:32

29:2
2 Kgs 24:12
Jer 22:24-28;
24:1

## Jeremiah Condemns Hananiah

**28** One day in late summer* of that same year—the fourth year of the reign of Zedekiah, king of Judah—Hananiah son of Azzur, a prophet from Gibeon, addressed me publicly in the Temple while all the priests and people listened. He said, ²"This is what the LORD of Heaven's Armies, the God of Israel, says: 'I will remove the yoke of the king of Babylon from your necks. ³Within two years I will bring back all the Temple treasures that King Nebuchadnezzar carried off to Babylon. ⁴And I will bring back Jehoiachin* son of Jehoiakim, king of Judah, and all the other captives that were taken to Babylon. I will surely break the yoke that the king of Babylon has put on your necks. I, the LORD, have spoken!'"

⁵Jeremiah responded to Hananiah as they stood in front of all the priests and people at the Temple. ⁶He said, "Amen! May your prophecies come true! I hope the LORD does everything you say. I hope he does bring back from Babylon the treasures of this Temple and all the captives. ⁷But listen now to the solemn words I speak to you in the presence of all these people. ⁸The ancient prophets who preceded you and me spoke against many nations, always warning of war, disaster, and disease. ⁹So a prophet who predicts peace must show he is right. Only when his predictions come true can we know that he is really from the LORD."

¹⁰Then Hananiah the prophet took the yoke off Jeremiah's neck and broke it in pieces. ¹¹And Hananiah said again to the crowd that had gathered, "This is what the LORD says: 'Just as this yoke has been broken, within two years I will break the yoke of oppression from all the nations now subject to King Nebuchadnezzar of Babylon.'" With that, Jeremiah left the Temple area.

¹²Soon after this confrontation with Hananiah, the LORD gave this message to Jeremiah: ¹³"Go and tell Hananiah, 'This is what the LORD says: You have broken a wooden yoke, but you have replaced it with a yoke of iron. ¹⁴The LORD of Heaven's Armies, the God of Israel, says: I have put a yoke of iron on the necks of all these nations, forcing them into slavery under King Nebuchadnezzar of Babylon. I have put everything, even the wild animals, under his control.'"

¹⁵Then Jeremiah the prophet said to Hananiah, "Listen, Hananiah! The LORD has not sent you, but the people believe your lies. ¹⁶Therefore, this is what the LORD says: 'You must die. Your life will end this very year because you have rebelled against the LORD.'"

¹⁷Two months later* the prophet Hananiah died.

## A Letter to the Exiles

**29** Jeremiah wrote a letter from Jerusalem to the elders, priests, prophets, and all the people who had been exiled to Babylon by King Nebuchadnezzar. ²This was after King Jehoiachin,* the queen mother, the court officials, the other officials of Judah, and all the craftsmen and artisans had been deported from Jerusalem. ³He sent the letter with Elasah son of Shaphan and Gemariah son of Hilkiah when they went to Babylon as King Zedekiah's ambassadors to Nebuchadnezzar. This is what Jeremiah's letter said:

⁴This is what the LORD of Heaven's Armies, the God of Israel, says to all the captives he has exiled to Babylon from Jerusalem: ⁵"Build homes, and plan to stay. Plant gardens,

28:1 Hebrew *In the fifth month,* of the ancient Hebrew lunar calendar. The fifth month in the fourth year of Zedekiah's reign occurred within the months of August and September 593 B.C. Also see note on 1:3. 28:4 Hebrew *Jeconiah,* a variant spelling of Jehoiachin. 28:17 Hebrew *In the seventh month of that same year.* See 28:1 and the note there. 29:2 Hebrew *Jeconiah,* a variant spelling of Jehoiachin.

---

**28:6-9** Hananiah had just come up with a prophecy everyone liked. He declared that God would soon bring relief from all their problems and oppressors. Jeremiah had to admit that Hananiah's words echoed his own wishes. He sincerely hoped Hananiah was right. But unfortunately, Hananiah's words were not from God. Positive or negative, God's words are exactly true. We, like Jeremiah, may honestly wish for results or benefits outside God's plans. But if we are going to be faithful to God, there will be times when we must disagree with our own wishes in order to speak the truth and be obedient to God.

**28:8-17** Jeremiah spoke the truth, but it was unpopular; Hananiah spoke lies, but his deceitful words brought false hope and comfort to the people. God had already outlined the marks of a true prophet (Deuteronomy 13; 18:20-22): A true prophet's predictions always come true, and his words never contradict previous revelation. Jeremiah's predictions were already coming

true, from Hananiah's death to the Babylonian invasions. But the people still preferred to listen to comforting lies rather than painful truth.

**29:4-7** Jeremiah wrote to the captives in Babylon (29:4-23) instructing them to move ahead with their lives and to pray for the pagan nation that enslaved them. Life cannot grind to a halt during troubled times. In an unpleasant or distressing situation, we must adjust and keep moving. You may find it difficult to pray for those in authority if they are evil, but that is when your prayers are most needed (1 Timothy 2:1, 2). When you enter times of trouble or sudden change, pray diligently and move ahead, doing whatever you can rather than giving up because of fear and uncertainty.

and eat the food they produce. 6Marry and have children. Then find spouses for them so that you may have many grandchildren. Multiply! Do not dwindle away! 7And work for the peace and prosperity of the city where I sent you into exile. Pray to the LORD for it, for its welfare will determine your welfare."

8This is what the LORD of Heaven's Armies, the God of Israel, says: "Do not let your prophets and fortune-tellers who are with you in the land of Babylon trick you. Do not listen to their dreams, 9because they are telling you lies in my name. I have not sent them," says the LORD.

10This is what the LORD says: "You will be in Babylon for seventy years. But then I will come and do for you all the good things I have promised, and I will bring you home again. 11For I know the plans I have for you," says the LORD. "They are plans for good and not for disaster, to give you a future and a hope. 12In those days when you pray, I will listen. 13If you look for me wholeheartedly, you will find me. 14I will be found by you," says the LORD. "I will end your captivity and restore your fortunes. I will gather you out of the nations where I sent you and will bring you home again to your own land."

15You claim that the LORD has raised up prophets for you in Babylon. 16But this is what the LORD says about the king who sits on David's throne and all those still living here in Jerusalem—your relatives who were not exiled to Babylon. 17This is what the LORD of Heaven's Armies says: "I will send war, famine, and disease upon them and make them like bad figs, too rotten to eat. 18Yes, I will pursue them with war, famine, and disease, and I will scatter them around the world. In every nation where I send them, I will make them an object of damnation, horror, contempt, and mockery. 19For they refuse to listen to me, though I have spoken to them repeatedly through the prophets I sent. And you who are in exile have not listened either," says the LORD.

20Therefore, listen to this message from the LORD, all you captives there in Babylon. 21This is what the LORD of Heaven's Armies, the God of Israel, says about your prophets—Ahab son of Kolaiah and Zedekiah son of Maaseiah—who are telling you lies in my name: "I will turn them over to Nebuchadnezzar* for execution before your eyes. 22Their terrible fate will become proverbial, so that the Judean exiles will curse someone by saying, 'May the LORD make you like Zedekiah and Ahab, whom the king of Babylon burned alive!' 23For these men have done terrible things among my people. They have committed adultery with their neighbors' wives and have lied in my name, saying things I did not command. I am a witness to this. I, the LORD, have spoken."

### A Message for Shemaiah

24The LORD sent this message to Shemaiah the Nehelamite in Babylon: 25"This is what the LORD of Heaven's Armies, the God of Israel, says: You wrote a letter on your own authority to

**29:6** Jer 16:1-4
**29:7** Ezra 6:10; Dan 4:27; 1 Tim 2:1-2
**29:10** 2 Chr 36:21-23; Jer 24:6-7; Dan 9:2; Zeph 2:7; Zech 7:5
**29:11** Ps 40:5; Isa 40:9-11; Jer 23:5-6; 30:9-10
**29:12** Ps 145:19; Jer 33:3
**29:13** Deut 4:29; 1 Chr 22:19; 2 Chr 22:9; Jer 24:7
**29:14** Deut 30:1-10; Isa 43:5-6; Jer 12:15; 16:14-15; 30:3
**29:17** Jer 24:3
**29:18** Isa 65:15; Jer 25:9; 42:18; Lam 2:15-16
**29:19** Jer 6:19; 26:5
**29:20** Jer 24:5; Ezek 11:9
**29:21** Jer 14:14-15; Lam 2:14
**29:22** Isa 65:15
**29:23** 2 Sam 13:12; Prov 5:21; Jer 5:8; 7:11
**29:25** 2 Kgs 25:18; Jer 21:1; 37:3

**29:21** Hebrew *Nebuchadrezzar*, a variant spelling of Nebuchadnezzar.

---

**29:10** Scholars differ on the exact dates of this 70-year period in Babylon. Some say it refers to the years 605–538 B.C., from the first deportation to Babylon to the arrival of the first exiles back in Jerusalem after Cyrus's freedom decree. Others point to the years 586–515 B.C., from the last deportation to Babylon and the destruction of the Temple until its rebuilding. A third possibility is that 70 years is an approximate number meaning a lifetime. All agree that God sent his people to Babylon for a long time, not the short captivity predicted by the false prophets.

**29:11** We're all encouraged by a leader who stirs us to move ahead, someone who believes we can do the task he has given and who will be with us all the way. God is that kind of leader. He knows the future, and his plans for us are good and full of hope. As long as God, who knows the future, provides our agenda and goes with us as we fulfill his mission, we can have boundless hope. This does not mean that we will be spared pain, suffering, or hardship, but that God will see us through to a glorious conclusion.

**29:12-14** God did not forget his people, even though they were captives in Babylon. He planned to give them a new beginning with a new purpose—to turn them into new people. In times of dire circumstances, it may appear as though God has forgotten

you. But God may be preparing you, as he did the people of Judah, for a new beginning with him at the center.

**29:13** According to God's wise plan, his people were to have a future and a hope; consequently, they could call upon him in confidence. Although the exiles were in a difficult place and time, they need not despair because they had God's presence, the privilege of prayer, and God's grace. If we seek him wholeheartedly, he will be found. Neither a strange land, sorrow, persecution, nor physical problems can break our fellowship with God.

**29:20-23** Why would Nebuchadnezzar decide to execute these two false prophets? In contrast to Jeremiah's message from God that the people should settle in Babylon and wait faithfully for seventy years to pass, the false prophets were inciting false hopes for a quick return to Jerusalem. This would have sounded like rebellion to the Babylonian king, who would have had little hesitation over killing uncooperative refugees.

**29:21** These false prophets, Ahab and Zedekiah, should not be confused with the kings who had the same names. Their family connections clearly identify them.

**29:24-28** These verses describe the reaction of Shemaiah, a false prophet exiled in 597 B.C. who had protested about

Zephaniah son of Maaseiah, the priest, and you sent copies to the other priests and people in Jerusalem. You wrote to Zephaniah,

26"The LORD has appointed you to replace Jehoiada as the priest in charge of the house of the LORD. You are responsible to put into stocks and neck irons any crazy man who claims to be a prophet. 27So why have you done nothing to stop Jeremiah from Anathoth, who pretends to be a prophet among you? 28Jeremiah sent a letter here to Babylon, predicting that our captivity will be a long one. He said, 'Build homes, and plan to stay. Plant gardens, and eat the food they produce.'"

29But when Zephaniah the priest received Shemaiah's letter, he took it to Jeremiah and read it to him. 30Then the LORD gave this message to Jeremiah: 31"Send an open letter to all the exiles in Babylon. Tell them, 'This is what the LORD says concerning Shemaiah the Nehelamite: Since he has prophesied to you when I did not send him and has tricked you into believing his lies, 32I will punish him and his family. None of his descendants will see the good things I will do for my people, for he has incited you to rebel against me. I, the LORD, have spoken!'"

## 5. Restoration is promised

**30** The LORD gave another message to Jeremiah. He said, 2"This is what the LORD, the God of Israel, says: Write down for the record everything I have said to you, Jeremiah. 3For the time is coming when I will restore the fortunes of my people of Israel and Judah. I will bring them home to this land that I gave to their ancestors, and they will possess it again. I, the LORD, have spoken!"

4This is the message the LORD gave concerning Israel and Judah. 5This is what the LORD says:

"I hear cries of fear;
  there is terror and no peace.
6 Now let me ask you a question:
  Do men give birth to babies?
Then why do they stand there, ashen-faced,
  hands pressed against their sides
  like a woman in labor?

7 In all history there has never been such a time of terror.
  It will be a time of trouble for my people Israel.*
  Yet in the end they will be saved!
8 For in that day,"
  says the LORD of Heaven's Armies,
"I will break the yoke from their necks
  and snap their chains.
Foreigners will no longer be their masters.

9    For my people will serve the LORD their God
  and their king descended from David—
    the king I will raise up for them.

10 "So do not be afraid, Jacob, my servant;
  do not be dismayed, Israel,"
  says the LORD.

**30:7** Hebrew *Jacob;* also in 30:10b, 18. See note on 5:20.

---

**Jeremiah's letter.** To discredit Jeremiah, Shemaiah accused him of false prophecy. Although Jeremiah's message was true and his words were from God, the people hated him because he told them to make the most of the exile. Jeremiah's truth from God offered temporary correction and long-range benefit, while the false teachers' lies offered only temporary comfort and long-range punishment.

**30:1ff** Chapters 30 and 31 show that Jeremiah spoke of hope and consolation as well as trouble and gloom. The people would one day be restored to their land, and God would make a new covenant with them to replace the one they broke. Whereas

once they sinned and disobeyed, eventually they would repent and obey.

**30:8, 9** Like Isaiah, Jeremiah associated events of the near future and those of the distant future. Reading these prophecies is like looking at several mountain peaks in a range. From a distance they look as though they are next to each other, when actually they are miles apart. Jeremiah presents near and distant events as if they will all happen soon. He sees the exile, but he sees also the future day when Christ will reign forever. The "king descended from David" refers to the Messiah (Luke 1:69).

"For I will bring you home again from distant lands,
    and your children will return from their exile.
Israel will return to a life of peace and quiet,
    and no one will terrorize them.
11 For I am with you and will save you,"
    says the LORD.
"I will completely destroy the nations where I have scattered you,
    but I will not completely destroy you.
I will discipline you, but with justice;
    I cannot let you go unpunished."

12 This is what the LORD says:
"Your injury is incurable—
    a terrible wound.
13 There is no one to help you
    or to bind up your injury.
No medicine can heal you.

**30:13**
Jer 14:19; 46:11

14 All your lovers—your allies—have left you
    and do not care about you anymore.
I have wounded you cruelly,
    as though I were your enemy.
For your sins are many,
    and your guilt is great.
15 Why do you protest your punishment—
    this wound that has no cure?
I have had to punish you
    because your sins are many
    and your guilt is great.

16 "But all who devour you will be devoured,
    and all your enemies will be sent into exile.
All who plunder you will be plundered,
    and all who attack you will be attacked.

**30:16**
Isa 14:2
Jer 2:3; 10:25

17 I will give you back your health
    and heal your wounds," says the LORD.
"For you are called an outcast—
    'Jerusalem* for whom no one cares.'"

**30:17**
Ps 107:20
Isa 56:8
Jer 8:22; 33:6

18 This is what the LORD says:
"When I bring Israel home again from captivity
    and restore their fortunes,
Jerusalem will be rebuilt on its ruins,
    and the palace reconstructed as before.

**30:18**
1 Chr 29:1, 19
Pss 48:3; 122:7
Jer 31:38-40

19 There will be joy and songs of thanksgiving,
    and I will multiply my people, not diminish them;
I will honor them, not despise them.
20     Their children will prosper as they did long ago.
I will establish them as a nation before me,
    and I will punish anyone who hurts them.

**30:19**
Isa 12:1; 51:3;
55:5; 60:9
Jer 17:26; 33:11

**30:17** Hebrew *Zion.*

---

**30:12, 13, 17** The medical language here conveys the idea that sin is terminal. Sinful people cannot be cured by being good or being religious. Beware of putting your confidence in useless cures while your sin spreads and causes you pain. God alone can cure the disease of sin, but you must be willing to let him do it.

**30:15** Judah protested its punishment, even though the sin that caused the pain was scandalous. But punishment is an opportunity for growth because it makes us aware of sin's consequences. The people should have asked how they could profit from their mistakes. Remember this the next time you are corrected.

**30:18** This prophecy that Jerusalem would be rebuilt was not completely fulfilled by the work of Ezra, Nehemiah, and Zerubbabel. The city was indeed rebuilt after the captivity, but the final restoration will occur when all believers are gathered in Christ's Kingdom. This restoration will include buildings (30:18), people (30:19), and rulers (30:21).

30:21
Exod 3:5
Num 16:5

²¹ They will have their own ruler again,
  and he will come from their own people.
I will invite him to approach me," says the LORD,
  "for who would dare to come unless invited?

30:22
Exod 6:7
Jer 32:38
Hos 2:23
Zech 13:9

²² You will be my people,
  and I will be your God."

30:23
Jer 23:19-20
30:24
Jer 4:8; 23:20

²³ Look! The LORD's anger bursts out like a storm,
  a driving wind that swirls down on the heads of the wicked.
²⁴ The fierce anger of the LORD will not diminish
  until it has finished all he has planned.
In the days to come
  you will understand all this.

### Hope for Restoration

31:1
Gen 17:7-8
Rom 11:26-28

**31** "In that day," says the LORD, "I will be the God of all the families of Israel, and they will be my people. ² This is what the LORD says:

"Those who survive the coming destruction
  will find blessings even in the barren land,
  for I will give rest to the people of Israel."

31:3
Deut 4:37; 7:8
Ps 25:6

³ Long ago the LORD said to Israel:
"I have loved you, my people, with an everlasting love.
  With unfailing love I have drawn you to myself.

31:4
Isa 30:32
Jer 24:6; 33:7

⁴ I will rebuild you, my virgin Israel.
  You will again be happy
  and dance merrily with your tambourines.

31:5
Ps 107:37
Isa 65:21
Ezek 28:26

⁵ Again you will plant your vineyards on the mountains of Samaria
  and eat from your own gardens there.
⁶ The day will come when watchmen will shout
  from the hill country of Ephraim,
'Come, let us go up to Jerusalem*
  to worship the LORD our God.'"

31:6
Isa 2:3
Mic 4:2

31:7
Pss 14:7; 28:9
Isa 37:31; 61:9

⁷ Now this is what the LORD says:
"Sing with joy for Israel.*
  Shout for the greatest of nations!
Shout out with praise and joy:
'Save your people, O LORD,
  the remnant of Israel!'

31:8
Deut 30:4
Isa 40:11; 43:6
Ezek 34:16
Mic 4:6

⁸ For I will bring them from the north
  and from the distant corners of the earth.
I will not forget the blind and lame,
  the expectant mothers and women in labor.
A great company will return!
⁹ Tears of joy will stream down their faces,
  and I will lead them home with great care.
They will walk beside quiet streams
  and on smooth paths where they will not stumble.
For I am Israel's father,
  and Ephraim is my oldest child.

31:6 Hebrew *Zion;* also in 31:12.   31:7 Hebrew *Jacob;* also in 31:11. See note on 5:20.

---

**30:21** This verse refers to the restoration after the Babylonian captivity as well as to the final restoration under Christ.

**31:1** This promise is to all the families of Israel, not only to the tribe of Judah. The restoration will include all people who trust God.

**31:3** God reaches toward his people with kindness motivated by deep and everlasting love. He is eager to do the best for them

if they will only let him. After many words of warning about sin, this reminder of God's magnificent love is a breath of fresh air. Rather than thinking of God with dread, look carefully and see him lovingly drawing us toward himself.

10 "Listen to this message from the LORD,
     you nations of the world;
     proclaim it in distant coastlands:
The LORD, who scattered his people,
     will gather them and watch over them
     as a shepherd does his flock.
11 For the LORD has redeemed Israel
     from those too strong for them.
12 They will come home and sing songs of joy on the heights of Jerusalem.
     They will be radiant because of the LORD's good gifts—
the abundant crops of grain, new wine, and olive oil,
     and the healthy flocks and herds.
Their life will be like a watered garden,
     and all their sorrows will be gone.
13 The young women will dance for joy,
     and the men—old and young—will join in the celebration.
I will turn their mourning into joy.
I will comfort them and exchange their sorrow for rejoicing.
14 The priests will enjoy abundance,
     and my people will feast on my good gifts.
     I, the LORD, have spoken!"

### Rachel's Sadness Turns to Joy
15 This is what the LORD says:

"A cry is heard in Ramah—
     deep anguish and bitter weeping.
Rachel weeps for her children,
     refusing to be comforted—
     for her children are gone."

16 But now this is what the LORD says:
"Do not weep any longer,
     for I will reward you," says the LORD.
"Your children will come back to you
     from the distant land of the enemy.
17 There is hope for your future," says the LORD.
     "Your children will come again to their own land.
18 I have heard Israel* saying,
'You disciplined me severely,
     like a calf that needs training for the yoke.
Turn me again to you and restore me,
     for you alone are the LORD my God.
19 I turned away from God,
     but then I was sorry.
I kicked myself for my stupidity!
     I was thoroughly ashamed of all I did in my younger days.'

20 "Is not Israel still my son,
     my darling child?" says the LORD.
"I often have to punish him,
     but I still love him.

**31:18** Hebrew *Ephraim*, referring to the northern kingdom of Israel; also in 31:20.

| | |
|---|---|
| **31:10** | Isa 40:11; 66:19 |
| **31:12** | Isa 2:2; 35:10; 58:11; 60:20; 65:19 Hos 2:22 Joel 3:18 Mic 4:1 John 16:22 |
| **31:13** | Ps 30:11 Isa 51:11; 61:3 Zech 8:4-5 |
| **31:15** | Ps 77:2 Jer 10:20 †Matt 2:17-18 |
| **31:16** | Isa 25:8; 30:19 Jer 30:3 Ezek 11:17 |
| **31:18** | Pss 80:3, 7, 19; 94:12 Jer 17:14 Hos 4:16 |
| **31:19** | Ezek 36:31 Luke 18:13 |
| **31:20** | Isa 55:7 Hos 11:8; 14:4 |

---

**31:14** This means that many sacrifices will be made at the Temple so that the priests will have a feast with their portion. It is also a symbol of life and prosperity (Psalm 36:8; 63:5; Isaiah 55:2).

**31:15** Rachel, Jacob's favorite wife, was the symbolic mother of the northern tribes, which were taken into captivity by the Assyrians. Rachel is pictured crying for the exiles at Ramah, a staging point of deportation. This verse is quoted in Matthew 2:18 to describe the sadness of the mothers of Bethlehem as the male children were killed. The weeping was great in both cases.

**31:18-20** These words picture grief and mourning. Although Israel, the northern kingdom, had sunk into the most degrading sins, God still loved the people. A remnant would turn to God by repenting of their sins, and God would forgive. God still loves you despite anything you may have done. He will forgive you if you turn back to him.

That's why I long for him
  and surely will have mercy on him.

**31:21**
Isa 48:20; 52:11

21 Set up road signs;
  put up guideposts.
Mark well the path
  by which you came.
Come back again, my virgin Israel;
  return to your towns here.
22 How long will you wander,
  my wayward daughter?
For the LORD will cause something new to happen—
  Israel will embrace her God.*"

**31:23**
Pss 48:1; 87:1
Isa 1:26

23 This is what the LORD of Heaven's Armies, the God of Israel, says: "When I bring them back from captivity, the people of Judah and its towns will again say, 'The LORD bless you, O righteous home, O holy mountain!' 24 Townspeople and farmers and shepherds alike will live together in peace and happiness. 25 For I have given rest to the weary and joy to the sorrowing."

**31:25**
Ps 107:9
John 4:14

26 At this, I woke up and looked around. My sleep had been very sweet.

**31:27**
Ezek 36:9-11
Hos 2:23

27 "The day is coming," says the LORD, "when I will greatly increase the human population and the number of animals here in Israel and Judah. 28 In the past I deliberately uprooted and tore down this nation. I overthrew it, destroyed it, and brought disaster upon it. But in the future I will just as deliberately plant it and build it up. I, the LORD, have spoken!

**31:28**
Jer 1:10
Dan 9:14

29 "The people will no longer quote this proverb:

**31:29**
Lam 5:7
Ezek 18:2

'The parents have eaten sour grapes,
  but their children's mouths pucker at the taste.'

**31:30**
Deut 24:16
Ezek 18:4, 20

30 All people will die for their own sins—those who eat the sour grapes will be the ones whose mouths will pucker.

**31:31-34**
†Heb 8:8-12

31 "The day is coming," says the LORD, "when I will make a new covenant with the people of Israel and Judah. 32 This covenant will not be like the one I made with their ancestors when I took them by the hand and brought them out of the land of Egypt. They broke that covenant, though I loved them as a husband loves his wife," says the LORD.

**31:31**
Jer 32:40
Ezek 37:26
Luke 22:20
1 Cor 11:25

33 "But this is the new covenant I will make with the people of Israel on that day," says the LORD. "I will put my instructions deep within them, and I will write them on their hearts. I will be their God, and they will be my people. 34 And they will not need to teach their neighbors, nor will they need to teach their relatives, saying, 'You should know the LORD.' For everyone, from the least to the greatest, will know me already," says the LORD. "And I will forgive their wickedness, and I will never again remember their sins."

**31:32**
Deut 1:31; 5:2-3

**31:33**
Heb 10:16

**31:34**
Isa 11:9; 43:25
Mic 7:18
Rom 11:27
1 Thes 4:9
†Heb 10:17
1 Jn 2:27

35 It is the LORD who provides the sun to light the day
  and the moon and stars to light the night,
  and who stirs the sea into roaring waves.
His name is the LORD of Heaven's Armies,
  and this is what he says:

**31:22** Hebrew *a woman will surround a man.*

---

**31:29, 30** The people tried to blame God's judgment on the sins of their parents. One person's sin does indeed affect other people, but all people are still held personally accountable for the sin in their own life (Deuteronomy 24:16; Ezekiel 18:2). What excuses do you use for your sins?

**31:33** God would write his law on their hearts rather than on tablets of stone, as he did the Ten Commandments. In 17:1 their sin was engraved on their hearts so that they wanted above all to disobey. This change seems to describe an experience very much like the new birth, with God taking the initiative. When we turn our life over to God, he, by his Holy Spirit, builds into us the desire to obey him.

**31:33** The old covenant, broken by the people, would be replaced by a new covenant. The foundation of this new covenant is Christ (Hebrews 8:6). It is revolutionary, involving not only Israel and Judah but even the Gentiles. It offers a unique personal relationship with God himself, with his laws written on individuals' hearts instead of on stone. Jeremiah looked forward to the day when Jesus would come to establish this covenant. But for us today, this covenant is here. We have the wonderful opportunity to make a fresh start and establish a permanent, personal relationship with God (see 29:11; 32:38-40).

**31:35-37** God has the power to do away with the laws of nature or even to do away with his people. But he will do neither. This is not a prediction; it is a promise. This is God's way of saying that he will not reject Israel any more than he will do away with nature's laws.

36 "I am as likely to reject my people Israel
    as I am to abolish the laws of nature!"
37 This is what the LORD says:
    "Just as the heavens cannot be measured
        and the foundations of the earth cannot be explored,
    so I will not consider casting them away
        for the evil they have done.
    I, the LORD, have spoken!

38 "The day is coming," says the LORD, "when all Jerusalem will be rebuilt for me, from the Tower of Hananel to the Corner Gate. 39A measuring line will be stretched out over the hill of Gareb and across to Goah. 40And the entire area—including the graveyard and ash dump in the valley, and all the fields out to the Kidron Valley on the east as far as the Horse Gate— will be holy to the LORD. The city will never again be captured or destroyed."

### Jeremiah's Land Purchase

**32** The following message came to Jeremiah from the LORD in the tenth year of the reign of Zedekiah,* king of Judah. This was also the eighteenth year of the reign of King Nebuchadnezzar.* 2Jerusalem was then under siege from the Babylonian army, and Jeremiah was imprisoned in the courtyard of the guard in the royal palace. 3King Zedekiah had put him there, asking why he kept giving this prophecy: "This is what the LORD says: 'I am about to hand this city over to the king of Babylon, and he will take it. 4King Zedekiah will be captured by the Babylonians* and taken to meet the king of Babylon face to face. 5He will take Zedekiah to Babylon, and I will deal with him there,' says the LORD. 'If you fight against the Babylonians, you will never succeed.'"

6At that time the LORD sent me a message. He said, 7"Your cousin Hanamel son of Shallum will come and say to you, 'Buy my field at Anathoth. By law you have the right to buy it before it is offered to anyone else.'"

8Then, just as the LORD had said he would, my cousin Hanamel came and visited me in the prison. He said, "Please buy my field at Anathoth in the land of Benjamin. By law you have the right to buy it before it is offered to anyone else, so buy it for yourself." Then I knew that the message I had heard was from the LORD.

9So I bought the field at Anathoth, paying Hanamel seventeen pieces* of silver for it. 10I signed and sealed the deed of purchase before witnesses, weighed out the silver, and paid him. 11Then I took the sealed deed and an unsealed copy of the deed, which contained the terms and conditions of the purchase, 12and I handed them to Baruch son of Neriah and grandson of Mahseiah. I did all this in the presence of my cousin Hanamel, the witnesses who had signed the deed, and all the men of Judah who were there in the courtyard of the guardhouse.

13Then I said to Baruch as they all listened, 14"This is what the LORD of Heaven's Armies, the God of Israel, says: 'Take both this sealed deed and the unsealed copy, and put them into a pottery jar to preserve them for a long time.' 15For this is what the LORD of Heaven's Armies, the God of Israel, says: 'Someday people will again own property here in this land and will buy and sell houses and vineyards and fields.'"

**31:36**
Ps 89:36-37
Isa 54:9-10
Jer 33:20-26
Amos 9:8-9

**31:37**
Isa 40:12
Jer 33:22, 24-26
Rom 11:2-5, 26-27

**31:38**
2 Chr 26:9
Neh 3:1; 12:39
Zech 14:10

**31:40**
2 Kgs 23:6
Neh 3:28
Joel 3:17
Zech 14:20

**32:1**
2 Kgs 25:1-2
Jer 39:1-2

**32:2**
Neh 3:25

**32:3**
Jer 21:4-7; 26:8-9;
34:2-3

**32:4**
2 Kgs 25:4-7
Jer 37:17; 39:4-7

**32:5**
Ezek 12:12-13;
17:9-10, 15

**32:7**
Lev 25:25
Ruth 4:3-4

**32:8**
1 Sam 9:16-17;
10:3-7

**32:9**
Gen 23:16
Matt 27:9-10

**32:10**
Ruth 4:1, 9
Isa 8:1-2

**32:15**
Jer 30:18; 31:5, 12
Amos 9:14-15
Zech 3:10

---

**32:1a** The tenth year of Zedekiah's reign and the eighteenth year of Nebuchadnezzar's reign was 587 B.C.
**32:1b** Hebrew *Nebuchadrezzar*, a variant spelling of Nebuchadnezzar; also in 32:28.   **32:4** Or *Chaldeans*; also in 32:5, 24, 25, 28, 29, 43.   **32:9** Hebrew *17 shekels*, about 7 ounces or 194 grams in weight.

---

**31:38-40** These points mark the boundaries of restored Jerusalem in the days of Nehemiah. Gareb and Goah are unknown. The graveyard and ash dump probably refer to the valley of Ben-Hinnom, where children were sacrificed in pagan worship.

**32:1-12** God told Jeremiah to buy a field outside Jerusalem. The city had been under siege for a year, and Jeremiah bought land that the soldiers occupied—certainly a poor

investment. In addition, Jeremiah was a prisoner in the palace. But Jeremiah was demonstrating his faith in God's promises to bring his people back and to rebuild Jerusalem.

**32:6-17** Trust doesn't come easy. It wasn't easy for Jeremiah to publicly buy land already captured by the enemy. But he trusted God. It wasn't easy for David to believe that he would become king, even after he was anointed. But he trusted God (1 Samuel 16–31). It wasn't easy for Moses to believe that he and his people would escape Egypt, even after God spoke to him from a burning bush. But he trusted God (Exodus 3:1–4:20). It isn't easy for us to believe that God can fulfill his "impossible" promises either, but we must trust him. God, who worked in the lives of biblical heroes, will work in our lives, too, if we will let him.

### Jeremiah's Prayer

16Then after I had given the papers to Baruch, I prayed to the LORD:

**32:17**
Gen 18:14
2 Kgs 19:15
Ps 102:25

**32:18**
Exod 34:6-7
Deut 7:9-10
1 Kgs 16:1-3
Matt 23:32-36

**32:19**
Ps 62:12
Isa 28:29
Matt 16:27
John 5:29

**32:21**
Deut 4:34; 26:8
1 Chr 17:21

**32:22**
Exod 13:5
Deut 1:8

**32:23**
Ezra 9:7
Dan 9:11-12

**32:24**
Josh 23:15-16
Ezek 14:21
Zech 1:6

17"O Sovereign LORD! You made the heavens and earth by your strong hand and powerful arm. Nothing is too hard for you! 18You show unfailing love to thousands, but you also bring the consequences of one generation's sin upon the next. You are the great and powerful God, the LORD of Heaven's Armies. 19You have all wisdom and do great and mighty miracles. You see the conduct of all people, and you give them what they deserve. 20You performed miraculous signs and wonders in the land of Egypt—things still remembered to this day! And you have continued to do great miracles in Israel and all around the world. You have made your name famous to this day.

21"You brought Israel out of Egypt with mighty signs and wonders, with a strong hand and powerful arm, and with overwhelming terror. 22You gave the people of Israel this land that you had promised their ancestors long before—a land flowing with milk and honey. 23Our ancestors came and conquered it and lived in it, but they refused to obey you or follow your word. They have not done anything you commanded. That is why you have sent this terrible disaster upon them.

24"See how the siege ramps have been built against the city walls! Through war, famine, and disease, the city will be handed over to the Babylonians, who will conquer it. Everything has happened just as you said. 25And yet, O Sovereign LORD, you have told me to buy the field—paying good money for it before these witnesses—even though the city will soon be handed over to the Babylonians."

### A Prediction of Jerusalem's Fall

**32:27**
Num 16:22; 27:16
Matt 19:26

**32:29**
2 Chr 36:19

**32:31**
1 Kgs 11:7-8
2 Kgs 21:4-7, 15;
23:27; 24:3-4
Matt 23:37

**32:32**
Ezra 9:7
Isa 1:23
Jer 2:26; 44:17, 21

**32:33**
2 Chr 36:15-16
Jer 25:3; 26:5;
35:15

**32:34**
Jer 7:30
Ezek 8:5

**32:35**
Lev 18:21; 20:2-5
2 Chr 28:2-3; 33:6
Acts 7:43

26Then this message came to Jeremiah from the LORD: 27"I am the LORD, the God of all the peoples of the world. Is anything too hard for me? 28Therefore, this is what the LORD says: I will hand this city over to the Babylonians and to Nebuchadnezzar, king of Babylon, and he will capture it. 29The Babylonians outside the walls will come in and set fire to the city. They will burn down all these houses where the people provoked my anger by burning incense to Baal on the rooftops and by pouring out liquid offerings to other gods. 30Israel and Judah have done nothing but wrong since their earliest days. They have infuriated me with all their evil deeds," says the LORD. 31"From the time this city was built until now, it has done nothing but anger me, so I am determined to get rid of it.

32"The sins of Israel and Judah—the sins of the people of Jerusalem, the kings, the officials, the priests, and the prophets—have stirred up my anger. 33My people have turned their backs on me and have refused to return. Even though I diligently taught them, they would not receive instruction or obey. 34They have set up their abominable idols right in my own Temple, defiling it. 35They have built pagan shrines to Baal in the valley of Ben-Hinnom, and there they sacrifice their sons and daughters to Molech. I have never commanded such a horrible deed; it never even crossed my mind to command such a thing. What an incredible evil, causing Judah to sin so greatly!

### A Promise of Restoration

**32:38**
†2 Cor 6:16

**32:39**
Deut 11:18-21
Ezek 37:25
John 17:21
Acts 4:32

36"Now I want to say something more about this city. You have been saying, 'It will fall to the king of Babylon through war, famine, and disease.' But this is what the LORD, the God of Israel, says: 37I will certainly bring my people back again from all the countries where I will scatter them in my fury. I will bring them back to this very city and let them live in peace and safety. 38They will be my people, and I will be their God. 39And I will give them one heart and one purpose: to worship me forever, for their own good and for the good of all

---

**32:17-25** After Jeremiah bought the field, he began to wonder if such a move was wise. He sought relief in prayer from his nagging doubts. In this prayer, Jeremiah affirmed that God is the Creator of heaven and earth (32:17), the wise Judge, who is aware of our conduct (32:19), and our Redeemer, who has great power (32:21). God loves us and sees our situation. Whenever we doubt God's wisdom or wonder if it is practical to obey him, we can review what we already know about him. Such thoughts and prayers will quiet our doubts and calm our fears.

**32:35** These pagan shrines were where the most important and grotesque part of Molech worship took place. Children were offered in sacrifice to this pagan god.

**32:36-42** God uses his power to accomplish *his* purposes through *his* people. God doesn't give you power to be all you want to be, but he gives you power to be all *he* wants you to be. The people of Israel had to learn that trusting God meant radically realigning their purposes and desires with his. God gave them "one heart" toward him (32:39). We must develop such singleness of heart and action to love God above anything else.

their descendants. [40]And I will make an everlasting covenant with them: I will never stop doing good for them. I will put a desire in their hearts to worship me, and they will never leave me. [41]I will find joy doing good for them and will faithfully and wholeheartedly re-plant them in this land.

[42]"This is what the LORD says: Just as I have brought all these calamities on them, so I will do all the good I have promised them. [43]Fields will again be bought and sold in this land about which you now say, 'It has been ravaged by the Babylonians, a desolate land where people and animals have all disappeared.' [44]Yes, fields will once again be bought and sold—deeds signed and sealed and witnessed—in the land of Benjamin and here in Jerusalem, in the towns of Judah and in the hill country, in the foothills of Judah* and in the Negev, too. For someday I will restore prosperity to them. I, the LORD, have spoken!"

## Promises of Peace and Prosperity

**33** While Jeremiah was still confined in the courtyard of the guard, the LORD gave him this second message: [2]"This is what the LORD says—the LORD who made the earth, who formed and established it, whose name is the LORD: [3]Ask me and I will tell you remark-able secrets you do not know about things to come. [4]For this is what the LORD, the God of Israel, says: You have torn down the houses of this city and even the king's palace to get materials to strengthen the walls against the siege ramps and swords of the enemy. [5]You expect to fight the Babylonians,* but the men of this city are already as good as dead, for I have determined to destroy them in my terrible anger. I have abandoned them because of all their wickedness.

[6]"Nevertheless, the time will come when I will heal Jerusalem's wounds and give it pros-perity and true peace. [7]I will restore the fortunes of Judah and Israel and rebuild their towns. [8]I will cleanse them of their sins against me and forgive all their sins of rebellion. [9]Then this city will bring me joy, glory, and honor before all the nations of the earth! The people of the world will see all the good I do for my people, and they will tremble with awe at the peace and prosperity I provide for them.

[10]"This is what the LORD says: You have said, 'This is a desolate land where people and an-imals have all disappeared.' Yet in the empty streets of Jerusalem and Judah's other towns, there will be heard once more [11]the sounds of joy and laughter. The joyful voices of bride-grooms and brides will be heard again, along with the joyous songs of people bringing thanksgiving offerings to the LORD. They will sing,

'Give thanks to the LORD of Heaven's Armies,
    for the LORD is good.
    His faithful love endures forever!'

For I will restore the prosperity of this land to what it was in the past, says the LORD.

[12]"This is what the LORD of Heaven's Armies says: This land—though it is now desolate and has no people and animals—will once more have pastures where shepherds can lead their flocks. [13]Once again shepherds will count their flocks in the towns of the hill country, the foothills of Judah,* the Negev, the land of Benjamin, the vicinity of Jerusalem, and all the towns of Judah. I, the LORD, have spoken!

[14]"The day will come, says the LORD, when I will do for Israel and Judah all the good things I have promised them.

[15] "In those days and at that time
    I will raise up a righteous descendant* from King David's line.
    He will do what is just and right throughout the land.

**32:44** Hebrew *the Shephelah.* **33:5** Or *Chaldeans.* **33:13** Hebrew *the Shephelah.* **33:15** Hebrew *a righteous branch.*

**32:44** The hill country is in western Palestine. The Negev is the southern part of Judah.

**33:1ff** God would restore Jerusalem, not because the people cried, but because it was part of his ultimate plan. The Babylonian disaster did not change God's purposes for his people. Although Jerusalem would be destroyed, it would be restored (after the 70-year captivity and in the end times when the Messiah will rule). God's justice is always tempered by his mercy.

**33:3** God assured Jeremiah that he had only to ask God and God would answer (see also Psalm 145:18; Isaiah 58:9; Matthew 7:7).

God is ready to answer our prayers, but we must ask for his assistance. Surely God could take care of our needs without our asking. But when we ask, we are acknowledging that he alone is God and that we cannot accomplish in our own strength all that is his domain to do. When we ask, we must humble ourselves, lay aside our willfulness and worry, and determine to obey him.

**33:15, 16** These verses refer to both the first and second comings of Christ. At his first coming he would set up his reign in the hearts of believers; at his second coming he will execute justice and righteousness throughout the whole earth. Christ is

### Cross-references (margin)

**32:40** Isa 55:3
**32:41** Deut 30:9; Isa 65:19; Amos 9:15
**32:42** Jer 31:28; Zech 8:14-15
**32:43** Ezek 37:11-14
**33:2** Exod 3:15; 15:3
**33:3** Ps 50:15; Isa 48:6; 55:6-7
**33:4** Isa 32:13-14
**33:5** Jer 21:10
**33:6** Isa 66:12; Jer 17:14
**33:7** Ps 85:1; Amos 9:14-15
**33:8** Ps 51:2; Jer 50:20; Heb 9:11-14
**33:9** Ps 40:3; Isa 62:2, 4; Jer 16:19; 24:6; Hos 3:5
**33:10** Isa 35:10
**33:12** Ezek 34:12-14; Zeph 2:6-7
**33:13** Lev 27:32; Jer 17:26; Luke 15:4
**33:14** Hag 2:6-9
**33:15** Ps 72:1-5; Isa 11:1-5

**33:16**
1 Cor 1:30
2 Cor 5:21
Phil 3:9

**33:17**
1 Kgs 2:4
Ps 89:29-37

**33:18**
Deut 18:1
Ezek 44:15
Heb 13:15

**33:20**
2 Sam 23:5
2 Chr 21:7
Ps 104:19-23
Isa 54:9

**33:22**
Gen 22:17

**33:24**
Neh 4:2-4
Ps 44:13-14
Isa 11:13
Ezek 36:2

**33:25**
Ps 74:16-17

**33:26**
Hos 2:23

**34:1**
2 Kgs 25:1
Jer 1:15
Dan 2:37-38

**34:2**
2 Chr 36:11-12
Jer 37:1-4

**34:3**
2 Kgs 25:4-7
Jer 21:7

**34:5**
2 Chr 16:14; 21:19

**34:7**
Josh 10:3, 10
2 Kgs 14:19
2 Chr 11:5-10

16 In that day Judah will be saved,
  and Jerusalem will live in safety.
And this will be its name:
  'The LORD Is Our Righteousness.'*

17For this is what the LORD says: David will have a descendant sitting on the throne of Israel forever. 18And there will always be Levitical priests to offer burnt offerings and grain offerings and sacrifices to me."

19Then this message came to Jeremiah from the LORD: 20"This is what the LORD says: If you can break my covenant with the day and the night so that one does not follow the other, 21only then will my covenant with my servant David be broken. Only then will he no longer have a descendant to reign on his throne. The same is true for my covenant with the Levitical priests who minister before me. 22And as the stars of the sky cannot be counted and the sand on the seashore cannot be measured, so I will multiply the descendants of my servant David and the Levites who minister before me."

23The LORD gave another message to Jeremiah. He said, 24"Have you noticed what people are saying?—'The LORD chose Judah and Israel and then abandoned them!' They are sneering and saying that Israel is not worthy to be counted as a nation. 25But this is what the LORD says: I would no more reject my people than I would change my laws that govern night and day, earth and sky. 26I will never abandon the descendants of Jacob or David, my servant, or change the plan that David's descendants will rule the descendants of Abraham, Isaac, and Jacob. Instead, I will restore them to their land and have mercy on them."

## 6. God's promised judgment arrives
### A Warning for Zedekiah

**34** King Nebuchadnezzar of Babylon came with all the armies from the kingdoms he ruled, and he fought against Jerusalem and the towns of Judah. At that time this message came to Jeremiah from the LORD: 2"Go to King Zedekiah of Judah, and tell him, 'This is what the LORD, the God of Israel, says: I am about to hand this city over to the king of Babylon, and he will burn it down. 3You will not escape his grasp but will be captured and taken to meet the king of Babylon face to face. Then you will be exiled to Babylon.

4"'But listen to this promise from the LORD, O Zedekiah, king of Judah. This is what the LORD says: You will not be killed in war 5but will die peacefully. People will burn incense in your memory, just as they did for your ancestors, the kings who preceded you. They will mourn for you, crying, "Alas, our master is dead!" This I have decreed, says the LORD.'"

6So Jeremiah the prophet delivered the message to King Zedekiah of Judah. 7At this time the Babylonian army was besieging Jerusalem, Lachish, and Azekah—the only fortified cities of Judah not yet captured.

**33:16** Hebrew *Yahweh Tsidqenu.*

---

**BABYLON ATTACKS JUDAH**
Zedekiah incurred Babylon's wrath in allying with Egypt (37:5) and not surrendering as God told him through Jeremiah (38:17). Nebuchadnezzar attacked Judah for the third and final time, moving systematically until all its cities fell. Jerusalem withstood siege for several months but was burned, as Jeremiah predicted (chapter 39).

the "righteous descendant" from King David's line, the man after God's own heart.

**33:18** As Christ fulfills the role of King, he also fulfills the role of Priest, maintaining constant fellowship with God and mediating for the people. This verse does not mean that actual priests will perform sacrifices, for sacrifices will no longer be necessary (Hebrews 10:4, 11, 12). Now that Christ is our High Priest, all believers are priests of God, and we can come before him personally.

**34:1ff** This chapter describes the fulfillment of many of Jeremiah's predictions. In the book of Jeremiah, many prophecies were both given and quickly fulfilled.

### Freedom for Hebrew Slaves

⁸This message came to Jeremiah from the Lord after King Zedekiah made a covenant with the people, proclaiming freedom for the slaves. ⁹He had ordered all the people to free their Hebrew slaves—both men and women. No one was to keep a fellow Judean in bondage. ¹⁰The officials and all the people had obeyed the king's command, ¹¹but later they changed their minds. They took back the men and women they had freed, forcing them to be slaves again.

¹²So the Lord gave them this message through Jeremiah: ¹³"This is what the Lord, the God of Israel, says: I made a covenant with your ancestors long ago when I rescued them from their slavery in Egypt. ¹⁴I told them that every Hebrew slave must be freed after serving six years. But your ancestors paid no attention to me. ¹⁵Recently you repented and did what was right, following my command. You freed your slaves and made a solemn covenant with me in the Temple that bears my name. ¹⁶But now you have shrugged off your oath and defiled my name by taking back the men and women you had freed, forcing them to be slaves once again.

¹⁷"Therefore, this is what the Lord says: Since you have not obeyed me by setting your countrymen free, I will set you free to be destroyed by war, disease, and famine. You will be an object of horror to all the nations of the earth. ¹⁸Because you have broken the terms of our covenant, I will cut you apart just as you cut apart the calf when you walked between its halves to solemnize your vows. ¹⁹Yes, I will cut you apart, whether you are officials of Judah or Jerusalem, court officials, priests, or common people—for you have broken your oath. ²⁰I will give you to your enemies, and they will kill you. Your bodies will be food for the vultures and wild animals.

²¹"I will hand over King Zedekiah of Judah and his officials to the army of the king of Babylon. And although Babylon's king has left Jerusalem for a while, ²²I will call the Babylonian armies back again. They will fight against this city and will capture it and burn it down. I will see to it that all the towns of Judah are destroyed, with no one living there."

### The Faithful Recabites

**35** This is the message the Lord gave Jeremiah when Jehoiakim son of Josiah was king of Judah: ²"Go to the settlement where the families of the Recabites live, and invite them to the Lord's Temple. Take them into one of the inner rooms, and offer them some wine."

³So I went to see Jaazaniah son of Jeremiah and grandson of Habazziniah and all his brothers and sons—representing all the Recabite families. ⁴I took them to the Temple, and we went into the room assigned to the sons of Hanan son of Igdaliah, a man of God. This room was located next to the one used by the Temple officials, directly above the room of Maaseiah son of Shallum, the Temple gatekeeper.

⁵I set cups and jugs of wine before them and invited them to have a drink, ⁶but they refused. "No," they said, "we don't drink wine, because our ancestor Jehonadab* son of Recab gave us this command: 'You and your descendants must never drink wine. ⁷And do not build houses or plant crops or vineyards, but always live in tents. If you follow these commands,

35:6 Hebrew *Jonadab*, a variant spelling of Jehonadab; also in 35:10, 14, 16, 18, 19. See 2 Kgs 10:15.

---

**Cross-references (margin):**

34:8 Neh 5:1-13
34:11 Hos 6:4
34:13 Deut 5:2-3, 27; Jer 31:32
34:14 Exod 21:2; 1 Kgs 9:22; 2 Kgs 17:13-14
34:15 Neh 10:29
34:16 Exod 20:7; 1 Sam 15:11
34:17 Lev 26:34-35; Deut 28:25, 64; Matt 7:2
34:18 Gen 15:10; Hos 6:7; Mic 7:1-5
34:20 1 Sam 17:46; Jer 19:7
34:21 2 Kgs 25:18-21; Ezek 17:16
34:22 Jer 44:22
35:1 2 Kgs 23:34-36; Dan 1:1
35:2 1 Kgs 6:5-6, 8; 1 Chr 2:55
35:4 1 Kgs 12:22; 1 Chr 9:18
35:5 Amos 2:12
35:6 Lev 10:9; 2 Kgs 10:15, 23; 1 Chr 2:55; Luke 1:15
35:7 Exod 20:12; Heb 11:9

---

**34:8, 9** Babylon had laid siege to Jerusalem, and the city was about to fall. Zedekiah finally decided to listen to Jeremiah and try to appease God—so he freed the slaves. He thought he could win God's favor with a kind act, but what he needed was a change of heart. The people had been disobeying God's law from the beginning (Exodus 21:2-11; Leviticus 25:39-55; Deuteronomy 15:12-18). When the siege was temporarily lifted, the people became bold and returned to their sins (34:11-17; 37:5, 11).

**34:15, 16** The people of Israel had a hard time keeping their promises to God. In the Temple, they would solemnly promise to obey God, but back in their homes and at work they wouldn't do it. God expressed his great displeasure. If you want to please God, make sure you keep your promises. God wants promises kept, not just piously made.

**34:18-20** Cutting a calf in two and walking between the halves was a customary way to ratify a contract (Genesis 15:9, 10). This action symbolized the judgment on anyone who broke the contract. God was saying, "You have broken the contract you made with me, so you know the judgment awaiting you!"

**35:1ff** The Recabites' code of conduct resembled that of the Nazirites, who took a special vow of dedication to God (Numbers 6). For 200 years they had obeyed their ancestor's vow to abstain from wine. While the rest of the nation was breaking its covenant with God, these people were steadfast in their commitment. God wanted the rest of his people to remain as committed to their covenant with him as the Recabites were to their vow. God had Jeremiah tempt the Recabites with wine to demonstrate their commitment and dedication. God knew they wouldn't break their vow.

**35:6** Jehonadab son of Recab had joined Jehu in purging the northern kingdom of Baal worship (2 Kings 10:15-28).

35:8
Prov 4:1-2, 10;
6:20
Col 3:20

35:9
Ps 37:16
1 Tim 6:6

35:11
2 Kgs 24:1-2
Dan 1:1-2

35:13
Isa 28:9-12

35:14
2 Chr 36:15
Isa 30:9

35:15
Deut 6:14
Jer 29:19
Ezek 18:30-32
Acts 26:20

35:16
Mal 1:6

35:17
Prov 1:24-25
Mic 3:12
Luke 13:34-35
Rom 10:21

35:18
Exod 20:12
Jer 15:19
Eph 6:1-3

35:19
Jer 15:19

36:1
Jer 25:1-3; 45:1

36:2
Jer 1:2-3, 5, 9-10;
25:9-29
Zech 5:1-2

36:3
Isa 55:7
Jer 18:8, 11; 26:3
Mark 4:12
Acts 3:19

36:4
Jer 32:12
Ezek 2:9

36:5
Jer 32:2

36:6
Zech 8:19

36:7
1 Kgs 8:33
2 Kgs 22:13
Jer 26:3

you will live long, good lives in the land.' 8So we have obeyed him in all these things. We have never had a drink of wine to this day, nor have our wives, our sons, or our daughters. 9We haven't built houses or owned vineyards or farms or planted crops. 10We have lived in tents and have fully obeyed all the commands of Jehonadab, our ancestor. 11But when King Nebuchadnezzar* of Babylon attacked this country, we were afraid of the Babylonian and Syrian* armies. So we decided to move to Jerusalem. That is why we are here."

12Then the LORD gave this message to Jeremiah: 13"This is what the LORD of Heaven's Armies, the God of Israel, says: Go and say to the people in Judah and Jerusalem, 'Come and learn a lesson about how to obey me. 14The Recabites do not drink wine to this day because their ancestor Jehonadab told them not to. But I have spoken to you again and again, and you refuse to obey me. 15Time after time I sent you prophets, who told you, "Turn from your wicked ways, and start doing things right. Stop worshiping other gods so that you might live in peace here in the land I have given to you and your ancestors." But you would not listen to me or obey me. 16The descendants of Jehonadab son of Recab have obeyed their ancestor completely, but you have refused to listen to me.'

17"Therefore, this is what the LORD God of Heaven's Armies, the God of Israel, says: 'Because you refuse to listen or answer when I call, I will send upon Judah and Jerusalem all the disasters I have threatened.'"

18Then Jeremiah turned to the Recabites and said, "This is what the LORD of Heaven's Armies, the God of Israel, says: 'You have obeyed your ancestor Jehonadab in every respect, following all his instructions.' 19Therefore, this is what the LORD of Heaven's Armies, the God of Israel, says: 'Jehonadab son of Recab will always have descendants who serve me.'"

### Baruch Reads the LORD's Messages

**36** During the fourth year that Jehoiakim son of Josiah was king in Judah,* the LORD gave this message to Jeremiah: 2"Get a scroll, and write down all my messages against Israel, Judah, and the other nations. Begin with the first message back in the days of Josiah, and write down every message, right up to the present time. 3Perhaps the people of Judah will repent when they hear again all the terrible things I have planned for them. Then I will be able to forgive their sins and wrongdoings."

4So Jeremiah sent for Baruch son of Neriah, and as Jeremiah dictated all the prophecies that the LORD had given him, Baruch wrote them on a scroll. 5Then Jeremiah said to Baruch, "I am a prisoner here and unable to go to the Temple. 6So you go to the Temple on the next day of fasting, and read the messages from the LORD that I have had you write on this scroll. Read them so the people who are there from all over Judah will hear them. 7Perhaps even yet they will turn from their evil ways and ask the LORD's forgiveness before it is too late. For the LORD has threatened them with his terrible anger."

8Baruch did as Jeremiah told him and read these messages from the LORD to the people at the Temple. 9He did this on a day of sacred fasting held in late autumn,* during the fifth year of the reign of Jehoiakim son of Josiah. People from all over Judah had come to Jerusalem to

35:11a Hebrew *Nebuchadrezzar*, a variant spelling of Nebuchadnezzar.   35:11b Or *Chaldean and Aramean.*
36:1 The fourth year of Jehoiakim's reign was 605 B.C.   36:9 Hebrew *in the ninth month*, of the ancient Hebrew lunar calendar (also in 36:22). The ninth month in the fifth year of Jehoiakim's reign occurred within the months of November and December 604 B.C. Also see note on 1:3.

---

**35:13-17** There is a vivid contrast between the Recabites and the other Israelites. (1) The Recabites kept their vows to a fallible human leader; the people of Israel broke their covenant with their infallible divine Leader. (2) Jehonadab told his family one time not to drink, and they obeyed; God commanded Israel constantly to turn from sin, and they refused. (3) The Recabites obeyed laws that dealt with temporal issues; Israel refused to obey God's laws that dealt with eternal issues. (4) The Recabites had obeyed for hundreds of years; Israel had disobeyed for hundreds of years. (5) The Recabites would be rewarded; Israel would be punished. We often are willing to observe customs merely for the sake of tradition; how much more should we obey God's Word because it is eternal.

**36:1ff** This happened in the summer of 605 B.C., shortly after Nebuchadnezzar's victory over the Egyptian army at Carchemish, before the events recorded in chapters 34 and 35.

**36:2-4** Most people in ancient times could neither read nor write, so those who could were highly esteemed. These men,

called scribes or teachers, held positions of great importance and were very respected for their knowledge. Baruch was Jeremiah's scribe. Writing was often done on vellum or papyrus sheets that were sewn or glued together and stored in long rolls called scrolls. After the Exile, scribes became teachers of the law. In New Testament times, the scribes formed a powerful political party.

**36:9** A time of fasting (when people abstained from eating food to show their humility and repentance) was often called during times of national emergency. Babylon was destroying city after city and closing in on Jerusalem. As the people came to the Temple, Baruch told them how to avert the coming tragedy, but they refused to listen.

attend the services at the Temple on that day. <sup>10</sup>Baruch read Jeremiah's words on the scroll to all the people. He stood in front of the Temple room of Gemariah, son of Shaphan the secretary. This room was just off the upper courtyard of the Temple, near the New Gate entrance.

<sup>11</sup>When Micaiah son of Gemariah and grandson of Shaphan heard the messages from the LORD, <sup>12</sup>he went down to the secretary's room in the palace where the administrative officials were meeting. Elishama the secretary was there, along with Delaiah son of Shemaiah, Elnathan son of Acbor, Gemariah son of Shaphan, Zedekiah son of Hananiah, and all the other officials. <sup>13</sup>When Micaiah told them about the messages Baruch was reading to the people, <sup>14</sup>the officials sent Jehudi son of Nethaniah, grandson of Shelemiah and great-grandson of Cushi, to ask Baruch to come and read the messages to them, too. So Baruch took the scroll and went to them. <sup>15</sup>"Sit down and read the scroll to us," the officials said, and Baruch did as they requested.

<sup>16</sup>When they heard all the messages, they looked at one another in alarm. "We must tell the king what we have heard," they said to Baruch. <sup>17</sup>"But first, tell us how you got these messages. Did they come directly from Jeremiah?"

<sup>18</sup>So Baruch explained, "Jeremiah dictated them, and I wrote them down in ink, word for word, on this scroll."

<sup>19</sup>"You and Jeremiah should both hide," the officials told Baruch. "Don't tell anyone where you are!" <sup>20</sup>Then the officials left the scroll for safekeeping in the room of Elishama the secretary and went to tell the king what had happened.

### King Jehoiakim Burns the Scroll

<sup>21</sup>The king sent Jehudi to get the scroll. Jehudi brought it from Elishama's room and read it to the king as all his officials stood by. <sup>22</sup>It was late autumn, and the king was in a winterized part of the palace, sitting in front of a fire to keep warm. <sup>23</sup>Each time Jehudi finished reading three or four columns, the king took a knife and cut off that section of the scroll. He then threw it into the fire, section by section, until the whole scroll was burned up. <sup>24</sup>Neither the king nor his attendants showed any signs of fear or repentance at what they heard. <sup>25</sup>Even when Elnathan, Delaiah, and Gemariah begged the king not to burn the scroll, he wouldn't listen.

<sup>26</sup>Then the king commanded his son Jerahmeel, Seraiah son of Azriel, and Shelemiah son of Abdeel to arrest Baruch and Jeremiah. But the LORD had hidden them.

### Jeremiah Rewrites the Scroll

<sup>27</sup>After the king had burned the scroll on which Baruch had written Jeremiah's words, the LORD gave Jeremiah another message. He said, <sup>28</sup>"Get another scroll, and write everything again just as you did on the scroll King Jehoiakim burned. <sup>29</sup>Then say to the king, 'This is what the LORD says: You burned the scroll because it said the king of Babylon would destroy this land and empty it of people and animals. <sup>30</sup>Now this is what the LORD says about King Jehoiakim of Judah: He will have no heirs to sit on the throne of David. His dead body will be thrown out to lie unburied—exposed to the heat of the day and the frost of the night. <sup>31</sup>I will punish him and his family and his attendants for their sins. I will pour out on them and on all the people of Jerusalem and Judah all the disasters I promised, for they would not listen to my warnings.'"

<sup>32</sup>So Jeremiah took another scroll and dictated again to his secretary, Baruch. He wrote everything that had been on the scroll King Jehoiakim had burned in the fire. Only this time he added much more!

---

**36:10**
Jer 26:10

**36:12**
Jer 26:22

**36:13**
2 Kgs 22:9-10

**36:16**
Amos 7:10-11
Acts 24:25

**36:18**
Jer 36:4

**36:19**
1 Kgs 17:3; 18:4
Jer 26:20-24

**36:21**
2 Kgs 22:9-10
2 Chr 34:18
Ezek 2:4-5

**36:22**
Amos 3:15

**36:24**
2 Kgs 19:1-2
Ps 36:1
Acts 5:34-39

**36:26**
1 Kgs 19:1-3, 10
Jer 15:20-21

**36:28**
Jer 28:13-14
Zech 1:5-6

**36:29**
Deut 29:19
Isa 30:10-11; 45:9
Jer 25:8-11; 26:9

**36:30**
2 Kgs 24:12-15
Jer 22:30

**36:31**
Deut 28:15-19
Prov 29:1
Jer 19:15

**36:32**
Exod 34:1

---

**36:10-32** God told Jeremiah to write his words on a scroll. Because he was not allowed to go to the Temple, Jeremiah asked his scribe, Baruch, to whom he had dictated the scroll to read it to the people gathered there. Baruch then read it to the officials, and finally Jehudi read it to the king himself. Although the king burned the scroll, he could not destroy the word of God. Today many people try to put God's Word aside or say that it contains errors and therefore cannot be trusted. People may reject God's Word, but they cannot destroy it. God's Word will stand forever (Psalm 119:89).

**36:25** Only three leaders protested this evil act of burning the scroll containing God's word. This shows how complacent and insensitive to God the people had become. Not only did the king reject God's word, he tried to destroy it. Speaking out against these actions took courage. Anyone who decides to live for God must be willing to stand for right even if almost everyone else turns away. It is in the climate of darkness and sin that genuine faith shines most brightly.

**36:30** Jehoiakim's son, Jehoiachin, was king for three months before he was taken into captivity, but this did not qualify as sitting "on the throne of David"—an expression that implied permanence. Jehoiakim did not secure a dynasty. Zedekiah, the next ruler, was Jehoiachin's uncle. Thus, the line of mortal human kings descended from David's son Solomon was finished, but in less than 600 years the eternal King would come through the descendants of Solomon's brother Nathan (see also the note on 22:30).

## Zedekiah Calls for Jeremiah

**37** Zedekiah son of Josiah succeeded Jehoiachin* son of Jehoiakim as the king of Judah. He was appointed by King Nebuchadnezzar* of Babylon. [2]But neither King Zedekiah nor his attendants nor the people who were left in the land listened to what the LORD said through Jeremiah.

[3]Nevertheless, King Zedekiah sent Jehucal son of Shelemiah, and Zephaniah the priest, son of Maaseiah, to ask Jeremiah, "Please pray to the LORD our God for us." [4]Jeremiah had not yet been imprisoned, so he could come and go among the people as he pleased.

[5]At this time the army of Pharaoh Hophra* of Egypt appeared at the southern border of Judah. When the Babylonian* army heard about it, they withdrew from their siege of Jerusalem.

[6]Then the LORD gave this message to Jeremiah: [7]"This is what the LORD, the God of Israel, says: The king of Judah sent you to ask me what is going to happen. Tell him, 'Pharaoh's army is about to return to Egypt, though he came here to help you. [8]Then the Babylonians* will come back and capture this city and burn it to the ground.'

[9]"This is what the LORD says: Do not fool yourselves into thinking that the Babylonians are gone for good. They aren't! [10]Even if you were to destroy the entire Babylonian army, leaving only a handful of wounded survivors, they would still stagger from their tents and burn this city to the ground!"

## Jeremiah Is Imprisoned

[11]When the Babylonian army left Jerusalem because of Pharaoh's approaching army, [12]Jeremiah started to leave the city on his way to the territory of Benjamin, to claim his share of the property among his relatives there.* [13]But as he was walking through the Benjamin Gate, a sentry arrested him and said, "You are defecting to the Babylonians!" The sentry making the arrest was Irijah son of Shelemiah, grandson of Hananiah.

[14]"That's not true!" Jeremiah protested. "I had no intention of doing any such thing." But Irijah wouldn't listen, and he took Jeremiah before the officials. [15]They were furious with Jeremiah and had him flogged and imprisoned in the house of Jonathan the secretary. Jonathan's house had been converted into a prison. [16]Jeremiah was put into a dungeon cell, where he remained for many days.

[17]Later King Zedekiah secretly requested that Jeremiah come to the palace, where the king asked him, "Do you have any messages from the LORD?"

"Yes, I do!" said Jeremiah. "You will be defeated by the king of Babylon."

[18]Then Jeremiah asked the king, "What crime have I committed? What have I done against you, your attendants, or the people that I should be imprisoned like this? [19]Where are your prophets now who told you the king of Babylon would not attack you or this land? [20]Listen, my lord the king, I beg you. Don't send me back to the dungeon in the house of Jonathan the secretary, for I will die there."

[21]So King Zedekiah commanded that Jeremiah not be returned to the dungeon. Instead, he was imprisoned in the courtyard of the guard in the royal palace. The king also commanded that Jeremiah be given a loaf of fresh bread every day as long as there was any left in the city. So Jeremiah was put in the palace prison.

**37:1a** Hebrew *Coniah,* a variant spelling of Jehoiachin.    **37:1b** Hebrew *Nebuchadrezzar,* a variant spelling of Nebuchadnezzar.    **37:5a** Hebrew *army of Pharaoh;* see 44:30.    **37:5b** Or *Chaldean;* also in 37:10, 11. **37:8** Or *Chaldeans;* also in 37:9, 13.    **37:12** Hebrew *to separate from there in the midst of the people.*

---

**37:1ff**  King Jehoiakim died on the way to Babylon (2 Chronicles 36:6). His son Jehoiachin was appointed king but was taken captive to Babylon three months later. Nebuchadnezzar then appointed Zedekiah as his vassal in Judah.

**37:2, 3**  King Zedekiah and his officials did not want to listen to Jeremiah's words, but they wanted the blessings of his prayers. They wanted a superficial religion that wouldn't cost anything. God is not pleased with those who come to him seeking only what they can get rather than seeking to have a relationship with him. We would not accept that kind of relationship with someone else, and we shouldn't expect God to accept it from us.

**37:5**  When Nebuchadnezzar besieged Jerusalem in 589 B.C., Pharaoh Hophra marched against him at Zedekiah's invitation. Jerusalem looked to Egypt for help in spite of Jeremiah's

warnings. But the Egyptians were no help, for as soon as the Babylonians turned on them, they retreated. Jeremiah's warnings had been correct.

**37:17**  Zedekiah teetered between surrender and resistance. Too frightened and weak to exercise authority, he asked Jeremiah to come secretly to the palace, perhaps hoping for some better news from God. Zedekiah was desperate. He wanted to hear a word from the Lord, but he feared the political ramifications of being caught talking to Jeremiah.

---

**37:1**
2 Kgs 24:17
1 Chr 3:15-16
2 Chr 36:9-10
Jer 22:24, 28
Ezek 17:12-21

**37:2**
2 Kgs 24:18-20
2 Chr 36:12
Prov 29:12

**37:3**
Jer 2:26-27; 21:1-2; 52:24

**37:5**
Ezek 17:15-16

**37:7**
Isa 30:1-3; 31:1-3
Jer 21:1-2
Ezek 17:17

**37:9**
Jer 29:8

**37:10**
Isa 30:17
Joel 2:11

**37:12**
Jer 32:8

**37:13**
Jer 18:18; 20:10
Zech 14:10
Acts 24:5-9, 13

**37:14**
Ps 27:12
Jer 40:4-6
Matt 5:11-12

**37:15**
Jer 18:23; 38:6
Matt 21:35
Acts 5:18
Heb 11:36

**37:17**
Jer 21:7; 38:14-16
Ezek 12:12-13; 17:19-21

**37:18**
1 Sam 24:9; 26:18
John 10:32
Acts 25:8, 10-11

**37:19**
Deut 32:37-38

**37:21**
Job 5:20
Ps 33:18-19
Isa 33:16
Jer 52:6

## Jeremiah in a Cistern

**38** Now Shephatiah son of Mattan, Gedaliah son of Pashhur, Jehucal* son of Shelemiah, and Pashhur son of Malkijah heard what Jeremiah had been telling the people. He had been saying, ²"This is what the LORD says: 'Everyone who stays in Jerusalem will die from war, famine, or disease, but those who surrender to the Babylonians* will live. Their reward will be life. They will live!' ³The LORD also says: 'The city of Jerusalem will certainly be handed over to the army of the king of Babylon, who will capture it.'"

⁴So these officials went to the king and said, "Sir, this man must die! That kind of talk will undermine the morale of the few fighting men we have left, as well as that of all the people. This man is a traitor!"

⁵King Zedekiah agreed. "All right," he said. "Do as you like. I can't stop you."

⁶So the officials took Jeremiah from his cell and lowered him by ropes into an empty cistern in the prison yard. It belonged to Malkijah, a member of the royal family. There was no water in the cistern, but there was a thick layer of mud at the bottom, and Jeremiah sank down into it.

⁷But Ebed-melech the Ethiopian,* an important court official, heard that Jeremiah was in the cistern. At that time the king was holding court at the Benjamin Gate, ⁸so Ebed-melech rushed from the palace to speak with him. ⁹"My lord the king," he said, "these men have done a very evil thing in putting Jeremiah the prophet into the cistern. He will soon die of hunger, for almost all the bread in the city is gone."

¹⁰So the king told Ebed-melech, "Take thirty of my men with you, and pull Jeremiah out of the cistern before he dies."

¹¹So Ebed-melech took the men with him and went to a room in the palace beneath the treasury, where he found some old rags and discarded clothing. He carried these to the cistern and lowered them to Jeremiah on a rope. ¹²Ebed-melech called down to Jeremiah, "Put these rags under your armpits to protect you from the ropes." Then when Jeremiah was ready, ¹³they pulled him out. So Jeremiah was returned to the courtyard of the guard—the palace prison—where he remained.

## Zedekiah Questions Jeremiah

¹⁴One day King Zedekiah sent for Jeremiah and had him brought to the third entrance of the LORD's Temple. "I want to ask you something," the king said. "And don't try to hide the truth."

¹⁵Jeremiah said, "If I tell you the truth, you will kill me. And if I give you advice, you won't listen to me anyway."

¹⁶So King Zedekiah secretly promised him, "As surely as the LORD our Creator lives, I will not kill you or hand you over to the men who want you dead."

¹⁷Then Jeremiah said to Zedekiah, "This is what the LORD God of Heaven's Armies, the God of Israel, says: 'If you surrender to the Babylonian officers, you and your family will live, and the city will not be burned down. ¹⁸But if you refuse to surrender, you will not escape! This city will be handed over to the Babylonians, and they will burn it to the ground.'"

**38:1** Hebrew *Jucal*, a variant spelling of Jehucal; see 37:3.   **38:2** Or *Chaldeans*; also in 38:18, 19, 23.
**38:7** Hebrew *the Cushite.*

**38:1**
Jer 21:8
**38:2**
Jer 21:9; 42:17
**38:3**
Jer 21:10; 32:3-5
**38:4**
1 Kgs 18:17-18
Jer 26:11
Amos 7:10
Acts 16:20-21
**38:5**
2 Sam 3:39
**38:6**
Pss 40:2;
69:1-2, 14
Jer 37:15-16
Zech 9:11
Acts 16:24
**38:9**
Jer 37:21; 52:6
**38:13**
Jer 37:21; 39:14-15
**38:14**
1 Kgs 22:16
Jer 21:1-2; 37:17
**38:15**
Luke 22:67-68
**38:16**
Isa 42:5
Jer 37:17
**38:17**
2 Kgs 25:27-30
Ps 80:7, 14
Jer 21:8-10;
27:12, 17
**38:18**
2 Kgs 25:4-10
Jer 27:8; 37:8

---

**38:4, 5** No wonder Judah was in turmoil: The king agreed with everybody. He listened to Jeremiah (37:21); then he agreed Jeremiah should be killed (38:5); and finally he rescued Jeremiah (38:10). Jeremiah was not popular; his words undermined the morale of the army and the people. Zedediah couldn't decide between public opinion and God's will. What is most influential in your life—what others say and think or what God wants?

**38:6** Officials put Jeremiah in a cistern to die. A cistern was a large hole in the ground lined with rocks to collect rainwater. The bottom would have been dark, damp, and, in this case, full of mud. Jeremiah could drown, die of exposure, or starve to death in the cistern.

**38:6** Judah's leaders persecuted Jeremiah repeatedly for faithfully proclaiming God's messages. For 40 years of faithful ministry, he received no acclaim, no love, no popular following. He was beaten, jailed, threatened, and even forced to leave his homeland. Only the pagan Babylonians showed him any respect (39:11, 12). God does not guarantee that his servants will escape persecution,

even when they are faithful. But God does promise that he will be with them and will give them strength to endure (2 Corinthians 1:3-7). As you minister to others, recognize that your service is for God and not just for human approval. God rewards our faithfulness, but not always during our lifetime.

**38:7, 8** The Benjamin Gate was one of Jerusalem's city gates where legal matters were handled. A palace official, Ebed-melech, had access to the king. When Ebed-melech heard of Jeremiah's plight, he went immediately to deal with the injustice.

**38:9-13** Ebed-melech feared God more than people. He alone among the palace officials stood up against the murder plot. His obedience could have cost him his life. Because he obeyed, however, he was spared when Jerusalem fell (39:15-18). You can either go along with the crowd or speak up for God. When someone is treated unkindly or unjustly, for example, reach out to that person with God's love. You may be the only one who does. And, when you are being treated unkindly yourself, be sure to thank God when he sends an "Ebed-melech" your way.

**38:19**
Isa 51:12-13; 57:11
Jer 39:9
John 12:42

**38:20**
Isa 55:3
Jer 7:23; 11:4, 8; 26:13

**38:22**
Jer 6:12; 8:10; 43:6

**38:23**
2 Kgs 25:7
Jer 39:6; 41:10

**38:26**
Jer 37:15-16, 20

**38:27**
1 Sam 10:15-16; 16:2-5

**38:28**
Jer 37:20-21; 39:13-14

**39:1**
2 Kgs 25:1-12

**39:2**
2 Kgs 25:4
Jer 52:7

**39:4**
2 Kgs 25:4
Isa 30:15-16
Jer 52:7
Amos 2:14

**39:5**
Jer 32:4-5; 52:8-9
Lam 4:20

**39:6**
Jer 24:8-10; 34:18-21; 52:10

**39:7**
2 Kgs 25:7
Jer 52:11
Ezek 12:13

**39:8**
2 Kgs 25:9-10
Neh 1:3

**39:9**
2 Kgs 25:11, 20
Jer 52:12-16, 26

**39:10**
2 Kgs 25:12

19"But I am afraid to surrender," the king said, "for the Babylonians may hand me over to the Judeans who have defected to them. And who knows what they will do to me!"

20Jeremiah replied, "You won't be handed over to them if you choose to obey the LORD. Your life will be spared, and all will go well for you. 21But if you refuse to surrender, this is what the LORD has revealed to me: 22All the women left in your palace will be brought out and given to the officers of the Babylonian army. Then the women will taunt you, saying,

'What fine friends you have!
    They have betrayed and misled you.
When your feet sank in the mud,
    they left you to your fate!'

23All your wives and children will be led out to the Babylonians, and you will not escape. You will be seized by the king of Babylon, and this city will be burned down."

24Then Zedekiah said to Jeremiah, "Don't tell anyone you told me this, or you will die! 25My officials may hear that I spoke to you, and they may say, 'Tell us what you and the king were talking about. If you don't tell us, we will kill you.' 26If this happens, just tell them you begged me not to send you back to Jonathan's dungeon, for fear you would die there."

27Sure enough, it wasn't long before the king's officials came to Jeremiah and asked him why the king had called for him. But Jeremiah followed the king's instructions, and they left without finding out the truth. No one had overheard the conversation between Jeremiah and the king. 28And Jeremiah remained a prisoner in the courtyard of the guard until the day Jerusalem was captured.

## The Fall of Jerusalem

**39** In January* of the ninth year of King Zedekiah's reign, King Nebuchadnezzar* came with his army to besiege Jerusalem. 2Two and a half years later, on July 18* in the eleventh year of Zedekiah's reign, the Babylonians broke through the wall, and the city fell. 3All the officers of the Babylonian army came in and sat in triumph at the Middle Gate: Nergal-sharezer of Samgar, and Nebo-sarsekim,* a chief officer, and Nergal-sharezer, the king's adviser, and all the other officers.

4When King Zedekiah and all the soldiers saw that the Babylonians had broken into the city, they fled. They waited for nightfall and then slipped through the gate between the two walls behind the king's garden and headed toward the Jordan Valley.*

5But the Babylonian* troops chased the king and caught him on the plains of Jericho. They took him to King Nebuchadnezzar of Babylon, who was at Riblah in the land of Hamath. There the king of Babylon pronounced judgment upon Zedekiah. 6He made Zedekiah watch as they slaughtered his sons and all the nobles of Judah. 7Then they gouged out Zedekiah's eyes, bound him in bronze chains, and led him away to Babylon.

8Meanwhile, the Babylonians burned Jerusalem, including the palace, and tore down the walls of the city. 9Then Nebuzaradan, the captain of the guard, sent to Babylon the rest of the people who remained in the city as well as those who had defected to him. 10But Nebuzaradan left a few of the poorest people in Judah, and he assigned them vineyards and fields to care for.

**39:1a** Hebrew *in the tenth month,* of the ancient Hebrew lunar calendar. A number of events in Jeremiah can be cross-checked with dates in surviving Babylonian records and related accurately to our modern calendar. This event occurred on January 15, 588 B.C.; see 52:4a and the note there.  **39:1b** Hebrew *Nebuchadrezzar,* a variant spelling of Nebuchadnezzar; also in 39:11.  **39:2** Hebrew *On the ninth day of the fourth month.* This day was July 18, 586 B.C.; also see note on 39:1a.  **39:3** Or *Nergal-sharezer, Samgar-nebo, Sarsekim.*  **39:4** Hebrew *the Arabah.*  **39:5** Or *Chaldean;* similarly in 39:8.

---

**38:27** The officials wanted accurate information, but not God's truth. They wanted to use this information against God, his prophet, and the king. But Jeremiah told the officials only what the king ordered him to say. We must not withhold God's truth from others, but we should withhold information that will be used to bring evil to God's people.

**39:1ff** Zedekiah, son of Josiah and last king of Judah, ruled 11 years, from 597 to 586 B.C. Zedekiah's two older brothers, Jehoahaz and Jehoiakim, and his nephew Jehoiachin ruled before him. When Jehoiachin was exiled to Babylon, Nebuchadnezzar made 21-year-old Mattaniah the king, changing his name to Zedekiah. Zedekiah rebelled against Nebuchadnezzar, who captured him, killed his sons in front of him, and then blinded

him and took him back to Babylon, where he later died (see 2 Kings 24–25; 2 Chronicles 36; and Jeremiah 52).

**39:5** Riblah was 200 miles north of Jerusalem. This was the Babylonian headquarters for ruling the region.

**39:10** Babylon had a shrewd foreign policy toward conquered lands. They deported the rich and powerful, leaving only the very poor in charge, thus making them grateful to their conquerors. This policy assured that conquered populations would be too loyal and too weak to revolt.

## Jeremiah Remains in Judah

¹¹King Nebuchadnezzar had told Nebuzaradan, the captain of the guard, to find Jeremiah. ¹²"See that he isn't hurt," he said. "Look after him well, and give him anything he wants." ¹³So Nebuzaradan, the captain of the guard; Nebushazban, a chief officer; Nergal-sharezer, the king's adviser; and the other officers of Babylon's king ¹⁴sent messengers to bring Jeremiah out of the prison. They put him under the care of Gedaliah son of Ahikam and grandson of Shaphan, who took him back to his home. So Jeremiah stayed in Judah among his own people.

¹⁵The LORD had given the following message to Jeremiah while he was still in prison: ¹⁶"Say to Ebed-melech the Ethiopian,* 'This is what the LORD of Heaven's Armies, the God of Israel, says: I will do to this city everything I have threatened. I will send disaster, not prosperity. You will see its destruction, ¹⁷but I will rescue you from those you fear so much. ¹⁸Because you trusted me, I will give you your life as a reward. I will rescue you and keep you safe. I, the LORD, have spoken!'"

**40** The LORD gave a message to Jeremiah after Nebuzaradan, the captain of the guard, had released him at Ramah. He had found Jeremiah bound in chains among all the other captives of Jerusalem and Judah who were being sent to exile in Babylon.

²The captain of the guard called for Jeremiah and said, "The LORD your God has brought this disaster on this land, ³just as he said he would. For these people have sinned against the LORD and disobeyed him. That is why it happened. ⁴But I am going to take off your chains and let you go. If you want to come with me to Babylon, you are welcome. I will see that you are well cared for. But if you don't want to come, you may stay here. The whole land is before you—go wherever you like. ⁵If you decide to stay, then return to Gedaliah son of Ahikam and grandson of Shaphan. He has been appointed governor of Judah by the king of Babylon. Stay there with the people he rules. But it's up to you; go wherever you like."

Then Nebuzaradan, the captain of the guard, gave Jeremiah some food and money and let him go. ⁶So Jeremiah returned to Gedaliah son of Ahikam at Mizpah, and he lived in Judah with the few who were still left in the land.

## Gedaliah Governs in Judah

⁷The leaders of the Judean guerrilla bands in the countryside heard that the king of Babylon had appointed Gedaliah son of Ahikam as governor over the poor people who were left behind in Judah—the men, women, and children who hadn't been exiled to Babylon. ⁸So they went to see Gedaliah at Mizpah. These included: Ishmael son of Nethaniah, Johanan and Jonathan sons of Kareah, Seraiah son of Tanhumeth, the sons of Ephai the Netophathite, Jezaniah son of the Maacathite, and all their men.

⁹Gedaliah vowed to them that the Babylonians* meant them no harm. "Don't be afraid to serve them. Live in the land and serve the king of Babylon, and all will go well for you," he promised. ¹⁰"As for me, I will stay at Mizpah to represent you before the Babylonians who come to meet with us. Settle in the towns you have taken, and live off the land. Harvest the grapes and summer fruits and olives, and store them away."

**39:16** Hebrew *the Cushite.*　　**40:9** Or *Chaldeans;* also in 40:10.

### Cross-references

**39:11**
Job 5:15-16
Jer 1:8; 15:20-21

**39:12**
1 Pet 3:13

**39:14**
2 Kgs 22:12, 14
Jer 26:24; 40:1-6

**39:16**
Jer 21:10
Zech 1:6

**39:17**
Pss 41:1-2;
50:14-15

**39:18**
Ps 34:22
Jer 17:7-8
Rom 10:11

**40:1**
Eph 6:20

**40:2**
Deut 29:24-28
Jer 22:8-9; 50:7

**40:3**
Dan 9:11

**40:4**
Gen 20:15
Jer 39:11, 12

**40:5**
2 Kgs 25:23

**40:6**
Jer 39:14

**40:7**
2 Kgs 25:23-24
Jer 39:10; 52:16

**40:8**
Jer 41:1

**40:9**
2 Kgs 25:24
Jer 27:11

**40:10**
Jer 35:19; 39:10

---

**39:11, 12** God had promised to rescue Jeremiah from his trouble (1:8). The superstitious Babylonians, who highly respected magicians and fortune-tellers, treated Jeremiah as a seer. Because he had been imprisoned by his own people, they assumed he was a traitor and on their side. They undoubtedly knew he had counseled cooperation with Babylon and predicted a Babylonian victory. So the Babylonians freed Jeremiah and protected him.

**39:13, 14** What a difference there is between Jeremiah's fate and Zedekiah's! Jeremiah was freed; Zedekiah was imprisoned. Jeremiah was saved because of his faith; Zedekiah was destroyed because of his fear. Jeremiah was treated with respect; Zedekiah was treated with contempt. Jeremiah was concerned for the people; Zedekiah was concerned for himself.

**39:17, 18** Ebed-melech had risked his life to save God's prophet Jeremiah (38:7-13). When Babylon conquered Jerusalem, God protected Ebed-melech from the Babylonians. God has special rewards for his faithful people, but not everyone will receive them in this life (see the note on 38:6).

**40–45** These six chapters cover events following Jerusalem's fall to Babylon.

**40:2, 3** The Babylonian captain of the guard, who did not know God, acknowledged that God had given the Babylonians victory. It is strange for people to recognize that God exists and does miracles and yet not personally accept him. Knowing God is more than knowing about him. Be sure you know him personally.

**40:4** Jeremiah was free to go anywhere. In Babylon he would have great comfort and power. In Judah he would continue to face hardship. In Babylon Jeremiah would have been favored by the Babylonians but hated by the Judean exiles. In Judah he would remain poor and unwanted, but the Judean remnant would know he was not a traitor. Jeremiah returned to Judah.

**40:6** Mizpah was a few miles north of Jerusalem. Not thoroughly destroyed by the Babylonians, Mizpah served as a refuge after the destruction of Jerusalem.

40:11
1 Sam 11:1
Isa 11:14; 16:4-5

40:12
Jer 43:5

[11]When the Judeans in Moab, Ammon, Edom, and the other nearby countries heard that the king of Babylon had left a few people in Judah and that Gedaliah was the governor, [12]they began to return to Judah from the places to which they had fled. They stopped at Mizpah to meet with Gedaliah and then went into the Judean countryside to gather a great harvest of grapes and other crops.

### A Plot against Gedaliah

40:13
Jer 25:21; 41:10

[13]Soon after this, Johanan son of Kareah and the other guerrilla leaders came to Gedaliah at Mizpah. [14]They said to him, "Did you know that Baalis, king of Ammon, has sent Ishmael son of Nethaniah to assassinate you?" But Gedaliah refused to believe them.

40:15
1 Sam 26:8
2 Sam 21:17
Jer 42:1-2

[15]Later Johanan had a private conference with Gedaliah and volunteered to kill Ishmael secretly. "Why should we let him come and murder you?" Johanan asked. "What will happen then to the Judeans who have returned? Why should the few of us who are still left be scattered and lost?"

40:16
Matt 10:16

[16]But Gedaliah said to Johanan, "I forbid you to do any such thing, for you are lying about Ishmael."

**EBED-MELECH**

During one of the bleakest moments in Jeremiah's life, God demonstrated his power by providing help from an unexpected source. Ebed-melech, a high-ranking African official in Zedekiah's court, risked his career and perhaps his life to rescue Jeremiah from a muddy cistern. This unsung Ethiopian represents a crowd of quiet heroes throughout Bible history who showed real courage and character. He made the most of his position in life by using it to serve God.

Spineless King Zedekiah had agreed to let Jeremiah's enemies arrange for the prophet's death. Though he had previously consulted with Jeremiah and even arranged for less harsh imprisonment, Zedekiah wavered under pressure. When certain influential voices demanded Jeremiah's life, Zedekiah offered no resistance. The plan involved lowering Jeremiah into an empty cistern and leaving him to die of starvation.

Ebed-melech's response shows us a radical and almost reckless pursuit of justice. He appealed directly to the king who was holding court in a public place. His boldness prodded Zedekiah to reverse his previous decision. Ebed-melech took the king's men, gathered the padding and ropes he would need, and hauled the shivering and slimy prophet out of the pit. The picture wasn't pretty, but the mission succeeded. Jeremiah later had the privilege of informing his Ethiopian rescuer that God would keep him safe during the fall and destruction of Jerusalem.

In whatever place you find yourself in life, continually ask God to help you see and respond to needs that you are uniquely placed to meet. Like Ebed-melech, you may experience fear along the way. But better to fear and act anyway than to live with the disappointment that fear prevented you from serving God and his people.

| | |
|---|---|
| **Strengths and accomplishments** | • Took Jeremiah's case before the king and secured his rescue<br>• Organized the extraction of the prophet from the quagmire-filled cistern<br>• Received God's guarantee of safety during the Babylonian destruction of Jerusalem |
| **Lessons from his life** | • The places we serve in life can often provide us with unique opportunities to serve God and his people<br>• We can trust God and act in spite of our fear<br>• God does not forget those who take a stand for him<br>• One bold person's actions may stem a tide of evil |
| **Vital statistics** | • Where: From Ethiopia, lived in Judah<br>• Occupation: Palace official in Judah<br>• Contemporaries: Jeremiah, Baruch, Zedekiah |
| **Key verse** | "Because you trusted me, I will give you your life as a reward. I will rescue you and keep you safe. I, the LORD, have spoken!" (Jeremiah 39:18). |

Ebed-melech's story is told in Jeremiah 38–39.

---

**40:13–41:3** Gedaliah, appointed governor of Judah, foolishly ignored the warnings of assassination. Ishmael, in the line of David, may have been angry that he had been passed over for leadership. This is similar to the chaotic political situation that Ezra and Nehemiah faced when they returned to rebuild the Temple and the city.

## The Murder of Gedaliah

**41** But in midautumn,* Ishmael son of Nethaniah and grandson of Elishama, who was a member of the royal family and had been one of the king's high officials, went to Mizpah with ten men to meet Gedaliah. While they were eating together, ²Ishmael and his ten men suddenly jumped up, drew their swords, and killed Gedaliah, whom the king of Babylon had appointed governor. ³Ishmael also killed all the Judeans and the Babylonian* soldiers who were with Gedaliah at Mizpah.

⁴The next day, before anyone had heard about Gedaliah's murder, ⁵eighty men arrived from Shechem, Shiloh, and Samaria to worship at the Temple of the LORD. They had shaved off their beards, torn their clothes, and cut themselves, and had brought along grain offerings and frankincense. ⁶Ishmael left Mizpah to meet them, weeping as he went. When he reached them, he said, "Oh, come and see what has happened to Gedaliah!"

⁷But as soon as they were all inside the town, Ishmael and his men killed all but ten of them and threw their bodies into a cistern. ⁸The other ten had talked Ishmael into letting them go by promising to bring him their stores of wheat, barley, olive oil, and honey that they had hidden away. ⁹The cistern where Ishmael dumped the bodies of the men he murdered was the large one dug by King Asa when he fortified Mizpah to protect himself against King Baasha of Israel. Ishmael son of Nethaniah filled it with corpses.

¹⁰Then Ishmael made captives of the king's daughters and the other people who had been left under Gedaliah's care in Mizpah by Nebuzaradan, the captain of the guard. Taking them with him, he started back toward the land of Ammon.

¹¹But when Johanan son of Kareah and the other guerrilla leaders heard about Ishmael's crimes, ¹²they took all their men and set out to stop him. They caught up with him at the large pool near Gibeon. ¹³The people Ishmael had captured shouted for joy when they saw Johanan and the other guerrilla leaders. ¹⁴And all the captives from Mizpah escaped and began to help Johanan. ¹⁵Meanwhile, Ishmael and eight of his men escaped from Johanan into the land of Ammon.

¹⁶Then Johanan son of Kareah and the other guerrilla leaders took all the people they had rescued in Gibeon—the soldiers, women, children, and court officials* whom Ishmael had captured after he killed Gedaliah. ¹⁷They took them all to the village of Geruth-kimham near Bethlehem, where they prepared to leave for Egypt. ¹⁸They were afraid of what the Babylonians* would do when they heard that Ishmael had killed Gedaliah, the governor appointed by the Babylonian king.

## Warning to Stay in Judah

**42** Then all the guerrilla leaders, including Johanan son of Kareah and Jezaniah* son of Hoshaiah, and all the people, from the least to the greatest, approached ²Jeremiah the prophet. They said, "Please pray to the LORD your God for us. As you can see, we are only a tiny remnant compared to what we were before. ³Pray that the LORD your God will show us what to do and where to go."

⁴"All right," Jeremiah replied. "I will pray to the LORD your God, as you have asked, and I will tell you everything he says. I will hide nothing from you."

⁵Then they said to Jeremiah, "May the LORD your God be a faithful witness against us if we refuse to obey whatever he tells us to do! ⁶Whether we like it or not, we will obey the LORD our God to whom we are sending you with our plea. For if we obey him, everything will turn out well for us."

⁷Ten days later the LORD gave his reply to Jeremiah. ⁸So he called for Johanan son of Kareah and the other guerrilla leaders, and for all the people, from the least to the greatest. ⁹He said to them, "You sent me to the LORD, the God of Israel, with your request, and this is his reply:

**41:1** 2 Kgs 25:25 Jer 39:14; 40:5-8, 13-14
**41:2** 2 Sam 3:27; 20:8-10 Pss 41:9; 109:5 John 13:18
**41:5** Deut 14:1 Josh 18:1 1 Kgs 16:24 Ps 78:60 Jer 16:6
**41:6** Jer 50:4
**41:7** Isa 59:7 Ezek 22:27; 33:24
**41:9** 1 Sam 13:6 1 Kgs 15:17-22 2 Chr 16:1-6 Heb 11:37-38
**41:10** Jer 40:11-12; 43:6
**41:11** Jer 40:7-8, 13-16
**41:12** 2 Sam 2:13
**41:15** Prov 28:17
**41:16** Jer 42:8, 14; 43:4-7
**41:17** 2 Sam 19:37-38
**41:18** Isa 57:11 Luke 12:4-5
**42:1** Jer 40:8, 12-13
**42:2** Deut 28:62 Isa 1:9 Acts 8:24
**42:3** Ps 86:11 Prov 3:6 Mic 4:2
**42:4** Ps 40:10 Jer 23:28
**42:5** Mic 1:2
**42:6** Exod 24:7 Deut 5:29
**42:9** 2 Kgs 22:15

**41:1** Hebrew *in the seventh month*, of the ancient Hebrew lunar calendar. This month occurred within the months of October and November 586 B.C; also see note on 39:1a.   **41:3** Or *Chaldean.*   **41:16** Or *eunuchs.*   **41:18** Or *Chaldeans.*   **42:1** Greek version reads *Azariah;* compare 43:2.

---

**41:4-9** The 80 men came from three cities of the northern kingdom to worship in Jerusalem. Ishmael probably killed them for the money and food they were carrying. Without a king, with no law and no loyalty to God, Judah was subjected to complete anarchy.

**41:16, 17** Johanan and his group were already on their way to Egypt, headed south from Gibeon, stopping first at Geruth-kimham, near Bethlehem. Their visit to Jeremiah (42:1-6) was hypocritical, as Jeremiah later told them (42:20).

**42:5, 6** Johanan and his associates spoke their own curse; Jeremiah merely elaborated on it. It was a tragic mistake to ask for God's guidance with no intention of following it. Be sure never to ask God for something that you know in your heart you really do not want. It is better not to pray than to pray hypocritically. God cannot be deceived.

**42:10**
Jer 31:28
Hos 11:8
Joel 2:13
Jon 3:10; 4:2

**42:11**
Ps 46:7, 11
Isa 43:5
Jer 41:18
Rom 8:31

**42:12**
Ps 106:45-46
Prov 16:7

**42:16**
Jer 44:13, 27

**42:17**
Jer 44:13-14, 28

**42:18**
2 Chr 36:16-19
Jer 29:18-19;
39:1-9

**42:19**
Deut 17:16
Ezek 2:5

**42:20**
Ezek 14:3

**42:21**
Deut 11:26
Ezek 2:7

**42:22**
Jer 43:11
Hos 9:6

**43:2**
2 Chr 36:13
Jer 5:12-13; 36:4,
10, 32; 38:4; 42:5

**43:4**
Jer 42:5-6, 10-12

**43:5**
Jer 40:11-12

**43:6**
Jer 40:7

**43:8**
Jer 44:1; 46:14
Ezek 30:18

**43:10**
Jer 25:8-9, 11;
27:6; 46:13

**43:11**
Isa 19:1-25
Ezek 29:19-20

**43:12**
Jer 46:25
Ezek 30:13

10"Stay here in this land. If you do, I will build you up and not tear you down; I will plant you and not uproot you. For I am sorry about all the punishment I have had to bring upon you. 11Do not fear the king of Babylon anymore,' says the LORD. 'For I am with you and will save you and rescue you from his power. 12I will be merciful to you by making him kind, so he will let you stay here in your land.'

13"But if you refuse to obey the LORD your God, and if you say, 'We will not stay here;' 14instead, we will go to Egypt where we will be free from war, the call to arms, and hunger,' 15then hear the LORD's message to the remnant of Judah. This is what the LORD of Heaven's Armies, the God of Israel, says: 'If you are determined to go to Egypt and live there, 16the very war and famine you fear will catch up to you, and you will die there. 17That is the fate awaiting every one of you who insists on going to live in Egypt. Yes, you will die from war, famine, and disease. None of you will escape the disaster I will bring upon you there.'

18"This is what the LORD of Heaven's Armies, the God of Israel, says: 'Just as my anger and fury have been poured out on the people of Jerusalem, so they will be poured out on you when you enter Egypt. You will be an object of damnation, horror, cursing, and mockery. And you will never see your homeland again.'

19"Listen, you remnant of Judah. The LORD has told you: 'Do not go to Egypt!' Don't forget this warning I have given you today. 20For you were not being honest when you sent me to pray to the LORD your God for you. You said, 'Just tell us what the LORD our God says, and we will do it!' 21And today I have told you exactly what he said, but you will not obey the LORD your God any better now than you have in the past. 22So you can be sure that you will die from war, famine, and disease in Egypt, where you insist on going."

## Jeremiah Taken to Egypt

**43** When Jeremiah had finished giving this message from the LORD their God to all the people, 2Azariah son of Hoshaiah and Johanan son of Kareah and all the other proud men said to Jeremiah, "You lie! The LORD our God hasn't forbidden us to go to Egypt! 3Baruch son of Neriah has convinced you to say this, because he wants us to stay here and be killed by the Babylonians* or be carried off into exile."

4So Johanan and the other guerrilla leaders and all the people refused to obey the LORD's command to stay in Judah. 5Johanan and the other leaders took with them all the people who had returned from the nearby countries to which they had fled. 6In the crowd were men, women, and children, the king's daughters, and all those whom Nebuzaradan, the captain of the guard, had left with Gedaliah. The prophet Jeremiah and Baruch were also included. 7The people refused to obey the voice of the LORD and went to Egypt, going as far as the city of Tahpanhes.

8Then at Tahpanhes, the LORD gave another message to Jeremiah. He said, 9"While the people of Judah are watching, take some large rocks and bury them under the pavement stones at the entrance of Pharaoh's palace here in Tahpanhes. 10Then say to the people of Judah, 'This is what the LORD of Heaven's Armies, the God of Israel, says: I will certainly bring my servant Nebuchadnezzar,* king of Babylon, here to Egypt. I will set his throne over these stones that I have hidden. He will spread his royal canopy over them. 11And when he comes, he will destroy the land of Egypt. He will bring death to those destined for death, captivity to those destined for captivity, and war to those destined for war. 12He will set fire to the temples of Egypt's gods; he will burn the temples and carry the idols away as plunder. He will pick clean the land of Egypt as a shepherd picks fleas from his cloak. And he himself will leave unharmed. 13He will break down the sacred pillars standing in the temple of the sun* in Egypt, and he will burn down the temples of Egypt's gods.'"

**43:3** Or *Chaldeans.*   **43:10** Hebrew *Nebuchadrezzar,* a variant spelling of Nebuchadnezzar.   **43:13** Or *in Heliopolis.*

---

**43:1-3** Johanan and his tiny band had come to Jeremiah for God's approval of their plan, not for God's direction. This is a recurring problem for some of us—seeking God's approval of our desires rather than asking him for guidance. It is not good to make plans apart from God's guidance, and it is not good to pray unless we are willing to accept God's answer.

**43:4-7** Afraid to obey the Lord, the people headed for Egypt, even forcing Jeremiah to go with them. (They thought that perhaps God would spare them if Jeremiah was with them.) Jeremiah had served as a prophet for 40 years. Many of his words had

already come true, and he had turned down an offer to live comfortably in Babylon, returning instead to his beloved people. But the people still rejected Jeremiah's advice. The response of our audience is not necessarily a measure of our success. Jeremiah was doing all God asked, but he had been called to minister to a very stubborn group of people.

**43:10-13** Nebuchadnezzar invaded Egypt in 568–567 B.C. Like Judah, Egypt rebelled against him and was quickly crushed. So much for the great empire on which Judah had constantly placed its hopes!

## Judgment for Idolatry

**44** This is the message Jeremiah received concerning the Judeans living in northern Egypt in the cities of Migdol, Tahpanhes, and Memphis,* and in southern Egypt* as well: ²"This is what the LORD of Heaven's Armies, the God of Israel, says: You saw the calamity I brought on Jerusalem and all the towns of Judah. They now lie deserted and in ruins. ³They provoked my anger with all their wickedness. They burned incense and worshiped other gods—gods that neither they nor you nor any of your ancestors had ever even known.

⁴"Again and again I sent my servants, the prophets, to plead with them, 'Don't do these horrible things that I hate so much.' ⁵But my people would not listen or turn back from their wicked ways. They kept on burning incense to these gods. ⁶And so my fury boiled over and fell like fire on the towns of Judah and into the streets of Jerusalem, and they are still a desolate ruin today.

⁷"And now the LORD God of Heaven's Armies, the God of Israel, asks you: Why are you destroying yourselves? For not one of you will survive—not a man, woman, or child among you who has come here from Judah, not even the babies in your arms. ⁸Why provoke my anger by burning incense to the idols you have made here in Egypt? You will only destroy yourselves and make yourselves an object of cursing and mockery for all the nations of the earth. ⁹Have you forgotten the sins of your ancestors, the sins of the kings and queens of Judah, and the sins you and your wives committed in Judah and Jerusalem? ¹⁰To this very hour you have shown no remorse or reverence. No one has chosen to follow my word and the decrees I gave to you and your ancestors before you.

¹¹"Therefore, this is what the LORD of Heaven's Armies, the God of Israel, says: I am determined to destroy every one of you! ¹²I will take this remnant of Judah—those who were determined to come here and live in Egypt—and I will consume them. They will fall here in Egypt, killed by war and famine. All will die, from the least to the greatest. They will be an object of damnation, horror, cursing, and mockery. ¹³I will punish them in Egypt just as I punished them in Jerusalem, by war, famine, and disease. ¹⁴Of that remnant who fled to Egypt, hoping someday to return to Judah, there will be no survivors. Even though they long to return home, only a handful will do so."

¹⁵Then all the women present and all the men who knew that their wives had burned incense to idols—a great crowd of all the Judeans living in northern Egypt and southern Egypt*—answered Jeremiah, ¹⁶"We will not listen to your messages from the LORD! ¹⁷We will do whatever we want. We will burn incense and pour out liquid offerings to the Queen of Heaven just as much as we like—just as we, and our ancestors, and our kings and officials have always done in the towns of Judah and in the streets of Jerusalem. For in those days we had plenty to eat, and we were well off and had no troubles! ¹⁸But ever since we quit burning incense to the Queen of Heaven and stopped worshiping her with liquid offerings, we have been in great trouble and have been dying from war and famine."

**44:1a** Hebrew *Noph.*    **44:1b** Hebrew *in Pathros.*    **44:15** Hebrew *in Egypt, in Pathros.*

### Cross references

**44:1**
Isa 19:13
Jer 43:7; 46:14

**44:2**
Isa 6:11
Mic 3:12

**44:3**
Deut 13:6; 32:17
Jer 32:30-32

**44:4**
Jer 32:34-35; 35:15
Ezek 8:10
Zech 7:7

**44:6**
Isa 51:17-20
Jer 7:17, 34

**44:7**
Jer 9:21
Ezek 33:11

**44:8**
1 Kgs 9:7-8
2 Kgs 17:15-17
2 Chr 7:19-20
Jer 11:12, 17
1 Cor 10:21-22

**44:9**
Jer 7:9-10, 17-18

**44:10**
Jer 6:15; 8:12

**44:11**
Lev 26:17
Amos 9:4

**44:12**
Isa 65:15
Jer 42:15-18, 22

**44:13**
Jer 24:10

**44:14**
Isa 10:20
Rom 9:27

**44:15**
Jer 5:1-5

**44:16**
Jer 8:6; 13:10

**44:17**
Exod 16:3
2 Kgs 17:16
Jer 7:18
Hos 2:5-9
Phil 3:19

**44:18**
Num 11:5-6
Mal 3:13-15

---

## ESCAPE TO EGYPT

With Judah in turmoil after the murder of Gedaliah, the people turned to Jeremiah for guidance. Jeremiah had God's answer, "Stay in this land." But the leaders disobeyed and went to Egypt, taking Jeremiah with them. In Egypt, Jeremiah told them they were in grave danger.

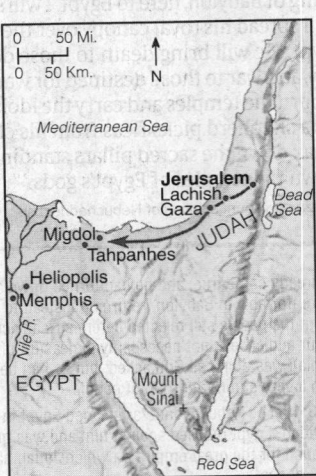

**44:1ff** This message, given in 580 B.C. while Jeremiah was in Egypt against his will, reminded the people that their idolatry had brought destruction on their land. Jeremiah told them that they would never return to Judah because the escape to Egypt had been against God's advice (42:9ff). But the people refused to learn any lessons from all the destruction their sins had caused.

**44:9, 10** When we forget a lesson or refuse to learn it, we risk repeating our mistakes. The people of Judah struggled with this; to forget their former sins was to repeat them. To fail to learn from failure is to assure future failure. Your past is your school of experience. Let your past mistakes point you to God's way.

**44:15-18** The farther we drift from God, the more confused our thinking becomes. Whatever spiritual life was left in the Israelites when they went to Egypt was lost as they sank into the depths of idolatry. (For more information on the "Queen of Heaven," see the note on 7:18.) The escape to Egypt had brought a change in their pagan worship habits, and they blamed their troubles on their neglect of their idols. But idol worship had started all their problems in the first place. The people refused to recognize the true source of their problems—departure from God's leading.

**44:19**
Num 30:6-7

**44:21**
Jer 11:13; 14:10
Ezek 8:10-11;
16:24
Hos 7:2

**44:22**
Isa 7:13
Jer 4:4; 25:11, 18,
38; 30:14

**44:23**
1 Kgs 9:9
Jer 7:13-15; 40:3
Dan 9:11-12

**44:24**
Jer 43:7

**44:25**
Ezek 20:39
Jas 1:13-15

**44:26**
Gen 22:16
Deut 32:40
Ps 50:16-17
Heb 6:13, 18

**44:27**
Jer 1:10

**44:28**
Isa 14:27; 46:9-10
Zech 1:5-6

**44:29**
Isa 40:8
Matt 24:15-16, 32

**44:30**
2 Kgs 25:4-7
Jer 46:25
Ezek 29:3

19"Besides," the women added, "do you suppose that we were burning incense and pouring out liquid offerings to the Queen of Heaven, and making cakes marked with her image, without our husbands knowing it and helping us? Of course not!"

20Then Jeremiah said to all of them, men and women alike, who had given him that answer, 21"Do you think the Lord did not know that you and your ancestors, your kings and officials, and all the people were burning incense to idols in the towns of Judah and in the streets of Jerusalem? 22It was because the Lord could no longer bear all the disgusting things you were doing that he made your land an object of cursing—a desolate ruin without inhabitants—as it is today. 23All these terrible things happened to you because you have burned incense to idols and sinned against the Lord. You have refused to obey him and have not followed his instructions, his decrees, and his laws."

24Then Jeremiah said to them all, including the women, "Listen to this message from the Lord, all you citizens of Judah who live in Egypt. 25This is what the Lord of Heaven's Armies, the God of Israel, says: 'You and your wives have said, "We will keep our promises to burn incense and pour out liquid offerings to the Queen of Heaven," and you have proved by your actions that you meant it. So go ahead and carry out your promises and vows to her!'

26"But listen to this message from the Lord, all you Judeans now living in Egypt: 'I have sworn by my great name,' says the Lord, 'that my name will no longer be spoken by any of the Judeans in the land of Egypt. None of you may invoke my name or use this oath: "As surely as the Sovereign Lord lives." 27For I will watch over you to bring you disaster and not good. Everyone from Judah who is now living in Egypt will suffer war and famine until all of you are dead. 28Only a small number will escape death and return to Judah from Egypt. Then all those who came to Egypt will find out whose words are true—mine or theirs!

29"'And this is the proof I give you,' says the Lord, 'that all I have threatened will happen to you and that I will punish you here.' 30This is what the Lord says: 'I will turn Pharaoh Hophra, king of Egypt, over to his enemies who want to kill him, just as I turned King Zedekiah of Judah over to King Nebuchadnezzar* of Babylon.'"

### A Message for Baruch

**45:1**
Jer 25:1;
36:4,18, 32

**45:3**
Ps 6:6
2 Cor 4:1, 16
Gal 6:9

**45:4**
Jer 18:7-10

**45:5**
Isa 66:16
Matt 6:25, 31-32
Rom 12:16

**45** The prophet Jeremiah gave a message to Baruch son of Neriah in the fourth year of the reign of Jehoiakim son of Josiah,* after Baruch had written down everything Jeremiah had dictated to him. He said, 2"This is what the Lord, the God of Israel, says to you, Baruch: 3You have said, 'I am overwhelmed with trouble! Haven't I had enough pain already? And now the Lord has added more! I am worn out from sighing and can find no rest.'

4"Baruch, this is what the Lord says: 'I will destroy this nation that I built. I will uproot what I planted. 5Are you seeking great things for yourself? Don't do it! I will bring great disaster upon all these people; but I will give you your life as a reward wherever you go. I, the Lord, have spoken!'"

### B. GOD'S JUDGMENT ON THE NATIONS (46:1—52:34)

All of Jeremiah's prophecies against foreign nations have been grouped together. Many of the people in these nations assumed that they were free from judgment and punishment for their sin. Following these prophecies is a historical appendix recounting the fall of Jerusalem. Just as Jerusalem received its punishment, these nations were certain to receive theirs as well. Those today who think that judgment will never touch them are forewarned.

**44:30** Hebrew *Nebuchadrezzar*, a variant spelling of Nebuchadnezzar.    **45:1** The fourth year of Jehoiakim's reign was 605 B.C.

---

When calamity forces you to examine your life, take a close look at God's instructions for you and be willing to humbly apply what you find there.

**44:28** After Jeremiah's forced move to Egypt, there is no word in the Bible about the events in the rest of his life.

**44:30** Pharaoh Hophra ruled Egypt from 588 to 569 B.C. and was killed by Ahmose, one of his generals, who was then crowned in his place.

**45:1ff** The event relating to this chapter is recorded in 36:1-8. The chapter was written in 605–604 B.C. Baruch was the scribe who recorded Jeremiah's words on a scroll.

**45:5** Baruch had long been serving this unpopular prophet, writing his book of struggles and judgments, and now he was upset. God told Baruch to take his eyes off himself and whatever rewards he thought he deserved. If Baruch did this, God would protect him. It is easy to lose the joy of serving our God when we take our eyes off him. The more we look away from God's purposes toward our own sacrifices, the more frustrated we will become. As you serve God, beware of focusing on what you are giving up. When this happens, ask God's forgiveness; then redirect your attention to the incomparable privilege of serving God.

## 1. Prophecies about foreign nations

**46** The following messages were given to Jeremiah the prophet from the LORD concerning foreign nations.

46:1
Jer 1:10
Ezek 29-32

### Messages about Egypt

2 This message concerning Egypt was given in the fourth year of the reign of Jehoiakim son of Josiah, the king of Judah, on the occasion of the battle of Carchemish* when Pharaoh Neco, king of Egypt, and his army were defeated beside the Euphrates River by King Nebuchadnezzar* of Babylon.

46:2
2 Kgs 23:29
2 Chr 35:20

3 "Prepare your shields,
   and advance into battle!

46:3
Joel 3:9

4 Harness the horses,
   and mount the stallions.
Take your positions.
   Put on your helmets.
Sharpen your spears,
   and prepare your armor.

5 But what do I see?
   The Egyptian army flees in terror.
The bravest of its fighting men run
   without a backward glance.
They are terrorized at every turn,"
   says the LORD.

46:5
Isa 42:17
Jer 6:25; 49:29
Ezek 39:18

6 "The swiftest runners cannot flee;
   the mightiest warriors cannot escape.
By the Euphrates River to the north,
   they stumble and fall.

46:6
Isa 30:16
Dan 11:18

7 "Who is this, rising like the Nile at floodtime,
   overflowing all the land?
8 It is the Egyptian army,
   overflowing all the land,
boasting that it will cover the earth like a flood,
   destroying cities and their people.

46:8
Isa 10:13; 37:24

9 Charge, you horses and chariots;
   attack, you mighty warriors of Egypt!
Come, all you allies from Ethiopia, Libya, and Lydia*
   who are skilled with the shield and bow!

46:9
Nah 2:4; 3:9

10 For this is the day of the Lord, the LORD of Heaven's Armies,
   a day of vengeance on his enemies.
The sword will devour until it is satisfied,
   yes, until it is drunk with your blood!
The Lord, the LORD of Heaven's Armies, will receive a sacrifice today
   in the north country beside the Euphrates River.

46:10
Isa 31:8; 34:6
Zeph 1:7

11 "Go up to Gilead to get medicine,
   O virgin daughter of Egypt!
But your many treatments
   will bring you no healing.

46:11
Jer 8:22; 30:13
Ezek 30:21-26
Nah 3:19

46:2a This event occurred in 605 B.C., during the fourth year of Jehoiakim's reign (according to the calendar system in which the new year begins in the spring). 46:2b Hebrew *Nebuchadrezzar*, a variant spelling of Nebuchadnezzar; also in 46:13, 26. 46:9 Hebrew *from Cush, Put, and Lud.*

---

46:1ff In this chapter, we gain several insights about God and his plan for this world. (1) Although God chose Israel for a special purpose, he loves all people and wants all to come to him. (2) God is holy and will not tolerate sin. (3) God's judgments are not based on prejudice and a desire for revenge but on fairness and justice. (4) God does not delight in judgment but in salvation. (5) God is impartial—he judges everyone by the same standard.

46:2 At the battle of Carchemish in 605 B.C., Babylon and Egypt, the two major world powers after Assyria's fall, clashed.

The Babylonians entered Carchemish by surprise and defeated Egypt. This battle, which passed world leadership to Babylon, was Nebuchadnezzar's first victory, establishing him in his new position as king of the Babylonian Empire. With Egypt's power declining, it was both poor strategy and disobedience to God for Judah to form an alliance with Egypt.

46:9 The soldiers from Ethiopia and Libya were from eastern and northern Africa. The men of Lydia may have been from Greece.

46:12
Jer 2:36
Nah 3:8-10

12 The nations have heard of your shame.
    The earth is filled with your cries of despair.
    Your mightiest warriors will run into each other
        and fall down together."

46:13
Isa 19:1
Jer 43:10-11

13 Then the LORD gave the prophet Jeremiah this message about King Nebuchadnezzar's plans to attack Egypt.

46:14
Jer 44:1
Nah 2:13

14 "Shout it out in Egypt!
    Publish it in the cities of Migdol, Memphis,* and Tahpanhes!
    Mobilize for battle,
        for the sword will devour everyone around you.

46:15
Pss 18:39; 68:1-2

15 Why have your warriors fallen?
    They cannot stand, for the LORD has knocked them down.

46:16
Lev 26:36-37
Jer 51:9

16 They stumble and fall over each other
    and say among themselves,
'Come, let's go back to our people,
    to the land of our birth.
    Let's get away from the sword of the enemy!'

46:17
1 Kgs 20:10-11
Isa 19:11-16

17 There they will say,
    'Pharaoh, the king of Egypt, is a loudmouth
        who missed his opportunity!'

46:18
1 Kgs 18:42
Ps 89:12
Jer 48:15

18 "As surely as I live," says the King,
    whose name is the LORD of Heaven's Armies,
    "one is coming against Egypt
        who is as tall as Mount Tabor,
        or as Mount Carmel by the sea!

46:19
Isa 20:4
Ezek 30:13

19 Pack up! Get ready to leave for exile,
    you citizens of Egypt!
The city of Memphis will be destroyed,
    without a single inhabitant.
20 Egypt is as sleek as a beautiful young cow,
    but a horsefly from the north is on its way!
21 Egypt's mercenaries have become like fattened calves.
    They, too, will turn and run,
    for it is a day of great disaster for Egypt,
        a time of great punishment.
22 Egypt flees, silent as a serpent gliding away.
    The invading army marches in;
        they come against her with axes like woodsmen.
23 They will cut down her people like trees," says the LORD,
    "for they are more numerous than locusts.
24 Egypt will be humiliated;
    she will be handed over to people from the north."

46:25
Isa 20:5-6
Jer 43:12-13
Ezek 30:13-16

46:26
Jer 44:30
Ezek 29:8-14;
32:11

46:27
Isa 41:13-14
Jer 23:3-4;
30:10-11; 50:19

25 The LORD of Heaven's Armies, the God of Israel, says: "I will punish Amon, the god of Thebes,* and all the other gods of Egypt. I will punish its rulers and Pharaoh, too, and all who trust in him. 26 I will hand them over to those who want them killed—to King Nebuchadnezzar of Babylon and his army. But afterward the land will recover from the ravages of war. I, the LORD, have spoken!

27 "But do not be afraid, Jacob, my servant;
    do not be dismayed, Israel.
For I will bring you home again from distant lands,
    and your children will return from their exile.

46:14 Hebrew *Noph*; also in 46:19.   46:25 Hebrew *of No.*

---

46:17 The Egyptian pharaoh was a "loudmouth" who "missed his opportunity" because, although he had come to help Jerusalem, he beat a hasty retreat when the Babylonians turned on him. Jeremiah had prophesied that Pharaoh Hophra would be killed by his enemies (44:30). This was fulfilled nearly 20 years later when his co-regent Ahmose led a revolt.

Israel* will return to a life of peace and quiet,
    and no one will terrorize them.
28 Do not be afraid, Jacob, my servant,
    for I am with you," says the LORD.
"I will completely destroy the nations to which I have exiled you,
    but I will not completely destroy you.
I will discipline you, but with justice;
    I cannot let you go unpunished."

**46:28**
Ps 46:7
Isa 43:2
Jer 10:24
Amos 9:8-9

## A Message about Philistia

**47** This is the LORD's message to the prophet Jeremiah concerning the Philistines of Gaza, before it was captured by the Egyptian army. 2 This is what the LORD says:

**47:1**
Jer 25:17, 20
Amos 1:6
Zeph 2:4

"A flood is coming from the north
    to overflow the land.
It will destroy the land and everything in it—
    cities and people alike.
People will scream in terror,
    and everyone in the land will wail.
3 Hear the clatter of stallions' hooves
    and the rumble of wheels as the chariots rush by.
Terrified fathers run madly,
    without a backward glance at their helpless children.

**47:2**
Isa 14:31

4 "The time has come for the Philistines to be destroyed,
    along with their allies from Tyre and Sidon.
Yes, the LORD is destroying the remnant of the Philistines,
    those colonists from the island of Crete.*
5 Gaza will be humiliated, its head shaved bald;
    Ashkelon will lie silent.
You remnant from the Mediterranean coast,*
    how long will you lament and mourn?

**47:4**
Gen 10:13-14
Isa 14:31; 23:5
Amos 9:7

**47:5**
Jer 25:19-20
Amos 1:7-8
Zeph 2:4, 7
Zech 9:5

6 "Now, O sword of the LORD,
    when will you be at rest again?
Go back into your sheath;
    rest and be still.

**47:6**
Jer 12:12

7 "But how can it be still
    when the LORD has sent it on a mission?
For the city of Ashkelon
    and the people living along the sea
    must be destroyed."

**47:7**
Ezek 14:17
Mic 6:9

## A Message about Moab

**48** This message was given concerning Moab. This is what the LORD of Heaven's Armies, the God of Israel, says:

**48:1**
Num 32:37-38
Jer 48:22-23
Ezek 25:9-10

"What sorrow awaits the city of Nebo;
    it will soon lie in ruins.
The city of Kiriathaim will be humiliated and captured;
    the fortress will be humiliated and broken down.
2 No one will ever brag about Moab again,
    for in Heshbon there is a plot to destroy her.

**48:2**
Isa 15:4-5;
16:13-14

**46:27** Hebrew *Jacob*. See note on 5:20.    **47:4** Hebrew *from Caphtor*.    **47:5** Hebrew *the plain*.

---

**46:28** God punished his people in order to bring them back to himself, and he punishes us to correct and purify us. No one welcomes punishment, but we should all welcome its results: correction and purity.

**47:1** Located on the coastal plain next to Judah, Philistia had always been a thorn in Israel's side. The two nations battled constantly. Other prophets who spoke against Philistia include Isaiah (14:28-32), Ezekiel (25:15-17), Amos (1:6-8), and Zephaniah (2:4-7).

**48:1** The Moabites were descendants of Lot through an incestuous relationship with one of his daughters (Genesis 19:30-37). They led the Israelites into idolatry (Numbers 25:1-3) and joined the bands of raiders Nebuchadnezzar sent into Judah in 602 B.C. They were later conquered by Babylon and disappeared as a nation.

'Come,' they say, 'we will cut her off from being a nation.'
The town of Madmen,* too, will be silenced;
the sword will follow you there.

³ Listen to the cries from Horonaim,
cries of devastation and great destruction.

⁴ All Moab is destroyed.
Her little ones will cry out.*

⁵ Her refugees weep bitterly,
climbing the slope to Luhith.
They cry out in terror,
descending the slope to Horonaim.

⁶ Flee for your lives!
Hide* in the wilderness!

⁷ Because you have trusted in your wealth and skill,
you will be taken captive.
Your god Chemosh, with his priests and officials,
will be hauled off to distant lands!

⁸ "All the towns will be destroyed,
and no one will escape—
either on the plateaus or in the valleys,
for the LORD has spoken.

⁹ Oh, that Moab had wings
so she could fly away,*
for her towns will be left empty,
with no one living in them.

¹⁰ Cursed are those who refuse to do the LORD's work,
who hold back their swords from shedding blood!

¹¹ "From his earliest history, Moab has lived in peace,
never going into exile.
He is like wine that has been allowed to settle.
He has not been poured from flask to flask,
and he is now fragrant and smooth.

¹² But the time is coming soon," says the LORD,
"when I will send men to pour him from his jar.
They will pour him out,
then shatter the jar!

¹³ At last Moab will be ashamed of his idol Chemosh,
as the people of Israel were ashamed of their gold calf at Bethel.*

¹⁴ "You used to boast, 'We are heroes,
mighty men of war.'

¹⁵ But now Moab and his towns will be destroyed.
His most promising youth are doomed to slaughter,"
says the King, whose name is the LORD of Heaven's Armies.

¹⁶ "Destruction is coming fast for Moab;
calamity threatens ominously.

¹⁷ You friends of Moab,
weep for him and cry!
See how the strong scepter is broken,
how the beautiful staff is shattered!

**48:5**
Isa 15:5

**48:7**
Num 21:29
Jer 9:23

**48:8**
Josh 13:10, 17, 21

**48:9**
Isa 16:2

**48:10**
1 Kgs 20:42

**48:11**
Zeph 1:12
Zech 1:15

**48:13**
1 Kgs 12:29
Isa 45:16
Hos 10:6

**48:14**
Ps 33:16-17
Isa 10:13-16

**48:15**
Jer 46:18; 50:27

**48:16**
Isa 13:22

**48:17**
Isa 14:5

48:2 *Madmen* sounds like the Hebrew word for "silence"; it should not be confused with the English word *madmen*. 48:4 Greek version reads *Her cries are heard as far away as Zoar.* 48:6 Or *Hide like a wild donkey*; or *Hide like a juniper shrub*; or *Be like* [the town of] *Aroer. The meaning of the Hebrew is uncertain.* 48:9 Or *Put salt on Moab, / for she will be laid waste.* 48:13 Hebrew *ashamed when they trusted in Bethel.*

**48:7** Chemosh was the main god of the nation of Moab (Numbers 21:29), and child sacrifice was an important part of his worship (2 Kings 3:26, 27). God's judgment made it clear that human-made resources and gods are no match for the Lord of Heaven's Armies.

**48:13** After Israel divided into northern and southern kingdoms, the northern kingdom set up gold calf idols in Bethel and Dan to keep people from going to worship in Jerusalem, capital of the southern kingdom (1 Kings 12:25-29).

18 "Come down from your glory
    and sit in the dust, you people of Dibon,
  for those who destroy Moab will shatter Dibon, too.
    They will tear down all your towers.
19 You people of Aroer,
    stand beside the road and watch.
  Shout to those who flee from Moab,
    'What has happened there?'

20 "And the reply comes back,
    'Moab lies in ruins, disgraced;
      weep and wail!
  Tell it by the banks of the Arnon River:
    Moab has been destroyed!'
21 Judgment has been poured out on the towns of the plateau—
    on Holon and Jahaz* and Mephaath,
22 on Dibon and Nebo and Beth-diblathaim,
23   on Kiriathaim and Beth-gamul and Beth-meon,
24 on Kerioth and Bozrah—
    all the towns of Moab, far and near.

25 "The strength of Moab has ended.
    His arm has been broken," says the LORD.
26 "Let him stagger and fall like a drunkard,
    for he has rebelled against the LORD.
  Moab will wallow in his own vomit,
    ridiculed by all.
27 Did you not ridicule the people of Israel?
    Were they caught in the company of thieves
    that you should despise them as you do?

28 "You people of Moab,
    flee from your towns and live in the caves.
  Hide like doves that nest
    in the clefts of the rocks.
29 We have all heard of the pride of Moab,
    for his pride is very great.
  We know of his lofty pride,
    his arrogance, and his haughty heart.
30 I know about his insolence,"
    says the LORD,
  "but his boasts are empty—
    as empty as his deeds.
31 So now I wail for Moab;
    yes, I will mourn for Moab.
  My heart is broken for the men of Kir-hareseth.*

32 "You people of Sibmah, rich in vineyards,
    I will weep for you even more than I did for Jazer.
  Your spreading vines once reached as far as the Dead Sea,*
    but the destroyer has stripped you bare!
  He has harvested your grapes and summer fruits.
33 Joy and gladness are gone from fruitful Moab.
    The presses yield no wine.

**48:18** Josh 13:9, 17; Isa 47:1

**48:19** Josh 12:2

**48:20** Num 21:13; Isa 16:7

**48:21** Josh 13:18; Isa 15:4

**48:23** Josh 13:19

**48:24** Amos 2:2

**48:25** Pss 10:15; 75:10; Zech 1:19-21

**48:27** Lam 2:15-17; Zeph 2:8

**48:28** Ps 55:6; Song 2:14; Isa 2:19

**48:29** Ps 138:6; Isa 16:6; Zeph 2:8

**48:31** Isa 15:5; 16:7, 11

**48:32** Isa 16:8-9

**48:33** Isa 16:10

**48:21** Hebrew *Jahzah*, a variant spelling of Jahaz.   **48:31** Hebrew *Kir-heres*, a variant spelling of Kir-hareseth; also in 48:36.   **48:32** Hebrew *the sea of Jazer.*

---

**48:29** Moab was condemned for its pride. God cannot tolerate pride because pride is taking personal credit for what God has done or looking down on others. God does not condemn our taking satisfaction in what we do (Ecclesiastes 3:22), but he stands against overestimates of our own importance. Romans 12:3 teaches us to have an honest estimate of ourselves.

**48:31** Kir-hareseth was a stronghold city in Moab. God's compassion reaches to all creation, even to his enemies.

No one treads the grapes with shouts of joy.
There is shouting, yes, but not of joy.

48:34
Gen 13:10
Isa 15:4-6

34"Instead, their awful cries of terror can be heard from Heshbon clear across to Elealeh and Jahaz; from Zoar all the way to Horonaim and Eglath-shelishiyah. Even the waters of Nimrim are dried up now.

48:36
Isa 16:11
48:37
Isa 15:2-3

35"I will put an end to Moab," says the LORD, "for the people offer sacrifices at the pagan shrines and burn incense to their false gods. 36My heart moans like a flute for Moab and Kir-hareseth, for all their wealth has disappeared. 37The people shave their heads and beards in mourning. They slash their hands and put on clothes made of burlap. 38There is crying and sorrow in every Moabite home and on every street. For I have smashed Moab like an old, unwanted jar. 39How it is shattered! Hear the wailing! See the shame of Moab! It has become an object of ridicule, an example of ruin to all its neighbors."

48:40
Jer 49:22

40This is what the LORD says:

"Look! The enemy swoops down like an eagle,
spreading his wings over Moab.

48:41
Jer 30:6; 49:22

41 Its cities will fall,
and its strongholds will be seized.
Even the mightiest warriors will be in anguish
like a woman in labor.

48:42
Ps 83:4
Jer 48:26

42 Moab will no longer be a nation,
for it has boasted against the LORD.

48:43
Isa 24:17
Lam 3:47

43 "Terror and traps and snares will be your lot,
O Moab," says the LORD.

48:44
1 Kgs 19:17
Amos 5:19

44 "Those who flee in terror will fall into a trap,
and those who escape the trap will step into a snare.
I will see to it that you do not get away,
for the time of your judgment has come,"
says the LORD.

48:45
Num 21:28-29
Ps 135:10-11

45 "The people flee as far as Heshbon
but are unable to go on.
For a fire comes from Heshbon,
King Sihon's ancient home,
to devour the entire land
with all its rebellious people.

48:46
Num 21:29

46 "O Moab, they weep for you!
The people of the god Chemosh are destroyed!
Your sons and your daughters
have been taken away as captives.

48:47
Jer 12:17; 49:39

47 But I will restore the fortunes of Moab
in days to come.
I, the LORD, have spoken!"

This is the end of Jeremiah's prophecy concerning Moab.

## A Message about Ammon

49:1
Ezek 25:2
Amos 1:13

**49** This message was given concerning the Ammonites. This is what the LORD says:

"Are there no descendants of Israel
to inherit the land of Gad?
Why are you, who worship Molech,*
living in its towns?

49:2
2 Sam 11:1
Isa 14:2
Ezek 21:28

2 In the days to come," says the LORD,
"I will sound the battle cry against your city of Rabbah.

**49:1** Hebrew *Malcam,* a variant spelling of Molech; also in 49:3.

**49:1** The Ammonites were descendants of Lot through an incestuous relationship with one of his daughters (as were the Moabites; see Genesis 19:30-38). They were condemned for stealing land from God's people and for worshiping the idol Molech, to whom they sacrificed children.

It will become a desolate heap of ruins,
    and the neighboring towns will be burned.
Then Israel will take back the land
    you took from her," says the LORD.

3 "Cry out, O Heshbon,
    for the town of Ai is destroyed.
Weep, O people of Rabbah!
    Put on your clothes of mourning.
Weep and wail, hiding in the hedges,
    for your god Molech, with his priests and officials,
    will be hauled off to distant lands.

**49:3**
Josh 7:2-5; 8:1-29
Jer 48:2, 7

4 You are proud of your fertile valleys,
    but they will soon be ruined.
You trusted in your wealth,
    you rebellious daughter,
    and thought no one could ever harm you.

**49:4**
Ps 62:10-11
Ezek 28:4-5
1 Tim 6:17

5 But look! I will bring terror upon you,"
    says the Lord, the LORD of Heaven's Armies.
"Your neighbors will chase you from your land,
    and no one will help your exiles as they flee.

**49:5**
Jer 16:16
Lam 4:15

6 But I will restore the fortunes of the Ammonites
    in days to come.
    I, the LORD, have spoken."

**49:6**
Jer 48:47; 49:39

## Messages about Edom

7 This message was given concerning Edom. This is what the LORD of Heaven's Armies says:

**49:7**
Gen 36:11, 15
Isa 34:5-6
Amos 1:12

"Is there no wisdom in Teman?
    Is no one left to give wise counsel?

8 Turn and flee!
    Hide in deep caves, you people of Dedan!
For when I bring disaster on Edom,*
    I will punish you, too!

**49:8**
Isa 21:13
Jer 25:23

9 Those who harvest grapes
    always leave a few for the poor.
If thieves came at night,
    they would not take everything.

**49:9**
Obad 1:5

10 But I will strip bare the land of Edom,
    and there will be no place left to hide.
Its children, its brothers, and its neighbors
    will all be destroyed,
    and Edom itself will be no more.

11 But I will protect the orphans who remain among you.
    Your widows, too, can depend on me for help."

**49:11**
Ps 68:5
Zech 7:10

12 And this is what the LORD says: "If the innocent must suffer, how much more must you! You will not go unpunished! You must drink this cup of judgment! 13 For I have sworn by my own name," says the LORD, "that Bozrah will become an object of horror and a heap of ruins; it will be mocked and cursed. All its towns and villages will be desolate forever."

**49:12**
Jer 25:15, 28-29
1 Pet 4:17

**49:13**
Isa 34:6, 9-15

14 I have heard a message from the LORD
    that an ambassador was sent to the nations to say,

**49:14**
Jer 50:14

**49:8** Hebrew *Esau*; also in 49:10.

---

**49:7** The Israelites descended from Jacob, and the Edomites descended from his twin brother, Esau; thus, both nations descended from their father, Isaac. There was constant conflict between these nations, and Edom rejoiced at the fall of Jerusalem (see the book of Obadiah). Teman, a town in the northern part of Edom, was known for its wisdom and was the hometown of Eliphaz, one of Job's friends (Job 2:11). But even the wisdom of Teman could not save Edom from God's wrath.

**49:8** Dedan was a flourishing city that supported caravan travel. God told its inhabitants to flee to the caves or they would also be destroyed. Teman and Dedan were at opposite ends of the country, so this shows the completeness of God's destruction of Edom. Bozrah (49:13) was a town in northern Edom.

"Form a coalition against Edom,
and prepare for battle!"

**49:15**
Luke 1:51
Obad 1:1-4

15 The LORD says to Edom,
"I will cut you down to size among the nations.
You will be despised by all.

**49:16**
Isa 14:13-15
Amos 9:2

16 You have been deceived
by the fear you inspire in others
and by your own pride.
You live in a rock fortress
and control the mountain heights.
But even if you make your nest among the peaks with the eagles,
I will bring you crashing down,"
says the LORD.

**49:17**
Jer 51:37
Ezek 35:7

17 "Edom will be an object of horror.
All who pass by will be appalled
and will gasp at the destruction they see there.

**49:18**
Gen 19:24-25
Deut 29:23
Amos 4:11

18 It will be like the destruction of Sodom and Gomorrah
and their neighboring towns," says the LORD.
"No one will live there;
no one will inhabit it.

**49:19**
Isa 46:9
Jer 50:44

19 I will come like a lion from the thickets of the Jordan,
leaping on the sheep in the pasture.
I will chase Edom from its land,
and I will appoint the leader of my choice.
For who is like me, and who can challenge me?
What ruler can oppose my will?"

**49:20**
Isa 14:24, 27
Mal 1:4-5

20 Listen to the LORD's plans against Edom
and the people of Teman.
Even the little children will be dragged off like sheep,
and their homes will be destroyed.

**49:21**
Ezek 26:15, 18

**49:22**
Isa 13:8
Jer 48:40-41

21 The earth will shake with the noise of Edom's fall,
and its cry of despair will be heard all the way to the Red Sea.*
22 Look! The enemy swoops down like an eagle,
spreading his wings over Bozrah.
Even the mightiest warriors will be in anguish
like a woman in labor.

### A Message about Damascus

**49:23**
Exod 15:15
Isa 10:9; 57:20
Jer 39:5
Amos 6:2
Nah 2:10

23 This message was given concerning Damascus. This is what the LORD says:

"The towns of Hamath and Arpad are struck with fear,
for they have heard the news of their destruction.
Their hearts are troubled
like a wild sea in a raging storm.
24 Damascus has become feeble,
and all her people turn to flee.
Fear, anguish, and pain have gripped her
as they grip a woman in labor.
25 That famous city, a city of joy,
will be forsaken!

**49:21** Hebrew *sea of reeds.*

---

**49:16** Edom was located in a rock fortress that today is known as Petra, in southern Jordan. Edom thought it was invincible because of its location. Edom was destroyed because of its pride. Pride destroys nations as well as individuals. It deludes us into thinking that we can take care of ourselves without God's help. Even serving God and others can lead us into pride. Take inventory of your life and service for God; ask God to point out and remove any pride you may be harboring.

**49:23-26** Damascus was the capital of Aram, north of Israel. This city was defeated by both Assyria and Babylon. Nebuchadnezzar attacked and defeated Damascus in 605 B.C. (Amos 1:4, 5). It is difficult to attribute the defeat of the army to a particular event, but God utterly destroyed Aram.

26 Her young men will fall in the streets and die.
   Her soldiers will all be killed,"
   says the LORD of Heaven's Armies.
27 "And I will set fire to the walls of Damascus
   that will burn up the palaces of Ben-hadad."

## A Message about Kedar and Hazor

28 This message was given concerning Kedar and the kingdoms of Hazor, which were attacked by King Nebuchadnezzar* of Babylon. This is what the LORD says:

"Advance against Kedar!
   Destroy the warriors from the East!
29 Their flocks and tents will be captured,
   and their household goods and camels will be taken away.
   Everywhere shouts of panic will be heard:
   'We are terrorized at every turn!'
30 Run for your lives," says the LORD.
   "Hide yourselves in deep caves, you people of Hazor,
   for King Nebuchadnezzar of Babylon has plotted against you
   and is preparing to destroy you.
31 "Go up and attack that complacent nation,"
   says the LORD.
   "Its people live alone in the desert
   without walls or gates.
32 Their camels and other livestock will all be yours.
   I will scatter to the winds these people
   who live in remote places.*
   I will bring calamity upon them
   from every direction," says the LORD.
33 "Hazor will be inhabited by jackals,
   and it will be desolate forever.
   No one will live there;
   no one will inhabit it."

## A Message about Elam

34 This message concerning Elam came to the prophet Jeremiah from the LORD at the beginning of the reign of King Zedekiah of Judah. 35 This is what the LORD of Heaven's Armies says:

"I will destroy the archers of Elam—
   the best of their forces.
36 I will bring enemies from all directions,
   and I will scatter the people of Elam to the four winds.
   They will be exiled to countries around the world.
37 I myself will go with Elam's enemies to shatter it.
   In my fierce anger, I will bring great disaster
   upon the people of Elam," says the LORD.
   "Their enemies will chase them with the sword
   until I have destroyed them completely.
38 I will set my throne in Elam," says the LORD,
   "and I will destroy its king and officials.
39 But I will restore the fortunes of Elam
   in days to come.
   I, the LORD, have spoken!"

49:26 Jer 50:30
49:27 1 Kgs 15:18-20; Amos 1:3-5
49:28 Isa 21:16-17
49:29 Jer 46:5
49:30 Jer 25:8-9, 24; 27:6
49:31 Judg 18:7; Isa 47:8
49:32 Jer 9:25-26; 25:23; Ezek 12:14-15
49:33 Isa 13:20-22; Zeph 2:9, 13-15
49:34 Gen 10:22; 2 Kgs 24:17-18; Isa 11:11; Dan 8:2
49:35 Isa 22:6; Jer 51:56
49:36 Ezek 5:10; Rev 7:1
49:37 Jer 6:19; 30:24
49:39 Jer 48:47

49:28 Hebrew Nebuchadrezzar, a variant spelling of Nebuchadnezzar; also in 49:30.   49:32 Or who clip the corners of their hair.

49:28 Kedar and Hazor were nomadic tribes east of Israel and south of Aram, in the desert. In 599 B.C. Nebuchadnezzar destroyed them.

49:34 Elam lay east of Babylon and was attacked by Nebuchadnezzar in 597 B.C. Later Elam became the nucleus of the Persian Empire (Daniel 8:2) and the residence of Darius.

49:38 The throne represents God's judgment and sovereignty. God would preside over Elam's destruction. He is the King over all kings, including Elam's.

### A Message about Babylon

**50** The Lord gave Jeremiah the prophet this message concerning Babylon and the land of the Babylonians.* ² This is what the Lord says:

50:1
Isa 13:1
Rev 14:8

"Tell the whole world,
and keep nothing back.
Raise a signal flag
to tell everyone that Babylon will fall!
Her images and idols* will be shattered.
Her gods Bel and Marduk will be utterly disgraced.

50:2
Isa 46:1
Jer 51:31

³ For a nation will attack her from the north
and bring such destruction that no one will live there again.
Everything will be gone;
both people and animals will flee.

50:3
Zeph 1:3

### Hope for Israel and Judah

⁴ "In those coming days,"
says the Lord,
"the people of Israel will return home
together with the people of Judah.
They will come weeping
and seeking the Lord their God.

50:4
Ezra 3:12-13
Isa 11:12-13
Jer 31:9
Hos 1:11

⁵ They will ask the way to Jerusalem*
and will start back home again.
They will bind themselves to the Lord
with an eternal covenant that will never be forgotten.

50:5
Isa 55:3
Jer 6:16; 32:40

⁶ "My people have been lost sheep.
Their shepherds have led them astray
and turned them loose in the mountains.
They have lost their way
and can't remember how to get back to the sheepfold.

50:6
Isa 53:6
Jer 13:16
Ezek 34:15-16
Matt 9:36

⁷ All who found them devoured them.
Their enemies said,
'We did nothing wrong in attacking them,
for they sinned against the Lord,
their true place of rest,
and the hope of their ancestors.'

50:7
Jer 17:13

⁸ "But now, flee from Babylon!
Leave the land of the Babylonians.
Like male goats at the head of the flock,
lead my people home again.

50:8
Jer 51:6
Rev 18:4

⁹ For I am raising up an army
of great nations from the north.
They will join forces to attack Babylon,
and she will be captured.
The enemies' arrows will go straight to the mark;
they will not miss!

¹⁰ Babylonia* will be looted
until the attackers are glutted with loot.
I, the Lord, have spoken!

50:10
Jer 51:24, 35

50:1 Or *Chaldeans;* also in 50:8, 25, 35, 45.   50:2 The Hebrew term (literally *round things*) probably alludes to dung.
50:5 Hebrew *Zion;* also in 50:28.   50:10 Or *Chaldea.*

---

50:1ff At the height of its power, the Babylonian Empire seemed invincible. But when Babylon had finished serving God's purpose of punishing Judah for her sins, it would be punished and crushed for its own. Babylon was destroyed in 539 B.C. by the Medo-Persians (Daniel 5:30, 31). Babylon is also used in Scripture as a symbol of all evil. This message can thus apply to the end times when God will wipe out all evil once and for all.

50:3 The nation from the north was Medo-Persia, an alliance of Media and Persia that would become the next world power. Cyrus took the city of Babylon by surprise and brought the nation to its knees in 539 B.C. (Daniel 5:30, 31). The complete destruction of the city was accomplished by later Persian kings.

## Babylon's Sure Fall

11 "You rejoice and are glad,
    you who plundered my chosen people.
You frisk about like a calf in a meadow
    and neigh like a stallion.

50:11
Jer 12:14; 46:20

12 But your homeland* will be overwhelmed
    with shame and disgrace.
You will become the least of nations—
    a wilderness, a dry and desolate land.

50:12
Jer 22:6

13 Because of the LORD's anger,
    Babylon will become a deserted wasteland.
All who pass by will be horrified
    and will gasp at the destruction they see there.

50:13
Jer 18:16

14 "Yes, prepare to attack Babylon,
    all you surrounding nations.
Let your archers shoot at her; spare no arrows.
    For she has sinned against the LORD.

50:14
Hab 2:8, 17

15 Shout war cries against her from every side.
    Look! She surrenders!
    Her walls have fallen.
It is the LORD's vengeance,
    so take vengeance on her.
    Do to her as she has done to others!

50:15
Ps 137:8

16 Take from Babylon all those who plant crops;
    send all the harvesters away.
Because of the sword of the enemy,
    everyone will run away and rush back to their own lands.

50:16
Jer 46:16

## Hope for God's People

17 "The Israelites are like sheep
    that have been scattered by lions.
First the king of Assyria ate them up.
    Then King Nebuchadnezzar* of Babylon cracked their bones."

50:17
2 Kgs 18:9-13;
24:1, 10-12

18 Therefore, this is what the LORD of Heaven's Armies,
    the God of Israel, says:
"Now I will punish the king of Babylon and his land,
    just as I punished the king of Assyria.

50:18
Isa 10:12
Nah 1:1; 3:7, 18-19

19 And I will bring Israel home again to its own land,
    to feed in the fields of Carmel and Bashan,
and to be satisfied once more
    in the hill country of Ephraim and Gilead.

20 In those days," says the LORD,
    "no sin will be found in Israel or in Judah,
    for I will forgive the remnant I preserve.

50:20
Jer 31:34
Mic 7:19

## The LORD's Judgment on Babylon

21 "Go up, my warriors, against the land of Merathaim
    and against the people of Pekod.
Pursue, kill, and completely destroy* them,
    as I have commanded you," says the LORD.

50:21
Ezek 23:23

22 "Let the battle cry be heard in the land,
    a shout of great destruction.

50:22
Jer 4:19-21

**50:12** Hebrew *your mother.*   **50:17** Hebrew *Nebuchadrezzar,* a variant spelling of Nebuchadnezzar.   **50:21** The Hebrew term used here refers to the complete consecration of things or people to the LORD, either by destroying them or by giving them as an offering.

---

**50:17-20** God would punish wicked Babylon as he punished Assyria for what it had done to Israel. Assyria was crushed by Babylon, which Assyria had once ruled. Babylon in turn would be crushed by Medo-Persia, formerly under its authority. These verses also look to the time when the Messiah will rule and Israel will be fully restored. No sin will then be found in Israel because God's people will seek him and be forgiven.

**50:21** Merathaim was located in southern Babylonia; Pekod was in eastern Babylonia.

**50:23**
Jer 51:20-24

23 Babylon, the mightiest hammer in all the earth,
    lies broken and shattered.
Babylon is desolate among the nations!

**50:24**
Job 9:4; 40:2, 9
Jer 48:43

24 Listen, Babylon, for I have set a trap for you.
    You are caught, for you have fought against the LORD.

**50:25**
Isa 13:4-5

25 The LORD has opened his armory
    and brought out weapons to vent his fury.
The terror that falls upon the Babylonians
    will be the work of the Sovereign LORD of Heaven's Armies.

**50:26**
Isa 14:23

26 Yes, come against her from distant lands.
    Break open her granaries.
Crush her walls and houses into heaps of rubble.
    Destroy her completely, and leave nothing!

**50:27**
Ps 37:13
Ezek 7:7

27 Destroy even her young bulls—
    it will be terrible for them, too!
Slaughter them all!
    For Babylon's day of reckoning has come.

**50:28**
Ps 149:6-9
Isa 48:20
Lam 1:10

28 Listen to the people who have escaped from Babylon,
    as they tell in Jerusalem
how the LORD our God has taken vengeance
    against those who destroyed his Temple.

**50:29**
Exod 10:3
Ps 137:8

29 "Send out a call for archers to come to Babylon.
    Surround the city so none can escape.
Do to her as she has done to others,
    for she has defied the LORD, the Holy One of Israel.

**50:30**
Jer 18:21

30 Her young men will fall in the streets and die.
    Her soldiers will all be killed,"
    says the LORD.

**50:31**
Nah 2:13

31 "See, I am your enemy, you arrogant people,"
    says the Lord, the LORD of Heaven's Armies.
"Your day of reckoning has arrived—
    the day when I will punish you.

**50:32**
Isa 10:12-15
Jer 21:14

32 O land of arrogance, you will stumble and fall,
    and no one will raise you up.
For I will light a fire in the cities of Babylon
    that will burn up everything around them."

**50:33**
Isa 14:17; 58:6

33 This is what the LORD of Heaven's Armies says:
"The people of Israel and Judah have been wronged.
    Their captors hold them and refuse to let them go.

**50:34**
Isa 14:3-7; 43:14
Mic 7:9

34 But the one who redeems them is strong.
    His name is the LORD of Heaven's Armies.
He will defend them
    and give them rest again in Israel.
But for the people of Babylon
    there will be no rest!

**50:35**
Jer 47:6
Dan 5:1-2, 7-8

35 "The sword of destruction will strike the Babylonians,"
    says the LORD.
"It will strike the people of Babylon—
    her officials and wise men, too.

**50:36**
Isa 44:25

36 The sword will strike her wise counselors,
    and they will become fools.

**50:32** Pride was Babylon's characteristic sin. Pride comes from feeling self-sufficient or believing that we don't need God. Proud nations or persons, however, will eventually fail because they refuse to recognize God as the ultimate power. Getting rid of pride is not easy, but if we can admit that it often rules us and ask God to forgive us, he will help us overcome it. The best antidote to pride is to focus our attention on the greatness and goodness of God.

The sword will strike her mightiest warriors,
  and panic will seize them.

<sup>37</sup> The sword will strike her horses and chariots
  and her allies from other lands,
    and they will all become like women.
The sword will strike her treasures,
  and they all will be plundered.

<sup>38</sup> The sword will even strike her water supply,
  causing it to dry up.
And why? Because the whole land is filled with idols,
  and the people are madly in love with them.

<sup>39</sup> "Soon Babylon will be inhabited by desert animals and hyenas.
  It will be a home for owls.
Never again will people live there;
  it will lie desolate forever.

<sup>40</sup> I will destroy it as I* destroyed Sodom and Gomorrah
  and their neighboring towns," says the LORD.
"No one will live there;
  no one will inhabit it.

<sup>41</sup> "Look! A great army is coming from the north.
  A great nation and many kings
  are rising against you from far-off lands.

<sup>42</sup> They are armed with bows and spears.
  They are cruel and show no mercy.
As they ride forward on horses,
  they sound like a roaring sea.
They are coming in battle formation,
  planning to destroy you, Babylon.

<sup>43</sup> The king of Babylon has heard reports about the enemy,
  and he is weak with fright.
Pangs of anguish have gripped him,
  like those of a woman in labor.

<sup>44</sup> "I will come like a lion from the thickets of the Jordan,
  leaping on the sheep in the pasture.
I will chase Babylon from its land,
  and I will appoint the leader of my choice.
For who is like me, and who can challenge me?
  What ruler can oppose my will?"

<sup>45</sup> Listen to the LORD's plans against Babylon
  and the land of the Babylonians.
Even the little children will be dragged off like sheep,
  and their homes will be destroyed.

<sup>46</sup> The earth will shake with the shout, "Babylon has been taken!"
  and its cry of despair will be heard around the world.

# 51

<sup>1</sup> This is what the LORD says:
"I will stir up a destroyer against Babylon
  and the people of Babylonia.*

<sup>2</sup> Foreigners will come and winnow her,
  blowing her away as chaff.

**50:37**
Ps 20:7-8
Jer 25:19-20; 48:41

**50:39**
Isa 13:20

**50:40**
Gen 19:24-25
Luke 17:28-30
2 Pet 2:6
Jude 1:7

**50:41**
Isa 13:2-5

**50:42**
Isa 13:17-18
Hab 1:8

**50:43**
Jer 30:6

**50:44**
Num 16:5
Job 41:10
Isa 46:9

**50:46**
Jer 10:10
Ezek 26:18

**51:1**
Jer 4:11-12

**51:2**
Jer 15:7
Matt 3:12

---

**50:40** Hebrew *as God*.  **51:1** Hebrew *of Leb-kamai*, a code name for Babylonia.

---

**50:39** Babylon remains a wasteland to this day. See also Isaiah 13:19-22.
**50:44-46** This invader was Cyrus, who attacked Babylon by surprise and overthrew it. The world was shocked that its greatest empire was overthrown so quickly. No earthly power, no matter how great, can last forever.

**51:2** To winnow is to separate the wheat from the chaff. When winnowers threw the mixture into the air, the wind blew away the worthless chaff while the wheat settled to the floor. Babylon would be blown away like chaff in the wind. (See also Matthew 3:12 where John the Baptist says Jesus will separate the wheat from the chaff.)

They will come from every side
   to rise against her in her day of trouble.

**51:3**
Jer 46:4

³ Don't let the archers put on their armor
   or draw their bows.
Don't spare even her best soldiers!
   Let her army be completely destroyed.*

⁴ They will fall dead in the land of the Babylonians,*
   slashed to death in her streets.

**51:5**
Isa 54:7-8
Jer 33:24-26

⁵ For the LORD of Heaven's Armies
   has not abandoned Israel and Judah.
He is still their God,
   even though their land was filled with sin
   against the Holy One of Israel."

**51:6**
Num 16:26
Rev 18:4

⁶ Flee from Babylon! Save yourselves!
   Don't get trapped in her punishment!
It is the LORD's time for vengeance;
   he will repay her in full.

**51:7**
Jer 25:15
Rev 14:8-10; 18:3

⁷ Babylon has been a gold cup in the LORD's hands,
   a cup that made the whole earth drunk.
The nations drank Babylon's wine,
   and it drove them all mad.

⁸ But suddenly Babylon, too, has fallen.
   Weep for her.
Give her medicine.
   Perhaps she can yet be healed.

**51:9**
Jer 46:16

⁹ We would have helped her if we could,
   but nothing can save her now.
Let her go; abandon her.
   Return now to your own land.
For her punishment reaches to the heavens;
   it is so great it cannot be measured.

**51:10**
Isa 40:2
Mic 7:9

¹⁰ The LORD has vindicated us.
   Come, let us announce in Jerusalem*
   everything the LORD our God has done.

**51:11**
Joel 3:9-10

¹¹ Sharpen the arrows!
   Lift up the shields!*
For the LORD has inspired the kings of the Medes
   to march against Babylon and destroy her.
This is his vengeance against those
   who desecrated his Temple.

**51:12**
Jer 4:28

¹² Raise the battle flag against Babylon!
   Reinforce the guard and station the watchmen.
Prepare an ambush,
   for the LORD will fulfill all his plans against Babylon.

**51:13**
Hab 2:9-11

¹³ You are a city by a great river,
   a great center of commerce,
but your end has come.
   The thread of your life is cut.

**51:14**
Nah 3:15

¹⁴ The LORD of Heaven's Armies has taken this vow
   and has sworn to it by his own name:
"Your cities will be filled with enemies,
   like fields swarming with locusts,
   and they will shout in triumph over you."

**51:3** The Hebrew term used here refers to the complete consecration of things or people to the LORD, either by destroying them or by giving them as an offering.  **51:4** Or *Chaldeans;* also in 51:54.  **51:10** Hebrew *Zion;* also in 51:24.  **51:11** Greek version reads *Fill up the quivers.*

**51:11** Cyrus, king of Persia, had allied himself with Babylon to defeat Nineveh (capital of the Assyrian Empire) in 612 B.C. Then the Medes joined Persia to defeat Babylon (539 B.C.).

*A Hymn of Praise to the LORD*

¹⁵ The LORD made the earth by his power,
    and he preserves it by his wisdom.
  With his own understanding
    he stretched out the heavens.
¹⁶ When he speaks in the thunder,
    the heavens are filled with water.
  He causes the clouds to rise over the earth.
  He sends the lightning with the rain
    and releases the wind from his storehouses.

¹⁷ The whole human race is foolish and has no knowledge!
    The craftsmen are disgraced by the idols they make,
  for their carefully shaped works are a fraud.
    These idols have no breath or power.
¹⁸ Idols are worthless; they are ridiculous lies!
    On the day of reckoning they will all be destroyed.
¹⁹ But the God of Israel* is no idol!
    He is the Creator of everything that exists,
  including his people, his own special possession.
    The LORD of Heaven's Armies is his name!

*Babylon's Great Punishment*

²⁰ "You* are my battle-ax and sword,"
    says the LORD.
  "With you I will shatter nations
    and destroy many kingdoms.
²¹ With you I will shatter armies—
    destroying the horse and rider,
    the chariot and charioteer.
²² With you I will shatter men and women,
    old people and children,
    young men and maidens.
²³ With you I will shatter shepherds and flocks,
    farmers and oxen,
    captains and officers.

²⁴ "I will repay Babylon
    and the people of Babylonia*
  for all the wrong they have done
    to my people in Jerusalem," says the LORD.

²⁵ "Look, O mighty mountain, destroyer of the earth!
    I am your enemy," says the LORD.
  "I will raise my fist against you,
    to knock you down from the heights.
  When I am finished,
    you will be nothing but a heap of burnt rubble.
²⁶ You will be desolate forever.
    Even your stones will never again be used for building.
  You will be completely wiped out,"
    says the LORD.

²⁷ Raise a signal flag to the nations.
    Sound the battle cry!
  Mobilize them all against Babylon.
    Prepare them to fight against her!

**51:15**
Ps 146:5-6
Jer 10:12-16
Rom 1:20

**51:16**
Job 37:2-5
Pss 18:13; 135:7
Jon 1:4

**51:17**
Isa 44:18-20
Hab 2:18-19

**51:19**
Jer 10:16

**51:20**
Mic 4:12-13

**51:21**
Exod 15:1

**51:22**
Isa 13:15-16, 18

**51:25**
Rev 8:8

**51:26**
Isa 13:19-22

**51:27**
Gen 8:4; 10:3
2 Kgs 19:37
Isa 13:2-5

**51:19** Hebrew *the Portion of Jacob.* See note on 5:20.   **51:20** Possibly Cyrus, whom God used to conquer Babylon. Compare Isa 44:28; 45:1.   **51:24** Or *Chaldea;* also in 51:35.

**51:17-19** It is foolish to trust in human-made images rather than in God. It is easy to think that the things we see and touch will bring us more security than God. But things rust, rot, and decay. God is eternal. Why put your trust in something that will disappear within a few years?

Bring out the armies of Ararat, Minni, and Ashkenaz.
Appoint a commander,
and bring a multitude of horses like swarming locusts!
28 Bring against her the armies of the nations—
led by the kings of the Medes
and all their captains and officers.

**51:29**
Jer 10:10
Amos 8:8

29 The earth trembles and writhes in pain,
for everything the LORD has planned against Babylon stands unchanged.
Babylon will be left desolate without a single inhabitant.

**51:30**
Ps 76:5
Isa 13:7-8; 45:1

30   Her mightiest warriors no longer fight.
They stay in their barracks, their courage gone.
They have become like women.
The invaders have burned the houses
and broken down the city gates.
31 The news is passed from one runner to the next
as the messengers hurry to tell the king
that his city has been captured.
32 All the escape routes are blocked.
The marshes have been set aflame,
and the army is in a panic.

**51:33**
Isa 21:10
Joel 3:13

33 This is what the LORD of Heaven's Armies,
the God of Israel, says:
"Babylon is like wheat on a threshing floor,
about to be trampled.
In just a little while
her harvest will begin."

**51:34**
Job 20:15
Ps 137:8
Isa 24:1-3

34 "King Nebuchadnezzar* of Babylon has eaten and crushed us
and drained us of strength.
He has swallowed us like a great monster
and filled his belly with our riches.
He has thrown us out of our own country.

**51:35**
Ps 137:8

35 Make Babylon suffer as she made us suffer,"
say the people of Zion.
"Make the people of Babylonia pay for spilling our blood,"
says Jerusalem.

### The LORD's Vengeance on Babylon

**51:36**
Ps 140:12
Rom 12:19

36 This is what the LORD says to Jerusalem:

"I will be your lawyer to plead your case,
and I will avenge you.
I will dry up her river,
as well as her springs,
37 and Babylon will become a heap of ruins,
haunted by jackals.
She will be an object of horror and contempt,
a place where no one lives.
38 Her people will roar together like strong lions.
They will growl like lion cubs.

**51:34** Hebrew *Nebuchadrezzar*, a variant spelling of Nebuchadnezzar.

---

**51:33** Grain was threshed on a threshing floor, where sheaves were brought from the field. The stalks of grain were distributed on the floor, a large level section of hard ground. There the grain was crushed to separate the kernels from the stalk; then the kernels were beaten with a wooden tool. Sometimes a wooden sledge was pulled over the grain by animals to break the kernels loose. Babylon would soon be trampled like grain on a threshing floor as God judged it for its sins.

**51:36** This verse may refer to an event accomplished by Cyrus, who took Babylon by surprise by diverting the river that ran through the city far upstream and walking beneath the city's fortifications on the dry riverbed. More likely it is saying that Babylon will be deprived of life-giving water. Unlike Jerusalem, Babylon will not be restored.

39 And while they lie inflamed with all their wine,
  I will prepare a different kind of feast for them.
I will make them drink until they fall asleep,
  and they will never wake up again,"
  says the Lord.

40 "I will bring them down
  like lambs to the slaughter,
  like rams and goats to be sacrificed.

41 "How Babylon* is fallen—
  great Babylon, praised throughout the earth!
Now she has become an object of horror
  among the nations.

42 The sea has risen over Babylon;
  she is covered by its crashing waves.

43 Her cities now lie in ruins;
  she is a dry wasteland
  where no one lives or even passes by.

44 And I will punish Bel, the god of Babylon,
  and make him vomit up all he has eaten.
The nations will no longer come and worship him.
  The wall of Babylon has fallen!

*A Message for the Exiles*

45 "Come out, my people, flee from Babylon.
  Save yourselves! Run from the Lord's fierce anger.

46 But do not panic; don't be afraid
  when you hear the first rumor of approaching forces.
For rumors will keep coming year by year.
  Violence will erupt in the land
  as the leaders fight against each other.

47 For the time is surely coming
  when I will punish this great city and all her idols.
Her whole land will be disgraced,
  and her dead will lie in the streets.

48 Then the heavens and earth will rejoice,
  for out of the north will come destroying armies
  against Babylon," says the Lord.

49 "Just as Babylon killed the people of Israel
  and others throughout the world,
  so must her people be killed.

50 Get out, all you who have escaped the sword!
  Do not stand and watch—flee while you can!
Remember the Lord, though you are in a far-off land,
  and think about your home in Jerusalem."

51 "We are ashamed," the people say.
  "We are insulted and disgraced
because the Lord's Temple
  has been defiled by foreigners."

52 "Yes," says the Lord, "but the time is coming
  when I will destroy Babylon's idols.
The groans of her wounded people
  will be heard throughout the land.

**51:41** Hebrew *Sheshach*, a code name for Babylon.

| Reference | |
|---|---|
| **51:39** | Ps 76:5 / Jer 25:27 |
| **51:42** | Dan 9:26 |
| **51:43** | Isa 13:20 |
| **51:44** | Ezra 1:7 / Isa 2:2 |
| **51:45** | Gen 19:12-16 / Isa 48:20 / Acts 2:40 |
| **51:46** | Isa 19:2 |
| **51:47** | Isa 21:9; 46:1-2 |
| **51:48** | Isa 44:23 / Rev 18:20 |
| **51:51** | Lam 1:10 |

**51:44** Bel is one of the names of Marduk, the chief god of the city of Babylon.

**51:51** The people were paralyzed with guilt over their past. The Babylonian armies had desecrated the Temple and the people were ashamed to return to Jerusalem. But God told them to return to the city because he would destroy Babylon for its sins.

51:53
Job 20:6-7

53 Though Babylon reaches as high as the heavens
    and makes her fortifications incredibly strong,
I will still send enemies to plunder her.
    I, the LORD, have spoken!

## Babylon's Complete Destruction

54 "Listen! Hear the cry of Babylon,
    the sound of great destruction from the land of the Babylonians.

51:55
Ps 69:2

55 For the LORD is destroying Babylon.
    He will silence her loud voice.
Waves of enemies pound against her;
    the noise of battle rings through the city.

51:56
Pss 76:3; 94:1-2

56 Destroying armies come against Babylon.
    Her mighty men are captured,
    and their weapons break in their hands.
For the LORD is a God who gives just punishment;
    he always repays in full.

51:57
Ps 76:5-6

57 I will make her officials and wise men drunk,
    along with her captains, officers, and warriors.
They will fall asleep
    and never wake up again!"
says the King, whose name is
    the LORD of Heaven's Armies.

51:58
Hab 2:13

58 This is what the LORD of Heaven's Armies says:
"The thick walls of Babylon will be leveled to the ground,
    and her massive gates will be burned.
The builders from many lands have worked in vain,
    for their work will be destroyed by fire!"

## Jeremiah's Message Sent to Babylon

59 The prophet Jeremiah gave this message to Seraiah son of Neriah and grandson of Mahseiah, a staff officer, when Seraiah went to Babylon with King Zedekiah of Judah. This was during the fourth year of Zedekiah's reign.* 60 Jeremiah had recorded on a scroll all the terrible disasters that would soon come upon Babylon—all the words written here. 61 He said

51:62
Isa 13:19-22
Ezek 35:9

51:63
Rev 18:21

51:64
Nah 1:8-9

to Seraiah, "When you get to Babylon, read aloud everything on this scroll. 62 Then say, 'LORD, you have said that you will destroy Babylon so that neither people nor animals will remain here. She will lie empty and abandoned forever.' 63 When you have finished reading the scroll, tie it to a stone and throw it into the Euphrates River. 64 Then say, 'In this same way Babylon and her people will sink, never again to rise, because of the disasters I will bring upon her.'"
    This is the end of Jeremiah's messages.

## 2. The fall of Jerusalem

52:1
2 Kgs 8:22;
24:18-20

52:2
Jer 36:30-31

52:3
2 Chr 36:13

52:4
2 Kgs 25:1-7
Jer 39:1

**52** Zedekiah was twenty-one years old when he became king, and he reigned in Jerusalem eleven years. His mother was Hamutal, the daughter of Jeremiah from Libnah. 2 But Zedekiah did what was evil in the LORD's sight, just as Jehoiakim had done. 3 These things happened because of the LORD's anger against the people of Jerusalem and Judah, until he finally banished them from his presence and sent them into exile.
    Zedekiah rebelled against the king of Babylon. 4 So on January 15,* during the ninth year

51:59 The fourth year of Zedekiah's reign was 593 B.C.    52:4a Hebrew *on the tenth day of the tenth month,* of the ancient Hebrew lunar calendar. A number of events in Jeremiah can be cross-checked with dates in surviving Babylonian records and related accurately to our modern calendar. This day was January 15, 588 B.C.

---

**51:59** Jeremiah could not visit Babylon, so he sent the message with Seraiah, the officer who cared for the comforts of the army. Seraiah was probably Baruch's brother (32:12).

**51:60-64** In this last of Jeremiah's messages, we find again the twin themes of God's sovereignty and his judgment. Babylon had been allowed to oppress the people of Israel, but Babylon itself would be judged. Although God brings good out of evil, he does not allow evil to remain unpunished. The wicked may succeed for a while, but resist the temptation to follow them or you may share in their judgment.

**52:1ff** This chapter provides more detail about the destruction of Jerusalem recorded in chapter 39 (similar material is found in 2 Kings 24:18–25:21). This appendix shows that Jeremiah's prophecies concerning the destruction of Jerusalem and the Babylonian captivity happened just as he predicted. For more information on Zedekiah, see the note on 39:1ff.

of Zedekiah's reign, King Nebuchadnezzar* of Babylon led his entire army against Jerusalem. They surrounded the city and built siege ramps against its walls. ⁵Jerusalem was kept under siege until the eleventh year of King Zedekiah's reign.

⁶By July 18 in the eleventh year of Zedekiah's reign,* the famine in the city had become very severe, and the last of the food was entirely gone. ⁷Then a section of the city wall was broken down, and all the soldiers fled. Since the city was surrounded by the Babylonians,* they waited for nightfall. Then they slipped through the gate between the two walls behind the king's garden and headed toward the Jordan Valley.*

⁸But the Babylonian troops chased King Zedekiah and caught him on the plains of Jericho, for his men had all deserted him and scattered. ⁹They took him to the king of Babylon at Riblah in the land of Hamath. There the king of Babylon pronounced judgment upon Zedekiah. ¹⁰He made Zedekiah watch as they slaughtered his sons and all the other officials of Judah. ¹¹Then they gouged out Zedekiah's eyes, bound him in bronze chains, and led him away to Babylon. Zedekiah remained there in prison until the day of his death.

### The Temple Destroyed

¹²On August 17 of that year,* which was the nineteenth year of King Nebuchadnezzar's reign, Nebuzaradan, the captain of the guard and an official of the Babylonian king, arrived in Jerusalem. ¹³He burned down the Temple of the Lord, the royal palace, and all the houses of Jerusalem. He destroyed all the important buildings* in the city. ¹⁴Then he supervised the entire Babylonian* army as they tore down the walls of Jerusalem on every side. ¹⁵Nebuzaradan, the captain of the guard, then took as exiles some of the poorest of the people, the rest of the people who remained in the city, the defectors who had declared their allegiance to the king of Babylon, and the rest of the craftsmen. ¹⁶But Nebuzaradan allowed some of the poorest people to stay behind in Judah to care for the vineyards and fields.

¹⁷The Babylonians broke up the bronze pillars in front of the Lord's Temple, the bronze water carts, and the great bronze basin called the Sea, and they carried all the bronze away to Babylon. ¹⁸They also took all the ash buckets, shovels, lamp snuffers, basins, dishes, and all the other bronze articles used for making sacrifices at the Temple. ¹⁹Nebuzaradan, the captain of the guard, also took the small bowls, incense burners, basins, pots, lampstands, dishes, bowls used for liquid offerings, and all the other articles made of pure gold or silver.

²⁰The weight of the bronze from the two pillars, the Sea with the twelve bronze oxen beneath it, and the water carts was too great to be measured. These things had been made for the Lord's Temple in the days of King Solomon. ²¹Each of the pillars was 27 feet tall and 18 feet in circumference.* They were hollow, with walls 3 inches thick.* ²²The bronze capital on top of each pillar was 7½ feet* high and was decorated with a network of bronze pomegranates all the way around. ²³There were 96 pomegranates on the sides, and a total of 100 on the network around the top.

²⁴Nebuzaradan, the captain of the guard, took with him as prisoners Seraiah the high priest, Zephaniah the priest of the second rank, and the three chief gatekeepers. ²⁵And from among the people still hiding in the city, he took an officer who had been in charge of the Judean army; seven of the king's personal advisers; the army commander's chief secretary, who was in charge of recruitment; and sixty other citizens. ²⁶Nebuzaradan, the captain of the guard, took them all to the king of Babylon at Riblah. ²⁷And there at Riblah, in the land of Hamath, the king of Babylon had them all put to death. So the people of Judah were sent into exile from their land.

²⁸The number of captives taken to Babylon in the seventh year of Nebuchadnezzar's reign* was 3,023. ²⁹Then in Nebuchadnezzar's eighteenth year* he took 832 more. ³⁰In Nebuchadnezzar's twenty-third year* he sent Nebuzaradan, the captain of the guard, who took 745 more—a total of 4,600 captives in all.

| Reference |
|---|
| 52:6 Jer 38:9 |
| 52:7 Jer 39:2, 4-7 |
| 52:8 Jer 21:7; 38:23 |
| 52:9 2 Kgs 25:6 Jer 39:5 |
| 52:10 Jer 39:6 |
| 52:11 Ezek 12:13 |
| 52:12 2 Kgs 25:8-21 |
| 52:13 2 Chr 36:19 Ps 74:6-8 Jer 39:8 |
| 52:14 2 Kgs 25:10 |
| 52:17 1 Kgs 7:15-36 |
| 52:18 1 Kgs 7:45 |
| 52:19 1 Kgs 7:50 |
| 52:20 1 Kgs 7:47 |
| 52:22 1 Kgs 7:20, 42 |
| 52:24 2 Kgs 25:18 Ezra 7:1 |
| 52:27 Jer 13:19 Mic 4:10 |
| 52:28 2 Kgs 24:2-3, 12-16 |

52:4b Hebrew *Nebuchadrezzar,* a variant spelling of Nebuchadnezzar; also in 52:12, 28, 29, 30. 52:6 Hebrew *By the ninth day of the fourth month* [in the eleventh year of Zedekiah's reign]. This day was July 18, 586 B.C.; also see note on 52:4a. 52:7a Or *the Chaldeans;* similarly in 52:8, 17. 52:7b Hebrew *the Arabah.* 52:12 Hebrew *On the tenth day of the fifth month,* of the ancient Hebrew lunar calendar. This day was August 17, 586 B.C.; also see note on 52:4a. 52:13 Or *destroyed the houses of all the important people.* 52:14 Or *Chaldean.* 52:21a Hebrew *18 cubits* [8.1 meters] *tall and 12 cubits* [5.4 meters] *in circumference.* 52:21b Hebrew *4 fingers thick* [8 centimeters]. 52:22 Hebrew *5 cubits* [2.3 meters]. 52:28 This exile in the seventh year of Nebuchadnezzar's reign occurred in 597 B.C. 52:29 This exile in the eighteenth year of Nebuchadnezzar's reign occurred in 586 B.C. 52:30 This exile in the twenty-third year of Nebuchadnezzar's reign occurred in 581 B.C.

52:8, 9 Riblah was 200 miles north of Jerusalem, located on the Orontes River in the region of Aram (or Syria). This was the Babylonian headquarters for ruling the entire region. Hamath was the district of Aram where the capital, Riblah, was located.

## Hope for Israel's Royal Line

**52:31**
2 Kgs 25:27-30
Ps 3:3

**52:33**
2 Sam 9:7, 13

31In the thirty-seventh year of the exile of King Jehoiachin of Judah, Evil-merodach ascended to the Babylonian throne. He was kind to* Jehoiachin and released him from prison on March 31 of that year.* 32He spoke kindly to Jehoiachin and gave him a higher place than all the other exiled kings in Babylon. 33He supplied Jehoiachin with new clothes to replace his prison garb and allowed him to dine in the king's presence for the rest of his life. 34So the Babylonian king gave him a regular food allowance as long as he lived. This continued until the day of his death.

**52:31a** Hebrew *He raised the head of.*   **52:31b** Hebrew *on the twenty-fifth day of the twelfth month,* of the ancient Hebrew lunar calendar. This day was March 31, 561 B.C.; also see note on 52:4a.

---

**52:31** Babylon's king showed kindness to Jehoiachin. In 561 B.C. Jehoiachin was released from prison and allowed to eat with the king. God continued to show kindness to the descendants of King David, even in exile.

**52:34** In the world's eyes, Jeremiah looked totally unsuccessful. He had no money, family, or friends. He prophesied the destruction of the nation, the capital city, and the Temple, but the political and religious leaders would not accept or follow his advice. No group of people liked him or listened to him. Yet as we look back,

we see that he successfully completed the work God gave him to do. Success must never be measured by popularity, fame, or fortune, for these are temporal measures. King Zedekiah, for example, lost everything by pursuing selfish goals. God measures our success with the yardsticks of obedience, faithfulness, and righteousness. If you are faithfully doing the work God has given you, you are successful in his eyes.

## VITAL STATISTICS

**PURPOSE:**
To teach people that to disobey God is to invite disaster, and to show that God suffers when his people suffer

**AUTHOR:**
Jeremiah

**ORIGINAL AUDIENCE:**
The exiled people of Judah

**DATE WRITTEN:**
Soon after the fall of Jerusalem in 586 B.C.

**SETTING:**
Jerusalem had been destroyed by Babylon and her people killed, tortured, or taken captive.

**KEY VERSE:**
"I have cried until the tears no longer come; my heart is broken. My spirit is poured out in agony as I see the desperate plight of my people. Little children and tiny babies are fainting and dying in the streets" (2:11).

**KEY PEOPLE:**
Jeremiah, the people of Jerusalem

**KEY PLACE:**
Jerusalem

**SPECIAL FEATURES:**
Three strands of Hebrew thought meet in Lamentations—prophecy, ritual, and wisdom. Lamentations is written in the rhythm and style of ancient Jewish funeral songs or chants. It contains five poems corresponding to the five chapters (see the second note on 3:1ff).

TEARS are defined simply as "drops of salty fluid flowing from the eyes." They can be caused by irritation or laughter but are usually associated with weeping, sorrow, and grief. When we cry, friends wonder what's wrong and try to console us. Babies cry for food; children cry at the loss of a pet; adults cry when confronted with trauma and death.

Jeremiah's grief ran deep. He is remembered as the "weeping prophet," and his tears flowed from a broken heart. As God's spokesman, he knew what lay ahead for Judah, his country, and for Jerusalem, the capital and "the city of God." God's judgment would fall and destruction would come. So Jeremiah wept. His tears were not self-centered, mourning over personal suffering or loss. He wept because the people had rejected their God—the God who had made them, loved them, and sought repeatedly to bless them. Jeremiah's heart was broken because he knew that the selfishness and sinfulness of the people would bring them much suffering and an extended exile. Jeremiah's tears were tears of empathy and sympathy. His heart was broken with those things that break God's heart.

Jeremiah's two books focus on one event—the destruction of Jerusalem. The book of Jeremiah predicts it, and Lamentations looks back on it. Known as the book of tears, Lamentations is a dirge, a funeral song written for the fallen city of Jerusalem.

What makes a person cry says a lot about that person—whether he or she is self-centered or God-centered. The book of Lamentations allows us to see what made Jeremiah sorrowful. As one of God's choice servants, he stands alone in the depth of his emotions, broken by his care for the people, his love for the nation, and his devotion to God.

What causes your tears? Do you weep because your selfish pride has been wounded or because the people around you lead sinful lives and reject the God who loves them dearly? Do you weep because you have lost something of value or because people all around you will suffer for their sinfulness? Our world is filled with injustice, poverty, war, and rebellion against God, all of which should move us to tears and to action. Read Lamentations and learn what it means to grieve with God.

## THE BLUEPRINT

1. Jeremiah mourns for Jerusalem (1:1–22)
2. God's anger at sin (2:1–22)
3. Hope in the midst of affliction (3:1–66)
4. God's anger is satisfied (4:1–22)
5. Jeremiah pleads for restoration (5:1–22)

Jeremiah grieves deeply because of the destruction of Jerusalem and the devastation of his nation. But in the middle of the book, in the depths of his grief, there shines a ray of hope. God's compassion is ever present. His faithfulness is great. Jeremiah realizes that it is only the Lord's mercy that has prevented total annihilation. This book shows us the serious consequences of sin and how we can still have hope in the midst of tragedy because God is able to turn it around for good. We see the timeless importance of prayer and confession of sin. We will all face tragedy in our life. But in the midst of our afflictions, there is hope in God.

## MEGATHEMES

| THEME | EXPLANATION | IMPORTANCE |
|---|---|---|
| *Destruction of Jerusalem* | Lamentations is a sad funeral song for the great capital city of the Jews. The Temple has been destroyed, the king is gone, and the people are in exile. God had warned that he would destroy them if they abandoned him. Now, afterward, the people realize their condition and confess their sin. | God's warnings are justified. He does what he says he will do. His punishment for sin is certain. Only by confessing and renouncing our sin can we turn to him for deliverance. How much better to do so before his warnings are fulfilled. |
| *God's Mercy* | God's compassion was at work even when the Israelites were experiencing the affliction of their Babylonian conquerors. Although the people had been unfaithful, God's faithfulness was great. He used this affliction to bring his people back to him. | God will always be faithful to his people. His merciful, refining work is evident even in affliction. At those times, we must pray for forgiveness and then turn to him for deliverance. |
| *Sin's Consequences* | God was angry at the prolonged rebellion by his people. Sin was the cause of their misery, and destruction was the result of their sin. The destruction of the nation shows the vanity of human glory and pride. | To continue in rebellion against God is to invite disaster. We must never trust our own leadership, resources, intelligence, or power more than God. If we do, we will experience consequences similar to Jerusalem's. |
| *Hope* | God's mercy in sparing some of the people offers hope for better days. One day, the people will be restored to a true and fervent relationship with God. | Only God can deliver us from sin. Without him there is no comfort or hope for the future. Because of Christ's death for us and his promise to return, we have a bright hope for tomorrow. |

## 1. Jeremiah mourns for Jerusalem

**1:1**
Isa 22:2
Jer 40:9

**1** * ¹ Jerusalem, once so full of people,
      is now deserted.
She who was once great among the nations
    now sits alone like a widow.
Once the queen of all the earth,
    she is now a slave.

**1:2**
Job 19:13-14
Pss 6:6; 77:2-6
Jer 2:25; 22:20-22
Mic 7:5

² She sobs through the night;
    tears stream down her cheeks.
Among all her lovers,
    there is no one left to comfort her.
All her friends have betrayed her
    and become her enemies.

**1:3**
Lev 26:39
Deut 28:64-67
2 Kgs 25:4-5

³ Judah has been led away into captivity,
    oppressed with cruel slavery.
She lives among foreign nations
    and has no place of rest.

**1** Each of the first four chapters of this book is an acrostic, laid out in the order of the Hebrew alphabet. The first word of each verse begins with a successive Hebrew letter. Chapters 1, 2, and 4 have one verse for each of the 22 Hebrew letters. Chapter 3 contains 22 stanzas of three verses each. Though chapter 5 has 22 verses, it is not an acrostic.

**1:1** This is the prophet Jeremiah's song of sorrow for Jerusalem's destruction. The nation of Judah had been utterly defeated, the Temple destroyed, and captives taken away to Babylon. Jeremiah's tears were for the suffering and humiliation of the people, but he also wept because God had rejected the people for their rebellious ways. Each year this book was read aloud to remind all the Jews that their great city fell because of their stubborn sinfulness.

**1:2** The term *lovers* refers to nations such as Egypt, to whom Judah kept turning for help. As the Babylonians closed in on Jerusalem, the nation of Judah turned away from God and sought help and protection from other nations instead.

Her enemies have chased her down,
    and she has nowhere to turn.

4 The roads to Jerusalem* are in mourning,
    for crowds no longer come to celebrate the festivals.
The city gates are silent,
    her priests groan,
her young women are crying—
    how bitter is her fate!

5 Her oppressors have become her masters,
    and her enemies prosper,
for the LORD has punished Jerusalem
    for her many sins.
Her children have been captured
    and taken away to distant lands.

6 All the majesty of beautiful Jerusalem*
    has been stripped away.
Her princes are like starving deer
    searching for pasture.
They are too weak to run
    from the pursuing enemy.

7 In the midst of her sadness and wandering,
    Jerusalem remembers her ancient splendor.
But now she has fallen to her enemy,
    and there is no one to help her.
Her enemy struck her down
    and laughed as she fell.

8 Jerusalem has sinned greatly,
    so she has been tossed away like a filthy rag.
All who once honored her now despise her,
    for they have seen her stripped naked and humiliated.
All she can do is groan
    and hide her face.

9 She defiled herself with immorality
    and gave no thought to her future.
Now she lies in the gutter
    with no one to lift her out.
"LORD, see my misery," she cries.
    "The enemy has triumphed."

10 The enemy has plundered her completely,
    taking every precious thing she owns.
She has seen foreigners violate her sacred Temple,
    the place the LORD had forbidden them to enter.

11 Her people groan as they search for bread.
    They have sold their treasures for food to stay alive.
"O LORD, look," she mourns,
    "and see how I am despised.

12 "Does it mean nothing to you, all you who pass by?
    Look around and see if there is any suffering like mine,

**1:4** Hebrew *Zion;* also in 1:17.    **1:6** Hebrew *of the daughter of Zion.*

**1:4**
Jer 9:11; 10:22
Lam 2:6-7
Joel 1:8-13

**1:5**
Ps 90:7-8
Ezek 8:17-18;
9:9-10

**1:6**
Jer 13:18

**1:7**
Jer 37:7
Lam 4:17

**1:8**
Isa 59:2-13

**1:9**
Ps 74:23
Eccl 4:1
Isa 3:8
Jer 13:17-18
Ezek 24:13

**1:10**
Ps 74:4-8
Isa 64:10-11
Jer 51:51

**1:11**
1 Sam 30:12

**1:12**
Isa 13:13
Jer 4:8; 18:16;
48:27

**1:9** The warning was loud and clear: If Judah played with fire, its people would get burned. Jerusalem foolishly took a chance and lost, refusing to believe that immoral living brings God's punishment. The ultimate consequence of sin is punishment (Romans 6:23). We can choose to ignore God's warnings, but as surely as judgment came upon Jerusalem, so it will come upon those who defy God. Are you listening to God's Word? Are you obeying it? Obedience is a sure sign of your love for God.

which the Lord brought on me
  when he erupted in fierce anger.

13 "He has sent fire from heaven that burns in my bones.
  He has placed a trap in my path and turned me back.
He has left me devastated,
  racked with sickness all day long.

14 "He wove my sins into ropes
  to hitch me to a yoke of captivity.
The Lord sapped my strength and turned me over to my enemies;
  I am helpless in their hands.

15 "The Lord has treated my mighty men
  with contempt.
At his command a great army has come
  to crush my young warriors.
The Lord has trampled his beloved city*
  like grapes are trampled in a winepress.

16 "For all these things I weep;
  tears flow down my cheeks.
No one is here to comfort me;
  any who might encourage me are far away.
My children have no future,
  for the enemy has conquered us."

17 Jerusalem reaches out for help,
  but no one comforts her.
Regarding his people Israel,*
  the Lord has said,
"Let their neighbors be their enemies!
  Let them be thrown away like a filthy rag!"

18 "The Lord is right," Jerusalem says,
  "for I rebelled against him.
Listen, people everywhere;
  look upon my anguish and despair,
for my sons and daughters
  have been taken captive to distant lands.

19 "I begged my allies for help,
  but they betrayed me.
My priests and leaders
  starved to death in the city,
even as they searched for food
  to save their lives.

20 "Lord, see my anguish!
  My heart is broken
and my soul despairs,
  for I have rebelled against you.

1:15 Hebrew *the virgin daughter of Judah.*   1:17 Hebrew *Jacob.* The names "Jacob" and "Israel" are often interchanged throughout the Old Testament, referring sometimes to the individual patriarch and sometimes to the nation.

1:14 At first, sin seems to offer freedom. But the liberty to do anything we want gradually becomes a desire to do everything. Then we become captive to sin, bound by its "yoke." Freedom from sin's captivity comes only from God. He gives us freedom, not to do anything we want, but to do what he knows is best for us. Strange as it may seem, true freedom comes in obeying God—following his guidance so that we can receive his best.
1:16 Jeremiah's sorrow expresses the sorrow of the nation. God is the comforter, but because of the people's sins, he had to turn away from them and become their judge. When we suffer the consequences of sin, repentance from the sin that caused the problem is the first and most important way to find relief.
1:19 Jerusalem's allies could not come to help because, like Jerusalem, they failed to seek God. Though these allies appeared strong, they were actually weak because God was not with them. Dependable assistance can come only from an ally whose power is from God. When you seek wise counsel, go to Christians who get their wisdom from the all-knowing God.

In the streets the sword kills,
>   and at home there is only death.

21 "Others heard my groans,
>   but no one turned to comfort me.
> When my enemies heard about my troubles,
>   they were happy to see what you had done.
> Oh, bring the day you promised,
>   when they will suffer as I have suffered.

1:21
Ps 35:15
Isa 14:5-6; 47:6
Jer 30:16

22 "Look at all their evil deeds, LORD.
>   Punish them,
> as you have punished me
>   for all my sins.
> My groans are many,
>   and I am sick at heart."

1:22
Neh 4:4-5
Ps 137:7-8

## 2. God's anger at sin

**2** ¹ The Lord in his anger
>   has cast a dark shadow over beautiful Jerusalem.*
> The fairest of Israel's cities lies in the dust,
>   thrown down from the heights of heaven.
> In his day of great anger,
>   the Lord has shown no mercy even to his Temple.*

2:1
Pss 99:5; 132:7
Isa 64:11
Ezek 28:14-16

² Without mercy the Lord has destroyed
>   every home in Israel.*
> In his anger he has broken down
>   the fortress walls of beautiful Jerusalem.*
> He has brought them to the ground,
>   dishonoring the kingdom and its rulers.

2:2
Pss 21:9; 89:39-40
Lam 3:43

³ All the strength of Israel
>   vanishes beneath his fierce anger.
> The Lord has withdrawn his protection
>   as the enemy attacks.
> He consumes the whole land of Israel
>   like a raging fire.

2:3
Ps 75:5, 10
Isa 42:25
Jer 21:14

⁴ He bends his bow against his people,
>   as though he were their enemy.
> His strength is used against them
>   to kill their finest youth.
> His fury is poured out like fire
>   on beautiful Jerusalem.*

2:4
Job 6:4; 16:13
Jer 7:20
Lam 3:12-13

⁵ Yes, the Lord has vanquished Israel
>   like an enemy.
> He has destroyed her palaces
>   and demolished her fortresses.
> He has brought unending sorrow and tears
>   upon beautiful Jerusalem.

2:5
Jer 52:13
Lam 2:2

⁶ He has broken down his Temple
>   as though it were merely a garden shelter.

2:6
Lam 1:4
Zeph 3:18

**2:1a** Hebrew *the daughter of Zion;* also in 2:8, 10, 18.   **2:1b** Hebrew *his footstool.*   **2:2a** Hebrew *Jacob;* also in 2:3b. See note on 1:17.   **2:2b** Hebrew *the daughter of Judah;* also in 2:5.   **2:4** Hebrew *on the tent of the daughter of Zion.*

**1:22** Babylon, although sinful, was God's instrument for punishing Judah and its capital, Jerusalem. The people of Jerusalem were pleading for God to punish sinful Babylon as he had punished them ("punish them, as you have punished me"). God would do this, for he had already passed judgment on Babylon (see Jeremiah 50:1-27).

**2:6** King Solomon's Temple in Jerusalem represented God's presence with the people (1 Kings 8:1-11). The Temple was the central place of worship. Many in Jeremiah's day assumed that God would never allow his Temple to be harmed. Its destruction symbolized God's rejection of his people—that he no longer lived among them.

The LORD has blotted out all memory
of the holy festivals and Sabbath days.
Kings and priests fall together
before his fierce anger.

**2:7** Ps 74:3-8 Isa 64:11 Ezek 7:20-22

7 The Lord has rejected his own altar;
he despises his own sanctuary.
He has given Jerusalem's palaces
to her enemies.
They shout in the LORD's Temple
as though it were a day of celebration.

**2:8** 2 Kgs 21:13 Isa 34:11 Amos 7:7-9

8 The LORD was determined
to destroy the walls of beautiful Jerusalem.
He made careful plans for their destruction,
then did what he had planned.
Therefore, the ramparts and walls
have fallen down before him.

**2:9** Neh 1:3 Jer 14:14; 23:16

9 Jerusalem's gates have sunk into the ground.
He has smashed their locks and bars.
Her kings and princes have been exiled to distant lands;
her law has ceased to exist.
Her prophets receive
no more visions from the LORD.

**2:10** Job 2:13 Isa 3:26 Amos 8:3 Jon 3:6-8

10 The leaders of beautiful Jerusalem
sit on the ground in silence.
They are clothed in burlap
and throw dust on their heads.
The young women of Jerusalem
hang their heads in shame.

**2:11** Jer 4:19 Lam 2:19

11 I have cried until the tears no longer come;
my heart is broken.
My spirit is poured out in agony
as I see the desperate plight of my people.
Little children and tiny babies
are fainting and dying in the streets.

**2:12** Job 30:16 Ps 42:4

12 They cry out to their mothers,
"We need food and drink!"
Their lives ebb away in the streets
like the life of a warrior wounded in battle.
They gasp for life
as they collapse in their mothers' arms.

**2:7** Our place of worship is not as important to God as our priorities in worship. A church building may be beautiful, but if its people don't sincerely follow God, the church will decay from within. The people of Judah, despite their stunning Temple, had rejected in their daily lives what they proclaimed in their worship rituals. Thus, their worship had turned into a mocking lie. When you worship, are you saying words you don't really mean? Do you pray for help you don't really believe will come? Do you express love for God you don't really have? Earnestly seek God and catch a fresh vision of his love and care. Then worship him wholeheartedly.

**2:9** Four powerful symbols and sources of security were lost: the protection of the *gates,* the leadership of the *kings and princes,* the guidance of the *law,* and the vision of the *prophets.* With those four factors present, the people were lulled into a false sense of security and felt comfortable with their sins. But after each was removed, the people were confronted with the

choice of repenting and returning to God or continuing on this path of suffering. Don't substitute symbols, even good ones, for the reality of a living, personal relationship with God himself.

**2:11** Jeremiah's tears were sincere and full of compassion. Sorrow does not mean that we lack faith or strength. There is nothing wrong with crying—Jesus himself felt sorrow and even wept (John 11:35). How do we react to the tearing down of our society and to moral degradation? This may not be as obvious as an invading enemy army, but the destruction is just as certain. We, too, should be deeply moved when we see the moral decay that surrounds us.

13 What can I say about you?
    Who has ever seen such sorrow?
 O daughter of Jerusalem,
    to what can I compare your anguish?
 O virgin daughter of Zion,
    how can I comfort you?
 For your wound is as deep as the sea.
    Who can heal you?

2:13
Lam 1:12

14 Your prophets have said
    so many foolish things, false to the core.
 They did not save you from exile
    by pointing out your sins.
 Instead, they painted false pictures,
    filling you with false hope.

2:14
Ezek 22:25, 28;
23:36
Mic 3:8

15 All who pass by jeer at you.
    They scoff and insult beautiful Jerusalem,* saying,
 "Is this the city called 'Most Beautiful in All the World'
    and 'Joy of All the Earth'?"

2:15
Job 27:23
Pss 48:2; 50:2
Jer 18:16

16 All your enemies mock you.
    They scoff and snarl and say,
 "We have destroyed her at last!
    We have long waited for this day,
    and it is finally here!"

2:16
Pss 22:13; 56:2
Lam 3:46
Obad 1:12-15

17 But it is the LORD who did just as he planned.
    He has fulfilled the promises of disaster
    he made long ago.
 He has destroyed Jerusalem without mercy.
    He has caused her enemies to gloat over her
    and has given them power over her.

2:17
Deut 28:43-44
Ps 89:42
Lam 1:5

18 Cry aloud* before the Lord,
    O walls of beautiful Jerusalem!
 Let your tears flow like a river
    day and night.
 Give yourselves no rest;
    give your eyes no relief.

2:18
Lam 2:8
Hos 7:14
Hab 2:11

19 Rise during the night and cry out.
    Pour out your hearts like water to the Lord.
 Lift up your hands to him in prayer,
    pleading for your children,
 for in every street
    they are faint with hunger.

2:19
1 Sam 1:15
Isa 51:20

20 "O LORD, think about this!
    Should you treat your own people this way?

2:20
Exod 32:11
Deut 9:26
Jer 23:11-12
Lam 4:13, 16

2:15 Hebrew *the daughter of Jerusalem.*    2:18 Hebrew *Their heart cried.*

---

2:14 False prophets were everywhere in Jeremiah's day. They gave counterfeit and misleading messages. While Jeremiah warned the people of coming destruction and lengthy captivity, the false prophets said that all was well so the people need not fear. All of Jeremiah's words came true because he was a true prophet of God (Jeremiah 14:14-16).

2:19 Chapter 1 describes Jerusalem's desolation and calls for God's revenge on his enemies. Chapter 2 includes a call for God's people to pour out their hearts in the Lord's presence. The people must turn from their sins; they must sincerely mourn over their wrongs against God (3:40-42). The people had much to cry about. Because of their stubborn rebellion against God, they had brought great suffering to all, especially to the innocent. Was this suffering God's fault? No, it was the fault of the wayward people. Sinful people brought destruction on themselves, but tragically, sin's consequences affected everyone—good and evil alike.

2:19 The people's suffering and sin should have brought them to the Lord, weeping for forgiveness. Only when our prideful, independent hearts are broken over sin can God come to our rescue. Just feeling sorry about experiencing sin's consequences does not bring forgiveness. But if we cry out to God in repentance, he will forgive us.

Should mothers eat their own children,
  those they once bounced on their knees?
Should priests and prophets be killed
  within the Lord's Temple?

2:21
2 Chr 36:17
Jer 6:11
Zech 11:6

21 "See them lying in the streets—
    young and old,
  boys and girls,
    killed by the swords of the enemy.
  You have killed them in your anger,
    slaughtering them without mercy.

2:22
Isa 24:17-18
Jer 16:2-4

22 "You have invited terrors from all around,
    as though you were calling them to a day of feasting.
  In the day of the LORD's anger,
    no one has escaped or survived.
  The enemy has killed all the children
    whom I carried and raised."

## 3. Hope in the midst of affliction

**3** ¹ I am the one who has seen the afflictions
    that come from the rod of the LORD's anger.

3:2
Jer 4:23

2 He has led me into darkness,
    shutting out all light.

3:3
Isa 5:25

3 He has turned his hand against me
    again and again, all day long.

3:4
Jer 50:17

4 He has made my skin and flesh grow old.
    He has broken my bones.
5 He has besieged and surrounded me
    with anguish and distress.
6 He has buried me in a dark place,
    like those long dead.

3:7
Jer 40:4

7 He has walled me in, and I cannot escape.
    He has bound me in heavy chains.
8 And though I cry and shout,
    he has shut out my prayers.

3:9
Isa 63:17

9 He has blocked my way with a high stone wall;
    he has made my road crooked.

10 He has hidden like a bear or a lion,
    waiting to attack me.

3:11
Hos 6:1

11 He has dragged me off the path and torn me in pieces,
    leaving me helpless and devastated.
12 He has drawn his bow
    and made me the target for his arrows.

13 He shot his arrows
    deep into my heart.

3:14
Lam 3:63

14 My own people laugh at me.
    All day long they sing their mocking songs.

---

**2:21, 22** This horrible scene could have been avoided. Jeremiah had warned the people for years that this day of destruction would come, and it broke his heart to see it fulfilled. We are always shocked when we hear of tragedy striking the innocent. But often innocent by-standers are victims of judgment on a nation. Sin has a way of causing great sorrow and devastation to many.

**3:1ff** In Jeremiah's darkest moment, his hope was strengthened with this assurance: God had been faithful and would continue to be faithful. Jeremiah saw both God's judgment and God's stead-

fast love. In the time of judgment, Jeremiah could still cling to God's love, just as in times of prosperity he had warned of God's judgment.

**3:1ff** In the original Hebrew, the first four chapters in Lamentations are acrostic poems. Each verse in each chapter begins with a successive letter of the Hebrew alphabet. Chapter 3 has 66 verses rather than 22 because it is a triple acrostic: The first three verses begin with the equivalent of *A*, the next three with *B*, and so on. This was a typical form of Hebrew poetry. Other examples of acrostics are Psalms 37, 119, and 145, and Proverbs 31:10-31.

<sup>15</sup> He has filled me with bitterness
and given me a bitter cup of sorrow to drink.

<sup>16</sup> He has made me chew on gravel.
He has rolled me in the dust.

<sup>17</sup> Peace has been stripped away,
and I have forgotten what prosperity is.

<sup>18</sup> I cry out, "My splendor is gone!
Everything I had hoped for from the Lord is lost!"

<sup>19</sup> The thought of my suffering and homelessness
is bitter beyond words.*

<sup>20</sup> I will never forget this awful time,
as I grieve over my loss.

<sup>21</sup> Yet I still dare to hope
when I remember this:

<sup>22</sup> The faithful love of the Lord never ends!*
His mercies never cease.

<sup>23</sup> Great is his faithfulness;
his mercies begin afresh each morning.

<sup>24</sup> I say to myself, "The Lord is my inheritance;
therefore, I will hope in him!"

<sup>25</sup> The Lord is good to those who depend on him,
to those who search for him.

<sup>26</sup> So it is good to wait quietly
for salvation from the Lord.

<sup>27</sup> And it is good for people to submit at an early age
to the yoke of his discipline:

<sup>28</sup> Let them sit alone in silence
beneath the Lord's demands.

<sup>29</sup> Let them lie face down in the dust,
for there may be hope at last.

<sup>30</sup> Let them turn the other cheek to those who strike them
and accept the insults of their enemies.

<sup>31</sup> For no one is abandoned
by the Lord forever.

<sup>32</sup> Though he brings grief, he also shows compassion
because of the greatness of his unfailing love.

<sup>33</sup> For he does not enjoy hurting people
or causing them sorrow.

<sup>34</sup> If people crush underfoot
all the prisoners of the land,

**3:15** Jer 9:15

**3:16** Prov 20:17

**3:17** Isa 59:11
Jer 12:12

**3:18** Job 17:15
Ezek 37:11

**3:19** Lam 3:5, 15

**3:22** Jer 3:12
Mal 3:6

**3:25** Isa 25:9; 26:9

**3:28** Jer 15:17

**3:29** Job 16:15; 40:4

**3:30** Isa 50:6
Matt 5:39

**3:31** Isa 54:7-10

**3:32** Hos 11:8

---

**3:19** Or *is wormwood and gall.*    **3:22** As in Syriac version; Hebrew reads *of the Lord keeps us from destruction.*

---

**3:21-23** Jeremiah saw one ray of hope in all the sin and sorrow surrounding him: "The faithful love of the Lord never ends. . . . Great is his faithfulness; his mercies begin afresh each morning." God willingly responds with help when we ask. Perhaps there is some sin in your life that you thought God would not forgive. God's steadfast love and mercy are greater than any sin, and he promises forgiveness.

**3:23** Jeremiah knew from personal experience about God's faithfulness. God had promised that punishment would follow disobedience, and it did. But God also had promised future restoration and blessing, and Jeremiah knew that God would keep that promise also. Trusting in God's faithfulness day by day makes us confident in his great promises for the future.

**3:27-33** To submit "to the yoke of his discipline" means to willingly come under God's discipline and learn what he wants to teach. This involves several important factors: (1) silent reflection on what God wants, (2) repentant humility, (3) self-control in the face of adversity, and (4) confident patience, depending on the divine Teacher to bring about loving lessons in our life. God has several long-term and short-term lessons for you right now. Are you doing your homework?

**3:30** This call to "turn the other cheek" reminds us that sometimes God calls us to suffer criticism and abuse for his purposes. Jesus taught his followers to turn the other cheek (Matthew 5:39), and he exemplified this at the highest level just before his crucifixion (Matthew 27:27-31; Luke 22:64; John 18:22; 19:3). This, however, should never be used to justify anyone's continued suffering of spousal or any other kind of abuse.

3:35
Prov 17:15

35 if they deprive others of their rights
      in defiance of the Most High,

3:36
Jer 22:3
Hab 1:13

36 if they twist justice in the courts—
      doesn't the Lord see all these things?

37 Who can command things to happen
      without the Lord's permission?

3:38
Job 2:10
Jer 32:42

38 Does not the Most High
      send both calamity and good?

3:39
Mic 7:9
Heb 12:5-6

39 Then why should we, mere humans, complain
      when we are punished for our sins?

3:40
2 Cor 13:5

40 Instead, let us test and examine our ways.
      Let us turn back to the LORD.

41 Let us lift our hearts and hands
      to God in heaven and say,

3:42
Neh 9:26
Jer 14:20

42 "We have sinned and rebelled,
      and you have not forgiven us.

43 "You have engulfed us with your anger, chased us down,
      and slaughtered us without mercy.

44 You have hidden yourself in a cloud
      so our prayers cannot reach you.

3:45
1 Cor 4:13

45 You have discarded us as refuse and garbage
      among the nations.

3:46
Lam 2:16

46 "All our enemies
      have spoken out against us.

3:47
Jer 48:43-44

47 We are filled with fear,
      for we are trapped, devastated, and ruined."

48 Tears stream from my eyes
      because of the destruction of my people!

49 My tears flow endlessly;
      they will not stop

50 until the LORD looks down
      from heaven and sees.

51 My heart is breaking
      over the fate of all the women of Jerusalem.

3:52
1 Sam 26:20

52 My enemies, whom I have never harmed,
      hunted me down like a bird.

3:53
Jer 37:16

53 They threw me into a pit
      and dropped stones on me.

3:54
Jon 2:3-5

54 The water rose over my head,
      and I cried out, "This is the end!"

55 But I called on your name, LORD,
      from deep within the pit.

3:56
Job 34:28

56 You heard me when I cried, "Listen to my pleading!
      Hear my cry for help!"

3:57
Isa 41:10-14

57 Yes, you came when I called;
      you told me, "Do not fear."

3:58
Jer 50:34; 51:36

58 Lord, you are my lawyer! Plead my case!
      For you have redeemed my life.

---

**3:39-42** Parents discipline children to produce right behavior. God disciplined Judah to produce right living and genuine worship. We must not complain about corrective or instructive discipline in our lives but learn from it, trusting God and being willing to change. We must allow God's correction to bring about the kind of behavior in our life that pleases him.

**3:52-57** At one point in his ministry, Jeremiah was thrown into an empty cistern, and he was left to die in the mire at the bottom (Jeremiah 38:6-13). But God rescued him. Jeremiah used this experience as a picture of the nation sinking into sin. If they turned to God, he would rescue them.

59 You have seen the wrong they have done to me, L ORD.
    Be my judge, and prove me right.
60 You have seen the vengeful plots
    my enemies have laid against me.

61 L ORD, you have heard the vile names they call me.
    You know all about the plans they have made.
62 My enemies whisper and mutter
    as they plot against me all day long.
63 Look at them! Whether they sit or stand,
    I am the object of their mocking songs.

64 Pay them back, L ORD,
    for all the evil they have done.
65 Give them hard and stubborn hearts,
    and then let your curse fall on them!
66 Chase them down in your anger,
    destroying them beneath the L ORD's heavens.

**3:61**
Lam 5:1

**3:62**
Ezek 36:3

**3:63**
Lam 3:14

**3:64**
Jer 51:24

**3:65**
Deut 2:30

## 4. God's anger is satisfied

**4** ¹How the gold has lost its luster!
    Even the finest gold has become dull.
The sacred gemstones
    lie scattered in the streets!

2 See how the precious children of Jerusalem,*
    worth their weight in fine gold,
are now treated like pots of clay
    made by a common potter.

3 Even the jackals feed their young,
    but not my people Israel.
They ignore their children's cries,
    like ostriches in the desert.

4 The parched tongues of their little ones
    stick to the roofs of their mouths in thirst.
The children cry for bread,
    but no one has any to give them.

5 The people who once ate the richest foods
    now beg in the streets for anything they can get.
Those who once wore the finest clothes
    now search the garbage dumps for food.

6 The guilt* of my people
    is greater than that of Sodom,
where utter disaster struck in a moment
    and no hand offered help.

**4:1**
2 Kgs 25:9-10

**4:2**
Isa 30:14
Jer 19:1, 11

**4:3**
Job 39:14-16
Lam 2:12

**4:4**
Jer 14:3

**4:5**
Jer 6:2
Amos 6:3-7

**4:6**
Gen 19:25
Jer 20:16
Ezek 16:48

**4:2** Hebrew *precious sons of Zion.*    **4:6** Or *punishment.*

---

**4:1ff** This chapter contrasts the situation before the siege of Jerusalem with the situation after the siege. The sights and sounds of prosperity were gone because of the people's sin. This chapter warns us not to assume that when life is going well, it will always stay that way. We must be careful not to glory in our prosperity or we will fall into spiritual poverty.

**4:1-10** When a city was under siege, the city wall—built for protection—sealed the people inside. They could not get out to the fields to get food and water because the enemy was camped around the city. As food in the city ran out, the people watched

their enemies harvest and eat the food in the fields. The siege was a test of wills to see which army could outlast the other. Jerusalem was under siege for two years. Life became so harsh that people even ate their own children, and dead bodies were left to rot in the streets. All hope was gone.

**4:6** The city of Sodom, destroyed by burning sulfur from heaven because of its wickedness (Genesis 18:20–19:29), became a symbol of God's ultimate judgment. Yet the guilt of Jerusalem was even greater than that of Sodom! Jeremiah wasn't comparing sins but acknowledging that Sodom had few of the advantages and blessings that the people of Jerusalem had enjoyed from God. Jerusalem's greater guilt was in turning away in spite of the city's countless God-given benefits.

**4:7**
Ps 51:7

7 Our princes once glowed with health—
   brighter than snow, whiter than milk.
Their faces were as ruddy as rubies,
   their appearance like fine jewels.*

**4:8**
Ps 102:5
Lam 5:10

8 But now their faces are blacker than soot.
   No one recognizes them in the streets.
Their skin sticks to their bones;
   it is as dry and hard as wood.

**4:9**
Lev 26:39

9 Those killed by the sword are better off •
   than those who die of hunger.
Starving, they waste away
   for lack of food from the fields.

**4:10**
Deut 28:53-55
2 Kgs 6:26-30
Lam 2:20

10 Tenderhearted women
   have cooked their own children.
They have eaten them
   to survive the siege.

**4:11**
Deut 32:22

11 But now the anger of the LORD is satisfied.
   His fierce anger has been poured out.
He started a fire in Jerusalem*
   that burned the city to its foundations.

**4:12**
Jer 21:13

12 Not a king in all the earth—
   no one in all the world—
would have believed that an enemy
   could march through the gates of Jerusalem.

**4:13**
Jer 2:30; 26:8-9
Ezek 22:26

13 Yet it happened because of the sins of her prophets
   and the sins of her priests,
who defiled the city
   by shedding innocent blood.

**4:14**
Deut 28:28-29
Isa 29:10; 56:10;
59:9-10

14 They wandered blindly
   through the streets,
so defiled by blood
   that no one dared touch them.

**4:15**
Lev 13:45-46
Jer 45:5

15 "Get away!" the people shouted at them.
   "You're defiled! Don't touch us!"
So they fled to distant lands
   and wandered among foreign nations,
   but none would let them stay.

**4:16**
Isa 9:14-16
Jer 52:24-27

16 The LORD himself has scattered them,
   and he no longer helps them.
People show no respect for the priests
   and no longer honor the leaders.

**4:17**
Jer 37:7
Ezek 29:16

17 We looked in vain for our allies
   to come and save us,
but we were looking to nations
   that could not help us.

4:7 Hebrew *like lapis lazuli*.   4:11 Hebrew *in Zion*.

---

**4:13-15** To be defiled or unclean meant to be unfit to enter the Temple or to worship before God. The priests and prophets should have been the most careful to maintain ceremonial purity so that they could continue to perform their duties before God. But many priests and prophets did evil and were defiled. As the nation's leaders, their example led the people into sin and caused the ultimate downfall of the nation and its capital city, Jerusalem.

**4:17** Judah had asked Egypt to help it fight the Babylonian army. Egypt gave Judah false hope by starting to help, but then it had retreated (Jeremiah 37:5-7). Jeremiah warned Judah not to ally itself with Egypt. He told the leaders to rely on God, but they refused to listen.

18 We couldn't go into the streets
    without danger to our lives.
  Our end was near; our days were numbered.
    We were doomed!

4:18
Jer 5:31; 16:16
Amos 8:2

19 Our enemies were swifter than eagles in flight.
    If we fled to the mountains, they found us.
  If we hid in the wilderness,
    they were waiting for us there.

4:19
Deut 28:49
Isa 5:26-28
Jer 4:13

20 Our king—the LORD's anointed, the very life of our nation—
    was caught in their snares.
  We had thought that his shadow
    would protect us against any nation on earth!

4:20
Jer 39:5
Ezek 12:12-13

21 Are you rejoicing in the land of Uz,
    O people of Edom?
  But you, too, must drink from the cup of the LORD's anger.
    You, too, will be stripped naked in your drunkenness.

4:21
Isa 34:7
Amos 1:11

22 O beautiful Jerusalem,* your punishment will end;
    you will soon return from exile.
  But Edom, your punishment is just beginning;
    soon your many sins will be exposed.

4:22
Isa 40:2
Jer 49:10

## 5. Jeremiah pleads for restoration

**5** ¹ LORD, remember what has happened to us.
    See how we have been disgraced!
  ² Our inheritance has been turned over to strangers,
    our homes to foreigners.
  ³ We are orphaned and fatherless.
    Our mothers are widowed.
  ⁴ We have to pay for water to drink,
    and even firewood is expensive.
  ⁵ Those who pursue us are at our heels;
    we are exhausted but are given no rest.
  ⁶ We submitted to Egypt and Assyria
    to get enough food to survive.
  ⁷ Our ancestors sinned, but they have died—
    and we are suffering the punishment they deserved!

  ⁸ Slaves have now become our masters;
    there is no one left to rescue us.
  ⁹ We hunt for food at the risk of our lives,
    for violence rules the countryside.
  ¹⁰ The famine has blackened our skin
    as though baked in an oven.
  ¹¹ Our enemies rape the women in Jerusalem*
    and the young girls in all the towns of Judah.

5:2
Isa 1:7
Hos 8:7-8
Zeph 1:13

5:7
Jer 14:20; 16:12

5:8
Neh 5:15
Zech 11:6

5:9
Jer 40:9-12

5:11
Isa 13:16
Zech 14:2

**4:22** Hebrew *O daughter of Zion.*   **5:11** Hebrew *in Zion.*

**4:20** King Zedekiah, although called "the LORD's anointed," had little spiritual depth and leadership power. Instead of putting his faith in God and listening to God's true prophet, Jeremiah, he listened to the false prophets. To make matters worse, the people chose to follow and trust in their king (2 Chronicles 36:11-16). They chose the path of complacency, wanting to feel secure rather than to follow the directives God was giving his people through Jeremiah. But the source of their confidence—King Zedekiah—was captured.

**4:21, 22** Edom was Judah's archenemy, even though they had a common ancestor, Isaac (see Genesis 25:19-26; 36:1). Edom had actively aided Babylon in the siege of Jerusalem. As a reward, Nebuchadnezzar gave the outlying lands of Judah to Edom. Jeremiah said that the nation of Edom would be judged for treachery against Judah—in essence, against its own relatives. (See also Jeremiah 49:7-22; Ezekiel 25:12-14; Amos 9:12; Obadiah 1:1-21.)

**5:1ff** At a time of grief, the true believer should turn to God in prayer. Here Jeremiah prayed for mercy for his people. At the end of his prayer, he wondered if God had "utterly rejected" his people because of his great anger toward them. But God would not stay angry with them forever. "You will not stay angry with your people forever, because you delight in showing unfailing love" (Micah 7:18).

<table>
<tr><td>

5:12
Isa 47:6

</td><td>

12 Our princes are being hanged by their thumbs,
    and our elders are treated with contempt.
13 Young men are led away to work at millstones,
    and boys stagger under heavy loads of wood.

</td></tr>
</table>

| 5:12<br>Isa 47:6 | 12 Our princes are being hanged by their thumbs,<br>   and our elders are treated with contempt.<br>13 Young men are led away to work at millstones,<br>   and boys stagger under heavy loads of wood. |
| 5:14<br>Isa 24:8<br>Jer 7:34 | 14 The elders no longer sit in the city gates;<br>   the young men no longer dance and sing. |
| 5:15<br>Jer 25:10<br>Amos 8:10 | 15 Joy has left our hearts;<br>   our dancing has turned to mourning.<br>16 The garlands have* fallen from our heads.<br>   Weep for us because we have sinned. |
| 5:17<br>Job 17:7<br>Isa 1:5 | 17 Our hearts are sick and weary,<br>   and our eyes grow dim with tears.<br>18 For Jerusalem* is empty and desolate,<br>   a place haunted by jackals. |
| 5:19<br>Pss 45:6; 102:12 | 19 But LORD, you remain the same forever!<br>   Your throne continues from generation to generation.<br>20 Why do you continue to forget us?<br>   Why have you abandoned us for so long? |
| 5:21<br>Ps 80:3<br>Isa 60:20-22<br>Jer 31:18 | 21 Restore us, O LORD, and bring us back to you again!<br>   Give us back the joys we once had!<br>22 Or have you utterly rejected us?<br>   Are you angry with us still? |

**5:16** Or *The crown has.*    **5:18** Hebrew *Mount Zion.*

---

**5:14** During peace and prosperity, the leaders and elders of the city would sit at the city gate and talk over politics, theology, and philosophy, and conduct business. As Jeremiah prayed, he saw fewer and fewer evidences of either the healthy interaction or the lighthearted dancing of their former lives under God's blessing. They had lost even the everyday events they had assumed would always be there. A lack of continual gratefulness to God often indicates that we are taking the goodness of life for granted.

**5:22** A high calling flouted by low living results in deep suffering. Lamentations gives us a portrait of the bitter suffering the people

of Jerusalem experienced when sin caught up with them and God turned his back on them. Every material goal they had lived for collapsed. But although God turned away from them because of their sin, he did not abandon them—that was their great hope. Despite their sinful past, God would restore them if they returned to him. Hope is found only in the Lord. Thus, our grief should turn us toward him, not away from him.

# EZEKIEL

## VITAL STATISTICS

**PURPOSE:**
To announce God's judgment on Israel and other nations and to foretell the eventual salvation of God's people

**AUTHOR:**
Ezekiel son of Buzi, a Zadokite priest

**ORIGINAL AUDIENCE:**
The Jews in captivity in Babylonia

**DATE WRITTEN:**
Approximately 571 B.C.

**SETTING:**
Ezekiel was a younger contemporary of Jeremiah. While Jeremiah ministered to the people still in Judah, Ezekiel prophesied to those already exiled in Babylonia after the defeat of Jehoiachin. He was taken there in 597 B.C.

**KEY VERSES:**
"For I will gather you up from all the nations and bring you home again to your land. Then I will sprinkle clean water on you, and you will be clean. Your filth will be washed away, and you will no longer worship idols. And I will give you a new heart, and I will put a new spirit in you. I will take out your stony, stubborn heart and give you a tender, responsive heart" (36:24–26).

**KEY PEOPLE:**
Ezekiel, Israel's leaders, Ezekiel's wife, Nebuchadnezzar, "the prince"

**KEY PLACES:**
Jerusalem, Babylon, and Egypt

A COMPUTER can be programmed to respond at your command. And by conditioning a dog with rewards and punishments, you can teach it to obey. But as every parent knows, children are not so easily taught. People have wills and must choose to submit, to follow the instructions of those who have authority over them. Surely discipline is part of the process—boys and girls should know that they will reap the consequences of disobedience.

God's children must learn to obey their heavenly Father. Created in his image, they have a choice, and God allows them to choose.

Ezekiel was a man who chose to obey God. Although he was a priest (1:3), he served as a Jewish "street preacher" in Babylon for 22 years, telling everyone about God's judgment and salvation, and calling them to repent and obey. And Ezekiel *lived* what he preached. During his ministry God told him to illustrate his messages with dramatic object lessons. Some of these acts included (1) lying on his side for 390 days during which he could eat only one eight-ounce meal a day cooked over manure, (2) shaving his head and beard, and (3) showing no sorrow when his wife died. He obeyed and faithfully proclaimed God's word.

God may not ask you to do anything quite so dramatic or difficult; but if he did, would you do it?

The book of Ezekiel chronicles the prophet's life and ministry. Beginning with his call as a prophet and commissioning as a "watchman for Israel" (chapters 1—3), Ezekiel immediately began to preach and demonstrate God's truth, as he predicted the approaching siege and destruction of Jerusalem (chapters 4—24). This devastation would be God's judgment for the people's idolatry. Ezekiel challenged them to turn from their wicked ways. In the next section, he spoke to the surrounding nations, prophesying that God would judge them for their sins as well (chapters 25—32). The book concludes with a message of hope, as Ezekiel proclaimed the faithfulness of God and foretold the future blessings for God's people (chapters 33—48).

As you read this exciting record, observe how Ezekiel fearlessly preached the word of God to the exiled Jews in the streets of Babylon, and hear the timeless truth of God's love and power. Think about each person's responsibility to trust God and about the inevitability of God's judgment against idolatry, rebellion, and indifference. Then commit yourself to obey God, whatever, wherever, and whenever he asks.

## THE BLUEPRINT

A. **MESSAGES OF DOOM**
(1:1—24:27)
1. Ezekiel's call
2. Visions of sin and judgment
3. Punishment is certain

While Jeremiah was prophesying in Jerusalem that the city would soon fall to the Babylonians, Ezekiel was giving the same message to the captives who were already in Babylon. Like those in Jerusalem, the captives stubbornly believed that Jerusalem would not fall and that they would soon return to their land. Ezekiel warned them that punishment was certain because of their sins and that God was purifying his people. God will always punish sin, whether we believe it or not.

B. **MESSAGES AGAINST FOREIGN NATIONS**
(25:1—32:32)

Ezekiel condemns the sinful actions of seven nations. The people in these nations were saying that God was obviously too weak to defend his people and the city of Jerusalem. But God was allowing his people to be defeated in order to punish them for their sins. These pagan nations, however, would face a similar fate, and then they would know that God is all-powerful. Those who dare to mock God today will also face a terrible fate.

C. **MESSAGES OF HOPE**
(33:1—48:35)
1. Restoring the people of God
2. Restoring the worship of God

After the fall of Jerusalem, Ezekiel delivered messages of future restoration and hope for the people. God is holy, but Jerusalem and the Temple had become defiled. The nation had to be cleansed through 70 years of captivity. Ezekiel gives a vivid picture of the unchangeable holiness of God. We, too, must gain a vision of the glory of God, a fresh sense of his greatness, as we face the struggles of daily life.

## MEGATHEMES

| THEME | EXPLANATION | IMPORTANCE |
|---|---|---|
| God's Holiness | Ezekiel saw a vision that revealed God's absolute moral perfection. God was spiritually and morally superior to members of Israel's corrupt and compromising society. Ezekiel wrote to let the people know that God in his holiness was also present in Babylon, not just in Jerusalem. | Because God is morally perfect, he can help us live above our tendency to compromise with this world. When we focus on his greatness, he gives us the power to overcome sin and to reflect his holiness. |
| Sin | Israel had sinned, and God's punishment came. The fall of Jerusalem and the Babylonian exile were used by God to correct the rebels and draw them back from their sinful way of life. Ezekiel warned them that not only was the nation responsible for sin but each individual was also accountable to God. | We cannot excuse ourselves from our responsibilities before God. We are accountable to God for our choices. Rather than neglect him, we must recognize sin for what it is—rebellion against God—and choose to follow him instead. |
| Restoration | Ezekiel consoles the people by telling them that the day will come when God will restore those who turn from sin. God will be their King and shepherd. He will give his people a new heart to worship him, and he will establish a new government and a new Temple. | The certainty of future restoration encourages believers in times of trial. But we must be faithful to God because we love him, not merely for what he can do for us. Is our faith in *him* or merely in our future benefits? |
| Leaders | Ezekiel condemned the shepherds (unfaithful priests and leaders), who led the people astray. By contrast, he served as a caring shepherd and a faithful watchman to warn the people about their sin. One day God's perfect shepherd, the Messiah, will lead his people. | Jesus is our perfect leader. If we truly want him to lead us, our devotion must be more than talk. If we are given the responsibility of leading others, we must take care of them even if it means sacrificing personal pleasure, happiness, time, or money. We are responsible for those we lead. |
| Worship | An angel gave Ezekiel a vision of the Temple in great detail. God's holy presence had departed from Israel and the Temple because of sin. The building of a future Temple portrays the return of God's glory and presence. God will cleanse his people and restore true worship. | All of God's promises will be fulfilled under the rule of the Messiah. The faithful followers will be restored to perfect fellowship with God and with one another. To be prepared for this time, we must focus on God. We do this through regular worship. Through worship we learn about God's holiness and the changes we must make in how we live. |

## A. MESSAGES OF DOOM (1:1—24:27)

Ezekiel prophesied to the exiles in Babylon. He had to dispel the false hope that Israel's captivity would be short, explain the reasons for the severe judgments on their nation, and bring a message of future hope. Although the people did not respond positively, they heard the messages and knew the truth. God's people were not left without explanation and direction, and neither are we.

### 1. Ezekiel's call

*A Vision of Living Beings*

**1** On July 31* of my thirtieth year,* while I was with the Judean exiles beside the Kebar River in Babylon, the heavens were opened and I saw visions of God. ²This happened during the fifth year of King Jehoiachin's captivity. ³(The LORD gave this message to Ezekiel son of Buzi, a priest, beside the Kebar River in the land of the Babylonians,* and he felt the hand of the LORD take hold of him.)

⁴As I looked, I saw a great storm coming from the north, driving before it a huge cloud that flashed with lightning and shone with brilliant light. There was fire inside the cloud, and in the middle of the fire glowed something like gleaming amber.* ⁵From the center of the cloud came four living beings that looked human, ⁶except that each had four faces and four wings. ⁷Their legs were straight, and their feet had hooves like those of a calf and shone like burnished bronze. ⁸Under each of their four wings I could see human hands. So each of the four beings had four faces and four wings. ⁹The wings of each living being touched the wings of the beings beside it. Each one moved straight forward in any direction without turning around.

**1:1**
Ezek 3:23; 40:2
Dan 8:1-2
Rev 4:1; 19:11
**1:2**
2 Kgs 24:12
**1:4**
Isa 21:1
Jer 23:19
**1:5**
Rev 4:6-8
**1:6**
Ezek 10:14, 21
**1:7**
Dan 10:6
Rev 1:15; 2:18
**1:8**
Ezek 10:8, 21
**1:9**
Ezek 10:22

**1:1a** Hebrew *On the fifth day of the fourth month,* of the ancient Hebrew lunar calendar. A number of dates in Ezekiel can be cross-checked with dates in surviving Babylonian records and related accurately to our modern calendar. This event occurred on July 31, 593 B.C. **1:1b** Or *in the thirtieth year.* **1:3** Or *Chaldeans.* **1:4** Or *like burnished metal;* also in 1:27.

---

**1:1** Ezekiel, born and raised in the land of Judah, was preparing to become a priest in God's Temple when the Babylonians attacked in 597 B.C. and carried him away along with 10,000 other captives (2 Kings 24:10-14). The nation was on the brink of complete destruction. Five years later, when Ezekiel was 30 (the normal age for becoming a priest), God called him to be a prophet. During the first six years when Ezekiel ministered in the land of the Babylonians (1:3), Jeremiah was preaching to the Jews still in Judah, and Daniel was serving in Nebuchadnezzar's court. The Kebar River connected to the Euphrates in Babylonia and was the location of a Jewish settlement of exiles.

**1:1** Why did the Jewish exiles in Babylonia need a prophet? God wanted Ezekiel to (1) help the exiles understand why they had been taken captive, (2) dispel the false hope that the captivity was going to be short, (3) bring a new message of hope, and (4) call the people to a new awareness of their dependence upon God.

**1:1** God communicated to Ezekiel in visions. A vision is a miraculous revelation of God's truth. These visions seem strange to

**EXILE IN BABYLON** Ezekiel worked for God right where he was—among the exiles in various colonies near the Kebar River in Babylonia. Jerusalem and its Temple lay over 500 miles away, but Ezekiel helped the people understand that, although they were far from home, they did not need to be far from God.

us because they are *apocalyptic.* This means that Ezekiel saw symbolic pictures that vividly conveyed an idea. Daniel and John were other Bible writers who used apocalyptic imagery. The people in exile had lost their perspective of God's purpose and presence, and Ezekiel came to them with a vision from God to show God's awesome glory and holiness and to warn the exiles of sin's consequences before it was too late.

**1:1ff** Ezekiel's latest dated message from God (29:17) was given in 571 B.C. He was taken captive during the second Babylonian invasion of Judah in 597 B.C. The Babylonians invaded Judah a third and final time in 586 B.C., completely destroying Jerusalem, burning the Temple, and deporting the rest of the people (see 2 Kings 25). Ezekiel dates all his messages from the year he was taken captive (597). His first prophecy to the exiles occurred four years after he arrived in Babylonia (593 B.C.).

**1:3** The name *Ezekiel* means "God is strong" or "God strengthens." In a very real sense, this sums up the basic message of the book: that in spite of the captivity, God's sovereign strength prevails, and he will judge his enemies and restore his true people.

**1:4ff** In this first vision, God called Ezekiel to be a prophet (see 2:5). Nothing in Ezekiel's previous experience had prepared him for such a display of God's glorious presence and power. The huge cloud flashed with lightning and was surrounded by a brilliant light. From the fire in the cloud came four living beings. They showed Ezekiel that Jerusalem's coming destruction was God's judgment of Judah for its sins. (These living beings are also seen in Revelation 4:6, 7.)

When Ezekiel received this vision, he was far away from the Temple in Jerusalem, the physical symbol of God's presence. Through this vision, he learned that God is present everywhere and that God's activities in heaven are shaping the events on earth.

**1:5-12** Each of the four living beings had four faces, symbolizing God's perfect nature. Some believe that the lion represented strength; the ox, diligent service; the human, intelligence; and the eagle, divinity. Others see these as the most majestic of God's creatures and say that they therefore represented God's whole creation. The early church fathers saw a connection between these beings and the four Gospels: the lion with Matthew, presenting

**1:10**
Ezek 10:14
Rev 4:7

**1:11**
Isa 6:2
Ezek 10:16, 19

**1:12**
Ezek 1:9, 20

**1:13**
Ps 104:4
Rev 4:5

**1:14**
Matt 24:27

**1:16**
Ezek 10:9-13

**1:17**
Ezek 1:12

**1:18**
Ezek 10:9-13
Rev 4:6, 8

**1:19**
Ezek 10:16-17, 19

**1:21**
Ezek 10:17

**1:22**
Ezek 10:1

**1:24**
2 Kgs 7:6
Ezek 10:5; 43:2
Dan 10:6
Rev 1:15; 19:6

**1:26**
Exod 24:10
Isa 6:1; 54:11
Ezek 10:1
Rev 1:13

**1:27**
Ezek 3:23

**1:28**
Rev 1:17; 4:3; 10:1

¹⁰Each had a human face in the front, the face of a lion on the right side, the face of an ox on the left side, and the face of an eagle at the back. ¹¹Each had two pairs of outstretched wings—one pair stretched out to touch the wings of the living beings on either side of it, and the other pair covered its body. ¹²They went in whatever direction the spirit chose, and they moved straight forward in any direction without turning around.

¹³The living beings looked like bright coals of fire or brilliant torches, and lightning seemed to flash back and forth among them. ¹⁴And the living beings darted to and fro like flashes of lightning.

¹⁵As I looked at these beings, I saw four wheels touching the ground beside them, one wheel belonging to each. ¹⁶The wheels sparkled as if made of beryl. All four wheels looked alike and were made the same; each wheel had a second wheel turning crosswise within it. ¹⁷The beings could move in any of the four directions they faced, without turning as they moved. ¹⁸The rims of the four wheels were tall and frightening, and they were covered with eyes all around.

¹⁹When the living beings moved, the wheels moved with them. When they flew upward, the wheels went up, too. ²⁰The spirit of the living beings was in the wheels. So wherever the spirit went, the wheels and the living beings also went. ²¹When the beings moved, the wheels moved. When the beings stopped, the wheels stopped. When the beings flew upward, the wheels rose up, for the spirit of the living beings was in the wheels.

²²Spread out above them was a surface like the sky, glittering like crystal. ²³Beneath this surface the wings of each living being stretched out to touch the others' wings, and each had two wings covering its body. ²⁴As they flew, their wings sounded to me like waves crashing against the shore or like the voice of the Almighty* or like the shouting of a mighty army. When they stopped, they let down their wings. ²⁵As they stood with wings lowered, a voice spoke from beyond the crystal surface above them.

²⁶Above this surface was something that looked like a throne made of blue lapis lazuli. And on this throne high above was a figure whose appearance resembled a man. ²⁷From what appeared to be his waist up, he looked like gleaming amber, flickering like a fire. And from his waist down, he looked like a burning flame, shining with splendor. ²⁸All around him was a glowing halo, like a rainbow shining in the clouds on a rainy day. This is what the glory of the LORD looked like to me. When I saw it, I fell face down on the ground, and I heard someone's voice speaking to me.

**1:24** Hebrew *Shaddai.*

---

**EZEKIEL**
served as a
prophet to
the exiles in
Babylon from
593–571 B.C.

*Climate of the times* . . . . . . Ezekiel and his people are taken to Babylon as captives. The Jews become foreigners in a strange land ruled by an authoritarian government.

*Main message.* . . . . . . . . . . Because of the people's sins, God allowed the nation of Judah to be destroyed. But there was still hope—God promised to restore the land to those who remained faithful to him.

*Importance of message* . . . God never forgets those who faithfully seek to obey him. They have a glorious future ahead.

*Contemporary prophets* . . . Daniel (605–536 B.C.), Habakkuk (612–589 B.C.), Jeremiah (627–586 B.C.).

---

Christ as the Lion of Judah; the ox with Mark, portraying Christ as the Servant; the human with Luke, portraying Christ as the perfect human; the eagle with John, portraying Christ as the Son of God, exalted and divine. The vision of John in Revelation 4 parallels Ezekiel's vision.

**1:16-18** Ezekiel described two wheels at right angles to each other, one on a north-south and the other on an east-west axis. Able to move anywhere, these wheels show that God is present everywhere and is able to see all things (1:18). God is not restricted to Jerusalem but rules all of life and history. Though the exiles had experienced great change, God was still in control.

**1:26** This figure "whose appearance resembled a man" revealed God's holiness and prepared Ezekiel for what God was about to tell him. The figure represented God himself on the throne. In a similar way, Christ revealed God in human form and prepared us for his message of salvation. Christ came into history in a real, human body.

**1:27, 28** The glory of the Lord appeared like fire and a glowing halo or rainbow to Ezekiel. Ezekiel fell face down, overwhelmed by the contrast between God's holiness and his own sinfulness and insignificance. Eventually every person will fall before God, either out of reverence and awe for his mercy or out of fear of his judgment. Based on the way you are living today, how will you respond to God's holiness?

**1:27, 28** The four living beings and the four wheels are powerful pictures of judgment, yet the rainbow over the throne symbolizes God's never-ending faithfulness to his people. Just as God sent a rainbow to Noah to symbolize his promise never again to destroy the earth by a flood (Genesis 9:8-17), so this rainbow symbolizes God's promise to preserve those who remain faithful to him. The purpose of God's judgment is to correct us and, ultimately, to allow perfect peace and righteousness to reign on the earth forever.

## Ezekiel's Call and Commission

**2** "Stand up, son of man," said the voice. "I want to speak with you." 2 The Spirit came into me as he spoke, and he set me on my feet. I listened carefully to his words. 3 "Son of man," he said, "I am sending you to the nation of Israel, a rebellious nation that has rebelled against me. They and their ancestors have been rebelling against me to this very day. 4 They are a stubborn and hard-hearted people. But I am sending you to say to them, 'This is what the Sovereign LORD says!' 5 And whether they listen or refuse to listen—for remember, they are rebels—at least they will know they have had a prophet among them.

6 "Son of man, do not fear them or their words. Don't be afraid even though their threats surround you like nettles and briers and stinging scorpions. Do not be dismayed by their dark scowls, even though they are rebels. 7 You must give them my messages whether they listen or not. But they won't listen, for they are completely rebellious! 8 Son of man, listen to what I say to you. Do not join them in their rebellion. Open your mouth, and eat what I give you."

9 Then I looked and saw a hand reaching out to me. It held a scroll, 10 which he unrolled. And I saw that both sides were covered with funeral songs, words of sorrow, and pronouncements of doom.

**3** The voice said to me, "Son of man, eat what I am giving you—eat this scroll! Then go and give its message to the people of Israel." 2 So I opened my mouth, and he fed me the scroll. 3 "Fill your stomach with this," he said. And when I ate it, it tasted as sweet as honey in my mouth.

4 Then he said, "Son of man, go to the people of Israel and give them my messages. 5 I am not sending you to a foreign people whose language you cannot understand. 6 No, I am not sending you to people with strange and difficult speech. If I did, they would listen! 7 But the people of Israel won't listen to you any more than they listen to me! For the whole lot of them are hard-hearted and stubborn. 8 But look, I have made you as obstinate and hard-hearted as they are. 9 I have made your forehead as hard as the hardest rock! So don't be afraid of them or fear their angry looks, even though they are rebels."

**2:2**
Dan 8:18
**2:3**
1 Sam 8:7-8
Jer 3:25
Dan 9:5-13
**2:4**
Isa 48:4
Jer 5:3
**2:5**
Matt 10:12-15
Luke 10:10-11
John 15:22
**2:6**
Isa 51:12
Jer 1:8
Mic 7:4
**2:8**
Jer 15:16
Rev 10:9
**2:9**
Jer 36:2
Rev 5:1-5; 10:8-11
**3:2**
Jer 25:17
**3:3**
Jer 6:11; 15:16
Rev 10:9-10
**3:5**
Jon 1:2; 3:2-4
Acts 26:17-18
**3:7**
John 15:20
**3:8**
Jer 1:18

---

**2:1** The immortal God addressed Ezekiel by calling him "son of man," emphasizing the distance between them. It is amazing that God chooses to work his divine will on earth through finite, imperfect beings. We are made from the dust of the ground, yet God chooses to place within us his life and breath and to ask us to serve him.

**2:2** We can only imagine what it was like for Ezekiel to experience this vision. Certainly there was much he did not understand, but Ezekiel knew that each part had significance because it came from God. When God saw Ezekiel's open and obedient attitude, he filled Ezekiel with his Spirit and gave Ezekiel power for the job ahead. God doesn't expect us to understand everything about him, but to be willing and obedient servants, faithful to what we know is true and right.

**2:3-5** The business world defines success in terms of giving customers what they want. Ezekiel, however, was called to give God's message to the people, whether they would listen or not. The measure of Ezekiel's success would not be how well the people responded, but how well he obeyed God and thus fulfilled God's purpose for him. Isaiah and Jeremiah also prophesied with little positive response (see Isaiah 6:9-12; Jeremiah 1:17-19). God's truth does not depend on how people respond. God will not judge us for how well others respond to our witness to our faith but for how faithful we have been. God always gives us the strength to accomplish what he asks us to do.

**2:4, 5** God called the people "stubborn and hard-hearted" because they refused to admit their sin. Rebelliousness was the nation's primary characteristic at this time. Even when God pointed out their wrongdoing, the people ignored the truth. Is God pointing at some sin in your life? Don't be stubborn—

confess your sin and begin to live for God. By obeying him now you will be ready for God's final review of your life (Matthew 25:31-46).

**2:6-8** God gave Ezekiel the difficult responsibility of presenting his message to ungrateful and abusive people. Sometimes we must be an example to or share our faith with unkind people. The Lord told Ezekiel not to be afraid, but to speak his words, whether or not the people would listen. He also wants us to tell the Good News, whether it's convenient or not (2 Timothy 4:2).

**2:6-10** Three times God told Ezekiel not to be afraid or dismayed. When God's Spirit is within us, we can lay aside our fears of rejection or ridicule. God's strength is powerful enough to help us live for him even under the heaviest criticism.

**2:9, 10** Ancient books were usually scrolls, one page (up to 30 feet long) rolled up simultaneously from both ends. Normally, scrolls had writing on only one side. But in this case, the warnings overflowed to the scroll's other side, showing the full measure of judgment about to descend on Judah.

**3:1-3** In his vision, Ezekiel ate God's message and found this spiritual food not only good for him but also sweet as honey (see Revelation 10:8-10 for a similar use of this image). If you "digest" God's Word, you will find that not only does it make you stronger in your faith, but its wisdom also sweetens your life. You need to feed yourself spiritually just as you do physically. This means doing more than simply giving God's Word a casual glance. You must make digesting God's Word a regular part of your life.

**3:8, 9** Belief in God is not a crutch for those too weak to stand on their own. God makes his followers strong enough to stand against anything or anyone, including those who hate what is right. Just as God gave Ezekiel tough faith ("as hard as the hardest rock"), he wants to give you the stability, perseverance, and insight you need to live up to the great task he has given you. Give yourself over to God's conditioning and let him get your life in shape.

3:10
Job 22:22

3:12
Ezek 8:3
Acts 2:2; 8:39

3:13
2 Sam 5:24
Ezek 1:15, 24;
10:5, 16-17

3:14
Ezek 8:1

3:17
Isa 52:8; 58:1; 62:6
Jer 6:17
Ezek 33:7-9

3:18
Ezek 33:6, 8

3:19
2 Kgs 17:13-14
Ezek 33:3, 9
Acts 18:6

3:20
Jer 6:21
Ezek 18:24; 33:18
Zeph 1:6

3:21
Acts 20:31

3:22
Acts 9:6

3:23
Ezek 1:1, 28
Acts 7:55

3:24
Ezek 2:2

3:25
Ezek 4:8

3:26
Luke 1:20, 22

[10]Then he added, "Son of man, let all my words sink deep into your own heart first. Listen to them carefully for yourself. [11]Then go to your people in exile and say to them, 'This is what the Sovereign LORD says!' Do this whether they listen to you or not."

[12]Then the Spirit lifted me up, and I heard a loud rumbling sound behind me. (May the glory of the LORD be praised in his place!)* [13]It was the sound of the wings of the living beings as they brushed against each other and the rumbling of their wheels beneath them.

[14]The Spirit lifted me up and took me away. I went in bitterness and turmoil, but the LORD's hold on me was strong. [15]Then I came to the colony of Judean exiles in Tel-abib, beside the Kebar River. I was overwhelmed and sat among them for seven days.

## A Watchman for Israel

[16]After seven days the LORD gave me a message. He said, [17]"Son of man, I have appointed you as a watchman for Israel. Whenever you receive a message from me, warn people immediately. [18]If I warn the wicked, saying, 'You are under the penalty of death,' but you fail to deliver the warning, they will die in their sins. And I will hold you responsible for their deaths. [19]If you warn them and they refuse to repent and keep on sinning, they will die in their sins. But you will have saved yourself because you obeyed me.

[20]"If righteous people turn away from their righteous behavior and ignore the obstacles I put in their way, they will die. And if you do not warn them, they will die in their sins. None of their righteous acts will be remembered, and I will hold you responsible for their deaths. [21]But if you warn righteous people not to sin and they listen to you and do not sin, they will live, and you will have saved yourself, too."

[22]Then the LORD took hold of me and said, "Get up and go out into the valley, and I will speak to you there." [23]So I got up and went, and there I saw the glory of the LORD, just as I had seen in my first vision by the Kebar River. And I fell face down on the ground.

[24]Then the Spirit came into me and set me on my feet. He spoke to me and said, "Go to your house and shut yourself in. [25]There, son of man, you will be tied with ropes so you cannot go out among the people. [26]And I will make your tongue stick to the roof of your mouth

3:12 A possible reading for this verse is *Then the Spirit lifted me up, and as the glory of the LORD rose from its place, I heard a loud rumbling sound behind me.*

---

**3:10, 11** Ezekiel needed to take God's words to heart before preaching them to others. God's message must sink deep into your heart and show in your actions before you can effectively help others understand and apply the gospel.

**3:14, 15** Ezekiel was bitter and angry, not at God, but at the sins and attitudes of the people. Ezekiel's extraordinary vision had ended, and he had to begin the tedious job of prophesying among his people, who cared little about God's messages. Before the Exile, the people had heard Jeremiah, but they would not listen. Here Ezekiel had to give a similar message, and he expected to be rejected as well. But Ezekiel had the vision of the four living beings and the wheels to back up his message. He had nothing to fear because God was with him. Despite knowing the probable outcome, Ezekiel obeyed God.

As we grow, we will have times of great joy when we feel close to God and times when sins, struggles, or everyday tasks overwhelm us. Like Ezekiel, we should obey God even when we don't feel like it. Don't let feelings hinder your obedience.

**3:15** Ezekiel sat quietly among the people for seven days. This was the customary period of mourning for the dead (Genesis 50:10; 1 Samuel 31:13; Job 2:13). Ezekiel was mourning for those who were spiritually dead. Tel-abib was the location of one of the settlements of Jews who were exiled from Jerusalem.

**3:17, 18** A watchman's job was to stand on the city wall and warn the people of approaching danger. Ezekiel's role was to be a spiritual watchman, warning the people of the judgment to come. Some think that the phrase "I will hold you responsible for their deaths" means that just as a watchman on the wall would pay with his life if he failed to warn the city of approaching enemies, Ezekiel would pay with his life if he refused to warn the people of coming judgment. Others believe this phrase simply means that God would hold Ezekiel accountable.

**3:18, 19** God had already told Ezekiel that the people would not listen, so why should he bother to tell them God's message? God

wanted the people to know they had been warned. Ezekiel's job was to obey God. We are responsible to tell others about God's judgment and his message of salvation, although we are not held responsible for how they respond. If we refuse to tell others what we know, however, God will judge us. Remember God's words to Ezekiel when you are tempted to remain silent among those who don't believe.

**3:18-21** In these verses, God is not talking about loss of salvation but rather about physical death. If the people back in Judah continued in their sins, they and their land and cities would be destroyed by Nebuchadnezzar's armies. If, on the other hand, the people would turn to God, God would spare them. God would hold Ezekiel responsible for his fellow Jews if he failed to warn them of the consequences of their sins. All people are individually responsible to God, but believers have a special responsibility to warn unbelievers of the consequences of rejecting God. If we fail to do this, God will hold us responsible for what happens to them. This should motivate us to begin sharing our faith with others—in word and deed—and to avoid becoming callous or unconcerned in our attitude.

**3:23** Ezekiel recognized his helplessness before God and fell face down in his presence. Sometimes our prosperity, popularity, or physical strength blinds us to our spiritual helplessness. But nothing we do on our own can accomplish much for God. Only when God is in control of our wills can we accomplish great tasks for him. The first step to being God's person is to admit that you need his help; then you can begin to see what God can really do in your life.

**3:24-27** Ezekiel was allowed to speak only when God had a message for the people. Thus, the people knew that whatever Ezekiel said was God's message. They did not have to wonder whether Ezekiel was speaking by God's authority or his own.

so that you will be speechless and unable to rebuke them, for they are rebels. ²⁷But when I give you a message, I will loosen your tongue and let you speak. Then you will say to them, 'This is what the Sovereign LORD says!' Those who choose to listen will listen, but those who refuse will refuse, for they are rebels.

## 2. Visions of sin and judgment
### A Sign of the Coming Siege

4 "And now, son of man, take a large clay brick and set it down in front of you. Then draw a map of the city of Jerusalem on it. ²Show the city under siege. Build a wall around it so no one can escape. Set up the enemy camp, and surround the city with siege ramps and battering rams. ³Then take an iron griddle and place it between you and the city. Turn toward the city and demonstrate how harsh the siege will be against Jerusalem. This will be a warning to the people of Israel.

⁴"Now lie on your left side and place the sins of Israel on yourself. You are to bear their sins for the number of days you lie there on your side. ⁵I am requiring you to bear Israel's sins for 390 days—one day for each year of their sin. ⁶After that, turn over and lie on your right side for 40 days—one day for each year of Judah's sin.

⁷"Meanwhile, keep staring at the siege of Jerusalem. Lie there with your arm bared and prophesy her destruction. ⁸I will tie you up with ropes so you won't be able to turn from side to side until the days of your siege have been completed.

⁹"Now go and get some wheat, barley, beans, lentils, millet, and emmer wheat, and mix them together in a storage jar. Use them to make bread for yourself during the 390 days you will be lying on your side. ¹⁰Ration this out to yourself, eight ounces* of food for each day, and eat it at set times. ¹¹Then measure out a jar* of water for each day, and drink it at set times. ¹²Prepare and eat this food as you would barley cakes. While all the people are watching, bake it over a fire using dried human dung as fuel and then eat the bread." ¹³Then the LORD said, "This is how Israel will eat defiled bread in the Gentile lands to which I will banish them!"

¹⁴Then I said, "O Sovereign LORD, must I be defiled by using human dung? For I have never been defiled before. From the time I was a child until now I have never eaten any animal that died of sickness or was killed by other animals. I have never eaten any meat forbidden by the law."

¹⁵"All right," the LORD said. "You may bake your bread with cow dung instead of human dung." ¹⁶Then he told me, "Son of man, I will make food very scarce in Jerusalem. It will be weighed out with great care and eaten fearfully. The water will be rationed out drop by drop, and the people will drink it with dismay. ¹⁷Lacking food and water, people will look at one another in terror, and they will waste away under their punishment.

### A Sign of the Coming Judgment

5 "Son of man, take a sharp sword and use it as a razor to shave your head and beard. Use a scale to weigh the hair into three equal parts. ²Place a third of it at the center of your map of Jerusalem. After acting out the siege, burn it there. Scatter another third across your

4:10 Hebrew *20 shekels* [228 grams].    4:11 Hebrew *1/6 of a hin* [about 1 pint or 0.6 liters].

| Ref | Cross-reference |
|---|---|
| 3:27 | Ezek 33:22 |
| 4:1 | Isa 20:2; Jer 13:1; 19:1 |
| 4:3 | Isa 8:18; 20:3; Jer 39:1-2 |
| 4:4 | Lev 10:17; Num 18:1 |
| 4:5 | Num 14:34 |
| 4:6 | Dan 9:24-26; Rev 11:2-3 |
| 4:7 | Ezek 21:2 |
| 4:8 | Ezek 3:25 |
| 4:9 | Exod 9:32; Isa 28:25 |
| 4:10 | Ezek 45:12 |
| 4:12 | Isa 36:12 |
| 4:13 | Dan 1:8; Hos 9:3 |
| 4:14 | Lev 17:15; 22:8; Deut 14:3-5; Isa 65:4; 66:17; Ezek 9:8; 20:49; Acts 10:14 |
| 4:16 | Lev 26:26; Isa 3:1; Lam 5:4; Ezek 5:16; 12:18-19 |
| 4:17 | Lev 26:39; Ezek 24:23; 33:10 |
| 5:1 | Lev 21:5; Isa 7:20; Dan 5:27 |
| 5:2 | Lev 26:33; Jer 39:1-2 |

**4:1ff** Ezekiel acted out the coming siege and fall of Jerusalem before it actually happened. God gave Ezekiel specific instructions about what to do and say and how to do and say it. Each detail had a specific meaning. Often we ignore or disregard the smaller details of God's Word, thinking God probably doesn't care. Like Ezekiel, we should want to obey God completely, even in the details.

**4:4-17** Ezekiel's unusual actions symbolically portrayed the fate of Jerusalem. He lay on his left side for 390 days to show that Israel would be imprisoned within the walls of the city. We know that Ezekiel did not have to lie on his side all day because these verses tell of other tasks God asked him to do during this time. The small amount of food he was allowed to eat represented the normal ration provided to those living in a city under siege by enemy armies. The food that was to be cooked over dried human dung was a symbol of Judah's spiritual uncleanness.

Certainly many people saw these spectacles and, in the process, heard Ezekiel's occasional speeches (3:27). How many would be willing to so dramatically portray the sins of our nation? We need to pray for greater boldness in our witness.

**4:12-14** Ezekiel asked God not to make him use human dung for fuel because it violated the laws for purity (Leviticus 21–22; Deuteronomy 23:12-14). As a priest, Ezekiel would have been careful to keep all these laws. To use human dung for fuel would paint a dramatic picture of ruin. If nothing was left in the city that could be burned, it would be impossible to continue to follow God's laws for sacrifices.

**5:1-10** Shaving one's head and beard signified mourning, humiliation, and repentance. God told Ezekiel to shave his head and beard and then to divide the hair into three parts, symbolizing what was going to happen to the people in Jerusalem (see 5:12). Along with verbal prophecies, God asked Ezekiel to use dramatic visual images to command the people's attention and to burn an indelible impression on their minds. Just as God gave Ezekiel creative ways to communicate his message to the exiles, we can

**5:3**
Jer 39:10
**5:4**
Jer 41:12
**5:5**
Jer 6:6
Lam 1:1

map and chop it with a sword. Scatter the last third to the wind, for I will scatter my people with the sword. ³Keep just a bit of the hair and tie it up in your robe. ⁴Then take some of these hairs out and throw them into the fire, burning them up. A fire will then spread from this remnant and destroy all of Israel.

⁵"This is what the Sovereign Lord says: This is an illustration of what will happen to Jerusalem. I placed her at the center of the nations, ⁶but she has rebelled against my regulations and decrees and has been even more wicked than the surrounding nations. She has refused to obey the regulations and decrees I gave her to follow.

⁷"Therefore, this is what the Sovereign Lord says: You people have behaved worse than your neighbors and have refused to obey my decrees and regulations. You have not even

**EZEKIEL**

Although Ezekiel's visions and prophecies were clear and vivid, very little is known about the prophet's personal life. He was among the thousands of young men deported from Judah to Babylon when King Jehoiachin surrendered. Until those tragic days, Ezekiel was being trained for the priesthood. But during the exile in Babylon, God called Ezekiel to be his prophet during one of Israel's darkest times.

Ezekiel experienced the same kind of shocking encounter with God that Isaiah had reported 150 years earlier. Like Isaiah, Ezekiel was never the same after his personal encounter with God. Although God's messages through both these prophets had many points in common, the conditions under which they lived were very different. Isaiah warned of the coming storm; Ezekiel spoke in the midst of the storm of national defeat that devastated his people. He announced that even Jerusalem would not escape destruction. In addition, during this time Ezekiel had to endure the pain of his wife's death.

God's description of Ezekiel as a watchman on the walls of the city captures the personal nature of his ministry. A watchman's job was dangerous. If he failed at his post, he and the entire city might be destroyed. His own safety depended on the quality of his work. The importance of each person's accountability before God was a central part of Ezekiel's message. He taught the exiles that God expected personal obedience and worship from each of them.

As in Ezekiel's day, it is easy for us today to forget that God has a personal interest in each one of us. We may feel insignificant or out of control when we look at world events. But knowing that God is ultimately in control, that he cares, and that he is willing to be known by us can bring a new sense of purpose to our lives. How do you measure your worth? Are you valuable because of your achievements and potential or because God, your Creator and Designer, declares you valuable?

**Strengths and accomplishments**
- Was a priest by training, a prophet by God's call
- Received vivid visions and delivered powerful messages
- Served as God's messenger during Israel's captivity in Babylon
- Became a tough and courageous man so he could reach a hard and stubborn people (Ezekiel 3:8)

**Lessons from his life**
- Even the repeated failures of his people will not prevent God's plan for the world from being fulfilled
- Each person's response to God determines his or her eternal destiny
- God has people through whom he can work even in seemingly hopeless situations

**Vital statistics**
- Where: Babylon
- Occupation: Prophet to the captives in Babylon
- Relatives: Father: Buzi. Wife: Unknown.
- Contemporaries: Jehoiachin, Jeremiah, Jehoiakim, Nebuchadnezzar

**Key verses**
"Then he added, 'Son of man, let all my words sink deep into your own heart first. Listen to them carefully for yourself. Then go to your people in exile and say to them, "This is what the Sovereign Lord says!" Do this whether they listen to you or not'" (Ezekiel 3:10, 11).

Ezekiel's story is told in the book of Ezekiel and 2 Kings 24:10-17.

creatively communicate the Good News about God to a lost generation.

**5:3, 4** The few strands of hair Ezekiel put in his robe symbolized the small remnant of faithful people whom God would preserve. But even some from this remnant would be judged and destroyed because their faith was not genuine. Where will you stand in the coming judgment? Matthew 7:22, 23 warns that many who believe they will be saved won't be. Make sure your commitment to the Lord is genuine.

**5:7** The people's wickedness was so great that they couldn't even be compared favorably with the pagan nations around them, not to mention how they would appear with respect to God's laws.

lived up to the standards of the nations around you. [8]Therefore, I myself, the Sovereign LORD, am now your enemy. I will punish you publicly while all the nations watch. [9]Because of your detestable idols, I will punish you like I have never punished anyone before or ever will again. [10]Parents will eat their own children, and children will eat their parents. I will punish you and scatter to the winds the few who survive.

[11]"As surely as I live, says the Sovereign LORD, I will cut you off completely. I will show you no pity at all because you have defiled my Temple with your vile images and detestable sins. [12]A third of your people will die in the city from disease and famine. A third of them will be slaughtered by the enemy outside the city walls. And I will scatter a third to the winds, chasing them with my sword. [13]Then at last my anger will be spent, and I will be satisfied. And when my fury against them has subsided, all Israel will know that I, the LORD, have spoken to them in my jealous anger.

[14]"So I will turn you into a ruin, a mockery in the eyes of the surrounding nations and to all who pass by. [15]You will become an object of mockery and taunting and horror. You will be a warning to all the nations around you. They will see what happens when the LORD punishes a nation in anger and rebukes it, says the LORD.

[16]"I will shower you with the deadly arrows of famine to destroy you. The famine will become more and more severe until every crumb of food is gone. [17]And along with the famine, wild animals will attack you and rob you of your children. Disease and war will stalk your land, and I will bring the sword of the enemy against you. I, the LORD, have spoken!"

## Judgment against Israel's Mountains

**6** Again a message came to me from the LORD: [2]"Son of man, turn and face the mountains of Israel and prophesy against them. [3]Proclaim this message from the Sovereign LORD against the mountains of Israel. This is what the Sovereign LORD says to the mountains and hills and to the ravines and valleys: I am about to bring war upon you, and I will smash your pagan shrines. [4]All your altars will be demolished, and your places of worship will be destroyed. I will kill your people in front of your idols.* [5]I will lay your corpses in front of your idols and scatter your bones around your altars. [6]Wherever you live there will be desolation, and I will destroy your pagan shrines. Your altars will be demolished, your idols will be smashed, your places of worship will be torn down, and all the religious objects you have made will be destroyed. [7]The place will be littered with corpses, and you will know that I alone am the LORD.

[8]"But I will let a few of my people escape destruction, and they will be scattered among the nations of the world. [9]Then when they are exiled among the nations, they will remember me. They will recognize how hurt I am by their unfaithful hearts and lustful eyes that long for their idols. Then at last they will hate themselves for all their detestable sins. [10]They will know that I alone am the LORD and that I was serious when I said I would bring this calamity on them.

[11]"This is what the Sovereign LORD says: Clap your hands in horror, and stamp your feet.

**6:4** The Hebrew term (literally *round things*) probably alludes to dung; also in 6:5, 6, 9, 13.

### Cross references

5:8
Jer 24:9
Zech 14:2

5:9
Dan 9:12
Matt 24:21

5:10
Lev 26:29
Jer 19:9
Amos 9:9
Zech 2:6; 7:14

5:11
Jer 7:9-11
Ezek 8:5-6, 16, 18

5:12
Jer 15:2; 44:27
Ezek 6:11-12;
12:14
Amos 9:9
Zech 2:6

5:13
Isa 1:24; 59:17
Lam 4:11
Ezek 36:6; 38:19

5:14
Pss 74:3-10; 79:1-4
Ezek 22:4

5:15
Isa 66:15-16
Jer 22:8-9
Ezek 25:17
1 Cor 10:11

5:16
Deut 32:23-24

6:2
Ezek 36:1

6:3
Ezek 36:4

6:4
Lev 26:30
2 Chr 14:5
Isa 27:9
Ezek 6:6

6:6
Zech 13:2

6:8
Isa 6:13
Jer 44:14, 28

6:9
Deut 30:2
Job 42:6
Ps 78:40
Isa 7:13; 43:24
Hos 11:8

---

**5:11** It was a serious sin to defile the Temple, God's sanctuary, by worshiping idols and practicing evil within its very walls. In the New Testament, we learn that God now makes his home *within* those who are his. Our body is God's temple (see 1 Corinthians 6:19). We defile God's temple today by allowing gossiping, bitterness, love of money, lying, or any other wrong actions or attitudes to be a part of our life. By asking the Holy Spirit's help, we can keep from defiling his temple, our body.

**5:13** Have you ever seen someone try to discipline a child by saying, "If you do that one more time . . ."? If the parent doesn't follow through, the child learns not to listen. Empty threats backfire. God was going to punish the Israelites for their blatant sins, and he wanted them to know that he would do what he said. The people learned the hard way that God always follows through on his word. Too many people ignore God's warnings, treating them as empty threats. Don't make the mistake of thinking God doesn't really mean what he says.

**6:1ff** This is the beginning of a two-part message. Remember that Ezekiel could speak only when giving messages from God. The message in chapter 6 is that Judah's idolatry will surely call

down God's judgment. The message in chapter 7 describes the nature of that judgment—utter destruction of the nation. Nevertheless God in his mercy saved a remnant. Ezekiel prophesies against the mountains of Israel because mountains were sites of the pagan shrines used to worship idols.

**6:8-10** A ray of light appears in this prophecy of darkness—God would spare a small group—a remnant—of people, but only after they had learned some hard lessons. God sometimes has to break a person in order to bring him or her to true repentance. The people needed to change their attitudes, but they wouldn't until God broke their hearts with humiliation, pain, suffering, and defeat. Does your heart long for God enough to change those areas displeasing him? Or will God have to break your heart?

**6:11** Prophets often used this threefold description of judgment upon Jerusalem—war, famine, and disease—as a way of saying that the destruction would be complete. War meant death in battle; famine came when enemies besieged a city; disease was always a danger during famine. Don't make the mistake of underestimating the extent of God's judgment. If you ignore the biblical warnings and turn away from God, his punishment awaits you.

**6:12**
Lam 4:11-12
Dan 9:7

**6:13**
1 Kgs 14:23
2 Kgs 16:4
Isa 57:5-7
Hos 4:13

**6:14**
Isa 5:25
Ezek 14:13

Cry out because of all the detestable sins the people of Israel have committed. Now they are going to die from war and famine and disease. ¹²Disease will strike down those who are far away in exile. War will destroy those who are nearby. And anyone who survives will be killed by famine. So at last I will spend my fury on them. ¹³They will know that I am the LORD when their dead lie scattered among their idols and altars on every hill and mountain and under every green tree and every great shade tree—the places where they offered sacrifices to their idols. ¹⁴I will crush them and make their cities desolate from the wilderness in the south to Riblah* in the north. Then they will know that I am the LORD."

### The Coming of the End

**7:2**
Ezek 11:13
Amos 8:2, 10

**7** Then this message came to me from the LORD: ²"Son of man, this is what the Sovereign LORD says to Israel:

"The end is here!
   Wherever you look—
east, west, north, or south—
   your land is finished.
³ No hope remains,
   for I will unleash my anger against you.
I will call you to account
   for all your detestable sins.

**7:4**
Ezek 6:7; 11:21;
22:31
Hos 9:7

⁴ I will turn my eyes away and show no pity.
   I will repay you for all your detestable sins.
Then you will know that I am the LORD.

**7:5**
2 Kgs 21:12-13
Nah 1:9

⁵ "This is what the Sovereign LORD says:
Disaster after disaster
   is coming your way!
⁶ The end has come.
   It has finally arrived.
   Your final doom is waiting!

**7:7**
Isa 22:5
Ezek 12:23-25, 28

⁷ O people of Israel, the day of your destruction is dawning.
   The time has come; the day of trouble is near.
Shouts of anguish will be heard on the mountains,
   not shouts of joy.

**6:14** As in some Hebrew manuscripts; most Hebrew manuscripts read *Diblah*.

---

| EZEKIEL'S ACTS OF OBEDIENCE | | |
|---|---|---|
| 2:1 | . . . . . . . . . . . . . . . . . . . . . . . . . . | Stood and received God's message |
| 3:24-27 | . . . . . . . . . . . . . . . . . . . . . | Shut himself inside his house |
| 3:27 | . . . . . . . . . . . . . . . . . . . . . . . . | Faithfully proclaimed God's message |
| 4:1ff | . . . . . . . . . . . . . . . . . . . . . . . | Drew a map of Jerusalem on a large brick (clay tablet) |
| 4:4, 5 | . . . . . . . . . . . . . . . . . . . . . . . | Lay on his left side for 390 days |
| 4:6 | . . . . . . . . . . . . . . . . . . . . . . . . . | Lay on his right side for 40 days |
| 4:9-17 | . . . . . . . . . . . . . . . . . . . . . . | Followed specific cooking instructions |
| 5:1-4 | . . . . . . . . . . . . . . . . . . . . . . . | Shaved his head and beard |
| 12:3-7 | . . . . . . . . . . . . . . . . . . . . . . | Left home to demonstrate exile |
| 13:1ff | . . . . . . . . . . . . . . . . . . . . . . | Spoke against false prophets |
| 19:1ff | . . . . . . . . . . . . . . . . . . . . . . | Sang a funeral song concerning the leaders |
| 21:2 | . . . . . . . . . . . . . . . . . . . . . . . . | Prophesied against Israel and the Temple |
| 21:19-23 | . . . . . . . . . . . . . . . . . . . . | Marked out two routes for Babylon's king |
| 24:16, 17 | . . . . . . . . . . . . . . . . . . . | Did not mourn his wife's death |

---

**6:14** The phrase "then they will know that I am the LORD" (or a variation of this phrase) occurs 65 times in the book of Ezekiel. The purpose of all God's punishment was not to take revenge but to impress upon the people the truth that the Lord is the only true and living God. People in Ezekiel's day were worshiping human-made idols and calling them gods. Today money, sex, and power have become idols for many. Punishment will come upon all who put other things ahead of God. It is easy to forget that the Lord alone is God, the supreme authority and the only source of eternal love and life. Remember that God may use the difficulties of your life to teach you that he alone is God.

8 Soon I will pour out my fury on you
    and unleash my anger against you.
I will call you to account
    for all your detestable sins.
9 I will turn my eyes away and show no pity.
    I will repay you for all your detestable sins.
Then you will know that it is I, the LORD,
    who is striking the blow.

10 "The day of judgment is here;
    your destruction awaits!
The people's wickedness and pride
    have blossomed to full flower.
11 Their violence has grown into a rod
    that will beat them for their wickedness.
None of these proud and wicked people will survive.
    All their wealth and prestige will be swept away.
12 Yes, the time has come;
    the day is here!
Buyers should not rejoice over bargains,
    nor sellers grieve over losses,
for all of them will fall
    under my terrible anger.
13 Even if the merchants survive,
    they will never return to their business.
For what God has said applies to everyone—
    it will not be changed!
Not one person whose life is twisted by sin
    will ever recover.

### The Desolation of Israel

14 "The trumpet calls Israel's army to mobilize,
    but no one listens,
    for my fury is against them all.
15 There is war outside the city
    and disease and famine within.
Those outside the city walls
    will be killed by enemy swords.
Those inside the city
    will die of famine and disease.
16 The survivors who escape to the mountains
    will moan like doves, weeping for their sins.
17 Their hands will hang limp,
    their knees will be weak as water.
18 They will dress themselves in burlap;
    horror and shame will cover them.
They will shave their heads
    in sorrow and remorse.

19 "They will throw their money in the streets,
    tossing it out like worthless trash.

**7:8**
Isa 42:25
Ezek 9:8; 14:19;
33:20; 36:19
Nah 1:6

**7:10**
Ps 89:32
Isa 10:5

**7:12**
Isa 5:13-14
Ezek 6:11-12
1 Cor 7:29-31
Jas 5:8-9

**7:14**
Jer 4:5

**7:15**
Jer 14:18

**7:16**
Isa 38:14; 59:11
Nah 2:7

**7:17**
Isa 13:7
Heb 12:12

**7:18**
Isa 15:3
Amos 8:10

**7:19**
Prov 11:4
Isa 2:20

---

**7:10, 11** In chapter 7, Ezekiel predicts the complete destruction of Israel. The wicked and proud will finally get what they deserve. If it seems as though God ignores the evil and proud people of our day, be assured that a day of judgment will come, just as it came for the people of Israel. God is waiting patiently for sinners to repent (see 2 Peter 3:9), but when his judgment comes, "none of these proud and wicked people will survive." What you decide about God now will determine your fate then.

**7:12, 13** The nation of Israel trusted in its prosperity and possessions instead of in God. So God planned to destroy the basis of its prosperity. Whenever we begin to trust in jobs, the economy, a political system, or military might for our security, we put God in the backseat.

**7:19** God's people had allowed their love of money to lead them into sin. For this, God would destroy them. Money has a strange power to lead people into sin. Paul said that "the love of money is the root of all kinds of evil" (1 Timothy 6:10). It is ironic that

> Their silver and gold won't save them
> on that day of the Lord's anger.
> It will neither satisfy nor feed them,
> for their greed can only trip them up.

**7:20**
Isa 30:22

> 20 They were proud of their beautiful jewelry
> and used it to make detestable idols and vile images.
> Therefore, I will make all their wealth
> disgusting to them.

**7:21**
2 Kgs 24:13

> 21 I will give it as plunder to foreigners,
> to the most wicked of nations,
> and they will defile it.

**7:22**
Jer 18:17

> 22 I will turn my eyes from them
> as these robbers invade and defile my treasured land.

**7:23**
Jer 27:2
Hos 4:2

> 23 "Prepare chains for my people,
> for the land is bloodied by terrible crimes.
> Jerusalem is filled with violence.

**7:24**
2 Chr 7:20

> 24 I will bring the most ruthless of nations
> to occupy their homes.
> I will break down their proud fortresses
> and defile their sanctuaries.
> 25 Terror and trembling will overcome my people.
> They will look for peace but not find it.

**7:26**
Jer 4:20; 18:18
Mic 3:6

> 26 Calamity will follow calamity;
> rumor will follow rumor.
> They will look in vain
> for a vision from the prophets.
> They will receive no teaching from the priests
> and no counsel from the leaders.
> 27 The king and the prince will stand helpless,
> weeping in despair,
> and the people's hands
> will tremble with fear.
> I will bring on them
> the evil they have done to others,
> and they will receive the punishment
> they so richly deserve.
> Then they will know that I am the Lord."

### Idolatry in the Temple

**8:2**
Ezek 1:4, 27-28

**8** Then on September 17,* during the sixth year of King Jehoiachin's captivity, while the leaders of Judah were in my home, the Sovereign Lord took hold of me. 2I saw a figure that appeared to be a man. From what appeared to be his waist down, he looked like a burning

**8:1** Hebrew *on the fifth day of the sixth month*, of the ancient Hebrew lunar calendar. This event occurred on September 17, 592 B.C.; also see note on 1:1.

---

we use a gift of God—money—to buy things that separate us from him. It is tragic that we spend so much money seeking to satisfy ourselves and so little time seeking God, the true source of satisfaction.

**7:20** God gave the people silver and gold, but they used that silver and gold to make idols. The resources God gives us should be used to do his work and carry out his will, but too often we use them to satisfy our own desires. When we abuse God's gifts or use resources selfishly, we miss the real purpose God had in mind. This is as shortsighted as idolatry.

**7:24** The people of Jerusalem took great pride in their buildings. The Temple itself was a source of pride (see 24:20, 21). This pride would be crushed when the evil and godless Babylonians destroyed Jerusalem's fortresses and sanctuaries. If you are going through a humiliating experience, God may be using that experience to weed out pride in your life.

**8:1ff** This prophecy's date corresponds to 592 B.C. The message of chapters 8–11 is directed specifically toward Jerusalem and its leaders. Chapter 8 records Ezekiel being taken in a vision from Babylon to the Temple in Jerusalem to see the great wickedness being practiced there. The people and their religious leaders were thoroughly corrupt. While Ezekiel's first vision (chapters 1–3) showed that judgment was from God, this vision showed that their sin was the reason for judgment.

**8:2** This figure could have been an angel or a manifestation of God himself. In Ezekiel's previous vision, a man with a similar appearance was pictured as God on his throne (1:26-28).

flame. From the waist up he looked like gleaming amber.* ³He reached out what seemed to be a hand and took me by the hair. Then the Spirit lifted me up into the sky and transported me to Jerusalem in a vision from God. I was taken to the north gate of the inner courtyard of the Temple, where there is a large idol that has made the LORD very jealous. ⁴Suddenly, the glory of the God of Israel was there, just as I had seen it before in the valley.

⁵Then the LORD said to me, "Son of man, look toward the north." So I looked, and there to the north, beside the entrance to the gate near the altar, stood the idol that had made the LORD so jealous.

⁶"Son of man," he said, "do you see what they are doing? Do you see the detestable sins the people of Israel are committing to drive me from my Temple? But come, and you will see even more detestable sins than these!" ⁷Then he brought me to the door of the Temple courtyard, where I could see a hole in the wall. ⁸He said to me, "Now, son of man, dig into the wall." So I dug into the wall and found a hidden doorway.

⁹"Go in," he said, "and see the wicked and detestable sins they are committing in there!" ¹⁰So I went in and saw the walls engraved with all kinds of crawling animals and detestable creatures. I also saw the various idols* worshiped by the people of Israel. ¹¹Seventy leaders of Israel were standing there with Jaazaniah son of Shaphan in the center. Each of them held an incense burner, from which a cloud of incense rose above their heads.

¹²Then the LORD said to me, "Son of man, have you seen what the leaders of Israel are doing with their idols in dark rooms? They are saying, 'The LORD doesn't see us; he has deserted our land!'" ¹³Then the LORD added, "Come, and I will show you even more detestable sins than these!"

¹⁴He brought me to the north gate of the LORD's Temple, and some women were sitting there, weeping for the god Tammuz. ¹⁵"Have you seen this?" he asked. "But I will show you even more detestable sins than these!"

¹⁶Then he brought me into the inner courtyard of the LORD's Temple. At the entrance to the sanctuary, between the entry room and the bronze altar, there were about twenty-five men with their backs to the sanctuary of the LORD. They were facing east, bowing low to the ground, worshiping the sun!

¹⁷"Have you seen this, son of man?" he asked. "Is it nothing to the people of Judah that they commit these detestable sins, leading the whole nation into violence, thumbing their noses at me, and provoking my anger? ¹⁸Therefore, I will respond in fury. I will neither pity nor spare them. And though they cry for mercy, I will not listen."

## The Slaughter of Idolaters

**9** Then the LORD thundered, "Bring on the men appointed to punish the city! Tell them to bring their weapons with them!" ²Six men soon appeared from the upper gate that faces north, each carrying a deadly weapon in his hand. With them was a man dressed in linen, who carried a writer's case at his side. They all went into the Temple courtyard and stood beside the bronze altar.

³Then the glory of the God of Israel rose up from between the cherubim, where it had

**8:3** Or *like burnished metal.*   **8:10** The Hebrew term (literally *round things*) probably alludes to dung.

**8:3** Ezek 3:12; 11:1 / Dan 5:5
**8:4** Ezek 1:27-28
**8:5** Ps 78:58 / Jer 3:2; 7:30; 32:34 / Ezek 8:3 / Zech 5:5
**8:6** 2 Kgs 23:4-5 / Ezek 5:11; 8:9, 17
**8:8** Isa 29:15
**8:10** Exod 20:4
**8:11** Num 11:16, 25; 16:17, 35 / Jer 19:1 / Luke 10:1
**8:14** Ezek 44:4; 46:9
**8:16** Deut 4:19; 17:3 / 2 Chr 29:6 / Job 31:26-28 / Jer 2:27; 44:17
**8:17** Jer 7:18-19 / Amos 3:10 / Mic 2:2
**8:18** Isa 1:15 / Jer 11:11 / Mic 3:4 / Zech 7:13
**9:2** Ezek 10:2
**9:3** Ezek 10:4; 11:22-23

**8:3-5** This "idol that has made the LORD very jealous" could be an image of Asherah, the Canaanite goddess of fertility, whose character encouraged sexual immorality and self-gratification. King Manasseh had placed such an idol in the Temple (2 Kings 21:7). King Josiah had burned the Asherah pole (2 Kings 23:6), but there were certainly many other idols around.

**8:6ff** In scene after scene, God revealed to Ezekiel the extent to which the people had embraced idolatry and wickedness. God's Spirit works within us in a similar way, revealing sin that lurks in our life. How comfortable would you feel if God held an open house in your life today?

**8:14** Tammuz was the Babylonian god of spring. He was the husband or lover of the goddess Ishtar. The followers of this cult believed that the green vegetation shriveled and died in the hot summer because Tammuz had died and descended into the underworld. Thus, the worshipers wept and mourned his death. In the springtime, when the new vegetation appeared, they rejoiced, believing that Tammuz had come back to life.

God was showing Ezekiel that many people were no longer worshiping the *true* God of life and vegetation. We must also be careful not to spend so much time thinking about the benefits of creation that we lose sight of the Creator.

**9:1ff** This chapter presents a picture of coming judgment. After Ezekiel had seen how corrupt Jerusalem had become, God called one man to spare the small minority that had been faithful. Then he called six men to slaughter the wicked people in the city. This judgment was ordered by God himself (9:5-7).

**9:2** The writer's case was a common object in Ezekiel's day. It included a long narrow board with a groove to hold the reed brush that was used to write on parchment, papyrus, or dried clay. The board had hollowed out areas for holding cakes of black and red ink that had to be moistened before use.

**9:3** What is God's glory? It is the manifestation of God's character—his ultimate power, transcendence, and moral perfection. God is completely above humans and their limitations. Yet God reveals himself to us so that we can worship and follow him.

**9:4**
Exod 12:7, 13
Ps 119:53, 136
Jer 13:17
2 Cor 1:22
2 Tim 2:19
Rev 7:2-3

**9:6**
2 Chr 36:17
Ezek 5:11; 8:11-12
Rev 9:4

**9:7**
Ezek 7:20-22

**9:8**
1 Chr 21:16
Amos 7:2-6

**9:9**
2 Kgs 21:16
Pss 10:11; 94:7
Isa 29:15
Ezek 7:23; 8:12;
22:2-3, 29
Mic 3:1-3; 7:3

**9:10**
Isa 65:6
Ezek 7:4; 8:18;
11:21; 24:14
Hos 9:7

**10:1**
Exod 24:10
Ezek 1:22, 26
Rev 4:2-3

**10:2**
Ps 18:10-13
Isa 6:6
Rev 8:5

**10:3**
Ezek 8:3, 16

**10:4**
Exod 40:34-35
Isa 6:1-4
Ezek 1:27-28; 9:3;
11:22-23

**10:5**
Job 40:9
Ezek 1:24
Rev 10:3

rested, and moved to the entrance of the Temple. And the LORD called to the man dressed in linen who was carrying the writer's case. ⁴He said to him, "Walk through the streets of Jerusalem and put a mark on the foreheads of all who weep and sigh because of the detestable sins being committed in their city."

⁵Then I heard the LORD say to the other men, "Follow him through the city and kill everyone whose forehead is not marked. Show no mercy; have no pity! ⁶Kill them all—old and young, girls and women and little children. But do not touch anyone with the mark. Begin right here at the Temple." So they began by killing the seventy leaders.

⁷"Defile the Temple!" the LORD commanded. "Fill its courtyards with corpses. Go!" So they went and began killing throughout the city.

⁸While they were out killing, I was all alone. I fell face down on the ground and cried out, "O Sovereign LORD! Will your fury against Jerusalem wipe out everyone left in Israel?"

⁹Then he said to me, "The sins of the people of Israel and Judah are very, very great. The entire land is full of murder; the city is filled with injustice. They are saying, 'The LORD doesn't see it! The LORD has abandoned the land!' ¹⁰So I will not spare them or have any pity on them. I will fully repay them for all they have done."

¹¹Then the man in linen clothing, who carried the writer's case, reported back and said, "I have done as you commanded."

## The LORD's Glory Leaves the Temple

**10** In my vision I saw what appeared to be a throne of blue lapis lazuli above the crystal surface over the heads of the cherubim. ²Then the LORD spoke to the man in linen clothing and said, "Go between the whirling wheels beneath the cherubim, and take a handful of burning coals and scatter them over the city." He did this as I watched.

³The cherubim were standing at the south end of the Temple when the man went in, and the cloud of glory filled the inner courtyard. ⁴Then the glory of the LORD rose up from above the cherubim and went over to the door of the Temple. The Temple was filled with this cloud of glory, and the courtyard glowed brightly with the glory of the LORD. ⁵The moving wings of the cherubim sounded like the voice of God Almighty* and could be heard even in the outer courtyard.

⁶The LORD said to the man in linen clothing, "Go between the cherubim and take some burning coals from between the wheels." So the man went in and stood beside one of the wheels. ⁷Then one of the cherubim reached out his hand and took some live coals from the fire burning among them. He put the coals into the hands of the man in linen clothing, and

**10:5** Hebrew *El-Shaddai.*

---

**9:3** Cherubim are an order of powerful angelic beings created to glorify God. They are associated with God's absolute holiness and moral perfection. God placed cherubim at the entrance of Eden to keep Adam and Eve out after they sinned (Genesis 3:24). Representations of cherubim were used to decorate the Tabernacle and Temple. The lid of the Ark of the Covenant, called the atonement cover, was adorned with two gold cherubim (Exodus 37:6-9). It was a symbol of the very presence of God. The cherubim seen by Ezekiel left the Temple along with the glory of God (chapter 10). Ezekiel then recognized them as the living beings he had seen in his first vision (see chapter 1).

**9:4, 5** God told the man with the writer's case to put a mark on those who were faithful to God. Their faithfulness was determined by their sorrow over their nation's sin. Those with the mark were spared when the six men began to destroy the wicked people. During the Exodus, the Israelites put a mark of blood on their doorframes to save them from death. In the final days, God will mark the foreheads of those destined for salvation (Revelation 7:3), and Satan will mark his followers (Revelation 13:16, 17), who, like him, are destined for destruction. When God punishes sin, he won't forget his promise to preserve his people.

**9:6** The spiritual leaders of Israel blatantly promoted their idolatrous beliefs, and the people abandoned God and followed them. Spiritual leaders are especially accountable to God because they are entrusted with the task of teaching the truth (see James 3:1). When they pervert the truth, they can lead countless people away from God and even cause a nation to fall. It is not surprising, then,

that when God began to judge the nation, he started at the Temple and worked outward (see 1 Peter 4:17). How sad it is that in the Temple, the one place where they should have been teaching God's truth, these men were teaching lies.

**9:9, 10** The people said that the Lord had abandoned the land and wouldn't see their sin. People have many convenient explanations to make it easier to sin: "It doesn't matter," "Everybody's doing it," or "Nobody will ever know." Do you find yourself making excuses for sin? Rationalizing sin makes it easier to commit, but rationalization does not convince God or cancel the punishment.

**10:1ff** Chapters 8–11 depict God's glory departing from the Temple. In 8:3, 4, his glory was over the north gate. It then moved to the entrance (9:3), then the south end of the Temple (10:3, 4), the east gate (10:18, 19; 11:1), and finally the mountain east of the Temple (11:23), probably the Mount of Olives. Because of the nation's sins, God's glory had departed.

**10:2** God's perfect holiness demands judgment for sin. The cherubim are mighty angels. The burning coals scattered over the city represent the purging of sin. For Jerusalem, this meant the destruction of all the people who blatantly sinned and refused to repent. Shortly after this prophecy, the Babylonians destroyed Jerusalem by fire (2 Kings 25:9; 2 Chronicles 36:19).

the man took them and went out. 8(All the cherubim had what looked like human hands under their wings.)

9I looked, and each of the four cherubim had a wheel beside him, and the wheels sparkled like beryl. 10All four wheels looked alike and were made the same; each wheel had a second wheel turning crosswise within it. 11The cherubim could move in any of the four directions they faced, without turning as they moved. They went straight in the direction they faced, never turning aside. 12Both the cherubim and the wheels were covered with eyes. The cherubim had eyes all over their bodies, including their hands, their backs, and their wings. 13I heard someone refer to the wheels as "the whirling wheels." 14Each of the four cherubim had four faces: the first was the face of an ox,* the second was a human face, the third was the face of a lion, and the fourth was the face of an eagle.

15Then the cherubim rose upward. These were the same living beings I had seen beside the Kebar River. 16When the cherubim moved, the wheels moved with them. When they lifted their wings to fly, the wheels stayed beside them. 17When the cherubim stopped, the wheels stopped. When they flew upward, the wheels rose up, for the spirit of the living beings was in the wheels.

18Then the glory of the LORD moved out from the door of the Temple and hovered above the cherubim. 19And as I watched, the cherubim flew with their wheels to the east gate of the LORD's Temple. And the glory of the God of Israel hovered above them.

20These were the same living beings I had seen beneath the God of Israel when I was by the Kebar River. I knew they were cherubim, 21for each had four faces and four wings and what looked like human hands under their wings. 22And their faces were just like the faces of the beings I had seen at the Kebar, and they traveled straight ahead, just as the others had.

## Judgment on Israel's Leaders

**11** Then the Spirit lifted me and brought me to the east gateway of the LORD's Temple, where I saw twenty-five prominent men of the city. Among them were Jaazaniah son of Azzur and Pelatiah son of Benaiah, who were leaders among the people.

2The Spirit said to me, "Son of man, these are the men who are planning evil and giving wicked counsel in this city. 3They say to the people, 'Is it not a good time to build houses? This city is like an iron pot. We are safe inside it like meat in a pot.*' 4Therefore, son of man, prophesy against them loudly and clearly."

5Then the Spirit of the LORD came upon me, and he told me to say, "This is what the LORD says to the people of Israel: I know what you are saying, for I know every thought that comes into your minds. 6You have murdered many in this city and filled its streets with the dead.

7"Therefore, this is what the Sovereign LORD says: This city is an iron pot all right, but the pieces of meat are the victims of your injustice. As for you, I will soon drag you from this pot. 8I will bring on you the sword of war you so greatly fear, says the Sovereign LORD. 9I will drive you out of Jerusalem and hand you over to foreigners, who will carry out my judgments against you. 10You will be slaughtered all the way to the borders of Israel. I will execute judgment on you, and you will know that I am the LORD. 11No, this city will not be an iron pot for you, and you will not be like meat safe inside it. I will judge you even to the borders of Israel, 12and you will know that I am the LORD. For you have refused to obey my decrees and regulations; instead, you have copied the standards of the nations around you."

**10:14** Hebrew *the face of a cherub;* compare 1:10.   **11:3** Hebrew *This city is the pot, and we are the meat.*

---

**10:9**
Ezek 1:16-17

**10:11**
Ezek 1:17

**10:12**
Ezek 1:18
Rev 4:6, 8

**10:14**
1 Kgs 7:27-30, 36
Ezek 1:6, 10; 10:21
Rev 4:7

**10:15**
Ezek 1:3-6, 19-21

**10:17**
Ezek 1:12

**10:18**
Ps 18:10

**10:19**
Ezek 1:22

**10:20**
Ezek 1:5, 26; 10:15

**10:21**
Ezek 1:6, 8; 10:14;
41:18-20

**10:22**
Ezek 1:10, 12

**11:1**
Ezek 8:3; 43:5

**11:2**
Isa 30:1
Mic 2:1

**11:3**
Jer 1:13
Ezek 24:3, 6
2 Pet 3:4

**11:4**
Ezek 3:4, 17

**11:5**
Jer 11:20; 17:10

**11:6**
Isa 1:15
Ezek 7:23; 22:2-6,
9, 12, 27
Matt 23:35

**11:7**
2 Kgs 25:18-22
Jer 52:24-27

**11:9**
Deut 28:36, 49-50
Ps 106:41

**11:10**
Num 34:8-9
Josh 13:5

**11:12**
Ezek 8:10, 14, 16;
18:8-9

---

**10:18** God's glory departed from the Temple and was never completely present again until Christ himself visited it in New Testament times. God's holiness required that he leave the Temple because the people had so defiled it. God had to completely destroy what people had perverted in order for true worship to be revived. We must commit ourselves, our families, our churches, and our nation to follow God faithfully so that we never have to experience God's abandoning us.

**11:1-4** God had abandoned his altar and Temple (chapters 9–11); here his judgment was complete as his glory stopped above the mountain east of the city (11:23). The city gate was where merchants and politicians conducted business, so the 25 men may have represented the nation's rulers. Because of their leadership positions, they were responsible for leading the people astray. They had wrongly said that they were secure from another attack

by the Babylonians. "This city is like an iron pot. We are safe inside it like meat in a pot" means they believed that they were the elite, the influential, the ones who would be protected from all harm. Without God, however, our situation is always precarious.

**11:5** God knew everything about the Israelites, even their thoughts. He also knows everything about us, even the sins we try to hide. Instead of worrying about people noticing how we look or what we do, we should care about what God thinks, for he sees everything. Trying to hide our thoughts and actions from God is futile. "Secret" sins are never secret from God. The only effective way to deal with our sins is to confess them and ask God to help us overcome them.

**11:12** From the time they entered the Promised Land, the Israelites were warned not to copy the customs and religious practices of other nations. Disobeying this command and following pagan

**11:13**
Ezek 9:8

¹³While I was still prophesying, Pelatiah son of Benaiah suddenly died. Then I fell face down on the ground and cried out, "O Sovereign LORD, are you going to kill everyone in Israel?"

### Hope for Exiled Israel

**11:15**
Ezek 33:24

**11:16**
Jer 29:7, 11

**11:17**
Isa 11:11-16
Jer 24:5-6

**11:18**
Ezek 5:11; 37:23

**11:19**
Jer 24:7; 32:39
Ezek 36:26
Zech 7:12
2 Cor 3:3

**11:20**
Ezek 36:27

**11:21**
Jer 16:18

¹⁴Then this message came to me from the LORD: ¹⁵"Son of man, the people still left in Jerusalem are talking about you and your relatives and all the people of Israel who are in exile. They are saying, 'Those people are far away from the LORD, so now he has given their land to us!'

¹⁶"Therefore, tell the exiles, 'This is what the Sovereign LORD says: Although I have scattered you in the countries of the world, I will be a sanctuary to you during your time in exile. ¹⁷I, the Sovereign LORD, will gather you back from the nations where you have been scattered, and I will give you the land of Israel once again.'

¹⁸"When the people return to their homeland, they will remove every trace of their vile images and detestable idols. ¹⁹And I will give them singleness of heart and put a new spirit within them. I will take away their stony, stubborn heart and give them a tender, responsive heart,* ²⁰so they will obey my decrees and regulations. Then they will truly be my people, and I will be their God. ²¹But as for those who long for vile images and detestable idols, I will repay them fully for their sins. I, the Sovereign LORD, have spoken!"

### The LORD's Glory Leaves Jerusalem

**11:22**
Ezek 10:19

**11:23**
Ezek 8:4
Zech 14:4

**11:24**
Ezek 8:3; 37:1

²²Then the cherubim lifted their wings and rose into the air with their wheels beside them, and the glory of the God of Israel hovered above them. ²³Then the glory of the LORD went up from the city and stopped above the mountain to the east.

²⁴Afterward the Spirit of God carried me back again to Babylonia,* to the people in exile there. And so ended the vision of my visit to Jerusalem. ²⁵And I told the exiles everything the LORD had shown me.

### 3. Punishment is certain
### Signs of the Coming Exile

**12:2**
Isa 6:9-10
Jer 5:21
Ezek 2:6-8
Matt 13:13-14
John 9:39-41

**12:3**
Jer 26:3; 36:3, 7
Luke 20:13
2 Tim 2:25

**12** Again a message came to me from the LORD: ²"Son of man, you live among rebels who have eyes but refuse to see. They have ears but refuse to hear. For they are a rebellious people.

³"So now, son of man, pretend you are being sent into exile. Pack the few items an exile could carry, and leave your home to go somewhere else. Do this right in front of the people so they can see you. For perhaps they will pay attention to this, even though they are such rebels.

**11:19** Hebrew *a heart of flesh.*   **11:24** Or *Chaldea.*

---

customs instead of God's laws always got them into trouble. Today, believers are still tempted to conform to the ways of the world. But we must get our standards of right and wrong from God, not from the popular trends of society.

**11:14ff** God promised the exiles in Babylonia that he would continue to be with them even though they were not in Jerusalem. This was a major concern to the Jews because they believed that God was present primarily in the Temple. But God assured them that he would continue to be their God regardless of where they were. In the midst of Ezekiel's burning message of judgment stands a cool oasis—God's promise to restore the faithful few to their homeland. God's arms are now open to receive those who will repent of their sins.

**11:15-21** God's messages through Ezekiel are full of irony. Here God says that the Jews in captivity are the righteous ones, and those in Jerusalem are the sinful and wicked ones. This was the opposite of the people's perception. Appearances can be deceiving. God will evaluate your life by your faith and obedience, not by your apparent earthly success. Furthermore, we should not judge others by outward appearances.

**11:16** God was a sanctuary for the righteous remnant. Idolatrous people, even though they worshiped in the Jerusalem Temple (11:15), would find no true sanctuary; but the faithful exiles, though they were far from home, would be protected by God. Likewise, our external circumstances do not truly indicate our standing with God. Those who appear safe and secure may be far from him, while those going through difficult times may be safely

under God's protection. We can depend on God to keep us safe if we pledge ourselves to his care.

**11:18, 19** "Singleness of heart" indicates a unanimous singleness of purpose. No longer will God's people seek many gods; they will be content with God. Their stony, stubborn hearts of stone will be radically transplanted with tender, responsive hearts (see Jeremiah 32:39; Ezekiel 18:31; 36:26). This new life can only be the work of the Holy Spirit. It is God's work, but we must recognize and turn from our sin. When we do, God will give us new motives, new guidelines, and new purpose. Have you received your new heart?

**11:23** God's glory left Jerusalem and stopped above a mountain on the east side of the city—almost certainly the Mount of Olives. Ezekiel 43:1-4 implies that God will return the same way he left, when he comes back to earth to set up his perfect Kingdom.

**12:1ff** Ezekiel played the role of a captive being led away to exile, portraying what was about to happen to King Zedekiah and the people remaining in Jerusalem. The exiles knew exactly what Ezekiel was doing because only six years earlier they had made similar preparations as they left Jerusalem for Babylonia. This was to show the people that they should not trust the king or the capital city to save them from the Babylonian army—only God could do that. And the exiles who hoped for an early return from exile would be disappointed. Ezekiel's graphic demonstration was proven correct to the last detail. But when he warned them, many refused to listen.

⁴Bring your baggage outside during the day so they can watch you. Then in the evening, as they are watching, leave your house as captives do when they begin a long march to distant lands. ⁵Dig a hole through the wall while they are watching and go out through it. ⁶As they watch, lift your pack to your shoulders and walk away into the night. Cover your face so you cannot see the land you are leaving. For I have made you a sign for the people of Israel."

⁷So I did as I was told. In broad daylight I brought my pack outside, filled with the things I might carry into exile. Then in the evening while the people looked on, I dug through the wall with my hands and went out into the night with my pack on my shoulder.

⁸The next morning this message came to me from the LORD: ⁹"Son of man, these rebels, the people of Israel, have asked you what all this means. ¹⁰Say to them, 'This is what the Sovereign LORD says: These actions contain a message for King Zedekiah in Jerusalem* and for all the people of Israel.' ¹¹Explain that your actions are a sign to show what will soon happen to them, for they will be driven into exile as captives.

¹²"Even Zedekiah will leave Jerusalem at night through a hole in the wall, taking only what he can carry with him. He will cover his face, and his eyes will not see the land he is leaving. ¹³Then I will throw my net over him and capture him in my snare. I will bring him to Babylon, the land of the Babylonians,* though he will never see it, and he will die there. ¹⁴I will scatter his servants and warriors to the four winds and send the sword after them. ¹⁵And when I scatter them among the nations, they will know that I am the LORD. ¹⁶But I will spare a few of them from death by war, famine, or disease, so they can confess all their detestable sins to their captors. Then they will know that I am the LORD."

¹⁷Then this message came to me from the LORD: ¹⁸"Son of man, tremble as you eat your food. Shake with fear as you drink your water. ¹⁹Tell the people, 'This is what the Sovereign LORD says concerning those living in Israel and Jerusalem: They will eat their food with trembling and sip their water in despair, for their land will be stripped bare because of their violence. ²⁰The cities will be destroyed and the farmland made desolate. Then you will know that I am the LORD.'"

### A New Proverb for Israel

²¹Again a message came to me from the LORD: ²²"Son of man, you've heard that proverb they quote in Israel: 'Time passes, and prophecies come to nothing.' ²³Tell the people, 'This is what the Sovereign LORD says: I will put an end to this proverb, and you will soon stop quoting it.' Now give them this new proverb to replace the old one: 'The time has come for every prophecy to be fulfilled!'

²⁴"There will be no more false visions and flattering predictions in Israel. ²⁵For I am the LORD! If I say it, it will happen. There will be no more delays, you rebels of Israel. I will fulfill my threat of destruction in your own lifetime. I, the Sovereign LORD, have spoken!"

²⁶Then this message came to me from the LORD: ²⁷"Son of man, the people of Israel are saying, 'He's talking about the distant future. His visions won't come true for a long, long time.' ²⁸Therefore, tell them, 'This is what the Sovereign LORD says: No more delay! I will now do everything I have threatened. I, the Sovereign LORD, have spoken!'"

### Judgment against False Prophets

**13** Then this message came to me from the LORD: ²"Son of man, prophesy against the false prophets of Israel who are inventing their own prophecies. Say to them, 'Listen to the word of the LORD. ³This is what the Sovereign LORD says: What sorrow awaits the false prophets who are following their own imaginations and have seen nothing at all!'

**12:10** Hebrew *the prince in Jerusalem;* similarly in 12:12. **12:13** Or *Chaldeans.*

**12:4**
2 Kgs 25:4
Jer 39:4; 52:7

**12:6**
Ezek 4:3; 24:24

**12:7**
Ezek 24:18

**12:9**
Ezek 2:5-8; 17:12; 24:19

**12:10**
2 Kgs 9:25
Isa 13:1
Mal 1:1

**12:11**
Jer 15:2; 52:15, 28-30

**12:12**
2 Kgs 25:4
Jer 39:4; 52:7

**12:13**
Isa 24:17
Jer 39:7; 52:11
Hos 7:12

**12:16**
Jer 22:8-9

**12:19**
Isa 6:11
Zech 7:14

**12:20**
Isa 7:23-24
Jer 25:9
Dan 9:17

**12:22**
Jer 5:12
Amos 6:3
2 Pet 3:3-4

**12:23**
Joel 2:11
Zeph 1:14

**12:24**
Jer 14:13-16
Zech 13:2-4

**12:25**
Num 14:28-34
Hab 1:5

**12:27**
Dan 10:14

**13:2**
Isa 9:15; 56:9-12
Jer 37:19

**13:3**
Jer 23:28-32
Lam 2:14

---

**12:10-12** Zedekiah, Judah's last king (597–586 B.C.), was reigning in Jerusalem when Ezekiel gave these messages from God. Ezekiel showed the people what would happen to Zedekiah. Jerusalem would be attacked again, and Zedekiah would join the exiles already in Babylon. Zedekiah would be unable to see because Nebuchadnezzar would have his eyes gouged out (2 Kings 25:3-7; Jeremiah 52:10, 11).

**12:21-28** These two short messages were warnings that God's words would come true—*soon!* Less than six years later, Jerusalem would be destroyed. Yet the people were skeptical. Unbelief and false security led them to believe it would never happen. The apostle Peter dealt with this problem in the church (2 Peter 3:9). It is dangerous to say Christ will never return or to regard his

coming as so far in the future as to be irrelevant today. All that God says is sure to happen. Don't dare assume that you have plenty of time to get right with God.

**13:1ff** This warning was directed against false prophets, whose messages were not from God but were lies intended to win popularity by saying whatever made the people happy. False prophets did not care about the truth as Ezekiel did. They lulled people into a false sense of security, making Ezekiel's job even more difficult. Beware of people who bend the truth in their quest for popularity and power.

**13:2, 3** The false prophets had a large following because they comforted the people and approved of their sinful actions. Lies are often attractive, and liars may have large followings. Today,

**13:5**
Ps 106:23
Isa 58:12

**13:6**
Jer 28:15; 29:8

4"O people of Israel, these prophets of yours are like jackals digging in the ruins. 5They have done nothing to repair the breaks in the walls around the nation. They have not helped it to stand firm in battle on the day of the LORD. 6Instead, they have told lies and made false predictions. They say, 'This message is from the LORD,' even though the LORD never sent them. And yet they expect him to fulfill their prophecies! 7Can your visions be anything but false if you claim, 'This message is from the LORD,' when I have not even spoken to you?

**13:8**
Nah 2:13

**13:9**
Ezra 2:59-63
Ps 69:28
Jer 20:3-6
Dan 12:1

8"Therefore, this is what the Sovereign LORD says: Because what you say is false and your visions are a lie, I will stand against you, says the Sovereign LORD. 9I will raise my fist against all the prophets who see false visions and make lying predictions, and they will be banished from the community of Israel. I will blot their names from Israel's record books, and they will never again set foot in their own land. Then you will know that I am the Sovereign LORD.

**13:10**
Jer 8:11; 50:6

10"This will happen because these evil prophets deceive my people by saying, 'All is peaceful' when there is no peace at all! It's as if the people have built a flimsy wall, and these prophets are trying to reinforce it by covering it with whitewash! 11Tell these whitewashers that their wall will soon fall down. A heavy rainstorm will undermine it; great hailstones and mighty winds will knock it down. 12And when the wall falls, the people will cry out, 'What happened to your whitewash?'

**13:13**
Exod 9:24-25
Ps 18:12-13
Rev 11:19; 16:21

**13:14**
Mic 1:6

**13:16**
Isa 57:21

13"Therefore, this is what the Sovereign LORD says: I will sweep away your whitewashed wall with a storm of indignation, with a great flood of anger, and with hailstones of fury. 14I will break down your wall right to its foundation, and when it falls, it will crush you. Then you will know that I am the LORD. 15At last my anger against the wall and those who covered it with whitewash will be satisfied. Then I will say to you: 'The wall and those who whitewashed it are both gone. 16They were lying prophets who claimed peace would come to Jerusalem when there was no peace. I, the Sovereign LORD, have spoken!'

### Judgment against False Women Prophets

**13:17**
Judg 4:4
2 Kgs 22:14
Luke 2:36
Acts 21:9
Rev 2:20

**13:18**
2 Pet 2:14

**13:19**
Prov 28:21
Jer 23:14, 17
Mic 3:5

17"Now, son of man, speak out against the women who prophesy from their own imaginations. 18This is what the Sovereign LORD says: What sorrow awaits you women who are ensnaring the souls of my people, young and old alike. You tie magic charms on their wrists and furnish them with magic veils. Do you think you can trap others without bringing destruction on yourselves? 19You bring shame on me among my people for a few handfuls of barley or a piece of bread. By lying to my people who love to listen to lies, you kill those who should not die, and you promise life to those who should not live.

**13:21**
Pss 91:3; 124:7

**13:22**
Amos 5:12
2 Pet 2:18-19

**13:23**
Mic 3:6
Zech 13:3

20"This is what the Sovereign LORD says: I am against all your magic charms, which you use to ensnare my people like birds. I will tear them from your arms, setting my people free like birds set free from a cage. 21I will tear off the magic veils and save my people from your grasp. They will no longer be your victims. Then you will know that I am the LORD. 22You have discouraged the righteous with your lies, but I didn't want them to be sad. And you have encouraged the wicked by promising them life, even though they continue in their sins. 23Because of all this, you will no longer talk of seeing visions that you never saw, nor will you make predictions. For I will rescue my people from your grasp. Then you will know that I am the LORD."

### The Idolatry of Israel's Leaders

**14:1**
2 Kgs 6:32

**14** Then some of the leaders of Israel visited me, and while they were sitting with me, 2this message came to me from the LORD: 3"Son of man, these leaders have set up idols* in their hearts. They have embraced things that will make them fall into sin. Why should I listen

**14:3** The Hebrew term (literally *round things*) probably alludes to dung; also in 14:4, 5, 6, 7.

---

for example, some spiritual leaders assure us that God promises his followers health and material success. This is comforting, but is it true? God's own Son did not have an easy life on earth. Make sure the messages you believe are consistent with what God teaches in his Word.

**13:10-12** These false prophets covered their lies (a "flimsy wall") with "whitewash"—a pleasing front. Such superficiality can't hold up under God's scrutiny.

**13:17** In the Bible, the gift of prophecy was given to women as well as men. Miriam (Exodus 15:20), Deborah (Judges 4:4), and Huldah (2 Kings 22:14) were prophets. But the women mentioned here are more like the medium of 1 Samuel 28:7, and they are condemned for discouraging the righteous (13:22).

**13:18** These magic charms and veils were used in witchcraft

practices as good luck charms, but they were used to ensnare the people in idolatry.

**14:3** God condemned the leaders for setting up idols in their hearts and then daring to come to God's prophet for advice. On the outside, they appeared to worship God, making regular visits to the Temple to offer sacrifices. But they were not sincere. It is easy for us to criticize the Israelites for worshiping idols when they so clearly needed God instead. But we have idols in our hearts when we pursue reputation, acceptance, wealth, or sensual pleasure with the intensity and commitment that should be reserved for serving God.

**14:3-5** For Hebrew writers, important functions of life were assigned to different physical organs. The heart was considered the core of a person's intellect and spirit. Because all people have to their requests? ⁴Tell them, 'This is what the Sovereign LORD says: The people of Israel have set up idols in their hearts and fallen into sin, and then they go to a prophet asking for a message. So I, the LORD, will give them the kind of answer their great idolatry deserves. ⁵I will do this to capture the minds and hearts of all my people who have turned from me to worship their detestable idols.'

⁶"Therefore, tell the people of Israel, 'This is what the Sovereign LORD says: Repent and turn away from your idols, and stop all your detestable sins. ⁷I, the LORD, will answer all those, both Israelites and foreigners, who reject me and set up idols in their hearts and so fall into sin, and who then come to a prophet asking for my advice. ⁸I will turn against such people and make a terrible example of them, eliminating them from among my people. Then you will know that I am the LORD.

⁹"And if a prophet is deceived into giving a message, it is because I, the LORD, have deceived that prophet. I will lift my fist against such prophets and cut them off from the community of Israel. ¹⁰False prophets and those who seek their guidance will all be punished for their sins. ¹¹In this way, the people of Israel will learn not to stray from me, polluting themselves with sin. They will be my people, and I will be their God. I, the Sovereign LORD, have spoken!'"

### The Certainty of the LORD's Judgment

¹²Then this message came to me from the LORD: ¹³"Son of man, suppose the people of a country were to sin against me, and I lifted my fist to crush them, cutting off their food supply and sending a famine to destroy both people and animals. ¹⁴Even if Noah, Daniel, and Job were there, their righteousness would save no one but themselves, says the Sovereign LORD.

¹⁵"Or suppose I were to send wild animals to invade the country, kill the people, and make the land too desolate and dangerous to pass through. ¹⁶As surely as I live, says the Sovereign LORD, even if those three men were there, they wouldn't be able to save their own sons or daughters. They alone would be saved, but the land would be made desolate.

¹⁷"Or suppose I were to bring war against the land, and I sent enemy armies to destroy both people and animals. ¹⁸As surely as I live, says the Sovereign LORD, even if those three men were there, they wouldn't be able to save their own sons or daughters. They alone would be saved.

¹⁹"Or suppose I were to pour out my fury by sending an epidemic into the land, and the disease killed people and animals alike. ²⁰As surely as I live, says the Sovereign LORD, even if Noah, Daniel, and Job were there, they wouldn't be able to save their own sons or daughters. They alone would be saved by their righteousness.

²¹"Now this is what the Sovereign LORD says: How terrible it will be when all four of these dreadful punishments fall upon Jerusalem—war, famine, wild animals, and disease—destroying all her people and animals. ²²Yet there will be survivors, and they will come here to join you as exiles in Babylon. You will see with your own eyes how wicked they are, and then you will feel better about what I have done to Jerusalem. ²³When you meet them and see their behavior, you will understand that these things are not being done to Israel without cause. I, the Sovereign LORD, have spoken!"

### Jerusalem—a Useless Vine

**15** Then this message came to me from the LORD: ²"Son of man, how does a grapevine compare to a tree? Is a vine's wood as useful as the wood of a tree? ³Can its wood be used for making things, like pegs to hang up pots and pans? ⁴No, it can only be used for fuel, and even as fuel, it burns too quickly. ⁵Vines are useless both before and after being put into the fire!

**Cross-references (margin):**
14:4 1 Kgs 21:20-24; 2 Kgs 1:16
14:5 Jer 2:11; Hos 10:2; Zech 7:12
14:6 1 Sam 7:3; Neh 1:9; Isa 30:22; 55:6-7
14:7 Exod 12:48; 20:10
14:8 Isa 65:15
14:9 Jer 6:14-15
14:11 Ezek 11:20; 44:10, 15
14:13 Ezek 15:8; 20:27
14:14 Gen 6:8; Job 1:1, 5; Dan 10:11; Heb 11:7
14:16 Gen 19:29
14:17 Ezek 5:12; 21:3-4; 25:13; Zeph 1:3
14:19 Jer 14:12; Ezek 5:12
14:21 Amos 4:6-10; Rev 6:4-8
14:22 Ezek 36:20
14:23 Jer 22:8-9
15:2 John 15:1-6
15:4 Heb 6:8

someone or something as the object of their heart's devotion, they have the potential for idolatry within them. God wants to recapture the hearts of his people. We must never let anything captivate our allegiance or imagination in such a way that it replaces or weakens our devotion to God.

**14:6-11** The people of Judah, although eager to accept the messages of false prophets, considered the presence of a few God-fearing men in the nation an insurance policy against disaster. In a pinch, they could always ask God's prophets for advice. We must remember that the relationship our pastor, family, or friends have with God will not protect us from the consequences of our own sins. Each person is responsible for his or her own

relationship with God. Is your faith personal and real, or are you resting in what others have done?

**14:14-19** Noah, Daniel, and Job were great men in Israel's history, renowned for their relationship with God and for their wisdom (see Genesis 6:8, 9; Daniel 2:47, 48; Job 1:1). Daniel had been taken into captivity during Babylon's first invasion of Judah in 605 B.C., eight years before Ezekiel was taken captive. At the time of Ezekiel's message, Daniel occupied a high government position in Babylon. But even these great men of God could not have saved the people of Judah because God had already passed judgment on the nation's pervasive evil.

**15:1ff** The messages given to Ezekiel in chapters 15–17 provided further evidence that God was going to destroy Jerusalem.

6 "And this is what the Sovereign LORD says: The people of Jerusalem are like grapevines growing among the trees of the forest. Since they are useless, I have thrown them on the fire to be burned. 7 And I will see to it that if they escape from one fire, they will fall into another. When I turn against them, you will know that I am the LORD. 8 And I will make the land desolate because my people have been unfaithful to me. I, the Sovereign LORD, have spoken!"

### Jerusalem—an Unfaithful Wife

**16** Then another message came to me from the LORD: 2 "Son of man, confront Jerusalem with her detestable sins. 3 Give her this message from the Sovereign LORD: You are nothing but a Canaanite! Your father was an Amorite and your mother a Hittite. 4 On the day you were born, no one cared about you. Your umbilical cord was not cut, and you were never washed, rubbed with salt, and wrapped in cloth. 5 No one had the slightest interest in you; no one pitied you or cared for you. On the day you were born, you were unwanted, dumped in a field and left to die.

6 "But I came by and saw you there, helplessly kicking about in your own blood. As you lay there, I said, 'Live!' 7 And I helped you to thrive like a plant in the field. You grew up and became a beautiful jewel. Your breasts became full, and your body hair grew, but you were still naked. 8 And when I passed by again, I saw that you were old enough for love. So I wrapped my cloak around you to cover your nakedness and declared my marriage vows. I made a covenant with you, says the Sovereign LORD, and you became mine.

9 "Then I bathed you and washed off your blood, and I rubbed fragrant oils into your skin. 10 I gave you expensive clothing of fine linen and silk, beautifully embroidered, and sandals made of fine goatskin leather. 11 I gave you lovely jewelry, bracelets, beautiful necklaces, 12 a ring for your nose, earrings for your ears, and a lovely crown for your head. 13 And so you were adorned with gold and silver. Your clothes were made of fine linen and were beautifully embroidered. You ate the finest foods—choice flour, honey, and olive oil—and became more beautiful than ever. You looked like a queen, and so you were! 14 Your fame soon spread throughout the world because of your beauty. I dressed you in my splendor and perfected your beauty, says the Sovereign LORD.

15 "But you thought your fame and beauty were your own. So you gave yourself as a prostitute to every man who came along. Your beauty was theirs for the asking. 16 You used the lovely things I gave you to make shrines for idols, where you played the prostitute. Unbelievable! How could such a thing ever happen? 17 You took the very jewels and gold and silver ornaments I had given you and made statues of men and worshiped them. This is adultery against me! 18 You used the beautifully embroidered clothes I gave you to dress your idols. Then you used my special oil and my incense to worship them. 19 Imagine it! You set before them as a sacrifice the choice flour, olive oil, and honey I had given you, says the Sovereign LORD.

20 "Then you took your sons and daughters—the children you had borne to me—and sacrificed them to your gods. Was your prostitution not enough? 21 Must you also slaughter my children by sacrificing them to idols? 22 In all your years of adultery and detestable sin, you have not once remembered the days long ago when you lay naked in a field, kicking about in your own blood.

### Cross references (margin)

**15:7**
Lev 26:17
1 Kgs 19:17
Isa 24:18
Amos 5:19; 9:1-4

**16:2**
Isa 58:1
Hos 8:1

**16:4**
Hos 2:3

**16:5**
Deut 32:10

**16:7**
Exod 1:7

**16:8**
Gen 22:16-18
Exod 19:5; 24:7-8
Ruth 3:9
Jer 2:2
Hos 2:18-20

**16:11**
Gen 24:22, 47
Isa 3:18-19

**16:12**
Jer 13:18

**16:13**
Deut 32:13-14
Ps 45:13-14

**16:14**
1 Kgs 10:1, 24
Ps 50:2
Lam 2:15

**16:15**
Isa 57:8
Jer 2:20
Ezek 27:3

**16:19**
Hos 2:8

**16:20**
Exod 13:2, 12
Ps 106:37-38
Jer 7:31

**16:21**
2 Kgs 17:17
Jer 19:5

---

The first message was about a vine, useless at first and even more useless after being burned. The people of Jerusalem were useless to God because of their idol worship, and so they would be destroyed and their cities burned. Isaiah also compared the nation of Israel to a vineyard (see Isaiah 5:1-7). Have you become apathetic and unfruitful to God? How can you begin fulfilling his plan for you?

**16:1ff** This message reminded Jerusalem of its former despised status among the Canaanite nations. Using the imagery of a young baby growing to mature womanhood, God reminded Jerusalem that he raised her from a lowly state to great glory as his bride. She betrayed God's trust and prostituted herself, however, by seeking alliances with pagan nations and adopting their customs. If we push God aside for anything, even education, family, career, or pleasure, we are abandoning him in the same way.

**16:3** *Canaan* was the name of the territory taken over by the children of Israel and *Canaanites* were the people who lived there. The Bible often uses this name to refer to all the corrupt pagan nations

of the region. The Amorites and Hittites, two Canaanite peoples, were known for their wickedness. But here God implies that his people are no better than the Canaanites.

**16:15** God cared for and loved Judah, only to have it turn away to other nations and their false gods. The nation had grown to maturity and become famous, but the people forgot who had given them their life (16:22). This is a picture of spiritual adultery (called apostasy—turning from the one true God). As you become wise and more mature, don't turn away from the one who truly loves you.

**16:20, 21** Child sacrifice had been practiced by the Canaanites long before Israel invaded their land, but it was strictly forbidden by God (Leviticus 20:1-3). By Ezekiel's time, however, the people were openly sacrificing their own children (2 Kings 16:3; 21:6). Jeremiah confirmed that this was a common practice (Jeremiah 7:31; 32:35). Because of such vile acts among the people and priesthood, the Temple became unfit for God to inhabit. When God left the Temple, he was no longer Judah's guide and protector.

<sup></sup>23"What sorrow awaits you, says the Sovereign LORD. In addition to all your other wickedness, 24you built a pagan shrine and put altars to idols in every town square. 25On every street corner you defiled your beauty, offering your body to every passerby in an endless stream of prostitution. 26Then you added lustful Egypt to your lovers, provoking my anger with your increasing promiscuity. 27That is why I struck you with my fist and reduced your boundaries. I handed you over to your enemies, the Philistines, and even they were shocked by your lewd conduct. 28You have prostituted yourself with the Assyrians, too. It seems you can never find enough new lovers! And after your prostitution there, you still were not satisfied. 29You added to your lovers by embracing Babylonia,* the land of merchants, but you still weren't satisfied.

30"What a sick heart you have, says the Sovereign LORD, to do such things as these, acting like a shameless prostitute. 31You build your pagan shrines on every street corner and your altars to idols in every square. In fact, you have been worse than a prostitute, so eager for sin that you have not even demanded payment. 32Yes, you are an adulterous wife who takes in strangers instead of her own husband. 33Prostitutes charge for their services—but not you! You give gifts to your lovers, bribing them to come and have sex with you. 34So you are the opposite of other prostitutes. You pay your lovers instead of their paying you!

### Judgment on Jerusalem's Prostitution

35"Therefore, you prostitute, listen to this message from the LORD! 36This is what the Sovereign LORD says: Because you have poured out your lust and exposed yourself in prostitution to all your lovers, and because you have worshiped detestable idols,* and because you have slaughtered your children as sacrifices to your gods, 37this is what I am going to do. I will gather together all your allies—the lovers with whom you have sinned, both those you loved and those you hated—and I will strip you naked in front of them so they can stare at you. 38I will punish you for your murder and adultery. I will cover you with blood in my jealous fury. 39Then I will give you to these many nations who are your lovers, and they will destroy you. They will knock down your pagan shrines and the altars to your idols. They will strip you and take your beautiful jewels, leaving you stark naked. 40They will band together in a mob to stone you and cut you up with swords. 41They will burn your homes and punish you in front of many women. I will stop your prostitution and end your payments to your many lovers.

42"Then at last my fury against you will be spent, and my jealous anger will subside. I will be calm and will not be angry with you anymore. 43But first, because you have not remembered your youth but have angered me by doing all these evil things, I will fully repay you for all of your sins, says the Sovereign LORD. For you have added lewd acts to all your detestable sins. 44Everyone who makes up proverbs will say of you, 'Like mother, like daughter.' 45For your mother loathed her husband and her children, and so do you. And you are exactly like your sisters, for they despised their husbands and their children. Truly your mother was a Hittite and your father an Amorite.

46"Your older sister was Samaria, who lived with her daughters in the north. Your younger sister was Sodom, who lived with her daughters in the south. 47But you have not merely sinned as they did. You quickly surpassed them in corruption. 48As surely as I live, says the Sovereign LORD, Sodom and her daughters were never as wicked as you and your daughters. 49Sodom's sins were pride, gluttony, and laziness, while the poor and needy suffered outside her door. 50She was proud and committed detestable sins, so I wiped her out, as you have seen.*

16:29 Or Chaldea.   16:36 The Hebrew term (literally round things) probably alludes to dung.   16:50 As in a few Hebrew manuscripts and Greek version; Masoretic Text reads as I have seen.

| | |
|---|---|
| **16:24** | Ps 78:58 |
| | Isa 57:5-7 |
| **16:25** | Prov 9:14 |
| **16:26** | Jer 7:18-19 |
| **16:27** | Isa 9:12 |
| **16:28** | 2 Kgs 16:7-18 |
| | 2 Chr 28:16-23 |
| **16:30** | Prov 9:13 |
| | Isa 3:9 |
| | Rev 17:1-6 |
| **16:31** | Isa 52:3 |
| **16:33** | Hos 8:9-10 |
| | Joel 3:3 |
| | Luke 15:30 |
| **16:36** | Jer 19:5 |
| | Ezek 20:31; 23:37 |
| **16:37** | Isa 47:3 |
| | Nah 3:5-6 |
| **16:38** | Ps 79:3, 5 |
| | Jer 18:21 |
| | Zeph 1:17 |
| | Rev 16:6 |
| **16:41** | 2 Kgs 25:9 |
| **16:42** | 2 Sam 24:25 |
| | Isa 40:1-2; 54:9-10 |
| **16:43** | Ps 78:42 |
| | Isa 63:10 |
| **16:45** | Isa 1:4 |
| **16:46** | Gen 13:11-13 |
| | Jer 3:8-11 |
| **16:47** | 1 Kgs 16:31 |
| | 2 Kgs 21:9 |
| | Ezek 5:6-7 |
| **16:48** | Matt 11:23-24 |
| **16:49** | Gen 13:10 |
| | Ps 138:6 |
| | Isa 22:13 |
| | Luke 12:16-20 |
| **16:50** | Gen 19:24-25 |

**16:27** The conduct of the Jews was so disgusting that even those who worshiped other gods, including their great enemy the Philistines, would have been ashamed to behave that way. The Jews outdid them in doing evil.

**16:44-52** The city of Sodom, a symbol of total corruption, was completely destroyed by God for its wickedness (Genesis 19:24, 25). Samaria, the capital of what had been the northern kingdom (Israel), was despised and rejected by the Jews in Judah. To be called a sister of Samaria and Sodom was bad enough, but to be called more wicked than they were meant that Judah's sins were an unspeakable abomination and that its doom was inevitable. The reason it was considered worse was not necessarily that Judah's

sins were worse but that Judah knew better. In that light, we who live in an age when God's message is made clear to us through the Bible are worse than Judah if we continue in sin (see Matthew 11:20-24).

**16:49** It is easy to judge and condemn Sodom, especially for its terrible sexual sins. Ezekiel reminded Judah, however, that Sodom was destroyed because of its pride, laziness, gluttony, and unconcern for the poor and needy. It is easy to be selective in what we consider gross sin. If we do not commit such horrible sins as adultery, homosexuality, stealing, and murder, we may think we are living good enough lives. But what about sins like pride, laziness, gluttony, and indifference to the needy? These

**16:51**
Jer 3:8-11
Matt 12:41-42

**16:53**
Isa 19:24-25

**16:54**
Jer 2:26

**16:57**
2 Kgs 16:5-7
2 Chr 28:5-6, 18-23
Hos 2:10; 7:1

**16:58**
Ezek 23:49

**16:59**
Isa 24:5

**16:60**
Jer 32:40

**16:62**
Jer 24:7

**16:63**
Ps 39:9
Dan 9:7-8
Rom 3:19

51"Even Samaria did not commit half your sins. You have done far more detestable things than your sisters ever did. They seem righteous compared to you. 52Shame on you! Your sins are so terrible that you make your sisters seem righteous, even virtuous.

53"But someday I will restore the fortunes of Sodom and Samaria, and I will restore you, too. 54Then you will be truly ashamed of everything you have done, for your sins make them feel good in comparison. 55Yes, your sisters, Sodom and Samaria, and all their people will be restored, and at that time you also will be restored. 56In your proud days you held Sodom in contempt. 57But now your greater wickedness has been exposed to all the world, and you are the one who is scorned—by Edom* and all her neighbors and by Philistia. 58This is your punishment for all your lewdness and detestable sins, says the LORD.

59"Now this is what the Sovereign LORD says: I will give you what you deserve, for you have taken your solemn vows lightly by breaking your covenant. 60Yet I will remember the covenant I made with you when you were young, and I will establish an everlasting covenant with you. 61Then you will remember with shame all the evil you have done. I will make your sisters, Samaria and Sodom, to be your daughters, even though they are not part of our covenant. 62And I will reaffirm my covenant with you, and you will know that I am the LORD. 63You will remember your sins and cover your mouth in silent shame when I forgive you of all that you have done. I, the Sovereign LORD, have spoken!"

## A Story of Two Eagles

**17:2**
Ezek 20:49; 24:3

**17:3**
Jer 22:23; 48:40
Dan 4:22

**17:5**
Deut 8:7-9
Isa 44:4

**17:7**
Ezek 31:4

**17** Then this message came to me from the LORD: 2"Son of man, give this riddle, and tell this story to the people of Israel. 3Give them this message from the Sovereign LORD:

"A great eagle with broad wings and long feathers,
    covered with many-colored plumage,
    came to Lebanon.
He seized the top of a cedar tree
4    and plucked off its highest branch.
He carried it away to a city filled with merchants.
    He planted it in a city of traders.
5 He also took a seedling from the land
    and planted it in fertile soil.
He placed it beside a broad river,
    where it could grow like a willow tree.
6 It took root there and
    grew into a low, spreading vine.
Its branches turned up toward the eagle,
    and its roots grew down into the ground.
It produced strong branches
    and put out shoots.
7 But then another great eagle came
    with broad wings and full plumage.
So the vine now sent its roots and branches
    toward him for water,
8 even though it was already planted in good soil
    and had plenty of water
so it could grow into a splendid vine
    and produce rich leaves and luscious fruit.

**16:57** As in many Hebrew manuscripts and Syriac version; Masoretic Text reads *Aram.*

sins may not be as shocking to you as the others, but they are also forbidden by God.

**16:59-63** Although the people had broken their promises and did not deserve anything but punishment, God would not break his promises. If the people turned back to him, he would again forgive them and renew his covenant. This covenant was put into effect when Jesus paid for everyone's sins by his death on the cross (Hebrews 10:8-10). No one is beyond the reach of God's forgiveness. Although we don't deserve anything but punishment for our sins, God's arms are still outstretched. He will not break his promise to give us salvation and forgiveness if we repent and turn to him.

**17:1ff** The first eagle in this chapter represents King Nebuchadnezzar of Babylon (see 17:12), who appointed or "planted" Zedekiah as king in Jerusalem. Zedekiah rebelled against this arrangement and tried to ally with Egypt, the second eagle, to battle against Babylon. This took place while Ezekiel, miles away in Babylon, was describing these events (explained in verses 10-21). Jeremiah, a prophet in Judah, was also warning Zedekiah not to form this alliance (Jeremiah 2:36, 37). Although many miles apart, the prophets had the same message because both spoke for God. God still directs his chosen spokespeople to speak his truth all around the world.

9 "So now the Sovereign LORD asks:
    Will this vine grow and prosper?
        No! I will pull it up, roots and all!
    I will cut off its fruit
        and let its leaves wither and die.
    I will pull it up easily
        without a strong arm or a large army.
10 But when the vine is transplanted,
    will it thrive?
    No, it will wither away
        when the east wind blows against it.
    It will die in the same good soil
        where it had grown so well."

### The Riddle Explained

11 Then this message came to me from the LORD: 12 "Say to these rebels of Israel: Don't you understand the meaning of this riddle of the eagles? The king of Babylon came to Jerusalem, took away her king and princes, and brought them to Babylon. 13 He made a treaty with a member of the royal family and forced him to take an oath of loyalty. He also exiled Israel's most influential leaders, 14 so Israel would not become strong again and revolt. Only by keeping her treaty with Babylon could Israel survive.

15 "Nevertheless, this man of Israel's royal family rebelled against Babylon, sending ambassadors to Egypt to request a great army and many horses. Can Israel break her sworn treaties like that and get away with it? 16 No! For as surely as I live, says the Sovereign LORD, the king of Israel will die in Babylon, the land of the king who put him in power and whose treaty he disregarded and broke. 17 Pharaoh and all his mighty army will fail to help Israel when the king of Babylon lays siege to Jerusalem again and destroys many lives. 18 For the king of Israel disregarded his treaty and broke it after swearing to obey; therefore, he will not escape.

19 "So this is what the Sovereign LORD says: As surely as I live, I will punish him for breaking my covenant and disregarding the solemn oath he made in my name. 20 I will throw my net over him and capture him in my snare. I will bring him to Babylon and put him on trial for this treason against me. 21 And all his best warriors* will be killed in battle, and those who survive will be scattered to the four winds. Then you will know that I, the LORD, have spoken.

22 "This is what the Sovereign LORD says: I will take a branch from the top of a tall cedar, and I will plant it on the top of Israel's highest mountain. 23 It will become a majestic cedar, sending forth its branches and producing seed. Birds of every sort will nest in it, finding shelter in the shade of its branches. 24 And all the trees will know that it is I, the LORD, who cuts the tall tree down and makes the short tree grow tall. It is I who makes the green tree wither and gives the dead tree new life. I, the LORD, have spoken, and I will do what I said!"

### The Justice of a Righteous God

**18** Then another message came to me from the LORD: 2 "Why do you quote this proverb concerning the land of Israel: 'The parents have eaten sour grapes, but their children's mouths pucker at the taste'? 3 As surely as I live, says the Sovereign LORD, you will not quote this proverb anymore in Israel. 4 For all people are mine to judge—both parents and children alike. And this is my rule: The person who sins is the one who will die.

17:21 Or *his fleeing warriors.* The meaning of the Hebrew is uncertain.

**Marginal references:**

17:10
Ezek 19:12-14
Hos 13:15

17:13
2 Kgs 24:15-17
2 Chr 36:13

17:14
Jer 27:12-17; 38:17

17:15
2 Kgs 24:20
2 Chr 36:13

17:16
Jer 52:11

17:17
Isa 36:6
Jer 37:7

17:18
1 Chr 29:24

17:20
Ezek 12:13; 20:36;
32:3

17:21
2 Kgs 25:5, 11
Amos 9:1-10

17:22
Pss 72:16; 80:15
Ezek 20:40
Zech 3:8; 4:12-14

17:24
Ps 96:12
Isa 55:12
Amos 9:11

18:2
Jer 31:29

18:4
Num 16:22; 27:16
Isa 42:5; 57:16

---

**17:10** This east wind was the hot, dry wind blowing off the desert, a wind that could wither a flourishing crop. The hot wind of Nebuchadnezzar's armies was about to overcome the nation of Judah.

**17:22, 23** Ezekiel's prophecy of judgment ends in hope. When the people put their hope in foreign alliances, they were disappointed. Only God could give them true hope. God said he would plant a branch, the Messiah, whose Kingdom would grow and become a shelter for all who come to him (see Isaiah 11:1-5). This prophecy was fulfilled at the coming of Jesus Christ.

**18:1ff** The people of Judah believed they were being punished for the sins of their ancestors, not their own. They thought this way

because this was the teaching of the Ten Commandments (Exodus 20:5). Instead, Ezekiel taught that the destruction of Jerusalem was due to the spiritual decay in previous generations. But this belief in the corporate life of Israel led to fatalism and irresponsibility. So Ezekiel gave God's new policy because the people had misconstrued the old one. God judges each person individually. Although we often suffer from the effects of sins committed by those who came before us, God does not punish us for someone else's sins, and we can't use their mistakes as an excuse for our sins. Each person is accountable to God for his or her actions.

In addition, some people of Judah used the corporate umbrella of God's blessing as an excuse for disobeying God. They thought that because of their righteous ancestors (18:5-9), they would live. God told them that they would not; they were the evil children of

**18:6**
Deut 4:19

**18:7**
Lev 19:13
Matt 25:35-40

**18:8**
Exod 22:25
Lev 25:36
Deut 23:19
Zech 8:16

**18:9**
Hab 2:4
Rom 1:17

**18:12**
2 Kgs 21:11
Isa 59:6-7
Amos 4:1

**18:13**
Ezek 33:4-5

**18:14**
2 Chr 29:6-10;
34:21

**18:16**
Job 31:16
Ps 41:1

**18:19**
Exod 20:5
Zech 1:3-6

**18:20**
Deut 24:16
Matt 16:27
Rom 2:6-9

**18:21**
Ezek 33:12, 19

**18:22**
Ps 18:20-24
Ezek 33:16
Mic 7:19

**18:23**
Ps 147:11
Ezek 33:11
2 Pet 3:9

**18:24**
1 Sam 15:11
Prov 21:16
Ezek 33:18
Gal 3:3-4

**18:25**
Gen 18:25
Deut 32:4
Ezek 33:17, 20
Zeph 3:5
Mal 3:13-15

**18:30**
Ezek 14:6; 33:11
Hos 12:6

5"Suppose a certain man is righteous and does what is just and right. 6He does not feast in the mountains before Israel's idols* or worship them. He does not commit adultery or have intercourse with a woman during her menstrual period. 7He is a merciful creditor, not keeping the items given as security by poor debtors. He does not rob the poor but instead gives food to the hungry and provides clothes for the needy. 8He grants loans without interest, stays away from injustice, is honest and fair when judging others, 9and faithfully obeys my decrees and regulations. Anyone who does these things is just and will surely live, says the Sovereign LORD.

10"But suppose that man has a son who grows up to be a robber or murderer and refuses to do what is right. 11And that son does all the evil things his father would never do—he worships idols on the mountains, commits adultery, 12oppresses the poor and helpless, steals from debtors by refusing to let them redeem their security, worships idols, commits detestable sins, 13and lends money at excessive interest. Should such a sinful person live? No! He must die and must take full blame.

14"But suppose that sinful son, in turn, has a son who sees his father's wickedness and decides against that kind of life. 15This son refuses to worship idols on the mountains and does not commit adultery. 16He does not exploit the poor, but instead is fair to debtors and does not rob them. He gives food to the hungry and provides clothes for the needy. 17He helps the poor,* does not lend money at interest, and obeys all my regulations and decrees. Such a person will not die because of his father's sins; he will surely live. 18But the father will die for his many sins—for being cruel, robbing people, and doing what was clearly wrong among his people.

19"'What?' you ask. 'Doesn't the child pay for the parent's sins?' No! For if the child does what is just and right and keeps my decrees, that child will surely live. 20The person who sins is the one who will die. The child will not be punished for the parent's sins, and the parent will not be punished for the child's sins. Righteous people will be rewarded for their own righteous behavior, and wicked people will be punished for their own wickedness. 21But if wicked people turn away from all their sins and begin to obey my decrees and do what is just and right, they will surely live and not die. 22All their past sins will be forgotten, and they will live because of the righteous things they have done.

23"Do you think that I like to see wicked people die? says the Sovereign LORD. Of course not! I want them to turn from their wicked ways and live. 24However, if righteous people turn from their righteous behavior and start doing sinful things and act like other sinners, should they be allowed to live? No, of course not! All their righteous acts will be forgotten, and they will die for their sins.

25"Yet you say, 'The Lord isn't doing what's right!' Listen to me, O people of Israel. Am I the one not doing what's right, or is it you? 26When righteous people turn from their righteous behavior and start doing sinful things, they will die for it. Yes, they will die because of their sinful deeds. 27And if wicked people turn from their wickedness, obey the law, and do what is just and right, they will save their lives. 28They will live because they thought it over and decided to turn from their sins. Such people will not die. 29And yet the people of Israel keep saying, 'The Lord isn't doing what's right!' O people of Israel, it is you who are not doing what's right, not I.

30"Therefore, I will judge each of you, O people of Israel, according to your actions, says

**18:6** The Hebrew term (literally *round things*) probably alludes to dung; also in 18:12, 15.    **18:17** Greek version reads *He refuses to do evil.*

---

righteous parents and, as such, would die (18:10-13). If, however, anyone returned to God, he or she would live (18:14-18).

**18:8** The law of Moses had rules about charging interest (Exodus 22:25; Leviticus 25:36; Deuteronomy 23:19, 20) to prevent God's people from taking advantage of the poor among them.

**18:12** Allowing people to "redeem their security" refers to lenders letting debtors use at night what they had pledged (often a cloak). Without their cloaks, debtors would be cold at night. (See Exodus 22:26 and Deuteronomy 24:10-13 for the giving of this law.)

**18:23** God is perfect love, but he also dispenses perfect justice. His perfect love causes him to be merciful to those who recognize their sin and turn back to him, but he cannot overlook those who willfully sin. Wicked people die both physically and spiritually. God takes no joy in their deaths; he would prefer that they turn to him and have eternal life. Likewise, we should not rejoice in the

misfortunes of nonbelievers. Instead, we should do all in our power to bring them to faith.

**18:25** A typical childish response to punishment is to say, "That isn't fair!" In reality, God is fair, but *we* have broken the rules. It is not God who must live up to our ideas of fairness; instead, we must live up to his. Don't spend your time looking for the loopholes in God's law. Instead, live up to God's standards.

**18:30-32** Ezekiel's solution to the problem of inherited guilt is for each person to turn to a changed life. This is God's work in us and not something we can do for ourselves. The Holy Spirit does it (Psalm 51:10-12). If we renounce our life's direction of sin and rebellion and turn to God, he will give us a new direction, a new love, and a new power to change. You can begin by faith, trusting in God's power to change your heart and mind. Then determine to live each day with him in control (Ephesians 4:22-24).

the Sovereign LORD. Repent, and turn from your sins. Don't let them destroy you! 31 Put all your rebellion behind you, and find yourselves a new heart and a new spirit. For why should you die, O people of Israel? 32 I don't want you to die, says the Sovereign LORD. Turn back and live!

**18:31**
Ps 51:10
Isa 1:16-17; 55:7
Acts 3:19

## A Funeral Song for Israel's Kings

**19** "Sing this funeral song for the princes of Israel:

**19:1**
2 Kgs 25:5-7

2 "What is your mother?
A lioness among lions!
She lay down among the young lions
and reared her cubs.

3 She raised one of her cubs
to become a strong young lion.
He learned to hunt and devour prey,
and he became a man-eater.

**19:3**
2 Kgs 23:31-34

4 Then the nations heard about him,
and he was trapped in their pit.
They led him away with hooks
to the land of Egypt.

**19:4**
2 Chr 36:4

5 "When the lioness saw
that her hopes for him were gone,
she took another of her cubs
and taught him to be a strong young lion.

6 He prowled among the other lions
and stood out among them in his strength.
He learned to hunt and devour prey,
and he, too, became a man-eater.

**19:6**
2 Kgs 24:9

7 He demolished fortresses*
and destroyed their towns and cities.
Their farms were desolated,
and their crops were destroyed.
The land and its people trembled in fear
when they heard him roar.

8 Then the armies of the nations attacked him,
surrounding him from every direction.
They threw a net over him
and captured him in their pit.

9 With hooks, they dragged him into a cage
and brought him before the king of Babylon.
They held him in captivity,
so his voice could never again be heard
on the mountains of Israel.

**19:9**
2 Kgs 24:15
2 Chr 36:6

10 "Your mother was like a vine
planted by the water's edge.
It had lush, green foliage
because of the abundant water.

**19:10**
Ps 80:8-11

11 Its branches became strong—
strong enough to be a ruler's scepter.

**19:7** As in Greek version; Hebrew reads *He knew widows.*

---

**19:1ff** Ezekiel used illustrations to communicate many of his messages. With the picture of the lioness and her cubs, he raised the curiosity of his listeners. The lioness symbolized the nation of Judah, and the two cubs were two of its kings. The first cub was King Jehoahaz, who had been taken captive to Egypt in 609 B.C. by Pharaoh Neco (2 Kings 23:31-33). The second cub was either King Jehoiachin, who had already been taken into captivity in Babylon (2 Kings 24:8ff), or King Zedekiah, who soon would be (2 Kings 25:7). This illustration showed that for Judah, there was no hope for a quick return from exile and no escape from the approaching Babylonian armies.

**19:11, 12** Not even the political and military might of Judah's kings could save the nation. Like branches of a vine, they would be cut off and uprooted by "the desert wind"—the powerful Babylonian army.

It grew very tall,
   towering above all others.
It stood out because of its height
   and its many lush branches.
12 But the vine was uprooted in fury
   and thrown down to the ground.
The desert wind dried up its fruit
   and tore off its strong branches,
so that it withered
   and was destroyed by fire.
13 Now the vine is transplanted to the wilderness,
   where the ground is hard and dry.
14 A fire has burst out from its branches
   and devoured its fruit.
Its remaining limbs are not
   strong enough to be a ruler's scepter.

"This is a funeral song, and it will be used in a funeral."

### The Rebellion of Israel

**20** On August 14,* during the seventh year of King Jehoiachin's captivity, some of the leaders of Israel came to request a message from the Lord. They sat down in front of me to wait for his reply. 2 Then this message came to me from the Lord: 3 "Son of man, tell the leaders of Israel, 'This is what the Sovereign Lord says: How dare you come to ask me for a message? As surely as I live, says the Sovereign Lord, I will tell you nothing!'

4 "Son of man, bring charges against them and condemn them. Make them realize how detestable the sins of their ancestors really were. 5 Give them this message from the Sovereign Lord: When I chose Israel—when I revealed myself to the descendants of Jacob in Egypt—I took a solemn oath that I, the Lord, would be their God. 6 I took a solemn oath that day that I would bring them out of Egypt to a land I had discovered and explored for them—a good land, a land flowing with milk and honey, the best of all lands anywhere. 7 Then I said to them, 'Each of you, get rid of the vile images you are so obsessed with. Do not defile yourselves with the idols* of Egypt, for I am the Lord your God.'

8 "But they rebelled against me and would not listen. They did not get rid of the vile images they were obsessed with, or forsake the idols of Egypt. Then I threatened to pour out my fury on them to satisfy my anger while they were still in Egypt. 9 But I didn't do it, for I acted to protect the honor of my name. I would not allow shame to be brought on my name among the surrounding nations who saw me reveal myself by bringing the Israelites out of Egypt. 10 So I brought them out of Egypt and led them into the wilderness. 11 There I gave them my decrees and regulations so they could find life by keeping them. 12 And I gave them my Sabbath days of rest as a sign between them and me. It was to remind them that I am the Lord, who had set them apart to be holy.

13 "But the people of Israel rebelled against me, and they refused to obey my decrees there in the wilderness. They wouldn't obey my regulations even though obedience would have given them life. They also violated my Sabbath days. So I threatened to pour out my fury on them, and I made plans to utterly consume them in the wilderness. 14 But again I held back in order to protect the honor of my name before the nations who had seen my power in

**19:12**
Jer 31:28
Ezek 17:10; 28:17
Hos 13:15
John 15:6

**19:13**
2 Kgs 24:12-16
Hos 2:3

**20:1**
Ezek 8:1, 11-12

**20:3**
Ezek 14:3

**20:4**
Ezek 16:2; 22:2

**20:5**
Exod 6:2-3, 7
Deut 7:6; 14:2
Ezek 6:2-9

**20:6**
Exod 33:3
Ps 48:2
Jer 33:24

**20:7**
Exod 20:2
Deut 29:16-18

**20:8**
Isa 63:10

**20:9**
Exod 32:11-14
Num 14:13

**20:11**
Exod 20:1-23
Lev 18:5

**20:12**
Exod 31:13, 17
Ezek 20:20

**20:13**
Num 14:11, 22
Isa 56:6

---

**20:1** Hebrew *In the fifth month, on the tenth day,* of the ancient Hebrew lunar calendar. This day was August 14, 591 B.C.; also see note on 1:1. **20:7** The Hebrew term (literally *round things*) probably alludes to dung; also in 20:8, 16, 18, 24, 31, 39.

---

**20:1ff** Here Ezekiel gives a panoramic view of Israel's history of rebellion. The emphasis is on God's attempts to bring the nation back to himself and on God's mercy for his constantly rebellious and disobedient people. Ezekiel gives the message that the people alone are responsible for the troubles and judgments they have experienced. Those who persist in rebellion God will purge out (20:38), while he will bring the faithful into the land of Israel. The reason: that "you will know that I am the Lord" (20:42).

**20:12, 13** The Sabbath, instituted by God at creation, was entrusted to Israel as a sign that God had created and redeemed them (Exodus 20:8-11; Deuteronomy 5:12-15). This day of rest

was a gift from a loving God, not a difficult obligation. But the people repeatedly violated the Sabbath and ignored God (see also 20:20, 21). It was meant to be a reminder that they were God's special people. Today many Christians celebrate the Lord's Day, Sunday, as their Sabbath. Whatever the day, we must be careful to fulfill God's purpose for the Sabbath. He wants us to rest, to refocus, and to remember him.

bringing Israel out of Egypt. 15But I took a solemn oath against them in the wilderness. I swore I would not bring them into the land I had given them, a land flowing with milk and honey, the most beautiful place on earth. 16For they had rejected my regulations, refused to follow my decrees, and violated my Sabbath days. Their hearts were given to their idols. 17Nevertheless, I took pity on them and held back from destroying them in the wilderness.

18"Then I warned their children not to follow in their parents' footsteps, defiling themselves with their idols. 19'I am the LORD your God,' I told them. 'Follow my decrees, pay attention to my regulations, 20and keep my Sabbath days holy, for they are a sign to remind you that I am the LORD your God.'

21"But their children, too, rebelled against me. They refused to keep my decrees and follow my regulations, even though obedience would have given them life. And they also violated my Sabbath days. So again I threatened to pour out my fury on them in the wilderness. 22Nevertheless, I withdrew my judgment against them to protect the honor of my name before the nations that had seen my power in bringing them out of Egypt. 23But I took a solemn oath against them in the wilderness. I swore I would scatter them among all the nations 24because they did not obey my regulations. They scorned my decrees by violating my Sabbath days and longing for the idols of their ancestors. 25I gave them over to worthless decrees and regulations that would not lead to life. 26I let them pollute themselves* with the very gifts I had given them, and I allowed them to give their firstborn children as offerings to their gods—so I might devastate them and remind them that I alone am the LORD.

## Judgment and Restoration

27"Therefore, son of man, give the people of Israel this message from the Sovereign LORD: Your ancestors continued to blaspheme and betray me, 28for when I brought them into the land I had promised them, they offered sacrifices on every high hill and under every green tree they saw! They roused my fury as they offered up sacrifices to their gods. They brought their perfumes and incense and poured out their liquid offerings to them. 29I said to them, 'What is this high place where you are going?' (This kind of pagan shrine has been called Bamah—'high place'—ever since.)

30"Therefore, give the people of Israel this message from the Sovereign LORD: Do you plan to pollute yourselves just as your ancestors did? Do you intend to keep prostituting yourselves by worshiping vile images? 31For when you offer gifts to them and give your little children to be burned as sacrifices,* you continue to pollute yourselves with idols to this day. Should I allow you to ask for a message from me, O people of Israel? As surely as I live, says the Sovereign LORD, I will tell you nothing.

32"You say, 'We want to be like the nations all around us, who serve idols of wood and stone.' But what you have in mind will never happen. 33As surely as I live, says the Sovereign LORD, I will rule over you with an iron fist in great anger and with awesome power. 34And in anger I will reach out with my strong hand and powerful arm, and I will bring you back* from the lands where you are scattered. 35I will bring you into the wilderness of the nations, and there I will judge you face to face. 36I will judge you there just as I did your ancestors in the wilderness after bringing them out of Egypt, says the Sovereign LORD. 37I will examine you carefully and hold you to the terms of the covenant. 38I will purge you of all those who rebel and revolt against me. I will bring them out of the countries where they are in exile, but they will never enter the land of Israel. Then you will know that I am the LORD.

20:25-26 Or *I gave them worthless decrees and regulations.... I polluted them.* 20:31 Or *and make your little children pass through the fire.* 20:34 Greek version reads *I will welcome you.* Compare 2 Cor 6:17.

---

**20:23, 24** At the very beginning of Israel's history, God clearly warned the people about the consequences of disobedience (Deuteronomy 28:15ff). When the people disobeyed, God let them experience those devastating consequences to remind them of the seriousness of their sins. If you choose to live for yourself, apart from God, you may experience similar destructive consequences. Even through such consequences, however, God may be drawing you to himself. Let your misfortunes bring you to your senses and to the merciful God before it is too late.

**20:25** These "worthless" decrees and regulations do not refer to any aspect of the laws of Moses—Ezekiel reinforces that law (20:11, 13, 21). Evidently the Jews had taken Exodus 13:12 and 22:29, the dedication of firstborn animals and chil-

dren, as a justification for child sacrifice to the Canaanite god Molech. God gave them over to this delusion to get them to acknowledge him, to jar their consciences, and to revitalize their faith (20:26).

**20:35-38** When the Israelites disobeyed God by refusing to enter the Promised Land the first time, God chose to purify his people by forcing them to wander in the wilderness until that entire generation died (Numbers 14:26-35). Here he promised to purge the nation of its rebellious people again as they crossed the vast wilderness from their captivity in Babylon. Only those who faithfully followed God would be able to return to their land. The purpose of this wilderness judgment would be to purge out all those who worshiped idols and to restore all those faithful to God.

### Cross-references (margin)

20:15 Ps 95:11
20:16 Ezek 11:21; 14:3-7
20:17 Jer 4:27; 5:18
20:18 Deut 4:3-4
20:19 Exod 6:7; 20:2 Deut 5:32
20:21 Num 25:1-3
20:22 Isa 48:9-11
20:23 Deut 28:64-68 Jer 15:4
20:24 Ezek 6:9
20:25 Ps 81:12 Rom 1:21-25, 28 2 Thes 2:9-11
20:26 Ezek 6:7; 20:30 Rom 11:8
20:30 Judg 2:19
20:31 Ps 106:37-39 Jer 7:31 Ezek 16:20
20:32 Jer 2:25; 44:17 Ezek 16:20
20:34 Jer 42:18; 44:6 Lam 2:4 †2 Cor 6:17
20:36 Deut 32:10 1 Cor 10:5-10
20:38 Ps 95:11 Ezek 34:17-22 Amos 9:9-10 Heb 4:3

**20:39**
Isa 1:12-15
Jer 44:25-26
Ezek 23:38-39

**20:40**
Isa 56:7; 60:7
Ezek 43:12, 27

**20:41**
Isa 27:12-13

**20:43**
Zech 12:10-14

39 "As for you, O people of Israel, this is what the Sovereign Lord says: Go right ahead and worship your idols, but sooner or later you will obey me and will stop bringing shame on my holy name by worshiping idols. 40 For on my holy mountain, the great mountain of Israel, says the Sovereign Lord, the people of Israel will someday worship me, and I will accept them. There I will require that you bring me all your offerings and choice gifts and sacrifices. 41 When I bring you home from exile, you will be like a pleasing sacrifice to me. And I will display my holiness through you as all the nations watch. 42 Then when I have brought you home to the land I promised with a solemn oath to give to your ancestors, you will know that I am the Lord. 43 You will look back on all the ways you defiled yourselves and will hate yourselves because of the evil you have done. 44 You will know that I am the Lord, O people of Israel, when I have honored my name by treating you mercifully in spite of your wickedness. I, the Sovereign Lord, have spoken!"

### Judgment against the Negev

**20:46**
Jer 13:19

**20:47**
Isa 9:18

**20:48**
Jer 7:20; 17:27

**20:49**
Matt 13:12-13
John 16:25

45 *Then this message came to me from the Lord: 46 "Son of man, turn and face the south* and speak out against it; prophesy against the brushlands of the Negev. 47 Tell the southern wilderness, 'This is what the Sovereign Lord says: Hear the word of the Lord! I will set you on fire, and every tree, both green and dry, will be burned. The terrible flames will not be quenched and will scorch everything from south to north. 48 And everyone in the world will see that I, the Lord, have set this fire. It will not be put out.'"

49 Then I said, "O Sovereign Lord, they are saying of me, 'He only talks in riddles!'"

### The Lord's Sword of Judgment

**21:2**
Ezek 20:46

**21:3**
Isa 57:1
Jer 21:13
Ezek 5:8
Nah 2:13; 3:5

**21:4**
Jer 12:12
Ezek 7:2; 20:47

**21:5**
1 Sam 3:12
Nah 1:9

**21:7**
Isa 13:7
Ezek 7:26

**21:9**
Deut 32:41

**21:10**
Isa 34:5-6

**21** 1 *Then this message came to me from the Lord: 2 "Son of man, turn and face Jerusalem and prophesy against Israel and her sanctuaries. 3 Tell her, 'This is what the Lord says: I am your enemy, O Israel, and I am about to unsheath my sword to destroy your people—the righteous and the wicked alike. 4 Yes, I will cut off both the righteous and the wicked! I will draw my sword against everyone in the land from south to north. 5 Everyone in the world will know that I am the Lord. My sword is in my hand, and it will not return to its sheath until its work is finished.'

6 "Son of man, groan before the people! Groan before them with bitter anguish and a broken heart. 7 When they ask why you are groaning, tell them, 'I groan because of the terrifying news I have heard. When it comes true, the boldest heart will melt with fear; all strength will disappear. Every spirit will faint; strong knees will become as weak as water. And the Sovereign Lord says: It is coming! It's on its way!'"

8 Then the Lord said to me, 9 "Son of man, give the people this message from the Lord:

"A sword, a sword
    is being sharpened and polished.
10 It is sharpened for terrible slaughter
    and polished to flash like lightning!
Now will you laugh?
Those far stronger than you have fallen beneath its power!*

20:45 Verses 20:45-49 are numbered 21:1-5 in Hebrew text.    20:46 Hebrew *toward Teman.*    21:1 Verses 21:1-32 are numbered 21:6-37 in Hebrew text.    21:10 The meaning of the Hebrew is uncertain.

---

**20:39** The Israelites were worshiping idols and giving gifts to God at the same time! They did not believe in their God as the one true God; instead, they worshiped him along with the other gods of the land. Perhaps they enjoyed the immoral pleasures of idol worship; or perhaps they didn't want to miss out on the benefits the idols might give them. Often people believe in God and give him gifts of church attendance or service, while still holding on to their idols of money, power, or pleasure, not wanting to miss out on any possible benefits. But God wants all of our life and all of our devotion; devotion to anything else is idol worship. Beware of trying to please God while also pursuing the pleasures of sin. You must choose one or the other.

**20:45-47** "The south" refers to Jerusalem and Judah. "The southern wilderness" is the region of the Negev, which is compared to a forest about to be destroyed by fire.

**20:49** Ezekiel was exasperated and discouraged. Many Israelites were complaining that he spoke only in riddles, so they refused

to listen. No matter how important our work or how significant our ministry, we will have moments of discouragement. Apparently God did not answer Ezekiel's plea; instead, he gave Ezekiel another message to proclaim. What has been discouraging you? Have you felt like giving up? Instead, continue doing what God has told you to do. He promises to reward the faithful (Mark 13:13). God's cure for discouragement may be another assignment. In serving others, we may find the renewal we need.

**21:1ff** The short message in 20:45-48 introduces the first of three messages about the judgments that would come upon Jerusalem: (1) the sword of the Lord (21:1-7); (2) the sharpened sword (21:8-17); (3) the sword of Nebuchadnezzar (21:18-22). The city would be destroyed because it was defiled. According to Jewish law, defiled objects were to be passed through fire in order to purify them (see Numbers 31:22, 23; Psalm 66:10-12; Proverbs 17:3). God's judgment is designed to purify; destruction is often a necessary part of that process.

¹¹ Yes, the sword is now being sharpened and polished;
  it is being prepared for the executioner.

¹² "Son of man, cry out and wail;
    pound your thighs in anguish,
  for that sword will slaughter my people and their leaders—
    everyone will die!

**21:12**
Joel 1:13

¹³ It will put them all to the test.
    What chance do they have?*
  says the Sovereign LORD.

¹⁴ "Son of man, prophesy to them
    and clap your hands.
  Then take the sword and brandish it twice,
    even three times,
  to symbolize the great massacre,
    the great massacre facing them on every side.

**21:14**
Lev 26:21, 24

¹⁵ Let their hearts melt with terror,
    for the sword glitters at every gate.
  It flashes like lightning
    and is polished for slaughter!

**21:15**
Josh 2:11
2 Sam 17:10
Jer 17:27

¹⁶ O sword, slash to the right,
    then slash to the left,
  wherever you will,
    wherever you want.

¹⁷ I, too, will clap my hands,
    and I will satisfy my fury.
  I, the LORD, have spoken!"

**21:17**
Ezek 5:13

## Omens for Babylon's King

¹⁸Then this message came to me from the LORD: ¹⁹"Son of man, make a map and trace two routes on it for the sword of Babylon's king to follow. Put a signpost on the road that comes out of Babylon where the road forks into two—²⁰one road going to Ammon and its capital, Rabbah, and the other to Judah and fortified Jerusalem. ²¹The king of Babylon now stands at the fork, uncertain whether to attack Jerusalem or Rabbah. He calls his magicians to look for omens. They cast lots by shaking arrows from the quiver. They inspect the livers of animal sacrifices. ²²The omen in his right hand says, 'Jerusalem!' With battering rams his soldiers will go against the gates, shouting for the kill. They will put up siege towers and build ramps against the walls. ²³The people of Jerusalem will think it is a false omen, because of their treaty with the Babylonians. But the king of Babylon will remind the people of their rebellion. Then he will attack and capture them.

**21:19**
Deut 3:11
Amos 1:14

**21:20**
Jer 49:2
Ezek 25:5
Amos 1:14

**21:21**
Num 23:23
Prov 16:33

**21:22**
Ezek 4:2; 26:9

**21:23**
Ezek 17:16-18;
29:16

²⁴"Therefore, this is what the Sovereign LORD says: Again and again you remind me of your sin and your guilt. You don't even try to hide it! In everything you do, your sins are obvious for all to see. So now the time of your punishment has come!

²⁵"O you corrupt and wicked prince of Israel, your final day of reckoning is here! ²⁶This is what the Sovereign LORD says:

**21:25**
Ps 37:13
Ezek 7:2-7

  "Take off your jeweled crown,
    for the old order changes.
  Now the lowly will be exalted,
    and the mighty will be brought down.

**21:26**
Ps 75:7
Jer 13:18
Ezek 16:12; 17:24

**21:13** The meaning of the Hebrew is uncertain.

---

**21:12** Pounding the thighs was a gesture of grief.

**21:18-23** Ammon evidently rebelled against Babylon about the same time as King Zedekiah of Judah. In 589 B.C. the nations of Judah and Ammon were among those who conspired against Babylon (Jeremiah 27:3). Ezekiel gave this message to the exiles who had heard the news and were again filled with hope of returning to their homeland. Ezekiel said that Babylon's king would march his armies into the region to stop the rebellion. Traveling from the north, he would stop at a fork in the road, one way lead-

ing to Rabbah, the capital of Ammon, and the other leading to Jerusalem, the capital of Judah. He had to decide which city to destroy. Just as Ezekiel predicted, King Nebuchadnezzar went to Jerusalem and besieged it.

**21:21** Nebuchadnezzar had two ways to get advice on the future. One was shaking arrows, much like drawing straws, to see which course of action was right; the second was having priests inspect the liver of a sacrificed animal to see if its shape and size would indicate a decision.

**21:27**
Ps 2:6
Jer 23:5-6
Ezek 34:24; 37:24
Hag 2:21-22

27 Destruction! Destruction!
I will surely destroy the kingdom.
And it will not be restored until the one appears
who has the right to judge it.
Then I will hand it over to him.

### A Message for the Ammonites

**21:28**
Isa 31:8
Jer 12:12
Zeph 2:8-10

28 "And now, son of man, prophesy concerning the Ammonites and their mockery. Give them this message from the Sovereign LORD:

"A sword, a sword
is drawn for your slaughter.
It is polished to destroy,
flashing like lightning!

**21:29**
Jer 27:9

29 Your prophets have given false visions,
and your fortune-tellers have told lies.
The sword will fall on the necks of the wicked
for whom the day of final reckoning has come.

**21:30**
Jer 47:6-7

30 "Now return the sword to its sheath,
for in your own country,
the land of your birth,
I will pass judgment upon you.

**21:31**
Ps 18:15
Nah 1:6
Hab 1:6, 10

31 I will pour out my fury on you
and blow on you with the fire of my anger.
I will hand you over to cruel men
who are skilled in destruction.

**21:32**
Ezek 25:10
Mal 4:1

32 You will be fuel for the fire,
and your blood will be spilled in your own land.
You will be utterly wiped out,
your memory lost to history,
for I, the LORD, have spoken!"

### The Sins of Jerusalem

**22** Now this message came to me from the LORD: 2 "Son of man, are you ready to judge Jerusalem? Are you ready to judge this city of murderers? Publicly denounce her detestable sins, 3 and give her this message from the Sovereign LORD: O city of murderers, doomed and damned—city of idols,* filthy and foul—4 you are guilty because of the blood you have shed. You are defiled because of the idols you have made. Your day of destruction has come! You have reached the end of your years. I will make you an object of mockery throughout the world. 5 O infamous city, filled with confusion, you will be mocked by people far and near.

**22:3**
Zeph 3:3
**22:4**
2 Kgs 21:16
**22:6**
Isa 1:23
**22:7**
Exod 22:22; 23:9
Prov 22:22-23
**22:9**
Hos 4:2, 10, 14
**22:10**
Lev 18:8, 19
**22:11**
Lev 18:15
2 Sam 13:14
**22:12**
Lev 19:13; 25:36
Deut 27:25
Mic 7:2-3

6 "Every leader in Israel who lives within your walls is bent on murder. 7 Fathers and mothers are treated with contempt. Foreigners are forced to pay for protection. Orphans and widows are wronged and oppressed among you. 8 You despise my holy things and violate my Sabbath days of rest. 9 People accuse others falsely and send them to their death. You are filled with idol worshipers and people who do obscene things. 10 Men sleep with their fathers' wives and have intercourse with women who are menstruating. 11 Within your walls live men who commit adultery with their neighbors' wives, who defile their daughters-in-law, or who rape their own sisters. 12 There are hired murderers, loan racketeers, and extortioners everywhere. They never even think of me and my commands, says the Sovereign LORD.

**22:3** The Hebrew term (literally *round things*) probably alludes to dung; also in 22:4.

**21:28** The Ammonites and Israelites were usually fighting with each other. God told the Israelites not to ally with foreign nations, but Judah and Ammon united against Babylon in 589 B.C. (Jeremiah 27:3). God first judged Judah when Nebuchadnezzar first went to Jerusalem (21:22); but Ammon would also be judged, not for allying with Judah, but for watching Jerusalem's destruction with insulting delight.

**22:1ff** Chapter 22 explains why Jerusalem's judgment would come (22:2-16), how it would come (22:17-22), and who would be affected by it (22:23-31).

**22:6-13** The leaders, whom God chose, were responsible for the moral climate of the nation. The same is true today (see James 3:1). Unfortunately, many of the sins mentioned here have been committed in recent years by Christian leaders. We are living in a time of unprecedented attacks by Satan. We must uphold our leaders in prayer, and leaders must seek accountability in order to help them maintain their moral and spiritual integrity.

13"But now I clap my hands in indignation over your dishonest gain and bloodshed. 14How strong and courageous will you be in my day of reckoning? I, the LORD, have spoken, and I will do what I said. 15I will scatter you among the nations and purge you of your wickedness. 16And when I have been dishonored among the nations because of you,* you will know that I am the LORD."

### The LORD's Refining Furnace

17Then this message came to me from the LORD: 18"Son of man, the people of Israel are the worthless slag that remains after silver is smelted. They are the dross that is left over—a useless mixture of copper, tin, iron, and lead. 19So tell them, 'This is what the Sovereign LORD says: Because you are all worthless slag, I will bring you to my crucible in Jerusalem. 20Just as copper, iron, lead, and tin are melted down in a furnace, I will melt you down in the heat of my fury. 21I will gather you together and blow the fire of my anger upon you, 22and you will melt like silver in fierce heat. Then you will know that I, the LORD, have poured out my fury on you.'"

### The Sins of Israel's Leaders

23Again a message came to me from the LORD: 24"Son of man, give the people of Israel this message: In the day of my indignation, you will be like a polluted land, a land without rain. 25Your princes* plot conspiracies just as lions stalk their prey. They devour innocent people, seizing treasures and extorting wealth. They make many widows in the land. 26Your priests have violated my instructions and defiled my holy things. They make no distinction between what is holy and what is not. And they do not teach my people the difference between what is ceremonially clean and unclean. They disregard my Sabbath days so that I am dishonored among them. 27Your leaders are like wolves who tear apart their victims. They actually destroy people's lives for money! 28And your prophets cover up for them by announcing false visions and making lying predictions. They say, 'My message is from the Sovereign LORD,' when the LORD hasn't spoken a single word to them. 29Even common people oppress the poor, rob the needy, and deprive foreigners of justice.

30"I looked for someone who might rebuild the wall of righteousness that guards the land. I searched for someone to stand in the gap in the wall so I wouldn't have to destroy the land, but I found no one. 31So now I will pour out my fury on them, consuming them with the fire of my anger. I will heap on their heads the full penalty for all their sins. I, the Sovereign LORD, have spoken!"

### The Adultery of Two Sisters

**23** This message came to me from the LORD: 2"Son of man, once there were two sisters who were daughters of the same mother. 3They became prostitutes in Egypt. Even as young girls, they allowed men to fondle their breasts. 4The older girl was named Oholah, and her sister was Oholibah. I married them, and they bore me sons and daughters. I am speaking of Samaria and Jerusalem, for Oholah is Samaria and Oholibah is Jerusalem.

**22:16** Or when you have been dishonored among the nations.   **22:25** As in Greek version; Hebrew reads prophets.

#### Cross-references
22:13 Prov 28:8; Isa 33:15; Amos 2:6-8
22:15 Deut 4:27; Zech 7:14
22:16 Ezek 6:4-7
22:18 Ps 119:119; Prov 17:3; Isa 1:22; 48:10; Jer 6:28
22:22 Ezek 20:8, 33; Hos 5:10
22:24 Jer 2:30; Ezek 24:13
22:25 Jer 2:34; 15:8; Hos 6:9
22:26 Lev 10:10; 1 Sam 2:12-17; Ezek 44:23; Hag 2:11-14
22:28 Jer 23:25-32; Ezek 13:6
22:29 Exod 23:9; Isa 5:7; Amos 3:10; Jas 5:4
22:30 Ps 106:23; Jer 5:1; Ezek 13:5
23:2 Jer 3:7-10; Ezek 16:46

---

**22:17-22** Precious metals are refined with intense heat to remove the impurities or slag. When heated, the slag rises to the top of the molten metal and is skimmed off and thrown away. The purpose of the invasion of Jerusalem was to refine the people, but the refining process showed that the people, like worthless slag, had nothing good in them.

**22:26** The priests were supposed to keep God's worship pure and teach the people right living. But the worship of God had become commonplace to them; they ignored the Sabbath, and they refused to teach the people. They no longer carried out their God-given duties (Leviticus 10:10, 11; Ezekiel 44:23). When doing God's work becomes no more important than any mundane task, we are no longer giving God the reverence he deserves. Instead of bringing God down to our sinful human level, we should live in ways that reflect his holiness.

**22:30** The wall spoken of here is not made of stones but of faithful people united in their efforts to resist evil. This wall was in disrepair because there was no one who could lead the people back to God. The feeble attempts to repair the gap—through religious rituals or messages based on opinion rather than God's will—were as worthless as whitewash, only covering the real problems. What the people really needed was total spiritual reconstruction! When we

give the appearance of loving God without living his way, we are covering up sins that could eventually damage us deeply. Don't use religion as a whitewash; repair your life by applying the principles of God's Word. Then you can join with others to "stand in the gap" and make a difference for God in the world.

**23:1ff** Ezekiel continued his discussion of the reasons for God's judgment by telling a further allegory. He compared the northern and southern kingdoms to two sisters who became prostitutes. The proud citizens of Jerusalem had long scorned their sister city of Samaria, thinking that they were superior. But God called both of these cities prostitutes—a shock to the people of Jerusalem, who thought they were righteous. Just as the imagery of this message was shocking and distasteful to the people, so our sins are repugnant to God.

**23:4-6** Oholah (meaning "her tent"), the northern kingdom of Israel, was lured away from God by the dashing Assyrians. The people of Israel coveted their youth, strength, power, wealth, and pleasure—the same qualities people think will bring happiness today.

**23:11ff** Oholibah (meaning "my tent is in her") was shown to be worse, because she did not learn from the judgment upon her sister but continued in her lust for the Assyrians and Babylonians. Therefore, her judgment was equally certain. Just as Oholibah

**23:5**
Ezek 16:28
Hos 8:9-10

**23:6**
Ezek 23:12, 23

**23:7**
Hos 5:3; 6:10

**23:8**
Exod 32:4
1 Kgs 12:28
2 Kgs 17:16

**23:9-10**
Ezek 16:37

**23:11**
Jer 3:8-11

**23:12**
2 Kgs 16:7

**23:14**
Ezek 8:10; 16:29

**23:16**
Matt 5:28

**23:17**
2 Kgs 24:17

**23:20**
Ezek 17:15

**23:21**
Jer 3:9

**23:23**
Gen 25:18
2 Kgs 20:14-17;
24:2
Job 1:17
Jer 50:21
Ezek 21:19

**23:24**
Jer 39:5-6

**23:25**
Ezek 8:17-18;
23:47
Zeph 1:18

**23:26**
Ezek 16:39

**23:27**
Ezek 16:41

**23:28**
Jer 21:7-10
Ezek 16:37

**23:29**
Deut 28:48

**23:30**
Ezek 6:9

**23:31**
2 Kgs 21:13

5 "Then Oholah lusted after other lovers instead of me, and she gave her love to the Assyrian officers. 6 They were all attractive young men, captains and commanders dressed in handsome blue, charioteers driving their horses. 7 And so she prostituted herself with the most desirable men of Assyria, worshiping their idols* and defiling herself. 8 For when she left Egypt, she did not leave her spirit of prostitution behind. She was still as lewd as in her youth, when the Egyptians slept with her, fondled her breasts, and used her as a prostitute.

9 "And so I handed her over to her Assyrian lovers, whom she desired so much. 10 They stripped her, took away her children as their slaves, and then killed her. After she received her punishment, her reputation was known to every woman in the land.

11 "Yet even though Oholibah saw what had happened to Oholah, her sister, she followed right in her footsteps. And she was even more depraved, abandoning herself to her lust and prostitution. 12 She fawned over all the Assyrian officers—those captains and commanders in handsome uniforms, those charioteers driving their horses—all of them attractive young men. 13 I saw the way she was going, defiling herself just like her older sister.

14 "Then she carried her prostitution even further. She fell in love with pictures that were painted on a wall—pictures of Babylonian* military officers, outfitted in striking red uniforms. 15 Handsome belts encircled their waists, and flowing turbans crowned their heads. They were dressed like chariot officers from the land of Babylonia.* 16 When she saw these paintings, she longed to give herself to them, so she sent messengers to Babylonia to invite them to come to her. 17 So they came and committed adultery with her, defiling her in the bed of love. After being defiled, however, she rejected them in disgust.

18 "In the same way, I became disgusted with Oholibah and rejected her, just as I had rejected her sister, because she flaunted herself before them and gave herself to satisfy their lusts. 19 Yet she turned to even greater prostitution, remembering her youth when she was a prostitute in Egypt. 20 She lusted after lovers with genitals as large as a donkey's and emissions like those of a horse. 21 And so, Oholibah, you relived your former days as a young girl in Egypt, when you first allowed your breasts to be fondled.

### The LORD's Judgment of Oholibah

22 "Therefore, Oholibah, this is what the Sovereign LORD says: I will send your lovers against you from every direction—those very nations from which you turned away in disgust. 23 For the Babylonians will come with all the Chaldeans from Pekod and Shoa and Koa. And all the Assyrians will come with them—handsome young captains, commanders, chariot officers, and other high-ranking officers, all riding their horses. 24 They will all come against you from the north* with chariots, wagons, and a great army prepared for attack. They will take up positions on every side, surrounding you with men armed with shields and helmets. And I will hand you over to them for punishment so they can do with you as they please. 25 I will turn my jealous anger against you, and they will deal harshly with you. They will cut off your nose and ears, and any survivors will then be slaughtered by the sword. Your children will be taken away as captives, and everything that is left will be burned. 26 They will strip you of your beautiful clothes and jewels. 27 In this way, I will put a stop to the lewdness and prostitution you brought from Egypt. You will never again cast longing eyes on those things or fondly remember your time in Egypt.

28 "For this is what the Sovereign LORD says: I will surely hand you over to your enemies, to those you loathe, those you rejected. 29 They will treat you with hatred and rob you of all you own, leaving you stark naked. The shame of your prostitution will be exposed to all the world. 30 You brought all this on yourself by prostituting yourself to other nations, defiling yourself with all their idols. 31 Because you have followed in your sister's footsteps, I will force you to drink the same cup of terror she drank.

**23:7** The Hebrew term (literally *round things*) probably alludes to dung; also in 23:30, 37, 39, 49.   **23:14** Or *Chaldean.*   **23:15** Or *Chaldea;* also in 23:16.   **23:24** As in Greek version; the meaning of the Hebrew is uncertain.

---

was privileged and should have known better, so we are privileged because we know about Christ. We need to be doubly sure that we follow him.

**23:12** "She fawned over all the Assyrian officers" probably means Judah excessively tried to please Assyria and may refer to Ahaz's paying protection money to Tiglath-pileser III (2 Kings 16:7, 8).

**23:16** An invitation to Babylonia was given by Hezekiah to the envoys from Babylon (2 Kings 20:12ff; Isaiah 39).

**23:17** At first, Judah made an alliance with Babylonia, but then changed its mind. During the reigns of Jehoiakim and Zedekiah, Judah looked to Egypt for help. Judah's unfaithfulness (its alliances with godless nations) cost it the only real protection it ever had—God.

**23:22-26** This predicts the last attack on Jerusalem that would destroy the city and bring to Babylonia the third wave of captives in 586 B.C. (2 Kings 25; Jeremiah 52). The first attack came in 605 B.C., the second in 597 B.C. Pekod, Shoa, and Koa were Babylonian allies.

<sup>32</sup> "Yes, this is what the Sovereign Lord says:

"You will drink from your sister's cup of terror,
 a cup that is large and deep.
It is filled to the brim
 with scorn and derision.
<sup>33</sup> Drunkenness and anguish will fill you,
 for your cup is filled to the brim with distress and desolation,
 the same cup your sister Samaria drank.
<sup>34</sup> You will drain that cup of terror
 to the very bottom.
Then you will smash it to pieces
 and beat your breast in anguish.
 I, the Sovereign Lord, have spoken!

<sup>35</sup> "And because you have forgotten me and turned your back on me, this is what the Sovereign Lord says: You must bear the consequences of all your lewdness and prostitution."

### The Lord's Judgment on Both Sisters

<sup>36</sup> The Lord said to me, "Son of man, you must accuse Oholah and Oholibah of all their detestable sins. <sup>37</sup> They have committed both adultery and murder—adultery by worshiping idols and murder by burning as sacrifices the children they bore to me. <sup>38</sup> Furthermore, they have defiled my Temple and violated my Sabbath day! <sup>39</sup> On the very day that they sacrificed their children to their idols, they boldly came into my Temple to worship! They came in and defiled my house.

<sup>40</sup> "You sisters sent messengers to distant lands to get men. Then when they arrived, you bathed yourselves, painted your eyelids, and put on your finest jewels for them. <sup>41</sup> You sat with them on a beautifully embroidered couch and put my incense and my special oil on a table that was spread before you. <sup>42</sup> From your room came the sound of many men carousing. They were lustful men and drunkards* from the wilderness, who put bracelets on your wrists and beautiful crowns on your heads. <sup>43</sup> Then I said, 'If they really want to have sex with old worn-out prostitutes like these, let them!' <sup>44</sup> And that is what they did. They had sex with Oholah and Oholibah, these shameless prostitutes. <sup>45</sup> But righteous people will judge these sister cities for what they really are—adulterers and murderers.

<sup>46</sup> "Now this is what the Sovereign Lord says: Bring an army against them and hand them over to be terrorized and plundered. <sup>47</sup> For their enemies will stone them and kill them with swords. They will butcher their sons and daughters and burn their homes. <sup>48</sup> In this way, I will put an end to lewdness and idolatry in the land, and my judgment will be a warning to others not to follow their wicked example. <sup>49</sup> You will be fully repaid for all your prostitution—your worship of idols. Yes, you will suffer the full penalty. Then you will know that I am the Sovereign Lord."

### The Sign of the Cooking Pot

**24** On January 15,* during the ninth year of King Jehoiachin's captivity, this message came to me from the Lord: <sup>2</sup> "Son of man, write down today's date, because on this very day the king of Babylon is beginning his attack against Jerusalem. <sup>3</sup> Then give these rebels an illustration with this message from the Sovereign Lord:

"Put a pot on the fire,
 and pour in some water.
<sup>4</sup> Fill it with choice pieces of meat—

**23:32** Ps 60:3; Ezek 5:14-15
**23:33** Jer 25:15
**23:34** Ps 75:8; Isa 51:17
**23:35** 1 Kgs 14:9; Neh 9:26; Hos 13:6
**23:36** Isa 58:1; Jer 1:10
**23:38** 2 Kgs 21:4, 7; Jer 17:27
**23:39** Jer 7:9-11
**23:40** 2 Kgs 9:30
**23:41** Jer 44:17
**23:42** Gen 24:30; Jer 51:7; Ezek 16:11-12, 49; Amos 6:3-6
**23:45** Ezek 16:38
**23:46** Jer 15:4; 24:9; 29:18; Ezek 16:38
**23:47** Jer 39:8
**23:49** Isa 59:18; Ezek 9:10
**24:2** 2 Kgs 25:1; Jer 39:1; 52:4
**24:3** Jer 1:13-14
**24:4** Mic 3:2-3

**23:42** Or *Sabeans.* **24:1** Hebrew *On the tenth day of the tenth month,* of the ancient Hebrew lunar calendar. This event occurred on January 15, 588 B.C.; also see note on 1:1.

---

**23:39** The Israelites went so far as to sacrifice their own children to idols and then to sacrifice to the Lord the same day. This made a mockery of worship. We cannot praise God and willfully sin at the same time. That would be like a person going to bed with a neighbor and then celebrating his or her wedding anniversary.

**24:1-14** Ezekiel gave this illustration in 588 B.C., about three years after the first of the previous messages (see 20:1, 2). The people in Judah thought they were the "choice pieces of meat" because they hadn't been taken into captivity in 597 when the Babylonians last invaded the land. Ezekiel used this illustration before (chapter 11) to show that, although the people thought they were safe and secure inside the cooking pot, this pot would actually be the place of their destruction. This message was given to the exiles in Babylonia the very day that the Babylonians attacked Jerusalem (24:2), beginning a siege that lasted over two years and resulted in the city's destruction. When God's punishment comes, it is relentless.

the rump and the shoulder
and all the most tender cuts.

⁵ Use only the best sheep from the flock,
and heap fuel on the fire beneath the pot.
Bring the pot to a boil,
and cook the bones along with the meat.

⁶ "Now this is what the Sovereign LORD says:
What sorrow awaits Jerusalem,
the city of murderers!
She is a cooking pot
whose corruption can't be cleaned out.
Take the meat out in random order,
for no piece is better than another.

⁷ For the blood of her murders
is splashed on the rocks.
It isn't even spilled on the ground,
where the dust could cover it!

⁸ So I will splash her blood on a rock
for all to see,
an expression of my anger
and vengeance against her.

⁹ "This is what the Sovereign LORD says:
What sorrow awaits Jerusalem,
the city of murderers!
I myself will pile up the fuel beneath her.
¹⁰ Yes, heap on the wood!
Let the fire roar to make the pot boil.
Cook the meat with many spices,
and afterward burn the bones.

¹¹ Now set the empty pot on the coals.
Heat it red hot!
Burn away the filth and corruption.
¹² But it's hopeless;
the corruption can't be cleaned out.
So throw it into the fire.

¹³ Your impurity is your lewdness
and the corruption of your idolatry.
I tried to cleanse you,
but you refused.
So now you will remain in your filth
until my fury against you has been satisfied.

¹⁴"I, the LORD, have spoken! The time has come, and I won't hold back. I will not change my mind, and I will have no pity on you. You will be judged on the basis of all your wicked actions, says the Sovereign LORD."

### The Death of Ezekiel's Wife

¹⁵Then this message came to me from the LORD: ¹⁶"Son of man, with one blow I will take away your dearest treasure. Yet you must not show any sorrow at her death. Do not weep; let

---

**24:6-13** The city of Jerusalem was like a pot so encrusted with sin that it would not come clean. God wanted to cleanse the lives of those who lived in Jerusalem, and he wants to cleanse our lives today. Sometimes he tries to purify us through difficulties and troublesome circumstances. When you face tough times, allow the sin to be burned from your life. Look at your problems as opportunities for your faith to grow. When these times come, unnecessary priorities and diversions are purged away. We can reexamine our lives so that we will do what really counts.

**24:15-18** God told Ezekiel that his wife would die and that he

should not grieve for her. Ezekiel obeyed God fully, even as Hosea did when he was told to marry a prostitute (Hosea 1:2, 3). In both cases, these unusual events were intended as symbolic acts to illustrate God's relationship with his people. Obeying God can carry a high price, but not obeying God will cost you more — eternal life. We should be wholehearted in our obedience to God as Ezekiel was. We can begin by doing all that God commands us to do, even when we don't feel like it. Are you willing to serve God as completely as Ezekiel did?

there be no tears. ¹⁷Groan silently, but let there be no wailing at her grave. Do not uncover your head or take off your sandals. Do not perform the usual rituals of mourning or accept any food brought to you by consoling friends."

**24:17**
Lev 21:10-12
2 Sam 15:30
Jer 16:7

¹⁸So I proclaimed this to the people the next morning, and in the evening my wife died. The next morning I did everything I had been told to do. ¹⁹Then the people asked, "What does all this mean? What are you trying to tell us?"

²⁰So I said to them, "A message came to me from the Lord, ²¹and I was told to give this message to the people of Israel. This is what the Sovereign Lord says: I will defile my Temple, the source of your security and pride, the place your heart delights in. Your sons and daughters whom you left behind in Judea will be slaughtered by the sword. ²²Then you will do as Ezekiel has done. You will not mourn in public or console yourselves by eating the food brought by friends. ²³Your heads will remain covered, and your sandals will not be taken off. You will not mourn or weep, but you will waste away because of your sins. You will mourn privately for all the evil you have done. ²⁴Ezekiel is an example for you; you will do just as he has done. And when that time comes, you will know that I am the Sovereign Lord."

**24:21**
Ps 27:4
Jer 16:11
Ezek 23:47

**24:23**
Job 27:15
Ps 78:64

**24:24**
Ezek 4:3
Luke 11:29-30

²⁵Then the Lord said to me, "Son of man, on the day I take away their stronghold—their joy and glory, their heart's desire, their dearest treasure—I will also take away their sons and daughters. ²⁶And on that day a survivor from Jerusalem will come to you in Babylon and tell you what has happened. ²⁷And when he arrives, your voice will suddenly return so you can talk to him, and you will be a symbol for these people. Then they will know that I am the Lord."

**24:25**
Pss 48:2; 122:1-9
Jer 7:4; 11:22

**24:26**
1 Sam 4:12
Job 1:15-19
Ezek 33:21-22

**24:27**
Ezek 3:26; 33:22

## B. MESSAGES AGAINST FOREIGN NATIONS (25:1—32:32)

These messages were given concerning seven nations that surrounded Judah. The Ammonites were judged because of their joy over the desecration of the Temple, the Moabites because they scorned Judah as special people, the Edomites because of their special hatred of the Jews, and the Philistines because of their vengeance. All these nations would soon realize that God is supreme. Nations today are also under limits imposed by God.

### A Message for Ammon

**25** Then this message came to me from the Lord: ²"Son of man, turn and face the land of Ammon and prophesy against its people. ³Give the Ammonites this message from the Sovereign Lord: Hear the word of the Sovereign Lord! Because you cheered when my Temple was defiled, mocked Israel in her desolation, and laughed at Judah as she went away into exile, ⁴I will allow nomads from the eastern deserts to overrun your country. They will set up their camps among you and pitch their tents on your land. They will harvest all your fruit and drink the milk from your livestock. ⁵And I will turn the city of Rabbah into a pasture for camels, and all the land of the Ammonites into a resting place for sheep and goats. Then you will know that I am the Lord.

**25:2**
Amos 1:13
Zeph 2:9

**25:4**
Deut 28:33, 51
Judg 6:3, 33
Isa 1:7

**25:5**
2 Sam 12:26
Jer 49:2
Zeph 2:14-15

---

**JUDAH'S ENEMIES**
Ammon, Moab, Edom, and Philistia, although once united with Judah against Babylon, had abandoned Judah and rejoiced to see its ruin. But these nations were as sinful as Judah and would also feel the sting of God's judgment.

**24:20-24** Ezekiel was not allowed to mourn for his dead wife in order to show his fellow exiles that they were not to mourn publicly over Jerusalem when it was destroyed. Any personal sorrow felt would soon be eclipsed by national sorrow over the horror of the city's total destruction. The individuals would waste away because of their sins, which caused the city's destruction.

**24:27** For some time Ezekiel had not been allowed to speak except when God gave him a message to deliver to the people (3:25-27). This restriction would soon end when Jerusalem was destroyed and all Ezekiel's prophecies about Judah and Jerusalem had come true (33:21, 22).

**25:1ff** Chapters 25–32 are God's word concerning the seven nations surrounding Judah. The judgments in these chapters are not simply the vengeful statements of Jews against their enemies; they are God's judgments on nations that failed to acknowledge the one true God and fulfill the good purposes God intended for them. The Ammonites were judged because of their joy over the desecration of the Temple (25:1-7), the Moabites because they found pleasure in Judah's wickedness (25:8-11), the Edomites because of their racial hatred for the Jews (25:12-14), and the Philistines because they sought revenge against Judah for defeating them in battle (25:15-17).

**25:5** Rabbah was the capital city of the Ammonites.

**25:6**
Job 27:23
Zeph 2:8, 10
**25:7**
Amos 1:14-15

6"This is what the Sovereign Lord says: Because you clapped and danced and cheered with glee at the destruction of my people, 7 I will raise my fist of judgment against you. I will give you as plunder to many nations. I will cut you off from being a nation and destroy you completely. Then you will know that I am the Lord.

### A Message for Moab

**25:8**
Isa 15:1
Jer 48:1
Amos 2:1
**25:9**
Num 32:37-38
Josh 13:17-20
1 Chr 5:8
Jer 48:23

8"This is what the Sovereign Lord says: Because the people of Moab have said that Judah is just like all the other nations, 9 I will open up their eastern flank and wipe out their glorious frontier towns—Beth-jeshimoth, Baal-meon, and Kiriathaim. 10And I will hand Moab over to nomads from the eastern deserts, just as I handed over Ammon. Yes, the Ammonites will no longer be counted among the nations. 11In the same way, I will bring my judgment down on the Moabites. Then they will know that I am the Lord.

### A Message for Edom

**25:13**
Gen 36:34
Jer 49:7
Mal 1:3-4
**25:14**
Ezek 34:11
Nah 1:2-4
Heb 10:30-31

12"This is what the Sovereign Lord says: The people of Edom have sinned greatly by avenging themselves against the people of Judah. 13Therefore, says the Sovereign Lord, I will raise my fist of judgment against Edom. I will wipe out its people and animals with the sword. I will make a wasteland of everything from Teman to Dedan. 14I will accomplish this by the hand of my people of Israel. They will carry out my vengeance with anger, and Edom will know that this vengeance is from me. I, the Sovereign Lord, have spoken!

### A Message for Philistia

**25:15**
Isa 14:29-31
Joel 3:4
Amos 1:6-8
Zeph 2:4-7
Zech 9:5-8
**25:16**
1 Sam 30:14

15"This is what the Sovereign Lord says: The people of Philistia have acted against Judah out of bitter revenge and long-standing contempt. 16Therefore, this is what the Sovereign Lord says: I will raise my fist of judgment against the land of the Philistines. I will wipe out the Kerethites and utterly destroy the people who live by the sea. 17I will execute terrible vengeance against them to punish them for what they have done. And when I have inflicted my revenge, they will know that I am the Lord."

### A Message for Tyre

**26:2**
2 Sam 5:11
Isa 23:1
Jer 25:22

**26:3**
Jer 50:42; 51:42

**26:4**
Isa 23:11
Amos 1:10

**26:7**
Dan 2:37, 47
Nah 2:3-4

**26** On February 3, during the twelfth year of King Jehoiachin's captivity,* this message came to me from the Lord: 2"Son of man, Tyre has rejoiced over the fall of Jerusalem, saying, 'Ha! She who was the gateway to the rich trade routes to the east has been broken, and I am the heir! Because she has been made desolate, I will become wealthy!'

3"Therefore, this is what the Sovereign Lord says: I am your enemy, O Tyre, and I will bring many nations against you, like the waves of the sea crashing against your shoreline. 4They will destroy the walls of Tyre and tear down its towers. I will scrape away its soil and make it a bare rock! 5 It will be just a rock in the sea, a place for fishermen to spread their nets, for I have spoken, says the Sovereign Lord. Tyre will become the prey of many nations, 6and its mainland villages will be destroyed by the sword. Then they will know that I am the Lord.

7"This is what the Sovereign Lord says: From the north I will bring King Nebuchadnezzar* of Babylon against Tyre. He is king of kings and brings his horses, chariots, charioteers,

26:1 Hebrew *In the eleventh year, on the first day of the month*, of the ancient Hebrew lunar calendar year. Since an element is missing in the date formula here, scholars have reconstructed this probable reading: *In the eleventh [month of the twelfth] year, on the first day of the month.* This reading would put this message on February 3, 585 B.C.; also see note on 1:1.   **26:7** Hebrew *Nebuchadrezzar*, a variant spelling of Nebuchadnezzar.

---

**25:9** These towns were on the northern border of Moab.

**25:12-14** The Edomites were blood brothers of the Jews, both nations having descended from Isaac (Genesis 25:19-26). Edom shared its northern border with Israel, and the two nations were always in conflict. The Edomites hated Israel so much that they rejoiced when Jerusalem, Israel's capital, was destroyed. Teman was in the northern part of Edom; Dedan was in the southern part. Thus, Ezekiel was saying that the entire country would be destroyed.

**25:16** The Kerethites originated in Crete, from which they take their name. They were either a clan of the Philistines or possibly a separate people who migrated from the Aegean to Palestine about the same time. The Kerethites and Philistines were closely intermixed once they were in Palestine and are often mentioned together.

**26:1ff** This message came to Ezekiel in 586 B.C. Chapters 26

and 27 are a prophecy against Tyre, the capital of Phoenicia, just north of Israel. Part of the city was on the coastline, and part was on a beautiful island. Tyre rejoiced when Jerusalem fell, because Tyre and Judah always competed for the lucrative trade that came through their lands from Egypt in the south and Mesopotamia to the north. Tyre dominated the sea trading routes, while Judah dominated the land caravan routes. After Judah was defeated, Tyre thought it had all the trade routes to itself. But this gloating didn't last long. In 586 B.C., Nebuchadnezzar attacked the city. It took him 15 years to capture Tyre (586-571) because the city's back side lay on the sea so fresh supplies could be shipped in daily.

and great army. 8First he will destroy your mainland villages. Then he will attack you by building a siege wall, constructing a ramp, and raising a roof of shields against you. 9He will pound your walls with battering rams and demolish your towers with sledgehammers. 10The hooves of his horses will choke the city with dust, and the noise of the charioteers and chariot wheels will shake your walls as they storm through your broken gates. 11His horsemen will trample through every street in the city. They will butcher your people, and your strong pillars will topple.

12"They will plunder all your riches and merchandise and break down your walls. They will destroy your lovely homes and dump your stones and timbers and even your dust into the sea. 13I will stop the music of your songs. No more will the sound of harps be heard among your people. 14I will make your island a bare rock, a place for fishermen to spread their nets. You will never be rebuilt, for I, the LORD, have spoken. Yes, the Sovereign LORD has spoken!

### The Effect of Tyre's Destruction

15"This is what the Sovereign LORD says to Tyre: The whole coastline will tremble at the sound of your fall, as the screams of the wounded echo in the continuing slaughter. 16All the seaport rulers will step down from their thrones and take off their royal robes and beautiful clothing. They will sit on the ground trembling with horror at your destruction. 17Then they will wail for you, singing this funeral song:

"O famous island city,
    once ruler of the sea,
    how you have been destroyed!
Your people, with their naval power,
    once spread fear around the world.
18 Now the coastlands tremble at your fall.
    The islands are dismayed as you disappear.

19"This is what the Sovereign LORD says: I will make Tyre an uninhabited ruin, like many others. I will bury you beneath the terrible waves of enemy attack. Great seas will swallow you. 20I will send you to the pit to join those who descended there long ago. Your city will lie in ruins, buried beneath the earth, like those in the pit who have entered the world of the dead. You will have no place of respect here in the land of the living. 21I will bring you to a terrible end, and you will exist no more. You will be looked for, but you will never again be found. I, the Sovereign LORD, have spoken!"

### The End of Tyre's Glory

**27** Then this message came to me from the LORD: 2"Son of man, sing a funeral song for Tyre, 3that mighty gateway to the sea, the trading center of the world. Give Tyre this message from the Sovereign LORD:

"You boasted, O Tyre,
    'My beauty is perfect!'
4 You extended your boundaries into the sea.
    Your builders made your beauty perfect.

| | |
|---|---|
| **26:8** | Jer 6:6; 32:24; 52:4 |
| **26:10** | Jer 39:3 |
| **26:11** | Isa 5:28; 26:5 |
| **26:12** | 2 Chr 32:27<br>Isa 23:8, 18 |
| **26:13** | Isa 24:8-9<br>Amos 6:5 |
| **26:14** | Deut 13:16<br>Isa 14:27 |
| **26:15** | Jer 49:21 |
| **26:16** | Ps 35:26<br>Jon 3:6 |
| **26:17** | Isa 14:12<br>Jer 48:39; 50:23 |
| **26:18** | Isa 23:5-7, 10-15 |
| **26:19** | Isa 8:7-8 |
| **26:20** | Ps 88:6<br>Jon 2:2, 6<br>Zech 2:8 |
| **26:21** | Ezek 27:36 |
| **27:2** | Jer 7:20; 9:10 |

---

**26:14** After a 15-year siege, Nebuchadnezzar could not conquer the part of Tyre located on the island; thus, certain aspects of the description in 26:12, 14 exceed the actual damage done to Tyre by Nebuchadnezzar. But the prophecy predicted what would happen to the island settlement later during the conquests of Alexander the Great. Alexander threw the rubble of the mainland city into the sea until it made a bridge to the island. Then he marched across the bridge and destroyed the island (332 B.C.). Today the island city is still a pile of rubble, a testimony to God's judgment.

**27:1ff** Chapter 27 is a funeral lament over Tyre's fall. It compares the city to a ship (27:1-9), mentions many of its trading partners (27:10-25), and then describes how the ship sank (27:26-36). Jesus spoke of Tyre in Matthew 11:22 as a city worthy of God's judgment.

**27:3, 4** The beauty of Tyre was the source of its pride, and Tyre's pride guaranteed its judgment. Conceit or pride in our own accomplishments should be a danger signal to us (see James 4:13-17). God is not against our taking pleasure or finding satisfaction in what we do; he is against arrogance and inflated self-esteem that looks down on others. We must acknowledge God as the basis and source of our life.

**27:5**
Deut 3:9
Song 4:8

5 You were like a great ship
    built of the finest cypress from Senir.*
They took a cedar from Lebanon
    to make a mast for you.

**27:6**
Num 21:33
Jer 22:20
Zech 11:2

6 They carved your oars
    from the oaks of Bashan.
Your deck of pine from the coasts of Cyprus*
    was inlaid with ivory.

**27:7**
Exod 25:4
Prov 7:16
Jer 10:9

7 Your sails were made of Egypt's finest linen,
    and they flew as a banner above you.
You stood beneath blue and purple awnings
    made bright with dyes from the coasts of Elishah.

**27:8**
Gen 10:18
1 Kgs 9:27
1 Chr 1:16

8 Your oarsmen came from Sidon and Arvad;
    your helmsmen were skilled men from Tyre itself.

**27:9**
1 Kgs 5:18

9 Wise old craftsmen from Gebal did the caulking.
    Ships from every land came with goods to barter for your trade.

10 "Men from distant Persia, Lydia, and Libya* served in your great army. They hung their shields and helmets on your walls, giving you great honor. 11 Men from Arvad and Helech stood on your walls. Your towers were manned by men from Gammad. Their shields hung on your walls, completing your beauty.

12 "Tarshish sent merchants to buy your wares in exchange for silver, iron, tin, and lead.

**27:13**
Gen 10:2-3
Isa 66:19
Ezek 38:2
Joel 3:3
Rev 18:13

13 Merchants from Greece,* Tubal, and Meshech brought slaves and articles of bronze to trade with you.

14 "From Beth-togarmah came riding horses, chariot horses, and mules, all in exchange for your goods.

**27:15**
Rev 18:12

15 Merchants came to you from Dedan.* Numerous coastlands were your captive markets; they brought payment in ivory tusks and ebony wood.

**27:16**
Ezek 16:13, 18

16 "Syria* sent merchants to buy your rich variety of goods. They traded turquoise, purple dyes, embroidery, fine linen, and jewelry of coral and rubies. 17 Judah and Israel traded for

**27:17**
Judg 11:33

your wares, offering wheat from Minnith, figs,* honey, olive oil, and balm.

**27:18**
Gen 14:15
Ezek 47:16-18

18 "Damascus sent merchants to buy your rich variety of goods, bringing wine from Helbon and white wool from Zahar. 19 Greeks from Uzal* came to trade for your merchandise. Wrought iron, cassia, and fragrant calamus were bartered for your wares.

**27:21**
Isa 21:13; 60:7

20 "Dedan sent merchants to trade their expensive saddle blankets with you. 21 The Arabians and the princes of Kedar sent merchants to trade lambs and rams and male goats in

**27:22**
Gen 10:7; 43:11
1 Kgs 10:2
Isa 60:6
Ezek 38:13

exchange for your goods. 22 The merchants of Sheba and Raamah came with all kinds of spices, jewels, and gold in exchange for your wares.

**27:23**
2 Kgs 19:12
Isa 37:12
Amos 1:5; 6:2

23 "Haran, Canneh, Eden, Sheba, Asshur, and Kilmad came with their merchandise, too. 24 They brought choice fabrics to trade—blue cloth, embroidery, and multicolored carpets rolled up and bound with cords. 25 The ships of Tarshish were your ocean caravans. Your island warehouse was filled to the brim!

### The Destruction of Tyre

**27:26**
Ps 48:7

26 "But look! Your oarsmen
    have taken you into stormy seas!
A mighty eastern gale
    has wrecked you in the heart of the sea!
27 Everything is lost—
    your riches and wares,
your sailors and pilots,
    your ship builders, merchants, and warriors.
On the day of your ruin,
    everyone on board sinks into the depths of the sea.
28 Your cities by the sea tremble
    as your pilots cry out in terror.

**27:29**
Rev 18:17-19

29 All the oarsmen abandon their ships;
    the sailors and pilots on shore come to stand on the beach.

**27:5** Or *Hermon.*   **27:6** Hebrew *Kittim.*   **27:10** Hebrew *Paras, Lud, and Put.*   **27:13** Hebrew *Javan.*
**27:15** Greek version reads *Rhodes.*   **27:16** Hebrew *Aram;* some manuscripts read *Edom.*   **27:17** The
meaning of the Hebrew is uncertain.   **27:19** Hebrew *Vedan and Javan from Uzal.* The meaning of the
Hebrew is uncertain.

³⁰ They cry aloud over you
and weep bitterly.
They throw dust on their heads
and roll in ashes.
³¹ They shave their heads in grief for you
and dress themselves in burlap.
They weep for you with bitter anguish
and deep mourning.
³² As they wail and mourn over you,
they sing this sad funeral song:
'Was there ever such a city as Tyre,
now silent at the bottom of the sea?
³³ The merchandise you traded
satisfied the desires of many nations.
Kings at the ends of the earth
were enriched by your trade.
³⁴ Now you are a wrecked ship,
broken at the bottom of the sea.
All your merchandise and crew
have gone down with you.
³⁵ All who live along the coastlands
are appalled at your terrible fate.
Their kings are filled with horror
and look on with twisted faces.
³⁶ The merchants among the nations
shake their heads at the sight of you,*
for you have come to a horrible end
and will exist no more.'"

### A Message for Tyre's King

**28** Then this message came to me from the LORD: ²"Son of man, give the prince of Tyre this message from the Sovereign LORD:

"In your great pride you claim, 'I am a god!
I sit on a divine throne in the heart of the sea.'
But you are only a man and not a god,
though you boast that you are a god.
³ You regard yourself as wiser than Daniel
and think no secret is hidden from you.
⁴ With your wisdom and understanding you have amassed great wealth—
gold and silver for your treasuries.
⁵ Yes, your wisdom has made you very rich,
and your riches have made you very proud.

⁶ "Therefore, this is what the Sovereign LORD says:
Because you think you are as wise as a god,
⁷ I will now bring against you a foreign army,
the terror of the nations.
They will draw their swords against your marvelous wisdom
and defile your splendor!

**27:36** Hebrew *hiss at you.*

---

**27:30**
1 Sam 4:12
2 Sam 1:2
Jon 3:6
Rev 18:19

**27:31**
Isa 16:9; 22:12
Ezek 7:18; 29:18

**27:32**
Rev 18:18

**27:34**
Zech 9:3-4

**27:36**
Ps 37:10, 36
Jer 49:17
Zeph 2:15

**28:2**
Ps 82:6-7
2 Thes 2:4

**28:3**
Dan 1:20

**28:4**
Zech 9:2-4

**28:5**
Job 31:24-25
Ps 52:7
Hos 12:7-8; 13:6

**28:6**
Exod 9:17

**28:7**
Dan 7:7
Hab 1:6-8

---

**28:1ff** Previously Ezekiel had prophesied against the city of Tyre (chapters 26–27). Here he focused his prophecy on Tyre's leader. The chief sin of Tyre's king was pride—believing himself to be a god. But Ezekiel also may have made a broader spiritual application, speaking about the spiritual king of Tyre, Satan, whom the people were really following (see the note on 28:12-19).

**28:2, 3** Daniel, an important official in Nebuchadnezzar's kingdom (14:14), was already renowned for his wisdom. Daniel proclaimed that all his wisdom came from God (Daniel 2:20-23). By contrast, the king of Tyre thought that he himself *was* a god. As truly wise people get closer to God, they recognize their need to depend on him for guidance.

**28:6-10** The enemy army that attacked Tyre was the Babylonian army under Nebuchadnezzar. This attack occurred in 573/572 B.C.

**28:8**
Ezek 27:26-27, 34

⁸ They will bring you down to the pit,
  and you will die in the heart of the sea,
    pierced with many wounds.
⁹ Will you then boast, 'I am a god!'
  to those who kill you?
To them you will be no god
  but merely a man!

**28:10**
1 Sam 17:26, 36
Ezek 31:18

¹⁰ You will die like an outcast*
    at the hands of foreigners.
  I, the Sovereign LORD, have spoken!"

**28:12**
Ezek 27:2

¹¹ Then this further message came to me from the LORD: ¹²"Son of man, sing this funeral song for the king of Tyre. Give him this message from the Sovereign LORD:

  "You were the model of perfection,
    full of wisdom and exquisite in beauty.

**28:13**
Gen 2:8
Exod 28:17-20;
39:10-21
Isa 51:3; 54:11-12

¹³ You were in Eden,
    the garden of God.
Your clothing was adorned with every precious stone*—
    red carnelian, pale-green peridot, white moonstone,
    blue-green beryl, onyx, green jasper,
    blue lapis lazuli, turquoise, and emerald—
  all beautifully crafted for you
    and set in the finest gold.
They were given to you
    on the day you were created.

**28:14**
Exod 25:17-20
Ezek 20:40

¹⁴ I ordained and anointed you
    as the mighty angelic guardian.*
You had access to the holy mountain of God
    and walked among the stones of fire.

**28:15**
Isa 14:12

¹⁵ "You were blameless in all you did
    from the day you were created
    until the day evil was found in you.

**28:16**
Ezek 8:17
Hab 2:8, 17

¹⁶ Your rich commerce led you to violence,
    and you sinned.
So I banished you in disgrace
    from the mountain of God.
I expelled you, O mighty guardian,
    from your place among the stones of fire.

**28:17**
Isa 19:11

¹⁷ Your heart was filled with pride
    because of all your beauty.
Your wisdom was corrupted
    by your love of splendor.
So I threw you to the ground
    and exposed you to the curious gaze of kings.

**28:18**
Amos 1:9-10
Mal 4:3

¹⁸ You defiled your sanctuaries
    with your many sins and your dishonest trade.
So I brought fire out from within you,
    and it consumed you.
I reduced you to ashes on the ground
    in the sight of all who were watching.

---

**28:10** Hebrew *will die the death of the uncircumcised.* **28:13** The identification of some of these gemstones is uncertain. **28:14** Hebrew *guardian cherub;* similarly in 28:16.

---

**28:12-19** Some of the phrases in this passage describing the human king of Tyre may describe Satan. Great care must be taken to interpret these verses with discernment. It is clear that at times Ezekiel describes this king in terms that could not apply to a mere human. This king had been in the Garden of Eden (28:13), had been "ordained and anointed . . . as the mighty angelic guardian" (28:14), and had access to the holy mountain of God (28:14), but was banished from there (28:16, 17). Ezekiel, therefore, may have been condemning not only the king of Tyre but Satan, who had motivated the king to sin.

<sup>19</sup> All who knew you are appalled at your fate.
    You have come to a terrible end,
    and you will exist no more."

### A Message for Sidon

<sup>20</sup>Then another message came to me from the LORD: <sup>21</sup>"Son of man, turn and face the city of Sidon and prophesy against it. <sup>22</sup>Give the people of Sidon this message from the Sovereign LORD:

28:21
Gen 10:15-19
Isa 23:2-4, 12

"I am your enemy, O Sidon,
    and I will reveal my glory by what I do to you.
When I bring judgment against you
    and reveal my holiness among you,
everyone watching will know
    that I am the LORD.
<sup>23</sup> I will send a plague against you,
    and blood will be spilled in your streets.
The attack will come from every direction,
    and your people will lie slaughtered within your walls.
Then everyone will know
    that I am the LORD.
<sup>24</sup> No longer will Israel's scornful neighbors
    prick and tear at her like briers and thorns.
For then they will know
    that I am the Sovereign LORD.

28:23
Jer 51:52
Ezek 38:22

28:24
Num 33:55
Josh 23:13
Isa 55:13

### Restoration for Israel

<sup>25</sup>"This is what the Sovereign LORD says: The people of Israel will again live in their own land, the land I gave my servant Jacob. For I will gather them from the distant lands where I have scattered them. I will reveal to the nations of the world my holiness among my people. <sup>26</sup>They will live safely in Israel and build homes and plant vineyards. And when I punish the neighboring nations that treated them with contempt, they will know that I am the LORD their God."

28:25
Ps 106:47
Isa 11:12-13
Jer 23:8

28:26
Jer 32:15, 43-44
Amos 9:13-14

### A Message for Egypt

**29** On January 7,* during the tenth year of King Jehoiachin's captivity, this message came to me from the LORD: <sup>2</sup>"Son of man, turn and face Egypt and prophesy against Pharaoh the king and all the people of Egypt. <sup>3</sup>Give them this message from the Sovereign LORD:

29:2
Isa 19:1-17
Jer 46:2-25

"I am your enemy, O Pharaoh, king of Egypt—
    you great monster, lurking in the streams of the Nile.
For you have said, 'The Nile River is mine;
    I made it for myself.'
<sup>4</sup> I will put hooks in your jaws
    and drag you out on the land
    with fish sticking to your scales.

29:3
Isa 27:1

29:4
2 Kgs 19:28
Isa 37:29
Ezek 38:4

**29:1** Hebrew *On the twelfth day of the tenth month,* of the ancient Hebrew lunar calendar. This event occurred on January 7, 587 B.C.; also see note on 1:1.

---

**28:20, 21** Sidon was another famous seaport, located about 25 miles north of Tyre. God charged this city with contempt for his people. Sidon's economy was bound to Tyre's, so when Tyre fell to Nebuchadnezzar, Sidon was doomed to follow.

**28:24-26** This promise that God's people will live in complete safety has yet to be fulfilled. While many were allowed to return from exile under Zerubbabel, Ezra, and Nehemiah, and although the political nation is restored today, the inhabitants do not yet live in complete safety (28:26). Therefore, this promise will have its ultimate fulfillment when Christ sets up his eternal Kingdom. Then all people who have been faithful to God will dwell together in harmony and complete safety.

**29:1ff** Chapters 29–32 contain seven prophecies, all dealing with judgment on Egypt. This is probably the first prophecy that was given by Ezekiel in 587 B.C. Hezekiah, Jehoiakim, and Zedekiah

(kings of Judah) had all sought help from Egypt despite God's warnings.

This prophecy was given for three key reasons: (1) Egypt was an ancient enemy of the Jews, having once enslaved them for more than 400 years; (2) Egypt worshiped many gods; (3) Egypt's wealth and power made it seem like a good ally. Egypt offered to help Judah only because of the benefits it hoped to receive from such an alliance. When the Egyptians didn't get what they hoped for, they bailed out of their agreement without regard to any promises they had made.

**29:2ff** Egypt had great artistic treasures, a flourishing civilization, and world-renowned military power. Unfortunately, it was also evil, egotistical, idolatrous, and it treated slaves cruelly. For those sins God condemned Egypt. At the battle of Carchemish in 605 B.C., Babylon crushed Egypt along with Assyria, its rivals for the position of world ruler.

**29:5**
Jer 7:33; 34:20

<sup>5</sup> I will leave you and all your fish
  stranded in the wilderness to die.
You will lie unburied on the open ground,
  for I have given you as food to the wild animals and birds.

**29:6**
Isa 36:6

<sup>6</sup> All the people of Egypt will know that I am the LORD,
  for to Israel you were just a staff made of reeds.

**29:7**
Jer 37:5-11
Ezek 17:15-17

<sup>7</sup> When Israel leaned on you,
  you splintered and broke
  and stabbed her in the armpit.
When she put her weight on you, you gave way,
  and her back was thrown out of joint.

**29:9**
Prov 18:12; 29:23

<sup>8</sup> "Therefore, this is what the Sovereign LORD says: I will bring an army against you, O Egypt, and destroy both people and animals. <sup>9</sup> The land of Egypt will become a desolate wasteland, and the Egyptians will know that I am the LORD.

"Because you said, 'The Nile River is mine; I made it,' <sup>10</sup> I am now the enemy of both you and your river. I will make the land of Egypt a totally desolate wasteland, from Migdol to Aswan, as far south as the border of Ethiopia.* <sup>11</sup> For forty years not a soul will pass that way, neither people nor animals. It will be completely uninhabited. <sup>12</sup> I will make Egypt desolate, and it will be surrounded by other desolate nations. Its cities will be empty and desolate for forty years, surrounded by other ruined cities. I will scatter the Egyptians to distant lands.

**29:11**
Jer 43:11-12

**29:12**
Jer 25:15-19;
27:6-11

**29:13**
Isa 19:22
Jer 46:26

<sup>13</sup> "But this is what the Sovereign LORD also says: At the end of the forty years I will bring the Egyptians home again from the nations to which they have been scattered. <sup>14</sup> I will restore the prosperity of Egypt and bring its people back to the land of Pathros in southern Egypt from which they came. But Egypt will remain an unimportant, minor kingdom. <sup>15</sup> It will be the lowliest of all the nations, never again great enough to rise above its neighbors.

**29:14**
Isa 11:11
Jer 44:1

**29:15**
Dan 11:42-43

**29:16**
Isa 30:1-3; 64:9
Hos 5:13; 8:13; 9:9

<sup>16</sup> "Then Israel will no longer be tempted to trust in Egypt for help. Egypt's shattered condition will remind Israel of how sinful she was to trust Egypt in earlier days. Then Israel will know that I am the Sovereign LORD."

### Nebuchadnezzar to Conquer Egypt

**29:17**
Ezek 24:1; 30:20

**29:18**
Jer 25:9; 27:6
Ezek 26:7-12

<sup>17</sup> On April 26, the first day of the new year,* during the twenty-seventh year of King Jehoiachin's captivity, this message came to me from the LORD: <sup>18</sup> "Son of man, the army of King Nebuchadnezzar* of Babylon fought so hard against Tyre that the warriors' heads were rubbed bare and their shoulders were raw and blistered. Yet Nebuchadnezzar and his army won no plunder to compensate them for all their work. <sup>19</sup> Therefore, this is what the Sovereign LORD says: I will give the land of Egypt to Nebuchadnezzar, king of Babylon. He will carry off its wealth, plundering everything it has so he can pay his army. <sup>20</sup> Yes, I have given him the land of Egypt as a reward for his work, says the Sovereign LORD, because he was working for me when he destroyed Tyre.

**29:19**
Jer 43:10-13
Ezek 30:10-12

**29:20**
Isa 10:6-7; 45:1-3

**29:21**
1 Sam 2:10
Pss 92:10; 132:17
Amos 3:7-8
Luke 21:15

<sup>21</sup> "And the day will come when I will cause the ancient glory of Israel to revive,* and then, Ezekiel, your words will be respected. Then they will know that I am the LORD."

**29:10** Hebrew *from Migdol to Syene as far as the border of Cush.*   **29:17** Hebrew *On the first day of the first month,* of the ancient Hebrew lunar calendar. This event occurred on April 26, 571 B.C.; also see note on 1:1.   **29:18** Hebrew *Nebuchadrezzar,* a variant spelling of Nebuchadnezzar; also in 29:19.   **29:21** Hebrew *I will cause a horn to sprout for the house of Israel.*

---

**29:9, 10** The Nile was Egypt's pride and joy, a life-giving river cutting through the middle of the desert. Rather than thanking God, however, Egypt declared, "The Nile River is mine; I made it." We do the same when we say, "This house is mine; I built it," or "I have brought myself to the place where I am today," or "I have built this church, business, or reputation from the ground up." These statements reveal our pride. Sometimes we take for granted what God has given us, thinking we have made it ourselves. Of course, we have put forth a lot of hard effort, but God supplied the resources, gave us the abilities, and provided us with the opportunities to make it happen. Instead of proclaiming our own greatness, as the Egyptians did, we should proclaim God's greatness and give him the credit. (Migdol is in the north of Egypt, and Aswan in the south. Thus, this meant all of Egypt.)

**29:13-16** This 40-year period of desolation in Egypt is hard to pinpoint. Nebuchadnezzar attacked Egypt around 572 B.C. and carried many people off to Babylon, while others fled for safety to surrounding nations. Approximately 33 years later, Cyrus, king of the Persian Empire, conquered Babylon and allowed the nations that Babylon had conquered to return to their homelands. Adding a possible seven-year regrouping and travel period, this could then make up that 40-year time period. Since that time, Egypt has never returned to its previous dominance as a world power.

**29:17, 18** This prophecy was given in 571 B.C. and is actually the latest prophecy in Ezekiel. Nebuchadnezzar had finally conquered Tyre after a long and costly 15-year siege (586–571 B.C.). He had not counted on such an expense, so he went south and conquered Egypt to make up for all he had lost in taking Tyre. Ezekiel placed this prophecy here to describe *who* would bring this punishment to Egypt. God was using Nebuchadnezzar, an evil man, as an instrument of his judgment on Tyre, Judah, and Egypt—evil nations themselves. When Babylon didn't recognize God's favor, he judged it, too.

*A Sad Day for Egypt*

**30** This is another message that came to me from the LORD: [2]"Son of man, prophesy and give this message from the Sovereign LORD:

**30:2**
Isa 13:6; 65:14
Joel 1:5, 11, 13, 15

"Weep and wail
for that day,
[3] for the terrible day is almost here—
the day of the LORD!
It is a day of clouds and gloom,
a day of despair for the nations.
[4] A sword will come against Egypt,
and those who are slaughtered will cover the ground.
Its wealth will be carried away
and its foundations destroyed.
The land of Ethiopia* will be ravished.
[5] Ethiopia, Libya, Lydia, all Arabia,*
and all their other allies
will be destroyed in that war.

**30:5**
Jer 25:20, 24

[6] "For this is what the LORD says:
All of Egypt's allies will fall,
and the pride of her power will end.
From Migdol to Aswan*
they will be slaughtered by the sword,
says the Sovereign LORD.
[7] Egypt will be desolate,
surrounded by desolate nations,
and its cities will be in ruins,
surrounded by other ruined cities.

**30:6**
Isa 20:3-6

[8] And the people of Egypt will know that I am the LORD
when I have set Egypt on fire
and destroyed all their allies.
[9] At that time I will send swift messengers in ships
to terrify the complacent Ethiopians.
Great panic will come upon them
on that day of Egypt's certain destruction.
Watch for it!
It is sure to come!

**30:8**
Ps 58:11
Amos 1:4, 7, 10-14

**30:9**
Isa 18:1-2
Ezek 32:9-10;
38:11

[10] "For this is what the Sovereign LORD says:
By the power of King Nebuchadnezzar* of Babylon,
I will destroy the hordes of Egypt.
[11] He and his armies—the most ruthless of all—
will be sent to demolish the land.
They will make war against Egypt
until slaughtered Egyptians cover the ground.
[12] I will dry up the Nile River
and sell the land to wicked men.
I will destroy the land of Egypt and everything in it
by the hands of foreigners.
I, the LORD, have spoken!

**30:12**
Ezek 29:3, 9

[13] "This is what the Sovereign LORD says:
I will smash the idols* of Egypt
and the images at Memphis.*

**30:13**
Isa 2:18
Jer 44:1; 46:14

---

**30:4** Hebrew *Cush*; similarly in 30:9. **30:5** Hebrew *Cush, Put, Lud, all Arabia, Cub. Cub* is otherwise unknown and may be another spelling for *Lub* (Libya). **30:6** Hebrew *to Syene.* **30:10** Hebrew *Nebuchadrezzar*, a variant spelling of Nebuchadnezzar. **30:13a** The Hebrew term (literally *round things*) probably alludes to dung. **30:13b** Hebrew *Noph*; also in 30:16.

---

**30:1-19** This is a lament for Egypt and its allies. Because of the Egyptians' pride and idolatry, they would be brought down.

**30:12** Egypt's pharaohs claimed that they had made the Nile—

the river on which the entire nation depended. If God dried up the Nile, the nation would be doomed.

**30:13-19** The list of cities to be destroyed shows the breadth

There will be no rulers left in Egypt;
    terror will sweep the land.

**30:14**
Ps 78:12, 43
Isa 19:11, 13

14 I will destroy southern Egypt,*
    set fire to Zoan,
    and bring judgment against Thebes.*

15 I will pour out my fury on Pelusium,*
    the strongest fortress of Egypt,
and I will stamp out
    the hordes of Thebes.

16 Yes, I will set fire to all Egypt!
    Pelusium will be racked with pain;
Thebes will be torn apart;
    Memphis will live in constant terror.

**30:17**
Gen 41:45

17 The young men of Heliopolis and Bubastis* will die in battle,
    and the women* will be taken away as slaves.

**30:18**
Lev 26:13
Jer 43:8-13

18 When I come to break the proud strength of Egypt,
    it will be a dark day for Tahpanhes, too.
A dark cloud will cover Tahpanhes,
    and its daughters will be led away as captives.

**30:19**
Ps 9:16
Ezek 5:8, 15

19 And so I will greatly punish Egypt,
    and they will know that I am the LORD."

### The Broken Arms of Pharaoh

**30:20**
Ezek 26:1

**30:21**
Pss 10:15; 37:17
Jer 30:13; 46:11

**30:22**
2 Kgs 24:7
Jer 37:7; 46:1-12,
21-25

**30:24**
Isa 45:1, 5
Zeph 2:12
Zech 10:12

**30:25**
Josh 8:18
1 Chr 21:16
Isa 5:25

20 On April 29,* during the eleventh year of King Jehoiachin's captivity, this message came to me from the LORD: 21"Son of man, I have broken the arm of Pharaoh, the king of Egypt. His arm has not been put in a cast so that it may heal. Neither has it been bound up with a splint to make it strong enough to hold a sword. 22 Therefore, this is what the Sovereign LORD says: I am the enemy of Pharaoh, the king of Egypt! I will break both of his arms—the good arm along with the broken one—and I will make his sword clatter to the ground. 23I will scatter the Egyptians to many lands throughout the world. 24I will strengthen the arms of Babylon's king and put my sword in his hand. But I will break the arms of Pharaoh, king of Egypt, and he will lie there mortally wounded, groaning in pain. 25 I will strengthen the arms of the king of Babylon, while the arms of Pharaoh fall useless to his sides. And when I put my sword in the hand of Babylon's king and he brings it against the land of Egypt, Egypt will know that I am the LORD. 26I will scatter the Egyptians among the nations, dispersing them throughout the earth. Then they will know that I am the LORD."

### Egypt Compared to Fallen Assyria

**31:2**
Nah 3:8-9

**31** On June 21,* during the eleventh year of King Jehoiachin's captivity, this message came to me from the LORD: 2"Son of man, give this message to Pharaoh, king of Egypt, and all his hordes:

**30:14a** Hebrew *Pathros.*    **30:14b** Hebrew *No;* also in 30:15, 16.    **30:15** Hebrew *Sin;* also in 30:16.    **30:17a** Hebrew of *Awen* and *Pi-beseth.*    **30:17b** Or *and her cities.*    **30:20** Hebrew *On the seventh day of the first month,* of the ancient Hebrew lunar calendar. This event occurred on April 29, 587 B.C.; also see note on 1:1.    **31:1** Hebrew *On the first day of the third month,* of the ancient Hebrew lunar calendar. This event occurred on June 21, 587 B.C.; also see note on 1:1.

---

of the destruction; the drying up of the Nile (30:12) shows how deep the devastation would reach. Egypt would be completely incapacitated. This was a clear message to Judah not to trust Egypt for help against the Babylonians.

**30:20, 21** This message came in 587 B.C. while Jerusalem was under attack from Babylon. Judah had rebelled against Babylon and made an alliance with Egypt in spite of God's warnings (Jeremiah 2:36, 37). Pharaoh Hophra made a halfhearted attempt to help Jerusalem, but when Nebuchadnezzar's army turned on him, he fled back to Egypt (Jeremiah 37:5-7). This defeat is what Ezekiel meant when he said that God had "broken the arm of Pharaoh."

**30:21-26** This prophecy was given to Ezekiel in 587 B.C. God destroyed Egypt's military superiority and gave it to Babylon. God allows nations to rise to power to accomplish a particular purpose, often beyond our immediate understanding. When

you read about armies and wars, don't despair. Remember that God is sovereign and in charge of everything, even military might. Besides praying for your military and government leaders, pray that God's greater purposes would be carried out and that his will would be done "on earth, as it is in heaven" (see Matthew 6:10).

**31:1ff** This message was given in 587 B.C. Ezekiel compared Egypt to Assyria, calling Assyria a great cedar tree. The Egyptians were to look at the fall of the mighty nation of Assyria (whose demise they had seen) as an example of what would happen to them. Just like Assyria, Egypt took pride in its strength and beauty; this would be its downfall. She would crash like a mighty tree and be sent to the grave. There is no permanence apart from God, even for a great society with magnificent culture and military power.

"To whom would you compare your greatness?
3 You are like mighty Assyria,
    which was once like a cedar of Lebanon,
with beautiful branches that cast deep forest shade
    and with its top high among the clouds.
4 Deep springs watered it
    and helped it to grow tall and luxuriant.
The water flowed around it like a river,
    streaming to all the trees nearby.

**31:4**
Ezek 17:5, 8
Rev 17:1, 15

5 This great tree towered high,
    higher than all the other trees around it.
It prospered and grew long thick branches
    because of all the water at its roots.

**31:5**
Ps 1:3

6 The birds nested in its branches,
    and in its shade all the wild animals gave birth.
All the great nations of the world
    lived in its shadow.

**31:6**
Ezek 17:23
Dan 4:12, 21
Matt 13:32

7 It was strong and beautiful,
    with wide-spreading branches,
for its roots went deep
    into abundant water.
8 No other cedar in the garden of God
    could rival it.
No cypress had branches to equal it;
    no plane tree had boughs to compare.
No tree in the garden of God
    came close to it in beauty.

**31:8**
Gen 2:8-9; 13:10
Ps 80:10
Isa 51:3

9 Because I made this tree so beautiful,
    and gave it such magnificent foliage,
it was the envy of all the other trees of Eden,
    the garden of God.

10 "Therefore, this is what the Sovereign LORD says: Because Egypt* became proud and arrogant, and because it set itself so high above the others, with its top reaching to the clouds, 11 I will hand it over to a mighty nation that will destroy it as its wickedness deserves. I have already discarded it. 12 A foreign army—the terror of the nations—has cut it down and left it fallen on the ground. Its branches are scattered across the mountains and valleys and ravines of the land. All those who lived in its shadow have gone away and left it lying there.

**31:10**
2 Chr 32:25
Isa 14:13-14
Dan 5:20

**31:11**
Deut 18:12
Dan 5:18-19
Nah 3:18

13 "The birds roost on its fallen trunk,
    and the wild animals lie among its branches.

**31:13**
Isa 18:6
Rev 19:17-18

14 Let the tree of no other nation
    proudly exult in its own prosperity,
though it be higher than the clouds
    and it be watered from the depths.
For all are doomed to die,
    to go down to the depths of the earth.
They will land in the pit
    along with everyone else on earth.

**31:14**
Num 16:30-33
Ps 63:9
Jon 2:2, 6
Eph 4:9

15 "This is what the Sovereign LORD says: When Assyria went down to the grave,* I made the deep springs mourn. I stopped its rivers and dried up its abundant water. I clothed Lebanon in black and caused the trees of the field to wilt. 16 I made the nations shake with fear at the sound of its fall, for I sent it down to the grave with all the others who descend to the pit. And all the other proud trees of Eden, the most beautiful and the best of Lebanon, the ones whose roots went deep into the water, took comfort to find it there with them in

**31:15**
Nah 2:8-10

**31:16**
Isa 14:8
Hag 2:7

31:10 Hebrew *you.*    31:15 Hebrew *to Sheol;* also in 31:16, 17.

---

31:9 "All the other trees of Eden" may refer to all the other nations of the world, which were jealous of Assyria's power and grandeur.    31:11 The "mighty nation" may refer to Babylon (see Daniel 2:37, 38).

**31:17**
Ps 9:17
Dan 4:11-12

**31:18**
Ps 52:7
Jer 9:25-26
Matt 13:19

the depths of the earth. [17]Its allies, too, were all destroyed and had passed away. They had gone down to the grave—all those nations that had lived in its shade.

[18]"O Egypt, to which of the trees of Eden will you compare your strength and glory? You, too, will be brought down to the depths with all these other nations. You will lie there among the outcasts* who have died by the sword. This will be the fate of Pharaoh and all his hordes. I, the Sovereign LORD, have spoken!"

## A Warning for Pharaoh

**32:2**
Jer 46:7-8
Nah 2:11-13

**32** On March 3,* during the twelfth year of King Jehoiachin's captivity, this message came to me from the LORD: [2]"Son of man, mourn for Pharaoh, king of Egypt, and give him this message:

"You think of yourself as a strong young lion among the nations,
    but you are really just a sea monster,
heaving around in your own rivers,
    stirring up mud with your feet.

**32:3**
Ezek 12:13

[3] Therefore, this is what the Sovereign LORD says:
I will send many people
    to catch you in my net
    and haul you out of the water.

**32:4**
Jer 8:2

[4] I will leave you stranded on the land to die.
    All the birds of the heavens will land on you,
and the wild animals of the whole earth
    will gorge themselves on you.
[5] I will scatter your flesh on the hills
    and fill the valleys with your bones.

**32:6**
Exod 7:17
Isa 34:3, 7
Rev 14:20

[6] I will drench the earth with your gushing blood
    all the way to the mountains,
    filling the ravines to the brim.

**32:7**
Prov 13:9
Amos 8:9

[7] When I blot you out,
    I will veil the heavens and darken the stars.
I will cover the sun with a cloud,
    and the moon will not give you its light.

**32:8**
Gen 1:14

[8] I will darken the bright stars overhead
    and cover your land in darkness.
    I, the Sovereign LORD, have spoken!

**32:9**
Exod 15:14-16
Rev 18:10-15

**32:10**
Ezek 26:16; 27:35

**32:11**
Jer 46:26

[9]"I will disturb many hearts when I bring news of your downfall to distant nations you have never seen. [10]Yes, I will shock many lands, and their kings will be terrified at your fate. They will shudder in fear for their lives as I brandish my sword before them on the day of your fall. [11]For this is what the Sovereign LORD says:

"The sword of the king of Babylon
    will come against you.

**32:12**
Ezek 28:7

[12] I will destroy your hordes with the swords of mighty warriors—
    the terror of the nations.
They will shatter the pride of Egypt,
    and all its hordes will be destroyed.
[13] I will destroy all your flocks and herds
    that graze beside the streams.
Never again will people or animals
    muddy those waters with their feet.

**31:18** Hebrew *among the uncircumcised.*   **32:1** Hebrew *On the first day of the twelfth month,* of the ancient Hebrew lunar calendar. This event occurred on March 3, 585 B.C.; also see note on 1:1.

**32:1ff** This prophecy was given in 585 B.C., two months after the news of Jerusalem's fall had reached the exiles in Babylon. Ezekiel prophesied numerous judgments upon many wicked nations. These judgments served a positive purpose: They showed that evil forces are continually being overcome and that one day God will overthrow all evil, making the world the perfect place he intended. They also serve as warnings that God alone

is sovereign. Even the mightiest rulers, like Pharaoh, will fall before God. All are accountable to him.

**32:2** Although Pharaoh thought of himself as a strong young lion, in God's eyes he was nothing but a crocodile ("sea monster") muddying the water. God's judgment would reduce Pharaoh to his true size. Anyone who defies God will face his judgment.

¹⁴ Then I will let the waters of Egypt become calm again,
    and they will flow as smoothly as olive oil,
    says the Sovereign Lord.
¹⁵ And when I destroy Egypt
    and strip you of everything you own
  and strike down all your people,
    then you will know that I am the Lord.

32:15
Exod 7:5; 14:4, 18
Ps 83:17-18

¹⁶ Yes, this is the funeral song
    they will sing for Egypt.
  Let all the nations mourn.
    Let them mourn for Egypt and its hordes.
    I, the Sovereign Lord, have spoken!"

32:16
2 Sam 3:33-34
2 Chr 35:25
Jer 9:17

### Egypt Falls into the Pit

¹⁷On March 17,* during the twelfth year, another message came to me from the Lord: ¹⁸"Son of man, weep for the hordes of Egypt and for the other mighty nations.* For I will send them down to the world below in company with those who descend to the pit. ¹⁹Say to them,

32:18
Jer 1:10
Hos 6:5

32:19
Jer 9:25-26

  'O Egypt, are you lovelier than the other nations?
  No! So go down to the pit and lie there among the outcasts.*'

²⁰The Egyptians will fall with the many who have died by the sword, for the sword is drawn against them. Egypt and its hordes will be dragged away to their judgment. ²¹Down in the grave* mighty leaders will mockingly welcome Egypt and its allies, saying, 'They have come down; they lie among the outcasts, hordes slaughtered by the sword.'

32:20
Ps 28:3

32:21
Isa 14:9-12
Luke 16:23-24

²²"Assyria lies there surrounded by the graves of its army, those who were slaughtered by the sword. ²³Their graves are in the depths of the pit, and they are surrounded by their allies. They struck terror in the hearts of people everywhere, but now they have been slaughtered by the sword.

32:23
Isa 14:15

²⁴"Elam lies there surrounded by the graves of all its hordes, those who were slaughtered by the sword. They struck terror in the hearts of people everywhere, but now they have descended as outcasts to the world below. Now they lie in the pit and share the shame of those who have gone before them. ²⁵They have a resting place among the slaughtered, surrounded by the graves of all their hordes. Yes, they terrorized the nations while they lived, but now they lie in shame with others in the pit, all of them outcasts, slaughtered by the sword.

32:24
Gen 10:22
Job 28:13
Ps 52:5
Jer 49:32-39

32:25
Ps 139:8

²⁶"Meshech and Tubal are there, surrounded by the graves of all their hordes. They once struck terror in the hearts of people everywhere. But now they are outcasts, all slaughtered by the sword. ²⁷They are not buried in honor like their fallen heroes, who went down to the grave* with their weapons—their shields covering their bodies* and their swords beneath their heads. Their guilt rests upon them because they brought terror to everyone while they were still alive.

32:26
Gen 10:2
Isa 66:19

32:27
Prov 14:32

²⁸"You too, Egypt, will lie crushed and broken among the outcasts, all slaughtered by the sword.

²⁹"Edom is there with its kings and princes. Mighty as they were, they also lie among those slaughtered by the sword, with the outcasts who have gone down to the pit.

32:29
Isa 34:5-15
Jer 49:7-22
Ezek 25:13

**32:17** Hebrew *On the fifteenth day of the month,* presumably in the twelfth month of the ancient Hebrew lunar calendar (see 32:1). This would put this message at the end of King Jehoiachin's twelfth year of captivity, on March 17, 585 B.C.; also see note on 1:1. Greek version reads *On the fifteenth day of the first month,* which would put this message on April 27, 586 B.C., at the beginning of Jehoiachin's twelfth year.    **32:18** The meaning of the Hebrew is uncertain.    **32:19** Hebrew *the uncircumcised;* also in 32:21, 24, 25, 26, 28, 29, 30, 32.    **32:21** Hebrew *in Sheol.*
**32:27a** Hebrew *to Sheol.*    **32:27b** The meaning of the Hebrew is uncertain.

---

**32:18** The Hebrews believed in an afterlife for all people, good and bad. Ezekiel predicted that Egypt would share the same fate as that of the evil nations already sent to the "pit." The words here are more poetic than doctrinal (see Job 24:19; Psalm 16:10; Isaiah 38:10, and the note on Matthew 25:46). The Egyptians had a preoccupation with the afterlife and built pyramids to ensure the pharaohs' comfort in the next life. God alone controls our future and life after death.

**32:21-32** In these verses, Ezekiel conducts a guided tour of the "grave"—the region of the afterlife. In the grave, all of God's enemies are condemned in judgment; many of them experience the fate they so quickly imposed on others. Though Babylon is not mentioned, Ezekiel's readers would have concluded that if all the other nations would be judged for their rebellion against God, Babylon would be judged as well. These words would comfort the captives.

**32:24-26** Elam was a nation of fierce warriors from the region east of Assyria. They were conquered by Nebuchadnezzar (Jeremiah 49:34-39) and eventually rebuilt themselves and became part of Persia. Meshech and Tubal were territories located in the eastern region of Asia Minor, now eastern and central Turkey. In chapters 38 and 39 they are described as allies of Gog, the chief prince of a confederacy. They are included with the evil nations that will be judged for fighting against God's people.

**32:30**
Jer 1:15; 25:26
Ezek 28:21-23;
38:15

**32:31**
Ezek 31:16

**33:2**
2 Sam 18:24-25
2 Kgs 9:17

**33:3**
Neh 4:18-20
Hos 8:1
Joel 2:1

**33:4**
Jer 6:17
Zech 1:4

**33:5**
Exod 9:19-21, 25
Heb 11:7

**33:6**
Isa 56:10

**33:7**
Isa 62:6-7
Jer 26:2

**33:10**
Lev 26:39
Isa 49:14

**33:11**
Hos 11:8
Acts 3:19
1 Tim 2:4
2 Pet 3:9

**33:12**
2 Chr 7:14

**33:13**
Heb 10:38
2 Pet 2:20-21

30 "All the princes of the north and the Sidonians are there with others who have died. Once a terror, they have been put to shame. They lie there as outcasts with others who were slaughtered by the sword. They share the shame of all who have descended to the pit.

31 "When Pharaoh and his entire army arrive, he will take comfort that he is not alone in having his hordes killed, says the Sovereign LORD. 32 Although I have caused his terror to fall upon all the living, Pharaoh and his hordes will lie there among the outcasts who were slaughtered by the sword. I, the Sovereign LORD, have spoken!"

## C. MESSAGES OF HOPE (33:1—48:35)

This section begins a new direction in Ezekiel's prophecies. Ezekiel is reminded that he is the nation's watchman. Before Jerusalem's fall, he told the people of their punishment and dispersion. Now he is to proclaim the hope of restoration, but even this message does not improve the people's response. They listen to him with curiosity and then live as they please. Today we have the good news of forgiveness, but how easy it is to ignore the message and continue to live sinful lives.

### 1. Restoring the people of God

#### Ezekiel as Israel's Watchman

**33** Once again a message came to me from the LORD: 2 "Son of man, give your people this message: 'When I bring an army against a country, the people of that land choose one of their own to be a watchman. 3 When the watchman sees the enemy coming, he sounds the alarm to warn the people. 4 Then if those who hear the alarm refuse to take action, it is their own fault if they die. 5 They heard the alarm but ignored it, so the responsibility is theirs. If they had listened to the warning, they could have saved their lives. 6 But if the watchman sees the enemy coming and doesn't sound the alarm to warn the people, he is responsible for their captivity. They will die in their sins, but I will hold the watchman responsible for their deaths.'

7 "Now, son of man, I am making you a watchman for the people of Israel. Therefore, listen to what I say and warn them for me. 8 If I announce that some wicked people are sure to die and you fail to tell them to change their ways, then they will die in their sins, and I will hold you responsible for their deaths. 9 But if you warn them to repent and they don't repent, they will die in their sins, but you will have saved yourself.

#### The Watchman's Message

10 "Son of man, give the people of Israel this message: You are saying, 'Our sins are heavy upon us; we are wasting away! How can we survive?' 11 As surely as I live, says the Sovereign LORD, I take no pleasure in the death of wicked people. I only want them to turn from their wicked ways so they can live. Turn! Turn from your wickedness, O people of Israel! Why should you die?

12 "Son of man, give your people this message: The righteous behavior of righteous people will not save them if they turn to sin, nor will the wicked behavior of wicked people destroy them if they repent and turn from their sins. 13 When I tell righteous people that they

---

**32:30** The princes of the north were probably the princes of the Phoenician city-states.

**32:32** After reading Ezekiel's prophecies against all these foreign nations, we may wonder if he was blindly loyal to his own nation. But Ezekiel spoke only when God gave him a message (3:27). Besides, God's prophets pronounced judgment on God's sinful people just as much as on God's enemies. But if Babylon was God's enemy, why isn't it mentioned in Ezekiel's judgments? Perhaps because (1) God wanted to foster a spirit of cooperation between the exiles and Babylon in order to preserve his people; (2) God was still using Babylon to refine his own people; (3) God wanted to use Daniel, a powerful official in Babylon, to draw the Babylonians to him.

**33:1ff** This chapter sets forth a new direction for Ezekiel's prophecies. Up to this point, Ezekiel has pronounced judgment upon Judah (chapters 1–24) and the surrounding evil nations (chapters 25–32) for their sins. After Jerusalem fell, he turned from messages of doom and judgment to messages of comfort, hope, and future restoration for God's people (chapters 33–48). God previously appointed Ezekiel to be a watchman, warning the nation of coming judgment (see 3:17-21). Here God appointed him to be a

watchman again, but this time he was to preach a message of hope. More warnings will come (33:23–34:10; 36:1-7), but these are part of the larger picture of hope. God will remember to bless those who are faithful to him. We must pay attention to both aspects of Ezekiel's message: warning and promise. Those who persist in rebelling against God should take warning. Those faithful to God should find encouragement and hope.

**33:10-12** The exiles were discouraged by their past sins. This is an important turning point in this book—elsewhere in Ezekiel the people had refused to face their sins. Here, they felt heavy guilt for rebelling against God for so many years. Therefore, God assured them of forgiveness if they repented. God wants *everyone* to turn to him. He looks at what we are and will become, not what we have been. God gives you the opportunity to turn to him if you will. Sincerely follow God, and ask him to forgive you when you fail.

**33:13** Past good deeds will not save a person who decides to turn to a life of sin. Some people think that if they do enough good deeds, they can hold on to the sins they don't want to give up. But it's useless to try to be good in some areas so you can be deliberately bad in others. God wants wholehearted love and obedience.

will live, but then they sin, expecting their past righteousness to save them, then none of their righteous acts will be remembered. I will destroy them for their sins. <sup>14</sup>And suppose I tell some wicked people that they will surely die, but then they turn from their sins and do what is just and right. <sup>15</sup>For instance, they might give back a debtor's security, return what they have stolen, and obey my life-giving laws, no longer doing what is evil. If they do this, then they will surely live and not die. <sup>16</sup>None of their past sins will be brought up again, for they have done what is just and right, and they will surely live.

<sup>17</sup>"Your people are saying, 'The Lord isn't doing what's right,' but it is they who are not do-ing what's right. <sup>18</sup>For again I say, when righteous people turn away from their righteous be-havior and turn to evil, they will die. <sup>19</sup>But if wicked people turn from their wickedness and do what is just and right, they will live. <sup>20</sup>O people of Israel, you are saying, 'The Lord isn't do-ing what's right.' But I judge each of you according to your deeds."

## Explanation of Jerusalem's Fall

<sup>21</sup>On January 8,* during the twelfth year of our captivity, a survivor from Jerusalem came to me and said, "The city has fallen!" <sup>22</sup>The previous evening the Lord had taken hold of me and given me back my voice. So I was able to speak when this man arrived the next morning.

<sup>23</sup>Then this message came to me from the Lord: <sup>24</sup>"Son of man, the scattered remnants of Judah living among the ruined cities keep saying, 'Abraham was only one man, yet he gained possession of the entire land. We are many; surely the land has been given to us as a possession.' <sup>25</sup>So tell these people, 'This is what the Sovereign Lord says: You eat meat with blood in it, you worship idols,* and you murder the innocent. Do you really think the land should be yours? <sup>26</sup>Murderers! Idolaters! Adulterers! Should the land belong to you?'

<sup>27</sup>"Say to them, 'This is what the Sovereign Lord says: As surely as I live, those living in the ruins will die by the sword. And I will send wild animals to eat those living in the open fields. Those hiding in the forts and caves will die of disease. <sup>28</sup>I will completely destroy the land and demolish her pride. Her arrogant power will come to an end. The mountains of Israel will be so desolate that no one will even travel through them. <sup>29</sup>When I have completely de-stroyed the land because of their detestable sins, then they will know that I am the Lord.'

<sup>30</sup>"Son of man, your people talk about you in their houses and whisper about you at the doors. They say to each other, 'Come on, let's go hear the prophet tell us what the Lord is say-ing!' <sup>31</sup>So my people come pretending to be sincere and sit before you. They listen to your words, but they have no intention of doing what you say. Their mouths are full of lustful words, and their hearts seek only after money. <sup>32</sup>You are very entertaining to them, like someone who sings love songs with a beautiful voice or plays fine music on an instrument. They hear what you say, but they don't act on it! <sup>33</sup>But when all these terrible things happen to them—as they certainly will—then they will know a prophet has been among them."

## The Shepherds of Israel

**34** Then this message came to me from the Lord: <sup>2</sup>"Son of man, prophesy against the shepherds, the leaders of Israel. Give them this message from the Sovereign Lord: What sorrow awaits you shepherds who feed yourselves instead of your flocks. Shouldn't

**33:14**
Isa 55:7
Ezek 18:27
Hos 14:1, 4
Mic 6:8

**33:15**
Lev 6:4-5
Num 5:6-8
Luke 19:8

**33:16**
Isa 1:18; 43:25
Ezek 18:22

**33:17**
Ezek 18:24-29

**33:21**
Jer 39:1-2
Ezek 24:1-2, 26

**33:22**
Luke 1:64

**33:24**
Isa 51:1-2
Jer 39:10
Acts 7:5
Rom 4:12

**33:25**
Lev 17:10-14
Deut 12:16, 23
Jer 7:9-10

**33:26**
Mic 2:1-2
Zeph 3:3

**33:27**
Isa 2:19
Jer 15:2-4

**33:28**
Jer 44:22
Ezek 6:14; 36:34

**33:29**
Isa 29:13; 58:2
Ezek 23:33, 35

**33:30**
Ezek 14:3

**33:31**
Isa 29:13
Matt 13:22
Luke 12:15
1 Jn 3:18

**33:32**
Mark 6:20

**33:33**
Ezek 2:5; 33:29

**34:2**
Jer 10:21; 23:1
Mic 3:1-3
John 10:11;
21:15-17

**33:21** Hebrew *On the fifth day of the tenth month,* of the ancient Hebrew lunar calendar. This event occurred on January 8, 585 B.C.; also see note on 1:1.   **33:25** The Hebrew term (literally *round things*) probably alludes to dung.

---

**33:15** While good deeds will not save us, our salvation must lead to righteous actions (see Ephesians 2:10; James 2:14-17). This includes restitution for past sins (as exemplified in the story of Zacchaeus, see Luke 19:1-10). God expects us to make restitu-tion, whenever necessary, for the wrongs we have committed.

**33:21, 22** Near the beginning of his ministry, Ezekiel had been unable to speak except to give specific messages from God (3:26, 27). After Ezekiel's prophecies came true and the false prophets were exposed, Ezekiel was again able to talk freely. No longer needing to prove himself, he was free to offer God's message of restoration and hope.

**33:30-32** The people refused to act upon Ezekiel's message. When people mock your witness for Christ or ignore your advice, don't give up. You cannot make someone accept the message of salvation. Your part is to be faithful in delivering it.

**33:31** In your heart, do you really love God? These people gave the appearance of following God, but they loved their money more.

Many today also give the outward impression of being religious while remaining inwardly greedy. Jesus warned that we cannot love God and money at the same time (Matthew 6:24). It's easy to say, "I surrender all" when we don't have much. It's when we start accumulating wealth that it becomes difficult to avoid loving it.

**33:32** The people were coming to listen to Ezekiel in order to be entertained. They listened to the message from the Lord but had no intention of putting it into practice. Many people regard church as entertainment. They enjoy the music, the people, and the activi-ties, but they don't take the messages to heart. They are apathetic toward serving the Lord. Have you reduced church services to the level of entertainment, or does your worship truly have an impact on your life? Listen to God's words and then obey—apply his words and put them into practice in your life.

**34:1ff** Ezekiel called the exiles "Israel," referring to all Jews in captivity from both the northern and southern kingdoms. Ezekiel criticized Israel's leaders for taking care of themselves rather than

**34:3**
Isa 56:11
Ezek 22:27
Zech 11:5, 16

**34:4**
Zech 11:15-16
Matt 9:36; 18:12-13
1 Pet 5:3

**34:5**
Jer 10:21; 23:2

**34:6**
Ps 142:4
1 Pet 2:25

**34:8**
Acts 20:29

shepherds feed their sheep? ³You drink the milk, wear the wool, and butcher the best animals, but you let your flocks starve. ⁴You have not taken care of the weak. You have not tended the sick or bound up the injured. You have not gone looking for those who have wandered away and are lost. Instead, you have ruled them with harshness and cruelty. ⁵So my sheep have been scattered without a shepherd, and they are easy prey for any wild animal. ⁶They have wandered through all the mountains and all the hills, across the face of the earth, yet no one has gone to search for them.

⁷"Therefore, you shepherds, hear the word of the LORD: ⁸As surely as I live, says the Sovereign LORD, you abandoned my flock and left them to be attacked by every wild animal. And though you were my shepherds, you didn't search for my sheep when they were lost. You took care of yourselves and left the sheep to starve. ⁹Therefore, you shepherds, hear the word of the LORD. ¹⁰This is what the Sovereign LORD says: I now consider these shepherds my enemies, and I will hold them responsible for what has happened to my flock. I will take away their right to feed the flock, and I will stop them from feeding themselves. I will rescue my flock from their mouths; the sheep will no longer be their prey.

### The Good Shepherd

**34:11**
John 10:16

**34:12**
Jer 23:3; 31:10
Joel 2:2
Luke 19:10

**34:13**
Isa 30:25
Ezek 36:29-30

**34:14**
Ps 23:2
John 10:9

**34:16**
Isa 10:16; 49:26

**34:17**
Zech 10:3
Matt 25:32

**34:18**
Num 16:9, 13
2 Sam 7:19

**34:21**
Deut 33:17
Luke 13:14-16

**34:22**
Jer 23:2-3
Zech 11:7-9

¹¹"For this is what the Sovereign LORD says: I myself will search and find my sheep. ¹²I will be like a shepherd looking for his scattered flock. I will find my sheep and rescue them from all the places where they were scattered on that dark and cloudy day. ¹³I will bring them back home to their own land of Israel from among the peoples and nations. I will feed them on the mountains of Israel and by the rivers and in all the places where people live. ¹⁴Yes, I will give them good pastureland on the high hills of Israel. There they will lie down in pleasant places and feed in the lush pastures of the hills. ¹⁵I myself will tend my sheep and give them a place to lie down in peace, says the Sovereign LORD. ¹⁶I will search for my lost ones who strayed away, and I will bring them safely home again. I will bandage the injured and strengthen the weak. But I will destroy those who are fat and powerful. I will feed them, yes—feed them justice!

¹⁷"And as for you, my flock, this is what the Sovereign LORD says to his people: I will judge between one animal of the flock and another, separating the sheep from the goats. ¹⁸Isn't it enough for you to keep the best of the pastures for yourselves? Must you also trample down the rest? Isn't it enough for you to drink clear water for yourselves? Must you also muddy the rest with your feet? ¹⁹Why must my flock eat what you have trampled down and drink water you have fouled?

²⁰"Therefore, this is what the Sovereign LORD says: I will surely judge between the fat sheep and the scrawny sheep. ²¹For you fat sheep pushed and butted and crowded my sick and hungry flock until you scattered them to distant lands. ²²So I will rescue my flock, and

---

| BAD SHEPHERDS VERSUS GOOD SHEPHERDS | Bad Shepherds | Good Shepherds |
|---|---|---|
| | Take care of themselves . . . . . . . . . . . . . . | Take care of their flock |
| | Worry about their own health. . . . . . . . . . . | Strengthen the weak and sick, search for the lost |
| | Rule harshly and brutally. . . . . . . . . . . . . . | Rule lovingly and gently |
| | Abandon and scatter the sheep. . . . . . . . . | Gather and protect the sheep |
| | Keep the best for themselves . . . . . . . . . . | Give their best to the sheep |

---

taking care of their people. He outlined their sins (34:1-6) and pronounced judgment upon them (34:7-10). Then he promised that a good shepherd (the Messiah) would come who would take care of the people as the other leaders were supposed to do (34:11-31). This beautiful message portrays the fate of the present shepherds, the work of the new shepherd, and the future of the sheep.

**34:4-6** God would judge the religious leaders because they were selfishly caught up in their own concerns and were neglecting their service to others. Spiritual leaders must be careful not to pursue self-development at the expense of broken, lost people. When we give too much attention to our own needs and ideas, we may push God aside and abandon those who depend on us.

**34:9, 10** Those shepherds who failed their flock would be removed from office and held responsible for what happened to

the people they were supposed to lead. Christian leaders must heed this warning and care for their flock, or total failure and judgment will be the result (see 1 Corinthians 9:24-27). True leadership focuses on helping others, not just on getting ahead.

**34:11-16** God promises to take over as shepherd of his scattered flock. When our leaders fail us, we must not despair but remember that God is in control and that he promises to return and care for his flock. Thus, we know that we can turn to God for help. He is still in control and can transform any tragic situation into good for his Kingdom (see Genesis 50:20; Romans 8:28).

**34:18, 19** A bad shepherd is not only selfish but destructive. A minister who muddies the waters for others by causing unnecessary fears, teaching false ideas, and acting sinfully is a detriment to his flock's spiritual nourishment.

they will no longer be abused. I will judge between one animal of the flock and another. ²³And I will set over them one shepherd, my servant David. He will feed them and be a shepherd to them. ²⁴And I, the LORD, will be their God, and my servant David will be a prince among my people. I, the LORD, have spoken!

**34:23**
Isa 40:11
Jer 23:4-6; 30:9
John 10:11

**34:24**
Jer 30:9

### The LORD's Covenant of Peace

²⁵"I will make a covenant of peace with my people and drive away the dangerous animals from the land. Then they will be able to camp safely in the wildest places and sleep in the woods without fear. ²⁶I will bless my people and their homes around my holy hill. And in the proper season I will send the showers they need. There will be showers of blessing. ²⁷The orchards and fields of my people will yield bumper crops, and everyone will live in safety. When I have broken their chains of slavery and rescued them from those who enslaved them, then they will know that I am the LORD. ²⁸They will no longer be prey for other nations, and wild animals will no longer devour them. They will live in safety, and no one will frighten them.

²⁹"And I will make their land famous for its crops, so my people will never again suffer from famines or the insults of foreign nations. ³⁰In this way, they will know that I, the LORD their God, am with them. And they will know that they, the people of Israel, are my people, says the Sovereign LORD. ³¹You are my flock, the sheep of my pasture. You are my people, and I am your God. I, the Sovereign LORD, have spoken!"

**34:25**
Isa 11:6-9
Jer 33:16
Hos 2:18

**34:26**
Gen 12:2
Deut 28:12
Isa 32:15; 44:3

**34:27**
Lev 26:13
Isa 52:2-3

**34:28**
Jer 30:10

**34:29**
Isa 60:21

**34:31**
Mic 7:14
John 10:11

### A Message for Edom

**35** Again a message came to me from the LORD: ²"Son of man, turn and face Mount Seir, and prophesy against its people. ³Give them this message from the Sovereign LORD:

"I am your enemy, O Mount Seir,
    and I will raise my fist against you
    to destroy you completely.
⁴ I will demolish your cities
    and make you desolate.
Then you will know that I am the LORD.

**35:2**
Gen 36:6-8

**35:3**
Jer 49:13, 17-18

**35:4**
Mal 1:2-4

⁵"Your eternal hatred for the people of Israel led you to butcher them when they were helpless, when I had already punished them for all their sins. ⁶As surely as I live, says the Sovereign LORD, since you show no distaste for blood, I will give you a bloodbath of your own. Your turn has come! ⁷I will make Mount Seir utterly desolate, killing off all who try to escape and any who return. ⁸I will fill your mountains with the dead. Your hills, your valleys, and your ravines will be filled with people slaughtered by the sword. ⁹I will make you desolate forever. Your cities will never be rebuilt. Then you will know that I am the LORD.

¹⁰"For you said, 'The lands of Israel and Judah will be ours. We will take possession of them. What do we care that the LORD is there!' ¹¹Therefore, as surely as I live, says the Sovereign LORD, I will pay back your angry deeds with my own. I will punish you for all your acts of anger, envy, and hatred. And I will make myself known to Israel* by what I do to you. ¹²Then you will know that I, the LORD, have heard every contemptuous word you spoke against the mountains of Israel. For you said, 'They are desolate; they have been given to us as food to eat!' ¹³In saying that, you boasted proudly against me, and I have heard it all!

¹⁴"This is what the Sovereign LORD says: The whole world will rejoice when I make you desolate. ¹⁵You rejoiced at the desolation of Israel's territory. Now I will rejoice at yours! You will be wiped out, you people of Mount Seir and all who live in Edom! Then you will know that I am the LORD.

**35:7**
Ezek 25:13

**35:8**
Isa 34:5-6

**35:9**
Jer 49:13

**35:10**
Ps 48:1-3

**35:11**
Pss 9:16; 137:7
Amos 1:11

**35:12**
Jer 50:7
Ezek 36:2

**35:13**
Isa 10:13-14
Ezek 36:3
Dan 11:36

**35:14**
Isa 44:23; 49:13
Jer 51:48

**35:15**
Isa 34:5-6
Lam 4:21
Obad 1:12, 15

**35:11** Hebrew *to them*; Greek version reads *to you.*

---

**34:23-31** In contrast to the present evil shepherds (leaders) of God's people (34:1-6), God will send a perfect shepherd, the Messiah ("my servant David"), who will take care of every need his people have and set up a Kingdom of perfect peace and justice (see Psalm 23; Jeremiah 23:5, 6; John 10:11; Hebrews 13:20, 21; Revelation 21). *Peace* here means more than the absence of conflict. It is contentment, fulfillment, and security.

**35:1ff** Ezekiel gave another prophecy against Edom (where Mount Seir was located); his first prophecy against Edom is found in 25:12-14. In this prophecy, Ezekiel is probably using Edom to represent *all* the nations opposed to God's people. Chapter 36

says that Israel will be restored, while this chapter says that Edom (God's enemies) will be made "desolate."

**35:2** Edom offered to help destroy Jerusalem and rejoiced when the city fell. Edom's long-standing hostility against God's people resulted in God's judgment.

**35:6-8** Ezekiel prophesied not only against the people of Edom but also against their mountains and land. Their home territory was Mount Seir. Mountains, symbols of strength and power, represented the pride of these people, who thought they could get away with evil. Their desire for revenge turned against them. Edom received the punishment it was so hasty to give out. God

36:2
Deut 32:13
Isa 58:14
Ezek 35:10
Hab 3:19

36:3
Jer 2:15; 51:34
Ezek 35:13

36:4
Deut 11:11
Ps 79:4
Jer 48:27

36:5
Isa 66:15-16
Jer 50:11
Mic 7:8

36:8
Isa 27:6
Ezek 17:22-23;
34:26-29

36:9
Lev 26:9
Ezek 28:26; 34:14

36:10
Isa 27:6; 49:17-22
Jer 31:27-28
Ezek 37:21-22

36:11
Jer 30:18
Ezek 16:55

36:13
Num 13:32

36:15
Isa 54:4
Jer 18:15

36:17
Jer 2:7

36:18
2 Chr 34:21, 25
Lam 2:4; 4:11
Ezek 22:18-20

36:19
Deut 28:64
Ezek 22:15
Amos 9:9
Rom 2:6

36:20
Isa 52:5
Jer 33:24
†Rom 2:24

36:21
Ps 74:18
Isa 48:9

36:22
Deut 9:5-7
Ps 106:8

## Restoration for Israel

**36** "Son of man, prophesy to Israel's mountains. Give them this message: O mountains of Israel, hear the word of the LORD! 2 This is what the Sovereign LORD says: Your enemies have taunted you, saying, 'Aha! Now the ancient heights belong to us!' 3 Therefore, son of man, give the mountains of Israel this message from the Sovereign LORD: Your enemies have attacked you from all directions, making you the property of many nations and the object of much mocking and slander. 4 Therefore, O mountains of Israel, hear the word of the Sovereign LORD. He speaks to the hills and mountains, ravines and valleys, and to ruined wastes and long-deserted cities that have been destroyed and mocked by the surrounding nations. 5 This is what the Sovereign LORD says: My jealous anger burns against these nations, especially Edom, because they have shown utter contempt for me by gleefully taking my land for themselves as plunder.

6 "Therefore, prophesy to the hills and mountains, the ravines and valleys of Israel. This is what the Sovereign LORD says: I am furious that you have suffered shame before the surrounding nations. 7 Therefore, this is what the Sovereign LORD says: I have taken a solemn oath that those nations will soon have their own shame to endure.

8 "But the mountains of Israel will produce heavy crops of fruit for my people—for they will be coming home again soon! 9 See, I care about you, and I will pay attention to you. Your ground will be plowed and your crops planted. 10 I will greatly increase the population of Israel, and the ruined cities will be rebuilt and filled with people. 11 I will increase not only the people, but also your animals. O mountains of Israel, I will bring people to live on you once again. I will make you even more prosperous than you were before. Then you will know that I am the LORD. 12 I will cause my people to walk on you once again, and you will be their territory. You will never again rob them of their children.

13 "This is what the Sovereign LORD says: The other nations taunt you, saying, 'Israel is a land that devours its own people and robs them of their children!' 14 But you will never again devour your people or rob them of their children, says the Sovereign LORD. 15 I will not let you hear those other nations insult you, and you will no longer be mocked by them. You will not be a land that causes its nation to fall, says the Sovereign LORD."

16 Then this further message came to me from the LORD: 17 "Son of man, when the people of Israel were living in their own land, they defiled it by the evil way they lived. To me their conduct was as unclean as a woman's menstrual cloth. 18 They polluted the land with murder and the worship of idols,* so I poured out my fury on them. 19 I scattered them to many lands to punish them for the evil way they had lived. 20 But when they were scattered among the nations, they brought shame on my holy name. For the nations said, 'These are the people of the LORD, but he couldn't keep them safe in his own land!' 21 Then I was concerned for my holy name, on which my people brought shame among the nations.

22 "Therefore, give the people of Israel this message from the Sovereign LORD: I am bringing you back, but not because you deserve it. I am doing it to protect my holy name, on which

**36:18** The Hebrew term (literally *round things*) probably alludes to dung; also in 36:25.

---

| OLD AND NEW COVENANTS | Old Covenant | New Covenant |
| --- | --- | --- |
| | Placed upon stone | Placed upon people's hearts |
| | Based on the law | Based on desire to love and serve God |
| | Must be taught | Known by all |
| | Legal relationship with God | Personal relationship with God |

---

has a way of allowing our treatment of others to boomerang on us. So be careful in your judgment of others (Matthew 7:1, 2).

**36:1ff** In this prophecy, Ezekiel said that Israel would be restored as a nation and would return to its own land. The mountains were symbolic of Israel's strength (see the note on 35:6-8). To the exiles in Babylon, this seemed impossible. This message again emphasized God's sovereignty and trustworthiness. He would first judge the nations used to punish Israel (36:1-7) and then restore his people (36:8-15).

**36:2** "The ancient heights" refers to the Promised Land—the land of Israel. Israel's enemies challenged not only their boundaries but also God's promises to Israel.

**36:21-23** Why did God want to protect his holy name—his reputation—among the nations of the world? God was concerned about the salvation of not only his people but also the whole world. To allow his people to remain in sin and be permanently destroyed by their enemies would lead other nations to conclude that their pagan gods were more powerful than Israel's God (Isaiah 48:11). Thus, to protect his holy name, God would return a remnant of his people to their land. God will not share his glory with false gods—he alone is the one true God. The people had the responsibility to represent God to the rest of the world. Believers today have that same responsibility. How do you represent God to your world?

you brought shame while you were scattered among the nations. ²³I will show how holy my great name is—the name on which you brought shame among the nations. And when I reveal my holiness through you before their very eyes, says the Sovereign LORD, then the nations will know that I am the LORD. ²⁴For I will gather you up from all the nations and bring you home again to your land.

²⁵"Then I will sprinkle clean water on you, and you will be clean. Your filth will be washed away, and you will no longer worship idols. ²⁶And I will give you a new heart, and I will put a new spirit in you. I will take out your stony, stubborn heart and give you a tender, responsive heart.* ²⁷And I will put my Spirit in you so that you will follow my decrees and be careful to obey my regulations.

²⁸"And you will live in Israel, the land I gave your ancestors long ago. You will be my people, and I will be your God. ²⁹I will cleanse you of your filthy behavior. I will give you good crops of grain, and I will send no more famines on the land. ³⁰I will give you great harvests from your fruit trees and fields, and never again will the surrounding nations be able to scoff at your land for its famines. ³¹Then you will remember your past sins and despise yourselves for all the detestable things you did. ³²But remember, says the Sovereign LORD, I am not doing this because you deserve it. O my people of Israel, you should be utterly ashamed of all you have done!

³³"This is what the Sovereign LORD says: When I cleanse you from your sins, I will repopulate your cities, and the ruins will be rebuilt. ³⁴The fields that used to lie empty and desolate in plain view of everyone will again be farmed. ³⁵And when I bring you back, people will say, 'This former wasteland is now like the Garden of Eden! The abandoned and ruined cities now have strong walls and are filled with people!' ³⁶Then the surrounding nations that survive will know that I, the LORD, have rebuilt the ruins and replanted the wasteland. For I, the LORD, have spoken, and I will do what I say.

³⁷"This is what the Sovereign LORD says: I am ready to hear Israel's prayers and to increase their numbers like a flock. ³⁸They will be as numerous as the sacred flocks that fill Jerusalem's streets at the time of her festivals. The ruined cities will be crowded with people once more, and everyone will know that I am the LORD."

## A Valley of Dry Bones

**37** The LORD took hold of me, and I was carried away by the Spirit of the LORD to a valley filled with bones. ²He led me all around among the bones that covered the valley floor. They were scattered everywhere across the ground and were completely dried out. ³Then he asked me, "Son of man, can these bones become living people again?"

"O Sovereign LORD," I replied, "you alone know the answer to that."

⁴Then he said to me, "Speak a prophetic message to these bones and say, 'Dry bones, listen to the word of the LORD! ⁵This is what the Sovereign LORD says: Look! I am going to put breath into you and make you live again! ⁶I will put flesh and muscles on you and cover you with skin. I will put breath into you, and you will come to life. Then you will know that I am the LORD.'"

36:26 Hebrew *a heart of flesh*.

**36:23**
Ps 126:2
Ezek 20:41; 39:7
**36:24**
Isa 43:5-6
**36:25**
Isa 52:15
Zech 13:1
John 3:5
Titus 3:5-6
Heb 10:22
**36:26**
Ps 51:10
2 Cor 5:17
**36:27**
Isa 59:21
Ezek 37:14
**36:28**
Jer 30:22
**36:29**
Ezek 34:27-29
Hos 2:21-23
**36:30**
Lev 26:4
**36:32**
Deut 9:5
**36:33**
Isa 58:12
Zech 8:7-8
**36:35**
Isa 51:3
**36:36**
Hos 14:4-7
**36:38**
1 Kgs 8:63
2 Chr 35:7-9
**37:1**
Jer 7:32–8:2
Acts 8:39
**37:3**
Deut 32:29
1 Sam 2:6
Isa 26:19
**37:4**
Isa 42:18
**37:5**
Ps 104:29-30
John 20:22
Eph 2:5
Rev 11:11
**37:6**
Joel 2:27; 3:17

---

**36:25-27** God promised to restore Israel not only physically but spiritually. To accomplish this, God would give them a new heart for following him and put his Spirit within them (see 11:19, 20; Psalm 51:7-11) to transform them and empower them to do his will. Again the new covenant was promised (16:61-63; 34:23-25), ultimately to be fulfilled in Christ. No matter how impure your life is right now, God offers you a fresh start. You can have your sins washed away, receive a new heart for God, and have his Spirit within you—if you accept God's promise. Why try to patch up your old life when you can have a new one?

**36:31, 32** God said his people should be ashamed of their sins. The people had become so callous that they had lost all sensitivity to sin. First they had to "remember" their sins, be ashamed of them, and finally repent of them (see James 4:8, 9). As we examine our life, we may find that we, too, have lost our sensitivity to certain sins. But as we measure ourselves against God's standards of right living, we will be ashamed. To regain sensitivity we must recognize our sin for what it is, be sorry for displeasing God, and ask his forgiveness. The Holy Spirit will guide us, making us responsive and receptive to God's truth (John 14:26; 16:8, 13).

**36:37, 38** God said that he was ready to answer Israel's prayers. We cannot expect God to answer our prayers, however, until we have received a new heart from him (36:26). Is your heart right with God?

**37:1ff** This vision illustrates the promise of chapter 36—new life and a nation restored, both physically and spiritually. The dry bones are a picture of the Jews in captivity—scattered and dead. The two pieces of wood (37:15-17) represent the reunion of the entire nation of Israel that had divided into northern and southern kingdoms after Solomon. The scattered exiles of both Israel and Judah would be released from the "graves" of exile and one day regathered in their homeland, with the Messiah as their leader. This vision has yet to be fulfilled. Ezekiel felt he was speaking to the dead as he preached to the exiles because they rarely responded to his message. But these dead bones responded! And just as God brought life to the dead bones, he would bring life again to his spiritually dead people.

**37:4, 5** The dry bones represented the people's spiritually dead condition. Your church may seem like a heap of dry bones to you, spiritually dead with no hope of vitality. But just

**37:7**
Jer 13:5-7

**37:9**
Ps 104:30
Hos 13:14

**37:10**
Jer 30:19
Rev 11:11

**37:11**
Ps 141:7
Isa 49:14

**37:12**
Deut 32:39
Isa 26:19
Hos 13:14
Amos 9:14-15

**37:14**
Joel 2:28-29

**37:16**
1 Kgs 12:16-20
2 Chr 10:17-19

**37:17**
Isa 11:13; 50:4
Hos 1:11

**37:21**
Isa 43:5-6
Ezek 39:27

**37:22**
Isa 11:13
Jer 50:4
Ezek 34:13-14
Hos 1:11

**37:23**
Ezek 11:18

**37:24**
Jer 30:21
Hos 3:5

**37:25**
Isa 11:1

**37:26**
Jer 30:19
Heb 13:20

**37:27**
Lev 26:11
†2 Cor 6:16

**37:28**
Exod 31:13
Zeph 3:15

7So I spoke this message, just as he told me. Suddenly as I spoke, there was a rattling noise all across the valley. The bones of each body came together and attached themselves as complete skeletons. 8Then as I watched, muscles and flesh formed over the bones. Then skin formed to cover their bodies, but they still had no breath in them.

9Then he said to me, "Speak a prophetic message to the winds, son of man. Speak a prophetic message and say, 'This is what the Sovereign LORD says: Come, O breath, from the four winds! Breathe into these dead bodies so they may live again.'"

10So I spoke the message as he commanded me, and breath came into their bodies. They all came to life and stood up on their feet—a great army.

11Then he said to me, "Son of man, these bones represent the people of Israel. They are saying, 'We have become old, dry bones—all hope is gone. Our nation is finished.' 12Therefore, prophesy to them and say, 'This is what the Sovereign LORD says: O my people, I will open your graves of exile and cause you to rise again. Then I will bring you back to the land of Israel. 13When this happens, O my people, you will know that I am the LORD. 14I will put my Spirit in you, and you will live again and return home to your own land. Then you will know that I, the LORD, have spoken, and I have done what I said. Yes, the LORD has spoken!'"

### Reunion of Israel and Judah

15Again a message came to me from the LORD: 16"Son of man, take a piece of wood and carve on it these words: 'This represents Judah and its allied tribes.' Then take another piece and carve these words on it: 'This represents Ephraim and the northern tribes of Israel.'* 17Now hold them together in your hand as if they were one piece of wood. 18When your people ask you what your actions mean, 19say to them, 'This is what the Sovereign LORD says: I will take Ephraim and the northern tribes and join them to Judah. I will make them one piece of wood in my hand.'

20"Then hold out the pieces of wood you have inscribed, so the people can see them. 21And give them this message from the Sovereign LORD: I will gather the people of Israel from among the nations. I will bring them home to their own land from the places where they have been scattered. 22I will unify them into one nation on the mountains of Israel. One king will rule them all; no longer will they be divided into two nations or into two kingdoms. 23They will never again pollute themselves with their idols* and vile images and rebellion, for I will save them from their sinful backsliding. I will cleanse them. Then they will truly be my people, and I will be their God.

24"My servant David will be their king, and they will have only one shepherd. They will obey my regulations and be careful to keep my decrees. 25They will live in the land I gave my servant Jacob, the land where their ancestors lived. They and their children and their grandchildren after them will live there forever, generation after generation. And my servant David will be their prince forever. 26And I will make a covenant of peace with them, an everlasting covenant. I will give them their land and increase their numbers,* and I will put my Temple among them forever. 27I will make my home among them. I will be their God, and they will be my people. 28And when my Temple is among them forever, the nations will know that I am the LORD, who makes Israel holy."

**37:16** Hebrew *This is Ephraim's wood, representing Joseph and all the house of Israel.* **37:23** The Hebrew term (literally *round things*) probably alludes to dung. **37:26** Hebrew reads *I will give them and increase their numbers;* Greek version lacks the entire phrase.

---

as God promised to restore his nation, he can restore any church, no matter how dry or dead it may be. Rather than give up, pray for renewal, for God can restore it to life. The hope and prayer of every church should be that God will put his Spirit into it (37:14). In fact, God is at work calling his people back to himself, bringing new life into dead churches.

**37:16** The first piece of wood was for Judah, being the leading tribe in the southern kingdom. The other was for Ephraim, the leading tribe in the northern kingdom.

**37:24, 25** The Messiah was often called David because he is David's descendant. David was a good king, but the Messiah would be the perfect King (Revelation 17:14; 19:16).

**37:26, 27** God's promise here goes beyond the physical and geographical restoration of Israel. He promises to breathe new spiritual life into his people so that their hearts and attitudes will be right with him and united with one another. This same process is described throughout God's Word as the cleansing and renewing of our hearts by God's Spirit (Titus 3:4-6).

## A Message for Gog

**38** This is another message that came to me from the LORD: ²"Son of man, turn and face Gog of the land of Magog, the prince who rules over the nations of Meshech and Tubal, and prophesy against him. ³Give him this message from the Sovereign LORD: Gog, I am your enemy! ⁴I will turn you around and put hooks in your jaws to lead you out with your whole army—your horses and charioteers in full armor and a great horde armed with shields and swords. ⁵Persia, Ethiopia, and Libya* will join you, too, with all their weapons. ⁶Gomer and all its armies will also join you, along with the armies of Beth-togarmah from the distant north, and many others.

⁷"Get ready; be prepared! Keep all the armies around you mobilized, and take command of them. ⁸A long time from now you will be called into action. In the distant future you will swoop down on the land of Israel, which will be enjoying peace after recovering from war and after its people have returned from many lands to the mountains of Israel. ⁹You and all your allies—a vast and awesome army—will roll down on them like a storm and cover the land like a cloud.

¹⁰"This is what the Sovereign LORD says: At that time evil thoughts will come to your mind, and you will devise a wicked scheme. ¹¹You will say, 'Israel is an unprotected land filled with unwalled villages! I will march against her and destroy these people who live in such confidence! ¹²I will go to those formerly desolate cities that are now filled with people who have returned from exile in many nations. I will capture vast amounts of plunder, for the people are rich with livestock and other possessions now. They think the whole world revolves around them!' ¹³But Sheba and Dedan and the merchants of Tarshish will ask, 'Do you really think the armies you have gathered can rob them of silver and gold? Do you think you can drive away their livestock and seize their goods and carry off plunder?'

¹⁴"Therefore, son of man, prophesy against Gog. Give him this message from the Sovereign LORD: When my people are living in peace in their land, then you will rouse yourself.* ¹⁵You will come from your homeland in the distant north with your vast cavalry and your mighty army, ¹⁶and you will attack my people Israel, covering their land like a cloud. At that time in the distant future, I will bring you against my land as everyone watches, and my holiness will be displayed by what happens to you, Gog. Then all the nations will know that I am the LORD.

¹⁷"This is what the Sovereign LORD asks: Are you the one I was talking about long ago, when I announced through Israel's prophets that in the future I would bring you against my people? ¹⁸But this is what the Sovereign LORD says: When Gog invades the land of Israel, my fury will boil over! ¹⁹In my jealousy and blazing anger, I promise a mighty shaking in the land of Israel on that day. ²⁰All living things—the fish in the sea, the birds of the sky, the animals of the field, the small animals that scurry along the ground, and all the people on earth—will quake in terror at my presence. Mountains will be thrown down; cliffs will crumble; walls will fall to the earth. ²¹I will summon the sword against you on all the hills of Israel, says the Sovereign LORD. Your men will turn their swords against each other. ²²I will punish you and your armies with disease and bloodshed; I will send torrential rain, hailstones, fire, and burning sulfur! ²³In this way, I will show my greatness and holiness, and I will make myself known to all the nations of the world. Then they will know that I am the LORD.

| |
|---|
| **38:2** Ezek 39:1 Rev 20:8-9 |
| **38:4** Isa 43:17 Ezek 39:2 Dan 11:40 |
| **38:5** Gen 10:6-7 Ezek 27:10; 30:4-5 |
| **38:6** Gen 10:2-3 Ezek 27:14 |
| **38:8** Isa 11:11 Ezek 34:13 |
| **38:9** Isa 5:28 Jer 4:13 Joel 2:2 |
| **38:10** Ps 36:4 Mic 2:1 |
| **38:11** Isa 37:24-25 Zech 2:4-5 |
| **38:12** Isa 10:6 Ezek 29:19 |
| **38:13** Isa 10:5-7 |
| **38:14** Jer 23:5-6 Zech 2:5, 8 |
| **38:16** Ezek 36:23 |
| **38:17** Isa 5:26-30; 34:1-6 |
| **38:18** Ps 18:7-8 |
| **38:19** Ezek 36:5-6 Joel 3:16 Hag 2:6-7 Heb 12:26-29 |
| **38:20** Jer 4:24 Nah 1:5-6 Zech 14:4-5 |
| **38:21** Judg 7:22 2 Chr 20:23 Hag 2:22 |
| **38:22** Ps 11:6 Zech 14:12-15 Rev 16:21 |

**38:5** Hebrew *Paras, Cush, and Put.*    **38:14** As in Greek version; Hebrew reads *then you will know.*

---

**38:1ff** In chapter 37, Ezekiel revealed how Israel (God's people) would be restored to their land from many parts of the world. Once Israel became strong, a confederacy of nations from the north would attack, led by Gog (see also Revelation 20:8). Their purpose would be to destroy God's people. Gog's allies would come from the mountainous area southeast of the Black Sea and southwest of the Caspian Sea (central Turkey), as well as from the area that is present-day Iran, Ethiopia, Libya, and possibly Russia. Gog could be a person (he sometimes is identified with Gyges, king of Lydia in 660 B.C.), or Gog could also be a symbol of all the evil in the world. Whether symbolic or literal, Gog represents the aggregate military might of all the forces opposed to God.

Many say that the battle Ezekiel described will occur at the end of human history, but there are many differences between the events described here and those in Revelation 20. Regardless of when this battle will occur, the message is clear: God will deliver his people—no enemy can stand before his mighty power.

**38:13** Sheba and Dedan, great trading centers in Arabia, would in effect say to Gog, "Who are you to usurp our position as the world's trade leaders?" Sheba and Dedan would then join this confederacy. Tarshish was the leading trade center in the west; many believe it was in Spain.

**38:21** God will directly intervene in the defense of Israel, unleashing severe natural disasters on the invaders from the north. In the end, the stricken pagan nations will turn on themselves in confusion and panic. All those who set themselves against God will be destroyed.

## The Slaughter of Gog's Hordes

**39** "Son of man, prophesy against Gog. Give him this message from the Sovereign LORD: I am your enemy, O Gog, ruler of the nations of Meshech and Tubal. ²I will turn you around and drive you toward the mountains of Israel, bringing you from the distant north. ³I will knock the bow from your left hand and the arrows from your right hand, and I will leave you helpless. ⁴You and your army and your allies will all die on the mountains. I will feed you to the vultures and wild animals. ⁵You will fall in the open fields, for I have spoken, says the Sovereign LORD. ⁶And I will rain down fire on Magog and on all your allies who live safely on the coasts. Then they will know that I am the LORD.

⁷"In this way, I will make known my holy name among my people of Israel. I will not let anyone bring shame on it. And the nations, too, will know that I am the LORD, the Holy One of Israel. ⁸That day of judgment will come, says the Sovereign LORD. Everything will happen just as I have declared it.

⁹"Then the people in the towns of Israel will go out and pick up your small and large shields, bows and arrows, javelins and spears, and they will use them for fuel. There will be enough to last them seven years! ¹⁰They won't need to cut wood from the fields or forests, for these weapons will give them all the fuel they need. They will plunder those who planned to plunder them, and they will rob those who planned to rob them, says the Sovereign LORD.

¹¹"And I will make a vast graveyard for Gog and his hordes in the Valley of the Travelers, east of the Dead Sea.* It will block the way of those who travel there, and they will change the name of the place to the Valley of Gog's Hordes. ¹²It will take seven months for the people of Israel to bury the bodies and cleanse the land. ¹³Everyone in Israel will help, for it will be a glorious victory for Israel when I demonstrate my glory on that day, says the Sovereign LORD.

¹⁴"After seven months, teams of men will be appointed to search the land for skeletons to bury, so the land will be made clean again. ¹⁵Whenever bones are found, a marker will be set up so the burial crews will take them to be buried in the Valley of Gog's Hordes. ¹⁶(There will be a town there named Hamonah, which means 'horde.') And so the land will finally be cleansed.

¹⁷"And now, son of man, this is what the Sovereign LORD says: Call all the birds and wild animals. Say to them: Gather together for my great sacrificial feast. Come from far and near to the mountains of Israel, and there eat flesh and drink blood! ¹⁸Eat the flesh of mighty men and drink the blood of princes as though they were rams, lambs, goats, and bulls—all fattened animals from Bashan! ¹⁹Gorge yourselves with flesh until you are glutted; drink blood until you are drunk. This is the sacrificial feast I have prepared for you. ²⁰Feast at my banquet table—feast on horses and charioteers, on mighty men and all kinds of valiant warriors, says the Sovereign LORD.

²¹"In this way, I will demonstrate my glory to the nations. Everyone will see the punishment I have inflicted on them and the power of my fist when I strike. ²²And from that time on the people of Israel will know that I am the LORD their God. ²³The nations will then know why Israel was sent away to exile—it was punishment for sin, for they were unfaithful to their God. Therefore, I turned away from them and let their enemies destroy them. ²⁴I turned my face away and punished them because of their defilement and their sins.

## Restoration for God's People

²⁵"So now, this is what the Sovereign LORD says: I will end the captivity of my people*; I will have mercy on all Israel, for I jealously guard my holy reputation! ²⁶They will accept responsibility for* their past shame and unfaithfulness after they come home to live in peace in their own land, with no one to bother them. ²⁷When I bring them home from the lands of

**39:11** Hebrew *the sea.*   **39:25** Hebrew *of Jacob.*   **39:26** A few Hebrew manuscripts read *They will forget.*

**39:1**
Ezek 38:2-4

**39:2**
Ezek 38:15

**39:3**
Pss 46:9; 76:3
Jer 21:4-5
Ezek 30:21-24
Hos 1:5

**39:4**
Isa 14:24-25
Ezek 29:5; 32:4-5

**39:6**
Jer 25:22
Ezek 30:8, 16;
38:22
Amos 1:4-7
Nah 1:6

**39:7**
Exod 20:7
Ezek 20:39

**39:9**
Ps 46:9

**39:10**
Isa 14:2
Mic 5:8
Hab 2:8

**39:13**
Jer 33:9
Ezek 28:22
Zeph 3:19-20

**39:17**
Isa 34:6-7
Jer 46:10
Zeph 1:7
Rev 19:17-18

**39:18**
Deut 32:14
Ps 22:12
Jer 51:40
Amos 4:1

**39:20**
Ps 76:5-6
Ezek 38:4
Hag 2:22
Rev 19:18

**39:21**
Exod 9:16
Ezek 38:16, 23

**39:23**
Isa 59:2
Ezek 36:18-19;
39:29

**39:24**
2 Kgs 17:7
Jer 2:17, 19; 4:18
Ezek 36:19

**39:25**
Jer 33:7
Ezek 34:13; 36:10
Hos 1:11

**39:26**
Ezek 34:25-28
Mic 4:4

**39:27**
Ezek 28:25-26

**39:1ff** The story of the battle continues. The defeat of the evil forces will be final and complete; they will be destroyed by divine intervention. Because of this victory, God's name will be known throughout the world. His glory will be evident, and the nations will understand that he alone is in charge of human history. God will clearly show his love for his people by restoring them to their homeland.

**39:12-16** Two themes are intertwined: God's total victory over his enemies, and the need to cleanse the land to make it holy. After the final battle, special crews will be appointed to give proper burial to the bodies of the dead enemies in order for the land to be cleansed. The land would have been defiled by unburied corpses. Those who would come in contact with the corpses out in the open would become ceremonially unclean (according to Numbers 19:14-16). There will be so many bodies that all kinds of birds will be called in order to help dispose of them (39:17-20). This message is exciting for us: With God on our side, we are assured of ultimate victory over his foes because God will fight on our behalf (see also Zephaniah 3:14-17; Romans 8:38, 39).

their enemies, I will display my holiness among them for all the nations to see. 28Then my people will know that I am the Lord their God, because I sent them away to exile and brought them home again. I will leave none of my people behind. 29And I will never again turn my face from them, for I will pour out my Spirit upon the people of Israel. I, the Sovereign Lord, have spoken!"

## 2. Restoring the worship of God
### The New Temple Area

**40** On April 28,* during the twenty-fifth year of our captivity—fourteen years after the fall of Jerusalem—the Lord took hold of me. 2In a vision from God he took me to the land of Israel and set me down on a very high mountain. From there I could see toward the south what appeared to be a city. 3As he brought me nearer, I saw a man whose face shone like bronze standing beside a gateway entrance. He was holding in his hand a linen measuring cord and a measuring rod.

4He said to me, "Son of man, watch and listen. Pay close attention to everything I show you. You have been brought here so I can show you many things. Then you will return to the people of Israel and tell them everything you have seen."

### The East Gateway
5I could see a wall completely surrounding the Temple area. The man took a measuring rod that was 10½ feet* long and measured the wall, and the wall was 10½ feet* thick and 10½ feet high.

6Then he went over to the eastern gateway. He climbed the steps and measured the threshold of the gateway; it was 10½ feet front to back.* 7There were guard alcoves on each side built into the gateway passage. Each of these alcoves was 10½ feet square, with a distance between them of 8¾ feet* along the passage wall. The gateway's inner threshold, which led to the entry room at the inner end of the gateway passage, was 10½ feet front to back. 8He also measured the entry room of the gateway.* 9It was 14 feet* across, with supporting columns

**40:1** Hebrew *At the beginning of the year, on the tenth day of the month*, of the ancient Hebrew lunar calendar. This event occurred on April 28, 573 B.C.; also see note on 1:1. **40:5a** Hebrew *6 long cubits* [3.2 meters], *each being a cubit* [18 inches or 45 centimeters] *and a handbreadth* [3 inches or 8 centimeters] *in length*. **40:5b** Hebrew *1 rod* [3.2 meters]; also in 40:5c, 7. **40:6** As in Greek version, which reads *1 rod* [3.2 meters] *deep*; Hebrew reads *1 rod deep, and 1 threshold, 1 rod deep*; also in 40:48. **40:7** Hebrew *5 cubits* [2.7 meters]; also in 40:8. **40:8** Many Hebrew manuscripts add *which faced inward toward the Temple; it was 1 rod* [10.5 feet or 3.2 meters] *deep*. 9Then he measured the entry room of the gateway.

**39:29** Isa 32:15; Ezek 36:27; 37:14; Joel 2:28-29; Acts 2:17
**40:1** 2 Kgs 25:1-7; Jer 39:1-9
**40:2** Ps 48:2; Ezek 20:40; Mic 4:1; Rev 21:10
**40:3** Dan 10:5-6; Zech 2:1-2; Rev 11:1; 21:15
**40:4** Jer 26:2; Ezek 43:10; 44:5; Acts 20:27
**40:5** Ezek 42:20
**40:6** Ezek 8:16; 11:1; 43:1
**40:7** 1 Kgs 6:5-10; 2 Chr 31:11; Jer 35:4; Ezek 40:29, 33, 36

**39:29** Both in this prophecy and in Joel 2:28, 29, God promises to pour out his Spirit on his people. The early church believed this began to be fulfilled at Pentecost, when God's Holy Spirit came to live in all believers (Acts 2:1-18).

**40:1ff** The building of the Temple envisioned a time of complete restoration to the exiles, a time when God would return to his people. The Temple was built from 520 to 515 B.C. (see Ezra 5–6) but fell short of Ezekiel's plan (Haggai 2:3; Zechariah 4:10). This vision of the Temple has been interpreted in four main ways: (1) This is the Temple Zerubbabel should have built from 520 to 515 B.C. and is the actual blueprint Ezekiel intended. But due to disobedience (43:2-10), it was never followed. (2) This is a literal Temple to be rebuilt during the millennial reign of Christ. (3) This Temple is symbolic of the true worship of God by the Christian church right now. (4) This Temple is symbolic of the future and eternal reign of God when his presence and blessing fill the earth.

Whether the Temple is literal or symbolic, it seems clear that this is a vision of God's final perfect Kingdom. This gave hope to the people of Ezekiel's time who had just seen their nation and its Temple destroyed with no hope of rebuilding it in the near future. The details given in this vision gave the people even more hope that what Ezekiel saw had come from God and would surely happen in the future.

**40:1ff** One argument against the view that Ezekiel's Temple is a literal building of the future is that sacrifices are mentioned (40:38-43). If the sacrifices were to be reinstituted in the last days, then Christ's final sacrifice would not have been final. The New Testament makes it clear that Christ died once and for all (Romans

6:10; Hebrews 9:12; 10:10, 18). Our sins have been removed; no further sacrifice is needed.

In Ezekiel's day, however, the only kind of worship the people knew was the kind that involved sacrifices and ceremonies as described in Exodus through Deuteronomy. Ezekiel had to explain the new order of worship in terms the people would understand. The next nine chapters tell how the Temple is the focal point of everything, showing that the ideal relationship with God is when all of life centers on him.

**40:1ff** Ezekiel explained God's dwelling place in words and images the people could understand. God wanted them to see the great splendor he had planned for those who lived faithfully. This kind of Temple was never built, but it was a vision intended to typify God's perfect plan for his people—the centrality of worship, the presence of the Lord, the blessings flowing from it, and the orderliness of worship and worship duties. Don't let the details obscure the point of this vision: One day all those who have been faithful to God will enjoy eternal life with him. Let the majesty of this vision lift you and teach you about the God you worship and serve.

**40:1–43:27** This vision came to Ezekiel in 573 B.C. Chapters 40–43 give the Temple's measurements and then describe how it would be filled with God's glory. Because Ezekiel was a priest, he would have been familiar with the furnishings and ceremonies of Solomon's Temple. As in Revelation 11:1, 2, the command to "measure" defines the areas God has marked out for special use. As you read all these details, remember that God is sovereign over all our worship and over the timetable for restoring the faithful to himself.

**40:3, 4** Who was this man? He was obviously not a human being, so he may have been the angel in 9:1-11 or one like him. Some say he may have been Christ himself because he speaks as God had been speaking to Ezekiel, calling him "son of man."

3½ feet* thick. This entry room was at the inner end of the gateway structure, facing toward the Temple.

¹⁰There were three guard alcoves on each side of the gateway passage. Each had the same measurements, and the dividing walls separating them were also identical. ¹¹The man measured the gateway entrance, which was 17½ feet* wide at the opening and 22¾ feet* wide in the gateway passage. ¹²In front of each of the guard alcoves was a 21-inch* curb. The alcoves themselves were 10½ feet* on each side.

¹³Then he measured the entire width of the gateway, measuring the distance between the back walls of facing guard alcoves; this distance was 43¾ feet.* ¹⁴He measured the dividing walls all along the inside of the gateway up to the entry room of the gateway; this distance was 105 feet.* ¹⁵The full length of the gateway passage was 87½ feet* from one end to the other. ¹⁶There were recessed windows that narrowed inward through the walls of the guard alcoves and their dividing walls. There were also windows in the entry room. The surfaces of the dividing walls were decorated with carved palm trees.

### The Outer Courtyard

¹⁷Then the man brought me through the gateway into the outer courtyard of the Temple. A stone pavement ran along the walls of the courtyard, and thirty rooms were built against the walls, opening onto the pavement. ¹⁸This pavement flanked the gates and extended out from the walls into the courtyard the same distance as the gateway entrance. This was the lower pavement. ¹⁹Then the man measured across the Temple's outer courtyard between the outer and inner gateways; the distance was 175 feet.*

### The North Gateway

²⁰The man measured the gateway on the north just like the one on the east. ²¹Here, too, there were three guard alcoves on each side, with dividing walls and an entry room. All the measurements matched those of the east gateway. The gateway passage was 87½ feet long and 43¾ feet wide between the back walls of facing guard alcoves. ²²The windows, the entry room, and the palm tree decorations were identical to those in the east gateway. There were seven steps leading up to the gateway entrance, and the entry room was at the inner end of the gateway passage. ²³Here on the north side, just as on the east, there was another gateway leading to the Temple's inner courtyard directly opposite this outer gateway. The distance between the two gateways was 175 feet.

### The South Gateway

²⁴Then the man took me around to the south gateway and measured its various parts, and they were exactly the same as in the others. ²⁵It had windows along the walls as the others did, and there was an entry room where the gateway passage opened into the outer courtyard. And like the others, the gateway passage was 87½ feet long and 43¾ feet wide between the back walls of facing guard alcoves. ²⁶This gateway also had a stairway of seven steps leading up to it, and an entry room at the inner end, and palm tree decorations along the dividing walls. ²⁷And here again, directly opposite the outer gateway, was another gateway that led into the inner courtyard. The distance between the two gateways was 175 feet.

### Gateways to the Inner Courtyard

²⁸Then the man took me to the south gateway leading into the inner courtyard. He measured it, and it had the same measurements as the other gateways. ²⁹Its guard alcoves, dividing walls, and entry room were the same size as those in the others. It also had windows along its walls and in the entry room. And like the others, the gateway passage was 87½ feet long and 43¾ feet wide. ³⁰(The entry rooms of the gateways leading into the inner courtyard were 14 feet* across and 43¾ feet wide.) ³¹The entry room to the south gateway faced into the outer courtyard. It had palm tree decorations on its columns, and there were eight steps leading to its entrance.

³²Then he took me to the east gateway leading to the inner courtyard. He measured it, and it had the same measurements as the other gateways. ³³Its guard alcoves, dividing walls, and entry room were the same size as those of the others, and there were windows along the

40:9a Hebrew 8 cubits [4.2 meters].   40:9b Hebrew 2 cubits [1.1 meters].   40:11a Hebrew 10 cubits [5.3 meters].
40:11b Hebrew 13 cubits [6.9 meters].   40:12a Hebrew 1 cubit [53 centimeters].   40:12b Hebrew 6 cubits
[3.2 meters].   40:13 Hebrew 25 cubits [13.3 meters]; also in 40:21, 25, 29, 30, 33, 36.   40:14 Hebrew 60 cubits
[31.8 meters]. Greek version reads 20 cubits [35 feet or 10.6 meters]. The meaning of the Hebrew in this verse is
uncertain.   40:15 Hebrew 50 cubits [26.5 meters]; also in 40:21, 25, 29, 33, 36.   40:19 Hebrew 100 cubits
[53 meters]; also in 40:23, 27, 47.   40:30 As in 40:9, which reads 8 cubits [14 feet or 4.2 meters]; here the Hebrew
reads 5 cubits [8 3/4 feet or 2.7 meters]. Some Hebrew manuscripts and the Greek version lack this entire verse.

walls and in the entry room. The gateway passage measured 87½ feet long and 43¾ feet wide. 34Its entry room faced into the outer courtyard. It had palm tree decorations on its columns, and there were eight steps leading to its entrance.

35Then he took me around to the north gateway leading to the inner courtyard. He measured it, and it had the same measurements as the other gateways. 36The guard alcoves, dividing walls, and entry room of this gateway had the same measurements as in the others and the same window arrangements. The gateway passage measured 87½ feet long and 43¾ feet wide. 37Its entry room faced into the outer courtyard, and it had palm tree decorations on the columns. There were eight steps leading to its entrance.

### Rooms for Preparing Sacrifices

38A door led from the entry room of one of the inner gateways into a side room, where the meat for sacrifices was washed. 39On each side of this entry room were two tables, where the sacrificial animals were slaughtered for the burnt offerings, sin offerings, and guilt offerings. 40Outside the entry room, on each side of the stairs going up to the north entrance, were two more tables. 41So there were eight tables in all—four inside and four outside—where the sacrifices were cut up and prepared. 42There were also four tables of finished stone for preparation of the burnt offerings, each 31½ inches square and 21 inches high.* On these tables were placed the butchering knives and other implements for slaughtering the sacrificial animals. 43There were hooks, each 3 inches* long, fastened to the foyer walls. The sacrificial meat was laid on the tables.

### Rooms for the Priests

44Inside the inner courtyard were two rooms,* one beside the north gateway, facing south, and the other beside the south* gateway, facing north. 45And the man said to me, "The room beside the north inner gate is for the priests who supervise the Temple maintenance. 46The room beside the south inner gate is for the priests in charge of the altar—the descendants of Zadok—for they alone of all the Levites may approach the LORD to minister to him."

### The Inner Courtyard and Temple

47Then the man measured the inner courtyard, and it was a square, 175 feet wide and 175 feet across. The altar stood in the courtyard in front of the Temple. 48Then he brought me to the entry room of the Temple. He measured the walls on either side of the opening to the entry room, and they were 8¾ feet thick. The entrance itself was 24½ feet wide, and the walls on each side of the entrance were an additional 5¼ feet long.* 49The entry room was 35 feet* wide and 21 feet* deep. There were ten steps leading up to it, with a column on each side.

**41** After that, the man brought me into the sanctuary of the Temple. He measured the walls on either side of its doorway, and they were 10½ feet* thick. 2The doorway was 17½ feet* wide, and the walls on each side of it were 8¾ feet* long. The sanctuary itself was 70 feet long and 35 feet wide.*

3Then he went beyond the sanctuary into the inner room. He measured the walls on either side of its entrance, and they were 3½ feet* thick. The entrance was 10½ feet wide, and the walls on each side of the entrance were 12¼ feet* long. 4The inner room of the sanctuary was 35 feet* long and 35 feet wide. "This," he told me, "is the Most Holy Place."

5Then he measured the wall of the Temple, and it was 10½ feet thick. There was a row of rooms along the outside wall; each room was 7 feet* wide. 6These side rooms were built in three levels, one above the other, with thirty rooms on each level. The supports for these side rooms rested on exterior ledges on the Temple wall; they did not extend into the wall. 7Each

**Cross-references (right margin):**
40:35 Ezek 44:4; 47:2
40:38 1 Kgs 6:8; 1 Chr 28:12; 2 Chr 4:6; Neh 13:5, 9; Ezek 41:10; 42:13
40:39 Lev 1:2-17; 4:2-3; 5:6; 6:6; 7:1-2; Ezek 46:2
40:42 Exod 20:25
40:44 1 Chr 6:31-32; 16:41-43; 25:1-7
40:45 Lev 8:35; 1 Chr 9:23
40:46 1 Kgs 2:35
40:48 1 Kgs 6:3
40:49 Jer 52:17-23; Rev 3:12
41:1 Ezek 40:2-3, 17
41:2 1 Kgs 6:2, 17; 2 Chr 3:3
41:4 Exod 26:33-34; 1 Kgs 6:20; 2 Chr 3:8; Heb 9:3-8
41:5 1 Kgs 6:5
41:6 1 Kgs 6:6, 10
41:7 1 Kgs 6:8

---

40:42 Hebrew 1½ cubits [80 centimeters] long and 1½ cubits wide and 1 cubit [53 centimeters] high.   40:43 Hebrew a handbreadth [8 centimeters].   40:44a As in Greek version; Hebrew reads rooms for singers.   40:44b As in Greek version; Hebrew reads east.   40:48 As in Greek version, which reads The entrance was 14 cubits [7.4 meters] wide, and the walls of the entrance were 3 cubits [1.6 meters] on each side; Hebrew lacks 14 cubits wide, and the walls of the entrance were.   40:49a Hebrew 20 cubits [10.6 meters].   40:49b As in Greek version, which reads 12 cubits [21 feet or 6.4 meters]; Hebrew reads 11 cubits [19¼ feet or 5.8 meters].   41:1 Hebrew 6 cubits [3.2 meters]; also in 41:3, 5.   41:2a Hebrew 10 cubits [5.3 meters].   41:2b Hebrew 5 cubits [2.7 meters]; also in 41:9, 11.   41:2c Hebrew 40 cubits [21.2 meters] long and 20 cubits [10.6 meters] wide.   41:3a Hebrew 2 cubits [1.1 meters].   41:3b Hebrew 7 cubits [3.7 meters].   41:4 Hebrew 20 cubits [10.6 meters]; also in 41:4b, 10.   41:5 Hebrew 4 cubits [2.1 meters].

---

**40:38, 39** The washing of the sacrifices was done according to the standards of preparation established in Leviticus 1:6-9. This washing was part of the process of presenting an acceptable sacrifice to God.

**41:4** God's holiness is a central theme throughout both the Old and New Testaments. The Most Holy Place was the innermost room in the Temple (Exodus 26:33, 34). This was where the Ark of the Covenant was kept and where God's glory was said to dwell. This room was entered only once a year by the high priest, who performed a ceremony to atone for the nation's sins.

level was wider than the one below it, corresponding to the narrowing of the Temple wall as it rose higher. A stairway led up from the bottom level through the middle level to the top level.

41:8
Ezek 40:5

⁸I saw that the Temple was built on a terrace, which provided a foundation for the side rooms. This terrace was 10½ feet* high. ⁹The outer wall of the Temple's side rooms was 8¾ feet thick. This left an open area between these side rooms ¹⁰and the row of rooms along the outer wall of the inner courtyard. This open area was 35 feet wide, and it went all the way around the Temple. ¹¹Two doors opened from the side rooms into the terrace yard, which was 8¾ feet wide. One door faced north and the other south.

41:10
Ezek 40:17

¹²A large building stood on the west, facing the Temple courtyard. It was 122½ feet wide and 157½ feet long, and its walls were 8¾ feet* thick. ¹³Then the man measured the Temple, and it was 175 feet* long. The courtyard around the building, including its walls, was an additional 175 feet in length. ¹⁴The inner courtyard to the east of the Temple was also 175 feet wide. ¹⁵The building to the west, including its two walls, was also 175 feet wide.

41:12
Ezek 42:1
Rev 21:27;
22:14-15
41:13
Ezek 40:47
41:15
Ezek 42:1, 10, 13
41:16
1 Kgs 6:4, 15
41:18
1 Kgs 6:29; 7:36
2 Chr 3:5
Ezek 10:18
41:19
Ezek 1:10; 10:14

The sanctuary, the inner room, and the entry room of the Temple ¹⁶were all paneled with wood, as were the frames of the recessed windows. The inner walls of the Temple were paneled with wood above and below the windows. ¹⁷The space above the door leading into the inner room, and its walls inside and out, were also paneled. ¹⁸All the walls were decorated with carvings of cherubim, each with two faces, and there was a carving of a palm tree between each of the cherubim. ¹⁹One face—that of a man—looked toward the palm tree on one side. The other face—that of a young lion—looked toward the palm tree on the other side. The figures were carved all along the inside of the Temple, ²⁰from the floor to the top of the walls, including the outer wall of the sanctuary.

41:21
1 Kgs 6:33
41:22
Exod 30:1-3, 8
Ezek 44:16
Mal 1:7, 12
Rev 8:3

²¹There were square columns at the entrance to the sanctuary, and the ones at the entrance of the Most Holy Place were similar. ²²There was an altar made of wood, 5¼ feet high and 3½ feet across.* Its corners, base, and sides were all made of wood. "This," the man told me, "is the table that stands in the Lord's presence."

41:23
1 Kgs 6:31-35
41:24
1 Kgs 6:34
41:26
Ezek 40:7-12

²³Both the sanctuary and the Most Holy Place had double doorways, ²⁴each with two swinging doors. ²⁵The doors leading into the sanctuary were decorated with carved cherubim and palm trees, just as on the walls. And there was a wooden roof at the front of the entry room to the Temple. ²⁶On both sides of the entry room were recessed windows decorated with carved palm trees. The side rooms along the outside wall also had roofs.

### Rooms for the Priests

42:1
Ezek 40:2-3, 17;
41:9, 12-15
42:2
Ezek 41:13
42:3
Ezek 40:17; 41:10
42:4
Ezek 46:19

**42** Then the man led me out of the Temple courtyard by way of the north gateway. We entered the outer courtyard and came to a group of rooms against the north wall of the inner courtyard. ²This structure, whose entrance opened toward the north, was 175 feet* long and 87½ feet* wide. ³One block of rooms overlooked the 35-foot* width of the inner courtyard. Another block of rooms looked out onto the pavement of the outer courtyard. The two blocks were built three levels high and stood across from each other. ⁴Between the two blocks of rooms ran a walkway 17½ feet* wide. It extended the entire 175 feet of the complex,* and all the doors faced north. ⁵Each of the two upper levels of rooms was narrower than the one beneath it because the upper levels had to allow space for walkways in front of them. ⁶Since there were three levels and they did not have supporting columns as in the courtyards, each of the upper levels was set back from the level beneath it.

42:6
Ezek 41:6
42:7
Ezek 41:13-14
42:9
Ezek 44:5; 46:19

⁷There was an outer wall that separated the rooms from the outer courtyard; it was 87½ feet long. ⁸This wall added length to the outer block of rooms, which extended for only 87½ feet, while the inner block—the rooms toward the Temple—extended for 175 feet. ⁹There was an eastern entrance from the outer courtyard to these rooms.

¹⁰On the south* side of the Temple there were two blocks of rooms just south of the inner courtyard between the Temple and the outer courtyard. These rooms were arranged just like the rooms on the north. ¹¹There was a walkway between the two blocks of rooms just like the complex on the north side of the Temple. This complex of rooms was the same length and

41:8 Hebrew *1 rod, 6 cubits* [3.2 meters].    41:12 Hebrew *70 cubits* [37.1 meters] *wide and 90 cubits* [47.7 meters] *long, and its walls were 5 cubits* [2.7 meters] *thick.*    41:13 Hebrew *100 cubits* [53 meters]; also in 41:13b, 14, 15.    41:22 Hebrew *3 cubits* [1.6 meters] *high and 2 cubits* [1.1 meters] *across.*    42:2a Hebrew *100 cubits* [53 meters]; also in 42:8.    42:2b Hebrew *50 cubits* [26.5 meters]; also in 42:7, 8.    42:3 Hebrew *20-cubit* [10.6-meter].    42:4a Hebrew *10 cubits* [5.3 meters].    42:4b As in Greek and Syriac versions, which read *its length was 100 cubits* [53 meters]; Hebrew reads *and a passage 1 cubit* [18 inches or 53 centimeters] *wide.*    42:10 As in Greek version; Hebrew reads *east.*

41:18  Cherubim are mighty angels.
41:22  The dimensions given would fit either the table of the    Bread of the Presence (Exodus 25:30) or the incense altar (Exodus 30:1-3).

width as the other one, and it had the same entrances and doors. The dimensions of each were identical. [12]So there was an entrance in the wall facing the doors of the inner block of rooms, and another on the east at the end of the interior walkway.

[13]Then the man told me, "These rooms that overlook the Temple from the north and south are holy. Here the priests who offer sacrifices to the LORD will eat the most holy offerings. And because these rooms are holy, they will be used to store the sacred offerings—the grain offerings, sin offerings, and guilt offerings. [14]When the priests leave the sanctuary, they must not go directly to the outer courtyard. They must first take off the clothes they wore while ministering, because these clothes are holy. They must put on other clothes before entering the parts of the building complex open to the public."

[15]When the man had finished measuring the inside of the Temple area, he led me out through the east gateway to measure the entire perimeter. [16]He measured the east side with his measuring rod, and it was 875 feet long.* [17]Then he measured the north side, and it was also 875 feet. [18]The south side was also 875 feet, [19]and the west side was also 875 feet. [20]So the area was 875 feet on each side with a wall all around it to separate what was holy from what was common.

## The LORD's Glory Returns

**43** After this, the man brought me back around to the east gateway. [2]Suddenly, the glory of the God of Israel appeared from the east. The sound of his coming was like the roar of rushing waters, and the whole landscape shone with his glory. [3]This vision was just like the others I had seen, first by the Kebar River and then when he came to destroy Jerusalem. I fell face down on the ground. [4]And the glory of the LORD came into the Temple through the east gateway.

[5]Then the Spirit took me up and brought me into the inner courtyard, and the glory of the LORD filled the Temple. [6]And I heard someone speaking to me from within the Temple, while the man who had been measuring stood beside me. [7]The LORD said to me, "Son of man, this is the place of my throne and the place where I will rest my feet. I will live here forever among the people of Israel. They and their kings will not defile my holy name any longer by their adulterous worship of other gods or by honoring the relics of their kings who have died. [8]They put their idol altars right next to mine with only a wall between them and me. They defiled my holy name by such detestable sin, so I consumed them in my anger. [9]Now let them stop worshiping other gods and honoring the relics of their kings, and I will live among them forever.

[10]"Son of man, describe to the people of Israel the Temple I have shown you, so they will be ashamed of all their sins. Let them study its plan, [11]and they will be ashamed* of what they have done. Describe to them all the specifications of the Temple—including its entrances and exits—and everything else about it. Tell them about its decrees and laws. Write down all these specifications and decrees as they watch so they will be sure to remember and follow them. [12]And this is the basic law of the Temple: absolute holiness! The entire top of the mountain where the Temple is built is holy. Yes, this is the basic law of the Temple.

### Cross-references (margin)

**42:13** Lev 6:25, 29; 7:6; 10:13-17; Num 18:9-10
**42:14** Exod 29:4-9; Isa 61:10; Zech 3:4-5
**42:15** Ezek 43:1
**42:16** Ezek 40:3, 5
**43:1** Ezek 10:19; 40:6; 44:1; 46:1
**43:2** Isa 6:3; Ezek 10:4, 18-19; Rev 1:15; 18:1
**43:3** Jer 1:10; Ezek 3:23
**43:4** Ezek 44:2
**43:5** 1 Kgs 8:10-11; 2 Cor 12:2-4
**43:7** Lev 26:30; Ps 47:8; Jer 16:18
**43:9** Ezek 18:30, 31
**43:10** Ezek 40:4
**43:11** Ezek 11:20; 12:3; 36:27; 44:5
**43:12** Ezek 40:2

**42:16** As in 45:2 and in Greek version at 42:17, which reads *500 cubits* [265 meters]; Hebrew reads *500 rods* [5,250 feet or 1,590 meters]; similarly in 42:17, 18, 19, 20.   **43:11** As in Greek version; Hebrew reads *if they are ashamed.*

---

**42:14** Approaching our holy God must not be taken lightly. The holy garments the priests were required to wear may symbolize the importance of having a holy heart when approaching God. The priests had to wear these special clothes in order to minister in the inner rooms of the Temple. Because the garments were holy, the priests had to change their clothes before going back out to the public.

**42:16-20** The perfect symmetry of Ezekiel's Temple may represent the order and harmony in God's future Kingdom.

**43:1ff** This is the culmination of chapters 40–42 because God's glory returns to the Temple. It reverses the negative tone of the book and serves as a fitting end for all the passages dealing with the blessings reserved for the restored remnant. All true believers should long for that moment when God's name will finally be glorified and he will live among his people forever.

**43:2** In 11:23, God's glory stopped over the Mount of Olives, to the east of Jerusalem, before leaving the city. This prophecy states that his glory would also return from the east.

**43:2-4** It was completely devastating for Ezekiel when God's glory departed (11:23) from his Temple, but he was overwhelmed with awe and joy beyond expression when he saw God's glory return.

**43:3** The Kebar River connected with the Euphrates River and was the location of a Jewish settlement of exiles in Babylonia.

**43:9-11** God's departure from the city had been a signal for the destruction of the city and the Temple. Now for God to return, his conditions had to be met: Idolatry had to be removed. Some commentators feel these verses indicate that Ezekiel was commanding the people of his day to build this Temple according to the designs and regulations that the angelic architect had given. But the people never repented and the conditions were not met, so the fulfillment was postponed.

**43:12** The basic law of God's Temple was holiness. In all he does, God is holy, perfect, and blameless. There is no trace of evil or sin in him. Just as God is holy, so we are to be holy (Leviticus 19:2; 1 Peter 1:15, 16). People are holy when they are devoted to

**43:13**
Exod 27:1-8
2 Chr 4:1

**43:15**
Exod 27:2
Lev 9:9
1 Kgs 1:49-50
Ps 118:27

**43:16**
Exod 27:1

**43:17**
Exod 20:26
Ezek 40:6

**43:18**
Exod 40:29
Lev 1:5, 11
Ezek 2:1
Heb 9:21-22

**43:19**
1 Kgs 2:35
Ezek 40:46; 44:15
Heb 7:27

**43:20**
Lev 8:15; 9:9

**43:21**
Exod 29:14
Lev 4:11-12
Heb 13:11

**43:23**
Exod 29:1

**43:24**
Lev 2:13
Mark 9:49-50
Col 4:6

**43:25**
Exod 29:35-37
Lev 8:33, 35

**43:27**
Lev 3:1; 9:1; 17:5
Ezek 20:40

**44:2**
Ezek 43:4

**44:3**
Gen 31:54
Exod 24:9-11
Zech 6:12-13

**44:4**
Ezek 1:28; 3:23

**44:5**
Deut 12:32; 32:46
Ezek 40:4;
43:10-11

**44:6**
Ezek 2:5-7; 3:9
1 Pet 4:3

## The Altar

13 "These are the measurements of the altar*: There is a gutter all around the altar 21 inches deep and 21 inches wide,* with a curb 9 inches* wide around its edge. And this is the height* of the altar: 14From the gutter the altar rises 3½ feet* to a lower ledge that surrounds the altar and is 21 inches* wide. From the lower ledge the altar rises 7 feet* to the upper ledge that is also 21 inches wide. 15The top of the altar, the hearth, rises another 7 feet higher, with a horn rising up from each of the four corners. 16The top of the altar is square, measuring 21 feet by 21 feet.* 17The upper ledge also forms a square, measuring 24½ feet by 24½ feet,* with a 21-inch gutter and a 10½-inch curb* all around the edge. There are steps going up the east side of the altar."

18Then he said to me, "Son of man, this is what the Sovereign LORD says: These will be the regulations for the burning of offerings and the sprinkling of blood when the altar is built. 19At that time, the Levitical priests of the family of Zadok, who minister before me, are to be given a young bull for a sin offering, says the Sovereign LORD. 20You will take some of its blood and smear it on the four horns of the altar, the four corners of the upper ledge, and the curb that runs around that ledge. This will cleanse and make atonement for the altar. 21Then take the young bull for the sin offering and burn it at the appointed place outside the Temple area.

22"On the second day, sacrifice as a sin offering a young male goat that has no physical defects. Then cleanse and make atonement for the altar again, just as you did with the young bull. 23When you have finished the cleansing ceremony, offer another young bull that has no defects and a perfect ram from the flock. 24You are to present them to the LORD, and the priests are to sprinkle salt on them and offer them as a burnt offering to the LORD.

25"Every day for seven days a male goat, a young bull, and a ram from the flock will be sacrificed as a sin offering. None of these animals may have physical defects of any kind. 26Do this each day for seven days to cleanse and make atonement for the altar, thus setting it apart for holy use. 27On the eighth day, and on each day afterward, the priests will sacrifice on the altar the burnt offerings and peace offerings of the people. Then I will accept you. I, the Sovereign LORD, have spoken!"

## The Prince, Levites, and Priests

**44** Then the man brought me back to the east gateway in the outer wall of the Temple area, but it was closed. 2And the LORD said to me, "This gate must remain closed; it will never again be opened. No one will ever open it and pass through, for the LORD, the God of Israel, has entered here. Therefore, it must always remain shut. 3Only the prince himself may sit inside this gateway to feast in the LORD's presence. But he may come and go only through the entry room of the gateway."

4Then the man brought me through the north gateway to the front of the Temple. I looked and saw that the glory of the LORD filled the Temple of the LORD, and I fell face down on the ground.

5And the LORD said to me, "Son of man, take careful notice. Use your eyes and ears, and listen to everything I tell you about the regulations concerning the LORD's Temple. Take careful note of the procedures for using the Temple's entrances and exits. 6And give these rebels, the people of Israel, this message from the Sovereign LORD: O people of Israel, enough of

---

**43:13a** Hebrew *measurements of the altar in long cubits, each being a cubit* [18 inches or 45 centimeters] *and a handbreadth* [3 inches or 8 centimeters] *in length.*   **43:13b** Hebrew *a cubit* [53 centimeters] *deep and a cubit wide.*   **43:13c** Hebrew *1 span* [23 centimeters].   **43:13d** As in Greek version; Hebrew reads *base.*   **43:14a** Hebrew *2 cubits* [1.1 meters].   **43:14b** Hebrew *1 cubit* [53 centimeters]; also in 43:14d.   **43:14c** Hebrew *4 cubits* [2.1 meters]; also in 43:15.   **43:16** Hebrew *12 cubits* [6.4 meters] *long and 12 cubits wide.*   **43:17a** Hebrew *14 cubits* [7.4 meters] *long and 14 cubits wide.*   **43:17b** Hebrew *a gutter of 1 cubit* [53 centimeters] *and a curb of 1/2 a cubit* [27 centimeters].

---

God and separated from sin. It is important to understand the concept of holiness in order that we may progress in our Christian growth.

**43:18-27** This vision was simultaneously flashing back to Mount Sinai and forward to Mount Calvary. When the people returned from exile, they would seek forgiveness through the sacrificial system instituted in Moses' day. Today, Christ's death has made the forgiveness of our sins possible, making us acceptable to God (Hebrews 9:9-15). God stands ready to forgive those who come to him in faith.

**44:2** Why was this east gate to remain closed? Several reasons have been suggested: (1) This was the gate through which God entered the Temple, and no one else could walk where God had

(43:4); (2) the closed gate indicated that God would never again leave the Temple (10:19; 11:23); (3) it would prevent people from worshiping the sun as it rises in the east from within the Temple grounds (8:16).

**44:3** Although Christ is called a prince (37:25), this prince is probably not Christ because he offers a sacrifice to God (46:4) and he can enter only by the "entry room of the gateway." He is a princely ruler of the city, but he is distinguished from other princes because he will be just and fair (see 45:9). Some, however, have understood this prince to be a prophetic image that anticipates the coming of Christ, who would offer himself as a sacrifice to God.

your detestable sins! [7] You have brought uncircumcised foreigners into my sanctuary— people who have no heart for God. In this way, you defiled my Temple even as you offered me my food, the fat and blood of sacrifices. In addition to all your other detestable sins, you have broken my covenant. [8] Instead of safeguarding my sacred rituals, you have hired foreigners to take charge of my sanctuary.

[9] "So this is what the Sovereign LORD says: No foreigners, including those who live among the people of Israel, will enter my sanctuary if they have not been circumcised and have not surrendered themselves to the LORD. [10] And the men of the tribe of Levi who abandoned me when Israel strayed away from me to worship idols* must bear the consequences of their unfaithfulness. [11] They may still be Temple guards and gatekeepers, and they may slaughter the animals brought for burnt offerings and be present to help the people. [12] But they encouraged my people to worship idols, causing Israel to fall into deep sin. So I have taken a solemn oath that they must bear the consequences for their sins, says the Sovereign LORD. [13] They may not approach me to minister as priests. They may not touch any of my holy things or the holy offerings, for they must bear the shame of all the detestable sins they have committed. [14] They are to serve as the Temple caretakers, taking charge of the maintenance work and performing general duties.

[15] "However, the Levitical priests of the family of Zadok continued to minister faithfully in the Temple when Israel abandoned me for idols. These men will serve as my ministers. They will stand in my presence and offer the fat and blood of the sacrifices, says the Sovereign LORD. [16] They alone will enter my sanctuary and approach my table to serve me. They will fulfill all my requirements.

[17] "When they enter the gateway to the inner courtyard, they must wear only linen clothing. They must wear no wool while on duty in the inner courtyard or in the Temple itself. [18] They must wear linen turbans and linen undergarments. They must not wear anything that would cause them to perspire. [19] When they return to the outer courtyard where the people are, they must take off the clothes they wear while ministering to me. They must leave them in the sacred rooms and put on other clothes so they do not endanger anyone by transmitting holiness to them through this clothing.

[20] "They must neither shave their heads nor let their hair grow too long. Instead, they must trim it regularly. [21] The priests must not drink wine before entering the inner courtyard. [22] They may choose their wives only from among the virgins of Israel or the widows of the priests. They may not marry other widows or divorced women. [23] They will teach my people the difference between what is holy and what is common, what is ceremonially clean and unclean.

[24] "They will serve as judges to resolve any disagreements among my people. Their decisions must be based on my regulations. And the priests themselves must obey my instructions and decrees at all the sacred festivals, and see to it that the Sabbaths are set apart as holy days.

[25] "A priest must not defile himself by being in the presence of a dead person unless it is his father, mother, child, brother, or unmarried sister. In such cases it is permitted. [26] Even then, he can return to his Temple duties only after being ceremonially cleansed and then waiting for seven days. [27] The first day he returns to work and enters the inner courtyard and the sanctuary, he must offer a sin offering for himself, says the Sovereign LORD.

[28] "The priests will not have any property or possession of land, for I alone am their special possession. [29] Their food will come from the gifts and sacrifices brought to the Temple by the people—the grain offerings, the sin offerings, and the guilt offerings. Whatever anyone

**44:10** The Hebrew term (literally *round things*) probably alludes to dung; also in 44:12.

**44:7**
Gen 17:14
Exod 12:43-49
Lev 22:25; 26:41
Jer 4:4; 9:26
**44:8**
Num 18:7
**44:9**
Joel 3:17
Zech 14:21
**44:10**
Num 18:23
2 Kgs 23:8-9
Ezek 22:26
**44:11**
Num 3:5-37;
4:1-33; 16:8-9;
18:2, 6
1 Chr 26:1
2 Chr 29:34
**44:12**
2 Kgs 16:10-16
Ezek 14:3-4
Hos 4:6; 5:1
**44:13**
Num 18:3
2 Kgs 23:9
**44:14**
Num 18:4, 6
1 Chr 23:28, 32
**44:15**
Num 18:7
Jer 33:18-22
Ezek 48:11
**44:17**
Exod 39:27-29
**44:18**
Exod 28:40, 42
**44:19**
Lev 16:23-24
**44:20**
Lev 21:5
Num 6:5
**44:21**
Lev 10:8-9
**44:22**
Lev 21:7, 13-15
**44:23**
Lev 10:10
Deut 33:10
**44:24**
Deut 17:8-9; 21:5
2 Chr 19:8-10
**44:25**
Lev 21:1-3
**44:26**
Num 19:13-19
**44:27**
Num 6:9-11
**44:28**
Num 18:20
Deut 10:9
Josh 13:33
**44:29**
Lev 27:21, 28
Num 18:9, 14-15
Josh 13:14

**44:9** Unbelievers would not be allowed to enter the Temple. Ezekiel's vision was for a restored, purified worship in which only those who prepared themselves physically and spiritually could participate. In 47:22, 23, we find that people from other nations are allowed to join in worship by accepting the standards of faith and practice declared in the law (see Leviticus 24:22; Numbers 15:29).

**44:15** Zadok's descendants are mentioned because many of the priests in Zadok's line had remained faithful to God, while others had become corrupt. Zadok supported God's choice of Solomon to succeed David and was therefore appointed high priest during

his reign (1 Kings 1:32-35; 2:27, 35). Zadok's descendants were considered the true priestly line throughout the time between the Old and New Testaments.

**44:20-31** These laws were originally given to God's people in the wilderness. They are recorded in the books of Exodus and Leviticus. They reveal the importance of approaching God respectfully, and they give guidelines for the priests to live above reproach so they could carry out their responsibility to teach the people "the difference between what is holy and what is common, what is ceremonially clean and unclean" (44:23).

44:30
Num 15:20; 18:12
2 Chr 31:4-6, 10

44:31
Lev 22:8
Deut 14:21

45:1
Josh 13:7; 14:2
Ps 16:5-6
Ezek 47:21; 48:8-9

45:2
Ezek 42:16-20

45:3
Ezek 48:10

45:4
Num 16:5
Ezek 40:45;
44:13-14; 48:10-11

45:5
Ezek 48:12-14

45:6
Ezek 48:15-16

45:7
Ezek 46:16-18;
48:21-22

45:8
Josh 11:23
Isa 11:3-5
Jer 23:5-6
Ezek 22:27; 46:18

45:9
Neh 5:1-5
Jer 6:7; 22:3
Zech 8:16

45:10
Lev 19:35-36
Deut 25:13-15
Prov 11:1; 16:11
Mic 6:10-11

45:12
Exod 30:13

45:15
Lev 1:4; 6:30

45:17
Lev 23:1-44
1 Kgs 8:62-64
2 Chr 31:3
Ezek 46:4-12

sets apart* for the LORD will belong to the priests. ³⁰The first of the ripe fruits and all the gifts brought to the LORD will go to the priests. The first samples of each grain harvest and the first of your flour must also be given to the priests so the LORD will bless your homes. ³¹The priests may not eat meat from any bird or animal that dies a natural death or that dies after being attacked by another animal.

### Division of the Land

**45** "When you divide the land among the tribes of Israel, you must set aside a section for the LORD as his holy portion. This piece of land will be 8⅓ miles long and 6⅔ miles wide.* The entire area will be holy. ²A section of this land, measuring 875 feet by 875 feet,* will be set aside for the Temple. An additional strip of land 87½ feet* wide is to be left empty all around it. ³Within the larger sacred area, measure out a portion of land 8⅓ miles long and 3⅓ miles wide.* Within it the sanctuary of the Most Holy Place will be located. ⁴This area will be holy, set aside for the priests who minister to the LORD in the sanctuary. They will use it for their homes, and my Temple will be located within it. ⁵The strip of sacred land next to it, also 8⅓ miles long and 3⅓ miles wide, will be a living area for the Levites who work at the Temple. It will be their possession and a place for their towns.*

⁶"Adjacent to the larger sacred area will be a section of land 8⅓ miles long and 1⅔ miles wide.* This will be set aside for a city where anyone in Israel can live.

⁷"Two special sections of land will be set apart for the prince. One section will share a border with the east side of the sacred lands and city, and the second section will share a border on the west side. Then the far eastern and western borders of the prince's lands will line up with the eastern and western boundaries of the tribal areas. ⁸These sections of land will be the prince's allotment. Then my princes will no longer oppress and rob my people; they will assign the rest of the land to the people, giving an allotment to each tribe.

### Rules for the Princes

⁹"For this is what the Sovereign LORD says: Enough, you princes of Israel! Stop your violence and oppression and do what is just and right. Quit robbing and cheating my people out of their land. Stop expelling them from their homes, says the Sovereign LORD. ¹⁰Use only honest weights and scales and honest measures, both dry and liquid.* ¹¹The homer* will be your standard unit for measuring volume. The ephah and the bath* will each measure one-tenth of a homer. ¹²The standard unit for weight will be the silver shekel.* One shekel will consist of twenty gerahs, and sixty shekels will be equal to one mina.*

### Special Offerings and Celebrations

¹³"You must give this tax to the prince: one bushel of wheat or barley for every 60* you harvest, ¹⁴one percent of your olive oil,* ¹⁵and one sheep or goat for every 200 in your flocks in Israel. These will be the grain offerings, burnt offerings, and peace offerings that will make atonement for the people who bring them, says the Sovereign LORD. ¹⁶All the people of Israel must join in bringing these offerings to the prince. ¹⁷The prince will be required to provide offerings that are given at the religious festivals, the new moon celebrations, the Sabbath days, and all other similar occasions. He will provide the sin offerings, burnt offerings, grain offerings, liquid offerings, and peace offerings to purify the people of Israel, making them right with the LORD.*

**44:29** The Hebrew term used here refers to the complete consecration of things or people to the LORD, either by destroying them or by giving them as an offering. **45:1** As in Greek version, which reads *25,000 cubits* [13.3 kilometers] *long and 20,000 cubits* [10.6 kilometers] *wide;* Hebrew reads *25,000 cubits long and 10,000 cubits* [3¹/₃ miles or 5.3 kilometers] *wide.* Compare 45:3, 5; 48:9. **45:2a** Hebrew *500 cubits* [265 meters] *by 500 cubits, a square.* **45:2b** Hebrew *50 cubits* [26.5 meters]. **45:3** Hebrew *25,000 cubits* [13.3 kilometers] *long and 10,000 cubits* [5.3 kilometers] *wide;* also in 45:5. **45:5** As in Greek version; Hebrew reads *They will have as their possession 20 rooms.* **45:6** Hebrew *25,000 cubits* [13.3 kilometers] *long and 5,000 cubits* [2.65 kilometers] *wide.* **45:10** Hebrew *use honest scales, an honest ephah, and an honest bath.* **45:11a** The *homer* measures about 40 gallons or 182 liters. **45:11b** The *ephah* is a dry measure; the *bath* is a liquid measure. **45:12a** The *shekel* weighs about 0.4 ounces or 11 grams. **45:12b** Elsewhere the *mina* is equated to 50 shekels. **45:13** Hebrew 1/6 *of an ephah from each homer of wheat and* 1/6 *of an ephah from each homer of barley.* **45:14** Hebrew *the portion of oil, measured by the bath, is* 1/10 *of a bath from each cor, which consists of 10 baths or 1 homer, for 10 baths are equivalent to a homer.* **45:17** Or *to make atonement for the people of Israel.*

---

**45:1-7** The land allotted to the Temple was in the center of the nation. God is central to life. He must be our first priority.

**45:9-12** Violence and oppression were two of the major social sins of the nation during this time (see Amos 5:10-13). In the new economy there would be plenty of land for the "prince" (45:7, 8) and no longer any basis for greed. Therefore, God commanded the princes and the people to do what was just and right, espe-

cially in their business dealings. Consider the ways that you measure goods, money, or services. If you are paid for an hour of work, be sure you work for a full hour. If you sell a bushel of apples, make sure it is a full bushel. God is completely trustworthy, and his followers should be, too.

**45:17** The conditions and regulations for these offerings are described in detail in Leviticus 1–7.

18"This is what the Sovereign LORD says: In early spring, on the first day of each new year,* sacrifice a young bull with no defects to purify the Temple. 19The priest will take blood from this sin offering and put it on the doorposts of the Temple, the four corners of the upper ledge of the altar, and the gateposts at the entrance to the inner courtyard. 20Do this also on the seventh day of the new year for anyone who has sinned through error or ignorance. In this way, you will purify* the Temple.

21"On the fourteenth day of the first month,* you must celebrate the Passover. This festival will last for seven days. The bread you eat during that time must be made without yeast. 22On the day of Passover the prince will provide a young bull as a sin offering for himself and the people of Israel. 23On each of the seven days of the feast he will prepare a burnt offering to the LORD, consisting of seven young bulls and seven rams without defects. A male goat will also be given each day for a sin offering. 24The prince will provide a basket of flour as a grain offering and a gallon of olive oil* with each young bull and ram.

25"During the seven days of the Festival of Shelters, which occurs every year in early autumn,* the prince will provide these same sacrifices for the sin offering, the burnt offering, and the grain offering, along with the required olive oil.

# 46

"This is what the Sovereign LORD says: The east gateway of the inner courtyard will be closed during the six workdays each week, but it will be open on Sabbath days and the days of new moon celebrations. 2The prince will enter the entry room of the gateway from the outside. Then he will stand by the gatepost while the priest offers his burnt offering and peace offering. He will bow down in worship inside the gateway passage and then go back out the way he came. The gateway will not be closed until evening. 3The common people will bow down and worship the LORD in front of this gateway on Sabbath days and the days of new moon celebrations.

4"Each Sabbath day the prince will present to the LORD a burnt offering of six lambs and one ram, all with no defects. 5He will present a grain offering of a basket of choice flour to go with the ram and whatever amount of flour he chooses to go with each lamb, and he is to offer one gallon of olive oil* for each basket of flour. 6At the new moon celebrations, he will bring one young bull, six lambs, and one ram, all with no defects. 7With the young bull he must bring a basket of choice flour for a grain offering. With the ram he must bring another basket of flour. And with each lamb he is to bring whatever amount of flour he chooses to give. With each basket of flour he must offer one gallon of olive oil.

8"The prince must enter the gateway through the entry room, and he must leave the same way. 9But when the people come in through the north gateway to worship the LORD during the religious festivals, they must leave by the south gateway. And those who entered through the south gateway must leave by the north gateway. They must never leave by the same gateway they came in, but must always use the opposite gateway. 10The prince will enter and leave with the people on these occasions.

11"So at the special feasts and sacred festivals, the grain offering will be a basket of choice flour with each young bull, another basket of flour with each ram, and as much flour as the prince chooses to give with each lamb. Give one gallon of olive oil with each basket of flour. 12When the prince offers a voluntary burnt offering or peace offering to the LORD, the east gateway to the inner courtyard will be opened for him, and he will offer his sacrifices as he does on Sabbath days. Then he will leave, and the gateway will be shut behind him.

13"Each morning you must sacrifice a one-year-old lamb with no defects as a burnt offering to the LORD. 14With the lamb, a grain offering must also be given to the LORD—about

**45:18**
Exod 12:2
Lev 16:16, 20;
22:20
Heb 9:14
**45:19**
Lev 16:18-20
**45:20**
Lev 4:27
Ps 19:12
**45:21**
Exod 12:18
Lev 23:5-8
Num 9:2-3;
28:16-17
**45:22**
Lev 4:14
**45:23**
Lev 23:8
Num 28:16-25
Job 42:8
**45:24**
Num 28:12-15
**45:25**
Lev 23:33-36
Num 29:12-38
**46:1**
Exod 20:9-10
Isa 66:23
Ezek 44:1-2
**46:2**
Ezek 44:3
**46:3**
Luke 1:10
**46:4**
Ezek 45:17
**46:5**
Ezek 45:24
**46:7**
Deut 16:17
**46:8**
Ezek 44:1-3
**46:9**
Ps 84:7
**46:10**
2 Chr 6:3; 7:4
Ps 42:4
**46:11**
Ezek 45:17
**46:12**
Lev 23:38
2 Chr 29:31
Ezek 44:3; 45:17
**46:13**
Isa 50:4
**46:14**
Exod 29:42
Num 28:5-6

**45:18** Hebrew *On the first day of the first month,* of the Hebrew calendar. This day in the ancient Hebrew lunar calendar occurred in March or April. **45:20** Or *will make atonement for.* **45:21** This day in the ancient Hebrew lunar calendar occurred in late March, April, or early May. **45:24** Hebrew *an ephah* [20 quarts or 22 liters] *of flour . . . and a hin* [3.8 liters] *of olive oil.* **45:25** Hebrew *the festival which begins on the fifteenth day of the seventh month* (see Lev 23:34). This day in the ancient Hebrew lunar calendar occurred in late September, October, or early November. **46:5** Hebrew *an ephah* [20 quarts or 22 liters] *of choice flour . . . a hin* [3.8 liters] *of olive oil;* similarly in 46:7, 11.

---

**45:21** The Passover was an annual seven-day festival instituted by God so that his people would remember when he brought them out of slavery in Egypt. On that first Passover night, the Lord passed over the homes marked by lamb's blood; he struck only the unmarked homes (see Exodus 11–12).

**45:25** This annual festival was celebrated in October. It com-

memorates God's protection of his people as they traveled through the wilderness from Egypt to the Promised Land (see Leviticus 23:33-43; Deuteronomy 16:13-17).

**46:1-15** Ezekiel continued to describe various aspects of daily worship. While allowing for diversity in worship, God prescribed order and continuity. This continuity gave a healthy rhythm to the spiritual life of his people.

46:15
Exod 29:42
Num 28:6
46:16
2 Chr 21:3
46:17
Lev 25:10

46:18
Ezek 45:8
Mic 2:1-2

46:20
Lev 2:4-7
2 Chr 35:13

47:1
Ps 46:4
Joel 2:13
Zech 13:1
Rev 22:1, 17
47:2
Ezek 44:1-4
47:3
Ezek 40:3
47:5
Isa 11:9
Hab 2:14
47:6
Ezek 40:4; 44:5
47:7
Isa 60:21; 61:3
Rev 22:2
47:8
Deut 3:17
Isa 35:6-7;
41:17-19; 44:3
47:9
Isa 12:3
John 4:14; 7:37-38
Rev 21:6
47:10
Num 34:6
2 Chr 20:2
Ps 104:25
Ezek 26:5; 48:28
Matt 13:47
Luke 5:5-9
47:12
Gen 2:9
Ps 1:3
Jer 17:8
Rev 22:2

three quarts of flour with a third of a gallon of olive oil* to moisten the choice flour. This will be a permanent law for you. ¹⁵The lamb, the grain offering, and the olive oil must be given as a daily sacrifice every morning without fail.

¹⁶"This is what the Sovereign Lord says: If the prince gives a gift of land to one of his sons as his inheritance, it will belong to him and his descendants forever. ¹⁷But if the prince gives a gift of land from his inheritance to one of his servants, the servant may keep it only until the Year of Jubilee, which comes every fiftieth year.* At that time the land will return to the prince. But when the prince gives gifts to his sons, those gifts will be permanent. ¹⁸And the prince may never take anyone's property by force. If he gives property to his sons, it must be from his own land, for I do not want any of my people unjustly evicted from their property."

## The Temple Kitchens

¹⁹In my vision, the man brought me through the entrance beside the gateway and led me to the sacred rooms assigned to the priests, which faced toward the north. He showed me a place at the extreme west end of these rooms. ²⁰He explained, "This is where the priests will cook the meat from the guilt offerings and sin offerings and bake the flour from the grain offerings into bread. They will do it here to avoid carrying the sacrifices through the outer courtyard and endangering the people by transmitting holiness to them."

²¹Then he brought me back to the outer courtyard and led me to each of its four corners. In each corner I saw an enclosure. ²²Each of these enclosures was 70 feet long and 52½ feet wide,* surrounded by walls. ²³Along the inside of these walls was a ledge of stone with fireplaces under the ledge all the way around. ²⁴The man said to me, "These are the kitchens to be used by the Temple assistants to boil the sacrifices offered by the people."

## The River of Healing

**47** In my vision, the man brought me back to the entrance of the Temple. There I saw a stream flowing east from beneath the door of the Temple and passing to the right of the altar on its south side. ²The man brought me outside the wall through the north gateway and led me around to the eastern entrance. There I could see the water flowing out through the south side of the east gateway.

³Measuring as he went, he took me along the stream for 1,750 feet* and then led me across. The water was up to my ankles. ⁴He measured off another 1,750 feet and led me across again. This time the water was up to my knees. After another 1,750 feet, it was up to my waist. ⁵Then he measured another 1,750 feet, and the river was too deep to walk across. It was deep enough to swim in, but too deep to walk through.

⁶He asked me, "Have you been watching, son of man?" Then he led me back along the riverbank. ⁷When I returned, I was surprised by the sight of many trees growing on both sides of the river. ⁸Then he said to me, "This river flows east through the desert into the valley of the Dead Sea.* The waters of this stream will make the salty waters of the Dead Sea fresh and pure. ⁹There will be swarms of living things wherever the water of this river flows. Fish will abound in the Dead Sea, for its waters will become fresh. Life will flourish wherever this water flows. ¹⁰Fishermen will stand along the shores of the Dead Sea. All the way from En-gedi to En-eglaim, the shores will be covered with nets drying in the sun. Fish of every kind will fill the Dead Sea, just as they fill the Mediterranean.* ¹¹But the marshes and swamps will not be purified; they will still be salty. ¹²Fruit trees of all kinds will grow along both sides of the river. The leaves of these trees will never turn brown and fall, and there will always be fruit on their branches. There will be a new crop every month, for they are watered by the river flowing from the Temple. The fruit will be for food and the leaves for healing."

46:14 Hebrew ¹/₆ of an ephah [3.7 liters] of flour with ¹/₃ of a hin [1.3 liters] of olive oil.  46:17 Hebrew until the Year of Release; see Lev 25:8-17.  46:22 Hebrew 40 cubits [21.2 meters] long and 30 cubits [15.9 meters] wide. 47:3 Hebrew 1,000 cubits [530 meters]; also in 47:4, 5.  47:8 Hebrew the sea.  47:10 Hebrew the great sea; also in 47:15, 17, 19, 20.

---

**47:1-12** This river is similar to the river mentioned in Revelation 22:1, 2. Both are associated with the river in the Garden of Eden (see Genesis 2:10). The river symbolizes life from God and the blessings that flow from his throne. It is a gentle, safe, deep river, expanding as it flows.

**47:8, 9** The valley of the Dead Sea is the geological depression in which the Dead Sea lies. The Dead Sea is a body of water so salty that nothing can live in it. The river will freshen the Dead Sea's water so it can support life. This is another picture of the

life-giving nature of the water that flows from God's Temple. God's power can transform us no matter how lifeless or corrupt we may be. Even when we feel messed up and beyond hope, his power can heal us.

**47:10** En-gedi and En-eglaim were on the western shore of the Dead Sea.

## Boundaries for the Land

13 This is what the Sovereign LORD says: "Divide the land in this way for the twelve tribes of Israel: The descendants of Joseph will be given two shares of land.* 14 Otherwise each tribe will receive an equal share. I took a solemn oath and swore that I would give this land to your ancestors, and it will now come to you as your possession.

15 "These are the boundaries of the land: The northern border will run from the Mediterranean toward Hethlon, then on through Lebo-hamath to Zedad; 16 then it will run to Berothah and Sibraim, which are on the border between Damascus and Hamath, and finally to Hazer-hatticon, on the border of Hauran. 17 So the northern border will run from the Mediterranean to Hazar-enan, on the border between Hamath to the north and Damascus to the south.

18 "The eastern border starts at a point between Hauran and Damascus and runs south along the Jordan River between Israel and Gilead, past the Dead Sea* and as far south as Tamar.* This will be the eastern border.

19 "The southern border will go west from Tamar to the waters of Meribah at Kadesh* and then follow the course of the Brook of Egypt to the Mediterranean. This will be the southern border.

20 "On the west side, the Mediterranean itself will be your border from the southern border to the point where the northern border begins, opposite Lebo-hamath.

21 "Divide the land within these boundaries among the tribes of Israel. 22 Distribute the land as an allotment for yourselves and for the foreigners who have joined you and are raising their families among you. They will be like native-born Israelites to you and will receive an allotment among the tribes. 23 These foreigners are to be given land within the territory of the tribe with whom they now live. I, the Sovereign LORD, have spoken!

## Division of the Land

**48** "Here is the list of the tribes of Israel and the territory each is to receive. The territory of Dan is in the extreme north. Its boundary line follows the Hethlon road to Lebo-hamath and then runs on to Hazar-enan on the border of Damascus, with Hamath to the north. Dan's territory extends all the way across the land of Israel from east to west.

2 "Asher's territory lies south of Dan's and also extends from east to west. 3 Naphtali's land lies south of Asher's, also extending from east to west. 4 Then comes Manasseh south of Naphtali, and its territory also extends from east to west. 5 South of Manasseh is Ephraim, 6 and then Reuben, 7 and then Judah, all of whose boundaries extend from east to west.

8 "South of Judah is the land set aside for a special purpose. It will be 8⅓ miles* wide and will extend as far east and west as the tribal territories, with the Temple at the center.

9 "The area set aside for the LORD's Temple will be 8⅓ miles long and 6⅔ miles wide.* 10 For the priests there will be a strip of land measuring 8⅓ miles long by 3⅓ miles wide,* with the LORD's Temple at the center. 11 This area is set aside for the ordained priests, the descendants of Zadok who served me faithfully and did not go astray with the people of Israel and the rest of the Levites. 12 It will be their special portion when the land is distributed, the most sacred land of all. Next to the priests' territory will lie the land where the other Levites will live.

13 "The land allotted to the Levites will be the same size and shape as that belonging to the priests—8⅓ miles long and 3⅓ miles wide. Together these portions of land will measure 8⅓ miles long by 6⅔ miles wide.* 14 None of this special land may ever be sold or traded or used by others, for it belongs to the LORD; it is set apart as holy.

### Cross references (margin)

47:13 Gen 48:5; Num 34:1-13; 1 Chr 5:1; Ezek 48:4-5
47:14 Gen 12:7; Deut 1:8; Ezek 20:5-6
47:15 Num 34:7-9; Ezek 48:1
47:16 Num 13:21; 1 Kgs 8:65
47:17 Num 34:9; Ezek 48:1
47:18 Gen 13:10-11; Num 34:10-12
47:19 Num 34:3-5; Deut 32:51; Isa 27:12
47:20 Num 34:6
47:22 Isa 14:1; 56:6-7; Acts 11:18; Rom 10:12; Eph 2:12-14; Col 3:11
48:1 Exod 1:1; Josh 19:40-48
48:2 Gen 30:12-13; Josh 19:24-31
48:3 Gen 30:7-8; Josh 19:32-39
48:4 Gen 30:22-24; 41:51; 48:5, 14-20; Josh 13:29-31; 17:1-11
48:5 Josh 16:5-10; 17:8-10, 14-18
48:6 Josh 13:15-21
48:7 Josh 15:1-63
48:8 Ezek 45:1-6; Rev 21:3, 22
48:10 Ezek 44:28; 45:4
48:11 Ezek 44:10-15
48:14 Lev 25:32-34

**47:13** It was important to retain twelve portions of land. Since Levi had no portion, the descendants of Joseph's sons, Ephraim and Manasseh, received land as two tribes. **47:18a** Hebrew *the eastern sea.* **47:18b** As in Greek version; Hebrew reads *you will measure.* **47:19** Hebrew *waters of Meribath-kadesh.* **48:8** Hebrew *25,000 cubits* [13.3 kilometers]. **48:9** As in one Greek manuscript and the Greek reading in 45:1: *25,000 cubits* [13.3 kilometers] *long and 20,000 cubits* [10.6 kilometers] *wide;* Hebrew reads *25,000 cubits long and 10,000 cubits* [3⅓ miles or 5.3 kilometers] *wide.* Similarly in 48:13b. Compare 45:1-5; 48:10-13. **48:10** Hebrew *25,000 cubits* [13.3 kilometers] *long by 10,000 cubits* [5.3 kilometers] *wide;* also in 48:13a. **48:13** See note on 48:9.

---

**47:22, 23** In the restoration there will be room for foreigners. The regulations of Leviticus 24:22 and Numbers 15:29 provided for this. Isaiah also taught it (Isaiah 56:3-8). The children of foreigners will even inherit property like Israelites. Anyone who accepts the standards and is willing to obey may enjoy the blessings of God's rule.

**48:1ff** The land would be divided into 13 parallel portions (one for each tribe plus a sacred district) that would stretch from the Jordan River or Dead Sea to the Mediterranean Sea. The division of the land shows that in God's Kingdom there is a place for all who believe in and obey the one true God (see John 14:1-6).

**48:15**
Ezek 42:20; 45:6
**48:16**
Rev 21:16

15"An additional strip of land 8⅓ miles long by 1⅔ miles wide,* south of the sacred Temple area, will be allotted for public use—homes, pasturelands, and common lands, with a city at the center. 16The city will measure 1½ miles* on each side—north, south, east, and west. 17Open lands will surround the city for 150 yards* in every direction. 18Outside the city there will be a farming area that stretches 3⅓ miles to the east and 3⅓ miles to the west* along the border of the sacred area. This farmland will produce food for the people working in the city. 19Those who come from the various tribes to work in the city may farm it. 20This entire area—including the sacred lands and the city—is a square that measures 8⅓ miles* on each side.

**48:21**
Ezek 34:24; 45:7
**48:23**
Gen 35:16-19
Josh 18:21-28
**48:24**
Gen 29:33; 49:5-7
Josh 19:1-9
**48:25**
Gen 30:14-18
Josh 19:17-23
**48:26**
Gen 30:19-20
Josh 19:10-16
**48:27**
Gen 30:10-11
Josh 13:24-28
Ezek 47:19-20
**48:28**
Num 34:6
**48:29**
Ezek 47:13-23

21"The areas that remain, to the east and to the west of the sacred lands and the city, will belong to the prince. Each of these areas will be 8⅓ miles wide, extending in opposite directions to the eastern and western borders of Israel, with the sacred lands and the sanctuary of the Temple in the center. 22So the prince's land will include everything between the territories allotted to Judah and Benjamin, except for the areas set aside for the sacred lands and the city.

23"These are the territories allotted to the rest of the tribes. Benjamin's territory lies just south of the prince's lands, and it extends across the entire land of Israel from east to west. 24South of Benjamin's territory lies that of Simeon, also extending across the land from east to west. 25Next is the territory of Issachar with the same eastern and western boundaries.

26"Then comes the territory of Zebulun, which also extends across the land from east to west. 27The territory of Gad is just south of Zebulun with the same borders to the east and west. 28The southern border of Gad runs from Tamar to the waters of Meribah at Kadesh* and then follows the Brook of Egypt to the Mediterranean.*

29"These are the allotments that will be set aside for each tribe's exclusive possession. I, the Sovereign LORD, have spoken!

### The Gates of the City

**48:31**
Rev 21:12-13

30"These will be the exits to the city: On the north wall, which is 1½ miles long, 31there will be three gates, each one named after a tribe of Israel. The first will be named for Reuben, the second for Judah, and the third for Levi. 32On the east wall, also 1½ miles long, the gates will be named for Joseph, Benjamin, and Dan. 33The south wall, also 1½ miles long, will have gates named for Simeon, Issachar, and Zebulun. 34And on the west wall, also 1½ miles long, the gates will be named for Gad, Asher, and Naphtali.

**48:35**
Isa 12:6; 24:23
Jer 3:17; 23:6;
33:16
Joel 3:21
Zech 2:10
Rev 21:3; 22:3

35"The distance around the entire city will be 6 miles.* And from that day the name of the city will be 'The LORD Is There.'*"

**48:15** Hebrew *25,000 cubits* [13.3 kilometers] *long by 5,000 cubits* [2.65 kilometers] *wide*.    **48:16** Hebrew *4,500 cubits* [2.4 kilometers]; also in 48:30, 32, 33, 34.    **48:17** Hebrew *250 cubits* [133 meters].    **48:18** Hebrew *10,000 cubits* [5.3 kilometers] *to the east and 10,000 cubits to the west*.    **48:20** Hebrew *25,000 cubits* [13.3 kilometers]; also in 48:21.    **48:28a** Hebrew *waters of Meribath-kadesh*.    **48:28b** Hebrew *the great sea*.    **48:35a** Hebrew *18,000 cubits* [9.6 kilometers].    **48:35b** Hebrew *Yahweh Shammah*.

---

**48:35** The book of Ezekiel begins by describing the holiness of God that Israel had despised and ignored. As a result, God's presence departed from the Temple, the city, and the people. The book ends with a detailed vision of the new Temple, the new city, and the new people—all demonstrating God's holiness. The pressures of everyday life may cause us to focus on the here and now and thus forget God. That is why worship is so important; it takes our eyes off our current worries, gives us a glimpse of God's holiness, and allows us to look toward his future Kingdom. God's presence makes everything glorious, and worship brings us into his presence.

# DANIEL

| Daniel | Ezekiel | Judah falls; | Daniel's |
| taken | becomes | Jerusalem is destroyed; | first |
| captive | a prophet | Jeremiah's ministry ends | vision |
| to Babylon | to exiles | 586 | 553 |
| 605 B.C. | 593 | | |

## VITAL STATISTICS

**PURPOSE:**
To give a historical account of the faithful Jews who lived in captivity and to show how God is in control of heaven and earth, directing the forces of nature, the destiny of nations, and the care of his people

**AUTHOR:**
Daniel

**ORIGINAL AUDIENCE:**
The other captives in Babylon

**DATE WRITTEN:**
Approximately 536 B.C., recording events that occurred from about 605–536 B.C.

**SETTING:**
Daniel had been taken captive and deported to Babylon by Nebuchadnezzar in 605 B.C. There he served in the government for about 70 years during the reigns of Nebuchadnezzar, Belshazzar, Darius, and Cyrus.

**KEY VERSE:**
"He [God] reveals deep and mysterious things and knows what lies hidden in darkness, though he is surrounded by light" (2:22).

**KEY PEOPLE:**
Daniel, Nebuchadnezzar, Shadrach, Meshach, Abednego, Belshazzar, Darius

**KEY PLACES:**
Nebuchadnezzar's palace, the blazing furnace, Belshazzar's feast, the den of lions

**SPECIAL FEATURES:**
Daniel's apocalyptic visions (chapters 7—12) give a glimpse of God's plan for the ages, including a direct prediction of the Messiah.

AN EARTHQUAKE shakes the foundation of our security; a tornado blows away a lifetime of treasures; an assassin's bullet changes national history; a drunk driver claims an innocent victim; a divorce shatters a home; terrorism frightens a nation. International and personal tragedies make our world seem a fearful place, overflowing with evil and seemingly out of control. And the litany of bombings, coups, murders, and natural disasters could cause us to think that God is absent or impotent. "Where is God?" we cry, engulfed by sorrow and despair.

Twenty-five centuries ago, Daniel could have despaired. He and thousands of his countrymen had been deported to a foreign land after Judah was conquered. Daniel found himself facing an egocentric despot and surrounded by idolaters. Instead of giving in or giving up, this courageous young man held fast to his faith in his God. Daniel knew that despite the circumstances, God was sovereign and was working out his plan for nations and individuals. The book of Daniel centers around this profound truth—the sovereignty of God.

After a brief account of Nebuchadnezzar's siege and defeat of Jerusalem, the scene quickly shifts to Daniel and his three friends, Hananiah, Mishael, and Azariah (Shadrach, Meshach, and Abednego). These men held prominent positions within the Babylonian government. Daniel, in particular, held such a position because of his ability to interpret the king's dreams that tell of God's unfolding plan (chapters 2 and 4). Sandwiched between the dreams is the fascinating account of Daniel's three friends and the furnace (chapter 3). Because they refused to bow down to an image of gold, they were condemned to a fiery death. But God intervened and spared their lives.

Belshazzar ruled Babylon after Nebuchadnezzar, and chapter 5 tells of his encounter with God's message written on a wall. Daniel, who was summoned to interpret the message, predicted Babylon's fall to the Medes and Persians. This prediction came true that very night, and Darius the Mede conquered the Babylonian kingdom.

Daniel became one of Darius's most trusted advisers. His privileged position angered other administrators, who plotted his death by convincing the king to outlaw prayer. In spite of the law, Daniel continued to pray to his sovereign Lord. As a result, he was condemned to die in a den of hungry lions. Again, God intervened, saving him, and shutting the mouths of the lions (chapter 6).

The book concludes with a series of visions that Daniel had during the reigns of Belshazzar (chapters 7—8), Darius (chapter 9), and Cyrus (chapters 10—12). These dreams dramatically outline God's future plans, beginning with Babylon and continuing to the end of the age. They give a preview of God's redemption and have been called the key to all biblical prophecy.

God is sovereign. He was in control in Babylon, and he has been moving in history, controlling the destinies of people ever since. And he is here now! Despite news reports or personal stress, we can be confident that God is in control. As you read Daniel, watch God work and find your security in his sovereignty.

| Babylon overthrown; Daniel thrown to lions 539 | First exiles return to Judah 538 | Daniel's ministry ends 536 |
|---|---|---|

## THE BLUEPRINT

A. DANIEL'S LIFE
(1:1—6:28)

Daniel and his three friends chose not to eat the king's food. They did not bow down to the king's image, even under penalty of death. Daniel continued to pray even though he knew he might be noticed and sentenced to death. These men are inspiring examples for us of how to live godly lives in a sinful world. When we face trials, we can expect God to also be with us through them. May God grant us similar courage to remain faithful under pressure.

B. DANIEL'S VISIONS
(7:1—12:13)

These visions gave the captives added confidence that God is in control of history. They were to wait patiently in faith and not worship the gods of Babylon or accept that society's way of life. God still rules over human activities. Evil will be overcome, so we should wait patiently and not give in to the temptations and pressures of the sinful way of life around us.

## MEGATHEMES

| THEME | EXPLANATION | IMPORTANCE |
|---|---|---|
| God Is in Control | God is all-knowing, and he is in charge of world events. God overrules and removes rebellious leaders who defy him. God will overcome evil; no one is exempt. But he will deliver the faithful who follow him. | Although nations vie for world control now, one day Christ's Kingdom will replace and surpass the kingdoms of this world. Our faith is sure because our future is secure in Christ. We must have courage and put our faith in God, who controls everything. |
| Purpose in Life | Daniel and his three friends are examples of dedication and commitment. They determined to serve God regardless of the consequences. They did not give in to pressures from an ungodly society because they had a clear purpose in life. | It is wise to make trusting and obeying God alone our true purpose in life. This will give us direction and peace in spite of the circumstances or consequences. We should disobey anyone who asks us to disobey God. Our first allegiance must be to God. |
| Perseverance | Daniel served for 70 years in a foreign land that was hostile to God, yet he did not compromise his faith in God. He was truthful, persistent in prayer, and disinterested in power for personal glory. | In order to fulfill your life's purpose, you need staying power. Don't let your Christian distinctness become blurred. Be relentless in your prayers, maintain your integrity, and be content to serve God wherever he puts you. |
| God's Faithfulness | God was faithful in Daniel's life. He delivered him from execution, from a den of lions, and from enemies who hated him. God cares for his people and deals patiently with them. | We can trust God to be with us through any trial. Because he has been faithful to us, we should remain faithful to him. |

## A. DANIEL'S LIFE (1:1—6:28)

While Ezekiel was ministering to the captives in Babylon, Daniel was drafted as a counselor to King Nebuchadnezzar. With God's help, Daniel interpreted two of the king's dreams, Daniel's three friends were rescued from certain death in the blazing furnace, and Daniel was rescued from a lions' den. Daniel's life is a picture of the triumph of faith. May God grant us this type of faith so that we may also live courageously each day.

**1:1**
2 Kgs 24:1
2 Chr 36:6

**1:2**
Isa 11:11
Jer 27:19-20
Zech 5:5-11

### Daniel in Nebuchadnezzar's Court

**1** During the third year of King Jehoiakim's reign in Judah,* King Nebuchadnezzar of Babylon came to Jerusalem and besieged it. ²The Lord gave him victory over King

1:1 This event occurred in 605 B.C., during the third year of Jehoiakim's reign (according to the calendar system in which the new year begins in the spring).

1:1, 2 Born during the middle of Josiah's reign (2 Kings 22–23), Daniel grew up during the king's reforms. During this time, Daniel probably heard Jeremiah, a prophet he quoted in 9:2. In 609 B.C. Josiah was killed in a battle against Egypt, and within four years, the southern kingdom of Judah had returned to its evil ways.

In 605 B.C. Nebuchadnezzar became king of Babylon. In September of that year, he swept into Palestine and surrounded

Jerusalem, making Judah his vassal state. To demonstrate his dominance, Nebuchadnezzar took many of Jerusalem's wisest men and most beautiful women to Babylon as captives. Daniel was among this group.

1:1, 2 Nebuchadnezzar, the supreme leader of Babylon, was feared throughout the world. When he invaded a country, defeat was certain. After a victory, the Babylonians usually took the most

Jehoiakim of Judah and permitted him to take some of the sacred objects from the Temple of God. So Nebuchadnezzar took them back to the land of Babylonia* and placed them in the treasure-house of his god.

³Then the king ordered Ashpenaz, his chief of staff, to bring to the palace some of the young men of Judah's royal family and other noble families, who had been brought to Babylon as captives. ⁴"Select only strong, healthy, and good-looking young men," he said. "Make sure they are well versed in every branch of learning, are gifted with knowledge and good judgment, and are suited to serve in the royal palace. Train these young men in the language and literature of Babylon.*" ⁵The king assigned them a daily ration of food and wine from his own kitchens. They were to be trained for three years, and then they would enter the royal service.

⁶Daniel, Hananiah, Mishael, and Azariah were four of the young men chosen, all from the tribe of Judah. ⁷The chief of staff renamed them with these Babylonian names:

Daniel was called Belteshazzar.
Hananiah was called Shadrach.
Mishael was called Meshach.
Azariah was called Abednego.

⁸But Daniel was determined not to defile himself by eating the food and wine given to them by the king. He asked the chief of staff for permission not to eat these unacceptable foods. ⁹Now God had given the chief of staff both respect and affection for Daniel. ¹⁰But he

**1:3**
Isa 39:7

**1:5**
Dan 1:8, 19

**1:6**
Ezek 14:14, 20;
28:3
Matt 24:15

**1:7**
Dan 2:49; 3:12-30;
4:8; 5:12

**1:8**
Lev 11:47
Deut 32:38
Ezek 4:13-14
Hos 9:3

**1:9**
Ps 106:46
Prov 16:7

1:2 Hebrew *the land of Shinar.*   1:4 Or *of the Chaldeans.*

---

talented and useful people back to Babylon and left only the poor behind to take whatever land they wanted and to live peacefully there (2 Kings 24:14). This system fostered great loyalty from conquered lands and ensured a steady supply of wise and talented people for civil service.

**1:2** At certain times God allows his work to suffer. In this instance, the Babylonians raided the Temple of God and took the worship articles to the temple of a god in Babylon. This god may have been Bel, also called Marduk, the chief god of the Babylonians. Those who loved the Lord must have felt disheartened and discouraged. We feel greatly disappointed when our churches suffer physical damage, split, close down for financial reasons, or are rocked by scandals. We do not know why God allows his church to experience these calamities. But like the people who witnessed the plundering of the Temple by the Babylonians, we must trust that God is in control and that he is watching over all who trust in him.

**1:4** The common language of Babylon was Aramaic, while the language of scholarship included the ancient and complicated Babylonian language. The academic program would have included mathematics, astronomy, history, science, and magic. These young men demonstrated not only aptitude but also discipline. This character trait, combined with integrity, served them well in their new culture.

**TAKEN TO BABYLON** Daniel, as a captive of Babylonian soldiers, faced a long and difficult march to a new land. The 500-mile trek, under harsh conditions, certainly tested his faith in God.

**1:7** Nebuchadnezzar changed the names of Daniel and his friends because he wanted to make them Babylonian—in their own eyes and in the eyes of the Babylonian people. New names would help them to be assimilated into the culture. Daniel means "God is my judge" in Hebrew; his name was changed to Belteshazzar, meaning "Bel, protect his life!" (Bel, also called Marduk, was the chief Babylonian god.) Hananiah means "the LORD shows grace"; his new name, Shadrach, probably means "under the command of Aku" (the moon god). Mishael means "who is like God?"; his new name, Meshach, probably means "who is like Aku?" Azariah means "the LORD helps"; his new name, Abednego, means "servant of Nego/Nebo" (or Nabu, the god of learning and writing). This was how the king attempted to change the religious loyalty of these young men from Judah's God to Babylon's gods.

**1:8** Daniel resolved not to eat this food, either because it was forbidden by Jewish law, such as pork (see Leviticus 11), or because accepting the king's food and drink was the first step toward depending on his gifts and favors. Although Daniel was in a culture that did not honor God, he still obeyed God's laws.

**1:8** Daniel "was determined" to be devoted to principle and to be committed to a course of action. When Daniel made up his mind not to defile himself, he was being true to a lifelong determination to do what was right and not to give in to the pressures around him. We, too, are often assaulted by pressures to compromise our standards and live more like the world around us. Merely wanting or preferring God's will and way is not enough to stand against the onslaught of temptation. Like Daniel, we must resolve to obey God.

**1:8** It is easier to resist temptation if you have thought through your convictions before the temptation arises. Daniel and his friends made their decision to be faithful to the laws of God before they were faced with the king's delicacies, so they did not hesitate to stick with their convictions. We will get into trouble if we have not previously decided where to draw the line. Before such situations arise, decide on your commitments and what you will do. Then when temptation comes, you will be ready to say no.

**1:9** God moved with an unseen hand to change the heart of this Babylonian official. The strong moral conviction of these four young men made an impact. God promises to be with his people in times of trial and temptation (Psalm 106:46; Isaiah 43:2-5; 1 Corinthians 10:13). His active intervention often comes just when we take a stand for him. Stand for God and trust him to protect you in ways you may not be able to see.

**1:10** Anything short of complete obedience meant execution for responded, "I am afraid of my lord the king, who has ordered that you eat this food and wine. If you become pale and thin compared to the other youths your age, I am afraid the king will have me beheaded."

¹¹Daniel spoke with the attendant who had been appointed by the chief of staff to look after Daniel, Hananiah, Mishael, and Azariah. ¹²"Please test us for ten days on a diet of vegetables and water," Daniel said. ¹³"At the end of the ten days, see how we look compared to the other young men who are eating the king's food. Then make your decision in light of what you see." ¹⁴The attendant agreed to Daniel's suggestion and tested them for ten days.

¹⁵At the end of the ten days, Daniel and his three friends looked healthier and better nourished than the young men who had been eating the food assigned by the king. ¹⁶So after that, the attendant fed them only vegetables instead of the food and wine provided for the others.

¹⁷God gave these four young men an unusual aptitude for understanding every aspect of literature and wisdom. And God gave Daniel the special ability to interpret the meanings of visions and dreams.

¹⁸When the training period ordered by the king was completed, the chief of staff brought all the young men to King Nebuchadnezzar. ¹⁹The king talked with them, and no one impressed him as much as Daniel, Hananiah, Mishael, and Azariah. So they entered the royal service. ²⁰Whenever the king consulted them in any matter requiring wisdom and balanced judgment, he found them ten times more capable than any of the magicians and enchanters in his entire kingdom.

²¹Daniel remained in the royal service until the first year of the reign of King Cyrus.*

**1:21** Cyrus began his reign (over Babylon) in 539 B.C.

### Cross-references

**1:12**
Dan 1:16

**1:15**
Exod 23:25
Prov 10:22

**1:16**
Dan 1:12

**1:17**
1 Kgs 3:12, 28
Job 32:8
Dan 1:20; 2:19; 7:1; 8:1

**1:19**
Gen 41:46
Jer 15:1
Dan 1:5

**1:20**
Num 14:22
Isa 19:3
Dan 1:17; 2:2, 27-28; 4:18; 5:7

**1:21**
Dan 6:28; 10:1

---

**DANIEL**
served as
a prophet to
the exiles in
Babylon from
605–536 B.C.

| | |
|---|---|
| Climate of the times . . . . . . . . . . . . | The people of Judah were captives in a strange land, feeling hopeless. |
| Main message. . . . . . . . . . . . . . . . . | God is sovereign over all human history, past, present, and future. |
| Importance of message . . . . . . . . . | We should spend less time wondering when future events will happen and more time learning how we should live now. |
| Contemporary prophets . . . . . . . . . | Jeremiah (627–586 B.C.), Habakkuk (612–589 B.C.), Ezekiel (593–571 B.C.) |

---

the officials who served Nebuchadnezzar. Even in such a small matter as this, the official feared for his life.

**1:12** The Babylonians were trying to change their *thinking* by giving them a Babylonian education, their *loyalty* by changing their names, and their *lifestyle* by changing their diet. Without compromising, Daniel found a way to live by God's standards in a culture that did not honor God. Wisely choosing to negotiate rather than to rebel, Daniel suggested an experimental 10-day diet of vegetables and water instead of the royal foods and wine the king offered. Without compromising, Daniel quickly thought of a practical, creative solution that saved his life and the lives of his companions. As God's people, we may adjust to our culture as long as we do not compromise God's laws.

**1:17** Daniel and his friends learned all they could about their new culture so they could do their work with excellence. But while they learned, they maintained steadfast allegiance to God, and God gave them skill and wisdom. Culture need not be God's enemy. If it does not violate his commands, it can aid in accomplishing his purpose. We who follow God are free to be competent leaders in our culture, but we are required to pledge our allegiance to God first.

**1:20** Nebuchadnezzar put Daniel and his friends on his staff of advisers. This staff included many "magicians and enchanters." These were astrologers who claimed to be able to tell the future through occult practices. They were masters at communicating their message so that it sounded authoritative—as though it came directly from their gods. In addition to knowledge, Daniel and his three friends had wisdom and understanding, given to

them by God. Thus, the king was far more pleased with them than with his magicians and enchanters. As we serve others, we must not merely pretend to have God's wisdom. Our wisdom will be genuine when we are rightly related to God.

**1:20** How did the captives survive in a foreign culture? They learned about the culture, achieved excellence in their work, served the people, prayed for God's help, and maintained their integrity. We may feel like foreigners whenever we experience change. Alien cultures come in many forms: a new job, a new school, a new neighborhood. We can use the same principles to help us adapt to our new surroundings without abandoning God.

**1:21** Daniel was one of the first captives taken to Babylon, and he lived to see the first exiles return to Jerusalem in 538 B.C. Throughout this time Daniel honored God, and God honored him. While serving as an adviser to the kings of Babylon, Daniel was God's spokesman to the Babylonian Empire. Babylon was a wicked nation, but it would have been much worse without Daniel's influence.

## Nebuchadnezzar's Dream

**2** One night during the second year of his reign,* Nebuchadnezzar had such disturbing dreams that he couldn't sleep. ²He called in his magicians, enchanters, sorcerers, and astrologers,* and he demanded that they tell him what he had dreamed. As they stood before the king, ³he said, "I have had a dream that deeply troubles me, and I must know what it means."

⁴Then the astrologers answered the king in Aramaic,* "Long live the king! Tell us the dream, and we will tell you what it means."

⁵But the king said to the astrologers, "I am serious about this. If you don't tell me what my dream was and what it means, you will be torn limb from limb, and your houses will be turned into heaps of rubble! ⁶But if you tell me what I dreamed and what the dream means, I will give you many wonderful gifts and honors. Just tell me the dream and what it means!"

⁷They said again, "Please, Your Majesty. Tell us the dream, and we will tell you what it means."

⁸The king replied, "I know what you are doing! You're stalling for time because you know I am serious when I say, ⁹'If you don't tell me the dream, you are doomed.' So you have conspired to tell me lies, hoping I will change my mind. But tell me the dream, and then I'll know that you can tell me what it means."

¹⁰The astrologers replied to the king, "No one on earth can tell the king his dream! And no king, however great and powerful, has ever asked such a thing of any magician, enchanter, or astrologer! ¹¹The king's demand is impossible. No one except the gods can tell you your dream, and they do not live here among people."

¹²The king was furious when he heard this, and he ordered that all the wise men of Babylon be executed. ¹³And because of the king's decree, men were sent to find and kill Daniel and his friends.

¹⁴When Arioch, the commander of the king's guard, came to kill them, Daniel handled the situation with wisdom and discretion. ¹⁵He asked Arioch, "Why has the king issued such a harsh decree?" So Arioch told him all that had happened. ¹⁶Daniel went at once to see the king and requested more time to tell the king what the dream meant.

**2:1** Gen 40:5-8; 41:1, 8; Esth 6:1; Job 33:15-17; Dan 6:18
**2:3** Dan 4:5
**2:4** Ezra 4:7; Isa 36:11; Dan 3:9; 5:10
**2:5** Ezra 6:11; Dan 2:12; 3:29
**2:6** Dan 2:48; 5:7, 16, 29
**2:9** Esth 4:11; Isa 41:23
**2:11** Gen 41:39; Exod 29:45; Isa 57:15; Dan 5:11
**2:12** Ps 76:10; Dan 2:5; 3:13
**2:13** Dan 1:19-20
**2:14** Dan 2:24

**2:1** The second year of Nebuchadnezzar's reign was 603 B.C. **2:2** Or *Chaldeans;* also in 2:4, 5, 10. **2:4** The original text from this point through chapter 7 is in Aramaic.

**2:1-11** Dreams were considered to be messages from the gods, and the astrologers were expected to interpret them. Usually the astrologers could give some sort of interpretation as long as they knew what the dream was about. This time, however, Nebuchadnezzar demanded to be told the dream also. God sent a series of dreams to Nebuchadnezzar with prophetic messages that could be revealed and understood only by a servant of God. People from other time periods who received dreams from God include Jacob (Genesis 28:10-15), Joseph (Genesis 37:5-11), Pharaoh's cup-bearer and his baker (Genesis 40), Pharaoh (Genesis 41), Solomon (1 Kings 3:5-15), and Joseph (Matthew 1:20-24).

**2:10, 11** The astrologers told the king that "no one on earth" could know the dreams of another person. What the king asked was humanly impossible. But Daniel could tell what the king had dreamed, and he could also give the interpretation because God was working through him. In daily life, we face many apparently impossible situations that would be hopeless if we had to handle them with our limited strength. But God specializes in working through us to achieve the impossible.

**2:10, 11** The astrologers were unable to persuade the king with any amount of logic or rational argument. The king asked for something impossible and didn't want anyone to change his mind. When power goes to a leader's head, whether at work, at home, or in the church, that leader may sometimes demand the impossible from subordinates. At times, he may motivate workers to achieve more than they thought they could. At other times, they may ignore his rantings and ravings. Just as Daniel dealt wisely in the situation, we can ask God to give us wisdom to know how to deal with unreasonable bosses.

**2:11** The astrologers admitted that their gods did not "live here among people." Of course their gods didn't—they didn't even exist! This exposed the limitations of the astrologers. They could invent interpretations of dreams but could not tell Nebuchadnezzar *what* he had dreamed. Although his request was unreasonable, Nebuchadnezzar was infuriated by their reply. It was not unusual in these times for astrologers to be in conflict with the king. They sometimes used their craft to gain political power.

**2:11** By answering that the gods "do not live here among people," the astrologers betrayed their concept of the gods. Theirs was a hollow religion, a religion of convenience. They believed in the gods, but that belief made no difference in their conduct. Today, many people profess to believe in God, but it is also a hollow belief. In essence, they are practical atheists because they don't listen to him or do what he says. Do you believe in God? He *does* live among people, and he wants to change your life.

**2:16-18** Daniel was at a crisis point. Imagine going to see the powerful, temperamental king who had just angrily ordered your death! Daniel did not shrink back in fear, however, but confidently believed God would tell him all the king wanted to know. When the king gave Daniel time to find the answer, Daniel found his three friends and they prayed. When you find yourself in a tight spot, share your needs with trusted friends who also believe in God's power. Prayer is more effective than panic. Panic confirms your hopelessness; prayer confirms your hope in God. Daniel's trust in God saved not only himself but also his three friends and all the other wise men of Babylon.

**2:18**
Gen 18:28
Isa 37:4
Jer 33:3
Ezek 36:27
Dan 2:23

**2:19**
Num 12:6
2 Kgs 6:8-12
Job 33:15-16
Dan 7:2, 7

**2:20**
1 Chr 29:11-12
Job 12:13
Pss 103:1-2; 113:2
Dan 2:21-23

**2:21**
1 Kgs 3:9-10; 4:29
Job 12:18-19
Ps 75:6-7
Dan 7:25
Jas 1:5

**2:22**
Job 12:22; 26:6
Ps 139:12
Isa 45:7
Jer 23:24
Dan 2:19, 28
Jas 1:17
1 Jn 1:5

**2:23**
Gen 31:42
Dan 2:21

**2:24**
Dan 2:12-13
Acts 27:24

**2:25**
Gen 41:14
Dan 1:6; 5:13; 6:13

**2:27**
Dan 2:2, 10-11;
5:7-8

**2:28**
Gen 40:8; 41:16
Dan 2:22, 45

¹⁷Then Daniel went home and told his friends Hananiah, Mishael, and Azariah what had happened. ¹⁸He urged them to ask the God of heaven to show them his mercy by telling them the secret, so they would not be executed along with the other wise men of Babylon. ¹⁹That night the secret was revealed to Daniel in a vision. Then Daniel praised the God of heaven. ²⁰He said,

"Praise the name of God forever and ever,
    for he has all wisdom and power.
²¹ He controls the course of world events;
    he removes kings and sets up other kings.
He gives wisdom to the wise
    and knowledge to the scholars.
²² He reveals deep and mysterious things
    and knows what lies hidden in darkness,
    though he is surrounded by light.
²³ I thank and praise you, God of my ancestors,
    for you have given me wisdom and strength.
You have told me what we asked of you
    and revealed to us what the king demanded."

### Daniel Interprets the Dream

²⁴Then Daniel went in to see Arioch, whom the king had ordered to execute the wise men of Babylon. Daniel said to him, "Don't kill the wise men. Take me to the king, and I will tell him the meaning of his dream."

²⁵Arioch quickly took Daniel to the king and said, "I have found one of the captives from Judah who will tell the king the meaning of his dream!"

²⁶The king said to Daniel (also known as Belteshazzar), "Is this true? Can you tell me what my dream was and what it means?"

²⁷Daniel replied, "There are no wise men, enchanters, magicians, or fortune-tellers who can reveal the king's secret. ²⁸But there is a God in heaven who reveals secrets, and he has shown King Nebuchadnezzar what will happen in the future. Now I will tell you your dream and the visions you saw as you lay on your bed.

---

## NEBUCHADNEZZAR'S DREAM FULFILLED

The large statue in Nebuchadnezzar's dream (2:24-45) represented the four kingdoms that would dominate as world powers. We recognize these as the Babylonian Empire, the Medo-Persian Empire, the Grecian Empire, and the Roman Empire. All of these will be crushed and brought to an end by the Kingdom of God, which will continue forever.

| Part | Material | Empire | Period of Domination |
|------|----------|--------|----------------------|
| Head | Gold | Babylonian | 606 B.C.–539 B.C. |
| Chest and Arms | Silver | Medo-Persian | 539 B.C.–331 B.C. |
| Belly and Thighs | Bronze | Grecian | 331 B.C.–146 B.C. |
| Legs and Feet | Iron and Clay | Roman | 146 B.C.–A.D. 476 |

---

**2:19-23** After Daniel asked God to reveal Nebuchadnezzar's dream to him, he saw a vision of the dream. Daniel's prayer was answered. Before rushing to Arioch with the news, Daniel took time to give God credit for all wisdom and power, thanking God for answering his request. How do you feel when your prayers are answered? Excited? Surprised? Relieved? There are times when we seek God in prayer and, after having been answered, dash off in our excitement, forgetting to give God credit for the answer. Match your persistence in prayer with gratitude when your requests are answered.

**2:21** If you know that you still have much to learn in life, and if you have ever wished that you knew more about how to deal with people, then look to God for wisdom. While educational institutions provide diplomas at great expense, God gives wisdom freely to all who ask. (See James 1:5 for more on asking God for wisdom.)

**2:21** When we see evil leaders who live long and good leaders

who die young, we may wonder if God is still in control. Daniel saw evil rulers with almost limitless power, but he knew that God "removes kings and sets up other kings" and that he controls everything that happens. God governs the world according to his purposes. You may be dismayed when you see evil people prosper, but God is in control. Let this knowledge give you confidence and peace no matter what happens.

**2:24** Daniel did not use his success to promote his own self-interest. He thought of others. When striving to succeed or survive, remember the needs of others.

**2:27-30** Before Daniel told the king anything else, he gave credit to God, explaining that he did not know the dream through his own wisdom but only because God revealed it. How easily we take credit for what God does through us! This robs God of the honor that he alone deserves. Instead, we should be like Daniel and point people to God so that we give him the glory.

29"While Your Majesty was sleeping, you dreamed about coming events. He who reveals secrets has shown you what is going to happen. 30And it is not because I am wiser than anyone else that I know the secret of your dream, but because God wants you to understand what was in your heart.

31"In your vision, Your Majesty, you saw standing before you a huge, shining statue of a man. It was a frightening sight. 32The head of the statue was made of fine gold. Its chest and arms were silver, its belly and thighs were bronze, 33its legs were iron, and its feet were a combination of iron and baked clay. 34As you watched, a rock was cut from a mountain, but not by human hands. It struck the feet of iron and clay, smashing them to bits. 35The whole statue was crushed into small pieces of iron, clay, bronze, silver, and gold. Then the wind blew them away without a trace, like chaff on a threshing floor. But the rock that knocked the statue down became a great mountain that covered the whole earth.

36"That was the dream. Now we will tell the king what it means. 37Your Majesty, you are the greatest of kings. The God of heaven has given you sovereignty, power, strength, and honor. 38He has made you the ruler over all the inhabited world and has put even the wild animals and birds under your control. You are the head of gold.

39"But after your kingdom comes to an end, another kingdom, inferior to yours, will rise to take your place. After that kingdom has fallen, yet a third kingdom, represented by bronze, will rise to rule the world. 40Following that kingdom, there will be a fourth one, as strong as iron. That kingdom will smash and crush all previous empires, just as iron smashes and crushes everything it strikes. 41The feet and toes you saw were a combination of iron and baked clay, showing that this kingdom will be divided. Like iron mixed with clay, it will have some of the strength of iron. 42But while some parts of it will be as strong as iron, other parts will be as weak as clay. 43This mixture of iron and clay also shows that these kingdoms will try to strengthen themselves by forming alliances with each other through intermarriage. But they will not hold together, just as iron and clay do not mix.

44"During the reigns of those kings, the God of heaven will set up a kingdom that will never be destroyed or conquered. It will crush all these kingdoms into nothingness, and it will stand forever. 45That is the meaning of the rock cut from the mountain, though not by human hands, that crushed to pieces the statue of iron, bronze, clay, silver, and gold. The great God was showing the king what will happen in the future. The dream is true, and its meaning is certain."

## Nebuchadnezzar Rewards Daniel

46Then King Nebuchadnezzar threw himself down before Daniel and worshiped him, and he commanded his people to offer sacrifices and burn sweet incense before him. 47The king said to Daniel, "Truly, your God is the greatest of gods, the Lord over kings, a revealer of mysteries, for you have been able to reveal this secret."

48Then the king appointed Daniel to a high position and gave him many valuable gifts. He made Daniel ruler over the whole province of Babylon, as well as chief over all his wise men. 49At Daniel's request, the king appointed Shadrach, Meshach, and Abednego to be in charge of all the affairs of the province of Babylon, while Daniel remained in the king's court.

**2:30**
Gen 41:16
Ps 139:2
Isa 43:3
Dan 1:17

**2:31**
Hab 1:7

**2:34**
Dan 8:25
Zech 4:6

**2:35**
Pss 1:4; 37:10
Isa 17:13
Hos 13:3

**2:37**
Isa 10:8; 47:5
Jer 27:6-7
Ezek 26:7
Hos 8:10

**2:38**
Ps 50:10

**2:40**
Dan 7:7, 23

**2:44**
Pss 2:9; 145:13
Isa 9:6-7; 60:12
Ezek 37:25
Mic 4:7

**2:45**
Gen 41:28, 32
Deut 10:17
2 Sam 7:22
Dan 2:29
Rev 22:6

**2:46**
Lev 26:31
Acts 10:25; 14:13
Rev 19:10; 22:8

**2:47**
Deut 10:17
Amos 3:7

**2:48**
Gen 41:39-43

**2:49**
Esth 2:19, 21
Amos 5:15

---

**2:31ff** The head of gold on the statue in the dream represented Nebuchadnezzar, ruler of the Babylonian Empire. The silver chest and two arms represented the Medo-Persian Empire, which conquered Babylon in 539 B.C. The belly and thighs of bronze were Greece and Macedonia under Alexander the Great, who conquered the Medo-Persian Empire (334–330 B.C.). The legs of iron represented Rome, which conquered the Greeks in 63 B.C. The feet of clay and iron represented the breakup of the Roman Empire, when the territory Rome ruled divided into a mixture of strong and weak nations. The type of metal in each part depicted the strength of the political power it represented. The rock cut out of the mountain depicted God's Kingdom, which would be ruled eternally by the Messiah, the King of kings. The dream revealed Daniel's God as the power behind all earthly kingdoms.

**2:44** God's Kingdom will never be destroyed. If you are upset by threats of war and the prosperity of evil leaders, remember that God, not world leaders, decides the outcome of history. Under

God's protection, God's Kingdom is indestructible. Those who trust in God are members of his Kingdom and are secure in him.

**2:47** Nebuchadnezzar honored Daniel and Daniel's God. If Daniel had taken the credit himself, the king would have honored only Daniel. Because Daniel gave God the credit, the king honored both of them. Part of our mission in this world is to show unbelievers what God is like. We can do that by acts of love and compassion; and if we give God credit for our actions, they will want to know more about him. Give thanks to God for what he is doing in and through you.

**2:49** After being named ruler over the whole province of Babylon and placed in charge of the wise men, Daniel requested that his companions, Shadrach, Meshach, and Abednego, be appointed as his assistants. Daniel knew that he could not handle such an enormous responsibility without capable assistants, so he chose the best men he knew—his three Hebrew companions. A competent leader never does all the work alone; he or she knows how to delegate and supervise. Moses, Israel's greatest

### Nebuchadnezzar's Gold Statue

**3:1**
Isa 46:6
Jer 16:20
Dan 2:31
Hab 2:19

**3:2**
Dan 3:3, 27; 6:1-7

**3:4**
Isa 40:9; 58:1
Dan 3:7; 4:1; 6:25
Rev 18:2

**3:5**
Dan 3:7, 10

**3:6**
Jer 29:22
Dan 3:11, 15, 21; 6:7
Matt 13:42
Rev 9:2; 14:11

**3** King Nebuchadnezzar made a gold statue ninety feet tall and nine feet wide* and set it up on the plain of Dura in the province of Babylon. ²Then he sent messages to the high officers, officials, governors, advisers, treasurers, judges, magistrates, and all the provincial officials to come to the dedication of the statue he had set up. ³So all these officials* came and stood before the statue King Nebuchadnezzar had set up.

⁴Then a herald shouted out, "People of all races and nations and languages, listen to the king's command! ⁵When you hear the sound of the horn, flute, zither, lyre, harp, pipes, and other musical instruments,* bow to the ground to worship King Nebuchadnezzar's gold statue. ⁶Anyone who refuses to obey will immediately be thrown into a blazing furnace."

⁷So at the sound of the musical instruments,* all the people, whatever their race or nation or language, bowed to the ground and worshiped the gold statue that King Nebuchadnezzar had set up.

**3:1** Aramaic *60 cubits* [27 meters] *tall and 6 cubits* [2.7 meters] *wide.* **3:3** Aramaic *the high officers, officials, governors, advisers, treasurers, judges, magistrates, and all the provincial officials.* **3:5** The identification of some of these musical instruments is uncertain. **3:7** Aramaic *the horn, flute, zither, lyre, harp, and other musical instruments.*

Daniel's early life demonstrates that there is more to being young than making mistakes. No characteristic wins the hearts of adults more quickly than wisdom in the words and actions of a young person. Daniel and his friends had been taken from their homes in Judah and exiled. Their futures were in doubt, but they all had personal traits that qualified them for jobs as servants in the king's palace. They took advantage of the opportunity without letting the opportunity take advantage of them.

Our first hint of Daniel's greatness comes in his quiet refusal to give up his convictions. He had applied God's will to his own life, and he resisted changing the good habits he had formed. Both his physical and spiritual diets were an important part of his relationship with God. He ate carefully and lived prayerfully. One of the benefits of being in training for royal service was eating food from the king's table. Daniel tactfully chose a simpler menu and proved it was a healthy choice. As with Daniel, mealtimes are obvious and regular tests of our efforts to control our appetites.

While Daniel limited his food intake, he indulged in prayer. He was able to communicate with God because he made it a habit. He put into practice his convictions, even when that meant being thrown into a den of hungry lions. His life proved he made the right choice.

Do you hold so strongly to your faith in God that whatever happens you will do what God says? Such conviction keeps you a step ahead of temptation; such conviction gives you wisdom and stability in changing circumstances. Prayerfully live out your convictions in everyday life and trust God for the results.

| | |
|---|---|
| **Strengths and accomplishments** | • Although young when deported, remained true to his faith<br>• Served as an adviser to two Babylonian kings and two Medo-Persian kings<br>• Was a man of prayer and a statesman with the gift of prophecy<br>• Survived the lions' den |
| **Lessons from his life** | • Quiet convictions often earn long-term respect<br>• Don't wait until you are in a tough situation to learn about prayer<br>• God can use people wherever they are |
| **Vital statistics** | • Where: Judah and the courts of both Babylon and Persia<br>• Occupation: A captive from Israel who became an adviser of kings<br>• Contemporaries: Shadrach, Meshach, Abednego, Nebuchadnezzar, Belshazzar, Darius, Cyrus |
| **Key verse** | "This man Daniel, whom the king named Belteshazzar, has exceptional ability and is filled with divine knowledge and understanding. He can interpret dreams, explain riddles, and solve difficult problems. Call for Daniel, and he will tell you what the writing means" (Daniel 5:12). |

Daniel's story is told in the book of Daniel. He is also mentioned in Matthew 24:15.

leader, shared the burden of administration with dozens of assistants. (This story is in Exodus 18:13-27.)

**3:1** In Babylon's religious culture, statues were frequently worshiped. Nebuchadnezzar hoped to use this huge image (90 feet high by 9 feet wide) as a strategy to unite the nation and solidify his power by centralizing worship. This gold statue may have been inspired by his dream. Instead of having only a head of gold, however, it was gold from head to toe. Nebuchadnezzar wanted his kingdom to last forever. When he made

the statue, Nebuchadnezzar showed that his devotion to Daniel's God was short-lived. He neither feared nor obeyed the God who was behind the dream.

**3:6** This blazing furnace was not a small oven for cooking dinner or heating a house; it was a huge industrial furnace that could have been used for baking bricks or smelting metals. The temperatures were hot enough to assure that no one could survive. The roaring flames could be seen leaping from its top opening, and a fiery blast killed the soldiers who went up to the large opening (3:22).

8But some of the astrologers* went to the king and informed on the Jews. 9They said to King Nebuchadnezzar, "Long live the king! 10You issued a decree requiring all the people to bow down and worship the gold statue when they hear the sound of the horn, flute, zither, lyre, harp, pipes, and other musical instruments. 11That decree also states that those who refuse to obey must be thrown into a blazing furnace. 12But there are some Jews—Shadrach, Meshach, and Abednego—whom you have put in charge of the province of Babylon. They pay no attention to you, Your Majesty. They refuse to serve your gods and do not worship the gold statue you have set up."

13Then Nebuchadnezzar flew into a rage and ordered that Shadrach, Meshach, and Abednego be brought before him. When they were brought in, 14Nebuchadnezzar said to them, "Is it true, Shadrach, Meshach, and Abednego, that you refuse to serve my gods or to worship the gold statue I have set up? 15I will give you one more chance to bow down and worship the statue I have made when you hear the sound of the musical instruments.* But if you refuse, you will be thrown immediately into the blazing furnace. And then what god will be able to rescue you from my power?"

16Shadrach, Meshach, and Abednego replied, "O Nebuchadnezzar, we do not need to defend ourselves before you. 17If we are thrown into the blazing furnace, the God whom we serve is able to save us. He will rescue us from your power, Your Majesty. 18But even if he doesn't, we want to make it clear to you, Your Majesty, that we will never serve your gods or worship the gold statue you have set up."

## The Blazing Furnace

19Nebuchadnezzar was so furious with Shadrach, Meshach, and Abednego that his face became distorted with rage. He commanded that the furnace be heated seven times hotter than usual. 20Then he ordered some of the strongest men of his army to bind Shadrach, Meshach, and Abednego and throw them into the blazing furnace. 21So they tied them up and threw them into the furnace, fully dressed in their pants, turbans, robes, and other garments. 22And because the king, in his anger, had demanded such a hot fire in the furnace, the flames killed the soldiers as they threw the three men in. 23So Shadrach, Meshach, and Abednego, securely tied, fell into the roaring flames.

24But suddenly, Nebuchadnezzar jumped up in amazement and exclaimed to his advisers, "Didn't we tie up three men and throw them into the furnace?"

"Yes, Your Majesty, we certainly did," they replied.

25"Look!" Nebuchadnezzar shouted. "I see four men, unbound, walking around in the fire unharmed! And the fourth looks like a god*!"

**3:8** Aramaic *Chaldeans.*   **3:15** Aramaic *the horn, flute, zither, lyre, harp, pipes, and other musical instruments.*
**3:25** Aramaic *like a son of the gods.*

### Cross-references (margin)

**3:8** Ezra 4:12-16 / Esth 3:8-9
**3:10** Dan 6:12
**3:13** Dan 2:12; 3:19
**3:14** Isa 46:1 / Dan 3:1; 4:8
**3:15** Exod 5:2 / Isa 36:18-20 / Jer 50:2 / Dan 2:47
**3:16** Dan 1:7; 3:12
**3:17** 1 Sam 17:37 / Ps 27:1-2 / Isa 26:3-4 / Jer 1:8
**3:18** Josh 24:15 / 1 Kgs 19:14 / Dan 3:28
**3:19** Lev 26:18-28
**3:22** Dan 2:15
**3:25** Isa 43:2 / Jer 1:8, 19

---

**3:12** We don't know if other Jews refused to fall down and worship the statue, but these three were singled out as public examples. Why didn't the three men just bow to the image and tell God that they didn't mean it? They had determined never to worship another god, and they courageously took their stand. As a result, they were condemned and led away to be executed. The men did not know whether they would be delivered from the fire; all they knew was that they would not fall down and worship an idol. Are you ready to take a stand for God no matter what? When you stand for God, you will stand out. It may be painful, and it may not always have a happy ending. Be prepared to say, "If he rescues me, or if he doesn't, I will serve only God."

**3:13** Nebuchadnezzar flew into a rage when anyone dared to disobey his commands. As the supreme ruler of Babylon, he expected absolute obedience. But his pride had caused him to go beyond his own authority. His demands were unjust and his reactions extreme. If you find yourself angered when people don't follow your directions, ask yourself, Why am I reacting this way? Your ego may be overly involved with your authority.

**3:15** The three men were given one more chance. Here are eight excuses they could have used to bow to the statue and save their lives: (1) We will fall down but not actually *worship* the idol. (2) We won't become idol worshipers but will worship it this one time, and then ask God for forgiveness. (3) The king has absolute power, and we must obey him. God will understand. (4) The king

appointed us—we owe this to him. (5) This is a foreign land, so God will excuse us for following the customs of the land. (6) Our ancestors set up idols in God's Temple! This isn't half as bad! (7) We're not hurting anybody. (8) If we get ourselves killed and some pagans take our high positions, they won't help our people in exile!

Although all these excuses sound sensible at first, they are dangerous rationalizations. To fall down and worship the image would violate God's command in Exodus 20:3, "You must not have any other god but me." It would also erase their testimony for God forever. Never again could they talk about the power of their God above all other gods. What excuses do you use for not standing up for him?

**3:16-18** Shadrach, Meshach, and Abednego were pressured to deny God, but they chose to be faithful to him no matter what happened! They trusted God to deliver them, but they were determined to be faithful regardless of the consequences. If God always rescued those who were true to him, Christians would not need faith. Their religion would be a great insurance policy, and there would be lines of selfish people ready to sign up. We should be faithful to serve God whether he intervenes on our behalf or not. Our eternal reward is worth any suffering we may have to endure first.

**3:25** It was obvious to those watching that this fourth person was supernatural. We cannot be certain who the fourth man was.

3:26
Deut 4:20
1 Kgs 8:51
3:27
Isa 43:2
Dan 3:2
Heb 11:34
3:28
Ps 34:7-8
Isa 37:36
Dan 3:25; 6:22
Acts 5:19; 12:7

26Then Nebuchadnezzar came as close as he could to the door of the flaming furnace and shouted: "Shadrach, Meshach, and Abednego, servants of the Most High God, come out! Come here!"

So Shadrach, Meshach, and Abednego stepped out of the fire. 27Then the high officers, officials, governors, and advisers crowded around them and saw that the fire had not touched them. Not a hair on their heads was singed, and their clothing was not scorched. They didn't even smell of smoke!

28Then Nebuchadnezzar said, "Praise to the God of Shadrach, Meshach, and Abednego!

## SHADRACH/MESHACH/ABEDNEGO

Friendships make life enjoyable and difficult times bearable. Friendships are tested and strengthened by hardships. Such was the relationship between three young Jewish men deported to Babylon along with Daniel. Shadrach, Meshach, and Abednego help us think about the real meaning of friendship. As much as these friends meant to each other, they never allowed their friendship to usurp God's place in their lives—not even in the face of death.

Together they silently defied King Nebuchadnezzar's order to fall down and worship his gold statue. They shared a courageous act, while others, eager to get rid of them, told the king that the three Jews were being disloyal. While this was not true, Nebuchadnezzar could not spare them without losing face.

This was the moment of truth. Death was about to end their friendship. A small compromise would have allowed them to live and go on enjoying each other, serving God, and serving their people while in this foreign land. But they were wise enough to see that compromise would have poisoned the very conviction that bound them so closely—each had a higher allegiance to God. So they did not hesitate to place their lives in the hands of God. The rest was victory!

When we leave God out of our most important relationships, we tend to expect those relationships to meet needs in us that only God can meet. Friends are helpful, but they cannot meet our deepest spiritual needs. Leaving God out of our relationships indicates how unimportant he really is in our own life. Our relationship with God should be important enough to touch our other relationships—especially our closest friendships.

| | |
|---|---|
| **Strengths and accomplishments** | • Stood with Daniel against eating food from the king's table<br>• Shared a friendship that stood the tests of hardship, success, wealth, and possible death<br>• Unwilling to compromise their convictions even in the face of death<br>• Survived the blazing furnace |
| **Lessons from their lives** | • There is great strength in real friendship<br>• It is important to stand with others with whom we share convictions<br>• God can be trusted even when we can't predict the outcome |
| **Vital statistics** | • Where: Babylon<br>• Occupations: King's servants and advisers<br>• Contemporaries: Daniel, Nebuchadnezzar |
| **Key verses** | "Shadrach, Meshach, and Abednego replied, 'O Nebuchadnezzar, we do not need to defend ourselves before you. If we are thrown into the blazing furnace, the God whom we serve is able to save us. He will rescue us from your power, Your Majesty. But even if he doesn't, we want to make it clear to you, Your Majesty, that we will never serve your gods or worship the gold statue you have set up'" (Daniel 3:16-18). |

The story of Shadrach (Hananiah), Meshach (Mishael), and Abednego (Azariah) is told in the book of Daniel.

---

It could have been an angel or a preincarnate appearance of Christ. In either case, God sent a heavenly visitor to accompany these faithful men during their time of great trial.

**3:25-30** God's deliverance of Shadrach, Meshach, and Abednego was a great victory of faith for the Jews in captivity. They were protected from harm, they were comforted in trial, God was glorified, and they were rewarded. Let us determine to be true to God no matter how difficult the pressure or punishment. God's protection transcends anything we could imagine.

**3:27** These young men had been completely untouched by the fire and heat. Only the rope that bound them had been burned. No human can bind us if God wants us to be free. The power available to us is the same that delivered Shadrach, Meshach, and Abednego and raised Christ from the dead (Ephesians 1:18-20). Trust God in every situation. There are eternal reasons for temporary trials, so be thankful that your destiny is in God's hands, not in human hands.

**3:28, 29** Nebuchadnezzar was not making a commitment here to serve the Hebrews' God alone. Instead, he was acknowledging that God is powerful, and he commanded his people not to speak against God. Nebuchadnezzar didn't tell the people to throw away all the other gods but to add this one to the list.

He sent his angel to rescue his servants who trusted in him. They defied the king's command and were willing to die rather than serve or worship any god except their own God. 29 Therefore, I make this decree: If any people, whatever their race or nation or language, speak a word against the God of Shadrach, Meshach, and Abednego, they will be torn limb from limb, and their houses will be turned into heaps of rubble. There is no other god who can rescue like this!"

**3:29**
Ezra 6:11
Dan 3:12, 15

30 Then the king promoted Shadrach, Meshach, and Abednego to even higher positions in the province of Babylon.

**3:30**
Dan 2:49; 3:12

## Nebuchadnezzar's Dream about a Tree

**4** 1*King Nebuchadnezzar sent this message to the people of every race and nation and language throughout the world:

**4:1**
Dan 6:25

"Peace and prosperity to you!

2"I want you all to know about the miraculous signs and wonders the Most High God has performed for me.

3 How great are his signs,
   how powerful his wonders!
His kingdom will last forever,
   his rule through all generations.

**4:3**
Deut 4:34
Ps 77:19
Isa 25:1
Dan 2:44; 4:34;
6:26

4*"I, Nebuchadnezzar, was living in my palace in comfort and prosperity. 5 But one night I had a dream that frightened me; I saw visions that terrified me as I lay in my bed. 6So I issued an order calling in all the wise men of Babylon, so they could tell me what my dream meant. 7When all the magicians, enchanters, astrologers,* and fortune-tellers came in, I told them the dream, but they could not tell me what it meant. 8At last Daniel came in before me, and I told him the dream. (He was named Belteshazzar after my god, and the spirit of the holy gods is in him.)

**4:4**
Ps 30:6
Isa 47:7-8

**4:5**
Dan 4:10, 13

**4:6**
Gen 41:8
Dan 2:2

9"I said to him, 'Belteshazzar, chief of the magicians, I know that the spirit of the holy gods is in you and that no mystery is too great for you to solve. Now tell me what my dream means.

**4:7**
Isa 44:25
Jer 27:9-10
Dan 2:7

10"'While I was lying in my bed, this is what I dreamed. I saw a large tree in the middle of the earth. 11 The tree grew very tall and strong, reaching high into the heavens for all the world to see. 12It had fresh green leaves, and it was loaded with fruit for all to eat. Wild animals lived in its shade, and birds nested in its branches. All the world was fed from this tree.

**4:8**
Dan 1:7; 4:9, 18

**4:9**
Gen 41:38
Ezek 28:3
Dan 1:20; 2:4-5,
47-48; 4:8; 5:11

**4:10**
Ezek 31:3-4

13"'Then as I lay there dreaming, I saw a messenger,* a holy one, coming down from heaven. 14The messenger shouted,

**4:12**
Jer 27:6-7
Ezek 31:7
Matt 13:32
Luke 13:19

"Cut down the tree and lop off its branches!
   Shake off its leaves and scatter its fruit!
Chase the wild animals from its shade
   and the birds from its branches.

**4:13**
Deut 33:2
Ps 89:7
Dan 8:13

15 But leave the stump and the roots in the ground,
   bound with a band of iron and bronze
   and surrounded by tender grass.
Now let him be drenched with the dew of heaven,
   and let him live with the wild animals among the plants of the field.

**4:14**
Jer 51:5-6
Ezek 31:10-14
Matt 3:10; 7:19
Rev 10:3; 18:2

**4:15**
Job 14:7-9

16 For seven periods of time,
   let him have the mind of a wild animal
   instead of the mind of a human.

**4:16**
Dan 7:25

4:1 Verses 4:1-3 are numbered 3:31-33 in Aramaic text.    4:4 Verses 4:4-37 are numbered 4:1-34 in Aramaic text.
4:7 Or *Chaldeans.*    4:13 Aramaic *a watcher;* also in 4:23.

---

**3:30** Where was Daniel in this story? The Bible doesn't say, but there are several possibilities: (1) He may have been on official business in another part of the kingdom. (2) He may have been present, but because he was a ruler, the officials didn't accuse him of not falling down and worshiping the image. (3) He may have been in the capital city handling the administration while Nebuchadnezzar was away. (4) He may have been considered exempt from bowing down to the image because of his reputation for interpreting dreams through his God. Whether Daniel was there or not, we can be sure that he would not have worshiped the statue.

**4:2, 3** Although Nebuchadnezzar praised Daniel's God, he still did not believe in him completely or submit to him alone (4:8). Many people attend church and use Christian language, but they really don't honor God with their lives. Profession doesn't always mean possession. Does your life match your profession of faith?

**4:17**
1 Sam 2:8
Ps 9:16
Dan 4:25; 11:21

17 For this has been decreed by the messengers*;
  it is commanded by the holy ones,
so that everyone may know
  that the Most High rules over the kingdoms of the world.
He gives them to anyone he chooses—
  even to the lowliest of people."

**4:18**
Gen 41:8
1 Kgs 14:2-3
Dan 4:7; 5:8

18 "'Belteshazzar, that was the dream that I, King Nebuchadnezzar, had. Now tell me what it means, for none of the wise men of my kingdom can do so. But you can tell me because the spirit of the holy gods is in you.'

**4:17** Aramaic *the watchers.*

---

**NEBUCHADNEZZAR**

Nebuchadnezzar was one world leader who decided he could get more cooperation from the people he conquered by letting them keep their gods. Their lands he took, their riches he robbed, their lives he controlled, but their idols he allowed them to worship, sometimes even worshiping them himself. Nebuchadnezzar's plan worked well, with one glaring exception. When he conquered the little nation of Judah, he met a God who demanded *exclusive* worship—not just his share among many gods. In a sense, Nebuchadnezzar had always been able to rule the gods. This new God was different; this God dared to claim that he had made Nebuchadnezzar all that he was. One of the great conquerors in history was himself conquered by his Creator.

The Bible allows us to note the ways in which God worked on Nebuchadnezzar. God allowed him victories, but he was accomplishing God's purposes. God allowed him to deport the best young Jewish leaders as his palace servants, while placing close to him a young man named Daniel, who would change the king's life. God allowed Nebuchadnezzar to attempt to kill three of his servants to teach the king that he did not really have power over life and death. God warned him of the dangers in his pride and then allowed Nebuchadnezzar to live through seven years of insanity before restoring him to the throne. God showed the king who was really in control!

These lessons are clear to us today because of our place in history. When our attention shifts to our own lives, we often find ourselves unable to see how God is working. But we do have the advantage of God's Word as our guide for today's challenges. We are commanded to obey God; we are also commanded to trust him. Trusting him covers those times when we are not sure about the outcome. God has entrusted us with this day; have we trusted him with our life?

| | |
|---|---|
| **Strengths and accomplishments** | • Greatest of the Babylonian kings<br>• Known as a builder of cities<br>• Described in the Bible as one of the foreign rulers God used for his purposes |
| **Weaknesses and mistakes** | • Thought of himself as a god and was persuaded to build a gold statue that all were to worship<br>• Became extremely proud, which led to a bout of insanity<br>• Tended to forget the demonstrations of God's power he had witnessed |
| **Lessons from his life** | • History records the actions of God's willing servants and those who were his unwitting tools<br>• A leader's greatness is affected by the quality of his advisers<br>• Uncontrolled pride is self-destructive |
| **Vital statistics** | • Where: Babylon<br>• Occupation: King<br>• Relatives: Father: Nabopolassar. Son: Evil-merodach. Grandson: Belshazzar.<br>• Contemporaries: Jeremiah, Ezekiel, Daniel, Jehoiakim, Jehoiachin |
| **Key verse** | "Now I, Nebuchadnezzar, praise and glorify and honor the King of heaven. All his acts are just and true, and he is able to humble the proud" (Daniel 4:37). |

Nebuchadnezzar's story is told in 2 Kings 24—25; 2 Chronicles 36; Jeremiah 21—52; Daniel 1—4.

---

**4:17** One of the most difficult lessons to learn is that God is sovereign. He is above all of those who are above us. He limits the power and authority of all the government, business, and religious leaders in the world. Those who live in freedom and with a relatively high degree of autonomy find this difficult to understand. While we may feel as though we are free to do what we please, God is sovereign over all of our plans and desires.

## Daniel Explains the Dream

[19]"Upon hearing this, Daniel (also known as Belteshazzar) was overcome for a time, frightened by the meaning of the dream. Then the king said to him, 'Belteshazzar, don't be alarmed by the dream and what it means.'

"Belteshazzar replied, 'I wish the events foreshadowed in this dream would happen to your enemies, my lord, and not to you! [20]The tree you saw was growing very tall and strong, reaching high into the heavens for all the world to see. [21]It had fresh green leaves and was loaded with fruit for all to eat. Wild animals lived in its shade, and birds nested in its branches. [22]That tree, Your Majesty, is you. For you have grown strong and great; your greatness reaches up to heaven, and your rule to the ends of the earth.

[23]"'Then you saw a messenger, a holy one, coming down from heaven and saying, "Cut down the tree and destroy it. But leave the stump and the roots in the ground, bound with a band of iron and bronze and surrounded by tender grass. Let him be drenched with the dew of heaven. Let him live with the animals of the field for seven periods of time."

[24]"'This is what the dream means, Your Majesty, and what the Most High has declared will happen to my lord the king. [25]You will be driven from human society, and you will live in the fields with the wild animals. You will eat grass like a cow, and you will be drenched with the dew of heaven. Seven periods of time will pass while you live this way, until you learn that the Most High rules over the kingdoms of the world and gives them to anyone he chooses. [26]But the stump and roots of the tree were left in the ground. This means that you will receive your kingdom back again when you have learned that heaven rules.

[27]"'King Nebuchadnezzar, please accept my advice. Stop sinning and do what is right. Break from your wicked past and be merciful to the poor. Perhaps then you will continue to prosper.'

## The Dream's Fulfillment

[28]"But all these things did happen to King Nebuchadnezzar. [29]Twelve months later he was taking a walk on the flat roof of the royal palace in Babylon. [30]As he looked out across the city, he said, 'Look at this great city of Babylon! By my own mighty power, I have built this beautiful city as my royal residence to display my majestic splendor.'

[31]"While these words were still in his mouth, a voice called down from heaven, 'O King Nebuchadnezzar, this message is for you! You are no longer ruler of this kingdom. [32]You will be driven from human society. You will live in the fields with the wild animals, and you will eat grass like a cow. Seven periods of time will pass while you live this way, until you learn that the Most High rules over the kingdoms of the world and gives them to anyone he chooses.'

[33]"That same hour the judgment was fulfilled, and Nebuchadnezzar was driven from human society. He ate grass like a cow, and he was drenched with the dew of heaven. He lived this way until his hair was as long as eagles' feathers and his nails were like birds' claws.

## Nebuchadnezzar Praises God

[34]"After this time had passed, I, Nebuchadnezzar, looked up to heaven. My sanity returned, and I praised and worshiped the Most High and honored the one who lives forever.

**4:19**
1 Sam 3:17
2 Sam 18:32
Dan 7:15, 28; 8:27

**4:22**
2 Sam 12:7
Jer 27:6-7
Dan 2:37-38

**4:24**
Job 40:11-12
Ps 107:40

**4:25**
Ps 75:7
Jer 27:5
Dan 4:17, 33; 5:21

**4:26**
Dan 4:31

**4:27**
Gen 41:33-37
1 Kgs 21:29
Ps 41:1-3
Prov 28:13
Isa 55:6-7
Ezek 18:21-22
Jon 3:9

**4:28**
Zech 1:6

**4:29**
2 Pet 3:9

**4:30**
Hab 2:4

**4:33**
Dan 4:25; 5:21

**4:34**
Ps 102:24
Jer 10:10
Dan 4:2; 5:18, 21
Rev 4:10; 10:6

---

**4:19** When Daniel understood Nebuchadnezzar's dream, he was stunned, and he wondered how to break the news. He told the king he wished what the dream foreshadowed would happen to the king's enemies and not to Nebuchadnezzar. How could Daniel be so deeply grieved at the fate of Nebuchadnezzar—the king who was responsible for the destruction of Daniel's home and nation? Daniel had forgiven Nebuchadnezzar, and so God was able to use Daniel. Very often when we have been wronged by someone, we find it difficult to forget the past. We may even be glad when that person suffers. Forgiveness means putting the past behind us. Can you love someone who has hurt you? Can you serve someone who mistreated you? Ask God to help you forgive, forget, and love. God may use you in an extraordinary way in that person's life!

**4:23ff** Although much of the world thought that Nebuchadnezzar was a mighty (even divine) king, God demonstrated that Nebu-

chadnezzar was an ordinary man. The king would go insane and become like an animal for a set period of time ("seven periods of time"). God humiliated Nebuchadnezzar to show that almighty God, not Nebuchadnezzar, was Lord of the nations. No matter how powerful a person may become, self-centered pride will push God from his or her life. Pride may be one of the most dangerous temptations you will face. Don't let your accomplishments cause you to forget God.

**4:27-33** Daniel pleaded with Nebuchadnezzar to change his ways, and God gave Nebuchadnezzar 12 months to do it. Unfortunately, there was no repentance in the heart of this proud king, and so the dream was fulfilled.

**4:34** Ancient kings tried to avoid mentioning their weaknesses or defeats in their monuments and official records. From Nebuchadnezzar's records, however, we can infer that for a time during his

His rule is everlasting,
   and his kingdom is eternal.
35 All the people of the earth
   are nothing compared to him.
He does as he pleases
   among the angels of heaven
   and among the people of the earth.
No one can stop him or say to him,
   'What do you mean by doing these things?'

36 "When my sanity returned to me, so did my honor and glory and kingdom. My advisers and nobles sought me out, and I was restored as head of my kingdom, with even greater honor than before.

37 "Now I, Nebuchadnezzar, praise and glorify and honor the King of heaven. All his acts are just and true, and he is able to humble the proud."

### The Writing on the Wall

**5** Many years later King Belshazzar gave a great feast for 1,000 of his nobles, and he drank wine with them. ²While Belshazzar was drinking the wine, he gave orders to bring in the gold and silver cups that his predecessor,* Nebuchadnezzar, had taken from the Temple in Jerusalem. He wanted to drink from them with his nobles, his wives, and his concubines. ³So they brought these gold cups taken from the Temple, the house of God in Jerusalem, and the king and his nobles, his wives, and his concubines drank from them. ⁴While they drank from them they praised their idols made of gold, silver, bronze, iron, wood, and stone.

⁵Suddenly, they saw the fingers of a human hand writing on the plaster wall of the king's palace, near the lampstand. The king himself saw the hand as it wrote, ⁶and his face turned pale with fright. His knees knocked together in fear and his legs gave way beneath him.

⁷The king shouted for the enchanters, astrologers,* and fortune-tellers to be brought before him. He said to these wise men of Babylon, "Whoever can read this writing and tell me what it means will be dressed in purple robes of royal honor and will have a gold chain placed around his neck. He will become the third highest ruler in the kingdom!"

⁸But when all the king's wise men had come in, none of them could read the writing or tell him what it meant. ⁹So the king grew even more alarmed, and his face turned pale. His nobles, too, were shaken.

¹⁰But when the queen mother heard what was happening, she hurried to the banquet hall. She said to Belshazzar, "Long live the king! Don't be so pale and frightened. ¹¹There is a man in your kingdom who has within him the spirit of the holy gods. During Nebuchadnezzar's reign, this man was found to have insight, understanding, and wisdom like that of

**Cross-references (left margin):**

**4:35** Job 42:2; Ps 135:6; Isa 40:17; 43:13; 45:9; Dan 6:27; Rom 9:20

**4:36** 2 Chr 33:12-13; Prov 22:4; Dan 2:31

**4:37** Exod 18:11; Ps 33:4-5; Matt 23:12

**5:1** Esth 1:3; Isa 22:12-14

**5:2** 2 Kgs 24:13; Ezra 1:7-11; Dan 1:2

**5:4** Rev 9:20

**5:6** Ps 69:23; Ezek 7:17; 21:7; Dan 7:28; Nah 2:10

**5:7** Gen 41:42-44; Isa 44:25; 47:13; Ezek 16:11; Dan 5:11, 16, 29; 6:2-3

**5:9** Job 18:11-14; Isa 21:2-4; Jer 6:24; Dan 5:6

**5:10** Dan 3:9; 6:6

**5:11** Gen 41:11-15; Dan 2:47; 4:8-9; 5:14

**5:2** Aramaic *father;* also in 5:11, 13, 18.   **5:7** Or *Chaldeans;* also in 5:11.

---

43-year reign he did not rule. The Bible, however, explains Nebuchadnezzar's pride and punishment.

**4:36** Nebuchadnezzar's pilgrimage with God is one of the themes of this book. In 2:47, he acknowledged that God revealed mysteries to Daniel. In 3:28, 29 he praised the God who rescued the three Hebrews. Despite Nebuchadnezzar's recognition that God exists and works great miracles, in 4:30 we see that he still did not acknowledge God as his Lord. We may recognize that God exists and does wonderful miracles, but so do many unbelievers! To be a child of God, you must invite him to be Lord of your life.

**5:1** Sixty-six years have elapsed since chapter 1, which tells of Nebuchadnezzar's second strike against Jerusalem in 605 B.C. Nebuchadnezzar died in 562 B.C. after a reign of 43 years. His son, Evil-merodach, ruled from 562 to 560 B.C.; his brother-in-law Neriglissar reigned four years from 560 to 556 B.C. After a two-month reign by Labashi-marduk in 556 B.C., the Babylonian Empire continued from 556 to 539 B.C. under the command of Nabonidus. Belshazzar was the son of Nabonidus. He co-reigned with his father from 553 to 539 B.C.

**5:1** Archaeologists have recently discovered Belshazzar's name on several documents. He ruled with his father, Nabonidus, stay-

ing home to administer the affairs of the kingdom while his father tried to reopen trade routes taken over by Cyrus and the Persians. Belshazzar was in charge of the city of Babylon when it was captured.

**5:7** Belshazzar served as co-regent with his father, Nabonidus. Thus, Nabonidus was the first ruler and his son Belshazzar, the second. The person who could read the writing would be given third place, which was the highest position and honor that Belshazzar could offer.

**5:8** Although the writing on the wall contained only three words in Aramaic, a language understood by Babylonians (see 2:4), the people could not determine its prophetic significance. God gave Daniel alone the ability to interpret the message of doom to Babylon. The wise men of the kingdom were ignorant of God's wisdom, no matter how great the reward. Daniel did not rush into the banquet hall with the others. His loyalty was to God, not money.

**5:10** This queen mother was either Nabonidus's wife or the wife of one of his predecessors, possibly even of Nebuchadnezzar. She was not Belshazzar's wife, because his wives were with him in the banquet hall.

the gods. Your predecessor, the king—your predecessor King Nebuchadnezzar—made him chief over all the magicians, enchanters, astrologers, and fortune-tellers of Babylon. [12]This man Daniel, whom the king named Belteshazzar, has exceptional ability and is filled with divine knowledge and understanding. He can interpret dreams, explain riddles, and solve difficult problems. Call for Daniel, and he will tell you what the writing means."

### Daniel Explains the Writing

[13]So Daniel was brought in before the king. The king asked him, "Are you Daniel, one of the exiles brought from Judah by my predecessor, King Nebuchadnezzar? [14]I have heard that you have the spirit of the gods within you and that you are filled with insight, understanding, and wisdom. [15]My wise men and enchanters have tried to read the words on the wall and tell me their meaning, but they cannot do it. [16]I am told that you can give interpretations and solve difficult problems. If you can read these words and tell me their meaning, you will be clothed in purple robes of royal honor, and you will have a gold chain placed around your neck. You will become the third highest ruler in the kingdom."

[17]Daniel answered the king, "Keep your gifts or give them to someone else, but I will tell you what the writing means. [18]Your Majesty, the Most High God gave sovereignty, majesty, glory, and honor to your predecessor, Nebuchadnezzar. [19]He made him so great that people of all races and nations and languages trembled before him in fear. He killed those he wanted to kill and spared those he wanted to spare. He honored those he wanted to honor and disgraced those he wanted to disgrace. [20]But when his heart and mind were puffed up with arrogance, he was brought down from his royal throne and stripped of his glory. [21]He was driven from human society. He was given the mind of a wild animal, and he lived among the wild donkeys. He ate grass like a cow, and he was drenched with the dew of heaven, until he learned that the Most High God rules over the kingdoms of the world and appoints anyone he desires to rule over them.

[22]"You are his successor,* O Belshazzar, and you knew all this, yet you have not humbled yourself. [23]For you have proudly defied the Lord of heaven and have had these cups from his Temple brought before you. You and your nobles and your wives and concubines have been drinking wine from them while praising gods of silver, gold, bronze, iron, wood, and stone—gods that neither see nor hear nor know anything at all. But you have not honored the God who gives you the breath of life and controls your destiny! [24]So God has sent this hand to write this message.

[25]"This is the message that was written: Mene, Mene, Tekel, and Parsin. [26]This is what these words mean:

Mene means 'numbered'—God has numbered the days of your reign and has brought it to an end.

[27] Tekel means 'weighed'—you have been weighed on the balances and have not measured up.

**5:22** Aramaic son.

| | |
|---|---|
| **5:12** | Dan 4:18 |
| **5:13** | Dan 1:1; 2:25 |
| **5:15** | Isa 47:12; Dan 5:8 |
| **5:16** | Gen 40:8 |
| **5:17** | 2 Kgs 5:16 |
| **5:18** | Jer 25:5-7; Dan 2:37; 4:2, 17; 5:21 |
| **5:19** | Prov 16:14; Dan 2:12; 3:6; 11:3 |
| **5:20** | Exod 9:17; Isa 14:13-15; Jer 13:18; Dan 4:30; Luke 18:14 |
| **5:21** | Exod 9:14-16; Ps 83:17-18; Ezek 17:24 |
| **5:22** | Exod 10:3; 2 Chr 33:23; 36:12 |
| **5:23** | 2 Kgs 14:10; Job 3:14; 12:10; Jer 10:23; 50:29; Dan 5:3-4; Hab 2:18-19 |
| **5:26** | Isa 13:6, 17; Jer 50:41-43 |
| **5:27** | Job 31:6; Ps 62:9 |

---

**5:17** The king offered Daniel beautiful gifts and great power if he would explain the writing, but Daniel turned him down. Daniel was not motivated by material rewards. His entire life had been characterized by doing right. Daniel was not showing disrespect in refusing the gifts, but he was growing older himself and knew the gifts would do him little good. Besides, being third highest ruler in a kingdom Daniel knew was about to be destroyed was not exactly motivating! Daniel wanted to show that he was giving an unbiased interpretation to the king. Doing right should be our first priority, not gaining power or rewards. Do you love God enough to do what is right, even if it means giving up personal rewards?

**5:21-23** Belshazzar knew Babylonian history, and so he knew how God had humbled Nebuchadnezzar. Nevertheless Belshazzar's feast was open defiance to God's authority as he took the

gold cups from God's Temple and drank from them (5:2-4). No one who understands that God is the Creator of the universe should be foolish enough to challenge him.

**5:22** Often kings would kill the bearer of bad news. But Daniel was not afraid to tell the truth to the king even though it was not what he wanted to hear. We should be just as courageous in telling the truth under pressure.

**5:23, 24** Belshazzar used the cups from the Temple for his party, and God condemned him for this act. We must not use for sinful purposes what has been dedicated to God. Today this would include church buildings, financial donations, and anything else that has been set apart for serving God. Be careful how you use what is God's.

**5:27** The writing on the wall was a message for all those who defy God. Although Belshazzar had power and wealth, his kingdom was totally corrupt, and he could not withstand the judgment of God. God's time of judgment comes for all people. If you have forgotten God and slipped into a sinful way of life, turn away from your sin now before he removes any opportunities

**5:28**
Isa 21:2; 45:1-2
Dan 5:31; 6:28

**5:30**
Isa 21:4-9
Jer 51:11, 31, 39,
57

**5:31**
Dan 6:1; 9:1

**6:1**
Esth 1:1

**6:2**
Ezra 4:22
Esth 7:4

**6:3**
Gen 41:40
Dan 5:12

**6:4**
Gen 43:18
Luke 23:14-15
Phil 2:15

**6:5**
Acts 24:13-16

**6:6**
Neh 2:3

**6:7**
Pss 59:3; 62:4;
64:2-6
Matt 12:14

**6:8**
Esth 1:19; 3:12
Isa 10:1
Matt 24:35

**6:9**
Pss 118:9; 146:3

28 *Parsin** means 'divided'—your kingdom has been divided and given to the Medes and Persians."

29 Then at Belshazzar's command, Daniel was dressed in purple robes, a gold chain was hung around his neck, and he was proclaimed the third highest ruler in the kingdom. 30 That very night Belshazzar, the Babylonian* king, was killed.*

31 *And Darius the Mede took over the kingdom at the age of sixty-two.

### Daniel in the Lions' Den

**6** 1 *Darius the Mede decided to divide the kingdom into 120 provinces, and he appointed a high officer to rule over each province. 2 The king also chose Daniel and two others as administrators to supervise the high officers and protect the king's interests. 3 Daniel soon proved himself more capable than all the other administrators and high officers. Because of Daniel's great ability, the king made plans to place him over the entire empire.

4 Then the other administrators and high officers began searching for some fault in the way Daniel was handling government affairs, but they couldn't find anything to criticize or condemn. He was faithful, always responsible, and completely trustworthy. 5 So they concluded, "Our only chance of finding grounds for accusing Daniel will be in connection with the rules of his religion."

6 So the administrators and high officers went to the king and said, "Long live King Darius! 7 We are all in agreement—we administrators, officials, high officers, advisers, and governors—that the king should make a law that will be strictly enforced. Give orders that for the next thirty days any person who prays to anyone, divine or human—except to you, Your Majesty—will be thrown into the den of lions. 8 And now, Your Majesty, issue and sign this law so it cannot be changed, an official law of the Medes and Persians that cannot be revoked." 9 So King Darius signed the law.

**5:28** Aramaic *Peres*, the singular of *Parsin*.   **5:30a** Or *Chaldean*.   **5:30b** The Persians and Medes conquered Babylon in October 539 B.C.   **5:31** Verse 5:31 is numbered 6:1 in Aramaic text.   **6:1** Verses 6:1-28 are numbered 6:2-29 in Aramaic text.

| KINGS DANIEL SERVED | Name | Empire | Story told in | Memorable event |
|---|---|---|---|---|
| | Nebuchad-nezzar | Babylonia | chapters 1–4 | Shadrach, Meshach, and Abednego thrown into blazing furnace; Nebuchadnezzar became insane for 7 years |
| | Belshazzar | Babylonia | chapters 5, 7–8 | Daniel read the writing on the wall, which signaled the end of the Babylonian Empire |
| | Darius | Medo-Persia | chapters 6, 9 | Daniel thrown into a lions' den |
| | Cyrus | Medo-Persia | chapters 10–12 | The exiles return to their homeland in Judah and their capital city, Jerusalem |

to repent. Ask God to forgive you, and begin to live by his standards of justice.

**5:28** The Medes and Persians joined forces to overthrow Babylon. This event was predicted in the second phase of Nebuchadnezzar's dream in chapter 2—the silver chest and arms.

**5:31** Darius and his soldiers entered Babylon by diverting the river that ran through the city, then walking in on the dry riverbed.

**5:31** This Darius is not to be confused with Darius I, mentioned in Ezra, Haggai, and Zechariah, or Darius II (the Persian), mentioned in Nehemiah. Darius the Mede is named only in the book of Daniel. Other records have no king between Belshazzar and Cyrus. Thus, Darius may have been (1) appointed by Cyrus to rule over Babylon as a province of Persia, (2) another name for Cyrus himself or for his son, Cambyses, or (3) a descendant of Xerxes I.

**6:1-3** At this time, Daniel was over 80 years old and one of Darius's top three administrators. Daniel was working with those who did not believe in his God, but he worked more efficiently and capably than all the rest. Thus, he attracted the attention of the pagan king and earned a place of respect. One of the best ways to influence non-Christian employers is to work diligently and responsibly. How well do you represent God to your employer?

**6:3, 4** Daniel made enemies at work by doing a good job. Perhaps you have had a similar experience. When you begin to

excel, you will find that coworkers may look for ways to hold you back and tear you down. How should you deal with those who would cheer at your downfall and even try to hasten it? Conduct your life above reproach. Then you will have nothing to hide, and your enemies will have a difficult time finding legitimate charges against you. Of course, this will not always save you from attacks, and, like Daniel, you will have to rely on God for protection.

**6:4, 5** The jealous administrators and officers couldn't find anything about Daniel's life to criticize, so they attacked his religion. If you face jealous critics because of your faith, be glad they're criticizing that part of your life—perhaps they had to focus on your religion as a last resort! Respond by continuing to believe and live as you should. Then remember that God is in control, fighting this battle for you.

**6:8, 9** In Babylon, the king's word *was* the law. In the Medo-Persian Empire, however, when a law was made, even the king couldn't change it. Darius was an effective government administrator, but he had a fatal flaw—pride. By appealing to his vanity, the men talked Darius into signing a law effectively making himself a god for 30 days. This law could not be broken—not even by an important official like Daniel. Another example of the irrevocable nature of the laws of the Medes and Persians appears in Esther 8:8.

10But when Daniel learned that the law had been signed, he went home and knelt down as usual in his upstairs room, with its windows open toward Jerusalem. He prayed three times a day, just as he had always done, giving thanks to his God. 11Then the officials went together to Daniel's house and found him praying and asking for God's help. 12So they went straight to the king and reminded him about his law. "Did you not sign a law that for the next thirty days any person who prays to anyone, divine or human—except to you, Your Majesty—will be thrown into the den of lions?"

"Yes," the king replied, "that decision stands; it is an official law of the Medes and Persians that cannot be revoked."

13Then they told the king, "That man Daniel, one of the captives from Judah, is ignoring you and your law. He still prays to his God three times a day."

14Hearing this, the king was deeply troubled, and he tried to think of a way to save Daniel. He spent the rest of the day looking for a way to get Daniel out of this predicament.

15In the evening the men went together to the king and said, "Your Majesty, you know that according to the law of the Medes and the Persians, no law that the king signs can be changed."

16So at last the king gave orders for Daniel to be arrested and thrown into the den of lions. The king said to him, "May your God, whom you serve so faithfully, rescue you."

17A stone was brought and placed over the mouth of the den. The king sealed the stone with his own royal seal and the seals of his nobles, so that no one could rescue Daniel. 18Then the king returned to his palace and spent the night fasting. He refused his usual entertainment and couldn't sleep at all that night.

19Very early the next morning, the king got up and hurried out to the lions' den. 20When he got there, he called out in anguish, "Daniel, servant of the living God! Was your God, whom you serve so faithfully, able to rescue you from the lions?"

21Daniel answered, "Long live the king! 22My God sent his angel to shut the lions' mouths so that they would not hurt me, for I have been found innocent in his sight. And I have not wronged you, Your Majesty."

23The king was overjoyed and ordered that Daniel be lifted from the den. Not a scratch was found on him, for he had trusted in his God.

24Then the king gave orders to arrest the men who had maliciously accused Daniel. He had them thrown into the lions' den, along with their wives and children. The lions leaped on them and tore them apart before they even hit the floor of the den.

25Then King Darius sent this message to the people of every race and nation and language throughout the world:

"Peace and prosperity to you!

26"I decree that everyone throughout my kingdom should tremble with fear before the God of Daniel.

**Cross references:**
6:10 1 Kgs 8:48-49; Pss 34:1; 95:6; 1 Thes 5:17-18
6:11 Ps 37:32-33; Dan 6:6
6:12 Esth 1:19; Acts 16:19-21
6:13 Esth 3:8; Acts 5:29
6:14 Mark 6:26
6:15 Esth 8:8; Ps 94:20-21
6:16 Job 5:19; Ps 37:39-40; Jer 38:5
6:17 Lam 3:53; Matt 27:66
6:18 2 Sam 12:16-17; Esth 6:1; Rev 18:22
6:20 Jer 32:17; Dan 3:17; Hos 12:6
6:22 Ps 91:11-13; Acts 12:11; 2 Tim 4:17; Heb 11:33
6:23 Ps 118:8; Isa 26:3; Dan 3:17, 28
6:24 Deut 19:18-19; 2 Kgs 14:6
6:25 Ezra 1:1-2; Esth 3:12; 8:9; Hos 1:10; 1 Pet 1:2
6:26 Ps 93:1-2

---

**6:10** Daniel stood alone. Although he knew about the law against praying to anyone except the king, he continued to pray three times a day as he always had. Daniel had a disciplined prayer life. Our prayers are usually interrupted, not by threats, but simply by the pressure of our schedules. Don't let threats or pressures cut into your prayer time. Pray regularly, no matter what, for prayer is your lifeline to God.

**6:10** Daniel made no attempt to hide his daily prayer routine from his enemies in government, even though he knew he would be disobeying the new law. Hiding his daily prayers would have been futile because surely the conspirators would have caught him at something else during the month. Also, hiding would have demonstrated that he was afraid of the other government officials. Daniel continued to pray because he could not look to the king for the guidance and strength that he needed during this difficult time. Only God could provide what he really needed.

**6:16** Lions roamed the countryside and forests in Mesopotamia, and the people feared them and greatly respected their power. Some kings hunted lions for sport. The Persians captured lions, keeping them in large parks where they were fed and attended. Lions were also used for executing people. But God has ways of delivering his people (6:22) that none of us can imagine. It is always premature to give up and give in to the pressure of unbelievers, because God has power they know nothing about. God can even shut the lions' mouths.

**6:16** Even unbelievers witnessed to Daniel's consistency. By his continual service, Daniel had demonstrated his faithful devotion to God. What can unbelievers determine about your life?

**6:21-23** The person who trusts in God and obeys his will is untouchable until God takes him or her. To trust God is to have immeasurable peace. God, who delivered Daniel, will deliver you. Do you trust him with your life?

**6:24** In accordance with Persian custom, this cruel punishment was transferred to those who had conspired against the king by provoking him into an unjust action (see also Esther 7:9, 10). The king's great anger resulted in the execution of the evil officials and their families. Evil deeds often backfire on those who plan cruelty.

**6:25-27** Nebuchadnezzar had come to believe that Israel's God was real because of the faithfulness of Daniel and his friends. Here Darius was also convinced of God's power because Daniel was faithful and God rescued him. Although Daniel was captive in a strange land, his devotion to God was a testimony to powerful rulers. If you find yourself in new surroundings, take the opportunity to testify about God's power in your life. Be faithful to God so he can use you to make an impact on others.

For he is the living God,
and he will endure forever.
His kingdom will never be destroyed,
and his rule will never end.
27 He rescues and saves his people;
he performs miraculous signs and wonders
in the heavens and on earth.
He has rescued Daniel
from the power of the lions."

6:27
Dan 4:3

28So Daniel prospered during the reign of Darius and the reign of Cyrus the Persian.*

## B. DANIEL'S VISIONS (7:1—12:13)
Daniel had many dreams and visions he did not understand. He dreamed of four beasts, which represented four kingdoms of the world, and of a ram and goat, which depicted two of those kingdoms in greater detail. Daniel's visions reveal that the Messiah will be the ruler of a spiritual Kingdom that will overpower and overshadow all other earthly kingdoms. These visions help us see that we should interpret all of history in light of God's eternal Kingdom.

### Daniel's Vision of Four Beasts

7:1
Job 33:14-16
Jer 36:4
Joel 2:28
7:2
Rev 7:1
7:3
Rev 13:1

7 Earlier, during the first year of King Belshazzar's reign in Babylon,* Daniel had a dream and saw visions as he lay in his bed. He wrote down the dream, and this is what he saw.
2In my vision that night, I, Daniel, saw a great storm churning the surface of a great sea, with strong winds blowing from every direction. 3Then four huge beasts came up out of the water, each different from the others.
4The first beast was like a lion with eagles' wings. As I watched, its wings were pulled off, and it was left standing with its two hind feet on the ground, like a human being. And it was given a human mind.
5Then I saw a second beast, and it looked like a bear. It was rearing up on one side, and it had three ribs in its mouth between its teeth. And I heard a voice saying to it, "Get up! Devour the flesh of many people!"
6Then the third of these strange beasts appeared, and it looked like a leopard. It had four bird's wings on its back, and it had four heads. Great authority was given to this beast.

7:7
Rev 12:3; 13:1

7Then in my vision that night, I saw a fourth beast—terrifying, dreadful, and very strong. It devoured and crushed its victims with huge iron teeth and trampled their remains beneath its feet. It was different from any of the other beasts, and it had ten horns.
8As I was looking at the horns, suddenly another small horn appeared among them. Three of the first horns were torn out by the roots to make room for it. This little horn had eyes like human eyes and a mouth that was boasting arrogantly.

6:28 Or *of Darius, that is, the reign of Cyrus the Persian.*   7:1 The first year of Belshazzar's reign (who was co-regent with his father, Nabonidus) was 556 B.C. (or perhaps as late as 553 B.C.).

---

7:1 Chronologically, this chapter takes place before chapter 5. At this time, Belshazzar had just been given a position of authority (553 B.C.), and Daniel was probably in his late sixties. The first six chapters of Daniel present history; the last six chapters are visions relating mainly to the future.

7:1ff Daniel had a vision of four huge beasts, each representing a world empire. This was similar to Nebuchadnezzar's dream in chapter 2. Nebuchadnezzar's dream covered the political aspects of the empires; Daniel's dream depicted their moral characteristics. These nations, which would reign over Israel, were evil and cruel; but Daniel also saw God's everlasting, indestructible Kingdom arrive and conquer them all.

7:4-8 The lion with eagles' wings represents Babylon with *its* swift conquests (statues of winged lions *have been* recovered from Babylon's ruins). The *bear that ravaged the lion* is Medo-Persia. The *three ribs in its mouth* represent the conquests of *three major enemies.* The leopard is Greece. Its wings show the swiftness of Alexander the Great's campaign as he conquered much of the civilized world in four years (334–330 B.C.). The leopard's four heads are the four divisions of the Greek Empire after Alexander's death.
    The fourth beast points to both Rome and the end times. Many

Bible scholars believe that the horns correspond to 10 kings who will reign shortly before God sets up his everlasting Kingdom. These 10 kings had still not come to power at the time of John's vision recorded in the book of Revelation (Revelation 17:12). The little horn is a future human ruler or the Antichrist (see also 2 Thessalonians 2:3, 4). God is illustrating the final end of all worldly kingdoms in contrast to his eternal Kingdom.

7:7 In the book of Revelation, John also recorded a vision of a scarlet beast that had seven heads and ten horns (Revelation 17:3). The angel told John that the ten horns were ten kings (Revelation 17:12). Most *likely these* would be ten rulers who will rule *under the Antichrist.* The number ten may be literal, or, *more likely* it symbolizes the totality of the powers on earth that will serve the Antichrist and war against Christ. In John's day, Rome was the world power, but would be followed by other powers. Whoever the ten kings are, they will give their power to the Antichrist and will make war against Christ and his followers.

⁹ I watched as thrones were put in place
    and the Ancient One* sat down to judge.
His clothing was as white as snow,
    his hair like purest wool.
He sat on a fiery throne
    with wheels of blazing fire,
¹⁰ and a river of fire was pouring out,
    flowing from his presence.
Millions of angels ministered to him;
    many millions stood to attend him.
Then the court began its session,
    and the books were opened.

¹¹I continued to watch because I could hear the little horn's boastful speech. I kept watching until the fourth beast was killed and its body was destroyed by fire. ¹²The other three beasts had their authority taken from them, but they were allowed to live a while longer.*

¹³As my vision continued that night, I saw someone like a son of man* coming with the clouds of heaven. He approached the Ancient One and was led into his presence. ¹⁴He was given authority, honor, and sovereignty over all the nations of the world, so that people of every race and nation and language would obey him. His rule is eternal—it will never end. His kingdom will never be destroyed.

### The Vision Is Explained

¹⁵I, Daniel, was troubled by all I had seen, and my visions terrified me. ¹⁶So I approached one of those standing beside the throne and asked him what it all meant. He explained it to me like this: ¹⁷"These four huge beasts represent four kingdoms that will arise from the earth. ¹⁸But in the end, the holy people of the Most High will be given the kingdom, and they will rule forever and ever."

¹⁹Then I wanted to know the true meaning of the fourth beast, the one so different from the others and so terrifying. It had devoured and crushed its victims with iron teeth and bronze claws, trampling their remains beneath its feet. ²⁰I also asked about the ten horns on the fourth beast's head and the little horn that came up afterward and destroyed three of the other horns. This horn had seemed greater than the others, and it had human eyes and a mouth that was boasting arrogantly. ²¹As I watched, this horn was waging war against God's holy people and was defeating them, ²²until the Ancient One—the Most High—came and judged in favor of his holy people. Then the time arrived for the holy people to take over the kingdom.

**7:9** Aramaic *an Ancient of Days;* also in 7:13, 22.  **7:12** Aramaic *for a season and a time.*  **7:13** Or *like a Son of Man.*

**7:9**
Ezek 1:13; 10:2, 6
Mark 9:3
Rev 1:14

**7:10**
Pss 50:3; 97:3
Isa 30:27
Dan 7:22, 26; 12:1
Rev 5:11; 20:11-15

**7:11**
Rev 19:20; 20:10

**7:13**
†Matt 26:64
†Mark 13:26
†Luke 21:27
Rev 1:13; 14:14

**7:14**
Pss 2:6-8; 72:17; 102:22
Dan 7:27
Eph 1:20-22
Heb 12:28
Rev 1:6

**7:16**
Dan 8:13-16; 10:5-6, 11-12
Zech 1:8-11
Rev 5:5; 7:13-14

**7:18**
Isa 60:12-14
Dan 7:22, 25, 27
Rev 2:26-27; 20:4

**7:21**
Rev 13:7

**7:22**
Dan 7:10
1 Cor 6:2-3

---

**7:9** Here the prophecy shifts to the end times. This judgment scene is similar to one that was seen by the apostle John (Revelation 1:14, 15). The Ancient One is almighty God, who assigns power to kingdoms and who will himself judge those kingdoms in the end.

**7:10** The book of Revelation records a similar picture of God with angels surrounding his throne. John recorded that there were "thousands and millions" (Revelation 5:11, 12). In other words, too many angels to count surround God's throne and minister to him. Created by God, angels are spiritual beings who help carry out his work on earth.

**7:10** The phrase "the books were opened" refers to judgment. Revelation refers to this final judgment where the "books were opened, including the Book of Life. And the dead were judged according to what they had done, as recorded in the books" (Revelation 20:12). The Book of Life is the heavenly registry of those who have accepted Christ's gift of salvation (Revelation 3:5). All believers' names are written in the Book of Life and they need not fear judgment. Unbelievers, however, will be judged *according* to their works, but their works, no matter how good, will not be *able* to save them.

**7:10** Daniel saw God judging *millions* of people as they stand before him. We all must stand before *almighty God* and give an account of our lives. If your life were judged by God today, what

would he say about it? How would he measure it against his will for you? We should live each day with the full awareness that we must appear before God to give account for how we used our life. How will your life measure up?

**7:11, 12** The slaying of the beast represents the fall of Rome. While this beast was destroyed, the other beasts were allowed to live for a period of time. The kingdoms (or their cultures) continued to be recognizable in some form; history did not end when God intervened with his judgment.

**7:13, 14** This one "like a son of man" is the Messiah. Jesus used this verse to refer to himself (Matthew 26:64; Luke 21:27; John 1:51). The clouds of heaven portray the Son of Man as divine; throughout the Bible, clouds represent his majesty and awesome presence. God's glory appeared in a cloud in Exodus 16:10 and 19:9 at the giving of the law at Sinai. Revelation also records Christ coming with the clouds of heaven (Revelation 1:7).

**7:18** The "holy people of the Most High" are the true Israel, the people ruled by the Messiah. Jesus Christ gave the Kingdom to the new Israel, his church, made up of all faithful believers. His coming ushered in the Kingdom of God, and all believers are its citizens (see also 7:22, 27). Although God may allow persecution to continue for a while, the destiny of his followers is to possess the Kingdom and be with him forever.

**7:21, 22** This "horn" that wages war against God's people is also

**7:24**
Rev 17:12

**7:25**
Dan 4:2; 11:36;
12:7
Rev 12:14; 13:6-7;
18:24

**7:26**
Rev 17:14; 19:2

**7:27**
Pss 2:6-12; 22:27;
86:9; 145:13
Isa 60:12
Dan 2:44; 4:34;
7:14, 18, 22
Luke 1:33
Rev 11:1, 5; 20:4

<sup>23</sup>Then he said to me, "This fourth beast is the fourth world power that will rule the earth. It will be different from all the others. It will devour the whole world, trampling and crushing everything in its path. <sup>24</sup>Its ten horns are ten kings who will rule that empire. Then another king will arise, different from the other ten, who will subdue three of them. <sup>25</sup>He will defy the Most High and oppress the holy people of the Most High. He will try to change their sacred festivals and laws, and they will be placed under his control for a time, times, and half a time.

<sup>26</sup>"But then the court will pass judgment, and all his power will be taken away and completely destroyed. <sup>27</sup>Then the sovereignty, power, and greatness of all the kingdoms under heaven will be given to the holy people of the Most High. His kingdom will last forever, and all rulers will serve and obey him."

<sup>28</sup>That was the end of the vision. I, Daniel, was terrified by my thoughts and my face was pale with fear, but I kept these things to myself.

### Daniel's Vision of a Ram and Goat

**8** <sup>1</sup>*During the third year of King Belshazzar's reign, I, Daniel, saw another vision, following the one that had already appeared to me. <sup>2</sup>In this vision I was at the fortress of Susa, in the province of Elam, standing beside the Ulai River.*

**8:2**
Gen 10:22; 14:1
Esth 1:2
Isa 11:11
Jer 25:25
Dan 7:2, 15

**8:3**
Dan 8:20

**8:4**
Deut 33:17
1 Kgs 22:11
Ezek 34:21

**8:5**
Dan 8:8, 21; 11:3

**8:8**
2 Chr 26:16
Dan 5:20; 7:2; 8:22
Rev 7:1

**8:9**
Dan 8:23;
11:16, 41

**8:10**
Jer 48:26, 42
Dan 7:7; 8:7; 11:31
Rev 12:4

<sup>3</sup>As I looked up, I saw a ram with two long horns standing beside the river.* One of the horns was longer than the other, even though it had grown later than the other one. <sup>4</sup>The ram butted everything out of his way to the west, to the north, and to the south, and no one could stand against him or help his victims. He did as he pleased and became very great.

<sup>5</sup>While I was watching, suddenly a male goat appeared from the west, crossing the land so swiftly that he didn't even touch the ground. This goat, which had one very large horn between its eyes, <sup>6</sup>headed toward the two-horned ram that I had seen standing beside the river, rushing at him in a rage. <sup>7</sup>The goat charged furiously at the ram and struck him, breaking off both his horns. Now the ram was helpless, and the goat knocked him down and trampled him. No one could rescue the ram from the goat's power.

<sup>8</sup>The goat became very powerful. But at the height of his power, his large horn was broken off. In the large horn's place grew four prominent horns pointing in the four directions of the earth. <sup>9</sup>Then from one of the prominent horns came a small horn whose power grew very great. It extended toward the south and the east and toward the glorious land of Israel. <sup>10</sup>Its power reached to the heavens, where it attacked the heavenly army, throwing some of the heavenly beings and some of the stars to the ground and trampling them.

8:1 The original text from this point through chapter 12 is in Hebrew. See note at 2:4.　　**8:2** Or *the Ulai Gate;* also in 8:16.　　**8:3** Or *the gate;* also in 8:6.

---

described in Revelation as the beast who is "allowed to wage war against God's people and to conquer them" (Revelation 13:7). For a while, the "horn" will defeat God's people. Yet, in reality, those who die for the faith will be the ultimate overcomers, for they will receive great rewards. In the end, however, the horn will be defeated by the Ancient One himself.

**7:24** The 10 horns, or 10 kings, are also mentioned in Revelation 17:12. There were also 10 toes in Nebuchadnezzar's vision (2:41, 42). While all do not agree concerning the identity of these 10 kings, we are reminded in Revelation 17:12-14 that these kings will make war against Christ, but, as the King of kings, he will conquer them. The other king mentioned here in verse 24 is the future man of lawlessness of 2 Thessalonians 2:3, 4.

**7:25** The exact meaning of this "time, times, and half a time" is debated. Many scholars believe that "time" means one year; "times" means two years; and "half a time" means half a year. Thus, this would refer to three and a half years. God's people will be placed under this king's control and the persecution will continue only a relatively short time. God has promised to give his Kingdom to his holy people.

**8:1** As with chapter 7, this chapter precedes chapter 5 chronologically; the dream probably occurred in 551 B.C. when Daniel was about 70 years old. Chapters 7 and 8 correspond to the first and third years of Belshazzar and belong chronologically between chapters 4 and 5. Chapter 9 took place at approximately the same time as chapter 6. It gives us more details about the Medo-Persian and Greek Empires, the two world powers that ruled after Babylonia.

**8:2** Susa was one of the capitals of the Babylonian Empire. Located in what is now Iran, Susa was a well-developed city. It was the winter capital of the Persian Empire and a mighty fortress. In his vision, Daniel saw himself in this important location. The earliest known code of law, the Code of Hammurabi, was found there. Susa rivaled Babylon itself in cultural sophistication.

**8:3** The two horns were the kings of Media and Persia (8:20). The longer horn represented the growing dominance of Persia in the Medo-Persian Empire.

**8:5-7** The goat represented Greece, and its large horn, Alexander the Great (8:21). This is an amazing prediction because Greece was not yet considered a world power when this prophecy was given. Alexander the Great conquered the world with great speed and military strategy, indicated by the goat's rapid movement. The shattering of both horns symbolized Alexander breaking both parts of the Medo-Persian Empire.

**8:8** Alexander the Great died in his thirties at the height of his power. His kingdom was split into four parts under four generals: Ptolemy I of Egypt and Palestine; Seleucus of Babylonia and Syria; Lysimachus of Asia Minor; and Antipater of Macedonia and Greece.

**8:9** Israel ("the glorious land") was attacked by Antiochus IV Epiphanes (the small horn) in the second century B.C. He was the eighth ruler of the Seleucid Empire (Babylonia and Syria). He overthrew Israel's high priest, looted the Temple, and replaced worship of God with a Greek form of worship. A further fulfillment of this prophecy of a powerful horn will occur in the future with the coming of the Antichrist (see 8:17, 19, 23; 11:36; 2 Thessalonians 2:4).

11 It even challenged the Commander of heaven's army by canceling the daily sacrifices offered to him and by destroying his Temple. 12 The army of heaven was restrained from responding to this rebellion. So the daily sacrifice was halted, and truth was overthrown. The horn succeeded in everything it did.*

13 Then I heard two holy ones talking to each other. One of them asked, "How long will the events of this vision last? How long will the rebellion that causes desecration stop the daily sacrifices? How long will the Temple and heaven's army be trampled on?"

14 The other replied, "It will take 2,300 evenings and mornings; then the Temple will be made right again."

## Gabriel Explains the Vision

15 As I, Daniel, was trying to understand the meaning of this vision, someone who looked like a man stood in front of me. 16 And I heard a human voice calling out from the Ulai River, "Gabriel, tell this man the meaning of his vision."

17 As Gabriel approached the place where I was standing, I became so terrified that I fell with my face to the ground. "Son of man," he said, "you must understand that the events you have seen in your vision relate to the time of the end."

18 While he was speaking, I fainted and lay there with my face to the ground. But Gabriel roused me with a touch and helped me to my feet.

19 Then he said, "I am here to tell you what will happen later in the time of wrath. What you have seen pertains to the very end of time. 20 The two-horned ram represents the kings of Media and Persia. 21 The shaggy male goat represents the king of Greece,* and the large horn between his eyes represents the first king of the Greek Empire. 22 The four prominent horns that replaced the one large horn show that the Greek Empire will break into four kingdoms, but none as great as the first.

23 "At the end of their rule, when their sin is at its height, a fierce king, a master of intrigue, will rise to power. 24 He will become very strong, but not by his own power. He will cause a shocking amount of destruction and succeed in everything he does. He will destroy powerful leaders and devastate the holy people. 25 He will be a master of deception and will become arrogant; he will destroy many without warning. He will even take on the Prince of princes in battle, but he will be broken, though not by human power.

26 "This vision about the 2,300 evenings and mornings* is true. But none of these things will happen for a long time, so keep this vision a secret."

27 Then I, Daniel, was overcome and lay sick for several days. Afterward I got up and performed my duties for the king, but I was greatly troubled by the vision and could not understand it.

## Daniel's Prayer for His People

**9** It was the first year of the reign of Darius the Mede, the son of Ahasuerus, who became king of the Babylonians.* 2 During the first year of his reign, I, Daniel, learned from reading the word of the LORD, as revealed to Jeremiah the prophet, that Jerusalem must lie desolate for seventy years.* 3 So I turned to the Lord God and pleaded with him in prayer and fasting. I also wore rough burlap and sprinkled myself with ashes.

8:11-12 The meaning of the Hebrew for these verses is uncertain.   8:21 Hebrew of Javan.   8:26 Hebrew about the evenings and mornings; compare 8:14.   9:1 Or the Chaldeans.   9:2 See Jer 25:11-12; 29:10.

---

8:11 The "Commander of heaven's army" here refers to a heavenly authority, perhaps an angel or even God himself (see also Joshua 5:13-15).

8:14 The phrase "evenings and mornings" means evening and morning sacrifices, and refers to the time from the desecration of the altar in the Temple by Antiochus IV Epiphanes to the restoration of Temple worship under Judas Maccabeus in 165 B.C.

8:16 Gabriel is an angel, the heavenly messenger God used to explain Daniel's visions (9:21). He also announced the birth of John the Baptist (Luke 1:11) and the Messiah (Luke 1:26).

8:17 The "time of the end," in this case, refers to the whole period from the end of the Exile until the second coming of Christ. Many of the events that would happen under Antiochus IV Epiphanes will be repeated on a broader scale just before Christ's second coming. During these times, God deals with Israel in a radically different way, with divine discipline coming through

Gentile nations. This time is sometimes referred to as the "period of the Gentiles" (Luke 21:24).

8:23 This fierce king describes both Antiochus IV Epiphanes and the Antichrist at the end of human history (Revelation 13:1-18).

8:25 This Prince of princes is God himself. No human power could defeat the king whom Daniel saw in his vision, but God would bring him down. Antiochus IV Epiphanes reportedly went insane and died in Persia in 164 B.C. God's power and justice will prevail, so we should never give up our faith or lose hope, no matter how powerful God's enemies may seem.

9:1 The vision in chapter 9 was given to Daniel during the same time period of chapter 6. This Darius is the person mentioned in chapter 6. The Ahasuerus (or Xerxes) mentioned here is not Esther's husband. The events described in the book of Esther happened about 50 years later.

9:2, 3 Daniel pleaded with God to bring about the promised

Cross-references: 8:11 Ezek 46:14; Dan 11:31, 36-37; 12:11. 8:12 Isa 59:14. 8:13 Pss 74:10; 79:5; Dan 4:13, 23; 12:6, 8; Luke 10:22; 21:24; Heb 10:29; Rev 6:10; 11:2. 8:14 Dan 7:25; 12:7, 11; Rev 11:2-3; 12:14; 13:5. 8:15 Dan 7:13; 10:16, 18. 8:16 Dan 9:21; Luke 1:19, 26. 8:17 Ezek 1:28; 6:2; 44:4; Dan 2:46; 8:19; 11:35, 40; Rev 1:17. 8:18 Ezek 2:2; Dan 10:9-10, 16, 18; Luke 9:32. 8:19 Dan 8:15-17. 8:24 Dan 8:11-13; 11:36; 12:7; Rev 13:3-9; 16:6; 17:12-17. 8:25 Job 34:20; Dan 2:34, 45. 8:27 Dan 7:28; 8:17; Hab 3:16. 9:1 Dan 5:31; 11:1. 9:2 2 Chr 36:21; Ezra 1:1; Jer 25:11; 29:10; Zech 7:5.

9:4
Deut 7:9, 21
Neh 9:32

9:5
Isa 53:6
Lam 1:18, 20

9:6
2 Chr 36:16
Jer 44:4-5, 21

9:7
Ezra 9:6-7
Jer 2:26-27; 3:25;
23:6; 33:16

9:9
Neh 9:17
Pss 106:43; 130:4

9:10
2 Kgs 17:13-15

9:11
Isa 1:2-4
Jer 8:5-10

9:12
Isa 44:26
Jer 44:2-6
Ezek 5:9
Zech 1:6

9:13
Lev 26:14-45
Deut 28:15-68
Isa 9:13
Jer 2:30; 5:3

9:15
Deut 5:15
Neh 9:10
Jer 32:20

9:16
Ps 87:1-3
Ezek 5:14
Joel 3:17
Zech 8:3

9:17
Num 6:24-26
Ps 80:3, 7, 19
Lam 5:18

9:18
Ps 80:14
Isa 37:17
Jer 7:12; 36:7

⁴I prayed to the LORD my God and confessed:

"O Lord, you are a great and awesome God! You always fulfill your covenant and keep your promises of unfailing love to those who love you and obey your commands. ⁵But we have sinned and done wrong. We have rebelled against you and scorned your commands and regulations. ⁶We have refused to listen to your servants the prophets, who spoke on your authority to our kings and princes and ancestors and to all the people of the land.

⁷"Lord, you are in the right; but as you see, our faces are covered with shame. This is true of all of us, including the people of Judah and Jerusalem and all Israel, scattered near and far, wherever you have driven us because of our disloyalty to you. ⁸O LORD, we and our kings, princes, and ancestors are covered with shame because we have sinned against you. ⁹But the Lord our God is merciful and forgiving, even though we have rebelled against him. ¹⁰We have not obeyed the LORD our God, for we have not followed the instructions he gave us through his servants the prophets. ¹¹All Israel has disobeyed your instruction and turned away, refusing to listen to your voice.

"So now the solemn curses and judgments written in the Law of Moses, the servant of God, have been poured down on us because of our sin. ¹²You have kept your word and done to us and our rulers exactly as you warned. Never has there been such a disaster as happened in Jerusalem. ¹³Every curse written against us in the Law of Moses has come true. Yet we have refused to seek mercy from the LORD our God by turning from our sins and recognizing his truth. ¹⁴Therefore, the LORD has brought upon us the disaster he prepared. The LORD our God was right to do all of these things, for we did not obey him.

¹⁵"O Lord our God, you brought lasting honor to your name by rescuing your people from Egypt in a great display of power. But we have sinned and are full of wickedness. ¹⁶In view of all your faithful mercies, Lord, please turn your furious anger away from your city Jerusalem, your holy mountain. All the neighboring nations mock Jerusalem and your people because of our sins and the sins of our ancestors.

¹⁷"O our God, hear your servant's prayer! Listen as I plead. For your own sake, Lord, smile again on your desolate sanctuary.

¹⁸"O my God, lean down and listen to me. Open your eyes and see our despair. See how your city—the city that bears your name—lies in ruins. We make this plea, not because we deserve help, but because of your mercy.

---

return of his people to their land. The prophet Jeremiah had written that God would not allow the captives to return to their land for 70 years (Jeremiah 25:11, 12; 29:10). Daniel knew of this prophecy and realized that this 70-year period was coming to an end.

**9:3ff** In Daniel's prayer for the nation he confessed his own sin, using the pronoun *we* throughout. In times of adversity, it's easy to blame others and excuse our own actions. If any Israelite was righteous, it was Daniel; and yet he confessed his sinfulness and need for God's forgiveness. Instead of looking for others to blame, first examine yourself and confess your own sins to God.

**9:3-19** Daniel knew how to pray. As he prayed, he fasted, confessed his sins, and pleaded that God would reveal his will. He prayed with complete surrender to God and with complete openness to what God was saying to him. When you pray, do you speak openly to God? Examine your attitude. Talk to God with openness, vulnerability, and honesty, and be ready for God's reply.

**9:4-6** The captives from Judah had rebelled against God. Their sins had led to their captivity. But God is merciful even to rebels if they confess their sins and return to him. Don't let your past disobedience keep you from returning to God. He is waiting for you and wants you to return to him.

**9:6** God had sent many prophets to speak to his people through the years, but their messages had been ignored. The truth had been too painful to hear. God still speaks clearly and accurately through the Bible, and he also speaks through preachers, teachers, and concerned friends. Sometimes the truth hurts, and we would rather hear words that soothe, even if they are false. If you are unwilling to accept God's message, maybe you are trying to avoid

making a painful change. Don't settle for a soothing lie that will bring harsh judgment. Accepting the truth even if it is painful can only help you.

**9:11-13** Daniel mentioned the curses outlined in Deuteronomy 28. God had given the people of Israel a choice: Obey me and receive blessings, or disobey me and face curses. The affliction was meant to turn the people to God. When we face difficult circumstances, we should ask ourselves if God has reason to send judgment. If we think so, we must seek his forgiveness. Then we can ask him to help us through our troubles.

**9:14** Daniel spoke about how God continually tried to bring Israel back to himself. Yet even after disaster struck them, they refused to obey him. God still uses circumstances, other people, and, most important, his Word to bring his people back to him. What would it take for God to get your attention?

**9:17-19** It would be a mistake to read the Bible as dry history and miss the deep personal feelings. In this section, Daniel was crying out to the Lord. He had a deep concern for his nation and his people. So often our prayers are without passion and true compassion for others. Are you willing to pray by pouring out your deep feelings to God?

**9:18** Daniel begged for mercy, not for help, because he knew that his people deserved God's wrath and punishment. God sends his help, not because we deserve it, but because he wants to show great mercy. If God would refuse to help us because of our sin, how could we complain? But when he sends mercy instead of the punishment we deserve, how can we withhold our praise and thanksgiving?

<sup>19</sup>"O Lord, hear. O Lord, forgive. O Lord, listen and act! For your own sake, do not delay, O my God, for your people and your city bear your name."

## Gabriel's Message about the Anointed One

<sup>20</sup>I went on praying and confessing my sin and the sin of my people, pleading with the LORD my God for Jerusalem, his holy mountain. <sup>21</sup>As I was praying, Gabriel, whom I had seen in the earlier vision, came swiftly to me at the time of the evening sacrifice. <sup>22</sup>He explained to me, "Daniel, I have come here to give you insight and understanding. <sup>23</sup>The moment you began praying, a command was given. And now I am here to tell you what it was, for you are very precious to God. Listen carefully so that you can understand the meaning of your vision.

<sup>24</sup>"A period of seventy sets of seven* has been decreed for your people and your holy city to finish their rebellion, to put an end to their sin, to atone for their guilt, to bring in everlasting righteousness, to confirm the prophetic vision, and to anoint the Most Holy Place.* <sup>25</sup>Now listen and understand! Seven sets of seven plus sixty-two sets of seven* will pass from the time the command is given to rebuild Jerusalem until a ruler—the Anointed One*—comes. Jerusalem will be rebuilt with streets and strong defenses,* despite the perilous times.

<sup>26</sup>"After this period of sixty-two sets of seven,* the Anointed One will be killed, appearing to have accomplished nothing, and a ruler will arise whose armies will destroy the city and the Temple. The end will come with a flood, and war and its miseries are decreed from that time to the very end. <sup>27</sup>The ruler will make a treaty with the people for a period of one set of seven,* but after half this time, he will put an end to the sacrifices and offerings. And as a climax to all his terrible deeds,* he will set up a sacrilegious object that causes desecration,* until the fate decreed for this defiler is finally poured out on him."

## Daniel's Vision of a Messenger

**10** In the third year of the reign of King Cyrus of Persia,* Daniel (also known as Belteshazzar) had another vision. He understood that the vision concerned events certain to happen in the future—times of war and great hardship.

<sup>2</sup>When this vision came to me, I, Daniel, had been in mourning for three whole weeks. <sup>3</sup>All that time I had eaten no rich food. No meat or wine crossed my lips, and I used no fragrant lotions until those three weeks had passed.

<sup>4</sup>On April 23,* as I was standing on the bank of the great Tigris River, <sup>5</sup>I looked up and saw a man dressed in linen clothing, with a belt of pure gold around his waist. <sup>6</sup>His body looked like a precious gem. His face flashed like lightning, and his eyes flamed like torches. His arms and feet shone like polished bronze, and his voice roared like a vast multitude of people.

**9:24a** Hebrew *seventy sevens.* **9:24b** Or *the Most Holy One.* **9:25a** Hebrew *Seven sevens plus sixty-two sevens.* **9:25b** Or *an anointed one;* similarly in 9:26. Hebrew reads *a messiah.* **9:25c** Or *and a moat,* or *and trenches.* **9:26** Hebrew *After sixty-two sevens.* **9:27a** Hebrew *for one seven.* **9:27b** Hebrew *And on the wing of abominations; the meaning of the Hebrew is uncertain.* **9:27c** Hebrew *an abomination of desolation.* **10:1** The third year of Cyrus's reign was 536 B.C. **10:4** Hebrew *On the twenty-fourth day of the first month,* of the ancient Hebrew lunar calendar. This date in the book of Daniel can be cross-checked with dates in surviving Persian records and can be related accurately to our modern calendar. This event occurred on April 23, 536 B.C.

### Cross-references (margin)

**9:19** Pss 44:23; 74:10-11
**9:20** Ps 145:18; Isa 6:5; 58:9
**9:21** Exod 29:39; 1 Kgs 18:36; Ezra 9:4
**9:22** Zech 1:9, 14
**9:23** Matt 24:15
**9:24** Lev 25:8; Num 14:34; 2 Chr 29:24; Isa 51:6, 8; 53:10; Rom 3:21; 5:10
**9:25** Isa 9:6; John 1:41; 4:25
**9:26** Isa 53:8; Matt 24:2; Mark 9:12; 13:2; Luke 19:43-44; 24:26
**9:27** Isa 10:23; 28:22; †Matt 24:15; †Mark 13:14; †Luke 21:20
**10:1** Dan 1:17, 21; 2:21; 6:28
**10:2** Ezra 9:4-5; Neh 1:4
**10:4** Ezek 1:3; Dan 8:2
**10:5** Jer 10:9; Ezek 9:2; Dan 12:6-7; Rev 1:13; 15:6
**10:6** Rev 1:14; 2:18

---

**9:23** Just as God answered Daniel's prayer, so we can have confidence that God hears and answers our prayers.

**9:24, 25** Each day of these 70 weeks ("seventy sets of seven") may represent one year. The Bible often uses round numbers to make a point, not to give an exact count. For example, Jesus said we are to forgive others "seventy times seven" (Matthew 18:22). He did not mean a literal 490 times, but that we should be abundantly forgiving. Similarly, some scholars see this figure of 70 weeks as a figurative time period. Others, however, interpret this time period as a literal 70 weeks or 490 years, observing that Christ's death came at the end of the 69 weeks (i.e., 483 years later). One interpretation places the 70th week as the seven years of the great tribulation, still in the future. Consequently the number would symbolize both the first and second comings of Christ.

**9:25** These "strong defenses" show that Jerusalem will be rebuilt as a complete, fully functioning city.

**9:26** The Messiah, the Anointed One, will be rejected and killed by his own people. His perfect eternal Kingdom will come later.

**9:26, 27** There has been much discussion on the numbers, times, and events in these verses, and there are three basic views: (1) The prophecy was fulfilled in the past at the desecration of the Temple by Antiochus IV Epiphanes from 168 to 167 B.C. (see 11:31); (2) it was fulfilled in the past at the destruction of the Temple by the Roman general Titus in A.D. 70 when one million Jews were killed; or (3) it is still to be fulfilled in the future under the Antichrist (see Matthew 24:15).

**10:1ff** This is Daniel's final vision (536 B.C.). In it, he was given further insight into the great spiritual battle between God's people and those who want to destroy them. There is also more detailed information on the future, specifically the struggles between the Ptolemies (kings of the south) and the Seleucids (kings of the north).

**10:1ff** Prior to this vision, Cyrus allowed the Jews to return to Jerusalem, but Daniel stayed in Babylon. Why didn't Daniel return to Jerusalem? He may have been too old to make the long, hazardous journey (he was over 80); his government duties could have prevented him; or God may have told him to stay behind to complete the work he was called to do.

**10:3** Daniel refrained from eating certain foods and using fragrant lotions because these were signs of feasting and rejoicing.

**10:5, 6** The man seen by Daniel was a heavenly being. Some commentators believe that this was an appearance of Christ (see Revelation 1:13-15), while others think it was an angel (because

**10:7**
2 Kgs 6:17
Ezek 12:18
Acts 9:7

**10:8**
Gen 32:24
Dan 7:28; 8:27
Hab 3:16

**10:9**
Gen 15:12
Dan 8:18

**10:10**
Jer 1:9

**10:11**
Job 4:14-15
Ezek 2:1
Dan 8:16-17

**10:12**
Dan 9:20-23;
10:2-3, 19

**10:13**
Dan 10:21; 12:1
Jude 1:9
Rev 12:7

**10:14**
Dan 2:28; 8:26;
12:4, 9

**10:15**
Ezek 24:27
Luke 1:20

**10:16**
Jer 1:9
Dan 7:15; 8:15

**10:17**
Exod 24:10-11
Isa 6:1-5

**10:18**
Isa 35:3-4

**10:19**
Josh 1:6-9
Judg 6:23
Isa 35:4; 43:1
Dan 10:12

**10:20**
Dan 8:21; 11:2

**10:21**
Dan 12:1, 4

**11:1**
Dan 5:31; 9:1

**11:2**
Dan 8:21, 26;
10:1, 20-21

⁷Only I, Daniel, saw this vision. The men with me saw nothing, but they were suddenly terrified and ran away to hide. ⁸So I was left there all alone to see this amazing vision. My strength left me, my face grew deathly pale, and I felt very weak. ⁹Then I heard the man speak, and when I heard the sound of his voice, I fainted and lay there with my face to the ground.

¹⁰Just then a hand touched me and lifted me, still trembling, to my hands and knees. ¹¹And the man said to me, "Daniel, you are very precious to God, so listen carefully to what I have to say to you. Stand up, for I have been sent to you." When he said this to me, I stood up, still trembling.

¹²Then he said, "Don't be afraid, Daniel. Since the first day you began to pray for understanding and to humble yourself before your God, your request has been heard in heaven. I have come in answer to your prayer. ¹³But for twenty-one days the spirit prince* of the kingdom of Persia blocked my way. Then Michael, one of the archangels,* came to help me, and I left him there with the spirit prince of the kingdom of Persia.* ¹⁴Now I am here to explain what will happen to your people in the future, for this vision concerns a time yet to come."

¹⁵While he was speaking to me, I looked down at the ground, unable to say a word. ¹⁶Then the one who looked like a man* touched my lips, and I opened my mouth and began to speak. I said to the one standing in front of me, "I am filled with anguish because of the vision I have seen, my lord, and I am very weak. ¹⁷How can someone like me, your servant, talk to you, my lord? My strength is gone, and I can hardly breathe."

¹⁸Then the one who looked like a man touched me again, and I felt my strength returning. ¹⁹"Don't be afraid," he said, "for you are very precious to God. Peace! Be encouraged! Be strong!"

As he spoke these words to me, I suddenly felt stronger and said to him, "Please speak to me, my lord, for you have strengthened me."

²⁰He replied, "Do you know why I have come? Soon I must return to fight against the spirit prince of the kingdom of Persia, and after that the spirit prince of the kingdom of Greece* will come. ²¹Meanwhile, I will tell you what is written in the Book of Truth. (No one helps me against these spirit princes except Michael, your spirit prince.* ¹¹:¹I have been standing beside Michael* to support and strengthen him since the first year of the reign of Darius the Mede.)

## Kings of the South and North

**11** ²"Now then, I will reveal the truth to you. Three more Persian kings will reign, to be succeeded by a fourth, far richer than the others. He will use his wealth to stir up everyone to fight against the kingdom of Greece.*

**10:13a** Hebrew *the prince;* also in 10:13c, 20.    **10:13b** Hebrew *the chief princes.*    **10:13c** As in one Greek version; Hebrew reads *and I was left there with the kings of Persia.* The meaning of the Hebrew is uncertain.    **10:16** As in most manuscripts of the Masoretic Text; one manuscript of the Masoretic Text and one Greek version read *Then something that looked like a human hand.*    **10:20** Hebrew *of Javan.*    **10:21** Hebrew *against these except Michael, your prince.*    **11:1** Hebrew *him.*    **11:2** Hebrew *of Javan.*

---

he required Michael's help—10:13). In either case, Daniel caught a glimpse of the battle between good and evil supernatural powers.

**10:10-18** Daniel was frightened by this vision, but the messenger reassured him. Daniel lost his speech, but the messenger's touch restored it. Daniel felt weak and helpless, but the messenger's words strengthened him. God can bring us healing when we are hurt, peace when we are troubled, and strength when we are weak. Trust God to minister to you as he did to Daniel.

**10:12, 13** Although God sent a messenger to Daniel, a powerful spiritual being ("the spirit prince of the kingdom of Persia") detained the messenger for three weeks. Daniel faithfully continued praying and fasting, and God's messenger eventually arrived, assisted by Michael, the archangel. Answers to our prayers may be hindered by unseen obstacles. Don't expect God's answers to come too easily or too quickly. Prayer may be challenged by evil forces, so pray fervently and pray earnestly. Then expect God to answer at the right time.

**10:20, 21** The heavenly warfare was to be directed against Persia and then Greece. Each of these nations was to have power over God's people. Both Persia and Greece were represented by evil "spirit princes," or demons. But God is in control of the past,

present, and future, and he has all events recorded in his "Book of Truth."

**11:2** The angelic messenger was revealing Israel's future (see 10:20, 21). Only God can reveal future events so clearly. God's work not only deals with the sweeping panorama of history but also focuses on the intricate details of people's lives. And his plans—whether for nations or individuals—are unshakable.

**11:2** The fourth Persian king may have been Xerxes I (also called Ahasuerus, 486–465 B.C.), who launched an all-out effort against Greece in 480 (Esther 1:1).

**11:2ff** Babylon was defeated by Medo-Persia. Medo-Persia was defeated by Greece under Alexander the Great, who conquered most of the Mediterranean and Middle Eastern lands. After Alexander's death, the empire was divided into four parts. The Ptolemies gained control of the southern section of Palestine, and the Seleucids took the northern part. Verses 2-20 show the conflict between the Ptolemies and Seleucids over control of Palestine in 300–200 B.C. Verses 21-35 describe the persecution of Israel under Antiochus IV Epiphanes. In verses 36-45 the prophecy shifts to the end times. Antiochus IV fades from view, and the Antichrist of the last days becomes the center of attention.

³"Then a mighty king will rise to power who will rule with great authority and accomplish everything he sets out to do. ⁴But at the height of his power, his kingdom will be broken apart and divided into four parts. It will not be ruled by the king's descendants, nor will the kingdom hold the authority it once had. For his empire will be uprooted and given to others.

⁵"The king of the south will increase in power, but one of his own officials will become more powerful than he and will rule his kingdom with great strength.

⁶"Some years later an alliance will be formed between the king of the north and the king of the south. The daughter of the king of the south will be given in marriage to the king of the north to secure the alliance, but she will lose her influence over him, and so will her father. She will be abandoned along with her supporters. ⁷But when one of her relatives* becomes king of the south, he will raise an army and enter the fortress of the king of the north and defeat him. ⁸When he returns to Egypt, he will carry back their idols with him, along with priceless articles of gold and silver. For some years afterward he will leave the king of the north alone.

⁹"Later the king of the north will invade the realm of the king of the south but will soon return to his own land. ¹⁰However, the sons of the king of the north will assemble a mighty army that will advance like a flood and carry the battle as far as the enemy's fortress.

¹¹"Then, in a rage, the king of the south will rally against the vast forces assembled by the king of the north and will defeat them. ¹²After the enemy army is swept away, the king of the south will be filled with pride and will execute many thousands of his enemies. But his success will be short lived.

¹³"A few years later the king of the north will return with a fully equipped army far greater than before. ¹⁴At that time there will be a general uprising against the king of the south. Violent men among your own people will join them in fulfillment of this vision, but they will not succeed. ¹⁵Then the king of the north will come and lay siege to a fortified city and capture it. The best troops of the south will not be able to stand in the face of the onslaught.

¹⁶"The king of the north will march onward unopposed; none will be able to stop him. He will pause in the glorious land of Israel,* intent on destroying it. ¹⁷He will make plans to come with the might of his entire kingdom and will form an alliance with the king of the south. He will give him a daughter in marriage in order to overthrow the kingdom from within, but his plan will fail.

¹⁸"After this, he will turn his attention to the coastland and conquer many cities. But a commander from another land will put an end to his insolence and cause him to retreat in shame. ¹⁹He will take refuge in his own fortresses but will stumble and fall and be seen no more.

²⁰"His successor will send out a tax collector to maintain the royal splendor. But after a very brief reign, he will die, though not from anger or in battle.

²¹"The next to come to power will be a despicable man who is not in line for royal succession. He will slip in when least expected and take over the kingdom by flattery and intrigue.

11:7 Hebrew *a branch from her roots.*   11:16 Hebrew *the glorious land.*

**11:3** Dan 5:19; 8:4-5, 21; 11:16, 36
**11:4** Jer 49:36; Ezek 37:9; Dan 7:2; 8:8; Zech 2:6; Rev 7:1
**11:5** Dan 11:9, 11, 14, 25, 40
**11:6** Dan 11:7, 13, 15, 40
**11:7** Dan 11:19, 38-39
**11:8** Isa 37:19; 46:1-2; Jer 43:12-13
**11:10** Isa 8:8; Jer 46:7-8; 51:42; Dan 11:26, 40
**11:13** Dan 4:16; 12:7
**11:15** Jer 6:6; Ezek 4:2; 17:17
**11:16** Josh 1:5; Dan 5:19; 8:9; 11:3, 36, 41
**11:17** 2 Kgs 12:17; Ezek 4:3, 7
**11:18** Gen 10:5; Isa 66:19; Zeph 2:11
**11:19** Pss 27:2; 37:36; Jer 46:6; Ezek 26:21
**11:20** Isa 60:17

---

**11:3** This mighty king of Greece was Alexander the Great, who conquered Medo-Persia and built a huge empire in only four years.

**11:4, 5** Eventually Alexander the Great's empire was divided into four nations. These four weaker nations were comprised of the following regions: (1) Egypt, (2) Babylonia and Syria, (3) Asia Minor, and (4) Macedonia and Greece. The king of Egypt ("the king of the south") was Ptolemy I or perhaps a reference to the Ptolemaic dynasty in general.

**11:6, 7** These prophecies seem to have been fulfilled many years later in the Seleucid wars between Egypt and Syria. In 252 B.C., Ptolemy II of Egypt ("the south") gave his daughter Berenice in marriage to Antiochus II of Syria ("the north")

to finalize a peace treaty between their two lands. But Berenice was murdered in Antioch by Antiochus II's former wife, Laodice. Berenice's brother, Ptolemy III, ascended the Egyptian throne and declared war against the Seleucids to avenge his sister's murder.

**11:9-11** The king of Syria ("the north") was Seleucus II, and the king of Egypt ("the south") was Ptolemy IV.

**11:13-16** This king of the north may have been Antiochus III (the Great). He defeated many Egyptian cities and established himself in Israel ("the glorious land"). He was later defeated by the Romans at Magnesia (11:18).

**11:17** The invader, Antiochus III, tried to bring peace between Egypt and Syria by having his daughter marry Ptolemy V Epiphanes of Egypt, but the plan failed.

**11:20** The successor to Antiochus III was Seleucus IV. He sent Heliodorus to collect money from the Temple treasury in Jerusalem.

**11:21** Seleucus IV was succeeded by his brother, Antiochus IV Epiphanes, who found favor with the Romans.

11:24
Num 13:20
Neh 9:25
Ezek 34:14

11:27
Pss 52:1; 64:6
Jer 9:3-5
Dan 11:35, 40
Hab 2:3
Acts 17:31

11:30
Gen 10:4
Num 24:24
Jer 2:10

11:31
Dan 8:11-13; 9:27;
12:11
Matt 24:15
Mark 13:14

11:32
Dan 11:21, 34
Mic 5:7-9
Zech 9:13-16;
10:3-6

11:33
Matt 24:9
John 16:2
Heb 11:36-38

11:34
Dan 11:21, 32
Matt 7:15
Rom 16:18

11:35
Deut 8:16
Prov 17:3
Dan 12:10
Zech 13:9
John 15:2

11:36
Deut 10:17
Ps 136:2
Isa 10:25; 14:13;
26:20
Dan 2:47; 5:20; 7:8,
11; 8:11;
9:27; 11:3
2 Thes 2:4
Rev 13:5-6

22Before him great armies will be swept away, including a covenant prince. 23With deceitful promises, he will make various alliances. He will become strong despite having only a handful of followers. 24Without warning he will enter the richest areas of the land. Then he will distribute among his followers the plunder and wealth of the rich—something his predecessors had never done. He will plot the overthrow of strongholds, but this will last for only a short while.

25Then he will stir up his courage and raise a great army against the king of the south. The king of the south will go to battle with a mighty army, but to no avail, for there will be plots against him. 26His own household will cause his downfall. His army will be swept away, and many will be killed. 27Seeking nothing but each other's harm, these kings will plot against each other at the conference table, attempting to deceive each other. But it will make no difference, for the end will come at the appointed time.

28"The king of the north will then return home with great riches. On the way he will set himself against the people of the holy covenant, doing much damage before continuing his journey.

29Then at the appointed time he will once again invade the south, but this time the result will be different. 30For warships from western coastlands* will scare him off, and he will withdraw and return home. But he will vent his anger against the people of the holy covenant and reward those who forsake the covenant.

31"His army will take over the Temple fortress, pollute the sanctuary, put a stop to the daily sacrifices, and set up the sacrilegious object that causes desecration.* 32He will flatter and win over those who have violated the covenant. But the people who know their God will be strong and will resist him.

33"Wise leaders will give instruction to many, but these teachers will die by fire and sword, or they will be jailed and robbed. 34During these persecutions, little help will arrive, and many who join them will not be sincere. 35And some of the wise will fall victim to persecution. In this way, they will be refined and cleansed and made pure until the time of the end, for the appointed time is still to come.

36"The king will do as he pleases, exalting himself and claiming to be greater than every god, even blaspheming the God of gods. He will succeed, but only until the time of wrath is completed. For what has been determined will surely take place. 37He will have no respect for the gods of his ancestors, or for the god loved by women, or for any other god, for he will boast that he is greater than them all. 38Instead of these, he will worship the god of fortresses—a god his ancestors never knew—and lavish on him gold, silver, precious stones,

11:30 Hebrew *from Kittim.*   11:31 Hebrew *the abomination of desolation.*

---

**11:22** The "great armies" refer to the way all opposition against Antiochus IV will be broken. The covenant prince may be the high priest Onias III, who was assassinated by Menelaus in 170 B.C.

**11:27** These two treacherous kings were probably Antiochus IV of Syria and Ptolemy VI of Egypt. Treachery and deceit are a power broker's way to position himself over someone else. When two power brokers try to gain the upper hand, it is a mutually weakening and self-destructive process. It is also futile because God ultimately holds all power in his hands.

**11:29-31** Antiochus IV would again invade "the south," but enemy ships would cause him to retreat. On his way back, he plundered Jerusalem, desecrated the Temple, and stopped the Jews' daily sacrifices. The Temple was desecrated when he sacrificed pigs on an altar erected in honor of Zeus. According to Jewish law, pigs were unclean and were not to be touched or eaten. To sacrifice a pig in the Temple was the worst kind of insult an enemy could level against the Jews. This happened from 168 to 167 B.C.

**11:32** This reference to those who have violated the covenant may include Menelaus, the high priest, who was won over by Antiochus and who conspired with him against the Jews who were loyal to God. The "people who know their God" may refer to the Maccabees and their sympathizers, but a further fulfillment may lie in the future.

**11:33, 34** Those who are wise will teach many, but they will also face great persecution. Difficult times show up our weaknesses

and our inability to cope. We want answers, leadership, and clear direction. During these times, God's Word begins to interest even those who would never look at it otherwise. We should look for opportunities to share God's Word in hard times. We must also be prepared to face persecution and rejection as we teach and preach.

**11:35** God's messenger described a time of trial when even wise believers would fall victim to persecution. If we persevere in our faith, any such experience will only refine us and make us stronger. Are you facing trials? Recognize them as opportunities to strengthen your faith. If you remain steadfast in these experiences, you will be stronger in your faith and closer to God.

**11:36-39** These verses could refer to Antiochus IV Epiphanes, Titus (the Roman general), or the Antichrist. Some of these events may have been fulfilled in the past, and some have yet to be fulfilled.

**11:37** The "god loved by women" may refer to Tammuz, a Babylonian fertility god. Tammuz is also mentioned in Ezekiel 8:14. In other words, this person won't recognize any deity or religions at all, not even pagan ones. Instead, he will proclaim himself to be divine and the ultimate power.

**11:38** The "god of fortresses" is believed by some to be Jupiter or Zeus. The implication is that this king will make *war* his god. More than all his predecessors, he will wage war and glorify its horrors.

and expensive gifts. 39Claiming this foreign god's help, he will attack the strongest fortresses. He will honor those who submit to him, appointing them to positions of authority and dividing the land among them as their reward.*

40"Then at the time of the end, the king of the south will attack the king of the north. The king of the north will storm out with chariots, charioteers, and a vast navy. He will invade various lands and sweep through them like a flood. 41He will enter the glorious land of Israel,* and many nations will fall, but Moab, Edom, and the best part of Ammon will escape. 42He will conquer many countries, and even Egypt will not escape. 43He will gain control over the gold, silver, and treasures of Egypt, and the Libyans and Ethiopians* will be his servants.

44"But then news from the east and the north will alarm him, and he will set out in great anger to destroy and obliterate many. 45He will stop between the glorious holy mountain and the sea and will pitch his royal tents. But while he is there, his time will suddenly run out, and no one will help him.

### The Time of the End

**12** "At that time Michael, the archangel* who stands guard over your nation, will arise. Then there will be a time of anguish greater than any since nations first came into existence. But at that time every one of your people whose name is written in the book will be rescued. 2Many of those whose bodies lie dead and buried will rise up, some to everlasting life and some to shame and everlasting disgrace. 3Those who are wise will shine as bright as the sky, and those who lead many to righteousness will shine like the stars forever. 4But you, Daniel, keep this prophecy a secret; seal up the book until the time of the end, when many will rush here and there, and knowledge will increase."

5Then I, Daniel, looked and saw two others standing on opposite banks of the river. 6One of them asked the man dressed in linen, who was now standing above the river, "How long will it be until these shocking events are over?"

7The man dressed in linen, who was standing above the river, raised both his hands toward heaven and took a solemn oath by the One who lives forever, saying, "It will go on for a time, times, and half a time. When the shattering of the holy people has finally come to an end, all these things will have happened."

8I heard what he said, but I did not understand what he meant. So I asked, "How will all this finally end, my lord?"

9But he said, "Go now, Daniel, for what I have said is kept secret and sealed until the time of the end. 10Many will be purified, cleansed, and refined by these trials. But the wicked will continue in their wickedness, and none of them will understand. Only those who are wise will know what it means.

**11:40** Isa 5:28
Jer 4:13
Dan 11:27, 35;
12:4, 9

**11:41** Jer 48:47; 49:6

**11:43** 2 Chr 12:3
Ezek 30:4-5
Nah 3:9

**11:45** Isa 65:25; 66:20
Dan 9:16, 20

**12:1** Jer 30:7
Ezek 5:9
Matt 24:21
Mark 13:19
Rev 16:18

**12:2** Isa 26:19
Ezek 37:12-14
Matt 25:46
John 5:28-29

**12:3** Isa 53:11
John 5:35

**12:4** Isa 8:16; 11:9
Rev 22:10

**12:6** Ezek 9:2
Zech 1:12-13
Matt 24:3
Mark 13:4

**12:7** Ezek 20:5
Luke 21:24
Rev 10:5-7; 12:14

**12:10** Isa 32:6-7
Rev 22:11

**11:39** Or *at a price.*    **11:41** Hebrew *the glorious land.*    **11:43** Hebrew *Cushites.*    **12:1** Hebrew *the great prince.*

---

**11:40** The Antichrist of the last days becomes the center of attention from this point through the rest of the book of Daniel.

**11:45** "The glorious holy mountain" is Mount Zion or the city of Jerusalem.

**12:1** Great suffering is in store for God's people throughout the years ahead. This way of describing the future is also used by Jeremiah (Jeremiah 30:7) and Jesus (Matthew 24:21ff). Yet the great suffering is tempered by a great promise of hope for true believers.

**12:2** This is a clear reference to the resurrection of both the righteous and the wicked, although the eternal destiny of each will be quite different. Up to this point in time, teaching about the resurrection was not common, although every Israelite believed that one day he or she would be included in the restoration of the new Kingdom. This reference to a bodily resurrection of both the saved and the lost was a sharp departure from common belief. (See also Job 19:25, 26; Psalm 16:10; and Isaiah 26:19 for other Old Testament references to the resurrection.)

**12:3** Many people try to be stars in the world of entertainment, only to find their stardom temporary. God tells us how we can be eternal "stars"—by being wise and leading many to God's righteousness. If we share our Lord with others, we can be true stars—radiantly beautiful in God's sight!

**12:4** Closing and sealing up the book meant that it was to be kept safe and preserved. This was to be done so that believers of all times could look back on God's work in history and find hope. Daniel did not understand the exact meaning of the times and events in his vision. We can see events as they unfold, for we are in the end times. The whole book will not be understood until the climax of earth's history.

**12:7** "Time, times, and half a time" may add up to 3 and a half years and may be taken as either literal or figurative.

**12:7** "The holy people" seem to be shattered again and again throughout history. God's recurring purpose in this is to break the pride and self-sufficiency of his rebellious people and to bring them to accept him as their Lord.

**12:10** Trials and persecutions make very little sense to us when we experience them, but they can purify us if we are willing to learn from them. After you come through a difficult time, seek to learn from it so that it can help you in the future. See Romans 5:3-5 for more on God's purpose in our sufferings.

**12:11**
Dan 9:27; 11:31
Matt 24:15
Mark 13:14

**12:12**
Rev 11:2; 12:6

**12:13**
Rev 14:13

¹¹"From the time the daily sacrifice is stopped and the sacrilegious object that causes desecration* is set up to be worshiped, there will be 1,290 days. ¹²And blessed are those who wait and remain until the end of the 1,335 days!

¹³"As for you, go your way until the end. You will rest, and then at the end of the days, you will rise again to receive the inheritance set aside for you."

**12:11** Hebrew *the abomination of desolation.*

**12:11** "The sacrilegious object that causes desecration" set up in the Temple refers to the altar of Zeus, where Antiochus IV Epiphanes sacrificed a pig. Some think it will have another fulfillment in the Antichrist and one of his horrible acts of evil (Matthew 24:15). However, this and the predictions at the early part of the chapter may refer specifically to Antiochus IV Epiphanes, and the rest of the prophecy may refer to the end times.

**12:11, 12** Either these are further calculations relating to the persecution of the Jews under Antiochus IV Epiphanes, or they refer to the end times. The abolishing of the daily sacrifices means the removal of worship of the true God, as well as oppression of believers. There is much speculation about these numbers in verses 11 and 12. The point is that this time of persecution has an end; God is in control of it, and he will be victorious over evil.

**12:13** The promise of resurrection was reaffirmed to Daniel. He would one day see the fulfillment of his words, but he was not to spend the rest of his life wondering what his visions might mean. Instead, he was to rest in the comfort of God's sovereignty and

look forward to the time when he would rise to receive and share eternal life with God. God does not reveal everything to us in this life. We must be content with the partial picture until he wants us to see more. He will tell us all we need to know.

**12:13** Daniel stands tall in the gallery of God's remarkable servants. Born of royal heritage, yet taken into captivity when only a teenager, Daniel determined to remain faithful to God in the land of his captivity. Even at great personal cost, Daniel spent his entire lifetime advising his captors with unusual wisdom. God chose him as his servant to record some of the events of the captivity and some significant events concerning the future. As an old man, having been faithful to God throughout his years, Daniel was assured by God that he would rise from the dead and receive his portion in God's eternal Kingdom. Faithfulness to God has a rich reward, not necessarily in this life, but most certainly in the life to come.

# HOSEA

## VITAL STATISTICS

**PURPOSE:**
To illustrate God's love for his sinful people

**AUTHOR:**
Hosea son of Beeri ("Hosea" means "salvation")

**ORIGINAL AUDIENCE:**
The people of Israel (the northern kingdom)

**DATE WRITTEN:**
Approximately 715 B.C., recording events from about 753–715 B.C.

**SETTING:**
Hosea began his ministry during the end of the prosperous but morally declining reign of Jeroboam II of Israel (the upper classes were doing well, but they were oppressing the poor). He prophesied until shortly after the fall of Samaria in 722 B.C.

**KEY VERSE:**
"Then the LORD said to me, 'Go and love your wife again, even though she commits adultery with another lover. This will illustrate that the LORD still loves Israel, even though the people have turned to other gods and love to worship them'" (3:1).

**KEY PEOPLE:**
Hosea, Gomer, their children

**KEY PLACES:**
The northern kingdom (Israel), Samaria, Ephraim

**SPECIAL FEATURES:**
Hosea employs many images from daily life: God is depicted as husband, lion, leopard, bear, dew, rain, moth, and others; Israel is pictured as wife, sick person, vine, grapes, early fruit, olive tree, woman in childbirth, oven, morning mist, chaff, and smoke, to name a few.

GROOMSMEN stand at attention as the music swells and the bride begins her long walk down the aisle, arm in arm with her father. The smiling, but nervous, husband-to-be follows every step, his eyes brimming with love. Then happy tears are shed, vows stated, and families merged. A wedding is a joyous celebration of love. It is the holy mystery of two becoming one, of beginning life together, and of commitment. Marriage is ordained by God and illustrates his relationship with his people. Thus, there is perhaps no greater tragedy than the violation of those sacred vows.

God told Hosea to find a wife and revealed to him ahead of time that she would be unfaithful to him. Although she would bear many children, some of these offspring would be fathered by others. In obedience to God, Hosea married Gomer. His relationship with her, her adultery, and their children became living, prophetic examples to Israel.

The book of Hosea is a love story—real, tragic, and true. Transcending the tale of young man and wife, it tells of God's love for his people and the response of his "bride." A covenant had been made, and God had been faithful. His love was steadfast, and his commitment unbroken. But Israel, like Gomer, was adulterous and unfaithful, spurning God's love and turning instead to false gods. Then after warning of judgment, God reaffirmed his love and offered reconciliation. His love and mercy were overflowing, but justice would be served.

The book begins with God's marriage instructions to Hosea. After Hosea's marriage, children were born, and each given a name signifying a divine message (chapter 1). Then, as predicted, Gomer left Hosea to pursue her lusts (chapter 2). But Hosea (whose name means "salvation") found her, redeemed her, and brought her home again, fully reconciled (chapter 3). Images of God's love, judgment, grace, and mercy were woven into their relationship. Next, God outlined his case against the people of Israel: Their sins would ultimately cause their destruction (chapters 4; 6—7; 12) and would rouse his anger, resulting in punishment (chapters 5; 8—10; 12—13). But even in the midst of Israel's immorality, God was merciful and offered hope, expressing his infinite love for his people (chapter 11) and the fact that their repentance would bring about blessing (chapter 14).

The book of Hosea dramatically portrays our God's constant and persistent love. As you read this book, watch the prophet submit himself willingly to his Lord's direction; grieve with him over the unfaithfulness of his wife and his people; and hear the clear warning of judgment. Then reaffirm your commitment to being God's person, faithful in your love and true to your vows.

| Tiglath-pileser III invades Israel 743 | Micah becomes a prophet to Judah 742 | Isaiah becomes a prophet to Judah 740 | | Israel (northern kingdom) falls 722 | Hosea's ministry ends 715 |
|---|---|---|---|---|---|

## THE BLUEPRINT

A. HOSEA'S WAYWARD WIFE (1:1—3:5)

Hosea was commanded by God to marry a woman who would be unfaithful to him and would cause him many heartaches. Just as Gomer lost interest in Hosea and ran after other lovers, we, too, can easily lose appreciation for our special relationship with God and pursue dreams and goals that do not include him. When we compromise our Christian lifestyles and adopt the ways of the world, we are being unfaithful.

B. GOD'S WAYWARD PEOPLE (4:1—14:9)
1. Israel's sinfulness
2. Israel's punishment
3. God's love for Israel

God wanted the people in the northern kingdom to turn from their sin and return to worshiping him alone, but they persisted in their wickedness. Throughout the book, Israel is described as ignorant of God, with no desire to please him. Israel did not understand God at all, just as Gomer did not understand Hosea. Like a loving husband or patient father, God wants people to know him and to turn to him daily.

## MEGATHEMES

| THEME | EXPLANATION | IMPORTANCE |
|---|---|---|
| The Nation's Sin | Just as Hosea's wife, Gomer, was unfaithful to him, so the nation of Israel had been unfaithful to God. Israel's idolatry was like adultery. They sought illicit relationships with Assyria and Egypt in pursuit of military might, and they mixed Baal worship with the worship of God. | Like Gomer, we can chase after other loves—love of power, pleasure, money, or recognition. The temptations in this world can be very seductive. Are we loyal to God, remaining completely faithful, or have other loves taken his rightful place? |
| God's Judgment | Hosea solemnly warned Judah against following Israel's example. Because Judah broke the covenant, turned away from God, and forgot her Maker, she experienced a devastating invasion and exile. Sin has terrible consequences. | Disaster surely follows ingratitude toward God and rebellion. The Lord is our only true refuge. If we harden our hearts against him, there is no safety or security anywhere else. We cannot escape God's judgment. |
| God's Love | Just as Hosea went after his unfaithful wife to bring her back, so the Lord pursues us with his love. His love is tender, loyal, unchanging, and undying. No matter what, God still loves us. | Have you forgotten God and become disloyal to him? Don't let prosperity diminish your love for him or let success blind you to your need for his love. |
| Restoration | Although God will discipline his people for sin, he encourages and restores those who have repented. True repentance opens the way to a new beginning. God forgives and restores. | There is still hope for those who turn back to God. No loyalty, achievement, or honor can be compared to loving him. Turn to the Lord while the offer is still good. No matter how far you have strayed, God is willing to forgive you. |

## A. HOSEA'S WAYWARD WIFE (1:1—3:5)

Hosea highlights the parallels between his relationship with Gomer and God's relationship with the nation of Israel. Although the people made a covenant with the one true God, they went after false gods. In the same way, Hosea married Gomer, knowing ahead of time that she would leave him. Hosea tenderly dealt with his wife in spite of her sin. And God was merciful toward the people of Israel despite their sins. God has not changed; he is still merciful and forgiving.

**1:1**
2 Chr 26:1-23;
27:1-9; 28:1-27;
29:1-32
Mic 1:1

**1** The LORD gave this message to Hosea son of Beeri during the years when Uzziah, Jotham, Ahaz, and Hezekiah were kings of Judah, and Jeroboam son of Jehoash* was king of Israel.

1:1 Hebrew *Joash,* a variant spelling of Jehoash.

1:1 Hosea was a prophet to the northern kingdom of Israel from 753 to 715 B.C. Under the reign of Jeroboam II, the northern kingdom had prospered materially but had decayed spiritually. The people were greedy and had adopted the moral behavior and idolatrous religion of the surrounding Canaanites.

Hosea's role was to show how the people of the northern king-

dom had been unfaithful to God, their "husband" and provider, and had married themselves to Baal and the gods of Canaan. He warned that unless they repented of their sin and turned back to God, they were headed for destruction. Hosea spoke of God's characteristics—his powerful love and justice—and how their practical experience of these should affect their lives and make

## Hosea's Wife and Children

2 When the LORD first began speaking to Israel through Hosea, he said to him, "Go and marry a prostitute,* so that some of her children will be conceived in prostitution. This will illustrate how Israel has acted like a prostitute by turning against the LORD and worshiping other gods."

3 So Hosea married Gomer, the daughter of Diblaim, and she became pregnant and gave Hosea a son. 4 And the LORD said, "Name the child Jezreel, for I am about to punish King Jehu's dynasty to avenge the murders he committed at Jezreel. In fact, I will bring an end to Israel's independence. 5 I will break its military power in the Jezreel Valley."

6 Soon Gomer became pregnant again and gave birth to a daughter. And the LORD said to Hosea, "Name your daughter Lo-ruhamah—'Not loved'—for I will no longer show love to the people of Israel or forgive them. 7 But I will show love to the people of Judah. I will free them from their enemies—not with weapons and armies or horses and charioteers, but by my power as the LORD their God."

8 After Gomer had weaned Lo-ruhamah, she again became pregnant and gave birth to a second son. 9 And the LORD said, "Name him Lo-ammi—'Not my people'—for Israel is not my people, and I am not their God.

10 *"Yet the time will come when Israel's people will be like the sands of the seashore—too many to count! Then, at the place where they were told, 'You are not my people,' it will be said, 'You are children of the living God.' 11 Then the people of Judah and Israel will unite together.

**1:2** Or *a promiscuous woman.*　　**1:10** Verses 1:10-11 are numbered 2:1-2 in Hebrew text.

**1:2**
Jer 3:1
Hos 2:5; 3:1

**1:4**
2 Kgs 10:1-28

**1:7**
Ps 44:3-7
Isa 30:18

**1:9**
†1 Pet 2:10

**1:10**
Gen 22:17; 32:12
Isa 63:16; 64:8
Jer 33:22
†Rom 9:26

**1:11**
Isa 11:12
Jer 30:21
Ezek 37:21-24
Hos 3:5

---

them return to God. Unfortunately, the people had broken their covenant with God, and they would receive the punishments God had promised (Deuteronomy 27–28).

**1:2, 3** Did God really order his prophet to marry a woman who was a prostitute? Some who find it difficult to believe God could make such a request view this story as an illustration, not a historical event. Many, however, think the story is historical and give one of these explanations: (1) According to God's law, a priest could not marry a prostitute or a divorced woman (Leviticus 21:7). However, Hosea was not a priest. (2) It is possible that Gomer was not a prostitute when Hosea married her and that God was letting Hosea know that Gomer would later turn to adultery and prostitution. In any case, Hosea knew ahead of time that his wife would be unfaithful and that their married life would become a living object lesson to the adulterous northern kingdom. Hosea's marriage to an unfaithful woman would illustrate God's relationship to the unfaithful nation of Israel.

**1:2, 3** It is difficult to imagine Hosea's feelings when God told him to marry a woman who would be unfaithful to him. He may not have wanted to do it, but he obeyed. God often required extraordinary obedience from his prophets who were facing extraordinary times. God may ask you to do something difficult and extraordinary, too. If he does, how will you respond? Will you obey him, trusting that he who knows everything has a special purpose for his request? Will you be able to accept the fact that the pain involved in obedience may benefit those you serve and not you personally?

**1:4, 5** Elijah had predicted that the family of Israel's King Ahab would be destroyed because of their wickedness (1 Kings 21:20-22), but Jehu went too far in carrying out God's command (2 Kings 10:1-11). Therefore, Jehu's dynasty would also be punished—in the Jezreel Valley, the very place where he carried out the massacre of Ahab's family. God's promise to put an end to Israel as an independent kingdom came true 25 years later when the Assyrians conquered the northern kingdom and carried the people into captivity.

**1:6, 8** In 1:3, we read that Gomer gave *Hosea* a son. In 1:6, Gomer gave birth to a daughter, and God called the child "your daughter" (referring to Hosea). However, in 1:8, we learn that Gomer gave birth to a second son, but there is no indication that Hosea was his natural father. The key to this part of the story is found in the names God chose for the children, showing his reaction to Israel's unfaithfulness. God's reaction to unfaithfulness is no different today. He wants our complete devotion.

**1:7** Israel and Judah had been a united kingdom under David and Solomon. After Solomon's death a civil dispute had arisen, and

the land was divided into a northern kingdom (Israel, whose capital was Samaria) and a southern kingdom (Judah, whose capital was Jerusalem). Although Hosea spoke mainly to the northern kingdom, his concern, like God's, was for the entire nation of Israelites including those from the kingdom of Judah. Just as Hosea prophesied, God helped Judah because Judah had a few kings who honored him. Shortly after defeating Israel, the Assyrian emperor Sennacherib invaded Judah and besieged Jerusalem. He was driven off by an angel's powerful and dramatic intervention (Isaiah 36–37).

**1:7** God said he would personally rescue the people of Judah from their enemies with no help from their weapons or armies. Although God asks us to do our part, we should remember that he is not limited to human effort. God often chooses to work through people, but only because it is good for *them.* He can accomplish all his purposes without any help from us if he so chooses. You are very important to God, but on your own you have neither the ability to fulfill nor the power to disrupt God's plans.

**1:9** Here God was in essence dissolving the covenant (Jeremiah 7:23). The name of the third child conveys the finality of God's judgment. God's warnings recorded in Deuteronomy 28:15-68 were beginning to come true: Israel was abandoning God, and in turn, he was leaving them alone and without his blessings.

**1:10** The Old Testament prophetic books sometimes use the word *Israel* to refer to the people of the united kingdom (north and south) and sometimes just to the northern kingdom. In talking about past events, Hosea usually thought of Israel as the northern kingdom with its capital in Samaria. But when Hosea spoke about future events relating to God's promises of restoration, it is difficult to understand his words as applying only to the northern kingdom because the exiled northerners would become hopelessly intermingled with their conquerors. Thus, most scholars see the promises of return as either: (1) conditional—the Israelites chose not to return to God, and therefore they were not entitled to the blessings included in the promises of restoration, or (2) unconditional—God's promises of restoration have been fulfilled in Jesus Christ, and therefore the church (the new Israel) receives his blessings (Romans 9:25, 26; 1 Peter 2:10).

**1:10, 11** Although Israel was unfaithful, God's commitment remained unchanged. This promise of a future reuniting confirmed the covenant made with Moses (Deuteronomy 30:1-10) and foreshadowed the prophecies of Jeremiah (Jeremiah 29:11-14; 31:31-40) and Ezekiel (Ezekiel 11:16-21). It was a prediction of the day when all the people of God will be united

They will choose one leader for themselves, and they will return from exile together. What a day that will be—the day of Jezreel*—when God will again plant his people in his land.

²:1*"In that day you will call your brothers Ammi—'My people.' And you will call your sisters Ruhamah—'The ones I love.'

### Charges against an Unfaithful Wife

**2** ² "But now bring charges against Israel—your mother—
for she is no longer my wife,
and I am no longer her husband.
Tell her to remove the prostitute's makeup from her face
and the clothing that exposes her breasts.

³ Otherwise, I will strip her as naked
as she was on the day she was born.
I will leave her to die of thirst,
as in a dry and barren wilderness.

⁴ And I will not love her children,
for they were conceived in prostitution.

⁵ Their mother is a shameless prostitute
and became pregnant in a shameful way.
She said, 'I'll run after other lovers
and sell myself to them for food and water,
for clothing of wool and linen,
and for olive oil and drinks.'

⁶ "For this reason I will fence her in with thornbushes.
I will block her path with a wall
to make her lose her way.

⁷ When she runs after her lovers,
she won't be able to catch them.
She will search for them
but not find them.

**1:11** *Jezreel* means "God plants."   **2:1** Verses 2:1-23 are numbered 2:3-25 in Hebrew text.

**2:2**
Isa 50:1
Hos 4:5

**2:3**
Isa 20:2-3;
32:13-14
Jer 14:3
Ezek 16:7, 22

**2:5**
Jer 2:25; 3:1-2
Ezek 23:16-17

**2:7**
Jer 2:2; 3:1
Ezek 23:4

---

**HOSEA**
served as a
prophet to Israel
(the northern
kingdom) from
753–715 B.C.

| | |
|---|---|
| *Climate of the times* . . . . . . | Israel's last six kings were especially wicked; they promoted heavy taxes, oppression of the poor, idol worship, and total disregard for God. Israel was subjected to Assyria and was forced to pay tribute, which depleted its few remaining resources. |
| *Main message.* . . . . . . . . . . | The people of Israel had sinned against God, as an adulterous woman sins against her husband. Judgment was sure to come for living in total disregard for God and fellow humans. Israel fell to Assyria in 722 B.C. |
| *Importance of message* . . . | When we sin, we sever our relationship with God, breaking our commitment to him. While all must answer to God for their sins, those who seek God's forgiveness are spared eternal judgment. |
| *Contemporary prophets* . . . | Jonah (793–753 B.C.), Amos (760–750 B.C.), Micah (742–687 B.C.), Isaiah (740–681 B.C.) |

---

under Christ. Today all believers everywhere are God's chosen people, "royal priests, a holy nation, God's very own possession" (see 1 Peter 2:9).

**1:11** Just as the other children's names carried significance, so did *Jezreel*. In verse 4, the name depicts divine judgment; here it represents planting. The name means "God plants." This was a sign of a new day and a new relationship between God and Israel.

**2:2ff** Israel's punishment and restoration are the themes of this chapter. As in a court case, the prostitute is brought to trial and found guilty. But after her punishment, she is joyfully and tenderly restored to God.

**2:5-7** The Israelites were thanking false gods (specifically Baal, the god whom they believed controlled weather and thus farming) for their food, shelter, and clothing, instead of the true God, who gave those blessings. Therefore, God would fence Israel in "with

thornbushes" and "block her path" by making the rewards of idol worship so disappointing that the people would be persuaded to turn back to God. Despite Israel's unfaithfulness, God was still faithful and merciful. He would continue to hold his arms out to his people, even to the point of placing obstacles in their wayward path to turn them back to him.

**2:7** Just as Gomer would return to her husband if she thought she would be better off with him, so people often return to God when they find life's struggle too difficult to handle. Returning to God out of desperation is better than rebelling against him, but it is better yet to turn to God out of gratitude for his care.

Then she will think,
'I might as well return to my husband,
for I was better off with him than I am now.'
8 She doesn't realize it was I who gave her everything she has—
the grain, the new wine, the olive oil;
I even gave her silver and gold.
But she gave all my gifts to Baal.

9 "But now I will take back the ripened grain and new wine
I generously provided each harvest season.
I will take away the wool and linen clothing
I gave her to cover her nakedness.
10 I will strip her naked in public,
while all her lovers look on.
No one will be able
to rescue her from my hands.
11 I will put an end to her annual festivals,
her new moon celebrations, and her Sabbath days—
all her appointed festivals.
12 I will destroy her grapevines and fig trees,
things she claims her lovers gave her.
I will let them grow into tangled thickets,
where only wild animals will eat the fruit.
13 I will punish her for all those times
when she burned incense to her images of Baal,
when she put on her earrings and jewels
and went out to look for her lovers
but forgot all about me,"
says the LORD.

*The LORD's Love for Unfaithful Israel*
14 "But then I will win her back once again.
I will lead her into the desert
and speak tenderly to her there.
15 I will return her vineyards to her
and transform the Valley of Trouble* into a gateway of hope.
She will give herself to me there,
as she did long ago when she was young,
when I freed her from her captivity in Egypt.
16 When that day comes," says the LORD,
"you will call me 'my husband'
instead of 'my master.'*

2:15 Hebrew *valley of Achor.*   2:16 Hebrew *'my baal.'*

**2:8** Ezek 16:18
Hos 8:4

**2:10** Ezek 16:37
Hos 8:7

**2:11** Isa 1:13-14
Jer 7:34; 16:9

**2:12** Jer 5:17; 8:13

**2:13** Jer 7:9
Ezek 23:40-42
Hos 4:13; 11:2

**2:14** Ezek 20:33-38

**2:15** Josh 7:26
Jer 2:1-3
Ezek 16:8, 22

**2:16** Isa 54:5

**2:8** Material possessions are success symbols in most societies. Israel was a wealthy nation at this time, and Gomer may have accumulated silver and gold. But Gomer didn't realize that Hosea had given her all she owned, just as Israel did not recognize God as the giver of blessings. Both Gomer and Israel used their possessions irresponsibly as they ran after other lovers and other gods. How do you use your possessions? Use what God has given you to honor him.

**2:12** The Israelites were so immersed in idolatry that they actually believed pagan gods gave them their vineyards and orchards. They had forgotten that the entire land was a gift from God (Deuteronomy 32:49). Today many people give credit to everything and everyone but God for their prosperity—luck, hard work, quick thinking, the right contacts. When *you* succeed, who gets the credit?

**2:13** Baal was the most important of the Canaanite gods, and his name came to be used to describe all the local deities worshiped throughout the land occupied by Israel. Unfortunately, the Israelites did not get rid of the idols and pagan worship centers as they had been commanded. Instead, they tolerated and frequently joined Baal

worshipers, often through the influence of corrupt kings. One Israelite king especially noted for his Baal worship was Ahab. The prophet Elijah, in a dramatic showdown with Ahab's hired prophets, proved God's power far superior to Baal's (1 Kings 18).

**2:14, 15** God was promising (1) to bring the people to the desert, a place free from distractions, so he could clearly communicate with them, and (2) to change what had been a time of trouble into a day of hope. The Valley of Trouble is the site where Achan had sinned by keeping forbidden war plunder (see Joshua 7). He had brought great disaster to Joshua's troops when they were attempting to conquer the land. God uses even our negative experiences to create opportunities to turn back to him. As you face problems and trials, remember that God speaks to you in the "desert" and not just in times of prosperity.

**2:16** Not until Judah's exile would the entire nation begin to come to its senses, give up its idols, and turn back to God; and not until that day when God rules through Jesus the Messiah will the relationship between God and his people be restored. In that day, God will no longer be like a master to them; he will be like a husband

<sup>17</sup> O Israel, I will wipe the many names of Baal from your lips,
    and you will never mention them again.
<sup>18</sup> On that day I will make a covenant
    with all the wild animals and the birds of the sky
    and the animals that scurry along the ground
        so they will not harm you.
    I will remove all weapons of war from the land,
        all swords and bows,
    so you can live unafraid
        in peace and safety.
<sup>19</sup> I will make you my wife forever,
    showing you righteousness and justice,
    unfailing love and compassion.

**2:18**
Lev 26:5-6
Job 5:23
Isa 2:4
Ezek 34:25;
39:1-10

**GOMER**

Gomer was a girl with a reputation. We don't know if she was already a working prostitute or was simply a promiscuous young woman by the time she met Hosea. But she was clearly a high risk for a lasting relationship. She must have been surprised and confused when, instead of propositioning her, Hosea arranged to marry her. By common cultural rule, the decisions were made by Hosea and Diblaim. Gomer may not even have been consulted. Her father was probably eager to remove an embarrassment from his life.

Hosea loved Gomer. Gomer seemed ambivalent toward her husband. Apparently, marriage simply changed the label on Gomer's behavior from promiscuity to adultery. She got pregnant three times, giving birth to two sons and a daughter. Hosea couldn't be sure if the children were his or had been fathered by other men, but he claimed them and named them as God instructed.

God's declarations about Israel overlap Hosea's struggle over Gomer's unfaithfulness. Sometime after the birth of their third child, Gomer became enslaved in prostitution. Hosea had to buy her freedom. He then insisted on her faithfulness.

What did Gomer think and feel during all this? How much did Hosea reveal to her about God's prediction that she would be unfaithful? How did she respond to Hosea's sacrificial faithfulness? We aren't told. After Hosea redeemed her, she isn't mentioned again. Her final appearance in the book leads to hopeful silence. If she responded to Hosea's love, they built a life together.

Probably the closest we come to feeling what Gomer felt are those times when we act unfaithfully toward God yet he continues to faithfully lavish his love on us. Gomer's shameful story turns out to be a thinly veiled version of our story. We know Gomer better than we might think at first, for she was what we are—sinners offered overwhelming grace!

| | |
|---|---|
| **Strength and accomplishment** | • May have traded a shameful past for a faithful future as a result of her husband's sacrificial love |
| **Weaknesses and mistakes** | • Developed a persistent promiscuous lifestyle resistant even to the responsibilities of motherhood<br>• Sold herself into sexual slavery |
| **Lessons from her life** | • Unfaithfulness damages our integrity but does not prevent someone else from loving us in spite of our failure<br>• God is committed to loving us even though he knows our waywardness and bent toward sin |
| **Vital statistics** | • Where: Israel<br>• Occupation: Wife, prostitute<br>• Relatives: Husband: Hosea. Father: Diblaim. Sons: Jezreel (God plants), Lo-ammi (Not my people). Daughter: Lo-ruhamah (Not loved). |
| **Key verse** | "When the LORD first began speaking to Israel through Hosea, he said to him, 'Go and marry a prostitute, so that some of her children will be conceived in prostitution. This will illustrate how Israel has acted like a prostitute by turning against the LORD and worshiping other gods'" (Hosea 1:2). |

Gomer's story is told in Hosea 1:1—3:5.

(Isaiah 54:4-8). The relationship will be deep and personal, the kind of relationship we can know, though imperfectly, in marriage.

**2:19, 20** The time will come when unfaithfulness will be impossible. God will bind us to himself in his perfect righteousness, justice, love, compassion, and faithfulness. God was promising a fresh new beginning, not just a temporary rewriting of a tired old covenant (see Jeremiah 31:31-34).

**2:19, 20** God's wedding gift to his people, both in Hosea's day and in our own, is his compassion. Through no merit of our own, God forgives us and makes us right with him. There is no way for us by our own efforts to reach God's high standards, but he graciously accepts us, forgives us, and draws us into a relationship with himself. In that relationship we have personal and intimate communion with him.

20 I will be faithful to you and make you mine,
    and you will finally know me as the LORD.

2:20
Jer 31:34
Hos 6:6; 13:4

21 "In that day, I will answer,"
    says the LORD.
    "I will answer the sky as it pleads for clouds.
    And the sky will answer the earth with rain.

2:21
Isa 55:10
Zech 8:12

22 Then the earth will answer the thirsty cries
    of the grain, the grapevines, and the olive trees.
    And they in turn will answer,
    'Jezreel'—'God plants!'

2:22
Jer 31:27
Joel 2:19

23 At that time I will plant a crop of Israelites
    and raise them for myself.
I will show love
    to those I called 'Not loved.'*
And to those I called 'Not my people,'*
    I will say, 'Now you are my people.'
And they will reply, 'You are our God!'"

2:23
†Rom 9:25
†1 Pet 2:10

## Hosea's Wife Is Redeemed

**3** Then the LORD said to me, "Go and love your wife again, even though she* commits adultery with another lover. This will illustrate that the LORD still loves Israel, even though the people have turned to other gods and love to worship them.*"

3:1
2 Sam 6:19
1 Chr 16:3
Song 2:5

2 So I bought her back for fifteen pieces of silver* and five bushels of barley and a measure of wine.* 3 Then I said to her, "You must live in my house for many days and stop your prostitution. During this time, you will not have sexual relations with anyone, not even with me.*"

3:2
Ruth 4:10

4 This shows that Israel will go a long time without a king or prince, and without sacrifices, sacred pillars, priests,* or even idols! 5 But afterward the people will return and devote themselves to the LORD their God and to David's descendant, their king.* In the last days, they will tremble in awe of the LORD and of his goodness.

3:4
Judg 17:6
3:5
Jer 50:4-5
Ezek 34:24

## B. GOD'S WAYWARD PEOPLE (4:1—14:9)

The rest of the book deals with Israel's sin and her impending judgment. Hosea points out the moral and spiritual decay of the nation. He describes the punishment awaiting the people and pleads with them to return to God. Although judgment and condemnation of sin are prevalent in the book, a strand of love and restoration runs throughout. Even in the midst of judgment, God is merciful and will restore those who repent and turn to him.

**2:23a** Hebrew *Lo-ruhamah;* see 1:6.   **2:23b** Hebrew *Lo-ammi;* see 1:9.   **3:1a** Or *Go and love a woman who.*
**3:1b** Hebrew *love their raisin cakes.*   **3:2a** Hebrew *15 shekels of silver,* about 6 ounces or 171 grams in weight.
**3:2b** As in Greek version, which reads *a homer of barley and a wineskin full of wine;* Hebrew reads *a homer*
[5 bushels or 182 liters] *of barley and a lethech* [2.5 bushels or 91 liters] *of barley.*   **3:3** Or *and I will live with you.*
**3:4** Hebrew *ephod,* the vest worn by the priest.   **3:5** Hebrew *to David their king.*

---

**3:1** This short chapter pictures the nation's exile and return. Israel would experience a time of purification in a foreign land, but God would still love the people and would be willing to accept them back. God commanded Hosea to show the same forgiving spirit to Gomer. Although Hosea had good reason to divorce Gomer, he was told to buy her back and love her.

**3:1** God asked Hosea to do something almost unthinkable— to buy back his adulterous, unrepentant wife and to continue to love her! When those who knew about Gomer's adultery heard Hosea say that God loved idolatrous Israel as much as Hosea loved Gomer, they must have been amazed. The people had heard God's words many times, but they felt the impact of those words when they saw them acted out in Hosea's merciful love for his wife.

**3:2** Apparently Gomer was on her own for a while. Needing to support herself, she must have either sold herself into slavery or become the mistress of another man. In either case, Hosea had to pay to get her back—although the required amount was pitifully small. Gomer was no longer worth much to anyone

except Hosea, but he loved her just as God loved Israel. No matter how low we sink, God is willing to buy us back— to redeem us—and to lift us up again.

**3:3** After this, Gomer is no longer mentioned by Hosea. This is explained in 3:4. Gomer's isolation showed how God would deal with the northern kingdom (5:6, 15). It is dangerous to rebel against God. If he were ever to withdraw his love and mercy, we would be without hope.

**3:4** God would separate the Israelites from their treasured idolatrous practices. The sacrifices, pillars, and priests mentioned were those used for idol worship. The priests served the idols; the idols were household gods, which were strictly forbidden for God's people.

**3:4, 5** The northern kingdom had rebelled against David's dynasty and had taken Jeroboam as their king (1 Kings 12–13). Their rebellion was both political and religious. At that time, they reverted back to the worship of gold idols. "David's descendant, their king" refers to the time of Messiah's rule when all people will bow before him in humility and submission. Those who won't accept Christ's blessings now will face his power and judgment later. How much better it is to love and follow Christ now than face his angry judgment later.

## 1. Israel's sinfulness

### *The LORD's Case against Israel*

**4:1**
Isa 59:4
Jer 7:28
Hos 12:2
Mic 6:2

**4** ¹ Hear the word of the LORD, O people of Israel!
    The LORD has brought charges against you, saying:
"There is no faithfulness, no kindness,
    no knowledge of God in your land.

**4:2**
Hos 6:8-9; 7:1-4;
10:4

² You make vows and break them;
    you kill and steal and commit adultery.
There is violence everywhere—
    one murder after another.

**4:3**
Isa 24:4; 33:9
Zeph 1:3

³ That is why your land is in mourning,
    and everyone is wasting away.
Even the wild animals, the birds of the sky,
    and the fish of the sea are disappearing.

**4:4**
Deut 17:12
Ezek 3:26
Amos 5:10, 13

⁴ "Don't point your finger at someone else
    and try to pass the blame!
My complaint, you priests,
    is with you.*

**4:4** Hebrew *Your people are like those with a complaint against the priests.*

---

**SPIRITUAL UNFAITHFULNESS**

Spiritual adultery and physical adultery are alike in many ways, and both are dangerous. God was disappointed with his people, because they had committed spiritual adultery against him, as Gomer had committed physical adultery against Hosea.

**Parallels**

Both spiritual and physical adultery are against God's law.

Both spiritual and physical adultery begin with disappointment and dissatisfaction—either real or imagined—with an already existing relationship.

Both spiritual and physical adultery begin with diverting affection from one object of devotion to another.

Both spiritual and physical adultery involve a process of deterioration; it is not usually an impulsive decision.

Both spiritual and physical adultery involve the creation of a fantasy about what a new object of love can do for you.

**The Danger**

When we break God's law in full awareness of what we're doing, our hearts become hardened to the sin, and our relationship with God is broken.

The feeling that God disappoints can lead you away from him. Feelings of disappointment and dissatisfaction are normal and, when endured, will pass.

The diverting of our affection is the first step in the blinding process that leads into sin.

The process is dangerous because you don't always realize it is happening until it is too late.

Such fantasy creates unrealistic expectations of what a new relationship can do and only leads to disappointment in all existing and future relationships.

---

**4:1ff** In this chapter, God brings a charge of disobedience against Israel. The religious leaders had failed to turn the people to God, and ritual prostitution had replaced right worship. The nation had declined spiritually and morally, breaking the laws that God had given them. The people found it easy to condemn Hosea's wife for her adultery. They were not so quick to see that *they* had been unfaithful to God.

**4:1-3** God explained the reasons for Israel's suffering. Their lawless behavior had brought the twin judgments of increased violence and ecological crisis. There is not always a direct cause-and-effect relationship between our actions and the problems we face. Nevertheless, when we are facing difficulties, we should seriously ask, Have I done anything sinful or irresponsible that has caused my suffering? If we discover that we are at fault, even partially, we must change our ways before God will help us.

**4:2** This verse may allude to the assassinations of kings during Hosea's lifetime. Shallum killed Zechariah (the king, not the prophet) and took the throne. Then Menahem killed Shallum and destroyed an entire city because it refused to accept him as king (2 Kings 15:8-16). God pointed out that even murder was being taken casually in Israel.

**4:4** We often blame others if we fear punishment for wrongdoing. Hosea warned the priests not to blame anyone else; the nation's sins were largely their fault. Israel's priests pointed out the people's sins, but God would not allow them to overlook their own irresponsible actions. Instead of instructing the nation in religion and morality, they had led the way toward idolatry and immorality. Their failure to lead the people in God's ways placed most of the blame for Israel's destruction on them. Knowing that God will not allow us to blame others for our sinfulness should cause us to admit our own sins. We are responsible for our own sinful actions. Beware of the tendency to blame others because it can keep you from feeling the need to repent.

**4:4-9** Hosea leveled his charges against the religious leaders. Who were these religious leaders? When Jeroboam I rebelled against Solomon's son Rehoboam and set up a rival kingdom in the north, he also set up his own religious system (see 1 Kings 12:25-33). In violation of God's law, he made two gold calves and told the people to worship them. He also appointed his own priests, who were not descendants of Aaron. At first the residents of the northern kingdom continued to worship God, even though they were doing it in the wrong way; but very soon they also began to worship Canaanite gods. Before long they had substituted Baal for God and no longer worshiped God at all. It is not surprising that Jeroboam's false priests were unable to preserve the true worship of God.

5 So you will stumble in broad daylight,
   and your false prophets will fall with you in the night.
   And I will destroy Israel, your mother.
6 My people are being destroyed
   because they don't know me.
   Since you priests refuse to know me,
   I refuse to recognize you as my priests.
   Since you have forgotten the laws of your God,
   I will forget to bless your children.
7 The more priests there are,
   the more they sin against me.
   They have exchanged the glory of God
   for the shame of idols.*

8 "When the people bring their sin offerings, the priests get fed.
   So the priests are glad when the people sin!
9 'And what the priests do, the people also do.'
   So now I will punish both priests and people
   for their wicked deeds.
10 They will eat and still be hungry.
   They will play the prostitute and gain nothing from it,
   for they have deserted the LORD
11    to worship other gods.

   "Wine has robbed my people
   of their understanding.
12 They ask a piece of wood for advice!
   They think a stick can tell them the future!
   Longing after idols
   has made them foolish.
   They have played the prostitute,
   serving other gods and deserting their God.
13 They offer sacrifices to idols on the mountaintops.
   They go up into the hills to burn incense
   in the pleasant shade of oaks, poplars, and terebinth trees.

   "That is why your daughters turn to prostitution,
   and your daughters-in-law commit adultery.
14 But why should I punish them
   for their prostitution and adultery?
   For your men are doing the same thing,
   sinning with whores and shrine prostitutes.
   O foolish people! You refuse to understand,
   so you will be destroyed.

| | |
|---|---|
| **4:5** | Ezek 14:3, 7 |
| | Hos 5:5 |
| **4:6** | Hos 4:14 |
| | Zech 11:8-9, 15-17 |
| | Mal 2:7-8 |
| **4:7** | Hos 10:1; 13:6 |
| | Hab 2:16 |
| **4:9** | Isa 24:2 |
| | Jer 5:31 |
| **4:11** | Isa 5:12; 28:7 |
| **4:12** | Jer 2:27 |
| **4:13** | Jer 2:20; 3:6 |
| | Ezek 6:13 |
| | Hos 2:13; 11:2 |
| **4:14** | Deut 23:17 |

**4:7** As in Syriac version and an ancient Hebrew tradition; Masoretic Text reads *I will turn their glory into shame.*

---

**4:6-9** God accused the religious leaders of keeping the people from knowing him. They were supposed to be spiritual leaders, but they had become leaders in wrongdoing. The people may have said to one another, "It must be OK if the priests do it." Spiritual leadership is a heavy responsibility. Whether you teach a church school class, hold a church office, or lead a Bible study, don't take your leadership responsibilities lightly. Be a leader who leads others to God.

**4:8** The priests were glad when the people sinned. Every time a person brought a sin offering, the priest received a portion of it. The more the people sinned, the more the priests received. Because they couldn't eat all of the offerings themselves, they sold some and gave some to their relatives. The priests profited from the continuation of sin; it gave them power and position in the community. So instead of trying to lead the people out of sin, they encouraged sin to increase their profits.

**4:10-12** The chief Canaanite gods, Baal and Asherah, represented the power of fertility and sexual reproduction. Not surprisingly, their worship included rituals with vile sexual practices. Male worshipers had sex with female temple prostitutes or female priests, and young women wishing to bear children had sex with male priests. But God said their efforts to increase fertility would not succeed.

**4:12** The "stick," or divining rod, was a way of attempting to tell the future. By divorcing themselves from God's authoritative religion centered in Jerusalem, inhabitants of the northern kingdom had effectively cut themselves off from God's word and from his way of forgiveness. The drive to be free from all restrictions can move us completely out of God's will.

<sup>15</sup> "Though you, Israel, are a prostitute,
may Judah avoid such guilt.
Do not join the false worship at Gilgal or Beth-aven,*
even though they take oaths there in the LORD's name.

4:16
Pss 23:2-3; 78:8
Isa 5:17; 7:25

<sup>16</sup> Israel is stubborn,
like a stubborn heifer.
So should the LORD feed her
like a lamb in a lush pasture?

4:17
Ps 81:12

<sup>17</sup> Leave Israel* alone,
because she is married to idolatry.
<sup>18</sup> When the rulers of Israel finish their drinking,
off they go to find some prostitutes.
They love shame more than honor.*

4:19
Hos 12:1; 13:15

<sup>19</sup> So a mighty wind will sweep them away.
Their sacrifices to idols will bring them shame.

## The Failure of Israel's Leaders

**5** <sup>1</sup> "Hear this, you priests.
Pay attention, you leaders of Israel.
Listen, you members of the royal family.
Judgment has been handed down against you.
For you have led the people into a snare
by worshiping the idols at Mizpah and Tabor.
<sup>2</sup> You have dug a deep pit to trap them at Acacia Grove.*
But I will settle with you for what you have done.

5:3
Amos 5:12

<sup>3</sup> I know what you are like, O Ephraim.
You cannot hide yourself from me, O Israel.
You have left me as a prostitute leaves her husband;
you are utterly defiled.

5:4
Hos 4:6, 14

<sup>4</sup> Your deeds won't let you return to your God.
You are a prostitute through and through,
and you do not know the LORD.

5:5
2 Kgs 17:19-20
Ezek 23:31-35

<sup>5</sup> "The arrogance of Israel testifies against her;
Israel and Ephraim will stumble under their load of guilt.
Judah, too, will fall with them.

5:6
Isa 1:15
Ezek 8:6
Mic 6:6-7

<sup>6</sup> When they come with their flocks and herds
to offer sacrifices to the LORD,
they will not find him,
because he has withdrawn from them.

5:7
Hos 2:4

<sup>7</sup> They have betrayed the honor of the LORD,
bearing children that are not his.
Now their false religion will devour them
along with their wealth.*

**4:15** Beth-aven means "house of wickedness"; it is being used as another name for Bethel, which means "house of God." **4:17** Hebrew Ephraim, referring to the northern kingdom of Israel. **4:18** As in Greek version; the meaning of the Hebrew is uncertain. **5:2** Hebrew at Shittim. The meaning of the Hebrew for this sentence is uncertain. **5:7** The meaning of the Hebrew is uncertain.

---

**4:15** God sent a warning to the southern kingdom of Judah that its priests should not become like those in Israel. (The southern kingdom was called Judah after its most powerful tribe.) Israel's priests who remained in the north had forgotten their spiritual heritage and had sold out to Baal. They were promoting idol worship and ritual prostitution. Israel would not escape punishment, but Judah could if it refused to follow Israel's example.

**4:19** The mighty wind that would sweep Israel away refers to the Assyrian invasion that would destroy the nation about 20 years later.

**5:1, 2** Mizpah and Tabor may have been sites prominent in the false worship of Baal. The leaders likely even encouraged the people to sin at these places. With both their civil and religious leaders hopelessly corrupt, the people of Israel did not have much

of a chance. They looked to their leaders for guidance, and they should have found it. Today we can often choose our own leaders, but we still need to be aware of whether they are taking us toward or away from God. God held the people responsible for what they did. Similarly, God holds us responsible for our actions and choices.

**5:3** Ephraim is another name for Israel, the northern kingdom, because Ephraim was the most powerful of the ten tribes in the north. In the same way, the southern kingdom was called Judah after its most powerful tribe.

**5:4** Persistent sin hardens a person's heart, making it difficult to repent. Deliberately choosing to disobey God can sear the conscience; each sin makes the next one easier to commit. Don't allow sin to groove a hard path deep within you. Steer as far away from sinful practices as possible.

8 "Sound the alarm in Gibeah!
  Blow the trumpet in Ramah!
Raise the battle cry in Beth-aven*!
  Lead on into battle, O warriors of Benjamin!
9 One thing is certain, Israel*:
  On your day of punishment,
  you will become a heap of rubble.

10 "The leaders of Judah have become like thieves.*
  So I will pour my anger on them like a waterfall.
11 The people of Israel will be crushed and broken by my judgment
  because they are determined to worship idols.*
12 I will destroy Israel as a moth consumes wool.
  I will make Judah as weak as rotten wood.

13 "When Israel and Judah saw how sick they were,
  Israel turned to Assyria—
to the great king there—
  but he could neither help nor cure them.
14 I will be like a lion to Israel,
  like a strong young lion to Judah.
  I will tear them to pieces!
I will carry them off,
  and no one will be left to rescue them.
15 Then I will return to my place
  until they admit their guilt and turn to me.
For as soon as trouble comes,
  they will earnestly search for me."

## 2. Israel's punishment
### A Call to Repentance

**6** 1 "Come, let us return to the LORD.
  He has torn us to pieces;
  now he will heal us.
He has injured us;
  now he will bandage our wounds.
2 In just a short time he will restore us,
  so that we may live in his presence.
3 Oh, that we might know the LORD!
  Let us press on to know him.
He will respond to us as surely as the arrival of dawn
  or the coming of rains in early spring."

4 "O Israel* and Judah,
  what should I do with you?" asks the LORD.
"For your love vanishes like the morning mist
  and disappears like dew in the sunlight.

**5:9**
Isa 28:1-4; 37:3
Hos 9:11-17

**5:10**
Deut 27:17
Pss 32:6; 93:3-4
Ezek 7:8

**5:12**
Ps 39:11
Isa 51:8

**5:13**
Jer 30:12

**5:14**
Pss 7:2; 50:22
Hos 13:7

**5:15**
Isa 64:7-9
Jer 2:27

**6:1**
Isa 30:26
Jer 50:4
Hos 14:4
Zeph 2:1-3

**6:3**
Isa 2:3
Joel 2:23
Mic 4:2

**6:4**
Ps 78:34-37
Hos 13:3

---

**5:8** Beth-aven means "house of wickedness"; it is being used as another name for Bethel, which means "house of God." **5:9** Hebrew Ephraim, referring to the northern kingdom of Israel; also in 5:11, 12, 13, 14. **5:10** Hebrew like those who move a boundary marker. **5:11** Or determined to follow human commands. The meaning of the Hebrew is uncertain. **6:4** Hebrew Ephraim, referring to the northern kingdom of Israel.

---

**5:8** Gibeah and Ramah were Israelite cities near Jerusalem. Hosea prophesied that these cities would sound the alarm of the coming judgment.

**5:13** During the reigns of Menahem and Hoshea, Israel turned to Assyria for help (2 Kings 15:19, 20; 17:3, 4). But even the great world powers of that time could not help Israel, for God himself had determined to judge the nation. If we neglect God's call to repentance, how can we escape? (See Hebrews 2:3.)

**6:1-3** This is presumption, not genuine repentance. The people did not understand the depth of their sins. They did not turn from idols, repent of their sins, or pledge to make changes. They thought that God's wrath would last only a few days; little did

they know that their nation would soon be taken into exile. Israel was interested in God only for the material benefits he provided; they did not value the eternal benefits that come from worshiping him. Before judging Israel, however, consider your attitude. What do you hope to gain from your religion? Do you "repent" easily, without seriously considering what changes need to take place in your life?

**6:4** God answered his people, pointing out that their profession of loyalty, like mist and dew, evaporated easily and had no substance. Many find it easy and comfortable to maintain the appearance of being committed without deep and sincere loyalty. If you profess loyalty to God, back it up with your actions.

**6:5**
Heb 4:12

⁵ I sent my prophets to cut you to pieces—
   to slaughter you with my words,
   with judgments as inescapable as light.

**6:6**
Matt 9:13; 12:7

⁶ I want you to show love,*
   not offer sacrifices.
I want you to know me*
   more than I want burnt offerings.
⁷ But like Adam,* you broke my covenant
   and betrayed my trust.

⁸ "Gilead is a city of sinners,
   tracked with footprints of blood.

**6:9**
Jer 7:9
Ezek 22:9

⁹ Priests form bands of robbers,
   waiting in ambush for their victims.
They murder travelers along the road to Shechem
   and practice every kind of sin.
¹⁰ Yes, I have seen something horrible in Ephraim and Israel:
   My people are defiled by prostituting themselves with other gods!

**6:11**
Jer 51:33
Joel 3:13

¹¹ "O Judah, a harvest of punishment is also waiting for you,
   though I wanted to restore the fortunes of my people.

### Israel's Love for Wickedness

**7:1**
Ezek 24:13

**7** ¹ "I want to heal Israel,* but its sins are too great.
   Samaria is filled with liars.
Thieves are on the inside
   and bandits on the outside!

**6:6a** Greek version translates this Hebrew term as *to show mercy.* Compare Matt 9:13; 12:7.  **6:6b** Hebrew *to know God.*  **6:7** Or *But at Adam.*  **7:1** Hebrew *Ephraim,* referring to the northern kingdom of Israel; also in 7:8, 11.

---

**OBEDIENCE VERSUS SACRIFICES**
God says many times that he doesn't want our gifts and sacrifices when we give them out of ritual or hypocrisy. God wants us first to love and obey him.

| | |
|---|---|
| 1 Samuel 15:22, 23 . . . . . . . . | Obedience is better than sacrifice. |
| Psalm 40:6-8 . . . . . . . . . . . . | God doesn't want sacrifices or offerings; he wants us to take joy in doing his will. |
| Psalm 51:16-19 . . . . . . . . . . | God isn't interested in sacrifice; he wants a broken and repentant heart. |
| Jeremiah 7:21-23 . . . . . . . . . | It isn't sacrifices God wants; he desires our obedience and promises that he will be our God and we will be his people. |
| Hosea 6:6 . . . . . . . . . . . . . . | God doesn't want sacrifices; he wants us to show love. He doesn't want offerings; he wants us to know him. |
| Amos 5:21-24 . . . . . . . . . . . | God hates pretense and hypocrisy; he wants to see justice roll on like a river. |
| Micah 6:6-8 . . . . . . . . . . . . | God is not satisfied with offerings; he wants us to do what is right, love mercy, and walk humbly with him. |
| Matthew 9:13 . . . . . . . . . . . | God doesn't want sacrifices; he wants us to be merciful. |

---

**6:6** Religious rituals can help people understand God and nourish their relationship with him. That is why God instituted circumcision and the sacrificial system in the Old Testament and baptism and the Lord's Supper in the New Testament. But a religious ritual is helpful only if it is carried out with an attitude of love for and obedience to God. If a person's heart is far from God, ritual will become empty mockery. God didn't want the Israelites' rituals; he wanted their worship. Why do you worship? What is the motive behind your "sacrifices" and "offerings"?

**6:7** One of Hosea's key themes is that Israel had broken the covenant God had made with them at Mount Sinai (Exodus 19–20). God wanted to make Israel a blessing and a light to all the nations (Genesis 12:2, 3; Isaiah 49:6); and if God's chosen people obeyed him and proclaimed him to the world, he would give them special blessings. If they broke the covenant, however, they would suffer severe penalties, as they should have known (see Deuteronomy 28:15-68). Sadly, the people broke the covenant and proved themselves unfaithful to God. How about you? Have you also broken faith with God? What about your forgotten promises to serve him?

**6:8, 9** Gilead was once a sacred place, but here it was corrupt. Shechem was once a city of refuge designated by Joshua (Joshua 20:1, 2, 7, 8); Gilead was a region that included Ramoth, also a city of refuge. At this time these areas were associated with murder and crime, with bands of evil priests lying in wait to murder travelers passing through the territory.

**6:11** So that the people of Judah would not become proud as they saw the northern kingdom's destruction, Hosea interjected a solemn warning about God's "harvest." God's Temple was in Judah (Jerusalem), and the people thought that what happened in Israel could never happen to them. But when they had become utterly corrupt, they, too, were led off into captivity (see 2 Kings 25).

**7:1, 2** God sees and knows everything. We, like Israel, often forget this. Thoughts like "No one will ever know," or "No one is watching" may tempt us to try to get away with sin. If you are facing difficult temptations, you will be less likely to give in if you remind yourself that God is watching. When faced with the opportunity to sin, remember that God sees everything.

2 Its people don't realize
    that I am watching them.
Their sinful deeds are all around them,
    and I see them all.

3 "The people entertain the king with their wickedness,
    and the princes laugh at their lies.
4 They are all adulterers,
    always aflame with lust.
They are like an oven that is kept hot
    while the baker is kneading the dough.
5 On royal holidays, the princes get drunk with wine,
    carousing with those who mock them.
6 Their hearts are like an oven
    blazing with intrigue.
Their plot smolders* through the night,
    and in the morning it breaks out like a raging fire.
7 Burning like an oven,
    they consume their leaders.
They kill their kings one after another,
    and no one cries to me for help.

8 "The people of Israel mingle with godless foreigners,
    making themselves as worthless as a half-baked cake!
9 Worshiping foreign gods has sapped their strength,
    but they don't even know it.
Their hair is gray,
    but they don't realize they're old and weak.
10 Their arrogance testifies against them,
    yet they don't return to the LORD their God
    or even try to find him.

11 "The people of Israel have become like silly, witless doves,
    first calling to Egypt, then flying to Assyria for help.
12 But as they fly about,
    I will throw my net over them
and bring them down like a bird from the sky.
    I will punish them for all the evil they do.*

13 "What sorrow awaits those who have deserted me!
    Let them die, for they have rebelled against me.
I wanted to redeem them,
    but they have told lies about me.
14 They do not cry out to me with sincere hearts.
    Instead, they sit on their couches and wail.
They cut themselves,* begging foreign gods for grain and new wine,
    and they turn away from me.
15 I trained them and made them strong,
    yet now they plot evil against me.

**7:2** Jer 2:19 · Hos 8:13

**7:3** Mic 7:3

**7:4** Jer 9:2; 23:10

**7:5** Isa 28:1

**7:7** Isa 64:7

**7:9** Isa 1:7

**7:10** Hos 5:5

**7:11** Hos 12:1

**7:12** Ezek 12:13

**7:13** Matt 23:37

**7:14** Amos 2:8

**7:15** Nah 1:9

---

**7:6** Hebrew *Their baker sleeps.*   **7:12** Hebrew *I will punish them because of what was reported against them in the assembly.*   **7:14** As in Greek version; Hebrew reads *They gather together.*

---

**7:6** "Their hearts are like an oven blazing with intrigue" refers to the lust for power and intrigue that was burning in these leaders' hearts. Three Israelite kings were assassinated during Hosea's lifetime—Zechariah, Shallum, and Pekahiah (2 Kings 15:8-26). The kings' foreign relations and domestic lives were ruined because they ignored God and his word.

**7:8** The people of Israel had intermarried with foreign people and had picked up their evil ways. When we spend a lot of time with unbelievers, either professionally or socially, we can easily pick up their attitudes and begin to imitate their actions. Beware of the influence they may have on you. Instead of drifting into bad habits, see if you can have a positive influence and point these people to God.

**7:10** Arrogance (pride) keeps a person from turning to God because arrogance claims no need of help from anyone, human or divine. Pride intensifies all our other sins because we cannot repent of any of them without first giving up our pride.

**7:11** Israel's King Menahem had paid Assyria to support him in power (2 Kings 15:19, 20); King Hoshea turned against Assyria and went to Egypt for help (2 Kings 17:4). Israel's kings went back and forth, allying themselves with different nations when they should have allied themselves with God.

**7:16**
Ps 78:57
Ezek 23:32
Hos 9:3, 6

16 They look everywhere except to the Most High.
    They are as useless as a crooked bow.
Their leaders will be killed by their enemies
    because of their insolence toward me.
Then the people of Egypt
    will laugh at them.

### Israel Harvests the Whirlwind

**8:1**
Hab 1:8

**8** 1 "Sound the alarm!
    The enemy descends like an eagle on the people of the LORD,
for they have broken my covenant
    and revolted against my law.
2 Now Israel pleads with me,
    'Help us, for you are our God!'
3 But it is too late.
The people of Israel have rejected what is good,
    and now their enemies will chase after them.

**8:4**
Hos 2:8; 13:10

4 The people have appointed kings without my consent,
    and princes without my knowledge.
By making idols for themselves from their silver and gold,
    they have brought about their own destruction.

**8:5**
Jer 13:27

5 "O Samaria, I reject this calf—
    this idol you have made.
My fury burns against you.
    How long will you be incapable of innocence?

**8:6**
Hos 13:2

6 This calf you worship, O Israel,
    was crafted by your own hands!
It is not God!
    Therefore, it must be smashed to bits.

**8:7**
Isa 66:15
Nah 1:3

7 "They have planted the wind
    and will harvest the whirlwind.
The stalks of grain wither
    and produce nothing to eat.
And even if there is any grain,
    foreigners will eat it.

**8:8**
Jer 51:34

8 The people of Israel have been swallowed up;
    they lie among the nations like an old discarded pot.

**8:9**
Jer 2:24
Ezek 16:33

9 Like a wild donkey looking for a mate,
    they have gone up to Assyria.
The people of Israel* have sold themselves—
    sold themselves to many lovers.

**8:9** Hebrew *Ephraim*, referring to the northern kingdom of Israel; also in 8:11.

---

**7:16** A crooked bow is unreliable. Its arrows miss the target, and its owner would be quite vulnerable in battle. Life without God is as unreliable as a crooked bow. Without God's direction, our thoughts are filled with lust, cheating, selfishness, and deceit. As long as we are warped by sin, we will never reach our true potential.

**7:16** People look everywhere except to God for happiness and fulfillment, pursuing possessions, recreation, and relationships. In reality, only God can truly satisfy the deep longings of the soul. Look first to heaven, to the Most High God. He will meet your *spiritual* needs, not all your materialistic wants.

**8:1-4** "The enemy descends like an eagle on the people of the LORD" refers to Assyria coming to attack Israel and take the people into captivity (2 Kings 15:28, 29). The people would call to God, but it would be too late because they had stubbornly refused to give up their idols. We, like Israel, often call on God to ease our pain without wanting him to change our behavior. And we, like Israel, may repent after it is too late to avoid the painful consequences of sin.

**8:5** Samaria was the capital of the northern kingdom, and sometimes it stands for the whole kingdom of Israel. Jeroboam I had set up worship of calf idols at Bethel and Dan and had encouraged the people to worship them (1 Kings 12:25-33). Thus, the people were worshiping the image of a created animal rather than the Creator.

**8:7** Crop yield is the result of good seed planted in good soil and given the proper proportions of sunlight, moisture, and fertilizer. A single seed can produce multiple fruit in good conditions. Israel, however, had sown its spiritual seed to the wind—it had invested itself in activities without substance. Like the wind that comes and goes, its idolatry and foreign alliances offered no protection. In seeking self-preservation apart from God, it had brought about its own destruction. Like a forceful whirlwind, God's judgment would come upon Israel by means of the Assyrians. When we seek security in anything except God, we expose ourselves to great danger. Without God there is no lasting security.

<sup>10</sup> But though they have sold themselves to many allies,
    I will now gather them together for judgment.
  Then they will writhe
    under the burden of the great king.

<sup>11</sup> "Israel has built many altars to take away sin,
    but these very altars became places for sinning!
<sup>12</sup> Even though I gave them all my laws,
    they act as if those laws don't apply to them.
<sup>13</sup> The people of Israel love their rituals of sacrifice,
    but to me their sacrifices are all meaningless.
  I will hold my people accountable for their sins,
    and I will punish them.
    They will return to Egypt.
<sup>14</sup> Israel has forgotten its Maker and built great palaces,
    and Judah has fortified its cities.
  Therefore, I will send down fire on their cities
    and will burn up their fortresses."

## Hosea Announces Israel's Punishment

**9** <sup>1</sup> O people of Israel,
    do not rejoice as other nations do.
  For you have been unfaithful to your God,
    hiring yourselves out like prostitutes,
    worshiping other gods on every threshing floor.
<sup>2</sup> So now your harvests will be too small to feed you.
    There will be no grapes for making new wine.
<sup>3</sup> You may no longer stay here in the LORD's land.
    Instead, you will return to Egypt,
  and in Assyria you will eat food
    that is ceremonially unclean.
<sup>4</sup> There you will make no offerings of wine to the LORD.
    None of your sacrifices there will please him.
  They will be unclean, like food touched by a person in mourning.
    All who present such sacrifices will be defiled.
  They may eat this food themselves,
    but they may not offer it to the LORD.
<sup>5</sup> What then will you do on festival days?
    How will you observe the LORD's festivals?

### Cross-references (side column)

8:10 Jer 42:2; Ezek 16:37; Hos 10:10

8:13 Hos 7:2; 1 Cor 4:5

8:14 Jer 17:27; Hos 2:13; 4:6; 13:6

9:1 Isa 22:12-13

9:2 Hos 2:9

9:3 Ezek 4:13

9:4 Exod 29:40; Hag 2:14

9:5 Hos 2:11; Joel 1:13

---

**8:11** The altars that were supposed to remove sin were actually increasing sin through their misuse in worshiping Baal.

**8:12** Though the laws were written for *them,* the people of Israel acted as if those laws didn't apply to them. It is easy to listen to a sermon and think of all the people we know who should be listening, or to read the Bible and think of those who should do what the passage teaches. The Israelites did this constantly, applying God's laws to others but not to themselves to avoid making needed changes. As you think of others who need to apply what you are hearing or reading, check to see if the same application could fit you. Apply the lessons to your own life first because often our own faults are the very first ones we see in others.

**8:13** The people's sacrifices had become mere ritual, and God refused to accept them. We have rituals, too: attending church, observing a regular quiet time, celebrating Christian holidays, praying before meals. Rituals give us security in a changing world. Because they are repeated often, they can drive God's lessons deep within us. But rituals can be abused. Beware if you find yourself observing a religious ritual for any of the following reasons: (1) to gain community approval, (2) to avoid the risks of

doing something different, (3) to make thought unnecessary, (4) to substitute for personal relationships, (5) to make up for bad behavior, (6) to earn God's favor. We should not reject the rituals of our worship, but we must be careful to think about why we do them. Focus on God, and perform every act with sincere devotion.

**8:13** In Egypt, the Israelites had been slaves (Exodus 1:11). The people would not literally return to Egypt, but they would return to slavery—this time scattered throughout the Assyrian Empire.

**8:14** Israel had placed its confidence in military strength, strong defenses, and economic stability, just as nations do today. But because of the people's inner moral decay, their apparent sources of strength were inadequate. There is a tendency in many nations toward removing all traces of God from daily life. But if a nation forgets its Maker, its strengths may prove worthless when put to the test.

**9:1** A threshing floor was a flat area, often built on a hilltop, where harvesters beat the wheat and separated it from the chaff. Often men would stay overnight at the threshing floor to protect their grain, so prostitutes would visit there. Because of the location of threshing floors in the hilltops, they began to be used as places to sacrifice to false gods.

**9:6**
Isa 5:6; 7:23
Hos 10:8

6 Even if you escape destruction from Assyria,
  Egypt will conquer you, and Memphis* will bury you.
  Nettles will take over your treasures of silver;
  thistles will invade your ruined homes.

**9:7**
Isa 10:3
Jer 10:15; 29:26
Lam 2:14
Ezek 7:2-7;
13:3, 10

7 The time of Israel's punishment has come;
  the day of payment is here.
  Soon Israel will know this all too well.
  Because of your great sin and hostility,
  you say, "The prophets are crazy
  and the inspired men are fools!"

8 The prophet is a watchman over Israel* for my God,
  yet traps are laid for him wherever he goes.
  He faces hostility even in the house of God.

**9:9**
Isa 31:6
Hos 7:2; 8:13

9 The things my people do are as depraved
  as what they did in Gibeah long ago.
  God will not forget.
  He will surely punish them for their sins.

**9:10**
Num 25:1-9
Jer 24:2

10 The LORD says, "O Israel, when I first found you,
  it was like finding fresh grapes in the desert.
  When I saw your ancestors,
  it was like seeing the first ripe figs of the season.
  But then they deserted me for Baal-peor,
  giving themselves to that shameful idol.
  Soon they became vile,
  as vile as the god they worshiped.

**9:11**
Hos 4:7

11 The glory of Israel will fly away like a bird,
  for your children will not be born
  or grow in the womb
  or even be conceived.

**9:12**
Hos 7:13

12 Even if you do have children who grow up,
  I will take them from you.
  It will be a terrible day when I turn away
  and leave you alone.

13 I have watched Israel become as beautiful as Tyre.
  But now Israel will bring out her children for slaughter."

14 O LORD, what should I request for your people?
  I will ask for wombs that don't give birth
  and breasts that give no milk.

**9:6** Memphis was the capital of northern Egypt.    **9:8** Hebrew *Ephraim*, referring to the northern kingdom of Israel;
also in 9:11, 13, 16.

---

**9:6** Israel's leaders vacillated between alliances with Egypt and alliances with Assyria. Hosea was saying that both were wrong. Breaking an alliance with untrustworthy Assyria and fleeing for help to the equally untrustworthy Egypt would not forestall Israel's destruction. Its only hope was to return to God.

**9:7** By the time Israel began to experience the consequences of its sins, it was no longer listening to God's messengers. Refusing to hear the truth from prophets who spoke out so clearly about its sins, the nation did not hear God's warnings about what was soon to happen. We all listen and read selectively, focusing on what seems to support our present lifestyle and ignoring a radical reordering of our priorities. In doing this, we are likely to miss the warning signs. Listen to people who think your approach is all wrong. Read articles that present viewpoints you would be unlikely to take. Ask yourself, Is God speaking to me through these speakers and writers? Is there something I need to change?

**9:9** A couple had stopped to stay overnight in Gibeah when some wicked men gathered around the house and demanded that the man come out so they could have sex with him. Instead, the traveler gave them his concubine. They raped and abused her all night

and then left her dead on the doorstep (Judges 19:14-30). That horrible act revealed the depths to which the people had sunk. Gibeah was destroyed for its evil (Judges 20:8-48), but Hosea said that the whole nation was now as evil as that city. Just as the city didn't escape punishment, neither would the nation.

**9:10** Baal-peor was the god of Peor, a mountain in Moab. In Numbers 22, Balaam, a prophet, was hired by King Balak of Moab to curse the Israelites as they were coming through his land. The Moabites enticed the Israelites into sexual sin and Baal worship. Before long, the Israelites became as corrupt as the gods they worshiped. People soon begin to copy the characteristics and lifestyles of those around them. What do you worship? Are you becoming more like God, or are you becoming more like the world?

**9:14** Hosea prayed this prayer when he foresaw the destruction that Israel's sins would bring (2 Kings 17:7-23). This vision of Israel's terrible fate moved him to pray that women would not get pregnant and that children would die as infants so they would not have to experience the tremendous suffering and pain that lay ahead.

15 The Lord says, "All their wickedness began at Gilgal;
  there I began to hate them.
I will drive them from my land
  because of their evil actions.
I will love them no more
  because all their leaders are rebels.
16 The people of Israel are struck down.
  Their roots are dried up,
    and they will bear no more fruit.
  And if they give birth,
    I will slaughter their beloved children."

17 My God will reject the people of Israel
  because they will not listen or obey.
They will be wanderers,
  homeless among the nations.

### The Lord's Judgment against Israel

**10** ¹ How prosperous Israel is—
  a luxuriant vine loaded with fruit.
But the richer the people get,
  the more pagan altars they build.
The more bountiful their harvests,
  the more beautiful their sacred pillars.
² The hearts of the people are fickle;
  they are guilty and must be punished.
The Lord will break down their altars
  and smash their sacred pillars.
³ Then they will say, "We have no king
  because we didn't fear the Lord.
But even if we had a king,
  what could he do for us anyway?"

⁴ They spout empty words
  and make covenants they don't intend to keep.
So injustice springs up among them
  like poisonous weeds in a farmer's field.

⁵ The people of Samaria tremble in fear
  for what might happen to their calf idol at Beth-aven.*
The people mourn and the priests wail,
  because its glory will be stripped away.*
⁶ This idol will be carted away to Assyria,
  a gift to the great king there.
Ephraim will be ridiculed and Israel will be shamed,
  because its people have trusted in this idol.
⁷ Samaria and its king will be cut off;
  they will float away like driftwood on an ocean wave.

*Cross-references (right margin):*
9:15 Isa 1:23; Hos 7:2; 12:2; Amos 4:4; 5:5
9:16 Ezek 24:21
10:1 1 Kgs 14:23; Isa 5:1-7; Ezek 15:1-5; Hos 8:11; 12:11
10:2 1 Kgs 18:21; Hos 10:8; Mic 5:13; Zeph 1:5
10:4 Ps 12:4; Hos 4:2
10:5 Hos 8:5
10:6 Hos 10:5

10:5a *Beth-aven* means "house of wickedness"; it is being used as another name for Bethel, which means "house of God." 10:5b Or *will be taken away into exile.*

---

**9:15** At Gilgal, both the political and the religious failure of the nation began. Here idols and kings were substituted for God. Saul, the united nation's first king, was crowned at Gilgal (1 Samuel 11:15), but by Hosea's time, Baal worship flourished there (4:15; 12:11).

**10:1** Israel prospered under Jeroboam II, gaining military and economic strength. But the more prosperous the nation became, the more love it lavished on idols. It seems as though the more God gives, the more we spend. We want bigger houses, better cars, and finer clothes. But the finest things the world offers line the pathway to destruction. As you prosper, consider where your money is going. Is it being used for God's purposes, or are you consuming it all on yourself?

**10:4** God was angry with the people of Israel for their insincere promises. Because the people did not keep their word, there were many lawsuits. People break their promises, but God always keeps his. Are you remaining true to your promises, both to other people and to God? If not, ask God for forgiveness and help to get back on track. Then be careful about the promises you make. Never make a promise unless you are sure you can keep it.

**10:5** *Beth-aven* means "house of wickedness," and it refers to Bethel ("house of God"), where false worship took place. If the Israelites' idols were really gods, they should have been able to protect them. How ironic that the people were fearing for their gods' safety! For more information on this calf idol, see the notes on 3:4, 5 and 8:5.

**10:8**
Hos 5:8; 9:6; 10:5
†Luke 23:30
Rev 6:16

8 And the pagan shrines of Aven,* the place of Israel's sin, will crumble.
Thorns and thistles will grow up around their altars.
They will beg the mountains, "Bury us!"
and plead with the hills, "Fall on us!"

9 The LORD says, "O Israel, ever since Gibeah,
there has been only sin and more sin!
You have made no progress whatsoever.
Was it not right that the wicked men of Gibeah were attacked?

**10:10**
Ezek 5:13

10 Now whenever it fits my plan,
I will attack you, too.
I will call out the armies of the nations
to punish you for your multiplied sins.

**10:11**
Jer 28:14

11 "Israel* is like a trained heifer treading out the grain—
an easy job she loves.
But I will put a heavy yoke on her tender neck.
I will force Judah to pull the plow
and Israel* to break up the hard ground.

**10:12**
Prov 11:18
Isa 45:8

12 I said, 'Plant the good seeds of righteousness,
and you will harvest a crop of love.
Plow up the hard ground of your hearts,
for now is the time to seek the LORD,
that he may come
and shower righteousness upon you.'

**10:13**
Ps 33:16
Gal 6:7-8

13 "But you have cultivated wickedness
and harvested a thriving crop of sins.
You have eaten the fruit of lies—
trusting in your military might,
believing that great armies
could make your nation safe.

**10:14**
2 Kgs 17:3

14 Now the terrors of war
will rise among your people.
All your fortifications will fall,
just as when Shalman destroyed Beth-arbel.
Even mothers and children
were dashed to death there.
15 You will share that fate, Bethel,
because of your great wickedness.
When the day of judgment dawns,
the king of Israel will be completely destroyed.

**10:8** *Aven* is a reference to Beth-aven; see 10:5a and the note there.    **10:11a** Hebrew *Ephraim,* referring to the northern kingdom of Israel.    **10:11b** Hebrew *Jacob.* The names "Jacob" and "Israel" are often interchanged throughout the Old Testament, referring sometimes to the individual patriarch and sometimes to the nation.

**10:9, 10** For information on what happened in Gibeah, see the note on 9:9 or read Judges 19 and 20. Gibeah stands for cruelty and sensuality, as in Judges, and for rebellion as in Saul's day (Gibeah was Saul's hometown; see 1 Samuel 10:5; 11:4).

**10:12** Hosea repeatedly uses illustrations about fields and crops. Here he envisions a plowed field. It is no longer stony and hard; it has been carefully prepared, and it is ready for planting. Is your life ready for God to work in it? You can break up the unplowed ground of your heart by acknowledging your sins and receiving God's forgiveness and guidance.

**10:13** The Israelites were taken in by the lie that military power could keep them safe. Believers today sometimes fall for lies. Those who lead others astray often follow these rules: Make it big; keep it simple; repeat it often. Believers can avoid falling for lies by asking: (1) Am I believing this because there is personal gain in it for me? (2) Am I discounting important facts? (3) Does this conflict with a direct command of Scripture? (4) Are there

any biblical parallels to the situation I'm facing that would help me know what to believe?

**10:14** Some say Shalman was Shalmaneser, king of Assyria; others say Shalman was Salmanu, a Moabite king mentioned in the inscriptions of Tiglath-pileser. Shalman had invaded Gilead around 740 B.C. and destroyed the city of Beth-arbel, killing many people, including women and children. This kind of cruelty was not uncommon in ancient warfare. Hosea was saying such would be Israel's fate.

**10:15** Because Israel had put its confidence in military might rather than in God, it would be destroyed by military power. Israel's king, who had led the people into idol worship, would be the first to fall. Divine judgment is *sometimes* swift, but it is *always* sure.

## 3. God's love for Israel

**11** ¹ "When Israel was a child, I loved him,
    and I called my son out of Egypt.
² But the more I* called to him,
    the farther he moved from me,
offering sacrifices to the images of Baal
    and burning incense to idols.
³ I myself taught Israel* how to walk,
    leading him along by the hand.
But he doesn't know or even care
    that it was I who took care of him.
⁴ I led Israel along
    with my ropes of kindness and love.
I lifted the yoke from his neck,
    and I myself stooped to feed him.

⁵ "But since my people refuse to return to me,
    they will return to Egypt
    and will be forced to serve Assyria.
⁶ War will swirl through their cities;
    their enemies will crash through their gates.
They will destroy them,
    trapping them in their own evil plans.
⁷ For my people are determined to desert me.
They call me the Most High,
    but they don't truly honor me.

⁸ "Oh, how can I give you up, Israel?
    How can I let you go?
How can I destroy you like Admah
    or demolish you like Zeboiim?
My heart is torn within me,
    and my compassion overflows.
⁹ No, I will not unleash my fierce anger.
    I will not completely destroy Israel,
for I am God and not a mere mortal.
    I am the Holy One living among you,
    and I will not come to destroy.

**11:1**
Exod 4:22
Hos 2:15; 12:9, 13;
13:4
Matt 2:15

**11:3**
Deut 1:31
Jer 30:17

**11:4**
Exod 16:32
Ps 78:25
Jer 31:2-3

**11:6**
Hos 13:16

**11:7**
Jer 8:5

**11:8**
Gen 14:8
Deut 29:23
Hos 6:4; 7:1

**11:9**
Deut 13:17
Isa 5:24; 12:6;
41:14
Jer 26:3

**11:2** As in Greek version; Hebrew reads *they.*   **11:3** Hebrew *Ephraim,* referring to the northern kingdom of Israel;
also in 11:8, 9, 12.

---

**11:1ff** In the final four chapters, Hosea shifts to the theme of God's intense love for Israel. God had always loved Israel as a parent loves a stubborn child, and that is why he would not release Israel from the consequences of its behavior. The Israelites were sinful, and they would be punished like a rebellious son brought by his parents before the elders (Deuteronomy 21:18-21). All through Israel's sad history, God repeatedly offered to restore the nation if it would only turn to him. By stubbornly refusing God's invitation, the northern kingdom had sealed its doom. It would be destroyed, never to rise again. Even so, Israel as a nation was not finished. A remnant of faithful Israelites would return to Jerusalem, where one day the Messiah would come, offering pardon and reconciliation to all who would faithfully follow him.

**11:3** God had consistently provided for his people, but they refused to see what he had done, and they showed no interest in thanking him. Ungratefulness is a common human fault. For example, when was the last time you thanked your parents for caring for you? your pastor for the service he gives your church? your child's teacher for the care taken with each day's activities? your heavenly Father for his guidance? Many of the benefits and privileges we enjoy are the result of loving actions done long ago. Look for hidden acts of nurturing, and thank those who make the world better through their love. But begin by thanking God for all his blessings.

**11:4** God's discipline requires times of leading and times of feeding. Sometimes the rope is taut; sometimes it is slack. God's discipline is always loving, and its object is always the well-being of the beloved. When you are called to discipline others—children, students, employees, or church members—do not be rigid. Vary your approach according to the goals you are seeking to accomplish. In each case, ask yourself, Does this person need guidance, or does he or she need to be nurtured?

**11:5** The northern kingdom survived for only two centuries after its break with Jerusalem. Its spiritual and political leaders did not help the people learn the way to God, so as a nation they would never repent. Hosea prophesied its downfall, which happened when Shalmaneser of Assyria conquered Israel in 722 B.C. Judah also would go into captivity, but a remnant would return to its homeland.

**11:8** Admah and Zeboiim were cities of the plain that had perished with Sodom and Gomorrah (Genesis 14:8; Deuteronomy 29:23).

**11:9** "I am God and not a mere mortal." It is easy for us to define God in terms of our own expectations and behavior. In so doing, we make him just slightly larger than ourselves. In reality, God is infinitely greater than we are. We should seek to become like him rather than attempt to remake him in our image.

**11:10**
Isa 31:4; 66:2, 5
Joel 3:16

10 For someday the people will follow me.
    I, the Lord, will roar like a lion.
And when I roar,
    my people will return trembling from the west.

**11:11**
Isa 11:11; 60:8

11 Like a flock of birds, they will come from Egypt.
    Trembling like doves, they will return from Assyria.
And I will bring them home again,"
    says the Lord.

### Charges against Israel and Judah

12 *Israel surrounds me with lies and deceit,
    but Judah still obeys God
    and is faithful to the Holy One.*

**12:1**
Gen 41:6
Jer 22:22
Ezek 17:10

**12** 1 *The people of Israel* feed on the wind;
    they chase after the east wind all day long.
They pile up lies and violence;
    they are making an alliance with Assyria
    while sending olive oil to buy support from Egypt.

**12:2**
Hos 4:1
Mic 6:2

2 Now the Lord is bringing charges against Judah.
    He is about to punish Jacob* for all his deceitful ways,
    and pay him back for all he has done.

**12:3**
Gen 25:26

3 Even in the womb,
    Jacob struggled with his brother;
when he became a man,
    he even fought with God.

**12:4**
Gen 28:13-15;
32:24-30; 35:10-15

4 Yes, he wrestled with the angel and won.
    He wept and pleaded for a blessing from him.
There at Bethel he met God face to face,
    and God spoke to him*—

**12:5**
Exod 3:15

5 the Lord God of Heaven's Armies,
    the Lord is his name!

**12:6**
Mic 7:7

6 So now, come back to your God.
    Act with love and justice,
    and always depend on him.

**11:12a** Verse 11:12 is numbered 12:1 in Hebrew text. **11:12b** Or *and Judah is unruly against God, the faithful Holy One.* The meaning of the Hebrew is uncertain. **12:1a** Verses 12:1-14 are numbered 12:2-15 in Hebrew text. **12:1b** Hebrew *Ephraim*, referring to the northern kingdom of Israel; also in 12:8, 14. **12:2** *Jacob* sounds like the Hebrew word for "deceiver." **12:4** As in Greek and Syriac versions; Hebrew reads *to us.*

---

**11:12** Unlike Israel, Judah had some fairly good kings—Asa, Jehoshaphat, Joash, Amaziah, Uzziah, Jotham, and especially Hezekiah and Josiah. Under some of these kings, God's law was dusted off and taught to the people. The priests continued to serve in God's appointed Temple in Jerusalem, and the festivals were celebrated at least some of the time. Unfortunately, the political or religious leaders were unable to completely wipe out idol worship and pagan rites (although Hezekiah and Josiah came close), which continued to fester until they eventually erupted and infected the whole country. Still, the influence of the good kings enabled Judah to survive more than 150 years longer than Israel, and that memory of their positive influence fortified a small group—a remnant—of faithful people who would one day return and restore their land and Temple.

**12:2-5** Jacob, whose name was later changed to Israel, was the common ancestor of all 12 tribes of Israel (both northern and southern kingdoms). Like the nations that descended from him, Jacob practiced deceit. Unlike Israel and Judah, however, he constantly searched for God. Jacob wrestled with the angel in order to be blessed, but his descendants thought their blessings came from their own successes. Jacob purged his house of idols (Genesis 35:2), but his descendants could not quit their idol worship.

**12:6** The two principles that Hosea called his nation to live by, love and justice, are at the very foundation of God's character. They are essential to his followers, but they are not easy to keep in balance. Some people are loving to the point that they excuse wrongdoing. Others are just to the extent that they forget love. Love without justice leaves people in their sins because it is not aiming at a higher standard. Justice without love drives people away from God because it has no heart. To specialize in one at the expense of the other is to distort our witness. Today's church, just like Hosea's nation, must live by both principles.

7 But no, the people are like crafty merchants
  selling from dishonest scales—
  they love to cheat.
8 Israel boasts, "I am rich!
  I've made a fortune all by myself!
  No one has caught me cheating!
  My record is spotless!"

9 "But I am the LORD your God,
  who rescued you from slavery in Egypt.
  And I will make you live in tents again,
  as you do each year at the Festival of Shelters.*
10 I sent my prophets to warn you
  with many visions and parables."

11 But the people of Gilead are worthless
  because of their idol worship.
  And in Gilgal, too, they sacrifice bulls;
  their altars are lined up like the heaps of stone
  along the edges of a plowed field.
12 Jacob fled to the land of Aram,
  and there he* earned a wife by tending sheep.
13 Then by a prophet
  the LORD brought Jacob's descendants* out of Egypt;
  and by that prophet
  they were protected.
14 But the people of Israel
  have bitterly provoked the LORD,
  so their Lord will now sentence them to death
  in payment for their sins.

### The LORD's Anger against Israel

**13** 1 When the tribe of Ephraim spoke,
  the people shook with fear,
  for that tribe was important in Israel.
  But the people of Ephraim sinned by worshiping Baal
  and thus sealed their destruction.
2 Now they continue to sin by making silver idols,
  images shaped skillfully with human hands.
  "Sacrifice to these," they cry,
  "and kiss the calf idols!"

**12:7**
Prov 11:1
Amos 8:5
Mic 6:11

**12:8**
Hos 13:6
Rev 3:17

**12:10**
2 Kgs 17:13
Ezek 17:2; 20:49

**12:12**
Gen 28:5; 29:20

**12:13**
Exod 14:19-22

**12:14**
2 Kgs 17:7-18

**13:1**
Hos 2:8-17

**13:2**
Isa 44:17-20; 46:6
Jer 10:2-5

**12:9** Hebrew *as in the days of your appointed feast.* **12:12** Hebrew *Israel.* See note on 10:11b. **12:13** Hebrew *brought Israel.* See note on 10:11b.

---

**12:7, 8** In Israel, dishonesty had become an accepted means of attaining wealth. Israelites who were financially successful could not imagine that God would consider them sinful. They thought that their wealth was a sign of God's approval, and they didn't bother to consider how they had gotten it. But God said that Israel's riches would not make up for its sin. Remember that God's measure of success is different from ours. He calls us to faithfulness, not to affluence. Character is more important to him than our purses.

**12:8** Rich people and nations often claim that their material success is due to their own hard work, initiative, and intelligence. Because they have bought whatever they wanted, they don't feel the need for God. They believe that their riches are their own and that they have the right to use them any way they please. If you find yourself feeling proud of your accomplishments, remember that all your opportunities, abilities, and resources come from God and that you hold them in sacred trust for him.

**12:9** Once a year the Israelites spent a week living in tents during the Festival of Shelters, which commemorated God's protection as they wandered in the wilderness for 40 years (see Deuteronomy 1:19–2:1). Here, because of their sin, God would cause them to live in tents again—this time not as part of a festival but in actual bondage.

**12:12** Hosea was using this reference to Jacob to say, "Don't forget your humble beginnings. What you have is not a result of your own efforts, but it is yours because God has been gracious to you."

**12:13** The prophet who brought Israel out of Egypt was Moses (Exodus 13:17-19).

**13:1** Israel, represented here by the northern tribe of Ephraim, had been great, but by Hosea's time the people had rebelled against God and had lost their authority among the nations. Greatness in the past is no guarantee of greatness in the future. It is good to remember what God has done for you and through you, but it is equally important to keep your relationship with him vital and up to date. Commit yourself to God moment by moment.

**13:3**
Ps 68:2
Isa 17:13
Dan 2:35
Hos 6:4

3 Therefore, they will disappear like the morning mist,
like dew in the morning sun,
like chaff blown by the wind,
like smoke from a chimney.

**13:4**
Exod 20:3
Isa 43:11; 45:21-22

4 "I have been the LORD your God
ever since I brought you out of Egypt.
You must acknowledge no God but me,
for there is no other savior.

**13:5**
Deut 2:7; 8:15;
32:10

5 I took care of you in the wilderness,
in that dry and thirsty land.

**13:6**
Hos 2:13; 4:6; 8:14

6 But when you had eaten and were satisfied,
you became proud and forgot me.
7 So now I will attack you like a lion,
like a leopard that lurks along the road.

**13:8**
Ps 50:22

8 Like a bear whose cubs have been taken away,
I will tear out your heart.
I will devour you like a hungry lioness
and mangle you like a wild animal.

9 "You are about to be destroyed, O Israel—
yes, by me, your only helper.

**13:10**
2 Kgs 17:4
Hos 8:4

10 Now where is* your king?
Let him save you!
Where are all the leaders of the land,
the king and the officials you demanded of me?

**13:11**
1 Sam 8:7
1 Kgs 14:7-10

11 In my anger I gave you kings,
and in my fury I took them away.

**13:12**
Deut 32:34-35
Rom 2:5

12 "Ephraim's guilt has been collected,
and his sin has been stored up for punishment.

**13:13**
Mic 4:9-10

13 Pain has come to the people
like the pain of childbirth,
but they are like a child
who resists being born.
The moment of birth has arrived,
but they stay in the womb!

**13:14**
Isa 25:8
Ezek 37:12-13
1 Cor 15:55
Phil 3:21

14 "Should I ransom them from the grave*?
Should I redeem them from death?

**13:10** As in Greek and Syriac versions and Latin Vulgate; Hebrew reads *I will be.* **13:14a** Hebrew *Sheol;* also in 13:14b.

---

**CYCLES OF JUDGMENT/ SALVATION IN HOSEA**

Judgment . . . . . . . . . . . . . 1:2-9; 2:2-13; 4:1–5:14; 6:4–11:7; 11:12–13:16
Salvation . . . . . . . . . . . . . . 1:10–2:1; 2:14–3:5; 5:15–6:3; 11:8-11; 14:1-9

God promises to judge, but he also promises mercy. Here you can see the cycles of judgment and salvation in Hosea. Prophecies of judgment are consistently followed by prophecies of forgiveness.

---

**13:4-6** When abundant possessions made Israel feel self-sufficient, it turned its back on God and forgot him. Self-sufficiency is as destructive today as it was in Hosea's time. Do you see your constant need of God's presence and help? Learn to rely on God, both in good times and bad. If you are traveling along a smooth and easy path right now, beware of forgetting who gave you your good fortune. Don't depend on your gifts; depend on the Giver. See Deuteronomy 6:10-12 and 8:7-20 for God's warning.

**13:11** God had warned the people of Israel that kings would cause more problems than they would solve, and he reluctantly gave them Saul as their first king (1 Samuel 8:4-22). The second king, David, was a good king, and Solomon, David's son, had his strengths. But after the nation divided in two, the northern king-

dom never had another good ruler. Evil kings led the nations deeper into idolatry and unwise political alliances. Eventually the evil kings destroyed the nation; with Hoshea, the northern kingdom's kings were cut off (2 Kings 17:1-6).

**13:12** Ephraim's (Israel's) sins were recorded for later punishment. All our sins are known and will be revealed at the day of judgment (2 Corinthians 5:10; Revelation 20:11-15). How will you live differently today knowing that everything you do will be revealed at the day of judgment?

**13:14** The apostle Paul used this passage to teach the resurrection of our bodies from death (1 Corinthians 15:55). For those who have trusted in Christ for deliverance from sin, death holds no threat of annihilation.

O death, bring on your terrors!
　　O grave, bring on your plagues!*
　　For I will not take pity on them.
15 Ephraim was the most fruitful of all his brothers,
　　but the east wind—a blast from the LORD—
　　will arise in the desert.
All their flowing springs will run dry,
　　and all their wells will disappear.
Every precious thing they own
　　will be plundered and carried away.
16 *The people of Samaria
　　must bear the consequences of their guilt
　　because they rebelled against their God.
They will be killed by an invading army,
　　their little ones dashed to death against the ground,
　　their pregnant women ripped open by swords."

## Healing for the Repentant

**14** ¹ *Return, O Israel, to the LORD your God,
　　for your sins have brought you down.
² Bring your confessions, and return to the LORD.
　　Say to him,
"Forgive all our sins and graciously receive us,
　　so that we may offer you our praises.*
³ Assyria cannot save us,
　　nor can our warhorses.
Never again will we say to the idols we have made,
　　'You are our gods.'
No, in you alone
　　do the orphans find mercy."

⁴ The LORD says,
"Then I will heal you of your faithlessness;
　　my love will know no bounds,
　　for my anger will be gone forever.
⁵ I will be to Israel
　　like a refreshing dew from heaven.
Israel will blossom like the lily;
　　it will send roots deep into the soil
　　like the cedars in Lebanon.
⁶ Its branches will spread out like beautiful olive trees,
　　as fragrant as the cedars of Lebanon.
⁷ My people will again live under my shade.
　　They will flourish like grain and blossom like grapevines.
　　They will be as fragrant as the wines of Lebanon.

**13:15**
Jer 51:36
Hos 10:1

**13:16**
2 Kgs 15:16

**14:2**
Mic 7:18-19
Heb 13:15

**14:3**
Pss 10:14; 68:5
Mic 5:10

**14:4**
Isa 57:18
Zeph 3:17

**14:5**
Song 2:1
Matt 6:28

**14:6**
Ps 52:8
Jer 11:16

**14:7**
Ps 91:1-4

13:14b Greek version reads *O death, where is your punishment? / O grave* [Hades], *where is your sting?* Compare 1 Cor 15:55.　**13:16** Verse 16 is numbered 14:1 in Hebrew text.　**14:1** Verses 14:1-9 are numbered 14:2-10 in Hebrew text.　**14:2** As in Greek and Syriac versions, which read *may repay the fruit of our lips;* Hebrew reads *may repay the bulls of our lips.*

---

**14:1ff** Verses 1-3 are Hosea's call to repent. Verses 4-8 are God's promise of restoration. God had to punish Israel for its gross and repeated violations of his law, but he would do so with a heavy heart. What God really wanted to do was restore the nation and make it prosper.

**14:1, 2** The people could return to God by asking him to forgive their sins. The same is true for us: We can pray Hosea's prayer and know our sins are forgiven because Christ died for them on the cross (John 3:16).
　　Forgiveness begins when we see the destructiveness of sin and the futility of life without God. Then we must admit we cannot save ourselves; our only hope is in God's mercy. When we seek forgiveness, we must recognize that we do not deserve

it and therefore cannot demand it. Our appeal must be for God's love and mercy, not for his justice. Although we cannot demand forgiveness, we can be confident that we have received it because God is gracious and loving and wants to restore us to himself, just as he wanted to restore Israel.

**14:3-8** When our will is weak, when our thinking is confused, and when our conscience is burdened with a load of guilt, we must remember that God cares for us continually; his love knows no bounds. When friends and family desert us, when coworkers don't understand us, and when we are tired of being good, God's love knows no bounds. When we can't see the way or seem to hear God's voice, and when we lack courage to go on, God's love knows no bounds. When our shortcomings and our awareness of our sins overcome us, God's love knows no bounds.

**14:8**
Isa 41:19

8 "O Israel,* stay away from idols!
　I am the one who answers your prayers and cares for you.
I am like a tree that is always green;
　all your fruit comes from me."

**14:9**
Ps 107:43
Isa 1:28; 26:7
Jer 9:12

9 Let those who are wise understand these things.
　Let those with discernment listen carefully.
The paths of the LORD are true and right,
　and righteous people live by walking in them.
But in those paths sinners stumble and fall.

**14:8** Hebrew *Ephraim*, referring to the northern kingdom of Israel.

---

**14:9** Hosea closes with an appeal to listen, learn, and benefit from God's word. To those receiving the Lord's message through Hosea, this meant the difference between life and death. For you, the reader of the book of Hosea, the choice is similar: You can either listen to the book's message and follow God's ways or refuse to walk along the Lord's path. But people who insist on following their own direction without God's guidance are in "total darkness" and "have no idea what they are stumbling over" (Proverbs 4:19). If you are lost, you can find the way by turning from your sin and following God.

**14:9** God's concern for *justice* that requires faithfulness and for *love* that offers forgiveness can be seen in his dealings with Hosea. We can err by forgetting God's love, feeling that our sins are hopeless; but we can also err by forgetting his wrath against our sins, thinking he will continue to accept us no matter how we act. *Forgiveness* is a key word: When God forgives us, he judges the sin but shows mercy to the sinner. We should never be afraid to come to God for a clean slate and a renewed life.

# JOEL

## VITAL STATISTICS

**PURPOSE:**
To warn Judah of God's impending judgment because of its sins and to urge the people to turn back to God

**AUTHOR:**
Joel son of Pethuel

**ORIGINAL AUDIENCE:**
The people of Judah (the southern kingdom)

**DATE WRITTEN:**
Probably during the time Joel may have prophesied, from approximately 835–796 B.C.

**SETTING:**
The people of Judah had become prosperous and complacent. Taking God for granted, they had turned to self-centeredness, idolatry, and sin. Joel warned them that this kind of life-style would inevitably bring God's judgment.

**KEY VERSES:**
"That is why the LORD says, 'Turn to me now, while there is time. Give me your hearts. Come with fasting, weeping, and mourning. Don't tear your clothing in your grief, but tear your hearts instead.' Return to the LORD your God, for he is merciful and compassionate, slow to get angry and filled with unfailing love. He is eager to relent and not punish" (2:12, 13).

**KEY PEOPLE:**
Joel, the people of Judah

**KEY PLACE:**
Jerusalem

A SINGLE bomb devastates a city, and the world is ushered into the nuclear age. A split atom—power and force such as we had never seen.

At a launch site, rockets roar and a payload is thrust into space. Discoveries dreamed of for centuries are ours as we begin to explore the edge of the universe.

Volcanos, earthquakes, tidal waves, hurricanes, and tornados unleash uncontrollable and unstoppable force. And we can only avoid them and then pick up the pieces.

Power, strength, might—we stand in awe at the natural and human-made display. But these forces cannot touch the power of omnipotent God. Creator of galaxies, atoms, and natural laws, the Sovereign Lord rules all there is and ever will be. How silly to live without him; how foolish to run and hide from him; how ridiculous to disobey him. But we do. Since Eden, we have sought independence from his control, as though we were gods and could plot our destiny. And he has allowed our rebellion. But soon *the day of the Lord* will come.

It is about this day that the prophet Joel speaks, and it is the theme of his book. On this day God will judge all unrighteousness and disobedience—all accounts will be settled and the crooked made straight.

We know very little about Joel—only that he was a prophet and the son of Pethuel. He may have lived in Jerusalem because his audience was Judah, the southern kingdom. Whoever he was, Joel speaks forthrightly and forcefully in this short and powerful book. His message is one of foreboding and warning, but it is also filled with hope. Joel states that our Creator, the omnipotent Judge, is also merciful, and he wants to bless all those who trust him.

Joel begins by describing a terrible plague of locusts that covers the land and devours the crops. The devastation wrought by these creatures is but a foretaste of the coming judgment of God, the "day of the LORD." Joel, therefore, urges the people to turn from their sin and turn back to God. Woven into this message of judgment and the need for repentance is an affirmation of God's kindness and the blessings he promises for all who follow him. In fact, "everyone who calls on the name of the LORD will be saved" (2:32).

As you read Joel, catch his vision of the power and might of God and of God's ultimate judgment of sin. Choose to follow, obey, and worship God alone as your sovereign Lord.

Jehoahaz
becomes
king of
Israel
814

Jehoash
becomes
king of
Israel
798

Joel's
ministry
ends
796?

## THE BLUEPRINT

1. The day of the locusts
   (1:1—2:27)
2. The day of the Lord
   (2:28—3:21)

The locust plague was only a foretaste of the judgment to come in the day of the Lord. This is a timeless call to repentance with the promise of blessing. Just as the people faced the tragedy of their crops being destroyed, we, too, will face tragic judgment if we live in sin. But God's grace is available to us both now and in that coming day.

## MEGATHEMES

| THEME | EXPLANATION | IMPORTANCE |
|---|---|---|
| Punishment | Like a destroying army of locusts, God's punishment for sin is overwhelming, dreadful, and unavoidable. When it comes, there will be no food, no water, no protection, and no escape. The day for settling accounts with God for how we have lived is fast approaching. | God is the one with whom we all must reckon—not nature, the economy, or a foreign invader. We can't ignore or offend God forever. We must pay attention to his message now, or we will face his anger later. |
| Forgiveness | God stood ready to forgive and restore all those who would come to him and turn away from sin. God wanted to shower his people with his love and restore them to a proper relationship with him. | Forgiveness comes by turning from sin and turning toward God. It is not too late to receive God's forgiveness. God's greatest desire is for you to come to him. |
| Promise of the Holy Spirit | Joel predicts the time when God will pour out his Holy Spirit on all people. It will be the beginning of new and fresh worship of God by those who believe in him, as well as the beginning of judgment on all who reject him. | God is in control. Justice and restoration are in his hands. The Holy Spirit confirms God's love for us just as he did for the first Christians (Acts 2). We must be faithful to God and place our life under the guidance and power of his Holy Spirit. |

## 1. The day of the locusts

**1** The LORD gave this message to Joel son of Pethuel.

*Mourning over the Locust Plague*

1:2
Jer 30:7
Joel 2:2, 16

2 Hear this, you leaders of the people.
   Listen, all who live in the land.
In all your history,
   has anything like this happened before?

1:3
Exod 10:2

3 Tell your children about it in the years to come,
   and let your children tell their children.
Pass the story down from generation to generation.

---

**1:1** Joel was a prophet to the nation of Judah, also known as the southern kingdom. Although the 12 tribes of Israel had been united under David and Solomon, after Solomon's death, the kingdom had divided into two parts. Two of the tribes—Judah and Benjamin—stayed loyal to David's line and accepted Solomon's son Rehoboam as king. They became the southern kingdom, also called Judah (after the larger tribe). The other ten tribes followed Jeroboam, set up a new kingdom with a new capital at Samaria, and called themselves Israel or the northern kingdom.

The book does not mention when Joel lived, but many believe that he prophesied during the reign of King Joash (835–796 B.C.). But the date of Joel's book is not nearly so important

as its timeless message: Sin brings God's judgment; yet with God's justice there is also great mercy.

**1:3** God urged parents to pass their history down to their children, telling over and over the important lessons they learned. One of the greatest gifts you can give young people is your life's story to help them repeat your successes and avoid your mistakes.

4 After the cutting locusts finished eating the crops,
    the swarming locusts took what was left!
After them came the hopping locusts,
    and then the stripping locusts,* too!

5 Wake up, you drunkards, and weep!
    Wail, all you wine-drinkers!
All the grapes are ruined,
    and all your sweet wine is gone.

6 A vast army of locusts* has invaded my land,
    a terrible army too numerous to count.
Its teeth are like lions' teeth,
    its fangs like those of a lioness.

7 It has destroyed my grapevines
    and ruined my fig trees,
stripping their bark and destroying it,
    leaving the branches white and bare.

8 Weep like a bride dressed in black,
    mourning the death of her husband.

9 For there is no grain or wine
    to offer at the Temple of the LORD.
So the priests are in mourning.
    The ministers of the LORD are weeping.

10 The fields are ruined,
    the land is stripped bare.
The grain is destroyed,
    the grapes have shriveled,
    and the olive oil is gone.

11 Despair, all you farmers!
    Wail, all you vine growers!
Weep, because the wheat and barley—
    all the crops of the field—are ruined.

12 The grapevines have dried up,
    and the fig trees have withered.
The pomegranate trees, palm trees, and apple trees—
    all the fruit trees—have dried up.
And the people's joy has dried up with them.

13 Dress yourselves in burlap and weep, you priests!
    Wail, you who serve before the altar!
Come, spend the night in burlap,
    you ministers of my God.
For there is no grain or wine
    to offer at the Temple of your God.

1:4 The precise identification of the four kinds of locusts mentioned here is uncertain.    1:6 Hebrew *A nation.*

**1:4** Deut 28:38-39 / Isa 33:4 / Nah 3:15-16

**1:6** Rev 9:3-10

**1:7** Isa 5:6 / Amos 4:9

**1:9** Hos 9:4

**1:10** Isa 24:4, 7

**1:11** Amos 5:16

**1:12** Song 2:3 / Hab 3:17-18 / Hag 2:19

**1:13** 1 Kgs 21:27 / Jer 4:8

---

**1:4** A locust plague can be as devastating as an invading army. Locusts gather in swarms too numerous to count (1:6) and fly several feet above the ground, seeming to darken the sun as they pass by (2:2). When they land, they devour almost every piece of vegetation (1:7-12), covering and entering everything in their path (2:9).

**1:4** Joel's detailed description has caused many to believe that he was referring to an actual locust plague that had come or was about to come upon the land. Another view is that the locusts symbolize an invading enemy army. In either case, the locusts represent devastation, and Joel's point was that God would punish the people because of their sin. Joel calls this judgment the "day of the LORD" (see the note on 1:15).

**1:5** The people's physical and moral senses were dulled, making them oblivious to sin. Joel called them to awaken from their complacency and admit their sins before it was too late. Otherwise everything would be destroyed, even the grapes that caused their drunkenness. Our times of peace and prosperity can lull us to sleep. We must never let material abundance hinder our spiritual readiness.

**1:9** Because of the devastation, there was no grain to make fine flour for the grain offerings and no wine for the drink offerings (see Leviticus 1 and 2 for a detailed explanation of these offerings).

**1:13** Mourners at a funeral would wear burlap clothing. Used here, it would be a sign of repentance.

**1:14**
Jon 3:8

¹⁴ Announce a time of fasting;
    call the people together for a solemn meeting.
Bring the leaders
    and all the people of the land
into the Temple of the LORD your God,
    and cry out to him there.

**1:15**
Isa 13:9
Jer 30:7
Ezek 7:2-13

¹⁵ The day of the LORD is near,
    the day when destruction comes from the Almighty.
How terrible that day will be!

**1:16**
Isa 3:7
Amos 4:6-7

¹⁶ Our food disappears before our very eyes.
    No joyful celebrations are held in the house of our God.

**1:17**
Isa 17:10-11

¹⁷ The seeds die in the parched ground,
    and the grain crops fail.
The barns stand empty,
    and granaries are abandoned.
¹⁸ How the animals moan with hunger!
    The herds of cattle wander about confused,
because they have no pasture.
    The flocks of sheep and goats bleat in misery.

**1:19**
Pss 50:15; 91:15
Mic 7:7

¹⁹ LORD, help us!
    The fire has consumed the wilderness pastures,
    and flames have burned up all the trees.

**1:20**
1 Kgs 17:7; 18:5
Ps 104:21

²⁰ Even the wild animals cry out to you
    because the streams have dried up,
    and fire has consumed the wilderness pastures.

### Locusts Invade like an Army

**2:1**
Zeph 1:16

**2** ¹ Sound the alarm in Jerusalem*!
    Raise the battle cry on my holy mountain!
Let everyone tremble in fear
    because the day of the LORD is upon us.

2:1 Hebrew *Zion;* also in 2:15, 23.

---

**JOEL**
served as a
prophet to
Judah, possibly
from 835–
796 B.C.

| | |
|---|---|
| Climate of the times . . . . . . . . | Wicked Queen Athaliah seized power in a bloody coup but was overthrown after a few years. Joash was crowned king, but he was only seven years old and in great need of spiritual guidance. Joash followed God in his early years but then turned away from him. |
| Main message . . . . . . . . . . . . | A plague of locusts had come to discipline the nation. Joel called the people to turn back to God before an even greater judgment occurred. |
| Importance of message . . . . . . | God judges all people for their sins, but he is merciful to those who turn to him and offers them eternal salvation. |
| Contemporary prophets . . . . . . | Elisha (848–797 B.C.), Jonah (793–753 B.C.) |

---

**1:14** A fast was a period of time when no food was eaten and people approached God with humility, sorrow for sin, and urgent prayer. In the Old Testament, people often would fast during times of calamity in order to focus their attention on God and to demonstrate their change of heart and their true devotion (see, for example, Judges 20:26; 1 Kings 21:27; Ezra 8:21; Jonah 3:5). This solemn meeting was a public religious gathering, called so that everyone could repent and pray to God for mercy.

**1:15** The "day of the LORD" is a common phrase in the Old Testament and in the book of Joel (see 2:1, 11, 31; 3:14). It always refers to some extraordinary happening, whether a present event (like a locust plague), an event in the near future (like the destruction of Jerusalem or the defeat of enemy nations), or the final period of history when God will defeat all the forces of evil.
Even when the day of the Lord refers to a present event, it also foreshadows the *final* day of the Lord. This final event of

history has two aspects to it: (1) the last judgment on all evil and sin and (2) the final reward for faithful believers. Righteousness and truth will prevail, but not before much suffering (Zechariah 14:1-3). If you trust the Lord, looking toward this final day should give you hope, because then all who are faithful will be united forever with God.

**1:15-19** Without God, destruction is sure. Those who have not personally accepted God's love and forgiveness will stand before him with no appeal. Be sure to avail yourself of God's love and mercy while you have the opportunity (2:32).

**2:1ff** Joel was still describing the devastating effects of the locust plague (see 2:25). The alarm showed that the crisis was at hand. However, Joel implied that the locust plague would be only the forerunner of an even greater crisis if the people didn't turn from their sins.

2 It is a day of darkness and gloom,
    a day of thick clouds and deep blackness.
Suddenly, like dawn spreading across the mountains,
    a great and mighty army appears.
Nothing like it has been seen before
    or will ever be seen again.

**2:2**
Dan 9:12

3 Fire burns in front of them,
    and flames follow after them.
Ahead of them the land lies
    as beautiful as the Garden of Eden.
Behind them is nothing but desolation;
    not one thing escapes.

**2:3**
Gen 2:8
Ps 105:34-35
Isa 51:3

4 They look like horses;
    they charge forward like warhorses.*

**2:4**
Rev 9:7

5 Look at them as they leap along the mountaintops.
    Listen to the noise they make—like the rumbling of chariots,
like the roar of fire sweeping across a field of stubble,
    or like a mighty army moving into battle.

**2:5**
Isa 5:24; 30:30
Rev 9:9

6 Fear grips all the people;
    every face grows pale with terror.
7 The attackers march like warriors
    and scale city walls like soldiers.
Straight forward they march,
    never breaking rank.

**2:6**
Isa 13:8
Jer 30:6

**2:7**
Isa 5:26-29

8 They never jostle each other;
    each moves in exactly the right position.
They break through defenses
    without missing a step.
9 They swarm over the city
    and run along its walls.
They enter all the houses,
    climbing like thieves through the windows.

**2:9**
Exod 10:6
Jer 9:21
John 10:1

10 The earth quakes as they advance,
    and the heavens tremble.
The sun and moon grow dark,
    and the stars no longer shine.

**2:10**
Isa 13:10
Nah 1:5
Matt 24:29; 27:51
†Mark 13:24-25

11 The Lord is at the head of the column.
    He leads them with a shout.
This is his mighty army,
    and they follow his orders.
The day of the Lord is an awesome, terrible thing.
    Who can possibly survive?

*A Call to Repentance*
12 That is why the Lord says,
    "Turn to me now, while there is time.
Give me your hearts.
    Come with fasting, weeping, and mourning.
13 Don't tear your clothing in your grief,
    but tear your hearts instead."

**2:12**
Deut 4:29-30

**2:13**
Exod 34:6
Amos 7:2-6

2:4 Or *like charioteers.*

---

**2:3** The Garden of Eden was Adam and Eve's first home (Genesis 2:8). Known for its beauty, it is used here to describe the beauty of the land prior to the devastation.

**2:12, 13** God told the people to turn to him while there was still time. Destruction would soon be upon them. Time is also running out for us. Because we don't know when our life will end, we

should trust and obey God now while we can. Don't let anything hinder you from turning to him.

**2:13** Deep remorse was often shown by tearing one's clothes. But God didn't want an outward display of penitence without true inward repentance (1 Samuel 16:7; Matthew 23:1-36). Be sure your attitude toward God is correct, not just your outward actions.

Return to the LORD your God,
for he is merciful and compassionate,
slow to get angry and filled with unfailing love.
He is eager to relent and not punish.

**2:14**
Hag 2:19

14 Who knows? Perhaps he will give you a reprieve,
sending you a blessing instead of this curse.
Perhaps you will be able to offer grain and wine
to the LORD your God as before.

**2:15**
Num 10:3
Joel 2:1

15 Blow the ram's horn in Jerusalem!
Announce a time of fasting;
call the people together
for a solemn meeting.

16 Gather all the people—
the elders, the children, and even the babies.
Call the bridegroom from his quarters
and the bride from her private room.

**2:17**
Pss 44:13; 79:10
Isa 37:20

17 Let the priests, who minister in the LORD's presence,
stand and weep between the entry room to the Temple and the altar.
Let them pray, "Spare your people, LORD!
Don't let your special possession become an object of mockery.
Don't let them become a joke for unbelieving foreigners who say,
'Has the God of Israel left them?'"

### The LORD's Promise of Restoration

**2:18**
Isa 60:10
Zech 1:14

18 Then the LORD will pity his people
and jealously guard the honor of his land.

**2:19**
Ezek 34:29; 36:15
Hos 2:21-22

19 The LORD will reply,
"Look! I am sending you grain and new wine and olive oil,
enough to satisfy your needs.
You will no longer be an object of mockery
among the surrounding nations.

**2:20**
Deut 11:24
Jer 1:14-15
Zech 14:8

20 I will drive away these armies from the north.
I will send them into the parched wastelands.
Those in the front will be driven into the Dead Sea,
and those at the rear into the Mediterranean.*
The stench of their rotting bodies will rise over the land."

Surely the LORD has done great things!

21    Don't be afraid, my people.
Be glad now and rejoice,
for the LORD has done great things.

**2:22**
Ps 65:12-13

22 Don't be afraid, you animals of the field,
for the wilderness pastures will soon be green.
The trees will again be filled with fruit;
fig trees and grapevines will be loaded down once more.

**2:23**
Ps 149:2
Hos 6:3
Zech 10:1

23 Rejoice, you people of Jerusalem!
Rejoice in the LORD your God!

**2:20** Hebrew *into the eastern sea, . . . into the western sea.*

---

**2:18** Joel reached a turning point in his message, moving from prophesying about an outpouring of God's judgment to prophesying about an outpouring of God's forgiveness and blessing. But this would come only if the people began to live as God wanted them to, giving up their sins. Where there is repentance, there is hope. This section of the book inspires that hope. Without it, Joel's prophecy could bring only despair. This promise of forgiveness should have encouraged the people to repent.

**2:20** Joel foresaw the invasion from the north by the armies of Assyria and Babylon, typified by the locusts.

**2:21** Joel contrasts the fear of God's judgment (2:1) with the joy of God's intervention (2:21). On the day of the Lord, sin will bring judgment, and only God's forgiveness will bring rejoicing. Unless you repent, your sin will result in punishment. Let God intervene in your life. Then you will be able to rejoice in that day because you will have nothing to fear. Before, there were fasting, plagues, and funeral dirges; then, there will be feasting, harvesting, and songs of praise. When God rules, his restoration will be complete. In the meantime, we must remember that God does not promise that all his followers will be prosperous now. When God pardons, he restores our relationship with him, but this does not guarantee individual wealth. Instead, God promises to meet the deepest needs of those who love him by loving us, forgiving us, giving us purpose in life, and giving us a caring Christian community.

For the rain he sends demonstrates his faithfulness.
Once more the autumn rains will come,
as well as the rains of spring.
24 The threshing floors will again be piled high with grain,
and the presses will overflow with new wine and olive oil.
25 The LORD says, "I will give you back what you lost
to the swarming locusts, the hopping locusts,
the stripping locusts, and the cutting locusts.*
It was I who sent this great destroying army against you.
26 Once again you will have all the food you want,
and you will praise the LORD your God,
who does these miracles for you.
Never again will my people be disgraced.
27 Then you will know that I am among my people Israel,
that I am the LORD your God, and there is no other.
Never again will my people be disgraced.

## 2. The day of the Lord
### The LORD's Promise of His Spirit
28* "Then, after doing all those things,
I will pour out my Spirit upon all people.
Your sons and daughters will prophesy.
Your old men will dream dreams,
and your young men will see visions.
29 In those days I will pour out my Spirit
even on servants—men and women alike.
30 And I will cause wonders in the heavens and on the earth—
blood and fire and columns of smoke.
31 The sun will become dark,
and the moon will turn blood red
before that great and terrible* day of the LORD arrives.
32 But everyone who calls on the name of the LORD
will be saved,
for some on Mount Zion in Jerusalem will escape,
just as the LORD has said.
These will be among the survivors
whom the LORD has called.

### Judgment against Enemy Nations
**3** 1* "At the time of those events," says the LORD,
"when I restore the prosperity of Judah and Jerusalem,
2 I will gather the armies of the world
into the valley of Jehoshaphat.*

**2:26**
Ps 67:5-7
Isa 45:17

**2:27**
Lev 26:11-12
Isa 45:5-6, 18
Joel 3:17, 21

**2:28-32**
†Acts 2:17-21

**2:29**
1 Cor 12:13
Gal 3:28

**2:30-31**
Joel 2:1, 10; 3:15
Matt 24:29
Mark 13:24-25

**2:32**
Isa 4:2
†Rom 10:13

**3:2**
Isa 66:16, 18
Ezek 36:1-5
Joel 3:12, 14

---

**2:25** The precise identification of the four kinds of locusts mentioned here is uncertain.   **2:28** Verses 2:28-32 are numbered 3:1-5 in Hebrew text.   **2:31** Greek version reads *glorious*.   **3:1** Verses 3:1-21 are numbered 4:1-21 in Hebrew text.   **3:2** *Jehoshaphat* means "the LORD judges."

---

**2:26, 27** If the Jews would never again experience a disaster like this locust plague ("never again will my people be disgraced"), how do we explain the captivity in Babylon, the Jews' slavery under the Greeks and Romans, and their persecution under Hitler? It is important not to take these verses out of context. This is still part of the "blessings" section of Joel's prophecy. Only if the people truly repented would they avoid a disaster like the one Joel had described. God's blessings are promised only to those who sincerely and consistently follow him. God does promise that after the final day of judgment, his people will never again experience this kind of disaster (Zechariah 14:9-11; Revelation 21).

**2:28-32** Peter quoted this passage (see Acts 2:16-21); the outpouring of the Spirit predicted by Joel occurred on Pentecost. While in the past God's Spirit seemed available to kings, prophets, and judges, Joel envisioned a time when the Spirit would be

available to every believer. Ezekiel also spoke of an outpouring of the Spirit (Ezekiel 39:28, 29). God's Spirit is available today to anyone who calls on the Lord for salvation (2:32).

**2:30** These "wonders" would give a hint or a picture of a coming event.

**2:31, 32** The "day of the LORD" is used here as God's appointed time to judge the nations (see the note on 1:15). Judgment and mercy go hand in hand. Joel had said that if the people repented, the Lord would save them from judgment (2:12-14). In this day of judgment and catastrophe, therefore, some will be saved. God's intention is not to destroy but to heal and to save. However, we must accept his salvation or we will certainly perish with the unrepentant.

**3:1, 2** The phrase "at the time of those events" refers to the time when those who call on the Lord will be saved (2:32). God will

There I will judge them
for harming my people, my special possession,
for scattering my people among the nations,
and for dividing up my land.
³ They threw dice* to decide which of my people
would be their slaves.
They traded boys to obtain prostitutes
and sold girls for enough wine to get drunk.

⁴"What do you have against me, Tyre and Sidon and you cities of Philistia? Are you trying to take revenge on me? If you are, then watch out! I will strike swiftly and pay you back for everything you have done. ⁵You have taken my silver and gold and all my precious treasures, and have carried them off to your pagan temples. ⁶You have sold the people of Judah and Jerusalem to the Greeks,* so they could take them far from their homeland.

⁷"But I will bring them back from all the places to which you sold them, and I will pay you back for everything you have done. ⁸I will sell your sons and daughters to the people of Judah, and they will sell them to the people of Arabia,* a nation far away. I, the LORD, have spoken!"

⁹ Say to the nations far and wide:
"Get ready for war!
Call out your best warriors.
Let all your fighting men advance for the attack.
¹⁰ Hammer your plowshares into swords
and your pruning hooks into spears.
Train even your weaklings to be warriors.
¹¹ Come quickly, all you nations everywhere.
Gather together in the valley."

And now, O LORD, call out your warriors!

¹² "Let the nations be called to arms.
Let them march to the valley of Jehoshaphat.
There I, the LORD, will sit
to pronounce judgment on them all.
¹³ Swing the sickle,
for the harvest is ripe.*
Come, tread the grapes,
for the winepress is full.
The storage vats are overflowing
with the wickedness of these people."

**3:3** Obad 1:11 / Nah 3:10

**3:4** Ezek 25:15-17

**3:5** 2 Kgs 12:18 / 2 Chr 21:16-17

**3:7** Isa 43:5-6 / Jer 23:8

**3:9** Isa 34:1 / Jer 46:3; 51:27 / Zech 14:2-3

**3:10** Isa 2:4 / Mic 4:3

**3:12** Ps 76:8-9 / Isa 3:13 / Joel 3:2, 14

**3:13** Hos 6:11 / Matt 13:39 / Mark 4:29 / Rev 14:15-19

**3:3** Hebrew *They cast lots.*  **3:6** Hebrew *to the peoples of Javan.*  **3:8** Hebrew *to the Sabeans.*  **3:13** Greek version reads *for the harvest time has come.* Compare Mark 4:29.

---

not only bless believers with everything they need; he will also bless them by destroying all evil and ending the pain and suffering on earth. This prophecy had three fulfillments: immediate, ongoing, and final. Its immediate interpretation could apply to King Jehoshaphat's recent battle against several enemy nations, including Moab and Ammon (2 Chronicles 20). Its ongoing fulfillment could be the partial restoration of the people to their land after the exile to Babylon. The final fulfillment will come in the great battle that precedes the Messiah's reign over the earth (Revelation 20:7-9).

**3:2** The geographic location of the valley of Jehoshaphat is not known, and some suggest it is being used as a symbol for the place where the Lord is to judge. Some think it may be a future valley created by the splitting of the Mount of Olives when the Messiah returns (Zechariah 14:4). The most important fact for us is that the name means "the LORD judges."

**3:4** Tyre and Sidon were major cities in Phoenicia to the northwest of Israel; Philistia was the nation southwest of Judah. Phoenicia and Philistia were small countries that rejoiced at the fall of

Judah and Israel because they would benefit from the increased trade. God would judge them for their wrong attitude.

**3:6** Jews were sold to Greeks, a pagan and unclean people. Some think this verse and 3:1 indicate that Joel lived after the captivity in Babylon (586 B.C.), when the Greek culture began to flourish. But archaeological studies have shown that the Greeks were trading with Phoenicia as early as 800 B.C. Also 3:4 mentions Tyre, Sidon, and Philistia. These places were contemporary with Judah before their captivity.

**3:8** The "people of Arabia" are also referred to as Sabeans, who came from Sheba, a nation in southwestern Arabia. One of Sheba's queens had visited Solomon over a century earlier (1 Kings 10:1-13). The Sabeans controlled the eastern trade routes.

<sup>14</sup> Thousands upon thousands are waiting in the valley of decision.
     There the day of the LORD will soon arrive.
<sup>15</sup> The sun and moon will grow dark,
     and the stars will no longer shine.
<sup>16</sup> The LORD's voice will roar from Zion
     and thunder from Jerusalem,
     and the heavens and the earth will shake.
     But the LORD will be a refuge for his people,
     a strong fortress for the people of Israel.

### Blessings for God's People

<sup>17</sup> "Then you will know that I, the LORD your God,
     live in Zion, my holy mountain.
     Jerusalem will be holy forever,
     and foreign armies will never conquer her again.
<sup>18</sup> In that day the mountains will drip with sweet wine,
     and the hills will flow with milk.
     Water will fill the streambeds of Judah,
     and a fountain will burst forth from the LORD's Temple,
     watering the arid valley of acacias.*
<sup>19</sup> But Egypt will become a wasteland
     and Edom will become a wilderness,
     because they attacked the people of Judah
     and killed innocent people in their land.

<sup>20</sup> "But Judah will be filled with people forever,
     and Jerusalem will endure through all generations.
<sup>21</sup> I will pardon my people's crimes,
     which I have not yet pardoned;
     and I, the LORD, will make my home
     in Jerusalem* with my people."

**3:18** Hebrew *valley of Shittim.*    **3:21** Hebrew *Zion.*

**Cross-references (margin):**
**3:14** Isa 34:2-8 / Joel 2:1; 3:2, 12
**3:15** Joel 2:10, 31
**3:16** Hos 11:10 / Amos 1:2
**3:17** Isa 11:9 / Ezek 20:40
**3:18** Exod 3:8 / Amos 9:13
**3:19** Amos 1:11 / Obad 1:10
**3:20** Ezek 37:25 / Amos 9:15
**3:21** Isa 4:4 / Ezek 36:25, 29

---

**3:14** Joel described multitudes waiting in the "valley of decision" (the valley of judgment of verses 2 and 12). Billions of people have lived on earth, and every one of them—dead, living, and yet to be born—will face judgment. Look around you. See your friends—those with whom you work and live. Have they received God's forgiveness? Have they been warned about sin's consequences? If we understand the severity of God's final judgment, we will want to take God's offer of hope to those we know.

**3:17** The last word will be God's; his ultimate sovereignty will be revealed in the end. We cannot predict when that end will come, but we can have confidence in his control over the world's events. The world's history, as well as our own pilgrimage, is in God's hands. We can be secure in his love and trust him to guide our decisions.

**3:18** The picture of this restored land is one of perfect beauty, similar to the Garden of Eden. The life-giving fountain flowing from the Lord's Temple illustrates the blessings that come from God. Those who trust in him will be forever fruitful. (See also Ezekiel 47:1-12; Revelation 22:1, 2.)

**3:19** Egypt and Edom were two of Israel's most persistent enemies. They represent all the nations hostile to God's people. God's promise that they would be destroyed is also a promise that all evil in the world will one day be destroyed.

**3:20, 21** The word *Judah* is used here to refer to all God's people—anyone who has called on the name of the Lord. There is full assurance of victory and peace for those who trust in God (2:32).

**3:21** Joel began with a prophecy about the destruction of the land and ended with a prophecy about its restoration. He began by stressing the need for repentance and ended with the promise of forgiveness that repentance brings. Joel was trying to convince the people to wake up (1:5), get rid of their complacency, and realize the danger of living apart from God. His message to us is that there is still time; anyone who calls on God's name can be saved (2:12-14, 32). Those who turn to God will enjoy the blessings mentioned in Joel's prophecy; those who refuse will face destruction.

# AMOS

WHEN we hear, "He's a man of God," we think of some famous evangelist, a "Reverend," a missionary, or the campus minister—professionals, Christian workers, those who preach and teach the Word as a vocation.

Surely Amos was a man of God, a person whose life was devoted to serving the Lord and whose lifestyle reflected this devotion—but he was a layperson. Herding sheep and tending sycamore-fig trees in the Judean countryside, Amos was not the son of a prophet; he was not the son of a priest. As a humble shepherd, he could have stayed in Tekoa, doing his job, providing for his family, and worshiping his God. But God gave Amos a vision of the future (1:1) and told him to take his message to Israel, the northern kingdom (7:15). Amos obeyed and thus proved he was a man of God.

Amos's message has impacted God's people throughout the centuries, and it needs to be heard today by individuals and nations. Though divided from their southern brothers and sisters in Judah, the northern Israelites were still God's people. But they were living beneath a pious veneer of religion, worshiping idols and oppressing the poor. Amos, a fiery, fearless, and honest shepherd from the south, confronted them with their sin and warned them of the impending judgment.

The book of Amos opens with this humble shepherd watching his sheep. God then gave him a vision of what was about to happen to the nation of Israel. God condemned all the nations who had sinned against him and harmed his people. Beginning with Aram, he moved quickly through Philistia, Tyre, Edom, Ammon, and Moab. All were condemned, and we can almost hear the Israelites shouting, "Amen!" And then, even Judah, Amos's homeland, was included in God's scathing denunciation (2:4, 5). How Amos's listeners must have enjoyed hearing those words! Suddenly, however, Amos turned to the people of Israel and pronounced God's judgment on *them*. The next four chapters enumerate and describe their sins. It is no wonder that Amaziah the priest intervened and tried to stop the preaching (7:10–13). Fearlessly, Amos continued to relate the visions of future judgment that God gave to him (chapters 8—9). After all the chapters on judgment, the book concludes with a message of hope. Eventually God will restore his people and make them great again (9:8–15).

As you read Amos's book, put yourself in the place of those Israelites and listen to God's message. Have you grown complacent? Have other concerns taken God's place in your life? Do you ignore those in need or oppress the poor? Picture yourself as Amos, faithfully doing what God calls you to do. You, too, can be God's person. Listen for his clear call and do what he says, wherever it leads.

## VITAL STATISTICS

**PURPOSE:**
To pronounce God's judgment upon Israel, the northern kingdom, for its complacency, idolatry, and oppression of the poor

**AUTHOR:**
Amos

**ORIGINAL AUDIENCE:**
The people of Israel (the northern kingdom)

**DATE WRITTEN:**
Probably during the reigns of Jeroboam II of Israel and Uzziah of Judah (approximately 760–750 B.C.)

**SETTING:**
The wealthy people of Israel were enjoying peace and prosperity. They were quite complacent and were oppressing the poor, even selling them into slavery. Soon, however, Israel would be conquered by Assyria, and the rich would themselves become slaves.

**KEY VERSE:**
"Instead, I want to see a mighty flood of justice, an endless river of righteous living" (5:24).

**KEY PEOPLE:**
Amos, Amaziah, Jeroboam II

**KEY PLACES:**
Bethel, Samaria

**SPECIAL FEATURES:**
Amos uses striking metaphors from his shepherding and farming experience—a loaded wagon (2:13), a roaring lion (3:8), a mutilated sheep (3:12), fat cows (4:1), and a basket of ripe fruit (8:1, 2).

## THE BLUEPRINT

1. Announcement of judgment
   (1:1—2:16)
2. Reasons for judgment
   (3:1—6:14)
3. Visions of judgment
   (7:1—9:15)

Amos speaks with brutal frankness in denouncing sin. He collided with the false religious leaders of his day and was not intimidated by priest or king. He continued to speak his message boldly. God requires truth and goodness, justice and righteousness, from all people and nations today as well. Many of the conditions in Israel during Amos's time are evident in today's society. We need Amos's courage to ignore danger and stand against sin.

## MEGATHEMES

| THEME | EXPLANATION | IMPORTANCE |
|---|---|---|
| *Everyone Answers to God* | Amos pronounced judgment from God on all the surrounding nations. Then he included Judah and Israel. God is in supreme control of all the nations. Everyone is accountable to him. | All people will have to account for their sin. When those who reject God seem to get ahead, don't envy their prosperity or feel sorry for yourself. Remember that we all must answer to God for how we live. |
| *Complacency* | Everyone was optimistic, business was booming, and people were happy (except for the poor and oppressed). With all the comfort and luxury came self-sufficiency and a false sense of security. But prosperity brought corruption and destruction. | A complacent present leads to a disastrous future. Don't congratulate yourself for the blessings and benefits you now enjoy. They are from God. If you are more satisfied with yourself than with God, remember that everything is meaningless without him. A self-sufficient attitude may be your downfall. |
| *Oppressing the Poor* | The wealthy and powerful people of Samaria, the capital of Israel, had become prosperous, greedy, and unjust. Illegal and immoral slavery came as the result of over-taxation and land-grabbing. There was also cruelty and indifference toward the poor. God is weary of greed and will not tolerate injustice. | God made all people; therefore, to ignore the poor is to ignore those whom God loves and whom Christ came to save. We must go beyond feeling bad for the poor and oppressed. We must act compassionately to stop injustice and to help care for those in need. |
| *Superficial Religion* | Although many people had abandoned real faith in God, they still pretended to be religious. They were carrying on superficial religious exercises instead of having spiritual integrity and practicing heartfelt obedience toward God. | Merely participating in ceremony or ritual falls short of true religion. God wants simple trust in him, not showy external actions. Don't settle for impressing others with external rituals when God wants heartfelt obedience and commitment. |

## 1. Announcement of judgment

**1** This message was given to Amos, a shepherd from the town of Tekoa in Judah. He received this message in visions two years before the earthquake, when Uzziah was king of Judah and Jeroboam II, the son of Jehoash,* was king of Israel.

² This is what he saw and heard:

> "The LORD's voice will roar from Zion
>     and thunder from Jerusalem!
> The lush pastures of the shepherds will dry up;
>     the grass on Mount Carmel will wither and die."

**1:1**
2 Sam 14:2
2 Kgs 14:23-29
Zech 14:5

**1:2**
Isa 42:13
Jer 12:4; 14:2
Amos 9:3

**1:1** Hebrew *Joash,* a variant spelling of Jehoash.

---

**1:1** Amos was a shepherd and fig grower from the southern kingdom (Judah), but he prophesied to the northern kingdom (Israel). Israel was politically at the height of its power with a prosperous economy, but the nation was spiritually corrupt. Idols were worshiped throughout the land and especially at Bethel, which was supposed to be the nation's religious center. Like Hosea, Amos was sent by God to denounce this social and religious corruption. About 30 or 40 years after Amos prophesied, Assyria destroyed the capital city, Samaria, and conquered Israel (722 B.C.). Uzziah reigned in Judah from 792–740; Jeroboam II reigned in Israel from 793–753.

**1:1** Tekoa, Amos's hometown, was located in the rugged sheep country of Judah, about 10 miles south of Jerusalem. Long before

Amos was born, a woman of Tekoa had helped reconcile David and his rebellious son, Absalom (2 Samuel 14:1-23).

**1:1** Amos raised sheep—not a particularly "spiritual" job; yet he became a channel of God's message to others. Your job may not cause you to feel spiritual or successful, but it is vital work if you are in the place God wants you to be. God can work through you to do extraordinary things, no matter how ordinary your occupation.

**1:1** The book of Zechariah and other historical records from this period mention an earthquake that occurred at this time (Zechariah 14:5).

**1:2** In the Bible, God is often pictured as a shepherd and his people as sheep. As a shepherd, God leads and protects his

### God's Judgment on Israel's Neighbors

³ This is what the LORD says:

"The people of Damascus have sinned again and again,*
and I will not let them go unpunished!
They beat down my people in Gilead
as grain is threshed with iron sledges.

⁴ So I will send down fire on King Hazael's palace,
and the fortresses of King Ben-hadad will be destroyed.
⁵ I will break down the gates of Damascus
and slaughter the people in the valley of Aven.
I will destroy the ruler in Beth-eden,
and the people of Aram will go as captives to Kir,"
says the LORD.

⁶ This is what the LORD says:

"The people of Gaza have sinned again and again,
and I will not let them go unpunished!
They sent whole villages into exile,
selling them as slaves to Edom.
⁷ So I will send down fire on the walls of Gaza,
and all its fortresses will be destroyed.

**1:8**
Isa 14:29-31
Jer 47:1-7
Ezek 25:16
Zeph 2:4-7
Zech 9:6

⁸ I will slaughter the people of Ashdod
and destroy the king of Ashkelon.
Then I will turn to attack Ekron,
and the few Philistines still left will be killed,"
says the Sovereign LORD.

**1:3** Hebrew *have committed three sins, even four;* also in 1:6, 9, 11, 13.

---

**AMOS**
served as a
prophet to Israel
(the northern
kingdom) from
760–750 B.C.

*Climate of the times* . . . . . . . Israel was enjoying peace and economic prosperity. But this
blessing had caused her to become a selfish, materialistic
society. Those who were well-off ignored the needs of those
less fortunate. The people were self-centered and indifferent
toward God.

*Main message* . . . . . . . . . . . Amos spoke against those who exploited or ignored the needy.

*Importance of message* . . . . . Believing in God is more than a matter of individual faith. God
calls all believers to work against injustices in society and
to aid those less fortunate.

*Contemporary prophets* . . . . . Jonah (793–753 B.C.), Hosea (753–715 B.C.)

---

flock. But here God is depicted as a ferocious lion ready to
devour those who are evil or unfaithful (see also Hosea 11:10).

**1:2** *Carmel* means "fertile field." It was a very fertile area. A
drought capable of drying up this area would have to be quite
severe.

**1:3** Damascus was the capital of Aram. In the past, Aram had
been one of Israel's most formidable enemies. After the defeat
of Aram by Assyria in 732 B.C. (2 Kings 16:9), Damascus was
no longer a real threat.

**1:3–2:6** Amos pronounced God's judgment on nation after
nation around Israel's borders—even Judah. Perhaps the people
of Israel cheered when they heard the rebukes leveled against
those nations. But then Amos proclaimed God's judgment on
the people of Israel. They could not excuse their own sin just
because the sins of their neighbors seemed worse. God is no
respecter of persons. He judges all people fairly and impartially.

**1:3–2:6** The accusation "The people . . . have sinned again and
again, and I will not let them go unpunished" echoes through
these verses as God evaluates nation after nation. Each nation had
persistently refused to follow God's commands. A sinful practice
can become a way of life. Ignoring or denying the problem will not

help us. We must begin the process of correction by confessing
our sins to God and asking him to forgive us. Otherwise we have
no hope but to continue our pattern of sin.

**1:4** King Hazael was king of Aram. Ben-hadad was Hazael's son
(2 Kings 13:24).

**1:5** The Arameans had been slaves in Kir, but here they were
free (9:7). Decreeing that the Arameans should go back to Kir
was like saying the Israelites should go back to Egypt as slaves
(Exodus 1).

**1:7, 8** Gaza, Ashdod, Ashkelon, and Ekron were four of the five
major cities of Philistia, an enemy who often threatened Israel.
The fifth city, Gath, had probably already been destroyed. Therefore, Amos was saying that the entire nation of Philistia would
be destroyed for its sins.

⁹This is what the LORD says:

"The people of Tyre have sinned again and again,
    and I will not let them go unpunished!
They broke their treaty of brotherhood with Israel,
    selling whole villages as slaves to Edom.
¹⁰ So I will send down fire on the walls of Tyre,
    and all its fortresses will be destroyed."

¹¹This is what the LORD says:

"The people of Edom have sinned again and again,
    and I will not let them go unpunished!
They chased down their relatives, the Israelites, with swords,
    showing them no mercy.
In their rage, they slashed them continually
    and were unrelenting in their anger.
¹² So I will send down fire on Teman,
    and the fortresses of Bozrah will be destroyed."

¹³This is what the LORD says:

"The people of Ammon have sinned again and again,
    and I will not let them go unpunished!
When they attacked Gilead to extend their borders,
    they ripped open pregnant women with their swords.
¹⁴ So I will send down fire on the walls of Rabbah,
    and all its fortresses will be destroyed.
The battle will come upon them with shouts,
    like a whirlwind in a mighty storm.
¹⁵ And their king* and his princes will go into exile together,"
    says the LORD.

**2** This is what the LORD says:

"The people of Moab have sinned again and again,*
    and I will not let them go unpunished!
They desecrated the bones of Edom's king,
    burning them to ashes.
² So I will send down fire on the land of Moab,
    and all the fortresses in Kerioth will be destroyed.
The people will fall in the noise of battle,
    as the warriors shout and the ram's horn sounds.
³ And I will destroy their king
    and slaughter all their princes,"
    says the LORD.

**1:15** Hebrew *malcam*, possibly referring to their god Molech.   **2:1** Hebrew *have committed three sins, even four;* also in 2:4, 6.

---

| | |
|---|---|
| **1:9** | 1 Kgs 5:1; 9:11-14<br>Isa 23:1-18 |
| **1:11** | Num 20:14-21<br>Isa 34:5-6; 63:1-3<br>Jer 49:7-22<br>Ezek 25:12-14<br>Mic 7:18 |
| **1:12** | Jer 49:7, 20 |
| **1:13** | 2 Kgs 15:16<br>Jer 49:1-6<br>Ezek 25:2-7<br>Hos 13:16 |
| **1:14** | Jer 49:2 |
| **1:15** | Jer 49:3 |
| **2:1** | Isa 15:1-9; 16:1-14<br>Jer 48:1-7<br>Zech 2:8-9 |
| **2:2** | Jer 48:24, 41, 45 |
| **2:3** | Isa 40:23 |

---

**1:9** Tyre was one of two major cities in Phoenicia. Several treaties had been made with this city, which supplied the cedar used to build David's palace and God's Temple (2 Samuel 5:11; 1 Kings 5).

**1:11, 12** Both Edom and Israel had descended from Isaac: Edom from Isaac's son Esau, and Israel from Esau's twin brother, Jacob (Genesis 25:19-28; 27). But these two nations, like the two brothers, were always fighting. Edom had rejoiced at Israel's misfortunes. As a result, God promised to destroy Edom completely, from Teman in the south to Bozrah in the north.

**1:13-15** The Ammonites had descended from an incestuous relationship between Lot and his younger daughter (Genesis 19:30-38). The Ammonites were hostile to Israel; and although Israel began to worship their idols, the Ammonites still attacked (Judges 10:6-8). After Saul had been anointed Israel's king, his first victory in battle was against the Ammonites (1 Samuel 11). Rabbah was Ammon's capital city. Amos's prophecy of Ammon's destruction was fulfilled through the Assyrian invasion.

**2:1-3** The Moabites had descended from an incestuous relationship between Lot and his older daughter (Genesis 19:30-37). Balak, king of Moab, had tried to hire the prophet Balaam to curse the Israelites so they could be defeated (Numbers 22–24). Balaam spoke the Lord's word of blessing instead, but some of the Moabites had succeeded in getting Israel to worship Baal (Numbers 25:1-3). The Moabites were known for their atrocities (2 Kings 3:26, 27). An archaeological artifact, the Moabite Stone, reveals that Moab was always ready to profit from the downfall of others.

## God's Judgment on Judah and Israel

2:4
Judg 2:17-20
2 Kgs 17:19

⁴This is what the LORD says:

"The people of Judah have sinned again and again,
and I will not let them go unpunished!
They have rejected the instruction of the LORD,
refusing to obey his decrees.
They have been led astray by the same lies
that deceived their ancestors.

2:5
Jer 17:27
Hos 8:14

⁵ So I will send down fire on Judah,
and all the fortresses of Jerusalem will be destroyed."

2:6
2 Kgs 18:12
Joel 3:3, 6

⁶This is what the LORD says:

"The people of Israel have sinned again and again,
and I will not let them go unpunished!
They sell honorable people for silver
and poor people for a pair of sandals.

2:7
Hos 4:14
Amos 5:12; 8:4

⁷ They trample helpless people in the dust
and shove the oppressed out of the way.
Both father and son sleep with the same woman,
corrupting my holy name.

2:8
Exod 22:26
Amos 4:1; 6:6

⁸ At their religious festivals,
they lounge in clothing their debtors put up as security.
In the house of their gods,*
they drink wine bought with unjust fines.

2:9
Ezek 17:9
Mal 4:1

⁹ "But as my people watched,
I destroyed the Amorites,
though they were as tall as cedars
and as strong as oaks.
I destroyed the fruit on their branches
and dug out their roots.

2:10
Exod 3:8; 12:51
Deut 2:7; 8:2-4

¹⁰ It was I who rescued you from Egypt
and led you through the desert for forty years,
so you could possess the land of the Amorites.

2:11
Num 6:2-3
Jer 7:25

¹¹ I chose some of your sons to be prophets
and others to be Nazirites.
Can you deny this, my people of Israel?"
asks the LORD.

2:8 Or their God.

---

**2:4-6** After Solomon died, the kingdom divided, and the tribes of Judah and Benjamin became the southern kingdom (Judah) under Solomon's son Rehoboam. The other 10 tribes became the northern kingdom (Israel) and followed Jeroboam, who had rebelled against Rehoboam.

God had punished other nations harshly for their evil actions and atrocities. But God also promised to judge both Israel and Judah because they ignored the revealed law of God. The other nations were ignorant, but Judah and Israel, God's people, knew what God wanted. Still they ignored him and joined pagan nations in worshiping idols. If we know God's Word and refuse to obey it, like Israel, our guilt is greater than those who are ignorant of it.

**2:4-6** Amos must have won over his audience as he proclaimed God's judgment against the evil nations surrounding Israel. But then he even spoke against his own nation, Judah, before focusing on God's indictment of Israel.

**2:6ff** God condemned Israel for five specific sins: (1) selling the poor as slaves (see Deuteronomy 15:7-11; Amos 8:6), (2) exploiting the poor (see Exodus 23:6; Deuteronomy 16:19), (3) engaging in perverse sexual sins (see Leviticus 20:11, 12), (4) taking illegal collateral for loans (see Exodus 22:26, 27; Deuteronomy 24:6, 12, 13), and (5) worshiping false gods (see Exodus 20:3-5).

**2:6, 7** Amos was speaking to the upper class. There was no middle class in the country—only the very rich and the very poor. The rich observed religious rituals. They gave extra tithes, went to places of worship, and offered sacrifices. But they were greedy and unjust, and they took advantage of the helpless. Be sure that you do not neglect the needs of the poor while you faithfully attend church and fulfill your religious obligations. God expects us to live out our faith—this means responding to those in need.

**2:9-11** The prophets were constantly challenging people to remember what God had done! When we read a list like this one, we are amazed at Israel's forgetfulness. But what would the prophets say about us? God's past faithfulness should have reminded the Israelites to obey him; likewise, what he has done for us should remind us to live for him.

**2:11** The Nazirites took a vow of service to God. The vow included abstaining from wine and never cutting their hair. But instead of being respected for their disciplined and temperate lives, they were being urged to break their vows. If the Nazirites were corrupted, there would remain little influence for good among the Israelites.

12 "But you caused the Nazirites to sin by making them drink wine,
   and you commanded the prophets, 'Shut up!'

2:12
Isa 30:10
Jer 11:21
Amos 7:13, 16

13 "So I will make you groan
   like a wagon loaded down with sheaves of grain.

14 Your fastest runners will not get away.
   The strongest among you will become weak.
   Even mighty warriors will be unable to save themselves.

2:14
Ps 33:16
Isa 30:16-17
Jer 9:23

15    The archers will not stand their ground.
   The swiftest runners won't be fast enough to escape.
   Even those riding horses won't be able to save themselves.

2:15
Isa 31:3
Jer 51:56
Ezek 39:3

16 On that day the most courageous of your fighting men
   will drop their weapons and run for their lives,"
   says the LORD.

## 2. Reasons for judgment

**3** Listen to this message that the LORD has spoken against you, O people of Israel and Judah—against the entire family I rescued from Egypt:

2 "From among all the families on the earth,
   I have been intimate with you alone.
   That is why I must punish you
   for all your sins."

3:2
Exod 19:5-6
Deut 7:6
Rom 2:9

### Witnesses against Guilty Israel

3 Can two people walk together
   without agreeing on the direction?

3:3
Gen 5:22; 6:9
Lev 26:23-24

4 Does a lion ever roar in a thicket
   without first finding a victim?
   Does a young lion growl in its den
   without first catching its prey?

3:4
Ps 104:21
Hos 11:10

5 Does a bird ever get caught in a trap
   that has no bait?
   Does a trap spring shut
   when there's nothing to catch?

6 When the ram's horn blows a warning,
   shouldn't the people be alarmed?
   Does disaster come to a city
   unless the LORD has planned it?

3:6
Isa 14:24-27
Jer 6:1
Hos 5:8

7 Indeed, the Sovereign LORD never does anything
   until he reveals his plans to his servants the prophets.

3:7
Gen 18:17
Dan 9:22-27
John 15:15

8 The lion has roared—
   so who isn't frightened?
   The Sovereign LORD has spoken—
   so who can refuse to proclaim his message?

3:8
Jer 20:9
Acts 4:20

---

**2:16** "That day" refers to the time when Assyria would attack Israel, destroy Samaria, and take the people captive (722 B.C.). This military defeat came only a few decades after this pronouncement.

**2:16** Television and movies are filled with images of people who seem to have no fear. Many today have modeled their lives after these images—they want to be tough. But God is not impressed with bravado. He says that even the toughest people will run in fear when God's judgment comes. Do you know people who think they can make it through life without God? Don't be swayed by their self-assured rhetoric. Recognize that God fears no one, and one day all people will fear him.

**3:2** God chose Israel to be the people through whom all other nations of the world could know him. He made this promise to Abraham, father of the Israelites (Genesis 12:1-3). Israel didn't have to do anything to be chosen; God had given them

this special privilege because he wanted to, not because they deserved special treatment (Deuteronomy 9:4-6). Pride in their privileged position, however, ruined Israel's sensitivity to the will of God and to the plight of others.

**3:3-6** With a series of seven rhetorical questions, Amos shows how two events can be linked together. Once one event takes place, the second will surely follow. Amos was showing that God's revelation to him was the sure sign that judgment would follow.

**3:6** This verse means that God himself would be sending disaster to Israel.

**3:7** Even in anger, God is merciful: He always warned his people through prophets before punishing them so they could not rationalize or complain when judgment came. Warnings about sin and judgment apply to people today just as they did to Israel. Because we have been warned about our sin, we have no excuse when

9 Announce this to the leaders of Philistia*
  and to the great ones of Egypt:
"Take your seats now on the hills around Samaria,
  and witness the chaos and oppression in Israel."

**3:10**
Ps 14:4
Jer 4:22
Hab 2:8-11
Zeph 1:9
Zech 5:3-4

10 "My people have forgotten how to do right,"
  says the Lord.
"Their fortresses are filled with wealth
  taken by theft and violence.
11 Therefore," says the Sovereign Lord,
  "an enemy is coming!
He will surround them and shatter their defenses.
  Then he will plunder all their fortresses."

**3:12**
1 Sam 17:34-37

12 This is what the Lord says:

"A shepherd who tries to rescue a sheep from a lion's mouth
  will recover only two legs or a piece of an ear.
So it will be for the Israelites in Samaria lying on luxurious beds,
  and for the people of Damascus reclining on couches.*

**3:13**
Ezek 2:7

13 "Now listen to this, and announce it throughout all Israel,*" says the Lord, the Lord God of Heaven's Armies.

**3:14**
Amos 4:4; 5:5-6

14 "On the very day I punish Israel for its sins,
  I will destroy the pagan altars at Bethel.
The horns of the altar will be cut off
  and fall to the ground.

**3:15**
Judg 3:20
1 Kgs 22:39
Jer 36:22

15 And I will destroy the beautiful homes of the wealthy—
  their winter mansions and their summer houses, too—
all their palaces filled with ivory,"
  says the Lord.

## Israel's Failure to Learn

**4:1**
Ps 22:12

**4** 1 Listen to me, you fat cows*
  living in Samaria,
you women who oppress the poor
  and crush the needy,
and who are always calling to your husbands,
  "Bring us another drink!"

**4:2**
Isa 37:29
Jer 16:16
Ezek 29:4; 38:4

2 The Sovereign Lord has sworn this by his holiness:
"The time will come when you will be led away
  with hooks in your noses.
Every last one of you will be dragged away
  like a fish on a hook!

**3:9** Hebrew *Ashdod.*   **3:12** The meaning of the Hebrew in this sentence is uncertain.   **3:13** Hebrew *the house of Jacob.* The names "Jacob" and "Israel" are often interchanged throughout the Old Testament, referring sometimes to the individual patriarch and sometimes to the nation.   **4:1** Hebrew *you cows of Bashan.*

---

punishment comes. Do not take lightly the warnings in God's Word about judgment. His warnings are a way of showing mercy to you.

**3:9** Amos pictured Philistia and Egypt summoned to witness Israel's great sins. Even Israel's most wicked and idolatrous neighbors would see God judge Israel.

**3:10** The people of Israel no longer knew how to do what was right. The more they sinned, the harder it was to remember what God wanted. The same is true for us. The longer we wait to deal with sin, the greater the hold it has on us. Finally, we forget what it means to do right. Are you on the verge of forgetting?

**3:11, 12** The enemy mentioned here was Assyria, which conquered Israel and did just as Amos predicted. The people were scattered to foreign lands, and foreigners were placed in the land to keep the peace. Israel's leaders had robbed their defenseless countrymen, and here they would be rendered defenseless by the

Assyrians. Amos added that even if the Israelites tried to repent, it would be too late. The destruction would be so complete that nothing of value would be left.

**3:14** God's judgment against Israel's altars shows that he was rejecting Israel's entire religious system because it was so polluted. The horns of the altar stood for protection (1 Kings 1:49-53), and the false altars would soon be gone. Then the people would have no sanctuary or protection (see 4:4) when judgment came.

**4:1** Israel's wealthy women were called "fat cows"—pampered, sleek, and well fed (see Psalm 22:12). These women selfishly pushed their husbands to oppress the helpless in order to support their lavish lifestyles. Be careful not to desire material possessions so much that you are willing to oppress others and displease God to get them.

3 You will be led out through the ruins of the wall;
　　you will be thrown from your fortresses,*"
　　says the LORD.

4 "Go ahead and offer sacrifices to the idols at Bethel.
　　Keep on disobeying at Gilgal.
Offer sacrifices each morning,
　　and bring your tithes every three days.
5 Present your bread made with yeast
　　as an offering of thanksgiving.
Then give your extra voluntary offerings
　　so you can brag about it everywhere!
This is the kind of thing you Israelites love to do,"
　　says the Sovereign LORD.

6 "I brought hunger to every city
　　and famine to every town.
But still you would not return to me,"
　　says the LORD.

7 "I kept the rain from falling
　　when your crops needed it the most.
I sent rain on one town
　　but withheld it from another.
Rain fell on one field,
　　while another field withered away.
8 People staggered from town to town looking for water,
　　but there was never enough.
But still you would not return to me,"
　　says the LORD.

9 "I struck your farms and vineyards with blight and mildew.
　　Locusts devoured all your fig and olive trees.
But still you would not return to me,"
　　says the LORD.

10 "I sent plagues on you
　　like the plagues I sent on Egypt long ago.
I killed your young men in war
　　and led all your horses away.*
The stench of death filled the air!
But still you would not return to me,"
　　says the LORD.

11 "I destroyed some of your cities,
　　as I destroyed* Sodom and Gomorrah.
Those of you who survived
　　were like charred sticks pulled from a fire.
But still you would not return to me,"
　　says the LORD.

| | |
|---|---|
| 4:5 | Lev 7:13; 22:18-21<br>Hos 9:1, 10 |
| 4:6 | Isa 3:1<br>Jer 14:18<br>Hag 2:17 |
| 4:7 | 1 Kgs 8:35-36<br>Zech 14:17 |
| 4:8 | 1 Kgs 18:5<br>Jer 14:3-4<br>Ezek 4:16<br>Mic 6:14<br>Hag 1:6 |
| 4:9 | Deut 28:22<br>Joel 2:25 |
| 4:10 | Exod 9:3-6<br>Lev 26:25<br>Isa 9:13<br>Jer 11:22; 18:21 |
| 4:11 | Gen 19:24-25<br>Jer 23:14 |

4:3 Or thrown out toward Harmon, possibly a reference to Mount Hermon.    4:10 Or and slaughtered your captured horses.    4:11 Hebrew as when God destroyed.

4:4 Amos sarcastically invited the people to sin in Bethel and Gilgal, where they worshiped idols instead of God. Bethel was where God had renewed his covenant to Abraham with Jacob (Genesis 28:10-22). At this time, Bethel was the religious center of the northern kingdom, and Jeroboam had placed an idol there to discourage the people from traveling to Jerusalem in the southern kingdom to worship (1 Kings 12:26-29). Gilgal was Israel's first campground after entering the Promised Land (Joshua 4:19). Here Joshua had renewed the covenant and the rite of circumcision, and the people had celebrated the Passover (Joshua 5:2-11). Saul was crowned Israel's first king in Gilgal (1 Samuel 11:15).

4:6-13 No matter how God warned the people—through famine, drought, blight, locusts, plagues, or war—they still ignored him. Because the Israelites didn't get the message, they would have to meet God face to face in judgment. No longer would they ignore God; they would have to face the one they had rejected, the one they had refused to obey when he commanded them to care for the poor. One day each of us will meet God face to face to give account for what we have done or refused to do. Are you prepared to meet him?

¹² "Therefore, I will bring upon you all the disasters I have announced.
   Prepare to meet your God in judgment, you people of Israel!"

**4:13**
Job 38:4-11
Pss 135:7; 139:2
Dan 2:28, 30
Amos 5:8; 8:9

¹³ For the LORD is the one who shaped the mountains,
   stirs up the winds, and reveals his thoughts to mankind.
He turns the light of dawn into darkness
   and treads on the heights of the earth.
The LORD God of Heaven's Armies is his name!

### A Call to Repentance

**5:1**
Jer 9:10
Ezek 19:1, 14

**5:2**
Isa 51:18
Jer 14:17; 50:32
Amos 8:14

**5** Listen, you people of Israel! Listen to this funeral song I am singing:

² "The virgin Israel has fallen,
   never to rise again!
She lies abandoned on the ground,
   with no one to help her up."

³ The Sovereign LORD says:

"When a city sends a thousand men to battle,
   only a hundred will return.
When a town sends a hundred,
   only ten will come back alive."

**5:4**
Deut 4:29;
32:46-47

⁴ Now this is what the LORD says to the family of Israel:

"Come back to me and live!
⁵ Don't worship at the pagan altars at Bethel;
   don't go to the shrines at Gilgal or Beersheba.
For the people of Gilgal will be dragged off into exile,
   and the people of Bethel will be reduced to nothing."

**5:6**
Deut 4:24

⁶ Come back to the LORD and live!
Otherwise, he will roar through Israel* like a fire,
   devouring you completely.
Your gods in Bethel
   won't be able to quench the flames.

**5:7**
Amos 2:3; 5:12;
6:12

⁷ You twist justice, making it a bitter pill for the oppressed.
   You treat the righteous like dirt.

**5:8**
Job 9:9; 12:22;
37:13; 38:31-34
Amos 9:6

⁸ It is the LORD who created the stars,
   the Pleiades and Orion.
He turns darkness into morning
   and day into night.
He draws up water from the oceans
   and pours it down as rain on the land.
The LORD is his name!

**5:9**
Amos 2:14
Mic 5:11

⁹ With blinding speed and power he destroys the strong,
   crushing all their defenses.

**5:10**
Amos 5:15

¹⁰ How you hate honest judges!
   How you despise people who tell the truth!

**5:6** Hebrew *the house of Joseph.*

---

**5:1** Amos shocked his listeners by singing a funeral song for them as though they had already been destroyed. The Israelites believed that their wealth and religious ritual made them secure, but Amos lamented their sure destruction.

**5:6** There is one sure remedy for a world that is sick and dying in sin: "Come back to the LORD and live!" Sin seeks to destroy, but hope is found in seeking God. In times of difficulty, seek God. In personal discomfort and struggle, seek God. When others are struggling, encourage them to seek God, too.

**5:7** The courts should have been places of justice where the poor and oppressed could find relief. Instead, they had become places of greed and injustice.

**5:8** Pleiades and Orion are star constellations. For thousands of years, navigators have staked lives and fortunes on the reliability of the stars. The constancy and orderliness of the heavens challenge us to look beyond them to their Creator.

**5:10-12** A society is in trouble when those who try to do right are hated for their commitment to justice. Any society that exploits the poor and defenseless or hates the truth is bent on destroying itself.

11 You trample the poor,
   stealing their grain through taxes and unfair rent.
Therefore, though you build beautiful stone houses,
   you will never live in them.
Though you plant lush vineyards,
   you will never drink wine from them.

5:11
Isa 59:15
Mic 6:15

12 For I know the vast number of your sins
   and the depth of your rebellions.
You oppress good people by taking bribes
   and deprive the poor of justice in the courts.

5:12
Isa 1:23
Amos 2:6

13 So those who are smart keep their mouths shut,
   for it is an evil time.

14 Do what is good and run from evil
   so that you may live!
Then the LORD God of Heaven's Armies will be your helper,
   just as you have claimed.

5:14
Mic 3:11

15 Hate evil and love what is good;
   turn your courts into true halls of justice.
Perhaps even yet the LORD God of Heaven's Armies
   will have mercy on the remnant of his people.*

5:15
Ps 97:10
Joel 2:14
Rom 12:9

16 Therefore, this is what the Lord, the LORD God of Heaven's Armies, says:

5:16
Amos 8:3, 10
Joel 1:8, 11

"There will be crying in all the public squares
   and mourning in every street.
Call for the farmers to weep with you,
   and summon professional mourners to wail.

17 There will be wailing in every vineyard,
   for I will destroy them all,"
says the LORD.

5:17
Isa 16:10

## Warning of Coming Judgment

18 What sorrow awaits you who say,
   "If only the day of the LORD were here!"
You have no idea what you are wishing for.
   That day will bring darkness, not light.

5:18
Isa 5:30
Jer 30:7
Joel 1:15; 2:1, 31

19 In that day you will be like a man who runs from a lion—
   only to meet a bear.
Escaping from the bear, he leans his hand against a wall in his house—
   and he's bitten by a snake.

5:19
Job 20:24

5:15 Hebrew the remnant of Joseph.

---

5:12 Why does God put so much emphasis on the way we treat the poor and needy? Because how we treat the poor reflects our true character. We know we can expect nothing in return. Do we, like Christ, give without thought of gain? We should treat the poor as we would like God to treat us.

5:12 Here are eight common excuses for not helping the poor and needy: (1) They don't deserve help. They got themselves into poverty; let them get themselves out. (2) God's call to help the poor applies to another time. (3) We don't know any people like this. (4) I have my own needs. (5) Any money I give will be wasted, stolen, or spent. The poor will never see it. (6) I may become a victim myself. (7) I don't know where to start, and I don't have time. (8) My little bit won't make any difference.
   Instead of making lame excuses, ask what can be done to help. Does your church have programs to help the needy? Could you volunteer to work with a community group that fights poverty? As one individual, you may not be able to accomplish much, but join with similarly motivated people and watch mountains begin to move.

5:15 If Israel were to sweep away the corrupt system of false

accusations, bribery, and corruption, and were to insist that only just decisions be given, this would show their change of heart. We dare not read this passage lightly or write it off simply as encouragement to be good. It is a command to reform our own legal and social system.

5:16 Failure to honor the dead was considered horrible in Israel, so loud weeping was common at funerals. Paid mourners, usually women, cried and mourned loudly with dirges and eulogies. Amos said there would be so many funerals that there would be a shortage of professional mourners, so farmers would be called from the fields to help (see also Jeremiah 9:17-20).

5:18 Here "the day of the LORD" means the imminent destruction by the Assyrian army as well as the future day of God's judgment. For the faithful, "the day of the LORD" will be glorious, but for the unfaithful it will be a day of darkness and doom. (See Joel 1:15 for more discussion of the day of the Lord.)

5:18-24 These people were calling for the day of the Lord, thinking it would bring an end to their troubles. But God said, "You have no idea what you are wishing for." This "day of the LORD" would bring justice, and justice would bring the punishment the people deserved for their sins.

**5:20**
Isa 13:10

20 Yes, the day of the LORD will be dark and hopeless,
   without a ray of joy or hope.

**5:21**
Lev 26:31
Isa 1:11-16
Jer 14:12
Hos 5:6
**5:22**
Isa 66:3

21 "I hate all your show and pretense—
   the hypocrisy of your religious festivals and solemn assemblies.
22 I will not accept your burnt offerings and grain offerings.
   I won't even notice all your choice peace offerings.
23 Away with your noisy hymns of praise!
   I will not listen to the music of your harps.

**5:24**
Jer 22:3
Mic 6:8

24 Instead, I want to see a mighty flood of justice,
   an endless river of righteous living.

25 "Was it to me you were bringing sacrifices and offerings during the forty years in the wilderness, Israel? 26 No, you served your pagan gods—Sakkuth your king god and Kaiwan your star god—the images you made for yourselves. 27 So I will send you into exile, to a land east of Damascus,*" says the LORD, whose name is the God of Heaven's Armies.

**6:1**
Exod 19:5
Isa 32:9-11

**6** 1 What sorrow awaits you who lounge in luxury in Jerusalem,*
      and you who feel secure in Samaria!
You are famous and popular in Israel,
   and people go to you for help.

**6:2**
Gen 10:10
1 Sam 17:23
2 Kgs 18:34
2 Chr 26:6
Isa 10:9

2 But go over to Calneh
   and see what happened there.
Then go to the great city of Hamath
   and down to the Philistine city of Gath.
You are no better than they were,
   and look at how they were destroyed.
3 You push away every thought of coming disaster,
   but your actions only bring the day of judgment closer.

**5:26-27** Greek version reads *No, you carried your pagan gods—the shrine of Molech, the star of your god Rephan, and the images you made for yourselves. So I will send you into exile, to a land east of Damascus.* Compare Acts 7:43.   **6:1** Hebrew *in Zion.*

---

**AMOS'S VISIONS**

| Vision/Reference | Significance |
|---|---|
| Swarm of locusts 7:1-3 | God was preparing punishment, which he delayed only because of Amos's intervention. |
| Fire 7:4-6 | God was preparing to devour the land, but Amos intervened on behalf of the people. |
| Wall and plumb line 7:7-9 | God would see if the people were crooked, and if they were, he would punish them. |
| Basket of ripe fruit 8:1ff | The people were ripe for punishment; though once beautiful, they were now rotten. |
| God standing by the altar 9:1ff | Punishment was executed. |

Amos had a series of visions concerning God's judgment on Israel. God was planning to judge Israel by sending a swarm of locusts or by sending fire. In spite of Amos's intercession on Israel's behalf, God would still carry out his judgment because Israel persisted in disobedience.

---

**5:21-23** God hates worship by people who go through the motions only for show. If we are living sinful lives and using religious rituals and traditions to make ourselves look good, God will despise our worship and not accept what we offer. He wants sincere hearts, not praise from hypocrites. When you worship at church, are you more concerned about your image or your attitude toward God?

**5:26** In days past, Israel had turned to worshiping stars and planets, preferring nature over nature's God (2 Kings 23:4, 5). Pagan religion allowed them to indulge in sexual immorality and to become wealthy through any means possible. Because they refused to worship and obey the one true God, they would cause their own destruction.

**5:27** Israel's captivity was indeed to a land east of Damascus—

the people were taken to Assyria. God's punishment was more than defeat; it was complete exile from their homeland.

**6:1-6** Amos leveled his attack at those living in complacency and luxury in both Israel and Judah. Great wealth and comfortable lifestyles may make people think they are secure, but God is not pleased if we isolate ourselves from others' needs. God wants us to care for others as he cares for us. His Kingdom has no place for selfishness or indifference. We must learn to put the needs of others before our wants. Using our wealth to help others is one way to guard against pride and complacency.

**6:2** Great cities to the east, north, and west had been destroyed because of their pride. What happened to them would happen to Israel because Israel's sin was just as great as theirs.

⁴ How terrible for you who sprawl on ivory beds
  and lounge on your couches,
eating the meat of tender lambs from the flock
  and of choice calves fattened in the stall.
⁵ You sing trivial songs to the sound of the harp
  and fancy yourselves to be great musicians like David.
⁶ You drink wine by the bowlful
  and perfume yourselves with fragrant lotions.
  You care nothing about the ruin of your nation.*
⁷ Therefore, you will be the first to be led away as captives.
  Suddenly, all your parties will end.

⁸The Sovereign LORD has sworn by his own name, and this is what he, the LORD God of Heaven's Armies, says:

"I despise the arrogance of Israel,*
  and I hate their fortresses.
I will give this city
  and everything in it to their enemies."

⁹(If there are ten men left in one house, they will all die. ¹⁰And when a relative who is responsible to dispose of the dead* goes into the house to carry out the bodies, he will ask the last survivor, "Is anyone else with you?" When the person begins to swear, "No, by . . . ," he will interrupt and say, "Stop! Don't even mention the name of the LORD.")

¹¹ When the LORD gives the command,
  homes both great and small will be smashed to pieces.

¹² Can horses gallop over boulders?
  Can oxen be used to plow them?
But that's how foolish you are when you turn justice into poison
  and the sweet fruit of righteousness into bitterness.
¹³ And you brag about your conquest of Lo-debar.*
  You boast, "Didn't we take Karnaim* by our own strength?"

¹⁴ "O people of Israel, I am about to bring an enemy nation against you,"
  says the LORD God of Heaven's Armies.
"They will oppress you throughout your land—
  from Lebo-hamath in the north
  to the Arabah Valley in the south."

## 3. Visions of judgment
*A Vision of Locusts*

**7** The Sovereign LORD showed me a vision. I saw him preparing to send a vast swarm of locusts over the land. This was after the king's share had been harvested from the fields and as the main crop was coming up. ²In my vision the locusts ate every green plant in sight. Then I said, "O Sovereign LORD, please forgive us or we will not survive, for Israel* is so small."

³So the LORD relented from this plan. "I will not do it," he said.

**Cross references:**
6:4 Ezek 34:2-3
6:5 1 Chr 15:16; 23:5; Isa 5:12
6:8 Lev 26:30
6:9 Amos 5:3
6:10 1 Sam 31:12; Amos 5:13; 8:3
6:11 Amos 3:15
6:12 Hos 10:4; Amos 5:7, 11-12
6:14 Num 34:7-8; 2 Kgs 14:25; Jer 5:15
7:1 Exod 10:12-16; Nah 3:15-17
7:2 Exod 10:15; Isa 37:4; Jer 14:7; 42:2; Ezek 9:8; 11:13

6:6 Hebrew *of Joseph.* 6:8 Hebrew *Jacob.* See note on 3:13. 6:10 Or *to burn the dead.* The meaning of the Hebrew is uncertain. 6:13a *Lo-debar* means "nothing." 6:13b *Karnaim* means "horns," a term that symbolizes strength. 7:2 Hebrew *Jacob;* also in 7:5. See note on 3:13.

6:4 Ivory was an imported luxury, rare and extremely expensive. Even a small amount of ivory symbolized wealth. Something as extravagant as a bed inlaid with ivory shows the gross waste of resources that should have been used to help the poor.

6:8-11 The people had built luxurious homes to flaunt their achievements. While it is not wrong to live in comfortable houses, we must not let them become sources of inflated pride and self-glorification. God gave our homes to us, and they are to be used for service, not just for show.

6:10 Amos gives us a picture of God's fearful judgment: The people hesitated to speak God's name, even during a time of grief, for fear that they would attract his attention and be judged also.

6:13, 14 Karnaim was a city northeast of Israel, an insignificant border town compared to the nation they were about to face, Assyria. Lebo-hamath was to the north, and the Arabah Valley to the south. The entire nation would be destroyed by Assyria (2 Kings 17).

7:1ff The following series of visions conveyed God's message to the people, using images that were familiar to them—locusts, fire, and a plumb line.

7:1-6 Twice Amos was shown a vision of Israel's impending punishment, and his immediate response was to pray that God would spare Israel. Prayer is a powerful privilege. Amos's prayers should remind us to pray for our nation.

## A Vision of Fire

7:4
Isa 66:15-16
Amos 2:5

⁴Then the Sovereign Lord showed me another vision. I saw him preparing to punish his people with a great fire. The fire had burned up the depths of the sea and was devouring the entire land. ⁵Then I said, "O Sovereign Lord, please stop or we will not survive, for Israel is so small."

7:6
Amos 7:3

⁶Then the Lord relented from this plan, too. "I will not do that either," said the Sovereign Lord.

## A Vision of a Plumb Line

7:8
Isa 28:17; 34:11
Amos 8:2

⁷Then he showed me another vision. I saw the Lord standing beside a wall that had been built using a plumb line. He was using a plumb line to see if it was still straight. ⁸And the Lord said to me, "Amos, what do you see?"

I answered, "A plumb line."

And the Lord replied, "I will test my people with this plumb line. I will no longer ignore all their sins. ⁹The pagan shrines of your ancestors* will be ruined, and the temples of Israel will be destroyed; I will bring the dynasty of King Jeroboam to a sudden end."

7:9
2 Kgs 15:8-10

## Amos and Amaziah

7:10
1 Kgs 12:31-32
2 Kgs 14:23-24

¹⁰Then Amaziah, the priest of Bethel, sent a message to Jeroboam, king of Israel: "Amos is hatching a plot against you right here on your very doorstep! What he is saying is intolerable. ¹¹He is saying, 'Jeroboam will soon be killed, and the people of Israel will be sent away into exile.'"

7:12
1 Sam 9:9
7:13
1 Kgs 12:29, 32;
13:1
Amos 2:12
Acts 4:17-18

¹²Then Amaziah sent orders to Amos: "Get out of here, you prophet! Go on back to the land of Judah, and earn your living by prophesying there! ¹³Don't bother us with your prophecies here in Bethel. This is the king's sanctuary and the national place of worship!"

7:14
1 Kgs 20:35
2 Kgs 2:3-7; 4:38

¹⁴But Amos replied, "I'm not a professional prophet, and I was never trained to be one.* I'm just a shepherd, and I take care of sycamore-fig trees. ¹⁵But the Lord called me away from my flock and told me, 'Go and prophesy to my people in Israel.' ¹⁶Now then, listen to this message from the Lord:

7:15
Jer 1:7
Ezek 2:3-4
7:16
Amos 7:13
Mic 2:6

"You say,
'Don't prophesy against Israel.
   Stop preaching against my people.*'
¹⁷ But this is what the Lord says:
'Your wife will become a prostitute in this city,
   and your sons and daughters will be killed.
Your land will be divided up,
   and you yourself will die in a foreign land.
And the people of Israel will certainly become captives in exile,
   far from their homeland.'"

7:17
Jer 14:16; 20:6
Hos 4:13-14

## A Vision of Ripe Fruit

8:2
Jer 24:1-3
Amos 7:8

**8** Then the Sovereign Lord showed me another vision. In it I saw a basket filled with ripe fruit. ²"What do you see, Amos?" he asked.

I replied, "A basket full of ripe fruit."

Then the Lord said, "Like this fruit, Israel is ripe for punishment! I will not delay their punishment again. ³In that day the singing in the Temple will turn to wailing. Dead bodies will be scattered everywhere. They will be carried out of the city in silence. I, the Sovereign Lord, have spoken!"

8:3
Hos 10:5-6
Amos 5:23

**7:9** Hebrew *of Isaac.*    **7:14** Or *I'm not a prophet nor the son of a prophet.*    **7:16** Hebrew *against the house of Isaac.*

---

**7:7-9** A plumb line is a device used to ensure the straightness of a wall. A wall that is not straight will eventually collapse. God wants people to be right with him; he wants the sin that makes us crooked removed immediately. God's Word is the plumb line that helps us be aware of our sin. How do you measure up to God's plumb line?

**7:10** Prophets like Amos were often seen as traitors and conspirators because they spoke out against the king and his advisers, questioning their authority and exposing their sin. The kings often saw the prophets as enemies rather than as God's spokesmen who were really trying to help them and the nation.

**7:10ff** Amaziah was the chief priest in Bethel, representing Israel's official religion. He was not concerned about hearing God's message; he was only worried about his own position. Maintaining his position was more important than listening to the truth. Don't let your desire for prestige, authority, or money keep you tied to a job or position you should leave. Don't let anything come between you and obeying God.

**7:14, 15** Without any special preparation, education, or upbringing, Amos obeyed God's call to "go and prophesy to my people in Israel." Obedience is the test of a faithful servant of God. Are you obeying God's call to you?

⁴ Listen to this, you who rob the poor
    and trample down the needy!
⁵ You can't wait for the Sabbath day to be over
    and the religious festivals to end
    so you can get back to cheating the helpless.
  You measure out grain with dishonest measures
    and cheat the buyer with dishonest scales.*
⁶ And you mix the grain you sell
    with chaff swept from the floor.
  Then you enslave poor people
    for one piece of silver or a pair of sandals.

⁷ Now the LORD has sworn this oath
    by his own name, the Pride of Israel*:
  "I will never forget
    the wicked things you have done!
⁸ The earth will tremble for your deeds,
    and everyone will mourn.
  The ground will rise like the Nile River at floodtime;
    it will heave up, then sink again.

⁹ "In that day," says the Sovereign LORD,
    "I will make the sun go down at noon
    and darken the earth while it is still day.
¹⁰ I will turn your celebrations into times of mourning
    and your singing into weeping.
  You will wear funeral clothes
    and shave your heads to show your sorrow—
  as if your only son had died.
    How very bitter that day will be!

¹¹ "The time is surely coming," says the Sovereign LORD,
    "when I will send a famine on the land—
  not a famine of bread or water
    but of hearing the words of the LORD.
¹² People will stagger from sea to sea
    and wander from border to border*
  searching for the word of the LORD,
    but they will not find it.
¹³ Beautiful girls and strong young men
    will grow faint in that day,
    thirsting for the LORD's word.
¹⁴ And those who swear by the shameful idols of Samaria—
    who take oaths in the name of the god of Dan
    and make vows in the name of the god of Beersheba*—
  they will all fall down,
    never to rise again."

**8:5**
Neh 13:15-21
Hos 12:7

**8:7**
Deut 33:26-29
Hos 7:2; 8:13

**8:8**
Pss 18:7; 114:3-7
Jer 46:8

**8:9**
Mic 3:6
Matt 27:45
Mark 15:33
Luke 23:44-45

**8:10**
Isa 15:2-3
Ezek 7:18
Amos 5:23; 6:4-7

**8:12**
Ezek 20:3, 31

**8:13**
Isa 41:17
Lam 1:18; 2:21
Hos 2:3

**8:14**
1 Kgs 12:28-29

**8:5** Hebrew *You make the ephah* [a unit for measuring grain] *small and the shekel* [a unit of weight] *great, and you deal falsely by using deceitful balances.*    **8:7** Hebrew *the pride of Jacob.* See note on 3:13.    **8:12** Hebrew *from north to east.*    **8:14** Hebrew *the way of Beersheba.*

**8:5, 6** These merchants were keeping the religious festivals, but not in spirit. They couldn't wait for the holy days and Sabbaths to be over so they could go back to making money. Their real interest was in enriching themselves, even if that meant cheating (shortchanging the quantity while boosting the price, or even selling chaff as wheat). Do you take a day to rest and worship God at least once a week, or is making money more important to you than anything else? When you give time to God, is your heart in your worship? Or is your religion only a front for unethical practices?

**8:11-13** The people had no appetite for God's word when prophets like Amos brought it. Because of their apathy, God said he would take away even the opportunity to hear his word. We have God's Word, the Bible. But many still look everywhere for answers to life's problems *except* in Scripture. You can help them by directing them to the Bible, showing them the parts that speak to their special needs and questions. God's Word is available to us. Let us help people know it before a time comes when they cannot find it.

### A Vision of God at the Altar

9:1
Zeph 2:14

**9** Then I saw a vision of the Lord standing beside the altar. He said,

"Strike the tops of the Temple columns,
so that the foundation will shake.
Bring down the roof
on the heads of the people below.
I will kill with the sword those who survive.
No one will escape!

9:2
Ps 139:7-10

2 "Even if they dig down to the place of the dead,*
I will reach down and pull them up.
Even if they climb up into the heavens,
I will bring them down.

9:3
Job 34:22
Ps 139:9-11
Isa 27:1
Jer 16:16

3 Even if they hide at the very top of Mount Carmel,
I will search them out and capture them.
Even if they hide at the bottom of the ocean,
I will send the sea serpent after them to bite them.

9:4
Lev 26:33
Jer 44:11

4 Even if their enemies drive them into exile,
I will command the sword to kill them there.
I am determined to bring disaster upon them
and not to help them."

9:5
Ps 46:2, 6
Isa 64:1

5 The Lord, the LORD of Heaven's Armies,
touches the land and it melts,
and all its people mourn.
The ground rises like the Nile River at floodtime,
and then it sinks again.

9:6
Ps 104:3, 6, 13

6 The LORD's home reaches up to the heavens,
while its foundation is on the earth.
He draws up water from the oceans
and pours it down as rain on the land.
The LORD is his name!

9:7
2 Chr 14:9, 12
Isa 20:4; 43:3

7 "Are you Israelites more important to me
than the Ethiopians?*" asks the LORD.
"I brought Israel out of Egypt,
but I also brought the Philistines from Crete*
and led the Arameans out of Kir.

9:8
Jer 5:10
Joel 2:32
Amos 7:17

8 "I, the Sovereign LORD,
am watching this sinful nation of Israel.

**9:2** Hebrew *to Sheol.*   **9:7a** Hebrew *the Cushites?*   **9:7b** Hebrew *Caphtor.*

---

**9:1** Judgment would begin at the altar, the center of the nation's life, the place where the people expected protection and blessing. This judgment would cover all 12 tribes. Commentators disagree concerning this altar. Some think it was the altar at Bethel; more likely it was the altar in the Temple in Jerusalem. God would destroy their base of security in order to bring them to himself. But in 9:11 he promises to restore his renewed people and their broken world.

**9:2-4** The "place of the dead" was the grave. The grave and Mount Carmel were symbols of inaccessibility. No one can escape God's judgment. This was good news for the faithful but bad news for the unfaithful. Whether we go to the mountaintops or the bottom of the sea, God will find us and judge us for our deeds. Amos pictured the judgment of the wicked as a sea serpent, relentlessly pursuing the condemned. For God's faithful followers, however, the judgment brings a new earth of peace and prosperity. Does God's judgment sound like good news or bad news to you?

**9:7** Ethiopia, south of Egypt, was a remote and exotic land to the Israelites. Crete was where the Philistines lived as they migrated

to Palestine. God would judge Israel no differently than he judges foreign nations. He is not the God of Israel only; he is God of the universe, and he controls all nations.

**9:8** Amos assured the Israelites that God would "never completely destroy" Israel—in other words, the punishment would not be permanent or total. God wants to redeem, not punish. But when punishment is necessary, he doesn't withhold it. Like a loving father, God disciplines those he loves in order to correct them. If God disciplines you, accept it as a sign of his love.

**9:8, 9** Although Assyria would destroy Israel and take the people into exile, some would be preserved. This exile had been predicted hundreds of years earlier (Deuteronomy 28:63-68). Although the nation would be purified through this invasion and captivity, not one true believer would be eternally lost. Our system of justice is not perfect, but God's is. Sinners will not get away, and the faithful will not be forgotten. True believers will not be lost.

I will destroy it
    from the face of the earth.
But I will never completely destroy the family of Israel,*"
    says the LORD.
9 "For I will give the command
    and will shake Israel along with the other nations
as grain is shaken in a sieve,
    yet not one true kernel will be lost.
10 But all the sinners will die by the sword—
    all those who say, 'Nothing bad will happen to us.'

**9:9**
Isa 30:28

## A Promise of Restoration

11 "In that day I will restore the fallen house* of David.
    I will repair its damaged walls.
From the ruins I will rebuild it
    and restore its former glory.
12 And Israel will possess what is left of Edom
    and all the nations I have called to be mine.*"
The LORD has spoken,
    and he will do these things.

**9:11**
Isa 16:5; 63:11

13 "The time will come," says the LORD,
    "when the grain and grapes will grow faster
      than they can be harvested.
Then the terraced vineyards on the hills of Israel
    will drip with sweet wine!
14 I will bring my exiled people of Israel
    back from distant lands,
and they will rebuild their ruined cities
    and live in them again.
They will plant vineyards and gardens;
    they will eat their crops and drink their wine.
15 I will firmly plant them there
    in their own land.
They will never again be uprooted
    from the land I have given them,"
    says the LORD your God.

**9:13**
Lev 26:5
Joel 3:18, 20

**9:14**
Isa 61:4
Jer 30:18; 31:28

**9:15**
Ezek 34:28

**9:8** Hebrew *the house of Jacob.* See note on 3:13.   **9:11a** Or *kingdom;* Hebrew reads *tent.*   **9:11b-12** Greek version reads *and restore its former glory, / so that the rest of humanity, including the Gentiles— / all those I have called to be mine—might seek me.* Compare Acts 15:16-17.

---

**9:11, 12** In the punishment, the house of David was reduced to a "fallen house." God's covenant with David stated that one of David's descendants would always sit on his throne (2 Samuel 7:12-16). The Exile made this promise seem impossible. But "in that day" God would raise up and restore the kingdom to its promised glory. This was a promise to both Israel and Judah, not to be fulfilled by an earthly, political ruler, but by the Messiah, who would renew the spiritual Kingdom and rule forever.

   James quoted these verses (Acts 15:16, 17), finding the promise fulfilled in Christ's resurrection and in the presence of both Jews and Gentiles in the church. "Possess what is left of Edom" envisions the messianic Kingdom, which will be universal and include Gentiles. When God brings in the Gentiles, he is restoring the ruins. After the Gentiles are called together, God will renew and restore the fortunes of the new Israel. All the land that was once under David's rule will again be part of God's nation.

**9:13** This verse describes a time of such an abundance of crops that the people won't be able to harvest them all.

**9:13-15** The Jews of Amos's day had lost sight of God's care and love for them. The rich were carefree and comfortable, refusing to help others in need. They observed their religious rituals in hopes of appeasing God, but they did not truly love him. Amos announced God's warnings of destruction for their evil ways.

   We must not assume that going to church and being good are enough. God expects our belief in him to affect all areas of our conduct and to extend to all people and circumstances. We should let Amos's words inspire us to live faithfully according to God's desires.

WRINKLED face, tiny hands with fingernail chips, folds of new skin, and miniature eyes, nose, and mouth—she's a newborn. After months of formation, she burst forth into the world and into her family. "She has her mother's eyes." "I can sure tell who her parents are." "Now that's your nose." Relatives and friends gaze into the little face and see her mom and dad. Mother and Father rejoice in their daughter, a miracle, a new member of the family. As loving parents, they will feed, protect, nurture, guide, and discipline her. This is their duty and joy.

God, too, has children—men and women whom he has chosen as his very own. There have always been individuals marked as his, but with Abraham he promised to build a nation. Israel was to be God's country, and her people, the Jews, his very own sons and daughters. Down through the centuries, God meted out discipline and punishment, but always with love and mercy. God, the eternal Father, protected and cared for his children.

Obadiah, the shortest book in the Old Testament, is a dramatic example of God's response to anyone who would harm his children. Edom was a mountainous nation, occupying the region southeast of the Dead Sea including Petra, the spectacular city discovered by archaeologists a few decades ago. As descendants of Esau (Genesis 25:19—27:45), the Edomites were blood relatives of Israel, and like their father, they were rugged, fierce, and proud warriors with a seemingly invincible mountain home. Of all people, they should have rushed to the aid of their northern brothers. Instead, however, they gloated over Israel's problems, captured and delivered fugitives to the enemy, and even looted Israel's countryside.

Obadiah gave God's message to the Edomites. Because of their indifference to and defiance of God, their cowardice and pride, and their treachery toward their relatives in Judah, they stood condemned and would be destroyed. The book begins with the announcement that disaster was coming to Edom (1:1–9). Despite their "impregnable" cliffs and mountains, they would not be able to escape God's judgment. Obadiah then gave the reasons for their destruction (1:10–14)—their blatant arrogance toward God and their persecution of God's children. This concise prophecy ends with a description of the day of the Lord, when judgment will fall on all who have harmed God's people (1:15–21).

Today, God's holy nation is his church—all who have trusted Christ for their salvation and have given their lives to him. These men and women are God's born-again and adopted children. As you read Obadiah, catch a glimpse of what it means to be God's child, under his love and protection. See how the heavenly Father responds to all who would attack those whom he loves.

## VITAL STATISTICS

**PURPOSE:**
To show that God judges those who have harmed his people

**AUTHOR:**
Obadiah. Very little is known about this man, whose name means "servant (or worshiper) of the LORD."

**ORIGINAL AUDIENCE:**
The Edomites and the Jews in Judah (the southern kingdom)

**DATE WRITTEN:**
Possibly during the reign of Jehoram in Judah, 855–840 B.C., or possibly during Jeremiah's ministry, 627–586 B.C.

**SETTING:**
Historically, Edom had constantly harassed the Jews. Prior to the time this book was written, they had participated in attacks against Judah. Given the dates above, this prophecy came after the division of Israel into the northern and southern kingdoms and before the conquering of Judah by Nebuchadnezzar in 586 B.C.

**KEY VERSE:**
"The day is near when I, the LORD, will judge all godless nations! As you have done to Israel, so it will be done to you. All your evil deeds will fall back on your own heads" (1:15).

**KEY PEOPLE:**
The Edomites

**KEY PLACES:**
Edom, Jerusalem

**SPECIAL FEATURES:**
The book of Obadiah uses vigorous poetic language and is written in the form of a dirge of doom.

## THE BLUEPRINT

1. Edom's destruction
   (1:1–16)
2. Israel's restoration
   (1:17–21)

The book of Obadiah shows the outcome of the ancient feud between Edom and Israel. Edom was proud of its high position, but God would bring her down. Those who are high and powerful today should not be overconfident in themselves, whether they are a nation, a corporation, a church, or a family. Just as Edom was destroyed for its pride, so will anyone be who lives in defiance of God.

## MEGATHEMES

| THEME | EXPLANATION | IMPORTANCE |
|-------|-------------|------------|
| Justice | Obadiah predicted that God would destroy Edom as punishment for standing by when Babylon invaded Judah. Because of their treachery, Edom's land would be given to Judah in the day when God rights the wrongs against his people. | God will judge and fiercely punish all who harm his people. We can be confident in God's final victory. He is our champion, and we can trust him to bring about true justice. |
| Pride | Because of their seemingly invincible rock fortress, the Edomites were proud and self-confident. But God humbled them and their nation disappeared from the face of the earth. | All those who defy God will meet their doom as Edom did. Any nation who trusts in its power, wealth, technology, or wisdom more than in God will be brought low. All who are proud will one day be shocked to discover that no one is exempt from God's justice. |

## 1. Edom's destruction

This is the vision that the Sovereign LORD revealed to Obadiah concerning the land of Edom.

**1:1**
Isa 34:5-15; 63:1-6
Jer 49:7-22

### Edom's Judgment Announced

We have heard a message from the LORD
  that an ambassador was sent to the nations to say,
"Get ready, everyone!
  Let's assemble our armies and attack Edom!"

2 The LORD says to Edom,
  "I will cut you down to size among the nations;
    you will be greatly despised.

**1:2**
Num 24:15-19

3 You have been deceived by your own pride
  because you live in a rock fortress
  and make your home high in the mountains.
  'Who can ever reach us way up here?'
    you ask boastfully.

**1:3**
Isa 16:6
Jer 49:15-16

4 But even if you soar as high as eagles
  and build your nest among the stars,

**1:4**
Job 39:26-30
Isa 14:12-15

---

**1:1** Obadiah was a prophet from Judah who told of God's judgment against the nation of Edom. There are two commonly accepted dates for this prophecy: (1) between 855 and 840 B.C., when King Jehoram and Jerusalem were attacked by a Philistine/Arab coalition (2 Chronicles 21:16ff); (2) 586 B.C., when Jerusalem was completely destroyed by the Babylonians (2 Kings 25; 2 Chronicles 36). Edom had rejoiced over the misfortunes of both Israel and Judah, and yet the Edomites and Jews descended from two brothers—Esau and Jacob (Genesis 25:19-26). But just as these two brothers were constantly fighting, so were Israel and Edom. God pronounced judgment on Edom for its callous and malicious actions toward his people.

**1:3** Edom was Judah's southern neighbor, sharing a common boundary. But neighbors are not always friends, and Edom liked nothing about Judah. Edom's capital at this time was Sela (perhaps the later city of Petra), a city considered impregnable because it was cut into rock cliffs and set in a canyon that could be entered only through a narrow gap. What Edom perceived as its strengths would be its downfall: (1) safety in their city (1:3, 4)—God would send them plummeting from the heights;

(2) pride in their self-sufficiency (1:4)—God would humble them; (3) wealth (1:5, 6)—thieves would steal all they had; (4) allies (1:7)—God would cause them to turn against Edom; (5) wisdom (1:8, 9)—the wise would be destroyed.

**1:3** The Edomites felt secure, and they were proud of their self-sufficiency. But they were fooling themselves because there is no lasting security apart from God. Is your security in objects or people? Ask yourself how much lasting security they really offer. Possessions and people can disappear in a moment, but God does not change. Only he can supply true security.

**1:4** The Edomites were proud of their city carved right into the rock. Today Sela, or Petra, is considered one of the marvels of the ancient world, but only as a tourist attraction. The Bible warns that pride is the surest route to self-destruction (Proverbs 16:18). Just as Petra and Edom fell, so will proud people fall. A humble person is more secure than a proud person because humility gives a more accurate perspective of oneself and the world.

**1:4-9** God did not pronounce these harsh judgments against Edom out of vengeance but in order to bring about justice. God is morally perfect and demands complete justice and fairness.

I will bring you crashing down,"
says the LORD.

**1:5-6**
Jer 49:9-10

5 "If thieves came at night and robbed you
(what a disaster awaits you!),
they would not take everything.
Those who harvest grapes
always leave a few for the poor.
But your enemies will wipe you out completely!
6 Every nook and cranny of Edom*
will be searched and looted.
Every treasure will be found and taken.

**1:7**
Isa 19:11-14
Jer 30:14

7 "All your allies will turn against you.
They will help to chase you from your land.
They will promise you peace
while plotting to deceive and destroy you.
Your trusted friends will set traps for you,
and you won't even know about it.

**1:8**
Job 5:12-14
Isa 19:3, 13-14;
29:14

8 At that time not a single wise person
will be left in the whole land of Edom,"
says the LORD.
"For on the mountains of Edom
I will destroy everyone who has understanding.

**1:9**
Jer 49:20-22
Amos 1:12-13

9 The mightiest warriors of Teman
will be terrified,
and everyone on the mountains of Edom
will be cut down in the slaughter.

## Reasons for Edom's Punishment

**1:10**
Ezek 25:12-14

10 "Because of the violence you did
to your close relatives in Israel,*
you will be filled with shame
and destroyed forever.

**1:11**
Ps 137:7
Joel 3:3
Nah 3:10

11 When they were invaded,
you stood aloof, refusing to help them.

**6** Hebrew *Esau;* also in 8b, 9, 18, 19, 21.    **10** Hebrew *your brother Jacob.* The names "Jacob" and "Israel" are often interchanged throughout the Old Testament, referring sometimes to the individual patriarch and sometimes to the nation.

---

**OBADIAH**
served as a
prophet to Judah
possibly around
853 B.C.

| | |
|---|---|
| Climate of the times . . . . . . . . | Edom was a constant thorn in Judah's side. The Edomites often participated in attacks initiated by other enemies. |
| Main message . . . . . . . . . . . . | God will judge Edom for its evil actions toward God's people. |
| Importance of message . . . . . . | Just as Edom was destroyed and disappeared as a nation, so God will destroy proud and wicked people. |
| Contemporary prophets . . . . . . | Elijah (875–848 B.C.), Micaiah (865–853 B.C.), Jehu (853 B.C.). |

---

The Edomites were simply getting what they deserved. Because they murdered, they would be murdered. Because they robbed, they would be robbed. Because they took advantage of others, they would be used. Don't talk yourself into sin, thinking that "nobody will know" or "I won't get caught." God knows all our sins, and he will be just.

**1:8** Edom was noted for its wise people. There is a difference, however, between human wisdom and God's wisdom. The Edomites may have been wise in the ways of the world, but they were foolish because they ignored and even mocked God.

**1:9** Eliphaz, one of Job's three friends (Job 2:11), was from Teman, about five miles east of Petra. Teman was named after Esau's grandson (Genesis 36:11).

**1:10, 11** The Israelites had descended from Jacob, and the Edomites, from his brother, Esau (Genesis 25:19-26). Instead of helping Israel and Judah when they were in need, Edom had allowed them to be destroyed and even had plundered what was left behind. Edom, therefore, acted like an enemy and would be punished. Anyone who does not help God's people is God's enemy. If you have withheld your help from someone in a time of need, this is sin (James 4:17). Sin includes not only what we do, but also what we refuse to do. Don't ignore or refuse to help those in need.

Foreign invaders carried off their wealth
and cast lots to divide up Jerusalem,
but you acted like one of Israel's enemies.

12 "You should not have gloated
when they exiled your relatives to distant lands.
You should not have rejoiced
when the people of Judah suffered such misfortune.
You should not have spoken arrogantly
in that terrible time of trouble.

13 You should not have plundered the land of Israel
when they were suffering such calamity.
You should not have gloated over their destruction
when they were suffering such calamity.
You should not have seized their wealth
when they were suffering such calamity.

14 You should not have stood at the crossroads,
killing those who tried to escape.
You should not have captured the survivors
and handed them over in their terrible time of trouble.

### Edom Destroyed, Israel Restored

15 "The day is near when I, the LORD,
will judge all godless nations!
As you have done to Israel,
so it will be done to you.
All your evil deeds
will fall back on your own heads.

16 Just as you swallowed up my people
on my holy mountain,
so you and the surrounding nations
will swallow the punishment I pour out on you.
Yes, all you nations will drink and stagger
and disappear from history.

1:12
Ezek 35:15
Mic 4:11

1:13
Ezek 35:5

1:15
Jer 50:29
Ezek 30:3
Joel 1:15
Hab 2:8

1:16
Jer 25:15; 49:12

| | | HISTORY OF THE CONFLICT BETWEEN ISRAEL AND EDOM |
|---|---|---|
| The nation of Israel descended from Jacob; the nation of Edom descended from Esau. | Genesis 25:23 | |
| Jacob and Esau struggled in their mother's womb | Genesis 25:19-26 | |
| Esau sold his birthright and blessing to Jacob | Genesis 25:29-34 | |
| Edom refused to let the Israelites pass through its land | Numbers 20:14-22 | |
| Israel's kings had constant conflict with Edom. | | |
| • Saul | 1 Samuel 14:47 | |
| • David | 2 Samuel 8:13, 14 | |
| • Solomon | 1 Kings 11:14-22 | |
| • Jehoram | 2 Kings 8:20-22; 2 Chronicles 21:8ff | |
| • Ahaz | 2 Chronicles 28:16 | |
| Edom urged Babylon to destroy Jerusalem | Psalm 137:7 | |

1:12 The Edomites were glad to see Judah in trouble. Their hatred made them want the nation destroyed. For their wrong attitudes and actions, God wiped out the Edomites. How often do you find yourself rejoicing at the misfortunes of others? Because God alone is the judge, we must never be happy about others' misfortunes, even if we think they deserve them (see Proverbs 24:17).

1:12-14 Of all Israel and Judah's neighbors, the Edomites were the only ones not promised any mercy from God. This was because they looted Jerusalem and rejoiced at the misfortunes of Israel and Judah. They betrayed their blood brothers in times of crisis and aided their brothers' enemies. (See also Psalm 137:7; Jeremiah 49:7-22; Ezekiel 25:12-14; Amos 1:11, 12.)

1:15 Why will God's judgment fall on all nations? Edom was not the only nation to rejoice at Judah's fall. All nations and individuals will be judged for the way they have treated God's people. Some nations today treat God's people favorably, while others are hostile toward them. God will judge all people according to the way they treat others, especially believers (Revelation 20:12, 13). Jesus talked about this in Matthew 25:31-46.

## 2. Israel's restoration

**1:17**
Isa 14:1-3
Amos 9:11-15

17 "But Jerusalem* will become a refuge for those who escape;
　　it will be a holy place.
And the people of Israel* will come back
　　to reclaim their inheritance.

**1:18**
Zech 12:6

18 The people of Israel will be a raging fire,
　　and Edom a field of dry stubble.
The descendants of Joseph will be a flame
　　roaring across the field, devouring everything.
There will be no survivors in Edom.
　　I, the LORD, have spoken!

**1:19**
Jer 31:5; 32:44

19 "Then my people living in the Negev
　　will occupy the mountains of Edom.
Those living in the foothills of Judah*
　　will possess the Philistine plains
　　and take over the fields of Ephraim and Samaria.
And the people of Benjamin
　　will occupy the land of Gilead.

**1:20**
1 Kgs 17:9

20 The exiles of Israel will return to their land
　　and occupy the Phoenician coast as far north as Zarephath.
The captives from Jerusalem exiled in the north*
　　will return home and resettle the towns of the Negev.

**1:21**
Ps 22:28
Zech 14:9
Rev 11:15; 19:6

21 Those who have been rescued* will go up to* Mount Zion in Jerusalem
　　to rule over the mountains of Edom.
And the LORD himself will be king!"

**17a** Hebrew *Mount Zion.*　**17b** Hebrew *house of Jacob;* also in 18. See note on 10.　**19** Hebrew *the Shephelah.*
**20** Hebrew *in Sepharad.*　**21a** As in Greek and Syriac versions; Hebrew reads *Rescuers.*　**21b** Or *from.*

**1:17-21** The Edomites were routed by Judas Maccabeus in 164 B.C. The nation no longer existed by the first century A.D. At the time of Obadiah's prophecy, Edom may have seemed more likely to survive than Judah. Yet Edom has vanished, and Judah still exists. This demonstrates the absolute certainty of God's word and of the punishment awaiting all who have mistreated God's people.

**1:19** The Negev was the southern part of Judah, a dry, hot region. The foothills were in the western part of Judah.

**1:20** The boundaries of the kingdom would be extended to include Phoenicia as far north as Zarephath, located between Tyre and Sidon on the Mediterranean coast.

**1:21** Obadiah brought God's message of judgment on Edom. God was displeased with both their inward and their outward rebellion. People today are much the same as people in Obadiah's time, filled with arrogance, envy, and dishonesty. We may wonder how much longer evil will continue. Regardless of sin's effects, however, God is in control. Don't despair or give up

hope. Know that when all is said and done, the Lord is still sovereign, and the confidence you place in him will not be in vain.

**1:21** Edom is an example to all the nations that are hostile to God. Nothing can break God's promise to protect his people from complete destruction. In the book of Obadiah we see four aspects of God's message of judgment: (1) Evil will certainly be punished; (2) those faithful to God have hope for a new future; (3) God is sovereign in human history; (4) God's ultimate purpose is to establish his eternal Kingdom. The Edomites had been cruel to God's people. They were arrogant and proud, and they took advantage of others' misfortunes. Any nation that mistreats people who obey God will be punished, regardless of how invincible they appear. Similarly we, as individuals, cannot allow ourselves to feel so comfortable with our wealth or security that we fail to help God's people. This is sin. And because God is just, sin will be punished.

# JONAH

## VITAL STATISTICS

**PURPOSE:**
To show the extent of God's grace—the message of salvation is for *all* people

**AUTHOR:**
Jonah son of Amittai

**ORIGINAL AUDIENCE:**
All the people of Israel

**DATE WRITTEN:**
Approximately 785–760 B.C.

**SETTING:**
Jonah preceded Amos and ministered under Jeroboam II, Israel's most powerful king (793–753 B.C.; see 2 Kings 14:23–25). Assyria was Israel's great enemy; it conquered Israel in 722 B.C. Nineveh's repentance must have been short-lived, for it was destroyed in 612 B.C.

**KEY VERSE:**
"But Nineveh has more than 120,000 people living in spiritual darkness, not to mention all the animals. Shouldn't I feel sorry for such a great city?" (4:11).

**KEY PEOPLE:**
Jonah, the ship's captain and crew

**KEY PLACES:**
Joppa, Nineveh

**SPECIAL FEATURES:**
This book is different from the other prophetic books because it tells the story of the prophet and does not center on his prophecies. In fact, only one verse summarizes his message to the people of Nineveh (3:4). Jonah is a historical narrative. It is also mentioned by Jesus as a picture of his death and resurrection (Matthew 12:38–42).

SIN runs rampant in society—daily headlines and overflowing prisons bear dramatic witness to that fact. With child abuse, pornography, serial killings, terrorism, anarchy, and ruthless dictatorships, the world seems to be filled to overflowing with violence, hatred, and corruption. Reading and hearing about these tragedies—and perhaps even experiencing them—we begin to understand the necessity of God's judgment. We may even find ourselves wishing for vengeance by any means upon the violent perpetrators. Surely they are beyond redemption! But suppose that in the midst of such thoughts, God told you to take the gospel to the worst of the offenders—how would you respond?

Jonah was given such a task. Assyria—a great but evil empire—was Israel's most dreaded enemy. The Assyrians flaunted their power before God and the world through numerous acts of heartless cruelty. So when Jonah heard God tell him to go to Assyria and call the people to repentance, he ran in the opposite direction.

The book of Jonah tells the story of this prophet's flight and how God stopped him and turned him around. But it is much more than a story of a man and a great fish. Jonah's story is a profound illustration of God's mercy and grace. No one deserved God's favor less than the people of Nineveh, Assyria's capital. Jonah knew this. But he knew that God would forgive and bless them if they would turn from their sin and worship him. Jonah also knew the power of God's message, that even through his own weak preaching, they would respond and be spared God's judgment. But Jonah hated the Assyrians, and he wanted vengeance, not mercy. So he ran the other way. Eventually, Jonah obeyed and preached in the streets of Nineveh, and the people repented and were delivered from judgment. Then Jonah sulked and complained to God, "Didn't I say before I left home that you would do this, LORD? That is why I ran away to Tarshish! I knew that you are a merciful and compassionate God, slow to get angry and filled with unfailing love. You are eager to turn back from destroying people" (4:2). In the end, God confronted Jonah about his self-centered values and lack of compassion, saying, "But Nineveh has more than 120,000 people living in spiritual darkness, not to mention all the animals. Shouldn't I feel sorry for such a great city?" (4:11).

As you read Jonah, see the full picture of God's love and compassion and realize that no one is beyond redemption. The gospel is for all who will repent and believe. Begin to pray for those who seem to be farthest from the Kingdom, and look for ways to tell them about God. Learn from the story of this reluctant prophet and determine to obey God, doing whatever he asks and going wherever he leads.

| Amos | Ashur-nirari V | Jonah's | | Israel |
| becomes | becomes | ministry | | falls to |
| a prophet | king of | ends | | Assyria |
| 760 | Assyria | 753 | | 722 |
| | 754 | | | |

## THE BLUEPRINT

1. Jonah forsakes his mission
   (1:1—2:10)
2. Jonah fulfills his mission
   (3:1—4:11)

Jonah was a reluctant prophet given a mission he found distasteful. He chose to run away from God rather than obey him. Like Jonah, we may have to do things in life that we don't want to do. Sometimes we find ourselves wanting to turn and run. But it is better to obey God than to defy him or run away. Often, in spite of our defiance, God in his mercy will give us another chance to serve him when we return to him.

## MEGATHEMES

| THEME | EXPLANATION | IMPORTANCE |
|---|---|---|
| God's Sovereignty | Although the prophet Jonah tried to run away from God, God was in control. By controlling the stormy seas and a great fish, God displayed his absolute, yet loving guidance. | Rather than running from God, trust him with your past, present, and future. Saying no to God quickly leads to disaster. Saying yes brings new understanding of God and his purpose in the world. |
| God's Message to All the World | God had given Jonah a purpose—to preach to the great Assyrian city of Nineveh. Jonah hated Nineveh, and so he responded with anger and indifference. Jonah had to learn that God loves all people. Through Jonah, God reminded Israel of its missionary purpose. | We must not limit our focus to our own people. God wants his people to proclaim his love in words and actions to the whole world. He wants us to be his missionaries wherever we are, wherever he sends us. |
| Repentance | When the reluctant preacher went to Nineveh, there was a great response. The people repented and turned to God. This was a powerful rebuke to the people of Israel, who thought they were better but refused to respond to God's message. God will forgive all those who turn from their sin. | God doesn't honor sham or pretense. He wants the sincere devotion of each person. It is not enough to share the privileges of Christianity; we must ask God to forgive us and to remove our sin. Refusing to repent shows that we still love our sin. |
| God's Compassion | God's message of love and forgiveness was not for the Jews alone. God loves all the people of the world. The Assyrians didn't deserve it, but God spared them when they repented. In his mercy, God did not reject Jonah for aborting his mission. God has great love, patience, and forgiveness. | God loves each of us, even when we fail him. But he also loves other people, including those not of our group, background, race, or denomination. When we accept his love, we must also learn to accept all those whom he loves. We will find it much easier to love others when we truly love God. |

### 1. Jonah forsakes his mission
*Jonah Runs from the LORD*

1:1
2 Kgs 14:25

**1** The LORD gave this message to Jonah son of Amittai: ²"Get up and go to the great city of Nineveh. Announce my judgment against it because I have seen how wicked its people are."

---

**1:1, 2** Jonah is mentioned in 2 Kings 14:25. He prophesied during the reign of Jeroboam II, the king of Israel from 793 to 753 B.C. He may have been a member of the company of prophets mentioned in connection with Elisha's ministry (2 Kings 2:3).

God told Jonah to preach to Nineveh, the most important city in Assyria, the rising world power of Jonah's day. Within 50 years, Nineveh would become the capital of the vast Assyrian Empire. Jonah doesn't say much about Nineveh's wickedness, but the prophet Nahum gives us more insight. Nahum says

that Nineveh was guilty of (1) evil plots against God (Nahum 1:9); (2) exploitation of the helpless (Nahum 2:12); (3) cruelty in war (Nahum 2:12, 13); (4) idolatry, prostitution, and witchcraft (Nahum 3:4). God told Jonah to go to Nineveh, about 500 miles northeast of Israel, to warn of judgment and to declare that the people could receive mercy and forgiveness if they repented.

³But Jonah got up and went in the opposite direction to get away from the LORD. He went down to the port of Joppa, where he found a ship leaving for Tarshish. He bought a ticket and went on board, hoping to escape from the LORD by sailing to Tarshish.

⁴But the LORD hurled a powerful wind over the sea, causing a violent storm that threatened to break the ship apart. ⁵Fearing for their lives, the desperate sailors shouted to their gods for help and threw the cargo overboard to lighten the ship.

But all this time Jonah was sound asleep down in the hold. ⁶So the captain went down after him. "How can you sleep at a time like this?" he shouted. "Get up and pray to your god! Maybe he will pay attention to us and spare our lives."

⁷Then the crew cast lots to see which of them had offended the gods and caused the terrible storm. When they did this, the lots identified Jonah as the culprit. ⁸"Why has this awful storm come down on us?" they demanded. "Who are you? What is your line of work? What country are you from? What is your nationality?"

⁹Jonah answered, "I am a Hebrew, and I worship the LORD, the God of heaven, who made the sea and the land."

¹⁰The sailors were terrified when they heard this, for he had already told them he was running away from the LORD. "Oh, why did you do it?" they groaned. ¹¹And since the storm was getting worse all the time, they asked him, "What should we do to you to stop this storm?"

¹²"Throw me into the sea," Jonah said, "and it will become calm again. I know that this terrible storm is all my fault."

**1:3** Acts 9:36
**1:5** 1 Kgs 18:26; Acts 27:18-19, 38
**1:6** Ps 107:28; Jon 3:8-9
**1:7** Josh 7:14, 18-19; 1 Sam 14:41-42
**1:8** Gen 47:3
**1:9** Gen 1:9; Ezra 1:2; 5:11; Neh 1:4; 9:6
**1:12** John 11:50

**1:3** Nineveh was a powerful and wicked city. Jonah had grown up hating the Assyrians and fearing their atrocities. His hatred was so strong that he didn't want them to receive God's mercy. Jonah was actually afraid the people would repent (4:2, 3). Jonah's attitude is representative of Israel's reluctance to share God's love and mercy with others, even though this was their God-given mission (Genesis 12:3). They, like Jonah, did not want non-Jews (Gentiles) to obtain God's favor.

**1:3** Jonah knew that God had a specific job for him, but he didn't want to do it. Tarshish could be one of any number of Phoenicia's western ports. Nineveh was toward the east. Jonah decided to go as far west as he could. When God gives us directions through his Word, sometimes we run in fear or in stubbornness, claiming that God is asking too much. It may have been fear or anger at the wideness of God's mercy that made Jonah run. But running got him into worse trouble. In the end, Jonah understood that it is best to do what God asks in the first place. But by then he had paid a costly price for running. It is far better to obey from the start.

**1:4** Before settling in the Promised Land, the Israelites had been nomads, wandering from place to place, seeking good pastureland for their flocks. Although they were not a seafaring people, their location along the Mediterranean Sea and near the neighboring maritime powers of Phoenicia and Philistia allowed much contact with ships and sailors. The ship Jonah sailed on was probably a large trading vessel with a deck.

**1:4** Jonah's disobedience to God endangered the lives of the ship's crew. We have a great responsibility to obey God's Word because our sin and disobedience can hurt others around us.

**1:4, 5** While the storm raged, Jonah was sound asleep below deck. Even as he ran from God, Jonah's actions apparently didn't bother his conscience. But the absence of guilt isn't always a barometer of whether we are doing right. Because we can deny reality, we cannot measure obedience by our feelings. Instead, we must compare what we do with God's standards for living.

**1:7** The crew cast lots to find the guilty person, relying on their superstition to give them the answer. Their system worked, but only because God intervened to let Jonah know that he couldn't run away.

**1:9-12** You cannot seek God's love and run from him at the same time. Jonah soon realized that no matter where he went, he couldn't get away from God. But before Jonah could return to God, he first had to stop going in the opposite direction. What has God told you to do? If you want more of God's love and power, you must be willing to carry out the responsibilities he gives you. You cannot say that you truly believe in God if you don't do what he says (1 John 2:3-6).

**1:12** Jonah knew that he had disobeyed and that the storm was his fault, but he didn't say anything until the crew cast lots and he lost the toss (1:7). Then Jonah was willing to give his life to save the sailors, although he had refused to do the same for the people of Nineveh. Jonah's hatred for the Assyrians had affected his perspective.

**JONAH'S ROUNDABOUT JOURNEY** God told Jonah to go to Nineveh, the capital of the Assyrian Empire. Many of Jonah's countrymen had experienced the atrocities of these fierce people. The last place Jonah wanted to go was on a missionary trip to Nineveh! So he went in the opposite direction. He boarded a ship in Joppa that was headed for Tarshish. But Jonah could not run from God.

13Instead, the sailors rowed even harder to get the ship to the land. But the stormy sea was too violent for them, and they couldn't make it. 14Then they cried out to the Lord, Jonah's God. "O Lord," they pleaded, "don't make us die for this man's sin. And don't hold us responsible for his death. O Lord, you have sent this storm upon him for your own good reasons."

**1:15**
Ps 89:9
Mark 4:41

15Then the sailors picked Jonah up and threw him into the raging sea, and the storm stopped at once! 16The sailors were awestruck by the Lord's great power, and they offered him a sacrifice and vowed to serve him.

**JONAH**

Few Old Testament personalities can compare in transparency with the prophet Jonah. We can see right through him. And most of what we see we don't like. He reminds us too much of ourselves: fearful, selfish, spiteful, and proud.

Even when Jonah wasn't physically running away from God, he was still resisting on the inside. He was quite capable of putting on a show of obedience to cover a seething internal mutiny. When he finally arrived in Nineveh with God's message, he delivered it as a summary judgment. He offered no way of escape. Jonah flatly declared the city's destruction.

Jonah knew (as he admitted later) that God was "a merciful and compassionate God, slow to get angry and filled with unfailing love . . . eager to turn back from destroying people" (4:2). He hoped the Ninevites wouldn't listen and was offended and resentful when they did. Jonah suffered under the painful mistake of assuming that he was the center of the universe.

Some people do not even think about God until they become angry. Discouragement, disappointment and disgust seem to clear away the haziness around God and we're all too eager to blame him for our troubles. God bluntly confronted Jonah with the reality of his disobedience, the pettiness of his demand for comfort, and the sinfulness of his blatant disregard for others. The wonderful character of God that Jonah wanted to withhold from the Ninevites, he himself had been taking for granted.

Fortunately, God will be just as blunt with us. He will shatter our comfort if that will place us in the best place to meet him. As long as we are surrounded by our sense of control and importance, we will not know God as God. What has God done lately in your life to open your eyes a little wider?

| | |
|---|---|
| **Strengths and accomplishments** | • Was sent (and finally went) to an enemy nation with God's message<br>• Survived an encounter with a large fish<br>• Was instrumental in the repentance of the population of a huge city, keeping it from destruction |
| **Weaknesses and mistakes** | • Thought he could avoid God's call in his life by running away<br>• Thought he could avoid God's call by sacrificing himself<br>• Thought he could avoid God's call by belligerent obedience<br>• Thought he could nullify God's call by sulking |
| **Lessons from his life** | • God cares deeply for us as well as for people we resent and hate<br>• God will accomplish his purposes, even through reluctant and unwilling servants<br>• God is patient with sinners and patient with his servants |
| **Vital statistics** | • Where: Gath-hepher<br>• Occupation: Prophet<br>• Relatives: Father: Amittai |
| **Key verse** | "But Jonah got up and went in the opposite direction to get away from the Lord. He went down to the port of Joppa, where he found a ship leaving for Tarshish. He bought a ticket and went on board, hoping to escape from the Lord by sailing to Tarshish" (Jonah 1:3). |

Jonah's story is told in the book of Jonah. He is also mentioned in 2 Kings 14:25; Matthew 12:39-41; 16:4; and Luke 11:29, 32.

**1:13** By trying to save Jonah's life, the pagan sailors showed more compassion than Jonah, because Jonah did not want to warn the Ninevites of the coming judgment of God. Believers should be ashamed when unbelievers show more concern and compassion than they do. God wants us to be concerned for all of his people, lost and saved.

**1:14-16** Jonah had disobeyed God. While he was running away, he stopped and submitted to God. Then the ship's crew began to worship God because they saw that the storm had stopped.

God is able to use even our mistakes to help others come to know him. It may be painful, but admitting our sins can be a powerful example to those who don't know God. Ironically, the pagan sailors did what the entire nation of Israel would not do—prayed to God and vowed to serve him.

¹⁷*Now the LORD had arranged for a great fish to swallow Jonah. And Jonah was inside the fish for three days and three nights.

**1:17**
Matt 12:40; 16:4

### Jonah's Prayer

**2** ¹*Then Jonah prayed to the LORD his God from inside the fish. ²He said,

"I cried out to the LORD in my great trouble,
and he answered me.
I called to you from the land of the dead,*
and LORD, you heard me!

**2:2**
Pss 18:4-6; 22:24

³ You threw me into the ocean depths,
and I sank down to the heart of the sea.
The mighty waters engulfed me;
I was buried beneath your wild and stormy waves.

**2:3**
Ps 42:7

⁴ Then I said, 'O LORD, you have driven me from your presence.
Yet I will look once more toward your holy Temple.'

**2:4**
1 Kgs 8:38
Pss 5:7; 31:22

⁵ "I sank beneath the waves,
and the waters closed over me.
Seaweed wrapped itself around my head.

**2:5**
Ps 69:1
Lam 3:54

⁶ I sank down to the very roots of the mountains.
I was imprisoned in the earth,
whose gates lock shut forever.
But you, O LORD my God,
snatched me from the jaws of death!

**2:6**
Pss 16:10; 30:3
Isa 38:17; 40:12

⁷ As my life was slipping away,
I remembered the LORD.

**2:7**
2 Chr 30:27
Pss 18:6; 77:10-11;
142:3

**1:17** Verse 1:17 is numbered 2:1 in Hebrew text.    **2:1** Verses 2:1-10 are numbered 2:2-11 in Hebrew text.
**2:2** Hebrew *from Sheol.*

---

| | |
|---|---|
| Climate of the times . . . . . . . . | Nineveh was the most important city in Assyria and would soon become the capital of the huge Assyrian Empire. But Nineveh was also a very wicked city. |
| Main message . . . . . . . . . . . . | Jonah, who hated the powerful and wicked Assyrians, was called by God to warn the Assyrians that they would receive judgment if they did not repent. |
| Importance of message . . . . . . | Jonah didn't want to go to Nineveh, so he tried to run from God. But God has ways of teaching us to obey and follow him. When Jonah preached, the city repented and God withheld his judgment. Even the most wicked will be saved if they truly repent of their sins and turn to God. |
| Contemporary prophets . . . . . . | Joel (835–796? B.C.), Amos (760–750 B.C.) |

**JONAH**
served as a
prophet to Israel
and Assyria from
793–753 B.C.

---

**1:17** Many have tried to dismiss this miraculous event as fiction, but the Bible does not describe it as a dream or a legend. We should not explain away this miracle as if we can pick and choose which of the miracles in the Bible to believe. That kind of attitude would allow us to question any part of the Bible and cause us to lose our trust in the Bible as God's true and reliable Word. Jonah's experience was used by Christ himself as an illustration of his death and resurrection (Matthew 12:39, 40).

**1:17** Jonah was sent by God to the Assyrians, ran from the task, and was swallowed by a great fish. The Bible tells us that he "was inside the fish for three days and three nights." Then he was delivered and went to Nineveh where the people responded with repentance. These events in Jonah's life were cited by Jesus. When the religious leaders demanded that Jesus give them a sign to prove his authority, Jesus said the only sign they would receive was the sign of Jonah: They would see Jesus swallowed by death and delivered after three days (Matthew 12:39-41; 16:4).

Jesus was making it very clear to the religious leaders of the day that their stubbornness to believe in him would be judged. The people of Nineveh responded to God's word spoken by Jonah,

but the religious leaders refused to believe God's word spoken by his very own Son. Often people of our generation demand a sign from God, but the only sign they will receive is the sign of Jonah—the death and resurrection of Christ.

**2:1ff** This is a prayer of thanksgiving, not a prayer for deliverance. Jonah was simply thankful that he had not drowned. He was delivered in a most spectacular way and was overwhelmed that he had escaped certain death. Even from inside the fish, Jonah's prayer was heard by God. We can pray anywhere and at any time, and God will hear us. Your sin is never too great, your predicament never too difficult, for God.

**2:1-7** Jonah said, "As my life was slipping away, I remembered the LORD" (2:7). Often we act the same way. When life is going well, we tend to take God for granted; but when we lose hope, we cry out to him. This kind of relationship with God can result only in an inconsistent, up-and-down spiritual life. A consistent, daily commitment to God promotes a solid relationship with him. Look to God during both the good and bad times, and you will have a stronger spiritual life.

**2:2** Jonah pictured his predicament inside the fish as though he had been buried alive.

And my earnest prayer went out to you
  in your holy Temple.
8 Those who worship false gods
  turn their backs on all God's mercies.
9 But I will offer sacrifices to you with songs of praise,
  and I will fulfill all my vows.
  For my salvation comes from the LORD alone."

**2:9**
Pss 3:8; 50:14;
68:20
Hos 14:2

10 Then the LORD ordered the fish to spit Jonah out onto the beach.

## 2. Jonah fulfills his mission
### Jonah Goes to Nineveh

**3:2**
Jer 1:17
Ezek 2:7

**3** Then the LORD spoke to Jonah a second time: 2 "Get up and go to the great city of Nineveh, and deliver the message I have given you."

**3:3**
Jon 1:2; 4:11

3 This time Jonah obeyed the LORD's command and went to Nineveh, a city so large that it took three days to see it all.* 4 On the day Jonah entered the city, he shouted to the crowds:

**3:4**
Matt 12:41
Luke 11:32

"Forty days from now Nineveh will be destroyed!" 5 The people of Nineveh believed God's message, and from the greatest to the least, they declared a fast and put on burlap to show their sorrow.

6 When the king of Nineveh heard what Jonah was saying, he stepped down from his throne and took off his royal robes. He dressed himself in burlap and sat on a heap of ashes.

**3:7**
2 Chr 20:3

7 Then the king and his nobles sent this decree throughout the city:

**3:8**
Ps 130:1-2
Jon 1:6, 14

"No one, not even the animals from your herds and flocks, may eat or drink anything at all. 8 People and animals alike must wear garments of mourning, and everyone must pray earnestly to God. They must turn from their evil ways and stop all their violence.

**3:9**
Joel 2:14

9 Who can tell? Perhaps even yet God will change his mind and hold back his fierce anger from destroying us."

**3:3** Hebrew *a great city to God, of three days' journey.*

---

**MIRACLES
IN THE BOOK
OF JONAH**

| | |
|---|---|
| God sent a violent storm. | 1:4 |
| God provided a great fish to swallow Jonah | 1:17 |
| God ordered the fish to spit up Jonah | 2:10 |
| God made a leafy plant to shade Jonah | 4:6 |
| God arranged for a worm to eat the plant | 4:7 |
| God arranged for a scorching wind to blow on Jonah | 4:8 |

---

**2:8** Those who worship worthless idols (false gods) forfeit God's grace and abandon any hope for mercy from the Lord. Any object of our devotion that replaces God is a lying vanity. We deceive ourselves with something that is ultimately empty and foolish. Make sure that nothing takes God's rightful place in your life.

**2:9** Obviously Jonah was not in a position to bargain with God. Instead, he simply thanked God for saving his life. Our troubles should cause us to cling tightly to God, not attempt to bargain our way out of the pain. We can thank and praise God for what he has already done for us, and for his love and mercy.

**2:9** It took a miracle of deliverance to get Jonah to do as God had commanded. As a prophet, Jonah was obligated to obey God's word, but he had tried to escape his responsibilities. At this time, he pledged to fulfill his vows. Jonah's story began with a tragedy, but a greater tragedy would have happened if God had allowed him to keep running. When you know God wants you to do something, don't run. God may not stop you as he did Jonah.

**3:1, 2** Jonah had run away from God but was given a second chance to participate in God's work. You may feel as though you are disqualified from serving God because of past mistakes. But serving God is not an earned position. No one qualifies for God's service, but God still asks us to carry out his work. You may yet have another chance.

**3:1, 2** Jonah was to preach only what God told him—a message of doom to one of the most powerful cities in the world. This was not the most desirable assignment, but those who bring God's word to others should not let social pressures or fear of people dictate their words. They are called to preach God's message and his truth, no matter how unpopular it may be.

**3:3** Nineveh was a huge city. The Hebrew text makes no distinction between the city proper (the walls of which were only about eight miles in circumference, accommodating a population of about 175,000 persons) and the administrative district of Nineveh that was about 30 to 60 miles across.

**3:4-9** God's word is for everyone. Despite the wickedness of the Ninevite people, they were open to God's message and repented immediately. If we simply proclaim God's message of salvation, we may be surprised at how many people will listen.

¹⁰When God saw what they had done and how they had put a stop to their evil ways, he changed his mind and did not carry out the destruction he had threatened.

3:10
Jer 18:8
Amos 7:3, 6

## Jonah's Anger at the LORD's Mercy

**4** This change of plans greatly upset Jonah, and he became very angry. ²So he complained to the LORD about it: "Didn't I say before I left home that you would do this, LORD? That is why I ran away to Tarshish! I knew that you are a merciful and compassionate God, slow to get angry and filled with unfailing love. You are eager to turn back from destroying people. ³Just kill me now, LORD! I'd rather be dead than alive if what I predicted will not happen."

4:2
Exod 34:6
Ps 86:5
Joel 2:13

⁴The LORD replied, "Is it right for you to be angry about this?"

4:3
1 Kgs 19:4
Job 6:8-9

⁵Then Jonah went out to the east side of the city and made a shelter to sit under as he waited to see what would happen to the city. ⁶And the LORD God arranged for a leafy plant to grow there, and soon it spread its broad leaves over Jonah's head, shading him from the sun. This eased his discomfort, and Jonah was very grateful for the plant.

⁷But God also arranged for a worm! The next morning at dawn the worm ate through the stem of the plant so that it withered away. ⁸And as the sun grew hot, God arranged for a scorching east wind to blow on Jonah. The sun beat down on his head until he grew faint and wished to die. "Death is certainly better than living like this!" he exclaimed.

4:7
Joel 1:12

4:8
Isa 49:10
Ezek 19:12
Hos 13:15

⁹Then God said to Jonah, "Is it right for you to be angry because the plant died?"

"Yes," Jonah retorted, "even angry enough to die!"

¹⁰Then the LORD said, "You feel sorry about the plant, though you did nothing to put it there. It came quickly and died quickly. ¹¹But Nineveh has more than 120,000 people living in spiritual darkness,* not to mention all the animals. Shouldn't I feel sorry for such a great city?"

4:11
Jon 1:2; 3:2; 3:10

4:11 Hebrew *people who don't know their right hand from their left.*

---

**3:10** The pagan people of Nineveh believed Jonah's message and repented. What a miraculous effect God's words had on those evil people! Their repentance stood in stark contrast to Israel's stubbornness. The people of Israel had heard many messages from the prophets, but they had refused to repent. The people of Nineveh only needed to hear God's message once. Jesus said that at the judgment, the people of Nineveh will stand up to condemn the Israelites for their failure to repent (Matthew 12:39-41). It is not our hearing God's word that pleases him, but our responding obediently to it.

**3:10** God responded in mercy by canceling his threatened destruction. God had said that any nation on which he had pronounced judgment would be saved if it repented (Jeremiah 18:7, 8). God forgave Nineveh, just as he had forgiven Jonah. The purpose of God's judgment is correction, not revenge. He is always ready to show compassion to anyone willing to seek him.

**4:1** Why did Jonah become angry when God spared Nineveh? The Jews did not want to share God's message with Gentile nations in Jonah's day, just as they resisted that role in Paul's day (1 Thessalonians 2:14-16). They had forgotten their original purpose as a nation—to be a blessing to the rest of the world by sharing God's message with other nations (Genesis 22:18). Jonah thought that God should not freely give his salvation to a wicked pagan nation. Yet this is exactly what God does for all who come to him today in faith.

**4:1, 2** Jonah revealed the reason for his reluctance to go to Nineveh (1:3). He didn't want the Ninevites forgiven; he wanted them destroyed. Jonah did not understand that the God of Israel was also the God of the whole world. Are you surprised when some unlikely person turns to God? Is it possible that your view is as narrow as Jonah's? We must not forget that, in reality, *we* do not deserve to be forgiven by God.

**4:3** Jonah had run from the job of delivering God's message of destruction to Nineveh (1:2, 3); then he wanted to die because the destruction wouldn't happen. How quickly Jonah had forgotten God's mercy for him when he was inside the fish (2:9, 10). Jonah was happy when God saved him, but he was angry when Nineveh was saved. Jonah was learning a valuable lesson about

God's mercy and forgiveness. God's forgiveness was not only for Jonah or for Israel alone; it extends to all who repent and believe.

**4:3** Jonah may have been more concerned about his own reputation than God's. He knew that if the people repented, none of his warnings to Nineveh would come true. This would embarrass him, although it would give glory to God. Are you more interested in getting glory for God or for yourself?

**4:5-11** God ministered tenderly to Jonah just as he had done to Nineveh and to Israel—and just as he does to us. God could have destroyed Jonah for his defiant anger, but instead he gently taught him a lesson. If we will obey God, he will lead us. His harsh judgment is reserved for those who persist in rebellion.

**4:9** Jonah was angry at the withering of the plant, but not over what could have happened to Nineveh. Most of us have cried at the death of a pet or when an object with sentimental value is broken, but have we cried over the fact that a friend does not know God? How easy it is to be more sensitive to our own interests than to the spiritual needs of people around us.

**4:10, 11** Sometimes people wish that judgment and destruction would come upon sinful people whose wickedness seems to demand immediate punishment. But God is more merciful than we can imagine. God feels compassion for the sinners we want judged, and he devises plans to bring them to himself. What is your attitude toward those who are especially wicked? Do you want them destroyed? Or do you wish that they could experience God's mercy and forgiveness?

**4:11** God spared the sailors when they pleaded for mercy. God saved Jonah when he prayed from inside the fish. God saved the people of Nineveh when they responded to Jonah's preaching. God answers the prayers of those who call upon him. God will always work his will, and he desires that all come to him, trust in him, and be saved. We can be saved if we heed God's warnings to us through his Word. If we respond in obedience, God will be gracious, and we will receive his mercy, not his punishment.

# MICAH

"I HATE YOU!" she screams and runs from the room. Words from a child thrown as emotional darts. Perhaps she learned the phrase from Mom and Dad, or maybe it just burst forth from that inner well of "sinful nature." Whatever the case, hate and love have become society's bywords, almost tired clichés, tossed carelessly at objects, situations, and even people.

The casual use of such words as *love* and *hate* has emptied them of their meaning. We no longer understand statements that describe a loving God who hates sin. So we picture God as gentle and kind—a cosmic pushover, and our concept of what he hates is tempered by our misconceptions and wishful thinking.

The words of the prophets stand in stark contrast to such misconceptions. God's hatred is real—burning, consuming, and destroying. He hates sin, and he stands as the righteous Judge, ready to mete out just punishment to all who defy his rule. God's love is also real. So real that he sent his Son, the Messiah, to save and accept judgment in the sinner's place. Love and hate are together—both unending, irresistible, and unfathomable.

In seven short chapters, Micah presents this true picture of God—the almighty Lord who hates sin and loves the sinner. Much of the book is devoted to describing God's judgment on Israel (the northern kingdom), on Judah (the southern kingdom), and on all the earth. This judgment will come "because of the rebellion of Israel and the sins of Judah" (1:5). And the prophet lists their despicable sins, including fraud (2:2), theft (2:8), greed (2:9), debauchery (2:11), oppression (3:3), hypocrisy (3:4), heresy (3:5), injustice (3:9), extortion and lying (6:12), murder (7:2), and other offenses. God's judgment will come.

In the midst of this overwhelming prediction of destruction, Micah gives hope and consolation because he also describes God's love. The truth is that judgment comes only after countless opportunities to repent, to turn back to true worship and obedience—"to do what is right, to love mercy, and to walk humbly with your God " (6:8). But even in the midst of judgment, God promises to deliver the small minority who have continued to follow him. He states, "Your king will lead you; the LORD himself will guide you" (2:13). The king, of course, is Jesus; and we read in 5:2 that he will be born as a baby in Bethlehem, an obscure Judean village.

As you read Micah, catch a glimpse of God's anger in action as he judges and punishes sin. See God's love in action as he offers eternal life to all who repent and believe. And then determine to join the faithful remnant of God's people, who live according to his will.

## VITAL STATISTICS

**PURPOSE:**
To warn God's people that judgment is coming and to offer pardon to all who repent

**AUTHOR:**
Micah, a native of Moresheth, near Gath, about 20 miles southwest of Jerusalem

**ORIGINAL AUDIENCE:**
The people of Israel (the northern kingdom) and of Judah (the southern kingdom)

**DATE WRITTEN:**
Possibly during the reigns of Jotham, Ahaz, and Hezekiah (742–687 B.C.)

**SETTING:**
The political situation is described in 2 Kings 15—20 and 2 Chronicles 26—30. Micah was a contemporary of Isaiah and Hosea.

**KEY VERSE:**
"No, O people, the LORD has told you what is good, and this is what he requires of you: to do what is right, to love mercy, and to walk humbly with your God" (6:8).

**KEY PEOPLE:**
The people of Samaria and Jerusalem

**KEY PLACES:**
Samaria, Jerusalem, Bethlehem

**SPECIAL FEATURES:**
This is a beautiful example of classical Hebrew poetry. There are three parts, each beginning with "Attention!" or "Listen" (1:2; 3:1; 6:1) and closing with a promise.

## THE BLUEPRINT

1. The trial of the capitals (1:1—2:13)
2. The trial of the leaders (3:1—5:15)
3. The trial of the people (6:1—7:20)

Micah emphasized the need for justice and peace. Like a lawyer, he set forth God's case against Israel and Judah, their leaders, and their people. Throughout the book are prophecies about Jesus, the Messiah, who will gather the people into one nation. He will be their King and Ruler, acting mercifully toward them. Micah makes it clear that God hates unkindness, idolatry, injustice, and empty ritual—and he still hates these today. But God is very willing to pardon the sins of any who repent.

## MEGATHEMES

| THEME | EXPLANATION | IMPORTANCE |
|---|---|---|
| Perverting Faith | God will judge the false prophets, dishonest leaders, and selfish priests in Israel and Judah. While they publicly carried out religious ceremonies, they were privately seeking to gain money and influence. To mix selfish motives with an empty display of religion is to pervert faith. | Don't try to mix your own selfish desires with true faith in God. One day God will reveal how foolish it is to substitute anything for loyalty to him. Coming up with your own private blend of religion will pervert your faith. |
| Oppression | Micah predicted ruin for all nations and leaders who were oppressive toward others. The upper classes oppressed and exploited the poor. Yet no one was speaking against them or doing anything to stop them. God will not put up with such injustice. | We dare not ask God to help us while we ignore those who are needy and oppressed, or while we silently condone the actions of those who oppress them. |
| The Messiah— King of Peace | God promised to provide a new King to bring strength and peace to his people. Hundreds of years before Christ's birth, God promised that the eternal King would be born in Bethlehem. It was God's great plan to restore his people through the Messiah. | Christ our King leads us just as God promised. But until his final judgment, his leadership is only visible among those who welcome his authority. We can have God's peace now by giving up our sins and welcoming him as King. |
| Pleasing God | Micah preached that God's greatest desire was not the offering of sacrifices at the Temple. God delights in faith that produces justice, love for others, and obedience to him. | True faith in God generates kindness, compassion, justice, and humility. We can please God by seeking these attributes in our work, our family, our church, and our neighborhood. |

## 1. The trial of the capitals

**1** The LORD gave this message to Micah of Moresheth during the years when Jotham, Ahaz, and Hezekiah were kings of Judah. The visions he saw concerned both Samaria and Jerusalem.

*1:1*
1 Chr 3:12-13
Jer 26:18

### Grief over Samaria and Jerusalem

2 Attention! Let all the people of the world listen!
Let the earth and everything in it hear.
The Sovereign LORD is making accusations against you;
the Lord speaks from his holy Temple.

*1:2*
Ps 50:7
Jer 6:19

3 Look! The LORD is coming!
He leaves his throne in heaven
and tramples the heights of the earth.

*1:3*
Isa 26:21
Amos 4:13

4 The mountains melt beneath his feet
and flow into the valleys
like wax in a fire,
like water pouring down a hill.

*1:4*
Ps 97:5
Isa 64:1-2
Nah 1:5

5 And why is this happening?
Because of the rebellion of Israel*—
yes, the sins of the whole nation.

*1:5*
2 Chr 34:3-4
Amos 8:14

1:5 Hebrew *Jacob*; also in 1:5b. The names "Jacob" and "Israel" are often interchanged throughout the Old Testament, referring sometimes to the individual patriarch and sometimes to the nation.

1:1 Micah and Isaiah lived at the same time, about 750–680 B.C., and undoubtedly knew of each other. Micah directed his message mainly to Judah, the southern kingdom, but he also had some words for Israel, the northern kingdom. Judah was enjoying great prosperity at this time. Of the three kings mentioned, Jotham (750–732) and Hezekiah (715–686) had tried to follow God (2 Kings 15:32-38; 18–20), but Ahaz (735–715) was one of the most evil kings ever to reign in Judah (2 Kings 16). Moresheth was a Judean village near Gath, on the border with Philistia.

1:3 "The heights of the earth" could simply mean "mountaintops" or may refer to the altars dedicated to various idols, usually placed in elevated areas (see also 1:5).

1:3-7 Although the 12 tribes of Israel had been united under David and Solomon, after Solomon's death, the kingdom had divided into two parts. Two of the tribes, Judah and Benjamin, stayed loyal to David's line and accepted Solomon's son as their king. They became the southern kingdom, also called Judah, with Jerusalem as their capital city. The other ten tribes became the northern kingdom, also called Israel, with Samaria as their capital city. The destruction of Samaria was literally fulfilled during Micah's lifetime, in 722 B.C. (2 Kings 17:1-18), just as he had predicted.

1:5 Two sins are identified in Micah's message: the perversion of worship (1:7; 3:5-7, 11; 5:12, 13) and injustice toward others (2:1, 2, 8, 9; 3:2, 3, 9-11; 7:2-6). Rampant in the capital cities, these sins infiltrated and infected the entire country.

Who is to blame for Israel's rebellion?
  Samaria, its capital city!
Where is the center of idolatry in Judah?
  In Jerusalem, its capital!

**1:6**
Jer 31:5
Ezek 13:14

6 "So I, the LORD, will make the city of Samaria
    a heap of ruins.
Her streets will be plowed up
    for planting vineyards.
I will roll the stones of her walls into the valley below,
    exposing her foundations.

**1:7**
Deut 9:21; 23:18
2 Chr 34:7

7 All her carved images will be smashed.
    All her sacred treasures will be burned.
These things were bought with the money
    earned by her prostitution,
and they will now be carried away
    to pay prostitutes elsewhere."

**1:8**
Isa 13:21-22;
20:2-4

8 Therefore, I will mourn and lament.
    I will walk around barefoot and naked.
I will howl like a jackal
    and moan like an owl.

**1:9**
Jer 30:11-15
Mic 1:12

9 For my people's wound
    is too deep to heal.
It has reached into Judah,
    even to the gates of Jerusalem.

10 Don't tell our enemies in Gath*;
    don't weep at all.
You people in Beth-leaphrah,*
    roll in the dust to show your despair.

**1:11**
Ezek 23:29

11 You people in Shaphir,*
    go as captives into exile—naked and ashamed.

**1:10a** *Gath* sounds like the Hebrew term for "tell." **1:10b** *Beth-leaphrah* means "house of dust." **1:11a** *Shaphir*
means "pleasant."

---

**MICAH**
served as a
prophet to
Judah from
742–687 B.C.

*Climate of the times* . . . . . . . King Ahaz set up pagan idols in the Temple and finally nailed
the Temple doors shut. Four different nations harassed Judah.
When Hezekiah became king, the nation began a slow road
to recovery and economic strength. Hezekiah probably heeded
much of Micah's advice.

*Main message* . . . . . . . . . . . Prediction of the fall of both the northern kingdom of Israel
and the southern kingdom of Judah. This was God's discipline
upon the people, actually showing how much he cared for
them. Hezekiah's good reign helped postpone Judah's
punishment.

*Importance ofmessage* . . . . . Choosing to live a life apart from God is making a commitment
to sin. Sin leads to judgment and death. God alone shows us
the way to eternal peace. His discipline often keeps us on the
right path.

*Contemporary prophets*. . . . . Hosea (753–715 B.C.), Isaiah (740–681 B.C.)

---

**1:9** Samaria's sins were incurable, and God's judgment on the
city had already begun. This sin was not like a gash in the skin but
more like a stab wound in a vital organ, causing an injury that
would soon prove fatal (Samaria was, in fact, destroyed early in
Micah's ministry). Tragically, Samaria's sin had influenced Jerusalem, and judgment would come to its very gates. This probably
refers to Sennacherib's siege in 701 B.C. (see 2 Kings 18–19).

**1:10-16** Micah declared God's judgment on city after city
because of the people's sins. The Hebrew of 1:10-13 includes a
clever wordplay (see the textual notes). Micah bitterly denounced

each town by using puns. *Shaphir* sounds like the Hebrew word
for "pleasant"; *Zaanan* sounds like the verb meaning "come out";
*Maroth* sounds like a word for "bitter." Read 1:11-12 aloud,
substituting the meaning for each city's name, and you will realize
the effect of Micah's word choice. Not all these cities can be identified now, but Lachish was on the border with Philistia and took
the brunt of the Assyrian invasion.

The people of Zaanan*
 dare not come outside their walls.
The people of Beth-ezel* mourn,
 for their house has no support.
12 The people of Maroth* anxiously wait for relief,
 but only bitterness awaits them
as the LORD's judgment reaches
 even to the gates of Jerusalem.

13 Harness your chariot horses and flee,
 you people of Lachish.*
You were the first city in Judah
 to follow Israel in her rebellion,
 and you led Jerusalem* into sin.
14 Send farewell gifts to Moresheth-gath*;
 there is no hope of saving it.
The town of Aczib*
 has deceived the kings of Israel.
15 O people of Mareshah,*
 I will bring a conqueror to capture your town.
And the leaders* of Israel
 will go to Adullam.

16 Oh, people of Judah, shave your heads in sorrow,
 for the children you love will be snatched away.
Make yourselves as bald as a vulture,
 for your little ones will be exiled to distant lands.

## Judgment against Wealthy Oppressors

2 ¹ What sorrow awaits you who lie awake at night,
 thinking up evil plans.
You rise at dawn and hurry to carry them out,
 simply because you have the power to do so.
2 When you want a piece of land,
 you find a way to seize it.
When you want someone's house,
 you take it by fraud and violence.
You cheat a man of his property,
 stealing his family's inheritance.

3 But this is what the LORD says:
"I will reward your evil with evil;
 you won't be able to pull your neck out of the noose.
You will no longer walk around proudly,
 for it will be a terrible time."

**1:12**
Job 30:26
Isa 59:9-11
Jer 8:15; 14:19

**1:13**
Josh 10:3

**1:14**
Josh 15:44

**1:15**
Josh 12:15;
15:35, 44

**1:16**
Prov 3:29-30
Isa 22:12

**2:1**
Prov 3:27
Isa 32:7
Hos 7:6-7

**2:2**
Isa 5:8

**2:3**
Isa 2:11-12
Jer 18:11

1:11b *Zaanan* sounds like the Hebrew term for "come out." 1:11c *Beth-ezel* means "adjoining house." 1:12 *Maroth* sounds like the Hebrew term for "bitter." 1:13a *Lachish* sounds like the Hebrew term for "team of horses." 1:13b Hebrew *the daughter of Zion.* 1:14a *Moresheth* sounds like the Hebrew term for "gift" or "dowry." 1:14b *Aczib* means "deception." 1:15a *Mareshah* sounds like the Hebrew term for "conqueror." 1:15b Hebrew *the glory.*

---

**1:13** The people of Lachish had influenced many to follow their evil example. They "led Jerusalem into sin." We often do the same when we sin. Regardless of whether you consider yourself a leader, your actions and words are observed by others who may choose to follow your example, whether you know it or not.

**1:14** Moresheth-gath was Micah's hometown (1:1).

**1:15** The terrain surrounding Adullam had numerous caves. Micah was warning that when the enemy approached, Judah's proud leaders would be forced to flee and hide in these caves.

**1:16** Micah pictured the devastating sorrow of parents seeing their children taken away to be slaves in a distant land. This happened frequently in both Israel and Judah, most horribly

when each nation was completely conquered—Israel in 722 B.C. and Judah in 586 B.C.

**2:1, 2** Micah spoke out against those who planned evil deeds at night and rose at dawn to do them. A person's thoughts and plans reflect his or her character. What do you think about as you lie down to sleep? Do your desires involve greed or stepping on others to achieve your goals? Evil thoughts lead to evil deeds.

**2:2** Micah warned against those who use their position to take advantage of others. Less than a century earlier, King Ahab of Israel had pouted because he couldn't get Naboth's vineyard. So his wife, Jezebel, had Naboth killed in order to give the garden to Ahab (1 Kings 21:1-16). This kind of injustice had spread throughout the nation and, like a disease, was destroying the people from the inside out.

**2:4**
Jer 6:12; 8:10
Hab 2:6

4 In that day your enemies will make fun of you
   by singing this song of despair about you:
   "We are finished,
      completely ruined!
   God has confiscated our land,
      taking it from us.
   He has given our fields
      to those who betrayed us.*"

**2:5**
Deut 32:8
Josh 18:4, 10

5 Others will set your boundaries then,
   and the LORD's people will have no say
      in how the land is divided.

*True and False Prophets*

**2:6**
Isa 30:10
Amos 2:12

6 "Don't say such things,"
   the people respond.*
"Don't prophesy like that.
   Such disasters will never come our way!"

**2:7**
Jer 15:16

7 Should you talk that way, O family of Israel?*
   Will the LORD's Spirit have patience with such behavior?
If you would do what is right,
   you would find my words comforting.

**2:8**
Jer 12:8
Mic 3:2-3; 7:2-3

8 Yet to this very hour
   my people rise against me like an enemy!
You steal the shirts right off the backs
   of those who trusted you,
making them as ragged as men
   returning from battle.

**2:9**
Jer 10:20

9 You have evicted women from their pleasant homes
   and forever stripped their children of all that God would give them.

**2:10**
Lev 18:24-28
Deut 12:9

10 Up! Begone!
   This is no longer your land and home,
for you have filled it with sin
   and ruined it completely.

**2:11**
Jer 5:31
Mic 3:5, 11

11 Suppose a prophet full of lies would say to you,
   "I'll preach to you the joys of wine and alcohol!"
That's just the kind of prophet you would like!

**2:4** Or *to those who took us captive.*   **2:6** Or *the prophets respond;* Hebrew reads *they prophesy.*   **2:7** Hebrew *O house of Jacob?* See note on 1:5a.

---

---

**2:5** Those who have been oppressing others will find the tables turned. They will end up not having any share in the decisions to divide the land because they won't have any surviving relatives.

**2:6, 7** If these messages seem harsh, remember that God did not want to take revenge on Israel; he wanted to get them back on the right path. The people had rejected what was true and right, and they needed stern discipline. Children may think discipline is harsh, but it helps keep them going in the right direction. If we only want God's comforting messages, we may miss what

he has for us. Listen whenever God speaks, even when the message is hard to take.

**2:11** The people liked the false prophets who told them only what they wanted to hear. Micah spoke against prophets who encouraged the people to feel comfortable in their sin. Preachers are popular when they don't ask too much of us and when they tell us our greed or lust might even be good for us. But a true teacher of God speaks the truth, regardless of what the listeners want to hear.

*Hope for Restoration*

12 "Someday, O Israel, I will gather you;
      I will gather the remnant who are left.
   I will bring you together again like sheep in a pen,
      like a flock in its pasture.
   Yes, your land will again
      be filled with noisy crowds!
13 Your leader will break out
      and lead you out of exile,
   out through the gates of the enemy cities,
      back to your own land.
   Your king will lead you;
      the LORD himself will guide you."

## 2. The trial of the leaders

*Judgment against Israel's Leaders*

**3** 1 I said, "Listen, you leaders of Israel!
         You are supposed to know right from wrong,
2 but you are the very ones
      who hate good and love evil.
   You skin my people alive
      and tear the flesh from their bones.
3 Yes, you eat my people's flesh,
      strip off their skin,
      and break their bones.
   You chop them up
      like meat for the cooking pot.
4 Then you beg the LORD for help in times of trouble!
      Do you really expect him to answer?
   After all the evil you have done,
      he won't even look at you!"

5 This is what the LORD says:
   "You false prophets are leading my people astray!
   You promise peace for those who give you food,
      but you declare war on those who refuse to feed you.
6 Now the night will close around you,
      cutting off all your visions.
   Darkness will cover you,
      putting an end to your predictions.
   The sun will set for you prophets,
      and your day will come to an end.
7 Then you seers will be put to shame,
      and you fortune-tellers will be disgraced.

**2:12**
Isa 11:11
Mic 4:7; 5:7; 7:18

**3:2**
Ezek 22:27

**3:3**
Ezek 11:7
Zeph 3:3

**3:4**
Deut 31:17
Isa 1:15; 59:2

**3:5**
Jer 6:14; 14:14-15

**3:6**
Isa 8:20-22; 29:10
Amos 8:9-10

**3:7**
Isa 44:25
Zech 13:4

**2:12, 13** Micah's prophecy telescopes two great events—Judah's return from captivity in Babylon, and the great gathering of all believers when the Messiah returns. God gave his prophets visions of various future events, but not necessarily the ability to discern when these events would happen. For example, they could not see the long period of time between the Babylonian captivity and the coming of the Messiah, but they could clearly see that the Messiah was coming. The purpose of this prophecy was not to predict exactly *how* this would occur but *that* it would. This gave the people hope and helped them turn from sin.

**3:1ff** Micah denounced the sins of the leaders, including priests and prophets—those responsible for teaching the people right from wrong. The leaders, who should have known the law and taught it to the people, had set the law aside and had become the worst of sinners. They were taking advantage of the very people they were supposed to serve. All sin is bad, but the sin that leads others astray is the worst of all.

**3:1** The dividing line between right and wrong often seems blurred, but spiritual leaders are supposed to help others see it. The Bible is God's guidebook to show us how to distinguish right and wrong. Spiritual leaders must understand the Bible's principles, teach them clearly, and exemplify them in their lives. While leaders cannot force people to do right, they should point them in that direction.

**3:2-4** The leaders had no compassion or respect for those they were supposed to serve. They were treating the people miserably in order to satisfy their own desires; then they had the gall to ask for God's help when they found themselves in trouble. We, like the leaders, should not treat God like a light switch to be turned on only as needed. Instead, we should always rely on him.

**3:5-7** Micah remained true to his calling and proclaimed God's words. In contrast, the false prophets' messages were geared to the favors they received. Not all those who claim to have

And you will cover your faces
because there is no answer from God."

**3:8**
Isa 58:1; 61:1-2

8 But as for me, I am filled with power—
with the Spirit of the LORD.
I am filled with justice and strength
to boldly declare Israel's sin and rebellion.
9 Listen to me, you leaders of Israel!
You hate justice and twist all that is right.

**3:10**
Jer 22:13-17
Ezek 22:25-28
Hab 2:9-12
**3:11**
Isa 48:2
Hos 4:18

10 You are building Jerusalem
on a foundation of murder and corruption.
11 You rulers make decisions based on bribes;
you priests teach God's laws only for a price;
you prophets won't prophesy unless you are paid.
Yet all of you claim to depend on the LORD.
"No harm can come to us," you say,
"for the LORD is here among us."

**3:12**
Jer 9:11; 26:18

12 Because of you, Mount Zion will be plowed like an open field;
Jerusalem will be reduced to ruins!
A thicket will grow on the heights
where the Temple now stands.

### The LORD's Future Reign

**4:1**
Pss 22:27; 86:9
Jer 3:17

**4** 1 In the last days, the mountain of the LORD's house
will be the highest of all—
the most important place on earth.
It will be raised above the other hills,
and people from all over the world will stream there to worship.

**4:2**
Ps 25:8-12
Isa 2:3; 4:3; 42:1-4
Jer 31:6
Zech 14:8-9

2 People from many nations will come and say,
"Come, let us go up to the mountain of the LORD,
to the house of Jacob's God.
There he will teach us his ways,
and we will walk in his paths."
For the LORD's teaching will go out from Zion;
his word will go out from Jerusalem.

**4:3**
Isa 11:3-5

3 The LORD will mediate between peoples
and will settle disputes between strong nations far away.
They will hammer their swords into plowshares
and their spears into pruning hooks.
Nation will no longer fight against nation,
nor train for war anymore.

**4:4**
Lev 26:6
Isa 40:5

4 Everyone will live in peace and prosperity,
enjoying their own grapevines and fig trees,
for there will be nothing to fear.

---

messages from God really do. Micah prophesied that one day
the false prophets would be shamed by their actions.

**3:8** Micah attributed the power of his ministry to the Spirit of the
Lord. Our power comes from the same source. Jesus told his
followers they would receive power to witness about him when
the Holy Spirit came on them (Acts 1:8). You can't witness effectively by relying on your own strength, because fear will keep you
from speaking out for God. Only by relying on the power of the
Holy Spirit can you live and witness for him.

**3:11** Micah warned the rulers, priests, and prophets of his day
to avoid bribes. Pastors today accept bribes when they allow those
who are big contributors to control the church. If fear of losing
money or members influences pastors to remain silent when they
should speak up for what is right, their churches are in danger.
We should remember that Judah was finally destroyed because
of the behavior of its religious leaders. A similar warning must
be directed at those who have money—*never* use your resources
to influence or manipulate God's ministers—that is bribery.

**3:12** Jerusalem would be destroyed just as Samaria was (1:6).
This happened in 586 B.C. when Nebuchadnezzar and the Babylonian army attacked the city (2 Kings 25). Although Micah blamed
the corrupt leaders, the people were not without fault. They
allowed the corruption to continue without turning to God or
calling for justice.

**4:1ff** The phrase "in the last days" describes the days when God
will reign over his perfect Kingdom (see 4:1-8). The "mountain
of the LORD's house" is Mount Zion. This will be an era of peace
and blessing, a time when war will be forever ended. We cannot
pinpoint its date, but God has promised that it *will* arrive (see
also Isaiah 2:2; Jeremiah 16:15; Joel 3:1ff; Zechariah 14:9-11;
Malachi 3:17, 18; Revelation 19—22).
    Verses 9-13 predicted the Babylonian captivity in 586 B.C.,
even before Babylon became a powerful empire. Just as God
promises a time of peace and prosperity, he also promises judgment and punishment for all who refuse to follow him. Both
results are certain.

The LORD of Heaven's Armies
   has made this promise!

5 Though the nations around us follow their idols,
   we will follow the LORD our God forever and ever.

### Israel's Return from Exile

6 "In that coming day," says the LORD,
   "I will gather together those who are lame,
     those who have been exiles,
     and those whom I have filled with grief.
7 Those who are weak will survive as a remnant;
   those who were exiles will become a strong nation.
Then I, the LORD, will rule from Jerusalem*
   as their king forever."

8 As for you, Jerusalem,
   the citadel of God's people,*
your royal might and power
   will come back to you again.
The kingship will be restored
   to my precious Jerusalem.

9 But why are you now screaming in terror?
   Have you no king to lead you?
Have your wise people all died?
   Pain has gripped you like a woman in childbirth.
10 Writhe and groan like a woman in labor,
   you people of Jerusalem,*
for now you must leave this city
   to live in the open country.
You will soon be sent in exile
   to distant Babylon.
But the LORD will rescue you there;
   he will redeem you from the grip of your enemies.

11 Now many nations have gathered against you.
   "Let her be desecrated," they say.
   "Let us see the destruction of Jerusalem.*"
12 But they do not know the LORD's thoughts
   or understand his plan.
These nations don't know
   that he is gathering them together
to be beaten and trampled
   like sheaves of grain on a threshing floor.
13 "Rise up and crush the nations, O Jerusalem!"*
   says the LORD.
"For I will give you iron horns and bronze hooves,
   so you can trample many nations to pieces.
You will present their stolen riches to the LORD,
   their wealth to the LORD of all the earth."

**4:5** 2 Kgs 17:29, 34

**4:6** Zeph 3:19

**4:7** Isa 9:6-7; 24:23

**4:8** Ps 48:12 Isa 1:26 Zech 9:10

**4:9** Jer 8:19

**4:10** 2 Kgs 20:18 Isa 48:20 Hos 2:14 Mic 7:8-12

**4:11** Isa 5:25-30

**4:12** Ps 147:19-20 Isa 55:8

**4:13** Isa 41:15-16; 60:9

---

**4:7** Hebrew *Mount Zion.*   **4:8** Hebrew *As for you, Migdal-eder, / the Ophel of the daughter of Zion.*   **4:10** Hebrew *O daughter of Zion.*   **4:11** Hebrew *of Zion.*   **4:13** Hebrew *"Rise up and thresh, O daughter of Zion."*

---

**4:9-13** Micah predicted the end of the kings. This was a drastic statement to the people of Judah who thought that their kingdom would last forever. Micah also said that Babylon would destroy the land of Judah and carry away its king, but that after a while God would help his people return to their land. This all happened just as Micah prophesied, and these events are recorded in 2 Chronicles 36:9-23 and Ezra 1–2.

**4:12** When God reveals the future, his purpose goes beyond satisfying our curiosity. He wants us to change our present behavior because of what we know about the future. Forever begins now; and a glimpse of God's plan for his followers should motivate us to serve him, no matter what the rest of the world may do.

**5:1**
Lam 3:30

# 5

¹*Mobilize! Marshal your troops!
　　The enemy is laying siege to Jerusalem.
They will strike Israel's leader
　in the face with a rod.

## A Ruler from Bethlehem

**5:2**
Jer 30:21
Zech 9:9
†Matt 2:6
John 1:1-2; 7:42

²* But you, O Bethlehem Ephrathah,
　are only a small village among all the people of Judah.
Yet a ruler of Israel will come from you,
　one whose origins are from the distant past.

**5:3**
Isa 10:20-22
Hos 11:8

³ The people of Israel will be abandoned to their enemies
　until the woman in labor gives birth.
Then at last his fellow countrymen
　will return from exile to their own land.

**5:4**
Isa 52:10

⁴ And he will stand to lead his flock with the LORD's strength,
　in the majesty of the name of the LORD his God.
Then his people will live there undisturbed,
　for he will be highly honored around the world.

**5:5**
Isa 8:7-8; 9:6

⁵　And he will be the source of peace.

When the Assyrians invade our land
　and break through our defenses,
we will appoint seven rulers to watch over us,
　eight princes to lead us.

**5:6**
Gen 10:8-11
Isa 37:36-37
Nah 2:11-13

⁶ They will rule Assyria with drawn swords
　and enter the gates of the land of Nimrod.
He will rescue us from the Assyrians
　when they pour over the borders to invade our land.

## The Remnant Purified

**5:7**
Deut 32:2

⁷ Then the remnant left in Israel*
　will take their place among the nations.
They will be like dew sent by the LORD
　or like rain falling on the grass,
which no one can hold back
　and no one can restrain.

**5:8**
Gen 49:9
Zech 10:5

⁸ The remnant left in Israel
　will take their place among the nations.
They will be like a lion among the animals of the forest,
　like a strong young lion among flocks of sheep and goats,

**5:1** Verse 5:1 is numbered 4:14 in Hebrew text.　**5:2** Verses 5:2-15 are numbered 5:1-14 in Hebrew text.
**5:7** Hebrew *in Jacob;* also in 5:8. See note on 1:5a.

---

**5:1** This leader was probably King Zedekiah, who was reigning in Jerusalem when Nebuchadnezzar conquered the city (2 Kings 25:1, 2). Zedekiah was the last of the kings in David's line to sit on the throne in Jerusalem. Micah said that the next king in David's line would be the Messiah, who would establish a Kingdom that would never end.

**5:1ff** Jerusalem's leaders were obsessed with wealth and position, but Micah prophesied that mighty Jerusalem, with all its wealth and power, would be besieged and destroyed. Its king could not save it. In contrast, Bethlehem, a tiny town, would be the birthplace of the only ruler who could save his people. This deliverer, the Messiah, would be born as a baby in Bethlehem (Luke 2:4-7) and eventually would reign as the eternal King (Revelation 19–22).

**5:2** Ephrathah was the district in which Bethlehem was located.

**5:2** This ruler is Jesus, the Messiah. Micah accurately predicted Christ's birthplace hundreds of years before Jesus was born. The promised eternal King in David's line, who would come to live as a man, had been alive forever—"whose origins are from the distant past." Although eternal, Christ entered human history as the man, Jesus of Nazareth.

**5:5** This chapter provides one of the clearest Old Testament prophecies of Christ's coming. The key descriptive phrase is "he will be the source of peace." In one of Christ's final talks he said, "I am leaving you with a gift—peace of mind and heart. And the peace I give is a gift the world cannot give. So don't be troubled or afraid" (John 14:27). Because of Christ's first coming, we have the opportunity to experience peace with God with no more fear of judgment and no more conflict and guilt. Christ's peace gives us assurance even though wars continue. At Christ's second coming, all wars and weapons will be destroyed (4:3-5).

**5:5** Micah's prophecy of seven rulers and eight princes is a figurative way of saying that the Messiah will raise up many good leaders when he returns to reign. This contrasts with Micah's words in chapter 3 about Judah's corrupt leaders. "The Assyrians" symbolically refer to all nations in every age that oppose God's people. These good leaders will help Christ defeat all evil in the world.

**5:6** The land of Nimrod is another name for Assyria, which, in this case, is a symbol of all the evil nations in the world.

pouncing and tearing as they go
    with no rescuer in sight.
9 The people of Israel will stand up to their foes,
    and all their enemies will be wiped out.

10 "In that day," says the LORD,
    "I will slaughter your horses
      and destroy your chariots.
11 I will tear down your walls
    and demolish your defenses.
12 I will put an end to all witchcraft,
    and there will be no more fortune-tellers.
13 I will destroy all your idols and sacred pillars,
    so you will never again worship the work of your own hands.
14 I will abolish your idol shrines with their Asherah poles
    and destroy your pagan cities.
15 I will pour out my vengeance
    on all the nations that refuse to obey me."

**5:10**
Hos 14:3
Zech 9:10

**5:11**
Isa 2:12-17
Hos 10:14

**5:12**
Deut 18:10-12

**5:14**
Exod 34:13

**5:15**
Isa 1:24; 65:12

## 3. The trial of the people
*The LORD's Case against Israel*

**6** Listen to what the LORD is saying:

"Stand up and state your case against me.
    Let the mountains and hills be called to witness your complaints.
2 And now, O mountains,
    listen to the LORD's complaint!
He has a case against his people.
    He will bring charges against Israel.

3 "O my people, what have I done to you?
    What have I done to make you tired of me?
    Answer me!
4 For I brought you out of Egypt
    and redeemed you from slavery.
    I sent Moses, Aaron, and Miriam to help you.
5 Don't you remember, my people,
    how King Balak of Moab tried to have you cursed
    and how Balaam son of Beor blessed you instead?
And remember your journey from Acacia Grove* to Gilgal,
    when I, the LORD, did everything I could
    to teach you about my faithfulness."

**6:2**
Hos 4:1; 12:2

**6:3**
Jer 2:5, 31

**6:4**
Exod 20:1-2
Ps 77:20

**6:5**
Num 22:5-6; 25:1
Josh 5:9-10

**6:5** Hebrew *Shittim*.

---

**5:10** When God rules in his eternal Kingdom, our strength and deliverance will not be found in military might but in God's almighty power. God will destroy all the weapons that people use for security. Armies will not be needed because God will rule in the heart of every person. Instead of being overwhelmed by fear of invasion or nuclear attack, we should have confidence in God.

**5:12-14** Idols, sacred pillars, and Asherah poles were all part of pagan worship.

**6:1ff** Here Micah pictures a courtroom. God, the Judge, tells his people what he requires of them and recites all the ways they have wronged both him and others. Chapters 4 and 5 are full of hope; chapters 6 and 7 proclaim judgment and appeal to the people to repent.

**6:1, 2** God called to the mountains to confirm the people's guilt. The mountains would serve as excellent witnesses, for it was in the high places that the people had built pagan altars and had sacrificed to false gods (1 Kings 14:23; Jeremiah 17:2, 3; Ezekiel 20:28).

**6:3** The people would never be able to answer this question

because God had done nothing wrong. In fact, God had been exceedingly patient with them, had always lovingly guided them, and had given them every opportunity to return to him. If God asked you, "What have I done to you?" how would you reply?

**6:5** The story of Balak and Balaam is found in Numbers 22–24. Acacia Grove was the Israelites' campsite east of the Jordan River just before they entered the Promised Land (Joshua 2:1). There the people received many of God's instructions about how to live. Gilgal, their first campsite after crossing the Jordan (Joshua 4:19), was where the people renewed their covenant with God (Joshua 5:3-9). These two places represent God's loving care for his people: his willingness both to protect them and to warn them about potential troubles. In Micah's day, the people had forgotten this covenant and its benefits and had turned away from God.

**6:5** God continued to be kind to his forgetful people, but their short memory and lack of thankfulness condemned them. When people refuse to see how fortunate they are and begin to take God's gifts for granted, they become self-centered. Regularly remember God's goodness and thank him. Remembering God's past protection will help you see his present provision.

**6:6**
Pss 40:6-8;
51:16-17

6 What can we bring to the LORD?
  What kind of offerings should we give him?
Should we bow before God
  with offerings of yearling calves?

**6:7**
Lev 18:21; 20:1-5
Ps 50:9
Isa 40:16

7 Should we offer him thousands of rams
  and ten thousand rivers of olive oil?
Should we sacrifice our firstborn children
  to pay for our sins?

**6:8**
Deut 10:12-13
Isa 57:15

8 No, O people, the LORD has told you what is good,
  and this is what he requires of you:
to do what is right, to love mercy,
  and to walk humbly with your God.

### Israel's Guilt and Punishment

9 Fear the LORD if you are wise!
  His voice calls to everyone in Jerusalem:
"The armies of destruction are coming;
  the LORD is sending them.*

**6:10**
Jer 5:26-27
Amos 3:10; 8:5

10 What shall I say about the homes of the wicked
  filled with treasures gained by cheating?
What about the disgusting practice
  of measuring out grain with dishonest measures?*

11 How can I tolerate your merchants
  who use dishonest scales and weights?

**6:12**
Isa 3:8

12 The rich among you have become wealthy
  through extortion and violence.
Your citizens are so used to lying
  that their tongues can no longer tell the truth.

**6:13**
Isa 1:7; 6:11

13 "Therefore, I will wound you!
  I will bring you to ruin for all your sins.

**6:14**
Lev 26:26
Isa 9:20; 30:6

14 You will eat but never have enough.
  Your hunger pangs and emptiness will remain.
And though you try to save your money,
  it will come to nothing in the end.
You will save a little,
  but I will give it to those who conquer you.

**6:15**
Deut 28:38-40
Jer 12:13
Amos 5:11
Zeph 1:13

15 You will plant crops
  but not harvest them.
You will press your olives
  but not get enough oil to anoint yourselves.
You will trample the grapes
  but get no juice to make your wine.

**6:16**
1 Kgs 16:25, 29-33
Jer 7:24; 18:15-16;
25:9

16 You keep only the laws of evil King Omri;
  you follow only the example of wicked King Ahab!
Therefore, I will make an example of you,
  bringing you to complete ruin.
You will be treated with contempt,
  mocked by all who see you."

**6:9** Hebrew *"Listen to the rod. / Who appointed it?"*   **6:10** Hebrew *of using the short ephah?* The ephah was a unit for measuring grain.

---

**6:6-8** Israel responded to God's request by trying to appease him with sacrifices, hoping he would then leave them alone. But sacrifices and other religious rituals aren't enough; God wants changed lives. He wants his people to be fair, just, merciful, and humble. God wants us to become *living* sacrifices (Romans 12:1, 2), not just doing religious deeds, but living rightly (Jeremiah 4:4; Hebrews 9:14). It is impossible to follow God consistently without his transforming love in our hearts.

**6:8** People have tried all kinds of ways to please God (6:6, 7), but God has made his wishes clear: He wants his people to do what is

right, love mercy, and walk humbly with him. In your efforts to please God, examine these areas on a regular basis. Are you fair in your dealings with people? Do you show mercy to those who wrong you? Are you learning humility?

**6:16** Omri reigned over Israel and led the people into idol worship (1 Kings 16:21-26). Ahab, his son, was Israel's most wicked king (1 Kings 16:29-33). If the people were following the commands and practices of these kings, they were in bad shape. Such pervasive evil was ripe for punishment.

## Misery Turned to Hope

**7** ¹ How miserable I am!
I feel like the fruit picker after the harvest
who can find nothing to eat.
Not a cluster of grapes or a single early fig
can be found to satisfy my hunger.

² The godly people have all disappeared;
not one honest person is left on the earth.
They are all murderers,
setting traps even for their own brothers.

³ Both their hands are equally skilled at doing evil!
Officials and judges alike demand bribes.
The people with influence get what they want,
and together they scheme to twist justice.

⁴ Even the best of them is like a brier;
the most honest is as dangerous as a hedge of thorns.
But your judgment day is coming swiftly now.
Your time of punishment is here, a time of confusion.

⁵ Don't trust anyone—
not your best friend or even your wife!

⁶ For the son despises his father.
The daughter defies her mother.
The daughter-in-law defies her mother-in-law.
Your enemies are right in your own household!

⁷ As for me, I look to the LORD for help.
I wait confidently for God to save me,
and my God will certainly hear me.

⁸ Do not gloat over me, my enemies!
For though I fall, I will rise again.
Though I sit in darkness,
the LORD will be my light.

⁹ I will be patient as the LORD punishes me,
for I have sinned against him.
But after that, he will take up my case
and give me justice for all I have suffered from my enemies.
The LORD will bring me into the light,
and I will see his righteousness.

¹⁰ Then my enemies will see that the LORD is on my side.
They will be ashamed that they taunted me, saying,
"So where is the LORD—
that God of yours?"
With my own eyes I will see their downfall;
they will be trampled like mud in the streets.

**7:1** Hos 9:10
**7:2** Isa 57:1; 59:7 Jer 5:26 Hos 5:1
**7:3** Prov 4:16-17
**7:4** Isa 10:3; 22:5 Ezek 2:6; 28:24 Nah 1:10
**7:5** Jer 9:4-5
**7:6** †Matt 10:35-36 †Luke 12:53
**7:7** Pss 4:3; 130:5
**7:8** Prov 24:15-16 Isa 9:2 Amos 9:11
**7:9** Ps 37:6 Jer 50:34
**7:10** Isa 51:23 Zech 10:5

**7:1ff** This chapter begins in gloom (7:1-6) and ends in hope (7:8-20). Micah watched as society rotted around him. Rulers demanded gifts; judges accepted bribes; corruption was universal. But God promised to lead the people out of the darkness of sin and into his light. Then the people would praise him for his faithfulness. God alone is perfectly faithful.

**7:1-4** Micah could not find an honest person anywhere in the land. Even today, fair-mindedness (uprightness, honesty, integrity) is difficult to find. Society rationalizes sin, and even believers sometimes compromise Christian principles in order to do what they want. It is easy to convince ourselves that we deserve a few breaks, especially when "everyone else" is doing it. But the standards for honesty come from God, not society. We are to be honest because God is truth, and we are to be like him.

**7:5, 6** Sin had affected the government leaders and society in general. Deceit and dishonesty had even ruined the family, the core of society. As a result, the only way left to purify the people was

God's judgment. This would draw the nation back to God and restore them from the inside out.

**7:7-10** Micah showed great faith in God both personally (7:7) and on Israel's behalf (7:8-10) as he proclaimed that (1) he would wait upon God because God hears and saves when help is needed, (2) God would bring his people through when times were tough, (3) Israel must be patient in punishment because God would bring them out of the darkness, and (4) their enemies would be punished. We, too, can have a relationship with God that can allow us to have confidence like Micah's. It doesn't take unusual talent; it simply takes faith in God and a willingness to act on that faith.

**7:9** Micah understood that if the people would be patient and obedient while they were being punished, God would forgive them and show his goodness again (Lamentations 3:39-41). Punishment does not mean rejection. The people were being punished in order to bring them back to God, not to send them away from him. When you face trials because of your sin, do not be angry with

**7:11**
Amos 9:11

11 In that day, Israel, your cities will be rebuilt,
    and your borders will be extended.

**7:12**
Isa 11:16; 19:23-25

12 People from many lands will come and honor you—
    from Assyria all the way to the towns of Egypt,
    from Egypt all the way to the Euphrates River,*
    and from distant seas and mountains.

**7:13**
Isa 3:10-11

13 But the land* will become empty and desolate
    because of the wickedness of those who live there.

### The LORD's Compassion on Israel

**7:14**
Amos 9:11

14 O LORD, protect your people with your shepherd's staff;
    lead your flock, your special possession.
    Though they live alone in a thicket
        on the heights of Mount Carmel,*
    let them graze in the fertile pastures of Bashan and Gilead
        as they did long ago.

**7:15**
Exod 3:20

15 "Yes," says the LORD,
    "I will do mighty miracles for you,
    like those I did when I rescued you
        from slavery in Egypt."

**7:16**
Mic 3:7

16 All the nations of the world will stand amazed
        at what the LORD will do for you.
    They will be embarrassed
        at their feeble power.
    They will cover their mouths in silent awe,
        deaf to everything around them.

**7:17**
Gen 3:14
Pss 9:20; 72:9

17 Like snakes crawling from their holes,
        they will come out to meet the LORD our God.
    They will fear him greatly,
        trembling in terror at his presence.

**7:18**
Jer 4:2; 32:41

18 Where is another God like you,
        who pardons the guilt of the remnant,
        overlooking the sins of his special people?
    You will not stay angry with your people forever,
        because you delight in showing unfailing love.

**7:19**
Isa 43:25
Jer 50:20

19 Once again you will have compassion on us.
        You will trample our sins under your feet
        and throw them into the depths of the ocean!

**7:20**
Gen 24:27; 32:10
Deut 7:8, 12
Luke 1:72

20 You will show us your faithfulness and unfailing love
        as you promised to our ancestors Abraham and Jacob long ago.

7:12 Hebrew *the river.*   7:13 Or *earth.*   7:14 Or *surrounded by a fruitful land.*

God or afraid that he has rejected you. Instead, turn away from your sin, turn to God, and continue to be patient and obedient.

**7:14** Bashan and Gilead were fertile areas east of the Jordan, previously the territory of Reuben, Gad, and the half-tribe of Manasseh.

**7:18** God delights to show his unfailing love! He does not forgive grudgingly but is glad when we repent, and he offers forgiveness to all who come back to him. Today you can confess your sins and receive his loving forgiveness. Don't be too proud to accept God's free offer.

**7:20** In an age when religion was making little difference in people's lives, Micah said that God expected his people to do what is right, love mercy, and walk humbly with him (6:8). He requires the same of Christians today. In a world that is unjust, we must act justly and do what is right. In a world of tough breaks, we must be merciful. In a world of pride and self-sufficiency, we must walk humbly with God. Only when we live according to God's way will we begin to affect our homes, our society, and our world.

# NAHUM

| | | | |
|---|---|---|---|
| Manasseh becomes king of Judah 697 B.C. | | Ashurbanipal becomes king of Assyria 669 | The fall of Thebes; Nahum becomes a prophet 663 |

## VITAL STATISTICS

**PURPOSE:**
To pronounce God's judgment on Assyria and to comfort Judah with this truth

**AUTHOR:**
Nahum

**ORIGINAL AUDIENCE:**
The people of Nineveh and of Judah (the southern kingdom)

**DATE WRITTEN:**
Sometime during Nahum's prophetic ministry (probably between 663 and 612 B.C.)

**SETTING:**
This particular prophecy took place after the fall of Thebes in 663 B.C. (see 3:8–10).

**KEY VERSES:**
"The LORD is good, a strong refuge when trouble comes. He is close to those who trust in him. But he will sweep away his enemies in an overwhelming flood. He will pursue his foes into the darkness of night. Why are you scheming against the LORD? He will destroy you with one blow; he won't need to strike twice!" (1:7–9).

**KEY PLACE:**
Nineveh

THE SHRILL whistle pierces the air, and all the action on the court abruptly stops. Pointing to the offending player, the referee shouts, "Foul!"

Rules, fouls, and penalties are part of any game and are regulated and enforced vigorously by referees, umpires, judges, and other officials. Every participant knows that boundaries must be set and behavior monitored, or the game will degenerate into chaos.

The world also has laws—boundaries and rules for living established by God. But men and women regularly flaunt these regulations, hiding their infractions or overpowering others and declaring that might makes right. God calls this sin—willful disobedience, rebellion against his control, or apathy. And at times it seems as though the violators succeed—no whistles blow, no fouls are called, and individual dictators rule. The truth is, however, that ultimately justice will be served in the world. God will settle all accounts.

Assyria was the most powerful nation on earth. Proud in their self-sufficiency and military might, they plundered, oppressed, and slaughtered their victims. One hundred years earlier, Jonah had preached in the streets of the great city Nineveh; the people had heard God's message and had turned from their evil. But generations later, evil was again reigning, and the prophet Nahum pronounced judgment on this wicked nation. Nineveh is called a "city of murder" (3:1), a city of cruelty (3:19), and the Assyrians are judged for their pride (2:13), idolatry (1:14), murder, lies, treachery, and social injustice (3:1–19). Nahum predicted that this proud and powerful nation would be utterly destroyed because of its sins. The end came within 50 years.

In this judgment of Assyria and its capital city, Nineveh, God is judging a sinful world. And the message is clear: Disobedience, rebellion, and injustice will not prevail but will be punished severely by a righteous and holy God, who rules over all the earth.

As you read Nahum, sense God's wrath as he avenges sin and brings about justice. Then decide to live under his guidance and within his rules, commands, and guidelines for life.

## THE BLUEPRINT

1. Nineveh's judge (1:1–15)
2. Nineveh's judgment (2:1—3:19)

Nineveh, the capital of the Assyrian Empire, is the subject of Nahum's prophecy. The news of its coming destruction was a relief for Judah, who was subject to Assyrian domination. No longer would Judah be forced to pay tribute as insurance against invasions. Judah was comforted to know that God was still in control. Nineveh is an example to all rulers and nations of the world today. God is sovereign over even those who are seemingly invincible. We can be confident that God's power and justice will one day conquer all evil.

## MEGATHEMES

| THEME | EXPLANATION | IMPORTANCE |
|---|---|---|
| God Judges | God would judge the city of Nineveh for its idolatry, arrogance, and oppression. Although Assyria was the leading military power in the world, God would completely destroy this "invincible" nation. God allows no person or power to usurp or scoff at his authority. | Anyone who remains arrogant and resists God's authority will face his anger. No ruler or nation will get away with rejecting him. No individual will be able to hide from his judgment. Yet those who keep trusting God will be kept safe forever. |
| God Rules | God rules over all the earth, even over those who don't acknowledge him. God is all-powerful, and no one can thwart his plans. God will overcome any who attempt to defy him. Human power is futile against God. | If you are impressed by or afraid of any weapons, armies, or powerful people, remember that God alone can truly rescue you from fear or oppression. We must place our confidence in God because he alone rules all of history, all the earth, and our life. |

### 1. Nineveh's judge

**1** This message concerning Nineveh came as a vision to Nahum, who lived in Elkosh.

*The LORD's Anger against Nineveh*

**1:2**
Exod 20:5
Deut 4:24; 32:35

2 The LORD is a jealous God,
    filled with vengeance and rage.
He takes revenge on all who oppose him
    and continues to rage against his enemies!

**1:3**
Exod 34:5-7
Pss 50:3; 104:3

3 The LORD is slow to get angry, but his power is great,
    and he never lets the guilty go unpunished.
He displays his power in the whirlwind and the storm.
    The billowing clouds are the dust beneath his feet.

**1:4**
Isa 33:9
Matt 8:26

4 At his command the oceans dry up,
    and the rivers disappear.
The lush pastures of Bashan and Carmel fade,
    and the green forests of Lebanon wither.

**1:5**
Exod 19:19
2 Sam 22:8-9

5 In his presence the mountains quake,
    and the hills melt away;
the earth trembles,
    and its people are destroyed.

---

**1:1** Nahum, like Jonah, was a prophet to Nineveh, the capital of the Assyrian Empire, and he prophesied between 663 and 612 B.C. Jonah had seen Nineveh repent a century earlier (see the book of Jonah), but the city had fallen back into wickedness. Assyria, the world power controlling the Fertile Crescent, seemed unstoppable. Its ruthless and savage warriors had already conquered Israel, the northern kingdom, and were causing great suffering in Judah. So Nahum proclaimed God's anger against Assyria's evil. Within a few decades, the mighty Assyrian Empire would be toppled by Babylon.

**1:1** Elkosh was a village thought by some to be in southwest Judah.

**1:2** God alone has the right to be jealous and to carry out vengeance. *Jealousy* and *vengeance* may be surprising terms to associate with God. When humans are jealous and take vengeance, they are usually acting in a spirit of selfishness. But it is appropriate for God to insist on our complete allegiance,

and it is just for him to punish unrepentant evildoers. His jealousy and vengeance are unmixed with selfishness. Their purpose is to remove sin and restore peace to the world (Deuteronomy 4:24; 5:9).

**1:3** God is slow to get angry, but when he is ready to punish, even the earth trembles. Often people avoid God because they see evildoers in the world and hypocrites in the church. They don't realize that because God is slow to anger, he gives his true followers time to share his love and truth with evildoers. But judgment *will* come; God will not allow sin to go unchecked forever. When people wonder why God doesn't punish evil immediately, help them remember that if he did, none of us would be here. We can all be thankful that God gives people time to turn to him.

**1:4** Bashan and Carmel were very fertile areas.

6 Who can stand before his fierce anger?
　Who can survive his burning fury?
His rage blazes forth like fire,
　and the mountains crumble to dust in his presence.

7 The LORD is good,
　a strong refuge when trouble comes.
He is close to those who trust in him.

8 But he will sweep away his enemies
　in an overwhelming flood.
He will pursue his foes
　into the darkness of night.

9 Why are you scheming against the LORD?
He will destroy you with one blow;
　he won't need to strike twice!

10 His enemies, tangled like thornbushes
　and staggering like drunks,
　will be burned up like dry stubble in a field.

11 Who is this wicked counselor of yours
　who plots evil against the LORD?

12 This is what the LORD says:
"Though the Assyrians have many allies,
　they will be destroyed and disappear.
O my people, I have punished you before,
　but I will not punish you again.

13 Now I will break the yoke of bondage from your neck
　and tear off the chains of Assyrian oppression."

14 And this is what the LORD says concerning the Assyrians in Nineveh:
"You will have no more children to carry on your name.
　I will destroy all the idols in the temples of your gods.
I am preparing a grave for you
　because you are despicable!"

15 *Look! A messenger is coming over the mountains with good news!
　He is bringing a message of peace.
Celebrate your festivals, O people of Judah,
　and fulfill all your vows,
for your wicked enemies will never invade your land again.
　They will be completely destroyed!

## 2. Nineveh's judgment
*The Fall of Nineveh*

**2** 1*Your enemy is coming to crush you, Nineveh.
　　Man the ramparts! Watch the roads!
Prepare your defenses! Call out your forces!

**Cross-references:**
1:6 1 Kgs 19:11
1:7 1 Chr 16:34; Pss 25:8; 100:5
1:8 Isa 8:7
1:9 Pss 2:1-4; 21:11
1:10 Isa 9:18; Mal 4:1
1:13 Isa 9:4; Jer 2:20
1:14 Nah 3:4-6
1:15 Isa 29:7-8; 40:9; 52:7; Rom 10:15

**1:15** Verse 1:15 is numbered 2:1 in Hebrew text.　**2:1** Verses 2:1-13 are numbered 2:2-14 in Hebrew text.

---

**1:6** No person on earth can safely defy God, the Almighty, the Creator of all the universe. God, who controls the sun, the galaxies, and the vast stretches beyond, also controls the rise and fall of nations. How could a small temporal kingdom like Assyria, no matter how powerful, challenge God's awesome power? If only Assyria could have looked ahead to see the desolate mound of rubble that it would become—yet God would still be alive and well! Don't defy God; he will be here forever with greater power than that of all armies and nations combined.

**1:6-8** To people who refuse to believe, God's punishment is like an angry fire. To those who love him, his mercy is a refuge, supplying all their needs without diminishing his supply. But to God's enemies he is an overwhelming flood that will sweep them away. The relationship we have with God is up to us. What kind of relationship will you choose?

**1:11** The one "who plots evil against the LORD" could have been (1) Ashurbanipal (669–627 B.C.), king of Assyria during much of Nahum's life and the one who brought Assyria to the zenith of its power; (2) Sennacherib (705–681), who openly defied God (2 Kings 18:13-35), epitomizing rebellion against God; (3) no one king in particular but the entire evil monarchy. The point is that Nineveh would be destroyed for rebelling against God.

**1:12-15** The good news for Judah, whom Assyria afflicted, was that its conquerors and tormentors would be destroyed and would never rise to torment it again. Nineveh was so completely wiped out that its ruins were not identified until 1845.

**2:1ff** This chapter predicts the events of 612 B.C., when the combined armies of the Babylonians and the Medes sacked seemingly impregnable Nineveh.

**2:2**
Isa 60:15
Ezek 37:21-23

2 Even though the destroyer has destroyed Judah,
    the LORD will restore its honor.
Israel's vine has been stripped of branches,
    but he will restore its splendor.

**2:3**
Ezek 23:14-15

3 Shields flash red in the sunlight!
    See the scarlet uniforms of the valiant troops!
Watch as their glittering chariots move into position,
    with a forest of spears waving above them.*

**2:4**
Jer 4:13
Nah 3:2

4 The chariots race recklessly along the streets
    and rush wildly through the squares.
They flash like firelight
    and move as swiftly as lightning.

**2:5**
Jer 46:12

5 The king shouts to his officers;
    they stumble in their haste,
    rushing to the walls to set up their defenses.
6 The river gates have been torn open!
    The palace is about to collapse!

**2:7**
Isa 32:12; 59:11

7 Nineveh's exile has been decreed,
    and all the servant girls mourn its capture.
They moan like doves
    and beat their breasts in sorrow.

**2:8**
Jer 46:5

8 Nineveh is like a leaking water reservoir!
    The people are slipping away.
"Stop, stop!" someone shouts,
    but no one even looks back.
9 Loot the silver!
    Plunder the gold!
There's no end to Nineveh's treasures—
    its vast, uncounted wealth.

**2:10**
Josh 2:11

10 Soon the city is plundered, empty, and ruined.
    Hearts melt and knees shake.
The people stand aghast,
    their faces pale and trembling.

**2:11**
Isa 5:29

11 Where now is that great Nineveh,
    that den filled with young lions?
It was a place where people—like lions and their cubs—
    walked freely and without fear.

**2:3** Greek and Syriac versions read *into position, / the horses whipped into a frenzy.*

---

**NAHUM**
served as
a prophet
to Judah from
663–612 B.C.

*Climate of the times.* . . . . . . Manasseh, one of Judah's most wicked kings, ruled the land. He openly defied God and persecuted God's people. Assyria, the world power at that time, made Judah one of its vassal states. The people of Judah wanted to be like the Assyrians, who seemed to have all the power and possessions they wanted.

*Main message.* . . . . . . . . . . The mighty empire of Assyria that oppressed God's people would soon tumble.

*Importance of message.* . . . . Those who do evil and oppress others will one day meet a bitter end.

*Contemporary prophets* . . . Zephaniah (640–621 B.C.)

---

**2:2** Assyria had plundered and crushed the northern kingdom (Israel) and had deported its people in 722 B.C. (2 Kings 17:3-6; 18:9-11). Assyria had also attacked the southern kingdom (Judah) and had forced it to pay tribute. These two separate kingdoms had been formed after Solomon's reign. A civil dispute with Solomon's son had caused ten of the tribes to set up their own kingdom. They had become the northern kingdom, while the remaining two tribes (Judah and Benjamin) stayed loyal to David's line and became the southern kingdom.

**2:6** This reference to the opening of river gates could refer either to the enemy flowing into Nineveh like a flood (1:8) or to an actual flood of water. Some scholars suggest that dam gates, which were found in archaeological excavations, were closed to dam up the river. When an enormous amount of water had been accumulated, the gates were opened, allowing the water to flood Nineveh.

12 The lion tore up meat for his cubs
        and strangled prey for his mate.
He filled his den with prey,
        his caverns with his plunder.

13 "I am your enemy!"
        says the Lord of Heaven's Armies.
"Your chariots will soon go up in smoke.
        Your young men* will be killed in battle.
Never again will you plunder conquered nations.
        The voices of your proud messengers will be heard no more."

| | 2:13 |
| --- | --- |
| | Ps 46:9 |

### The Lord's Judgment against Nineveh

**3** ¹ What sorrow awaits Nineveh,
        the city of murder and lies!
She is crammed with wealth
        and is never without victims.

2 Hear the crack of whips,
        the rumble of wheels!
Horses' hooves pound,
        and chariots clatter wildly.

3 See the flashing swords and glittering spears
        as the charioteers charge past!
There are countless casualties,
        heaps of bodies—
so many bodies that
        people stumble over them.

4 All this because Nineveh,
        the beautiful and faithless city,
mistress of deadly charms,
        enticed the nations with her beauty.
She taught them all her magic,
        enchanting people everywhere.

5 "I am your enemy!"
        says the Lord of Heaven's Armies.
"And now I will lift your skirts
        and show all the earth your nakedness and shame.

6 I will cover you with filth
        and show the world how vile you really are.

7 All who see you will shrink back and say,
        'Nineveh lies in ruins.
Where are the mourners?'
        Does anyone regret your destruction?"

8 Are you any better than the city of Thebes,*
        situated on the Nile River, surrounded by water?
She was protected by the river on all sides,
        walled in by water.

| | 3:1 |
| --- | --- |
| | Ezek 24:6-9 |

| | 3:2 |
| --- | --- |
| | Nah 2:3-4 |

| | 3:3 |
| --- | --- |
| | Isa 34:13 |

| | 3:4 |
| --- | --- |
| | Isa 47:9 |
| | Rev 17:1-6; 18:2-3 |

| | 3:5 |
| --- | --- |
| | Isa 47:3 |

| | 3:6 |
| --- | --- |
| | Job 9:31 |
| | Isa 14:16 |

| | 3:7 |
| --- | --- |
| | Isa 51:19 |
| | Jer 15:5 |

| | 3:8 |
| --- | --- |
| | Isa 19:6-8 |
| | Jer 46:25 |
| | Ezek 30:14-16 |

**2:13** Hebrew *young lions.*    **3:8** Hebrew *No-amon;* also in 3:10.

---

**2:12–3:1** The major source of wealth for the Assyrian economy was the plunder taken from other nations. The Assyrians had taken the food of innocent people to maintain their luxurious standard of living, depriving others to supply their excesses. Depriving innocent people to support the luxury of a few is a sin that angers God. As Christians we must stand firm against this common but evil practice.

**2:13** God had given the people of Nineveh a chance to repent, which they did after hearing Jonah (see the book of Jonah). But they had returned to their sin, and its consequences were destroying them. There is a point for people, cities, and nations after which there is no turning back; Assyria had passed that point. We must warn others to repent while there is still time.

**3:4** Nineveh had used its beauty, prestige, and power to seduce other nations. Like a harlot, she had enticed them into false friendships. Then when the other nations relaxed, thinking Assyria was a friend, Assyria destroyed and plundered them. Beautiful and impressive on the outside, Nineveh was vicious and deceitful on the inside. Beneath attractive facades sometimes lie seduction and death. Don't let an institution, company, movement, or person seduce you into lowering your standards or compromising your moral principles.

**3:8-10** Thebes was a city in Egypt, the previous world power, that had stood in the path of Assyria's expansion in the south. The Assyrians had conquered Thebes 51 years before this prophecy was given. To Judah, surrounded to the north and south by

**3:9**
Isa 20:5-6
Jer 46:9

9 Ethiopia* and the land of Egypt
    gave unlimited assistance.
The nations of Put and Libya
    were among her allies.

**3:10**
2 Kgs 8:12
Ps 137:9
Hos 13:16

10 Yet Thebes fell,
    and her people were led away as captives.
Her babies were dashed to death
    against the stones of the streets.
Soldiers threw dice* to get Egyptian officers as servants.
    All their leaders were bound in chains.

**3:11**
Isa 49:26
Jer 25:15-27

11 And you, Nineveh, will also stagger like a drunkard.
    You will hide for fear of the attacking enemy.
12 All your fortresses will fall.
    They will be devoured like the ripe figs
that fall into the mouths
    of those who shake the trees.

**3:13**
Isa 19:16
Jer 50:37; 51:30

13 Your troops will be as weak
    and helpless as women.
The gates of your land will be opened wide to the enemy
    and set on fire and burned.

**3:14**
2 Chr 32:3-4
Nah 2:1

14 Get ready for the siege!
    Store up water!
    Strengthen the defenses!
Go into the pits to trample clay,
    and pack it into molds,
    making bricks to repair the walls.

**3:15**
Isa 66:15-16
Joel 1:4

15 But the fire will devour you;
    the sword will cut you down.
The enemy will consume you like locusts,
    devouring everything they see.
There will be no escape,
    even if you multiply like swarming locusts.
16 Your merchants have multiplied
    until they outnumber the stars.
But like a swarm of locusts,
    they strip the land and fly away.
17 Your guards* and officials are also like swarming locusts
    that crowd together in the hedges on a cold day.
But like locusts that fly away when the sun comes up,
    all of them will fly away and disappear.

**3:18**
1 Kgs 22:17
Ps 76:5-6
Isa 56:10
Jer 50:18

18 Your shepherds are asleep, O Assyrian king;
    your princes lie dead in the dust.
Your people are scattered across the mountains
    with no one to gather them together.

**3:19**
Jer 30:13
Lam 2:15
Mic 1:9

19 There is no healing for your wound;
    your injury is fatal.
All who hear of your destruction
    will clap their hands for joy.
Where can anyone be found
    who has not suffered from your continual cruelty?

**3:9** Hebrew *Cush*.  **3:10** Hebrew *They cast lots*.  **3:17** Or *princes*.

Assyria, the situation appeared hopeless. But God said that the same atrocities done in Thebes would happen in Nineveh.

**3:8-10** No power on earth can protect us from God's judgment or be a suitable substitute for his power in our lives. Thebes and Assyria put their trust in alliances and military power, but history would show that these were inadequate. Don't insist on learning through personal experience; instead, learn the lessons history has already taught. Put your trust in God above all else.

**3:19** All the nations hated to be ruled by the merciless Assyrians, but the nations wanted to be like Assyria—powerful, wealthy, prestigious—and they courted Assyria's friendship. In the same way, we don't like the idea of being ruled harshly, so we do what we can to stay on good terms with a powerful leader. And deep down, we would like to have that power. But power is seductive, so we should not try to get or hold on to it. Those who lust after power will be powerfully destroyed, as was the mighty Assyrian Empire.

# HABAKKUK

## VITAL STATISTICS

**PURPOSE:**
To show that God is still in control of the world despite the apparent triumph of evil

**AUTHOR:**
Habakkuk

**ORIGINAL AUDIENCE:**
The people of Judah (the southern kingdom)

**DATE WRITTEN:**
Between 612 and 589 B.C.

**SETTING:**
Babylon was becoming the dominant world power and Judah would soon feel Babylon's destructive force.

**KEY VERSE:**
"I have heard all about you, LORD. I am filled with awe by your amazing works. In this time of our deep need, help us again as you did in years gone by. And in your anger, remember your mercy" (3:2).

**KEY PEOPLE:**
Habakkuk, the Babylonians

**KEY PLACE:**
Judah

FROM innocent childhood queries to complex university discussions, life is filled with questions. Asking how and why and when, we probe beneath the surface to find satisfying answers. But not all questions have answers wrapped and neatly tied. These unanswered interrogations create more questions and nagging, spirit-destroying doubt. Some choose to live with their doubts, ignoring them and moving on with life. Others become cynical and hardened. But many reject those options and continue to ask, looking for answers.

Habakkuk was a man who sought answers. Troubled by what he observed, he asked difficult questions. These questions were not merely intellectual exercises or bitter complaints. Habakkuk saw a dying world, and it broke his heart. Why is there evil in the world? Why do the wicked seem to be winning? He boldly and confidently took his complaints directly to God. And God answered with an avalanche of proof and prediction.

The prophet's questions and God's answers are recorded in this book. As we turn the pages, we are immediately confronted with his urgent cries, "How long, O LORD, must I call for help? But you do not listen! 'Violence is everywhere!' I cry, but you do not come to save" (1:2). In fact, most of the first chapter is devoted to his questions. As chapter two begins, Habakkuk declares that he will wait to hear God's answers to his complaints. Then God begins to speak, telling the prophet to write his answer plainly so that all will see and understand. It may seem, God says, as though the wicked triumph, but eventually they will be judged, and righteousness will prevail. Judgment may not come quickly, but it *will* come. God's answers fill chapter two. Then Habakkuk concludes his book with a prayer of triumph. With questions answered and a new understanding of God's power and love, Habakkuk rejoices in who God is and in what he will do. "Yet I will rejoice in the LORD! I will be joyful in the God of my salvation! The Sovereign LORD is my strength! He makes me as surefooted as a deer, able to tread upon the heights" (3:18, 19).

Listen to the profound questions that Habakkuk boldly brings to God, and realize that you can also bring your complaints and inquiries to him. Listen to God's answers and rejoice that he is at work in the world and in your life.

## THE BLUEPRINT

1. Habakkuk's complaints (1:1—2:20)
2. Habakkuk's prayer (3:1–19)

When Habakkuk was troubled, he brought his concerns directly to God. After receiving God's answers, he responded with a prayer of faith. Habakkuk's example is one that should encourage us as we struggle to move from doubt to faith. We don't have to be afraid to ask questions of God. The problem is not with God and his ways but with our limited understanding of him.

## MEGATHEMES

| THEME | EXPLANATION | IMPORTANCE |
|---|---|---|
| Struggle and Doubt | Habakkuk asked God why the wicked in Judah were not being punished for their sin. He couldn't understand why a just God would allow such evil to exist. God promised to use the Babylonians to punish Judah. When Habakkuk cried out for answers in his time of struggle, God answered him with words of hope. | God wants us to come to him with our struggles and doubts. His answers may not be what we expect, however. God sustains us by revealing himself to us. Trusting him leads to quiet hope, not bitter resignation. |
| God's Sovereignty | Habakkuk asked God why he would use the wicked Babylonians to punish his people. God said that he would also punish the Babylonians after they had fulfilled his purpose. | God is still in control of this world in spite of the apparent triumph of evil. God doesn't overlook sin. One day he will rule the whole earth with perfect justice. |
| Hope | God is the Creator; he is all-powerful. He has a plan, and he will carry it out. He will punish sin. He is our strength and our place of safety. We can have confidence that he will love us and guard our relationship with him forever. | Hope means going beyond our unpleasant daily experiences to the joy of knowing God. We live by trusting in him, not by the benefits, happiness, or success we may experience in this life. Our hope comes from God. |

## 1. Habakkuk's complaints

**1**
1:1
Isa 13:1
Nah 1:1

This is the message that the prophet Habakkuk received in a vision.

*Habakkuk's Complaint*

1:2
Pss 13:1-4; 22:1-2
Jer 14:9

2 How long, O LORD, must I call for help?
     But you do not listen!
"Violence is everywhere!" I cry,
     but you do not come to save.

1:3
Jer 20:8

3 Must I forever see these evil deeds?
     Why must I watch all this misery?
Wherever I look,
     I see destruction and violence.
I am surrounded by people
     who love to argue and fight.

1:4
Pss 22:12; 119:126
Isa 5:20

4 The law has become paralyzed,
     and there is no justice in the courts.
The wicked far outnumber the righteous,
     so that justice has become perverted.

*The LORD's Reply*

1:5
Isa 29:9
†Acts 13:41

5 The LORD replied,

"Look around at the nations;
     look and be amazed!*

1:5 Greek version reads *Look, you mockers; / look and be amazed and die.* Compare Acts 13:41.

1:1 Habakkuk lived in Judah during the reign of Jehoiakim (2 Kings 23:36–24:5). He prophesied between the fall of Nineveh (the capital of Assyria) in 612 B.C. and the Babylonian invasion of Judah in 588 B.C. With Assyria in disarray, Babylon was becoming the dominant world power. This book records the prophet's dialogue with God concerning the questions, Why does God often seem indifferent in the face of evil? and Why do evil people seem to go unpunished? While other prophetic books brought God's word to people, this book brought people's questions to God. A "vision" is a message from God.

1:2-4 Saddened by the violence and corruption he saw around him, Habakkuk poured out his heart to God. Today injustice is still rampant, but don't let your concern cause you to doubt God or rebel against him. Instead, consider the message that God gave Habakkuk and recognize God's long-range plans and purposes. Realize that God is doing right, even when you do not understand why he works as he does.

1:5 God responded to Habakkuk's questions and concerns by stating that he would do amazing acts that would astound Habakkuk. When circumstances around us become almost unbearable,

For I am doing something in your own day,
    something you wouldn't believe
    even if someone told you about it.
6 I am raising up the Babylonians,*
    a cruel and violent people.
They will march across the world
    and conquer other lands.

**1:6**
Deut 28:49
2 Kgs 24:2

7 They are notorious for their cruelty
    and do whatever they like.

**1:7**
Jer 39:5-9

8 Their horses are swifter than cheetahs*
    and fiercer than wolves at dusk.
Their charioteers charge from far away.
    Like eagles, they swoop down to devour their prey.

**1:8**
Jer 4:13

9 "On they come, all bent on violence.
    Their hordes advance like a desert wind,
    sweeping captives ahead of them like sand.
10 They scoff at kings and princes
    and scorn all their fortresses.
They simply pile ramps of earth
    against their walls and capture them!

**1:10**
2 Kgs 25:6-7
2 Chr 36:6
Jer 32:24; 33:4-5
Ezek 26:7-11

11 They sweep past like the wind
    and are gone.
But they are deeply guilty,
    for their own strength is their god."

**1:11**
Jer 4:11-12

### Habakkuk's Second Complaint

12 O Lord my God, my Holy One, you who are eternal—
    surely you do not plan to wipe us out?
O Lord, our Rock, you have sent these Babylonians to correct us,
    to punish us for our many sins.

**1:12**
Deut 32:4, 30-31

13 But you are pure and cannot stand the sight of evil.
    Will you wink at their treachery?
Should you be silent while the wicked
    swallow up people more righteous than they?

**1:13**
Ps 50:21
1 Pet 1:15-16

14 Are we only fish to be caught and killed?
    Are we only sea creatures that have no leader?
15 Must we be strung up on their hooks
    and caught in their nets while they rejoice and celebrate?

**1:15**
Jer 16:16

**1:6** Or *Chaldeans.*   **1:8** Or *leopards.*

---

we wonder if God has forgotten us. But remember, he is in control. God has a plan and will judge evildoers in his time. If we are truly humble, we will be willing to accept God's answers and await his timing.

**1:5ff** God told the inhabitants of Jerusalem that they would be utterly amazed at what he was about to do. The people would, in fact, see a series of unbelievable events: (1) Their own independent and prosperous kingdom, Judah, would suddenly become a vassal nation; (2) Egypt, a world power for centuries, would be crushed almost overnight; (3) Nineveh, the capital of the Assyrian Empire, would be so completely ransacked that people would forget where it had been; and (4) the Babylonians would rise to power. Though these words were indeed amazing, the people saw them fulfilled during their lifetime.

**1:6** The Babylonians, who lived northwest of the Persian Gulf, made a rapid rise to power around 630 B.C. They began to assert themselves against the Assyrian Empire and by 605 B.C. had conquered Assyria and Egypt to become the strongest world power. But they were as wicked as the Assyrians, for they loved

to collect captives (1:9), were proud of their warfare tactics (1:10), and trusted in their military strength (1:11).

**1:10** Armies were able to take walled cities by building earthen ramps—heaping mounds of earth against the walls.

**1:11** Babylon was proud of its military might, strategies, armies, and weapons. With no regard for humanity, the armies brought home riches, plunder, prisoners, and tribute from the nations they conquered. Such is the essence of idolatry—asking the gods we make to help us get all we want. The essence of Christianity is asking the God *who made us* to help us give all we can in service to him. The goal of idolatry is self-glory; the aim of Christianity is God's glory.

**1:13** Judah's forthcoming punishment would be at the hands of the Babylonians. Habakkuk was appalled that God would use a nation even more wicked than Judah to punish it. But the Babylonians did not know they were being used by God to help Judah return to him, and Babylon's pride in its victories would be its downfall. Evil is self-destructive, and it is never beyond God's control. God may use whatever unusual instrument he chooses to correct or punish us. When we deserve punishment or correction, how can we complain about the kind of discipline God uses on us?

**1:16**
Jer 44:17-18

> 16 Then they will worship their nets
>     and burn incense in front of them.
> "These nets are the gods who have made us rich!"
>     they will claim.

**1:17**
Isa 14:6

> 17 Will you let them get away with this forever?
>     Will they succeed forever in their heartless conquests?

**2** ¹ I will climb up to my watchtower
>        and stand at my guardpost.
> There I will wait to see what the LORD says
>     and how he* will answer my complaint.

### The LORD's Second Reply

**2:2**
Deut 27:8
Isa 8:1
Rev 1:19

> 2 Then the LORD said to me,
>
> "Write my answer plainly on tablets,
>     so that a runner can carry the correct message to others.

**2:3**
Dan 8:17-19;
9:24-27; 10:1, 14
†Heb 10:37

> 3 This vision is for a future time.
>     It describes the end, and it will be fulfilled.
> If it seems slow in coming, wait patiently,
>     for it will surely take place.
>     It will not be delayed.

**2:4**
Pss 10:4; 49:17-20
Prov 3:6; 16:3
†Rom 1:17
†Gal 3:11
†Heb 10:38

> 4 "Look at the proud!
>     They trust in themselves, and their lives are crooked.
>     But the righteous will live by their faithfulness to God.*
> 5 Wealth* is treacherous,
>     and the arrogant are never at rest.

**2:1** As in Syriac version; Hebrew reads *I*.   **2:3b-4** Greek version reads *If the vision is delayed, wait patiently, / for it will surely come and not delay. / ⁴I will take no pleasure in anyone who turns away. / But the righteous person will live by my faith.* Compare Rom 1:17; Gal 3:11; Heb 10:37-38.   **2:5a** As in Dead Sea Scroll 1QpHab; other Hebrew manuscripts read *Wine*.

---

**HABAKKUK**
served as a
prophet to
Judah from
612–589 B.C.

| | |
|---|---|
| Climate of the times. . . . . . . | Judah's last four kings were wicked men who rejected God and oppressed their own people. Babylon invaded Judah twice before finally destroying it in 586 B.C. It was a time of fear, oppression, persecution, lawlessness, and immorality. |
| Main message. . . . . . . . . . | Habakkuk couldn't understand why God seemed to do nothing about the wickedness in society. Then he realized that faith in God alone would supply the answers to his questions. |
| Importance of message. . . . | Instead of questioning the ways of God, we should realize that he is totally just and we should have faith that he is in control and that one day evil will be utterly destroyed. |
| Contemporary prophets . . . | Jeremiah (627–586 B.C.), Daniel (605–536 B.C.), Ezekiel (593–571 B.C.) |

---

**2:1** The watchman and watchtower, often used by the prophets to show an attitude of expectation (Isaiah 21:8, 11; Jeremiah 6:17; Ezekiel 3:17), are pictures of Habakkuk's attitude of patient waiting and watching for God's response. Stone watchtowers were built on city walls or ramparts so that watchmen could see people (enemies or messengers) approaching their city while still at a distance. Watchtowers were also erected in vineyards to help guard the ripening grapes (Isaiah 5:2). Habakkuk wanted to be in the best position to receive God's message.

**2:2ff** This chapter records God's answers to Habakkuk's questions: (1) How long would evil prevail (1:2, 3)? (2) Why was Babylon chosen to punish Judah (1:13)? God said that the judgment, though slow to come, was certain. Although God used Babylon against Judah, he knew Babylon's sins and would punish it in due time.

**2:3** Evil and injustice seem to have the upper hand in the world. Like Habakkuk, Christians often feel angry and discouraged as they see what goes on. Habakkuk complained vigorously to God

about the situation. God's answer to Habakkuk is the same answer he would give us, "If it seems slow in coming, wait patiently, for it will surely take place." It isn't easy to be patient, but it helps to remember that God hates sin even more than we do. Punishment of sin will certainly come. As God told Habakkuk, "Wait patiently." We must trust God even when we don't under-stand why events occur as they do.

**2:4** The wicked Babylonians trusted in themselves and would fall; but the righteous will live by their faithfulness to God. This verse has inspired countless Christians. Paul quotes it in Romans 1:17 and Galatians 3:11. The writer of Hebrews quotes it in 10:38, just before the famous chapter on faith. And it is helpful to all Christians who must live through difficult times without seeing signs of hope. Christians must trust that God is directing all things according to his purposes.

They open their mouths as wide as the grave,*
and like death, they are never satisfied.
In their greed they have gathered up many nations
and swallowed many peoples.

6 "But soon their captives will taunt them.
They will mock them, saying,
'What sorrow awaits you thieves!
Now you will get what you deserve!
You've become rich by extortion,
but how much longer can this go on?'

**2:6**
Isa 14:4-5, 10
Jer 50:13, 34-35
Hab 2:9, 12, 15, 19

7 Suddenly, your debtors will take action.
They will turn on you and take all you have,
while you stand trembling and helpless.

**2:7**
Prov 29:1

8 Because you have plundered many nations,
now all the survivors will plunder you.
You committed murder throughout the countryside
and filled the towns with violence.

**2:8**
Isa 33:1
Zech 2:8-9

9 "What sorrow awaits you who build big houses
with money gained dishonestly!
You believe your wealth will buy security,
putting your family's nest beyond the reach of danger.

**2:9**
Jer 22:13

10 But by the murders you committed,
you have shamed your name and forfeited your lives.
11 The very stones in the walls cry out against you,
and the beams in the ceilings echo the complaint.

**2:11**
Josh 24:27
Luke 19:40

12 "What sorrow awaits you who build cities
with money gained through murder and corruption!
13 Has not the LORD of Heaven's Armies promised
that the wealth of nations will turn to ashes?
They work so hard,
but all in vain!

**2:12**
Mic 3:10
Hab 2:9, 15, 19

**2:13**
Isa 50:11

14 For as the waters fill the sea,
the earth will be filled with an awareness
of the glory of the LORD.

**2:14**
Pss 22:27; 86:9
Isa 11:9
Zech 14:9

15 "What sorrow awaits you who make your neighbors drunk!
You force your cup on them
so you can gloat over their shameful nakedness.

**2:15**
Hos 7:5

16 But soon it will be your turn to be disgraced.
Come, drink and be exposed!*
Drink from the cup of the LORD's judgment,
and all your glory will be turned to shame.

**2:16**
Jer 25:15-16

17 You cut down the forests of Lebanon.
Now you will be cut down.
You destroyed the wild animals,
so now their terror will be yours.
You committed murder throughout the countryside
and filled the towns with violence.

**2:17**
Jer 51:35

18 "What good is an idol carved by man,
or a cast image that deceives you?

**2:18**
Isa 42:17
Jer 2:27-28; 50:2

**2:5b** Hebrew as Sheol.   **2:16** Dead Sea Scrolls and Greek and Syriac versions read and stagger!

---

**2:9-13** Babylon's riches had come from the misfortunes of others, but these riches would only be fuel for the fire. The victims and their cities would cry out against Babylon. Money is not evil, but God condemns the love of riches and the evil means of acquiring them (1 Timothy 6:10). Be careful not to hunger for wealth so much that you lose your appetite for God. Do not allow money to take the place of family, friends, or God.

**2:18** Idolatry may seem like a sin that modern people do not commit. But idolatry is not just bowing down to idols; it is trusting in what one has made and, therefore, in one's own power as creator and sustainer. If we say we worship God but put our trust in bank accounts, homes, businesses, and organizations, then we are idolaters. Do you trust God more than you trust what your hands have made?

How foolish to trust in your own creation—
a god that can't even talk!

<sup>19</sup> What sorrow awaits you who say to wooden idols,
'Wake up and save us!'
To speechless stone images you say,
'Rise up and teach us!'
Can an idol tell you what to do?
They may be overlaid with gold and silver,
but they are lifeless inside.

<sup>20</sup> But the LORD is in his holy Temple.
Let all the earth be silent before him."

## 2. Habakkuk's prayer

**3** This prayer was sung by the prophet Habakkuk*:

<sup>2</sup> I have heard all about you, LORD.
I am filled with awe by your amazing works.
In this time of our deep need,
help us again as you did in years gone by.
And in your anger,
remember your mercy.

<sup>3</sup> I see God moving across the deserts from Edom,*
the Holy One coming from Mount Paran.*
His brilliant splendor fills the heavens,
and the earth is filled with his praise.
<sup>4</sup> His coming is as brilliant as the sunrise.
Rays of light flash from his hands,
where his awesome power is hidden.
<sup>5</sup> Pestilence marches before him;
plague follows close behind.
<sup>6</sup> When he stops, the earth shakes.
When he looks, the nations tremble.
He shatters the everlasting mountains
and levels the eternal hills.
He is the Eternal One!
<sup>7</sup> I see the people of Cushan in distress,
and the nation of Midian trembling in terror.

<sup>8</sup> Was it in anger, LORD, that you struck the rivers
and parted the sea?
Were you displeased with them?
No, you were sending your chariots of salvation!
<sup>9</sup> You brandished your bow
and your quiver of arrows.
You split open the earth with flowing rivers.

**Cross references (left margin):**

**2:19**
1 Kgs 18:26-29
Jer 10:4-5

**2:20**
Zeph 1:7
Zech 2:13

**3:2**
Pss 78:38-39; 85:6
Isa 54:8
Jer 10:7

**3:3**
Deut 5:24
Pss 48:10; 113:4;
148:13

**3:4**
Job 26:14
Pss 18:12; 104:1

**3:5**
Exod 12:29-30
Deut 32:24-25

**3:7**
Exod 15:14

**3:8**
Exod 7:19-20

**3:1** Hebrew adds *according to shigionoth*, probably indicating the musical setting for the prayer. **3:3a** Hebrew *Teman.* **3:3b** Hebrew adds *selah*; also in 3:9, 13. The meaning of this Hebrew term is uncertain; it is probably a musical or literary term.

**2:20** Idols have no life, no personhood, no power; they are empty chunks of wood or stone. Temples built to idols are equally empty; no one lives there. But the Lord *is* in his Temple. He is real, alive, and powerful. He is truly and fully God. Idolaters command their idols to save them, but we who worship the living God come to him in silent awe and reverence. We acknowledge that God is in control and knows what he is doing. Idols remain silent because they cannot answer. The living God, by contrast, speaks through his Word. Approach God reverently and wait silently to hear what he has to say.

**3:1ff** Habakkuk praised God for answering his questions. Evil will not triumph forever; God is in control, and he can be completely trusted to vindicate those who are faithful to him. We must patiently wait for him to act (3:16).

**3:2** Habakkuk knew that God was going to discipline the people of Judah and that it wasn't going to be a pleasant experience. But Habakkuk accepted God's will, asking for help and mercy. Habakkuk did not ask to escape the discipline, but he accepted the truth that Judah needed to learn a lesson. God still disciplines in love to bring his children back to him (Hebrews 12:5, 6). Accept God's discipline gladly, and ask him to help you change.

10 The mountains watched and trembled.
    Onward swept the raging waters.
The mighty deep cried out,
    lifting its hands to the LORD.
11 The sun and moon stood still in the sky
    as your brilliant arrows flew
    and your glittering spear flashed.

12 You marched across the land in anger
    and trampled the nations in your fury.
13 You went out to rescue your chosen people,
    to save your anointed ones.
You crushed the heads of the wicked
    and stripped their bones from head to toe.
14 With his own weapons,
    you destroyed the chief of those
who rushed out like a whirlwind,
    thinking Israel would be easy prey.
15 You trampled the sea with your horses,
    and the mighty waters piled high.

16 I trembled inside when I heard this;
    my lips quivered with fear.
My legs gave way beneath me,*
    and I shook in terror.
I will wait quietly for the coming day
    when disaster will strike the people who invade us.
17 Even though the fig trees have no blossoms,
    and there are no grapes on the vines;
even though the olive crop fails,
    and the fields lie empty and barren;
even though the flocks die in the fields,
    and the cattle barns are empty,
18 yet I will rejoice in the LORD!
    I will be joyful in the God of my salvation!
19 The Sovereign LORD is my strength!
    He makes me as surefooted as a deer,*
    able to tread upon the heights.

(For the choir director: This prayer is to be accompanied by stringed instruments.)

**3:16** Hebrew *Decay entered my bones.*   **3:19** Or *He gives me the speed of a deer.*

*Cross-references (right margin):*
**3:10** Ps 93:3
**3:12** Isa 41:15
**3:13** Ps 110:6
**3:14** Judg 7:22; Dan 11:40
**3:15** Hab 3:8
**3:17** Jer 5:17; Joel 1:10-12; Amos 4:9
**3:18** Ps 97:12; Isa 12:2; Luke 1:47; Phil 4:4
**3:19** Pss 18:13; 46:1-5

---

**3:17-19** Crop failure and the death of animals would devastate Judah. But Habakkuk affirmed that even in the times of starvation and loss, he would still rejoice in the Lord. Habakkuk's feelings were not controlled by the events around him but by faith in God's ability to give him strength. When nothing makes sense, and when troubles seem more than you can bear, remember that God gives strength. Take your eyes off your difficulties and look to God.

**3:19** God will give his followers strength and confidence in difficult times. They will run surefooted as deer across rough and dangerous terrain. At the proper time, God will bring about his justice and completely rid the world of evil. In the meantime, God's people need to live in the strength of his Spirit, confident in his ultimate victory over evil.

**3:19** The note to the choir director was to be used when this passage was sung as a psalm in Temple worship.

**3:19** Habakkuk had asked God why evil people prosper while the righteous suffer. God's answer: They don't, not in the long run. Habakkuk saw his own limitations in contrast to God's unlimited power and control of all the world's events. God is alive and in control of the world and its events. We cannot see all that God is doing, and we cannot see all that God will do. But we can be assured that he is God and will do what is right. Knowing this can give us confidence and hope in a confusing world.

# ZEPHANIAH

OVERWHELMING grief, prolonged distress, incessant abuse, continual persecution, and imminent punishment breed hopelessness and despair. "If only," we cry, as we search our mind for a way out and look to the skies for rescue. With just a glimmer of hope, we would take courage and carry on.

Hope is the silver shaft of sun breaking through the storm-darkened sky, words of comfort in the intensive care unit, the first spring bird perched on a snow-covered twig, and the finish line in sight. It is a rainbow, a song, a loving touch. Hope is knowing God and resting in his love.

As God's prophet, Zephaniah was bound to speak the truth. This he did clearly, thundering certain judgment and horrible punishment for all who would defy the Lord. God's awful wrath would sweep away everything in the land and destroy it. "'I will sweep away people and animals alike. I will sweep away the birds of the sky and the fish in the sea. I will reduce the wicked to heaps of rubble, and I will wipe humanity from the face of the earth,' says the LORD" (1:3). No living thing in the land would escape. And that terrible day was coming soon: "That terrible day of the LORD is near. Swiftly it comes—a day of bitter tears, a day when even strong men will cry out. It will be a day when the LORD's anger is poured out—a day of terrible distress and anguish, a day of ruin and desolation, a day of darkness and gloom, a day of clouds and blackness" (1:14, 15). We can sense the oppression and depression his listeners must have felt. They were judged guilty, and they were doomed.

But in the midst of this terrible pronouncement, there is hope. The first chapter of Zephaniah's prophecy is filled with terror. In chapter two, however, a whispered promise appears. "Seek the LORD, all who are humble, and follow his commands. Seek to do what is right and to live humbly. Perhaps even yet the LORD will protect you—protect you from his anger" (2:3). And a few verses later we read of "the remnant of the tribe of Judah" (2:7) who will be restored.

Finally in chapter three, the quiet refrain grows to a crescendo as God's salvation and deliverance for those who are faithful to him is declared. "Sing, O daughter of Zion; shout aloud, O Israel! Be glad and rejoice with all your heart, O daughter of Jerusalem! For the LORD will remove his hand of judgment and will disperse the armies of your enemy. And the LORD himself, the King of Israel, will live among you! At last your troubles will be over, and you will never again fear disaster" (3:14, 15). This is true hope, grounded in the knowledge of God's justice and in his love for his people.

As you read Zephaniah, listen carefully to the words of judgment. God does not take sin lightly, and it will be punished. But be encouraged by the words of hope—our God reigns, and he will rescue his own. Decide to be part of that faithful remnant of souls who humbly worship and obey the living Lord.

## VITAL STATISTICS

**PURPOSE:**
To shake the people of Judah out of their complacency and urge them to return to God

**AUTHOR:**
Zephaniah

**ORIGINAL AUDIENCE:**
The people of Judah (the southern kingdom)

**DATE WRITTEN:**
Probably near the end of Zephaniah's ministry (640–621 B.C.), when King Josiah's great reforms began

**SETTING:**
King Josiah of Judah was attempting to reverse the evil trends set by the two previous kings of Judah—Manasseh and Amon. Josiah was able to extend his influence because no strong superpower was dominating the world at that time (Assyria was declining rapidly). Zephaniah's prophecy may have been the motivating factor in Josiah's reform. Zephaniah was a contemporary of Jeremiah.

**KEY VERSE:**
"Seek the LORD, all who are humble, and follow his commands. Seek to do what is right and to live humbly. Perhaps even yet the LORD will protect you—protect you from his anger on that day of destruction" (2:3).

**KEY PLACE:**
Jerusalem

## THE BLUEPRINT

1. The day of judgment (1:1—3:8)
2. The day of hope (3:9–20)

Zephaniah warned the people of Judah that if they refused to repent, the entire nation, including the beloved city of Jerusalem, would be lost. The people knew that God would eventually bless them, but Zephaniah made it clear that there would be judgment first, then blessing. This judgment would not be merely punishment for sin, but it would also be a means of purifying the people. Though we live in a fallen world surrounded by evil, we can hope in the perfect Kingdom of God to come, and we can allow any punishment that touches us now to purify us from sin.

## MEGATHEMES

| THEME | EXPLANATION | IMPORTANCE |
|---|---|---|
| Day of Judgment | Destruction was coming because Judah had forsaken the Lord. The people worshiped Baal, Molech, and the stars in heaven. Even the priests mixed pagan practices with faith in God. God's punishment for sin was on the way. | To escape God's judgment we must listen to him, accept his correction, trust him, and seek his guidance. If we accept him as our Lord, we can escape his condemnation. |
| Indifference to God | Although there had been occasional attempts at renewal, Judah had no sorrow for its sins. The people were prosperous, and they no longer cared about God. God's demands for righteous living seemed irrelevant to the people, whose security and wealth made them complacent. | Don't let material comfort be a barrier to your commitment to God. Prosperity can lead to an attitude of proud self-sufficiency. We need to admit that money won't save us and that we cannot save ourselves. Only God can save us. |
| Day of Cheer | The day of judgment will also be a day of cheer. God will judge all those who mistreat his people. He will purify his people, purging away all sin and evil. God will restore his people and give them hope. | When people are purged of sin, there is great relief and hope. No matter how difficult our experience now, we can look forward to the day of celebration when God will completely restore us. It will truly be a day to rejoice! |

## 1. The day of judgment

**1** The LORD gave this message to Zephaniah when Josiah son of Amon was king of Judah. Zephaniah was the son of Cushi, son of Gedaliah, son of Amariah, son of Hezekiah.

1:1
2 Kgs 22:1–23:28
2 Chr 34:1–35:26

### Coming Judgment against Judah

2 "I will sweep away everything
   from the face of the earth," says the LORD.

1:2
Isa 6:11

3 "I will sweep away people and animals alike.
   I will sweep away the birds of the sky and the fish in the sea.
I will reduce the wicked to heaps of rubble,*
   and I will wipe humanity from the face of the earth," says the LORD.

1:3
Isa 6:11-12
Jer 4:25; 9:10

4 "I will crush Judah and Jerusalem with my fist
   and destroy every last trace of their Baal worship.
I will put an end to all the idolatrous priests,
   so that even the memory of them will disappear.

1:4
2 Kgs 23:4-7

5 For they go up to their roofs
   and bow down to the sun, moon, and stars.
They claim to follow the LORD,
   but then they worship Molech,* too.

1:5
1 Kgs 11:33

**1:3** The meaning of the Hebrew is uncertain. **1:5** Hebrew *Malcam*, a variant spelling of Molech; or it could possibly mean *their king*.

**1:1** Zephaniah prophesied in the days of Josiah king of Judah (640–609 B.C.). Josiah followed God, and during his reign the Book of the Law was discovered in the Temple. After reading it, Josiah began a great religious revival in Judah (2 Kings 22:1–23:25). Zephaniah helped fan the revival by warning the people that judgment would come if they did not turn from their sins. Although this great revival turned the nation back to God, it did not fully eliminate idolatry and lasted only a short time. Just four years after Josiah's death, Nebuchadnezzar swept into Palestine and took the first wave of Israelite captives into exile.

**1:2ff** The people of Judah were clearly warned by the highest authority of all—God. They refused to listen, either because they doubted God's prophet and thus did not believe that the message was from God, or because they doubted God himself and thus did not believe that he would do what he said. If we refuse to listen to God's Word, the Bible, we are as shortsighted as the people of Judah, and like them, we will be punished.

**1:4** When the Israelites arrived in the Promised Land, God had commanded that they completely rid the land of its pagan inhabitants who worshiped idols. But the Israelites failed to do so, and gradually they began to worship the Canaanites' gods.

The Canaanites believed in many gods that represented many aspects of life, and the chief god was Baal, symbolizing strength and fertility. God was extremely angry when his people turned from him to Baal.

**1:4-6** Idols have been worshiped down through history. More than just a stone statue, an idol can be anything reverenced more than God. Thus, idol worship is prevalent even today: People trust in themselves, money, or power and not in God. But ultimately all idols will prove worthless, and the true God will prevail. Seek God first (Matthew 6:33), and have no other gods before him (Exodus 20:3).

**1:5** The people had become polytheistic, worshiping the Lord *and* all the other gods of the land. They added the "best" of pagan worship to the worship of God. But God commands that he alone be worshiped (Exodus 20:1-5); thus, the people committed a horrible sin. One of these other gods was Molech, the national god of the Ammonites. The worship of Molech included child sacrifice, an abominable sin. From the time of Moses, the Israelites had been warned about worshiping this false god (Leviticus 18:21; 20:5), but they refused to take heed. Because of their sins, God would destroy them.

**1:6**
Isa 1:4; 9:13

6 And I will destroy those who used to worship me
   but now no longer do.
They no longer ask for the Lord's guidance
   or seek my blessings."

**1:7**
Isa 34:6
Hab 2:20
Zech 2:13

7 Stand in silence in the presence of the Sovereign Lord,
   for the awesome day of the Lord's judgment is near.
The Lord has prepared his people for a great slaughter
   and has chosen their executioners.*

**1:8**
Isa 24:21-23

8 "On that day of judgment,"
   says the Lord,
"I will punish the leaders and princes of Judah
   and all those following pagan customs.

**1:9**
Amos 3:10

9 Yes, I will punish those who participate in pagan worship ceremonies,
   and those who fill their masters' houses with violence and deceit.

**1:10**
2 Chr 33:14
Neh 3:3; 12:39

10 "On that day," says the Lord,
   "a cry of alarm will come from the Fish Gate
and echo throughout the New Quarter of the city.*
   And a great crash will sound from the hills.
11 Wail in sorrow, all you who live in the market area,
   for all the merchants and traders will be destroyed.

**1:12**
Jer 16:16-17
Amos 6:1

12 "I will search with lanterns in Jerusalem's darkest corners
   to punish those who sit complacent in their sins.
They think the Lord will do nothing to them,
   either good or bad.

**1:13**
Deut 28:30
Amos 5:11

13 So their property will be plundered,
   their homes will be ransacked.
They will build new homes
   but never live in them.

**1:7** Hebrew *has prepared a sacrifice and sanctified his guests.*    **1:10** Or *the Second Quarter,* a newer section
of Jerusalem. Hebrew reads *the Mishneh.*

---

**ZEPHANIAH**
served as a
prophet to
Judah from
640–621 B.C.

*Climate of the times.* . . . . . . Josiah was the last good king in Judah. His bold
attempts to reform the nation and turn it back to God
were probably influenced by Zephaniah.

*Main message.* . . . . . . . . . . A day will come when God, as judge, will severely
punish all nations. But after judgment, he will show
mercy to all who have been faithful to him.

*Importance of message.* . . . We will all be judged for our disobedience to God;
but if we remain faithful to him, he will show us mercy.

*Contemporary prophet* . . . . Jeremiah (627–586 B.C.)

---

**1:7** A day of judgment and great slaughter occurred during the
lifetime of these people when Babylon invaded the land. The
prophet saw these prophecies as future events, but he could not
see when or in what order these events would take place. Many
think that these prophecies have a double fulfillment—one for the
near future (soon after the prophecy was made) and another for
the distant future (possibly during the end times). Some scholars
believe that these prophecies of judgment refer to events entirely
in the future.

**1:8, 9** Following pagan customs involved not only imitating
foreign ways but also worshiping foreign gods. Leaders who
should have been good examples to the people were adopting
foreign practices and thus showing their contempt for the Lord
by ignoring his commands against adopting the pagan culture.

**1:12** God would search the city with lanterns and punish those
who deserved punishment. Because they did not search their
own hearts and because they were content with the moral chaos

around them and indifferent to God, God would use the Babylonians to judge them. Within 20 years, the Babylonians would enter
Jerusalem, drag people out of hiding, and take them captive or kill
them. No one would escape God's judgment; there would be no
place to hide.

**1:12-14** Some people think of God as an indulgent heavenly
grandfather, nice to have around but not a real force in shaping
modern life. They don't believe in his power or his coming judgment. But God is holy, and therefore he will actively judge and
justly punish everyone who is content to live in sin, indifferent
to him, or unconcerned about justice. When people are indifferent to God, they tend to think that he is indifferent to them and
their sin. They will be surprised to find that the "terrible day of
the Lord is near."

They will plant vineyards
  but never drink wine from them.

14 "That terrible day of the LORD is near.
    Swiftly it comes—
a day of bitter tears,
  a day when even strong men will cry out.

15 It will be a day when the LORD's anger is poured out—
    a day of terrible distress and anguish,
a day of ruin and desolation,
  a day of darkness and gloom,
a day of clouds and blackness,
16     a day of trumpet calls and battle cries.
  Down go the walled cities
    and the strongest battlements!

17 "Because you have sinned against the LORD,
    I will make you grope around like the blind.
Your blood will be poured into the dust,
    and your bodies will lie rotting on the ground."

18 Your silver and gold will not save you
    on that day of the LORD's anger.
For the whole land will be devoured
    by the fire of his jealousy.
He will make a terrifying end
    of all the people on earth.*

### A Call to Repentance

**2** ¹ Gather together—yes, gather together,
      you shameless nation.
2 Gather before judgment begins,
    before your time to repent is blown away like chaff.
  Act now, before the fierce fury of the LORD falls
    and the terrible day of the LORD's anger begins.

3 Seek the LORD, all who are humble,
    and follow his commands.
  Seek to do what is right
    and to live humbly.
  Perhaps even yet the LORD will protect you—
    protect you from his anger on that day of destruction.

### Judgment against Philistia

4 Gaza and Ashkelon will be abandoned,
    Ashdod and Ekron torn down.
5 And what sorrow awaits you Philistines*
    who live along the coast and in the land of Canaan,
  for this judgment is against you, too!

**1:18** Or *the people living in the land.*   **2:5** Hebrew *Kerethites.*

---

| Ref | |
|---|---|
| **1:14** | Ezek 7:16-18 |
| **1:15** | Isa 22:5 / Joel 2:2 |
| **1:16** | Isa 2:12-15 / Jer 4:19 |
| **1:17** | Deut 28:28-29 / Pss 79:3; 83:10 / Isa 59:10 / Jer 8:2; 9:22 |
| **1:18** | Zeph 3:8 |
| **2:1** | 2 Chr 20:4 / Jer 3:3; 6:15 / Joel 1:14 |
| **2:2** | Zeph 1:18 |
| **2:3** | Ps 57:1 / Amos 5:6, 14-15 |
| **2:4** | Amos 1:6-8 / Zech 9:5 |
| **2:5** | Isa 14:29, 31 |

---

**1:14-18** The day of the Lord was near; the Babylonians would soon come and destroy Jerusalem. The day of the Lord is also near for us. God promises a final judgment, a day of worldwide destruction (Revelation 20:12-15). The Babylonian conquest occurred just as surely and horribly as Zephaniah had predicted. And God's final day of judgment is also sure—but so is your ability to save. To be spared from judgment, recognize that you have sinned, that your sin will bring judgment, that you cannot save yourself, and that God alone can save you.

**1:18** Money is not evil in itself, but it is useless to save us. In this life, money can warp our perspective, giving us feelings of security and power. Just as the Israelites' wealth could not save them from the Babylonian invasion, so at the final judgment, our riches will be worthless. Only Christ's redemptive work on our behalf matters for eternity. Christ alone will ransom us if we believe in him. Don't trust money; trust Christ.

**2:1-3** There was still time for the people to avert God's judgment. They simply had to turn from their sins, humble themselves, and obey God. The Old Testament prophets announced news of destruction, but they also offered the only means of escape and protection—turning from sin and walking with God (see also Micah 6:8).

**2:4** The four cities mentioned here are in Philistia, the nation southwest of Judah on the coast of the Mediterranean Sea. Age-

The LORD will destroy you
    until not one of you is left.
⁶ The Philistine coast will become a wilderness pasture,
    a place of shepherd camps
    and enclosures for sheep and goats.

**2:7**
Isa 32:14
Zeph 3:20

⁷ The remnant of the tribe of Judah will pasture there.
    They will rest at night in the abandoned houses in Ashkelon.
For the LORD their God will visit his people in kindness
    and restore their prosperity again.

### Judgment against Moab and Ammon

**2:8**
Ezek 25:3, 8

⁸ "I have heard the taunts of the Moabites
    and the insults of the Ammonites,
mocking my people
    and invading their borders.

**2:9**
Isa 11:14; 15:1-9

⁹ Now, as surely as I live,"
    says the LORD of Heaven's Armies, the God of Israel,
"Moab and Ammon will be destroyed—
    destroyed as completely as Sodom and Gomorrah.
Their land will become a place of stinging nettles,
    salt pits, and eternal desolation.
The remnant of my people will plunder them
    and take their land."

**2:10**
Isa 16:6-10
Jer 48:28-31
Zeph 2:8
**2:11**
Joel 2:11
Zeph 1:4; 3:4

¹⁰ They will receive the wages of their pride,
    for they have scoffed at the people of the LORD of Heaven's Armies.
¹¹ The LORD will terrify them
    as he destroys all the gods in the land.
Then nations around the world will worship the LORD,
    each in their own land.

### Judgment against Ethiopia and Assyria

**2:12**
Isa 20:3-4

¹² "You Ethiopians* will also be slaughtered
    by my sword," says the LORD.

**2:12** Hebrew *Cushites.*

---

old enemies of Israel from the days of Joshua, the Philistines were known for their cruelty. God judged these cities for their idolatry and their constant taunting of Israel. These four cities were four of the five capitals. The fifth (Gath) had probably already been destroyed.

**2:7** All the prophets, even while prophesying doom and destruction, speak of "the remnant"—a small group of God's people who remain faithful to him and whom God will restore to the land. Although God said he would destroy Judah, he also promised to save some, thus keeping his original covenant to preserve Abraham's descendants (Genesis 17:4-8). Because God is holy, he cannot allow sin to continue. But God is also faithful to his promises. He cannot stay angry forever with Israel or with you, if you are his child, because he loves his children and always seeks their good.

**2:8** The Moabites and Ammonites lived to the east of Judah, and they often ridiculed and attacked Judah. These nations worshiped Chemosh and Molech (1 Kings 11:7). Moab's king once sacrificed his son on the city wall to stop an invasion (2 Kings 3:26, 27). God would judge these nations for their wickedness and for their treatment of his people.

**2:8-11** Judah had been taunted and mocked by the neighboring nations, Moab and Ammon, but God reminded them that he had "heard the taunts" (2:8), and that the taunters would be punished for their pride (2:10). At times the whole world seems to mock God and those who have faith in him. When you are ridiculed, remember that God hears and will answer. Eventually, in God's timing, justice will be carried out.

**2:9** The nations of Moab and Ammon trace their roots to Lot's incest with his daughters after escaping the destruction of evil Sodom and Gomorrah (Genesis 19). Ironically, Moab and Ammon would be the same kind of perpetual wasteland that God had made those evil cities. Sodom and Gomorrah were so completely destroyed that their exact location is still unknown.

**2:12** Ethiopia, at the southern end of the Red Sea, controlled Egypt at this time. No one can escape deserved judgment. The Ethiopians were also "slaughtered by my sword" when the Babylonians invaded Egypt in 605 B.C. (See Isaiah 18 and Ezekiel 30:9 for other prophecies concerning Ethiopia.)

13 And the LORD will strike the lands of the north with his fist,
   destroying the land of Assyria.
He will make its great capital, Nineveh, a desolate wasteland,
   parched like a desert.

2:13
Nah 3:7

14 The proud city will become a pasture for flocks and herds,
   and all sorts of wild animals will settle there.
The desert owl and screech owl will roost on its ruined columns,
   their calls echoing through the gaping windows.
Rubble will block all the doorways,
   and the cedar paneling will be exposed to the weather.

2:14
Isa 34:11

15 This is the boisterous city,
   once so secure.
"I am the greatest!" it boasted.
   "No other city can compare with me!"
But now, look how it has become an utter ruin,
   a haven for wild animals.
Everyone passing by will laugh in derision
   and shake a defiant fist.

2:15
1 Kgs 9:7-8
Isa 22:2-7; 32:14;
47:8

## Jerusalem's Rebellion and Redemption

**3** ¹ What sorrow awaits rebellious, polluted Jerusalem,
   the city of violence and crime!

3:1
Jer 6:6

² No one can tell it anything;
   it refuses all correction.
It does not trust in the LORD
   or draw near to its God.

3:2
Ps 78:22
Jer 5:3

³ Its leaders are like roaring lions
   hunting for their victims.
Its judges are like ravenous wolves at evening time,
   who by dawn have left no trace of their prey.

3:3
Ezek 22:6-12

⁴ Its prophets are arrogant liars seeking their own gain.
   Its priests defile the Temple by disobeying God's instructions.

3:4
Ezek 22:26
Mal 2:7-9

⁵ But the LORD is still there in the city,
   and he does no wrong.
Day by day he hands down justice,
   and he does not fail.
But the wicked know no shame.

3:5
Jer 3:3

---

**2:13** Zephaniah mentioned the large nation to the south and then moved to the nation that invaded from the north, Assyria. Though declining, Assyria was still the strongest military power of the day, dominating the world for three centuries and destroying any nation in its path. Nineveh, the large capital city, was considered impregnable. However, just as Zephaniah predicted, Nineveh was wiped out in 612 B.C. by the Babylonians, who would become the next world power.

**2:13-15** To predict the destruction of Nineveh 10 years before it happened would be equivalent to predicting the destruction of London, Tokyo, Paris, or New York. Nineveh was the ancient Near Eastern center for culture, technology, and beauty. It had great libraries, buildings, and a vast irrigation system that created lush gardens in the city. The city wall was 60 miles long, 100 feet high, and over 30 feet wide and was fortified with 1,500 towers. Yet the entire city was destroyed so completely that its very existence was questioned until it was discovered, with great difficulty, by 19th-century archaeologists. Nineveh had indeed become as desolate and dry as the desert.

**3:1ff** After predicting the destruction of the surrounding nations, Zephaniah returned to the problem at hand—sin in Jerusalem. The city of God, and God's people themselves, had become "polluted"—as sinful as their pagan neighbors. The people pretended to worship and serve God, but in their hearts they had rejected him and continued to be complacent

about their sins. They no longer cared about the consequences of turning away from God.

**3:2** Do you know people who refuse to listen when someone disagrees with their opinions? Their root problem is pride—inflated self-esteem. God's people had become so proud that they would not even listen to God's voice. Do you find it difficult to listen to the spiritual counsel of others or God's words from the Bible? Don't let pride make you unable or unwilling to let God work in your life. You will be more willing to listen when you consider how weak and sinful you really are compared to God.

**3:3, 4** Leading God's people is a privilege and a responsibility. Through Zephaniah, God rebuked many different leaders in Jerusalem—judges, prophets, and priests—because of their callous disobedience, irresponsibility, and sin. If you are a leader in the church, consider yourself in a privileged position, but be careful. God holds you responsible for the purity of your actions, the quality of your example, and the truth of your words.

**3:5** Jerusalem's citizens, of all people, had no excuse for their sins. Jerusalem, where the Temple was located, was the religious center of the nation. But even though the people didn't follow God, God was still there in the city, present in the midst of corruption, persecution, and unbelief. No matter how spiritually desolate the world seems, God is here, and he is at work. Ask yourself, What is he doing now, and how can I be part of his work?

**3:6**
Zeph 2:5

6 "I have wiped out many nations,
    devastating their fortress walls and towers.
Their streets are now deserted;
    their cities lie in silent ruin.
There are no survivors—
    none at all.

**3:7**
Hos 9:9

7 I thought, 'Surely they will have reverence for me now!
    Surely they will listen to my warnings.
Then I won't need to strike again,
    destroying their homes.'
But no, they get up early
    to continue their evil deeds.

**3:8**
Ps 27:14
Ezek 38:14-23
Zeph 1:18

8 Therefore, be patient," says the LORD.
    "Soon I will stand and accuse these evil nations.
For I have decided to gather the kingdoms of the earth
    and pour out my fiercest anger and fury on them.
All the earth will be devoured
    by the fire of my jealousy.

## 2. The day of hope

**3:9**
Ps 22:27

9 "Then I will purify the speech of all people,
    so that everyone can worship the LORD together.

**3:10**
Ps 68:31
Isa 60:7

10 My scattered people who live beyond the rivers of Ethiopia*
    will come to present their offerings.

**3:11**
Isa 11:9

11 On that day you will no longer need to be ashamed,
    for you will no longer be rebels against me.
I will remove all proud and arrogant people from among you.
    There will be no more haughtiness on my holy mountain.

**3:12**
Nah 1:7

12 Those who are left will be the lowly and humble,
    for it is they who trust in the name of the LORD.

**3:13**
Hos 2:18
Mic 4:7
Rev 14:5

13 The remnant of Israel will do no wrong;
    they will never tell lies or deceive one another.
They will eat and sleep in safety,
    and no one will make them afraid."

14 Sing, O daughter of Zion;
    shout aloud, O Israel!
Be glad and rejoice with all your heart,
    O daughter of Jerusalem!

**3:15**
Isa 33:22
Ezek 37:26-28
Zech 8:3

15 For the LORD will remove his hand of judgment
    and will disperse the armies of your enemy.

**3:10** Hebrew *Cush.*

**3:7** We may wonder how the Israelites could have had such clear warnings and still not turn to God. The problem was that they had allowed sin to so harden them that they no longer cared to follow God. They refused to heed God's warnings, and they refused to repent. The more God punished them, the more they sinned. If you are living in disobedience to God now, your heart may grow hard, and you may lose all desire for God.

**3:8** In the last days, God will judge all people according to what they have done (Revelation 20:12). Justice will prevail; evildoers will be punished; and the obedient will be blessed. Don't try to avenge yourself. Be patient, and God's justice will come.

**3:9** God will purify speech and unify language so that all his people from all nations will be able to worship him together. In the new earth, all believers will be able to understand each other; the confusion of languages at the tower of Babel will be reversed (Genesis 11). God will purify our hearts, so that the words coming from our lips will be pure as well.

**3:10** The "scattered people" refers to Jews dispersed beyond the rivers of Ethiopia. It symbolizes that all Jews, no matter how far they have been scattered, will return to worship God.

**3:11, 12** God will remove the proud people and leave the lowly and humble. God is opposed to the proud and arrogant of every generation. But those who are lowly and humble, both physically and spiritually, will be rewarded because they trust in God. Self-reliance and arrogance have no place among God's people or in his Kingdom.

**3:14-18** The Lord himself will remove his hand of judgment, disperse Israel's enemies, and come to live among his people. He will give them gladness. Zephaniah points out that gladness results when we allow God to be with us. We do that by faithfully following him and obeying his commands. Then God rejoices over us with singing. If you want to be happy, draw close to the source of happiness by obeying God.

And the LORD himself, the King of Israel,
    will live among you!
At last your troubles will be over,
    and you will never again fear disaster.
16 On that day the announcement to Jerusalem will be,
    "Cheer up, Zion! Don't be afraid!
17 For the LORD your God is living among you.
    He is a mighty savior.
    He will take delight in you with gladness.
        With his love, he will calm all your fears.*
        He will rejoice over you with joyful songs."

18 "I will gather you who mourn for the appointed festivals;
    you will be disgraced no more.*
19 And I will deal severely with all who have oppressed you.
    I will save the weak and helpless ones;
    I will bring together
        those who were chased away.
    I will give glory and fame to my former exiles,
        wherever they have been mocked and shamed.
20 On that day I will gather you together
    and bring you home again.
    I will give you a good name, a name of distinction,
        among all the nations of the earth,
    as I restore your fortunes before their very eyes.
        I, the LORD, have spoken!"

**3:16**
Isa 35:3-4
Heb 12:12-13
**3:17**
Isa 62:5; 63:1

**3:19**
Isa 60:14
Ezek 34:16

**3:20**
Isa 56:5; 66:22
Ezek 37:12
Zeph 2:7

**3:17** Or *He will be silent in his love.* Greek and Syriac versions read *He will renew you with his love.*
**3:18** The meaning of the Hebrew for this verse is uncertain.

---

**3:20** "Before their very eyes" does not necessarily mean that this promise would be fulfilled during Zephaniah's generation. Rather, it means that the restoration will be an obvious work of the Lord.

**3:20** The message of doom in the beginning of the book becomes a message of hope by the end. There will be a new day when God will bless his people. If the leaders in the church today were to hear a message from a prophet of God, the message would probably resemble the book of Zephaniah. Under Josiah's religious reforms, the people did return to God *outwardly,* but their hearts were far from him. Zephaniah encouraged the nation to gather together and pray for salvation. We must also ask ourselves: Is our reform merely an outward show, or is it changing our hearts and lives? We need to gather together and pray, to walk humbly with God, to do what is right, and to hear the message of hope regarding the new world to come.

# HAGGAI

PRESSURES, demands, expectations, and tasks push in from all sides and assault our schedules. Do this! Be there! Finish that! Call them! Everyone seems to want something from us—family, friends, employer, school, church, clubs. Soon we have little left to give as we run out of energy and time. We find ourselves rushing through life, attending to the necessary, the immediate, and the urgent. The important is all too often left in the dust. Our problem is not the volume of demands or lack of scheduling skills, but values—what is *truly* important to us.

Our values and priorities are reflected in how we use our resources—time, money, strength, and talent. Often our actions belie our words. We say God is number one, but then we relegate him to a lesser number on our "to do" lists.

Twenty-five centuries ago, a voice was heard, calling men and women to the right priorities. Haggai knew what was important and what had to be done, and he challenged God's people to respond.

In 586 B.C., the armies of Babylon had destroyed the Temple in Jerusalem—God's house, the symbol of his presence. In 538 B.C. King Cyrus decreed that Jews could return to their beloved city and rebuild the Temple. So they traveled to Jerusalem and began the work. But then they forgot their purpose and lost their priorities, as opposition and apathy brought the work to a standstill (Ezra 4:4, 5). Then Haggai spoke, calling them back to God's values: "Why are you living in luxurious houses while my house lies in ruins?" (1:4). The people were more concerned with their own needs than with doing God's will, and, as a result, they suffered. Then Haggai called them to action: "This is what the LORD of Heaven's Armies says: Look at what's happening to you! Now go up into the hills, bring down timber, and rebuild my house. Then I will take pleasure in it and be honored, says the LORD" (1:7, 8). And God's message through his servant Haggai became the catalyst for finishing the work.

Although Haggai is a small book, it is filled with challenge and promise, reminding us of God's claim on our lives and our priorities. As you read Haggai, imagine him walking the streets and alleys of Jerusalem, urging the people to get back to doing God's work. And listen to Haggai speaking to you, urging you to reorder your priorities in accordance with God's will. What has God told you to do? Put all else aside and obey him.

## VITAL STATISTICS

**PURPOSE:**
To call the people to complete the rebuilding of the Temple

**AUTHOR:**
Haggai

**ORIGINAL AUDIENCE:**
The people living in Jerusalem and those who had returned from exile

**DATE WRITTEN:**
520 B.C.

**SETTING:**
The Temple in Jerusalem had been destroyed in 586 B.C. Cyrus had allowed the Jews to return to their homeland and rebuild their temple in 538 B.C. They had begun the work but had been unable to complete it. Through the ministry of Haggai and Zechariah, the Temple was completed (520–516 B.C.).

**KEY VERSE:**
"Why are you living in luxurious houses while my house lies in ruins?" (1:4).

**KEY PEOPLE:**
Haggai, Zerubbabel, Jeshua

**KEY PLACE:**
Jerusalem

**SPECIAL FEATURES:**
Haggai was the first of the postexilic prophets. The other two were Zechariah and Malachi. The literary style of this book is simple and direct.

## THE BLUEPRINT

1. The call to rebuild the Temple (1:1–15)
2. Encouragement to complete the Temple (2:1–23)

When the exiles first returned from Babylon, they set about rebuilding the Temple right away. Although they began with the right attitudes, they slipped back into wrong behavior, and the work came to a standstill. We need to be on guard to keep our priorities straight. Remain active in your service to God and continue to put first things first.

## MEGATHEMES

| THEME | EXPLANATION | IMPORTANCE |
|---|---|---|
| *Right Priorities* | God had given the Jews the assignment to finish the Temple in Jerusalem when they returned from captivity. After 15 years, they still had not completed it. They were more concerned about building their own homes than finishing God's work. Haggai told them to get their priorities straight. | It is easy to make other priorities more important than doing God's work. But God wants us to follow through and build up his Kingdom. Don't stop and don't make excuses. Set your heart on what is right and do it. Get your priorities straight. |
| *God's Encouragement* | Haggai encouraged the people as they worked. He assured them of the divine presence of the Holy Spirit and of final victory, and instilled in them the hope that the Messiah would reign. | If God gives you a task, don't be afraid to get started. His resources are infinite. God will help you complete it by giving you encouragement from others along the way. |

## 1. The call to rebuild the Temple

**1** On August 29* of the second year of King Darius's reign, the LORD gave a message through the prophet Haggai to Zerubbabel son of Shealtiel, governor of Judah, and to Jeshua* son of Jehozadak, the high priest.

**1:1**
Ezra 2:2; 3:8;
5:1-2; 6:6-14
Zech 6:11

²"This is what the LORD of Heaven's Armies says: The people are saying, 'The time has not yet come to rebuild the house of the LORD.'"

³Then the LORD sent this message through the prophet Haggai: ⁴"Why are you living in luxurious houses while my house lies in ruins? ⁵This is what the LORD of Heaven's Armies says: Look at what's happening to you! ⁶You have planted much but harvest little. You eat but are not satisfied. You drink but are still thirsty. You put on clothes but cannot keep warm. Your wages disappear as though you were putting them in pockets filled with holes!

**1:4**
Hag 1:9

**1:6**
Hag 1:9; 2:16

⁷"This is what the LORD of Heaven's Armies says: Look at what's happening to you! ⁸Now go up into the hills, bring down timber, and rebuild my house. Then I will take pleasure in it and be honored, says the LORD. ⁹You hoped for rich harvests, but they were poor. And when you brought your harvest home, I blew it away. Why? Because my house lies in ruins, says the LORD of Heaven's Armies, while all of you are busy building your own fine houses. ¹⁰It's because of you that the heavens withhold the dew and the earth produces no crops. ¹¹I have called for a drought on your fields and hills—a drought to wither the grain and grapes and olive trees and all your other crops, a drought to starve you and your livestock and to ruin everything you have worked so hard to get."

**1:8**
Ezra 3:7-13
Ps 132:13-14
Hag 2:7, 9

**1:9**
Isa 40:7
Hag 1:4

**1:10**
Deut 28:24
1 Kgs 8:35-36; 17:1
Joel 1:18-20

**1:11**
Deut 28:22-24

**1:1a** Hebrew *On the first day of the sixth month*, of the ancient Hebrew lunar calendar. A number of dates in Haggai can be cross-checked with dates in surviving Persian records and related accurately to our modern calendar. This event occurred on August 29, 520 B.C.   **1:1b** Hebrew *Joshua*, a variant spelling of Jeshua; also in 1:12, 14.

**1:1** Zerubbabel, governor of Judah, and Jeshua, the high priest, were key leaders in rebuilding the Temple. They had already reestablished the altar, but work on the Temple had slowed. Haggai gave a message to these outstanding leaders and to the exiles who had returned from Babylon, encouraging them to complete the rebuilding of the Temple in Jerusalem.

**1:1ff** The Jews who had returned from Babylon in 538 B.C. to rebuild the Temple in Jerusalem were not able to finish their work because they were hindered by their enemies. After opposition put a halt to progress, no further work had been done on the Temple for over 10 years. In August 520 B.C., Haggai delivered a message to encourage the people to rebuild the Temple. Haggai was probably born in captivity in Babylon and returned to Jerusalem with Zerubbabel in 538 B.C. (Ezra 1–2). Haggai and Zechariah, two prophets who encouraged the Temple rebuilding, are mentioned in Ezra 5:1.

**1:2-15** Haggai encouraged the people to finish rebuilding the Temple. Opposition from hostile neighbors had caused them to feel discouraged and to neglect the Temple and thus neglect God. But Haggai's message turned them around and motivated them to pick up their tools and continue the work they had begun.

**1:3-6** God asked his people how they could live in luxury when his house was lying in ruins. The Temple was the focal point of Judah's relationship with God, but it was still demolished.

Instead of rebuilding the Temple, the people put their energies into beautifying their own homes. However, the harder the people worked for themselves, the less they had, because they ignored their spiritual lives. The same happens to us. If we put God first, he will provide for our deepest needs. If we put him in any other place, all our efforts will be futile. Caring only for your physical needs while ignoring your relationship with God will lead to ruin.

**1:6** Because the people had not given God first place in their lives, their work was not fruitful or productive, and their material possessions did not satisfy. While they concentrated on building and beautifying their own homes, God's blessing was withheld because they no longer put him first. Moses had predicted that this would be the result if the people neglected God (Deuteronomy 28:38-45).

**1:9** Judah's problem was confused priorities. Like Judah, our priorities involving occupation, family, and God's work are often confused. Jobs, homes, vacations, and leisure activities may rank higher on our list of importance than God. What is most important to you? Where is God on your list of priorities?

**1:11** Grain, grapes for wine, and olives for oil were Israel's major crops. The people depended on these for security while neglecting the worship of God. As a result, God would send a drought to destroy their livelihood and call them back to himself.

### Obedience to God's Call

**1:12**
Ps 112:1
Isa 50:10
Hag 1:1

**1:13**
Mal 2:7; 3:1

**1:14-15**
Ezra 5:2
Neh 4:6
Hag 1:1

¹²Then Zerubbabel son of Shealtiel, and Jeshua son of Jehozadak, the high priest, and the whole remnant of God's people began to obey the message from the LORD their God. When they heard the words of the prophet Haggai, whom the LORD their God had sent, the people feared the LORD. ¹³Then Haggai, the LORD's messenger, gave the people this message from the LORD: "I am with you, says the LORD!"

¹⁴So the LORD sparked the enthusiasm of Zerubbabel son of Shealtiel, governor of Judah, and the enthusiasm of Jeshua son of Jehozadak, the high priest, and the enthusiasm of the whole remnant of God's people. They began to work on the house of their God, the LORD of Heaven's Armies, ¹⁵on September 21* of the second year of King Darius's reign.

### 2. Encouragement to complete the Temple

*The New Temple's Diminished Splendor*

**2:3**
Ezra 3:12

**2:4**
Deut 31:23
Acts 7:9
Eph 6:10-12

**2:5**
Exod 29:45-46
Neh 9:10
Isa 63:11, 14

**2:6**
Ezek 38:19
†Heb 12:26

**2:7**
1 Kgs 8:11
Isa 60:4-9

**2** Then on October 17 of that same year,* the LORD sent another message through the prophet Haggai. ²"Say this to Zerubbabel son of Shealtiel, governor of Judah, and to Jeshua* son of Jehozadak, the high priest, and to the remnant of God's people there in the land: ³'Does anyone remember this house—this Temple—in its former splendor? How, in comparison, does it look to you now? It must seem like nothing at all! ⁴But now the LORD says: Be strong, Zerubbabel. Be strong, Jeshua son of Jehozadak, the high priest. Be strong, all you people still left in the land. And now get to work, for I am with you, says the LORD of Heaven's Armies. ⁵My Spirit remains among you, just as I promised when you came out of Egypt. So do not be afraid.'

⁶"For this is what the LORD of Heaven's Armies says: In just a little while I will again shake the heavens and the earth, the oceans and the dry land. ⁷I will shake all the nations, and the

**1:15** Hebrew *on the twenty-fourth day of the sixth month,* of the ancient Hebrew lunar calendar. This event occurred on September 21, 520 B.C.; also see note on 1:1a. **2:1** Hebrew *on the twenty-first day of the seventh month,* of the ancient Hebrew lunar calendar. This event (in the second year of Darius's reign) occurred on October 17, 520 B.C.; also see note on 1:1a. **2:2** Hebrew *Joshua,* a variant spelling of Jeshua; also in 2:4.

---

**HAGGAI** served as a prophet to Judah about 520 B.C., after the return from exile.

*Climate of the times* . . . . . . The people of Judah had been exiled to Babylon in 586 B.C., and Jerusalem and the Temple had been destroyed. Under Cyrus, king of Persia, the Jews were allowed to return to Judah and rebuild their Temple.

*Main message* . . . . . . . . . The people returned to Jerusalem to begin rebuilding the Temple, but they hadn't finished. Haggai's message encouraged the people to finish rebuilding God's Temple.

*Importance of message* . . . The Temple lay half-finished while the people lived in beautiful homes. Haggai warned them against putting their possessions and jobs ahead of God. We must put God first in our lives.

*Contemporary prophet* . . . . Zechariah (520–480 B.C.)

---

**1:14, 15** The people began rebuilding the Temple just 23 days after Haggai's first message. Rarely did a prophet's message produce such a quick response. How often we hear a sermon and respond, "That was an excellent point—I ought to do that," only to leave church and forget to act. These people put their words into action. When you hear a good sermon or lesson, ask what you should *do* about it, and then make plans to put it into practice.

**2:1-9** This is Haggai's second message. It was given during the Festival of Shelters in October 520 B.C. The older people could remember the incredible beauty of Solomon's Temple, destroyed 66 years earlier. Many were discouraged because the rebuilt Temple was inferior to Solomon's. But Haggai encouraged them with God's message that the glory of this Temple would surpass that of its predecessor. The most important part of the Temple is God's presence. Some 500 years later, Jesus Christ would walk in the Temple courts.

**2:4** "Be strong . . . now get to work, for I am with you." Judah's people had returned to worshiping God, and God had promised to bless their efforts. But it was time for them to *work*. We must be people of prayer, Bible study, and worship, but eventually we must get out and *do* the work God has prepared for us. He wants to change the world through us, his ambassadors. God has given

you a job to do in the church, at your place of employment, and at home. The time has come to take courage and get going because God is with you!

**2:5** The Israelites had been led from captivity in Egypt to their Promised Land. They were God's chosen people, guided and cared for by his Holy Spirit. Although God had punished them for their sins, he kept his promise and never left them (Exodus 29:45, 46). No matter what difficulties we face or how frustrating our work may be, God's Spirit is with us.

**2:6-9** The focus shifts from the local Temple being rebuilt in Jerusalem to the worldwide reign of the Messiah on earth. The words "in just a little while" are not limited to the immediate historical context; they refer to God's control of history—he can act anytime he chooses. God will act *in his time* (see also Hebrews 12:26, 27).

**2:7** When God promised to shake all the nations with his judgment, he was speaking of both his present judgment on evil nations and future judgment during the last days.

treasures of all the nations will be brought to this Temple. I will fill this place with glory, says the LORD of Heaven's Armies. ⁸The silver is mine, and the gold is mine, says the LORD of Heaven's Armies. ⁹The future glory of this Temple will be greater than its past glory, says the LORD of Heaven's Armies. And in this place I will bring peace. I, the LORD of Heaven's Armies, have spoken!"

## Blessings Promised for Obedience

¹⁰On December 18* of the second year of King Darius's reign, the LORD sent this message to the prophet Haggai: ¹¹"This is what the LORD of Heaven's Armies says. Ask the priests this question about the law: ¹²'If one of you is carrying some meat from a holy sacrifice in his robes and his robe happens to brush against some bread or stew, wine or olive oil, or any other kind of food, will it also become holy?'"

The priests replied, "No."

¹³Then Haggai asked, "If someone becomes ceremonially unclean by touching a dead person and then touches any of these foods, will the food be defiled?"

And the priests answered, "Yes."

¹⁴Then Haggai responded, "That is how it is with this people and this nation, says the LORD. Everything they do and everything they offer is defiled by their sin. ¹⁵Look at what was happening to you before you began to lay the foundation of the LORD's Temple. ¹⁶When you hoped for a twenty-bushel crop, you harvested only ten. When you expected to draw fifty gallons from the winepress, you found only twenty. ¹⁷I sent blight and mildew and hail to destroy everything you worked so hard to produce. Even so, you refused to return to me, says the LORD.

¹⁸"Think about this eighteenth day of December, the day* when the foundation of the LORD's Temple was laid. Think carefully. ¹⁹I am giving you a promise now while the seed is still in the barn.* You have not yet harvested your grain, and your grapevines, fig trees, pomegranates, and olive trees have not yet produced their crops. But from this day onward I will bless you."

## Promises for Zerubbabel

²⁰On that same day, December 18,* the LORD sent this second message to Haggai: ²¹"Tell Zerubbabel, the governor of Judah, that I am about to shake the heavens and the earth. ²²I will overturn royal thrones and destroy the power of foreign kingdoms. I will overturn their chariots and riders. The horses will fall, and their riders will kill each other.

²³"But when this happens, says the LORD of Heaven's Armies, I will honor you, Zerubbabel son of Shealtiel, my servant. I will make you like a signet ring on my finger, says the LORD, for I have chosen you. I, the LORD of Heaven's Armies, have spoken!"

**2:10** Hag 1:15
**2:12** Exod 29:37; Ezek 44:19; Matt 23:19
**2:13** Num 19:11-12, 22
**2:14** Prov 15:8; Isa 1:11-15
**2:15** Ezra 3:10; 4:24; Hag 1:5
**2:16** Hag 1:9
**2:18** Hag 2:10
**2:21** Hag 2:6; Heb 12:26
**2:22** Mic 5:10

2:10 Hebrew *On the twenty-fourth day of the ninth month*, of the ancient Hebrew lunar calendar (similarly in 2:18). This event occurred on December 18, 520 B.C.; also see note on 1:1a.   2:18 Or *On this eighteenth day of December, think about the day.*   2:19 Hebrew *Is the seed yet in the barn?*   2:20 Hebrew *On the twenty-fourth day of the [ninth] month*; see note on 2:10.

**2:8, 9** God wanted the Temple to be rebuilt, and he had the gold and silver to do it, but he needed willing hands. God has chosen to do his work through people. He provides the resources, but willing hands must do the work. Are your hands available for God's work in the world?

**2:10-19** The point of this message (delivered in December 520 B.C.) is that holiness will not rub off on others, but contamination will. As the people began to obey God, God promised to encourage and prosper them. But they needed to understand that activities in the Temple would not clean up their sin; only repentance and obedience could do that. If we insist on harboring wrong attitudes and sins or on maintaining close relationships with sinful people, we will be defiled. Holy living will come only when we are empowered by God's Holy Spirit.

**2:14** When a child eats spaghetti sauce, very soon his or her face, hands, and clothes become red. Sin and selfish attitudes produce the same result—they stain everything they touch. Even good deeds done for God can be tainted by sinful attitudes. The only remedy is God's cleansing.

**2:16** For many years, the grain had only given 50 percent of the expected yield, and wine had done even worse.

**2:18, 19** The people relaid the Temple foundation, and immedi-

ately God blessed them. He did not wait for the project to be completed. God often sends his encouragement and approval with our first few obedient steps. He is eager to bless us!

**2:20-23** Haggai's final message acknowledged that he was merely the messenger who brings the word of the Lord. It is addressed to Zerubbabel, the governor of Judah.

**2:23** A signet ring was used to guarantee the authority and authenticity of a letter. It served as a signature when pressed in soft wax on a written document. God was reaffirming and guaranteeing his promise of a Messiah through David's line (Matthew 1:12).

**2:23** God closed his message to Zerubbabel with this tremendous affirmation: "I have chosen you." Such a proclamation applies to us as well: Each of us has been chosen by God (Ephesians 1:4). This truth should make us see how much God loves us and motivate us to work for him. When you feel down, remind yourself: God has chosen me!

**2:23** Haggai's message to the people sought to get their priorities straight, help them quit worrying, and motivate them to rebuild the Temple. Like them, we often place a higher priority on our personal comfort than on God's work and true worship. But God is pleased and promises strength and guidance when we give him first place in our life.

# ZECHARIAH

THE FUTURE—that vast uncharted sea of the unknown, holding joy or terror, comfort or pain, love or loneliness. Some people fear the days to come, wondering what evils lurk in the shadows; others consult seers and future-telling charlatans, trying desperately to discover its secrets. But tomorrow's story is known only to God and to those special messengers called prophets, to whom God has revealed a chapter or two.

A prophet's primary task was to proclaim the word of the Lord, pointing out sin, explaining its consequences, and calling men and women to repentance and obedience. Elijah, Elisha, Isaiah, Jeremiah, Ezekiel, Hosea, and Amos stand with scores of others who faithfully delivered God's message despite rejection, ridicule, and persecution. And at times they were given prophetic visions foretelling coming events.

Nestled near the end of the Old Testament, among what are known as "minor prophets," is the book of Zechariah. As one of three postexilic prophets, along with Haggai and Malachi, Zechariah ministered to the small remnant of Jews who had returned to Judah to rebuild the Temple and their nation. Like Haggai, he encouraged the people to finish rebuilding the Temple, but his message went far beyond those physical walls and contemporary issues. With spectacular apocalyptic imagery and graphic detail, Zechariah told of the Messiah, the one whom God would send to rescue his people and to reign over all the earth. Zechariah is one of our most important prophetic books, giving detailed messianic references that were clearly fulfilled in the life of Jesus Christ. The rebuilding of the Temple, he says, was just the first act in the drama of the end times and the ushering in of the messianic age. Zechariah proclaimed a stirring message of hope to these ex-captives and exiles—their King was coming!

Jesus is Messiah, the promised "great deliverer" of Israel. Unlike Zechariah's listeners, we can look back at Christ's ministry and mission. As you study Zechariah's prophecy, you will see details of Christ's life that were written 500 years before their fulfillment. Read and stand in awe of our God, who keeps his promises. But there is also a future message that has not yet been fulfilled—the return of Christ at the end of the age. As you read Zechariah, think through the implications of this promised event. *Your King is coming,* and he will reign forever and ever.

God knows and controls the future. We may never see more than a moment ahead, but we can be secure if we trust in him. Read Zechariah and strengthen your faith in God—he alone is your hope and security.

## VITAL STATISTICS

**PURPOSE:**
To give hope to God's people by revealing God's future deliverance through the Messiah

**AUTHOR:**
Zechariah

**ORIGINAL AUDIENCE:**
The Jews in Jerusalem who had returned from their captivity in Babylon

**DATE WRITTEN:**
Chapters 1—8 were written approximately 520–518 B.C. Chapters 9—14 were written around 480 B.C.

**SETTING:**
The exiles had returned from Babylon to rebuild the Temple, but the work had been thwarted and stalled. Haggai and Zechariah confronted the people with their task and encouraged them to complete it.

**KEY VERSES:**
"Rejoice, O people of Zion! Shout in triumph, O people of Jerusalem! Look, your king is coming to you. He is righteous and victorious, yet he is humble, riding on a donkey— riding on a donkey's colt. . . . Your king will bring peace to the nations. His realm will stretch from sea to sea and from the Euphrates River to the ends of the earth" (9:9, 10).

**KEY PEOPLE:**
Zerubbabel, Jeshua

**KEY PLACE:**
Jerusalem

**SPECIAL FEATURES:**
This book is the most apocalyptic and messianic of all the minor prophets.

---

## THE BLUEPRINT

A. MESSAGES WHILE REBUILDING THE TEMPLE (1:1—8:23)
   1. Zechariah's night visions
   2. Zechariah's words of encouragement

Zechariah encouraged the people to put away the sin in their lives and to continue rebuilding the Temple. His visions described the judgment of Israel's enemies, the blessings to Jerusalem, and the need for God's people to remain pure—avoiding hypocrisy, superficiality, and sin. Zechariah's visions provided hope for the people. We also need to carefully follow the instruction to remain pure until Christ returns.

B. MESSAGES AFTER
   COMPLETING THE TEMPLE
   (9:1—14:21)

Besides encouragement and hope, Zechariah's messages were also a warning that God's messianic Kingdom would not begin as soon as the Temple was complete. Israel's enemies would be judged and the King would come, but God's people would themselves face many difficult circumstances before experiencing the blessing of the messianic Kingdom. We, too, may face much sorrow, disappointment, and distress before coming into Christ's eternal Kingdom.

## MEGATHEMES

| THEME | EXPLANATION | IMPORTANCE |
|---|---|---|
| God's Jealousy | God was angry at his people for ignoring his prophets through the years, and he was concerned that they not follow the careless and false leaders who exploited them. Disobedience was the root of their problems and the cause of their misery. God was jealous for their devotion to him. | God is jealous for our devotion. To avoid Israel's ruin, don't walk in their steps. Don't reject God, follow false teachers, or lead others astray. Turn to God, faithfully obey his commands, and make sure you are leading others correctly. |
| Rebuild the Temple | The Jews were discouraged. They were free from exile, yet the Temple was not completed. Zechariah encouraged them to rebuild it. God would both protect his workmen and empower them by his Holy Spirit to carry out his work. | More than the rebuilding of the Temple was at stake—the people were staging the first act in God's wonderful drama of the end times. Those of us who love God must complete his work. To do so we must have the Holy Spirit's help. God will empower us with his Spirit. |
| The King Is Coming | The Messiah will come both to rescue people from sin and to reign as King. He will establish his Kingdom, conquer all his enemies, and rule over all the earth. Everything will one day be under his loving and powerful control. | The Messiah came as a servant to die for us. He will return as a victorious King. At that time, he will usher in peace throughout the world. Submit to his leadership now to be ready for the King's triumphant return. |
| God's Protection | There was opposition to God's plan in Zechariah's day, and he prophesied future times of trouble. But God's Word endures. God remembers the covenants he makes with his people. He cares for his people and will deliver them from all the world powers that oppress them. | Although evil is still present, God's infinite love and personal care have been demonstrated through the centuries. God keeps his promises. Although our bodies may be destroyed, we need never fear our ultimate destiny if we love and obey him. |

## A. MESSAGES WHILE REBUILDING THE TEMPLE (1:1—8:23)

Zechariah begins by describing eight visions that came to him at night. Then he gives a collection of messages about the crowning of Jeshua, answers to questions of feasting and fasting, and encouragement to continue rebuilding the Temple. We, too, can be inspired to continue following God in faithfulness throughout our life.

### 1. Zechariah's night visions

*A Call to Return to the LORD*

**1** In November* of the second year of King Darius's reign, the LORD gave this message to the prophet Zechariah son of Berekiah and grandson of Iddo:

² "I, the LORD, was very angry with your ancestors. ³ Therefore, say to the people, 'This is what the LORD of Heaven's Armies says: Return to me, and I will return to you, says the LORD of Heaven's Armies.' ⁴ Don't be like your ancestors who would not listen or pay attention when the earlier prophets said to them, 'This is what the LORD of Heaven's Armies says: Turn from your evil ways, and stop all your evil practices.'

1:1
Ezra 4:24; 5:1
Neh 12:4, 16

1:2
2 Chr 36:16

1:3
Isa 31:6
Mal 3:7

1:4
2 Chr 24:19;
29:6-10; 36:15
Jer 6:17; 11:6-8

**1:1** Hebrew *In the eighth month.* A number of dates in Zechariah can be cross-checked with dates in surviving Persian records and related accurately to our modern calendar. This month of the ancient Hebrew lunar calendar occurred within the months of October and November 520 B.C.

**1:1** Born in Babylon during the Exile, Zechariah was a fairly young man when he returned to Jerusalem in 538 B.C. King Cyrus of Persia had defeated Babylon in 539 and had decreed that captives in exile could return to their homelands. Zechariah and Haggai were among the first to leave. Zechariah, a prophet and a priest, began ministering at the same time as the prophet Haggai (520–518 B.C.). His first prophecy was delivered two months after Haggai's first prophecy.

Like Haggai, Zechariah encouraged the people to continue rebuilding the Temple, whose reconstruction had been halted for

nearly 10 years. Zechariah combated the people's spiritual apathy, despair over pressures from their enemies, and discouragement about the smaller scale of the new Temple foundation. Neglect of our spiritual priorities can be just as devastating today to fulfilling God's purpose.

**1:2-6** The familiar phrase "Like father, like son" implies that children turn out like their parents. But here, God warned Israel *not* to be like their forefathers, who disobeyed him and reaped the consequences—his punishment. We are responsible before God for our actions. We can't use our heredity or environment as

1:6
Jer 12:16-17
Lam 2:17

5 "Where are your ancestors now? They and the prophets are long dead. 6 But everything I said through my servants the prophets happened to your ancestors, just as I said. As a result, they repented and said, 'We have received what we deserved from the LORD of Heaven's Armies. He has done what he said he would do.'"

### A Man among the Myrtle Trees

7 Three months later, on February 15,* the LORD sent another message to the prophet Zechariah son of Berekiah and grandson of Iddo.

1:8
Neh 8:15
Isa 41:19; 55:13
Zech 6:2-3
Rev 6:4
1:9
Zech 2:3

8 In a vision during the night, I saw a man sitting on a red horse that was standing among some myrtle trees in a small valley. Behind him were riders on red, brown, and white horses. 9 I asked the angel who was talking with me, "My lord, what do these horses mean?"

"I will show you," the angel replied.

10 The rider standing among the myrtle trees then explained, "They are the ones the LORD has sent out to patrol the earth."

1:11
Isa 14:7

11 Then the other riders reported to the angel of the LORD, who was standing among the myrtle trees, "We have been patrolling the earth, and the whole earth is at peace."

1:12
Ps 74:10
Isa 64:9-12
Jer 25:11-12
Dan 9:2
1:13
Isa 40:1-2
Zech 4:1

12 Upon hearing this, the angel of the LORD prayed this prayer: "O LORD of Heaven's Armies, for seventy years now you have been angry with Jerusalem and the towns of Judah. How long until you again show mercy to them?" 13 And the LORD spoke kind and comforting words to the angel who talked with me.

1:14
Zech 1:17; 8:2
1:15
Ps 123:4
Amos 1:11

14 Then the angel said to me, "Shout this message for all to hear: 'This is what the LORD of Heaven's Armies says: My love for Jerusalem and Mount Zion is passionate and strong. 15 But I am very angry with the other nations that are now enjoying peace and security. I was only a little angry with my people, but the nations inflicted harm on them far beyond my intentions.

1:16
Ezra 6:14-15
Isa 54:8-10
Zech 2:10

16 "'Therefore, this is what the LORD says: I have returned to show mercy to Jerusalem. My Temple will be rebuilt, says the LORD of Heaven's Armies, and measurements will be taken for the reconstruction of Jerusalem.*'

1:17
Isa 44:26; 51:3

17 "Say this also: 'This is what the LORD of Heaven's Armies says: The towns of Israel will again overflow with prosperity, and the LORD will again comfort Zion and choose Jerusalem as his own.'"

1:7 Hebrew *On the twenty-fourth day of the eleventh month, the month of Shebat, in the second year of Darius.* This event occurred on February 15, 519 B.C.; also see note on 1:1.    1:16 Hebrew *and the measuring line will be stretched out over Jerusalem.*

---

**ZECHARIAH** served as a prophet to Judah about 520 B.C., after the return from exile.

| | |
|---|---|
| Climate of the times . . . . . . . . . . . . | The exiles had returned from captivity to rebuild their Temple. But work on the Temple had stalled, and the people were ignoring their service to God. |
| Main message . . . . . . . . . . . . . . . . . | Zechariah, like Haggai, encouraged the people to finish rebuilding the Temple. His visions gave the people hope. He told the people of a future king who would one day establish an eternal Kingdom. |
| Importance of message . . . . . . . . . | Even in times of discouragement and despair, God is working out his plan. God protects and guides us; we must trust and follow him. |
| Contemporary prophet . . . . . . . . . . | Haggai (approximately 520 B.C.) |

---

excuses for our sins. We are free to choose, and individually we must return to God and follow him.

**1:5, 6** The words God had spoken through his prophets a century earlier, before the captivity, also applied to Zechariah's generation, and they are still relevant for us. Because God's Word endures, we must read, study, and apply what is preserved for us in Scripture. Learn the lessons of God's Word so you will not have to repeat the mistakes of others.

**1:7-17** The man among the myrtle trees was the angel of the Lord (1:11). The horses and their colors were symbols of God's involvement in world governments. The full meaning of the colors is unknown, although the red horse is often associated with war and the white horse with final victory.

**1:11** The angel of the Lord saw that all the nations were secure and at peace, while Israel was still oppressed and despised.

But God was planning a change. He had released his people, and he would allow them to return and rebuild his Temple.

**1:12** Seventy years was the time that God had decreed for Israel to remain in captivity (Jeremiah 25:11; 29:10). This time was over, and the angel asked God to act swiftly to complete the promised return of his people to Jerusalem.

**1:13** God's people had lived under his judgment for 70 years during their captivity in Babylon. But here God spoke words of comfort and assurance. God promises that when we return to him, he will heal us (Hosea 6:1). If you feel wounded and crushed by the events of your life, turn to God so he can heal and comfort you.

**1:15** Although the pagan nations afflicted God's people beyond his intentions, God was not powerless to stop them. God used these nations to punish his sinful people. When the nations went beyond his plans by trying to destroy Israel as a nation, he intervened.

## Four Horns and Four Blacksmiths

18*Then I looked up and saw four animal horns. 19"What are these?" I asked the angel who was talking with me.

He replied, "These horns represent the nations that scattered Judah, Israel, and Jerusalem."

20Then the LORD showed me four blacksmiths. 21"What are these men coming to do?" I asked.

The angel replied, "These four horns—these nations—scattered and humbled Judah. Now these blacksmiths have come to terrify those nations and throw them down and destroy them."

## Future Prosperity of Jerusalem

**2** 1*When I looked again, I saw a man with a measuring line in his hand. 2"Where are you going?" I asked.

He replied, "I am going to measure Jerusalem, to see how wide and how long it is."

3Then the angel who was with me went to meet a second angel who was coming toward him. 4The other angel said, "Hurry, and say to that young man, 'Jerusalem will someday be so full of people and livestock that there won't be room enough for everyone! Many will live outside the city walls. 5Then I, myself, will be a protective wall of fire around Jerusalem, says the LORD. And I will be the glory inside the city!'"

## The Exiles Are Called Home

6The LORD says, "Come away! Flee from Babylon in the land of the north, for I have scattered you to the four winds. 7Come away, people of Zion, you who are exiled in Babylon!"

8After a period of glory, the LORD of Heaven's Armies sent me* against the nations who plundered you. For he said, "Anyone who harms you harms my most precious possession.* 9I will raise my fist to crush them, and their own slaves will plunder them." Then you will know that the LORD of Heaven's Armies has sent me.

10The LORD says, "Shout and rejoice, O beautiful Jerusalem,* for I am coming to live among you. 11Many nations will join themselves to the LORD on that day, and they, too, will be my people. I will live among you, and you will know that the LORD of Heaven's Armies sent me to you. 12The land of Judah will be the LORD's special possession in the holy land, and he will once again choose Jerusalem to be his own city. 13Be silent before the LORD, all humanity, for he is springing into action from his holy dwelling."

## Cleansing for the High Priest

**3** Then the angel showed me Jeshua* the high priest standing before the angel of the LORD. The Accuser, Satan,* was there at the angel's right hand, making accusations against Jeshua. 2And the LORD said to Satan, "I, the LORD, reject your accusations, Satan. Yes, the

**1:19** 1 Kgs 22:11
**1:20** Isa 44:12; 54:16
**1:21** Ps 75:10; Zech 1:18-19
**2:1** Ezek 40:3-5
**2:2** Jer 31:39; Rev 21:15-17
**2:5** Zech 2:10-11
**2:6** Isa 48:20; Jer 3:18; 31:10
**2:8** Deut 32:10; Isa 60:7-14
**2:11** Mic 4:2
**2:12** Deut 32:9; Zech 1:17
**2:13** Ps 78:65; Hab 2:20; Zeph 1:7
**3:1** Ezra 5:2; Job 1:6-12; Ps 109:6; Hag 1:1; Zech 6:11
**3:2** 2 Chr 6:6; Amos 4:11; Zech 2:12; Jude 1:23

**1:18** Verses 1:18-21 are numbered 2:1-4 in Hebrew text.   **2:1** Verses 2:1-13 are numbered 2:5-17 in Hebrew text.   **2:8a** The meaning of the Hebrew is uncertain.   **2:8b** Hebrew *Anyone who touches you touches the pupil of his eye.*   **2:10** Hebrew *O daughter of Zion.*   **3:1a** Hebrew *Joshua,* a variant spelling of Jeshua; also in 3:3, 4, 6, 8, 9.   **3:1b** Hebrew *The satan;* similarly in 3:2.

---

**1:18-21** The horns were the four world powers that oppressed Israel—Egypt, Assyria, Babylon, and Medo-Persia. The four blacksmiths (1:20) were the nations used to overthrow Israel's enemies. God raised them up to judge the oppressors of his people.

**2:1** The man with the measuring line symbolizes the hope of a rebuilt Jerusalem and a restored people. The man would be measuring to mark out the boundaries for a foundation (see 1:16; and Jeremiah 31:38-40).

**2:6, 7** Many of the captive Israelites did not return to Jerusalem because they had become accustomed to the security and wealth they had in Babylon. But Zechariah instructed them to leave Babylon quickly. This was an urgent request because Babylon would be destroyed and its decadent culture would cause God's people to forget their spiritual priorities. A vast majority of the Israelites rejected these warnings and remained in Babylon.

**2:8** Believers are precious to God (Psalm 116:15); they are his very own children (Psalm 103:13). Treating any believer unkindly is the same as treating God that way. As Jesus told his disciples, when we help others we are helping him; when we neglect or abuse them, we are neglecting or abusing him (Matthew 25:34-46). Be

careful, therefore, how you treat fellow believers—that is the way you are treating God.

**2:9-12** *Me* (2:9) may refer to the Messiah, who, in the end, will judge all who have oppressed God's people. God promises to live among his people, and he says that many nations will come to know him (John 1:14; Revelation 21:3).

**2:11, 12** God did not forget his words to Abraham, "All the families on earth will be blessed through you" (Genesis 12:3). Abraham, the father of the nation of Israel, was promised that his descendants would bless the whole world. Since the coming of Jesus, the Messiah, this promise is being fulfilled—people from all nations are coming to God through him.

**3:1** Jeshua was Israel's high priest when the remnant returned to Jerusalem and began rebuilding the walls (Haggai 1:1, 12; 2:4).

**3:1-3** Satan accused Jeshua, who here represents the nation of Israel. The accusations were accurate—Jeshua stood in "filthy" clothes (sins). Yet God revealed his mercy, stating that he chose to save his people in spite of their sin. Satan is always accusing people of their sins before God (Job 1:6). But he greatly misunderstands the breadth of God's mercy and forgiveness toward those who believe in him. Satan the Accuser will ultimately be

LORD, who has chosen Jerusalem, rebukes you. This man is like a burning stick that has been snatched from the fire."

3:3
Ezra 9:15

3:4
Isa 43:25; 61:10
Zech 3:9

³Jeshua's clothing was filthy as he stood there before the angel. ⁴So the angel said to the others standing there, "Take off his filthy clothes." And turning to Jeshua he said, "See, I have taken away your sins, and now I am giving you these fine new clothes."

⁵Then I said, "They should also place a clean turban on his head." So they put a clean priestly turban on his head and dressed him in new clothes while the angel of the LORD stood by.

---

| ZECHARIAH'S VISIONS | Vision | Reference | Significance |
|---|---|---|---|
| | Zechariah sees messengers reporting to God that the surrounding nations that have oppressed Judah are living in careless and sinful ease. | 1:7-17 | Israel was asking, "Why isn't God punishing the wicked?" Wicked nations may prosper, but not forever. God will bring upon them the judgment they deserve. |
| | Zechariah sees four horns, representing the four world powers that oppressed and scattered the people of Judah and Israel. Then he sees four blacksmiths who will throw down the horns. | 1:18-21 | God will do what he promised. After the evil nations have carried out his will in punishing his people, God will destroy these nations for their sin. |
| | Zechariah sees a man measuring the city of Jerusalem. The city will one day be full of people, and God himself will be a wall around the city. | 2:1-13 | The city will be restored in God's future Kingdom. God will keep his promise to protect his people. |
| | Zechariah sees Jeshua the high priest standing before God. Jeshua's filthy clothes are exchanged for fine new clothes; Satan's accusations against him are rejected by God. | 3:1-10 | The story of Jeshua the high priest pictures how the filthy clothes of sin are replaced with the pure linen of God's righteousness. Christ has taken our clothes of sin and replaced them with God's righteousness. (See Ephesians 4:24; 1 John 1:9.) |
| | Zechariah sees a lampstand that is continually kept burning by an unlimited reservoir of oil. This picture reminds the people that it is only through God's Spirit that they will succeed, not by their own might and resources. | 4:1-14 | The Spirit of God is given without measure. Human effort does not make a difference. The work of God is not accomplished in human strength. |
| | Zechariah sees a flying scroll, which represents God's curse. | 5:1-4 | By God's word and Spirit, every person will be judged. The individual's sin is the focus here, not the sins of the nation. God's curse is a symbol of destruction; all sin will be judged and removed. |
| | Zechariah sees a vision of a woman in a basket. She represents the wickedness of the nations. The angel packed the woman back into the basket and sent her back to Babylon. | 5:5-11 | Sins of the individual were judged in the last vision (5:1-4); now sin is being removed from society. Sin has to be eradicated in order to clean up the nation and the individual. |
| | Zechariah sees a vision of four horses and chariots. The horses represent God's judgment on the world—one is sent north, the direction from which most of Judah's enemies came. The other horses are patrolling the world, ready to execute judgment at God's command. | 6:1-8 | Judgment will come upon those who oppress God's people—it will come in God's time and at his command. |

---

destroyed (Revelation 12:10), while everyone who is a believer will be saved (John 3:16). To be prepared, we can ask God to remove our clothing of sin and dress us with his goodness.

**3:2** God punished Judah through the fire of great trials, but he rescued the nation before it was completely destroyed, like "a burning stick that has been snatched from the fire."

**3:2-4** Zechariah's vision graphically portrays how we receive God's mercy. We do nothing ourselves. God removes our filthy clothes (sins), then provides us with fine, new clothes (the righ-

teousness and holiness of God—2 Corinthians 5:21; Ephesians 4:24; Revelation 19:8). All we need to do is repent and ask God to forgive us. When Satan tries to make you feel dirty and unworthy, remember that the clean clothes of Christ's righteousness make you worthy to draw near to God.

**3:5-7** The Greek name for Jeshua is Jesus, meaning "the LORD saves." He is seen here as a symbol of Jesus, the Messiah.

⁶Then the angel of the Lord spoke very solemnly to Jeshua and said, ⁷"This is what the Lord of Heaven's Armies says: If you follow my ways and carefully serve me, then you will be given authority over my Temple and its courtyards. I will let you walk among these others standing here.

⁸"Listen to me, O Jeshua the high priest, and all you other priests. You are symbols of things to come. Soon I am going to bring my servant, the Branch. ⁹Now look at the jewel I have set before Jeshua, a single stone with seven facets.* I will engrave an inscription on it, says the Lord of Heaven's Armies, and I will remove the sins of this land in a single day.

¹⁰"And on that day, says the Lord of Heaven's Armies, each of you will invite your neighbor to sit with you peacefully under your own grapevine and fig tree."

### A Lampstand and Two Olive Trees

**4** Then the angel who had been talking with me returned and woke me, as though I had been asleep. ²"What do you see now?" he asked.

I answered, "I see a solid gold lampstand with a bowl of oil on top of it. Around the bowl are seven lamps, each having seven spouts with wicks. ³And I see two olive trees, one on each side of the bowl." ⁴Then I asked the angel, "What are these, my lord? What do they mean?"

⁵"Don't you know?" the angel asked.

"No, my lord," I replied.

⁶Then he said to me, "This is what the Lord says to Zerubbabel: It is not by force nor by strength, but by my Spirit, says the Lord of Heaven's Armies. ⁷Nothing, not even a mighty mountain, will stand in Zerubbabel's way; it will become a level plain before him! And when Zerubbabel sets the final stone of the Temple in place, the people will shout: 'May God bless it! May God bless it!'*"

⁸Then another message came to me from the Lord: ⁹"Zerubbabel is the one who laid the foundation of this Temple, and he will complete it. Then you will know that the Lord of Heaven's Armies has sent me. ¹⁰Do not despise these small beginnings, for the Lord rejoices to see the work begin, to see the plumb line in Zerubbabel's hand."

(The seven lamps* represent the eyes of the Lord that search all around the world.)

¹¹Then I asked the angel, "What are these two olive trees on each side of the lampstand, ¹²and what are the two olive branches that pour out golden oil through two gold tubes?"

**3:7**
1 Kgs 3:14
Isa 62:9

**3:8**
Isa 4:2; 8:18; 11:1;
53:2
Jer 33:15
Ezek 12:11
Zech 6:12

**3:10**
1 Kgs 4:25
Mic 4:4

**4:1**
Zech 1:9

**4:2**
Exod 25:31, 37
Rev 4:5

**4:3**
Zech 4:11-12, 14
Rev 11:4

**4:5**
Zech 1:9

**4:6**
Isa 11:2-4
Hos 1:7
Hag 2:4-5
Eph 6:17

**4:7**
Ezra 3:11-13
Jer 51:25

**4:9**
Ezra 3:8-10; 5:16
Zech 6:12-15

**4:10**
Amos 7:2, 7-8
Hag 2:3
Zech 3:9
Rev 1:12

**3:9** Hebrew *seven eyes.*   **4:7** Hebrew *'Grace, grace to it.'*   **4:10** Or *The seven facets* (see 3:9); Hebrew reads *These seven.*

---

**3:7-10** There was no priesthood during the Exile, so it had to be reinstated upon the return to the land. In this vision, Jeshua is installed as high priest. One of the high priest's duties was to offer a sacrifice on the Day of Atonement to make amends for all the sins of the people. The priest was the mediator between God and the nation. Thus, he represented the coming Messiah (Isaiah 11:1), who would change the entire order of God's dealing with people's sin (Hebrews 10:8-14 explains this in detail). Jesus, the Messiah, was the High Priest who offered, once for all, the sacrifice of himself to take away our sins. In the new order, every Christian is a priest, offering a holy, cleansed life to God (1 Peter 2:9; Revelation 5:10).

**3:8, 9** The "Branch" refers to the Messiah. The meaning of the stone with seven facets is unclear. It could mean (1) the Branch himself as the foundation stone of the Temple, (2) the rock struck by Moses that produced water for the Israelites (Numbers 20:7-11), or (3) the renewed spiritual priesthood of the church (1 Peter 2:5). These verses were fulfilled hundreds of years later by Jesus Christ. God said, "I will remove the sins of this land in a single day," and this was fulfilled in Christ who "suffered for our sins once for all time . . . to bring you safely home to God" (1 Peter 3:18). You cannot remove your sins by your own effort. You must allow God to remove them through Christ.

**3:10** God promises that each person will have his or her own place of security during Christ's reign (see also Micah 4:4).

**4:1-3** The gold lampstand with a bowl and seven lamps on it represents a steady supply of oil, signifying that God's power would be reflected in the light. Oil was obtained from crushed olives and used in bowls with wicks to produce light. The two olive trees stood for the priestly and royal offices.

**4:6** Zerubbabel was given the responsibility of rebuilding the Temple in Jerusalem (Ezra 3:2, 8; Haggai 1:1; 2:23). While the prophets Haggai and Zechariah gave the moral and spiritual encouragement to resume work on the Temple, Zerubbabel saw that the task was carried out. As the work was being completed, the prophets encouraged Zerubbabel and told him of a time when spiritual apathy and foreign oppression would forever be abolished.

**4:6** Many people believe that to survive in this world a person must be tough, strong, unbending, and harsh. But God says, "Not by force nor by strength, but by my Spirit." The key words are "by my Spirit." It is *only* through God's Spirit that anything of lasting value is accomplished. The returned exiles were indeed weak—harassed by their enemies, tired, discouraged, and poor. But actually they had God on their side! As you live for God, determine not to trust in your own strength or abilities. Instead, depend on God and work in the power of his Spirit! (See also Hosea 1:7.)

**4:9** The Temple was completed in 516 B.C. (Ezra 6:14, 15).

**4:10** Many of the older Jews were disheartened when they realized this new Temple would not match the size and splendor of the previous Temple built during King Solomon's reign. But bigger and more beautiful is not always better. What you do for God may seem small and insignificant at the time, but God rejoices in what is right, not necessarily in what is big. Be faithful in the small opportunities. Begin where you are and do what you can, and leave the results to God.

4:14
Exod 29:7
Isa 61:1-3
Dan 9:24-26
Mic 4:13
Zech 3:1-7
Rev 11:4

13 "Don't you know?" he asked.

"No, my lord," I replied.

14 Then he said to me, "They represent the two heavenly beings who stand in the court of the Lord of all the earth."

## A Flying Scroll

5:1
Jer 36:1-6
Ezek 2:9-10

**5** I looked up again and saw a scroll flying through the air. 2 "What do you see?" the angel asked.

"I see a flying scroll," I replied. "It appears to be about 30 feet long and 15 feet wide.*"

5:3
Exod 20:15
Jer 26:6
Mal 3:8-9

3 Then he said to me, "This scroll contains the curse that is going out over the entire land. One side of the scroll says that those who steal will be banished from the land; the other side says that those who swear falsely will be banished from the land. 4 And this is what the LORD

5:4
Lev 14:34-45
Jer 2:26
Hab 2:9-11
Mal 3:5

of Heaven's Armies says: I am sending this curse into the house of every thief and into the house of everyone who swears falsely using my name. And my curse will remain in that house and completely destroy it—even its timbers and stones."

## A Woman in a Basket

5:5
Zech 1:9

5 Then the angel who was talking with me came forward and said, "Look up and see what's coming."

5:6
Lev 19:36
Amos 8:5

6 "What is it?" I asked.

He replied, "It is a basket for measuring grain,* and it's filled with the sins* of everyone throughout the land."

5:8
Hos 12:7
Mic 6:11

7 Then the heavy lead cover was lifted off the basket, and there was a woman sitting inside it. 8 The angel said, "The woman's name is Wickedness," and he pushed her back into the basket and closed the heavy lid again.

9 Then I looked up and saw two women flying toward us, gliding on the wind. They had wings like a stork, and they picked up the basket and flew into the sky.

10 "Where are they taking the basket?" I asked the angel.

5:11
Gen 10:10
Isa 11:11
Dan 1:2

11 He replied, "To the land of Babylonia,* where they will build a temple for the basket. And when the temple is ready, they will set the basket there on its pedestal."

## Four Chariots

6:1
Zech 1:18; 6:5
6:2
Rev 6:4-5
6:3
Rev 6:2

**6** Then I looked up again and saw four chariots coming from between two bronze mountains. 2 The first chariot was pulled by red horses, the second by black horses, 3 the third by white horses, and the fourth by powerful dappled-gray horses. 4 "And what are these, my lord?" I asked the angel who was talking with me.

6:5
Ezek 37:9
Dan 7:2
Rev 7:1

5 The angel replied, "These are the four spirits* of heaven who stand before the Lord of all the earth. They are going out to do his work. 6 The chariot with black horses is going north, the chariot with white horses is going west,* and the chariot with dappled-gray horses is going south."

6:6
Ezek 1:4
Dan 11:5-6, 9, 40

7 The powerful horses were eager to set out to patrol the earth. And the LORD said, "Go and patrol the earth!" So they left at once on their patrol.

6:8
Jer 1:14-15
Ezek 5:13

8 Then the LORD summoned me and said, "Look, those who went north have vented the anger of my Spirit* there in the land of the north."

**5:2** Hebrew *20 cubits* [9 meters] *long and 10 cubits* [4.5 meters] *wide.* **5:6a** Hebrew *an ephah* [20 quarts or 22 liters]; also in 5:7, 8, 9, 10, 11. **5:6b** As in Greek version; Hebrew reads *the appearance.* **5:11** Hebrew *the land of Shinar.* **6:5** Or *the four winds.* **6:6** Hebrew *is going after them.* **6:8** Hebrew *have given my Spirit rest.*

---

**4:14** The two heavenly beings may be Jeshua and Zerubbabel, dedicated for this special task. Also note that in Revelation 11:3, two witnesses arise to prophesy to the nations during the time of tribulation. These witnesses will be killed but will rise again.

**5:1-9** The judgment of the flying scroll was leveled against those who violated God's law, specifically by stealing and lying (5:1-4). The woman in a basket personified wickedness, and so this vision showed that wickedness would be not only severely punished (the vision of the flying scroll) but also banished (the vision of the woman in a basket, 5:6-9).

**5:9-11** The woman in a basket was carried away "to the land of Babylonia," which had become a symbol for the center of world idolatry and wickedness. This woman was a picture to Zechariah that wickedness and sin would be taken away from Israel and one day sin would be removed from the entire earth. When Christ

died, he removed sin's power and penalty. When we trust Christ to forgive us, he removes the penalty of sin and gives us the power to overcome sin in our life. When Christ returns, he will remove all sin from the earth, allowing people to live in eternal safety and security.

**6:1-8** The four chariots were similar to the four horsemen in the first vision. These chariots represent the four angels of God's judgment on the earth.

**6:6, 8** The black horses that went north executed God's judgment in the north country. God is angry with sin and with the wicked (Psalm 7:11), and his anger is expressed in judgment. As much as we like to concentrate on God's love and mercy, anger and judgment are also part of his righteous character. If you have unconfessed or habitual sin in your life, confess it and turn away from it. Confession releases God's mercy, but refusing to repent invites his judgment.

## 2. Zechariah's words of encouragement
### The Crowning of Jeshua

9 Then I received another message from the LORD: 10 "Heldai, Tobijah, and Jedaiah will bring gifts of silver and gold from the Jews exiled in Babylon. As soon as they arrive, meet them at the home of Josiah son of Zephaniah. 11 Accept their gifts, and make a crown* from the silver and gold. Then put the crown on the head of Jeshua* son of Jehozadak, the high priest. 12 Tell him, 'This is what the LORD of Heaven's Armies says: Here is the man called the Branch. He will branch out from where he is and build the Temple of the LORD. 13 Yes, he will build the Temple of the LORD. Then he will receive royal honor and will rule as king from his throne. He will also serve as priest from his throne,* and there will be perfect harmony between his two roles.'

14 "The crown will be a memorial in the Temple of the LORD to honor those who gave it—Heldai,* Tobijah, Jedaiah, and Josiah* son of Zephaniah."

15 People will come from distant lands to rebuild the Temple of the LORD. And when this happens, you will know that my messages have been from the LORD of Heaven's Armies. All this will happen if you carefully obey what the LORD your God says.

### A Call to Justice and Mercy

7 On December 7* of the fourth year of King Darius's reign, another message came to Zechariah from the LORD. 2 The people of Bethel had sent Sharezer and Regemmelech,* along with their attendants, to seek the LORD's favor. 3 They were to ask this question of the prophets and the priests at the Temple of the LORD of Heaven's Armies: "Should we continue to mourn and fast each summer on the anniversary of the Temple's destruction,* as we have done for so many years?"

4 The LORD of Heaven's Armies sent me this message in reply: 5 "Say to all your people and your priests, 'During these seventy years of exile, when you fasted and mourned in the summer and in early autumn,* was it really for me that you were fasting? 6 And even now in your holy festivals, aren't you eating and drinking just to please yourselves? 7 Isn't this the same message the LORD proclaimed through the prophets in years past when Jerusalem and the towns of Judah were bustling with people, and the Negev and the foothills of Judah* were well populated?'"

8 Then this message came to Zechariah from the LORD: 9 "This is what the LORD of Heaven's Armies says: Judge fairly, and show mercy and kindness to one another. 10 Do not oppress widows, orphans, foreigners, and the poor. And do not scheme against each other.

6:9 Zech 1:1; 7:1; 8:1
6:10 Ezra 7:14-16; 8:26-30
6:12 Isa 4:2-3; 11:1 Jer 23:5-6 Zech 3:8; 4:6-9
6:13 Ps 110:4 Isa 9:6; 11:10
6:15 Isa 56:6-8; 60:10 Zech 3:7
7:2 Zech 8:21
7:3 Ezra 3:10-12
7:5 Isa 58:5 Zech 1:12 Matt 5:16; 6:2, 5, 16; 23:5
7:7 Jer 17:26; 22:21 Zech 1:4
7:9 Mic 6:8 Zech 8:16
7:10 Exod 22:22 Deut 24:14-18 Prov 22:22-23 Zech 8:17

6:11a As in Greek and Syriac versions; Hebrew reads crowns.  6:11b Hebrew Joshua, a variant spelling of Jeshua.  6:13 Or There will be a priest by his throne.  6:14a As in Syriac version (compare 6:10); Hebrew reads Helem.  6:14b As in Syriac version (compare 6:10); Hebrew reads Hen.  7:1 Hebrew On the fourth day of the ninth month, the month of Kislev, of the ancient Hebrew lunar calendar. This event occurred on December 7, 518 B.C.; also see note on 1:1.  7:2 Or Bethel-sharezer had sent Regemmelech.  7:3 Hebrew mourn and fast in the fifth month. The Temple had been destroyed in the fifth month of the ancient Hebrew lunar calendar (August 586 B.C.); see 2 Kgs 25:8.  7:5 Hebrew fasted and mourned in the fifth and seventh months. The fifth month of the ancient Hebrew lunar calendar usually occurs within the months of July and August. The seventh month usually occurs within the months of September and October; both the Day of Atonement and the Festival of Shelters were celebrated in the seventh month.  7:7 Hebrew the Shephelah.

6:9-15 This vision is about the Messiah, the King-Priest. In the days of the kings and after the Exile, Judah's government was to be ruled by two distinct persons—the king, ruling the nation's political life, and the high priest, ruling its religious life. Kings and priests had often been corrupt. God was telling Zechariah that someone worthy of the crown would come to rule as both king ("rule as king from his throne") and priest ("as priest from his throne"). This was an unlikely combination for that day.

6:15 Some of God's promises are conditional—we must obey him to receive them. The rebuilding of the Temple required careful obedience. God would protect the people as long as they obeyed. Casual or occasional obedience, the result of a halfhearted or divided commitment, would not lead to blessing. Many of God's blessings come to us as a result of diligent obedience. Inconsistent obedience can't produce consistent blessing.

7:1ff The fourth year of King Darius's reign was 518 B.C. For the previous 70 years, the people had been holding a fast in August to remember the destruction of Jerusalem. Because Jerusalem was being rebuilt, they came to the Temple to ask if they had to continue this annual fast. God did not answer their question directly. Instead, he told them that their acts of justice and mercy were more important than their fasting. What he wanted from his people was true justice in their dealings and mercy and compassion for the weak.

7:5-7 The Israelites had lost their sincere desire for a loving relationship with God. Zechariah told them that they had been fasting without a proper attitude of repentance or worship. They fasted and mourned during their exile with no thought of God or their sins that had caused it in the first place. When you go to church, pray, or have fellowship with other believers, are you doing these things from habit or for what you can get out of them? God says that an attitude of worship without a sincere desire to know and love him will lead to ruin.

7:7 The Negev was the southern part of Judah.

**7:11**
Ps 58:4-5
Jer 8:5
Acts 7:57

**7:12**
Neh 9:30
Jer 17:1
Ezek 3:9
Dan 9:11-12

**7:13**
Prov 1:24-28
Isa 1:15
Jer 11:10-14

**7:14**
Deut 28:64
Jer 12:10; 23:19;
44:6

**8:3**
Zech 2:10

**8:4**
Isa 65:20-22

**8:5**
Jer 30:19-20

**8:6**
Ps 118:23
Jer 32:17, 27

**8:7**
Ps 107:2-3
Isa 11:11; 43:5
Amos 9:14-15

**8:8**
Ezek 37:28
Zech 2:11; 10:10

**8:9**
Ezra 5:1; 6:14
Hag 2:4

**8:10**
Isa 19:2
Amos 3:6; 9:4
Hag 1:6-11;
2:16-19

**8:11**
Isa 12:1

**8:12**
Gen 27:28

**8:13**
Ps 72:17
Jer 29:18
Dan 9:11
Zech 14:11

¹¹"Your ancestors refused to listen to this message. They stubbornly turned away and put their fingers in their ears to keep from hearing. ¹²They made their hearts as hard as stone, so they could not hear the instructions or the messages that the LORD of Heaven's Armies had sent them by his Spirit through the earlier prophets. That is why the LORD of Heaven's Armies was so angry with them.

¹³"Since they refused to listen when I called to them, I would not listen when they called to me, says the LORD of Heaven's Armies. ¹⁴As with a whirlwind, I scattered them among the distant nations, where they lived as strangers. Their land became so desolate that no one even traveled through it. They turned their pleasant land into a desert."

## Promised Blessings for Jerusalem

**8** Then another message came to me from the LORD of Heaven's Armies: ²"This is what the LORD of Heaven's Armies says: My love for Mount Zion is passionate and strong; I am consumed with passion for Jerusalem!

³"And now the LORD says: I am returning to Mount Zion, and I will live in Jerusalem. Then Jerusalem will be called the Faithful City; the mountain of the LORD of Heaven's Armies will be called the Holy Mountain.

⁴"This is what the LORD of Heaven's Armies says: Once again old men and women will walk Jerusalem's streets with their canes and will sit together in the city squares. ⁵And the streets of the city will be filled with boys and girls at play.

⁶"This is what the LORD of Heaven's Armies says: All this may seem impossible to you now, a small remnant of God's people. But is it impossible for me? says the LORD of Heaven's Armies.

⁷"This is what the LORD of Heaven's Armies says: You can be sure that I will rescue my people from the east and from the west. ⁸I will bring them home again to live safely in Jerusalem. They will be my people, and I will be faithful and just toward them as their God.

⁹"This is what the LORD of Heaven's Armies says: Be strong and finish the task! Ever since the laying of the foundation of the Temple of the LORD of Heaven's Armies, you have heard what the prophets have been saying about completing the building. ¹⁰Before the work on the Temple began, there were no jobs and no money to hire people or animals. No traveler was safe from the enemy, for there were enemies on all sides. I had turned everyone against each other.

¹¹"But now I will not treat the remnant of my people as I treated them before, says the LORD of Heaven's Armies. ¹²For I am planting seeds of peace and prosperity among you. The grapevines will be heavy with fruit. The earth will produce its crops, and the heavens will release the dew. Once more I will cause the remnant in Judah and Israel to inherit these blessings. ¹³Among the other nations, Judah and Israel became symbols of a cursed nation. But no longer! Now I will rescue you and make you both a symbol and a source of blessing. So don't be afraid. Be strong, and get on with rebuilding the Temple!

---

**7:11, 12** Zechariah explained to the people that their ancestors brought God's great wrath on themselves by hardening their hearts. Any sin seems more natural the second time—as we become hardened, each repetition is easier. Ignoring or refusing God's warning hardens you each time you do wrong. Read God's Word and apply it to your life. Sensitivity and submission to God's Word can soften your heart and allow you to live as you should.

**8:3** One day Christ will reign in his Kingdom on earth. There all his people will live with him. This truth should encourage us to look forward to the Messiah's reign.

**8:4, 5** In troubled times, the very old and very young are the first to suffer and die. But both groups are plentiful in this vision, filling the streets with their normal everyday activities. This is a sign of the complete peace and prosperity of God's new earth.

**8:6** The remnant was the small group of exiles who had returned from Babylon to rebuild Jerusalem and the Temple. Struggling to survive in the land, they became discouraged over the opposition they often faced from hostile neighbors. It was hard to believe that one day God himself would reign from this city and that their land would enjoy great peace and prosperity. Our God is all-powerful; he can do anything! When confronting seemingly

impossible tasks or situations, remember that "with God everything is possible" (Matthew 19:26).

**8:8** The covenant relationship will be renewed, and the whole community will be filled with the presence of God. This promise of forgiveness and restoration extends to all God's people wherever they may be found. (For other references to this promise, see Exodus 6:6, 7; 19:5, 6; 29:45; Leviticus 26:12; Deuteronomy 7:6; Jeremiah 31:1, 33.)

**8:9** God had to give the Temple workers a little push to get them moving. They had heard the prophets' words of encouragement; at this time they needed to stop just listening and get to work. We need to listen to what God says, but after he has made our course of action plain, we need to "be strong" and do what he wants.

**8:13-15** For more than 15 years, God and his prophets had been urging the people to finish building the Temple. Here again, God encouraged them with visions of the future. We may be tempted to slow down for many reasons: People aren't responding; we feel physically or emotionally drained; the workers are uncooperative; the work is distasteful, too difficult, or not worth the effort. God's promises about the future should encourage us *now*. He knows what the results of our labors will be, and thus he can give us a perspective that will help us continue in our work for him.

¹⁴"For this is what the LORD of Heaven's Armies says: I was determined to punish you when your ancestors angered me, and I did not change my mind, says the LORD of Heaven's Armies. ¹⁵But now I am determined to bless Jerusalem and the people of Judah. So don't be afraid. ¹⁶But this is what you must do: Tell the truth to each other. Render verdicts in your courts that are just and that lead to peace. ¹⁷Don't scheme against each other. Stop your love of telling lies that you swear are the truth. I hate all these things, says the LORD."

¹⁸Here is another message that came to me from the LORD of Heaven's Armies. ¹⁹"This is what the LORD of Heaven's Armies says: The traditional fasts and times of mourning you have kept in early summer, midsummer, autumn, and winter* are now ended. They will become festivals of joy and celebration for the people of Judah. So love truth and peace.

²⁰"This is what the LORD of Heaven's Armies says: People from nations and cities around the world will travel to Jerusalem. ²¹The people of one city will say to the people of another, 'Come with us to Jerusalem to ask the LORD to bless us. Let's worship the LORD of Heaven's Armies. I'm determined to go.' ²²Many peoples and powerful nations will come to Jerusalem to seek the LORD of Heaven's Armies and to ask for his blessing.

²³"This is what the LORD of Heaven's Armies says: In those days ten men from different nations and languages of the world will clutch at the sleeve of one Jew. And they will say, 'Please let us walk with you, for we have heard that God is with you.'"

## B. MESSAGES AFTER COMPLETING THE TEMPLE (9:1—14:21)

After the Temple was completed, Zechariah gave several prophecies about Israel's future, which describe the first and second comings of Jesus Christ. This book contains more about the person, work, and glory of Christ than the other minor prophets combined. Israel's King would come, but he would be rejected by his people. They would later repent and be restored to God. The King who is coming is our King. May we be found faithful and pure in his sight when we meet him face to face.

### Judgment against Israel's Enemies

**9** This is the message* from the LORD against the land of Aram* and the city of Damascus, for the eyes of humanity, including all the tribes of Israel, are on the LORD.

² Doom is certain for Hamath,
    near Damascus,
and for the cities of Tyre and Sidon,
    though they are so clever.
³ Tyre has built a strong fortress
    and has made silver and gold
    as plentiful as dust in the streets!
⁴ But now the Lord will strip away Tyre's possessions
    and hurl its fortifications into the sea,
    and it will be burned to the ground.
⁵ The city of Ashkelon will see Tyre fall
    and will be filled with fear.

**8:14** Jer 4:28; 29:11-14
Ezek 24:14
**8:15** Jer 29:11
**8:16** †Eph 4:25
**8:17** Zech 5:3-4; 7:10
Mal 3:5
**8:19** Isa 12:1
Zech 7:3-5; 8:16
Luke 1:74-75
**8:20** Zech 2:11; 14:16
**8:22** Isa 49:6, 22-23;
60:3-12
**8:23** Isa 45:14; 60:14
**9:1** Amos 1:3-5
**9:2** Jer 49:23
Ezek 28:3-5
**9:3** Josh 19:29
**9:4** Isa 23:1-7
Ezek 27:32;
28:16, 18

---

**8:19** Hebrew *in the fourth, fifth, seventh, and tenth months.* The fourth month of the ancient Hebrew lunar calendar usually occurs within the months of June and July. The fifth month usually occurs within the months of July and August. The seventh month usually occurs within the months of September and October. The tenth month usually occurs within the months of December and January.   **9:1a** Hebrew *An Oracle: The message.*   **9:1b** Hebrew *land of Hadrach.*

---

**8:14-17** God promised to give his people rich rewards, reassuring them that despite the punishments they had endured, he would not change his mind to bless them. But he also said they had a job to do: "This is what you must do." God will be faithful, but we also have responsibilities: to tell the truth, exercise justice, and live peacefully. If you expect God to do his part, be sure to do yours.

**8:19-22** There will come a time when fasting for sins will be replaced by feasting and joy. People from all nations will "seek the LORD of Heaven's Armies." This was also promised in 2:11.

**8:23** In the past, Jerusalem had often borne the brunt of cruel jokes from other nations (8:13). The city was not respected; its citizens had sinned so much that God let them be kicked around by their enemies. But eventually, says Zechariah, Jerusalem will be a holy place—highly respected throughout the world because its people will have a change of heart toward God. People from

other nations will see how God has rewarded his people for their faithfulness and want to be included in their great blessings.

**9:1-17** The last six chapters of the book are two messages delivered late in Zechariah's life. These messages point to the Messiah and his second coming. Some of these prophecies were fulfilled before the Messiah came, perhaps by Alexander the Great; others were fulfilled during the Messiah's time on earth; and others will be fulfilled when he returns. Those who oppressed Jerusalem—Aram, Philistia, Phoenicia—would be crushed. Zion's promised King would come—first as a servant on a donkey's colt, later as a powerful ruler and judge.

**9:5-7** Zechariah mentions four key cities in Philistia: Ashkelon, Gaza, and Ekron would be destroyed, and Ashdod would be overtaken by foreigners. This would happen because of their great evil and idolatry. But those left in the land would be adopted into Israel as a new clan, as the Jebusites were. (When David conquered

Gaza will shake with terror,
as will Ekron, for their hopes will be dashed.
Gaza's king will be killed,
and Ashkelon will be deserted.
⁶ Foreigners will occupy the city of Ashdod.
I will destroy the pride of the Philistines.
⁷ I will grab the bloody meat from their mouths
and snatch the detestable sacrifices from their teeth.
Then the surviving Philistines will worship our God
and become like a clan in Judah.*
The Philistines of Ekron will join my people,
as the ancient Jebusites once did.

**9:8**
Isa 52:1; 54:14

⁸ I will guard my Temple
and protect it from invading armies.
I am watching closely to ensure
that no more foreign oppressors overrun my people's land.

### Zion's Coming King

**9:9**
Ps 97:6-8
Isa 9:6-7; 57:15
Jer 23:5-6
Zech 2:10
†Matt 21:5
†John 12:15

⁹ Rejoice, O people of Zion!*
Shout in triumph, O people of Jerusalem!
Look, your king is coming to you.
He is righteous and victorious,*
yet he is humble, riding on a donkey—
riding on a donkey's colt.

**9:10**
Ps 72:17
Isa 57:18-19
Mic 4:2-10; 5:4

¹⁰ I will remove the battle chariots from Israel*
and the warhorses from Jerusalem.
I will destroy all the weapons used in battle,
and your king will bring peace to the nations.
His realm will stretch from sea to sea
and from the Euphrates River* to the ends of the earth.*

**9:11**
Exod 24:8
Heb 10:29

¹¹ Because of the covenant I made with you,
sealed with blood,
I will free your prisoners
from death in a waterless dungeon.

**9:12**
Isa 61:7
Joel 3:16

¹² Come back to the place of safety,
all you prisoners who still have hope!
I promise this very day
that I will repay two blessings for each of your troubles.

**9:13**
Ps 45:3
Jer 51:20
Joel 3:6-8

¹³ Judah is my bow,
and Israel is my arrow.
Jerusalem* is my sword,
and like a warrior, I will brandish it against the Greeks.*

**9:7** Hebrew *and will become a leader in Judah.*   **9:9a** Hebrew *O daughter of Zion!*   **9:9b** Hebrew *and is being vindicated.*   **9:10a** Hebrew *Ephraim,* referring to the northern kingdom of Israel; also in 9:13.   **9:10b** Hebrew *the river.*   **9:10c** Or *the end of the land.*   **9:13a** Hebrew *Zion.*   **9:13b** Hebrew *the sons of Javan.*

Jerusalem, he did not wipe out the Jebusites, but absorbed them into Judah.)

**9:8** Several centuries after Zechariah's day, Antiochus IV Epiphanes would invade Israel; and in A.D. 70, Titus, a Roman general, would completely destroy the Temple. This promise, therefore, may have been conditional upon the people's obedience. The day will come, however, when God's people will never again have to worry about invading enemies (Joel 3:17).

**9:9** The triumphal entry of Jesus riding into Jerusalem (Matthew 21:1-11) was predicted here more than 500 years before it happened. Just as this prophecy was fulfilled when Jesus came to earth, so the prophecies of his second coming are just as certain to come true. We are to be ready for his return, for he is coming!

**9:10** When we view two distant mountains, they appear to be close together, perhaps even to touch each other. But as we approach them, we can see that they are, in fact, far apart, even

separated by a huge valley. This is the situation with many Old Testament prophecies. Verse 9 was clearly fulfilled in Christ's first coming, but verse 10 can now be seen to refer to his second coming. At that time all nations will be subject to Christ, and his rule will extend over the whole earth. In Philippians 2:9-11, we are told that at that time every knee will bow to Christ and every tongue will confess him as Lord.

**9:11** Covenants in Old Testament times were sealed or confirmed with blood, much as we would sign our name to a contract. The old covenant was sealed by the blood of sacrifices, pointing ahead to the blood Christ would shed at Calvary, his "signature" that confirmed God's new covenant with his people. Because God had made a covenant with these people, he delivered them from the "waterless dungeon," the cistern-like prison of exile.

<sup>14</sup> The LORD will appear above his people;
  his arrows will fly like lightning!
The Sovereign LORD will sound the ram's horn
  and attack like a whirlwind from the southern desert.

<sup>15</sup> The LORD of Heaven's Armies will protect his people,
  and they will defeat their enemies by hurling great stones.
They will shout in battle as though drunk with wine.
  They will be filled with blood like a bowl,
  drenched with blood like the corners of the altar.

<sup>16</sup> On that day the LORD their God will rescue his people,
  just as a shepherd rescues his sheep.
They will sparkle in his land
  like jewels in a crown.

<sup>17</sup> How wonderful and beautiful they will be!
  The young men will thrive on abundant grain,
  and the young women will flourish on new wine.

### The LORD Will Restore His People

**10** <sup>1</sup> Ask the LORD for rain in the spring,
  for he makes the storm clouds.
And he will send showers of rain
  so every field becomes a lush pasture.

<sup>2</sup> Household gods give worthless advice,
  fortune-tellers predict only lies,
and interpreters of dreams pronounce
  falsehoods that give no comfort.
So my people are wandering like lost sheep;
  they are attacked because they have no shepherd.

<sup>3</sup> "My anger burns against your shepherds,
  and I will punish these leaders.*
For the LORD of Heaven's Armies has arrived
  to look after Judah, his flock.
He will make them strong and glorious,
  like a proud warhorse in battle.

<sup>4</sup> From Judah will come the cornerstone,
  the tent peg,
the bow for battle,
  and all the rulers.

<sup>5</sup> They will be like mighty warriors in battle,
  trampling their enemies in the mud under their feet.
Since the LORD is with them as they fight,
  they will overthrow even the enemy's horsemen.

<sup>6</sup> "I will strengthen Judah and save Israel*;
  I will restore them because of my compassion.

**10:3** Or *these male goats.*   **10:6** Hebrew *save the house of Joseph.*

---

**9:14** 
Ps 18:14
Isa 27:13; 31:5

**9:15** 
Zech 12:6

**9:16** 
Isa 62:3

**10:1** 
Jer 10:13
Hos 6:3
Joel 2:23-24

**10:2** 
Ezek 34:5, 8
Mic 3:6-11
Matt 9:36
Mark 6:34

**10:3** 
Ezek 34:2, 7, 12

**10:5** 
2 Sam 22:43

**10:6** 
Isa 54:8

---

**9:14-17** After Solomon's reign, the kingdom was divided into the northern kingdom (called Israel or Ephraim) and the southern kingdom (called Judah, with Jerusalem as the capital). This prophecy says that all Israel, north and south, will someday be reunited. The first part of this chapter tells how God will help his people avoid war; here God explains that he will come to help his people when war is inevitable. Verses 14-16 explain how the Jews will win over the Greeks, but it is also a figurative picture of the ultimate future victory over evil by God's people.

**10:2** We often create idols of money, power, fame, or success, and then we expect them to give us happiness and security. But these idols can't supply what we need any more than a stone image can make it rain. How foolish it is to trust in idols. Instead, trust God's promises for your future.

**10:4** Zechariah's prophecy, more than 500 years before Christ's

first coming, called Christ the "cornerstone" (see also Isaiah 28:16), the "tent peg" (Isaiah 22:23), the "bow for battle," and a ruler who was a man of action (see also Genesis 49:10; Micah 5:2). This Messiah would be strong, stable, victorious, and trustworthy—in all ways, the answer to Israel's problems. Only in the Messiah will all the promises to God's people be fulfilled.

**10:6** Judah refers to the southern kingdom, and Israel refers to the northern kingdom. One day God will unite all his people. This verse tells about God's reuniting of the Jews (see also Jeremiah 31:10). This was a startling idea. The people of the northern kingdom of Israel were so completely absorbed into other cultures after their captivity in 722 B.C. that a regathering could only be accomplished by God.

**10:6, 12** God promises to strengthen his people. When we stay closely connected to God, his Spirit will enable us to do his will,

It will be as though I had never rejected them,
    for I am the LORD their God, who will hear their cries.
7 The people of Israel* will become like mighty warriors,
    and their hearts will be made happy as if by wine.
Their children, too, will see it and be glad;
    their hearts will rejoice in the LORD.

8 When I whistle to them, they will come running,
    for I have redeemed them.
From the few who are left,
    they will grow as numerous as they were before.

9 Though I have scattered them like seeds among the nations,
    they will still remember me in distant lands.
They and their children will survive
    and return again to Israel.

10 I will bring them back from Egypt
    and gather them from Assyria.
I will resettle them in Gilead and Lebanon
    until there is no more room for them all.

11 They will pass safely through the sea of distress,*
    for the waves of the sea will be held back,
    and the waters of the Nile will dry up.
The pride of Assyria will be crushed,
    and the rule of Egypt will end.

12 By my power* I will make my people strong,
    and by my authority they will go wherever they wish.
    I, the LORD, have spoken!"

**11** ¹ Open your doors, Lebanon,
    so that fire may devour your cedar forests.
² Weep, you cypress trees, for all the ruined cedars;
    the most majestic ones have fallen.
Weep, you oaks of Bashan,
    for the thick forests have been cut down.
³ Listen to the wailing of the shepherds,
    for their rich pastures are destroyed.
Hear the young lions roaring,
    for their thickets in the Jordan Valley are ruined.

### The Good and Evil Shepherds

⁴This is what the LORD my God says: "Go and care for the flock that is intended for slaughter. ⁵The buyers slaughter their sheep without remorse. The sellers say, 'Praise the LORD! Now I'm rich!' Even the shepherds have no compassion for them. ⁶Likewise, I will no longer have pity on the people of the land," says the LORD. "I will let them fall into each other's hands and into the hands of their king. They will turn the land into a wilderness, and I will not rescue them."

10:7 Hebrew *of Ephraim.*   10:11 Or *the sea of Egypt,* referring to the Red Sea.   10:12 Hebrew *In the LORD.*

### Cross-references (margin)

**10:8**
Isa 5:26; 7:18-19
Jer 33:22
Ezek 36:11

**10:9**
1 Kgs 8:47-48
Ezek 6:9

**10:10**
Isa 11:11-16;
49:19-21

**10:11**
Isa 19:5-7
Ezek 30:13
Zeph 2:13

**10:12**
Mic 4:5

**11:1**
Ezek 31:3

**11:3**
Jer 2:15; 25:34-36;
50:44

**11:5**
Jer 50:7
Ezek 34:2-6
Hos 12:8
1 Tim 6:9

**11:6**
Isa 9:19-21
Jer 13:14
Zech 8:10; 14:13

---

despite the obstacles. When we stray away from God, we will be cut off from our power source.

**10:10** This pictured return from Egypt and Assyria was a symbolic way of saying that the people would be returned from all the countries where they had been dispersed. Egypt and Assyria evoked memories of slavery and separation.

**10:11** The "sea of distress" refers to the Red Sea, through which the Israelites were miraculously delivered from Egypt. As the Israelites returned once again from Egypt and other lands, they would be protected by God's miraculous power.

**11:4-17** In this message, God told Zechariah to act out the roles of two different kinds of shepherds. The first type of shepherd demonstrated how God would reject his people (the sheep) because they rejected him (11:4-14). The second type of shep-

herd demonstrated how God would let his people fall into the clutches of evil shepherds (11:15-17). (See Ezekiel 34 for a detailed portrayal of the evil shepherds of Israel.)

**11:4** God told Zechariah to take a job as shepherd of a flock of sheep being fattened for slaughter. The Messiah would shepherd God's people during a time of spiritual and political confusion. The flock represented the people feeding on their own greed and evil desires until they were ripe for God's judgment.

⁷So I cared for the flock intended for slaughter—the flock that was oppressed. Then I took two shepherd's staffs and named one Favor and the other Union. ⁸I got rid of their three evil shepherds in a single month.

But I became impatient with these sheep, and they hated me, too. ⁹So I told them, "I won't be your shepherd any longer. If you die, you die. If you are killed, you are killed. And let those who remain devour each other!"

¹⁰Then I took my staff called Favor and cut it in two, showing that I had revoked the covenant I had made with all the nations. ¹¹That was the end of my covenant with them. The suffering flock was watching me, and they knew that the LORD was speaking through my actions.

¹²And I said to them, "If you like, give me my wages, whatever I am worth; but only if you want to." So they counted out for my wages thirty pieces of silver.

¹³And the LORD said to me, "Throw it to the potter*"—this magnificent sum at which they valued me! So I took the thirty coins and threw them to the potter in the Temple of the LORD.

¹⁴Then I took my other staff, Union, and cut it in two, showing that the bond of unity between Judah and Israel was broken.

¹⁵Then the LORD said to me, "Go again and play the part of a worthless shepherd. ¹⁶This illustrates how I will give this nation a shepherd who will not care for those who are dying, nor look after the young,* nor heal the injured, nor feed the healthy. Instead, this shepherd will eat the meat of the fattest sheep and tear off their hooves.

¹⁷ "What sorrow awaits this worthless shepherd
    who abandons the flock!
The sword will cut his arm
    and pierce his right eye.
His arm will become useless,
    and his right eye completely blind."

### Future Deliverance for Jerusalem

**12** This* message concerning the fate of Israel came from the LORD: "This message is from the LORD, who stretched out the heavens, laid the foundations of the earth, and formed the human spirit. ²I will make Jerusalem like an intoxicating drink that makes the nearby nations stagger when they send their armies to besiege Jerusalem and Judah. ³On that day I will make Jerusalem an immovable rock. All the nations will gather against it to try to move it, but they will only hurt themselves.

⁴"On that day," says the LORD, "I will cause every horse to panic and every rider to lose his nerve. I will watch over the people of Judah, but I will blind all the horses of their enemies. ⁵And the clans of Judah will say to themselves, 'The people of Jerusalem have found strength in the LORD of Heaven's Armies, their God.'

**11:7** Pss 90:17; 133:1
Ezek 37:16-23

**11:8** Hos 5:7

**11:9** Ps 69:22-28
Jer 15:2-3

**11:10** Jer 14:21

**11:12-13** †Matt 27:9-10
Acts 1:18-19

**11:14** Zech 11:6

**11:15** Zech 11:17

**11:16** Jer 23:2, 22
Ezek 34:2-6

**11:17** Zech 10:2; 11:15

**12:1** Job 26:7
Jer 51:15
Heb 1:10-12

**12:2** Ps 75:8
Isa 51:17, 22-23

**12:3** Dan 2:34-35, 44-45
Matt 21:44

**11:13** Syriac version reads *into the treasury;* also in 11:13b. Compare Matt 27:6-10.    **11:16** Or *the scattered.*
**12:1** Hebrew *An Oracle: This.*

---

**11:7** Zechariah took two shepherd's staffs and named them "Favor" and "Union." He broke the first one ("Favor") to show that God's gracious covenant with his people was broken. He broke the second one ("Union") to show that "the bond of unity between Judah and Israel was broken" (11:14).

**11:8** The identity of the three evil shepherds is not known. But God knew they were unfit to shepherd his people, and so he removed them.

**11:12** To pay this shepherd 30 pieces of silver was an insult—this was the price paid to an owner for a slave gored by an ox (Exodus 21:32). This is also the amount Judas received for betraying Jesus (Matthew 27:3-10). The priceless Messiah was sold for the price of a slave.

**11:13** Potters were in the lowest social class. "This magnificent sum" (a sarcastic comment) was so little that it could be thrown to the potters. It is significant that the 30 pieces of silver paid to Judas for betraying Jesus were returned to the Temple and used to buy a potter's field (Matthew 27:3-10).

**11:14** Because the people had rejected the Messiah, God would reject them—symbolized by Zechariah breaking the staff called

"Union." Not long after Zechariah's time, the Jews began to divide into numerous factions: Pharisees, Sadducees, Essenes, Herodians, and Zealots. The discord among these groups was a key factor leading to the destruction of Jerusalem in A.D. 70.

**11:15-17** Israel would not only reject the true shepherd; it would accept instead a worthless shepherd. This shepherd would serve his own concerns rather than the concerns of his flock and would destroy rather than defend them. Condemnation is his rightful fate because he trusted his arm (military might) and his right eye (intellect). God would destroy both areas.

**11:17** It is a great tragedy for God's people when their leaders fail to care for them adequately. God holds leaders particularly accountable for the condition of his people. The New Testament tells church leaders, "Not many of you should become teachers in the church, for we who teach will be judged more strictly" (James 3:1). If God puts you in a position of leadership, remember that it is also a place of great responsibility.

**12:1-14** This chapter pictures the final siege against the people of Jerusalem.

**12:3, 4** This speaks of a great future battle against Jerusalem. Some say it is Armageddon, the last great battle on earth. Those

**12:6**
Isa 10:16-18
Obad 1:18

⁶"On that day I will make the clans of Judah like a flame that sets a woodpile ablaze or like a burning torch among sheaves of grain. They will burn up all the neighboring nations right and left, while the people living in Jerusalem remain secure.

**12:7**
Amos 9:11

⁷"The LORD will give victory to the rest of Judah first, before Jerusalem, so that the people of Jerusalem and the royal line of David will not have greater honor than the rest of Judah.

**12:8**
Exod 14:19
Lev 26:8
Ps 82:6
Mic 7:8
Zech 9:14-15

⁸On that day the LORD will defend the people of Jerusalem; the weakest among them will be as mighty as King David! And the royal descendants will be like God, like the angel of the LORD who goes before them! ⁹For on that day I will begin to destroy all the nations that come against Jerusalem.

**12:10**
Joel 2:28-29
John 19:34-37
Rev 1:7

¹⁰"Then I will pour out a spirit* of grace and prayer on the family of David and on the people of Jerusalem. They will look on me whom they have pierced and mourn for him as for an only son. They will grieve bitterly for him as for a firstborn son who has died. ¹¹The

**12:11**
Matt 24:30

sorrow and mourning in Jerusalem on that day will be like the great mourning for Hadad-rimmon in the valley of Megiddo.

¹²"All Israel will mourn, each clan by itself, and with the husbands separate from their wives. The clan of David will mourn alone, as will the clan of Nathan, ¹³the clan of Levi, and the clan of Shimei. ¹⁴Each of the surviving clans from Judah will mourn separately, and with the husbands separate from their wives.

## A Fountain of Cleansing

**13:1**
Num 19:9-22

**13** "On that day a fountain will be opened for the dynasty of David and for the people of Jerusalem, a fountain to cleanse them from all their sins and impurity.

**13:2**
Exod 23:13
1 Kgs 22:22

²"And on that day," says the LORD of Heaven's Armies, "I will erase idol worship throughout the land, so that even the names of the idols will be forgotten. I will remove from the land both the false prophets and the spirit of impurity that came with them. ³If anyone

**13:3**
Deut 13:6-11
Jer 23:25

continues to prophesy, his own father and mother will tell him, 'You must die, for you have prophesied lies in the name of the LORD.' And as he prophesies, his own father and mother will stab him.

**13:4**
2 Kgs 1:8
Matt 3:4

⁴"On that day people will be ashamed to claim the prophetic gift. No one will pretend to be a prophet by wearing prophet's clothes. ⁵He will say, 'I'm no prophet; I'm a farmer. I began

**13:5**
Amos 7:14

working for a farmer as a boy.' ⁶And if someone asks, 'Then what about those wounds on your chest?*' he will say, 'I was wounded at my friends' house!'

## The Scattering of the Sheep

**13:7**
Isa 40:11; 53:4-5
†Matt 26:31
†Mark 14:27

⁷ "Awake, O sword, against my shepherd,
        the man who is my partner,"
    says the LORD of Heaven's Armies.

**12:10** Or *the Spirit.*   **13:6** Hebrew *wounds between your hands?*

who oppose God's people will not prevail forever. Eventually, evil, pain, and oppression will be abolished once and for all.

**12:7** As water flows downhill, so a city's influence usually flows to its surrounding countryside. But this time, the countryside of Judah would have priority over Jerusalem so that the people of Jerusalem would not become proud. Don't think that you must witness to only "important" people—professional athletes, movie stars, and prominent businesspeople. Christ came to seek and save the lost (Luke 19:10), even the "down-and-out" lost. We must be careful to avoid spiritual pride, or we, like Jerusalem, may be the last to know what God is doing.

**12:10** The Holy Spirit was poured out at Pentecost, 50 days after Christ's resurrection (see Acts 2). Zechariah calls the Spirit "a spirit of grace and prayer." It is this Spirit who convicts us of sin, reveals to us God's righteousness and judgment, and helps us as we pray. "And the Holy Spirit helps us in our weakness. For example, we don't know what God wants us to pray for. But the Holy Spirit prays for us with groanings that cannot be expressed in words" (Romans 8:26). Ask God to fill you with his Spirit.

**12:10-14** Eventually *all* people will realize that Jesus, the man who was pierced and killed, is indeed the Messiah. There will be an awakening, with sorrow for sin and genuine revival. The crucified Messiah will be clearly revealed (Philippians 2:10; Revelation 5:13).

**12:11** Hadad-rimmon could refer to the place near the plain of

Megiddo, where King Josiah was killed. Josiah's death was greatly mourned by his people (see 2 Chronicles 35:22-25).

**12:12-14** These verses are saying that all Israel will mourn—king, prophet, priest, and people. Each family will go into private mourning, husbands and wives by themselves, to face their sorrow.

**13:1ff** There will be a never-ending supply of God's mercy, forgiveness, and cleansing power. This picture of a fountain is similar to the never-ending stream flowing out from the Temple (Ezekiel 47:1). The fountain is used in Scripture to symbolize God's forgiveness. In John 4, Jesus tells of his "living water" that satisfies completely. Are you spiritually thirsty? Do you need to experience God's forgiveness? Drink from the fountain—ask Jesus to forgive you and give you his salvation.

**13:2-6** This chapter pictures the final days of the earth as we know it. For God's new era to begin, there must be a cleansing—all evil must be abolished. Therefore, idols will be banished, and false prophets will be ashamed of themselves and no longer try to deceive God's people.

**13:7** Just before his arrest, Jesus quoted from this verse, referring to himself and his disciples (Matthew 26:31, 32). He knew beforehand that his disciples would scatter when he was arrested. The Roman "sword" was the military power that put Christ to death.

"Strike down the shepherd,
and the sheep will be scattered,
and I will turn against the lambs.
8 Two-thirds of the people in the land
will be cut off and die," says the LORD.
"But one-third will be left in the land.
9 I will bring that group through the fire
and make them pure.
I will refine them like silver
and purify them like gold.
They will call on my name,
and I will answer them.
I will say, 'These are my people,'
and they will say, 'The LORD is our God.'"

**13:8**
Zech 11:6-9

**13:9**
Isa 48:10
Hos 2:23
Zech 12:10

### The LORD Will Rule the Earth

**14** Watch, for the day of the LORD is coming when your possessions will be plundered right in front of you! 2I will gather all the nations to fight against Jerusalem. The city will be taken, the houses looted, and the women raped. Half the population will be taken into captivity, and the rest will be left among the ruins of the city.

3 Then the LORD will go out to fight against those nations, as he has fought in times past. 4On that day his feet will stand on the Mount of Olives, east of Jerusalem. And the Mount of Olives will split apart, making a wide valley running from east to west. Half the mountain will move toward the north and half toward the south. 5 You will flee through this valley, for it will reach across to Azal.* Yes, you will flee as you did from the earthquake in the days of King Uzziah of Judah. Then the LORD my God will come, and all his holy ones with him.*

6 On that day the sources of light will no longer shine,* 7yet there will be continuous day! Only the LORD knows how this could happen. There will be no normal day and night, for at evening time it will still be light.

8On that day life-giving waters will flow out from Jerusalem, half toward the Dead Sea and half toward the Mediterranean,* flowing continuously in both summer and winter.

9And the LORD will be king over all the earth. On that day there will be one LORD—his name alone will be worshiped.

10All the land from Geba, north of Judah, to Rimmon, south of Jerusalem, will become one vast plain. But Jerusalem will be raised up in its original place and will be inhabited all the way from the Benjamin Gate over to the site of the old gate, then to the Corner Gate, and from the Tower of Hananel to the king's winepresses. 11And Jerusalem will be filled, safe at last, never again to be cursed and destroyed.

**14:1**
Mal 4:1

**14:4**
Ezek 11:23
Mic 1:3-4
Zech 4:7

**14:5**
Isa 29:6
Matt 16:27; 25:31
Jude 1:14

**14:6**
Acts 2:16, 20

**14:7**
Rev 21:23-25; 22:5

**14:8**
Ezek 47:1-12
John 7:37-38
Rev 22:1-2

**14:9**
Deut 6:4
Ps 47:7
Zech 9:9

**14:10**
2 Kgs 14:13

**14:11**
Ps 48:8
Rev 22:3

**14:5a** The meaning of the Hebrew is uncertain. **14:5b** As in Greek version; Hebrew reads *with you.* **14:6** Hebrew *there will be no light, no cold or frost.* The meaning of the Hebrew is uncertain. **14:8** Hebrew *half toward the eastern sea and half toward the western sea.*

**13:8, 9** This "third" was a remnant, a small part of the whole. Throughout the history of Israel, whenever the whole nation seemed to turn against God, God said that a righteous remnant still trusted and followed him. These believers were refined like silver and gold through the fire of their difficult circumstances. Determine to be part of God's remnant, that small part of the whole that is obedient to him. Obey God no matter what the rest of the world does. This may mean trials and troubles at times; but as fire purifies gold and silver, you will be purified and made more like Christ.

**14:1** Many times in the Bible we are encouraged to watch for the day of the Lord. What if you knew exactly when this would happen? Would you live differently? Christ could return at any

moment. Be ready for him by studying the Scriptures carefully and by making sure that you live as he intends—in obedience and spiritual readiness.

**14:1-21** This chapter portrays the eventual triumph of the Messiah over all the earth and his reign over God's people. But the chronological order of these future events is not clear. They show that God has various ways of dealing with his people. Now we are to watch as the events unfold and God provides an escape for his people.

**14:4** On the Mount of Olives, Jesus spoke with his disciples about the end times (Matthew 24). Near this mountain, an angel promised that Jesus would return in the same manner as he had left (Acts 1:11; see also Ezekiel 11:23).

**14:5** Only God's people will escape God's punishment (Matthew 24:16-20). In this time of confusion, God will clearly know who his people are. (See the note on Amos 1:1 concerning the earthquake in King Uzziah's day.)

**14:10** Jerusalem is honored as the city of God and the focal point of all the world's worship. Jerusalem's elevation is a dramatic way of showing God's supremacy.

¹²And the LORD will send a plague on all the nations that fought against Jerusalem. Their people will become like walking corpses, their flesh rotting away. Their eyes will rot in their sockets, and their tongues will rot in their mouths. ¹³On that day they will be terrified, stricken by the LORD with great panic. They will fight their neighbors hand to hand. ¹⁴Judah, too, will be fighting at Jerusalem. The wealth of all the neighboring nations will be captured—great quantities of gold and silver and fine clothing. ¹⁵This same plague will strike the horses, mules, camels, donkeys, and all the other animals in the enemy camps.

¹⁶In the end, the enemies of Jerusalem who survive the plague will go up to Jerusalem each year to worship the King, the LORD of Heaven's Armies, and to celebrate the Festival of Shelters. ¹⁷Any nation in the world that refuses to come to Jerusalem to worship the King, the LORD of Heaven's Armies, will have no rain. ¹⁸If the people of Egypt refuse to attend the festival, the LORD will punish them with the same plague that he sends on the other nations who refuse to go. ¹⁹Egypt and the other nations will all be punished if they don't go to celebrate the Festival of Shelters.

²⁰On that day even the harness bells of the horses will be inscribed with these words: HOLY TO THE LORD. And the cooking pots in the Temple of the LORD will be as sacred as the basins used beside the altar. ²¹In fact, every cooking pot in Jerusalem and Judah will be holy to the LORD of Heaven's Armies. All who come to worship will be free to use any of these pots to boil their sacrifices. And on that day there will no longer be traders* in the Temple of the LORD of Heaven's Armies.

14:21 Hebrew *Canaanites*.

**14:14** Zech 12:2

**14:16** Isa 60:6-9; 66:18-21

**14:20** Exod 39:30 Ezek 46:20

**14:21** Neh 8:10 Rom 14:6-7 1 Cor 10:31

---

**14:16** This Festival of Shelters is the only festival still appropriate during the Messiah's reign. The Passover was fulfilled in Christ's death; the Day of Atonement, in acceptance of Christ's salvation; the Festival of First Harvest, in his resurrection; and Pentecost, with the arrival of the Holy Spirit. But the Festival of Shelters, a festival of thanksgiving, celebrates the harvest of human souls for the Lord. Jesus may have alluded to it in John 4:35.

**14:20, 21** In the future, even such common objects as horses' bells and cooking pots will be holy. This vision of a restored, holy Jerusalem stands in contrast to its broken walls and unpleasant living conditions. One day God would fulfill the people's dreams for Jerusalem beyond what they could imagine. God wants to do much more for us than we can imagine (Ephesians 3:20). As we walk with him, we will discover this day by day.

**14:21** Zechariah was speaking to a people who were enduring hardships: They were being harassed by neighbors; they were discouraged over their small numbers and seemingly inadequate Temple; and their worship was apathetic. But God said, "My love for Jerusalem and Mount Zion is passionate and strong" (1:14). He promised to restore their land, their city, and their Temple. Like other prophets, Zechariah blended prophecies of the present, near future, and final days into one sweeping panorama. Through his message we learn that our hope is found in God and his Messiah, who are in complete control of the world.

# MALACHI

| First exiles return to Jerusalem 538 B.C. | Temple reconstruction begins 536 | Haggai, Zechariah become prophets 520 | Temple completed 516 |
|---|---|---|---|

## VITAL STATISTICS

**PURPOSE:**
To confront the people with their sins and to restore their relationship with God

**AUTHOR:**
Malachi

**ORIGINAL AUDIENCE:**
The people in Jerusalem

**DATE WRITTEN:**
Approximately 430 B.C.

**SETTING:**
Malachi, Haggai, and Zechariah were postexilic prophets to Judah (the southern kingdom). Haggai and Zechariah rebuked the people for their failure to rebuild the Temple. Malachi confronted them with their neglect of the Temple and their false worship.

**KEY VERSES:**
"The day of judgment is coming, burning like a furnace. . . . But for you who fear my name, the Sun of Righteousness will rise with healing in his wings. And you will go free, leaping with joy like calves let out to pasture" (4:1, 2).

**KEY PEOPLE:**
Malachi, the priests

**KEY PLACES:**
Jerusalem, the Temple

**SPECIAL FEATURES:**
Malachi's literary style employs a dramatic use of questions asked by God and his people (for example, see 3:7, 8).

A VASE shatters, brushed by a careless elbow; a toy breaks, handled roughly by young fingers; fabric rips, pulled by strong and angry hands. Spills and rips take time to clean up, effort to repair, and money to replace, but far more costly are shattered relationships. Unfaithfulness, untruths, hateful words, and forsaken vows tear delicate personal bonds and inflict wounds not easily healed. Most tragic, however, is a broken relationship with God.

God loves perfectly and completely. And his love is a love of action—giving, guiding, and guarding. He is altogether faithful, true to his promises to his chosen people. But consistently they spurn their loving God, breaking the covenant, following other gods, and living for themselves. So their relationship with him is shattered.

But the breach is not irreparable; all hope is not lost. God can heal and mend and reweave the fabric. Forgiveness is available. And that is grace.

This is the message of Malachi, God's prophet in Jerusalem. His words reminded the Jews, God's chosen nation, of their willful disobedience, beginning with the priests (1:1—2:9) and then including every person (2:10—3:15). They had shown contempt for God's name (1:6), offered defiled sacrifices (1:7–14), led others into sin (2:7–9), broken God's laws (2:11–16), called evil "good" (2:17), kept God's tithes and offerings for themselves (3:8, 9), and become arrogant (3:13–15). The relationship was broken, and judgment and punishment would be theirs. In the midst of this wickedness, however, a faithful few—the remnant—still loved and honored God. God would shower his blessings upon these men and women (3:16–18).

Malachi paints a stunning picture of Israel's unfaithfulness that clearly shows the people to be worthy of punishment, but woven throughout this message is hope—the possibility of forgiveness. This is beautifully expressed in 4:2–"But for you who fear my name, the Sun of Righteousness will rise with healing in his wings. And you will go free, leaping with joy like calves let out to pasture."

Malachi concludes with a promise of the coming of "the prophet Elijah," who will offer God's forgiveness to all people through repentance and faith (4:5, 6).

The book of Malachi forms a bridge between the Old Testament and the New Testament. As you read Malachi, see yourself as the recipient of this word of God to his people. Evaluate the depth of your commitment, the sincerity of your worship, and the direction of your life. Then allow God to restore your relationship with him through his love and forgiveness.

## THE BLUEPRINT

1. The sinful priests
   (1:1—2:9)
2. The sinful people
   (2:10—3:15)
3. The faithful few
   (3:16—4:6)

Malachi rebuked the people and the priests for neglecting the worship of God and failing to live according to his will. The priests were corrupt; how could they lead the people? They had become stumbling blocks instead of spiritual leaders. The men were divorcing their wives and marrying pagan women; how could they have godly children? Their relationship to God had become inconsequential. If our relationship with God is unimportant, we need to take stock of ourselves by setting aside our sinful habits, putting the Lord first, and giving God our best each day.

| Ezra | Nehemiah | Malachi |
|------|----------|---------|
| comes to | comes to | becomes |
| Jerusalem | Jerusalem | a prophet |
| 458 | 445 | 430 |

## MEGATHEMES

| THEME | EXPLANATION | IMPORTANCE |
|-------|-------------|------------|
| God's Love | God loves his people even when they ignore or disobey him. He has great blessings to bestow on those who are faithful to him. His love never ends. | Because God loves us so much, he hates hypocrisy and careless living. This kind of living denies him the relationship he wants to have with us. What we give and how we live reflects the sincerity of our love for God. |
| The Sin of the Priests | Malachi singled out the priests for condemnation. They knew what God required, yet their sacrifices were unworthy and their service was insincere; they were lazy, arrogant, and insensitive. They had a casual attitude toward the worship of God and observance of God's standards. | If religious leaders go wrong, how will the people be led? We are all leaders in some capacity. Don't neglect your responsibilities or be ruled by what is convenient. Neglect and insensitivity are acts of disobedience. God wants leaders who are faithful and sincere. |
| The Sin of the People | The people had not learned the lesson of the Exile, nor had they listened to the prophets. Men were callously divorcing their faithful wives to marry younger pagan women. This was against God's law because it disobeyed his commands about marriage and threatened the religious training of the children. But pride had hardened the hearts of the people. | God deserves our very best honor, respect, and faithfulness. But sin hardens our heart to our true condition. Pride is unwarranted self-esteem; it is setting your own judgment above God's and looking down on others. Don't let pride keep you from giving God your devotion, money, marriage, and family. |
| The Lord's Coming | God's love for his faithful people is demonstrated by the Messiah's coming. The Messiah will lead the people to the realization of all their fondest hopes. The day of the Lord's coming will be a day of comfort and healing for a faithful few, and a day of judgment for those who reject him. | At Christ's first coming, he refined and purified all those who believed in him. Upon his return, he will expose and condemn those who are proud, insensitive, or unprepared. Yet God is able to heal and forgive. Forgiveness is available to all who come to him. |

## 1. The sinful priests

1:2-3
†Rom 9:13

**1** This is the message* that the LORD gave to Israel through the prophet Malachi.*

### The LORD's Love for Israel

2 "I have always loved you," says the LORD.

But you retort, "Really? How have you loved us?"

And the LORD replies, "This is how I showed my love for you: I loved your ancestor Jacob, 3 but I rejected his brother, Esau, and devastated his hill country. I turned Esau's inheritance into a desert for jackals."

1:1a Hebrew *An Oracle: The message.*  1:1b *Malachi* means "my messenger."

1:1  Malachi, the last Old Testament prophet, preached after Haggai, Zechariah, and Nehemiah—about 430 B.C. The Temple had been rebuilt for almost a century, and the people were losing their enthusiasm for worship. Apathy and disillusionment had set in because the exciting messianic prophecies of Isaiah, Jeremiah, and Micah had not been fulfilled. Many of the sins that had brought the downfall of Jerusalem in 586 B.C. were still being practiced in Judah. Malachi confronted the hypocrites with their sins by portraying a graphic dialogue between a righteous God and his hardened people.

1:2  God's first message through Malachi was "I have always loved you." Although this message applied specifically to Israel, it is a message of hope for all people in all times. Unfortunately, many people are cynical about God's love, using political and economic progress as a measure of success. Because the government was corrupt and the economy poor, the Israelites assumed that God didn't love them. They were wrong. God loves all people because he made them; however, his *eternal* rewards go only to those who are faithful to him.

1:2-5  The phrase "I rejected . . . Esau" does not refer to Esau's eternal destiny. It simply means that God chose Jacob, not his brother Esau, to be the one through whom the nation of Israel and the Messiah would come (see Romans 9:10-13). God allowed Esau to father a nation, but this nation, Edom, later became one of Israel's chief enemies. The story of Jacob and Esau is found in Genesis 25:19-26. Because God chose Jacob and his descendants as the nation through whom the world would be blessed, God cared for them in a special way. Ironically, they rejected God after he chose them.

⁴Esau's descendants in Edom may say, "We have been shattered, but we will rebuild the ruins."

But the LORD of Heaven's Armies replies, "They may try to rebuild, but I will demolish them again. Their country will be known as 'The Land of Wickedness,' and their people will be called 'The People with Whom the LORD Is Forever Angry.' ⁵When you see the destruction for yourselves, you will say, 'Truly, the LORD's greatness reaches far beyond Israel's borders!'"

### Unworthy Sacrifices

⁶The LORD of Heaven's Armies says to the priests: "A son honors his father, and a servant respects his master. If I am your father and master, where are the honor and respect I deserve? You have shown contempt for my name!

"But you ask, 'How have we ever shown contempt for your name?'

⁷"You have shown contempt by offering defiled sacrifices on my altar.

"Then you ask, 'How have we defiled the sacrifices?*'

"You defile them by saying the altar of the LORD deserves no respect. ⁸When you give blind animals as sacrifices, isn't that wrong? And isn't it wrong to offer animals that are crippled and diseased? Try giving gifts like that to your governor, and see how pleased he is!" says the LORD of Heaven's Armies.

⁹"Go ahead, beg God to be merciful to you! But when you bring that kind of offering, why should he show you any favor at all?" asks the LORD of Heaven's Armies.

¹⁰"How I wish one of you would shut the Temple doors so that these worthless sacrifices could not be offered! I am not pleased with you," says the LORD of Heaven's Armies, "and I will not accept your offerings. ¹¹But my name is honored* by people of other nations from morning till night. All around the world they offer* sweet incense and pure offerings in honor of my name. For my name is great among the nations," says the LORD of Heaven's Armies.

¹²"But you dishonor my name with your actions. By bringing contemptible food, you are saying it's all right to defile the Lord's table. ¹³You say, 'It's too hard to serve the LORD,' and you turn up your noses at my commands," says the LORD of Heaven's Armies. "Think of it! Animals that are stolen and crippled and sick are being presented as offerings! Should I accept from you such offerings as these?" asks the LORD.

¹⁴"Cursed is the cheat who promises to give a fine ram from his flock but then sacrifices a defective one to the Lord. For I am a great king," says the LORD of Heaven's Armies, "and my name is feared among the nations!

---

**1:4** Isa 9:10

**1:5** Pss 35:27; 48:1

**1:6** Exod 20:12 Deut 31:12 Isa 1:2

**1:7** Lev 21:6-8

**1:8** Lev 1:3 Deut 15:21

**1:9** Lev 23:33-44 Ps 51:17

**1:10** Isa 1:13 Jer 14:12

**1:11** Ps 113:3 Isa 60:6-7

**1:13** Isa 43:22-24

**1:14** Exod 12:5 Lev 22:18-21 Ps 72:8-11

---

**1:7** As in Greek version; Hebrew reads *defiled you?*   **1:11a** Or *will be honored.*   **1:11b** Or *will offer.*

---

**1:6ff** God charged the priests with failing to honor him (to the point of despising his name) and failing to be good spiritual examples to the people. The Temple had been rebuilt in 516 B.C., and worship was being conducted there, but the priests did not worship God properly. They were not following his laws for the sacrifices. Ezra the priest had sparked a great revival around 458 B.C. However, by Malachi's time, the nation's leaders had once again fallen away from God, and the people right along with them. The worship of God was no longer from heartfelt adoration; instead, it was simply a burdensome job for the priests.

**1:6-8** God's law required that only perfect animals be offered to God (see, for example, Leviticus 1:3). But these priests were allowing the people to offer blind, crippled, and diseased animals to God. God accused them of dishonoring him by offering imperfect sacrifices, and he was greatly displeased. The New Testament says that our lives should be living sacrifices to God (Romans 12:1). If we give God only our leftover time, money, and energy, we repeat the same sin as these worshipers, who didn't want to bring anything valuable to God. What we give God reflects our true attitude toward him.

**1:7, 8** The people sacrificed to God wrongly through (1) expedience—being as cheap as possible, (2) neglect—not caring how they offered the sacrifice, and (3) outright disobedience—sacrificing their own way and not as God had commanded. Their methods of giving showed their real attitudes toward God. How about your attitude? Do expedience, neglect, or disobedience characterize your giving?

**1:10** As intermediaries between God and the people, priests were responsible for reflecting God's attitudes and character. By accepting imperfect sacrifices, they were leading the people to believe that God accepted those sacrifices as well. But God says, "I am not pleased with you." As Christians, we are often in the same position as these priests because we reflect God to our friends and family. What image of God's character and attitudes do they see in you? If you casually accept sin, you are like these priests in Malachi's day, and God is not pleased with you.

**1:11** A theme that can be heard throughout the Old Testament is affirmed in this book: "My name is honored by people of other nations." God had a chosen people, the Jews, through whom he planned to save and bless the entire world. Today God still wants to save and bless the world through all who believe in him—Jews and Gentiles. Christians are now his chosen people, and our offering to the Lord is our life. Are you available to God to be used in making his name honored by the nations? This mission begins in our home and in our neighborhood, but it doesn't stop there. We must work and pray so that God's name will be honored everywhere.

**1:13** Worship was "too hard" according to these priests. Some people think that following God is supposed to make life more comfortable. They are looking for a God of convenience. The truth is that it takes commitment and hard work to live by God's high standards. We may have to face poverty or suffering. But if serving God is more important to us than anything else, what we give up is nothing compared to what we gain—eternal life with God.

## A Warning to the Priests

**2** "Listen, you priests—this command is for you! ²Listen to me and make up your minds to honor my name," says the LORD of Heaven's Armies, "or I will bring a terrible curse against you. I will curse even the blessings you receive. Indeed, I have already cursed them, because you have not taken my warning to heart. ³I will punish your descendants and splatter your faces with the manure from your festival sacrifices, and I will throw you on the manure pile. ⁴Then at last you will know it was I who sent you this warning so that my covenant with the Levites can continue," says the LORD of Heaven's Armies.

⁵"The purpose of my covenant with the Levites was to bring life and peace, and that is what I gave them. This required reverence from them, and they greatly revered me and stood in awe of my name. ⁶They passed on to the people the truth of the instructions they received from me. They did not lie or cheat; they walked with me, living good and righteous lives, and they turned many from lives of sin.

⁷"The words of a priest's lips should preserve knowledge of God, and people should go to him for instruction, for the priest is the messenger of the LORD of Heaven's Armies. ⁸But you priests have left God's paths. Your instructions have caused many to stumble into sin. You have corrupted the covenant I made with the Levites," says the LORD of Heaven's Armies. ⁹"So I have made you despised and humiliated in the eyes of all the people. For you have not obeyed me but have shown favoritism in the way you carry out my instructions."

## 2. The sinful people

### A Call to Faithfulness

¹⁰Are we not all children of the same Father? Are we not all created by the same God? Then why do we betray each other, violating the covenant of our ancestors?

**2:4**
Num 3:12

**2:5**
Num 25:12

**2:6**
Deut 33:10

**2:7**
Lev 10:11
Num 27:21
Deut 17:8-11

**2:8**
Neh 13:29
Isa 9:16
Ezek 44:10

**2:9**
Deut 1:17
1 Sam 2:30

**2:10**
Exod 19:5
Josh 24:3
Jer 31:9

---

**MALACHI** served as a prophet to Judah about 430 B.C. He was the last of the Old Testament prophets.

| | |
|---|---|
| Climate of the times. . . . . . . . . . | The city of Jerusalem and the Temple had been rebuilt for almost a century, but the people had become complacent in their worship of God. |
| Main message. . . . . . . . . . . . . | The people's relationship with God was broken because of their sin, and they would soon be punished. But the few who repented would receive God's blessing, highlighted in his promise to send a Messiah. |
| Importance of message . . . . . . . | Hypocrisy, neglecting God, and careless living have devastating consequences. Serving and worshiping God must be the primary focus of our life, both now and in eternity. |
| Contemporary prophets. . . . . . . | None |

---

**2:1, 2** God warned the priests that if they did not honor his name, he would punish them. Like these priests, we, too, are called to honor God's name—to worship him. This means acknowledging God for who he is—the almighty Creator of the universe, who alone is perfect and who reaches down to sinful people with perfect love. According to this definition, are you honoring God's name?

**2:1, 2** The priests didn't take seriously God's priority, even though he had reminded them through his word many times. How do you find out what is most important to God? Begin by loving him with all your heart, soul, and strength (Deuteronomy 6:5). This means listening to what God says in his Word and then setting your heart, mind, and will on doing what he says. When we love God, his Word becomes a shining light that guides our daily activities. The priests in Malachi's day had stopped loving God, and thus they did not know nor care what he wanted.

**2:4-6** The Levites "walked with [God]," and "turned many from lives of sin" (2:6). Levi was the ancestor of the tribe of Levites, the tribe set apart for service to God (Numbers 1:47-54). The Levites became God's ministers, first in the Tabernacle, then in the Temple. In these verses, God was addressing the priests who were from this tribe, admonishing them for corrupting the laws he gave their ancestor Levi and not following his example.

**2:7, 8** Malachi was angry at the priests because, although they were to be God's messengers, they did not know God's will. And this lack of knowledge caused them to lead God's people astray.

Their ignorance was willful and inexcusable. Pastors and leaders of God's people *must* know God's Word—what it says, what it means, and how it applies to daily life. How much time do you spend in God's Word?

**2:9** The priests had allowed influential and favored people to break the law. The priests were so dependent on these people for support that they could not afford to confront them when they did wrong. In your church, are certain people allowed to do wrong without criticism? There should be no double standard based on wealth or position. Let your standards be those presented in God's Word. Playing favorites is contemptible in God's sight (see James 2:1-9).

**2:10-16** The people were being unfaithful. Though not openly saying they rejected God, they were living as if he did not exist. Men were marrying pagan women who worshiped idols. Divorce was common, occurring for no reason other than a desire for change. People acted as if they could do anything without being punished. And they wondered why God refused to accept their offerings and bless them (2:13)! We cannot successfully separate our dealings with God from the rest of our life. He must be Lord of all.

¹¹Judah has been unfaithful, and a detestable thing has been done in Israel and in Jerusalem. The men of Judah have defiled the LORD's beloved sanctuary by marrying women who worship idols. ¹²May the LORD cut off from the nation of Israel* every last man who has done this and yet brings an offering to the LORD of Heaven's Armies.

¹³Here is another thing you do. You cover the LORD's altar with tears, weeping and groaning because he pays no attention to your offerings and doesn't accept them with pleasure. ¹⁴You cry out, "Why doesn't the LORD accept my worship?" I'll tell you why! Because the LORD witnessed the vows you and your wife made when you were young. But you have been unfaithful to her, though she remained your faithful partner, the wife of your marriage vows.

¹⁵Didn't the LORD make you one with your wife? In body and spirit you are his.* And what does he want? Godly children from your union. So guard your heart; remain loyal to the wife of your youth. ¹⁶"For I hate divorce!" says the LORD, the God of Israel. "To divorce your wife is to overwhelm her with cruelty,*" says the LORD of Heaven's Armies. "So guard your heart; do not be unfaithful to your wife."

¹⁷You have wearied the LORD with your words.

"How have we wearied him?" you ask.

You have wearied him by saying that all who do evil are good in the LORD's sight, and he is pleased with them. You have wearied him by asking, "Where is the God of justice?"

## The Coming Day of Judgment

**3** "Look! I am sending my messenger, and he will prepare the way before me. Then the Lord you are seeking will suddenly come to his Temple. The messenger of the covenant, whom you look for so eagerly, is surely coming," says the LORD of Heaven's Armies.

²"But who will be able to endure it when he comes? Who will be able to stand and face him when he appears? For he will be like a blazing fire that refines metal, or like a strong soap that bleaches clothes. ³He will sit like a refiner of silver, burning away the dross. He will purify the Levites, refining them like gold and silver, so that they may once again offer acceptable sacrifices to the LORD. ⁴Then once more the LORD will accept the offerings brought to him by the people of Judah and Jerusalem, as he did in the past.

⁵"At that time I will put you on trial. I am eager to witness against all sorcerers and adulterers and liars. I will speak against those who cheat employees of their wages, who oppress widows and orphans, or who deprive the foreigners living among you of justice, for these people do not fear me," says the LORD of Heaven's Armies.

---

**2:12** Hebrew *from the tents of Jacob.* The names "Jacob" and "Israel" are often interchanged throughout the Old Testament, referring sometimes to the individual patriarch and sometimes to the nation. **2:15** Or *Didn't the one LORD make us and preserve our life and breath?* or *Didn't the one LORD make her, both flesh and spirit?* The meaning of the Hebrew is uncertain. **2:16** Hebrew *to cover one's garment with violence.*

---

**2:11** Ezra 9:1-2 / Jer 3:7-9

**2:14** Prov 5:18

**2:15** Gen 2:24 / Matt 19:4-6 / 1 Cor 7:10, 14

**2:16** Matt 5:31; 19:6-8 / Mark 10:4-5

**2:17** Isa 5:20; 43:22, 24 / Zeph 1:12

**3:1** †Matt 11:10 / †Mark 1:2 / †Luke 7:27

**3:2** Ezek 22:14 / Matt 3:10-12 / Rev 6:17

**3:3** Dan 12:10

**3:4** 2 Chr 7:3 / Ps 51:19

**3:5** Exod 22:22 / Jer 7:9 / Jas 5:4

---

**2:11, 12** After the Temple had been rebuilt and the walls completed, the people were excited to see past prophecies coming true. But as time passed, the prophecies about the destruction of God's enemies and a coming Messiah were not immediately fulfilled. The people became discouraged, and they grew complacent about obeying all of God's laws. This complacency gradually led to blatant sin, such as marriage to those who worshiped idols. Ezra and Nehemiah also had confronted this problem years earlier (Ezra 9–10; Nehemiah 13:23-31).

**2:14** The people were complaining about their adverse circumstances when they had only themselves to blame. People often try to avoid guilt feelings by shifting the blame. But this doesn't solve the problem. When you face problems, look first at yourself. If you changed your attitude or behavior, would the problem be solved?

**2:14, 15** Divorce in these times was practiced exclusively by men. They were disloyal to their wives and ignored the wedding vows they had made before God, thus corrupting his purpose for them to rear godly children who love the Lord. Not only were men unfaithful to their wives, but they also were ignoring the fact that this bonding relationship was an illustration of their union with God.

**2:15, 16** "Guard your heart; remain loyal to the wife of your youth" means to have the same commitment to marriage that God has to his promises for his people. Our passion should be reserved exclusively for our spouse.

**2:17–3:6** God was tired of the way the people had cynically twisted his truths. He would punish those who insisted that because God was silent, he approved of their actions or at least would never punish them. God would also punish those who professed a counterfeit faith while acting sinfully (see 3:5).

**3:1** There are two messengers in this verse. The first is usually understood to be John the Baptist (Matthew 11:10; Luke 7:27). The second messenger is Jesus, the Messiah, for whom both Malachi and John the Baptist prepared the way.

**3:2, 3** In the process of refining metals, the raw metal is heated with fire until it melts. The impurities separate from it and rise to the surface. They are skimmed off, leaving the pure metal. Without this heating and melting, there could be no purifying. As the impurities are skimmed off the top, the reflection of the worker appears in the clear, pure surface. As we are purified by God, his reflection in our life will become more and more clear to those around us. God says that the Levites (Israel's leaders) should be especially open to his purification process in their lives. The strong soap was alkali used to whiten cloth, also used here as a symbol of the purifying process.

### A Call to Repentance

6"I am the LORD, and I do not change. That is why you descendants of Jacob are not already destroyed. 7Ever since the days of your ancestors, you have scorned my decrees and failed to obey them. Now return to me, and I will return to you," says the LORD of Heaven's Armies.

"But you ask, 'How can we return when we have never gone away?'

8"Should people cheat God? Yet you have cheated me!

"But you ask, 'What do you mean? When did we ever cheat you?'

"You have cheated me of the tithes and offerings due to me. 9You are under a curse, for your whole nation has been cheating me. 10Bring all the tithes into the storehouse so there will be enough food in my Temple. If you do," says the LORD of Heaven's Armies, "I will open the windows of heaven for you. I will pour out a blessing so great you won't have enough room to take it in! Try it! Put me to the test! 11Your crops will be abundant, for I will guard them from insects and disease.* Your grapes will not fall from the vine before they are ripe," says the LORD of Heaven's Armies. 12"Then all nations will call you blessed, for your land will be such a delight," says the LORD of Heaven's Armies.

13"You have said terrible things about me," says the LORD.

"But you say, 'What do you mean? What have we said against you?'

14"You have said, 'What's the use of serving God? What have we gained by obeying his commands or by trying to show the LORD of Heaven's Armies that we are sorry for our sins? 15From now on we will call the arrogant blessed. For those who do evil get rich, and those who dare God to punish them suffer no harm.'"

**3:7** Zech 1:3

**3:8** Neh 13:11

**3:12** Deut 28:3-12 Isa 61:9; 62:4

**3:14-15** Ps 73:13

3:11 Hebrew *from the devourer.*

---

**GIVING A TENTH**
Many ancient peoples observed the practice of tithing—that is, giving a tenth of their earnings (or produce, harvest, etc.) back to a leader or a god. Malachi reminded the people of God's command to tithe. The first instance is Abraham's tithe to Melchizedek.

| | |
|---|---|
| The Israelites were required to tithe of their crops, fruit, and herds. | Leviticus 27:30-32 |
| The tithe was received by the Levites to support them. | Numbers 18:21, 24 |
| The Levites, in turn, gave "a tithe of the tithe" to support the priests. | Numbers 18:26-29; Nehemiah 10:39 |
| The Israelites were to bring their tithes to Jerusalem, and offering them came in the form of a ritual meal in which Levites were invited to share. If Jerusalem was too far for a person to transport the tithe, he could take the tithe there in the form of money. Every third year the tithe could be offered in one's local area, but the person was still to go to Jerusalem to worship. | Deuteronomy 12:5-7, 11-19; 14:22-29; 26:12-15 |
| God promises blessings for those who faithfully tithe, and he says that refusing to tithe is like robbing him. | Malachi 3:8-12 |
| Tithing, without love for or obedience to God, amounts to nothing more than a meaningless ritual. | Matthew 23:23; Luke 11:42 |

---

**3:7** God's patience seems endless! Throughout history, his people have disobeyed, even scorned, his laws, but he has always been willing to accept them back. Here, however, the people have the nerve to imply that they never disobeyed ("How can we return when we have never gone away?")! Many people have turned their backs on forgiveness and restoration because they have refused to admit their sin. Don't follow their example. God is ready to return to us if we are willing to return to him.

**3:8-12** Malachi urged the people to stop holding back their tithes, to stop cheating God. The tithing system began during the time of Moses (Leviticus 27:30-34; Deuteronomy 14:22). The Levites received some of the tithe because they could not possess land of their own (Numbers 18:20, 21). During Malachi's day, the people were not giving tithes, so the Levites went to work to earn a living, thereby neglecting their God-given responsibilities to care for the Temple and for the service of worship. Everything we have is from God; so when we refuse to return to him a part of what he has given, we rob him. Do you selfishly want to keep 100 percent of what God gives, or are you willing to return at least 10 percent to help advance God's Kingdom?

**3:8-12** The people of Malachi's day ignored God's command to give a tithe of their income to his Temple. They may have feared losing what they had worked so hard to get, but in this they misjudged God. "Give, and you will receive," he says (Luke 6:38). When we give, we must remember that the blessings God promises are not always material and may not be experienced completely here on earth, but we will certainly receive them in our future life with him.

**3:10** The "storehouse" was a place in the Temple for storing grain and other food given as tithes. The priests lived off these gifts. We also need to give from the plenty that God has given us in order to support those who serve God by ministering to the spiritual needs of others.

**3:13-15** These verses describe the people's arrogant attitude toward God. When we ask, "What's the use of serving God?" we are really asking, "What good does it do for *me?*" Our focus is selfish. Our real question should be, "What good does it do for God?" We must serve God just because he is God and deserves to be served.

## 3. The faithful few

### The LORD's Promise of Mercy

16Then those who feared the LORD spoke with each other, and the LORD listened to what they said. In his presence, a scroll of remembrance was written to record the names of those who feared him and always thought about the honor of his name.

17"They will be my people," says the LORD of Heaven's Armies. "On the day when I act in judgment, they will be my own special treasure. I will spare them as a father spares an obedient child. 18Then you will again see the difference between the righteous and the wicked, between those who serve God and those who do not."

### The Coming Day of Judgment

**4** 1*The LORD of Heaven's Armies says, "The day of judgment is coming, burning like a furnace. On that day the arrogant and the wicked will be burned up like straw. They will be consumed—roots, branches, and all.

2"But for you who fear my name, the Sun of Righteousness will rise with healing in his wings.* And you will go free, leaping with joy like calves let out to pasture. 3On the day when I act, you will tread upon the wicked as if they were dust under your feet," says the LORD of Heaven's Armies.

4"Remember to obey the Law of Moses, my servant—all the decrees and regulations that I gave him on Mount Sinai* for all Israel.

5"Look, I am sending you the prophet Elijah before the great and dreadful day of the LORD arrives. 6His preaching will turn the hearts of fathers to their children, and the hearts of children to their fathers. Otherwise I will come and strike the land with a curse."

**4:1** Verses 4:1-6 are numbered 3:19-24 in Hebrew text. **4:2** Or *the sun of righteousness will rise with healing in its wings.* **4:4** Hebrew *Horeb,* another name for Sinai.

**3:16**
Ps 56:8

**3:17**
Neh 13:22
1 Pet 2:9

**3:18**
Ps 58:11

**4:1**
Isa 5:24
Mal 3:2

**4:2**
Isa 30:26; 35:6

**4:3**
Mic 7:10

**4:4**
Deut 4:1

**4:5**
Matt 11:14
Mark 9:11-13
Luke 1:17
John 1:21

**4:6**
Isa 11:4
Luke 1:17
Rev 19:15

---

**3:16** God will remember those who remain faithful to him, and who love, fear, honor, and respect him.

**3:17** God's special treasure are those faithful to him. This fulfills the promise he made in the covenant to his people (Exodus 19:5). According to 1 Peter 2:9, believers are God's very own possession. Have you committed your life to God for safekeeping?

**4:2** In the day of the Lord, God's wrath toward the wicked will burn like a furnace (4:1). But he will be like the healing warmth of the sun to those who love and obey him. John the Baptist prophesied that with the coming of Jesus, the dawn was about to break with light for those in sin's darkness (Luke 1:76-79). In Isaiah 60:20 and Revelation 21:23, 24, we learn that no light will be needed in God's holy city, because God himself will be the light.

**4:2ff** These last verses of the Old Testament are filled with hope. Regardless of how life looks now, God controls the future, and everything will be made right. We who have loved and served God look forward to a joyful celebration. This hope for the future becomes ours when we trust God with our lives.

**4:4** These decrees and regulations, given to Moses at Mount Sinai, were the foundation of the nation's civil, moral, and ceremonial life (Exodus 20; Deuteronomy 4:5, 6). We still must obey the moral laws because they apply to all generations.

**4:5, 6** Elijah was one of the greatest prophets who ever lived (his story is recorded in 1 Kings 17—2 Kings 2). With Malachi's

death, the voice of God's prophets would be silent for 400 years. Then a prophet would come, like Elijah, to herald the Messiah's coming (Matthew 17:10-13; Luke 1:17). This prophet was John the Baptist. John prepared people's hearts for Jesus by urging people to repent of their sins. Christ's coming would bring not only unity and peace but also judgment on those who refused to turn from their sins.

**4:6** Malachi gives us practical guidelines about commitment to God: God deserves the best we have to offer (1:7-10). We must be willing to change our wrong ways of living (2:1, 2). We should make our family a lifelong priority (2:13-16). We should be sensitive to God's refining process in our life (3:3). We should tithe our income (3:8-12). There is no room for pride (3:13-15).

Malachi closes his messages by pointing to that great final day of judgment. For those who are committed to God, judgment day will be a day of joy because it will usher in eternity in God's presence. Those who have ignored God will be "straw," to be burned up (4:1). To help the people prepare for that day of judgment, God would send a prophet like Elijah (John the Baptist), who would prepare the way for Jesus, the Messiah. The New Testament begins with this prophet calling the people to turn from their sins to God. Such a commitment to God demands great sacrifice on our part, but we can be sure it will be worth it all in the end.

THE INTERLUDE in our English Bible is scarcely noticeable. A simple turn of the page and you leave behind the Old Testament to enter the New Testament. If you are reading the Bible chronologically, like a story, you find that the first chapter of Matthew re-acquaints you with characters you've already come to know and admire: Abraham, Isaac, Jacob, David, and more. Yet a new character—indeed, a person who will claim to be the main character of the entire Bible—is now introduced: Jesus Christ.

You'll also soon notice that the world in which Jesus travels bears little resemblance to the one left behind in Malachi. The Eastern empires of the Israelites' captivity—Babylon, Assyria, and Persia—no longer dominate the region. Instead, a new power has risen in the West: the empire of Rome. Its boundaries extend from the Mediterranean to North Africa and even Europe. Its ruler in Palestine, a cruel and self-serving king named Herod, sits enthroned over the Jews.

You will recall that the northern kingdom of Israel had been taken into captivity by Assyria, and then the southern kingdom of Judah later went into captivity in Babylon. All of this occurred because the people had sinned and refused to remain faithful to God. The prophets had warned the people over and over, but they refused to believe. In Malachi, the Israelites had recently returned to Judah and their capital city from Babylonian captivity and rebuilt the Temple, their center of worship. Under the guidance of priests and prophets, the community's leaders since ancient times, they had sought to repopulate the land, drive out their enemies, and learn again how to worship God in the way he desired. In Matthew, however, the Jews are settled and secure under the Pax Romana, the peace of Rome. They no longer worship in the Temple alone but also in dozens of synagogues scattered throughout the country's towns and villages. Priests continue to provide leadership, but the people now look to a new array of religious authorities as well, including Pharisees, Sadducees, and teachers of religious law (also known as scribes). Over all of these authorities sits a governing body called the high council (or Sanhedrin), which functions something like a religious Supreme Court.

Most noticeable, perhaps, is the lack of prophets. Whereas Malachi had followed a succession of prophets going back hundreds of years, not a single divine spokesperson appeared before the nation during the years between the Old and New Testaments. Anyone who claimed to be a prophet was proven to be an imposter. For more than 400 years, the heavens seemed closed to the nation of Israel. They heard nothing from God.

Nothing but silence.

Then, one ordinary night in the tiny village of Bethlehem, Jesus was born. With his first cries, God's voice once again graced the land. For Jews with ears to hear and eyes to see, it became clear throughout Jesus' life that he was the Son of God, the Savior for whom they had been waiting. God had used the years of silence to prepare the perfect time and place for Jesus' arrival. During the years between the Testaments—years of war and upheaval, flawed heroes and unfulfilled hopes—God had set the stage for the final era of salvation history, an era of Good News for Jews and Gentiles alike.

---

**THE PERSIAN PERIOD (539–336 B.C.)**

In the very first year of his reign, Cyrus the king of Persia had freed the Israelites from their captivity and encouraged them to return to their homeland (Ezra 1). His successor, King Darius, continued Persia's pro-Israel policy, even threatening with capital punishment those who hindered the Israelites from rebuilding their Temple and resettling their land (Ezra 6). The Jews dwelt in relative peace.

However, several key developments began to reshape their practice of religion. Likely as a result of their many years in exile, the Jews began to worship in local synagogues spread throughout the Persian empire. They continued this new practice in their own land, even after the Temple was rebuilt. Although priests served in the Temple and performed the required sacrifices, worship in the synagogues centered on the study of the Law, and teachers of religious law became the influential preservers and interpreters of the law. People with questions about God became more likely to turn to a teacher of the law than a priest.

During this time, the Israelites also came into religious conflict with the Samaritans. Descendants of Israelites who had been left behind during the Babylonian exile, the Samaritans had intermarried with Babylonians, Syrians, and others. As a result, their worship grew syncretistic, incorporating elements of pagan religions with worship of Yahweh, the God of Israel. While the Jews rebuilt the Temple in Jerusalem, the Samaritans built a rival temple in the north. The ensuing religious and ethnic strife between Jews and Samaritans proved to be long lasting, which made it all the more amazing when Jesus later took the time to speak to an adulterous Samaritan woman (John 4).

---

**THE HELLENISTIC PERIOD (336–165 B.C.)**

With the fall of Persia to Alexander the Great, the age of the great Eastern empires ended. Western might came to dominate the Mediterranean and Middle East. Indeed, the Greek empire became the largest the world had ever seen, extending even into western India. Although Alexander the Great died young amidst suspicious circumstances, his empire continued under the rule of his generals, who split it into four sections. Ptolemy Soter claimed both Egypt and Israel.

Politically, little changed for the Jews under Greek and Ptolemaic rule. They continued to live and worship under the authority of a distant and foreign ruler, much as they had for generations. Culturally, however, they became more and more influenced by Greek (Hellenistic) civilization. Alexander's strategy for preserving his empire had been to unite the diverse, subjugated peoples around a common culture. The Ptolemaic dynasty carried out this policy with vigor, promoting Greek language and thought by all possible means. Thousands of Jews were forcibly resettled in Alexandria. Although Jews both at home and abroad resisted adapting to Greek religion, they couldn't escape all aspects of Hellenistic influence. They soon began to speak Greek, the trade language of the empire. Their worship came to reflect a Greek preference for aesthetics over content. More significantly, a group of Jewish scholars during this time translated the Old Testament from its original Hebrew into Greek. Called the Septuagint, this Greek translation came to be widely used by Jews everywhere. Jesus himself later quoted from the Septuagint, as did many New Testament authors.

In 198 B.C., the Syrian section of the empire overthrew the Egyptian section. For the first time, Israel came under the rule of a leader who tried to stamp out Judaism completely. Antiochus Epiphanes desecrated the Temple, forbade sacrifices to Yahweh, outlawed circumcision, forced Jews to eat pork, and canceled Sabbaths and feast days. Some Jews attempted to conciliate Antiochus and cooperate with his demands; others resisted. These two groups were known as the Hellenists and the Hasidim (pious ones), forerunners of the Pharisees. Also, a group loyal to the high priest emerged, the precursors of the Sadducees.

The conflict in Israel finally reached a boiling point when an elderly priest named Mattathias refused to offer a required pagan sacrifice. Mattathias killed a Syrian officer and a reprobate Jew, fled to the hills, and called faithful Jews everywhere to join him in rebellion. During the ensuing guerrilla war, Mattathias's son, Judas Maccabeus, eventually overcame the Syrians and achieved independence for Israel—its last period of self-rule until the emergence of the modern state of Israel in 1948.

**THE MACCABEAN PERIOD (165–63 B.C.)**

However, independence proved to be both short-lived and disastrous. As the political dynasty of the Maccabees, also called the Hasmoneans, assumed both the throne and the office of high priest, the nation became beset by infighting. The Sadducees supported Hasmonean rulers as both kings and priests, whereas the Pharisees insisted that a true king could only be a descendant of David and a priest could only be a descendant of Aaron. The founder of the Essenes (the community which preserved for posterity the Dead Sea Scrolls) may have also founded his Qumran community around this time, in reaction against the Hasmoneans. As successive rulers became more and more unpopular (for example, Alexander Janneas was pelted by Jews at a festival when he attempted to perform his priestly duties—he responded by massacring 6,000 of them) the country became increasingly unstable.

Israelite factions turned to mercenaries and outside nations for support. By the time the growing Roman empire turned its attention toward Israel, the nation was able to offer little resistance. In 63 B.C., Pompey sacked Jerusalem. Soon the Jews were once again under the command of a foreign ruler, in this case an Idumean named Antipater who had been installed by Rome. Antipater's son, Herod the Great, followed him as king of the Jews, and it was under his rule that Jesus was born—and that all the Jewish boys in Bethlehem under the age of two were killed.

**THE ROMAN PERIOD (63 B.C.– A.D. 135)**

Finally, God's silence ended. As Matthew opens his Gospel, the Jews are now unwilling subjects of the Roman empire. They are allowed freedom of worship and limited authority in overseeing their own affairs. But they long for more. They read the prophecies of the Old Testament and watch expectantly for the promised Messiah. They dream about the day that Israel will once again be the powerful nation it was under King David. They worship under the guidance of the high priest, dispute religious matters in the high council, struggle to survive under Rome, and all the while await the coming Savior. Yet they expect a warrior, and not the baby lying in a manger that God's angels announce.

And Jesus will never live up to their expectations. Both of the main religious factions will disapprove of him. The Pharisees are the legalists of the day. They devote themselves to the law of Moses and apply it strictly to everyday life. They believe in the supernatural, angels, and the resurrection. They take their religious traditions seriously, so they cannot accept Jesus' disregard for their rules and his claim to forgive sins. The Sadducees are the rationalists of the day. They are skeptical toward religion. Although they believe in a literal interpretation of Moses' law, they do not allow it to have much impact on their everyday lives. They deny the supernatural and the resurrection; they focus on temporal, political concerns. They see Jesus primarily as a threat, a rabble-rouser who might catch the attention of Rome and thus imperil the nation.

In the end, these factions come to agree on one point, at least—that Jesus must be killed. They work together in the high council to sentence him. They stir up crowds and pressure the Roman authorities to have Jesus crucified. They succeed. Yet in the end, it was God's plan that ultimately succeeded. His suffering Servant lived and died as the payment for sin, and he rose again as the hope of the world.

Looking back on the years between the Old and New Testaments, it is clear that God brought about the perfect political and religious setting for the work of his Son. Instigated by the Jewish religious factions the Romans put Jesus to death. The power and highway system of Rome allowed the message of his resurrection to spread. And through the writing of the New Testament, the Greek language proclaimed the gospel in a tongue nearly everyone could understand. As Paul wrote in Galatians 4:4: "When the right time came, God sent his Son."

Turn the page. The New Testament tells the story.

# new TESTAMENT

# MATTHEW

## VITAL STATISTICS

**PURPOSE:**
To prove that Jesus is the Messiah, the eternal King

**AUTHOR:**
Matthew (Levi)

**ORIGINAL AUDIENCE:**
Matthew wrote especially to the Jews.

**DATE WRITTEN:**
Approximately A.D. 60–65

**SETTING:**
Matthew was a Jewish tax collector who became one of Jesus' disciples. This Gospel forms the connecting link between the Old and New Testaments because of its emphasis on the fulfillment of prophecy.

**KEY VERSE:**
"Don't misunderstand why I have come. I did not come to abolish the law of Moses or the writings of the prophets. No, I came to accomplish their purpose" (5:17).

**KEY PEOPLE:**
Jesus, Mary, Joseph, John the Baptist, the disciples, the religious leaders, Caiaphas, Pilate, Mary Magdalene

**KEY PLACES:**
Bethlehem, Jerusalem, Capernaum, Galilee, Judea

**SPECIAL FEATURES:**
Matthew is filled with messianic language ("Son of David" is used throughout) and Old Testament references (53 quotes and 76 other references). This Gospel was not written as a chronological account; its purpose is to present the clear evidence that Jesus is the Messiah, the Savior.

AS the motorcade slowly winds through the city, thousands pack the sidewalks hoping to catch a glimpse. Marching bands with great fanfare announce the arrival, and protective agents scan the crowd and run alongside the limousine. Pomp, ceremony, protocol—modern symbols of position and evidences of importance—herald the arrival of a head of state. Whether they are leaders by birth or election, we honor and respect them.

The Jews waited for a leader who had been promised centuries before by prophets. They believed that this leader—the Messiah ("anointed one")—would rescue them from their Roman oppressors and establish a new kingdom. As their king, he would rule the world with justice. Many Jews, however, overlooked prophecies that also spoke of this king as a suffering servant who would be rejected and killed. It is no wonder, then, that few recognized Jesus as the Messiah. How could this humble carpenter's son from Nazareth be their king? But Jesus was and is the King of all the earth!

Matthew (Levi) was one of Jesus' 12 disciples. Once he was a despised tax collector, but his life was changed by this man from Galilee. Matthew wrote this Gospel to his fellow Jews to prove that Jesus is the Messiah and to explain God's Kingdom.

Matthew begins his account by giving Jesus' genealogy. He then tells of Jesus' birth and early years, including the family's escape to Egypt from the murderous Herod and their return to Nazareth. Following Jesus' baptism by John (3:16, 17) and his defeat of Satan in the wilderness, Jesus began his public ministry by calling his first disciples and giving the Sermon on the Mount (chapters 5—7). Matthew shows Christ's authority by reporting his miracles of healing the sick and the demon-possessed, and even raising the dead.

Despite opposition from the Pharisees and others in the religious establishment (chapters 12—15), Jesus continued to teach concerning the Kingdom of Heaven (chapters 16—20). During this time, Jesus spoke with his disciples about his imminent death and resurrection (16:21) and revealed his true identity to Peter, James, and John (17:1–5). Near the end of his ministry, Jesus entered Jerusalem in a triumphant procession (21:1–11). But soon opposition mounted, and Jesus knew that his death was near. So he taught his disciples about the future—what they could expect before his return (chapter 24) and how to live until then (chapter 25).

In Matthew's finale (chapters 26—28), he focuses on Jesus' final days on earth—the Last Supper, his prayer in Gethsemane, the betrayal by Judas, the flight of the disciples, Peter's denial, the trials before Caiaphas and Pilate, Jesus' final words on the cross, and his burial in a borrowed tomb. But the story does not end there, for the Messiah rose from the dead—conquering death and then telling his followers to continue his work by making disciples in all nations.

As you read this Gospel, listen to Matthew's clear message: Jesus is the Christ, the King of kings and Lord of lords. Celebrate his victory over evil and death, and make Jesus the Lord of your life.

| | | Pontius | Jesus | Jesus | Jesus | Jesus is |
|---|---|---|---|---|---|---|
| Tiberius | | Pilate | begins | chooses | feeds | crucified, |
| Caesar | | appointed | his | twelve | 5,000 | rises again, |
| becomes | | governor | ministry | disciples | 29 | and ascends |
| emperor | | 26 | 26/27 | 28 | | 30 |
| 14 | | | | | | |

## THE BLUEPRINT

A.  BIRTH AND PREPARATION
    OF JESUS, THE KING
    (1:1—4:11)

The people of Israel were waiting for the Messiah, their king. Matthew begins his book by showing how Jesus Christ was a descendant of David. But Matthew goes on to show that God did not send Jesus to be an earthly king but a heavenly King. His Kingdom would be much greater than David's because it would never end. Even at Jesus' birth, many recognized him as a King. Herod, the ruler, as well as Satan, was afraid of Jesus' kingship and tried to stop him, but others worshiped him and brought royal gifts. We must be willing to recognize Jesus for who he really is and worship him as King of our life.

B.  MESSAGE AND MINISTRY OF
    JESUS, THE KING (4:12—25:46)
    1. Jesus begins his ministry
    2. Jesus gives the Sermon on the Mount
    3. Jesus performs many miracles
    4. Jesus teaches about the Kingdom
    5. Jesus encounters differing reactions
       to his ministry
    6. Jesus faces conflict with the
       religious leaders
    7. Jesus teaches on the Mount of Olives

Jesus gave the Sermon on the Mount, directions for living in his Kingdom. He also told many parables about the difference between his Kingdom and the kingdoms of earth. Forgiveness, peace, and putting others first are some of the characteristics that make one great in the Kingdom of God. And to be great in God's Kingdom, we must live by God's standards right now. Jesus came to show us how to live as faithful subjects in his Kingdom.

C.  DEATH AND RESURRECTION
    OF JESUS, THE KING
    (26:1—28:20)

Jesus was formally presented to the nation of Israel but was rejected. How strange for the King to be accused, arrested, and crucified. But Jesus demonstrated his power, even over death, through his resurrection and gained access for us into his Kingdom. With all this evidence that Jesus is God's Son, we, too, should accept him as our Lord.

## MEGATHEMES

| THEME | EXPLANATION | IMPORTANCE |
|---|---|---|
| Jesus Christ, the King | Jesus is revealed as the King of kings. His miraculous birth, his life and teaching, his miracles, and his triumph over death show his true identity. | Jesus cannot be equated with any person or power. He is the supreme ruler of time and eternity, heaven and earth, humans and angels. We should give him his rightful place as King of our lives. |
| The Messiah | Jesus was the Messiah, the one for whom the Jews had waited to deliver them from Roman oppression. Yet, tragically, they didn't recognize him when he came because his kingship was not what they expected. The true purpose of God's anointed deliverer was to die for all people to free them from sin's oppression. | Because Jesus was sent by God, we can trust him with our lives. It is worth everything we have to acknowledge him and give ourselves to him, because he came to be our Messiah, our Savior. |
| Kingdom of God | Jesus came to earth to begin his Kingdom. His full Kingdom will be realized at his return and will be made up of anyone who has faithfully followed him. | The way to enter God's Kingdom is by faith—believing in Christ to save us from sin and change our lives. We must do the work of his Kingdom now to be prepared for his return. |

| | | |
|---|---|---|
| Teachings | Jesus taught the people through sermons, illustrations, and parables. Through his teachings, he showed the true ingredients of faith and how to guard against a fruit-less and hypocritical life. | Jesus' teachings show us how to prepare for life in his eternal Kingdom by living properly right now. He lived what he taught, and we, too, must practice what we preach. |
| Resurrection | When Jesus rose from the dead, he rose in power as the true King. In his victory over death, he established his credentials as King and his power and authority over evil. | The Resurrection shows Jesus' all-powerful life for us—not even death could stop his plan of offering eternal life. Those who believe in Jesus can hope for a resurrection like his. Our role is to tell his story to all the earth so that everyone may share in his victory. |

# KEY PLACES IN MATTHEW

Jesus' earthly story begins in the town of Bethlehem in the Roman province of Judea (2:1). A threat to kill the infant king led Joseph to take his family to Egypt (2:14). When they returned, God led them to settle in Nazareth in Galilee (2:22, 23). At about age 30, Jesus was baptized in the Jordan River and was tempted by Satan in the Judean wilderness (3:13; 4:1). Jesus set up his base of operations in Capernaum (4:12, 13) and from there ministered throughout Israel, telling parables, teaching about the Kingdom, and healing the sick. He traveled to the region of the Gadarenes around Gadara and healed two demon-possessed men (8:28ff); fed over 5,000 people with five loaves and two fish on the shores of Galilee near Bethsaida (14:15ff); healed the sick in Gennesaret (14:34ff); ministered to the Gentiles in Tyre and Sidon (15:21ff); visited Caesarea Philippi, where Peter declared him to be the Messiah (16:13ff); and taught in Perea, east of the Jordan (19:1). As he set out on his last visit to Jerusalem, he told the disciples what would happen to him there (20:17ff). He spent some time in Jericho (20:29) and then stayed in Bethany at night as he went back and forth to Jerusalem during his last week (21:17ff). In Jerusalem he would be crucified, but he would rise again.

The broken lines (—·—·—) indicate modern boundaries.

## A. BIRTH AND PREPARATION OF JESUS, THE KING (1:1—4:11)

Matthew opens his Gospel with a genealogy to prove that Jesus is a descendant of both King David and Abraham, just as the Old Testament had predicted. Jesus' birth didn't go unnoticed, for both shepherds and wise men came to worship him. The Jewish people were waiting for the Messiah to appear. However, after he was born, the Jews didn't recognize him because they were looking for a different kind of king.

### The Record of Jesus' Ancestors (3/Luke 3:23-28)

**1:1**
Gen 22:18
2 Sam 7:12-14
1 Chr 17:11
Pss 89:3-4; 132:11
Isa 9:6; 11:1
Matt 22:42
John 7:42
Rom 1:3
Gal 3:16
Rev 22:16

**1 ** This is a record of the ancestors of Jesus the Messiah, a descendant of David* and of Abraham:

2 Abraham was the father of Isaac.
  Isaac was the father of Jacob.
  Jacob was the father of Judah and his brothers.

**1:2**
Gen 21:3, 12;
25:26; 29:35
1 Chr 1:34

3 Judah was the father of Perez and Zerah (whose mother was Tamar).
  Perez was the father of Hezron.
  Hezron was the father of Ram.*

**1:3**
Gen 38:29-30
Ruth 4:12, 18-19
1 Chr 2:4-5, 9

4 Ram was the father of Amminadab.
  Amminadab was the father of Nahshon.
  Nahshon was the father of Salmon.

**1:4-5**
Ruth 4:13, 17-22
1 Chr 2:10-12, 15
Heb 11:31

5 Salmon was the father of Boaz (whose mother was Rahab).
  Boaz was the father of Obed (whose mother was Ruth).
  Obed was the father of Jesse.

**1:6**
Ruth 4:17, 22
2 Sam 12:24
1 Chr 2:13-15

6 Jesse was the father of King David.
  David was the father of Solomon (whose mother was Bathsheba, the widow of Uriah).

**1:7-10**
1 Chr 3:10-14

7 Solomon was the father of Rehoboam.
  Rehoboam was the father of Abijah.
  Abijah was the father of Asa.*
8 Asa was the father of Jehoshaphat.
  Jehoshaphat was the father of Jehoram.*
  Jehoram was the father* of Uzziah.
9 Uzziah was the father of Jotham.
  Jotham was the father of Ahaz.
  Ahaz was the father of Hezekiah.
10 Hezekiah was the father of Manasseh.
  Manasseh was the father of Amon.*
  Amon was the father of Josiah.

1:1 Greek *Jesus the Messiah, son of David.*   1:3 Greek *Aram*, a variant spelling of Ram; also in 1:4. See 1 Chr 2:9-10.   1:7 Greek *Asaph*, a variant spelling of Asa; also in 1:8. See 1 Chr 3:10.   1:8a Greek *Joram*, a variant spelling of Jehoram; also in 1:8b. See 1 Kgs 22:50 and note at 1 Chr 3:11.   1:8b Or *ancestor;* also in 1:11.   1:10 Greek *Amos*, a variant spelling of Amon; also in 1:10b. See 1 Chr 3:14.

**1:1** Presenting this record of ancestors (called a genealogy) was one of the most interesting ways that Matthew could begin a book for a Jewish audience. Because a person's family line proved his or her standing as one of God's chosen people, Matthew began by showing that Jesus was a descendant of Abraham, the father of all Jews, and a direct descendant of David, fulfilling Old Testament prophecies about the Messiah's line. The facts of this ancestry were carefully preserved. This is the first of many proofs recorded by Matthew to show that Jesus is the true Messiah.

**1:1ff** More than 400 years had passed since the last Old Testament prophecies, and faithful Jews all over the world were still waiting for the Messiah (Luke 3:15). Matthew wrote this book to Jews to present Jesus as King and Messiah, the promised descendant of David who would reign forever (Isaiah 11:1-5). The Gospel of Matthew links the Old and New Testaments and contains many references that show how Jesus fulfilled Old Testament prophecy.

**1:1ff** Jesus entered human history when the land of Palestine was controlled by Rome and considered an insignificant outpost of the vast and mighty Roman Empire. The presence of Roman soldiers in Israel gave the Jews military peace, but at the price of oppression, slavery, injustice, and immorality. Into this kind of world came the promised Messiah.

**1:1-17** In the first 17 verses we meet 46 people whose lifetimes span 2,000 years. All were ancestors of Jesus, but they varied considerably in personality, spirituality, and experience. Some were heroes of faith—like Abraham, Isaac, Ruth, and David. Some had shady reputations—like Rahab and Tamar. Many were very ordinary—like Hezron, Ram, Nahshon, and Akim. And others were evil—like Manasseh and Abijah. God's work in history is not limited by human failures or sins, and he works through ordinary people. Just as God used all kinds of people to bring his Son into the world, he uses all kinds today to accomplish his will. And God wants to use you.

**1:3-6** Matthew's inclusion of four particular women (Tamar, Rahab, Ruth, and Bathsheba) reveals his concern to do more than relay historical data. These women raise both ethnic and ethical questions. At least two of them were not Israelites by birth and all four of them had reputations that could have made them unmentionable in an ancestral tree. Yet this was the line into which God's Son was born. Jesus' genealogy makes it clear, not that there were a few disreputable people in his family, but that all of them were sinners. God sent his Son as Savior of *all* people—Jews, Gentiles, men, and women. No matter what the sins of the people, God's plan was never thwarted. It continues to unfold. That plan includes you.

¹¹ Josiah was the father of Jehoiachin* and his brothers (born at the time of the exile to Babylon).

¹² After the Babylonian exile:
Jehoiachin was the father of Shealtiel.
Shealtiel was the father of Zerubbabel.

¹³ Zerubbabel was the father of Abiud.
Abiud was the father of Eliakim.
Eliakim was the father of Azor.

¹⁴ Azor was the father of Zadok.
Zadok was the father of Akim.
Akim was the father of Eliud.

¹⁵ Eliud was the father of Eleazar.
Eleazar was the father of Matthan.
Matthan was the father of Jacob.

¹⁶ Jacob was the father of Joseph, the husband of Mary.
Mary gave birth to Jesus, who is called the Messiah.

¹⁷All those listed above include fourteen generations from Abraham to David, fourteen from David to the Babylonian exile, and fourteen from the Babylonian exile to the Messiah.

### An Angel Appears to Joseph (8)

¹⁸This is how Jesus the Messiah was born. His mother, Mary, was engaged to be married to Joseph. But before the marriage took place, while she was still a virgin, she became pregnant through the power of the Holy Spirit. ¹⁹Joseph, her fiancé, was a good man and did not want to disgrace her publicly, so he decided to break the engagement* quietly.

²⁰As he considered this, an angel of the Lord appeared to him in a dream. "Joseph, son of David," the angel said, "do not be afraid to take Mary as your wife. For the child within her was conceived by the Holy Spirit. ²¹And she will have a son, and you are to name him Jesus,* for he will save his people from their sins."

²²All of this occurred to fulfill the Lord's message through his prophet:

**1:11** Greek *Jeconiah,* a variant spelling of Jehoiachin; also in 1:12. See 2 Kgs 24:6 and note at 1 Chr 3:16.
**1:19** Greek *to divorce her.* **1:21** *Jesus* means "The LORD saves."

*Cross-references:*
**1:11** 2 Kgs 24:14-16 / 1 Chr 3:15-16 / Jer 27:20 / Dan 1:1-2
**1:12** 1 Chr 3:17, 19 / Ezra 3:2
**1:16** Matt 27:17, 22 / Luke 2:11
**1:18** Luke 1:27, 35 / Gal 4:4
**1:19** Deut 24:1
**1:20** Luke 1:35
**1:21** Luke 1:31; 2:11, 21 / Acts 5:31; 13:23 / Heb 7:25

---

**1:11** The exile to Babylon occurred in 586 B.C. when Nebuchadnezzar, king of Babylon, conquered Judah, destroyed Jerusalem, and took thousands of people captive.

**1:16** Because Mary was a virgin when she became pregnant, Matthew lists Joseph only as the husband of Mary, not the father of Jesus. Matthew's genealogy gives Jesus' legal (or royal) lineage through Joseph. Mary's ancestral line is recorded in Luke 3:23-38. Both Mary and Joseph were direct descendants of David.

Matthew traced the genealogy back to Abraham, while Luke traced it back to Adam. Matthew wrote to the Jews, so Jesus was shown as a descendant of their father, Abraham. Luke wrote to the Gentiles, so he emphasized Jesus as the Savior of all people.

**1:17** Matthew breaks Israel's history into three sets of 14 generations, but there were probably more generations than those listed here. Genealogies often compressed history, meaning that not every generation of ancestors was specifically listed. Thus, the phrase *the father of* can also be translated "the ancestor of."

**1:18** Jewish marriage involved three basic steps. First, the two families agreed to the union. Second, a public announcement was made. At this point, the couple was "engaged." This was similar to engagement today except that their relationship could be broken only through death or divorce (even though sexual relations were not yet permitted). Third, the couple was married and began living together. Because Mary and Joseph were engaged, Mary's apparent unfaithfulness carried a severe social stigma. According to Jewish civil law, Joseph had a right to divorce her, and the Jewish authorities could have had her stoned to death (Deuteronomy 22:23, 24).

**1:18** Why is the Virgin Birth important to the Christian faith? Jesus Christ, God's Son, had to be free from the sinful nature passed on to all other human beings by Adam. Because Jesus

was born of a woman, he was a human being; but as the Son of God, Jesus was born without any trace of human sin. Jesus is both fully human and fully divine.

Because Jesus lived as a man, we know that he fully understands our experiences and struggles (Hebrews 4:15, 16). Because he is God, he has the power and authority to deliver us from sin (Colossians 2:13-15). We can tell Jesus all our thoughts, feelings, and needs. He has been where we are now, and he has the ability to help.

**1:19** Joseph was faced with a difficult choice after discovering that Mary was pregnant. Perhaps Joseph thought he had only two options: divorce Mary quietly or have her stoned. But God gave a third option—marry her (1:20-23). In view of the circumstances, this had not occurred to Joseph. But God often shows us that there are more options available than we think. Although Joseph seemed to be doing the right thing by breaking the engagement, only God's guidance helped him make the best decision. But that did not make it an easy decision. Consenting to marry Mary surely cast doubt on his own innocence regarding the pregnancy, as well as leaving them both with a social stigma they would carry for the rest of their lives. Yet Joseph chose to obey the angel's command (1:24). When our decisions affect the lives of others, we must always seek God's wisdom and then be willing to follow through no matter how difficult it may be.

**1:20** The conception and birth of Jesus Christ are supernatural events beyond human logic or reasoning. Because of this, God sent angels to help certain people understand the significance of what was happening (see 2:13, 19; Luke 1:11, 26; 2:9).

Angels are spiritual beings created by God who help carry out his work on earth. They bring God's messages to people (Luke 1:26), protect God's people (Daniel 6:22), offer encouragement (Genesis 16:7ff), give guidance (Exodus 14:19), carry out punish-

**1:23**
†Isa 7:14; 8:8, 10
John 1:14
1 Tim 3:16

23 "Look! The virgin will conceive a child!
    She will give birth to a son,
and they will call him Immanuel,*
    which means 'God is with us.'"

**1:23** Isa 7:14; 8:8, 10 (Greek version).

---

**JOSEPH**

The strength of what we believe is measured by how much we are willing to suffer for those beliefs. Joseph was a man with strong beliefs. He was prepared to do what was right, despite the pain he knew it would cause. But Joseph had another trait: He not only tried to do what was right, he also tried to do it in the right way.

When Mary told Joseph about her pregnancy, Joseph knew the child was not his. His respect for Mary's character and the explanation she gave him, as well as her attitude toward the expected child, must have made it hard to think his bride had done something wrong. Still, someone else was the child's father—and it was mind-boggling to accept that the "someone else" was God.

Joseph decided he had to break the engagement, but he was determined to do it in a way that would not cause public shame to Mary. He intended to act with justice and love.

At this point, God sent a messenger to Joseph to confirm Mary's story and open another way of obedience for Joseph—to take Mary as his wife. Joseph obeyed God, married Mary, and honored her virginity until the baby was born.

We do not know how long Joseph lived his role as Jesus' earthly father—he is last mentioned when Jesus was 12 years old. But Joseph trained his son in the trade of carpentry, made sure he had good spiritual training in Nazareth, and took the whole family on the yearly trip to Jerusalem for the Passover, which Jesus continued to observe during his adult years.

Joseph knew Jesus was someone special from the moment he heard the angel's words. His strong belief in that fact and his willingness to follow God's leading empowered him to be Jesus' chosen earthly father.

| | |
|---|---|
| **Strengths and accomplishments** | • A man of integrity<br>• A descendant of King David<br>• Jesus' legal and earthly father<br>• A person sensitive to God's guidance and willing to do God's will no matter what the consequence |
| **Lessons from his life** | • God honors integrity<br>• Social position is of little importance when God chooses to use us<br>• Being obedient to the guidance we have from God leads to more guidance from him<br>• Feelings are not accurate measures of the rightness or wrongness of an action |
| **Vital statistics** | • Where: Nazareth, Bethlehem<br>• Occupation: Carpenter<br>• Relatives: Wife: Mary. Children: Jesus, James, Joses, Judas, Simon, and daughters.<br>• Contemporaries: Herod the Great, John the Baptist, Simeon, Anna |
| **Key verses** | "Joseph, her fiancé, was a good man and did not want to disgrace her publicly, so he decided to break the engagement quietly. As he considered this, an angel of the Lord appeared to him in a dream. 'Joseph, son of David,' the angel said, 'do not be afraid to take Mary as your wife. For the child within her was conceived by the Holy Spirit'" (Matthew 1:19-20). |

Joseph's story is told in Matthew 1:16–2:23; Luke 1:26–2:52.

---

ment (2 Samuel 24:16), patrol the earth (Zechariah 1:9-14), and fight the forces of evil (2 Kings 6:16-18; Revelation 20:1, 2). There are both good and bad angels (Revelation 12:7), but because bad angels are allied with the devil, or Satan, they have considerably less power and authority than good angels. Eventually the main role of angels will be to offer continuous praise to God (Revelation 7:11, 12).

**1:20-23** The angel declared to Joseph that Mary's child was conceived by the Holy Spirit and would be a son. This reveals an important truth about Jesus—he is both God and human. The infinite, unlimited God took on the limitations of humanity so he could live and die for the salvation of all who would believe in him.

*Jesus* means "the Lord saves." Jesus came to earth to save us

because we can't save ourselves from sin and its consequences. No matter how good we are, we can't eliminate the sinful nature present in all of us. Only Jesus can do that. Jesus didn't come to help people save themselves; he came to be their Savior from the power and penalty of sin. Thank Christ for his death on the cross for your sin, and then ask him to take control of your life. Your new life begins at that moment.

Jesus would fulfill the prophecy of Isaiah, for he would be *Immanuel* ("God is with us," see Isaiah 7:14). Jesus was God in the flesh; thus, God was literally among us, "with us." Through the Holy Spirit, Christ is present today in the life of every believer. Perhaps not even Isaiah understood how far-reaching the meaning of *Immanuel* would be.

24When Joseph woke up, he did as the angel of the Lord commanded and took Mary as his wife. 25But he did not have sexual relations with her until her son was born. And Joseph named him Jesus.

**1:25**
Luke 1:31

### Visitors Arrive from Eastern Lands (12)

**2** Jesus was born in Bethlehem in Judea, during the reign of King Herod. About that time some wise men* from eastern lands arrived in Jerusalem, asking, 2"Where is the newborn king of the Jews? We saw his star as it rose,* and we have come to worship him."

**2:1**
Luke 1:5; 2:4-7

**2:2**
Num 24:17

3King Herod was deeply disturbed when he heard this, as was everyone in Jerusalem. 4He called a meeting of the leading priests and teachers of religious law and asked, "Where is the Messiah supposed to be born?"

Jer 23:5
Matt 2:9
Rev 22:16

5"In Bethlehem in Judea," they said, "for this is what the prophet wrote:

**2:5**
John 7:42

**2:1** Or *royal astrologers;* Greek reads *magi;* also in 2:7, 16.   **2:2** Or *star in the east.*

---

**1:24** Joseph changed his plans quickly after learning that Mary had not been unfaithful to him (1:19). He obeyed God and proceeded with the marriage plans. Although others may have disapproved of his decision, Joseph went ahead with what he knew was right. Sometimes we avoid doing what is right because of what others might think. Like Joseph, we must choose to obey God rather than seek the approval of others.

**2:1** Bethlehem is a small town five miles south of Jerusalem. It sits on a high ridge over 2,000 feet above sea level. It is mentioned in more detail in the Gospel of Luke. Luke also explains why Joseph and Mary were in Bethlehem when Jesus was born, rather than in Nazareth, their hometown.

**2:1** The land of Israel was divided into four political districts and several lesser territories. Judea was to the south, Samaria in the middle, Galilee to the north, and Idumea to the southwest. Bethlehem of Judea (also called Judah, 2:6) had been prophesied as the Messiah's birthplace (Micah 5:2). Jerusalem was also in Judea and was the seat of government for Herod the Great, king over all four political districts. After Herod's death, the districts were divided among three separate rulers (see the note on 2:19-22). Although he was a ruthless, evil man who murdered many in his own family, Herod the Great supervised the renovation of the Temple, making it much larger and more beautiful. This made him popular with many Jews. Jesus would visit Jerusalem many times because the great Jewish festivals were held there.

**2:1, 2** Not much is known about these "wise men." We don't know where they came from or how many there were. Tradition says they were men of high position from Parthia, near the site of ancient Babylon. How did they know that the star represented the Messiah? (1) They could have been Jews who remained in

### THE FLIGHT TO EGYPT

Herod planned to kill the baby Jesus, whom he perceived to be a future threat to his position. Warned of this treachery in a dream, Joseph took his family to Egypt until Herod's death, which occurred a year or two later. They then planned to return to Judea, but God led them instead to Nazareth in Galilee.

Babylon after the Exile and knew the Old Testament predictions of the Messiah's coming. (2) They may have been eastern astrologers who studied ancient manuscripts from around the world. Because of the Jewish exile centuries earlier, they would have had copies of the Old Testament in their land. (3) They may have had a special message from God directing them to the Messiah. Some scholars say these wise men were each from a different land, representing the entire world bowing before Jesus. These men from faraway lands recognized Jesus as the Messiah when most of God's chosen people in Israel did not. Matthew pictures Jesus as the King over the whole world, not just Judea.

**2:1, 2** The wise men traveled thousands of miles to see the king of the Jews. When they finally found him, they responded with joy, worship, and gifts. This is so different from the approach people often take today. We expect God to come looking for us, to explain himself, prove who he is, and give *us* gifts. But those who are wise still seek and worship Jesus today, not for what they can get, but for who he is.

**2:2** The wise men said they saw Jesus' star. Balaam referred to a coming "star . . . from Jacob" (Numbers 24:17). Some say this star may have been a conjunction of Jupiter, Saturn, and Mars in 6 B.C., and others offer other explanations. But couldn't God, who created the heavens, have created a special star to signal the arrival of his Son? Whatever the nature of the star, these wise men traveled thousands of miles searching for a king, and they found him.

**2:3** Herod the Great was quite disturbed when the wise men asked about a newborn king of the Jews because (1) Herod was not the rightful heir to the throne of David; therefore, many Jews hated him as a usurper. If Jesus really was an heir, trouble would arise. (2) Herod was ruthless, and because of his many enemies, he was suspicious that someone would try to overthrow him. (3) Herod didn't want the Jews, a religious people, to unite around a religious figure. (4) If these wise men were of Jewish descent and from Parthia (the most powerful region next to Rome), they would have welcomed a Jewish king who could swing the balance of power away from Rome. The land of Israel, far from Rome, would have been easy prey for a nation trying to gain more control.

The text tells us that not only was Herod disturbed, but so was everyone in Jerusalem. When Jesus was born into the world, people immediately began to react. His presence did not soothe and comfort most people; instead, it startled and disturbed them. In some he awakened spiritual longings; in others, fear and insecurity. Things have not changed that much. Jesus still disturbs people. If it is true that God entered our world when Jesus was born, we dare not sit idly by ignoring and rationalizing our inaction. We must acknowledge Jesus as the rightful King of our lives.

**2:4-6** The leading priests and teachers of religious law were aware of Micah 5:2 and other prophecies about the Messiah. Matthew repeatedly highlighted their knowledge and unbelief. The wise men's news troubled Herod because he knew that the Jewish people expected the Messiah to come soon (Luke 3:15). Most Jews expected the Messiah to be a great military and

**2:6**
†Mic 5:2

6 'And you, O Bethlehem in the land of Judah,
    are not least among the ruling cities* of Judah,
for a ruler will come from you
    who will be the shepherd for my people Israel.'*"

7 Then Herod called for a private meeting with the wise men, and he learned from them the time when the star first appeared. 8 Then he told them, "Go to Bethlehem and search carefully for the child. And when you find him, come back and tell me so that I can go and worship him, too!"

**2:9**
Matt 2:2

9 After this interview the wise men went their way. And the star they had seen in the east guided them to Bethlehem. It went ahead of them and stopped over the place where the

**2:11**
Ps 72:10
Isa 60:6

child was. 10 When they saw the star, they were filled with joy! 11 They entered the house and saw the child with his mother, Mary, and they bowed down and worshiped him. Then they opened their treasure chests and gave him gifts of gold, frankincense, and myrrh.

**2:12**
Matt 2:22

12 When it was time to leave, they returned to their own country by another route, for God had warned them in a dream not to return to Herod.

### The Escape to Egypt (13)

**2:13**
Matt 1:20; 2:19

13 After the wise men were gone, an angel of the Lord appeared to Joseph in a dream. "Get up! Flee to Egypt with the child and his mother," the angel said. "Stay there until I tell you to return, because Herod is going to search for the child to kill him."

**2:6a** Greek *the rulers.*    **2:6b** Mic 5:2; 2 Sam 5:2.

---

**GOSPEL
ACCOUNTS
FOUND ONLY
IN MATTHEW**

| Passage | Subject |
|---|---|
| 1:20-24 . . . . . . . . . . . . . . . . . . . . . . . . | Joseph's dream* |
| 2:1-12 . . . . . . . . . . . . . . . . . . . . . . . . | The visit of the wise men |
| 2:13-15 . . . . . . . . . . . . . . . . . . . . . . . . | Escape to Egypt* |
| 2:16-18 . . . . . . . . . . . . . . . . . . . . . . . . | Slaughter of the male children* |
| 27:3-10 . . . . . . . . . . . . . . . . . . . . . . . . | The death of Judas* |
| 27:19 . . . . . . . . . . . . . . . . . . . . . . . . | The dream of Pilate's wife |
| 27:52 . . . . . . . . . . . . . . . . . . . . . . . . | The other resurrections |
| 28:11-15 . . . . . . . . . . . . . . . . . . . . . . . . | The bribery of the guards |
| 28:19, 20 . . . . . . . . . . . . . . . . . . . . . . | The baptism emphasis in the great commission* |

Matthew records nine special events that are not mentioned in any of the other Gospels. In each case, the most apparent reason for Matthew's choice has to do with his purpose in communicating the gospel to Jewish people. Five cases are fulfillments of Old Testament prophecies (marked with asterisks above). The other four would have been of particular interest to the Jews of Matthew's day.

---

political deliverer, like Alexander the Great. Herod's counselors would have told Herod this. No wonder this ruthless man took no chances and ordered all the baby boys in Bethlehem killed (2:16)!

**2:6** Most religious leaders believed in a literal fulfillment of all Old Testament prophecy; therefore, they believed the Messiah would be born in Bethlehem as foreseen by the prophet Micah seven centuries earlier (Micah 5:2). Ironically, when Jesus was born, these same religious leaders became his greatest enemies. When the Messiah for whom they had been waiting finally came, they didn't recognize him.

**2:8** Herod did not want to worship Christ—he was lying. This was a trick to get the wise men to return to him and reveal the whereabouts of the newborn king. Herod's plan was to kill Jesus.

**2:11** Jesus was probably one or two years old when the wise men found him. By this time, Mary and Joseph were married, living in a house, and intending to stay in Bethlehem for a while. For more on Joseph and Mary's stay there, see the note on Luke 2:39.

**2:11** The wise men gave these expensive gifts as worthy acknowledgement for a future king. Bible students have seen in the gifts symbols of Christ's identity and what he would accomplish. Gold was a gift for royalty; frankincense was a gift for deity; and myrrh

was a spice used to anoint a body for burial. These gifts may have provided the financial resources for the trip to Egypt and back.

**2:11** The wise men brought gifts and worshiped Jesus for who he was. This is the essence of true worship—honoring Christ for who he is and being willing to give him what is valuable to you. Worship God because he is the perfect, just, and almighty Creator of the universe, worthy of the best you have to give.

**2:12** After finding Jesus and worshiping him, the wise men were warned by God not to return through Jerusalem as they had intended. Finding Jesus may mean that your life must take a different direction, one that is responsive and obedient to God's Word. In what ways has Jesus affected the direction of your life?

**2:13** This was the second dream or vision that Joseph received from God. Joseph's first dream revealed that Mary's child would be the Messiah (1:20, 21). His second dream told him how to protect the child's life. Although Joseph was not Jesus' natural father, he was Jesus' legal father and was responsible for his safety and well-being. Divine guidance comes only to prepared hearts. Joseph remained receptive to God's guidance.

¹⁴That night Joseph left for Egypt with the child and Mary, his mother, ¹⁵and they stayed there until Herod's death. This fulfilled what the Lord had spoken through the prophet: "I called my Son out of Egypt."*

**2:15**
†Hos 11:1

¹⁶Herod was furious when he realized that the wise men had outwitted him. He sent soldiers to kill all the boys in and around Bethlehem who were two years old and under, based on the wise men's report of the star's first appearance. ¹⁷Herod's brutal action fulfilled what God had spoken through the prophet Jeremiah:

¹⁸ "A cry was heard in Ramah—
　　weeping and great mourning.
　Rachel weeps for her children,
　　refusing to be comforted,
　　for they are dead."*

**2:18**
†Jer 31:15

### The Return to Nazareth (14)

¹⁹When Herod died, an angel of the Lord appeared in a dream to Joseph in Egypt. ²⁰"Get up!" the angel said. "Take the child and his mother back to the land of Israel, because those who were trying to kill the child are dead."

**2:19**
Matt 1:20; 2:12
**2:20**
Exod 4:19

²¹So Joseph got up and returned to the land of Israel with Jesus and his mother. ²²But when he learned that the new ruler of Judea was Herod's son Archelaus, he was afraid to go there. Then, after being warned in a dream, he left for the region of Galilee. ²³So the family went and lived in a town called Nazareth. This fulfilled what the prophets had said: "He will be called a Nazarene."

**2:22**
Matt 2:12
**2:23**
Luke 2:39
John 1:45-46
Acts 4:10; 24:5

### John the Baptist Prepares the Way for Jesus (16/Mark 1:1-8; Luke 3:1-17)

**3** In those days John the Baptist came to the Judean wilderness and began preaching. His message was, ²"Repent of your sins and turn to God, for the Kingdom of Heaven is near."* ³The prophet Isaiah was speaking about John when he said,

**3:2**
Matt 4:17; 10:7
Mark 1:15
**3:3**
†Isa 40:3
Mal 3:1
Luke 1:76

**2:15** Hos 11:1.　**2:18** Jer 31:15.　**3:2** Or *has come,* or *is coming soon.*

---

**2:14, 15** Going to Egypt was not unusual because there were colonies of Jews in several major Egyptian cities. These colonies had developed during the time of the great captivity (see Jeremiah 43–44). There is an interesting parallel between this flight to Egypt and Israel's history. As an infant nation, Israel went to Egypt, just as Jesus did as a child. God led Israel out (Hosea 11:1); God brought Jesus back. Both events show God working to save his people.

**2:16** Herod, the king of the Jews, killed all the boys under two years of age in an obsessive attempt to kill Jesus, the newborn king. He stained his hands with blood, but he did not harm Jesus. Herod was king by a human appointment; Jesus was King by a divine appointment. No one can thwart God's plans.

**2:16** Herod was afraid that this newborn king would one day take his throne. He completely misunderstood the reason for Christ's coming. Jesus didn't want Herod's throne; he wanted to be king of Herod's life. Jesus wanted to give Herod eternal life, not take away his present life. Today people are often afraid that Christ wants to take things away when, in reality, he wants to give them real freedom, peace, and joy. Don't fear Christ—give him the throne of your life.

**2:17, 18** Rachel had been the favored wife of Jacob, one of the great men of God in the Old Testament. As such, she was considered the mother of a nation. From Jacob's 12 sons had come the 12 tribes of Israel. Rachel was buried near Bethlehem (Genesis 35:19). For more about the significance of this verse, see the note on Jeremiah 31:15, from which this verse was quoted.

**2:19-22** Herod the Great died in 4 B.C. of an incurable disease. Rome trusted him but didn't trust his sons. Herod knew that Rome wouldn't give his successor as much power, so he divided his kingdom into three parts, one for each son. Archelaus received Judea, Samaria, and Idumea; Herod Antipas received Galilee and Perea; Herod Philip II received Traconitis. Archelaus, a violent man, began his reign by slaughtering 3,000 influential people. Nine years later, he was banished. God didn't want Joseph's family to go into the region of this evil ruler.

**2:23** Nazareth sat in the hilly area of southern Galilee near the crossroads of great caravan trade routes. The town itself was rather small. The Roman garrison in charge of Galilee was housed there. The people of Nazareth had constant contact with people from all over the world, so world news reached them quickly. The people of Nazareth had an attitude of independence that many of the Jews despised. This may have been why Nathanael commented "Nazareth! . . . Can anything good come from Nazareth?" (John 1:46).

**2:23** The Old Testament does not record this specific statement, "He will be called a Nazarene." Many scholars believe, however, that Matthew is referring to Isaiah 11:1, where the Hebrew word for "branch" is similar to the word for "Nazarene." Or he may be referring to a prophecy unrecorded in the Bible. In any case, Matthew paints the picture of Jesus as the true Messiah announced by God through the prophets; and he makes the point that Jesus, the Messiah, had unexpectedly humble beginnings, just as the Old Testament had predicted (see Micah 5:2).

**3:1, 2** Almost 30 years had passed since the events of chapter 2. Here John the Baptist burst onto the scene. His theme was "Repent of your sins." The people needed to repent—make a 180-degree turn—from the kind of self-centeredness that leads to wrong actions, such as lying, cheating, stealing, gossiping, taking revenge, abusing, and indulging in sexual immorality. A person who turns from sin stops rebelling and begins following God's way of living prescribed in his Word. The first step in turning to God is to admit your sin, as John urged. Then God will receive you and help you live the way he wants. Remember that only God can get rid of sin. He doesn't expect us to clean up our lives *before* we come to him.

**3:1, 2** John the Baptist's Profile is found in John 1, p. 1749.

**3:2** The Kingdom of Heaven began when God himself entered human history as a man. Today Jesus Christ reigns in the hearts of believers, but the Kingdom of Heaven will not be fully realized until all evil in the world is judged and removed. Christ came to earth first as a suffering servant; he will come again as king and judge to rule victoriously over all the earth.

**3:3** The prophecy quoted is Isaiah 40:3. Isaiah was one of the

"He is a voice shouting in the wilderness,
  'Prepare the way for the LORD's coming!
    Clear the road for him!'"*

**3:4**
Lev 11:22
2 Kgs 1:8

⁴John's clothes were woven from coarse camel hair, and he wore a leather belt around his waist. For food he ate locusts and wild honey. ⁵People from Jerusalem and from all of Judea

**3:3** Isa 40:3 (Greek version).

---

**HEROD**

The Bible records history. It has proven itself an accurate and reliable record of people, events, and places. Independent historical accounts verify the Bible's descriptions and details of many famous lives. One of these was the father of the Herodian family, Herod the Great.

Herod is remembered as a builder of cities and the lavish rebuilder of the Temple in Jerusalem. But he also destroyed people. He showed little greatness in either his personal actions or his character. He was ruthless in ruling his territory. His suspicions and jealousy led to the murder of several of his children and the death of his wife Mariamne.

Herod's title, king of the Jews, was granted by Rome but never accepted by the Jewish people. He was not part of the Davidic family line, and he was only partly Jewish. Although Israel benefited from Herod's lavish efforts to repair the Temple in Jerusalem, he won little admiration because he also rebuilt various pagan temples. Herod's costly attempt to gain the loyalty of the people failed because it was superficial. His only loyalty was to himself.

Because his royal title was not genuine, Herod was constantly worried about losing his position. His actions when hearing from the wise men about their search for the new king are consistent with all that we know about Herod. He planned to locate and kill the child before he could become a threat. The murder of innocent children that followed is a tragic lesson in what can happen when actions are motivated by selfishness. Herod's suspicions did not spare even his own family. His life was self-destructive.

| | |
|---|---|
| **Strengths and accomplishments** | • Was given the title king of the Jews by the Romans<br>• Held on to his power for more than 30 years<br>• Was an effective, though ruthless, ruler<br>• Sponsored a great variety of large building projects |
| **Weaknesses and mistakes** | • Tended to treat those around him with fear, suspicion, and jealousy<br>• Had several of his own children and at least one wife killed<br>• Ordered the killing of the baby boys in Bethlehem<br>• Although claiming to be a God-worshiper, he was still involved in many forms of pagan religion |
| **Lessons from his life** | • Great power brings neither peace nor security<br>• No one can prevent God's plans from being carried out<br>• Superficial loyalty does not impress people or God |
| **Vital statistics** | • Occupation: King of Judea from 37 to 4 B.C.<br>• Relatives: Father: Antipater. Sons: Archelaus, Antipater, Antipas, Philip, and others. Wives: Doris, Mariamne, and others.<br>• Contemporaries: Zechariah, Elizabeth, Mary, Joseph, Mark Antony, Augustus |
| **Key verse** | "Herod was furious when he realized that the wise men had outwitted him. He sent soldiers to kill all the boys in and around Bethlehem who were two years old and under" (Matthew 2:16). |

Herod the Great is mentioned in Matthew 2:1-22 and Luke 1:5.

---

greatest prophets of the Old Testament and one of the most quoted in the New. Like Isaiah, John was a prophet who urged the people to confess their sins and live for God. Both prophets taught that the message of repentance is good news to those who listen and seek the healing forgiveness of God's love, but terrible news to those who refuse to listen and thus cut off their only hope.

**3:3** John the Baptist *prepared* the way for Jesus by preparing others to welcome him. People who do not know Jesus need to get ready to meet him. We can prepare them by explaining their need for forgiveness, demonstrating Christ's teachings by our conduct, and telling them how Christ can give their lives meaning. We can "clear the road for him" by correcting misconceptions that might be hindering people from coming to Christ. Someone you know may be open to a relationship with Christ. How are you helping those around you to welcome Jesus?

**3:4** John was markedly different from other religious leaders of his day. While many were greedy, selfish, and preoccupied with

winning the praise of the people, John was concerned only with the praise of God. Having separated himself from the evil and hypocrisy of his day, John lived differently from other people to show that his message was new. John not only preached God's law, he *lived* it. Do you practice what you preach? Could people discover what you believe by observing the way you live?

**3:4-6** John must have presented a strange image! Many people came to hear this preacher, who wore odd clothes and ate unusual food. Some probably came simply out of curiosity and ended up turning from their sins as they listened to his powerful message. People may be curious about your Christian life-style and values. You can use their simple curiosity as an opener to share how Christ makes a difference in you.

**3:5** Why did John attract so many people? He was the first true prophet in 400 years. He publicly blasted both Herod and the religious leaders, daring words that fascinated the common people. But John also had a strong message for his audience: They, too, and all over the Jordan Valley went out to see and hear John. 6And when they confessed their sins, he baptized them in the Jordan River.

7But when he saw many Pharisees and Sadducees coming to watch him baptize,* he denounced them. "You brood of snakes!" he exclaimed. "Who warned you to flee God's coming wrath? 8Prove by the way you live that you have repented of your sins and turned to God. 9Don't just say to each other, 'We're safe, for we are descendants of Abraham.' That means nothing, for I tell you, God can create children of Abraham from these very stones. 10Even now the ax of God's judgment is poised, ready to sever the roots of the trees. Yes, every tree that does not produce good fruit will be chopped down and thrown into the fire.

11"I baptize with* water those who repent of their sins and turn to God. But someone is coming soon who is greater than I am—so much greater that I'm not worthy even to be his slave and carry his sandals. He will baptize you with the Holy Spirit and with fire.* 12He is ready to separate the chaff from the wheat with his winnowing fork. Then he will clean up the threshing area, gathering the wheat into his barn but burning the chaff with never-ending fire."

**3:7**
Matt 12:34; 23:33
Luke 3:7
John 8:44
Rom 5:9
Eph 5:6
Col 3:6

**3:9**
John 8:33, 37, 39
Rom 4:12

**3:10**
Matt 7:19
Luke 13:7
John 15:6

**3:11**
John 1:26-27, 31, 33
Acts 1:5; 2:3-4; 13:24; 19:4

**3:12**
Matt 13:30

3:7 Or *coming to be baptized.*   3:11a Or *in.*   3:11b Or *in the Holy Spirit and in fire.*

---

were sinners and needed to turn from their sins. His words were powerful and true. The people were expecting a prophet like Elijah (Malachi 4:5; Luke 1:17), and John seemed to be the one!

**3:6** When you wash dirty hands, the results are immediately visible. But turning from sins (repentance) happens inside with a cleansing that isn't seen right away. So John used a symbolic action that people could see: baptism. The Jews used baptism to initiate converts, so John's audience was familiar with the rite. Here, baptism was used as a sign of repentance and forgiveness. Turning from sins implies a change in behavior, turning from sin toward God. Have you turned from sin in your life? Can others see the difference it makes in you? A changed life with new and different behavior makes your repentance real and visible.

**3:6** The Jordan River is about 70 miles long, its main section stretching between the Sea of Galilee and the Dead Sea. Jerusalem lies about 20 miles west of the Jordan. This river was Israel's eastern border, and many significant events in the nation's history took place there. It was by the Jordan River that the Israelites renewed their covenant with God before entering the Promised Land (Joshua 1—2). Here John the Baptist calls them to renew their covenant with God again, this time through baptism.

**3:7** The Jewish religious leaders were divided into several groups. Two of the most prominent groups were the Pharisees and the Sadducees. The Pharisees separated themselves from

anything non-Jewish and carefully followed both the Old Testament laws and the oral traditions handed down through the centuries. The Sadducees believed the Pentateuch alone (Genesis—Deuteronomy) to be God's Word. They were descended mainly from priestly nobility, while the Pharisees came from all classes of people. The two groups disliked each other greatly, and both opposed Jesus. John the Baptist criticized the Pharisees for being legalistic and hypocritical, following the letter of the law while ignoring its true intent. He criticized the Sadducees for using religion to advance their political position. For more information on these two groups, see the chart in Mark 2, p. 1617.

**3:8** John the Baptist called people to more than words or ritual; he told them to change their behavior. "Prove by the way you live that you have repented of your sins" means that God looks beyond our words and religious activities to see if our conduct backs up what we say, and he judges our words by the actions that accompany them. Do your actions match your words?

**3:9, 10** Just as a fruit tree is expected to bear fruit, God's people should produce a crop of good deeds. God has no use for people who call themselves Christians but who live otherwise. Like many people in John's day who were God's people in name only, we are of no value if we are Christians in name only. If others can't see our faith in the way we treat them, we may not be God's people at all.

**3:10** God's message hasn't changed since the Old Testament: People will be judged for their unproductive lives. God calls us to be *active* in our obedience. John compared people who claim they believe God but don't live for God to unproductive trees that will be cut down. To be productive for God, we must obey his teachings, resist temptation, actively serve and help others, and share our faith. How productive are you for God?

**3:11** John baptized people as a sign that they had asked God to forgive their sins and had decided to live as he wanted them to live. Baptism was an *outward* sign of commitment. To be effective, it had to be accompanied by an *inward* change of attitude leading to a changed life—the work of the Holy Spirit. John said that Jesus would baptize with the Holy Spirit and fire. This looked ahead to Pentecost (Acts 2), when the Holy Spirit would be sent by Jesus in the form of tongues of fire, empowering his followers to preach the Good News. John's statement also symbolizes the work of the Holy Spirit in bringing God's judgment on those who refuse to turn from their sins. Everyone will one day be baptized—either now by God's Holy Spirit or later by the fire of his judgment.

**3:12** A winnowing fork is a pitchfork used to toss wheat in the air to separate grain from chaff. The grain is the part of the plant that is useful; chaff is the worthless outer shell. Because it is useless, chaff is burned; grain, however, is gathered.

**JESUS BEGINS HIS MINISTRY**

From his childhood home, Nazareth, Jesus set out to begin his earthly ministry. He was baptized by John the Baptist in the Jordan River, tempted by Satan in the wilderness, and then returned to Galilee. Between the temptation and his move to Capernaum (4:12, 13), he ministered in Judea, Samaria, and Galilee (see John 1—4).

Mediterranean Sea
GALILEE
N
Capernaum • Sea of Galilee
Nazareth •
DECAPOLIS (Ten Towns)
Jordan River
SAMARIA
Bethany •
Jerusalem •
Wilderness
PEREA
JUDEA
Dead Sea
IDUMEA
0   20 Mi.
0   20 Km.

**The Baptism of Jesus** (**17**/Mark 1:9-11; Luke 3:21-22)

13 Then Jesus went from Galilee to the Jordan River to be baptized by John. 14 But John tried to talk him out of it. "I am the one who needs to be baptized by you," he said, "so why are you coming to me?"

15 But Jesus said, "It should be done, for we must carry out all that God requires.*"So John agreed to baptize him.

16 After his baptism, as Jesus came up out of the water, the heavens were opened* and he saw the Spirit of God descending like a dove and settling on him. 17 And a voice from heaven said, "This is my dearly loved Son, who brings me great joy."

**3:13-17**
Mark 1:9-11
Luke 3:21-22
John 1:31-34
**3:16**
Isa 11:2
**3:17**
Gen 22:2
Ps 2:7
Isa 42:1
Matt 12:18; 17:5
Mark 9:7
Luke 9:35

**3:15** Or *for we must fulfill all righteousness.*  **3:16** Some manuscripts read *opened to him.*

---

**THE PHARISEES AND SADDUCEES**
The Pharisees and Sadducees were the two major religious groups in Israel at the time of Christ. The Pharisees were more religiously minded, while the Sadducees were more politically minded. Although the groups disliked and distrusted each other, they became allies in their common hatred for Jesus.

| Name | Positive Characteristics | Negative Characteristics |
|---|---|---|
| PHARISEES | • Were committed to obeying all of God's commands<br>• Were admired by the common people for their apparent piety<br>• Believed in a bodily resurrection and eternal life<br>• Believed in angels and demons | • Behaved as though their own religious rules were just as important as God's rules for living<br>• Their piety was often hypocritical, and their efforts often forced others to try to live up to standards they themselves could not live up to<br>• Believed that salvation came from perfect obedience to the law and was not based on forgiveness of sins<br>• Became so obsessed with obeying their legal interpretations in every detail that they completely ignored God's message of mercy and grace<br>• Were more concerned with appearing to be good than obeying God |
| SADDUCEES | • Believed strongly in the law of Moses and in Levitical purity<br>• Were more practically minded than the Pharisees | • Relied on logic while placing little importance on faith<br>• Did not believe all the Old Testament was God's Word<br>• Did not believe in a bodily resurrection or eternal life<br>• Did not believe in angels or demons<br>• Were often willing to compromise their values with the Romans and others in order to maintain their status and influential positions |

---

"Winnowing" is often used as a picture of God's judgment. Unrepentant people will be judged and discarded because they are worthless in doing God's work; those who repent and believe will be saved and used by God.

**3:13-15** John had been explaining that Jesus' baptism would be much greater than his, when suddenly Jesus came to him and asked to be baptized! John felt unqualified. He wanted Jesus to baptize *him.* Why did Jesus ask to be baptized? It was not for repentance for sin because Jesus never sinned. "We must carry out all that God requires" refers to accomplishing God's mission. Jesus saw his baptism as advancing God's work. Jesus was baptized because (1) he was confessing sin on behalf of the nation, as Nehemiah, Ezra, Moses, and Daniel had done; (2) he was showing support for what John was doing; (3) he was inaugurating his public ministry; (4) he was identifying with the penitent people of God, not with the critical Pharisees who were only watching. Jesus, the perfect man, didn't need baptism for sin, but he accepted baptism in obedient service to the Father, and God showed his approval.

**3:15** Put yourself in John's shoes. Your work is going well, people are taking notice, everything is growing. But you know that the purpose of your work is to prepare the people for Jesus (John 1:35-37). Then Jesus arrives, and his coming tests your integrity. Will you be able to turn your followers over to him? John passed the test by publicly baptizing Jesus. Soon

he would say, "He must become greater and greater, and I must become less and less" (John 3:30). Can we, like John, put our egos and profitable work aside in order to point others to Jesus? Are we willing to lose some of our status so that everyone will benefit?

**3:16, 17** The doctrine of the Trinity, which appeared later in church history, teaches that God is three persons and yet one in essence. In this passage, all three persons of the Trinity are present and active. God the Father speaks; God the Son is baptized; God the Holy Spirit descends on Jesus. God is one, yet in three persons at the same time. This is one of God's incomprehensible mysteries. Other Bible references that speak of the Father, Son, and Holy Spirit are Matthew 28:19; John 15:26; 1 Corinthians 12:4-13; 2 Corinthians 13:14; Ephesians 2:18; 1 Thessalonians 1:2-5; and 1 Peter 1:2.

*Satan Tempts Jesus in the Wilderness* (**18**/Mark 1:12-13; Luke 4:1-13)

**4** Then Jesus was led by the Spirit into the wilderness to be tempted there by the devil. ²For forty days and forty nights he fasted and became very hungry.

³During that time the devil* came and said to him, "If you are the Son of God, tell these stones to become loaves of bread."

⁴But Jesus told him, "No! The Scriptures say,

'People do not live by bread alone,
   but by every word that comes from the mouth of God.'*"

⁵Then the devil took him to the holy city, Jerusalem, to the highest point of the Temple, ⁶and said, "If you are the Son of God, jump off! For the Scriptures say,

'He will order his angels to protect you.
And they will hold you up with their hands
   so you won't even hurt your foot on a stone.'*"

⁷Jesus responded, "The Scriptures also say, 'You must not test the LORD your God.'*"

**4:1**
Gen 3:1-7
1 Thes 3:5
**4:2**
Exod 34:28
1 Kgs 19:8
**4:4**
†Deut 8:3
**4:6**
†Ps 91:11-12
**4:7**
†Deut 6:16

**4:3** Greek *the tempter.*   **4:4** Deut 8:3.   **4:6** Ps 91:11-12.   **4:7** Deut 6:16.

---

**4:1** This time of testing showed that Jesus really was the Son of God, able to overcome the devil and his temptations. A person has not shown true obedience if he or she has never had an opportunity to disobey. We read in Deuteronomy 8:2 that God led Israel into the wilderness to humble and test them. God wanted to see whether or not his people would really obey him. We, too, will be tested. Because we know that testing will come, we should be alert and ready for it. Remember, your convictions are only strong if they hold up under pressure!

**4:1** The devil, also called Satan, tempted Eve in the Garden of Eden, and here he tempted Jesus in the wilderness. Satan is a fallen angel. He is *real,* not symbolic, and is constantly fighting against those who follow and obey God. Satan's temptations are real, and he is always trying to get us to live his way or our way rather than God's way. Jesus will one day reign over all creation, but Satan tried to force his hand and get him to declare his kingship prematurely. If Jesus had given in, his mission on earth—to die for our sins and give us the opportunity to have eternal life—would have been lost. When temptations seem especially strong, or when you think you can rationalize giving in, consider whether Satan may be trying to block God's purposes for your life or for someone else's life.

**4:1ff** This temptation by the devil shows us that Jesus was human, and it gave Jesus the opportunity to reaffirm God's plan for his ministry. It also gives us an example to follow when we are tempted. Jesus' temptation was an important demonstration of his sinlessness. He would face temptation and not give in.

Although we may feel dirty after being tempted, we should remember that temptation itself is not sin. We sin when we give in and disobey God. Remembering this will help us turn away from the temptation.

**4:1ff** Jesus wasn't tempted inside the Temple or at his baptism but in the wilderness, where he was tired, alone, and hungry, and thus most vulnerable. The devil often tempts us when we are vulnerable—when we are under physical or emotional stress (for example, lonely, tired, weighing big decisions, or faced with uncertainty). But he also likes to tempt us through our strengths, where we are most susceptible to pride (see the note on Luke 4:3ff). We must guard at all times against his attacks.

**4:1-10** The devil's temptations focused on three crucial areas: (1) physical needs and desires, (2) possessions and power, and (3) pride (see 1 John 2:15, 16 for a similar list). But Jesus did not give in. Hebrews 4:15 says that Jesus "faced all of the same testings we do, yet he did not sin." He knows firsthand what we are experiencing, and he is willing and able to help us in our struggles. When you are tempted, turn to him for strength.

**4:3, 4** Jesus was hungry and weak after fasting for 40 days, but he chose not to use his divine power to satisfy his natural desire for food. Food, hunger, and eating are good, but the timing was wrong. Jesus was in the wilderness to fast, not to eat. And because Jesus had given up the unlimited, independent use of his divine power in order to experience humanity fully, he wouldn't use his power to change the stones to bread. We also may be tempted to satisfy a perfectly normal desire in a wrong way or at the wrong time. If we indulge in sex before marriage or if we steal to get food, we are trying to satisfy God-given desires in wrong ways. Remember, many of your desires are normal and good, but God wants you to satisfy them in the right way and at the right time.

**4:3, 4** Jesus was able to resist all of the devil's temptations because he not only knew Scripture, but he also obeyed it. Ephesians 6:17 says that God's Word is a sword to use in spiritual combat. Knowing Bible verses is an important step in helping us resist the devil's attacks, but we must also obey the Bible. Note that Satan had memorized Scripture, but he failed to obey it. Knowing and obeying the Bible helps us follow God's desires rather than the devil's.

**4:5** The Temple was the religious center of the Jewish nation and the place where the people expected the Messiah to arrive (Malachi 3:1). Herod the Great had renovated the Temple in hopes of gaining the Jews' confidence. The Temple was the tallest building in the area, and this "highest point" was probably the corner wall that jutted out of the hillside, overlooking the valley below. From this spot, Jesus could see all of Jerusalem behind him and the country for miles in front of him.

**4:5-7** God is not our magician in the sky ready to perform on request. In response to Satan's temptations, Jesus said not to put God to a test (Deuteronomy 6:16). You may want to ask God to do something to prove his existence or his love for you. Jesus once taught through a parable that people who don't believe what is written in the Bible won't believe even if someone were to come back from the dead to warn them (Luke 16:31)! God wants us to live by faith, not by magic. Don't try to manipulate God by asking for signs.

**4:6** The devil used Scripture to try to convince Jesus to sin! Sometimes friends or associates will present attractive and convincing reasons why you should try something you know is wrong. They may even find Bible verses that *seem* to support their viewpoint. Study the Bible carefully, especially the broader contexts of specific verses, so that you understand God's principles for living and what he wants for your life. Only if you really understand what the *whole* Bible says will you be able to recognize errors of interpretation when people take verses out of context and twist them to say what they want them to say.

⁸Next the devil took him to the peak of a very high mountain and showed him all the kingdoms of the world and their glory. ⁹"I will give it all to you," he said, "if you will kneel down and worship me."

**4:10**
†Deut 6:13

¹⁰ "Get out of here, Satan," Jesus told him. "For the Scriptures say,

'You must worship the LORD your God
   and serve only him.'*"

**4:11**
Luke 22:43
Heb 1:14
Jas 4:7

¹¹ Then the devil went away, and angels came and took care of Jesus.

## B. MESSAGE AND MINISTRY OF JESUS, THE KING (4:12—25:46)
Matthew features Jesus' sermons. The record of Jesus' actions is interspersed with great passages of his teaching. This section of Matthew is topical rather than chronological. Matthew records for us the Sermon on the Mount, the parables of the Kingdom, Jesus' teachings on forgiveness, and parables about the end of the age.

### 1. Jesus begins his ministry
*Jesus Preaches in Galilee* (**30**/Mark 1:14-15; Luke 4:14-15; John 4:43-45)
¹²When Jesus heard that John had been arrested, he left Judea and returned to Galilee. ¹³He went first to Nazareth, then left there and moved to Capernaum, beside the Sea of

**4:10** Deut 6:13.

---

| THE TEMPTATIONS | Temptation | Real needs used as basis for temptation | Possible doubts that made the temptations real | Potential weaknesses Satan sought to exploit | Jesus' answer |
|---|---|---|---|---|---|
| | Make bread | Physical need: Hunger | Would God provide food? | Hunger, impatience, need to "prove his sonship" | Deuteronomy 8:3 "Depend on God" Focus: God's purpose |
| | Dare God to rescue you (based on misapplied Scripture, Psalm 91:11, 12) | Emotional need: Security | Would God protect? | Pride, insecurity, need to test God | Deuteronomy 6:16 "Don't test God" Focus: God's plan |
| | Worship me! (Satan) | Psychological need: significance, power, achievement | Would God rule? | Desire for quick power, easy solutions, need to prove equality with God | Deuteronomy 6:13 "No compromise with evil" Focus: God's person |

As if going through a final test of preparation, Jesus was tempted by Satan in the wilderness. Three specific parts of the Temptation are listed by Matthew. They are familiar because we face the same kinds of temptations. As the chart shows, temptation is often the combination of a real need and a possible doubt that creates an inappropriate desire. Jesus demonstrates both the importance and effectiveness of knowing and applying Scripture to combat temptation.

---

**4:8, 9** Did the devil have the power to give Jesus the nations of the world? Didn't God, the Creator of the world, have control over these nations? The devil may have been lying about his implied power, or he may have based his offer on his temporary control and free rein over the earth because of humanity's sinfulness. The temptation before Jesus was to take the world as a political ruler right then, without carrying out his plan to save the world from sin. Satan was trying to distort Jesus' perspective by making him focus on worldly power and not on God's plans.

**4:8-10** The devil offered the whole world to Jesus if Jesus would only kneel down and worship him. Today the devil offers us the world by trying to entice us with materialism and power. We can resist temptations the same way Jesus did. If you find yourself craving something that the world offers, quote Jesus' words to the devil: "You must worship the LORD your God and serve only him."

**4:11** Angels, like these who waited on Jesus, have a significant role as God's messengers. These spiritual beings were involved in Jesus' life on earth by (1) announcing Jesus' birth to Mary,

(2) reassuring Joseph, (3) naming Jesus, (4) announcing Jesus' birth to the shepherds, (5) protecting Jesus by sending his family to Egypt, and (6) ministering to Jesus in Gethsemane. For more on angels, see the note on 1:20.

**4:12, 13** Jesus moved from Nazareth, his hometown, to Capernaum, about 20 miles farther north. Capernaum became Jesus' home base during his ministry in Galilee. Jesus probably moved (1) to get away from intense opposition in Nazareth, (2) to have an impact on the greatest number of people (Capernaum was a busy city, and Jesus' message could reach more people and spread more quickly), and (3) to utilize extra resources and support for his ministry.

Jesus' move fulfilled the prophecy of Isaiah 9:1, 2, which states that the Messiah would be a light to the land of Zebulun and Naphtali, the region of Galilee where Capernaum was located. Zebulun and Naphtali were two of the original 12 tribes of Israel.

Galilee, in the region of Zebulun and Naphtali. [14]This fulfilled what God said through the prophet Isaiah:

[15] "In the land of Zebulun and of Naphtali,
>      beside the sea, beyond the Jordan River,
>      in Galilee where so many Gentiles live,
[16] the people who sat in darkness
>      have seen a great light.
> And for those who lived in the land where death casts its shadow,
>      a light has shined."*

[17]From then on Jesus began to preach, "Repent of your sins and turn to God, for the Kingdom of Heaven is near.*"

**4:15-16**
†Isa 9:1-2; 42:6-7
Luke 2:32

**4:17**
Matt 3:2; 10:7

### Four Fishermen Follow Jesus (33/Mark 1:16-20)

[18]One day as Jesus was walking along the shore of the Sea of Galilee, he saw two brothers—Simon, also called Peter, and Andrew—throwing a net into the water, for they fished for a living. [19]Jesus called out to them, "Come, follow me, and I will show you how to fish for people!" [20]And they left their nets at once and followed him.

[21]A little farther up the shore he saw two other brothers, James and John, sitting in a boat with their father, Zebedee, repairing their nets. And he called them to come, too. [22]They immediately followed him, leaving the boat and their father behind.

**4:19**
Matt 16:17-18
John 1:42

**4:20**
Mark 10:28
Luke 18:28

### Jesus Preaches throughout Galilee (36/Mark 1:35-39; Luke 4:42-44)

[23]Jesus traveled throughout the region of Galilee, teaching in the synagogues and announcing the Good News about the Kingdom. And he healed every kind of disease and illness. [24]News about him spread as far as Syria, and people soon began bringing to him all who were sick. And whatever their sickness or disease, or if they were demon possessed or epileptic or paralyzed—he healed them all. [25]Large crowds followed him wherever he went—people from Galilee, the Ten Towns,* Jerusalem, from all over Judea, and from east of the Jordan River.

**4:23**
Matt 9:35
Mark 1:39
Luke 4:15

**4:15-16** Isa 9:1-2 (Greek version).    **4:17** Or *has come*, or *is coming soon*.    **4:25** Greek *Decapolis*.

---

**4:14-16** By quoting from the book of Isaiah, Matthew continues to tie Jesus' ministry to the Old Testament. This was helpful for his Jewish readers, who were familiar with these Scriptures. In addition, it shows the unity of God's purposes as he works with his people throughout all ages.

**4:17** The "Kingdom of Heaven" has the same meaning as the "Kingdom of God" in Mark and Luke. Matthew uses this phrase because the Jews, out of their intense reverence and respect, did not pronounce God's name. The Kingdom of Heaven is still near because it has arrived in our heart. See the note on 3:2 for more on the Kingdom of Heaven.

**4:17** Jesus started his ministry with the same message people had heard John the Baptist say: "Repent of your sins." The message is the same today as when Jesus and John gave it. Becoming a follower of Christ means turning away from our self-centeredness and "self" control and turning our life over to Christ's direction and control.

**4:18** The Sea of Galilee is really a large lake. About 30 fishing towns surrounded it during Jesus' day, and Capernaum was the largest.

**4:18-20** These men already knew Jesus. He had talked to Peter and Andrew previously (John 1:35-42) and had been preaching in the area. When Jesus called them, they knew what kind of man he was and were willing to follow him. Jesus told Peter and Andrew to leave their fishing business and begin fishing "for people," helping others find God. Jesus was calling them away from their productive trade to be productive spiritually. We all need to fish for souls. If we practice Christ's teachings and share the Good News with others, we will be able to draw those around us to Christ like a fisherman who pulls fish into his boat with nets.

**4:21, 22** James and his brother, John, along with Peter and Andrew, were the first disciples that Jesus called to work with him. Jesus' call motivated these men to get up and leave their jobs—immediately. They didn't make excuses about why it wasn't a good time. They left at once and followed. Jesus calls each of us to follow him. When Jesus asks us to serve him, we must be like the disciples and do it at once.

**4:23** Jesus was teaching, preaching, and healing. These were the three main aspects of his ministry. *Teaching* shows Jesus' concern for understanding; *preaching* shows his concern for commitment; and *healing* shows his concern for wholeness. His miracles of healing authenticated his teaching and preaching, proving that he truly was from God.

**4:23** Jesus soon developed a powerful preaching ministry and often spoke in the synagogues. Most towns that had 10 or more Jewish families had a synagogue. The building served as a religious gathering place on the Sabbath and as a school during the week. The leader of the synagogue was not a preacher as much as an administrator. His job was to find and invite rabbis to teach and preach. It was customary to invite visiting rabbis like Jesus to speak.

**4:23, 24** Jesus preached the gospel—the Good News—to everyone who wanted to hear it. The Good News is that the Kingdom of Heaven has come, that God is with us, and that he cares for us. Christ can heal us, not just of physical sickness, but of spiritual sickness as well. There's no sin or problem too great or too small for him to handle. Jesus' words were good news because they offered freedom, hope, peace of heart, and eternal life with God.

**4:25** The "Ten Towns" was a league of 10 Gentile cities east of the Sea of Galilee, joined together for better trade and mutual defense. The word about Jesus was out, and Jews and Gentiles were coming long distances to hear him.

## 2. Jesus gives the Sermon on the Mount

*Jesus Gives the Beatitudes* (**49**/Luke 6:17-26)

5:1
Luke 6:12
John 6:3
5:3-12
Luke 6:20-23
5:3
Isa 57:15
Matt 25:34

**5** One day as he saw the crowds gathering, Jesus went up on the mountainside and sat down. His disciples gathered around him, ² and he began to teach them.

³ "God blesses those who are poor and realize their need for him,*
for the Kingdom of Heaven is theirs.

5:3 Greek *poor in spirit.*

---

**KEY LESSONS FROM THE SERMON ON THE MOUNT**

| Beatitude | Old Testament anticipation | Clashing worldly values | God's reward | How to develop this attitude |
|---|---|---|---|---|
| Realize need for God (5:3) | Isaiah 57:15 | Pride and personal independence | Kingdom of Heaven | James 4:7-10 |
| Mourn (5:4) | Isaiah 61:1, 2 | Happiness at any cost | Comfort (2 Corinthians 1:4) | Psalm 51 James 4:7-10 |
| Humble (5:5) | Psalm 37:5-11 | Power | Inherit the earth | Matthew 11:27-30 |
| Hunger and thirst for justice (5:6) | Isaiah 11:4, 5; 42:1-4 | Pursuing personal needs | Satisfied | John 16:5-11 Philippians 3:7-11 |
| Merciful (5:7) | Psalm 41:1 | Strength without feeling | Be shown mercy | Ephesians 5:1, 2 |
| Pure hearts (5:8) | Psalms 24:3, 4; 51:10 | Deception is acceptable | See God | 1 John 3:1-3 |
| Work for peace (5:9) | Isaiah 57:18, 19; 60:17 | Personal peace is pursued without concern for the world's chaos | Be called children of God | Romans 12:9-21 Hebrews 12:10, 11 |
| Persecuted (5:10) | Isaiah 52:13; 53:12 | Weak commitments | Kingdom of Heaven | 2 Timothy 3:12 |

In his longest recorded sermon, Jesus began by describing the traits he was looking for in his followers. He said that God blesses those who live out those traits. Each beatitude is an almost direct contradiction of society's typical way of life. In the last beatitude, Jesus even points out that a serious effort to develop these traits is bound to create opposition. The best example of each trait is found in Jesus himself. If our goal is to become like him, applying the Beatitudes will challenge the way we live each day.

---

**5:1ff** Matthew 5–7 is called the Sermon on the Mount because Jesus gave it on a hillside near Capernaum. This "sermon" probably covered several days of preaching. In it, Jesus proclaimed his attitude toward the law. Position, authority, and money are not important in his Kingdom—what matters is faithful obedience from the heart. The Sermon on the Mount challenged the proud and legalistic religious leaders of the day. It called them back to the messages of the Old Testament prophets, who, like Jesus, taught that heartfelt obedience is more important than legalistic observance.

**5:1, 2** Enormous crowds were following Jesus—he was the talk of the town, and everyone wanted to see him. The disciples, who were the closest associates of this popular man, were certainly tempted to feel important, proud, and possessive. Being with Jesus gave them not only prestige but also opportunity for receiving money and power.

The crowds were gathering once again. But before speaking to them, Jesus pulled his disciples aside and warned them about the temptations they would face as his associates. Don't expect fame and fortune, Jesus was saying, but mourning, hunger, and persecution. Nevertheless, Jesus assured his disciples that they would be rewarded—but perhaps not in this life. There may be times when following Jesus will bring us great popularity. If we don't live by Jesus' words in this sermon, we will find

ourselves using God's message only to promote our personal interests.

**5:3-5** Jesus began his sermon with words that seem to contradict each other. But God's way of living usually contradicts the world's. If you want to live for God, you must be ready to say and do what seems strange to the world. You must be willing to give when others take, to love when others hate, to help when others abuse. By giving up your own rights in order to serve others, you will one day receive everything God has in store for you.

**5:3-12** The Beatitudes can be understood in at least four ways: (1) They are a code of ethics for the disciples and a standard of conduct for all believers. (2) They contrast Kingdom values (what is eternal) with worldly values (what is temporary). (3) They contrast the superficial "faith" of the Pharisees with the real faith that Christ demands. (4) They show how the Old Testament expectations will be fulfilled in the new Kingdom. These Beatitudes are not multiple choice—pick what you like and leave the rest. They must be taken as a whole. They describe what we should be like as Christ's followers.

**5:3-12** Each beatitude tells how to be *blessed* by God. *Blessed* means more than happiness. It implies the fortunate or enviable state of those who are in God's Kingdom. The Beatitudes don't promise laughter, pleasure, or earthly prosperity. Being "blessed"

<sup>4</sup> God blesses those who mourn,
    for they will be comforted.

<sup>5</sup> God blesses those who are humble,
    for they will inherit the whole earth.

<sup>6</sup> God blesses those who hunger and thirst for justice,*
    for they will be satisfied.

<sup>7</sup> God blesses those who are merciful,
    for they will be shown mercy.

<sup>8</sup> God blesses those whose hearts are pure,
    for they will see God.

<sup>9</sup> God blesses those who work for peace,
    for they will be called the children of God.

<sup>10</sup> God blesses those who are persecuted for doing right,
    for the Kingdom of Heaven is theirs.

<sup>11</sup>"God blesses you when people mock you and persecute you and lie about you* and say all sorts of evil things against you because you are my followers. <sup>12</sup>Be happy about it! Be very glad! For a great reward awaits you in heaven. And remember, the ancient prophets were persecuted in the same way.

### Jesus Teaches about Salt and Light (50)

<sup>13</sup> "You are the salt of the earth. But what good is salt if it has lost its flavor? Can you make it salty again? It will be thrown out and trampled underfoot as worthless.

<sup>14</sup>"You are the light of the world—like a city on a hilltop that cannot be hidden. <sup>15</sup>No one lights a lamp and then puts it under a basket. Instead, a lamp is placed on a stand, where it gives light to everyone in the house. <sup>16</sup>In the same way, let your good deeds shine out for all to see, so that everyone will praise your heavenly Father.

### Jesus Teaches about the Law (51)

<sup>17</sup>"Don't misunderstand why I have come. I did not come to abolish the law of Moses or the writings of the prophets. No, I came to accomplish their purpose. <sup>18</sup>I tell you the truth, until

**5:6** Or *for righteousness.*   **5:11** Some manuscripts do not include *and lie about you.*

**5:4**
Isa 61:2-3

**5:5**
Ps 37:11

**5:6**
Isa 55:1-2

**5:7**
Matt 18:33
Jas 2:13

**5:8**
Ps 24:3-4

**5:9**
Heb 12:14
Jas 3:18

**5:10**
2 Tim 2:12
1 Pet 3:14

**5:11**
Matt 10:22
1 Pet 4:14

**5:12**
Acts 7:52
Heb 11:32-38
Jas 5:10

**5:13**
Mark 9:50
Luke 14:34-35

**5:15**
Mark 4:21
Luke 8:16; 11:33

**5:16**
Eph 5:8-9
1 Pet 2:12

**5:17**
Rom 3:31

**5:18**
Luke 16:17; 21:33

---

by God means the experience of hope and joy, independent of outward circumstances. To find hope and joy, the deepest form of happiness, follow Jesus no matter what the cost.

**5:3-12** With Jesus' announcement that the Kingdom was near (4:17), people were naturally asking, "How do I qualify to be in God's Kingdom?" Jesus said that God's Kingdom is organized differently from worldly kingdoms. In the Kingdom of Heaven, wealth and power and authority are unimportant. Kingdom people seek different blessings and benefits, and they have different attitudes. Are your attitudes a carbon copy of the world's selfishness, pride, and lust for power, or do they reflect the humility and self-sacrifice of Jesus, your king?

**5:11, 12** Jesus said to be happy when we're persecuted for our faith. Persecution can be good because (1) it takes our eyes off earthly rewards, (2) it strips away superficial belief, (3) it strengthens the faith of those who endure, and (4) our attitude through it serves as an example to others who follow. We can be comforted knowing that God's greatest prophets were persecuted (Elijah, Jeremiah, Daniel). The fact that we are being persecuted proves that we have been faithful; faithless people would be unnoticed. In the future God will reward the faithful by receiving them into his eternal Kingdom, where there is no more persecution.

**5:13** If a seasoning has no flavor, it has no value. If Christians make no effort to affect the world around them, they are of little value to God. If we are too much like the world, we are worthless. Christians should not blend in with everyone else. Instead, we should affect others positively, just as seasoning brings out the best flavor in food.

**5:14-16** Can you hide a city that is sitting on top of a mountain? Its light at night can be seen for miles. If we live for Christ, we will glow like lights, showing others what Christ is like. We hide

our light by (1) being quiet when we should speak, (2) going along with the crowd, (3) denying the light, (4) letting sin dim our light, (5) not explaining our light to others, or (6) ignoring the needs of others. Be a beacon of truth—don't shut your light off from the rest of the world.

**5:17** God's moral and ceremonial laws were given to help people love God with all their hearts and minds. Throughout Israel's history, however, these laws had often been misquoted and misapplied. By Jesus' time, religious leaders had turned the laws into a confusing mass of rules. When Jesus talked about a new way to understand God's law, he was actually trying to bring people back to its *original* purpose. Jesus did not speak against the law itself but against the abuses and excesses to which it had been subjected (see John 1:17).

**5:17-20** If Jesus did not come to abolish the law, does that mean all the Old Testament laws still apply to us today? In the Old Testament, there were three categories of law: ceremonial, civil, and moral.

(1) The *ceremonial law* related specifically to Israel's worship (see Leviticus 1:2, 3, for example). Its primary purpose was to point forward to Jesus Christ; these laws, therefore, were no longer necessary after Jesus' death and resurrection. While we are no longer bound by ceremonial law, the principles behind them—to worship and love a holy God—still apply. Jesus was often accused by the Pharisees of violating ceremonial law.

(2) The *civil law* applied to daily living in Israel (see Deuteronomy 24:10, 11, for example). Because modern society and culture are so radically different from that time and setting, all of these guidelines cannot be followed specifically. But the principles behind the commands are timeless and should guide our conduct. Jesus demonstrated these principles by example.

(3) The *moral law* (such as the Ten Commandments) is the direct command of God, and it requires strict obedience (see

**5:19**
Jas 2:10

heaven and earth disappear, not even the smallest detail of God's law will disappear until its purpose is achieved. ¹⁹So if you ignore the least commandment and teach others to do the same, you will be called the least in the Kingdom of Heaven. But anyone who obeys God's laws and teaches them will be called great in the Kingdom of Heaven.

²⁰"But I warn you—unless your righteousness is better than the righteousness of the teachers of religious law and the Pharisees, you will never enter the Kingdom of Heaven!

### Jesus Teaches about Anger (52)

**5:21**
†Exod 20:13
†Deut 5:17
Matt 19:18
Mark 10:19
Luke 18:20
Rom 13:9
Jas 2:11

**5:22**
Eph 4:26
Jas 1:19-20
1 Jn 3:15

²¹"You have heard that our ancestors were told, ' You must not murder. If you commit murder, you are subject to judgment.'* ²²But I say, if you are even angry with someone,* you are subject to judgment! If you call someone an idiot,* you are in danger of being brought before the court. And if you curse someone,* you are in danger of the fires of hell.*

²³"So if you are presenting a sacrifice* at the altar in the Temple and you suddenly remember that someone has something against you, ²⁴leave your sacrifice there at the altar. Go and be reconciled to that person. Then come and offer your sacrifice to God.

**5:21** Exod 20:13; Deut 5:17. **5:22a** Some manuscripts add *without cause.* **5:22b** Greek uses an Aramaic term of contempt: *If you say to your brother, 'Raca.'* **5:22c** Greek *if you say, 'You fool.'* **5:22d** Greek *Gehenna;* also in 5:29, 30. **5:23** Greek *gift;* also in 5:24.

---

**SIX WAYS TO THINK LIKE CHRIST**

| Reference | Example | It's not enough to | We must also |
|---|---|---|---|
| 5:21, 22 | Murder | Avoid killing | Avoid anger and hatred |
| 5:23-26 | Sacrifices | Offer regular gifts | Have right relationships with God and others |
| 5:27-30 | Adultery | Avoid adultery | Keep our hearts from lusting and be faithful |
| 5:31, 32 | Divorce | Be legally married | Live out marriage commitments |
| 5:33-37 | Vows | Keep a vow | Avoid casual and irresponsible commitments to God |
| 5:38-47 | Revenge | Seek justice for ourselves | Show mercy and love to others |

We, more often than not, avoid the extreme sins but regularly commit the types of sins with which Jesus was most concerned. In these six examples, our real struggle with sin is exposed. Jesus pointed out what kind of lives would be required of his followers. Are you living as Jesus taught?

---

Exodus 20:13, for example). The moral law reveals the nature and will of God, and it still applies today. Jesus obeyed the moral law completely.

**5:19** Some of those in the crowd were experts at telling others what to do, but they missed the central point of God's laws themselves. Jesus made it clear, however, that obeying God's laws is more important than explaining them. It's much easier to study God's laws and tell others to obey them than to put them into practice. How are you doing at obeying God *yourself?*

**5:20** The Pharisees were exacting and scrupulous in their attempts to follow their laws. So how could Jesus reasonably call us to greater righteousness than theirs? The Pharisees' weakness was that they were content to obey the laws outwardly without allowing God to change their hearts (or attitudes). They looked pious, but they were far from the Kingdom of Heaven. God judges our hearts as well as our deeds, for it is in the heart that our real allegiance lies.

Jesus was saying that his listeners needed a different kind of righteousness altogether (out of love for God), not just a more intense version of the Pharisees' obedience (which was mere legal compliance). Our righteousness must (1) come from what God does in us, not what we can do by ourselves, (2) be God-centered, not self-centered, (3) be based on reverence for God, not approval from people, and (4) go beyond keeping the law to living by the principles behind the law. We should be just as concerned about our attitudes that people don't see as about our actions that are seen by all.

**5:21, 22** When Jesus said, "But I say," he was not doing away with the law or adding his own beliefs. Rather, he was

giving a fuller understanding of why God made that law in the first place. For example, Moses said, "You must not murder" (Exodus 20:13); Jesus taught that we should not even become angry enough to murder, for then we have already committed murder in our heart. The Pharisees read this law and, not having literally murdered anyone, felt that they had obeyed it. Yet they were angry enough with Jesus that they would soon plot his death, though they would not do the dirty work themselves. We miss the intent of God's Word when we read his rules for living without trying to understand why he made them. When do you keep God's rules but close your eyes to his intent?

**5:21, 22** Killing is a terrible sin, but *anger* is a great sin, too, because it also violates God's command to love. Anger in this case refers to a seething, brooding bitterness against someone. It is a dangerous emotion that always threatens to leap out of control, leading to violence, emotional hurt, increased mental stress, and spiritual damage. Anger keeps us from developing a spirit pleasing to God. Have you ever been proud that you didn't strike out and say what was really on your mind? Self-control is good, but Christ wants us to practice thought-control as well. Jesus said that we will be held accountable even for our attitudes.

**5:23, 24** Broken relationships can hinder our relationship with God. If we have a problem or grievance with a friend, we should resolve the problem as soon as possible. We are hypocrites if we claim to love God while we hate others. Our attitudes toward others reflect our relationship with God (1 John 4:20).

25 "When you are on the way to court with your adversary, settle your differences quickly. Otherwise, your accuser may hand you over to the judge, who will hand you over to an officer, and you will be thrown into prison. 26 And if that happens, you surely won't be free again until you have paid the last penny.*

### Jesus Teaches about Lust (53)

27 "You have heard the commandment that says, 'You must not commit adultery.'* 28 But I say, anyone who even looks at a woman with lust has already committed adultery with her in his heart. 29 So if your eye—even your good eye*—causes you to lust, gouge it out and throw it away. It is better for you to lose one part of your body than for your whole body to be thrown into hell. 30 And if your hand—even your stronger hand*—causes you to sin, cut it off and throw it away. It is better for you to lose one part of your body than for your whole body to be thrown into hell.

### Jesus Teaches about Divorce (54)

31 "You have heard the law that says, 'A man can divorce his wife by merely giving her a written notice of divorce.'* 32 But I say that a man who divorces his wife, unless she has been unfaithful, causes her to commit adultery. And anyone who marries a divorced woman also commits adultery.

### Jesus Teaches about Vows (55)

33 "You have also heard that our ancestors were told, 'You must not break your vows; you must carry out the vows you make to the LORD.'* 34 But I say, do not make any vows! Do not say, 'By heaven!' because heaven is God's throne. 35 And do not say, 'By the earth!' because the earth is his footstool. And do not say, 'By Jerusalem!' for Jerusalem is the city of the great King. 36 Do not even say, 'By my head!' for you can't turn one hair white or black. 37 Just say a simple, 'Yes, I will,' or 'No, I won't.' Anything beyond this is from the evil one.

**5:25-26**
Matt 18:34-35
Luke 12:58-59

**5:27**
†Exod 20:14
†Deut 5:18
Matt 19:18
Mark 10:19
Luke 18:20
Rom 13:9
Jas 2:11

**5:29-30**
Matt 18:8-9
Mark 9:43-47

**5:31**
†Deut 24:1
Matt 19:7
Mark 10:4

**5:32**
1 Cor 7:10-11

**5:33**
Lev 19:12
Num 30:2
Deut 23:21

**5:34**
Isa 66:1
Jas 5:12

**5:35**
Isa 66:1

**5:37**
Jas 5:12

**5:26** Greek *the last kodrantes* [i.e., quadrans].   **5:27** Exod 20:14; Deut 5:18.   **5:29** Greek *your right eye.*
**5:30** Greek *your right hand.*   **5:31** Deut 24:1.   **5:33** Num 30:2.

---

**5:25, 26** In Jesus' day, someone who couldn't pay a debt was thrown into prison until the debt was paid. Unless someone came to pay the debt for the prisoner, he or she would probably die there. It is practical advice to resolve our differences with our enemies before their anger causes more trouble (Proverbs 25:8-10). You may not get into a disagreement that takes you to court, but even small conflicts mend more easily if you try to make peace right away. In a broader sense, these verses advise us to get things right with our brothers and sisters before we have to stand before God.

**5:27, 28** The Old Testament law said that it is wrong for a person to have sex with someone other than his or her spouse (Exodus 20:14). But Jesus said that the *desire* to have sex with someone other than your spouse is mental adultery and thus sin. Jesus emphasized that if the *act* is wrong, then so is the *intention*. To be faithful to your spouse with your body but not your mind is to break the trust so vital to a strong marriage. Jesus is condemning not natural interest in the opposite sex or even healthy sexual desire but the deliberate and repeated filling of one's mind with fantasies that would be evil if acted out.

**5:27, 28** Some think that if lustful thoughts are sin, why shouldn't a person go ahead and do the lustful actions, too? Acting out sinful desires is harmful in several ways: (1) It causes people to excuse sin rather than to stop sinning; (2) it destroys marriages; (3) it is deliberate rebellion against God's Word; (4) it always hurts someone else in addition to the sinner. Sinful actions are more dangerous than sinful desires, and that is why desires should not be acted out. Nevertheless, sinful desires are just as damaging to obedience. Left unchecked, wrong desires will result in wrong actions and turn people away from God.

**5:29, 30** When Jesus said to get rid of your hand or your eye, he was speaking figuratively. He didn't mean literally to gouge out your eye, because even a blind person can lust. But if that were the only choice, it would be better to go into heaven with one eye or hand than to go to hell with two. We sometimes tolerate sins in our life that, left unchecked, could eventually destroy us. It is better to experience the pain of removal (getting rid of a bad habit or some-

thing we treasure, for instance) than to allow the sin to bring judgment and condemnation. Examine your life for anything that causes you to sin, and take every necessary action to remove it.

**5:31, 32** Divorce is as hurtful and destructive today as in Jesus' day. God intends marriage to be a lifetime commitment (Genesis 2:24). When entering into marriage, people should never consider divorce an option for solving problems or a way out of a relationship that seems dead. In these verses, Jesus is also attacking those who purposefully abuse the marriage contract, using divorce to satisfy their lustful desire to marry someone else. Are your actions today helping your marriage grow stronger, or are you tearing it apart?

**5:32** Jesus said that divorce is not permissible except for unfaithfulness. This does not mean that divorce should automatically occur when a spouse commits adultery. The word translated "unfaithful" implies a sexually immoral lifestyle, not a confessed and repented act of adultery. Those who discover that their partner has been unfaithful should first make every effort to forgive, reconcile, and restore their relationship. We are always to look for reasons to restore the marriage relationship rather than for excuses to leave it.

**5:33ff** Here, Jesus was emphasizing the importance of telling the truth. People were breaking vows and using sacred language casually and carelessly. Keeping vows and promises is important; it builds trust and makes committed human relationships possible. The Bible condemns making vows or taking oaths casually, giving your word while knowing that you won't keep it, or swearing falsely in God's name (Exodus 20:7; Leviticus 19:12; Numbers 30:1, 2; Deuteronomy 19:16-20). Vows are needed in certain situations only because we live in a sinful society that breeds distrust.

**5:33-37** Vows were common, but Jesus told his followers not to use them—their word alone should be enough (see James 5:12). Are you known as a person of your word? Truthfulness seems so rare that we feel we must end our statements with "I promise." If we tell the truth all the time, we will have less pressure to back up our words with an oath or promise.

5:38
†Exod 21:24
†Lev 24:20
†Deut 19:21

5:39
1 Cor 6:7
1 Pet 3:9

5:40
1 Cor 6:7

5:42
Deut 15:8

5:43
†Lev 19:18
Luke 10:27
Rom 13:9

5:44
Exod 23:4-5
Luke 23:34

5:48
Luke 6:36
1 Pet 1:16

## Jesus Teaches about Revenge (56)

38 "You have heard the law that says the punishment must match the injury: 'An eye for an eye, and a tooth for a tooth.'*39 But I say, do not resist an evil person! If someone slaps you on the right cheek, offer the other cheek also. 40 If you are sued in court and your shirt is taken from you, give your coat, too. 41 If a soldier demands that you carry his gear for a mile,* carry it two miles. 42 Give to those who ask, and don't turn away from those who want to borrow.

## Jesus Teaches about Loving Enemies (57/Luke 6:27-36)

43 "You have heard the law that says, 'Love your neighbor'* and hate your enemy. 44 But I say, love your enemies!* Pray for those who persecute you! 45 In that way, you will be acting as true children of your Father in heaven. For he gives his sunlight to both the evil and the good, and he sends rain on the just and the unjust alike. 46 If you love only those who love you, what reward is there for that? Even corrupt tax collectors do that much. 47 If you are kind only to your friends,* how are you different from anyone else? Even pagans do that. 48 But you are to be perfect, even as your Father in heaven is perfect.

**5:38** Greek *the law that says: 'An eye for an eye and a tooth for a tooth.'* Exod 21:24; Lev 24:20; Deut 19:21. **5:41** Greek *milion* [4,854 feet or 1,478 meters]. **5:43** Lev 19:18. **5:44** Some manuscripts add *Bless those who curse you. Do good to those who hate you.* Compare Luke 6:27-28. **5:47** Greek *your brothers.*

---

| JESUS AND THE OLD TESTAMENT LAW | Reference | Examples of Old Testament mercy in justice: |
|---|---|---|
| | Leviticus 19:18 . . . . . . . . . . . . | "Do not seek revenge or bear a grudge against a fellow Israelite, but love your neighbor as yourself. I am the LORD." |
| | Proverbs 24:28, 29 . . . . . . . . . | "Don't testify against your neighbors without cause; don't lie about them. And don't say, 'Now I can pay them back for what they've done to me! I'll get even with them!'" |
| | Proverbs 25:21, 22 . . . . . . . . . | "If your enemies are hungry, give them food to eat. If they are thirsty, give them water to drink. You will heap burning coals of shame on their heads, and the LORD will reward you." |
| | Lamentations 3:30, 31 . . . . . . . | "Let them turn the other cheek to those who strike them and accept the insults of their enemies. For no one is abandoned by the Lord forever." |

What seems to be a case of Jesus contradicting the laws of the Old Testament deserves a careful look. It is too easy to overlook how much mercy was written into the Old Testament laws. Above are several examples. What God designed as a system of justice with mercy had been distorted over the years into a license for revenge. It was this misapplication of the law that Jesus attacked.

---

**5:38** God's purpose behind this law was an expression of mercy. The law was given to judges and said, in effect, "Make the punishment fit the crime." It was not a guide for personal revenge (Exodus 21:23-25; Leviticus 24:19, 20; Deuteronomy 19:21). These laws were given to *limit* vengeance and help the court administer punishment that was neither too strict nor too lenient. Some people, however, were using this phrase to justify their vendettas against others. People still try to excuse their acts of revenge by saying, "I was just doing to him what he did to me."

**5:38-42** When we are wronged, often our first reaction is to get even. Instead, Jesus said we should do *good* to those who wrong us! Our desire should not be to keep score but to love and forgive. This is not natural—it is supernatural. Only God can give us the strength to love as he does. Instead of planning vengeance, pray for those who hurt you.

**5:39-44** To many Jews of Jesus' day, these statements were offensive. Any Messiah who would turn the other cheek was not the military leader they wanted to lead a revolt against Rome. Since they were under Roman oppression, they wanted retaliation against their enemies, whom they hated. But Jesus suggested a new, radical response to injustice: Instead of demanding rights, give them up freely! According to Jesus, it is more important to *give* justice and mercy than to receive it.

**5:43, 44** By telling us not to retaliate, Jesus keeps us from taking the law into our own hands. By loving and praying for our enemies, we can overcome evil with good.

The Pharisees interpreted Leviticus 19:18 as teaching that they should love only those who love in return, and Psalms 139:19-22 and 140:9-11 as meaning that they should hate their enemies. But Jesus says we are to love our enemies. If you love your enemies and treat them well, you will truly show that Jesus is Lord of your life. This is possible only for those who give themselves fully to God, because only he can deliver people from natural selfishness. We must trust the Holy Spirit to help us *show* love to those for whom we may not *feel* love.

**5:48** How can we be perfect? (1) *In character:* In this life we cannot be flawless, but we can aspire to be as much like Christ as possible. (2) *In holiness:* Like the Pharisees, we are to separate ourselves from the world's sinful values. But unlike the Pharisees, we are to be devoted to God's desires rather than our own and carry his love and mercy into the world. (3) *In maturity:* We can't achieve Christlike character and holy living all at once, but we must grow toward maturity and wholeness. Just as we expect different behavior from a baby, a child, a teenager, and an adult, so God expects different behavior from us, depending on our stage of spiritual development. (4) *In love:* We can seek to love others as completely as God loves us.

We can be perfect if our behavior is appropriate for our maturity level—perfect, yet with much room to grow. Our tendency to sin must never deter us from striving to be more like Christ. Christ calls all of his disciples to excel, to rise above mediocrity, and to mature in every area, becoming like him. Those who strive to become perfect will one day be perfect, even as Christ is perfect (1 John 3:2, 3).

## Jesus Teaches about Giving to the Needy (58)

**6** "Watch out! Don't do your good deeds publicly, to be admired by others, for you will lose the reward from your Father in heaven. ² When you give to someone in need, don't do as the hypocrites do—blowing trumpets in the synagogues and streets to call attention to their acts of charity! I tell you the truth, they have received all the reward they will ever get. ³ But when you give to someone in need, don't let your left hand know what your right hand is doing. ⁴Give your gifts in private, and your Father, who sees everything, will reward you.

**6:1-2**
Matt 23:5

**6:4**
Matt 6:6, 18

## Jesus Teaches about Prayer (59)

⁵"When you pray, don't be like the hypocrites who love to pray publicly on street corners and in the synagogues where everyone can see them. I tell you the truth, that is all the reward they will ever get. ⁶But when you pray, go away by yourself, shut the door behind you, and pray to your Father in private. Then your Father, who sees everything, will reward you.

⁷"When you pray, don't babble on and on as people of other religions do. They think their prayers are answered merely by repeating their words again and again. ⁸ Don't be like them, for your Father knows exactly what you need even before you ask him! ⁹ Pray like this:

Our Father in heaven,
     may your name be kept holy.
¹⁰ May your Kingdom come soon.
May your will be done on earth,
     as it is in heaven.
¹¹ Give us today the food we need,*
¹² and forgive us our sins,
     as we have forgiven those who sin against us.

**6:5**
Matt 6:16; 23:5
Luke 18:10-14

**6:6**
2 Kgs 4:33
Isa 26:20

**6:7**
Eccl 5:1-2

**6:8**
Matt 6:32
Luke 12:30

**6:9-13**
Luke 11:2-4

**6:9**
1 Pet 1:17

**6:10**
Matt 26:39, 42
Luke 22:42

**6:11**
Prov 30:8
John 6:32

**6:11** Or *Give us today our food for the day;* or *Give us today our food for tomorrow.*

---

**6:2** The term *hypocrites,* as used here, describes people who do good acts for appearances only—not out of compassion or other good motives. Their actions may be good, but their motives are hollow. These empty acts are their only reward, but God will reward those who are sincere in their faith.

**6:3** When Jesus says not to tell your left hand what your right hand is doing, he is teaching that our motives for giving to God and to others must be pure. It is easy to give with mixed motives, to do something for someone if it will benefit us in return. But believers should avoid all scheming and give for the pleasure of giving and as a response to God's love. Why do *you* give?

**6:3, 4** It's easier to do what's right when we gain recognition and praise. To be sure our motives are not selfish, we should do our good deeds quietly or in secret, with no thought of reward. Jesus says we should check our motives in three areas: generosity (6:4), prayer (6:6), and fasting (6:18). Those acts should not be self-centered but God-centered, done not to make us look good but to make God look good. The reward God promises is not material, and it is never given to those who seek it. Doing something only for ourselves is not a loving sacrifice. With your next good deed, ask, Would I still do this if no one would ever know I did it?

**6:5, 6** Some people, especially the religious leaders, wanted to be seen as "holy," and public prayer was one way to get attention. Jesus saw through their self-righteous acts, however, and taught that the essence of prayer is not public style but private communication with God. There is a place for public prayer, but to pray only where others will notice you indicates that your real audience is not God.

**6:6** Some have concluded that Jesus' directions about private prayer call into question all public prayer. Jesus' own practice indicates this wasn't his intention. The Gospels record Jesus at prayer both privately (14:23) and publicly (14:18, 19). Again, Jesus was drawing attention to the motives behind actions. The point really wasn't a choice between public and private prayer but between heartfelt and hypocritical prayer. When asked to pray in public, focus on addressing God, not on how you're coming across to others.

**6:7, 8** Repeating the same words over and over like a magic incantation is no way to ensure that God will hear your prayer. It's not wrong to come to God many times with the same requests—Jesus encourages *persistent* prayer. But he condemns the shallow repetition of words that are not offered with a sincere heart. We can never pray too much if our prayers are honest and sincere. Before you start to pray, make sure you mean what you say.

**6:9** This is often called the Lord's Prayer because Jesus gave it to the disciples as a model for them (and us) to keep in mind as we pray. Jesus provided a pattern to be imitated as well as duplicated. We should praise God, pray for his work in the world, pray for our daily needs, and pray for help in our daily struggles. To what extent do you use the items in the Lord's Prayer to guide your own prayer times?

**6:9** The phrase "Our Father in heaven" indicates that God is not only majestic and holy but also personal and loving. The first line of this model prayer is a statement of praise and a commitment to hallow, or honor, God's holy name. We can honor God's name by being careful to use it respectfully. If we use God's name lightly, we aren't remembering God's holiness.

**6:10** The phrase "May your Kingdom come soon" is a reference to God's spiritual reign, not Israel's freedom from Rome. God's Kingdom was announced in the covenant with Abraham (8:11; Luke 13:28), is present in Christ's reign in believers' hearts (Luke 17:21), and will be complete when all evil is destroyed and God establishes the new heaven and earth (Revelation 21:1).

**6:10** When we pray "May your will be done," we are not resigning ourselves to fate but praying that God's perfect purpose will be accomplished in this world as well as in the next. And how does God accomplish his will on earth? He does it largely through people willing to obey him. This part of the prayer allows us to offer ourselves as doers of God's will, asking him to guide, lead, and give us the means to accomplish his purposes.

**6:11** When we pray "Give us today the food we need," we are acknowledging that God is our sustainer and provider. It is a misconception to think that we provide for our needs ourselves. We must trust God *daily* to provide what he knows we need.

**6:13**
Luke 22:40, 46
John 17:15

13 And don't let us yield to temptation,*
      but rescue us from the evil one.*

**6:14**
Mark 11:25
Eph 4:32
Col 3:13

14 "If you forgive those who sin against you, your heavenly Father will forgive you. 15 But if you refuse to forgive others, your Father will not forgive your sins.

**6:15**
Matt 18:35

### Jesus Teaches about Fasting (60)

**6:16**
Isa 58:5
Matt 6:5; 23:5

16 "And when you fast, don't make it obvious, as the hypocrites do, for they try to look miserable and disheveled so people will admire them for their fasting. I tell you the truth, that is the only reward they will ever get. 17 But when you fast, comb your hair and wash your face.

**6:18**
Matt 6:4, 6

18 Then no one will notice that you are fasting, except your Father, who knows what you do in private. And your Father, who sees everything, will reward you.

### Jesus Teaches about Money (61)

**6:19**
Prov 23:4
Jas 5:2-3

19 "Don't store up treasures here on earth, where moths eat them and rust destroys them, and where thieves break in and steal. 20 Store your treasures in heaven, where moths and rust

**6:20**
Matt 19:21
Mark 10:21
Luke 18:22
1 Tim 6:19

cannot destroy, and thieves do not break in and steal. 21 Wherever your treasure is, there the desires of your heart will also be.

22 "Your eye is a lamp that provides light for your body. When your eye is good, your whole body is filled with light. 23 But when your eye is bad, your whole body is filled with darkness.

**6:23**
Matt 20:15
Mark 7:22

And if the light you think you have is actually darkness, how deep that darkness is!

24 "No one can serve two masters. For you will hate one and love the other; you will be devoted to one and despise the other. You cannot serve both God and money.

**6:13a** Or *And keep us from being tested.* **6:13b** Or *from evil.* Some manuscripts add *For yours is the kingdom and the power and the glory forever. Amen.*

---

**SEVEN REASONS NOT TO WORRY**

| | |
|---|---|
| 6:25 . . . . . . . . . . . . | The same God who created life in you can be trusted with the details of your life. |
| 6:26 . . . . . . . . . . . . | Worrying about the future hampers your efforts for today. |
| 6:27 . . . . . . . . . . . . | Worrying is more harmful than helpful. |
| 6:28-30 . . . . . . . . . . | God does not ignore those who depend on him. |
| 6:31, 32 . . . . . . . . . | Worrying shows a lack of faith in and understanding of God. |
| 6:33 . . . . . . . . . . . . | Worrying keeps us from real challenges God wants us to pursue. |
| 6:34 . . . . . . . . . . . . | Living one day at a time keeps us from being consumed with worry. |

---

**6:13** God sometimes allows us to be tested by temptation. As disciples, we should pray to be delivered from these trying times and for deliverance from Satan ("the evil one") and his deceit. All Christians struggle with temptation. Sometimes it is so subtle that we don't even realize what is happening to us. God has promised that he won't allow us to be tempted beyond what we can bear (1 Corinthians 10:13). Ask God to help you recognize temptation and to give you strength to overcome it and choose God's way instead. For more on temptation, see the notes on 4:1.

**6:14, 15** Jesus gives a startling warning about forgiveness: If we refuse to forgive others, God will also refuse to forgive us. Why? Because when we don't forgive others, we are denying our common ground as sinners in need of God's forgiveness. God's forgiveness of sin is not the direct result of our forgiving others, but it is based on our realizing what forgiveness means (see Ephesians 4:32). It is easy to ask God for forgiveness but difficult to grant it to others. Whenever we ask God to forgive us for sin, we should ask, Have I forgiven the people who have wronged me?

**6:16** Fasting—going without food in order to spend time in prayer—is noble *and* difficult. It gives us time to pray, teaches self-discipline, reminds us that we can live with a lot less, and helps us appreciate God's gifts. Jesus was not condemning fasting, but hypocrisy—fasting in order to gain public approval. Fasting was mandatory for the Jewish people once a year on the Day of Atonement (Leviticus 23:32). The Pharisees voluntarily fasted twice a week to impress the people with their "holiness." Jesus commended acts of self-sacrifice done quietly and sincerely.

He wanted people to adopt spiritual disciplines for the right reasons, not from a selfish desire for praise.

**6:20** Storing treasures in heaven is not limited to tithing but is accomplished by all acts of obedience to God. There is a sense in which giving our money to God's work is like investing in heaven. But we should seek to please God not only in our giving but also in fulfilling God's purposes in all we do.

**6:21** Jesus made it clear that having the wrong treasures leads to our hearts being in the wrong place. What we treasure the most controls us, whether we admit it or not. If possessions or money become too important to us, we must reestablish control or get rid of items. Jesus calls for a decision that allows us to live contentedly with whatever we have because we have chosen eternal values over temporary, earthly treasures.

**6:22, 23** Spiritual vision is our capacity to see clearly what God wants us to do and to see the world from his point of view. But this spiritual insight can be easily clouded. Self-serving desires, interests, and goals block that vision. Serving God is the best way to restore it. A "good" eye is one that is fixed on God.

**6:24** Jesus says we can have only one master. We live in a materialistic society where many people serve money. They spend all their lives collecting and storing it, only to die and leave it behind. Their desire for money and what it can buy far outweighs their commitment to God and spiritual matters. Whatever you store up, you will spend much of your time and energy thinking about. Don't fall into the materialistic trap, because "the love of money is the root of all kinds of evil" (1 Timothy 6:10). Can you honestly say that God, and not money, is your master? One test is to ask

## Jesus Teaches about Worry (62)

25 "That is why I tell you not to worry about everyday life—whether you have enough food and drink, or enough clothes to wear. Isn't life more than food, and your body more than clothing? 26 Look at the birds. They don't plant or harvest or store food in barns, for your heavenly Father feeds them. And aren't you far more valuable to him than they are? 27 Can all your worries add a single moment to your life?

28 "And why worry about your clothing? Look at the lilies of the field and how they grow. They don't work or make their clothing, 29 yet Solomon in all his glory was not dressed as beautifully as they are. 30 And if God cares so wonderfully for wildflowers that are here today and thrown into the fire tomorrow, he will certainly care for you. Why do you have so little faith?

31 "So don't worry about these things, saying, 'What will we eat? What will we drink? What will we wear?' 32 These things dominate the thoughts of unbelievers, but your heavenly Father already knows all your needs. 33 Seek the Kingdom of God* above all else, and live righteously, and he will give you everything you need.

34 "So don't worry about tomorrow, for tomorrow will bring its own worries. Today's trouble is enough for today.

| | |
|---|---|
| **6:25** | Phil 4:6 / 1 Tim 6:6, 8 / 1 Pet 5:7 |
| **6:26** | Job 38:41 |
| **6:29** | 1 Kgs 10:4-7 |
| **6:30** | Matt 8:26; 14:31; 16:8 |
| **6:32** | Matt 6:8 / Luke 12:30 |
| **6:33** | Ps 37:4, 25 / Mark 10:29-30 |
| **6:34** | Exod 16:4 |

## Jesus Teaches about Judging Others (63/Luke 6:37-42)

**7** "Do not judge others, and you will not be judged. 2 For you will be treated as you treat others.* The standard you use in judging is the standard by which you will be judged.*

3 "And why worry about a speck in your friend's eye* when you have a log in your own? 4 How can you think of saying to your friend,* 'Let me help you get rid of that speck in your eye,' when you can't see past the log in your own eye? 5 Hypocrite! First get rid of the log in your own eye; then you will see well enough to deal with the speck in your friend's eye.

6 "Don't waste what is holy on people who are unholy.* Don't throw your pearls to pigs! They will trample the pearls, then turn and attack you.

| | |
|---|---|
| **7:1-2** | Luke 6:37-42 / Rom 2:1-3; 14:4 / 1 Cor 4:5; 5:12 / Jas 4:11-12 |
| **7:3-5** | Luke 6:37-38, 41-42 |

**6:33** Some manuscripts do not include *of God.*   **7:2a** Or *For God will judge you as you judge others.*   **7:2b** Or *The measure you give will be the measure you get back.*   **7:3** Greek *your brother's eye;* also in 7:5.   **7:4** Greek *your brother.*   **7:6** Greek *Don't give the sacred to dogs.*

---

yourself which one occupies more of your thoughts, time, and efforts.

**6:24** Jesus contrasted heavenly values with earthly values when he explained that our first loyalty should be to those things that do not fade, cannot be stolen or used up, and never wear out. We should not be fascinated with our possessions, lest *they* possess *us.* God alone deserves to be our master. Either we store our treasures with God (6:20, 21), focus our "eyes" on him (6:22, 23), and serve him alone—or else we do not serve him at all. Where does your ultimate allegiance lie?

**6:25** Because of the ill effects of worry, Jesus tells us not to worry about those needs that God promises to supply. Worry may (1) damage your health, (2) disrupt your productivity, (3) negatively affect the way you treat others, and (4) reduce your ability to trust in God. How many ill effects of worry are you experiencing? Here is the difference between worry and genuine concern—worry immobilizes, but concern moves you to action.

**6:33** To "seek the Kingdom of God above all else" means to put God first in your life, to fill your thoughts with his desires, to take his character for your pattern, and to serve and obey him in everything. What is really important to you? People, objects, goals, and other desires all compete for priority. Any of these can quickly become most important to you if you don't actively choose to give God first place in *every* area of your life.

**6:34** Planning for tomorrow is time well spent; worrying about tomorrow is time wasted. Sometimes it's difficult to tell the difference. Careful planning is thinking ahead about goals, steps, and schedules, and trusting in God's guidance. When done well, planning can help alleviate worry. Worriers, by contrast, are consumed by fear and find it difficult to trust God. They let their

plans interfere with their relationship with God. Don't let worries about tomorrow affect your relationship with God today.

**7:1, 2** Jesus tells us to examine our own motives and conduct instead of judging others. The traits that bother us in others are often the habits we have ourselves. Our bad habits and behavior patterns are the very ones that we most want to change in others. Do you find it easy to magnify others' faults while excusing your own? If you are ready to criticize someone, check to see if you deserve the same criticism. Judge yourself first, and then lovingly forgive and help your neighbor.

**7:1-5** Jesus' statement, "Do not judge others," is against the kind of hypocritical, judgmental attitude that tears others down in order to build oneself up. It is not a blanket statement to overlook wrong behavior of others but a call to be *discerning* rather than negative. Jesus said to expose false prophets (7:15-23), and Paul taught that we should exercise church discipline (1 Corinthians 5:1, 2) and trust God to be the final Judge (1 Corinthians 4:3-5).

**7:6** Pigs were unclean animals according to God's law (Deuteronomy 14:8). Anyone who touched an unclean animal became "ceremonially unclean" and could not go to the Temple to worship until the uncleanness was removed. Jesus says that we should not entrust holy teachings to unholy or unclean people. It is futile to try to teach holy concepts to people who don't want to listen and will only tear apart what we say. We should not stop giving God's Word to unbelievers, but we should be wise and discerning in our witnessing, so that we will not be wasting our time.

**7:7, 8** Jesus tells us to persist in pursuing God. People often give up after a few halfhearted efforts and conclude that God cannot be found. But knowing God takes faith, focus, and follow-through, and Jesus assures us that we will be rewarded. Don't give up in your efforts to seek God. Continue to ask him for more knowledge, patience, wisdom, love, and understanding. He will give them to you.

### Jesus Teaches about Asking, Looking, Knocking (64)

**7:7-11**
Luke 11:9-13
**7:7**
Matt 21:22
Mark 11:24
Luke 11:9-13
John 14:13-14;
15:7; 16:23-24
Jas 1:5-6
1 Jn 3:21-22;
5:14-15

7 "Keep on asking, and you will receive what you ask for. Keep on seeking, and you will find. Keep on knocking, and the door will be opened to you. 8 For everyone who asks, receives. Everyone who seeks, finds. And to everyone who knocks, the door will be opened.

9 "You parents—if your children ask for a loaf of bread, do you give them a stone instead? 10 Or if they ask for a fish, do you give them a snake? Of course not! 11 So if you sinful people know how to give good gifts to your children, how much more will your heavenly Father give good gifts to those who ask him.

### The Golden Rule

**7:12**
Luke 6:31
Rom 13:8-10
Gal 5:14

12 "Do to others whatever you would like them to do to you. This is the essence of all that is taught in the law and the prophets.

### Jesus Teaches about the Way to Heaven (65)

**7:14**
John 14:6
Acts 14:22

13 "You can enter God's Kingdom only through the narrow gate. The highway to hell* is broad, and its gate is wide for the many who choose that way. 14 But the gateway to life is very narrow and the road is difficult, and only a few ever find it.

### Jesus Teaches about Fruit in People's Lives (66/Luke 6:43-45)

**7:15**
Jer 23:16
Matt 24:11, 24
Luke 6:26
Acts 20:29
Rom 16:17
2 Pet 2:1
1 Jn 4:1
**7:16-20**
Matt 12:33

15 "Beware of false prophets who come disguised as harmless sheep but are really vicious wolves. 16 You can identify them by their fruit, that is, by the way they act. Can you pick grapes from thornbushes, or figs from thistles? 17 A good tree produces good fruit, and a bad tree produces bad fruit. 18 A good tree can't produce bad fruit, and a bad tree can't produce good fruit. 19 So every tree that does not produce good fruit is chopped down and thrown into the fire. 20 Yes, just as you can identify a tree by its fruit, so you can identify people by their actions.

### Jesus Teaches about Building on a Solid Foundation (67/Luke 6:46-49)

**7:21**
Luke 6:46
Jas 1:22
**7:22**
Acts 19:13-15

21 "Not everyone who calls out to me, 'Lord! Lord!' will enter the Kingdom of Heaven. Only those who actually do the will of my Father in heaven will enter. 22 On judgment day many will say to me, 'Lord! Lord! We prophesied in your name and cast out demons in your name

**7:13** Greek *The road that leads to destruction.*

**7:9, 10** The children in Jesus' example asked their father for bread and fish—good and necessary items. If the children had asked for a poisonous snake, would the wise father have granted the request? Sometimes God knows we are praying for "snakes" and does not give us what we ask for, even though we persist in our prayers. Nor will God give us "stones" or "snakes" instead of what we need. As we learn to know God better as a loving Father, we learn to ask for what is good for us, and then he grants it.

**7:11** Christ is showing us the heart of God the Father. God is not selfish, begrudging, or stingy, and we don't have to beg or grovel as we come with our requests. He is a loving Father, who understands, cares, and comforts. If humans can be kind, imagine how kind God, the Creator of kindness, can be.

**7:11** Jesus used the expression "you sinful people" to contrast sinful and fallible human beings with the holy and perfect God.

**7:12** This is commonly known as the Golden Rule. In many religions it is stated negatively: "Don't do to others what you don't want done to you." By stating it positively, Jesus made it more significant. It is not very hard to refrain from harming others; it is much more difficult to take the initiative in doing something good for them. The Golden Rule, as Jesus formulated it, is the foundation of active goodness and mercy—the kind of love God shows to us every day. Think of a good and merciful action you can do today.

**7:13, 14** The gate that leads to eternal life (John 10:7-9) is called "narrow." This does not mean that it is difficult to become a Christian but that there is only *one* way to eternal life with God and that only a few decide to walk that road. Believing in Jesus is the only way to heaven, because he alone died for our sins and made us right before God. Living his way may not be popular, but it is true and right. Thank God there is one way!

**7:15** False prophets were common in Old Testament times. They prophesied only what the king and the people wanted to

hear, claiming it was God's message. Jesus indicates that false prophets were just as prevalent in his time. False teachers are just as common today. Jesus says to beware of those whose words sound religious but who are motivated by money, fame, or power. You can tell who they are because in their teaching they minimize Christ and glorify themselves.

**7:20** We should evaluate teachers' words by examining their lives. Just as trees are consistent in the kind of fruit they produce, good teachers consistently exhibit good behavior and high moral character as they seek to live out the truths of Scripture. This does not mean we should have witch-hunts, throwing out Sunday school teachers, pastors, and others who are less than perfect. Every one of us is subject to sin, and we must show the same mercy to others that we expect for ourselves. When Jesus talks about worthless trees, he means teachers who deliberately teach false doctrine. We must examine the teachers' motives, the direction they are taking, and the results they are seeking.

**7:21** Some self-professed athletes can "talk" a great game, but that tells you nothing about their athletic skills. And not everyone who talks about heaven belongs to God's Kingdom. Jesus is more concerned about our *walk* than our *talk*. He wants us to *do* right, not just *say* the right words. What you do cannot be separated from what you believe.

**7:21-23** Jesus exposed those people who sounded religious but had no personal relationship with him. On "judgment day" only our relationship with Christ—our acceptance of him as Savior and our obedience to him—will matter. Many people think that if they are "good" people and say religious things, they will be rewarded with eternal life. In reality, faith in Christ is what will count at the judgment.

**7:22** "Judgment day" is the final day of reckoning when God will settle all accounts, judging sin and rewarding faith.

and performed many miracles in your name.' 23But I will reply, 'I never knew you. Get away from me, you who break God's laws.'

24"Anyone who listens to my teaching and follows it is wise, like a person who builds a house on solid rock. 25 Though the rain comes in torrents and the floodwaters rise and the winds beat against that house, it won't collapse because it is built on bedrock. 26But anyone who hears my teaching and doesn't obey it is foolish, like a person who builds a house on sand. 27 When the rains and floods come and the winds beat against that house, it will collapse with a mighty crash."

28 When Jesus had finished saying these things, the crowds were amazed at his teaching, 29for he taught with real authority—quite unlike their teachers of religious law.

### 3. Jesus performs many miracles

*Jesus Heals a Man with Leprosy* (38/Mark 1:40-45; Luke 5:12-16)

**8** Large crowds followed Jesus as he came down the mountainside. 2Suddenly, a man with leprosy approached him and knelt before him. "Lord," the man said, "if you are willing, you can heal me and make me clean."

3Jesus reached out and touched him. "I am willing," he said. "Be healed!" And instantly the leprosy disappeared. 4 Then Jesus said to him, "Don't tell anyone about this. Instead, go to the priest and let him examine you. Take along the offering required in the law of Moses for those who have been healed of leprosy.* This will be a public testimony that you have been cleansed."

*A Roman Officer Demonstrates Faith* (68/Luke 7:1-10)

5When Jesus returned to Capernaum, a Roman officer* came and pleaded with him, 6"Lord, my young servant* lies in bed, paralyzed and in terrible pain."

7Jesus said, "I will come and heal him."

**8:4** See Lev 14:2-32. **8:5** Greek *a centurion;* similarly in 8:8, 13. **8:6** Or *child;* also in 8:13.

---

**7:23**
Matt 25:12, 41
Luke 13:25-27

**7:24**
2 Tim 2:19
Jas 1:22

**7:26**
Jas 1:23

**7:27**
Ezek 13:10-12

**7:28**
Matt 13:54
Mark 1:22; 6:2
Luke 4:32
John 7:46

**8:4**
Lev 14:1-32

**8:5-7**
John 4:43-54

---

**7:24** To build "on solid rock" means to be a hearing, responding disciple, not a phony, superficial one. Practicing obedience becomes the solid foundation to weather the storms of life. See James 1:22-27 for more on putting into practice what we hear.

**7:24-27** The two lives Jesus compares at the end of the Sermon on the Mount have several points in common: they both build, they both hear Jesus' teaching, and they both experience the same set of circumstances in life. The difference between them isn't caused by ignorance but by one ignoring what Jesus said. Externally, their lives may look similar; but the lasting, structural differences will be revealed by the storms of life. The immediate differences in your life when you follow Jesus may not be obvious, but eventually they will turn out to affect even

**JESUS' MIRACULOUS POWER DISPLAYED**
Jesus finished the sermon he had given on a hillside near Galilee and returned to Capernaum. As he and his disciples crossed the Sea of Galilee, Jesus calmed a fierce storm. Then, in the Gentile Gadarene region, Jesus commanded demons to come out of two men.

your eternal destiny. To what degree does your life reflect the directions Jesus gave in this sermon?

**7:26, 27** Like a house of cards, the fool's life crumbles. Most people do not deliberately seek to build on a false or inferior foundation; instead, they just don't think about their life's purpose. Many people are headed for destruction, not out of stubbornness but out of thoughtlessness. Part of our responsibility as believers is to help others stop and think about where their lives are headed and to point out the consequences of ignoring Christ's message.

**7:29** The teachers of religious law (religious scholars) often cited traditions and quoted authorities to support their arguments and interpretations. But Jesus spoke with a new authority—his own. He didn't need to quote anyone because he was the original Word (John 1:1).

**8:2, 3** Leprosy, like AIDS today, was a terrifying disease because there was no known cure. In Jesus' day, the Greek word for "leprosy" was used for a variety of similar diseases, and some forms were contagious. If a person contracted the contagious type, a priest declared him a leper and banished him from his home and city. The leper was sent to live in a community with other lepers until he either got better or died. Yet when the leper begged Jesus to heal him, Jesus reached out and touched him, even though his skin was covered with the dread disease.

Sin is also an incurable disease—and we all have it. Only Christ's healing touch can miraculously take away our sins and restore us to real living. But first, just like the leper, we must realize our inability to cure ourselves and ask for Christ's saving help.

**8:4** The law required a healed leper to be examined by the priest (Leviticus 14). Jesus wanted this man to give his story firsthand to the priest to prove that his leprosy was completely gone so that he could be restored to his community.

**8:5, 6** The Roman officer could have let many obstacles stand between him and Jesus—pride, doubt, money, language, distance, time, self-sufficiency, power, race. But he didn't. If he did

**8:8**
Ps 107:20

8But the officer said, "Lord, I am not worthy to have you come into my home. Just say the word from where you are, and my servant will be healed. 9I know this because I am under the authority of my superior officers, and I have authority over my soldiers. I only need to say, 'Go,' and they go, or 'Come,' and they come. And if I say to my slaves, 'Do this,' they do it."

**8:10-12**
Ps 107:3
Matt 13:41-42;
21:43
Acts 10:45; 11:18;
14:27
Eph 3:6

10When Jesus heard this, he was amazed. Turning to those who were following him, he said, "I tell you the truth, I haven't seen faith like this in all Israel! 11And I tell you this, that many Gentiles will come from all over the world—from east and west—and sit down with Abraham, Isaac, and Jacob at the feast in the Kingdom of Heaven. 12But many Israelites—those for whom the Kingdom was prepared—will be thrown into outer darkness, where there will be weeping and gnashing of teeth."

**8:13**
Matt 9:29; 15:28
John 4:50-51

13Then Jesus said to the Roman officer, "Go back home. Because you believed, it has happened." And the young servant was healed that same hour.

### Jesus Heals Peter's Mother-in-Law and Many Others
(**35**/Mark 1:29-34; Luke 4:38-41)

14When Jesus arrived at Peter's house, Peter's mother-in-law was sick in bed with a high fever. 15But when Jesus touched her hand, the fever left her. Then she got up and prepared a meal for him.

16That evening many demon-possessed people were brought to Jesus. He cast out the evil spirits with a simple command, and he healed all the sick. 17This fulfilled the word of the Lord through the prophet Isaiah, who said,

**8:17**
†Isa 53:4

"He took our sicknesses
and removed our diseases."*

### Jesus Teaches about the Cost of Following Him (**122**/Luke 9:51-62)

18When Jesus saw the crowd around him, he instructed his disciples to cross to the other side of the lake.

19Then one of the teachers of religious law said to him, "Teacher, I will follow you wherever you go."

20But Jesus replied, "Foxes have dens to live in, and birds have nests, but the Son of Man* has no place even to lay his head."

**8:17** Isa 53:4.   **8:20** "Son of Man" is a title Jesus used for himself.

---

not let these barriers block his approach to Jesus, we don't need to either. What keeps you from Christ?

**8:8-12** This Roman officer (also called a centurion) was a career military officer in the Roman army with control over 100 soldiers. Roman soldiers, of all people, were hated by the Jews for their oppression, control, and ridicule. Yet this man's genuine faith amazed Jesus! This hated Gentile's faith put to shame the pompous piety of many of the Jewish religious leaders.

**8:10-12** Jesus told the crowd that many religious Jews who should be in the Kingdom would be excluded because of their lack of faith. Entrenched in their religious traditions, they could not accept Christ and his new message. We must be careful not to become so set in our religious habits that we expect God to work only in specified ways. Don't limit God by your mind-set and lack of faith.

**8:11, 12** Faithful people of God from "all over the world" will be gathered to feast with the Messiah (Isaiah 25:6; 55). The Jews should have known that when the Messiah came, his blessings would be for Gentiles too (see Isaiah 66:12, 19). But this message came as a shock because they were too wrapped up in their own affairs and destiny. In claiming God's promises, we must not apply them so personally or culturally that we forget to see what God wants to do to reach *all* the people he loves.

**8:11, 12** Matthew emphasizes this universal theme—Jesus' message is for everyone. The Old Testament prophets knew this (see Isaiah 56:3, 6-8; 66:12, 19; Malachi 1:11), but many New Testament Jewish leaders chose to ignore it. Each individual has to choose to accept or reject the Good News, and no one can become part of God's Kingdom on the basis of heritage or connections. Having Christian parents is a wonderful blessing,

but it won't guarantee you eternal life. *You* must believe in and follow Christ.

**8:14, 15** Peter's mother-in-law gives us a beautiful example to follow. Her response to Jesus' touch was to wait on Jesus and his disciples—immediately. Has God ever helped you through a dangerous or difficult situation? If so, you should ask, How can I express my gratitude to him? Because God has promised us all the rewards of his Kingdom, we should look for ways to serve him and his followers now.

**8:16, 17** Matthew continues to show Jesus' kingly nature. Through a single touch, Jesus healed (8:3, 15); when he spoke a single word, evil spirits fled his presence (8:16). Jesus has authority over all evil powers and all earthly disease. He also has power and authority to conquer sin. Sickness and evil are consequences of living in a fallen world. But in the future, when God removes all sin, there will be no more sickness and death. Jesus' healing miracles were a taste of what the whole world will one day experience in God's Kingdom.

**8:19, 20** Following Jesus is not always easy or comfortable. Often it means great cost and sacrifice, with no earthly rewards or security. Jesus didn't have a place to call home. You may find that following Christ costs you popularity, friendships, leisure time, or treasured habits. But while the cost of following Christ is high, the value of being Christ's disciple is even higher. Discipleship is an investment that lasts for eternity and yields incredible rewards.

21Another of his disciples said, "Lord, first let me return home and bury my father." 22But Jesus told him, "Follow me now. Let the spiritually dead bury their own dead.*"

8:22
Matt 9:9
Mark 2:14
Luke 9:59
John 1:43; 21:19

### Jesus Calms the Storm (87/Mark 4:35-41; Luke 8:22-25)

23Then Jesus got into the boat and started across the lake with his disciples. 24Suddenly, a fierce storm struck the lake, with waves breaking into the boat. But Jesus was sleeping. 25The disciples went and woke him up, shouting, "Lord, save us! We're going to drown!"

26Jesus responded, "Why are you afraid? You have so little faith!" Then he got up and rebuked the wind and waves, and suddenly there was a great calm.

8:26
Pss 89:10;
107:25-32
Matt 6:30

27The disciples were amazed. "Who is this man?" they asked. "Even the winds and waves obey him!"

### Jesus Sends Demons into a Herd of Pigs (88/Mark 5:1-20; Luke 8:26-29)

28When Jesus arrived on the other side of the lake, in the region of the Gadarenes,* two men who were possessed by demons met him. They lived in a cemetery and were so violent that no one could go through that area.

29They began screaming at him, "Why are you interfering with us, Son of God? Have you come here to torture us before God's appointed time?"

8:29
Mark 1:24
Luke 4:34
2 Pet 2:4

30There happened to be a large herd of pigs feeding in the distance. 31So the demons begged, "If you cast us out, send us into that herd of pigs."

32 "All right, go!" Jesus commanded them. So the demons came out of the men and entered the pigs, and the whole herd plunged down the steep hillside into the lake and drowned in the water.

**8:22** Greek *Let the dead bury their own dead.* **8:28** Other manuscripts read *Gerasenes;* still others read *Gergesenes.* Compare Mark 5:1; Luke 8:26.

---

**8:21, 22** It is possible that this disciple was not asking permission to go to his father's funeral but rather to put off following Jesus until his elderly father died. Perhaps he was the firstborn son and wanted to be sure to claim his inheritance. Perhaps he didn't want to face his father's wrath if he left the family business to follow an itinerant preacher. Whether his concern was financial security, family approval, or something else, he did not want to commit himself to Jesus just yet. Jesus, however, would not accept his excuse.

Jesus was always direct with those who wanted to follow him. He made sure they counted the cost and set aside any conditions they might have for following him. As God's Son, Jesus did not hesitate to demand complete loyalty. Even family loyalty was not to take priority over the demands of obedience. His direct challenge forces us to ask ourselves about our own priorities in following him. The decision to follow Jesus should not be put off, even though other loyalties compete for our attention. Nothing should be placed above a total commitment to living for him.

**8:23** The boat used here was probably the kind familiar to many of Jesus' disciples who were fishermen. Josephus, an ancient historian, wrote that there were usually more than 300 fishing boats on the Sea of Galilee at one time. This boat was large enough to hold Jesus and his 12 disciples and was powered both by oars and sails. During a storm, however, the sails were taken down to keep them from ripping and to make the boat easier to control.

**8:24** The Sea of Galilee is an unusual body of water. It is relatively small (13 miles long, 7 miles wide), but it is 150 feet deep, and the shoreline is 680 feet below sea level. Sudden storms can appear over the surrounding mountains with little warning, stirring the water into violent 20-foot waves. The disciples had not foolishly set out in a storm. They had been caught without warning, and their danger was great.

**8:25** Although the disciples had witnessed many miracles, they panicked in this storm. As experienced sailors, they knew its danger; what they did not know was that Christ could control the forces of nature. We often encounter storms in our life, where we feel God can't or won't work. When we truly understand who God is, however, we will realize that he controls both the storms of nature and the storms of the troubled heart. Jesus' power that calmed this storm can also help us deal with the problems we

face. Jesus is willing to help if we only ask him. We should never discount his power even in terrible trials.

**8:28** The region of the Gadarenes is located southeast of the Sea of Galilee, near the town of Gadara, one of the most important cities of the region (see map). Gadara was a member of the Ten Towns (see the note on Mark 5:20), towns with independent governments that were largely inhabited by Gentiles. This explains the herd of pigs (8:30), for the Jews did not raise pigs because pigs were considered unclean and thus unfit to eat.

**8:28** Demon-possessed people are under the control of one or more demons. Demons are fallen angels who joined Satan in his rebellion against God and are now evil spirits under Satan's control. They help Satan tempt people to sin and have great destructive powers. But whenever they are confronted by Jesus, they lose their power. These demons recognized Jesus as God's Son (8:29), but they didn't think they had to obey him. Just believing is not enough (see James 2:19 for a discussion of belief and demons). Faith is more than belief. By faith, you accept what Jesus has done for you, receive him as the only one who can save you from sin, and live out your faith by obeying his commands.

**8:28** Matthew says there were two demon-possessed men, while Mark and Luke refer only to one. Apparently Mark and Luke mention only the man who did the talking.

**8:28** According to Jewish ceremonial laws, the men Jesus encountered were unclean in three ways: They were Gentiles (non-Jews), they were demon possessed, and they lived in a cemetery. Jesus helped them anyway. We should not turn our backs on people who are "unclean" or repulsive to us or who violate our moral standards and religious beliefs. Instead, we must realize that every human individual is a unique creation of God, needing to be touched by his love.

**8:29** The Bible tells us that at the end of the world the devil and his angels will be thrown into the lake of fire that burns with sulfur (Revelation 20:10). When the demons asked if Jesus had come to torture them "before God's appointed time," they showed they knew their ultimate fate.

**8:32** When the demons entered the pigs, they drove the animals into the sea. The demons' action proves their destructive intent—if they could not destroy the men, they would destroy the pigs. Jesus' action, by contrast, shows the value he places on each human life.

**8:34**
Acts 16:39

³³The herdsmen fled to the nearby town, telling everyone what happened to the demon-possessed men. ³⁴Then the entire town came out to meet Jesus, but they begged him to go away and leave them alone.

### Jesus Heals a Paralyzed Man (**39**/Mark 2:1-12; Luke 5:17-26)

**9** Jesus climbed into a boat and went back across the lake to his own town. ²Some people brought to him a paralyzed man on a mat. Seeing their faith, Jesus said to the paralyzed man, "Be encouraged, my child! Your sins are forgiven."

**MATTHEW**

More than any other disciple, Matthew had a clear idea of how much it would cost to follow Jesus, yet he did not hesitate a moment. When he left his tax-collecting booth, he guaranteed himself unemployment. For several of the other disciples, there was always fishing to return to, but for Matthew, there was no turning back.

Two changes happened to Matthew when he decided to follow Jesus. First, Jesus gave him a new life. He not only belonged to a new group; he belonged to the Son of God. He was not just accepting a different way of life; he was now an accepted person. For a despised tax collector, that change must have been wonderful! Second, Jesus gave Matthew a new purpose for his skills. When he followed Jesus, the only tool from his past job that he carried with him was his pen. From the beginning, God had made him a record keeper. Jesus' call eventually allowed him to put his skills to their finest work. Matthew was a keen observer, and he undoubtedly recorded what he saw going on around him. The Gospel that bears his name came as a result.

Matthew's experience points out that each of us, from the beginning, is one of God's works in progress. Much of what God has for us he gives long before we are able to consciously respond to him. He trusts us with skills and abilities ahead of schedule. He has made each of us capable of being his servant. When we trust him with what he has given us, we begin a life of real adventure. Matthew couldn't have known that God would use the very skills he had sharpened as a tax collector to record the greatest story ever lived. And God has no less meaningful a purpose for each one of us. Have you recognized Jesus saying to you, "Follow me"? What has been your response?

| | |
|---|---|
| **Strengths and accomplishments** | • Was one of Jesus' 12 disciples<br>• Responded immediately to Jesus' call<br>• Invited many friends to his home to meet Jesus<br>• Compiled the Gospel of Matthew<br>• Clarified for his Jewish audience Jesus' fulfillment of Old Testament prophecies |
| **Lessons from his life** | • Jesus consistently accepted people from every level of society<br>• Matthew was given a new life, and his God-given skills of record keeping and attention to detail were given a new purpose<br>• Having been accepted by Jesus, Matthew immediately tried to bring others into contact with Jesus |
| **Vital statistics** | • Where: Capernaum<br>• Occupations: Tax collector, disciple of Jesus<br>• Relative: Father: Alphaeus<br>• Contemporaries: Jesus, Pilate, Herod, other disciples |
| **Key verse** | "As Jesus was walking along, he saw a man named Matthew sitting at his tax collector's booth. 'Follow me and be my disciple,' Jesus said to him. So Matthew got up and followed him" (Matthew 9:9). |

Matthew's story is told in the Gospels. He is also mentioned in Acts 1:13.

---

**8:34** Why did the people ask Jesus to leave? Unlike their own pagan gods, Jesus could not be contained, controlled, or appeased. They feared Jesus' supernatural power, a power that they had never before witnessed. And they were upset about losing a herd of pigs more than they were glad about the deliverance of the demon-possessed men. Are you more concerned about property and programs than people? Human beings are created in God's image and have eternal value. How foolish and yet how easy it is to value possessions, investments, and even animals above human life. Would you rather have Jesus leave you than finish his work in you?

**9:1** "His own town" was Capernaum, a good choice for Jesus' base of operations. It was a wealthy city due to fishing and trade. Situated on the Sea of Galilee in a densely populated area, Capernaum housed the Roman garrison that kept peace in the region.

The city was a cultural melting pot, greatly influenced by Greek and Roman manners, dress, architecture, and politics.

**9:2** Among the first words Jesus said to the paralyzed man were "Your sins are forgiven." Then he healed the man. We must be careful not to concentrate more on God's power to heal physical sickness than on his power to forgive spiritual sickness in the form of sin. Jesus saw that even more than physical health, this man needed spiritual health. Spiritual health comes only from Jesus' healing touch.

**9:2** Both the man's body and his spirit were paralyzed—he could not walk, and he did not know Jesus. But the man's spiritual state was Jesus' first concern. If God does not heal us or someone we love, we need to remember that physical healing is not Christ's only concern. We will all be completely healed in Christ's coming Kingdom; but first we have to come to know Jesus.

³But some of the teachers of religious law said to themselves, "That's blasphemy! Does he think he's God?"

⁴Jesus knew* what they were thinking, so he asked them, "Why do you have such evil thoughts in your hearts? ⁵Is it easier to say 'Your sins are forgiven,' or 'Stand up and walk'? ⁶So I will prove to you that the Son of Man* has the authority on earth to forgive sins." Then Jesus turned to the paralyzed man and said, "Stand up, pick up your mat, and go home!"

⁷And the man jumped up and went home! ⁸Fear swept through the crowd as they saw this happen. And they praised God for sending a man with such great authority.*

**9:3**
Matt 26:65
John 10:33

**9:4**
Matt 12:25
Luke 6:8; 9:47;
11:17

**9:6-8**
Matt 15:31
Luke 7:16
Acts 9:33-35

### Jesus Eats with Sinners at Matthew's House (40/Mark 2:13-17; Luke 5:27-32)

⁹As Jesus was walking along, he saw a man named Matthew sitting at his tax collector's booth. "Follow me and be my disciple," Jesus said to him. So Matthew got up and followed him.

¹⁰Later, Matthew invited Jesus and his disciples to his home as dinner guests, along with many tax collectors and other disreputable sinners. ¹¹But when the Pharisees saw this, they asked his disciples, "Why does your teacher eat with such scum?*"

¹²When Jesus heard this, he said, "Healthy people don't need a doctor—sick people do." ¹³Then he added, "Now go and learn the meaning of this Scripture: 'I want you to show mercy, not offer sacrifices.'* For I have come to call not those who think they are righteous, but those who know they are sinners."

**9:11**
Matt 11:19
Luke 5:30; 15:1-2;
19:7

**9:13**
†Hos 6:6
Mic 6:6-8
Matt 12:7
Luke 19:10
1 Tim 1:15

### Religious Leaders Ask Jesus about Fasting (41/Mark 2:18-22; Luke 5:33-39)

¹⁴One day the disciples of John the Baptist came to Jesus and asked him, "Why don't your disciples fast* like we do and the Pharisees do?"

¹⁵Jesus replied, "Do wedding guests mourn while celebrating with the groom? Of course not. But someday the groom will be taken away from them, and then they will fast.

¹⁶"Besides, who would patch old clothing with new cloth? For the new patch would shrink and rip away from the old cloth, leaving an even bigger tear than before.

**9:15**
John 3:29

9:4 Some manuscripts read *saw*.   9:6 "Son of Man" is a title Jesus used for himself.   9:8 Greek *for giving such authority to human beings.*   9:11 Greek *with tax collectors and sinners?*   9:13 Hos 6:6 (Greek version).
9:14 Some manuscripts read *fast often.*

---

**9:3** Blaspheming is claiming to be God and applying his characteristics to yourself. The religious leaders rightly saw that Jesus was claiming to be God. What they did not understand was that he *is* God and thus has the authority to heal and to forgive sins.

**9:5, 6** It's easy to tell someone his sins are forgiven; it's a lot more difficult to reverse a case of paralysis! Jesus backed up his words by healing the man's legs. Jesus' action showed that his words were true; he had the power to forgive as well as to heal. Talk is cheap, but our words lack meaning if our actions do not back them up. We can say we love God or others, but if we are not taking practical steps to demonstrate that love, our words are empty and meaningless. How well do your actions back up what you say?

**9:9** Matthew was a Jew who was appointed by the Romans to be the area's tax collector. He collected taxes from the citizens as well as from merchants passing through town. Tax collectors were expected to take a commission on the taxes they collected, but most of them overcharged and kept the profits. Thus, tax collectors were hated by the Jews because of their reputation for cheating and because of their support of Rome.

**9:9** When Jesus called Matthew to be one of his disciples, Matthew got up and followed, leaving a lucrative career. When God calls you to follow or obey him, do you do it with as much abandon as Matthew? Sometimes the decision to follow Christ requires difficult or painful choices. Like Matthew, we must decide to leave behind those things that would keep us from following Christ.

**9:10-13** When he visited Matthew, Jesus hurt his own reputation among the religious elites in order to reach out to those who were lost. Matthew's reputation hadn't yet caught up with his new life as a disciple, but he became a bridge for Jesus' message to Matthew's past associates. We should not be afraid to reach out to

people who are living in sin. God's message changes people— and their friends, too!

**9:11, 12** The Pharisees constantly tried to trap Jesus, and they thought his association with these "lowlifes" was the perfect opportunity. They were more concerned with their own appearance of holiness than with helping people, with criticism than encouragement, with outward respectability than practical help. But God is concerned for all people, including the sinful and hurting ones. The Christian life is not a popularity contest! Following Jesus' example, we should share the Good News with the poor, immoral, lonely, and outcast, not just the rich, moral, popular, and powerful.

**9:13** Those who are sure that they are good enough can't be saved because the first step in following Jesus is acknowledging our need and admitting that we don't have all the answers. For more on "I want you to show mercy, not offer sacrifices," see the chart in Hosea 7, p. 1413.

**9:14** John's disciples fasted (went without food) as a sign of mourning for sin and preparation for the Messiah's coming. Jesus' disciples did not need to fast because he is the Messiah and was with them! Jesus did not condemn fasting—he himself fasted (4:2). He emphasized that fasting must be done for the right reasons.

**9:14** John the Baptist's message was harsh, and it focused on law. When people look at God's law and compare themselves to it, they realize how far they fall short and how badly they need to repent. Jesus' message focused on life, the result of turning from sin and turning to him. John's disciples had the right start, but they needed to take the next step and trust in Jesus. Where is your focus—on law or on Christ?

**9:15** The arrival of the Kingdom of Heaven was like a wedding feast with Jesus as the groom. His disciples, therefore, were filled

17"And no one puts new wine into old wineskins. For the old skins would burst from the pressure, spilling the wine and ruining the skins. New wine is stored in new wineskins so that both are preserved."

### Jesus Heals a Bleeding Woman and Restores a Girl to Life
(**89**/Mark 5:21-43; Luke 8:40-56)

18As Jesus was saying this, the leader of a synagogue came and knelt before him. "My daughter has just died," he said, "but you can bring her back to life again if you just come and lay your hand on her."

19So Jesus and his disciples got up and went with him. 20Just then a woman who had suffered for twelve years with constant bleeding came up behind him. She touched the fringe of his robe, 21for she thought, "If I can just touch his robe, I will be healed."

22Jesus turned around, and when he saw her he said, "Daughter, be encouraged! Your faith has made you well." And the woman was healed at that moment.

23When Jesus arrived at the official's home, he saw the noisy crowd and heard the funeral music. 24"Get out!" he told them. "The girl isn't dead; she's only asleep." But the crowd laughed at him. 25After the crowd was put outside, however, Jesus went in and took the girl by the hand, and she stood up! 26The report of this miracle swept through the entire countryside.

### Jesus Heals the Blind and Mute (**90**)

27After Jesus left the girl's home, two blind men followed along behind him, shouting, "Son of David, have mercy on us!"

28They went right into the house where he was staying, and Jesus asked them, "Do you believe I can make you see?"

"Yes, Lord," they told him, "we do."

29Then he touched their eyes and said, "Because of your faith, it will happen." 30Then their eyes were opened, and they could see! Jesus sternly warned them, "Don't tell anyone about this." 31But instead, they went out and spread his fame all over the region.

**9:22**
Matt 9:29
Mark 10:52
Luke 7:50; 17:19
Acts 3:16

**9:23**
2 Chr 35:25
Jer 9:17-18

**9:24**
John 11:11-13

**9:27**
Matt 20:29-31
Mark 10:47

**9:30**
Mark 7:36

**9:31**
Mark 7:36

---

with joy. It would not be right to mourn or fast when the groom was present.

**9:17** In Bible times wine was not kept in glass bottles but in goatskins sewn around the edges to form watertight bags. New wine expanded as it fermented, stretching its wineskin. After the wine had aged, the stretched skin would burst if more new wine was poured into it. New wine, therefore, was always put into new wineskins.

Jesus used this description to explain that he had not come to patch up the old religious system of Judaism with its rules and traditions. His purpose was to bring in something new, though it had been prophesied for centuries. This new message, the Good News, said that Jesus Christ, God's Son, came to earth to offer all people forgiveness of sins and reconciliation with God. The Good News did not fit into the old rigid legalistic system of religion. It needed a fresh start. The message will always remain "new" because it must be accepted and applied in every generation. When we follow Christ, we must be prepared for new ways to live, new ways to look at people, and new ways to serve.

**9:18** Mark and Luke say this man's name was Jairus (Mark 5:22; Luke 8:41). As leader of the synagogue, Jairus was responsible for administration—looking after the building, supervising worship, running the school on weekdays, and finding rabbis to teach on the Sabbath. For more information on synagogues, read the first note on Mark 1:21.

**9:20-22** This woman had suffered for 12 years with a hemorrhage (perhaps a menstrual disorder). In our times of desperation, we don't have to worry about the correct way to reach out to God. Like this woman, we can simply reach out in faith. He will respond.

**9:22** God changed a situation that had been a problem for years. Like the leper and the demon-possessed men (see the note on 8:2, 3 and the second note on 8:28), this woman was considered unclean. For 12 years, she, too, had been one of the "untouchables" and had not been able to lead a normal life. But Jesus changed that and restored her. Sometimes we are tempted

to give up on people or situations that have not changed for many years. God can change what seems unchangeable, giving new purpose and hope.

**9:23-26** The synagogue leader didn't come to Jesus until his daughter was dead—it was too late for anyone else to help. But Jesus simply went to the girl and raised her! In our lives, Christ can make a difference when it seems too late for anyone else to help. He can bring healing to broken relationships, release from addicting habits, and forgiveness and healing to emotional scars. If your situation looks hopeless, remember that Christ can do the impossible.

**9:27** "Son of David" was a popular way of addressing Jesus as the Messiah because it was known that the Messiah would be a descendant of David (Isaiah 9:7). This is the first time the title is used in Matthew. Jesus' ability to give sight to the blind was prophesied in Isaiah 29:18; 35:5; 42:7.

**9:27-30** Jesus didn't respond immediately to the blind men's pleas. He waited to see if they had faith. Not everyone who says he wants help really believes God can help him. Jesus may have waited and questioned these men to emphasize and increase their faith. When you think that God is too slow in answering your prayers, consider that he might be testing you as he did the blind men. Do you believe that God can help you? Do you *really* want his help?

**9:28** These blind men were persistent. They went right into the house where Jesus was staying. They knew Jesus could heal them, and they would let nothing stop them from finding him. That's real faith in action. If you believe Jesus is the answer to your every need, don't let anything or anyone stop you from reaching out to him.

**9:30** Jesus told the people to keep quiet about his healings because he did not want to be known only as a miracle worker. He healed because he had compassion on people, but he also wanted to bring *spiritual* healing to a sin-sick world.

³²When they left, a demon-possessed man who couldn't speak was brought to Jesus. ³³So Jesus cast out the demon, and then the man began to speak. The crowds were amazed. "Nothing like this has ever happened in Israel!" they exclaimed.

³⁴But the Pharisees said, "He can cast out demons because he is empowered by the prince of demons."

### Jesus Urges the Disciples to Pray for Workers (92)

³⁵Jesus traveled through all the towns and villages of that area, teaching in the synagogues and announcing the Good News about the Kingdom. And he healed every kind of disease and illness. ³⁶When he saw the crowds, he had compassion on them because they were confused and helpless, like sheep without a shepherd. ³⁷He said to his disciples, "The harvest is great, but the workers are few. ³⁸So pray to the Lord who is in charge of the harvest; ask him to send more workers into his fields."

### Jesus Sends Out the Twelve Disciples (93/Mark 6:7-13; Luke 9:1-6)

**10** Jesus called his twelve disciples together and gave them authority to cast out evil* spirits and to heal every kind of disease and illness. ²Here are the names of the twelve apostles:

   first, Simon (also called Peter),
   then Andrew (Peter's brother),
   James (son of Zebedee),
   John (James's brother),
³ Philip,
   Bartholomew,
   Thomas,
   Matthew (the tax collector),
   James (son of Alphaeus),
   Thaddaeus,*
⁴ Simon (the zealot*),
   Judas Iscariot (who later betrayed him).

**10:1** Greek *unclean*. **10:3** Other manuscripts read *Lebbaeus*; still others read *Lebbaeus who is called Thaddaeus*. **10:4** Greek *the Cananean*, an Aramaic term for Jewish nationalists.

**9:32-33**
Matt 12:22
Mark 7:32, 35;
9:17, 25
Luke 11:14

**9:34**
Matt 12:24
Mark 3:22
Luke 11:15

**9:35**
Matt 4:23

**9:36**
†Num 27:17
†2 Chr 18:16
†Zech 10:2
Mark 6:34

**9:37-38**
Luke 10:2
John 4:35

**10:2-4**
John 1:40-49
Acts 1:13

**10:4**
Matt 26:25; 27:3
Mark 14:44

---

**9:32** While Jesus was on earth, demonic forces were especially active. Although we cannot always be sure why or how demon possession occurs, it causes both physical and mental problems. In this case, the demon made the man unable to talk. For more on demons and demon possession, read the notes on 8:28 and Mark 1:23.

**9:34** In chapter 9, the Pharisees accuse Jesus of four different sins: blasphemy, befriending outcasts, pride, and serving Satan. Matthew shows how Jesus was maligned by those who should have received him most gladly. Why did the Pharisees do this? (1) Jesus bypassed their religious authority. (2) He weakened their control over the people. (3) He challenged their cherished beliefs. (4) He exposed their insincere motives.

While the Pharisees questioned, debated, and dissected Jesus, people were being healed and lives changed right in front of them. Their skepticism was based not on insufficient evidence but on jealousy of Jesus' popularity.

**9:36** Jesus was overwhelmed with compassionate pity for the people. His response echoes the deep inner mercy of God, often described in the Old Testament. Ezekiel also compared Israel to sheep without a shepherd (Ezekiel 34:5, 6). Jesus came to be the Shepherd, the one who could show people how to avoid life's pitfalls (see John 10:14).

**9:37, 38** Jesus looked at the crowds following him and referred to them as a field ripe for harvest. Many people are ready to give their lives to Christ if someone would show them how. Jesus commands us to pray that people will respond to this need for workers. Often, when we pray for something, God answers our prayers by using *us*. Be prepared for God to use you to show another person the way to him.

**10:1** Jesus *called* his 12 disciples. He didn't draft them, force them, or ask them to volunteer; he chose them to serve him in a special way. Christ calls us today. He doesn't twist our arms and make us do something we don't want to do. We can choose to join him or remain behind. When Christ calls you to follow him, how do you respond?

**10:2-4** The list of Jesus' 12 disciples doesn't give us many details—probably because there weren't many impressive details to tell. Jesus called people from all walks of life—fishermen, political activists, tax collectors. He called common people and uncommon leaders; rich and poor; educated and uneducated. Today, many people think only certain people are fit to follow Christ, but this was not the attitude of the Master himself. God can use anyone, no matter how insignificant he or she appears. When you feel small and useless, remember that God uses ordinary people to do his extraordinary work.

**10:3** Bartholomew is probably another name for Nathanael, whom we meet in John 1:45-51. Thaddaeus is also known as Judas son of James. The disciples are also listed in Mark 3:16-19; Luke 6:14-16; and Acts 1:13.

**10:4** Simon the Zealot may have been a member of the Zealots, a radical political party working for the violent overthrow of Roman rule in Israel.

**10:5**
2 Kgs 17:24
John 4:9

**10:6**
Jer 50:6
Matt 15:24

**10:7**
Matt 3:2; 4:17

**10:9-10**
1 Cor 9:14
1 Tim 5:18

**10:15**
Gen 18:20—19:29
Matt 11:23-24
2 Pet 2:6
Jude 1:7

⁵ Jesus sent out the twelve apostles with these instructions: "Don't go to the Gentiles or the Samaritans, ⁶ but only to the people of Israel—God's lost sheep. ⁷ Go and announce to them that the Kingdom of Heaven is near.* ⁸ Heal the sick, raise the dead, cure those with leprosy, and cast out demons. Give as freely as you have received!

⁹ "Don't take any money in your money belts—no gold, silver, or even copper coins. ¹⁰ Don't carry a traveler's bag with a change of clothes and sandals or even a walking stick. Don't hesitate to accept hospitality, because those who work deserve to be fed.

¹¹ "Whenever you enter a city or village, search for a worthy person and stay in his home until you leave town. ¹² When you enter the home, give it your blessing. ¹³ If it turns out to be a worthy home, let your blessing stand; if it is not, take back the blessing. ¹⁴ If any household or town refuses to welcome you or listen to your message, shake its dust from your feet as you leave. ¹⁵ I tell you the truth, the wicked cities of Sodom and Gomorrah will be better off than such a town on the judgment day.

**10:7** Or *has come*, or *is coming soon*.

| COUNTING THE COST OF FOLLOWING CHRIST | Who may oppose us? | Natural response | Possible pressures | Needed truth |
|---|---|---|---|---|
| | GOVERNMENT 10:18-19 | | Threats 10:26 | → The truth will be revealed (10:26) |
| | RELIGIOUS PEOPLE 10:17 | Fear and worry | Physical harm 10:28 | → Our soul cannot be harmed (10:28) |
| | | | Public ridicule 10:22 | → God himself will acknowledge us if we acknowledge him (10:32) |
| | FAMILY 10:21 | | Rejection by loved ones 10:34-37 | → God's love can sustain us (10:31) |

Jesus helped his disciples prepare for the rejection many of them would experience by being Christians. Being God's person will usually create reactions from others who are resisting him.

**10:5, 6** Why didn't Jesus send the disciples to the Gentiles or the Samaritans? A Gentile is anyone who is not a Jew. The Samaritans were a race that resulted from intermarriage between Jews and Gentiles after the Old Testament captivities (see 2 Kings 17:24). Jesus asked his disciples to go only to the Jews because he came *first* to the Jews (Romans 1:16). God chose them to tell the rest of the world about him. Jewish disciples and apostles preached the Good News of the risen Christ all around the Roman Empire, and soon Gentiles were pouring into the church. The Bible clearly teaches that God's message of salvation is for *all* people, regardless of race, sex, or national origin (Genesis 12:3; Isaiah 25:6; 56:3-7; Malachi 1:11; Acts 10:34, 35; Romans 3:29, 30; Galatians 3:28).

**10:7** The Jews were waiting for the Messiah to usher in his Kingdom. They hoped for a political and military kingdom that would free them from Roman rule and bring back the days of glory under David and Solomon. But Jesus was talking about a spiritual Kingdom. The Good News today is that the Kingdom is still *near*. Jesus, the Messiah, has already begun his Kingdom on earth in the hearts of his followers. One day the Kingdom will be fully realized. Then evil will be destroyed and all people will live in peace with one another.

**10:8** Jesus gave the disciples a principle to guide their actions as they ministered to others: "Give as freely as you have received." Because God has showered us with his blessings, we should give generously to others of our time, love, and possessions.

**10:10** Jesus said that those who minister are to be cared for. The disciples could expect food and shelter in return for the spiritual service they provided. Who ministers to you? Make sure you take care of the pastors, missionaries, and teachers who serve God by serving you (see 1 Corinthians 9:9, 10; 1 Timothy 5:17).

**10:10** Mark's account (6:8) says to take a walking stick, and Matthew and Luke (9:3) say not to. Jesus may have meant that they were not to take an *extra* pair of sandals, walking stick, and bag. In any case, the principle was that they were to go out ready for duty and travel, unencumbered by excess material goods.

**10:14** Why did Jesus tell his disciples to shake the dust off their feet if a city or home didn't welcome them? When leaving Gentile cities, pious Jews often shook the dust from their feet to show their separation from Gentile practices. If the disciples shook the dust of a *Jewish* town from their feet, it would show their separation from Jews who rejected their Messiah. This gesture was to show the people that they were making a wrong choice—that the opportunity to choose Christ might not present itself again. Are you receptive to teaching from God? If you ignore the Spirit's prompting, you may not get another chance.

**10:15** The cities of Sodom and Gomorrah were destroyed by fire from heaven because of their wickedness (Genesis 19:24, 25). Those who reject the Good News when they hear it will be worse off than the wicked people of these destroyed cities, who never heard the Good News at all.

## Jesus Prepares the Disciples for Persecution (94)

16"Look, I am sending you out as sheep among wolves. So be as shrewd as snakes and harmless as doves. 17But beware! For you will be handed over to the courts and will be flogged with whips in the synagogues. 18You will stand trial before governors and kings because you are my followers. But this will be your opportunity to tell the rulers and other unbelievers about me.* 19When you are arrested, don't worry about how to respond or what to say. God will give you the right words at the right time. 20For it is not you who will be speaking—it will be the Spirit of your Father speaking through you.

21"A brother will betray his brother to death, a father will betray his own child, and children will rebel against their parents and cause them to be killed. 22And all nations will hate you because you are my followers.* But everyone who endures to the end will be saved. 23When you are persecuted in one town, flee to the next. I tell you the truth, the Son of Man* will return before you have reached all the towns of Israel.

24"Students* are not greater than their teacher, and slaves are not greater than their master. 25Students are to be like their teacher, and slaves are to be like their master. And since I, the master of the household, have been called the prince of demons,* the members of my household will be called by even worse names!

26"But don't be afraid of those who threaten you. For the time is coming when everything that is covered will be revealed, and all that is secret will be made known to all. 27What I tell you now in the darkness, shout abroad when daybreak comes. What I whisper in your ear, shout from the housetops for all to hear!

28"Don't be afraid of those who want to kill your body; they cannot touch your soul. Fear only God, who can destroy both soul and body in hell.* 29What is the price of two sparrows—one copper coin*? But not a single sparrow can fall to the ground without your Father knowing it. 30And the very hairs on your head are all numbered. 31So don't be afraid; you are more valuable to God than a whole flock of sparrows.

32"Everyone who acknowledges me publicly here on earth, I will also acknowledge before my Father in heaven. 33But everyone who denies me here on earth, I will also deny before my Father in heaven.

34"Don't imagine that I came to bring peace to the earth! I came not to bring peace, but a sword.

**10:16** Luke 10:3 Acts 20:29
**10:17** Acts 5:40; 22:19; 26:11
**10:19-20** Luke 12:11-12 Acts 4:8
**10:21** Mic 7:6
**10:22** John 15:21
**10:24** John 13:16; 15:20
**10:26** Mark 4:22
**10:28** Isa 8:12-13 Heb 10:31
**10:29** Luke 12:6
**10:30** 1 Sam 14:45 2 Sam 14:11 Luke 21:18 Acts 27:34
**10:32** Rom 10:9 Rev 3:5
**10:33** Mark 8:38 Luke 9:26 2 Tim 2:12

**10:18** Or *But this will be your testimony against the rulers and other unbelievers.* **10:22** Greek *on account of my name.* **10:23** "Son of Man" is a title Jesus used for himself. **10:24** Or *Disciples.* **10:25** Greek *Beelzeboul;* other manuscripts read *Beezeboul;* Latin version reads *Beelzebub.* **10:28** Greek *Gehenna.* **10:29** Greek *one assarion* [i.e., one "as," a Roman coin equal to 1/16 of a denarius].

**10:16** The opposition of the Pharisees would be like ravaging wolves. The disciples' only hope would be to look to their Shepherd for protection. We may face similar hostility. Like the disciples, we are not to be sheeplike in our attitude but sensible and prudent. We are not to be gullible pawns, but neither are we to be deceitful connivers. We must find a balance between wisdom and vulnerability to accomplish God's work.

**10:17, 18** Later the disciples experienced these hardships (Acts 5:40; 12:1-3), not only from without (governments, courts), but also from within (friends, family; 10:21). Living for God often brings on persecution, but with it comes the opportunity to tell the Good News of salvation. In times of persecution, we can be confident because Jesus has "overcome the world" (John 16:33). And those who endure to the end will be saved (Matthew 10:22).

**10:19, 20** Jesus told the disciples that when arrested for preaching the Good News, they should not worry about what to say in their defense—God's Spirit would speak through them. This promise was fulfilled in Acts 4:8-14 and elsewhere. Some mistakenly think this means we don't have to prepare to present the Good News because God will take care of everything. Scripture teaches, however, that we are to make carefully prepared, thoughtful statements (Colossians 4:6). Jesus is telling us not to stop preparing but to stop worrying.

**10:22** Enduring to the end is not a way to be saved but the evidence that a person is really committed to Jesus. Persistence is not a means to earn salvation; it is the by-product of a truly devoted life.

**10:25** The prince of demons was Satan, also known as Beelzebub and the lord of flies. The Pharisees accused Jesus of using Satan's power to drive out demons (see 12:24). Good is sometimes labeled evil. If Jesus, who is perfect, was called evil, his followers should expect that similar accusations will be directed at them. But those who endure will be vindicated (10:22).

**10:29-31** Jesus said that God is aware of everything that happens even to sparrows, and you are far more valuable to him than they are. You are so valuable that God sent his only Son to die for you (John 3:16). Because God places such value on you, you need never fear personal threats or difficult trials. These can't shake God's love or dislodge his Spirit from within you.

This doesn't mean, however, that God will take away all your troubles (see 10:16). The real test of value is how well something holds up under the wear, tear, and stress of everyday life. Those who stand up for Christ in spite of their troubles truly have lasting value and will receive great rewards (see 5:11, 12).

**10:32** Anyone who acknowledges Jesus Christ (that is, publicly confesses faith in or declares allegiance to him) will be acknowledged by Christ before his Father in heaven. Jesus' followers would face earthly courts of law where they would have to publicly claim to belong to Jesus Christ, usually at their peril (10:17-25). Genuine discipleship always involves acknowledging Jesus Christ, whether or not we face pressure and persecution.

**10:34** Jesus did not come to bring the kind of peace that glosses over deep differences just for the sake of superficial harmony. Conflict and disagreement will arise between those who choose to follow Christ and those who don't. Yet we can look forward to

**10:35-36**
†Mic 7:6

³⁵ 'I have come to set a man against his father,
    a daughter against her mother,
    and a daughter-in-law against her mother-in-law.

**10:37**
Luke 14:26

³⁶   Your enemies will be right in your own household!'*

**10:38**
Mark 8:34
Luke 9:23; 14:27

³⁷ "If you love your father or mother more than you love me, you are not worthy of being mine; or if you love your son or daughter more than me, you are not worthy of being mine.

**10:39**
Matt 16:25
Mark 8:35
Luke 9:24; 17:33
John 12:25

³⁸ If you refuse to take up your cross and follow me, you are not worthy of being mine. ³⁹ If you cling to your life, you will lose it; but if you give up your life for me, you will find it.

**10:40**
John 12:44; 13:20

⁴⁰ "Anyone who receives you receives me, and anyone who receives me receives the Father who sent me. ⁴¹If you receive a prophet as one who speaks for God,* you will be given the same reward as a prophet. And if you receive righteous people because of their righteousness, you will be given a reward like theirs. ⁴²And if you give even a cup of cold water to one of the least of my followers, you will surely be rewarded."

**10:41**
1 Kgs 17:9-24
2 Kgs 4:8-37

### 4. Jesus teaches about the Kingdom
*Jesus Eases John's Doubt* (**70**/Luke 7:18-35)

**11** When Jesus had finished giving these instructions to his twelve disciples, he went out to teach and preach in towns throughout the region.

²John the Baptist, who was in prison, heard about all the things the Messiah was doing. So he sent his disciples to ask Jesus, ³"Are you the Messiah we've been expecting,* or should we keep looking for someone else?"

**11:3**
Mal 3:1

**11:5**
Isa 35:4-6;
42:7, 18; 61:1
Luke 4:18-19

⁴Jesus told them, "Go back to John and tell him what you have heard and seen—⁵the blind see, the lame walk, the lepers are cured, the deaf hear, the dead are raised to life, and the Good News is being preached to the poor. ⁶And tell him, 'God blesses those who do not turn away because of me.*' "

**11:6**
Matt 13:57

**11:7**
Matt 3:5

⁷As John's disciples were leaving, Jesus began talking about him to the crowds. " What kind of man did you go into the wilderness to see? Was he a weak reed, swayed by every breath of wind? ⁸Or were you expecting to see a man dressed in expensive clothes? No, people with expensive clothes live in palaces. ⁹Were you looking for a prophet? Yes, and he is more than a prophet. ¹⁰John is the man to whom the Scriptures refer when they say,

**11:9**
Matt 14:5; 21:26
Luke 1:76

**11:10**
Exod 23:20
†Mal 3:1
Mark 1:2
Luke 7:27

'Look, I am sending my messenger ahead of you,
    and he will prepare your way before you.'*

**10:35-36** Mic 7:6.  **10:41** Greek *receive a prophet in the name of a prophet.*  **11:3** Greek *Are you the one who is coming?*  **11:6** Or *who are not offended by me.*  **11:10** Mal 3:1.

---

the day when all conflict will be resolved. For other verses on Jesus as peacemaker, see Isaiah 9:6; Matthew 5:9; John 14:27.

**10:34-39** Christian commitment may separate friends and loved ones. In saying this, Jesus was not encouraging disobedience to parents or conflict at home. Rather, he was showing that his presence demands a decision. Because some will follow Christ and some won't, conflict will inevitably arise. As we take up our cross and follow him, our different values, morals, and goals will set us apart from others. Christ calls us to a higher mission than to find comfort and tranquility in this life. Love of family is a law of God, but even this love can be self-serving and used as an excuse not to serve God or do his work. Don't neglect your family, but remember that your commitment to God is even more important. God should be your first priority.

**10:38** To take up our cross and follow Jesus means to be willing to publicly identify with him, to experience certain opposition, and to be willing to face even suffering and death for his sake.

**10:39** This verse is a positive and negative statement of the same truth: Clinging to this life may cause us to forfeit the best from Christ in this world *and* in the next. The more we love this life's rewards (leisure, power, popularity, financial security), the more we will discover how empty they really are. The best way to enjoy life, therefore, is to loosen our greedy grasp on earthly rewards so that we can be free to follow Christ. In doing so, we will inherit eternal life and begin at once to experience the benefits of following Christ.

**10:42** How much we love God can be measured by how well we treat others. Jesus' example of giving a cup of cold water to a thirsty child is a good model of unselfish service. A child usually can't or won't return a favor. God notices every good deed we do or don't do as if he were the one receiving it. Is there something unselfish you can do for someone else today? Although no one else may see you, God will notice.

**11:2, 3** John had been put in prison by Herod. Herod had married his own sister-in-law, and John publicly rebuked Herod's flagrant sin (14:3-5). John's Profile is found in John 1, p. 1749. Herod's Profile is found in Mark 6, p. 1629.

**11:4-6** As John sat in prison, he began to have some doubts about whether Jesus really was the Messiah. If John's purpose was to prepare people for the coming Messiah (3:3), and if Jesus really was that Messiah, then why was John in prison when he could have been preaching to the crowds, preparing their hearts?

Jesus answered John's doubts by pointing to the acts of healing the blind, lame, and deaf, curing the lepers, raising the dead, and preaching the Good News to the poor. With so much evidence, Jesus' identity was obvious. If you sometimes doubt your salvation, the forgiveness of your sins, or God's work in your life, look at the evidence in Scripture and the changes in your life. When you doubt, don't turn away from Christ; turn *to* him.

11 "I tell you the truth, of all who have ever lived, none is greater than John the Baptist. Yet even the least person in the Kingdom of Heaven is greater than he is! 12 And from the time John the Baptist began preaching until now, the Kingdom of Heaven has been forcefully advancing,* and violent people are attacking it. 13 For before John came, all the prophets and the law of Moses looked forward to this present time. 14 And if you are willing to accept what I say, he is Elijah, the one the prophets said would come.* 15 Anyone with ears to hear should listen and understand!

16 "To what can I compare this generation? It is like children playing a game in the public square. They complain to their friends,

17 'We played wedding songs,
    and you didn't dance,
so we played funeral songs,
    and you didn't mourn.'

18 For John didn't spend his time eating and drinking, and you say, 'He's possessed by a demon.' 19 The Son of Man,* on the other hand, feasts and drinks, and you say, 'He's a glutton and a drunkard, and a friend of tax collectors and other sinners!' But wisdom is shown to be right by its results."

## Jesus Promises Rest for the Soul (71)

20 Then Jesus began to denounce the towns where he had done so many of his miracles, because they hadn't repented of their sins and turned to God. 21 "What sorrow awaits you, Korazin and Bethsaida! For if the miracles I did in you had been done in wicked Tyre and Sidon, their people would have repented of their sins long ago, clothing themselves in burlap and throwing ashes on their heads to show their remorse. 22 I tell you, Tyre and Sidon will be better off on judgment day than you.

23 "And you people of Capernaum, will you be honored in heaven? No, you will go down to the place of the dead.* For if the miracles I did for you had been done in wicked Sodom, it would still be here today. 24 I tell you, even Sodom will be better off on judgment day than you."

25 At that time Jesus prayed this prayer: "O Father, Lord of heaven and earth, thank you for hiding these things from those who think themselves wise and clever, and for revealing them to the childlike. 26 Yes, Father, it pleased you to do it this way!

27 "My Father has entrusted everything to me. No one truly knows the Son except the Father, and no one truly knows the Father except the Son and those to whom the Son chooses to reveal him."

**11:12-13** Luke 16:16

**11:14** Mal 4:5 / Matt 17:10-13 / Mark 9:11-13 / Luke 1:17 / John 1:21

**11:15** Matt 13:9, 43 / Mark 4:9, 23 / Luke 8:8; 14:35 / Rev 2:7

**11:18** Matt 3:4 / Luke 1:15

**11:19** Matt 9:11, 14

**11:21-22** Isa 23:1-8 / Ezek 26–28 / Joel 3:4-8 / Amos 1:9-10 / Zech 9:2-4 / Matt 10:15

**11:23** †Isa 14:13, 15

**11:25-27** Eph 1:17-18

**11:27** Matt 28:18 / John 3:35; 10:15; 17:2, 25-26

**11:12** Or the Kingdom of Heaven has suffered from violence.   **11:14** See Mal 4:5.   **11:19** "Son of Man" is a title Jesus used for himself.   **11:23** Greek to Hades.

**11:11** No person ever fulfilled his God-given purpose better than John. Yet in God's coming Kingdom all members will have a greater spiritual heritage than John because they will have seen and known Christ and his finished work on the cross.

**11:12** There are three common views about the meaning of this verse: (1) Jesus may have been referring to a vast movement toward God, the momentum that began with John's preaching. (2) He may have been reflecting the Jewish activists' expectation that God's Kingdom would come through a violent overthrow of Rome. (3) Or he may have meant that entering God's Kingdom takes courage, unwavering faith, determination, and endurance because of the growing opposition leveled at Jesus' followers. In any case, Jesus was pointing out that John's ministry had ushered in the Kingdom of Heaven.

**11:14** John was not a resurrected Elijah, but he took on Elijah's prophetic role—boldly confronting sin and pointing people to God (Malachi 3:1). See Elijah's Profile in 1 Kings 17, p. 545.

**11:16-19** Jesus condemned the attitude of his generation. No matter what he said or did, they took the opposite view. They were cynical and skeptical because he challenged their comfortable, secure, and self-centered lives. Too often we justify our inconsistencies because listening to God may require us to change the way we live.

**11:21-24** Tyre, Sidon, and Sodom were ancient cities with a long-standing reputation for wickedness (Genesis 18–19; Ezekiel 27–28). Each was destroyed by God for its evil. The people of Bethsaida, Korazin, and Capernaum saw Jesus firsthand, and yet they stubbornly refused to repent of their sins and believe in him. Jesus said that if some of the wickedest cities in the world had seen him, they would have repented. Because Bethsaida, Korazin, and Capernaum saw Jesus and didn't believe, they would suffer even greater punishment than would the wicked cities that didn't see Jesus. Similarly, nations and cities with churches on every corner and Bibles in every home will have no excuse on judgment day if they do not repent and believe.

**11:25** Jesus mentioned two kinds of people in his prayer: the "wise and clever"—arrogant in their own knowledge—and the "childlike"—humbly open to receive the truth of God's Word. Are you wise in your own eyes, or do you seek the truth in childlike faith, realizing that only God holds all the answers?

**11:27** In the Old Testament, know means more than knowledge. It implies an intimate relationship. The communion between God the Father and God the Son is the core of their relationship. For anyone else to know God, God must reveal himself to that person, by the Son's choice. How fortunate we are that Jesus

**11:29**
†Jer 6:16
**11:30**
1 Jn 5:3

²⁸ Then Jesus said, "Come to me, all of you who are weary and carry heavy burdens, and I will give you rest. ²⁹ Take my yoke upon you. Let me teach you, because I am humble and gentle at heart, and you will find rest for your souls. ³⁰ For my yoke is easy to bear, and the burden I give you is light."

**12:2**
Exod 20:10
Deut 5:14
Luke 13:14; 14:3
John 5:10; 7:23;
9:16
**12:3**
1 Sam 21:1-6
**12:4**
Lev 24:5-9
**12:5**
Num 28:9-10
**12:6**
Matt 12:41-42
Luke 11:31-32
**12:7**
Mic 6:6-8

### The Disciples Pick Wheat on the Sabbath (45/Mark 2:23-28; Luke 6:1-5)

**12** At about that time Jesus was walking through some grainfields on the Sabbath. His disciples were hungry, so they began breaking off some heads of grain and eating them. ²But some Pharisees saw them do it and protested, "Look, your disciples are breaking the law by harvesting grain on the Sabbath."

³ Jesus said to them, "Haven't you read in the Scriptures what David did when he and his companions were hungry?⁴ He went into the house of God, and he and his companions broke the law by eating the sacred loaves of bread that only the priests are allowed to eat. ⁵ And haven't you read in the law of Moses that the priests on duty in the Temple may work on the Sabbath?⁶ I tell you, there is one here who is even greater than the Temple!⁷ But you would not have condemned my innocent disciples if you knew the meaning of this Scripture: 'I want you to show mercy, not offer sacrifices.'*⁸ For the Son of Man* is Lord, even over the Sabbath!"

**12:7** Hos 6:6 (Greek version).    **12:8** "Son of Man" is a title Jesus used for himself.

has clearly revealed God to us, as well as his truth and how we can know him.

**11:28-30** A yoke is a heavy wooden harness that fits over the shoulders of an ox or oxen. It is attached to a piece of equipment the oxen are to pull. A person may be carrying heavy burdens of (1) sin, (2) excessive demands of religious leaders (23:4; Acts 15:10), (3) oppression and persecution, or (4) weariness in the search for God.

Jesus frees people from all these burdens. The rest that Jesus promises is love, healing, and peace with God, not the end of all labor. A relationship with God changes meaningless, wearisome toil into spiritual productivity and purpose.

**11:30** In what sense was Jesus' yoke easy? The yoke emphasizes the challenges, work, and difficulties of partnering with Christ in life. Responsibilities weigh us down, even the effort of staying true to God. But Jesus' yoke remains easy compared to the crushing alternative.

Jesus doesn't offer a life of luxurious ease—the yoke is still an oxen's tool for working hard. But it's a shared yoke, with weight falling on bigger shoulders than yours. Someone with more pulling power is up front helping. Suddenly you are participating in life's responsibilities with a great Partner—and now that frown can turn into a smile, and that gripe into a song.

**12:1, 2** The Pharisees had established 39 categories of actions forbidden on the Sabbath, based on interpretations of God's law and on Jewish custom. Harvesting was one of those forbidden actions. By picking wheat and rubbing it in their hands, the disciples were technically harvesting, according to the Pharisees. Jesus and the disciples were picking grain because they were hungry, not because they wanted to harvest the grain for a profit. They were not working on the Sabbath. The Pharisees, however, could not (and did not want to) see beyond their law's technicalities. They had no room for compassion, and they were determined to accuse Jesus of wrongdoing.

**12:4** This story is recorded in 1 Samuel 21:1-6. The Bread of the Presence was replaced every week, and the old loaves were eaten by the priests. The loaves given to David were the old loaves that had just been replaced with fresh ones. Although the priests were the only ones allowed to eat this bread, God did not punish David because his need for food was more important than the priestly regulations. Jesus was saying, "If you condemn me, you must also condemn David," something the religious leaders could never do without causing a great uproar among the people. Jesus was not condoning disobedience to God's laws. Instead, he was emphasizing discernment and compassion in enforcing the laws.

**12:5** The Ten Commandments require that the Sabbath be kept holy (Exodus 20:8-11). The Pharisees had interpreted that to require a long list of actions that could not be done on the Sabbath, forcing the people to "rest." That was the *letter* of the law. But because the *purpose* of the Sabbath is to rest and to worship God, the priests were allowed to work by performing sacrifices and conducting worship services. This "Sabbath work" was serving and worshiping God. Jesus always emphasized the intent of the law, the meaning behind the letter. The Pharisees had lost the spirit of the law and were rigidly demanding that the letter (and their interpretation of it) be obeyed.

**12:6** The Pharisees were so concerned about religious rituals that they missed the whole purpose of the Temple—to bring people to God. And because Jesus Christ is even greater than the Temple, how much better can he bring people to God. God is far more important than the created instruments of worship. If we become more concerned with the means of worship than with the one we worship, we will miss God even as we think we are worshiping him.

**12:7** Jesus repeated to the Pharisees words the Jewish people had heard time and again throughout their history (1 Samuel 15:22, 23; Psalm 40:6-8; Isaiah 1:11-17; Jeremiah 7:21-23; Hosea 6:6). Our heart attitude toward God comes first. Only then can we properly obey and observe religious regulations and rituals.

**12:8** When Jesus said he was master of the Sabbath, he claimed to be greater than the law and above the law. To the Pharisees, this was heresy. They did not realize that Jesus, the divine Son of God, had created the Sabbath. The Creator is always greater than his creation; thus, Jesus had the authority to overrule their traditions and regulations.

### Jesus Heals a Man's Hand on the Sabbath (46/Mark 3:1-6; Luke 6:6-11)

9 Then Jesus went over to their synagogue, 10 where he noticed a man with a deformed hand. The Pharisees asked Jesus, "Does the law permit a person to work by healing on the Sabbath?" (They were hoping he would say yes, so they could bring charges against him.)

11 And he answered, "If you had a sheep that fell into a well on the Sabbath, wouldn't you work to pull it out? Of course you would. 12 And how much more valuable is a person than a sheep! Yes, the law permits a person to do good on the Sabbath."

13 Then he said to the man, "Hold out your hand." So the man held out his hand, and it was restored, just like the other one! 14 Then the Pharisees called a meeting to plot how to kill Jesus.

### Large Crowds Follow Jesus (47/Mark 3:7-12)

15 But Jesus knew what they were planning. So he left that area, and many people followed him. He healed all the sick among them, 16 but he warned them not to reveal who he was. 17 This fulfilled the prophecy of Isaiah concerning him:

18 "Look at my Servant, whom I have chosen.
   He is my Beloved, who pleases me.
I will put my Spirit upon him,
   and he will proclaim justice to the nations.
19 He will not fight or shout
   or raise his voice in public.
20 He will not crush the weakest reed
   or put out a flickering candle.
   Finally he will cause justice to be victorious.
21 And his name will be the hope
   of all the world."*

### Religious Leaders Accuse Jesus of Getting His Power from Satan (74/Mark 3:20-30)

22 Then a demon-possessed man, who was blind and couldn't speak, was brought to Jesus. He healed the man so that he could both speak and see. 23 The crowd was amazed and asked, "Could it be that Jesus is the Son of David, the Messiah?"

24 But when the Pharisees heard about the miracle, they said, "No wonder he can cast out demons. He gets his power from Satan,* the prince of demons."

**12:18-21** Isa 42:1-4 (Greek version for 42:4).    **12:24** Greek *Beelzeboul;* also in 12:27. Other manuscripts read *Beezeboul;* Latin version reads *Beelzebub.*

---

**Side references:**

**12:10**
Luke 13:14; 14:3
John 9:16

**12:11**
Luke 14:5
**12:12**
Matt 6:26; 10:31

**12:18-21**
†Isa 42:1-4

**12:22-23**
Matt 9:32-33

**12:24**
Matt 9:34

---

**12:10** As they pointed to the man with the deformed hand, the Pharisees tried to trick Jesus by asking him if it was legal to heal on the Sabbath. Their Sabbath rules said that people could be helped on the Sabbath only if their lives were in danger. Jesus healed on the Sabbath several times, and none of those healings were in response to emergencies. If Jesus had waited until another day, he would have been submitting to the Pharisees' authority, showing that their petty rules were equal to God's law. If he healed the man on the Sabbath, the Pharisees could claim that because Jesus broke their rules, his power was not from God. But Jesus made it clear how ridiculous and petty their rules were. God is a God of people, not rules. The best time to reach out to someone is when he or she needs help.

**12:10-12** The Pharisees placed their laws above human need. They were so concerned about Jesus breaking one of their rules that they did not care about the man's deformed hand. What is your attitude toward others? If your convictions don't allow you to help certain people, your convictions may not be in tune with God's Word. Don't allow rule keeping to blind you to human need.

**12:14** The Pharisees plotted Jesus' death because they were proud, fearful, and outraged. Jesus had overruled their authority

(Luke 6:11) and had exposed their evil attitudes in front of the entire crowd in the synagogue. Jesus had showed that the Pharisees were more loyal to their religious system than to God.

**12:15** Up to this point, Jesus had been aggressively confronting the Pharisees' hypocrisy. Here he decided to withdraw from the synagogue before a major confrontation developed because it was not yet time for him to die. Jesus had many lessons still to teach his disciples and the people.

**12:16** Jesus did not want those he healed to tell others about his miracles because he didn't want the people coming to him for the wrong reasons. That would hinder his teaching ministry and arouse false hopes about an earthly kingdom. But the news of Jesus' miracles spread, and many came to see for themselves (see Mark 3:7, 8).

**12:17-21** The people expected the Messiah to be a king. This quotation from Isaiah's prophecy (Isaiah 42:1-4) showed that the Messiah was indeed a king, but it illustrated what *kind* of king— a gentle ruler who brings justice to the nations. Like the crowd in Jesus' day, we may want Christ to rule as a king and bring great and visible victories in our life. But often Christ's work is quiet, and it happens according to *his* perfect timing, not ours.

**12:24** The Pharisees had already accused Jesus of being empowered by the prince of demons (9:34). They were trying to discredit him by using an emotional argument. Refusing to believe that Jesus came from God, they said he was in league with Satan. Jesus easily exposed the foolishness of their argument.

**12:25**
Matt 9:4

**12:27**
Matt 9:34
Acts 19:13

**12:28**
Acts 10:38

**12:30**
Mark 9:40
Luke 9:50

**12:31-32**
Mark 3:28-30
Luke 12:10

**12:33**
Matt 7:16-20
Luke 6:43-45

**12:34**
Matt 3:7; 23:33

**12:38**
Matt 16:1
Mark 8:11-12
Luke 11:16
John 2:18; 6:30
1 Cor 1:22

**12:38-42**
Matt 16:4

**12:40**
Jon 1:17

**12:41**
Jon 1:2; 3:5

25Jesus knew their thoughts and replied, "Any kingdom divided by civil war is doomed. A town or family splintered by feuding will fall apart. 26And if Satan is casting out Satan, he is divided and fighting against himself. His own kingdom will not survive. 27And if I am empowered by Satan, what about your own exorcists? They cast out demons, too, so they will condemn you for what you have said. 28But if I am casting out demons by the Spirit of God, then the Kingdom of God has arrived among you. 29For who is powerful enough to enter the house of a strong man like Satan and plunder his goods? Only someone even stronger—someone who could tie him up and then plunder his house.

30"Anyone who isn't with me opposes me, and anyone who isn't working with me is actually working against me.

31"So I tell you, every sin and blasphemy can be forgiven—except blasphemy against the Holy Spirit, which will never be forgiven. 32Anyone who speaks against the Son of Man can be forgiven, but anyone who speaks against the Holy Spirit will never be forgiven, either in this world or in the world to come.

33"A tree is identified by its fruit. If a tree is good, its fruit will be good. If a tree is bad, its fruit will be bad. 34You brood of snakes! How could evil men like you speak what is good and right? For whatever is in your heart determines what you say. 35A good person produces good things from the treasury of a good heart, and an evil person produces evil things from the treasury of an evil heart. 36And I tell you this, you must give an account on judgment day for every idle word you speak. 37The words you say will either acquit you or condemn you."

*Religious Leaders Ask Jesus for a Miraculous Sign* (75)
38One day some teachers of religious law and Pharisees came to Jesus and said, "Teacher, we want you to show us a miraculous sign to prove your authority."

39But Jesus replied, "Only an evil, adulterous generation would demand a miraculous sign; but the only sign I will give them is the sign of the prophet Jonah. 40For as Jonah was in the belly of the great fish for three days and three nights, so will the Son of Man be in the heart of the earth for three days and three nights.

41"The people of Nineveh will stand up against this generation on judgment day and

---

**12:25** In the Incarnation, Jesus gave up the complete and unlimited use of his supernatural abilities. But he still had profound insight into human nature. His discernment stopped the religious leaders' attempts to trick him. The resurrected Christ knows all our thoughts. This can be comforting because he knows what we really mean when we speak to him. It can be threatening because we cannot hide from him, and he knows any selfish motives.

**12:29** At Jesus' birth, Satan's power and control were disrupted. In the wilderness Jesus overcame Satan's temptations, and at the Resurrection he defeated Satan's ultimate weapon—death. Eventually Satan will be constrained forever (Revelation 20:10), and evil will no longer pervade the earth. Jesus has complete power and authority over Satan and all his forces.

**12:30** It is impossible to be neutral about Christ. Anyone who is not actively following him has chosen to reject him. Any person who tries to remain neutral in the struggle of good against evil is choosing to be separated from God, who alone is good. To refuse to follow Christ is to choose to be on Satan's team.

**12:31, 32** The Pharisees had blasphemed against the Spirit by attributing the power by which Christ did miracles to Satan (12:24) instead of the Holy Spirit. The unpardonable sin is the deliberate refusal to acknowledge God's power in Christ. It indicates a deliberate and irreversible hardness of heart. Sometimes believers worry that they have accidentally committed this unforgivable sin. But only those who have turned their backs on God and rejected all faith have any need to worry. Jesus said they can't be forgiven—not because their sin is worse than any other but because they will never ask for forgiveness. Whoever rejects the prompting of the Holy Spirit removes himself or herself from the only force that can lead him or her to repentance and restoration to God.

**12:34-36** Jesus reminds us that what we say reveals what is in our heart. What kinds of words come from your mouth? That is an indication of what is in your heart. You can't solve your heart problem, however, just by cleaning up your speech. You must

allow the Holy Spirit to fill you with new attitudes and motives; then your speech will be cleansed at its source.

**12:38-40** The Pharisees were asking for another miraculous sign, but they were not sincerely seeking to know Jesus. Jesus knew they had already seen enough miraculous proof to convince them that he was the Messiah if they would just open their hearts. But they had already decided not to believe in him, and more miracles would not change that.

Many people have said, "If I could just see a real miracle, then I could really believe in God." But Jesus' response to the Pharisees applies to us. We have plenty of evidence—Jesus' birth, death, resurrection, and ascension, and centuries of his work in believers around the world. Instead of looking for additional evidence or miracles, accept what God has already given and move forward. He may use your life as evidence to reach another person.

**12:39-41** Jonah was a prophet sent to the Assyrian city of Nineveh (see the book of Jonah). Because Assyria was such a cruel and warlike nation, Jonah tried to run from his assignment and ended up spending three days in the belly of a huge fish. When Jonah got out, he grudgingly went to Nineveh, preached God's message, and saw the city repent. By contrast, when Jesus came to his people, they refused to repent. Here Jesus is clearly saying that his resurrection will prove he is the Messiah. Three days after his death, Jesus will come back to life, just as Jonah was given a new chance at life after three days in the fish.

**12:41, 42** In Jonah's day, Nineveh was the capital of the Assyrian Empire, and it was as evil as it was powerful (Jonah 1:2). But the entire city repented at Jonah's preaching. The queen of Sheba traveled far to see Solomon, king of Israel, and learn about his great wisdom (1 Kings 10:1-10; also see the note on Luke 11:31, 32 for more on the queen of Sheba). These Gentiles recognized the truth about God when it was presented to them, unlike the religious leaders, who ignored the truth even though it stared them in the face. How have you responded to the evidence and truth that you have?

condemn it, for they repented of their sins at the preaching of Jonah. Now someone greater than Jonah is here—but you refuse to repent. 42 The queen of Sheba* will also stand up against this generation on judgment day and condemn it, for she came from a distant land to hear the wisdom of Solomon. Now someone greater than Solomon is here—but you refuse to listen.

43 "When an evil* spirit leaves a person, it goes into the desert, seeking rest but finding none. 44 Then it says, 'I will return to the person I came from.' So it returns and finds its former home empty, swept, and in order. 45 Then the spirit finds seven other spirits more evil than itself, and they all enter the person and live there. And so that person is worse off than before. That will be the experience of this evil generation."

### Jesus Describes His True Family (76/Mark 3:31-35; Luke 8:19-21)

46As Jesus was speaking to the crowd, his mother and brothers stood outside, asking to speak to him. 47 Someone told Jesus, "Your mother and your brothers are outside, and they want to speak to you."*

48Jesus asked, "Who is my mother? Who are my brothers?"49 Then he pointed to his disciples and said, "Look, these are my mother and brothers.50 Anyone who does the will of my Father in heaven is my brother and sister and mother!"

### Jesus Tells the Parable of the Four Soils (77/Mark 4:1-9; Luke 8:4-8)

**13** Later that same day Jesus left the house and sat beside the lake. 2A large crowd soon gathered around him, so he got into a boat. Then he sat there and taught as the people stood on the shore. 3He told many stories in the form of parables, such as this one:

"Listen! A farmer went out to plant some seeds. 4 As he scattered them across his field, some seeds fell on a footpath, and the birds came and ate them.5 Other seeds fell on shallow soil with underlying rock. The seeds sprouted quickly because the soil was shallow.6 But the plants soon wilted under the hot sun, and since they didn't have deep roots, they died.7 Other seeds fell among thorns that grew up and choked out the tender plants.8 Still other seeds fell on fertile soil, and they produced a crop that was thirty, sixty, and even a hundred times as much as had been planted!9 Anyone with ears to hear should listen and understand."

### Jesus Explains the Parable of the Four Soils (78/Mark 4:10-25; Luke 8:9-18)

10His disciples came and asked him, "Why do you use parables when you talk to the people?"

11He replied, "You are permitted to understand the secrets* of the Kingdom of Heaven, but others are not.12 To those who listen to my teaching, more understanding will be given, and they will have an abundance of knowledge. But for those who are not listening, even what little understanding they have will be taken away from them.13 That is why I use these parables,

**12:42** Greek *The queen of the south.*   **12:43** Greek *unclean.*   **12:47** Some manuscripts do not include verse 47. Compare Mark 3:32 and Luke 8:20.   **13:11** Greek *the mysteries.*

---

**12:43-45** Jesus was describing the attitude of the nation of Israel and the religious leaders in particular. Just cleaning up one's life without filling it with God leaves plenty of room for Satan to enter. The book of Ezra records how the people rid themselves of idolatry but failed to replace it with love for God and obedience to him. Ridding our life of sin is the first step. We must also take the second step: filling our life with God's Word and the Holy Spirit. Unfilled and complacent people are easy targets for Satan.

**12:46-50** Jesus was not denying his responsibility to his earthly family. On the contrary, he criticized the religious leaders for not following the Old Testament command to honor their parents (15:1-9). He provided for his mother's security as he hung on the cross (John 19:25-27). His mother and brothers were present in the upper room at Pentecost (Acts 1:14). Instead, Jesus was pointing out that spiritual relationships are as binding as physical ones, and he was paving the way for a new community of believers (the universal church), our spiritual family.

**13:2, 3** Jesus used many stories, or parables (13:34), when speaking to the crowds. These stories compare something familiar to something unfamiliar, helping us understand spiritual truth by using everyday objects and relationships. Jesus' parables compel

listeners to discover truth, while at the same time concealing the truth from those too lazy or too stubborn to see it. To those who are honestly searching, the truth becomes clear. We must be careful not to read too much into parables, forcing them to say what they don't mean. Each parable has a central meaning unless otherwise specified by Jesus.

**13:8** This parable should encourage spiritual "farmers"—those who teach, preach, and seek to lead others to the Lord. The farmer sowed good seed, but not all the seed sprouted; even the plants that grew had varying yields. Don't be discouraged if you do not always see results as you faithfully teach the Word. Belief cannot be forced to follow a mathematical formula (i.e., a 4:1 ratio of seeds planted to seeds sprouted). Rather, it is a miracle of God's Holy Spirit using your words to produce faith in Christ.

**13:9, 10** Human ears hear many sounds, but there is a deeper kind of listening that results in spiritual understanding. When speaking in parables, Jesus was not hiding truth from sincere seekers, because those who were receptive to spiritual truth understood the illustrations. To others they were only stories without meaning.

**13:12** This phrase means that we are responsible to use well what we have. When people reject Jesus, their hardness of heart drives away or renders useless even the little understanding they had.

---

**12:42**
1 Kgs 10:1-10
2 Chr 9:1-12
Matt 12:6

**12:45**
2 Pet 2:20

**12:46**
Mark 6:3
John 2:12; 7:3-5
Acts 1:14

**12:50**
John 15:14

**13:9**
Matt 11:15; 13:43

**13:11**
Matt 11:25; 16:17
1 Cor 2:10, 14
Col 1:27
1 Jn 2:20, 27

**13:12**
Matt 25:29
Mark 4:25
Luke 19:26

**13:13**
Jer 5:21

For they look, but they don't really see.
They hear, but they don't really listen or understand.

13:14-15
†Isa 6:9-10

14 This fulfills the prophecy of Isaiah that says,

'When you hear what I say,
    you will not understand.
When you see what I do,
    you will not comprehend.
15 For the hearts of these people are hardened,
    and their ears cannot hear,
and they have closed their eyes—
    so their eyes cannot see,
and their ears cannot hear,
    and their hearts cannot understand,
and they cannot turn to me
    and let me heal them.'*

13:17
John 8:56
Heb 11:13
1 Pet 1:10-12

16 "But blessed are your eyes, because they see; and your ears, because they hear. 17 I tell you the truth, many prophets and righteous people longed to see what you see, but they didn't see it. And they longed to hear what you hear, but they didn't hear it.

18 "Now listen to the explanation of the parable about the farmer planting seeds: 19 The seed that fell on the footpath represents those who hear the message about the Kingdom and don't understand it. Then the evil one comes and snatches away the seed that was planted in their hearts. 20 The seed on the rocky soil represents those who hear the message and immediately receive it with joy. 21 But since they don't have deep roots, they don't last long. They fall away as soon as they have problems or are persecuted for believing God's

13:22
Matt 19:23
Luke 12:16-21
1 Tim 6:9-10, 17

word. 22 The seed that fell among the thorns represents those who hear God's word, but all too quickly the message is crowded out by the worries of this life and the lure of wealth, so no fruit is produced. 23 The seed that fell on good soil represents those who truly hear and understand God's word and produce a harvest of thirty, sixty, or even a hundred times as much as had been planted!"

### Jesus Tells the Parable of the Weeds (80)

13:24
Mark 4:26-29

24 Here is another story Jesus told: "The Kingdom of Heaven is like a farmer who planted good seed in his field. 25 But that night as the workers slept, his enemy came and planted weeds among the wheat, then slipped away. 26 When the crop began to grow and produce grain, the weeds also grew.

27 "The farmer's workers went to him and said, 'Sir, the field where you planted that good seed is full of weeds! Where did they come from?'

28 "'An enemy has done this!' the farmer exclaimed.

"'Should we pull out the weeds?' they asked.

13:30
Matt 3:12

29 "'No,' he replied, 'you'll uproot the wheat if you do. 30 Let both grow together until the harvest. Then I will tell the harvesters to sort out the weeds, tie them into bundles, and burn them, and to put the wheat in the barn.'"

**13:14-15** Isa 6:9-10 (Greek version).

---

**13:22** How easy it is to agree with Christ with no intention of obeying. It is easy to denounce worries of this life and the deceitfulness of wealth and still do nothing to change our ways. In light of eternal life with God, are your present worries justified? If you had everything you could want but forfeited eternal life with God, would those things be so desirable?

**13:23** The four types of soil represent different responses to God's message. People respond differently because they are in different states of readiness. Some are hardened, others are shallow, others are contaminated by distracting worries, and some are receptive. How has God's Word taken root in your life? What kind of soil are you?

**13:24ff** Jesus gives the meaning of this parable in verses 36-43. All the parables in this chapter teach us about God and his Kingdom. They explain what the Kingdom is really like as opposed to our expectations of it. The Kingdom of Heaven is not a geographic

location but a spiritual realm where God rules and where we share in his eternal life. We join that Kingdom when we trust in Christ as Savior.

**13:30** The young weeds and the young blades of wheat look the same and can't be distinguished until they are grown and ready for harvest. Weeds (unbelievers) and wheat (believers) must live side by side in this world. God allows unbelievers to remain for a while, just as a farmer allows weeds to remain in his field so the surrounding wheat isn't uprooted with them. At the harvest, however, the weeds will be uprooted and thrown away. God's harvest (judgment) of all people is coming. We are to make ourselves ready by making sure that our faith is sincere.

### Jesus Tells the Parable of the Mustard Seed (81/Mark 4:30-34)

31 Here is another illustration Jesus used: "The Kingdom of Heaven is like a mustard seed planted in a field. 32 It is the smallest of all seeds, but it becomes the largest of garden plants; it grows into a tree, and birds come and make nests in its branches."

**13:32**
Ps 104:12
Ezek 17:23; 31:6

### Jesus Tells the Parable of the Yeast (82)

33 Jesus also used this illustration: "The Kingdom of Heaven is like the yeast a woman used in making bread. Even though she put only a little yeast in three measures of flour, it permeated every part of the dough."

**13:33**
Luke 13:20-21
1 Cor 5:6
Gal 5:9

34 Jesus always used stories and illustrations like these when speaking to the crowds. In fact, he never spoke to them without using such parables. 35 This fulfilled what God had spoken through the prophet:

**13:34**
John 16:25

**13:35**
†Ps 78:2

"I will speak to you in parables.
I will explain things hidden since the creation of the world.*"

### Jesus Explains the Parable of the Weeds (83)

36 Then, leaving the crowds outside, Jesus went into the house. His disciples said, "Please explain to us the story of the weeds in the field."

**13:36**
Matt 15:15

37 Jesus replied, "The Son of Man* is the farmer who plants the good seed. 38 The field is the world, and the good seed represents the people of the Kingdom. The weeds are the people who belong to the evil one. 39 The enemy who planted the weeds among the wheat is the devil. The harvest is the end of the world,* and the harvesters are the angels.

**13:38**
John 8:44
1 Jn 3:10

**13:39**
Joel 3:13
Rev 14:15

40 "Just as the weeds are sorted out and burned in the fire, so it will be at the end of the world. 41 The Son of Man will send his angels, and they will remove from his Kingdom everything that causes sin and all who do evil. 42 And the angels will throw them into the fiery furnace, where there will be weeping and gnashing of teeth. 43 Then the righteous will shine like the sun in their Father's Kingdom. Anyone with ears to hear should listen and understand!

**13:41**
Matt 24:31
Mark 13:27

**13:42**
Matt 8:12; 13:50;
22:13; 24:51; 25:30
Luke 13:28

### Jesus Tells the Parable of the Hidden Treasure (84)

44 "The Kingdom of Heaven is like a treasure that a man discovered hidden in a field. In his excitement, he hid it again and sold everything he owned to get enough money to buy the field.

**13:44**
Phil 3:7-8

**13:35** Some manuscripts do not include *of the world.* Ps 78:2.   **13:37** "Son of Man" is a title Jesus used for himself.
**13:39** Or *the age;* also in 13:40, 49.

---

**13:31, 32** The mustard seed was the smallest seed a farmer used. Jesus used this parable to show that the Kingdom has small beginnings but will grow and produce great results.

**13:33** In other Bible passages, yeast is used as a symbol of evil or uncleanness. Here it is a positive symbol of growth.

#### NAZARETH REJECTS JESUS

Chronologically, this return to Nazareth occurred after Jesus was in the Gadarene region and healed the demon-possessed men (8:28-34), then recrossed the sea to Capernaum. From there he traveled to Nazareth, where he had grown up, only to discover that the people refused to believe he was the Christ.

Although yeast looks like a minor ingredient, it permeates the whole loaf. Although the Kingdom began small and was nearly invisible, it would soon grow and have a great impact on the world.

**13:40-43** At the end of the world, angels will separate the evil from the good. There are true and false believers in churches today, but we should be cautious in our judgments because only Christ is qualified to make the final separation. If you start judging, you may damage some of the good "plants." It's more important to judge our own response to God than to analyze others' responses.

**13:42** Jesus often uses these terms to refer to the coming judgment. The weeping indicates sorrow or remorse, and gnashing of teeth shows extreme anxiety or pain. Those who say they don't care what happens to them after they die don't realize what they are saying. They will be punished for living in selfishness and indifference to God.

**13:43** Those who will shine like the sun in God's Kingdom stand in contrast to those who receive his judgment. A similar illustration is used in Daniel 12:3.

**13:44** The Kingdom of Heaven is more valuable than anything else we can have, and a person must be willing to give up everything to obtain it. The man who discovered the treasure hidden in the field stumbled upon it by accident but knew its value when he found it. Although the transaction cost the man everything, he paid nothing for the priceless treasure itself. It came free, with the field. Nothing is more precious than the Kingdom of Heaven; yet God gives it to us as a gift.

### Jesus Tells the Parable of the Pearl Merchant (85)
45 "Again, the Kingdom of Heaven is like a merchant on the lookout for choice pearls.
46 When he discovered a pearl of great value, he sold everything he owned and bought it!

### Jesus Tells the Parable of the Fishing Net (86)

**13:47**
Matt 22:10

47 "Again, the Kingdom of Heaven is like a fishing net that was thrown into the water and caught fish of every kind. 48When the net was full, they dragged it up onto the shore, sat down, and sorted the good fish into crates, but threw the bad ones away. 49 That is the way it will be at the end of the world. The angels will come and separate the wicked people from the righteous, 50 throwing the wicked into the fiery furnace, where there will be weeping and gnashing of teeth. 51Do you understand all these things?"

**13:50**
Matt 8:12; 13:42;
22:13; 24:51; 25:30
Luke 13:28

"Yes," they said, "we do."

52Then he added, "Every teacher of religious law who becomes a disciple in the Kingdom of Heaven is like a homeowner who brings from his storeroom new gems of truth as well as old."

## 5. Jesus encounters differing reactions to his ministry
### The People of Nazareth Refuse to Believe (91/Mark 6:1-6)

**13:53**
Matt 7:28
**13:54**
John 7:15
**13:55**
Matt 12:46
Luke 3:23
John 6:42
**13:57**
Luke 4:24
John 4:44

53When Jesus had finished telling these stories and illustrations, he left that part of the country. 54He returned to Nazareth, his hometown. When he taught there in the synagogue, everyone was amazed and said, "Where does he get this wisdom and the power to do miracles?" 55Then they scoffed, "He's just the carpenter's son, and we know Mary, his mother, and his brothers—James, Joseph,* Simon, and Judas. 56All his sisters live right here among us. Where did he learn all these things?" 57And they were deeply offended and refused to believe in him.

Then Jesus told them, "A prophet is honored everywhere except in his own hometown and among his own family." 58And so he did only a few miracles there because of their unbelief.

### Herod Kills John the Baptist (95/Mark 6:14-29; Luke 9:7-9)

**14** When Herod Antipas, the ruler of Galilee,* heard about Jesus, 2 he said to his advisers, "This must be John the Baptist raised from the dead! That is why he can do such miracles."

**14:3**
Luke 3:19-20
**14:4**
Lev 18:16; 20:21

3 For Herod had arrested and imprisoned John as a favor to his wife Herodias (the former wife of Herod's brother Philip). 4 John had been telling Herod, "It is against God's law for you

**13:55** Other manuscripts read *Joses;* still others read *John.*   **14:1** Greek *Herod the tetrarch.* Herod Antipas was a son of King Herod and was ruler over Galilee.

---

**13:45, 46** In this parable, the Kingdom of Heaven is not the precious pearl, but the merchant. In contrast to the previous picture, Jesus is now displaying another aspect of the Kingdom. The contrast becomes vivid in the transaction—the Kingdom pays the ultimate price to possess the pearl, the price God was willing to pay to redeem us.

**13:47-49** The parable of the fishing net has the same meaning as the parable of the wheat and weeds. We are to obey God and tell others about his grace and goodness, but we cannot dictate who is part of the Kingdom of Heaven and who is not. This sorting will be done at the last judgment by those infinitely more qualified than we.

**13:52** Anyone who understands God's real purpose in the law as revealed in the Old Testament has a real treasure. The Old Testament points the way to Jesus, the Messiah. Jesus always upheld its authority and relevance. But there is a double benefit for those who understand Jesus' teaching about the Kingdom of Heaven. This was a new treasure that Jesus was revealing. Both the old and new teaching give practical guidelines for faith and for living in the world. The teachers of religious law, however, were trapped in the old and blind to the new. They were looking for a future kingdom *preceded* by judgment. Jesus, however, taught that the Kingdom was *now,* and the judgment was future. The religious leaders were looking for a physical and temporal kingdom (via military rebellion and physical rule), but they were blind to the spiritual significance of the Kingdom that Christ brought.

**13:55** The residents of Jesus' hometown had known Jesus since he was a young child and were acquainted with his family; they

could not bring themselves to believe in his message. They were too close to the situation. Jesus had come to them as a prophet, one who challenged them to respond to unpopular spiritual truth. They did not listen to the timeless message because they could not see beyond the man.

**13:57** Jesus was not the first prophet to be rejected in his own country. Jeremiah experienced rejection in his hometown, even by members of his own family (Jeremiah 12:5, 6).

**13:58** Jesus did few miracles in his hometown "because of their unbelief." Unbelief blinds people to the truth and robs them of hope. These people missed the Messiah. How does your faith measure up? If you can't see God's work, perhaps it is because of your unbelief. Believe, ask God for a mighty work in your life, and expect him to act. Look with the eyes of faith.

**14:1** Herod Antipas was one of three rulers over the four districts of Palestine. His territory included the regions of Galilee and Perea. He was the son of Herod the Great, who ordered the killing of the babies in Bethlehem (2:16). He heard Jesus' case before Jesus' crucifixion (Luke 23:6-12). His Profile is found in Mark 6, p. 1629.

**14:2** For more information on John the Baptist, see his Profile in John 1, p. 1749.

**14:3** Philip, Herod's half brother, was another of Palestine's three rulers. His territories were Iturea and Traconitis, northeast of the Sea of Galilee (Luke 3:1). Philip's wife, Herodias, left Philip to live with Herod Antipas. John the Baptist condemned the two for living immorally (see Mark 6:17, 18).

to marry her." 5Herod wanted to kill John, but he was afraid of a riot, because all the people believed John was a prophet.

**14:5**
Matt 11:9; 21:26

6But at a birthday party for Herod, Herodias's daughter performed a dance that greatly pleased him, 7so he promised with a vow to give her anything she wanted. 8At her mother's urging, the girl said, "I want the head of John the Baptist on a tray!" 9Then the king regretted what he had said; but because of the vow he had made in front of his guests, he issued the necessary orders. 10So John was beheaded in the prison, 11 and his head was brought on a tray and given to the girl, who took it to her mother. 12Later, John's disciples came for his body and buried it. Then they went and told Jesus what had happened.

**14:10**
Matt 17:12
**14:12**
Acts 8:2

### Jesus Feeds Five Thousand (96/Mark 6:30-44; Luke 9:10-17; John 6:1-15)
13As soon as Jesus heard the news, he left in a boat to a remote area to be alone. But the crowds heard where he was headed and followed on foot from many towns. 14 Jesus saw the huge crowd as he stepped from the boat, and he had compassion on them and healed their sick.

**14:14**
Matt 9:36
Mark 1:41
Heb 2:17-18; 4:15;
5:1-3

15That evening the disciples came to him and said, "This is a remote place, and it's already getting late. Send the crowds away so they can go to the villages and buy food for themselves."

16But Jesus said, "That isn't necessary—you feed them."

17 "But we have only five loaves of bread and two fish!" they answered.

**14:16-20**
2 Kgs 4:42-44

18 "Bring them here," he said. 19Then he told the people to sit down on the grass. Jesus took the five loaves and two fish, looked up toward heaven, and blessed them. Then, breaking the loaves into pieces, he gave the bread to the disciples, who distributed it to the people. 20They all ate as much as they wanted, and afterward, the disciples picked up twelve baskets of leftovers. 21About 5,000 men were fed that day, in addition to all the women and children!

**14:19-22**
Matt 15:35-39
Mark 8:6-10

### Jesus Walks on Water (97/Mark 6:45-52; John 6:16-21)
22Immediately after this, Jesus insisted that his disciples get back into the boat and cross to the other side of the lake, while he sent the people home. 23After sending them home, he went up into the hills by himself to pray. Night fell while he was there alone.

**14:23**
Luke 9:28

24Meanwhile, the disciples were in trouble far away from land, for a strong wind had risen, and they were fighting heavy waves. 25About three o'clock in the morning* Jesus came toward them, walking on the water. 26When the disciples saw him walking on the water, they were terrified. In their fear, they cried out, "It's a ghost!"

**14:26**
Luke 24:37

**14:25** Greek *In the fourth watch of the night.*

---

**14:9** Herod did not want to kill John the Baptist, but he gave the order so that he wouldn't be embarrassed in front of his guests. How easy it is to give in to the crowd and to let ourselves be pressured into doing wrong. Don't get in a situation where it will be too embarrassing to do what is right. Determine to do what is right, no matter how embarrassing or painful it may be.

**14:13, 14** Jesus sought solitude after the news of John's death. Sometimes we may need to deal with our grief alone. Jesus did not dwell on his grief but returned to the ministry he came to do.

**14:14** Jesus performed some miracles as signs of his identity. He used other miracles to teach important truths. But here we read that he healed people because he "had compassion on them." Jesus was, and is, a loving, caring, and feeling person. When you are suffering, remember that Jesus hurts with you. He has compassion on you.

**JESUS WALKS ON THE SEA**
The miraculous feeding of the 5,000 occurred on the shores of the Sea of Galilee near Bethsaida. Jesus then sent his disciples across the lake. Several hours later they encountered a storm, and Jesus came to them—walking on the water. The boat then landed at Gennesaret.

**14:19-21** Jesus multiplied five loaves and two fish to feed over 5,000 people. What he was originally given seemed insufficient, but in his hands it became more than enough. We often feel that our contribution to Jesus is meager, but he can use and multiply whatever we give him, whether it is talent, time, or treasure. It is when we give them to Jesus that our resources are multiplied.

**14:21** The text states that there were 5,000 men present, *besides* women and children. Therefore, the total number of people Jesus fed could have been 10,000 to 15,000. The number of men is listed separately because in the Jewish culture of the day, men and women usually ate separately when in public. The children ate with the women.

**14:23** Seeking solitude was an important priority for Jesus (see also 14:13). He made room in his busy schedule to be alone with the Father. Spending time with God in prayer nurtures a vital

27But Jesus spoke to them at once. "Don't be afraid,"he said. "Take courage. I am here!*"

28Then Peter called to him, "Lord, if it's really you, tell me to come to you, walking on the water."

29 "Yes, come," Jesus said.

So Peter went over the side of the boat and walked on the water toward Jesus. 30But when he saw the strong* wind and the waves, he was terrified and began to sink. "Save me, Lord!" he shouted.

31Jesus immediately reached out and grabbed him. "You have so little faith," Jesus said. "Why did you doubt me?"

32When they climbed back into the boat, the wind stopped. 33Then the disciples worshiped him. "You really are the Son of God!" they exclaimed.

### Jesus Heals All Who Touch Him (98/Mark 6:53-56)

34After they had crossed the lake, they landed at Gennesaret. 35When the people recognized Jesus, the news of his arrival spread quickly throughout the whole area, and soon people were bringing all their sick to be healed. 36They begged him to let the sick touch at least the fringe of his robe, and all who touched him were healed.

### Jesus Teaches about Inner Purity (102/Mark 7:1-23)

**15** 1Some Pharisees and teachers of religious law now arrived from Jerusalem to see Jesus. They asked him, 2"Why do your disciples disobey our age-old tradition? For they ignore our tradition of ceremonial hand washing before they eat."

3Jesus replied, "And why do you, by your traditions, violate the direct commandments of God? 4 For instance, God says, 'Honor your father and mother,'* and 'Anyone who speaks disrespectfully of father or mother must be put to death.'*5 But you say it is all right for people to say to their parents, 'Sorry, I can't help you. For I have vowed to give to God what I would have given to you.'6 In this way, you say they don't need to honor their parents.* And so you cancel the word of God for the sake of your own tradition. 7 You hypocrites! Isaiah was right when he prophesied about you, for he wrote,

**14:27** Or *The 'I AM' is here*; Greek reads *I am*. See Exod 3:14.  **14:30** Some manuscripts do not include *strong*. **15:4a** Exod 20:12; Deut 5:16.  **15:4b** Exod 21:17 (Greek version); Lev 20:9 (Greek version).  **15:6** Greek *their father*; other manuscripts read *their father or their mother*.

**Marginal cross-references:**

14:31
Matt 6:30

14:33
Ps 2:7
Matt 16:16; 26:63; 27:54
Mark 1:1
Luke 22:70
John 1:49; 6:69
Rom 1:4

14:36
Matt 9:20-21

15:2
Luke 11:38

15:4
†Exod 20:12; 21:17
†Lev 20:9
†Deut 5:16
Matt 19:19
Mark 10:19
Luke 18:20
Eph 6:2

---

relationship with him and equips us to meet life's challenges and struggles. Develop the discipline of spending time alone with God. It will help you grow spiritually and become more and more like Christ.

**14:28** Peter was not putting Jesus to the test, something we are told not to do (4:7). Instead, he was the only one in the boat to react in faith. His impulsive request led him to experience a rather unusual demonstration of God's power. Peter started to sink because he took his eyes off Jesus and focused on the high waves around him. His faith wavered when he realized what he was doing. We probably will not walk on water, but we may walk through tough situations. If we focus on the waves of difficult circumstances around us without faith in Jesus to help, we, too, may despair and sink. To maintain your faith when situations are difficult, focus on Jesus' power rather than on your inadequacies.

**14:30, 31** Although we start out with good intentions, sometimes our faith falters. This doesn't necessarily mean we have failed. When Peter's faith faltered, he reached out to Christ, the only one who could help. He was afraid, but he still looked to Christ. When you are apprehensive about the troubles around you and doubt Christ's presence or ability to help, remember that he is always with you and is the *only* one who can really help.

**14:34** Gennesaret was located on the west side of the Sea of Galilee in a fertile, well-watered area.

**14:35, 36** The people recognized Jesus as a great healer, but how many understood who he truly was? They came to Jesus for physical healing, but did they come for spiritual healing? They came to prolong their lives on earth, not to seek eternal life. People may follow Jesus to learn valuable lessons from his life or in hopes of finding relief from pain. But we miss Jesus' whole message if we seek him only to heal our bodies but not our souls, if we look to him for help only in this life, rather than for his eter-

nal plan for us. Only when we understand the real Jesus Christ can we appreciate how he can truly change our life.

**14:36** Jewish men wore fringe on the lower edges of their robes according to God's command (Deuteronomy 22:12). By Jesus' day, elaborate versions of this fringe were seen as a sign of holiness (23:5). There is no indication that the fringe on Jesus' robe was anything more than typical. It was natural that people seeking healing should reach out and touch the fringe of his robe. But as one sick woman learned, healing came from faith and not from Jesus' robe (9:19-22).

**15:1, 2** The Pharisees and teachers of religious law came from Jerusalem, the center of Jewish authority, to scrutinize Jesus' activities. Over the centuries since the Jews' return from Babylonian captivity, hundreds of religious traditions had been added to God's laws. The Pharisees and teachers of religious law considered them all equally important. Many traditions are not bad in themselves. Certain religious traditions can add richness and meaning to life. But we must not assume that because our traditions have been practiced for years, they should be elevated to a sacred standing. God's principles never change, and his law doesn't need additions. Traditions should help us understand God's laws better, not become laws themselves.

**15:5, 6** This was the practice of *Corban* (literally, "offering"; see Mark 7:11). Anyone who made a Corban vow was required to dedicate money to God's Temple that otherwise would have gone to support his parents. Corban had become a religiously acceptable way to neglect parents, circumventing the child's responsibility to them. Although the action—giving money to God—seemed worthy and no doubt conferred prestige on the giver, many people who took the Corban vow were disregarding God's command to care for needy parents. These religious leaders were ignoring God's clear command to honor their parents.

8 'These people honor me with their lips,
   but their hearts are far from me.
9 Their worship is a farce,
   for they teach man-made ideas as commands from God.'* "

10 Then Jesus called to the crowd to come and hear. "Listen," he said, "and try to understand. 11It's not what goes into your mouth that defiles you; you are defiled by the words that come out of your mouth."

12 Then the disciples came to him and asked, "Do you realize you offended the Pharisees by what you just said?"

13Jesus replied, "Every plant not planted by my heavenly Father will be uprooted, 14 so ignore them. They are blind guides leading the blind, and if one blind person guides another, they will both fall into a ditch."

15Then Peter said to Jesus, "Explain to us the parable that says people aren't defiled by what they eat."

16 "Don't you understand yet?" Jesus asked. 17 "Anything you eat passes through the stomach and then goes into the sewer. 18 But the words you speak come from the heart—that's what defiles you. 19 For from the heart come evil thoughts, murder, adultery, all sexual immorality, theft, lying, and slander. 20 These are what defile you. Eating with unwashed hands will never defile you."

### Jesus Sends a Demon Out of a Girl (103/Mark 7:24-30)

21 Then Jesus left Galilee and went north to the region of Tyre and Sidon. 22A Gentile* woman who lived there came to him, pleading, "Have mercy on me, O Lord, Son of David! For my daughter is possessed by a demon that torments her severely."

23But Jesus gave her no reply, not even a word. Then his disciples urged him to send her away. "Tell her to go away," they said. "She is bothering us with all her begging."

24Then Jesus said to the woman, "I was sent only to help God's lost sheep—the people of Israel."

15:8-9 Isa 29:13 (Greek version).    15:22 Greek *Canaanite*.

**15:8-9**
†Isa 29:13

**15:9**
Col 2:20-22

**15:11**
Matt 12:34
Acts 10:14-15

**15:13**
Isa 60:21; 61:3
John 15:2
1 Cor 3:9

**15:14**
Matt 23:16, 24
Luke 6:39
Rom 2:19

**15:18**
Matt 12:34
Jas 3:6

**15:19**
Rom 1:29-31
1 Cor 5:10-11;
6:9-10
Gal 5:19-21

**15:24**
Matt 10:6
Rom 15:8

---

**15:8, 9** The prophet Isaiah also criticized hypocrites (Isaiah 29:13), and Jesus applied Isaiah's words to these religious leaders. The Pharisees knew a lot about God, but they didn't know God. When we claim to honor God while our heart is far from him, our worship means nothing. It is not enough to study about religion or even to study the Bible; it is not enough to act religious. Our actions and our attitudes must be sincere. If they are not, Isaiah's words also describe us.

**15:11** Jesus was referring to the Jewish regulations concerning food and drink. This verse could be paraphrased: "You aren't made unclean by eating nonkosher food! It is what you *say* and *think*

### MINISTRY IN PHOENICIA

After preaching again in Capernaum, Jesus left Galilee for Phoenicia, where he preached in Tyre and Sidon. On his return, he traveled through the region of Decapolis (Ten Towns), fed the 4,000 beside the sea, then crossed to Magadan.

that makes you unclean!" This statement offended the Pharisees, who were very concerned about what people ate and drank.

**15:13, 14** Jesus told his disciples to leave the Pharisees alone because the Pharisees were blind to God's truth. Anyone who listened to their teaching would risk spiritual blindness as well. Not all religious leaders clearly see God's truth. Make sure that those you listen to and learn from are those with good spiritual eyesight—they teach and follow the principles of Scripture.

**15:15** Later Peter would be faced with the issue of clean and unclean food (see the notes on 15:11 and Acts 10:12). Then he would learn that nothing should be a barrier to proclaiming the Good News to the Gentiles (non-Jews).

**15:16-20** We work hard to keep our outward appearance attractive, but what is deep down in our heart (where others can't see) is more important to God. What are you like inside? When people become Christians, God makes them different on the inside. He will continue the process of change inside them if they only ask. God wants us to have healthy thoughts and motives, not just healthy bodies.

**15:23** Puzzled by Jesus' silence, the disciples asked him to get rid of the woman because she was bothering them with her persistent begging. They showed no compassion for her or sensitivity to her needs. It is possible to become so occupied with spiritual matters that we become oblivious to the needs around us. This may be true especially if we are prejudiced against needy people or if they cause us inconvenience. Instead of being annoyed, be aware of the opportunities that surround you, and make an effort to look for ways to minister to others.

**15:24** Jesus' words do not contradict the truth that God's message is for all people (Psalm 22:27; Isaiah 56:7; Matthew 28:19; Romans 15:9-12). After all, when Jesus said these words, he was in Gentile territory on a mission to Gentile people. He ministered to Gentiles on many other occasions also. Jesus was simply telling

**15:25**
Matt 8:2

25 But she came and worshiped him, pleading again, "Lord, help me!"

26 Jesus responded, "It isn't right to take food from the children and throw it to the dogs."

27 She replied, "That's true, Lord, but even dogs are allowed to eat the scraps that fall beneath their masters' table."

**15:28**
Matt 8:10

28 "Dear woman," Jesus said to her, "your faith is great. Your request is granted." And her daughter was instantly healed.

### Jesus Heals Many People (**104**/Mark 7:31-37)

**15:30**
Isa 35:5-6
Matt 4:23; 11:5
Luke 7:22

29 Jesus returned to the Sea of Galilee and climbed a hill and sat down. 30 A vast crowd brought to him people who were lame, blind, crippled, those who couldn't speak, and many others. They laid them before Jesus, and he healed them all. 31 The crowd was amazed! Those who hadn't been able to speak were talking, the crippled were made well, the lame were walking, and the blind could see again! And they praised the God of Israel.

### Jesus Feeds Four Thousand (**105**/Mark 8:1-10)

**15:32**
Matt 9:36

32 Then Jesus called his disciples and told them, "I feel sorry for these people. They have been here with me for three days, and they have nothing left to eat. I don't want to send them away hungry, or they will faint along the way."

**15:33**
Mark 6:37
John 6:5

33 The disciples replied, "Where would we get enough food here in the wilderness for such a huge crowd?"

**15:34-37**
Matt 14:17-20
Mark 6:38-43
Luke 9:13-17
John 6:9-13

34 Jesus asked, "How much bread do you have?"

They replied, "Seven loaves, and a few small fish."

35 So Jesus told all the people to sit down on the ground. 36 Then he took the seven loaves and the fish, thanked God for them, and broke them into pieces. He gave them to the disciples, who distributed the food to the crowd.

**15:37**
Matt 16:10
**15:38**
Matt 14:21
Mark 6:44

37 They all ate as much as they wanted. Afterward, the disciples picked up seven large baskets of leftover food. 38 There were 4,000 men who were fed that day, in addition to all the women and children. 39 Then Jesus sent the people home, and he got into a boat and crossed over to the region of Magadan.

### Leaders Demand a Miraculous Sign (**106**/Mark 8:11-13)

**16:1**
Matt 12:38
Luke 11:16
John 6:30

**16** One day the Pharisees and Sadducees came to test Jesus, demanding that he show them a miraculous sign from heaven to prove his authority.

**16:2-3**
Luke 12:54-56

2 He replied, "You know the saying, 'Red sky at night means fair weather tomorrow; 3 red sky in the morning means foul weather all day.' You know how to interpret the weather signs in the sky, but you don't know how to interpret the signs of the times!* 4 Only an evil,

**16:4**
Matt 12:39
Luke 11:29

**16:2-3** Several manuscripts do not include any of the words in 16:2-3 after *He replied.*

---

the woman that Jews were to have the first opportunity to accept him as the Messiah because God wanted them to present the message of salvation to the rest of the world (see Genesis 12:3). Jesus was not rejecting the Gentile woman. He may have wanted to test her faith, or he may have wanted to use the situation as another opportunity to teach that faith is available to all people.

**15:26-28** *Dog* was a term the Jews commonly applied to Gentiles because the Jews considered these pagan people no more likely than dogs to receive God's blessing. Jesus was not degrading the woman by using this term; he was reflecting the Jews' attitude so as to contrast it with his own. The woman did not argue. Instead, using Jesus' choice of words, she agreed to be considered a dog as long as she could receive God's blessing for her daughter. Ironically, many Jews would lose God's blessing and salvation because they rejected Jesus, and many Gentiles would find salvation because they recognized and accepted him.

**15:29-31** A vast crowd was brought to Jesus to be healed, and he healed them all. Jesus is still able to heal people who are suffering physically, emotionally, and spiritually, and we can be the ones who bring suffering people to him. Whom do you know that needs Christ's healing touch? You can bring them to Jesus through prayer or through explaining to them the reason for the hope that you have (1 Peter 3:15). Then let Christ do the healing.

**15:32ff** This feeding of 4,000 is a separate event from the feeding of the 5,000 (14:13-21), confirmed by Mark 8:19, 20. This was the beginning of Jesus' expanded ministry to the Gentiles.

**15:33** Jesus had already fed more than 5,000 people with five loaves and two fish. Here, in a similar situation, the disciples were again perplexed. How easily we throw up our hands in despair when faced with difficult situations. Like the disciples, we often forget that if God has cared for us in the past, he will do the same now. When facing a difficult situation, remember that God cares for you and trust him to work faithfully again.

**16:1** The Pharisees and Sadducees were Jewish religious leaders of two different parties, and their views were diametrically opposed on many issues. The Pharisees carefully followed their religious rules and traditions, believing that this was the way to God. They also believed in the authority of all Scripture and in the resurrection of the dead. The Sadducees accepted only the books of Moses as Scripture and did not believe in life after death. In Jesus, however, these two groups had a common enemy, and they joined forces to try to kill him. For more information on the Pharisees and Sadducees, see the charts in chapter 3, p. 1541 and Mark 2, p. 1617.

**16:1** The Pharisees and Sadducees demanded a sign "from heaven." They tried to explain away Jesus' other miracles as sleight of hand, coincidence, or use of evil power, but they believed that only God could do a sign in the sky. This, they were sure, would be a feat beyond Jesus' power. Although Jesus could have easily impressed them, he refused. He knew that even a miracle in the sky would not convince them he was the Messiah because they had already decided not to believe in him.

adulterous generation would demand a miraculous sign, but the only sign I will give them is the sign of the prophet Jonah.*" Then Jesus left them and went away.

### Jesus Warns against Wrong Teaching (107/Mark 8:14-21)

5Later, after they crossed to the other side of the lake, the disciples discovered they had forgotten to bring any bread. 6 "Watch out!" Jesus warned them. "Beware of the yeast of the Pharisees and Sadducees."

7At this they began to argue with each other because they hadn't brought any bread. 8Jesus knew what they were saying, so he said, "You have so little faith! Why are you arguing with each other about having no bread?9 Don't you understand even yet? Don't you remember the 5,000 I fed with five loaves, and the baskets of leftovers you picked up?10 Or the 4,000 I fed with seven loaves, and the large baskets of leftovers you picked up?11 Why can't you understand that I'm not talking about bread? So again I say, 'Beware of the yeast of the Pharisees and Sadducees.' "

12Then at last they understood that he wasn't speaking about the yeast in bread, but about the deceptive teaching of the Pharisees and Sadducees.

### Peter Says Jesus Is the Messiah (109/Mark 8:27-30; Luke 9:18-20)

13When Jesus came to the region of Caesarea Philippi, he asked his disciples, "Who do people say that the Son of Man is?"*

14 "Well," they replied, "some say John the Baptist, some say Elijah, and others say Jeremiah or one of the other prophets."

15Then he asked them, "But who do you say I am?"

16Simon Peter answered, "You are the Messiah,* the Son of the living God."

17 Jesus replied, "You are blessed, Simon son of John,* because my Father in heaven has revealed this to you. You did not learn this from any human being. 18 Now I say to you that

**16:6** Luke 12:1

**16:9** Matt 14:14-21 Mark 6:34-44 Luke 9:11-17 John 6:1-13

**16:10** Matt 15:32-38 Mark 8:1-9

**16:11** Luke 12:1

**16:14** Mark 6:14-15

**16:16** Matt 1:16; 14:33 Mark 14:61 John 1:34, 49; 6:69; 11:27; 20:31

**16:18** John 1:42 1 Cor 3:11 Eph 2:20-22; 4:15-16 1 Pet 2:4-5

16:4 Greek *the sign of Jonah*.   16:13 "Son of Man" is a title Jesus used for himself.   16:16 Or *the Christ. Messiah* (a Hebrew term) and *Christ* (a Greek term) both mean "the anointed one."   16:17 Greek *Simon bar-Jonah;* see John 1:42; 21:15-17.

---

**16:4** By using the sign of Jonah, who was inside a great fish for three days, Jesus was predicting his death and resurrection (see also 12:38-42).

**16:4** Many people, like these Jewish leaders, say they want to see a miracle so that they can believe. But Jesus knew that miracles never convince the skeptical. Jesus had been healing, raising people from the dead, and feeding thousands, and still people wanted him to prove himself. Do you doubt Christ because you haven't *seen* a miracle? Do you expect God to prove himself to you personally before you believe? Jesus says, "Blessed are those who believe without seeing me" (John 20:29). We have miracles recorded in the Old and New Testaments, 2,000 years of church history, and the witness of thousands. With all this

evidence, those who won't believe are either too proud or too stubborn. If you simply step forward in faith and believe, then you will begin to see the miracles that God can do in your life!

**16:12** Yeast is put into bread to make it rise, and it takes only a little to affect a whole batch of dough. Jesus used yeast as an example of how a small amount of evil can affect a large group of people. The wrong teachings of the Pharisees and Sadducees were leading many people astray. Beware of the tendency to say, "How can this little wrong possibly affect anyone?"

**16:13** Caesarea Philippi was located several miles north of the Sea of Galilee, in the territory ruled by Philip. The influence of Greek and Roman culture was everywhere, and pagan temples and idols abounded. When Philip became ruler, he rebuilt and renamed the city after the emperor (Caesar) and himself. The city was originally called Caesarea, the same name as the capital city of Philip's brother Herod's territory.

**16:13-17** The disciples answered Jesus' question with the common view—that Jesus was one of the great prophets come back to life. This belief may have stemmed from Deuteronomy 18:18, where God said he would raise up a prophet from among the people. (John the Baptist's Profile is in John 1, p. 1749; Elijah's Profile is in 1 Kings 17, p. 545; and Jeremiah's Profile is in Jeremiah 2, p. 1201.) Peter, however, confessed Jesus as divine and as the promised and long-awaited Messiah. If Jesus were to ask you this question, how would you answer? Is he your Lord and Messiah?

**16:18** The rock on which Jesus would build his church has been identified as (1) Jesus himself (his work of salvation by dying for us on the cross); (2) Peter (the first great leader in the church at Jerusalem); (3) the confession of faith that Peter gave and that all subsequent true believers would give. It seems most likely that the rock refers to Peter as the leader of the church. Just as Peter had revealed the true identity of Christ, so Jesus revealed Peter's identity and role.

Later, Peter reminds Christians that they are the church built

**JOURNEY TO CAESAREA PHILIPPI**

Jesus left Magadan, crossed the lake, and landed in Bethsaida. There he healed a man who had been born blind. From there, he and his disciples went to Caesarea Philippi, where Peter confessed Jesus as the Messiah and Son of God.

you are Peter (which means 'rock'),* and upon this rock I will build my church, and all the powers of hell* will not conquer it. ¹⁹ And I will give you the keys of the Kingdom of Heaven. Whatever you forbid* on earth will be forbidden in heaven, and whatever you permit* on earth will be permitted in heaven."

²⁰Then he sternly warned the disciples not to tell anyone that he was the Messiah.

### Jesus Predicts His Death the First Time (110/Mark 8:31–9:1; Luke 9:21-27)

²¹From then on Jesus* began to tell his disciples plainly that it was necessary for him to go to Jerusalem, and that he would suffer many terrible things at the hands of the elders, the leading priests, and the teachers of religious law. He would be killed, but on the third day he would be raised from the dead.

²² But Peter took him aside and began to reprimand him* for saying such things. "Heaven forbid, Lord," he said. "This will never happen to you!"

²³ Jesus turned to Peter and said, "Get away from me, Satan! You are a dangerous trap to me. You are seeing things merely from a human point of view, not from God's."

²⁴Then Jesus said to his disciples, "If any of you wants to be my follower, you must turn from your selfish ways, take up your cross, and follow me. ²⁵ If you try to hang on to your life, you will lose it. But if you give up your life for my sake, you will save it. ²⁶ And what do you benefit if you gain the whole world but lose your own soul?* Is anything worth more than

**16:19**
Isa 22:22
Matt 18:18
John 20:23
Rev 1:18; 3:7

**16:21**
John 2:19
1 Cor 15:3-4

**16:23**
Matt 4:10

**16:24**
Matt 10:38
Luke 14:27

**16:25**
Matt 10:39
Luke 17:33
John 12:25

**16:26**
Ps 49:7-9
Matt 4:8-9

**16:18a** Greek *that you are Peter.*  **16:18b** Greek *and the gates of Hades.*  **16:19a** Or *bind,* or *lock.*  **16:19b** Or *loose,* or *open.*  **16:21** Some manuscripts read *Jesus the Messiah.*  **16:22** Or *began to correct him.*  **16:26** Or *your self?* also in 16:26b.

---

on the foundation of the apostles and prophets, with Jesus Christ as the cornerstone (1 Peter 2:4-6). All believers are joined into this church by faith in Jesus Christ as Savior, the same faith that Peter expressed here (see also Ephesians 2:20, 21). Jesus praised Peter for his confession of faith. It is faith like Peter's that is the foundation of Christ's Kingdom.

**16:19** The meaning of this verse has been a subject of debate for centuries. Some say the "keys" represent the authority to carry out church discipline, legislation, and administration (18:15-18), while others say the keys give the authority to announce the forgiveness of sins (John 20:23). Still others say the keys may be the opportunity to bring people to the Kingdom of Heaven by presenting them with the message of salvation found in God's Word (Acts 15:7-9). The religious leaders thought they held the keys of the Kingdom, and they tried to shut some people out. We cannot decide to open or close the Kingdom of Heaven for others, but God uses us to help others find the way inside. To all who believe in Christ and obey his words, the Kingdom doors are swung wide open.

**16:20** Jesus warned the disciples not to publicize Peter's confession because they did not yet fully understand the kind of Messiah he had come to be—not a military commander but a suffering servant. They needed to come to a full understanding of Jesus and their mission as disciples before they could proclaim it to others in a way that would not cause a rebellion. They would have a difficult time understanding what Jesus came to do until his earthly mission was complete.

**16:21** The phrase "From then on" marks a turning point. In 4:17 it signaled Jesus' announcement of the Kingdom of Heaven. Here it points to his new emphasis on his death and resurrection. The disciples still didn't grasp Jesus' true purpose because of their preconceived notions about what the Messiah should be. This is the first of three times that Jesus predicted his death (see 17:22, 23; 20:18 for others).

**16:21-28** This passage corresponds to Daniel's prophecies: The Messiah would be cut off (Daniel 9:26); there would be a period of trouble (Daniel 9:27); and the king would come in glory (Daniel 7:13, 14). The disciples would endure the same suffering as their King and, like him, would be rewarded in the end.

**16:22** Peter, Jesus' friend and devoted follower who had just eloquently proclaimed Jesus' true identity, sought to protect him from the suffering he prophesied. But if Jesus hadn't

suffered and died, Peter would have died in his sins. Great temptations can come from those who love us and seek to protect us. Be cautious of advice from a friend who says, "Surely God doesn't want you to face this." Often our most difficult temptations come from those who are only trying to protect us from discomfort.

**16:23** In his wilderness temptations, Jesus heard the message that he could achieve greatness without dying (4:9). Here he heard the same message from Peter. Peter had just recognized Jesus as Messiah; here, however, he forsook God's perspective and evaluated the situation from a human one. Satan is always trying to get us to leave God out of the picture. Jesus rebuked Peter for this attitude.

**16:24** When Jesus used this picture of his followers taking up their crosses to follow him, the disciples knew what he meant. Crucifixion was a common Roman method of execution, and condemned criminals had to carry their cross through the streets to the execution site. Following Jesus, therefore, meant a true commitment, the risk of death, and no turning back (see 10:39).

**16:25** The possibility of losing their lives was very real for the disciples as well as for Jesus. Real discipleship implies real commitment—pledging our whole existence to his service. If we try to save our physical life from death, pain, or discomfort, we may risk losing eternal life. If we protect ourselves from the pain God calls us to suffer, we begin to die spiritually and emotionally. Our lives turn inward, and we lose our intended purpose. When we give our life in service to Christ, however, we discover the real purpose of living.

**16:26** When we don't know Christ, we make choices as though there were no afterlife. In reality, this life is just the introduction to eternity. How we live this brief span determines our eternal state. What we accumulate on earth has no value in gaining eternal life. Even the highest social or civic honors cannot earn us entrance into heaven. Evaluate your lifestyle from an eternal perspective, and you will find your values and decisions changing.

your soul? 27 For the Son of Man will come with his angels in the glory of his Father and will judge all people according to their deeds. 28And I tell you the truth, some standing here right now will not die before they see the Son of Man coming in his Kingdom."

16:27
Prov 24:12
Matt 25:31
Rev 22:12

## Jesus Is Transfigured on the Mountain (111/Mark 9:2-13; Luke 9:28-36)

**17** Six days later Jesus took Peter and the two brothers, James and John, and led them up a high mountain to be alone. 2As the men watched, Jesus' appearance was transformed so that his face shone like the sun, and his clothes became as white as light. 3Suddenly, Moses and Elijah appeared and began talking with Jesus.

17:2
2 Pet 1:16-18

4Peter exclaimed, "Lord, it's wonderful for us to be here! If you want, I'll make three shelters as memorials*—one for you, one for Moses, and one for Elijah."

5But even as he spoke, a bright cloud overshadowed them, and a voice from the cloud said, "This is my dearly loved Son, who brings me great joy. Listen to him." 6The disciples were terrified and fell face down on the ground.

17:5
Ps 2:7
Matt 3:17; 12:18
Mark 1:11
Luke 3:22
2 Pet 1:17

7Then Jesus came over and touched them. "Get up," he said. "Don't be afraid." 8And when they looked up, Moses and Elijah were gone, and they saw only Jesus.

9As they went back down the mountain, Jesus commanded them, "Don't tell anyone what you have seen until the Son of Man* has been raised from the dead."

10Then his disciples asked him, "Why do the teachers of religious law insist that Elijah must return before the Messiah comes?*"

17:10-11
Mal 4:5-6
Luke 1:16-17

11Jesus replied, "Elijah is indeed coming first to get everything ready. 12 But I tell you, Elijah has already come, but he wasn't recognized, and they chose to abuse him. And in the same way they will also make the Son of Man suffer." 13Then the disciples realized he was talking about John the Baptist.

17:12
Matt 11:14

## Jesus Heals a Demon-Possessed Boy (112/Mark 9:14-29; Luke 9:37-43)

14At the foot of the mountain, a large crowd was waiting for them. A man came and knelt before Jesus and said, 15 "Lord, have mercy on my son. He has seizures and suffers terribly. He often falls into the fire or into the water. 16 So I brought him to your disciples, but they couldn't heal him."

**17:4** Greek *three tabernacles*. **17:9** "Son of Man" is a title Jesus used for himself. **17:10** Greek *that Elijah must come first?*

---

**16:27** Jesus Christ has been given the authority to judge all the earth (Romans 14:9-11; Philippians 2:9-11). Although his judgment is already working in our lives, there is a future, final judgment when Christ returns (25:31-46) and everyone's life will be reviewed and evaluated. This will not be confined to unbelievers; Christians, too, will face a judgment. Their eternal destiny is secure, but Jesus will look at how they handled gifts, opportunities, and responsibilities in order to determine their heavenly rewards. At the time of judgment, God will deliver the righteous and condemn the wicked. We should not judge others' salvation; that is God's work.

**16:28** Because all the disciples died *before* Christ's return, many believe that Jesus' words were fulfilled at the Transfiguration when Peter, James, and John saw his glory (17:1-3). Others say this statement refers to the Resurrection (Matthew 28; Mark 16; Luke 24; John 20) and Ascension of Jesus (Acts 1). Still others believe that Pentecost (Acts 2) and the beginning of Christ's church fulfilled Jesus' words. In any case, certain disciples were eyewitnesses to the power and glory of Christ's Kingdom.

**17:1ff** The Transfiguration was a vision, a brief glimpse of the true glory of the King (16:27, 28). This was a special revelation of Jesus' divinity to three of the disciples, and it was God's divine affirmation of everything Jesus had done and was about to do.

**17:3** The Transfiguration was a foretaste of heaven; the participants were doing something worth noting—talking together. In God's world, interactions count highly. People are individuals, with minds, hearts, and opinions. People are also part of a wider whole, connected by relationships built on sharing between whole persons. Friendship is the key. Make time and opportunities to talk with others. Good conversations act as training for eternity.

**17:3-5** Moses and Elijah were the two greatest prophets in the Old Testament. Moses represents the law, or the old covenant.

He wrote the Pentateuch, and he predicted the coming of a great prophet (Deuteronomy 18:15-19). Elijah represents the prophets who foretold the coming of the Messiah (Malachi 4:5, 6). Moses' and Elijah's presence with Jesus confirmed Jesus' messianic mission: to fulfill God's law and the words of God's prophets. Just as God's voice in the cloud over Mount Sinai gave authority to his law (Exodus 19:9), God's voice at the Transfiguration gave authority to Jesus' words.

**17:4** Peter wanted to build three memorials for these three great men. Peter had the right idea about Christ, but his timing was wrong. Peter wanted to act, but this was a time for worship and adoration. He wanted to memorialize the moment, but he was supposed to learn and move on.

**17:5** Jesus is more than just a great leader, a good example, a good influence, or a great prophet. He is the Son of God. When you understand this profound truth, the only adequate response is worship. When you have a correct understanding of Christ, you will obey him.

**17:9** Jesus told Peter, James, and John not to tell anyone what they had seen until after his resurrection because Jesus knew that they didn't fully understand it and could not explain what they didn't understand. Their question (17:10ff) revealed their misunderstandings. They knew that Jesus was the Messiah, but they had much more to learn about the significance of his death and resurrection.

**17:10-12** Based on Malachi 4:5, 6, the teachers of the Old Testament law believed that Elijah must appear before the Messiah would appear. Jesus referred to John the Baptist, not to the Old Testament prophet Elijah. John the Baptist took on Elijah's prophetic role, boldly confronting sin and pointing people to God. Malachi had prophesied that a prophet like Elijah would come (Malachi 4:5).

**17:17**
Deut 32:5, 20

**17:18**
Matt 8:13; 9:22;
15:28

**17:20**
Matt 21:21
Mark 11:23
Luke 17:6
1 Cor 13:2

17 Jesus said, "You faithless and corrupt people! How long must I be with you? How long must I put up with you? Bring the boy here to me." 18Then Jesus rebuked the demon in the boy, and it left him. From that moment the boy was well.

19Afterward the disciples asked Jesus privately, "Why couldn't we cast out that demon?"

20 "You don't have enough faith," Jesus told them. "I tell you the truth, if you had faith even as small as a mustard seed, you could say to this mountain, 'Move from here to there,' and it would move. Nothing would be impossible.*"

### Jesus Predicts His Death the Second Time (113/Mark 9:30-32; Luke 9:44-45)

22After they gathered again in Galilee, Jesus told them, "The Son of Man is going to be betrayed into the hands of his enemies. 23He will be killed, but on the third day he will be raised from the dead." And the disciples were filled with grief.

### Peter Finds the Coin in the Fish's Mouth (114)

**17:24**
Exod 30:13

**17:25**
Matt 22:17-22
Rom 13:7

24On their arrival in Capernaum, the collectors of the Temple tax* came to Peter and asked him, "Doesn't your teacher pay the Temple tax?"

25"Yes, he does," Peter replied. Then he went into the house.

But before he had a chance to speak, Jesus asked him, "What do you think, Peter?* Do kings tax their own people or the people they have conquered?*"

26"They tax the people they have conquered," Peter replied.

"Well, then," Jesus said, "the citizens are free! 27However, we don't want to offend them, so go down to the lake and throw in a line. Open the mouth of the first fish you catch, and you will find a large silver coin.* Take it and pay the tax for both of us."

### The Disciples Argue about Who Would Be the Greatest (115/Mark 9:33-37; Luke 9:46-48)

**18** About that time the disciples came to Jesus and asked, "Who is greatest in the Kingdom of Heaven?"

**17:20** Some manuscripts add verse 21, *But this kind of demon won't leave except by prayer and fasting.* Compare Mark 9:29.   **17:24** Greek *the two-drachma [tax]*; also in 17:24b. See Exod 30:13-16; Neh 10:32-33.   **17:25a** Greek *Simon?*   **17:25b** Greek *their sons or others?*   **17:27** Greek *a stater* [a Greek coin equivalent to four drachmas].

---

**17:17** The disciples had been given the authority to do the healing, but they had not yet learned how to appropriate the power of God. Jesus' frustration is with the unbelieving and unresponsive generation. His disciples were merely a reflection of that attitude in this instance. Jesus' purpose was not to criticize the disciples but to encourage them to greater faith.

**17:17-20** The disciples had been unable to cast out this demon, and they asked Jesus why. He said their faith was too small. It is the power of God, plus our faith, that moves mountains. The mustard seed was the smallest particle imaginable. Jesus said that even faith as small or undeveloped as a mustard seed would have been sufficient. Perhaps the disciples had tried to cast out the demon with their own ability rather than God's. There is great potential in even a little faith when we trust in God's power to act. If we feel weak or powerless as Christians, we should examine our faith, making sure we are trusting God's power, not our own ability to produce results.

**17:20** Jesus wasn't condemning the disciples for substandard faith; he was trying to show how important faith would be in their future ministry. If you are facing a problem that seems as big and immovable as a mountain, turn your eyes from the mountain and look to Christ for more faith. Only then will you be able to overcome the obstacles that may stand in your way.

**17:22, 23** Once again Jesus predicted his death (see also 16:21); but more important, he told them of his resurrection. Unfortunately, the disciples heard only the first part of Jesus' words and became discouraged. They couldn't understand that Jesus wanted to go back to Jerusalem, where he would walk right into trouble.

The disciples didn't fully comprehend the purpose of Jesus' death and resurrection until Pentecost (Acts 2). They didn't know that Jesus' death and resurrection would make his Kingdom possible. We shouldn't get upset at ourselves for being unable to understand everything about Jesus. After all, the disciples spent three years with him, saw his miracles, heard his words, and still

had difficulty understanding. Despite their questions and doubts, however, they believed. We should do no less.

**17:24** All Jewish males had to pay a Temple tax to support Temple upkeep (Exodus 30:11-16). Tax collectors set up booths to collect these taxes. Only Matthew records this incident—perhaps because he had been a tax collector himself.

**17:24-27** Peter answered a question without really knowing the answer, putting Jesus and the disciples in an awkward position. Jesus used this situation, however, to emphasize his kingly role. Just as kings pay no taxes and collect none from their family, Jesus, the King, owed no taxes. But Jesus supplied the tax payment for both himself and Peter rather than offend those who didn't understand his kingship. Although Jesus supplied the tax money, Peter had to go and get it. Ultimately all that we have comes to us from God's supply, but he may want us to be active in the process.

**17:24-27** As God's people, we are foreigners on earth because our loyalty is always to our real King—Jesus. Still we have to cooperate with the authorities and be responsible citizens. An ambassador to another country keeps the local laws in order to represent well the one who sent him. We are Christ's ambassadors (2 Corinthians 5:20). Are you being a good foreign ambassador for him to this world?

**18:1** From Mark's Gospel we learn that Jesus precipitated this conversation by asking the disciples what they had been discussing among themselves earlier (Mark 9:33, 34).

**18:1-4** Jesus used a child to help his self-centered disciples get the point. We are not to be *childish* (like the disciples, arguing over petty issues) but *childlike*, with humble and sincere hearts. In what areas of your life do you tend to struggle with childishness? In what ways are you making progress with childlikeness?

2 Jesus called a little child to him and put the child among them. 3 Then he said, "I tell you the truth, unless you turn from your sins and become like little children, you will never get into the Kingdom of Heaven. 4 So anyone who becomes as humble as this little child is the greatest in the Kingdom of Heaven.

5 "And anyone who welcomes a little child like this on my behalf* is welcoming me. 6 But if you cause one of these little ones who trusts in me to fall into sin, it would be better for you to have a large millstone tied around your neck and be drowned in the depths of the sea.

### Jesus Warns against Temptation (117/Mark 9:42-50)

7 "What sorrow awaits the world, because it tempts people to sin. Temptations are inevitable, but what sorrow awaits the person who does the tempting. 8 So if your hand or foot causes you to sin, cut it off and throw it away. It's better to enter eternal life with only one hand or one foot than to be thrown into eternal fire with both of your hands and feet. 9 And if your eye causes you to sin, gouge it out and throw it away. It's better to enter eternal life with only one eye than to have two eyes and be thrown into the fire of hell.*

### Jesus Warns against Looking Down on Others (118)

10 "Beware that you don't look down on any of these little ones. For I tell you that in heaven their angels are always in the presence of my heavenly Father.*

12 "If a man has a hundred sheep and one of them wanders away, what will he do? Won't he leave the ninety-nine others on the hills and go out to search for the one that is lost? 13 And if he finds it, I tell you the truth, he will rejoice over it more than over the ninety-nine that didn't wander away! 14 In the same way, it is not my heavenly Father's will that even one of these little ones should perish.

### Jesus Teaches How to Treat a Believer Who Sins (119)

15 "If another believer* sins against you,* go privately and point out the offense. If the other person listens and confesses it, you have won that person back. 16 But if you are unsuccessful, take one or two others with you and go back again, so that everything you say may be confirmed by two or three witnesses. 17 If the person still refuses to listen, take your case to the church. Then if he or she won't accept the church's decision, treat that person as a pagan or a corrupt tax collector.

18 "I tell you the truth, whatever you forbid* on earth will be forbidden in heaven, and whatever you permit* on earth will be permitted in heaven.

**18:5** Greek *in my name.* **18:9** Greek *the Gehenna of fire.* **18:10** Some manuscripts add verse 11, *And the Son of Man came to save those who are lost.* Compare Luke 19:10. **18:15a** Greek *If your brother.* **18:15b** Some manuscripts do not include *against you.* **18:18a** Or *bind,* or *lock.* **18:18b** Or *loose,* or *open.*

**18:3**
Matt 19:14
Mark 10:15
Luke 18:17
1 Pet 2:2

**18:4**
Matt 20:26-27
Mark 10:43-44
Luke 22:26

**18:5**
Matt 10:40
Luke 10:16
John 13:20

**18:6-9**
1 Cor 8:12-13

**18:8-9**
Matt 5:29-30

**18:10**
Acts 12:15
Heb 1:14

**18:15**
Lev 19:17
Gal 6:1
Jas 5:19-20

**18:16**
†Deut 19:15
2 Cor 13:1
1 Tim 5:19

**18:17**
1 Cor 6:1-6

**18:18**
Matt 16:19
John 20:23

**18:3, 4** The disciples had become so preoccupied with the organization of Jesus' earthly kingdom that they had lost sight of its divine purpose. Instead of seeking a place of service, they sought positions of advantage. It is easy to lose our eternal perspective and compete for promotions or status in the church. It is difficult, but healthy, to identify with "children"—weak and dependent people with no status or influence.

**18:6** Children are trusting by nature. Because they trust adults, they are easily led to faith in Christ. God holds parents and other adults accountable for how they influence these little ones. Jesus warned that anyone who turns little children away from faith in him will receive severe punishment.

**18:7ff** Jesus warned the disciples about two ways to cause others to sin: tempting them (18:7-9) and neglecting or demeaning them (18:10-14). As leaders, we are to help young people or new believers avoid anything or anyone that could cause them to stumble in their faith and lead them to sin. We must never take lightly the spiritual education and protection of those young in age or young in the faith.

**18:8, 9** We must remove stumbling blocks that cause us to sin. This does not mean to cut off a part of the body. For the church it means that any person, program, or teaching that threatens the spiritual growth of the body must be removed. For the individual, any relationship, practice, or activity that leads to sin should be stopped. Jesus says it would be better to go to heaven with one hand than to hell with both. Sin, of course, affects more than our hands; it affects our mind and hearts.

**18:12-14** Just as a shepherd is concerned enough about one lost sheep to go search the hills for it, so God is concerned about every human being he has created (he "does not want anyone to be destroyed," 2 Peter 3:9). If you come in contact with children in your neighborhood who need Christ, steer them toward him by your example, your words, and your acts of kindness.

**18:15-17** These are Jesus' guidelines for dealing with those who sin against us. They were meant for (1) Christians, not unbelievers, (2) sins committed against *you* and not others, and (3) conflict resolution in the context of the church, not the community at large. Jesus' words are not a license for a frontal attack on every person who hurts or slights us. They are not a license to start a destructive gossip campaign or to call for a church trial. They are designed to reconcile those who disagree so that all Christians can live in harmony.

When someone wrongs us, we often do the opposite of what Jesus recommends. We turn away in hatred or resentment, seek revenge, or engage in gossip. By contrast, we should go to that person *first,* as difficult as that may be. Then we should forgive that person as often as he or she needs it (18:21, 22). This will create a much better chance of restoring the relationship.

**18:18** This *forbidding* and *permitting* refers to the decisions of the church in conflicts. Among believers, there should need to be no court of appeals beyond the church. Ideally, the church's decisions should be God-guided and based on discernment of his Word. Believers have the responsibility, therefore, to bring their problems to the church, and the church has the responsibility

**18:19**
Matt 7:7; 21:22
Mark 11:24
John 15:7; 16:23
1 Jn 3:22; 5:14-15

**18:20**
Matt 28:20
John 14:23

**18:21-22**
Luke 17:3-4

**18:23**
Matt 25:19

**18:25**
Lev 25:39
2 Kgs 4:1
Neh 5:5

**18:27**
Luke 7:42

**18:34**
Matt 5:25-26
Luke 12:58-59

**18:35**
Matt 6:15
Mark 11:25
Eph 4:32
Col 3:13

19 "I also tell you this: If two of you agree here on earth concerning anything you ask, my Father in heaven will do it for you. 20 For where two or three gather together as my followers,* I am there among them."

### Jesus Tells the Parable of the Unforgiving Debtor (120)

21 Then Peter came to him and asked, "Lord, how often should I forgive someone* who sins against me? Seven times?"

22 "No, not seven times," Jesus replied, "but seventy times seven!*

23 "Therefore, the Kingdom of Heaven can be compared to a king who decided to bring his accounts up to date with servants who had borrowed money from him. 24 In the process, one of his debtors was brought in who owed him millions of dollars.* 25 He couldn't pay, so his master ordered that he be sold—along with his wife, his children, and everything he owned—to pay the debt.

26 "But the man fell down before his master and begged him, 'Please, be patient with me, and I will pay it all.' 27 Then his master was filled with pity for him, and he released him and forgave his debt.

28 "But when the man left the king, he went to a fellow servant who owed him a few thousand dollars.* He grabbed him by the throat and demanded instant payment.

29 "His fellow servant fell down before him and begged for a little more time. 'Be patient with me, and I will pay it,' he pleaded. 30 But his creditor wouldn't wait. He had the man arrested and put in prison until the debt could be paid in full.

31 "When some of the other servants saw this, they were very upset. They went to the king and told him everything that had happened. 32 Then the king called in the man he had forgiven and said, ' You evil servant! I forgave you that tremendous debt because you pleaded with me. 33 Shouldn't you have mercy on your fellow servant, just as I had mercy on you?' 34 Then the angry king sent the man to prison to be tortured until he had paid his entire debt.

35 "That's what my heavenly Father will do to you if you refuse to forgive your brothers and sisters* from your heart."

**18:20** Greek *gather together in my name.*    **18:21** Greek *my brother.*    **18:22** Or *seventy-seven times.*    **18:24** Greek *10,000 talents* [375 tons or 340 metric tons of silver].    **18:28** Greek *100 denarii.* A denarius was equivalent to a laborer's full day's wage.    **18:35** Greek *your brother.*

---

**JESUS AND FORGIVENESS**

| Jesus forgave . . . | Reference |
|---|---|
| the paralyzed man lowered on a mat through the roof | Matthew 9:2-8 |
| the woman caught in adultery | John 8:3-11 |
| the woman who anointed his feet with perfume | Luke 7:44-50 |
| Peter, for denying he knew Jesus | John 18:15-18, 25-27; 21:15-19 |
| the criminal on the cross | Luke 23:39-43 |
| the people who crucified him | Luke 23:34 |

Jesus not only taught frequently about forgiveness, he also demonstrated his own willingness to forgive. Here are several examples that should be an encouragement to recognize his willingness to forgive us also.

---

to use God's guidance in seeking to resolve conflicts. Handling problems God's way will have an impact now and for eternity.

**18:19, 20** Jesus looked ahead to a new day when he would be present with his followers not in body, but through his Holy Spirit. In the body of believers (the church), the sincere agreement of two people in prayer is more powerful than the superficial agreement of thousands, because Christ's Holy Spirit is with them. Two or more believers, *filled with the Holy Spirit,* will pray according to God's will, not their own; thus, their requests will be granted.

**18:22** The rabbis taught that people should forgive those who offend them—but only three times. Peter, trying to be especially generous, asked Jesus if seven (the "perfect" number) was enough times to forgive someone. But Jesus answered, "Seventy times seven," meaning that we shouldn't even keep track of how many times we forgive someone. We

should always forgive those who are truly repentant, no matter how many times they ask.

**18:30** In Bible times, serious consequences awaited those who could not pay their debts. A person lending money could seize the borrower who couldn't pay and force him or his family to work until the debt was paid. The debtor could also be thrown into prison, or his family could be sold into slavery to help pay off the debt. It was hoped that the debtor, while in prison, would sell off his landholdings or that relatives would pay the debt. If not, the debtor could remain in prison for life.

**18:35** Because God has forgiven all our sins, we should not withhold forgiveness from others. As we realize how completely Christ has forgiven us, it should produce an attitude of forgiveness toward others. When we don't forgive others, we are setting ourselves above Christ's law of love.

## 6. Jesus faces conflict with the religious leaders

*Jesus Teaches about Marriage and Divorce* (**173**/Mark 10:1-12)

**19** When Jesus had finished saying these things, he left Galilee and went down to the region of Judea east of the Jordan River. ²Large crowds followed him there, and he healed their sick.

³Some Pharisees came and tried to trap him with this question: "Should a man be allowed to divorce his wife for just any reason?"

⁴ "Haven't you read the Scriptures?" Jesus replied. "They record that from the beginning 'God made them male and female.'* ⁵And he said, 'This explains why a man leaves his father and mother and is joined to his wife, and the two are united into one.'* ⁶ Since they are no longer two but one, let no one split apart what God has joined together."

⁷"Then why did Moses say in the law that a man could give his wife a written notice of divorce and send her away?"* they asked.

⁸ Jesus replied, "Moses permitted divorce only as a concession to your hard hearts, but it was not what God had originally intended. ⁹And I tell you this, whoever divorces his wife and marries someone else commits adultery—unless his wife has been unfaithful.*"

¹⁰ Jesus' disciples then said to him, "If this is the case, it is better not to marry!"

¹¹ "Not everyone can accept this statement," Jesus said. "Only those whom God helps. ¹²Some are born as eunuchs, some have been made eunuchs by others, and some choose not to marry* for the sake of the Kingdom of Heaven. Let anyone accept this who can."

*Jesus Blesses the Children* (**174**/Mark 10:13-16; Luke 18:15-17)

¹³One day some parents brought their children to Jesus so he could lay his hands on them and pray for them. But the disciples scolded the parents for bothering him.

¹⁴ But Jesus said, "Let the children come to me. Don't stop them! For the Kingdom of Heaven belongs to those who are like these children." ¹⁵And he placed his hands on their heads and blessed them before he left.

**19:2**
Matt 4:23

**19:3**
Matt 5:31

**19:4**
†Gen 1:27; 5:2

**19:5**
†Gen 2:24
1 Cor 6:16
Eph 5:31

**19:7**
†Deut 24:1
Matt 5:31

**19:9**
Matt 5:32
Luke 16:18
1 Cor 7:10-11

**19:11**
1 Cor 7:7-9, 17

**19:12**
1 Cor 7:32, 34

**19:14**
Matt 18:2-3

**19:4** Gen 1:27; 5:2.  **19:5** Gen 2:24.  **19:7** See Deut 24:1.  **19:9** Some manuscripts add *And anyone who marries a divorced woman commits adultery.* Compare Matt 5:32.  **19:12** Greek *and some make themselves eunuchs.*

---

**19:3-12** John had been put in prison and killed, at least in part for his public opinions on marriage and divorce, so the Pharisees hoped to trap Jesus, too. They were trying to trick Jesus by having him choose sides in a theological controversy. Two schools of thought represented two opposing views of divorce. One group supported divorce for almost any reason. The other believed that divorce could be allowed only for marital unfaithfulness. This conflict hinged on how each group interpreted Deuteronomy 24:1-4. In his answer, however, Jesus focused on marriage rather than divorce. He pointed out that God intended marriage to be permanent and gave four reasons for the importance of marriage (19:4-6).

**19:4-6** Today, many homosexuals want to commit to "marry" with the blessing of the church. Reasons for homosexual feelings and desires are complex and serious. Christians should not trivialize the situation or flippantly condemn the homosexual person. But Jesus made God's ideal very plain: At creation he approved one kind of marriage bond, man to woman. These become one flesh—one before God. See Romans 1:24-27 for further discussion.

Where does that leave homosexual marriage? At best, it is a human invention without any biblical precedent. God created man and woman. Heterosexual monogamy is God's plan for marriage—the best plan, the only one.

**19:7, 8** This law is found in Deuteronomy 24:1-4. In Moses' day, as well as in Jesus' day, the practice of marriage fell far short of God's intention. The same is true today. Jesus said that Moses gave this law only because of the people's hard hearts—permanent marriage was God's intention. But because sinful human nature made divorce inevitable, Moses instituted some

laws to help its victims. These were civil laws designed especially to protect the women who, in that culture, were quite vulnerable when living alone. Because of Moses' law, a man could no longer just throw his wife out—he had to write a formal letter of dismissal. This was a radical step toward civil rights, for it made men think twice about divorce. God designed marriage to be indissoluble. Instead of looking for reasons to leave each other, husbands and wives should concentrate on how to stay together (19:3-9).

**19:10-12** Although divorce was relatively easy in Old Testament times (19:7), it is not what God originally intended. Couples should decide against divorce from the start and build their marriage on mutual commitment. There are also many good reasons for not marrying, one being to have more time to work for God's Kingdom. Don't assume that God wants everyone to marry. For many it may be better if they don't. Be sure that you prayerfully seek God's will before you make the lifelong commitment of marriage.

**19:12** A "eunuch" is an emasculated male—a man with no testicles. Jesus' point here is that some people have physical limitations that prevent their marrying, while others choose not to marry because, in their particular situation, they can serve God better as single people. Jesus was not teaching us to avoid marriage because it is inconvenient or takes away our freedom. That would be selfishness. A good reason to remain single is to use the time and freedom to serve God. Paul elaborates on this in 1 Corinthians 7.

**19:13-15** The disciples must have forgotten what Jesus had said about children (18:4-6). Jesus wanted little children to come to him because he loves them and because they have a guileless trust in God. All people need childlike faith in God. The receptiveness of little children was a great contrast to the stubbornness of the religious leaders, who let their education and sophistication stand in the way of the simple faith needed to believe in Jesus.

## Jesus Speaks to the Rich Young Man (175/Mark 10:17-31; Luke 18:18-30)

**19:16**
Matt 19:29
Luke 10:25

16Someone came to Jesus with this question: "Teacher,* what good deed must I do to have eternal life?"

**19:17**
Lev 18:5
Luke 10:28

17 "Why ask me about what is good?" Jesus replied. "There is only One who is good. But to answer your question—if you want to receive eternal life, keep* the commandments."

**19:18**
†Exod 20:12-16
†Deut 5:17-21

18"Which ones?" the man asked.

And Jesus replied: "'You must not murder. You must not commit adultery. You must not steal. You must not testify falsely. 19Honor your father and mother. Love your neighbor as yourself.'* "

**19:19**
Exod 20:12
†Lev 19:18
Deut 5:16
Matt 5:43-44; 22:39
Luke 10:27
Rom 13:9

20"I've obeyed all these commandments," the young man replied. "What else must I do?"

**19:21**
Acts 2:45; 4:34-37

21Jesus told him, "If you want to be perfect, go and sell all your possessions and give the money to the poor, and you will have treasure in heaven. Then come, follow me."

**19:23**
Matt 13:22
1 Tim 6:9-10

22 But when the young man heard this, he went away sad, for he had many possessions.

23Then Jesus said to his disciples, "I tell you the truth, it is very hard for a rich person to enter the Kingdom of Heaven. 24I'll say it again—it is easier for a camel to go through the eye of a needle than for a rich person to enter the Kingdom of God!"

**19:26**
Gen 18:14
Job 42:2
Jer 32:17
Zech 8:6

25The disciples were astounded. "Then who in the world can be saved?" they asked.

26Jesus looked at them intently and said, "Humanly speaking, it is impossible. But with God everything is possible."

**19:27**
Matt 4:19

27Then Peter said to him, "We've given up everything to follow you. What will we get?"

**19:16** Some manuscripts read *Good Teacher.* **19:17** Some manuscripts read *continue to keep.* **19:18-19** Exod 20:12-16; Deut 5:16-20; Lev 19:18.

---

**19:16** To this man seeking assurance of eternal life, Jesus pointed out that salvation does not come from good deeds unaccompanied by love for God. The man needed a whole new starting point. Instead of adding another commandment to keep or good deed to perform, the young man needed to submit humbly to the lordship of Christ.

**19:17ff** In response to the young man's question about what good deed he needed to do in order to be assured of eternal life, Jesus told him to keep God's Ten Commandments. Jesus then listed six of them, all referring to relationships with others. When the young man replied that he had kept the commandments, Jesus told him that he must do something more—sell everything and give the money to the poor. Jesus' statement exposed the man's weakness. In reality, his wealth was his god, his idol, and he would not give it up. Thus, he violated the first and greatest commandment (Exodus 20:3; Matthew 22:36-40).

**19:21** When Jesus told this young man that he would "be perfect" if he gave everything he had to the poor, Jesus wasn't speaking in the temporal, human sense. He was explaining how to be justified and made whole or complete in God's sight.

**19:21** Should all believers sell everything they own? No. We are responsible to care for our own needs and the needs of our families so as not to be a burden on others. We should, however, be willing to give up anything if God asks us to do so. This kind of attitude allows nothing to come between us and God and keeps us from using our God-given wealth selfishly. If you are relieved by the fact that Christ did not tell all his followers to sell all their possessions, then you may be too attached to what you have.

**19:22** We cannot love God with all our heart and yet keep our money to ourselves. Loving him totally means using our money in ways that please him.

**19:24-26** Because it is impossible for a camel to go through the eye of a needle, it appears impossible for a rich person to get into the Kingdom of Heaven. The disciples were astounded. They thought that if anyone could be saved, it would be the rich, whom their culture considered especially blessed by God. Jesus explained, however, that "with God everything is possible" (19:26). Even rich people can enter the Kingdom if God brings them in. Faith in Christ, not in self or riches, is what counts. On what are you counting for salvation?

**19:27** In the Bible, God gives rewards to his people according to his justice. In the Old Testament, obedience often brought reward in this life (Deuteronomy 28), but obedience and immediate reward are not always linked. If they were, good people would always be rich, and suffering would always be a sign of sin. As believers, our reward is God's presence and power through his indwelling Holy Spirit. Later, in eternity, we will be rewarded for our faith and service. If material rewards in this life came to us for every faithful deed, we would be tempted to boast about our achievements and act out of wrong motivations.

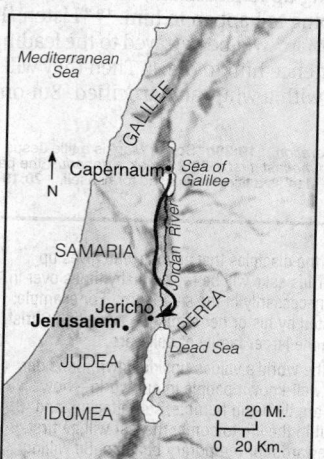

### JESUS TRAVELS TOWARD JERUSALEM

Jesus left Galilee for the last time—heading toward Jerusalem and death. He again crossed the Jordan, spending some time in Perea before going on to Jericho.

28 Jesus replied, "I assure you that when the world is made new* and the Son of Man* sits upon his glorious throne, you who have been my followers will also sit on twelve thrones, judging the twelve tribes of Israel. 29 And everyone who has given up houses or brothers or sisters or father or mother or children or property, for my sake, will receive a hundred times as much in return and will inherit eternal life. 30 But many who are the greatest now will be least important then, and those who seem least important now will be the greatest then.*

**19:28**
Luke 22:28-30
Rev 3:21

**19:30**
Matt 20:16
Mark 10:31
Luke 13:30

## Jesus Tells the Parable of the Vineyard Workers (176)

**20** "For the Kingdom of Heaven is like the landowner who went out early one morning to hire workers for his vineyard. 2 He agreed to pay the normal daily wage* and sent them out to work.

**20:1**
Matt 21:28, 33

3 "At nine o'clock in the morning he was passing through the marketplace and saw some people standing around doing nothing. 4 So he hired them, telling them he would pay them whatever was right at the end of the day. 5 So they went to work in the vineyard. At noon and again at three o'clock he did the same thing.

6 "At five o'clock that afternoon he was in town again and saw some more people standing around. He asked them, 'Why haven't you been working today?'

7 "They replied, 'Because no one hired us.'

"The landowner told them, 'Then go out and join the others in my vineyard.'

8 "That evening he told the foreman to call the workers in and pay them, beginning with the last workers first. 9 When those hired at five o'clock were paid, each received a full day's wage. 10 When those hired first came to get their pay, they assumed they would receive more. But they, too, were paid a day's wage. 11 When they received their pay, they protested to the owner, 12 'Those people worked only one hour, and yet you've paid them just as much as you paid us who worked all day in the scorching heat.'

**20:8**
Lev 19:13
Deut 24:15

13 "He answered one of them, 'Friend, I haven't been unfair! Didn't you agree to work all day for the usual wage? 14 Take your money and go. I wanted to pay this last worker the same as you. 15 Is it against the law for me to do what I want with my money? Should you be jealous because I am kind to others?'

**20:15**
Deut 15:9

**20:16**
Matt 19:30
Mark 10:31
Luke 13:30

16 "So those who are last now will be first then, and those who are first will be last."

## Jesus Predicts His Death the Third Time (177/Mark 10:32-34; Luke 18:31-34)

17 As Jesus was going up to Jerusalem, he took the twelve disciples aside privately and told them what was going to happen to him. 18 "Listen," he said, "we're going up to Jerusalem, where the Son of Man* will be betrayed to the leading priests and the teachers of religious law. They will sentence him to die. 19 Then they will hand him over to the Romans* to be mocked, flogged with a whip, and crucified. But on the third day he will be raised from the dead."

**20:18-19**
Matt 16:21;
17:22-23
Luke 9:22
Acts 2:23

**19:28a** Or *in the regeneration.* **19:28b** "Son of Man" is a title Jesus used for himself. **19:30** Greek *But many who are first will be last; and the last, first.* **20:2** Greek *a denarius,* the payment for a full day's labor; similarly in 20:9, 10, 13. **20:18** "Son of Man" is a title Jesus used for himself. **20:19** Greek *the Gentiles.*

---

**19:29** Jesus assured the disciples that anyone who gives up something valuable for his sake will be repaid many times over in this life, although not necessarily in the same form. For example, a person may be rejected by his or her family for accepting Christ, but he or she will gain the larger family of believers.

**19:30** Jesus turned the world's values upside down. Consider the most powerful or well-known people in our world—how many got where they are by being humble, self-effacing, and gentle? Not many! But in the life to come, the last will be first. Don't forfeit eternal rewards for temporary benefits. Be willing to make sacrifices now for greater rewards later. Be willing to accept human disapproval, while knowing that you have God's approval.

**20:1ff** Jesus further clarified the membership rules of the Kingdom of Heaven: Entrance is by God's grace alone. In this parable, God is the landowner and believers are the workers. This parable speaks especially to those who feel superior because of heritage or position, to those who feel superior because they have spent

so much time with Christ, and to new believers as reassurance of God's grace.

**20:15** This parable is not about rewards but about salvation. It is a strong teaching about *grace,* God's generosity. We shouldn't begrudge those who turn to God in the last moments of life, because, in reality, *no one* deserves eternal life.

Many people we don't expect to see in the Kingdom will be there. The criminal who repented as he was dying (Luke 23:40-43) will be there along with people who have believed and served God for many years. Do you resent God's gracious acceptance of the despised, the outcast, and the sinners who have turned to him for forgiveness? Have you ever been jealous of what God has given to another person? Instead, focus on God's gracious benefits to you, and be thankful for what you have.

**20:17-19** Jesus predicted his death and resurrection for the third time (see 16:21 and 17:22, 23 for the first two times). But the disciples still didn't accept and believe what he meant. They continued to argue over their positions in Christ's Kingdom (20:20-28).

### Jesus Teaches about Serving Others (178/Mark 10:35-45)

**20:21**
Matt 19:28

20Then the mother of James and John, the sons of Zebedee, came to Jesus with her sons. She knelt respectfully to ask a favor. 21 "What is your request?" he asked.

She replied, "In your Kingdom, please let my two sons sit in places of honor next to you, one on your right and the other on your left."

**20:22**
Matt 26:39, 42
Mark 14:36
Luke 22:42
John 18:11

22 But Jesus answered by saying to them, "You don't know what you are asking! Are you able to drink from the bitter cup of suffering I am about to drink?"

"Oh yes," they replied, "we are able!"

**20:23**
Acts 12:2
Rev 1:9

23 Jesus told them, "You will indeed drink from my bitter cup. But I have no right to say who will sit on my right or my left. My Father has prepared those places for the ones he has chosen."

**20:26**
Matt 23:11
Mark 9:35
Luke 9:48

24When the ten other disciples heard what James and John had asked, they were indignant. 25 But Jesus called them together and said, "You know that the rulers in this world lord it over their people, and officials flaunt their authority over those under them. 26 But among

**20:28**
Isa 53:10
Phil 2:7
1 Tim 2:6
1 Pet 1:18-19

you it will be different. Whoever wants to be a leader among you must be your servant, 27 and whoever wants to be first among you must become your slave. 28 For even the Son of Man came not to be served but to serve others and to give his life as a ransom for many."

### Jesus Heals Two Blind Beggars (179/Mark 10:46-52; Luke 18:35-43)

29As Jesus and the disciples left the town of Jericho, a large crowd followed behind. 30Two blind men were sitting beside the road. When they heard that Jesus was coming that way, they began shouting, "Lord, Son of David, have mercy on us!"

31"Be quiet!" the crowd yelled at them.

But they only shouted louder, "Lord, Son of David, have mercy on us!"

32When Jesus heard them, he stopped and called, "What do you want me to do for you?"

33"Lord," they said, "we want to see!" 34Jesus felt sorry for them and touched their eyes. Instantly they could see! Then they followed him.

---

**20:20** The mother of James and John came to Jesus and "knelt respectfully to ask a favor." She gave Jesus worship, but her real motive was to get something from him. Too often this happens in our churches and in our life. We play religious games, expecting God to give us something in return. True worship, however, adores and praises Christ for who he is and for what he has done.

**20:20** The mother of James and John asked Jesus to give her sons special positions in his Kingdom. Parents naturally want to see their children promoted and honored, but this desire is dangerous if it causes them to stand in the way of God's specific will for their children. God may have different work in mind for them—perhaps not as glamorous but just as important. Thus, parents' desires for their children's advancement must be held in check as they pray that God's will be done in their children's lives.

**20:20** According to 27:56, the mother of James and John was at the cross when Jesus was crucified. Some have suggested that she was the sister of Mary, the mother of Jesus. A close family relationship may have prompted her to make this request for her sons.

**20:22** James, John, and their mother failed to grasp Jesus' previous teachings on rewards (19:16-30) and eternal life (20:1-16). They failed to understand the suffering they must face before living in the glory of God's Kingdom. The "cup" was the suffering and crucifixion that Christ faced. Both James and John would also face great suffering. James would be put to death for his faith, and John would be exiled.

**20:23** Jesus was showing that he was under the authority of the Father, who alone makes the decisions about leadership in heaven. Such rewards are not granted as favors. They are for those who have maintained their commitment to Jesus in spite of severe trials.

**20:24** The other disciples were upset with James and John for trying to grab the top positions. *All* the disciples wanted to be the greatest (18:1), but Jesus taught them that the greatest person in

God's Kingdom is the servant of all. Authority is given, not for self-importance, ambition, or respect, but for useful service to God and his creation.

**20:27** Jesus described leadership from a new perspective. Instead of using people, we are to serve them. Jesus' mission was to serve others and to give his life away. A real leader has a servant's heart. Servant leaders appreciate others' worth and realize that they're not above any job. If you see something that needs to be done, don't wait to be asked. Take the initiative and do it like a faithful servant.

**20:28** A "ransom" was the price paid to release a slave from bondage. Jesus often told his disciples that he must die, but here he told them why—to redeem all people from the bondage of sin and death. The disciples thought that as long as Jesus was alive, he could save them. But Jesus revealed that only his death would save them and the world.

**20:29-34** Matthew records that there were two blind men, while Mark and Luke mention only one. This is probably the same event, but Mark and Luke singled out the more vocal of the two men.

**20:30** The blind men called Jesus "Son of David" because the Jews knew that the Messiah would be a descendant of David (see Isaiah 9:6, 7; 11:1; Jeremiah 23:5, 6). These blind beggars could *see* that Jesus was the long-awaited Messiah, while the religious leaders who witnessed Jesus' miracles were blind to his identity, refusing to open their eyes to the truth. Seeing with your eyes doesn't guarantee seeing with your heart.

**20:32, 33** Although Jesus was concerned about the coming events in Jerusalem, he demonstrated what he had just told the disciples about service (20:28) by stopping to care for the blind men.

## Jesus Rides into Jerusalem on a Donkey
(183/Mark 11:1-11; Luke 19:28-44; John 12:12-19)

**21** As Jesus and the disciples approached Jerusalem, they came to the town of Bethphage on the Mount of Olives. Jesus sent two of them on ahead. ² "Go into the village over there," he said. "As soon as you enter it, you will see a donkey tied there, with its colt beside it. Untie them and bring them to me. ³If anyone asks what you are doing, just say, 'The Lord needs them,' and he will immediately let you take them."

⁴This took place to fulfill the prophecy that said,

5 "Tell the people of Jerusalem,*
   'Look, your King is coming to you.
He is humble, riding on a donkey—
   riding on a donkey's colt.'"*

**21:5**
†Isa 62:11
†Zech 9:9

⁶The two disciples did as Jesus commanded. ⁷They brought the donkey and the colt to him and threw their garments over the colt, and he sat on it.*

⁸Most of the crowd spread their garments on the road ahead of him, and others cut branches from the trees and spread them on the road. ⁹Jesus was in the center of the procession, and the people all around him were shouting,

**21:9**
†Pss 118:25-26;
148:1
Luke 13:35

"Praise God* for the Son of David!
   Blessings on the one who comes in the name of the LORD!
   Praise God in highest heaven!"*

**21:11**
Luke 7:16, 39
John 1:21, 25;
6:14; 7:40; 9:17

¹⁰The entire city of Jerusalem was in an uproar as he entered. "Who is this?" they asked. ¹¹And the crowds replied, "It's Jesus, the prophet from Nazareth in Galilee."

## Jesus Clears the Temple Again (184/Mark 11:12-19; Luke 19:45-48)
¹²Jesus entered the Temple and began to drive out all the people buying and selling animals for sacrifice. He knocked over the tables of the money changers and the chairs of those selling doves. ¹³He said to them, "The Scriptures declare, 'My Temple will be called a house of prayer,' but you have turned it into a den of thieves!" *

**21:13**
†Isa 56:7
†Jer 7:11

¹⁴The blind and the lame came to him in the Temple, and he healed them. ¹⁵The leading priests and the teachers of religious law saw these wonderful miracles and heard even the children in the Temple shouting, "Praise God for the Son of David."

**21:14**
Isa 35:5-6
**21:15**
Matt 21:9

**21:5a** Greek *Tell the daughter of Zion.* Isa 62:11.   **21:5b** Zech 9:9.   **21:7** Greek *over them, and he sat on them.*
**21:9a** Greek *Hosanna,* an exclamation of praise that literally means "save now"; also in 21:9b, 15.   **21:9b** Pss
118:25-26; 148:1.   **21:13** Isa 56:7; Jer 7:11.

---

**21:2-5** Matthew mentions a donkey and a colt, while the other Gospels mention only the colt. This was the same event, but Matthew focuses on the prophecy in Zechariah 9:9, where a donkey and a colt are mentioned. He shows how Jesus' actions fulfilled the prophet's words, thus giving another indication that Jesus was indeed the Messiah. When Jesus entered Jerusalem on a donkey's colt, he affirmed his messianic royalty as well as his humility. On the practical side, what better way to lead an unbroken colt for its first ride down a crowded road than to have its mother with it?

**PREPARATION FOR THE TRIUMPHAL ENTRY**
On their way from Jericho, Jesus and the disciples neared Bethphage, on the slope of the Mount of Olives, just outside Jerusalem. Two disciples went into the village, as Jesus told them, to bring back a donkey and its colt. Jesus rode into Jerusalem on the colt, an unmistakable sign of his kingship.

Mediterranean Sea
GALILEE
N
Sea of Galilee
SAMARIA
Jordan River
Jericho
Mount of Olives
**Jerusalem**
Bethphage
Bethany
PEREA
Dead Sea
JUDEA
IDUMEA
0   20 Mi.
0   20 Km.

**21:8** This verse is one of the few places where the Gospels record that Jesus' glory is recognized on earth. Jesus boldly rode as the King of peace, and the crowd gladly joined him. But these same people would bow to political pressure and desert him in just a few days. Today we celebrate this event on Palm Sunday. That day should remind us to guard against superficial acclaim for Christ.

**21:12** This is the second time Jesus cleared the Temple (see John 2:13-17). Merchants and money changers set up their booths in the Court of the Gentiles in the Temple, crowding out the Gentiles who had come from all over the civilized world to worship God. The merchants sold sacrificial animals at high prices, taking advantage of those who had come long distances. The money changers exchanged all international currency for the special Temple coins—the only money the merchants would accept. They often deceived foreigners who didn't know the exchange rates. Their commercialism in God's house frustrated people's attempts at worship. This, of course, greatly angered Jesus. Any practice that interferes with worshiping God should be stopped.

21:16
†Ps 8:2
But the leaders were indignant. 16They asked Jesus, "Do you hear what these children are saying?"

21:17
Mark 11:1
John 11:1, 18; 12:1
"Yes," Jesus replied. "Haven't you ever read the Scriptures? For they say, 'You have taught children and infants to give you praise.'*" 17Then he returned to Bethany, where he stayed overnight.

### Jesus Says the Disciples Can Pray for Anything (188/Mark 11:20-26)
18In the morning, as Jesus was returning to Jerusalem, he was hungry, 19and he noticed a fig tree beside the road. He went over to see if there were any figs, but there were only leaves. Then he said to it, "May you never bear fruit again!" And immediately the fig tree withered up.

21:21
Matt 17:20
Luke 17:6
1 Cor 13:2
Jas 1:6
20The disciples were amazed when they saw this and asked, "How did the fig tree wither so quickly?"

21Then Jesus told them, "I tell you the truth, if you have faith and don't doubt, you can do things like this and much more. You can even say to this mountain, 'May you be lifted up and thrown into the sea,' and it will happen. 22 You can pray for anything, and if you have faith, you will receive it."

21:22
Matt 7:7-11
John 14:13-14

### Religious Leaders Challenge Jesus' Authority (189/Mark 11:27-33; Luke 20:1-8)
21:23
Acts 4:7
23When Jesus returned to the Temple and began teaching, the leading priests and elders came up to him. They demanded, "By what authority are you doing all these things? Who gave you the right?"

24 "I'll tell you by what authority I do these things if you answer one question," Jesus replied. 25 "Did John's authority to baptize come from heaven, or was it merely human?"

They talked it over among themselves. "If we say it was from heaven, he will ask us why we didn't believe John. 26But if we say it was merely human, we'll be mobbed because the people believe John was a prophet." 27 So they finally replied, "We don't know."

21:26
Matt 11:9

And Jesus responded, "Then I won't tell you by what authority I do these things.

### Jesus Tells the Parable of the Two Sons (190)
21:28
Luke 15:11
28 "But what do you think about this? A man with two sons told the older boy, 'Son, go out and work in the vineyard today.' 29The son answered, 'No, I won't go,' but later he changed his mind and went anyway. 30 Then the father told the other son, 'You go,' and he said, 'Yes, sir, I will.' But he didn't go.

31 "Which of the two obeyed his father?"

They replied, "The first."*

21:16 Ps 8:2.   21:29-31 Other manuscripts read *"The second."* In still other manuscripts the first son says "Yes" but does nothing, the second son says "No" but then repents and goes, and the answer to Jesus' question is that the second son obeyed his father.

---

21:19 Why did Jesus curse the fig tree? This was not a thoughtless, angry act but an acted-out parable. Jesus was showing his anger at religion without substance. Just as the fig tree looked good from a distance but was fruitless on close examination, so the Temple looked impressive at first glance, but its sacrifices and other activities were hollow because they were not done to worship God sincerely (see 21:43). If you only appear to have faith without putting it to work in your life, you are like the fig tree that withered and died because it bore no fruit. Genuine faith means bearing fruit for God's Kingdom. For more information about the fig tree, see the note on Mark 11:13-26.

21:21 Many have wondered about Jesus' statement that if we have faith and don't doubt, we can move mountains. Jesus, of course, was not suggesting that his followers use prayer as "magic" and perform capricious "mountain moving" acts. Instead, he was making a strong point about the disciples' (and our) lack of faith. What kinds of mountains do you face? Have you talked to God about them? How strong is your faith?

21:22 This verse is not a guarantee that we can get *anything* we want simply by asking Jesus and believing. God does not grant requests that would hurt us or others or that would violate his own nature or will. Jesus' statement is not a blank check. To be fulfilled, our requests must be in harmony with the principles of God's Kingdom. The stronger our belief, the more likely our

prayers will be in line with God's will, and then God will be happy to grant them.

21:23-27 The Pharisees demanded to know where Jesus got his authority. If Jesus said his authority came from God, they would accuse him of blasphemy. If he said that he was acting on his own authority, the crowds would be convinced that the Pharisees had the greater authority. But Jesus answered them with a seemingly unrelated question that exposed their real motives. They didn't really want an answer to their question; they only wanted to trap him. Jesus showed that the Pharisees wanted the truth only if it supported their own views and causes.

21:25 For more information on John the Baptist, see Matthew 3 and his Profile in John 1, p. 1749.

21:30 The son who said he would obey and then didn't represented many of the people of Israel in Jesus' day, particularly the religious leaders. They said they wanted to do God's will, but they constantly disobeyed. They were phony, just going through the motions. It is dangerous to pretend to obey God when our heart is far from him because God knows our true intentions. Our actions must match our words.

Then Jesus explained his meaning: "I tell you the truth, corrupt tax collectors and prostitutes will get into the Kingdom of God before you do. [32] For John the Baptist came and showed you the right way to live, but you didn't believe him, while tax collectors and prostitutes did. And even when you saw this happening, you refused to believe him and repent of your sins.

**21:32**
Matt 3:1-12
Luke 3:12-13;
7:29-30

### Jesus Tells the Parable of the Evil Farmers (191/Mark 12:1-12; Luke 20:9-19)

[33] "Now listen to another story. A certain landowner planted a vineyard, built a wall around it, dug a pit for pressing out the grape juice, and built a lookout tower. Then he leased the vineyard to tenant farmers and moved to another country. [34] At the time of the grape harvest, he sent his servants to collect his share of the crop. [35] But the farmers grabbed his servants, beat one, killed one, and stoned another. [36] So the landowner sent a larger group of his servants to collect for him, but the results were the same.

**21:33**
Isa 5:1-2

**21:35**
Matt 23:34, 37

[37] "Finally, the owner sent his son, thinking, 'Surely they will respect my son.'

[38] "But when the tenant farmers saw his son coming, they said to one another, 'Here comes the heir to this estate. Come on, let's kill him and get the estate for ourselves!' [39] So they grabbed him, dragged him out of the vineyard, and murdered him.

[40] "When the owner of the vineyard returns," Jesus asked, "what do you think he will do to those farmers?"

[41] The religious leaders replied, "He will put the wicked men to a horrible death and lease the vineyard to others who will give him his share of the crop after each harvest."

**21:41**
Matt 8:11-12
Luke 21:24
Acts 13:46

[42] Then Jesus asked them, "Didn't you ever read this in the Scriptures?

'The stone that the builders rejected
    has now become the cornerstone.
This is the Lord's doing,
    and it is wonderful to see.'*

**21:42**
†Ps 118:22-23
Isa 28:16
Acts 4:11
Eph 2:20
1 Pet 2:6-7

[43] I tell you, the Kingdom of God will be taken away from you and given to a nation that will produce the proper fruit. [44] Anyone who stumbles over that stone will be broken to pieces, and it will crush anyone it falls on.*"

**21:44**
Isa 8:14-15
Dan 2:34-35, 44-45

[45] When the leading priests and Pharisees heard this parable, they realized he was telling the story against them—they were the wicked farmers. [46] They wanted to arrest him, but they were afraid of the crowds, who considered Jesus to be a prophet.

**21:46**
Matt 21:26

### Jesus Tells the Parable of the Wedding Dinner (192)

**22** Jesus also told them other parables. He said, [2] "The Kingdom of Heaven can be illustrated by the story of a king who prepared a great wedding feast for his son. [3] When the banquet was ready, he sent his servants to notify those who were invited. But they all refused to come!

**22:3**
Matt 21:34

[4] "So he sent other servants to tell them, 'The feast has been prepared. The bulls and fattened cattle have been killed, and everything is ready. Come to the banquet!' [5] But the guests he had invited ignored them and went their own way, one to his farm, another to his business. [6] Others seized his messengers and insulted them and killed them.

**22:4**
Matt 21:36

**22:6**
Matt 21:35

**21:42** Ps 118:22-23.   **21:44** This verse is not included in some early manuscripts. Compare Luke 20:18.

---

**21:33ff** The main elements in this parable are (1) the landowner—God, (2) the vineyard—Israel, (3) the tenant farmers—the Jewish religious leaders, (4) the landowner's servants—the prophets and priests who remained faithful to God and preached to Israel, (5) the son—Jesus (21:38), and (6) the other tenants—the Gentiles. Jesus was exposing the religious leaders' murderous plot (21:45).

**21:37** In trying to reach us with his love, God finally sent his own Son. Jesus' perfect life, his words of truth, and his sacrifice of love are meant to cause us to listen to him and to follow him as Lord. If we ignore God's gracious gift of his Son, we reject God himself.

**21:42** Jesus refers to himself as "the stone that the builders rejected." Although Jesus was rejected by many of his people,

he will become the cornerstone of his new building, the church (see Acts 4:11; 1 Peter 2:7).

**21:44** Jesus used this metaphor to show that one truth can affect people in different ways, depending on how they relate to it (see Isaiah 8:14, 15; 28:16; Daniel 2:34, 44, 45). Ideally they will build on it; many, however, will trip over it. And at the Last Judgment God's enemies will be crushed by it. In the end, Christ, the "building block," will become the "crushing stone." He offers mercy and forgiveness *now* and promises judgment later. We should choose him now!

**22:1-14** In this culture, two invitations were expected when banquets were given. The first asked the guests to attend; the second announced that all was ready. In this story the king invited his guests three times, and each time they rejected his invitation. God wants us to join him at his banquet, which will last for eternity. That's why he sends us invitations again and again. Have you accepted his invitation?

22:7
Luke 19:27
22:8
Acts 13:46
22:10
Matt 13:47-48

22:12
Matt 20:13; 26:50
22:13
Matt 8:12; 25:30
22:14
2 Pet 1:10
Rev 17:14

7 "The king was furious, and he sent out his army to destroy the murderers and burn their town. 8 And he said to his servants,' The wedding feast is ready, and the guests I invited aren't worthy of the honor. 9 Now go out to the street corners and invite everyone you see.' 10 So the servants brought in everyone they could find, good and bad alike, and the banquet hall was filled with guests.

11 "But when the king came in to meet the guests, he noticed a man who wasn't wearing the proper clothes for a wedding. 12 'Friend,' he asked, 'how is it that you are here without wedding clothes?' But the man had no reply. 13 Then the king said to his aides, 'Bind his hands and feet and throw him into the outer darkness, where there will be weeping and gnashing of teeth.'

14 "For many are called, but few are chosen."

### Religious Leaders Question Jesus about Paying Taxes
(193/Mark 12:13-17; Luke 20:20-26)

15 Then the Pharisees met together to plot how to trap Jesus into saying something for which he could be arrested. 16 They sent some of their disciples, along with the supporters of Herod, to meet with him. "Teacher," they said, "we know how honest you are. You teach the way of God truthfully. You are impartial and don't play favorites. 17 Now tell us what you think about this: Is it right to pay taxes to Caesar or not?"

22:17
Matt 17:25

18 But Jesus knew their evil motives. "You hypocrites!" he said. "Why are you trying to trap me? 19 Here, show me the coin used for the tax." When they handed him a Roman coin,* 20 he asked, "Whose picture and title are stamped on it?"

22:21
Rom 13:7

21 "Caesar's," they replied.

"Well, then," he said, "give to Caesar what belongs to Caesar, and give to God what belongs to God."

22 His reply amazed them, and they went away.

### Religious Leaders Question Jesus about the Resurrection
(194/Mark 12:18-27; Luke 20:27-40)

22:23
Acts 23:8
1 Cor 15:12
22:24
†Deut 25:5-6

23 That same day Jesus was approached by some Sadducees—religious leaders who say there is no resurrection from the dead. They posed this question: 24 "Teacher, Moses said, 'If a man dies without children, his brother should marry the widow and have a child who will carry on the brother's name.'* 25 Well, suppose there were seven brothers. The oldest one married and then died without children, so his brother married the widow. 26 But the second brother also died, and the third brother married her. This continued with all seven

22:19 Greek *a denarius.*   22:24 Deut 25:5-6.

---

**22:11, 12** It was customary for wedding guests to be given wedding clothes to wear to the banquet. It was unthinkable to refuse to wear these clothes. That would insult the host, who could only assume that the guest was arrogant and thought he didn't need these clothes, or that he did not want to take part in the wedding celebration. The wedding clothes picture the righteousness needed to enter God's Kingdom—the total acceptance in God's eyes that Christ gives every believer. Christ has provided these clothes of righteousness for everyone, but each person must choose to put them on in order to enter the King's banquet (eternal life). There is an open invitation, but we must be ready. For more on the imagery of clothes of righteousness and salvation, see Psalm 132:16; Isaiah 61:10; Zechariah 3:3-5; Revelation 3:4, 5; 19:7, 8.

**22:15-17** The Pharisees, a religious group, opposed the Roman occupation of Palestine. The supporters of Herod, a political party, supported Herod Antipas and the policies instituted by Rome. Normally these two groups were bitter enemies, but here they united against Jesus. Thinking they had a foolproof plan to corner him, together their representatives asked Jesus about paying Roman taxes. If Jesus agreed that it was right to pay taxes to Caesar, the Pharisees would say he was opposed to God, the only King they recognized. If Jesus said the taxes should not be paid, the supporters of Herod would hand him over to Herod on the charge of rebellion. In this case the Pharisees were not motivated by love for God's laws, and Herod's supporters were not motivated by love for Roman justice. Jesus' answer exposed their evil motives and embarrassed them both.

**22:17** The Jews were required to pay taxes to support the Roman government. They hated this taxation because the money went directly into Caesar's treasury, where some of it went to support the pagan temples and decadent lifestyle of the Roman aristocracy. Caesar's image on the coins was a constant reminder of Israel's subjection to Rome.

**22:21** Jesus avoided this trap by showing that we have dual citizenship (1 Peter 2:17). Our citizenship in the nation requires that we pay money for the services and benefits we receive. Our citizenship in the Kingdom of Heaven requires that we pledge to God our ultimate obedience and commitment.

**22:23ff** After the Pharisees and supporters of Herod had failed to trap Jesus, the Sadducees smugly stepped in to try. They did not believe in the resurrection because the Pentateuch (Genesis—Deuteronomy) has no direct teaching on it. The Pharisees had never been able to come up with a convincing argument from the Pentateuch for the resurrection, and the Sadducees thought they had trapped Jesus for sure. But Jesus was about to show them otherwise (see 22:31, 32 for Jesus' answer).

**22:24** The law said that when a woman's husband died without having a son, the man's brother had a responsibility to marry and care for the widow (Deuteronomy 25:5, 6). This law protected women who were left alone, because in that culture they usually had no other means to support themselves.

of them. 27Last of all, the woman also died. 28So tell us, whose wife will she be in the resurrection? For all seven were married to her."

29 Jesus replied, "Your mistake is that you don't know the Scriptures, and you don't know the power of God. 30 For when the dead rise, they will neither marry nor be given in marriage. In this respect they will be like the angels in heaven.

31 "But now, as to whether there will be a resurrection of the dead—haven't you ever read about this in the Scriptures? Long after Abraham, Isaac, and Jacob had died, God said,* 32 'I am the God of Abraham, the God of Isaac, and the God of Jacob.'* So he is the God of the living, not the dead."

33 When the crowds heard him, they were astounded at his teaching.

### Religious Leaders Question Jesus about the Greatest Commandment
(195/Mark 12:28-34)
34But when the Pharisees heard that he had silenced the Sadducees with his reply, they met together to question him again. 35One of them, an expert in religious law, tried to trap him with this question: 36"Teacher, which is the most important commandment in the law of Moses?"

37 Jesus replied, "'You must love the LORD your God with all your heart, all your soul, and all your mind.'* 38This is the first and greatest commandment. 39A second is equally important: 'Love your neighbor as yourself.'* 40 The entire law and all the demands of the prophets are based on these two commandments."

### Religious Leaders Cannot Answer Jesus' Question
(196/Mark 12:35-37; Luke 20:41-44)
41Then, surrounded by the Pharisees, Jesus asked them a question: 42"What do you think about the Messiah? Whose son is he?"

They replied, "He is the son of David."

43 Jesus responded, "Then why does David, speaking under the inspiration of the Spirit, call the Messiah 'my Lord'? For David said,

44 'The LORD said to my Lord,
  Sit in the place of honor at my right hand
    until I humble your enemies beneath your feet.'*

45Since David called the Messiah 'my Lord,' how can the Messiah be his son?"

46No one could answer him. And after that, no one dared to ask him any more questions.

22:29 John 20:9

22:32 †Exod 3:6, 15-16 Acts 7:32

22:33 Matt 7:28; 13:54 Mark 11:18

22:35 Luke 10:25

22:37 †Deut 6:5

22:39 †Lev 19:18 Matt 5:43; 19:19 Mark 12:31 Luke 10:27 Rom 13:9

22:40 Matt 7:12 Luke 10:25-28 Rom 13:10

22:43 2 Sam 23:2 Acts 2:30 2 Pet 1:20-21

22:44 †Ps 110:1 Acts 2:34-35 Heb 1:13

22:46 Mark 12:34 Luke 20:40

22:31 Greek *read about this? God said.*   22:32 Exod 3:6.   22:37 Deut 6:5.   22:39 Lev 19:18.   22:44 Ps 110:1.

---

**22:29, 30** The Sadducees asked Jesus what marriage would be like in heaven. Jesus said it was more important to understand God's power than know what heaven will be like. In every generation and culture, ideas of eternal life tend to be based on images and experiences of present life. Jesus answered that these faulty ideas are caused by ignorance of God's Word. We must not make up our own ideas about eternity and heaven by thinking of it and God in human terms. We should concentrate more on our relationship with God than about what heaven will look like. Eventually we will find out, and it will be far beyond our greatest expectations.

**22:31, 32** Because the Sadducees accepted only the Pentateuch as God's divine Word, Jesus answered them from the book of Exodus (3:6). God would not have said, "I *am* the God of Abraham, the God of Isaac, and the God of Jacob" if God thought of Abraham, Isaac, and Jacob as dead. From God's perspective, they are alive. Jesus' use of the present tense pointed to the resurrection and the eternal life that all believers enjoy in him.

**22:34** We might think the Pharisees would have been glad to see the Sadducees silenced. The question that the Sadducees had always used to trap them was finally answered by Jesus. But the Pharisees were too proud to be impressed. Jesus'

answer gave them a theological victory over the Sadducees, but they were more interested in defeating Jesus than in learning the truth.

**22:35-40** The Pharisees, who had classified over 600 laws, often tried to distinguish the more important from the less important. So one of them, an "expert in religious law," asked Jesus to identify the most important law. Jesus quoted from Deuteronomy 6:5 and Leviticus 19:18. By fulfilling these two commands, a person keeps all the others. They summarize the Ten Commandments and the other Old Testament moral laws.

**22:37-40** Jesus said that if we truly love God and our neighbor, we will naturally keep the commandments. This is looking at God's law positively. Rather than worrying about all we should *not* do, we should concentrate on all we *can* do to show our love for God and others.

**22:41-45** The Pharisees, Sadducees, and supporters of Herod had asked their questions. Then Jesus turned the tables and asked them a penetrating question—who they thought the Messiah was. The Pharisees knew that the Messiah would be a descendant of David, but they did not understand that he would be God himself. Jesus quoted from Psalm 110:1 to show that the Messiah would be greater than David. (Hebrews 1:13 uses the same text as proof of Christ's deity.) The most important question we will ever answer is what we believe about Christ. Other theological questions are irrelevant until we believe that Jesus is who he said he is.

23:2
Ezra 7:6, 25
Neh 8:1-4

23:4
Luke 11:46
Acts 15:20
Gal 6:13

23:5
Exod 13:9
Num 15:37-40
Deut 6:8

23:11
Matt 20:26-27
Mark 9:35;
10:43-45
Luke 9:48; 22:26

23:12
Job 22:29
Prov 29:23
Ezek 21:26
Luke 14:11; 18:14

23:13
Luke 11:52

## Jesus Warns against the Religious Leaders (197/Mark 12:38-40; Luke 20:45-47)

**23** Then Jesus said to the crowds and to his disciples, 2 "The teachers of religious law and the Pharisees are the official interpreters of the law of Moses.* 3 So practice and obey whatever they tell you, but don't follow their example. For they don't practice what they teach. 4 They crush people with unbearable religious demands and never lift a finger to ease the burden.

5 "Everything they do is for show. On their arms they wear extra wide prayer boxes with Scripture verses inside, and they wear robes with extra long tassels.* 6 And they love to sit at the head table at banquets and in the seats of honor in the synagogues. 7 They love to receive respectful greetings as they walk in the marketplaces, and to be called 'Rabbi.'*

8 "Don't let anyone call you 'Rabbi,' for you have only one teacher, and all of you are equal as brothers and sisters.* 9 And don't address anyone here on earth as 'Father,' for only God in heaven is your spiritual Father. 10 And don't let anyone call you 'Teacher,' for you have only one teacher, the Messiah. 11 The greatest among you must be a servant. 12 But those who exalt themselves will be humbled, and those who humble themselves will be exalted.

## Jesus Condemns the Religious Leaders (198)

13 "What sorrow awaits you teachers of religious law and you Pharisees. Hypocrites! For you shut the door of the Kingdom of Heaven in people's faces. You won't go in yourselves, and you don't let others enter either.*

**23:2** Greek *and the Pharisees sit in the seat of Moses.* **23:5** Greek *They enlarge their phylacteries and lengthen their tassels.* **23:7** *Rabbi,* from Aramaic, means "master" or "teacher." **23:8** Greek *brothers.* **23:13** Some manuscripts add verse 14, *What sorrow awaits you teachers of religious law and you Pharisees. Hypocrites! You shamelessly cheat widows out of their property and then pretend to be pious by making long prayers in public. Because of this, you will be severely punished.* Compare Mark 12:40 and Luke 20:47.

---

**THE SEVEN SORROWS**

| | |
|---|---|
| 23:13 | Not letting others enter the Kingdom of Heaven and not entering yourselves |
| 23:15 | Converting people away from God to be like yourselves |
| 23:16-22 | Blindly leading God's people to follow man-made traditions instead of God's Word |
| 23:23, 24 | Involving yourself in every last detail and ignoring what is really important: justice, mercy, and faith |
| 23:25, 26 | Keeping up appearances while your private world is corrupt |
| 23:27, 28 | Acting spiritual to cover up sin |
| 23:29-36 | Pretending to have learned from past history, but your present behavior shows you have learned nothing |

Jesus mentioned seven ways to guarantee God's anger, when he told the religious leaders, "What sorrow awaits you." These seven statements were strong and unforgettable. They are still applicable anytime we become so involved in perfecting the practice of religion that we forget that God is also concerned with mercy, real love, and forgiveness.

---

**23:2, 3** The Pharisees' traditions and their interpretations and applications of the laws had become as important to them as God's law itself. Their laws were not all bad—some were beneficial. Problems arose when the religious leaders (1) held that man-made rules were equal to God's laws, (2) told the people to obey these rules but did not do so themselves, or (3) obeyed the rules, not to honor God, but to make themselves look good. Usually Jesus did not condemn what the Pharisees taught but what they *were*—hypocrites.

**23:5** These "prayer boxes" were leather boxes containing Scripture verses. Very religious people wore these boxes on their foreheads and arms in order to obey Deuteronomy 6:8 and Exodus 13:9, 16. But the prayer boxes had been made extra wide and had become more important for the status they gave than for the truth they contained.

**23:5-7** Jesus again exposed the hypocritical attitudes of the religious leaders. They knew the Scriptures but did not live by them. They didn't care about *being* holy—just *looking* holy in order to receive people's admiration and praise. Today, like the Pharisees, many people say they know the Bible but do not let it change their lives. They say they follow Jesus, but they don't live by his standards of love. We must make sure that our actions match our beliefs.

**23:5-7** People desire positions of leadership not only in business but also in the church. It is dangerous when love for position grows stronger than loyalty to God. This is what happened to the Pharisees and teachers of religious law. Jesus condemned leaders who serve themselves rather than others.

**23:11, 12** Jesus challenged society's norms. To him, greatness comes from serving—giving of yourself to help God and others. Service keeps us aware of others' needs, and it stops us from focusing only on ourselves. Jesus came as a servant. What kind of greatness do you seek?

**23:13, 14** Being a religious leader in Jerusalem was very different from being a pastor in a secular society today. Israel's history, culture, and daily life centered around its relationship with God. The religious leaders were the best known, most powerful, and most respected of all leaders. Jesus made these stinging accusations because the leaders' hunger for more power, money, and status had made them lose sight of God, and their blindness was spreading to the whole nation.

¹⁵ "What sorrow awaits you teachers of religious law and you Pharisees. Hypocrites! For you cross land and sea to make one convert, and then you turn that person into twice the child of hell* you yourselves are!

¹⁶ "Blind guides! What sorrow awaits you! For you say that it means nothing to swear 'by God's Temple,' but that it is binding to swear 'by the gold in the Temple.' ¹⁷ Blind fools! Which is more important—the gold or the Temple that makes the gold sacred? ¹⁸ And you say that to swear 'by the altar' is not binding, but to swear 'by the gifts on the altar' is binding. ¹⁹ How blind! For which is more important—the gift on the altar or the altar that makes the gift sacred? ²⁰ When you swear 'by the altar,' you are swearing by it and by everything on it. ²¹ And when you swear 'by the Temple,' you are swearing by it and by God, who lives in it. ²² And when you swear 'by heaven,' you are swearing by the throne of God and by God, who sits on the throne.

²³ "What sorrow awaits you teachers of religious law and you Pharisees. Hypocrites! For you are careful to tithe even the tiniest income from your herb gardens,* but you ignore the more important aspects of the law—justice, mercy, and faith. You should tithe, yes, but do not neglect the more important things. ²⁴ Blind guides! You strain your water so you won't accidentally swallow a gnat, but you swallow a camel!*

²⁵ "What sorrow awaits you teachers of religious law and you Pharisees. Hypocrites! For you are so careful to clean the outside of the cup and the dish, but inside you are filthy—full of greed and self-indulgence! ²⁶ You blind Pharisee! First wash the inside of the cup and the dish,* and then the outside will become clean, too.

²⁷ "What sorrow awaits you teachers of religious law and you Pharisees. Hypocrites! For you are like whitewashed tombs—beautiful on the outside but filled on the inside with dead people's bones and all sorts of impurity. ²⁸ Outwardly you look like righteous people, but inwardly your hearts are filled with hypocrisy and lawlessness.

²⁹ "What sorrow awaits you teachers of religious law and you Pharisees. Hypocrites! For you build tombs for the prophets your ancestors killed, and you decorate the monuments of the godly people your ancestors destroyed. ³⁰ Then you say, 'If we had lived in the days of our ancestors, we would never have joined them in killing the prophets.'

³¹ "But in saying that, you testify against yourselves that you are indeed the descendants of those who murdered the prophets. ³² Go ahead and finish what your ancestors started. ³³ Snakes! Sons of vipers! How will you escape the judgment of hell?

³⁴ "Therefore, I am sending you prophets and wise men and teachers of religious law. But you will kill some by crucifixion, and you will flog others with whips in your synagogues, chasing them from city to city. ³⁵ As a result, you will be held responsible for the murder of all godly people of all time—from the murder of righteous Abel to the murder of Zechariah son of Barachiah, whom you killed in the Temple between the sanctuary and the altar. ³⁶ I tell you the truth, this judgment will fall on this very generation.

23:15 Greek *of Gehenna;* also in 23:33.   23:23 Greek *tithe the mint, the dill, and the cumin.*   23:24 See Lev 11:4, 23, where gnats and camels are both forbidden as food.   23:26 Some manuscripts do not include *and the dish.*

**23:16**
Isa 9:16
Matt 5:33-35; 15:14
Rom 2:19

**23:19**
Exod 29:37
**23:21**
1 Kgs 8:13
Ps 26:8
**23:22**
Ps 11:4
Isa 66:1
Matt 5:34
Acts 7:49
**23:23**
Lev 27:30
Hos 6:6
Mic 6:8
Zech 7:9
Luke 11:42
**23:24**
Matt 23:16
**23:25**
Mark 7:4
**23:27**
Luke 11:44
Acts 23:3
**23:28**
Luke 16:15

**23:31**
Acts 7:52
**23:33**
Matt 3:7; 12:34
Luke 3:7
**23:34**
Matt 10:23
Acts 7:52; 22:19
2 Cor 11:23-25
1 Thes 2:15
**23:35**
Gen 4:8
2 Chr 24:20-21
Zech 1:1
Heb 11:4

---

**23:15** The Pharisees' converts were attracted to religion, not to God. By getting caught up in the details of their additional laws and regulations, they completely missed God, to whom the laws pointed. A religion of works puts pressure on people to surpass others in what they know and do. Thus, a hypocritical teacher was likely to have students who were even more hypocritical. We must make sure we are not creating Pharisees by emphasizing outward obedience at the expense of inner renewal.

**23:23, 24** It's possible to obey the details of the laws but still be disobedient in our general behavior. For example, we could be very precise and faithful about giving 10 percent of our money to God but refuse to give one minute of our time in helping others. Tithing is important, but giving a tithe does not exempt us from fulfilling God's other directives.

**23:24** The Pharisees strained their water so they wouldn't accidentally swallow a gnat—an unclean insect according to the law. Meticulous about the details of ceremonial cleanliness, they nevertheless had lost their perspective on inner purity—in essence, they would then swallow a camel and not even notice. They were ceremonially clean on the outside but had corrupt hearts.

**23:25-28** Jesus condemned the Pharisees and religious leaders for outwardly appearing upright and holy but inwardly remaining full of corruption and greed. Living our Christianity merely as a show for others is like washing only the outside of a cup. When we are clean on the inside, our cleanliness on the outside won't be a sham.

**23:34-36** These prophets, wise men, and teachers were probably leaders in the early church who were persecuted, scourged, and killed, as Jesus predicted. The people of Jesus' generation said they would not act as their fathers did in killing the prophets whom God had sent to them (23:30), but they were about to kill the Messiah himself and his faithful followers. Thus, they would become guilty of all the righteous blood shed through the centuries.

**23:35** Jesus summarized the history of Old Testament martyrdom. Abel was the first martyr (Genesis 4); Zechariah was the last mentioned in the Hebrew Bible, which ended with 2 Chronicles. Zechariah is a classic example of a man of God who was killed by those who claimed to be God's people (see 2 Chronicles 24:20, 21).

## Jesus Grieves over Jerusalem Again (199)

37 "O Jerusalem, Jerusalem, the city that kills the prophets and stones God's messengers! How often I have wanted to gather your children together as a hen protects her chicks beneath her wings, but you wouldn't let me.³⁸ And now, look, your house is abandoned and desolate.*³⁹ For I tell you this, you will never see me again until you say, 'Blessings on the one who comes in the name of the LORD!'* "

## 7. Jesus teaches on the Mount of Olives

### Jesus Tells about the Future (201/Mark 13:1-23; Luke 21:5-24)

**24** As Jesus was leaving the Temple grounds, his disciples pointed out to him the various Temple buildings. ²But he responded, "Do you see all these buildings? I tell you the truth, they will be completely demolished. Not one stone will be left on top of another!"

³Later, Jesus sat on the Mount of Olives. His disciples came to him privately and said, "Tell us, when will all this happen? What sign will signal your return and the end of the world?*"

⁴Jesus told them, "Don't let anyone mislead you,⁵ for many will come in my name, claiming, 'I am the Messiah.' They will deceive many.⁶ And you will hear of wars and threats of wars, but don't panic. Yes, these things must take place, but the end won't follow immediately.⁷ Nation will go to war against nation, and kingdom against kingdom. There will be famines and earthquakes in many parts of the world.⁸ But all this is only the first of the birth pains, with more to come.

⁹ "Then you will be arrested, persecuted, and killed. You will be hated all over the world because you are my followers.*¹⁰ And many will turn away from me and betray and hate each other.¹¹ And many false prophets will appear and will deceive many people.¹² Sin will be rampant everywhere, and the love of many will grow cold.¹³ But the one who endures to

**23:39**
†Ps 118:26
Matt 21:9
Mark 11:10
Luke 19:38

**24:2**
Luke 19:44

**24:3**
Matt 13:39; 28:20
Luke 17:30

**24:4**
Mark 13:5

**24:5**
Matt 24:11, 23-24
John 5:43
1 Jn 2:18

**24:6**
Dan 2:28-29

**24:7**
Isa 19:2

**24:9-14**
Matt 10:17-22

**24:9**
John 16:2

**24:11**
Matt 24:5, 24

**23:38** Some manuscripts do not include *and desolate.*  **23:39** Ps 118:26.  **24:3** Or *the age?*  **24:9** Greek *on account of my name.*

**23:37** Jesus wanted to gather his people together as a hen protects her chicks under her wings, but they wouldn't let him. Jesus also wants to protect us if we will just come to him. Many times we hurt and don't know where to turn. We reject Christ's help because we don't think he can give us what we need. But who knows our needs better than our Creator? Those who turn to Jesus will find that he helps and comforts as no one else can.

**23:37** Jerusalem was the capital city of God's chosen people, the ancestral home of David, Israel's greatest king, and the location of the Temple, the earthly dwelling place of God. It was intended to be the center of worship of the true God and a symbol of justice to all people. But Jerusalem had become blind to God and insensitive to human need. Here we see the depth of Jesus' feelings for lost people and for his beloved city, which would soon be destroyed.

**24:1, 2** Although no one knows exactly what this Temple looked like, it must have been beautiful. Herod had helped the Jews remodel and beautify it, no doubt to stay on friendly terms with his subjects. Next to the inner Temple, where the sacred objects were kept and the sacrifices offered, there was a large area called the Court of the Gentiles (where the money changers and merchants had their booths). Outside these courts were long porches. Solomon's Colonnade was 1,562 feet long, decorated with 160 columns stretching along its 921-foot length. Gazing at this glorious and massive structure, the disciples found Jesus' words about its destruction difficult to believe. But the Temple was indeed destroyed only 40 years later when the Romans sacked Jerusalem in A.D. 70.

**24:3ff** Jesus was sitting on the Mount of Olives, the very place where the prophet Zechariah had predicted that the Messiah would stand when he came to establish his Kingdom (Zechariah 14:4). It was a fitting place for the disciples to ask Jesus when he would come in power and what they could expect then. Jesus' reply emphasized the events that would take place before the end of the age. He pointed out that his disciples should be less concerned with knowing the exact date and more concerned with being prepared—living God's way consistently so that no matter when Jesus came, they would be ready.

**24:4** The disciples asked Jesus for the sign of his coming and of the end of the age. Jesus' first response was "Don't let anyone mislead you." The fact is that whenever we look for signs, we become very susceptible to being deceived. There are many "false prophets" (24:11, 24) around with counterfeit signs of spiritual power and authority. The only sure way to keep from being deceived is to focus on Christ and his words. Don't look for special signs, and don't spend time looking at other people. Look at Christ.

**24:9-13** You may not be facing intense persecution now, but Christians in other parts of the world are. As you hear about Christians suffering for their faith, remember that they are your brothers and sisters in Christ. Pray for them. Ask God what you can do to help them in their troubles. When one part of the body suffers, the *whole* body suffers. But when all the parts join together to ease the suffering, the whole body benefits (1 Corinthians 12:26).

**24:11** The Old Testament frequently mentions false prophets (see 2 Kings 3:13; Isaiah 44:25; Jeremiah 23:16; Ezekiel 13:2, 3; Micah 3:5; Zechariah 13:2). False prophets claimed to receive messages from God, but they preached a "health and wealth" message. They said what the people wanted to hear, even when the nation was not following God as it should. There were false prophets in Jesus' day, and we have them today. They are the popular leaders who tell people what they want to hear, such as "God wants you to be rich," "Do whatever your desires tell you," or "There is no such thing as sin or hell." Jesus said false teachers would come, and he warned his disciples, as he warns us, not to listen to their dangerous words.

**24:12** With false teaching and loose morals comes a particularly destructive disease—the loss of true love for God and others. Sin cools your love for God and others by turning your focus on yourself. You cannot truly love if you think only of yourself.

the end will be saved. 14And the Good News about the Kingdom will be preached through-out the whole world, so that all nations* will hear it; and then the end will come.

15 "The day is coming when you will see what Daniel the prophet spoke about—the sacrilegious object that causes desecration* standing in the Holy Place." (Reader, pay attention!) 16 "Then those in Judea must flee to the hills. 17A person out on the deck of a roof must not go down into the house to pack. 18A person out in the field must not return even to get a coat. 19 How terrible it will be for pregnant women and for nursing mothers in those days. 20And pray that your flight will not be in winter or on the Sabbath. 21 For there will be greater anguish than at any time since the world began. And it will never be so great again. 22In fact, unless that time of calamity is shortened, not a single person will survive. But it will be shortened for the sake of God's chosen ones.

23 "Then if anyone tells you, 'Look, here is the Messiah,' or 'There he is,' don't believe it. 24For false messiahs and false prophets will rise up and perform great signs and wonders so as to deceive, if possible, even God's chosen ones. 25 See, I have warned you about this ahead of time.

### Jesus Tells about His Return (202/Mark 13:24-31; Luke 21:25-33)

26 "So if someone tells you, 'Look, the Messiah is out in the desert,' don't bother to go and look. Or, 'Look, he is hiding here,' don't believe it! 27For as the lightning flashes in the east and shines to the west, so it will be when the Son of Man* comes. 28 Just as the gathering of vultures shows there is a carcass nearby, so these signs indicate that the end is near.*

29 "Immediately after the anguish of those days,

the sun will be darkened,
    the moon will give no light,
the stars will fall from the sky,
    and the powers in the heavens will be shaken.*

30And then at last, the sign that the Son of Man is coming will appear in the heavens, and there will be deep mourning among all the peoples of the earth. And they will see the Son of Man coming on the clouds of heaven with power and great glory.* 31And he will send out his angels with the mighty blast of a trumpet, and they will gather his chosen ones from all over the world*—from the farthest ends of the earth and heaven.

32 "Now learn a lesson from the fig tree. When its branches bud and its leaves begin to sprout, you know that summer is near. 33 In the same way, when you see all these things, you can know his return is very near, right at the door. 34 I tell you the truth, this generation* will not pass from the scene until all these things take place. 35 Heaven and earth will disappear, but my words will never disappear.

24:14 Matt 28:19; Rev 3:10; 16:14
24:15 Dan 9:27; 11:31; 12:11
24:17 Luke 17:31
24:21 Dan 12:1; Joel 2:2; Rev 3:10; 7:14
24:23-24 Luke 17:21-23; 2 Thes 2:9-10; 1 Jn 4:1-3; Rev 13:13-14
24:26-27 Luke 17:23-24
24:28 Luke 17:37; Rev 19:17
24:29 Isa 13:10; 34:4; Ezek 32:7; Joel 2:10, 31; 3:15; Rev 6:12-13
24:30 †Dan 7:13; Zech 12:10-14; Rev 1:7
24:31 1 Cor 15:52; 1 Thes 4:16; Rev 8:2; 11:15
24:33 Jas 5:9
24:34 Matt 16:28
24:35 Matt 5:18; Luke 16:17

24:14 Or all peoples.   24:15 Greek the abomination of desolation. See Dan 9:27; 11:31; 12:11.   24:27 "Son of Man" is a title Jesus used for himself.   24:28 Greek Wherever the carcass is, the vultures gather.   24:29 See Isa 13:10; 34:4; Joel 2:10.   24:30 See Dan 7:13.   24:31 Greek from the four winds.   24:34 Or this age, or this nation.

24:14 Jesus said that before he returns, the Good News about the Kingdom (the message of salvation) would be preached throughout the world. This was the disciples' mission—and it is ours today. Jesus talked about the end times and final judgment to show his followers the urgency of spreading the Good News of salvation to everyone.

24:15, 16 What was "the sacrilegious object that causes desecration" mentioned by both Daniel and Jesus? Rather than one specific object, event, or person, it could be seen as any deliberate attempt to mock and deny the reality of God's presence. Daniel's prediction came true in 168 B.C. when Antiochus Epiphanes sacrificed a pig to Zeus on the sacred Temple altar (Daniel 9:27; 11:30, 31). Jesus' words were remembered in A.D. 70 when Titus placed an idol on the site of the burned Temple after destroying Jerusalem. In the end times the Antichrist will set up an image of himself and order everyone to worship it (2 Thessalonians 2:4; Revelation 13:14, 15). These are all abominations to God.

24:21, 22 Jesus, talking about the end times, telescoped near future and far future events, as did the Old Testament prophets. Many of these persecutions have already occurred; more are yet to come. But God is in control of even the length of persecutions. He will not forget his people. This is all we need to know about the future to motivate us to live rightly now.

24:23, 24 Jesus' warnings about false teachers still hold true. Upon close examination it becomes clear that many nice-sounding messages don't agree with God's message in the Bible. Only a solid foundation in God's Word can equip us to perceive the errors and distortions in false teaching.

24:24-28 In times of persecution even strong believers will find it difficult to be loyal. To keep from being deceived by false messiahs, we must understand that Jesus' return will be unmistakable (Mark 13:26); no one will doubt that it is he. If you have to be told that the Messiah has come, then he hasn't (24:27). Christ's coming will be obvious to everyone.

24:30 The nations of the earth will mourn because unbelievers will suddenly realize they have chosen the wrong side. Everything they have scoffed about will be happening, and it will be too late for them.

### Jesus Tells about Remaining Watchful (**203**/Mark 13:32-37; Luke 21:34-38)

**24:36**
Acts 1:7
1 Thes 5:1-2

36 "However, no one knows the day or hour when these things will happen, not even the angels in heaven or the Son himself.* Only the Father knows.

**24:37-39**
Gen 6:9–7:24

37 "When the Son of Man returns, it will be like it was in Noah's day. 38 In those days before the flood, the people were enjoying banquets and parties and weddings right up to the time Noah entered his boat. 39 People didn't realize what was going to happen until the flood came and swept them all away. That is the way it will be when the Son of Man comes.

**24:40-41**
Luke 17:34-35

40 "Two men will be working together in the field; one will be taken, the other left. 41 Two women will be grinding flour at the mill; one will be taken, the other left.

**24:42**
Matt 25:13
Luke 12:40
1 Thes 5:6
Rev 3:3; 16:15

42 "So you, too, must keep watch! For you don't know what day your Lord is coming. 43 Understand this: If a homeowner knew exactly when a burglar was coming, he would keep watch and not permit his house to be broken into. 44 You also must be ready all the time, for the Son of Man will come when least expected.

45 "A faithful, sensible servant is one to whom the master can give the responsibility of managing his other household servants and feeding them. 46 If the master returns and finds that the servant has done a good job, there will be a reward. 47 I tell you the truth, the master will put that servant in charge of all he owns. 48 But what if the servant is evil and thinks, 'My master won't be back for a while,' 49 and he begins beating the other servants, partying, and getting drunk? 50 The master will return unannounced and unexpected, 51 and he will cut the servant to pieces and assign him a place with the hypocrites. In that place there will be weeping and gnashing of teeth.

**24:51**
Matt 8:12; 25:30

### Jesus Tells the Parable of the Ten Bridesmaids (**204**)

**25:1**
Luke 12:35-38

**25** "Then the Kingdom of Heaven will be like ten bridesmaids* who took their lamps and went to meet the bridegroom. 2 Five of them were foolish, and five were wise. 3 The five who were foolish didn't take enough olive oil for their lamps, 4 but the other five were wise enough to take along extra oil. 5 When the bridegroom was delayed, they all became drowsy and fell asleep.

**25:5**
1 Thes 5:6

6 "At midnight they were roused by the shout, 'Look, the bridegroom is coming! Come out and meet him!'

**25:8**
Luke 12:35-40

7 "All the bridesmaids got up and prepared their lamps. 8 Then the five foolish ones asked the others, 'Please give us some of your oil because our lamps are going out.'

9 "But the others replied, ' We don't have enough for all of us. Go to a shop and buy some for yourselves.'

**25:10**
Luke 13:24-25
Rev 19:9

10 "But while they were gone to buy oil, the bridegroom came. Then those who were ready went in with him to the marriage feast, and the door was locked. 11 Later, when the other five bridesmaids returned, they stood outside, calling, 'Lord! Lord! Open the door for us!'

**25:13**
Matt 24:42, 44
Mark 13:35
Luke 12:40

12 "But he called back, 'Believe me, I don't know you!'

13 "So you, too, must keep watch! For you do not know the day or hour of my return.

**24:36** Some manuscripts do not include *or the Son himself.*   **25:1** Or *virgins;* also in 25:7, 11.

---

**24:36** It is good that we don't know exactly when Christ will return. If we knew the precise date, we might be tempted to be lazy in our work for Christ. Worse yet, we might plan to keep sinning and then turn to God right at the end. Heaven is not our only goal; we have work to do here. And we must keep on doing it until death or until we see the unmistakable return of our Savior.

**24:40-42** Christ's second coming will be swift and sudden. There will be no opportunity for last-minute repentance or bargaining. The choice we have already made will determine our eternal destiny.

**24:44** Jesus' purpose in telling about his return is not to stimulate predictions and calculations about the date but to warn us to be prepared. Will you be ready? The only safe choice is to obey him *today* (24:46).

**24:45-47** Jesus asks us to spend the time of waiting taking care of his people and doing his work here on earth, both within the church and outside it. This is the best way to prepare for Christ's return.

**24:51** "Weeping and gnashing of teeth" is a phrase used to describe despair. God's coming judgment is as certain as Jesus' return to earth.

**25:1ff** Jesus told the following parables to clarify further what it means to be ready for his return and how to live until he comes. In the story of the 10 bridesmaids (25:1-13), we are taught that every person is responsible for his or her own spiritual condition. The story of the three servants (25:14-30) shows the necessity of using well what God has entrusted to us. The parable of the sheep and goats (25:31-46) stresses the importance of serving others in need. No parable by itself *completely* describes our preparation. Instead, each paints one part of the whole picture.

**25:1ff** This parable is about a wedding. On the wedding day the bridegroom went to the bride's house for the ceremony; then the bride and groom, along with a great procession, returned to the groom's house, where a feast took place, often lasting a full week.

These 10 bridesmaids were waiting to join the procession, and they hoped to take part in the marriage feast. But when the groom didn't come at the expected time, five of them were out of lamp oil. By the time they had purchased extra oil, it was too late to join the feast.

When Jesus returns to take his people to heaven, we must be ready. Spiritual preparation cannot be bought or borrowed at the last minute. Our relationship with God must be our own.

## Jesus Tells the Parable of the Loaned Money (205)

14 "Again, the Kingdom of Heaven can be illustrated by the story of a man going on a long trip. He called together his servants and entrusted his money to them while he was gone. 15 He gave five bags of silver* to one, two bags of silver to another, and one bag of silver to the last—dividing it in proportion to their abilities. He then left on his trip.

16 "The servant who received the five bags of silver began to invest the money and earned five more. 17 The servant with two bags of silver also went to work and earned two more. 18 But the servant who received the one bag of silver dug a hole in the ground and hid the master's money.

19 "After a long time their master returned from his trip and called them to give an account of how they had used his money. 20 The servant to whom he had entrusted the five bags of silver came forward with five more and said, 'Master, you gave me five bags of silver to invest, and I have earned five more.'

21 "The master was full of praise. ' Well done, my good and faithful servant. You have been faithful in handling this small amount, so now I will give you many more responsibilities. Let's celebrate together!*'

22 "The servant who had received the two bags of silver came forward and said, 'Master, you gave me two bags of silver to invest, and I have earned two more.'

23 "The master said, 'Well done, my good and faithful servant. You have been faithful in handling this small amount, so now I will give you many more responsibilities. Let's celebrate together!'

24 "Then the servant with the one bag of silver came and said, 'Master, I knew you were a harsh man, harvesting crops you didn't plant and gathering crops you didn't cultivate. 25 I was afraid I would lose your money, so I hid it in the earth. Look, here is your money back.'

26 "But the master replied, 'You wicked and lazy servant! If you knew I harvested crops I didn't plant and gathered crops I didn't cultivate, 27 why didn't you deposit my money in the bank? At least I could have gotten some interest on it.'

28 "Then he ordered, ' Take the money from this servant, and give it to the one with the ten bags of silver. 29 To those who use well what they are given, even more will be given, and they will have an abundance. But from those who do nothing, even what little they have will be taken away. 30 Now throw this useless servant into outer darkness, where there will be weeping and gnashing of teeth.'

## Jesus Tells about the Final Judgment (206)

31 "But when the Son of Man* comes in his glory, and all the angels with him, then he will sit upon his glorious throne. 32 All the nations* will be gathered in his presence, and he will separate the people as a shepherd separates the sheep from the goats. 33 He will place the sheep at his right hand and the goats at his left.

25:15 Greek *talents;* also throughout the story. A talent is equal to 75 pounds or 34 kilograms.   25:21 Greek *Enter into the joy of your master* [or *your Lord*]; also in 25:23.   25:31 "Son of Man" is a title Jesus used for himself. 25:32 Or *peoples.*

**25:15** Matt 18:24-25 / Rom 12:3, 6

**25:19** Matt 18:23

**25:21** Matt 24:45-46 / Luke 16:10

**25:29** Matt 13:12 / Mark 4:25 / Luke 8:18

**25:30** Matt 8:12 / Luke 13:28

**25:31** Dan 7:13 / Zech 14:5 / Rev 20:11

**25:32** Ezek 34:17, 20 / Rev 20:12

**25:33** Luke 12:32

**25:15** The master divided the money among his servants according to their abilities. No one received more or less than he could handle. If he failed in his assignment, his excuse could not be that he was overwhelmed. Failure would indicate only laziness or hatred toward the master. The bags of silver represent any kind of resource we are given. God gives us time, gifts, and other resources according to our abilities, and he expects us to invest them wisely until he returns. We are responsible to use well what God has given us. The issue is not how much we have but how well we use what we have.

**25:21** Jesus is coming back—we know this is true. Does this mean we must quit our jobs in order to serve God? No, it means we are to use our time, talents, and treasures diligently in order to serve God completely in whatever we do. For a few people, this may mean changing professions. For most of us, it means doing our daily work out of love for God.

**25:24-30** This last man was thinking only of himself. He hoped to play it safe and protect himself from his hard master, but he was judged for his self-centeredness. We must not make excuses to avoid doing what God calls us to do. If God truly is our Master, we must obey willingly. Our time, abilities, and money aren't

ours in the first place—we are caretakers, not owners. When we ignore, squander, or abuse what we are given, we are rebellious and deserve to be punished.

**25:29, 30** This parable describes the consequences of two attitudes toward Christ's return. The person who diligently prepares for it by investing his or her time and talents to serve God will be rewarded. The person who has no heart for the work of the Kingdom will be punished. God rewards faithfulness. Those who bear no fruit for God's Kingdom cannot expect to be treated the same as those who are faithful.

**25:31-46** God will separate his obedient followers from pretenders and unbelievers. The real evidence of our belief is the way we act. To treat all persons we encounter as if they were Jesus is no easy task. What we do for others demonstrates what we really think about Jesus' words to us: Feed the hungry, give the homeless a place to stay, look after the sick. How well do your actions separate you from pretenders and unbelievers?

**25:32** Jesus used sheep and goats to picture the division between believers and unbelievers. Sheep and goats often grazed together but were separated when it came time to shear the sheep. Ezekiel 34:17-24 also refers to the separation of sheep and goats.

**25:34**
Luke 22:30
1 Cor 15:50
Gal 5:21

**25:35-36**
Isa 58:7
Heb 13:3
Jas 2:15-16

34 "Then the King will say to those on his right, 'Come, you who are blessed by my Father, inherit the Kingdom prepared for you from the creation of the world. 35 For I was hungry, and you fed me. I was thirsty, and you gave me a drink. I was a stranger, and you invited me into your home. 36 I was naked, and you gave me clothing. I was sick, and you cared for me. I was in prison, and you visited me.'

37 "Then these righteous ones will reply, 'Lord, when did we ever see you hungry and feed you? Or thirsty and give you something to drink? 38 Or a stranger and show you hospitality? Or naked and give you clothing? 39 When did we ever see you sick or in prison and visit you?'

**25:40**
Prov 19:17
Matt 10:40, 42

**25:41**
Matt 7:23
Mark 9:48
2 Pet 2:4
Rev 20:10

40 "And the King will say, 'I tell you the truth, when you did it to one of the least of these my brothers and sisters,* you were doing it to me!'

41 "Then the King will turn to those on the left and say, 'Away with you, you cursed ones, into the eternal fire prepared for the devil and his demons.*42 For I was hungry, and you didn't feed me. I was thirsty, and you didn't give me a drink. 43 I was a stranger, and you didn't invite me into your home. I was naked, and you didn't give me clothing. I was sick and in prison, and you didn't visit me.'

**25:45**
Prov 14:31; 17:5

**25:46**
Dan 12:2
John 3:15, 36; 5:29
Acts 13:46-48
Rom 2:7-8
Gal 6:8

44 "Then they will reply, 'Lord, when did we ever see you hungry or thirsty or a stranger or naked or sick or in prison, and not help you?'

45 "And he will answer, 'I tell you the truth, when you refused to help the least of these my brothers and sisters, you were refusing to help me.'

46 "And they will go away into eternal punishment, but the righteous will go into eternal life."

## C. DEATH AND RESURRECTION OF JESUS, THE KING (26:1—28:20)

After facing much opposition for his teaching, Jesus is betrayed by Judas, denied by the disciples, crucified, and he dies. Three days later he rises from the dead and appears to the disciples, confirming that he is indeed King over life and death. The long-awaited King has brought in his Kingdom, but it is different than expected, for he reigns in our heart until the day he comes again to establish a new and perfect world.

### Religious Leaders Plot to Kill Jesus (207/Mark 14:1-2; Luke 22:1-2)

**26:2**
Exod 12:1-27

**26** When Jesus had finished saying all these things, he said to his disciples, 2 "As you know, Passover begins in two days, and the Son of Man* will be handed over to be crucified."

**26:3**
Ps 2:2
John 11:47-53
Acts 4:6

3 At that same time the leading priests and elders were meeting at the residence of Caiaphas, the high priest, 4 plotting how to capture Jesus secretly and kill him. 5 "But not during the Passover celebration," they agreed, "or the people may riot."

25:40 Greek *my brothers.*   25:41 Greek *his angels.*   26:2 "Son of Man" is a title Jesus used for himself.

---

**25:34-40** This parable describes acts of mercy we all can do every day. These acts do not depend on wealth, ability, or intelligence; they are simple acts freely given and freely received. We have no excuse to neglect those who have deep needs, and we cannot hand over this responsibility to the church or government. Jesus demands our personal involvement in caring for others' needs (Isaiah 58:7).

**25:40** There has been much discussion about the identity of the "brothers and sisters." Some have said they are the Jews; others say they are all Christians; still others say they are suffering people everywhere. Such a debate is much like the lawyer's earlier question to Jesus, "Who is my neighbor?" (Luke 10:29). The point of this parable is not the *who,* but the *what*—the importance of serving where service is needed. The focus of this parable is that we should love every person and serve anyone we can. Such love for others glorifies God by reflecting our love for him.

**25:46** Eternal punishment takes place in hell (the lake of fire, or Gehenna), the place of punishment after death for all those who refuse to repent. In the Hebrew, three words were used in connection with eternal punishment.

(1) *Sheol,* or "the grave," was used in the Hebrew Old Testament to mean the place of the dead, generally thought to be under the earth. (In the Hebrew, this word occurs in Job 24:19; Psalm 16:10; Isaiah 38:10.)

(2) *Hades* is the Greek word for the underworld, the realm

of the dead. It is the word used in the New Testament for Sheol. (In the Greek, this word occurs in Matthew 16:18; Revelation 1:18; 20:13, 14.)

(3) *Gehenna,* or hell, was named after the valley of Ben-Hinnom near Jerusalem, where children were sacrificed by fire to the pagan gods (see 2 Kings 23:10; 2 Chronicles 28:3). This is the place of eternal fire (Matthew 5:22; 10:28; Mark 9:43; Luke 12:5; James 3:6; Revelation 19:20) prepared for the devil, his angels, and all those who do not believe in God (25:46; Revelation 20:9, 10). This is the final and eternal state of the wicked after the resurrection and the Last Judgment.

When Jesus warns against unbelief, he is trying to save us from agonizing, eternal punishment.

**26:3** Caiaphas was the ruling high priest during Jesus' ministry. He was the son-in-law of Annas, the previous high priest. The Roman government had taken over the process of appointing all political and religious leaders. Caiaphas served for 18 years, longer than most high priests, suggesting that he was gifted at cooperating with the Romans. He was the first to recommend Jesus' death in order to "save" the nation (John 11:49, 50).

**26:3-5** This was a deliberate plot to kill Jesus. Without this plot, there would have been no groundswell of popular opinion against him. In fact, because of Jesus' popularity, the religious leaders were afraid to arrest him during the Passover. They did not want their actions to incite a riot.

### A Woman Anoints Jesus with Perfume (182/Mark 14:3-9; John 12:1-11)

6Meanwhile, Jesus was in Bethany at the home of Simon, a man who had previously had leprosy. 7While he was eating,* a woman came in with a beautiful alabaster jar of expensive perfume and poured it over his head.

8The disciples were indignant when they saw this. "What a waste!" they said. 9"It could have been sold for a high price and the money given to the poor."

10 But Jesus, aware of this, replied, "Why criticize this woman for doing such a good thing to me? 11You will always have the poor among you, but you will not always have me. 12She has poured this perfume on me to prepare my body for burial. 13I tell you the truth, wherever the Good News is preached throughout the world, this woman's deed will be remembered and discussed."

**26:11**
Deut 15:11

### Judas Agrees to Betray Jesus (208/Mark 14:10-11; Luke 22:3-6)

14Then Judas Iscariot, one of the twelve disciples, went to the leading priests 15and asked, "How much will you pay me to betray Jesus to you?" And they gave him thirty pieces of silver. 16From that time on, Judas began looking for an opportunity to betray Jesus.

**26:14-16**
John 11:57
**26:15**
Exod 21:32
Zech 11:12

### Disciples Prepare for the Passover (209/Mark 14:12-16; Luke 22:7-13)

17On the first day of the Festival of Unleavened Bread, the disciples came to Jesus and asked, "Where do you want us to prepare the Passover meal for you?"

18 "As you go into the city," he told them, "you will see a certain man. Tell him, ' The Teacher says: My time has come, and I will eat the Passover meal with my disciples at your house.' " 19So the disciples did as Jesus told them and prepared the Passover meal there.

**26:17**
Exod 12:18-20
Deut 16:5-8

### Jesus and the Disciples Share the Last Supper
### (211/Mark 14:17-25; Luke 22:14-30; John 13:21-30)

20When it was evening, Jesus sat down at the table* with the twelve disciples.* 21While they were eating, he said, "I tell you the truth, one of you will betray me."

**26:7** Or *reclining.*   **26:20a** Or *Jesus reclined.*   **26:20b** Some manuscripts read *the Twelve.*

---

**26:6-13** Matthew and Mark put this event just before the Last Supper, while John has it just before the Triumphal Entry. Of the three, John places this event in the most likely chronological order. We must remember that the main purpose of the Gospel writers was to give an accurate record of Jesus' message, not to present an exact chronological account of his life. Matthew and Mark may have chosen to place this event here to contrast the complete devotion of Mary with the betrayal of Judas, the next event they record in their Gospels.

**26:7** This woman was Mary, the sister of Martha and Lazarus, who lived in Bethany (John 12:1-3). Alabaster jars were carved from a translucent gypsum. These jars were used to hold perfumed oil.

**VISIT IN BETHANY**

Chronologically, the events of Matthew 26:6-13 precede the events of 21:1ff. In 20:29, Jesus left Jericho, heading toward Jerusalem. Then he arrived in Bethany, where a woman anointed him. From there he went toward Bethphage, where two of his disciples got the colt that he would ride into Jerusalem.

**26:8** All the disciples were indignant, but John's Gospel singles out Judas Iscariot as especially so (John 12:4).

**26:11** Here Jesus brought back to mind Deuteronomy 15:11: "There will always be some in the land who are poor." This statement does not justify ignoring the needs of the poor. Scripture continually exhorts us to care for the needy. The passage in Deuteronomy continues: "That is why I am commanding you to share freely with the poor and with other Israelites in need." Rather, by saying this, Jesus highlighted the special sacrifice Mary made for him.

**26:14, 15** Why would Judas want to betray Jesus? Judas, like the other disciples, expected Jesus to start a political rebellion and overthrow Rome. As treasurer, Judas certainly assumed (as did the other disciples—see Mark 10:35-37) that he would be given an important position in Jesus' new government. But when Jesus praised Mary for pouring out perfume worth a year's salary, Judas may have realized that Jesus' Kingdom was not physical or political but spiritual. Judas's greedy desire for money and status could not be realized if he followed Jesus, so he betrayed Jesus in exchange for money and favor from the religious leaders.

**26:15** Matthew alone records the exact amount of money Judas accepted to betray Jesus—30 silver coins, the price of a slave (Exodus 21:32). The religious leaders had planned to wait until after the Passover to take Jesus, but with Judas's unexpected offer, they accelerated their plans.

**26:17** The Passover took place on one night and at one meal, but the Festival of Unleavened Bread, which was celebrated with it, continued for a week. The people removed all yeast from their homes in commemoration of their ancestors' exodus from Egypt, when they did not have time to let the bread dough rise. Thousands of people poured into Jerusalem from all over the Roman Empire for this festival. For more information on how the Passover was celebrated, see the notes on Mark 14:1 and in Exodus 12.

26:23
Ps 41:9

26:24
Ps 22:7-8, 16-18
Isa 53:8-9
Luke 24:25-27, 46
1 Pet 1:10-11

26:28
Exod 24:8
Jer 31:31
Zech 9:11
Heb 9:20

²² Greatly distressed, each one asked in turn, "Am I the one, Lord?"

²³ He replied, "One of you who has just eaten from this bowl with me will betray me. ²⁴ For the Son of Man must die, as the Scriptures declared long ago. But how terrible it will be for the one who betrays him. It would be far better for that man if he had never been born!"

²⁵ Judas, the one who would betray him, also asked, "Rabbi, am I the one?"
And Jesus told him, "You have said it."

²⁶ As they were eating, Jesus took some bread and blessed it. Then he broke it in pieces and gave it to the disciples, saying, "Take this and eat it, for this is my body."

²⁷ And he took a cup of wine and gave thanks to God for it. He gave it to them and said, "Each of you drink from it, ²⁸ for this is my blood, which confirms the covenant* between

26:28 Some manuscripts read *the new covenant.*

---

**MARY** — LAZARUS'S SISTER

Hospitality is an art. Making sure a guest is welcomed, warmed, and well fed requires creativity, organization, and teamwork. Their ability to accomplish these goals makes Mary and her sister, Martha, one of the best hospitality teams in the Bible. Their frequent guest was Jesus Christ.

For Mary, hospitality meant giving more attention to the guest himself than to the needs he might have. She would rather talk than cook. She was more interested in her guest's words than in the cleanliness of her home or the timeliness of her meals. She let her older sister, Martha, take care of those details. Mary's approach to events shows her to be mainly a "responder." She did little preparation—her role was participation. Unlike her sister, who had to learn to stop and listen, Mary needed to learn that action is often appropriate and necessary.

We first meet Mary during a visit Jesus paid to her home. She simply sat at his feet and listened. When Martha became irritated at her sister's lack of help, Jesus stated that Mary's choice to enjoy his company was the most appropriate response at the time. Our last glimpse of Mary shows her to have become a woman of thoughtful and worshipful action. Again she was at Jesus' feet, washing them with perfume and wiping them with her hair. She seemed to understand, better even than the disciples, why Jesus was going to die. Jesus said her act of worship would be told everywhere, along with the gospel, as an example of costly service.

What kind of hospitality does Jesus receive from your life? Are you so busy planning and running your life that you neglect precious time with him? Or do you respond to him by listening to his Word, then finding ways to worship him with your life? It is that kind of hospitality he longs for from each of us.

| | |
|---|---|
| **Strengths and accomplishments** | • Perhaps the only person who understood and accepted Jesus' coming death, taking time to anoint his body while he was still living<br>• Learned when to listen and when to act |
| **Lessons from her life** | • The busyness of serving God can become a barrier to knowing him personally<br>• Small acts of obedience and service have widespread effects |
| **Vital statistics** | • Where: Bethany<br>• Relatives: Sister: Martha. Brother: Lazarus. |
| **Key verses** | "'She has poured this perfume on me to prepare my body for burial. I tell you the truth, wherever the Good News is preached throughout the world, this woman's deed will be remembered and discussed'" (Matthew 26:12-13). |

Mary's story is told in Matthew 26:6-13; Mark 14:3-9; Luke 10:38-42; John 11:17-45; 12:1-11.

---

**26:23** In Jesus' time, some food was eaten from a common bowl into which everyone dipped their hand.

**26:26** Each name we use for this sacrament brings out a different dimension to it. It is the *Lord's Supper* because it commemorates the Passover meal Jesus ate with his disciples; it is the *Eucharist* (thanksgiving) because in it we thank God for Christ's work for us; it is *Communion* because through it we commune with God and with other believers. As we eat the bread and drink the wine, we should be quietly reflective as we recall Jesus' death and his promise to come again, grateful for God's wonderful gift to us, and joyful as we meet with Christ and the body of believers.

**26:28** How does Jesus' blood relate to the new covenant? People under the old covenant (those who lived before Jesus) could approach God only through a priest and an animal sacri-

fice. Now all people can come directly to God through faith because Jesus' death has made us acceptable in God's eyes (Romans 3:21-24).

The old covenant was a shadow of the new (Jeremiah 31:31; Hebrews 8:1ff), pointing forward to the day when Jesus himself would be the final and ultimate sacrifice for sin. Rather than an unblemished lamb slain on the altar, the perfect Lamb of God was slain on the cross, a sinless sacrifice, so that our sins could be forgiven once and for all. All those who believe in Christ receive that forgiveness.

God and his people. It is poured out as a sacrifice to forgive the sins of many. [29] Mark my words—I will not drink wine again until the day I drink it new with you in my Father's Kingdom."

**26:29**
Acts 10:41

[30] Then they sang a hymn and went out to the Mount of Olives.

**26:30**
Pss 113–118

### Jesus Again Predicts Peter's Denial (222/Mark 14:26-31)

[31] On the way, Jesus told them, "Tonight all of you will desert me. For the Scriptures say,

'God will strike* the Shepherd,
    and the sheep of the flock will be scattered.'

**26:31**
†Zech 13:7
John 16:32

[32] But after I have been raised from the dead, I will go ahead of you to Galilee and meet you there."

**26:32**
Matt 28:7

[33] Peter declared, "Even if everyone else deserts you, I will never desert you."

**26:34**
Matt 26:69-75
Mark 14:66-72
Luke 22:56-62
John 18:25-27

[34] Jesus replied, "I tell you the truth, Peter—this very night, before the rooster crows, you will deny three times that you even know me."

[35] "No!" Peter insisted. "Even if I have to die with you, I will never deny you!" And all the other disciples vowed the same.

**26:35**
John 13:37

### Jesus Agonizes in the Garden (223/Mark 14:32-42; Luke 22:39-46)

[36] Then Jesus went with them to the olive grove called Gethsemane, and he said, "Sit here while I go over there to pray." [37] He took Peter and Zebedee's two sons, James and John, and he became anguished and distressed. [38] He told them, "My soul is crushed with grief to the point of death. Stay here and keep watch with me."

**26:36**
John 18:1

**26:38**
†Pss 42:6; 43:5
John 12:27

[39] He went on a little farther and bowed with his face to the ground, praying, "My Father! If it is possible, let this cup of suffering be taken away from me. Yet I want your will to be done, not mine."

**26:39**
Matt 20:22
John 5:30; 6:38
Heb 5:7-8

**26:31** Greek *I will strike.* Zech 13:7.

---

**THE PASSOVER MEAL AND GETHSEMANE**  Jesus, who would soon be the final Passover Lamb, ate the traditional Passover meal with his disciples in the upper room of a house in Jerusalem. During the meal they partook of the bread and wine, which would be the elements of future Communion celebrations, and then went out to the Garden of Gethsemane on the Mount of Olives.

**26:29** Again Jesus assured his disciples of victory over death and of their future with him. The next few hours would bring apparent defeat, but soon they would experience the power of the Holy Spirit and witness the great spread of the Good News. And one day they would all be together again in God's new Kingdom.

**26:30** It is possible that the hymn the disciples sang was from Psalms 115–118, the traditional psalms sung as part of the Passover meal.

**26:35** All the disciples declared that they would die before denying Jesus. A few hours later, however, they all scattered. Talk is cheap. It is easy to say we are devoted to Christ, but our claims are meaningful only when they are tested in the crucible of persecution. How strong is your faith? Is it strong enough to stand up under intense trial?

**26:37, 38** Jesus was in great anguish over his approaching physical pain, separation from the Father, and death for the sins of the world. The divine course was set, but he, in his human nature, still struggled (Hebrews 5:7-9). Because of the anguish Jesus experienced, he can relate to our suffering. Jesus' strength to obey came from his relationship with God the Father, who is also the source of our strength (John 17:11, 15, 16, 21, 26).

**26:39** Jesus was not rebelling against his Father's will when he asked that the cup of suffering and separation be taken away. In fact, he reaffirmed his desire to do God's will by saying, "Yet I want your will to be done, not mine." His prayer reveals to us his terrible suffering. His agony was worse than death because he paid for *all* sin by being separated from God. The sinless Son of God took our sins upon himself to save us from suffering and separation.

**26:39** In times of suffering people sometimes wish they knew the future, or they wish they could understand the reason for their anguish. Jesus knew what lay ahead of him, and he knew the reason. Even so, his struggle was intense—more wrenching than any struggle we will ever have to face. What does it take to be able to say, "I want your will to be done"? It takes firm trust in God's plans; it takes prayer and obedience each step of the way.

**26:41**
Matt 6:13

40 Then he returned to the disciples and found them asleep. He said to Peter, "Couldn't you watch with me even one hour? 41 Keep watch and pray, so that you will not give in to temptation. For the spirit is willing, but the body is weak!"

42 Then Jesus left them a second time and prayed, "My Father! If this cup cannot be taken away* unless I drink it, your will be done." 43 When he returned to them again, he found them sleeping, for they couldn't keep their eyes open.

**26:45**
John 12:23-27;
13:1; 17:1

44 So he went to pray a third time, saying the same things again. 45 Then he came to the disciples and said, "Go ahead and sleep. Have your rest. But look—the time has come. The Son of Man is betrayed into the hands of sinners. 46 Up, let's be going. Look, my betrayer is here!"

### Jesus Is Betrayed and Arrested (224/Mark 14:43-52; Luke 22:47-53; John 18:1-11)

47 And even as Jesus said this, Judas, one of the twelve disciples, arrived with a crowd of men armed with swords and clubs. They had been sent by the leading priests and elders of the people. 48 The traitor, Judas, had given them a prearranged signal: "You will know which one to arrest when I greet him with a kiss." 49 So Judas came straight to Jesus. "Greetings, Rabbi!" he exclaimed and gave him the kiss.

**26:52**
Gen 9:6
Rev 13:10

50 Jesus said, "My friend, go ahead and do what you have come for."

Then the others grabbed Jesus and arrested him. 51 But one of the men with Jesus pulled out his sword and struck the high priest's slave, slashing off his ear.

**26:53**
2 Kgs 6:16-17
Ps 91:11
Dan 7:10

52 "Put away your sword," Jesus told him. "Those who use the sword will die by the sword. 53 Don't you realize that I could ask my Father for thousands* of angels to protect us, and he

**26:54**
Ps 22:7-8, 16-18
Isa 53:8-9
Luke 24:25-27, 46
1 Pet 1:10-11

would send them instantly? 54 But if I did, how would the Scriptures be fulfilled that describe what must happen now?"

**26:56**
Isa 53:7
Zech 13:7
Matt 26:31

55 Then Jesus said to the crowd, "Am I some dangerous revolutionary, that you come with swords and clubs to arrest me? Why didn't you arrest me in the Temple? I was there teaching every day. 56 But this is all happening to fulfill the words of the prophets as recorded in the Scriptures." At that point, all the disciples deserted him and fled.

### Caiaphas Questions Jesus (226/Mark 14:53-65)

**26:58**
Mark 14:66
Luke 22:55
John 18:15

57 Then the people who had arrested Jesus led him to the home of Caiaphas, the high priest, where the teachers of religious law and the elders had gathered. 58 Meanwhile, Peter

**26:42** Greek *If this cannot pass.*    **26:53** Greek *twelve legions.*

---

**BETRAYED!**

| | |
|---|---|
| Delilah betrayed Samson to the Philistines. | Judges 16:16-21 |
| Absalom betrayed David, his father | 2 Samuel 15:10-16 |
| Jehu betrayed Joram and killed him | 2 Kings 9:14-27 |
| Officials betrayed Joash and killed him. | 2 Kings 12:20, 21 |
| Judas betrayed Jesus. | Matthew 26:46-56 |

Scripture records a number of occasions on which a person or group was betrayed. The tragedies caused by these violations of trust are a strong lesson about the importance of keeping our commitments.

---

**26:40, 41** Jesus used Peter's drowsiness to warn him about the kinds of temptation he would soon face. The way to overcome temptation is to keep alert and pray. Keeping alert means being aware of the possibilities of temptation, sensitive to the subtleties, and spiritually equipped to fight it. Because temptation strikes where we are most vulnerable, we can't resist it alone. Prayer is essential because God's strength can shore up our defenses and defeat Satan's power.

**26:48** Judas had told the crowd to arrest the man he kissed. This was not an arrest by Roman soldiers under Roman law but an arrest by the religious leaders. Judas pointed Jesus out, not because Jesus was hard to recognize, but because Judas had agreed to be the formal accuser in case a trial was called. Judas was able to lead the group to one of Jesus' retreats, where no onlookers would interfere with the arrest.

**26:51-53** The man who cut off the servant's ear was Peter (John 18:10). Peter was trying to prevent what he saw as *defeat*. He didn't realize that Jesus had to die in order to gain *victory*. But

Jesus demonstrated perfect commitment to his Father's will. His Kingdom would not be advanced with swords but with faith and obedience. Luke 22:51 records that Jesus then touched the servant's ear and healed him.

**26:55** Although the religious leaders could have arrested Jesus at any time, they came at night because they were afraid of the crowds that followed him each day (see 26:5).

**26:56** A few hours earlier, this band of men had said they would rather die than desert their Lord (see the note on 26:35).

**26:57** Earlier in the evening, Jesus had been questioned by Annas (the former high priest and the father-in-law of Caiaphas). Annas then sent Jesus to Caiaphas's home to be questioned (John 18:12-24). Because of their haste to complete the trial and see Jesus die before the Sabbath, less than 24 hours away, the religious leaders met in Caiaphas's home at night instead of waiting for daylight and meeting in the Temple.

followed him at a distance and came to the high priest's courtyard. He went in and sat with the guards and waited to see how it would all end.

59 Inside, the leading priests and the entire high council* were trying to find witnesses who would lie about Jesus, so they could put him to death. 60 But even though they found many who agreed to give false witness, they could not use anyone's testimony. Finally, two men came forward 61 who declared, "This man said, 'I am able to destroy the Temple of God and rebuild it in three days.'"

62 Then the high priest stood up and said to Jesus, "Well, aren't you going to answer these charges? What do you have to say for yourself?" 63 But Jesus remained silent. Then the high priest said to him, "I demand in the name of the living God—tell us if you are the Messiah, the Son of God."

64 Jesus replied, "You have said it. And in the future you will see the Son of Man seated in the place of power at God's right hand* and coming on the clouds of heaven."*

65 Then the high priest tore his clothing to show his horror and said, "Blasphemy! Why do we need other witnesses? You have all heard his blasphemy. 66 What is your verdict?"

"Guilty!" they shouted. "He deserves to die!"

67 Then they began to spit in Jesus' face and beat him with their fists. And some slapped him, 68 jeering, "Prophesy to us, you Messiah! Who hit you that time?"

### Peter Denies Knowing Jesus (227/Mark 14:66-72; Luke 22:54-65; John 18:25-27)
69 Meanwhile, Peter was sitting outside in the courtyard. A servant girl came over and said to him, "You were one of those with Jesus the Galilean."

70 But Peter denied it in front of everyone. "I don't know what you're talking about," he said.

71 Later, out by the gate, another servant girl noticed him and said to those standing around, "This man was with Jesus of Nazareth.*"

**26:59** Greek *the Sanhedrin.* **26:64a** Greek *seated at the right hand of the power.* See Ps 110:1. **26:64b** See Dan 7:13. **26:71** Or *Jesus the Nazarene.*

*Cross-references:*
**26:60** Deut 19:15; Ps 27:12
**26:61** Matt 27:40; John 2:19; Acts 6:14
**26:63** Matt 16:16-18
**26:64** Ps 110:1; †Dan 7:13; Matt 24:30; Rev 1:7
**26:65-66** Lev 24:16; John 19:7
**26:67** Isa 50:6; 53:5

---

**26:59** The high council was the most powerful religious and political body of the Jewish people. Although the Romans controlled Israel's government, they gave the people power to handle religious disputes and some civil disputes, so the high council made many of the local decisions affecting daily life. But a death sentence had to be approved by the Romans (John 18:31).

**26:60, 61** The high council tried to find witnesses who would distort some of Jesus' teachings. Finally, they found two witnesses who distorted Jesus' words about the Temple (see John 2:19). They claimed that Jesus had said he could destroy the Temple—a blasphemous boast. Actually Jesus had said, "Destroy this temple, and in three days I will raise it up" (John 2:19). Jesus, of course, had been talking about his body, not the building. Ironically, the religious leaders were about to destroy Jesus' body just as he had said, and three days later he would rise from the dead.

**26:64** Jesus declared his royalty in no uncertain terms. In calling himself the Son of Man, Jesus was claiming to be the Messiah, as his listeners well knew. He knew this declaration would be his undoing, but he did not panic. He was calm, courageous, and determined.

**26:65, 66** The high priest accused Jesus of blasphemy—calling himself God. To the Jews, this was a great crime, punishable by death (Leviticus 24:16). The religious leaders refused even to consider that Jesus' words might be true. They had decided to kill Jesus, and in so doing, they sealed their own fate as well as his. Like the members of the high council, you must decide whether Jesus' words are blasphemy or truth. Your decision has eternal implications.

**26:69ff** There were three stages to Peter's denial. First, he acted confused and tried to divert attention from himself by changing the subject. Second, using an oath he denied that he knew Jesus. Third, he swore that he did not know Jesus. Believers who deny Christ often begin doing so subtly by pretending not to know him. When opportunities to discuss religious issues come up, they walk away or pretend they don't know the answers. With only a little more pressure, they can be induced to deny flatly their relationship with Christ. If you find yourself subtly diverting conversation so you don't have to talk about Christ, watch out. You may be on the road to denying him.

Antonia Fortress
(later Praetorium?)

Mount of Olives

Temple

Garden of Gethsemane

Hasmonean Palace

Herod's Royal Palace

Herod's Lower Palace

UPPER CITY

Caiaphas's House?

JERUSALEM

Traditional Upper Room?

LOWER CITY

N

0        .1 Mi.
0        .1 Km.

**JESUS' TRIAL** After Judas singled Jesus out for arrest, the mob took Jesus first to Caiaphas, the high priest. This trial, a mockery of justice, ended at daybreak with their decision to kill him; but the Jews needed Rome's permission for the death sentence. Jesus was taken to Pilate (who was probably in the Praetorium), then to Herod (Luke 23:5–12), and back to Pilate, who sentenced him to die.

72Again Peter denied it, this time with an oath. "I don't even know the man," he said.

73A little later some of the other bystanders came over to Peter and said, "You must be one of them; we can tell by your Galilean accent."

74Peter swore, "A curse on me if I'm lying—I don't know the man!" And immediately the rooster crowed.

75Suddenly, Jesus' words flashed through Peter's mind: "Before the rooster crows, you will deny three times that you even know me." And he went away, weeping bitterly.

**26:75**
Matt 26:34
Mark 14:30
Luke 22:34
John 13:38

*The Council of Religious Leaders Condemns Jesus* (**228**/Mark 15:1; Luke 22:66-71)

**27** Very early in the morning the leading priests and the elders of the people met again to lay plans for putting Jesus to death. 2Then they bound him, led him away, and took him to Pilate, the Roman governor.

**27:1-2**
Mark 15:1
Luke 23:1-2
John 18:28

---

**PETER**

Jesus' first words to Simon Peter were "Come, follow me" (Mark 1:17). His last words to him were "Follow me" (John 21:22). Every step of the way between those two challenges, Peter never failed to follow—even though he often stumbled.

When Jesus entered Peter's life, this plain fisherman became a new person with new goals and new priorities. He did not become a perfect person, however, and he never stopped being Simon Peter. We may wonder what Jesus saw in Simon that made him greet this potential disciple with a new name: Peter—the "rock." Impulsive Peter certainly didn't act like a rock much of the time. But when Jesus chose his followers, he wasn't looking for models; he was looking for real people. He chose people who could be changed by his love, and then he sent them out to communicate that his acceptance was available to anyone—even to those who often fail.

We may wonder what Jesus sees in us when he calls us to follow him. But we know Jesus accepted Peter, and, in spite of his failures, Peter went on to do great things for God. Are you willing to keep following Jesus, even when you fail?

| | |
|---|---|
| **Strengths and accomplishments** | • Became the recognized leader among Jesus' disciples—one of the inner group of three<br>• Was the first great voice of the gospel during and after Pentecost<br>• Probably knew Mark and gave him information for the Gospel of Mark<br>• Wrote 1 and 2 Peter |
| **Weaknesses and mistakes** | • Often spoke without thinking; was brash and impulsive<br>• During Jesus' trial, denied three times that he even knew Jesus<br>• Later found it hard to treat Gentile Christians as equals |
| **Lessons from his life** | • Enthusiasm has to be backed up by faith and understanding, or it fails<br>• God's faithfulness can compensate for our greatest unfaithfulness<br>• It is better to be a follower who sometimes fails than one who fails to follow |
| **Vital statistics** | • Occupations: Fisherman, disciple<br>• Relatives: Father: John. Brother: Andrew.<br>• Contemporaries: Jesus, Pilate, Herod |
| **Key verse** | "Now I say to you that you are Peter (which means 'rock'), and upon this rock I will build my church, and all the powers of hell will not conquer it" (Matthew 16:18). |

Peter's story is told in the Gospels and the book of Acts. He is mentioned in Galatians 1:18 and 2:7-14; and he wrote the books of 1 and 2 Peter.

---

**26:72-74** That Peter denied that he knew Jesus, using an oath and swearing, does not mean he used foul language. This was the kind of swearing that a person does in a court of law. Peter was swearing that he did not know Jesus and was invoking a curse on himself if his words were untrue. In effect he was saying, "May God strike me dead if I am lying."

**27:1, 2** The religious leaders had to persuade the Roman government to sentence Jesus to death because they did not have the authority to do it themselves. The Romans had taken away the religious leaders' authority to inflict capital punishment. Politically, it looked better for the religious leaders anyway if someone else was responsible for killing Jesus. They wanted the death to appear Roman sponsored so the crowds couldn't blame them. The Jewish leaders had arrested Jesus on theological grounds—blasphemy. Because this charge would be thrown out of a Roman court, how-

ever, they had to come up with a political reason for Jesus' death. Their strategy was to show Jesus as a rebel who claimed to be a king and thus a threat to Caesar.

**27:2** Pilate was the Roman governor for the regions of Samaria and Judea from A.D. 26 to 36. Jerusalem was located in Judea. Pilate took special pleasure in demonstrating his authority over the Jews; for example, he impounded money from the Temple treasuries to build an aqueduct. Pilate was not popular, but the religious leaders had no other way to get rid of Jesus than to go to him. Ironically, when Jesus, a Jew, came before him for trial, Pilate found him innocent. He could not find a single fault in Jesus, nor could he contrive one.

### Judas Hangs Himself (229)

³When Judas, who had betrayed him, realized that Jesus had been condemned to die, he was filled with remorse. So he took the thirty pieces of silver back to the leading priests and the elders. ⁴"I have sinned," he declared, "for I have betrayed an innocent man."

"What do we care?" they retorted. "That's your problem."

⁵Then Judas threw the silver coins down in the Temple and went out and hanged himself. ⁶The leading priests picked up the coins. "It wouldn't be right to put this money in the Temple treasury," they said, "since it was payment for murder."* ⁷After some discussion they finally decided to buy the potter's field, and they made it into a cemetery for foreigners. ⁸That is why the field is still called the Field of Blood. ⁹This fulfilled the prophecy of Jeremiah that says,

"They took* the thirty pieces of silver—
    the price at which he was valued by the people of Israel,
¹⁰ and purchased the potter's field,
    as the Lord directed.*"

### Jesus Stands Trial before Pilate (230/Mark 15:2-5; Luke 23:1-5; John 18:28-38)

¹¹Now Jesus was standing before Pilate, the Roman governor. "Are you the king of the Jews?" the governor asked him.

Jesus replied, "You have said it."

¹²But when the leading priests and the elders made their accusations against him, Jesus remained silent. ¹³"Don't you hear all these charges they are bringing against you?" Pilate demanded. ¹⁴But Jesus made no response to any of the charges, much to the governor's surprise.

### Pilate Hands Jesus Over to Be Crucified
(232/Mark 15:6-15; Luke 23:13-25; John 18:39–19:16)

¹⁵Now it was the governor's custom each year during the Passover celebration to release one prisoner to the crowd—anyone they wanted. ¹⁶This year there was a notorious prisoner, a man named Barabbas.* ¹⁷As the crowds gathered before Pilate's house that morning, he asked them, "Which one do you want me to release to you—Barabbas, or Jesus who is called the Messiah?" ¹⁸(He knew very well that the religious leaders had arrested Jesus out of envy.)

¹⁹Just then, as Pilate was sitting on the judgment seat, his wife sent him this message: "Leave that innocent man alone. I suffered through a terrible nightmare about him last night."

**27:3**
Matt 26:14-15

**27:5-10**
Acts 1:18-19

**27:9-10**
†Jer 32:6-9
†Zech 11:12-13

**27:12**
Isa 53:7
Matt 26:63
John 19:9
1 Pet 2:22
**27:14**
Mark 14:61

**27:19**
Job 33:14-16

---

**27:6** Greek *since it is the price for blood.*   **27:9** Or *I took.*   **27:9-10** Greek *as the Lord directed me.* Zech 11:12-13; Jer 32:6-9.   **27:16** Some manuscripts read *Jesus Barabbas;* also in 27:17.

---

**27:3, 4** Jesus' formal accuser (see 26:48 note) wanted to drop his charges, but the religious leaders refused to halt the trial. When he betrayed Jesus, perhaps Judas was trying to force Jesus' hand to get him to lead a revolt against Rome. This did not work, of course. Whatever his reason, Judas changed his mind, but it was too late. Many of the plans we set into motion cannot be reversed. It is best to think of the potential consequences before we launch into an action we may later regret.

**27:4** The priests' job was to teach people about God and act as intercessors for them, helping administer the sacrifices to cover their sins. Judas returned to the priests, exclaiming that he had sinned. Rather than helping him find forgiveness, however, the priests said, "That's your problem." Not only had they rejected the Messiah, they had rejected their role as priests.

**27:5** According to Matthew, Judas hanged himself. Acts 1:18, however, says that he fell and burst open. The best explanation is that the limb from which he was hanging broke, and the resulting fall split open his body.

**27:6** These leading priests felt no guilt in giving Judas money to betray an innocent man, but when Judas returned the money, the priests couldn't accept it because it was wrong to accept payment for murder! Their hatred for Jesus had caused them to lose all sense of right and wrong.

**27:9, 10** This prophecy is found specifically in Zechariah 11:12, 13 but may also have been taken from Jeremiah 18:1-4; 19:1-11;

or 32:6-15. In Old Testament times, Jeremiah was considered the collector of some of the prophets' writings, so perhaps his name is cited rather than Zechariah.

**27:12** Standing before Pilate, the religious leaders accused Jesus of a different crime than the ones for which they had arrested him. They arrested him for blasphemy (claiming to be God), but that charge would mean nothing to the Romans. So the religious leaders had to accuse Jesus of crimes that would have concerned the Roman government, such as encouraging the people not to pay taxes, claiming to be a king, and causing riots. These accusations were not true, but the religious leaders were determined to kill Jesus, and they broke several commandments in order to do so.

**27:14** Jesus' silence fulfilled the words of the prophet (Isaiah 53:7). Pilate was amazed that Jesus didn't try to defend himself. He recognized the obvious plot against Jesus and wanted to let him go, but Pilate was already under pressure from Rome to keep peace in his territory. The last thing he needed was a rebellion over this quiet and seemingly insignificant man.

**27:15, 16** Barabbas had taken part in a rebellion against the Roman government (Mark 15:7). Although an enemy to Rome, he may have been a hero to the Jews. Ironically, Barabbas was guilty of the crime for which Jesus was accused.

**27:19** For a leader who was supposed to administer justice, Pilate proved to be more concerned about political expediency

**27:20**
Acts 3:14

20 Meanwhile, the leading priests and the elders persuaded the crowd to ask for Barabbas to be released and for Jesus to be put to death. 21So the governor asked again, "Which of these two do you want me to release to you?"

The crowd shouted back, "Barabbas!"

**27:22**
Matt 1:16

22 Pilate responded, "Then what should I do with Jesus who is called the Messiah?"

They shouted back, "Crucify him!"

23"Why?" Pilate demanded. "What crime has he committed?"

But the mob roared even louder, "Crucify him!"

**27:24**
Deut 21:5-9
Ps 26:6

24Pilate saw that he wasn't getting anywhere and that a riot was developing. So he sent for a bowl of water and washed his hands before the crowd, saying, "I am innocent of this man's blood. The responsibility is yours!"

**27:25**
Acts 5:28

25And all the people yelled back, "We will take responsibility for his death—we and our children!"*

**27:26**
Isa 53:5
John 19:1

26So Pilate released Barabbas to them. He ordered Jesus flogged with a lead-tipped whip, then turned him over to the Roman soldiers to be crucified.

### Roman Soldiers Mock Jesus (233/Mark 15:16-20)

27Some of the governor's soldiers took Jesus into their headquarters* and called out the en-

**27:29**
Ps 22:8
Isa 53:3
John 19:2-3

tire regiment. 28They stripped him and put a scarlet robe on him. 29They wove thorn branches into a crown and put it on his head, and they placed a reed stick in his right hand as a scepter. Then they knelt before him in mockery and taunted, "Hail! King of the Jews!"

**27:30**
Isa 50:6

30And they spit on him and grabbed the stick and struck him on the head with it. 31When they were finally tired of mocking him, they took off the robe and put his own clothes on

**27:31**
Isa 53:7

him again. Then they led him away to be crucified.

**27:25** Greek *"His blood be on us and on our children."*  **27:27** Or *into the Praetorium.*

---

**THE SEVEN**
**LAST WORDS**
**OF JESUS ON**
**THE CROSS**

"Father, forgive them, for they don't know what they are doing." ........................................ Luke 23:34

"I assure you, today you will be with me in paradise." ......... Luke 23:43

Speaking to Mary and John: "Dear woman, here is your son.... Here is your mother.".......................... John 19:26, 27

"My God, my God, why have you abandoned me?".......... Matthew 27:46; Mark 15:34

"I am thirsty.".................................... John 19:28

"It is finished!".................................. John 19:30

"Father, I entrust my spirit into your hands!"................. Luke 23:46

The statements that Jesus made from the cross have been treasured by all who have followed him as Lord. They demonstrate both his humanity and his divinity. They also capture the last moments of all that Jesus went through to gain our forgiveness.

---

than about doing what was right. He had several opportunities to make the right decision. His conscience told him Jesus was innocent; Roman law said an innocent man should not be put to death; and his wife had a nightmare that caused her to encourage her husband to let Jesus go. Pilate had no good excuse to condemn Jesus, but he was afraid of the crowd.

**27:21** Crowds are fickle. They loved Jesus on Sunday because they thought he was going to inaugurate his Kingdom. Then they hated him on Friday when his power appeared broken. In the face of the mass uprising against Jesus, his friends were afraid to speak up.

**27:24** At first Pilate hesitated to give the religious leaders permission to crucify Jesus. He perceived that they were simply jealous of a teacher who was more popular with the people than they were. But when the Jews threatened to report Pilate to Caesar (John 19:12), Pilate became afraid. Historical records indicate that the Jews had already threatened to lodge a formal complaint against Pilate for his stubborn flouting of their traditions—and such a complaint would most likely have led to his recall by Rome. His job was in jeopardy. The Roman government could not afford to put large numbers of troops in all the

regions under their control, so one of Pilate's main duties was to do whatever was necessary to maintain peace.

**27:24** In making no decision, Pilate made the decision to let the crowds crucify Jesus. Although he washed his hands, the guilt remained. Washing your hands of a tough situation doesn't cancel your guilt. It merely gives you a false sense of peace. Don't make excuses—take responsibility for the decisions you make.

**27:27** A regiment was a division of the Roman legion, containing about 200 men.

### Jesus Is Led Away to Be Crucified (234/Mark 15:21-24; Luke 23:26-31; John 19:17)

32Along the way, they came across a man named Simon, who was from Cyrene,* and the soldiers forced him to carry Jesus' cross. 33And they went out to a place called Golgotha (which means "Place of the Skull"). 34The soldiers gave him wine mixed with bitter gall, but when he had tasted it, he refused to drink it.

**27:34**
Ps 69:21

### Jesus Is Placed on the Cross (235/Mark 15:25-32; Luke 23:32-43; John 19:18-27)

35After they had nailed him to the cross, the soldiers gambled for his clothes by throwing dice.* 36Then they sat around and kept guard as he hung there. 37A sign was fastened above Jesus' head, announcing the charge against him. It read: "This is Jesus, the King of the Jews." 38Two revolutionaries* were crucified with him, one on his right and one on his left.

**27:35**
†Ps 22:18

**27:38**
Isa 53:12

39The people passing by shouted abuse, shaking their heads in mockery. 40"Look at you now!" they yelled at him. "You said you were going to destroy the Temple and rebuild it in three days. Well then, if you are the Son of God, save yourself and come down from the cross!"

41The leading priests, the teachers of religious law, and the elders also mocked Jesus. 42"He saved others," they scoffed, "but he can't save himself! So he is the King of Israel, is he? Let him come down from the cross right now, and we will believe in him! 43He trusted God, so let God rescue him now if he wants him! For he said, 'I am the Son of God.'" 44Even the revolutionaries who were crucified with him ridiculed him in the same way.

**27:39**
Pss 22:7; 109:25
Lam 2:15

**27:40**
Matt 26:61
John 2:19-20

### Jesus Dies on the Cross (236/Mark 15:33-41; Luke 23:44-49; John 19:28-37)

45At noon, darkness fell across the whole land until three o'clock. 46At about three o'clock, Jesus called out with a loud voice,"*Eli, Eli,* lema sabachthani?*" which means"My God, my God, why have you abandoned me?"*

**27:45**
Amos 8:9

**27:46**
†Ps 22:1

**27:32** *Cyrene* was a city in northern Africa.   **27:35** Greek *by casting lots.* A few late manuscripts add *This fulfilled the word of the prophet: "They divided my garments among themselves and cast lots for my robe."* See Ps 22:18.   **27:38** Or *criminals;* also in 27:44.   **27:46a** Some manuscripts read *Eloi, Eloi.*   **27:46b** Ps 22:1.

---

Golgotha □
(other possible site)

Antonia Fortress
(later Praetorium?)

Traditional
Golgotha □

Temple

Hasmonean
Palace □

Herod's
Royal
Palace □

Herod's □
Lower
Palace

UPPER CITY

Caiaphas's
House?

**JERUSALEM**

Traditional
Upper
□ Room?

LOWER CITY

N

0          .1 Mi.

0          .1 Km.

**THE WAY OF THE CROSS**   The Roman soldiers took Jesus into their headquarters at the Praetorium and mocked him, dressing him in a scarlet robe and a crown of thorns. They then led him to the crucifixion site outside the city. He was so weakened by his beatings that he could not carry his cross, and a man from Cyrene was forced to carry it to Golgotha.

**27:32**   Condemned prisoners had to carry their own crosses to the execution site. Jesus, weakened from the beatings he had received, was physically unable to carry his cross any farther. Thus, a bystander, Simon, was forced to do so. Simon was from Cyrene, in northern Africa, and was probably one of the thousands of Jews visiting Jerusalem for the Passover.

**27:33**   Some scholars say Golgotha ("Place of the Skull") derives its name from its appearance. Golgotha may have been a regular place of execution in a prominent public place outside the city. Executions held there would serve as a deterrent to criminals.

**27:34**   Wine mixed with gall was offered to Jesus to help reduce his pain, but Jesus refused to drink it. Gall is generally understood to be a narcotic that was used to deaden pain. Jesus would suffer fully conscious and with a clear mind.

**27:35**   The soldiers customarily took the clothing of those they crucified. These soldiers threw dice and divided Jesus' clothing among themselves, fulfilling the prophecy made by David. Much of Psalm 22 parallels Jesus' crucifixion.

**27:40**   This accusation was used against Jesus in his trial by the high council (26:61). It is ironic that Jesus was in the very process of fulfilling his own prophecy. Because Jesus is the Son of God, who always obeys the will of the Father, he did not come down from the cross.

**27:44**   Later one of these criminals repented. Jesus promised that the repentant criminal would join him in paradise (Luke 23:39-43).

**27:45**   We do not know how this darkness occurred, but it is clear that God caused it. Nature testified to the gravity of Jesus' death, while Jesus' friends and enemies alike fell silent in the encircling gloom. The darkness on that Friday afternoon was both physical and spiritual.

**27:46**   Jesus was not questioning God; he was quoting the first line of Psalm 22—a deep expression of the anguish he felt when he took on the sins of the world, which caused him to be separated from his Father. *This* was what Jesus dreaded as he prayed

47Some of the bystanders misunderstood and thought he was calling for the prophet Elijah. 48One of them ran and filled a sponge with sour wine, holding it up to him on a reed stick so he could drink. 49But the rest said, "Wait! Let's see whether Elijah comes to save him."*

50Then Jesus shouted out again, and he released his spirit. 51At that moment the curtain in the sanctuary of the Temple was torn in two, from top to bottom. The earth shook, rocks split apart, 52and tombs opened. The bodies of many godly men and women who had died were raised from the dead. 53They left the cemetery after Jesus' resurrection, went into the holy city of Jerusalem, and appeared to many people.

54The Roman officer* and the other soldiers at the crucifixion were terrified by the earthquake and all that had happened. They said, "This man truly was the Son of God!"

55And many women who had come from Galilee with Jesus to care for him were watching from a distance. 56Among them were Mary Magdalene, Mary (the mother of James and Joseph), and the mother of James and John, the sons of Zebedee.

### Jesus Is Laid in the Tomb (237/Mark 15:42-47; Luke 23:50-56; John 19:38-42)

57As evening approached, Joseph, a rich man from Arimathea who had become a follower of Jesus, 58went to Pilate and asked for Jesus' body. And Pilate issued an order to release it to him. 59Joseph took the body and wrapped it in a long sheet of clean linen cloth. 60He placed it in his own new tomb, which had been carved out of the rock. Then he rolled a great stone across the entrance and left. 61Both Mary Magdalene and the other Mary were sitting across from the tomb and watching.

**27:49** Some manuscripts add *And another took a spear and pierced his side, and out flowed water and blood.* Compare John 19:34. **27:54** Greek *The centurion.*

**Marginal references:**

**27:48**
Ps 69:21
John 19:29-30

**27:51**
Exod 26:31-33
Heb 10:19-20

**27:52**
Ezek 37:12

**27:55-56**
Luke 8:2-3

**27:60**
Matt 28:2
Mark 16:3-4
Luke 24:2
John 20:1

---

**HOW JESUS' TRIAL WAS ILLEGAL**

1. Even before the trial began, it had been determined that Jesus must die (Mark 14:1; John 11:50). There was no "innocent until proven guilty" approach.

2. False witnesses were sought to testify against Jesus (Matthew 26:59). Usually the religious leaders went through an elaborate system of screening witnesses to ensure justice.

3. No defense for Jesus was sought or allowed (Luke 22:67-71).

4. The trial was conducted at night (Mark 14:53-65; 15:1), which was illegal according to the religious leaders' own laws.

5. The high priest put Jesus under oath, but then incriminated him for what he said (Matthew 26:63-66).

6. Cases involving such serious charges were to be tried only in the high council's regular meeting place, not in the high priest's home (Mark 14:53-65).

The religious leaders were not interested in giving Jesus a fair trial. In their minds, Jesus had to die. This blind obsession led them to pervert the justice they were appointed to protect. Above are many examples of the actions taken by the religious leaders that were illegal according to their own laws.

---

to God in the garden to take the cup from him (26:39). The physical agony was horrible, but even worse was the period of spiritual separation from God. Jesus suffered this double death so that we would never have to experience eternal separation from God.

**27:47** The bystanders misinterpreted Jesus' words and thought he was calling for Elijah. Because Elijah ascended into heaven without dying (2 Kings 2:11), they thought he would return again to rescue them from great trouble (Malachi 4:5). At their annual Passover meal, each family set an extra place for Elijah in expectation of his return.

**27:51** The Temple had three main parts: the courts, the Holy Place (where only the priests could enter), and the Most Holy Place (where only the high priest could enter, and only once a year, to atone for the sins of the nation—Leviticus 16:1-35). The curtain separating the Holy Place from the Most Holy Place was torn in two at Christ's death, symbolizing that the barrier between God and humanity was removed. Now all people are free to approach God because of Christ's sacrifice for our sins (see Hebrews 9:1-14; 10:19-22).

**27:52, 53** Christ's death was accompanied by at least four

miraculous events: darkness, the tearing in two of the curtain in the Temple, an earthquake, and dead people rising from their tombs. Jesus' death, therefore, could not have gone unnoticed. Everyone knew something significant had happened.

**27:57, 58** Joseph of Arimathea was a secret disciple of Jesus. He was a religious leader, an honored member of the high council (Mark 15:43). Joseph courageously asked to take Jesus' body from the cross and to bury it. The disciples who publicly followed Jesus had fled, but this Jewish leader, who followed Jesus in secret, came forward and did what was right.

**27:60** The tomb where Jesus was laid was probably a man-made cave cut out of one of the many limestone hills in the area. These caves were often large enough to walk into.

### Guards Are Posted at the Tomb (238)

62 The next day, on the Sabbath,* the leading priests and Pharisees went to see Pilate. 63 They told him, "Sir, we remember what that deceiver once said while he was still alive: 'After three days I will rise from the dead.' 64 So we request that you seal the tomb until the third day. This will prevent his disciples from coming and stealing his body and then telling everyone he was raised from the dead! If that happens, we'll be worse off than we were at first."

65 Pilate replied, "Take guards and secure it the best you can." 66 So they sealed the tomb and posted guards to protect it.

27:63
Matt 12:40; 16:21;
17:23; 20:19
Mark 8:31; 9:31;
10:34
Luke 9:22; 18:33

27:64
Matt 28:13

27:66
Dan 6:17

### Jesus Rises from the Dead (239/Mark 16:1-8; Luke 24:1-12; John 20:1-10)

**28** Early on Sunday morning,* as the new day was dawning, Mary Magdalene and the other Mary went out to visit the tomb.

2 Suddenly there was a great earthquake! For an angel of the Lord came down from heaven, rolled aside the stone, and sat on it. 3 His face shone like lightning, and his clothing was as white as snow. 4 The guards shook with fear when they saw him, and they fell into a dead faint.

5 Then the angel spoke to the women. "Don't be afraid!" he said. "I know you are looking for Jesus, who was crucified. 6 He isn't here! He is risen from the dead, just as he said would happen. Come, see where his body was lying. 7 And now, go quickly and tell his disciples that he has risen from the dead, and he is going ahead of you to Galilee. You will see him there. Remember what I have told you."

28:3
Dan 7:9; 10:5-6

28:6
Matt 12:40; 16:21;
17:23; 20:19
Mark 8:31; 9:31;
10:34
Luke 9:22; 18:33;
24:7

28:7
Matt 26:32
Mark 14:28; 16:7

### Jesus Appears to the Women (241)

8 The women ran quickly from the tomb. They were very frightened but also filled with great joy, and they rushed to give the disciples the angel's message. 9 And as they went, Jesus met them and greeted them. And they ran to him, grasped his feet, and worshiped him. 10 Then Jesus said to them, "Don't be afraid! Go tell my brothers to leave for Galilee, and they will see me there."

28:10
John 20:17
Rom 8:29
Heb 2:11-13, 17

### Religious Leaders Bribe the Guards (242)

11 As the women were on their way, some of the guards went into the city and told the leading priests what had happened. 12 A meeting with the elders was called, and they decided to give

27:62 Or *On the next day, which is after the Preparation.*    28:1 Greek *After the Sabbath, on the first day of the week.*

---

**27:64-66** The religious leaders took Jesus' resurrection claims more seriously than the disciples did. The disciples didn't remember Jesus' teaching about his resurrection (20:17-19); but the religious leaders remembered and took steps they thought would prevent it (or at least a fabrication of it). Because of his claims, they were almost as afraid of Jesus after his death as when he was alive. They tried to take every precaution that his body would remain in the tomb. Because the tomb was hewn out of rock in the side of a hill, there was only one entrance. The tomb was sealed by stringing a cord across the stone that was rolled over the entrance. The cord was sealed at each end with clay. But the religious leaders took a further precaution, asking that guards be placed at the tomb's entrance. The Pharisees failed to understand that no rock, seal, guard, or army could prevent the Son of God from rising again.

**28:1** The other Mary was not Jesus' mother. She could have been the wife of Clopas (John 19:25). Or, she may have been Jesus' aunt, the mother of James and John (Matthew 27:56).

**28:2** The stone was not rolled aside so Jesus could get out, but so others could get in and see that Jesus had indeed risen from the dead, just as he had promised.

**28:5-7** The angel who announced the good news of the Resurrection to the women gave them four messages: (1) *Don't be afraid.* The reality of the Resurrection brings joy, not fear. When you are afraid, remember the empty tomb. (2) *He isn't here.* Jesus is not dead and is not to be looked for among the dead. He is alive, with his people. (3) *Come, see.* The women could check the evidence themselves. The tomb was empty then, and it is empty today. The Resurrection is a historical fact. (4) *Go*

*quickly and tell.* They were to spread the joy of the Resurrection. We, too, are to spread the great news about Jesus' resurrection.

**28:6** Jesus' resurrection is the key to the Christian faith. Why? (1) Just as he promised, Jesus rose from the dead. We can be confident, therefore, that he will accomplish all he has promised. (2) Jesus' bodily resurrection shows us that the living Christ is ruler of God's eternal Kingdom, not a false prophet or impostor. (3) We can be certain of our resurrection because he was resurrected. Death is not the end—there is future life. (4) The power that brought Jesus back to life is available to us to bring our spiritually dead selves back to life. (5) The Resurrection is the basis for the church's witness to the world. Jesus is more than just a human leader; he is the Son of God.

**28:10** By "brothers," Jesus probably meant his disciples. This showed that he had forgiven them, even after they had denied and deserted him. Jesus told the women to pass a message on to the disciples—that he would meet them in Galilee, as he had previously told them (Mark 14:28). But the disciples, afraid of the religious leaders, stayed hidden behind locked doors in Jerusalem (John 20:19). So Jesus met them first there (Luke 24:36) and then later in Galilee (John 21).

**28:11-15** Jesus' resurrection was already causing a great stir in Jerusalem. A group of women was moving quickly through the streets, looking for the disciples to tell them the amazing news that Jesus was alive. At the same time, a group of religious leaders was plotting how to cover up the Resurrection.

Today there is still a great stir over the Resurrection, and there are still only two choices: to believe that Jesus rose from the dead, or to be closed to the truth—denying it, ignoring it, or trying to explain it away.

**28:13**
Matt 27:64

the soldiers a large bribe. 13 They told the soldiers, "You must say, 'Jesus' disciples came during the night while we were sleeping, and they stole his body.' 14If the governor hears about it, we'll stand up for you so you won't get in trouble." 15So the guards accepted the bribe and said what they were told to say. Their story spread widely among the Jews, and they still tell it today.

### Jesus Gives the Great Commission (248/Mark 16:15-18)

**28:18**
John 3:35; 13:3;
17:2
Eph 1:20-22
Phil 2:9-10

**28:19**
Luke 24:47
Acts 1:8; 2:38

16Then the eleven disciples left for Galilee, going to the mountain where Jesus had told them to go. 17 When they saw him, they worshiped him—but some of them doubted! 18 Jesus came and told his disciples, "I have been given all authority in heaven and on earth. 19 Therefore, go and make disciples of all the nations,* baptizing them in the name of the Father and the Son and the Holy Spirit. 20 Teach these new disciples to obey all the commands I have given you. And be sure of this: I am with you always, even to the end of the age."

**28:19** Or *all peoples.*

**28:18** God gave Jesus authority over heaven and earth. On the basis of that authority, Jesus told his disciples to make more disciples as they preached, baptized, and taught. With this same authority, Jesus still commands us to tell others the Good News and make them disciples for the Kingdom.

**28:18-20** When someone is dying or leaving us, his or her last words are very important. Jesus left the disciples with these last words of instruction: They were under his authority; they were to make more disciples; they were to baptize and teach these new disciples to obey Christ; Christ would be with them always. Whereas in previous missions Jesus had sent his disciples only to the Jews (10:5, 6), their mission from now on would be worldwide. Jesus is Lord of the earth, and he died for the sins of people from all nations.

We are to go—whether it is next door or to another country—and make disciples. It is not an option but a command to all who call Jesus "Lord." We are not all evangelists in the formal sense, but we have all received gifts that we can use to help fulfill the great commission. As we obey, we have comfort in the knowledge that Jesus is always with us.

**28:19** Jesus' words affirm the reality of the Trinity. Some people accuse theologians of making up the concept of the Trinity and reading it into Scripture. As we see here, the concept comes

directly from Jesus himself. He did not say baptize them in the *names,* but in the *name* of the Father, Son, and Holy Spirit. The word *Trinity* does not occur in Scripture, but it well describes the three-in-one nature of the Father, Son, and Holy Spirit.

**28:19** The disciples were to baptize people because baptism unites believers with Jesus Christ in their death to sin and their resurrection to new life. Baptism symbolizes submission to Christ, a willingness to live God's way, and identification with God's covenant people.

**28:20** How is Jesus "with" us? Jesus was with the disciples physically until he ascended into heaven and then spiritually through the Holy Spirit (Acts 1:4). The Holy Spirit would be Jesus' presence that would never leave them (John 14:26). Jesus continues to be with us today through his Spirit.

**28:20** The Old Testament prophecies and genealogies in the book of Matthew present Jesus' credentials for being King of the world—not a military or political leader, as the disciples had originally hoped, but a spiritual King who can overcome all evil and rule in the heart of every person. If we refuse to serve the King faithfully, we are disloyal subjects, fit only to be banished from the Kingdom. We must make Jesus King of our life and worship him as our Savior, King, and Lord.

# MARK

## VITAL STATISTICS

**PURPOSE:**
To present the person, work, and teachings of Jesus

**AUTHOR:**
John Mark. He was not one of the 12 disciples, but he accompanied Paul on his first missionary journey (Acts 13:13).

**ORIGINAL AUDIENCE:**
The Christians in Rome, where the Gospel was written

**DATE WRITTEN:**
Between A.D. 55 and 65

**SETTING:**
The Roman Empire under Tiberius Caesar. The empire, with its common language and excellent transportation and communication systems, was ripe to hear Jesus' message, which spread quickly from nation to nation.

**KEY VERSE:**
"For even the Son of Man came not to be served but to serve others and to give his life as a ransom for many" (10:45).

**KEY PEOPLE:**
Jesus, the 12 disciples, Pilate, the Jewish religious leaders

**KEY PLACES:**
Capernaum, Nazareth, Caesarea Philippi, Jericho, Bethany, Mount of Olives, Jerusalem, Golgotha

**SPECIAL FEATURES:**
Mark was probably the first Gospel written. The other Gospels quote all but 31 verses of Mark. Mark records more miracles than does any other Gospel.

WE'RE number one! . . . The greatest, strongest, prettiest . . . champions! Daily such proclamations boldly assert claims of supremacy. Everyone wants to be associated with a winner. Losers are those who finish less than first. In direct contrast are the words of Jesus: "And whoever wants to be first must be the slave of everyone else. For even the Son of Man came here not to be served but to serve others and to give his life as a ransom for many" (10:44, 45). Jesus *is* the greatest—God incarnate, our Messiah—but he entered history as a servant.

This is the message of Mark. Written to encourage Roman Christians and to prove beyond a doubt that Jesus is the Messiah, Mark presents a rapid succession of vivid pictures of Jesus in action—his true identity revealed by what he does, not necessarily by what he says. It is Jesus on the move.

Omitting the birth of Jesus, Mark begins with John the Baptist's preaching. Then, moving quickly past Jesus' baptism, temptation in the wilderness, and call of the disciples, Mark takes us directly into Jesus' public ministry. We see Jesus confronting a demon, healing a man with leprosy, and forgiving and healing the paralyzed man lowered into Jesus' presence by friends.

Next, Jesus calls Matthew (Levi) and has dinner with him and his questionable associates. This initiates the conflict with the Pharisees and other religious leaders, who condemn Jesus for eating with sinners and breaking the Sabbath.

In chapter 4, Mark pauses to give a sample of Jesus' teaching—the parable of the farmer and the illustration of the mustard seed—and then plunges back into the action. Jesus calms the waves, drives out demons, and raises Jairus's daughter from the dead.

After returning to Nazareth for a few days and experiencing rejection in his hometown, Jesus commissions the disciples to spread the Good News everywhere. Opposition from Herod and the Pharisees increases, and John the Baptist is beheaded. But Jesus continues to move, feeding 5,000, reaching out to the woman from Syrian Phoenicia, healing the deaf man, and feeding 4,000.

Finally, it is time to reveal his true identity to the disciples. Do they really know who Jesus is? Peter proclaims him Messiah but then promptly shows that he does not understand Jesus' mission. After the Transfiguration, Jesus continues to teach and heal, confronting the Pharisees about divorce and the rich young man about eternal life. Blind Bartimaeus is healed.

Events move rapidly toward a climax. The Last Supper, the betrayal, the Crucifixion, and the Resurrection are dramatically portrayed, along with more examples of Jesus' teachings. Mark shows us Jesus—moving, serving, sacrificing, and saving! As you read Mark, be ready for action, be open for God's move in your life, and be challenged to move into your world to serve.

## THE BLUEPRINT

**A. BIRTH AND PREPARATION OF JESUS, THE SERVANT (1:1–13)**

Jesus did not arrive unannounced or unexpected. The Old Testament prophets had clearly predicted the coming of a great one, sent by God himself, who would offer salvation and eternal peace to Israel and the entire world. Then came John the Baptist, who announced that the long-awaited Messiah had finally come and would soon be among the people. In God's work in the world today, Jesus does not come unannounced or unexpected. Yet many still reject him. We have the witness of the Bible, but some choose to ignore it, just as many ignored John the Baptist in his day.

**B. MESSAGE AND MINISTRY OF JESUS, THE SERVANT (1:14—13:37)**
1. Jesus' ministry in Galilee
2. Jesus' ministry beyond Galilee
3. Jesus' ministry in Jerusalem

Jesus had all the power of God: He raised the dead, gave sight to the blind, restored deformed bodies, and quieted stormy seas. But with all this power, Jesus came to humanity as a servant. We can use his life as a pattern for how to live today. As Jesus served God and others, so should we.

**C. DEATH AND RESURRECTION OF JESUS, THE SERVANT (14:1—16:20)**

Jesus came as a servant, so many did not recognize or acknowledge him as the Messiah. We must be careful that we also don't reject God or his will because he doesn't quite fit our image of what God should be.

## MEGATHEMES

| THEME | EXPLANATION | IMPORTANCE |
|---|---|---|
| Jesus Christ | Jesus Christ alone is the Son of God. In Mark, Jesus demonstrates his divinity by overcoming disease, demons, and death. Although he had the power to be king of the earth, Jesus chose to obey the Father and die for us. | When Jesus rose from the dead, he proved that he was God, that he could forgive sin, and that he has the power to change our lives. By trusting in him for forgiveness, we can begin a new life with him as our guide. |
| Servant | As the Messiah, Jesus fulfilled the prophecies of the Old Testament by coming to earth. He did not come as a conquering king; he came as a servant. He helped people by telling them about God and healing them. Even more, by giving his life as a sacrifice for sin, he performed the ultimate act of service. | Because of Jesus' example, we should be willing to serve God and others. Real greatness in Christ's Kingdom is shown by service and sacrifice. Ambition or love of power or position should not be our motive; instead, we should do God's work because we love him. |
| Miracles | Mark records more of Jesus' miracles than sermons. Jesus is clearly a man of power and action, not just words. Jesus did miracles to convince the people who he was and to confirm to the disciples his true identity— God. | The more convinced we become that Jesus is God, the more we will see his power and his love. His mighty works show us he is able to save anyone regardless of his or her past. His miracles of forgiveness bring healing, wholeness, and changed lives to those who trust him. |
| Spreading the Gospel | Jesus directed his public ministry to the Jews first. When the Jewish leaders opposed him, Jesus also went to the non-Jewish world, healing and preaching. Roman soldiers, Syrians, and other Gentiles heard the Good News. Many believed and followed him. Jesus' final message to his disciples challenged them to go into all the world and preach the gospel of salvation. | Jesus crossed national, racial, and economic barriers to spread his Good News. Jesus' message of faith and forgiveness is for the whole world—not just our church, neighborhood, or nation. We must reach out beyond our own people and needs to fulfill the worldwide vision of Jesus Christ so that people everywhere may hear this great message and be saved from sin and death. |

## A. BIRTH AND PREPARATION OF JESUS, THE SERVANT (1:1–13)

Mark, the shortest of the four Gospels, opens with Jesus' baptism and temptation. Moving right into action, Mark quickly prepares us for Christ's ministry. The Gospel of Mark is concise, straightforward, and chronological.

*John the Baptist Prepares the Way for Jesus* (**16**/Matthew 3:1-12; Luke 3:1-18)

**1** This is the Good News about Jesus the Messiah, the Son of God.* It began ²just as the prophet Isaiah had written:

"Look, I am sending my messenger ahead of you,
   and he will prepare your way.*
³ He is a voice shouting in the wilderness,
   'Prepare the way for the LORD's coming!
   Clear the road for him!'*"

⁴This messenger was John the Baptist. He was in the wilderness and preached that people should be baptized to show that they had repented of their sins and turned to God to be forgiven. ⁵All of Judea, including all the people of Jerusalem, went out to see and hear John. And when they confessed their sins, he baptized them in the Jordan River. ⁶His clothes were woven from coarse camel hair, and he wore a leather belt around his waist. For food he ate locusts and wild honey.

⁷John announced: "Someone is coming soon who is greater than I am—so much greater that I'm not even worthy to stoop down like a slave and untie the straps of his sandals. ⁸I baptize you with* water, but he will baptize you with the Holy Spirit!"

**1:1** Some manuscripts do not include *the Son of God*.   **1:2** Mal 3:1.   **1:3** Isa 40:3 (Greek version).   **1:8** Or *in*; also in 1:8b.

**Cross-references (right margin):**
1:1
Ps 2:7
Matt 1:1
John 1:34
1 Jn 4:15
1:2-3
†Isa 40:3
†Mal 3:1
John 1:23
1:4
Acts 13:24; 19:4
1:6
Lev 11:22
2 Kgs 1:8
Zech 13:4
1:7
Acts 13:25
1:8
Joel 2:28
Acts 2:4; 10:45; 11:16

---

**1:1** When you experience the excitement of a big event, you naturally want to tell someone. Telling the story can bring back that original thrill as you relive the experience. Reading Mark's first words, you can sense his excitement. Picture yourself in the crowd as Jesus heals and teaches. Imagine yourself as one of the disciples. Respond to his words of love and encouragement. And remember that Jesus came for us who live today as well as for those who lived 2,000 years ago.

**1:1** Mark was not one of the 12 disciples of Jesus, but he probably knew Jesus personally. Mark wrote his Gospel in the form of a fast-paced story, like a popular novel. The book portrays Jesus as a man who backed up his words with action that constantly proved who he is—the Son of God. Because Mark wrote his Gospel for Christians in Rome, where many gods were worshiped, he wanted his readers to know that Jesus is *the one true* Son of God.

Without God's revelation, our finite minds cannot comprehend the infinite. But because of what we know about Jesus (thanks to writers like Mark), we can understand what God is like. Mark gave the "punch line" of his Gospel in the very first verse, but both Jesus' enemies and his disciples would not get it until Jesus' resurrection. For us who read Mark today, the message is clear that we must not ignore or reject Jesus Christ.

**1:2, 3** Isaiah was one of the greatest prophets of the Old Testament. The second half of the book of Isaiah is devoted to the promise of salvation. Isaiah wrote about the coming of the Messiah, Jesus Christ, and the man who would announce his coming, John the Baptist. John's call to "clear the road for him" meant that people should give up their selfish way of living, renounce their sins, seek God's forgiveness, and establish a relationship with God by believing and obeying his words as found in Scripture (Isaiah 1:18-20; 57:15).

**1:2, 3** Mark 1:2, 3 is a composite quotation, taken first from Malachi 3:1 and then from Isaiah 40:3.

**1:2-4** Hundreds of years earlier, the prophet Isaiah had predicted that John the Baptist and Jesus would come. Isaiah's words comforted many people as they looked forward to the Messiah, and knowing that God keeps his promises can comfort you, too. As you read the book of Mark, realize that it is more than just a story; it is part of God's Word. In it God is revealing to you his plans for human history—and offering the Good News of his salvation to you.

**1:3** John the Baptist prepared the way for Jesus. People who do not know Jesus need to be prepared to meet him. We can "prepare the way" by explaining their need for forgiveness, demonstrating Christ's teaching by our conduct, and telling them how Christ can give their lives meaning. We can "clear the road for him" by correcting misconceptions that might be hindering people form approaching Christ. Someone you know may be open to a relationship with Christ. What can you do to prepare the way for this person?

**1:4** Why does the Gospel of Mark begin with the story of John the Baptist and not mention the story of Jesus' birth? Important Roman officials of this day were always preceded by an announcer or herald. When the herald arrived in town, the people knew that someone of prominence would soon arrive. Because Mark's audience was primarily Roman Christians, he began his book with John the Baptist, whose mission it was to announce the coming of Jesus, the most important man who ever lived. Roman Christians would have been less interested in Jesus' birth than in this messenger who prepared the way.

**1:4** In John's ministry, baptism was a visible sign that a person had decided to change his or her life, giving up a sinful and selfish way of living and turning to God. John took a known custom and gave it new meaning. The Jews often baptized non-Jews who had converted to Judaism. But to baptize a Jew as a sign of repentance was a radical departure from Jewish custom. The early church took baptism a step further, associating it with Jesus' death and resurrection (see, for example, Romans 6:3, 4; 1 Peter 3:21).

**1:5** Jesus came at a time in history when the entire civilized world was relatively peaceful under Roman rule, travel was easy, and there was a common language. The news about Jesus' life, death, and resurrection could spread quickly throughout the vast Roman Empire.

In Israel, people were ready for Jesus, too, and they flocked to hear this wilderness preacher. There had been no God-sent prophets for 400 years, since the days of Malachi (who wrote the last book of the Old Testament). Anticipation was growing that a great prophet, or the Messiah prophesied in the Old Testament, would soon come (see Luke 3:15).

**1:5** The purpose of John's preaching was to prepare people to accept Jesus as God's Son. When John challenged the people to confess sin individually, he signaled the start of a new way to relate to God.

# KEY PLACES IN MARK

Sidon

LEBANON

N

Tyre · Caesarea Philippi

PHOENICIA

Mediterranean Sea

SYRIA

GALILEE

Capernaum · Bethsaida
Gennesaret · Sea of Galilee
Dalmanutha ·

Nazareth ·

DECAPOLIS
(Region of Ten Towns)

ISRAEL

SAMARIA

Jordan River

Jericho ·
Jerusalem · + Mount of Olives
Bethphage · · Bethany

JORDAN

Dead Sea

JUDEA

IDUMEA

0        20 Mi.

0        20 Km.

The broken lines (—·—·—) indicate modern boundaries.

Of the four Gospels, Mark's narrative is the most chronological—that is, most of the stories are positioned in the order they actually occurred. Though the shortest of the four, the Gospel of Mark contains the most events; it is action-packed. Most of this action centers in Galilee, where Jesus began his ministry. Capernaum served as his base of operation (1:21; 2:1; 9:33), from which he would go out to cities like Bethsaida, where he healed a blind man (8:22ff); Gennesaret, where he performed many healings (6:53ff); Tyre and Sidon (to the far north), where he healed many, drove out demons, and met the woman from Syrian Phoenicia (3:8; 7:24ff); and Caesarea Philippi, where Peter declared him to be the Messiah (8:27ff). After his ministry in Galilee and the surrounding regions, Jesus headed for Jerusalem (10:1). Before going there, Jesus told his disciples three times that he would be crucified there and then come back to life (8:31; 9:31; 10:33, 34).

---

Is change needed in your life before you can hear and understand Jesus' message? You have to admit that you need forgiveness before you can accept it. To prepare to receive Christ, repent. Turn away from the world's dead-end attractions, sinful temptations, and harmful attitudes, and turn to God. He can give you a new start.

**1:6** John dressed much like the prophet Elijah (2 Kings 1:8) in order to distinguish himself from the religious leaders, whose flowing robes reflected their great pride in their position (12:38). John's striking appearance reinforced his striking message.

**1:7, 8** Although John was the first genuine prophet in 400 years, Jesus the Messiah would be infinitely greater than he.

John was pointing out how insignificant he was compared to the one who was coming. John was not even worthy of being his slave. What John began, Jesus finished. What John prepared, Jesus fulfilled.

**1:8** John said Jesus would baptize them with the Holy Spirit, sending the Holy Spirit to live within each believer. John's baptism with water prepared a person to receive Christ's message. This baptism demonstrated repentance, humility, and willingness to turn from sin. This was the *beginning* of the spiritual process. When Jesus baptizes with the Holy Spirit, the entire person is transformed by the Spirit's power. Jesus offers to us both forgiveness of sin and the power to live for him.

*The Baptism of Jesus* (**17**/Matthew 3:13-17; Luke 3:21-22)

9 One day Jesus came from Nazareth in Galilee, and John baptized him in the Jordan River. 10 As Jesus came up out of the water, he saw the heavens splitting apart and the Holy Spirit descending on him* like a dove. 11 And a voice from heaven said, "You are my dearly loved Son, and you bring me great joy."

**1:11**
Gen 22:2
Ps 2:7
Isa 42:1
Matt 12:18; 17:5
Mark 9:7
Luke 9:35
2 Pet 1:17

*Satan Tempts Jesus in the Wilderness* (**18**/Matthew 4:1-11; Luke 4:1-13)

12 The Spirit then compelled Jesus to go into the wilderness, 13 where he was tempted by Satan for forty days. He was out among the wild animals, and angels took care of him.

### B. MESSAGE AND MINISTRY OF JESUS, THE SERVANT (1:14—13:37)

Mark tells us dramatic, action-packed stories. He gives us the most vivid account of Christ's activities. He features facts and actions, rather than teachings. The way Jesus lived his life is the perfect example of how we should live our lives today.

### 1. Jesus' ministry in Galilee

*Jesus Preaches in Galilee* (**30**/Matthew 4:12-17; Luke 4:14-15; John 4:43-45)

14 Later on, after John was arrested, Jesus went into Galilee, where he preached God's Good News.* 15 "The time promised by God has come at last!" he announced. "The Kingdom of God is near! Repent of your sins and believe the Good News!"

**1:14**
Mark 6:17-18
**1:15**
Gal 4:4
Eph 1:10

*Four Fishermen Follow Jesus* (**33**/Matthew 4:18-22)

16 One day as Jesus was walking along the shore of the Sea of Galilee, he saw Simon* and his brother Andrew throwing a net into the water, for they fished for a living. 17 Jesus called out to them, "Come, follow me, and I will show you how to fish for people!" 18 And they left their nets at once and followed him.

**1:10** Or *toward him,* or *into him.*   **1:14** Some manuscripts read *the Good News of the Kingdom of God.*   **1:16** *Simon* is called "Peter" in 3:16 and thereafter.

---

**1:9** Jesus grew up in Nazareth, where he had lived since he was a young boy (Matthew 2:22, 23). Nazareth was a small town in Galilee, located about halfway between the Sea of Galilee and the Mediterranean Sea. The city was despised and avoided by many Jews (John 1:46). Nazareth was a crossroads for trade routes and had contact with many cultures.

**1:9** If John's baptism was for repentance from sin, why was Jesus baptized? While even the greatest prophets (Isaiah, Jeremiah, Ezekiel) had to confess their sinfulness and need for repentance, Jesus didn't need to admit sin—he was sinless. Although Jesus didn't need forgiveness, he was baptized for the following reasons: (1) to begin his mission to bring the message of salvation to all people; (2) to show support for John's ministry; (3) to identify with our humanness and sin; (4) to give us an example to follow.

**1:10, 11** The Spirit descended like a dove on Jesus, and the voice from heaven proclaimed the Father's approval of Jesus as

**JESUS BEGINS HIS MINISTRY**

When Jesus came from his home in Nazareth to begin his ministry, he first took two steps in preparation—baptism by John in the Jordan River and temptation by Satan in the rough Judean wilderness. After the temptations, Jesus returned to Galilee and later set up his home base in Capernaum.

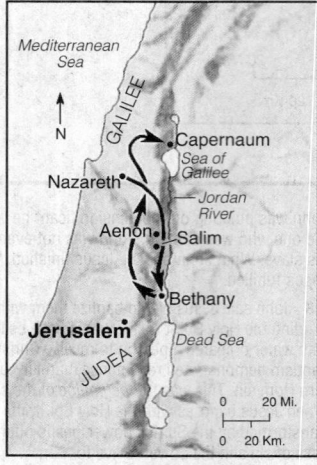

Mediterranean Sea
N
GALILEE
Capernaum
Sea of Galilee
Nazareth
Jordan River
Aenon
Salim
Bethany
**Jerusalem**
Dead Sea
JUDEA
0    20 Mi.
0    20 Km.

his divine Son. Here we see all three members of the Trinity together—God the Father, God the Son, and God the Holy Spirit. (See also Matthew 28:19; Luke 1:35; John 15:26; 1 Corinthians 12:4-13; 2 Corinthians 13:14; Ephesians 2:18; 1 Thessalonians 1:2-5; 1 Peter 1:2.)

**1:11** The dove and the voice from heaven were signs that Jesus was the Messiah. Many people want something tangible, visible, and "real" before they will believe. So Jesus did healings and other miracles, and God raised him from the dead. Still people doubt.

Will visible signs convince anyone? The "sign" that really brings us to faith is the power of God's message to answer the cry of the heart. To the confused, God offers a mind enlightened by faith. To the depressed, God offers a reason for joy. To the lonely, God offers eternal companionship. Don't look for a spectacular visible sign; instead, seek a cleansed and renewed life as evidence of his presence.

**1:12, 13** Satan is an angel who rebelled against God. He is real, not symbolic, and is constantly working against God and those who obey him. Satan tempted Eve in the garden and persuaded her to sin; he tempted Jesus in the wilderness and did not persuade him to fall. To be tempted is not a sin. Tempting others or giving in to temptation *is* sin. For a more detailed account of Jesus' temptation, read Matthew 4:1-11.

**1:12, 13** To identify fully with human beings, Jesus had to endure Satan's temptations. Although Jesus is God, he is also man. And as fully human, he was not exempt from Satan's attacks. Because Jesus faced temptations and overcame them, he can assist us in two important ways: (1) as an example of how to face temptation without sinning, and (2) as a helper who knows just what we need because he went through the same experience (Hebrews 4:15).

**1:16-20** We often assume that Jesus' disciples were great men of faith from the first time they met Jesus. But they had to grow in their faith just as all believers do (14:48-50, 66-72; John 14:1-9; 20:26-29). This is apparently not the only time Jesus called Peter (Simon), James, and John to follow him (see Luke 5:1-11 and John 1:35-42 for two other times). Although it took time for Jesus' call and his message to get through, the disciples *followed.* In the same way, we may question and falter, but we must never stop following Jesus.

**1:19**
Matt 10:2
Mark 3:17; 10:35
Luke 5:10

¹⁹A little farther up the shore Jesus saw Zebedee's sons, James and John, in a boat repairing their nets. ²⁰He called them at once, and they also followed him, leaving their father, Zebedee, in the boat with the hired men.

### Jesus Teaches with Authority (34/Luke 4:31-37)

²¹Jesus and his companions went to the town of Capernaum. When the Sabbath day came,

**1:22**
Matt 7:28-29

he went into the synagogue and began to teach. ²²The people were amazed at his teaching, for he taught with real authority—quite unlike the teachers of religious law.

**1:24**
Matt 8:29
John 6:69

²³Suddenly, a man in the synagogue who was possessed by an evil* spirit began shouting, ²⁴"Why are you interfering with us, Jesus of Nazareth? Have you come to destroy us? I know who you are—the Holy One of God!"

**1:26**
Mark 9:20

²⁵Jesus cut him short. "Be quiet! Come out of the man," he ordered. ²⁶At that, the evil spirit screamed, threw the man into a convulsion, and then came out of him.

²⁷Amazement gripped the audience, and they began to discuss what had happened. "What sort of new teaching is this?" they asked excitedly. "It has such authority! Even evil spirits obey his orders!" ²⁸The news about Jesus spread quickly throughout the entire region of Galilee.

### Jesus Heals Peter's Mother-in-Law and Many Others (35/Matthew 8:14-17; Luke 4:38-41)

²⁹After Jesus left the synagogue with James and John, they went to Simon and Andrew's home. ³⁰Now Simon's mother-in-law was sick in bed with a high fever. They told Jesus about her right away. ³¹So he went to her bedside, took her by the hand, and helped her sit up. Then the fever left her, and she prepared a meal for them.

³²That evening after sunset, many sick and demon-possessed people were brought to

**1:23** Greek *unclean;* also in 1:26, 27.

---

**1:17** Fishing was a major industry around the Sea of Galilee. Fishing with nets was the most common method. Jesus called the disciples to fish for people with the same energy they had used to fish for food. The gospel would be like a net, lifting people from dark waters into the light of day and transforming their lives. How can God use you to fish for people's souls? How can you train new converts to find new seas and cast new nets where waters have never been fished before? The gospel makes missionaries of all God's people. Where are you casting your net?

**1:21** Jesus had recently moved to Capernaum from Nazareth (Matthew 4:12, 13). Capernaum was a thriving town with great wealth as well as great sin and decadence. Because it was the headquarters for many Roman troops, pagan influences from all over the Roman Empire were pervasive. This was an ideal place for Jesus to challenge both Jews and non-Jews with the Good News of God's Kingdom.

**1:21, 22** Because the Temple in Jerusalem was too far for many Jews to travel to regularly for worship, many towns had synagogues serving both as places of worship and as schools. Beginning in the days of Ezra, about 450 B.C., a group of 10 Jewish families could start a synagogue. There, during the week, Jewish boys were taught the Old Testament law and Jewish religion. Girls could not attend. Each Saturday, the Sabbath, the Jewish men would gather to listen to a rabbi teach from the Scriptures. Because there was no permanent rabbi or teacher, it was customary for the synagogue leader to ask visiting teachers to speak. This is why Jesus often taught in the synagogues in the towns he visited. While the Jewish teachers often quoted from well-known rabbis to give their words more authority, Jesus didn't have that need. Because Jesus is God, he knew exactly what the Scriptures said and meant. He was the ultimate authority.

**1:23** Evil spirits, or demons, are ruled by Satan. They work to tempt people to sin. They were not created by Satan because God is the Creator of all. Rather they are fallen angels who joined Satan in his rebellion. Though not all disease comes from Satan, demons can cause a person to become mute, deaf, blind, or insane. But in every case where demons confronted Jesus, they lost their power. Thus, God limits what evil spirits can do; they

can do nothing without his permission. During Jesus' life on earth, demons were allowed to be very active to demonstrate once and for all Christ's power and authority over them.

**1:23ff** Some people dismiss all accounts of demon possession as a primitive way to describe mental illness. Although throughout history mental illness has often been wrongly diagnosed as demon possession, clearly a hostile outside force controlled the man described here. Mark emphasized Jesus' conflict with evil powers to show his superiority over them, so he recorded many stories about Jesus driving out evil spirits. Jesus didn't have to conduct an elaborate exorcism ritual. His word was enough to send out the evil spirit.

**1:23, 24** The evil spirit knew at once that Jesus was the Holy One sent from God. By including this event in his Gospel, Mark was establishing Jesus' credentials, showing that even the spiritual underworld recognized Jesus as the Messiah.

**1:29-31** Each Gospel writer had a slightly different perspective as he wrote; thus, the comparable stories in the Gospels often highlight different details. In Matthew, Jesus touched the woman's hand. In Mark, he helped her up. In Luke, he spoke to the fever, and it left her. The accounts do not conflict. Just as four people might witness the same event and all recount different details, so each Gospel writer simply emphasized different details of this story.

**1:32, 33** The people came to Jesus in the evening after sunset. That day had been the Sabbath (1:21), their day of rest, lasting from sunset Friday to sunset Saturday. The Jewish leaders had proclaimed that it was against the law to be healed on the Sabbath (Matthew 12:10; Luke 13:14). The people didn't want to break this law or the Jewish law that prohibited traveling on the Sabbath, so they waited until sunset. After the sun went down on Saturday, the crowds were free to find Jesus so he could heal them.

Jesus. 33 The whole town gathered at the door to watch. 34 So Jesus healed many people who were sick with various diseases, and he cast out many demons. But because the demons knew who he was, he did not allow them to speak.

**1:34**
Mark 3:12

### Jesus Preaches throughout Galilee (36/Matthew 4:23-25; Luke 4:42-44)

35 Before daybreak the next morning, Jesus got up and went out to an isolated place to pray. 36 Later Simon and the others went out to find him. 37 When they found him, they said, "Everyone is looking for you."

38 But Jesus replied, "We must go on to other towns as well, and I will preach to them, too. That is why I came." 39 So he traveled throughout the region of Galilee, preaching in the synagogues and casting out demons.

**1:38**
Isa 61:1

**1:39**
Matt 4:23; 9:35

### Jesus Heals a Man with Leprosy (38/Matthew 8:1-4; Luke 5:12-16)

40 A man with leprosy came and knelt in front of Jesus, begging to be healed. "If you are willing, you can heal me and make me clean," he said.

41 Moved with compassion,* Jesus reached out and touched him. "I am willing," he said. "Be healed!" 42 Instantly the leprosy disappeared, and the man was healed. 43 Then Jesus sent him on his way with a stern warning: 44 "Don't tell anyone about this. Instead, go to the priest and let him examine you. Take along the offering required in the law of Moses for those who have been healed of leprosy.* This will be a public testimony that you have been cleansed."

**1:44**
Lev 14:1-32

45 But the man went and spread the word, proclaiming to everyone what had happened. As a result, large crowds soon surrounded Jesus, and he couldn't publicly enter a town anywhere. He had to stay out in the secluded places, but people from everywhere kept coming to him.

### Jesus Heals a Paralyzed Man (39/Matthew 9:1-8; Luke 5:17-26)

**2** When Jesus returned to Capernaum several days later, the news spread quickly that he was back home. 2 Soon the house where he was staying was so packed with visitors that there was no more room, even outside the door. While he was preaching God's word to them, 3 four men arrived carrying a paralyzed man on a mat. 4 They couldn't bring him to

**2:2**
Eph 2:17
Heb 2:3

**1:41** Some manuscripts read *Moved with anger.*    **1:44** See Lev 14:2-32.

---

**1:34** Why didn't Jesus want the demons to reveal who he was? (1) By commanding the demons to remain silent, Jesus proved his authority and power over them. (2) Jesus wanted the people to believe he was the Messiah because of what he said and did, not because of the demons' words. (3) Jesus wanted to reveal his identity as the Messiah according to his timetable, not according to Satan's timetable. Satan wanted the people to follow Jesus around for what they could get out of him, not because he was the Son of God who could truly set them free from sin's guilt and power.

**1:35-37** Were the disciples impatient that Jesus prayed in solitude while so much ministry waited to be done? How would you have responded if you had been the one to find Jesus in prayer? It's easy to be so caught up with ministry that you neglect times of solitude, individual worship, and prayer. Perhaps you need to redesign your schedule to find time for earnest prayer. It is vitally important to: (1) seek the Lord before your busy schedule takes over your thoughts; (2) withdraw from noise and demands so you can focus on God; (3) take Jesus' attitude of regular communion with the Father; (4) reflect on the priorities Jesus had for his life; (5) determine to pray on a more regular basis, not just in times of crisis. If prayer was important for Jesus, then it must be important for his followers. Pray—even if you have to get up very early in the morning to do it!

**1:39** The Romans divided the land of Israel into three separate regions: Galilee, Samaria, and Judea. Galilee was the northernmost region, an area about 60 miles long and 30 miles wide. Jesus did much of his ministry in this area, an ideal place for him to teach because there were over 250 towns concentrated there, with many synagogues.

**1:40, 41** In keeping with the law in Leviticus 13 and 14, Jewish leaders declared people with leprosy unclean. This meant that lepers were unfit to participate in any religious or social activity. Because the law said that contact with any unclean person made a person unclean, too, some people even threw rocks at lepers to keep them at a safe distance. Even the mention of the name of this disabling disease terrified people. How astounding it was, then, when Jesus reached out and touched this man who had leprosy.

The real value of a person is inside, not outside. Although a person's body may be diseased or deformed, the person inside is no less valuable to God. In a sense, we are all people with leprosy because we have all been deformed by the ugliness of sin. By sending his Son, Jesus, God has touched us, giving us the opportunity to be healed.

**1:43, 44** Although leprosy was incurable, many different types of skin diseases were classified together as "leprosy." According to the Old Testament laws about leprosy (Leviticus 13–14), when a leper was cured, he or she had to go to a priest to be examined. Then the leper was to give a thank offering at the Temple. Jesus adhered to these laws by sending the man to the priest, demonstrating Jesus' complete regard for God's law. Sending a healed leper to a priest was also a way to verify Jesus' great miracle to the community.

**2:3** The paralyzed man's need moved his friends to action, and they brought him to Jesus. When you recognize someone's need, do you act? Many people have physical and spiritual needs you can meet, either by yourself or with others who are also concerned. Human need moved these four men; let it also move you to compassionate action.

**2:4** The crowd that had gathered made it impossible to bring the paralyzed man close to Jesus. Successful churches or busy Christians can be oblivious to needy people who want to see

**2:5**
Luke 7:48

**2:7**
Ps 130:3-4
Isa 43:25

Jesus because of the crowd, so they dug a hole through the roof above his head. Then they lowered the man on his mat, right down in front of Jesus. ⁵Seeing their faith, Jesus said to the paralyzed man, "My child, your sins are forgiven."

⁶But some of the teachers of religious law who were sitting there thought to themselves, ⁷"What is he saying? This is blasphemy! Only God can forgive sins!"

| PROMINENT JEWISH RELIGIOUS AND POLITICAL GROUPS | Name and Selected References | Description | Agreement with Jesus | Disagreement with Jesus |
|---|---|---|---|---|
| | PHARISEES<br>Matthew 5:20<br>Matthew 23:1-36<br>Luke 6:2<br>Luke 7:36-47 | Strict group of religious Jews who advocated obedience to the most minute portions of the Jewish law and traditions. Very influential in the synagogues. | Respect for the law, belief in the resurrection of the dead, committed to obeying God's will. | Rejected Jesus' claim to be Messiah because he did not follow all their traditions and associated with notoriously wicked people. |
| | SADDUCEES<br>Matthew 3:7<br>Matthew 16:11, 12<br>Mark 12:18 | Wealthy, upper class, Jewish priestly party. Rejected the authority of the Bible beyond the five books of Moses. Profited from business in the Temple. They, along with the Pharisees, were one of the two major parties of the Jewish high council. | Showed great respect for the five books of Moses, as well as the sanctity of the Temple. | Denied the resurrection of the dead. Thought the Temple could also be used as a place to transact business. |
| | TEACHERS OF RELIGIOUS LAW<br>Matthew 7:29<br>Mark 2:6<br>Mark 2:16 | Professional interpreters of the law—who especially emphasized the traditions. Many teachers of religious law were Pharisees. | Respect for the law. Committed to obeying God. | Denied Jesus' authority to reinterpret the law. Rejected Jesus as Messiah because he did not obey all of their traditions. |
| | SUPPORTERS OF HEROD<br>Matthew 22:16<br>Mark 3:6<br>Mark 12:13 | A Jewish political party of King Herod's supporters. | Unknown. In the Gospels they tried to trap Jesus with questions and plotted to kill him. | Afraid of Jesus causing political instability. They saw Jesus as a threat to their political future at a time when they were trying to regain from Rome some of their lost political power. |
| | ZEALOTS<br>Luke 6:15<br>Acts 1:14 | A fiercely dedicated group of Jewish patriots determined to end Roman rule in Israel. | Concerned about the future of Israel. Believed in the Messiah but did not recognize Jesus as the one sent by God. | Believed that the Messiah must be a political leader who would deliver Israel from Roman occupation. |
| | ESSENES<br>none | Jewish monastic group practicing ritual purity and personal holiness. | Emphasized justice, honesty, commitment. | Believed ceremonial rituals made them righteous. |

Jesus. In some churches, if the crowd is too thick and too disinterested, a needy person will simply wander away. How sad when the people in a church are so preoccupied with their own relationships and agendas that they don't even see those who are trying to get in. That should never happen. Where Jesus is present, may the faces of the faithful reflect his love, may their hands extend to greet all newcomers and seekers as friends, and may they open a way for others to come in.

**2:4** Houses in Bible times were built of stone. They had flat roofs made of mud mixed with straw. Outside stairways led to the roofs. These friends may have carried the paralyzed man up the outside stairs to the roof. They then could easily have taken apart the mud and straw mixture to make a hole through which to lower their friend to Jesus.

**2:6, 7** The teachers of religious law were in a perfect position, sitting where they could observe and criticize. Some sitting Christians follow their example. Is the music at church too fast or too loud? Is the sermon too long or too short? Do people aggravate you by sitting in your pew or dressing too casually? How much time do you spend worshiping in church and how much time do you spend complaining and criticizing? How about trying a little healthy activism—the kind that gets involved to work with fellow believers toward real progress on common goals, such as sharing the Good News, helping the needy, and building strong and caring disciples of Christ. Are you criticizing the church or changing the world?

8Jesus knew immediately what they were thinking, so he asked them, "Why do you question this in your hearts? 9Is it easier to say to the paralyzed man 'Your sins are forgiven,' or 'Stand up, pick up your mat, and walk'? 10So I will prove to you that the Son of Man* has the authority on earth to forgive sins." Then Jesus turned to the paralyzed man and said, 11"Stand up, pick up your mat, and go home!"

**2:8**
Matt 16:8

12And the man jumped up, grabbed his mat, and walked out through the stunned onlookers. They were all amazed and praised God, exclaiming, "We've never seen anything like this before!"

**2:12**
Matt 9:33

### Jesus Eats with Sinners at Matthew's House (40/Matthew 9:9-13; Luke 5:27-32)

13Then Jesus went out to the lakeshore again and taught the crowds that were coming to him. 14As he walked along, he saw Levi son of Alphaeus sitting at his tax collector's booth. "Follow me and be my disciple," Jesus said to him. So Levi got up and followed him.

**2:14**
John 1:43

15Later, Levi invited Jesus and his disciples to his home as dinner guests, along with many tax collectors and other disreputable sinners. (There were many people of this kind among Jesus' followers.) 16But when the teachers of religious law who were Pharisees* saw him eating with tax collectors and other sinners, they asked his disciples, "Why does he eat with such scum?*"

17When Jesus heard this, he told them, "Healthy people don't need a doctor—sick people do. I have come to call not those who think they are righteous, but those who know they are sinners."

**2:17**
Luke 19:10
1 Tim 1:15

### Religious Leaders Ask Jesus about Fasting (41/Matthew 9:14-17; Luke 5:33-39)

18Once when John's disciples and the Pharisees were fasting, some people came to Jesus and asked, "Why don't your disciples fast like John's disciples and the Pharisees do?"

19Jesus replied, "Do wedding guests fast while celebrating with the groom? Of course not. They can't fast while the groom is with them. 20But someday the groom will be taken away from them, and then they will fast.

**2:19**
John 3:29
Rev 19:7
**2:20**
Luke 17:22

21"Besides, who would patch old clothing with new cloth? For the new patch would shrink and rip away from the old cloth, leaving an even bigger tear than before.

**2:10** "Son of Man" is a title Jesus used for himself.  **2:16a** Greek *the scribes of the Pharisees.*  **2:16b** Greek *with tax collectors and sinners?*

---

**2:8-11** Before saying to the paralyzed man, "Stand up," Jesus said, "Your sins are forgiven." To the Jewish leaders this statement was blasphemous—claiming to do something only God could do. According to the law, the punishment for this sin was death (Leviticus 24:15, 16). The religious leaders understood correctly that Jesus was claiming divine prerogatives, but their judgment was wrong. Jesus was not blaspheming; his claim was true. Jesus is God, and he proved his claim by healing the paralyzed man (2:9-12).

**2:10** This is the first time in Mark that Jesus is referred to as the "Son of Man," a title emphasizing that Jesus is fully human. The title, *Son of God* (see, for example, John 20:31) emphasizes that he is fully God. As God's Son, Jesus has the authority to forgive sin. As a man, he can identify with our deepest needs and sufferings and help us overcome sin (see also the note on 8:31).

**2:14** Levi is another name for Matthew, the disciple who wrote the Gospel of Matthew. See Matthew's Profile in Matthew 9, p. 1557 for more information.

**2:14** Capernaum (2:1) was a key military center for Roman troops as well as a thriving business community. Several major highways intersected in Capernaum, with merchants passing through from as far away as Egypt to the south and Mesopotamia to the north. Levi (Matthew), a Jew, worked for the Romans as the area's tax collector, collecting taxes from citizens as well as from merchants passing through town. Tax collectors were expected to take a commission on the taxes they collected. Most of them overcharged and vastly enriched themselves. Tax collectors were despised by the Jews because of their reputation for cheating and their support of Rome.

**2:16, 17** The self-righteous Pharisees were indignant that Jesus would eat a meal with such sinners. But Jesus gladly associated with sinners because he loved them and because he knew that they needed to hear what he had to say. Jesus spent time with whoever needed or wanted to hear his message—poor, rich, bad, good. We, too, must befriend those who need Christ, even if they do not seem to be ideal companions. Are there people you have been neglecting because of their reputation? They may be the ones who most need to see and hear the message of Christ's love in and from you.

**2:18ff** John the Baptist had two goals: to lead people to repent of their sin, and to prepare them for Christ's coming. John's message was sobering, so he and his followers fasted. Fasting is both an outward sign of humility and regret for sin, and an inner discipline that clears the mind and keeps the spirit alert. Fasting empties the body of food; repentance empties the life of sin. Jesus' disciples did not need to fast to prepare for his coming because he was with them. Jesus did not condemn fasting, however. He himself fasted for 40 days (Matthew 4:2). Nevertheless, Jesus emphasized fasting with the right motives. The Pharisees fasted twice a week to show others how holy they were. Jesus explained that if people fast only to impress others, they will be twisting the purpose of fasting.

**2:19** Jesus compared himself to a groom. In the Bible, the image of a bride is often used for God's people, and the image of a groom for the God who loves them (Isaiah 62:5; Matthew 25:1-13; Revelation 21:2).

**2:21** Jesus did not come to patch up the old religious system of Judaism with its rules and traditions. His purpose was to fulfill it and start something new (though this "new" thing had been prophesied for centuries). Jesus Christ, God's Son, came to earth to offer all people forgiveness of sins and reconciliation with God. This new Good News did not fit into the old rigid legalistic system

**2:22**
Gal 3:1-3

22"And no one puts new wine into old wineskins. For the wine would burst the wineskins, and the wine and the skins would both be lost. New wine calls for new wineskins."

### The Disciples Pick Wheat on the Sabbath (**45**/Matthew 12:1-8; Luke 6:1-5)

**2:23**
Deut 23:25

23One Sabbath day as Jesus was walking through some grainfields, his disciples began breaking off heads of grain to eat. 24But the Pharisees said to Jesus, "Look, why are they breaking the law by harvesting grain on the Sabbath?"

**2:25-26**
1 Sam 21:1-7

25Jesus said to them, "Haven't you ever read in the Scriptures what David did when he and his companions were hungry? 26He went into the house of God (during the days when Abiathar was high priest) and broke the law by eating the sacred loaves of bread that only the priests are allowed to eat. He also gave some to his companions."

**2:27**
Exod 23:12
Deut 5:14
John 7:21-24

27Then Jesus said to them, "The Sabbath was made to meet the needs of people, and not people to meet the requirements of the Sabbath. 28So the Son of Man is Lord, even over the Sabbath!"

### Jesus Heals a Man's Hand on the Sabbath (**46**/Matthew 12:9-14; Luke 6:6-11)

**3** Jesus went into the synagogue again and noticed a man with a deformed hand. 2Since it was the Sabbath, Jesus' enemies watched him closely. If he healed the man's hand, they planned to accuse him of working on the Sabbath.

3Jesus said to the man with the deformed hand, "Come and stand in front of everyone." 4Then he turned to his critics and asked, "Does the law permit good deeds on the Sabbath, or is it a day for doing evil? Is this a day to save life or to destroy it?" But they wouldn't answer him.

**3:5**
Mark 6:52; 8:17

5He looked around at them angrily and was deeply saddened by their hard hearts. Then he said to the man, "Hold out your hand." So the man held out his hand, and it was

---

of religion. It needed a fresh start. The message will always remain "new" because it must be accepted and applied in every generation. When you follow Christ, be prepared for new ways to live, new ways to look at people, and new ways to serve.

**2:22** A wineskin was a goatskin sewed together at the edges to form a watertight bag. New wine, expanding as it aged, stretched the wineskin. New wine, therefore, could not be put into a wineskin that had already been stretched, or the taut skin would burst.

The Pharisees had become rigid like old wineskins. They could not accept faith in Jesus that would not be contained or limited by man-made ideas or rules. Your heart, like a wineskin, can become rigid and prevent you from accepting the new life that Christ offers. Keep your heart pliable and open to accepting the life-changing truths of Christ.

**2:23** Jesus and his disciples were not stealing when they picked the grain. Leviticus 19:9, 10 and Deuteronomy 23:25 say that farmers were to leave the edges of their fields unharvested so that some of their crops could be picked by travelers and by the poor. Just as walking on a sidewalk is not trespassing on private property, picking heads of grain at the edge of a field was not stealing.

**2:24** God's law said that crops should not be harvested on the Sabbath (Exodus 34:21). This law prevented farmers from becoming greedy and ignoring God on the Sabbath. It also protected laborers from being overworked.

The Pharisees interpreted the action of Jesus and his disciples—picking the grain and eating it as they walked through the fields—as harvesting; and so they judged Jesus a lawbreaker. But Jesus and the disciples clearly were not harvesting the grain for personal gain; they were simply looking for something to eat. The Pharisees were so focused on the words of the rule that they missed its intent.

**2:25-28** Jesus used the example of David to point out how ridiculous the Pharisees' accusations were (this incident occurred in 1 Samuel 21:1-6). God created the Sabbath for our benefit; we are restored both physically and spiritually when we take time to rest and to focus on God. For the Pharisees, Sabbath rules had become more important than Sabbath rest. Both David and Jesus understood that the intent of God's law is to promote love for God and others.

The Christian faith involves many rules that are meant to be

governed by love. That makes love the highest rule, but it also moves Christians toward personal sacrifice, discipline, and responsibility—scarce resources in today's world. When confronted with rules of your own or others' making, ask: (1) Does the rule serve God's purposes? (2) Does the rule reveal God's character? (3) Does the rule help people get into God's family, or keep them out? (4) Does the rule have biblical roots that can be supported in the context of all of Scripture? Good rules pass all four tests.

**2:26** The "sacred loaves of bread" (called the Bread of the Presence) were set before God on a table in the Holy Place in the Tabernacle (and later in the Temple). Every Sabbath, 12 freshly-baked loaves of bread were set out, and the priests ate the old loaves. See Exodus 25:30 and Leviticus 24:5-9 for more about the Bread of the Presence.

**3:2** Already many of the religious leaders had turned against Jesus and become his "enemies." They were jealous of his popularity, his miracles, and the authority in his teaching and actions. They valued their status in the community and their opportunity for personal gain so much that they lost sight of their goal as religious leaders—to point people toward God. Of all people, the Pharisees should have recognized the Messiah, but they refused to acknowledge him because they were not willing to give up their treasured position and power. When Jesus exposed their attitudes, he became their enemy instead of their Messiah, and they began looking for ways to turn the people against him.

**3:5** Jesus was angry about the Pharisees' uncaring attitudes. Anger itself is not wrong. It depends on what makes us angry and what we do with our anger. Too often we express our anger in selfish and harmful ways. By contrast, Jesus expressed his anger by correcting a problem—healing the man's hand. Use your anger to find constructive solutions rather than to tear people down.

# THE TWELVE

| Name | Occupation | Outstanding Characteristics | Major Events in His Life |
|---|---|---|---|
| SIMON PETER (son of John) | Fisherman | Impulsive; later—bold in preaching about Jesus | One of three in core group of disciples; recognized Jesus as the Messiah; denied Christ and repented; preached Pentecost sermon; a leader of the Jerusalem church; baptized Gentiles; wrote 1 and 2 Peter. |
| JAMES (son of Zebedee), he and his brother, John, were called the "Sons of Thunder" | Fisherman | Ambitious, short-tempered, judgmental, deeply committed to Jesus | Also in core group; he and his brother, John, asked Jesus for places of honor in his Kingdom; wanted to call fire down to destroy a Samaritan village; first disciple to be martyred. |
| JOHN (son of Zebedee), James's brother, and "the disciple Jesus loved" | Fisherman | Ambitious, judgmental, later—very loving | Third disciple in core group; asked Jesus for a place of honor in his Kingdom; wanted to call down fire on a Samaritan village; a leader of the Jerusalem church; wrote the Gospel of John, 1, 2, 3 John, and Revelation. |
| ANDREW (Peter's brother) | Fisherman | Eager to bring others to Jesus | Accepted John the Baptist's testimony about Jesus; told Peter about Jesus; he and Philip told Jesus that Greeks wanted to see him. |
| PHILIP | Fisherman | Questioning attitude | Told Nathanael about Jesus; wondered how Jesus could feed the 5,000; asked Jesus to show his followers God the Father; he and Andrew told Jesus that Greeks wanted to see him. |
| NATHANAEL | Unknown | Honest and straightforward | Initially rejected Jesus because Jesus was from Nazareth but acknowledged him as the "Son of God" and "King of Israel" when they met. |
| MATTHEW (Levi) | Tax collector | Despised outcast because of his dishonest career | Abandoned his corrupt (and financially profitable) way of life to follow Jesus; invited Jesus to a party with his notorious friends; wrote the Gospel of Matthew. |
| THOMAS (the Twin) | Unknown | Courage and doubt | Suggested the disciples go with Jesus to Bethany—even if it meant death; asked Jesus about where he was going; refused to believe Jesus was risen until he could see Jesus alive and touch his wounds. |
| JAMES (son of Alphaeus) | Unknown | Unknown | Became one of Jesus' disciples. |
| THADDAEUS (Judas son of James) | Unknown | Unknown | Asked Jesus why he would reveal himself to his followers and not to the world. |
| SIMON THE ZEALOT | Unknown | Fierce patriotism | Became a disciple of Jesus. |
| JUDAS ISCARIOT | Unknown | Treacherous and greedy | Became one of Jesus' disciples; betrayed Jesus; committed suicide. |

Jesus' faithful disciples were ordinary men who became extraordinary because of Jesus Christ. Despite their confusion and lack of understanding during his lifetime, they became powerful witnesses to his resurrection. Their lives were transformed by God's power. The story of Jesus' disciples does not end with the Gospels. It continues in the book of Acts and many of the letters.

# DISCIPLES

| What Jesus Said about Him | A Key Lesson from His Life | Selected References |
| --- | --- | --- |
| Named him Peter, "rock"; called him "Satan" when he urged Jesus to reject the cross; said he would fish for people; he received revelation from God; he would deny Jesus; he would later be crucified for his faith. | Christians falter at times, but when they return to Jesus, he forgives them and strengthens their faith | Matthew 4:18-20 Mark 8:29-33 Luke 22:31-34 John 21:15-19 Acts 2:14-41 Acts 10:1—11:18 |
| Called James and John "Sons of Thunder"; said he would fish for people; would drink the cup Jesus drank. | Christians must be willing to die for Jesus. | Mark 3:17 Mark 10:35-40 Luke 9:52-56 Acts 12:1, 2 |
| Called John and James "Sons of Thunder"; said he would fish for people; would drink the cup Jesus drank; would take care of Jesus' mother after Jesus' death. | The transforming power of the love of Christ is available to all. | Mark 1:19 Mark 10:35-40 Luke 9:52-56 John 19:26, 27 John 21:20-24 |
| Said he would fish for people. | Christians are to tell other people about Jesus. | Matthew 4:18-20 John 1:35-42; 6:8, 9 John 12:20-24 |
| Asked if Philip realized that to know and see him was to know and see the Father. | God uses our questions to teach us. | Matthew 10:3 John 1:43-46; 6:2-7 John 12:20-22 John 14:8-11 |
| Called him "a true son of Israel" and "an honest man." | Jesus respects honesty in people— even if they challenge him because of it. | Mark 3:18 John 1:45-51 John 21:1-13 |
| Called him to be a disciple. | Christianity is not for people who think they're already good; it is for people who know they've failed and want help. | Matthew 9:9-13 Mark 2:15-17 Luke 5:27-32 |
| Said Thomas believed because he actually saw Jesus after the Resurrection. | Even when Christians experience serious doubts, Jesus reaches out to them to restore their faith. | Matthew 10:3 John 14:5; 20:24-29 John 21:1-13 |
| Unknown | Unknown | Matthew 10:3 Mark 3:18 Luke 6:15 |
| Unknown | Christians follow Jesus because they believe in him; they do not always understand the details of God's plan. | Matthew 10:3 Mark 3:18 John 14:22 |
| Unknown | If we are willing to give up our plans for the future, we can participate in Jesus' plans. | Matthew 10:4 Mark 3:18 Luke 6:15 |
| Called him "a devil"; said Judas would betray Jesus. | It is not enough to be familiar with Jesus' teachings. Jesus' true followers love and obey him. | Matthew 26:20-25 Luke 22:47, 48 John 12:4-8 |

restored! 6At once the Pharisees went away and met with the supporters of Herod to plot how to kill Jesus.

3:6
Matt 22:15-16
Mark 12:13

## Large Crowds Follow Jesus (47/Matthew 12:15-21)

7Jesus went out to the lake with his disciples, and a large crowd followed him. They came from all over Galilee, Judea, 8Jerusalem, Idumea, from east of the Jordan River, and even from as far north as Tyre and Sidon. The news about his miracles had spread far and wide, and vast numbers of people came to see him.

3:7-8
Matt 4:25

9Jesus instructed his disciples to have a boat ready so the crowd would not crush him. 10He had healed many people that day, so all the sick people eagerly pushed forward to touch him. 11And whenever those possessed by evil* spirits caught sight of him, the spirits would throw them to the ground in front of him shrieking, "You are the Son of God!" 12But Jesus sternly commanded the spirits not to reveal who he was.

3:10
Mark 4:1
3:11-12
Mark 1:24-25, 34
Luke 4:41
Acts 16:16-17

## Jesus Chooses the Twelve Disciples (48/Luke 6:12-16)

13Afterward Jesus went up on a mountain and called out the ones he wanted to go with him. And they came to him. 14Then he appointed twelve of them and called them his apostles.* They were to accompany him, and he would send them out to preach, 15giving them authority to cast out demons. 16These are the twelve he chose:

3:14
Mark 6:30
3:16
Matt 16:17-18
John 1:42

Simon (whom he named Peter),
17 James and John (the sons of Zebedee, but Jesus nicknamed them "Sons of Thunder"*),
18 Andrew,
   Philip,
   Bartholomew,
   Matthew,
   Thomas,
   James (son of Alphaeus),
   Thaddaeus,
   Simon (the zealot*),
19 Judas Iscariot (who later betrayed him).

3:17
Luke 9:54

3:11 Greek *unclean;* also in 3:30.   3:14 Some manuscripts do not include *and called them his apostles.*
3:17 Greek *whom he named Boanerges, which means Sons of Thunder.*   3:18 Greek *the Cananean,* an Aramaic term for Jewish nationalists.

---

3:6 The Pharisees were a Jewish religious group that zealously followed the Old Testament laws as well as their own religious traditions. They were highly respected in the community, but they hated Jesus because he challenged their proud attitudes and dishonorable motives.

The supporters of Herod were a Jewish political party that hoped to restore Herod the Great's line to the throne. Jesus was a threat to them as well because he challenged their political ambitions. These two groups were normally at odds, but they joined forces against Jesus.

3:6 The Pharisees had accused Jesus of breaking their law that said medical attention could be given to no one on the Sabbath except in matters of life and death. Ironically, the Pharisees themselves were breaking God's law by plotting murder.

3:7-11 The evil spirits knew that Jesus was the Son of God, but they had no intention of following him. Many people followed Jesus but didn't understand his true purpose for coming. Some people came for miracles, some came to hear his teaching, but they didn't understand the way of the cross. Knowing about Jesus, or even believing that he is God's Son, does not guarantee salvation. You must also follow and obey him (see James 2:17).

3:12 Jesus warned the evil spirits not to reveal his identity because he did not want them to reinforce a popular misconception. The huge crowds were looking for a political and military leader who would free them from Rome's control, and they thought that the Messiah predicted by the Old Testament prophets would be this kind of man. Jesus wanted to teach the people about the kind of Messiah he really was—one who was far different from their expectations. Christ's Kingdom is spiritual. It begins with the overthrow of sin in people's hearts, not with the overthrow of governments.

3:13 What does it mean to hear the "call" of God? First, God calls you to faith in Jesus. You will know this call by the growing desire in your heart to settle the matter of peace with God speedily. Respond to him—answer with a grateful, "Yes, Lord, I need you!"

Second, God calls you to service in Jesus' name. Wherever you are (and sometimes you need to move), whatever you're doing (and sometimes you need to upgrade your skills), God has a place of service for you. Jesus calls you and he wants you. Answer this call thoughtfully, seriously, in consultation with other Christians, saying, "Yes, Lord, I love you and will follow you!"

3:14 From the hundreds of people who followed him from place to place, Jesus chose 12 to be his *apostles. Apostle* means "messenger or authorized representative." Why did Jesus choose 12 disciples? The number 12 corresponds to the 12 tribes of Israel (Matthew 19:28), showing the continuity between the old religious system and the new one based on Jesus' message. Many people followed Jesus, but these 12 received the most intense training.

Jesus did not choose these 12 to be his associates and companions because of their faith; their faith often faltered. He didn't choose them because of their talent and ability; no one stood out with unusual ability. The disciples represented a wide range of backgrounds and life experiences, but apparently they had no more leadership potential than those who were not chosen. The one characteristic they all shared was their willingness to obey Jesus. After Jesus' ascension, they were filled with the Holy Spirit and empowered to carry out special roles in the growth of the early church. We should not disqualify ourselves from service to Christ because we do not have the expected credentials. Being a good disciple is simply a matter of following Jesus with a willing heart.

## Religious Leaders Accuse Jesus of Getting His Power from Satan (74/Matthew 12:22-37)

20One time Jesus entered a house, and the crowds began to gather again. Soon he and his disciples couldn't even find time to eat. 21When his family heard what was happening, they tried to take him away. "He's out of his mind," they said.

3:22
John 7:20;
8:48, 52;
10:20

22But the teachers of religious law who had arrived from Jerusalem said, "He's possessed by Satan,* the prince of demons. That's where he gets the power to cast out demons."

23Jesus called them over and responded with an illustration. "How can Satan cast out Satan?" he asked. 24"A kingdom divided by civil war will collapse. 25Similarly, a family splintered by feuding will fall apart. 26And if Satan is divided and fights against himself,

3:27
Isa 49:24-25

how can he stand? He would never survive. 27Let me illustrate this further. Who is powerful enough to enter the house of a strong man like Satan and plunder his goods? Only someone even stronger—someone who could tie him up and then plunder his house.

3:28-30
Luke 12:10
1 Jn 5:16

28"I tell you the truth, all sin and blasphemy can be forgiven, 29but anyone who blasphemes the Holy Spirit will never be forgiven. This is a sin with eternal consequences." 30He told them this because they were saying, "He's possessed by an evil spirit."

## Jesus Describes His True Family (76/Matthew 12:46-50; Luke 8:19-21)

3:31
Mark 6:3
John 7:3-5

31Then Jesus' mother and brothers came to see him. They stood outside and sent word for him to come out and talk with them. 32There was a crowd sitting around Jesus, and someone said, "Your mother and your brothers* are outside asking for you."

3:34
John 20:17
Rom 8:29
Heb 2:11

33Jesus replied, "Who is my mother? Who are my brothers?" 34Then he looked at those around him and said, "Look, these are my mother and brothers. 35Anyone who does God's will is my brother and sister and mother."

**3:22** Greek *Beezeboul;* other manuscripts read *Beezeboul;* Latin version reads *Beelzebub.*   **3:32** Some manuscripts add *and sisters.*

---

**3:21** With the crowds pressing in on him, Jesus didn't even take time to eat. Because of this, his friends and family came to take charge of him (3:31, 32), thinking he had gone "over the edge" as a religious fanatic. They were concerned for him, but they missed the point of his ministry. Even those who were closest to Jesus were slow to understand who he was and what he had come to do.

**3:21** The family may be the most difficult place to be a witness for Jesus. To be the first or only Christian may go against the grain. Your faith may be misinterpreted as criticism. Your zeal may be misunderstood. You may be accused of being a hypocrite because other areas of your life still fall short of Christ's ideals. Uncommitted people may view your new commitment to the Bible as unreasonable bigotry.

Family members require the most patience. They see you at your worst when your guard is down. Remember that Christ's family rejected and ridiculed him. Jesus knows what you face by trying to be a witness for him in your own family. Stay true to your faith. Don't respond negatively to the attacks that may come. Over time, your love for your family will have a positive effect.

**3:22-27** These teachers of the law brought a nonsensical accusation against Jesus. They tried to say that Jesus was driving out demons by the power of the prince of demons—in other words, that Jesus' power came from Satan, not God. They wanted the people to believe that Jesus himself was possessed (3:30). This would disprove his claim as the Messiah and place him instead in league with the devil.

The more effective you are in your Christian life, the more extreme will be the attacks of the enemy. Even the most ridiculous accusation will convince some when it's cleverly packaged to sound sincere and concerned. Stand firm for the truth, even when clever attacks come.

**3:27** Although God permits Satan to work in our world, God is still in control. Because he is God, Jesus has power over Satan and is able to drive out demons, thus ending their terrible work in people's lives. One day Satan will be bound forever (Revelation 20:10).

**3:28, 29** Christians sometimes wonder if they have committed this sin of blaspheming the Holy Spirit. Christians need not worry because this sin is attributing to the devil the work of the Holy Spirit. It reveals a heart attitude of unbelief and unrepentance. Deliberate, ongoing rejection of the work of the Holy Spirit is blasphemy because it is rejecting God himself. The religious leaders accused Jesus of blasphemy, but ironically they were the guilty ones when they looked Jesus in the face and accused him of being possessed by Satan.

**3:31-35** Jesus' mother was Mary (Luke 1:30, 31), and his brothers were probably the other children Mary and Joseph had after Jesus (see also 6:3). Some Christians believe the ancient tradition that Jesus was Mary's only child. If this is true, the "brothers" were possibly cousins (cousins were often called brothers in those days). Some have offered yet another suggestion: When Joseph married Mary, he was a widower, and these were his children by his first marriage. Most likely, however, these were Jesus' half brothers (see Mark 6:3, 4).

Jesus' family did not yet fully understand his ministry, as can be seen in 3:21. Jesus explained that in our spiritual family, the relationships are ultimately more important and longer lasting than those formed in our physical families.

**3:33-35** God's family is accepting and doesn't exclude anyone. Although Jesus cared for his mother and brothers, he also cared for all those who loved him. Jesus did not show partiality; he allowed everyone the privilege of obeying God and becoming part of his family. In our increasingly computerized, impersonal world, warm relationships among members of God's family take on major importance. The church should give the loving, personalized care that many people find nowhere else.

*Jesus Tells the Parable of the Four Soils* (**77**/Matthew 13:1-9; Luke 8:4-8)

**4** Once again Jesus began teaching by the lakeshore. A very large crowd soon gathered around him, so he got into a boat. Then he sat in the boat while all the people remained on the shore. ²He taught them by telling many stories in the form of parables, such as this one:

³"Listen! A farmer went out to plant some seed. ⁴ As he scattered it across his field, some of the seed fell on a footpath, and the birds came and ate it. ⁵ Other seed fell on shallow soil with underlying rock. The seed sprouted quickly because the soil was shallow. ⁶ But the plant soon wilted under the hot sun, and since it didn't have deep roots, it died.⁷ Other seed fell among thorns that grew up and choked out the tender plants so they produced no grain. ⁸ Still other seeds fell on fertile soil, and they sprouted, grew, and produced a crop that was thirty, sixty, and even a hundred times as much as had been planted!"⁹ Then he said, "Anyone with ears to hear should listen and understand."

*Jesus Explains the Parable of the Four Soils* (**78**/Matthew 13:10-23; Luke 8:9-18)

¹⁰Later, when Jesus was alone with the twelve disciples and with the others who were gathered around, they asked him what the parables meant.

¹¹He replied, "You are permitted to understand the secret* of the Kingdom of God. But I use parables for everything I say to outsiders, ¹² so that the Scriptures might be fulfilled:

'When they see what I do,
    they will learn nothing.
When they hear what I say,
    they will not understand.
Otherwise, they will turn to me
    and be forgiven.'*"

¹³Then Jesus said to them, "If you can't understand the meaning of this parable, how will you understand all the other parables? ¹⁴ The farmer plants seed by taking God's word to others. ¹⁵ The seed that fell on the footpath represents those who hear the message, only to have Satan come at once and take it away. ¹⁶ The seed on the rocky soil represents those who hear the message and immediately receive it with joy. ¹⁷ But since they don't have deep roots, they don't last long. They fall away as soon as they have problems or are persecuted for believing God's word. ¹⁸ The seed that fell among the thorns represents others who hear God's word, ¹⁹ but all too quickly the message is crowded out by the worries of this life, the

**4:11** Greek *mystery.*   **4:12** Isa 6:9-10 (Greek version).

**4:2**
Mark 4:33-34

**4:9**
Matt 11:15
Mark 4:23

**4:12**
†Isa 6:9-10
John 12:39-40
Acts 28:26-27

**4:14**
Eph 3:8
Jas 1:18
1 Pet 1:23-25

**4:15**
2 Cor 4:4
1 Pet 5:8

**4:19**
1 Tim 6:9-10, 17
1 Jn 2:15-17

---

**4:2** Jesus taught the people by telling stories called parables, using familiar scenes to explain spiritual truths. This method of teaching compels the listener to think. It conceals the truth from those who are too stubborn or prejudiced to hear what is being taught. Most parables have one main point, so we must be careful not to go beyond what Jesus intended to teach.

**4:3** Seed was planted by hand. As the farmer walked across the field, he threw handfuls of seed onto the ground from a large bag slung across his shoulders. The plants did not grow in neat rows as they do with today's machine planting. No matter how skillful, no farmer could keep some of his seed from falling on the footpath, from being scattered among rocks and thorns, or from being carried off by the wind. So the farmer would throw the seed liberally, and enough would fall on good ground to ensure the harvest.

**4:9** The hearing Jesus wants from us is not the kind we use when we listen to background music or when someone starts to recount a long story we've already heard. To truly "hear" Jesus' words is to believe them, to use them immediately in decisions and attitudes, and to base life on them—your recreation and work, family plans and money matters, praying and singing. To hear Jesus' words is to make Jesus your true Lord. What is Jesus saying to you?

**4:14-20** This parable should encourage spiritual "sowers"— those who teach, preach, and lead others. The farmer sowed

good seed, but not all the seed sprouted, and even the plants that grew had varying yields. Don't be discouraged if you do not always see results as you faithfully teach the Word. Some people do not understand God's truth because they are not ready for it. God reveals truth to people who will act on it and make it visible in their lives. When you talk with people about God, be aware that they will not understand if they are not yet ready. Be patient, taking every chance to tell them more about God and praying that the Holy Spirit will open their minds and hearts to receive the truth and act on it. Productivity is in God's hands.

**4:14-20** The four soils represent four different ways people respond to God's message. Usually we think that Jesus was talking about four different kinds of people. But he may also have been talking about (1) different times or phases in a person's life or (2) how we willingly apply God's message to some areas of our life but resist applying it to others. For example, you may be open to God about your future but closed concerning how you spend your money. You may respond like good soil to God's demand for worship but rocky soil to his demand to give to people in need. Strive to be like good soil in every area of your life at all times.

**4:19** Worries of this life, the lure of wealth, and the desire for things plagued first-century disciples just as they do us today. How easy it is for our daily routines to become overcrowded. A life packed with materialistic pursuits crowds out God's Word and leaves us unfruitful for him. Stay free so you can hear God when he speaks.

lure of wealth, and the desire for other things, so no fruit is produced. 20 And the seed that fell on good soil represents those who hear and accept God's word and produce a harvest of thirty, sixty, or even a hundred times as much as had been planted!"

**4:21-25**
Matt 5:15
**4:22**
Matt 10:26
Luke 12:2
**4:23**
Matt 11:15; 13:43
**4:25**
Matt 13:12; 25:29
Luke 19:26

21 Then Jesus asked them, "Would anyone light a lamp and then put it under a basket or under a bed? Of course not! A lamp is placed on a stand, where its light will shine. 22 For everything that is hidden will eventually be brought into the open, and every secret will be brought to light. 23 Anyone with ears to hear should listen and understand."

24 Then he added, "Pay close attention to what you hear. The closer you listen, the more understanding you will be given*—and you will receive even more. 25 To those who listen to my teaching, more understanding will be given. But for those who are not listening, even what little understanding they have will be taken away from them."

### Jesus Tells the Parable of the Growing Seed (79)

**4:26-27**
1 Cor 3:6-7

26 Jesus also said, "The Kingdom of God is like a farmer who scatters seed on the ground. 27 Night and day, while he's asleep or awake, the seed sprouts and grows, but he does not understand how it happens. 28 The earth produces the crops on its own. First a leaf blade pushes through, then the heads of wheat are formed, and finally the grain ripens. 29 And as soon as the grain is ready, the farmer comes and harvests it with a sickle, for the harvest time has come."

**4:28-29**
Matt 9:37-38
Rev 14:15

### Jesus Tells the Parable of the Mustard Seed (81/Matthew 13:31-32)

**4:32**
Ezek 17:23; 31:6
Dan 4:12, 21

30 Jesus said, "How can I describe the Kingdom of God? What story should I use to illustrate it? 31 It is like a mustard seed planted in the ground. It is the smallest of all seeds, 32 but it becomes the largest of all garden plants; it grows long branches, and birds can make nests in its shade."

**4:33**
Matt 13:34-35
**4:34**
John 16:25

33 Jesus used many similar stories and illustrations to teach the people as much as they could understand. 34 In fact, in his public ministry he never taught without using parables; but afterward, when he was alone with his disciples, he explained everything to them.

### Jesus Calms the Storm (87/Matthew 8:23-27; Luke 8:22-25)

35 As evening came, Jesus said to his disciples, "Let's cross to the other side of the lake." 36 So they took Jesus in the boat and started out, leaving the crowds behind (although other boats followed). 37 But soon a fierce storm came up. High waves were breaking into the boat, and it began to fill with water.

38 Jesus was sleeping at the back of the boat with his head on a cushion. The disciples woke him up, shouting, "Teacher, don't you care that we're going to drown?"

**4:24** Or *The measure you give will be the measure you get back.*

---

**4:21** Many Christians today are hidden from sight, reluctant to be identified as Christians. Such a Christian is like a brand-new light that never leaves the carton it came in. If a lamp doesn't help people see, it isn't worth much. Does your life show other people how to find God and how to live for him? If not, ask what "baskets" have hidden your light. Complacency, resentment, embarrassment, stubbornness of heart, or disobedience could keep you from shining. What do you need to do to let your light shine?

**4:24, 25** The light of Jesus' truth is revealed to us, not hidden. But we may not be able to see or to use all of that truth right now. Only as we put God's teachings into practice will we understand and see more of the truth. The truth is clear, but our ability to understand is imperfect. As we obey, we will sharpen our vision and increase our understanding (see James 1:22-25).

**4:25** Jesus' words may have been directed to the Jews who had no understanding of Jesus and would lose even what they had— their privileged status as God's people. Or Jesus might have meant that when people reject him, their hardness of heart drives away or renders useless even the little understanding they had; thus, any opportunity to share in God's Kingdom will eventually be taken away completely. To understand Jesus' message, people must listen and respond. Those who listen casually, for whatever reason, will miss the point.

**4:26-29** God promises that his harvest will be magnificent and prolific—the best fruit ever grown. Your witness may be weak and your efforts may seem to influence so few, but the Word of God is a powerful growth agent. Keep your eyes on the great harvest to come and don't let bad soil or weeds discourage you from faithful service and witness.

**4:30-32** Jesus used this parable to explain that although Christianity had very small beginnings, it would grow into a worldwide community of believers. When you feel alone in your stand for Christ, realize that God is building a worldwide Kingdom. He has faithful followers in every part of the world. Your faith, no matter how small, can join with that of others to accomplish great things.

**4:35-38** The "lake" is the Sea of Galilee, a body of water 680 feet below sea level and surrounded by hills. Winds blowing across the land intensify close to the sea, often causing violent and unexpected storms. The disciples were seasoned fishermen, who had spent their lives fishing on this huge lake, but during this squall they panicked.

**4:37** Problems occur in every area of life. The disciples needed rest, but they encountered a terrible storm. The Christian life may have more stormy weather than calm seas. As Christ's follower, be prepared for the storms that will surely come. Do not surrender to the stress, but remain resilient and recover from setbacks. With faith in Christ, you can pray, trust, and move ahead. When a squall approaches, lean into the wind and trust God.

³⁹When Jesus woke up, he rebuked the wind and said to the waves, "Silence! Be still!" **4:39**
Suddenly the wind stopped, and there was a great calm. ⁴⁰Then he asked them, "Why are  Pss 65:8;
you afraid? Do you still have no faith?"                                                107:25-32

⁴¹The disciples were absolutely terrified. "Who is this man?" they asked each other.  **4:41**
"Even the wind and waves obey him!"                                                      Ps 33:8-9

### Jesus Sends Demons into a Herd of Pigs (88/Matthew 8:28-34; Luke 8:26-39)

**5** So they arrived at the other side of the lake, in the region of the Gerasenes.* ²When
Jesus climbed out of the boat, a man possessed by an evil* spirit came out from a cemetery to meet him. ³This man lived among the burial caves and could no longer be restrained,
even with a chain. ⁴Whenever he was put into chains and shackles—as he often was—he
snapped the chains from his wrists and smashed the shackles. No one was strong enough to
subdue him. ⁵Day and night he wandered among the burial caves and in the hills, howling
and cutting himself with sharp stones.

⁶When Jesus was still some distance away, the man saw him, ran to meet him, and bowed
low before him. ⁷With a shriek, he screamed, "Why are you interfering with me, Jesus, Son  **5:7-8**
of the Most High God? In the name of God, I beg you, don't torture me!" ⁸For Jesus had  Acts 16:17
already said to the spirit, "Come out of the man, you evil spirit."

⁹Then Jesus demanded, "What is your name?"

And he replied, "My name is Legion, because there are many of us inside this man."
¹⁰Then the evil spirits begged him again and again not to send them to some distant place.

¹¹There happened to be a large herd of pigs feeding on the hillside nearby. ¹²"Send us
into those pigs," the spirits begged. "Let us enter them."

¹³So Jesus gave them permission. The evil spirits came out of the man and entered the
pigs, and the entire herd of about 2,000 pigs plunged down the steep hillside into the lake
and drowned in the water.

5:1 Other manuscripts read *Gadarenes;* still others read *Gergesenes.* See Matt 8:28; Luke 8:26.  **5:2** Greek *unclean;*
also in 5:8, 13.

---

**4:41** The disciples lived with Jesus, but they underestimated
him. They did not see that his power applied to their very own
situation. Jesus has been with his people for 20 centuries, and
yet we, like the disciples, underestimate his power to handle
crises in our lives. The disciples did not yet know enough about
Jesus. We cannot make the same excuse.

**5:1, 2** Although we cannot be sure why demon possession
occurs, we know that evil spirits can use the human body to
distort and destroy people's relationship with God and likeness
to him. Even today, demons are dangerous, powerful, and
destructive. While it is important to recognize their evil activity,
we should avoid any curiosity about or involvement with
demonic forces or the occult (Deuteronomy 18:10-12). If we

**HEALING
A DEMON-
POSSESSED
MAN**

From Capernaum,
Jesus and his
disciples crossed
the Sea of Galilee.
A storm blew up
unexpectedly,
but Jesus calmed
it. Landing in the
region of the
Gerasenes, Jesus
sent demons out
of a man and into
a herd of pigs that
plunged over the
steep bank into
the lake.

resist the devil and his influences, he will flee from us
(James 4:7).

**5:7** The demon screamed at Jesus, "Why are you interfering
with me?" It was a shriek of fear, defense, and rebellion
against God. No one today would like to admit to being demon
possessed, but most of our society, like the demon, is screaming at God, the church, and Christian values, "Why are you
interfering with me? Get out of my life!" When people reject
Jesus Christ and his authority, they put themselves on the side
of the demons and are heading in the same direction. Every
person must ask: Will I choose autonomy and self-will leading
to destruction, or will I choose Christ's loving leadership over
my life, giving me forgiveness, healing from sin, cleansing, and
true freedom? The answer has eternal implications.

**5:9** The evil spirit said its name was Legion. A legion was the
largest unit of the Roman army, consisting of 3,000 to 6,000
soldiers. This man was possessed by many demons.

**5:10** Mark often highlights the supernatural struggle between
Jesus and Satan. The demons' goal was to control the humans
they inhabited; Jesus' goal was to give people freedom from
sin and Satan's control. The demons knew they had no power
over Jesus, so they simply begged not to be sent to some
distant place ("the bottomless pit" in Luke 8:31). Jesus granted
their request to enter into the herd of pigs (5:13), but ended
their destructive work in people. Perhaps Jesus let the demons
destroy the pigs to demonstrate his own superiority over a very
powerful yet destructive force. He could have sent them to hell,
but he did not because the time for judgment had not yet come.
In the end, the devil and all his demons will be sent into eternal
fire (Matthew 25:41).

**5:11** According to Old Testament law (Leviticus 11:7), pigs were
unclean animals. This meant that they could not be eaten or even
touched by a Jew. This incident took place southeast of the Sea
of Galilee in the region of the Gerasenes, a Gentile region, which
explains how a herd of pigs could be involved.

**5:15**
Matt 4:24

14The herdsmen fled to the nearby town and the surrounding countryside, spreading the news as they ran. People rushed out to see what had happened. 15A crowd soon gathered around Jesus, and they saw the man who had been possessed by the legion of demons. He was sitting there fully clothed and perfectly sane, and they were all afraid. 16Then those who had seen what happened told the others about the demon-possessed man and the pigs. 17And the crowd began pleading with Jesus to go away and leave them alone.

**5:18**
Ps 116:12

**5:20**
Ps 116:16
Isa 63:7
1 Tim 1:13-14

18As Jesus was getting into the boat, the man who had been demon possessed begged to go with him. 19But Jesus said, "No, go home to your family, and tell them everything the Lord has done for you and how merciful he has been." 20So the man started off to visit the Ten Towns* of that region and began to proclaim the great things Jesus had done for him; and everyone was amazed at what he told them.

**5:20** Greek Decapolis.

---

**THE TOUCH OF JESUS**
What kind of people did Jesus associate with? Whom did he consider important enough to touch? Here we see many of the people Jesus came to know. Some reached out to him; he reached out to them all. Regardless of how great or unknown, rich or poor, young or old, sinner or saint—Jesus cares equally for all. No person is beyond the loving touch of Jesus.

| Jesus talked with . . . | Reference |
|---|---|
| A despised tax collector | Matthew 9:9 |
| An insane hermit | Mark 5:1-15 |
| The Roman governor | Mark 15:1-15 |
| A young boy | Mark 9:17-27 |
| A prominent religious leader | John 3:1-21 |
| A homemaker | Luke 10:38-42 |
| An expert in religious law | Matthew 22:35 |
| A criminal | Luke 23:40-43 |
| A synagogue leader | Mark 5:22 |
| Fishermen | Matthew 4:18-20 |
| A king | Luke 23:7-11 |
| A poor widow | Luke 7:11-17; 21:1-4 |
| A Roman captain | Luke 7:1-10 |
| A group of children | Mark 10:13-16 |
| A prophet | Matthew 3 |
| An adulterous woman | John 8:1-11 |
| The Jewish high council | Luke 22:66-71 |
| A sick woman | Mark 5:25-34 |
| A rich man | Mark 10:17-23 |
| A blind beggar | Mark 10:46 |
| Jewish political leaders | Mark 12:13 |
| A group of women | Luke 8:2, 3 |
| The high priest | Matthew 26:62-68 |
| An outcast with leprosy | Luke 17:11-19 |
| A government official | John 4:46-53 |
| A young girl | Mark 5:41, 42 |
| A traitor | John 13:1-3, 27 |
| A helpless and paralyzed man | Mark 2:1-12 |
| An angry mob of soldiers and guards | John 18:3-9 |
| A woman from a foreign land | Mark 7:25-30 |
| A doubting follower | John 20:24-29 |
| An enemy who hated him | Acts 9:1-9 |
| A Samaritan woman | John 4:1-26 |

---

**5:17** After such a wonderful miracle of saving a man's life, why did the people want Jesus to leave? They were undoubtedly afraid of his supernatural power. They may have also feared that Jesus would continue destroying their pigs—their livelihood. They would rather give up Jesus than lose their source of income and security.

**5:19** Jesus told this man to tell his friends about the miraculous healing. Most of the time, Jesus urged those he healed to keep quiet. Why the difference? (1) The demon-possessed man had been alone and unable to speak. Telling others what Jesus did for him would prove that he was healed. (2) This was mainly a Gentile and pagan area, so Jesus was not expecting great crowds to follow him or religious leaders to hinder him. (3) By sending the man away with this good news, Jesus was expanding his ministry to people who were not Jews.

**5:19, 20** This man had been demon possessed but became a living example of Jesus' power. He wanted to go with Jesus, but Jesus told him to go home and share his story with his friends. If you have experienced Jesus' power in your life, are you, like this man, enthusiastically sharing the good news with those around you? Just as we would tell others about a doctor who cured a physical disease, we should tell about Christ who cures our sin.

**5:20** These Ten Towns were located southeast of the Sea of Galilee. Ten cities, each with its own independent government, formed an alliance for protection and for increased trade opportunities. These cities had been settled several centuries earlier by Greek traders and immigrants. Although Jews also lived in the area, they were not in the majority. Many people from the Ten Towns followed Jesus (Matthew 4:25).

## Jesus Heals a Bleeding Woman and Restores a Girl to Life
(89/Matthew 9:18-26; Luke 8:40-56)

<sup>21</sup>Jesus got into the boat again and went back to the other side of the lake, where a large crowd gathered around him on the shore. <sup>22</sup>Then a leader of the local synagogue, whose name was Jairus, arrived. When he saw Jesus, he fell at his feet, <sup>23</sup>pleading fervently with him. "My little daughter is dying," he said. "Please come and lay your hands on her; heal her so she can live."

<sup>24</sup>Jesus went with him, and all the people followed, crowding around him. <sup>25</sup>A woman in the crowd had suffered for twelve years with constant bleeding. <sup>26</sup>She had suffered a great deal from many doctors, and over the years she had spent everything she had to pay them, but she had gotten no better. In fact, she had gotten worse. <sup>27</sup>She had heard about Jesus, so she came up behind him through the crowd and touched his robe. <sup>28</sup>For she thought to herself, "If I can just touch his robe, I will be healed." <sup>29</sup>Immediately the bleeding stopped, and she could feel in her body that she had been healed of her terrible condition.

<sup>30</sup>Jesus realized at once that healing power had gone out from him, so he turned around in the crowd and asked, "Who touched my robe?"

<sup>31</sup>His disciples said to him, "Look at this crowd pressing around you. How can you ask, 'Who touched me?'"

<sup>32</sup>But he kept on looking around to see who had done it. <sup>33</sup>Then the frightened woman, trembling at the realization of what had happened to her, came and fell to her knees in front of him and told him what she had done. <sup>34</sup>And he said to her, "Daughter, your faith has made you well. Go in peace. Your suffering is over."

<sup>35</sup>While he was still speaking to her, messengers arrived from the home of Jairus, the leader of the synagogue. They told him, "Your daughter is dead. There's no use troubling the Teacher now."

<sup>36</sup>But Jesus overheard* them and said to Jairus, "Don't be afraid. Just have faith."

<sup>37</sup>Then Jesus stopped the crowd and wouldn't let anyone go with him except Peter, James, and John (the brother of James). <sup>38</sup>When they came to the home of the synagogue leader, Jesus saw much commotion and weeping and wailing. <sup>39</sup>He went inside and asked, "Why all this commotion and weeping? The child isn't dead; she's only asleep."

<sup>40</sup>The crowd laughed at him. But he made them all leave, and he took the girl's father and mother and his three disciples into the room where the girl was lying. <sup>41</sup>Holding her hand, he said to her, *"Talitha koum,"* which means "Little girl, get up!" <sup>42</sup>And the girl, who was twelve years old, immediately stood up and walked around! They were overwhelmed and totally amazed. <sup>43</sup>Jesus gave them strict orders not to tell anyone what had happened, and then he told them to give her something to eat.

**5:36** Or *ignored.*

| | |
|---|---|
| **5:23** | Matt 8:3; Mark 6:5; 7:32; 8:23, 25; Luke 4:40; 13:13; Acts 9:12, 17; 28:8 |
| **5:25** | Lev 15:25-30 |
| **5:27** | Mark 3:10; Acts 19:11-12 |
| **5:30** | Luke 6:19 |
| **5:34** | Mark 10:52; Luke 7:50; 17:19; 18:42; Acts 14:9 |
| **5:36** | John 11:25-40 |
| **5:39** | John 11:11 |
| **5:40** | Acts 9:40 |
| **5:41-42** | Luke 7:14 |
| **5:43** | Matt 8:4; Mark 1:44; 7:36 |

**5:22** Jesus went back across the Sea of Galilee, probably landing at Capernaum. Jairus was the elected leader of the local synagogue, responsible for supervising worship, running the weekly school, and caring for the building. Many synagogue leaders had close ties to the Pharisees. It is likely, therefore, that some synagogue rulers had been pressured not to support Jesus. For Jairus to bow before Jesus was a significant and perhaps daring act of respect and worship.

**5:25-34** This woman had a seemingly incurable condition causing her to bleed constantly. This may have been a menstrual or uterine disorder that would have made her ritually unclean (Leviticus 15:25-27) and excluded her from most social contact. She desperately wanted Jesus to heal her, but she knew that her bleeding would cause Jesus to be unclean under Jewish law if she touched him. Sometimes we feel that our problems will keep us from God. But he is always ready to help, no matter how impossible the problem seems to us. We should never allow our fear to keep us from approaching him.

**5:31** It was virtually impossible to get close to Jesus, but one woman fought her way desperately through the crowd in order to touch him. As soon as she did, she was healed. What a difference between the crowds who are curious about Jesus and the few who reach out and touch him! Today, many people are vaguely familiar with Jesus, but nothing in their lives is changed or bettered by this passing acquaintance. It is only faith that releases God's healing power. Move beyond curiosity. Reach out to Christ in faith. That touch will change your life forever.

**5:35, 36** Jairus's crisis made him feel confused, afraid, and without hope. Jesus' words to Jairus in the midst of crisis speak to us as well: "Don't be afraid. Just have faith." In Jesus, there is both hope and promise. The next time you feel hopeless and afraid, look at your problem from Jesus' point of view. Then don't be afraid; just have faith.

**5:38** Loud weeping and wailing were customary at a person's death. Lack of them was the ultimate disgrace and disrespect. Some people, usually women, made mourning a profession and were paid by the dead person's family to weep over the body. On the day of death, the body was carried through the streets, followed by mourners, family members, and friends.

**5:39, 40** The mourners laughed at Jesus when he said, "The child isn't dead; she's only asleep." The girl was dead, but Jesus used the image of sleep to indicate that her condition was temporary and that she would be restored.

Jesus tolerated the crowd's abuse in order to teach an important lesson about maintaining hope and trust in him. Today, most of the world laughs at Christ's claims. When you are belittled for expressing faith in Jesus and hope for eternal life, remember that unbelievers don't see from God's perspective. For a clear statement about life after death, see 1 Thessalonians 4:13, 14.

**5:41, 42** Jesus not only demonstrated great power, he also showed tremendous compassion. Jesus' power over nature, evil spirits, and death was motivated by compassion—for a demon-possessed man who lived among tombs, a diseased woman, and the family of a dead girl. The rabbis of the day

*The People of Nazareth Refuse to Believe* (**91**/Matthew 13:53-58)

**6** Jesus left that part of the country and returned with his disciples to Nazareth, his home-town. ²The next Sabbath he began teaching in the synagogue, and many who heard him were amazed. They asked, "Where did he get all this wisdom and the power to perform such miracles?" ³Then they scoffed, "He's just a carpenter, the son of Mary* and the brother of James, Joseph,* Judas, and Simon. And his sisters live right here among us." They were deeply offended and refused to believe in him.

⁴Then Jesus told them, "A prophet is honored everywhere except in his own hometown

**6:2**
John 7:15

**6:3**
John 6:42

**6:4**
John 4:44

**6:3a** Some manuscripts read *He's just the son of the carpenter and of Mary.*   **6:3b** Most manuscripts read *Joses;* see Matt 13:55.

---

**HEROD ANTIPAS**

Most people dislike having their sins pointed out, especially in public. The shame of being exposed is often stronger than the guilt brought on by the wrongdoing. Herod Antipas was a man experiencing both guilt and shame.

Herod's ruthless ambition was public knowledge, as was his illegal marriage to his brother's wife, Herodias. One man made Herod's sin a public issue. That man was John the Baptist. John had been preaching in the wilderness, and thousands flocked to hear him. Apparently it was no secret that John had rebuked Herod for his adulterous marriage. Herodias was particularly anxious to have John silenced. As a solution, Herod imprisoned John.

Herod liked John. John was probably one of the few people he met who spoke only the truth to him. But the truth about his sin was a bitter pill to swallow, and Herod wavered at the point of conflict: He couldn't afford to have John constantly reminding the people of their leader's sinfulness, but he was afraid to have John killed. He put off the choice. Eventually Herodias forced his hand, and John was executed. Of course, this only served to increase Herod's guilt.

Upon hearing about Jesus, Herod immediately identified him with John. He couldn't decide what to do about Jesus. He didn't want to repeat the mistake he had made with John, so he tried to threaten Jesus just before Jesus' final journey to Jerusalem. When the two met briefly during Jesus' trial, Jesus would not speak to Herod. Herod had proved himself a poor listener to John, and Jesus had nothing to add to John's words. Herod responded with spite and mocking. Having rejected the messenger, he found it easy to reject the Messiah.

For each person, God chooses the best possible ways to reveal himself. He uses his Word, various circumstances, our minds, or other people to get our attention. He is persuasive and persistent but never forces himself on us. To miss or resist God's message, as did Herod, is a tragedy. How aware are you of God's attempts to enter your life? Have you welcomed him?

| | |
|---|---|
| **Strengths and accomplishments** | • Built the city of Tiberias and oversaw other architectural projects<br>• Ruled the region of Galilee for the Romans |
| **Weaknesses and mistakes** | • Consumed with his quest for power<br>• Put off decisions or made wrong ones under pressure<br>• Divorced his wife to marry the wife of his half brother, Philip<br>• Imprisoned John the Baptist and later ordered his execution<br>• Had a minor part in the execution of Jesus |
| **Lessons from his life** | • A life motivated by ambition is usually characterized by self-destruction<br>• Opportunities to do good usually come to us in the form of choices to be made |
| **Vital statistics** | • Where: Jerusalem<br>• Occupation: Roman ruler of the region of Galilee and Perea<br>• Relatives: Father: Herod the Great. Mother: Malthace. First wife: daughter of Aretas IV. Second wife: Herodias.<br>• Contemporaries: John the Baptist, Jesus, Pilate |
| **Key verse** | "Herod was greatly disturbed whenever he talked with John, but even so, he liked to listen to him" (Mark 6:20). |

Herod Antipas's story is told in the Gospels. He is also mentioned in Acts 4:27; 13:1.

---

considered such people unclean. Polite society avoided them. But Jesus reached out and helped.

**5:43** Jesus told the girl's parents not to spread the news of the miracle. He wanted the facts to speak for themselves, and the time was not yet right for a major confrontation with the religious leaders. Jesus still had much to accomplish, and he didn't want people following him just to see his miracles.

**6:4** Jesus said that a prophet (in other words, a worker for God) is never honored in his hometown. But that doesn't make his work any less important. A person doesn't need to be respected or honored to be useful to God. If friends, neighbors, or family don't respect your Christian work, don't let their rejection keep you from serving God.

and among his relatives and his own family." 5And because of their unbelief, he couldn't do any miracles among them except to place his hands on a few sick people and heal them. 6And he was amazed at their unbelief.

**6:5**
Matt 9:18

### Jesus Sends Out the Twelve Disciples (93/Matthew 10:1-15; Luke 9:1-6)

Then Jesus went from village to village, teaching the people. 7And he called his twelve disciples together and began sending them out two by two, giving them authority to cast out evil* spirits. 8He told them to take nothing for their journey except a walking stick—no food, no traveler's bag, no money.* 9He allowed them to wear sandals but not to take a change of clothes.

**6:7**
Luke 10:1

**6:8-9**
Matt 10:9-10
Luke 9:3; 10:4

10"Wherever you go," he said, "stay in the same house until you leave town. 11But if any place refuses to welcome you or listen to you, shake its dust from your feet as you leave to show that you have abandoned those people to their fate."

**6:10**
Luke 10:7

**6:11**
Luke 10:11
Acts 13:51

12So the disciples went out, telling everyone they met to repent of their sins and turn to God. 13And they cast out many demons and healed many sick people, anointing them with olive oil.

**6:13**
Luke 10:34
Jas 5:14

### Herod Kills John the Baptist (95/Matthew 14:1-12; Luke 9:7-9)

14Herod Antipas, the king, soon heard about Jesus, because everyone was talking about him. Some were saying,* "This must be John the Baptist raised from the dead. That is why he can do such miracles." 15Others said, "He's the prophet Elijah." Still others said, "He's a prophet like the other great prophets of the past."

**6:15**
Matt 16:14

16When Herod heard about Jesus, he said, "John, the man I beheaded, has come back from the dead."

17For Herod had sent soldiers to arrest and imprison John as a favor to Herodias. She had been his brother Philip's wife, but Herod had married her. 18John had been telling Herod,

**6:17-18**
Lev 18:15-16;
20:21
Luke 3:19-20

**6:7** Greek *unclean.*    **6:8** Greek *no copper coins in their money belts.*    **6:14** Some manuscripts read *He was saying.*

---

**6:5** Jesus could have done greater miracles in Nazareth, but he chose not to because of the people's pride and unbelief. The miracles he did had little effect on the people because they did not accept his message or believe that he was from God. Therefore, Jesus looked elsewhere, seeking those who would respond to his miracles and message.

**6:7** The disciples were sent out in pairs. Individually they could have reached more areas of the country, but this was not Christ's plan. The advantages in going out by twos include: (1) They could strengthen and encourage each other. (2) They could provide comfort in rejection. (3) They could give each other discernment, and fewer mistakes would be made. (4) They could stir each other to action as a counter to idleness or indifference. Our strength comes from God, but he meets many of our needs through our teamwork with others. As you serve Christ, don't try to go it alone.

**6:8, 9** Mark records that the disciples were instructed to take nothing with them *except* walking sticks, while Matthew and Luke record that Jesus told them *not* to take walking sticks. One explanation is that Matthew and Luke were referring to a club used for protection, whereas Mark was talking about a shepherd's crook. In any case, the point in all three accounts is the same—the disciples were to leave at once, without extensive preparation, trusting in God's care rather than in their own resources.

**6:11** Pious Jews shook the dust from their feet after passing through Gentile cities or territory to show their separation from Gentile influences and practices. When the disciples shook the dust from their feet after leaving a *Jewish* town, it was a vivid sign that they wished to remain separate from people who had rejected Jesus and his message. Jesus made it clear that all who heard the gospel were responsible for what they did with it. The disciples were not to blame if the message was rejected, as long as they had faithfully and carefully presented it. We are not responsible when others reject Christ's message of salvation, but we do have the responsibility to share the Good News clearly and faithfully.

**6:14, 15** Herod, along with many others, wondered who Jesus really was. Unable to accept Jesus' claim to be God's Son, many people made up their own explanations for his power and authority. Herod thought that Jesus was John the Baptist come back to life, while those who were familiar with the Old Testament thought he was Elijah (Malachi 4:5). Still others believed that Jesus was a teaching prophet in the tradition of Moses, Isaiah, or Jeremiah. Today people still have to make up their minds about Jesus. Some think that if they can name what he is—prophet, teacher, good man—they can weaken the power of his claim on their lives. But what they *think* does not change who Jesus *is.*

**6:17-19** Palestine was divided into four territories, each with a different ruler. Herod Antipas, called Herod in the Gospels, was ruler over Galilee; his brother Philip ruled over Traconitis and Iturea. Philip's wife was Herodias, but she had left him to marry

**PREACHING IN GALILEE**
After returning to his hometown, Nazareth, from Capernaum, Jesus preached in the villages of Galilee and sent his disciples out to preach as well. After meeting back in Capernaum, they left by boat to rest, only to be met by the crowds who followed the boat along the shore.

Mediterranean Sea

GALILEE

N

Capernaum • Bethsaida
Nazareth •   *Sea of Galilee*

Jordan River

**Jerusalem**

Dead Sea

0    20 Mi.

0    20 Km.

"It is against God's law for you to marry your brother's wife." [19]So Herodias bore a grudge against John and wanted to kill him. But without Herod's approval she was powerless, [20]for Herod respected John; and knowing that he was a good and holy man, he protected him. Herod was greatly disturbed whenever he talked with John, but even so, he liked to listen to him.

[21]Herodias's chance finally came on Herod's birthday. He gave a party for his high government officials, army officers, and the leading citizens of Galilee. [22]Then his daughter, also named Herodias,* came in and performed a dance that greatly pleased Herod and his guests. "Ask me for anything you like," the king said to the girl, "and I will give it to you." [23]He even vowed, "I will give you whatever you ask, up to half my kingdom!"

6:23
Esth 5:3-6; 7:2

[24]She went out and asked her mother, "What should I ask for?"

Her mother told her, "Ask for the head of John the Baptist!"

[25]So the girl hurried back to the king and told him, "I want the head of John the Baptist, right now, on a tray!"

[26]Then the king deeply regretted what he had said; but because of the vows he had made in front of his guests, he couldn't refuse her. [27]So he immediately sent an executioner to the prison to cut off John's head and bring it to him. The soldier beheaded John in the prison, [28]brought his head on a tray, and gave it to the girl, who took it to her mother. [29]When John's disciples heard what had happened, they came to get his body and buried it in a tomb.

### Jesus Feeds Five Thousand (**96**/Matthew 14:13-21; Luke 9:10-17; John 6:1-15)

6:30
Luke 9:10; 10:17
6:31
Mark 3:20

[30]The apostles returned to Jesus from their ministry tour and told him all they had done and taught. [31]Then Jesus said, "Let's go off by ourselves to a quiet place and rest awhile." He said this because there were so many people coming and going that Jesus and his apostles didn't even have time to eat.

6:34
†Num 27:17
†1 Kgs 22:17
†2 Chr 18:16
†Zech 10:2
Matt 9:36

[32]So they left by boat for a quiet place, where they could be alone. [33]But many people recognized them and saw them leaving, and people from many towns ran ahead along the shore and got there ahead of them. [34]Jesus saw the huge crowd as he stepped from the boat, and he had compassion on them because they were like sheep without a shepherd. So he began teaching them many things.

**6:22** Some manuscripts read *the daughter of Herodias herself.*

---

| **REAL LEADERSHIP** Mark gives us some of the best insights into Jesus' character. | Herod as a leader | Jesus as a leader |
|---|---|---|
| | Selfish | Compassionate |
| | Murderer | Healer |
| | Immoral | Just and good |
| | Political opportunist | Servant |
| | King over small territory | King over all creation |

---

Herod Antipas. When John confronted the two for committing adultery, Herodias formulated a plot to kill him. Instead of trying to get rid of her sin, Herodias tried to get rid of the one who brought it to public attention. This is also exactly what the religious leaders were trying to do to Jesus.

**6:18** Christians today face a world of moral compromise. Secular power sets standards that correspond to majority vote; Christian standards, however, begin and end with God's Word. To be faithful to God's Word, we must stand up against what is morally wrong. Responsible Christians must choose their battles. Start with prayers for wisdom, then prayers for courage. Once your battle is chosen, speak and act as a faithful follower of the living God. Witness with strength; move mountains by faith; overcome in love. Show the compromised world a little of John's stubbornness, fortitude, and faith.

**6:20** Herod arrested John the Baptist under pressure from his wife and advisers. Though Herod respected John's integrity, in the end Herod had John killed because of pressure from his peers and family. What you do under pressure often shows what you are really like.

**6:22, 23** As a ruler under Roman authority, Herod had no kingdom to give. The offer of half his kingdom was Herod's way to say

that he would give Herodias's daughter almost anything she wanted. When Herodias asked for John's head, Herod would have been greatly embarrassed in front of his guests if he had denied her request. Words are powerful. Because they can lead to great sin, we should use them with great care.

**6:30** Mark uses the word *apostles* here and in 3:14. *Apostle* means "one sent" as messenger, authorized agent, or missionary. The word became an official title for Jesus' 12 disciples after his death and resurrection (Acts 1:25, 26; Ephesians 2:20).

**6:31** When the disciples had returned from their mission, Jesus took them away to rest. Doing God's work is very important, but Jesus recognized that to do it effectively we need periodic rest and renewal. Jesus and his disciples, however, did not always find it easy to get the rest they needed!

**6:34** This crowd was as pitiful as a flock of sheep without a shepherd. Sheep are easily scattered; without a shepherd they are in grave danger. Jesus was the Shepherd who could teach them what they needed to know and keep them from straying from God. See Psalm 23; Isaiah 40:11; Ezekiel 34:5ff; and John 10:11-16 for descriptions of the good shepherd.

³⁵Late in the afternoon his disciples came to him and said, "This is a remote place, and it's already getting late. ³⁶Send the crowds away so they can go to the nearby farms and villages and buy something to eat."

³⁷But Jesus said, "You feed them."

"With what?" they asked. "We'd have to work for months to earn enough money* to buy food for all these people!"

³⁸"How much bread do you have?" he asked. "Go and find out."

They came back and reported, "We have five loaves of bread and two fish."

³⁹Then Jesus told the disciples to have the people sit down in groups on the green grass. ⁴⁰So they sat down in groups of fifty or a hundred.

⁴¹Jesus took the five loaves and two fish, looked up toward heaven, and blessed them. Then, breaking the loaves into pieces, he kept giving the bread to the disciples so they could distribute it to the people. He also divided the fish for everyone to share. ⁴²They all ate as much as they wanted, ⁴³and afterward, the disciples picked up twelve baskets of leftover bread and fish. ⁴⁴A total of 5,000 men and their families were fed from those loaves!

### Jesus Walks on Water (97/Matthew 14:22-23; John 6:16-21)

⁴⁵Immediately after this, Jesus insisted that his disciples get back into the boat and head across the lake to Bethsaida, while he sent the people home. ⁴⁶After telling everyone good-bye, he went up into the hills by himself to pray.

⁴⁷Late that night, the disciples were in their boat in the middle of the lake, and Jesus was alone on land. ⁴⁸He saw that they were in serious trouble, rowing hard and struggling against the wind and waves. About three o'clock in the morning* Jesus came toward them, walking on the water. He intended to go past them, ⁴⁹but when they saw him walking on the water, they cried out in terror, thinking he was a ghost. ⁵⁰They were all terrified when they saw him.

But Jesus spoke to them at once. "Don't be afraid," he said. "Take courage! I am here!*"

⁵¹Then he climbed into the boat, and the wind stopped. They were totally amazed, ⁵²for they still didn't understand the significance of the miracle of the loaves. Their hearts were too hard to take it in.

**6:37** Greek *It would take 200 denarii.* A denarius was equivalent to a laborer's full day's wage.    **6:48** Greek *About the fourth watch of the night.*    **6:50** Or *The 'I Am' is here;* Greek reads *I am.* See Exod 3:14.

**6:37**
2 Kgs 4:42-44
Matt 15:33
Mark 8:4

**6:38**
Matt 15:34
Mark 8:5

**6:41**
Matt 14:19

**6:52**
Mark 8:17-21

---

**6:37-42** When Jesus asked the disciples to provide food for over 5,000 people, they were amazed and said it would take a small fortune to feed such a crowd. How do you react when you are given an impossible task? A situation that seems impossible with human resources is simply an opportunity for God. The disciples did everything they could by gathering the available food and organizing the people into groups. Then, in answer to prayer, God did the impossible. When facing a seemingly impossible task, do what you can and ask God to do the rest. He may see fit to make the impossible happen.

**6:37-42** Why did Jesus bother to feed these people? He could just as easily have sent them on their way. Jesus does not ignore needs, however. He is concerned with every aspect of our lives—the physical as well as the spiritual.

We might well ask why the church has taken so lightly the command, "You feed them." Jesus' compassion for these hungry people is recorded in all four Gospels. For people who are desperately hungry, there is no better way for us to show God's love to them than to help to provide for their physical needs. As we work to bring wholeness to people's lives, we must never ignore the fact that all of us have both physical and spiritual needs. It is impossible to minister effectively to the spiritual need without considering the physical need. (See also James 2:14-17.)

**6:49, 50** The disciples were afraid, but Jesus' presence calmed their fears. When you experience fear, do you try to deal with it yourself, or do you let Jesus deal with it? In times of fear and uncertainty, it is calming to know that Christ is always with you (Matthew 28:20). To recognize Christ's presence is the antidote for fear.

**6:52** The disciples didn't want to believe, perhaps because (1) they couldn't accept the fact that this human named Jesus was really the Son of God; (2) they dared not believe that the Messiah would choose them as his followers; (3) they still did not understand the real purpose for Jesus' coming to earth. Their disbelief took the form of misunderstanding. Even after watching Jesus miraculously feed 5,000 people, they still could not take the final step of faith and believe that he was God's Son. If they had, they would not have been amazed that Jesus could walk on water.

**JESUS WALKS ON THE WATER**
After feeding the people who had followed to hear him at Bethsaida, Jesus sent the people home, sent his disciples by boat toward Bethsaida, and went to pray. The disciples encountered a storm, and Jesus walked to them on the water. They landed at Gennesaret.

Mediterranean Sea

N

Bethsaida
Gennesaret
Sea of Galilee
Jordan River

Jerusalem

Dead Sea

0   20 Mi.
0   20 Km.

### Jesus Heals All Who Touch Him (**98**/Matthew 14:34-36)

**6:56**
Matt 9:20
Mark 5:27
Luke 8:44

53After they had crossed the lake, they landed at Gennesaret. They brought the boat to shore 54and climbed out. The people recognized Jesus at once, 55and they ran throughout the whole area, carrying sick people on mats to wherever they heard he was. 56Wherever he went—in villages, cities, or the countryside—they brought the sick out to the marketplaces. They begged him to let the sick touch at least the fringe of his robe, and all who touched him were healed.

### Jesus Teaches about Inner Purity (**102**/Matthew 15:1-20)

**7:2**
Luke 11:38
Acts 10:14, 28

**7:3**
Gal 1:14
Col 2:8

**7:4**
Matt 23:25
Luke 11:39

**7:6-7**
†Isa 29:13
Col 2:22

**7** One day some Pharisees and teachers of religious law arrived from Jerusalem to see Jesus. 2They noticed that some of his disciples failed to follow the Jewish ritual of hand washing before eating. 3(The Jews, especially the Pharisees, do not eat until they have poured water over their cupped hands,* as required by their ancient traditions. 4Similarly, they don't eat anything from the market until they immerse their hands* in water. This is but one of many traditions they have clung to—such as their ceremonial washing of cups, pitchers, and kettles.*)

5So the Pharisees and teachers of religious law asked him, "Why don't your disciples follow our age-old tradition? They eat without first performing the hand-washing ceremony."

6Jesus replied, "You hypocrites! Isaiah was right when he prophesied about you, for he wrote,

'These people honor me with their lips,
　　but their hearts are far from me.
7　Their worship is a farce,
　　for they teach man-made ideas as commands from God.'*

**7:3** Greek *have washed with the fist.*　**7:4a** Some manuscripts read *sprinkle themselves.*　**7:4b** Some manuscripts add *and dining couches.*　**7:7** Isa 29:13 (Greek version).

---

| GOSPEL ACCOUNTS FOUND ONLY IN MARK | Section | Topic | Significance |
|---|---|---|---|
| | 4:26-29 | Story of the growing seed | We must share the Good News of Jesus with other people, but only God makes it grow in their lives. |
| | 7:31-37 | Jesus heals a deaf man who could hardly talk | Jesus cares about our physical as well as spiritual needs. |
| | 8:22-26 | Jesus heals the blind man at Bethsaida | Jesus is considerate because he makes sure this man's sight is fully restored. |

---

Is your heart hardened against Jesus? Even Christians can be hard-hearted to Jesus' word. We can be informed about what his Word says, and we can be amazed at how he has worked in other people's lives, but we can refuse to believe he will come to our aid in our time of trouble. Such a reaction is not unbelief, but willful, hard-hearted rejection of Christ's ability to help. Instead, "take courage," and trust that he is there for you.

**6:53** Gennesaret was a small fertile plain located on the west side of the Sea of Galilee. Capernaum, Jesus' home, sat at the northern edge of this plain.

**7:1ff** The religious leaders sent some investigators from their headquarters in Jerusalem to check up on Jesus. The delegation didn't like what they found, however, because Jesus scolded them for keeping the law and the traditions in order to look holy instead of to honor God. The prophet Isaiah accused the religious leaders of his day of doing the same thing (Isaiah 29:13). Jesus used Isaiah's words to accuse these men.

**7:3, 4** Mark explained these Jewish rituals because he was writing to a non-Jewish audience. Before each meal, devout Jews performed a short ceremony, washing their hands and arms in a specific way. The disciples did not have dirty hands, but they were simply not carrying out this traditional cleansing. The Pharisees thought this ceremony cleansed them from any contact they might have had with anything considered unclean. Jesus said they were wrong in thinking they were acceptable to God just because they were clean on the outside.

**7:4** Christians become like Pharisees when they worry that contact with unbelievers may leave them tainted—avoiding "worldly" places where sinners hang out or rejecting books or speakers whose ideas do not conform to theirs. Some Christians and some Pharisees have a lot in common: Both would try to stop Jesus from working certain places or talking to certain people. Jesus wants us to go out into the world and make contact. Jesus didn't intend for us to withdraw, purify ourselves, and never reach out.

**7:6, 7** Hypocrisy is pretending to be something you are not and have no intention of being. Jesus called the Pharisees hypocrites because they worshiped God for the wrong reasons. Their worship was not motivated by love but by a desire to attain profit, to appear holy, and to increase their status. We become hypocrites when we (1) pay more attention to reputation than to character, (2) carefully follow certain religious practices while allowing our hearts to remain distant from God, and (3) emphasize our virtues but others' sins.

[8]For you ignore God's law and substitute your own tradition."

[9]Then he said, "You skillfully sidestep God's law in order to hold on to your own tradition. [10]For instance, Moses gave you this law from God: 'Honor your father and mother,'* and 'Anyone who speaks disrespectfully of father or mother must be put to death.'* [11]But you say it is all right for people to say to their parents, 'Sorry, I can't help you. For I have vowed to give to God what I would have given to you.'* [12]In this way, you let them disregard their needy parents. [13]And so you cancel the word of God in order to hand down your own tradition. And this is only one example among many others."

[14]Then Jesus called to the crowd to come and hear. "All of you listen," he said, "and try to understand. [15]It's not what goes into your body that defiles you; you are defiled by what comes from your heart.*"

[17]Then Jesus went into a house to get away from the crowd, and his disciples asked him what he meant by the parable he had just used. [18]"Don't you understand either?" he asked. "Can't you see that the food you put into your body cannot defile you? [19]Food doesn't go into your heart, but only passes through the stomach and then goes into the sewer." (By saying this, he declared that every kind of food is acceptable in God's eyes.)

[20]And then he added, "It is what comes from inside that defiles you. [21]For from within, out of a person's heart, come evil thoughts, sexual immorality, theft, murder, [22]adultery, greed, wickedness, deceit, lustful desires, envy, slander, pride, and foolishness. [23]All these vile things come from within; they are what defile you."

**7:9**
Isa 24:4-5

**7:10**
†Exod 20:12; 21:17
†Lev 20:9
†Deut 5:16
1 Tim 5:8

**7:15**
1 Cor 8:8
1 Tim 4:4

**7:17**
Mark 9:28

**7:19**
Acts 10:15; 11:9
Rom 14:1-12
Col 2:16
1 Tim 4:3-5

**7:21-22**
Rom 1:29-31
Gal 5:19-21
Titus 1:15

## 2. Jesus' ministry beyond Galilee

*Jesus Sends a Demon Out of a Girl* (**103**/Matthew 15:21-28)

[24]Then Jesus left Galilee and went north to the region of Tyre.* He didn't want anyone to know which house he was staying in, but he couldn't keep it a secret. [25]Right away a woman

**7:10a** Exod 20:12; Deut 5:16. **7:10b** Exod 21:17 (Greek version); Lev 20:9 (Greek version). **7:11** Greek *'What I would have given to you is Corban' (that is, a gift).* **7:15** Some manuscripts add verse 16, *Anyone with ears to hear should listen and understand.* Compare 4:9, 23. **7:24** Some manuscripts add *and Sidon.*

---

**7:8, 9** The Pharisees had added hundreds of their own rules and regulations to God's holy laws, and then they tried to force people to follow these rules. These men claimed to know God's will in every detail of life. There are still religious leaders today who add rules and regulations to God's Word, causing much confusion among believers. It is idolatry to claim that your interpretation of God's Word is as important as God's Word itself. It is especially dangerous to set up unbiblical standards for *others* to follow. Instead, look to Christ for guidance about your own behavior, and let him lead others in the details of their lives.

**7:8, 9** Jesus wasn't against all tradition, but he was against those who made their traditions as important, if not more important, than God's Word. Good traditions shine a spotlight on God's Word, move us to obedient service, and help our hearts sing. They explain

### MINISTRY IN PHOENICIA

Jesus' ministry was to all people— first to Jews but also to Gentiles. Jesus took his disciples from Galilee to Tyre and Sidon, large cities in Phoenicia, where he healed a Gentile woman's daughter.

and reinforce the teachings of God. God's Word should always be the focus, and tradition a means of bringing that Word alive. Celebrate your traditions with the prayer that Christ would be exalted. Change your traditions if they become more important than God's Word.

**7:10, 11** The Pharisees used God as an excuse to avoid helping their families. They thought it was more important to put money in the Temple treasury than to help their needy parents, although God's law specifically says to honor fathers and mothers (Exodus 20:12) and to care for those in need (Leviticus 25:35-43). (For vowing to give money to God, see the note on Matthew 15:5, 6.) We should give money and time to God, but we must never use God as an excuse to neglect our responsibilities. Helping those in need is one of the most important ways to honor God.

**7:18, 19** As they interpreted the dietary laws (Leviticus 11), the Jews believed they could be clean before God because of what they refused to eat. Jesus pointed out that sin begins in the attitudes and intentions of the inner person. Jesus did not degrade the law, but he paved the way for the change made clear in Acts 10:9-29 when God removed the cultural restrictions regarding food. While being concerned about what we put into our bodies is a good, healthy practice, very few people are as stringent about what they put into their minds through reading or watching television. Jesus was more concerned about mind-set and thought processes than about food laws. Do you worry about what foods you eat, but put "junk food" in your mind?

**7:20-23** An evil action begins with a single thought. Allowing our mind to dwell on lust, envy, hatred, or revenge will lead to sin. Don't defile yourself by focusing on evil. Instead, follow Paul's advice in Philippians 4:8 and think about what is true, honorable, right, pure, lovely, and admirable.

**7:24** Jesus traveled about 30 miles to Tyre. The cities of Tyre and Sidon were port cities on the Mediterranean Sea north of Israel. Both had flourishing trade and were very wealthy. They were proud, historic Canaanite cities.

In David's day, Tyre was on friendly terms with Israel (2 Samuel 5:11), but soon afterward the city became known for its wicked-who had heard about him came and fell at his feet. Her little girl was possessed by an evil* spirit, 26and she begged him to cast out the demon from her daughter.

Since she was a Gentile, born in Syrian Phoenicia, 27Jesus told her, "First I should feed the children—my own family, the Jews.* It isn't right to take food from the children and throw it to the dogs."

28She replied, "That's true, Lord, but even the dogs under the table are allowed to eat the scraps from the children's plates."

29"Good answer!" he said. "Now go home, for the demon has left your daughter." 30And when she arrived home, she found her little girl lying quietly in bed, and the demon was gone.

### Jesus Heals Many People (104/Matthew 15:29-31)

31Jesus left Tyre and went up to Sidon before going back to the Sea of Galilee and the region of the Ten Towns.* 32A deaf man with a speech impediment was brought to him, and the people begged Jesus to lay his hands on the man to heal him.

**7:33**
Mark 8:23
John 9:6

**7:34**
Matt 14:19
Mark 6:41
John 11:41; 17:1

33Jesus led him away from the crowd so they could be alone. He put his fingers into the man's ears. Then, spitting on his own fingers, he touched the man's tongue. 34Looking up to heaven, he sighed and said, *"Ephphatha,"* which means, *"Be opened!"* 35Instantly the man could hear perfectly, and his tongue was freed so he could speak plainly!

**7:36**
Matt 8:4

**7:37**
Isa 35:5-6

36Jesus told the crowd not to tell anyone, but the more he told them not to, the more they spread the news. 37They were completely amazed and said again and again, "Everything he does is wonderful. He even makes the deaf to hear and gives speech to those who cannot speak."

### Jesus Feeds Four Thousand (105/Matthew 15:32-39)

**8:1-10**
Mark 6:32-44

**8:2**
Matt 9:36

**8** About this time another large crowd had gathered, and the people ran out of food again. Jesus called his disciples and told them, 2"I feel sorry for these people. They have been here with me for three days, and they have nothing left to eat. 3If I send them home hungry, they will faint along the way. For some of them have come a long distance."

**8:4**
Num 11:21-22
2 Kgs 4:42-43

4His disciples replied, "How are we supposed to find enough food to feed them out here in the wilderness?"

5Jesus asked, "How much bread do you have?"

"Seven loaves," they replied.

**7:25** Greek *unclean.*   **7:27** Greek *Let the children eat first.*   **7:31** Greek *Decapolis.*

---

ness. Its king even claimed to be God (Ezekiel 28:1ff). Tyre rejoiced when Jerusalem was destroyed in 586 B.C., because without Israel's competition, Tyre's trade and profits would increase. It was into this evil and materialistic culture that Jesus brought his message.

**7:26** This woman is called a Gentile, born in Syrian Phoenicia. Mark's designation refers to her political background. His Roman audience would easily identify her by the part of the empire that was her home.

**7:27, 28** On the surface, Jesus' words may seem harsh and unsympathetic, but the woman recognized them as a wide-open door to God's throne. Jesus did not use the negative term for "dogs" that referred to scavengers (the word sometimes used by Jews to refer to Gentiles); instead, he used the term for a household pet. The woman took the cue and added to his analogy of pets under a family dining table. Her attitude was expectant and hopeful, not prickly or hypersensitive. She knew what she wanted and she believed Jesus could provide. We could learn from this woman's singular purpose and optimistic resilience. Jesus really does want to meet our needs. When we pray, we're talking to a friend.

**7:29** This miracle shows that Jesus' power over demons is so great that he doesn't need to be present physically in order to free someone. His power transcends any distance.

**7:34** When Jesus said, "Be opened!" he used language that this deaf man would understand. The healing message was personal and unique. Whoever thought spittle might be the conduit of a miracle? If there is only one means of witness in your church (sermons, for instance), many people likely will not hear. Churches need lots of different methods to meet diverse needs. Let musi-

cians play, singers sing, actors act, and writers write. Let each creative Christian tell the story. Jesus used spit and mud; surely we can find windows to the minds and hearts of people as well.

**8:1ff** This is a different miracle from the feeding of the 5,000 described in chapter 6. At that time, those fed were mostly Jews. This time Jesus was ministering to a non-Jewish crowd in the Gentile region of the Ten Towns. Jesus' actions and message were beginning to have an impact on large numbers of Gentiles. That Jesus would compassionately minister to non-Jews was very reassuring to Mark's primarily Roman audience.

**8:1-3** Do you ever feel that God is so busy with important concerns that he can't possibly be aware of your needs? Just as Jesus was concerned about these people's need for food, he is concerned about our daily needs. At another time Jesus said, "Your heavenly Father already knows all your needs" (Matthew 6:32). Do you have concerns that you think would not interest God? Nothing is too large for him to handle and no need too small to escape his interest.

**8:4** How could the disciples experience so many of Jesus' miracles and yet be so slow to comprehend who he was? They had already seen Jesus feed over 5,000 people with five loaves and two fish (6:35-44), yet here they doubted whether he could feed another large group.

Sometimes we are also slow to catch on. Although Christ has brought us through trials and temptations in the past, we don't believe that he will do so in the future. Is your heart too closed to take in all that God can do for you? Don't be like the disciples. Remember what Christ has done, and have faith that he will do it again.

⁶So Jesus told all the people to sit down on the ground. Then he took the seven loaves, thanked God for them, and broke them into pieces. He gave them to his disciples, who distributed the bread to the crowd. ⁷A few small fish were found, too, so Jesus also blessed these and told the disciples to distribute them.

**8:7**
Matt 14:19

⁸They ate as much as they wanted. Afterward, the disciples picked up seven large baskets of leftover food. ⁹There were about 4,000 people in the crowd that day, and Jesus sent them home after they had eaten. ¹⁰Immediately after this, he got into a boat with his disciples and crossed over to the region of Dalmanutha.

**8:10**
Matt 15:39

## Leaders Demand a Miraculous Sign (106/Matthew 16:1-4)
¹¹When the Pharisees heard that Jesus had arrived, they came and started to argue with him. Testing him, they demanded that he show them a miraculous sign from heaven to prove his authority.

**8:11-21**
Luke 11:16, 29
John 6:30

¹²When he heard this, he sighed deeply in his spirit and said, "Why do these people keep demanding a miraculous sign? I tell you the truth, I will not give this generation any such sign." ¹³So he got back into the boat and left them, and he crossed to the other side of the lake.

## Jesus Warns against Wrong Teaching (107/Matthew 16:5-12)
¹⁴But the disciples had forgotten to bring any food. They had only one loaf of bread with them in the boat. ¹⁵As they were crossing the lake, Jesus warned them, "Watch out! Beware of the yeast of the Pharisees and of Herod."

**8:15**
Luke 12:1

¹⁶At this they began to argue with each other because they hadn't brought any bread. ¹⁷Jesus knew what they were saying, so he said, "Why are you arguing about having no bread? Don't you know or understand even yet? Are your hearts too hard to take it in? ¹⁸ 'You have eyes—can't you see? You have ears—can't you hear?'* Don't you remember anything at all? ¹⁹When I fed the 5,000 with five loaves of bread, how many baskets of leftovers did you pick up afterward?"

**8:17**
Isa 6:9-10
Mark 6:52

**8:18**
†Jer 5:21
Ezek 12:2
Matt 13:13

"Twelve," they said.

**8:19**
Mark 6:41-44
Luke 9:17
John 6:13

²⁰"And when I fed the 4,000 with seven loaves, how many large baskets of leftovers did you pick up?"

"Seven," they said.

**8:20**
Matt 15:37

²¹"Don't you understand yet?" he asked them.

## Jesus Restores Sight to a Blind Man (108)
²²When they arrived at Bethsaida, some people brought a blind man to Jesus, and they begged him to touch the man and heal him. ²³Jesus took the blind man by the hand and led him out of the village. Then, spitting on the man's eyes, he laid his hands on him and asked, "Can you see anything now?"

**8:23**
Mark 7:33
John 9:6

²⁴The man looked around. "Yes," he said, "I see people, but I can't see them very clearly. They look like trees walking around."

**8:18** Jer 5:21.

---

**8:6** Jesus gave thanks for the food, and he serves as a model for us. Life is a gift, and the nourishment life requires, while it comes from the work of many hands, conveys God's material blessing. Mealtime provides an opportunity to thank God for daily needs met, for taste and beauty, and for human company and divine companionship. Giving thanks keeps us from regarding a plate of food as a trough, our stomachs as bottomless pits, and our gathering to eat as a bothersome interruption. Keep up the good tradition of praying and thanking God before your meals. Let your gratefulness to God be genuine.

**8:11** The Pharisees had tried to explain away Jesus' previous miracles by claiming they were done by luck, coincidence, or evil power. Here they demanded a sign from heaven—something only God could do. Jesus refused their demand because he knew that even this kind of miracle would not convince them. They had already decided not to believe. Hearts can become so hard that even the most convincing facts and demonstrations will not change them.

**8:15** Mark mentions the yeast of the Pharisees and of Herod, while Matthew talks about the yeast of the Pharisees and Sad-

ducees. Mark's audience, mostly non-Jews, would have known about Herod but not necessarily about the Jewish religious sect of the Sadducees. Thus, Mark quoted the part of Jesus' statement that his readers would understand. This reference to Herod may mean the supporters of Herod, a group of Jews who supported the king. Many supporters of Herod were also Sadducees. Yeast in this passage symbolizes evil. Just as only a small amount of yeast is needed to make a batch of bread rise, so the hard-heartedness of the religious and political leaders could permeate and contaminate the entire society and make it rise up against Jesus.

**8:17, 18** Jesus rebuked the disciples for their hard hearts. Today the Hardhearts believe: (1) that poverty is always caused by laziness; helping the poor only enables them; (2) that worship is best conducted in one way—our way—which has worked very well for forty years, thank you, and need not be changed; (3) that evangelism doesn't apply; people will never change anyway, so we don't need to do it. Joining the Hardhearts requires only one pledge: You must refuse to listen to Jesus' questions. Don't be a Hardheart. Be open to Christ's truth. Let him soften your heart.

25 Then Jesus placed his hands on the man's eyes again, and his eyes were opened. His sight was completely restored, and he could see everything clearly. 26 Jesus sent him away, saying, "Don't go back into the village on your way home."

**8:26**
Matt 8:4

### Peter Says Jesus Is the Messiah (**109**/Matthew 16:13-20; Luke 9:18-20)

27 Jesus and his disciples left Galilee and went up to the villages near Caesarea Philippi. As they were walking along, he asked them, "Who do people say I am?"

**8:27-30**
John 6:67-71

28 "Well," they replied, "some say John the Baptist, some say Elijah, and others say you are one of the other prophets."

**8:28**
Matt 14:2

29 Then he asked them, "But who do you say I am?"

Peter replied, "You are the Messiah.*"

**8:29**
Matt 16:20
Luke 9:20
John 6:69; 11:27

30 But Jesus warned them not to tell anyone about him.

### Jesus Predicts His Death the First Time (**110**/Matthew 16:21-28; Luke 9:21-27)

31 Then Jesus began to tell them that the Son of Man* must suffer many terrible things and be rejected by the elders, the leading priests, and the teachers of religious law. He would be killed, but three days later he would rise from the dead. 32 As he talked about this openly with his disciples, Peter took him aside and began to reprimand him for saying such things.*

33 Jesus turned around and looked at his disciples, then reprimanded Peter. "Get away from me, Satan!" he said. "You are seeing things merely from a human point of view, not from God's."

**8:29** Or *the Christ. Messiah* (a Hebrew term) and *Christ* (a Greek term) both mean "the anointed one." **8:31** "Son of Man" is a title Jesus used for himself. **8:32** Or *began to correct him.*

---

**8:25** Why did Jesus touch the man a second time before he could see? This miracle was not too difficult for Jesus, but he chose to do it in stages, possibly to show the disciples that some healing would be gradual rather than instantaneous or to demonstrate that spiritual truth is not always perceived clearly at first. Before Jesus left, however, the man was healed completely.

**8:27** Caesarea Philippi was an especially pagan city known for its worship of Greek gods and its temples devoted to the ancient god Pan. The ruler Philip, referred to in 6:17, changed the city's name from Caesarea to Caesarea Philippi so that it would not be confused with the coastal city of Caesarea (Acts 8:40), the capital of the territory ruled by his brother Herod Antipas. This pagan city where many gods were recognized was a fitting place for Jesus to ask the disciples to recognize him as the Son of God.

**8:28** For the story of John the Baptist, see Mark 1:1-11 and 6:14-29. For the story of Elijah, see 1 Kings 17–20 and 2 Kings 1–2.

**8:29** Jesus asked the disciples who other people thought he was; then he asked them the same question. It is not enough to know what others say about Jesus: You must know, understand, and accept for yourself that he is the Messiah. You must move from curiosity to commitment, from admiration to adoration.

**8:30** Why did Jesus warn his own disciples not to tell anyone the truth about him? Jesus knew they needed more instruction about the work he would accomplish through his death and resurrection. Without more teaching, the disciples would have only half the picture. When they confessed Jesus as the Christ, they still didn't know all that it meant.

**8:31** The name for Jesus, *Son of Man,* is Jesus' most common title for himself. It comes from Daniel 7:13, where the Son of Man is a heavenly figure who, in the end times, has authority and power. The name refers to Jesus as the Messiah, the representative man, the human agent of God who is vindicated by God. In this passage, *Son of Man* is linked closely with Peter's confession of Jesus as the Christ and confirms its messianic significance.

From this point on, Jesus spoke plainly and directly to his disciples about his death and resurrection. He began to prepare them for what was going to happen to him by telling them three times that he would soon die (8:31; 9:31; 10:33, 34).

**8:32, 33** In this moment, Peter was not considering God's purposes but only his own natural human desires and feelings. Peter wanted Christ to be king, but not the suffering servant

prophesied in Isaiah 53. He was ready to receive the glory of following the Messiah but not the persecution.

The Christian life is not a paved road to wealth and ease. It often involves hard work, persecution, deprivation, and deep suffering. Peter saw only part of the picture. Don't repeat his mistake. Instead, focus on the good that God can bring out of apparent evil and the Resurrection that follows the Crucifixion.

**8:33** Peter was often the spokesman for all the disciples. In singling him out, Jesus may have been addressing all of them indirectly. Unknowingly, the disciples were trying to prevent Jesus from going to the cross and thus fulfilling his mission on earth. Satan also tempted Jesus to avoid the way of the cross (Matthew 4). Whereas Satan's motives were evil, the disciples were motivated by love and admiration for Jesus. Nevertheless, the disciples' job was not to guide and protect Jesus but to follow him. Only after Jesus' death and resurrection would they fully understand why he had to die.

**CONTINUED MINISTRY**
After taking a roundabout way back to Galilee through Decapolis (the Ten Towns), Jesus returned to Dalmanutha where Jewish leaders questioned his authority. From there he went to Bethsaida and on to Caesarea Philippi. Here he talked with his disciples about his authority and coming events.

34Then, calling the crowd to join his disciples, he said, "If any of you wants to be my follower, you must turn from your selfish ways, take up your cross, and follow me. 35If you try to hang on to your life, you will lose it. But if you give up your life for my sake and for the sake of the Good News, you will save it. 36And what do you benefit if you gain the whole world but lose your own soul?* 37Is anything worth more than your soul? 38If anyone is ashamed of me and my message in these adulterous and sinful days, the Son of Man will be ashamed of that person when he returns in the glory of his Father with the holy angels."

**8:34**
Matt 10:38
Luke 14:27

**8:35**
Matt 10:39
Luke 17:33
John 12:25

**8:38**
Matt 10:33
Luke 12:9

**9** Jesus went on to say, "I tell you the truth, some standing here right now will not die before they see the Kingdom of God arrive in great power!"

### Jesus is Transfigured on the Mountain (111/Matthew 17:1-13; Luke 9:28-36)

2Six days later Jesus took Peter, James, and John, and led them up a high mountain to be alone. As the men watched, Jesus' appearance was transformed, 3and his clothes became dazzling white, far whiter than any earthly bleach could ever make them. 4Then Elijah and Moses appeared and began talking with Jesus.

**9:2-10**
2 Pet 1:17-18

**9:3**
Dan 7:9
Matt 28:3

5Peter exclaimed, "Rabbi, it's wonderful for us to be here! Let's make three shelters as memorials*—one for you, one for Moses, and one for Elijah." 6He said this because he didn't really know what else to say, for they were all terrified.

7Then a cloud overshadowed them, and a voice from the cloud said, "This is my dearly loved Son. Listen to him." 8Suddenly, when they looked around, Moses and Elijah were gone, and they saw only Jesus with them.

**9:7**
Exod 40:34
Deut 18:15
Heb 1:2; 2:3; 12:25

9As they went back down the mountain, he told them not to tell anyone what they had seen until the Son of Man* had risen from the dead. 10So they kept it to themselves, but they often asked each other what he meant by "rising from the dead."

**8:36** Or *your self?* also in 8:37.   **9:5** Greek *three tabernacles.*   **9:9** "Son of Man" is a title Jesus used for himself.

---

**8:34** The Romans, Mark's original audience, knew what taking up the cross meant. Death on a cross was a form of execution used by Rome for dangerous criminals. A prisoner carried his own cross to the place of execution, signifying submission to Rome's power.

Jesus used the image of carrying a cross to illustrate the ultimate submission required of his followers. He is not against pleasure, nor was he saying that we should seek pain needlessly. Jesus was talking about the heroic effort needed to follow him moment by moment, to do his will even when the work is difficult and the future looks bleak.

**8:35** We should be willing to lose our life for the sake of the Good News, not because our life is useless but because nothing—not even life itself—can compare to what we gain with Christ. Jesus wants us to *choose* to follow him rather than to lead a life of sin and self-satisfaction. He wants us to stop trying to control our own destiny and to let him direct us. This makes good sense because, as the Creator, Christ knows better than we do what real life is about. He asks for submission, not self-hatred; he asks us only to lose our self-centered determination to be in charge.

**8:36, 37** Many people spend all their energy seeking pleasure. Jesus said, however, that worldliness, which is centered on possessions, position, or power, is ultimately worthless. Whatever you have on earth is only temporary; it cannot be exchanged for your soul. If you work hard at getting what you want, you might eventually have a "pleasurable" life, but in the end you will find it hollow and empty. Are you willing to make the pursuit of God more important than the selfish pursuits? Follow Jesus, and you will know what it means to live abundantly now and to have eternal life as well.

**8:38** Jesus constantly turns the world's perspective upside down with talk of first and last, saving and losing. Here he gives us a choice. We can reject Jesus now and be rejected by him at his second coming, or we can accept him now and be accepted by him then. Rejecting Christ may help us escape shame for the time being, but it will guarantee an eternity of shame later.

**9:1** What did Jesus mean when he said that some of the disciples would see the Kingdom of God arrive in power? There are

several possibilities. He could have been foretelling his transfiguration, resurrection and ascension, the coming of the Holy Spirit at Pentecost, or his second coming. The Transfiguration is a strong possibility because Mark immediately tells that story. In the Transfiguration (9:2-8), Peter, James, and John saw Jesus glorified as the Son of God (2 Peter 1:16).

**9:2** We don't know why Jesus singled out Peter, James, and John for this special revelation of his glory and purity. Perhaps they were the ones most ready to understand and accept this great truth. These three disciples were the inner circle of the group of 12. They were among the first to hear Jesus' call (1:16-19). They headed the Gospel lists of disciples (3:16). And they were present at certain healings where others were excluded (Luke 8:51).

**9:2** Jesus took the disciples to either Mount Hermon or Mount Tabor. A mountain was often associated with closeness to God and readiness to receive his words. God had appeared to both Moses (Exodus 24:12-18) and Elijah (1 Kings 19:8-18) on mountains.

**9:3ff** The Transfiguration revealed Christ's divine nature. God's voice exalted Jesus above Moses and Elijah as the long-awaited Messiah with full divine authority. Moses represented the law, and Elijah, the prophets. Their appearance showed Jesus as the fulfillment of both the Old Testament law and the prophetic promises.

Jesus was not a reincarnation of Elijah or Moses. He was not merely one of the prophets. As God's only Son, he far surpasses them in authority and power. Many voices try to tell us how to live and how to know God personally. Some of these are helpful, many are not. We must first listen to the Bible, and then evaluate all other authorities in light of God's revelation.

**9:9, 10** Jesus told Peter, James, and John not to speak about what they had seen because they would not fully understand it until Jesus had risen from the dead. Then they would realize that only through dying could Jesus show his power over death and his authority to be King of all. The disciples would not be powerful witnesses for God until they had grasped this truth.

It was natural for the disciples to be confused about Jesus' death and resurrection because they could not see into the future. We, on the other hand, have God's revealed Word, the Bible, to

11 Then they asked him, "Why do the teachers of religious law insist that Elijah must return before the Messiah comes?*"

9:13
Ps 22:6-7
Isa 50:6; 53:3
Matt 11:14

12 Jesus responded, "Elijah is indeed coming first to get everything ready. Yet why do the Scriptures say that the Son of Man must suffer greatly and be treated with utter contempt? 13 But I tell you, Elijah has already come, and they chose to abuse him, just as the Scriptures predicted."

*Jesus Heals a Demon-Possessed Boy (112/Matthew 17:14-21; Luke 9:37-43)*
14 When they returned to the other disciples, they saw a large crowd surrounding them, and some teachers of religious law were arguing with them. 15 When the crowd saw Jesus, they were overwhelmed with awe, and they ran to greet him.

16 "What is all this arguing about?" Jesus asked.

17 One of the men in the crowd spoke up and said, "Teacher, I brought my son so you could heal him. He is possessed by an evil spirit that won't let him talk. 18 And whenever this spirit seizes him, it throws him violently to the ground. Then he foams at the mouth and grinds his teeth and becomes rigid.* So I asked your disciples to cast out the evil spirit, but they couldn't do it."

19 Jesus said to them,* "You faithless people! How long must I be with you? How long must I put up with you? Bring the boy to me."

9:20
Mark 1:26

20 So they brought the boy. But when the evil spirit saw Jesus, it threw the child into a violent convulsion, and he fell to the ground, writhing and foaming at the mouth.

21 "How long has this been happening?" Jesus asked the boy's father.

He replied, "Since he was a little boy. 22 The spirit often throws him into the fire or into water, trying to kill him. Have mercy on us and help us, if you can."

9:23
Matt 21:21
Mark 11:23-24
Luke 17:6
John 11:40
Acts 14:9
9:24
Luke 17:5
9:25
Acts 10:38
9:26
Mark 1:26
9:27
Matt 8:15

23 "What do you mean, 'If I can'?" Jesus asked. "Anything is possible if a person believes."

24 The father instantly cried out, "I do believe, but help me overcome my unbelief!"

25 When Jesus saw that the crowd of onlookers was growing, he rebuked the evil* spirit. "Listen, you spirit that makes this boy unable to hear and speak," he said. "I command you to come out of this child and never enter him again!"

26 Then the spirit screamed and threw the boy into another violent convulsion and left him. The boy appeared to be dead. A murmur ran through the crowd as people said, "He's dead." 27 But Jesus took him by the hand and helped him to his feet, and he stood up.

28 Afterward, when Jesus was alone in the house with his disciples, they asked him, "Why couldn't we cast out that evil spirit?"

29 Jesus replied, "This kind can be cast out only by prayer.*"

**9:11** Greek *that Elijah must come first?*   **9:18** Or *becomes weak.*   **9:19** Or *said to his disciples.*   **9:25** Greek *unclean.*   **9:29** Some manuscripts read *by prayer and fasting.*

give us the full meaning of Jesus' death and resurrection. We have no excuse for our unbelief.

**9:11-13** When Jesus said that Elijah had already come, he was speaking of John the Baptist (Matthew 17:11-13), who had fulfilled the role prophesied for Elijah.

**9:12, 13** It was difficult for the disciples to grasp the idea that their Messiah would have to suffer. The Jews who studied the Old Testament prophecies expected the Messiah to be a great king like David, who would overthrow the enemy, Rome. Their vision was limited to their own time and experience. They did not understand that the values of God's eternal Kingdom were different from the values of the world. They wanted relief from their present problems, but deliverance from sin is far more important than deliverance from physical suffering or political oppression. Our understanding and appreciation of Jesus must go beyond what he can do for us here and now.

**9:18** As the three disciples came down from the mountain with Jesus, they passed from a reassuring experience of God's presence to a frightening experience of evil. The beauty they had just seen must have made the ugliness seem even uglier. As our spiritual vision improves and allows us to see and understand God better, we will also be able to see and understand evil better. We would be overcome by its horror if we did not have Jesus with us to take us through it safely. Don't be afraid to confront evil and suffering, no matter how ugly or horrible. Jesus goes with you.

**9:18** Why couldn't the disciples cast out the evil spirit? In 6:13 we read that they cast out demons while on their mission to the villages. Perhaps they had special authority only for that trip, or perhaps their faith was faltering. Mark tells this story to show that the battle with Satan is a difficult, ongoing struggle. Victory over sin and temptation comes through faith in Jesus Christ, not through our own efforts.

**9:23** Jesus' words do not mean that we can automatically obtain anything we want if we just think positively. Jesus meant that anything is *possible* if we believe, because nothing is too difficult for God. We cannot have everything we pray for as if by magic, but with faith, we can have everything we need to serve him.

**9:24** The attitude of trust and confidence that the Bible calls *belief* or *faith* (Hebrews 11:1, 6) is not something we can obtain without help. Faith is a gift from God (Ephesians 2:8, 9). No matter how much faith we have, we never reach the point of being self-sufficient. Faith is not stored away like money in the bank. Growing in faith is a constant process of daily renewing our trust in Jesus.

**9:29** The disciples would often face difficult situations that could be resolved only through prayer. Prayer is the key that unlocks faith in our life. Effective prayer needs both the attitude of complete dependence and the action of asking. Prayer demonstrates our reliance on God as we humbly invite him to fill us with faith and power. There is no substitute for prayer, especially in circumstances that seem impossible.

### Jesus Predicts His Death the Second Time (113/Matthew 17:22-23; Luke 9:44-45)

³⁰Leaving that region, they traveled through Galilee. Jesus didn't want anyone to know he was there, ³¹for he wanted to spend more time with his disciples and teach them. He said to them, "The Son of Man is going to be betrayed into the hands of his enemies. He will be killed, but three days later he will rise from the dead."³²They didn't understand what he was saying, however, and they were afraid to ask him what he meant.

**9:31**
Matt 16:21
Mark 8:31
Luke 9:22

### The Disciples Argue about Who Would Be the Greatest (115/Matthew 18:1-6; Luke 9:46-48)

³³After they arrived at Capernaum and settled in a house, Jesus asked his disciples, "What were you discussing out on the road?" ³⁴But they didn't answer, because they had been arguing about which of them was the greatest. ³⁵He sat down, called the twelve disciples over to him, and said, "Whoever wants to be first must take last place and be the servant of everyone else."

**9:34**
Luke 22:24
**9:35**
Matt 20:27

³⁶Then he put a little child among them. Taking the child in his arms, he said to them, ³⁷"Anyone who welcomes a little child like this on my behalf* welcomes me, and anyone who welcomes me welcomes not only me but also my Father who sent me."

**9:37**
Matt 10:40
Luke 10:16
John 13:20

### The Disciples Forbid Another to Use Jesus' Name (116/Luke 9:49-50)

³⁸John said to Jesus, "Teacher, we saw someone using your name to cast out demons, but we told him to stop because he wasn't in our group."

**9:38-41**
Num 11:26-29
**9:39**
1 Cor 12:3

³⁹"Don't stop him!" Jesus said. "No one who performs a miracle in my name will soon be able to speak evil of me. ⁴⁰Anyone who is not against us is for us. ⁴¹If anyone gives you even a cup of water because you belong to the Messiah, I tell you the truth, that person will surely be rewarded.

**9:40**
Matt 12:30
Luke 11:23
**9:41**
Matt 10:42

### Jesus Warns against Temptation (117/Matthew 18:7-9)

⁴²"But if you cause one of these little ones who trusts in me to fall into sin, it would be better for you to be thrown into the sea with a large millstone hung around your neck. ⁴³If your hand causes you to sin, cut it off. It's better to enter eternal life with only one hand than to go into the unquenchable fires of hell* with two hands.* ⁴⁵If your foot causes you to sin, cut it

**9:43**
Matt 5:30; 18:8

**9:37** Greek *in my name.* **9:43a** Greek *Gehenna;* also in 9:45, 47. **9:43b** Some manuscripts add verse 44, *'where the maggots never die and the fire never goes out.'* See 9:48.

---

**9:30, 31** Leaving Caesarea Philippi, Jesus began his last tour through the region of Galilee.

**9:34** The disciples, caught up in their constant struggle for personal success, were embarrassed to answer Jesus' question. It is always painful to compare our motives with Christ's. It is not wrong for believers to be industrious or ambitious, but when ambition pushes aside obedience and service, it becomes sin. We are all like the disciples and even like the Pharisees in this regard. Pride or insecurity can cause us to overvalue position and prestige. In God's Kingdom, such motives are destructive. The only safe ambition is directed toward Christ's Kingdom, not our own advancement. We must renounce pride and status seeking. They are Satan's tools, not Christ's.

**9:35** Serving others is real leadership. Jesus described leadership from a new perspective. Instead of *using* people, we are to *serve* them. Jesus' mission was to serve others and to give his life away. A real leader has a servant's heart. Servant leaders appreciate others' worth and realize that they're not above any job. If you see something that needs to be done, don't wait to be asked; take the initiative and do it like a faithful servant. Don't approach life expecting high positions, honors, and special privileges. Look instead for ways to help others.

**9:36, 37** Jesus taught the disciples to welcome children. This was a new approach in a society where children were usually treated as second-class citizens. It is important not only to treat children well but also to teach them about Jesus. Children's ministries should never be regarded as less important than those for adults.

**9:38-40** Jesus was not saying that being indifferent or neutral toward him is as good as being committed. As he explained in Matthew 12:30, "Anyone who isn't with me opposes me, and

anyone who isn't working with me is actually working against me." In both cases, Jesus was pointing out that neutrality toward him is not possible. Nevertheless his followers will not all resemble each other or belong to the same groups. People who are on Jesus' side have the same goal of building up the Kingdom of God, and they should not let their differences interfere with this goal. Those who share a common faith in Christ should cooperate. People don't have to be just like us to be following Jesus with us.

**9:41, 42** Luke 9:48 states, "Whoever is the least among you is the greatest." In Jesus' eyes, whoever welcomes a child welcomes Jesus; giving a cup of cold water to a person in need is the same as giving an offering to God. By contrast, harming others or failing to care for them is a sin, even if they are unimportant people in the world's eyes. It is possible for thoughtless, selfish people to gain a measure of worldly greatness, but lasting greatness is measured by God's standards. What do you use as your measure—personal achievement or unselfish service?

**9:42** This caution against harming little ones in the faith applies both to what we do individually as teachers and examples and to what we allow to fester in our Christian fellowship. Our thoughts and actions must be motivated by love (1 Corinthians 13), and we must be careful about judging others (Matthew 7:1-5; Romans 14:1—15:4). However, we also have a responsibility to confront flagrant sin within the church (1 Corinthians 5:12, 13).

**9:43ff** This startling language is not meant to promote self-mutilation, but instead stresses the importance of cutting sin out of your life. Painful self-discipline is required of his true followers. Giving up a relationship, job, or habit that is against God's will may seem just as painful as cutting off a hand, but Christ is worth any possible loss or discomfort. Nothing should stand in the way of faith. We must be ruthless in removing sin

**9:47**
Matt 5:29

off. It's better to enter eternal life with only one foot than to be thrown into hell with two feet.* 47 And if your eye causes you to sin, gouge it out. It's better to enter the Kingdom of God with only one eye than to have two eyes and be thrown into hell,48 'where the maggots never die and the fire never goes out.'*

**9:50**
Matt 5:13
Luke 14:34
Rom 12:18
Col 4:6

49 "For everyone will be tested with fire.* 50 Salt is good for seasoning. But if it loses its flavor, how do you make it salty again? You must have the qualities of salt among yourselves and live in peace with each other."

### Jesus Teaches about Marriage and Divorce (173/Matthew 19:1-12)

**10** Then Jesus left Capernaum and went down to the region of Judea and into the area east of the Jordan River. Once again crowds gathered around him, and as usual he was teaching them.

2 Some Pharisees came and tried to trap him with this question: "Should a man be allowed to divorce his wife?"

3 Jesus answered them with a question: "What did Moses say in the law about divorce?"

**10:4**
†Deut 24:1-3

4 "Well, he permitted it," they replied. "He said a man can give his wife a written notice of divorce and send her away."*

**10:6**
†Gen 1:27; 5:2

**10:7-8**
†Gen 2:24
1 Cor 6:16
Eph 5:31

5 But Jesus responded, "He wrote this commandment only as a concession to your hard hearts. 6 But 'God made them male and female'* from the beginning of creation. 7 'This explains why a man leaves his father and mother and is joined to his wife,*8 and the two are united into one.'* Since they are no longer two but one,9 let no one split apart what God has joined together."

**9:45** Some manuscripts add verse 46, *'where the maggots never die and the fire never goes out.'* See 9:48.
**9:48** Isa 66:24.   **9:49** Greek *salted with fire;* other manuscripts add *and every sacrifice will be salted with salt.*
**10:4** See Deut 24:1.   **10:6** Gen 1:27; 5:2.   **10:7** Some manuscripts do not include *and is joined to his wife.*
**10:7-8** Gen 2:24.

---

from our lives now in order to avoid suffering for eternity. Make your choices from an eternal perspective.

**9:50** Jesus used salt to illustrate three qualities that should be found in his people: (1) *We should remember God's faithfulness,* just as salt when used with a sacrifice recalled God's covenant with his people (Leviticus 2:13). (2) *We should make a difference in the "flavor" of the world we live in,* just as salt changes meat's flavor (see Matthew 5:13). (3) *We should counteract the moral decay in society,* just as salt preserves food from decay. When we lose this desire to "salt" the earth with the love and message of God, we become useless to him.

**10:2** The Pharisees were trying to trap Jesus with their question. If he supported divorce, he would be upholding the Pharisees' procedures, and they doubted that he would do that. If Jesus spoke against divorce, however, some members of the crowd would dislike his position; some may have even used the law to their advantage to divorce their wives. More important, he might incur the wrath of Herod, who had already killed John the Baptist for speaking out against divorce and adultery (6:17-28). This is what the Pharisees wanted.

The Pharisees saw divorce as a legal issue rather than a spiritual one. Jesus used this test as an opportunity to review God's intended purpose for marriage and to expose the Pharisees' selfish motives. They were not thinking about what God intended for marriage and were quoting Moses unfairly and out of context. Jesus showed these legal experts how superficial their knowledge really was.

**10:5-9** God allowed divorce as a concession to people's sinfulness. Unfortunately, the Pharisees used Deuteronomy 24:1 as a proof text for the sanctioning of divorce. Jesus explained that divorce was not God's ideal; instead, God wants married people to consider their marriage permanent. Don't enter marriage with the option of getting out. Your marriage is more likely to be happy if from the outset you are committed to permanence. Don't be hardhearted like these Pharisees, but be hardheaded in your determination, with God's help, to stay together.

That said, we know that in our world, divorce is sometimes necessary (for physical survival, for well-being of children, etc.). Jesus clearly gave God's ideal for marriage in Genesis priority

over Moses' permission for divorce. Jesus did not cancel Moses' teaching, however. For possible exceptions, see Matthew 5:32 and 19:9, where Jesus permitted divorce when the spouse had been unfaithful; and 1 Corinthians 7:15, where Paul recognized divorce when the unbelieving partner leaves the marriage. Divorce is wrong; it severs a holy union. But divorce is permitted. Jesus did not elaborate on the permissible reasons, but his high view of marriage surely requires that divorce be a last resort to avoid greater disaster.

**10:6-9** Women were often treated as property. Marriage and divorce were regarded as transactions similar to buying and selling land. But Jesus condemned this attitude, clarifying God's original intention—that marriage bring oneness (Genesis 2:24). Jesus held up God's ideal for marriage and told his followers to live by that ideal.

**FINAL TRIP TO JUDEA**
Jesus quietly left Capernaum, heading toward the borders of Judea before crossing the Jordan River. He preached there before going to Jericho. This trip from Galilee was his last; he would not return before his death.

¹⁰Later, when he was alone with his disciples in the house, they brought up the subject again. ¹¹He told them, "Whoever divorces his wife and marries someone else commits adultery against her. ¹²And if a woman divorces her husband and marries someone else, she commits adultery."

### Jesus Blesses the Children (174/Matthew 19:13-15; Luke 18:15-17)

¹³One day some parents brought their children to Jesus so he could touch and bless them. But the disciples scolded the parents for bothering him.

¹⁴When Jesus saw what was happening, he was angry with his disciples. He said to them, "Let the children come to me. Don't stop them! For the Kingdom of God belongs to those who are like these children. ¹⁵I tell you the truth, anyone who doesn't receive the Kingdom of God like a child will never enter it." ¹⁶Then he took the children in his arms and placed his hands on their heads and blessed them.

### Jesus Speaks to the Rich Young Man (175/Matthew 19:16-30; Luke 18:18-30)

¹⁷As Jesus was starting out on his way to Jerusalem, a man came running up to him, knelt down, and asked, "Good Teacher, what must I do to inherit eternal life?"

¹⁸"Why do you call me good?" Jesus asked. "Only God is truly good. ¹⁹But to answer your question, you know the commandments: 'You must not murder. You must not commit adultery. You must not steal. You must not testify falsely. You must not cheat anyone. Honor your father and mother.'*"

²⁰"Teacher," the man replied, "I've obeyed all these commandments since I was young."

²¹Looking at the man, Jesus felt genuine love for him. "There is still one thing you haven't done," he told him. "Go and sell all your possessions and give the money to the poor, and you will have treasure in heaven. Then come, follow me."

²²At this the man's face fell, and he went away sad, for he had many possessions.

²³Jesus looked around and said to his disciples, "How hard it is for the rich to enter the Kingdom of God!" ²⁴This amazed them. But Jesus said again, "Dear children, it is very hard* to enter the Kingdom of God. ²⁵In fact, it is easier for a camel to go through the eye of a needle than for a rich person to enter the Kingdom of God!"

**10:19** Exod 20:12-16; Deut 5:16-20.   **10:24** Some manuscripts read *very hard for those who trust in riches.*

---

**10:11**
Matt 5:32
Luke 16:18
1 Cor 7:10-11

**10:15**
Matt 18:3

**10:16**
Mark 9:36

**10:19**
†Exod 20:12-16
†Deut 5:16-20
Rom 13:9

**10:21**
Matt 6:19-20
Luke 12:33
Acts 2:44-45

**10:24**
Matt 7:13-14
John 3:5

---

**10:13-16** Jesus was often criticized for spending too much time with the wrong people—children, tax collectors, and sinners (Matthew 9:11; Luke 15:1, 2; 19:7). Some, including the disciples, thought Jesus should be spending more time with important leaders and the devout because this was the way to improve his position and avoid criticism. But Jesus didn't need to improve his position. He was God, and he wanted to speak to those who needed him most.

**10:14** To feel secure, all children need is a loving look and gentle touch from someone who cares. They believe us because they trust us. Jesus said that people should trust in him with this kind of childlike faith. We do not have to understand all the mysteries of the universe; it should be enough to know that God loves us and provides forgiveness for our sin.

**10:15** How can you "receive the Kingdom of God like a child"? Adults considering the Christian faith for the first time will have life experiences that take them way past the ability to be as innocent as children. Jesus does not ask us to put aside our experiences, but he does require a change of attitude: adult self-sufficiency must recognize its need for the sovereign God; adult moral defensiveness must humble itself before the holy God; and adult skeptical toughness must soften before the loving God. Children do not feel supremely powerful, perfectly righteous, or totally autonomous. These are adult fantasies. Coming to Jesus means to accept his goodness on your behalf, confess your need, and commit your life to his tender guidance.

**10:17-23** This man wanted to be sure he would get eternal life, so he asked what he could *do*. He said he'd never once broken any of the laws Jesus mentioned (10:19), and perhaps he had even kept the Pharisees' additional regulations as well. But Jesus lovingly broke through the man's pride with a challenge that brought out his true motives: "Go and sell all your possessions and give the money to the poor." This challenge exposed the barrier that could

keep this man out of the Kingdom: his love of money. Money represented his pride of accomplishment and self-effort. Ironically, his attitude made him unable to keep the first commandment: to let nothing be more important than God (Exodus 20:3). He could not meet the one requirement Jesus gave—to turn his whole heart and life over to God. The man came to Jesus wondering what he could do; he left seeing what he was unable to do. What barriers are keeping you from turning your life over to Christ?

**10:18** When Jesus asked this question, he was saying, "Do you really know the one to whom you are talking?" Because only God is truly good, the man was calling Jesus "God," whether or not he realized it.

**10:21** What does your money mean to you? Although Jesus wanted this man to sell everything and give his money to the poor, this does not mean that all believers should sell all their possessions. Most of his followers did not sell everything, although they used their possessions to serve others. Instead, this incident shows us that we must not let our possessions or money keep us from following Jesus. We must remove all barriers to serving him fully. If Jesus asked, could you give up your house? your car? your level of income? your position on the ladder of promotion? Your reaction may show your attitude toward money—whether it is your servant or your master.

**10:21** Jesus showed genuine love for this man, even though he knew that the man might not follow him. Love is able to give tough advice; it doesn't hedge on the truth. Christ loved us enough to die for us, and he also loves us enough to talk straight to us. If his love were superficial, he would give us only his approval; but because his love is complete, he gives us life-changing challenges.

**10:23** Jesus said it was very difficult for the rich to enter the Kingdom of God because the rich, having their basic physical needs met, often become self-reliant. When they feel empty, they buy something new to try to fill the void that only God can fill.

26The disciples were astounded. "Then who in the world can be saved?" they asked.

27Jesus looked at them intently and said, "Humanly speaking, it is impossible. But not with God. Everything is possible with God."

28Then Peter began to speak up. "We've given up everything to follow you," he said.

29"Yes," Jesus replied, "and I assure you that everyone who has given up house or brothers or sisters or mother or father or children or property, for my sake and for the Good News, 30will receive now in return a hundred times as many houses, brothers, sisters, mothers, children, and property—along with persecution. And in the world to come that person will have eternal life. 31But many who are the greatest now will be least important then, and those who seem least important now will be the greatest then.*"

### Jesus Predicts His Death the Third Time (177/Matthew 20:17-19; Luke 18:31-34)

32They were now on the way up to Jerusalem, and Jesus was walking ahead of them. The disciples were filled with awe, and the people following behind were overwhelmed with fear. Taking the twelve disciples aside, Jesus once more began to describe everything that was about to happen to him. 33"Listen," he said, "we're going up to Jerusalem, where the Son of Man* will be betrayed to the leading priests and the teachers of religious law. They will sentence him to die and hand him over to the Romans.* 34They will mock him, spit on him, flog him with a whip, and kill him, but after three days he will rise again."

### Jesus Teaches about Serving Others (178/Matthew 20:20-28)

35Then James and John, the sons of Zebedee, came over and spoke to him. "Teacher," they said, "we want you to do us a favor."

36"What is your request?" he asked.

37They replied, "When you sit on your glorious throne, we want to sit in places of honor next to you, one on your right and the other on your left."

38But Jesus said to them, "You don't know what you are asking! Are you able to drink from the bitter cup of suffering I am about to drink? Are you able to be baptized with the baptism of suffering I must be baptized with?"

39"Oh yes," they replied, "we are able!"

Then Jesus told them, "You will indeed drink from my bitter cup and be baptized with my baptism of suffering. 40But I have no right to say who will sit on my right or my left. God has prepared those places for the ones he has chosen."

41When the ten other disciples heard what James and John had asked, they were indignant.

**Cross-references (left margin):**

10:27 Gen 18:14; Job 42:2; Mark 14:36

10:28 Mark 1:18

10:30 2 Tim 3:12

10:31 Matt 20:16; Luke 13:30

10:33 Matt 16:21; 17:22-23; Mark 8:31; 9:31; Luke 24:7

10:34 Isa 50:6

10:38 Luke 12:50; John 18:11

10:39 Acts 12:2; Rev 1:9

---

10:31 Greek *But many who are first will be last; and the last, first.* 10:33a "Son of Man" is a title Jesus used for himself. 10:33b Greek *the Gentiles.*

---

Their abundance and self-sufficiency become their deficiency. The person who has everything on earth can still lack what is most important—eternal life.

**10:26** The disciples were amazed. Was not wealth a blessing from God, a reward for being good? This misconception is still common today. Although many believers enjoy material prosperity, many others live in poverty. Wealth is not a sign of faith or of partiality on God's part.

**10:29, 30** Jesus assured the disciples that anyone who gives up something valuable for his sake will be repaid a hundred times over in this life, although not necessarily in the same way. For example, someone may be rejected by his family for accepting Christ, but he or she will gain the larger family of believers. Along with these rewards, however, we experience persecution because the world hates God. Jesus emphasized persecution to make sure that people do not selfishly follow him only for the rewards.

**10:31** Jesus explained that in the world to come, the values of this world will be reversed. Those who seek status and importance here will have none in heaven. Those who are humble here will be great in heaven. The corrupt condition of our society encourages confusion in values. We are bombarded by messages that tell us how to be important and how to feel good, and Jesus' teaching about service to others seems alien. But those who have humbly served others are most qualified to be great in heaven.

**10:33, 34** Jesus' death and resurrection should have come as no surprise to the disciples. Here he clearly explained to them what would happen to him. Unfortunately, they didn't really hear what he was saying. Jesus said he was the Messiah, but they thought the Messiah would be a conquering king. He spoke to them of resurrection, but they heard only his words about death. Because Jesus often spoke in parables, the disciples may have thought that his words on death and resurrection were another parable they weren't astute enough to understand. Jesus' predictions of his death and resurrection show that these events were God's plan from the beginning and not accidents.

**10:35** Mark records that John and James went to Jesus with their request; in Matthew, their mother also made the request. Apparently mother and sons were in agreement in requesting honored places in Christ's Kingdom.

**10:37** The disciples, like most Jews of that day, had the wrong idea of the Messiah's Kingdom as predicted by the Old Testament prophets. They thought Jesus would establish an earthly kingdom that would free Israel from Rome's oppression. James and John wanted honored places in it. But Jesus' Kingdom is not of this world; it is not centered in palaces and thrones but in the hearts and lives of his followers. The disciples did not understand this until after Jesus' resurrection.

**10:38, 39** James and John said they were willing to face any trial for Christ. Both did suffer: James died as a martyr (Acts 12:2), and John was forced to live in exile (Revelation 1:9). It is easy to say we will endure anything for Christ, and yet most of us complain about the most minor problems. We may say that we are willing to suffer for Christ, but are we willing to suffer the minor irritations that sometimes come with serving others?

42 So Jesus called them together and said, "You know that the rulers in this world lord it over their people, and officials flaunt their authority over those under them. 43 But among you it will be different. Whoever wants to be a leader among you must be your servant, 44 and whoever wants to be first among you must be the slave of everyone else. 45 For even the Son of Man came not to be served but to serve others and to give his life as a ransom for many."

*10:42*
Luke 22:25-27
1 Pet 5:3

*10:43-44*
Matt 23:11
Mark 9:35
Luke 22:26

*10:45*
Matt 20:28
John 13:14
Phil 2:7
1 Tim 2:5-6
Titus 2:14

### Jesus Heals a Blind Beggar (179/Matthew 20:29-34; Luke 18:35-43)

46 Then they reached Jericho, and as Jesus and his disciples left town, a large crowd followed him. A blind beggar named Bartimaeus (son of Timaeus) was sitting beside the road. 47 When Bartimaeus heard that Jesus of Nazareth was nearby, he began to shout, "Jesus, Son of David, have mercy on me!"

48 "Be quiet!" many of the people yelled at him.

But he only shouted louder, "Son of David, have mercy on me!"

49 When Jesus heard him, he stopped and said, "Tell him to come here."

So they called the blind man. "Cheer up," they said. "Come on, he's calling you!" 50 Bartimaeus threw aside his coat, jumped up, and came to Jesus.

51 "What do you want me to do for you?" Jesus asked.

"My rabbi,*" the blind man said, "I want to see!"

52 And Jesus said to him, "Go, for your faith has healed you." Instantly the man could see, and he followed Jesus down the road.*

*10:47*
Isa 11:1
Jer 23:5-6
Matt 9:27; 15:22

*10:52*
Matt 9:22
Mark 5:34
Luke 7:50; 8:48;
17:19

### 3. Jesus' ministry in Jerusalem

*Jesus Rides into Jerusalem on a Young Donkey*
**(183/Matthew 21:1-11; Luke 19:28-44; John 12:12-19)**

**11** As Jesus and his disciples approached Jerusalem, they came to the towns of Bethphage and Bethany on the Mount of Olives. Jesus sent two of them on ahead. 2 "Go into that

*11:2*
1 Sam 6:7
Zech 9:9

**10:51** Greek uses the Hebrew term *Rabboni*.     **10:52** Or *on the way*.

---

**10:42-45** James and John wanted the highest positions in Jesus' Kingdom. But Jesus told them that true greatness comes in serving others. Peter, one of the disciples who had heard this message, expands the thought in 1 Peter 5:1-4.

Businesses, organizations, and institutions measure greatness by personal achievement. In Christ's Kingdom, however, service is the way to get ahead. The desire to be on top will hinder, not help. Rather than seeking to have your needs met, look for ways that you can minister to the needs of others.

**10:45** This verse reveals not only the motive for Jesus' ministry but also the basis for our salvation. A ransom was the price paid to release a slave. Jesus paid a ransom for us because we could not pay it ourselves. His death released all of us from our slavery to sin. The disciples thought Jesus' life and power would save them from Rome; Jesus said his *death* would save them from sin,

an even greater slavery than Rome's. More about the ransom Jesus paid for us is found in 1 Peter 1:18, 19.

**10:46** Jericho was a popular resort city rebuilt by Herod the Great in the Judean desert, not far from the Jordan River crossing. Jesus was on his way to Jerusalem (10:32), and, after crossing over from Perea, he would naturally enter Jericho.

**10:46** Beggars were a common sight in most towns. Because most occupations of that day required physical labor, anyone with a crippling disease or disability was at a severe disadvantage and was usually forced to beg, even though God's laws commanded care for such needy people (Leviticus 25:35-38). Blindness was considered a curse from God for sin (John 9:2), but Jesus refuted this idea when he reached out to heal the blind.

**10:47** "Son of David" was a popular way of addressing Jesus as the Messiah, because it was known that the Messiah would be a descendant of King David (Isaiah 9:7). The fact that Bartimaeus called Jesus the Son of David shows that he recognized Jesus as the Messiah. His faith in Jesus as the Messiah brought about his healing.

**10:47** We do not know how long Bartimaeus had been blind, but it only took a moment for him to decide to call on Jesus for help. Jesus met many spiritually blind people—religious leaders, family members, people in the crowd. Though their eyes were fine, they could not see the truth about Jesus. But blind Bartimaeus heard the report that Jesus was coming and boldly cried out.

In coming to Jesus, we need Bartimaeus's boldness. We must overcome our reticence and doubts and take the step to call on him. Bartimaeus had not seen Jesus' miracles, but he responded in faith to what he had heard. We have heard Jesus described in the Gospels. May we be like those of whom Peter wrote, "You love him even though you have never seen him. Though you do not see him now, you trust him; and you rejoice with a glorious, inexpressible joy" (1 Peter 1:8).

**11:1, 2** This was Sunday of the week that Jesus would be crucified, and the great Passover festival was about to begin. Jews came to Jerusalem from all over the Roman world during this week-long celebration to remember the great exodus from Egypt

**JESUS NEARS JERUSALEM**
Leaving Jericho, Jesus headed toward acclaim, then crucifixion, in Jerusalem. During his last week, he stayed outside the city in Bethany, a village on the eastern slope of the Mount of Olives, entering Jerusalem to teach, eat the Passover, and finally be crucified.

village over there," he told them. "As soon as you enter it, you will see a young donkey tied there that no one has ever ridden. Untie it and bring it here.³ If anyone asks, 'What are you doing?' just say, 'The Lord needs it and will return it soon.'"

⁴The two disciples left and found the colt standing in the street, tied outside the front door. ⁵As they were untying it, some bystanders demanded, "What are you doing, untying that colt?" ⁶They said what Jesus had told them to say, and they were permitted to take it. ⁷Then they brought the colt to Jesus and threw their garments over it, and he sat on it.

⁸Many in the crowd spread their garments on the road ahead of him, and others spread leafy branches they had cut in the fields. ⁹Jesus was in the center of the procession, and the people all around him were shouting,

> "Praise God!*
> Blessings on the one who comes in the name of the LORD!
> ¹⁰ Blessings on the coming Kingdom of our ancestor David!
> Praise God in highest heaven!"*

**11:9-10**
†Pss 118:25-26;
148:1

**11:11**
Matt 21:10, 17

¹¹So Jesus came to Jerusalem and went into the Temple. After looking around carefully at everything, he left because it was late in the afternoon. Then he returned to Bethany with the twelve disciples.

**11:9** Greek *Hosanna*, an exclamation of praise that literally means "save now"; also in 11:10.
**11:9-10** Pss 118:25-26; 148:1.

| KEY CHARACTERISTICS OF CHRIST IN THE GOSPELS | Characteristic | Reference |
|---|---|---|
| | Jesus is the Son of God . . . . . . . . . . . . . . . . . | Matthew 16:15, 16; Mark 1:1; Luke 22:70, 71; John 8:24 |
| | Jesus is God who became human . . . . . . . . . | John 1:1, 2, 14; 20:28 |
| | Jesus is the Christ, the Messiah . . . . . . . . . . | Matthew 26:63, 64; Mark 14:61, 62; Luke 9:20; John 4:25, 26 |
| | Jesus came to help sinners . . . . . . . . . . . . . . | Matthew 9:13; Luke 5:32 |
| | Jesus has power to forgive sins . . . . . . . . . . . | Mark 2:9-12; Luke 24:47 |
| | Jesus has authority over death . . . . . . . . . . . | Matthew 28:5, 6; Mark 5:22-24, 35-42; Luke 24:5, 6; John 11:1-44 |
| | Jesus has power to give eternal life . . . . . . . . | John 10:28; 17:2 |
| | Jesus healed the sick . . . . . . . . . . . . . . . . . . | Matthew 8:5-13; Mark 1:32-34; Luke 5:12-15; John 9:1-7 |
| | Jesus taught with authority . . . . . . . . . . . . . | Matthew 7:29; Mark 1:21, 22 |
| | Jesus was compassionate . . . . . . . . . . . . . . . | Matthew 9:36; Mark 1:41; 8:2 |
| | Jesus experienced sorrow . . . . . . . . . . . . . . . | Matthew 26:38; John 11:35 |
| | Jesus never disobeyed God . . . . . . . . . . . . . . | Matthew 3:15; John 8:46 |

(see Exodus 12:37-51). Many in the crowds had heard of or seen Jesus and were hoping he would come to the Temple (John 11:55-57).

Jesus did come, not as a warring king on a horse or in a chariot, but as a gentle and peaceable King on a donkey's colt, just as Zechariah 9:9 had predicted. Jesus knew that those who would hear him teach at the Temple would return to their homes throughout the world and announce the coming of the Messiah.

**11:9, 10** The people exclaimed "Praise God!" because they recognized that Jesus was fulfilling the prophecy in Zechariah 9:9 (see also Psalms 24:7-10; 118:26). They spoke of David's kingdom because of God's words to David in 2 Samuel 7:12-14. The crowd correctly saw Jesus as the fulfillment of these prophecies, but they did not understand where Jesus' kingship would lead him. This same crowd cried out, "Crucify him!" when Jesus stood on trial only a few days later.

**11:10** Like those who witnessed Jesus' victory parade into Jerusalem, we have expectations for what we think God should do to make life better, safer, and more enjoyable. Like excited spectators, we can't wait to see suffering stopped, injustice corrected, and prosperity begun. Like the people on the road

to Jerusalem that day, we have much to learn about Jesus' death and resurrection. We must not let our personal desires catch us up in the celebration and shouting lest we miss the meaning of true discipleship. In our excitement and celebration, we must remember that following Christ involves hardships. It may include suffering, even death.

**11:11-21** In this passage, two unusual incidents are related: the cursing of the fig tree and the clearing of the Temple. The cursing of the fig tree was an acted-out parable related to the clearing of the Temple. The Temple was supposed to be a place of worship, but true worship had disappeared. The fig tree showed promise of fruit, but it produced none. Jesus was showing his anger at religious life without substance. If you claim to have faith without putting it to work in your life, you are like the barren fig tree. Genuine faith has great potential; ask God to help you bear fruit for his Kingdom.

*Jesus Clears the Temple Again* (**184**/Matthew 21:12-17; Luke 19:45-48)

12 The next morning as they were leaving Bethany, Jesus was hungry. 13 He noticed a fig tree in full leaf a little way off, so he went over to see if he could find any figs. But there were only leaves because it was too early in the season for fruit. 14 Then Jesus said to the tree, "May no one ever eat your fruit again!" And the disciples heard him say it.

15 When they arrived back in Jerusalem, Jesus entered the Temple and began to drive out the people buying and selling animals for sacrifices. He knocked over the tables of the money changers and the chairs of those selling doves, 16 and he stopped everyone from using the Temple as a marketplace.* 17 He said to them, "The Scriptures declare, 'My Temple will be called a house of prayer for all nations,' but you have turned it into a den of thieves."*

**11:17**
†Isa 56:7
†Jer 7:11

18 When the leading priests and teachers of religious law heard what Jesus had done, they began planning how to kill him. But they were afraid of him because the people were so amazed at his teaching.

**11:18**
Matt 21:46
Mark 12:12
Luke 20:19

19 That evening Jesus and the disciples left* the city.

*Jesus Says the Disciples Can Pray for Anything* (**188**/Matthew 21:18-22)

20 The next morning as they passed by the fig tree he had cursed, the disciples noticed it had withered from the roots up. 21 Peter remembered what Jesus had said to the tree on the previous day and exclaimed, "Look, Rabbi! The fig tree you cursed has withered and died!"

22 Then Jesus said to the disciples, "Have faith in God. 23 I tell you the truth, you can say to this mountain, 'May you be lifted up and thrown into the sea,' and it will happen. But you must really believe it will happen and have no doubt in your heart. 24 I tell you, you can pray for anything, and if you believe that you've received it, it will be yours. 25 But when you are praying, first forgive anyone you are holding a grudge against, so that your Father in heaven will forgive your sins, too.*"

**11:22**
Matt 17:20
Luke 17:6

**11:24**
Matt 7:7

**11:25**
Matt 5:23; 6:14

**11:16** Or *from carrying merchandise through the Temple.* **11:17** Isa 56:7; Jer 7:11. **11:19** Greek *they left;* other manuscripts read *he left.* **11:25** Some manuscripts add verse 26, *But if you refuse to forgive, your Father in heaven will not forgive your sins.* Compare Matt 6:15.

---

**11:13-26** Fig trees, a popular source of inexpensive food in Israel, require three years from the time they are planted until they can bear fruit. Each tree yields a great amount of fruit twice a year, in late spring and in early autumn. This incident occurred early in the spring when the leaves were beginning to bud. The figs normally grow as the leaves fill out, but this tree, though full of leaves, had no figs. The tree looked promising but offered no fruit. Jesus' harsh words to the fig tree could be applied to the nation of Israel. Fruitful in appearance only, Israel was spiritually barren.

**11:15-17** Jesus became angry, but he did not sin. There is a place for righteous indignation. Christians are right to be upset about sin and injustice and should take a stand against them. Unfortunately, believers are often passive about these important issues and instead get angry over personal insults and petty irritations. Make sure your anger is directed toward the right issues.

**11:15-17** Money changers and merchants did big business during Passover. Those who came from foreign countries had to have their money changed into Temple currency because this was the only money accepted for the Temple tax and for the purchase of sacrificial animals. Often the inflated exchange rate enriched the money changers, and the exorbitant prices of animals made the merchants wealthy. Their stalls were set up in the Temple's Court of the Gentiles, making it all but impossible for non-Jews to spend any time in worship (Isaiah 56:6, 7). Jesus became angry because God's house of worship had become a place of extortion and a barrier to Gentiles who wanted to worship.

**11:22, 23** The kind of prayer that moves mountains is prayer for the fruitfulness of God's Kingdom. It would seem impossible to move a mountain into the sea, so Jesus used that illustration to show that God can do the impossible. God will answer your prayers but not as a result of your positive mental attitude. Other conditions must be met: (1) You must be a believer; (2) you must not hold a grudge against another person; (3) you must not pray with selfish motives; (4) your request must be for the good of God's Kingdom. To pray effectively, you need faith in God, not faith in the object of your request. If you focus only on your request, you will be left with nothing if your request is refused.

**11:24** Jesus, our example, prayed, "Everything is possible for you. . . . Yet I want your will to be done, not mine" (14:36). Our prayers are often motivated by our own interests and desires. We like to hear that we can have anything. But Jesus prayed with

**CLEARING THE TEMPLE** On Monday morning of his last week, Jesus left Bethany, entered Jerusalem, and cleared the Temple of money changers and merchants.

Labels on map: Antonia Fortress (later Praetorium?); to Bethphage and Bethany; Temple; Hasmonean Palace; Herod's Lower Palace; Herod's Royal Palace; UPPER CITY; Caiaphas's House?; JERUSALEM; Traditional Upper Room?; LOWER CITY

*Religious Leaders Challenge Jesus' Authority* (**189**/Matthew 21:23-27; Luke 20:1-8)
27 Again they entered Jerusalem. As Jesus was walking through the Temple area, the leading priests, the teachers of religious law, and the elders came up to him. 28 They demanded, "By what authority are you doing all these things? Who gave you the right to do them?"

29 "I'll tell you by what authority I do these things if you answer one question," Jesus replied. 30 "Did John's authority to baptize come from heaven, or was it merely human? Answer me!"

31 They talked it over among themselves. "If we say it was from heaven, he will ask why we didn't believe John. 32 But do we dare say it was merely human?" For they were afraid of what the people would do, because everyone believed that John was a prophet. 33 So they finally replied, "We don't know."

And Jesus responded, "Then I won't tell you by what authority I do these things."

*Jesus Tells the Parable of the Evil Farmers* (**191**/Matthew 21:33-46; Luke 20:9-19)

**12** Then Jesus began teaching them with stories: "A man planted a vineyard. He built a wall around it, dug a pit for pressing out the grape juice, and built a lookout tower. Then he leased the vineyard to tenant farmers and moved to another country. 2 At the time of the grape harvest, he sent one of his servants to collect his share of the crop. 3 But the farmers grabbed the servant, beat him up, and sent him back empty-handed. 4 The owner then sent another servant, but they insulted him and beat him over the head. 5 The next servant he sent was killed. Others he sent were either beaten or killed, 6 until there was only one left—his son whom he loved dearly. The owner finally sent him, thinking, 'Surely they will respect my son.'

7 "But the tenant farmers said to one another, 'Here comes the heir to this estate. Let's kill him and get the estate for ourselves!' 8 So they grabbed him and murdered him and threw his body out of the vineyard.

9 "What do you suppose the owner of the vineyard will do?" Jesus asked. "I'll tell you—he will come and kill those farmers and lease the vineyard to others. 10 Didn't you ever read this in the Scriptures?

'The stone that the builders rejected
　　has now become the cornerstone.
11 This is the LORD's doing,
　　and it is wonderful to see.'*"

12 The religious leaders* wanted to arrest Jesus because they realized he was telling the story against them—they were the wicked farmers. But they were afraid of the crowd, so they left him and went away.

**12:10-11** Ps 118:22-23.　**12:12** Greek *They.*

**Margin references (left column):**

11:32
Matt 14:5; 21:46

12:1
Isa 5:1-2

12:5
2 Chr 24:21;
36:15-16
Neh 9:26
Matt 23:34-37
Acts 7:52
1 Thes 2:15

12:6
Rom 8:3
Gal 4:4

12:8
Heb 13:12

12:10-11
†Ps 118:22-23
Acts 4:11
Rom 9:33
Eph 2:20
1 Pet 2:5-7

12:12
Mark 11:18

---

*God's* interests in mind. When we pray, we can express our desires, but we should want his will above ours. Check yourself to see if your prayers focus on your interests or God's.

**11:25** Forgiving others is tough work—so much so that many people would rather do something totally distasteful than offer forgiveness to someone who has wronged them. For a person to pray while bearing a grudge, however, is like a tree sprouting leaves and bearing no fruit (11:13). True faith changes the heart. Real prayer dismantles pride and vengeance, filling the holes with love. Real faith seeks peace. For our churches to have prayer power, there must be harmony and forgiveness evident in the body of believers. Let go of hurts, abandon grudges, and forgive others.

**11:27-33** The religious leaders were in a quandary. They had wanted to trap Jesus with a question that would show him to be either a blasphemer or a weird fanatic. Instead, Jesus had countered their question with a question about John the Baptist. Now they would have to try to save face. They had not stood up for John or tried to get him released—John had irritated them just as Jesus was doing (see Matthew 3:7-10). Always cloaked in self-interest, these religious leaders were only concerned about position and reputation; they weren't looking for the truth. In John 3:19, Jesus summed up this attitude: "People loved the darkness more than the light, for their actions were evil." People who reject

Jesus' claims have a greater problem than intellectual doubt; they are rebelling against Christ's control of their lives. They try to ask tricky questions, but don't really want an answer. Sincere seekers, however, will find the truth (Matthew 7:7, 8).

**11:30** For more information, see John the Baptist's Profile in John 1, p. 1749.

**12:1ff** In this parable, the man who planted the vineyard is God; the vineyard is the nation Israel; the tenant farmers are Israel's religious leaders; the servants are the prophets and priests who remained faithful to God; the son is Jesus; and the others are the Gentiles. The religious leaders not only frustrated their nation's purpose but also killed those who were trying to fulfill it. They were so jealous and possessive that they ignored the welfare of the very people they were supposed to be bringing to God. By telling this story, Jesus exposed the religious leaders' plot to kill him and warned that their sins would be punished.

**12:10, 11** Jesus referred to himself as the stone rejected by the builders. Although he would be rejected by most of the Jewish leaders, he would become the cornerstone of a new "building," the church (Acts 4:11, 12). The cornerstone was used as a base to make sure the other stones of the building were straight and level. Likewise, Jesus' life and teaching would be the church's foundation.

## Religious Leaders Question Jesus about Paying Taxes
(193/Matthew 22:15-22; Luke 20:20-26)

13Later the leaders sent some Pharisees and supporters of Herod to trap Jesus into saying something for which he could be arrested. 14"Teacher," they said, "we know how honest you are. You are impartial and don't play favorites. You teach the way of God truthfully. Now tell us—is it right to pay taxes to Caesar or not? 15Should we pay them, or shouldn't we?"

Jesus saw through their hypocrisy and said, "Why are you trying to trap me? Show me a Roman coin,* and I'll tell you." 16When they handed it to him, he asked, "Whose picture and title are stamped on it?"

"Caesar's," they replied.

17"Well, then," Jesus said, "give to Caesar what belongs to Caesar, and give to God what belongs to God."

**12:17**
Rom 13:7

His reply completely amazed them.

## Religious Leaders Question Jesus about the Resurrection
(194/Matthew 22:23-33; Luke 20:27-40)

18Then Jesus was approached by some Sadducees—religious leaders who say there is no resurrection from the dead. They posed this question: 19"Teacher, Moses gave us a law that if a man dies, leaving a wife without children, his brother should marry the widow and have a child who will carry on the brother's name.* 20Well, suppose there were seven brothers. The oldest one married and then died without children. 21So the second brother married the widow, but he also died without children. Then the third brother married her. 22This continued with all seven of them, and still there were no children. Last of all, the woman also died. 23So tell us, whose wife will she be in the resurrection? For all seven were married to her."

**12:18-27**
Acts 23:8
1 Cor 15:12
**12:19**
†Gen 38:8
†Deut 25:5

24Jesus replied, "Your mistake is that you don't know the Scriptures, and you don't know the power of God. 25 For when the dead rise, they will neither marry nor be given in marriage. In this respect they will be like the angels in heaven.

**12:25**
1 Cor 15:42, 49, 52

**12:15** Greek *a denarius.*   **12:19** See Deut 25:5-6.

---

**12:13** The Pharisees were primarily a religious group concerned with ritual purity; the supporters of Herod were a Jewish political group that approved of Herod's compromises with Rome. The Pharisees did not like Jesus because he exposed their hypocrisy. The supporters of Herod also saw Jesus as a threat. Supporters of the dynasty of Herod the Great, they had lost political control when, as a result of reported unrest, Rome deposed Archelaus (Herod's son with authority over Judea), and replaced him with a Roman governor. The supporters of Herod feared that Jesus would cause still more instability in Judea and that Rome might react by never allowing the Roman leaders to step down and be replaced by a descendant of Herod.

**12:14** Anyone who avoided paying taxes faced harsh penalties. The Jews hated to pay taxes to Rome because the money supported their oppressors and symbolized their subjection. Much of the tax money also went to maintain the pagan temples and luxurious lifestyles of Rome's upper class. The Pharisees and supporters of Herod hoped to trap Jesus with this tax question. A yes would mean he supported Rome, which would turn the people against him. A no would bring accusations of treason and rebellion against Rome and could lead to civil penalties.

**12:17** Jesus avoided the trick question by showing that believers have dual citizenship (1 Peter 2:17). Our citizenship in the nation requires that we pay money for the services and benefits we receive. Our citizenship in the Kingdom of Heaven requires that we pledge to God our primary obedience and commitment. (See Acts 4:18, 19 and 5:29 for discussions on obeying God rather than people.) As God's followers, we have legitimate obligations to both God and the government. But it is important to keep our priorities straight. When the two authorities conflict, our duty to God always must come before our duty to the government. The coin bearing the emperor's image should be given to the emperor; our lives, bearing God's image, belong to God. Are you giving to God what is rightfully his?

**12:18-23** After the Pharisees and supporters of Herod failed to trap Jesus with their tax question, the Sadducees stepped in with a question they were sure would stump him. This was a question that they had successfully used against the Pharisees, who could not come up with an answer. The Sadducees did not believe in life after death because the Pentateuch (Genesis—Deuteronomy) had no direct teaching about it, and the writings of Moses were the only Scriptures they followed. But Jesus was about to point out that Moses' books support the idea of eternal life (12:26).

**12:19** According to Old Testament law, when a man died without a son, his brother had to marry the widow and produce children to care for her and allow the family line to continue. The first son of this marriage was considered the heir of the dead man (Deuteronomy 25:5, 6).

**12:24** What life will be like after the resurrection is far beyond our ability to understand or imagine (Isaiah 64:4; 1 Corinthians 2:9). We need not be afraid of eternal life because of the unknowns, however. Instead of wondering what God's coming Kingdom will be like, we should concentrate on our relationship with Christ right now because in the new Kingdom, we will be with him. If we learn to love and trust Christ *now*, we will not be afraid of what he has in store for us then.

**12:25-27** Jesus' statement does not mean that people won't recognize their spouses in the coming Kingdom. It simply means that God's new order will not be an extension of this life and that the same physical and natural rules won't apply. Jesus' comment in verse 25 was not intended to be the final word on marriage in heaven; instead, this response was Jesus' refusal to answer the Sadducees' riddle and fall into their trap. Sidestepping their question about the much-married woman, he gave a definitive answer to their real question about the doctrine of resurrection. Because the Sadducees believed only in the Pentateuch (Genesis—Deuteronomy), Jesus quoted from Exodus 3:6 to prove that there is life after death. God spoke of Abraham, Isaac, and Jacob years after their deaths as if they *still lived.* God's covenant with all people exists beyond death.

**12:26**
†Exod 3:6
**12:27**
Matt 22:32
Luke 20:38

26 "But now, as to whether the dead will be raised—haven't you ever read about this in the writings of Moses, in the story of the burning bush? Long after Abraham, Isaac, and Jacob had died, God said to Moses,* 'I am the God of Abraham, the God of Isaac, and the God of Jacob.'* 27 So he is the God of the living, not the dead. You have made a serious error."

### Religious Leaders Question Jesus about the Greatest Commandment (195/Matthew 22:34-40)

**12:29-30**
†Deut 6:4-5
†Josh 22:5
Luke 10:27
**12:31**
†Lev 19:18
Rom 13:9
Gal 5:14
Jas 2:8
**12:32**
†Deut 4:35, 39; 6:4
1 Cor 8:4-6

28One of the teachers of religious law was standing there listening to the debate. He realized that Jesus had answered well, so he asked, "Of all the commandments, which is the most important?"

29Jesus replied, "The most important commandment is this: 'Listen, O Israel! The Lᴏʀᴅ our God is the one and only Lᴏʀᴅ. 30 And you must love the Lᴏʀᴅ your God with all your heart, all your soul, all your mind, and all your strength.'* 31 The second is equally important: 'Love your neighbor as yourself.'* No other commandment is greater than these."

32 The teacher of religious law replied, "Well said, Teacher. You have spoken the truth by

**12:26a** Greek *in the story of the bush? God said to him.*    **12:26b** Exod 3:6.    **12:29-30** Deut 6:4-5.    **12:31** Lev 19:18.

---

**WHAT JESUS SAID ABOUT LOVE**

In Mark 12:28 a teacher of religious law asked Jesus which of all the commandments was the most important to follow. Jesus mentioned two commandments, one from Deuteronomy 6:5, the other from Leviticus 19:18. Both had to do with love. Why is love so important? Jesus said that all of the commandments were given for two simple reasons: to help us love God and love others as we should.

| What else did Jesus say about love? | Reference |
|---|---|
| God loves us | John 3:16 |
| We are to love God | Matthew 22:37 |
| Because God loves us, he cares for us | Matthew 6:25-34 |
| God wants everyone to know how much he loves them | John 17:23 |
| God loves even those who hate him; we are to do the same | Matthew 5:43-47; Luke 6:35 |
| God seeks out even those most alienated from him | Luke 15 |
| God must be our first love | Matthew 6:24; 10:37 |
| We love God when we obey him | John 14:21; 15:10 |
| God loves Jesus, his Son | John 5:20; 10:17 |
| Jesus loves God | John 14:31 |
| Those who refuse Jesus don't have God's love | John 5:41-44 |
| Jesus loves us just as God loves Jesus | John 15:9 |
| Jesus proved his love for us by dying on the cross so that we could live eternally with him | John 3:14, 15; 15:13, 14 |
| The love between God and Jesus is the perfect example of how we are to love others | John 17:21-26 |
| We are to love one another (John 13:34, 35) and demonstrate that love | Matthew 5:40-42; 10:42 |
| We are *not* to love the praise of people (John 12:43), selfish recognition (Matthew 23:6), earthly belongings (Luke 6:19-31), or anything more than God | Luke 16:13 |
| Jesus' love extends to each individual | Mark 10:21; John 10:11-15 |
| Jesus wants us to love him through the good and through the difficult times | Matthew 26:31-35 |
| Jesus wants our love to be genuine | John 21:15-17 |

---

**12:28** By Jesus' time, the Jews had accumulated hundreds of laws—613 by one historian's count. Some religious leaders tried to distinguish between major and minor laws, and some taught that all laws were equally binding and that it was dangerous to make any distinctions. This teacher's question could have provoked controversy among these groups, but Jesus' answer summarized all of God's laws.

**12:29-31** God's laws are not burdensome. They can be reduced to two simple principles: Love God and love others. These commands are from the Old Testament (Deuteronomy 6:5; Leviticus 19:18). When you love God completely and care for others as you care for yourself, then you have fulfilled the intent of the Ten Commandments and the other Old Testament laws. According to Jesus, these two commandments summarize all God's laws. Let

them rule your thoughts, decisions, and actions. When you are uncertain about what to do, ask yourself which course of action best demonstrates love for God and love for others.

**12:32-34** This Pharisee had grasped the intent of God's law— that true obedience comes from the heart. Because all the Old Testament commands lead to Christ, his next step was faith in Jesus himself. This, however, was the most difficult step to take. We do not know if this Pharisee ever became a true believer, but we must remember that being "close" to being a Christian is infinitely far away if a person never commits to Christ. Salvation cannot rest on intellectual knowledge alone. You must repent, follow Christ, and be made a new person by his Holy Spirit. Don't be content with being close; take the step and make the commitment.

saying that there is only one God and no other. 33And I know it is important to love him with all my heart and all my understanding and all my strength, and to love my neighbor as myself. This is more important than to offer all of the burnt offerings and sacrifices required in the law."

12:33
†Lev 19:18
Mic 6:6-8

34Realizing how much the man understood, Jesus said to him, "You are not far from the Kingdom of God." And after that, no one dared to ask him any more questions.

12:34
Matt 22:46
Luke 20:40

## Religious Leaders Cannot Answer Jesus' Question
**(196**/Matthew 22:41-46; Luke 20:41-44)
35Later, as Jesus was teaching the people in the Temple, he asked, "Why do the teachers of religious law claim that the Messiah is the son of David? 36For David himself, speaking under the inspiration of the Holy Spirit, said,

12:36
2 Sam 23:2
†Ps 110:1

'The LORD said to my Lord,
Sit in the place of honor at my right hand
until I humble your enemies beneath your feet.'*

37Since David himself called the Messiah 'my Lord,' how can the Messiah be his son?" The large crowd listened to him with great delight.

12:37
Rom 1:3; 9:5
Rev 22:16

## Jesus Warns against the Religious Leaders **(197**/Matthew 23:1-12; Luke 20:45-47)
38Jesus also taught: "Beware of these teachers of religious law! For they like to parade around in flowing robes and receive respectful greetings as they walk in the marketplaces. 39And how they love the seats of honor in the synagogues and the head table at banquets. 40Yet they shamelessly cheat widows out of their property and then pretend to be pious by making long prayers in public. Because of this, they will be more severely punished."

12:39
Luke 11:43

## A Poor Widow Gives All She Has **(200**/Luke 21:1-4)
41Jesus sat down near the collection box in the Temple and watched as the crowds dropped in their money. Many rich people put in large amounts. 42Then a poor widow came and dropped in two small coins.*

12:41
2 Kgs 12:9
John 8:20

43Jesus called his disciples to him and said, "I tell you the truth, this poor widow has given more than all the others who are making contributions. 44For they gave a tiny part of their surplus, but she, poor as she is, has given everything she had to live on."

12:43-44
2 Cor 8:12

## Jesus Tells about the Future **(201**/Matthew 24:1-25; Luke 21:5-24)

**13** As Jesus was leaving the Temple that day, one of his disciples said, "Teacher, look at these magnificent buildings! Look at the impressive stones in the walls."

2Jesus replied, "Yes, look at these great buildings. But they will be completely demolished. Not one stone will be left on top of another!"

13:2
Luke 19:44

3Later, Jesus sat on the Mount of Olives across the valley from the Temple. Peter, James, John, and Andrew came to him privately and asked him, 4"Tell us, when will all this happen? What sign will show us that these things are about to be fulfilled?"

**12:36** Ps 110:1. **12:42** Greek *two lepta, which is a kodrantes* [i.e., a quadrans].

---

**12:35-37** Jesus quoted Psalm 110:1 to show that David considered the Messiah to be his Lord, not just his descendant. The religious leaders did not understand that the Messiah would be far more than a human descendant of David; he would be God himself in human form.

**12:38-40** Jesus again exposed the religious leaders' impure motives. The teachers received no pay, so they depended on the hospitality extended by devout Jews. Some of them used this custom to exploit people, cheating the poor out of everything they had and taking advantage of the rich. Through their pious actions they hoped to gain status, recognition, and respect.

**12:38-40** Jesus warned against trying to make a good impression. These teachers of religious law were religious hypocrites who had no love for God. True followers of Christ are not distinguished by showy spirituality. Reading the Bible, praying in public, or following church rituals can be phony if the motive for doing them is to be noticed or honored. Let your actions be consistent with your beliefs. Live for Christ, even when no one is looking.

**12:41** There were several boxes in the Temple where money could be placed. Some were for collecting the Temple tax from

Jewish males; the others were for freewill offerings. This particular collection box was probably in the Court of the Women.

**12:41-44** This widow gave all she had to live on, in contrast to the way most people handle their money. When we consider giving a certain percentage of our income a great accomplishment, we resemble those who gave "a tiny part of their surplus." Here, Jesus was admiring generous and sacrificial giving. As believers, we should consider increasing our giving—whether of money, time, or talents—to a point beyond convenience or calculation.

**13:1, 2** About 15 years before Jesus was born (20 B.C.), Herod the Great began to remodel and rebuild the Temple, which had stood for nearly 500 years since the days of Ezra (Ezra 6:14, 15). Herod made the Temple one of the most beautiful buildings in Jerusalem, not to honor God, but to appease the Jews whom he ruled. The magnificent building project was not completely finished until A.D. 64. Jesus' prophecy that not one stone would be left on another was fulfilled in A.D. 70, when the Romans completely destroyed the Temple and the entire city of Jerusalem.

**13:3ff** The disciples wanted to know when the Temple would be destroyed. Jesus gave them a prophetic picture of that time,

**13:5**
2 Thes 2:3, 10-12
1 Tim 4:1
2 Tim 3:13
1 Jn 4:6

**13:6**
John 5:43

**13:8**
2 Chr 15:6
Isa 19:2

**13:10**
Rom 10:18

**13:11**
Matt 10:19-20
Luke 12:11-12

**13:12**
Mic 7:6

**13:13**
Matt 10:22
John 15:18-21

⁵ Jesus replied, "Don't let anyone mislead you, ⁶ for many will come in my name, claiming, 'I am the Messiah.'* They will deceive many. ⁷ And you will hear of wars and threats of wars, but don't panic. Yes, these things must take place, but the end won't follow immediately. ⁸ Nation will go to war against nation, and kingdom against kingdom. There will be earthquakes in many parts of the world, as well as famines. But this is only the first of the birth pains, with more to come.

⁹ "When these things begin to happen, watch out! You will be handed over to the local councils and beaten in the synagogues. You will stand trial before governors and kings because you are my followers. But this will be your opportunity to tell them about me.* ¹⁰ For the Good News must first be preached to all nations.* ¹¹ But when you are arrested and stand trial, don't worry in advance about what to say. Just say what God tells you at that time, for it is not you who will be speaking, but the Holy Spirit.

¹² "A brother will betray his brother to death, a father will betray his own child, and children will rebel against their parents and cause them to be killed. ¹³ And everyone will hate you because you are my followers.* But the one who endures to the end will be saved.

**13:6** Greek *claiming, 'I am.'*    **13:9** Or *But this will be your testimony against them.*    **13:10** Or *all peoples.*
**13:13** Greek *on account of my name.*

---

| **JESUS' PROPHECIES IN THE OLIVET DISCOURSE** | *Type of Prophecy* | *Old Testament References* | *Other New Testament References* |
|---|---|---|---|
| | *The Last Days* | | |
| | Mark 13:1-23 | Daniel 9:26, 27 | John 15:21 |
| | Matthew 24:1-28 | Daniel 11:31 | Revelation 11:2 |
| | Luke 21:5-24 | Joel 2:2 | 1 Timothy 4:1, 2 |
| | *The Second Coming of Christ* | | |
| | Mark 13:24-27 | Isaiah 13:6-10 | Revelation 6:12 |
| | Luke 21:25-28 | Ezekiel 32:7 | Mark 14:62 |
| | Matthew 24:29-31 | Daniel 7:13, 14 | 1 Thessalonians 4:16 |

In Mark 13, often called the Olivet discourse, Jesus talked a lot about two things: the end times and his second coming. Jesus was not trying to encourage his disciples to speculate about exactly when he would return by sharing these prophecies with them. Instead, he urges all his followers to be watchful and prepared for his coming. If we serve Jesus faithfully now, we will be ready when he returns.

---

including events leading up to it. He also talked about future events connected with his return to earth to judge all people. Jesus predicted both near and distant events without putting them in chronological order. Some of the disciples lived to see the destruction of Jerusalem in A.D. 70. This event would assure them that everything else Jesus predicted would also happen.

Jesus warned his followers about the future so that they could learn how to live in the present. Many predictions Jesus made in this passage have not yet been fulfilled. He did not make them so that we would guess when they might be fulfilled but to help us to be spiritually alert and prepared at all times as we wait for his return.

**13:3, 4** The Mount of Olives rises above Jerusalem to the east. From its slopes a person can look down into the city and see the Temple. Zechariah 14:1-4 predicts that the Messiah will stand on this very mountain when he returns to set up his eternal Kingdom.

**13:5-7** What are the signs of the end times? There have been people in every generation since Christ's resurrection claiming to know exactly when Jesus would return. No one has been right yet, however, because Christ will return on God's timetable, not ours. Jesus predicted that before his return, many believers would be misled by false teachers claiming to have revelations from God.

According to Scripture, one clear sign of Christ's return will be his unmistakable appearance in the clouds, which will be seen by all people (13:26; Revelation 1:7). In other words, you do not have to wonder whether a certain person is the Messiah or whether these are the "end times." When Jesus returns, *you will know* beyond a doubt, because it will be evident to all true

believers. Beware of groups who claim special knowledge of Christ's return because no one knows when that time will be (13:32). Be cautious about saying, "This is it!" but be bold in your total commitment to have your heart and life ready for Christ's return.

**13:9-11** As the early church began to grow, most of the disciples experienced the kind of persecution Jesus was talking about. Since the time of Christ, Christians have been persecuted in their own lands and on foreign mission fields. Though you may be safe from persecution now, your vision of God's Kingdom must not be limited by what happens only to you. A glance at a newspaper will reveal that many Christians in other parts of the world daily face hardships and persecution. Persecutions are an opportunity for Christians to witness for Christ to those opposed to him. God's desire is that the Good News be proclaimed to everyone in spite of persecution.

**13:11** Jesus was teaching the kind of attitude we should have when we must take a stand for the Good News. We don't have to be fearful or defensive about our faith because the Holy Spirit will be present to give us the right words to say.

**13:13** To believe in Jesus and "endure to the end" will take perseverance because our faith will be challenged and opposed. Severe trials will sift true Christians from fair-weather believers. Enduring to the end does not earn salvation for us but marks us as already saved. The assurance of our salvation will keep us strong in times of persecution.

¹⁴"The day is coming when you will see the sacrilegious object that causes desecration* standing where he* should not be." (Reader, pay attention!) "Then those in Judea must flee to the hills. ¹⁵A person out on the deck of a roof must not go down into the house to pack. ¹⁶A person out in the field must not return even to get a coat. ¹⁷How terrible it will be for pregnant women and for nursing mothers in those days. ¹⁸And pray that your flight will not be in winter. ¹⁹For there will be greater anguish in those days than at any time since God created the world. And it will never be so great again. ²⁰In fact, unless the Lord shortens that time of calamity, not a single person will survive. But for the sake of his chosen ones he has shortened those days.

²¹"Then if anyone tells you, 'Look, here is the Messiah,' or 'There he is,' don't believe it. ²²For false messiahs and false prophets will rise up and perform signs and wonders so as to deceive, if possible, even God's chosen ones. ²³Watch out! I have warned you about this ahead of time!

### Jesus Tells about His Return (202/Matthew 24:26-35; Luke 21:25-33)

²⁴"At that time, after the anguish of those days,

the sun will be darkened,
    the moon will give no light,
²⁵ the stars will fall from the sky,
    and the powers in the heavens will be shaken.*

²⁶Then everyone will see the Son of Man* coming on the clouds with great power and glory.*²⁷And he will send out his angels to gather his chosen ones from all over the world*—from the farthest ends of the earth and heaven.

²⁸"Now learn a lesson from the fig tree. When its branches bud and its leaves begin to sprout, you know that summer is near. ²⁹In the same way, when you see all these things taking place, you can know that his return is very near, right at the door. ³⁰I tell you the truth, this generation* will not pass from the scene before all these things take place. ³¹Heaven and earth will disappear, but my words will never disappear.

### Jesus Tells about Remaining Watchful (203/Matthew 24:36-51; Luke 21:34-38)

³²"However, no one knows the day or hour when these things will happen, not even the angels in heaven or the Son himself. Only the Father knows. ³³And since you don't know when that time will come, be on guard! Stay alert*!

13:14a Greek the abomination of desolation. See Dan 9:27; 11:31; 12:11.    13:14b Or it.    13:24-25 See Isa 13:10; 34:4; Joel 2:10.    13:26a "Son of Man" is a title Jesus used for himself.    13:26b See Dan 7:13.    13:27 Greek from the four winds.    13:30 Or this age, or this nation.    13:33 Some manuscripts add and pray.

**Cross-references (right margin):**

13:14
†Dan 9:27;
11:31; 12:11
Matt 24:15
2 Thes 2:3

13:17
Luke 23:29

13:19
Dan 9:26; 12:1
Joel 2:2
Rev 7:14

13:21
Luke 17:23

13:22
Deut 13:1-3
2 Thes 2:9-10
Rev 13:13

13:24-25
†Isa 13:10; 34:4
Ezek 32:7-8
†Joel 2:10, 31; 3:15
Rev 6:12-14; 8:12

13:26
†Dan 7:13
Matt 16:27
Rev 1:7

13:27
Deut 30:4
Zech 2:6

13:31
Matt 5:18
Luke 16:17

13:32
Acts 1:7

13:33-37
Matt 25:13-14
Luke 12:35-40
Rom 13:11
Eph 6:17-18
Col 4:2
1 Thes 5:6

---

**13:14** The "sacrilegious object that causes desecration" refers to the desecration of the Temple by God's enemies. This happened repeatedly in Israel's history: in 597 B.C. when Nebuchadnezzar looted the Temple and took Judean captives to Babylon (2 Chronicles 36); in 168 B.C. when Antiochus Epiphanes sacrificed a pig to Zeus on the sacred Temple altar (Daniel 9:27; 11:30, 31); in A.D. 70 when the Roman general Titus placed an idol on the site of the burned-out Temple after the destruction of Jerusalem. Just a few years after Jesus gave this warning, in A.D. 38, the emperor Caligula made plans to put his own statue in the Temple, but he died before this could be carried out.

**13:17** Some Christian couples who are contemplating pregnancy have been discouraged by this verse. They wonder if kids should be brought into a world filled with sin, evil, and terror. Jesus was not making a general warning against pregnancy, however. Many times in history have had risks and drawbacks; no place or time is perfect. We must remember that God will look out for the welfare of our children as he has looked out for us.

**13:20** The "chosen ones" are God's chosen people, those who are saved. See Romans 8:29, 30 and Ephesians 1:4, 5 for more on God's choice.

**13:22, 23** Is it possible for Christians to be deceived? Yes. So convincing will be the arguments and proofs from deceivers in the end times that it will be difficult *not* to fall away from Christ. If we are prepared, Jesus says, we can remain faithful. But if we are not prepared, we will turn away. To penetrate the disguises of false teachers we can ask: (1) Have their predictions come true, or do they have to revise them to fit what's already happened? (2) Does any teaching utilize a small section of the Bible to the neglect of the whole? (3) Does the teaching contradict what the Bible says about God? (4) Are the practices meant to glorify the teacher or Christ? (5) Do the teachings promote hostility toward other Christians?

**13:31** The truth that heaven and earth will disappear is all that much more believable in our age of nuclear power and terrorism. Jesus tells us, however, that even though the earth will pass away, the truth of his words will never be changed or abolished. God and his Word provide the only stability in our unstable world. How shortsighted people are who spend all their time and energy learning about this temporary world and accumulating its possessions, while neglecting the Bible and its eternal truths!

**13:32** When Jesus said that even he did not know the time of the end, he was affirming his humanity. Of course God the Father knows the time, and Jesus and the Father are one. But when Jesus became a man, he voluntarily gave up the unlimited use of his divine attributes.

The emphasis of this verse is not on Jesus' lack of knowledge, but rather on the fact that no one knows. It is God the Father's secret to be revealed when he wills. No one can predict by Scripture or science the exact day of Jesus' return. Jesus is teaching that preparation, not calculation, is needed.

**13:33, 34** Months of planning go into a wedding, the birth of a baby, a career change, a speaking engagement, the purchase of a home. Do you place the same importance on preparing for Christ's return, the most important event in your life? Its results

34 "The coming of the Son of Man can be illustrated by the story of a man going on a long trip. When he left home, he gave each of his slaves instructions about the work they were to do, and he told the gatekeeper to watch for his return. 35 You, too, must keep watch! For you don't know when the master of the household will return—in the evening, at midnight, before dawn, or at daybreak. 36 Don't let him find you sleeping when he arrives without warning. 37 I say to you what I say to everyone: Watch for him!"

### C. DEATH AND RESURRECTION OF JESUS, THE SERVANT (14:1—16:20)

Mark tells us about Jesus' ultimate deed of servanthood—dying for us on the cross. Jesus died for our sin so we wouldn't have to. Now we can have eternal fellowship with God instead of eternal suffering and death. When first written in Rome, this Gospel was encouraging to Roman Christians during times of persecution. Christ's victory through suffering can encourage us during difficult times, too.

*Religious Leaders Plot to Kill Jesus* (**207**/Matthew 26:1-5; Luke 22:1-2)

**14:1-2**
John 11:55-57

**14** It was now two days before Passover and the Festival of Unleavened Bread. The leading priests and the teachers of religious law were still looking for an opportunity to capture Jesus secretly and kill him. 2 "But not during the Passover celebration," they agreed, "or the people may riot."

*A Woman Anoints Jesus with Perfume* (**182**/Matthew 26:6-13; John 12:1-11)

**14:3**
Luke 7:37-38

3Meanwhile, Jesus was in Bethany at the home of Simon, a man who had previously had leprosy. While he was eating,* a woman came in with a beautiful alabaster jar of expensive perfume made from essence of nard. She broke open the jar and poured the perfume over his head.

14:3 Or *reclining.*

---

will last for eternity. You dare not postpone your preparations because you do not know when his return will occur. The way to prepare is to study God's Word and live by its instructions each day. Only then will you be ready.

**13:35-37** Mark 13 tells us how to live while we wait for Christ's return: (1) We are not to be misled by confusing claims or speculative interpretations of what will happen (13:5, 6). (2) We should not be afraid to tell people about Christ, despite what they might say or do to us (13:9-11). (3) We must stand firm by faith and not be surprised by persecution (13:13). (4) We must be morally alert, obedient to the commands for living found in God's Word. This chapter was not given to promote discussions on prophetic timetables but to stimulate right living for God in a world where he is largely ignored.

**14:1** The Passover commemorated the night the Israelites were freed from Egypt (Exodus 12), when God "passed over" homes marked by the blood of a lamb while killing firstborn sons in unmarked homes. The day of Passover was followed by a seven-day festival called the Festival of Unleavened Bread. This, too, recalled the Israelites' quick escape from Egypt when they didn't have time to let their bread rise, so they baked it without yeast (leaven). On this holiday, Jewish families still gather for a special meal that includes lamb, wine, bitter herbs, and unleavened bread.

**14:2** The Jews were preparing to observe Passover, a time of remembrance for families to celebrate when the blood of lambs had saved their ancestors. But some of the religious leaders had another agenda. Jesus had disrupted their security, revealed their sham, and opposed their authority. Now they would put him away. But the world is controlled by our all-wise God, not puny politicians. God would turn the religious leaders' murder plot into the greatest blessing that mankind would ever know. Another Lamb would be slain, and his blood would save all people. When grief or disaster seem to be dominating, remember that your life is in God's hands and remember what Jesus did for you.

**14:3** Bethany is located on the eastern slope of the Mount of Olives (Jerusalem is on the western side). This town was the home of Jesus' friends Lazarus, Mary, and Martha, who were also present at this dinner (John 11:2). The woman who anointed Jesus' feet was Mary, Lazarus and Martha's sister (John 12:1-3).

**14:3-9** Matthew and Mark placed this event just before the Last

Supper, while John placed it a week earlier, just before the Triumphal Entry. It must be remembered that the main purpose of the Gospel writers was not to present an exact chronological account of Christ's life but to give an accurate record of his message. Matthew and Mark may have chosen to place this event here to contrast the complete devotion of Mary with the betrayal of Judas, the next event in both Gospels.

**UPPER ROOM AND GETHSEMANE** Jesus and the disciples ate the traditional Passover meal in an upper room in the city and then went to the Mount of Olives into a garden called Gethsemane. In the cool of the evening, Jesus prayed for strength to face the trial and suffering ahead.

⁴Some of those at the table were indignant. "Why waste such expensive perfume?" they asked. ⁵"It could have been sold for a year's wages\* and the money given to the poor!" So they scolded her harshly.

⁶But Jesus replied, "Leave her alone. Why criticize her for doing such a good thing to me? ⁷You will always have the poor among you, and you can help them whenever you want to. But you will not always have me. ⁸She has done what she could and has anointed my body for burial ahead of time. ⁹I tell you the truth, wherever the Good News is preached throughout the world, this woman's deed will be remembered and discussed."

**14:7** Deut 15:11

**14:8** John 19:40

### Judas Agrees to Betray Jesus (208/Matthew 26:14-16; Luke 22:3-6)

¹⁰Then Judas Iscariot, one of the twelve disciples, went to the leading priests to arrange to betray Jesus to them. ¹¹They were delighted when they heard why he had come, and they promised to give him money. So he began looking for an opportunity to betray Jesus.

### Disciples Prepare for the Passover (209/Matthew 26:17-19; Luke 22:7-13)

¹²On the first day of the Festival of Unleavened Bread, when the Passover lamb is sacrificed, Jesus' disciples asked him, "Where do you want us to go to prepare the Passover meal for you?"

**14:12** Exod 12:14-21 Deut 16:1-4 1 Cor 5:7-8

¹³So Jesus sent two of them into Jerusalem with these instructions: "As you go into the city, a man carrying a pitcher of water will meet you. Follow him. ¹⁴At the house he enters, say to the owner, 'The Teacher asks: Where is the guest room where I can eat the Passover meal with my disciples?' ¹⁵He will take you upstairs to a large room that is already set up. That is where you should prepare our meal." ¹⁶So the two disciples went into the city and found everything just as Jesus had said, and they prepared the Passover meal there.

**14:14** Exod 12:8 Lev 23:5

### Jesus and the Disciples Share the Last Supper
**(211/Matthew 26:20-30; Luke 22:14-30; John 13:21-30)**

¹⁷In the evening Jesus arrived with the twelve disciples.\* ¹⁸As they were at the table\* eating, Jesus said, "I tell you the truth, one of you eating with me here will betray me."

**14:18** †Ps 41:9

¹⁹Greatly distressed, each one asked in turn, "Am I the one?"

²⁰He replied, "It is one of you twelve who is eating from this bowl with me. ²¹For the Son of Man\* must die, as the Scriptures declared long ago. But how terrible it will be for the one who betrays him. It would be far better for that man if he had never been born!"

**14:21** Ps 22:1-21 Isa 53:3-8

²²As they were eating, Jesus took some bread and blessed it. Then he broke it in pieces and gave it to the disciples, saying, "Take it, for this is my body."

**14:22-25** 1 Cor 11:23-25

²³And he took a cup of wine and gave thanks to God for it. He gave it to them, and they all

**14:23** 1 Cor 10:16

**14:5** Greek *for 300 denarii.* A denarius was equivalent to a laborer's full day's wage. **14:17** Greek *the Twelve.* **14:18** Or *As they reclined.* **14:21** "Son of Man" is a title Jesus used for himself.

---

**14:4, 5** Where Mark says "some of those at the table," John specifically mentions Judas (John 12:4, 5). Judas's indignation over Mary's act of worship was based not on concern for the poor but on greed. Because Judas was the treasurer of Jesus' ministry and had embezzled funds (John 12:6), he no doubt wanted the perfume sold so that he could benefit from the proceeds.

**14:6, 7** Jesus was not saying that we should neglect the poor, nor was he justifying indifference to them. (For Jesus' teaching about the poor, see Matthew 6:2-4; Luke 6:20, 21; 14:13, 21; 18:22.) Jesus was praising Mary for her unselfish act of worship. The essence of worshiping Christ is to regard him with utmost love, respect, and devotion and to be willing to sacrifice to him what is most precious.

**14:10** Why would Judas want to betray Jesus? Very likely, Judas expected Jesus to start a political rebellion and overthrow Rome. As treasurer, Judas certainly assumed (as did the other disciples, see 10:35-37) that he would be given an important position in Jesus' new government. But when Jesus praised Mary for pouring out the perfume, thought to be worth a day's salary, Judas finally began to realize that Jesus' Kingdom was not physical or political. Judas's greedy desire for money and status could not be fulfilled if he followed Jesus, so he betrayed him in exchange for money and favor from the religious leaders.

**14:13** The two men Jesus sent were Peter and John (Luke 22:8).

**14:14, 15** Many homes had large upstairs rooms, sometimes with stairways both inside and outside the house. The preparations for the Passover would have included setting the table and buying and preparing the Passover lamb, unleavened bread, sauces, and other ceremonial food and drink.

**14:19** Judas, the very man who would betray Jesus, was at the table with the others. Judas had already determined to betray Jesus, but in cold-blooded hypocrisy he shared the fellowship of this meal. It is easy to become enraged or shocked by what Judas did; yet professing commitment to Christ and then denying him with one's life is also betraying him. It is denying Christ's love to disobey him; it is denying his truth to distrust him; it is denying his deity to reject his authority. Do your words and actions match?

**14:20** It was often the practice to eat from a common bowl. Meat or bread was dipped into a bowl filled with sauce often made from fruit.

**14:22-25** Mark records the origin of the Last Supper, which is still celebrated in worship services today. Jesus and his disciples ate a meal, sang psalms, read Scripture, and prayed. Then Jesus took two traditional parts of the Passover meal, the passing of bread and the drinking of wine, and gave them new meaning as representations of his body and blood. He used the bread and wine to explain the significance of what he was about to do on the cross. For more on the significance of the Last Supper, see 1 Corinthians 11:23-29.

The Last Supper is remembered by different terms. Each name

## JUDAS ISCARIOT

It is easy to overlook the fact that Jesus chose Judas to be his disciple. We may also forget that while Judas betrayed Jesus, *all* the disciples abandoned him. With the other disciples, Judas shared a persistent misunderstanding of Jesus' mission. They all expected Jesus to make the right political moves. When he kept talking about dying, they all felt varying degrees of anger, fear, and disappointment. They didn't understand why they had been chosen if Jesus' mission was doomed to fail.

The exact motivation behind Judas's betrayal is unknown. What is clear is that Judas allowed his desires to place him in a position where Satan could manipulate him. Judas accepted payment to set Jesus up for the religious leaders. He identified Jesus for the guards in the dimly lit Garden of Gethsemane. It is possible that he was trying to force Jesus' hand: Would Jesus now rebel against Rome and set up a new political government?

Whatever his plan, though, at some point Judas realized he didn't like the way things were turning out. He tried to undo the evil he had done by returning the money to the priests, but it was too late. The wheels of God's sovereign plan had been set into motion. How sad that Judas ended his life in despair without ever experiencing the gift of reconciliation God could give even to him through Jesus Christ.

Human feelings toward Judas have always been mixed. Some have fervently hated him for his betrayal. Others have pitied him for not realizing what he was doing. A few have tried to make him a hero for his part in ending Jesus' earthly mission. Some have questioned God's fairness in allowing one man to bear such guilt. While there are many feelings about Judas, there are some facts to consider as well. He, by his own choice, betrayed God's Son into the hands of soldiers (Luke 22:48). He was a thief (John 12:6). Jesus knew that Judas's life of evil would not change (John 6:70). Judas's betrayal of Jesus was part of God's sovereign plan (Psalm 41:9; Zechariah 11:12-13; Matthew 20:18; 26:20-25; Acts 1:16, 20).

In betraying Jesus, Judas made the greatest mistake in history. But the fact that Jesus knew Judas would betray him doesn't mean that Judas was a puppet of God's will. Judas made the choice. God knew what that choice would be and confirmed it. Judas didn't lose his relationship with Jesus; rather, he never found Jesus in the first place. He is called "the one headed for destruction" (John 17:12) because he was never saved.

Judas does us a favor if he makes us think a second time about our commitment to God and the presence of God's Spirit within us. Are we true disciples and followers, or uncommitted pretenders? We can choose despair and death, or we can choose repentance, forgiveness, hope, and eternal life. Judas's betrayal sent Jesus to the cross to guarantee that second choice, our only chance. Will we accept Jesus' free gift, or, like Judas, betray him?

| | |
|---|---|
| **Strengths and accomplishments** | • He was chosen as one of the 12 disciples; the only non-Galilean<br>• He was in charge of the disciples' funds<br>• He was able to recognize the evil in his betrayal of Jesus |
| **Weaknesses and mistakes** | • He was greedy (John 12:6)<br>• He betrayed Jesus<br>• He committed suicide instead of seeking forgiveness |
| **Lessons from his life** | • Evil plans and motives leave us open to being used by Satan for even greater evil<br>• The consequences of evil are so devastating that even small lies and little wrongdoings have serious results<br>• God's plan and his purposes are worked out even in the worst possible events |
| **Vital statistics** | • Where: Possibly from the town of Kerioth<br>• Occupation: Disciple of Jesus<br>• Relative: Father: Simon<br>• Contemporaries: Jesus, Pilate, Herod, the other 11 disciples |
| **Key verses** | "Then Satan entered into Judas Iscariot, who was one of the twelve disciples, and he went to the leading priests and captains of the Temple guard to discuss the best way to betray Jesus to them" (Luke 22:3-4). |

Judas's story is told in the Gospels. He is also mentioned in Acts 1:18-19.

---

believers use for this sacrament brings out a different dimension to it. It is the "Lord's Supper" because it commemorates the Passover meal that Jesus ate with his disciples; it is the "Eucharist" (thanksgiving) because in it we thank God for Christ's work for us; it is "Communion" because through it we commune with God and with other believers. As we eat the bread and drink the wine, we should be quietly reflective as we recall Jesus' death and his promise to come again, grateful for God's wonderful gift to us, and joyful as we meet with Christ and the body of believers.

**14:23** Whatever name your church uses for this event (Communion, Lord's Supper, or Eucharist) and on whatever

schedule you celebrate it, the importance is that through celebrating Communion together believers experience the presence of Christ. The celebration of Communion: (1) humbles us before God. We confess our sin and restate our need for Christ to guide us. (2) reminds us that we are forgiven. We remember that his shed blood paid the price. (3) expresses our oneness in Christ. We are unified in our faith. (4) encourages us to recommit. We are reminded to pledge ourselves to serve him who died for us.

drank from it. [24]And he said to them, "This is my blood, which confirms the covenant* between God and his people. It is poured out as a sacrifice for many. [25] I tell you the truth, I will not drink wine again until the day I drink it new in the Kingdom of God."

[26]Then they sang a hymn and went out to the Mount of Olives.

### Jesus Again Predicts Peter's Denial (222/Matthew 26:31-35)

[27]On the way, Jesus told them, "All of you will desert me. For the Scriptures say,

'God will strike* the Shepherd,
    and the sheep will be scattered.'

**14:27**
†Zech 13:7

[28] But after I am raised from the dead, I will go ahead of you to Galilee and meet you there." [29]Peter said to him, "Even if everyone else deserts you, I never will."

**14:28**
Mark 16:7

[30]Jesus replied, "I tell you the truth, Peter—this very night, before the rooster crows twice, you will deny three times that you even know me."

[31]"No!" Peter declared emphatically. "Even if I have to die with you, I will never deny you!" And all the others vowed the same.

### Jesus Agonizes in the Garden (223/Matthew 26:36-46; Luke 22:39-46)

[32]They went to the olive grove called Gethsemane, and Jesus said, "Sit here while I go and pray." [33]He took Peter, James, and John with him, and he became deeply troubled and distressed. [34]He told them, "My soul is crushed with grief to the point of death. Stay here and keep watch with me."

**14:33**
Matt 17:1
Mark 9:2
Luke 9:28

**14:34**
†Pss 42:6; 43:5
John 12:27

[35]He went on a little farther and fell to the ground. He prayed that, if it were possible, the awful hour awaiting him might pass him by. [36] "Abba, Father," * he cried out, "everything is possible for you. Please take this cup of suffering away from me. Yet I want your will to be done, not mine."

**14:36**
Matt 20:22
John 5:30; 6:38;
18:11
Rom 8:15
Gal 4:6

[37]Then he returned and found the disciples asleep. He said to Peter, "Simon, are you asleep? Couldn't you watch with me even one hour? [38] Keep watch and pray, so that you will not give in to temptation. For the spirit is willing, but the body is weak."

**14:38**
Rom 7:22-23

[39]Then Jesus left them again and prayed the same prayer as before. [40]When he returned to them again, he found them sleeping, for they couldn't keep their eyes open. And they didn't know what to say.

[41]When he returned to them the third time, he said, "Go ahead and sleep. Have your rest. But no—the time has come. The Son of Man is betrayed into the hands of sinners. [42] Up, let's be going. Look, my betrayer is here!"

**14:24** Some manuscripts read *the new covenant.*   **14:27** Greek *I will strike.* Zech 13:7.   **14:36** *Abba* is an Aramaic term for "father."

---

**14:24** Jesus' death for us on the cross seals a new covenant between God and us. The old covenant involved forgiveness of sins through the blood of an animal sacrifice (Exodus 24:6-8). But instead of a spotless lamb on the altar, Jesus offered himself, the spotless Lamb of God, as a sacrifice that would forgive sin once and for all. Jesus was the final sacrifice for sins, and his blood sealed the new covenant between God and us. Now all of us can come to God through Jesus, in full confidence that God will hear us and save us from our sins.

**14:26** The hymn they sang was most likely taken from Psalms 115–118, traditionally sung at the Passover meal.

**14:27-31** This was the second time in the same evening that Jesus predicted the disciples' denial and desertion, which probably explains their strong reaction (14:31). For Jesus' earlier prediction, see Luke 22:31-34 and John 13:36-38.

**14:31** Peter was so emphatic. It is easy to say we are devoted to Christ, but our claims are meaningful only when they are tested in the crucible of persecution. How strong is your faith? Is it strong enough to stand up under intense trial? We need the Holy Spirit, not boastfulness and human resolve. We must never discount our vulnerability to pride, greed, or even indifference.

**14:35, 36** Was Jesus trying to get out of his task? Jesus expressed his true feelings, but he did not deny or rebel against God's will. He reaffirmed his desire to do what God wanted. Jesus' prayer highlights the terrible suffering he had to endure—an agony so much more magnified because he had to take on the sins of the whole world. This "cup" was the agony of alienation from God, his Father, at the cross (Hebrews 5:7-9). The sinless Son of God took on our sins and was separated for a while from God so that we could be eternally saved.

**14:36** While praying, Jesus was aware of what doing the Father's will would cost him. He understood the suffering he was about to encounter, and he did not want to have to endure the horrible experience. But Jesus prayed, "Yet I want your will to be done, not mine." Anything worth having costs something. What does your commitment to God cost you? We must be willing to pay any price to gain what is priceless—eternal life.

**14:38** You may not face execution for your faith, but you probably face many problems that wear you down. You deal with irritating people whom you must love and serve; you face the burden of unfinished tasks or lack of obvious results; you cope with helpers who let you down or fail to comprehend. Remember that in times of great stress, you are vulnerable to temptation, even if you have a willing spirit. Jesus explained how to resist: (1) *Keep watch* (14:34)—stay awake and be morally vigilant. (2) *Pray to God* (14:35)—this is how you maintain your vigilance. (3) *Seek support of friends and loved ones* (14:33, 37, 40, 41)—this is how you build up your resistance and help others; when one is weak, others are strong. (4) *Focus on the purpose God has given you* (14:36)—this is how you do God's will and not your own.

## Jesus Is Betrayed and Arrested
(**224**/Matthew 26:47-56; Luke 22:47-53; John 18:1-11)

⁴³And immediately, even as Jesus said this, Judas, one of the twelve disciples, arrived with a crowd of men armed with swords and clubs. They had been sent by the leading priests, the teachers of religious law, and the elders. ⁴⁴The traitor, Judas, had given them a prearranged signal: "You will know which one to arrest when I greet him with a kiss. Then you can take him away under guard." ⁴⁵As soon as they arrived, Judas walked up to Jesus. "Rabbi!" he exclaimed, and gave him the kiss.

⁴⁶Then the others grabbed Jesus and arrested him. ⁴⁷But one of the men with Jesus pulled out his sword and struck the high priest's slave, slashing off his ear.

⁴⁸Jesus asked them, "Am I some dangerous revolutionary, that you come with swords and clubs to arrest me?⁴⁹ Why didn't you arrest me in the Temple? I was there among you teaching every day. But these things are happening to fulfill what the Scriptures say about me."

⁵⁰Then all his disciples deserted him and ran away. ⁵¹One young man following behind was clothed only in a long linen shirt. When the mob tried to grab him, ⁵²he slipped out of his shirt and ran away naked.

**14:47**
John 18:10

**14:49**
Isa 53:7-9
Luke 24:44

**14:50**
Ps 88:8
John 16:32

---

| MAJOR EVENTS OF PASSION WEEK | Day | Event | References |
|---|---|---|---|
| Sunday through Wednesday Jesus spent each night in Bethany, just two miles east of Jerusalem on the opposite slope of the Mount of Olives. He probably stayed at the home of Mary, Martha, and Lazarus. Jesus spent Thursday night praying in the Garden of Gethsemane. Friday and Saturday nights Jesus' body lay in the garden tomb. | Sunday | Triumphal Entry into Jerusalem | Matthew 21:1-11; Mark 11:1-10; Luke 19:29-40; John 12:12-19 |
| | Monday | Jesus clears the Temple | Matthew 21:12, 13; Mark 11:15-17; Luke 19:45, 46 |
| | Tuesday | Jesus' authority challenged in the Temple | Matthew 21:23-27; Mark 11:27-33; Luke 20:1-8 |
| | | Jesus teaches in stories and confronts the Jewish leaders | Matthew 21:28–23:36; Mark 12:1-40; Luke 20:9-47 |
| | | Greeks ask to see Jesus | John 12:20-26 |
| | | The Olivet discourse | Matthew 24; Mark 13; Luke 21:5-38 |
| | | Judas agrees to betray Jesus | Matthew 26:14-16; Mark 14:10, 11; Luke 22:3-6 |
| | Wednesday | The Bible does not say what Jesus did on this day; he probably remained in Bethany with his disciples | |
| | Thursday | The Last Supper | Matthew 26:26-29; Mark 14:22-25; Luke 22:14-20 |
| | | Jesus speaks to the disciples in the upper room | John 13–17 |
| | | Jesus struggles in Gethsemane | Matthew 26:36-46; Mark 14:32-42; Luke 22:39-46; John 18:1 |
| | | Jesus is betrayed and arrested | Matthew 26:47-56; Mark 14:43-52; Luke 22:47-53; John 18:2-12 |
| | Friday | Jesus is tried by Jewish and Roman authorities and is denied by Peter | Matthew 26:57–27:2, 11-31; Mark 14:53–15:20; Luke 22:54–23:25; John 18:13–19:16 |
| | | Jesus is crucified | Matthew 27:31-56; Mark 15:20-41; Luke 23:26-49; John 19:17-30 |
| | Sunday | The Resurrection | Matthew 28:1-10; Mark 16:1-11; Luke 24:1-12; John 20:1-18 |

---

**14:43-45** Judas was given a contingent of police and soldiers (John 18:3) in order to seize Jesus and bring him before the religious court for trial. The religious leaders had issued a warrant for Jesus' arrest, and Judas was acting as Jesus' official accuser.

**14:47** According to John 18:10, the person who pulled out a sword was Peter. Luke 22:51 records that Jesus immediately healed the man's ear and prevented any further bloodshed.

**14:50** Just hours earlier, these disciples had vowed never to desert Jesus (14:31).

**14:51, 52** Tradition says that this young man may have been John Mark, the writer of this Gospel. The incident is not mentioned in any of the other accounts.

### Caiaphas Questions Jesus (226/Matthew 26:57-68)

53 They took Jesus to the high priest's home where the leading priests, the elders, and the teachers of religious law had gathered. 54 Meanwhile, Peter followed him at a distance and went right into the high priest's courtyard. There he sat with the guards, warming himself by the fire.

55 Inside, the leading priests and the entire high council* were trying to find evidence against Jesus, so they could put him to death. But they couldn't find any. 56 Many false witnesses spoke against him, but they contradicted each other. 57 Finally, some men stood up and gave this false testimony: 58 "We heard him say, 'I will destroy this Temple made with human hands, and in three days I will build another, made without human hands.'" 59 But even then they didn't get their stories straight!

60 Then the high priest stood up before the others and asked Jesus, "Well, aren't you going to answer these charges? What do you have to say for yourself?" 61 But Jesus was silent and made no reply. Then the high priest asked him, "Are you the Messiah, the Son of the Blessed One?"

62 Jesus said, "I AM.* And you will see the Son of Man seated in the place of power at God's right hand* and coming on the clouds of heaven.*"

63 Then the high priest tore his clothing to show his horror and said, "Why do we need other witnesses? 64 You have all heard his blasphemy. What is your verdict?"

"Guilty!" they all cried. "He deserves to die!"

65 Then some of them began to spit at him, and they blindfolded him and beat him with their fists. "Prophesy to us," they jeered. And the guards slapped him as they took him away.

### Peter Denies Knowing Jesus
(227/Matthew 26:69-75; Luke 22:54-65; John 18:25-27)
66 Meanwhile, Peter was in the courtyard below. One of the servant girls who worked for the high priest came by 67 and noticed Peter warming himself at the fire. She looked at him closely and said, "You were one of those with Jesus of Nazareth.*"

14:55 Greek *the Sanhedrin.* 14:62a Or *The 'I AM' is here; or I am the LORD.* See Exod 3:14. 14:62b Greek *at the right hand of the power.* See Ps 110:1. 14:62c See Dan 7:13. 14:67 Or *Jesus the Nazarene.*

**Cross-references (right margin):**

14:54
Matt 26:3
John 18:18

14:56
Ps 35:11
Prov 6:16-19;
19:5

14:58
Mark 15:29
John 2:19

14:61
Isa 53:7
1 Pet 2:23

14:62
†Ps 110:1
†Dan 7:13
Matt 16:27; 24:30
Mark 8:38; 13:26
Acts 1:11
1 Thes 4:16
2 Thes 1:7
Rev 1:7; 22:20

14:63
Lev 10:6; 21:10
Num 14:6

14:64
Lev 24:16
John 19:7

14:65
Isa 50:6; 53:5

---

**JESUS' TRIAL** From Gethsemane, Jesus' trial began at the home of Caiaphas, the high priest. Jesus was then taken to Pilate, the Roman governor. Luke records that Pilate sent him to Herod, who was in Jerusalem—presumably in one of his two palaces (Luke 23:5-12). Herod sent him back to Pilate, who handed Jesus over to be crucified.

**14:53ff** This trial by the high council had two phases. A small group met at night (John 18:12-24), and then the full high council met at daybreak (Luke 22:66-71). They tried Jesus for religious offenses, such as calling himself the Son of God, which, according to law, was blasphemy. The trial was fixed: These religious leaders had already decided to kill Jesus (Luke 22:2).

**14:55** The Romans controlled Israel, but the Jews were given some authority over religious and minor civil disputes. The Jewish ruling body, the high council, was made up of 71 of Israel's religious leaders. It was assumed that these men would be just. Instead, they showed great injustice in the trial of Jesus, even to the point of making up lies to use against him (14:57).

**14:58** The statement that the false witnesses finally agreed to use as an accusation twisted Jesus' actual words. Jesus did not say, "I will destroy this Temple with human hands"; he said, "Destroy this temple, and in three days I will raise it up" (John 2:19). Jesus was not talking about Herod's Temple but about his own body.

**14:60-64** To the first question, Jesus made no reply because it was based on confusing and erroneous evidence. Not answering was wiser than trying to clarify the fabricated accusations. But if Jesus had refused to answer the second question, it could have been taken as a denial of his mission. Instead, his answer predicted a powerful role reversal. Sitting at God's right hand in the place of power, he would come to judge his accusers, and they would have to answer *his* questions (Psalm 110:1; Revelation 20:11-13).

**14:66, 67** Caiaphas's home, where Jesus was tried (14:53), was part of a huge palace with several courtyards. John was apparently acquainted with the high priest, and he was let into the courtyard along with Peter (John 18:15, 16).

68But Peter denied it. "I don't know what you're talking about," he said, and he went out into the entryway. Just then, a rooster crowed.*

69When the servant girl saw him standing there, she began telling the others, "This man is definitely one of them!" 70But Peter denied it again.

A little later some of the other bystanders confronted Peter and said, "You must be one of them, because you are a Galilean."

71Peter swore, "A curse on me if I'm lying—I don't know this man you're talking about!" 72And immediately the rooster crowed the second time.

Suddenly, Jesus' words flashed through Peter's mind: "Before the rooster crows twice, you will deny three times that you even know me." And he broke down and wept.

## The Council of Religious Leaders Condemns Jesus
(228/Matthew 27:1-2; Luke 22:66-71)

**15** Very early in the morning the leading priests, the elders, and the teachers of religious law—the entire high council*—met to discuss their next step. They bound Jesus, led him away, and took him to Pilate, the Roman governor.

## Jesus Stands Trial before Pilate
(230/Matthew 27:11-14; Luke 23:1-5; John 18:28-37)

2Pilate asked Jesus, "Are you the king of the Jews?"

Jesus replied, "You have said it."

3Then the leading priests kept accusing him of many crimes, 4and Pilate asked him, "Aren't you going to answer them? What about all these charges they are bringing against you?" 5But Jesus said nothing, much to Pilate's surprise.

**14:68** Some manuscripts do not include *Just then, a rooster crowed.* **15:1** Greek *the Sanhedrin;* also in 15:43.

Side references:
14:70 Acts 2:7
14:72 Mark 14:30
15:1 Matt 27:1; Luke 23:1; John 18:28
15:5 Isa 53:7; Mark 14:60-61; Luke 23:9

---

**WHY DID JESUS HAVE TO DIE?**

| | |
|---|---|
| The Problem | We have all done things that are wrong, and we have failed to obey God's laws. Because of this, we have been separated from God our Creator. Separation from God is death; but, by ourselves, we can do nothing to become united with God. |
| Why Jesus Could Help | Jesus was not only a man; he was God's unique Son. Because Jesus never disobeyed God and never sinned, only he can bridge the gap between the sinless God and sinful people. |
| The Solution | Jesus freely offered his life for us, dying on the cross in our place, taking all our wrongdoing upon himself, and saving us from the consequences of sin—including God's judgment and death. |
| The Results | Jesus took our past, present, and future sins upon himself so that we could have new life. Because all our wrongdoing is forgiven, we are reconciled to God. Furthermore, Jesus' resurrection from the dead is the proof that his substitutionary sacrifice on the cross was acceptable to God, and his resurrection has become the source of new life for those who believe that Jesus is the Son of God. All who believe in him may have this new life and live it in union with him. |

---

**14:71** It is easy to get angry at the high council and the Roman governor for their injustice in condemning Jesus, but Peter and the rest of the disciples also contributed to Jesus' pain by deserting him (14:50). While most of us may not be like the Jewish and Roman leaders, we are like the disciples because all of us have been guilty of denying Christ as Lord in vital areas of our lives. We may pride ourselves that we have not committed certain sins, but we are all guilty of sin. Don't try to excuse yourself by pointing at others whose sins seem worse than yours.

**15:1** Why did the Jewish leaders send Jesus to Pilate, the Roman governor? The Romans had taken away the Jews' right to inflict capital punishment; so in order for Jesus to be condemned to death, he had to be sentenced by a Roman leader. The Jewish leaders wanted Jesus executed on a cross, a method of death that they believed brought a curse from God (see Deuteronomy 21:23). They hoped to persuade the people that Jesus was cursed, not blessed, by God.

**15:3, 4** The Jewish leaders had to fabricate new accusations against Jesus when they brought him before Pilate. The charge of blasphemy would mean nothing to the Roman governor, so they accused Jesus of three other crimes: (1) encouraging the people to not pay their taxes to Rome, (2) claiming he was a king—"the King of the Jews," and (3) causing riots all over the countryside. Tax evasion, treason, and terrorism—all these would be cause for Pilate's concern (see also Luke 23:2).

**15:5** Why didn't Jesus answer Pilate's questions? It would have been futile to answer, and the time had come to give his life to save the world. Jesus had no reason to try to prolong the trial or save himself. His was the ultimate example of self-assurance and peace, which no ordinary criminal could imitate. Nothing would stop him from completing the work he had come to earth to do (Isaiah 53:7).

## Pilate Hands Jesus Over to Be Crucified
(**232**/Matthew 27:15-26; Luke 23:13-25; John 18:38–19:16)

⁶Now it was the governor's custom each year during the Passover celebration to release one prisoner—anyone the people requested. ⁷One of the prisoners at that time was Barabbas, a revolutionary who had committed murder in an uprising. ⁸The crowd went to Pilate and asked him to release a prisoner as usual.

⁹"Would you like me to release to you this 'King of the Jews'?" Pilate asked. ¹⁰(For he realized by now that the leading priests had arrested Jesus out of envy.) ¹¹But at this point the leading priests stirred up the crowd to demand the release of Barabbas instead of Jesus. ¹²Pilate asked them, "Then what should I do with this man you call the king of the Jews?"

¹³They shouted back, "Crucify him!"

¹⁴"Why?" Pilate demanded. "What crime has he committed?"

But the mob roared even louder, "Crucify him!"

¹⁵So to pacify the crowd, Pilate released Barabbas to them. He ordered Jesus flogged with a lead-tipped whip, then turned him over to the Roman soldiers to be crucified.

15:11
Acts 3:14

15:15
Isa 53:6

## Roman Soldiers Mock Jesus (**233**/Matthew 27:27-31)

¹⁶The soldiers took Jesus into the courtyard of the governor's headquarters (called the Praetorium) and called out the entire regiment. ¹⁷They dressed him in a purple robe, and they wove thorn branches into a crown and put it on his head. ¹⁸Then they saluted him and taunted, "Hail! King of the Jews!" ¹⁹And they struck him on the head with a reed stick, spit on him, and dropped to their knees in mock worship. ²⁰When they were finally tired of mocking him, they took off the purple robe and put his own clothes on him again. Then they led him away to be crucified.

---

**15:7** Barabbas was arrested for his part in a rebellion against the Roman government, and, although he had committed a murder, he may have been a hero among the Jews. The fiercely independent Jews hated to be ruled by pagan Romans. They hated paying taxes to support the despised government and its gods. Most of the Roman authorities who had to settle Jewish disputes hated the Jews in return. The time was ripe for rebellion.

**15:8** This crowd was most likely a group of people loyal to the Jewish leaders. But where were the disciples and the crowds who days earlier had shouted, "Praise God in highest heaven"

**JESUS' ROUTE TO GOLGOTHA** After being sentenced by Pilate, Jesus was taken from the praetorium to Golgotha, a place outside the city, for crucifixion.

(11:10)? Jesus' sympathizers were afraid of the Jewish leaders, so they went into hiding. Another possibility is that the multitude included many people who were in the Palm Sunday parade but who turned against Jesus when they saw that he was not going to be an earthly conqueror and their deliverer from Rome.

**15:10** The Jewish leaders hated Pilate, but they went to him for the favor of condemning Jesus to crucifixion. Pilate could see that this was a frame-up. Why else would these people, who hated him and the Roman Empire he represented, ask him to convict one of their fellow Jews of treason and give him the death penalty?

**15:13** Crucifixion was the Roman penalty for rebellion. Only slaves or those who were not Roman citizens could be crucified. If Jesus died by crucifixion, he would die the death of a rebel and slave, not of the king he claimed to be. This is just what the Jewish religious leaders wanted and the reason they whipped the mob into a frenzy. In addition, crucifixion would put the responsibility for killing Jesus on the Romans.

**15:15** The region of Judea where Pilate ruled as governor was little more than a hot and dusty outpost of the Roman Empire. Because Judea was so far from Rome, Pilate was given just a small army. His primary job was to keep the peace. We know from historical records that Pilate had already been warned about other uprisings in his region. Although he may have seen no guilt in Jesus and no reason to condemn him to death, Pilate wavered when the Jews in the crowd threatened to report him to Caesar (John 19:12). Such a report, accompanied by a riot, could cost him his position and hopes for advancement.

Although Jesus was innocent according to Roman law, Pilate caved in to political pressure. He abandoned what he knew was right. Trying to second-guess the Jewish leaders, Pilate gave a decision that would please everyone while keeping himself safe. When we ignore God's clear statements of right and wrong and make decisions based on the preferences of our audience, we fall into compromise and lawlessness. God promises to honor those who do right, not those who make everyone happy.

**15:19** The brutal guards, the power-hungry governor, and the conniving religious leaders had the upper hand. But they did not know the true power and authority of this man they were torturing and had condemned to death. Worldly powers and philosophies that mock Jesus' lordship will not be so arrogant when Jesus

## Jesus Is Led Away to Be Crucified
**(234**/Matthew 27:32-34; Luke 23:26-31; John 19:17)

15:23
Ps 69:21

²¹A passerby named Simon, who was from Cyrene,* was coming in from the countryside just then, and the soldiers forced him to carry Jesus' cross. (Simon was the father of Alexander and Rufus.) ²²And they brought Jesus to a place called Golgotha (which means "Place of the Skull"). ²³They offered him wine drugged with myrrh, but he refused it.

## Jesus Is Placed on the Cross
**(235**/Matthew 27:35-44; Luke 23:32-43; John 19:18-27)

15:24
†Ps 22:18
15:25
John 19:14

²⁴Then the soldiers nailed him to the cross. They divided his clothes and threw dice* to decide who would get each piece. ²⁵It was nine o'clock in the morning when they crucified

**15:21** *Cyrene* was a city in northern Africa.    **15:24** Greek *cast lots.* See Ps 22:18.

**PILATE**

In Jesus' day, any death sentence had to be approved by the Roman official in charge of the administrative district. Pontius Pilate was governor of the province of Judea, where Jerusalem was located. When the Jewish leaders had Jesus in their power and wanted to kill him, they had to obtain Pilate's permission. So it happened that early one morning Pilate found a crowd at his door demanding a man's death.

Pilate's relationship with the Jews had always been stormy. His Roman toughness and fairness had been weakened by cynicism, compromises, and mistakes. On several occasions his actions had deeply offended the religious leaders. The resulting riots and chaos must have made Pilate wonder what he had gotten himself into. He was trying to control people who treated their Roman conquerors without respect. Jesus' trial was another episode in Pilate's ongoing problems.

For Pilate, there was never a doubt about Jesus' innocence. Three separate times he declared Jesus not guilty. He couldn't understand why these people wanted to kill Jesus, but his fear of the Jews' political pressure made him decide to allow Jesus' crucifixion. Because of the people's threat to inform the emperor that Pilate hadn't eliminated a rebel against Rome, Pilate went against what he knew was right. In desperation, he chose to do wrong.

We share a common humanity with Pilate. At times we know what is right but choose what is wrong. He had his moment in history, and now we have ours. What have we done with our opportunities and responsibilities? What judgment have we passed on Jesus?

| | |
|---|---|
| **Strength and accomplishment** | • Roman governor of Judea |
| **Weaknesses and mistakes** | • He failed in his attempt to rule a people who were defeated militarily but never dominated by Rome<br>• His constant political struggles made him a cynical and uncaring compromiser, susceptible to pressure<br>• Although he realized Jesus was innocent, he bowed to the public demand for his execution |
| **Lessons from his life** | • Great evil can happen when truth is at the mercy of political pressures<br>• Resisting the truth leaves a person without purpose or direction |
| **Vital statistics** | • Where: Judea<br>• Occupation: Roman governor of Judea<br>• Relative: Wife: unnamed<br>• Contemporaries: Jesus, Caiaphas, Herod |
| **Key verses** | "'What is truth?' Pilate asked. Then he went out again to the people and told them, 'He is not guilty of any crime. But you have a custom of asking me to release one prisoner each year at Passover. Would you like me to release this "King of the Jews"?'" (John 18:38-39). |

Pilate's story is told in the Gospels. He is also mentioned in Acts 3:13; 4:27; 13:28; 1 Timothy 6:13.

returns in judgment (see Philippians 2:10, 11). When you feel that unjust people who have control and viewpoints hostile to Christianity are carrying the day, rest assured that Jesus holds the highest place and will return in glory.

**15:21** Colonies of Jews existed outside Judea. Simon had made a Passover pilgrimage to Jerusalem all the way from Cyrene in North Africa. His sons, Alexander and Rufus, are mentioned here probably because they became well known in the early church (Romans 16:13).

**15:24** Throwing dice was a way of making a decision by chance. The soldiers gambled to decide who would receive Jesus' clothing.

Roman soldiers had the right to take for themselves the clothing of those crucified. This act fulfilled the prophecy of Psalm 22:18.

**15:25** Crucifixion was a feared and shameful form of execution. The victim was forced to carry his cross along the longest possible route to the crucifixion site as a warning to bystanders. There were several shapes for crosses and several different methods of crucifixion. Jesus was nailed to the cross; condemned men were sometimes tied to their crosses with ropes. In either case, death came by suffocation as the person lost strength and the weight of the body made breathing more and more difficult.

him. 26A sign announced the charge against him. It read, "The King of the Jews." 27Two revolutionaries* were crucified with him, one on his right and one on his left.*

29The people passing by shouted abuse, shaking their heads in mockery. "Ha! Look at you now!" they yelled at him. "You said you were going to destroy the Temple and rebuild it in three days. 30Well then, save yourself and come down from the cross!"

31The leading priests and teachers of religious law also mocked Jesus. "He saved others," they scoffed, "but he can't save himself! 32Let this Messiah, this King of Israel, come down from the cross so we can see it and believe him!" Even the men who were crucified with Jesus ridiculed him.

*15:29*
Pss 22:7; 109:2
Mark 14:58
John 2:19

*15:32*
Zeph 3:15

### Jesus Dies on the Cross (236/Matthew 27:45-56; Luke 23:44-49; John 19:28-37)

33At noon, darkness fell across the whole land until three o'clock. 34Then at three o'clock Jesus called out with a loud voice, *"Eloi, Eloi, lema sabachthani?"* which means "My God, my God, why have you abandoned me?"*

35Some of the bystanders misunderstood and thought he was calling for the prophet Elijah. 36One of them ran and filled a sponge with sour wine, holding it up to him on a reed stick so he could drink. "Wait!" he said. "Let's see whether Elijah comes to take him down!"

37Then Jesus uttered another loud cry and breathed his last. 38And the curtain in the sanctuary of the Temple was torn in two, from top to bottom.

39When the Roman officer* who stood facing him* saw how he had died, he exclaimed, "This man truly was the Son of God!"

40Some women were there, watching from a distance, including Mary Magdalene, Mary (the mother of James the younger and of Joseph*), and Salome. 41They had been followers of Jesus and had cared for him while he was in Galilee. Many other women who had come with him to Jerusalem were also there.

*15:34*
†Ps 22:1

*15:36*
Ps 69:21

*15:38*
Exod 26:31-33
Heb 10:19-20

*15:40-41*
Luke 8:2-3

### Jesus Is Laid in the Tomb (237/Matthew 27:57-61; Luke 23:50-56; John 19:38-42)

42This all happened on Friday, the day of preparation,* the day before the Sabbath. As evening approached, 43Joseph of Arimathea took a risk and went to Pilate and asked for Jesus'

*15:43*
Luke 2:25, 38

15:27a Or Two criminals. 15:27b Some manuscripts add verse 28, And the Scripture was fulfilled that said, "He was counted among those who were rebels." See Isa 53:12; also compare Luke 22:37. 15:34 Ps 22:1. 15:39a Greek the centurion; similarly in 15:44, 45. 15:39b Some manuscripts add heard his cry and. 15:40 Greek Joses; also in 15:47. See Matt 27:56. 15:42 Greek It was the day of preparation.

**15:26** A sign stating the condemned man's crime was often placed on a cross as a warning. Because Jesus was never found guilty, the only accusation placed on his sign was the "crime" of being King of the Jews.

**15:27** Luke records that one of these revolutionaries repented before his death, and Jesus promised that man that he would be with him in paradise (Luke 23:39-43).

**15:31** Jesus could have saved himself, but he endured this suffering because of his love for us. He could have chosen not to take the pain and humiliation; he could have killed those who mocked him. But he suffered through it all because he loved even his enemies. We had a significant part in the drama that dark afternoon because our sins were on the cross, too. Jesus died on that cross for us, and the penalty for our sins was paid by his death. The only adequate response we can make is to confess our sins and gratefully accept the fact that Jesus paid for them so we wouldn't have to. Don't insult God with indifference toward the greatest act of genuine love in history.

**15:32** When James and John had asked Jesus for the places of honor next to him in his Kingdom, Jesus had told them that they didn't know what they were asking (10:35-39). Here, as Jesus was preparing to inaugurate his Kingdom through his death, the places on his right and on his left were taken by dying men—criminals. As Jesus explained to his two power-hungry disciples, a person who wants to be close to Jesus must be prepared to suffer and die as he himself was doing. The way to the Kingdom is the way of the cross. If we want the glory of the Kingdom, we must be willing to be united with the crucified Christ.

**15:34** Jesus did not ask this question in surprise or despair. He was quoting the first line of Psalm 22. The whole psalm is a prophecy expressing the deep agony of the Messiah's death for the world's sin. Jesus knew that he would be temporarily separated from God the moment he took upon himself the sins of the world. This separation was what he had dreaded as he prayed in Gethsemane. The physical agony was horrible, but the spiritual alienation from God was the ultimate torture.

**15:37** Jesus' loud cry may have been his last words, "It is finished" (John 19:30).

**15:38** A heavy curtain hung in front of the Temple room called the Most Holy Place, a place reserved by God for himself. Symbolically, the curtain separated the holy God from sinful people. The room was entered only once a year, on the Day of Atonement, by the high priest as he made a sacrifice to gain forgiveness for the sins of all the people. When Jesus died, the curtain was torn in two, showing that his death for our sins had opened up the way for us to approach our holy God. Read Hebrews 9 for a more complete explanation.

**15:42ff** The Sabbath began at sundown on Friday and ended at sundown on Saturday. Jesus died just a few hours before sundown on Friday. It was against Jewish law to do physical work or to travel on the Sabbath. It was also against Jewish law to let a dead body remain exposed overnight (Deuteronomy 21:23). Joseph came to bury Jesus' body before the Sabbath began. If Jesus had died on the Sabbath when Joseph was unavailable, his body would have been taken down by the Romans. Had the Romans taken Jesus' body, no Jews could have confirmed his death, and opponents could have disputed his resurrection.

body. (Joseph was an honored member of the high council, and he was waiting for the Kingdom of God to come.) 44Pilate couldn't believe that Jesus was already dead, so he called for the Roman officer and asked if he had died yet. 45The officer confirmed that Jesus was dead, so Pilate told Joseph he could have the body. 46Joseph bought a long sheet of linen cloth. Then he took Jesus' body down from the cross, wrapped it in the cloth, and laid it in a tomb that had been carved out of the rock. Then he rolled a stone in front of the entrance. 47Mary Magdalene and Mary the mother of Joseph saw where Jesus' body was laid.

**15:46**
Acts 13:29

---

| EVIDENCE THAT JESUS ACTUALLY DIED AND AROSE | Proposed Explanations for Empty Tomb | Evidence against These Explanations | References |
|---|---|---|---|
| This evidence demonstrates Jesus' uniqueness in history and proves that he is God's Son. No one else was able to predict his own resurrection and then accomplish it. | Jesus was only unconscious and later revived. | A Roman soldier told Pilate that Jesus was dead. | Mark 15:44, 45 |
| | | The Roman soldiers did not break Jesus' legs because he had already died, and one of them pierced Jesus' side with a spear. | John 19:32-34 |
| | | Joseph of Arimathea and Nicodemus wrapped Jesus' body and placed it in the tomb. | John 19:38-40 |
| | The women made a mistake and went to the wrong tomb. | Mary Magdalene and Mary the mother of Joseph saw Jesus placed in the tomb. | Matthew 27:59-61 Mark 15:47 Luke 23:55 |
| | Unknown thieves stole Jesus' body. | On Sunday morning Peter and John also went to the same tomb. | John 20:3-9 |
| | The disciples stole Jesus' body. | The tomb was sealed and guarded by Roman soldiers. | Matthew 27:65, 66 |
| | | The disciples were ready to die for their faith. Stealing Jesus' body would have been admitting that their faith was meaningless. | Acts 12:2 |
| | The religious leaders stole Jesus' body to produce it later. | If the religious leaders had taken Jesus' body, they would have produced it to stop the rumors of his resurrection. | None |

---

**15:42, 43** After Jesus died on the cross, Joseph of Arimathea asked for his body and then sealed it in a new tomb. Although an honored member of the high council, Joseph was a secret disciple of Jesus. Not all the Jewish leaders hated Jesus. Joseph risked his reputation to give a proper burial to his Lord. It is frightening to risk one's reputation even for what is right. If your Christian witness endangers your reputation, remember Joseph. Today he is remembered with admiration in the Christian church. How many other members of the Jewish high council can you name?

**15:44** Pilate was surprised that Jesus had died so quickly, so he asked an officer to verify the report. Today, in an effort to deny the Resurrection, there are those who say that Jesus didn't really die. His death, however, was confirmed by the officer, Pilate, Joseph of Arimathea, the religious leaders, and the women who witnessed his burial. Jesus suffered actual physical death on the cross.

**15:46** This tomb was probably a cave carved out from a hill. It was large enough to walk into. Joseph wrapped Jesus' body, placed it in the tomb, and rolled a heavy stone across the entrance. The religious leaders also watched where Jesus was buried. They stationed guards by the tomb and sealed the stone to make sure that no one would steal Jesus' body and claim he had risen from the dead (Matthew 27:62-66).

**15:47** These women could do very little. They couldn't speak before the high council in Jesus' defense; they couldn't appeal to Pilate; they couldn't stand against the crowds; they couldn't overpower the Roman guards. But they did what they could.

They stayed at the cross when the disciples had fled, they followed Jesus' body to its tomb, and they prepared spices for his body. Because these women used the opportunities they had, they were the first to witness the Resurrection. God blessed their devotion and diligence. As believers, we should take advantage of the opportunities we have and do what we *can* for Christ, instead of worrying about what we cannot do.

## Jesus Rises from the Dead (**239**/Matthew 28:1-7; Luke 24:1-12; John 20:1-10)

**16** Saturday evening, when the Sabbath ended, Mary Magdalene, Mary the mother of James, and Salome went out and purchased burial spices so they could anoint Jesus' body. ²Very early on Sunday morning,* just at sunrise, they went to the tomb. ³On the way they were asking each other, "Who will roll away the stone for us from the entrance to the tomb?" ⁴But as they arrived, they looked up and saw that the stone, which was very large, had already been rolled aside.

⁵When they entered the tomb, they saw a young man clothed in a white robe sitting on the right side. The women were shocked, ⁶but the angel said, "Don't be alarmed. You are looking for Jesus of Nazareth,* who was crucified. He isn't here! He is risen from the dead! Look, this is where they laid his body. ⁷Now go and tell his disciples, including Peter, that Jesus is going ahead of you to Galilee. You will see him there, just as he told you before he died."

⁸The women fled from the tomb, trembling and bewildered, and they said nothing to anyone because they were too frightened.*

**16:1**
Luke 23:56
John 19:39-40
**16:3**
Mark 15:46

**16:5**
John 20:12
Acts 1:10; 10:30
**16:6**
Acts 2:23-32
1 Cor 15:4-12
**16:7**
Matt 26:32
John 21:1

### [Shorter Ending of Mark]

Then they briefly reported all this to Peter and his companions. Afterward Jesus himself sent them out from east to west with the sacred and unfailing message of salvation that gives eternal life. Amen.

### [Longer Ending of Mark]

## Jesus Appears to Mary Magdalene (**240**/John 20:11-18)

⁹After Jesus rose from the dead early on Sunday morning, the first person who saw him was Mary Magdalene, the woman from whom he had cast out seven demons. ¹⁰She went to the disciples, who were grieving and weeping, and told them what had happened. ¹¹But when she told them that Jesus was alive and she had seen him, they didn't believe her.

**16:9-11**
Matt 28:1-10
John 20:11-18

## Jesus Appears to Two Believers Traveling on the Road (**243**/Luke 24:13-34)

¹²Afterward he appeared in a different form to two of his followers who were walking from Jerusalem into the country. ¹³They rushed back to tell the others, but no one believed them.

**16:12-13**
Luke 24:13-35

**16:2** Greek *on the first day of the week;* also in 16:9.   **16:6** Or *Jesus the Nazarene.*   **16:8** The most reliable early manuscripts of the Gospel of Mark end at verse 8. Other manuscripts include various endings to the Gospel. A few include both the "shorter ending" and the "longer ending." The majority of manuscripts include the "longer ending" immediately after verse 8.

---

**16:1, 2** The women purchased the spices on Saturday evening after the Sabbath had ended so they could go to the tomb early the next morning and anoint Jesus' body as a sign of love, devotion, and respect. Bringing spices to the tomb was like bringing flowers to a grave today. These women faced two overwhelming problems as they set out to honor Jesus' body, however. The Roman guards and the huge rock in the tomb's doorway. Impossible obstacles. So what did these women expect to accomplish that early Sunday morning? Yet urged on by love and gratitude, they walked on—even as they wondered the same questions aloud.

The church's mission—to send the gospel to all the world—is fraught with overwhelming obstacles. Any one of them appears devastating. Against human stubbornness, disease, danger, terrorism, loneliness, sin, greed, and even church strife and corruption, what can a few missionaries hope to accomplish? Yet like these solitary women, we go out with love and gratitude for Jesus and leave the big obstacles to God.

**16:5** Mark says that one angel met the women at the tomb, while Luke mentions two angels. Each Gospel writer chose to highlight different details as he explained the same story, just as eyewitnesses to a news story each may highlight a different aspect of that event. Mark probably emphasized only the angel who spoke. The unique emphasis of each Gospel shows that the four accounts were written independently. This should give us confidence that all four are true and reliable.

**16:6** The Resurrection is vitally important for many reasons: (1) Jesus kept his promise to rise from the dead, so we can believe he will keep all his other promises. (2) The Resurrection ensures that the ruler of God's eternal Kingdom will be the living Christ, not just an idea, hope, or dream. (3) Christ's resurrection gives us the assurance that we also will be resurrected. (4) The power of God that brought Christ's body back from the dead is available to us to bring our morally and spiritually dead selves back to life so that we can change and grow (1 Corinthians 15:12-19). (5) The Resurrection provides the substance of the church's witness to the world. We do not merely tell lessons from the life of a good teacher; we proclaim the reality of the resurrection of Jesus Christ.

**16:7** The angel made special mention of Peter to show that, in spite of Peter's denials, Jesus had not disowned or deserted him. Jesus had great responsibilities for Peter to fulfill in the church that was not yet in existence.

**16:7** The angel told the disciples to meet Jesus in Galilee "as he told you" (see 14:28). This is where Jesus had called most of them and had said they would "fish for people" (Matthew 4:19), and it would be where this mission would be restated (John 21). But the disciples, filled with fear, remained behind locked doors in Jerusalem (John 20:19). Jesus met them first in Jerusalem (Luke 24:36) and later in Galilee (John 21). Then he returned to Jerusalem, where he ascended into heaven from the Mount of Olives (Acts 1:12).

### Jesus Appears to Thomas (245/John 20:24-31)

16:14-18
Matt 28:16-20
Luke 24:36-49
John 20:19-23
Acts 1:6-8

¹⁴Still later he appeared to the eleven disciples as they were eating together. He rebuked them for their stubborn unbelief because they refused to believe those who had seen him after he had been raised from the dead.*

### Jesus Gives the Great Commission (248/Matthew 28:16-20)

16:16
Acts 2:38;
16:31, 33

16:17
Acts 2:4, 11; 8:7;
10:46; 16:18; 19:6

16:18
Luke 10:19
Acts 28:3-6

¹⁵And then he told them, "Go into all the world and preach the Good News to everyone. ¹⁶ Anyone who believes and is baptized will be saved. But anyone who refuses to believe will be condemned.¹⁷ These miraculous signs will accompany those who believe: They will cast out demons in my name, and they will speak in new languages.*¹⁸ They will be able to handle snakes with safety, and if they drink anything poisonous, it won't hurt them. They will be able to place their hands on the sick, and they will be healed."

### Jesus Ascends into Heaven (250/Luke 24:50-53)

16:19-20
Luke 24:50-53
Acts 1:9-11

16:19
Rom 8:34
Col 3:1
Heb 1:3

¹⁹When the Lord Jesus had finished talking with them, he was taken up into heaven and sat down in the place of honor at God's right hand. ²⁰And the disciples went everywhere and preached, and the Lord worked through them, confirming what they said by many miraculous signs.

**16:14** Some early manuscripts add: *And they excused themselves, saying, "This age of lawlessness and unbelief is under Satan, who does not permit God's truth and power to conquer the evil [unclean] spirits. Therefore, reveal your justice now." This is what they said to Christ. And Christ replied to them, "The period of years of Satan's power has been fulfilled, but other dreadful things will happen soon. And I was handed over to death for those who have sinned, so that they may return to the truth and sin no more, and so they may inherit the spiritual, incorruptible, and righteous glory in heaven."* **16:17** Or *new tongues;* some manuscripts do not include *new.*

---

**16:15** Jesus told his disciples to go into all the world, telling everyone that he had paid the penalty for sin and that those who believe in him can be forgiven and live eternally with God. Christians today in all parts of the world are telling this Good News to people who haven't heard about Christ. The driving power that carries missionaries around the world and sets Christ's church in motion is the faith that comes from the Resurrection. Do you ever feel as though you don't have the skill or determination to be a witness for Christ? You must personally realize that Jesus rose from the dead and lives for you today. As you grow in your relationship with Christ, he will give you both the opportunities and the inner strength to tell his message.

**16:16** It is not the water of baptism that saves but God's grace accepted through faith in Christ. Because of Jesus' response to the criminal on the cross who died with him, we know it is possible to be saved without being baptized (Luke 23:43). Baptism alone, without faith, does not guarantee that a person will go to heaven. Those who refuse to accept Jesus as their Savior will be condemned, regardless of whether or not they have been baptized.

**16:18** There are times when God intervenes miraculously to protect his followers. Occasionally he gives them special powers.

Paul handled a snake safely (Acts 28:5), and the disciples healed the sick (Matthew 10:1; Acts 3:7, 8). This does not mean, however, that we should test God by putting ourselves in dangerous situations or try to tempt the laws of nature. No one should build a religion on a portion of Scripture. God calls us to live as new citizens in the eternal Kingdom and to witness by word and service to God's love and power. Our witness should center on Jesus, not on superhero-type stunts.

**16:19** When Jesus ascended into heaven, his physical presence left the disciples (Acts 1:9). Jesus' sitting at God's right hand signifies the completion of his work, his authority as God, and his coronation as King.

**16:20** Mark's Gospel emphasizes Christ's power as well as his servanthood. Jesus' life and teaching turned the world upside down and continue to do so. The world sees power as a way to gain control over others. But Jesus, with all authority and power in heaven and earth, chose to serve others. He held children in his arms, healed the sick, washed the disciples' feet, and died for the sins of the world. Jesus' followers today receive this same power to serve. As believers, we are called to be servants of Christ. As Christ served, so we are to serve.

# LUKE

## VITAL STATISTICS

**PURPOSE:**
To present an accurate account of the life of Christ and to present Christ as the perfect human and Savior

**AUTHOR:**
Luke—a doctor (Colossians 4:14), a Greek, and Gentile Christian. He is the only known Gentile author in the New Testament. Luke was a close friend and companion of Paul. He also wrote Acts, and the two books go together.

**ORIGINAL AUDIENCE:**
Theophilus ("one who loves God"), Gentiles

**DATE WRITTEN:**
About A.D. 60

**SETTING:**
Luke wrote from Rome or possibly from Caesarea.

**KEY VERSES:**
"Jesus responded, 'Salvation has come to this home today, for this man has shown himself to be a true son of Abraham. For the Son of Man came to seek and save those who are lost'" (19:9, 10).

**KEY PEOPLE:**
Jesus, Elizabeth, Zechariah, John the Baptist, Mary, the disciples, Herod the Great, Pilate, Mary Magdalene

**KEY PLACES:**
Bethlehem, Galilee, Judea, Jerusalem

**SPECIAL FEATURES:**
This is the most comprehensive of the Gospels. The general vocabulary and diction show that the author was educated. He makes frequent references to illnesses and diagnoses. Luke stresses Jesus' relationships with people; emphasizes prayer, miracles, and angels; records inspired hymns of praise; gives a prominent place to women. Most of 9:51–18:35 is not found in any other Gospel.

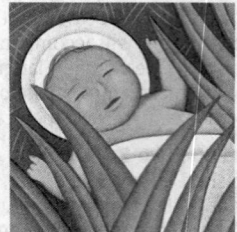

EVERY birth is a miracle, and every child is a gift from God. But nearly 20 centuries ago, the miracle of miracles occurred. A baby was born, but he was the Son of God. The Gospels tell of this birth, but Dr. Luke, as though he were the attending physician, provides most of the details surrounding this awesome occasion. With a divine Father and a human mother, Jesus entered history—God in the flesh.

Luke affirms Jesus' divinity, but the real emphasis of his book is on Jesus' humanity—Jesus, the Son of God, is also the Son of Man. As a doctor, Luke was a man of science, and as a Greek, he was a man of detail. It is not surprising, then, that he begins by outlining his extensive research and explaining that he is reporting the facts (1:1–4). Luke also was a close friend and traveling companion of Paul, so he could interview the other disciples, had access to other historical accounts, and was an eyewitness to the birth and growth of the early church. His Gospel and book of Acts are reliable, historical documents.

Luke's story begins with angels appearing to Zechariah and then to Mary, telling them of the upcoming births of their sons. From Zechariah and Elizabeth would come John the Baptist, who would prepare the way for Christ. And Mary would conceive a child by the Holy Spirit and bear Jesus, the Son of God. Soon after John's birth, Caesar Augustus declared a census, and so Mary and Joseph traveled to Bethlehem, the town of David, their ancient ancestor. There the child was born. Angels announced the joyous event to shepherds, who rushed to the manger. When the shepherds left, they went praising God and spreading the news. Eight days later, Jesus was circumcised and then dedicated to God in the Temple, where Simeon and Anna confirmed Jesus' identity as the Savior, their Messiah.

Luke gives us a glimpse of Jesus at age 12—discussing theology with the Jewish teachers of the law at the Temple (2:41–52). Eighteen years later Jesus went out in the wilderness to be baptized by John the Baptist before beginning his public ministry (3:1–23). At this point, Luke traces Jesus' genealogy on his stepfather Joseph's side, through David and Abraham back to Adam, underscoring Jesus' identity as the Son of Man (3:23–38).

After the Temptation (4:1–13), Jesus returned to Galilee to preach, teach, and heal (4:14ff). During this time, he began gathering his group of 12 disciples (5:1–11, 27–29). Later Jesus commissioned the disciples and sent them out to proclaim the Kingdom of God. When they returned, Jesus revealed to them his mission, his true identity, and what it meant to be his disciple (9:18–62). His mission would take him to Jerusalem (9:51–53), where he would be rejected, tried, and crucified.

While Jesus carried his own cross to Golgotha, some women in Jerusalem wept for him, but Jesus told them to weep for themselves and for their children (23:28). Luke's Gospel does not end in sadness, however. It concludes with the thrilling account of Jesus' resurrection from the dead, his appearances to the disciples, and his promise to send the Holy Spirit (24:1–53). Read Luke's beautifully written and accurate account of the life of Jesus, Son of Man and Son of God. Then praise God for sending the Savior—our risen and triumphant Lord—for all people.

## THE BLUEPRINT

A. BIRTH AND PREPARATION OF JESUS, THE SAVIOR (1:1—4:13)

From an infant who could do nothing on his own, Jesus grew to become completely able to fulfill his mission on earth. He was fully human, developing in all ways like us. Yet he remained fully God. He took no shortcuts and was not isolated from the pressures and temptations of life. There are no shortcuts for us either as we prepare for lives of service to God.

B. MESSAGE AND MINISTRY OF JESUS, THE SAVIOR (4:14—21:38)
1. Jesus' ministry in Galilee
2. Jesus' ministry on the way to Jerusalem
3. Jesus' ministry in Jerusalem

Jesus taught great crowds of people, especially through parables, which are stories that illustrate great truths. But only those with ears to hear will understand. We should pray that God's Spirit would help us understand the implications of these truths for our lives so we can become more and more like Jesus.

C. DEATH AND RESURRECTION OF JESUS, THE SAVIOR (22:1—24:53)

The Savior of the world was arrested and executed. But death could not destroy him, and Jesus came back to life and ascended to heaven. In Luke's careful, historical account, we receive the facts about Jesus' resurrection. We must not only believe that these facts are true, but we must also trust Christ as our Savior. It is shortsighted to neglect the facts, but how sad it is to accept the facts and neglect the forgiveness that Jesus offers to each of us.

## MEGATHEMES

| THEME | EXPLANATION | IMPORTANCE |
|---|---|---|
| Jesus Christ, the Savior | Luke describes how God's Son entered human history. Jesus lived as the perfect example of a human. After a perfect ministry, he provided a perfect sacrifice for our sin so we could be saved. | Jesus is our perfect leader and Savior. He offers forgiveness to all who will accept him as Lord of their lives and believe that what he says is true. |
| History | Luke was a medical doctor and historian. He put great emphasis on dates and details, connecting Jesus to events and people in history. | Luke gives details so we can believe in the reliability of the history of Jesus' life. Even more important, we can believe with certainty that Jesus is God. |
| People | Jesus was deeply interested in people and relationships. He showed warm concern for his followers and friends—men, women, and children. | Jesus' love for people is good news for everyone. His message is for all people in every nation. Each one of us has an opportunity to respond to him in faith. |
| Compassion | As a perfect human, Jesus showed tender sympathy to the poor, the despised, the hurt, and the sinful. No one was rejected or ignored by him. | Jesus is more than a good teacher—he cares for you. Because of his deep love for you, he can satisfy your needs. |
| Holy Spirit | The Holy Spirit was present at Jesus' birth, baptism, ministry, and resurrection. As a perfect example for us, Jesus lived in dependence on the Holy Spirit. | The Holy Spirit was sent by God as confirmation of Jesus' authority. The Holy Spirit is given to enable people to live for Christ. By faith we can have the indwelling Holy Spirit's presence and power to witness and to serve. |

## A. BIRTH AND PREPARATION OF JESUS, THE SAVIOR (1:1—4:13)

Luke gives us the most detailed account of Jesus' birth. In describing Jesus' birth, childhood, and development, Luke lifts up the humanity of Jesus. Our Savior was the ideal human. Fully prepared, the ideal human was now ready to live the perfect life.

**1:1-2**
John 15:27
Acts 1:21-22
Heb 2:3
2 Pet 1:16
1 Jn 1:1-4

### Luke's Purpose in Writing (1)

**1** Many people have set out to write accounts about the events that have been fulfilled among us. ²They used the eyewitness reports circulating among us from the early

---

**1:1, 2** Luke tells Jesus' story from the unique perspective of a Gentile, a physician, and the first historian of the early church. Though not an eyewitness of Jesus' ministry, Luke nevertheless was concerned that eyewitness accounts be preserved accurately and that the foundations of Christian belief be transmitted intact to the next generation. In Luke's Gospel are many of Jesus' parables. In addition, more than any other Gospel, it gives specific instances of Jesus' concern for women.

disciples.* ³Having carefully investigated everything from the beginning, I also have
decided to write a careful account for you, most honorable Theophilus, ⁴so you can be
certain of the truth of everything you were taught.

1:3
Acts 1:1

### An Angel Promises the Birth of John to Zechariah (4)

⁵When Herod was king of Judea, there was a Jewish priest named Zechariah. He was a member of the priestly order of Abijah, and his wife, Elizabeth, was also from the priestly line of
Aaron. ⁶Zechariah and Elizabeth were righteous in God's eyes, careful to obey all of the
Lord's commandments and regulations. ⁷They had no children because Elizabeth was unable to conceive, and they were both very old.

1:5
1 Chr 24:10
2 Chr 31:2
Matt 2:1

⁸One day Zechariah was serving God in the Temple, for his order was on duty that week.
⁹As was the custom of the priests, he was chosen by lot to enter the sanctuary of the Lord and
burn incense. ¹⁰While the incense was being burned, a great crowd stood outside, praying.

1:8
1 Chr 24:19
2 Chr 8:14

1:9
Exod 30:7

¹¹While Zechariah was in the sanctuary, an angel of the Lord appeared to him, standing
to the right of the incense altar. ¹²Zechariah was shaken and overwhelmed with fear when
he saw him. ¹³But the angel said, "Don't be afraid, Zechariah! God has heard your prayer.
Your wife, Elizabeth, will give you a son, and you are to name him John. ¹⁴You will have great
joy and gladness, and many will rejoice at his birth, ¹⁵for he will be great in the eyes of the
Lord. He must never touch wine or other alcoholic drinks. He will be filled with the Holy
Spirit, even before his birth.* ¹⁶And he will turn many Israelites to the Lord their God.

1:15
Num 6:3
Judg 13:4
Jer 1:5
Matt 11:11

1:16
Mal 4:5-6

1:2 Greek *from those who from the beginning were servants of the word.*    1:15 Or *even from birth.*

---

**1:1-4** There was a lot of interest in Jesus, and many people had written firsthand accounts about him. Luke may have used these accounts and all other available resources as material for an accurate and complete account of Jesus' life, teachings, and ministry. Because truth was important to Luke, he relied heavily on eyewitness accounts. Christianity doesn't say, "Close your eyes and believe," but rather, "Check it out for yourself." The Bible encourages you to investigate its claims thoroughly (John 1:46; 21:24; Acts 17:11, 12) because your conclusion about Jesus is a life-and-death matter.

**1:1-4** *Theophilus* means "one who loves God." The book of Acts, also written by Luke, is likewise addressed to Theophilus. This preface may be a general dedication to all Christian readers. Theophilus may have been Luke's patron, who helped to finance the book's writing. More likely, Theophilus was a Roman acquaintance of Luke's with a strong interest in the new Christian religion.

**1:3, 4** As a medical doctor, Luke knew the importance of being thorough. He used his skills in observation and analysis to thoroughly investigate the stories about Jesus. His diagnosis: The Good News of Jesus Christ is true! You can read Luke's account of Jesus' life with confidence that it was written by a clear thinker and a thoughtful researcher. Because the Good News is founded on historical truth, our spiritual growth must involve careful, disciplined, and thorough investigation of God's Word so that we can understand how God has acted in history. If this kind of study is not part of your life, find a pastor, teacher, or even a book to help you get started and to guide you in this important part of Christian growth.

**1:5** This was Herod the Great, confirmed by the Roman Senate as king of the Jews. Only half-Jewish himself and eager to please his Roman superiors, Herod expanded and beautified the Jerusalem Temple—but he placed a Roman eagle over the entrance. When he helped the Jews, it was for political purposes and not because he cared about their God. Later, Herod the Great would order a massacre of infants in a futile attempt to kill the infant Jesus, whom some were calling the new "king of the Jews" (Matthew 2:2).

**1:5** A Jewish priest was a minister of God who worked at the Temple managing its upkeep, teaching the people the Scriptures, and directing the worship services. At this time there were about 20,000 priests throughout the country—far too many to minister in the Temple at one time. Therefore the priests were divided into 24 separate groups of about 1,000 each, according to David's instructions (1 Chronicles 24:3-19).

Zechariah was a member of the order of Abijah, on duty this particular week. Each morning a priest was to enter the Holy Place in the Temple and burn incense. The priests would cast lots to decide who would enter the inner sanctuary, and one day the lot fell to Zechariah. But it was not by chance that Zechariah was on duty and that he was chosen that day to enter the Holy Place—perhaps a once-in-a-lifetime opportunity. God was guiding the events of history to prepare the way for Jesus to come to earth.

**1:6** Zechariah and Elizabeth didn't merely go through the motions in following God's laws; they backed up their outward compliance with inward obedience. Unlike the religious leaders whom Jesus called hypocrites, Zechariah and Elizabeth did not stop with the letter of the law. Their obedience was from the heart, and that is why they are called "righteous in God's eyes."

**1:7** God answers prayer in his own way and in his own time. He worked in an "impossible" situation—Elizabeth's age and barrenness—to bring about the fulfillment of all the prophecies concerning the Messiah. If you want to have your prayers answered, you must be open to what God can do in impossible situations. And you must wait for God to work in his way and in his time.

**1:9** Incense was burned in the Temple twice daily (Exodus 30:7-10). When the people saw the smoke from the burning incense, they prayed. The smoke drifting heavenward symbolized their prayers ascending to God's throne.

**1:11, 12** Angels are spirit beings who live in God's presence and do his will. Only two angels are mentioned by name in Scripture—Michael and Gabriel—but there are many who act as God's messengers. Here, Gabriel (1:19) delivered a special message to Zechariah. This was not a dream or a vision. The angel appeared in visible form and spoke audible words to the priest.

**1:13** While burning incense on the altar, Zechariah was also praying, most likely for the coming of the Messiah to his people. How odd it must have seemed that the angel would say that his prayer was answered and Zechariah would soon have a son. Yet the greatest desire of Zechariah's heart—to have a son—would come true. At the same time, the answer to the nation's prayer for the Messiah would also come true. Zechariah's son would grow up to prepare the way for the Messiah.

**1:13** *John* means "the Lord is gracious," and *Jesus* means "the Lord saves." Both names were prescribed by God, not

# KEY PLACES IN LUKE

The broken lines (—·—·—) indicate modern boundaries.

Luke begins his account in the Temple in Jerusalem, giving us the background for the birth of John the Baptist, then moves on to the town of Nazareth and the story of Mary, chosen to be Jesus' mother (1:26ff). As a result of Caesar's call for a census, Mary and Joseph had to travel to Bethlehem, where Jesus was born in fulfillment of prophecy (2:1ff). Jesus grew up in Nazareth and began his earthly ministry by being baptized by John (3:21, 22) and tempted by Satan (4:1ff). Much of his ministry focused on Galilee: He set up his "home" in Capernaum (4:31ff), and from there he taught throughout the region (8:1ff). Later he visited Gerasa (also called Gadara), where he healed a demon-possessed man (8:36ff). He fed more than 5,000 people with one lunch on the shores of the Sea of Galilee near Bethsaida (9:10ff). Jesus always traveled to Jerusalem for the major festivals, and he enjoyed visiting friends in nearby Bethany (10:38ff). He healed 10 men with leprosy on the border between Galilee and Samaria (17:11) and helped a dishonest tax collector in Jericho turn his life around (19:1ff). The little villages of Bethphage and Bethany on the Mount of Olives were Jesus' resting places during his last days on earth. He was crucified outside Jerusalem's walls, but he would rise again. Two of Jesus' followers walking on the road leading to Emmaus were among the first to see the resurrected Christ (24:13ff).

chosen by human parents. Throughout the Gospels, God acts graciously and saves his people. He will not withhold salvation from anyone who sincerely comes to him.

**1:15** John was set apart for special service to God. He may have been forbidden to drink wine as part of the Nazirite vow, an ancient vow of consecration to God (see Numbers 6:1-8). Samson (Judges 13) was under the Nazirite vow, and Samuel may have been also (1 Samuel 1:11).

**1:15** This is Luke's first mention of the Holy Spirit, the third Person of the Trinity; Luke refers to the Holy Spirit more than any other Gospel writer. Because Luke also wrote the book of Acts, we know he was thoroughly informed about the work of the

Holy Spirit. Luke recognized and emphasized the Holy Spirit's work in directing the beginnings of Christianity and in guiding the early church. The presence of the Spirit was God's gift to the entire church at Pentecost. Prior to that, God's Spirit was given to the faithful for special tasks. We need the Holy Spirit's help to do God's work effectively.

<sup>17</sup>He will be a man with the spirit and power of Elijah. He will prepare the people for the coming of the Lord. He will turn the hearts of the fathers to their children,* and he will cause those who are rebellious to accept the wisdom of the godly."

<sup>18</sup>Zechariah said to the angel, "How can I be sure this will happen? I'm an old man now, and my wife is also well along in years."

<sup>19</sup>Then the angel said, "I am Gabriel! I stand in the very presence of God. It was he who sent me to bring you this good news! <sup>20</sup>But now, since you didn't believe what I said, you will be silent and unable to speak until the child is born. For my words will certainly be fulfilled at the proper time."

<sup>21</sup>Meanwhile, the people were waiting for Zechariah to come out of the sanctuary, wondering why he was taking so long. <sup>22</sup>When he finally did come out, he couldn't speak to them. Then they realized from his gestures and his silence that he must have seen a vision in the sanctuary.

<sup>23</sup>When Zechariah's week of service in the Temple was over, he returned home. <sup>24</sup>Soon afterward his wife, Elizabeth, became pregnant and went into seclusion for five months. <sup>25</sup>"How kind the Lord is!" she exclaimed. "He has taken away my disgrace of having no children."

## An Angel Promises the Birth of Jesus to Mary (5)

<sup>26</sup>In the sixth month of Elizabeth's pregnancy, God sent the angel Gabriel to Nazareth, a village in Galilee, <sup>27</sup>to a virgin named Mary. She was engaged to be married to a man named Joseph, a descendant of King David. <sup>28</sup>Gabriel appeared to her and said, "Greetings, favored woman! The Lord is with you!*"

<sup>29</sup>Confused and disturbed, Mary tried to think what the angel could mean. <sup>30</sup>"Don't be afraid, Mary," the angel told her, "for you have found favor with God! <sup>31</sup>You will conceive and give birth to a son, and you will name him Jesus. <sup>32</sup>He will be very great and will be called the Son of the Most High. The Lord God will give him the throne of his ancestor David. <sup>33</sup>And he will reign over Israel* forever; his Kingdom will never end!"

**1:17** See Mal 4:5-6.  **1:28** Some manuscripts add *Blessed are you among women.*  **1:33** Greek *over the house of Jacob.*

| | |
|---|---|
| **1:17** Matt 17:11-13 | |
| **1:18** Gen 18:11 | |
| **1:19** Dan 8:16; 9:21 | |
| **1:20** Ezek 3:26 | |
| **1:25** Gen 30:23 Isa 4:1 | |
| **1:26** Matt 2:23 | |
| **1:27** Matt 1:16, 18 Luke 2:5 | |
| **1:31** Isa 7:14 Matt 1:21-23 | |
| **1:32** Isa 9:6-7; 16:5 Jer 23:5 Phil 2:10 1 Tim 6:15 | |
| **1:33** Ps 89:3-4 Isa 9:7 Jer 33:17 Dan 2:44; 7:14, 27 Heb 1:8 | |

---

**1:17** John's role was to be almost identical to that of an Old Testament prophet: to encourage people to turn away from sin and back to God. John is often compared to the great prophet Elijah, who was known for standing up to evil rulers (Malachi 4:5; Matthew 11:14; 17:10-13). See Elijah's Profile in 1 Kings 17, p. 545.

**1:18-20** When told he would have a son, Zechariah doubted the angel's word. From Zechariah's human perspective, his doubts were understandable—but with God, anything is possible. What God promises, he delivers. And God delivers *on time!* You can have complete confidence that God will keep his promises. Their fulfillment may not be the next day, but they will be "at the proper time." If you are waiting for God to answer some request or to fill some need, remain patient. No matter how impossible God's promises may seem, what he has said in his Word will come true at the right time.

**1:21** The people were waiting outside for Zechariah to come out and pronounce the customary blessing upon them as found in Numbers 6:24-26.

**1:25** Zechariah and Elizabeth were both godly people, yet they were suffering. Some Jews at that time did not believe in a bodily resurrection, so their hope of immortality was in their children. In addition, children cared for their parents in their old age and added to the family's financial security and social status. Children were considered a blessing, and childlessness was seen as a curse. Zechariah and Elizabeth had been childless for many years, and at this time they were too old to expect any change in their situation. They felt humiliated and hopeless. But God was waiting for the right time to encourage them and take away their disgrace.

**1:26** Gabriel appeared not only to Zechariah and to Mary but also to the prophet Daniel more than 500 years earlier (Daniel 8:15-17; 9:21). Each time Gabriel appeared, he brought important messages from God.

**1:26** Nazareth, Joseph and Mary's hometown, was a long way from Jerusalem, the center of Jewish life and worship. Located on a major trade route, Nazareth was frequently visited by Gentile merchants and Roman soldiers. It was known for its independent and aloof attitude. Jesus was born in Bethlehem but grew up in Nazareth. Nevertheless the people of Nazareth would reject him as the Messiah (4:22-30).

**1:27, 28** Mary was young, poor, female—all characteristics that, to the people of her day, would make her seem unusable by God for any major task. But God chose Mary for one of the most important acts of obedience he has ever demanded of anyone. You may feel that your ability, experience, or education makes you an unlikely candidate for God's service. Don't limit God's choices. He can use you if you trust him.

**1:30, 31** God's favor does not automatically bring instant success or fame. His blessing on Mary, the honor of being the mother of the Messiah, would lead to much pain: her peers would ridicule her; her fiancé would come close to leaving her; her son would be rejected and murdered. But through her son would come the world's only hope, and this is why Mary has been praised by countless generations. Her submission was part of God's plan to bring about our salvation. If sorrow weighs you down and dims your hope, think of Mary and wait patiently for God to finish working out his plan.

**1:31** *Jesus*, a Greek form of the Hebrew name *Joshua*, was a common name meaning "the LORD saves." Just as Joshua had led Israel into the Promised Land (see Joshua 1:1, 2), so Jesus would lead his people into eternal life. The symbolism of his name was not lost on the people of his day, who took names seriously and saw them as a source of power. In Jesus' name, people were healed, demons were banished, and sins were forgiven.

**1:32, 33** Centuries earlier, God had promised David that David's kingdom would last forever (2 Samuel 7:16). This promise was

**1:35**
Matt 1:20
Mark 1:1
John 1:34; 20:31
Rom 1:4

³⁴Mary asked the angel, "But how can this happen? I am a virgin."

³⁵The angel replied, "The Holy Spirit will come upon you, and the power of the Most High will overshadow you. So the baby to be born will be holy, and he will be called the Son of God. ³⁶What's more, your relative Elizabeth has become pregnant in her old age! People used to say she was barren, but she has conceived a son and is now in her sixth month. ³⁷For nothing is impossible with God.*"

**1:37** Some manuscripts read *For the word of God will never fail.*

**ZECHARIAH**

Zechariah, a Jewish priest, was told before anyone else that God was setting in motion his own visit to earth. Zechariah and his wife, Elizabeth, were known for their personal holiness. They were well suited to doing a special work for God. But they shared the pain of not having children, and in Jewish culture this was considered not having God's blessing. Zechariah and Elizabeth were old, and they had stopped even asking for children.

One day while on duty at the Temple in Jerusalem, Zechariah received an unexpected blessing. He was chosen to be the priest who would enter the Holy Place to offer incense to God for the people. Suddenly, much to his surprise and terror, he found himself face to face with an angel. The angel's message was too good to be true! But the news of the coming Savior was eclipsed by doubts about his own ability to father the child the angel promised him. His age spoke more loudly than God's promise. As a result, God prevented Zechariah from speaking until the promise became a reality.

The record of the prayer in Luke 1 is our last glimpse of Zechariah. Like so many of God's most faithful servants, he passed quietly from the scene once his part was done. He becomes our hero for those times when we doubt God and yet are willing to obey. We gain hope from Zechariah's story that God can do great things through anyone who is available to him.

| | |
|---|---|
| **Strengths and accomplishments** | • Known as a righteous man<br>• Was a priest of God<br>• One of the few people to be directly addressed by an angel<br>• Fathered John the Baptist |
| **Weakness and mistake** | • Momentarily doubted the angel's promise of a son because of his own old age |
| **Lessons from his life** | • Physical limitations do not limit God<br>• God accomplishes his will, often in unexpected ways |
| **Vital statistics** | • Occupation: Priest<br>• Relatives: Wife: Elizabeth. Son: John the Baptist. |
| **Key verses:** | "Zechariah and Elizabeth were righteous in God's eyes, careful to obey all of the Lord's commandments and regulations. They had no children because Elizabeth was unable to conceive, and they were both very old" (Luke 1:6-7). |

Zechariah's story is told in Luke 1.

fulfilled in the coming of Jesus, a direct descendant of David, whose Kingdom will never end.

**1:34** The birth of Jesus to a virgin is a miracle that many people find hard to believe. These three facts can aid our faith: (1) Luke was a medical doctor, and he knew perfectly well how babies are made. It would have been just as hard for him to believe in a virgin birth as it is for us, yet he reports it as fact. (2) Luke was a painstaking researcher who based his Gospel on eyewitness accounts. Tradition holds that he talked with Mary about the events he recorded in the first two chapters. This is Mary's story, not a fictional invention. (3) Christians and Jews, who worship God as the Creator of the universe, should have no doubts that God has the power to create a child in a virgin's womb.

**1:35** Why is the Virgin Birth important to the Christian faith? Jesus was born without the sin that entered the world through Adam. He was born holy, just as Adam was created sinless. In contrast to Adam, who disobeyed God, Jesus obeyed God and was thus able to face sin's consequences in our place and make us acceptable to God (Romans 5:14-19). Jesus Christ, God's Son, had to be free from the sinful nature passed on to all other human beings by Adam. Because Jesus was born of a woman, he was a human being; but as the Son of God, Jesus was born

without any trace of human sin. Jesus is both fully human and fully divine. Because Jesus lived as a man, human beings know that he fully understands their experiences and struggles (Hebrews 4:15-16). Because he is God, he has the power and authority to deliver people from sin (Colossians 2:13-15). People can tell Jesus all their thoughts, feelings, and needs. He has been where they are, and he has the ability to help.

38Mary responded, "I am the Lord's servant. May everything you have said about me come true." And then the angel left her.

## Mary Visits Elizabeth (6)

39A few days later Mary hurried to the hill country of Judea, to the town 40where Zechariah lived. She entered the house and greeted Elizabeth. 41At the sound of Mary's greeting, Elizabeth's child leaped within her, and Elizabeth was filled with the Holy Spirit.

42Elizabeth gave a glad cry and exclaimed to Mary, "God has blessed you above all women, and your child is blessed. 43Why am I so honored, that the mother of my Lord should visit me? 44When I heard your greeting, the baby in my womb jumped for joy. 45You are blessed because you believed that the Lord would do what he said."

## The Magnificat: Mary's Song of Praise

46Mary responded,

"Oh, how my soul praises the Lord.
47   How my spirit rejoices in God my Savior!
48 For he took notice of his lowly servant girl,
         and from now on all generations will call me blessed.
49 For the Mighty One is holy,
         and he has done great things for me.
50 He shows mercy from generation to generation
         to all who fear him.
51 His mighty arm has done tremendous things!
         He has scattered the proud and haughty ones.
52 He has brought down princes from their thrones
         and exalted the humble.
53 He has filled the hungry with good things
         and sent the rich away with empty hands.
54 He has helped his servant Israel
         and remembered to be merciful.
55 For he made this promise to our ancestors,
         to Abraham and his children forever."

56Mary stayed with Elizabeth about three months and then went back to her own home.

**1:41**
Gen 25:22
Luke 1:15

**1:42**
Judg 5:24

**1:43**
Luke 2:11

**1:46-55**
1 Sam 2:1-10
Ps 34:2-3

**1:47**
1 Tim 1:1; 2:3
Titus 1:3; 2:10; 3:4

**1:48**
1 Sam 1:11

**1:49**
Ps 111:9

**1:50**
Ps 103:13, 17

**1:51**
2 Sam 22:28
Ps 89:10

**1:52**
Job 5:12;
12:19

**1:53**
1 Sam 2:5
Ps 107:9

**1:54**
Ps 98:3
Isa 41:8

**1:55**
Gen 17:7; 22:17

---

**1:38** A young unmarried girl who became pregnant risked disaster. Unless the father of the child agreed to marry her, she would probably remain unmarried for life. If her own father rejected her, she could be forced into begging or prostitution in order to earn her living. And Mary, with her story about becoming pregnant by the Holy Spirit, risked being considered crazy as well. Still Mary said, despite the possible risks, "May everything you have said about me come true." When Mary said that, she didn't know about the tremendous opportunity she would have. She only knew that God was asking her to serve him, and she willingly obeyed. Don't wait to see the bottom line before offering your life to God. Offer yourself willingly, even when the outcome seems disastrous.

**1:38** God's announcement of the birth of a special child was met with various responses throughout Scripture. Sarah, Abraham's wife, laughed (Genesis 18:9-15). Zechariah doubted (Luke 1:18). By contrast, Mary graciously submitted. She believed the angel's words and agreed to bear the child, even under humanly impossible circumstances. God is able to do the impossible. Our response to his demands should not be laughter or doubt but willing acceptance.

**1:41-43** Apparently the Holy Spirit told Elizabeth that Mary's child was the Messiah because Elizabeth called her young relative "the mother of my Lord" as she greeted her. As Mary rushed off to visit her relative, she must have been wondering if the events of the last few days had been real. Elizabeth's greeting must have strengthened her faith. Mary's pregnancy may have seemed impossible, but her wise relative believed in the Lord's faithfulness and rejoiced in Mary's blessed condition.

**1:42, 43** Even though she herself was pregnant with a long-awaited son, Elizabeth could have envied Mary, whose son would

be even greater than her own. Instead, she was filled with joy that the mother of her Lord would visit her. Have you ever envied people whom God has apparently singled out for special blessing? A cure for jealousy is to rejoice with those individuals, realizing that God uses his people in ways best suited to his purpose.

**1:46-55** This song is often called the *Magnificat*, the first word in the Latin translation of this passage. Mary's song has often been used as the basis for choral music and hymns. Like Hannah, the mother of Samuel (1 Samuel 2:1-10), Mary glorified God in song for what he was going to do for the world through her. Notice that in both songs, God is pictured as a champion of the poor, the oppressed, and the despised.

**1:48** When Mary said, "From now on all generations will call me blessed," was she being proud? No, she was recognizing and accepting the gift God had given her. Pride is refusing to accept God's gifts or taking credit for what God has done; humility is accepting the gifts and using them to praise and serve God. Don't deny, belittle, or ignore your gifts. Thank God for them and use them to his glory.

**1:54, 55** God kept his promise to Abraham to be merciful to God's people forever (Genesis 22:16-18). Christ's birth fulfilled the promise, and Mary understood this. She was not surprised when her special son eventually announced that he was the Messiah. She had known Jesus' mission from before his birth. Some of God's promises to Israel are found in 2 Samuel 22:50, 51; Psalms 89:2-4; 103:17, 18; Micah 7:18-20.

**1:56** Because travel was difficult, long visits were customary. Mary must have been a great help to Elizabeth, who was experiencing the discomforts of a first pregnancy in old age.

## John the Baptist Is Born (7)

57 When it was time for Elizabeth's baby to be born, she gave birth to a son. 58 And when her neighbors and relatives heard that the Lord had been very merciful to her, everyone rejoiced with her.

59 When the baby was eight days old, they all came for the circumcision ceremony. They wanted to name him Zechariah, after his father. 60 But Elizabeth said, "No! His name is John!"

61 "What?" they exclaimed. "There is no one in all your family by that name." 62 So they used gestures to ask the baby's father what he wanted to name him. 63 He motioned for a writing tablet, and to everyone's surprise he wrote, "His name is John." 64 Instantly Zechariah could speak again, and he began praising God.

65 Awe fell upon the whole neighborhood, and the news of what had happened spread throughout the Judean hills. 66 Everyone who heard about it reflected on these events and asked, "What will this child turn out to be?" For the hand of the Lord was surely upon him in a special way.

## Zechariah's Prophecy

67 Then his father, Zechariah, was filled with the Holy Spirit and gave this prophecy:

68 "Praise the Lord, the God of Israel,
    because he has visited and redeemed his people.
69 He has sent us a mighty Savior*
    from the royal line of his servant David,
70 just as he promised
    through his holy prophets long ago.
71 Now we will be saved from our enemies
    and from all who hate us.
72 He has been merciful to our ancestors
    by remembering his sacred covenant—

1:69 Greek *has raised up a horn of salvation for us.*

**Margin references:**
1:59 Gen 17:12; Lev 12:3; Luke 2:21; Phil 3:5
1:66 Luke 2:19; Acts 11:21
1:67 Joel 2:28
1:68 Pss 41:13; 72:18; 106:48; 111:9
1:69 1 Sam 2:1-10; Pss 18:2; 132:17; Ezek 29:21
1:70 Jer 23:5; Acts 3:21; Rom 1:2-4
1:71 Ps 106:10
1:72-73 Pss 105:8-9; 106:45-46

---

**GOD'S UNUSUAL METHODS OF COMMUNICATING**
One of the best ways to understand God's willingness to communicate to people is to note the various methods, some of them quite unexpected, that he has used to give his message.

| Person/Group | Method | Reference |
|---|---|---|
| Jacob, Zechariah, Mary, shepherds | Angels | Genesis 32:22-32; Luke 1:13, 30; 2:10 |
| Jacob, Joseph, a baker, a cup-bearer, Pharaoh, Isaiah, Joseph, the wise men | Dreams | Genesis 28:10-22; 37:5-10; 40:5; 41:7, 8; Isaiah 1:1; Matthew 1:20; 2:12, 13 |
| Belshazzar | Writing on the wall | Daniel 5:5-9 |
| Balaam | Talking donkey | Numbers 22:21-35 |
| People of Israel | Pillars of cloud and fire | Exodus 13:21, 22 |
| Jonah | Being swallowed by a fish | Jonah 2 |
| Abraham, Moses, Jesus at his baptism, Paul | Verbally | Genesis 12:1-4; Exodus 7:8; Matthew 3:13-17; Acts 18:9 |
| Moses | Fire | Exodus 3:2 |
| Us | God's Son | Hebrews 1:1, 2 |

---

1:59 The circumcision ceremony was an important event to the family of a Jewish baby boy. God commanded circumcision when he was beginning to form his holy nation (Genesis 17:4-14), and he had reaffirmed it through Moses (Leviticus 12:1-3). This ceremony was a time of joy when friends and family members would celebrate the baby's becoming part of God's covenant nation.

1:59 Family lines and family names were important to the Jews. The people naturally assumed the child would receive Zechariah's name or at least a family name. They were surprised, therefore, that both Elizabeth and Zechariah wanted to name the boy John. This was the name the angel had given them (see 1:13).

1:62 Zechariah's relatives talked to him by gestures because he was apparently deaf as well as speechless and had not heard what his wife had said.

1:67-79 Zechariah praised God with his first words after months of silence. In a song that is often called the *Benedictus* after the first words in the Latin translation of this passage, Zechariah prophesied the coming of a Savior who would redeem his people and predicted that his son, John, would prepare the Messiah's way. All the Old Testament prophecies were coming true—no wonder Zechariah praised God! The Messiah would come in Zechariah's lifetime, and his son had been chosen to pave the way.

1:72, 73 This was God's promise to Abraham to bless all peoples through him (see Genesis 12:3). It would be fulfilled through the Messiah, Abraham's descendant.

73 the covenant he swore with an oath
  to our ancestor Abraham.
74 We have been rescued from our enemies
  so we can serve God without fear,
75 in holiness and righteousness
  for as long as we live.

76 "And you, my little son,
  will be called the prophet of the Most High,
  because you will prepare the way for the Lord.
77 You will tell his people how to find salvation
  through forgiveness of their sins.
78 Because of God's tender mercy,
  the morning light from heaven is about to break upon us,*
79 to give light to those who sit in darkness and in the shadow of death,
  and to guide us to the path of peace."

80 John grew up and became strong in spirit. And he lived in the wilderness until he began his public ministry to Israel.

*1:73-74* Gen 22:16-18

*1:75* Eph 4:24

*1:76* Isa 40:3 Mal 3:1

*1:77* Jer 31:34

*1:78* Mal 4:2

*1:79* Isa 9:2; 58:8; 60:1-2 Matt 4:16

*1:80* Luke 2:40, 52

## Jesus Is Born in Bethlehem (9)

**2** At that time the Roman emperor, Augustus, decreed that a census should be taken throughout the Roman Empire. 2(This was the first census taken when Quirinius was governor of Syria.) 3All returned to their own ancestral towns to register for this census. 4And because Joseph was a descendant of King David, he had to go to Bethlehem in Judea, David's ancient home. He traveled there from the village of Nazareth in Galilee. 5He took with him Mary, his fiancée, who was now obviously pregnant.

*2:1-7* Matt 1:18-25

*2:5* Luke 1:27

1:78 Or *the Morning Light from Heaven is about to visit us.*

---

**1:76** Zechariah had just recalled hundreds of years of God's sovereign work in history, beginning with Abraham and going on into eternity. Then, in tender contrast, he personalized the story. His son had been chosen for a key role in the drama of the ages. Although God has unlimited power, he chooses to work through frail humans who begin as helpless babies. Don't minimize what God can do through those who are faithful to him.

**1:80** Why did John live out in the wilderness? Prophets used the isolation of the uninhabited wilderness to enhance their spiritual growth and to focus their message on God. By being in the wilderness, John remained separate from the economic and political powers so that he could aim his message against them. He also remained separate from the hypocritical religious leaders of his day. His message was different from theirs, and his life proved it.

**THE JOURNEY TO BETHLEHEM**
Caesar's decree for a census of the entire Roman Empire made it necessary for Joseph and Mary to leave their hometown, Nazareth, and journey the 70 miles to the Judean village of Bethlehem.

**2:1** Luke is the only Gospel writer who related the events he recorded to world history. His account was addressed to a predominantly Greek audience that would have been interested in and familiar with the political situation. Palestine was under the rule of the Roman Empire with Emperor Caesar Augustus, the first Roman emperor, in charge. The Roman rulers, considered to be like gods, stood in contrast to the tiny baby in a manger who was truly God in the flesh.

**2:1** A Roman census (registration) was taken to aid military conscription or tax collection. The Jews weren't required to serve in the Roman army, but they could not avoid paying taxes. Augustus's decree went out in God's perfect timing and according to God's perfect plan to bring his Son into the world.

**2:1-6** The Romans ruled the civilized world at this time. By contrast, Joseph controlled very little. Against his better judgment and political convictions, he complied with the Roman order to make a long trip just to pay his taxes. His fiancée, who had to go with him, was about to give birth.

The Romans were in control insofar as human authority can get its way by exerting human power. But the Romans did not recognize their limitations. In reality, God controls the world. In all times and places, he works his will. By the decree of Emperor Augustus, Jesus was born in the very town prophesied for his birth (Micah 5:2), even though his parents did not live there. Joseph and Mary were both descendants of David. The Old Testament is filled with prophecies that the Messiah would be born in David's royal line (see, for example, Isaiah 11:1; Jeremiah 33:15; Ezekiel 37:24; Hosea 3:5). Rome made the decree, just as God intended.

**2:4, 5** Sometimes we think to ourselves, "I'm being obedient, so why aren't things going better?" We face discomfort or inconvenience and immediately think either that we have misread God's will or that God has made a mistake. But watch this quiet couple as they head toward Bethlehem. God did not soften Joseph's bumpy road, but strengthened him. God did not provide a luxurious inn for Joseph and Mary, but brought his Son into the world in humble surroundings. When we do God's will, we are not guaranteed comfort and convenience. But we are

2:6
Matt 1:25
Gal 4:4

⁶And while they were there, the time came for her baby to be born. ⁷She gave birth to her first child, a son. She wrapped him snugly in strips of cloth and laid him in a manger, because there was no lodging available for them.

### Shepherds Visit Jesus (10)

⁸That night there were shepherds staying in the fields nearby, guarding their flocks of sheep. ⁹Suddenly, an angel of the Lord appeared among them, and the radiance of the Lord's glory surrounded them. They were terrified, ¹⁰but the angel reassured them. "Don't be afraid!" he said. "I bring you good news that will bring great joy to all people. ¹¹The Savior—yes, the Messiah, the Lord—has been born today in Bethlehem, the city of David! ¹²And you will recognize him by this sign: You will find a baby wrapped snugly in strips of cloth, lying in a manger."

2:9
Acts 5:19

2:11
John 4:42; 20:31

2:13
Ps 103:20
Rev 5:11

¹³Suddenly, the angel was joined by a vast host of others—the armies of heaven—praising God and saying,

2:14
Isa 57:19
Luke 19:38

¹⁴ "Glory to God in highest heaven,
    and peace on earth to those with whom God is pleased."

---

**DOUBTERS IN THE BIBLE**

| Doubter | Doubtful Moment | Reference |
|---|---|---|
| Abraham | When told he would be a father in old age | Genesis 17:17 |
| Sarah | When she heard she would be a mother in old age | Genesis 18:12 |
| Moses | When told to return to Egypt to lead the people | Exodus 3:10-15 |
| Israelites | Whenever they faced difficulties in the wilderness | Exodus 16:1-3 |
| Gideon | When told he would be a judge and leader | Judges 6:14-23 |
| Zechariah | When told he would be a father in old age | Luke 1:18 |
| Thomas | When told Jesus had risen from the dead | John 20:24, 25 |

Many of the people God used to accomplish great things started out as real doubters. With all of them, God showed great patience. Honest doubt was not a bad starting point as long as they didn't stay there. How great a part does doubt have in your willingness to trust God?

---

promised that everything, even discomfort and inconvenience, has meaning in God's plan. He will guide you and provide all you need. Like Joseph, live each day by faith, trusting that God is in charge.

**2:7** Strips of cloth were used to keep a baby warm and give him a sense of security. These cloths were believed to protect his internal organs. The custom of wrapping infants this way is still practiced in many Mid-eastern countries.

**2:7** This mention of the manger is the basis for the traditional belief that Jesus was born in a stable. Stables were often caves with feeding troughs (mangers) carved into the rock walls. Despite popular Christmas card pictures, the surroundings were dark and dirty. This was not the atmosphere the Jews expected as the birthplace of the Messiah-King. They thought their promised Messiah would be born in royal surroundings. We should not limit God by our expectations. He is at work wherever he is needed in our sin-darkened and dirty world.

**2:7** Although our first picture of Jesus is as a baby in a manger, it must not be our last. The Christ child in the manger is the subject of a beautiful Christmas scene, but we must not leave him there. This tiny, helpless baby lived an amazing life, died for us, ascended to heaven, and will return to earth as King of kings. Christ will rule the world and judge all people according to their decisions about him. Do you still picture Jesus as a baby in a manger—or is he your Lord? Make sure you don't underestimate Jesus. Let him grow up in your life.

**2:8** God continued to reveal the news about his Son, but not to those we might expect. Luke records that Jesus' birth was announced to shepherds in the fields. These may have been the shepherds who supplied the lambs for the Temple sacrifices that were performed for the forgiveness of sin. Here the angels invited these shepherds to greet the Lamb of God (John 1:36), who would take away the sins of the world forever.

**2:8-15** What a birth announcement! The shepherds were terrified, but their fear turned to joy as the angels announced the Messiah's birth. First the shepherds ran to see the baby; then they spread the word. Jesus is *your* Messiah, *your* Savior. Do you look forward to meeting him in prayer and in his Word each day? Have you discovered a Lord so wonderful that you can't help sharing your joy with your friends?

**2:9, 10** The greatest event in history had just happened! The Messiah had been born! For ages the Jews had waited for this, and when it finally occurred, the announcement came to humble shepherds. The Good News about Jesus is that he comes to all, including the plain and the ordinary. He comes to anyone with a heart humble enough to accept him. Whoever you are, whatever you do, you can have Jesus in your life. Don't think you need extraordinary qualifications—he accepts you as you are.

**2:11-14** Some of the Jews were waiting for a savior to deliver them from Roman rule; others hoped the Christ (Messiah) would deliver them from physical ailments. But Jesus, while healing their illnesses and establishing a spiritual Kingdom, delivered them from sin. His work is more far-reaching than anyone could imagine. Christ paid the price for sin and opened the way to peace with God. He offers us more than temporary political or physical changes—he offers us new hearts that will last for eternity.

**2:14** The story of Jesus' birth resounds with music that has inspired composers for 2,000 years. The angels' song, often called the *Gloria* after its first word in the Latin translation, is the basis for many modern choral works, traditional Christmas carols, and ancient liturgical chants.

<sup>15</sup>When the angels had returned to heaven, the shepherds said to each other, "Let's go to Bethlehem! Let's see this thing that has happened, which the Lord has told us about."

<sup>16</sup>They hurried to the village and found Mary and Joseph. And there was the baby, lying in the manger. <sup>17</sup>After seeing him, the shepherds told everyone what had happened and what the angel had said to them about this child. <sup>18</sup>All who heard the shepherds' story were astonished, <sup>19</sup>but Mary kept all these things in her heart and thought about them often. <sup>20</sup>The shepherds went back to their flocks, glorifying and praising God for all they had heard and seen. It was just as the angel had told them.

**2:17**
Luke 2:10-12
**2:19**
Luke 2:51

### Mary and Joseph Bring Jesus to the Temple (11)

<sup>21</sup>Eight days later, when the baby was circumcised, he was named Jesus, the name given him by the angel even before he was conceived.

<sup>22</sup>Then it was time for their purification offering, as required by the law of Moses after the birth of a child; so his parents took him to Jerusalem to present him to the Lord. <sup>23</sup>The law of the Lord says, "If a woman's first child is a boy, he must be dedicated to the LORD."* <sup>24</sup>So they offered the sacrifice required in the law of the Lord—"either a pair of turtledoves or two young pigeons."*

**2:21**
Gen 17:12
Lev 12:3
Matt 1:21
**2:22**
Lev 12:2-6
**2:23**
†Exod 13:2, 12, 15
**2:24**
†Lev 5:11; 12:8

### The Prophecy of Simeon

<sup>25</sup>At that time there was a man in Jerusalem named Simeon. He was righteous and devout and was eagerly waiting for the Messiah to come and rescue Israel. The Holy Spirit was upon him <sup>26</sup>and had revealed to him that he would not die until he had seen the Lord's Messiah. <sup>27</sup>That day the Spirit led him to the Temple. So when Mary and Joseph came to present the baby Jesus to the Lord as the law required, <sup>28</sup>Simeon was there. He took the child in his arms and praised God, saying,

**2:25**
†Isa 40:1; 49:13
**2:26**
Ps 89:48
John 8:51
Heb 11:5

<sup>29</sup> "Sovereign Lord, now let your servant die in peace,
     as you have promised.
<sup>30</sup> I have seen your salvation,
<sup>31</sup>     which you have prepared for all people.
<sup>32</sup> He is a light to reveal God to the nations,
     and he is the glory of your people Israel!"

**2:30-31**
Isa 40:5; 52:10
Acts 4:12
**2:32**
Isa 42:6-7; 46:13;
49:6

<sup>33</sup>Jesus' parents were amazed at what was being said about him. <sup>34</sup>Then Simeon blessed them, and he said to Mary, the baby's mother, "This child is destined to cause many in Israel to fall, but he will be a joy to many others. He has been sent as a sign from God, but many will oppose him. <sup>35</sup>As a result, the deepest thoughts of many hearts will be revealed. And a sword will pierce your very soul."

**2:34**
Isa 8:14
1 Cor 1:23
1 Pet 2:7-8

**2:23** Exod 13:2.    **2:24** Lev 12:8.

---

**2:21-24** Jewish families went through several ceremonies soon after a baby's birth: (1) *Circumcision.* Every boy was circumcised and named on the eighth day after birth (Leviticus 12:3; Luke 1:59, 60). Circumcision symbolized the Jews' separation from Gentiles and their unique relationship with God (see the note on 1:59). (2) *Redemption of the firstborn.* A firstborn son was presented to God one month after birth (Exodus 13:2, 11-16; Numbers 18:15, 16). The ceremony included buying back—"redeeming"—the child from God through an offering. This way, the parents acknowledged that the child belonged to God, who alone has the power to give life. (3) *Purification of the mother.* For 40 days after the birth of a son and 80 days after the birth of a daughter, the mother was cere-monially unclean and could not enter the Temple. At the end of her time of separation, the parents were to bring a lamb for a burnt offering and a dove or pigeon for a sin offering. The priest would sacrifice these animals and declare her to be clean. If a lamb was too expensive, the parents could bring a second dove or pigeon instead. This is what Mary and Joseph did.

Jesus was God's Son, but his family carried out these ceremo-nies according to God's law. Jesus was not born above the law; instead, he fulfilled it perfectly.

**2:28-32** When Mary and Joseph brought Jesus to the Temple to be dedicated to God, they met an old man who told them what their child would become. Simeon's song is often called the *Nunc*

*Dimittis,* from the first words of its Latin translation. Simeon could die in peace because he had seen the Messiah.

**2:32** The Jews were well acquainted with the Old Testament prophecies that spoke of the Messiah's blessings to their nation. They did not always give equal attention to the prophecies stating that he would bring salvation to the entire world, not just the Jews (see, for example, Isaiah 49:6). Many thought that Christ had come to save only his own people. Luke made sure his Greek audience understood that Christ had come to save *all* who believe, Gentiles as well as Jews.

**2:33** Joseph and Mary were amazed when this old man took their son into his arms and spoke such stunning words. Simeon said that Jesus was a gift from God, and he recognized Jesus as the Messiah who would be a light to the entire world. This was at least the second time that Mary had been greeted with a prophecy about her son; the first time was when Elizabeth had welcomed her as the mother of her Lord (1:42-45).

**2:34, 35** Simeon prophesied that Jesus would have a paradox-ical effect on Israel. Some would fall because of him (see Isaiah 8:14, 15), while others would rise (see Malachi 4:2). With Jesus, there would be no neutral ground: People would either joyfully accept him or totally reject him. As Jesus' mother, Mary would be grieved by the widespread rejection he would face. This is the first note of sorrow in Luke's Gospel.

### The Prophecy of Anna

2:37
1 Tim 5:5

2:38
Isa 52:9
Luke 1:68; 24:21

2:39
Matt 2:23

2:40
Luke 1:80

36Anna, a prophet, was also there in the Temple. She was the daughter of Phanuel from the tribe of Asher, and she was very old. Her husband died when they had been married only seven years. 37Then she lived as a widow to the age of eighty-four.* She never left the Temple but stayed there day and night, worshiping God with fasting and prayer. 38She came along just as Simeon was talking with Mary and Joseph, and she began praising God. She talked about the child to everyone who had been waiting expectantly for God to rescue Jerusalem.

39When Jesus' parents had fulfilled all the requirements of the law of the Lord, they returned home to Nazareth in Galilee. 40There the child grew up healthy and strong. He was filled with wisdom, and God's favor was on him.

### Jesus Speaks with the Religious Teachers (15)

2:41
Exod 12:24-27
Deut 16:1-8

41Every year Jesus' parents went to Jerusalem for the Passover festival. 42When Jesus was twelve years old, they attended the festival as usual. 43After the celebration was over, they started home to Nazareth, but Jesus stayed behind in Jerusalem. His parents didn't miss him at first, 44because they assumed he was among the other travelers. But when he didn't show up that evening, they started looking for him among their relatives and friends.

45When they couldn't find him, they went back to Jerusalem to search for him there. 46Three days later they finally discovered him in the Temple, sitting among the religious teachers, listening to them and asking questions. 47All who heard him were amazed at his understanding and his answers.

2:47
Matt 7:28
John 7:15

2:37 Or *She had been a widow for eighty-four years.*

---

**TO FEAR OR NOT TO FEAR**

| Person | Reference | Person | Reference |
|---|---|---|---|
| Abraham | Genesis 15:1 | Zechariah | Luke 1:13 |
| Moses | Numbers 21:34 | Mary | Luke 1:30 |
| | Deuteronomy 3:2 | Shepherds | Luke 2:10 |
| Joshua | Joshua 8:1 | Peter | Luke 5:10 |
| Jeremiah | Lamentations 3:57 | Paul | Acts 27:23, 24 |
| Daniel | Daniel 10:12, 19 | John | Revelation 1:17, 18 |

People in the Bible who were confronted by God or his angels all had one consistent response—fear. To each of them, God's response was always the same—don't be afraid. As soon as they sensed that God accepted them and wanted to communicate with them, their fear subsided. He had given them freedom to be his friends. He has given you the same freedom.

---

2:36 Although Simeon and Anna were very old, they had never lost their hope that they would see the Messiah. Led by the Holy Spirit, they were among the first to bear witness to Jesus. In the Jewish culture, elders were respected; thus, because of Simeon's and Anna's ages, their prophecies carried extra weight. In contrast, our society values youthfulness over wisdom, and contributions by the elderly are often ignored. As Christians, we should reverse those values wherever we can. Encourage older people to share their wisdom and experience. Listen carefully when they speak. Offer them your friendship, and help them find ways to continue to serve God.

2:36, 37 Anna was called a prophet, indicating that she was unusually close to God. Prophets did not necessarily predict the future. Their main role was to speak for God, proclaiming his truth.

2:39 Did Mary and Joseph return immediately to Nazareth, or did they remain in Bethlehem for a time (as implied in Matthew 2)? Apparently there is a gap of several years between verses 38 and 39—ample time for them to find a place to live in Bethlehem, flee to Egypt to escape Herod's wrath, and return to Nazareth when it was safe to do so.

2:41, 42 According to God's law, every male was required to go to Jerusalem three times a year for the great festivals (Deuteronomy 16:16). In the spring, the Passover was celebrated, followed immediately by the weeklong Festival of Unleavened Bread. Pass-

over commemorated the night of the Jews' escape from Egypt when God had killed the Egyptian firstborn but had passed over Israelite homes (see Exodus 12:21-36). Passover was the most important of the three annual festivals.

2:43-45 At age 12, Jesus was considered almost an adult, so he probably didn't spend a lot of time with his parents during the festival. Those who attended these festivals often traveled in caravans for protection from robbers along the Palestine roads. The women and children usually would travel at the front of the caravan, with the men bringing up the rear. A 12-year-old boy conceivably could have been in either group, so both Mary and Joseph probably assumed that Jesus was with the other one. But when the caravan left Jerusalem, Jesus stayed behind, absorbed in his discussion with the religious leaders.

2:46, 47 The Temple courts were famous throughout Judea as a place of learning. The apostle Paul studied in Jerusalem, perhaps in the Temple courts, under Gamaliel, one of its foremost teachers (Acts 22:3). At the time of the Passover, the greatest rabbis of the land would assemble to teach and to discuss great truths among themselves. The coming Messiah would no doubt have been a popular discussion topic, for everyone was expecting him soon. Jesus would have been eager to listen and to ask probing questions. It was not his youth but the depth of his wisdom that astounded these teachers.

⁴⁸His parents didn't know what to think. "Son," his mother said to him, "why have you done this to us? Your father and I have been frantic, searching for you everywhere."

⁴⁹"But why did you need to search?" he asked. "Didn't you know that I must be in my Father's house?"* ⁵⁰But they didn't understand what he meant.

⁵¹Then he returned to Nazareth with them and was obedient to them. And his mother stored all these things in her heart.

⁵²Jesus grew in wisdom and in stature and in favor with God and all the people.

### John the Baptist Prepares the Way for Jesus (16/Matthew 3:1-12; Mark 1:1-8)

**3** It was now the fifteenth year of the reign of Tiberius, the Roman emperor. Pontius Pilate was governor over Judea; Herod Antipas was ruler* over Galilee; his brother Philip was ruler* over Iturea and Traconitis; Lysanias was ruler over Abilene. ²Annas and Caiaphas were the high priests. At this time a message from God came to John son of Zechariah, who was living in the wilderness. ³Then John went from place to place on both sides of the Jordan River, preaching that people should be baptized to show that they had repented of their sins and turned to God to be forgiven. ⁴Isaiah had spoken of John when he said,

"He is a voice shouting in the wilderness,
'Prepare the way for the LORD's coming!
    Clear the road for him!

**2:49** Or *"Didn't you realize that I should be involved with my Father's affairs?"*   **3:1a** Greek *Herod was tetrarch.* Herod Antipas was a son of King Herod.   **3:1b** Greek *tetrarch;* also in 3:1c.

---

**2:48** Luke 3:23; 4:22
**2:49** John 2:16
**2:50** Mark 9:32
**2:51** Luke 2:19
**2:52** 1 Sam 2:26 / Prov 3:4 / Luke 1:80
**3:2** Luke 1:80
**3:3** Acts 13:24; 19:4
**3:4-6** †Isa 40:3-5

---

**2:48** Mary had to let go of her child and let him become a man, God's Son, the Messiah. Fearful that she hadn't been careful enough with this God-given child, she searched frantically for him. But she was looking for a boy, not the young man who was in the Temple astounding the religious leaders with his questions. Letting go of people or projects we have nurtured can be very difficult. It is both sweet and painful to see our children growing into adults, our students into teachers, our subordinates into managers, our inspirations into institutions. But when the time comes we must step back and let go—in spite of the hurt. Then our protégés can exercise their wings, take flight, and soar to the heights God intended for them.

**2:49, 50** This is the first mention of Jesus' awareness that he was God's Son. But even though he knew his real Father, Jesus did not reject his earthly parents. He went back to Nazareth with them and lived under their authority for another 18 years. God's people do not despise human relationships or family responsibilities. If the Son of God obeyed his human parents, how much more should we honor our family members! Don't use commitment to God's work to justify neglecting your family.

**2:50** Jesus' parents didn't understand what he meant about his Father's house. They didn't realize he was making a distinction between his earthly father and his heavenly Father. Jesus knew that he had a unique relationship with God. Although Mary and Joseph knew he was God's Son, they didn't understand what his mission would involve. Besides, they had to raise him, along with his brothers and sisters (Matthew 13:55, 56), as a normal child. They knew he was unique, but they did not know what was going on in his mind.

**2:52** The Bible does not record any events of the next 18 years of Jesus' life, but Jesus undoubtedly was learning and maturing. As the oldest in a large family, he undoubtedly assisted Joseph in his carpentry work. Joseph may have died during this time, leaving Jesus to provide for the family. The normal routines of daily life gave Jesus a solid understanding of the Judean people.

**2:52** The second chapter of Luke shows us that although Jesus was unique, he had a normal childhood and adolescence. In terms of development, he went through the same progression we do. He grew physically and mentally, he related to other people, and he was loved by God. A full human life is balanced. Thus it was important to Jesus—and it should be important to all believers— to develop fully and harmoniously in each of these key areas: physical, mental, social, and spiritual.

**3:1** Tiberius, the Roman emperor, ruled from A.D. 14 to 37. Pilate was the Roman governor responsible for the province of Judea; Herod Antipas and Philip were half brothers and sons of the cruel Herod the Great, who had been dead more than 20 years. Antipas, Philip, Pilate, and Lysanias apparently had equal powers in governing their separate territories. All were subject to Rome and responsible for keeping peace in their respective lands.

**3:2** Jewish law provided for only one high priest. He was appointed from Aaron's line and held his position for life. By this time, however, the religious system had been corrupted, and the Roman government was appointing its own religious leaders to maintain greater control over the Jews. Apparently the Roman authorities had deposed the Jewish-appointed Annas and had replaced him with Annas's son-in-law, Caiaphas. Nevertheless Annas retained his title (see Acts 4:6) and probably also much of the power it carried. Because the Jews believed the high priest's position to be for life, they would have continued to call Annas their high priest.

**3:2** This is John the Baptist, whose birth story is told in chapter 1. See his Profile in John 1, p. 1749.

**3:2** Pilate, Herod, and Caiaphas were the most powerful leaders in Palestine, but they were upstaged by a wilderness prophet from rural Judea. God chose to speak through the loner, John the Baptist, who has gone down in history as greater than any of the rulers of his day. How often people judge others by the superficial standards of power, wealth, and beauty, and miss the truly great people through whom God works! Greatness is measured not by what you have but by your faith in God. Like John, give yourself entirely to God so God's power can work through you.

**3:3** To turn to God to receive forgiveness from sins implies turning *away* from sins. We can't just say we believe and then live any way we choose (see 3:7, 8); neither can we simply live a morally correct life without a personal relationship with God because that cannot bring forgiveness from sin. Determine to rid your life of any sins God points out, and then determine to live in a way that pleases him.

**3:4, 5** In John's day, before a king would take a trip, messengers would tell those he was planning to visit to prepare the roads for him. Similarly John told his listeners to make their lives ready so the Lord could come to them. This does not mean that you must get rid of all your sin or wrongdoing before you can accept Christ; rather, when you accept him, he takes care of all your sinfulness. To "prepare the way" means clearing aside the baggage of the past and the doubts of the present in order to let the King come into your life. He'll take it from there.

<sup></sup>
**5** The valleys will be filled,
   and the mountains and hills made level.
The curves will be straightened,
   and the rough places made smooth.
**6** And then all people will see
   the salvation sent from God.'"*

**3:6**
Luke 2:30-31
Acts 28:28
Titus 2:11

**3:7**
Matt 12:34; 23:33

**3:8**
John 8:33, 37, 39
Acts 3:25

**7** When the crowds came to John for baptism, he said, "You brood of snakes! Who warned you to flee God's coming wrath? **8** Prove by the way you live that you have repented of your

**3:4-6** Isa 40:3-5 (Greek version).

In societies like Israel, in which a woman's value was largely measured by her ability to bear children, to be without children often led to personal hardship and public shame. For Elizabeth, a childless old age was a painful and lonely time but still she remained faithful to God.

Both Elizabeth and Zechariah came from priestly families. For two weeks each year, Zechariah had to go to the Temple in Jerusalem to attend to his priestly duties. After one of those trips, Zechariah returned home excited but speechless. He had to write down his good news, because he couldn't give it any other way. And what a wonderful surprise he had for his wife: Their faded dream would become an exciting reality! Soon Elizabeth became pregnant, and she knew her child was a long-hoped-for gift from God.

News traveled fast among the family. Seventy miles to the north, in Nazareth, Elizabeth's relative Mary also unexpectedly became pregnant. Within days after the angel's message that she would bear the Messiah, Mary went to visit Elizabeth. They were instantly bound together by the unique gifts God had given them. Elizabeth knew that Mary's son would be even greater than her own, for John would be the messenger for Mary's son.

When her baby was born, Elizabeth insisted on his God-given name: John. Zechariah's written agreement freed his tongue, and everyone in town wondered what would become of this obviously special child.

Elizabeth whispered her praise as she cared for God's gift. Knowing about Mary must have made her marvel at God's timing. Things had worked out even better than she could have planned. We, too, need to remember that God is in control of every situation. When did you last pause to recognize God's timing in the events of your life?

**ELIZABETH**

| | |
|---|---|
| **Strengths and accomplishments** | • Known as a deeply spiritual woman<br>• Showed no doubts about God's ability to fulfill his promise<br>• Mother of John the Baptist<br>• The first woman besides Mary to hear of the coming Savior |
| **Lessons from her life** | • God does not forget those who have been faithful to him<br>• God's timetable and methods do not have to conform to what we expect |
| **Vital statistics** | • Occupation: Homemaker<br>• Relatives: Husband: Zechariah. Son: John the Baptist. Relative: Mary.<br>• Contemporaries: Joseph, Herod the Great |
| **Key verses** | "Why am I so honored, that the mother of my Lord should visit me? When I heard your greeting, the baby in my womb jumped for joy. You are blessed because you believed that the Lord would do what he said" (Luke 1:43-45). |

Elizabeth's story is told in Luke 1:5-80.

**3:6** This book was written to a non-Jewish audience. Luke quoted from Isaiah to show that salvation is for "all people," not just the Jews (Isaiah 40:3-5; 52:10). John the Baptist called everyone to prepare to meet Jesus. That includes you, no matter what your nationality, social standing, religious affiliation, or political position. God is calling to all people. Don't let feelings of being an outsider cause you to hold back. No one who wants to follow Jesus is an outsider in God's Kingdom.

**3:7-9** Some people wanted to be baptized by John so they could escape eternal punishment, but they were not really repenting from sin nor were they willing to change the way they lived. John had harsh words for such people. He knew that God values reformation above ritual. Confession of sins and a changed life are inseparable. Faith without deeds is dead (James 2:14-26). Jesus also spoke harsh words to the respectable religious leaders who lacked the

willingness to repent. They wanted to be known as religious authorities and they wanted eternal life, but they didn't want to repent of their sins. Thus, their lives were unproductive. Turning from sin must be tied to action. Following Jesus means more than saying the right words; it means acting on what he says.

**3:8** Many of John's hearers were shocked when he said that being Abraham's descendants was not enough to ensure salvation. The religious leaders relied more on family than on faith for their standing with God. For them, religion was inherited. But a personal relationship with God cannot be handed down from parents to children. Everyone has to make a personal decision of whether or not to trust Christ. Don't rely on someone else's faith for your salvation. Have you made that personal decision to trust Christ?

sins and turned to God. Don't just say to each other, 'We're safe, for we are descendants of Abraham.' That means nothing, for I tell you, God can create children of Abraham from these very stones. 9Even now the ax of God's judgment is poised, ready to sever the roots of the trees. Yes, every tree that does not produce good fruit will be chopped down and thrown into the fire."

10The crowds asked, "What should we do?"

11John replied, "If you have two shirts, give one to the poor. If you have food, share it with those who are hungry."

12Even corrupt tax collectors came to be baptized and asked, "Teacher, what should we do?"

13He replied, "Collect no more taxes than the government requires."

14"What should we do?" asked some soldiers.

John replied, "Don't extort money or make false accusations. And be content with your pay."

15Everyone was expecting the Messiah to come soon, and they were eager to know whether John might be the Messiah. 16John answered their questions by saying, "I baptize you with* water; but someone is coming soon who is greater than I am—so much greater that I'm not even worthy to be his slave and untie the straps of his sandals. He will baptize you with the Holy Spirit and with fire.* 17He is ready to separate the chaff from the wheat with his winnowing fork. Then he will clean up the threshing area, gathering the wheat into his barn but burning the chaff with never-ending fire." 18John used many such warnings as he announced the Good News to the people.

### Herod Puts John in Prison (26)

19John also publicly criticized Herod Antipas, the ruler of Galilee,* for marrying Herodias, his brother's wife, and for many other wrongs he had done. 20So Herod put John in prison, adding this sin to his many others.

3:16a Or in.   3:16b Or in the Holy Spirit and in fire.   3:19 Greek Herod the tetrarch.

**Marginal cross-references:**
3:9 Matt 7:19; John 15:6
3:11 Jas 2:15; 1 Jn 3:17
3:12 Luke 7:29
3:13 Luke 19:8
3:14 Exod 23:1; Lev 19:11
3:16 Mark 1:4; John 1:26-27, 33; Acts 1:5; 2:3; 11:16; 13:25; 19:4
3:17 Matt 13:30
3:19-20 Matt 14:3; Mark 6:17

---

**3:11-14** John's message demanded at least three specific responses: (1) Share what you have with those who need it, (2) whatever your job is, do it well and with fairness, and (3) be content with your earnings. John had not been commissioned to bring comforting messages to those who lived sinful lives; he was calling the people to right living as he prepared the way for their Messiah. What changes can you make in sharing what you have, doing your work honestly and well, and being content?

**3:12** Tax collectors were notorious for their dishonesty. Romans gathered funds for their government by farming out the collection privilege. Tax collectors earned their own living by adding a sizable sum—whatever they could get away with—to the total and keeping this money for themselves. Unless the people revolted and risked Roman retaliation, they had to pay whatever was demanded. Obviously the people hated the tax collectors, who were generally corrupt and greedy. Yet, said John, God would accept even these men; God desires to pour out mercy on those who confess their sins and then to give them strength to live changed lives.

**3:12-14** John's message took root in unexpected places—among the poor, the dishonest, and even the hated occupation army. These people were painfully aware of their needs and they were honestly seeking to know what to do to change their lives. Did anyone follow John's advice? Surely some did, and their softened hearts became ready to receive the message of the One who was to come.

**3:14** These soldiers were the Roman troops sent to keep peace in this distant province. Many of them oppressed the poor and used their power to take advantage of all the people. John called them to turn from their sins and change their ways.

**3:15** Israel had not seen a prophet for more than 400 years. It was widely believed that when the Messiah would come, prophecy would reappear (Joel 2:28, 29; Malachi 3:1; 4:5). When John burst onto the scene, the people were excited. He was obviously a great prophet, and they were sure that the eagerly awaited age of the Messiah had come. Some, in fact, thought John himself was the

Messiah. John spoke like the prophets of old, saying that the people must turn from their sin to God to avoid punishment and to experience his mercy and approval. This is a message for all times and places, but John spoke it with particular urgency; he was preparing the people for the coming Messiah.

**3:16** John's baptism with water symbolized the washing away of sins. His baptism followed his message of repentance and reformation. Jesus' baptism with fire equips one with power to do God's will. The baptism with the Holy Spirit was first given at Pentecost (Acts 2) when the Holy Spirit came upon believers in the form of tongues of fire, empowering them to proclaim Jesus' resurrection in many languages. The baptism with fire also symbolizes the work of the Holy Spirit in bringing God's judgment on those who refuse to repent.

**3:17** John warned of impending judgment by comparing those who refuse to live for God to chaff, the useless outer husk of the grain. By contrast, John compared those who repent and reform their lives to the nourishing wheat itself. The winnowing fork was a pitchfork used to toss wheat so that the kernels would separate from the husks. Those who refuse to be used by God will be discarded because they have no value in furthering God's work. Those who repent and believe, however, hold great value in God's eyes because they are beginning a new life of productive service for him.

**3:19, 20** In these two verses Luke flashes forward to continue his explanation about John the Baptist. (See the Harmony of the Gospels for the chronological order of events.) This is Herod Antipas (see Mark 6, p. 1629 for his Profile). Herodias was Herod's niece and also his brother's wife. She would treacherously plot John the Baptist's death (Matthew 14:1-12). The Herods were a murderous and deceitful family. Rebuking a tyrannical Roman official who could imprison and execute him was extremely dangerous, yet that is what John did. Herod seemingly would have the last word, but the story is not finished. At the Last Judgment, Herod, not John, will face God's punishment—for eternity.

## The Baptism of Jesus (**17**/Matthew 3:13-17; Mark 1:9-11)

**3:22**
Gen 22:2
Ps 2:7
Isa 42:1
Matt 12:18; 17:5
Mark 9:7
Luke 9:35
2 Pet 1:17

²¹One day when the crowds were being baptized, Jesus himself was baptized. As he was praying, the heavens opened, ²² and the Holy Spirit, in bodily form, descended on him like a dove. And a voice from heaven said, "You are my dearly loved Son, and you bring me great joy.*"

**3:22** Some manuscripts read *my Son, and today I have become your Father.*

## SIMEON/ANNA

When Joseph and Mary took the eight-day-old Jesus to the Temple for his circumcision, they had two unexpected but delightful encounters. Well-worn examples of patient waiting met them—Simeon and Anna. Both of these godly saints recognized Jesus' identity as the Messiah. Simeon and Anna give us a picture of godly expectation in an environment ripe with expectations.

Simeon was certain he would see the Messiah before he died. We don't know how surprised he was to discover the Savior as a baby in Mary's arms. We do know that he recognized Jesus and gave God praise for his faithfulness. When Simeon saw the baby, he considered his life complete.

Simeon's exuberance caught Anna's attention. She was another regular in the Temple. Anna's brief marriage ended in widowhood and she spent the remainder of her eighty-four plus years serving as a prophetess. Anna overheard Simeon's prophecy about Jesus and immediately added her own excited words of praise for the Savior.

Anna discovered that God can make every passage of life meaningful and useful. The long years of widowhood were also effective years of worship and service. Both she and Simeon dedicated their lives to God and were rewarded in ways we can only fully appreciate if we are willing to live the same way.

As you interact with people at various stages of life today, think about the development of your relationship with God. When talking to a younger person, ask yourself: "How was God involved in my life at that age?" When noticing someone older ask: "How do I want my relationship with God to mature by that point in my life?"

| | |
|---|---|
| **Strengths and accomplishments** | • Exercised faithful anticipation regarding God's promised Messiah<br>• Did not hesitate to give praise to God for his work in the world<br>• Both spoke from the powerful authority of their faith and age |
| **Lessons from their lives** | • God does give to some of his faithful followers a deeper insight and clarity about his plans<br>• There were those in Israel who did recognize Jesus<br>• Advancing age does not invalidate a person's usefulness in God's purposes |
| **Vital statistics** | • Where: Jerusalem<br>• Contemporaries: Joseph, Mary, Herod the Great |
| **Key verses** | "The Holy Spirit was upon [Simeon] and had revealed to him that he would not die until he had seen the Lord's Messiah. . . . [Anna] never left the Temple but stayed there day and night, worshiping God with fasting and prayer" (Luke 2:25-26, 37). |

Simeon and Anna's stories are told in Luke 2:21-38.

**3:21** Luke emphasizes Jesus' human nature. Jesus was born to humble parents, a birth unannounced except to shepherds and foreigners. This baptism recorded here was the first public declaration of Jesus' ministry. Instead of going to Jerusalem and identifying with the established religious leaders, Jesus went to a river and identified with those who were repenting of sin. When Jesus, at age 12, had visited the Temple, he had understood his mission (2:49). Eighteen years later, at his baptism, he began carrying it out. And as Jesus prayed, God spoke and confirmed his decision to act. God was breaking into human history through Jesus the Christ.

**3:21, 22** Theologians have long been troubled by Jesus' allowing himself to be baptized by John. After all, this baptism was for sinners. Why, then, did Jesus do it? He did it because he is both God and human—he underwent baptism and even death as only a human could; he lived a sinless life and rose from the dead as only God could. This baptism by John in the Jordan River was another step in his identification with us sinful people; and the arrival of the dove signifies God's approval. Now Jesus would officially begin his ministry as God's beloved Son walking

the dusty roads of Israel. When you are hurting, depressed, broken, remember: You have a Savior who understands your humanity. When you sin, remember: He has paid the price for your disobedience.

**3:21, 22** This is one of several places in Scripture where all the members of the Trinity are mentioned—Father, Son, and Holy Spirit. In the traditional words of the church, the one God exists in three persons but one substance, coeternal and coequal. No explanation can adequately portray the power and intricacy of this unique relationship. There are no perfect analogies in nature because there is no other relationship like the Trinity.

## The Record of Jesus' Ancestors (3/Matthew 1:1-17)

23 Jesus was about thirty years old when he began his public ministry.

Jesus was known as the son of Joseph.
Joseph was the son of Heli.
24 Heli was the son of Matthat.
Matthat was the son of Levi.
Levi was the son of Melki.
Melki was the son of Jannai.
Jannai was the son of Joseph.
25 Joseph was the son of Mattathias.
Mattathias was the son of Amos.
Amos was the son of Nahum.
Nahum was the son of Esli.
Esli was the son of Naggai.
26 Naggai was the son of Maath.
Maath was the son of Mattathias.
Mattathias was the son of Semein.
Semein was the son of Josech.
Josech was the son of Joda.
27 Joda was the son of Joanan.
Joanan was the son of Rhesa.
Rhesa was the son of Zerubbabel.
Zerubbabel was the son of Shealtiel.
Shealtiel was the son of Neri.
28 Neri was the son of Melki.
Melki was the son of Addi.
Addi was the son of Cosam.
Cosam was the son of Elmadam.
Elmadam was the son of Er.
29 Er was the son of Joshua.
Joshua was the son of Eliezer.
Eliezer was the son of Jorim.
Jorim was the son of Matthat.
Matthat was the son of Levi.
30 Levi was the son of Simeon.
Simeon was the son of Judah.
Judah was the son of Joseph.
Joseph was the son of Jonam.
Jonam was the son of Eliakim.
31 Eliakim was the son of Melea.
Melea was the son of Menna.
Menna was the son of Mattatha.
Mattatha was the son of Nathan.
Nathan was the son of David.
32 David was the son of Jesse.
Jesse was the son of Obed.
Obed was the son of Boaz.

**3:23**
Luke 4:22
John 6:42

**3:27**
1 Chr 3:17
Ezra 3:2

**3:31-33**
Ruth 4:18-22
1 Sam 16:1, 13
2 Sam 5:14
1 Chr 2:9-12; 3:5

---

**3:23** Imagine the Savior of the world working in a small-town carpenter's shop until he was 30 years old! It seems incredible that Jesus would have been content to remain in Nazareth all that time, but he patiently trusted his Father's timing for his life and ministry. Thirty was the prescribed age for priests to begin their ministry (Numbers 4:3). Joseph was 30 years old when he

began serving the king of Egypt (Genesis 41:46), and David was 30 years old when he began to reign over Judah (2 Samuel 5:4). Age 30, then, was a good time to begin an important task in the Jewish culture. Like Jesus, we need to resist the temptation to jump ahead before receiving the Spirit's direction. Are you waiting and wondering what your next step should be? Don't jump ahead—trust God's timing.

**3:23-38** Matthew's genealogy goes back to Abraham and shows that Jesus was related to all Jews (Matthew 1). Luke's genealogy goes back to Adam, showing that Jesus is related to all human beings. This is consistent with Luke's picture of Jesus as the Savior of the whole world.

Boaz was the son of Salmon.*
Salmon was the son of Nahshon.
33 Nahshon was the son of Amminadab.
Amminadab was the son of Admin.
Admin was the son of Arni.*
Arni was the son of Hezron.
Hezron was the son of Perez.
Perez was the son of Judah.
34 Judah was the son of Jacob.
Jacob was the son of Isaac.
Isaac was the son of Abraham.
Abraham was the son of Terah.
Terah was the son of Nahor.
35 Nahor was the son of Serug.
Serug was the son of Reu.
Reu was the son of Peleg.
Peleg was the son of Eber.
Eber was the son of Shelah.

**3:34-36**
Gen 11:10-26
1 Chr 1:24-27

**3:32** Greek *Sala*, a variant spelling of Salmon; also in 3:32b. See Ruth 4:22.   **3:33** Some manuscripts read *Amminadab was the son of Aram. Arni* and *Aram* are alternate spellings of Ram. See 1 Chr 2:9-10.

**M**otherhood is a painful privilege. Young Mary of Nazareth had the unique privilege of being mother to the very Son of God. Yet the pains and pleasures of her motherhood can be understood by mothers everywhere. Mary was the only human present at Jesus' birth who also witnessed his death. She saw him arrive as her baby son, and she watched him die as her Savior.

Until Gabriel's unexpected visit, Mary's life was quite satisfactory. She had recently become engaged to a carpenter, Joseph, and was anticipating married life. But her life was about to change forever.

Angels don't usually make appointments before visiting. Feeling as if she were being congratulated for winning the grand prize in a contest she had never entered, Mary found the angel's greeting puzzling and his presence frightening. What she heard next was the news almost every woman in Israel hoped to hear—that her child would be the Messiah, God's promised Savior. Mary did not doubt the message but rather asked how pregnancy would be possible. Gabriel told her the baby would be God's Son. Her answer was the one God waits in vain to hear from so many other people: "I am the Lord's servant. May everything you have said about me come true" (Luke 1:38). Later her song of joy shows us how well she knew God, for her thoughts were filled with his words from the Old Testament.

When he was eight days old Jesus was taken to the Temple to be dedicated to God. There Joseph and Mary were met by two devout people, Simeon and Anna, who recognized the child as the Messiah and praised God. Simeon directed some words to Mary that must have come to her mind many times in the years that followed: "A sword will pierce your very soul" (Luke 2:35). A big part of her painful privilege of motherhood would be to see her son rejected and crucified by the people he came to save.

We can imagine that even if she had known all she would suffer as Jesus' mother, Mary would still have given the same response. Are you, like Mary, available to be used by God?

| | |
|---|---|
| **Strengths and accomplishments** | • The mother of Jesus, the Messiah<br>• The one human who was with Jesus from birth to death<br>• Willing to be available to God<br>• Knew and applied Old Testament Scriptures |
| **Lessons from her life** | • God's best servants are often ordinary people who make themselves available to him<br>• God's plans involve extraordinary events in ordinary people's lives<br>• A person's character is revealed by his or her response to the unexpected |
| **Vital statistics** | • Where: Nazareth, Bethlehem<br>• Occupation: Homemaker<br>• Relatives: Husband: Joseph. Relatives: Zechariah and Elizabeth. Children: Jesus, James, Joseph, Judas, Simon, and daughters. |
| **Key verse** | "Mary responded, 'I am the Lord's servant. May everything you have said about me come true.' And then the angel left her" (Luke 1:38). |

Mary's story is told throughout the Gospels. She is also mentioned in Acts 1:14.

36 Shelah was the son of Cainan.
   Cainan was the son of Arphaxad.
   Arphaxad was the son of Shem.
   Shem was the son of Noah.
   Noah was the son of Lamech.
37 Lamech was the son of Methuselah.
   Methuselah was the son of Enoch.
   Enoch was the son of Jared.
   Jared was the son of Mahalalel.
   Mahalalel was the son of Kenan.
38 Kenan was the son of Enosh.*
   Enosh was the son of Seth.
   Seth was the son of Adam.
   Adam was the son of God.

**3:36-38**
Gen 4:25–5:32
1 Chr 1:1-4

**3:38**
Gen 1:26-27;
2:7; 5:1-2

### Satan Tempts Jesus in the Wilderness (18/Matthew 4:1-11; Mark 1:12-13)

**4** Then Jesus, full of the Holy Spirit, returned from the Jordan River. He was led by the Spirit in the wilderness,* 2 where he was tempted by the devil for forty days. Jesus ate nothing all that time and became very hungry.

3 Then the devil said to him, "If you are the Son of God, tell this stone to become a loaf of bread."

**4:1**
Isa 11:2; 61:1
**4:2**
Exod 34:28
1 Kgs 19:8
Heb 4:15

**3:38** Greek *Enos,* a variant spelling of Enoch; also in 3:38b. See Gen 5:6.   **4:1** Some manuscripts read *into the wilderness.*

**4:1** Sometimes we feel that if the Holy Spirit leads us, it will always be "beside peaceful streams" (Psalm 23:2). But that is not necessarily true. He led Jesus into the wilderness for a long and difficult time of testing, and he may also lead us into difficult situations. When facing trials, first make sure you haven't brought them on yourself through sin or unwise choices. If you find no sin to confess or unwise behavior to change, then ask God to strengthen you for your test. Finally, be careful to follow faithfully wherever the Holy Spirit leads.

**4:1, 2** The devil, who tempted Adam and Eve in the garden, also tempted Jesus in the wilderness. Satan is a real being, a created but rebellious fallen angel, and not a symbol or an idea. He constantly fights against God and those who follow and obey God. Jesus was a prime target for the devil's temptations. Satan had succeeded with Adam and Eve, and he hoped to succeed with Jesus as well.

**4:1-13** Knowing and obeying God's Word is an effective weapon against temptation, the only *offensive* weapon provided in the

Christian's "armor" (Ephesians 6:17). Jesus used Scripture to counter Satan's attacks, and so should we. But to use it effectively, we must have faith in God's promises because Satan also knows Scripture and is adept at twisting it to suit his purposes. Obeying the Scriptures is more important than simply having a verse to quote, so read them daily and apply them to your life. Then your "sword" will always be sharp.

**4:2** Why was it necessary for Jesus to be tempted? First, temptation is part of the human experience. For Jesus to be fully human, for him to understand us completely, he had to face temptation (see Hebrews 4:15). Second, Jesus had to undo Adam's work. Adam, though created perfect, gave in to temptation and passed sin on to the whole human race. Jesus, by contrast, resisted Satan. His victory offers salvation to all of Adam's descendants (see Romans 5:12-19).

**4:3** Satan may tempt us to doubt Christ's true identity. He knows that once we begin to question whether or not Jesus is God, it's far easier to get us to do what he wants. Times of questioning can help us sort out our beliefs and strengthen our faith, but those times can also be dangerous. If you are dealing with doubt, be aware that you are especially vulnerable to temptation. Even as you search for answers, protect yourself by meditating on the unshakable truths of God's Word.

**4:3** Sometimes what we are tempted to do isn't wrong in itself. Turning a stone into bread wasn't necessarily bad. The sin was not in the act but in the reason behind it. The devil was trying to get Jesus to take a shortcut, to solve Jesus' immediate problem at the expense of his long-range goals, to seek comfort at the sacrifice of his discipline. Satan often works that way—persuading us to take action, even right action, for the wrong reason or at the wrong time. The fact that something is not wrong in itself does not mean that it is good for you at a given time. Many people sin by attempting to fulfill legitimate desires outside of God's will or ahead of his timetable. First ask: Is the Holy Spirit leading me to do this or is Satan trying to get me off the track?

**4:3ff** Often we are tempted not through our weaknesses, but through our strengths. The devil tempted Jesus where he was strong. Jesus had power over stones, the kingdoms of the world, and even angels, and Satan wanted him to use that power without regard for his mission. When we give in to the devil and wrongly use our strengths, we become proud and self-reliant. Trusting in our own powers, we feel little need of God. To avoid this trap, we

### JESUS' TEMPTATION AND RETURN TO GALILEE

Jesus was tempted by Satan in the rough Judean wilderness before returning to his boyhood home, Nazareth. John's Gospel tells of Jesus' journeys in Galilee, Samaria, and Judea (see John 1–4) before he moved to Capernaum to set up his base of operations (see Matthew 4:12, 13).

Mediterranean Sea
GALILEE
N
Capernaum
Sea of Galilee
Nazareth
Jordan River
DECAPOLIS (Ten Towns)
SAMARIA
Wilderness
PEREA
Jerusalem
Dead Sea
JUDEA
IDUMEA

0    20 Mi.
0    20 Km.

4:4
†Deut 8:3

4:6
Matt 28:18
John 12:31; 14:30
1 Jn 5:19
Rev 13:2

4:8
†Deut 6:13; 10:20

4:10-11
†Ps 91:11-12

4:12
†Deut 6:16

4:13
Heb 4:15

4But Jesus told him, "No! The Scriptures say, 'People do not live by bread alone.'*"

5Then the devil took him up and revealed to him all the kingdoms of the world in a moment of time. 6"I will give you the glory of these kingdoms and authority over them," the devil said, "because they are mine to give to anyone I please. 7I will give it all to you if you will worship me."

8Jesus replied, "The Scriptures say,

'You must worship the LORD your God
    and serve only him.'*"

9Then the devil took him to Jerusalem, to the highest point of the Temple, and said, "If you are the Son of God, jump off! 10For the Scriptures say,

'He will order his angels to protect and guard you.
11 And they will hold you up with their hands
    so you won't even hurt your foot on a stone.'*"

12Jesus responded, "The Scriptures also say, 'You must not test the LORD your God.'*"
13When the devil had finished tempting Jesus, he left him until the next opportunity came.

## B. MESSAGE AND MINISTRY OF JESUS, THE SAVIOR (4:14—21:38)
Luke accurately records the actions and teachings of Christ, helping us understand the way of salvation. Much unique material appears in Luke, especially the parables of Jesus. Jesus came to teach us how to live and how to find salvation. How carefully, then, we should study the words and life of our Savior.

### 1. Jesus' ministry in Galilee
*Jesus Preaches in Galilee* (**30**/Matthew 4:12-17; Mark 1:14-15; John 4:43-45)
14Then Jesus returned to Galilee, filled with the Holy Spirit's power. Reports about him spread quickly through the whole region. 15He taught regularly in their synagogues and was praised by everyone.

### *Jesus Is Rejected at Nazareth* (**32**)
16When he came to the village of Nazareth, his boyhood home, he went as usual to the synagogue on the Sabbath and stood up to read the Scriptures. 17The scroll of Isaiah the prophet was handed to him. He unrolled the scroll and found the place where this was written:

4:4 Deut 8:3.   4:8 Deut 6:13.   4:10-11 Ps 91:11-12.   4:12 Deut 6:16.

---

must realize that all our strengths are God's gifts to us, and we must dedicate those strengths to his service.

**4:6, 7** The devil arrogantly hoped to succeed in his rebellion against God by diverting Jesus from his mission and winning his worship. "This world is mine, not God's," he was saying, "and if you hope to do anything worthwhile here, you'll need to follow my instructions." Jesus didn't argue with Satan about who owns the world, but Jesus refused to validate Satan's claim by worshiping him. Jesus knew that he would redeem the world through giving up his life on the cross, not through making an alliance with a corrupt angel.

**4:9-11** Here the devil misinterpreted Scripture. The intention of Psalm 91 is to show God's protection of his people, not to incite them to use God's power for sensational or foolish displays.

**4:13** Christ's defeat of the devil in the wilderness was decisive but not final. Throughout his ministry, Jesus would confront Satan in many forms. Too often we see temptation as once and for all. In reality, we need to be constantly on guard against the devil's ongoing attacks. Where are you most susceptible to temptation right now? How are you preparing to withstand it?

**4:13** What would it take for you to "sell out"? What is there in life that would cause you to compromise your faith? Whatever it is—sexual temptation, financial inducement, fear of alienating or offending someone—it will be placed in your path at some point. The enemy wants to destroy believers or at least neutralize them through sin, shame, and guilt. When that temptation rears its seductive head, do what Jesus did: rely on the Word of God and stand fast in your commitment to worship God alone, above all else. No matter the cost or the sacrifice, no matter how

appealing the come-on, believers must follow Jesus' example and stand strong.

**4:15, 16** Synagogues were very important in Jewish religious life. During the Exile when the Jews no longer had their Temple, synagogues were established as places of worship on the Sabbath and as schools for young boys during the week. Synagogues continued to exist even after the Temple was rebuilt. A synagogue could be set up in any town with at least 10 Jewish families. It was administered by one leader and an assistant. At the synagogue, the leader often would invite a visiting rabbi to read from the Scriptures and to teach. Itinerant rabbis, like Jesus, were always welcome to speak to those gathered each Sabbath in the synagogues. The apostle Paul also took advantage of this practice (see Acts 13:5; 14:1).

**4:16** Jesus went to the synagogue "as usual." Even though he was the perfect Son of God and his local synagogue undoubtedly left much to be desired, Jesus attended services every week. His example makes our excuses for not attending church sound weak and self-serving. Make regular worship a part of your life.

**4:17-21** Jesus was quoting from Isaiah 61:1, 2. Isaiah pictures the deliverance of Israel from exile in Babylon as a Year of Jubilee when all debts are cancelled, all slaves are freed, and all property is returned to original owners (Leviticus 25). But the release from Babylonian exile had not brought the expected fulfillment; they were still a conquered and oppressed people. So Isaiah must have been referring to a future messianic age. Jesus boldly announced, "The Scripture you've just heard has been fulfilled this very day!" Jesus was proclaiming himself as the one who would bring this Good News to pass, but he would do so in a way that the people were not yet able to grasp.

18 "The Spirit of the Lord is upon me,
> for he has anointed me to bring Good News to the poor.
He has sent me to proclaim that captives will be released,
> that the blind will see,
that the oppressed will be set free,
19   and that the time of the Lord's favor has come.*"

20He rolled up the scroll, handed it back to the attendant, and sat down. All eyes in the synagogue looked at him intently. 21 Then he began to speak to them. "The Scripture you've just heard has been fulfilled this very day!"

22Everyone spoke well of him and was amazed by the gracious words that came from his lips. "How can this be?" they asked. "Isn't this Joseph's son?"

23 Then he said, "You will undoubtedly quote me this proverb: 'Physician, heal yourself'—meaning, 'Do miracles here in your hometown like those you did in Capernaum.' 24But I tell you the truth, no prophet is accepted in his own hometown.

25 "Certainly there were many needy widows in Israel in Elijah's time, when the heavens were closed for three and a half years, and a severe famine devastated the land. 26 Yet Elijah was not sent to any of them. He was sent instead to a foreigner—a widow of Zarephath in the land of Sidon. 27And there were many lepers in Israel in the time of the prophet Elisha, but the only one healed was Naaman, a Syrian."

28When they heard this, the people in the synagogue were furious. 29 Jumping up, they mobbed him and forced him to the edge of the hill on which the town was built. They intended to push him over the cliff, 30 but he passed right through the crowd and went on his way.

### Jesus Teaches with Authority (34/Mark 1:21-28)

31 Then Jesus went to Capernaum, a town in Galilee, and taught there in the synagogue every Sabbath day. 32 There, too, the people were amazed at his teaching, for he spoke with authority.

33Once when he was in the synagogue, a man possessed by a demon—an evil* spirit—began shouting at Jesus, 34"Go away! Why are you interfering with us, Jesus of Nazareth? Have you come to destroy us? I know who you are—the Holy One of God!"

35 Jesus cut him short. "Be quiet! Come out of the man," he ordered. At that, the demon threw the man to the floor as the crowd watched; then it came out of him without hurting him further.

36Amazed, the people exclaimed, "What authority and power this man's words possess! Even evil spirits obey him, and they flee at his command!" 37 The news about Jesus spread through every village in the entire region.

4:18-19 Or and to proclaim the acceptable year of the Lord. Isa 61:1-2 (Greek version); 58:6.   4:33 Greek unclean; also in 4:36.

**Cross-references (right margin):**

4:18-19
†Isa 61:1-2

4:19
Lev 25:8-10
2 Cor 6:2

4:22
Luke 2:47
John 6:42; 7:15

4:23
Matt 4:13; 11:23
Mark 1:21-28;
2:1-12

4:24
Matt 13:57
Mark 6:4
John 4:44

4:25-26
1 Kgs 17:1-9; 18:1
Jas 5:17

4:27
2 Kgs 5:1-14

4:29
Num 15:35
Acts 7:58
Heb 13:12

4:30
John 8:59

4:31
Matt 4:13-16
John 2:12

4:32
Matt 7:28-29
John 7:46

4:34
Luke 4:41
John 6:69

4:35
Luke 4:39-41

---

**4:24** Even Jesus himself was not accepted as a prophet in his hometown. Many people have a similar attitude. Don't be surprised if your Christian life and faith are not easily understood or accepted by those who know you well. Because they know your background, your failures, and your foibles, they may not see past those to the new person you have become. Let God work in your life, pray to be a positive witness for him, and be patient.

**4:28** Jesus' remarks angered the people of Nazareth because he was saying that God sometimes chose to reach Gentiles rather than Jews. Jesus implied that his hearers were as unbelieving as the citizens of the northern kingdom of Israel in the days of Elijah and Elisha, a time notorious for its great wickedness.

**4:31** Jesus had recently moved to Capernaum from Nazareth (Matthew 4:13). Capernaum was a thriving city with great wealth as well as great decadence. Because it was the headquarters for many Roman troops, word about Jesus could spread all over the Roman Empire from there.

**4:33** A man possessed by a demon was in the synagogue where Jesus was teaching. This man made his way into the place of worship and verbally abused Jesus. It is naive to think that we will be sheltered from evil in the church. Satan is happy to invade our presence wherever and whenever he can. But Jesus' authority is much greater than Satan's, and where Jesus is present, demons cannot stay for long.

**4:34-36** The people were amazed at Jesus' authority to drive out demons—evil spirits ruled by Satan and sent to harass people, tempt them to sin, and ultimately destroy them. Demons are fallen angels who have joined Satan in rebellion against God. Jesus faced many demons during his time on earth, and he always exerted authority over them. Not only did the evil spirit leave this man; Luke records that the man was not even injured.

While we may not often see cases of demon possession today, it does still exist. However, we would not doubt that evil permeates our world. We need not be fearful, however. Jesus' power is far greater than Satan's. The first step toward conquering fear of evil is to recognize Jesus' authority and power. He has overcome all evil, including Satan himself.

### Jesus Heals Peter's Mother-in-Law and Many Others
**(35/Matthew 8:14-17; Mark 1:29-34)**

38After leaving the synagogue that day, Jesus went to Simon's home, where he found Simon's mother-in-law very sick with a high fever. "Please heal her," everyone begged. 39Standing at her bedside, he rebuked the fever, and it left her. And she got up at once and prepared a meal for them.

40As the sun went down that evening, people throughout the village brought sick family members to Jesus. No matter what their diseases were, the touch of his hand healed every one. 41Many were possessed by demons; and the demons came out at his command, shouting, "You are the Son of God!" But because they knew he was the Messiah, he rebuked them and refused to let them speak.

### Jesus Preaches throughout Galilee (36/Matthew 4:23-25; Mark 1:35-39)

42Early the next morning Jesus went out to an isolated place. The crowds searched everywhere for him, and when they finally found him, they begged him not to leave them. 43But he replied, "I must preach the Good News of the Kingdom of God in other towns, too, because that is why I was sent." 44So he continued to travel around, preaching in synagogues throughout Judea.*

### Jesus Provides a Miraculous Catch of Fish (37)

**5** One day as Jesus was preaching on the shore of the Sea of Galilee,* great crowds pressed in on him to listen to the word of God. 2He noticed two empty boats at the water's edge, for the fishermen had left them and were washing their nets. 3Stepping into one of the boats, Jesus asked Simon,* its owner, to push it out into the water. So he sat in the boat and taught the crowds from there.

4When he had finished speaking, he said to Simon, "Now go out where it is deeper, and let down your nets to catch some fish."

5"Master," Simon replied, "we worked hard all last night and didn't catch a thing. But if you say so, I'll let the nets down again." 6And this time their nets were so full of fish they began to tear! 7A shout for help brought their partners in the other boat, and soon both boats were filled with fish and on the verge of sinking.

**4:44** Some manuscripts read *Galilee*.    **5:1** Greek *Lake Gennesaret*, another name for the Sea of Galilee. **5:3** *Simon* is called "Peter" in 6:14 and thereafter.

Margin references: 4:40-41 Matt 8:16-17; Mark 1:32-34 / 4:41 Mark 3:11 / 4:42-44 Matt 4:23 / 4:43 Luke 8:1 / 4:44 Matt 4:23; Mark 1:39 / 5:4 John 21:6 / 5:5 John 21:3 / 5:6 John 21:11

**4:39** Jesus healed Simon's (Peter's) mother-in-law so completely that not only did the fever leave but her strength was restored, and immediately she got up and took care of others' needs. What a beautiful attitude of service she showed! God gives us health so that we may serve others.

**4:40** The people came to Jesus when the sun was setting because this was the Sabbath (4:31), their day of rest. Sabbath lasted from sunset on Friday to sunset on Saturday. The people didn't want to break the law that prohibited travel on the Sabbath, so they waited until the sun set on the Sabbath before coming to Jesus. Then, as Luke the physician notes, they came with all kinds of diseases, and Jesus healed each one.

**4:40** When you've faced a particularly difficult time, what helped you most? While some may have said kind words, most likely it was the presence of a friend and his or her touch. A hug, an arm around your shoulder, or even just a hand laid gently on top of yours—these simple wordless gestures mean so much to those in pain. In healing the sick and the demon possessed, Jesus had already demonstrated that he could heal with just a word (4:39). Yet here in Capernaum, Luke records that the touch of Jesus' hand healed the sick. Why not just speak a word and heal the whole crowd at once? Why go to all the trouble of treating each person individually, face-to-face? Because human touch is so very important. Does someone need a touch from you today?

**4:41** Why didn't Jesus want the demons to reveal who he was? (1) Jesus commanded them to remain silent to show his authority over them. (2) Jesus wanted his listeners to believe he was the Messiah because of his words, not because of the demons' words. (3) Jesus was going to reveal his identity according to God's timetable, and he would not be pushed by Satan's evil

plans. The demons called Jesus "Son of God" or "the Holy One sent from God" (4:34) because they knew he was the Christ. But Jesus was going to show himself to be the suffering servant before he became the great King. To reveal his identity as King too soon would stir up the crowds with the wrong expectations of what he had come to do.

**4:42** Jesus had to get up very early just to get some time alone. If Jesus needed solitude for prayer and refreshment, how much more is this true for us? Don't become so busy that life turns into a flurry of activity leaving no room for quiet fellowship alone with God. No matter how much you have to do, you should always have time for prayer.

**4:43** The Kingdom of God is Good News! It was Good News to the Jews because they had been awaiting the coming of the promised Messiah ever since the Babylonian captivity. It is Good News for us also because it means freedom from slavery to sin and selfishness. The Kingdom of God is here and now because the Holy Spirit lives in the hearts of believers. Yet it is also in the future because Jesus will return to reign over a perfect Kingdom, where sin and evil will no longer exist.

**5:2** Fishermen on the Sea of Galilee used nets, often bell-shaped ones with lead weights around the edges. A net would be thrown flat onto the water, and the lead weights would cause it to sink around the fish. Then the fishermen would pull on a cord, drawing the net around the fish. Nets had to be kept in good condition, so they would be washed to remove weeds and then mended.

[8]When Simon Peter realized what had happened, he fell to his knees before Jesus and said, "Oh, Lord, please leave me—I'm too much of a sinner to be around you." [9]For he was awestruck by the number of fish they had caught, as were the others with him. [10]His partners, James and John, the sons of Zebedee, were also amazed.

Jesus replied to Simon, "Don't be afraid! From now on you'll be fishing for people!" [11]And as soon as they landed, they left everything and followed Jesus.

### Jesus Heals a Man with Leprosy (38/Matthew 8:1-4; Mark 1:40-45)

[12]In one of the villages, Jesus met a man with an advanced case of leprosy. When the man saw Jesus, he bowed with his face to the ground, begging to be healed. "Lord," he said, "if you are willing, you can heal me and make me clean."

[13]Jesus reached out and touched him. "I am willing," he said. "Be healed!" And instantly the leprosy disappeared. [14]Then Jesus instructed him not to tell anyone what had happened. He said, "Go to the priest and let him examine you. Take along the offering required in the law of Moses for those who have been healed of leprosy.* This will be a public testimony that you have been cleansed."

[15]But despite Jesus' instructions, the report of his power spread even faster, and vast crowds came to hear him preach and to be healed of their diseases. [16]But Jesus often withdrew to the wilderness for prayer.

### Jesus Heals a Paralyzed Man (39/Matthew 9:1-8; Mark 2:1-12)

[17]One day while Jesus was teaching, some Pharisees and teachers of religious law were sitting nearby. (It seemed that these men showed up from every village in all Galilee and Judea, as well as from Jerusalem.) And the Lord's healing power was strongly with Jesus.

[18]Some men came carrying a paralyzed man on a sleeping mat. They tried to take him inside to Jesus, [19]but they couldn't reach him because of the crowd. So they went up to the roof and took off some tiles. Then they lowered the sick man on his mat down into the crowd, right in front of Jesus. [20]Seeing their faith, Jesus said to the man, "Young man, your sins are forgiven."

5:14 See Lev 14:2-32.

**Cross references (right margin):**
5:8 Gen 18:27; Job 42:5-6
5:11 Matt 19:27
5:14 Lev 14:2-32
5:15 Matt 9:26
5:20 Luke 7:48

---

**5:8** Simon Peter was awestruck at this miracle, and his first response was to realize his own insignificance in comparison to this man's greatness. Peter knew that Jesus had healed the sick and driven out demons, but he was amazed that Jesus cared about his day-to-day routine and understood his needs. God is interested not only in saving us but also in helping us in our daily activities.

**5:11** God has two requirements for coming to him. Like Peter, we must recognize our own sinfulness. Then, like these fishermen, we must realize that we can't save ourselves and that we need help. If we know that Jesus is the only one who can help us, we will be ready to leave everything and follow him.

**5:11** This was the disciples' second call. After the first call (Matthew 4:18-22; Mark 1:16-20), Peter, Andrew, James, and John had gone back to fishing. They continued to watch Jesus, however, as he established his authority in the synagogue, healed the sick, and drove out demons. Here he also established his authority in their lives—he met them on their level and helped them in their work. From this point on, they left their nets and remained with Jesus. For us, following Jesus means more than just acknowledging him as Savior. We must leave our past behind and commit our future to him.

**5:12** Leprosy was a feared disease because there was no known cure for it, and some forms of it were highly contagious. Leprosy had a similar emotional impact and terror associated with it as AIDS does today. (Sometimes called Hansen's disease, leprosy still exists in a less contagious form that can be treated.) The priests monitored the disease, banishing lepers who were in a contagious stage to prevent the spread of infection and readmitting lepers whose disease was in remission. Because leprosy destroys the nerve endings, lepers often would unknowingly damage their fingers, toes, and noses. This man with leprosy had an advanced case, so he undoubtedly had lost much bodily tissue. Still, he believed that Jesus could heal him of every trace of the disease. And Jesus did just that, reaching out to touch this untouchable, contagious, man in order to restore him. For more on the power of touch, see the second note on 4:40.

**5:16** People were flocking to hear Jesus preach and to have their diseases healed, but Jesus made sure he often withdrew to quiet, solitary places to pray. Many things clamor for our attention, and we often run ourselves ragged attending to them. Like Jesus, however, we should take time to withdraw to a quiet and deserted place to pray. Strength comes from God, and we can only be strengthened by spending time with him.

**5:17** The religious leaders spent much time defining and discussing the huge body of religious tradition that had been accumulating for more than 400 years since the Jews' return from exile. They were so concerned with these man-made traditions, in fact, that they often lost sight of Scripture. Here these leaders felt threatened because Jesus challenged their sincerity and because the people were flocking to him.

**5:18, 19** In Bible times, houses were built of stone and had flat roofs made of mud mixed with straw. Outside stairways led to the roof. These men carried their friend up the stairs to the roof, where they took apart as much as was necessary to lower him in front of Jesus.

**5:18-20** It wasn't the paralyzed man's faith that impressed Jesus but the faith of his friends. Jesus responded to their faith and healed the man. For better or worse, our faith affects others. We cannot make another person a Christian, but we can do much through our words, actions, and love to give him or her a chance to respond. Look for opportunities to bring your friends to the living Christ.

**5:21**
Isa 43:25; 55:7
Luke 7:49

**5:22**
Luke 6:8; 9:47

**5:24-25**
John 5:8-9

21 But the Pharisees and teachers of religious law said to themselves, "Who does he think he is? That's blasphemy! Only God can forgive sins!"

22 Jesus knew what they were thinking, so he asked them, "Why do you question this in your hearts? 23 Is it easier to say 'Your sins are forgiven,' or 'Stand up and walk'? 24 So I will prove to you that the Son of Man* has the authority on earth to forgive sins." Then Jesus turned to the paralyzed man and said, "Stand up, pick up your mat, and go home!"

25 And immediately, as everyone watched, the man jumped up, picked up his mat, and went home praising God. 26 Everyone was gripped with great wonder and awe, and they praised God, exclaiming, "We have seen amazing things today!"

*Jesus Eats with Sinners at Matthew's House* (**40**/Matthew 9:9-13; Mark 2:13-17)
27 Later, as Jesus left the town, he saw a tax collector named Levi sitting at his tax collector's booth. "Follow me and be my disciple," Jesus said to him. 28 So Levi got up, left everything, and followed him.

**5:29-30**
Luke 15:1-2

29 Later, Levi held a banquet in his home with Jesus as the guest of honor. Many of Levi's fellow tax collectors and other guests also ate with them. 30 But the Pharisees and their teachers of religious law complained bitterly to Jesus' disciples, "Why do you eat and drink with such scum?*"

31 Jesus answered them, "Healthy people don't need a doctor—sick people do. 32 I have come to call not those who think they are righteous, but those who know they are sinners and need to repent."

*Religious Leaders Ask Jesus about Fasting* (**41**/Matthew 9:14-17; Mark 2:18-22)
33 One day some people said to Jesus, "John the Baptist's disciples fast and pray regularly, and so do the disciples of the Pharisees. Why are your disciples always eating and drinking?"

**5:34**
John 3:29

**5:35**
Luke 9:22; 17:22

34 Jesus responded, "Do wedding guests fast while celebrating with the groom? Of course not. 35 But someday the groom will be taken away from them, and then they will fast."

36 Then Jesus gave them this illustration: "No one tears a piece of cloth from a new garment and uses it to patch an old garment. For then the new garment would be ruined, and the new patch wouldn't even match the old garment.

**5:24** "Son of Man" is a title Jesus used for himself.　**5:30** Greek *with tax collectors and sinners?*

---

**5:21** When Jesus told the paralyzed man his sins were forgiven, the Jewish leaders accused Jesus of blasphemy—claiming to be God or to do what only God can do. In Jewish law, blasphemy was punishable by death (Leviticus 24:16). In labeling Jesus' claim to forgive sins blasphemous, the religious leaders showed they did not understand that Jesus *is* God, and that he has God's power to heal both the body and the soul. Forgiveness of sins was a sign that the messianic age had come (Isaiah 40:2; Joel 2:32; Micah 7:18, 19; Zechariah 13:1).

**5:24** God offers the same forgiveness given to the paralytic to all who believe. The Greek word *aphiemi,* translated "forgiven," means to leave or let go, to give up a debt, to send away from oneself. Forgiveness means that a relationship has been renewed despite a wrong that has been done. But the act cannot be erased or changed. The notion of *aphiemi,* however, goes far beyond human forgiveness, for it includes the "putting away" of sin in two ways: (1) The law and justice are satisfied because Jesus paid the penalty that sin deserved; thus, sins can no longer be held against a believer. (2) The guilt caused by sin is removed and replaced with Christ's righteousness. Believers are so forgiven that, in God's eyes, it is as if they had never sinned. Do you carry a heavy burden for sins you have committed? Confess all to Christ and receive *aphiemi*—ultimate forgiveness.

**5:27** For more about Levi (who was also named Matthew), the disciple and author of the Gospel of Matthew, see his Profile in Matthew 9, p. 1557.

**5:28, 29** Levi left a lucrative, though probably dishonest, tax-collecting business to follow Jesus. Then he responded as Jesus would want all his followers to do. He held a banquet for his fellow tax collectors and other notorious "sinners" so they could meet Jesus, too. Levi, who left behind a material fortune in order to gain a spiritual fortune, was proud to be associated with Jesus.

**5:30-32** The Pharisees wrapped their sin in respectability. They made themselves appear good by publicly doing good deeds and pointing at the sins of others. Jesus chose to spend time not with these proud, self-righteous religious leaders, but with people who sensed their own sin and knew that they were not good enough for God. In order to come to God, we must repent; in order to renounce our sin, we must first acknowledge it.

**5:35** Jesus knew his death was coming. After that time, fasting would be in order. Although he was fully human, Jesus knew he was God and why he had come—to die for the sins of the world.

**5:36-39** "Wineskins" were goatskins sewn together at the edges to form watertight bags. Because new wine expands as it ages, it had to be put in new, pliable wineskins. A used skin, having become more rigid, would burst and spill the wine. Like old wineskins, the Pharisees were too rigid to accept Jesus, who could not be contained in their traditions or rules. Christianity required new approaches, new traditions, new structures. Our church programs and ministries should not be so structured that they have no room for a fresh touch of the Spirit, a new method, or a new idea. We, too, must be careful that our heart does not become so rigid that it prevents us from accepting new ways of thinking that Christ brings. We need to keep our heart pliable so we can accept Jesus' life-changing message.

37 "And no one puts new wine into old wineskins. For the new wine would burst the wineskins, spilling the wine and ruining the skins. 38 New wine must be stored in new wineskins. 39 But no one who drinks the old wine seems to want the new wine. 'The old is just fine,' they say."

## The Disciples Pick Wheat on the Sabbath (45/Matthew 12:1-8; Mark 2:23-28)

**6** One Sabbath day as Jesus was walking through some grainfields, his disciples broke off heads of grain, rubbed off the husks in their hands, and ate the grain. 2 But some Pharisees said, "Why are you breaking the law by harvesting grain on the Sabbath?"

3 Jesus replied, "Haven't you read in the Scriptures what David did when he and his companions were hungry? 4 He went into the house of God and broke the law by eating the sacred loaves of bread that only the priests can eat. He also gave some to his companions." 5 And Jesus added, "The Son of Man* is Lord, even over the Sabbath."

## Jesus Heals a Man's Hand on the Sabbath (46/Matthew 12:9-14; Mark 3:1-6)

6 On another Sabbath day, a man with a deformed right hand was in the synagogue while Jesus was teaching. 7 The teachers of religious law and the Pharisees watched Jesus closely. If he healed the man's hand, they planned to accuse him of working on the Sabbath.

8 But Jesus knew their thoughts. He said to the man with the deformed hand, "Come and stand in front of everyone." So the man came forward. 9 Then Jesus said to his critics, "I have a question for you. Does the law permit good deeds on the Sabbath, or is it a day for doing evil? Is this a day to save life or to destroy it?"

10 He looked around at them one by one and then said to the man, "Hold out your hand." So the man held out his hand, and it was restored! 11 At this, the enemies of Jesus were wild with rage and began to discuss what to do with him.

## Jesus Chooses the Twelve Disciples (48/Mark 3:13-19)

12 One day soon afterward Jesus went up on a mountain to pray, and he prayed to God all night. 13 At daybreak he called together all of his disciples and chose twelve of them to be apostles. Here are their names:

6:5 "Son of Man" is a title Jesus used for himself.

**6:1**
Deut 23:25
**6:2**
John 5:10
**6:3-4**
1 Sam 21:6
**6:4**
Lev 24:5-9
**6:7**
Luke 14:1
**6:8**
Luke 5:22; 9:47
**6:13**
John 6:70

---

**6:1, 2** Jewish legal tradition had 39 categories of activities forbidden on the Sabbath, and harvesting was one of them. The teachers of religious law even went so far as to describe different methods of harvesting. One method was to rub the heads of grain between the hands, as the disciples were doing here. God's law said farmers were to leave the edges of their fields unplowed so travelers and the poor could eat from this bounty (Deuteronomy 23:25); thus, the disciples were not guilty of stealing grain. Neither were they breaking the Sabbath by doing their daily work on it. In fact, though they may have been violating the Pharisees' rules, they were not breaking any divine law.

**6:3-5** Each week 12 consecrated loaves of bread, representing the 12 tribes of Israel, would be placed on a table in the Temple. This bread was called the Bread of the Presence. After its use in the Temple, it was to be eaten only by priests. Jesus, accused of Sabbath breaking, referred to a well-known story about David (1 Samuel 21:1-6). On one occasion, when fleeing from Saul, David and his men had eaten this sacred bread. Their need had been more important than ceremonial regulations. Jesus was appealing to the same principle: Human need is more important than human regulations and rules. By comparing himself and his disciples with David and his men, Jesus was saying, "If you condemn me, you must also condemn David."

**6:5** When Jesus said that he was "Lord, even over the Sabbath," he meant that he had the authority to overrule the Pharisees' traditions and regulations because he had created the Sabbath. The Creator is always greater than the creation.

**6:6, 7** According to the tradition of the religious leaders, no healing could be done on the Sabbath. Healing, they said, was practicing medicine, and a person could not practice his or her profession on the Sabbath. The religious leaders were more concerned about protecting their laws than freeing a person from painful suffering. The religious leaders were more concerned with negatives: what

rules should not be broken, what activities should not be done. Jesus was positive: doing good and helping those in need.

Which would an objective observer say is more characteristic of your Christianity—the positives or the negatives? Are you more concerned about what people shouldn't be doing than you are about advancing God's Kingdom? Is your way of being a Christian the only way? And what about your church? The Pharisees thought their religious system had all the answers. They could not accept Jesus because he did not fit into their system. Beware of thinking that you or your church has all the answers. No religious system is big enough to contain Christ completely or to fulfill perfectly all his desires for the world. Christianity is the most positive force to ever hit this planet. Make sure you don't let it degenerate into a bunch of negatives.

**6:11** Jesus' enemies were furious. Not only had he read their minds; he also had flouted their laws and exposed the hatred in their hearts. Ironically, their hatred, combined with their zeal for the law, drove them to plot murder—an act that was clearly against their law.

**6:12** The Gospel writers note that before every important event in Jesus' life, he would take time to go off by himself and pray. This time Jesus was preparing to choose his inner circle, the 12 apostles. Make sure that all your important decisions are grounded in prayer.

**6:13** Jesus had many *disciples* (learners), but he chose only 12 *apostles* (messengers). The apostles were his inner circle to whom he gave special training and whom he sent out with his own authority. These were the men who started the Christian church. In the Gospels these 12 men are usually called the disciples, but in the book of Acts they are called apostles.

**6:13-16** Jesus selected "ordinary" men with a mixture of backgrounds and personalities to be his disciples. Today, God calls "ordinary" people together to build his church, teach salvation's

**6:14-15**
Acts 1:13

14 Simon (whom he named Peter),
Andrew (Peter's brother),
James,
John,
Philip,
Bartholomew,
15 Matthew,
Thomas,
James (son of Alphaeus),
Simon (who was called the zealot),
16 Judas (son of James),
Judas Iscariot (who later betrayed him).

### Jesus Gives the Beatitudes (49/Matthew 5:1-12)

17When they came down from the mountain, the disciples stood with Jesus on a large, level area, surrounded by many of his followers and by the crowds. There were people from all over Judea and from Jerusalem and from as far north as the seacoasts of Tyre and Sidon.
18They had come to hear him and to be healed of their diseases; and those troubled by evil* spirits were healed. 19Everyone tried to touch him, because healing power went out from him, and he healed everyone.
20Then Jesus turned to his disciples and said,

**6:19**
Matt 9:20
Mark 5:30
**6:20-23**
Matt 5:1-12

"God blesses you who are poor,
for the Kingdom of God is yours.
21 God blesses you who are hungry now,
for you will be satisfied.
God blesses you who weep now,
for in due time you will laugh.

**6:21**
Isa 55:1; 61:3
Rev 7:16-17

**6:22**
John 15:19; 16:2
1 Pet 4:14

22What blessings await you when people hate you and exclude you and mock you and curse you as evil because you follow the Son of Man. 23 When that happens, be happy! Yes, leap for joy! For a great reward awaits you in heaven. And remember, their ancestors treated the ancient prophets that same way.

**6:23**
2 Chr 36:16
Acts 5:41; 7:52
Jas 1:2

**6:24**
Jas 5:1

24 "What sorrow awaits you who are rich,
for you have your only happiness now.
25 What sorrow awaits you who are fat and prosperous now,
for a time of awful hunger awaits you.
What sorrow awaits you who laugh now,
for your laughing will turn to mourning and sorrow.

**6:25**
Isa 5:22; 65:13

**6:18** Greek *unclean.*

---

message, and serve others out of love. Alone we may feel unqualified to serve Christ effectively, but together we make up a group strong enough to serve God in any way. Ask for patience to accept the diversity of people in your church, and build on the variety of strengths represented in your group.

**6:14-16** The disciples are not always listed by the same names. For example, Simon is sometimes called Peter or Cephas. Matthew is also known as Levi. Bartholomew is thought to be the same person as Nathanael (John 1:45). Judas the son of James is also called Thaddaeus.

**6:19** Once word of Jesus' healing power spread, crowds gathered just to touch him. For many, he had become a magician or a symbol of good fortune. Instead of desiring God's pardon and love, they only wanted physical healing or a chance to see spectacular events. Some people still see God as a cosmic magician and consider prayer as a way to get God to do his tricks. But God is not a magician—he is the Master. Prayer is not a way for us to control God; it is a way for us to put ourselves under his control.

**6:20ff** This may be Luke's account of the sermon that Matthew records in Matthew 5–7, or it may be that Jesus gave similar sermons on several different occasions. Some believe that this was not one sermon, but a composite based on Jesus' customary teachings.

**6:20-23** These verses are called the *Beatitudes,* from the Latin word meaning "blessing." They describe what it means to be Christ's follower, give standards of conduct, and contrast Kingdom values with worldly values, showing what Christ's followers can expect from the world and what God will give them. In addition, they contrast fake piety with true humility. They also show how Old Testament expectations are fulfilled in God's Kingdom.

**6:21** Some believe that the hunger about which Jesus spoke is a hunger for righteousness (Matthew 5:6). Others say this is physical hunger. In any case, in a nation where riches were seen as a sign of God's favor, Jesus startled his hearers by pronouncing blessings on the hungry. In doing so, however, he was in line with an ancient tradition. The Old Testament is filled with texts proclaiming God's concern for the poor and needy. See, for example, 1 Samuel 2:5; Psalm 146:7; Isaiah 58:6, 7; and Jesus' own mother's prayer in Luke 1:53.

**6:24** If you are trying to find fulfillment only through riches, wealth may be the only reward you will ever get—and it does not last. We should not seek comfort now at the expense of eternal life.

<sup>26</sup> What sorrow awaits you who are praised by the crowds,
  for their ancestors also praised false prophets.

**6:26**
Jas 4:4

### Jesus Teaches about Loving Enemies (57/Matthew 5:43-48)

<sup>27</sup> "But to you who are willing to listen, I say, love your enemies! Do good to those who hate you. <sup>28</sup> Bless those who curse you. Pray for those who hurt you. <sup>29</sup> If someone slaps you on one cheek, offer the other cheek also. If someone demands your coat, offer your shirt also. <sup>30</sup> Give to anyone who asks; and when things are taken away from you, don't try to get them back. <sup>31</sup> Do to others as you would like them to do to you.

**6:27**
Prov 25:21
Rom 12:20

**6:28**
Rom 12:14

**6:30**
Deut 15:7-8, 10

<sup>32</sup> "If you love only those who love you, why should you get credit for that? Even sinners love those who love them! <sup>33</sup> And if you do good only to those who do good to you, why should you get credit? Even sinners do that much! <sup>34</sup> And if you lend money only to those who can repay you, why should you get credit? Even sinners will lend to other sinners for a full return.

**6:31**
Matt 7:12

**6:33-35**
Lev 25:35-36

<sup>35</sup> "Love your enemies! Do good to them. Lend to them without expecting to be repaid. Then your reward from heaven will be very great, and you will truly be acting as children of the Most High, for he is kind to those who are unthankful and wicked. <sup>36</sup> You must be compassionate, just as your Father is compassionate.

**6:36**
Matt 5:48

### Jesus Teaches about Judging Others (63/Matthew 7:1-6)

<sup>37</sup> "Do not judge others, and you will not be judged. Do not condemn others, or it will all come back against you. Forgive others, and you will be forgiven. <sup>38</sup> Give, and you will receive. Your gift will return to you in full—pressed down, shaken together to make room for more, running over, and poured into your lap. The amount you give will determine the amount you get back.*"

**6:38**
Ps 79:12
Mark 4:24

<sup>39</sup> Then Jesus gave the following illustration: "Can one blind person lead another? Won't they both fall into a ditch? <sup>40</sup> Students* are not greater than their teacher. But the student who is fully trained will become like the teacher.

**6:39**
Matt 15:14

**6:40**
Matt 10:24-25
John 13:16; 15:20

<sup>41</sup> "And why worry about a speck in your friend's eye* when you have a log in your own? <sup>42</sup> How can you think of saying, 'Friend,* let me help you get rid of that speck in your eye,' when you can't see past the log in your own eye? Hypocrite! First get rid of the log in your own eye; then you will see well enough to deal with the speck in your friend's eye.

### Jesus Teaches about Fruit in People's Lives (66/Matthew 7:15-20)

<sup>43</sup> "A good tree can't produce bad fruit, and a bad tree can't produce good fruit. <sup>44</sup> A tree is identified by its fruit. Figs are never gathered from thornbushes, and grapes are not picked

**6:44**
Matt 12:33

**6:38** Or *The measure you give will be the measure you get back.*  **6:40** Or *Disciples.*  **6:41** Greek *your brother's eye;* also in 6:42.  **6:42** Greek *Brother.*

---

**6:26** Many false prophets lived during Old Testament times. They were praised by kings and crowds because their predictions—prosperity and victory in war—were exactly what the people wanted to hear. But popularity is no guarantee of truth, and human flattery does not bring God's approval. Sadness lies ahead for those who chase after the crowd's praise rather than God's truth.

**6:27** The Jews despised the Romans because they oppressed God's people, but Jesus told the people to love these enemies. Such words turned many away from Christ. Jesus wasn't talking about having affection for enemies; he was talking about an act of the will. You can't "fall into" this kind of love—it takes conscious effort. Loving our enemies means acting in their best interests. We can pray for them, and we can think of ways to help them. Jesus loves the whole world, even though the world is in rebellion against God. Jesus asks us to follow his example by loving our enemies. Grant your enemies the same respect and rights as you desire for yourself.

**6:37, 38** A forgiving spirit demonstrates that a person has received God's forgiveness. Jesus used the picture of measuring grain in a basket to ensure the full amount. If we are critical rather than compassionate, we will also receive criticism. If we treat others generously, graciously, and compassionately, however, these qualities will come back to us in full measure. We are to love others, not judge them.

**6:39, 40** Make sure you're following the right teachers and leaders, because you will go no farther than they do. Look for leaders who will show you more about faith and whose guidance you can trust.

**6:41** Jesus doesn't mean we should ignore wrongdoing, but we should not be so worried about others' sins that we overlook our own. We often rationalize our sins by pointing out the same mistakes in others. What kinds of specks in others' eyes are the easiest for you to criticize? Remember your own "logs" when you feel like criticizing, and you may find that you have less to say.

**6:42** We should not be so afraid of the label *hypocrite* that we stand still in our Christian life, hiding our faith and making no attempts to grow. A person who tries to do right but often fails is not a hypocrite. Neither are those who fulfill their duty even when they don't feel like doing it. Often it is necessary and good to set aside our desires in order to do what needs to be done. It is not hypocrisy to be weak in faith. A hypocrite is a person who only puts on religious behavior in order to gain attention, approval, or admiration from others.

**6:45** Jesus reminds us that our speech and actions reveal our true underlying beliefs, attitudes, and motivations. The good impressions we try to make cannot last if we are being deceptive. What is in your heart will come out in your speech and behavior.

from bramble bushes. 45 A good person produces good things from the treasury of a good heart, and an evil person produces evil things from the treasury of an evil heart. What you say flows from what is in your heart.

### Jesus Teaches about Building on a Solid Foundation (67/Matthew 7:21-29)

**6:46**
Mal 1:6
Matt 7:21

46 "So why do you keep calling me 'Lord, Lord!' when you don't do what I say? 47 I will show you what it's like when someone comes to me, listens to my teaching, and then follows it. 48 It is like a person building a house who digs deep and lays the foundation on solid rock. When the floodwaters rise and break against that house, it stands firm because it is well built. 49 But anyone who hears and doesn't obey is like a person who builds a house without a foundation. When the floods sweep down against that house, it will collapse into a heap of ruins."

### A Roman Officer Demonstrates Faith (68/Matthew 8:5-13)

**7:2**
John 4:47

**7** When Jesus had finished saying all this to the people, he returned to Capernaum. 2 At that time the highly valued slave of a Roman officer* was sick and near death. 3 When the officer heard about Jesus, he sent some respected Jewish elders to ask him to come and heal his slave. 4 So they earnestly begged Jesus to help the man. "If anyone deserves your help, he does," they said, 5 "for he loves the Jewish people and even built a synagogue for us."

**7:5**
Acts 10:2

6 So Jesus went with them. But just before they arrived at the house, the officer sent some friends to say, "Lord, don't trouble yourself by coming to my home, for I am not worthy of such an honor. 7 I am not even worthy to come and meet you. Just say the word from where you are, and my servant will be healed. 8 I know this because I am under the authority of my superior officers, and I have authority over my soldiers. I only need to say, 'Go,' and they go, or 'Come,' and they come. And if I say to my slaves, 'Do this,' they do it."

**7:7**
Ps 107:20

9 When Jesus heard this, he was amazed. Turning to the crowd that was following him, he said, "I tell you, I haven't seen faith like this in all Israel!" 10 And when the officer's friends returned to his house, they found the slave completely healed.

**7:2** Greek *a centurion;* similarly in 7:6.

---

**6:46-49** Why would people build a house without a foundation? Perhaps to save time and avoid the hard work of preparing the stone. Possibly because the waterfront scenery is more attractive or because beach houses have higher social status than cliff houses. Perhaps because they want to join their friends who have already settled in sandy areas. Maybe because they haven't heard about the violent storms coming, because they have discounted the reports, or because they think disaster can't happen to them. Whatever their reason, those with no foundation are shortsighted, and they will be sorry. Obeying God is like building a house on a strong, solid foundation that stands firm when storms come. When life is calm, our foundations don't seem to matter. But when crises come, our foundations are tested. Be sure your life is built on the solid foundation of knowing and trusting Jesus Christ.

**7:1ff** This passage marks a turning point in Luke's account of Jesus' ministry. Up to this point, Jesus has dealt exclusively with the Jews; here he begins to include the Gentiles. Notice who the main characters are in this short drama: the Jewish elders, a Roman officer, and the officer's slave—very different racial and religious backgrounds, and vastly different standings on the social ladder. Jesus broke through all those barriers, all the way to the sick man's need. The gospel travels well across ethnic, racial, national, and religious barriers. Are you willing to work through them as well? Jesus was no respecter of artificial divisions, and we should follow his example. Reach out to those whom Jesus came to save.

**7:2** This Roman officer was a centurion, meaning he was a captain in charge of 100 men. The officer heard about Jesus, so obviously also heard about Jesus' healing power. He sent a request through some of the Jewish elders on behalf of his slave. He may have heard about the healing of the Roman official's son (which probably occurred earlier, see John 4:46-54). He knew Jesus had the power to heal his slave.

**7:3** Matthew 8:5 says the Roman officer visited Jesus himself, while Luke 7:3 says he sent Jewish elders to present his request to Jesus. In those days, dealing with a person's messengers was

considered the same as dealing with the one who had sent them. Thus, in dealing with the messengers, Jesus was dealing with the officer. For his Jewish audience, Matthew emphasized the Roman soldier's faith. For his Gentile audience, Luke highlighted the good relationship between the Jewish elders and the Roman officer. This army captain daily delegated work and sent groups on missions, so this was how he chose to get his message to Jesus.

**7:9** The Roman officer didn't come to Jesus, and he didn't expect Jesus to come to him. Just as this officer did not need to be present to have his orders carried out, so Jesus didn't need to be present to heal. The officer's faith was especially amazing because he was a Gentile who had not been brought up to know a loving God. Hence Jesus' comment.

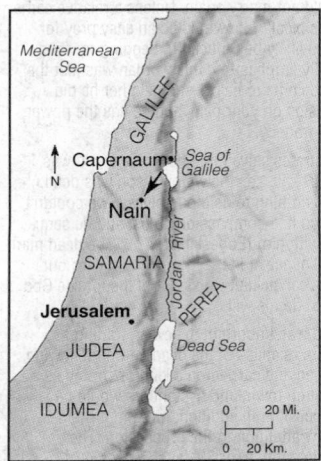

### JESUS RAISES A WIDOW'S SON FROM THE DEAD

Jesus traveled to Nain and met a funeral procession leaving the village. A widow's only son had died, but Jesus brought the young man back to life. This miracle, recorded only in Luke, reveals Jesus' compassion for people's needs.

## Jesus Raises a Widow's Son from the Dead (69)

[11]Soon afterward Jesus went with his disciples to the village of Nain, and a large crowd followed him. [12]A funeral procession was coming out as he approached the village gate. The young man who had died was a widow's only son, and a large crowd from the village was with her. [13]When the Lord saw her, his heart overflowed with compassion. "Don't cry!" he said. [14]Then he walked over to the coffin and touched it, and the bearers stopped. "Young man," he said, "I tell you, get up." [15]Then the dead boy sat up and began to talk! And Jesus gave him back to his mother.

[16]Great fear swept the crowd, and they praised God, saying, "A mighty prophet has risen among us," and "God has visited his people today." [17]And the news about Jesus spread throughout Judea and the surrounding countryside.

**7:11-16**
1 Kgs 17:17-24
2 Kgs 4:32-37

**7:13**
Luke 8:52

**7:14**
Luke 8:54
John 11:43
Acts 9:40

**7:16**
Luke 1:65-68

## Jesus Eases John's Doubt (70/Matthew 11:1-19)

[18]The disciples of John the Baptist told John about everything Jesus was doing. So John called for two of his disciples, [19]and he sent them to the Lord to ask him, "Are you the Messiah we've been expecting,* or should we keep looking for someone else?"

[20]John's two disciples found Jesus and said to him, "John the Baptist sent us to ask, 'Are you the Messiah we've been expecting, or should we keep looking for someone else?'"

[21]At that very time, Jesus cured many people of their diseases, illnesses, and evil spirits, and he restored sight to many who were blind. [22]Then he told John's disciples, "Go back to John and tell him what you have seen and heard—the blind see, the lame walk, the lepers are cured, the deaf hear, the dead are raised to life, and the Good News is being preached to the poor. [23]And tell him, 'God blesses those who do not turn away because of me.*'"

[24]After John's disciples left, Jesus began talking about him to the crowds. "What kind of man did you go into the wilderness to see? Was he a weak reed, swayed by every breath of wind? [25]Or were you expecting to see a man dressed in expensive clothes? No, people who wear beautiful clothes and live in luxury are found in palaces. [26]Were you looking for a prophet? Yes, and he is more than a prophet. [27]John is the man to whom the Scriptures refer when they say,

**7:19**
Mal 3:1-3

**7:22**
†Isa 29:18-19;
35:5-6;
42:18; 61:1
Luke 4:18

**7:26**
Luke 1:76

**7:27**
†Exod 23:20
†Mal 3:1

'Look, I am sending my messenger ahead of you,
    and he will prepare your way before you.'*

[28]I tell you, of all who have ever lived, none is greater than John. Yet even the least person in the Kingdom of God is greater than he is!"

**7:28**
Luke 1:15

**7:19** Greek *Are you the one who is coming?* Also in 7:20.   **7:23** Or *who are not offended by me.*   **7:27** Mal 3:1.

---

**7:11-15** The widow's situation was serious. She had lost her husband, and now her only son had died—her last means of support. The crowd of mourners would go home, and she would be left penniless and alone. The widow was probably past the age of childbearing and would not marry again. Unless a relative came to her aid, her future was bleak. She would be an easy prey for swindlers, and she would likely be reduced to begging for food. In fact, as Luke repeatedly emphasizes, this woman was just the kind of person Jesus had come to help—and help her he did. Jesus has great compassion on your pain, and he has the power to bring hope out of any tragedy.

**7:11-17** This story illustrates salvation. The whole world was dead in sin (Ephesians 2:1), just as the widow's son was dead. Being dead, we could do nothing to help ourselves—we couldn't even ask for help. But God had compassion on us, and he sent Jesus to raise us to life with him (Ephesians 2:4-7). The dead man did not earn his second chance at life, and we cannot earn our new life in Christ. But we can accept God's gift of life, praise God for it, and use our lives to do his will.

**7:12** Honoring the dead was important in Jewish tradition. A funeral procession, with relatives of the dead person following the body that was wrapped and carried on a kind of stretcher, would make its way through town, and bystanders would be expected to join the procession. In addition, hired mourners would cry aloud and draw attention to the procession. The family's mourning would continue for 30 days.

**7:16** The people thought of Jesus as a prophet because, like the Old Testament prophets, he boldly proclaimed God's message and sometimes raised the dead. Both Elijah and Elisha raised children from the dead (1 Kings 17:17-24; 2 Kings 4:18-37). The people were correct in thinking that Jesus was a prophet, but he is much more—he was God himself.

**7:18-23** John was confused because the reports he received about Jesus were unexpected and incomplete. John's doubts were natural, and Jesus didn't rebuke him for them. Instead, he responded in a way that John would understand: Jesus explained that he had accomplished what the Messiah was supposed to accomplish. God can handle our doubts, and he welcomes our questions. Do you have questions about Jesus—about who he is or what he expects of you? Admit them to yourself and to God, and begin looking for answers. Only as you face your doubts honestly can you begin to resolve them.

**7:20-22** The proofs listed here for Jesus being the Messiah are significant. They consist of observable deeds, not theories—actions that Jesus' contemporaries saw and reported for us to read today. The prophets had said that the Messiah would do these very acts (see Isaiah 35:5, 6; 61:1). These physical proofs helped John—and will help all of us—to recognize who Jesus is.

**7:28** Of all people, no one fulfilled his God-given purpose better than John. Yet in God's Kingdom, all who come after John have a greater spiritual heritage because they have clearer knowledge of the purpose of Jesus' death and resurrection. John was the last to

**7:29-30**
Matt 21:32
Luke 3:7, 12

29 When they heard this, all the people—even the tax collectors—agreed that God's way was right,* for they had been baptized by John. 30 But the Pharisees and experts in religious law rejected God's plan for them, for they had refused John's baptism.

31 "To what can I compare the people of this generation?" Jesus asked. "How can I describe them? 32 They are like children playing a game in the public square. They complain to their friends,

'We played wedding songs,
    and you didn't dance,
so we played funeral songs,
    and you didn't weep.'

**7:33**
Luke 1:15

**7:35**
1 Cor 1:24

33 For John the Baptist didn't spend his time eating bread or drinking wine, and you say, 'He's possessed by a demon.' 34 The Son of Man,* on the other hand, feasts and drinks, and you say, 'He's a glutton and a drunkard, and a friend of tax collectors and other sinners!' 35 But wisdom is shown to be right by the lives of those who follow it.*"

### A Sinful Woman Anoints Jesus' Feet (72)

**7:36-50**
Matt 26:6-13
Mark 14:3-9
John 12:1-8

**7:37**
Luke 8:2

36 One of the Pharisees asked Jesus to have dinner with him, so Jesus went to his home and sat down to eat.* 37 When a certain immoral woman from that city heard he was eating there, she brought a beautiful alabaster jar filled with expensive perfume. 38 Then she knelt behind him at his feet, weeping. Her tears fell on his feet, and she wiped them off with her hair. Then she kept kissing his feet and putting perfume on them.

**7:39**
Matt 21:11

39 When the Pharisee who had invited him saw this, he said to himself, "If this man were a prophet, he would know what kind of woman is touching him. She's a sinner!"

40 Then Jesus answered his thoughts. "Simon," he said to the Pharisee, "I have something to say to you."

"Go ahead, Teacher," Simon replied.

**7:42**
Matt 18:27
Col 2:13

41 Then Jesus told him this story: "A man loaned money to two people—500 pieces of silver* to one and 50 pieces to the other. 42 But neither of them could repay him, so he kindly forgave them both, canceling their debts. Who do you suppose loved him more after that?"

43 Simon answered, "I suppose the one for whom he canceled the larger debt."

**7:44**
Gen 18:4
1 Tim 5:10

"That's right," Jesus said. 44 Then he turned to the woman and said to Simon, "Look at this woman kneeling here. When I entered your home, you didn't offer me water to wash the dust from my feet, but she has washed them with her tears and wiped them with her hair.

**7:29** Or *praised God for his justice.* **7:34** "Son of Man" is a title Jesus used for himself. **7:35** Or *But wisdom is justified by all her children.* **7:36** Or *and reclined.* **7:41** Greek *500 denarii.* A denarius was equivalent to a laborer's full day's wage.

---

function like the Old Testament prophets, the last to prepare the people for the coming messianic age. Jesus was not contrasting the man John with individual Christians; he was contrasting life before Christ with life in the fullness of Christ's Kingdom.

**7:29, 30** The common people, including the tax collectors (who embodied evil in most people's minds) heard John's message and repented. In contrast, the Pharisees and experts in the law—religious leaders—rejected his words. Wanting to live their own way, they justified their own point of view and refused to listen to other ideas. They "rejected God's plan for them." They were so close to Jesus, and yet so far away. The truth stood before them, and they rejected it. What have you done with the truth you read in God's Word?

**7:31-35** The religious leaders hated both John and Jesus, but they did not bother to be consistent in their faultfinding. They criticized John the Baptist because he fasted and drank no wine; they criticized Jesus because he ate heartily and drank wine with tax collectors and sinners. Their real objection to both men, of course, had nothing to do with dietary habits. What the Pharisees and experts in the law couldn't stand was being exposed for their hypocrisy.

**7:33, 34** The Pharisees weren't troubled by their inconsistency toward John the Baptist and Jesus. They were good at justifying their "wisdom." Most of us can find compelling reasons to do or believe whatever suits our purposes. If we do not examine our

ideas in the light of God's truth, however, we may be just as obviously self-serving as the Pharisees.

**7:36ff** A similar incident occurred later in Jesus' ministry (see Matthew 26:6-13; Mark 14:3-9; John 12:1-11).

**7:38** Although the woman was not an invited guest, she entered the house anyway and knelt behind Jesus at his feet. In Jesus' day, it was customary to recline while eating. Dinner guests would lie on couches with their heads near the table, propping themselves up on one elbow and stretching their feet out behind them. The woman could easily anoint Jesus' feet without approaching the table.

**7:44ff** Again Luke contrasts the Pharisees with sinners—and again the sinners come out ahead. Simon had committed several social errors in neglecting to wash Jesus' feet (a courtesy extended to guests because sandaled feet got very dirty), anoint his head with oil, and offer him the kiss of greeting. Did Simon perhaps feel that he was too good for Jesus? Was he trying to give Jesus a subtle put-down? Whatever the case, the contrast is vivid. The sinful woman lavished tears, expensive perfume, and kisses on her Savior. In this story it is the grateful immoral woman, and not the religious leader, whose sins were forgiven. Although God's grace through faith is what saves us, and not acts of love or generosity, this woman's act demonstrated her true faith, and Jesus honored her.

[45] You didn't greet me with a kiss, but from the time I first came in, she has not stopped kissing my feet. [46] You neglected the courtesy of olive oil to anoint my head, but she has anointed my feet with rare perfume.

[47] "I tell you, her sins—and they are many—have been forgiven, so she has shown me much love. But a person who is forgiven little shows only little love." [48] Then Jesus said to the woman, "Your sins are forgiven."

[49] The men at the table said among themselves, "Who is this man, that he goes around forgiving sins?"

[50] And Jesus said to the woman, "Your faith has saved you; go in peace."

### Women Accompany Jesus and the Disciples (73)

**8** Soon afterward Jesus began a tour of the nearby towns and villages, preaching and announcing the Good News about the Kingdom of God. He took his twelve disciples with him, [2] along with some women who had been cured of evil spirits and diseases. Among them were Mary Magdalene, from whom he had cast out seven demons; [3] Joanna, the wife of Chuza, Herod's business manager; Susanna; and many others who were contributing from their own resources to support Jesus and his disciples.

### Jesus Tells the Parable of the Four Soils (77/Matthew 13:1-9; Mark 4:1-9)

[4] One day Jesus told a story in the form of a parable to a large crowd that had gathered from many towns to hear him: [5] "A farmer went out to plant his seed. As he scattered it across his field, some seed fell on a footpath, where it was stepped on, and the birds ate it. [6] Other seed fell among rocks. It began to grow, but the plant soon wilted and died for lack of moisture. [7] Other seed fell among thorns that grew up with it and choked out the tender plants. [8] Still other seed fell on fertile soil. This seed grew and produced a crop that was a hundred times as much as had been planted!" When he had said this, he called out, "Anyone with ears to hear should listen and understand."

### Jesus Explains the Parable of the Four Soils (78/Matthew 13:10-23; Mark 4:10-25)

[9] His disciples asked him what this parable meant. [10] He replied, "You are permitted to understand the secrets* of the Kingdom of God. But I use parables to teach the others so that the Scriptures might be fulfilled:

'When they look, they won't really see.
    When they hear, they won't understand.'*

**8:10a** Greek *mysteries.*   **8:10b** Isa 6:9 (Greek version).

---

**Cross-references (margin):**

**7:45** Rom 16:16; 1 Cor 16:20; 2 Cor 13:12; 1 Thes 5:26; 1 Pet 5:14

**7:46** 2 Sam 12:20; Ps 23:5

**7:48-49** Luke 5:20-21

**7:50** Matt 9:22

**8:1** Matt 4:23

**8:2** Matt 27:55-56; Mark 15:40-41; Luke 23:49

**8:3** Matt 14:1

**8:10** †Isa 6:9-10

---

**7:47** Overflowing love is the natural response to forgiveness and the appropriate consequence of faith. But only those who realize the depth of their sin can appreciate the complete forgiveness that God offers them. Jesus has rescued all of his followers, whether they were once extremely wicked or conventionally good, from eternal death. Do you appreciate the wideness of God's mercy? Are you grateful for his forgiveness?

**7:49, 50** The Pharisees believed that only God could forgive sins, so they wondered why this man, Jesus, was saying that the woman's sins were forgiven. They did not grasp the fact that Jesus was indeed God. (See also 5:17-26 and notes there.)

**8:2, 3** Jesus lifted women up from degradation and servitude to the joy of fellowship and service. In Jewish culture, women were not supposed to learn from rabbis. By allowing these women to travel with him, Jesus was showing that all people are equal under God. These women supported Jesus' ministry with their own money. They owed a great debt to him because he had driven demons out of some and had healed others.

**8:2, 3** Here we catch a glimpse of a few of the people behind the scenes in Jesus' ministry. The ministry of those in the foreground is often supported by those whose work is less visible but just as essential. Offer your resources to God, whether or not you will be on center stage.

**8:4** Jesus often communicated spiritual truth through short stories (called parables). These stories describe a familiar object or situation and give it a startling new twist. By linking the known with the hidden and forcing listeners to think, parables can point to spiritual truths. A parable compels listeners to discover the truth for themselves, and it conceals the truth from those too lazy or dull to understand it. In reading Jesus' parables, we must be careful not to read too much into them. Most have only one point and one meaning.

**8:5** Why would a farmer allow precious seed to land on the footpath, on rocks, or among thorns? This is not an irresponsible farmer scattering seeds at random. He is using the acceptable method of seeding a large field—tossing it by handfuls as he walks through the field. His goal is to get as much seed as possible to take root in good soil, but waste is inevitable as some falls or is blown into less productive areas. That some of the seed produces no crop is not the fault of the faithful farmer or of the seed. The yield depends on the condition of the soil where the seed falls. It is our responsibility to spread the seed (God's message), but we should not give up when some of our efforts fail. Remember, not every seed falls on good soil.

**8:10** Why didn't the crowds understand Jesus' words? Perhaps they were looking for a military leader or a political Messiah and could not fit his gentle teaching style into their preconceived idea. Perhaps they were afraid of pressure from religious leaders and did not want to look too deeply into Jesus' words. God told Isaiah that people would listen without understanding and watch without learning anything (Isaiah 6:9), and that kind of reaction confronted Jesus. The story of the farmer was an accurate picture of the people's reaction to the rest of his stories.

**8:11**
1 Pet 1:23

**8:12**
1 Cor 1:21

**8:14**
Matt 19:23
1 Tim 6:9, 10
2 Tim 4:10

**8:16**
Matt 5:15
Luke 11:33

**8:17**
Matt 10:26

**8:18**
Matt 25:29
Luke 19:26

11 "This is the meaning of the parable: The seed is God's word.12 The seeds that fell on the footpath represent those who hear the message, only to have the devil come and take it away from their hearts and prevent them from believing and being saved.13 The seeds on the rocky soil represent those who hear the message and receive it with joy. But since they don't have deep roots, they believe for a while, then they fall away when they face temptation. 14 The seeds that fell among the thorns represent those who hear the message, but all too quickly the message is crowded out by the cares and riches and pleasures of this life. And so they never grow into maturity.15 And the seeds that fell on the good soil represent honest, good-hearted people who hear God's word, cling to it, and patiently produce a huge harvest.

16 "No one lights a lamp and then covers it with a bowl or hides it under a bed. A lamp is placed on a stand, where its light can be seen by all who enter the house.17 For all that is secret will eventually be brought into the open, and everything that is concealed will be brought to light and made known to all.

18 "So pay attention to how you hear. To those who listen to my teaching, more understanding will be given. But for those who are not listening, even what they think they understand will be taken away from them."

### Jesus Describes His True Family (76/Matthew 12:46-50; Mark 3:31-35)
19 Then Jesus' mother and brothers came to see him, but they couldn't get to him because of the crowd. 20 Someone told Jesus, "Your mother and your brothers are outside, and they want to see you."

21 Jesus replied, "My mother and my brothers are all those who hear God's word and obey it."

---

**JESUS AND WOMEN**

As a non-Jew recording the words and works of Jesus' life, Luke demonstrates a special sensitivity to other "outsiders" with whom Jesus came into contact. For instance, Luke records five events involving women that are not mentioned in the other Gospels. In first-century Jewish culture, women were usually treated as second-class citizens with few of the rights men had. But Jesus crossed those barriers, and Luke showed the special care Jesus had for women. Jesus treated all people with equal respect. The above passages tell of his encounters with women.

---

**8:11-15** "Footpath" people, like many of the religious leaders, refuse to believe God's message. "Rocky soil" people, like many in the crowds who followed Jesus, believe his message but never get around to doing anything about it. "Thorn patch" people, overcome by worries and the lure of materialism, leave no room in their lives for God. "Good soil" people, in contrast to all the other groups, follow Jesus no matter what the cost. Which type of soil are you?

**8:16, 17** When the light of the truth about Jesus illuminates us, we have the duty to shine that light to help others. Our witness for Christ should be public, not hidden. We should not keep the benefits for ourselves alone but pass them on to others. In order to be helpful, we need to be well placed. Seek opportunities to shine your light when unbelievers need help to see.

**8:18** Applying God's Word helps us grow. This is a principle of growth in physical, mental, and spiritual life. For example,

a muscle, when exercised, will grow stronger, but an unused muscle will grow weak and flabby. If you are not growing stronger, you are growing weaker; it is impossible for you to stand still. How are you using what God has taught you?

**8:21** Jesus' true family is comprised of those who hear *and* obey his words. Hearing without obeying is not enough. As Jesus loved his mother (see John 19:25-27), so he loves us. Christ offers us an intimate family relationship with him (Romans 8:14-16).

### Jesus Calms the Storm (87/Matthew 8:23-27; Mark 4:35-41)

22One day Jesus said to his disciples, "Let's cross to the other side of the lake." So they got into a boat and started out. 23As they sailed across, Jesus settled down for a nap. But soon a fierce storm came down on the lake. The boat was filling with water, and they were in real danger.

24The disciples went and woke him up, shouting, "Master, Master, we're going to drown!"

When Jesus woke up, he rebuked the wind and the raging waves. Suddenly the storm stopped and all was calm. 25Then he asked them, "Where is your faith?"

The disciples were terrified and amazed. "Who is this man?" they asked each other. "When he gives a command, even the wind and waves obey him!"

### Jesus Sends Demons into a Herd of Pigs (88/Matthew 8:28-34; Mark 5:1-20)

26So they arrived in the region of the Gerasenes,* across the lake from Galilee. 27As Jesus was climbing out of the boat, a man who was possessed by demons came out to meet him. For a long time he had been homeless and naked, living in a cemetery outside the town.

28As soon as he saw Jesus, he shrieked and fell down in front of him. Then he screamed, "Why are you interfering with me, Jesus, Son of the Most High God? Please, I beg you, don't torture me!" 29For Jesus had already commanded the evil* spirit to come out of him. This spirit had often taken control of the man. Even when he was placed under guard and put in chains and shackles, he simply broke them and rushed out into the wilderness, completely under the demon's power.

**8:28**
Matt 8:29
Mark 1:23-24

30Jesus demanded, "What is your name?"

"Legion," he replied, for he was filled with many demons. 31The demons kept begging Jesus not to send them into the bottomless pit.*

**8:31**
Rev 9:1-2, 11; 20:3

32There happened to be a large herd of pigs feeding on the hillside nearby, and the demons begged him to let them enter into the pigs.

So Jesus gave them permission. 33Then the demons came out of the man and entered the pigs, and the entire herd plunged down the steep hillside into the lake and drowned.

**8:26** Other manuscripts read *Gadarenes;* still others read *Gergesenes;* also in 8:37. See Matt 8:28; Mark 5:1.
**8:29** Greek *unclean.*   **8:31** Or *the abyss,* or *the underworld.*

---

**8:23** The Sea of Galilee (actually a large lake) is even today the scene of fierce storms, sometimes with waves as high as 20 feet. Jesus' disciples were not frightened without cause. Even though several of them were expert fishermen and knew how to handle a boat, their peril was real.

**8:23-25** When caught in the storms of life, it is easy to think that God has lost control and that we're at the mercy of the winds of fate. In reality, God is sovereign. He controls the history of the world as well as our personal destiny. Just as Jesus calmed the waves, he can calm whatever storms you may face.

**HEALING A DEMON-POSSESSED MAN**

As he traveled through Galilee, Jesus told many parables and met many people, as recorded in Matthew and Mark. Later, from Capernaum, Jesus and the disciples set out in a boat, only to encounter a fierce storm. Jesus calmed the storm and, when they landed, exorcised a "legion" of demons.

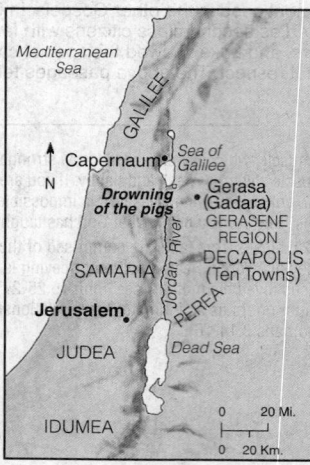

Mediterranean Sea
GALILEE
Capernaum
Sea of Galilee
N
Drowning of the pigs
Gerasa (Gadara)
GERASENE REGION
DECAPOLIS (Ten Towns)
Jordan River
SAMARIA
PEREA
Jerusalem
JUDEA
Dead Sea
IDUMEA
0    20 Mi.
0    20 Km.

**8:26** The region of the Gerasenes was a Gentile region southeast of the Sea of Galilee, location of the Ten Towns. These were Greek cities that belonged to no country and were self-governing. Although Jews would not have raised pigs because the Jewish religion labeled them unclean, the Gentiles had no such aversion.

**8:27, 28** These demons recognized Jesus and his authority immediately. They knew who Jesus was and what his great power could do to them. Demons, Satan's messengers, are powerful and destructive. Still active today, they attempt to distort and destroy people's relationship with God. Demons and demon possession are real. It is vital that believers recognize the power of Satan and his demons, but we shouldn't let curiosity lead us to get involved with demonic forces (Deuteronomy 18:10-12). Demons are powerless against those who trust in Jesus. If we resist the devil, he will leave us alone (James 4:7).

**8:29-31** The demons begged Jesus to spare them from the bottomless pit, which is also mentioned in Revelation 9:1 and 20:1-3 as the place of confinement for Satan and his messengers. The demons, of course, knew all about this place of confinement, and they didn't want to go there.

**8:30** The demon's name was Legion. A legion was the largest unit in the Roman army, having between 3,000 and 6,000 soldiers. The man was possessed by not one but many demons.

**8:33** Why didn't Jesus just destroy these demons—or send them to the bottomless pit? Because the time for such work had not yet come. He healed many people of the destructive effects of demon possession, but he did not yet destroy demons. The same question could be asked today—why doesn't Jesus stop all the evil in the world? His time for that has not yet come. But it will come. The book of Revelation portrays the future victory of Jesus over Satan, his demons, and all evil.

**8:33-37** A man had been freed from the devil's power, but the people in the town thought only about their livestock. People have

³⁴When the herdsmen saw it, they fled to the nearby town and the surrounding country-side, spreading the news as they ran. ³⁵People rushed out to see what had happened. A crowd soon gathered around Jesus, and they saw the man who had been freed from the demons. He was sitting at Jesus' feet, fully clothed and perfectly sane, and they were all afraid. ³⁶Then those who had seen what happened told the others how the demon-possessed man had been healed. ³⁷And all the people in the region of the Gerasenes begged Jesus to go away and leave them alone, for a great wave of fear swept over them.

So Jesus returned to the boat and left, crossing back to the other side of the lake. ³⁸The man who had been freed from the demons begged to go with him. But Jesus sent him home, saying, ³⁹ "No, go back to your family, and tell them everything God has done for you." So he went all through the town proclaiming the great things Jesus had done for him.

### Jesus Heals a Bleeding Woman and Restores a Girl to Life
**(89**/Matthew 9:18-26; Mark 5:21-43)
⁴⁰On the other side of the lake the crowds welcomed Jesus, because they had been waiting for him. ⁴¹Then a man named Jairus, a leader of the local synagogue, came and fell at Jesus' feet, pleading with him to come home with him. ⁴²His only daughter,* who was about twelve years old, was dying.

As Jesus went with him, he was surrounded by the crowds. ⁴³A woman in the crowd had suffered for twelve years with constant bleeding,* and she could find no cure. ⁴⁴Coming up behind Jesus, she touched the fringe of his robe. Immediately, the bleeding stopped.

⁴⁵ "Who touched me?" Jesus asked.

Everyone denied it, and Peter said, "Master, this whole crowd is pressing up against you."

⁴⁶But Jesus said, "Someone deliberately touched me, for I felt healing power go out from me." ⁴⁷When the woman realized that she could not stay hidden, she began to tremble and fell to her knees in front of him. The whole crowd heard her explain why she had touched him and that she had been immediately healed. ⁴⁸ "Daughter," he said to her, "your faith has made you well. Go in peace."

⁴⁹While he was still speaking to her, a messenger arrived from the home of Jairus, the leader of the synagogue. He told him, "Your daughter is dead. There's no use troubling the Teacher now."

**8:42** Or *His only child, a daughter.*    **8:43** Some manuscripts add *having spent everything she had on doctors.*

---

**8:37**
Acts 16:39

**8:43**
Lev 15:25-30

**8:46**
Luke 5:17; 6:19

**8:48**
Matt 9:22
Mark 5:34
Luke 7:50; 17:19;
18:42

---

always tended to value financial gain above needy people. Much injustice and oppression, both at home and abroad, is the direct result of some individual's or company's urge to get rich. People are continually being sacrificed to the god of money. Don't think more highly of "pigs" than of people.

**8:38, 39** Often Jesus would ask those he healed to be quiet about the healing, but he urged this man to return to his family and tell them what God had done for him. Why? (1) Jesus knew the man would be an effective witness to those who knew his previous condition and could attest to the miraculous healing. (2) Jesus wanted to expand his ministry by introducing his message into this Gentile area. (3) Jesus knew that the Gentiles, since they were not expecting a Messiah, would not divert his ministry by trying to crown him king. (In fact, the people in this region had asked him to go away.) When God touches your life, don't be afraid to share the wonderful events with your family and friends.

**8:41** The synagogue was the local center of worship. The synagogue leader was responsible for administration, building maintenance, and worship supervision. It would have been quite unusual for a respected synagogue leader to fall at the feet of an itinerant preacher and beg him to heal his daughter. Jesus honored this man's humble faith (8:50, 54-56).

**8:43-48** Many people surrounded Jesus as he made his way toward Jairus's house. It was virtually impossible to get through the multitude, but one woman fought her way desperately through the crowd in order to touch Jesus. As soon as she did so, she was healed. What a difference there is between the crowds that are curious about Jesus and the few who reach out and touch him! Today, many people are familiar with who Jesus

is, but nothing in their lives is changed by knowing he is God's Son. It is only faith in Christ that releases God's healing power. Are you just curious about God, or do you reach out to him in faith, knowing that his mercy will bring healing to your body, soul, and spirit?

**8:45, 46** Certainly Jesus knew who had touched him—he knew that someone had intentionally touched him in order to receive some sort of healing. Jesus wanted the woman to step forward and identify herself. To let her slip away would have meant a lost opportunity for Jesus to teach her that his cloak did not have magical properties, it had been her faith in him that had healed her. He may also have wanted to teach the crowds a lesson. According to Jewish law, a man who touched a menstruating woman became ceremonially unclean (Leviticus 15:19-28). This was true whether her bleeding was normal or, as in this woman's case, the result of an abnormal condition. To protect themselves from such defilement, Jewish men carefully avoided touching, speaking to, or even looking at women. By contrast, Jesus proclaimed to hundreds of people that this "unclean" woman had touched him—and then he healed her. In Jesus' mind, this suffering woman was not to be overlooked. As God's creation, she deserved attention and respect.

⁵⁰But when Jesus heard what had happened, he said to Jairus, "Don't be afraid. Just have faith, and she will be healed."

⁵¹When they arrived at the house, Jesus wouldn't let anyone go in with him except Peter, John, James, and the little girl's father and mother. ⁵²The house was filled with people weeping and wailing, but he said, "Stop the weeping! She isn't dead; she's only asleep."

⁵³But the crowd laughed at him because they all knew she had died. ⁵⁴Then Jesus took her by the hand and said in a loud voice, "My child, get up!"⁵⁵And at that moment her life* returned, and she immediately stood up! Then Jesus told them to give her something to eat. ⁵⁶Her parents were overwhelmed, but Jesus insisted that they not tell anyone what had happened.

**8:52**
Luke 7:13

**8:54**
Luke 7:14

**8:56**
Matt 8:4
Mark 7:36
Luke 5:14

## Jesus Sends Out the Twelve Disciples (93/Matthew 10:1-15; Mark 6:7-13)

**9** One day Jesus called together his twelve disciples* and gave them power and authority to cast out all demons and to heal all diseases. ²Then he sent them out to tell everyone about the Kingdom of God and to heal the sick. ³ "Take nothing for your journey,"he instructed them. "Don't take a walking stick, a traveler's bag, food, money,* or even a change of clothes.⁴ Wherever you go, stay in the same house until you leave town.⁵ And if a town refuses to welcome you, shake its dust from your feet as you leave to show that you have abandoned those people to their fate."

**9:3**
Luke 10:4; 22:35
**9:4**
Luke 10:5-7
**9:5**
Luke 10:10-11
Acts 13:51

⁶So they began their circuit of the villages, preaching the Good News and healing the sick.

## Herod Kills John the Baptist (95/Matthew 14:1-12; Mark 6:14-29)

⁷When Herod Antipas, the ruler of Galilee,* heard about everything Jesus was doing, he was puzzled. Some were saying that John the Baptist had been raised from the dead. ⁸Others thought Jesus was Elijah or one of the other prophets risen from the dead.

**9:8**
Matt 11:14

**8:55** Or *her spirit.*  **9:1** Greek *the Twelve;* other manuscripts read *the twelve apostles.*  **9:3** Or *silver coins.* **9:7** Greek *Herod the tetrarch.* Herod Antipas was a son of King Herod and was ruler over Galilee.

---

**8:50** Anyone with a child can readily put himself or herself emotionally in Jairus's place. His daughter had died while they were on the way home. Luke did not record it, but the poor man probably cried out in grief. Jesus surely felt the father's very human grief. Jesus said, "Don't be afraid. Just have faith." Again, Luke didn't record Jairus's reaction to these words, but Jairus must have had at least some flicker of hope because he did complete his mission in bringing Jesus to his house. When you experience intense grief over the loss of a loved one, breakup of a marriage, loss of a job, or rejection of a close friend, don't abandon hope. Don't turn away from the one Person who can help you. Do what Jairus did: Don't be afraid; just have faith. Your hope is found in the resurrected Lord, the one with power over life and death.

**8:56** Jesus told the parents not to talk about their daughter's healing because he knew the facts would speak for themselves. Jesus was concerned for his ministry. He did not want to be known as just a miracle worker; he wanted people to listen to his words that could heal their broken spiritual lives.

**9:1-10** Note Jesus' methods of leadership. He empowered his disciples (9:1), gave them specific instructions so they knew what to do (9:3, 4), told them how to deal with tough times (9:5), and held them accountable (9:10). As you lead others, study the Master Leader's pattern. Which of these elements do you need to incorporate into your leadership?

**9:2** Jesus announced his Kingdom by both preaching and healing, and he sent his disciples out to do the same. If he had limited himself to preaching, people might have seen his Kingdom as spiritual only. If he had healed without preaching, people might not have realized the spiritual importance of his mission. Most of his listeners expected a Messiah who would bring wealth and power to their nation; they preferred material benefits to spiritual discernment. The truth about Jesus is that he is both God and man, both spiritual and physical; and the salvation that he offers is both for the soul and the body. Any group or teaching that emphasizes soul at the expense of body, or body at the expense of soul, is in danger of distorting Jesus' Good News.

**9:3, 4** Why were the disciples instructed to depend on others while they went from town to town preaching the Good News?

Their purpose was to blanket Judea with Jesus' message, and by traveling light they could move quickly. Their dependence on others had other good effects as well: (1) It clearly showed that the Messiah had not come to offer wealth to his followers. (2) It forced the disciples to rely on God's power and not on their own provision. (3) It involved the villagers and made them more eager to hear the message. This was an excellent approach for the disciples' short-term mission; it was not intended, however, to be a permanent way of life for them.

**9:4** The disciples were told to stay in only one home in each town because they were not to offend their hosts by moving to a home that was more comfortable or socially prominent. To remain in one home was not a burden for the homeowner, because the disciples' stay in each community was short. (See also 10:7.)

**9:5** Shaking the dust of certain towns from their feet had deep cultural implications. Pious Jews would do this after passing through Gentile cities to show their separation from Gentile practices. If the disciples were to shake the dust of a *Jewish* town from their feet, it would show their separation from Jews who rejected their Messiah. This action also would show that the disciples were not responsible for how the people responded to their message. Neither are we responsible if we have carefully and truthfully presented Christ but our message is rejected. Like the disciples, we must move on to others whom God desires to reach.

**9:7** For more information on Herod Antipas, see his Profile in Mark 6, p. 1629.

**9:7, 8** People found accepting Jesus as the Son of God so difficult that they tried to come up with other solutions—most of which sound quite unbelievable to us. Many thought that Jesus must be someone who had come back to life, perhaps John the Baptist or another prophet. Some suggested that he was Elijah, the great prophet who had not died but had been taken to heaven in a chariot of fire (2 Kings 2:1-11). Very few found the correct answer, as Peter did (9:20). Many people today still have difficulty accepting Jesus as the fully human yet fully divine Son of God. People are still trying to find alternate explanations—a great prophet, a radical political leader, a self-

**9:9**
Luke 23:8

⁹"I beheaded John," Herod said, "so who is this man about whom I hear such stories?" And he kept trying to see him.

*Jesus Feeds Five Thousand* (**96**/Matthew 14:13-21; Mark 6:30-44; John 6:1-15)
¹⁰When the apostles returned, they told Jesus everything they had done. Then he slipped quietly away with them toward the town of Bethsaida. ¹¹But the crowds found out where he was going, and they followed him. He welcomed them and taught them about the Kingdom of God, and he healed those who were sick.

¹²Late in the afternoon the twelve disciples came to him and said, "Send the crowds away to the nearby villages and farms, so they can find food and lodging for the night. There is nothing to eat here in this remote place."

Jesus singled out three of his 12 disciples for special training. James, his brother John, and Peter made up this inner circle. Each eventually played a key role in the early church. Peter became a great speaker, John became a major writer, and James was the first of the 12 disciples to die for his faith.

The fact that his name is always mentioned before John's indicates that James was the older brother. Zebedee, their father, owned a fishing business in which they worked alongside Peter and Andrew. When Peter, Andrew, and John left Galilee to see John the Baptist, James stayed back with the boats and fishing nets. Later, when Jesus called them, James was as eager as his partners to follow.

James enjoyed being in the inner circle of Jesus' disciples, but he misunderstood Jesus' purpose. He and his brother even tried to secure their role in Jesus' Kingdom by asking Jesus to promise them each a special position. Like the other disciples, James had a limited view of what Jesus was doing on earth, picturing only an earthly kingdom that would overthrow Rome and restore Israel's former glory. But above all, James wanted to be with Jesus. He had found the right leader, even though he was still on the wrong timetable. It took Jesus' death and resurrection to correct his view.

James was the first of the 12 disciples to die for the gospel. He was willing to die because he knew Jesus had conquered death, the doorway to eternal life. Our expectations about life will be limited if this life is all we can see. Jesus promised eternal life to those willing to trust him. If we believe this promise, he will give us the courage to stand for him even during dangerous times.

| | |
|---|---|
| **Strengths and accomplishments** | • One of the 12 disciples<br>• One of a special inner circle of three with Peter and John<br>• First of the 12 disciples to be killed for his faith |
| **Weaknesses and mistakes** | • Two outbursts from James indicate struggles with temper (Luke 9:54) and selfishness (Mark 10:37). Both times, he and his brother, John, spoke as one |
| **Lesson from his life** | • Loss of life is not too heavy a price to pay for following Jesus |
| **Vital statistics** | • Where: Galilee<br>• Occupations: Fisherman, disciple<br>• Relatives: Father: Zebedee. Mother: Salome. Brother: John.<br>• Contemporaries: Jesus, Pilate, Herod Agrippa |
| **Key verses** | "Then James and John, the sons of Zebedee, came over and spoke to him. 'Teacher,' they said, 'we want you to do us a favor.' 'What is your request?' he asked. They replied, 'When you sit on your glorious throne, we want to sit in places of honor next to you, one on your right and the other on your left'" (Mark 10:35-37). |

James's story is told in the Gospels. He is also mentioned in Acts 1:13 and 12:2.

deceived rabble-rouser. None of these explanations can account for Jesus' miracles or especially his glorious resurrection. In the end, the attempts to explain away Jesus are far more difficult to believe than the truth.

**9:9** For the story of why Herod had John beheaded, see Mark 6:14-29.

**9:10, 11** Jesus had tried to slip quietly away from the crowds, but they found out where he was going and followed him. Instead of showing impatience at this interruption, Jesus welcomed the people and ministered to their needs. How do you see people who interrupt your schedule—as nuisances or as the reason for your life and ministry?

**9:11** The Kingdom of God was a focal point of Jesus' teaching. He explained that it was not just a future Kingdom; it was among them, embodied in him, the Messiah. Even though the Kingdom will not be complete until Jesus comes again in glory, we do not have to wait to experience it. The Kingdom of God begins in the hearts of those who believe in Jesus (17:21). It is as present with us today as it was with the Judeans over 2,000 years ago.

13But Jesus said, "You feed them."

"But we have only five loaves of bread and two fish," they answered. "Or are you expecting us to go and buy enough food for this whole crowd?" 14For there were about 5,000 men there.

Jesus replied, "Tell them to sit down in groups of about fifty each." 15So the people all sat down. 16Jesus took the five loaves and two fish, looked up toward heaven, and blessed them. Then, breaking the loaves into pieces, he kept giving the bread and fish to the disciples so they could distribute it to the people. 17They all ate as much as they wanted, and afterward, the disciples picked up twelve baskets of leftovers!

**9:17**
2 Kgs 4:44

### Peter Says Jesus Is the Messiah (109/Matthew 16:13-20; Mark 8:27-30)

18One day Jesus left the crowds to pray alone. Only his disciples were with him, and he asked them, "Who do people say I am?"

19"Well," they replied, "some say John the Baptist, some say Elijah, and others say you are one of the other ancient prophets risen from the dead."

20Then he asked them, "But who do you say I am?"

Peter replied, "You are the Messiah* sent from God!"

**9:19**
Luke 9:7-8
**9:20**
John 6:68-69

### Jesus Predicts His Death the First Time (110/Matthew 16:21-28; Mark 8:31–9:1)

21Jesus warned his disciples not to tell anyone who he was. 22 "The Son of Man* must suffer many terrible things," he said. "He will be rejected by the elders, the leading priests, and the teachers of religious law. He will be killed, but on the third day he will be raised from the dead."

23Then he said to the crowd, "If any of you wants to be my follower, you must turn from your selfish ways, take up your cross daily, and follow me. 24If you try to hang on to your life, you will lose it. But if you give up your life for my sake, you will save it. 25And what do you benefit if you gain the whole world but are yourself lost or destroyed? 26If anyone is ashamed of me and my message, the Son of Man will be ashamed of that person when he

**9:23**
Matt 10:38
Luke 14:27
**9:24**
Matt 10:39
Luke 17:33
John 12:25
**9:26**
Matt 10:33
Luke 12:9
2 Tim 2:12

9:20 Or *the Christ. Messiah* (a Hebrew term) and *Christ* (a Greek term) both mean "the anointed one."  9:22 "Son of Man" is a title Jesus used for himself.

---

**9:13, 14** When the disciples expressed concern about where the crowd of thousands would eat, Jesus offered a surprising solution: "You feed them." The disciples protested, focusing their attention on what they didn't have (food and money). Do you think God would ask you to do something that you and he together couldn't handle? Don't let your lack of resources blind you to God's power.

**9:16, 17** Why did Jesus bother to feed these people? He could just as easily have sent them on their way, but Jesus does not ignore needs. He is concerned with every aspect of life—the physical as well as the spiritual. As we work to bring wholeness to people's lives, we must never ignore the fact that all of us have both physical and spiritual needs. It is impossible to minister effectively to one type of need without considering the other.

**9:18-20** The Christian faith goes beyond knowing what others believe. It requires us to hold beliefs for ourselves. When Jesus asks, "Who do you say I am?" he wants us to take a stand. Who do *you* say Jesus is?

**9:21** Jesus told his disciples not to tell anyone that he was the Christ because at this point they didn't fully understand the significance of that confession—nor would anyone else. Everyone still expected the Messiah to come as a conquering king. But even though Jesus was the Messiah, he still had to suffer, be rejected by the leaders, be killed, and rise from the dead. When the disciples saw all this happen to Jesus, they would understand what the Messiah had come to do. Only then would they be equipped to share the Good News that the Messiah had come and brought his Kingdom to people's hearts.

**9:22** This was the turning point in Jesus' instruction to his disciples. From then on he began teaching clearly and specifically what they could expect, so that they would not be surprised when it happened. He explained that he would not *now* be the

conquering Messiah because he first had to suffer, die, and rise again. But one day he would return in great glory to set up his eternal Kingdom.

**9:23** To take up the cross meant to carry one's own cross to the place of crucifixion. Many Galileans had been killed that way by the Romans—and Jesus would face it as well. With this word picture, Christ presented a clear and challenging description of the Christian life. Being his disciple means putting aside selfish desires, shouldering one's "cross" every day, and following him. It is simple and yet so demanding. For the original Twelve, this meant literal suffering and death. For believers today, it means understanding that we belong to him and that we live to serve his purposes. Consider this: Do you think of your relationship with God primarily in terms of what's in it for you (which is considerable) or in terms of what you can do for him? Are you willing to deny yourself, take up your cross daily, and follow him? Anything less is not discipleship; it is merely superficial lip service. (See also the note on 14:27.)

**9:24, 25** If this present life is most important to you, you will do everything you can to protect it. You will not want to do anything that might endanger your safety, health, or comfort. By contrast, if following Jesus is most important, you may find yourself in unsafe, unhealthy, and uncomfortable places. You may risk death, but you will not fear it because you know that Jesus will raise you to eternal life. Nothing material can compensate for the loss of eternal life. Jesus' disciples are not to use their lives on earth merely to please themselves; they should spend their lives serving God and others.

**9:26** Luke's Greek audience would have had difficulty understanding a God who could die, just as Jesus' Jewish audience would have been perplexed by a Messiah who would let himself be captured and killed. Both would be ashamed of Jesus if they did not look past his death to his glorious resurrection and second coming. Then they would see Jesus, not as a loser, returns in his glory and in the glory of the Father and the holy angels. 27 I tell you the truth, some standing here right now will not die before they see the Kingdom of God."

### Jesus Is Transfigured on the Mountain (111/Matthew 17:1-13; Mark 9:2-13)

28About eight days later Jesus took Peter, John, and James up on a mountain to pray. 29And as he was praying, the appearance of his face was transformed, and his clothes became dazzling white. 30Suddenly, two men, Moses and Elijah, appeared and began talking with Jesus. 31They were glorious to see. And they were speaking about his exodus from this world, which was about to be fulfilled in Jerusalem.

32Peter and the others had fallen asleep. When they woke up, they saw Jesus' glory and the two men standing with him. 33As Moses and Elijah were starting to leave, Peter, not even knowing what he was saying, blurted out, "Master, it's wonderful for us to be here! Let's make three shelters as memorials*—one for you, one for Moses, and one for Elijah." 34But even as he was saying this, a cloud overshadowed them, and terror gripped them as the cloud covered them.

35Then a voice from the cloud said, "This is my Son, my Chosen One.* Listen to him." 36When the voice finished, Jesus was there alone. They didn't tell anyone at that time what they had seen.

### Jesus Heals a Demon-Possessed Boy (112/Matthew 17:14-21; Mark 9:14-29)

37The next day, after they had come down the mountain, a large crowd met Jesus. 38A man in the crowd called out to him, "Teacher, I beg you to look at my son, my only child. 39An evil spirit keeps seizing him, making him scream. It throws him into convulsions so that he foams at the mouth. It batters him and hardly ever leaves him alone. 40I begged your disciples to cast out the spirit, but they couldn't do it."

41Jesus said, "You faithless and corrupt people! How long must I be with you and put up with you?" Then he said to the man, "Bring your son here."

42As the boy came forward, the demon knocked him to the ground and threw him into a violent convulsion. But Jesus rebuked the evil* spirit and healed the boy. Then he gave him back to his father. 43Awe gripped the people as they saw this majestic display of God's power.

### Jesus Predicts His Death the Second Time (113/Matthew 17:22-23; Mark 9:30-32)

While everyone was marveling at everything he was doing, Jesus said to his disciples, 44 "Listen to me and remember what I say. The Son of Man is going to be betrayed into the hands of his enemies." 45But they didn't know what he meant. Its significance was hidden from them, so they couldn't understand it, and they were afraid to ask him about it.

9:33 Greek *three tabernacles.* 9:35 Some manuscripts read *This is my dearly loved Son.* 9:42 Greek *unclean.*

---

but as the Lord of the universe, who through his death brought salvation to those who believe.

**9:27** When Jesus said some would not die without seeing the Kingdom, he may have been referring to: (1) Peter, James, and John, who would witness the Transfiguration eight days later; (2) all who would witness the Resurrection and Ascension; (3) all who would take part in the spread of the church after Pentecost. Jesus' listeners would not have to wait for another, future Messiah. The Kingdom was among them, and would soon come in power.

**9:29, 30** Jesus took Peter, James, and John to the top of a mountain to show them who he really was—not merely a great prophet, but God's own Son. Moses, representing the Law, and Elijah, representing the Prophets, appeared with Jesus. Then God's voice singled out Jesus as the long-awaited Messiah, who possessed divine authority. Jesus would fulfill both the Law and the Prophets (Matthew 5:17).

**9:33** When Peter suggested making three shelters, he may have been thinking of the Festival of Shelters, where shelters were set up to commemorate the Exodus, God's deliverance of the Israelites from slavery in Egypt. Peter wanted to keep Moses and Elijah with them, but this was not what God wanted. Peter's desire to build memorials for Jesus, Moses, and Elijah may also show his understanding that real faith is built on three cornerstones: the Law, the Prophets, and Jesus. But Peter grew in his understanding, and eventually he would write of Jesus as the "cornerstone" of the church (1 Peter 2:6).

**9:35** As God's Son, Jesus has God's power and authority; thus, his words should be our final authority. If a person's teaching is true, it will agree with Jesus' teachings. Don't be hasty to seek advice and guidance from merely human sources and thereby neglect Christ's message. Test everything you hear against Jesus' words and you will not be led astray. If we believe he is God's Son, then we surely will want to do what he says.

**9:37-39** Peter, James, and John experienced a wonderful moment on the mountain, and they probably didn't want to leave. Sometimes we too have such an inspiring experience that we want to stay where we are—away from the reality and problems of our daily life. Knowing that struggles await us in the valley encourages us to linger on the mountaintop. Yet staying on top of a mountain prohibits our ministering to others. Instead of becoming spiritual giants, we would soon become dwarfed by our self-centeredness. We need times of retreat and renewal but only so we can return to minister to the world. Our faith must make sense off the mountain as well as on it.

**9:40** Why couldn't the disciples cast out the evil spirit? For a possible answer, see the note on Mark 9:18.

**9:45, 46** The disciples didn't understand Jesus' words about his death. They still thought of Jesus as only an earthly king, and they were concerned about their places in the Kingdom he would set up. So they ignored Jesus' words about his death and began arguing about who would be the greatest.

### The Disciples Argue about Who Would Be the Greatest
(115/Matthew 18:1-6; Mark 9:33-37)
46Then his disciples began arguing about which of them was the greatest. 47But Jesus knew their thoughts, so he brought a little child to his side. 48Then he said to them, "Anyone who welcomes a little child like this on my behalf* welcomes me, and anyone who welcomes me also welcomes my Father who sent me. Whoever is the least among you is the greatest."

**9:47**
Matt 9:4
**9:48**
Matt 10:40
Luke 10:16

### The Disciples Forbid Another to Use Jesus' Name (116/Mark 9:38-41)
49John said to Jesus, "Master, we saw someone using your name to cast out demons, but we told him to stop because he isn't in our group."
   50But Jesus said, "Don't stop him! Anyone who is not against you is for you."

**9:50**
Matt 12:30
Luke 11:23

## 2. Jesus' ministry on the way to Jerusalem
### Jesus Teaches about the Cost of Following Him (122/Matthew 8:18-22)
51As the time drew near for him to ascend to heaven, Jesus resolutely set out for Jerusalem. 52He sent messengers ahead to a Samaritan village to prepare for his arrival. 53But the people of the village did not welcome Jesus because he was on his way to Jerusalem. 54When James and John saw this, they said to Jesus, "Lord, should we call down fire from heaven to burn them up*?" 55But Jesus turned and rebuked them.* 56So they went on to another village.

**9:51**
Mark 16:19
Luke 13:22; 17:11;
18:31; 19:28
**9:54**
2 Kgs 1:10, 12

   57As they were walking along, someone said to Jesus, "I will follow you wherever you go."
   58But Jesus replied, "Foxes have dens to live in, and birds have nests, but the Son of Man has no place even to lay his head."
   59He said to another person, "Come, follow me."
   The man agreed, but he said, "Lord, first let me return home and bury my father."
   60But Jesus told him, "Let the spiritually dead bury their own dead!* Your duty is to go and preach about the Kingdom of God."

**9:60**
Matt 3:2
**9:61**
1 Kgs 19:20

   61Another said, "Yes, Lord, I will follow you, but first let me say good-bye to my family."
   62But Jesus told him, "Anyone who puts a hand to the plow and then looks back is not fit for the Kingdom of God."

**9:62**
Phil 3:13

**9:48** Greek *in my name.*   **9:54** Some manuscripts add *as Elijah did.*   **9:55** Some manuscripts add an expanded conclusion to verse 55 and an additional sentence in verse 56: *And he said, "You don't realize what your hearts are like. 56For the Son of Man has not come to destroy people's lives, but to save them."*   **9:60** Greek *Let the dead bury their own dead.*

---

**9:48** Our care for others is a measure of our greatness. How much concern do you show for others? This is a vital question that can accurately measure your greatness in God's eyes. How have you expressed your care for others lately, especially the helpless, the needy, the poor—those who can't return your love and concern? Your honest answer to that question will give you a good idea of your real greatness.

**9:49, 50** The disciples were jealous. Nine of them together had been unable to cast out a single evil spirit (9:40), but when they saw a man who was not one of their group casting out demons, they told him to stop. Our pride is hurt when someone else succeeds where we have failed, but Jesus says there is no room for such jealousy in the spiritual warfare of his Kingdom. Share Jesus' open-arms attitude toward Christian workers outside your group. Rejoice when they are able to bring people to Christ.

**9:51** Although Jesus knew he would face persecution and death in Jerusalem, he was determined to go there. That kind of resolve should characterize our lives as well. When God gives us a course of action, we must move steadily toward our destination, regardless of the potential hazards that await us there.

**9:53** After Assyria invaded Israel, the northern kingdom, and resettled it with its own people (2 Kings 17:24-41), the mixed race that developed became known as the Samaritans. "Pure-bred" Jews hated these "half-breeds," and the Samaritans in turn hated the Jews. So many tensions arose between the two peoples that Jewish travelers between Galilee and southern Judea often would walk around rather than through Samaritan territory, even though this would lengthen their trip considerably. Jesus held no such prejudices, and he sent messengers ahead to get things ready in a Samaritan village. But the village refused to welcome these Jewish travelers who were headed for Jerusalem.

**9:54** When the Samaritan village did not welcome Jesus and his disciples, James and John didn't want to stop at shaking the dust from their feet (9:5). They wanted to retaliate by calling down fire from heaven on the people, as Elijah had done on the servants of a wicked king of Israel (2 Kings 1). When others reject or scorn us, we, too, may feel like retaliating. We must remember that judgment belongs to God, and we must not expect him to use his power to carry out personal vendettas.

**9:59** Luke does not say whether the father is already dead or terminally ill. It seems likely that if the father were dead, the son would have been fulfilling the burial duties. Jesus was saying that true discipleship requires instant action. Jesus did not teach people to forsake responsibilities to family, but he often gave commands to people in light of their real motives. Perhaps this man wanted to delay following Christ and was using his father as an excuse. Following Jesus has a cost, and each of us must be ready to serve, even when it requires sacrifice.

**9:62** What does Jesus want from us? Total dedication, not half-hearted commitment. We can't pick and choose among Jesus' ideas and follow him selectively; we have to accept the cross along with the crown. We must count the cost and be willing to abandon everything else that has given us security—without looking back. With our focus on Jesus, we should allow nothing to distract us from following him.

## Jesus Sends Out Seventy-Two Messengers (130)

**10:1**
Mark 6:7

**10:2**
Matt 9:37-38
John 4:35

**10:3**
Matt 10:16

**10:4**
2 Kgs 4:29
Luke 9:3

**10:7**
1 Cor 9:6-14
1 Tim 5:18

**10:9**
Matt 3:2

**10:12**
Gen 19:24-25
Matt 10:15

**10** The Lord now chose seventy-two* other disciples and sent them ahead in pairs to all the towns and places he planned to visit. ²These were his instructions to them: "The harvest is great, but the workers are few. So pray to the Lord who is in charge of the harvest; ask him to send more workers into his fields.³ Now go, and remember that I am sending you out as lambs among wolves. ⁴ Don't take any money with you, nor a traveler's bag, nor an extra pair of sandals. And don't stop to greet anyone on the road.

⁵ "Whenever you enter someone's home, first say, 'May God's peace be on this house.' ⁶ If those who live there are peaceful, the blessing will stand; if they are not, the blessing will return to you.⁷ Don't move around from home to home. Stay in one place, eating and drinking what they provide. Don't hesitate to accept hospitality, because those who work deserve their pay.

⁸ "If you enter a town and it welcomes you, eat whatever is set before you.⁹ Heal the sick, and tell them, 'The Kingdom of God is near you now.'¹⁰ But if a town refuses to welcome you, go out into its streets and say,¹¹ 'We wipe even the dust of your town from our feet to show that we have abandoned you to your fate. And know this—the Kingdom of God is near!' ¹² I assure you, even wicked Sodom will be better off than such a town on judgment day.

**10:1** Some manuscripts read *seventy;* also in 10:17.

---

**A COLLECTION OF ATTITUDES ABOUT OTHERS' NEEDS**

To the expert in religious law . . . . . . . . the wounded man was a subject to discuss.
To the bandits. . . . . . . . . . . . . . . . . . . the wounded man was someone to use and exploit.
To the religious men . . . . . . . . . . . . . . the wounded man was a problem to be avoided.
To the innkeeper· · · · · · · · · · · · · · · · · the wounded man was a customer to serve for a fee.
To the Samaritan . . . . . . . . . . . . . . . . the wounded man was a human being worth being cared for and loved.
To Jesus . . . . . . . . . . . . . . . . . . . . . . . all of them and all of us were worth dying for.

Confronting the needs of others brings out various attitudes in us. Jesus used the story of the good but despised Samaritan to make clear what attitude was acceptable to him. If we are honest, we often will find ourselves in the place of the expert in religious law, needing to learn again who our neighbor is. Note these different attitudes toward the wounded man.

---

**10:1, 2** Far more than 12 people had been following Jesus. Here Jesus designated a group of 72 to prepare a number of towns for his later visit. These disciples were not unique in their qualifications. They were not better educated, more capable, or of higher status than Jesus' other followers. What prepared them for this mission was that they had been equipped with Jesus' power and a vision to reach all the people. It is important to dedicate our skills to God's Kingdom, but we must also be equipped with his power and have a clear vision of what he wants us to do.

**10:2** Christian service has no unemployment. God has work enough for everyone. Jesus encouraged the disciples not just to do the work but also to pray for workers. Part of every missionary's job is to pray for new workers and to help newcomers learn the ropes. Whatever your role in God's work, pray today for more helpers. Believers are not always to work alone. God wants them to pray, recruit, and equip others to join them as they explore opportunities to serve Jesus. Some people, as soon as they understand the gospel, want to go to convert people immediately. Jesus gave a different approach: begin by mobilizing people to pray. And before praying for unsaved people, pray that other concerned disciples will join you in reaching out to them. God will lead you to an important responsibility, but prayer comes first.

**10:3** Jesus said he was sending his disciples out "as lambs among wolves." They would have to be careful because they would surely meet with opposition. We, too, are sent into the world like lambs among wolves. Be alert, and remember to face your enemies, not with aggression but with love and gentleness. A dangerous mission requires sincere commitment.

**10:7** Jesus' direction to stay in one house avoided certain problems. Shifting from house to house could offend the families who

first took them in. Some families might begin to compete for the disciples' presence, and some might think they weren't good enough to hear their message. If the disciples appeared not to appreciate the hospitality offered them, the town might not accept Jesus when he followed them there. In addition, by staying in one place, the disciples would not have to worry continually about getting good accommodations. They could settle down and focus on their appointed task. (See also 9:4.)

**10:7** Jesus told his disciples to accept hospitality graciously because their work entitled them to it. Ministers of the Good News deserve to be supported, and our responsibility is to make sure they have what they need. There are several ways to encourage those who serve God in his church: (1) See that they have an adequate salary; (2) see that they are supported emotionally—plan special times to express appreciation for something they have done; (3) lift their spirits with special surprises from time to time. Our ministers deserve to know we are giving to them cheerfully and generously.

**10:8, 9** Jesus gave two rules for the disciples to follow as they traveled. They were to eat what was set before them—that is, they were to accept hospitality without being picky—and they were to heal the sick. Because of the healings, people would be willing to listen to the Good News.

**10:12** Sodom was an evil city that God had destroyed because of its great sinfulness (Genesis 19). The city's name is often used to symbolize wickedness and immorality. Sodom will suffer on judgment day, but cities who saw the Messiah and rejected him will suffer even more.

13 "What sorrow awaits you, Korazin and Bethsaida! For if the miracles I did in you had been done in wicked Tyre and Sidon, their people would have repented of their sins long ago, clothing themselves in burlap and throwing ashes on their heads to show their remorse. 14 Yes, Tyre and Sidon will be better off on judgment day than you. 15And you people of Capernaum, will you be honored in heaven? No, you will go down to the place of the dead.*"

10:14
Isa 23
Ezek 26–28

10:15
†Isa 14:13, 15

16Then he said to the disciples, "Anyone who accepts your message is also accepting me. And anyone who rejects you is rejecting me. And anyone who rejects me is rejecting God, who sent me."

10:16
Matt 10:40
John 5:23
1 Thes 4:8

### The Seventy-Two Messengers Return (131)

17When the seventy-two disciples returned, they joyfully reported to him, "Lord, even the demons obey us when we use your name!"

18 "Yes," he told them, "I saw Satan fall from heaven like lightning! 19 Look, I have given you authority over all the power of the enemy, and you can walk among snakes and scorpions and crush them. Nothing will injure you. 20But don't rejoice because evil spirits obey you; rejoice because your names are registered in heaven."

10:18
John 12:31
Rev 12:8-9

10:20
Exod 32:32
Isa 4:3
Phil 4:3
Rev 3:5

21At that same time Jesus was filled with the joy of the Holy Spirit, and he said, "O Father, Lord of heaven and earth, thank you for hiding these things from those who think themselves wise and clever, and for revealing them to the childlike. Yes, Father, it pleased you to do it this way.

22 "My Father has entrusted everything to me. No one truly knows the Son except the Father, and no one truly knows the Father except the Son and those to whom the Son chooses to reveal him."

10:22
Matt 28:18
John 1:18; 3:35

23Then when they were alone, he turned to the disciples and said, "Blessed are the eyes that see what you have seen. 24I tell you, many prophets and kings longed to see what you see, but they didn't see it. And they longed to hear what you hear, but they didn't hear it."

10:24
1 Pet 1:10-14

### Jesus Tells the Parable of the Good Samaritan (132)

25One day an expert in religious law stood up to test Jesus by asking him this question: "Teacher, what should I do to inherit eternal life?"

26Jesus replied, "What does the law of Moses say? How do you read it?"

10:15 Greek *to Hades.*

---

10:13 Korazin was a city near the Sea of Galilee, probably about two miles north of Capernaum. Tyre and Sidon were cities destroyed by God as punishment for their wickedness (see Ezekiel 26–28).

10:15 Capernaum was Jesus' base for his Galilean ministry. The city was located at an important crossroads used by traders and the Roman army, so a message proclaimed in Capernaum was likely to go far. Many people of Capernaum did not understand Jesus' miracles or believe his teaching, however, and the city was included among those who would be judged for rejecting him.

10:17-20 The disciples had seen tremendous results as they ministered in Jesus' name and with his authority. They were elated by the victories they had witnessed, and Jesus shared their enthusiasm. He helped them get their priorities right, however, by reminding them of their most important victory— that their names were registered in heaven. This honor was more important than any of their accomplishments. As we see God's wonders at work in and through us, we should not lose sight of the greatest wonder of all—our heavenly citizenship.

10:18, 19 Jesus may have been looking ahead to his victory over Satan at the cross. John 12:31, 32 indicates that Satan would be judged and driven out at the time of Jesus' death. On the other hand, Jesus may have been warning his disciples against pride. Perhaps he was referring to Isaiah 14:12-17, which begins, "How you are fallen from heaven, O shining star, son of the morning!" Some interpreters identify this verse with Satan and explain that Satan's pride led to all the evil we see on earth today. To Jesus' disciples, who were thrilled with their power over evil spirits ("snakes and scorpions"), he may have been giving this stern

warning: "Yours is the kind of pride that led to Satan's downfall. Be careful!"

10:21 Jesus thanked God that spiritual truth was for everyone and not just for the elite. Many of life's rewards seem to go to the intelligent, the rich, the good looking, or the powerful, but the Kingdom of God is equally available to all, regardless of position or abilities. We come to Jesus, not through strength or brains, but through childlike trust. Jesus is not opposed to engaging in scholarly pursuits; he is opposed to spiritual pride (being wise in one's own eyes). Join Jesus in thanking God that we all have equal access to him. Trust in God's grace, not in your personal qualifications, for your citizenship in the Kingdom.

10:22 Christ's mission was to reveal God the Father to people. His words brought difficult ideas down to earth. He explained God's love through stories, teachings, and, most of all, his life. By examining Jesus' actions, principles, and attitudes, we can understand God more clearly.

10:23, 24 Old Testament men of God, such as David and Isaiah, made many God-inspired predictions that Jesus fulfilled. As Peter later wrote, these prophets wondered what their words meant and when they would be fulfilled (1 Peter 1:10-13). The disciples had the fantastic opportunity of being eyewitnesses to the fulfillment of those prophecies. For many months, however, they took Jesus for granted, not really listening to him or obeying him. We also have a privileged position: the legacy of 2,000 years of church history, the availability of the Bible in hundreds of languages and translations, and access to many excellent pastors and speakers. Yet often we take these for granted. Remember, with privilege comes responsibility. Because we are privileged to know so much about Christ, we must be careful to follow him.

**10:27**
†Deut 6:5
†Lev 19:18

**10:28**
Lev 18:5
Rom 10:5

**10:29**
Luke 16:15

27 The man answered, "'You must love the LORD your God with all your heart, all your soul, all your strength, and all your mind.' And, 'Love your neighbor as yourself.'"*

28 "Right!" Jesus told him. "Do this and you will live!"

29 The man wanted to justify his actions, so he asked Jesus, "And who is my neighbor?"

30 Jesus replied with a story: "A Jewish man was traveling from Jerusalem down to Jericho, and he was attacked by bandits. They stripped him of his clothes, beat him up, and left him half dead beside the road.

10:27 Deut 6:5; Lev 19:18.

---

**MARTHA**

Many older brothers and sisters have an irritating tendency to take charge, a habit developed while growing up. We can easily see this pattern in Martha, the older sister of Mary and Lazarus. She was used to being in control.

The fact that Martha, Mary, and Lazarus are remembered for their hospitality takes on added significance when we note that hospitality was a social requirement in their culture. It was considered shameful to turn anyone away from your door. Apparently Martha's family met this requirement very well.

Martha worried about details. She wished to please, to serve, to do the right thing—but she often succeeded in making everyone around her uncomfortable. Perhaps as the oldest she feared shame if her home did not measure up to expectations. She tried to do everything she could to make sure that wouldn't happen. As a result, she found it hard to relax and enjoy her guests and even harder to accept Mary's lack of cooperation in all the preparations. Martha's frustration was so intense that she finally asked Jesus to settle the matter. He gently corrected her attitude and showed her that her priorities, though good, were not the best. The personal attention she gave her guests should be more important than the comforts she tried to provide for them.

Later, following her brother Lazarus's death, Martha could hardly help being herself. When she heard Jesus was finally coming, she rushed out to meet him and expressed her inner conflict of disappointment and hope. Jesus pointed out that her hope was too limited. He was not only Lord over death; he was the resurrection and the life! Moments later, Martha again spoke without thinking, pointing out that four-day-old corpses are well on their way to decomposition. Her awareness of details sometimes kept her from seeing the whole picture, but Jesus was consistently patient with her.

In our last picture of Martha, she is once again serving a meal to Jesus and his disciples. She has not stopped serving. But the Bible records her silence this time. She has begun to learn what her younger sister already knew—that worship begins with silence and listening.

| | |
|---|---|
| **Strengths and accomplishments** | • Known as a hospitable homemaker<br>• Believed in Jesus with growing faith<br>• Had a strong desire to do everything exactly right |
| **Weaknesses and mistakes** | • Expected others to agree with her priorities<br>• Was overly concerned with details<br>• Tended to feel sorry for herself when her efforts were not recognized<br>• Limited Jesus' power to this life |
| **Lessons from her life** | • Getting caught up in details can make us forget the main reasons for our actions<br>• There is a proper time to listen to Jesus and a proper time to work for him |
| **Vital statistics** | • Where: Bethany<br>• Relatives: Sister: Mary. Brother: Lazarus. |
| **Key verse** | "But Martha was distracted by the big dinner she was preparing. She came to Jesus and said, 'Lord, doesn't it seem unfair to you that my sister just sits here while I do all the work? Tell her to come and help me'" (Luke 10:40). |

Martha's story is told in Luke 10:38-42 and John 11:17-45.

---

**10:27** This expert in religious law was quoting Deuteronomy 6:5 and Leviticus 19:18. He correctly understood that the law demanded total devotion to God and love for one's neighbor. Jesus talked more about these laws elsewhere (see Matthew 19:16-22 and Mark 10:17-22).

**10:27-37** The legal expert viewed the wounded man as a topic for discussion; the bandits, as an object to exploit; the priest, as a problem to avoid; and the Temple assistant, as an object of curiosity. Only the Samaritan treated him as a person to love.

From the illustration we learn three principles about loving our neighbor: (1) Lack of love is often easy to justify, even though it is never right; (2) our neighbor is anyone of any race, creed, or social background who is in need; (3) love means acting to meet the person's need. Wherever you live, needy people are close by. There is no good reason for refusing to help.

31 "By chance a priest came along. But when he saw the man lying there, he crossed to the other side of the road and passed him by. 32 A Temple assistant* walked over and looked at him lying there, but he also passed by on the other side.

10:31
Lev 21:1-3

33 "Then a despised Samaritan came along, and when he saw the man, he felt compassion for him. 34 Going over to him, the Samaritan soothed his wounds with olive oil and wine and bandaged them. Then he put the man on his own donkey and took him to an inn, where he took care of him. 35 The next day he handed the innkeeper two silver coins,* telling him, ' Take care of this man. If his bill runs higher than this, I'll pay you the next time I'm here.'

36 "Now which of these three would you say was a neighbor to the man who was attacked by bandits?" Jesus asked.

37 The man replied, "The one who showed him mercy."
Then Jesus said, "Yes, now go and do the same."

## Jesus Visits Martha and Mary (133)

38 As Jesus and the disciples continued on their way to Jerusalem, they came to a certain village where a woman named Martha welcomed him into her home. 39 Her sister, Mary, sat at the Lord's feet, listening to what he taught. 40 But Martha was distracted by the big dinner she was preparing. She came to Jesus and said, "Lord, doesn't it seem unfair to you that my sister just sits here while I do all the work? Tell her to come and help me."

10:38
John 11:1; 12:2-3

10:41
Matt 6:25-34
Luke 12:11, 22

41 But the Lord said to her, "My dear Martha, you are worried and upset over all these details! 42 There is only one thing worth being concerned about. Mary has discovered it, and it will not be taken away from her."

10:42
Ps 27:4
Phil 3:13-14

## Jesus Teaches His Disciples about Prayer (134)

**11** Once Jesus was in a certain place praying. As he finished, one of his disciples came to him and said, "Lord, teach us to pray, just as John taught his disciples."

11:1
Luke 3:21

2 Jesus said, "This is how you should pray:*

11:2-4
Matt 6:9-13

"Father, may your name be kept holy.
    May your Kingdom come soon.
3 Give us each day the food we need,*
4 and forgive us our sins,
    as we forgive those who sin against us.
And don't let us yield to temptation.*"

11:4
Matt 18:35
Mark 11:25

**10:32** Greek *A Levite.* **10:35** Greek *two denarii.* A denarius was equivalent to a laborer's full day's wage. **11:2** Some manuscripts add additional phrases from the Lord's Prayer as it reads in Matt 6:9-13. **11:3** Or *Give us each day our food for the day;* or *Give us each day our food for tomorrow.* **11:4** Or *And keep us from being tested.*

---

**10:33** A deep hatred existed between Jews and Samaritans. The Jews saw themselves as pure descendants of Abraham, while the Samaritans were a mixed race produced when Jews from the northern kingdom intermarried with other peoples after Israel's exile (see also the note on 9:53). To this legal expert, the person least likely to act correctly would be the Samaritan. In fact, he did not even say the word *Samaritan* in answer to Jesus' question. This expert's attitude betrayed his lack of the very thing that he had earlier said the law commanded—love.

### JESUS VISITS MARY AND MARTHA

After teaching throughout Galilee, Jesus returned to Jerusalem for the Festival of Shelters (John 7:2ff). He spoke in Jerusalem and then visited his friends Mary and Martha in Bethany, a tiny village on the eastern slope of the Mount of Olives.

**10:38-42** Mary and Martha both loved Jesus. On this occasion they were both serving him. But Martha thought Mary's style of serving was inferior to hers. She didn't realize that in her desire to serve, she was actually neglecting her guest. Are you so busy doing things *for* Jesus that you're not spending any time *with* him? Don't let your service become self-serving. Jesus did not blame Martha for being concerned about household chores. He was only asking her to set priorities. Service to Christ can degenerate into mere busywork that is totally devoid of devotion to God.

**11:2-13** Notice the order in this prayer. First, Jesus praised God; then he made his requests. Praising God first puts us in the right frame of mind to tell him about our needs. Too often our prayers are more like shopping lists than conversations. These verses focus on three aspects of prayer: its content (11:2-4), our persistence (11:5-10), and God's faithfulness (11:11-13).

**11:3** God's provision is daily, not all at once. We cannot store it up and then cut off communication with God. And we dare not be self-satisfied. If you are running low on strength, ask yourself, How long have I been away from the Source?

**11:4** When Jesus taught his disciples to pray, he made forgiveness the cornerstone of their relationship with God. God has forgiven our sins; we must now forgive those who have wronged us. To remain unforgiving shows we have not understood that we

**11:7**
Matt 26:10
Luke 18:5
Gal 6:17

**11:8**
Luke 18:1-6

**11:13**
Jas 1:17

**11:15**
Matt 9:34

**11:16**
Matt 12:38; 16:1

**11:17**
Matt 9:4

**11:20**
Exod 8:19

**11:22**
Isa 49:24; 53:12

⁵Then, teaching them more about prayer, he used this story: "Suppose you went to a friend's house at midnight, wanting to borrow three loaves of bread. You say to him, ⁶ 'A friend of mine has just arrived for a visit, and I have nothing for him to eat.' ⁷ And suppose he calls out from his bedroom, 'Don't bother me. The door is locked for the night, and my family and I are all in bed. I can't help you.'⁸ But I tell you this—though he won't do it for friendship's sake, if you keep knocking long enough, he will get up and give you whatever you need because of your shameless persistence.*

⁹ "And so I tell you, keep on asking, and you will receive what you ask for. Keep on seeking, and you will find. Keep on knocking, and the door will be opened to you. ¹⁰ For everyone who asks, receives. Everyone who seeks, finds. And to everyone who knocks, the door will be opened.

¹¹ "You fathers—if your children ask* for a fish, do you give them a snake instead?¹² Or if they ask for an egg, do you give them a scorpion? Of course not! ¹³ So if you sinful people know how to give good gifts to your children, how much more will your heavenly Father give the Holy Spirit to those who ask him."

### Jesus Answers Hostile Accusations (135)

¹⁴One day Jesus cast out a demon from a man who couldn't speak, and when the demon was gone, the man began to speak. The crowds were amazed, ¹⁵ but some of them said, "No wonder he can cast out demons. He gets his power from Satan,* the prince of demons." ¹⁶ Others, trying to test Jesus, demanded that he show them a miraculous sign from heaven to prove his authority.

¹⁷He knew their thoughts, so he said, "Any kingdom divided by civil war is doomed. A family splintered by feuding will fall apart. ¹⁸ You say I am empowered by Satan. But if Satan is divided and fighting against himself, how can his kingdom survive? ¹⁹And if I am empowered by Satan, what about your own exorcists? They cast out demons, too, so they will condemn you for what you have said. ²⁰ But if I am casting out demons by the power of God,* then the Kingdom of God has arrived among you.²¹ For when a strong man like Satan is fully armed and guards his palace, his possessions are safe—²² until someone even stronger attacks and overpowers him, strips him of his weapons, and carries off his belongings.

²³ "Anyone who isn't with me opposes me, and anyone who isn't working with me is actually working against me.

**11:8** Or *in order to avoid shame,* or *so his reputation won't be damaged.* **11:11** Some manuscripts add *for bread, do you give them a stone? Or [if they ask].* **11:15** Greek *Beelzeboul;* also in 11:18, 19. Other manuscripts read *Beezeboul;* Latin version reads *Beelzebub.* **11:20** Greek *by the finger of God.*

---

ourselves deeply need to be forgiven. Think of some people who have wronged you. Have you forgiven them? How will God deal with you if he treats you as you treat others?

**11:8** Persistence, or boldness, in prayer overcomes *our* insensitivity, not God's. To practice persistence does more to change our heart and mind than his, and it helps us understand and express the intensity of our need. Persistence in prayer helps us recognize God's work.

**11:13** Even though good fathers make mistakes, they treat their children well. How much better our perfect heavenly Father treats his children! The most important gift he could ever give us is the Holy Spirit (Acts 2:1-4), whom he promised to give all believers after his death, resurrection, and return to heaven (John 15:26).

**11:14-23** A similar and possibly separate event is reported in Matthew 12:22-45 and Mark 3:20-30. The event described by Luke happened in Judea, while the other took place in Galilee. According to Luke, Jesus spoke to the crowds; in Matthew and Mark, he accused the Pharisees.

**11:15-20** Some of the Pharisees' followers also were exorcists—that is, they drove out demons. The Pharisees' accusations were becoming more desperate. To accuse Jesus of being empowered by Satan, the prince of demons, because Jesus was driving out demons was also to say that the Pharisees' own exorcists were doing Satan's work. Jesus turned the religious leaders' accusation against them. Jesus first dismissed their claim as absurd (Why would the devil drive out his own demons?). Then he engaged in a little irony ("What about your own exorcists?"). Finally, he

concluded that his work of driving out demons proved that the Kingdom of God had arrived.

Satan, who had controlled the kingdom of this world for thousands of years, was now being controlled and overpowered by Jesus and the Kingdom of Heaven. Jesus' Kingdom began to come into power at Jesus' birth and grew as he resisted the wilderness temptations. It established itself through his teachings and healings, blossomed in victory at his resurrection and at Pentecost, and will become permanent and universal at his second coming.

**11:21, 22** Jesus may have been referring to Isaiah 49:24-26. Regardless of how great Satan's power is, Jesus is stronger still. He will overpower Satan and dispose of him for eternity (see Revelation 20:2, 10).

**11:23** How does this verse relate to 9:50: "Anyone who is not against you is for you"? In the earlier passage, Jesus was talking about a person who was driving out demons in Jesus' name. Those who fight evil, he was saying, are on the same side as the one driving out demons in Jesus' name. Here, by contrast, he was talking about the conflict between God and the devil. In this battle, if a person is not on God's side, he or she is on Satan's side. There is no neutral ground. Because God has already won the battle, why be on the losing side? If you aren't actively for Christ, you are against him.

24 "When an evil* spirit leaves a person, it goes into the desert, searching for rest. But when it finds none, it says, 'I will return to the person I came from.' 25 So it returns and finds that its former home is all swept and in order. 26 Then the spirit finds seven other spirits more evil than itself, and they all enter the person and live there. And so that person is worse off than before."

27 As he was speaking, a woman in the crowd called out, "God bless your mother—the womb from which you came, and the breasts that nursed you!"

28 Jesus replied, "But even more blessed are all who hear the word of God and put it into practice."

### Jesus Warns against Unbelief (136)

29 As the crowd pressed in on Jesus, he said, "This evil generation keeps asking me to show them a miraculous sign. But the only sign I will give them is the sign of Jonah. 30 What happened to him was a sign to the people of Nineveh that God had sent him. What happens to the Son of Man* will be a sign to these people that he was sent by God.

31 "The queen of Sheba* will stand up against this generation on judgment day and condemn it, for she came from a distant land to hear the wisdom of Solomon. Now someone greater than Solomon is here—but you refuse to listen. 32 The people of Nineveh will also stand up against this generation on judgment day and condemn it, for they repented of their sins at the preaching of Jonah. Now someone greater than Jonah is here—but you refuse to repent.

### Jesus Teaches about the Light Within (137)

33 "No one lights a lamp and then hides it or puts it under a basket.* Instead, a lamp is placed on a stand, where its light can be seen by all who enter the house.

34 "Your eye is a lamp that provides light for your body. When your eye is good, your whole body is filled with light. But when it is bad, your body is filled with darkness. 35 Make sure that the light you think you have is not actually darkness. 36 If you are filled with light, with no dark corners, then your whole life will be radiant, as though a floodlight were filling you with light."

### Jesus Criticizes the Religious Leaders (138)

37 As Jesus was speaking, one of the Pharisees invited him home for a meal. So he went in and took his place at the table.* 38 His host was amazed to see that he sat down to eat without first performing the hand-washing ceremony required by Jewish custom. 39 Then the Lord said to him, "You Pharisees are so careful to clean the outside of the cup and the dish, but inside you are filthy—full of greed and wickedness! 40 Fools! Didn't God make the inside as well as the outside? 41 So clean the inside by giving gifts to the poor, and you will be clean all over.

**Cross-references (right margin):**
- 11:24-26 / Matt 12:43-45
- 11:27 / Luke 1:28, 42, 48
- 11:28 / Luke 6:47; 8:21
- 11:29-32 / Matt 12:38-42 / 1 Cor 1:22
- 11:30 / Jon 1:17; 2:10
- 11:31 / 1 Kgs 10:1-10 / 2 Chr 9:1-12
- 11:32 / Jon 3:5, 8, 10
- 11:33 / Matt 5:15 / Luke 8:16
- 11:34-36 / Matt 6:22-23
- 11:38 / Mark 7:3-4
- 11:39 / Matt 23:25 / Mark 7:20-23
- 11:41 / Luke 12:33

11:24 Greek *unclean*.   11:30 "Son of Man" is a title Jesus used for himself.   11:31 Greek *The queen of the south*.
11:33 Some manuscripts do not include *or puts it under a basket*.   11:37 Or *and reclined*.

---

**11:24-26** Jesus was illustrating an unfortunate human tendency: Our desire to reform often does not last long. In Israel's history, almost as soon as a good king would pull down idols, a bad king would set them up again. It is not enough to be emptied of evil; we must then be filled with the power of the Holy Spirit to accomplish God's new purpose in our life (see also Matthew 12:43-45; Galatians 5:22).

**11:27, 28** Jesus was speaking to people who put extremely high value on family ties. Their genealogies were important guarantees that they were part of God's chosen people. A man's value came from his ancestors, and a woman's value came from the sons she bore. Jesus' response to the woman meant that a person's obedience to God is more important than his or her place on the family tree. Consistent obedience is more important than the honor of bearing a respected son.

**11:29, 30** What was the sign of Jonah? God had asked Jonah to preach repentance to the Gentiles (non-Jews). Jesus was affirming Jonah's message. Salvation is not only for Jews but for all people. Matthew 12:40 adds another explanation: Jesus would die and rise after three days, just as the prophet Jonah was rescued after three days in the belly of the great fish.

**11:29-32** The cruel, warlike men of Nineveh, capital of Assyria, repented when Jonah preached to them—and Jonah did not even care about them. The pagan queen of Sheba praised the God of

Israel when she heard Solomon's wisdom, and Solomon was full of faults. By contrast, Jesus, the perfect Son of God, came to people that he loved dearly—but they rejected him. Thus, God's chosen people made themselves more liable to judgment than either a notoriously wicked nation or a powerful pagan queen. Compare 10:12-15, where Jesus says the evil cities of Sodom, Tyre, and Sidon will be judged less harshly than the cities in Judea and Galilee that rejected Jesus' message.

**11:31, 32** The people of Nineveh and the queen of Sheba had turned to God with far less evidence than Jesus was giving his listeners—and far less than we have today. We have eyewitness reports of the risen Jesus, the continuing power of the Holy Spirit unleashed at Pentecost, easy access to the Bible, and knowledge of 2,000 years of Christ's acts through his church. With the knowledge and insight available to us, our response to Christ ought to be even more complete and wholehearted.

**11:33-36** The lamp is Christ; the eye represents spiritual understanding and insight. Evil desires make the eye less sensitive and blot out the light of Christ's presence. If you have a hard time seeing God at work in the world and in your life, check your vision. Are any sinful desires blinding you to Christ?

**11:37-39** The hand-washing ceremony was done not for health reasons but as a symbol of washing away any contamination from touching anything unclean. Not only did the Pharisees make

**11:42**
Lev 27:30
Matt 23:23

**11:43**
Matt 23:6-7
Mark 12:38-39

**11:44**
Matt 23:27-28

**11:46**
Matt 23:4

**11:47**
Matt 23:29-32

**11:48**
Acts 7:51-53; 8:1

**11:49-51**
Matt 23:34-36
1 Cor 1:24, 30

**11:51**
Gen 4:8
2 Chr 24:20-21

**11:52**
Matt 23:13

**11:54**
Luke 20:20

42 "What sorrow awaits you Pharisees! For you are careful to tithe even the tiniest income from your herb gardens,* but you ignore justice and the love of God. You should tithe, yes, but do not neglect the more important things.

43 "What sorrow awaits you Pharisees! For you love to sit in the seats of honor in the synagogues and receive respectful greetings as you walk in the marketplaces. 44 Yes, what sorrow awaits you! For you are like hidden graves in a field. People walk over them without knowing the corruption they are stepping on."

45 "Teacher," said an expert in religious law, "you have insulted us, too, in what you just said."

46 "Yes," said Jesus, "what sorrow also awaits you experts in religious law! For you crush people with unbearable religious demands, and you never lift a finger to ease the burden. 47 What sorrow awaits you! For you build monuments for the prophets your own ancestors killed long ago. 48 But in fact, you stand as witnesses who agree with what your ancestors did. They killed the prophets, and you join in their crime by building the monuments! 49 This is what God in his wisdom said about you:* 'I will send prophets and apostles to them, but they will kill some and persecute the others.'

50 "As a result, this generation will be held responsible for the murder of all God's prophets from the creation of the world—51 from the murder of Abel to the murder of Zechariah, who was killed between the altar and the sanctuary. Yes, it will certainly be charged against this generation.

52 "What sorrow awaits you experts in religious law! For you remove the key to knowledge from the people. You don't enter the Kingdom yourselves, and you prevent others from entering."

53 As Jesus was leaving, the teachers of religious law and the Pharisees became hostile and tried to provoke him with many questions. 54 They wanted to trap him into saying something they could use against him.

**11:42** Greek *tithe the mint, the rue, and every herb.*  **11:49** Greek *Therefore, the wisdom of God said.*

---

a public show of their washing, but they also commanded everyone else to follow a practice originally intended only for the priests.

**11:41** The Pharisees loved to think of themselves as "clean," but their stinginess toward God and the poor proved that they were not as clean as they thought. How do you use the resources God has entrusted to you? Are you generous in meeting the needs around you? Your generosity reveals much about the purity of your heart.

**11:42** Rationalizing not helping others is easy because we have already given to the church, but a person who follows Jesus should share with needy neighbors. While tithing is important to the life of the church, our compassion must not stop there. Where we can help, we should help.

**11:42-52** Jesus criticized the Pharisees and the experts in religious law harshly because they (1) washed their outsides but not their insides, (2) remembered to give a tenth of even their garden herbs but neglected justice, (3) loved praise and attention, (4) loaded people down with burdensome religious demands, (5) would not accept the truth about Jesus, and (6) prevented others from believing the truth. They went wrong by focusing on outward appearances and ignoring the inner condition of their hearts. People do the same when their service comes from a desire to be seen rather than from a pure heart that is full of love for others. People may sometimes be fooled, but God isn't. Don't be a Christian on the outside only. Bring your inner life under God's control and your outer life will naturally reflect him.

**11:44** The Old Testament laws said a person who touched a grave was unclean (Numbers 19:16). Jesus accused the Pharisees of making others unclean by their spiritual rottenness. Like unmarked graves hidden in a field, the Pharisees corrupted everyone who came in contact with them.

**11:46** These "religious demands" were the details the Pharisees had added to God's law. To the commandment, "Remember to observe the Sabbath day by keeping it holy" (Exodus 20:8), for example, they had added instructions regarding how far a person

could walk on the Sabbath, which kinds of knots could be tied, and how much weight could be carried. Healing a person was considered unlawful work on the Sabbath although rescuing a trapped animal was permitted (14:5). No wonder Jesus condemned their additions to the law.

**11:49** God's prophets have been persecuted and murdered throughout history. But this generation was rejecting more than a human prophet—they were rejecting God himself. This quotation is not from the Old Testament. Jesus, the greatest prophet of all, was directly giving them God's message.

**11:51** Abel's death is recorded in Genesis 4:8. For more about him, see his Profile in Genesis 5, p. 15. Zechariah's death is recorded in 2 Chronicles 24:20-22 (the last book in the Hebrew canon). Why would all these sins come upon this particular generation? Because they were rejecting the Messiah himself, the one to whom all their history and prophecy were pointing.

**11:52** How did the legal experts remove the "key to knowledge"? Through their erroneous interpretations of Scripture and their added man-made rules, they made God's truth hard to understand and practice. On top of that, these men were bad examples, arguing their way out of the demanding rules they placed on others. Caught up in a religion of their own making, they could no longer lead the people to God. They had closed the door of God's love to the people and had thrown away the key.

**11:53, 54** The teachers of religious law and the Pharisees hoped to arrest Jesus for blasphemy, heresy, and lawbreaking. They were enraged by Jesus' words about them, but they couldn't arrest him for merely speaking words. They had to find a legal way to get rid of Jesus.

## Jesus Speaks against Hypocrisy (139)

**12** Meanwhile, the crowds grew until thousands were milling about and stepping on each other. Jesus turned first to his disciples and warned them, "Beware of the yeast of the Pharisees—their hypocrisy.² The time is coming when everything that is covered up will be revealed, and all that is secret will be made known to all.³ Whatever you have said in the dark will be heard in the light, and what you have whispered behind closed doors will be shouted from the housetops for all to hear!

⁴ "Dear friends, don't be afraid of those who want to kill your body; they cannot do any more to you after that.⁵ But I'll tell you whom to fear. Fear God, who has the power to kill you and then throw you into hell.* Yes, he's the one to fear.

⁶ "What is the price of five sparrows—two copper coins*? Yet God does not forget a single one of them.⁷ And the very hairs on your head are all numbered. So don't be afraid; you are more valuable to God than a whole flock of sparrows.

⁸ "I tell you the truth, everyone who acknowledges me publicly here on earth, the Son of Man* will also acknowledge in the presence of God's angels.⁹ But anyone who denies me here on earth will be denied before God's angels.¹⁰ Anyone who speaks against the Son of Man can be forgiven, but anyone who blasphemes the Holy Spirit will not be forgiven.

¹¹ "And when you are brought to trial in the synagogues and before rulers and authorities, don't worry about how to defend yourself or what to say,¹² for the Holy Spirit will teach you at that time what needs to be said."

**12:1**
Matt 16:6, 11-12
**12:2**
Mark 4:22

**12:4**
John 15:14-15
**12:5**
Heb 10:31
**12:8**
Luke 15:10
Rev 3:5
**12:9**
Mark 8:38
Luke 9:26
2 Tim 2:12
**12:10**
Matt 12:31-32
Mark 3:28-29
1 Jn 5:16
**12:11-12**
Matt 10:19-20
Mark 13:11
Luke 21:12-15

## Jesus Tells the Parable of the Rich Fool (140)

¹³ Then someone called from the crowd, "Teacher, please tell my brother to divide our father's estate with me."

**12:5** Greek *Gehenna*.    **12:6** Greek *two assaria* [Roman coins equal to ¹/16 of a denarius].    **12:8** "Son of Man" is a title Jesus used for himself.

---

**12:1, 2** As Jesus watched the huge crowds waiting to hear him, he warned his disciples against hypocrisy—trying to appear holy when one's heart is far from God. The Pharisees could not keep their attitudes hidden forever. Their selfishness would act like yeast, and soon they would expose themselves for what they really were—power-hungry impostors, not devoted religious leaders. It is easy to be angry at the blatant hypocrisy of the Pharisees, but each of us must resist the temptation to settle for the appearance of respectability when our hearts are far from God.

**12:1, 2** What are the signs of hypocrisy? (1) Hypocrisy is knowing the truth but not obeying it. People can say they follow Jesus, but not be obedient to his Word. (2) Hypocrisy is living a self-serving life. People may desire leadership only because they love position and control, not because they want to serve others. (3) Hypocrisy reduces faith to rigid rules. People can end up worshiping their own rules and regulations about what they think God wants instead of worshiping God himself. (4) Hypocrisy is outward conformity without inner reality. People can obey the details but still be disobedient in general behavior. For example, a person may carefully tithe his income, but be rude and obnoxious to his coworkers.

Many non-Christians use the supposed (or real) hypocrisy of Christians as an excuse to stay away from God and the church. Look carefully at your life. You are not perfect; therefore, at times an action or behavior might provide the ammunition for someone to label you a hypocrite. However, you must discern your own heart. Consider the signs of hypocrisy noted above and make sure you are not guilty. Then ask God to help you live rightly.

**12:4, 5** Fear of opposition or ridicule can weaken our witness for Christ. Often we cling to peace and comfort, even at the cost of our walk with God. Jesus reminds us here that we should fear God who controls eternal, not merely temporal, consequences. Don't allow fear of a person or group to keep you from standing up for Christ.

**12:7** Our true value is God's estimate of our worth, not our peers' estimate. Other people evaluate and categorize us according to how we perform, what we achieve, and how we look. But God cares for us, as he does for all of his creatures, because we belong to him. Thus, we can face life without fear; we are very valuable to God.

**12:8, 9** We deny Jesus when we (1) hope no one will find out we are Christians, (2) decide *not* to speak up for what is right, (3) are silent about our relationship with God, (4) blend into society, and (5) accept our culture's non-Christian values. By contrast, we acknowledge him when we (1) live moral, upright, Christ-honoring lives, (2) look for opportunities to share our faith with others, (3) help others in need, (4) take a stand for justice, (5) love others, (6) acknowledge our loyalty to Christ, and (7) use our lives and resources to carry out his desires rather than our own.

**12:10** Jesus said that blasphemy against the Holy Spirit is unforgivable. This has worried many sincere Christians, but it does not need to. The unforgivable sin is attributing to Satan the work that the Holy Spirit accomplishes (see the notes on Matthew 12:31, 32; Mark 3:28, 29). Thus, it is the deliberate and ongoing rejection of the Holy Spirit's work and even of God himself. A person who has committed this sin is far from God and totally unaware of any sin at all. If you fear you have committed this sin, be assured that your very concern shows that you have not sinned in this way.

**12:11, 12** The disciples knew they could never get the upper hand in a religious dispute with the well-educated Jewish leaders. Nevertheless, they would not be left unprepared. Jesus promised that the Holy Spirit would give them the appropriate words in their time of need. The disciples' testimony might not make them look impressive, but it would still point out God's work in the world through Jesus' life. We need to pray for opportunities to witness for Christ, and then trust him to help us with our words. This promise of the Spirit's help, however, does not compensate for lack of preparation. Remember that these disciples had three years of personal instruction and practical application. We need to study God's Word. Then God will bring his truths to mind when we most need them, helping us present them in the most effective way.

**12:13ff** Problems like this were often brought to rabbis for them to settle. Jesus' response, though not directed to the topic, is not a change of subject. Rather, Jesus is pointing to a higher issue—a correct attitude toward the accumulation of wealth. Life is more than material goods; far more important is our relationship with God. Jesus put his finger on this questioner's heart. When we bring problems to God in prayer, he often responds in the same way, showing us how we need to change and grow in our attitude

**12:14**
Exod 2:14
Acts 7:27, 35

**12:15**
Job 20:20; 31:24
Ps 62:10
1 Tim 6:9-10

**12:19**
Prov 27:1
1 Cor 15:32
Jas 5:1-5

**12:20**
Job 27:8
Ps 39:6-7

14Jesus replied, "Friend, who made me a judge over you to decide such things as that?" 15Then he said, "Beware! Guard against every kind of greed. Life is not measured by how much you own."

16Then he told them a story: "A rich man had a fertile farm that produced fine crops.17 He said to himself, 'What should I do? I don't have room for all my crops.'18 Then he said, 'I know! I'll tear down my barns and build bigger ones. Then I'll have room enough to store all my wheat and other goods.19 And I'll sit back and say to myself, "My friend, you have enough stored away for years to come. Now take it easy! Eat, drink, and be merry!" '

20 "But God said to him, 'You fool! You will die this very night. Then who will get everything you worked for?'

21 "Yes, a person is a fool to store up earthly wealth but not have a rich relationship with God."

### Jesus Warns about Worry (141)

**12:24**
Job 38:41
Ps 147:9

22Then, turning to his disciples, Jesus said, "That is why I tell you not to worry about everyday life—whether you have enough food to eat or enough clothes to wear.23 For life is more than food, and your body more than clothing.24 Look at the ravens. They don't plant or harvest or store food in barns, for God feeds them. And you are far more valuable to him than any birds!25 Can all your worries add a single moment to your life?26 And if worry can't accomplish a little thing like that, what's the use of worrying over bigger things?

**12:27**
1 Kgs 10:1-10

27 "Look at the lilies and how they grow. They don't work or make their clothing, yet Solomon in all his glory was not dressed as beautifully as they are.28 And if God cares so wonderfully for flowers that are here today and thrown into the fire tomorrow, he will certainly care for you. Why do you have so little faith?

**12:30**
Matt 6:8

29 "And don't be concerned about what to eat and what to drink. Don't worry about such things.30 These things dominate the thoughts of unbelievers all over the world, but your Father already knows your needs.31 Seek the Kingdom of God above all else, and he will give you everything you need.

**12:32**
Luke 22:29

32 "So don't be afraid, little flock. For it gives your Father great happiness to give you the Kingdom.

**12:33**
Matt 19:21
Acts 2:45

33 "Sell your possessions and give to those in need. This will store up treasure for you in heaven! And the purses of heaven never get old or develop holes. Your treasure will be safe;

---

toward the problem. This answer is often not the one we were looking for, but it is more effective in helping us trace God's hand in our life.

**12:15** Jesus says that the good life has nothing to do with being wealthy, so be on guard against greed (desire for what we don't have). This is the exact opposite of what society usually says. Advertisers spend millions of dollars to entice us to think that if we buy more and more of their products, we will be happier, more fulfilled, more comfortable. How do you respond to the constant pressure to buy? Learn to tune out expensive enticements and concentrate instead on the truly fulfilled life—living in a relationship with God and doing his work.

**12:16-21** The rich man in Jesus' story died before he could begin to use what was stored in his big barns. Planning for retirement—preparing for life *before* death—is wise, but neglecting life *after* death is disastrous. If you accumulate wealth only to enrich yourself, with no concern for helping others, you will enter eternity empty-handed.

**12:18-20** Why do you save money? Are you saving for retirement? to buy more expensive cars or toys? to be secure? Jesus challenges us to think beyond earthbound goals and to use what we have been given for God's Kingdom. Faith, service, and obedience are the way to become rich toward God.

**12:22-34** Jesus commands us not to worry. But how can we avoid it? Only faith can free us from the anxiety caused by greed and covetousness. Working and planning responsibly is good; dwelling on all the ways our planning could go wrong is bad. Worry is pointless because it can't fill any of our needs; worry is foolish because the Creator of the universe loves us and knows what we need. He promises to meet all our real needs but not necessarily all our desires.

Overcoming worry requires: (1) Simple trust in God, your heavenly Father. This trust is expressed by praying to him rather than worrying. (2) Perspective on your problems. This can be gained by developing a strategy for addressing and correcting your problems. (3) A support team to help. Find some believers who will pray for you to find wisdom and strength to deal with your worries.

**12:31** Seeking the Kingdom of God above all else means making Jesus the Lord and King of your life. He must control every area—your work, play, plans, relationships. Is the Kingdom only one of your many concerns, or is it central to all you do? Are you holding back any areas of your life from God's control? As Lord and Creator, he wants to help provide what you need as well as guide how you use what he provides.

**12:33** Money seen as an end in itself quickly traps us and cuts us off from both God and the needy. The key to using money wisely is to see how much we can use for God's purposes, not how much we can accumulate for ourselves. Does God's love touch your wallet? Does your money free you to help others? If so, you are storing up lasting treasures in heaven. If your financial goals and possessions hinder you from giving generously, loving others, or serving God, sell what you must to bring your life into line with his purposes.

no thief can steal it and no moth can destroy it. 34Wherever your treasure is, there the desires of your heart will also be.

## Jesus Warns about Preparing for His Coming (142)

35"Be dressed for service and keep your lamps burning, 36 as though you were waiting for your master to return from the wedding feast. Then you will be ready to open the door and let him in the moment he arrives and knocks. 37The servants who are ready and waiting for his return will be rewarded. I tell you the truth, he himself will seat them, put on an apron, and serve them as they sit and eat! 38He may come in the middle of the night or just before dawn.* But whenever he comes, he will reward the servants who are ready.

39"Understand this: If a homeowner knew exactly when a burglar was coming, he would not permit his house to be broken into. 40You also must be ready all the time, for the Son of Man will come when least expected."

41Peter asked, "Lord, is that illustration just for us or for everyone?"

42And the Lord replied, "A faithful, sensible servant is one to whom the master can give the responsibility of managing his other household servants and feeding them. 43If the master returns and finds that the servant has done a good job, there will be a reward. 44I tell you the truth, the master will put that servant in charge of all he owns. 45But what if the servant thinks, 'My master won't be back for a while,' and he begins beating the other servants, partying, and getting drunk? 46The master will return unannounced and unexpected, and he will cut the servant in pieces and banish him with the unfaithful.

47"And a servant who knows what the master wants, but isn't prepared and doesn't carry out those instructions, will be severely punished. 48But someone who does not know, and then does something wrong, will be punished only lightly. When someone has been given much, much will be required in return; and when someone has been entrusted with much, even more will be required.

## Jesus Warns about Coming Division (143)

49 "I have come to set the world on fire, and I wish it were already burning! 50I have a terrible baptism of suffering ahead of me, and I am under a heavy burden until it is accomplished. 51 Do you think I have come to bring peace to the earth? No, I have come to divide people against each other! 52From now on families will be split apart, three in favor of me, and two against—or two in favor and three against.

12:38 Greek in the second or third watch.

| | |
|---|---|
| 12:35-36 | Matt 25:1-13 Mark 13:33-37 |
| 12:35 | †Exod 12:11 |
| 12:37 | Luke 17:7-8 John 13:4 |
| 12:39 | 1 Thes 5:2 Rev 16:15 |
| 12:40 | Mark 13:33 |
| 12:47 | Deut 25:2 Jas 4:17 |
| 12:48 | Lev 5:17 Num 15:27-30 |
| 12:50 | Mark 10:38-39 |

---

**12:34** If you concentrate your money in your business, your thoughts will center on making the business profitable. If you direct it toward other people, you will become concerned with their welfare. Where do you put your time, money, and energy? What do you think about most? How should you change the way you use your resources in order to reflect Kingdom values more accurately?

**12:35-40** Jesus repeatedly said that he would leave this world but would return at some future time (see Matthew 24–25; John 14:1-3). He also said that a Kingdom was being prepared for his followers. Many Greeks envisioned this as a heavenly, idealized, spiritual Kingdom. Jews—like Isaiah and John, the writer of Revelation—saw it as a restored earthly Kingdom.

**12:40** Christ's return at an unexpected time is not a trap, a trick by which God hopes to catch us off guard. In fact, God is delaying his return so more people will have the opportunity to follow him (see 2 Peter 3:9). Before Christ's return, we have time to live out our beliefs and to reflect Jesus' love as we relate to others.

People who are ready for their Lord's return are (1) not hypocritical but sincere (12:1), (2) not fearful but ready to witness (12:4-9), (3) not worried but trusting (12:25, 26), (4) not greedy but generous (12:34), (5) not lazy but diligent (12:37). May your life be more like Christ's so that when he comes, you will be ready to greet him joyfully.

**12:42-44** Jesus promises a reward for those who have been faithful to the Master. While we sometimes experience immediate and material rewards for our obedience to God, this is not always the case. If so, we would be tempted to boast about our achievements and only do good for what we get. Jesus said that if we

look for rewards now, we will lose them later (see Mark 8:36). Our heavenly rewards will be the most accurate reflection of what we have done on earth, and they will be far greater than we can imagine.

**12:48** Jesus has told us how to live until he comes: We must watch for him, work diligently, and obey his commands. Such attitudes are especially necessary for leaders. Watchful and faithful leaders will be given increased opportunities and responsibilities. The more resources, talents, and understanding we have, the more we are required to use them effectively. God will not hold us responsible for gifts he has not given us, but all of us have been given enough gifts and duties to keep us busy until Jesus returns.

**12:50** The "baptism of suffering" to which Jesus referred was his coming crucifixion. Jesus was dreading the physical pain, of course, but even worse would be the spiritual pain of complete separation from God that would accompany his death for the sins of the world.

**12:51-53** In these strange and unsettling words, Jesus revealed that his coming often results in conflict. Because he demands a response, families may be split apart when some choose to follow him and others refuse to do so. Jesus allows no middle ground. He demands loyalty and commitment, sometimes to the point of severing other relationships. Are you willing to risk your family's disapproval in order to follow the Lord?

**12:54-57** For most of recorded history, the world's principal occupation was farming. The farmer depended directly on the weather for his livelihood. He needed just the right amounts of sun and rain—not too much, not too little—to make his living, and he grew skilled at interpreting natural signs. Jesus was

**12:53**
†Mic 7:6

<sup>53</sup> 'Father will be divided against son
     and son against father;
mother against daughter
     and daughter against mother;
and mother-in-law against daughter-in-law
     and daughter-in-law against mother-in-law.'*"

### Jesus Warns about the Future Crisis (144)

**12:54-56**
Matt 16:2-3

<sup>54</sup>Then Jesus turned to the crowd and said, "When you see clouds beginning to form in the west, you say, 'Here comes a shower.' And you are right. <sup>55</sup> When the south wind blows, you say, 'Today will be a scorcher.' And it is. <sup>56</sup> You fools! You know how to interpret the weather signs of the earth and sky, but you don't know how to interpret the present times.

**12:58-59**
Matt 5:25-26

<sup>57</sup> "Why can't you decide for yourselves what is right? <sup>58</sup> When you are on the way to court with your accuser, try to settle the matter before you get there. Otherwise, your accuser may drag you before the judge, who will hand you over to an officer, who will throw you into prison. <sup>59</sup> And if that happens, you won't be free again until you have paid the very last penny.*"

### Jesus Calls the People to Repent (145)

**13:2**
John 9:2-3

**13:3**
Ps 7:12

**13:4**
John 9:7, 11

**13:6**
Matt 21:19
Mark 11:12-14

**13:7**
Hab 3:17
Matt 3:10

**13** About this time Jesus was informed that Pilate had murdered some people from Galilee as they were offering sacrifices at the Temple. <sup>2</sup> "Do you think those Galileans were worse sinners than all the other people from Galilee?" Jesus asked. "Is that why they suffered? <sup>3</sup> Not at all! And you will perish, too, unless you repent of your sins and turn to God. <sup>4</sup> And what about the eighteen people who died when the tower in Siloam fell on them? Were they the worst sinners in Jerusalem? <sup>5</sup> No, and I tell you again that unless you repent, you will perish, too."

<sup>6</sup>Then Jesus told this story: "A man planted a fig tree in his garden and came again and again to see if there was any fruit on it, but he was always disappointed. <sup>7</sup> Finally, he said to

**12:53** Mic 7:6.    **12:59** Greek *last lepton* [the smallest Jewish coin].

---

**SEVEN
SABBATH
MIRACLES**

Over the centuries, the Jewish religious leaders had added rule after rule to God's law. For example, God's law said the Sabbath is a day of rest (Exodus 20:10, 11). But the religious leaders added to that law, creating one that said, "You cannot heal on the Sabbath" because that is "work." Seven times Jesus healed people on the Sabbath. In doing this, he was challenging these religious leaders to look beyond their rules to their true purpose—to honor God by helping those in need. Would God have been pleased if Jesus had ignored these people?

---

announcing an earthshaking event that would be much more important than the year's crops—the coming of God's Kingdom. Just as dark clouds forewarn of a rainstorm, there were signs that the Kingdom would soon arrive. But Jesus' hearers, though skilled at interpreting weather signs, were intentionally ignoring the signs of the times.

**13:1-5** Pilate may have killed the Galileans because he thought they were rebelling against Rome; those killed by the tower in Siloam may have been working for the Romans on an aqueduct there. The Pharisees, who were opposed to using force to deal with Rome, would have said that the Galileans killed by Pilate deserved to die for rebelling. The Zealots, a group of anti-Roman terrorists, would have said the aqueduct workers deserved to die for cooperating. Jesus dismissed the idea that accidents or human cruelties were God's judgment on especially bad sinners. Neither the Galileans nor the workers should be blamed for their calamities. Whether a person is killed in a tragic accident or

miraculously survives is not a measure of righteousness. Everyone has to die. Jesus did not explain why some live and some die tragically; instead he pointed to everyone's need for repentance. No matter how or when it occurs, death is not the end. Jesus promises that those who believe in him will not perish but have eternal life (John 3:16).

**13:6-9** In the Old Testament, a fruitful tree was often used as a symbol of godly living (see, for example, Psalm 1:3 and Jeremiah 17:7, 8). Jesus pointed out what would happen to the other kind of tree—the kind that took valuable time and space and still produced nothing for the patient gardener. By this illustration Jesus warned his listeners that God would not tolerate forever their lack of productivity. (Luke 3:9 records John the Baptist's version of the same message.) Have you been enjoying God's special treatment without giving anything in return? If so, respond to the Gardener's patient care and begin to bear the fruit God has created you to produce.

his gardener, 'I've waited three years, and there hasn't been a single fig! Cut it down. It's just taking up space in the garden.'

8 "The gardener answered, 'Sir, give it one more chance. Leave it another year, and I'll give it special attention and plenty of fertilizer. 9 If we get figs next year, fine. If not, then you can cut it down.'"

13:8
2 Pet 3:9, 15

### Jesus Heals the Crippled Woman (146)

10 One Sabbath day as Jesus was teaching in a synagogue, 11 he saw a woman who had been crippled by an evil spirit. She had been bent double for eighteen years and was unable to stand up straight. 12 When Jesus saw her, he called her over and said, "Dear woman, you are healed of your sickness!" 13 Then he touched her, and instantly she could stand straight. How she praised God!

13:10
Matt 4:23

13:13
Mark 5:23

14 But the leader in charge of the synagogue was indignant that Jesus had healed her on the Sabbath day. "There are six days of the week for working," he said to the crowd. "Come on those days to be healed, not on the Sabbath."

13:14
Exod 20:9-10
Deut 5:13-14
Matt 12:10
Mark 3:2
Luke 6:7
John 5:16

15 But the Lord replied, "You hypocrites! Each of you works on the Sabbath day! Don't you untie your ox or your donkey from its stall on the Sabbath and lead it out for water? 16 This dear woman, a daughter of Abraham, has been held in bondage by Satan for eighteen years. Isn't it right that she be released, even on the Sabbath?"

13:15
Luke 14:5

13:16
Luke 19:9

17 This shamed his enemies, but all the people rejoiced at the wonderful things he did.

### Jesus Teaches about the Kingdom of God (147)

18 Then Jesus said, "What is the Kingdom of God like? How can I illustrate it? 19 It is like a tiny mustard seed that a man planted in a garden; it grows and becomes a tree, and the birds make nests in its branches."

20 He also asked, "What else is the Kingdom of God like? 21 It is like the yeast a woman used in making bread. Even though she put only a little yeast in three measures of flour, it permeated every part of the dough."

### Jesus Teaches about Entering the Kingdom (153)

22 Jesus went through the towns and villages, teaching as he went, always pressing on toward Jerusalem. 23 Someone asked him, "Lord, will only a few be saved?"

He replied, 24 "Work hard to enter the narrow door to God's Kingdom, for many will try to enter but will fail. 25 When the master of the house has locked the door, it will be too late. You will stand outside knocking and pleading, 'Lord, open the door for us!' But he will reply, 'I don't know you or where you come from.' 26 Then you will say, 'But we ate and drank with you, and you taught in our streets.' 27 And he will reply, 'I tell you, I don't know you or where you come from. Get away from me, all you who do evil.'

13:24
Mark 10:25
1 Tim 6:12

13:25
Matt 25:10-11

13:27
†Ps 6:8
Matt 25:12

---

**13:10-17** Why was healing considered work? The religious leaders saw healing as part of a doctor's profession, and practicing one's profession on the Sabbath was prohibited. The synagogue leader could not see beyond the law to Jesus' compassion in healing this crippled woman. Jesus shamed him and the other leaders by pointing out their hypocrisy. They would untie their animals and care for them, but they refused to rejoice when a human being was freed from Satan's bondage.

**13:16** In our fallen world, disease and disability are common. Their causes are many and often multiple—inadequate nutrition, contact with a source of infection, lowered defenses, and even direct attack by Satan. Whatever the immediate cause of our illness, we can trace its original source to Satan, the author of all the evil in our world. The Good News is that Jesus is more powerful than the devil or any disease. He often brings physical healing in this life; and when he returns, he will put an end to all disease and disability.

**13:18-21** The general expectation among Jesus' hearers was that the Messiah would come as a great king and leader, freeing the nation from Rome and restoring Israel's former glory. But Jesus said his Kingdom was beginning quietly. Like the tiny mustard seed that grows into an enormous tree, or the spoonful of yeast that makes the bread dough double in size, the Kingdom of God would eventually push outward until the whole world was changed.

**13:22** This is the second time Luke reminds us that Jesus was intentionally going to Jerusalem (the other time is in 9:51). Jesus knew he was on his way to die, but he continued preaching to large crowds. The prospect of death did not deter Jesus from his mission.

**13:24, 25** Finding salvation requires more concentrated effort than most people are willing to put forth. Obviously we cannot save ourselves—there is no way we can work ourselves into God's favor. We "work hard to enter" through the narrow door by earnestly desiring to know Jesus and diligently striving to follow him whatever the cost. We dare not put off making this decision because the door will not stay open forever.

**13:26, 27** The people were eager to know who would be in God's Kingdom. Jesus explained that, although many people know something about God, only a few have acknowledged their sins and accepted his forgiveness. We may not necessarily see the people we expect to find in the Kingdom of God. Some perfectly respectable religious leaders claiming allegiance to Jesus will not be there because they were not true followers and secretly were morally corrupt. Just listening to Jesus' words or admiring his miracles is not enough. We must turn from sin and trust in God to save us.

13:29
Ps 107:3
Isa 43:5; 49:12;
59:19
Rev 14:15; 21:13;
22:16

13:30
Matt 19:30; 20:16
Mark 10:31

28 "There will be weeping and gnashing of teeth, for you will see Abraham, Isaac, Jacob, and all the prophets in the Kingdom of God, but you will be thrown out. 29 And people will come from all over the world—from east and west, north and south—to take their places in the Kingdom of God. 30 And note this: Some who seem least important now will be the greatest then, and some who are the greatest now will be least important then.*"

### Jesus Grieves over Jerusalem (154)

31 At that time some Pharisees said to him, "Get away from here if you want to live! Herod Antipas wants to kill you!"

13:33
Matt 16:21

32 Jesus replied, "Go tell that fox that I will keep on casting out demons and healing people today and tomorrow; and the third day I will accomplish my purpose. 33 Yes, today, tomorrow, and the next day I must proceed on my way. For it wouldn't do for a prophet of God to be killed except in Jerusalem!

13:34-35
Luke 19:41-44

13:35
†Ps 118:26
Jer 12:7; 22:5
Luke 19:38

34 "O Jerusalem, Jerusalem, the city that kills the prophets and stones God's messengers! How often I have wanted to gather your children together as a hen protects her chicks beneath her wings, but you wouldn't let me. 35 And now, look, your house is abandoned. And you will never see me again until you say, 'Blessings on the one who comes in the name of the LORD!'*"

### Jesus Heals a Man with Swollen Limbs (155)

14:1
Luke 7:36; 11:37

14:3
Luke 6:9

14:5
Matt 12:11

**14** One Sabbath day Jesus went to eat dinner in the home of a leader of the Pharisees, and the people were watching him closely. 2 There was a man there whose arms and legs were swollen.* 3 Jesus asked the Pharisees and experts in religious law, "Is it permitted in the law to heal people on the Sabbath day, or not?" 4 When they refused to answer, Jesus touched the sick man and healed him and sent him away. 5 Then he turned to them and said, "Which of you doesn't work on the Sabbath? If your son* or your cow falls into a pit, don't you rush to get him out?" 6 Again they could not answer.

### Jesus Teaches about Humility (156)

14:7
Matt 23:6

14:8-11
Prov 25:6-7

7 When Jesus noticed that all who had come to the dinner were trying to sit in the seats of honor near the head of the table, he gave them this advice: 8 "When you are invited to a wedding feast, don't sit in the seat of honor. What if someone who is more distinguished than you has also been invited? 9 The host will come and say, 'Give this person your seat.' Then you will be embarrassed, and you will have to take whatever seat is left at the foot of the table!

10 "Instead, take the lowest place at the foot of the table. Then when your host sees you, he will come and say, 'Friend, we have a better place for you!' Then you will be honored in front

---

**13:30** Greek *Some are last who will be first, and some are first who will be last.* **13:35** Ps 118:26. **14:2** Or *who had dropsy.* **14:5** Some manuscripts read *donkey.*

---

**13:29** God's Kingdom will include people from every part of the world. Israel's rejection of Jesus as Messiah would not stop God's plan. True Israel includes all people who believe in Christ. This was an important fact for Luke to stress as he was directing his Good News to a Gentile audience (see also Romans 4:16-25; Galatians 3:6-9).

**13:30** God's Kingdom will have many surprises. Some who are despised now will be greatly honored then; some influential people here will be left outside the gates. Many "great" people on this earth (in God's eyes) are virtually ignored by the rest of the world. What matters to God is not a person's earthly popularity, status, wealth, heritage, or power but his or her commitment to Christ. How do your values match those of the Bible? Put God in first place, and you will join people from all over the world who will take their places at the feast in the Kingdom of Heaven.

**13:31-33** The Pharisees weren't interested in protecting Jesus from danger; they were trying to trap him themselves. The Pharisees urged Jesus to leave because they wanted to stop him from going to Jerusalem, not because they feared Herod. But Jesus' life, work, and death would not be determined by Herod or the Pharisees. His life was planned and directed by God himself, and his mission would unfold in God's time and according to God's plan.

**13:33** Why was Jesus focusing on Jerusalem? Jerusalem, the city of God, symbolized the entire nation. It was Israel's largest

city, the nation's spiritual and political capital, and Jews from around the world frequently visited it. But Jerusalem had a history of rejecting God's prophets (1 Kings 19:10; 2 Chronicles 24:19; Jeremiah 2:30; 26:20-23). It would reject the Messiah, just as it had rejected his forerunners.

**14:1-6** Earlier Jesus had been invited to a Pharisee's home for discussion (7:36). This time a prominent Pharisee invited Jesus to his home specifically to trap him into saying or doing something for which he could be arrested. It may be surprising to see Jesus on the Pharisees' turf after he had denounced them so many times. But he was not afraid to face them, even though he knew that their purpose was to trick him into breaking their laws.

**14:7-11** Jesus advised people not to rush for the best places at a feast. People today are just as eager to raise their social status, whether by being with the right people, dressing for success, or driving the right car. Whom do you try to impress? Rather than aiming for prestige, look for a place where you can serve. If God wants you to serve on a wider scale, he will invite you to take a higher place.

**14:7-14** Jesus taught two lessons here. First, he spoke to the guests, telling them not to seek places of honor. Service is more important in God's Kingdom than status. Second, he told the host not to be exclusive about whom he invited. God opens his Kingdom to everyone.

of all the other guests. ¹¹For those who exalt themselves will be humbled, and those who humble themselves will be exalted."

¹²Then he turned to his host. "When you put on a luncheon or a banquet," he said, "don't invite your friends, brothers, relatives, and rich neighbors. For they will invite you back, and that will be your only reward. ¹³Instead, invite the poor, the crippled, the lame, and the blind. ¹⁴Then at the resurrection of the righteous, God will reward you for inviting those who could not repay you."

### Jesus Tells the Parable of the Great Feast (157)

¹⁵Hearing this, a man sitting at the table with Jesus exclaimed, "What a blessing it will be to attend a banquet* in the Kingdom of God!"

¹⁶Jesus replied with this story: "A man prepared a great feast and sent out many invitations. ¹⁷When the banquet was ready, he sent his servant to tell the guests, 'Come, the banquet is ready.' ¹⁸But they all began making excuses. One said, 'I have just bought a field and must inspect it. Please excuse me.' ¹⁹Another said, 'I have just bought five pairs of oxen, and I want to try them out. Please excuse me.' ²⁰Another said, 'I now have a wife, so I can't come.'

²¹"The servant returned and told his master what they had said. His master was furious and said, 'Go quickly into the streets and alleys of the town and invite the poor, the crippled, the blind, and the lame.' ²²After the servant had done this, he reported, 'There is still room for more.' ²³So his master said, 'Go out into the country lanes and behind the hedges and urge anyone you find to come, so that the house will be full. ²⁴For none of those I first invited will get even the smallest taste of my banquet.'"

### Jesus Teaches about the Cost of Being a Disciple (158)

²⁵A large crowd was following Jesus. He turned around and said to them, ²⁶"If you want to be my disciple, you must hate everyone else by comparison—your father and mother, wife and children, brothers and sisters—yes, even your own life. Otherwise, you cannot be my disciple. ²⁷And if you do not carry your own cross and follow me, you cannot be my disciple.

²⁸"But don't begin until you count the cost. For who would begin construction of a building without first calculating the cost to see if there is enough money to finish it? ²⁹Otherwise, you might complete only the foundation before running out of money, and then everyone would laugh at you. ³⁰They would say, 'There's the person who started that building and couldn't afford to finish it!'

**14:15** Greek *to eat bread.*

---

**Cross references (right margin):**

**14:11**
Matt 23:12
Luke 18:14

**14:14**
Acts 24:15

**14:20**
Deut 24:5
1 Cor 7:33

**14:24**
Matt 21:43
Acts 13:46

**14:26**
Deut 33:9
Matt 16:24
Mark 8:34
Luke 9:23; 18:29
John 12:25

**14:27**
Matt 10:38; 16:24
Mark 8:34
Luke 9:23

---

**14:11** How can we humble ourselves? Some people try to give the appearance of humility in order to manipulate others. Others think that humility means putting themselves down. Truly humble people compare themselves only with Christ, realize their sinfulness, and understand their limitations. On the other hand, they also recognize their gifts and strengths and are willing to use them as Christ directs. Humility is not self-degradation; it is realistic self-assessment and commitment to serve.

**14:15-24** The man sitting at the table with Jesus envisioned the glory of God's Kingdom, but he did not yet understand how to have a share in it. In Jesus' story, many people turned down the invitation to the banquet because the timing was inconvenient. We, too, may resist or delay responding to God's invitation, and our excuses may sound reasonable—work duties, family responsibilities, financial needs, or other reasons. Nevertheless, God's invitation is the most important event in your life, no matter how inconveniently it may be timed. Are you making excuses to avoid responding to God's call? Jesus reminds us that the time will come when God will pull his invitation and offer it to others—then it will be too late to get into the banquet.

**14:16ff** The custom was to send two invitations to a party: the first to announce the event and the second to tell the guests that everything was ready. The guests in Jesus' story insulted the host by making excuses when he issued the second invitation. In Israel's history, God's first invitation came from Moses and the prophets; the second came from his Son. The religious leaders accepted the first invitation. They believed that God had called them to be his people, but they insulted God by refusing to accept his Son. Thus, as the master in the story sent his servant into the

streets to invite the needy to his banquet, so God sent his Son to a whole world of needy people to tell them that God's Kingdom had arrived and was ready for them.

**14:16ff** In this chapter we read Jesus' words against seeking status and in favor of hard work and even suffering. Let us not lose sight of the end result of all our humility and self-sacrifice—a joyous banquet with our Lord! God never asks us to suffer for the sake of suffering. He never asks us to give up something good unless he plans to replace it with something even better. Jesus is not calling us to join him in a labor camp but in a feast—the wedding feast of the Lamb (Revelation 19:6-9), when God and his beloved church will be joined forever.

**14:27** Jesus' audience was well aware of what it meant to carry one's own cross. When the Romans led a criminal to his execution site, he was forced to carry the cross on which he would die. This showed his submission to Rome and warned observers that they had better submit, too. Jesus made this statement to get the crowds to think through their enthusiasm for him. He encouraged those who were superficial either to go deeper or to turn back. Following Christ means total submission to him—perhaps even to the point of death. (See also the note on 9:23.)

**14:28-30** When a builder doesn't count the cost or estimates it inaccurately, the building may be left uncompleted. Will you abandon the Christian life after a little while because you did not count the cost of commitment to Jesus? What are those costs? Christians may face loss of social status or wealth. They may have to give up control of their money, their time, or their career. They may be hated, separated from their family, and even put to death. Following Christ does not mean a trouble-free life. We must care-

31 "Or what king would go to war against another king without first sitting down with his counselors to discuss whether his army of 10,000 could defeat the 20,000 soldiers marching against him? 32 And if he can't, he will send a delegation to discuss terms of peace while the enemy is still far away. 33 So you cannot become my disciple without giving up everything you own.

34 "Salt is good for seasoning. But if it loses its flavor, how do you make it salty again? 35 Flavorless salt is good neither for the soil nor for the manure pile. It is thrown away. Anyone with ears to hear should listen and understand!"

### Jesus Tells the Parable of the Lost Sheep (159)

**15** Tax collectors and other notorious sinners often came to listen to Jesus teach. 2 This made the Pharisees and teachers of religious law complain that he was associating with such sinful people—even eating with them!

3 So Jesus told them this story: 4 "If a man has a hundred sheep and one of them gets lost, what will he do? Won't he leave the ninety-nine others in the wilderness and go to search for the one that is lost until he finds it? 5 And when he has found it, he will joyfully carry it home on his shoulders. 6 When he arrives, he will call together his friends and neighbors, saying, 'Rejoice with me because I have found my lost sheep.' 7 In the same way, there is more joy in heaven over one lost sinner who repents and returns to God than over ninety-nine others who are righteous and haven't strayed away!

### Jesus Tells the Parable of the Lost Coin (160)

8 "Or suppose a woman has ten silver coins* and loses one. Won't she light a lamp and sweep the entire house and search carefully until she finds it? 9 And when she finds it, she will call in her friends and neighbors and say, 'Rejoice with me because I have found my lost coin.' 10 In the same way, there is joy in the presence of God's angels when even one sinner repents."

### Jesus Tells the Parable of the Lost Son (161)

11 To illustrate the point further, Jesus told them this story: "A man had two sons. 12 The younger son told his father, 'I want my share of your estate now before you die.' So his father agreed to divide his wealth between his sons.

**15:8** Greek *ten drachmas*. A drachma was the equivalent of a full day's wage.

---

**Side margin references:**

14:33
Phil 3:7-8

14:34
Matt 5:13
Mark 9:50

14:35
Matt 11:15

15:1
Matt 9:11
Luke 5:29
Gal 2:12

15:12
Deut 21:17

---

fully count the cost of becoming Christ's disciples so that we will firmly hold to our faith and won't be tempted later to turn back.

**14:34** Salt can lose its flavor. When it gets wet and then dries, nothing is left but a tasteless residue. Many Christians blend into the world and avoid the cost of standing up for Christ. But Jesus says if Christians lose their distinctive saltiness, they become worthless. Just as salt flavors and preserves food, we are to preserve the good in the world and bring new flavor to life. This requires careful planning, willing sacrifice, and unswerving commitment to Christ's Kingdom. But if a Christian fails to be "salty," he or she fails to represent Christ in the world. How salty are you?

**15:2** Why were the Pharisees and teachers of religious law bothered that Jesus associated with these people? The religious leaders were always careful to stay "clean" according to Old Testament law. In fact, they went well beyond the law in their avoidance of certain people and situations and in their ritual washings. By contrast, Jesus took their concept of "cleanness" lightly. He risked defilement by touching those who had leprosy and by neglecting to wash in the Pharisees' prescribed manner, and he showed complete disregard for their sanctions against associating with certain classes of people. He came to offer salvation to sinners and to show that God loves them. Jesus didn't worry about the accusations. Instead, he continued going to those who needed him, regardless of the effect these rejected people might have on his reputation. How are you following Jesus' example?

**15:3-6** It may seem foolish for the shepherd to leave 99 sheep to go search for just one. But the shepherd knew that the 99 would be safe in the sheepfold, whereas the lost sheep was in danger. Because each sheep was of high value, the shepherd knew that it was worthwhile to search diligently for the lost one. God's love for the individual is so great that he seeks out each one and rejoices

when he or she is found. Jesus associated with sinners because he wanted to bring the lost sheep—people considered beyond hope— the Good News of God's Kingdom. Before you were a believer, God sought you; and he is still seeking those who are yet lost.

**15:4, 5** We may be able to understand a God who would forgive sinners who come to him for mercy. But a God who tenderly searches for sinners and then joyfully forgives them must possess an extraordinary love! This is the kind of love that prompted Jesus to come to earth to search for lost people and save them. This is the kind of extraordinary love that God has for you.

**15:8-10** Palestinian women received 10 silver coins as a wedding gift. Besides their monetary value, these coins held sentimental value like that of a wedding ring, and to lose one would be extremely distressing. Just as a woman would rejoice at finding her lost coin, so the angels rejoice over a repentant sinner. Each individual is precious to God. He grieves over every loss and rejoices whenever one of his children is found and brought into the Kingdom. Perhaps we would have more joy in our churches if we shared Jesus' love and concern for the lost, diligently seeking them, and rejoicing when they come to the Savior.

**15:12** The younger son's share of the estate would have been one-third, with the older son receiving two-thirds (Deuteronomy 21:17). In most cases he would have received this at his father's death, although fathers sometimes chose to divide up their inheritance early and retire from managing their estates. What is unusual here is that the younger one initiated the division of the estate. This showed arrogant disregard for his father's authority as head of the family.

13 "A few days later this younger son packed all his belongings and moved to a distant land, and there he wasted all his money in wild living. 14 About the time his money ran out, a great famine swept over the land, and he began to starve. 15 He persuaded a local farmer to hire him, and the man sent him into his fields to feed the pigs. 16 The young man became so hungry that even the pods he was feeding the pigs looked good to him. But no one gave him anything.

17 "When he finally came to his senses, he said to himself, 'At home even the hired servants have food enough to spare, and here I am dying of hunger! 18 I will go home to my father and say, "Father, I have sinned against both heaven and you, 19 and I am no longer worthy of being called your son. Please take me on as a hired servant."'

**15:18**
Ps 51:4

20 "So he returned home to his father. And while he was still a long way off, his father saw him coming. Filled with love and compassion, he ran to his son, embraced him, and kissed him. 21 His son said to him, 'Father, I have sinned against both heaven and you, and I am no longer worthy of being called your son.*'

**15:20**
Gen 45:14-15; 46:29

22 "But his father said to the servants, 'Quick! Bring the finest robe in the house and put it on him. Get a ring for his finger and sandals for his feet. 23 And kill the calf we have been fattening. We must celebrate with a feast, 24 for this son of mine was dead and has now returned to life. He was lost, but now he is found.' So the party began.

**15:22**
Gen 41:42
Zech 3:4
Rev 6:11

**15:24**
Eph 2:1, 5; 5:14

25 "Meanwhile, the older son was in the fields working. When he returned home, he heard music and dancing in the house, 26 and he asked one of the servants what was going on. 27 'Your brother is back,' he was told, 'and your father has killed the fattened calf. We are celebrating because of his safe return.'

28 "The older brother was angry and wouldn't go in. His father came out and begged him, 29 but he replied, 'All these years I've slaved for you and never once refused to do a single thing you told me to. And in all that time you never gave me even one young goat for a feast with my friends. 30 Yet when this son of yours comes back after squandering your money on prostitutes, you celebrate by killing the fattened calf!'

31 "His father said to him, 'Look, dear son, you have always stayed by me, and everything I have is yours. 32 We had to celebrate this happy day. For your brother was dead and has come back to life! He was lost, but now he is found!'"

**15:31**
Prov 29:3
John 17:10, 24

**15:21** Some manuscripts add *Please take me on as a hired servant.*

---

**15:15, 16** According to Moses' law, pigs were unclean animals (Leviticus 11:2-8; Deuteronomy 14:8). This meant that pigs could not be eaten or used for sacrifices. To protect themselves from defilement, Jews would not even touch pigs. For a Jew to stoop to feeding pigs was a great humiliation, and for this young man to eat food that the pigs had touched was to be degraded beyond belief. The younger son had truly sunk to the depths.

**15:17** The younger son, like many who are rebellious and immature, wanted to be free to live as he pleased, and he had to hit bottom before he came to his senses. It often takes great sorrow and tragedy to cause people to look to the only One who can help them—Jesus. Are you trying to live life your own way, selfishly pushing aside any responsibility or commitment that gets in your way? Stop and look before you hit bottom. You will save yourself and your family much grief.

**15:20** In the two preceding stories, the seeker actively looked for the coin and the sheep, which could not return by themselves. In this story, the father watched and waited. He was dealing with a human being with a will of his own, but he was ready to greet his son if he returned. In the same way, God's love is constant and patient and welcoming. He will search for us and give us opportunities to respond, but he will not force us to come to him. Like the father in this story, God waits patiently for us to come to our senses.

**15:24** The sheep was lost because it foolishly wandered away (15:4); the coin was lost through no fault of its own (15:8); and the son left out of selfishness (15:12). God's great love reaches out and finds sinners no matter why or how they got lost.

**15:25-31** The older brother found great difficulty in accepting his younger brother when he returned, and it is just as difficult to accept "younger brothers and sisters" today. People who repent after leading notoriously sinful lives are often held in suspicion; churches are sometimes unwilling to admit them to membership. Instead, we should rejoice like the angels in heaven when an unbeliever repents and turns to God. Like the father, accept repentant sinners wholeheartedly and give them the support and encouragement that they need to grow in Christ.

**15:30** In the story of the lost son, the father's response is contrasted with the older brother's. The father forgave because he was filled with love. The son refused to forgive because he was bitter. His resentment rendered him just as lost to the father's love as his younger brother had been. Don't let anything keep you from forgiving others. If you are refusing to forgive people, you are missing a wonderful opportunity to experience joy and share it with others. Make your joy grow: Forgive somebody who has hurt you.

**15:32** In Jesus' story, the older brother represents the Pharisees, who were angry and resentful that sinners were being welcomed into God's Kingdom. "After all," the Pharisees must have thought, "we have sacrificed and done *so much* for God." How easy it is to resent God's gracious forgiveness of others whom we consider to be far worse sinners than ourselves. But if our self-righteousness gets in the way of rejoicing when others come to Jesus, we are no better than the Pharisees.

*Jesus Tells the Parable of the Shrewd Manager* (**162**)

**16:1**
Luke 15:13, 30

**16** Jesus told this story to his disciples: "There was a certain rich man who had a manager handling his affairs. One day a report came that the manager was wasting his employer's money.² So the employer called him in and said, ' What's this I hear about you? Get your report in order, because you are going to be fired.'

³ "The manager thought to himself, 'Now what? My boss has fired me. I don't have the strength to dig ditches, and I'm too proud to beg.⁴ Ah, I know how to ensure that I'll have plenty of friends who will give me a home when I am fired.'

⁵ "So he invited each person who owed money to his employer to come and discuss the situation. He asked the first one, 'How much do you owe him?'⁶ The man replied, 'I owe him 800 gallons of olive oil.' So the manager told him, ' Take the bill and quickly change it to 400 gallons.*'

⁷ "'And how much do you owe my employer?' he asked the next man. 'I owe him 1,000 bushels of wheat,' was the reply. 'Here,' the manager said, 'take the bill and change it to 800 bushels.*'

**16:8**
John 12:36
Eph 5:8
1 Thes 5:5

⁸ "The rich man had to admire the dishonest rascal for being so shrewd. And it is true that the children of this world are more shrewd in dealing with the world around them than are the children of the light.⁹ Here's the lesson: Use your worldly resources to benefit others and make friends. Then, when your earthly possessions are gone, they will welcome you to an eternal home.*

**16:10-12**
Matt 25:20-30
Luke 19:17-26

¹⁰ "If you are faithful in little things, you will be faithful in large ones. But if you are dishonest in little things, you won't be honest with greater responsibilities.¹¹ And if you are untrustworthy about worldly wealth, who will trust you with the true riches of heaven? ¹² And if you are not faithful with other people's things, why should you be trusted with things of your own?

**16:13**
Matt 6:24

**16:14**
Luke 23:35
1 Tim 3:3

**16:15**
Prov 24:12
Matt 23:28
Luke 8:9-14

**16:16**
Matt 11:12-13

**16:17**
Matt 5:18

¹³ "No one can serve two masters. For you will hate one and love the other; you will be devoted to one and despise the other. You cannot serve both God and money."

¹⁴ The Pharisees, who dearly loved their money, heard all this and scoffed at him. ¹⁵ Then he said to them, "You like to appear righteous in public, but God knows your hearts. What this world honors is detestable in the sight of God.

¹⁶ "Until John the Baptist, the law of Moses and the messages of the prophets were your guides. But now the Good News of the Kingdom of God is preached, and everyone is eager to get in.*¹⁷ But that doesn't mean that the law has lost its force. It is easier for heaven and earth to disappear than for the smallest point of God's law to be overturned.

**16:6** Greek *100 baths . . . 50 [baths].*   **16:7** Greek *100 korous . . . 80 [korous].*   **16:9** Or *you will be welcomed into eternal homes.*   **16:16** Or *everyone is urged to enter in.*

---

**16:1-8** Our use of money is a good test of the lordship of Christ. (1) Money belongs to God, not us; let us use our resources wisely, (2) Money can be used for good or evil; let us use ours for good. (3) Money has a lot of power, let us use it carefully and thoughtfully. We must use our material goods in a way that will foster faith and obedience (see 12:33, 34).

**16:9** We are to make wise use of the financial opportunities we have, not to earn heaven but to help people find Christ. If we use our money to help those in need or to help others find Christ, our earthly investment will bring eternal benefit. When we obey God's will, the unselfish use of possessions will follow.

**16:10, 11** Our integrity is often put on the line in money matters. God calls us to be honest even in small details we could easily ignore. Heaven's riches are far more valuable than earthly wealth. But if we are not trustworthy with our money here (no matter how much or little we have), we will be unfit to handle the vast riches of God's Kingdom. See that you maintain your integrity in all matters, whether big or small.

**16:13** Money can easily take God's place in your life. It can become your master. How can you tell if you are a slave to money? Ask yourself: Do I think and worry about it frequently? Do I give up doing what I should do or would like to do in order to make more money? Do I spend a great deal of my time caring for my possessions? Is it hard for me to give money away? Am I in debt?

Money is a hard and deceptive master. Wealth promises power and control, but often it cannot deliver. Great fortunes can be made—and lost—overnight, and no amount of money can provide health, happiness, or eternal life. How much better it is to let God be your master. His servants have peace of mind and security, both now and forever.

**16:14** Because the Pharisees loved money, they took exception to Jesus' teaching. We live in an age that measures people's worth by how much money they make. Do you scoff at Jesus' warnings against serving money? Do you try to explain them away? Do you apply them to someone else? Unless we take Jesus' statements seriously, we may be acting like Pharisees ourselves.

**16:15** The Pharisees acted piously to get praise from others, but God knew what was in their hearts. They considered their wealth to be a sign of God's approval. God detested their wealth because it caused them to abandon true spirituality. Though prosperity may earn people's praise, it must never substitute for devotion and service to God.

**16:16, 17** John the Baptist's ministry was the dividing line between the Old and New Testaments (John 1:15-18). With the arrival of Jesus came the realization of all the prophets' hopes. Jesus emphasized that his Kingdom fulfilled the law (the Old Testament); it did not cancel it (Matthew 5:17). His was not a new system but the culmination of the old. The same God who worked through Moses was working through Jesus.

18 "For example, a man who divorces his wife and marries someone else commits adultery. And anyone who marries a woman divorced from her husband commits adultery."

### Jesus Tells about the Rich Man and the Beggar (163)

19 Jesus said, "There was a certain rich man who was splendidly clothed in purple and fine linen and who lived each day in luxury. 20 At his gate lay a poor man named Lazarus who was covered with sores. 21 As Lazarus lay there longing for scraps from the rich man's table, the dogs would come and lick his open sores.

22 "Finally, the poor man died and was carried by the angels to be with Abraham.* The rich man also died and was buried, 23 and his soul went to the place of the dead.* There, in torment, he saw Abraham in the far distance with Lazarus at his side.

24 "The rich man shouted, 'Father Abraham, have some pity! Send Lazarus over here to dip the tip of his finger in water and cool my tongue. I am in anguish in these flames.'

25 "But Abraham said to him, 'Son, remember that during your lifetime you had everything you wanted, and Lazarus had nothing. So now he is here being comforted, and you are in anguish. 26 And besides, there is a great chasm separating us. No one can cross over to you from here, and no one can cross over to us from there.'

27 "Then the rich man said, 'Please, Father Abraham, at least send him to my father's home. 28 For I have five brothers, and I want him to warn them so they don't end up in this place of torment.'

29 "But Abraham said, 'Moses and the prophets have warned them. Your brothers can read what they wrote.'

30 "The rich man replied, 'No, Father Abraham! But if someone is sent to them from the dead, then they will repent of their sins and turn to God.'

31 "But Abraham said, 'If they won't listen to Moses and the prophets, they won't listen even if someone rises from the dead.'"

### Jesus Tells about Forgiveness and Faith (164)

**17** One day Jesus said to his disciples, "There will always be temptations to sin, but what sorrow awaits the person who does the tempting! 2 It would be better to be thrown into the sea with a millstone hung around your neck than to cause one of these little ones to fall into sin. 3 So watch yourselves!

"If another believer* sins, rebuke that person; then if there is repentance, forgive. 4 Even if that person wrongs you seven times a day and each time turns again and asks forgiveness, you must forgive."

**16:22** Greek *into Abraham's bosom.*   **16:23** Greek *to Hades.*   **17:3** Greek *If your brother.*

---

**16:18**
Matt 5:32; 19:9
Mark 10:11-12
1 Cor 7:10-11

**16:22**
Matt 8:11

**16:24**
Luke 3:8

**16:25**
Luke 6:24

**16:28**
Acts 18:5

**16:29**
Luke 24:27, 44
John 1:45; 5:45-47
Acts 15:21

**16:31**
Matt 6:24
John 11:44-48

**17:1-3**
Matt 18:7
Mark 9:42

**17:3**
Matt 18:15

---

**16:18** Most religious leaders of Jesus' day permitted a man to divorce his wife for nearly any reason. Jesus' teaching about divorce went beyond Moses' (Deuteronomy 24:1-4). Stricter than any of the then-current schools of thought, Jesus' teachings shocked his hearers (see Matthew 19:10) just as they shake today's readers. Jesus says in no uncertain terms that marriage is a lifetime commitment. To leave your spouse for another person may be legal, but it is adultery in God's eyes. As you think about marriage, remember that God intends it to be a permanent commitment.

**16:19-31** The Pharisees considered wealth to be a proof of a person's righteousness. Jesus startled them with this story in which a diseased beggar is rewarded and a rich man is punished. The rich man did not go to hell because of his wealth but because he was selfish, refusing to feed Lazarus, take him in, or care for him. The rich man was hard-hearted in spite of his great blessings. The amount of money we have is not as important as the way we use it. What is your attitude toward your money and possessions? Do you hoard them selfishly, or do you use them to help others?

**16:20** This Lazarus is merely a character in a story and should not be confused with the Lazarus whom Jesus raised from the dead in John 11.

**16:29-31** The rich man thought that his five brothers would surely believe a messenger who had been raised from the dead. But Jesus said that if they did not believe Moses and the proph-

ets, who spoke constantly of caring for the poor, not even a resurrection would convince them. Notice the irony in Jesus' statement; on his way to Jerusalem to die, he was fully aware that even when he had risen from the dead, most of the religious leaders would not accept him. They were set in their ways, and neither Scripture nor God's Son himself would shake them loose.

**17:1-3** Jesus warned about God's wrath for those who offend, abuse, or lead astray the little ones. Jesus warns any predators who would hurt children in any way. How appropriate such a warning is in this day when corruption enters our homes every day in many television programs or on the internet. While Christians must guard against physical abuse, they also must be aware of and work against the mental and spiritual corruption that unfiltered television and unsupervised internet surfing can bring.

Jesus' warning envisions an additional group, however. The "little ones" can be new disciples. Indifference to the training and treatment of new Christians can leave them theologically vulnerable. Make the follow-through care of recent converts and new members a high priority in your church.

**17:3, 4** To rebuke does not mean to point out every sin we see; it means to bring sin to a person's attention with the purpose of restoring him or her to God and to fellow humans. When you feel you must rebuke another Christian for a sin, check your attitudes before you speak. Do you love that person? Are you willing to forgive? Unless rebuke is tied to forgiveness, it will not help the sinning person.

**17:5**
Mark 9:24

**17:6**
Matt 17:20; 21:21

**17:10**
1 Cor 9:16

⁵The apostles said to the Lord, "Show us how to increase our faith."

⁶The Lord answered, "If you had faith even as small as a mustard seed, you could say to this mulberry tree, 'May you be uprooted and thrown into the sea,' and it would obey you!

⁷ "When a servant comes in from plowing or taking care of sheep, does his master say, 'Come in and eat with me'?⁸ No, he says, 'Prepare my meal, put on your apron, and serve me while I eat. Then you can eat later.'⁹ And does the master thank the servant for doing what he was told to do? Of course not. ¹⁰ In the same way, when you obey me you should say, 'We are unworthy servants who have simply done our duty.'"

### Jesus Heals Ten Men with Leprosy (169)

**17:11**
Luke 9:51-52;
13:22

**17:12**
Lev 13:46

**17:14**
Lev 14:2-3
Luke 5:14

**17:16**
Matt 10:5

**17:19**
Matt 9:22
Luke 7:50; 18:42

¹¹As Jesus continued on toward Jerusalem, he reached the border between Galilee and Samaria. ¹²As he entered a village there, ten lepers stood at a distance, ¹³crying out, "Jesus, Master, have mercy on us!"

¹⁴He looked at them and said, "Go show yourselves to the priests."* And as they went, they were cleansed of their leprosy.

¹⁵One of them, when he saw that he was healed, came back to Jesus, shouting, "Praise God!" ¹⁶He fell to the ground at Jesus' feet, thanking him for what he had done. This man was a Samaritan.

¹⁷Jesus asked, "Didn't I heal ten men? Where are the other nine?¹⁸ Has no one returned to give glory to God except this foreigner?" ¹⁹And Jesus said to the man, "Stand up and go. Your faith has healed you.*"

**17:14** See Lev 14:2-32.   **17:19** Or *Your faith has saved you.*

---

**17:5, 6** The disciples' request was genuine; they wanted the faith necessary for such radical forgiveness. But Jesus didn't directly answer their question because the amount of faith is not as important as its genuineness. What is faith? It is complete trust and loyalty to God that results in a willingness to do his will. Faith is not something we use to put on a show for others. It is complete and humble obedience to God's will, readiness to do whatever he calls us to do. The amount of faith isn't as important as the right kind of faith—faith in our all-powerful God.

**17:6** A mustard seed is small, but it is alive and growing. Almost invisible at first, the seed will begin to spread, first under the ground and then visibly. Like a tiny seed, a small amount of genuine faith in God will take root and grow. Although each change will be gradual and imperceptible, soon this faith will have produced major results that will uproot and destroy competing loyalties. We don't need more faith; a tiny seed of faith is enough if it is alive and growing.

**17:7-10** If we have obeyed God, we have only done our duty, and we should regard it as a privilege. Do you sometimes feel that you deserve extra credit for serving God? Remember, obedience is not something extra we do; it is our duty. Jesus is not suggesting that our service is meaningless or useless, nor is he advocating doing away with rewards. He is attacking unwarranted self-esteem and spiritual pride.

**17:11-14** Because leprosy was contagious, people who had leprosy were required to try to stay away from other people and to announce their presence if they had to come near. Sometimes leprosy would go into remission. If a leper thought his leprosy had gone away, he was supposed to present himself to a priest, who could declare him clean (Leviticus 14). Jesus sent the 10 lepers to the priest *before* they were healed—and they went! They responded in faith, and Jesus healed them on the way. Is your trust in God so strong that you act on what he says even before you see evidence that it will work?

**17:16** Jesus healed all 10 lepers, but only one returned to thank him. It is possible to receive God's great gifts with an ungrateful spirit—9 of the 10 men did so. Only the thankful man, however, learned that his faith had played a role in his healing; and only grateful Christians grow in understanding

God's grace. God does not demand that we thank him, but he is pleased when we do so. And he uses our responsiveness to teach us more about himself.

**17:16** Not only was this man a leper, he was also a Samaritan—a race despised by the Jews as idolatrous half-breeds (see the note on 10:33). Once again Luke is pointing out that God's grace is for everybody.

### LAST TRIP FROM GALILEE

Jesus left Galilee for the last time—he would not return before his death. He passed through Samaria, met and healed 10 men who had leprosy, and continued to Jerusalem. He spent some time east of the Jordan (Mark 10:1) before going to Jericho (Luke 19:1).

## Jesus Teaches about the Coming of the Kingdom of God (170)

20One day the Pharisees asked Jesus, "When will the Kingdom of God come?"

Jesus replied, "The Kingdom of God can't be detected by visible signs.* 21 You won't be able to say, 'Here it is!' or 'It's over there!' For the Kingdom of God is already among you.*"

22Then he said to his disciples, "The time is coming when you will long to see the day when the Son of Man returns,* but you won't see it. 23 People will tell you, 'Look, there is the Son of Man,' or 'Here he is,' but don't go out and follow them. 24 For as the lightning flashes and lights up the sky from one end to the other, so it will be on the day when the Son of Man comes. 25 But first the Son of Man must suffer terribly* and be rejected by this generation.

26 "When the Son of Man returns, it will be like it was in Noah's day. 27 In those days, the people enjoyed banquets and parties and weddings right up to the time Noah entered his boat and the flood came and destroyed them all.

28 "And the world will be as it was in the days of Lot. People went about their daily business—eating and drinking, buying and selling, farming and building—29 until the morning Lot left Sodom. Then fire and burning sulfur rained down from heaven and destroyed them all. 30 Yes, it will be 'business as usual' right up to the day when the Son of Man is revealed. 31 On that day a person out on the deck of a roof must not go down into the house to pack. A person out in the field must not return home. 32 Remember what happened to Lot's wife! 33 If you cling to your life, you will lose it, and if you let your life go, you will save it. 34 That night two people will be asleep in one bed; one will be taken, the other left. 35 Two women will be grinding flour together at the mill; one will be taken, the other left.*"

37"Where will this happen, Lord?"* the disciples asked.

Jesus replied, "Just as the gathering of vultures shows there is a carcass nearby, so these signs indicate that the end is near."*

## Jesus Tells the Parable of the Persistent Widow (171)

**18** One day Jesus told his disciples a story to show that they should always pray and never give up. 2 "There was a judge in a certain city," he said, "who neither feared God nor cared about people. 3 A widow of that city came to him repeatedly, saying, 'Give me justice in this dispute with my enemy.' 4 The judge ignored her for a while, but finally he said to himself, 'I don't fear God or care about people, 5 but this woman is driving me crazy. I'm going to see that she gets justice, because she is wearing me out with her constant requests!'"

**17:20**
John 3:3; 18:36

**17:23**
Mark 13:21
Luke 17:21; 21:8

**17:24**
1 Tim 6:15

**17:25**
Matt 16:21
Mark 8:31
Luke 9:22

**17:26-27**
Matt 24:37-39

**17:28**
Gen 19:1-28

**17:30**
2 Thes 1:7

**17:31**
Matt 24:17-18
Mark 13:15-16

**17:33**
Matt 10:39; 16:25
Mark 8:35
Luke 9:24
John 12:25

**17:35**
Matt 24:41

**17:37**
Matt 24:28

**18:1**
Rom 12:12
Col 4:2
1 Thes 5:17

**18:5**
Luke 11:7-8

**17:20** Or *by your speculations.* **17:21** Or *is within you,* or *is in your grasp.* **17:22** Or *long for even one day with the Son of Man.* "Son of Man" is a title Jesus used for himself. **17:25** Or *suffer many things.* **17:35** Some manuscripts add verse 36, *Two men will be working in the field; one will be taken, the other left.* Compare Matt 24:40. **17:37a** Greek *"Where, Lord?"* **17:37b** Greek *"Wherever the carcass is, the vultures gather."*

---

**17:20, 21** The Pharisees asked when God's Kingdom would come, not knowing that it had already arrived. The Kingdom of God is not like an earthly kingdom with geographical boundaries. Instead, it begins with the work of God's Spirit in people's lives and in relationships. We must resist looking to institutions or programs for evidence of the progress of God's Kingdom. Instead, we should look for what God is doing in people's hearts.

**17:23, 24** Many will claim to be the Messiah, and many will claim that the Son of Man has returned—and people will believe them. Jesus warns us never to take such reports seriously, no matter how convincing they may sound. When Jesus returns, his power and presence will be evident to everyone. No one will need to spread the message because all will see for themselves.

**17:23-36** Life will be going on as usual on the day Christ returns. No warning will sound. Most people will be going about their everyday tasks, indifferent to the demands of God. They will be as surprised by Christ's return as the people in Noah's day were by the Flood (Genesis 6–8) or the people in Lot's day by the destruction of Sodom (Genesis 19). We don't know the time of Christ's return, but we do know that he is coming. He may come today, tomorrow, or centuries in the future. Whenever Christ comes, we must be morally and spiritually ready. Live as if Jesus were returning today.

**17:26-35** Jesus warned against false security. We are to abandon the values and attachments of this world in order to be ready for Christ's return. His return will happen suddenly,

and when he comes, there will be no second chances. Some will be taken to be with him; the rest will be left behind.

**17:33** Those clinging to this life are those seeking to escape physical persecution. Those who live for themselves display these common attitudes: (1) *Materialism*—I want it and work hard to get it. All that I see is real. Unseen things are merely ideas and dreams. (2) *Individualism*—I work hard for me, and you work hard for you. I may make it; you may not. That's your problem, not mine. (3) *Skepticism*—Anything I'm not convinced about can't be important. Everything important to know I can figure out. Those who have these attitudes may protect themselves, but they will lose the spiritual dimension to their lives. Keep your commitment to Christ at full strength. Then you'll be ready when he returns.

**17:37** To answer the disciples' question, Jesus quoted a familiar proverb. One vulture circling overhead does not mean much, but a gathering of vultures means that a carcass is nearby. Likewise, one sign of the end may not be significant, but when many signs occur, the Second Coming is near.

**18:1** To persist in prayer and not give up does not mean endless repetition or painfully long prayer sessions. Constant prayer means keeping our requests continually before God as we live for him day by day, believing he will answer. When we live by faith, we are not to give up. God may delay answering, but his delays always have good reasons. As we persist in prayer, we grow in character, faith, and hope.

**18:3** Widows and orphans were among the most vulnerable

18:7
Rev 6:10

6Then the Lord said, "Learn a lesson from this unjust judge.7 Even he rendered a just decision in the end. So don't you think God will surely give justice to his chosen people who cry out to him day and night? Will he keep putting them off?8 I tell you, he will grant justice to them quickly! But when the Son of Man* returns, how many will he find on the earth who have faith?"

18:8
1 Tim 4:1

### Jesus Tells the Parable of Two Men Who Prayed (172)

9 Then Jesus told this story to some who had great confidence in their own righteousness and scorned everyone else: 10 "Two men went to the Temple to pray. One was a Pharisee, and the other was a despised tax collector. 11 The Pharisee stood by himself and prayed this prayer*: 'I thank you, God, that I am not a sinner like everyone else. For I don't cheat, I don't sin, and I don't commit adultery. I'm certainly not like that tax collector!12 I fast twice a week, and I give you a tenth of my income.'

18:11
Matt 6:5

18:12
Matt 23:23

13 "But the tax collector stood at a distance and dared not even lift his eyes to heaven as he prayed. Instead, he beat his chest in sorrow, saying, 'O God, be merciful to me, for I am a sinner.'14 I tell you, this sinner, not the Pharisee, returned home justified before God. For those who exalt themselves will be humbled, and those who humble themselves will be exalted."

18:14
Matt 23:12
Luke 14:11

### Jesus Blesses the Children (174/Matthew 19:13-15; Mark 10:13-16)

15One day some parents brought their little children to Jesus so he could touch and bless them. But when the disciples saw this, they scolded the parents for bothering him.

16Then Jesus called for the children and said to the disciples, "Let the children come to me. Don't stop them! For the Kingdom of God belongs to those who are like these children. 17 I tell you the truth, anyone who doesn't receive the Kingdom of God like a child will never enter it."

18:17
Matt 18:3

### Jesus Speaks to the Rich Young Man (175/Matthew 19:16-30; Mark 10:17-31)

18Once a religious leader asked Jesus this question: "Good Teacher, what should I do to inherit eternal life?"

19 "Why do you call me good?" Jesus asked him. "Only God is truly good.20 But to answer your question, you know the commandments: 'You must not commit adultery. You must not murder. You must not steal. You must not testify falsely. Honor your father and mother.'*"

18:20
†Exod 20:13-16
†Deut 5:17-20

21The man replied, "I've obeyed all these commandments since I was young."

18:8 "Son of Man" is a title Jesus used for himself.   18:11 Some manuscripts read *stood and prayed this prayer to himself.*   18:20 Exod 20:12-16; Deut 5:16-20.

---

of all God's people, and both Old Testament prophets and New Testament apostles insisted that these needy people be properly cared for. See, for example, Exodus 22:22-24; Isaiah 1:17; 1 Timothy 5:3; James 1:27.

**18:6, 7** If godless judges respond to constant pressure, how much more will a great and loving God respond to us? If we know he loves us, we can believe he will hear our cries for help.

**18:10** The people who lived near Jerusalem often would go to the Temple to pray. The Temple was the center of their worship.

**18:11-14** The Pharisee did not go to the Temple to pray to God but to announce to all within earshot how good he was. The tax collector went recognizing his sin and begging for mercy. Self-righteousness is dangerous. It leads to pride, causes a person to despise others, and prevents him or her from learning anything from God. The tax collector's prayer should be our prayer because we all need God's mercy every day. Don't let pride in your achievements cut you off from God.

**18:15, 16** It was customary for a mother to bring her children to a rabbi for a blessing, and that is why these mothers gathered around Jesus. The disciples, however, thought the children were unworthy of the Master's time—less important than whatever else he was doing. But Jesus welcomed them because little children have the kind of faith and trust needed to enter God's Kingdom. It is important that we introduce our children to Jesus.

**18:17** How does someone "receive the Kingdom of God like a child"? It means having the simple, trusting attitude that children show to adults on whom they depend. Jesus wants his people to enjoy prayer by delighting in his company. Find ways in a busy day to read the Bible enthusiastically, seek God's help in any problem, rely on him for guidance, and trust him explicitly. Children do all that with adults who love them. How much more should believers have that attitude toward Jesus, who loves them.

**18:18ff** This leader sought reassurance, some way of knowing for sure that he had eternal life. He wanted Jesus to measure and grade his qualifications or to give him some task he could do to assure his own immortality. So Jesus gave him a task— the one thing the rich man knew he could not do. "Then who in the world can be saved?" the bystanders asked. "No one can, by his or her own achievements," Jesus' answer implied. "What is impossible for people is possible with God." Salvation cannot be earned—it is God's gift (see Ephesians 2:8-10).

**18:18, 19** Jesus' question to the leader who came and called him "Good Teacher" was, in essence, "Do you know who I am?" Undoubtedly the man did not catch the implications of Jesus' reply—that the man was right in calling him good because Jesus truly is God.

22 When Jesus heard his answer, he said, "There is still one thing you haven't done. Sell all your possessions and give the money to the poor, and you will have treasure in heaven. Then come, follow me."

23 But when the man heard this he became very sad, for he was very rich.

24 When Jesus saw this,* he said, "How hard it is for the rich to enter the Kingdom of God! 25 In fact, it is easier for a camel to go through the eye of a needle than for a rich person to enter the Kingdom of God!"

26 Those who heard this said, "Then who in the world can be saved?"

27 He replied, "What is impossible for people is possible with God."

28 Peter said, "We've left our homes to follow you."

29 "Yes," Jesus replied, "and I assure you that everyone who has given up house or wife or brothers or parents or children, for the sake of the Kingdom of God, 30 will be repaid many times over in this life, and will have eternal life in the world to come."

### Jesus Predicts His Death the Third Time (177/Matthew 20:17-19; Mark 10:32-34)

31 Taking the twelve disciples aside, Jesus said, "Listen, we're going up to Jerusalem, where all the predictions of the prophets concerning the Son of Man will come true. 32 He will be handed over to the Romans,* and he will be mocked, treated shamefully, and spit upon. 33 They will flog him with a whip and kill him, but on the third day he will rise again."

34 But they didn't understand any of this. The significance of his words was hidden from them, and they failed to grasp what he was talking about.

### Jesus Heals a Blind Beggar (179/Matthew 20:29-34; Mark 10:46-52)

35 As Jesus approached Jericho, a blind beggar was sitting beside the road. 36 When he heard the noise of a crowd going past, he asked what was happening. 37 They told him that Jesus the Nazarene* was going by. 38 So he began shouting, "Jesus, Son of David, have mercy on me!"

39 "Be quiet!" the people in front yelled at him.

But he only shouted louder, "Son of David, have mercy on me!"

40 When Jesus heard him, he stopped and ordered that the man be brought to him. As the man came near, Jesus asked him, 41 "What do you want me to do for you?"

"Lord," he said, "I want to see!"

42 And Jesus said, "All right, receive your sight! Your faith has healed you." 43 Instantly the man could see, and he followed Jesus, praising God. And all who saw it praised God, too.

**18:24** Some manuscripts read *When Jesus saw how sad the man was.* **18:32** Greek *the Gentiles.* **18:37** Or *Jesus of Nazareth.*

**18:22**
Matt 6:20

**18:28**
Matt 4:19

**18:31**
Ps 22
Isa 53
Luke 9:51;
24:25-27, 44

**18:32**
Matt 16:21
Luke 9:22, 44

**18:38**
Matt 9:27

**18:41**
Mark 10:36

**18:42**
Matt 9:22
Luke 7:50; 17:19

**18:43**
Luke 19:37

---

**18:22, 23** This man's wealth made his life comfortable and gave him power and prestige. By telling him to sell everything he owned, Jesus was touching the very basis of his security and identity. The man did not understand that he would be even more secure if he followed Jesus than he was with all his wealth. Jesus does not ask believers to sell everything they have, although this may be his will for some. He does ask us all, however, to get rid of anything that has become more important in life than God. If your possessions take first place in your life, it would be better for you to get rid of them.

**18:26-30** Peter and the other disciples had paid a high price— leaving their homes and jobs—to follow Jesus. But Jesus reminded Peter that following him has its benefits as well as its sacrifices. Any believer who has had to give up something to follow Christ will be repaid in this life as well as in the next. For example, if you must give up a secure job, you will find that God offers a secure relationship with himself now and forever. If you must give up your family's approval, you will gain the love of the family of God. The disciples had begun to pay the price of following Jesus, and he said they would be rewarded. Don't dwell on what you have given up; think about what you have gained and give thanks for it. You can never outgive God.

**18:31-34** Some predictions about what would happen to Jesus are found in Psalm 41:9 (betrayal); Psalm 22:16-18 and Isaiah 53:4-7 (crucifixion); Psalm 16:10 (resurrection). The disciples didn't understand Jesus, apparently because they were focusing on what he had said about his death and were ignoring what he had said about his resurrection. Even though Jesus had spoken plainly, they would not grasp the significance of his words until they saw the risen Christ face to face.

**18:35** Beggars often would wait along the roads near cities because that was where they could contact the most people. Usually disabled in some way, beggars were unable to earn a living. Medical help was not available for their problems, and people tended to ignore their obligation to care for the needy (Leviticus 25:35-38). Thus, beggars had little hope of escaping their degrading way of life. But this blind beggar took hope in the Messiah. He shamelessly cried out for Jesus' attention, and Jesus said that his faith allowed him to see. No matter how desperate your situation may seem, if you call out to Jesus in faith, he will help you.

**18:38** The blind man called Jesus "Son of David," a title for the Messiah (Isaiah 11:1-3). This means that he understood Jesus to be the long-awaited Messiah. It is interesting to note that a poor and blind beggar could *see* that Jesus was the Messiah, while the religious leaders who saw his miracles were blinded to his identity and refused to recognize him as the Messiah.

### Jesus Brings Salvation to Zacchaeus's Home (180)

**19:1**
Luke 18:35

**19** Jesus entered Jericho and made his way through the town. ²There was a man there named Zacchaeus. He was the chief tax collector in the region, and he had become very rich. ³He tried to get a look at Jesus, but he was too short to see over the crowd. ⁴So he ran ahead and climbed a sycamore-fig tree beside the road, for Jesus was going to pass that way.

**19:4**
1 Kgs 10:27
1 Chr 27:28

⁵When Jesus came by, he looked up at Zacchaeus and called him by name. "Zacchaeus!" he said. "Quick, come down! I must be a guest in your home today."

⁶Zacchaeus quickly climbed down and took Jesus to his house in great excitement and joy. ⁷But the people were displeased. "He has gone to be the guest of a notorious sinner," they grumbled.

**19:7**
Matt 9:11
Luke 5:30; 15:2

⁸Meanwhile, Zacchaeus stood before the Lord and said, "I will give half my wealth to the poor, Lord, and if I have cheated people on their taxes, I will give them back four times as much!"

**19:8**
Exod 22:1
Num 5:7
Luke 3:12-13

⁹Jesus responded, "Salvation has come to this home today, for this man has shown himself to be a true son of Abraham. ¹⁰For the Son of Man* came to seek and save those who are lost."

**19:9**
Matt 9:13
Acts 16:31-34
1 Tim 1:15

### Jesus Tells the Parable of the King's Ten Servants (181)

**19:11-27**
Matt 25:14-30

¹¹The crowd was listening to everything Jesus said. And because he was nearing Jerusalem, he told them a story to correct the impression that the Kingdom of God would begin right

**19:11**
Acts 1:6

**19:10** "Son of Man" is a title Jesus used for himself.

---

---

**19:1-10** To finance their great world empire, the Romans levied heavy taxes on all nations under their control. The Jews opposed these taxes because they supported a secular government and its pagan gods, but they were still forced to pay. Tax collectors were among the most unpopular people in Israel. Jews by birth, they chose to work for Rome and were considered traitors. Besides, it was common knowledge that tax collectors were making themselves rich by gouging their fellow Jews. No wonder the people muttered when Jesus went home with the tax collector Zacchaeus. But despite the fact that Zacchaeus was both a cheater and a turncoat, Jesus loved him; and in response, this tax collector was converted. In every society, certain groups of people are considered "untouchable" because of their political views, their immoral behavior, or their lifestyle. We should not give in to social pressure to avoid these people. Jesus loves them, and they need to hear his Good News.

**19:8** Judging from the crowd's reaction to him, Zacchaeus must have been a very crooked tax collector. After he met Jesus, however, he realized that his life needed straightening out. By giving to the poor and making restitution—with generous interest—to those he had cheated, Zacchaeus demonstrated inner change by outward action. Following Jesus in your head or heart alone is not enough. You must show your faith by changed behavior. Has your faith resulted in action? What changes do you need to make?

**19:9, 10** When Jesus said Zacchaeus was a son of Abraham and yet was lost, he must have shocked his hearers in at least two ways: (1) They would not have liked to acknowledge that this unpopular tax collector was a fellow son of Abraham, and (2) they would not have wished to admit that sons of Abraham could be lost. But a person is not saved because of a good heritage or condemned by a bad one; faith is more important than genealogy. Jesus came to save all the lost, regardless of their background or previous way of life. Through faith, the lost can be forgiven and made new.

**19:11ff** The people still hoped for a political leader who would set up an earthly kingdom and get rid of Roman domination. Jesus' story showed that his Kingdom would not take this form right away. First, he would go away for a while, and his followers would need to be faithful and productive during his absence. Upon his return, Jesus would inaugurate a Kingdom more powerful and just than anything they could expect or imagine.

**19:11ff** This story showed Jesus' followers what they were to do during the time between Jesus' departure and his second coming. Because we live in that time period, it applies directly to us. We have been given excellent resources to build and expand God's Kingdom. Jesus expects us to use these talents so that they multiply and the Kingdom grows. He asks each of us to account for what we do with his gifts. While awaiting the coming of the Kingdom of God in glory, we must do Christ's work.

away. 12He said, "A nobleman was called away to a distant empire to be crowned king and then return.13 Before he left, he called together ten of his servants and divided among them ten pounds of silver,* saying, 'Invest this for me while I am gone.'14 But his people hated him and sent a delegation after him to say, 'We do not want him to be our king.'

19:12
Mark 13:34

15 "After he was crowned king, he returned and called in the servants to whom he had given the money. He wanted to find out what their profits were.16 The first servant reported, 'Master, I invested your money and made ten times the original amount!'

17 "'Well done!' the king exclaimed. 'You are a good servant. You have been faithful with the little I entrusted to you, so you will be governor of ten cities as your reward.'

19:17
Luke 16:10

18 "The next servant reported, 'Master, I invested your money and made five times the original amount.'

19 "'Well done!' the king said. 'You will be governor over five cities.'

20 "But the third servant brought back only the original amount of money and said, 'Master, I hid your money and kept it safe.21 I was afraid because you are a hard man to deal with, taking what isn't yours and harvesting crops you didn't plant.'

22 "'You wicked servant!' the king roared. 'Your own words condemn you. If you knew that I'm a hard man who takes what isn't mine and harvests crops I didn't plant,23 why didn't you deposit my money in the bank? At least I could have gotten some interest on it.'

19:22
Job 15:6
Matt 12:37

24 "Then, turning to the others standing nearby, the king ordered, 'Take the money from this servant, and give it to the one who has ten pounds.'

25 "'But, master,' they said, 'he already has ten pounds!'

26 "'Yes,' the king replied, 'and to those who use well what they are given, even more will be given. But from those who do nothing, even what little they have will be taken away.27 And as for these enemies of mine who didn't want me to be their king—bring them in and execute them right here in front of me.'"

19:26
Matt 13:12
Mark 4:25
Luke 8:18
19:27
Luke 19:14

## 3. Jesus' ministry in Jerusalem
### Jesus Rides into Jerusalem on a Young Donkey
**(183**/Matthew 21:1-11; Mark 11:1-11; John 12:12-19)

28After telling this story, Jesus went on toward Jerusalem, walking ahead of his disciples. 29As he came to the towns of Bethphage and Bethany on the Mount of Olives, he sent two disciples ahead. 30 "Go into that village over there,"he told them. "As you enter it, you will see a young donkey tied there that no one has ever ridden. Untie it and bring it here.31 If anyone asks, 'Why are you untying that colt?' just say, 'The Lord needs it.'"

32So they went and found the colt, just as Jesus had said. 33And sure enough, as they were untying it, the owners asked them, "Why are you untying that colt?"

34And the disciples simply replied, "The Lord needs it." 35So they brought the colt to Jesus and threw their garments over it for him to ride on.

**19:13** Greek *ten minas;* one mina was worth about three months' wages.

---

**LAST WEEK IN JERUSALEM**
As they approached Jerusalem from Jericho (19:1), Jesus and the disciples came to the villages of Bethany and Bethphage, nestled on the eastern slope of the Mount of Olives, only a few miles outside Jerusalem. Jesus stayed in Bethany during the nights of that last week, entering Jerusalem during the day.

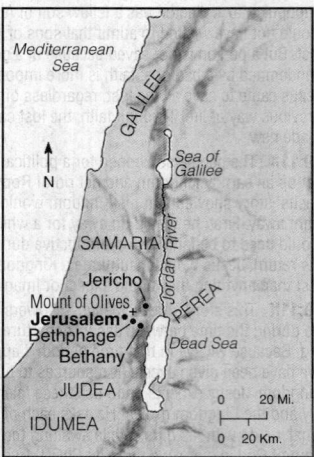

**19:20-27** Why was the king so hard on this man who had not increased the money? He punished the man because (1) he didn't share his master's interest in the Kingdom, (2) he didn't trust his master's intentions, (3) his only concern was for himself, and (4) he did nothing to use the money. Like the king in this story, God has given you gifts to use for the benefit of his Kingdom. Do you want the Kingdom to grow? Do you trust God to govern it fairly? Are you as concerned for others' welfare as you are for your own? Are you willing to use faithfully what he has entrusted to you?

**19:30-35** By this time Jesus was extremely well known. Everyone coming to Jerusalem for the Passover festival had heard of him, and, for a time, the popular mood was favorable toward him. "The Lord needs it" was all the disciples had to say, and the colt's owners gladly turned their animal over to them.

**19:35-38** Christians celebrate this event on Palm Sunday. The people lined the road, praising God, waving palm branches, and throwing their cloaks in front of the colt as it passed before them. "Long live the King" was the meaning behind their joyful shouts, because they knew that Jesus was intentionally fulfilling the prophecy in Zechariah 9:9: "Look, your king is coming to you. He is righteous and victorious, yet he is humble, riding on a donkey—riding on a donkey's colt." To announce that he was indeed the Messiah,

**19:36**
2 Kgs 9:13

³⁶As he rode along, the crowds spread out their garments on the road ahead of him. ³⁷When he reached the place where the road started down the Mount of Olives, all of his followers began to shout and sing as they walked along, praising God for all the wonderful miracles they had seen.

**19:38**
†Pss 118:25-26;
148:1
Luke 2:14; 13:35

³⁸ "Blessings on the King who comes in the name of the Lᴏʀᴅ!
    Peace in heaven, and glory in highest heaven!"*

³⁹But some of the Pharisees among the crowd said, "Teacher, rebuke your followers for saying things like that!"

**19:40**
Hab 2:11
**19:43**
Isa 29:3
Jer 6:6
Ezek 4:2
Luke 21:20
**19:44**
Ps 137:9
Luke 21:6

⁴⁰He replied, "If they kept quiet, the stones along the road would burst into cheers!"

⁴¹But as he came closer to Jerusalem and saw the city ahead, he began to weep. ⁴² "How I wish today that you of all people would understand the way to peace. But now it is too late, and peace is hidden from your eyes. ⁴³Before long your enemies will build ramparts against your walls and encircle you and close in on you from every side. ⁴⁴They will crush you into the ground, and your children with you. Your enemies will not leave a single stone in place, because you did not accept your opportunity for salvation."

### Jesus Clears the Temple Again (**184**/Matthew 21:12-17; Mark 11:12-19)

**19:46**
†Isa 56:7
†Jer 7:11

⁴⁵Then Jesus entered the Temple and began to drive out the people selling animals for sacrifices. ⁴⁶He said to them, "The Scriptures declare, 'My Temple will be a house of prayer,' but you have turned it into a den of thieves."*

**19:47**
Matt 26:55
Luke 21:37; 22:53
John 18:20

⁴⁷After that, he taught daily in the Temple, but the leading priests, the teachers of religious law, and the other leaders of the people began planning how to kill him. ⁴⁸But they could think of nothing, because all the people hung on every word he said.

### Religious Leaders Challenge Jesus' Authority (**189**/Matthew 21:23-27; Mark 11:27-33)

**20:2**
John 2:18
Acts 4:7; 7:27
**20:4**
Mark 1:4

**20** One day as Jesus was teaching the people and preaching the Good News in the Temple, the leading priests, the teachers of religious law, and the elders came up to him. ²They demanded, "By what authority are you doing all these things? Who gave you the right?"

³"Let me ask you a question first," he replied. ⁴"Did John's authority to baptize come from heaven, or was it merely human?"

**20:6**
Luke 7:29

⁵They talked it over among themselves. "If we say it was from heaven, he will ask why we didn't believe John. ⁶But if we say it was merely human, the people will stone us because they are convinced John was a prophet." ⁷So they finally replied that they didn't know.

⁸And Jesus responded, "Then I won't tell you by what authority I do these things."

**19:38** Pss 118:26; 148:1.   **19:46** Isa 56:7; Jer 7:11.

---

Jesus chose a *time* when all Israel would be gathered at Jerusalem, a *place* where huge crowds could see him, and a *way* of proclaiming his mission that was unmistakable. The people went wild. They were sure their liberation was at hand.

**19:38** The people who were praising God for giving them a king had the wrong idea about Jesus. They expected him to be a national leader who would restore their nation to its former glory; thus, they were deaf to the words of their prophets and blind to Jesus' real mission. When it became apparent that Jesus was not going to fulfill their hopes, many people turned against him.

**19:39, 40** The Pharisees thought the crowd's words were sacrilegious and blasphemous. They didn't want someone challenging their power and authority, and they didn't want a revolt that would bring the Roman army down on them. So they asked Jesus to keep his people quiet. But Jesus said that if the people were quiet, the stones would burst into cheers. Why? Not because Jesus was setting up a powerful political kingdom but because he was establishing God's eternal Kingdom, a reason for the greatest celebration of all.

**19:41-44** The Jewish leaders had rejected their King (19:47). They had gone too far. They had refused God's offer of salvation in Jesus Christ when they were visited by God himself, and soon their nation would suffer. God did not turn away from the Jewish people who obeyed him, however, and he continues to offer salvation to the people he loves, both Jews and Gentiles.

Eternal life is within your reach; accept it while the opportunity is still offered.

**19:43, 44** About 40 years after Jesus said these words, they came true. In A.D. 66, the Jews revolted against Roman control. Three years later Titus, son of the emperor Vespasian, was sent to crush the rebellion. Roman soldiers attacked Jerusalem and broke through the northern wall but still couldn't take the city. Finally, they laid siege to it, and in A.D. 70 they were able to enter the severely weakened city and burn it. Six hundred thousand Jews were killed during Titus's onslaught.

**19:47** Who were the "other leaders of the people"? This group probably included wealthy leaders in politics, commerce, and law. They had several reasons for wanting to get rid of Jesus. He had damaged business in the Temple by driving the merchants out. In addition, he was preaching against injustice, and his teachings often favored the poor over the rich. Furthermore, his great popularity was in danger of attracting Rome's attention, and the leaders of Israel wanted as little as possible to do with Rome.

**20:1-8** This group of leaders wanted to get rid of Jesus, so they tried to trap him with their question. If Jesus would answer that his authority came from God—if he stated openly that he was the Messiah and the Son of God—they would accuse him of blasphemy and bring him to trial. Jesus did not let himself be caught. Instead, he turned the question on them. Thus, he exposed their motives and avoided their trap.

*Jesus Tells the Parable of the Evil Farmers* (**191**/Matthew 21:33-46; Mark 12:1-12)

⁹Now Jesus turned to the people again and told them this story: "A man planted a vineyard, leased it to tenant farmers, and moved to another country to live for several years. ¹⁰At the time of the grape harvest, he sent one of his servants to collect his share of the crop. But the farmers attacked the servant, beat him up, and sent him back empty-handed. ¹¹So the owner sent another servant, but they also insulted him, beat him up, and sent him away empty-handed. ¹²A third man was sent, and they wounded him and chased him away.

¹³ "'What will I do?' the owner asked himself. 'I know! I'll send my cherished son. Surely they will respect him.'

¹⁴"But when the tenant farmers saw his son, they said to each other, 'Here comes the heir to this estate. Let's kill him and get the estate for ourselves!' ¹⁵So they dragged him out of the vineyard and murdered him.

"What do you suppose the owner of the vineyard will do to them?" Jesus asked. ¹⁶"I'll tell you—he will come and kill those farmers and lease the vineyard to others."

"How terrible that such a thing should ever happen," his listeners protested.

¹⁷Jesus looked at them and said, "Then what does this Scripture mean?

'The stone that the builders rejected
    has now become the cornerstone.'*

¹⁸Everyone who stumbles over that stone will be broken to pieces, and it will crush anyone it falls on."

¹⁹The teachers of religious law and the leading priests wanted to arrest Jesus immediately because they realized he was telling the story against them—they were the wicked farmers. But they were afraid of the people's reaction.

*Religious Leaders Question Jesus about Paying Taxes*
(**193**/Matthew 22:15-22; Mark 12:13-17)

²⁰Watching for their opportunity, the leaders sent spies pretending to be honest men. They tried to get Jesus to say something that could be reported to the Roman governor so he would arrest Jesus. ²¹"Teacher," they said, "we know that you speak and teach what is right and are not influenced by what others think. You teach the way of God truthfully. ²²Now tell us—is it right for us to pay taxes to Caesar or not?"

²³He saw through their trickery and said, ²⁴"Show me a Roman coin.* Whose picture and title are stamped on it?"

"Caesar's," they replied.

²⁵"Well then," he said, "give to Caesar what belongs to Caesar, and give to God what belongs to God."

²⁶So they failed to trap him by what he said in front of the people. Instead, they were amazed by his answer, and they became silent.

**20:17** Ps 118:22.    **20:24** Greek *a denarius.*

### Marginal references

**20:9-19** Isa 5:1-7
**20:10-12** 2 Chr 36:15-16
**20:14** Heb 1:2
**20:17** †Ps 118:22; Acts 4:11
**20:18** Isa 8:14-15; Dan 2:34, 35
**20:25** Luke 23:2; Rom 13:6-7

---

**20:9-16** The characters in this story are easily identified. Even the religious leaders understood it. The owner of the vineyard is God; the vineyard is Israel; the tenant farmers are the religious leaders; the servants are the prophets and priests God sent to Israel; the son is the Messiah, Jesus; the others are the Gentiles. Jesus' parable indirectly answered the religious leaders' question about his authority; it also showed them that he knew about their plan to kill him.

**20:17-19** Quoting Psalm 118:22, Jesus showed the unbelieving leaders that even their rejection of the Messiah had been prophesied in Scripture. Ignoring the cornerstone was dangerous. A person could be tripped or crushed (judged and punished). Jesus' comments were veiled, but the religious leaders had no trouble interpreting them. They immediately wanted to arrest him.

**20:18** The word "broken" conjures up uniformly negative images: broken bones, broken hearts, broken toys. You don't want something you value to be broken. Conversely, in God's dictionary, brokenness is not only good but also essential. He uses only people whose hearts, volition, and pride have been broken. Jesus gives a double warning: those who stumble over that stone—himself—"will be broken to pieces," while it will crush anyone it falls on. God offers a choice of "brokennesses." Those who cast

themselves on Jesus, submitting their wills and all that they are to him, will be broken by him of arrogance, hard-heartedness, and self-centeredness. It is not a pleasant process but an absolutely necessary one. For those who do not submit to him, he will ultimately "fall on them," an experience that can only be described as "crushing." The choice is yours: broken before him, or crushed by him.

**20:20-26** Jesus turned his enemies' attempt to trap him into a powerful lesson: As God's followers, we have legitimate obligations to both God and the government. But it is important to keep our priorities straight. When the two authorities conflict, our duty to God always must come before our duty to the government.

**20:22** This was a loaded question. The Jews were enraged at having to pay taxes to Rome, thus supporting the pagan government and its gods. They hated the system that allowed tax collectors to charge exorbitant rates and keep the extra for themselves. If Jesus said they should pay taxes, they would call him a traitor to their nation and their religion. But if he said they should not, they could report him to Rome as a rebel. Jesus' questioners thought they had him this time, but he outwitted them again.

**20:24** This Roman coin was a denarius, the usual pay for one day's work.

### Religious Leaders Question Jesus about the Resurrection
(**194**/Matthew 22:23-33; Mark 12:18-27)

**20:27**
Acts 23:8

**20:28**
†Deut 25:5

27 Then Jesus was approached by some Sadducees—religious leaders who say there is no resurrection from the dead. 28 They posed this question: "Teacher, Moses gave us a law that if a man dies, leaving a wife but no children, his brother should marry the widow and have a child who will carry on the brother's name.* 29 Well, suppose there were seven brothers. The oldest one married and then died without children. 30 So the second brother married the widow, but he also died. 31 Then the third brother married her. This continued with all seven of them, who died without children. 32 Finally, the woman also died. 33 So tell us, whose wife will she be in the resurrection? For all seven were married to her!"

**20:36**
John 1:12
Gal 4:5-7
1 Jn 3:1-2

34 Jesus replied, "Marriage is for people here on earth. 35 But in the age to come, those worthy of being raised from the dead will neither marry nor be given in marriage. 36 And they will never die again. In this respect they will be like angels. They are children of God and children of the resurrection.

**20:37**
†Exod 3:6

37 "But now, as to whether the dead will be raised—even Moses proved this when he wrote about the burning bush. Long after Abraham, Isaac, and Jacob had died, he referred to the Lord* as 'the God of Abraham, the God of Isaac, and the God of Jacob.'* 38 So he is the God of the living, not the dead, for they are all alive to him."

39 "Well said, Teacher!" remarked some of the teachers of religious law who were standing there. 40 And then no one dared to ask him any more questions.

### Religious Leaders Cannot Answer Jesus' Question
(**196**/Matthew 22:41-46; Mark 12:35-37)

**20:42-43**
†Ps 110:1

41 Then Jesus presented them with a question. "Why is it," he asked, "that the Messiah is said to be the son of David? 42 For David himself wrote in the book of Psalms:

'The Lord said to my Lord,
    Sit in the place of honor at my right hand
43 until I humble your enemies,
    making them a footstool under your feet.'*

44 Since David called the Messiah 'Lord,' how can the Messiah be his son?"

### Jesus Warns against the Religious Leaders (**197**/Matthew 23:1-12; Mark 12:38-40)
45 Then, with the crowds listening, he turned to his disciples and said, 46 "Beware of these teachers of religious law! For they like to parade around in flowing robes and love to receive

**20:28** See Deut 25:5-6.   **20:37a** Greek *when he wrote about the bush. He referred to the Lord.*   **20:37b** Exod 3:6.
**20:42-43** Ps 110:1.

---

**20:27-38** The Sadducees, a group of conservative religious leaders, honored only the Pentateuch—Genesis through Deuteronomy—as Scripture. They also did not believe in a resurrection of the dead because they could find no mention of it in those books. The Sadducees decided to try their hand at tricking Jesus, so they brought him a question that they probably had used successfully to stump the Pharisees. After addressing their question about marriage, Jesus answered their *real* question about the resurrection. Basing his answer on the writings of Moses—an authority they respected—he upheld belief in the resurrection.

**20:34, 35** Jesus' statement does not mean that people will not recognize their spouses in heaven. It simply means that we must not think of heaven as an extension of life as we now know it. Our relationships in this life are limited by time, death, and sin. We don't know everything about our resurrection life, but Jesus affirms that relationships will be different from what we are used to here and now.

**20:37, 38** Jesus answered the Sadducees' question, then he went beyond it to the real issue. People may ask you tough religious questions, such as "How can a loving God allow people to starve?" "If God knows what I'm going to do, do I have any free choice?" If they do, follow Jesus' example. First, answer them to the best of your ability; then look for the real issue: hurt over a personal tragedy, for example, or difficulty in making a decision. Often the spoken question is only a test, not of your ability to answer hard questions, but of your willingness to listen and care.

**20:41-44** The Pharisees and Sadducees had asked their questions. Then Jesus turned the tables and asked them a question that went right to the heart of the matter—what they thought about the Messiah's identity. The Pharisees knew that the Messiah would be a descendant of David, but they did not understand that he would be more than a human descendant—he would be God in the flesh. Jesus quoted from Psalm 110:1 to show that David knew that the Messiah would be both human and divine. The Pharisees expected only a human ruler to restore Israel's greatness as in the days of David and Solomon.

The central issue of life is what we believe about Jesus. Other spiritual questions are irrelevant unless we first decide to believe that Jesus is who he said he is. The Pharisees and Sadducees could not do this. They remained confused over Jesus' identity.

**20:45-47** The teachers of religious law loved the benefits associated with their position, and they sometimes cheated the poor in order to get even more benefits. Every job has its rewards, but gaining rewards should never become more important than doing the job faithfully. God will punish people who use their position of responsibility to cheat others. Use whatever resources you have been given to help others and not just yourself.

respectful greetings as they walk in the marketplaces. And how they love the seats of honor in the synagogues and the head table at banquets. 47 Yet they shamelessly cheat widows out of their property and then pretend to be pious by making long prayers in public. Because of this, they will be severely punished."

## A Poor Widow Gives All She Has (200/Mark 12:41-44)

**21** While Jesus was in the Temple, he watched the rich people dropping their gifts in the collection box. 2 Then a poor widow came by and dropped in two small coins.*

3 "I tell you the truth," Jesus said, "this poor widow has given more than all the rest of them. 4 For they have given a tiny part of their surplus, but she, poor as she is, has given everything she has."

## Jesus Tells about the Future (201/Matthew 24:1-25; Mark 13:1-23)

5 Some of his disciples began talking about the majestic stonework of the Temple and the memorial decorations on the walls. But Jesus said, 6 "The time is coming when all these things will be completely demolished. Not one stone will be left on top of another!"

**21:6**
Luke 19:44

7 "Teacher," they asked, "when will all this happen? What sign will show us that these things are about to take place?"

8 He replied, "Don't let anyone mislead you, for many will come in my name, claiming, 'I am the Messiah,'* and saying, 'The time has come!' But don't believe them. 9 And when you hear of wars and insurrections, don't panic. Yes, these things must take place first, but the end won't follow immediately." 10 Then he added, "Nation will go to war against nation, and kingdom against kingdom. 11 There will be great earthquakes, and there will be famines and plagues in many lands, and there will be terrifying things and great miraculous signs from heaven.

**21:8**
Luke 17:23

**21:10**
2 Chr 15:6
Isa 19:2

12 "But before all this occurs, there will be a time of great persecution. You will be dragged into synagogues and prisons, and you will stand trial before kings and governors because you are my followers. 13 But this will be your opportunity to tell them about me.* 14 So don't worry in advance about how to answer the charges against you, 15 for I will give you the right words and such wisdom that none of your opponents will be able to reply or refute you! 16 Even those closest to you—your parents, brothers, relatives, and friends—will betray you. They will even kill some of you. 17 And everyone will hate you because you are my followers.* 18 But not a hair of your head will perish! 19 By standing firm, you will win your souls.

**21:12**
Acts 12:4

**21:13**
Phil 1:12

**21:14**
Luke 12:11-12

**21:15**
Acts 6:10

**21:18**
Matt 10:30

**21:2** Greek *two lepta* [the smallest of Jewish coins]. **21:8** Greek *claiming, 'I am.'* **21:13** Or *This will be your testimony against them.* **21:17** Greek *on account of my name.*

---

**20:47** How strange to think that the teachers of religious law would receive the worst punishment. But behind their appearance of holiness and respectability, they were arrogant, crafty, selfish, and uncaring. Jesus exposed their evil hearts. He showed that despite their pious words, they were neglecting God's laws and doing as they pleased. Religious deeds do not cancel sin. Jesus said that God's most severe judgment awaited these teachers because they should have been living examples of mercy and justice.

**21:1, 2** Jesus was in the area of the Temple called the Court of Women. In this area were seven boxes in which worshipers could deposit their Temple tax and six boxes for freewill offerings, like the one this woman gave. This widow was not only poor but had few resources for making money. Her small gift was a sacrifice, but she gave it willingly.

**21:1-4** In contrast to the way most of us handle our money, this widow gave all she had to live on. When we consider ourselves generous in giving a small percentage of our income to the Lord, we resemble those who gave "a tiny part of their surplus." Here, Jesus admired the woman's generous and sacrificial giving. As believers, we should consider increasing our giving—whether money, time, or talents—to a point beyond mere convenience or comfort.

**21:5, 6** The Temple the disciples were admiring was not Solomon's Temple—that had been destroyed by the Babylonians early in the sixth century B.C. This Temple had been built by Ezra after the return from exile later in the sixth century B.C., desecrated by the Seleucids in the second century B.C., reconsecrated by the

Maccabees soon afterward, and enormously expanded by Herod the Great over a 46-year period. It was a beautiful, imposing structure with a significant history, but Jesus said that it would be completely destroyed. This happened in A.D. 70 when the Roman army burned Jerusalem.

**21:7ff** Jesus did not leave his disciples unprepared for the difficult years ahead. He warned them about false messiahs, natural disasters, and persecutions; however, he assured the disciples that he would be with them to protect them and make his Kingdom known through them. In the end, Jesus promised that he would return in power and glory to save them. Jesus' warnings and promises to his disciples also apply to us as we look forward to his return.

**21:12, 13** These persecutions soon began. Luke recorded many of them in the book of Acts. Paul wrote from prison that he suffered gladly because it helped him know Christ better and do Christ's work for the church (Philippians 3:10; Colossians 1:24). The early church thrived despite intense persecution. In fact, late in the second century the church father Tertullian wrote, "The blood of Christians is seed," because opposition helped spread Christianity.

**21:14-19** Jesus warned that in the coming persecutions his followers would be betrayed by their family members and friends. Christians of every age have had to face this possibility. It is reassuring to know that even when we feel completely abandoned, the Holy Spirit will stay with us. He will comfort us, protect us, and give us the words we need. This assurance can give us the courage and hope to stand firm for Christ no matter how difficult the situation.

**21:18** Jesus was *not* saying that believers would be exempt from physical harm or death during the persecutions. Remember that

**21:22**
Deut 32:35
Dan 9:24-27
Hos 9:7

**21:23**
1 Cor 7:26, 28

**21:24**
Isa 5:5; 63:18
Dan 8:13
2 Pet 3:10, 12
Rev 11:2

20 "And when you see Jerusalem surrounded by armies, then you will know that the time of its destruction has arrived. 21 Then those in Judea must flee to the hills. Those in Jerusalem must get out, and those out in the country should not return to the city. 22 For those will be days of God's vengeance, and the prophetic words of the Scriptures will be fulfilled. 23 How terrible it will be for pregnant women and for nursing mothers in those days. For there will be disaster in the land and great anger against this people. 24 They will be killed by the sword or sent away as captives to all the nations of the world. And Jerusalem will be trampled down by the Gentiles until the period of the Gentiles comes to an end.

### Jesus Tells about His Return (202/Matthew 24:26-35; Mark 13:24-31)

**21:26**
†Isa 34:4

**21:27**
†Dan 7:13
Matt 26:64
Rev 1:7; 14:14

25 "And there will be strange signs in the sun, moon, and stars. And here on earth the nations will be in turmoil, perplexed by the roaring seas and strange tides. 26 People will be terrified at what they see coming upon the earth, for the powers in the heavens will be shaken. 27 Then everyone will see the Son of Man* coming on a cloud with power and great glory.* 28 So when all these things begin to happen, stand and look up, for your salvation is near!"

29 Then he gave them this illustration: "Notice the fig tree, or any other tree. 30 When the leaves come out, you know without being told that summer is near. 31 In the same way, when you see all these things taking place, you can know that the Kingdom of God is near. 32 I tell you the truth, this generation will not pass from the scene until all these things have taken place. 33 Heaven and earth will disappear, but my words will never disappear.

**21:33**
Isa 40:6-8
Matt 5:18

### Jesus Tells about Remaining Watchful (203/Matthew 24:36-51; Mark 13:32-37)

**21:34**
Matt 24:48-50
Rom 13:13
1 Thes 5:3

**21:36**
Mark 13:33

**21:37**
Luke 19:47; 22:39
John 8:1-2

34 "Watch out! Don't let your hearts be dulled by carousing and drunkenness, and by the worries of this life. Don't let that day catch you unaware, 35 like a trap. For that day will come upon everyone living on the earth. 36 Keep alert at all times. And pray that you might be strong enough to escape these coming horrors and stand before the Son of Man."

37 Every day Jesus went to the Temple to teach, and each evening he returned to spend the night on the Mount of Olives. 38 The crowds gathered at the Temple early each morning to hear him.

**21:27a** "Son of Man" is a title Jesus used for himself.    **21:27b** See Dan 7:13.

---

many of the disciples were martyred. Rather he was saying that none of his followers would suffer spiritual or eternal loss. On earth, everyone will die, but believers in Jesus will be saved for eternal life.

**21:24** The "period of the Gentiles" began with Babylon's destruction of Jerusalem in 586 B.C. and the exile of the Jewish people. Israel was no longer an independent nation but was under the control of Gentile rulers. In Jesus' day, Israel was governed by the Roman Empire, and a Roman general would destroy the city in A.D. 70. Jesus was saying that the domination of God's people by his enemies would continue until God decided to end it. The "period of the Gentiles" refers not just to the repeated destructions of Jerusalem but also to the continuing and mounting persecution of God's people until the end.

**21:28** The picture of the coming persecutions and natural disasters is gloomy, but ultimately it is a cause not for worry but for great joy. As believers see these events happening, they will know that the return of their Messiah is near, and they can look forward to his reign of justice and peace. Rather than being terrified by what is happening in our world, we should confidently await Christ's return to bring justice and restoration to his people.

**21:34-36** Jesus told the disciples to keep a constant watch for his return. Although nearly 2,000 years have passed since he spoke these words, their truth remains: Christ is coming again, and we need to watch and be spiritually fit. This means working faithfully at the tasks God has given us. Don't let your mind and spirit be dulled by careless living, drinking, or foolishly pursuing pleasure. Don't let the cares of this life weigh you down. Be ready to move at God's command.

**21:36** Only days after telling the disciples to pray that they might escape persecution, Jesus himself asked God to spare him the agonies of the cross, if that was God's will (22:41, 42). It is abnormal to *want* to suffer, but as Jesus' followers, we must be willing to suffer if by doing so we can help build God's Kingdom. We have

two wonderful promises to help us as we suffer: God will always be with us (Matthew 28:20), and he will one day rescue us and give us eternal life (Revelation 21:1-4).

THE TEMPLE
IN JESUS' DAY

to Jerusalem

Slaughtering places

COURT OF ISRAEL          to Mount of Olives

Most Holy Place                    Barrier

Steps

SOLOMON'S COLONNADE

Altar     COURT OF      Storage areas
Holy Place  THE WOMEN    for wood, tools,
                          oil, grain
COURT OF THE PRIESTS

COURT OF THE GENTILES

ROYAL PORCH

## C. DEATH AND RESURRECTION OF JESUS, THE SAVIOR (22:1—24:53)

The perfect man was a high ideal in Greek culture. Written with Greeks in mind, Luke's Gospel shows how Jesus was the perfect man given as the perfect sacrifice for the sin of all people. Christ is the ideal human—the perfect model for us to follow. We must stand in awe of his character, which met humanity's highest ideals as well as God's demand for an atonement for sin. He is, at one and the same time, our model and our Savior.

### Religious Leaders Plot to Kill Jesus (207/Matthew 26:1-5; Mark 14:1-2)

**22** The Festival of Unleavened Bread, which is also called Passover, was approaching. ²The leading priests and teachers of religious law were plotting how to kill Jesus, but they were afraid of the people's reaction.

### Judas Agrees to Betray Jesus (208/Matthew 26:14-16; Mark 14:10-11)

³Then Satan entered into Judas Iscariot, who was one of the twelve disciples, ⁴and he went to the leading priests and captains of the Temple guard to discuss the best way to betray Jesus to them. ⁵They were delighted, and they promised to give him money. ⁶So he agreed and began looking for an opportunity to betray Jesus so they could arrest him when the crowds weren't around.

**22:3**
John 13:2, 27
Acts 1:17
**22:5**
Zech 11:12
1 Tim 6:10

### Disciples Prepare for the Passover (209/Matthew 26:17-19; Mark 14:12-16)

⁷Now the Festival of Unleavened Bread arrived, when the Passover lamb is sacrificed. ⁸Jesus sent Peter and John ahead and said, "Go and prepare the Passover meal, so we can eat it together."

⁹"Where do you want us to prepare it?" they asked him.

¹⁰He replied, "As soon as you enter Jerusalem, a man carrying a pitcher of water will meet you. Follow him. At the house he enters, ¹¹say to the owner, 'The Teacher asks: Where is the guest room where I can eat the Passover meal with my disciples?' ¹²He will take you upstairs to a large room that is already set up. That is where you should prepare our meal." ¹³They went off to the city and found everything just as Jesus had said, and they prepared the Passover meal there.

**22:8**
Exod 12:8-11

**22:10**
1 Sam 10:2-7

### Jesus and the Disciples Share the Last Supper
(211/Matthew 26:20-30; Mark 14:17-26; John 13:21-30)

¹⁴When the time came, Jesus and the apostles sat down together at the table.* ¹⁵Jesus said, "I have been very eager to eat this Passover meal with you before my suffering begins. ¹⁶For I tell you now that I won't eat this meal again until its meaning is fulfilled in the Kingdom of God."

¹⁷Then he took a cup of wine and gave thanks to God for it. Then he said, "Take this and share it among yourselves. ¹⁸For I will not drink wine again until the Kingdom of God has come."

**22:15-20**
1 Cor 11:23-26
**22:16**
Luke 14:15

**22:14** Or *reclined together.*

---

**22:1** All Jewish males over the age of 12 were required to go to Jerusalem for the Passover festival, which was followed by a seven-day celebration called the Festival of Unleavened Bread. For these festivals, Jews from all over the Roman Empire would converge on Jerusalem to celebrate one of the most important events in their history. To learn more about the Passover and the Festival of Unleavened Bread, see the first note on Mark 14:1.

**22:3** Satan's part in the betrayal of Jesus does not remove any of the responsibility from Judas. Disillusioned because Jesus was talking about dying rather than about setting up his Kingdom, Judas may have been trying to force Jesus' hand and make him use his power to prove he was the Messiah. Or perhaps Judas, not understanding Jesus' mission, no longer believed that Jesus was God's chosen one. (For more information on Judas, see his Profile in Mark 14, p. 1655.) Whatever Judas thought, Satan assumed that Jesus' death would end his mission and thwart God's plan. Like Judas, he did not know that Jesus' death and resurrection were the most important parts of God's plan all along.

**22:7, 8** The Passover meal included the sacrifice of a lamb because of the association with the Jews' exodus from Egypt. When the Jews were getting ready to leave, God told them to kill a lamb and paint its blood on the doorframes of their houses.

They then were to prepare the meat for food. Peter and John had to buy and prepare the lamb as well as the unleavened bread, herbs, wine, and other ceremonial food.

**22:10** Ordinarily women, not men, would go to the well and bring home the water. So this man with the water pitcher would have stood out in the crowd.

**22:14-18** The Passover commemorated Israel's escape from Egypt when the blood of a lamb painted on their doorframes had saved their firstborn sons from death. This event foreshadowed Jesus' work on the cross. As the spotless Lamb of God, his blood would be spilled in order to save his people from the penalty of death brought by sin.

**22:17, 20** Luke mentions two cups of wine, while Matthew and Mark mention only one. In the traditional Passover meal, wine is served four times. Christ spoke the words about his body and his blood when he offered the fourth and last cup.

**22:17-20** Christians differ in their interpretation of the meaning of the commemoration of the Lord's Supper. There are three main views: (1) The bread and wine actually become Christ's body and blood; (2) the bread and wine remain unchanged, yet Christ is spiritually present by faith in and through them; (3) the bread and wine, which remain unchanged, are lasting memorials of Christ's sacrifice. No matter which view they favor, all Christians agree

**22:19**
Luke 24:30
Acts 27:35

**22:20**
Exod 24:8
Jer 31:31-34
Heb 9:15-18

**22:21**
Ps 41:9
John 13:21

**22:22**
Acts 2:23; 4:28

¹⁹He took some bread and gave thanks to God for it. Then he broke it in pieces and gave it to the disciples, saying, "This is my body, which is given for you. Do this to remember me."

²⁰After supper he took another cup of wine and said, "This cup is the new covenant between God and his people—an agreement confirmed with my blood, which is poured out as a sacrifice for you.*

²¹"But here at this table, sitting among us as a friend, is the man who will betray me. ²² For it has been determined that the Son of Man* must die. But what sorrow awaits the one who betrays him." ²³ The disciples began to ask each other which of them would ever do such a thing.

²⁴Then they began to argue among themselves about who would be the greatest among

**22:19-20** Some manuscripts do not include 22:19b-20, *which is given for you . . . which is poured out as a sacrifice for you.*   **22:22** "Son of Man" is a title Jesus used for himself.

---

| JESUS' TRIAL | Event | Probable Reasons | References |
|---|---|---|---|
| | Trial before Annas (powerful ex-high priest) | Although no longer the high priest, he may have still wielded much power | John 18:13-23 |
| | Trial before Caiaphas (the ruling high priest) | To gather evidence for the full high council hearing to follow | Matthew 26:57-68 Mark 14:53-65 Luke 22:54, 63-65 John 18:24 |
| | Trial before the high council (Sanhedrin) | Formal religious trial and condemnation to death | Matthew 27:1 Mark 15:1 Luke 22:66-71 |
| | Trial before Pilate (highest Roman authority) | All death sentences needed Roman approval | Matthew 27:2, 11-14 Mark 15:1-5 Luke 23:1-6 John 18:28-38 |
| | Trial before Herod (ruler of Galilee) | A courteous and guilt-sharing act by Pilate because Jesus was from Galilee, Herod's district | Luke 23:7-12 |
| | Trial before Pilate | Pilate's last effort to avoid condemning an obviously innocent man | Matthew 27:15-26 Mark 15:6-15 Luke 23:13-25 John 18:39–19:16 |

Jesus' trial was actually a series of hearings, carefully controlled to accomplish the death of Jesus. The verdict was predecided, but certain "legal" procedures were necessary. A lot of effort went into condemning and crucifying an innocent man. Jesus went through an unfair trial in our place so that we would not have to face a fair trial and receive the well-deserved punishment for our sins.

---

that the Lord's Supper commemorates Christ's death on the cross for our sins and points to the coming of his Kingdom in glory. When we partake of it, we show our deep gratitude for Christ's work on our behalf, and our faith is strengthened.

**22:19** Jesus asked the disciples to eat the broken bread to remember him. He wanted them to remember his sacrifice, the basis for forgiveness of sins, and also his friendship, which they could continue to enjoy through the work of the Holy Spirit. Although the exact meaning of Communion has been strongly debated throughout church history, Christians still take bread and wine in order to remember their Lord and Savior, Jesus Christ. Do not neglect participating in the Lord's Supper. Let it remind you of what Christ did for you.

**22:20** In Old Testament times, God agreed to forgive people's sins if they would bring animals for the priests to sacrifice. When this sacrificial system was inaugurated, the covenant between God and his people was sealed with the blood of animals (Exodus 24:8). But animal blood did not in itself remove sin (only God can forgive sin), and animal sacrifices had to be repeated day after day and year after year. Jesus instituted a "new covenant" (agreement) between God and his people. Under this new covenant, Jesus would die in the place of sinners. Unlike the blood of animals, his blood (because he is God) would remove the sins of all who put their faith in him. Jesus' sacrifice would never have to be repeated; it would be good for all eternity (Hebrews

9:23-28). The prophets looked forward to this new covenant that would fulfill the old sacrificial agreement (Jeremiah 31:31-34), and John the Baptist called Jesus "the Lamb of God who takes away the sin of the world" (John 1:29).

**22:21** From the accounts of Mark and John, we know that the betrayer was Judas Iscariot. Although the other disciples were confused by Jesus' words, Judas knew what Jesus meant.

**22:24** The most important event in human history was about to take place, and the disciples were still arguing about their prestige in the Kingdom! Looking back, we see that this was no time to worry about status. But the disciples, wrapped up in their own concerns, did not perceive what Jesus had been trying to tell them about his approaching death and resurrection. What are your major concerns today? Twenty years from now, as you look back, will these worries look petty and inappropriate? Get your eyes off yourself and get ready for Christ's coming into human history for the second time.

**22:24-27** The world's system of leadership is very different from leadership in God's Kingdom. Worldly leaders are often selfish and arrogant as they claw their way to the top. (Some kings in the ancient world gave themselves the title "Benefactor," friend of the people.) But among Christians, the leader is to be the one who *serves* best. There are different styles of leadership—some lead through public speaking, some through administering, some them. 25 Jesus told them, "In this world the kings and great men lord it over their people, yet they are called 'friends of the people.' 26 But among you it will be different. Those who are the greatest among you should take the lowest rank, and the leader should be like a servant. 27 Who is more important, the one who sits at the table or the one who serves? The one who sits at the table, of course. But not here! For I am among you as one who serves.

28 "You have stayed with me in my time of trial. 29 And just as my Father has granted me a Kingdom, I now grant you the right 30 to eat and drink at my table in my Kingdom. And you will sit on thrones, judging the twelve tribes of Israel.

**22:26**
Matt 23:11
Mark 9:35
1 Pet 5:5
**22:27**
John 13:4-16

### Jesus Predicts Peter's Denial (212/John 13:31-38)

31 "Simon, Simon, Satan has asked to sift each of you like wheat. 32 But I have pleaded in prayer for you, Simon, that your faith should not fail. So when you have repented and turned to me again, strengthen your brothers."

33 Peter said, "Lord, I am ready to go to prison with you, and even to die with you."

34 But Jesus said, "Peter, let me tell you something. Before the rooster crows tomorrow morning, you will deny three times that you even know me."

35 Then Jesus asked them, "When I sent you out to preach the Good News and you did not have money, a traveler's bag, or an extra pair of sandals, did you need anything?"

"No," they replied.

36 "But now," he said, "take your money and a traveler's bag. And if you don't have a sword, sell your cloak and buy one! 37 For the time has come for this prophecy about me to be fulfilled: 'He was counted among the rebels.'* Yes, everything written about me by the prophets will come true."

38 "Look, Lord," they replied, "we have two swords among us."

"That's enough," he said.

**22:31**
Job 1:6-12
Amos 9:9
**22:32**
John 17:9, 15;
21:15
**22:33**
John 11:16
**22:35**
Matt 10:9-10
Luke 9:3

**22:37**
†Isa 53:12

### Jesus Agonizes in the Garden (223/Matthew 26:36-46; Mark 14:32-42)

39 Then, accompanied by the disciples, Jesus left the upstairs room and went as usual to the Mount of Olives. 40 There he told them, "Pray that you will not give in to temptation."

41 He walked away, about a stone's throw, and knelt down and prayed, 42 "Father, if you are willing, please take this cup of suffering away from me. Yet I want your will to be done, not mine." 43 Then an angel from heaven appeared and strengthened him. 44 He prayed more fervently, and he was in such agony of spirit that his sweat fell to the ground like great drops of blood.*

45 At last he stood up again and returned to the disciples, only to find them asleep, exhausted from grief. 46 "Why are you sleeping?" he asked them. "Get up and pray, so that you will not give in to temptation."

**22:40**
Matt 6:13

22:37 Isa 53:12.    22:43-44 Verses 43 and 44 are not included in many ancient manuscripts.

---

through relationships—but every Christian leader needs a servant's heart. Ask the people you lead how you can serve them better.

**22:31, 32** Satan wanted to crush Simon Peter and the other disciples like grains of wheat. He hoped to find only chaff and blow it away. But Jesus assured Peter that his faith, although it would falter, would not be destroyed. It would be renewed, and Peter would become a powerful leader.

**22:33, 34** Jesus told the disciples that one of them would betray him and that calamity awaited the traitor (22:22). Jesus then told Peter that he would deny that he knew Jesus. Later, however, Peter would repent and receive a commission to feed Jesus' lambs (John 21:15). Betraying and denying—one is just about as bad as the other. But Judas and Peter had entirely different fates because one repented.

**22:35-38** Here Jesus reversed his earlier advice regarding how to travel (9:3). The disciples were to bring bags, money, and swords. They would be facing hatred and persecution and would need to be prepared. When Jesus said, "That's enough," he may have meant it was not time to think of using swords. In either case, mention of a sword vividly communicated the trials they would soon face.

**22:39** The Mount of Olives was located just to the east of Jerusalem. Jesus went up the southwestern slope to an olive grove called Gethsemane, which means "oil press."

**22:40** Jesus asked the disciples to pray that they would not fall into temptation because he knew that he would soon be leaving them. Jesus also knew that they would need extra strength to face the temptations ahead—temptations to run away or to deny their relationship with him. They were about to see Jesus die. Would they still think he was the Messiah? The disciples' strongest temptation would undoubtedly be to think they had been deceived.

**22:41, 42** Was Jesus trying to get out of his mission? It is never wrong to express our true feelings to God. Jesus exposed his dread of the coming trials, but he also reaffirmed his commitment to do what God wanted. The cup he spoke of meant the terrible agony he knew he would endure—not only the horror of the crucifixion but, even worse, the total separation from God that he would have to experience in order to die for the world's sins.

**22:44** Only Luke tells us that Jesus' sweat resembled drops of blood. Jesus was in extreme agony, but he did not give up or give in. He went ahead with the mission for which he had come.

**22:46** These disciples were asleep. How tragic it is that many Christians act as though they are sound asleep when it comes to devotion to Christ and service for him. Don't be found insensitive to or unprepared for Christ's work.

### Jesus Is Betrayed and Arrested
(**224**/Matthew 26:47-56; Mark 14:43-52; John 18:1-11)

47 But even as Jesus said this, a crowd approached, led by Judas, one of the twelve disciples. Judas walked over to Jesus to greet him with a kiss. 48 But Jesus said, "Judas, would you betray the Son of Man with a kiss?"

49 When the other disciples saw what was about to happen, they exclaimed, "Lord, should we fight? We brought the swords!" 50 And one of them struck at the high priest's slave, slashing off his right ear.

51 But Jesus said, "No more of this." And he touched the man's ear and healed him.

52 Then Jesus spoke to the leading priests, the captains of the Temple guard, and the elders who had come for him. "Am I some dangerous revolutionary," he asked, "that you come with swords and clubs to arrest me? 53 Why didn't you arrest me in the Temple? I was there every day. But this is your moment, the time when the power of darkness reigns."

**22:53**
Luke 19:47
John 7:30

### Peter Denies Knowing Jesus
(**227**/Matthew 26:69-75; Mark 14:66-72; John 18:25-27)

54 So they arrested him and led him to the high priest's home. And Peter followed at a distance. 55 The guards lit a fire in the middle of the courtyard and sat around it, and Peter joined them there. 56 A servant girl noticed him in the firelight and began staring at him. Finally she said, "This man was one of Jesus' followers!"

57 But Peter denied it. "Woman," he said, "I don't even know him!"

58 After a while someone else looked at him and said, "You must be one of them!"

"No, man, I'm not!" Peter retorted.

59 About an hour later someone else insisted, "This must be one of them, because he is a Galilean, too."

60 But Peter said, "Man, I don't know what you are talking about." And immediately, while he was still speaking, the rooster crowed.

61 At that moment the Lord turned and looked at Peter. Suddenly, the Lord's words

**22:61**
Luke 7:13

---

**22:47** A kiss was and still is the traditional greeting among men in certain parts of the world. In this case, it was also the agreed-upon signal to point out Jesus (Matthew 26:48). It is ironic that a gesture of greeting would be the means of betrayal. It was a hollow gesture because of Judas's treachery. Have any of your religious practices become empty gestures? We still betray Christ when our acts of service or giving are insincere or carried out merely for show.

**22:50** We learn from the Gospel of John that the man who cut off the servant's ear was Peter (John 18:10).

**22:53** The religious leaders had not arrested Jesus in the Temple for fear of a riot. Instead, they came secretly at night, under the influence of the power of darkness—Satan himself. Although it looked as if Satan was getting the upper hand, everything was proceeding according to God's plan. It was time for Jesus to die.

**22:54** Jesus was immediately taken to the high priest's home, even though this was the middle of the night. The Jewish leaders were in a hurry—they wanted to complete the execution before the Sabbath and get on with the Passover celebration. This residence was a palace with outer walls enclosing a courtyard, where servants and soldiers warmed themselves around a fire.

**22:55** Peter's experiences in the next few hours would change his life. He would change from a halfhearted follower to a repentant disciple, and finally to the kind of person Christ could use to build his church. For more information on Peter, see his Profile in Matthew 27, p. 1603.

**22:60** Sin, like cancer, has a way of growing if unchecked. Notice the progression of Peter's denials: In 22:57, he denied knowing Jesus; in 22:58, he denied being one of his followers; in 22:60, he denied even knowing what they were talking about. Sin has a way of spreading. As it does, the cover-up gets bigger as well. The time to get a grip on sin and its cancerous effects is in the very beginning, before it has time to multiply its poisons in your life. Better yet, kill it before it even begins. Confess your sins or your desire to sin to the Lord, and ask his help to avoid Peter's mistakes.

**JESUS' TRIAL** Taken from Gethsemane, Jesus first appeared before the Jewish high council, which had convened at daybreak at Caiaphas's house. From there he went to Pilate, the Roman governor; then to Herod, tetrarch of Galilee, who was visiting in Jerusalem; and back to Pilate, who, in desperation, sentenced Jesus to die.

flashed through Peter's mind: "Before the rooster crows tomorrow morning, you will deny three times that you even know me." 62And Peter left the courtyard, weeping bitterly.

63The guards in charge of Jesus began mocking and beating him. 64They blindfolded him and said, "Prophesy to us! Who hit you that time?" 65And they hurled all sorts of terrible insults at him.

*The Council of Religious Leaders Condemns Jesus* (228/Matthew 27:1-2; Mark 15:1)
66At daybreak all the elders of the people assembled, including the leading priests and the teachers of religious law. Jesus was led before this high council,* 67and they said, "Tell us, are you the Messiah?"

But he replied, "If I tell you, you won't believe me. 68And if I ask you a question, you won't answer. 69But from now on the Son of Man will be seated in the place of power at God's right hand.*"

70They all shouted, "So, are you claiming to be the Son of God?"

And he replied, "You say that I am."

71"Why do we need other witnesses?" they said. "We ourselves heard him say it."

*Jesus Stands Trial before Pilate*
(230/Matthew 27:11-14; Mark 15:2-5; John 18:28-37)
**23** Then the entire council took Jesus to Pilate, the Roman governor. 2They began to state their case: "This man has been leading our people astray by telling them not to pay their taxes to the Roman government and by claiming he is the Messiah, a king."

3So Pilate asked him, "Are you the king of the Jews?"

Jesus replied, "You have said it."

4Pilate turned to the leading priests and to the crowd and said, "I find nothing wrong with this man!"

5Then they became insistent. "But he is causing riots by his teaching wherever he goes—all over Judea, from Galilee to Jerusalem!"

*Jesus Stands Trial before Herod* (231)
6"Oh, is he a Galilean?" Pilate asked. 7When they said that he was, Pilate sent him to Herod Antipas, because Galilee was under Herod's jurisdiction, and Herod happened to be in Jerusalem at the time.

8Herod was delighted at the opportunity to see Jesus, because he had heard about him and had been hoping for a long time to see him perform a miracle. 9He asked Jesus question after question, but Jesus refused to answer. 10Meanwhile, the leading priests and the teachers of religious law stood there shouting their accusations. 11Then Herod and his soldiers began mocking and ridiculing Jesus. Finally, they put a royal robe on him and sent him back to Pilate. 12(Herod and Pilate, who had been enemies before, became friends that day.)

**22:66** Greek *before their Sanhedrin.*   **22:69** See Ps 110:1.

**22:69**
Ps 110:1
Dan 7:13
Acts 7:56
**22:70**
Matt 4:3

**23:2**
John 19:12

**23:4**
1 Tim 6:13

**23:8**
Luke 9:9
**23:9**
John 19:9

**23:12**
Acts 4:27

---

**22:62** Peter wept bitterly, not only because he realized that he had denied his Lord, the Messiah, but also because he had turned away from a very dear friend, a person who had loved and taught him for three years. Peter had said that he would *never* deny Christ, despite Jesus' prediction (Mark 14:29-31; Luke 22:33, 34). But when frightened, he went against all he had boldly promised. Unable to stand up for his Lord for even 12 hours, he had failed as a disciple and as a friend. We need to be aware of our own breaking points and not become overconfident or self-sufficient. If we fail him, we must remember that Christ can use those who recognize their failure. From this humiliating experience Peter learned much that would help him later when he assumed leadership of the young church.

**22:70** Jesus in effect agreed that he was the Son of God when he simply turned the high priest's question around by saying, "You say that I am." And Jesus identified himself with God by using a familiar title for God found in the Old Testament: "I AM" (Exodus 3:14). The high priest recognized Jesus' claim and could accuse him of blasphemy. For any other human this claim would have been blasphemy, but in this case it was true. Blasphemy, the sin of claiming to be God or of attacking God's authority and majesty in any way, was punishable by death. The Jewish leaders had the evidence they wanted.

**23:1** Pilate was the Roman governor of Judea, where Jerusalem

was located. He had a reputation for seeming to take special pleasure in harassing the Jews. For example, Pilate had taken money from the Temple treasury and had used it to build an aqueduct. And he had insulted the Jewish religion by bringing imperial images into the city. As Pilate well knew, such acts could backfire. If the people were to lodge a formal complaint against his administration, Rome might remove him from his post. Pilate was already beginning to feel insecure in his position when the Jewish leaders brought Jesus to trial. Would he continue to badger the Jews and risk his political future, or would he give in to their demands and condemn a man who, he was quite sure, was innocent? That was the question facing Pilate that springtime Friday morning nearly 2,000 years ago. For more about Pilate, see his Profile in Mark 15, p. 1661.

**23:7** Herod Antipas was in Jerusalem that weekend for the Passover celebration. (This was the Herod who had killed John the Baptist.) Pilate hoped to pass Jesus off on Herod because he knew that Jesus had lived and worked in Galilee. But Herod was not much help. He was curious about Jesus and enjoyed making fun of him. But when Herod sent Jesus back to Pilate, it was with the verdict of "not guilty." For more about Herod Antipas, see his Profile in Mark 6, p. 1629.

**23:12** Herod was the part-Jewish ruler of Galilee and Perea. Pilate was the Roman governor of Judea and Samaria. Those four

## Pilate Hands Jesus Over to Be Crucified
(232/Matthew 27:15-26; Mark 15:6-15; John 18:39–19:16)

13 Then Pilate called together the leading priests and other religious leaders, along with the people, 14and he announced his verdict. "You brought this man to me, accusing him of leading a revolt. I have examined him thoroughly on this point in your presence and find him innocent. 15Herod came to the same conclusion and sent him back to us. Nothing this man has done calls for the death penalty. 16So I will have him flogged, and then I will release him."*

18Then a mighty roar rose from the crowd, and with one voice they shouted, "Kill him, and release Barabbas to us!" 19(Barabbas was in prison for taking part in an insurrection in Jerusalem against the government, and for murder.) 20Pilate argued with them, because he wanted to release Jesus. 21But they kept shouting, "Crucify him! Crucify him!"

22For the third time he demanded, "Why? What crime has he committed? I have found no reason to sentence him to death. So I will have him flogged, and then I will release him."

23But the mob shouted louder and louder, demanding that Jesus be crucified, and their voices prevailed. 24So Pilate sentenced Jesus to die as they demanded. 25As they had requested, he released Barabbas, the man in prison for insurrection and murder. But he turned Jesus over to them to do as they wished.

## Jesus Is Led Away to Be Crucified
(234/Matthew 27:32-34; Mark 15:21-24; John 19:17)

26As they led Jesus away, a man named Simon, who was from Cyrene,* happened to be coming in from the countryside. The soldiers seized him and put the cross on him and

**23:16**
John 19:1
Acts 16:37

**23:18**
Acts 3:13-14

---

**23:16** Some manuscripts add verse 17, *Now it was necessary for him to release one prisoner to them during the Passover celebration.* Compare Matt 27:15; Mark 15:6; John 18:39.   **23:26** *Cyrene* was a city in northern Africa.

---

provinces, together with several others, had been united under Herod the Great. But when Herod died in 4 B.C., the kingdom was divided among his sons. Archelaus, the son who had received Judea and Samaria, was removed from office within 10 years, and his provinces were then ruled by a succession of Roman governors, of whom Pilate was the fifth.

Herod Antipas had two advantages over Pilate: He came from a hereditary part-Jewish monarchy and he had held his position much longer. But Pilate had two advantages over Herod: He was a Roman citizen and an envoy of the emperor, and his position was created to replace that of Herod's ineffective half brother. It is not surprising that the two men were uneasy around each other. Jesus' trial, however, brought them together. Because Pilate recognized Herod's authority over Galilee, Herod stopped feeling threatened by the Roman politician. And because neither man knew what to do in this predicament, their common problem united them.

**23:13-25** Pilate wanted to release Jesus, but the crowd loudly demanded his death; so Pilate sentenced Jesus to die. No doubt Pilate did not want to risk losing his position, which may already have been shaky, by allowing a riot to occur in his province. As a career politician, he knew the importance of compromise, and he saw Jesus more as a political threat than as a human being with rights and dignity.

When the stakes are high, it is difficult to stand up for what is right, and it is easy to see our opponents as problems to be solved rather than as people to be respected. Had Pilate been a man of real courage, he would have released Jesus no matter what the consequences. But the crowd roared, and Pilate buckled. We are like Pilate when we know what is right but decide not to do it. When you have a difficult decision to make, don't discount the effects of peer pressure. Realize beforehand that the right decision could have unpleasant consequences: social rejection, career derailment, public ridicule. Then think of Pilate and resolve to stand up for what is right no matter what other people pressure you to do.

**23:15** Jesus was tried six times, by both Jewish and Roman authorities, but he was never convicted of a crime deserving death. Today, no one can find fault in Jesus. But just like Pilate, Herod, and the religious leaders, many still refuse to acknowledge him as Lord.

**23:18, 19** Barabbas had been part of a rebellion against the Roman government (Mark 15:7). As a political insurgent, he was no doubt a hero among some of the Jews. How ironic it is that Barabbas, who was released, was guilty of the very crime Jesus was accused of (23:14).

**23:18, 19** Who was Barabbas? Jewish men had names that identified them with their fathers. Simon Peter, for example, is called Simon son of John (Matthew 16:17). Barabbas is never identified by his given name, and this name is not much help either—*barabbas* means "son of *Abba*" (or "son of daddy"). He could have been anybody's son—and that's just the point. Barabbas, son of an unnamed father, committed a crime. Because Jesus died in his place, this man was set free. We, too, are sinners and criminals who have broken God's holy law. Like Barabbas, we deserve to die. But Jesus has died in our place, for our sins, and we have been set free. We don't have to be "very important people" to accept our freedom in Christ. In fact, thanks to Jesus, God adopts us all as his own sons and daughters and gives us the right to call him our dear Father (see Galatians 4:4-6).

**23:22** When Pilate said he would have Jesus flogged, he was referring to a punishment that could have killed Jesus. The usual procedure was to bare the upper half of the victim's body and tie his hands to a pillar before whipping him with a three-pronged whip. The number of lashes was determined by the severity of the crime; up to 40 were permitted under Jewish law. After being flogged, Jesus also endured other agonies as recorded in Matthew and Mark. He was slapped, struck with fists, and mocked. A crown of thorns was placed on his head, and he was beaten with a stick and stripped before being hung on the cross.

**23:23, 24** Pilate did not want to give Jesus the death sentence. He thought the Jewish leaders were simply jealous men who wanted to get rid of a rival. When they threatened to report Pilate to Caesar (John 19:12), however, Pilate became frightened. Historical records indicate that Pilate had already been warned by Roman authorities about tensions in this region. The last thing he needed was a riot in Jerusalem at Passover time, when the city was crowded with Jews from all over the empire. So Pilate turned Jesus over to the mob to do with as they pleased.

made him carry it behind Jesus. 27A large crowd trailed behind, including many grief-stricken women. 28But Jesus turned and said to them, "Daughters of Jerusalem, don't weep for me, but weep for yourselves and for your children. 29For the days are coming when they will say, 'Fortunate indeed are the women who are childless, the wombs that have not borne a child and the breasts that have never nursed.' 30People will beg the mountains, 'Fall on us,' and plead with the hills, 'Bury us.'* 31For if these things are done when the tree is green, what will happen when it is dry?*"

### Jesus Is Placed on the Cross
(235/Matthew 27:35-44; Mark 15:25-32; John 19:18-27)

32Two others, both criminals, were led out to be executed with him. 33When they came to a place called The Skull,* they nailed him to the cross. And the criminals were also crucified—one on his right and one on his left.

34Jesus said, "Father, forgive them, for they don't know what they are doing."* And the soldiers gambled for his clothes by throwing dice.*

35The crowd watched and the leaders scoffed. "He saved others," they said, "let him save himself if he is really God's Messiah, the Chosen One." 36The soldiers mocked him, too, by offering him a drink of sour wine. 37They called out to him, "If you are the King of the Jews, save yourself!" 38A sign was fastened above him with these words: "This is the King of the Jews."

39One of the criminals hanging beside him scoffed, "So you're the Messiah, are you? Prove it by saving yourself—and us, too, while you're at it!"

23:29 Luke 21:23
23:30 Isa 2:19 †Hos 10:8 Rev 6:16
23:32 Isa 53:12 Matt 27:38 Mark 15:27 John 19:18
23:34 †Ps 22:18
23:35 Ps 22:17
23:36 Pss 22:7; 69:21 Matt 27:48

23:30 Hos 10:8.  23:31 Or *If these things are done to me, the living tree, what will happen to you, the dry tree?*
23:33 Sometimes rendered *Calvary*, which comes from the Latin word for "skull."  23:34a This sentence is not included in many ancient manuscripts.  23:34b Greek *by casting lots.* See Ps 22:18.

---

**23:27-29** Luke alone mentions the tears of the Jewish women while Jesus was being led through the streets to his execution. Jesus told them not to weep for him but for themselves. He knew that in only about 40 years, Jerusalem and the Temple would be destroyed by the Romans.

**23:31** This proverb is difficult to interpret. Some feel it means:

**JESUS LED AWAY TO DIE**  As Jesus was led away through the streets of Jerusalem, he could no longer carry his cross, and Simon of Cyrene was given the burden. Jesus was crucified, along with common criminals, on a hill outside Jerusalem.

If the innocent Jesus (green tree) suffered at the hands of the Romans, what would happen to the guilty Jews (dry tree)?

**23:32, 33** The place called The Skull, or Golgotha, was probably a hill outside Jerusalem along a main road. The Romans executed people publicly as examples to the people.

**23:32, 33** When James and John asked Jesus for the places of honor next to him in his Kingdom, he told them they didn't know what they were asking (Mark 10:35-39). Here, as Jesus was preparing to inaugurate his Kingdom through his death, the places on his right and on his left were taken by dying men—criminals. As Jesus explained to his two position-conscious disciples, a person who wants to be close to Jesus must be prepared to suffer and die. The way to the Kingdom is the way of the cross.

**23:34** Jesus asked God to forgive the people who were putting him to death—Jewish leaders, Roman politicians and soldiers, bystanders—and God answered that prayer by opening up the way of salvation even to Jesus' murderers. Jesus was suffering the most horrible, painful death ever devised by sinful man, and he looked at the people responsible for his suffering and prayed for their forgiveness. The Roman officer and soldiers who witnessed the Crucifixion said, "This man truly was the Son of God!" (Matthew 27:54). Soon many priests were converted to the Christian faith (Acts 6:7). Because we are all sinners, we all played a part in putting Jesus to death. The good news is that God is gracious. He will forgive us and give us new life through his Son.

**23:34** Roman soldiers customarily divided up the clothing of executed criminals among themselves. When they gambled for Jesus' clothes, they fulfilled the prophecy in Psalm 22:18.

**23:38** This sign was meant to be ironic. A king, stripped and executed in public view, had obviously lost his kingdom forever. But Jesus, who turns the world's wisdom upside down, was just coming into his Kingdom. His death and resurrection would strike the deathblow to Satan's rule and establish Christ's eternal authority over the earth. Few people reading the sign that bleak afternoon understood its real meaning, but the sign was absolutely true. All was not lost. Jesus is King of the Jews—and of the Gentiles and the whole universe.

**23:39-43** As this man was about to die, he turned to Christ for forgiveness, and Christ accepted him. This shows that our deeds

23:43
2 Cor 12:3-4
Rev 2:7

⁴⁰But the other criminal protested, "Don't you fear God even when you have been sentenced to die? ⁴¹We deserve to die for our crimes, but this man hasn't done anything wrong." ⁴²Then he said, "Jesus, remember me when you come into your Kingdom."

⁴³And Jesus replied, "I assure you, today you will be with me in paradise."

### Jesus Dies on the Cross (236/Matthew 27:45-56; Mark 15:33-41; John 19:28-37)

23:45
Exod 26:31-33
Heb 9:3, 8;
10:19-20
23:46
†Ps 31:5

⁴⁴By this time it was about noon, and darkness fell across the whole land until three o'clock. ⁴⁵The light from the sun was gone. And suddenly, the curtain in the sanctuary of the Temple was torn down the middle. ⁴⁶Then Jesus shouted, "Father, I entrust my spirit into your hands!"* And with those words he breathed his last.

23:48
Luke 18:13

23:49
Ps 38:11

⁴⁷When the Roman officer* overseeing the execution saw what had happened, he worshiped God and said, "Surely this man was innocent.*" ⁴⁸And when all the crowd that came to see the crucifixion saw what had happened, they went home in deep sorrow.* ⁴⁹But Jesus' friends, including the women who had followed him from Galilee, stood at a distance watching.

### Jesus Is Laid in the Tomb (237/Matthew 27:57-61; Mark 15:42-47; John 19:38-42)

⁵⁰Now there was a good and righteous man named Joseph. He was a member of the Jewish high council, ⁵¹but he had not agreed with the decision and actions of the other religious leaders. He was from the town of Arimathea in Judea, and he was waiting for the Kingdom of

23:53
Luke 19:30

God to come. ⁵²He went to Pilate and asked for Jesus' body. ⁵³Then he took the body down from the cross and wrapped it in a long sheet of linen cloth and laid it in a new tomb that had been carved out of rock. ⁵⁴This was done late on Friday afternoon, the day of preparation,* as the Sabbath was about to begin.

23:55
Luke 8:2; 23:49
23:56
Exod 12:16; 20:10
Lev 23:8

⁵⁵As his body was taken away, the women from Galilee followed and saw the tomb where his body was placed. ⁵⁶Then they went home and prepared spices and ointments to anoint his body. But by the time they were finished the Sabbath had begun, so they rested as required by the law.

### Jesus Rises from the Dead (239/Matthew 28:1-7; Mark 16:1-8; John 20:1-10)

24:1
John 20:19
1 Cor 16:2

**24** But very early on Sunday morning* the women went to the tomb, taking the spices they had prepared. ²They found that the stone had been rolled away from the

---

23:46 Ps 31:5.   23:47a Greek the centurion.   23:47b Or righteous.   23:48 Greek went home beating their breasts.
23:54 Greek It was the day of preparation.   24:1 Greek But on the first day of the week, very early in the morning.

---

don't save us—our faith in Christ does. It is never too late to turn to God. Even in his misery, Jesus had mercy on this criminal who decided to believe in him. Our lives would be much more useful and fulfilling if we turn to God early, but even those who repent at the very last moment will be with God in paradise.

**23:42, 43** The dying criminal had more faith than the rest of Jesus' followers put together. Although the disciples continued to love Jesus, their hopes for the Kingdom were shattered. Most of them had gone into hiding. As one of his followers sadly said two days later, "We had hoped he was the Messiah who had come to rescue Israel" (24:21). By contrast, the criminal looked at the man who was dying next to him and said, "Jesus, remember me when you come into your Kingdom." By all appearances, the Kingdom was finished. How awe-inspiring is the faith of this man who alone saw beyond the present shame to the coming glory!

**23:44** Darkness covered the entire land for about three hours in the middle of the day. All nature seemed to mourn over the stark tragedy of the death of God's Son.

**23:45** This significant event symbolized Christ's work on the cross. The Temple had three parts: the courts for all the people; the Holy Place, where only priests could enter; and the Most Holy Place, where the high priest alone could enter once a year to atone for the sins of the people. It was in the Most Holy Place that the Ark of the Covenant, and God's presence with it, rested. The curtain that was torn was the one that closed off the Most Holy Place from view. At Christ's death, the barrier between God and humanity was split in two. Now all people can approach God directly through Christ (Hebrews 9:1-14; 10:19-22).

**23:50-52** Joseph of Arimathea was a wealthy and honored member of the Jewish high council. He was also a secret disciple of Jesus (John 19:38). The disciples who had publicly followed Jesus

fled, but Joseph boldly took a stand that could have cost him dearly. He cared enough about Jesus to ask for his body so he could give it a proper burial.

**23:53** The tomb was likely a man-made cave cut out of one of the many limestone hills in the area around Jerusalem. Such a tomb was large enough to walk into. After burial, a large stone would have been rolled across the entrance (John 20:1).

**23:55** The Galilean women followed Joseph to the tomb, so they knew exactly where to find Jesus' body when they returned after the Sabbath with their spices and perfumes. These women could not do "great" things for Jesus—they were not permitted to stand up before the Jewish high council or the Roman governor and testify on his behalf—but they did what they could. They stayed at the cross when most of the disciples had fled, and they got ready to anoint their Lord's body. Because of their devotion, they were the first to know about the Resurrection. As believers, we may feel we can't do much for Jesus. But we are called to take advantage of the opportunities given us, doing what we *can* do and not worrying about what we cannot do.

**24:1** The women brought spices to the tomb as we would bring flowers—as a sign of love and respect. The women went home and kept the Sabbath as the law required, from sundown Friday to sundown Saturday, before gathering up their spices and perfumes and returning to the tomb.

**24:1-9** The two angels (appearing as "two men . . . clothed in dazzling robes") asked the women why they were looking in a tomb for someone who was alive. Often we run into people who are looking for God among the dead. They study the Bible as a mere historical document and go to church as if going to a memorial service. But Jesus is not among the dead—he lives! He reigns in the hearts of Christians, and he is the head of his church. Do you look for Jesus entrance. ³So they went in, but they didn't find the body of the Lord Jesus. ⁴As they stood there puzzled, two men suddenly appeared to them, clothed in dazzling robes.

⁵The women were terrified and bowed with their faces to the ground. Then the men asked, "Why are you looking among the dead for someone who is alive? ⁶He isn't here! He is risen from the dead! Remember what he told you back in Galilee, ⁷that the Son of Man* must be betrayed into the hands of sinful men and be crucified, and that he would rise again on the third day."

⁸Then they remembered that he had said this. ⁹So they rushed back from the tomb to tell his eleven disciples—and everyone else—what had happened. ¹⁰It was Mary Magdalene, Joanna, Mary the mother of James, and several other women who told the apostles what had happened. ¹¹But the story sounded like nonsense to the men, so they didn't believe it. ¹²However, Peter jumped up and ran to the tomb to look. Stooping, he peered in and saw the empty linen wrappings; then he went home again, wondering what had happened.

*Jesus Appears to Two Believers Traveling on the Road* (**243**/Mark 16:12-13)
¹³That same day two of Jesus' followers were walking to the village of Emmaus, seven miles* from Jerusalem. ¹⁴As they walked along they were talking about everything that had happened. ¹⁵As they talked and discussed these things, Jesus himself suddenly came and began walking with them. ¹⁶But God kept them from recognizing him.

¹⁷He asked them, "What are you discussing so intently as you walk along?"

They stopped short, sadness written across their faces. ¹⁸Then one of them, Cleopas, replied, "You must be the only person in Jerusalem who hasn't heard about all the things that have happened there the last few days."

¹⁹ "What things?" Jesus asked.

"The things that happened to Jesus, the man from Nazareth," they said. "He was a prophet who did powerful miracles, and he was a mighty teacher in the eyes of God and all the people. ²⁰But our leading priests and other religious leaders handed him over to be condemned to death, and they crucified him. ²¹We had hoped he was the Messiah who had come to rescue Israel. This all happened three days ago.

24:7 "Son of Man" is a title Jesus used for himself.    24:13 Greek *60 stadia* [11.1 kilometers].

**Cross-references (right margin):**

24:3
Mark 16:19
Acts 1:21; 4:33

24:4
Acts 1:10

24:6
Matt 16:21
Luke 9:22

24:8
John 2:22

24:10
Matt 27:56
Luke 8:1-3

24:11
Mark 16:11

24:12
John 20:3-7

24:15
Matt 18:20

24:16
John 20:14; 21:4

24:18
John 19:25

24:20
Luke 23:13

24:21
Luke 1:68
Acts 1:6

---

among the living? Do you expect him to be active in the world and in the church? Look for signs of his power—they are all around you.

**24:6, 7**  The angels reminded the women that Jesus had accurately predicted all that had happened to him (9:22, 44; 18:31-33).

**24:6, 7**  The resurrection of Jesus from the dead is the central fact of Christian history. On it, the church is built; without it, there would be no Christian church today. Jesus' resurrection is unique. Other religions have strong ethical systems, concepts about paradise and the afterlife, and various holy scriptures. Only Christianity has a God who became human, literally died for his people, and was raised again in power and glory to rule his church forever.

Why is the Resurrection so important? (1) Because Christ was raised from the dead, we know that the Kingdom of Heaven has broken into earth's history. Our world is now headed for redemption, not disaster. God's mighty power is at work destroying sin, creating new lives, and preparing us for Jesus' second coming. (2) Because of the Resurrection, we know that death has been conquered and we, too, will be raised from the dead to live forever with Christ. (3) The Resurrection gives authority to the church's witness in the world. Look at the early evangelistic sermons in the book of Acts: The apostles' most important message was the proclamation that Jesus Christ had been raised from the dead! (4) The Resurrection gives meaning to the church's sacrament of the Lord's Supper. Like Jesus' followers on the Emmaus Road, we break bread with our risen Lord, who comes in power to save us. (5) The Resurrection helps us find meaning even in great tragedy. No matter what happens to us as we walk with the Lord, the Resurrection gives us hope for the future. (6) The Resurrection assures us that Christ is alive and ruling his Kingdom. He is not a legend; he is alive and real. (7) God's power that brought Jesus back from the dead is available to us so that we can live for him in an evil world.

Christians can look very different from one another, and they can hold widely varying beliefs about politics, lifestyle, and even theology. But one central belief unites and inspires all true Chris-

tians: Jesus Christ rose from the dead! (For more on the importance of the Resurrection, see 1 Corinthians 15:3-7, 12-58.)

**24:11, 12**  People who hear about the Resurrection for the first time may need time before they can comprehend this amazing story. Like the disciples, they may pass through four stages of belief: (1) At first, they may think it is a fairy tale, impossible to believe. (2) Like Peter, they may check out the facts but still be puzzled about what happened. (3) Only when they encounter Jesus personally will they be able to accept the fact of the Resurrection. (4) Then, as they commit themselves to Jesus and devote their lives to serving him, they will begin fully to understand the reality of his presence with them.

**24:12**  From John 20:3, 4, we learn that another disciple ran to the tomb with Peter. That other disciple was almost certainly John, the author of the fourth Gospel.

**24:13ff**  The two followers returning to Emmaus at first missed the significance of history's greatest event because they were too focused on their disappointments and problems. In fact, they didn't recognize Jesus when he was walking beside them. To compound the problem, they were walking in the wrong direction—away from the fellowship of believers in Jerusalem. We are likely to miss Jesus and withdraw from the strength found in other believers when we become preoccupied with our dashed hopes and frustrated plans. Only when we are looking for Jesus in our midst will we experience the power and help he can bring.

**24:18**  The news about Jesus' crucifixion had spread throughout Jerusalem. Because this was Passover week, Jews visiting the city from all over the Roman Empire now knew about his death. This was not a small, insignificant event, affecting only the disciples— the whole nation was interested.

**24:21**  These followers from Emmaus had been counting on Jesus to redeem Israel, that is, to rescue the nation from its enemies. Most Jews believed that the Old Testament prophecies pointed to a

**24:22-23**
Matt 28:1-8
Mark 16:1-8

22 "Then some women from our group of his followers were at his tomb early this morning, and they came back with an amazing report. 23 They said his body was missing, and they had seen angels who told them Jesus is alive! 24 Some of our men ran out to see, and sure enough, his body was gone, just as the women had said."

**24:26**
Matt 26:24
Luke 24:7, 44
John 12:23-24;
13:31-32
Acts 17:3
Heb 2:10; 5:5

25 Then Jesus said to them, "You foolish people! You find it so hard to believe all that the prophets wrote in the Scriptures. 26 Wasn't it clearly predicted that the Messiah would have to suffer all these things before entering his glory?" 27 Then Jesus took them through the writings of Moses and all the prophets, explaining from all the Scriptures the things concerning himself.

28 By this time they were nearing Emmaus and the end of their journey. Jesus acted as if he were going on, 29 but they begged him, "Stay the night with us, since it is getting late." So he went home with them. 30 As they sat down to eat,* he took the bread and blessed it. Then he broke it and gave it to them. 31 Suddenly, their eyes were opened, and they recognized him. And at that moment he disappeared!

**24:34**
1 Cor 15:5

32 They said to each other, "Didn't our hearts burn within us as he talked with us on the road and explained the Scriptures to us?" 33 And within the hour they were on their way back to Jerusalem. There they found the eleven disciples and the others who had gathered with them, 34 who said, "The Lord has really risen! He appeared to Peter.*"

### Jesus Appears to His Disciples (244/John 20:19-23)

35 Then the two from Emmaus told their story of how Jesus had appeared to them as they were walking along the road, and how they had recognized him as he was breaking the bread. 36 And just as they were telling about it, Jesus himself was suddenly standing there

**24:30** Or *As they reclined.*   **24:34** Greek *Simon.*

---

military and political Messiah; they didn't realize that the Messiah had come to redeem people from slavery to sin. When Jesus died, therefore, they lost all hope. They didn't understand that Jesus' death offered the greatest hope possible.

**24:24** These followers knew that the tomb was empty but didn't understand that Jesus had risen, and they were filled with sadness. Despite the women's witness, which was verified by some of the disciples, and despite the biblical prophecies of this very event, they still didn't believe. Today the Resurrection still catches people by surprise. In spite of 2,000 years of evidence and witness, many people refuse to believe. What more will it take? For these disciples it took the living Jesus in their midst. For many people today, it takes the presence of alive Christians.

**24:25** Even though these Jewish men knew the biblical prophecies well, they failed to understand that Christ's suffering was his path to glory. They could not understand why God had not intervened to save Jesus from the cross. They were so caught up in the world's admiration of political power and military might that they were blind to God's Kingdom values—that the last will be first, and that life grows out of death. The world has not changed its values. The suffering servant is no more popular today than he was 2,000 years ago. But we have not only the witness of the Old Testament prophets; we also have the witness of the New Testament apostles and the history of the Christian church testifying to Jesus' victory over death. Will we confront the values of our culture and put our faith in Jesus? Or will we foolishly continue to ignore this Good News?

**24:25-27** After the two followers had explained their sadness and confusion, Jesus responded by going to Scripture and applying it to his ministry. When we are puzzled by questions or problems, we, too, can go to Scripture and find authoritative help. If we, like these two, do not understand what the Bible means, we can turn to other believers who know the Bible and have the wisdom to apply it to our situation.

**24:27** Beginning with the promised offspring in Genesis (Genesis 3:15) and going through the suffering servant in Isaiah (Isaiah 53), the pierced one in Zechariah (Zechariah 12:10), and the messenger of the covenant in Malachi (Malachi 3:1), Jesus reintroduced these disciples to the Old Testament. Christ is the thread woven through all the Scriptures, the central theme that binds them together. Following are several key passages Jesus may have mentioned on

this walk to Emmaus: Genesis 3; 12; Psalms 22; 69; 110; Isaiah 53; Jeremiah 31; Zechariah 9; 13; Malachi 3.

**24:33, 34** Paul also mentions that Jesus appeared to Peter alone (1 Corinthians 15:5). This appearance is not further described in the Gospels. Jesus showed individual concern for Peter because Peter felt completely unworthy after denying his Lord. But Peter repented, and Jesus approached him and forgave him. Soon God would use Peter in building Christ's church (see the first half of the book of Acts).

**24:36-43** Jesus' body wasn't a figment of the imagination or the appearance of a ghost—the disciples touched him, and he ate food. On the other hand, his body wasn't a restored human body like Lazarus's (John 11)—he was able to appear and disappear. Jesus' resurrected body was immortal. This is the kind of body we will be given at the resurrection of the dead (see 1 Corinthians 15:42-50).

**ON THE ROAD TO EMMAUS**
After Jesus' death, two of his followers were walking from Jerusalem back toward Emmaus when a stranger joined them. During dinner in Emmaus, Jesus revealed himself to them and then disappeared. They immediately returned to Jerusalem to tell the disciples the good news that Jesus was alive!

among them. "Peace be with you," he said. ³⁷But the whole group was startled and frightened, thinking they were seeing a ghost!

³⁸"Why are you frightened?" he asked. "Why are your hearts filled with doubt? ³⁹Look at my hands. Look at my feet. You can see that it's really me. Touch me and make sure that I am not a ghost, because ghosts don't have bodies, as you see that I do." ⁴⁰As he spoke, he showed them his hands and his feet.

⁴¹Still they stood there in disbelief, filled with joy and wonder. Then he asked them, "Do you have anything here to eat?" ⁴²They gave him a piece of broiled fish, ⁴³and he ate it as they watched.

### Jesus Appears to the Disciples in Jerusalem (249)

⁴⁴Then he said, "When I was with you before, I told you that everything written about me in the law of Moses and the prophets and in the Psalms must be fulfilled." ⁴⁵Then he opened their minds to understand the Scriptures. ⁴⁶And he said, "Yes, it was written long ago that the Messiah would suffer and die and rise from the dead on the third day. ⁴⁷It was also written that this message would be proclaimed in the authority of his name to all the nations,* beginning in Jerusalem: 'There is forgiveness of sins for all who repent.' ⁴⁸You are witnesses of all these things.

⁴⁹"And now I will send the Holy Spirit, just as my Father promised. But stay here in the city until the Holy Spirit comes and fills you with power from heaven."

### Jesus Ascends into Heaven (250/Mark 16:19-20)

⁵⁰Then Jesus led them to Bethany, and lifting his hands to heaven, he blessed them. ⁵¹While he was blessing them, he left them and was taken up to heaven. ⁵²So they worshiped him and then returned to Jerusalem filled with great joy. ⁵³And they spent all of their time in the Temple, praising God.

**24:44**
Luke 24:27

**24:47**
Acts 2:38; 10:43;
13:38; 26:18
**24:48**
John 15:27

**24:49**
Acts 2:1-4

**24:50-53**
Mark 16:19
Acts 1:4-14
**24:53**
Acts 2:46; 3:1; 5:42

---

**24:44** Many days may have elapsed between verses 43 and 44 because Jesus and his followers traveled to Galilee and back before he returned to heaven (Matthew 28:16; John 21). In his second book, Acts, Luke makes it clear that Jesus spent 40 days with his disciples between his resurrection and ascension.

**24:44-46** The writings by Moses, the prophets, and in the Psalms refers to the entire Old Testament. In other words, the entire Old Testament points to the Messiah. For example, his role as prophet was foretold in Deuteronomy 18:15-20; his sufferings were prophesied in Psalm 22 and Isaiah 53; his resurrection was predicted in Psalm 16:9-11 and Isaiah 53:10, 11.

**24:45** Jesus opened these people's minds to understand the Scriptures. The Holy Spirit still does this in our life today when we study the Bible. Have you ever wondered how to understand a difficult Bible passage? Besides reading surrounding passages, asking other people, and consulting reference works, pray that the Holy Spirit will open your mind to understand, giving you the needed insight to put God's Word into action in your life.

**24:47** Luke wrote to the Greek-speaking world. He wanted them to know that Christ's message of God's love and forgiveness should go to all the world. We must never ignore the worldwide scope of Christ's Good News. God wants all the world to hear the Good News of salvation.

**24:50-53** As the disciples stood and watched, Jesus began rising into the air, and soon he disappeared into heaven. Seeing Jesus leave must have been frightening, but the disciples knew that Jesus would keep his promise to send the Holy Spirit to be with them. This same Jesus, who lived with the disciples, who died and was buried, and who rose from the dead, loves us and

promises to be with us always. We can get to know him better by studying the Scriptures, praying, and allowing the Holy Spirit to make us more like Jesus.

**24:51** Jesus' physical presence left the disciples when he returned to heaven (Acts 1:9), but the Holy Spirit soon came to comfort them and empower them to spread the Good News of salvation (Acts 2:1-4). Today Jesus' work of salvation is complete, and he is sitting at God's right hand, where he has authority over heaven and earth.

**24:53** Luke's Gospel portrays Jesus as a perfect life lived according to God's plan. As a child, he was obedient to his parents and amazed the religious leaders in the Temple. As an adult, he served God and others through preaching and healing, and finally, as a condemned man, he suffered without complaint. This portrayal of Jesus was well suited to Luke's Greek audience, who placed high value on being an example and improving oneself, and who often discussed the meaning of perfection. The Greeks, however, had a difficult time understanding the spiritual importance of the physical world. To them, the spiritual was always more important than the physical. To help them understand the God-man, who united the spiritual and the physical, Luke emphasized that Jesus was not a phantom but a real human being who healed people and fed them because he was concerned with their physical health as well as the state of their souls.

As believers living according to God's plan, we, too, should obey our Lord in every detail as we seek to bring wholeness to people's bodies and souls. If others want to know how to live a perfect life, we can point them to Jesus.

## KEY PLACES IN JOHN

The broken lines (— · — ·) indicate modern boundaries.

John's story begins as John the Baptist ministers near Bethany east of the Jordan (1:28ff). Jesus also begins his ministry, talking to some of the men who would later become his 12 disciples. Jesus' ministry in Galilee began with a visit to a wedding in Cana (2:1ff). Then he went to Capernaum, which became his new home (2:12). He journeyed to Jerusalem for the special festivals (2:13) and there met with Nicodemus, a religious leader (3:1ff). When Jesus left Judea, he traveled through Samaria and ministered to the Samaritans (4:1ff). Jesus did miracles in Galilee (4:46ff) and in Judea and Jerusalem (5:1ff). We follow him as he fed 5,000 near Bethsaida beside the Sea of Galilee (Sea of Tiberias) (6:1ff), walked on the water to his frightened disciples (6:16ff), preached through Galilee (7:1), returned to Jerusalem (7:2ff), preached beyond the Jordan in Perea (10:40), raised Lazarus from the dead in Bethany (11:1ff), and finally entered Jerusalem for the last time to celebrate the Passover with his disciples and give them key teachings about what was to come and how they should act. His last hours before his crucifixion were spent in the city (13:1ff), in a grove of olive trees (the Garden of Gethsemane) (18:1ff), and finally in various buildings in Jerusalem during his trial (18:12ff). He would be crucified, but he would rise again as he had promised.

# JOHN

## VITAL STATISTICS

PURPOSE:
To prove conclusively that Jesus is the Son of God and that all who believe in him will have eternal life

AUTHOR:
John the apostle, son of Zebedee, brother of James, called a "Son of Thunder"

ORIGINAL AUDIENCE:
New Christians and searching non-Christians

DATE WRITTEN:
Probably A.D. 85–90

SETTING:
Written after the destruction of Jerusalem in A.D. 70 and before John's exile to the island of Patmos

KEY VERSES:
"The disciples saw Jesus do many other miraculous signs in addition to the ones recorded in this book. But these are written so that you may continue to believe that Jesus is the Messiah, the Son of God, and that by believing in him you will have life by the power of his name" (20:30, 31).

KEY PEOPLE:
Jesus, John the Baptist, the disciples, Mary, Martha, Lazarus, Jesus' mother, Pilate, Mary Magdalene

KEY PLACES:
Judean countryside, Samaria, Galilee, Bethany, Jerusalem

SPECIAL FEATURES:
Of the eight miracles recorded, six are unique (among the Gospels) to John, as is the "Upper Room Discourse" (chapters 14–17). Over 90 percent of John is unique to his Gospel—John does not contain a genealogy or any record of Jesus' birth, childhood, temptation, transfiguration, appointment of the disciples, nor any account of Jesus' parables, ascension, or great commission.

HE SPOKE, and galaxies whirled into place, stars burned the heavens, and planets began orbiting their suns—words of awesome, unlimited, unleashed power. He spoke again, and the waters and lands were filled with plants and creatures, running, swimming, growing, and multiplying—words of animating, breathing, pulsing life. Again he spoke, and man and woman were formed, thinking, speaking, and loving—words of personal and creative glory. Eternal, infinite, unlimited—he was, is, and always will be the Maker and Lord of all that exists.

And then he came in the flesh to a speck in the universe called planet Earth. The mighty Creator became a part of the creation, limited by time and space and susceptible to aging, sickness, and death. But love propelled him, and so he came to rescue and save those who were lost and to give them the gift of eternity. He is the Word; he is Jesus, the Messiah.

It is this truth that the apostle John brings to us in this book. John's Gospel is not a life of Christ; it is a powerful argument for the incarnation, a conclusive demonstration that Jesus was, and is, the very heaven-sent Son of God and the only source of eternal life.

John discloses Jesus' identity with his very first words, "In the beginning the Word already existed. The Word was with God, and the Word was God. He existed in the beginning with God" (1:1, 2); and the rest of the book continues the theme. John, the eyewitness, chose eight of Jesus' miracles (or miraculous signs, as he calls them) to reveal his divine/human nature and his life-giving mission. These signs are (1) turning water to wine (2:1–11), (2) healing the official's son (4:46–54), (3) healing the lame man at the pool of Bethesda (5:1–9), (4) feeding the 5,000 with just a few loaves and fish (6:1–14), (5) walking on the water (6:15–21), (6) restoring sight to the blind man (9:1–41), (7) raising Lazarus from the dead (11:1–44), and, after the Resurrection, (8) giving the disciples an overwhelming catch of fish (21:1–14).

In every chapter Jesus' deity is revealed. And Jesus' true identity is underscored through the titles he is given—the Word, the only Son, Lamb of God, Son of God, true bread, life, resurrection, vine. And the formula is "I am." When Jesus uses this phrase, he affirms his preexistence and eternal deity. Jesus says, *I am* the bread of life (6:35); *I am* the light of the world (8:12; 9:5); *I am* the gate (10:7); *I am* the good shepherd (10:11, 14); *I am* the resurrection and the life (11:25); *I am* the way, the truth, and the life (14:6); and *I am* the true vine (15:1).

The greatest sign, of course, is the Resurrection, and John provides a stirring eyewitness account of finding the empty tomb. Then he records various post-Resurrection appearances by Jesus.

John, the devoted follower of Christ, has given us a personal and powerful look at Jesus Christ, the eternal Son of God. As you read his story, commit yourself to believe in and follow him.

## THE BLUEPRINT

A. BIRTH AND PREPARATION OF JESUS, THE SON OF GOD (1:1—2:12)

John makes it clear that Jesus is not just a man; he is the eternal Son of God. He is the light of the world because he offers this gift of eternal life to all people. How blind and foolish to call Jesus nothing more than an unusually good man or moral teacher. Yet we sometimes act as if this were true when we casually toss around his words and go about living our own way. If Jesus is the eternal Son of God, we should pay attention to his divine identity and life-giving message.

B. MESSAGE AND MINISTRY OF JESUS, THE SON OF GOD (2:13—12:50)
1. Jesus encounters belief and unbelief from the people
2. Jesus encounters conflict with the religious leaders
3. Jesus encounters crucial events in Jerusalem

Jesus meets with individuals, preaches to great crowds, trains his disciples, and debates with the religious leaders. The message that he is the Son of God receives a mixed reaction. Some worship him, some are puzzled, some shrink back, and some move to silence him. We see the same varied reactions today. Times have changed, but people's hearts remain hard. May we see ourselves in these encounters Jesus had with people, and may our response be to worship and follow him.

C. DEATH AND RESURRECTION OF JESUS, THE SON OF GOD (13:1—21:25)
1. Jesus teaches his disciples
2. Jesus completes his mission

Jesus carefully instructed the disciples how to continue to believe even after his death, yet they could not take it in. After he died and the first reports came back that Jesus was alive, the disciples could not believe it. Thomas is especially remembered as one who refused to believe even when he heard the eyewitness accounts from other disciples. May we not be like Thomas, demanding a physical face-to-face encounter, but may we accept the eyewitness testimony of the disciples that John has recorded in this Gospel.

## MEGATHEMES

| THEME | EXPLANATION | IMPORTANCE |
|---|---|---|
| Jesus Christ, Son of God | John shows us that Jesus is unique as God's special Son, yet he is fully God. Because he is fully God, Jesus is able to reveal God to us clearly and accurately. | Because Jesus is God's Son, we can perfectly trust what he says. By trusting him, we can gain an open mind to understand God's message and fulfill his purpose in our lives. |
| Eternal Life | Because Jesus is God, he lives forever. Before the world began, he lived with God, and he will reign forever with him. In John we see Jesus revealed in power and magnificence even before his resurrection. | Jesus offers eternal life to us. We are invited to begin living in a personal, eternal relationship with him now. Although we must grow old and die, by trusting him we can have a new life that lasts forever. |
| Belief | John records eight specific signs, or miracles, that show the nature of Jesus' power and love. We see his power over everything created, and we see his love of all people. These signs encourage us to believe in him. | Believing is active, living, and continuous trust in Jesus as God. When we believe in his life, his words, his death, and his resurrection, we are cleansed from sin and receive power to follow him. But we must respond to him by believing. |
| Holy Spirit | Jesus taught his disciples that the Holy Spirit would come after he ascended from earth. The Holy Spirit would then indwell, guide, counsel, and comfort those who follow Jesus. Through the Holy Spirit, Christ's presence and power are multiplied in all who believe. | Through God's Holy Spirit, we are drawn to him in faith. We must know the Holy Spirit to understand all Jesus taught. We can experience Jesus' love and guidance as we allow the Holy Spirit to do his work in us. |
| Resurrection | On the third day after he died, Jesus rose from the dead. This was verified by his disciples and many eyewitnesses. This reality changed the disciples from frightened deserters to dynamic leaders in the new church. This fact is the foundation of the Christian faith. | We can be changed as the disciples were and have confidence that our bodies will one day be raised to live with Christ forever. The same power that raised Christ to life can give us the ability to follow Christ each day. |

## A. BIRTH AND PREPARATION OF JESUS, THE SON OF GOD (1:1—2:12)

In this Gospel, John provides clear evidence that Jesus is the Son of God and that by believing in him we may have eternal life. John also provides unique material about Jesus' birth. He did not come into being when he was born, because he is eternal.

### God Became a Human (2)

**1** ¹ In the beginning the Word already existed.
　　　The Word was with God,
　　and the Word was God.
² He existed in the beginning with God.
³ God created everything through him,
　　and nothing was created except through him.
⁴ The Word gave life to everything that was created,*
　　and his life brought light to everyone.
⁵ The light shines in the darkness,
　　and the darkness can never extinguish it.*

⁶ God sent a man, John the Baptist,* ⁷ to tell about the light so that everyone might believe because of his testimony. ⁸ John himself was not the light; he was simply a witness to tell about the light. ⁹ The one who is the true light, who gives light to everyone, was coming into the world.

¹⁰ He came into the very world he created, but the world didn't recognize him. ¹¹ He came to his own people, and even they rejected him. ¹² But to all who believed him and accepted him, he gave the right to become children of God. ¹³ They are reborn—not with a physical birth resulting from human passion or plan, but a birth that comes from God.

**1:1**
Gen 1:1
Phil 2:6
1 Jn 5:20

**1:3**
1 Cor 8:6
Col 1:16-17
Heb 1:2

**1:4**
John 3:15-16, 36;
6:35, 48; 8:12;
1 Jn 5:12, 20

**1:9**
1 Jn 2:8

**1:12**
Rom 8:15-16, 29
1 Jn 3:1, 23

**1:3-4** Or and nothing that was created was created except through him. The Word gave life to everything.
**1:5** Or and the darkness has not understood it.   **1:6** Greek a man named John.

---

**1:1** What Jesus taught and what he did are tied inseparably to who he is. John shows Jesus as fully human and fully God. Although Jesus took upon himself full humanity and lived as a man, he never ceased to be the eternal God who has always existed, the Creator and Sustainer of all things, and the source of eternal life. This is the truth about Jesus, and the foundation of all truth. If we cannot or do not believe this basic truth, we will not have enough faith to trust our eternal destiny to him. That is why John wrote this Gospel—to build faith and confidence in Jesus Christ so that we may believe that he truly was and is the Son of God (20:30, 31).

**1:1** John wrote to believers everywhere, both Jews and non-Jews (Gentiles). As one of Jesus' 12 disciples, John writes with credibility and the details of an eyewitness. His book is not a biography (like the book of Luke); it is a thematic presentation of Jesus' life. Many in John's original audience had a Greek background. Greek culture encouraged worship of many mythological gods, whose supernatural characteristics were as important to Greeks as genealogies were to Jews. John shows that Jesus is not only different from but superior to these gods of mythology.

**1:1ff** What does John mean by "the Word"? *The Word* was a term used by theologians and philosophers, both Jews and Greeks, in many different ways. In Hebrew Scripture, *the Word* was an agent of creation (Psalm 33:6), the source of God's message to his people through the prophets (Hosea 4:1), and God's law, his standard of holiness (Psalm 119:11). In Greek philosophy, *the Word* was the principle of reason that governed the world, or the thought still in the mind, while in Hebrew thought, *the Word* was another expression for God. John's description shows clearly that he is speaking of Jesus (see especially 1:14)—a human being he knew and loved, but at the same time the Creator of the universe, the ultimate revelation of God, the living picture of God's holiness, the one who "holds all creation together" (Colossians 1:17). To Jewish readers, to say this man Jesus "was God" was blasphemous. To Greek readers, "the Word became human" (1:14) was unthinkable. To John, this new understanding of the Word was the Good News of Jesus Christ.

**1:3** When God created, he made something from nothing. Because we are created beings, we have no basis for pride.

Remember that you exist only because God made you, and you have special gifts only because God gave them to you. With God you are something valuable and unique; apart from God you are nothing, and if you try to live without him, you will be abandoning the purpose for which you were made.

**1:3-5** Do you ever feel that your life is too complex for God to understand? Remember, God created the entire universe, and nothing is too difficult for him. God created you; he is alive today, and his love is bigger than any problem you may face.

**1:4, 5** "The darkness can never extinguish it" means the darkness of evil never has and never will overcome God's light. Jesus Christ is the Creator of life, and his life brings light to humankind. In his light, we see ourselves as we really are (sinners in need of a Savior). When we follow Jesus, the true Light, we can avoid walking blindly and falling into sin. He lights the path ahead of us so we can see how to live. He removes the darkness of sin from our lives. In what ways have you allowed the light of Christ to shine into your life? Let Christ guide your life, and you'll never need to stumble in darkness.

**1:6-8** For more information on John the Baptist, see his Profile on page 1749.

**1:8** We, like John the Baptist, are not the source of God's light; we merely reflect that light. Jesus Christ is the true Light; he helps us see our way to God and shows us how to walk along that way. But Christ has chosen to reflect his light through his followers to an unbelieving world, perhaps because unbelievers are not able to bear the full blazing glory of his light firsthand. The word *witness* indicates our role as reflectors of Christ's light. We are never to present ourselves as the light to others, but are always to point them to Christ, the Light.

**1:10, 11** Although Christ created the world, the people he created didn't recognize him (1:10). Even the people chosen by God to prepare the rest of the world for the Messiah rejected him (1:11), although the entire Old Testament pointed to his coming.

**1:12, 13** All who welcome Jesus Christ as Lord of their lives are reborn spiritually, receiving new life from God. Through faith in Christ, this new birth changes us from the inside out—rearrang-

**1:14**
Gal 4:4
Phil 2:6-8
Col 2:9
1 Tim 3:16
1 Jn 1:1; 4:2-3

¹⁴So the Word became human* and made his home among us. He was full of unfailing love and faithfulness.* And we have seen his glory, the glory of the Father's one and only Son.

**1:14a** Greek *became flesh.*    **1:14b** Or *grace and truth;* also in 1:17.

---

**JOHN THE BAPTIST**

There's no getting around it—John the Baptist was unique. He wore odd clothes and ate strange food and preached an unusual message to the Judeans who went out to the waste-lands to see him.

But John did not aim at uniqueness for its own sake. Instead, he aimed at obedience. He knew he had a specific role to play in the world—announcing the coming of the Savior—and he put all his energies into this task. Luke tells us that John was in the wilderness when God's word of direction came to him. John was ready and waiting. The angel who had announced John's birth to Zechariah had made it clear that this child was to be a Nazirite—one set apart for God's service. John remained faithful to that calling.

This wild-looking man had no power or position in the Jewish political system, but he spoke with almost irresistible authority. People were moved by his words because he spoke the truth, challenging them to turn from their sins and baptizing them as a symbol of their repentance. They responded by the hundreds. But even as people crowded to him, he pointed beyond himself, never forgetting that his main role was to announce the coming of the Savior.

The words of truth that moved many to repentance goaded others to resistance and resentment. John even challenged Herod to admit his sin. Herodias, the woman Herod had married illegally, decided to get rid of this wilderness preacher. Although she was able to have him killed, she was not able to stop his message. The one John had announced was already on the move. John had accomplished his mission.

God has given each of us a purpose for living, and we can trust him to guide us. John did not have the complete Bible as we know it today, but he focused his life on the truth he knew from the available Old Testament Scriptures. Likewise, we can discover in God's Word the truths he wants us to know. And as these truths work in us, others will be drawn to him. God can use you in a way he can use no one else. Let him know your willingness to follow him today.

| | |
|---|---|
| **Strengths and accomplishments** | • The God-appointed messenger to announce the arrival of Jesus<br>• A preacher whose theme was repentance<br>• A fearless confronter<br>• Known for his remarkable lifestyle<br>• Uncompromising |
| **Lessons from his life** | • God does not guarantee an easy or safe life to those who serve him<br>• Doing what God desires is the greatest possible life investment<br>• Standing for the truth is more important than life itself |
| **Vital statistics** | • Where: Judea<br>• Occupation: Prophet<br>• Relatives: Father: Zechariah. Mother: Elizabeth. Distant relative: Jesus.<br>• Contemporaries: Herod, Herodias |
| **Key verse** | "I tell you the truth, of all who have ever lived, none is greater than John the Baptist. Yet even the least person in the Kingdom of Heaven is greater than he is!" (Matthew 11:11). |

John's story is told in all four Gospels. His coming was predicted in Isaiah 40:3 and Malachi 4:5; and he is mentioned in Acts 1:5, 22; 10:37; 11:16; 13:24, 25; 18:25; 19:3, 4.

---

ing our attitudes, desires, and motives. Being born makes you physically alive and places you in your parents' family (1:13). Being born of God makes you spiritually alive and puts you in God's family (1:12). Have you asked Christ to make you a new person? This fresh start in life is available to all who believe in Christ.

**1:14** "The Word became human." By doing so, Christ became (1) *the perfect teacher*—in Jesus' life we see how God thinks and therefore how we should think (Philippians 2:5-11); (2) *the perfect example*—as a model of what we are to become, he shows us how to live and gives us the power to live that way (1 Peter 2:21); (3) *the perfect sacrifice*—Jesus came as a sacrifice for all sins, and his death satisfied God's requirements for the removal of sin (Colossians 1:15-23).

**1:14** "The Father's one and only Son" means Jesus is God's only and unique Son. The emphasis is on *unique.* Jesus is one of a kind and enjoys a relationship with God. He is unlike all believers, who are called "children of God."

**1:14** When Jesus was conceived, God became a man. He was not part man and part God; he was completely human and completely divine (Colossians 2:9). Before Christ came, people could know God partially. After Christ came, people could know God fully because he became visible and tangible in Christ. Christ is the perfect expression of God in human form. The two most common errors people make about Jesus are to minimize his humanity or to minimize his divinity. Jesus is both God and man.

¹⁵John testified about him when he shouted to the crowds, "This is the one I was talking about when I said, 'Someone is coming after me who is far greater than I am, for he existed long before me.'"

¹⁶From his abundance we have all received one gracious blessing after another.* ¹⁷For the law was given through Moses, but God's unfailing love and faithfulness came through Jesus Christ. ¹⁸No one has ever seen God. But the unique One, who is himself God,* is near to the Father's heart. He has revealed God to us.

### John the Baptist Declares His Mission (19)

¹⁹This was John's testimony when the Jewish leaders sent priests and Temple assistants* from Jerusalem to ask John, "Who are you?" ²⁰He came right out and said, "I am not the Messiah."

²¹"Well then, who are you?" they asked. "Are you Elijah?"

"No," he replied.

"Are you the Prophet we are expecting?"*

"No."

²²"Then who are you? We need an answer for those who sent us. What do you have to say about yourself?"

²³John replied in the words of the prophet Isaiah:

"I am a voice shouting in the wilderness,
  'Clear the way for the LORD's coming!'"*

²⁴Then the Pharisees who had been sent ²⁵asked him, "If you aren't the Messiah or Elijah or the Prophet, what right do you have to baptize?"

²⁶John told them, "I baptize with* water, but right here in the crowd is someone you do not recognize. ²⁷Though his ministry follows mine, I'm not even worthy to be his slave and untie the straps of his sandal."

²⁸This encounter took place in Bethany, an area east of the Jordan River, where John was baptizing.

1:16 Or received the grace of Christ rather than the grace of the law; Greek reads received grace upon grace.
1:18 Some manuscripts read But the one and only Son.   1:19 Greek and Levites.   1:21 Greek Are you the Prophet? See Deut 18:15, 18; Mal 4:5-6.   1:23 Isa 40:3.   1:26 Or in; also in 1:31, 33.

**Cross References:**
1:16 Col 2:9-10
1:17 Exod 31:18; 34:28; John 7:19
1:18 Exod 33:20; 2 Cor 4:4, 6; Col 1:15
1:19-28 Matt 3:1-12; Mark 1:2-8; Luke 3:1-16
1:20 Luke 3:15; John 3:28
1:21 Deut 18:15; Mal 4:5; Matt 11:14
1:23 †Isa 40:3
1:26 Mal 3:1; Matt 3:11; Mark 1:8; Luke 3:16
1:27 Mark 1:7; John 1:15; Acts 13:25
1:28 John 3:26; 10:40

---

**1:17** Law and grace (the combination of God's "unfailing love and faithfulness") are both aspects of God's nature that he uses in dealing with us. Moses emphasized God's law and justice, while Jesus Christ came to highlight God's mercy, love, faithfulness, and forgiveness. Moses could only be the giver of the law, while Christ came to fulfill the law (Matthew 5:17). The nature and will of God were revealed in the law; now the nature and will of God are revealed in Jesus Christ. Rather than coming through cold stone tablets, God's revelation now comes through a person's life. As we get to know Christ better, our understanding of God will increase.

**1:18** God communicated through various people in the Old Testament, usually prophets who were told to give specific messages. But no one ever *saw* God. Jesus is both God and the Father's unique Son. In Christ, God revealed his nature and essence in a way that could be seen and touched. In Christ, God became a man who lived on earth.

**1:19** The priests and Temple assistants (also called Levites) were respected religious leaders in Jerusalem. Priests served in the Temple, and Temple assistants helped them. The Pharisees (1:24) were a group that both John the Baptist and Jesus often denounced. Many of them outwardly obeyed God's laws to look pious, while inwardly their hearts were filled with pride and greed. The Pharisees believed that their own oral traditions were just as important as God's inspired Word. For more information on the Pharisees, see the charts in Matthew 3, p. 1541 and Mark 2, p. 1617.

These leaders came to see John the Baptist for several reasons: (1) Their duty as guardians of the faith included investigating any new teaching or movement (Deuteronomy 13:1-5;

18:20-22). (2) They wanted to find out if John had the credentials of a prophet. (3) John had quite a following, and it was growing. They were probably jealous and wanted to see why this man was so popular.

**1:21-23** In the religious leaders' minds, there were four options regarding John the Baptist's identity: He was (1) the Prophet foretold by Moses (Deuteronomy 18:15), (2) Elijah (Malachi 4:5), (3) the Messiah, or (4) a false prophet. John denied being the first three personages. Instead, he called himself, in the words of the Old Testament prophet Isaiah, "The voice of someone shouting, 'Clear the way through the wilderness for the LORD!'" (Isaiah 40:3). The leaders kept pressing John to say who he was because people were expecting the Messiah to come (Luke 3:15). But John emphasized only *why* he had come—to prepare the way for the Messiah. The Pharisees missed the point. They wanted to know who John was, but John wanted to prepare them to recognize who Jesus was.

**1:25, 26** John was baptizing Jews. The Essenes (a strict, monastic sect of Judaism) practiced baptism for purification, but normally only non-Jews (Gentiles) were baptized when they converted to Judaism. When the Pharisees questioned John's authority to baptize, they were asking who gave John the right to treat God's chosen people like Gentiles. John said, "I baptize with water"— he was merely helping the people perform a symbolic act of repentance. But soon one would come who would truly *forgive* sins, something only the Son of God—the Messiah—could do.

**1:27** John the Baptist said he was not even worthy to be Christ's slave. But according to Luke 7:28, Jesus said that John was the greatest of all prophets. If such a great person felt inadequate even to be Christ's slave, how much more should we lay aside our pride to serve Christ! When we truly understand who Christ is, our pride and self-importance melt away.

### John the Baptist Proclaims Jesus as the Messiah (20)

**1:29**
Isa 53:7
1 Cor 5:7
1 Pet 1:19

29 The next day John saw Jesus coming toward him and said, "Look! The Lamb of God who takes away the sin of the world! 30 He is the one I was talking about when I said, 'A man is coming after me who is far greater than I am, for he existed long before me.' 31 I did not recognize him as the Messiah, but I have been baptizing with water so that he might be revealed to Israel."

**1:32**
Matt 3:16
Mark 1:10
Luke 3:22

**1:33**
Luke 3:16
Acts 1:5

**1:34**
John 1:49; 10:36

32 Then John testified, "I saw the Holy Spirit descending like a dove from heaven and resting upon him. 33 I didn't know he was the one, but when God sent me to baptize with water, he told me, 'The one on whom you see the Spirit descend and rest is the one who will baptize with the Holy Spirit.' 34 I saw this happen to Jesus, so I testify that he is the Chosen One of God.*"

### The First Disciples Follow Jesus (21)

35 The following day John was again standing with two of his disciples. 36 As Jesus walked by, John looked at him and declared, "Look! There is the Lamb of God!" 37 When John's two disciples heard this, they followed Jesus.

38 Jesus looked around and saw them following. "What do you want?" he asked them.

They replied, "Rabbi" (which means "Teacher"), "where are you staying?"

39 "Come and see," he said. It was about four o'clock in the afternoon when they went with him to the place where he was staying, and they remained with him the rest of the day.

**1:34** Some manuscripts read *the Son of God.*

---

**1:29** Every morning and evening, a lamb was sacrificed in the Temple for the sins of the people (Exodus 29:38-42). Isaiah 53:7 prophesied that the Messiah, God's servant, would be led to the slaughter like a lamb. To pay the penalty for sin, a life had to be given—and God chose to provide the sacrifice himself. The sins of the world were removed when Jesus died as the perfect sacrifice. This is the way our sins are forgiven (1 Corinthians 5:7). The "sin of the world" means everyone's sin, the sin of each individual. Jesus paid the price of *your* sin by his death. You can receive forgiveness by confessing your sin to him and asking for his forgiveness.

**1:30** Although John the Baptist was a well-known preacher who attracted large crowds, he was content for Jesus to take the higher place. This is true humility, the basis for greatness in preaching, teaching, or any other work we do for Christ. When you are content to do what God wants you to do and let Jesus Christ be honored for it, God will do great things through you.

**1:31-34** At Jesus' baptism, John the Baptist had declared Jesus to be the Messiah. At that time God had given John a sign to show him that Jesus truly had been sent from God (1:33). John and Jesus were related (see Luke 1:36), so John probably knew who he was. But it wasn't until Jesus' baptism that John understood that Jesus was the Messiah. Jesus' baptism is described in Matthew 3:13-17; Mark 1:9-11; and Luke 3:21, 22.

**1:33** John the Baptist's baptism with water was preparatory, because it was for repentance and symbolized the washing away of sins. Jesus, by contrast, would baptize with the Holy Spirit. He would send the Holy Spirit upon all believers, empowering them to live and to teach the message of salvation. This outpouring of the Spirit came after Jesus had risen from the dead and ascended into heaven (see 20:22; Acts 2).

**1:34** John the Baptist's job was to point people to Jesus, their long-awaited Messiah. Today people are looking for someone to give them security in an insecure world. Our job is to point them to Christ and to show that he is the one whom they seek.

**1:35ff** These new disciples used several names for Jesus: Lamb of God (1:36), Rabbi (1:38), Messiah (1:41), Son of God (1:49), and King of Israel (1:49). As they got to know Jesus, their appreciation for him grew. The more time we spend getting to know Christ, the more we will understand and appreciate who he is. We may be drawn to him for his teaching, but we will come to know him as the Son of God. Although these disciples made this

verbal shift in a few days, they would not fully understand Jesus until three years later (Acts 2). What they so easily professed had to be worked out in experience. We may find that words of faith come easily, but deep appreciation for Christ comes with living by faith.

**1:37** One of the two disciples was Andrew (1:40). The other was probably John, the writer of this book. Why did these disciples leave John the Baptist? Because that's what John wanted them to do—he was pointing the way to Jesus, the one John had prepared them to follow. These were Jesus' first disciples, along with Simon Peter (1:42) and Nathanael (1:45).

**1:38** When the two disciples began to follow Jesus, he asked them, "What do you want?" Following Christ is not enough; we must follow him for the right reasons. To follow Christ for our own purposes would be asking Christ to follow us—to align with us to support and advance our cause, not his. We must examine our motives for following him. Are we seeking his glory or ours?

### JESUS' FIRST TRAVELS

After his baptism by John in the Jordan River and the temptation by Satan in the wilderness (see the map in Mark 1, p. 1613), Jesus returned to Galilee. He visited Nazareth, Cana, and Capernaum, and then returned to Jerusalem for the Passover.

40Andrew, Simon Peter's brother, was one of these men who heard what John said and then followed Jesus. 41Andrew went to find his brother, Simon, and told him, "We have found the Messiah" (which means "Christ"*).

42Then Andrew brought Simon to meet Jesus. Looking intently at Simon, Jesus said, "Your name is Simon, son of John—but you will be called Cephas" (which means "Peter"*).

43The next day Jesus decided to go to Galilee. He found Philip and said to him, "Come, follow me." 44Philip was from Bethsaida, Andrew and Peter's hometown.

45Philip went to look for Nathanael and told him, "We have found the very person Moses* and the prophets wrote about! His name is Jesus, the son of Joseph from Nazareth."

46"Nazareth!" exclaimed Nathanael. "Can anything good come from Nazareth?"

"Come and see for yourself," Philip replied.

47As they approached, Jesus said, "Now here is a genuine son of Israel—a man of complete integrity."

48"How do you know about me?" Nathanael asked.

Jesus replied, "I could see you under the fig tree before Philip found you."

49Then Nathanael exclaimed, "Rabbi, you are the Son of God—the King of Israel!"

50Jesus asked him, "Do you believe this just because I told you I had seen you under the fig tree? You will see greater things than this." 51Then he said, "I tell you the truth, you will all see heaven open and the angels of God going up and down on the Son of Man, the one who is the stairway between heaven and earth.*"

## Jesus Turns Water into Wine (22)

**2** The next day* there was a wedding celebration in the village of Cana in Galilee. Jesus' mother was there, 2and Jesus and his disciples were also invited to the celebration. 3The wine supply ran out during the festivities, so Jesus' mother told him, "They have no more wine."

4"Dear woman, that's not our problem," Jesus replied. "My time has not yet come."

**1:41** Messiah (a Hebrew term) and Christ (a Greek term) both mean "the anointed one." **1:42** The names Cephas (from Aramaic) and Peter (from Greek) both mean "rock." **1:45** Greek Moses in the law. **1:51** Greek going up and down on the Son of Man; see Gen 28:10-17. "Son of Man" is a title Jesus used for himself. **2:1** Greek On the third day; see 1:35, 43.

**1:40**
Matt 4:18-22
Mark 1:16
Luke 5:2-11

**1:41**
Ps 2:2
John 4:25

**1:42**
Matt 16:18
1 Cor 15:5
1 Pet 2:5

**1:43**
John 6:5-6;
12:20-22

**1:45**
Gen 3:15
Num 21:8-9; 24:17
Deut 18:15, 18
Isa 7:14; 11:1-10;
52:10, 13; 53:1-12
Jer 23:5-6; 30:9
Ezek 34:23-24;
37:24-25
Hos 11:1
Mic 5:2
Zech 3:8-9;
6:12-13; 9:9
Mal 3:1; 4:2, 5

**1:49**
2 Sam 7:14
Ps 2:2
John 1:34; 20:31

**1:51**
Gen 28:12

**2:1**
John 1:35, 43

**2:4**
John 7:30; 8:20

---

**1:40-42** Andrew accepted John the Baptist's testimony about Jesus and immediately went to tell his brother, Simon, about him. There was no question in Andrew's mind that Jesus was the Messiah. Not only did he tell his brother, but he was also eager to introduce others to Jesus (see 6:8, 9; 12:22). How many people in your life have heard you talk about your relationship with Jesus?

**1:42** Jesus saw not only who Simon was, but who he would become. That is why he gave him a new name—Cephas in Aramaic, Peter in Greek (the name means "a rock"). Peter is not presented as rock-solid throughout the Gospels, but he became a solid rock in the days of the early church, as we learn in the book of Acts. By giving Simon a new name, Jesus introduced a change in character. For more on Simon Peter, see his Profile in Matthew 27, p. 1603.

**1:46** Nazareth was despised by the Jews because a Roman army garrison was located there. Some have speculated that an aloof attitude or a poor reputation in morals and religion on the part of the people of Nazareth led to Nathanael's harsh comment. Nathanael's hometown was Cana, about four miles from Nazareth.

**1:46** When Nathanael heard that the Messiah was from Nazareth, he was surprised. Philip responded, "Come and see for yourself." Fortunately for Nathanael, he went to meet Jesus and became a disciple. If he had stuck to his prejudice without investigating further, he would have missed the Messiah! Don't let people's stereotypes about Christ cause them to miss his power and love. Invite them to come and see who Jesus really is.

**1:47-49** Jesus knew about Nathanael before the two ever met. Jesus also knows what we are really like. An honest person will feel comfortable with the thought that Jesus knows him or her through and through. A dishonest person will feel uncomfortable. You can't pretend to be something you're not. God knows the real you and wants you to follow him.

**1:51** This is a reference to Jacob's dream recorded in Genesis 28:12. As the unique God-man, Jesus would be the ladder between heaven and earth. Jesus is not saying that this would be a physical experience (that they would see the ladder with their eyes) like the Transfiguration, but that they would have spiritual insight into Jesus' true nature and purpose for coming.

**2:1, 2** Jesus was on a mission to save the world, the greatest mission in the history of humankind. Yet he took time to attend a wedding and take part in its festivities. We may be tempted to think we should not take time out from our "important" work for social occasions. But maybe these social occasions are part of our mission. Jesus valued these wedding festivities because they involved people, and Jesus came to be with people. Our mission can often be accomplished in joyous times of celebration with others. Bring balance to your life by bringing Jesus into times of pleasure as well as times of work.

**2:1-3** Weddings in Jesus' day were week-long festivals. Banquets would be prepared for many guests, and the week would be spent celebrating the new life of the married couple. Often the whole town was invited, and everybody would come—it was considered an insult to refuse an invitation to a wedding. To accommodate many people, careful planning was needed. To run out of wine was more than embarrassing; it broke the strong unwritten laws of hospitality. Jesus was about to respond to a heartfelt need.

**2:4** Mary was probably not asking Jesus to do a miracle; she was simply hoping that her son would help solve this major problem and find some wine. Tradition says that Joseph, Mary's husband, was dead, so she probably was used to asking for her son's help in certain situations. Jesus' answer to Mary is difficult to understand, but maybe that is the point. Although Mary did not understand what Jesus was going to do, she trusted him to do what was right. Those who believe in Jesus but run into situations they

2:6
Mark 7:3-4
John 3:25

2:9
John 4:46

2:11
John 2:23; 3:2;
4:54; 6:14; 11:47;
12:37

⁵ But his mother told the servants, "Do whatever he tells you."

⁶ Standing nearby were six stone water jars, used for Jewish ceremonial washing. Each could hold twenty to thirty gallons.* ⁷ Jesus told the servants, "Fill the jars with water." When the jars had been filled, ⁸ he said, "Now dip some out, and take it to the master of ceremonies." So the servants followed his instructions.

⁹ When the master of ceremonies tasted the water that was now wine, not knowing where it had come from (though, of course, the servants knew), he called the bridegroom over. ¹⁰ "A host always serves the best wine first," he said. "Then, when everyone has had a lot to drink, he brings out the less expensive wine. But you have kept the best until now!"

¹¹ This miraculous sign at Cana in Galilee was the first time Jesus revealed his glory. And his disciples believed in him.

**2:6** Greek *2 or 3 measures* [75 to 113 liters].

**NICODEMUS**

God specializes in finding and changing people we consider out of reach. It took a while for Nicodemus to come out of the dark, but God was patient with this "undercover" believer.

Afraid of being discovered, Nicodemus made an appointment to see Jesus at night. Daylight conversations between Pharisees and Jesus tended to be antagonistic, but Nicodemus really wanted to learn. He probably got a lot more than he expected—a challenge to a new life! We know very little about Nicodemus, but we know that he left that evening's encounter a changed man. He came away with a whole new understanding of both God and himself.

Nicodemus next appears as part of the Jewish high council (7:50). As the group discussed ways to eliminate Jesus, Nicodemus raised the question of justice. Although his objection was overruled, he had spoken up. He had begun to change.

Our last picture of Nicodemus shows him joining Joseph of Arimathea in asking for Jesus' body in order to provide for its burial (19:39). Realizing what he was risking, Nicodemus was making a bold move. He was continuing to grow.

God looks for steady growth, not instant perfection. How well does your present level of spiritual growth match up with how long you have known Jesus?

| | |
|---|---|
| **Strengths and accomplishments** | • One of the few religious leaders who believed in Jesus<br>• A member of the powerful Jewish high council<br>• A Pharisee who was attracted by Jesus' character and miracles<br>• Joined with Joseph of Arimathea in burying Jesus |
| **Weakness and mistake** | • Limited by his fear of being publicly exposed as Jesus' follower |
| **Lessons from his life** | • Unless we are born again, we can never be part of the Kingdom of God<br>• God is able to change those we might consider unreachable<br>• God is patient, but persistent<br>• If we are available, God can use us |
| **Vital statistics** | • Where: Jerusalem<br>• Occupation: Religious leader<br>• Contemporaries: Jesus, Annas, Caiaphas, Pilate, Joseph of Arimathea |
| **Key verse** | "'What do you mean?' exclaimed Nicodemus. 'How can an old man go back into his mother's womb and be born again?'" (John 3:4). |

Nicodemus's story is told in John 3:1-21; 7:50-52; and 19:39-40.

cannot understand must continue to trust that he will work in the best way.

**2:5** Mary submitted to Jesus' way of doing things. She recognized that Jesus was more than her human son—he was the Son of God. When we bring our problems to Christ, we may think we know how he should take care of them. But he may have a completely different plan. Like Mary, we should submit and allow him to deal with the problem as he sees best.

**2:6** The six stone water jars were normally used for ceremonial washing. When full, the pots would hold 20 to 30 gallons. According to the Jews' ceremonial law, people became symbolically unclean by touching objects of everyday life. Before eating, the Jews would pour water over their hands to cleanse themselves of any bad influences associated with what they had touched.

**2:10** People look everywhere but to God for excitement and meaning. For some reason, they expect God to be dull and life-

less. Just as the wine Jesus made was the best, so life in him is better than life on our own. Why wait until everything else runs out before trying God? Why save the best until last?

**2:11** When the disciples saw Jesus' miracle, they believed. The miracle showed his power over nature and revealed the way he would go about his ministry—helping others, speaking with authority, and being in personal touch with people.

Miracles are not merely superhuman events, but events that demonstrate God's power. Almost every miracle Jesus did was a renewal of fallen creation—restoring sight, making the lame walk, even restoring life to the dead. Believe in Christ not because he is a superman but because he is the God who continues his creation, even in those of us who are poor, weak, crippled, orphaned, blind, deaf, or with some other desperate need.

¹²After the wedding he went to Capernaum for a few days with his mother, his brothers, and his disciples.

2:12<br>Matt 12:46-50

## B. MESSAGE AND MINISTRY OF JESUS, THE SON OF GOD (2:13—12:50)

John stresses the deity of Christ. He gives us eight miracles that serve as signs that Jesus is the Messiah. In this section he records Jesus describing himself as the bread of life, the water of life, the light of the world, the gate, and the good shepherd. John provides teachings of Jesus found nowhere else. This is the most theological of the four Gospels.

### 1. Jesus encounters belief and unbelief from the people

*Jesus Clears the Temple* (23)

¹³It was nearly time for the Jewish Passover celebration, so Jesus went to Jerusalem. ¹⁴In the Temple area he saw merchants selling cattle, sheep, and doves for sacrifices; he also saw dealers at tables exchanging foreign money. ¹⁵Jesus made a whip from some ropes and chased them all out of the Temple. He drove out the sheep and cattle, scattered the money changers' coins over the floor, and turned over their tables. ¹⁶Then, going over to the people who sold doves, he told them, "Get these things out of here. Stop turning my Father's house into a marketplace!"

2:13-22<br>Matt 21:12-17<br>Mark 11:15-19<br>Luke 19:45-48

2:16<br>Luke 2:49

¹⁷Then his disciples remembered this prophecy from the Scriptures: "Passion for God's house will consume me."*

2:17<br>†Ps 69:9

¹⁸But the Jewish leaders demanded, "What are you doing? If God gave you authority to do this, show us a miraculous sign to prove it."

¹⁹"All right," Jesus replied. "Destroy this temple, and in three days I will raise it up."

2:19<br>Matt 26:61; 27:40<br>Mark 14:58<br>Acts 6:14

**2:17** Or *"Concern for God's house will be my undoing."* Ps 69:9.

---

**2:12** Capernaum became Jesus' home base during his ministry in Galilee. Located on a major trade route, it was an important city in the region, with a Roman garrison and a customs station. At Capernaum, Matthew was called to be a disciple (Matthew 9:9). The city was also the home of several other disciples (Matthew 4:13-19) and a high-ranking government official (4:46). It had at least one major synagogue. Although Jesus made this city his base of operations in Galilee, he condemned it for the people's unbelief (Matthew 11:23; Luke 10:15).

**2:13** The Passover celebration took place yearly at the Temple in Jerusalem. Every Jewish male was expected to make a pilgrimage to Jerusalem during this time (Deuteronomy 16:16). This was a week-long festival—the Passover was one day, and the Festival of Unleavened Bread lasted the rest of the week. The entire week commemorated the freeing of the Jews from slavery in Egypt (Exodus 12:1-13).

**2:13** Jerusalem was both the religious and the political seat of Palestine, and the place where the Messiah was expected to arrive. The Temple was located there, and many Jewish families from all over the world would travel to Jerusalem during the key festivals. The Temple was on an imposing site, a hill overlooking the city. Solomon had built the first Temple on this same site almost 1,000 years earlier (959 B.C.), but his Temple had been destroyed by the Babylonians (2 Kings 25). The Temple was rebuilt in 515 B.C., and Herod the Great had enlarged and remodeled it.

**2:14** The Temple area was always crowded during Passover with thousands of out-of-town visitors. The religious leaders crowded it even further by allowing money changers and merchants to set up booths in the Court of the Gentiles. They rationalized this practice as a convenience for the worshipers and as a way to make money for Temple upkeep. But the religious leaders did not seem to care that the Court of the Gentiles was so full of merchants that foreigners found it difficult to worship. And worship was the main purpose for visiting the Temple. No wonder Jesus was angry!

**2:14** The Temple tax had to be paid in local currency, so foreigners had to have their money changed. But the money changers often charged exorbitant exchange rates. The people also were required to make sacrifices for sins. Because of the long journey, many could not bring their own animals. Some who brought animals had them rejected for imperfections. So animal merchants conducted a flourishing business in the Temple courtyard. The price of sacrificial animals was much higher in the Temple area than elsewhere. Jesus was angry at the dishonest, greedy practices of the money changers and merchants, and he particularly disliked their presence on the Temple grounds. They were making a mockery of God's house of worship.

**2:14ff** John records this first clearing, or cleansing, of the Temple. A second clearing occurred at the end of Jesus' ministry, about three years later, and that event is recorded in Matthew 21:12-17; Mark 11:12-19; Luke 19:45-48.

**2:14-16** God's Temple was being misused by people who had turned it into a marketplace. They had forgotten, or didn't care, that God's house is a place of worship, not a place for making a profit. Our attitude toward the church is wrong if we see it as a place for personal contacts or business advantage. Make sure you attend church to worship God.

**2:15, 16** Jesus was obviously angry at the merchants who exploited those who had come to God's house to worship. There is a difference between uncontrolled rage and righteous indignation—yet both are called anger. We must be very careful how we use the powerful emotion of anger. It is right to be angry about injustice and sin; it is wrong to be angry over trivial personal offenses.

**2:15, 16** Jesus made a whip and chased out the money changers. Does his example permit us to use violence against wrongdoers? Certain authority is granted to some, but not to all. For example, the authority to use weapons and restrain people is granted to police officers, but not to the general public. The authority to imprison people is granted to judges, but not to individual citizens. Jesus had God's authority, something we cannot have. While we want to live like Christ, we should never try to claim his authority where it has not been given to us.

**2:17** Jesus took the evil acts in the Temple as an insult against God, and thus, he did not deal with them halfheartedly. He was consumed with righteous anger against such flagrant disrespect for God.

**2:19, 20** The Jews understood Jesus to mean the Temple out of which he had just driven the merchants and money changers. This was the Temple Zerubbabel had built over 500 years earlier, but Herod the Great had begun remodeling it, making it much larger and far more beautiful. It had been 46 years since this remodeling had started (20 B.C.), and it still wasn't completely finished. They understood Jesus' words to mean that this imposing building could be torn down and rebuilt in three days, and they were startled.

**2:21**
John 10:38;
14:2, 10; 17:21
1 Cor 3:16; 6:19

**2:22**
Luke 24:6-8
John 12:16; 14:26

**2:23**
John 7:31;
11:47-48

**3:1-2**
John 7:50; 19:39

**3:2**
Matt 22:16
Acts 2:22; 10:38

**3:3**
John 1:13

**3:5**
Ezek 36:26-27
Titus 3:5
2 Pet 1:11

**3:6**
John 1:13
Rom 8:15-16
1 Cor 15:50
Gal 4:6

20"What!" they exclaimed. "It has taken forty-six years to build this Temple, and you can rebuild it in three days?" 21But when Jesus said "this temple," he meant his own body. 22After he was raised from the dead, his disciples remembered he had said this, and they believed both the Scriptures and what Jesus had said.

### Nicodemus Visits Jesus at Night (24)

23Because of the miraculous signs Jesus did in Jerusalem at the Passover celebration, many began to trust in him. 24But Jesus didn't trust them, because he knew human nature. 25No one needed to tell him what mankind is really like.

**3** There was a man named Nicodemus, a Jewish religious leader who was a Pharisee. 2After dark one evening, he came to speak with Jesus. "Rabbi," he said, "we all know that God has sent you to teach us. Your miraculous signs are evidence that God is with you."

3Jesus replied, "I tell you the truth, unless you are born again,* you cannot see the Kingdom of God."

4"What do you mean?" exclaimed Nicodemus. "How can an old man go back into his mother's womb and be born again?"

5Jesus replied, "I assure you, no one can enter the Kingdom of God without being born of water and the Spirit.* 6Humans can reproduce only human life, but the Holy Spirit gives

**3:3** Or *born from above;* also in 3:7. **3:5** Or *and spirit.* The Greek word for *Spirit* can also be translated *wind;* see 3:8.

---

**2:21, 22** Jesus was not talking about the Temple made of stones, but about his body. His listeners didn't realize it, but Jesus was greater than the Temple (Matthew 12:6). His words would take on meaning for his disciples after his resurrection. That Christ so perfectly fulfilled this prediction became the strongest proof for his claims to be God.

**2:23-25** The Son of God knows all about human nature. Jesus was well aware of the truth of Jeremiah 17:9, which states, "The human heart is the most deceitful of all things, and desperately wicked. Who really knows how bad it is?" Jesus was discerning, and he knew that the faith of some followers was superficial. Some of the same people claiming to believe in Jesus at this time would later yell "Crucify him!" It's easy to believe when it is exciting and everyone else believes the same way. But keep your faith firm even when it isn't popular to follow Christ.

**3:1** Nicodemus was a Pharisee and a member of the ruling council (called the high council, or the Sanhedrin). The Pharisees were a group of religious leaders whom Jesus and John the Baptist often criticized for being hypocrites (see the note on Matthew 3:7 for more on the Pharisees). Most Pharisees were intensely jealous of Jesus because he undermined their authority and challenged their views. But Nicodemus was searching, and he believed that Jesus had some answers. A learned teacher himself, he came to Jesus to be taught. No matter how intelligent and well educated you are, you must come to Jesus with an open mind and heart so he can teach you the truth about God.

**3:1ff** Nicodemus came to Jesus personally, although he could have sent one of his assistants. He wanted to examine Jesus for himself to separate fact from rumor. Perhaps Nicodemus was afraid of what his peers, the Pharisees, would say about his visit, so he came after dark. Later, when he understood that Jesus was truly the Messiah, he spoke up boldly in his defense (7:50, 51). Like Nicodemus, we must examine Jesus for ourselves—others cannot do it for us. Then, if we believe he is who he says, we will want to speak up for him.

**3:3** What did Nicodemus know about the Kingdom? From the Bible he knew it would be ruled by God, it would be restored on earth, and it would incorporate God's people. Jesus revealed to this devout Pharisee that the Kingdom would come to the whole world (3:16), not just the Jews, and that Nicodemus wouldn't be a part of it unless he was personally born again (3:5). This was a revolutionary concept: The Kingdom is personal, not national or ethnic, and its entrance requirements are repentance and spiritual rebirth. Jesus later taught that God's Kingdom has *already begun* in the hearts of believers (Luke 17:21). It will be fully realized when Jesus returns again to judge the world and abolish evil forever (Revelation 21–22).

**3:5, 6** "Being born of water and the Spirit" could refer to (1) the contrast between physical birth (water) and spiritual birth (Spirit), or (2) being regenerated by the Spirit and signifying that rebirth by Christian baptism. The water may also represent the cleansing action of God's Holy Spirit (Titus 3:5). Nicodemus undoubtedly would have been familiar with God's promise in Ezekiel 36:25, 26. Jesus was explaining the importance of a spiritual rebirth, saying that people don't enter the Kingdom by living a better life, but by being spiritually reborn.

**3:6** Who is the Holy Spirit? God is three persons in one—the Father, the Son, and the Holy Spirit. God became a man in Jesus so that Jesus could die for our sins. Jesus rose from the dead to offer salvation to all people through spiritual renewal and rebirth. When Jesus ascended into heaven, his physical presence left the earth, but he promised to send the Holy Spirit so that his spiritual presence would still be among humankind (see Luke 24:49). The Holy Spirit first became available to all believers at Pentecost (Acts 2). Whereas in Old Testament days the Holy Spirit empowered specific individuals for specific purposes, now all believers have the power of the Holy Spirit available to them. For more on the Holy Spirit, read 14:16-28; Romans 8:9; 1 Corinthians 12:13; and 2 Corinthians 1:22.

**THE VISIT IN SAMARIA** Jesus went to Jerusalem for the Passover, cleared the Temple, and talked with Nicodemus, a religious leader, about eternal life. He then left Jerusalem and traveled in Judea. On his way to Galilee, he visited Sychar and other villages in Samaria. Unlike most Jews of the day, he did not try to avoid the region of Samaria.

*Mediterranean Sea*

N

Cana • • Capernaum

*Sea of Galilee*

Nazareth •

GALILEE

Jordan River

Mount Ebal
SAMARIA
Mount Gerizim
Sychar
**Jerusalem**

PEREA

JUDEA

*Dead Sea*

IDUMEA

0       20 Mi.

0       20 Km.

birth to spiritual life.* [7] So don't be surprised when I say, ' You* must be born again.' [8] The wind blows wherever it wants. Just as you can hear the wind but can't tell where it comes from or where it is going, so you can't explain how people are born of the Spirit."

[9] "How are these things possible?" Nicodemus asked.

[10] Jesus replied, "You are a respected Jewish teacher, and yet you don't understand these things? [11] I assure you, we tell you what we know and have seen, and yet you won't believe our testimony. [12] But if you don't believe me when I tell you about earthly things, how can you possibly believe if I tell you about heavenly things? [13] No one has ever gone to heaven and returned. But the Son of Man* has come down from heaven. [14] And as Moses lifted up the bronze snake on a pole in the wilderness, so the Son of Man must be lifted up, [15] so that everyone who believes in him will have eternal life.*

[16] "For God loved the world so much that he gave his one and only Son, so that everyone who believes in him will not perish but have eternal life. [17] God sent his Son into the world not to judge the world, but to save the world through him.

[18] "There is no judgment against anyone who believes in him. But anyone who does not believe in him has already been judged for not believing in God's one and only Son. [19] And the judgment is based on this fact: God's light came into the world, but people loved the darkness more than the light, for their actions were evil. [20] All who do evil hate the light and refuse to go near it for fear their sins will be exposed. [21] But those who do what is right come to the light so others can see that they are doing what God wants.*"

## John the Baptist Tells More about Jesus (25)

[22] Then Jesus and his disciples left Jerusalem and went into the Judean countryside. Jesus spent some time with them there, baptizing people.

[23] At this time John the Baptist was baptizing at Aenon, near Salim, because there was plenty of water there; and people kept coming to him for baptism. [24] (This was before John was thrown into prison.) [25] A debate broke out between John's disciples and a certain Jew*

**3:8** Eccl 11:5

**3:13** John 6:38, 42 Eph 4:8-10

**3:14** Num 21:8-9 John 8:28; 12:34

**3:15** John 20:31 1 Jn 5:11-12

**3:16** Rom 5:8; 8:32 1 Jn 4:9-10; 5:13

**3:17** John 12:47

**3:18** John 5:24

**3:19** John 1:5, 9; 8:12; 9:5; 12:46

**3:20** Eph 5:11-13

**3:21** 1 Jn 1:6

**3:22** John 3:26; 4:1-2

**3:24** Matt 4:12

**3:6** Greek *what is born of the Spirit is spirit.* **3:7** The Greek word for *you* is plural; also in 3:12. **3:13** Some manuscripts add *who lives in heaven.* "Son of Man" is a title Jesus used for himself. **3:15** Or *everyone who believes will have eternal life in him.* **3:21** Or *can see God at work in what he is doing.* **3:25** Some manuscripts read *some Jews.*

**3:8** Jesus explained that we cannot control the work of the Holy Spirit. He works in ways we cannot predict or understand. Just as you did not control your physical birth, so you cannot control your spiritual birth. It is a gift from God through the Holy Spirit (Romans 8:16; 1 Corinthians 2:10-12; 1 Thessalonians 1:5, 6).

**3:10, 11** This Jewish teacher of the Bible knew the Old Testament thoroughly, but he didn't understand what it said about the Messiah. Knowledge is not salvation. You should know the Bible, but even more important, you should understand the God whom the Bible reveals and the salvation that God offers.

**3:14, 15** When the Israelites were wandering in the wilderness, God sent a plague of snakes to punish the people for their rebellious attitudes. Those doomed to die from snakebite could be healed by obeying God's command to look up at the elevated bronze snake and by believing that God would heal them if they did (see Numbers 21:8, 9). Similarly, our salvation happens when we look up to Jesus, believing he will save us. God has provided this way for us to be healed of sin's deadly bite.

**3:16** The message of the Good News comes to a focus in this verse. God's love is not static or self-centered; it reaches out and draws others in. Here God sets the pattern of true love, the basis for all love relationships—when you love someone dearly, you are willing to give freely to the point of self-sacrifice. God paid dearly with the life of his Son, the highest price he could pay. Jesus accepted our punishment, paid the price for our sins, and then offered us the new life that he had bought for us. When we share the Good News with others, our love must be like Jesus'—willingly giving up our own comfort and security so that others might join us in receiving God's love.

**3:16** Some people are repulsed by the idea of eternal life because their lives are miserable. But eternal life is not an extension of a person's miserable, mortal life; eternal life is God's life embodied in Christ given to all believers now as a guarantee that they will live forever. In eternal life there is no death, sickness, enemy, evil,

or sin. When we don't know Christ, we make choices as though this life is all we have. In reality, this life is just the introduction to eternity. Receive this new life by faith and begin to evaluate all that happens from an eternal perspective.

**3:16** To "believe" is more than intellectual agreement that Jesus is God. It means to put our trust and confidence in him that he alone can save us. It is to put Christ in charge of our present plans and eternal destiny. Believing is both trusting his words as reliable, and relying on him for the power to change. If you have never trusted Christ, let this promise of everlasting life be yours—and believe.

**3:18** People often try to protect themselves from their fears by putting their faith in something they do or have: good deeds, skill or intelligence, money or possessions. But only God can save us from the one thing that we really need to fear—eternal condemnation. We believe in God by recognizing the insufficiency of our own efforts to find salvation and by asking him to do his work in us. When Jesus talks about unbelievers, he means those who reject or ignore him completely, not those who have momentary doubts.

**3:19-21** Many people don't want their lives exposed to God's light because they are afraid of what will be revealed. They don't want to be changed. Don't be surprised when these same people are threatened by your desire to obey God and do what is right, because they are afraid that the light in you may expose some of the darkness in their lives. Rather than giving in to discouragement, keep praying that they will come to see how much better it is to live in light than in darkness.

**3:25ff** Some people look for points of disagreement so they can sow seeds of discord, discontent, and doubt. John the Baptist ended this theological argument by focusing on his devotion to Christ. It is divisive to try to force others to believe our way. Instead, let's witness about what Christ has done for us. How can anyone argue with us about that?

**3:26**
John 1:7, 34

**3:27**
1 Cor 4:7
Heb 5:4

**3:28**
Mal 3:1

**3:29**
Matt 9:15
Rev 21:9

**3:31**
1 Jn 4:5

**3:33**
1 Jn 5:10

**3:34**
Luke 4:18

**3:35**
John 5:20; 15:9

**3:36**
John 3:16
1 Jn 5:12-13

over ceremonial cleansing. ²⁶So John's disciples came to him and said, "Rabbi, the man you met on the other side of the Jordan River, the one you identified as the Messiah, is also baptizing people. And everybody is going to him instead of coming to us."

²⁷John replied, "No one can receive anything unless God gives it from heaven. ²⁸You yourselves know how plainly I told you, 'I am not the Messiah. I am only here to prepare the way for him.' ²⁹It is the bridegroom who marries the bride, and the best man is simply glad to stand with him and hear his vows. Therefore, I am filled with joy at his success. ³⁰He must become greater and greater, and I must become less and less.

³¹"He has come from above and is greater than anyone else. We are of the earth, and we speak of earthly things, but he has come from heaven and is greater than anyone else.* ³²He testifies about what he has seen and heard, but how few believe what he tells them! ³³Anyone who accepts his testimony can affirm that God is true. ³⁴For he is sent by God. He speaks God's words, for God gives him the Spirit without limit. ³⁵The Father loves his Son and has put everything into his hands. ³⁶And anyone who believes in God's Son has eternal life. Anyone who doesn't obey the Son will never experience eternal life but remains under God's angry judgment."

### Jesus Talks to a Woman at the Well (27)

**4:1**
John 3:22, 26

**4:4**
Matt 10:5
Luke 9:52

**4:5-6**
Gen 33:19; 48:22
Josh 24:32

**4** Jesus* knew the Pharisees had heard that he was baptizing and making more disciples than John ²(though Jesus himself didn't baptize them—his disciples did). ³So he left Judea and returned to Galilee.

⁴He had to go through Samaria on the way. ⁵Eventually he came to the Samaritan village of Sychar, near the field that Jacob gave to his son Joseph. ⁶Jacob's well was there; and Jesus,

**3:31** Some manuscripts do not include *and is greater than anyone else.* **4:1** Some manuscripts read *The Lord.*

---

**3:26** John the Baptist's disciples were disturbed because people were following Jesus instead of John. It is easy to grow jealous of the popularity of another person's ministry. But we must remember that our true mission is to influence people to follow Christ, not us.

**3:27** Why did John the Baptist continue to baptize after Jesus came onto the scene? Why didn't he become a disciple, too? John explained that because God had given him his work, he had to continue it until God called him to do something else. John's main purpose was to point people to Christ. Even with Jesus beginning his own ministry, John could still turn people to Jesus.

**3:30** John's willingness to decrease in importance shows unusual humility. Pastors and other Christian leaders can be tempted to focus more on the success of their ministries than on Christ. Beware of those who put more emphasis on their own achievements than on God's Kingdom.

**3:31-35** Jesus' testimony was trustworthy because he had come from heaven and was speaking of what he had seen there. His words were the very words of God. Your whole spiritual life depends on your answer to one question: Who is Jesus Christ? If you accept Jesus as only a prophet or teacher, you have to reject his teaching, for he claimed to be God's Son, even God himself. The heartbeat of John's Gospel is the dynamic truth that Jesus Christ is God's Son, the Messiah, the Savior, who existed from the beginning and will continue to live forever. This same Jesus has invited us to accept him and live with him eternally. When we understand who Jesus is, we are compelled to believe what he said.

**3:34** God's Spirit was upon Jesus without measure or limit. Thus, Jesus was the highest revelation of God to humanity (Hebrews 1:2).

**3:36** Jesus says that those who believe in him *have* (not *will have*) eternal life. To receive eternal life is to join in God's life, which by nature is eternal. Thus, eternal life begins at the moment of spiritual rebirth.

**3:36** John, the author of this Gospel, has been demonstrating that Jesus is the true Son of God. Jesus sets before us the greatest choice in life. We are responsible to decide today whom we will obey (Joshua 24:15), and God wants us to choose him and

life (Deuteronomy 30:15-20). God's angry judgment refers to his final rejection of those who reject him. To put off the choice is to choose not to follow Christ. Indecision is a fatal decision.

**4:1-3** Already opposition was rising against Jesus, especially from the Pharisees. They resented Jesus' popularity as well as his message, which challenged much of their teachings. Because Jesus was just beginning his ministry, it wasn't yet time to confront these leaders openly; so he left Jerusalem and traveled north toward Galilee.

**4:4** To go from the territory of Judea to Galilee meant passing through a central territory called Samaria. Most Jews did everything they could to avoid traveling through Samaria. The reason goes way back into their history.

After the northern kingdom, with its capital at Samaria, fell to the Assyrians, many Jews were deported to Assyria, and foreigners were brought in to settle the land and help keep the peace (2 Kings 17:24). The intermarriage between those foreigners and the remaining Jews resulted in a mixed race, impure in the opinion of Jews who lived in the southern kingdom. Thus, the pure Jews hated this mixed race, called Samaritans, because they felt that their fellow Jews who had intermarried had betrayed their people and nation. The Samaritans had set up an alternate center for worship on Mount Gerizim (4:20) to parallel the Temple at Jerusalem, but it had been destroyed 150 years earlier. While there was long-standing prejudice between Jews and Samaritans, Jesus did not live by such restrictions. The route through Samaria was shorter, and that was the route he took.

**4:5-7** Jacob's well was on the property originally owned by Jacob (Genesis 33:18, 19). It was not a spring-fed well, but a well into which water seeped from rain and dew, collecting at the bottom. Wells were almost always located outside the city along the main road. Twice each day, morning and evening, women came to draw water. This woman came at noon, however, probably to avoid meeting people who knew her reputation. Jesus gave this woman an extraordinary message about fresh and pure water that would quench her spiritual thirst forever.

tired from the long walk, sat wearily beside the well about noontime. ⁷Soon a Samaritan woman came to draw water, and Jesus said to her, "Please give me a drink." ⁸He was alone at the time because his disciples had gone into the village to buy some food.

⁹The woman was surprised, for Jews refuse to have anything to do with Samaritans.* She said to Jesus, "You are a Jew, and I am a Samaritan woman. Why are you asking me for a drink?"

¹⁰Jesus replied, "If you only knew the gift God has for you and who you are speaking to, you would ask me, and I would give you living water."

¹¹"But sir, you don't have a rope or a bucket," she said, "and this well is very deep. Where would you get this living water? ¹²And besides, do you think you're greater than our ancestor Jacob, who gave us this well? How can you offer better water than he and his sons and his animals enjoyed?"

¹³Jesus replied, "Anyone who drinks this water will soon become thirsty again. ¹⁴But those who drink the water I give will never be thirsty again. It becomes a fresh, bubbling spring within them, giving them eternal life."

¹⁵"Please, sir," the woman said, "give me this water! Then I'll never be thirsty again, and I won't have to come here to get water."

¹⁶"Go and get your husband," Jesus told her.

¹⁷"I don't have a husband," the woman replied.

Jesus said, "You're right! You don't have a husband— ¹⁸for you have had five husbands, and you aren't even married to the man you're living with now. You certainly spoke the truth!"

¹⁹"Sir," the woman said, "you must be a prophet. ²⁰So tell me, why is it that you Jews insist that Jerusalem is the only place of worship, while we Samaritans claim it is here at Mount Gerizim,* where our ancestors worshiped?"

²¹Jesus replied, "Believe me, dear woman, the time is coming when it will no longer matter whether you worship the Father on this mountain or in Jerusalem. ²²You Samaritans know very little about the one you worship, while we Jews know all about him, for salvation comes through the Jews. ²³But the time is coming—indeed it's here now—when true worshipers will worship the Father in spirit and in truth. The Father is looking for those who will worship him that way. ²⁴For God is Spirit, so those who worship him must worship in spirit and in truth."

**4:7**
Gen 24:17
1 Kgs 17:10

**4:9**
Ezra 4:1-3; 9–10
Matt 10:5
Luke 9:52-53
John 8:48
Acts 10:48

**4:10**
Isa 12:3; 44:3
Jer 2:13; 17:13
John 7:37-39
1 Cor 12:13
Rev 7:17; 21:6;
22:17

**4:14**
John 6:35; 7:38

**4:15**
John 6:34

**4:19**
Matt 21:46
John 7:40; 9:17

**4:20**
Deut 11:29;
12:5-14
Josh 8:33

**4:21**
Mal 1:11
1 Tim 2:8

**4:22**
2 Kgs 17:28-41
Isa 2:3
Rom 3:1-2; 9:4-5

**4:23-24**
2 Cor 3:17-18
Phil 3:3

**4:9** Some manuscripts do not include this sentence.     **4:20** Greek *on this mountain*.

---

**4:7-9**  This woman (1) was a Samaritan, a member of the hated mixed race, (2) was known to be living in sin, and (3) was in a public place. No respectable Jewish man would talk to a woman under such circumstances. But Jesus did. The Good News is for every person, no matter what his or her race, social position, or past sins. We must be prepared to share this Good News at any time and in any place. Jesus crossed all barriers to share the Good News, and we who follow him must do no less.

**4:10**  What did Jesus mean by "living water"? In the Old Testament, many verses speak of thirsting after God as one thirsts for water (Psalm 42:1; Isaiah 55:1; Jeremiah 2:13; Zechariah 13:1). God is called the fountain of life (Psalm 36:9) and the fountain of living water (Jeremiah 17:13). In saying he would bring living water that could forever quench a person's thirst for God, Jesus was claiming to be the Messiah. Only the Messiah could give this gift that satisfies the soul's desire.

**4:13-15**  Many spiritual functions parallel physical functions. As our bodies hunger and thirst, so do our souls. But our souls need *spiritual* food and water. The woman confused the two kinds of water, perhaps because no one had ever talked with her about her spiritual hunger and thirst before. We would not think of depriving our bodies of food and water when they hunger or thirst. Why then should we deprive our souls? The living Word, Jesus Christ, and the written Word, the Bible, can satisfy our hungry and thirsty souls.

**4:15**  The woman mistakenly believed that if she received the water Jesus offered, she would not have to return to the well each day. She was interested in Jesus' message because she thought it could make her life easier. But if that were always the case, people

would accept Christ's message for the wrong reasons. Christ did not come to take away challenges, but to change us on the inside and to empower us to deal with problems from God's perspective.

**4:16-20**  When this woman discovered that Jesus knew all about her private life, she quickly changed the subject. Often people become uncomfortable when the conversation is too close to home, and they try to talk about something else. As we witness, we should gently guide the conversation back to Christ. His presence exposes sin and makes people squirm, but only Christ can forgive sins and give new life.

**4:20-24**  The woman brought up a popular theological issue— the correct place to worship. But her question was a smoke screen to keep Jesus away from her deepest need. Jesus directed the conversation to a much more important point: The *location* of worship is not nearly as important as the *attitude* of the worshipers.

**4:22**  When Jesus said, "Salvation comes through the Jews," he meant that only through the Jewish Messiah would the whole world find salvation. God had promised that through the Jewish race the whole earth would be blessed (Genesis 12:3). The Old Testament prophets had called the Jews to be a light to the other nations of the world, bringing them to a knowledge of God; and they had predicted the Messiah's coming. The woman at the well may have known of these passages and was expecting the Messiah, but she didn't realize that she was talking to him!

**4:24**  "God is Spirit" means he is not a physical being limited to one place. He is present everywhere, and he can be worshiped anywhere, at any time. It is not where we worship that counts, but how we worship. Is your worship genuine and true? Do you have the Holy Spirit's help? How does the Holy Spirit help us worship?

**4:25**
Deut 18:15

**4:26**
Mark 14:61-62
John 9:37

25 The woman said, "I know the Messiah is coming—the one who is called Christ. When he comes, he will explain everything to us."

26 Then Jesus told her, "I Am the Messiah!"*

### Jesus Tells about the Spiritual Harvest (28)

27 Just then his disciples came back. They were shocked to find him talking to a woman, but none of them had the nerve to ask, "What do you want with her?" or "Why are you talking to her?" 28 The woman left her water jar beside the well and ran back to the village, telling everyone,

**4:29**
Matt 9:37
John 7:26

29 "Come and see a man who told me everything I ever did! Could he possibly be the Messiah?" 30 So the people came streaming from the village to see him.

31 Meanwhile, the disciples were urging Jesus, "Rabbi, eat something."

32 But Jesus replied, "I have a kind of food you know nothing about."

33 "Did someone bring him food while we were gone?" the disciples asked each other.

**4:34**
John 5:30, 36;
6:38; 17:4

**4:35**
Matt 9:37
Luke 10:2

**4:37**
Job 31:8
Mic 6:15

34 Then Jesus explained: "My nourishment comes from doing the will of God, who sent me, and from finishing his work. 35 You know the saying, 'Four months between planting and harvest.' But I say, wake up and look around. The fields are already ripe* for harvest. 36 The harvesters are paid good wages, and the fruit they harvest is people brought to eternal life. What joy awaits both the planter and the harvester alike! 37 You know the saying, 'One plants and another harvests.' And it's true. 38 I sent you to harvest where you didn't plant; others had already done the work, and now you will get to gather the harvest."

### Many Samaritans Believe in Jesus (29)

39 Many Samaritans from the village believed in Jesus because the woman had said, "He told me everything I ever did!" 40 When they came out to see him, they begged him to stay in their village. So he stayed for two days,

**4:42**
Luke 2:11
1 Jn 4:14

41 long enough for many more to hear his message and believe. 42 Then they said to the woman, "Now we believe, not just because of what you told us, but because we have heard him ourselves. Now we know that he is indeed the Savior of the world."

### Jesus Preaches in Galilee (30/Matthew 4:12-17; Mark 1:14-15; Luke 4:14-15)

**4:44**
Matt 13:57
Luke 4:24

43 At the end of the two days, Jesus went on to Galilee. 44 He himself had said that a prophet is not honored in his own hometown. 45 Yet the Galileans welcomed him, for they had been in Jerusalem at the Passover celebration and had seen everything he did there.

### Jesus Heals a Government Official's Son (31)

**4:46**
John 2:1-11

46 As he traveled through Galilee, he came to Cana, where he had turned the water into wine. There was a government official in nearby Capernaum whose son was very sick. 47 When he

**4:26** Or *"The 'I Am' is here"*; or *"I am the Lord"*; Greek reads *"I am, the one speaking to you."* See Exod 3:14.
**4:35** Greek *white.*

---

The Holy Spirit prays for us (Romans 8:26), teaches us the words of Christ (14:26), and tells us we are loved (Romans 5:5).

**4:34** The "nourishment" about which Jesus was speaking was his spiritual nourishment. It includes more than Bible study, prayer, and attending church. Spiritual nourishment also comes from doing God's will and helping to bring his work of salvation to completion. We are nourished not only by what we take in, but also by what we give out for God. In 17:4, Jesus refers to completing God's work on earth.

**4:35** Sometimes Christians excuse themselves from witnessing by saying that their family or friends aren't ready to believe. Jesus, however, makes it clear that around us a continual harvest waits to be reaped. Don't let Jesus find you making excuses. Look around. You will find people ready to hear God's Word.

**4:36-38** The wages Jesus offers are the joy of working for him and seeing the harvest of believers. These wages come to planter and harvester alike because both find joy in seeing new believers come into Christ's Kingdom. The phrase "others had already done the work" (4:38) may refer to the Old Testament prophets and to John the Baptist, who paved the way for the Good News.

**4:39** The Samaritan woman immediately shared her experience with others. Despite her reputation, many took her invitation and came out to meet Jesus. Perhaps there are sins in our past of which we're ashamed. But Christ changes us. As people see

these changes, they become curious. Use these opportunities to introduce them to Christ.

**JESUS RETURNS TO GALILEE**
Jesus stayed in Sychar for two days, then went on to Galilee. He visited Nazareth and various towns in Galilee before arriving in Cana. From there he spoke the word of healing, and a government official's son in Capernaum was healed. The Gospel of Matthew tells us Jesus then settled in Capernaum (Matthew 4:12, 13).

heard that Jesus had come from Judea to Galilee, he went and begged Jesus to come to Capernaum to heal his son, who was about to die.

48Jesus asked, "Will you never believe in me unless you see miraculous signs and wonders?"

49The official pleaded, "Lord, please come now before my little boy dies."

50Then Jesus told him, "Go back home. Your son will live!" And the man believed what Jesus said and started home.

51While the man was on his way, some of his servants met him with the news that his son was alive and well. 52He asked them when the boy had begun to get better, and they replied, "Yesterday afternoon at one o'clock his fever suddenly disappeared!" 53Then the father realized that that was the very time Jesus had told him, "Your son will live." And he and his entire household believed in Jesus. 54This was the second miraculous sign Jesus did in Galilee after coming from Judea.

### Jesus Heals a Lame Man by a Pool (42)

**5** Afterward Jesus returned to Jerusalem for one of the Jewish holy days. 2Inside the city, near the Sheep Gate, was the pool of Bethesda,* with five covered porches. 3Crowds of sick people—blind, lame, or paralyzed—lay on the porches.* 5One of the men lying there had been sick for thirty-eight years. 6When Jesus saw him and knew he had been ill for a long time, he asked him, "Would you like to get well?"

7"I can't, sir," the sick man said, "for I have no one to put me into the pool when the water bubbles up. Someone else always gets there ahead of me."

8Jesus told him, "Stand up, pick up your mat, and walk!"

9Instantly, the man was healed! He rolled up his sleeping mat and began walking! But this miracle happened on the Sabbath, 10so the Jewish leaders objected. They said to the man who was cured, "You can't work on the Sabbath! The law doesn't allow you to carry that sleeping mat!"

**4:48**
1 Cor 1:22

**4:50**
Matt 8:13
Mark 7:29

**4:53**
Acts 11:14;
16:14-15

**4:54**
John 2:11

**5:1**
Lev 23:1-2
Deut 16:1
John 2:13

**5:2**
Neh 3:1; 12:39

**5:8**
Matt 9:6
Mark 2:11
Luke 5:24

**5:10**
Neh 13:15-20
Jer 17:21
Matt 12:2

**5:2** Other manuscripts read *Beth-zatha;* still others read *Bethsaida.* **5:3** Some manuscripts add an expanded conclusion to verse 3 and all of verse 4: *waiting for a certain movement of the water,* 4*for an angel of the Lord came from time to time and stirred up the water. And the first person to step in after the water was stirred was healed of whatever disease he had.*

---

**4:46-49** This government official was probably an officer in Herod's service. He had walked 20 miles to see Jesus and addressed him as "Lord," putting himself under Jesus even though he had legal authority over Jesus.

**4:48** This miracle was more than a favor to one official; it was a sign to all the people. John's Gospel was written to all humankind to urge faith in Christ. Here a government official had faith that Jesus could do what he claimed. The official believed; *then* he saw a miraculous sign.

**4:50** This government official not only believed Jesus could heal; he also obeyed Jesus by returning home, thus demonstrating his

**JESUS TEACHES IN JERUSALEM**
Between chapters 4 and 5 of John, Jesus ministered throughout Galilee, especially in Capernaum. He had been calling certain men to follow him, but it wasn't until after this trip to Jerusalem (5:1) that he chose his 12 disciples from among them.

faith. It isn't enough for us to say we believe that Jesus can take care of our problems. We need to act as if he can. When you pray about a need or problem, live as though you believe Jesus can do what he says.

**4:51** Jesus' miracles were not mere illusions. Although the official's son was 20 miles away, he was healed when Jesus spoke the word. Distance was no problem because Christ has mastery over space. We can never put so much space between ourselves and Christ that he can no longer help us.

**4:53** Notice how the official's faith grew. First, he believed enough to ask Jesus to help his son. Second, he believed Jesus' assurance that his son would live, and he acted on it. Third, he and his whole house believed in Jesus. Faith is a gift that grows as we use it.

**5:1** Three festivals (or "holy days") required all Jewish males to come to Jerusalem: (1) the Festival of Passover and Unleavened Bread, (2) the Festival of Pentecost (also called the Festival of Harvest or the Festival of Weeks), and (3) the Festival of Shelters.

**5:6** After 38 years, this man's problem had become a way of life. No one had ever helped him. He had no hope of ever being healed. The man's situation looked hopeless. But no matter how trapped you feel in your infirmities, God can minister to your deepest needs. Don't let a problem or hardship cause you to lose hope. God may have special work for you to do in spite of your condition, or even because of it. Many have ministered effectively to hurting people because they have triumphed over their own hurts.

**5:10** According to the Pharisees, carrying a mat on the Sabbath was work and was therefore unlawful. It did not break an Old Testament law, but it broke the Pharisees' *interpretation* of God's command to "remember to observe the Sabbath day by keeping it holy" (Exodus 20:8). This was just one of hundreds of rules they had added to the Old Testament law.

**5:10** A man who hadn't walked for 38 years had been healed, but the Pharisees were more concerned about their petty rules than the life and health of a human being. The Jewish leaders saw both a

**5:14**
John 8:11

**5:18**
Phil 2:6
Titus 2:13
2 Pet 1:1
1 Jn 5:21

**5:19**
John 8:28; 12:49;
14:10

**5:21**
John 11:25

[11]But he replied, "The man who healed me told me, 'Pick up your mat and walk.'"

[12]"Who said such a thing as that?" they demanded.

[13]The man didn't know, for Jesus had disappeared into the crowd. [14]But afterward Jesus found him in the Temple and told him, "Now you are well; so stop sinning, or something even worse may happen to you." [15]Then the man went and told the Jewish leaders that it was Jesus who had healed him.

### Jesus Claims to Be the Son of God (43)

[16]So the Jewish leaders began harassing* Jesus for breaking the Sabbath rules. [17]But Jesus replied, "My Father is always working, and so am I." [18]So the Jewish leaders tried all the harder to find a way to kill him. For he not only broke the Sabbath, he called God his Father, thereby making himself equal with God.

[19]So Jesus explained, "I tell you the truth, the Son can do nothing by himself. He does only what he sees the Father doing. Whatever the Father does, the Son also does. [20]For the Father loves the Son and shows him everything he is doing. In fact, the Father will show him how to do even greater works than healing this man. Then you will truly be astonished. [21]For just as the Father gives life to those he raises from the dead, so the Son gives life to anyone he wants. [22]In addition, the Father judges no one. Instead, he has given the Son absolute authority to

**5:16** Or *persecuting.*

---

| THE CLAIMS OF CHRIST | Jesus claimed to be: | Matthew | Mark | Luke | John |
|---|---|---|---|---|---|
| Those who read the life of Christ are faced with one unavoidable question—was Jesus God? Part of any reasonable conclusion has to include the fact that he did claim to be God. We have no other choice but to agree or disagree with his claim. Eternal life is at stake in the choice. | the fulfillment of Old Testament prophecies | 5:17; 14:33; 16:16, 17; 26:31, 53-56; 27:43 | 14:21, 61, 62 | 4:16-21; 7:18-23; 18:31; 22:37; 24:44 | 2:22; 5:45-47; 6:45; 7:40; 10:34-36; 13:18; 15:25; 20:9 |
| | the Son of Man | 8:20; 12:8; 16:27; 19:28; 20:18, 19; 24:27, 44; 25:31; 26:2, 45, 64 | 8:31, 38; 9:9; 10:45; 14:41 | 6:22; 7:33, 34; 12:8; 17:22; 18:8, 31; 19:10; 21:36 | 1:51; 3:13, 14; 6:27, 53; 12:23, 34 |
| | the Son of God | 11:27; 14:33; 16:16, 17; 27:43 | 3:11, 12; 14:61, 62 | 8:28; 10:22 | 1:18; 3:35, 36; 5:18-26; 6:40; 10:36; 11:4; 17:1; 19:7 |
| | the Messiah/ the Christ | 23:9, 10; 26:63, 64 | 8:29, 30 | 4:41; 23:1, 2; 24:25-27 | 4:25, 26; 10:24, 25; 11:27 |
| | Teacher/Master | 26:18 | | | 13:13, 14 |
| | one with authority to forgive | | 2:1-12 | 7:48, 49 | |
| | Lord | | 5:19 | | 13:13, 14; 20:28, 29 |
| | Savior | | | 19:10 | 3:17; 10:9 |

---

mighty miracle of healing and a broken rule. They threw the miracle aside as they focused their attention on the broken rule, because the rule was more important to them than the miracle. It is easy to get so caught up in our man-made structures and rules that we forget the people involved. Are your guidelines for living God-made or man-made? Are they helping people, or have they become needless stumbling blocks?

**5:14** This man had been lame, or paralyzed, and suddenly he could walk. This was a great miracle. But he needed an even greater miracle—to have his sins forgiven. The man was delighted to be physically healed, but he had to turn from his sins and seek God's forgiveness to be spiritually healed. God's forgiveness is the greatest gift you will ever receive. Don't neglect his gracious offer.

**5:17** If God stopped every kind of work on the Sabbath, nature would fall into chaos, and sin would overrun the world. Genesis

2:2 says that God rested on the seventh day, but this can't mean that he stopped doing good. Jesus wanted to teach that when the opportunity to do good presents itself, it should not be ignored, even on the Sabbath.

**5:17ff** Jesus was identifying himself with God, his Father. There could be no doubt as to his claim to be God. Jesus does not leave us the option to believe in God while ignoring God's Son (5:23). The Pharisees also called God their Father, but they realized Jesus was claiming a unique relationship with him. In response to Jesus' claim, the Pharisees had two choices: to believe him, or to accuse him of blasphemy. They chose the second.

**5:19-23** Because of his unity with God, Jesus lived as God wanted him to live. Because of our identification with Jesus, we must honor him and live as he wants us to live. The question "What would Jesus do?" may help us make the right choices.

judge, [23]so that everyone will honor the Son, just as they honor the Father. Anyone who does not honor the Son is certainly not honoring the Father who sent him.

[24]"I tell you the truth, those who listen to my message and believe in God who sent me have eternal life. They will never be condemned for their sins, but they have already passed from death into life.

[25]"And I assure you that the time is coming, indeed it's here now, when the dead will hear my voice—the voice of the Son of God. And those who listen will live. [26]The Father has life in himself, and he has granted that same life-giving power to his Son. [27]And he has given him authority to judge everyone because he is the Son of Man.* [28]Don't be so surprised! Indeed, the time is coming when all the dead in their graves will hear the voice of God's Son, [29]and they will rise again. Those who have done good will rise to experience eternal life, and those who have continued in evil will rise to experience judgment. [30]I can do nothing on my own. I judge as God tells me. Therefore, my judgment is just, because I carry out the will of the one who sent me, not my own will.

### Jesus Supports His Claim (44)

[31]"If I were to testify on my own behalf, my testimony would not be valid. [32]But someone else is also testifying about me, and I assure you that everything he says about me is true. [33]In fact, you sent investigators to listen to John the Baptist, and his testimony about me was true. [34]Of course, I have no need of human witnesses, but I say these things so you might be saved. [35]John was like a burning and shining lamp, and you were excited for a while about his message. [36]But I have a greater witness than John—my teachings and my miracles. The Father gave me these works to accomplish, and they prove that he sent me. [37]And the Father who sent me has testified about me himself. You have never heard his voice or seen him face to face, [38]and you do not have his message in your hearts, because you do not believe me—the one he sent to you.

[39]"You search the Scriptures because you think they give you eternal life. But the Scriptures point to me! [40]Yet you refuse to come to me to receive this life.

[41]"Your approval means nothing to me, [42]because I know you don't have God's love within you. [43]For I have come to you in my Father's name, and you have rejected me. Yet if others come in their own name, you gladly welcome them. [44]No wonder you can't believe! For you gladly honor each other, but you don't care about the honor that comes from the one who alone is God.*

[45]"Yet it isn't I who will accuse you before the Father. Moses will accuse you! Yes, Moses, in whom you put your hopes. [46]If you really believed Moses, you would believe me, because he wrote about me. [47]But since you don't believe what he wrote, how will you believe what I say?"

**5:27** "Son of Man" is a title Jesus used for himself.   **5:44** Some manuscripts read *from the only One*.

**5:23**
1 Jn 2:23
**5:24**
John 3:15;
20:30-31
1 Jn 3:14; 5:13
**5:25**
John 4:21; 6:63, 68
**5:26**
John 1:4; 6:57
1 Jn 5:11-12
**5:27**
John 9:39
Acts 10:42; 17:31
**5:29**
Dan 12:2
Matt 25:46
Acts 24:15
**5:30**
John 5:19; 6:38
**5:31**
John 8:13-14
**5:32**
John 8:18
**5:36**
John 10:25, 38;
14:11; 15:24
1 Jn 5:9
**5:37**
Deut 4:12
John 1:18; 8:18
1 Tim 1:17
**5:38**
1 Jn 2:14
**5:39**
Luke 24:27, 44
Acts 13:27
Rom 2:17-20
**5:41**
John 12:43
**5:45**
John 9:28
Rom 2:17
**5:46**
Gen 3:15
Deut 18:15, 18
Luke 24:27, 44
Acts 26:22-23
**5:47**
Luke 16:31

---

**5:24** "Eternal life"—living forever with God—begins when you accept Jesus Christ as Savior. At that moment, new life begins in you (2 Corinthians 5:17). It is a completed transaction. You still will face physical death, but when Christ returns again, your body will be resurrected to live forever (1 Corinthians 15).

**5:25** In saying that the dead will hear his voice, Jesus was talking about the spiritually dead who hear, understand, and accept him. Those who accept Jesus, the Word, will have eternal life. Jesus was also talking about the physically dead. He raised several dead people while he was on earth, and at his second coming, "the Christians who have died" will rise to meet him (1 Thessalonians 4:16).

**5:26** God is the source and Creator of life, for there is no life apart from God, here or hereafter. The life in us is a gift from him (see Deuteronomy 30:20; Psalm 36:9). Because Jesus is eternally existent with God, the Creator, he, too, is "the life" (14:6) through whom we may live eternally (see 1 John 5:11).

**5:27** The Old Testament mentioned three signs of the coming Messiah. In this chapter, John shows that Jesus has fulfilled all three signs. Authority to judge is given to him as the Son of Man (cf. 5:27 with Daniel 7:13, 14). The lame and sick are healed (cf. 5:20, 21 with Isaiah 35:6; Jeremiah 31:8, 9). The dead are raised to life (cf. 5:21, 28 with Deuteronomy 32:39; 1 Samuel 2:6; 2 Kings 5:7).

**5:29** Those who have rebelled against Christ will be resurrected, too, but they will hear God's judgment against them and will be sentenced to eternity apart from him. There are those who wish to live well on earth, ignore God, and then see death as final rest. Jesus does not allow unbelieving people to see death as the end of it all. There is a judgment to face.

**5:31ff** Jesus claimed to be equal with God (5:18), to give eternal life (5:24), to be the source of life (5:26), and to judge sin (5:27). These statements make it clear that Jesus was claiming to be divine—an almost unbelievable claim, but one that was supported by another witness, John the Baptist.

**5:39, 40** The religious leaders knew what the Bible said but failed to apply its words to their lives. They knew the teachings of the Scriptures but failed to see the Messiah to whom the Scriptures pointed. They knew the rules but missed the Savior. Entrenched in their own religious system, they refused to let the Son of God change their lives. Don't become so involved in "religion" that you miss Christ.

**5:41** Whose praise do you seek? The religious leaders enjoyed great prestige in Israel, but their stamp of approval meant nothing to Jesus. He was concerned about God's approval. This is a good principle for us. If even the highest officials in the world approve of our actions and God does not, we should be concerned. But if God approves, even though others don't, we should be content.

**5:45** The Pharisees prided themselves on being the true follow-

### Jesus Feeds Five Thousand (96/Matthew 14:13-21; Mark 6:30-44; Luke 9:10-17)

**6** After this, Jesus crossed over to the far side of the Sea of Galilee, also known as the Sea of Tiberias. ²A huge crowd kept following him wherever he went, because they saw his miraculous signs as he healed the sick. ³Then Jesus climbed a hill and sat down with his disciples around him. ⁴(It was nearly time for the Jewish Passover celebration.) ⁵Jesus soon saw a huge crowd of people coming to look for him. Turning to Philip, he asked, "Where can we buy bread to feed all these people?" ⁶He was testing Philip, for he already knew what he was going to do.

⁷Philip replied, "Even if we worked for months, we wouldn't have enough money* to feed them!"

⁸Then Andrew, Simon Peter's brother, spoke up. ⁹"There's a young boy here with five barley loaves and two fish. But what good is that with this huge crowd?"

¹⁰"Tell everyone to sit down," Jesus said. So they all sat down on the grassy slopes. (The men alone numbered about 5,000.) ¹¹Then Jesus took the loaves, gave thanks to God, and distributed them to the people. Afterward he did the same with the fish. And they all ate as much as they wanted. ¹²After everyone was full, Jesus told his disciples, "Now gather the leftovers, so that nothing is wasted." ¹³So they picked up the pieces and filled twelve baskets with scraps left by the people who had eaten from the five barley loaves.

¹⁴When the people saw him* do this miraculous sign, they exclaimed, "Surely, he is the Prophet we have been expecting!"* ¹⁵When Jesus saw that they were ready to force him to be their king, he slipped away into the hills by himself.

### Jesus Walks on Water (97/Matthew 14:22-33; Mark 6:45-52)

¹⁶That evening Jesus' disciples went down to the shore to wait for him. ¹⁷But as darkness fell and Jesus still hadn't come back, they got into the boat and headed across the lake toward

**6:7** Greek *Two hundred denarii would not be enough.* A denarius was equivalent to a laborer's full day's wage.
**6:14a** Some manuscripts read *Jesus.* **6:14b** See Deut 18:15, 18; Mal 4:5-6.

**Cross-references (left margin):**
6:4 John 11:55
6:5 John 1:43
6:8 John 1:40
6:9 2 Kgs 4:43 John 21:9, 13
6:14 Deut 18:15, 18 Acts 3:22; 7:37

---

ers of their ancestor Moses. They were trying to follow every one of his laws to the letter, and they even added some of their own. Jesus' warning that Moses would accuse them stung them to fury. Moses wrote about Jesus (Genesis 3:15; Numbers 21:9; 24:17; Deuteronomy 18:15), yet the religious leaders refused to believe Jesus when he came.

**6:5** If anyone knew where to get food, it would have been Philip because he was from Bethsaida, a town about nine miles away (1:44). Jesus was testing Philip to strengthen his faith. By asking for a human solution (knowing that there was none), Jesus highlighted the powerful and miraculous act that he was about to perform.

**6:5-7** When Jesus asked Philip where they could buy a great amount of bread, Philip started assessing the probable cost. Jesus wanted to teach him that financial resources are not the most important ones. We can limit what God does in us by assuming what is and is not possible. Is there some impossible task that you believe God wants you to do? Don't let your estimate of what can't be done keep you from taking on the task. God can do the miraculous; trust him to provide the resources.

**6:8, 9** The disciples are contrasted with the youngster who brought what he had. They certainly had more resources than the boy, but they knew they didn't have enough, so they didn't give anything at all. The boy gave what little he had, and it made all the difference. If we offer nothing to God, he will have nothing to use. But he can take what little we have and turn it into something great.

**6:8, 9** In performing his miracles, Jesus usually preferred to work through people. Here he took what a young child offered and used it to accomplish one of the most spectacular miracles recorded in the Gospels. Age is no barrier to Christ. Never think you are too young or old to be of service to him.

**6:13** There is a lesson in the leftovers. God gives in abundance. He takes whatever we can offer him in time, ability, or resources and multiplies its effectiveness beyond our wildest expectations. If you take the first step in making yourself available to God, he

will show you how greatly you can be used to advance the work of his Kingdom.

**6:14** "The Prophet" is the one prophesied by Moses (Deuteronomy 18:15).

*Map labels: Mediterranean Sea, GALILEE, Capernaum, Bethsaida, Gennesaret, Sea of Galilee, Jordan River, SAMARIA, PEREA, Jerusalem, JUDEA, Dead Sea, IDUMEA, N, 0 20 Mi., 0 20 Km.*

**JESUS WALKS ON THE WATER**
Jesus fed the 5,000 on a hill near the Sea of Galilee at Bethsaida. The disciples set out across the sea toward Capernaum. But they encountered a storm— and Jesus came walking to them on the water! The boat landed at Gennesaret (Mark 6:53); from there they went back to Capernaum.

Capernaum. ¹⁸Soon a gale swept down upon them, and the sea grew very rough. ¹⁹They had rowed three or four miles* when suddenly they saw Jesus walking on the water toward the boat. They were terrified, ²⁰but he called out to them, "Don't be afraid. I am here!*" ²¹Then they were eager to let him in the boat, and immediately they arrived at their destination!

**6:19**
Job 9:8
**6:20**
Matt 14:27

### Jesus Is the True Bread from Heaven (99)

²²The next day the crowd that had stayed on the far shore saw that the disciples had taken the only boat, and they realized Jesus had not gone with them. ²³Several boats from Tiberias landed near the place where the Lord had blessed the bread and the people had eaten. ²⁴So when the crowd saw that neither Jesus nor his disciples were there, they got into the boats and went across to Capernaum to look for him. ²⁵They found him on the other side of the lake and asked, "Rabbi, when did you get here?"

**6:23**
John 6:11

²⁶Jesus replied, "I tell you the truth, you want to be with me because I fed you, not because you understood the miraculous signs. ²⁷But don't be so concerned about perishable things like food. Spend your energy seeking the eternal life that the Son of Man* can give you. For God the Father has given me the seal of his approval."

**6:27**
Matt 3:17; 17:5
Mark 1:11; 9:7
Luke 3:22
John 1:33; 4:14;
6:50-51, 54, 58
Acts 2:22
Rom 6:23

²⁸They replied, "We want to perform God's works, too. What should we do?"

²⁹Jesus told them, "This is the only work God wants from you: Believe in the one he has sent."

**6:29**
1 Jn 3:23

³⁰They answered, "Show us a miraculous sign if you want us to believe in you. What can you do? ³¹After all, our ancestors ate manna while they journeyed through the wilderness! The Scriptures say, 'Moses gave them bread from heaven to eat.'*"

**6:31**
Exod 16:15
Num 11:7-9
Neh 9:15
†Pss 78:24; 105:40

³²Jesus said, "I tell you the truth, Moses didn't give you bread from heaven. My Father did. And now he offers you the true bread from heaven. ³³The true bread of God is the one who comes down from heaven and gives life to the world."

**6:33**
John 6:41, 50

³⁴"Sir," they said, "give us that bread every day."

³⁵Jesus replied, "I am the bread of life. Whoever comes to me will never be hungry again. Whoever believes in me will never be thirsty. ³⁶But you haven't believed in me even though you have seen me. ³⁷However, those the Father has given me will come to me, and I will never reject them. ³⁸For I have come down from heaven to do the will of God who sent me, not to do my own will. ³⁹And this is the will of God, that I should not lose even one of all those he has given me, but that I should raise them up at the last day. ⁴⁰For it is my Father's will that all who see his Son and believe in him should have eternal life. I will raise them up at the last day."

**6:35**
John 4:14; 6:48;
7:37-38
**6:37**
John 10:28-29;
17:2, 24
**6:38**
John 4:34; 5:30
**6:39**
John 10:28-29;
17:12; 18:9
**6:40**
John 12:45

**6:19** Greek *25 or 30 stadia* [4.6 or 5.5 kilometers].   **6:20** Or *The 'I Aᴍ' is here;* Greek reads *I am.* See Exod 3:14.
**6:27** "Son of Man" is a title Jesus used for himself.   **6:31** Exod 16:4; Ps 78:24.

**6:18** The Sea of Galilee is 650 feet below sea level, 150 feet deep, and surrounded by hills. These physical features make it subject to sudden windstorms that would cause extremely high waves. Such storms were expected on this lake, but they were nevertheless frightening. When Jesus came to the disciples during a storm, walking on the water (three and a half miles from shore), he told them not to be afraid. We often face spiritual and emotional storms and feel tossed about like a small boat on a big lake. In spite of terrifying circumstances, if we trust our lives to Christ for his safe-keeping, he will give us peace in any storm.

**6:18, 19** The disciples, terrified, probably thought they were seeing a ghost (Mark 6:49). But if they had thought about all they had already seen Jesus do, they could have accepted this miracle. They were frightened—they didn't expect Jesus to come, and they weren't prepared for his help. Faith is a mind-set that *expects* God to act. When we act on this expectation, we can overcome our fears.

**6:26** Jesus criticized the people who followed him only for the physical and temporal benefits and not for the satisfying of their spiritual hunger. Many people use religion to gain prestige, comfort, or even political votes. But those are self-centered motives. True believers follow Jesus simply because they know he has the truth and his way is the way to live.

**6:28, 29** Many sincere seekers for God are puzzled about what he wants them to do. The religions of the world are people's attempts to answer this question. But Jesus' reply is brief and simple: We

must believe on him whom God has sent. Satisfying God does not come from the work we *do,* but from whom we *believe.* The first step involves accepting that Jesus is who he claims to be. All spiritual development is built on this affirmation. Declare to Jesus, "You are the Messiah, the Son of the living God" (Matthew 16:16), and embark on a life of belief that is satisfying to your Creator.

**6:35** People eat bread to satisfy physical hunger and to sustain physical life. We can satisfy spiritual hunger and sustain spiritual life only by a right relationship with Jesus Christ. No wonder he called himself the bread of life. But bread must be eaten to sustain life, and Christ must be invited into our daily walk to sustain spiritual life.

**6:37, 38** Jesus did not work independently of God the Father, but in union with him. This should give us even more assurance of being welcomed into God's presence and being protected by him. Jesus' purpose was to do the will of God, not to satisfy Jesus' human desires. When we follow Jesus, we should have the same purpose.

**6:39** Jesus said he would not lose even one person whom the Father had given him. Thus, anyone who makes a sincere commitment to believe in Jesus Christ as Savior is secure in God's promise of eternal life. Christ will not let his people be overcome by Satan and lose their salvation (see also 17:12; Philippians 1:6).

**6:40** Those who put their faith in Christ will be resurrected from physical death to eternal life with God when Christ comes again (see 1 Corinthians 15:52; 1 Thessalonians 4:16).

## The People Disagree That Jesus Is from Heaven (100)

<sup>41</sup>Then the people* began to murmur in disagreement because he had said, "I am the bread that came down from heaven."<sup>42</sup>They said, "Isn't this Jesus, the son of Joseph? We know his father and mother. How can he say, 'I came down from heaven'?"

<sup>43</sup>But Jesus replied, "Stop complaining about what I said. <sup>44</sup> For no one can come to me unless the Father who sent me draws them to me, and at the last day I will raise them up.<sup>45</sup> As it is written in the Scriptures,* 'They will all be taught by God.' Everyone who listens to the Father and learns from him comes to me. <sup>46</sup> (Not that anyone has ever seen the Father; only I, who was sent from God, have seen him.)

<sup>47</sup> "I tell you the truth, anyone who believes has eternal life. <sup>48</sup> Yes, I am the bread of life! <sup>49</sup> Your ancestors ate manna in the wilderness, but they all died. <sup>50</sup> Anyone who eats the bread from heaven, however, will never die. <sup>51</sup>I am the living bread that came down from heaven. Anyone who eats this bread will live forever; and this bread, which I will offer so the world may live, is my flesh."

<sup>52</sup>Then the people began arguing with each other about what he meant. "How can this man give us his flesh to eat?" they asked.

<sup>53</sup>So Jesus said again, "I tell you the truth, unless you eat the flesh of the Son of Man and drink his blood, you cannot have eternal life within you. <sup>54</sup> But anyone who eats my flesh and drinks my blood has eternal life, and I will raise that person at the last day. <sup>55</sup> For my flesh is true food, and my blood is true drink. <sup>56</sup> Anyone who eats my flesh and drinks my blood remains in me, and I in him. <sup>57</sup> I live because of the living Father who sent me; in the same way, anyone who feeds on me will live because of me. <sup>58</sup> I am the true bread that came down from heaven. Anyone who eats this bread will not die as your ancestors did (even though they ate the manna) but will live forever."

<sup>59</sup>He said these things while he was teaching in the synagogue in Capernaum.

## Many Disciples Desert Jesus (101)

<sup>60</sup>Many of his disciples said, "This is very hard to understand. How can anyone accept it?"

<sup>61</sup>Jesus was aware that his disciples were complaining, so he said to them, "Does this offend you? <sup>62</sup> Then what will you think if you see the Son of Man ascend to heaven again? <sup>63</sup> The Spirit alone gives eternal life. Human effort accomplishes nothing. And the very words I have spoken to you are spirit and life. <sup>64</sup> But some of you do not believe me." (For Jesus knew from the beginning which ones didn't believe, and he knew who would betray him.) <sup>65</sup>Then he said, "That is why I said that people can't come to me unless the Father gives them to me."

**6:41** Greek *Jewish people;* also in 6:52. **6:45** Greek *in the prophets.* Isa 54:13.

### Cross-references

**6:41** John 6:33, 35, 51
**6:42** Luke 4:22; John 7:27-28
**6:44** Jer 31:3; John 6:65; 12:32
**6:45** †Isa 54:13; Jer 31:33-34; 1 Thes 4:9; Heb 8:10-11
**6:46** John 1:18; 5:37
**6:47** John 3:15-16, 36
**6:48** John 6:35, 41, 51, 58
**6:51** John 10:10-11; Heb 10:10
**6:54** John 6:39-40, 44
**6:56** John 14:20; 15:4-7; 17:21-23; 1 Jn 2:24; 3:24
**6:57** John 5:26
**6:58** John 6:31
**6:62** Acts 1:9-11; Eph 4:8
**6:63** Rom 8:2; 1 Cor 15:45; 1 Pet 3:18
**6:64** John 13:11
**6:65** John 6:44

---

**6:41** Some of the people grumbled in disagreement because they could not accept Jesus' claim of divinity. They saw him only as a carpenter from Nazareth. They refused to believe that Jesus was God's divine Son, and they could not tolerate his message. Many people reject Christ because they say they cannot believe he is the Son of God. In reality, the demands that Christ makes for their loyalty and obedience are what they can't accept. So to protect themselves from the message, they reject the messenger.

**6:44** God, not people, plays the most active role in salvation. When someone chooses to believe in Jesus' Christ as Savior, he or she does so only in response to the urging of God's Holy Spirit. God does the urging; then we decide whether or not to believe. Thus, no one can believe in Jesus without God's help.

**6:45** Jesus was alluding to an Old Testament view of the messianic Kingdom in which all people are taught directly by God (Isaiah 54:13; Jeremiah 31:31-34). He was stressing the importance of not merely hearing, but learning. We are taught by God through the Bible, our experiences, the thoughts the Holy Spirit brings, and relationships with other Christians. Are you open to God's teaching?

**6:47** As used here, *believes* means "continues to believe." We do not believe merely once; we keep on believing in and trusting Jesus.

**6:47ff** The religious leaders frequently asked Jesus to prove to them why he was better than the prophets they already had. Jesus here referred to the manna that Moses had given their ancestors in the wilderness (see Exodus 16). This bread was physical and temporal. The people ate it, and it sustained them for a day. But they had to get more bread every day, and this bread could not keep them from dying. Jesus, who is much greater than Moses, offers himself as the spiritual bread from heaven that satisfies completely and leads to eternal life.

**6:51** How can Jesus give us his flesh as bread to eat? To eat living bread means to accept Christ into our lives and become united with him. We are united with Christ in two ways: (1) by believing in his death (the sacrifice of his flesh) and resurrection and (2) by devoting ourselves to living as he requires, depending on his teaching for guidance and trusting in the Holy Spirit for power.

**6:56** This was a shocking message—to eat flesh and drink blood sounded cannibalistic. The idea of drinking any blood, let alone human blood, was repugnant to the religious leaders because the law forbade it (Leviticus 17:10, 11). Jesus was not talking about literal blood, of course. He was saying that his life had to become their own, but they could not accept this concept. The Gospel writers as well as the apostle Paul used the body and blood imagery in talking about Communion (see 1 Corinthians 11:23-26).

**6:63, 65** The Holy Spirit gives spiritual life; without the work of the Holy Spirit, we cannot even see our need for new life (14:17). All spiritual renewal begins and ends with God. He reveals truth to us, lives within us, and then enables us to respond to that truth.

66At this point many of his disciples turned away and deserted him. 67Then Jesus turned to the Twelve and asked, "Are you also going to leave?"

68Simon Peter replied, "Lord, to whom would we go? You have the words that give eternal life. 69We believe, and we know you are the Holy One of God.*"

70Then Jesus said, "I chose the twelve of you, but one is a devil." 71He was speaking of Judas, son of Simon Iscariot, one of the Twelve, who would later betray him.

**6:68**
John 6:63

**6:69**
Matt 16:16
Mark 1:24; 8:29
Luke 9:20
1 Jn 2:20

## 2. Jesus encounters conflict with the religious leaders

### Jesus' Brothers Ridicule Him (121)

**7** After this, Jesus traveled around Galilee. He wanted to stay out of Judea, where the Jewish leaders were plotting his death. 2But soon it was time for the Jewish Festival of Shelters, 3and Jesus' brothers said to him, "Leave here and go to Judea, where your followers can see your miracles! 4You can't become famous if you hide like this! If you can do such wonderful things, show yourself to the world!" 5For even his brothers didn't believe in him.

6Jesus replied, "Now is not the right time for me to go, but you can go anytime. 7The world can't hate you, but it does hate me because I accuse it of doing evil. 8You go on. I'm not going* to this festival, because my time has not yet come." 9After saying these things, Jesus remained in Galilee.

**7:1**
John 5:18; 7:19;
8:37, 40

**7:2**
Lev 23:34
Deut 16:16

**7:3**
Matt 12:46

**7:6**
John 2:4; 7:30;
8:20

**7:7**
John 15:18

### Jesus Teaches Openly at the Temple (123)

10But after his brothers left for the festival, Jesus also went, though secretly, staying out of public view. 11The Jewish leaders tried to find him at the festival and kept asking if anyone had seen him. 12There was a lot of grumbling about him among the crowds. Some argued, "He's a good man," but others said, "He's nothing but a fraud who deceives the people." 13But no one had the courage to speak favorably about him in public, for they were afraid of getting in trouble with the Jewish leaders.

**7:11**
John 11:56

**7:12**
John 7:40-43

**7:13**
John 9:22-23

**6:69** Other manuscripts read *you are the Christ, the Holy One of God;* still others read *you are the Christ, the Son of God;* and still others read *you are the Christ, the Son of the living God.*   **7:8** Some manuscripts read *not yet going.*

---

**6:66** Why did Jesus' words cause many of his followers to desert him? (1) They may have realized that he wasn't going to be the conquering Messiah-King they expected. (2) He refused to give in to their self-centered requests. (3) He emphasized faith, not deeds. (4) His teachings were difficult to understand, and some of his words were offensive. As we grow in our faith, we may be tempted to turn away because Jesus' lessons are difficult. Will your response be to give up, ignore certain teachings, or reject Christ? Instead, ask God to show you what the teachings mean and how they apply to your life. Then have the courage to act on God's truth.

**6:67** There is no middle ground with Jesus. When he asked the disciples if they would also leave, he was showing that they could either accept or reject him. Jesus was not trying to repel people with his teachings. He was simply telling the truth. The more the people heard Jesus' real message, the more they divided into two camps—the honest seekers who wanted to understand more, and those who rejected Jesus because they didn't like what they had heard.

**6:67, 68** After many of Jesus' followers had deserted him, he asked the 12 disciples if they were also going to leave. Peter replied, "To whom would we go?" In his straightforward way, Peter answered for all of us—there is no other way. Though there are many philosophies and self-styled authorities, Jesus alone has the words of eternal life. People look everywhere for eternal life and miss Christ, the only source. Stay with him, especially when you are confused or feel alone.

**6:70** In response to Jesus' message, some people left; others stayed and truly believed; and some, like Judas, stayed but tried to use Jesus for personal gain. Many people today turn away from Christ. Others pretend to follow, going to church for status, approval of family and friends, or business contacts. But there are only two real responses to Jesus—you either accept him or reject him. How have you responded to Christ?

**6:71** For more information on Judas, see his Profile in Mark 14, p. 1655.

**7:2** The Festival of Shelters is described in Leviticus 23:33ff. This event occurred in October, about six months after the Passover celebration mentioned in John 6:2-5. The festival commemorated the days when the Israelites wandered in the wilderness and lived in shelters (Leviticus 23:43).

**7:3-5** Jesus' brothers had a difficult time believing in him. Some of these brothers would eventually become leaders in the church (James, for example), but for several years they were embarrassed by Jesus. After Jesus died and rose again, they finally believed. We today have every reason to believe because we have the full record of Jesus' miracles, death, and resurrection. We also have the evidence of what the Good News has done in people's lives through the centuries. Don't miss this opportunity to believe in God's Son.

**7:7** Because the world hated Jesus, we who follow him can expect that many people will hate us as well. If circumstances are going too well, ask if you are following Christ as you should. We can be grateful when life goes well, but we must make sure it is not at the cost of following Jesus halfheartedly or not at all.

**7:10** Jesus came with the greatest gift ever offered, so why did he often act secretly? The religious leaders hated him, and many would refuse his gift of salvation, no matter what he said or did. The more Jesus taught and worked publicly, the more these leaders would cause trouble for him and his followers. So it was necessary for Jesus to teach and work as quietly as possible. Many people today have the privilege of teaching, preaching, and worshiping publicly with little persecution. These believers should be grateful and make the most of their opportunities to proclaim the Good News.

**7:13** The Jewish religious leaders had a great deal of power over the common people. Apparently these leaders couldn't do much to Jesus at this time, but they threatened anyone who might publicly support him, most likely with excommunication. Excommunication from the synagogue was one of the reprisals for believing in Jesus (9:22). To a Jew, this was a severe punishment.

<sup>14</sup>Then, midway through the festival, Jesus went up to the Temple and began to teach. <sup>15</sup>The people* were surprised when they heard him. "How does he know so much when he hasn't been trained?" they asked.

<sup>16</sup>So Jesus told them, "My message is not my own; it comes from God who sent me. <sup>17</sup>Anyone who wants to do the will of God will know whether my teaching is from God or is merely my own. <sup>18</sup>Those who speak for themselves want glory only for themselves, but a person who seeks to honor the one who sent him speaks truth, not lies. <sup>19</sup>Moses gave you the law, but none of you obeys it! In fact, you are trying to kill me."

<sup>20</sup>The crowd replied, "You're demon possessed! Who's trying to kill you?"

<sup>21</sup>Jesus replied, "I did one miracle on the Sabbath, and you were amazed. <sup>22</sup>But you work on the Sabbath, too, when you obey Moses' law of circumcision. (Actually, this tradition of circumcision began with the patriarchs, long before the law of Moses.) <sup>23</sup>For if the correct time for circumcising your son falls on the Sabbath, you go ahead and do it so as not to break the law of Moses. So why should you be angry with me for healing a man on the Sabbath? <sup>24</sup>Look beneath the surface so you can judge correctly."

<sup>25</sup>Some of the people who lived in Jerusalem started to ask each other, "Isn't this the man they are trying to kill? <sup>26</sup>But here he is, speaking in public, and they say nothing to him. Could our leaders possibly believe that he is the Messiah? <sup>27</sup>But how could he be? For we know where this man comes from. When the Messiah comes, he will simply appear; no one will know where he comes from."

<sup>28</sup>While Jesus was teaching in the Temple, he called out, "Yes, you know me, and you know where I come from. But I'm not here on my own. The one who sent me is true, and you don't know him. <sup>29</sup>But I know him because I come from him, and he sent me to you." <sup>30</sup>Then the leaders tried to arrest him; but no one laid a hand on him, because his time* had not yet come.

<sup>31</sup>Many among the crowds at the Temple believed in him. "After all," they said, "would you expect the Messiah to do more miraculous signs than this man has done?"

### *Religious Leaders Attempt to Arrest Jesus* (124)

<sup>32</sup>When the Pharisees heard that the crowds were whispering such things, they and the leading priests sent Temple guards to arrest Jesus. <sup>33</sup>But Jesus told them, "I will be with you only a little longer. Then I will return to the one who sent me. <sup>34</sup>You will search for me but not find me. And you cannot go where I am going."

<sup>35</sup>The Jewish leaders were puzzled by this statement. "Where is he planning to go?" they asked. "Is he thinking of leaving the country and going to the Jews in other lands?* Maybe he will even teach the Greeks! <sup>36</sup>What does he mean when he says, 'You will search for me but not find me,' and 'You cannot go where I am going'?"

**7:15** Greek *Jewish people.*   **7:30** Greek *his hour.*   **7:35** Or *the Jews who live among the Greeks?*

**Cross-references (left margin):**

**7:15** Matt 13:54; Luke 2:47; Acts 4:13

**7:16** John 8:28; 12:49; 14:10

**7:18** John 5:41, 44; 8:50, 54

**7:19** John 1:17; 7:1, 25; 8:37-40

**7:20** John 8:48, 52; 10:20

**7:21-22** Gen 17:10-13; Lev 12:3

**7:23** John 5:8-10, 16; Acts 7:8

**7:24** Isa 11:3-4; John 8:15

**7:27** John 9:29

**7:28-29** John 8:26, 55; 17:25

**7:30** John 8:20

**7:31** John 2:23; 8:30; 10:42; 11:45; 12:11, 42

**7:33** John 13:33; 16:5

**7:34** John 8:21; 13:33

---

**7:13** Everyone was talking about Jesus! But when it came time to speak up for him in public, no one said a word. All were afraid. Fear can stifle our witness. Although many people talk about Christ in church, when it comes to making a public statement about their faith, they are often embarrassed. Jesus says that he will acknowledge us before God if we acknowledge him before others (Matthew 10:32). Be courageous! Speak up for Christ!

**7:16-18** Those who attempt to know God's will and do it will know intuitively that Jesus was telling the truth about himself. Have you ever listened to religious speakers and wondered if they were telling the truth? Test them: (1) Their words should agree with, not contradict, the Bible; (2) their words should point to God and his will, not to themselves.

**7:19** The Pharisees spent their days trying to achieve holiness by keeping the meticulous rules that they had added to God's laws. Jesus' accusation that they didn't keep Moses' laws stung them deeply. In spite of their pompous pride in themselves and their rules, they did not even fulfill a legalistic religion, for they were living far below what the law of Moses required. Murder was certainly against the law. Jesus' followers should do *more* than the moral law requires, not by adding to its requirements, but by going beyond and beneath the mere dos and don'ts of the law to the spirit of the law.

**7:20** Most of the people were probably not aware of the plot to kill Jesus (5:18). There was a small group looking for the right opportunity to kill him, but most were still trying to decide what they believed about him.

**7:21-23** According to Moses' law, circumcision was to be performed eight days after a baby's birth (Genesis 17:9-14; Leviticus 12:3). This rite was carried out on all Jewish males to demonstrate their identity as part of God's covenant people. If the eighth day after birth was a Sabbath, the circumcision would still be performed (even though it was considered work). While the religious leaders allowed certain exceptions to Sabbath laws, they allowed none to Jesus, who was simply showing mercy to those who needed healing.

**7:26** This chapter shows the many reactions people had toward Jesus. They called him a good man (7:12), a fraud (7:12), demon possessed (7:20), the Messiah (7:26), and the Prophet, whose coming had been predicted by Moses (7:40). We must make up our own minds about who Jesus is, knowing that whatever we decide will have eternal consequences.

**7:27** There was a popular tradition that the Messiah would simply appear. But those who believed this tradition were ignoring the Scriptures that clearly predicted the Messiah's birthplace (Micah 5:2).

37On the last day, the climax of the festival, Jesus stood and shouted to the crowds, "Anyone who is thirsty may come to me! 38 Anyone who believes in me may come and drink! For the Scriptures declare, 'Rivers of living water will flow from his heart.'"* 39(When he said "living water," he was speaking of the Spirit, who would be given to everyone believing in him. But the Spirit had not yet been given,* because Jesus had not yet entered into his glory.)

40When the crowds heard him say this, some of them declared, "Surely this man is the Prophet we've been expecting."* 41Others said, "He is the Messiah." Still others said, "But he can't be! Will the Messiah come from Galilee? 42For the Scriptures clearly state that the Messiah will be born of the royal line of David, in Bethlehem, the village where King David was born."* 43So the crowd was divided about him. 44Some even wanted him arrested, but no one laid a hand on him.

45When the Temple guards returned without having arrested Jesus, the leading priests and Pharisees demanded, "Why didn't you bring him in?"

46"We have never heard anyone speak like this!" the guards responded.

47"Have you been led astray, too?" the Pharisees mocked. 48"Is there a single one of us rulers or Pharisees who believes in him? 49This foolish crowd follows him, but they are ignorant of the law. God's curse is on them!"

50Then Nicodemus, the leader who had met with Jesus earlier, spoke up. 51"Is it legal to convict a man before he is given a hearing?" he asked.

52They replied, "Are you from Galilee, too? Search the Scriptures and see for yourself—no prophet ever comes* from Galilee!"

_____

[*The most ancient Greek manuscripts do not include John 7:53–8:11.*]

53Then the meeting broke up, and everybody went home.

### Jesus Forgives an Adulterous Woman (125)

**8** Jesus returned to the Mount of Olives, 2but early the next morning he was back again at the Temple. A crowd soon gathered, and he sat down and taught them. 3As he was speaking, the teachers of religious law and the Pharisees brought a woman who had been caught in the act of adultery. They put her in front of the crowd.

**7:37-38** Or *"Let anyone who is thirsty come to me and drink.* 38*For the Scriptures declare, 'Rivers of living water will flow from the heart of anyone who believes in me.'"* **7:39** Some manuscripts read *But as yet there was no Spirit.* Still others read *But as yet there was no Holy Spirit.* **7:40** See Deut 18:15, 18; Mal 4:5-6. **7:42** See Mic 5:2. **7:52** Some manuscripts read *the prophet does not come.*

| Reference | Cross-references |
|---|---|
| **7:37** | Isa 55:1; John 4:10, 14; 6:35; Rev 22:17 |
| **7:38** | Prov 18:4; Isa 58:11; Ezek 47:1-10; Joel 3:18 |
| **7:39** | John 14:17-18; 16:7; 20:22; Rom 8:9; 1 Cor 15:45; 2 Cor 3:17 |
| **7:40** | Deut 18:15; John 6:14 |
| **7:41** | John 1:46 |
| **7:42** | 2 Sam 7:12; Mic 5:2; Matt 1:1; 2:5-10; Luke 2:4 |
| **7:44** | John 7:30 |
| **7:46** | Matt 7:28 |
| **7:48** | John 12:42 |
| **7:50** | John 3:1-2; 19:39 |
| **7:51** | Deut 1:16 |
| **7:52** | Isa 9:1-2; Matt 4:14-16; John 1:46 |
| **8:2** | Matt 26:55 |

**7:38** Jesus' words, "come and drink," alluded to the theme of many Bible passages that talk about the Messiah's life-giving blessings (Isaiah 12:2, 3; 44:3, 4; 58:11). In promising to give the Holy Spirit to all who believed, Jesus was claiming to be the Messiah, for that was something only the Messiah could do.

**7:38** Jesus used the term *living water* in 4:10 to indicate eternal life. Here he uses the term to refer to the Holy Spirit. The two go together: Wherever the Holy Spirit is accepted, he brings eternal life. Jesus teaches more about the Holy Spirit in chapters 14–16. The Holy Spirit empowered Jesus' followers at Pentecost (Acts 2) and has since been available to all who believe in Jesus as Savior.

**7:40-44** The crowd was asking questions about Jesus. Some believed, others were hostile, and others disqualified Jesus as the Messiah because he was from Nazareth, not Bethlehem (Micah 5:2). But he *was* born in Bethlehem (Luke 2:1-7), although he grew up in Nazareth. He may have had a pronounced Galilean accent. If they had looked more carefully, they would not have jumped to the wrong conclusions. When you search for God's truth, make sure you look carefully and thoughtfully at the Bible with an open heart and mind. Don't jump to conclusions before knowing more of what the Bible says.

**7:44-46** Although the Romans ruled Palestine, they gave the Jewish religious leaders authority over minor civil and religious affairs. The religious leaders supervised their own Temple guards and gave the officers power to arrest anyone causing a disturbance or breaking any of their ceremonial laws. Because these leaders had developed hundreds of trivial laws, it was almost impossible for anyone, even the leaders themselves, not to break, neglect, or ignore at least a few of them some of the time. But

these Temple guards couldn't find one reason to arrest Jesus. And as they listened to Jesus to try to find evidence, they couldn't help hearing the wonderful words he said.

**7:46-49** The Jewish leaders saw themselves as an elite group that alone had the truth, and they resisted the truth about Christ because it wasn't *theirs* to begin with. It is easy to think that we have the truth and that those who disagree with us do not have any truth at all. But God's truth is available to everyone. Don't copy the Pharisees' self-centered and narrow attitude.

**7:50-52** This passage offers additional insight into Nicodemus, the Pharisee who visited Jesus at night (chapter 3). Apparently Nicodemus had become a secret believer. Since most of the Pharisees hated Jesus and wanted to kill him, Nicodemus risked his reputation and high position even though he only spoke up indirectly for Jesus. His statement was bold, and the Pharisees immediately became suspicious. After Jesus' death, Nicodemus brought spices for his body (19:39). That is the last time he is mentioned in Scripture.

**7:51** Nicodemus confronted the Pharisees with their failure to keep their own laws. The Pharisees were losing ground—the Temple guards came back impressed by Jesus (7:46), and one of the Pharisees' own, Nicodemus, was defending him. With their hypocritical motives being exposed and their prestige slowly eroding, they began to move to protect themselves. Pride would interfere with their ability to reason, and soon they would become obsessed with getting rid of Jesus just to save face. What was good and right no longer mattered.

**8:3-6** The Jewish leaders had already disregarded the law by arresting the woman without the man. The law required that both

**8:5**
Lev 20:10
Deut 22:22-24
Job 31:11
**8:6**
Matt 22:15
**8:7**
Deut 17:7

4"Teacher," they said to Jesus, "this woman was caught in the act of adultery. 5The law of Moses says to stone her. What do you say?"

6They were trying to trap him into saying something they could use against him, but Jesus stooped down and wrote in the dust with his finger. 7They kept demanding an answer, so he stood up again and said, "All right, but let the one who has never sinned throw the first stone!" 8Then he stooped down again and wrote in the dust.

9When the accusers heard this, they slipped away one by one, beginning with the oldest, until only Jesus was left in the middle of the crowd with the woman. 10Then Jesus stood up again and said to the woman, "Where are your accusers? Didn't even one of them condemn you?"

**8:11**
John 5:14

11"No, Lord," she said.

And Jesus said, "Neither do I. Go and sin no more."

---

### Jesus Is the Light of the World (126)

**8:12**
Isa 9:1-2
John 1:4-5, 9; 3:19;
9:5; 12:35-36, 46
2 Cor 4:6
**8:14**
John 7:28; 9:29

12Jesus spoke to the people once more and said, "I am the light of the world. If you follow me, you won't have to walk in darkness, because you will have the light that leads to life."

13The Pharisees replied, "You are making those claims about yourself! Such testimony is not valid."

14Jesus told them, "These claims are valid even though I make them about myself. For I know where I came from and where I am going, but you don't know this about me. 15You judge me by human standards, but I do not judge anyone. 16 And if I did, my judgment would be correct in every respect because I am not alone. The Father* who sent me is with me. 17Your own law says that if two people agree about something, their witness is accepted as fact.* 18 I am one witness, and my Father who sent me is the other."

**8:16**
John 5:30
**8:17-18**
Deut 17:6; 19:15
John 5:37
1 Jn 5:7-9
**8:19**
John 14:7, 9
**8:20**
Mark 12:41
John 7:30

19"Where is your father?" they asked.

Jesus answered, "Since you don't know who I am, you don't know who my Father is. If you knew me, you would also know my Father." 20Jesus made these statements while he was teaching in the section of the Temple known as the Treasury. But he was not arrested, because his time* had not yet come.

**8:16** Some manuscripts read *The One.*    **8:17** See Deut 19:15.    **8:20** Greek *his hour.*

---

parties to adultery be stoned (Leviticus 20:10; Deuteronomy 22:22). The leaders were using the woman as a trap so they could trick Jesus. If Jesus said the woman should not be stoned, they would accuse him of violating Moses' law. If he urged them to execute her, they would report him to the Romans, who did not permit the Jews to carry out their own executions (18:31).

**8:7** This is a significant statement about judging others. Because Jesus upheld the legal penalty for adultery, stoning, he could not be accused of being against the law. But by saying that only a sinless person could throw the first stone, he highlighted the importance of compassion and forgiveness. When others are caught in sin, are you quick to pass judgment? To do so is to act as though you have never sinned. It is God's role to judge, not ours. Our role is to show forgiveness and compassion.

**8:9** When Jesus said that only someone who had not sinned should throw the first stone, the leaders slipped quietly away, from oldest to youngest. Evidently the older men were more aware of their sins than the younger. Age and experience often temper youthful self-righteousness. But whatever your age, take an honest look at your life. Recognize your sinful nature, and look for ways to help others rather than hurt them.

**8:11** Jesus didn't condemn the woman accused of adultery, but neither did he ignore or condone her sin. He told her to leave her life of sin. Jesus stands ready to forgive any sin in your life, but confession and repentance mean a change of heart. With God's help we can accept Christ's forgiveness and stop our wrongdoing.

**8:12** To understand what Jesus meant by "the light of the world," see the note on 1:4, 5.

**8:12** Jesus was speaking in the Treasury—the part of the Temple where the offerings were put (8:20) and where candles burned to

symbolize the pillar of fire that led the people of Israel through the wilderness (Exodus 13:21, 22). In this context, Jesus called himself the light of the world. The pillar of fire represented God's presence, protection, and guidance. Likewise, Jesus brings God's presence, protection, and guidance. Is he the light of *your* world?

**8:12** What does it mean to follow Christ? As a soldier follows his captain, so we should follow Christ, our commander. As a slave follows his master, so we should follow Christ, our Lord. As we follow the advice of a trusted counselor, so we should follow Jesus' commands to us in Scripture. As we follow the laws of our nation, so we should follow the laws of the Kingdom of Heaven.

**8:13, 14** The Pharisees thought Jesus was either a lunatic or a liar. Jesus provided them with a third alternative: He was telling the truth. Because most of the Pharisees refused to consider the third alternative, they never recognized him as Messiah and Lord. If you are seeking to know who Jesus is, do not close any door before looking through it honestly. Only with an open mind will you know the truth that he is Messiah and Lord.

**8:13-18** The Pharisees argued that Jesus' claim was legally invalid because he had no other witnesses. Jesus responded that his confirming witness was God himself. Jesus and the Father made two witnesses, the number required by the law (Deuteronomy 19:15).

**8:20** The Temple Treasury was located in the Court of Women. In this area, 13 collection boxes were set up to receive money offerings. Seven of the boxes were for the Temple tax; the other 6 were for freewill offerings. On another occasion, a widow placed her money in one of these boxes, and Jesus taught a profound lesson from her action (Luke 21:1-4).

## Jesus Warns of Coming Judgment (127)

²¹Later Jesus said to them again, "I am going away. You will search for me but will die in your sin. You cannot come where I am going."

²²The people* asked, "Is he planning to commit suicide? What does he mean, 'You cannot come where I am going'?"

²³Jesus continued, "You are from below; I am from above. You belong to this world; I do not. ²⁴That is why I said that you will die in your sins; for unless you believe that I AM who I claim to be,* you will die in your sins."

²⁵"Who are you?" they demanded.

Jesus replied, "The one I have always claimed to be.* ²⁶I have much to say about you and much to condemn, but I won't. For I say only what I have heard from the one who sent me, and he is completely truthful." ²⁷But they still didn't understand that he was talking about his Father.

²⁸So Jesus said, "When you have lifted up the Son of Man on the cross, then you will understand that I AM he.* I do nothing on my own but say only what the Father taught me. ²⁹And the one who sent me is with me—he has not deserted me. For I always do what pleases him." ³⁰Then many who heard him say these things believed in him.

## Jesus Speaks about God's True Children (128)

³¹Jesus said to the people who believed in him, "You are truly my disciples if you remain faithful to my teachings. ³²And you will know the truth, and the truth will set you free."

³³"But we are descendants of Abraham," they said. "We have never been slaves to anyone. What do you mean, 'You will be set free'?"

³⁴Jesus replied, "I tell you the truth, everyone who sins is a slave of sin. ³⁵A slave is not a permanent member of the family, but a son is part of the family forever. ³⁶So if the Son sets you free, you are truly free. ³⁷Yes, I realize that you are descendants of Abraham. And yet some of you are trying to kill me because there's no room in your hearts for my message. ³⁸I am telling you what I saw when I was with my Father. But you are following the advice of your father."

³⁹"Our father is Abraham!" they declared.

"No," Jesus replied, "for if you were really the children of Abraham, you would follow his example.* ⁴⁰Instead, you are trying to kill me because I told you the truth, which I heard from God. Abraham never did such a thing. ⁴¹No, you are imitating your real father."

They replied, "We aren't illegitimate children! God himself is our true Father."

⁴²Jesus told them, "If God were your Father, you would love me, because I have come to you from God. I am not here on my own, but he sent me. ⁴³Why can't you understand what I am saying? It's because you can't even hear me! ⁴⁴For you are the children of your father the devil, and you love to do the evil things he does. He was a murderer from the beginning. He has always hated the truth, because there is no truth in him. When he lies, it is consistent with his character; for he is a liar and the father of lies. ⁴⁵So when I tell the truth, you just

**8:21**
John 7:34, 36;
13:33

**8:22**
John 7:35

**8:23**
John 3:31; 17:14

**8:24**
Exod 3:14-15
John 4:26;
8:28, 58; 13:19

**8:26**
John 3:32-34;
12:49

**8:28**
John 3:14; 5:19;
8:24; 12:32

**8:29**
John 4:34; 6:38;
8:16; 14:10; 16:32

**8:30**
John 7:31

**8:31**
John 15:7
2 Jn 1:9

**8:32**
Rom 8:2
2 Cor 3:17
Gal 5:1, 13

**8:33**
Matt 3:9
Luke 3:8

**8:34**
Rom 6:16, 20
2 Pet 2:19

**8:35**
Gen 21:10
Gal 4:30

**8:39**
Matt 3:9
John 8:33
Gal 3:7, 14, 29

**8:41**
Deut 32:6
Isa 63:16; 64:8
Mal 1:6

**8:42**
1 Jn 5:1

**8:44**
Gen 3:4; 4:9
1 Jn 3:8

**8:45**
John 18:37

**8:22** Greek *Jewish people*; also in 8:31, 48, 52, 57.  **8:24** Greek *unless you believe that I am.* See Exod 3:14.
**8:25** Or *Why do I speak to you at all?*  **8:28** Greek *When you have lifted up the Son of Man, then you will know that I am.* "Son of Man" is a title Jesus used for himself.  **8:39** Some manuscripts read *if you are really the children of Abraham, follow his example.*

---

**8:24** People will die in their sins if they reject Christ, because they are rejecting the only way to be rescued from sin. Sadly, many are so taken up with the values of this world that they are blind to the priceless gift Christ offers. Where are you looking? Don't focus on this world's values and miss what is most valuable—eternal life with God.

**8:32** Jesus himself is the truth that sets us free (8:36). He is the source of truth, the perfect standard of what is right. He frees us from continued slavery to sin, from self-deception, and from deception by Satan. He shows us clearly the way to eternal life with God. Thus, Jesus does not give us freedom to do what we want, but freedom to follow God. As we seek to serve God, Jesus' perfect truth frees us to be all that God meant us to be.

**8:34, 35** Sin has a way of enslaving us, controlling us, dominating us, and dictating our actions. Jesus can free you from this slavery that keeps you from becoming the person God created you to be. If sin is restraining, mastering, or enslaving you, Jesus can break its power over your life.

**8:41** Jesus made a distinction between illegitimate children and true children. The religious leaders were descendants of Abraham (founder of the Jewish nation) and therefore claimed to be children of God. But their actions showed them to be true children of Satan, for they lived under Satan's guidance. True children of Abraham (faithful followers of God) would not act as they did. Your church membership and family connections will not make you a true child of God. Your true father is the one you imitate and obey.

**8:43** The religious leaders were unable to understand because they refused to listen. Satan used their stubbornness, pride, and prejudices to keep them from believing in Jesus.

**8:44, 45** The attitudes and actions of these leaders clearly identified them as followers of Satan. They may not have been conscious of this, but their hatred of truth, their lies, and their murderous intentions indicated how much control the devil had over them. They were his tools in carrying out his plans; they spoke the very same language of lies. Satan still uses people to obstruct God's work (Genesis 4:8; Romans 5:12; 1 John 3:12).

8:47
1 Jn 4:6

naturally don't believe me! [46]Which of you can truthfully accuse me of sin? And since I am telling you the truth, why don't you believe me? [47]Anyone who belongs to God listens gladly to the words of God. But you don't listen because you don't belong to God."

### Jesus States He Is Eternal (129)

[48]The people retorted, "You Samaritan devil! Didn't we say all along that you were possessed by a demon?"

8:50
John 5:41
8:51
John 5:24;
11:25-26
8:53
John 4:12
8:54
John 16:14; 17:5
8:55
John 7:28-29;
15:10
8:56
Gen 18:18;
22:17-18
Matt 13:17
Heb 11:13
8:58
Exod 3:14
Isa 43:10, 13
John 1:1; 8:24, 28

[49]"No," Jesus said, "I have no demon in me. For I honor my Father—and you dishonor me. [50]And though I have no wish to glorify myself, God is going to glorify me. He is the true judge. [51]I tell you the truth, anyone who obeys my teaching will never die!"

[52]The people said, "Now we know you are possessed by a demon. Even Abraham and the prophets died, but you say, 'Anyone who obeys my teaching will never die!' [53]Are you greater than our father Abraham? He died, and so did the prophets. Who do you think you are?"

[54]Jesus answered, "If I want glory for myself, it doesn't count. But it is my Father who will glorify me. You say, 'He is our God,'*' [55]but you don't even know him. I know him. If I said otherwise, I would be as great a liar as you! But I do know him and obey him. [56]Your father Abraham rejoiced as he looked forward to my coming. He saw it and was glad."

[57]The people said, "You aren't even fifty years old. How can you say you have seen Abraham?*"

[58]Jesus answered, "I tell you the truth, before Abraham was even born, I Am!*" [59]At that point they picked up stones to throw at him. But Jesus was hidden from them and left the Temple.

### Jesus Heals the Man Who Was Born Blind (148)

9:2
Exod 20:5
Ezek 18:20
Luke 13:2
John 9:34
9:3
John 11:4
9:4
John 5:17; 11:9;
12:35
9:5
Isa 49:6
John 1:4-5, 9; 8:12;
12:46
9:6
Mark 8:23

**9** As Jesus was walking along, he saw a man who had been blind from birth. [2]"Rabbi," his disciples asked him, "why was this man born blind? Was it because of his own sins or his parents' sins?"

[3]"It was not because of his sins or his parents' sins," Jesus answered. "This happened so the power of God could be seen in him. [4]We must quickly carry out the tasks assigned us by the one who sent us.* The night is coming, and then no one can work. [5]But while I am here in the world, I am the light of the world."

[6]Then he spit on the ground, made mud with the saliva, and spread the mud over the

8:54 Some manuscripts read *your God.*  8:57 Some manuscripts read *How can you say Abraham has seen you?*  8:58 Or *before Abraham was even born, I have always been alive;* Greek reads *before Abraham was, I am.* See Exod 3:14.  9:4 Other manuscripts read *I must quickly carry out the tasks assigned me by the one who sent me;* still others read *We must quickly carry out the tasks assigned us by the one who sent me.*

---

**8:46, 47** In a number of places Jesus intentionally challenged his listeners to test him. He welcomed those who wanted to question his claims and character as long as they were willing to follow through on what they discovered. Jesus' challenge clarifies the two most frequent reasons that people miss when encountering him: (1) They never accept his challenge to test him, or (2) they test him but are not willing to believe what they discover. Have you made either of those mistakes?

**8:51** When Jesus says those who obey won't die, he is talking about spiritual death, not physical death. Even physical death, however, will eventually be overcome. Those who follow Christ will be raised to live eternally with him.

**8:56** God told Abraham, the father of the Jewish nation, that through him all nations would be blessed (Genesis 12:1-7; 15:1-21). Abraham had been able to see this through the eyes of faith. Jesus, a descendant of Abraham, blessed all people through his death, resurrection, and offer of salvation.

**8:58** This is one of the most powerful statements uttered by Jesus. When he said that he existed before Abraham was born, he undeniably proclaimed his divinity. Not only did Jesus say that he existed before Abraham; he also applied God's holy name (*I Am*—Exodus 3:14) to himself. This claim demands a response. It cannot be ignored. The Jewish leaders tried to stone Jesus for blasphemy because he claimed equality with God. But Jesus *is* God. How have you responded to Jesus, the Son of God?

**8:59** In accordance with the law given in Leviticus 24:16, the religious leaders were ready to stone Jesus for claiming to be God. They well understood what Jesus was claiming, and because they

didn't believe he was God, they charged him with blasphemy. It is ironic that *they* were really the blasphemers, cursing and attacking the very God they claimed to serve!

**9:1ff** In chapter 9, we see four different reactions to Jesus. The neighbors revealed surprise and skepticism; the Pharisees showed disbelief and prejudice; the parents believed but kept quiet for fear of excommunication; and the healed man showed consistent, growing faith. Each reaction to Jesus allowed the man to reach a clearer understanding of the one who had healed him.

**9:2, 3** A common belief in Jewish culture was that calamity or suffering was the result of some great sin. But Christ used this man's suffering to teach about faith and to glorify God. We live in a fallen world where good behavior is not always rewarded and bad behavior not always punished. Therefore, innocent people sometimes suffer. If God took suffering away whenever we asked, we would follow him for comfort and convenience, not out of love and devotion. Regardless of the reasons for our suffering, Jesus has the power to help us deal with it. When you suffer from a disease, tragedy, or disability, try not to ask, Why did this happen to me? or What did I do wrong? Instead, ask God to give you strength for the trial and a clearer perspective on what is happening.

**9:6** When Jesus spit on the ground and made mud in order to repair the man's eyes, he was working with original materials. Genesis 2:7 states that God formed Adam's body from the dust of the ground. Jesus was demonstrating a creator's awareness of the materials he first used to shape the human body.

blind man's eyes. [7]He told him, "Go wash yourself in the pool of Siloam" (Siloam means "sent"). So the man went and washed and came back seeing!

[8]His neighbors and others who knew him as a blind beggar asked each other, "Isn't this the man who used to sit and beg?" [9]Some said he was, and others said, "No, he just looks like him!"

But the beggar kept saying, "Yes, I am the same one!"

[10]They asked, "Who healed you? What happened?"

[11]He told them, "The man they call Jesus made mud and spread it over my eyes and told me, 'Go to the pool of Siloam and wash yourself.' So I went and washed, and now I can see!"

[12]"Where is he now?" they asked.

"I don't know," he replied.

## Religious Leaders Question the Blind Man (149)

[13]Then they took the man who had been blind to the Pharisees, [14]because it was on the Sabbath that Jesus had made the mud and healed him. [15]The Pharisees asked the man all about it. So he told them, "He put the mud over my eyes, and when I washed it away, I could see!"

[16]Some of the Pharisees said, "This man Jesus is not from God, for he is working on the Sabbath." Others said, "But how could an ordinary sinner do such miraculous signs?" So there was a deep division of opinion among them.

[17]Then the Pharisees again questioned the man who had been blind and demanded, "What's your opinion about this man who healed you?"

The man replied, "I think he must be a prophet."

[18]The Jewish leaders still refused to believe the man had been blind and could now see, so they called in his parents. [19]They asked them, "Is this your son? Was he born blind? If so, how can he now see?"

[20]His parents replied, "We know this is our son and that he was born blind, [21]but we don't know how he can see or who healed him. Ask him. He is old enough to speak for himself." [22]His parents said this because they were afraid of the Jewish leaders, who had announced that anyone saying Jesus was the Messiah would be expelled from the synagogue. [23]That's why they said, "He is old enough. Ask him."

[24]So for the second time they called in the man who had been blind and told him, "God should get the glory for this,* because we know this man Jesus is a sinner."

[25]"I don't know whether he is a sinner," the man replied. "But I know this: I was blind, and now I can see!"

[26]"But what did he do?" they asked. "How did he heal you?"

[27]"Look!" the man exclaimed. "I told you once. Didn't you listen? Why do you want to hear it again? Do you want to become his disciples, too?"

[28]Then they cursed him and said, "You are his disciple, but we are disciples of Moses! [29]We know God spoke to Moses, but we don't even know where this man comes from."

[30]"Why, that's very strange!" the man replied. "He healed my eyes, and yet you don't know where he comes from? [31]We know that God doesn't listen to sinners, but he is ready to hear those who worship him and do his will. [32]Ever since the world began, no one has been able to open the eyes of someone born blind. [33]If this man were not from God, he couldn't have done it."

**9:24** Or *Give glory to God, not to Jesus;* Greek reads *Give glory to God.*

### Cross-references

**9:7**
2 Kgs 5:10
Isa 35:5

**9:8**
Acts 3:10

**9:14**
Luke 13:14
John 5:9

**9:16**
John 3:2; 7:43

**9:17**
Matt 21:11

**9:22**
Luke 6:22
John 7:13; 12:42;
16:2; 19:38
Acts 5:13

**9:24**
Josh 7:19

**9:28**
John 5:45

**9:29**
John 8:14

**9:31**
Job 27:8-9
Pss 34:15; 66:18;
145:19
Prov 15:29
Isa 1:15
Jer 11:11; 14:12
Mic 3:4
Zech 7:13

**9:33**
John 3:2

---

**9:7** The pool of Siloam was built by Hezekiah. His workers constructed an underground tunnel from a spring outside the city walls to carry water into the city. Thus, the people could always get water without fear of being attacked. This was especially important during times of siege (see 2 Kings 20:20; 2 Chronicles 32:30).

**9:13-17** While the Pharisees conducted investigations and debated about Jesus, people were being healed and lives were being changed. The Pharisees' skepticism was based not on insufficient evidence, but on jealousy of Jesus' popularity and his influence on the people.

**9:14-16** The Jewish Sabbath, Saturday, was the weekly holy day of rest. The Pharisees had made a long list of specific dos and don'ts regarding the Sabbath. Kneading the mud and healing the man were considered work and therefore were forbidden. Jesus

may have purposely made the clay in order to emphasize his teaching about the Sabbath—that it is right to care for others' needs even if it involves working on a day of rest.

**9:25** By now the man who had been blind had heard the same questions over and over. He did not know how or why he was healed, but he knew that his life had been miraculously changed and he was not afraid to tell the truth. You don't need to know all the answers in order to share Christ with others. It is important to tell them how he has changed your life. Then trust that God will use your words to help others believe in him, too.

**9:28, 34** The man's new faith was severely tested by some of the authorities. He was cursed and evicted from the synagogue. Persecution may come when you follow Jesus. You may lose friends; you may even lose your life. But no one can ever take away the eternal life that Jesus gives you.

9:34
John 9:2

34"You were born a total sinner!" they answered. "Are you trying to teach us?" And they threw him out of the synagogue.

### Jesus Teaches about Spiritual Blindness (150)

35When Jesus heard what had happened, he found the man and asked, "Do you believe in the Son of Man?*"

36The man answered, "Who is he, sir? I want to believe in him."

9:37
John 4:26

37 "You have seen him," Jesus said, "and he is speaking to you!"

38"Yes, Lord, I believe!" the man said. And he worshiped Jesus.

9:39
Luke 4:18

39Then Jesus told him,* "I entered this world to render judgment—to give sight to the blind and to show those who think they see* that they are blind."

9:40
Rom 2:19

40Some Pharisees who were standing nearby heard him and asked, "Are you saying we're blind?"

9:41
John 15:22

41"If you were blind, you wouldn't be guilty," Jesus replied. "But you remain guilty because you claim you can see.

10:2
Acts 20:28

### Jesus Is the Good Shepherd (151)

10:4
Ps 80:2
John 10:27

**10** "I tell you the truth, anyone who sneaks over the wall of a sheepfold, rather than going through the gate, must surely be a thief and a robber! 2 But the one who enters through the gate is the shepherd of the sheep. 3 The gatekeeper opens the gate for him, and the sheep recognize his voice and come to him. He calls his own sheep by name and leads them out. 4 After he has gathered his own flock, he walks ahead of them, and they follow him because they know his voice. 5 They won't follow a stranger; they will run from him because they don't know his voice."

10:6
John 16:25

10:7
John 14:6

10:8
Jer 23:1-2
Ezek 34:2-3

10:9
Ps 118:20
John 14:6

6 Those who heard Jesus use this illustration didn't understand what he meant, 7 so he explained it to them: "I tell you the truth, I am the gate for the sheep. 8 All who came before me* were thieves and robbers. But the true sheep did not listen to them. 9 Yes, I am the gate. Those who come in through me will be saved.* They will come and go freely and will find good pastures. 10 The thief's purpose is to steal and kill and destroy. My purpose is to give them a rich and satisfying life.

10:10
John 5:40
Acts 20:29
2 Pet 2:1

10:11
Isa 40:11
Ezek 34:11-16, 23
Heb 13:20
1 Pet 2:25
1 Jn 3:16
Rev 7:17

11"I am the good shepherd. The good shepherd sacrifices his life for the sheep. 12 A hired hand will run when he sees a wolf coming. He will abandon the sheep because they don't belong to him and he isn't their shepherd. And so the wolf attacks them and scatters the flock. 13 The hired hand runs away because he's working only for the money and doesn't really care about the sheep.

10:14
2 Tim 2:19

10:15
Matt 11:27

14 "I am the good shepherd; I know my own sheep, and they know me, 15 just as my Father knows me and I know the Father. So I sacrifice my life for the sheep. 16 I have other sheep,

10:16
Isa 56:8
Ezek 37:24
John 11:52
Eph 2:14-18

9:35 Some manuscripts read the Son of God? "Son of Man" is a title Jesus used for himself.   9:38-39a Some manuscripts do not include "Yes, Lord, I believe!" the man said. And he worshiped Jesus. Then Jesus told him.   9:39b Greek those who see.   10:8 Some manuscripts do not include before me.   10:9 Or will find safety.

---

9:38 This man gained not only physical sight but also spiritual sight as he recognized Jesus first as a prophet (9:17), then as his Lord. When you turn to Christ, you begin to see him differently. The longer you walk with him, the better you will understand who he is. Peter tells us to "grow in the grace and knowledge of our Lord and Savior Jesus Christ" (2 Peter 3:18). If you want to know more about Jesus, keep trusting him in every area of life.

9:40, 41 The Pharisees were shocked that Jesus thought they were spiritually blind. Jesus countered by saying that it was only blindness (stubbornness and stupidity) that could excuse their behavior. To those who remained open and recognized how sin had truly blinded them from knowing the truth, he gave spiritual understanding and insight. But he rejected those who had become complacent, self-satisfied, and blind.

10:1 At night, sheep were often gathered into a sheepfold to protect them from thieves, weather, or wild animals. The sheep-folds were caves, sheds, or open areas surrounded by walls made of stones or branches. The shepherd often slept across the door-way of the fold to protect the sheep. Just as a shepherd cares for his sheep, Jesus, the good shepherd, cares for his flock (those who follow him). The prophet Ezekiel, in predicting the coming of the Messiah, called him a shepherd (Ezekiel 34:23).

10:7 In the sheepfold, the shepherd functioned as a gate, letting the sheep in and protecting them. Jesus is the gate to God's salvation for us. He offers access to safety and security. Christ is our protector. Some people resent that Jesus is the gate, the only way of access to God. But Jesus is God's Son—why should we seek any other way or want to customize a different approach to God? (See also the notes on 14:6.)

10:10 In contrast to the thief who takes life, Jesus gives life. The life he gives right now is abundantly rich and full. It is eternal, yet it begins immediately. Life in Christ is lived on a higher plane because of his overflowing forgiveness, love, and guidance. Have you taken Christ's offer of life?

10:11, 12 A hired hand tends the sheep for money, while the shepherd does it out of love. The shepherd owns the sheep and is committed to them. Jesus is not merely doing a job; he is committed to love us and even lay down his life for us. False teachers and false prophets do not have this commitment.

10:16 The "other sheep" were non-Jews. Jesus came to save Gentiles as well as Jews. This is an insight into his worldwide mission—to die for the sins of the world. People tend to want to restrict God's blessings to their own group, but Jesus refuses to be limited by the fences we build.

too, that are not in this sheepfold. I must bring them also. They will listen to my voice, and there will be one flock with one shepherd.

¹⁷"The Father loves me because I sacrifice my life so I may take it back again. ¹⁸No one can take my life from me. I sacrifice it voluntarily. For I have the authority to lay it down when I want to and also to take it up again. For this is what my Father has commanded."

¹⁹When he said these things, the people* were again divided in their opinions about him. ²⁰Some said, "He's demon possessed and out of his mind. Why listen to a man like that?" ²¹Others said, "This doesn't sound like a man possessed by a demon! Can a demon open the eyes of the blind?"

### Religious Leaders Surround Jesus at the Temple (152)

²²It was now winter, and Jesus was in Jerusalem at the time of Hanukkah, the Festival of Dedication. ²³He was in the Temple, walking through the section known as Solomon's Colonnade. ²⁴The people surrounded him and asked, "How long are you going to keep us in suspense? If you are the Messiah, tell us plainly."

²⁵Jesus replied, "I have already told you, and you don't believe me. The proof is the work I do in my Father's name. ²⁶But you don't believe me because you are not my sheep. ²⁷My sheep listen to my voice; I know them, and they follow me. ²⁸I give them eternal life, and they will never perish. No one can snatch them away from me, ²⁹for my Father has given them to me, and he is more powerful than anyone else.* No one can snatch them from the Father's hand. ³⁰The Father and I are one."

³¹Once again the people picked up stones to kill him. ³²Jesus said, "At my Father's direction I have done many good works. For which one are you going to stone me?"

³³They replied, "We're stoning you not for any good work, but for blasphemy! You, a mere man, claim to be God."

³⁴Jesus replied, "It is written in your own Scriptures* that God said to certain leaders of the people, 'I say, you are gods!'* ³⁵And you know that the Scriptures cannot be altered. So if

**10:17-18**
Phil 2:8-9
Heb 5:8; 7:16

**10:23**
Acts 3:11; 5:12
**10:24**
Luke 22:67
**10:25**
John 5:36; 10:38;
14:11
**10:26**
John 8:47
**10:28**
John 6:37, 39;
17:12
**10:29**
John 14:28
17:2, 6, 24
**10:30**
John 1:1; 10:38;
14:8-11; 17:21-24
**10:33**
Lev 24:16
Matt 26:63-66
John 1:1, 18;
5:18; 20:28
Rom 9:5
Phil 2:6
Titus 2:13
2 Pet 1:1
1 Jn 5:20
**10:34**
†Ps 82:6

**10:19** Greek *Jewish people;* also in 10:24, 31.   **10:29** Other manuscripts read *for what my Father has given me is more powerful than anything;* still others read *for regarding that which my Father has given me, he is greater than all.* **10:34a** Greek *your own law.*   **10:34b** Ps 82:6.

---

**10:17, 18** Jesus' death and resurrection, as part of God's plan for the salvation of the world, were under God's full control. No one could kill Jesus without his consent.

**10:19, 20** If Jesus had been merely a man, his claims to be God would have proven him insane. But his miracles proved his words true—he really was God. The Jewish leaders could not see beyond their own prejudices, and they looked at Jesus only from a human perspective—Jesus confined in a human box. But Jesus was not limited by their restricted vision.

**10:22, 23** Hanukkah commemorated the cleansing of the Temple under Judas Maccabeus in 164 B.C. after Antiochus

**MINISTRY EAST OF THE JORDAN**
Jesus had been in Jerusalem for the Festival of Shelters (7:2); then he preached in various towns, probably in Judea, before returning to Jerusalem for Hanukkah. He again angered the religious leaders, who tried to arrest him, but he left the city and went to the region east of the Jordan to preach.

Epiphanes had defiled it by sacrificing a pig on the altar of burnt offering. The festival was celebrated toward the end of December.

**10:23** Solomon's Colonnade was a roofed walkway supported by large stone columns, just inside the walls of the Temple courtyard.

**10:24** Many people asking for proof do so for the wrong reasons. Most of these questioners didn't want to follow Jesus in the way that required them to submit to his leadership. They hoped that Jesus would declare himself Messiah for perverted reasons. They, along with the disciples and everyone else in the Jewish nation, would have been delighted to have him drive out the Romans. Many of them didn't think he was going to do that, however. These doubters hoped he would identify himself so they could accuse him of telling lies (as the Pharisees did in 8:13).

**10:28, 29** Just as a shepherd protects his sheep, Jesus protects his people from eternal harm. While believers can expect to suffer on earth, Satan cannot harm their souls or take away their eternal life with God. There are many reasons to be afraid here on earth because this is the devil's domain (1 Peter 5:8). But if you choose to follow Jesus, he will give you everlasting safety.

**10:30** This is the clearest statement of Jesus' divinity he ever made. Jesus and his Father are not the same person, but they are one in essence and nature. Thus, Jesus is not merely a good teacher—he is God. His claim to be God was unmistakable. The religious leaders wanted to kill him because their laws said that anyone claiming to be God should die. Nothing could persuade them that Jesus' claim was true.

**10:31** The Jewish leaders attempted to carry out the directive found in Leviticus 24:16 regarding those who blaspheme (claim to be God). They intended to stone Jesus.

**10:34-36** Jesus referred to Psalm 82:6, where the Israelite rulers and judges are called "gods" (see also Exodus 4:16; 7:1). If God called the Israelite leaders gods because they were agents of

10:36
John 5:17-20

those people who received God's message were called 'gods,' ³⁶why do you call it blasphemy when I say, 'I am the Son of God'? After all, the Father set me apart and sent me into the world. ³⁷Don't believe me unless I carry out my Father's work. ³⁸But if I do his work, believe in the evidence of the miraculous works I have done, even if you don't believe me. Then you will know and understand that the Father is in me, and I am in the Father."

³⁹Once again they tried to arrest him, but he got away and left them. ⁴⁰He went beyond the Jordan River near the place where John was first baptizing and stayed there awhile. ⁴¹And many followed him. "John didn't perform miraculous signs," they remarked to one another, "but everything he said about this man has come true." ⁴²And many who were there believed in Jesus.

10:42
John 2:23; 7:31;
8:30; 11:45;
12:11, 42

### 3. Jesus encounters crucial events in Jerusalem
*Lazarus Becomes Sick and Dies* (165)

11:1
Matt 21:17
Luke 10:38

**11** A man named Lazarus was sick. He lived in Bethany with his sisters, Mary and Martha. ²This is the Mary who later poured the expensive perfume on the Lord's feet and wiped them with her hair.* Her brother, Lazarus, was sick. ³So the two sisters sent a message to Jesus telling him, "Lord, your dear friend is very sick."

11:2
John 12:3

11:4
John 9:3

⁴But when Jesus heard about it he said, "Lazarus's sickness will not end in death. No, it happened for the glory of God so that the Son of God will receive glory from this." ⁵So although Jesus loved Martha, Mary, and Lazarus, ⁶he stayed where he was for the next two days. ⁷Finally, he said to his disciples, "Let's go back to Judea."

**11:2** This incident is recorded in chapter 12.

| | Reference | Name | Significance |
|---|---|---|---|
| **THE NAMES OF JESUS** In different settings, Jesus gave himself names that pointed to special roles he was ready to fulfill for people. Some of these refer back to the Old Testament promises of the Messiah. Others were ways to help people understand him. | 6:27 | Son of Man | Jesus' favorite reference to himself. It emphasized his humanity—but the way he used it, it was a claim to divinity. |
| | 6:35 | Bread of life | Refers to his life-giving role—that he is the only source of eternal life. |
| | 8:12 | Light of the world | Light is a symbol of spiritual truth. Jesus is the universal answer for people's need of spiritual truth. |
| | 10:7 | Gate for the sheep | Jesus is the only way into God's Kingdom. |
| | 10:11 | Good shepherd | Jesus appropriated the prophetic images of the Messiah pictured in the Old Testament. This is a claim to divinity, focusing on Jesus' love and guidance. |
| | 11:25 | The resurrection and the life | Not only is Jesus the source of life; he is the power over death. |
| | 14:6 | The way, the truth, and the life | Jesus is the method, the message, and the meaning for all people. With this title, he summarized his purpose in coming to earth. |
| | 15:1 | The true vine | This title has an important second part, "you are the branches." As in so many of his other names, Jesus reminds us that just as branches gain life from the vine and cannot live apart from it, so we are completely dependent on Christ for spiritual life. |

God's revelation and will, how could it be blasphemy for Jesus to call himself the Son of God? Jesus was rebuking the religious leaders, because he is the Son of God in a unique, unparalleled relationship of oneness with the Father.

**10:35** "The Scriptures cannot be altered" is a clear statement of the truth of the Bible. If we accept Christ as Lord, we also must accept his testimony to the Bible as God's Word.

**11:1** The village of Bethany was located about two miles east of Jerusalem on the road to Jericho. It was near enough to Jerusalem for Jesus and the disciples to be in danger, but far enough away so as not to attract attention prematurely.

**11:3** As their brother grew very sick, Mary and Martha turned to Jesus for help. They believed in his ability to help because they had seen his miracles. We, too, know of Jesus' miracles,

both from Scripture and through changed lives we have seen. When we need extraordinary help, Jesus offers extraordinary resources. We should not hesitate to ask him for assistance.

**11:4** Any trial a believer faces can ultimately bring glory to God because God can bring good out of any bad situation (Genesis 50:20; Romans 8:28). When trouble comes, do you grumble, complain, and blame God, or do you see your problems as opportunities to honor him?

**11:5-7** Jesus loved this family and often stayed with them. He knew their pain but did not respond immediately. His delay had a specific purpose. God's timing, especially his delays, may make us think he is not answering or is not answering the way we want. But he will meet all our needs according to his perfect schedule and purpose (Philippians 4:19). Patiently await his timing.

8But his disciples objected. "Rabbi," they said, "only a few days ago the people* in Judea were trying to stone you. Are you going there again?"

9Jesus replied, "There are twelve hours of daylight every day. During the day people can walk safely. They can see because they have the light of this world. 10But at night there is danger of stumbling because they have no light." 11Then he said, "Our friend Lazarus has fallen asleep, but now I will go and wake him up."

12The disciples said, "Lord, if he is sleeping, he will soon get better!" 13They thought Jesus meant Lazarus was simply sleeping, but Jesus meant Lazarus had died.

14So he told them plainly, "Lazarus is dead. 15And for your sakes, I'm glad I wasn't there, for now you will really believe. Come, let's go see him."

16Thomas, nicknamed the Twin,* said to his fellow disciples, "Let's go, too—and die with Jesus."

### Jesus Comforts Mary and Martha (166)

17When Jesus arrived at Bethany, he was told that Lazarus had already been in his grave for four days. 18Bethany was only a few miles* down the road from Jerusalem, 19and many of the people had come to console Martha and Mary in their loss. 20When Martha got word that Jesus was coming, she went to meet him. But Mary stayed in the house. 21Martha said to Jesus, "Lord, if only you had been here, my brother would not have died. 22But even now I know that God will give you whatever you ask."

23Jesus told her, "Your brother will rise again."

24"Yes," Martha said, "he will rise when everyone else rises, at the last day."

25Jesus told her, "I am the resurrection and the life.* Anyone who believes in me will live, even after dying. 26Everyone who lives in me and believes in me will never ever die. Do you believe this, Martha?"

27"Yes, Lord," she told him. "I have always believed you are the Messiah, the Son of God, the one who has come into the world from God." 28Then she returned to Mary. She called Mary aside from the mourners and told her, "The Teacher is here and wants to see you." 29So Mary immediately went to him.

30Jesus had stayed outside the village, at the place where Martha met him. 31When the people who were at the house consoling Mary saw her leave so hastily, they assumed she was going to Lazarus's grave to weep. So they followed her there. 32When Mary arrived and saw Jesus, she fell at his feet and said, "Lord, if only you had been here, my brother would not have died."

**11:8** John 8:59; 10:31
**11:9** John 9:4
**11:10** John 12:35
**11:11** Dan 12:2; Matt 9:24; 27:52; Mark 5:39; Luke 8:52; Acts 7:60; 1 Cor 11:30
**11:16** Matt 10:3; John 14:5; 20:24-28; 21:2; Acts 1:3
**11:20** Luke 10:38-42
**11:22** John 16:30
**11:23-24** Dan 12:2; John 5:28-29; Acts 24:15; Phil 3:21; 1 Thes 4:14
**11:25** John 1:4; 3:36; 5:21; 6:39-40; 14:6; Col 1:18; 3:4; 1 Jn 1:1-2; 5:10-11; Rev 1:17-18
**11:26** John 8:51
**11:27** Matt 16:16; John 6:14

**11:8** Greek *Jewish people;* also in 11:19, 31, 33, 36, 45, 54.   **11:16** Greek *Thomas, who was called Didymus.*
**11:18** Greek *was about 15 stadia* [about 2.8 kilometers].   **11:25** Some manuscripts do not include *and the life.*

---

**11:9, 10** "Daylight" symbolizes the knowledge of God's will and reliance on his guidance, and "night," the absence of this knowledge combined with self-reliance. When we move ahead in darkness, we will be likely to stumble.

### JESUS RAISES LAZARUS

Jesus had been preaching in the villages beyond the Jordan, probably in Perea, when he received the news of Lazarus's sickness. Jesus did not leave immediately, but waited two days before returning to Judea. He knew Lazarus would be dead when he arrived in Bethany, but he was going to do a great miracle.

**11:14, 15** If Jesus had been with Lazarus during the final moments of Lazarus's sickness, he might have healed him rather than let him die. But Lazarus died so that Jesus' power over death could be shown to his disciples and others. The raising of Lazarus was an essential display of his power, and the resurrection from the dead is a crucial belief of the Christian faith. Jesus not only raised himself from the dead (10:18), but he has the power to raise others.

**11:16** We often remember Thomas as "the doubter," because he doubted Jesus' resurrection (John 20:25). But here he demonstrated love and courage. The disciples knew the dangers of going with Jesus to Jerusalem, and they tried to talk him out of it. Thomas merely expressed what all of them felt. When their objections failed, they were willing to go, even though it appeared they might have to die with Jesus. They may not have understood why Jesus would be killed, but they were loyal. There are unknown dangers in doing God's work. It is wise to consider the high cost of being Jesus' disciple.

**11:25, 26** Jesus has power over life and death as well as power to forgive sins. This is because he is the Creator of life (see 14:6). He who *is* life can surely restore life. Whoever believes in Christ has a spiritual life that death cannot conquer or diminish in any way. When we realize his power and how wonderful his offer to us really is, how can we not commit our lives to him? To those of us who believe, what wonderful assurance and certainty we have: "Since I live, you too will live" (14:19).

**11:27** Martha is best known for being too busy to sit down and

³³ When Jesus saw her weeping and saw the other people wailing with her, a deep anger welled up within him,* and he was deeply troubled. ³⁴ "Where have you put him?" he asked them.

**11:35**
Luke 19:41
**11:37**
John 9:6-7

They told him, "Lord, come and see." ³⁵ Then Jesus wept. ³⁶ The people who were standing nearby said, "See how much he loved him!" ³⁷ But some said, "This man healed a blind man. Couldn't he have kept Lazarus from dying?"

### Jesus Raises Lazarus from the Dead (167)

**11:39**
John 11:17

³⁸ Jesus was still angry as he arrived at the tomb, a cave with a stone rolled across its entrance. ³⁹ "Roll the stone aside," Jesus told them.

But Martha, the dead man's sister, protested, "Lord, he has been dead for four days. The smell will be terrible."

**11:41**
Matt 11:25

⁴⁰ Jesus responded, "Didn't I tell you that you would see God's glory if you believe?" ⁴¹ So they rolled the stone aside. Then Jesus looked up to heaven and said, "Father, thank you for

**11:33** Or *he was angry in his spirit.*

---

**LAZARUS**

The details surrounding death may vary, but the reality is universal. Scenes like Lazarus's funeral in Bethany are repeated many times around the world each day. A grieving family gathers at a graveside. Friends agonize over what to say. Their helpless silence, downcast eyes, and shuffling feet provide more distraction than comfort. When death is unexpected, the whys hang in the air like choking smog.

Drawn by grief and duty, people came from Jerusalem and the surrounding area to pay their last respects to a citizen of Bethany. Jesus' friend Lazarus was dead. His brief sickness proved stronger than any available medicine. Jesus had been sent for, but had failed to arrive in time. Death didn't wait. Following the wisdom of hot countries, the body was soon wrapped and buried. Four days later, Jesus arrived.

Lazarus's sisters Mary and Martha reacted in shock. Grief-stricken, they struggled to understand why Jesus had delayed in coming. We have no idea how Lazarus reacted to his own death. In fact, we don't have a record of a single word he said. We do know that he listened to Jesus. Even when the curtain of death was between them, Lazarus responded to Jesus' voice. He came hobbling out of his cave-tomb, still wrapped in the grave clothes. Jesus raised him from the dead!

When all is said and done, only what God accomplished through us will really matter. We will take little credit. Jesus worked in and around Lazarus just as he does with us. We have Christ's invitation to participate in his work, but we must not forget that he will do much more than we will know. Meanwhile, we delight in what Christ does with the little we have to offer him.

Lazarus's resurrection poses an important question: When you die, do you fully expect that your next conscious experience will be hearing the voice of Jesus call you by name?

| | |
|---|---|
| **Strengths and accomplishments** | • Regularly hosted Jesus in his home<br>• Raised from the dead by Jesus after four days in the grave |
| **Lessons from his life** | • Once we have given God ownership of our lives, we can't predict what he will do with them<br>• Jesus' circle of relationships went beyond the 12 disciples<br>• Jesus declared that the events surrounding Lazarus's sickness and death would glorify God |
| **Vital statistics** | • Where: Bethany<br>• Relatives: Sisters: Mary and Martha |
| **Key verse** | "But when Jesus heard about it he said, 'Lazarus's sickness will not end in death. No, it happened for the glory of God so that the Son of God will receive glory from this'" (John 11:4). |

Lazarus's role as an "active spectator" is recorded in John 11:1–12:11.

---

talk with Jesus (Luke 10:38-42). But here we see her as a woman of deep faith. Her statement of faith is exactly the response that Jesus wants from us.

**11:33-37** John stresses that we have a God who cares. When Jesus saw the weeping and wailing, he too wept openly. Perhaps he empathized with their grief, or perhaps he was troubled at their unbelief. In either case, Jesus showed that he cares enough for us to weep with us in our sorrow. This portrait contrasts with the Greek concept of God that was popular in that day—a God with no emotions and no messy involvement with humans. Here we

see many of Jesus' emotions—compassion, indignation, sorrow, even frustration. He often expressed deep emotion, and we must never be afraid to reveal our true feelings to him. He understands them, for he experienced them. Be honest, and don't try to hide anything from your Savior. He cares.

**11:38** Tombs at this time were usually caves carved in the limestone rock of a hillside. A tomb was often large enough for people to walk inside. Several bodies would be placed in one tomb. After burial, a large stone was rolled across the entrance to the tomb.

hearing me. ⁴²You always hear me, but I said it out loud for the sake of all these people standing here, so that they will believe you sent me." ⁴³Then Jesus shouted, "Lazarus, come out!" ⁴⁴And the dead man came out, his hands and feet bound in graveclothes, his face wrapped in a headcloth. Jesus told them, "Unwrap him and let him go!"

**11:42**
John 12:30
**11:43**
Luke 7:14

### Religious Leaders Plot to Kill Jesus (168)

⁴⁵Many of the people who were with Mary believed in Jesus when they saw this happen. ⁴⁶But some went to the Pharisees and told them what Jesus had done. ⁴⁷Then the leading priests and Pharisees called the high council* together. "What are we going to do?" they asked each other. "This man certainly performs many miraculous signs. ⁴⁸If we allow him to go on like this, soon everyone will believe in him. Then the Roman army will come and destroy both our Temple* and our nation."

**11:47**
Matt 26:3-5

⁴⁹Caiaphas, who was high priest at that time,* said, "You don't know what you're talking about! ⁵⁰You don't realize that it's better for you that one man should die for the people than for the whole nation to be destroyed."

**11:49**
Matt 26:3
**11:50**
John 18:13-14

⁵¹He did not say this on his own; as high priest at that time he was led to prophesy that Jesus would die for the entire nation. ⁵²And not only for that nation, but to bring together and unite all the children of God scattered around the world.

**11:51**
Exod 28:30
Num 27:21

⁵³So from that time on, the Jewish leaders began to plot Jesus' death. ⁵⁴As a result, Jesus stopped his public ministry among the people and left Jerusalem. He went to a place near the wilderness, to the village of Ephraim, and stayed there with his disciples.

**11:52**
Isa 49:6
John 10:16
1 Jn 2:2

⁵⁵It was now almost time for the Jewish Passover celebration, and many people from all over the country arrived in Jerusalem several days early so they could go through the purification ceremony before Passover began. ⁵⁶They kept looking for Jesus, but as they stood around in the Temple, they said to each other, "What do you think? He won't come for Passover, will he?" ⁵⁷Meanwhile, the leading priests and Pharisees had publicly ordered that anyone seeing Jesus must report it immediately so they could arrest him.

**11:53**
Matt 26:4
**11:55**
Exod 12:13
2 Chr 30:17-19
Matt 26:1-2
Mark 14:1

### A Woman Anoints Jesus with Perfume (182/Matthew 26:6-13; Mark 14:3-9)

**12** Six days before the Passover celebration began, Jesus arrived in Bethany, the home of Lazarus—the man he had raised from the dead. ²A dinner was prepared in Jesus' honor. Martha served, and Lazarus was among those who ate* with him. ³Then Mary took a twelve-ounce jar* of expensive perfume made from essence of nard, and she anointed Jesus' feet with it, wiping his feet with her hair. The house was filled with the fragrance.

**12:1**
John 11:1
**12:2**
Luke 10:38-42
**12:3**
Luke 7:37-38

**11:47** Greek *the Sanhedrin.*   **11:48** Or *our position;* Greek reads *our place.*   **11:49** Greek *that year;* also in 11:51.
**12:2** Or *who reclined.*   **12:3** Greek *took 1 litra [327 grams].*

---

**TIME WITH THE DISCIPLES**
Lazarus's return to life became the last straw for the religious leaders, who were bent on killing Jesus. So Jesus stopped his public ministry and took his disciples away from Jerusalem to Ephraim. From there they returned to Galilee for a while (see the map in Luke 17, p. 1723).

**11:44** Jesus raised others from the dead, including Jairus's daughter (Matthew 9:18-26; Mark 5:42, 43; Luke 8:40-56) and a widow's son (Luke 7:11-15).

**11:45-53** Even when confronted point-blank with the power of Jesus' deity, some refused to believe. These eyewitnesses not only rejected Jesus; they plotted his murder. They were so hardened that they preferred to reject God's Son rather than admit that they were wrong. They preferred "closure" instead of being open to God's marvelous power. Beware of pride. If we allow it to grow, it can lead us into enormous sin.

**11:48** The Jewish leaders knew that if they didn't stop Jesus, the Romans would lash out against all of them. Rome gave partial freedom to the Jews as long as they were quiet and obedient. Jesus' miracles often caused a disturbance. The leaders feared that Rome's displeasure would bring additional hardship to their nation.

**11:51** John regarded Caiaphas's statement as a prophecy. As high priest, Caiaphas was used by God to explain Jesus' death even though Caiaphas didn't realize what he was doing.

**12:3** Essence of nard was a fragrant ointment imported from the mountains of India. Thus, it was very expensive. The amount Mary used was worth a year's wages.

**12:4**
John 6:71

**12:6**
John 13:29

**12:7**
John 19:40

**12:8**
Deut 15:11

⁴But Judas Iscariot, the disciple who would soon betray him, said, ⁵"That perfume was worth a year's wages.* It should have been sold and the money given to the poor." ⁶Not that he cared for the poor—he was a thief, and since he was in charge of the disciples' money, he often stole some for himself.

⁷Jesus replied, "Leave her alone. She did this in preparation for my burial. ⁸You will always have the poor among you, but you will not always have me."

**12:5** Greek *worth 300 denarii.* A denarius was equivalent to a laborer's full day's wage.

---

**CAIAPHAS**

Caiaphas was the leader of the religious group called the Sadducees. Educated and wealthy, they were politically influential in the nation. As the elite group, they were on fairly good terms with Rome. They hated Jesus because he endangered their secure lifestyles and taught a message they could not accept. A kingdom in which leaders *served* had no appeal to them.

Caiaphas's usual policy was to remove any threats to his power by whatever means necessary. For Caiaphas, whether Jesus should die was not in question; the only point to be settled was *when* his death should take place. Not only did Jesus have to be captured and tried; the Jewish high council also needed Roman approval before they could carry out the death sentence. Caiaphas's plans were unexpectedly helped by Judas's offer to betray Christ.

Caiaphas did not realize that his schemes were actually part of a wonderful plan God was carrying out. Caiaphas's willingness to sacrifice another man to preserve his own security was decidedly selfish. By contrast, Jesus' willingness to die for us was a clear example of loving self-sacrifice. Caiaphas thought he had won the battle as Jesus hung on the cross, but he did not count on the Resurrection!

Caiaphas's mind was closed. He couldn't accept the Resurrection even when the evidence was overwhelming, and he attempted to silence those whose lives had been forever changed by the risen Christ (Matthew 28:12, 13). Caiaphas represents those people who will not believe because they think it will cost them too much to accept Jesus as Lord. They choose the fleeting power, prestige, and pleasures of this life instead of the eternal life God offers those who receive his Son. What is your choice?

| | |
|---|---|
| **Strength and accomplishment** | • High priest for 18 years |
| **Weaknesses and mistakes** | • One of the most directly responsible persons for Jesus' death<br>• Used his office as a means to power and personal security<br>• Planned Jesus' capture, carried out his illegal trial, pressured Pilate to approve the Crucifixion, attempted to prevent the Resurrection, and later tried to cover up the fact of the Resurrection<br>• Kept up religious appearances while compromising with Rome<br>• Involved in the later persecution of Christians |
| **Lessons from his life** | • God uses even the twisted motives and actions of his enemies to bring about his will<br>• When we cover selfish motives with spiritual objectives and words, God still sees our intentions |
| **Vital statistics** | • Where: Jerusalem<br>• Occupation: High priest<br>• Relative: Father-in-law: Annas<br>• Contemporaries: Jesus, Pilate, Herod Antipas |
| **Key verses** | "Caiaphas, who was high priest at that time, said, 'You don't know what you're talking about! You don't realize that it's better for you that one man should die for the people than for the whole nation to be destroyed'" (John 11:49-50). |

Caiaphas is mentioned in Matthew 26:57; Luke 3:2; John 11; 18; and in Acts 4:6.

---

**12:4-6** Judas often dipped into the disciples' money bag for his own use. Quite likely, Jesus knew what Judas was doing (2:24, 25; 6:64), but never did or said anything about it. Similarly, when we choose the way of sin, God may not immediately do anything to stop us, but this does not mean he approves of our actions. What we deserve will come.

**12:5, 6** Judas used a pious phrase to hide his true motives. But Jesus knew what was in his heart. Judas's life had become a lie, and the devil was gaining more and more control over him (13:27). Satan is the father of lies, and a lying character opens the door to his influence. Jesus' knowledge of us should

make us want to keep our actions consistent with our words. Because we have nothing to fear with him, we should have nothing to hide.

**12:7, 8** This act and Jesus' response to it do not teach us to ignore the poor so we can spend money extravagantly for Christ. This was a unique act for a specific occasion—an anointing that anticipated Jesus' burial and a public declaration of faith in him as Messiah. Jesus' words should have taught Judas a valuable lesson about the worth of money. Unfortunately, Judas did not take heed; soon he would sell his Master's life for 30 pieces of silver.

⁹When all the people* heard of Jesus' arrival, they flocked to see him and also to see Lazarus, the man Jesus had raised from the dead. ¹⁰Then the leading priests decided to kill Lazarus, too, ¹¹for it was because of him that many of the people had deserted them* and believed in Jesus.

**12:10**
Luke 16:31

### Jesus Rides into Jerusalem on a Young Donkey
(**183**/Matthew 21:1-11; Mark 11:1-11; Luke 19:28-44)
¹²The next day, the news that Jesus was on the way to Jerusalem swept through the city. A large crowd of Passover visitors ¹³took palm branches and went down the road to meet him. They shouted,

**12:13**
Lev 23:40
†Ps 118:25-26
Zeph 3:15

"Praise God!*
Blessings on the one who comes in the name of the LORD!
Hail to the King of Israel!"*

¹⁴Jesus found a young donkey and rode on it, fulfilling the prophecy that said:

¹⁵ "Don't be afraid, people of Jerusalem.*
Look, your King is coming,
riding on a donkey's colt."*

**12:15**
Isa 35:4
†Zech 9:9

¹⁶His disciples didn't understand at the time that this was a fulfillment of prophecy. But after Jesus entered into his glory, they remembered what had happened and realized that these things had been written about him.

**12:16**
John 2:22; 7:39

¹⁷Many in the crowd had seen Jesus call Lazarus from the tomb, raising him from the dead, and they were telling others* about it. ¹⁸That was the reason so many went out to meet him—because they had heard about this miraculous sign. ¹⁹Then the Pharisees said to each other, "There's nothing we can do. Look, everyone* has gone after him!"

**12:17**
John 11:43-44
**12:18**
John 12:11; 19:37

### Jesus Explains Why He Must Die (**185**)
²⁰Some Greeks who had come to Jerusalem for the Passover celebration ²¹paid a visit to Philip, who was from Bethsaida in Galilee. They said, "Sir, we want to meet Jesus." ²²Philip told Andrew about it, and they went together to ask Jesus.

**12:21**
John 1:43-44
**12:23**
John 13:32; 17:1

²³Jesus replied, "Now the time has come for the Son of Man* to enter into his glory. ²⁴I tell you the truth, unless a kernel of wheat is planted in the soil and dies, it remains alone. But its death will produce many new kernels—a plentiful harvest of new lives. ²⁵Those who

**12:24**
1 Cor 15:36
**12:25**
Matt 10:39
Luke 9:24; 17:33

**12:9** Greek *Jewish people;* also in 12:11. **12:11** Or *had deserted their traditions;* Greek reads *had deserted.* **12:13a** Greek *Hosanna,* an exclamation of praise adapted from a Hebrew expression that means "save now." **12:13b** Ps 118:25-26; Zeph 3:15. **12:15a** Greek *daughter of Zion.* **12:15b** Zech 9:9. **12:17** Greek *were testifying.* **12:19** Greek *the world.* **12:23** "Son of Man" is a title Jesus used for himself.

---

**12:10, 11** The leading priests' blindness and hardness of heart caused them to sink ever deeper into sin. They rejected the Messiah and planned to kill him, and then plotted to murder Lazarus as well. One sin leads to another. From the Jewish leaders' point of view, they could accuse Jesus of blasphemy because he claimed equality with God. But Lazarus had done nothing of the kind. They wanted Lazarus dead simply because he was a living witness to Jesus' power. This is a warning to us to avoid sin. Sin leads to more sin, a downward spiral that can be stopped only by repentance and the power of the Holy Spirit to change our behavior.

**12:13** Jesus began his last week on earth by riding into Jerusalem on a donkey under a canopy of palm branches, with crowds hailing him as their king. To announce that he was indeed the Messiah, Jesus chose a *time* when all Israel would be gathered at Jerusalem, a *place* where huge crowds could see him, and a *way* of proclaiming his mission that was unmistakable. On Palm Sunday we celebrate Jesus' Triumphal Entry into Jerusalem as Lord of lords and King of Peace.

**12:13** The people who were praising God for giving them a king had the wrong idea about Jesus. They were sure he would be a national leader who would restore their nation to its former glory, and thus, they were deaf to the words of their prophets and blind to Jesus' real mission. When it became apparent that Jesus was not going to fulfill their hopes, many people turned against him.

**12:16** After Jesus' resurrection, the disciples understood for the first time many of the prophecies that they had missed along the

way. Jesus' words and actions took on new meaning and made more sense. In retrospect, the disciples saw how Jesus had led them into a deeper and better understanding of his truth. Stop now and think about the events in your life leading up to where you are now. How has God led you to this point? As you grow older, you will look back and see God's involvement more clearly than you do now.

**12:18** The people flocked to Jesus because they had heard about his great miracle in raising Lazarus from the dead. Their adoration was short-lived and their commitment shallow, for in a few days they would do nothing to stop his crucifixion. Devotion based only on curiosity or popularity fades quickly.

**12:20, 21** These Greeks probably were converts to the Jewish faith. They may have gone to Philip because, though he was a Jew, he had a Greek name.

**12:23-25** This is a beautiful picture of the necessary sacrifice of Jesus. Unless a kernel of wheat is planted in the soil, it will not become a blade of wheat producing many more seeds. Jesus had to die to pay the penalty for our sin, but also to show his power over death. His resurrection proves he has eternal life. Because Jesus is God, Jesus can give this same eternal life to all who believe in him.

**12:25** We must be so committed to living for Christ that we should "care nothing" for our lives by comparison. This does not mean that we long to die or that we are careless or destructive with the life God has given, but that we are willing to die if doing

**12:26**
John 14:3; 17:24

**12:27**
Ps 6:3
Matt 26:38
Mark 14:34

**12:28**
Matt 3:17; 17:5
Mark 1:11; 9:7
Luke 3:22; 9:35
2 Pet 1:17-18

**12:31**
John 14:30; 16:11
Eph 2:2

**12:32**
John 3:14; 6:44

**12:34**
Pss 89:4, 36; 110:4
Isa 9:7
Ezek 37:25
Dan 7:14

love their life in this world will lose it. Those who care nothing for their life in this world will keep it for eternity. 26 Anyone who wants to be my disciple must follow me, because my servants must be where I am. And the Father will honor anyone who serves me.

27 "Now my soul is deeply troubled. Should I pray, 'Father, save me from this hour'? But this is the very reason I came! 28 Father, bring glory to your name."

Then a voice spoke from heaven, saying, "I have already brought glory to my name, and I will do so again." 29 When the crowd heard the voice, some thought it was thunder, while others declared an angel had spoken to him.

30 Then Jesus told them, "The voice was for your benefit, not mine. 31 The time for judging this world has come, when Satan, the ruler of this world, will be cast out. 32 And when I am lifted up from the earth, I will draw everyone to myself." 33 He said this to indicate how he was going to die.

34 The crowd responded, "We understood from Scripture* that the Messiah would live forever. How can you say the Son of Man will die? Just who is this Son of Man, anyway?"

**12:34** Greek *from the law.*

---

| GREAT EXPECTATIONS | What was expected | What Jesus did | Reference |
|---|---|---|---|
| *Jesus Does the Unexpected* Wherever he went, Jesus exceeded people's expectations. | A man looked for healing. | Jesus also forgave his sins. | Mark 2:1-12 |
| | The disciples were expecting an ordinary day of fishing. | They found the Savior. | Luke 5:1-11 |
| | A widow was resigned to bury her dead son. | Jesus restored her son to life. | Luke 7:11-17 |
| | The religious leaders wanted a miracle. | Jesus offered them the Creator of miracles. | Matthew 12:38-45 |
| | A woman who wanted to be healed touched Jesus. | Jesus helped her see it was her faith that had healed her. | Mark 5:25-34 |
| | The disciples thought the crowd should be sent home because there was no food. | Jesus used a small meal to feed thousands, and there were leftovers! | John 6:1-15 |
| | The crowds looked for a political leader to set up a new kingdom to overthrow Rome's control. | Jesus offered them an eternal, spiritual kingdom to overthrow sin's control. | A theme throughout the Gospels |
| | The disciples wanted to eat the Passover meal with Jesus, their Master. | Jesus washed their feet, showing that he was also their servant. | John 13:1-20 |
| | The religious leaders wanted Jesus killed and got their wish. | But Jesus rose from the dead! | John 11:53; 19:30; 20:1-29 |

---

so will glorify Christ. We must disown the tyrannical rule of our own self-centeredness. By laying aside our striving for advantage, security, and pleasure, we can serve God lovingly and freely. Releasing control of our lives and transferring control to Christ bring eternal life and genuine joy.

**12:26** Many believed that Jesus came for the Jews only. But when Jesus said, "Anyone who wants to be my disciple must follow me," he was talking to these Greeks as well. No matter who the sincere seekers are, Jesus welcomes them. His message is for everyone. Don't allow social or racial differences to become barriers to the Good News. Take the Good News to all people.

**12:27** Jesus knew his crucifixion lay ahead, and because he was human, he dreaded it. He knew he would have to take the sins of the world on himself, and he knew this would separate him from his Father. He wanted to be delivered from this horrible death, but he knew that God sent him into the world to die for our sins, in our place. Jesus said no to his human desires in order to obey his Father and glorify him. Although we will never have to face such a difficult and awesome task, we are still called to obedience. Whatever the Father asks, we should do his will and bring glory to his name.

**12:31** The ruler of this world is Satan, an angel who rebelled against God. Satan is real, not symbolic, and is constantly work-

ing against God and those who obey him. Satan tempted Eve in the garden and persuaded her to sin; he tempted Jesus in the wilderness and did not persuade him to fall (Matthew 4:1-11). Satan has great power, but people can be delivered from his reign of spiritual darkness because of Christ's victory on the cross. Satan is powerful, but Jesus is much more powerful. Jesus' resurrection shattered Satan's deathly power (Colossians 1:13, 14). To overcome Satan we need faithful allegiance to God's Word, determination to stay away from sin, and the support of other believers.

**12:32-34** The crowd could not believe what Jesus was saying about the Messiah. They were waving palm branches for a victorious Messiah who would set up a political, earthly kingdom that would never end. From their reading of certain Scriptures, they thought the Messiah would never die (Psalms 89:35, 36; 110:4; Isaiah 9:7). Other passages, however, showed that he would die (Isaiah 53:5-9). Jesus' words did not mesh with their concept of the Messiah. First he had to suffer and die—then he would one day set up his eternal Kingdom. What kind of Messiah, or Savior, are you seeking? Beware of trying to force Jesus into your own mold—he won't fit.

35 Jesus replied, "My light will shine for you just a little longer. Walk in the light while you can, so the darkness will not overtake you. Those who walk in the darkness cannot see where they are going. 36 Put your trust in the light while there is still time; then you will become children of the light."

After saying these things, Jesus went away and was hidden from them.

*Most of the People Do Not Believe in Jesus* (186)

37 But despite all the miraculous signs Jesus had done, most of the people still did not believe in him. 38 This is exactly what Isaiah the prophet had predicted:

"LORD, who has believed our message?
To whom has the LORD revealed his powerful arm?"*

39 But the people couldn't believe, for as Isaiah also said,

40 "The Lord has blinded their eyes
    and hardened their hearts—
so that their eyes cannot see,
    and their hearts cannot understand,
and they cannot turn to me
    and have me heal them."*

41 Isaiah was referring to Jesus when he said this, because he saw the future and spoke of the Messiah's glory. 42 Many people did believe in him, however, including some of the Jewish leaders. But they wouldn't admit it for fear that the Pharisees would expel them from the synagogue. 43 For they loved human praise more than the praise of God.

*Jesus Summarizes His Message* (187)

44 Jesus shouted to the crowds, "If you trust me, you are trusting not only me, but also God who sent me. 45 For when you see me, you are seeing the one who sent me. 46 I have come as a light to shine in this dark world, so that all who put their trust in me will no longer remain in the dark. 47 I will not judge those who hear me but don't obey me, for I have come to save the world and not to judge it. 48 But all who reject me and my message will be judged on the day of judgment by the truth I have spoken. 49 I don't speak on my own authority. The Father who sent me has commanded me what to say and how to say it. 50 And I know his commands lead to eternal life; so I say whatever the Father tells me to say."

12:38 Isa 53:1.   12:40 Isa 6:10.

**12:35, 36** Jesus said he would be with them in person for only a short time, and they should take advantage of his presence while they had it. Like a light shining in a dark place, he would point out the way they should walk. If they walked in his light, they would become "children of the light," revealing the truth and pointing people to God. As Christians, we are to be Christ's light bearers, letting his light shine through us. How brightly is your light shining? Can others see Christ in your actions?

**12:37, 38** Jesus had performed many miracles, but most people still didn't believe in him. Likewise, many today won't believe despite all God does. Don't be discouraged if your witness for Christ doesn't turn as many to him as you'd like. Your job is to continue as a faithful witness. You are responsible to reach out to others, but they are responsible for their own decisions.

**12:39-41** People in Jesus' time, like those in the time of Isaiah, would not believe despite the evidence (12:37). As a result, God hardened their hearts. Does that mean God intentionally prevented these people from believing in him? No, he simply confirmed their own choices. After a lifetime of resisting God, they had become so set in their ways that they wouldn't even try to understand Jesus' message. For such people, it is virtually impossible to come to God—their hearts have been permanently hardened. Other instances of hardened hearts because of constant stubbornness are recorded in Exodus 9:12, Romans 1:24-28, and 2 Thessalonians 2:8-12.

**12:42, 43** Along with those who refused to believe, many believed but refused to admit it. This is just as bad, and Jesus had strong words for such people (see Matthew 10:32, 33). People who will not take a stand for Jesus are afraid of rejection or ridicule. Many Jewish leaders wouldn't admit to faith in Jesus because they feared excommunication from the synagogue (which was their livelihood) and loss of their prestigious place in the community. But the praise of others is fickle and short-lived. We should be much more concerned about God's eternal acceptance than about the temporary approval of other people.

**12:45** We often wonder what God is like. How can we know the Creator when he doesn't make himself visible? Jesus said plainly that those who see him see God, because he *is* God. If you want to know what God is like, study the person and words of Jesus Christ.

**12:48** The purpose of Jesus' first mission on earth was not to judge people, but to show them the way to find salvation and eternal life. When he comes again, one of his main purposes will be to judge people for how they lived on earth. Christ's words that we would *not* accept and obey will condemn us. On the day of judgment, those who accepted Jesus and lived his way will be raised to eternal life (1 Corinthians 15:51-57; 1 Thessalonians 4:15-18; Revelation 21:1-7), and those who rejected Jesus and lived any way they pleased will face eternal punishment (Revelation 20:11-15). Decide now which side you'll be on, for the consequences of your decision last forever.

## C. DEATH AND RESURRECTION OF JESUS, THE SON OF GOD (13:1—21:25)

John begins his Gospel with eternity and ends with Jesus coming to earth again. He features Jesus teaching his disciples privately just before his arrest and death. We see, clearly, the deep love Jesus has for the believer and the peace that comes from faith. Knowing the love Jesus has for believers, we, too, should believe and allow Jesus to forgive our sins. Only then will we experience peace in a world filled with turmoil.

### 1. Jesus teaches his disciples

*Jesus Washes the Disciples' Feet* (210)

**13:1**
John 16:28; 17:1

**13:2**
Luke 22:3
John 6:70-71

**13** Before the Passover celebration, Jesus knew that his hour had come to leave this world and return to his Father. He had loved his disciples during his ministry on earth, and now he loved them to the very end.* ²It was time for supper, and the devil had already prompted Judas,* son of Simon Iscariot, to betray Jesus. ³Jesus knew that the Father

**13:1** Or *he showed them the full extent of his love.*    **13:2** Or *the devil had already intended for Judas.*

---

**JOHN**

Being loved is the most powerful motivation in the world! Our ability to love is often shaped by our experience of love. We usually love others as we have been loved.

Some of the greatest statements about God's loving nature were written by a man who experienced God's love in a unique way. John, Jesus' disciple, expressed his relationship to the Son of God by calling himself "the disciple Jesus loved" (John 21:20). Although Jesus' love is clearly communicated in all the Gospels, in John's Gospel it is a central theme. Because his own experience of Jesus' love was so strong and personal, John was sensitive to those words and actions of Jesus that illustrated how the one who *is* love loved others.

Jesus knew John fully and loved him fully. He gave John and his brother James the nickname "Sons of Thunder" (Mark 3:17), perhaps from an occasion when the brothers asked Jesus for permission to "call down fire from heaven" on a village that had refused to welcome Jesus and the disciples (Luke 9:54). In John's Gospel and letters, we see the great God of love, while the thunder of God's justice bursts from the pages of Revelation.

Jesus confronts each of us as he confronted John. We cannot know the depth of Jesus' love unless we are willing to face the fact that he knows us completely. Otherwise we are fooled into believing he must love the people we pretend to be, not the sinners we actually are. John and all the disciples convince us that God is able and willing to accept us as we are. Being aware of God's love is a great motivator for change. His love is not given in exchange for our efforts; his love frees us to really live. Have you accepted that love?

| | |
|---|---|
| **Strengths and accomplishments** | • One of John the Baptist's disciples before following Jesus<br>• One of the 12 disciples and, with Peter and James, one of the inner three that were closest to Jesus<br>• Wrote five New Testament books: the Gospel of John; 1, 2, and 3 John; and Revelation |
| **Weaknesses and mistakes** | • Along with James, shared a tendency to outbursts of selfishness and anger<br>• Asked for a special position in Jesus' Kingdom |
| **Lessons from his life** | • Those who realize how much they are loved are able to love much<br>• When God changes a life, he does not take away personality characteristics, but puts them to effective use in his service |
| **Vital statistics** | • Occupations: Fisherman, disciple<br>• Relatives: Father: Zebedee. Mother: Salome. Brother: James.<br>• Contemporaries: Jesus, Pilate, Herod |
| **Key verses** | "Dear friends, I am not writing a new commandment for you; rather it is an old one you have had from the very beginning. This old commandment—to love one another—is the same message you heard before. Yet it is also new. Jesus lived the truth of this commandment, and you also are living it. For the darkness is disappearing, and the true light is already shining" (1 John 2:7-8). |

John's story is told throughout the Gospels, Acts, and Revelation.

---

**13:1** Jesus knew he would be betrayed by one of his disciples, denied by another, and deserted by all of them for a time. Still he "loved them to the very end." God knows us completely, as Jesus knew his disciples (2:24, 25; 6:64). He knows the sins we have committed and the ones we will yet commit. Still, he loves us. How do you respond to that kind of love?

**13:1ff** Chapters 13–17 tell us what Jesus said to his disciples on the night before his death. These words were all spoken in one

evening when, with only the disciples as his audience, he gave final instructions to prepare them for his death and resurrection, events that would change their lives forever.

**13:1-3** For more information on Judas Iscariot, see his Profile in Mark 14, p. 1655.

**13:1-17** Jesus was the model servant, and he showed his servant attitude to his disciples. Washing guests' feet was a job for a household servant to carry out when guests arrived. But had given him authority over everything and that he had come from God and would return to God. [4]So he got up from the table, took off his robe, wrapped a towel around his waist, [5]and poured water into a basin. Then he began to wash the disciples' feet, drying them with the towel he had around him.

[6]When Jesus came to Simon Peter, Peter said to him, "Lord, are you going to wash my feet?"

[7]Jesus replied, "You don't understand now what I am doing, but someday you will."

[8]"No," Peter protested, "you will never ever wash my feet!"

Jesus replied, "Unless I wash you, you won't belong to me."

[9]Simon Peter exclaimed, "Then wash my hands and head as well, Lord, not just my feet!"

[10]Jesus replied, "A person who has bathed all over does not need to wash, except for the feet,* to be entirely clean. And you disciples are clean, but not all of you." [11]For Jesus knew who would betray him. That is what he meant when he said, "Not all of you are clean."

[12]After washing their feet, he put on his robe again and sat down and asked, "Do you understand what I was doing? [13]You call me 'Teacher' and 'Lord,' and you are right, because that's what I am. [14]And since I, your Lord and Teacher, have washed your feet, you ought to wash each other's feet. [15]I have given you an example to follow. Do as I have done to you. [16]I tell you the truth, slaves are not greater than their master. Nor is the messenger more important than the one who sends the message. [17]Now that you know these things, God will bless you for doing them.

[18]"I am not saying these things to all of you; I know the ones I have chosen. But this fulfills the Scripture that says, 'The one who eats my food has turned against me.'* [19]I tell you this beforehand, so that when it happens you will believe that I AM the Messiah.* [20]I tell you the truth, anyone who welcomes my messenger is welcoming me, and anyone who welcomes me is welcoming the Father who sent me."

### Jesus and the Disciples Share the Last Supper
(**211**/Matthew 26:20-30; Mark 14:17-26; Luke 22:14-30)

[21]Now Jesus was deeply troubled,* and he exclaimed, "I tell you the truth, one of you will betray me!"

[22]The disciples looked at each other, wondering whom he could mean. [23]The disciple Jesus loved was sitting next to Jesus at the table.* [24]Simon Peter motioned to him to ask, "Who's he talking about?" [25]So that disciple leaned over to Jesus and asked, "Lord, who is it?"

[26]Jesus responded, "It is the one to whom I give the bread I dip in the bowl." And when he had dipped it, he gave it to Judas, son of Simon Iscariot. [27]When Judas had eaten the bread, Satan entered into him. Then Jesus told him, "Hurry and do what you're going to do."

**Cross-references (margin):**

**13:4** Luke 12:37; 22:27
**13:5** Luke 7:44 / John 12:3
**13:8** Ezek 36:25 / 1 Cor 6:11 / Eph 5:26 / Titus 3:5
**13:10** John 15:3
**13:11** John 6:64, 70-71; 13:2
**13:13** 1 Cor 12:3
**13:14** Luke 22:27 / 1 Tim 5:10 / 1 Pet 5:5
**13:15** Phil 2:5-7 / 1 Pet 5:3-5 / 1 Jn 2:6; 3:16
**13:17** Jas 1:25
**13:18** †Ps 41:9
**13:20** Matt 10:40 / Luke 10:16
**13:23** John 19:26
**13:25** John 21:20
**13:27** Luke 22:3 / John 13:2

---

**13:10** Some manuscripts do not include *except for the feet.* **13:18** Ps 41:9. **13:19** Or *that the 'I AM' has come;* or *that I am the LORD;* Greek reads *that I am.* See Exod 3:14. **13:21** Greek *was troubled in his spirit.* **13:23** Greek *was reclining on Jesus' bosom.* The "disciple Jesus loved" was probably John.

---

Jesus wrapped a towel around his waist, as the lowliest slave would do, and washed and dried his disciples' feet. If even he, God in the flesh, is willing to serve, we his followers must also be servants, willing to serve in any way that glorifies God. Are you willing to follow Christ's example of serving? Whom can you serve today? There is a special blessing for those who not only agree that humble service is Christ's way, but who also follow through and do it (13:17).

**13:6, 7** Imagine being Peter and watching Jesus wash the others' feet, all the while moving closer to you. Seeing his Master behave like a slave must have confused Peter. He still did not understand Jesus' teaching that to be a leader, a person must be a servant. This is not a comfortable passage for leaders who find it hard to serve those beneath them. How do you treat those who work under you (whether children, employees, or volunteers)?

**13:8, 9** When Jesus responded: "Unless I wash you, you won't belong to me," he may have meant (1) that unless he washed away Peter's sins by his death on the cross, then Peter could have no relationship with him, or (2) that unless Peter submitted to him and allowed Jesus to minister in this way, Peter would never learn the lesson of humility. Either way, Peter seemed to grasp the significance of Jesus' words, for he then wanted to be bathed completely: "Then wash my hands and head as well, Lord, not just my feet!"

**13:12ff** Jesus did not wash his disciples' feet just to get them to be nice to each other. His far greater goal was to extend his mission on earth after he was gone. These men were to move into the world serving God, serving each other, and serving all people to whom they took the message of salvation.

**13:22** Judas was not the obvious betrayer. After all, he was the one the disciples trusted to keep the money (12:6; 13:29).

**13:26** The honored guest at a meal was often singled out like this.

**13:27** Satan's part in the betrayal of Jesus does not remove any of the responsibility from Judas. Disillusioned because Jesus was talking about dying rather than setting up his Kingdom, Judas may have been trying to force Jesus' hand and make him use his power to prove he was the Messiah. Or perhaps Judas, not understanding Jesus' mission, no longer believed Jesus was God's chosen one. Whatever Judas thought, Satan assumed that Jesus' death would end his mission and thwart God's plan. Like Judas, Satan did not know that Jesus' death was the most important part of God's plan all along.

**13:27-38** John describes these few moments in clear detail. We can see that Jesus knew exactly what was going to happen. He knew about Judas and about Peter, but he did not change the situation, nor did he stop loving them. In the same way, Jesus knows exactly what you will do to hurt him. Yet he still loves you

13:29
John 12:6
13:30
Luke 22:53

28None of the others at the table knew what Jesus meant. 29Since Judas was their treasurer, some thought Jesus was telling him to go and pay for the food or to give some money to the poor. 30So Judas left at once, going out into the night.

### Jesus Predicts Peter's Denial (212/Luke 22:31-38)

13:34
Lev 19:18
Eph 5:2
1 Thes 4:9
1 Pet 1:22
1 Jn 2:8; 3:23;
4:10-11

13:35
1 Jn 3:14; 4:20

13:36-38
Matt 26:33-35
Mark 14:29-31
Luke 22:33-34

13:36
John 21:18
2 Pet 1:14

31As soon as Judas left the room, Jesus said, "The time has come for the Son of Man* to enter into his glory, and God will be glorified because of him. 32 And since God receives glory because of the Son,* he will soon give glory to the Son. 33 Dear children, I will be with you only a little longer. And as I told the Jewish leaders, you will search for me, but you can't come where I am going. 34 So now I am giving you a new commandment: Love each other. Just as I have loved you, you should love each other. 35 Your love for one another will prove to the world that you are my disciples."

36Simon Peter asked, "Lord, where are you going?"

And Jesus replied, "You can't go with me now, but you will follow me later."

37"But why can't I come now, Lord?" he asked. "I'm ready to die for you."

38Jesus answered, "Die for me? I tell you the truth, Peter—before the rooster crows tomorrow morning, you will deny three times that you even know me.

### Jesus Is the Way to the Father (213)

14:2
Ps 90:1
John 2:16, 19-21

**14** "Don't let your hearts be troubled. Trust in God, and trust also in me. 2 There is more than enough room in my Father's home.* If this were not so, would I have told you that I am going to prepare a place for you?*3 When everything is ready, I will come and get you, so that you will always be with me where I am. 4 And you know the way to where I am going."

14:6
John 1:4, 14, 16;
8:32; 10:10; 11:25
Rom 5:2
Eph 2:18
Heb 10:20
1 Jn 5:20

5"No, we don't know, Lord," Thomas said. "We have no idea where you are going, so how can we know the way?"

6Jesus told him, "I am the way, the truth, and the life. No one can come to the Father except through me. 7 If you had really known me, you would know who my Father is.* From now on, you do know him and have seen him!"

14:7
John 6:46; 8:19
1 Jn 2:13

**13:31** "Son of Man" is a title Jesus used for himself. **13:32** Some manuscripts do not include *And since God receives glory because of the Son.* **14:2a** Or *There are many rooms in my Father's house.* **14:2b** Or *If this were not so, I would have told you that I am going to prepare a place for you.* Some manuscripts read *If this were not so, I would have told you. I am going to prepare a place for you.* **14:7** Some manuscripts read *If you have really known me, you will know who my Father is.*

---

unconditionally and will forgive you whenever you ask him. Judas couldn't understand this, and his life ended tragically. Peter understood, and despite his shortcomings, his life ended triumphantly because he never let go of his faith in the one who loved him.

**13:34** To love others was not a new commandment (see Leviticus 19:18), but to love others as much as Christ loved others was revolutionary. Now we are to love others based on Jesus' sacrificial love for us. Such love will not only bring unbelievers to Christ; it will also keep believers strong and united in a world hostile to God. Jesus was a living example of God's love, as we are to be living examples of Jesus' love.

**13:34, 35** Jesus says that our Christlike love will show we are his disciples. Do people see petty bickering, jealousy, and division in your church? Or do they know you are Jesus' followers by your love for one another?

Love is more than simply warm feelings; it is an attitude that reveals itself in action. How can we love others as Jesus loves us? By helping when it's not convenient, by giving when it hurts, by devoting energy to others' welfare rather than our own, by absorbing hurts from others without complaining or fighting back. This kind of loving is hard to do. That is why people notice when you do it and know you are empowered by a supernatural source. The Bible has another beautiful description of love in 1 Corinthians 13.

**13:37, 38** Peter proudly told Jesus that he was ready to die for him. But Jesus corrected him. He knew Peter would deny that he knew Jesus that very night to protect himself (18:15-18, 25-27). In our enthusiasm, it is easy to make promises, but God knows the extent of our commitment. Paul tells us not to think of ourselves more highly than we ought (Romans 12:3). Instead of

bragging, demonstrate your commitment step by step as you grow in your knowledge of God's Word and in your faith.

**14:1-3** Jesus' words show that the way to eternal life, though unseen, is secure—as secure as your trust in Jesus. He has already prepared the way to eternal life. The only issue that may still be unsettled is your willingness to believe.

**14:2, 3** There are few verses in Scripture that describe eternal life, but these few verses are rich with promises. Here Jesus says, "I am going to prepare a place for you," and "I will come and get you." We can look forward to eternal life because Jesus has promised it to all who believe in him. Although the details of eternity are unknown, we need not fear because Jesus is preparing for us and will spend eternity with us.

**14:5, 6** This is one of the most basic and important passages in Scripture. How can we know the way to God? Only through Jesus. Jesus is the way because he is both God and man. By uniting our lives with his, we are united with God. Trust Jesus to take you to the Father, and all the benefits of being God's child will be yours.

**14:6** Jesus says he is the *only* way to God the Father. Some people may argue that this way is too narrow. In reality, it is wide enough for the whole world, if the world chooses to accept it. Instead of worrying about how limited it sounds to have only one way, we should be saying, "Thank you, God, for providing a sure way to get to you!"

**14:6** As the *way,* Jesus is our path to the Father. As the *truth,* he is the reality of all God's promises. As the *life,* he joins his divine life to ours, both now and eternally. Jesus is, in truth, the only living way to the Father.

8Philip said, "Lord, show us the Father, and we will be satisfied."

9Jesus replied, "Have I been with you all this time, Philip, and yet you still don't know who I am? Anyone who has seen me has seen the Father! So why are you asking me to show him to you? 10Don't you believe that I am in the Father and the Father is in me? The words I speak are not my own, but my Father who lives in me does his work through me. 11Just believe that I am in the Father and the Father is in me. Or at least believe because of the work you have seen me do.

12"I tell you the truth, anyone who believes in me will do the same works I have done, and even greater works, because I am going to be with the Father. 13You can ask for anything in my name, and I will do it, so that the Son can bring glory to the Father. 14Yes, ask me for anything in my name, and I will do it!

### Jesus Promises the Holy Spirit (214)

15"If you love me, obey* my commandments. 16And I will ask the Father, and he will give you another Advocate,* who will never leave you. 17He is the Holy Spirit, who leads into all truth. The world cannot receive him, because it isn't looking for him and doesn't recognize him. But you know him, because he lives with you now and later will be in you.* 18No, I will not abandon you as orphans—I will come to you. 19Soon the world will no longer see me, but you will see me. Since I live, you also will live. 20When I am raised to life again, you will know that I am in my Father, and you are in me, and I am in you. 21Those who accept my commandments and obey them are the ones who love me. And because they love me, my Father will love them. And I will love them and reveal myself to each of them."

22Judas (not Judas Iscariot, but the other disciple with that name) said to him, "Lord, why are you going to reveal yourself only to us and not to the world at large?"

23Jesus replied, "All who love me will do what I say. My Father will love them, and we will come and make our home with each of them. 24Anyone who doesn't love me will not obey me. And remember, my words are not my own. What I am telling you is from the Father who

14:15 Other manuscripts read *you will obey;* still others read *you should obey.*    14:16 Or *Comforter,* or *Encourager,* or *Counselor.* Greek reads *Paraclete;* also in 14:26.    14:17 Some manuscripts read *and is in you.*

**14:9**
John 1:14, 18;
12:45
2 Cor 4:4
Col 1:15
Heb 1:3

**14:10**
John 5:19; 10:38;
17:11, 21-24

**14:16**
John 14:26; 15:26

**14:17**
Rom 8:15-16
1 Jn 3:24

**14:18**
Rom 8:9-11
2 Cor 3:17-18

**14:20**
John 10:38; 15:4-5;
16:16, 23; 17:21-24

**14:21**
John 15:10; 16:27
1 Jn 2:5
2 Jn 1:6

**14:22**
Luke 6:16
Acts 10:41

**14:23**
Ps 91:1
John 15:10
Eph 3:17
1 Jn 4:16; 5:3
Rev 3:20; 21:3

**14:24**
John 7:16; 14:10

---

**14:9** Jesus is the visible, tangible image of the invisible God. He is the complete revelation of what God is like. Jesus explained to Philip, who wanted to see the Father, that to know Jesus is to know God. The search for God, for truth and reality, ends in Christ. (See also Colossians 1:15; Hebrews 1:1-4.)

**14:12, 13** Jesus is not saying that his disciples would do greater works—after all, raising the dead is about as amazing as you can get. Rather, the disciples, working in the power of the Holy Spirit, would carry the Good News of God's Kingdom out of Palestine and into the whole world.

**14:14** When Jesus says we can ask for anything, we must remember that our asking must be in his name—that is, according to God's character and will. God will not grant requests contrary to his nature or his will, and we cannot use his name as a magic formula to fulfill our selfish desires. If we are sincerely following God and seeking to do his will, then our requests will be in line with what he wants, and he will grant them. (See also 15:16; 16:23.)

**14:15, 16** Jesus was soon going to leave the disciples, but he would remain with them. How could this be? The Advocate—the Spirit of God himself—would come after Jesus was gone to care for and guide the disciples. The regenerating power of the Spirit came on the disciples just before Jesus' ascension (20:22), and the Spirit was poured out on all the believers at Pentecost (Acts 2), shortly after Jesus ascended to heaven. The Holy Spirit is the very presence of God within us and all believers, helping us live as God wants and building Christ's church on earth. By faith we can appropriate the Spirit's power each day.

**14:16** The word translated "Advocate" combines the ideas of comfort and counsel. The word could also be translated Comforter, Encourager, or Counselor. The Holy Spirit is a powerful person on our side, working for and with us.

**14:17ff** The following chapters teach these truths about the Holy Spirit: He will never leave us (14:16); the world at large

cannot receive him (14:17); he lives with us and in us (14:17); he teaches us (14:26); he reminds us of Jesus' words (14:26; 15:26); he convinces us of sin, shows us God's righteousness, and announces God's judgment on evil (16:8); he guides us into truth and gives insight into future events (16:13); he brings glory to Christ (16:14). The Holy Spirit has been active among people from the beginning of time, but after Pentecost (Acts 2) he came to live in all believers. Many people are unaware of the Holy Spirit's activities, but to those who hear Christ's words and understand the Spirit's power, the Spirit gives a whole new way to look at life.

**14:18** When Jesus said, "I will come to you," he meant it. Although Jesus ascended to heaven, he sent the Holy Spirit to live in believers, and to have the Holy Spirit is to have Jesus himself.

**14:19-21** Sometimes people wish they knew the future so they could prepare for it. God has chosen not to give us this knowledge. He alone knows what will happen, but he tells us all we need to know to *prepare* for the future. When we live by his standards, he will not leave us; he will come to us, he will be in us, and he will show himself to us. God knows what will happen, and because he will be with us through it all, we need not fear. We don't have to know the future to have faith in God; we have to have faith in God to be secure about the future.

**14:21** Jesus said that his followers show their love for him by obeying him. Love is more than lovely words; it is commitment and conduct. If you love Christ, then prove it by obeying what he says in his Word.

**14:22, 23** Because the disciples were still expecting Jesus to establish an earthly kingdom and overthrow Rome, they found it hard to understand why he did not tell the world at large that he was the Messiah. Not everyone, however, could understand Jesus' message. Ever since Pentecost, the Good News of the Kingdom has been proclaimed in the whole world, and yet not everyone is receptive to it. Jesus saves the deepest revelations of himself for those who love and obey him.

**14:26**
John 1:33; 15:26;
16:7; 20:22
1 Jn 2:20, 27

**14:27**
John 16:33; 20:19
Phil 4:7
Col 3:15

**14:29**
John 13:19

**14:30**
John 12:31

**14:31**
John 10:18; 12:49

sent me. ²⁵ I am telling you these things now while I am still with you. ²⁶ But when the Father sends the Advocate as my representative—that is, the Holy Spirit—he will teach you everything and will remind you of everything I have told you.

²⁷ "I am leaving you with a gift—peace of mind and heart. And the peace I give is a gift the world cannot give. So don't be troubled or afraid. ²⁸ Remember what I told you: I am going away, but I will come back to you again. If you really loved me, you would be happy that I am going to the Father, who is greater than I am. ²⁹ I have told you these things before they happen so that when they do happen, you will believe.

³⁰ "I don't have much more time to talk to you, because the ruler of this world approaches. He has no power over me, ³¹ but I will do what the Father requires of me, so that the world will know that I love the Father. Come, let's be going.

### Jesus Teaches about the Vine and the Branches (215)

**15:3**
John 17:17
Eph 5:26

**15:4**
John 6:56

**15:6**
Matt 3:10; 7:19;
13:42

**15:8**
Matt 5:16

**15** "I am the true grapevine, and my Father is the gardener. ² He cuts off every branch of mine that doesn't produce fruit, and he prunes the branches that do bear fruit so they will produce even more. ³ You have already been pruned and purified by the message I have given you. ⁴ Remain in me, and I will remain in you. For a branch cannot produce fruit if it is severed from the vine, and you cannot be fruitful unless you remain in me.

⁵ "Yes, I am the vine; you are the branches. Those who remain in me, and I in them, will produce much fruit. For apart from me you can do nothing. ⁶ Anyone who does not remain in me is thrown away like a useless branch and withers. Such branches are gathered into a pile to be burned. ⁷ But if you remain in me and my words remain in you, you may ask for anything you want, and it will be granted! ⁸ When you produce much fruit, you are my true disciples. This brings great glory to my Father.

---

**14:26** Jesus promised the disciples that the Holy Spirit would help them remember what he had been teaching them. This promise ensures the validity of the New Testament. The disciples were eyewitnesses of Jesus' life and teachings, and the Holy Spirit helped them remember without taking away their individual perspectives. We can be confident that the Gospels are accurate records of what Jesus taught and did (see 1 Corinthians 2:10-14). The Holy Spirit can help us in the same way. As we study the Bible, we can trust him to plant truth in our mind, convince us of God's will, and remind us when we stray from it.

**14:27** The end result of the Holy Spirit's work in our lives is deep and lasting peace. Unlike worldly peace, which is usually defined as the absence of conflict, this peace is confident assurance in any circumstance; with Christ's peace, we have no need to fear the present or the future. Sin, fear, uncertainty, doubt, and numerous other forces are at war within us. The peace of God moves into our hearts and lives to restrain these hostile forces and offer comfort in place of conflict. Jesus says he will give us that peace if we are willing to accept it from him. If your life is full of stress, allow the Holy Spirit to fill you with Christ's peace (see Philippians 4:6, 7 for more on experiencing God's peace).

**14:28** As God the Son, Jesus willingly submits to God the Father. On earth, Jesus also submitted to many of the physical limitations of his humanity (Philippians 2:6).

**14:30, 31** Although Satan, the ruler of this world, was unable to overpower Jesus (Matthew 4), he still had the arrogance to try. Satan's power exists only because God allows him to act. But because Jesus is sinless, Satan has no power over him. If we obey Jesus and align ourselves closely with God's purposes, Satan can have no power over us.

**14:31** "Come, let's be going" suggests that chapters 15–17 may have been spoken en route to the Garden of Gethsemane. Another view is that Jesus was asking the disciples to get ready to leave the upper room, but they did not actually do so until 18:1.

**15:1** The grapevine is a prolific plant; a single vine supports numerous branches and bears many grapes. In the Old Testament, grapes symbolized Israel's fruitfulness in doing God's work on the earth (Psalm 80:8; Isaiah 5:1-7; Ezekiel 19:10-14). In the Passover meal, the fruit of the vine symbolized God's goodness to his people.

**15:1ff** Christ is the vine, and God is the gardener who cares for the branches to make them fruitful. The branches are all those who claim to be followers of Christ. The fruitful branches are true believers who by their living union with Christ produce much fruit. But those who become unproductive—those who turn back from following Christ after making a superficial commitment—will be separated from the vine. Unproductive followers are as good as dead and will be cut off and tossed aside.

**15:2, 3** Jesus makes a distinction between two kinds of pruning: (1) cutting off and (2) cutting back branches. Fruitful branches are cut back to promote growth. In other words, God must sometimes discipline us to strengthen our character and faith. But branches that don't bear fruit are cut off at the trunk not only because they are worthless but also because they often infect the rest of the tree. People who don't bear fruit for God or who try to block the efforts of God's followers will be cut off from his life-giving power.

**15:5** "Fruit" is not limited to soul winning. In this chapter, answered prayer, joy, and love are mentioned as fruit (15:7, 11, 12). Galatians 5:22-24 and 2 Peter 1:5-8 describe additional fruit: qualities of Christian character.

**15:5, 6** Remaining in Christ means (1) believing that he is God's Son (1 John 4:15), (2) receiving him as Savior and Lord (John 1:12), (3) doing what God says (1 John 3:24), (4) continuing to believe the Good News (1 John 2:24), and (5) relating in love to the community of believers, Christ's body (John 15:12).

**15:5-8** Many people try to be good, honest people who do what is right. But Jesus says that the only way to live a truly good life is to stay close to him, like a branch attached to the vine. Apart from Christ our efforts are unfruitful. Are you receiving the nourishment and life offered by Christ, the vine? If not, you are missing a special gift he has for you.

**15:8** When a vine produces "much fruit," God is glorified, for daily he sent the sunshine and rain to make the crops grow, and constantly he nurtured each tiny plant and prepared it to blossom. What a moment of glory for the Lord of the harvest when the harvest is brought into the barns, mature and ready for use! He made it all happen! This farming analogy shows how God is glorified when people come into a right relationship with him and begin to "produce much fruit" in their lives.

9"I have loved you even as the Father has loved me. Remain in my love. 10 When you obey my commandments, you remain in my love, just as I obey my Father's commandments and remain in his love. 11 I have told you these things so that you will be filled with my joy. Yes, your joy will overflow! 12 This is my commandment: Love each other in the same way I have loved you. 13 There is no greater love than to lay down one's life for one's friends. 14 You are my friends if you do what I command. 15 I no longer call you slaves, because a master doesn't confide in his slaves. Now you are my friends, since I have told you everything the Father told me. 16 You didn't choose me. I chose you. I appointed you to go and produce lasting fruit, so that the Father will give you whatever you ask for, using my name. 17 This is my command: Love each other.

### Jesus Warns about the World's Hatred (216)

18 "If the world hates you, remember that it hated me first. 19 The world would love you as one of its own if you belonged to it, but you are no longer part of the world. I chose you to come out of the world, so it hates you. 20 Do you remember what I told you? 'A slave is not greater than the master.' Since they persecuted me, naturally they will persecute you. And if they had listened to me, they would listen to you. 21 They will do all this to you because of me, for they have rejected the one who sent me. 22 They would not be guilty if I had not come and spoken to them. But now they have no excuse for their sin. 23 Anyone who hates me also hates my Father. 24 If I hadn't done such miraculous signs among them that no one else could do, they would not be guilty. But as it is, they have seen everything I did, yet they still hate me and my Father. 25 This fulfills what is written in their Scriptures*: 'They hated me without cause.'

26 "But I will send you the Advocate*—the Spirit of truth. He will come to you from the Father and will testify all about me. 27 And you must also testify about me because you have been with me from the beginning of my ministry.

**16** "I have told you these things so that you won't abandon your faith. 2 For you will be expelled from the synagogues, and the time is coming when those who kill you will think they are doing a holy service for God. 3 This is because they have never known the Father or me. 4 Yes, I'm telling you these things now, so that when they happen, you will remember my warning. I didn't tell you earlier because I was going to be with you for a while longer.

15:25 Greek *in their law.* Pss 35:19; 69:4.   15:26 Or *Comforter,* or *Encourager,* or *Counselor.* Greek reads *Paraclete.*

| | |
|---|---|
| **15:9** | John 3:35 |
| **15:10** | John 14:15 |
| **15:11** | John 17:13 / 1 Jn 1:4 |
| **15:12** | John 13:34 |
| **15:13** | John 10:11 / Rom 5:6-8 |
| **15:16** | Rom 1:13 / Phil 1:22 |
| **15:18** | John 7:7 / 1 Jn 3:13 |
| **15:19** | John 17:14 / 1 Jn 4:5 |
| **15:21** | Matt 5:11 / 1 Pet 4:14 |
| **15:22** | John 9:41 |
| **15:24** | John 5:36; 9:41 |
| **15:25** | †Pss 35:19; 69:4 |
| **15:26** | John 14:17 / 1 Jn 5:7 |
| **16:2** | John 9:22 |
| **16:3** | John 15:21 |
| **16:4** | John 13:19 |

**15:11** When things are going well, we feel elated. When hardships come, we sink into depression. But true joy transcends the rolling waves of circumstance. Joy comes from a consistent relationship with Jesus Christ. When our lives are intertwined with his, he will help us walk through adversity without sinking into debilitating lows and manage prosperity without moving into deceptive highs. The joy of living with Jesus Christ daily will keep us levelheaded, no matter how high or low our circumstances.

**15:12, 13** We are to love each other as Jesus loved us, and he loved us enough to give his life for us. We may not have to die for someone, but there are other ways to practice sacrificial love: listening, helping, encouraging, giving. Think of someone in particular who needs this kind of love today. Give all the love you can, and then try to give a little more.

**15:15** Because Jesus Christ is Lord and Master, he should call us servants; instead, he calls us friends. How comforting and reassuring to be chosen as Christ's friends! Because he is Lord and Master, we owe him our unqualified obedience, but most of all, Jesus asks us to obey him because we love him.

**15:16** Jesus made the first choice—to love and to die for us, to invite us to live with him forever. We make the next choice—

to accept or reject his offer. Without *his* choice, we would have no choice to make.

**15:17** Christians will get plenty of hatred from the world; from each other we need love and support. Do you allow small problems to get in the way of loving other believers? Jesus commands that you love them, and he will give you the strength to do it.

**15:26** Once again Jesus offers hope. The Holy Spirit gives strength to endure the unreasonable hatred and evil in our world and the hostility many have toward Christ. This is especially comforting for those facing persecution.

**15:26** Jesus uses two names for the Holy Spirit—"Advocate" and "Spirit of truth." The word *Advocate* conveys the helping, encouraging, and strengthening work of the Spirit. *Spirit of truth* points to the teaching, illuminating, and reminding work of the Spirit. The Holy Spirit ministers to both the head and the heart, and both dimensions are important.

**16:1-16** In his last moments with his disciples, Jesus (1) warned them about further persecution, (2) told them where, when, and why he was going, and (3) assured them that they would not be left alone, but that the Spirit would come. Jesus knew what lay ahead, and he did not want the disciples' faith shaken or destroyed. God wants you to know you are not alone. You have the Holy Spirit to comfort you, teach you truth, and help you.

**16:2** Saul (who later became Paul), under the authority of the high priest, went through the land hunting down and persecuting Christians, convinced that he was doing the right thing (Acts 9:1, 2; 26:9-11).

### Jesus Teaches about the Holy Spirit (217)

**16:5**
John 7:33; 13:36
**16:7**
John 14:26; 15:26
**16:9**
John 15:22
**16:10**
Acts 3:14; 7:52
Rom 1:17
1 Pet 3:18
**16:11**
John 12:31
**16:13**
John 14:17, 26
**16:15**
John 17:10

⁵ "But now I am going away to the one who sent me, and not one of you is asking where I am going. ⁶ Instead, you grieve because of what I've told you. ⁷ But in fact, it is best for you that I go away, because if I don't, the Advocate* won't come. If I do go away, then I will send him to you. ⁸ And when he comes, he will convict the world of its sin, and of God's righteousness, and of the coming judgment. ⁹ The world's sin is that it refuses to believe in me. ¹⁰ Righteousness is available because I go to the Father, and you will see me no more. ¹¹ Judgment will come because the ruler of this world has already been judged.

¹² "There is so much more I want to tell you, but you can't bear it now. ¹³ When the Spirit of truth comes, he will guide you into all truth. He will not speak on his own but will tell you what he has heard. He will tell you about the future. ¹⁴ He will bring me glory by telling you whatever he receives from me. ¹⁵ All that belongs to the Father is mine; this is why I said, 'The Spirit will tell you whatever he receives from me.'

### Jesus Teaches about Using His Name in Prayer (218)

**16:16**
John 14:18-24

¹⁶ "In a little while you won't see me anymore. But a little while after that, you will see me again."

¹⁷ Some of the disciples asked each other, "What does he mean when he says, 'In a little while you won't see me, but then you will see me,' and 'I am going to the Father'? ¹⁸ And what does he mean by 'a little while'? We don't understand."

**16:20**
Mark 16:10
Luke 23:27
John 20:20
**16:21**
Isa 13:8; 21:3;
26:17
Acts 13:33
Col 1:18
**16:22**
Isa 66:14
John 20:20
**16:23**
John 14:20; 16:26
**16:24**
John 15:11
**16:25**
Ps 78:2
John 10:6
**16:27**
John 8:42; 14:21;
17:8
**16:28**
John 13:3

¹⁹ Jesus realized they wanted to ask him about it, so he said, "Are you asking yourselves what I meant? I said in a little while you won't see me, but a little while after that you will see me again. ²⁰ I tell you the truth, you will weep and mourn over what is going to happen to me, but the world will rejoice. You will grieve, but your grief will suddenly turn to wonderful joy. ²¹ It will be like a woman suffering the pains of labor. When her child is born, her anguish gives way to joy because she has brought a new baby into the world. ²² So you have sorrow now, but I will see you again; then you will rejoice, and no one can rob you of that joy. ²³ At that time you won't need to ask me for anything. I tell you the truth, you will ask the Father directly, and he will grant your request because you use my name. ²⁴ You haven't done this before. Ask, using my name, and you will receive, and you will have abundant joy.

²⁵ "I have spoken of these matters in figures of speech, but soon I will stop speaking figuratively and will tell you plainly all about the Father. ²⁶ Then you will ask in my name. I'm not saying I will ask the Father on your behalf,²⁷ for the Father himself loves you dearly because you love me and believe that I came from God.*²⁸ Yes, I came from the Father into the world, and now I will leave the world and return to the Father."

**16:7** Or *Comforter*, or *Encourager*, or *Counselor*. Greek reads *Paraclete*.   **16:27** Some manuscripts read *from the Father*.

---

**16:5** Although the disciples had asked Jesus about his death (13:36; 14:5), they had never wondered about its meaning. They were mostly concerned about themselves. If Jesus went away, what would become of them?

**16:7** Unless Jesus did what he came to do, there would be no Good News. If he did not die, he could not remove our sins; he could not rise again and defeat death. If he did not go back to the Father, the Holy Spirit would not come. Christ's presence on earth was limited to one place at a time. His leaving meant he could be present to the whole world through the Holy Spirit.

**16:8-11** Three important tasks of the Holy Spirit are (1) convicting the world of its sin and calling it to repentance, (2) revealing the standard of God's righteousness to anyone who believes, because Christ would no longer be physically present on earth, and (3) demonstrating Christ's judgment over Satan.

**16:9** According to Jesus, not believing in him is *sin.*

**16:10, 11** Christ's death on the cross made a personal relationship with God available to us. When we confess our sin, God declares us righteous and delivers us from judgment for our sins.

**16:13** The truth into which the Holy Spirit guides us is the truth about Christ. The Spirit also helps us through patient practice to discern right from wrong.

**16:13** Jesus said the Holy Spirit would tell them "about the future"—the nature of their mission, the opposition they would face, and the final outcome of their efforts. They didn't fully understand these promises until the Holy Spirit came after Jesus' death and resurrection. Then the Holy Spirit revealed truths to the disciples that they wrote down in the books that now form the New Testament.

**16:16** Jesus was referring to his death, now only a few hours away, and his resurrection three days later.

**16:20** What a contrast between the disciples and the world! The world rejoiced as the disciples wept, but the disciples would see Jesus again (in three days) and rejoice. The world's values are often the opposite of God's values. This can cause Christians to feel like misfits. But even if life is difficult now, one day we will rejoice. Keep your eye on the future and on God's promises!

**16:23-27** Jesus is talking about a new relationship between the believer and God. Previously, people approached God through priests. After Jesus' resurrection, any believer could approach God directly. A new day has dawned and now all believers are priests, talking with God personally and directly (see Hebrews 10:19-23). We approach God, not because of our own merit, but because Jesus, our great High Priest, has made us acceptable to God.

29 Then his disciples said, "At last you are speaking plainly and not figuratively. 30 Now we understand that you know everything, and there's no need to question you. From this we believe that you came from God."

31 Jesus asked, "Do you finally believe? 32 But the time is coming—indeed it's here now—when you will be scattered, each one going his own way, leaving me alone. Yet I am not alone because the Father is with me. 33 I have told you all this so that you may have peace in me. Here on earth you will have many trials and sorrows. But take heart, because I have overcome the world."

## Jesus Prays for Himself (219)

**17** After saying all these things, Jesus looked up to heaven and said, "Father, the hour has come. Glorify your Son so he can give glory back to you. 2 For you have given him authority over everyone. He gives eternal life to each one you have given him. 3 And this is the way to have eternal life—to know you, the only true God, and Jesus Christ, the one you sent to earth. 4 I brought glory to you here on earth by completing the work you gave me to do. 5 Now, Father, bring me into the glory we shared before the world began.

## Jesus Prays for His Disciples (220)

6 "I have revealed you* to the ones you gave me from this world. They were always yours. You gave them to me, and they have kept your word. 7 Now they know that everything I have is a gift from you, 8 for I have passed on to them the message you gave me. They accepted it and know that I came from you, and they believe you sent me.

9 "My prayer is not for the world, but for those you have given me, because they belong to you. 10 All who are mine belong to you, and you have given them to me, so they bring me glory. 11 Now I am departing from the world; they are staying in this world, but I am coming to you. Holy Father, you have given me your name;* now protect them by the power of your name so that they will be united just as we are. 12 During my time here, I protected them by the power of the name you gave me.* I guarded them so that not one was lost, except the one headed for destruction, as the Scriptures foretold.

13 "Now I am coming to you. I told them many things while I was with them in this world so they would be filled with my joy. 14 I have given them your word. And the world hates

**Cross references (right margin):**
16:32 Zech 13:7; Matt 26:31; John 8:29
16:33 John 14:27; Rom 5:1; 8:37; 1 Jn 5:4
17:1 John 13:31
17:2 Matt 28:18; John 6:37, 39
17:3 Phil 3:8; 1 Jn 5:20
17:5 John 1:1-2; 17:24; Phil 2:6
17:6 John 17:26
17:8 John 13:3; 16:30
17:9 1 Jn 5:19
17:10 John 16:15
17:11 John 10:30; 17:21; Gal 3:28
17:12 John 6:39
17:13 John 7:33; 15:11
17:14 John 15:18-19

**17:6** Greek *have revealed your name;* also in 17:26. **17:11** Some manuscripts read *you have given me these [disciples].* **17:12** Some manuscripts read *I protected those you gave me, by the power of your name.*

---

**16:30** The disciples believed Jesus' words because they were convinced that he knew everything. But their belief was only a first step toward the great faith they would receive when the Holy Spirit came to live in them.

**16:31-33** As Christians, we should expect continuing tension with an unbelieving world that is "out of sync" with Christ, his Good News, and his people. At the same time, we can expect our relationship with Christ to produce peace and comfort because we are "in sync" with him.

**16:32** The disciples scattered after Jesus was arrested (see Mark 14:50). Jesus accepted their statement of faith even though he knew their weakness. He knew they would have to grow into people whose words and lives matched even to the point of death. He takes us through the same process. How well are you living out what you say you believe about Jesus?

**16:33** Jesus summed up all he had told them this night, tying together themes from 14:27-29; 16:1-4; and 16:9-11. With these words he told his disciples to take courage. In spite of the inevitable struggles they would face, they would not be alone. Jesus does not abandon us to our struggles either. If we remember that the ultimate victory has already been won, we can claim the peace of Christ in the most troublesome times.

**17:1ff** This entire chapter is Jesus' prayer. From it, we learn that the world is a tremendous battleground where the forces under Satan's power and those under God's authority are at war. Satan and his forces are motivated by bitter hatred for Christ and his forces. Jesus prayed for his disciples, including those of us who follow him today. He prayed that God would keep his chosen believers safe from Satan's power, setting them apart and making them pure and holy, uniting them through his truth.

**17:3** How do we get eternal life? Jesus tells us clearly here—by knowing God the Father himself through his Son, Jesus Christ. Eternal life requires entering into a personal relationship with God in Jesus Christ. When we admit our sin and turn away from it, Christ's love lives in us by the Holy Spirit.

**17:5** Before Jesus came to earth, he was one with God. At this point, when his mission on earth was almost finished, Jesus was asking his Father to restore him to his original place of honor and authority. Jesus' resurrection and ascension—and Stephen's dying exclamation (Acts 7:56)—attest that Jesus did return to his exalted position at the right hand of God.

**17:10** What did Jesus mean when he said "they bring me glory"? God's glory is the revelation of his character and presence. The lives of Jesus' disciples reveal his character, and he is present to the world through them. Does your life reveal Jesus' character and presence?

**17:11** Jesus was asking that the disciples be united in harmony and love as the Father, Son, and Holy Spirit are united—the strongest of all unions. (See the notes on 17:21-23.)

**17:12** Judas was "the one headed for destruction," who was lost because he betrayed Jesus and never sought forgiveness (see Psalm 41:9).

**17:13** Joy is a common theme in Christ's teachings—he wants us to be joyful (see 15:11; 16:24). The key to immeasurable joy is living in intimate contact with Christ, the source of all joy. When we do, we will experience God's special care and protection and see the victory God brings even when defeat seems certain.

**17:14** The world hates Christians because Christians' values differ from the world's. Because Christ's followers don't cooperate with the world by joining in their sin, they are living accusations

**17:15**
1 Jn 5:18

**17:17**
John 15:3

**17:18**
John 20:21

**17:19**
Heb 2:11

them because they do not belong to the world, just as I do not belong to the world. ¹⁵ I'm not asking you to take them out of the world, but to keep them safe from the evil one. ¹⁶ They do not belong to this world any more than I do. ¹⁷Make them holy by your truth; teach them your word, which is truth. ¹⁸ Just as you sent me into the world, I am sending them into the world. ¹⁹And I give myself as a holy sacrifice for them so they can be made holy by your truth.

### Jesus Prays for Future Believers (221)

**17:20**
John 17:9

**17:21**
John 10:38
Gal 3:28

**17:22**
John 17:11

**17:23**
John 16:27; 17:5

**17:24**
John 1:14; 12:26

**17:25**
Matt 11:27

**17:26**
John 15:9

²⁰ "I am praying not only for these disciples but also for all who will ever believe in me through their message. ²¹I pray that they will all be one, just as you and I are one—as you are in me, Father, and I am in you. And may they be in us so that the world will believe you sent me.

²² "I have given them the glory you gave me, so they may be one as we are one. ²³ I am in them and you are in me. May they experience such perfect unity that the world will know that you sent me and that you love them as much as you love me. ²⁴ Father, I want these whom you have given me to be with me where I am. Then they can see all the glory you gave me because you loved me even before the world began!

²⁵ "O righteous Father, the world doesn't know you, but I do; and these disciples know you sent me. ²⁶ I have revealed you to them, and I will continue to do so. Then your love for me will be in them, and I will be in them."

### 2. Jesus completes his mission
#### Jesus Is Betrayed and Arrested
(224/Matthew 26:47-56; Mark 14:43-52; Luke 22:47-53)

**18:1**
2 Sam 15:23
Matt 26:36
Mark 14:32

**18:3**
John 7:32, 45

**18** After saying these things, Jesus crossed the Kidron Valley with his disciples and entered a grove of olive trees. ²Judas, the betrayer, knew this place, because Jesus had often gone there with his disciples. ³ The leading priests and Pharisees had given Judas a contingent of Roman soldiers and Temple guards to accompany him. Now with blazing torches, lanterns, and weapons, they arrived at the olive grove.

---

against the world's immorality. The world follows Satan's agenda, and Satan is the avowed enemy of Jesus and his people.

**17:17** A follower of Christ becomes pure and holy through believing and obeying the Word of God (Hebrews 4:12). He or she has already accepted forgiveness through Christ's sacrificial death (Hebrews 7:26, 27). But daily application of God's Word has a purifying effect on our minds and hearts. Scripture points out sin, motivates us to confess, renews our relationship with Christ, and guides us back to the right path.

**17:18** Jesus didn't ask God to take believers *out* of the world but instead to use them *in* the world. Because Jesus sends us into the world, we should not try to escape from the world, nor should we avoid all relationships with non-Christians. We are called to be salt and light (Matthew 5:13-16), and we are to do the work that God sent us to do.

**17:20** Jesus prayed for all who would follow him, including you and others you know. He prayed for unity (17:11), protection from the evil one (17:15), and holiness (17:17). Knowing that Jesus prayed for us should give us confidence as we work for his Kingdom.

**17:21-23** Jesus' great desire for his disciples was that they would become one. He wanted them unified as a powerful witness to the reality of God's love. Are you helping to unify the body of Christ, the church? You can pray for other Christians, avoid gossip, build others up, work together in humility, give your time and money, exalt Christ, and refuse to get sidetracked arguing over divisive matters.

**17:21-23** Jesus prayed for unity among believers based on the believers' unity with him and the Father. Christians can know unity among themselves if they are living in union with God. For example, each branch living in union with the vine is united with all other branches doing the same.

**18:3** The Jewish religious leaders were given authority by the Romans to make arrests for minor infractions. The Roman

soldiers may not have participated in the arrest but accompanied the Temple guards to make sure matters didn't get out of control.

**BETRAYAL IN THE GARDEN** After eating the Passover meal in the upper room, Jesus and his disciples went to Gethsemane, where Judas led the Temple guard to arrest Jesus. Jesus was then taken to Caiaphas's house for his first of many trials.

4Jesus fully realized all that was going to happen to him, so he stepped forward to meet them. " Who are you looking for?" he asked.

5"Jesus the Nazarene,"* they replied.

"I Am he,"* Jesus said. (Judas, who betrayed him, was standing with them.) 6As Jesus said "I Am he," they all drew back and fell to the ground! 7Once more he asked them, " Who are you looking for?"

And again they replied, "Jesus the Nazarene."

8"I told you that I Am he," Jesus said. "And since I am the one you want, let these others go." 9He did this to fulfill his own statement: "I did not lose a single one of those you have given me."*

10Then Simon Peter drew a sword and slashed off the right ear of Malchus, the high priest's slave. 11But Jesus said to Peter, "Put your sword back into its sheath. Shall I not drink from the cup of suffering the Father has given me?"

### Annas Questions Jesus (225)

12So the soldiers, their commanding officer, and the Temple guards arrested Jesus and tied him up. 13First they took him to Annas, the father-in-law of Caiaphas, the high priest at that time.* 14Caiaphas was the one who had told the other Jewish leaders, "It's better that one man should die for the people."

15Simon Peter followed Jesus, as did another of the disciples. That other disciple was acquainted with the high priest, so he was allowed to enter the high priest's courtyard with Jesus. 16Peter had to stay outside the gate. Then the disciple who knew the high priest spoke to the woman watching at the gate, and she let Peter in. 17The woman asked Peter, "You're not one of that man's disciples, are you?"

"No," he said, "I am not."

18Because it was cold, the household servants and the guards had made a charcoal fire. They stood around it, warming themselves, and Peter stood with them, warming himself.

19Inside, the high priest began asking Jesus about his followers and what he had been teaching them. 20Jesus replied, "Everyone knows what I teach. I have preached regularly in the synagogues and the Temple, where the people* gather. I have not spoken in secret. 21Why are you asking me this question? Ask those who heard me. They know what I said."

18:4 John 6:64
18:9 John 6:39; 17:12
18:10 Luke 22:36, 38
18:11 Matt 20:22; 26:39 Mark 10:38; 14:36 Luke 22:42
18:12-14 Matt 26:57-58 Mark 14:53-54 Luke 22:54
18:13 Luke 3:2 John 18:24
18:16-18 Matt 26:69-70 Mark 14:66-68 Luke 22:55-57
18:18 Mark 14:54, 67
18:19-24 Matt 26:59-68 Mark 14:55-65 Luke 22:63-71
18:20 Matt 26:55 John 7:26

18:5a Or *Jesus of Nazareth*; also in 18:7.   18:5b Or *"The 'I Am' is here"*; or *"I am the Lord"*; Greek reads *I am*; also in 18:6, 8. See Exod 3:14.   18:9 See John 6:39 and 17:12.   18:13 Greek *that year.*   18:20 Greek *Jewish people*; also in 18:38.

18:4, 5 John does not record Judas's kiss of greeting (Matthew 26:49; Mark 14:45; Luke 22:47, 48), but Judas's kiss marked a turning point for the disciples. With Jesus' arrest, each one's life would be radically different. For the first time, Judas openly betrayed Jesus before the other disciples. For the first time, Jesus' loyal disciples ran away from him (Matthew 26:56). The band of disciples would undergo severe testing before they were transformed from hesitant followers to dynamic leaders.

18:5, 6 The men may have been startled by the boldness of Jesus' question or by the words "I Am he," a declaration of his divinity (Exodus 3:14). Or perhaps they were overcome by his obvious power and authority.

18:10, 11 Trying to protect Jesus, Peter pulled a sword and wounded the high priest's slave. But Jesus told Peter to put away his sword and allow God's plan to unfold. At times it is tempting to take matters into our own hands, to force the issue. Most often such moves lead to sin. Instead, we must trust God to work out his plan. Think of it—if Peter had had his way, Jesus would not have gone to the cross, and God's plan of redemption would have been thwarted. Luke records that Jesus touched the man's ear and healed him (Luke 22:51).

18:11 "The cup" refers to the suffering, isolation, and death that Jesus would have to endure in order to atone for the sins of the world.

18:12, 13 Jesus was immediately taken to the high priest's residence, even though this was the middle of the night. The religious leaders were in a hurry—they wanted to complete the execution before the Sabbath and get on with the Passover celebration. This residence was a palace whose outer walls enclosed a court-

yard, where servants and soldiers could warm themselves around a fire.

18:13 Both Annas and Caiaphas had been high priests. Annas was Israel's high priest from A.D. 6 to 15, when he was deposed by Roman rulers. Caiaphas, Annas's son-in-law, was appointed high priest from A.D. 18 to 36/37. According to Jewish law, the office of high priest was held for life. Many Jews, therefore, still considered Annas the high priest and still called him by that title. But although Annas retained much authority among the Jews, Caiaphas made the final decisions.

Both Caiaphas and Annas cared more about their political ambitions than about their responsibility to lead the people to God. Though religious leaders, they had become evil. As the nation's spiritual leaders, they should have been sensitive to God's revelation. They should have known that Jesus was the Messiah about whom the Scriptures spoke, and they should have pointed the people to him. But when deceitful men and women pursue evil, they want to eliminate all opposition. Instead of honestly evaluating Jesus' claims based on their knowledge of Scripture, these religious leaders sought to further their own selfish ambitions and were even willing to kill God's Son, if that's what it took, to do it.

18:15, 16 The other disciple is probably John, the author of this Gospel. He knew the high priest and identified himself to the woman at the door. Because of his connections, John got himself and Peter into the courtyard. But Peter refused to identify himself as Jesus' follower. Peter's experiences in the next few hours would change his life. For more information about Peter, see his Profile in Matthew 27, p. 1603.

18:19ff During the night, Jesus had a pretrial hearing before Annas prior to being taken to Caiaphas and the entire high council

**18:22**
John 19:3

**18:23**
Matt 5:39
Acts 23:2-5

**18:24**
Matt 26:3

22 Then one of the Temple guards standing nearby slapped Jesus across the face. "Is that the way to answer the high priest?" he demanded.

23 Jesus replied, "If I said anything wrong, you must prove it. But if I'm speaking the truth, why are you beating me?"

24 Then Annas bound Jesus and sent him to Caiaphas, the high priest.

### Peter Denies Knowing Jesus
(**227**/Matthew 26:69-75; Mark 14:66-72; Luke 22:54-65)
25 Meanwhile, as Simon Peter was standing by the fire warming himself, they asked him again, "You're not one of his disciples, are you?"

He denied it, saying, "No, I am not."

| THE SIX STAGES OF JESUS' TRIAL Although Jesus' trial lasted less than 18 hours, he was taken to six different hearings. | Before Jewish Authorities | Preliminary Hearing before Annas (John 18:12-24) | Because the office of high priest was for life, Annas was still the "official" high priest in the eyes of the Jews, even though the Romans had appointed another. Thus, Annas still carried much weight in the high council. |
|---|---|---|---|
| | | Hearing before Caiaphas (Matthew 26:57-68) | Like the hearing before Annas, this hearing was conducted at night in secrecy. It was full of illegalities that made a mockery of justice (see the chart in Matthew 27, p. 1607). |
| | Before Roman Authorities | Trial before the High Council (Matthew 27:1, 2) | Just after daybreak, 70 members of the high council met to rubber-stamp their approval of the previous hearings to make them appear legal. The purpose of this trial was not to determine justice, but to justify their own preconceptions of Jesus' guilt. |
| | | First Hearing before Pilate (Luke 23:1-5) | The religious leaders had condemned Jesus to death on religious grounds, but only the Roman government could grant the death penalty. Thus, they took Jesus to Pilate, the Roman governor, and accused him of treason and rebellion, crimes for which the Roman government gave the death penalty. Pilate saw at once that Jesus was innocent, but he was afraid about the uproar being caused by the religious leaders. |
| | | Hearing before Herod (Luke 23:6-12) | Because Jesus' home was in the region of Galilee, Pilate sent Jesus to Herod Antipas, the ruler of Galilee, who was in Jerusalem for the Passover celebration. Herod was eager to see Jesus do a miracle, but when Jesus remained silent, Herod wanted nothing to do with him and sent him back to Pilate. |
| | | Last Hearing before Pilate (Luke 23:13-25) | Pilate didn't like the religious leaders. He wasn't interested in condemning Jesus because he knew Jesus was innocent. However, he knew that another uprising in his district might cost him his job. First he tried to compromise with the religious leaders by having Jesus beaten, an illegal action in itself. But finally he gave in and handed Jesus over to be executed. Pilate's self-interest was stronger than his sense of justice. |

(Mark 14:53-65). The religious leaders knew they had no grounds for charging Jesus, so they tried to build evidence against him by using false witnesses (Mark 14:55-59).

**18:22-27** We can easily blame the high council for their injustice in condemning Jesus, but we must remember that Peter and the rest of the disciples also contributed to Jesus' pain by deserting and denying him (Matthew 26:56, 75). While most of us are not like the religious leaders, we are all like the disciples, for all of us have been guilty of denying that Christ is Lord in vital areas of our lives or of keeping secret our identity as believers in times of pressure. Don't excuse yourself by pointing at others whose sins seem worse than yours. Instead, come to Jesus for forgiveness and healing.

**18:25** The other three Gospels say that Peter's three denials happened near a fire in the courtyard outside Caiaphas's palace. John places the first denial outside Annas's home and the other two denials outside Caiaphas's home. This was very likely the

same courtyard. The high priest's compound was large, and Annas and Caiaphas undoubtedly lived near each other.

**18:25-27** Imagine standing outside while Jesus, your Lord and Master, is questioned. Imagine watching this man, whom you have come to believe is the long-awaited Messiah, being abused and beaten. Naturally Peter was confused and afraid. It is a serious sin to deny Christ, but Jesus forgave Peter (21:15-17). No sin is too great for Jesus to forgive if you are truly repentant. He will forgive even your worst sin if you turn from it and ask his pardon.

26 But one of the household slaves of the high priest, a relative of the man whose ear Peter had cut off, asked, "Didn't I see you out there in the olive grove with Jesus?" 27 Again Peter denied it. And immediately a rooster crowed.

18:27
John 13:38

### Jesus Stands Trial before Pilate

(230/Matthew 27:11-14; Mark 15:2-5; Luke 23:1-5)

28 Jesus' trial before Caiaphas ended in the early hours of the morning. Then he was taken to the headquarters of the Roman governor.* His accusers didn't go inside because it would defile them, and they wouldn't be allowed to celebrate the Passover. 29 So Pilate, the governor, went out to them and asked, "What is your charge against this man?"

30 "We wouldn't have handed him over to you if he weren't a criminal!" they retorted.

31 "Then take him away and judge him by your own law," Pilate told them.

"Only the Romans are permitted to execute someone," the Jewish leaders replied. 32 (This fulfilled Jesus' prediction about the way he would die.*)

18:32
Matt 20:19
John 12:32

33 Then Pilate went back into his headquarters and called for Jesus to be brought to him. "Are you the king of the Jews?" he asked him.

18:33
Luke 23:3
John 19:9

34 Jesus replied, "Is this your own question, or did others tell you about me?"

35 "Am I a Jew?" Pilate retorted. "Your own people and their leading priests brought you to me for trial. Why? What have you done?"

36 Jesus answered, "My Kingdom is not an earthly kingdom. If it were, my followers would fight to keep me from being handed over to the Jewish leaders. But my Kingdom is not of this world."

18:36
Matt 26:53
Luke 17:21
John 6:15

**18:28** Greek *to the Praetorium;* also in 18:33.   **18:32** See John 12:32-33.

---

**18:27** This fulfilled Jesus' words to Peter after he promised he would never deny him (Mark 14:31; John 13:38).

**18:28** By Jewish law, entering the house of a Gentile would cause a Jewish person to be ceremonially defiled. As a result, he could not take part in worship at the Temple or celebrate the festivals until he was restored to a state of "cleanness." Afraid of being

**JESUS' TRIAL AND CRUCIFIXION**   Jesus was taken from trial before the Jewish high council to trial before the Roman governor, Pilate, in Pilate's palace. Pilate sent him to Herod (Luke 23:5-12), but Herod just returned Jesus to Pilate. Responding to threats from the mob, Pilate finally turned Jesus over to be crucified.

defiled, these men stayed outside the house where they had taken Jesus for trial. They kept the ceremonial requirements of their religion while harboring murder and treachery in their hearts.

**18:29** This Roman governor, Pilate, was in charge of Judea (the region where Jerusalem was located) from A.D. 26 to 36. Pilate was unpopular with the Jews because he had raided the Temple treasuries for money to build an aqueduct. He did not like the Jews, but when Jesus, the King of the Jews, stood before him, Pilate found him innocent.

**18:30** Pilate knew what was going on; he knew that the religious leaders hated Jesus, and he did not want to act as their executioner. They could not sentence him to death themselves—permission had to come from a Roman leader. But Pilate initially refused to sentence Jesus without sufficient evidence. Jesus' life became a pawn in a political power struggle.

**18:31ff** Pilate made four attempts to deal with Jesus: (1) He tried to put the responsibility on someone else (18:31); (2) he tried to find a way of escape so he could release Jesus (18:39); (3) he tried to compromise by having Jesus flogged rather than handing him over to die (19:1-3); and (4) he tried a direct appeal to the sympathy of the accusers (19:15). Everyone has to decide what to do with Jesus. Pilate tried to let everyone else decide for him—and in the end, he lost.

**18:32** This prediction is recorded in Matthew 20:19 and John 12:32, 35. Crucifixion was a common method of execution for criminals who were not Roman citizens.

**18:34** If Pilate was asking this question in his role as the Roman governor, he would have been inquiring whether Jesus was setting up a rebel government. But the Jews were using the word *king* to mean their religious ruler, the Messiah. Israel was a captive nation, under the authority of the Roman Empire. A rival king might have threatened Rome; a Messiah could have been a purely religious leader.

**18:36, 37** Pilate asked Jesus a straightforward question, and Jesus answered clearly. Jesus is a King, but one whose Kingdom is not of this world. There seems to have been no question in Pilate's mind that Jesus spoke the truth and was innocent of any crime. It also seems apparent that while recognizing the truth, Pilate chose to reject it. It is a tragedy when we fail to recognize the truth. It is a greater tragedy when we recognize the truth but fail to heed it.

**18:37**
John 8:47
1 Jn 4:6

37Pilate said, "So you are a king?"

Jesus responded, "You say I am a king. Actually, I was born and came into the world to testify to the truth. All who love the truth recognize that what I say is true."

### Pilate Hands Jesus Over to Be Crucified
(**232**/Matthew 27:15-26; Mark 15:6-15; Luke 23:13-25)

38"What is truth?" Pilate asked. Then he went out again to the people and told them, "He is not guilty of any crime. 39But you have a custom of asking me to release one prisoner each year at Passover. Would you like me to release this 'King of the Jews'?"

40But they shouted back, "No! Not this man. We want Barabbas!" (Barabbas was a revolutionary.)

**19:1**
Isa 50:6; 53:5

**19:3**
John 18:22

**19:4**
Luke 23:4
John 18:38

**19:6**
John 18:31

**19:7**
Lev 24:16
Matt 26:63-66

**19:11**
Rom 13:1

**19:12**
Luke 23:2
Acts 17:7

**19** Then Pilate had Jesus flogged with a lead-tipped whip. 2The soldiers wove a crown of thorns and put it on his head, and they put a purple robe on him. 3"Hail! King of the Jews!" they mocked, as they slapped him across the face.

4Pilate went outside again and said to the people, "I am going to bring him out to you now, but understand clearly that I find him not guilty." 5Then Jesus came out wearing the crown of thorns and the purple robe. And Pilate said, "Look, here is the man!"

6When they saw him, the leading priests and Temple guards began shouting, "Crucify him! Crucify him!"

"Take him yourselves and crucify him," Pilate said. "I find him not guilty."

7The Jewish leaders replied, "By our law he ought to die because he called himself the Son of God."

8When Pilate heard this, he was more frightened than ever. 9He took Jesus back into the headquarters* again and asked him, "Where are you from?" But Jesus gave no answer. 10"Why don't you talk to me?" Pilate demanded. "Don't you realize that I have the power to release you or crucify you?"

11Then Jesus said, "You would have no power over me at all unless it were given to you from above. So the one who handed me over to you has the greater sin."

12Then Pilate tried to release him, but the Jewish leaders shouted, "If you release this

**19:9** Greek *the Praetorium.*

---

**18:38** Pilate was cynical; he thought that all truth was relative. To many government officials, truth was whatever the majority of people agreed with or whatever helped advance their own personal power and political goals. When there is no standard or acknowledgement of truth, there is no basis for moral right and wrong. Justice becomes whatever works or whatever helps those in power. In Jesus and his Word we have a standard for truth and for our moral behavior.

**18:40** Barabbas was a rebel against Rome, and although he had committed murder, he was probably a hero among the Jews. The Jews hated being governed by Rome and paying taxes to the despised government. Barabbas, who had led a rebellion and failed, was released instead of Jesus, the only one who could truly help Israel. For more on Barabbas, see the note on Luke 23:18, 19.

**19:1ff** To grasp the full picture of Jesus' crucifixion, read John's perspective along with the other three accounts in Matthew 27, Mark 15, and Luke 23. Each writer adds meaningful details, but each has the same message—Jesus died on the cross, in fulfillment of Old Testament prophecy, so that we could be saved from our sins and be given eternal life.

**19:1-3** Flogging could have killed Jesus. The usual procedure was to bare the upper half of the victim's body and tie his hands to a pillar before whipping him with a three-pronged whip, with pieces of lead in the prongs. The number of lashes was determined by the severity of the crime; up to 40 were permitted under Jewish law (Deuteronomy 25:3). After being flogged, Jesus also endured other agonies recorded here and in the other Gospels.

**19:2-5** The soldiers went beyond their orders to whip Jesus—they also mocked his claim to royalty by placing a crown on his head and a royal robe on his shoulders.

**19:7** The truth finally came out—the religious leaders had not brought Jesus to Pilate because he was causing rebellion against

Rome, but because they thought he had broken their religious laws. Blasphemy, one of the most serious crimes in Jewish law, deserved the death penalty. Accusing Jesus of blasphemy would give credibility to their case in the eyes of Jews; accusing Jesus of treason would give credibility to their case in the eyes of the Romans. They didn't care which accusation Pilate listened to, as long as he would cooperate with them in killing Jesus.

**19:10** Throughout the trial we see that Jesus was in control, not Pilate or the religious leaders. Pilate vacillated, the Jewish leaders reacted out of hatred and anger, but Jesus remained composed. He knew the truth, he knew God's plan, and he knew the reason for his trial. Despite the pressure and persecution, Jesus remained unmoved. It was really Pilate and the religious leaders who were on trial, not Jesus. When you are questioned or ridiculed because of your faith, remember that while you may be on trial before your accusers, they are on trial before God.

**19:11** When Jesus said the man who delivered him to Pilate was guiltier than Pilate, he was not excusing Pilate for reacting to the political pressure placed on him. Pilate was responsible for his decision about Jesus. Caiaphas and the other religious leaders were guilty of a greater sin because they premeditated Jesus' murder.

**19:12, 13** This veiled threat by the Jewish leaders pressured Pilate into allowing Jesus to be crucified. As Roman governor of the area, Pilate was expected to keep the peace. Because Rome could not afford to keep large numbers of troops in the outlying regions, they maintained control by crushing rebellions immediately with brute force. Pilate was afraid that reports to Caesar of insurrection in his region would cost Pilate his job and perhaps even his life. When we face a tough decision, we can take the easy way out, or we can stand for what is right regardless of the cost. If we know the good we ought to do and don't do it, we sin (James 4:17).

man, you are no 'friend of Caesar.'* Anyone who declares himself a king is a rebel against Caesar."

13 When they said this, Pilate brought Jesus out to them again. Then Pilate sat down on the judgment seat on the platform that is called the Stone Pavement (in Hebrew, *Gabbatha*). 14 It was now about noon on the day of preparation for the Passover. And Pilate said to the people,* "Look, here is your king!"

15 "Away with him," they yelled. "Away with him! Crucify him!"

"What? Crucify your king?" Pilate asked.

"We have no king but Caesar," the leading priests shouted back.

16 Then Pilate turned Jesus over to them to be crucified.

### Jesus Is Led Away to Be Crucified
(**234**/Matthew 27:32-37; Mark 15:21-24; Luke 23:26-31)
So they took Jesus away. 17 Carrying the cross by himself, he went to the place called Place of the Skull (in Hebrew, *Golgotha*).

### Jesus Is Placed on the Cross
(**235**/Matthew 27:35-44; Mark 15:25-32; Luke 23:32-43)
18 There they nailed him to the cross. Two others were crucified with him, one on either side, with Jesus between them. 19 And Pilate posted a sign on the cross that read, "Jesus of Nazareth,* the King of the Jews." 20 The place where Jesus was crucified was near the city, and the sign was written in Hebrew, Latin, and Greek, so that many people could read it.

21 Then the leading priests objected and said to Pilate, "Change it from 'The King of the Jews' to 'He said, I am King of the Jews.'"

22 Pilate replied, "No, what I have written, I have written."

23 When the soldiers had crucified Jesus, they divided his clothes among the four of them. They also took his robe, but it was seamless, woven in one piece from top to bottom. 24 So they said, "Rather than tearing it apart, let's throw dice* for it." This fulfilled the Scripture that says, "They divided my garments among themselves and threw dice for my clothing."* So that is what they did.

25 Standing near the cross were Jesus' mother, and his mother's sister, Mary (the wife of Clopas), and Mary Magdalene. 26 When Jesus saw his mother standing there beside the disciple he loved, he said to her, "Dear woman, here is your son." 27 And he said to this disciple, "Here is your mother." And from then on this disciple took her into his home.

**19:13**
Matt 27:19

**19:24**
†Ps 22:18
**19:25**
Matt 27:55-56
Mark 15:40-41
Luke 8:2; 23:49
**19:26**
John 2:4; 13:23;
20:2; 21:7, 20

**19:12** "Friend of Caesar" is a technical term that refers to an ally of the emperor.    **19:14** Greek *Jewish people;* also in 19:20.    **19:19** Or *Jesus the Nazarene.*    **19:24a** Greek *cast lots.*    **19:24b** Ps 22:18.

---

**19:13** The Stone Pavement was part of the Tower of Antonia bordering the northwest corner of the Temple complex.

**19:15** The Jewish leaders were so desperate to get rid of Jesus that, despite their intense hatred for Rome, they shouted, "We have no king but Caesar." How ironic that they feigned allegiance to Rome while rejecting their own Messiah! Their own words condemned them, for God was to be their only true King, and they had abandoned every trace of loyalty to him. The priests had truly lost their reason for existence—instead of turning people to God, they claimed allegiance to Rome in order to kill their Messiah.

**19:17** The Place of the Skull was probably a hill outside Jerusalem along a main road. Many executions took place here so the Romans could use them as an example to the people.

**19:18** Crucifixion was a Roman form of execution. The condemned man was forced to carry his cross along a main road to the execution site, as a warning to the people. Types of crosses and methods of crucifixion varied. Jesus was nailed to his cross; some people were tied with ropes. Death came by suffocation because the weight of the body made breathing difficult as the victim lost strength. Crucifixion was a hideously slow and painful death.

**19:19** This sign was meant to be ironic. A king, stripped nearly naked and executed in public view, had obviously lost his kingdom forever. But Jesus, who turns the world's wisdom upside down,

was just coming into his Kingdom. His death and resurrection would strike the deathblow to Satan's rule and would establish Jesus' eternal authority over the earth. Few people reading the sign that bleak afternoon understood its real meaning, but the sign was absolutely true. All was not lost. Jesus was King of the Jews—and of the Gentiles, and of the whole universe.

**19:20** The sign was written in three languages: Hebrew for the native Jews, Latin for the Roman occupation forces, and Greek for foreigners and Jews visiting from other lands. In a double irony, the multi-lingual sign declared that Jesus was Lord of all.

**19:23, 24** Roman soldiers in charge of crucifixions customarily took for themselves the clothes of the condemned men. They divided Jesus' clothing, throwing dice to determine who would get his seamless garment, the most valuable piece of clothing. This fulfilled the prophecy in Psalm 22:18.

**19:25-27** Even while dying on the cross, Jesus was concerned about his family. He instructed John to care for Mary, Jesus' mother. Our families are precious gifts from God, and we should value and care for them under all circumstances. Neither Christian work nor key responsibilities in any job or position excuse us from caring for our families. What can you do today to show your love to your family?

**19:27** Jesus asked his close friend John, the writer of this Gospel, to care for Jesus' mother, Mary, whose husband, Joseph, must have been dead by this time. Why didn't Jesus assign this task to his brothers? As the oldest son, Jesus entrusted his mother to a person who stayed with him at the cross—and that was John.

## Jesus Dies on the Cross (236/Matthew 27:45-56; Mark 15:33-41; Luke 23:44-49)

**19:28**
†Pss 22:15; 69:21

²⁸Jesus knew that his mission was now finished, and to fulfill Scripture he said, "I am thirsty."*²⁹A jar of sour wine was sitting there, so they soaked a sponge in it, put it on a hyssop branch, and held it up to his lips. ³⁰When Jesus had tasted it, he said, "It is finished!" Then he bowed his head and released his spirit.

**19:30**
Job 19:26-27

**19:31**
Deut 21:22-23

³¹It was the day of preparation, and the Jewish leaders didn't want the bodies hanging there the next day, which was the Sabbath (and a very special Sabbath, because it was the Passover). So they asked Pilate to hasten their deaths by ordering that their legs be broken.

**19:28** See Pss 22:15; 69:21.

**MARY MAGDALENE**

The absence of women among the 12 disciples has bothered a few people. But it is clear that there were many women among Jesus' followers. It is also clear that Jesus did not treat women as others in his culture did; he treated them with dignity, as people with worth.

Mary of Magdala was an early follower of Jesus who certainly deserves to be called a disciple. An energetic, impulsive, caring woman, she not only traveled with Jesus, but also contributed to the needs of the group. She was present at the Crucifixion and was on her way to anoint Jesus' body on Sunday morning when she discovered the empty tomb. Mary was the first to see Jesus after his resurrection.

Mary Magdalene is a heartwarming example of thankful living. Her life was miraculously freed by Jesus when he drove seven demons out of her. In every glimpse we have of her, she was acting out her appreciation for the freedom Christ had given her. That freedom allowed her to stand under Christ's cross when all the disciples except John were hiding in fear. After Jesus' death, she intended to give his body every respect. Like the rest of Jesus' followers, she never expected his bodily resurrection—but she was overjoyed to discover it.

Mary's faith was not complicated, but it was direct and genuine. She was more eager to believe and obey than to understand everything. Jesus honored her childlike faith by appearing to her first and by entrusting her with the first message of his resurrection.

| | |
|---|---|
| **Strengths and accomplishments** | • Contributed to the needs of Jesus and his disciples<br>• One of the few faithful followers present at Jesus' death on the cross<br>• First to see the risen Christ |
| **Weakness and mistake** | • Jesus had to drive seven demons out of her |
| **Lessons from her life** | • Those who are obedient grow in understanding<br>• Women are vital to Jesus' ministry<br>• Jesus relates to women as he created them—as equal reflectors of God's image |
| **Vital statistics** | • Where: Magdala, Jerusalem<br>• Occupation: We are not told, but she seems to have been wealthy<br>• Contemporaries: Jesus, the 12 disciples, Mary, Martha, Lazarus, Jesus' mother Mary |
| **Key verse** | "After Jesus rose from the dead early on Sunday morning, the first person who saw him was Mary Magdalene, the woman from whom he had cast out seven demons" (Mark 16:9). |

Mary Magdalene's story is told in Matthew 27–28; Mark 15–16; Luke 23–24; and John 19–20. She is also mentioned in Luke 8:2.

**19:29** This sour wine was a cheap wine that the Roman soldiers drank while waiting for those crucified to die.

**19:30** Until this time, a complicated system of sacrifices had atoned for sins. Sin separates people from God, and only through the sacrifice of an animal, a substitute, could people be forgiven and become clean before God. But people sin continually, so frequent sacrifices were required. Jesus, however, became the final and ultimate sacrifice for sin. The word *finished* is the same as "paid in full." Jesus came to *finish* God's work of salvation (4:34; 17:4), to pay the full penalty for our sins. With his death, the complex sacrificial system ended because Jesus took all sin upon himself. Now we can freely approach God because of what Jesus did for us. Those who believe in Jesus' death and resurrection can live eternally with God and escape the penalty that comes from sin.

**19:31** It was against God's law to leave the body of a dead person exposed overnight (Deuteronomy 21:23), and it was also against the law to work after sundown on Friday, when the Sabbath began. This is why the religious leaders urgently wanted to get Jesus' body off the cross and buried by sundown.

**19:31-35** These Romans were experienced soldiers. They knew from many previous crucifixions whether a man was dead or alive. There was no question that Jesus was dead when they checked him, so they decided not to break his legs as they had done to the other victims. Piercing his side and seeing the sudden flow of blood and water (indicating that the sac surrounding the heart and the heart itself had been pierced) was further proof of his death. Some people say Jesus didn't really die, that he only passed out—and that's how he came back to life. But we have the witness of an impartial party, the Roman soldiers, that Jesus died on the cross (see Mark 15:44, 45).

Then their bodies could be taken down. 32 So the soldiers came and broke the legs of the two men crucified with Jesus. 33 But when they came to Jesus, they saw that he was already dead, so they didn't break his legs. 34 One of the soldiers, however, pierced his side with a spear, and immediately blood and water flowed out. 35 (This report is from an eyewitness giving an accurate account. He speaks the truth so that you also can believe.*) 36 These things happened in fulfillment of the Scriptures that say, "Not one of his bones will be broken,"* 37 and "They will look on the one they pierced."*

**19:35**
John 20:30-31;
21:24
1 Jn 1:1

**19:36**
†Exod 12:46
Num 9:12
†Ps 34:20

**19:37**
†Zech 12:10
Rev 1:7

## Jesus Is Laid in the Tomb (237/Matthew 27:56-61; Mark 15:42-47; Luke 23:50-56)

38 Afterward Joseph of Arimathea, who had been a secret disciple of Jesus (because he feared the Jewish leaders), asked Pilate for permission to take down Jesus' body. When Pilate gave permission, Joseph came and took the body away. 39 With him came Nicodemus, the man who had come to Jesus at night. He brought about seventy-five pounds* of perfumed ointment made from myrrh and aloes. 40 Following Jewish burial custom, they wrapped Jesus' body with the spices in long sheets of linen cloth. 41 The place of crucifixion was near a garden, where there was a new tomb, never used before. 42 And so, because it was the day of preparation for the Jewish Passover* and since the tomb was close at hand, they laid Jesus there.

**19:39**
John 3:1-2; 7:50

**19:40**
Luke 24:12
John 20:5-7

## Jesus Rises from the Dead (239/Matthew 28:1-7; Mark 16:1-8; Luke 24:1-12)

**20** Early on Sunday morning,* while it was still dark, Mary Magdalene came to the tomb and found that the stone had been rolled away from the entrance. 2 She ran and found Simon Peter and the other disciple, the one whom Jesus loved. She said, "They have taken the Lord's body out of the tomb, and we don't know where they have put him!"

**20:2**
John 13:23

3 Peter and the other disciple started out for the tomb. 4 They were both running, but the other disciple outran Peter and reached the tomb first. 5 He stooped and looked in and saw the linen wrappings lying there, but he didn't go in. 6 Then Simon Peter arrived and went inside. He also noticed the linen wrappings lying there, 7 while the cloth that had covered Jesus' head was folded up and lying apart from the other wrappings. 8 Then the disciple who had reached the tomb first also went in, and he saw and believed—9 for until then they still hadn't understood the Scriptures that said Jesus must rise from the dead. 10 Then they went home.

**20:3**
Luke 24:12

**20:5**
John 19:40

**20:7**
John 11:44

**20:9**
John 2:22

**19:35** Some manuscripts read *can continue to believe.* **19:36** Exod 12:46; Num 9:12; Ps 34:20. **19:37** Zech 12:10. **19:39** Greek *100 litras* [32.7 kilograms]. **19:42** Greek *because of the Jewish day of preparation.* **20:1** Greek *On the first day of the week.*

---

**19:32** The Roman soldiers would break victims' legs to hasten the death process. When a person hung on a cross, death came by suffocation, but the victim could push against the cross with his legs to hold up his body and keep breathing. With broken legs, he would suffocate almost immediately.

**19:34, 35** The graphic details of Jesus' death are especially important in John's record because he was an eyewitness.

**19:36, 37** Jesus died as the lambs for the Passover meal were being slain. Not a bone was to be broken in these sacrificial lambs (Exodus 12:46; Numbers 9:12). Jesus, the Lamb of God, was the perfect sacrifice for the sins of the world (1 Corinthians 5:7).

**19:38, 39** Four people were changed in the process of Jesus' death. The criminal, dying on the cross beside Jesus, asked Jesus to include him in his Kingdom (Luke 23:39-43). The Roman officer proclaimed that Jesus was surely the Son of God (Mark 15:39). Joseph and Nicodemus, members of the Jewish high council and secret followers of Jesus (7:50-52), came out of hiding. These men were changed more by Jesus' death than by his life. They realized who Jesus was, and that realization brought out their belief, proclamation, and action. When confronted with Jesus and his death, we should be changed—to believe, proclaim, and act.

**19:38-42** Joseph of Arimathea and Nicodemus were secret followers of Jesus. They were afraid to make this allegiance known because of their positions in the Jewish community. Joseph was a leader and honored member of the Jewish high council. Nicodemus, also a member of the high council, had come to Jesus by night (3:1) and later tried to defend him before the other religious leaders (7:50-52). Yet they risked their reputations to provide for Jesus' burial. Are you a secret believer? Do you hide your faith from your friends and fellow workers? This is an appropriate time to step out of hiding and let others know whom you follow.

**19:42** As they buried Jesus, Nicodemus and Joseph had to hurry to avoid working on the Sabbath, which began Friday evening at sundown. This tomb was probably a cave carved out of the stone hillside. It was large enough for a person to walk into, so Joseph and Nicodemus carried Jesus' body into it. A large stone was rolled in front of the entrance.

**20:1** Other women came to the tomb along with Mary Magdalene. The other Gospel accounts give their names. For more information on Mary Magdalene, see her Profile on page 1797.

**20:1** The stone was not rolled away from the entrance to the tomb so Jesus could get out. He could have left easily without moving the stone. It was rolled away so others could get *in* and see that Jesus was gone.

**20:1ff** People who hear about the Resurrection for the first time may need time before they can comprehend this amazing story. Like Mary and the disciples, they may pass through four stages of belief. (1) At first, they may think the story is a fabrication, impossible to believe (20:2). (2) Like Peter, they may check out the facts and still be puzzled about what happened (20:6). (3) Only when they encounter Jesus personally are they able to accept the fact of the Resurrection (20:16). (4) Then, as they commit themselves to the risen Lord and devote their lives to serving him, they begin to understand fully the reality of his presence with them (20:28).

**20:6, 7** The linen wrappings were left as if Jesus' body had simply vacated them. The cloth that covered Jesus' head was still rolled up in the shape of a head, and it was at about the right distance from the wrappings that had enveloped Jesus' body. A grave robber couldn't possibly have made off with Jesus' body and left the linens as if they were still shaped around it.

**20:9** As further proof that the disciples did not fabricate this story, we find that Peter and John were surprised that Jesus was

## Jesus Appears to Mary Magdalene (240/Mark 16:9-11)

**20:11-18**
Mark 16:9-11

**20:12**
Mark 16:5
Luke 24:4

**20:14**
Mark 16:9
Luke 24:16
John 21:4

¹¹Mary was standing outside the tomb crying, and as she wept, she stooped and looked in. ¹²She saw two white-robed angels, one sitting at the head and the other at the foot of the place where the body of Jesus had been lying. ¹³"Dear woman, why are you crying?" the angels asked her.

"Because they have taken away my Lord," she replied, "and I don't know where they have put him."

¹⁴She turned to leave and saw someone standing there. It was Jesus, but she didn't recognize him. ¹⁵ "Dear woman, why are you crying?" Jesus asked her. "Who are you looking for?"

She thought he was the gardener. "Sir," she said, "if you have taken him away, tell me where you have put him, and I will go and get him."

¹⁶"Mary!" Jesus said.

She turned to him and cried out, "Rabboni!" (which is Hebrew for "Teacher").

---

**THOMAS**

Thomas, so often remembered as "Doubting Thomas," deserves to be respected for his faith. He was a doubter, but his doubts had a purpose—he wanted to know the truth. Thomas did not idolize his doubts; he gladly believed when given reasons to do so. He expressed his doubts fully and had them answered completely. Doubting was only his way of responding, not his way of life.

Although our glimpses of Thomas are brief, his character comes through with consistency. He struggled to be faithful to what he knew, despite what he felt. At one point, when it was plain to everyone that Jesus' life was in danger, only Thomas put into words what most were feeling, "Let's go, too—and die with Jesus" (John 11:16). He didn't hesitate to follow Jesus.

We don't know why Thomas was absent the first time Jesus appeared to the disciples after the Resurrection, but he was reluctant to believe their witness to Christ's resurrection. Not even 10 friends could change his mind!

We can doubt without having to live a doubting way of life. Doubt encourages rethinking. Its purpose is more to sharpen the mind than to change it. Doubt can be used to pose the question, get an answer, and push for a decision. But doubt was never meant to be a permanent condition. Doubt is one foot lifted, poised to step forward or backward. There is no motion until the foot comes down.

When you experience doubt, take encouragement from Thomas. He didn't stay in his doubt but allowed Jesus to bring him to belief. Take encouragement also from the fact that countless other followers of Christ have struggled with doubts. The answers God gave them may help you, too. Don't settle into doubts, but move on from them to decision and belief. Find another believer with whom you can share your doubts. Silent doubts rarely find answers.

| | |
|---|---|
| **Strengths and accomplishments** | • One of Jesus' 12 disciples<br>• Intense both in doubt and belief<br>• A loyal and honest man |
| **Weaknesses and mistakes** | • Along with the others, abandoned Jesus at his arrest<br>• Refused to believe the others' claims to have seen Christ and demanded proof<br>• Struggled with a pessimistic outlook |
| **Lessons from his life** | • Jesus does not reject doubts that are honest and directed toward belief<br>• Better to doubt out loud than to disbelieve in silence |
| **Vital statistics** | • Where: Galilee, Judea, Samaria<br>• Occupation: Disciple of Jesus<br>• Contemporaries: Jesus, other disciples, Herod, Pilate |
| **Key verses** | "Then he said to Thomas, 'Put your finger here and look at my hands. Put your hand into the wound in my side. Don't be faithless any longer. Believe!' 'My Lord and my God!' Thomas exclaimed" (John 20:27-28). |

Thomas's story is told in the Gospels. He is also mentioned in Acts 1:13.

---

not in the tomb. When John saw the linen wrappings looking like an empty cocoon from which Jesus had emerged, he believed that Jesus had risen. It wasn't until after they had seen the empty tomb that they remembered what the Scriptures and Jesus had said—he would die, but he would also rise again!

**20:9** Jesus' resurrection is the key to the Christian faith. Why? (1) Just as he said, Jesus rose from the dead. We can be confident, therefore, that he will accomplish all he has promised.

(2) Jesus' bodily resurrection shows us that the living Christ, not a false prophet or imposter, is ruler of God's eternal Kingdom. (3) We can be certain of our own resurrection because Jesus was resurrected. Death is not the end—there is future life. (4) The divine power that brought Jesus back to life is now available to us to bring our spiritually dead selves back to life. (5) The Resurrection is the basis for the church's witness to the world.

¹⁷"Don't cling to me," Jesus said, "for I haven't yet ascended to the Father. But go find my brothers and tell them, 'I am ascending to my Father and your Father, to my God and your God.'"

¹⁸Mary Magdalene found the disciples and told them, "I have seen the Lord!" Then she gave them his message.

20:17
Matt 28:10
John 16:28
Rom 8:29
Col 1:18
Heb 2:11

### Jesus Appears to His Disciples (244/Luke 24:36-43)

¹⁹That Sunday evening* the disciples were meeting behind locked doors because they were afraid of the Jewish leaders. Suddenly, Jesus was standing there among them! "Peace be with you," he said. ²⁰As he spoke, he showed them the wounds in his hands and his side. They were filled with joy when they saw the Lord! ²¹Again he said, "Peace be with you. As the Father has sent me, so I am sending you." ²²Then he breathed on them and said, "Receive the Holy Spirit. ²³If you forgive anyone's sins, they are forgiven. If you do not forgive them, they are not forgiven."

20:19-23
Matt 28:16-20
Luke 24:36-49
20:20
John 16:20-22
20:21
Matt 28:19
John 17:18
20:22
John 7:37-39;
14:16-18, 26

### Jesus Appears to Thomas (245/Mark 16:14)

²⁴One of the twelve disciples, Thomas (nicknamed the Twin),* was not with the others when Jesus came. ²⁵They told him, "We have seen the Lord!"

But he replied, "I won't believe it unless I see the nail wounds in his hands, put my fingers into them, and place my hand into the wound in his side."

²⁶Eight days later the disciples were together again, and this time Thomas was with them. The doors were locked; but suddenly, as before, Jesus was standing among them. "Peace be with you," he said. ²⁷Then he said to Thomas, "Put your finger here, and look at my hands. Put your hand into the wound in my side. Don't be faithless any longer. Believe!"

²⁸"My Lord and my God!" Thomas exclaimed.

²⁹Then Jesus told him, "You believe because you have seen me. Blessed are those who believe without seeing me."

20:24
John 11:16

20:28
John 1:1, 18;
10:30; 14:9
Col 2:9
Titus 2:13
2 Pet 1:1
1 Jn 5:20
20:29
1 Pet 1:8

20:19 Greek *In the evening of that day, the first day of the week.*   20:24 Greek *Thomas, who was called Didymus.*

---

**20:17** Mary did not want to lose Jesus again. She had not yet understood the Resurrection. Perhaps she thought this was his promised second coming (14:3). But Jesus did not want to be detained at the tomb. If he did not ascend to heaven, the Holy Spirit could not come. Both he and Mary had important work to do.

**20:18** Mary didn't recognize Jesus at first. Her grief had blinded her; she couldn't see him because she didn't expect to see him. Then he spoke her name, and immediately she recognized him. Imagine the love that flooded her heart when she heard her Savior saying her name. Jesus is near you, and he is calling your name. Can you, like Mary, regard him as your Lord?

**20:18** Mary did not meet the risen Christ until she had discovered the empty tomb. She responded with joy and obedience by going to tell the disciples. We cannot meet Christ until we discover that he is indeed alive, that his tomb is empty. Are you filled with joy by this good news, and do you share it with others?

**20:21** Jesus again identified himself with his Father. He told the disciples by whose authority he did his work. Then he passed the job to his disciples of spreading the Good News of salvation around the world. Whatever God has asked you to do, remember: (1) Your authority comes from God, and (2) Jesus has demonstrated by words and actions how to accomplish the job he has given you. As the Father sent Jesus, Jesus sends his followers . . . and you.

**20:22** This may have been a special filling of the Holy Spirit for the disciples, a foretaste of what all believers would experience from the time of Pentecost (Acts 2) and forever after. To do God's work, we need the guidance and power of the Holy Spirit. We must avoid trying to do his work in our own strength.

**20:22** There is life in the breath of God. Man was created but did not come alive until God breathed into him the breath of life (Genesis 2:7). God's first breath made man different from all other forms of creation. Now, through the breath of Jesus, God imparted eternal, spiritual life. With this inbreathing came the power to do God's will on earth.

**20:23** Jesus was giving the disciples their Spirit-powered and Spirit-guided mission—to preach the Good News about Jesus so people's sins might be forgiven. The disciples did not have the power to forgive sins (only God can forgive sins), but Jesus gave them the privilege of telling new believers that their sins *have been* forgiven because they have accepted Jesus' message (see the note on Matthew 16:19). All believers have this same privilege. We can announce forgiveness of sins with certainty when we ourselves have found repentance and faith.

**20:24-29** Have you ever wished you could actually see Jesus, touch him, and hear his words? Are there times you want to sit down with him and get his advice? Thomas wanted Jesus' physical presence. But God's plan is wiser. He has not limited himself to one physical body; he wants to be present with you at all times. Even now he is with you in the form of the Holy Spirit. You can talk to him, and you can find his words to you in the pages of the Bible. He can be as real to you as he was to Thomas.

**20:25-28** Jesus wasn't hard on Thomas for his doubts. Despite his skepticism, Thomas was still loyal to the believers and to Jesus himself. Some people need to doubt before they believe. If doubt leads to questions, and questions lead to answers, and if the answers are accepted, then doubt has done good work. It is when doubt becomes stubbornness and stubbornness becomes a prideful lifestyle that doubt harms faith. When you doubt, don't stop there. Let your doubt deepen your faith as you continue to search for the answer.

**20:27** Jesus' resurrected body was unique. It was not the same kind of flesh and blood Lazarus had when he came back to life. Jesus' body was no longer subject to the same laws of nature as before his death. He could appear in a locked room; yet he was not a ghost or apparition because he could be touched and could eat. Jesus' resurrection was *literal* and *physical*—he was not a disembodied spirit.

**20:29** Some people think they would believe in Jesus if they could see a definite sign or miracle. But Jesus says we are blessed if we can believe without seeing. We have all the proof we need in

20:30
John 21:25

20:31
John 3:15; 19:35
1 Jn 5:13

30The disciples saw Jesus do many other miraculous signs in addition to the ones recorded in this book. 31But these are written so that you may continue to believe* that Jesus is the Messiah, the Son of God, and that by believing in him you will have life by the power of his name.

## Jesus Appears to Seven Disciples (246)

21:2
John 1:45-51;
11:16; 20:24

21:3
Luke 5:5

21:4
Luke 24:16
John 20:14

21:6
Luke 5:4-7

21:7
John 13:23

21:9
John 18:18

21:14
John 20:19, 26

**21** Later, Jesus appeared again to the disciples beside the Sea of Galilee.* This is how it happened. 2Several of the disciples were there—Simon Peter, Thomas (nicknamed the Twin),* Nathanael from Cana in Galilee, the sons of Zebedee, and two other disciples.

3Simon Peter said, "I'm going fishing."

"We'll come, too," they all said. So they went out in the boat, but they caught nothing all night.

4At dawn Jesus was standing on the beach, but the disciples couldn't see who he was. 5He called out, "Fellows,* have you caught any fish?"

"No," they replied.

6Then he said, "Throw out your net on the right-hand side of the boat, and you'll get some!" So they did, and they couldn't haul in the net because there were so many fish in it.

7Then the disciple Jesus loved said to Peter, "It's the Lord!" When Simon Peter heard that it was the Lord, he put on his tunic (for he had stripped for work), jumped into the water, and headed to shore. 8The others stayed with the boat and pulled the loaded net to the shore, for they were only about a hundred yards* from shore. 9When they got there, they found breakfast waiting for them—fish cooking over a charcoal fire, and some bread.

10"Bring some of the fish you've just caught," Jesus said. 11So Simon Peter went aboard and dragged the net to the shore. There were 153 large fish, and yet the net hadn't torn.

12"Now come and have some breakfast!" Jesus said. None of the disciples dared to ask him, "Who are you?" They knew it was the Lord. 13Then Jesus served them the bread and the fish. 14This was the third time Jesus had appeared to his disciples since he had been raised from the dead.

**20:31** Some manuscripts read *that you may believe.* **21:1** Greek *Sea of Tiberias*, another name for the Sea of Galilee. **21:2** Greek *Thomas, who was called Didymus.* **21:5** Greek *Children.* **21:8** Greek *200 cubits* [90 meters].

---

JESUS'
APPEARANCES
AFTER HIS
RESURRECTION

| | |
|---|---|
| Mary Magdalene | Mark 16:9-11; John 20:11-18 |
| The other women at the tomb | Matthew 28:8-10 |
| Peter in Jerusalem | Luke 24:34; 1 Corinthians 15:5 |
| The two travelers on the road | Mark 16:12, 13; Luke 24:13-35 |
| Ten disciples behind closed doors | Mark 16:14; Luke 24:36-43; John 20:19-25 |
| All the disciples, with Thomas (excluding Judas Iscariot) | John 20:26-31; 1 Corinthians 15:5 |
| Seven disciples while fishing | John 21:1-14 |
| Eleven disciples on the mountain | Matthew 28:16-20 |
| A crowd of 500 | 1 Corinthians 15:6 |
| Jesus' brother James | 1 Corinthians 15:7 |
| Those who watched Jesus ascend into heaven | Luke 24:44-49; Acts 1:3-8 |

The truth of Christianity rests heavily on the Resurrection. If Jesus rose from the grave, who saw him? How trustworthy were the witnesses? Those who claimed to have seen the risen Jesus went on to turn the world upside down. Most of them also died for being followers of Christ. People rarely die for halfhearted belief. These are the people who saw Jesus risen from the grave.

---

the words of the Bible and the testimony of believers. A physical appearance would not make Jesus any more real to us than he is now.

**20:30, 31** To understand the life and mission of Jesus more fully, all we need to do is study the Gospels. John tells us that his Gospel records only a few of the many events in Jesus' life on earth. But the Good News includes everything we need to know to believe that Jesus is the Messiah, the Son of God, through whom we receive eternal life.

**21:1ff** This chapter tells how Jesus commissioned Peter. Perhaps Peter needed special encouragement after his denial—he may have felt completely worthless. Verses 1-14 set the scene for Jesus' conversation with Peter.

**21:7** Only John ("the disciple Jesus loved") recognized Jesus in the dim morning light, undoubtedly because Jesus had performed a similar miracle earlier (Luke 5:1-11).

## Jesus Challenges Peter (247)

15After breakfast Jesus asked Simon Peter, "Simon son of John, do you love me more than these?*"

"Yes, Lord," Peter replied, "you know I love you."

"Then feed my lambs," Jesus told him.

16Jesus repeated the question: "Simon son of John, do you love me?"

"Yes, Lord," Peter said, "you know I love you."

"Then take care of my sheep," Jesus said.

17A third time he asked him, "Simon son of John, do you love me?"

Peter was hurt that Jesus asked the question a third time. He said, "Lord, you know everything. You know that I love you."

Jesus said, "Then feed my sheep.

18"I tell you the truth, when you were young, you were able to do as you liked; you dressed yourself and went wherever you wanted to go. But when you are old, you will stretch out your hands, and others* will dress you and take you where you don't want to go." 19Jesus said this to let him know by what kind of death he would glorify God. Then Jesus told him, "Follow me."

20Peter turned around and saw behind them the disciple Jesus loved—the one who had leaned over to Jesus during supper and asked, "Lord, who will betray you?" 21Peter asked Jesus, "What about him, Lord?"

22Jesus replied, "If I want him to remain alive until I return, what is that to you? As for you, follow me." 23So the rumor spread among the community of believers* that this disciple wouldn't die. But that isn't what Jesus said at all. He only said, "If I want him to remain alive until I return, what is that to you?"

24This disciple is the one who testifies to these events and has recorded them here. And we know that his account of these things is accurate.

25Jesus also did many other things. If they were all written down, I suppose the whole world could not contain the books that would be written.

21:15 Or more than these others do?   21:18 Some manuscripts read and another one.   21:23 Greek the brothers.

**21:15**
Matt 26:33

**21:16**
Acts 20:28
Heb 13:20-21
1 Pet 5:2-3

**21:17**
John 13:38; 16:30

**21:19**
John 13:36
2 Pet 1:14

**21:20**
John 13:23, 25

**21:22**
Matt 16:27

**21:24**
John 15:27; 19:35
1 Jn 1:1-3
3 Jn 1:12

**21:25**
John 20:30

---

**21:15-17** In this beach scene, Jesus led Peter through an experience that would remove the cloud of his denial. Peter had denied Jesus three times. Three times Jesus asked Peter if he loved him. When Peter answered yes, Jesus told him to feed his sheep. It is one thing to say you love Jesus, but the real test is willingness to serve him. Peter had repented, and here Jesus was asking him to commit his life. Peter's life changed when he finally realized who Jesus was. His occupation changed from fisherman to evangelist; his identity changed from impetuous to "rock"; and his relationship to Jesus changed—he was forgiven, and he finally understood the significance of Jesus' words about his death and resurrection.

**21:15-17** Jesus asked Peter three times if he loved him. The first time Jesus said, "Do you love (Greek agape: volitional, self-sacrificial love) me more than these?" The second time, Jesus focused on Peter alone and still used the word translated into Greek, agape. The third time, Jesus used the word translated into Greek, phileo (signifying affection, affinity, or brotherly love) and asked, in effect, "Are you even my friend?" Each time Peter responded with the word translated into Greek as phileo. Jesus doesn't settle for quick, superficial answers. He has a way of getting to the heart of the matter. Peter had to face his true feelings and motives when Jesus confronted him. How would you respond if Jesus asked you, "Do you love me? Do you really love me? Are you even my friend?"

**21:18, 19** This was a prediction of Peter's death by crucifixion. Tradition indicates that Peter was crucified for his faith—upside down because he did not feel worthy of dying as his Lord did. Despite what Peter's future held, Jesus told him to follow him. We may be uncertain and fearful about our future. But if we know God is in control, we can confidently follow Christ.

**21:21, 22** Peter asked Jesus how John would die. Jesus replied that Peter should not concern himself with that. We tend to compare our lives to others, whether to rationalize our own level of devotion to Christ or to question God's justice. Jesus responds to us as he did to Peter: "What is that to you? As for you, follow me."

**21:23** Early church history reports that after John spent several years as an exile on the island of Patmos, he returned to Ephesus where he died as an old man, near the end of the first century.

**21:25** John's stated purpose for writing his Gospel was to show that Jesus was the Son of God (20:31). He clearly and systematically presented the evidence for Jesus' claims. When evidence is presented in the courtroom, those who hear it must make a choice. Those who read the Gospel of John must also make a choice—is Jesus the Son of God, or isn't he? You are the jury. The evidence has been clearly presented. You must decide. Read John's Gospel and believe!

# 250 EVENTS IN THE LIFE OF CHRIST/ A HARMONY OF THE GOSPELS

All four books in the Bible that tell the story of Jesus Christ—Matthew, Mark, Luke, and John—stand alone, emphasizing a unique aspect of Jesus' life. But when these are blended into one complete account, or harmonized, we gain new insights about the life of Christ.

This harmony combines the four Gospels into a single chronological account of Christ's life on earth. It includes every chapter and verse of each Gospel, leaving nothing out.

The harmony is divided into 250 events. The title of each event is identical to the title found in the corresponding Gospel. Parallel passages found in more than one Gospel have identical titles, helping you to identify them quickly.

Each of the 250 events in the harmony is numbered. The number of the event corresponds to the number next to the title in the Bible text. When reading one of the Gospel accounts, you will notice, at times, that some numbers are missing or out of sequence. The easiest way to locate these events is to refer to the harmony.

In addition, if you are looking for a particular event in the life of Christ, the harmony can help you locate it more rapidly than paging through all four Gospels. Each of the 250 events has a distinctive title keyed to the main emphasis of the passage to help you locate and remember the events.

This harmony will help you to better visualize the travels of Jesus, study the four Gospels comparatively, and appreciate the unity of their message.

## I. BIRTH AND PREPARATION OF JESUS CHRIST

|  | Matthew | Mark | Luke | John |
|---|---|---|---|---|
| 1. Luke's purpose in writing |  |  | 1:1-4 |  |
| 2. God became a human |  |  |  | 1:1-18 |
| 3. The record of Jesus' ancestors | 1:1-17 |  | 3:23-38 |  |
| 4. An angel promises the birth of John to Zechariah |  |  | 1:5-25 |  |
| 5. An angel promises the birth of Jesus to Mary |  |  | 1:26-38 |  |
| 6. Mary visits Elizabeth |  |  | 1:39-56 |  |
| 7. John the Baptist is born |  |  | 1:57-80 |  |
| 8. An angel appears to Joseph | 1:18-25 |  |  |  |
| 9. Jesus is born in Bethlehem |  |  | 2:1-7 |  |
| 10. Shepherds visit Jesus |  |  | 2:8-20 |  |
| 11. Mary and Joseph bring Jesus to the Temple |  |  | 2:21-40 |  |
| 12. Visitors arrive from eastern lands | 2:1-12 |  |  |  |
| 13. The escape to Egypt | 2:13-18 |  |  |  |
| 14. The return to Nazareth | 2:19-23 |  |  |  |
| 15. Jesus speaks with the religious teachers |  |  | 2:41-52 |  |
| 16. John the Baptist prepares the way for Jesus | 3:1-12 | 1:1-8 | 3:1-18 |  |
| 17. The baptism of Jesus | 3:13-17 | 1:9-11 | 3:21, 22 |  |
| 18. Satan tempts Jesus in the wilderness | 4:1-11 | 1:12, 13 | 4:1-13 |  |
| 19. John the Baptist declares his mission |  |  |  | 1:19-28 |
| 20. John the Baptist proclaims Jesus as the Messiah |  |  |  | 1:29-34 |
| 21. The first disciples follow Jesus |  |  |  | 1:35-51 |
| 22. Jesus turns water into wine |  |  |  | 2:1-12 |

## II. MESSAGE AND MINISTRY OF JESUS CHRIST

| | Matthew | Mark | Luke | John |
|---|---|---|---|---|
| 23. Jesus clears the Temple | | | | 2:13-25 |
| 24. Nicodemus visits Jesus at night | | | | 3:1-21 |
| 25. John the Baptist tells more about Jesus | | | | 3:22-36 |
| 26. Herod puts John in prison | | | 3:19, 20 | |
| 27. Jesus talks to a woman at the well | | | | 4:1-26 |
| 28. Jesus tells about the spiritual harvest | | | | 4:27-38 |
| 29. Many Samaritans believe in Jesus | | | | 4:39-42 |
| 30. Jesus preaches in Galilee | 4:12-17 | 1:14, 15 | 4:14, 15 | 4:43-45 |
| 31. Jesus heals a government official's son | | | | 4:46-54 |
| 32. Jesus is rejected at Nazareth | | | 4:16-30 | |
| 33. Four fishermen follow Jesus | 4:18-22 | 1:16-20 | | |
| 34. Jesus teaches with authority | | 1:21-28 | 4:31-37 | |
| 35. Jesus heals Peter's mother-in-law and many others | 8:14-17 | 1:29-34 | 4:38-41 | |
| 36. Jesus preaches throughout Galilee | 4:23-25 | 1:35-39 | 4:42-44 | |
| 37. Jesus provides a miraculous catch of fish | | | 5:1-11 | |
| 38. Jesus heals a man with leprosy | 8:1-4 | 1:40-45 | 5:12-16 | |
| 39. Jesus heals a paralyzed man | 9:1-8 | 2:1-12 | 5:17-26 | |
| 40. Jesus eats with sinners at Matthew's house | 9:9-13 | 2:13-17 | 5:27-32 | |
| 41. Religious leaders ask Jesus about fasting | 9:14-17 | 2:18-22 | 5:33-39 | |
| 42. Jesus heals a lame man by a pool | | | | 5:1-15 |
| 43. Jesus claims to be the Son of God | | | | 5:16-30 |
| 44. Jesus supports his claim | | | | 5:31-47 |
| 45. The disciples pick wheat on the Sabbath | 12:1-8 | 2:23-28 | 6:1-5 | |
| 46. Jesus heals a man's hand on the Sabbath | 12:9-14 | 3:1-6 | 6:6-11 | |
| 47. Large crowds follow Jesus | 12:15-21 | 3:7-12 | | |
| 48. Jesus chooses the twelve disciples | | 3:13-19 | 6:12-16 | |
| 49. Jesus gives the Beatitudes | 5:1-12 | | 6:17-26 | |
| 50. Jesus teaches about salt and light | 5:13-16 | | | |
| 51. Jesus teaches about the law | 5:17-20 | | | |
| 52. Jesus teaches about anger | 5:21-26 | | | |
| 53. Jesus teaches about lust | 5:27-30 | | | |
| 54. Jesus teaches about divorce | 5:31, 32 | | | |
| 55. Jesus teaches about vows | 5:33-37 | | | |
| 56. Jesus teaches about revenge | 5:38-42 | | | |
| 57. Jesus teaches about loving enemies | 5:43-48 | | 6:27-36 | |
| 58. Jesus teaches about giving to the needy | 6:1-4 | | | |
| 59. Jesus teaches about prayer | 6:5-15 | | | |
| 60. Jesus teaches about fasting | 6:16-18 | | | |
| 61. Jesus teaches about money | 6:19-24 | | | |
| 62. Jesus teaches about worry | 6:25-34 | | | |
| 63. Jesus teaches about judging others | 7:1-6 | | 6:37-42 | |
| 64. Jesus teaches about asking, looking, knocking | 7:7-12 | | | |
| 65. Jesus teaches about the way to heaven | 7:13, 14 | | | |
| 66. Jesus teaches about fruit in people's lives | 7:15-20 | | 6:43-45 | |
| 67. Jesus teaches about building on a solid foundation | 7:21-29 | | 6:46-49 | |
| 68. A Roman officer demonstrates faith | 8:5-13 | | 7:1-10 | |
| 69. Jesus raises a widow's son from the dead | | | 7:11-17 | |
| 70. Jesus eases John's doubt | 11:1-19 | | 7:18-35 | |
| 71. Jesus promises rest for the soul | 11:20-30 | | | |
| 72. A sinful woman anoints Jesus' feet | | | 7:36-50 | |
| 73. Women accompany Jesus and the disciples | | | 8:1-3 | |
| 74. Religious leaders accuse Jesus of getting his power from Satan | 12:22-37 | 3:20-30 | | |
| 75. Religious leaders ask Jesus for a miracle | 12:38-45 | | | |
| 76. Jesus describes his true family | 12:46-50 | 3:31-35 | 8:19-21 | |
| 77. Jesus tells the parable of the four soils | 13:1-9 | 4:1-9 | 8:4-8 | |
| 78. Jesus explains the parable of the four soils | 13:10-23 | 4:10-25 | 8:9-18 | |
| 79. Jesus tells the parable of the growing seed | | 4:26-29 | | |
| 80. Jesus tells the parable of the weeds | 13:24-30 | | | |
| 81. Jesus tells the parable of the mustard seed | 13:31, 32 | 4:30-34 | | |
| 82. Jesus tells the parable of the yeast | 13:33-35 | | | |
| 83. Jesus explains the parable of the weeds | 13:36-43 | | | |
| 84. Jesus tells the parable of hidden treasure | 13:44 | | | |

|                                                                      | Matthew   | Mark     | Luke     | John    |
|----------------------------------------------------------------------|-----------|----------|----------|---------|
| 85. Jesus tells the parable of the pearl merchant                    | 13:45, 46 |          |          |         |
| 86. Jesus tells the parable of the fishing net                       | 13:47-52  |          |          |         |
| 87. Jesus calms the storm                                            | 8:23-27   | 4:35-41  | 8:22-25  |         |
| 88. Jesus sends demons into a herd of pigs                           | 8:28-34   | 5:1-20   | 8:26-39  |         |
| 89. Jesus heals a bleeding woman and restores<br>a girl to life      | 9:18-26   | 5:21-43  | 8:40-56  |         |
| 90. Jesus heals the blind and mute                                   | 9:27-34   |          |          |         |
| 91. The people of Nazareth refuse to believe                         | 13:53-58  | 6:1-6    |          |         |
| 92. Jesus urges the disciples to pray for workers                    | 9:35-38   |          |          |         |
| 93. Jesus sends out the twelve disciples                             | 10:1-15   | 6:7-13   | 9:1-6    |         |
| 94. Jesus prepares the disciples for persecution                     | 10:16-42  |          |          |         |
| 95. Herod kills John the Baptist                                     | 14:1-12   | 6:14-29  | 9:7-9    |         |
| 96. Jesus feeds five thousand                                        | 14:13-21  | 6:30-44  | 9:10-17  | 6:1-15  |
| 97. Jesus walks on water                                             | 14:22-33  | 6:45-52  |          | 6:16-21 |
| 98. Jesus heals all who touch him                                    | 14:34-36  | 6:53-56  |          |         |
| 99. Jesus is the true bread from heaven                              |           |          |          | 6:22-40 |
| 100. The people disagree that Jesus is from heaven                   |           |          |          | 6:41-59 |
| 101. Many disciples desert Jesus                                     |           |          |          | 6:60-71 |
| 102. Jesus teaches about inner purity                                | 15:1-20   | 7:1-23   |          |         |
| 103. Jesus sends a demon out of a girl                               | 15:21-28  | 7:24-30  |          |         |
| 104. Jesus heals many people                                         | 15:29-31  | 7:31-37  |          |         |
| 105. Jesus feeds four thousand                                       | 15:32-39  | 8:1-10   |          |         |
| 106. Leaders demand a miraculous sign                                | 16:1-4    | 8:11-13  |          |         |
| 107. Jesus warns against wrong teaching                              | 16:5-12   | 8:14-21  |          |         |
| 108. Jesus restores sight to a blind man                             |           | 8:22-26  |          |         |
| 109. Peter says Jesus is the Messiah                                 | 16:13-20  | 8:27-30  | 9:18-20  |         |
| 110. Jesus predicts his death the first time                         | 16:21-28  | 8:31-9:1 | 9:21-27  |         |
| 111. Jesus is transfigured on the mountain                           | 17:1-13   | 9:2-13   | 9:28-36  |         |
| 112. Jesus heals a demon-possessed boy                               | 17:14-21  | 9:14-29  | 9:37-43  |         |
| 113. Jesus predicts his death the second time                        | 17:22, 23 | 9:30-32  | 9:44, 45 |         |
| 114. Peter finds the coin in the fish's mouth                        | 17:24-27  |          |          |         |
| 115. The disciples argue about who would be the greatest             | 18:1-6    | 9:33-37  | 9:46-48  |         |
| 116. The disciples forbid another to use Jesus' name                 |           | 9:38-41  | 9:49, 50 |         |
| 117. Jesus warns against temptation                                  | 18:7-9    | 9:42-50  |          |         |
| 118. Jesus warns against looking down on others                      | 18:10-14  |          |          |         |
| 119. Jesus teaches how to treat a believer who sins                  | 18:15-20  |          |          |         |
| 120. Jesus tells the parable of the unforgiving debtor               | 18:21-35  |          |          |         |
| 121. Jesus' brothers ridicule him                                    |           |          |          | 7:1-9   |
| 122. Jesus teaches about the cost of following him                   | 8:18-22   |          | 9:51-62  |         |
| 123. Jesus teaches openly at the Temple                              |           |          |          | 7:10-31 |
| 124. Religious leaders attempt to arrest Jesus                       |           |          |          | 7:32-52 |
| 125. Jesus forgives an adulterous woman                              |           |          |          | 8:1-11  |
| 126. Jesus is the light of the world                                 |           |          |          | 8:12-20 |
| 127. Jesus warns of coming judgment                                  |           |          |          | 8:21-30 |
| 128. Jesus speaks about God's true children                          |           |          |          | 8:31-47 |
| 129. Jesus states he is eternal                                      |           |          |          | 8:48-59 |
| 130. Jesus sends out seventy-two messengers                          |           |          | 10:1-16  |         |
| 131. The seventy-two messengers return                               |           |          | 10:17-24 |         |
| 132. Jesus tells the parable of the Good Samaritan                   |           |          | 10:25-37 |         |
| 133. Jesus visits Martha and Mary                                    |           |          | 10:38-42 |         |
| 134. Jesus teaches his disciples about prayer                        |           |          | 11:1-13  |         |
| 135. Jesus answers hostile accusations                               |           |          | 11:14-28 |         |
| 136. Jesus warns against unbelief                                    |           |          | 11:29-32 |         |
| 137. Jesus teaches about the light within                            |           |          | 11:33-36 |         |
| 138. Jesus criticizes the religious leaders                          |           |          | 11:37-54 |         |
| 139. Jesus speaks against hypocrisy                                  |           |          | 12:1-12  |         |
| 140. Jesus tells the parable of the rich fool                        |           |          | 12:13-21 |         |
| 141. Jesus warns about worry                                         |           |          | 12:22-34 |         |
| 142. Jesus warns about preparing for his coming                      |           |          | 12:35-48 |         |
| 143. Jesus warns about coming division                               |           |          | 12:49-53 |         |
| 144. Jesus warns about the future crisis                             |           |          | 12:54-59 |         |
| 145. Jesus calls the people to repent                                |           |          | 13:1-9   |         |
| 146. Jesus heals the crippled woman                                  |           |          | 13:10-17 |         |
| 147. Jesus teaches about the Kingdom of God                          |           |          | 13:18-21 |         |
| 148. Jesus heals the man who was born blind                          |           |          |          | 9:1-12  |
| 149. Religious leaders question the blind man                        |           |          |          | 9:13-34 |

|                                                                      | Matthew | Mark | Luke | John |
|----------------------------------------------------------------------|---------|------|------|------|
| 150. Jesus teaches about spiritual blindness                         |         |      |      | 9:35-41 |
| 151. Jesus is the good shepherd                                      |         |      |      | 10:1-21 |
| 152. Religious leaders surround Jesus at the Temple                  |         |      |      | 10:22-42 |
| 153. Jesus teaches about entering the Kingdom                        |         |      | 13:22-30 | |
| 154. Jesus grieves over Jerusalem                                    |         |      | 13:31-35 | |
| 155. Jesus heals a man with swollen limbs                            |         |      | 14:1-6 | |
| 156. Jesus teaches about humility                                    |         |      | 14:7-14 | |
| 157. Jesus tells the parable of the great feast                      |         |      | 14:15-24 | |
| 158. Jesus teaches about the cost of being a disciple                |         |      | 14:25-35 | |
| 159. Jesus tells the parable of the lost sheep                       |         |      | 15:1-7 | |
| 160. Jesus tells the parable of the lost coin                        |         |      | 15:8-10 | |
| 161. Jesus tells the parable of the lost son                         |         |      | 15:11-32 | |
| 162. Jesus tells the parable of the shrewd manager                   |         |      | 16:1-18 | |
| 163. Jesus tells about the rich man and the beggar                   |         |      | 16:19-31 | |
| 164. Jesus tells about forgiveness and faith                         |         |      | 17:1-10 | |
| 165. Lazarus becomes sick and dies                                   |         |      |      | 11:1-16 |
| 166. Jesus comforts Mary and Martha                                  |         |      |      | 11:17-37 |
| 167. Jesus raises Lazarus from the dead                              |         |      |      | 11:38-44 |
| 168. Religious leaders plot to kill Jesus                            |         |      |      | 11:45-57 |
| 169. Jesus heals ten men with leprosy                                |         |      | 17:11-19 | |
| 170. Jesus teaches about the coming of the Kingdom of God            |         |      | 17:20-37 | |
| 171. Jesus tells the parable of the persistent widow                 |         |      | 18:1-8 | |
| 172. Jesus tells the parable of two men who prayed                   |         |      | 18:9-14 | |
| 173. Jesus teaches about marriage and divorce                        | 19:1-12 | 10:1-12 | | |
| 174. Jesus blesses the children                                      | 19:13-15 | 10:13-16 | 18:15-17 | |
| 175. Jesus speaks to the rich young man                              | 19:16-30 | 10:17-31 | 18:18-30 | |
| 176. Jesus tells the parable of the vineyard workers                 | 20:1-16 | | | |
| 177. Jesus predicts his death the third time                         | 20:17-19 | 10:32-34 | 18:31-34 | |
| 178. Jesus teaches about serving others                              | 20:20-28 | 10:35-45 | | |
| 179. Jesus heals a blind beggar                                      | 20:29-34 | 10:46-52 | 18:35-43 | |
| 180. Jesus brings salvation to Zacchaeus's home                      |         |      | 19:1-10 | |
| 181. Jesus tells the parable of the king's ten servants              |         |      | 19:11-27 | |
| 182. A woman anoints Jesus with perfume                              | 26:6-13 | 14:3-9 | | 12:1-11 |
| 183. Jesus rides into Jerusalem on a young donkey                    | 21:1-11 | 11:1-11 | 19:28-44 | 12:12-19 |
| 184. Jesus clears the Temple again                                   | 21:12-17 | 11:12-19 | 19:45-48 | |
| 185. Jesus explains why he must die                                  |         |      |      | 12:20-36 |
| 186. Most of the people do not believe in Jesus                      |         |      |      | 12:37-43 |
| 187. Jesus summarizes his message                                    |         |      |      | 12:44-50 |
| 188. Jesus says the disciples can pray for anything                  | 21:18-22 | 11:20-26 | | |
| 189. Religious leaders challenge Jesus' authority                    | 21:23-27 | 11:27-33 | 20:1-8 | |
| 190. Jesus tells the parable of the two sons                         | 21:28-32 | | | |
| 191. Jesus tells the parable of the evil farmers                     | 21:33-46 | 12:1-12 | 20:9-19 | |
| 192. Jesus tells the parable of the wedding feast                    | 22:1-14 | | | |
| 193. Religious leaders question Jesus about paying taxes             | 22:15-22 | 12:13-17 | 20:20-26 | |
| 194. Religious leaders question Jesus about the resurrection         | 22:23-33 | 12:18-27 | 20:27-40 | |
| 195. Religious leaders question Jesus about the greatest commandment | 22:34-40 | 12:28-34 | | |
| 196. Religious leaders cannot answer Jesus' question                 | 22:41-46 | 12:35-37 | 20:41-44 | |
| 197. Jesus warns against the religious leaders                       | 23:1-12 | 12:38-40 | 20:45-47 | |
| 198. Jesus condemns the religious leaders                            | 23:13-36 | | | |
| 199. Jesus grieves over Jerusalem again                              | 23:37-39 | | | |
| 200. A poor widow gives all she has                                  |         | 12:41-44 | 21:1-4 | |
| 201. Jesus tells about the future                                    | 24:1-25 | 13:1-23 | 21:5-24 | |
| 202. Jesus tells about his return                                    | 24:26-35 | 13:24-31 | 21:25-33 | |
| 203. Jesus tells about remaining watchful                            | 24:36-51 | 13:32-37 | 21:34-38 | |
| 204. Jesus tells the parable of the ten bridesmaids                  | 25:1-13 | | | |
| 205. Jesus tells the parable of the loaned money                     | 25:14-30 | | | |
| 206. Jesus tells about the final judgment                            | 25:31-46 | | | |

## III. DEATH AND RESURRECTION OF JESUS CHRIST

| | | | | |
|---|---|---|---|---|
| 207. Religious leaders plot to kill Jesus | 26:1-5 | 14:1, 2 | 22:1, 2 | |
| 208. Judas agrees to betray Jesus | 26:14-16 | 14:10, 11 | 22:3-6 | |
| 209. Disciples prepare for the Passover | 26:17-19 | 14:12-16 | 22:7-13 | |

|  | Matthew | Mark | Luke | John |
|---|---|---|---|---|
| 210. Jesus washes the disciples' feet |  |  |  | 13:1-20 |
| 211. Jesus and the disciples share the Last Supper | 26:20-30 | 14:17-26 | 22:14-30 | 13:21-30 |
| 212. Jesus predicts Peter's denial |  |  | 22:31-38 | 13:31-38 |
| 213. Jesus is the way to the Father |  |  |  | 14:1-14 |
| 214. Jesus promises the Holy Spirit |  |  |  | 14:15-31 |
| 215. Jesus teaches about the vine and the branches |  |  |  | 15:1-17 |
| 216. Jesus warns about the world's hatred |  |  |  | 15:18–16:4 |
| 217. Jesus teaches about the Holy Spirit |  |  |  | 16:5-15 |
| 218. Jesus teaches about using his name in prayer |  |  |  | 16:16-33 |
| 219. Jesus prays for himself |  |  |  | 17:1-5 |
| 220. Jesus prays for his disciples |  |  |  | 17:6-19 |
| 221. Jesus prays for future believers |  |  |  | 17:20-26 |
| 222. Jesus again predicts Peter's denial | 26:31-35 | 14:27-31 |  |  |
| 223. Jesus agonizes in the garden | 26:36-46 | 14:32-42 | 22:39-46 |  |
| 224. Jesus is betrayed and arrested | 26:47-56 | 14:43-52 | 22:47-53 | 18:1-11 |
| 225. Annas questions Jesus |  |  |  | 18:12-24 |
| 226. Caiaphas questions Jesus | 26:57-68 | 14:53-65 |  |  |
| 227. Peter denies knowing Jesus | 26:69-75 | 14:66-72 | 22:54-65 | 18:25-27 |
| 228. The council of religious leaders condemns Jesus | 27:1, 2 | 15:1 | 22:66-71 |  |
| 229. Judas hangs himself | 27:3-10 |  |  |  |
| 230. Jesus stands trial before Pilate | 27:11-14 | 15:2-5 | 23:1-5 | 18:28-37 |
| 231. Jesus stands trial before Herod |  |  | 23:6-12 |  |
| 232. Pilate hands Jesus over to be crucified | 27:15-26 | 15:6-15 | 23:13-25 | 18:38–19:16 |
| 233. Roman soldiers mock Jesus | 27:27-31 | 15:16-20 |  |  |
| 234. Jesus is led away to be crucified | 27:32-34 | 15:21-24 | 23:26-31 | 19:17 |
| 235. Jesus is placed on the cross | 27:35-44 | 15:25-32 | 23:32-43 | 19:18-27 |
| 236. Jesus dies on the cross | 27:45-56 | 15:33-41 | 23:44-49 | 19:28-37 |
| 237. Jesus is laid in the tomb | 27:57-61 | 15:42-47 | 23:50-56 | 19:38-42 |
| 238. Guards are posted at the tomb | 27:62-66 |  |  |  |
| 239. Jesus rises from the dead | 28:1-7 | 16:1-8 | 24:1-12 | 20:1-10 |
| 240. Jesus appears to Mary Magdalene |  | 16:9-11 |  | 20:11-18 |
| 241. Jesus appears to the women | 28:8-10 |  |  |  |
| 242. Religious leaders bribe the guards | 28:11-15 |  |  |  |
| 243. Jesus appears to two believers traveling on the road |  | 16:12, 13 | 24:13-34 |  |
| 244. Jesus appears to his disciples |  |  | 24:35-43 | 20:19-23 |
| 245. Jesus appears to Thomas |  | 16:14 |  | 20:24-31 |
| 246. Jesus appears to seven disciples |  |  |  | 21:1-14 |
| 247. Jesus challenges Peter |  |  |  | 21:15-25 |
| 248. Jesus gives the great commission | 28:16-20 | 16:15-18 |  |  |
| 249. Jesus appears to the disciples in Jerusalem |  |  | 24:44-49 |  |
| 250. Jesus ascends into heaven |  | 16:19, 20 | 24:50-53 |  |

**COMPARISON OF THE FOUR GOSPELS**

All four Gospels present the life and teachings of Jesus. Each book, however, focuses on a unique facet of Jesus and his character. To understand more about the specific characteristics of Jesus, read any one of the four Gospels.

|  | Matthew | Mark | Luke | John |
|---|---|---|---|---|
| Jesus is . . . | The promised King | The Servant of God | The Son of Man | The Son of God |
| The original readers were . . . | Jews | Gentiles, Romans | Greeks | Christians throughout the world |
| Significant themes . . . | Jesus is the Messiah because he fulfilled Old Testament prophecy | Jesus backed up his words with action | Jesus was God but also fully human | Belief in Jesus is required for salvation |
| Character of the writer . . . | Teacher | Storyteller | Historian | Theologian |
| Greatest emphasis is on . . . | Jesus' sermons and words | Jesus' miracles and actions | Jesus' humanity | The principles of Jesus' teaching |

I. Teaching Parables
  A. About the Kingdom of God
    1. The Soils (Matthew 13:3-8; Mark 4:3-8; Luke 8:5-8)
    2. The Weeds (Matthew 13:24-30)
    3. The Mustard Seed (Matthew 13:31, 32; Mark 4:30-32; Luke 13:18, 19)
    4. The Yeast (Matthew 13:33; Luke 13:20, 21)
    5. The Treasure (Matthew 13:44)
    6. The Pearl (Matthew 13:45, 46)
    7. The Fishing Net (Matthew 13:47-50)
    8. The Growing Seed (Mark 4:26-29)
  B. About Service and Obedience
    1. The Workers in the Vineyard (Matthew 20:1-16)
    2. The Loaned Money (Matthew 25:14-30)
    3. The Nobleman's Servants (Luke 19:11-27)
    4. The Servant's Role (Luke 17:7-10)
  C. About Prayer
    1. The Friend at Midnight (Luke 11:5-8)
    2. The Unjust Judge (Luke 18:1-8)
  D. About Neighbors
    1. The Good Samaritan (Luke 10:30-37)
  E. About Humility
    1. The Wedding Feast (Luke 14:7-11)
    2. The Proud Pharisee and the Corrupt Tax Collector (Luke 18:9-14)
  F. About Wealth
    1. The Rich Fool (Luke 12:16-21)
    2. The Great Feast (Luke 14:16-24)
    3. The Shrewd Manager (Luke 16:1-9)
II. Gospel Parables
  A. About God's Love
    1. The Lost Sheep (Matthew 18:12-14; Luke 15:3-7)
    2. The Lost Coin (Luke 15:8-10)
    3. The Lost Son (Luke 15:11-32)
  B. About Thankfulness
    1. The Forgiven Debts (Luke 7:41-43)
III. Parables of Judgment and the Future
  A. About Christ's Return
    1. The Ten Bridesmaids (Matthew 25:1-13)
    2. The Faithful and Sensible Servants (Matthew 24:45-51; Luke 12:42-48)
    3. The Traveling Homeowner (Mark 13:34-37)
  B. About God's Values
    1. The Two Sons (Matthew 21:28-32)
    2. The Evil Farmers (Matthew 21:33-41; Mark 12:1-9; Luke 20:9-16)
    3. The Unproductive Fig Tree (Luke 13:6-9)
    4. The Wedding Feast (Matthew 22:1-14)
    5. The Unforgiving Debtor (Matthew 18:23-35)

**THE PARABLES
OF JESUS**

**JESUS' MIRACLES**

John and the other Gospel writers were able to record only a fraction of the people who were touched and healed by Jesus. But enough of Jesus' words and works have been saved so that we also might be able to know him and be his disciples in this day. Here is a list of the miracles that are included in the Gospels. They were supernatural events that pointed people to God, and they were acts of love by one who is love.

|                                          | Matthew        | Mark             | Luke            | John    |
|------------------------------------------|----------------|------------------|-----------------|---------|
| Five thousand people are fed             | 14:15-21       | 6:35-44          | 9:12-17         | 6:5-14  |
| Calming the storm                        | 8:23-27        | 4:35-41          | 8:22-25         |         |
| Demons sent into the pigs                | 8:28-34        | 5:1-20           | 8:26-39         |         |
| Jairus's daughter raised                 | 9:18, 23-26    | 5:22-24, 35-43   | 8:41, 42, 49-56 |         |
| A sick woman is healed                   | 9:20-22        | 5:25-34          | 8:43-48         |         |
| Jesus heals a paralytic                  | 9:1-8          | 2:1-12           | 5:17-26         |         |
| A leper is healed at Gennesaret          | 8:1-4          | 1:40-45          | 5:12-15         |         |
| Peter's mother-in-law healed             | 8:14-17        | 1:29-31          | 4:38, 39        |         |
| A deformed hand is restored              | 12:9-13        | 3:1-5            | 6:6-10          |         |
| A boy with an evil spirit is healed      | 17:14-21       | 9:14-29          | 9:37-42         |         |
| Jesus walks on the water                 | 14:22-33       | 6:45-52          |                 | 6:16-21 |
| Blind Bartimaeus receives sight          | 20:29-34       | 10:46-52         | 18:35-43        |         |
| A girl is freed from a demon             | 15:21-28       | 7:24-30          |                 |         |
| Four thousand are fed                    | 15:32-38       | 8:1-9            |                 |         |
| Cursing the fig tree                     | 21:18-22       | 11:12-14, 20-24  |                 |         |
| A Roman officer's servant is healed      | 8:5-13         |                  | 7:1-10          |         |
| An evil spirit is sent out of a man      |                | 1:23-27          | 4:33-36         |         |
| A mute demoniac is healed                | 12:22          |                  | 11:14           |         |
| Two blind men find sight                 | 9:27-31        |                  |                 |         |
| Jesus heals the mute man                 | 9:32, 33       |                  |                 |         |
| A coin in a fish's mouth                 | 17:24-27       |                  |                 |         |
| A deaf and mute man is healed            |                | 7:31-37          |                 |         |
| A blind man sees at Bethsaida            |                | 8:22-26          |                 |         |
| The first miraculous catch of fish       |                |                  | 5:1-11          |         |
| A widow's son is raised                  |                |                  | 7:11-16         |         |
| A crippled woman is healed               |                |                  | 13:10-17        |         |
| Jesus heals a sick man                   |                |                  | 14:1-6          |         |
| Ten lepers are healed                    |                |                  | 17:11-19        |         |
| Jesus restores a man's ear               |                |                  | 22:49-51        |         |
| Jesus turns water into wine              |                |                  |                 | 2:1-11  |
| An official's son is healed at Cana      |                |                  |                 | 4:46-54 |
| A lame man is healed                     |                |                  |                 | 5:1-16  |
| Jesus heals a man born blind             |                |                  |                 | 9:1-7   |
| Lazarus is raised from the dead          |                |                  |                 | 11:1-45 |
| The second miraculous catch of fish      |                |                  |                 | 21:1-14 |

| | Old Testament Prophecies | New Testament Fulfillment |
|---|---|---|
| 1. Messiah was to be born in Bethlehem | Micah 5:2 | Matthew 2:1-6<br>Luke 2:1-20 |
| 2. Messiah was to be born of a virgin | Isaiah 7:14 | Matthew 1:18-25<br>Luke 1:26-38 |
| 3. Messiah was to be a prophet like Moses | Deuteronomy 18:15, 18, 19 | John 7:40 |
| 4. Messiah was to enter Jerusalem in triumph | Zechariah 9:9 | Matthew 21:1-9<br>John 12:12-16 |
| 5. Messiah was to be rejected by his own people | Isaiah 53:1, 3 | Matthew 26:3, 4<br>John 12:37-43<br>Acts 4:1-12 |
| 6. Messiah was to be betrayed by one of his followers | Psalm 118:22<br>Psalm 41:9 | Matthew 26:14-16, 47-50<br>Luke 22:19-23 |
| 7. Messiah was to be tried and condemned | Isaiah 53:8 | Matthew 27:1, 2<br>Luke 23:1-25 |
| 8. Messiah was to be silent before his accusers | Isaiah 53:7 | Matthew 27:12-14<br>Mark 15:3, 4<br>Luke 23:8-10 |
| 9. Messiah was to be struck and spat on by his enemies | Isaiah 50:6 | Matthew 26:67; 27:30<br>Mark 14:65 |
| 10. Messiah was to be mocked and insulted | Psalm 22:7, 8 | Matthew 27:39-44<br>Luke 23:11, 35 |
| 11. Messiah was to die by crucifixion | Psalm 22:14, 16, 17 | Matthew 27:31<br>Mark 15:20, 25 |
| 12. Messiah was to suffer with criminals and pray for his enemies | Isaiah 53:12 | Matthew 27:38<br>Mark 15:27, 28<br>Luke 23:32-34 |
| 13. Messiah was to be given sour wine | Psalm 69:21 | Matthew 27:34<br>John 19:28-30 |
| 14. Others were to throw dice for Messiah's garments | Psalm 22:18 | Matthew 27:35<br>John 19:23, 24 |
| 15. Messiah's bones were not to be broken | Exodus 12:46 | John 19:31-36 |
| 16. Messiah was to die as a sacrifice for sin | Isaiah 53:5, 6, 8, 10, 11, 12 | John 1:29; 11:49-52<br>Acts 10:43; 13:38, 39 |
| 17. Messiah was to be raised from the dead | Psalm 16:10 | Matthew 28:1-10<br>Acts 2:22-32 |
| 18. Messiah is now at God's right hand | Psalm 110:1 | Mark 16:19<br>Luke 24:50, 51 |

**MESSIANIC PROPHECIES AND FULFILLMENTS**

For the Gospel writers, one of the main reasons for believing in Jesus was the way his life fulfilled the Old Testament prophecies about the Messiah. Following is a list of some of the main prophecies.

# KEY PLACES IN ACTS

Modern names and boundaries are shown in gray.

The apostle Paul, whose missionary journeys fill much of this book, traveled tremendous distances as he tirelessly spread the gospel across much of the Roman Empire. His combined trips, by land and sea, equal more than 13,000 air miles.

**1 Judea**  Jesus ascended to heaven from the Mount of Olives, outside Jerusalem, and his followers returned to the city to await the infilling of the Holy Spirit, which occurred at Pentecost. Peter gave a powerful sermon that was heard by Jews from across the empire. The Jerusalem church grew, but Stephen was martyred for his faith by Jewish leaders who did not believe in Jesus (1:1—7:60).

**2 Samaria**  After Stephen's death, persecution of Christians intensified, but it caused the believers to leave Jerusalem and spread the gospel to other cities in the empire. Philip took the gospel into Samaria, and even to a man from Ethiopia (8:1–40).

**3 Syria**  Paul (Saul) began his story as a persecutor of Christians, only to be met by Jesus himself on the road to Damascus. He became a believer, but his new faith caused opposition, so he returned to Tarsus, his home, for safety. Barnabas sought out Paul in Tarsus and brought him to the church in Antioch of Syria, where they worked together. Meanwhile, Peter had received a vision that led him to Caesarea, where he presented the gospel to a Gentile family, who became believers (9:1—12:25).

**4 Cyprus and Galatia**  Paul and Barnabas were dedicated by the church in Antioch of Syria for God's work of spreading the gospel to other cities. They set off on their first missionary journey through Cyprus and Galatia (13:1—14:28).

**5 Jerusalem**  Controversy between Jewish Christians and Gentile Christians over the matter of keeping the law led to a special council, with delegates from the churches in Antioch and Jerusalem meeting in Jerusalem. Together, they resolved the conflict and the news was taken back to Antioch (15:1–35).

**6 Macedonia**  Barnabas traveled to Cyprus while Paul took a second missionary journey. He revisited the churches in Galatia and headed toward Ephesus, but the Holy Spirit said no. So he turned north toward Bithynia and Pontus but again was told not to go. He then received the "Macedonian call," and followed the Spirit's direction into the cities of Macedonia (15:36—17:14).

**7 Achaia**  Paul traveled from Macedonia to Athens and Corinth in Achaia, then traveled by ship to Ephesus before returning to Caesarea, Jerusalem, and finally back to Antioch (17:15—18:22).

**8 Ephesus**  Paul's third missionary journey took him back through Cilicia and Galatia, this time straight to Ephesus in Asia. He visited other cities in Asia before going back to Macedonia and Achaia. He returned to Jerusalem by ship, despite his knowledge that arrest awaited him there (18:23—23:30).

**9 Caesarea**  Paul was arrested in Jerusalem and taken to Antipatris, then on to Caesarea under Roman guard. Paul always took advantage of any opportunity to share the gospel, and he did so before many Gentile leaders. Because Paul appealed his case to Caesar, he began the long journey to Rome (23:31—26:32).

**10 Rome**  After storms, layovers in Crete, and shipwreck on the island of Malta, Paul arrived in Sicily and finally in Italy, where he traveled by land, under guard, to his long-awaited destination: Rome, the capital of the empire (27:1—28:31).

# ACTS

## VITAL STATISTICS

**PURPOSE:**
To give an accurate account of the birth and growth of the Christian church

**AUTHOR:**
Luke (a Gentile physician)

**ORIGINAL AUDIENCE:**
Theophilus

**DATE WRITTEN:**
Between A.D. 63 and 70

**SETTING:**
Acts is the connecting link between Christ's life and the life of the church, between the Gospels and the Letters.

**KEY VERSE:**
"But you will receive power when the Holy Spirit comes upon you. And you will be my witnesses, telling people about me everywhere—in Jerusalem, throughout Judea, in Samaria, and to the ends of the earth" (1:8).

**KEY PEOPLE:**
Peter, John, James, Stephen, Philip, Paul, Barnabas, Cornelius, James (Jesus' brother), Timothy, Lydia, Silas, Titus, Apollos, Agabus, Ananias, Felix, Festus, Agrippa, Luke

**KEY PLACES:**
Jerusalem, Samaria, Lydda, Joppa, Antioch, Cyprus, Pisidian Antioch, Iconium, Lystra, Derbe, Philippi, Thessalonica, Berea, Athens, Corinth, Ephesus, Caesarea, Malta, Rome

**SPECIAL FEATURES:**
Acts is a sequel to the Gospel of Luke. Because Acts ends so abruptly, Luke may have planned to write a third book, continuing the story.

WITH a flick of a match, friction occurs and a spark leaps from match to tinder. A small flame burns the edges and grows, fueled by wood and air. Heat builds, and soon the kindling is licked by reddish orange tongues. Higher and wider it spreads, consuming the wood. The flame has become a fire.

Nearly 2,000 years ago, a match was struck in Palestine. At first, just a few in that corner of the world were touched and warmed, but the fire spread beyond Jerusalem and Judea out to the world and to all people. Acts provides an eyewitness account of the flame and fire—the birth and spread of the church. Beginning in Jerusalem with a small group of disciples, the message traveled across the Roman Empire. Empowered by the Holy Spirit, this courageous band preached, taught, healed, and demonstrated love in synagogues, schools, homes, marketplaces, and courtrooms, and on streets, hills, ships, and desert roads—wherever God sent them, lives and history were changed.

Written by Luke as a sequel to his Gospel, Acts is an accurate historical record of the early church. But Acts is also a theological book, with lessons and living examples of the work of the Holy Spirit, church relationships and organization, the implications of grace, and the law of love. And Acts is an apologetic work, building a strong case for the validity of Christ's claims and promises.

The book of Acts begins with the outpouring of the promised Holy Spirit and the commencement of the proclamation of the gospel of Jesus Christ. This Spirit-inspired evangelism began in Jerusalem and eventually spread to Rome, covering most of the Roman Empire. The gospel first went to the Jews, but they, as a nation, rejected it. A remnant of Jews, of course, gladly received the Good News. But the continual rejection of the gospel by the vast majority of the Jews led to the ever-increasing proclamation of the gospel to the Gentiles. This was according to Jesus' plan: The gospel was to go from Jerusalem, to Judea, to Samaria, and to the ends of the earth (1:8). This, in fact, is the pattern that the Acts narrative follows. The glorious proclamation began in Jerusalem (chapters 1—7), went to Judea and Samaria (chapters 8 and following), and to the countries beyond Judea (11:19; 13:4 and on to the end of Acts). The second half of Acts is focused primarily on Paul's missionary journeys to many countries north of the Mediterranean Sea. He, with his companions, took the gospel first to the Jews and then to the Gentiles. Some of the Jews believed, and many of the Gentiles received the Good News with joy. New churches were started, and new believers began to grow in the Christian life.

As you read Acts, put yourself in the place of the disciples: Identify with them as they are filled with the Holy Spirit, and experience the thrill of seeing thousands respond to the gospel message. Sense their commitment as they give every ounce of talent and treasure to Christ. And as you read, watch the Spirit-led boldness of these first-century believers, who through suffering and in the face of death take every opportunity to tell of their crucified and risen Lord. Then decide to be a twenty-first-century version of those men and women of God.

| Paul's third missionary journey 53–57 | Nero becomes emperor 54 | Paul imprisoned in Caesarea 57–59 | Paul's journey to Rome 59 | Paul released from prison 62 | Paul martyred 67? | Rome destroys Jerusalem 70 |
| --- | --- | --- | --- | --- | --- | --- |

## THE BLUEPRINT

A. PETER'S MINISTRY
(1:1—12:25)
  1. Establishment of the church
  2. Expansion of the church

After the resurrection of Jesus Christ, Peter preached boldly and performed many miracles. Peter's actions demonstrate vividly the source and effects of Christian power. Because of the Holy Spirit, God's people were empowered so they could accomplish their tasks. The Holy Spirit is still available to empower believers today. We should turn to the Holy Spirit to give us the strength, courage, and insight to accomplish our work for God.

B. PAUL'S MINISTRY
(13:1—28:31)
  1. First missionary journey
  2. The council at Jerusalem
  3. Second missionary journey
  4. Third missionary journey
  5. Paul on trial

Paul's missionary adventures show us the progress of Christianity. The gospel could not be confined to one corner of the world. This was a faith that offered hope to all humanity. We, too, should venture forth and share in this heroic task to witness for Christ in all the world.

## MEGATHEMES

| THEME | EXPLANATION | IMPORTANCE |
| --- | --- | --- |
| Church Beginnings | Acts is the history of how Christianity was founded and organized and solved its problems. The community of believers began by faith in the risen Christ and in the power of the Holy Spirit, who enabled them to witness, to love, and to serve. | New churches are continually being founded. By faith in Jesus Christ and through the power of the Holy Spirit, the church can be a vibrant agent for change. As we face new problems, Acts gives important remedies for solving them. |
| Holy Spirit | The church did not start or grow by its own power or enthusiasm. The disciples were empowered by God's Holy Spirit. He was the promised Advocate and Guide sent when Jesus went to heaven. | The Holy Spirit's work demonstrated that Christianity was supernatural. Thus, the church became more Holy Spirit conscious than problem conscious. By faith, any believer can claim the Holy Spirit's power to do Christ's work. |
| Church Growth | Acts presents the history of a dynamic, growing community of believers from Jerusalem to Syria, Africa, Asia, and Europe. In the first century, Christianity spread from believing Jews to non-Jews in 39 cities and 30 countries, islands, or provinces. | When the Holy Spirit works, there is movement, excitement, and growth. He gives us the motivation, energy, and ability to get the gospel to the whole world. How are you fitting into God's plan for spreading Christianity? What is your place in this movement? |
| Witnessing | Peter, John, Philip, Paul, Barnabas, and thousands more witnessed to their new faith in Christ. By personal testimony, preaching, or defense before authorities, they told the story with boldness and courage to groups of all sizes. | We are God's people, chosen to be part of his plan to reach the world. In love and by faith, we can have the Holy Spirit's help as we witness or preach. Witnessing is also beneficial to us because it strengthens our faith as we confront those who challenge it. |
| Opposition | Through imprisonment, beatings, plots, and riots, Christians were persecuted by both Jews and Gentiles. But the opposition became a catalyst for the spread of Christianity. Growth during times of oppression showed that Christianity was not the work of humans, but of God. | God can work through any opposition. When persecution from hostile unbelievers comes, realize that it has come because you have been a faithful witness and you have looked for the opportunity to present the Good News about Christ. Seize the opportunities that opposition brings. |

## A. PETER'S MINISTRY (1:1—12:25)

The book of Acts begins where the Gospels leave off, reporting the actions of the apostles and the work of the Holy Spirit. Beginning in Jerusalem, the church is established and grows rapidly, then faces intense persecution, which drives the believers out into the surrounding areas. Through this dispersion, Samaritans and Gentiles hear the Good News and believe.

### 1. Establishment of the church

*The Promise of the Holy Spirit*

**1** In my first book* I told you, Theophilus, about everything Jesus began to do and teach ²until the day he was taken up to heaven after giving his chosen apostles further instructions through the Holy Spirit. ³During the forty days after his crucifixion, he appeared to the apostles from time to time, and he proved to them in many ways that he was actually alive. And he talked to them about the Kingdom of God.

⁴Once when he was eating with them, he commanded them, "Do not leave Jerusalem until the Father sends you the gift he promised, as I told you before. ⁵John baptized with* water, but in just a few days you will be baptized with the Holy Spirit."

*The Ascension of Jesus*

⁶So when the apostles were with Jesus, they kept asking him, "Lord, has the time come for you to free Israel and restore our kingdom?"

1:1 The reference is to the Gospel of Luke.   1:5 Or *in;* also in 1:5b.

**1:1**
Luke 1:3
**1:3**
Luke 24:33-36
John 20:19, 26;
21:1, 14
**1:4**
Luke 24:49
John 14:16-17, 26
Acts 2:33
**1:5**
Luke 3:16

---

**1:1** In the book of Acts, Luke continues the story he began in his Gospel, covering the 30 years after Jesus was taken up into heaven. During that short time the church was established, and the Good News of salvation was spread throughout the world, even to the capital of the Roman Empire. Those preaching the Good News, though ordinary people with human frailties and limitations, were empowered by the Holy Spirit to take it all over the world. In the book of Acts we learn about the nature of the church and how we, like these early believers, can turn our world upside down (17:6).

**1:1ff** Verses 1-11 are the bridge between the events recorded in the Gospels and the events marking the beginning of the church. Jesus spent 40 days teaching his disciples, and they were drastically changed. Before the Resurrection, they had argued with each other and had deserted their Lord. One of them (Peter) even lied about knowing Jesus. Here, in a series of meetings with the living, resurrected Christ, the disciples had many questions answered. They became convinced of the Resurrection, learned about the Kingdom of God, and discovered their power source—the Holy Spirit. By reading the Bible, we can sit with the resurrected Christ in his school of discipleship. By believing in him, we can receive his power through the Holy Spirit to be new people. By joining with other Christians, we can take part in doing his work on earth.

**1:1-3** Luke says that the disciples were eyewitnesses to all that had happened to Jesus Christ—his life before his crucifixion, and the 40 days after his resurrection as he taught them more about the Kingdom of God. Today people still doubt Jesus' resurrection. But Jesus appeared to the disciples on many occasions after his resurrection, proving that he was alive. Consider the change the Resurrection made in the disciples' lives. At Jesus' death, they had scattered, disillusioned, and fearing for their lives. After seeing the resurrected Christ, they became fearless and risked everything to spread the Good News about him around the world. They faced imprisonment, beatings, rejection, and martyrdom, yet they never compromised their mission. These men would not have risked—and in some cases, given—their lives for something they knew was a fraud. They knew Jesus was alive, and the early church was fired with their enthusiasm to tell others. We need to know this so we can have confidence in their testimony. Twenty centuries later we can still be confident that our faith is based on fact.

**1:3** Jesus explained that his coming inaugurated the Kingdom of God. When he returned to heaven, God's Kingdom would remain in the hearts of all believers through the presence of the Holy Spirit. But the Kingdom of God will not be fully realized until Jesus Christ returns to judge all people and remove all evil from the world. Until that time believers are to work to spread God's Kingdom across

the world. The book of Acts records how this work was begun. What the early church started, we must continue.

**1:4, 5** The *Trinity* is a description of the unique relationship of God the Father, the Son, and the Holy Spirit. If Jesus had stayed on earth, his physical presence would have limited the spread of the Good News because physically he could be in only one place at a time. After Christ was taken up into heaven, he would be spiritually present everywhere through the Holy Spirit. The Holy Spirit was sent so that God would be with and within his followers after Christ returned to heaven. The Spirit would comfort them, guide them to know his truth, remind them of Jesus' words, give them the right words to say, and fill them with power (see John 14–16).

**1:5** At Pentecost (2:1-4) the Holy Spirit was made available to all who believed in Jesus. We receive the Holy Spirit (are baptized with him) when we receive Jesus Christ as our Savior. The baptism of the Holy Spirit must be understood in the light of his total work in Christians.

(1) The Spirit marks the beginning of the Christian experience. We cannot be Christians without his Spirit (Romans 8:9); we cannot be joined to Christ without his Spirit (1 Corinthians 6:17); we cannot be adopted as his children without his Spirit (Romans 8:14-17; Galatians 4:6, 7); we cannot be in the body of Christ except by baptism in the Spirit (1 Corinthians 12:13).

(2) The Spirit is the power of our new lives. He begins a life-long process of change making us more like Christ (Galatians 3:3; Philippians 1:6). When we receive Christ by faith, we begin an immediate personal relationship with God. The Holy Spirit works in us to help us become like Christ.

(3) The Spirit unites the Christian community in Christ (Ephesians 2:19-22). The Holy Spirit can be experienced by all, and he works through all (1 Corinthians 12:11; Ephesians 4:4).

**1:6** During the years of Jesus' ministry on earth, the disciples continually wondered about his Kingdom. When would it come? What would be their role? In the traditional view, the Messiah would be an earthly conqueror who would free Israel from Rome. But the Kingdom Jesus spoke about was, first of all, a *spiritual* Kingdom established in the hearts and lives of believers (Luke 17:21). God's presence and power dwell in believers in the person of the Holy Spirit.

**1:6, 7** Like other Jews, the disciples chafed under their Roman rulers. They wanted Jesus to free Israel from Roman power and then become their king. Jesus replied that God the Father sets the timetable for all events—worldwide, national, and personal. If you want changes in your life that God hasn't yet made, don't become impatient. Instead, trust God's timetable.

**1:7**
Matt 24:36
1 Thes 5:1-2

**1:8**
Luke 24:48
John 15:27
Acts 2:1-4

**1:9**
Mark 16:19

**1:11**
Rev 1:7

**1:12**
Luke 24:50, 52

**1:13**
Matt 10:2-4
Mark 3:16-19
Luke 6:14-16

**1:14**
Acts 2:42

**1:16**
Ps 41:9

**1:17**
John 6:70-71
Acts 1:24-25

**1:18**
Matt 27:3-8

⁷He replied, "The Father alone has the authority to set those dates and times, and they are not for you to know. ⁸But you will receive power when the Holy Spirit comes upon you. And you will be my witnesses, telling people about me everywhere—in Jerusalem, throughout Judea, in Samaria, and to the ends of the earth."

⁹After saying this, he was taken up into a cloud while they were watching, and they could no longer see him. ¹⁰As they strained to see him rising into heaven, two white-robed men suddenly stood among them. ¹¹"Men of Galilee," they said, "why are you standing here staring into heaven? Jesus has been taken from you into heaven, but someday he will return from heaven in the same way you saw him go!"

## Matthias Replaces Judas

¹²Then the apostles returned to Jerusalem from the Mount of Olives, a distance of half a mile.* ¹³When they arrived, they went to the upstairs room of the house where they were staying.

Here are the names of those who were present: Peter, John, James, Andrew, Philip, Thomas, Bartholomew, Matthew, James (son of Alphaeus), Simon (the Zealot), and Judas (son of James). ¹⁴They all met together and were constantly united in prayer, along with Mary the mother of Jesus, several other women, and the brothers of Jesus.

¹⁵During this time, when about 120 believers* were together in one place, Peter stood up and addressed them. ¹⁶"Brothers," he said, "the Scriptures had to be fulfilled concerning Judas, who guided those who arrested Jesus. This was predicted long ago by the Holy Spirit, speaking through King David. ¹⁷Judas was one of us and shared in the ministry with us." ¹⁸(Judas had bought a field with the money he received for his treachery. Falling headfirst there, his body split open, spilling out all his intestines. ¹⁹The news of his death spread to all the people of Jerusalem, and they gave the place the Aramaic name *Akeldama,* which means "Field of Blood.")

**1:12** Greek *a Sabbath day's journey.*   **1:15** Greek *brothers.*

---

**1:8** The "power" believers receive from the Holy Spirit includes courage, boldness, confidence, insight, ability, and authority. The disciples would need all these gifts to fulfill their mission. If you believe in Jesus Christ as your Savior, you can experience the power of the Holy Spirit in your life.

**1:8** Jesus had instructed his disciples to witness to people of all nations about him (Matthew 28:19, 20). But they were told to wait first for the Holy Spirit (Luke 24:49). God has important work for you to do for him, but you must do it by the power of the Holy Spirit. We often like to get on with the job, even if it means running ahead of God. But waiting is sometimes part of God's plan. Are you waiting and listening for God's complete instructions, or are you running ahead of his plans? We need God's timing and power to be truly effective.

**1:8** This verse describes a series of ever-widening circles. The Good News was to spread, geographically, from Jerusalem, into Judea and Samaria, and finally to the ends of the earth. It would begin with the devout Jews in Jerusalem and Samaria, spread to the mixed race in Samaria, and, finally, be offered to Gentiles all over the world. God's Good News has not reached its final destination if someone in your family, your workplace, your school, or your community hasn't heard the Good News about Jesus Christ. Make sure that you are contributing in some way to the ever-widening circle of God's loving message.

**1:9-11** After 40 days with his disciples (1:3), Jesus returned to heaven. It was important for the disciples to see Jesus taken up into heaven; they knew without a doubt that he was God and that his home was in heaven. The two white-robed men were angels who proclaimed to the disciples that one day Jesus would return in the same way he had gone—bodily and visibly. History is not haphazard or cyclical; it is moving toward a specific point—the return of Jesus to judge and rule over the earth. We should be ready for his sudden return (1 Thessalonians 5:2), not by standing around "staring into heaven," but by working hard to share the Good News so that others will be able to share in God's great blessings.

**1:12, 13** After Christ was taken up into heaven, the disciples

immediately returned to Jerusalem and had a prayer meeting. Jesus had said they would be baptized with the Holy Spirit in a few days, so they waited and prayed. When you face a difficult task, an important decision, or a baffling dilemma, don't rush into the work and just hope it comes out the way it should. Instead, make your first step prayer for the Holy Spirit's power and guidance.

**1:13** A "Zealot" could mean anyone zealous for the Jewish law. The Zealots may have been a radical political party working for the violent overthrow of Roman rule in Israel.

**1:14** At this time, Jesus' brothers were with the disciples. During Jesus' lifetime, they had not believed he was the Messiah (John 7:5), but his resurrection must have convinced them. Jesus' special appearance to James, one of his brothers, may have been an especially significant event in their conversion (see 1 Corinthians 15:7).

**1:15-26** This was the first church business meeting. The small group of 11 had already grown to more than 120. The main order of business was to appoint a new disciple, or apostle, as the 11 were now called. While the apostles waited, they were doing what they could—praying, seeking God's guidance, and getting organized. Waiting for God to work does not mean sitting around doing nothing. We must do what we can, while we can, as long as we don't run ahead of God.

**1:16, 17** How could someone who had been with Jesus daily betray him? Judas had received the same calling and teaching as everyone else. But he had chosen to reject Christ. Judas hardened his heart and joined in the plot with Jesus' enemies to put him to death. Judas remained unrepentant to the end, and he finally committed suicide. Although Jesus predicted this would happen, it was Judas's choice. Those privileged to be *close* to the truth are not necessarily *committed* to the truth. See Judas's Profile in Mark 14, p. 1655 for more information on his life.

**1:18** Matthew says that Judas hanged himself (Matthew 27:5); Acts says that he fell. The traditional explanation is that when Judas hanged himself, the rope or branch broke, Judas fell, and his body burst open.

20Peter continued, "This was written in the book of Psalms, where it says, 'Let his home become desolate, with no one living in it.' It also says, 'Let someone else take his position.'*

21"So now we must choose a replacement for Judas from among the men who were with us the entire time we were traveling with the Lord Jesus—22from the time he was baptized by John until the day he was taken from us. Whoever is chosen will join us as a witness of Jesus' resurrection."

23So they nominated two men: Joseph called Barsabbas (also known as Justus) and Matthias. 24Then they all prayed, "O Lord, you know every heart. Show us which of these men you have chosen 25as an apostle to replace Judas in this ministry, for he has deserted us and gone where he belongs." 26Then they cast lots, and Matthias was selected to become an apostle with the other eleven.

### The Holy Spirit Comes

**2** On the day of Pentecost* all the believers were meeting together in one place. 2Suddenly, there was a sound from heaven like the roaring of a mighty windstorm, and it filled the house where they were sitting. 3Then, what looked like flames or tongues of fire appeared and settled on each of them. 4And everyone present was filled with the Holy Spirit and began speaking in other languages,* as the Holy Spirit gave them this ability.

5At that time there were devout Jews from every nation living in Jerusalem. 6When they heard the loud noise, everyone came running, and they were bewildered to hear their own languages being spoken by the believers.

7They were completely amazed. "How can this be?" they exclaimed. "These people are all from Galilee, 8and yet we hear them speaking in our own native languages! 9Here we are—Parthians, Medes, Elamites, people from Mesopotamia, Judea, Cappadocia, Pontus, the province of Asia, 10Phrygia, Pamphylia, Egypt, and the areas of Libya around Cyrene, visitors from Rome 11(both Jews and converts to Judaism), Cretans, and Arabs. And we all hear these people speaking in our own languages about the wonderful things God has done!" 12They stood there amazed and perplexed. "What can this mean?" they asked each other.

13But others in the crowd ridiculed them, saying, "They're just drunk, that's all!"

**1:20** Pss 69:25; 109:8.   **2:1** The Festival of Pentecost came 50 days after Passover (when Jesus was crucified).
**2:4** Or *in other tongues.*

**1:20**
†Pss 69:25; 109:8

**1:21-22**
Mark 1:9-11

**1:24**
Acts 6:6

**1:26**
Prov 16:33

**2:1**
Lev 23:15-21
Deut 16:9-11
Acts 1:14; 20:16

**2:2**
Acts 4:31

**2:4**
Mark 16:17
Acts 4:31;
10:44-46; 19:6
1 Cor 12:10; 13:1

**2:7**
Acts 1:11

**2:9**
Acts 16:6; 19:10
1 Pet 1:1

**2:10**
Matt 27:32
Acts 13:13; 16:6

**2:13**
1 Cor 14:23
Eph 5:18

---

**1:21, 22** Many consistently followed Jesus throughout his ministry on earth. The 12 disciples were his inner circle, but others shared the disciples' deep love for and commitment to Jesus.

**1:21-25** The apostles had to choose a replacement for Judas Iscariot. They outlined specific criteria for making the choice. After finalists were chosen, the apostles prayed, asking God to guide the selection process. This gives us a good example of how to proceed when we are making important decisions. Set up criteria consistent with the Bible, examine the alternatives, and pray for wisdom and guidance to reach a wise decision.

**1:26** The disciples became *apostles. Disciple* means "follower or learner," and *apostle* means "messenger or missionary." These men now had the special assignment of spreading the Good News of Jesus' death and resurrection.

**2:1** Held 50 days after Passover, Pentecost was also called the Festival of First Harvest. It was one of three major annual festivals (Deuteronomy 16:16), a festival of thanksgiving for the harvested crops. Jesus was crucified at Passover time, and he ascended 40 days after his resurrection. The Holy Spirit came 50 days after the Resurrection, 10 days after the Ascension. Jews of many nations had gathered in Jerusalem for this festival. Thus, Peter's speech (2:14ff) was given to an international audience, and it resulted in a worldwide harvest of new believers—the first converts to Christianity.

**2:3, 4** This was a fulfillment of John the Baptist's words about the Holy Spirit's baptizing with fire (Luke 3:16) and of the prophet Joel's words about the outpouring of the Holy Spirit (Joel 2:28, 29).

Why tongues of fire? Tongues symbolize speech and the communication of the Good News. Fire symbolizes God's purifying presence, which burns away the undesirable elements of our lives and sets our hearts aflame to ignite the lives of others. On Mount Sinai, God confirmed the validity of the Old Testament law with fire

from heaven (Exodus 19:16-18). At Pentecost, God confirmed the validity of the Holy Spirit's ministry by sending fire. At Mount Sinai, fire came down on one place; at Pentecost, fire came down on many believers, symbolizing that God's presence is available to all who believe in him.

**2:3, 4** God made his presence known to this group of believers in a spectacular way—roaring wind (2:2), fire, and his Holy Spirit. Would you like God to reveal himself to you in such recognizable ways? He may do so, but be wary of forcing your expectations on God. In 1 Kings 19:10-13, Elijah also needed a message from God. First came a great wind, then an earthquake, and finally a fire. But God's message came in a "gentle whisper." God may use dramatic methods to work in your life—or he may speak in gentle whispers. Wait patiently and always listen.

**2:4-11** These people literally spoke in other languages as the Spirit gave them ability—a miraculous attention-getter for the international crowd gathered in town for the festival. All the nationalities represented recognized their own languages being spoken. More than miraculous speaking drew people's attention, however; they saw the presence and power of the Holy Spirit. The apostles continued to minister in the Holy Spirit's power wherever they went.

**2:7, 8** Christianity is not limited to any race or group of people. Christ offers salvation to all people without regard to nationality. Visitors in Jerusalem were surprised to hear the apostles and other believers speaking in languages other than their own, but they need not have been. God works all kinds of miracles to spread the Good News, using many languages as he calls all kinds of people to become his followers. No matter what your race, color, nationality, or language, God speaks to you. Are you listening?

**2:9-11** Why are all these places mentioned? This is a list of many lands from which Jews had come to the festivals in Jerusalem. These Jews were not originally from Palestine because their

**A JOURNEY THROUGH THE BOOK OF ACTS**

Beginning with a brief summary of Jesus' last days on earth with his disciples, his ascension, and the selection of a replacement for Judas Iscariot, Luke moves quickly to his subject— the spread of the gospel and the growth of the church. Pentecost, highlighted by the filling of the Holy Spirit (2:1-13) and Peter's powerful sermon (2:14-42), was the beginning. Then the Jerusalem church grew daily through the bold witness of Peter and John and the love of the believers (2:43–4:37). The infant church was not without problems, however, with external opposition (resulting in imprisonment, beatings, and death) and internal deceit and complaining. Greek-speaking Jewish believers were appointed to help with the administration of the church to free the apostles to preach. Stephen and Philip were among the first deacons, and Stephen became the church's first martyr (5:1–8:3).

Instead of stopping Christianity, opposition and persecution served as catalysts for its spread because the believers took the message with them wherever they fled (8:4). Soon there were converts throughout **Samaria** and even in **Ethiopia** (8:5-40).

At this point, Luke introduces us to a bright young Jew, zealous for the law and intent on ridding Judaism of the Jesus heresy. But on the way to **Damascus** to capture believers, Saul was converted when he was confronted in person by the risen Christ (9:1-9). Through the ministry of Ananias and the sponsorship of Barnabas, Saul (Paul) was welcomed into the fellowship and then sent to **Tarsus** for safety (9:10-30).

Meanwhile, the church continued to thrive throughout **Judea, Galilee,** and **Samaria**. Luke recounts Peter's preaching and how Peter healed Aeneas in **Lydda** and Dorcas in **Joppa** (9:31-43). While in **Joppa,** Peter learned through a vision that he could take the gospel to the "unclean" Gentiles. Peter understood, and he faithfully shared the truth with Cornelius, whose entire household became believers (chapter 10). This was startling news to the **Jerusalem** church; but when Peter told his story, they praised God for his plan for *all* people to hear the Good News (11:1-18). This pushed the church into even wider circles as the message was preached to Greeks in **Antioch,** where Barnabas went to encourage the believers. Then he went on to **Tarsus** to find Saul (11:20-26).

To please the Jewish leaders, Herod joined in the persecution of the **Jerusalem** church, killing James (John's brother) and imprisoning Peter. But God freed Peter, and Peter walked from prison to a prayer meeting on his behalf at John Mark's house (chapter 12).

Here Luke shifts the focus to Paul's ministry. Commissioned by the **Antioch** church for a missionary tour (13:1-3), Paul and Barnabas took the gospel to **Cyprus** and south **Galatia** with great success (13:4–14:28). But the Jewish-Gentile controversy still smoldered, and with so many Gentiles responding to Christ, the controversy threatened to divide the church. So a council met in **Jerusalem** to rule on the relationship of Gentile Christians to the Old Testament laws. After hearing both sides, James (Jesus' brother and the leader of the Jerusalem church) resolved the issue and sent messengers to the churches with the decision (15:1-31).

After the council, Paul and Silas preached in **Antioch.** Then they left for **Syria** and **Cilicia** as Barnabas and Mark sailed for **Cyprus** (15:35-41). On this second missionary journey, Paul and Silas traveled throughout **Macedonia** and **Achaia,** establishing churches in **Philippi, Thessalonica, Berea, Corinth,** and **Ephesus** before returning to **Antioch** (16:1–18:22). Luke also tells of the ministry of Apollos (18:24-28).

On Paul's third missionary trip, he traveled through **Galatia, Phrygia, Macedonia,** and **Achaia,** encouraging and teaching the believers (19:1–21:9). During this time, he felt compelled to go to **Jerusalem;** and although he was warned by Agabus and others of impending imprisonment (21:10-12), he continued his journey in that direction.

While in **Jerusalem,** Paul was accosted in the Temple by an angry mob and taken into protective custody by the Roman commander (21:17–22:29). Now we see Paul as a prisoner and on trial before the Jewish high council (23:1-9), Governor Felix (23:23–24:27), and Festus and Agrippa (25:1–26:32). In each case, Paul gave a strong and clear witness for his Lord.

Because Paul appealed to Caesar, however, he was sent to **Rome** for the final hearing of his case. But on the way, the ship was destroyed in a storm, and the sailors and prisoners had to swim ashore. Even in this circumstance Paul shared his faith (27:1–28:10). Eventually the journey continued and Paul arrived in Rome, where he was held under house arrest while awaiting trial (28:11-31).

Luke ends Acts abruptly with the encouraging word that Paul had freedom in his captivity as he talked to visitors and guards, "boldly proclaiming the Kingdom of God and teaching about the Lord Jesus Christ. And no one tried to stop him" (28:31).

---

ancestors had been dispersed to other parts of the world through captivities and persecutions. Very likely, some of the Jews who responded to Peter's message returned to their homelands with God's Good News of salvation. Thus, God prepared the way for the spread of the Good News. As you read Acts, you will see how the way was often prepared for Paul and other messengers by people who had become believers at Pentecost. The church at Rome, for example, was probably begun by such Jewish believers.

**2:12** When the gathered crowd recognized that something supernatural was taking place, they naturally wanted an explanation. At this point, Peter stepped forward and explained the truth about

God. This should be the pattern in our lives as well. Hopefully we are living in such a way that people will see Christ in us. If we *do* shine and sparkle (Matthew 5:14; Philippians 2:15) and if we are "salty" (Matthew 5:13), we will get the attention of others. They will surely want to know what is so attractive and different about us. Then we can explain our "Christian hope" (1 Peter 3:15). What is different about your life? What supernatural evidence would cause someone to stop you and say, "What can this mean?"

### Peter Preaches to the Crowd

14 Then Peter stepped forward with the eleven other apostles and shouted to the crowd, "Listen carefully, all of you, fellow Jews and residents of Jerusalem! Make no mistake about this. 15 These people are not drunk, as some of you are assuming. Nine o'clock in the morning is much too early for that. 16 No, what you see was predicted long ago by the prophet Joel:

17 'In the last days,' God says,
    'I will pour out my Spirit upon all people.
    Your sons and daughters will prophesy.
        Your young men will see visions,
        and your old men will dream dreams.
18 In those days I will pour out my Spirit
    even on my servants—men and women alike—
    and they will prophesy.
19 And I will cause wonders in the heavens above
    and signs on the earth below—
    blood and fire and clouds of smoke.
20 The sun will become dark,
    and the moon will turn blood red
    before that great and glorious day of the LORD arrives.
21 But everyone who calls on the name of the LORD
    will be saved.'*

22 "People of Israel, listen! God publicly endorsed Jesus the Nazarene* by doing powerful miracles, wonders, and signs through him, as you well know. 23 But God knew what would happen, and his prearranged plan was carried out when Jesus was betrayed. With the help of lawless Gentiles, you nailed him to a cross and killed him. 24 But God released him from the horrors of death and raised him back to life, for death could not keep him in its grip. 25 King David said this about him:

'I see that the LORD is always with me.
    I will not be shaken, for he is right beside me.
26 No wonder my heart is glad,
    and my tongue shouts his praises!
    My body rests in hope.

**2:17-21** Joel 2:28-32.   **2:22** Or *Jesus of Nazareth.*

Side references:
**2:17-21** †Joel 2:28-32
**2:18** Num 11:29; 1 Cor 12:10
**2:20** Matt 24:29
**2:21** Rom 10:13
**2:22** John 3:2
**2:23** 1 Pet 1:20
**2:24** Acts 3:15
**2:25-28** †Ps 16:8-11; Acts 13:30-35

---

**2:14** Peter had been an unstable leader during Jesus' ministry, letting his bravado be his downfall, even denying that he knew Jesus (John 18:15-18, 25-27). But Christ had forgiven and restored him (John 21). This was a new Peter, humble but bold. His confidence came from the Holy Spirit, who made him a powerful and dynamic speaker. Have you ever felt as if you've made such bad mistakes that God could never forgive and use you? No matter what sins you have committed, God promises to forgive you and make you useful for his Kingdom. Allow him to forgive you and use you effectively to serve him.

**2:14ff** Peter tells the people that they should listen to the testimony of the believers because the Old Testament prophecies concerning Jesus had been entirely fulfilled in him (2:14-21), because Jesus is the Messiah (2:25-36), and because the risen Christ could change their lives (2:37-40).

**2:16-21** Not everything mentioned in Joel 2:28, 29 was happening that particular morning. The "last days" include all the days between Christ's first and second comings and is another way of saying "from now on." "That great and glorious day of the LORD" (2:20) denotes the whole Christian age. Even Moses yearned for the Lord to put his Spirit upon everyone (Numbers 11:29). At Pentecost the Holy Spirit was released throughout the entire world—to men, women, slaves, Jews, Gentiles. Now *everyone* can receive the Spirit. This was a revolutionary thought for first-century Jews.

**2:23** Everything that happened to Jesus was under God's control. His plans were never disrupted by the Roman government or the Jewish officials. This was especially comforting to those facing oppression during the time of the early Christian church.

**2:24** Peter spoke forthrightly about the Resurrection. As Peter preached, the events of Christ's death and resurrection were still hot news, less than two months old. Christ's execution had been carried out in public before many witnesses. His empty tomb was available for inspection just a short distance away. If Christ had not truly died, Peter's message would have been laughed at or ignored. If Christ had not been resurrected, authorities could have produced his body and put an end to this new faith. But Peter and the apostles had witnessed the risen Christ. Changed men, they announced the news with great passion and conviction.

Our faith and our credibility also rest on the truth of the empty tomb. Why? For a number of important reasons. According to the apostle Paul in 1 Corinthians 15, the resurrection of Christ means that he is the Son of God and that his word can be trusted. It means that his sacrifice for sin was acceptable to God, so we can be completely forgiven. It means that our Savior is alive and active, able to help us in times of need. It also means that one day we, too, will conquer death. The Christian faith rests on the basic fact of the empty tomb. Don't neglect this essential part of the gospel when you share your faith with others.

**2:25-32** Peter quoted from Psalm 16:8-11—a psalm written by David. He explained that David was not writing about himself because David died and was buried (2:29). Instead, he was writing as a prophet (2:30) who spoke of the Messiah who would be

27 For you will not leave my soul among the dead*
    or allow your Holy One to rot in the grave.
28 You have shown me the way of life,
    and you will fill me with the joy of your presence.'*

29 "Dear brothers, think about this! You can be sure that the patriarch David wasn't referring to himself, for he died and was buried, and his tomb is still here among us. 30 But he was a prophet, and he knew God had promised with an oath that one of David's own descendants would sit on his throne. 31 David was looking into the future and speaking of the Messiah's resurrection. He was saying that God would not leave him among the dead or allow his body to rot in the grave.

32 "God raised Jesus from the dead, and we are all witnesses of this. 33 Now he is exalted to the place of highest honor in heaven, at God's right hand. And the Father, as he had promised, gave him the Holy Spirit to pour out upon us, just as you see and hear today. 34 For David himself never ascended into heaven, yet he said,

'The LORD said to my Lord,
    "Sit in the place of honor at my right hand
35 until I humble your enemies,
    making them a footstool under your feet."'*

36 "So let everyone in Israel know for certain that God has made this Jesus, whom you crucified, to be both Lord and Messiah!"

37 Peter's words pierced their hearts, and they said to him and to the other apostles, "Brothers, what should we do?"

38 Peter replied, "Each of you must repent of your sins and turn to God, and be baptized in the name of Jesus Christ for the forgiveness of your sins. Then you will receive the gift of the Holy Spirit. 39 This promise is to you, and to your children, and even to the Gentiles*—all who have been called by the Lord our God." 40 Then Peter continued preaching for a long time, strongly urging all his listeners, "Save yourselves from this crooked generation!"

41 Those who believed what Peter said were baptized and added to the church that day—about 3,000 in all.

### The Believers Form a Community

42 All the believers devoted themselves to the apostles' teaching, and to fellowship, and to sharing in meals (including the Lord's Supper*), and to prayer.

43 A deep sense of awe came over them all, and the apostles performed many miraculous signs and wonders. 44 And all the believers met together in one place and shared everything they had. 45 They sold their property and possessions and shared the money with those in

**Marginal cross-references:**

**2:29** 1 Kgs 2:10 / Acts 13:36
**2:30** 2 Sam 7:12-14 / †Pss 89:4; 132:11
**2:31** †Ps 16:10
**2:33** John 14:26 / Acts 1:4, 8 / Eph 4:8 / Phil 2:9
**2:34-35** †Ps 110:1
**2:36** Acts 5:30-31
**2:37** Acts 16:30
**2:38** Mark 16:16 / Acts 3:19; 8:12; 22:16
**2:39** Isa 44:3; 57:19 / Eph 2:13
**2:40** Deut 32:5 / Phil 2:15
**2:42** Acts 20:7
**2:44-45** Acts 4:32-37

**2:27** Greek *in Hades;* also in 2:31. **2:25-28** Ps 16:8-11 (Greek version). **2:34-35** Ps 110:1. **2:39** Or *and to people far in the future;* Greek reads *and to those far away.* **2:42** Greek *the breaking of bread;* also in 2:46.

---

resurrected. The emphasis here is that Jesus' body was *not* left to rot in the grave but was, in fact, resurrected and glorified.

**2:37** After Peter's powerful, Spirit-filled message, the people were deeply moved and asked, "What should we do?" This is the basic question we must ask. It is not enough to be sorry for our sins. We must repent, ask God to forgive us, and then live like forgiven people. Has God spoken to you through his Word or through the words of another believer? Like Peter's audience, ask God what you should do, and then obey.

**2:38, 39** If you want to follow Christ, you must "repent of your sins, turn to God, and be baptized in the name of Jesus Christ." To repent means to turn from sin, to change the direction of your life from selfishness and rebellion against God's laws. At the same time, you must *turn to* Christ, depending on him for forgiveness, mercy, guidance, and purpose. We cannot save ourselves—only God can save us. Baptism identifies us with Christ and with the community of believers. It is a condition of discipleship and a sign of faith.

**2:40-43** About 3,000 people became new believers when Peter preached the Good News about Christ. These new Christians

were united with the other believers, taught by the apostles, and included in the prayer meetings and fellowship. New believers in Christ need to be in groups, where they can learn God's Word, pray, and mature in the faith. If you have just begun a relationship with Christ, seek out other believers for fellowship, prayer, and teaching. This is the way to grow.

**2:44** Recognizing the other believers as brothers and sisters in the family of God, the Christians in Jerusalem shared all they had so that all could benefit from God's gifts. It is tempting—especially if we have material wealth—to cut ourselves off from one another, concerning ourselves with only our interests and enjoying only our own little piece of the world. But as part of God's spiritual family, it is our responsibility to help one another in every way possible. God's family works best when its members work together.

need. 46They worshiped together at the Temple each day, met in homes for the Lord's Supper, and shared their meals with great joy and generosity*—47all the while praising God and enjoying the goodwill of all the people. And each day the Lord added to their fellowship those who were being saved.

**2:47**
Acts 4:4; 6:7
Rom 14:18

### Peter Heals a Crippled Beggar

**3** Peter and John went to the Temple one afternoon to take part in the three o'clock prayer service. 2As they approached the Temple, a man lame from birth was being carried in. Each day he was put beside the Temple gate, the one called the Beautiful Gate, so he could beg from the people going into the Temple. 3When he saw Peter and John about to enter, he asked them for some money.

**3:1**
Acts 10:3, 9, 30
**3:2**
Acts 14:8

4Peter and John looked at him intently, and Peter said, "Look at us!" 5The lame man looked at them eagerly, expecting some money. 6But Peter said, "I don't have any silver or gold for you. But I'll give you what I have. In the name of Jesus Christ the Nazarene,* get up and* walk!"

**3:4**
Acts 13:9; 14:9
**3:6**
Acts 4:10

7Then Peter took the lame man by the right hand and helped him up. And as he did, the man's feet and ankles were instantly healed and strengthened. 8He jumped up, stood on his feet, and began to walk! Then, walking, leaping, and praising God, he went into the Temple with them.

**3:8**
John 5:14
**3:9**
Acts 4:16, 21

9All the people saw him walking and heard him praising God. 10When they realized he was the lame beggar they had seen so often at the Beautiful Gate, they were absolutely astounded! 11They all rushed out in amazement to Solomon's Colonnade, where the man was holding tightly to Peter and John.

**3:10**
John 9:8
**3:11**
John 10:23
Acts 5:12

### Peter Preaches in the Temple

12Peter saw his opportunity and addressed the crowd. "People of Israel," he said, "what is so surprising about this? And why stare at us as though we had made this man walk by our own power or godliness? 13For it is the God of Abraham, Isaac, and Jacob—the God of all our ancestors—who has brought glory to his servant Jesus by doing this. This is the same Jesus whom you handed over and rejected before Pilate, despite Pilate's decision to release him. 14You rejected this holy, righteous one and instead demanded the release of a murderer. 15You killed the author of life, but God raised him from the dead. And we are witnesses of this fact!

**3:13**
†Exod 3:6, 15
Matt 22:32
Acts 5:30; 7:32
**3:15**
Acts 2:24; 5:30

**2:46** Or *and sincere hearts.*   **3:6a** Or *Jesus Christ of Nazareth.*   **3:6b** Some manuscripts do not include *get up and.*

---

**2:46** A common misconception about the first Christians (who were Jews) was that they rejected the Jewish religion. But these believers saw Jesus' message and resurrection as the fulfillment of everything they knew and believed from the Old Testament. The Jewish believers at first did not separate themselves from the rest of the Jewish community. They still went to the Temple and synagogues for worship and instruction in the Scriptures. But their belief in Jesus created great friction with Jews who didn't believe that Jesus was the Messiah. Thus, believing Jews were forced to meet in private homes for Communion, prayer, and teaching about Christ. By the end of the first century, many of these Jewish believers were excommunicated from their synagogues.

**2:47** A healthy Christian community attracts people to Christ. The Jerusalem church's zeal for worship and brotherly love was contagious. A healthy, loving church will grow in numbers. What are you doing to make your church the kind of place that will attract others to Christ?

**3:1** The Jews observed three times of prayer—morning (9:00 AM), afternoon (3:00 PM), and evening (sunset). At these times devout Jews and Gentiles who believed in God often would go to the Temple to pray. Peter and John were going to the Temple for the afternoon prayer service.

**3:2** The Beautiful Gate was an entrance to the Temple, not to the city. It was one of the favored entrances, and many people passed through it on their way to worship. Giving money to beggars was considered praiseworthy in the Jewish religion. So the beggar wisely placed himself where he would be seen by the most people who were on their way to worship at the Temple.

**3:5, 6** The lame man asked for money, but Peter gave him something much better—the use of his legs. We often ask God to solve a small problem, but he wants to give us a whole new life and help

for *all* our problems. He may say, "I've got something even better for you." You may ask God for what you want, but don't be surprised when he gives you what you really *need.*

**3:6** "In the name of Jesus Christ" means "by the authority of Jesus Christ." The apostles were doing this healing through the Holy Spirit's power, not their own.

**3:7-10** In his excitement, the formerly lame man began to jump and walk around. He also praised God! Then others were awed by God's power. Don't forget to thank people who help you, but also remember to praise God for his care and protection.

**3:11** Solomon's Colonnade was part of the Temple complex built by King Herod the Great in an attempt to strengthen his relationship with the Jews. A colonnade is an entrance or porch supported by columns. Jesus taught and performed miracles in the Temple many times. When the apostles went to the Temple, they were undoubtedly in close proximity to the same religious leaders who had conspired to put Jesus to death.

**3:11ff** Peter had an audience, and he capitalized on the opportunity to share Jesus Christ. He clearly presented his message by telling (1) who Jesus was, (2) how the Jews had rejected him, (3) why their rejection was fatal, and (4) what they needed to do to change the situation. Peter told the crowd that they still had a choice; God still offered them the opportunity to believe and receive Jesus as their Messiah and as their Lord. Displays of God's mercy and grace, such as the healing of this lame man, often create teachable moments. Pray to have courage like Peter to see these opportunities and to use them to speak up for Christ.

**3:13-15** Pilate had decided to release Jesus, but the people had clamored to have Barabbas, a murderer, released instead (see Luke 23:13-25). When Peter said, "You killed," he meant it literally. Jesus' trial and death had occurred right there in Jeru-

**3:17**
Luke 23:34
Acts 13:27
1 Tim 1:13

**3:18**
Pss 22; 41:9;
69:4, 21
Isa 50:6; 53:4-11
Zech 12:10; 13:7
Luke 24:27, 44, 46

**3:19**
Acts 2:38; 26:20

**3:21**
Luke 1:70

**3:22**
†Deut 18:15, 18
John 1:20-21;
7:40-41, 52

**3:23**
Lev 23:29
Deut 18:19

**3:25**
†Gen 22:18; 26:4
Rom 9:4-8

**3:26**
Acts 13:46
Rom 1:16

**4:1**
Luke 22:4

¹⁶"Through faith in the name of Jesus, this man was healed—and you know how crippled he was before. Faith in Jesus' name has healed him before your very eyes.

¹⁷"Friends,* I realize that what you and your leaders did to Jesus was done in ignorance. ¹⁸But God was fulfilling what all the prophets had foretold about the Messiah—that he must suffer these things. ¹⁹Now repent of your sins and turn to God, so that your sins may be wiped away. ²⁰Then times of refreshment will come from the presence of the Lord, and he will again send you Jesus, your appointed Messiah. ²¹For he must remain in heaven until the time for the final restoration of all things, as God promised long ago through his holy prophets. ²²Moses said, 'The Lᴏʀᴅ your God will raise up for you a Prophet like me from among your own people. Listen carefully to everything he tells you.'* ²³Then Moses said, 'Anyone who will not listen to that Prophet will be completely cut off from God's people.'*

²⁴"Starting with Samuel, every prophet spoke about what is happening today. ²⁵You are the children of those prophets, and you are included in the covenant God promised to your ancestors. For God said to Abraham, 'Through your descendants* all the families on earth will be blessed.' ²⁶When God raised up his servant, Jesus, he sent him first to you people of Israel, to bless you by turning each of you back from your sinful ways."

## Peter and John before the Council

**4** While Peter and John were speaking to the people, they were confronted by the priests, the captain of the Temple guard, and some of the Sadducees. ²These leaders were very disturbed that Peter and John were teaching the people that through Jesus there is a

**3:17** Greek *Brothers.*   **3:22** Deut 18:15.   **3:23** Deut 18:19; Lev 23:29.   **3:25** Greek *your seed;* see Gen 12:3; 22:18.

---

salem only weeks earlier. It wasn't an event of the distant past—most of these people had heard about it, and some may very well have taken part in condemning Jesus.

**3:15** The religious leaders thought they had put an end to Jesus when they crucified him. But their confidence was shaken when Peter told them that Jesus was alive again and that this time they could not harm him. Peter's message emphasized that (1) the people and their religious leaders had killed Jesus (3:17), (2) God had brought him back to life, and (3) the apostles had been witnesses of this fact. After pointing out the sin and injustice of these leaders, Peter showed the significance of the Resurrection, God's triumph and power over death.

**3:16** Jesus, not the apostles, received the glory for the healing of the lame man. In those days a man's name represented his character; it stood for his authority and power. By using Jesus' name, Peter showed who gave him the authority and power to heal. The apostles did not emphasize what *they* could do but what God could do through them. Jesus' name is not to be used as magic—it must be used in faith. When we pray in Jesus' name, we must remember that it is Christ himself, not merely the sound of his name, who gives our prayers their power.

**3:18** Some of these prophecies are in Psalm 22, Isaiah 50:6, and Isaiah 53. Peter was explaining the kind of Messiah God had sent to earth. The Jews had expected a great ruler, not a suffering servant.

**3:19** John the Baptist had prepared the way for Jesus by preaching that people should turn from their sins. The apostles' message of salvation also included the call to repent—acknowledging personal sin and turning from it. Many people want the benefits of being identified with Christ without admitting their own disobedience and repenting. The key to forgiveness is confessing your sin and turning from it (see 2:38).

**3:19, 20** When we repent, God promises not only to cleanse us of our sins but to bring spiritual refreshment. Turning away from sin may at first seem painful because it is hard to break old habits and give up certain sins. But God will give you a better way. As Hosea promised, "Oh, that we might know the Lᴏʀᴅ! Let us press on to know him. He will respond to us as surely as the arrival of dawn or the coming of rains in early spring" (Hosea 6:3). Do you feel a need to be refreshed?

**3:21** The time when God will bring the "final restoration of all things" refers to the Second Coming, the Last Judgment, and the removal of sin from the world.

**3:21, 22** Most Jews thought that Joshua was this Prophet predicted by Moses (Deuteronomy 18:15). Peter was saying that the Prophet was Jesus Christ. Peter wanted to show that their long-awaited Messiah had come! He and all the apostles were calling the Jewish nation to realize what they had done to their Messiah, to repent, and to believe. From this point on in Acts, we see many Jews rejecting the Good News. So the message went also to the Gentiles, many of whom were open to receive Jesus.

**3:24** The prophet Samuel had lived during the transition between the judges and the kings of Israel, and he had been seen as the first in a succession of prophets. Samuel anointed David king, founding David's royal line, from which the Messiah eventually came. All the prophets pointed to a future Messiah. For more on Samuel, see his Profile in 1 Samuel 7, p. 419.

**3:25** God had promised Abraham that he would bless the world through Abraham's descendants, the Jewish race (Genesis 12:3), from which the Messiah would come. God intended the Jewish nation to be a separate and holy nation that would teach the world about God, introduce the Messiah, and then carry on his work in the world. After the days of Solomon, the nation gave up its mission to tell the world about God. Here, too, in apostolic times as well as in the time Jesus spent on earth, the Jews rejected their Messiah.

**4:1** These priests had special influence and were often close relatives of the high priest. The captain of the Temple guard was the leader of the guards who were stationed around the Temple to ensure order. The Sadducees were members of a small but powerful Jewish religious sect that did not believe in the resurrection of the dead. They were the religious leaders who stood to gain financially by cooperating with the Romans. Most of those who planned and carried out Jesus' arrest and crucifixion were from these three groups.

**4:2, 3** Peter and John spoke to the people during the afternoon prayer time. The Sadducees moved in quickly to investigate. Because they did not believe in the Resurrection, they were understandably disturbed with what the apostles were saying. Peter and John were refuting one of their fundamental beliefs and thus threatening their authority as religious teachers. Even though the nation was under Roman rule, the Sadducees had almost unlimited power over the Temple grounds. Thus, they were able to arrest Peter and John for no other reason than teaching something that contradicted their beliefs.

resurrection of the dead. ³They arrested them and, since it was already evening, put them in jail until morning. ⁴But many of the people who heard their message believed it, so the number of believers now totaled about 5,000 men, not counting women and children.*

⁵The next day the council of all the rulers and elders and teachers of religious law met in Jerusalem. ⁶Annas the high priest was there, along with Caiaphas, John, Alexander, and other relatives of the high priest. ⁷They brought in the two disciples and demanded, "By what power, or in whose name, have you done this?"

⁸Then Peter, filled with the Holy Spirit, said to them, "Rulers and elders of our people, ⁹are we being questioned today because we've done a good deed for a crippled man? Do you want to know how he was healed? ¹⁰Let me clearly state to all of you and to all the people of Israel that he was healed by the powerful name of Jesus Christ the Nazarene,* the man you crucified but whom God raised from the dead. ¹¹For Jesus is the one referred to in the Scriptures, where it says,

'The stone that you builders rejected
    has now become the cornerstone.'*

¹²There is salvation in no one else! God has given no other name under heaven by which we must be saved."

¹³The members of the council were amazed when they saw the boldness of Peter and John, for they could see that they were ordinary men with no special training in the Scriptures. They also recognized them as men who had been with Jesus. ¹⁴But since they could see the man who had been healed standing right there among them, there was nothing the council could say. ¹⁵So they ordered Peter and John out of the council chamber* and conferred among themselves.

¹⁶"What should we do with these men?" they asked each other. "We can't deny that they have performed a miraculous sign, and everybody in Jerusalem knows about it. ¹⁷But to keep them from spreading their propaganda any further, we must warn them not to speak to anyone in Jesus' name again." ¹⁸So they called the apostles back in and commanded them never again to speak or teach in the name of Jesus.

**4:3** Acts 5:18
**4:4** Acts 4:21
**4:6** Matt 26:3; Luke 3:2
**4:7** Matt 21:23
**4:10** Acts 2:24; 3:6
**4:11** †Ps 118:22; Isa 28:16; Matt 21:42; 1 Pet 2:4, 7
**4:12** Matt 1:21; Acts 10:43; 1 Tim 2:5
**4:13** Matt 11:25
**4:15** Acts 5:34-35
**4:16** John 11:47; Acts 3:6-10
**4:17-19** Acts 5:28-29

**4:4** Greek *5,000 adult males*.    **4:10** Or *Jesus Christ of Nazareth*.    **4:11** Ps 118:22.    **4:15** Greek *the Sanhedrin*.

---

**4:3** Seldom will sharing the Good News send us to jail as it did Peter and John. Still, we run risks in trying to win others to Christ. We might be willing to face a night in jail if it would bring 5,000 people to Christ, but shouldn't we also be willing to suffer for the sake of even one? What do you risk in witnessing—rejection, persecution? Whatever the risks, realize that nothing done for God is ever wasted.

**4:5, 6** The rulers, elders, and teachers of religious law made up the Jewish high council—the same council that had condemned Jesus to death (Luke 22:66). It had 70 members plus the current high priest, who presided over the group. The Sadducees held a majority in this ruling group. These were the wealthy, intellectual, and powerful men of Jerusalem. Jesus' followers stood before the same high council that Jesus had.

**4:6** Annas had been deposed as high priest by the Romans, who then had appointed Caiaphas, Annas's son-in-law, in his place. Because the Jews considered the office of high priest a lifetime position, however, they still called Annas by that title and gave him respect and authority within the high council. Annas and Caiaphas had played significant roles in Jesus' trial (John 18:24, 28). They were not pleased that the man they thought they had sacrificed for the good of the nation (John 11:49-51) had followers who were just as persistent and promised to be just as troublesome as he had been.

**4:7** The high council asked Peter and John by what power they had healed the man (3:6, 7) and by what authority they preached (3:12-26). The actions and words of Peter and John threatened these religious leaders, who, for the most part, were more interested in their reputations and positions than in God. Through the help of the Holy Spirit (Mark 13:11), Peter spoke boldly before the council, actually putting the council on trial by showing them that the one they had crucified had risen again. Instead of being defensive, the apostles went on the offensive, boldly speaking out for God and presenting the Good News to these leaders.

**4:11** The cornerstone unites two walls at the corner of a building and holds the building together. Peter said that the Jews rejected Christ, but now Christ had become the cornerstone of the church (Psalm 118:22; Mark 12:10; 1 Peter 2:7). Without him there would be no church because it wouldn't be able to stand.

**4:12** Many people react negatively to the fact that there is no other name than that of Jesus to call on for salvation. Yet this is not something the church decided; it is the specific teaching of Jesus himself (John 14:6). If God designated Jesus to be the Savior of the world, no one else can be his equal. Christians are to be open-minded on many issues but not on how we are saved from sin. No other religious teacher could die for our sins; no other religious teacher came to earth as God's only Son; no other religious teacher rose from the dead. Our focus should be on Jesus, whom God provided as the way to have an eternal relationship with himself. There is no other name or way!

**4:13** Knowing that Peter and John were untrained, the council was amazed at what being with Jesus had done for them. A changed life convinces people of Christ's power. One of your greatest testimonies is the difference others see in your life and attitudes since you have believed in Christ.

**4:13-18** Although the evidence was overwhelming and irrefutable (changed lives and a healed man), the religious leaders refused to believe in Christ and continued to try to suppress the truth. Don't be surprised if some people reject you and your positive witness for Christ. When minds are closed, even the clearest presentation of the facts can't open them. But don't give up either. Pray for those people and continue to spread the Good News.

<sup></sup>19But Peter and John replied, "Do you think God wants us to obey you rather than him? 20We cannot stop telling about everything we have seen and heard."

21The council then threatened them further, but they finally let them go because they didn't know how to punish them without starting a riot. For everyone was praising God 22 for this miraculous sign—the healing of a man who had been lame for more than forty years.

### The Believers Pray for Courage

23As soon as they were freed, Peter and John returned to the other believers and told them what the leading priests and elders had said. 24When they heard the report, all the believers lifted their voices together in prayer to God: "O Sovereign Lord, Creator of heaven and earth, the sea, and everything in them—25you spoke long ago by the Holy Spirit through our ancestor David, your servant, saying,

'Why were the nations so angry?
    Why did they waste their time with futile plans?
26 The kings of the earth prepared for battle;
    the rulers gathered together
against the LORD
    and against his Messiah.'*

27"In fact, this has happened here in this very city! For Herod Antipas, Pontius Pilate the governor, the Gentiles, and the people of Israel were all united against Jesus, your holy servant, whom you anointed. 28But everything they did was determined beforehand according to your will. 29And now, O Lord, hear their threats, and give us, your servants, great boldness in preaching your word. 30Stretch out your hand with healing power; may miraculous signs and wonders be done through the name of your holy servant Jesus."

31After this prayer, the meeting place shook, and they were all filled with the Holy Spirit. Then they preached the word of God with boldness.

### The Believers Share Their Possessions

32All the believers were united in heart and mind. And they felt that what they owned was not their own, so they shared everything they had. 33 The apostles testified powerfully to the resurrection of the Lord Jesus, and God's great blessing was upon them all. 34There were no needy people among them, because those who owned land or houses would sell them 35 and bring the money to the apostles to give to those in need.

4:25-26 Or *his anointed one;* or *his Christ.* Ps 2:1-2.

Margin references: 4:20 1 Jn 1:1, 3 | 4:24 †Exod 20:11 †Ps 146:6 | 4:25-26 †Ps 2:1-2 | 4:27 Isa 61:1 Acts 3:13 | 4:28 Acts 2:23 | 4:29 Eph 6:19 | 4:30 Acts 5:12 | 4:31 Acts 2:4; 16:26 | 4:32 Acts 2:44 | 4:33-35 Acts 2:45-47

**4:20** We may sometimes be afraid to share our faith in Christ because people may feel uncomfortable or reject us. But Peter and John's zeal for the Lord was so strong that they could not keep quiet, even when threatened. If your courage to witness for God has weakened, pray that your boldness may increase. Remember Jesus' promise, "Everyone who acknowledges me publicly here on earth, I will also acknowledge before my Father in heaven" (Matthew 10:32).

**4:24-30** Notice how the believers prayed. First, they praised God; then they told God their specific problem and asked for his help. They did not ask God to remove the problem but to help them deal with it. We can follow this model when we pray. We may ask God to remove our problems, and he may choose to do so. But we must recognize that often he will leave a problem but give us the strength and courage to deal with it.

**4:27** Herod Antipas had been appointed by the Romans to rule over the territory of Galilee. For more information on Herod, see his Profile in Mark 6, p. 1629. Pontius Pilate was the Roman governor over Judea. He bowed to pressure from the crowd and sentenced Jesus to death. For more information on Pilate, see his Profile in Mark 15, p. 1661.

**4:28** God is the sovereign Lord of all events, who rules history to fulfill his purposes. What his will determines, his power carries out. No leader, army, government, or council can stand in God's way.

**4:29-31** Boldness is not reckless impulsiveness. Boldness requires courage to press on through our fears and do what we know is right. How can we be more bold? Like the disciples,

we need to pray with others. To gain boldness, you can (1) pray for the power of the Holy Spirit to give you courage, (2) look for opportunities in your family and neighborhood to talk about Christ, (3) realize that rejection, social discomfort, and embarrassment are not necessarily persecution, and (4) start where you are by being bolder in small ways.

**4:32** Differences of opinion are inevitable among human personalities and can actually be helpful if handled well. But spiritual unity is essential—loyalty, commitment, and love for God and his Word. Without spiritual unity, the church could not survive. Paul wrote the letter of 1 Corinthians to urge the church in Corinth toward greater unity.

**4:32** None of these Christians felt that what they had was their own, so they were able to give and share, eliminating poverty among them. They would not let a brother or sister suffer when others had plenty. How do you feel about your possessions? We should adopt the attitude that everything we have comes from God, and we are only sharing what is already his.

**4:32-35** The early church was able to share possessions and property as a result of the unity brought by the Holy Spirit working in and through the believers' lives. This way of living is different from communism because (1) the sharing was voluntary; (2) it didn't involve *all* private property but only as much as was needed; (3) it was not a membership requirement in order to be a part of the church. The spiritual unity and generosity of these early believers attracted others to them. This organizational structure is not a biblical command, but it offers vital principles for us to follow.

36For instance, there was Joseph, the one the apostles nicknamed Barnabas (which means "Son of Encouragement"). He was from the tribe of Levi and came from the island of Cyprus. 37He sold a field he owned and brought the money to the apostles.

4:36
Acts 9:27; 11:19-
30; 12:25; 13:2

## Ananias and Sapphira

5 But there was a certain man named Ananias who, with his wife, Sapphira, sold some property. 2He brought part of the money to the apostles, claiming it was the full amount. With his wife's consent, he kept the rest.

5:2
Acts 4:34-35, 37

3Then Peter said, "Ananias, why have you let Satan fill your heart? You lied to the Holy Spirit, and you kept some of the money for yourself. 4The property was yours to sell or not sell, as you wished. And after selling it, the money was also yours to give away. How could you do a thing like this? You weren't lying to us but to God!"

5:3
Deut 23:21
John 13:2

5As soon as Ananias heard these words, he fell to the floor and died. Everyone who heard about it was terrified. 6Then some young men got up, wrapped him in a sheet, and took him out and buried him.

5:5
Acts 2:43

7About three hours later his wife came in, not knowing what had happened. 8Peter asked her, "Was this the price you and your husband received for your land?"

"Yes," she replied, "that was the price."

9And Peter said, "How could the two of you even think of conspiring to test the Spirit of the Lord like this? The young men who buried your husband are just outside the door, and they will carry you out, too."

5:9
1 Cor 10:9

10Instantly, she fell to the floor and died. When the young men came in and saw that she was dead, they carried her out and buried her beside her husband. 11Great fear gripped the entire church and everyone else who heard what had happened.

## The Apostles Heal Many

12The apostles were performing many miraculous signs and wonders among the people. And all the believers were meeting regularly at the Temple in the area known as Solomon's Colonnade. 13But no one else dared to join them, even though all the people had high regard for them. 14Yet more and more people believed and were brought to the Lord—crowds of both men and women. 15As a result of the apostles' work, sick people were brought out into the streets on beds and mats so that Peter's shadow might fall across some of them as he went by. 16Crowds came from the villages around Jerusalem, bringing their sick and those possessed by evil* spirits, and they were all healed.

5:12
Mark 16:15-20
John 10:23
Acts 3:10
Heb 2:4

5:13
Acts 2:47

**5:16** Greek unclean.

---

**4:36** Barnabas (Joseph) was a respected leader of the church. He was a Levite by birth, a member of the Jewish tribe that carried out Temple duties. But his family had moved to Cyprus, so Barnabas didn't serve in the Temple. He traveled with Paul on Paul's first missionary journey (13:1ff). For more information on Barnabas, see his Profile in chapter 13, p. 1849.

**5:1ff** In Acts 5:1–8:3 we see both internal and external problems facing the early church. Inside, the church had dishonesty (5:1-11), greed (5:3), and administrative headaches (6:1-7). Outside, the church was being pressured by persecution. While church leaders were careful and sensitive in dealing with the internal problems, they could not do much to prevent the external pressures. Through it all, the leaders kept their focus on what was most important—spreading the Good News of Jesus Christ.

**5:3** Even after the Holy Spirit had come, the believers were not immune to Satan's temptations. Although Satan was defeated by Christ at the cross, he was still actively trying to make the believers stumble—as he does today (Ephesians 6:12; 1 Peter 5:8). Satan's overthrow is inevitable, but it will not occur until the last days, when Christ returns to judge the world (Revelation 20:10).

**5:3ff** The sin Ananias and Sapphira committed was not stinginess or holding back part of the money—it was their choice whether or not to sell the land and how much to give. Their sin was lying to God and God's people, saying they gave the whole amount but holding back some for themselves and trying to make themselves appear more generous than they really were. This act was judged harshly because dishonesty, greed, and covetousness are destructive in a church, preventing the Holy Spirit from work-

ing effectively. All lying is bad, but when we lie to try to deceive God and accuse God of being harsh. "I thought God and his people about our relationship with him, we destroy our testimony for Christ.

**5:11** Some read the account of Ananias and Sapphira being struck down and accuse God of being harsh. "I thought God was supposed to be loving and forgiving. I thought all that wrath stuff was for Old Testament times." With an emphasis on grace and mercy, it's easy to overlook the equally important truth of God's holiness. We must remember that God has not changed (Malachi 3:6). He still hates sin as much as he ever did. God's judgment of Ananias and Sapphira produced shock and fear among the believers, making them realize how seriously God regards sin in the church.

**5:14** What makes Christianity attractive? It is easy to be drawn to churches because of programs, good speakers, size, beautiful facilities, or fellowship. People were attracted to the early church, however, by expressions of God's power at work; the generosity, sincerity, honesty, and unity of the members; and the character of the leaders. Have our standards slipped? God wants to add believers to his church, not just newer and better programs or larger and fancier facilities.

**5:15, 16** People who passed within Peter's shadow were healed, not by Peter's shadow, but by God's power working through Peter. What did these miraculous healings do for the early church? (1) They attracted new believers; (2) they confirmed the truth of the apostles' teaching; and (3) they demonstrated that the power of the Messiah, who had been crucified and risen, was now with his followers.

## The Apostles Meet Opposition

**5:17**
Acts 4:1, 2

**5:19**
Acts 12:7-10

**5:20**
John 6:63, 68

**5:21**
Acts 4:5-6

17 The high priest and his officials, who were Sadducees, were filled with jealousy. 18 They arrested the apostles and put them in the public jail. 19 But an angel of the Lord came at night, opened the gates of the jail, and brought them out. Then he told them, 20 "Go to the Temple and give the people this message of life!"

21 So at daybreak the apostles entered the Temple, as they were told, and immediately began teaching.

When the high priest and his officials arrived, they convened the high council*—the full assembly of the elders of Israel. Then they sent for the apostles to be brought from the jail for trial. 22 But when the Temple guards went to the jail, the men were gone. So they returned to the council and reported, 23 "The jail was securely locked, with the guards standing outside, but when we opened the gates, no one was there!"

**5:24**
Acts 4:1

24 When the captain of the Temple guard and the leading priests heard this, they were perplexed, wondering where it would all end. 25 Then someone arrived with startling news: "The men you put in jail are standing in the Temple, teaching the people!"

**5:26**
Matt 14:5; 21:26

**5:28**
Matt 23:35; 27:25
Acts 2:23; 4:18;
7:52

**5:29**
Acts 4:19

**5:30**
Acts 10:39

**5:31**
Acts 2:33
Heb 2:10

**5:32**
Luke 24:28
John 15:26-27

**5:33**
Acts 7:54

**5:34**
Acts 22:3

26 The captain went with his Temple guards and arrested the apostles, but without violence, for they were afraid the people would stone them. 27 Then they brought the apostles before the high council, where the high priest confronted them. 28 "Didn't we tell you never again to teach in this man's name?" he demanded. "Instead, you have filled all Jerusalem with your teaching about him, and you want to make us responsible for his death!"

29 But Peter and the apostles replied, "We must obey God rather than any human authority. 30 The God of our ancestors raised Jesus from the dead after you killed him by hanging him on a cross.* 31 Then God put him in the place of honor at his right hand as Prince and Savior. He did this so the people of Israel would repent of their sins and be forgiven. 32 We are witnesses of these things and so is the Holy Spirit, who is given by God to those who obey him."

33 When they heard this, the high council was furious and decided to kill them. 34 But one member, a Pharisee named Gamaliel, who was an expert in religious law and respected by all the people, stood up and ordered that the men be sent outside the council chamber for a

**5:21** Greek *Sanhedrin;* also in 5:27, 41.   **5:30** Greek *on a tree.*

---

**5:17, 18** The apostles experienced power to do miracles, great boldness in preaching, and God's presence in their lives; yet they were not free from hatred and persecution. They were arrested, put in jail, beaten, and slandered by community leaders. Faith in God does not make troubles disappear; it makes troubles appear less frightening because it puts them in the right perspective. Don't expect everyone to react favorably when you share something as dynamic as your faith in Christ. Some will be jealous, afraid, or threatened. Expect some negative reactions, and remember that you must be more concerned about serving God than about the reactions of people (see 5:29).

**5:19** The angel of the Lord gave the apostles a command that, when followed, would lead to a brutal flogging (5:40). If that strikes you as odd, it is probably because of the prevailing idea among many believers that obedience inevitably leads to blessing (defined as "a problem-free, blissful existence"). Serious students of the Bible know, however, that obeying God often results in pain and suffering. They also recognize that being persecuted for Christ is a deeper kind of blessing. What biblical commands, if obeyed, might result in discomfort for you today? Will you commit to live them out anyway?

**5:21** Suppose someone threatened to kill you if you didn't stop talking about God. You might be tempted to keep quiet. But after being threatened by powerful leaders, arrested, jailed, and miraculously released, the apostles went back to preaching. This was nothing less than God's power working through them (4:13)! When we are convinced of the truth of Christ's resurrection and have experienced the presence and power of his Holy Spirit, we will also have the confidence to speak out for Christ.

**5:21** The Temple at daybreak was a busy place. Many people stopped at the Temple to pray and worship at sunrise. The apostles were already there, ready to tell them the Good News of new life in

Jesus Christ. Also at daybreak, the 70 men of the high council (also called the Sanhedrin) were gathering, preparing to question the apostles. This was going to be no small trial. The religious leaders would do anything to stop these apostles from challenging their authority, threatening their secure position, and exposing their hypocritical motives to the people.

**5:29** The apostles knew their priorities. While we should try to live at peace with everyone (Romans 12:18), conflict with the world and its authorities is sometimes inevitable for a Christian (John 15:18). There will be situations where you cannot obey both God and people. Then you must obey God and trust his Word. Let Jesus' words in Luke 6:22 encourage you: "What blessings await you when people hate you and exclude you and mock you and curse you as evil because you follow the Son of Man."

**5:34** The Pharisees were the other major party in the Jewish high council with the Sadducees (5:17). The Pharisees were the strict keepers of the law—not only God's law but hundreds of other rules they had added to God's law. They were careful about outward purity, but many had hearts full of impure motives. Jesus confronted the Pharisees often during his ministry on earth. Oddly enough, a Pharisee named Gamaliel became an unexpected ally for the apostles, although he probably did not support their teachings. He was a distinguished member of the high council and a teacher. While Gamaliel may have saved the apostles' lives, his real intentions probably were to prevent a division in the council and to avoid arousing the Romans. The apostles were popular among the people, and killing them might start a riot. Gamaliel's advice to the council gave the apostles some breathing room to continue their work. The council decided to wait, hoping that this would all fade away harmlessly. They couldn't have been more wrong. Ironically, Paul, later one of the greatest apostles, had been one of Gamaliel's students (22:3).

while. 35 Then he said to his colleagues, "Men of Israel, take care what you are planning to do to these men! 36Some time ago there was that fellow Theudas, who pretended to be someone great. About 400 others joined him, but he was killed, and all his followers went their various ways. The whole movement came to nothing. 37After him, at the time of the census, there was Judas of Galilee. He got people to follow him, but he was killed, too, and all his followers were scattered.

38"So my advice is, leave these men alone. Let them go. If they are planning and doing these things merely on their own, it will soon be overthrown. 39But if it is from God, you will not be able to overthrow them. You may even find yourselves fighting against God!"

40The others accepted his advice. They called in the apostles and had them flogged. Then they ordered them never again to speak in the name of Jesus, and they let them go.

41 The apostles left the high council rejoicing that God had counted them worthy to suffer disgrace for the name of Jesus.* 42And every day, in the Temple and from house to house, they continued to teach and preach this message: "Jesus is the Messiah."

### Seven Men Chosen to Serve

**6** But as the believers* rapidly multiplied, there were rumblings of discontent. The Greek-speaking believers complained about the Hebrew-speaking believers, saying that their widows were being discriminated against in the daily distribution of food.

2So the Twelve called a meeting of all the believers. They said, "We apostles should spend our time teaching the word of God, not running a food program. 3And so, brothers, select seven men who are well respected and are full of the Spirit and wisdom. We will give them this responsibility. 4Then we apostles can spend our time in prayer and teaching the word."

5Everyone liked this idea, and they chose the following: Stephen (a man full of faith and the Holy Spirit), Philip, Procorus, Nicanor, Timon, Parmenas, and Nicolas of Antioch (an

**5:36**
Acts 21:38

**5:37**
Luke 2:1-2; 13:1-2

**5:39**
Prov 21:30
Isa 46:10
**5:40**
Matt 10:17
Mark 13:9
**5:41**
Matt 5:10-12
John 15:21
1 Pet 4:13
**5:42**
Acts 2:46

**6:1**
Acts 2:45; 4:35
1 Tim 5:3

**6:3**
1 Tim 3:7-8
**6:4**
Acts 1:14
**6:5**
Acts 21:8

**5:41** Greek *for the name.*    **6:1** Greek *disciples;* also in 6:2, 7.

---

**5:39** Gamaliel presented some sound advice about reacting to religious movements. Unless adherents in these groups endorse obviously dangerous doctrines or practices, it is often wiser to be tolerant rather than repressive. Sometimes only time will tell if they are presenting merely human ideas or if God is trying to say something through them. The next time a group promotes differing religious ideas, consider Gamaliel's advice, just in case you "find yourselves fighting against God."

**5:40-42** Peter and John had been warned repeatedly not to preach, but they continued in spite of the threats. We, too, should live as Christ has asked us to, sharing our faith no matter what the cost. We may not be beaten or thrown in jail, but we may be ridiculed, ostracized, or slandered. To what extent are you willing to suffer for the sake of sharing the Good News with others?

**5:41** Have you ever thought of persecution as a blessing, as something worth rejoicing about? This beating suffered by Peter and John was the first time any of the apostles had been physically abused for their faith. These men knew how Jesus had suffered, and they praised God that he had allowed them to be persecuted like their Lord. If you are mocked or persecuted for your faith, it isn't because you're doing something wrong but because God has counted you "worthy to suffer disgrace for the name of Jesus."

**5:42** Home Bible studies are not new. As the believers needed to grow in their new faith, home Bible studies met their needs, as well as serving as a means to introduce new people to the Christian faith. During later times of persecution, meeting in homes became the primary method of passing on Bible knowledge. Christians throughout the world still use this approach when under persecution and as a way to build up believers.

**6:1** When we read the descriptions of the early church—the miracles, the sharing and generosity, the fellowship—we may wish we could have been a part of this "perfect" church. In reality, the early church had problems just as we do today. No church has ever been or will ever be perfect until Christ and his followers are united at his second coming. All churches have problems. If

your church's shortcomings distress you, ask yourself: Would a perfect church allow me to be a member? Then do what you can to make your church better. A church does not have to be perfect to advance the cause of Christ.

**6:1ff** Another internal problem developed in the early church between the Hebrew-speaking Christians (probably local Jews who had been converted) and the Greek-speaking Christians (probably Jews from other lands who had been converted at Pentecost). The Greek-speaking Christians complained that their widows were being unfairly treated. This favoritism was probably not intentional but was more likely caused by the language barrier. To correct the situation, the apostles put seven respected Greek-speaking men in charge of the food distribution program. This solved the problem and allowed the apostles to keep their focus on teaching and preaching the Good News about Jesus.

**6:2** "The Twelve" are the 11 original disciples plus Matthias, who had been chosen to replace Judas Iscariot (1:26).

**6:2-4** As the early church increased in size, so did its needs. One great need was to organize the distribution of food to the poor. The apostles needed to focus on preaching, so they chose others to administer the food program. Each person has a vital part to play in the life of the church (see 1 Corinthians 12). If you are in a position of leadership and find yourself overwhelmed by responsibilities, determine *your* God-given abilities and priorities and then find others to help. If you are not in leadership, you have gifts that can be used by God in various areas of the church's ministry. Offer these gifts in service to him.

**6:3** This administrative task was not taken lightly. Notice the requirements for the men who were to handle the food program: They were to be well respected and full of the Holy Spirit and wisdom. People who carry heavy responsibilities and work closely with others should have these qualities. We must look for spiritually mature and wise men and women to lead our churches.

**6:4** The apostles' priorities were correct. The ministry of the Word should never be neglected because of administrative burdens. Pastors should not try, or be expected to try, to do everything. Instead, the work of the church should be spread out among its members.

**6:6**
Num 8:10
Acts 1:24; 13:3
1 Tim 4:14

**6:7**
Acts 12:24; 19:20;
21:20

**6:9**
Matt 27:32

**6:10**
Luke 21:15

**6:11**
Matt 26:59-61

**6:13**
Acts 7:48; 21:28

**6:14**
John 2:19-21
Acts 21:21

**7:2**
Gen 11:31–12:1;
15:7
Acts 22:1

**7:3**
†Gen 12:1

**7:4**
Gen 12:5
Heb 11:8

**7:5**
Gen 12:7; 13:15;
15:2, 18; 17:8; 24:7

**7:6**
†Gen 15:13-14

**7:7**
Exod 3:12

earlier convert to the Jewish faith). ⁶These seven were presented to the apostles, who prayed for them as they laid their hands on them.

⁷So God's message continued to spread. The number of believers greatly increased in Jerusalem, and many of the Jewish priests were converted, too.

### Stephen Is Arrested

⁸Stephen, a man full of God's grace and power, performed amazing miracles and signs among the people. ⁹But one day some men from the Synagogue of Freed Slaves, as it was called, started to debate with him. They were Jews from Cyrene, Alexandria, Cilicia, and the province of Asia. ¹⁰None of them could stand against the wisdom and the Spirit with which Stephen spoke.

¹¹So they persuaded some men to lie about Stephen, saying, "We heard him blaspheme Moses, and even God." ¹²This roused the people, the elders, and the teachers of religious law. So they arrested Stephen and brought him before the high council.*

¹³The lying witnesses said, "This man is always speaking against the holy Temple and against the law of Moses. ¹⁴We have heard him say that this Jesus of Nazareth* will destroy the Temple and change the customs Moses handed down to us."

¹⁵At this point everyone in the high council stared at Stephen, because his face became as bright as an angel's.

### Stephen Addresses the Council

**7** Then the high priest asked Stephen, "Are these accusations true?"

²This was Stephen's reply: "Brothers and fathers, listen to me. Our glorious God appeared to our ancestor Abraham in Mesopotamia before he settled in Haran.* ³God told him, 'Leave your native land and your relatives, and come into the land that I will show you.'* ⁴So Abraham left the land of the Chaldeans and lived in Haran until his father died. Then God brought him here to the land where you now live.

⁵"But God gave him no inheritance here, not even one square foot of land. God did promise, however, that eventually the whole land would belong to Abraham and his descendants—even though he had no children yet. ⁶God also told him that his descendants would live in a foreign land, where they would be oppressed as slaves for 400 years. ⁷'But I will punish the nation that enslaves them,' God said, 'and in the end they will come out and worship me here in this place.'*

**6:12** Greek *Sanhedrin;* also in 6:15.   **6:14** Or *Jesus the Nazarene.*   **7:2** *Mesopotamia* was the region now called Iraq. *Haran* was a city in what is now called Syria.   **7:3** Gen 12:1.   **7:5-7** Gen 12:7; 15:13-14; Exod 3:12.

---

**6:6** Spiritual leadership is serious business and must not be taken lightly by the church or its leaders. In the early church, the chosen men were commissioned (by prayer and laying on of hands) by the apostles. Laying hands on someone, an ancient Jewish practice, was a way to set a person apart for special service (see Numbers 27:23; Deuteronomy 34:9).

**6:7** Jesus had told the apostles that they were to witness first in Jerusalem (1:8). In a short time, their message had infiltrated the entire city and all levels of society. Even some Jewish priests were being converted, an obvious violation of the wishes of the high council that would endanger their position.

**6:7** The word of God spread like ripples on a pond where, from a single center, each wave touches the next, spreading wider and farther. The Good News still spreads this way today. You don't have to change the world single-handedly; it is enough just to be part of the wave, touching those around you, who in turn will touch others until all have felt the movement. Don't ever feel that your part is insignificant or unimportant.

**6:9** This was a group of Jewish slaves who had been freed by Rome and had formed their own synagogue in Jerusalem.

**6:11** These men lied about Stephen, causing him to be arrested and brought before the Jewish high council. The Sadducees, the dominant party in the council, accepted and studied only the writings of Moses (Genesis—Deuteronomy). In their view, to speak blasphemy against Moses was a crime. But from Stephen's speech (chapter 7), we learn that this accusation was false. Stephen based his review of Israel's history on Moses' writings.

**6:14** When Stephen was brought before the council of religious leaders, the accusation against him was the same that the religious leaders had used against Jesus (Matthew 26:59-61). The group falsely accused Stephen of wanting to change Moses' customs, because they knew that the Sadducees, who controlled the council, believed *only* in Moses' laws.

**7:1** This high priest was probably Caiaphas, the same man who had earlier questioned and condemned Jesus (John 18:24).

**7:2ff** Stephen launched into a long speech about Israel's relationship with God. From Old Testament history he showed that the Jews had constantly rejected God's message and his prophets and that this council had rejected the Messiah, God's Son. He made three main points: (1) Israel's history is the history of God's acts in the world; (2) people worshiped God long before there was a Temple, because God does not live in a Temple; and (3) Jesus' death was just one more example of Israel's rebellion against and rejection of God.

**7:2ff** Stephen didn't really defend himself. Instead, he took the offensive, seizing the opportunity to summarize his teaching about Jesus. Stephen was accusing these religious leaders of failing to obey God's laws—the laws they prided themselves in following so meticulously. This was the same accusation that Jesus had leveled against them. When we witness for Christ, we don't need to be on the defensive. Instead, we can simply share our faith.

8"God also gave Abraham the covenant of circumcision at that time. So when Abraham became the father of Isaac, he circumcised him on the eighth day. And the practice was continued when Isaac became the father of Jacob, and when Jacob became the father of the twelve patriarchs of the Israelite nation.

9"These patriarchs were jealous of their brother Joseph, and they sold him to be a slave in Egypt. But God was with him 10and rescued him from all his troubles. And God gave him favor before Pharaoh, king of Egypt. God also gave Joseph unusual wisdom, so that Pharaoh appointed him governor over all of Egypt and put him in charge of the palace.

11"But a famine came upon Egypt and Canaan. There was great misery, and our ancestors ran out of food. 12Jacob heard that there was still grain in Egypt, so he sent his sons—our ancestors—to buy some. 13The second time they went, Joseph revealed his identity to his brothers,* and they were introduced to Pharaoh. 14Then Joseph sent for his father, Jacob, and all his relatives to come to Egypt, seventy-five persons in all. 15So Jacob went to Egypt. He died there, as did our ancestors. 16Their bodies were taken to Shechem and buried in the tomb Abraham had bought for a certain price from Hamor's sons in Shechem.

17"As the time drew near when God would fulfill his promise to Abraham, the number of our people in Egypt greatly increased. 18But then a new king came to the throne of Egypt who knew nothing about Joseph. 19This king exploited our people and oppressed them, forcing parents to abandon their newborn babies so they would die.

20"At that time Moses was born—a beautiful child in God's eyes. His parents cared for him at home for three months. 21When they had to abandon him, Pharaoh's daughter adopted him and raised him as her own son. 22Moses was taught all the wisdom of the Egyptians, and he was powerful in both speech and action.

23"One day when Moses was forty years old, he decided to visit his relatives, the people of Israel. 24He saw an Egyptian mistreating an Israelite. So Moses came to the man's defense and avenged him, killing the Egyptian. 25Moses assumed his fellow Israelites would realize that God had sent him to rescue them, but they didn't.

26"The next day he visited them again and saw two men of Israel fighting. He tried to be a peacemaker. 'Men,' he said, 'you are brothers. Why are you fighting each other?'

27"But the man in the wrong pushed Moses aside. 'Who made you a ruler and judge over us?' he asked. 28'Are you going to kill me as you killed that Egyptian yesterday?' 29When Moses heard that, he fled the country and lived as a foreigner in the land of Midian. There his two sons were born.

30"Forty years later, in the desert near Mount Sinai, an angel appeared to Moses in the flame of a burning bush. 31When Moses saw it, he was amazed at the sight. As he went to take a closer look, the voice of the LORD called out to him, 32'I am the God of your ancestors—the God of Abraham, Isaac, and Jacob.' Moses shook with terror and did not dare to look.

33"Then the LORD said to him, 'Take off your sandals, for you are standing on holy ground. 34I have certainly seen the oppression of my people in Egypt. I have heard their groans and have come down to rescue them. Now go, for I am sending you back to Egypt.'*

**7:8** Gen 17:10-14; 21:2-4; 25:26; 35:23-26

**7:9** Gen 37:28; 39:2 Ps 105:17

**7:10** Gen 41:37-43 Ps 105:21

**7:11** Gen 41:54

**7:12** Gen 42:1-2

**7:13** Gen 45:1-4

**7:14** Gen 45:9-10; 46:26-27 Deut 10:22

**7:15** Gen 46:5-7; 49:33 Exod 1:6

**7:16** Gen 23:16-20

**7:17-18** †Exod 1:7-8 Ps 105:24

**7:19** Exod 1:10-11, 22

**7:20** Exod 2:2 Heb 11:23

**7:21** Exod 2:3-10

**7:22** 1 Kgs 4:30 Isa 19:11

**7:23-24** Exod 2:11-12

**7:26-28** †Exod 2:13-14

**7:29** Exod 2:15

**7:30-31** Exod 3:1-4

**7:32-34** †Exod 3:4-10

**7:13** Other manuscripts read *Joseph was recognized by his brothers.*   **7:31-34** Exod 3:5-10.

---

**7:8** Circumcision was a sign of the promise or covenant God made with Abraham and the entire nation of Israel (Genesis 17:9-13). Because Stephen summarized Israel's history, he told how this covenant fared during that time. Stephen pointed out that God always had kept his side of the promise, but Israel had failed again and again to uphold its end. Although the Jews in Stephen's day still circumcised their baby boys, they failed to obey God. The people's hearts were far from God. Their lack of faith and lack of obedience showed that they had failed to keep their part of the covenant.

**7:8** The Jewish rite of circumcision, like Israel's regular sacrifices and annual feasts, was intended to be a very meaningful event. As with all religious rituals, circumcision was designed to serve as an outer symbol of an inner reality. Those who participated

thoughtfully would be reminded of profound spiritual truths. But we know from our own experiences of repeating the church creeds, saying the Lord's Prayer, or celebrating ordinances like baptism and the Lord's Supper, that it is difficult to avoid merely going through the motions. We are often guilty of participating passively and mindlessly in religious exercises. Make it your goal to give God your full attention (body, soul, and spirit) the next time you pray, take Communion, or take part in a church ceremony.

**7:17** Stephen's review of Jewish history gives a clear testimony of God's faithfulness and sovereignty. Despite the continued failures of his chosen people and the swirling world events, God was working out his plan. When faced by a confusing array of circumstances, remember that (1) God is in control—nothing surprises him; (2) this world is not all there is—it will pass away, but God is eternal; (3) God is just, and he will make things right—punishing the wicked and rewarding the faithful; (4) God wants to use you (like Joseph, Moses, and Stephen) to make a difference in the world.

**7:35**
†Exod 2:14

**7:36**
Exod 7:3; 12:41

**7:37**
†Deut 18:15
Acts 3:22

**7:38**
Exod 19:1-6
Deut 32:45-47

35"So God sent back the same man his people had previously rejected when they demanded, 'Who made you a ruler and judge over us?' Through the angel who appeared to him in the burning bush, God sent Moses to be their ruler and savior. 36And by means of many wonders and miraculous signs, he led them out of Egypt, through the Red Sea, and through the wilderness for forty years.

37"Moses himself told the people of Israel, 'God will raise up for you a Prophet like me from among your own people.'* 38Moses was with our ancestors, the assembly of God's people in the wilderness, when the angel spoke to him at Mount Sinai. And there Moses received life-giving words to pass on to us.*

**7:37** Deut 18:15.   **7:38** Some manuscripts read *to you.*

---

**STEPHEN**

Around the world, the gospel has most often taken root in places prepared by the blood of martyrs. But before people can *give* their lives for the gospel, they must first *live* their lives for the gospel. One way God trains his servants is to place them in insignificant positions. Their desire to serve Christ is translated into the reality of serving others.

Long before violent persecution broke out against Christians, there was already social ostracism. Jews who accepted Jesus as Messiah were usually cut off from their families. As a result, the believers depended on each other for support. The sharing of homes, food, and resources was both a practical and necessary mark of the early church. Eventually, the number of believers made it necessary to organize the sharing. People were being overlooked. There were complaints. Those chosen to help manage were chosen for their integrity, wisdom, and sensitivity to God.

Stephen was an effective administrator and messenger before becoming a martyr. He was named one of the managers of food distribution in the early church. And besides being a good administrator, Stephen was also a powerful speaker. When confronted in the Temple by various antagonistic groups, Stephen's logic in responding was convincing. This is clear from the defense he made before the Jewish high council. He presented a summary of the Jews' own history and made powerful applications that stung his listeners. During his defense Stephen must have known he was speaking his own death sentence. Members of the council could not stand to have their evil motives exposed. They stoned him to death while he prayed for their forgiveness. His final words show how much like Jesus he had become in just a short time. His death had a lasting impact on young Saul (Paul) of Tarsus, who would move from being a violent persecutor of Christians to being one of the greatest champions of the gospel the church has known.

Stephen's life is a continual challenge to all Christians. Because he was the first to die for the faith, his sacrifice raises questions: How many risks do we take in being Jesus' followers? Would we be willing to die for him? Are we really willing to live for him?

| | |
|---|---|
| **Strengths and accomplishments** | • One of seven leaders chosen to supervise food distribution to the needy in the early church<br>• Known for his spiritual qualities of faith, wisdom, grace, and power; also known for the Spirit's presence in his life<br>• Outstanding leader, teacher, and debater<br>• First to give his life for the gospel |
| **Lessons from his life** | • Striving for excellence in small assignments prepares one for greater responsibilities<br>• Real understanding of God always leads to practical and compassionate actions toward people |
| **Vital statistics** | • Occupation: Organizer of food distribution<br>• Contemporaries: Paul, Caiaphas, Gamaliel, the apostles |
| **Key verses** | "As they stoned him, Stephen prayed, 'Lord Jesus, receive my spirit.' He fell to his knees, shouting, 'Lord, don't charge them with this sin!' And with that, he died" (Acts 7:59-60). |

Stephen's story is told in Acts 6:3–8:2. He is also mentioned in Acts 11:19; 22:20.

---

**7:37** The Jews originally thought this "Prophet" was Joshua. But Moses was prophesying about the coming Messiah (Deuteronomy 18:15). Peter also quoted this verse in referring to the Messiah (3:22).

**7:38** Stephen used the word *ekklesia* (translated "assembly") to describe the congregation or people of God in the wilderness. This word means "called-out ones" and was used by the first-century Christians to describe their own community or "assembly." Stephen's point was that the giving of the law through

Moses to the Jews was the sign of the covenant. By *obedience,* then, they would continue to be God's covenant people. But because they disobeyed (7:39), they broke the covenant and forfeited their right to be the chosen people.

**7:38** From Galatians 3:19 and Hebrews 2:2, it appears that God had given the law to Moses through angels. Exodus 31:18 says God wrote the Ten Commandments himself ("written by the finger of God"). Apparently God used angelic messengers as mediators to deliver his law to Moses.

39"But our ancestors refused to listen to Moses. They rejected him and wanted to return to Egypt. 40They told Aaron, 'Make us some gods who can lead us, for we don't know what has become of this Moses, who brought us out of Egypt.' 41So they made an idol shaped like a calf, and they sacrificed to it and celebrated over this thing they had made. 42Then God turned away from them and abandoned them to serve the stars of heaven as their gods! In the book of the prophets it is written,

'Was it to me you were bringing sacrifices and offerings
    during those forty years in the wilderness, Israel?
43 No, you carried your pagan gods—
    the shrine of Molech,
    the star of your god Rephan,
    and the images you made to worship them.
So I will send you into exile
    as far away as Babylon.'*

44"Our ancestors carried the Tabernacle* with them through the wilderness. It was constructed according to the plan God had shown to Moses. 45Years later, when Joshua led our ancestors in battle against the nations that God drove out of this land, the Tabernacle was taken with them into their new territory. And it stayed there until the time of King David.

46"David found favor with God and asked for the privilege of building a permanent Temple for the God of Jacob.* 47But it was Solomon who actually built it. 48However, the Most High doesn't live in temples made by human hands. As the prophet says,

49 'Heaven is my throne,
    and the earth is my footstool.
Could you build me a temple as good as that?'
    asks the Lord.
'Could you build me such a resting place?
50    Didn't my hands make both heaven and earth?'*

51"You stubborn people! You are heathen* at heart and deaf to the truth. Must you forever resist the Holy Spirit? That's what your ancestors did, and so do you! 52Name one prophet your ancestors didn't persecute! They even killed the ones who predicted the coming of the Righteous One—the Messiah whom you betrayed and murdered. 53You deliberately disobeyed God's law, even though you received it from the hands of angels."

54The Jewish leaders were infuriated by Stephen's accusation, and they shook their fists at him in rage.* 55But Stephen, full of the Holy Spirit, gazed steadily into heaven and saw the glory of God, and he saw Jesus standing in the place of honor at God's right hand. 56And he told them, "Look, I see the heavens opened and the Son of Man standing in the place of honor at God's right hand!"

**7:39** Num 14:3
**7:40** †Exod 32:1, 23
**7:42-43** †Amos 5:25-27
**7:44** Exod 25:9, 40 Heb 8:5
**7:45** Josh 3:14-17; 18:1; 23:9 2 Sam 7:2, 6
**7:46** 2 Sam 7:2-16 1 Kgs 8:17 Ps 132:1-5
**7:47** 1 Kgs 6:1-38
**7:48** 2 Chr 2:6 Isa 57:15 Eph 2:22 1 Pet 2:5
**7:49-50** †Isa 66:1-2
**7:51** Exod 32:9; 33:3, 5
**7:52** Matt 23:30-34
**7:53** Gal 3:19
**7:55** Heb 1:3, 13
**7:56** Matt 3:16

**7:42-43** Amos 5:25-27 (Greek version).   **7:44** Greek *the tent of witness*.   **7:46** Some manuscripts read *the house of Jacob*.   **7:49-50** Isa 66:1-2.   **7:51** Greek *uncircumcised*.   **7:54** Greek *they were grinding their teeth against him*.

**7:43** Here Stephen gave more details of the idolatry referred to in 7:40. These were idols worshiped by Israel during their wilderness wanderings (Exodus 32:4). Molech was the god associated with child sacrifice, and Rephan was an Egyptian god. Amos also names Assyrian deities worshiped by Israel (Amos 5:25-27).

**7:44-50** Stephen had been accused of speaking against the Temple (6:13). Although he recognized the importance of the Temple, he knew that it was not more important than God. God is not limited; he lives not only in a house of worship but also in those who are open to receive him (Isaiah 66:1, 2). Solomon knew this when he prayed at the dedication of the Temple (2 Chronicles 6:18). God wants to live in us. Is he living in you?

**7:52** Indeed, many prophets were persecuted and killed: Uriah (Jeremiah 26:20-23); Jeremiah (Jeremiah 38:1-6); Isaiah (tradition says he was killed by King Manasseh; see 2 Kings 21:16); Amos (Amos 7:10-13); Zechariah (not the author of the Bible book but the son of Jehoiada the priest; see 2 Chronicles 24:20-22); Elijah (1 Kings 19:1, 2). Jesus also told a parable about how the Jews had constantly rejected God's messages and persecuted his messengers (Luke 20:9-19).

**7:55-58** Stephen saw the glory of God and Jesus, the Messiah, standing at God's right hand. Stephen's words are similar to Jesus' words spoken before the high council (Matthew 26:64; Mark 14:62; Luke 22:69). Stephen's vision supported Jesus' claim and angered the Jewish leaders who had condemned Jesus to death for blasphemy. They would not tolerate Stephen's words, so they dragged him out and killed him. People may not kill us for witnessing about Christ, but they may let us know they don't want to hear the truth and try to silence us. Keep honoring God in your conduct and words; though many may turn against you and your message, some will follow Christ. Remember, Stephen's death had a profound impact on Paul, who later became the world's greatest missionary. Even those who oppose you now may later turn to Christ.

7:58
Lev 24:14-16
Deut 17:7
7:59
Ps 31:5
Luke 23:46
7:60
Luke 23:34

57 Then they put their hands over their ears and began shouting. They rushed at him 58 and dragged him out of the city and began to stone him. His accusers took off their coats and laid them at the feet of a young man named Saul.*

59 As they stoned him, Stephen prayed, "Lord Jesus, receive my spirit." 60 He fell to his knees, shouting, "Lord, don't charge them with this sin!" And with that, he died.

8:1
Acts 7:58

**8** Saul was one of the witnesses, and he agreed completely with the killing of Stephen.

## 2. Expansion of the church
### Persecution Scatters the Believers

A great wave of persecution began that day, sweeping over the church in Jerusalem; and all the believers except the apostles were scattered through the regions of Judea and Samaria.

8:3
Acts 9:1; 22:4;
26:9-11
1 Cor 15:9
Gal 1:13

2 (Some devout men came and buried Stephen with great mourning.) 3 But Saul was going everywhere to destroy the church. He went from house to house, dragging out both men and women to throw them into prison.

### Philip Preaches in Samaria

8:4
Acts 8:1; 11:19
8:5
Acts 6:5; 21:8

4 But the believers who were scattered preached the Good News about Jesus wherever they went. 5 Philip, for example, went to the city of Samaria and told the people there about the Messiah. 6 Crowds listened intently to Philip because they were eager to hear his message

7:58 Saul is later called Paul; see 13:9.

---

**THE EFFECTS OF STEPHEN'S DEATH**

Stephen's death was not in vain. Below are some of the events that were by-products (either directly or indirectly) of the persecution that began with Stephen's martyrdom.

1. Philip's evangelistic tour (Acts 8:4-40)
2. Paul's (Saul's) conversion (Acts 9:1-30)
3. Peter's missionary tour (Acts 9:32–11:18)
4. The church in Antioch of Syria founded (Acts 11:19ff)

---

**7:58** Saul is also called Paul (see 13:9), the great missionary who wrote many of the letters in the New Testament. Saul was his Hebrew name; Paul, his Greek name, was used as he began his ministry to the Gentiles. When Luke introduces him, Paul was going everywhere persecuting Jesus' followers. This is in great contrast to the Paul about whom Luke wrote for most of the book of Acts, describing him as a devoted follower of Christ and a gifted preacher. Paul was uniquely qualified to talk to the Jews about Jesus because he had once persecuted those who believed in him and understood how the opposition felt. Paul is a powerful example of a person who was thought impossible for God to reach and change.

**7:59** The penalty for blasphemy, speaking irreverently about God, was death by stoning (Leviticus 24:14). The religious leaders, who were furious, had Stephen stoned without a trial. They did not understand that Stephen's words were true because they were not seeking the truth. They only wanted support for their own views.

**7:60** As Stephen died, he spoke words very similar to Jesus' words on the cross (Luke 23:34). For telling others the good news of Jesus' death, burial, and resurrection the members of the early church were persecuted. Sometimes, as in the case of Stephen, they were even put to death. Christ had promised his followers that living for him would lead to trouble (see Luke 21:12-19). This is still true. If we boldly live out our faith, the light of our lives will expose the sinfulness of others. Our words of truth will pierce their souls. Some will be convicted and yield to the leading of the Spirit. Others will become angry and hardened in their hatred of the truth. As Jesus said, "They will do all this to you because of me, for they have rejected the One who sent me" (John 15:21). We shouldn't be surprised or abandon our faith when we are persecuted.

**8:1-4** Persecution pushed the Christians beyond Jerusalem and into Judea and Samaria, thus fulfilling the second part of Jesus' command (see 1:8). The persecution helped spread the Good News. God would bring great results from the believers' suffering.

**8:4** Persecution forced the believers out of their homes in Jerusalem, and along with them went the Good News. Sometimes we have to become uncomfortable before we'll move. We may not want to experience it, but discomfort may be best for us because God may be working through our hurts. When you are tempted to complain about uncomfortable or painful circumstances, stop and ask if God might be preparing you for a special task.

**8:5** This is not the apostle Philip (see John 1:43, 44) but a Greek-speaking Jew, "full of the Spirit and wisdom" (6:3), who was one of the seven men chosen to help with the food distribution program in the church (6:5).

**8:5** Israel had been divided into three main regions: Galilee in the north, Samaria in the middle, and Judea in the south. The city of Samaria (in the region of Samaria) had been the capital of the northern kingdom of Israel in the days of the divided kingdom before it was conquered by Assyria in 722 B.C. During that war, the Assyrian king had taken many captives, leaving only the poorest people in the land and resettling it with foreigners. These foreigners had intermarried with the Jews who were left, and the mixed race became known as Samaritans. The Samaritans were considered half-breeds by the "pure" Jews in the southern kingdom of Judah, and the two groups hated each other intensely. But Jesus himself went into Samaria (John 4), and he commanded his followers to spread the Good News there (1:8).

and see the miraculous signs he did. ⁷Many evil* spirits were cast out, screaming as they left their victims. And many who had been paralyzed or lame were healed. ⁸So there was great joy in that city.

⁹A man named Simon had been a sorcerer there for many years, amazing the people of Samaria and claiming to be someone great. ¹⁰Everyone, from the least to the greatest, often spoke of him as "the Great One—the Power of God." ¹¹They listened closely to him because for a long time he had astounded them with his magic.

¹²But now the people believed Philip's message of Good News concerning the Kingdom of God and the name of Jesus Christ. As a result, many men and women were baptized. ¹³Then Simon himself believed and was baptized. He began following Philip wherever he went, and he was amazed by the signs and great miracles Philip performed.

¹⁴When the apostles in Jerusalem heard that the people of Samaria had accepted God's message, they sent Peter and John there. ¹⁵As soon as they arrived, they prayed for these new believers to receive the Holy Spirit. ¹⁶The Holy Spirit had not yet come upon any of them, for they had only been baptized in the name of the Lord Jesus. ¹⁷Then Peter and John laid their hands upon these believers, and they received the Holy Spirit.

¹⁸When Simon saw that the Spirit was given when the apostles laid their hands on people, he offered them money to buy this power. ¹⁹"Let me have this power, too," he exclaimed, "so that when I lay my hands on people, they will receive the Holy Spirit!"

²⁰But Peter replied, "May your money be destroyed with you for thinking God's gift can be bought! ²¹You can have no part in this, for your heart is not right with God. ²²Repent of your wickedness and pray to the Lord. Perhaps he will forgive your evil thoughts, ²³for I can see that you are full of bitter jealousy and are held captive by sin."

**8:7** Matt 10:1 Mark 6:7; 16:17
**8:9** Acts 5:36; 13:6
**8:12** Acts 2:38
**8:13** Acts 19:11
**8:14** Acts 8:1
**8:15** Acts 2:38; 19:2
**8:16** Acts 10:44
**8:17** Acts 6:6; 19:6
**8:20** Matt 10:8
**8:21** Ps 78:37
**8:23** Deut 29:17-18 Isa 58:6

**8:7** Greek *unclean.*

---

**8:7** Jesus encountered and drove out many evil spirits during his ministry on earth. Evil spirits, or demons, are ruled by Satan. Most scholars believe that demons are fallen angels who joined Satan in his rebellion against God. They can cause a person to be mute, deaf, blind, or insane and also tempt people to sin. Although they can be powerful, they are not able to read our minds and cannot be everywhere at once. Demons are real and active, but Jesus has given authority over them to his followers. Although Satan is allowed to work in our world, God is in complete control. He can drive demons out and end their destructive work in people's lives. Eventually Satan and his demons will be thrown into the lake of fire, forever ending their evil work in the world (Revelation 20:10).

**8:9-11** In the days of the early church, sorcerers and magicians were numerous and influential. They worked wonders, performed healings and exorcisms, and practiced astrology. Their wonders may simply have been magic tricks, or the sorcerers may have

been empowered by Satan (Matthew 24:24; 2 Thessalonians 2:9). Simon had done so many wonders that some even thought that he was the Messiah; but his powers did not come from God (see 8:18-24).

**8:14** Peter and John were sent to Samaria to find out whether or not the Samaritans were truly becoming believers. The Jewish Christians, even the apostles, were still unsure whether Gentiles (non-Jews) and half-Jews could receive the Holy Spirit. It wasn't until Peter's experience with Cornelius (chapter 10) that the apostles became fully convinced that the Holy Spirit was for all people. John had asked Jesus if they should call fire down from heaven to burn up a Samaritan village that refused to welcome them (Luke 9:51-55). Here he and Peter went to the Samaritans to pray with them.

**8:15-17** This was a crucial moment for the spread of the Good News and for the growth of the church. Peter and John had to go to Samaria to help keep this new group of believers from becoming separated from other believers. When Peter and John saw the Lord working in these people, they were assured that the Holy Spirit worked through *all* believers—Gentiles and mixed races as well as "pure" Jews.

**8:15-17** Many scholars believe that God chose to give this dramatic filling of his Spirit as a sign at this special moment in history—the spread of the Good News into Samaria through the powerful, effective preaching of believers. Normally, the Holy Spirit enters a person's life at conversion. This was a special event. The pouring out of the Spirit would happen again with Cornelius and his family (10:44-47), a sign that the uncircumcised Gentiles could receive the Good News.

**8:18-23** "Everything has a price" seems to be true in our world of bribes, wealth, and materialism. Simon thought he could buy the Holy Spirit's power, but Peter harshly rebuked him. Why? The only way to receive God's power is to do what Peter told Simon to do—repent, ask God for forgiveness, and be filled with his Spirit. No amount of money can buy salvation, forgiveness of sin, or God's power. These are only gained by repentance and belief in Christ as Savior. In addition, Simon apparently wanted that ability for selfish reasons: to have power, to make money, or to gain prestige. God doesn't give us abilities to enhance our own lives. He grants us gifts so that we may bring him glory by

**PHILIP'S MINISTRY**

To escape persecution in Jerusalem, Philip fled to Samaria, where he continued preaching the gospel. While he was there, an angel commanded him to meet an Ethiopian official on the road between Jerusalem and Gaza. The man became a believer before continuing on to Ethiopia. Philip then went from Azotus to Caesarea.

8:24
Exod 8:8
Num 21:7

24"Pray to the Lord for me," Simon exclaimed, "that these terrible things you've said won't happen to me!"

25After testifying and preaching the word of the Lord in Samaria, Peter and John returned to Jerusalem. And they stopped in many Samaritan villages along the way to preach the Good News.

### Philip and the Ethiopian Eunuch

8:26
Acts 5:19; 6:5

8:27
1 Kgs 8:41-43
Ps 68:31
Isa 56:3-5
Zeph 3:10

26As for Philip, an angel of the Lord said to him, "Go south* down the desert road that runs from Jerusalem to Gaza." 27So he started out, and he met the treasurer of Ethiopia, a eunuch of great authority under the Kandake, the queen of Ethiopia. The eunuch had gone to Jerusalem to worship, 28and he was now returning. Seated in his carriage, he was reading aloud from the book of the prophet Isaiah.

29The Holy Spirit said to Philip, "Go over and walk along beside the carriage."

30Philip ran over and heard the man reading from the prophet Isaiah. Philip asked, "Do you understand what you are reading?"

31The man replied, "How can I, unless someone instructs me?" And he urged Philip to come up into the carriage and sit with him.

8:26 Or *Go at noon.*

| MISSIONARIES OF THE NEW TESTAMENT AND THEIR JOURNEYS | Name | Journey's Purpose | Scripture Reference in Acts |
|---|---|---|---|
| | Philip | One of the first to preach the gospel outside Jerusalem | 8:4-40 |
| | Peter and John | Visited new Samaritan believers to encourage them | 8:14-25 |
| | Paul (journey to Damascus) | Set out to capture Christians but was captured by Christ | 9:1-25 |
| | Peter | Led by God to one of the first Gentile families to become Christians—Cornelius's family | 9:32–10:48 |
| | Barnabas | Went to Antioch as an encourager; traveled on to Tarsus to bring Paul back to Antioch; took famine relief to Jerusalem | 11:25-30 |
| | Barnabas, Paul, John Mark | Left Antioch for Cyprus, Pamphylia, and Galatia on the first missionary journey | 13:1–14:28 |
| | Barnabas and John Mark | Left Antioch for Cyprus after a disagreement with Paul | 15:36-41 |
| | Paul, Silas, Timothy, Luke | Left Antioch to revisit churches in Galatia; then traveled on to Asia, Macedonia, and Achaia on the second missionary journey | 15:36–18:22 |
| | Apollos | Left Alexandria for Ephesus; learned the complete gospel story from Priscilla and Aquila; preached in Athens and Corinth | 18:24-28 |
| | Paul, Timothy, Erastus | Revisited churches in Galatia, Asia, Macedonia, and Achaia on the third major missionary journey | 18:23; 19:1–21:14 |

building up others. When you find yourself wishing for an ability that would put you into the limelight or somehow enrich you personally, check your motives. Instead of sitting around wishing for talents you don't have, spend your time serving God and others with the gifts you *do* possess.

**8:24** The last time a parent or friend rebuked you, were you hurt, angry, or defensive? Learn a lesson from Simon and his reaction to what Peter told him. He exclaimed, "Pray to the Lord for me." If you are rebuked for a serious mistake, it is for your good. Admit your error, repent quickly, and ask for prayer.

**8:26** Philip was having a successful preaching ministry to great crowds in Samaria (8:5-8), but he obediently left that ministry to travel on a desert road. Because Philip went where God sent him, Ethiopia was opened up to the Good News. Follow God's leading, even if it seems like a demotion. At first you may not understand his plans, but the results will prove that God's way is right.

**8:27** Ethiopia is located in Africa south of Egypt. The eunuch was obviously very dedicated to God because he had traveled

such a long distance to worship in Jerusalem. The Jews had contact with Ethiopia in ancient days (Psalm 68:31; Jeremiah 38:7), so this man may have been a Gentile convert to Judaism. Because he was in charge of the treasury of Ethiopia, this man's conversion brought Christianity into the power structures of another government. This is the beginning of the witness "to the ends of the earth" (1:8). See the prophecy in Isaiah 56:3-8 for words about foreigners and eunuchs.

**8:29-35** Philip found the Ethiopian man reading Scripture. Taking advantage of this opportunity to explain the Good News, Philip asked the man if he understood what he was reading. Philip (1) followed the Spirit's leading, (2) began the discussion from where the man was (immersed in the prophecies of Isaiah), and (3) explained how Jesus Christ fulfilled Isaiah's prophecies. When we share the Good News, we should start where the other person's concerns are focused. Then we can show how God's Word applies to those concerns.

32 The passage of Scripture he had been reading was this:

> "He was led like a sheep to the slaughter.
> And as a lamb is silent before the shearers,
> he did not open his mouth.
> 33 He was humiliated and received no justice.
> Who can speak of his descendants?
> For his life was taken from the earth."*

**8:32-33**
†Isa 53:7-8

34 The eunuch asked Philip, "Tell me, was the prophet talking about himself or someone else?" 35 So beginning with this same Scripture, Philip told him the Good News about Jesus. 36 As they rode along, they came to some water, and the eunuch said, "Look! There's some water! Why can't I be baptized?"* 38 He ordered the carriage to stop, and they went down into the water, and Philip baptized him.

**8:35**
Luke 24:27
Acts 18:28

**8:36**
Acts 10:47

39 When they came up out of the water, the Spirit of the Lord snatched Philip away. The eunuch never saw him again but went on his way rejoicing. 40 Meanwhile, Philip found himself farther north at the town of Azotus. He preached the Good News there and in every town along the way until he came to Caesarea.

**8:39**
1 Kgs 18:12
2 Kgs 2:16
Ezek 3:12

### Saul's Conversion

**9** Meanwhile, Saul was uttering threats with every breath and was eager to kill the Lord's followers.* So he went to the high priest. 2 He requested letters addressed to the synagogues in Damascus, asking for their cooperation in the arrest of any followers of the Way he found there. He wanted to bring them—both men and women—back to Jerusalem in chains.

**9:1-29**
//Acts 22:3-21;
26:9-18

**9:1**
Acts 8:3

**9:2**
Acts 9:14; 22:4

3 As he was approaching Damascus on this mission, a light from heaven suddenly shone down around him. 4 He fell to the ground and heard a voice saying to him, "Saul! Saul! Why are you persecuting me?"

**9:3**
Acts 22:6-7;
26:12-13
1 Cor 15:8

**8:32-33** Isa 53:7-8 (Greek version).   **8:36** Some manuscripts add verse 37, *"You can," Philip answered, "if you believe with all your heart." And the eunuch replied, "I believe that Jesus Christ is the Son of God."*   **9:1** Greek *disciples.*

---

**8:35** Some think that the Old Testament is not relevant today, but Philip led this man to faith in Jesus Christ by using the Old Testament. Jesus Christ is found in the pages of both the Old and New Testaments. God's entire Word is applicable to all people in all ages. Don't avoid or neglect to use the Old Testament. It, too, is God's Word.

**8:38** Baptism was a sign of identification with Christ and with the Christian community. Although Philip was the only witness, it was still important for the eunuch to take this step.

**8:39, 40** Why was Philip suddenly transported to a different city? This miraculous sign showed the urgency of bringing the

Gentiles to belief in Christ. Azotus is Ashdod, one of the ancient Philistine capitals. Philip probably lived in Caesarea for the next 20 years (21:8).

**9:2** Saul (later called Paul) was so zealous for his Jewish beliefs that he began a persecution campaign against anyone who believed in Christ ("followers of the Way"). Why would the Jews in Jerusalem want to persecute Christians as far away as Damascus? There are several possibilities: (1) to seize the Christians who had fled, (2) to prevent the spread of Christianity to other major cities, (3) to keep the Christians from causing any trouble with Rome, (4) to advance Saul's career and build his reputation as a true Pharisee, zealous for the law, (5) to unify the factions of Judaism by giving them a common enemy.

**9:2-5** As Saul traveled to Damascus, pursuing Christians, he was confronted by the risen Christ and brought face to face with the truth of the Good News. Sometimes God breaks into a life in a spectacular manner, and sometimes conversion is a quiet experience. Beware of people who insist that you must have a particular type of conversion experience. The right way to come to faith in Jesus is whatever way God brings *you.*

**9:3** Damascus, a key commercial city, was located about 150 miles northeast of Jerusalem in the Roman province of Syria. Several trade routes linked Damascus to other cities throughout the Roman world. Saul may have thought that by stamping out Christianity in Damascus, he could prevent its spread to other areas.

**9:3-5** Paul refers to this experience as the start of his new life in Christ (1 Corinthians 9:1; 15:8; Galatians 1:15, 16). At the center of this wonderful experience was Jesus Christ. Paul did not see a vision; he saw the risen Christ himself (9:17). Paul acknowledged Jesus as Lord, confessed his own sin, surrendered his life to Christ, and resolved to obey him. True conversion comes from a personal encounter with Jesus Christ and leads to a new life in relationship with him.

**SAUL TRAVELS TO DAMASCUS**
Many Christians fled Jerusalem when persecution began after Stephen's death, seeking refuge in other cities and countries. Saul tracked them down, even traveling 150 miles to Damascus in Syria to bring Christians back in chains to Jerusalem. But as he neared the ancient city, he discovered that God had other plans for him (9:15).

**9:5**
Acts 5:39

**9:7**
Dan 10:7
Acts 22:9; 26:14

**9:10**
Acts 10:3; 11:5;
12:9; 22:12

**9:11**
Acts 21:39

**9:13**
Acts 26:10

⁵"Who are you, lord?" Saul asked.

And the voice replied, "I am Jesus, the one you are persecuting! ⁶Now get up and go into the city, and you will be told what you must do."

⁷The men with Saul stood speechless, for they heard the sound of someone's voice but saw no one! ⁸Saul picked himself up off the ground, but when he opened his eyes he was blind. So his companions led him by the hand to Damascus. ⁹He remained there blind for three days and did not eat or drink.

¹⁰Now there was a believer* in Damascus named Ananias. The Lord spoke to him in a vision, calling, "Ananias!"

"Yes, Lord!" he replied.

¹¹The Lord said, "Go over to Straight Street, to the house of Judas. When you get there, ask for a man from Tarsus named Saul. He is praying to me right now. ¹²I have shown him a vision of a man named Ananias coming in and laying hands on him so he can see again."

¹³"But Lord," exclaimed Ananias, "I've heard many people talk about the terrible things

**9:10** Greek *disciple;* also in 9:26, 36.

---

Jesus' last words to his followers were a command to take the gospel everywhere, but they seemed reluctant to leave Jerusalem. It took intense persecution to scatter the believers from Jerusalem and into Judea and Samaria, where Jesus had instructed them to go. Philip, one of the men in charge of food distribution, left Jerusalem and, like most Jewish Christians, spread the gospel wherever he went; but unlike most of them, he did not limit his audience to other Jews. He went directly to Samaria—the last place many Jews would go due to age-old prejudice.

The Samaritans responded in large numbers. When word got back to Jerusalem, Peter and John were sent to evaluate Philip's ministry. They quickly became involved themselves, seeing firsthand God's acceptance of those who previously were considered unacceptable.

In the middle of all this success and excitement, God directed Philip out to the desert for an appointment with an Ethiopian eunuch, another foreigner, who had been in Jerusalem. Philip went immediately. His effectiveness in sharing the gospel with this man placed a Christian in a significant position in a distant country and may well have had an effect on an entire nation.

Philip ended up in Caesarea, where events allowed him to be Paul's host many years later. Paul, who, as the leading persecutor of the Christians, had been instrumental in pushing Philip and others out of Jerusalem, had himself become an effective believer. Philip began the conversion of the Gentiles, which was continued across the entire Roman Empire by Paul.

Whether or not you are a follower of Christ, Philip's life presents a challenge. To those still outside the gospel, he is a reminder that the gospel is for you also. To those who have accepted Christ, he is a reminder that we are not free to disqualify anyone from hearing about Jesus. How much like Philip would your neighbors say you are?

| | |
|---|---|
| **Strengths and accomplishments** | • One of the seven organizers of food distribution in the early church<br>• Became an evangelist, one of the first traveling missionaries<br>• One of the first to obey Jesus' command to take the gospel to all people<br>• A careful student of the Bible who could explain its meaning clearly |
| **Lessons from his life** | • God finds great and various uses for those willing to obey wholeheartedly<br>• The gospel is universal Good News<br>• The whole Bible, not just the New Testament, helps us understand more about Jesus<br>• Both mass response (the Samaritans) and individual response (the man from Ethiopia) to the gospel are valuable |
| **Vital statistics** | • Occupations: Organizer of food distribution, evangelist<br>• Relatives: Four daughters<br>• Contemporaries: Paul, Stephen, the apostles |
| **Key verse** | "So beginning with this same Scripture, Philip told him the Good News about Jesus" (Acts 8:35). |

Philip's story is told in Acts 6:1-7; 8:5-40; 21:8-10.

---

**9:5** Saul thought he was pursuing heretics, but he was persecuting Jesus himself. Anyone who persecutes believers today is also guilty of persecuting Jesus (see Matthew 25:40, 45) because believers are the body of Christ on earth.

**9:13, 14** "Not him, Lord; that's impossible. He could never become a Christian!" In essence, that's what Ananias said when

God told him of Saul's conversion. After all, Saul had pursued believers to their death. Despite these understandable feelings, Ananias obeyed God and ministered to Saul. We must not limit God—he can do anything. We must obey and follow God's leading, even when he leads us to difficult people and places.

this man has done to the believers* in Jerusalem! ¹⁴And he is authorized by the leading priests to arrest everyone who calls upon your name."

¹⁵But the Lord said, "Go, for Saul is my chosen instrument to take my message to the Gentiles and to kings, as well as to the people of Israel. ¹⁶ And I will show him how much he must suffer for my name's sake."

¹⁷So Ananias went and found Saul. He laid his hands on him and said, "Brother Saul, the Lord Jesus, who appeared to you on the road, has sent me so that you might regain your sight and be filled with the Holy Spirit." ¹⁸Instantly something like scales fell from Saul's eyes, and he regained his sight. Then he got up and was baptized. ¹⁹Afterward he ate some food and regained his strength.

### Saul in Damascus and Jerusalem
Saul stayed with the believers* in Damascus for a few days. ²⁰And immediately he began preaching about Jesus in the synagogues, saying, "He is indeed the Son of God!"

²¹All who heard him were amazed. "Isn't this the same man who caused such devastation among Jesus' followers in Jerusalem?" they asked. "And didn't he come here to arrest them and take them in chains to the leading priests?"

²²Saul's preaching became more and more powerful, and the Jews in Damascus couldn't refute his proofs that Jesus was indeed the Messiah. ²³After a while some of the Jews plotted together to kill him. ²⁴They were watching for him day and night at the city gate so they could murder him, but Saul was told about their plot. ²⁵So during the night, some of the other believers* lowered him in a large basket through an opening in the city wall.

²⁶When Saul arrived in Jerusalem, he tried to meet with the believers, but they were all afraid of him. They did not believe he had truly become a believer! ²⁷Then Barnabas brought him to the apostles and told them how Saul had seen the Lord on the way to Damascus and how the Lord had spoken to Saul. He also told them that Saul had preached boldly in the name of Jesus in Damascus.

**9:15**
Acts 13:2
Rom 1:1
Gal 1:15-16
1 Tim 1:12

**9:16**
Acts 20:23; 21:11
2 Cor 11:23-27

**9:17**
Acts 13:52;
22:12-13
1 Cor 9:1; 15:8

**9:19**
Acts 26:20

**9:21**
Acts 8:3

**9:22**
Acts 18:28

**9:23**
Acts 23:12

**9:24**
Acts 20:3;
23:16, 20
2 Cor 11:32

**9:25**
1 Sam 19:12
2 Cor 11:33

**9:26**
Acts 22:17
Gal 1:17-18

**9:27**
Acts 4:36

**9:13** Greek *God's holy people;* also in 9:32, 41.  **9:19** Greek *disciples;* also in 9:26, 38.  **9:25** Greek *his disciples.*

---

**9:15, 16** Faith in Christ brings great blessings but often great suffering, too. Paul would suffer for his faith (see 2 Corinthians 11:23-27). God calls us to commitment, not to comfort. He promises to be with us *through* suffering and hardship, not to spare us from them.

**9:17** Ananias found Saul, as he had been instructed, and greeted him as "Brother Saul." Ananias feared this meeting because Saul had come to Damascus to capture the believers and take them as prisoners to Jerusalem (9:2). In obedience to the Holy Spirit, however, Ananias greeted Saul lovingly. It is not always easy to love others, especially when we are afraid of them or doubt their motives. Nevertheless we must follow Jesus' command (John 13:34) and Ananias's example, showing loving acceptance to other believers.

**9:17, 18** Although Acts makes no mention of a special filling of the Holy Spirit for Saul, his changed life and subsequent accomplishments bear strong witness to the Holy Spirit's presence and power in him. Evidently, the Holy Spirit had filled Saul when he received his sight and was baptized. See the second note on 8:15-17 for more on the filling of the Holy Spirit.

**9:20** Immediately after receiving his sight and spending some time with the believers in Damascus, Saul went to the synagogue to tell the Jews about Jesus Christ. Some Christians counsel new believers to wait until they are thoroughly grounded in their faith before attempting to share the Good News. Saul spent time with other believers to learn about Jesus before beginning his worldwide ministry, but he did not wait to witness. Although we should not rush into a ministry unprepared, we do not need to wait before telling others what has happened to us.

**9:21, 22** Saul's arguments were powerful because he was a brilliant scholar. Even more convincing, however, was his changed life. People knew that what Saul taught was real because they could see the evidence in the way he lived. It is important to know what the Bible teaches and how to defend the faith, but your life should back up your words.

**9:23** According to Galatians 1:17, 18, Paul left Damascus and traveled to Arabia, the desert region just southeast of Damascus, where he lived for three years. It is unclear whether his three-year stay occurred between verses 22 and 23 or between verses 25 and 26. Some commentators say that "after a while" could mean a long period of time. They suggest that when Paul returned to Damascus, the governor under Aretas ordered his arrest (2 Corinthians 11:32) in an effort to keep peace with influential Jews.

The other possibility is that Paul's night escape occurred during his first stay in Damascus, just after his conversion, when the Pharisees were especially upset over his defection from their

**SAUL'S RETURN TO TARSUS**
At least three years elapsed between Acts 9:22 and 9:26. After time alone in Arabia (see Galatians 1:16–18), Saul (Paul) returned to Damascus and then to Jerusalem. The apostles were reluctant to believe that this former persecutor could have become one of them. Saul escaped to Caesarea, where he caught a ship and returned to Tarsus.

PAUL

No person, apart from Jesus himself, shaped the history of Christianity like the apostle Paul. Even before he was a believer, his actions were significant. His frenzied persecution of Christians following Stephen's death got the church started in obeying Christ's final command to take the gospel worldwide. Paul's personal encounter with Jesus changed his life. He never lost his fierce intensity, but from then on it was channeled for the gospel.

Paul was very religious. His training under Gamaliel was the finest available. His intentions and efforts were sincere. He was a good Pharisee who knew the Bible and sincerely believed that this Christian movement was dangerous to Judaism. Thus, Paul hated the Christian faith and persecuted Christians without mercy.

Paul got permission to travel to Damascus to capture Christians and bring them back to Jerusalem. But God stopped him in his hurried tracks on the Damascus road. Paul personally met Jesus Christ, and his life was never the same.

Until Paul's conversion, little had been done about carrying the gospel to non-Jews. Philip had preached in Samaria and to an Ethiopian man; Cornelius, a Gentile, was converted under Peter; and in Antioch of Syria, some Greeks had joined the believers. When Barnabas was sent from Jerusalem to check on this situation, he went to Tarsus to find Paul and bring him to Antioch, and together they worked among the believers there. They were then sent on a missionary journey, the first of three Paul would take that would carry the gospel across the Roman Empire.

The thorny issue of whether Gentile believers had to obey Jewish laws before they could become Christians caused many problems in the early church. Paul worked hard to convince the Jews that Gentiles were acceptable to God, but he spent even more time convincing the Gentiles that they were acceptable to God. The lives Paul touched were changed and challenged by meeting Christ through him.

God did not waste any part of Paul—his background, his training, his citizenship, his mind, or even his weaknesses. Are you willing to let God do the same for you? You will never know all he can do with you until you allow him to have all that you are!

| | |
|---|---|
| **Strengths and accomplishments** | • Transformed by God from a persecutor of Christians to a preacher for Christ<br>• Preached for Christ throughout the Roman Empire on three missionary journeys<br>• Wrote letters to various churches, which became part of the New Testament<br>• Was never afraid to face an issue head-on and deal with it<br>• Was sensitive to God's leading and, despite his strong personality, always did as God directed<br>• Is often called the apostle to the Gentiles |
| **Weaknesses and mistakes** | • Witnessed and approved of Stephen's stoning<br>• Set out to destroy Christianity by persecuting Christians |
| **Lessons from his life** | • The Good News is that forgiveness and eternal life are available to all people and are gifts of God's grace through faith in Christ<br>• Obedience results from a relationship with God, but obedience will never create or earn that relationship<br>• Real freedom doesn't come until we no longer have to prove our freedom<br>• God does not waste our time; he will use our past and present so we may serve him with our future |
| **Vital statistics** | • Where: Born in Tarsus but became a world traveler for Christ<br>• Occupations: Trained as a Pharisee, learned the tentmaking trade, served as a missionary<br>• Contemporaries: Gamaliel, Stephen, the apostles, Luke, Barnabas, Timothy |
| **Key verses** | "For to me, living means living for Christ, and dying is even better. But if I live, I can do more fruitful work for Christ. So I really don't know which is better. I'm torn between two desires: I long to go and be with Christ, which would be far better for me. But for your sakes, it is better that I continue to live" (Philippians 1:21-24). |

Paul's story is told in Acts 7:58—28:31 and throughout his New Testament letters.

---

ranks. He would have fled to Arabia to spend time alone with God and to let the Jewish religious leaders cool down. Regardless of which theory is correct, there was a period of at least three years between Paul's conversion (9:3-6) and his trip to Jerusalem (9:26).

**9:26, 27** It is difficult to change your reputation, and Saul had a terrible reputation with the Christians. But Barnabas, a Jewish convert (mentioned in 4:36), became the bridge between Saul

and the apostles. New Christians (especially those with tarnished reputations) need sponsors, people who will come alongside, encourage, teach, and introduce them to other believers. In what ways can you become a Barnabas to new believers?

**9:27** Galatians 1:18, 19 explains that Paul was in Jerusalem only 15 days and that he met only with Peter and James.

²⁸So Saul stayed with the apostles and went all around Jerusalem with them, preaching boldly in the name of the Lord. ²⁹He debated with some Greek-speaking Jews, but they tried to murder him. ³⁰When the believers* heard about this, they took him down to Caesarea and sent him away to Tarsus, his hometown.

³¹The church then had peace throughout Judea, Galilee, and Samaria, and it became stronger as the believers lived in the fear of the Lord. And with the encouragement of the Holy Spirit, it also grew in numbers.

### Peter Heals Aeneas and Raises Dorcas

³²Meanwhile, Peter traveled from place to place, and he came down to visit the believers in the town of Lydda. ³³There he met a man named Aeneas, who had been paralyzed and bedridden for eight years. ³⁴Peter said to him, "Aeneas, Jesus Christ heals you! Get up, and roll up your sleeping mat!" And he was healed instantly. ³⁵Then the whole population of Lydda and Sharon saw Aeneas walking around, and they turned to the Lord.

³⁶There was a believer in Joppa named Tabitha (which in Greek is Dorcas*). She was always doing kind things for others and helping the poor. ³⁷About this time she became ill and died. Her body was washed for burial and laid in an upstairs room. ³⁸But the believers had heard that Peter was nearby at Lydda, so they sent two men to beg him, "Please come as soon as possible!"

³⁹So Peter returned with them; and as soon as he arrived, they took him to the upstairs room. The room was filled with widows who were weeping and showing him the coats and other clothes Dorcas had made for them. ⁴⁰But Peter asked them all to leave the room; then he knelt and prayed. Turning to the body he said, "Get up, Tabitha." And she opened her eyes! When she saw Peter, she sat up! ⁴¹He gave her his hand and helped her up. Then he called in the widows and all the believers, and he presented her to them alive.

⁴²The news spread through the whole town, and many believed in the Lord. ⁴³And Peter stayed a long time in Joppa, living with Simon, a tanner of hides.

### Cornelius Calls for Peter

**10** In Caesarea there lived a Roman army officer* named Cornelius, who was a captain of the Italian Regiment. ²He was a devout, God-fearing man, as was everyone in his

**9:31** Acts 8:1
**9:32** Acts 8:14
**9:34** Acts 3:6; 4:10
**9:35** Acts 2:41
**9:36** 1 Tim 2:10 Titus 3:8
**9:40** 1 Kgs 17:19-23 2 Kgs 4:32-36 Matt 9:25 John 11:43
**9:42** Acts 2:41
**9:43** Acts 10:6
**10:1-2** Acts 8:40; 27:1, 3

**9:30** Greek *brothers.* **9:36** The names *Tabitha* in Aramaic and *Dorcas* in Greek both mean "gazelle." **10:1** Greek *a centurion;* similarly in 10:22.

---

**9:29, 30** In these short sentences we can see two characteristics of Paul, even as a new believer in Christ: He was bold, and he stirred up controversy. These would characterize Paul's ministry the rest of his life.

**9:30** Saul's visit to Tarsus helped quiet conflicts with the Jews and allowed him time to prove his commitment. After Saul, the most zealous persecutor, was converted, the church enjoyed a brief time of peace.

**PETER'S MINISTRY**
Peter traveled to the ancient crossroads town of Lydda, where he healed crippled Aeneas. The believers in Joppa, an old port city, sent for him after a wonderful woman died. Peter went and brought her back to life. While in Joppa, Peter had a vision that led him to take the gospel to Cornelius, a Gentile, in Caesarea.

**9:36** The important harbor city of Joppa sits 125 feet above sea level overlooking the Mediterranean Sea. Joppa was the town into which the cedars of Lebanon had been floated to be shipped to Jerusalem for use in the Temple construction (2 Chronicles 2:16; Ezra 3:7). The prophet Jonah had left the port of Joppa on his ill-fated trip (Jonah 1:3).

**9:36-42** Tabitha made an enormous impact on her community by "always doing kind things for others and helping the poor," by making coats and other garments (9:39). When she died, the room was filled with mourners, very likely many of the people she had helped. And when she was brought back to life, the news raced through the town. God uses great preachers like Peter and Paul, but he also uses those who have gifts of kindness like Tabitha. Rather than wishing you had other gifts, make good use of the gifts God has given you.

**9:43** In Joppa, Peter stayed at the home of Simon, a tanner of hides—a leatherworker. Leatherworkers made animal hides into leather. It is significant that Peter was at Simon's house because leatherworking involved contact with dead animals, and Jewish law considered it an "unclean" occupation. Peter was already beginning to break down his prejudice against people who were not of his kind and who had customs that did not adhere to Jewish religious traditions.

**10:1** This Caesarea, sometimes called Palestinian Caesarea, was located on the coast of the Mediterranean Sea, 32 miles north of Joppa. The largest and most important port city on the Mediterranean in Palestine, Caesarea served as the capital of the Roman province of Judea. This was the first city to have Gentile Christians and a non-Jewish church.

**10:1** This Roman officer was a centurion—a commander of 100 soldiers. Although stationed in Caesarea, Cornelius would

10:3
Acts 3:1

10:4
2 Chr 7:15
Rev 8:4

household. He gave generously to the poor and prayed regularly to God. ³One afternoon about three o'clock, he had a vision in which he saw an angel of God coming toward him. "Cornelius!" the angel said.

⁴Cornelius stared at him in terror. "What is it, sir?" he asked the angel.

## GREAT ESCAPES IN THE BIBLE

| Who escaped | Reference | What happened | What the escape accomplished | Application |
|---|---|---|---|---|
| Jacob | Genesis 31:1-55 | Fled from his father-in-law, Laban, after almost 20 years of service | Allowed Jacob to return home for Isaac's death and for reconciliation with Esau, his brother | A time away from home often puts the really important things into perspective |
| Moses | Exodus 2:11-15 | Fled Egypt after killing an Egyptian in defense of a fellow Israelite | Saved his own life and began another part of God's training | God fits even our mistakes into his plan |
| Israelites | Exodus 12:28-42 | Escaped Egypt after 430 years, most of that time in slavery | God confirmed his choice of Abraham's descendants | God will not forget his promises |
| Spies | Joshua 2:1-24 | Escaped searchers in Jericho by hiding in Rahab's house | Prepared the destruction of Jericho and preserved Rahab, who would become one of David's ancestors—as well as an ancestor of Jesus | God's plan weaves lives together in a pattern beyond our understanding |
| Ehud | Judges 3:15-30 | Escaped undetected after assassinating the Moabite king Eglon | Broke the control of Moab over Israel and began 80 years of peace | Punishments by God are often swift and deadly |
| Samson | Judges 16:1-3 | Escaped a locked city by ripping the gates from their hinges | Merely postponed Samson's self-destruction because of his lack of self-control | Without dependence on God and his guidance, even great ability is wasted |
| Elijah | 1 Kings 19:1-18 | Fled into the wilderness out of fear of Queen Jezebel | Preserved Elijah's life but also displayed his human weakness | Even at moments of real success, our personal weaknesses are our greatest challenges |
| Saul (Paul) | Acts 9:23-25 | Lowered over the wall in a basket to get out of Damascus | Saved this new Christian for great service to God | God has a purpose for every life, which leads to a real adventure for those willing to cooperate |
| Peter | Acts 12:1-11 | Freed from prison by an angel | Saved Peter for God's further plans for his life | God can use extraordinary means to carry out his plan—often when we least expect it |
| Paul and Silas | Acts 16:22-40 | Chains loosened and doors opened by an earthquake, but they chose not to leave the prison | Pointed out the powerlessness of humans before God | When our dependence and attention are focused on God rather than our problems, he is able to offer help in unexpected ways |

probably return soon to Rome. Thus, his conversion was a major stepping-stone for spreading the Good News to the empire's capital city.

**10:2** What will happen to the heathen who have never heard about Christ? This question is often asked about God's justice. Cornelius wasn't a believer in Christ, but he was seeking God and was reverent and generous. Therefore, God sent Peter to tell Cornelius about Christ. This shows that God "rewards those who sincerely seek him" (Hebrews 11:6). Cornelius's story demonstrates God's willingness to use extraordinary means to reach those who desire to know him. Those who sincerely seek God will find him! God made Cornelius's knowledge complete.

**10:3** Cornelius had a vision featuring a heavenly messenger. God spoke to other Bible characters through a variety of means—the burning bush of Moses (Exodus 3:1-4); the talking donkey of Balaam (Numbers 22:21-30); the gentle whisper heard by Elijah (1 Kings 19:11-14); the strange object lessons of Jeremiah (Jeremiah 13:1-11). Simply put, God speaks to his people in remarkably different ways—through the written Scriptures, through the words of others, through circumstances and events. It is up to us to listen, to be perceptive, to be alert. What is God trying to say to you today?

And the angel replied, "Your prayers and gifts to the poor have been received by God as an offering! 5Now send some men to Joppa, and summon a man named Simon Peter. 6He is staying with Simon, a tanner who lives near the seashore."

10:6
Acts 9:43

7As soon as the angel was gone, Cornelius called two of his household servants and a devout soldier, one of his personal attendants. 8He told them what had happened and sent them off to Joppa.

### Peter Visits Cornelius

9The next day as Cornelius's messengers were nearing the town, Peter went up on the flat roof to pray. It was about noon, 10and he was hungry. But while a meal was being prepared, he fell into a trance. 11He saw the sky open, and something like a large sheet was let down by its four corners. 12In the sheet were all sorts of animals, reptiles, and birds. 13Then a voice said to him, "Get up, Peter; kill and eat them."

10:9-32
//Acts 11:5-14
10:11
Ezek 1:1-3
Matt 3:16
Acts 7:56

14"No, Lord," Peter declared. "I have never eaten anything that our Jewish laws have declared impure and unclean.*"

10:14
Lev 11:1-47
Ezek 4:14

15But the voice spoke again: "Do not call something unclean if God has made it clean." 16The same vision was repeated three times. Then the sheet was suddenly pulled up to heaven.

10:15
Matt 15:11
Rom 14:14, 17, 20
1 Cor 10:25
1 Tim 4:3-4
Titus 1:15

17Peter was very perplexed. What could the vision mean? Just then the men sent by Cornelius found Simon's house. Standing outside the gate, 18they asked if a man named Simon Peter was staying there.

19Meanwhile, as Peter was puzzling over the vision, the Holy Spirit said to him, "Three men have come looking for you. 20Get up, go downstairs, and go with them without hesitation. Don't worry, for I have sent them."

10:19
Acts 11:12; 13:2
10:20
Acts 15:7-9

21So Peter went down and said, "I'm the man you are looking for. Why have you come?"

22They said, "We were sent by Cornelius, a Roman officer. He is a devout and God-fearing man, well respected by all the Jews. A holy angel instructed him to summon you to his house so that he can hear your message." 23So Peter invited the men to stay for the night. The next day he went with them, accompanied by some of the brothers from Joppa.

10:22
Acts 10:2
10:23
Acts 10:45; 11:12

24They arrived in Caesarea the following day. Cornelius was waiting for them and had called together his relatives and close friends. 25As Peter entered his home, Cornelius fell at his feet and worshiped him. 26But Peter pulled him up and said, "Stand up! I'm a human being just like you!" 27So they talked together and went inside, where many others were assembled.

10:24
Acts 8:40
10:25-26
Acts 14:13-15
Rev 19:10; 22:9

28Peter told them, "You know it is against our laws for a Jewish man to enter a Gentile home like this or to associate with you. But God has shown me that I should no longer think of anyone as impure or unclean. 29So I came without objection as soon as I was sent for. Now tell me why you sent for me."

10:28
John 4:9
Acts 11:3; 15:9

30Cornelius replied, "Four days ago I was praying in my house about this same time, three o'clock in the afternoon. Suddenly, a man in dazzling clothes was standing in front of me. 31He told me, 'Cornelius, your prayer has been heard, and your gifts to the poor have been noticed by God! 32Now send messengers to Joppa, and summon a man named Simon Peter. He is staying in the home of Simon, a tanner who lives near the seashore.' 33So I sent for you at once, and it was good of you to come. Now we are all here, waiting before God to hear the message the Lord has given you."

10:30-33
Acts 10:1-8

10:14 Greek anything common and unclean.

---

10:12 According to Jewish law, certain foods were forbidden to be eaten (see Leviticus 11). The food laws made it difficult for Jews to eat with Gentiles without risking defilement. In fact, the Gentiles themselves were often seen as "unclean." Peter's vision meant that he should not look upon the Gentiles as inferior people whom God would not redeem. Before having the vision, Peter would have thought that a Gentile Roman officer could not become a follower of Christ. Afterward he understood that it was his responsibility to go with the messengers into a Gentile home and tell Cornelius the Good News of salvation in Jesus Christ.

10:15, 16 Steeped in Jewish tradition and filled with certain biases, Peter was convinced his views on the Gentiles were correct. It took a three-part heavenly vision for God to change Peter's mind. One of the most basic and practical lessons from this encounter is that when God speaks, we must not challenge what he says. Doubting God is the rebellion of Eden. When God says something is so, we must not debate with him. The right response is humble submission to his revealed truth. Are you trying to argue with God over some point that he has already made clear?

10:21, 22 Cornelius was religious, devoted, generous, respected, and sincere (10:1, 2). However, he was still spiritually separated from God. Because he needed to understand the gospel, God sent Peter to present to him the truth about salvation. Be careful not to equate earnestness with righteousness before God. We are brought into right standing with God by faith in Christ alone. Have you trusted in Jesus? Are you sharing with others—even those who seem religious—the truth that Christ is the only way to God?

**10:34**
Deut 10:17
Rom 2:11
Col 3:25

**10:35**
Acts 15:9

**10:36**
Rom 5:1
Eph 2:17

**10:38**
Luke 4:18-19

### The Gentiles Hear the Good News

34Then Peter replied, "I see very clearly that God shows no favoritism. 35In every nation he accepts those who fear him and do what is right. 36This is the message of Good News for the people of Israel—that there is peace with God through Jesus Christ, who is Lord of all. 37You know what happened throughout Judea, beginning in Galilee, after John began preaching his message of baptism. 38And you know that God anointed Jesus of Nazareth with the Holy Spirit and with power. Then Jesus went around doing good and healing all who were oppressed by the devil, for God was with him.

**CORNELIUS**

The early days of Christianity were exciting as God's Spirit moved and people's lives were changed. Converts were pouring in from surprising backgrounds. Even the dreaded Saul (Paul) became a Christian, and non-Jews were responding to the Good News about Jesus. Among the first of these was the Roman captain Cornelius.

Because of frequent outbreaks of violence, Roman soldiers had to be stationed throughout Israel to keep the peace. But most Romans, hated as conquerors, did not get along well in the nation. As an army officer, Cornelius was in a difficult position. He represented Rome, but his home was in Caesarea. During his years in Israel, he himself had been conquered by the God of Israel. He had a reputation as a godly man who put his faith into action, and he was respected by the Jews.

Four significant aspects of Cornelius's character are noted in Acts: (1) He actively sought God, (2) he revered God, (3) he was generous in meeting other people's needs, and (4) he prayed. God told him to send for Peter, because Peter would give him more knowledge about the God he was already seeking to please.

When Peter entered Cornelius's home, Peter broke a whole list of Jewish rules. Peter confessed he wasn't comfortable, but here was an eager audience, and he couldn't hold back his message. He had no sooner started sharing the gospel when God gave overwhelming approval by filling that Roman family with his Holy Spirit. Peter saw he had no choice but to baptize them and welcome them as equals in the growing Christian church. Another step had been taken in carrying the gospel to the whole world.

Cornelius is a welcome example of God's willingness to use extraordinary means to reach those who desire to know him. He does not play favorites, and he does not hide from those who want to find him. God sent his Son because he loves the whole world—and that includes Peter, Cornelius, and you.

| | |
|---|---|
| **Strengths and accomplishments** | • A godly and generous Roman<br>• Well-respected by the Jews even though he was an officer in the occupying army<br>• He responded to God and encouraged his family to do the same<br>• His conversion helped the young church realize that the Good News was for all people, both Jews and Gentiles |
| **Lessons from his life** | • God reaches those who want to know him<br>• The gospel is for all people<br>• There are people everywhere eager to believe<br>• When we are willing to seek the truth and be obedient to the light God gives us, God will reward us richly |
| **Vital statistics** | • Where: Caesarea<br>• Occupation: Roman army officer<br>• Contemporaries: Peter, Philip, the apostles |
| **Key verse** | "He was a devout, God-fearing man, as was everyone in his household. He gave generously to the poor and prayed regularly to God" (Acts 10:2). |

Cornelius's story is told in Acts 10:1–11:18.

**10:34, 35** Perhaps the greatest barrier to the spread of the Good News in the first century was the Jewish-Gentile conflict. Most of the early believers were Jewish, and they thought it scandalous even to think of associating with Gentiles. But God told Peter to take the Good News to a Roman, and Peter obeyed despite his background and personal feelings. (Later Peter struggled with this again—see Galatians 2:11-14.) God was making it clear that the Good News of Christ is for everyone! We should not allow any barrier—language, culture, race, geography, economic level, or educational level—to keep us from telling others about Christ.

**10:35** Every nation has people who are restless for God, ready to receive the Good News—but someone must take it to them.

Seeking God is not enough—people must find him. How then shall seekers find God without someone to point the way? Is God asking you to show someone the way to him? (See Romans 10:14, 15.)

**10:37-43** Peter's brief and powerful sermon contains a concise statement of the Good News: Jesus' perfect life of servanthood; his death on the cross; his resurrection, personally witnessed and experienced by Peter; Jesus' fulfillment of the Scriptures; the necessity of personal faith in him. A sermon or witness for Christ does not need to be long to be effective. It should be Spirit-led and should center on Christ, the way and the truth and the life.

<sup>39</sup>"And we apostles are witnesses of all he did throughout Judea and in Jerusalem. They put him to death by hanging him on a cross,* <sup>40</sup>but God raised him to life on the third day. Then God allowed him to appear, <sup>41</sup>not to the general public,* but to us whom God had chosen in advance to be his witnesses. We were those who ate and drank with him after he rose from the dead. <sup>42</sup>And he ordered us to preach everywhere and to testify that Jesus is the one appointed by God to be the judge of all—the living and the dead. <sup>43</sup>He is the one all the prophets testified about, saying that everyone who believes in him will have their sins forgiven through his name."

**10:39**
Luke 24:48
**10:40-41**
John 21:12-13

**10:42**
Matt 28:19
2 Cor 5:10
**10:43**
Isa 53:11
Jer 31:34

### The Gentiles Receive the Holy Spirit

<sup>44</sup>Even as Peter was saying these things, the Holy Spirit fell upon all who were listening to the message. <sup>45</sup>The Jewish believers* who came with Peter were amazed that the gift of the Holy Spirit had been poured out on the Gentiles, too. <sup>46</sup>For they heard them speaking in other tongues* and praising God.

Then Peter asked, <sup>47</sup>"Can anyone object to their being baptized, now that they have received the Holy Spirit just as we did?" <sup>48</sup>So he gave orders for them to be baptized in the name of Jesus Christ. Afterward Cornelius asked him to stay with them for several days.

**10:44**
Acts 11:15; 15:8
**10:46**
Mark 16:17
Acts 2:4; 19:6
**10:47**
Acts 8:36; 11:17
**10:48**
Acts 2:38; 19:5

### Peter Explains His Actions

**11** Soon the news reached the apostles and other believers* in Judea that the Gentiles had received the word of God. <sup>2</sup>But when Peter arrived back in Jerusalem, the Jewish believers* criticized him. <sup>3</sup>"You entered the home of Gentiles* and even ate with them!" they said.

<sup>4</sup>Then Peter told them exactly what had happened. <sup>5</sup>"I was in the town of Joppa," he said, "and while I was praying, I went into a trance and saw a vision. Something like a large sheet was let down by its four corners from the sky. And it came right down to me. <sup>6</sup>When I looked inside the sheet, I saw all sorts of tame and wild animals, reptiles, and birds. <sup>7</sup>And I heard a voice say, 'Get up, Peter; kill and eat them.'

<sup>8</sup>"No, Lord,' I replied. 'I have never eaten anything that our Jewish laws have declared impure or unclean.*'

<sup>9</sup>"But the voice from heaven spoke again: 'Do not call something unclean if God has made it clean.' <sup>10</sup>This happened three times before the sheet and all it contained was pulled back up to heaven.

<sup>11</sup>"Just then three men who had been sent from Caesarea arrived at the house where we were staying. <sup>12</sup>The Holy Spirit told me to go with them and not to worry that they were

**11:3**
Acts 10:28
Gal 2:12

**11:5-14**
//Acts 10:9-32

**11:12**
Acts 10:23, 45

**10:39** Greek *on a tree.* **10:41** Greek *the people.* **10:45** Greek *The faithful ones of the circumcision.* **10:46** Or *in other languages.* **11:1** Greek *brothers.* **11:2** Greek *those of the circumcision.* **11:3** Greek *of uncircumcised men.* **11:8** Greek *anything common or unclean.*

---

**10:43** Two examples of prophets testifying about Jesus and his forgiveness of sins are Isaiah 52:13–53:12 and Ezekiel 36:25, 26.

**10:45** Cornelius and Peter were very different people. Cornelius was wealthy, a Gentile, and a military man. Peter was a Jewish fisherman turned preacher. But God's plan included both of them. In Cornelius's house that day, a new chapter in Christian history was written as a Jewish Christian leader and a Gentile Christian convert each discovered something significant about the other. Cornelius needed Peter in order to hear the Good News and know the way of salvation. Peter needed Cornelius in order to know that Gentiles were included in God's plan. You and another believer may also need each other to understand how God works!

**10:47, 48** In this case, the people were baptized *after* they received the Holy Spirit, publicly declaring their allegiance to Christ and identification with the Christian community.

**10:48** Cornelius wanted Peter to stay with him for several days. He was a new believer and realized his need for teaching and fellowship. Are you as eager to learn more about Christ? Recognize your need to be with mature Christians, and strive to learn from them.

**11:1-3** A Gentile was anyone who was not a Jew. Most Jewish believers thought that God offered salvation only to the Jews because God had given his law to them (Exodus 19–20). A group in Jerusalem believed that Gentiles could be saved, but only if they followed all the Jewish laws and traditions—in essence, if they

first became Jews before becoming Christians. Both groups were mistaken. God chose the Jews and taught them his laws so they could bring the message of salvation to *all* people (see Genesis 12:3; Psalm 22:27; Isaiah 42:4; 49:6; 56:3-7; 60:1-3; Jeremiah 16:19-21; Zechariah 2:11; Malachi 1:11; Romans 15:9-12).

**11:2-18** When Peter brought the news of Cornelius's conversion back to Jerusalem, the believers were shocked that Peter had eaten with Gentiles. After they heard the whole story, however, they praised God (11:18). Their reactions teach us how to handle disagreements with other Christians. Before judging the behavior of fellow believers, it is important to hear them out. The Holy Spirit may have something important to teach us through them.

**11:8** God had promised throughout Scripture that he would reach the nations. This began with his general promise to Abraham (Genesis 12:3; 18:18) and became very specific in Malachi's statement: "But my name is honored by people of other nations from morning till night" (Malachi 1:11). But this was an extremely difficult truth for Jews, even Jewish believers, to accept. The Jewish believers understood how certain prophecies were fulfilled in Christ, but they overlooked other Old Testament teachings. Too often we are inclined to accept only the parts of God's Word that appeal to us and support our own agendas, ignoring the teachings we don't like. We must accept all of God's Word as absolute truth.

**11:12ff** Peter's defense for eating with Gentiles was a simple

11:13
Acts 10:30-32

11:14
Acts 10:22, 44;
16:31

11:15
Acts 2:4

11:16
Acts 1:5

11:17
Acts 10:47

11:18
Acts 13:48

11:19
Acts 8:1-4; 13:1;
14:25-27; 15:3

11:21
Luke 1:66
Acts 2:41

11:22
Acts 4:36

11:23
Acts 13:43; 14:26;
15:40; 20:24

11:24
Acts 2:41

Gentiles. These six brothers here accompanied me, and we soon entered the home of the man who had sent for us. ¹³He told us how an angel had appeared to him in his home and had told him, 'Send messengers to Joppa, and summon a man named Simon Peter. ¹⁴He will tell you how you and everyone in your household can be saved!'

¹⁵"As I began to speak," Peter continued, "the Holy Spirit fell on them, just as he fell on us at the beginning. ¹⁶Then I thought of the Lord's words when he said, 'John baptized with* water, but you will be baptized with the Holy Spirit.' ¹⁷And since God gave these Gentiles the same gift he gave us when we believed in the Lord Jesus Christ, who was I to stand in God's way?"

¹⁸When the others heard this, they stopped objecting and began praising God. They said, "We can see that God has also given the Gentiles the privilege of repenting of their sins and receiving eternal life."

### The Church in Antioch of Syria

¹⁹Meanwhile, the believers who had been scattered during the persecution after Stephen's death traveled as far as Phoenicia, Cyprus, and Antioch of Syria. They preached the word of God, but only to Jews. ²⁰However, some of the believers who went to Antioch from Cyprus and Cyrene began preaching to the Gentiles* about the Lord Jesus. ²¹The power of the Lord was with them, and a large number of these Gentiles believed and turned to the Lord.

²²When the church at Jerusalem heard what had happened, they sent Barnabas to Antioch. ²³When he arrived and saw this evidence of God's blessing, he was filled with joy, and he encouraged the believers to stay true to the Lord. ²⁴Barnabas was a good man, full of the Holy Spirit and strong in faith. And many people were brought to the Lord.

**11:16** Or *in;* also in 11:16b.   **11:20** Greek *the Hellenists* (i.e., those who speak Greek); other manuscripts read *the Greeks.*

---

restatement of what happened. He brought six witnesses with him to back him up, and then he quoted Jesus' promise about the coming of the Holy Spirit (11:16). These Gentiles' lives had been changed, and that was all the evidence Peter and the other believers needed. Changed lives are an equally powerful evidence today.

**11:16** Jesus had also demonstrated clearly that he and his message were for all people. He had preached in Samaria (John 4:1-42); in the region of the Gerasenes, populated by Greeks (Mark 5:1-20); and he even had reached out to Romans (Luke 7:1-10). The apostles shouldn't have been surprised that they were called to do the same.

**11:18** The intellectual questions ended, and the theological discussion stopped with the report that God had given the Holy Spirit to the Gentiles. This was a turning point for the early church. They had to accept those whom God had chosen, even if they were Gentiles. But joy over the conversion of Gentiles was not unanimous. This continued to be a struggle for some Jewish Christians throughout the first century.

**11:20, 21** In Antioch, Christianity was launched on its worldwide mission and there the believers aggressively preached to the Gentiles (non-Jews who did not worship God). Philip had preached in Samaria, but the Samaritans were part Jewish (8:5); Peter had preached to Cornelius, but he already worshiped God (10:2). Believers who were scattered after the outbreak of persecution in Jerusalem spread the Good News to other Jews in the lands they fled to (11:19). The seeds of this missionary work had been sown after Stephen's death. At this time, the believers began actively sharing the Good News with Gentiles.

**11:22** With the exception of Jerusalem, Antioch of Syria played a more important role in the early church than any other city. After Rome and Alexandria, Antioch was the largest city in the Roman world. In Antioch the first Gentile church was founded, and there the believers were first called Christians (11:26). Paul used the city as his home base during his missionary journeys. Antioch was the center of worship for several pagan cults that promoted sexual immorality and other forms of evil common to pagan religions. It was also a vital

commercial center—the gateway to the eastern world. Antioch was a key city both to Rome and to the early church.

**11:22-26** Barnabas presents a wonderful example of how to help new Christians. He demonstrated strong faith; he ministered joyfully with kindness and encouragement; he taught new believers further lessons about God (see 9:26-30). Remember Barnabas when you see new believers, and think of ways to help them grow in their faith.

### BARNABAS AND SAUL IN ANTIOCH

Persecution scattered the believers into Phoenicia, Cyprus, and Antioch, and the gospel went with them. Most spoke only to Jews, but in Antioch, some Gentiles were converted. The church sent Barnabas to investigate, and he was pleased with what he found. Barnabas went to Tarsus to bring Saul (Paul) back to Antioch.

25 Then Barnabas went on to Tarsus to look for Saul. 26When he found him, he brought him back to Antioch. Both of them stayed there with the church for a full year, teaching large crowds of people. (It was at Antioch that the believers* were first called Christians.)

27During this time some prophets traveled from Jerusalem to Antioch. 28One of them named Agabus stood up in one of the meetings and predicted by the Spirit that a great famine was coming upon the entire Roman world. (This was fulfilled during the reign of Claudius.) 29So the believers in Antioch decided to send relief to the brothers and sisters* in Judea, everyone giving as much as they could. 30This they did, entrusting their gifts to Barnabas and Saul to take to the elders of the church in Jerusalem.

### James Is Killed and Peter Is Imprisoned

**12** About that time King Herod Agrippa* began to persecute some believers in the church. 2He had the apostle James (John's brother) killed with a sword. 3When Herod saw how much this pleased the Jewish people, he also arrested Peter. (This took place during the Passover celebration.*) 4Then he imprisoned him, placing him under the guard of four squads of four soldiers each. Herod intended to bring Peter out for public trial after the Passover. 5But while Peter was in prison, the church prayed very earnestly for him.

### Peter's Miraculous Escape from Prison

6The night before Peter was to be placed on trial, he was asleep, fastened with two chains between two soldiers. Others stood guard at the prison gate. 7Suddenly, there was a bright light in the cell, and an angel of the Lord stood before Peter. The angel struck him on the side to awaken him and said, "Quick! Get up!" And the chains fell off his wrists. 8Then the angel told him, "Get dressed and put on your sandals." And he did. "Now put on your coat and follow me," the angel ordered.

9So Peter left the cell, following the angel. But all the time he thought it was a vision. He didn't realize it was actually happening. 10They passed the first and second guard posts and

**11:25**
†Acts 9:30

**11:27**
Acts 13:1; 15:32

**11:29**
Rom 15:26

**11:30**
Acts 12:25
1 Pet 5:1

**12:2**
Matt 4:21; 20:23

**12:4-10**
Acts 5:18-25
**12:5**
Eph 6:18

**12:7**
Acts 5:19

**12:9**
Acts 9:10
**12:10**
Acts 5:19; 16:26

11:26 Greek *disciples;* also in 11:29.   **11:29** Greek *the brothers.*   **12:1** Greek *Herod the king.* He was the nephew of Herod Antipas and a grandson of Herod the Great.   **12:3** Greek *the days of unleavened bread.*

---

**11:25** Saul had been sent to his home in Tarsus for protection after his conversion had caused an uproar among the Jewish leaders in Jerusalem (9:26-30). He stayed there for several years before Barnabas brought him to help the church at Antioch.

**11:26** The young church at Antioch was a curious mixture of Jews (who spoke Greek or Aramaic) and Gentiles. It is significant that this is the first place where the believers were called Christians (or "Christ-ones") because all they had in common was Christ—not race, culture, or even language. Christ's love crosses all boundaries and unites all people.

**11:26** Barnabas and Saul stayed at Antioch for a full year, teaching the new believers. They could have left for other cities, but they saw the importance of follow-up and training. Have you helped someone believe in Christ? Spend time teaching and encouraging that person. Are you a new believer? Remember, you are just beginning your Christian life. Your faith needs to grow and mature through consistent Bible study and teaching.

**11:27, 28** Prophets were found not only in the Old Testament but also in the early church. Their role was to present God's will to the people and to instruct them in God's word. Sometimes, like Agabus, they also had the gift of predicting the future.

**11:28, 29** Serious food shortages occurred during the reign of the Roman emperor Claudius (A.D. 41–54) because of a drought that had extended across much of the Roman Empire for many years. It is significant that the church in Antioch assisted the church in Jerusalem. The daughter church had grown enough to be able to help the established church.

**11:29** The people of Antioch were motivated to give generously because they cared about the needs of others. This is the cheerful giving that the Bible commends (2 Corinthians 9:7). Reluctant giving reflects a lack of concern for people. Focus your concern on the needy, and you will be motivated to give.

**12:1** King Herod Agrippa I was the son of Aristobulus and grandson of Herod the Great. His sister was Herodias, who had

been responsible for the death of John the Baptist (see Mark 6:17-28). Herod Agrippa I was part Jewish. The Romans had appointed him to rule over most of Palestine, including the territories of Galilee, Perea, Judea, and Samaria. He persecuted the Christians in order to please the Jewish leaders who opposed them, hoping that would solidify his position. Agrippa I died suddenly in A.D. 44 (see 12:20-23). His death was also recorded by the historian Josephus.

**12:2** James and John were two of Jesus' original 12 disciples. They had asked Jesus for special recognition in his Kingdom (Mark 10:35-40). Jesus had said that to be a part of his Kingdom would mean suffering with him (drink from the same cup—Mark 10:38, 39). James and John did indeed suffer—Herod executed James, and later John was exiled (see Revelation 1:9).

**12:2-11** Why did God allow James to die and yet miraculously save Peter? Life is full of difficult questions like this. Why is one child physically disabled and another child athletically gifted? Why do people die before realizing their potential? Questions like these we cannot possibly answer in this life because we do not see all that God sees. He has chosen to allow evil in this world for a time. But we can trust God's leading because he has promised to destroy all evil eventually. In the meantime, we know that God will help us use our suffering to strengthen us and glorify him. For more on this question, see the notes on Job 1:1ff; 2:10; 3:23-26.

**12:3-5** Herod had Peter arrested during the Passover celebration. This was a strategic move, since more Jews were in the city than usual, and Herod could impress the most people. Herod's plan undoubtedly was to execute Peter, but the believers were praying for Peter's safety. The earnest prayer of the church significantly affected the outcome of these events. Prayer changes things, so pray often and with confidence.

**12:7** God sent an angel to rescue Peter. Angels are God's messengers. They are divinely created beings with supernatural power, and they sometimes take on human appearance in order came to the iron gate leading to the city, and this opened for them all by itself. So they passed through and started walking down the street, and then the angel suddenly left him.

**12:11**
Ps 34:7
Dan 3:28; 6:22
2 Pet 2:9

¹¹Peter finally came to his senses. "It's really true!" he said. "The Lord has sent his angel and saved me from Herod and from what the Jewish leaders* had planned to do to me!"

**12:12**
Acts 12:25; 15:37
Col 4:10
1 Pet 5:13

¹²When he realized this, he went to the home of Mary, the mother of John Mark, where many were gathered for prayer. ¹³He knocked at the door in the gate, and a servant girl named Rhoda came to open it. ¹⁴When she recognized Peter's voice, she was so overjoyed that, instead of opening the door, she ran back inside and told everyone, "Peter is standing at the door!"

**12:11** Or *the Jewish people.*

---

For good or evil, families have lasting and powerful influence on their children. Traits and qualities are passed on to the next generation, and often with the mistakes and sins of the parents being repeated by the children. Four generations of the Herod family are mentioned in the Bible. Each leader left his evil mark: Herod the Great murdered Bethlehem's baby boys; Herod Antipas was involved in Jesus' trial and John the Baptist's execution; Herod Agrippa I murdered the apostle James; and Herod Agrippa II was one of Paul's judges.

Herod Agrippa I related fairly well to his Jewish subjects. He had a Jewish grandmother of royal blood (Mariamne), which allowed the people to accept him—though grudgingly. As a youth, Agrippa I had been temporarily imprisoned by the emperor Tiberias, but he was now trusted by Rome and got along well with the emperors Caligula and Claudius.

An unexpected opportunity for Herod to gain new favor with the Jews was created by the Christian movement. Gentiles began to be accepted into the church in large numbers. Many Jews had been tolerating this new movement as a sect within Judaism, but its rapid growth alarmed them. Persecution of Christians was revived, and even the apostles were not spared. James was killed, and Peter was thrown into prison.

But soon Herod made a fatal error. During a visit to Caesarea, the people called him a god, and he accepted their praise. Herod was immediately struck with a painful disease, and he died within a week.

Like his grandfather and uncle before him, and his son after him, Herod Agrippa I came close to the truth but missed it. Because religion was important only as an aspect of politics, he had no reverence and no qualms about taking praise that only God should receive. His mistake is a common one. Whenever we become proud of our own abilities and accomplishments, not recognizing them as gifts from God, we repeat Herod's sin.

**HEROD AGRIPPA I**

| | |
|---|---|
| **Strengths and accomplishments** | • Capable administrator and negotiator<br>• Managed to maintain good relations with the Jews in his region and with Rome |
| **Weaknesses and mistakes** | • Arranged the murder of the apostle James<br>• Imprisoned Peter with plans to execute him<br>• Allowed the people to praise him as a god |
| **Lessons from his life** | • Those who set themselves against God are doomed to ultimate failure<br>• There is great danger in accepting praise that only God deserves<br>• Family traits can influence children toward great good or great evil |
| **Vital statistics** | • Where: Jerusalem<br>• Occupation: Roman-appointed king of the Jews<br>• Relatives: Grandfather: Herod the Great. Father: Aristobulus. Uncle: Herod Antipas. Sister: Herodias. Wife: Cypros. Son: Herod Agrippa II. Daughters: Bernice, Mariamne, Drusilla.<br>• Contemporaries: Emperors Tiberias, Caligula, and Claudius. James, Peter, the apostles. |
| **Key verse** | "Instantly, an angel of the Lord struck Herod with a sickness, because he accepted the people's worship instead of giving the glory to God. So he was consumed with worms and died" (Acts 12:23). |

Herod Agrippa I's story is told in Acts 12:1-23.

---

to talk to people. Angels should not be worshiped because they are not divine. They are God's servants, just as we are.

**12:12** John Mark wrote the Gospel of Mark. His mother's house was large enough to accommodate a meeting of many believers. An upstairs room in this house may have been the location of Jesus' Last Supper with his disciples (Luke 22:8ff).

**12:13-15** The prayers of the group of believers were answered, even as they prayed. But when the answer arrived at the door, they didn't believe it. We should be people of faith who believe that God answers the prayers of those who seek his will. When you pray, believe you'll get an answer. And when the answer comes, don't be surprised; be thankful!

15"You're out of your mind!" they said. When she insisted, they decided, "It must be his angel."

12:15
Matt 18:10

16Meanwhile, Peter continued knocking. When they finally opened the door and saw him, they were amazed. 17He motioned for them to quiet down and told them how the Lord had led him out of prison. "Tell James and the other brothers what happened," he said. And then he went to another place.

12:17
Acts 15:13; 21:18

18At dawn there was a great commotion among the soldiers about what had happened to Peter. 19Herod Agrippa ordered a thorough search for him. When he couldn't be found, Herod interrogated the guards and sentenced them to death. Afterward Herod left Judea to stay in Caesarea for a while.

12:19
Acts 8:40; 16:27

### The Death of Herod Agrippa

20Now Herod was very angry with the people of Tyre and Sidon. So they sent a delegation to make peace with him because their cities were dependent upon Herod's country for food. The delegates won the support of Blastus, Herod's personal assistant, 21and an appointment with Herod was granted. When the day arrived, Herod put on his royal robes, sat on his throne, and made a speech to them. 22The people gave him a great ovation, shouting, "It's the voice of a god, not of a man!"

12:22
Ezek 28:2
12:23
1 Sam 25:38
2 Sam 24:16-17
2 Kgs 19:35
Dan 5:20

23Instantly, an angel of the Lord struck Herod with a sickness, because he accepted the people's worship instead of giving the glory to God. So he was consumed with worms and died.

24Meanwhile, the word of God continued to spread, and there were many new believers.

12:24
Acts 6:7; 19:20

25When Barnabas and Saul had finished their mission to Jerusalem, they returned,* taking John Mark with them.

12:25
Acts 11:29-30

## B. PAUL'S MINISTRY (13:1—28:31)

The book focuses now on the ministry to the Gentiles and the spread of the church around the world, and Paul replaces Peter as the central figure in the book. Paul completes three missionary journeys and ends up being imprisoned in Jerusalem and transported to Rome. The book of Acts ends abruptly, showing that the history of the church is not yet complete. We are to be a part of the sequel.

## 1. First missionary journey

### Barnabas and Saul Are Commissioned

**13** Among the prophets and teachers of the church at Antioch of Syria were Barnabas, Simeon (called "the black man"*), Lucius (from Cyrene), Manaen (the childhood companion of King Herod Antipas*), and Saul. 2One day as these men were worshiping the Lord and fasting, the Holy Spirit said, "Dedicate Barnabas and Saul for the special work to

13:1
Acts 11:27
Rom 16:21
13:2
Gal 1:15-16

12:25 Or *mission, they returned to Jerusalem.* Other manuscripts read *mission, they returned from Jerusalem;* still others read *mission, they returned from Jerusalem to Antioch.*   **13:1a** Greek *who was called Niger.*   **13:1b** Greek *Herod the tetrarch.*

---

**12:17** This James was Jesus' brother, who became a leader in the Jerusalem church (15:13; Galatians 1:19). The James who was killed (12:2) was John's brother and one of the original 12 disciples.

**12:19** Under Roman law, guards who allowed a prisoner to escape were subject to the same punishment the prisoner was to receive. Thus, these 16 guards were sentenced to death.

**12:19** The Jews considered Jerusalem their capital, but the Romans made Caesarea their headquarters in Palestine. That is where Herod Agrippa I lived.

**12:20** These coastal cities, Tyre and Sidon, were free and self-governing but economically dependent on Judea (see the map in the introduction to Acts for their location). We don't know why Herod had quarreled with them, but now representatives from those cities were trying to appease him through his personal assistant.

**12:23** Herod died a horrible death accompanied by intense pain; he was literally eaten alive, from the inside out, by worms. Pride is a serious sin, and in this case, God chose to punish it immediately. God does not immediately punish all sin, but he *will* judge everyone (Hebrews 9:27). Accept Christ's offer of forgiveness today. No one can afford to wait.

**12:25** John Mark was Barnabas's cousin (Colossians 4:10). His mother, Mary, often would open her home to the apostles (12:12), so John Mark would have been exposed to most of the great men and teachings of the early church. Later, John Mark joined Paul and Barnabas on their first missionary journey, but for unknown reasons, he left them in the middle of the trip. John Mark was criticized by Paul for abandoning the mission (15:37-39), but he wrote the Gospel of Mark and was later acclaimed by Paul as a vital help in the growth of the early church (2 Timothy 4:11).

**13:1** What variety there is in the church! The common thread among these five men was their deep faith in Christ. We must never exclude anyone whom Christ has called to follow him. Like the early church, if believers today do their part to reach out to all who are lost, church congregations will eventually be comprised of people from different racial and cultural backgrounds. When this happens, we most often see our propensity to label and categorize. We are most comfortable with those who are just like us. Clearly, at the root of these tendencies is the ugly sin of prejudice. The more we understand the gospel and embrace God's version of the body of Christ, however, the more we will begin to transcend these differences. More than merely getting along, we will be able to honestly and authentically say from our hearts that we love each other.

**13:2, 3** The church dedicated Barnabas and Saul to the work God had for them. To *dedicate* means "to set apart" for a special

**13:3**
Acts 6:6

which I have called them." ³So after more fasting and prayer, the men laid their hands on them and sent them on their way.

### Paul's First Missionary Journey

**13:5**
Acts 9:20; 12:12

⁴So Barnabas and Saul were sent out by the Holy Spirit. They went down to the seaport of Seleucia and then sailed for the island of Cyprus. ⁵There, in the town of Salamis, they went to the Jewish synagogues and preached the word of God. John Mark went with them as their assistant.

**JOHN MARK**

Mistakes are effective teachers. Their consequences have a way of making lessons painfully clear. But those who learn from their mistakes are wise. John Mark was a good learner who just needed some time and encouragement.

Mark was eager to do the right thing, but he had trouble staying with a task. In his Gospel, Mark mentions a young man (probably referring to himself) who fled in such fear during Jesus' arrest that he left his clothes behind. This tendency to run showed up later when Paul and Barnabas took him as their assistant on their first missionary journey. At their second stop, Mark left them and returned to Jerusalem. It was a decision Paul did not easily accept. In preparing for their second journey two years later, Barnabas again suggested Mark as a traveling companion, but Paul flatly refused. As a result, the team was divided. Barnabas took Mark with him, and Paul chose Silas. Barnabas was patient with Mark, and the young man repaid his investment. Paul and Mark were later reunited, and the older apostle became a close friend of the young disciple.

Mark was a valuable companion to three early Christian leaders: Barnabas, Paul, and Peter. The material in Mark's Gospel seems to have come mostly from Peter. Mark's role as an assistant allowed him to be an observer. He heard Peter's accounts of the years with Jesus over and over, and he was one of the first to put Jesus' life in writing.

Barnabas played a key role in Mark's life. He stood beside the young man despite his failure, giving him patient encouragement. Mark challenges us to learn from our mistakes and appreciate the patience of others. Is there a "Barnabas" in your life you need to thank for his or her encouragement to you?

| | |
|---|---|
| **Strengths and accomplishments** | • Wrote the Gospel of Mark<br>• Provided his family's home as one of the main meeting places for the Christians in Jerusalem<br>• Persisted beyond his youthful mistakes<br>• Was an assistant and traveling companion to three of the greatest early missionaries |
| **Weaknesses and mistakes** | • Probably the nameless young man described in the Gospel of Mark who fled in panic when Jesus was arrested<br>• Left Paul and Barnabas for unknown reasons during the first missionary journey |
| **Lessons from his life** | • Personal maturity usually comes from a combination of time and mistakes<br>• Mistakes are not usually as important as what can be learned from them<br>• Effective living is not measured as much by what we accomplish as by what we overcome in order to accomplish it<br>• Encouragement can change a person's life |
| **Vital statistics** | • Where: Jerusalem<br>• Occupations: Missionary-in-training, Gospel writer, traveling companion<br>• Relatives: Mother: Mary. Cousin: Barnabas.<br>• Contemporaries: Paul, Peter, Timothy, Luke, Silas |
| **Key verse** | "Only Luke is with me. Bring Mark with you when you come, for he will be helpful to me in my ministry" (Paul writing in 2 Timothy 4:11). |

John Mark's story is told in Acts 12:25–13:13 and 15:36-39. He is also mentioned in Colossians 4:10; 2 Timothy 4:11; Philemon 1:24; 1 Peter 5:13.

purpose. We, too, should dedicate our pastors, missionaries, and Christian workers for their tasks. We can also dedicate ourselves to use our time, money, and talents for God's work. Ask God what he wants you to set apart for him.

**13:2, 3** This was the beginning of Saul's (Paul, see 13:9) first missionary journey. The church was involved in sending Paul and Barnabas, but it was God's plan. Why did Paul and Barnabas go where they did? (1) The Holy Spirit led them. (2) They followed the

communication routes of the Roman Empire, making travel easier. (3) They visited key population and cultural centers to reach as many people as possible. (4) They went to cities with synagogues, speaking first to the Jews in hopes that they would see Jesus as the Messiah and help spread the Good News to everyone.

**13:4** Located in the Mediterranean Sea, the island of Cyprus, with a large Jewish population, was Barnabas's home. Their first stop was in familiar territory.

⁶Afterward they traveled from town to town across the entire island until finally they reached Paphos, where they met a Jewish sorcerer, a false prophet named Bar-Jesus. ⁷He had attached himself to the governor, Sergius Paulus, who was an intelligent man. The governor invited Barnabas and Saul to visit him, for he wanted to hear the word of God. ⁸But Elymas, the sorcerer (as his name means in Greek), interfered and urged the governor to pay no attention to what Barnabas and Saul said. He was trying to keep the governor from believing.

⁹Saul, also known as Paul, was filled with the Holy Spirit, and he looked the sorcerer in the eye. ¹⁰Then he said, "You son of the devil, full of every sort of deceit and fraud, and enemy of all that is good! Will you never stop perverting the true ways of the Lord? ¹¹Watch now, for the Lord has laid his hand of punishment upon you, and you will be struck blind. You will not see the sunlight for some time." Instantly mist and darkness came over the man's eyes, and he began groping around begging for someone to take his hand and lead him.

¹²When the governor saw what had happened, he became a believer, for he was astonished at the teaching about the Lord.

### Paul Preaches in Antioch of Pisidia

¹³Paul and his companions then left Paphos by ship for Pamphylia, landing at the port town of Perga. There John Mark left them and returned to Jerusalem. ¹⁴But Paul and Barnabas traveled inland to Antioch of Pisidia.*

On the Sabbath they went to the synagogue for the services. ¹⁵After the usual readings from the books of Moses* and the prophets, those in charge of the service sent them this message: "Brothers, if you have any word of encouragement for the people, come and give it."

¹⁶So Paul stood, lifted his hand to quiet them, and started speaking. "Men of Israel," he said, "and you God-fearing Gentiles, listen to me.

13:6 Matt 7:15; Acts 8:9
13:8 2 Tim 3:8
13:9 Acts 2:4
13:10 Hos 14:9; Matt 13:38; John 8:44
13:11 2 Kgs 6:18; Acts 9:8
13:13 Acts 12:12; 15:38
13:14 Acts 14:19, 21
13:15 Acts 15:21
13:16 Acts 12:17; 13:26

13:13-14 *Pamphylia* and *Pisidia* were districts in what is now Turkey.   13:15 Greek *from the law.*

**13:6, 7** Sergius Paulus functioned as the governor of the island. Such leaders often kept private sorcerers. Bar-Jesus realized that if Sergius Paulus believed in Jesus, he would soon be out of a job.
**13:9, 10** Here is where Saul is first called Paul.
**13:10** The Holy Spirit led Paul to confront Bar-Jesus with his sin. There is a time to be nice and a time to confront. Ask God to show you the difference and to give you the courage to do what is right.
**13:13** No reason is given why John Mark left Paul and Barnabas. Some suggestions are: (1) He was homesick; (2) he resented the change in leadership from Barnabas (his cousin) to Paul; (3) he became ill (an illness that may have affected all of them—see Galatians 4:13); (4) he was unable to withstand the rigors and dangers of the missionary journey; (5) he may have planned to go only that far but had not communicated this to Paul and Barnabas. Paul implicitly accused John Mark of lacking courage and commitment,

refusing to take him along on another journey (see 15:37, 38). It is clear from Paul's later letters, however, that he grew to respect Mark (Colossians 4:10) and that he needed Mark in his work (2 Timothy 4:11).
**13:14** Antioch of Pisidia was a different city from Antioch of Syria, where there was already a flourishing church (11:26). This Antioch, in the region of Pisidia, was a hub of good roads and trade, with a large Jewish population.
**13:14** When they went to a new city to witness for Christ, Paul and Barnabas would go first to the synagogue. The Jews who were there believed in God and diligently studied the Scriptures. Tragically, however, many could not accept Jesus as the promised Messiah because they had the wrong idea of what the Messiah should be. He was not, as they desired, a military king who would overthrow Rome's control but a servant-king who would defeat sin in people's hearts. (Only later, when Christ returns, will he judge the nations of the world.) Paul and Barnabas did not separate themselves from the synagogues but tried to show clearly that the very Scriptures the Jews studied pointed to Jesus.
**13:14, 15** What happened in a synagogue service? First, the *Shema* was recited (this is Deuteronomy 6:4, which Jews repeated several times daily). Certain prayers were spoken; then there was a reading from the law (the books of Genesis through Deuteronomy), a reading from the Prophets intending to illustrate the law, and a sermon. Those in charge of the service decided who would lead the service and give the sermon. A different person was chosen to lead each week. Since it was customary for the synagogue leader to invite visiting rabbis to speak, Paul and Barnabas usually had an open door when they first went to a synagogue. But as soon as they spoke about Jesus as Messiah, the door would often slam shut. They were usually not invited back by the religious leaders, and sometimes they would be thrown out of town!
**13:16ff** Paul's message to the Jews in the synagogue in Antioch began with an emphasis on God's covenant with Israel. This was a point of agreement, because all Jews were proud to be God's chosen people. Then Paul explained how the Good News fulfilled the covenant. Some Jews found this message hard to swallow.

**MINISTRY IN CYPRUS** The leaders of the church in Antioch chose Paul and Barnabas to take the gospel westward. Along with John Mark, they boarded ship at Seleucia and set out across the Mediterranean for Cyprus. They preached in Salamis, the largest city, and went across the island to Paphos.

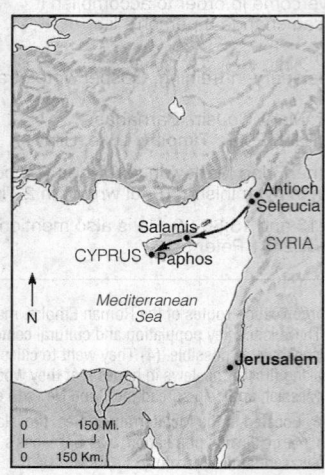

13:17
Exod 6:6-7
Deut 7:6-8

13:18
Exod 16:35
Num 14:34

13:19
Deut 7:1

13:20
Judg 2:16
1 Sam 3:20

13:21
1 Sam 8:5; 9:1-2;
10:21-24

17"The God of this nation of Israel chose our ancestors and made them multiply and grow strong during their stay in Egypt. Then with a powerful arm he led them out of their slavery. 18He put up with them* through forty years of wandering in the wilderness. 19Then he destroyed seven nations in Canaan and gave their land to Israel as an inheritance. 20All this took about 450 years.

"After that, God gave them judges to rule until the time of Samuel the prophet. 21Then the people begged for a king, and God gave them Saul son of Kish, a man of the tribe of Benjamin, who reigned for forty years. 22But God removed Saul and replaced him with David, a man about whom God said, 'I have found David son of Jesse, a man after my own heart. He will do everything I want him to do.'*

13:18 Some manuscripts read *He cared for them;* compare Deut 1:31.   13:22 1 Sam 13:14.

Every group needs an "encourager" because everyone needs encouragement at one time or another. However, the value of encouragement is often missed because it tends to be private rather than public. In fact, people most need encouragement when they feel most alone. A man named Joseph was such an encourager that he earned the nickname "Son of Encouragement," or Barnabas, from the Jerusalem Christians.

Barnabas was drawn to people he could encourage, and he was a great help to those around him. It is delightful that wherever Barnabas encouraged Christians, non-Christians flocked to become believers!

Barnabas's actions were crucial to the early church. In a way, we can thank him for most of the New Testament. God used his relationship with Paul at one point and with Mark at another to keep these two men going when either might have failed. Barnabas did wonders with encouragement!

When Paul arrived in Jerusalem for the first time following his conversion, the local Christians were understandably reluctant to welcome him. They thought his story was a trick to capture more Christians. But Barnabas proved willing to risk his life to meet with Paul and then convince the others that their former enemy was now a vibrant believer in Jesus. We can only wonder what might have happened to Paul without Barnabas.

It was Barnabas who encouraged Mark to go with him and Paul to Antioch. Mark joined them on their first missionary journey but decided during the trip to return home. Later, Barnabas wanted to invite Mark to join them for another journey, but Paul would not agree. As a result, the partners went separate ways, Barnabas with Mark and Paul with Silas. This actually doubled the missionary effort. Barnabas's patient encouragement was a huge boost for the effectiveness of Mark's eventual ministry. Paul and Mark were later reunited in missionary efforts.

As Barnabas's life shows, we are often presented with situations where there is someone who needs encouragement. Our tendency, however, is to criticize instead. It may be important at times to point out someone's shortcomings, but before we have the right to do this, we must build that person's trust through encouragement. Will you take the opportunity to encourage those with whom you come in contact today?

| | |
|---|---|
| **Strengths and accomplishments** | • One of the first to sell possessions to help the Christians in Jerusalem<br>• First to travel with Paul as a missionary team<br>• Was an encourager, as his nickname shows, and thus one of the most quietly influential people in the early days of Christianity<br>• Called an apostle, although not one of the original 12 |
| **Weakness and mistake** | • Like Peter, temporarily stayed aloof from Gentile believers until Paul corrected him |
| **Lessons from his life** | • Encouragement is one of the most effective ways to help<br>• Sooner or later, true obedience to God will involve risk<br>• There is always someone who needs encouragement |
| **Vital statistics** | • Where: Cyprus, Jerusalem, Antioch<br>• Occupations: Missionary, teacher<br>• Relatives: Aunt: Mary. Cousin: John Mark.<br>• Contemporaries: Peter, Silas, Paul, Herod Agrippa I |
| **Key verses** | "When he arrived and saw this evidence of God's blessing, he was filled with joy, and he encouraged the believers to stay true to the Lord. Barnabas was a good man, full of the Holy Spirit and strong in faith. And many people were brought to the Lord" (Acts 11:23-24). |

Barnabas's story is told in Acts 4:36-37; 9:27–15:39. He is also mentioned in 1 Corinthians 9:6; Galatians 2:1, 9, 13; Colossians 4:10.

23"And it is one of King David's descendants, Jesus, who is God's promised Savior of Israel! 24Before he came, John the Baptist preached that all the people of Israel needed to repent of their sins and turn to God and be baptized. 25As John was finishing his ministry he asked, 'Do you think I am the Messiah? No, I am not! But he is coming soon—and I'm not even worthy to be his slave and untie the sandals on his feet.'

26"Brothers—you sons of Abraham, and also you God-fearing Gentiles—this message of salvation has been sent to us! 27 The people in Jerusalem and their leaders did not recognize Jesus as the one the prophets had spoken about. Instead, they condemned him, and in doing this they fulfilled the prophets' words that are read every Sabbath. 28They found no legal reason to execute him, but they asked Pilate to have him killed anyway.

29"When they had done all that the prophecies said about him, they took him down from the cross* and placed him in a tomb. 30But God raised him from the dead! 31And over a period of many days he appeared to those who had gone with him from Galilee to Jerusalem. They are now his witnesses to the people of Israel.

32"And now we are here to bring you this Good News. The promise was made to our ancestors, 33and God has now fulfilled it for us, their descendants, by raising Jesus. This is what the second psalm says about Jesus:

'You are my Son.
   Today I have become your Father.*'

34For God had promised to raise him from the dead, not leaving him to rot in the grave. He said, 'I will give you the sacred blessings I promised to David.'* 35Another psalm explains it more fully: 'You will not allow your Holy One to rot in the grave.'* 36This is not a reference to David, for after David had done the will of God in his own generation, he died and was buried with his ancestors, and his body decayed. 37No, it was a reference to someone else— someone whom God raised and whose body did not decay.

38*"Brothers, listen! We are here to proclaim that through this man Jesus there is forgiveness for your sins. 39Everyone who believes in him is declared right with God—something the law of Moses could never do. 40Be careful! Don't let the prophets' words apply to you. For they said,

41 'Look, you mockers,
      be amazed and die!
For I am doing something in your own day,
      something you wouldn't believe
      even if someone told you about it.'*"

13:29 Greek *from the tree.*   13:33 Or *Today I reveal you as my Son.* Ps 2:7.   13:34 Isa 55:3.   13:35 Ps 16:10.
13:38 English translations divide verses 38 and 39 in various ways.   13:41 Hab 1:5 (Greek version).

**Cross-references (right margin):**

13:23
2 Sam 7:12
Isa 11:1
Luke 2:11
13:24
Mark 1:4-5
13:25
Mark 1:7
John 1:20
13:27
Acts 3:17
13:28
Matt 27:22-23
Acts 3:14
13:29
Matt 27:59-60
Luke 23:52-53
13:30
Matt 28:6
Acts 2:24
13:31
Luke 24:48
Acts 1:11
1 Cor 15:5
13:32
Rom 1:2-4
13:33
†Ps 2:7
Heb 1:5; 5:5
13:34
†Isa 55:3
13:35
†Ps 16:10
13:37
Acts 2:24
13:39
Rom 3:28; 10:4
13:41
†Hab 1:5

---

**13:23-31** Because Paul was speaking to devout Jews, he began by reminding them about the covenant, Abraham, David, and other familiar themes. Later, when speaking to the Greek philosophers in Athens (17:22-32), he would begin by talking about what he had observed in their city. In both cases, however, he centered the sermon around Christ and emphasized the Resurrection. When you share the Good News, begin where your audience is—then tell them about Christ.

**13:38, 39** This is the focus of the Good News: Forgiveness of sins and freedom from guilt are available through faith in Christ to all people—including *you*. Have you received this forgiveness? Are you refreshed each day by the thought that you are right with God?

**MINISTRY IN PAMPHYLIA AND GALATIA** Paul, Barnabas, and John Mark left Paphos and landed at Perga in the humid region of Pamphylia, a narrow strip of land between the sea and the Taurus Mountains. John Mark left them in Perga, but Paul and Barnabas traveled up the steep road into the higher elevation of Pisidia in Galatia. When the Jews rejected his message, Paul preached to Gentiles, and the Jews drove Paul and Barnabas out of the Pisidian city of Antioch.

42As Paul and Barnabas left the synagogue that day, the people begged them to speak about these things again the next week. 43Many Jews and devout converts to Judaism followed Paul and Barnabas, and the two men urged them to continue to rely on the grace of God.

### Paul Turns to the Gentiles

44The following week almost the entire city turned out to hear them preach the word of the Lord. 45But when some of the Jews saw the crowds, they were jealous; so they slandered Paul and argued against whatever he said.

46Then Paul and Barnabas spoke out boldly and declared, "It was necessary that we first preach the word of God to you Jews. But since you have rejected it and judged yourselves unworthy of eternal life, we will offer it to the Gentiles. 47For the Lord gave us this command when he said,

'I have made you a light to the Gentiles,
    to bring salvation to the farthest corners of the earth.'*"

48When the Gentiles heard this, they were very glad and thanked the Lord for his message; and all who were chosen for eternal life became believers. 49So the Lord's message spread throughout that region.

50Then the Jews stirred up the influential religious women and the leaders of the city, and they incited a mob against Paul and Barnabas and ran them out of town. 51So they shook the dust from their feet as a sign of rejection and went to the town of Iconium. 52And the believers* were filled with joy and with the Holy Spirit.

### Paul and Barnabas in Iconium

**14** The same thing happened in Iconium.* Paul and Barnabas went to the Jewish synagogue and preached with such power that a great number of both Jews and Greeks became believers. 2Some of the Jews, however, spurned God's message and poisoned the minds of the Gentiles against Paul and Barnabas. 3But the apostles stayed there a long time,

**13:47** Isa 49:6.  **13:52** Greek *the disciples*.  **14:1** *Iconium*, as well as *Lystra* and *Derbe* (14:6), were towns in what is now Turkey.

**13:45**
Acts 8:6
1 Pet 4:4
Jude 1:10
**13:46**
Acts 18:6
**13:47**
†Isa 49:6
Luke 2:32
**13:48**
Rom 8:29-30
Eph 1:4-5, 11
1 Pet 1:2
**13:51**
Matt 10:14
Mark 6:11
Luke 9:5; 10:11
Acts 18:6
**13:52**
1 Pet 1:8
**14:1**
Acts 13:45
**14:2**
2 Tim 3:11
**14:3**
Heb 2:4

---

**13:42-45** The Jewish leaders undoubtedly brought theological arguments against Paul and Barnabas, but Luke tells us that the real reason for their hostility was that "they were jealous." When we see others succeeding where we haven't or receiving the affirmation we crave, it is hard to rejoice with them. Jealousy is a natural reaction. But how tragic it is when our jealous feelings make us try to stop God's work. If a work is God's work, rejoice in it—no matter who is doing it.

**13:46** Why was it necessary for the Good News to go first to the Jews? God planned that through the Jewish nation *all* the world would know of God (Genesis 12:3). Paul, a Jew himself, loved his people (Romans 9:1-5) and wanted to give them every opportunity to join him in proclaiming God's salvation. Unfortunately, many Jews did not recognize Jesus as Messiah, and they did not understand that God was offering salvation to anyone, Jew or Gentile, who comes to him through faith in Christ.

**13:47** God had planned for Israel to be this light (Isaiah 49:6). Through Israel came Jesus, the light of the nations (Luke 2:32). This light would spread out and enlighten the Gentiles.

**13:50** Instead of accepting the truth, the Jewish leaders stirred up opposition and ran Paul and Barnabas out of town. When confronted by a disturbing truth, people often turn away and refuse to listen. When God's Spirit points out needed changes in our lives, we must listen to him. Otherwise we may be pushing the truth so far away that it no longer affects us.

**13:51** Often Jews would shake the dust off their feet when leaving a Gentile town on the way back to their own land. This symbolized cleansing themselves from the contamination of those who did not worship God. For Paul and Barnabas to do this to Jews demonstrated that Jews who rejected the Good News were not truly part of Israel and were no better than pagans. Jesus had told his disciples to shake from their feet the dust of any town that would not accept or listen to them (Mark 6:11). The disciples were not to blame if the message was rejected, as long as they had faithfully

presented it. When we share Christ carefully and sensitively, God does not hold us responsible for the other person's decision.

**14:3, 4** We may wish we could perform a miraculous act that would convince everyone once and for all that Jesus is the Lord. But we see here that even if we could perform a miracle, it wouldn't convince everyone. God gave these men power to do great wonders as confirmation of the message of grace, but people were still divided. Don't spend your time and energy wishing for miracles. Sow your seeds of the Good News on the best ground you can find in the best way you can, and leave the convincing to the Holy Spirit.

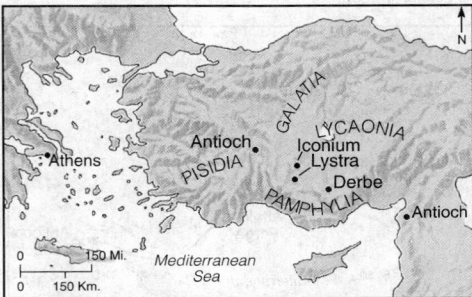

**CONTINUED MINISTRY IN GALATIA** Paul and Barnabas, thrown out of Antioch in Pisidia, descended the mountains, going east into Lycaonia. They went first to Iconium, a commercial center on the road between Asia and Syria. After preaching there, they had to flee to Lystra, 25 miles south. Paul was stoned in Lystra, but he and Barnabas traveled the 50 miles to Derbe, a border town. The pair then boldly retraced their steps.

preaching boldly about the grace of the Lord. And the Lord proved their message was true by giving them power to do miraculous signs and wonders. [4]But the people of the town were divided in their opinion about them. Some sided with the Jews, and some with the apostles.

[5]Then a mob of Gentiles and Jews, along with their leaders, decided to attack and stone them. [6]When the apostles learned of it, they fled to the region of Lycaonia—to the towns of Lystra and Derbe and the surrounding area. [7]And there they preached the Good News.

### Paul and Barnabas in Lystra and Derbe

[8]While they were at Lystra, Paul and Barnabas came upon a man with crippled feet. He had been that way from birth, so he had never walked. He was sitting [9]and listening as Paul preached. Looking straight at him, Paul realized he had faith to be healed. [10]So Paul called to him in a loud voice, "Stand up!" And the man jumped to his feet and started walking.

[11]When the crowd saw what Paul had done, they shouted in their local dialect, "These men are gods in human form!" [12]They decided that Barnabas was the Greek god Zeus and that Paul was Hermes, since he was the chief speaker. [13]Now the temple of Zeus was located just outside the town. So the priest of the temple and the crowd brought bulls and wreaths of flowers to the town gates, and they prepared to offer sacrifices to the apostles.

[14]But when the apostles Barnabas and Paul heard what was happening, they tore their clothing in dismay and ran out among the people, shouting, [15]"Friends,* why are you doing this? We are merely human beings—just like you! We have come to bring you the Good News that you should turn from these worthless things and turn to the living God, who made heaven and earth, the sea, and everything in them. [16]In the past he permitted all the nations to go their own ways, [17]but he never left them without evidence of himself and his goodness. For instance, he sends you rain and good crops and gives you food and joyful hearts." [18]But even with these words, Paul and Barnabas could scarcely restrain the people from sacrificing to them.

[19]Then some Jews arrived from Antioch and Iconium and won the crowds to their side. They stoned Paul and dragged him out of town, thinking he was dead. [20]But as the believers* gathered around him, he got up and went back into the town. The next day he left with Barnabas for Derbe.

**14:15** Greek *Men.*   **14:20** Greek *disciples;* also in 14:22, 28.

---

**14:4** Acts 28:24
**14:5** Acts 14:19; 20:3 2 Tim 3:11
**14:6** Matt 10:23
**14:8** Acts 3:2
**14:10** Acts 3:8
**14:11** Acts 28:6
**14:15** Exod 20:11 Ps 146:6 Matt 16:16 Acts 10:26 1 Thes 1:9 Rev 14:7
**14:16** Ps 81:12
**14:17** Ps 147:8 Rom 1:20
**14:19** Acts 13:45 2 Cor 11:25 2 Tim 3:11

---

**14:6** Iconium (14:1), Lystra, and Derbe were three cities Paul visited in the southern part of the region of Galatia. Paul probably wrote a letter to these churches—the letter to the Galatians—because many Jewish Christians were claiming that non-Jewish Christians couldn't be saved unless they followed Jewish laws and customs. Paul's letter refuted this and brought the believers back to a right understanding of faith in Jesus (see Galatians 3:3, 5). Paul may have written his letter soon after leaving the region (see the note on 14:28).

**THE END OF THE FIRST JOURNEY**   From Antioch in Pisidia, Paul and Barnabas went down the mountains back to Pamphylia on the coast. Stopping first in Perga, where they had landed, they went west to Attalia, the main port that sent goods from Asia to Syria and Egypt. There they found a ship bound for Seleucia, the port of Antioch in Syria. This ended their first missionary journey.

**14:11, 12** Zeus and Hermes (also known as Jupiter and Mercury) were two popular gods in the Roman world. People from Lystra claimed that these gods had once visited their city. According to legend, no one had offered them hospitality except an old couple, so Zeus and Hermes had killed the rest of the people and rewarded the old couple. When the citizens of Lystra saw the miracles of Paul and Barnabas, they assumed that the gods were revisiting them. Remembering the story of what had happened to the previous citizens, they immediately honored Paul and Barnabas and showered them with gifts.

**14:15-18** Responding to the people of Lystra, Paul and Barnabas reminded them that God never leaves himself "without evidence of himself and his goodness." Rain and good crops, for example, are evidence of his goodness. Later Paul wrote that this evidence in nature leaves people without an excuse for unbelief (Romans 1:20). When in doubt about God, look around and you will see abundant evidence that he is at work in the world.

**14:18, 19** Only days after the people in Lystra had thought that Paul and Barnabas were gods and wanted to offer sacrifices to them, they stoned Paul and left him for dead. That's human nature. Jesus understood how fickle crowds can be (John 2:24, 25). When many people approve of us, we feel good, but that should never cloud our thinking or affect our decisions. We should not live to please the crowd—especially in our spiritual lives. Be like Jesus. Know the nature of the crowd and don't put your trust in it. Put your trust in God alone.

**14:18-20** Paul and Barnabas were persistent in their preaching of the Good News, considering the cost to themselves to be nothing in comparison with obedience to Christ. They had just narrowly escaped being stoned in Iconium (14:1-7), but Jews from Antioch and Iconium tracked Paul down, stoned him, and left him for dead. But Paul got up and went back into the city to preach the Good

### Paul and Barnabas Return to Antioch of Syria

14:22
2 Tim 3:12

21After preaching the Good News in Derbe and making many disciples, Paul and Barnabas returned to Lystra, Iconium, and Antioch of Pisidia, 22where they strengthened the believers. They encouraged them to continue in the faith, reminding them that we must suffer many hardships to enter the Kingdom of God. 23Paul and Barnabas also appointed elders in every church. With prayer and fasting, they turned the elders over to the care of the Lord, in whom they had put their trust. 24Then they traveled back through Pisidia to Pamphylia. 25They preached the word in Perga, then went down to Attalia.

14:26
Acts 13:1-3
14:27
1 Cor 16:9
Col 4:3
Rev 3:8

26Finally, they returned by ship to Antioch of Syria, where their journey had begun. The believers there had entrusted them to the grace of God to do the work they had now completed. 27Upon arriving in Antioch, they called the church together and reported everything God had done through them and how he had opened the door of faith to the Gentiles, too. 28And they stayed there with the believers for a long time.

## 2. The council at Jerusalem

15:1
Lev 12:3
Gal 5:2
15:2
Acts 11:30
Gal 2:1-10
15:3
Acts 11:19; 14:27

**15** While Paul and Barnabas were at Antioch of Syria, some men from Judea arrived and began to teach the believers*: "Unless you are circumcised as required by the law of Moses, you cannot be saved." 2Paul and Barnabas disagreed with them, arguing vehemently. Finally, the church decided to send Paul and Barnabas to Jerusalem, accompanied by some local believers, to talk to the apostles and elders about this question. 3The church sent the delegates to Jerusalem, and they stopped along the way in Phoenicia and Samaria to visit the believers. They told them—much to everyone's joy—that the Gentiles, too, were being converted.

**15:1** Greek *brothers;* also in 15:3, 23, 32, 33, 36, 40.

---

News. That's commitment! Being a disciple of Christ calls for total commitment. As Christians, we no longer belong to ourselves but to our Lord, for whom we are called to suffer.

**14:21, 22** Paul and Barnabas returned to visit the believers in all the cities where they had recently been threatened and physically attacked. These men knew the dangers they faced, yet they believed that they had a responsibility to encourage the new believers. No matter how inconvenient or uncomfortable the task may seem, we must always support new believers who need our help and encouragement. It was not convenient or comfortable for Jesus to go to the cross for us!

**14:23** Part of the reason that Paul and Barnabas risked their lives to return to these cities was to organize the churches' leadership. They were not just following up on a loosely knit group; they were helping the believers get organized with spiritual leaders who could help them grow. Churches grow under Spirit-led leaders, both laypersons and pastors. Pray for your church leaders and support them; and if God puts his finger on you, humbly accept the responsibility of a leadership role in your church.

**14:28** Paul probably wrote his letter to the Galatians while he was staying in Antioch (A.D. 48 or 49) after completing his first missionary journey. There are several theories as to what part of Galatia Paul was addressing, but most agree that Iconium, Lystra, and Derbe were part of that region for which the letter was intended. Galatians was probably written before the Jerusalem council (Acts 15), because in the letter the question of whether Gentile believers should be required to follow Jewish law was not yet resolved. The council met to solve that problem.

**15:1** The question of whether Gentile believers should obey the law of Moses in order to be saved was extremely critical at this point in Christianity's history and could have potentially split the early church if not handled carefully. The controversy had intensified with the success of the new Gentile churches. The Judaizers in the Jerusalem church were led by converted Pharisees (15:5) who preferred a legalistic religion to one based on faith alone. If the Judaizers had won, the Gentiles would have been required to be circumcised and, in effect, converted to Judaism. This would have confined Christianity to simply being another sect within Judaism.

There is something of a "Pharisee" in each one of us. We may unwittingly mistake upholding tradition, structure, and legal requirements for obeying God. Make sure the gospel brings freedom and life, not rules and ceremonies, to those you are trying to reach.

**15:2ff** The delegates to the council at Jerusalem came from the churches in Jerusalem and Antioch. The conversion of Gentiles was raising an urgent question for the early church: The real problem for the Jewish Christians was not whether Gentiles could be saved but whether Gentile believers also had to adhere to the laws of Moses and other Jewish traditions. The test of following these laws was circumcision. One group of Jewish Christians insisted that following the law, including submitting to the rite of circumcision, was necessary for salvation. The Gentiles, however, did not think they needed to become Jewish first in order to become Christians. The Jewish Christians also were worried because soon Gentile Christians would outnumber Jewish Christians. And they were afraid of weakening moral standards among believers if they did not follow Jewish laws. So Paul and Barnabas discussed this problem with the leaders of the church. Paul, Barnabas, and the other church leaders believed that the Old Testament law was very important but was not a prerequisite to salvation. The law cannot save; only by grace through faith in Jesus Christ can a person be saved. The council upheld the conviction expressed by Paul and Barnabas that following the Jewish laws, including being circumcised, was not essential for salvation.

**15:2ff** It is helpful to see how the churches in Antioch and Jerusalem resolved their conflict: (1) The church in Antioch sent a delegation to help seek a solution; (2) the delegates met with the church leaders to give their reports and set another date to continue the discussion; (3) Paul and Barnabas gave their report; (4) James summarized the reports and drew up the decision; (5) everyone agreed to abide by the decision; (6) the council sent a letter with delegates back to Antioch to report the decision.

This is a wise way to handle conflicts within the church. Problems must be confronted, and all sides of the argument should be given a fair hearing. The discussion should be held in the presence of leaders who are spiritually mature and trustworthy to make wise decisions. Everyone should then abide by the decisions.

**PAUL'S FIRST MISSIONARY JOURNEY** (ACTS 13:1—14:28)

**PAUL'S SECOND MISSIONARY JOURNEY** (ACTS 15:36—18:22)

**PAUL'S THIRD MISSIONARY JOURNEY**  (ACTS 18:23—21:16)

**PAUL'S JOURNEY TO ROME**  (ACTS 21:17—28:31)

⁴When they arrived in Jerusalem, Barnabas and Paul were welcomed by the whole church, including the apostles and elders. They reported everything God had done through them. ⁵But then some of the believers who belonged to the sect of the Pharisees stood up and insisted, "The Gentile converts must be circumcised and required to follow the law of Moses."

⁶So the apostles and elders met together to resolve this issue. ⁷At the meeting, after a long discussion, Peter stood and addressed them as follows: "Brothers, you all know that God chose me from among you some time ago to preach to the Gentiles so that they could hear the Good News and believe. ⁸God knows people's hearts, and he confirmed that he accepts Gentiles by giving them the Holy Spirit, just as he did to us. ⁹He made no distinction between us and them, for he cleansed their hearts through faith. ¹⁰So why are you now challenging God by burdening the Gentile believers* with a yoke that neither we nor our ancestors were able to bear? ¹¹We believe that we are all saved the same way, by the undeserved grace of the Lord Jesus."

¹²Everyone listened quietly as Barnabas and Paul told about the miraculous signs and wonders God had done through them among the Gentiles.

¹³When they had finished, James stood and said, "Brothers, listen to me. ¹⁴Peter* has told you about the time God first visited the Gentiles to take from them a people for himself. ¹⁵And this conversion of Gentiles is exactly what the prophets predicted. As it is written:

¹⁶ 'Afterward I will return
    and restore the fallen house* of David.
I will rebuild its ruins
    and restore it,
¹⁷ so that the rest of humanity might seek the LORD,
    including the Gentiles—
    all those I have called to be mine.
The LORD has spoken—
¹⁸    he who made these things known so long ago.'*

¹⁹"And so my judgment is that we should not make it difficult for the Gentiles who are turning to God. ²⁰Instead, we should write and tell them to abstain from eating food offered to idols, from sexual immorality, from eating the meat of strangled animals, and from consuming blood. ²¹For these laws of Moses have been preached in Jewish synagogues in every city on every Sabbath for many generations."

**15:10** Greek *disciples.*   **15:14** Greek *Symeon.*   **15:16** Or *kingdom;* Greek reads *tent.*   **15:16-18** Amos 9:11-12 (Greek version); Isa 45:21.

### Cross-references

**15:5** Acts 15:11

**15:7-8** Acts 2:4; 10:44; 11:15

**15:9** Acts 10:43; Rom 10:12

**15:10** Matt 23:4; Gal 5:1

**15:11** Rom 3:24; Eph 2:5-8

**15:12** Acts 14:27; 15:4

**15:13** Acts 12:17

**15:14** Acts 15:7-9

**15:16-17** †Amos 9:11-12

**15:18** Isa 45:21

**15:20** Gen 9:4; Exod 20:3-4; Lev 3:17; Deut 12:16; 1 Cor 8:7; 10:7

**15:21** Acts 13:15

---

**15:10** If the law was a yoke that the Jews could not bear, how did having the law help them throughout their history? Paul wrote that the law was a guide that pointed out their sins so they could repent and return to God and right living (see Galatians 3:24, 25). It was, and still is, impossible to obey the law completely.

**15:13** This James is Jesus' brother. He became the leader of the church in Jerusalem and wrote the book of James.

**15:16-18** Despite the compelling experiences of Peter, Barnabas, and Paul, James turned to God's Word as the ultimate test of truth. This should be the way we evaluate events. We all have beliefs (some of them fervent), we all have experiences, and our tendency is to want to measure others by our yardstick. It is common for believers to think that their experiences, their convictions, are true and should be the norm. Different ideas are thought to be inferior or invalid. Ultimately, however, what matters is what God's Word says. The more we know God's Word, the more we read it, study it, memorize it, and meditate on it, the better we will be able to discern what is right and best in times of controversy or doctrinal disagreement.

**15:19-21** James's judgment was that Gentile believers did not have to be circumcised, but they should stay away from food sacrificed to idols, from sexual immorality (a common part of idol worship), and from consuming blood (reflecting the biblical teaching that the life is in the blood—Leviticus 17:14) or eating meat of strangled animals. If Gentile Christians would abstain from these practices, they would please God and get along better with their Jewish brothers and sisters in Christ. Of course, other actions were inappropriate for believers, but the Jews were especially concerned about these four. This compromise helped the church grow unhindered by the cultural differences of Jews and Gentiles.

**THE JERUSALEM COUNCIL**
A dispute arose when some Jewish believers taught that Gentile believers had to be circumcised to be saved. Paul and Barnabas went to Jerusalem to discuss this situation with the leaders there. After the Jerusalem council made its decision, Paul and Barnabas returned to Antioch with the news.

*The Letter for Gentile Believers*

**15:22**
Acts 15:27; 16:19
1 Pet 5:12

22 Then the apostles and elders together with the whole church in Jerusalem chose delegates, and they sent them to Antioch of Syria with Paul and Barnabas to report on this decision. The men chosen were two of the church leaders*—Judas (also called Barsabbas) and Silas. 23 This is the letter they took with them:

**15:22** Greek *were leaders among the brothers.*

---

**THE FIRST CHURCH CONFERENCE**

| Group | Position | Reasons |
|---|---|---|
| Judaizers (some Jewish Christians) | Gentiles must become Jewish first to be eligible for salvation | 1. They were devout, practicing Jews who found it difficult to set aside a tradition of gaining merit with God by keeping the law. |
| | | 2. They thought grace was too easy for the Gentiles. |
| | | 3. They were afraid of seeming too non-Jewish in the practice of their new faith—which could lead to death. |
| | | 4. The demands on the Gentiles were a way of maintaining control and authority in the movement. |
| Gentile Christians | Faith in Christ as Savior is the only requirement for salvation | 1. To submit to Jewish demands would be to doubt what God had already done for them by grace alone. |
| | | 2. They resisted exchanging their pagan rituals for a system of Jewish rituals—neither of which had power to save. |
| | | 3. They sought to obey Christ by baptism (rather than by circumcision) as a sign of their new faith. |
| Peter and James | Faith is the only requirement, but there must be evidence of change by rejecting the old lifestyle | 1. They tried to distinguish between what was true from God's Word versus what was just human tradition. |
| | | 2. They had Christ's command to preach to all the world. |
| | | 3. They wanted to preserve unity. |
| | | 4. They saw that Christianity could never survive as just a sect within Judaism. |

As long as most of the first Christians were Jewish, there was little difficulty in welcoming new believers; however, Gentiles (non-Jews) began to accept Jesus' offer of salvation. The evidence in their lives and the presence of God's Spirit in them showed that God was accepting them. Some of the early Christians believed that non-Jewish Christians needed to meet certain conditions before they could be worthy to accept Christ. The issue could have destroyed the church, so a conference was called in Jerusalem, and the issue was formally settled there, although it continued to be a problem for many years following. Above is an outline of the three points of view at the conference.

---

When we share our message across cultural and economic boundaries, we must be sure that the requirements for faith we set up are God's, not people's.

**15:19-21** The early church experienced the difficulty of bringing together diverse peoples. Jews and Gentiles had so little in common! Different histories, traditions, practices, customs, cultures, languages. How do you possibly take such dissimilar groups and make them one? One solution is to decide not to, to decide that it is impossible. So you segregate, isolate, and study each other with suspicion. This response profoundly affects Christianity's effectiveness and attractiveness. When there is snobbery or a judgmental atmosphere, the church betrays the teachings of Christ and loses all appeal.

The other solution is to submit our prejudices and presuppositions to the greater purposes of God. When we imitate him (Ephesians 5:1), we become tolerant, understanding, and accepting. However, such tolerance is not meant to include sinful lifestyles.

James mentioned a few laws that the Gentile believers should keep, with an understanding that basic morality and living for God would cover the rest. When believers of different races, ethnic backgrounds, and social strata come together in love and worship of the Savior, nothing gives greater glory to God or provides a more compelling witness.

**15:22** Later, Silas accompanied Paul on Paul's second missionary journey in place of Barnabas, who visited different cities with John Mark.

**15:23-29** This letter answered their questions and brought great joy to the Gentile Christians in Antioch (15:31). Beautifully written, it appeals to the Holy Spirit's guidance and explains what is to be done as though the readers already knew it. Believers should be careful not only in what they say but also in how they say it. We may be correct in our content, but we can lose our audience by our tone of voice or by our attitude.

"This letter is from the apostles and elders, your brothers in Jerusalem. It is written to the Gentile believers in Antioch, Syria, and Cilicia. Greetings!

24"We understand that some men from here have troubled you and upset you with their teaching, but we did not send them! 25So we decided, having come to complete agreement, to send you official representatives, along with our beloved Barnabas and Paul, 26who have risked their lives for the name of our Lord Jesus Christ. 27We are sending Judas and Silas to confirm what we have decided concerning your question.

28"For it seemed good to the Holy Spirit and to us to lay no greater burden on you than these few requirements: 29You must abstain from eating food offered to idols, from consuming blood or the meat of strangled animals, and from sexual immorality. If you do this, you will do well. Farewell."

30The messengers went at once to Antioch, where they called a general meeting of the believers and delivered the letter. 31And there was great joy throughout the church that day as they read this encouraging message.

32Then Judas and Silas, both being prophets, spoke at length to the believers, encouraging and strengthening their faith. 33They stayed for a while, and then the believers sent them back to the church in Jerusalem with a blessing of peace.* 35Paul and Barnabas stayed in Antioch. They and many others taught and preached the word of the Lord there.

### 3. Second missionary journey
#### Paul and Barnabas Separate
36After some time Paul said to Barnabas, "Let's go back and visit each city where we previously preached the word of the Lord, to see how the new believers are doing." 37Barnabas agreed and wanted to take along John Mark. 38But Paul disagreed strongly, since John Mark had deserted them in Pamphylia and had not continued with them in their work. 39Their disagreement was so sharp that they separated. Barnabas took John Mark with him and sailed for Cyprus. 40Paul chose Silas, and as he left, the believers entrusted him to the Lord's gracious care. 41Then he traveled throughout Syria and Cilicia, strengthening the churches there.

#### Paul's Second Missionary Journey
**16** Paul went first to Derbe and then to Lystra, where there was a young disciple named Timothy. His mother was a Jewish believer, but his father was a Greek. 2Timothy

**15:33** Some manuscripts add verse 34, *But Silas decided to stay there.*

15:24
Gal 1:7; 5:10

15:26
Acts 14:19
1 Cor 15:30

15:32
Acts 11:27; 13:1

15:36
Acts 13:4, 13-14, 51; 14:1, 6, 24-25

15:37
Acts 12:12, 25

15:38
Acts 13:13

16:1
Acts 14:6
Phil 2:19-22
2 Tim 1:2, 5-6; 3:15

---

**15:31** The debate over circumcision could have split the church, but Paul, Barnabas, and the Jews in Antioch made the right decision—they sought counsel from the church leaders and from God's Word. Our differences should be settled the same way—by seeking wise counsel and abiding by the decisions. Don't let disagreements divide you from other believers.

**THE SECOND JOURNEY BEGINS** Paul and Silas set out on a second missionary journey to visit the cities Paul had preached in earlier. This time they set out by land rather than sea, traveling the Roman road through Cilicia and the Cilician Gates—a gorge through the Taurus Mountains—then northwest toward Derbe, Lystra, and Iconium. The Spirit told them not to go into Asia, so they turned northward toward Bithynia. Again the Spirit said no, so they turned west through Mysia to the harbor city of Troas.

**15:36-39** Paul and Barnabas disagreed sharply over Mark. Paul didn't want to take him along because he had left them earlier (13:13). This disagreement caused the two great preachers to form two teams, opening up two missionary endeavors instead of one. God works even through conflict and disagreements. Later, Mark became vital to Paul's ministry (Colossians 4:10). Christians do not always agree, but problems can be solved by agreeing to disagree and letting God work his will.

**15:40** Paul's second missionary journey, this time with Silas as his co-worker, began approximately three years after his first one ended. The two visited many of the cities covered on Paul's first journey, plus others. This journey laid the groundwork for the church in Greece.

**15:40** Silas had been involved in the Jerusalem council and had been one of the two men chosen to represent the Jerusalem church by taking the letter and decision back to Antioch (15:22). Paul, from the Antioch church, chose Silas, from the Jerusalem church, and they traveled together to many cities to spread the Good News. This teamwork demonstrated the church's unity after the decision at the Jerusalem council.

**16:1** Timothy is the first second-generation Christian mentioned in the New Testament. His mother, Eunice, and grandmother Lois (2 Timothy 1:5) had become believers and had faithfully influenced him for the Lord. Although Timothy's father apparently was not a Christian, the faithfulness of Timothy's mother and grandmother prevailed. Never underestimate the effect of godly parenting on a child.

**16:2, 3** Timothy and his mother, Eunice, were from Lystra. Eunice had probably heard Paul's preaching when he was there during his first missionary journey (14:6-18). Timothy was the

**16:3**
Gal 2:3-5

was well thought of by the believers* in Lystra and Iconium, ³ so Paul wanted him to join them on their journey. In deference to the Jews of the area, he arranged for Timothy to be circumcised before they left, for everyone knew that his father was a Greek. ⁴ Then they went from town to town, instructing the believers to follow the decisions made by the apostles and elders in Jerusalem. ⁵ So the churches were strengthened in their faith and grew larger every day.

**16:5**
Acts 9:31

**16:2** Greek *brothers;* also in 16:40.

**SILAS**

The lives of the first Christian missionaries can be described with many words, but *boring* is not one of them. There were days of great excitement as men and women who had never heard of Jesus responded to the gospel. There were dangerous journeys over land and sea. Health risks and hunger were part of the daily routine. And there was open and hostile resistance to Christianity in many cities. Silas was one of the first missionaries, and he found out that serving Jesus Christ was certainly not boring!

Silas's name appears in Acts at the end of the first church council on the Jewish/Gentile problem. The majority of early Christians were Jews who realized that Jesus was the fulfillment of God's Old Testament promises to his people; however, the universal application of those promises had been overlooked. Thus, many felt that becoming Jewish was a prerequisite to becoming a Christian. The idea that God could accept a Gentile pagan was too incredible. But Gentiles began to accept Christ as Savior, and the transformation of their lives and the presence of God's Spirit confirmed their conversions. Some Jews were still reluctant, however, and insisted these new Christians take on various Jewish customs. The issue came to a boiling point at the Jerusalem council but was peacefully resolved. Silas was one of the representatives from Jerusalem sent with Paul and Barnabas back to Antioch with an official letter of welcome and acceptance to the Gentile Christians. Having fulfilled this mission, Silas returned to Jerusalem. Within a short time, however, he was back in Antioch at Paul's request to join him on his second missionary journey.

Paul, Silas, and Timothy began a far-ranging ministry that included some exciting adventures. Paul and Silas spent a night singing in a Philippian jail after being severely beaten. An earthquake, the loosing of their chains, and the resulting panic led to the conversion of their jailer and his family. Later, they narrowly missed another beating in Thessalonica, prevented by an evening escape. In Berea there was more trouble, but Silas and Timothy stayed to teach the young believers, while Paul traveled on to Athens. The team was finally reunited in Corinth. In each place they visited, they left behind a small group of Christians.

Silas leaves the story as suddenly as he entered it. Peter mentions him as the coauthor of 1 Peter, but we do not know when he joined Peter. He was an effective believer before leaving Jerusalem, and he doubtless continued to minister after his work with Paul was completed. He took advantage of opportunities to serve God and was not discouraged by the setbacks and opposition he met along the way. Silas, though not the most famous of the early missionaries, was certainly a hero worth imitating.

| | |
|---|---|
| **Strengths and accomplishments** | • A leader in the Jerusalem church<br>• Represented the church in carrying the "acceptance letter" prepared by the Jerusalem council to the Gentile believers in Antioch<br>• Was closely associated with Paul from the second missionary journey on<br>• Sang songs of praise to God while in jail with Paul in Philippi<br>• Worked as a writing secretary for both Paul and Peter |
| **Lessons from his life** | • Partnership is a significant part of effective ministry<br>• God never guarantees that his servants will not suffer<br>• Obedience to God will often mean giving up what makes us feel secure |
| **Vital statistics** | • Where: Roman citizen living in Jerusalem<br>• Occupation: One of the first career missionaries<br>• Contemporaries: Paul, Timothy, Peter, Mark, Barnabas |
| **Key verses** | "So we decided, having come to complete agreement, to send you official representatives, along with our beloved Barnabas and Paul, who have risked their lives for the name of our Lord Jesus Christ. We are sending Judas and Silas to confirm what we have decided concerning your question" (Acts 15:25-27). |

Silas's story is told in Acts 15:22–19:10. He is also mentioned in 2 Corinthians 1:19; 1 Thessalonians 1:1; 2 Thessalonians 1:1; 1 Peter 5:12.

son of a Jewish mother and Greek father—to the Jews, a half-breed like a Samaritan. So Paul asked Timothy to be circumcised to remove some of the stigma he may have had with Jewish believers. Timothy was not required to be circumcised (the

Jerusalem council had decided that—chapter 15), but he voluntarily did this to overcome any barriers to his witness for Christ. Sometimes we need to go beyond the call of duty in order to further the Kingdom of God.

## A Call from Macedonia

⁶Next Paul and Silas traveled through the area of Phrygia and Galatia, because the Holy Spirit had prevented them from preaching the word in the province of Asia at that time. ⁷Then coming to the borders of Mysia, they headed north for the province of Bithynia,* but again the Spirit of Jesus did not allow them to go there. ⁸So instead, they went on through Mysia to the seaport of Troas.

16:7
Rom 8:9
Phil 1:19

16:8
2 Cor 2:12
2 Tim 4:13

⁹That night Paul had a vision: A man from Macedonia in northern Greece was standing there, pleading with him, "Come over to Macedonia and help us!" ¹⁰So we* decided to leave for Macedonia at once, having concluded that God was calling us to preach the Good News there.

16:9
Rom 15:26

## Lydia of Philippi Believes in Jesus

¹¹We boarded a boat at Troas and sailed straight across to the island of Samothrace, and the next day we landed at Neapolis. ¹²From there we reached Philippi, a major city of that district of Macedonia and a Roman colony. And we stayed there several days.

16:11
2 Cor 2:12

16:12
Phil 1:1
1 Thes 2:2

¹³On the Sabbath we went a little way outside the city to a riverbank, where we thought people would be meeting for prayer, and we sat down to speak with some women who had gathered there. ¹⁴One of them was Lydia from Thyatira, a merchant of expensive purple cloth, who worshiped God. As she listened to us, the Lord opened her heart, and she accepted what Paul was saying. ¹⁵She was baptized along with other members of her household, and she asked us to be her guests. "If you agree that I am a true believer in the Lord," she said, "come and stay at my home." And she urged us until we agreed.

16:14
Rev 1:11; 2:18, 24

16:6-7 *Phrygia, Galatia, Asia, Mysia,* and *Bithynia* were all districts in what is now Turkey.    16:10 Luke, the writer of this book, here joined Paul and accompanied him on his journey.

---

**16:6** We don't know how the Holy Spirit told Paul that he and his companions should not go into Asia. It may have been through a prophet, a vision, an inner conviction, or some other circumstance. To know God's will does not mean we must hear his voice. He leads in different ways. When you are seeking God's will, (1) make sure your plan is in harmony with God's Word; (2) ask mature Christians for their advice; (3) check your own motives to see if you are seeking to do what you want or what you think God wants; (4) pray for God to open and close the doors as he desires.

**16:7-9** The "Spirit of Jesus" is another name for the Holy Spirit. The Holy Spirit had closed the door twice for Paul, so Paul must have wondered which geographical direction to take in spreading the Good News. Then, in a vision (16:9), Paul was given definite direction, and he and his companions obediently traveled into Macedonia. The Holy Spirit guides us to the right places, but he also guides us away from the wrong places. As we seek God's will, we need to know what God wants us to do and where he

wants us to go, but we also need to know what God does not want us to do and where he does not want us to go.

**16:10** The use of the pronoun *we* indicates that Luke, the author of the Gospel of Luke and of this book, joined Paul, Silas, and Timothy on their journey. He was an eyewitness to most of the remaining incidents recorded in this book.

**16:12** Philippi was the key city in the region of Macedonia (northern Greece today). Paul founded a church during this visit (A.D. 50–51). Later, Paul wrote a letter to the church, the book of Philippians, probably from a prison in Rome (A.D. 61). The letter was personal and tender, showing Paul's deep love for and friendship with the believers there. In it he thanked them for a gift they had sent, alerted them to a coming visit by Timothy and Epaphroditus, urged the church to clear up any disunity, and encouraged the believers not to give in to persecution.

**16:13** Inscribed on the arches outside the city of Philippi was a prohibition against bringing an unrecognized religion into the city; therefore, this prayer meeting was held outside the city, beside the river.

**16:13, 14** After following the Holy Spirit's leading into Macedonia, Paul made his first evangelistic contact with a small group of women. Paul never allowed gender or cultural boundaries to keep him from preaching the Good News. He preached to these women, and Lydia, an influential merchant, believed. This opened the way for ministry in that region. God often worked in and through women in the early church.

**16:14** Lydia was a merchant of purple cloth, so she was probably wealthy. Purple cloth was valuable and expensive. It was often worn as a sign of nobility or royalty.

**16:14ff** Luke highlights the stories of three individuals who became believers through Paul's ministry in Philippi: Lydia, the influential businesswoman (16:14), the demon-possessed slave girl (16:16-18), and the jailer (16:27-30). The Good News was affecting all strata of society, just as it does today.

**16:15** Why was Lydia's household baptized after Lydia responded in faith to the Good News? Baptism was a public sign of identification with Christ and the Christian community. Although all members of her household may not have chosen to follow Christ (we don't know), it was now a Christian home.

**16:15** Lydia practically begged for the opportunity to host Paul

**PAUL TRAVELS TO MACEDONIA**   At Troas, Paul received the Macedonian call (16:9), and he, Silas, Timothy, and Luke boarded a ship. They sailed to the island of Samothrace, then on to Neapolis, the port for the city of Philippi. Philippi sat on the Egnatian Way, a main transportation artery connecting the eastern provinces with Italy.

## Paul and Silas in Prison

**16:16**
Deut 18:10-11
1 Sam 28:3, 7

¹⁶One day as we were going down to the place of prayer, we met a demon-possessed slave girl. She was a fortune-teller who earned a lot of money for her masters. ¹⁷She followed Paul and the rest of us, shouting, "These men are servants of the Most High God, and they have come to tell you how to be saved."

**16:18**
Mark 16:17
Acts 19:13

¹⁸This went on day after day until Paul got so exasperated that he turned and said to the demon within her, "I command you in the name of Jesus Christ to come out of her." And instantly it left her.

¹⁹Her masters' hopes of wealth were now shattered, so they grabbed Paul and Silas and

---

Almost everywhere Paul and Silas traveled, they found people open to the gospel message. When they arrived in Philippi they met just such a disciple-in-the-making. Her name was Lydia.

Lydia's business as a dealer in fine purple cloth and dye probably means she was wealthy. No husband is mentioned, but she was responsible for a household. Lydia was also a spiritual searcher. She was among the Gentile women who gathered outside Philippi on each Sabbath to pray to the God of the Jews. One eventful day, Paul and Silas visited the group.

Lydia's attendance at the prayer gathering demonstrated her willingness to respond to as much about God as she knew. God responded to her quest by providing her with more truth. When she heard the Good News about Jesus Christ, she listened and believed. She is remembered as Paul's first European convert.

Luke described with swift strokes the first two steps in Lydia's life as a disciple: (1) She was baptized, (2) she brought the rest of the members of her household to Paul and they apparently believed as well, because they were baptized as well. Lydia's response was both inward and outward. She immediately understood that her new faith created all kinds of opportunities for practical application. Then, as now, the gospel had life-changing effects. The first actions of new believers often indicate how deeply they have understood and received the gift of salvation. The Christian life is a gift we continue to receive by sharing it with others.

Thinking of Lydia, how would you describe the initial effects of the gospel in your life? When you accepted Christ, what changes did others notice in you? How did Christ's presence affect your behavior? To what degree has your life continued to display that gratefulness you felt when you first believed?

| | |
|---|---|
| **Strengths and accomplishments** | • Successful businesswoman<br>• The first convert to Christianity in Philippi, and therefore, Europe<br>• Brought her entire household to hear about Jesus, and all were baptized as a result<br>• Provided housing in Philippi for Paul and Silas |
| **Lessons from her life** | • God rewards those who honestly seek him<br>• One of the marks of conversion is care for others—physically and spiritually |
| **Vital statistics** | • Where: From Thyatira, living in Philippi<br>• Occupation: Merchant specializing in costly purple cloth<br>• Relatives: A household that was baptized with her |
| **Key verse** | "One of them was Lydia from Thyatira, a merchant of expensive purple cloth, who worshiped God. As she listened to us, the Lord opened her heart, and she accepted what Paul was saying" (Acts 16:14). |

The events surrounding Lydia's conversion are found in Acts 16:11-40.

---

and Silas in her home. Rather than seeing the men as a burden and their presence as a disruption of her family and business routine, Lydia laid out the welcome mat. The notion of hospitality is related to the word "hospital." In other words, we practice hospitality when we generously and cordially throw open the doors of our homes to care for others. In hospitality, we nurture, strengthen, and serve. The result is that others find physical, spiritual, and emotional help. When they leave us, they are healthier and more whole than when they came. Is this your practice? Is your home a "hospital" for hurting or needy souls?

**16:16** This girl's fortune-telling ability came from evil spirits. Fortune-telling was a common practice in Greek and Roman culture. There were many superstitious methods by which people thought they could foretell future events, from interpreting omens in nature to communicating with the spirits of the dead. This young slave girl had an evil spirit, and she made her master rich by interpreting signs and telling people their fortunes. The master was exploiting her unfortunate condition for personal gain.

**16:17, 18** What the slave girl said was true, although the source of her knowledge was a demon. Why did a demon announce the truth about Paul, and why did this annoy Paul? If Paul accepted the demon's words, he would appear to be linking the Good News with demon-related activities. This would damage his message about Christ. Truth and evil do not mix.

**16:19** Faced with the loss of their slave girl's fortune-telling ability, the Philippian entrepreneurs were furious. Never mind that Paul and Silas were speaking eternal truths, never mind that the poor slave girl had been delivered from an awful existence; these men could only bemoan their economic loss! The gospel would also later hurt Ephesian idol makers financially (chapter 19), resulting in a citywide riot. When people care more about their own economic well being than the glory of God and the salvation of lost souls, it is a clear sign of idolatry, greed, and worldliness.

dragged them before the authorities at the marketplace. 20"The whole city is in an uproar because of these Jews!" they shouted to the city officials. 21"They are teaching customs that are illegal for us Romans to practice."

22A mob quickly formed against Paul and Silas, and the city officials ordered them stripped and beaten with wooden rods. 23They were severely beaten, and then they were thrown into prison. The jailer was ordered to make sure they didn't escape. 24So the jailer put them into the inner dungeon and clamped their feet in the stocks.

25Around midnight Paul and Silas were praying and singing hymns to God, and the other prisoners were listening. 26Suddenly, there was a massive earthquake, and the prison was shaken to its foundations. All the doors immediately flew open, and the chains of every prisoner fell off! 27The jailer woke up to see the prison doors wide open. He assumed the prisoners had escaped, so he drew his sword to kill himself. 28But Paul shouted to him, "Stop! Don't kill yourself! We are all here!"

29The jailer called for lights and ran to the dungeon and fell down trembling before Paul and Silas. 30Then he brought them out and asked, "Sirs, what must I do to be saved?"

31They replied, "Believe in the Lord Jesus and you will be saved, along with everyone in your household." 32And they shared the word of the Lord with him and with all who lived in his household. 33Even at that hour of the night, the jailer cared for them and washed their wounds. Then he and everyone in his household were immediately baptized. 34He brought them into his house and set a meal before them, and he and his entire household rejoiced because they all believed in God.

35The next morning the city officials sent the police to tell the jailer, "Let those men go!" 36So the jailer told Paul, "The city officials have said you and Silas are free to leave. Go in peace."

37But Paul replied, "They have publicly beaten us without a trial and put us in prison— and we are Roman citizens. So now they want us to leave secretly? Certainly not! Let them come themselves to release us!"

38When the police reported this, the city officials were alarmed to learn that Paul and Silas were Roman citizens. 39So they came to the jail and apologized to them. Then they brought them out and begged them to leave the city. 40When Paul and Silas left the prison, they returned to the home of Lydia. There they met with the believers and encouraged them once more. Then they left town.

**16:20**
Acts 17:6
**16:21**
Esth 3:8
**16:22**
2 Cor 11:25
1 Thes 2:2
**16:25**
Eph 5:19
**16:26**
Acts 5:19; 12:10
**16:27**
Acts 12:18-19
**16:30**
Acts 2:37
**16:31**
John 3:15
Acts 11:14
**16:37**
Acts 22:25
**16:38**
Acts 22:29
**16:39**
Matt 8:34
**16:40**
Acts 16:14

---

**16:22-25** Paul and Silas were stripped, beaten, and placed in stocks in the inner cell. Stocks were made of two boards joined with iron clamps, leaving holes just big enough for the ankles. The prisoner's legs were placed across the lower board, and then the upper board was closed over them. Sometimes both wrists and ankles were placed in stocks. Paul and Silas, who had committed no crime and who were peaceful men, were put in stocks designed for holding the most dangerous prisoners in absolute security. Despite this dismal situation, they praised God, praying and singing as the other prisoners listened. No matter what our circumstances, we should praise God. Others may come to Christ because of our example.

**16:27** The jailer drew his sword to kill himself because jailers were responsible for their prisoners and would be held accountable for their escape.

**16:30, 31** Paul and Silas's reputation in Philippi was well known. When the jailer realized his own condition and need, he risked everything to find the answer. The Good News of salvation is simply expressed: Believe in the Lord Jesus, and you will be saved (see Romans 10:9; 1 Corinthians 12:3; Ephesians 2:8, 9; Philippians 2:11). When we recognize Jesus as Lord and trust in him with our entire life, salvation is assured to us. If you have never trusted in Jesus to save you, do so quickly. Your life can be filled with joy, just as the jailer's was (16:34).

**16:31-34** Paul and Silas took the family unit seriously. So the offer of salvation was made to the jailer's entire household— family and servants. Yet it was not the jailer's faith that saved them; they all needed to come to Jesus in faith and believe in him in the same way the jailer had. His entire family did believe and all were saved. Pray that God will use you to introduce Jesus to your family and that they will come to believe in him.

**16:37, 38** Paul refused to take his freedom and run. He wanted to teach the city officials in Philippi a lesson and to protect the other believers from the treatment he and Silas had received. The word would spread that Paul and Silas had been found innocent and freed by the leaders, expressing the truth that believers should not be persecuted—especially if they were Roman citizens. Roman citizenship carried with it certain privileges. These Philippian

**MINISTRY IN MACEDONIA**
Luke stayed in Philippi while Paul, Silas, and Timothy continued on the Egnatian Way to Amphipolis, Apollonia, and Thessalonica. But trouble arose in Thessalonica, and they fled to Berea. When their enemies from Thessalonica pursued them, Paul set out by sea to Athens, leaving Silas and Timothy to encourage the believers.

## Paul Preaches in Thessalonica

**17** Paul and Silas then traveled through the towns of Amphipolis and Apollonia and came to Thessalonica, where there was a Jewish synagogue. ²As was Paul's custom, he went to the synagogue service, and for three Sabbaths in a row he used the Scriptures to reason with the people. ³He explained the prophecies and proved that the Messiah must suffer and rise from the dead. He said, "This Jesus I'm telling you about is the Messiah." ⁴Some of the Jews who listened were persuaded and joined Paul and Silas, along with many God-fearing Greek men and quite a few prominent women.*

⁵But some of the Jews were jealous, so they gathered some troublemakers from the marketplace to form a mob and start a riot. They attacked the home of Jason, searching for Paul and Silas so they could drag them out to the crowd.* ⁶Not finding them there, they dragged out Jason and some of the other believers* instead and took them before the city council. "Paul and Silas have caused trouble all over the world," they shouted, "and now they are here disturbing our city, too. ⁷And Jason has welcomed them into his home. They are all guilty of treason against Caesar, for they profess allegiance to another king, named Jesus."

⁸The people of the city, as well as the city council, were thrown into turmoil by these reports. ⁹So the officials forced Jason and the other believers to post bond, and then they released them.

**17:2**
Acts 9:20; 13:14;
17:10, 17

**17:3**
Luke 24:26
Acts 3:18; 9:22;
18:5

**17:5**
Rom 16:21
1 Thes 2:14

**17:6**
Acts 16:20-21

**17:7**
Luke 23:2
John 19:12

17:4 Some manuscripts read *quite a few of the wives of the leading men.*   17:5 Or *the city council.*   17:6 Greek *brothers;* also in 17:10, 14.

---

| THE BOOKS | | | | |
|---|---|---|---|---|
| **THE BOOKS OF THE NEW TESTAMENT: WHEN WERE THEY WRITTEN?** Dates are approximate. | Galatians . . . . . . . . . . A.D. 49 | Philemon . . . . . . 60 | Acts . . . . . . . . . 66/68 | |
| | James. . . . . . . . . . . . 49 | Philippians . . . . . 61 | 2 Peter . . . . . . . . 66/68 | |
| | 1, 2 Thessalonians . . . 51/52 | Matthew . . . . . . . 61/64 | 2 Timothy . . . . . . 66/67 | |
| | 1, 2 Corinthians . . . . . 55 | Luke . . . . . . . . . . 61/64 | Hebrews . . . . . . . 68/70 | |
| | Romans . . . . . . . . . . 57 | 1 Timothy . . . . . . 64 | John . . . . . . . . . 85 | |
| | Mark . . . . . . . . . . . . 58/60 | Titus . . . . . . . . . . 64 | 1, 2, 3 John . . . . 85/90 | |
| | Ephesians . . . . . . . . 60 | 1 Peter . . . . . . . . 64/65 | Revelation . . . . . 95 | |
| | Colossians . . . . . . . . 60 | Jude . . . . . . . . . 65 | | |

---

authorities were alarmed because it was illegal to whip a Roman citizen. In addition, every citizen had the right to a fair trial, which Paul and Silas had not been given.

**17:1** Thessalonica was one of the wealthiest and most influential cities in Macedonia. This is the first city Paul visited where his teachings attracted a large group of socially prominent citizens. The church he planted grew quickly, but from A.D. 50 to 51, Paul was forced out of the city by a mob (17:5, 6, 10). He later sent Timothy back to Thessalonica to see how the Christians were doing. Soon afterward, Paul wrote two letters to the Thessalonian believers (1 and 2 Thessalonians), encouraging them to remain faithful and to refuse to listen to false teachers who tried to refute their beliefs.

**17:1, 2** A synagogue, a group of Jews who gathered for teaching and prayer, could be established wherever 10 Jewish males lived. Paul's regular practice was to preach in synagogues as long as the Jews allowed it. Often those who weren't Jews would come to these services and hear Paul's preaching. For a description of a synagogue service, see the note on 13:14, 15.

**17:2, 3** When Paul spoke in the synagogues, he wisely began by talking about Old Testament writings and explaining how the Messiah fulfilled them, moving from the known to the unknown. This is a good strategy for us. When we witness for Christ, we should begin where people are, affirming the truth they do know, and then we can present Christ, the one who is truth.

**17:5** The Jewish leaders didn't try to refute the theology of Paul and Silas, but they were jealous of the popularity of these itinerant preachers. Their motives for causing the riot were rooted in personal jealousy, not doctrinal purity.

**17:6** We don't know much about Jason except that he evidently was the local host and sponsor of Paul and Silas; thus, he took

the heat for all the problems. Jason is just one of many "unsung heroes" who faithfully played their part to help spread the Good News. Because of Jason's courage, Paul and Silas were able to minister more effectively. You may not receive much attention (in fact, you may receive only grief) for your service for Christ. But God wants to use you. Lives will be changed because of your courage and faithfulness.

**17:6** What a reputation these early Christians had! The power of the Good News revolutionized lives, broke down all social barriers, threw open prison doors, caused people to care deeply for one another, and stirred them to worship God. Our world needs to be turned upside down, to be transformed. The Good News doesn't merely improve programs and encourage good conduct; it dynamically transforms lives. Take courage and ask God how you can help spread his Good News throughout *your* world.

**17:7** The Jewish leaders had to concoct charges against Paul and Silas that would be heard by the city government. The Romans did not care about theological disagreements between the Jews and these preachers. Treason, however, was a serious offense in the Roman Empire. Paul and Silas were not advocating rebellion against Roman law, but their loyalty to another king sounded suspicious.

**17:8, 9** Jason posted bond—putting up cash for freedom. By doing so, he promised that the trouble would cease or his own property and possibly his own life would be taken.

## Paul and Silas in Berea

¹⁰That very night the believers sent Paul and Silas to Berea. When they arrived there, they went to the Jewish synagogue. ¹¹And the people of Berea were more open-minded than those in Thessalonica, and they listened eagerly to Paul's message. They searched the Scriptures day after day to see if Paul and Silas were teaching the truth. ¹²As a result, many Jews believed, as did many of the prominent Greek women and men.

¹³But when some Jews in Thessalonica learned that Paul was preaching the word of God in Berea, they went there and stirred up trouble. ¹⁴The believers acted at once, sending Paul on to the coast, while Silas and Timothy remained behind. ¹⁵Those escorting Paul went with him all the way to Athens; then they returned to Berea with instructions for Silas and Timothy to hurry and join him.

## Paul Preaches in Athens

¹⁶While Paul was waiting for them in Athens, he was deeply troubled by all the idols he saw everywhere in the city. ¹⁷He went to the synagogue to reason with the Jews and the God-fearing Gentiles, and he spoke daily in the public square to all who happened to be there.

¹⁸He also had a debate with some of the Epicurean and Stoic philosophers. When he told them about Jesus and his resurrection, they said, "What's this babbler trying to say with these strange ideas he's picked up?" Others said, "He seems to be preaching about some foreign gods."

¹⁹Then they took him to the high council of the city.* "Come and tell us about this new teaching," they said. ²⁰"You are saying some rather strange things, and we want to know what it's all about." ²¹(It should be explained that all the Athenians as well as the foreigners in Athens seemed to spend all their time discussing the latest ideas.)

²²So Paul, standing before the council,* addressed them as follows: "Men of Athens, I notice that you are very religious in every way, ²³for as I was walking along I saw your many shrines. And one of your altars had this inscription on it: 'To an Unknown God.' This God, whom you worship without knowing, is the one I'm telling you about.

**17:19** Or *the most learned society of philosophers in the city.* Greek reads *the Areopagus.*    **17:22** Traditionally rendered *standing in the middle of Mars Hill;* Greek reads *standing in the middle of the Areopagus.*

Cross-references (right margin):
**17:11** John 5:39
**17:13** Acts 14:19
**17:14** Matt 10:23
**17:15** Acts 18:5; 1 Thes 3:1
**17:17** Acts 18:19
**17:18** 1 Cor 1:22
**17:23** John 4:22

---

**17:11** How do you evaluate sermons and teachings? The people in Berea searched the Scriptures for themselves to verify the message they heard. Always compare what you hear with what the Bible says. A preacher or teacher who gives God's true message will never contradict or explain away anything that is found in God's Word.

**17:16** Athens, with its magnificent buildings and many gods, was a center for Greek culture, philosophy, and education. Philosophers and educated men were always ready to hear something new, so they invited Paul to speak to them at the meeting of the high council of the city (17:18, 19).

**17:16** Paul was "troubled by all the idols he saw everywhere in the city." The word translated "troubled" is the Greek word "paroxysm," meaning "sudden, violent emotion." Paul was filled with a combination of anger and grief. Seeing people spiritually lost, blinded by Satan, and trapped in a pagan culture caused Paul to be in a state of emotional upheaval. Though highly educated, the Athenians were ignorant of the one true God. It's interesting to note that Paul turned his internal turmoil into positive action: he looked for opportunities to share the truth about Jesus. Does the lostness of people move you to action? And if so, do you seek opportunities to share the gospel?

**17:18** The Epicureans and Stoics were the dominant philosophers in Greek culture. The Epicureans believed that seeking happiness or pleasure was the primary goal of life. By contrast, the Stoics placed thinking above feeling and tried to live in harmony with nature and reason, suppressing their desire for pleasure. Thus, they were very disciplined.

**17:19** For a time the council met on a low hill in Athens near the Acropolis. As Paul stood there and spoke about the one true God, his audience could look down on the city and see the many idols representing gods that Paul knew were worthless.

**17:22** Paul was well prepared to speak to this group. He came from Tarsus, an educational center, and had the training and knowledge to present his beliefs clearly and persuasively. Paul was a rabbi, taught by the finest scholar of his day, Gamaliel, and he had spent much of his life thinking and reasoning through the Scriptures.

It is not enough to teach or preach with conviction. Like Paul, we must be prepared. The more we know about the Bible, what it means, and how to apply it to life, the more convincing our words will be. This does not mean that we should avoid presenting the Good News until we feel adequately prepared. We should use what we have learned but always seek to know more in order to be an effective witness and be able to respond to people's questions and arguments.

**17:22ff** Paul's address is a good example of how to communicate the Good News. Paul did not begin by reciting Jewish history, as he usually did, for this would have been meaningless to his Greek audience. He began by building a case for the one true God, using examples they understood (17:22, 23). The Athenians had built an idol to the unknown god for fear of missing blessings or receiving punishment. Paul's opening statement to the men of Athens was about their unknown god. Paul was not endorsing this god but using the inscription as a point of entry for his witness to the one true God. Then he established common ground by emphasizing what they agreed on about God (17:24-29). Finally, he moved his message to the person of Christ, centering on the Resurrection (17:30, 31). When you witness to others, you can follow Paul's approach: Use examples, establish common ground, and then move people toward a decision about Jesus Christ.

**17:23** Paul explained the one true God to these educated men of Athens; although these men were, in general, very religious, they did not know God. Today we have a "Christian" society, but to most people, God is still unknown. We need to proclaim who he is and make clear what he did for everyone through his

**17:24**
1 Kgs 8:27
Isa 42:5
Acts 7:48

**17:25**
Ps 50:12
Isa 42:5

**17:26**
Deut 32:8

**17:27**
Isa 55:6
Jer 23:23-24

**17:29**
Isa 40:18-25
Rom 1:23

**17:30**
Acts 14:16

24"He is the God who made the world and everything in it. Since he is Lord of heaven and earth, he doesn't live in man-made temples, 25 and human hands can't serve his needs—for he has no needs. He himself gives life and breath to everything, and he satisfies every need. 26 From one man* he created all the nations throughout the whole earth. He decided beforehand when they should rise and fall, and he determined their boundaries.

27 "His purpose was for the nations to seek after God and perhaps feel their way toward him and find him—though he is not far from any one of us. 28 For in him we live and move and exist. As some of your* own poets have said, 'We are his offspring.' 29 And since this is true, we shouldn't think of God as an idol designed by craftsmen from gold or silver or stone.

30 "God overlooked people's ignorance about these things in earlier times, but now he

**17:26** Greek *From one;* other manuscripts read *From one blood.* **17:28** Some manuscripts read *our.*

One of the essential qualities of a good doctor is compassion. People need to know that their doctor cares. Even if he or she doesn't know what is wrong or isn't sure what to do, real concern is always a doctor's good medicine. Doctor Luke was a person of compassion.

Although we know few facts of his life, Luke has left us a strong impression of himself by what he wrote. In his Gospel, he emphasizes Jesus Christ's compassion. He vividly recorded both the power demonstrated by Christ's life and the care with which Christ treated people. Luke highlighted the relationships Jesus had with women. His writing in Acts is full of sharp verbal pictures of real people caught up in the greatest events of history.

Luke was also a doctor. He had a traveling medical practice as Paul's companion. Since the gospel was often welcomed with whips and stones, the doctor was undoubtedly seldom without patients. It is even possible that Paul's "thorn in the flesh" was some kind of physical ailment that needed Luke's regular attention (see 2 Corinthians 12:7). Paul deeply appreciated Luke's skills and faithfulness.

God also made special use of Luke as the historian of the early church. Repeatedly, the details of Luke's descriptions have been proven accurate. The first words in his Gospel indicate his interest in the truth.

Luke's compassion reflected his Lord's. Luke's skill as a doctor helped Paul. His passion for the facts as he recorded the life of Christ, the spread of the early church, and the lives of Christianity's missionaries gives us dependable sources for the basis of our faith. He accomplished all this while staying out of the spotlight. Perhaps his greatest example is the challenge to greatness even when we are not the center of attention.

| | |
|---|---|
| **Strengths and accomplishments** | • A humble, faithful, and useful companion of Paul<br>• A well-educated and trained physician<br>• A careful and exact historian<br>• Writer of both the Gospel of Luke and the book of Acts |
| **Lessons from his life** | • The words we leave behind will be a lasting picture of who we are<br>• Even the most successful person needs the personal care of others<br>• Excellence is shown by how we work when no one is noticing |
| **Vital statistics** | • Where: Probably met Paul in Troas<br>• Occupations: Doctor, historian, traveling companion<br>• Contemporaries: Paul, Timothy, Silas, Peter |
| **Key verses** | "Many people have set out to write accounts about the events that have been fulfilled among us. They used the eyewitness reports circulating among us from the early disciples. Having carefully investigated everything from the beginning, I also have decided to write a careful account for you, most honorable Theophilus, so you can be certain of the truth of everything you were taught" (Luke 1:1-4). |

Luke includes himself in the *we* sections of Acts 16–28. He is also mentioned in Luke 1:3; Acts 1:1; Colossians 4:14; 2 Timothy 4:11; Philemon 1:24.

Son, Jesus Christ. We cannot assume that even religious people around us truly know Jesus or understand the importance of faith in him.

**17:27, 28** God is in his creation and close to every one of us. But he is not trapped in his creation—he is transcendent. God is the Creator, not the creation. This means that God is sovereign and in control, while at the same time he is close and personal. Let the Creator of the universe rule your life.

**17:30, 31** Paul did not leave his message unfinished. He confronted his listeners with Jesus' resurrection and its meaning

to all people—either blessing or punishment. The Greeks had no concept of judgment. Most of them preferred worshiping many gods instead of just one, and the concept of resurrection was unbelievable and offensive to them. Paul did not hold back the truth, however, no matter what they might think of it. Paul often changed his approach to fit his audience, but he never changed his basic message.

commands everyone everywhere to repent of their sins and turn to him. 31For he has set a
day for judging the world with justice by the man he has appointed, and he proved to everyone who this is by raising him from the dead."

32When they heard Paul speak about the resurrection of the dead, some laughed in contempt, but others said, "We want to hear more about this later." 33That ended Paul's discussion with them, 34but some joined him and became believers. Among them were
Dionysius, a member of the council,* a woman named Damaris, and others with them.

### Paul Meets Priscilla and Aquila in Corinth

**18** Then Paul left Athens and went to Corinth.* 2There he became acquainted with a Jew
named Aquila, born in Pontus, who had recently arrived from Italy with his wife,
Priscilla. They had left Italy when Claudius Caesar deported all Jews from Rome. 3Paul lived
and worked with them, for they were tentmakers* just as he was.

4Each Sabbath found Paul at the synagogue, trying to convince the Jews and Greeks alike.
5And after Silas and Timothy came down from Macedonia, Paul spent all his time preaching
the word. He testified to the Jews that Jesus was the Messiah. 6But when they opposed and
insulted him, Paul shook the dust from his clothes and said, "Your blood is upon your own
heads—I am innocent. From now on I will go preach to the Gentiles."

**17:31**
Ps 96:13
Acts 10:42

**18:2**
Rom 16:3
1 Cor 16:19
**18:3**
Acts 20:34
1 Cor 4:12; 9:15
**18:5**
Acts 17:3; 18:28
**18:6**
Matt 10:14
Acts 13:45-46;
20:26

**17:34** Greek *an Areopagite.*   **18:1** *Athens* and *Corinth* were major cities in Achaia, the region in the southern portion
of the Greek peninsula.   **18:3** Or *leatherworkers.*

**MINISTRY IN
CORINTH AND
EPHESUS**
Paul left Athens
and traveled on
to Corinth, one
of the greatest
commercial
centers of the
empire, located
on a narrow neck
of land offering
direct passage
between the
Aegean and Adri-
atic seas. When
Paul left from the
port of Corinth
at Cenchrea, he
visited Ephesus.
He then traveled
to Caesarea, from
where he went on
to Jerusalem to
report on his trip
before returning
to Antioch.

**17:32-34** Paul's speech received a mixed reaction: Some
laughed, some wanted more information, and a few believed.
Don't hesitate to tell others about Christ because you fear that
some will not believe you. Don't expect a unanimously positive
response to your witnessing. Even if only a few believe, it's worth
the effort.

**18:1** Corinth was the political and commercial center of Greece,
surpassing Athens in importance. It had a reputation for great
wickedness and immorality. A temple to Aphrodite, goddess of
love and war, had been built on the large hill behind the city. In
this popular religion, people worshiped the goddess by giving

money to the temple and taking part in sexual acts with male
and female temple prostitutes. Paul found Corinth a challenge
and a great ministry opportunity. Later, he would write a series
of letters to the Corinthians dealing in part with the problems of
immorality. Two of these letters are 1 and 2 Corinthians.

**18:2, 3** Each Jewish boy learned a trade and tried to earn his
living with it. Paul and Aquila had been trained in tentmaking,
cutting and sewing the woven cloth of goats' hair into tents.
Tents were used to house soldiers, so these tents may have been
sold to the Roman army. As a tentmaker, Paul was able to go
wherever God led him, carrying his livelihood with him. The word
*tentmaker* in Greek was also used to describe a leatherworker.

**18:6** Paul told the Jews he had done all he could for them.
Because they had rejected Jesus as their Messiah, he would go
to the Gentiles, who would be more receptive.

**18:8**
1 Cor 1:14

⁷Then he left and went to the home of Titius Justus, a Gentile who worshiped God and lived next door to the synagogue. ⁸Crispus, the leader of the synagogue, and everyone in his household believed in the Lord. Many others in Corinth also heard Paul, became believers, and were baptized.

**18:9-10**
Isa 41:10
Jer 1:18

⁹One night the Lord spoke to Paul in a vision and told him, "Don't be afraid! Speak out! Don't be silent! ¹⁰For I am with you, and no one will attack and harm you, for many people in this city belong to me." ¹¹So Paul stayed there for the next year and a half, teaching the word of God.

¹²But when Gallio became governor of Achaia, some Jews rose up together against Paul and brought him before the governor for judgment. ¹³They accused Paul of "persuading people to worship God in ways that are contrary to our law."

---

**AQUILA & PRISCILLA**

Some married couples know how to make the most of life. They complement each other, capitalize on each other's strengths, and form an effective team. Their united efforts affect those around them. Aquila and Priscilla were such a couple. They are never mentioned separately in the Bible. In marriage and ministry, they operated as one.

Priscilla and Aquila met Paul in Corinth during his second missionary journey. They had just been expelled from Rome by Emperor Claudius's decree against Jews. Their home was as movable as the tents they made to support themselves. They opened their home to Paul, and he joined them in tentmaking. He shared with them his wealth of spiritual wisdom.

Priscilla and Aquila made the most of their spiritual education. They listened carefully to sermons and evaluated what they heard. When they heard Apollos speak, they were impressed by his ability but realized that his information was not complete. Instead of open confrontation, the couple quietly took Apollos home and shared with him what he needed to know. Until then, Apollos had only been aware of John the Baptist's message about Christ. Priscilla and Aquila told him about Jesus' life, death, and resurrection, and the reality of God's indwelling Spirit. He continued to preach powerfully—but now with the full story.

As for Priscilla and Aquila, they went on using their home as a warm place for training and worship. Back in Rome years later, they hosted one of the house churches that developed.

In an age when the focus is mostly on what happens *between* a husband and wife, Aquila and Priscilla are an example of what can happen *through* a husband and wife. Their effectiveness together is the result of their good relationship with each other. Their hospitality opened the doorway of salvation to many. The Christian home is still one of the best tools for spreading the gospel. Do guests find Christ in your home?

| | |
|---|---|
| **Strengths and accomplishments** | • Outstanding husband/wife team who ministered in the early church<br>• Supported themselves by tentmaking while serving Christ<br>• Close friends of Paul<br>• Explained to Apollos the full message of Christ |
| **Lessons from their lives** | • Couples can have an effective ministry together<br>• The home is a valuable tool for evangelism<br>• Every believer needs to be well educated in the faith, whatever his or her role in the church |
| **Vital statistics** | • Where: Originally from Rome, moved to Corinth, then Ephesus<br>• Occupation: Tentmakers<br>• Contemporaries: Emperor Claudius, Paul, Timothy, Apollos |
| **Key verses** | "Give my greetings to Priscilla and Aquila, my co-workers in the ministry of Christ Jesus. In fact, they once risked their lives for me. I am thankful to them, and so are all the Gentile churches" (Romans 16:3-4). |

Their story is told in Acts 18. They are also mentioned in Romans 16:3-5; 1 Corinthians 16:19; 2 Timothy 4:19.

---

**18:10** In a vision, Christ told Paul that he had many people in Corinth. Sometimes we can feel alone or isolated, especially when we see wickedness all around us or are persecuted for our faith. Usually, however, there are others in the neighborhood or community who also follow Christ. Ask God to lead you to them.

**18:10, 11** Others who became Christians in Corinth were Phoebe (Romans 16:1—Cenchrea was the port city of Corinth), Tertius (Romans 16:22), Erastus (Romans 16:23), Quartus (Romans 16:23), Chloe (1 Corinthians 1:11), Gaius (1 Corinthians 1:14), Stephanas and his household (1 Corinthians 1:15), Fortunatus (1 Corinthians 16:17), and Achaicus (1 Corinthians 16:17).

**18:11** During the year and a half that Paul stayed in Corinth, he established a church and wrote two letters to the believers in Thessalonica (the books of 1 and 2 Thessalonians). Although

Paul had been in Thessalonica for only a short time (17:1-15), he commended the believers there for their loving deeds, strong faith, and endurance inspired by hope. While encouraging them to stay away from immorality, he dealt with the themes of salvation, suffering, and the second coming of Jesus Christ. Paul told them to continue to work hard while they awaited Christ's return.

**18:12** Gallio served as governor of Achaia (modern Greece) in A.D. 51 and was the brother of Seneca the philosopher. He became consul in A.D. 55.

**18:13** Paul was charged with promoting a religion not approved by Roman law. This charge amounted to treason. Paul was not encouraging obedience to a human king other than Caesar (see 17:7), nor was he speaking against the Roman Empire. Instead, he was speaking about Christ's eternal Kingdom.

14But just as Paul started to make his defense, Gallio turned to Paul's accusers and said, "Listen, you Jews, if this were a case involving some wrongdoing or a serious crime, I would have a reason to accept your case. 15But since it is merely a question of words and names and your Jewish law, take care of it yourselves. I refuse to judge such matters." 16And he threw them out of the courtroom.

**18:15**
John 18:31

17The crowd* then grabbed Sosthenes, the leader of the synagogue, and beat him right there in the courtroom. But Gallio paid no attention.

**18:17**
Acts 18:8
1 Cor 1:1

### Paul Returns to Antioch of Syria

18Paul stayed in Corinth for some time after that, then said good-bye to the brothers and sisters* and went to nearby Cenchrea. There he shaved his head according to Jewish custom, marking the end of a vow. Then he set sail for Syria, taking Priscilla and Aquila with him.

**18:18**
Num 6:18
Acts 21:24
Rom 16:1

19They stopped first at the port of Ephesus, where Paul left the others behind. While he was there, he went to the synagogue to reason with the Jews. 20They asked him to stay longer, but he declined. 21As he left, however, he said, "I will come back later,* God willing." Then he set sail from Ephesus. 22The next stop was at the port of Caesarea. From there he went up and visited the church at Jerusalem* and then went back to Antioch.

**18:19**
Eph 1:1
Rev 1:11; 2:1

**18:21**
Jas 4:15

**18:22**
Acts 8:40; 11:19

23After spending some time in Antioch, Paul went back through Galatia and Phrygia, visiting and strengthening all the believers.*

**18:23**
Acts 16:6

### Apollos Instructed at Ephesus

24Meanwhile, a Jew named Apollos, an eloquent speaker who knew the Scriptures well, had arrived in Ephesus from Alexandria in Egypt. 25He had been taught the way of the Lord, and he taught others about Jesus with an enthusiastic spirit* and with accuracy. However, he knew only about John's baptism. 26When Priscilla and Aquila heard him preaching boldly in the synagogue, they took him aside and explained the way of God even more accurately.

**18:24**
Acts 19:1
1 Cor 1:12; 4:6;
16:12
Titus 3:13

**18:25**
Acts 19:3

27Apollos had been thinking about going to Achaia, and the brothers and sisters in Ephesus encouraged him to go. They wrote to the believers in Achaia, asking them to welcome him. When he arrived there, he proved to be of great benefit to those who, by God's grace, had believed. 28He refuted the Jews with powerful arguments in public debate. Using the Scriptures, he explained to them that Jesus was the Messiah.

**18:27**
2 Cor 3:1

**18:28**
Acts 9:22

**18:17** Greek *Everyone;* other manuscripts read *All the Greeks.* **18:18** Greek *brothers;* also in 18:27. **18:21** Some manuscripts read *"I must by all means be at Jerusalem for the upcoming festival, but I will come back later."* **18:22** Greek *the church.* **18:23** Greek *disciples;* also in 18:27. **18:25** Or *with enthusiasm in the Spirit.*

---

**18:14-16** This was an important judicial decision for the spread of the Good News in the Roman Empire. Judaism was a recognized religion under Roman law. As long as Christians were seen as part of Judaism, the court refused to hear cases brought against them. If they had claimed to be a new religion, they could easily have been outlawed by the government. In effect, Gallio was saying, "I don't understand all your terminology and finer points of theology. Handle the matter yourself and don't bother me."

**18:17** Crispus had been the leader of the synagogue, but he and his family were converted and joined the Christians (18:8). Sosthenes had been chosen to take his place. The mob could have been Greeks venting their feelings against the Jews for causing turmoil, or the crowd may have included some Jews. In any case, they beat Sosthenes for losing the case and leaving the synagogue worse off than before. A person named Sosthenes is mentioned in 1 Corinthians 1:1, and many believe this was the same man who, in time, became a convert and a companion of Paul.

**18:18** This vow Paul took was probably a temporary Nazirite vow that ended with shaving of the head and offering the hair as a sacrifice (Numbers 6:18).

**18:22** This verse marks the end of Paul's second missionary journey and the beginning of the third, which lasted from A.D. 53 to 57. Leaving the church at Antioch (his home base), Paul headed toward Ephesus, but along the way he revisited the churches in Galatia and Phrygia (18:23). The heart of this trip was a lengthy stay (two to three years) in Ephesus. Before returning to Jerusalem, he also visited believers in Macedonia and Greece.

**18:24-26** Apollos had heard only what John the Baptist had said about Jesus (see Luke 3:1-18), so his message was not the complete story. John focused on repentance from sin, the first step.

But the whole message is to repent from sin and then believe in Christ. Apollos did not know about Jesus' life, crucifixion, and resurrection. Nor did he know about the coming of the Holy Spirit. Priscilla and Aquila explained the way of salvation to him.

**18:27, 28** Apollos was from Alexandria in Egypt, the second most important city in the Roman Empire, and the home of a great university. Alexandria had a thriving Jewish population. Apollos was a scholar, orator, and debater; and after his knowledge about Christ was made more complete, God greatly used these gifts to strengthen and encourage the church. Reason is a powerful tool in the right hands and in the right situation. Apollos used the gift of reason to convince many in Greece of the truth of the Good News.

As often happens however, abilities sometimes cause division because of jealousy, pride, or other problems. Apollos's abilities eventually created a problem. Some of the Corinthians became more enamored with Apollos than with his message. There is no evidence to suggest that Apollos encouraged this behavior, and Paul never blamed Apollos for this development. Still, Paul eventually had to confront the Corinthians about their divisiveness (see 1 Corinthians 1:12, 13). Be glad for God's gifts but always remember that they are given to bring honor to him. *He* is the point! *His* glory is the issue! Use the gift, but more than that, praise the Giver of the gifts and use them to his glory.

**18:27, 28** Not all the work of a minister or missionary is drudgery, setback, or suffering. Chapter 18 is triumphant, showing victories in key cities and the addition of exciting new leaders such as Priscilla, Aquila, and Apollos to the church. Rejoice in the victories Christ brings, and don't let the hazards create a negative mind-set.

## 4. Third missionary journey

19:1
Acts 18:24
19:2
John 7:39; 20:22
Acts 8:16

**19** While Apollos was in Corinth, Paul traveled through the interior regions until he reached Ephesus, on the coast, where he found several believers.* 2"Did you receive the Holy Spirit when you believed?" he asked them.

"No," they replied, "we haven't even heard that there is a Holy Spirit."

**19:1** Greek *disciples;* also in 19:9, 30.

Some people have an amazing natural talent for public speaking. Some even have a great message to go along with it. When Apollos arrived in Ephesus shortly after Paul's departure, he made an immediate impact. He spoke boldly in public, interpreting and applying the Old Testament Scriptures effectively. He debated opponents of Christianity forcefully and effectively. It didn't take long for him to be noticed by Priscilla and Aquila.

The couple quickly realized that Apollos did not have the whole story. His preaching was based on the Old Testament and John the Baptist's message. He was probably urging people to repent and prepare for the coming Messiah. Priscilla and Aquila took him home with them and brought him up to date on all that had happened. As they told him of Jesus' life, death, and resurrection, and the coming of the Holy Spirit, Apollos must have seen Scripture after Scripture become clear. He was filled with new energy and boldness now that he knew the complete gospel.

Apollos next decided to travel to Achaia. His friends in Ephesus were able to send along a glowing letter of introduction. He quickly became the verbal champion of the Christians in Corinth, debating the opponents of the gospel in public. As often happens, Apollos's abilities eventually created a problem. Some of the Corinthians began to follow Apollos rather than his message. Paul had to confront the Corinthians about their divisiveness. They had been forming little groups named after their favorite preacher. Apollos left Corinth and hesitated to return. Paul wrote warmly of Apollos as a fellow minister who had "watered" the seeds of the gospel that Paul had planted in Corinth. Paul last mentions Apollos briefly to Titus. Apollos was still a traveling representative of the gospel who deserved Titus's help.

Although his natural abilities could have made him proud, Apollos proved himself willing to learn. God used Priscilla and Aquila, fresh from months of learning from Paul, to give Apollos the complete gospel. Because Apollos did not hesitate to be a student, he became an even better teacher. How much does your willingness to learn affect God's efforts to help you become all he wants you to be?

| | |
|---|---|
| **Strengths and accomplishments** | • A gifted and persuasive preacher and apologist in the early church<br>• Willing to be taught<br>• One of the possible candidates for the unknown author of Hebrews |
| **Lessons from his life** | • Effective communication of the gospel includes an accurate message delivered with God's power<br>• A clear verbal defense of the gospel can be a real encouragement to believers, while convincing unbelievers of its truth |
| **Vital statistics** | • Where: From Alexandria in Egypt<br>• Occupations: Traveling preacher, apologist<br>• Contemporaries: Priscilla, Aquila, Paul |
| **Key verses** | "He had been taught the way of the Lord, and he taught others about Jesus with an enthusiastic spirit and with accuracy. However, he knew only about John's baptism. When Priscilla and Aquila heard him preaching boldly in the synagogue, they took him aside and explained the way of God even more accurately" (Acts 18:25-26). |

Apollos's story is told in Acts 18:24–19:1. He is also mentioned in 1 Corinthians 1:12; 3:4-6, 22; 4:1, 6; 16:12; Titus 3:13.

---

**19:1** Ephesus was the capital and leading business center of the Roman province of Asia (part of present-day Turkey). A hub of sea and land transportation, it ranked with Antioch of Syria and Alexandria in Egypt as one of the great cities on the Mediterranean Sea. Paul stayed in Ephesus for a little over two years. There he wrote his first letter to the Corinthians to counter several problems the church in Corinth was facing. Later, while imprisoned in Rome, Paul wrote a letter to the Ephesian church (the book of Ephesians).

**19:2-4** John's baptism was a sign of repentance from sin only, not a sign of new life in Christ. Like Apollos (18:24-26), these Ephesian believers needed further instruction about the message and ministry of Jesus Christ. They believed in Jesus as the Messiah, but they did not understand the significance of the work of the Holy Spirit. Becoming a Christian involves turning from sin

(repentance) and turning to Christ (faith). These believers were incomplete.

In the book of Acts, believers received the Holy Spirit in a variety of ways. Usually the Holy Spirit would fill a person as soon as he or she professed faith in Christ. Here that filling happened later because these disciples' knowledge was incomplete. God was confirming to these believers, who did not initially know about the Holy Spirit, that they were a part of the church. The Holy Spirit's filling endorsed them as believers.

Pentecost was the formal outpouring of the Holy Spirit on the church. The other outpourings in the book of Acts were God's way of uniting new believers to the church. The mark of the true church is not merely right doctrine but right actions, the true evidence of the Holy Spirit's work.

3"Then what baptism did you experience?" he asked.

And they replied, "The baptism of John."

4Paul said, "John's baptism called for repentance from sin. But John himself told the people to believe in the one who would come later, meaning Jesus."

5As soon as they heard this, they were baptized in the name of the Lord Jesus. 6Then when Paul laid his hands on them, the Holy Spirit came on them, and they spoke in other tongues* and prophesied. 7There were about twelve men in all.

## Paul Ministers in Ephesus

8Then Paul went to the synagogue and preached boldly for the next three months, arguing persuasively about the Kingdom of God. 9But some became stubborn, rejecting his message and publicly speaking against the Way. So Paul left the synagogue and took the believers with him. Then he held daily discussions at the lecture hall of Tyrannus. 10This went on for the next two years, so that people throughout the province of Asia—both Jews and Greeks—heard the word of the Lord.

11God gave Paul the power to perform unusual miracles. 12When handkerchiefs or aprons that had merely touched his skin were placed on sick people, they were healed of their diseases, and evil spirits were expelled.

13A group of Jews was traveling from town to town casting out evil spirits. They tried to use the name of the Lord Jesus in their incantation, saying, "I command you in the name of Jesus, whom Paul preaches, to come out!" 14Seven sons of Sceva, a leading priest, were doing this. 15But one time when they tried it, the evil spirit replied, "I know Jesus, and I know Paul, but who are you?" 16Then the man with the evil spirit leaped on them, overpowered them, and attacked them with such violence that they fled from the house, naked and battered.

17The story of what happened spread quickly all through Ephesus, to Jews and Greeks alike. A solemn fear descended on the city, and the name of the Lord Jesus was greatly honored. 18Many who became believers confessed their sinful practices. 19A number of them who had been practicing sorcery brought their incantation books and burned them at a

19:6 Or *in other languages*.

19:3 Acts 18:25
19:4 Mark 1:4
19:5 Acts 8:12, 16; 10:48 Gal 3:27
19:6 Acts 2:4; 10:44, 46
19:8 Acts 28:23
19:10 Acts 20:31
19:11 Mark 16:20
19:12 Acts 5:15-16
19:13 Matt 12:27 Mark 9:38 Luke 9:49
19:15 Mark 1:24, 34 Luke 4:34, 41
19:17 Acts 5:5, 11
19:19 Deut 18:10-14

---

**19:6** When Paul laid his hands on these disciples, they received the Holy Spirit, just as the disciples had at Pentecost, resulting in outward, visible signs of the Holy Spirit's presence. This also had happened when the Holy Spirit had come on the Gentiles (non-Jews, see 10:45-47). Much has been made about this passage and others in Acts that depict believers speaking in tongues. Some have uncomfortably downplayed or dismissed these historical events. Others have tried to duplicate them. Few issues have prompted more argument and confusion or split more churches. We should remember that tongues-speaking is not the central theme of the book of Acts. The point of Luke's history is the faithful communication of the gospel to the ends of the earth. If we want to be doers of the Word (James 1:22), we will faithfully be involved in the same process of evangelism. Seek to share your faith in the power of the

Holy Spirit (1:8) and leave it up to God to give you whatever experiences he thinks you need.

**19:9** Paul spoke in a lecture hall at this school. Such halls were used in the morning for teaching philosophy, but they were empty during the hot part of the day (about 11 AM to 4 PM). Because many people did not work during those hours, they would come to hear Paul's preaching.

**19:10** "The province of Asia" refers to Asia Minor or modern-day Turkey. During this time, Paul and his coworkers spread the Good News throughout the land.

**19:13** These Jews traveled from town to town making a living by claiming to heal people and drive out demons. Often they would recite a whole list of names in their incantation to be sure of including the right deity. Here they were trying to use Jesus' name in an effort to match Paul's power.

**19:13-16** Some Ephesians engaged in exorcism and occult practices for profit (see 19:18, 19). The sons of Sceva were impressed by Paul, whose power to drive out demons came from God's Holy Spirit, not from witchcraft, and was obviously more powerful than theirs. They discovered, however, that no one can control or duplicate God's power. These men were calling on the name of Jesus without knowing him personally. The power to change people comes from Christ. It cannot be tapped by reciting his name like a magic charm. God works his power only through those he chooses.

**19:18, 19** Ephesus was a center for black magic and other occult practices. The people cooked up magical formulas to give them wealth, happiness, and success in marriage. Superstition and sorcery were commonplace. God clearly forbids such practices (Deuteronomy 18:9-13). You cannot be a believer and hold on to the occult, black magic, or sorcery. Once you begin to dabble in these areas, you may become obsessed by them because Satan is very powerful. But God's power is even greater (1 John 4:4; Revelation 20:10). If you are mixed up in the occult, learn a lesson from the Ephesians and get rid of anything that could trap you in such practices.

**PAUL TAKES A THIRD JOURNEY** What prompted Paul's third journey may have been the need to correct any misunderstandings in the churches Paul had planted. So he hurried north, then west, returning to many of the cities he had previously visited. This time, however, he stayed on a more direct westward route toward Ephesus.

19:20
Acts 6:7; 12:24

19:21
Acts 23:11
Rom 15:25
1 Cor 16:5

19:22
Rom 16:23
2 Tim 4:20

19:23
2 Cor 1:8

19:24
Acts 16:16

19:26
Ps 115:4
Isa 44:10-20
Jer 10:3-5
Acts 17:29
1 Cor 8:4

19:28
Acts 18:19

19:29
Acts 20:4
Rom 16:23
1 Cor 1:14
Col 4:10
Phlm 1:24

19:32
Acts 21:34

19:33
1 Tim 1:20

19:37
Rom 2:22

public bonfire. The value of the books was several million dollars.* 20So the message about the Lord spread widely and had a powerful effect.

21Afterward Paul felt compelled by the Spirit* to go over to Macedonia and Achaia before going to Jerusalem. "And after that," he said, "I must go on to Rome!" 22He sent his two assistants, Timothy and Erastus, ahead to Macedonia while he stayed awhile longer in the province of Asia.

### The Riot in Ephesus

23About that time, serious trouble developed in Ephesus concerning the Way. 24It began with Demetrius, a silversmith who had a large business manufacturing silver shrines of the Greek goddess Artemis.* He kept many craftsmen busy. 25He called them together, along with others employed in similar trades, and addressed them as follows:

"Gentlemen, you know that our wealth comes from this business. 26But as you have seen and heard, this man Paul has persuaded many people that handmade gods aren't really gods at all. And he's done this not only here in Ephesus but throughout the entire province! 27Of course, I'm not just talking about the loss of public respect for our business. I'm also concerned that the temple of the great goddess Artemis will lose its influence and that Artemis—this magnificent goddess worshiped throughout the province of Asia and all around the world—will be robbed of her great prestige!"

28At this their anger boiled, and they began shouting, "Great is Artemis of the Ephesians!" 29Soon the whole city was filled with confusion. Everyone rushed to the amphitheater, dragging along Gaius and Aristarchus, who were Paul's traveling companions from Macedonia. 30Paul wanted to go in, too, but the believers wouldn't let him. 31Some of the officials of the province, friends of Paul, also sent a message to him, begging him not to risk his life by entering the amphitheater.

32Inside, the people were all shouting, some one thing and some another. Everything was in confusion. In fact, most of them didn't even know why they were there. 33The Jews in the crowd pushed Alexander forward and told him to explain the situation. He motioned for silence and tried to speak. 34But when the crowd realized he was a Jew, they started shouting again and kept it up for about two hours: "Great is Artemis of the Ephesians! Great is Artemis of the Ephesians!"

35At last the mayor was able to quiet them down enough to speak. "Citizens of Ephesus," he said. "Everyone knows that Ephesus is the official guardian of the temple of the great Artemis, whose image fell down to us from heaven. 36Since this is an undeniable fact, you should stay calm and not do anything rash. 37You have brought these men here, but they have stolen nothing from the temple and have not spoken against our goddess.

38"If Demetrius and the craftsmen have a case against them, the courts are in session and the officials can hear the case at once. Let them make formal charges. 39And if there are

19:19 Greek *50,000 pieces of silver*, each of which was the equivalent of a day's wage.    19:21 Or *decided in his spirit*.    19:24 *Artemis* is otherwise known as Diana.

---

19:21  Why did Paul say he had to go to Rome? Wherever he went, he could see Rome's influence. Paul wanted to take the message of Christ to the world's center of influence and power.

19:22  Paul later wrote letters to Timothy: the books of 1 and 2 Timothy. Erastus was a committed follower of Christ who was not only Paul's helpful assistant but also Corinth's city treasurer (see Romans 16:23).

19:23  "The Way" refers to those who followed the way of Christ—the Christians.

19:24  Artemis was a goddess of fertility. She was represented by a carved female figure with many breasts. A large statue of Artemis (which was said to have come from heaven, 19:35) was in the great temple at Ephesus. That temple was one of the wonders of the ancient world. The festival of Artemis involved wild orgies and carousing. Obviously the religious and commercial life of Ephesus reflected the city's worship of this pagan deity.

19:25-27  When Paul preached in Ephesus, Demetrius and his fellow craftsmen did not quarrel with his doctrine. Their anger boiled because his preaching threatened their profits. They made silver shrines of the Ephesian goddess Artemis. The craftsmen knew that if people started believing in God and discarding the idols, their livelihood would suffer.

19:27  Demetrius's strategy for stirring up a riot was to appeal to his fellow workmen's love of money and then to encourage them to hide their greed behind the mask of patriotism and religious loyalty. The rioters couldn't see the selfish motives for their rioting; instead, they saw themselves as heroes for the sake of their land and beliefs.

19:29-31  Paul often sought others to help him in his work. On this occasion, his traveling companions were Aristarchus (who would accompany him on other journeys; see 20:3, 4 and 27:1, 2), and Gaius (probably not the same Gaius mentioned in Romans 16:23 and 1 Corinthians 1:14). Paul wanted to go to the amphitheater to defend his companions, but the other believers wouldn't let him go, fearing for his safety. The officials who begged him not to risk his life were government officials responsible for the religious and political order of the region. Paul's message had reached all levels of society, crossing all social barriers and giving Paul friends in high places.

19:33, 34  The mob had become anti-Jewish as well as anti-Christian. This Alexander may have been pushed forward by the Jews as a spokesman to explain that the Jews had no part in the Christian community and thus were not involved in the economic problem of the silversmiths.

complaints about other matters, they can be settled in a legal assembly. ⁴⁰I am afraid we are in danger of being charged with rioting by the Roman government, since there is no cause for all this commotion. And if Rome demands an explanation, we won't know what to say." ⁴¹*Then he dismissed them, and they dispersed.

### Paul Goes to Macedonia and Greece

**20** When the uproar was over, Paul sent for the believers* and encouraged them. Then he said good-bye and left for Macedonia. ²While there, he encouraged the believers in all the towns he passed through. Then he traveled down to Greece, ³where he stayed for three months. He was preparing to sail back to Syria when he discovered a plot by some Jews against his life, so he decided to return through Macedonia.

⁴Several men were traveling with him. They were Sopater son of Pyrrhus from Berea; Aristarchus and Secundus from Thessalonica; Gaius from Derbe; Timothy; and Tychicus and Trophimus from the province of Asia. ⁵They went on ahead and waited for us at Troas. ⁶After the Passover* ended, we boarded a ship at Philippi in Macedonia and five days later joined them in Troas, where we stayed a week.

**20:1** Acts 16:9-10

**20:3** Acts 9:23-24; 23:12 2 Cor 11:26

**20:4** Acts 16:1; 19:29; 21:29 Eph 6:21 2 Tim 4:20 Titus 3:12

**20:6** Acts 16:8, 10

### Paul's Final Visit to Troas

⁷On the first day of the week, we gathered with the local believers to share in the Lord's Supper.* Paul was preaching to them, and since he was leaving the next day, he kept talking until midnight. ⁸The upstairs room where we met was lighted with many flickering lamps. ⁹As Paul spoke on and on, a young man named Eutychus, sitting on the windowsill, became very drowsy. Finally, he fell sound asleep and dropped three stories to his death below. ¹⁰Paul went down, bent over him, and took him into his arms. "Don't worry," he said, "he's alive!" ¹¹Then they all went back upstairs, shared in the Lord's Supper,* and ate together. Paul continued talking to them until dawn, and then he left. ¹²Meanwhile, the young man was taken home unhurt, and everyone was greatly relieved.

**20:7** Acts 2:42, 46 1 Cor 16:2 Rev 1:10

**20:10** 1 Kgs 17:21 2 Kgs 4:34 Matt 9:23-24

### Paul Meets the Ephesian Elders

¹³Paul went by land to Assos, where he had arranged for us to join him, while we traveled by ship. ¹⁴He joined us there, and we sailed together to Mitylene. ¹⁵The next day we sailed past the island of Kios. The following day we crossed to the island of Samos, and* a day later we arrived at Miletus.

**20:15** 2 Tim 4:20

**19:41** Some translations include verse 41 as part of verse 40.  **20:1** Greek *disciples*.  **20:6** Greek *the days of unleavened bread*.  **20:7** Greek *to break bread*.  **20:11** Greek *broke the bread*.  **20:15** Some manuscripts read *and having stayed at Trogyllium*.

---

**19:40** The city of Ephesus was under the domination of the Roman Empire. The main responsibility of the local city leaders was simply to maintain peace and order. If they failed to control the people, Rome would remove the appointed officials from office. The entire town could also be put under martial law, taking away many civic freedoms.

**THROUGH MACEDONIA AND ACHAIA**
A riot in Ephesus sent Paul to Troas, then through Macedonia to the region of Achaia. In Achaia he went to Corinth to deal with problems there. Paul had planned to sail from Corinth straight to Antioch of Syria, but a plot against his life was discovered. So he retraced his steps through Macedonia.

**19:41** The riot in Ephesus convinced Paul that it was time to move on. But it also showed that the law still provided some protection for Christians as they challenged the worship of the goddess Artemis and the most idolatrous religion in Asia.

**20:1-3** While in Greece, Paul spent much of his time in Corinth. From there he wrote the letter to the Romans. Although Paul had not yet been to Rome, believers had already started a church there (2:10; 18:2). Paul wrote to tell the church that he planned to visit the Roman believers. The letter to the Romans is a theological essay on the meaning of faith and salvation, an explanation of the relation between Jews and Gentiles in Christ, and a list of practical guidelines for the church.

**20:4** These men who were traveling with Paul represented churches that Paul had started in Asia. Each man was carrying an offering from his home church to be given to the believers in Jerusalem. Having each man deliver the gift gave the gifts a personal touch and strengthened the unity of the believers. This was also an effective way to teach the church about giving, because the men were able to report back to their churches the way God was working through their giving. Paul discussed this gift in one of his letters to the Corinthian church (see 2 Corinthians 8:1-21).

**20:5, 6** The use of *us* and *we* shows that this is where Luke again joined the group. The last *we* occurred in chapter 16.

**20:6** Jewish believers celebrated the Passover (which was immediately followed by the Festival of Unleavened Bread) according to Moses' instructions (see Exodus 12:43-51) even if they couldn't be at Jerusalem for the occasion.

**20:8, 9** The "flickering lamps" were candles in lanterns. The combination of the heat from the candles and the number of people

16Paul had decided to sail on past Ephesus, for he didn't want to spend any more time in the province of Asia. He was hurrying to get to Jerusalem, if possible, in time for the Festival of Pentecost. 17But when we landed at Miletus, he sent a message to the elders of the church at Ephesus, asking them to come and meet him.

18When they arrived he declared, "You know that from the day I set foot in the province of Asia until now 19I have done the Lord's work humbly and with many tears. I have endured the trials that came to me from the plots of the Jews. 20I never shrank back from telling you what you needed to hear, either publicly or in your homes. 21I have had one message for Jews and Greeks alike—the necessity of repenting from sin and turning to God, and of having faith in our Lord Jesus.

22"And now I am bound by the Spirit* to go to Jerusalem. I don't know what awaits me, 23except that the Holy Spirit tells me in city after city that jail and suffering lie ahead. 24But my life is worth nothing to me unless I use it for finishing the work assigned me by the Lord Jesus—the work of telling others the Good News about the wonderful grace of God.

25"And now I know that none of you to whom I have preached the Kingdom will ever see me again. 26I declare today that I have been faithful. If anyone suffers eternal death, it's not my fault,* 27for I didn't shrink from declaring all that God wants you to know.

28"So guard yourselves and God's people. Feed and shepherd God's flock—his church, purchased with his own blood*—over which the Holy Spirit has appointed you as elders.* 29I know that false teachers, like vicious wolves, will come in among you after I leave, not sparing the flock. 30Even some men from your own group will rise up and distort the truth in order to draw a following. 31Watch out! Remember the three years I was with you—my constant watch and care over you night and day, and my many tears for you.

32"And now I entrust you to God and the message of his grace that is able to build you up and give you an inheritance with all those he has set apart for himself.

**20:18** Acts 18:19-21; 19:1-41
**20:21** Acts 2:38; 26:18
**20:22** Acts 19:21
**20:23** Acts 9:16; 21:4, 11
**20:24** Acts 21:13; 2 Tim 4:7
**20:26** Acts 18:6
**20:28** Ps 74:2; John 21:15-17; 1 Pet 5:2
**20:29** Matt 7:15; John 10:12
**20:30** 1 Jn 2:19
**20:31** Acts 19:10
**20:32** Deut 33:3-4; Acts 26:18; Eph 1:18; Col 1:12; 3:24; 1 Pet 1:4

**20:22** Or *by my spirit,* or *by an inner compulsion;* Greek reads *by the spirit.*    **20:26** Greek *I am innocent of the blood of all.*    **20:28a** Or *with the blood of his own [Son].*    **20:28b** Greek *overseers.*

---

gathered in the upstairs room probably made the room very warm. This no doubt helped Eutychus fall asleep, as well as the fact that Paul spoke for a long time. Eutychus was probably between the ages of 8 to 14 years old (the age of a "young man").

**20:16** Paul had missed attending the Passover in Jerusalem, so he was especially interested in arriving on time for Pentecost, which was 50 days after Passover. He was carrying with him gifts for the Jerusalem believers from churches in Asia and Greece (see Romans 15:25, 26; 1 Corinthians 16:1ff; 2 Corinthians 8–9). The Jerusalem church was experiencing difficult times. Paul may have been anxious to deliver this gift to the believers at Pentecost because it was a day of celebration and thanksgiving to God for his provision.

**20:18-21** The way of the believer is not an easy road; being a Christian does not solve or remove all problems. Paul served humbly and "with many tears," but he never quit, never gave up. The message of salvation was so important that he never missed an opportunity to share it. And although he preached his message in different ways to fit different audiences, the message remained the same: Repent and turn to Christ by faith. The Christian life will have its rough times, tears, and sorrows, as well as joys, but we should always be ready to tell others what good things God has done for us. His blessings far outweigh life's difficulties.

**20:23** The Holy Spirit showed Paul that he would be imprisoned and experience suffering. Even knowing this, Paul did not shrink from fulfilling his mission. His strong character was a good example to the Ephesian elders, some of whom would also suffer for Christ.

**20:24** We often feel that life is a failure unless we're getting a lot out of it: recognition, fun, money, success. But Paul considered life worth *nothing* unless he used it for God's work. What he put *into* life was far more important than what he got out of it. Which is more important to you—what you get out of life, or what you put into it?

**20:24** Single-mindedness is a quality needed by anyone who wishes to do God's work. Paul was a single-minded person, and

the most important goal of his life was to tell others about Christ (Philippians 3:7-13). It is no wonder that Paul was the greatest missionary who ever lived. God is looking for more men and women who will focus on that one great task God has given them to do.

**20:31, 36-38** Paul's relationship with these believers is a beautiful example of Christian fellowship. He had cared for them and loved them, even cried over their needs. They responded with love and care for him and sorrow over his leaving. They had prayed together and comforted one another. Like Paul, you can build strong relationships with other Christians by sharing, caring, sorrowing, rejoicing, and praying with them. You will gather others around you only by giving yourself away to them.

**PAUL TRAVELS FROM TROAS TO MILETUS**
From Troas, Paul traveled overland to Assos, then boarded a ship to Mitylene and Samos on its way to Miletus. He summoned the elders of the Ephesian church to say farewell to them, because he knew he would probably not see them again.

33"I have never coveted anyone's silver or gold or fine clothes. 34You know that these hands of mine have worked to supply my own needs and even the needs of those who were with me. 35And I have been a constant example of how you can help those in need by working hard. You should remember the words of the Lord Jesus:'It is more blessed to give than to receive.'"

36When he had finished speaking, he knelt and prayed with them. 37They all cried as they embraced and kissed him good-bye. 38They were sad most of all because he had said that they would never see him again. Then they escorted him down to the ship.

### Paul's Journey to Jerusalem

**21** After saying farewell to the Ephesian elders, we sailed straight to the island of Cos. The next day we reached Rhodes and then went to Patara. 2There we boarded a ship sailing for Phoenicia. 3We sighted the island of Cyprus, passed it on our left, and landed at the harbor of Tyre, in Syria, where the ship was to unload its cargo.

4We went ashore, found the local believers,* and stayed with them a week. These believers prophesied through the Holy Spirit that Paul should not go on to Jerusalem. 5When we returned to the ship at the end of the week, the entire congregation, including women* and children, left the city and came down to the shore with us. There we knelt, prayed, 6and said our farewells. Then we went aboard, and they returned home.

7The next stop after leaving Tyre was Ptolemais, where we greeted the brothers and sisters* and stayed for one day. 8The next day we went on to Caesarea and stayed at the home

**21:4** Greek *disciples;* also in 21:16.  **21:5** Or *wives.*  **21:7** Greek *brothers;* also in 21:17.

**20:33**
1 Sam 12:3
1 Cor 9:11
2 Cor 7:2; 11:9;
12:14-17
**20:34**
Acts 18:3
1 Cor 4:12
1 Thes 2:9
**20:35**
1 Thes 4:11
**20:36**
Acts 21:5
**21:1**
Acts 16:10

**21:4**
Acts 20:23; 21:11
**21:5**
Acts 20:36

**21:8**
Acts 6:5; 8:26, 40
Eph 4:11
2 Tim 4:5

**PAUL RETURNS TO JERUSALEM** The ship sailed from Miletus to Cos, Rhodes, and Patara. Paul and his companions then boarded a cargo ship bound for Phoenicia. They passed Cyprus and landed at Tyre, then Ptolemais, and finally Caesarea, where Paul disembarked and returned by land to Jerusalem.

**20:33** Paul was satisfied with whatever he had, wherever he was, as long as he could do God's work. Examine your attitudes toward wealth and comfort. If you focus more on what you don't have than on what you do have, it's time to reexamine your priorities and put God's work back in first place.

**20:34** Paul was a tentmaker, and he supported himself with this trade. Paul did not work to become rich but to be free from being dependent on anyone. He supported himself as well as others who traveled with him (he mentions this in some of his letters; see Philippians 4:11-13; 1 Thessalonians 2:9).

**20:35** These words of Jesus are not recorded in the Gospels. Obviously, not all of Jesus' words were written down (John 21:25); this saying may have been passed on orally through the apostles.

**21:4** Did Paul disobey the Holy Spirit by going to Jerusalem? No. More likely, the Holy Spirit warned these believers about the suffering that Paul would face in Jerusalem. They drew the conclusion that he should not go there because of that danger. This is supported by 21:10-12, where the local believers, after hearing that Paul would be turned over to the Romans, begged him to turn back.

**21:8** This is the Philip mentioned in 6:5 and 8:26-40.

**21:9**
Joel 2:28
Acts 2:17

**21:10**
Acts 11:28

**21:11**
Acts 20:23; 21:33

of Philip the Evangelist, one of the seven men who had been chosen to distribute food. 9He had four unmarried daughters who had the gift of prophecy.

10Several days later a man named Agabus, who also had the gift of prophecy, arrived from Judea. 11He came over, took Paul's belt, and bound his own feet and hands with it. Then he said, "The Holy Spirit declares, 'So shall the owner of this belt be bound by the Jewish leaders in Jerusalem and turned over to the Gentiles.'" 12When we heard this, we and the local believers all begged Paul not to go on to Jerusalem.

**21:13**
Acts 20:24

**21:14**
Matt 26:39

13But he said, "Why all this weeping? You are breaking my heart! I am ready not only to be jailed at Jerusalem but even to die for the sake of the Lord Jesus." 14When it was clear that we couldn't persuade him, we gave up and said, "The Lord's will be done."

## 5. Paul on trial
### Paul Arrives at Jerusalem

15After this we packed our things and left for Jerusalem. 16Some believers from Caesarea accompanied us, and they took us to the home of Mnason, a man originally from Cyprus and one of the early believers. 17When we arrived, the brothers and sisters in Jerusalem welcomed us warmly.

**21:19**
Acts 15:12

**21:20**
Acts 15:1, 5
Gal 3:10-11

**21:21**
Acts 16:3
Gal 2:3

18The next day Paul went with us to meet with James, and all the elders of the Jerusalem church were present. 19After greeting them, Paul gave a detailed account of the things God had accomplished among the Gentiles through his ministry.

20After hearing this, they praised God. And then they said, "You know, dear brother, how many thousands of Jews have also believed, and they all follow the law of Moses very seriously. 21But the Jewish believers here in Jerusalem have been told that you are teaching all the Jews who live among the Gentiles to turn their backs on the laws of Moses. They've heard that you teach them not to circumcise their children or follow other Jewish customs. 22What should we do? They will certainly hear that you have come.

**21:23**
Acts 18:18

**21:24**
Num 6:5, 13-20

23"Here's what we want you to do. We have four men here who have completed their vow. 24Go with them to the Temple and join them in the purification ceremony, paying for them to have their heads ritually shaved. Then everyone will know that the rumors are all false and that you yourself observe the Jewish laws.

**21:25**
Acts 15:19-29

25"As for the Gentile believers, they should do what we already told them in a letter: They should abstain from eating food offered to idols, from consuming blood or the meat of strangled animals, and from sexual immorality."

---

**21:9** Obviously the gift of prophecy was given to both men and women. Women actively participated in God's work (2:17; Philippians 4:3). Other women who prophesied include Miriam (Exodus 15:20), Deborah (Judges 4:4), Huldah (2 Kings 22:14), Isaiah's wife (Isaiah 8:3), and Anna (Luke 2:36-38).

**21:10** Fifteen years earlier, Agabus had predicted the famine in Jerusalem (11:27-29).

**21:13, 14** Paul knew he would be imprisoned in Jerusalem. Although his friends pleaded with him to not go there, he knew that he had to because God wanted him to. No one enjoys pain, but a faithful disciple wants above all else to please God. Our desire to please God should overshadow our desire to avoid hardship and suffering. When we really want to do God's will, we must accept all that comes with it—even the pain. Then we can say with Paul's companions, "The Lord's will be done."

**21:18** James, Jesus' brother, was the leader of the Jerusalem church (15:13-21; Galatians 1:19; 2:9).

**21:21** The Jerusalem council (Acts 15) had settled the issue of circumcision for Gentile believers. Evidently a rumor said that Paul had gone far beyond their decision, even forbidding Jews to circumcise their children. This, of course, was not true, so Paul willingly submitted to Jewish custom to show that he was not working against the council's decision and that he was still Jewish in his lifestyle. Sometimes we must go the second mile to avoid offending others, especially when not doing so would hinder God's work.

**21:23, 24** Because Paul was going to participate with the four men in the vow (apparently he had been asked to pay for some of the required expenses), he would need to take part in the purifi-

cation ceremony for entering the Temple (Numbers 6:9-20). Paul submitted himself to this Jewish custom to keep peace in the Jerusalem church. Although Paul was a man of strong convictions, he was willing to compromise on nonessential points, becoming all things to all people so that he might save some (1 Corinthians 9:19-23). Often churches split over disagreements about minor issues or traditions. Like Paul, we should remain firm on Christian essentials but flexible on nonessentials. Of course, no one should violate his or her true convictions, but sometimes we need to honor Christ by mutual submission for the sake of the Good News.

**21:23, 24** The Jewish laws can be thought of in two ways. Paul rejected one way and accepted the other. (1) Paul rejected the idea that the Old Testament laws bring salvation to those who keep them. Salvation is freely given by God's gracious act. We receive salvation through faith. The laws are of no value for salvation except to show us our sin. (2) Paul accepted the view that the Old Testament laws prepare for and teach about the coming of Jesus Christ. Christ fulfilled the law and released us from its burden of guilt. But the law still teaches many valuable principles and provides guidelines for grateful living. Paul was not observing the laws in order to be saved. He was simply keeping the laws as custom to avoid offending those he wished to reach with the Good News (see Romans 3:21-31; 7:4-6; 13:9, 10). For more on the law, see Galatians 3:23-29; 4:21-31, and the chart in Galatians 3, p. 1989.

## Paul Is Arrested

26So Paul went to the Temple the next day with the other men. They had already started the purification ritual, so he publicly announced the date when their vows would end and sacrifices would be offered for each of them.

21:26
Num 6:1-21
1 Cor 9:20

27The seven days were almost ended when some Jews from the province of Asia saw Paul in the Temple and roused a mob against him. They grabbed him, 28yelling, "Men of Israel, help us! This is the man who preaches against our people everywhere and tells everybody to disobey the Jewish laws. He speaks against the Temple—and even defiles this holy place by bringing in Gentiles.\*" 29(For earlier that day they had seen him in the city with Trophimus, a Gentile from Ephesus,\* and they assumed Paul had taken him into the Temple.)

21:27
Acts 24:18; 26:21
21:28
Matt 24:15
Acts 6:13; 24:5-6
21:29
Acts 20:4
2 Tim 4:20

30The whole city was rocked by these accusations, and a great riot followed. Paul was grabbed and dragged out of the Temple, and immediately the gates were closed behind him. 31As they were trying to kill him, word reached the commander of the Roman regiment that all Jerusalem was in an uproar. 32He immediately called out his soldiers and officers\* and ran down among the crowd. When the mob saw the commander and the troops coming, they stopped beating Paul.

21:32
Acts 23:27

33Then the commander arrested him and ordered him bound with two chains. He asked the crowd who he was and what he had done. 34Some shouted one thing and some another. Since he couldn't find out the truth in all the uproar and confusion, he ordered that Paul be taken to the fortress. 35As Paul reached the stairs, the mob grew so violent the soldiers had to lift him to their shoulders to protect him. 36And the crowd followed behind, shouting, "Kill him, kill him!"

21:33
Acts 20:23
Eph 6:20

21:36
Luke 23:18
John 19:15
Acts 22:22

## Paul Speaks to the Crowd

37As Paul was about to be taken inside, he said to the commander, "May I have a word with you?"

"Do you know Greek?" the commander asked, surprised. 38"Aren't you the Egyptian who led a rebellion some time ago and took 4,000 members of the Assassins out into the desert?"

39"No," Paul replied, "I am a Jew and a citizen of Tarsus in Cilicia, which is an important city. Please, let me talk to these people." 40The commander agreed, so Paul stood on the stairs and motioned to the people to be quiet. Soon a deep silence enveloped the crowd, and he addressed them in their own language, Aramaic.\*

21:39
Acts 9:11; 22:3
21:40
Acts 26:14

**22** "Brothers and esteemed fathers," Paul said, "listen to me as I offer my defense." 2When they heard him speaking in their own language,\* the silence was even greater.

22:1
Acts 7:2

3Then Paul said, "I am a Jew, born in Tarsus, a city in Cilicia, and I was brought up and educated here in Jerusalem under Gamaliel. As his student, I was carefully trained in our Jewish laws and customs. I became very zealous to honor God in everything I did, just like all of you today. 4And I persecuted the followers of the Way, hounding some to death, arresting both men and women and throwing them in prison. 5The high priest and the whole council of elders can testify that this is so. For I received letters from them to our Jewish brothers in Damascus, authorizing me to bring the Christians from there to Jerusalem, in chains, to be punished.

22:3-21
//Acts 9:1-29;
26:9-18
22:3
Acts 5:34-40
Rom 10:2
22:4
Acts 8:3; 9:2

**21:28** Greek *Greeks.* **21:29** Greek *Trophimus, the Ephesian.* **21:32** Greek *centurions.* **21:40** Or *Hebrew.*
**22:2** Greek *in Aramaic,* or *in Hebrew.*

---

**21:31** Because Jerusalem was under Roman control, an uproar in the city would be investigated by Roman authorities. The commander of the troops at this time was Claudius Lysias (23:26). He was head of a regiment (a special group, part of a legion) of Roman soldiers and was the senior Roman official in Jerusalem.

**21:37, 38** By speaking in Greek, Paul showed that he was a cultured, educated man and not just a common rebel starting riots in the streets. The language grabbed the commander's attention and gave Paul protection and the opportunity to give his defense.

**21:38** The historian Josephus wrote of an Egyptian who had led a revolt of 4,000 people in Jerusalem in A.D. 54 and then had disappeared. The commander assumed that Paul was this rebel.

**21:40–22:2** Paul was speaking in Aramaic, the common language among Palestinian Jews. He used Aramaic not only to

communicate in the language of his listeners but also to show that he was a devout Jew and had respect for the Jewish laws and customs. Paul spoke Greek to the Roman officials and Aramaic to the Jews.

**22:3** Gamaliel was the most honored rabbi of the first century. He was well known and respected as an expert on religious law and as a voice for moderation (5:34). Paul was showing his credentials as a well-educated man trained under the most respected Jewish rabbi.

**22:3, 4** By saying that at one time he was as zealous for God as any of his listeners, Paul was acknowledging their sincere motives behind their desire to kill him, pointing out that he had done the same to Christian leaders a few years earlier. Paul always tried to establish common ground with his audience before launching into

**22:6**
Acts 9:2-8;
26:12-13

6"As I was on the road, approaching Damascus about noon, a very bright light from heaven suddenly shone down around me. 7I fell to the ground and heard a voice saying to me, 'Saul, Saul, why are you persecuting me?'

8"'Who are you, lord?' I asked.

**22:9**
Acts 9:7; 26:13

"And the voice replied, 'I am Jesus the Nazarene,* the one you are persecuting.' 9The people with me saw the light but didn't understand the voice speaking to me.

10"I asked, 'What should I do, Lord?'

"And the Lord told me, 'Get up and go into Damascus, and there you will be told everything you are to do.'

**22:11**
Acts 9:8

**22:12**
Acts 9:17

11"I was blinded by the intense light and had to be led by the hand to Damascus by my companions. 12A man named Ananias lived there. He was a godly man, deeply devoted to the law, and well regarded by all the Jews of Damascus. 13He came and stood beside me and said, 'Brother Saul, regain your sight.' And that very moment I could see him!

**22:14**
Acts 3:13
1 Cor 15:8

**22:15**
Acts 26:16

**22:16**
Acts 2:38
Rom 10:13
1 Cor 6:11
Heb 10:22

14"Then he told me, 'The God of our ancestors has chosen you to know his will and to see the Righteous One and hear him speak. 15For you are to be his witness, telling everyone what you have seen and heard. 16What are you waiting for? Get up and be baptized. Have your sins washed away by calling on the name of the Lord.'

17"After I returned to Jerusalem, I was praying in the Temple and fell into a trance. 18I saw a vision of Jesus* saying to me, 'Hurry! Leave Jerusalem, for the people here won't accept your testimony about me.'

**22:19**
Acts 8:3; 22:4-5;
26:9-11

**22:20**
Acts 7:57–8:1

19"'But Lord,' I argued, 'they certainly know that in every synagogue I imprisoned and beat those who believed in you. 20And I was in complete agreement when your witness Stephen was killed. I stood by and kept the coats they took off when they stoned him.'

**22:21**
Acts 9:15; 13:2
Rom 15:15-16

21"But the Lord said to me, 'Go, for I will send you far away to the Gentiles!'"

**22:22**
Acts 21:36; 25:24

22The crowd listened until Paul said that word. Then they all began to shout, "Away with such a fellow! He isn't fit to live!" 23They yelled, threw off their coats, and tossed handfuls of dust into the air.

### Paul Reveals His Roman Citizenship

**22:25**
Acts 16:37

24The commander brought Paul inside and ordered him lashed with whips to make him confess his crime. He wanted to find out why the crowd had become so furious. 25When they tied Paul down to lash him, Paul said to the officer* standing there, "Is it legal for you to whip a Roman citizen who hasn't even been tried?"

26When the officer heard this, he went to the commander and asked, "What are you doing? This man is a Roman citizen!"

27So the commander went over and asked Paul, "Tell me, are you a Roman citizen?"

"Yes, I certainly am," Paul replied.

28"I am, too," the commander muttered, "and it cost me plenty!"

Paul answered, "But I am a citizen by birth!"

**22:29**
Acts 16:38

29The soldiers who were about to interrogate Paul quickly withdrew when they heard he was a Roman citizen, and the commander was frightened because he had ordered him bound and whipped.

**22:8** Or *Jesus of Nazareth.*  **22:18** Greek *him.*  **22:25** Greek *the centurion;* also in 22:26.

---

a full-scale defense of Christianity. When you witness for Christ, first identify yourself with your audience. They will be much more likely to listen if they feel a common bond with you.

**22:6ff** After gaining a hearing and establishing common ground with his audience, Paul gave his testimony. He shared how he had come to faith in Christ. Sound reasoning is good, but it is also important to simply share what Christ has done in our lives. No matter how we present the message, however, not everyone will accept it, as Paul knew. We must faithfully and responsibly present the Good News and leave the results to God.

**22:21, 22** These people listened intently to Paul, but the word *Gentiles* brought out all their anger and exposed their pride. They were supposed to be a light to the Gentiles, telling them about the one true God. But they had renounced that mission by becoming separatist and exclusive. God's plan, however, would not be thwarted; the Gentiles were hearing the Good News through Jewish Christians, such as Paul and Peter.

**22:25-28** Paul's question stopped the officer because by law a Roman citizen could not be punished until he had been proven guilty of a crime. Paul had been born a Roman citizen, whereas the commander had purchased his citizenship. Buying citizenship was a common practice and a good source of income for the Roman government. Bought citizenship was considered inferior to citizenship by birth.

### Paul before the High Council

³⁰The next day the commander ordered the leading priests into session with the Jewish high council.* He wanted to find out what the trouble was all about, so he released Paul to have him stand before them.

# 23

Gazing intently at the high council,* Paul began: "Brothers, I have always lived before God with a clear conscience!"

²Instantly Ananias the high priest commanded those close to Paul to slap him on the mouth. ³But Paul said to him, "God will slap you, you corrupt hypocrite!* What kind of judge are you to break the law yourself by ordering me struck like that?"

⁴Those standing near Paul said to him, "Do you dare to insult God's high priest?"

⁵"I'm sorry, brothers. I didn't realize he was the high priest," Paul replied, "for the Scriptures say, 'You must not speak evil of any of your rulers.'*"

⁶Paul realized that some members of the high council were Sadducees and some were Pharisees, so he shouted, "Brothers, I am a Pharisee, as were my ancestors! And I am on trial because my hope is in the resurrection of the dead!"

⁷This divided the council—the Pharisees against the Sadducees—⁸for the Sadducees say there is no resurrection or angels or spirits, but the Pharisees believe in all of these. ⁹So there was a great uproar. Some of the teachers of religious law who were Pharisees jumped up and began to argue forcefully. "We see nothing wrong with him," they shouted. "Perhaps a spirit or an angel spoke to him." ¹⁰As the conflict grew more violent, the commander was afraid they would tear Paul apart. So he ordered his soldiers to go and rescue him by force and take him back to the fortress.

¹¹That night the Lord appeared to Paul and said, "Be encouraged, Paul. Just as you have been a witness to me here in Jerusalem, you must preach the Good News in Rome as well."

### The Plan to Kill Paul

¹²The next morning a group of Jews* got together and bound themselves with an oath not to eat or drink until they had killed Paul. ¹³There were more than forty of them in the conspiracy. ¹⁴They went to the leading priests and elders and told them, "We have bound ourselves with an oath to eat nothing until we have killed Paul. ¹⁵So you and the high council should ask the commander to bring Paul back to the council again. Pretend you want to examine his case more fully. We will kill him on the way."

¹⁶But Paul's nephew—his sister's son—heard of their plan and went to the fortress and told Paul. ¹⁷Paul called for one of the Roman officers* and said, "Take this young man to the commander. He has something important to tell him."

22:30 Greek Sanhedrin. 23:1 Greek Sanhedrin; also in 23:6, 15, 20, 28. 23:3 Greek you whitewashed wall. 23:5 Exod 22:28. 23:12 Greek the Jews. 23:17 Greek centurions; also in 23:23.

**23:1** Acts 24:16; 1 Cor 4:4; 2 Cor 1:12; 1 Tim 3:9; Heb 13:18; 1 Pet 3:16, 21 **23:2** John 18:22; Acts 24:1 **23:3** Lev 19:15; Ezek 13:10-15; John 7:51 **23:5** †Exod 22:28 **23:6** Acts 26:5; Phil 3:5 **23:8** Matt 22:23; Mark 12:18; Luke 20:27 **23:9** Acts 22:7; 25:25 **23:11** Acts 18:9; 27:24; 28:23 **23:12** Acts 9:23 **23:14-15** Acts 25:3 **23:16** Acts 21:34

**22:30** Paul used his times of persecution as an opportunity to witness. Even his enemies were creating a platform for him to address the entire Jewish high council. If we are sensitive to the Holy Spirit's leading, we will see increased opportunities to share our faith, even in the face of opposition.

**23:2-5** Josephus, a respected first-century historian, described Ananias as profane, greedy, and hot-tempered. Paul's outburst came as a result of the illegal command that Ananias had given. Ananias had violated Jewish law by assuming that Paul was guilty without a trial and ordering his punishment (see Deuteronomy 19:15). Paul didn't recognize Ananias as the high priest, probably because Ananias's command broke the law he was pledged to represent. As Christians, we are to represent Christ. If someone we know says, "I didn't know you were a Christian," we have failed to represent him as we should. We are not merely Christ's followers; we are his representative to others.

**23:6-8** The Sadducees and Pharisees were two groups of religious leaders but with strikingly different beliefs. The Pharisees believed in a bodily resurrection, but the Sadducees did not. The Sadducees adhered only to Genesis through Deuteronomy, which contain no explicit teaching on resurrection. Paul's words moved the debate away from himself and toward their festering controversy about resurrection. The Jewish council was split.

**23:6-8** Paul's sudden insight that the council was a mixture of Sadducees and Pharisees is an example of the insight that Jesus promises to believers (Mark 13:9-11). God will help us when we are under fire for our faith. Like Paul, we should always be ready to present our testimony. The Holy Spirit will give us the courage to speak boldly.

**23:14, 15** When the Pharisee/Sadducee controversy died down, the religious leaders refocused their attention on Paul. To these leaders, politics and position had become more important than God. They were ready to plan another murder, just as they had done with Jesus. But as always, God was in control.

**23:16** This is the only biblical reference to a member of Paul's family. Some scholars believe that Paul's family had disowned him when he became a Christian. Paul wrote of having suffered the loss of everything for Christ (Philippians 3:8). His nephew was able to see him, even though Paul was in protective custody, because Roman prisoners were accessible to their relatives and friends, who could bring them food and other amenities.

**23:16-22** It is easy to overlook children, assuming that they aren't old enough to do much for the Lord. But this young man played an important part in protecting Paul's life. God can use anyone, of any age, who is willing to yield to him. Jesus made it clear that children are important (Matthew 18:2-6). Give children the importance God gives them.

¹⁸So the officer did, explaining, "Paul, the prisoner, called me over and asked me to bring this young man to you because he has something to tell you."

¹⁹The commander took his hand, led him aside, and asked, "What is it you want to tell me?"

²⁰Paul's nephew told him, "Some Jews are going to ask you to bring Paul before the high council tomorrow, pretending they want to get some more information. ²¹But don't do it! There are more than forty men hiding along the way ready to ambush him. They have vowed not to eat or drink anything until they have killed him. They are ready now, just waiting for your consent."

²²"Don't let anyone know you told me this," the commander warned the young man.

### Paul Is Sent to Caesarea

**23:23**
Acts 8:40

²³Then the commander called two of his officers and ordered, "Get 200 soldiers ready to leave for Caesarea at nine o'clock tonight. Also take 200 spearmen and 70 mounted troops. ²⁴Provide horses for Paul to ride, and get him safely to Governor Felix." ²⁵Then he wrote this letter to the governor:

**23:27**
Acts 21:30-33;
22:25-29

²⁶"From Claudius Lysias, to his Excellency, Governor Felix: Greetings!

**23:28**
Acts 22:30

²⁷"This man was seized by some Jews, and they were about to kill him when I arrived with the troops. When I learned that he was a Roman citizen, I removed him to safety. ²⁸Then I took him to their high council to try to learn the basis of the accusations against him. ²⁹I soon discovered the charge was something regarding their religious

**23:29**
Acts 18:14-15;
25:18-19; 26:31;
28:18

---

**UNSUNG HEROES IN ACTS**

When we think of the success of the early church, we often think of the work of the apostles. But the church could have died if it hadn't been for the unsung heroes, the men and women who through some small but committed act moved the church forward.

| Hero | Reference | Heroic Action |
|---|---|---|
| Crippled man | 3:9-12 | After his healing, he praised God. As the crowds gathered to see what happened, Peter used the opportunity to tell many about Jesus. |
| Five deacons | 6:2-5 | Everyone has heard of Stephen, and many know of Philip, but there were five other men chosen to be deacons. They not only laid the foundation for service in the church, but their hard work also gave the apostles the time they needed to preach the gospel. |
| Ananias | 9:10-19 | He had the responsibility of being the first to demonstrate Christ's love to Saul (Paul) after his conversion. |
| Cornelius | 10:30-35 | His example showed Peter that the gospel was for *all* people, Jews and Gentiles. |
| Rhoda | 12:13-15 | Her persistence brought Peter inside Mary's home, where he would be safe. |
| James | 15:13-21 | He took command of the Jerusalem council and had the courage and discernment to help form a decision that would affect literally millions of Christians over many generations. |
| Lydia | 16:13-15 | She opened her home to Paul, from which he led many to Christ and founded a church in Philippi. |
| Jason | 17:5-9 | He risked his life for the gospel by allowing Paul to stay in his home. He stood up for what was true and right, even though he faced persecution for it. |
| Paul's nephew | 23:16-24 | He saved Paul's life by telling officials of a murder plot. |
| Julius | 27:1, 43 | He spared Paul when the other soldiers wanted to kill him. |

---

**23:23, 24** The Roman commander ordered Paul sent to Caesarea. Jerusalem was the seat of Jewish government, but Caesarea was the Roman headquarters for the area. God works in amazing and amusing ways. God could have used any number of ways to get Paul to Caesarea, but he chose to use the Roman army to deliver Paul from his enemies. God's ways are not our ways. Ours are limited; his are not. Don't limit God by asking him to respond your way. When God intervenes, things will work out much better than you could ever anticipate.

**23:26** Felix was the Roman governor of Judea from A.D. 52 to 59. This was the same position Pontius Pilate had held. While the Jews were given much freedom to govern themselves, the governor ran the army, kept the peace, and gathered the taxes.

**23:26** How did Luke know what was written in the letter from Claudius Lysias? In his concern for historical accuracy, Luke used many sources to make sure that his writings were correct (see Luke 1:1-4). This letter was probably read aloud in court when Paul came before Felix to answer the Jews' accusations. Also, because Paul was a Roman citizen, a copy may have been given to him as a courtesy.

law—certainly nothing worthy of imprisonment or death. ³⁰But when I was informed of a plot to kill him, I immediately sent him on to you. I have told his accusers to bring their charges before you."

³¹So that night, as ordered, the soldiers took Paul as far as Antipatris. ³²They returned to the fortress the next morning, while the mounted troops took him on to Caesarea. ³³When they arrived in Caesarea, they presented Paul and the letter to Governor Felix. ³⁴He read it and then asked Paul what province he was from. "Cilicia," Paul answered.

³⁵"I will hear your case myself when your accusers arrive," the governor told him. Then the governor ordered him kept in the prison at Herod's headquarters.*

### Paul Appears before Felix

**24** Five days later Ananias, the high priest, arrived with some of the Jewish elders and the lawyer* Tertullus, to present their case against Paul to the governor. ²When Paul was called in, Tertullus presented the charges against Paul in the following address to the governor:

"You have provided a long period of peace for us Jews and with foresight have enacted reforms for us. ³For all of this, Your Excellency, we are very grateful to you. ⁴But I don't want to bore you, so please give me your attention for only a moment. ⁵We have found this man to be a troublemaker who is constantly stirring up riots among the Jews all over the world. He is a ringleader of the cult known as the Nazarenes. ⁶Furthermore, he was trying to desecrate the Temple when we arrested him.* ⁸You can find out the truth of our accusations by examining him yourself." ⁹Then the other Jews chimed in, declaring that everything Tertullus said was true.

¹⁰The governor then motioned for Paul to speak. Paul said, "I know, sir, that you have been a judge of Jewish affairs for many years, so I gladly present my defense before you. ¹¹You can quickly discover that I arrived in Jerusalem no more than twelve days ago to worship at the Temple. ¹²My accusers never found me arguing with anyone in the Temple, nor stirring up a riot in any synagogue or on the streets of the city. ¹³These men cannot prove the things they accuse me of doing.

¹⁴"But I admit that I follow the Way, which they call a cult. I worship the God of our ancestors, and I firmly believe the Jewish law and everything written in the prophets. ¹⁵I have the same hope in God that these men have, that he will raise both the righteous and the unrighteous. ¹⁶Because of this, I always try to maintain a clear conscience before God and all people.

**23:30**
Acts 24:19; 25:16

**23:33**
Acts 8:40
**23:34**
Acts 6:9; 21:39; 22:3
**23:35**
Acts 25:16

**24:1**
Acts 23:2, 24-30, 35

**24:3**
Acts 23:26; 26:25
**24:5**
Mark 1:24
Acts 16:20; 17:6; 24:14
**24:6**
Acts 21:28, 30
**24:9**
1 Thes 2:16

**24:11**
Acts 21:27
**24:13**
Acts 25:7
**24:14**
Acts 9:2; 26:22
**24:15**
Dan 12:2
Matt 22:31-32
John 5:28-29
Acts 23:6; 28:20
**24:16**
Acts 23:1

---

**23:35** Greek *Herod's Praetorium.* **24:1** Greek *some elders and an orator.* **24:6** Some manuscripts add an expanded conclusion to verse 6, all of verse 7, and an additional phrase in verse 8: *We would have judged him by our law, ⁷but Lysias, the commander of the garrison, came and violently took him away from us, ⁸commanding his accusers to come before you.*

---

**24:1** The accusers arrived: Ananias, the high priest; Tertullus, the lawyer; and several Jewish leaders. They traveled 60 miles to Caesarea, the Roman center of government, to bring their false accusations against Paul. Their murder plot had failed (23:12-15), but they persisted in trying to kill him. This attempt at murder was both premeditated and persistent.

**24:2ff** Tertullus was a special orator called to present the religious leaders' case before the Roman governor. He made three accusations against Paul: (1) He was a troublemaker, stirring up riots among the Jews around the world; (2) he was the ringleader of an unrecognized religious cult, which was against Roman law; (3) he had tried to desecrate the Temple. The religious leaders hoped that these accusations would persuade Felix to execute Paul in order to keep the peace in Palestine.

**24:5** While the charge that Paul was a troublemaker was insulting to Paul, it was too vague to be a substantive legal charge. "The Nazarenes" refers to the Christians—named here after Jesus' hometown of Nazareth.

**24:10ff** Tertullus and the religious leaders seemed to have a strong argument against Paul, but Paul refuted their accusations point by point. Paul was also able to present the Good News through his defense. Paul's accusers were unable to present specific evidence to support their general accusations. For example, Paul was accused of starting trouble among the Jews in the province of Asia (24:18, 19), but the Jews in the province of Asia (western Turkey) were not present to confirm this. This is another example of Paul using every opportunity to witness for Christ (see 24:14, 24).

**IMPRISONMENT IN CAESAREA**
Paul brought news of his third journey to the elders of the Jerusalem church, who rejoiced at his ministry. But Paul's presence soon stirred up the Jews, who persuaded the Romans to arrest him. A plot to kill Paul was uncovered, so Paul was taken by night to Antipatris and then transferred to the provincial prison in Caesarea.

**24:17**
Acts 11:29-30
Rom 15:25-28
1 Cor 16:1-4
2 Cor 8:1-4
Gal 2:10

**24:18**
Acts 21:26-27

**24:21**
Acts 23:6

17"After several years away, I returned to Jerusalem with money to aid my people and to offer sacrifices to God. 18My accusers saw me in the Temple as I was completing a purification ceremony. There was no crowd around me and no rioting. 19But some Jews from the province of Asia were there—and they ought to be here to bring charges if they have anything against me! 20Ask these men here what crime the Jewish high council* found me guilty of, 21except for the one time I shouted out, 'I am on trial before you today because I believe in the resurrection of the dead!'"

**24:23**
Acts 27:3;
28:16, 30

22At that point Felix, who was quite familiar with the Way, adjourned the hearing and said, "Wait until Lysias, the garrison commander, arrives. Then I will decide the case." 23He ordered an officer* to keep Paul in custody but to give him some freedom and allow his friends to visit him and take care of his needs.

**24:25**
Acts 10:42
Gal 5:23
2 Pet 1:6

24A few days later Felix came back with his wife, Drusilla, who was Jewish. Sending for Paul, they listened as he told them about faith in Christ Jesus. 25As he reasoned with them about righteousness and self-control and the coming day of judgment, Felix became frightened. "Go away for now," he replied. "When it is more convenient, I'll call for you again." 26He also hoped that Paul would bribe him, so he sent for him quite often and talked with him.

**24:27**
Acts 25:9, 14

27After two years went by in this way, Felix was succeeded by Porcius Festus. And because Felix wanted to gain favor with the Jewish people, he left Paul in prison.

### Paul Appears before Festus

**25:1**
Acts 24:27

**25:2**
Acts 24:1; 25:15

**25:3**
Acts 23:15

**25:5**
Acts 23:30

**25** Three days after Festus arrived in Caesarea to take over his new responsibilities, he left for Jerusalem, 2where the leading priests and other Jewish leaders met with him and made their accusations against Paul. 3They asked Festus as a favor to transfer Paul to Jerusalem (planning to ambush and kill him on the way). 4But Festus replied that Paul was at Caesarea and he himself would be returning there soon. 5So he said, "Those of you in authority can return with me. If Paul has done anything wrong, you can make your accusations."

**25:6**
Acts 25:17

**25:7**
Acts 24:5-6, 13

**25:8**
Acts 6:13; 24:12;
28:17

**25:9**
Acts 24:27

6About eight or ten days later Festus returned to Caesarea, and on the following day he took his seat in court and ordered that Paul be brought in. 7When Paul arrived, the Jewish leaders from Jerusalem gathered around and made many serious accusations they couldn't prove.

8Paul denied the charges. "I am not guilty of any crime against the Jewish laws or the Temple or the Roman government," he said.

9Then Festus, wanting to please the Jews, asked him, "Are you willing to go to Jerusalem and stand trial before me there?"

**24:20** Greek *Sanhedrin.*   **24:23** Greek *a centurion.*

---

**24:22** Felix had been governor for six years and would have known about the Christians ("the Way"), a topic of conversation among the Roman leaders. The Christians' peaceful lifestyles had already proven to the Romans that Christians didn't go around starting riots.

**24:25** Paul's talk with Felix became so personal that Felix grew frightened. Felix, like Herod Antipas (Mark 6:17, 18), had taken another man's wife. Paul's words were interesting until they focused on "righteousness and self-control and the coming day of judgment." Many people will be glad to discuss the Good News with you as long as it doesn't touch their lives too personally. When it does, some will resist or run. But this is what the Good News is all about—God's power to change lives. The Good News is not effective until it moves from principles and doctrine into a life-changing dynamic. When someone resists or runs from your witness, you have undoubtedly succeeded in making the Good News personal.

**24:27** The Jews were in the majority, and the Roman political leaders wanted to defer to them to help keep the peace. Paul seemed to incite problems among the Jews everywhere he went. By keeping him in prison, Felix left office on good terms with the Jews. Felix lost his job as governor and was called back to Rome. Porcius Festus took over as governor in late 59 or early 60. He was more just than Felix, who had kept Paul in prison for two years, in hopes that perhaps Paul would bribe him and that,

by detaining Paul, the Jews would be kept happy. When Festus came into office, he immediately ordered Paul's trial to resume.

**24:27** Though God had promised that Paul would preach the gospel in Rome (23:11), the great apostle had to endure more than two years of Felix's refusal to decide his fate. In addition to this custody, Paul was subjected to other long stretches of time during which he could do little but trust God and wait for him to act. What do you do when it comes to the issue of waiting on God? Do you become anxious? angry? discouraged? Few things test our patience and faith like being forced to wait—which perhaps explains why our sovereign God often puts us in situations where we have no other choice.

**25:1-9** Although two years had passed, the Jewish leaders still were looking for a way to kill Paul. They told Festus about Paul and tried to convince him to hold the trial in Jerusalem (so they could prepare an ambush). But God and Paul thwarted their schemes again.

¹⁰But Paul replied, "No! This is the official Roman court, so I ought to be tried right here. You know very well I am not guilty of harming the Jews. ¹¹If I have done something worthy of death, I don't refuse to die. But if I am innocent, no one has a right to turn me over to these men to kill me. I appeal to Caesar!"

¹²Festus conferred with his advisers and then replied, "Very well! You have appealed to Caesar, and to Caesar you will go!"

¹³A few days later King Agrippa arrived with his sister, Bernice,* to pay their respects to Festus. ¹⁴During their stay of several days, Festus discussed Paul's case with the king. "There is a prisoner here," he told him, "whose case was left for me by Felix. ¹⁵When I was in Jerusalem, the leading priests and Jewish elders pressed charges against him and asked me to condemn him. ¹⁶I pointed out to them that Roman law does not convict people without a trial. They must be given an opportunity to confront their accusers and defend themselves.

¹⁷"When his accusers came here for the trial, I didn't delay. I called the case the very next day and ordered Paul brought in. ¹⁸But the accusations made against him weren't any of the crimes I expected. ¹⁹Instead, it was something about their religion and a dead man named Jesus, who Paul insists is alive. ²⁰I was at a loss to know how to investigate these things, so I asked him whether he would be willing to stand trial on these charges in Jerusalem. ²¹But Paul appealed to have his case decided by the emperor. So I ordered that he be held in custody until I could arrange to send him to Caesar."

²²"I'd like to hear the man myself," Agrippa said.

And Festus replied, "You will—tomorrow!"

### Paul Speaks to Agrippa

²³So the next day Agrippa and Bernice arrived at the auditorium with great pomp, accompanied by military officers and prominent men of the city. Festus ordered that Paul be brought in. ²⁴Then Festus said, "King Agrippa and all who are here, this is the man whose death is demanded by all the Jews, both here and in Jerusalem. ²⁵But in my opinion he has done nothing deserving death. However, since he appealed his case to the emperor, I have decided to send him to Rome.

²⁶"But what shall I write the emperor? For there is no clear charge against him. So I have brought him before all of you, and especially you, King Agrippa, so that after we examine him, I might have something to write. ²⁷For it makes no sense to send a prisoner to the emperor without specifying the charges against him!"

**26** Then Agrippa said to Paul, "You may speak in your defense."
So Paul, gesturing with his hand, started his defense: ²"I am fortunate, King Agrippa, that you are the one hearing my defense today against all these accusations made by the Jewish leaders, ³for I know you are an expert on all Jewish customs and controversies. Now please listen to me patiently!

**25:13** Greek *Agrippa the king and Bernice arrived.*

| | |
|---|---|
| **25:10** | Acts 25:21 |
| **25:11** | Acts 26:32; 28:19 |
| **25:14** | Acts 24:27 |
| **25:15** | Acts 25:1-2 |
| **25:16** | Acts 23:30 |
| **25:18-19** | Acts 18:14-15; 23:29 |
| **25:21** | Acts 25:11-12 |
| **25:22** | Acts 9:15 |
| **25:24** | Acts 22:22 |
| **25:25** | Acts 23:9 |

---

**25:10, 11** Paul knew that he was innocent of the charges against him and could appeal to Caesar's judgment. He knew his rights as a Roman citizen and as an innocent person. Paul had met his responsibilities as a Roman, and so he had the opportunity to claim Rome's protection. Every Roman citizen had the right to appeal to Caesar. This didn't mean that Caesar himself would hear the case but that the citizen's case would be tried by the highest courts in the empire. Festus saw Paul's appeal as a way to send him out of the country and thus pacify the Jews. Paul wanted to go to Rome to preach the Good News (Romans 1:10), and he knew that his appeal would give him the opportunity. To go to Rome as a prisoner was better than not to go there at all.

**25:13** This was Herod Agrippa II, son of Herod Agrippa I and a descendant of Herod the Great. He had power over the Temple, controlled the Temple treasury, and could appoint and remove the high priest. Bernice was the sister of Herod Agrippa II. She had married her uncle, Herod Chalcis, had become mistress

to her brother Agrippa II, and then had become mistress to the emperor Vespasian's son, Titus. Here Agrippa and Bernice were making an official visit to Festus. Agrippa, of Jewish descent, could help clarify Paul's case for the Roman governor. Agrippa and Festus were anxious to cooperate in governing their neighboring territories.

**25:19** Even though Festus knew little about Christianity, he somehow sensed that the Resurrection was central to Christian belief.

**25:23ff** Paul was in prison, but that didn't stop him from making the most of his situation. Military officers and prominent city leaders met in the auditorium with Agrippa to hear this case. Paul saw this new audience as yet another opportunity to present the Good News. Rather than complain about your present situation, look for ways to use every opportunity to serve God and share him with others. Your problems may be opportunities in disguise.

**26:3ff** This speech is a good example of Paul's powerful oratory. Beginning with a compliment to Agrippa, he told his story, including the resurrection of Christ, and the royal audience was spellbound.

26:4
Gal 1:13
Phil 3:5-6

26:6
Gen 3:15; 22:18
Deut 18:15
Isa 7:14; 9:6-7
Jer 23:5-6; 33:14
Ezek 34:23; 37:24
Dan 9:24
Mal 3:1; 4:2

26:7
Phil 3:11
1 Thes 3:10

26:8
Dan 12:2
Acts 23:6

26:9
John 15:21; 16:2
1 Tim 1:13

26:10
Acts 8:3; 22:4-5

26:12-18
//Acts 9:1-19;
22:6-16

26:14
Acts 9:7

26:16
Acts 22:14-15
Gal 1:12
Col 1:25
1 Tim 1:12

4"As the Jewish leaders are well aware, I was given a thorough Jewish training from my earliest childhood among my own people and in Jerusalem. 5If they would admit it, they know that I have been a member of the Pharisees, the strictest sect of our religion. 6Now I am on trial because of my hope in the fulfillment of God's promise made to our ancestors. 7In fact, that is why the twelve tribes of Israel zealously worship God night and day, and they share the same hope I have. Yet, Your Majesty, they accuse me for having this hope! 8Why does it seem incredible to any of you that God can raise the dead?

9"I used to believe that I ought to do everything I could to oppose the very name of Jesus the Nazarene.* 10Indeed, I did just that in Jerusalem. Authorized by the leading priests, I caused many believers* there to be sent to prison. And I cast my vote against them when they were condemned to death. 11Many times I had them punished in the synagogues to get them to curse Jesus.* I was so violently opposed to them that I even chased them down in foreign cities.

12"One day I was on such a mission to Damascus, armed with the authority and commission of the leading priests. 13About noon, Your Majesty, as I was on the road, a light from heaven brighter than the sun shone down on me and my companions. 14We all fell down, and I heard a voice saying to me in Aramaic,* 'Saul, Saul, why are you persecuting me? It is useless for you to fight against my will.*'

15"'Who are you, lord?' I asked.

"And the Lord replied, 'I am Jesus, the one you are persecuting. 16Now get to your feet! For I have appeared to you to appoint you as my servant and witness. You are to tell the world

26:9 Or *Jesus of Nazareth.*   26:10 Greek *many of God's holy people.*   26:11 Greek *to blaspheme.*   26:14a Or *Hebrew.*   26:14b Greek *It is hard for you to kick against the oxgoads.*

---

Like great-grandfather, like grandfather, like father, like son—this tells the story of Herod Agrippa II. He inherited the character flaws of generations of powerful men. Each son followed his father in weaknesses, mistakes, and missed opportunities to know God. Each generation had a confrontation with God but failed to realize the importance of the moment. Herod Agrippa's great-uncle, Herod Antipas, actually met Jesus during his trial but failed to see Jesus for who he was. Agrippa II heard the gospel from Paul but considered the message mild entertainment. He found it humorous that Paul actually tried to convince him to become a Christian.

Like so many before and after, Agrippa II stopped within hearing distance of the Kingdom of God. He left himself without excuse. He heard the gospel but decided it wasn't worth responding to personally. Sadly, his mistake is not uncommon. Many who read his story also will not believe. Their problem, like his, is not really that the gospel isn't convincing or that they don't need to know God personally; it is that they choose not to respond.

What has been your response to the gospel? Has it turned your life around and given you the hope of eternal life, or has it been a message to resist or reject? Perhaps it has just been entertainment. It may seem like too great a price to give God control of your life, but the price is minimal compared to living apart from him for eternity because you have chosen not to be his child.

**HEROD AGRIPPA II**

| | |
|---|---|
| **Strengths and accomplishments** | • Last of the Herod dynasty that ruled parts of Palestine from 40 B.C. to A.D. 100<br>• Continued his father's success in mediating between Rome and Palestine<br>• Continued the family tradition of building and improving cities |
| **Weaknesses and mistakes** | • Was not convinced by the gospel and consciously rejected it<br>• Carried on an incestuous relationship with his sister Bernice |
| **Lessons from his life** | • Families pass on both positive and negative influences to children<br>• There are no guarantees of multiple opportunities to respond to God |
| **Vital statistics** | • Occupation: Ruler of northern and eastern Palestine<br>• Relatives: Great-grandfather: Herod the Great. Father: Herod Agrippa I. Great-uncle: Herod Antipas. Sisters: Bernice, Drusilla.<br>• Contemporaries: Paul, Felix, Festus, Peter, Luke |
| **Key verse** | "Agrippa interrupted him. 'Do you think you can persuade me to become a Christian so quickly?'" (Acts 26:28). |

Herod Agrippa II's story is told in Acts 25:13–26:32.

what you have seen and what I will show you in the future. [17]And I will rescue you from both your own people and the Gentiles. Yes, I am sending you to the Gentiles [18] to open their eyes, so they may turn from darkness to light and from the power of Satan to God. Then they will receive forgiveness for their sins and be given a place among God's people, who are set apart by faith in me.'

[19]"And so, King Agrippa, I obeyed that vision from heaven. [20]I preached first to those in Damascus, then in Jerusalem and throughout all Judea, and also to the Gentiles, that all must repent of their sins and turn to God—and prove they have changed by the good things they do. [21]Some Jews arrested me in the Temple for preaching this, and they tried to kill me. [22]But God has protected me right up to this present time so I can testify to everyone, from the least to the greatest. I teach nothing except what the prophets and Moses said would happen— [23]that the Messiah would suffer and be the first to rise from the dead, and in this way announce God's light to Jews and Gentiles alike."

[24]Suddenly, Festus shouted, "Paul, you are insane. Too much study has made you crazy!"

[25]But Paul replied, "I am not insane, Most Excellent Festus. What I am saying is the sober truth. [26]And King Agrippa knows about these things. I speak boldly, for I am sure these events are all familiar to him, for they were not done in a corner! [27]King Agrippa, do you believe the prophets? I know you do—"

[28]Agrippa interrupted him. "Do you think you can persuade me to become a Christian so quickly?"*

[29]Paul replied, "Whether quickly or not, I pray to God that both you and everyone here in this audience might become the same as I am, except for these chains."

[30]Then the king, the governor, Bernice, and all the others stood and left. [31]As they went out, they talked it over and agreed, "This man hasn't done anything to deserve death or imprisonment."

[32]And Agrippa said to Festus, "He could have been set free if he hadn't appealed to Caesar."

## Paul Sails for Rome

**27** When the time came, we set sail for Italy. Paul and several other prisoners were placed in the custody of a Roman officer* named Julius, a captain of the Imperial Regiment. [2]Aristarchus, a Macedonian from Thessalonica, was also with us. We left on a ship whose home port was Adramyttium on the northwest coast of the province of Asia;* it was scheduled to make several stops at ports along the coast of the province.

[3]The next day when we docked at Sidon, Julius was very kind to Paul and let him go ashore to visit with friends so they could provide for his needs. [4]Putting out to sea from there, we encountered strong headwinds that made it difficult to keep the ship on course, so we sailed north of Cyprus between the island and the mainland. [5]Keeping to the open sea,

**26:17**
Acts 13:46-48;
22:21
Rom 11:13; 15:16
Gal 1:15-16; 2:7-9
1 Tim 2:7
2 Tim 1:11

**26:18**
Isa 35:5;
42:7, 16; 61:1
Luke 1:77, 79
Eph 1:11; 5:8
Col 1:13
1 Pet 2:9

**26:20**
Matt 3:8
Acts 9:19-29

**26:21**
Acts 21:30-31

**26:22**
Luke 24:27, 44

**26:23**
Isa 42:6; 49:6
Luke 24:46-47
Rom 1:3-4
1 Cor 15:20
Col 1:18
Rev 1:5

**26:24**
1 Cor 4:10

**26:26**
John 18:20
Acts 26:3

**26:31**
Acts 23:9, 29

**26:32**
Acts 25:11

**27:1**
Acts 25:12

**27:2**
Acts 19:29; 20:4

**27:3**
Matt 11:21
Acts 24:23; 27:43;
28:2, 16

26:28 Or "A little more, and your arguments would make me a Christian."   27:1 Greek centurion; similarly in 27:6, 11, 31, 43.   27:2 Asia was a Roman province in what is now western Turkey.

**26:17, 18** Paul took every opportunity to remind his audience that the Gentiles had an equal share in God's inheritance. This inheritance is the promise and blessing of the covenant that God had made with Abraham (see Ephesians 2:19; 1 Peter 1:3, 4). Paul's mission was to preach the Good News to the Gentiles.

**26:24** Paul was risking his life for a message that was offensive to the Jews and unbelievable to the Gentiles. Jesus received the same response to his message (Mark 3:21; John 10:20). To a worldly, materialistic mind, it seems insane to risk so much to gain what seems to be so little. But as you follow Christ, you soon discover that one's most prized possessions cannot compare to even the smallest eternal reward.

**26:26** Paul was appealing to the *facts:* People were still alive who had heard Jesus and seen his miracles; the empty tomb could still be seen; and the Christian message was turning the world upside down (17:6). The history of Jesus' life and the early church are facts that still confront us today. We still have eyewitness accounts of Jesus' life recorded in the Bible as well as historical and archaeological records of the early church to study. Examine the events and facts as verified by many witnesses. Strengthen your faith with the truth of these accounts.

**26:28, 29** Agrippa responded to Paul's presentation with a sarcastic remark. Paul didn't react to the brush-off but made a personal appeal to which he hoped all his listeners would respond. Paul's response is a good example for us as we tell others about God's plan of salvation. A sincere personal appeal or personal testimony can show the depth of our concern and break through hardened hearts.

**26:28, 29** Paul's heart is revealed here in his words: He was more concerned for the salvation of these strangers than for the removal of his own chains. Ask God to give you a burning desire to see others come to Christ—a desire so strong that it overshadows your problems.

**27:1, 2** Use of the pronoun *we* indicates that Luke accompanied Paul on this journey. Aristarchus is the man who had been dragged into the theater at the beginning of the riot in Ephesus (19:29; 20:4; Philemon 1:24).

**27:1-3** Julius, a Roman army officer, was assigned to guard Paul. Obviously he had to remain close to Paul at all times. Through this contact, Julius developed a respect for Paul. He gave Paul a certain amount of freedom (27:3) and later spared his life (27:43). How would your character look, up close and personal?

we passed along the coast of Cilicia and Pamphylia, landing at Myra, in the province of Lycia. [6]There the commanding officer found an Egyptian ship from Alexandria that was bound for Italy, and he put us on board.

27:6
Acts 28:11

[7]We had several days of slow sailing, and after great difficulty we finally neared Cnidus. But the wind was against us, so we sailed across to Crete and along the sheltered coast of the island, past the cape of Salmone. [8]We struggled along the coast with great difficulty and finally arrived at Fair Havens, near the town of Lasea. [9]We had lost a lot of time. The weather was becoming dangerous for sea travel because it was so late in the fall,* and Paul spoke to the ship's officers about it.

27:9
Lev 16:29-31

[10]"Men," he said, "I believe there is trouble ahead if we go on—shipwreck, loss of cargo, and danger to our lives as well." [11]But the officer in charge of the prisoners listened more to the ship's captain and the owner than to Paul. [12]And since Fair Havens was an exposed harbor—a poor place to spend the winter—most of the crew wanted to go on to Phoenix, farther up the coast of Crete, and spend the winter there. Phoenix was a good harbor with only a southwest and northwest exposure.

### The Storm at Sea

[13]When a light wind began blowing from the south, the sailors thought they could make it. So they pulled up anchor and sailed close to the shore of Crete. [14]But the weather changed abruptly, and a wind of typhoon strength (called a "northeaster") burst across the island and blew us out to sea. [15]The sailors couldn't turn the ship into the wind, so they gave up and let it run before the gale.

27:14
Mark 4:37

[16]We sailed along the sheltered side of a small island named Cauda,* where with great difficulty we hoisted aboard the lifeboat being towed behind us. [17]Then the sailors bound ropes around the hull of the ship to strengthen it. They were afraid of being driven across to

27:9 Greek *because the fast was now already gone by.* This fast was associated with the Day of Atonement (*Yom Kippur*), which occurred in late September or early October.   27:16 Some manuscripts read *Clauda.*

**THE TRIP TOWARD ROME**
Paul began his 2,000-mile trip to Rome at Caesarea. To avoid the open seas, the ship followed the coastline. At Myra, Paul was put on a vessel bound for Italy. It arrived with difficulty at Cnidus, then went to Crete, landing at the port of Fair Havens. The next stop was Phoenix, but the ship was blown south around the island of Cauda, then drifted for two weeks until it was shipwrecked on the island of Malta.

27:9 Ships in ancient times had no compasses, so they navigated by the stars. Overcast weather made sailing almost impossible and very dangerous. Sailing was doubtful in September and impossible by November. This event occurred in October (A.D. 59).

27:12 Although this was not the best time to sail, the ship's captain and the owner of the ship didn't want to spend the winter in Lasea, or Fair Havens, so the officer took a chance. At first the winds and weather were favorable, but then the deadly storm arose.

27:17 Binding ropes around the hull of the ship meant passing ropes under the ship to hold it together. Syrtis was on the northern coast of Africa.

the sandbars of Syrtis off the African coast, so they lowered the sea anchor to slow the ship and were driven before the wind. ¹⁸The next day, as gale-force winds continued to batter the ship, the crew began throwing the cargo overboard. ¹⁹The following day they even took some of the ship's gear and threw it overboard. ²⁰The terrible storm raged for many days, blotting out the sun and the stars, until at last all hope was gone.

²¹No one had eaten for a long time. Finally, Paul called the crew together and said, "Men, you should have listened to me in the first place and not left Crete. You would have avoided all this damage and loss. ²²But take courage! None of you will lose your lives, even though the ship will go down. ²³For last night an angel of the God to whom I belong and whom I serve stood beside me, ²⁴and he said, 'Don't be afraid, Paul, for you will surely stand trial before Caesar! What's more, God in his goodness has granted safety to everyone sailing with you.' ²⁵So take courage! For I believe God. It will be just as he said. ²⁶But we will be shipwrecked on an island."

### The Shipwreck

²⁷About midnight on the fourteenth night of the storm, as we were being driven across the Sea of Adria,* the sailors sensed land was near. ²⁸They dropped a weighted line and found that the water was 120 feet deep. But a little later they measured again and found it was only 90 feet deep.* ²⁹At this rate they were afraid we would soon be driven against the rocks along the shore, so they threw out four anchors from the back of the ship and prayed for daylight.

³⁰Then the sailors tried to abandon the ship; they lowered the lifeboat as though they were going to put out anchors from the front of the ship. ³¹But Paul said to the commanding officer and the soldiers, "You will all die unless the sailors stay aboard." ³²So the soldiers cut the ropes to the lifeboat and let it drift away.

³³Just as day was dawning, Paul urged everyone to eat. "You have been so worried that you haven't touched food for two weeks," he said. ³⁴"Please eat something now for your own good. For not a hair of your heads will perish." ³⁵Then he took some bread, gave thanks to God before them all, and broke off a piece and ate it. ³⁶Then everyone was encouraged and began to eat—³⁷all 276 of us who were on board. ³⁸After eating, the crew lightened the ship further by throwing the cargo of wheat overboard.

³⁹When morning dawned, they didn't recognize the coastline, but they saw a bay with a beach and wondered if they could get to shore by running the ship aground. ⁴⁰So they cut off the anchors and left them in the sea. Then they lowered the rudders, raised the foresail, and headed toward shore. ⁴¹But they hit a shoal and ran the ship aground too soon. The bow of the ship stuck fast, while the stern was repeatedly smashed by the force of the waves and began to break apart.

⁴²The soldiers wanted to kill the prisoners to make sure they didn't swim ashore and escape. ⁴³But the commanding officer wanted to spare Paul, so he didn't let them carry out their plan. Then he ordered all who could swim to jump overboard first and make for land. ⁴⁴The others held on to planks or debris from the broken ship.* So everyone escaped safely to shore.

**27:18**
Jon 1:5

**27:21**
Acts 27:10

**27:23**
Acts 18:9; 23:11
2 Tim 4:17

**27:24**
Acts 23:11

**27:25**
Rom 4:20-21

**27:26**
Acts 28:1

**27:34**
Matt 10:30
Luke 12:7

**27:35**
Matt 14:19

**27:38**
Jon 1:5
Acts 27:18

**27:41**
2 Cor 11:25

**27:43-44**
Acts 27:22, 24

27:27 The *Sea of Adria* includes the central portion of the Mediterranean.    27:28 Greek *20 fathoms . . . 15 fathoms* [37 meters . . . 27 meters].    27:44 Or *or were helped by members of the ship's crew.*

---

**27:21**  Why would Paul talk to the crew this way? Paul was not taunting them with an "I told you so" but was reminding them that, with God's guidance, he had predicted this very problem (27:10). In the future, they listened to him (27:30-32), and their lives were spared because of it.

**27:27**  The Sea of Adria referred to the central part of the Mediterranean Sea between Italy, Crete, and the northern coast of Africa.

**27:28**  These weighted lines had marks on them so that when the weight hit the bottom, the sailors could tell the depth of the water from the marks on the line.

**27:29**  In the middle of a midnight squall, the passengers and crew (led by Paul) did all they could possibly do—they dropped

some anchors to try to stop the runaway ship. Then they prayed. Of course, Paul alone was praying to the one God who could do anything about their situation. This is a good reminder for us. We must never rely solely on our own wisdom or skills. But it is equally wrong to sit and do nothing when there are still actions we can take to overcome certain problems. Do all that you can to fix the problem. Then trust God to do his part.

**27:42, 43**  The soldiers would pay with their own lives if any of their prisoners escaped. Their instinctive reaction was to kill the prisoners so they wouldn't get away. Julius, the officer, was impressed with Paul and wanted to save his life. Julius was the highest ranking official; therefore, he could make this decision. This act preserved Paul for his later ministry in Rome and fulfilled Paul's prediction that all the people on the ship would be saved (27:22).

## Paul on the Island of Malta

28:1
Acts 27:26, 39

**28** Once we were safe on shore, we learned that we were on the island of Malta. ²The people of the island were very kind to us. It was cold and rainy, so they built a fire on the shore to welcome us.

³As Paul gathered an armful of sticks and was laying them on the fire, a poisonous snake, driven out by the heat, bit him on the hand. ⁴The people of the island saw it hanging from his hand and said to each other, "A murderer, no doubt! Though he escaped the sea, justice will not permit him to live." ⁵But Paul shook off the snake into the fire and was unharmed. ⁶The people waited for him to swell up or suddenly drop dead. But when they had waited a long time and saw that he wasn't harmed, they changed their minds and decided he was a god.

28:4
Luke 13:2, 4
28:5
Mark 16:18
Luke 10:19
28:6
Acts 14:11

⁷Near the shore where we landed was an estate belonging to Publius, the chief official of the island. He welcomed us and treated us kindly for three days. ⁸As it happened, Publius's father was ill with fever and dysentery. Paul went in and prayed for him, and laying his hands on him, he healed him. ⁹Then all the other sick people on the island came and were healed. ¹⁰As a result we were showered with honors, and when the time came to sail, people supplied us with everything we would need for the trip.

28:8
Jas 5:14-15

---

**PAUL'S JOURNEY TO ROME**

| Reference | What Happened |
|---|---|
| 21:30-34 . . . . . . . . | When Paul arrived in Jerusalem, a riot broke out. Seeing the riot, Roman soldiers put Paul into protective custody. Paul asked for a chance to defend himself to the people. His speech was interrupted by the crowd when he told about what God was doing in the lives of Gentiles. |
| 22:24, 25 . . . . . . . | A Roman commander ordered a beating to get a confession from Paul. Paul claimed Roman citizenship and escaped the whip. |
| 22:30 . . . . . . . . . | Paul was brought before the Jewish high council. Because of his Roman citizenship, he was rescued from the religious leaders who wanted to kill him. |
| 23:10 . . . . . . . . . | The Roman commander put Paul back under protective custody. |
| 23:21-24 . . . . . . . | Due to a plot to kill Paul, the commander transferred him to Caesarea, which was under Governor Felix's control. |
| 23:35 . . . . . . . . . | Paul was in prison until the Jews arrived to accuse him. Paul defended himself before Felix. |
| 24:25, 26 . . . . . . . | Paul was in prison for two years, speaking occasionally to Felix and Drusilla. |
| 24:27 . . . . . . . . . | Felix was replaced by Festus. |
| 25:1, 10 . . . . . . . | New accusations were brought against Paul—Jews wanted him back in Jerusalem for a trial. Paul claimed his right to a hearing before Caesar. |
| 25:12 . . . . . . . . . | Festus promised to send him to Rome. |
| 25:13, 14 . . . . . . . | Festus discussed Paul's case with Herod Agrippa II. |
| 26:1 . . . . . . . . . . | Agrippa and Festus heard Paul speak. Paul again told his story. |
| 26:24-28 . . . . . . . | Agrippa interrupted with a sarcastic rejection of the gospel. |
| 26:30-32 . . . . . . . | Group consensus was that Paul was guilty of nothing and could have been released if he had not appealed to Rome. |
| 27:1, 2 . . . . . . . . . | Paul left for Rome, courtesy of the Roman Empire. |

One of Paul's most important journeys was to Rome, but he didn't get there the way he expected. It turned out to be more of a legal journey than a missionary journey. Through a series of legal trials and transactions, Paul was delivered to Rome, where his presentation of the gospel would even penetrate the walls of the emperor's palace. Sometimes when our plans don't work out as we want them to, they work out even better than we expected.

---

**28:1, 2** The island of Malta is 60 miles south of Sicily. It had excellent harbors and was ideally located for trade. The islanders on Malta were of Phoenician ancestry.

**28:3** God had promised safe passage to Paul (27:23-25), and he would let nothing stop his servant. The poisonous snake that bit Paul was unable to harm him. Our life is in God's hands, to continue on or to come to an end in his good timing. God still had work for Paul to do.

**28:6** These people were very superstitious and believed in many gods. When they saw that Paul was unhurt by the poisonous snake, they thought he was a god. A similar assessment is reported in 14:11-18.

**28:7, 8** Paul continued to minister to others, even as a shipwrecked prisoner. On this trip alone, the Roman army officer, the chief official of Malta, and many others were affected. It is no wonder that the Good News spread like wildfire.

## Paul Arrives at Rome

¹¹It was three months after the shipwreck that we set sail on another ship that had wintered at the island—an Alexandrian ship with the twin gods* as its figurehead. ¹²Our first stop was Syracuse,* where we stayed three days. ¹³From there we sailed across to Rhegium.* A day later a south wind began blowing, so the following day we sailed up the coast to Puteoli. ¹⁴There we found some believers,* who invited us to spend a week with them. And so we came to Rome.

**28:11**
Acts 27:6

¹⁵The brothers and sisters* in Rome had heard we were coming, and they came to meet us at the Forum* on the Appian Way. Others joined us at The Three Taverns.* When Paul saw them, he was encouraged and thanked God.

¹⁶When we arrived in Rome, Paul was permitted to have his own private lodging, though he was guarded by a soldier.

**28:16**
Acts 24:23; 27:23

## Paul Preaches at Rome under Guard

¹⁷Three days after Paul's arrival, he called together the local Jewish leaders. He said to them, "Brothers, I was arrested in Jerusalem and handed over to the Roman government, even though I had done nothing against our people or the customs of our ancestors. ¹⁸The Romans tried me and wanted to release me, because they found no cause for the death sentence. ¹⁹But when the Jewish leaders protested the decision, I felt it necessary to appeal to Caesar, even though I had no desire to press charges against my own people. ²⁰I asked you to come here today so we could get acquainted and so I could explain to you that I am bound with this chain because I believe that the hope of Israel—the Messiah—has already come."

**28:17**
Acts 24:12-13;
25:8

**28:18**
Acts 23:29

**28:19**
Acts 25:11

**28:20**
Acts 26:6

²¹They replied, "We have had no letters from Judea or reports against you from anyone who has come here. ²²But we want to hear what you believe, for the only thing we know about this movement is that it is denounced everywhere."

**28:22**
Acts 24:14

²³So a time was set, and on that day a large number of people came to Paul's lodging. He explained and testified about the Kingdom of God and tried to persuade them about Jesus from the Scriptures. Using the law of Moses and the books of the prophets, he spoke to them from morning until evening. ²⁴Some were persuaded by the things he said, but others did not believe. ²⁵And after they had argued back and forth among themselves, they left with this final word from Paul: "The Holy Spirit was right when he said to your ancestors through Isaiah the prophet,

**28:24**
Acts 14:4

---

**28:11** The *twin gods* were the Roman gods Castor and Pollux.   **28:12** *Syracuse* was on the island of Sicily.
**28:13** *Rhegium* was on the southern tip of Italy.   **28:14** Greek *brothers.*   **28:15a** Greek *brothers.*   **28:15b** *The Forum* was about 43 miles (70 kilometers) from Rome.   **28:15c** *The Three Taverns* was about 35 miles (57 kilometers) from Rome.

---

**28:15**   Where did the Roman believers come from? The Good News had spread to Rome by various methods. Many Jews who lived in Rome would visit Jerusalem for religious festivals. Some had been present at Pentecost (2:10), had believed in Jesus, and had brought the message back to Rome. Also, Paul had written his letter to the Romans before this time.

### PAUL ARRIVES IN ROME

The shipwreck occurred on Malta, where the ship's company spent three months. Finally, another ship gave them passage for the 100 miles to Syracuse, capital of Sicily, then sailed on to Rhegium, finally dropping anchor at Puteoli. Paul was taken to the Forum on the Appian Way and to The Three Taverns before arriving in Rome.

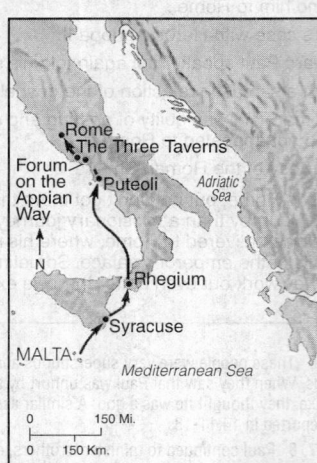

**28:15**   The Forum on the Appian Way was a town about 43 miles south of Rome; The Three Taverns was located about 35 miles south of Rome. A *tavern* was a shop or a place that provided food and lodging for travelers. The Christians openly went to meet Paul and encourage him.

**28:17**   The decree of Claudius expelling Jews from Rome (18:2) must have been temporary because Jewish leaders were back in Rome.

**28:17-20**   Paul wanted to preach the Good News in Rome, and he eventually got there—in chains, through shipwreck, and after many trials. Although he may have wished for an easier passage, he knew that God had blessed him greatly in allowing him to meet the believers in Rome and preach the message to both Jews and Gentiles in that great city. In all things, God worked for Paul's good (Romans 8:28). You can trust God to do the same for you. God may not make you comfortable or secure, but he will provide the opportunity to do his work.

**28:22**   Christians were denounced everywhere by the Romans because they were seen as a threat to the Roman establishment. They believed in one God, whereas the Romans had many gods, including Caesar. The Christians were committed to an authority higher than Caesar.

**28:23**   Paul used the Old Testament to teach the Jews that Jesus was the Messiah, the fulfillment of God's promises. The book of

**28:26-27**
†Isa 6:9-10
John 12:39-40

26 'Go and say to this people:
> When you hear what I say,
> > you will not understand.
> When you see what I do,
> > you will not comprehend.
27 For the hearts of these people are hardened,
> > and their ears cannot hear,
> > and they have closed their eyes—
> so their eyes cannot see,
> > and their ears cannot hear,
> > and their hearts cannot understand,
> and they cannot turn to me
> > and let me heal them.'*

**28:28**
Pss 67:2; 98:3
Luke 3:6
Acts 13:46

**28:30**
Acts 28:16

28So I want you to know that this salvation from God has also been offered to the Gentiles, and they will accept it."*

30For the next two years, Paul lived in Rome at his own expense.* He welcomed all who visited him, 31boldly proclaiming the Kingdom of God and teaching about the Lord Jesus Christ. And no one tried to stop him.

**28:26-27** Isa 6:9-10 (Greek version).    **28:28** Some manuscripts add verse 29, *And when he had said these words, the Jews departed, greatly disagreeing with each other.*    **28:30** Or *in his own rented quarters.*

---

Romans, written 10 years earlier, reveals Paul's ongoing dialogue with the Jews in Rome.

**28:30** Paul remained in Rome under guard (28:16) in a rented house for two years (28:30). There sat the greatest apostle and spokesman for Christianity—unable to move freely and minister as he desired. However, Paul didn't complain or despair. He simply did what he could. Able to receive visitors, he taught, preached, and counseled even while he was confined to quarters. He wrote letters, commonly called his Prison Letters, to the Ephesians, Colossians, and Philippians—letters that have impacted millions of believers down through the centuries. He also wrote personal letters, such as the one to Philemon. Luke was with Paul in Rome (2 Timothy 4:11). Timothy often visited him (Philippians 1:1; Colossians 1:1; Philemon 1:1), as did Tychicus (Ephesians 6:21), Epaphroditus (Philippians 4:18), and Mark (Colossians 4:10). Paul witnessed to the whole Roman guard (Philippians 1:13) and was involved with the Roman believers. If you find yourself in a "negative" or unpleasant situation, look for ways to redeem the circumstances. There is never a time or place in which you can't glorify and serve God.

**28:30** Tradition says that Paul was released after two years of house arrest in Rome and that he then left on a fourth missionary journey. Some reasons for this tradition are as follows: (1) Luke does not give us an account of Paul's trial before Caesar, and Luke was a detailed chronicler; (2) the prosecution had two years to bring the case to trial, and time may have run out; (3) in his letter to the Philippians, written during his imprisonment in Rome, Paul implied that he would soon be released and would do further traveling; (4) Paul mentions several places where he intended to take the Good News, but he never visited those places in his first three journeys; (5) early Christian literature talks plainly about other travels by Paul.

During his time of freedom, Paul may have continued to travel extensively, even going to Spain (see Romans 15:24, 28) and back to the churches in Greece. The books of 1 Timothy and Titus were written during this time. Later, Paul was imprisoned again, probably in Rome, where he wrote his last letter (2 Timothy).

**28:31** Why does the book of Acts end here and so abruptly? The book is not about the life of Paul but about the spread of the Good News, and that had been clearly presented. God apparently thought it was not necessary for someone to write an additional book describing the continuing history of the early church. Now that the Good News had been preached and established at the center of trade and government, it would spread across the world.

**28:31** The book of Acts deals with the history of the Christian church and its expansion in ever-widening circles touching Jerusalem, Antioch, Ephesus, and Rome—the most influential cities in the Western world. Acts also shows the mighty miracles and testimonies of the heroes and martyrs of the early church—Peter, Stephen, James, Paul. All the ministry was prompted and held together by the Holy Spirit working in the lives of ordinary people—merchants, travelers, slaves, jailers, church leaders, males, females, Gentiles, Jews, rich, poor. Many unsung heroes of the faith continued the work, through the Holy Spirit, in succeeding generations, changing the world with a changeless message: Jesus Christ is Savior and Lord of all who call on him. Today we can be the unsung heroes in the continuing story of the spread of the Good News. It is that same message that we Christians are to take to our world so that many more may hear and believe.

# ROMANS

## VITAL STATISTICS

**PURPOSE:**
To introduce Paul to the Romans and to give a sample of his message before he arrives in Rome

**AUTHOR:**
Paul

**ORIGINAL AUDIENCE:**
The Christians in Rome

**DATE WRITTEN:**
About A.D. 57, from Corinth, as Paul was preparing for his visit to Jerusalem.

**SETTING:**
Apparently Paul had finished his work in the east, and he planned to visit Rome on his way to Spain after first bringing a collection to Jerusalem for the poor Christians there (15:23–28). The Roman church was mostly Jewish but also contained a great number of Gentiles.

**KEY VERSE:**
"Therefore, since we have been made right in God's sight by faith, we have peace with God because of what Jesus Christ our Lord has done for us" (5:1).

**KEY PEOPLE:**
Paul, Phoebe

**KEY PLACE:**
Rome

**SPECIAL FEATURES:**
Paul wrote Romans as an organized and carefully presented statement of his faith—it does not have the form of a typical letter. He does, however, spend considerable time greeting people in Rome at the end of the letter.

KNOWLEDGEABLE and experienced, the district attorney makes his case. Calling key witnesses to the stand, he presents the evidence. After discrediting the testimonies of witnesses for the defense by skillfully cross-examining them, he concludes with an airtight summary and stirring challenge for the jury. The announced verdict is no surprise. "Guilty" states the foreman, and justice is served.

The apostle Paul was intelligent, articulate, and committed to his calling. Like a skilled lawyer, he presented the case for the gospel clearly and forthrightly in his letter to the believers in Rome.

Paul had heard of the church at Rome, but he had not yet been there, nor had any of the other apostles. Evidently the church had been started by Jews who had come to faith during Pentecost (Acts 2). They had spread the gospel on their return to Rome, and the church had grown.

Although many barriers separated them, Paul felt a bond with these believers in Rome. They were his brothers and sisters in Christ, and he longed to see them face to face. He had never met most of the believers there, yet he loved them. He sent this letter to introduce himself and to make a clear declaration of the faith.

After a brief introduction, Paul presents the facts of the gospel (1:3) and declares his allegiance to it (1:16, 17). He continues by building an airtight case for the lostness of humanity and the necessity for God's intervention (1:18—3:20).

Then Paul presents the Good News: Salvation is available to all, regardless of a person's identity, sin, or heritage. We are saved by *grace* (unearned, undeserved favor from God) through *faith* (complete trust) in Christ and his finished work. Through him we can stand before God justified, "not guilty" (3:21—5:21). With this foundation Paul moves directly into a discussion of the freedom that comes from being saved—freedom from the power of sin (6:1–23), freedom from the domination of the law (7:1–25), freedom to become like Christ and discover God's limitless love (8:1–39).

Speaking directly to his Jewish brothers and sisters, Paul shares his concern for them and explains how they fit into God's plan (9:1—11:12). God has made the way for Jews and Gentiles to be united in the body of Christ; both groups can praise God for his wisdom and love (11:13–36).

Paul explains what it means to live in complete submission to Christ: Use spiritual gifts to serve others (12:3–8), genuinely love others (12:9–21), and be good citizens (13:1–14). Freedom must be guided by love as we build each other up in the faith, being sensitive and helpful to those who are weak (14:1—15:4). Paul stresses unity, especially between Gentiles and Jews (15:5–13). He concludes by reviewing his reasons for writing, outlining his personal plans (15:22–33), greeting his friends, and giving a few final thoughts and greetings from his traveling companions (16:1–27).

As you read Romans, reexamine your commitment to Christ, and reconfirm your relationships with other believers in Christ's body.

## THE BLUEPRINT

A. WHAT TO BELIEVE
(1:1—11:36)
1. Sinfulness of humanity
2. Forgiveness of sin through Christ
3. Freedom from sin's grasp
4. Israel's past, present, and future

Paul clearly sets forth the foundations of the Christian faith. All people are sinful; Christ died to forgive sin; we are made right with God through faith; this begins a new life with a new relationship with God. Like a sports team that constantly reviews the basics, we will be greatly helped in our faith by keeping close to these foundations. If we study Romans carefully, we will never be at a loss to know what to believe.

B. HOW TO BEHAVE
(12:1—16:27)
1. Personal responsibility
2. Personal notes

Paul gives clear, practical guidelines for the believers in Rome. The Christian life is not abstract theology unconnected with life, but it has practical implications that will affect how we choose to behave each day. It is not enough merely to know the gospel; we must let it transform our life and let God impact every aspect of our lives.

## MEGATHEMES

| THEME | EXPLANATION | IMPORTANCE |
|---|---|---|
| Sin | Sin means refusing to do God's will and failing to do all that God wants. Since Adam's rebellion against God, our nature is to disobey him. Our sin cuts us off from God. Sin causes us to want to live our own way rather than God's way. Because God is morally perfect, just, and fair, he is right to condemn sin. | Each person has sinned, either by rebelling against God or by ignoring his will. No matter what our background or how hard we try to live good and moral lives, we cannot earn salvation or remove our sin. Only Christ can save us. |
| Salvation | Our sin points out our need to be forgiven and cleansed. Although we don't deserve it, God, in his kindness, reached out to love and forgive us. He provides the way for us to be saved. Christ's death paid the penalty for our sin. | It is good news that God saves us from our sin. But in order to enter into a wonderful new relationship with God, we must believe that Jesus died for us and that he forgives all our sin. |
| Growth | By God's power, believers are sanctified—made holy. This means we are set apart from sin, enabled to obey and to become more like Christ. When we are growing in our relationship with Christ, the Holy Spirit frees us from the demands of the law and from fear of judgment. | Because we are free from sin's control, the law's demands, and fear of God's punishment, we can grow in our relationship with Christ. By trusting in the Holy Spirit and allowing him to help us, we can overcome sin and temptation. |
| Sovereignty | God oversees and cares about his people—past, present, and future. God's ways of dealing with people are always fair. Because God is in charge of all creation, he can save whomever he wills. | Because of God's mercy, both Jews and Gentiles can be saved. We all must respond to his mercy and accept his gracious offer of forgiveness. Because he is sovereign, let him reign in your heart. |
| Service | When our purpose is to give credit to God for his love, power, and perfection in all we do, we can serve him properly. Serving him unifies all believers and enables them to show love and sensitivity to others. | None of us can be fully Christlike by ourselves—it takes the entire body of Christ to fully express Christ. By actively and vigorously building up other believers, Christians can be a symphony of service to God. |

## A. WHAT TO BELIEVE (1:1—11:36)

Paul begins his message to the Romans by vividly portraying the sinfulness of all people, explaining how forgiveness is available through faith in Christ, and showing what believers experience in life through their new faith. In this section, we learn of the centrality of faith to becoming a Christian and to living the Christian life. Apart from faith, we have no hope in life.

### 1. Sinfulness of humanity

*Greetings from Paul*

**1** This letter is from Paul, a slave of Christ Jesus, chosen by God to be an apostle and sent out to preach his Good News. ²God promised this Good News long ago through his prophets in the holy Scriptures. ³The Good News is about his Son. In his earthly life he was born into King David's family line, ⁴and he was shown to be* the Son of God when he was raised from the dead by the power of the Holy Spirit.* He is Jesus Christ our Lord. ⁵Through Christ, God has given us the privilege* and authority as apostles to tell Gentiles everywhere what God has done for them, so that they will believe and obey him, bringing glory to his name.

⁶And you are included among those Gentiles who have been called to belong to Jesus Christ. ⁷I am writing to all of you in Rome who are loved by God and are called to be his own holy people.

May God our Father and the Lord Jesus Christ give you grace and peace.

**1:3**
Matt 1:1; 22:42
Rom 9:5
2 Tim 2:8

**1:4**
Acts 13:33
Rom 8:11

**1:5**
Acts 9:15
Rom 16:26
Gal 1:16
Eph 3:8-9

**1:7**
1 Cor 1:2
2 Cor 1:1
Gal 1:3
Eph 1:1

**1:4a** Or *and was designated.*   **1:4b** Or *by the Spirit of holiness;* or *in the new realm of the Spirit.*   **1:5** Or *the grace.*

**1:1** Paul wrote this letter to the church in Rome. Neither he nor the other church leaders, James and Peter, had yet been to Rome. Most likely, the Roman church had been established by believers who had been at Jerusalem for Pentecost (Acts 2:10) and by travelers who had heard the Good News in other places and had brought it back to Rome (for example, Priscilla and Aquila, Acts 18:2; Romans 16:3-5). Paul wrote the letter to the Romans during his ministry in Corinth (at the end of his third missionary journey just before returning to Jerusalem—Acts 20:3; Romans 15:25) to encourage the believers and to express his desire to visit them someday (within three years he would). The Roman church had no New Testament because the Gospels were not yet being circulated in their final written form. Thus, this letter may well have been the first piece of Christian literature the Roman believers had seen. Written to both Jewish and Gentile Christians, the letter to the Romans is a systematic presentation of the Christian faith.

**1:1** When Paul, a devout Jew who had at first persecuted the Christians, became a believer, God used him to spread the Good News throughout the world. Although he was a prisoner, Paul did eventually preach in Rome (Acts 28), perhaps even to Caesar himself. Paul's Profile is found in Acts 9, p. 1837.

**1:1** Paul humbly calls himself a slave of Christ Jesus and an apostle ("one who is sent"). For a Roman citizen—which Paul was—to choose to be a slave was unthinkable. But Paul chose to be completely dependent on and obedient to his beloved Master. What is your attitude toward Christ, your Master? Our willingness to serve and obey Jesus Christ enables us to be useful and usable servants to do work for him—work that really matters. Obedience begins as we renounce other masters, identify ourselves with Jesus, discover his will and live according to it, and consciously turn away from conflicting interests, even if these interests have been important to us in the past.

**1:2** Some of the prophecies predicting the Good News regarding Jesus Christ are found in Genesis 12:3; Psalms 16:10; 40:6-10; 118:22; Isaiah 11:1ff; Zechariah 9:9-11; 12:10; Malachi 4:1-6.

**1:3, 4** Paul states that Jesus is the Son of God, the promised Messiah, and the resurrected Lord. Paul calls Jesus a descendant of King David to emphasize that Jesus truly had fulfilled the Old Testament Scriptures predicting that the Messiah would come from David's line. With this statement of faith, Paul declares his agreement with the teaching of all Scripture and of the apostles.

**1:3-5** Here Paul summarizes the Good News about Jesus Christ, who (1) came as a human by natural descent, (2) was part of the Jewish royal line through David, (3) died and was raised from the dead, and (4) opened the door for God's grace and kindness to be poured out on us. The book of Romans is an expansion of these themes.

**1:5** Christians have both a privilege and a great responsibility. Paul and the apostles received the privilege of being called, but they also received the authority and the responsibility to share with others what God has done. God also graciously forgives our sins when we believe in him as Lord. In doing this, we are committing ourselves to begin a new life. Paul's new life also involved a God-given responsibility: to witness about God's Good News to the world as a missionary. God may or may not call you to be a foreign missionary, but he does call you (and all believers) to be Christ's ambassador and to witness to the changed life that Jesus Christ has begun in you.

**1:6** Jews and Christians alike stood against the idolatrous Roman religions, and Roman officials often confused the two groups. This was especially easy to do since the Christian church in Rome could have been originally composed of Jewish converts who had attended Pentecost in Jerusalem (see Acts 2:1ff). By the time Paul wrote this letter to the Romans, however, many Gentiles had joined the church. The Jews and the Gentiles needed to know the relationship between Judaism and Christianity.

**1:6, 7** Paul says that those who become Christians are invited by Jesus Christ to (1) belong to God's family, and (2) be his very own people. What a wonderful expression of what it means to be a Christian! In being reborn into God's family we have the greatest experience of love and the greatest inheritance. Because of all that God has done for us, we strive to be his holy people.

**1:7** Rome was the capital of the Roman Empire that had spread over most of Europe, North Africa, and the Near East. In New Testament times, Rome was experiencing a golden age. The city was wealthy, literary, and artistic. It was a cultural center, but it was also morally decadent. The Romans worshiped many pagan gods, and even some of the emperors were worshiped. In stark contrast to the Romans, the followers of Christ believed in only one God and lived by his high moral standards.

Christianity was also at odds with the Romans' dependence on military strength. Many Romans were naively pragmatic, believing that any means to accomplish the intended task was good. And for them, nothing worked better than physical might. The Romans trusted in their strong military power to protect them against all enemies. Christians in every age need to be reminded that God is the only permanent source of our security and salvation, and at the same time he is "our Father"!

**1:8**
Rom 16:19
1 Thes 1:8

**1:9**
Eph 1:16
Phil 1:8-9
1 Thes 2:5
2 Tim 1:3

**1:10**
Rom 15:23, 32

**1:11**
Rom 15:23

**1:13**
John 15:16
Rom 15:22

## God's Good News

⁸Let me say first that I thank my God through Jesus Christ for all of you, because your faith in him is being talked about all over the world. ⁹God knows how often I pray for you. Day and night I bring you and your needs in prayer to God, whom I serve with all my heart* by spreading the Good News about his Son.

¹⁰One of the things I always pray for is the opportunity, God willing, to come at last to see you. ¹¹For I long to visit you so I can bring you some spiritual gift that will help you grow strong in the Lord. ¹²When we get together, I want to encourage you in your faith, but I also want to be encouraged by yours.

¹³I want you to know, dear brothers and sisters,* that I planned many times to visit you, but I was prevented until now. I want to work among you and see spiritual fruit, just as I have

**1:9** Or *in my spirit.*   **1:13** Greek *brothers.*

---

**THE GOSPEL GOES TO ROME**
When Paul wrote his letter to the church in Rome, he had not yet been there, but he had taken the gospel "from Jerusalem all the way to Illyricum" (15:19). He planned to visit and preach in Rome one day and hoped to continue to take the gospel farther west—even to Spain.

---

**1:8** Paul uses the phrase "I thank my God through Jesus Christ" to emphasize the point that Christ is the one and only mediator between us and God. Through Christ, God sends his love and forgiveness to us; through Christ, we send our thanks to God (see 1 Timothy 2:5).

**1:8** The Roman Christians, at the Western world's political power center, were highly visible. Fortunately, their reputation was excellent; their strong faith was making itself known around the world. When people talk about your congregation or your denomination, what do they say? Are their comments accurate? Would you rather they noticed other features? What is the best way to get the public to recognize your faith?

**1:9, 10** When you pray continually about a concern, don't be surprised at how God answers. Paul prayed to visit Rome so he could teach the Christians there. When he finally arrived in Rome, it was as a prisoner (see Acts 28:16). Paul prayed for a safe trip, and he did arrive safely—after getting arrested, slapped in the face, shipwrecked, and bitten by a poisonous snake. When we sincerely pray, God will answer—although in his timing and sometimes in ways we do not expect.

**1:11-13** A reading of the first few verses of Romans relates Paul's ardent desire to visit Rome and the sovereign hand of God

that had prevented him from getting there for quite some time. The combination of these two factors—Paul's impassioned desire to go to Rome and God's sovereign "no"—resulted in his sitting down to write this letter to the Romans. This letter is a powerful exposition of the Christian faith and has helped countless millions of believers across the centuries since Paul first penned it to the group of believers in Rome. Perhaps there are some "no's" in our lives that God is planning to use greatly if we would just faithfully do what lies directly ahead of us instead of worrying about why we didn't get our way.

**1:13** By the end of his third missionary journey, Paul had traveled through Syria, Galatia, Asia, Macedonia, and Achaia. The churches in these areas were made up mostly of Gentile believers.

seen among other Gentiles. ¹⁴For I have a great sense of obligation to people in both the civilized world and the rest of the world,* to the educated and uneducated alike. ¹⁵So I am eager to come to you in Rome, too, to preach the Good News.

¹⁶For I am not ashamed of this Good News about Christ. It is the power of God at work, saving everyone who believes—the Jew first and also the Gentile.* ¹⁷This Good News tells us how God makes us right in his sight. This is accomplished from start to finish by faith. As the Scriptures say, "It is through faith that a righteous person has life."*

### God's Anger at Sin

¹⁸But God shows his anger from heaven against all sinful, wicked people who suppress the truth by their wickedness.* ¹⁹They know the truth about God because he has made it obvious to them. ²⁰For ever since the world was created, people have seen the earth and sky. Through everything God made, they can clearly see his invisible qualities—his eternal power and divine nature. So they have no excuse for not knowing God.

**1:14** 1 Cor 9:16
**1:16** Acts 3:26; 1 Cor 1:18, 24
**1:17** †Hab 2:4; Rom 3:21-22; Gal 3:11; Heb 10:38
**1:18** Eph 5:6; Col 3:6
**1:20** Job 12:7-9; Ps 19:1

**1:14** Greek to Greeks and barbarians. **1:16** Greek also the Greek. **1:17** Or "The righteous will live by faith." Hab 2:4. **1:18** Or who, by their wickedness, prevent the truth from being known.

---

**1:14** What was Paul's obligation? After his experience with Christ on the road to Damascus (Acts 9), his whole life was consumed with spreading the Good News of salvation. His obligation was to people of the entire world. He met his obligation by proclaiming Christ's salvation to people—across all cultural, social, racial, and economic lines, both Jews and Gentiles. We also are obligated to Christ because he took the punishment we deserve for our sins. Although we cannot repay Christ for all he has done, we can demonstrate our gratitude by showing his love to others.

**1:15** Paul was eager to preach the gospel. Is our Christian service done in a spirit of eagerness? Or do we serve out of habit, a feeling of obligation, or perhaps even with a feeling of reluctant duty (much like a child who has to take a bath)? When we fully understand what Christ has done for us and what he offers to others, we will be motivated to share the Good News. Ask God to rekindle that fresh eager attitude that wants to obey him and to tell others about Christ.

**1:16** Paul was not ashamed because his message was the Good News about Christ. It was a message of salvation, it had life-changing power, and it was for everyone. When you are tempted to be ashamed, remember what the Good News is all about. If you focus on God and on what God is doing in the world rather than on your own inadequacy, you won't be ashamed or embarrassed.

**1:16** Why did the message go to the Jews first? They had been God's special people for more than 2,000 years, ever since God chose Abraham and promised great blessings to his descendants (Genesis 12:1-3). God did not choose the Jews because they deserved to be chosen (Deuteronomy 7:7, 8; 9:4-6) but because he wanted to show his love and mercy to them, for it would be through them that his Messiah would come into the world. God chose them, not to play favorites, but so that they would tell the world about his plan of salvation.

For centuries the Jews had been learning about God by obeying his laws, keeping his festivals, and living according to his moral principles. Often they would forget God's promises and laws; often they would have to be disciplined; but still they had a precious heritage of belief in the one true God. Of all the people on earth, the Jews should have been the most ready to welcome the Messiah and to understand his mission and message—and some of them did (see Luke 2:25, 36-38). Of course, the disciples and the great apostle Paul were faithful Jews who recognized in Jesus God's most precious gift to the human race.

**1:17** The Good News shows us both how righteous God is in his plan for us to be saved and also how we may be made fit for eternal life. By trusting Christ, our relationship with God is made right. "From start to finish," God declares us to be right with him because of faith and faith alone. Paul then quotes from Habakkuk 2:4 to show that as we trust God, we are saved; we have life both now and forever.

**1:18** Why is God angry at sinful people? Because they have substituted the truth about him with a lie (1:25). They have stifled the truth God naturally reveals to all people in order to believe anything that supports their own self-centered lifestyles. God cannot tolerate sin because his nature is morally perfect. He cannot ignore or condone willful rebellion. God wants to remove the sin and restore the sinner—and he is able to, as long as the sinner does not stubbornly distort or reject the truth. But God shows his anger against those who persist in sinning. Make sure you are not pursuing a lie rather than the true God. Don't suppress the truth about him merely to protect your own lifestyle.

**1:18ff** Romans 1:18–3:20 develops Paul's argument that no one can claim by his or her own efforts or merit to be good in God's sight—not the masses, not the Romans, not even the Jews. All people everywhere deserve God's condemnation for their sin.

**1:18-20** In these verses, Paul answers a common objection to belief in God: How could a loving God send anyone to hell, especially someone who has never heard about Christ? In fact, says Paul, God has revealed himself plainly in the creation to all people. And yet people reject even this basic knowledge of God. Also, all people have an inner sense of what God requires, but they choose not to live up to it. Put another way, people's moral standards are always better than their behavior. If people suppress God's truth in order to live their own way, they have no excuse. They know the truth, and they will have to endure the consequences of ignoring it.

**1:18-20** Some people wonder why we need missionaries if people can know about God through nature (the creation). The answer: (1) Although people know that God exists, their wickedness blinds them to the truth. Missionaries sensitively expose their sin and point them to Christ. (2) Although people may believe there is a God, they refuse to commit themselves to him. Missionaries help persuade them by sharing God's Word and by pointing out the dangerous consequences of their actions. (3) Missionaries help the church obey the great commission of our Lord (Matthew 28:19, 20). (4) Most important, although nature reveals God, people need to be told about Jesus and how, through him, they can have a personal relationship with God.

Knowing that God exists is not enough. People must learn that God is loving and that he sent his Son to demonstrate his love for us (5:8). They must be shown how to accept God's forgiveness of their sins. (See also 10:14, 15.)

**1:19** Does anyone have an excuse for not believing in God? The Bible answers an emphatic no. God has revealed what he is like in and through his creation. Every person, therefore, either accepts or rejects God. Don't be fooled. When the day comes for God to judge your response to him, no excuses will be accepted. Begin today to give your devotion and worship to him.

**1:20** What kind of God does nature reveal? Nature shows us a God of might, intelligence, and intricate detail; a God of order and beauty; a God who controls powerful forces. That is *general* revelation. Through *special* revelation (the Bible and the coming of

**1:21**
2 Kgs 17:15
Eph 4:17-18

**1:22**
Jer 10:14
1 Cor 1:20

**1:23**
Deut 4:15-19
Ps 106:20

**1:24**
Acts 14:16

**1:26**
1 Thes 4:5

²¹Yes, they knew God, but they wouldn't worship him as God or even give him thanks. And they began to think up foolish ideas of what God was like. As a result, their minds became dark and confused. ²²Claiming to be wise, they instead became utter fools. ²³And instead of worshiping the glorious, ever-living God, they worshiped idols made to look like mere people and birds and animals and reptiles.

²⁴So God abandoned them to do whatever shameful things their hearts desired. As a result, they did vile and degrading things with each other's bodies. ²⁵They traded the truth about God for a lie. So they worshiped and served the things God created instead of the Creator himself, who is worthy of eternal praise! Amen. ²⁶That is why God abandoned

---

**WHAT IS FAITH?**

*Faith* is a word with many meanings. It can mean faithfulness (Matthew 24:45). It can mean absolute trust, as shown by some of the people who came to Jesus for healing (Luke 7:2-10). It can mean confident hope (Hebrews 11:1). Or, as James points out, it can even mean a barren belief that does not result in good deeds (James 2:14-26). What does Paul mean when, in Romans, he speaks of "saving faith"?

We must be very careful to understand faith as Paul uses the word because he ties faith so closely to salvation. It is *not* something we must do in order to earn salvation—if that were true, then faith would be just one more deed, and Paul clearly states that human deeds can never save us (Galatians 2:16). Instead, faith is a gift God gives us *because* he is saving us (Ephesians 2:8). It is God's grace, not our faith, that saves us. In his mercy, however, when he saves us, he gives us faith—a relationship with his Son that helps us become like him. Through the faith he gives us, he carries us from death into life (John 5:24).

Even in Old Testament times, grace, not deeds, was the basis of salvation. As Hebrews points out, "it is not possible for the blood of bulls and goats to take away sins" (10:4). God intended for his people to look beyond the animal sacrifices to him, but all too often they instead put their confidence in fulfilling the requirements of the law—that is, performing the required sacrifices. When Jesus triumphed over death, he canceled the charges against us and opened the way to the Father (Colossians 2:12-15). Because he is merciful, he offers us faith. How tragic if we turn faith into a deed and try to develop it on our own! We can never come to God through our own faith any more than his Old Testament people could come through their own sacrifices. Instead, we must accept his gracious offer with thanksgiving and allow him to plant the seed of faith within us.

---

Jesus), we learn about God's love and forgiveness and the promise of eternal life. God has graciously given us many sources that we might come to believe in him.

**1:20** God reveals his divine nature and personal qualities through creation, even though creation's testimony has been distorted by the Fall. Adam's sin resulted in a divine curse upon the whole natural order (Genesis 3:17-19); thorns and thistles were an immediate result, and natural disasters have been common from Adam's day to ours. In Romans 8:19-21, Paul says that nature itself is eagerly awaiting its own redemption from the effects of sin (see Revelation 22:3).

**1:21-23** How could intelligent people turn to idolatry? Idolatry begins when people reject what they know about God. Instead of looking to him as the creator and sustainer of life, they see themselves as the center of the universe. They soon invent "gods" that are convenient projections of their own selfish ideas. These gods may be wooden figures, or they may also be goals or things we pursue, such as money, power, or possessions. They may even be misrepresentations of God himself—making God in our image, instead of the reverse. The common denominator is this: Idolaters worship the things God made rather than God himself. Is there anything you feel you can't live without? Is there any priority greater than God? Do you have a dream you would sacrifice everything to realize? Does God take first place in your life? Do you worship God or idols of your own making?

**1:21-32** Paul clearly portrays the inevitable downward spiral into sin. First, people reject God; next, they make up their own ideas of what a god should be and do; then they fall into every kind of wickedness: greed, hate, envy, murder, quarreling, deception, malicious behavior, and gossip. Finally, they grow to hate God and encourage others to do so. God does not cause this steady progression toward evil. Rather, when people reject him, he allows them to live as they choose. God gives them over to or

permits them to experience the natural consequences of their sin. Once caught in the downward spiral, no one can pull himself or herself out. Sinners must trust Christ alone to deliver them from destruction.

**1:23** When Paul says that people worshiped idols made to look like people or animals instead of worshiping God, he seems to deliberately state people's wickedness in the terms used in the Genesis narrative of Adam's fall (see Genesis 3:1-24). When people worship the creature instead of the Creator, they lose sight of their own identity as those who are higher than the animals—made in the image of God.

**1:24-32** These people chose to reject God, and God allowed them to do it. God does not usually stop us from making wrong choices. He lets us choose independence from him, even though he knows that in time we will become slaves to our own rebellious life-style and lose our freedom not to sin. Does life without God look like freedom to you? Look more closely. There is no worse slavery than slavery to sin.

**1:25** People tend to believe lies that reinforce their own selfish, personal beliefs. Today, more than ever, we need to know what the basis is for our beliefs. With TV, music, movies, and the rest of the media often presenting sinful lifestyles and unwholesome values, we find ourselves constantly bombarded by attitudes and beliefs that are totally opposed to the Bible. Be careful about what influences you use to form your opinions. The Bible is the only standard of truth. Evaluate all other opinions in light of its teachings.

**1:26, 27** God's plan for sexual relationships is his ideal for his creation. Unfortunately, sin distorts the natural use of God's gifts. Sin often means not only denying God but also denying the way we are made. When people say that any sex act is acceptable as long as nobody gets hurt, they are fooling themselves. In the long run (and often in the short run), sexual sin them to their shameful desires. Even the women turned against the natural way to have sex and instead indulged in sex with each other. <sup>27</sup>And the men, instead of having normal sexual relations with women, burned with lust for each other. Men did shameful things with other men, and as a result of this sin, they suffered within themselves the penalty they deserved.

1:27
Lev 18:22; 20:13
1 Cor 6:9

<sup>28</sup>Since they thought it foolish to acknowledge God, he abandoned them to their foolish thinking and let them do things that should never be done. <sup>29</sup>Their lives became full of every kind of wickedness, sin, greed, hate, envy, murder, quarreling, deception, malicious behavior, and gossip. <sup>30</sup>They are backstabbers, haters of God, insolent, proud, and boastful. They invent new ways of sinning, and they disobey their parents. <sup>31</sup>They refuse to understand, break their promises, are heartless, and have no mercy. <sup>32</sup>They know God's justice requires that those who do these things deserve to die, yet they do them anyway. Worse yet, they encourage others to do them, too.

1:30
2 Tim 3:2
1:31
2 Tim 3:3
1:32
Rom 6:23

## God's Judgment of Sin

**2** You may think you can condemn such people, but you are just as bad, and you have no excuse! When you say they are wicked and should be punished, you are condemning yourself, for you who judge others do these very same things. <sup>2</sup>And we know that God, in his justice, will punish anyone who does such things. <sup>3</sup>Since you judge others for doing these things, why do you think you can avoid God's judgment when you do the same things? <sup>4</sup>Don't you see how wonderfully kind, tolerant, and patient God is with you? Does this mean nothing to you? Can't you see that his kindness is intended to turn you from your sin?

<sup>5</sup>But because you are stubborn and refuse to turn from your sin, you are storing up terrible punishment for yourself. For a day of anger is coming, when God's righteous judgment will be revealed. <sup>6</sup>He will judge everyone according to what they have done. <sup>7</sup>He will give

2:1
Matt 7:1
2:4
Rom 9:22
2 Pet 3:9, 15
2:5
Ps 110:5
2:6
†Ps 62:12
Matt 16:27
2:7
Matt 25:46
2 Tim 4:14

---

hurts people—individuals, families, whole societies. Because sex is such a powerful and essential part of what it means to be human, it must be treated with great respect. Sexual desires are of such importance that the Bible gives them special attention and counsels more careful restraint and self-control than with any other desire. One of the clearest indicators of a society or person in rebellion against God is the rejection of God's guidelines for the use of sex.

**1:26, 27** Homosexuality (to turn against or abandon natural relations of sex) was as widespread in Paul's day as it is in ours. God is willing to receive anyone who comes to him in faith, and Christians should love and accept others no matter what their background. Yet, homosexuality is strictly forbidden in Scripture (Leviticus 18:22). Homosexuality is considered an acceptable practice by many in our world today—even by some churches. But society does not set the standard for God's law. Homosexuals believe that their desires are normal and that they have a right to express them. But God does not encourage us to fulfill all our desires (even normal ones). Those desires that violate his laws must be controlled.

If you have these desires, you can and must resist acting upon them. Consciously avoid places or activities you know will kindle temptations. Don't underestimate the power of Satan to tempt you, or the potential for serious harm if you continue to yield to these temptations. Remember, God can and will forgive sexual sins just as he forgives other sins. Surrender yourself to God, asking him to show you the way out of sin and into the light of his freedom and his love. Prayer, Bible study, and loving support of Christians in a Bible-believing church can help you to gain strength to resist these powerful temptations. If you are already deeply involved in homosexual behavior, seek help from a trustworthy, professional, Christian counselor.

**1:32** How were these people aware that God's justice would require death? All human beings are created in God's image; thus, we have a basic moral nature and a conscience. This truth is understood beyond religious circles. Psychologists, for example, say that the rare person who has no conscience has a serious personality disorder that is extremely difficult to treat. Most people instinctively know when they do wrong—but they may not care. Some people will even risk an early death for the

freedom to indulge their desires now. "I know it's wrong, but I really want it," they say; or "I know it's dangerous, but it's worth the risk." For such people, part of the "fun" is going against God's law, the community's moral standards, common sense, or their own sense of right and wrong. But deep down inside they know that sin deserves the punishment of death (6:23).

**2:1** Whenever we find ourselves feeling justifiably angry about someone's sin, we should be careful. We need to speak out against sin, but we must do so in a spirit of humility. Often the sins we notice most clearly in others are the ones that have taken root in us. If we look closely at ourselves, we may find that we are committing the same sins in more socially acceptable forms. For example, a person who gossips may be very critical of others who gossip about him or her.

**2:1ff** When Paul's letter was read in the Roman church, no doubt many heads nodded as he condemned idol worshipers, homosexual practices, and violent people. But what surprise his listeners must have felt when he turned on them and said in effect, "You are just as bad, and you have no excuse!" Paul was emphatically stressing that we have all sinned repeatedly, and there is no way apart from Christ to be saved from sin's consequences.

**2:4** In his kindness, God holds back his judgment, giving people time to turn from their sin. It is easy to mistake God's patience for approval of the wrong way we are living. Self-evaluation is difficult, and it is even more difficult to bring ourselves to God and let him tell us where we need to change. But as Christians we must ask God to point out our sins, so that he can heal them. Unfortunately, we are more likely to be amazed at God's patience with others than humbled at his patience with us.

**2:5-11** Although God does not usually punish us immediately for sin, his eventual judgment is certain. We don't know exactly when it will happen, but we know that no one will escape that final encounter with the Creator. For more on judgment, see John 12:48 and Revelation 20:11-15.

**2:7** Paul says that those who patiently and persistently *do* God's will find eternal life. He is not contradicting his previous statement that salvation comes by faith alone (1:16, 17). We are not saved by good deeds, but when we commit our life fully to God, eternal life to those who keep on doing good, seeking after the glory and honor and immortality that God offers. ⁸But he will pour out his anger and wrath on those who live for themselves, who refuse to obey the truth and instead live lives of wickedness. ⁹There will be trouble and calamity for everyone who keeps on doing what is evil—for the Jew first and also for the Gentile.* ¹⁰But there will be glory and honor and peace from God for all who do good—for the Jew first and also for the Gentile. ¹¹For God does not show favoritism.

¹²When the Gentiles sin, they will be destroyed, even though they never had God's written law. And the Jews, who do have God's law, will be judged by that law when they fail to obey it. ¹³For merely listening to the law doesn't make us right with God. It is obeying the law that makes us right in his sight. ¹⁴Even Gentiles, who do not have God's written law, show that they know his law when they instinctively obey it, even without having heard it. ¹⁵They demonstrate that God's law is written in their hearts, for their own conscience and thoughts either accuse them or tell them they are doing right. ¹⁶And this is the message I proclaim— that the day is coming when God, through Christ Jesus, will judge everyone's secret life.

### The Jews and the Law

¹⁷You who call yourselves Jews are relying on God's law, and you boast about your special relationship with him. ¹⁸You know what he wants; you know what is right because you have been taught his law. ¹⁹You are convinced that you are a guide for the blind and a light for people who are lost in darkness. ²⁰You think you can instruct the ignorant and teach children the ways of God. For you are certain that God's law gives you complete knowledge and truth.

²¹Well then, if you teach others, why don't you teach yourself? You tell others not to steal, but do you steal? ²²You say it is wrong to commit adultery, but do you commit adultery? You condemn idolatry, but do you use items stolen from pagan temples?* ²³You are so proud of knowing the law, but you dishonor God by breaking it. ²⁴No wonder the Scriptures say, "The Gentiles blaspheme the name of God because of you."*

**2:8**
2 Thes 2:12

**2:11**
Gal 2:6
Eph 6:9
Col 3:25

**2:13**
Matt 7:21
John 13:17
Jas 1:22-25

**2:14**
Acts 10:35

**2:16**
Acts 10:42
Rom 16:25
2 Tim 2:8

**2:17**
Mic 3:11

**2:20**
2 Tim 3:5

**2:21**
Matt 23:3-4

**2:24**
†Isa 52:5
Ezek 36:20

2:9 Greek *also for the Greek;* also in 2:10.   2:22 Greek *do you steal from temples?*   2:24 Isa 52:5 (Greek version).

---

**SALVATION'S FREEWAY**
Verses in Romans that describe the way to salvation.

Romans 3:23 . . . . . . . Everyone has sinned.

Romans 6:23 . . . . . . . The penalty for our sin is death.

Romans 5:8 . . . . . . . . Jesus Christ died for sin.

Romans 10:8-10. . . . . To be forgiven for our sin, we must believe and confess that Jesus is Lord. Salvation comes through Jesus Christ.

---

we want to please him and do his will. As such, our good deeds are a grateful *response* to what God has done, not a prerequisite to earning his favor.

**2:12-15** People are condemned not for what they don't know but for what they do with what they know. Those who know God's written Word and his law will be judged by them. Those who have never seen a Bible still know right from wrong, and they will be judged because they violated those standards that their own consciences dictated. God's law is written within them.

**2:12-15** If you traveled around the world, you would find evidence in every society and culture of God's moral law. For example, all cultures prohibit murder, and yet in all societies that law has been broken. We belong to a stubborn, sinful race. We know what is right, but we insist on doing what is wrong. It is not enough to know what is right; we must also do it. Admit to yourself and to God that you frequently fail to live up to your own standards (much less to God's standards). That's the first step to forgiveness and healing.

**2:17ff** Paul continues to argue that all stand guilty before God. After describing the fate of the unbelieving, pagan Gentiles, he moves to admonish God's people. Despite their knowledge of God's will, they were guilty because they, too, refuse to live by it. Those of us who have grown up in Christian families may know what God's Word says. But Paul says that if we do not live up to what we know, we are no better off than unbelievers.

**2:21, 22** Paul explained to the Jews that they needed to teach *themselves*, not others, by their law. They knew the law so well that they had learned how to excuse their own actions while criticizing others. But the law is more than a set of rules—it is a guideline for living according to God's will. It is also a reminder that we cannot please God without a proper relationship to him. As Jesus pointed out, withholding what rightfully belongs to someone else is stealing (Mark 7:9-13), and anyone who even looks at a woman with lust in his eye has committed adultery with her in his heart (Matthew 5:27, 28). Before we accuse others, we must look at ourselves and see if sin, in any form, exists within us.

**2:21-27** These verses are a scathing criticism of hypocrisy. It is much easier to tell others how to behave than to behave properly ourselves. It is easier to say the right words than to allow them to take root in our own life. Do you ever advise others to do something you are unwilling to do yourself? Make sure that your actions match your words.

**2:24** If you claim to be one of God's people, your life should reflect what God is like. When you disobey God, you dishonor his name. People may even blaspheme or profane God's name because of you. What do people think about God as they watch your life?

25 The Jewish ceremony of circumcision has value only if you obey God's law. But if you don't obey God's law, you are no better off than an uncircumcised Gentile. 26 And if the Gentiles obey God's law, won't God declare them to be his own people? 27 In fact, uncircumcised Gentiles who keep God's law will condemn you Jews who are circumcised and possess God's law but don't obey it.

28 For you are not a true Jew just because you were born of Jewish parents or because you have gone through the ceremony of circumcision. 29 No, a true Jew is one whose heart is right with God. And true circumcision is not merely obeying the letter of the law; rather, it is a change of heart produced by God's Spirit. And a person with a changed heart seeks praise* from God, not from people.

**2:25**
Gal 5:3
**2:28**
Matt 3:9
John 8:39
Gal 6:15
**2:29**
Deut 30:6
John 5:44
Rom 7:6
2 Cor 3:6; 10:18
Phil 3:3
Col 2:11
1 Pet 3:4

## God Remains Faithful

**3** Then what's the advantage of being a Jew? Is there any value in the ceremony of circumcision? 2 Yes, there are great benefits! First of all, the Jews were entrusted with the whole revelation of God.*

3 True, some of them were unfaithful; but just because they were unfaithful, does that mean God will be unfaithful? 4 Of course not! Even if everyone else is a liar, God is true. As the Scriptures say about him,

**3:2**
Deut 4:7-8
Ps 147:19-20
Acts 7:38
**3:4**
†Ps 51:4

"You will be proved right in what you say,
   and you will win your case in court."*

5 "But," some might say, "our sinfulness serves a good purpose, for it helps people see how righteous God is. Isn't it unfair, then, for him to punish us?" (This is merely a human point of view.) 6 Of course not! If God were not entirely fair, how would he be qualified to judge the world? 7 "But," someone might still argue, "how can God condemn me as a sinner if my dishonesty highlights his truthfulness and brings him more glory?" 8 And some people even slander us by claiming that we say, "The more we sin, the better it is!" Those who say such things deserve to be condemned.

**3:5**
Rom 5:8
**3:7**
Rom 9:19
**3:8**
Rom 6:1

## All People Are Sinners

9 Well then, should we conclude that we Jews are better than others? No, not at all, for we have already shown that all people, whether Jews or Gentiles,* are under the power of sin. 10 As the Scriptures say,

**3:9**
Rom 1:18–2:24
**3:10-12**
†Pss 14:1-3; 53:1-3

**2:29** Or *receives praise.* **3:2** Greek *the oracles of God.* **3:4** Ps 51:4 (Greek version). **3:9** Greek *or Greeks.*

---

**2:25-29** *Circumcision* refers to the sign of God's special covenant with his people. All Jewish males were required to submit to this rite (Genesis 17:9-14). According to Paul, being a circumcised Jew meant nothing if the person didn't obey God's laws. On the other hand, the uncircumcised Gentiles would receive God's love and approval if they kept God's law. Paul goes on to explain that a true Jew (one who pleases God) is not someone who has been circumcised but someone whose heart is right with God and obeys him.

**2:28, 29** To be a Jew meant you were in God's family, an heir to all his promises. Yet Paul made it clear that membership in God's family is based on internal, not external, qualities. All whose hearts are right with God are true Jews—that is, part of God's family (see also Galatians 3:7). Attending church or being baptized, confirmed, or accepted for membership is not enough, just as submitting to circumcision was not enough for the Jews. God desires our heartfelt devotion and obedience (see also Deuteronomy 10:16; Jeremiah 4:4).

**3:1ff** In this chapter Paul contends that everyone stands guilty before God. Paul has dismantled the common excuses of people who refuse to admit they are sinners: (1) "There is no God" or "I follow my conscience" (1:18-32); (2) "I'm not as bad as other people" (2:1-16); (3) "I'm a church member" or "I'm a religious person" (2:17-29). No one will be exempt from God's judgment of sin. Every person must accept the fact that he or she is sinful and condemned before God and receive God's wonderful gift of salvation.

**3:1ff** What a depressing picture Paul is painting! All of us—pagan Gentiles, humanitarians, and religious people—are

condemned by our own actions. The law, which God gave to show the way to live, holds up our evil deeds to public view. Is there any hope for us? Yes, says Paul. The law condemns us, it is true, but the law is not the basis of our hope. God himself is. He, in his righteousness and wonderful love, offers us eternal life. We receive our salvation not through law but through faith in Jesus Christ. We do not—cannot—earn it; we accept it as a gift from our loving heavenly Father.

**3:2** The Jewish nation had great benefits. (1) They were entrusted with God's laws ("the whole revelation of God," Exodus 19–20; Deuteronomy 4:8). (2) They were the race through whom the Messiah came to earth (Isaiah 11:1-10; Matthew 1:1-17). (3) They were the beneficiaries of covenants with God himself (Genesis 17:1-16; Exodus 19:3-6). But these privileges did not make them better than anyone else (see 3:9). In fact, because of them the Jews were even more responsible to live up to God's requirements.

**3:5-8** Some may think they don't have to worry about sin because (1) it's God's job to forgive; (2) God is so loving that he won't judge; (3) sin isn't so bad—it teaches valuable lessons; or (4) we need to stay in touch with the culture around us. It is far too easy to take God's grace for granted. But God cannot overlook sin. No matter how many excuses they make, sinners will have to answer to God for their sin.

**3:10-12** Paul is referring to Psalm 14:1-3. "No one is righteous" means "no one is innocent." Every person is valuable in God's eyes because God created us in his image, and he loves us. But no one is good enough (that is, no one can earn right standing with God). Though we are valuable, we have fallen into sin. But

"No one is righteous—
not even one.
11 No one is truly wise;
no one is seeking God.
12 All have turned away;
all have become useless.
No one does good,
not a single one."*

**3:13**
†Pss 5:9; 140:3

13 "Their talk is foul, like the stench from an open grave.
Their tongues are filled with lies."
"Snake venom drips from their lips."*

**3:14**
†Ps 10:7

14     "Their mouths are full of cursing and bitterness."*

**3:15-17**
†Isa 59:7-8

15 "They rush to commit murder.
16     Destruction and misery always follow them.

**3:18**
†Ps 36:1

17 They don't know where to find peace."*
18     "They have no fear of God at all."*

**3:19**
Rom 2:12

19Obviously, the law applies to those to whom it was given, for its purpose is to keep people from having excuses, and to show that the entire world is guilty before God. 20For no one can ever be made right with God by doing what the law commands. The law simply shows us how sinful we are.

**3:20**
Ps 143:2
Rom 4:15; 7:7
Gal 2:16; 3:11

## 2. Forgiveness of sin through Christ
*Christ Took Our Punishment*

**3:21**
Rom 1:2, 17; 9:30

21But now God has shown us a way to be made right with him without keeping the requirements of the law, as was promised in the writings of Moses* and the prophets long ago. 22We are made right with God by placing our faith in Jesus Christ. And this is true for everyone who believes, no matter who we are.

**3:22**
Rom 4:11; 10:4, 12
Gal 2:16
Col 3:11

**3:10-12** Pss 14:1-3; 53:1-3 (Greek version).   **3:13** Pss 5:9 (Greek version); 140:3.   **3:14** Ps 10:7 (Greek version).
**3:15-17** Isa 59:7-8.   **3:18** Ps 36:1.   **3:21** Greek *in the law.*

**CRUCIAL CONCEPTS IN ROMANS**

| | |
|---|---|
| ELECTION. . . . . . . . . . . . . . . Romans 9:10-13 | God's choice of an individual or group for a specific purpose or destiny. |
| JUSTIFICATION. . . . . . . . . . Romans 4:25; 5:18 | God's act of declaring us "not guilty" for our sins, making us "right" with him. |
| PROPITIATION . . . . . . . . . . Romans 3:25 | The removal of God's punishment for sin through the perfect sacrifice of Jesus Christ. |
| REDEMPTION. . . . . . . . . . . Romans 3:24; 8:23 | Jesus Christ has paid the price so we can go free. The price of sin is death; Jesus paid the price. |
| SANCTIFICATION . . . . . . . . Romans 5:2; 15:16 | Becoming more and more like Jesus Christ through the work of the Holy Spirit. |
| GLORIFICATION . . . . . . . . . Romans 8:18, 19, 30 | The ultimate state of the believer after death when he or she becomes like Christ (1 John 3:2). |

God, through Jesus his Son, has redeemed us and offers to forgive us if we turn to him in faith.

**3:10-18** Paul uses these Old Testament references to show that humanity in general, in its present sinful condition, is unacceptable before God. Have you ever thought to yourself, "Well, I'm not too bad. I'm a pretty good person"? Look at these verses and see if any of them apply to you. Have you ever lied? Have you ever hurt someone's feelings by your words or tone of voice? Are you bitter toward anyone? Do you become angry with those who strongly disagree with you? In thought, word, and deed, you, like everyone else in the world, stand guilty before God. We must remember who we are in his sight—alienated sinners. Don't deny that you are a sinner. Instead, allow your desperate need to point you toward Christ.

**3:19** The last time someone accused you of wrongdoing, what was your reaction? Denial, argument, and defensiveness? The entire world will be silent before God. No excuses or arguments will remain. Have you reached the point with God where you are

ready to hang up your defenses and await his decision? If you haven't, stop now and admit your sin to him. If you have, the following verses are truly good news for you!

**3:20, 31** In these verses we see two functions of God's law. First, it shows us where we go wrong. Because of the law, we know that we are helpless sinners and that we must come to Jesus Christ for mercy. Second, the moral code revealed in the law can serve to guide our actions by holding up God's moral standards. We do not earn salvation by keeping the law (no one except Christ ever kept or could keep God's law perfectly), but we do please God when our life conforms to his revealed will for us.

**3:21-29** After all this bad news about our sinfulness and God's condemnation, Paul gives the wonderful news. There is a way to be declared not guilty—by trusting Jesus Christ to take away our sins. Trusting means putting our confidence in Christ to forgive our sins, to make us right with God, and to empower us to live the way he taught us. God's solution is available to all of us regardless of our background or past behavior.

23For everyone has sinned; we all fall short of God's glorious standard. 24Yet God, with un-deserved kindness, declares that we are righteous. He did this through Christ Jesus when he freed us from the penalty for our sins. 25For God presented Jesus as the sacrifice for sin. Peo-ple are made right with God when they believe that Jesus sacrificed his life, shedding his blood. This sacrifice shows that God was being fair when he held back and did not punish those who sinned in times past, 26for he was looking ahead and including them in what he would do in this present time. God did this to demonstrate his righteousness, for he himself is fair and just, and he declares sinners to be right in his sight when they believe in Jesus.

27Can we boast, then, that we have done anything to be accepted by God? No, because our acquittal is not based on obeying the law. It is based on faith. 28So we are made right with God through faith and not by obeying the law.

29After all, is God the God of the Jews only? Isn't he also the God of the Gentiles? Of course he is. 30There is only one God, and he makes people right with himself only by faith, whether they are Jews or Gentiles.* 31Well then, if we emphasize faith, does this mean that we can forget about the law? Of course not! In fact, only when we have faith do we truly fulfill the law.

### The Faith of Abraham

4 Abraham was, humanly speaking, the founder of our Jewish nation. What did he discover about being made right with God? 2If his good deeds had made him acceptable to God, he would have had something to boast about. But that was not God's way. 3For the Scriptures tell us, "Abraham believed God, and God counted him as righteous because of his faith."*

4When people work, their wages are not a gift, but something they have earned. 5But people are counted as righteous, not because of their work, but because of their faith in God

3:30 Greek *whether they are circumcised or uncircumcised.*   4:3 Gen 15:6.

**3:24**
Eph 2:8
Heb 9:12

**3:25**
Lev 16:10
Heb 9:12-14
1 Pet 1:19
1 Jn 4:10

**3:27**
Rom 2:17; 4:2
1 Cor 1:29-31

**3:28**
Acts 13:39

**3:29**
Rom 10:12
Gal 3:28

**3:31**
Matt 5:17

**4:2**
1 Cor 1:31

**4:3**
†Gen 15:6
Gal 3:6
Jas 2:23

**4:4**
Rom 11:6
Gal 2:16

---

**3:23** Some sins seem bigger than others because their obvious consequences are much more serious. Murder, for example, seems to us to be worse than hatred, and adultery seems worse than pride. But this does not mean that because we only commit "little" sins we deserve eternal life. All sins make us sinners, and all sins cut us off from our holy God. All sins, therefore, lead to death (because they disqualify us from living with God), regard-less of how great or small they seem. Don't minimize "little" sins or overrate "big" sins. They all separate us from God, but they all can be forgiven.

**3:24** Paul explains that God declares that we are righteous. When a judge in a court of law declares the defendant not guilty, all the charges are removed from his record. Legally, it is as if the person had never been accused. When God forgives our sins, our record is wiped clean. From his perspective, it is as though we had never sinned. He could do this because Jesus took the penalty that we deserved. Christ purchased our freedom from sin, and the price was his life.

**3:25** Christ died in our place, for our sins. God is justifiably angry at sinners. They have rebelled against him and cut them-selves off from his life-giving power. But God declares Christ's death to be the appropriate, designated sacrifice for our sin. Christ then stands in our place, having paid the penalty of death for our sin, and he completely satisfies God's demands. His sacrifice brings pardon, deliverance, and freedom.

**3:25, 26** What happened to people who lived before Christ came and died for sin? If God condemned sinners, was he being unfair? If he saved the righteous, was Christ's sacrifice unnecessary? Paul shows that God forgave all human sin at the cross of Jesus. Old Testament believers looked forward in faith to Christ's coming and were saved, even though they did not know Jesus' name or the details of his earthly life. Unlike the Old Testament believers, you know about the God who loved the world so much that he gave his own Son (John 3:16). Have you put your trust in him?

**3:27, 28** Most religions require specific duties that must be performed to make a person acceptable to a god. Christianity is unique in that no good deed that we do will make us right with God. No amount of human achievement or personal goodness

will close the gap between God's moral perfection and our imperfect daily performance. Good deeds are important, but they will not earn us eternal life. We are saved only by trusting in what God has done for us (see Ephesians 2:8-10).

**3:28** Why does God save us by faith alone? (1) Faith eliminates the pride of human effort, because faith is not a deed that we do. (2) Faith exalts what God has done, not what we do. (3) Faith admits that we can't keep the law or measure up to God's stan-dards—we need help. (4) Faith is based on our relationship with God, not our performance for God.

**3:31** There were some misunderstandings between the Jewish and Gentile Christians in Rome. Worried Jewish Christians were asking Paul, "Does faith wipe out everything Judaism stands for? Does it cancel our Scriptures, put an end to our customs, declare that God is no longer working through us?" (This is essentially the question used to open chapter 3.) "Of course not!" says Paul. When we understand the way of salvation through faith, we understand the Jewish religion better. We know why Abraham was chosen, why the law was given, and why God worked patiently with Israel for centuries. Faith does not wipe out the Old Testament. Rather, it makes God's dealings with the Jewish people understandable. In chapter 4, Paul will expand on this theme (see also 5:20, 21; 8:3, 4; 13:9, 10; Galatians 3:24-29; and 1 Timothy 1:8 for more on this concept).

**4:1-3** The Jews were proud to be descendants of Abraham. Paul uses Abraham as a good example of someone who was saved by faith. By emphasizing faith, Paul is not saying that God's law is unimportant (4:13) but that it is impossible to be saved simply by obeying it. For more about Abraham, see his Profile in Genesis 18, p. 33.

**4:5** When some people learn that they are saved by God through faith, they start to worry. "Do I have enough faith?" they wonder. "Is my faith strong enough to save me?" These people miss the point. It is Jesus Christ who saves us, not *our* feelings or actions, and he is strong enough to save us no matter how weak our faith is. Jesus offers us salvation as a gift because he loves us, not because we have earned it through our powerful faith. What, then, is the role of faith? Faith is believing and trusting in Jesus Christ and reaching out to accept his wonderful gift of salvation.

who forgives sinners. 6David also spoke of this when he described the happiness of those who are declared righteous without working for it:

**4:7-8**
†Ps 32:1-2
2 Cor 5:19

7 "Oh, what joy for those
   whose disobedience is forgiven,
   whose sins are put out of sight.
8 Yes, what joy for those
   whose record the LORD has cleared of sin."*

**4:9**
Gen 15:6
Rom 3:30

9Now, is this blessing only for the Jews, or is it also for uncircumcised Gentiles?* Well, we have been saying that Abraham was counted as righteous by God because of his faith. 10But how did this happen? Was he counted as righteous only after he was circumcised, or was it before he was circumcised? Clearly, God accepted Abraham before he was circumcised!

**4:11**
Gen 17:10-11

11Circumcision was a sign that Abraham already had faith and that God had already accepted him and declared him to be righteous—even before he was circumcised. So Abraham is the spiritual father of those who have faith but have not been circumcised. They are counted as righteous because of their faith. 12And Abraham is also the spiritual father of those who have been circumcised, but only if they have the same kind of faith Abraham had before he was circumcised.

**4:13**
Gen 18:18;
22:17-18
Gal 3:29

13Clearly, God's promise to give the whole earth to Abraham and his descendants was based not on his obedience to God's law, but on a right relationship with God that comes by faith. 14If God's promise is only for those who obey the law, then faith is not necessary and the promise is pointless. 15For the law always brings punishment on those who try to obey it. (The only way to avoid breaking the law is to have no law to break!)

**4:14**
Gal 3:18

**4:15**
Rom 3:20; 7:12
1 Cor 15:55-56
Gal 3:10

16So the promise is received by faith. It is given as a free gift. And we are all certain to receive it, whether or not we live according to the law of Moses, if we have faith like Abraham's. For Abraham is the father of all who believe. 17That is what the Scriptures mean when God told him, "I have made you the father of many nations."* This happened because Abraham believed in the God who brings the dead back to life and who creates new things out of nothing.

**4:16**
Gal 3:7

**4:17**
†Gen 17:5
Isa 48:13
John 5:21
1 Cor 1:28

18Even when there was no reason for hope, Abraham kept hoping—believing that he would become the father of many nations. For God had said to him, "That's how many descendants you will have!"* 19And Abraham's faith did not weaken, even though, at about 100 years of age, he figured his body was as good as dead—and so was Sarah's womb.

**4:18**
†Gen 15:5

**4:19**
Gen 17:17; 18:11
Heb 11:11

20Abraham never wavered in believing God's promise. In fact, his faith grew stronger,

**4:7-8** Ps 32:1-2 (Greek version).   **4:9** Greek *is this blessing only for the circumcised, or is it also for the uncircumcised?*   **4:17** Gen 17:5.   **4:18** Gen 15:5.

---

**4:6-8** What can we do to get rid of guilt? King David was guilty of terrible sins—adultery, murder, lying—and yet he experienced the joy of forgiveness. We, too, can have this joy when we (1) quit denying our guilt and recognize that we have sinned, (2) admit our guilt to God and ask for his forgiveness, and (3) let go of our guilt and believe that God has forgiven us. This can be difficult when a sin has taken root in our life over many years, when it is very serious, or when it involves others. We must remember that Jesus is willing and able to forgive every sin. In view of the tremendous price he paid on the cross, it is arrogant to think that there is any sin too great for him to forgive. Even though our faith is weak, our conscience is sensitive, and our memory haunts us, God's Word declares that sins confessed are sins forgiven (1 John 1:9).

**4:10-12** Circumcision was a sign to others and a personal seal or certification for the Jews that they were God's special people. Circumcision of all Jewish boys set apart the Jewish people from the nations that worshiped other gods; thus, it was a very important ceremony. God gave the blessing and the command for this ceremony to Abraham (Genesis 17:9-14).

Paul's point here is that the ritual of circumcision did not earn Abraham his acceptance by God; he had been blessed long before the circumcision ceremony was introduced. Abraham found favor with God by faith alone, before he was circumcised. Genesis 12:1-3 tells of God's call to Abraham when he was 75 years old; the circumcision ceremony was introduced when

he was 99 (Genesis 17:1-14). Ceremonies and rituals serve as reminders of our faith as well as instruct new or young believers, but we should not think that they give us any special merit before God. They are outward signs and seals that demonstrate inner belief and trust. The focus of our faith should be on Christ and his saving work, not on our own actions.

**4:16** Paul explains that Abraham had pleased God through faith alone before he had ever heard about the rituals that would become so important to the Jewish people. We, too, are saved by faith plus nothing. It is not by loving God and doing good that we are saved; neither is it by faith plus love or by faith plus good deeds. We are saved only through faith in Christ, trusting him to forgive all our sins. For more on Abraham, see his Profile in Genesis 18, p. 33.

**4:17** The promise (or covenant) God gave Abraham stated that Abraham would be the father of many nations (Genesis 17:2-4) and that the entire world would be blessed through him (Genesis 12:3). This promise was fulfilled in Jesus Christ. Jesus was from Abraham's line, and truly the whole world was blessed through him.

and in this he brought glory to God. [21]He was fully convinced that God is able to do whatever he promises. [22]And because of Abraham's faith, God counted him as righteous. [23]And when God counted him as righteous, it wasn't just for Abraham's benefit. It was recorded [24]for our benefit, too, assuring us that God will also count us as righteous if we believe in him, the one who raised Jesus our Lord from the dead. [25]He was handed over to die because of our sins, and he was raised to life to make us right with God.

### Faith Brings Joy

**5** Therefore, since we have been made right in God's sight by faith, we have peace with God because of what Jesus Christ our Lord has done for us. [2]Because of our faith, Christ has brought us into this place of undeserved privilege where we now stand, and we confidently and joyfully look forward to sharing God's glory.

[3]We can rejoice, too, when we run into problems and trials, for we know that they help us develop endurance. [4]And endurance develops strength of character, and character strengthens our confident hope of salvation. [5]And this hope will not lead to disappointment. For we know how dearly God loves us, because he has given us the Holy Spirit to fill our hearts with his love.

[6]When we were utterly helpless, Christ came at just the right time and died for us sinners. [7]Now, most people would not be willing to die for an upright person, though someone might perhaps be willing to die for a person who is especially good. [8]But God showed his great love for us by sending Christ to die for us while we were still sinners. [9]And since we have been made right in God's sight by the blood of Christ, he will certainly save us from God's condemnation. [10]For since our friendship with God was restored by the death of his Son while we were still his enemies, we will certainly be saved through the life of his Son. [11]So now we can rejoice in our wonderful new relationship with God because our Lord Jesus Christ has made us friends of God.

**4:22**
[†]Gen 15:6
Rom 4:3

**4:24**
1 Pet 1:21

**4:25**
Isa 53:4-5
Rom 8:30
1 Cor 15:17
2 Cor 5:15
1 Pet 1:21

**5:1**
Rom 3:28

**5:2**
Eph 2:18; 3:12

**5:3**
Matt 5:12

**5:5**
2 Cor 1:22
Gal 4:6
Eph 1:13
Phil 1:20

**5:6**
Gal 4:4
Eph 5:2

**5:8**
John 3:16
1 Jn 4:10

**5:9**
Rom 1:18; 2:5, 8

**5:10**
Rom 8:34
2 Cor 5:18-19
Eph 2:3

---

**4:21** Abraham never doubted that God would fulfill his promise. Abraham's life was marked by mistakes, sins, and failures as well as by wisdom and goodness, but he consistently trusted God. His faith was strengthened by the obstacles he faced, and his life was an example of faith in action. If he had looked only at his own resources for subduing Canaan and founding a nation, he would have given up in despair. But Abraham looked to God, obeyed him, and waited for God to fulfill his word.

**4:25** When we accept Jesus Christ as our Savior, an exchange takes place. We give him our sins, and he forgives us and makes us right with God (see 2 Corinthians 5:21). There is nothing we can do to earn this. Only through Christ can we be made right in God's eyes. What an incredible bargain this is for us! But sadly, many still choose to pass up this gift to continue "enjoying" their sin.

**5:1** We are now at peace *with God*, which may differ from peaceful feelings such as calmness and tranquility. Peace with God means that we have been reconciled with him. There is no more hostility between us, no sin blocking our relationship with him. Peace with God is possible only because Jesus paid the price for our sins through his death on the cross.

**5:1-5** These verses introduce a section that contains some difficult concepts. To understand the next four chapters, it helps to keep in mind the two-sided reality of the Christian life. On the one hand, we are complete in Christ (our acceptance with him is secure). On the other hand, we are growing in Christ (we are becoming more and more like him). At one and the same time we have the status of kings and the duties of slaves. We feel both the presence of Christ and the pressure of sin. We enjoy the peace that comes from being made right with God, but we still face daily problems that often help us grow. If we remember these two sides of the Christian life, we will not grow discouraged as we face temptations and problems. Instead, we will learn to depend on the power available to us from Christ, who lives in us by the Holy Spirit.

**5:2** Paul states that, as believers, we now have entered into a place of undeserved privilege. Not only has God declared us not guilty; he has drawn us close to himself. Instead of being enemies, we have become his friends—in fact, his own children (John 15:15; Galatians 4:5).

**5:3, 4** For first-century Christians, suffering was the rule rather than the exception. Paul tells us that in the future we will *become*, but until then we must *overcome*. This means we will experience difficulties that help us grow. We rejoice in suffering, not because we like pain or deny its tragedy, but because we know God is using life's difficulties and Satan's attacks to build our character. The problems that we run into will develop our perseverance—which in turn will strengthen our character, deepen our trust in God, and give us greater confidence about the future. You probably find your patience tested in some way every day. Thank God for those opportunities to grow, and deal with them in his strength (see also James 1:2-4; 1 Peter 1:6, 7).

**5:5, 6** All three members of the Trinity are involved in salvation. The Father loved us so much that he sent his Son to bridge the gap between us (John 3:16). The Father and the Son send the Holy Spirit to fill our life with love and to enable us to live by his power (Acts 1:8). With all this loving care, how can we do less than serve him completely!

**5:6** We were weak and helpless because we could do nothing on our own to save ourselves. Someone had to come and rescue us. Christ came at exactly the right time in history—according to God's own schedule. God controls all history, and he controlled the timing, method, and events surrounding Jesus' death.

**5:8** *While we were still sinners*—these are amazing words. God sent Jesus Christ to die for us, not because we were good enough, but just because he loved us. Whenever you feel uncertain about God's love for you, remember that he loved you even before you turned to him.

**5:9, 10** The love that caused Christ to die is the same love that sends the Holy Spirit to live in us and guide us every day. The power that raised Christ from the dead is the same power that saved you and is available to you in your daily life. Be assured that, having begun a life with Christ, you have a reserve of power and love to call on each day for help to meet every challenge or trial. You can pray for God's power and love as you need it.

**5:11** God is holy, and he will not be associated with sin. All people are sinful and so they are separated from God. In addition,

### Adam and Christ Contrasted

**5:12**
Gen 2:17; 3:19
1 Cor 15:21-22

**5:13**
Rom 4:15

**5:14**
1 Cor 15:22, 45

¹²When Adam sinned, sin entered the world. Adam's sin brought death, so death spread to everyone, for everyone sinned. ¹³Yes, people sinned even before the law was given. But it was not counted as sin because there was not yet any law to break. ¹⁴Still, everyone died—from the time of Adam to the time of Moses—even those who did not disobey an explicit commandment of God, as Adam did. Now Adam is a symbol, a representation of Christ, who was yet to come. ¹⁵But there is a great difference between Adam's sin and God's gracious gift. For the sin of this one man, Adam, brought death to many. But even greater is God's wonderful grace and his gift of forgiveness to many through this other man, Jesus Christ. ¹⁶And the result of God's gracious gift is very different from the result of that one man's sin. For Adam's sin led to condemnation, but God's free gift leads to our being made right with God, even though we are guilty of many sins.

**5:17**
1 Cor 15:21

¹⁷For the sin of this one man, Adam, caused death to rule over many. But even greater is God's wonderful grace and his gift of righteousness, for all who receive it will live in triumph over sin and death through this one man, Jesus Christ.

**5:18**
Isa 53:11
1 Cor 15:22

**5:19**
Phil 2:8

¹⁸Yes, Adam's one sin brings condemnation for everyone, but Christ's one act of righteousness brings a right relationship with God and new life for everyone. ¹⁹Because one person disobeyed God, many became sinners. But because one other person obeyed God, many will be made righteous.

**5:20**
Rom 4:15; 7:8
Gal 3:19

**5:21**
Rom 6:23

²⁰God's law was given so that all people could see how sinful they were. But as people sinned more and more, God's wonderful grace became more abundant. ²¹So just as sin ruled over all people and brought them to death, now God's wonderful grace rules instead, giving us right standing with God and resulting in eternal life through Jesus Christ our Lord.

---

**WHAT WE HAVE AS GOD'S CHILDREN**

| What we have as Adam's children | What we have as God's children |
| --- | --- |
| Ruin 5:9 | Rescue 5:8 |
| Sin 5:12, 15, 21 | Righteousness 5:18 |
| Death 5:12, 16, 21 | Eternal life 5:17, 21 |
| Separation from God 5:18 | Relationship with God 5:11, 19 |
| Disobedience 5:12, 19 | Obedience 5:19 |
| Judgment 5:18 | Deliverance 5:10, 11 |
| Law 5:20 | Grace 5:20 |

---

all sin deserves punishment. Instead of punishing us with the death we deserve, however, Christ took our sins upon himself and took our punishment by dying on the cross. Now we can rejoice in God. Through faith in *Christ's* work, we become close to God (friends) rather than being enemies and outcasts.

**5:12** How can we be declared guilty for something Adam did thousands of years ago? Many feel it isn't fair for God to judge us because of Adam's sin. Yet each of us confirms our heritage with Adam by our own sins every day. We have the same sinful nature and are prone to rebel against God, and we are judged for the sins *we* commit. Because we are sinners, it isn't fairness we need—it is mercy.

**5:13, 14** Paul has shown that keeping the law does not bring salvation. Here he adds that breaking the law is not what brings death. Death is the result of Adam's sin and of the sins we all commit, even if they don't resemble Adam's. Paul reminds his readers that for thousands of years the law had not yet been explicitly given, and yet people died. The law was added, he explains in 5:20, to help people see their sinfulness, to show them the seriousness of their offenses, and to drive them to God for mercy and pardon. This was true in Moses' day, and it is still true today. Sin is a deep discrepancy between who we are and who we were created to be. The law points out our sin and places the responsibility for it squarely on our shoulders. But the law offers no remedy. When we are convicted of sin, we must turn to Jesus Christ for healing.

**5:14** Adam was the counterpart of Christ. Just as Adam was a representative of created humanity, so is Christ the representative of a new spiritual humanity.

**5:15-19** We were all born into Adam's physical family—the family line that leads to certain death. All of us have reaped the results of Adam's sin. We have inherited his guilt, a sinful nature (the tendency to sin), and God's punishment. Because of Jesus, however, we can trade judgment for forgiveness. Christ offers us the opportunity to be born into his spiritual family—the family line that begins with forgiveness and leads to eternal life. If we do nothing, we receive death through Adam; but if we come to God by faith, we receive life through Christ. To which family line do you now belong?

**5:20** As a sinner, separated from God, you see his law from below, as a ladder to be climbed to get to God. Perhaps you have repeatedly tried to climb it, only to fall to the ground every time you have advanced one or two rungs. Or perhaps the sheer height of the ladder seems so overwhelming that you have never even started up. In either case, what relief you should feel to see Jesus offering with open arms to lift you above the ladder of the law, to take you directly to God! Once Jesus lifts you into God's presence, you are free to obey—out of love, not necessity, and through God's power, not your own. You know that if you stumble, you will not fall back to the ground. Instead, you will be caught and held in Christ's loving arms.

## 3. Freedom from sin's grasp

*Sin's Power Is Broken*

**6** Well then, should we keep on sinning so that God can show us more and more of his wonderful grace? [2]Of course not! Since we have died to sin, how can we continue to live in it? [3]Or have you forgotten that when we were joined with Christ Jesus in baptism, we joined him in his death? [4]For we died and were buried with Christ by baptism. And just as Christ was raised from the dead by the glorious power of the Father, now we also may live new lives.

[5]Since we have been united with him in his death, we will also be raised to life as he was. [6]We know that our old sinful selves were crucified with Christ so that sin might lose its power in our lives. We are no longer slaves to sin. [7]For when we died with Christ we were set free from the power of sin. [8]And since we died with Christ, we know we will also live with him. [9]We are sure of this because Christ was raised from the dead, and he will never die again. Death no longer has any power over him. [10]When he died, he died once to break the power of sin. But now that he lives, he lives for the glory of God. [11]So you also should consider yourselves to be dead to the power of sin and alive to God through Christ Jesus.

[12]Do not let sin control the way you live;* do not give in to sinful desires. [13]Do not let any part of your body become an instrument of evil to serve sin. Instead, give yourselves completely to God, for you were dead, but now you have new life. So use your whole body as an instrument to do what is right for the glory of God. [14]Sin is no longer your master, for you no longer live under the requirements of the law. Instead, you live under the freedom of God's grace.

**6:1** Rom 3:5-8

**6:2** Rom 8:13 Col 2:20; 3:3

**6:4** Eph 4:22-24 Col 2:12; 3:10

**6:5** Phil 3:10-11 Col 2:12; 3:1

**6:6** Gal 2:20; 5:24 Col 2:12

**6:7** 1 Pet 4:1

**6:11** Rom 7:4 Col 2:20; 3:3

**6:13** Rom 12:1 2 Cor 5:14

**6:14** Rom 7:4, 6; 8:2, 12 Gal 5:18 1 Jn 3:16

**6:12** Or *Do not let sin reign in your body, which is subject to death.*

---

**6:1-8:39** This section deals with *sanctification*—the change God makes in our life as we grow in the faith. Chapter 6 explains that believers are free from sin's control. Chapter 7 discusses the continuing struggle believers have with sin. Chapter 8 describes how we can have victory over sin.

**6:1, 2** If God loves to forgive, why not give him more to forgive? If forgiveness is guaranteed, do we have the freedom to sin as much as we want to? Paul's forceful answer is *Of course not!* Such an attitude—deciding ahead of time to take advantage of God—shows that a person does not understand the seriousness of sin. God's forgiveness does not make sin less serious; his Son's death for sin shows us the dreadful seriousness of sin. Jesus paid with his life so we could be forgiven. The availability of God's mercy must not become an excuse for careless living and moral laxness.

**6:1-4** In the church of Paul's day, immersion was the usual form of baptism; that is, new Christians were completely "buried" in water. They understood baptism to symbolize the death and burial of the old way of life. Coming up out of the water symbolized resurrection to new life with Christ. If we think of our old, sinful life as dead and buried, we have a powerful motive to resist sin. We can consciously choose to treat the desires and temptations of the old nature as if they were dead. Then we can continue to enjoy our wonderful new life with Jesus (see Galatians 3:27 and Colossians 2:12 and 3:1-4 for more on this concept).

**6:5ff** Because we are united with Christ in his death, our evil desires and bondage to sin died with him. Now, united by faith with him in his resurrection life, we have unbroken fellowship with God and freedom from sin's hold on us. For more on the difference between our new life in Christ and our old sinful nature, read Ephesians 4:21-24 and Colossians 3:3-15.

**6:6, 7** The power of sin over us died with Christ on the cross. Our "old sinful selves," our sinful nature, died once and for all, so we are freed from its power. The "power of sin" refers to our rebellious sin-loving nature inherited from Adam. Though we often willingly cooperate with our sinful nature, it is not us but the sin in us that is evil. And it is this power of sin at work in our life that is defeated. Paul has already stated that through faith

in Christ we stand righteous before God. Here Paul emphasizes that we need no longer live under sin's power. God does not take us out of the world or make us robots—we will still feel like sinning, and sometimes we will sin. The difference is that before we were saved we were slaves to our sinful nature, but now we can choose to live for Christ (see Galatians 2:20).

**6:8, 9** Because of Christ's death and resurrection, his followers need never fear death. That assurance frees us to enjoy fellowship with him and to do his will. This will affect all our activities—work and worship, play, Bible study, quiet times, and times of caring for others. When you know that you don't have to fear death, you will experience a new vigor in life.

**6:11** "Consider yourselves to be dead to the power of sin" means that we should regard our old sinful nature as dead and unresponsive to sin. Because of our union and identification with Christ, we no longer want to pursue our old plans, desires, and goals. Now we want to live for the glory of God. As we start this new life, the Holy Spirit will help us become all that Christ wants us to be.

**6:12** How can we keep this command to not let sin control the way we live, to not give in to its desires? We can take the following steps: (1) Identify our personal weaknesses, (2) recognize the things that tempt us, (3) stay away from sources of temptation, (4) practice self-restraint, (5) consciously invest our time in good habits and service, and (5) lean on God's strength and grace.

**6:13** When Paul uses the term "instrument of evil," he uses a word that can refer to a tool or a weapon. Our skills, capabilities, and bodies can serve many purposes, good or bad. In sin, every part of our bodies are vulnerable. In Christ, every part can be an instrument for service. It is the one to whom we offer our service that makes the difference. We are like lasers that can burn destructive holes in steel plates or do delicate cataract surgery. Will you give yourself completely to God, asking him to put you to good use for his glory?

**6:14, 15** If we're no longer under the law but under grace, are we now free to sin and disregard the Ten Commandments? Paul says, "Of course not!" When we were under the law, sin was our master—the law does not justify us or help us overcome sin. But now that we are bound to Christ, he is our Master, and he gives us power to do good rather than evil.

<sup>15</sup>Well then, since God's grace has set us free from the law, does that mean we can go on sinning? Of course not! <sup>16</sup>Don't you realize that you become the slave of whatever you choose to obey? You can be a slave to sin, which leads to death, or you can choose to obey God, which leads to righteous living. <sup>17</sup>Thank God! Once you were slaves of sin, but now you wholeheartedly obey this teaching we have given you. <sup>18</sup>Now you are free from your slavery to sin, and you have become slaves to righteous living.

<sup>19</sup>Because of the weakness of your human nature, I am using the illustration of slavery to help you understand all this. Previously, you let yourselves be slaves to impurity and lawlessness, which led ever deeper into sin. Now you must give yourselves to be slaves to righteous living so that you will become holy.

<sup>20</sup>When you were slaves to sin, you were free from the obligation to do right. <sup>21</sup>And what was the result? You are now ashamed of the things you used to do, things that end in eternal doom. <sup>22</sup>But now you are free from the power of sin and have become slaves of God. Now you do those things that lead to holiness and result in eternal life. <sup>23</sup>For the wages of sin is death, but the free gift of God is eternal life through Christ Jesus our Lord.

### No Longer Bound to the Law

**7** Now, dear brothers and sisters*—you who are familiar with the law—don't you know that the law applies only while a person is living? <sup>2</sup>For example, when a woman marries,

**7:1** Greek *brothers;* also in 7:4.

**Marginal references:**

**6:16**
John 8:34
2 Pet 2:19
**6:17**
2 Tim 1:13
**6:18**
John 8:32
**6:21**
Rom 7:5; 8:6, 13
**6:22**
John 8:32
Rom 8:2
1 Cor 7:22
1 Pet 1:9; 2:16
**6:23**
Matt 25:46
John 3:16; 17:2
Rom 5:21
Gal 6:8

**7:2**
1 Cor 7:39

| WHAT HAS GOD DONE ABOUT SIN? | He has given us | | Principle | Importance |
|---|---|---|---|---|
| | New life | 6:2, 3 | Sin's power is broken. | We can be certain that sin's power is broken. |
| | | 6:4 | Sin-loving nature is buried. | |
| | | 6:6 | You are no longer under sin's control. | |
| | New nature | 6:5 | Now you share his new life. | We can see ourselves as unresponsive to the old power and alive to the new. |
| | | 6:11 | Look upon your old self as dead; instead, be alive to God. | |
| | New freedom | 6:12 | Do not let sin control you. | We can commit ourselves to obey Christ in perfect freedom. |
| | | 6:13 | Give yourselves completely to God. | |
| | | 6:14 | You are free. | |
| | | 6:16 | You can choose your own master. | |

**6:16-18** All people have a master and pattern themselves after him. Without Jesus, we would have no choice; we would be enslaved to sin, and the results would be guilt, suffering, and separation from God. Thanks to Jesus, however, we can now choose God as our Master. Following him, we can enjoy new life and learn how to work for him. Are you still serving your first master, sin? Or have you chosen God?

**6:17** To "wholeheartedly obey" means to give yourself fully to God, to love him "with all your heart, all your soul, and all your mind" (Matthew 22:37). And yet so often our efforts to know and obey God's commands can best be described as "halfhearted." How do you rate your heart's obedience? God wants to give you the power to obey him with all your heart.

**6:17** The "teaching" they were to obey refers to the Good News that Jesus died for their sins and was raised to give them new life. Many believe that this refers to the early church's statement of faith found in 1 Corinthians 15:1-11.

**6:19-22** It is impossible to be neutral. Every person has a master—either God or sin. A Christian is not someone who cannot sin but someone who is no longer a slave to sin. He or she belongs to God.

**6:23** You are free to choose between two masters, but you are not free to adjust the consequences of your choice. Each of the two masters pays with his own kind of currency. The currency of sin is eternal death. That is all you can expect or hope for in life without God. Christ's currency is eternal life—new life with God that begins on earth and continues forever with God. What choice have you made?

**6:23** Eternal life is a gift from God. If it is a gift, then it is not something that we earn, nor something that must be paid back. Consider the foolishness of someone who receives a gift given out of love and then offers to pay for it. A gift cannot be purchased by the recipient. A more appropriate response to a loved one who offers a gift is graceful acceptance with gratitude. Our salvation is a gift of God, not something of our own doing (Ephesians 2:8, 9). He saved us because of his mercy, not because of any good things that we have done (Titus 3:5). How much more we should accept with thanksgiving the gift that God has freely given to us.

**7:1ff** Paul shows that the law is powerless to save the sinner (7:7-14), the lawkeeper (7:15-22), and even the person with a new nature (7:23-25). The sinner is condemned by the law; the lawkeeper can't live up to it; and the person with the new nature finds his or her obedience to the law sabotaged by the effects of the old nature. Once again Paul declares that salvation cannot be found by obeying the law. No matter who we are, only Jesus Christ can set us free.

**7:2-6** Paul uses marriage to illustrate our relationship to the law. When a spouse dies, the law of marriage no longer applies. Because we have died with Christ, the law can no longer condemn us. Since we are united with Christ, his Spirit enables us to produce good deeds for God. We now serve God, not by obeying a set of rules, but out of renewed hearts and minds that overflow with love for him.

the law binds her to her husband as long as he is alive. But if he dies, the laws of marriage no longer apply to her. ³So while her husband is alive, she would be committing adultery if she married another man. But if her husband dies, she is free from that law and does not commit adultery when she remarries.

⁴So, my dear brothers and sisters, this is the point: You died to the power of the law when you died with Christ. And now you are united with the one who was raised from the dead. As a result, we can produce a harvest of good deeds for God. ⁵When we were controlled by our old nature,* sinful desires were at work within us, and the law aroused these evil desires that produced a harvest of sinful deeds, resulting in death. ⁶But now we have been released from the law, for we died to it and are no longer captive to its power. Now we can serve God, not in the old way of obeying the letter of the law, but in the new way of living in the Spirit.

### God's Law Reveals Our Sin

⁷Well then, am I suggesting that the law of God is sinful? Of course not! In fact, it was the law that showed me my sin. I would never have known that coveting is wrong if the law had not said, "You must not covet."* ⁸But sin used this command to arouse all kinds of covetous desires within me! If there were no law, sin would not have that power. ⁹At one time I lived without understanding the law. But when I learned the command not to covet, for instance, the power of sin came to life, ¹⁰and I died. So I discovered that the law's commands, which were supposed to bring life, brought spiritual death instead. ¹¹Sin took advantage of those commands and deceived me; it used the commands to kill me. ¹²But still, the law itself is holy, and its commands are holy and right and good.

¹³But how can that be? Did the law, which is good, cause my death? Of course not! Sin used what was good to bring about my condemnation to death. So we can see how terrible sin really is. It uses God's good commands for its own evil purposes.

### Struggling with Sin

¹⁴So the trouble is not with the law, for it is spiritual and good. The trouble is with me, for I am all too human, a slave to sin. ¹⁵I don't really understand myself, for I want to do what is

**7:5** Greek *When we were in the flesh.*    **7:7** Exod 20:17; Deut 5:21.

**7:3**
Luke 16:18
**7:4**
Rom 6:6; 8:2
Gal 5:18
Col 2:14
1 Pet 2:24
**7:5**
Rom 6:21; 8:8
Gal 5:19-21
**7:6**
2 Cor 3:6
Gal 5:22
Phil 3:3
**7:7**
†Exod 20:17
†Deut 5:21
Rom 4:15
**7:8**
Rom 4:15
**7:10**
Lev 18:5
Rom 10:5
2 Cor 3:7
Gal 3:12
**7:11**
Gen 3:13
Heb 3:13
**7:12**
1 Tim 1:8
**7:14**
1 Kgs 21:20-25
Rom 3:9; 6:6
**7:15**
Gal 5:17

---

**7:4** When a person dies to the old life and accepts Christ as Savior, a new life begins. An unbeliever's life is centered on his or her own personal gratification. Those who don't follow Christ have only their own self-determination as their source of power. By contrast, God is at the center of a Christian's life. God supplies the power for a Christian's daily living. Believers find that their whole way of looking at the world changes when they come to Christ.

**7:6** Some people try to earn their way to God by keeping a set of rules (obeying the Ten Commandments, attending church faithfully, or doing good deeds), but all they earn for their efforts is frustration and discouragement. However, because of Christ's sacrifice, the way to God is already open, and we can become his children simply by putting our faith in him. No longer trying to reach God by keeping rules, we can become more and more like Jesus as we live for him day by day. Let the Holy Spirit turn your eyes away from your own performance and toward Jesus. He will free you to serve him out of love and gratitude. This is "living in the Spirit."

**7:6** Keeping the rules, laws, and customs of Christianity doesn't save us. Even if we could keep our actions pure, we would still be doomed because our hearts and minds are perverse and rebellious. Like Paul, we can find no relief in the synagogue or church until we look to Jesus Christ himself for our salvation—which he gives us freely. When we do come to Jesus, we are flooded with relief and gratitude. Will we keep the rules any better? Most likely, but we will be motivated by love and gratitude, not by the desire to get God's approval. We will not be merely submitting to an external code, but we will willingly and lovingly seek to do God's will.

**7:9-11** Where there is no law, there is no sin, because people cannot know that their actions are sinful unless a law forbids those actions. God's law makes people realize that they are sinners doomed to die, yet it offers no help. Sin is real, and it is dangerous. Imagine a sunny day at the beach. You plunge into the surf; then you notice a sign on the pier: "No swimming. Sharks."

Your day is ruined. Is it the sign's fault? Are you angry with the people who put it up? The law is like the sign. It is essential, and we are grateful for it—but it doesn't get rid of the sharks.

**7:11, 12** Sin deceives people by misusing the law. The law was holy, expressing God's nature and will for people. In the Garden of Eden (Genesis 3), the serpent deceived Eve, changing her focus from the freedom she had to the one restriction God had made. Ever since then, we have all been rebels. Sin looks good to us precisely because God has said it is wrong. When we are tempted to rebel, we need to look at the law from a wider perspective—in the light of God's grace and mercy. If we focus on his great love for us, we will understand that he only restricts us from actions and attitudes that ultimately will harm us.

**7:15** Paul shares three lessons that he learned in trying to deal with his sinful desires: (1) Knowledge of the rules is not the answer (7:9). Paul felt fine as long as he did not understand what the law demanded. When he learned the truth, he knew he was doomed. (2) Self-determination (struggling in one's own strength) doesn't succeed (7:15). Paul found himself sinning in ways that weren't even attractive to him. (3) Becoming a Christian does not stamp out all sin and temptation from a person's life (7:22-25).

Being born again takes a moment of faith, but becoming like Christ is a lifelong process. Paul compares Christian growth to a strenuous race or fight (1 Corinthians 9:24-27; 2 Timothy 4:7). Thus, as Paul has been emphasizing since the beginning of this letter, *no one* in the world is innocent; no one deserves to be saved—not the pagan who doesn't know God's laws, not the person who knows them and tries to keep them. All of us must depend totally on the work of Christ for our salvation. We cannot earn it by our good behavior.

**7:15** This is more than the cry of one desperate man; it describes the experience of all Christians struggling against sin or trying to please God by keeping rules and laws without the Spirit's help. We must never underestimate the power of sin and attempt to fight it in

7:18
Gen 6:5; 8:21
John 3:6
Rom 8:3

7:22
Pss 1:2; 40:8

7:23
Gal 5:17
Jas 4:1
1 Pet 2:11

7:24
Rom 6:6; 8:2

7:25
Rom 6:16, 22
1 Cor 15:57
2 Cor 2:14

right, but I don't do it. Instead, I do what I hate. [16]But if I know that what I am doing is wrong, this shows that I agree that the law is good. [17]So I am not the one doing wrong; it is sin living in me that does it.

[18]And I know that nothing good lives in me, that is, in my sinful nature.* I want to do what is right, but I can't. [19]I want to do what is good, but I don't. I don't want to do what is wrong, but I do it anyway. [20]But if I do what I don't want to do, I am not really the one doing wrong; it is sin living in me that does it.

[21]I have discovered this principle of life—that when I want to do what is right, I inevitably do what is wrong. [22]I love God's law with all my heart. [23]But there is another power* within me that is at war with my mind. This power makes me a slave to the sin that is still within me. [24]Oh, what a miserable person I am! Who will free me from this life that is dominated by sin and death? [25]Thank God! The answer is in Jesus Christ our Lord. So you see how it is: In my mind I really want to obey God's law, but because of my sinful nature I am a slave to sin.

### Life in the Spirit

8:1
Rom 8:34

8:2
Rom 8:11
2 Cor 3:6
Gal 2:19; 5:1

8:3
Acts 13:38
2 Cor 5:21
Phil 2:7
Heb 2:14; 4:15

8:4
Gal 5:16, 25

8:5
Gal 5:19-22

8:6
Rom 6:23
Gal 6:8

8:9
John 14:17-18, 23
Gal 4:6
Phil 1:19
1 Pet 1:11

**8** So now there is no condemnation for those who belong to Christ Jesus. [2]And because you belong to him, the power* of the life-giving Spirit has freed you* from the power of sin that leads to death. [3]The law of Moses was unable to save us because of the weakness of our sinful nature.* So God did what the law could not do. He sent his own Son in a body like the bodies we sinners have. And in that body God declared an end to sin's control over us by giving his Son as a sacrifice for our sins. [4]He did this so that the just requirement of the law would be fully satisfied for us, who no longer follow our sinful nature but instead follow the Spirit.

[5]Those who are dominated by the sinful nature think about sinful things, but those who are controlled by the Holy Spirit think about things that please the Spirit. [6]So letting your sinful nature control your mind leads to death. But letting the Spirit control your mind leads to life and peace. [7]For the sinful nature is always hostile to God. It never did obey God's laws, and it never will. [8]That's why those who are still under the control of their sinful nature can never please God.

[9]But you are not controlled by your sinful nature. You are controlled by the Spirit if you have the Spirit of God living in you. (And remember that those who do not have the Spirit of

**7:18** Greek *my flesh;* also in 7:25.   **7:23** Greek *law;* also in 7:23b.   **8:2a** Greek *the law;* also in 8:2b.   **8:2b** Some manuscripts read *me.*   **8:3** Greek *our flesh;* similarly in 8:4, 5, 6, 7, 8, 9, 12.

---

our own strength. Satan is a crafty tempter, and we have an amazing ability to make excuses. Instead of trying to overcome sin with our own human willpower, we must take hold of God's provision for victory over sin: the Holy Spirit, who lives within us and gives us power. And when we fall, he lovingly reaches out to help us up.

**7:23-25** The "power within" is the sin nature deep within us. This is our vulnerability to sin; it refers to everything within us that is more loyal to our old way of selfish living than to God.

**7:23-25** There is great tension in daily Christian experience. The conflict is that we agree with God's commands but cannot do them. As a result, we are painfully aware of our sin. This inward struggle with sin was as real for Paul as it is for us. From Paul we learn what to do about it. Whenever he felt overwhelmed by the spiritual battle, he would return to the beginnings of his spiritual life, remembering how he had been freed from sin by Jesus Christ. When we feel confused and overwhelmed by sin's appeal, let us claim the freedom Christ gave us. His power can lift us to victory.

**8:1** "Not guilty; let him go free." What would those words mean to you if you were on death row? The fact is that the whole human race *is* on death row, justly condemned for repeatedly breaking God's holy law. Without Jesus we would have no hope at all. But thank God! He has declared us not guilty and has offered us freedom from sin and power to do his will.

**8:2** This life-giving Spirit is the Holy Spirit. He was present at the creation of the world (Genesis 1:2), and he is the power behind the rebirth of every Christian. He gives us the power we need to live the Christian life. For more about the Holy Spirit, read the notes on John 3:6; Acts 1:3; 1:4, 5; 1:5.

**8:3** Jesus gave himself as a sacrifice for our sins. In Old Testa-

ment times, animal sacrifices were continually offered at the Temple. The sacrifices showed the Israelites the seriousness of sin: Blood had to be shed before sins could be pardoned (see Leviticus 17:11). But the blood of animals could not really remove sins (Hebrews 10:4). The sacrifices could only point to Jesus' sacrifice, which paid the penalty for all sins.

**8:5, 6** Paul divides people into two categories: those who are dominated by their sinful nature, and those who are controlled by the Holy Spirit. All of us would be in the first category if Jesus hadn't offered us a way out. Once we have said yes to Jesus, we will want to continue following him, because his way brings life and peace. Daily we must consciously choose to center our life on God. Use the Bible to discover God's guidelines, and then follow them. In every perplexing situation, ask yourself, What would Jesus want me to do? When the Holy Spirit points out what is right, do it eagerly. For more on our sinful nature versus our new life in Christ, see 6:6-8; Ephesians 4:22-24; Colossians 3:3-15.

**8:9** Have you ever worried about whether or not you really are a Christian? A Christian is anyone who has the Spirit of God living in him or her. If you have sincerely trusted Christ for your salvation and acknowledged him as Lord, then the Holy Spirit lives within you and you are a Christian. You can be assured that you have the Holy Spirit because Jesus promised that he would send him. Since you now believe that Jesus Christ is God's Son and that eternal life comes through him (1 John 5:5), you will begin to act as Christ directs (Romans 8:5; Galatians 5:22, 23); you will find help in your daily problems and in your praying (Romans 8:26, 27); you will be empowered to serve God and do his will (Acts 1:8; Romans 12:6ff); and you will become part of God's plan to build up his church (Ephesians 4:12, 13).

Christ living in them do not belong to him at all.) ¹⁰And Christ lives within you, so even though your body will die because of sin, the Spirit gives you life* because you have been made right with God. ¹¹The Spirit of God, who raised Jesus from the dead, lives in you. And just as God raised Christ Jesus from the dead, he will give life to your mortal bodies by this same Spirit living within you.

¹²Therefore, dear brothers and sisters,* you have no obligation to do what your sinful nature urges you to do. ¹³For if you live by its dictates, you will die. But if through the power of the Spirit you put to death the deeds of your sinful nature,* you will live. ¹⁴For all who are led by the Spirit of God are children* of God.

¹⁵So you have not received a spirit that makes you fearful slaves. Instead, you received God's Spirit when he adopted you as his own children.* Now we call him, "Abba, Father."* ¹⁶For his Spirit joins with our spirit to affirm that we are God's children. ¹⁷And since we are his children, we are his heirs. In fact, together with Christ we are heirs of God's glory. But if we are to share his glory, we must also share his suffering.

### The Future Glory

¹⁸Yet what we suffer now is nothing compared to the glory he will reveal to us later. ¹⁹For all creation is waiting eagerly for that future day when God will reveal who his children really are. ²⁰Against its will, all creation was subjected to God's curse. But with eager hope, ²¹the creation looks forward to the day when it will join God's children in glorious freedom from death and decay. ²²For we know that all creation has been groaning as in the pains of childbirth right up to the present time. ²³And we believers also groan, even though we have the Holy Spirit within us as a foretaste of future glory, for we long for our bodies to be released from sin and suffering. We, too, wait with eager hope for the day when God will give us our full rights as his adopted children,* including the new bodies he has promised us. ²⁴We were given this hope when we were saved. (If we already have something, we don't need to hope* for it. ²⁵But if we look forward to something we don't yet have, we must wait patiently and confidently.)

**8:10** Or *your spirit is alive.*   **8:12** Greek *brothers;* also in 8:29.   **8:13** Greek *deeds of the body.*   **8:14** Greek *sons;* also in 8:19.   **8:15a** Greek *you received a spirit of sonship.*   **8:15b** *Abba* is an Aramaic term for "father."   **8:23** Greek *wait anxiously for sonship.*   **8:24** Some manuscripts read *wait.*

Marginal cross-references:

**8:10**
John 14:20; 15:5;
17:23, 26
2 Cor 13:5
Col 1:26-27
**8:11**
Rom 6:5
1 Cor 6:14; 15:45
**8:13**
Gal 6:8
Col 3:5
**8:14**
John 1:12
Gal 3:26
Rev 21:7
**8:15**
Gal 4:5-6
**8:16**
2 Cor 1:22
Eph 1:13
**8:17**
Gal 3:29; 4:7
**8:18**
2 Cor 4:17
Col 3:4
1 Pet 1:6-7
**8:19**
2 Pet 3:13
1 Jn 3:2
**8:20**
Gen 3:17-19
**8:21**
Acts 3:21
2 Pet 3:13
Rev 21:1
**8:22**
Jer 12:4
**8:23**
2 Cor 1:22; 5:5
Phil 3:21

---

**8:11** The Holy Spirit is God's promise or guarantee of eternal life for those who believe in him. The Spirit is within us now by faith, and by faith we are certain to live with Christ forever. See Romans 8:23; 1 Corinthians 6:14; 2 Corinthians 4:14; 1 Thessalonians 4:14.

**8:13** When we turn away from sin's appeal in the Holy Spirit's power, regarding sin as dead, we can ignore temptation when it comes (see 6:11; Galatians 5:24).

**8:14-17** Paul uses adoption to illustrate the believer's new relationship with God. In Roman culture, the adopted person lost all rights in his old family and gained all the rights of a legitimate child in his new family. He became a full heir to his new father's estate. Likewise, when a person becomes a Christian, he or she gains all the privileges and responsibilities of a child in God's family. One of these outstanding privileges is being led by the Spirit (see Galatians 4:5, 6). We may not always feel as though we belong to God, but the Holy Spirit is our witness. His inward presence reminds us of who we are and encourages us with God's love (5:5).

**8:14-17** We are no longer like "fearful slaves"; instead, we are the Master's children. What a privilege! Because we are God's children, we share in great treasures as co-heirs. God has already given us his best gifts: his Son, his Holy Spirit, forgiveness, and eternal life; and he encourages us to ask him for whatever we need.

**8:17** There is a price for being identified with Jesus. Along with being "heirs of God's glory," Paul also mentions the suffering that Christians must face. What kinds of suffering are we to endure? For first-century believers, there was economic and social persecution, and some even faced death. We, too, must pay a price for following Jesus. In many parts of today's world, Christians face pressures just as severe as those faced by Christ's first followers. Even in countries where Christianity is tolerated or encouraged, Christians must not become complacent. To live as Jesus did—serving others, giving up one's rights, resisting pressures to conform

to the world—always exacts a price. Nothing we suffer, however, can compare to the great price that Jesus paid to save us.

**8:19-22** Sin has caused all creation to fall from the perfect state in which God created it. The world is in bondage to death and decay so that it cannot fulfill its intended purpose. One day all creation will be liberated and transformed. Until that time it waits in eager expectation for the resurrection of God's children.

**8:19-22** Christians see the world as it is—physically decaying and spiritually infected with sin. But Christians do not need to be pessimistic, because they have hope for future glory. They look forward to the new heaven and new earth that God has promised, and they wait for God's new order that will free the world from sin, sickness, and evil. In the meantime, Christians go with Christ into the world where they heal people's bodies and souls and fight the evil effects of sin in the world.

**8:23** We will be resurrected with glorified bodies like the body Christ now has in heaven (see 1 Corinthians 15:25-58). We have the "foretaste," the first installment or down payment of future glory—the Holy Spirit—as a guarantee of our resurrection life (see 2 Corinthians 1:22; 5:5; Ephesians 1:14).

**8:24, 25** It is natural for children to trust their parents, even though parents sometimes fail to keep their promises. Our heavenly Father, however, never makes promises he won't keep. Nevertheless his plan may take more time than we expect. What are we waiting for? New bodies, a new heaven and new earth, rest and rewards, our eternal family and home, the absence of sin and suffering, and being face to face with Jesus! Rather than acting like impatient children as we wait for God's will to unfold, we need to have confidence in God's perfect timing and wisdom.

**8:24, 25** In Romans, Paul presents the idea that salvation is past, present, and future. It is past because we *were* saved the moment we believed in Jesus Christ as Savior (3:21-26; 5:1-11; 6:1-11, 22,

**8:26**
John 14:16

**8:27**
1 Cor 4:5

**8:28**
Eph 1:11; 3:11
2 Tim 1:9

**8:29**
Eph 1:5
Col 1:18
2 Tim 2:19
Heb 1:6
1 Pet 1:2

**8:31**
Ps 118:6

**8:32**
John 3:16
Rom 4:25; 5:8

**8:33**
Isa 50:8

**8:34**
Ps 110:1
1 Jn 2:1

**8:35**
1 Cor 4:11
2 Cor 11:26-27

**8:36**
†Ps 44:22

**8:37**
John 16:33
1 Cor 15:57
1 Jn 5:4

26And the Holy Spirit helps us in our weakness. For example, we don't know what God wants us to pray for. But the Holy Spirit prays for us with groanings that cannot be expressed in words. 27And the Father who knows all hearts knows what the Spirit is saying, for the Spirit pleads for us believers* in harmony with God's own will. 28And we know that God causes everything to work together* for the good of those who love God and are called according to his purpose for them. 29For God knew his people in advance, and he chose them to become like his Son, so that his Son would be the firstborn* among many brothers and sisters. 30And having chosen them, he called them to come to him. And having called them, he gave them right standing with himself. And having given them right standing, he gave them his glory.

## Nothing Can Separate Us from God's Love

31What shall we say about such wonderful things as these? If God is for us, who can ever be against us? 32Since he did not spare even his own Son but gave him up for us all, won't he also give us everything else? 33Who dares accuse us whom God has chosen for his own? No one—for God himself has given us right standing with himself. 34Who then will condemn us? No one—for Christ Jesus died for us and was raised to life for us, and he is sitting in the place of honor at God's right hand, pleading for us.

35Can anything ever separate us from Christ's love? Does it mean he no longer loves us if we have trouble or calamity, or are persecuted, or hungry, or destitute, or in danger, or threatened with death? 36(As the Scriptures say, "For your sake we are killed every day; we are being slaughtered like sheep."*) 37No, despite all these things, overwhelming victory is ours through Christ, who loved us.

**8:27** Greek *for God's holy people.*   **8:28** Some manuscripts read *And we know that everything works together.*
**8:29** Or *would be supreme.*   **8:36** Ps 44:22.

---

23); our new life (eternal life) begins at that moment. And it is present because we *are being* saved; this is the process of sanctification (see the note on 6:1–8:39). But at the same time, we have not fully received all the benefits and blessings of salvation that will be ours when Christ's new Kingdom is completely established. That's our future salvation. While we can be confident of our salvation, we still look ahead with hope and trust toward that complete change of body and personality that lies beyond this life, when we will be like Christ (1 John 3:2).

**8:26, 27** As a believer, you are not left to your own resources to cope with problems. Even when you don't know the right words to pray, the Holy Spirit prays with and for you, and God answers. With God helping you pray, you don't need to be afraid to come before him. Ask the Holy Spirit to intercede for you "in harmony with God's own will." Then, when you bring your requests to God, trust that he will always do what is best.

**8:28** God works in "everything"—not just isolated incidents—for our good. This does not mean that all that happens to us is good. Evil is prevalent in our fallen world, but God is able to turn every circumstance around for our long-range good. Note that God is not working to make us happy but to fulfill his purpose. Note also that this promise is not for everybody. It can be claimed only by those who love God and are called by him, that is, those whom the Holy Spirit convinces to receive Christ. Such people have a new perspective, a new mind-set. They trust in God, not in worldly treasures; their security is in heaven, not on earth. Their faith in God does not waver in pain and persecution because they know God is with them.

**8:29** God's ultimate goal for us is to make us like Christ (1 John 3:2). As we become more and more like him, we discover our true selves, the persons we were created to be. How can we become like Christ? By reading and heeding the Word, by studying his life on earth through the Gospels, by spending time in prayer, by being filled with his Spirit, and by doing his work in the world.

**8:29, 30** Some believe these verses mean that before the beginning of the world, God chose certain people to receive his gift of salvation. They point to verses such as Ephesians 1:11, which says that God "chose us in advance, and he makes everything work out according to his plan." Others believe that God knew in advance who would respond to him, and upon those he set his mark (he chose them). What is clear is that God's *purpose* for people was not an afterthought; it was settled before the foundation of the world. People are to serve and honor God. If you believe in Christ, you can rejoice in the fact that God has always known you. God's love is eternal. His wisdom and power are supreme. He will guide and protect you until you one day stand in his presence.

**8:30** *Called* means "summoned or invited." For more on "right standing" (also called justification) and receiving his glory, see the chart in chapter 3, p. 1899.

**8:31-34** Do you ever think that because you aren't good enough for God, he will not save you? Do you ever feel as if salvation is for everyone else but you? Then these verses are especially for you. If God gave his Son for you, he isn't going to hold back the gift of salvation! If Christ gave his life for you, he isn't going to turn around and condemn you! He will not withhold anything you need to live for him. The book of Romans is more than a theological explanation of God's redeeming grace—it is a letter of comfort and confidence addressed to you.

**8:34** Paul says that Jesus is pleading for us in heaven. God has acquitted us and has removed our sin and guilt, so it is Satan, not God, who accuses us. When he does, Jesus, our advocate, sits at God's right hand to present our case. For more on the concept of Christ as our advocate, see the notes on Hebrews 4:14; 4:15.

**8:35, 36** These words were written to a church that would soon undergo terrible persecution. In just a few years, Paul's hypothetical situations would turn into painful realities. This passage reaffirms God's profound love for his people. No matter what happens to us, no matter where we are, we can never be separated from his love. Suffering should not drive us away from God but help us to identify with him and allow his love to heal us.

**8:35-39** These verses contain one of the most comforting promises in all Scripture. Believers have always had to face hardships in many forms: persecution, illness, imprisonment, and even death. These sometimes cause them to fear that they have been abandoned by Christ. But Paul exclaims that it is *impossible* to be separated from Christ. His death for us is proof of his unconquerable love. Nothing can separate us from Christ's presence. God tells us how great his love is so that we will feel totally secure in him. If we believe these overwhelming assurances, we will not be afraid.

38And I am convinced that nothing can ever separate us from God's love. Neither death nor life, neither angels nor demons,* neither our fears for today nor our worries about tomorrow—not even the powers of hell can separate us from God's love. 39No power in the sky above or in the earth below—indeed, nothing in all creation will ever be able to separate us from the love of God that is revealed in Christ Jesus our Lord.

## 4. Israel's past, present, and future
### God's Selection of Israel

**9** With Christ as my witness, I speak with utter truthfulness. My conscience and the Holy Spirit confirm it. 2My heart is filled with bitter sorrow and unending grief 3 for my people, my Jewish brothers and sisters.* I would be willing to be forever cursed—cut off from Christ!—if that would save them. 4They are the people of Israel, chosen to be God's adopted children.* God revealed his glory to them. He made covenants with them and gave them his law. He gave them the privilege of worshiping him and receiving his wonderful promises. 5Abraham, Isaac, and Jacob are their ancestors, and Christ himself was an Israelite as far as his human nature is concerned. And he is God, the one who rules over everything and is worthy of eternal praise! Amen.*

6Well then, has God failed to fulfill his promise to Israel? No, for not all who are born into the nation of Israel are truly members of God's people! 7Being descendants of Abraham doesn't make them truly Abraham's children. For the Scriptures say, "Isaac is the son through whom your descendants will be counted,"* though Abraham had other children, too. 8This means that Abraham's physical descendants are not necessarily children of God. Only the children of the promise are considered to be Abraham's children. 9For God had promised, "I will return about this time next year, and Sarah will have a son."*

10This son was our ancestor Isaac. When he married Rebekah, she gave birth to twins.* 11But before they were born, before they had done anything good or bad, she received a message from God. (This message shows that God chooses people according to his own purposes; 12he calls people, but not according to their good or bad works.) She was told, "Your older son will serve your younger son."* 13In the words of the Scriptures, "I loved Jacob, but I rejected Esau."*

14Are we saying, then, that God was unfair? Of course not! 15For God said to Moses,

"I will show mercy to anyone I choose,
   and I will show compassion to anyone I choose."*

16So it is God who decides to show mercy. We can neither choose it nor work for it.

**8:38** Greek *nor rulers.* **9:3** Greek *my brothers.* **9:4** Greek *chosen for sonship.* **9:5** Or *May God, the one who rules over everything, be praised forever. Amen.* **9:7** Gen 21:12. **9:9** Gen 18:10, 14. **9:10** Greek *she conceived children through this one man.* **9:12** Gen 25:23. **9:13** Mal 1:2-3. **9:15** Exod 33:19.

### Cross-references
**8:38** John 10:28; Col 3:3
**8:39** Rom 5:3-8
**9:1** 1 Tim 2:7
**9:3** Exod 32:32
**9:4** Exod 4:22; Deut 4:13; 7:6; Eph 2:12
**9:5** John 1:1, 18; Rom 1:3; Titus 2:13; 2 Pet 1:1; 1 Jn 5:20
**9:6** Num 23:19; Rom 2:28; Gal 6:16
**9:7** †Gen 21:12; Heb 11:18
**9:8** Rom 8:14; Gal 3:16; 4:23
**9:9** †Gen 18:10, 14
**9:10** Gen 25:21
**9:12** †Gen 25:23
**9:13** †Mal 1:2-3
**9:14** Deut 32:4
**9:15** †Exod 33:19
**9:16** Eph 2:8

---

**8:38** *Powers* are unseen forces of evil in the universe, forces like Satan and his fallen angels (see Ephesians 6:12). In Christ we are super-conquerors, and his love will protect us from any such forces.

**9:1-3** Paul expressed concern for his Jewish brothers and sisters by saying that he would willingly take their punishment if that would save them. While the only one who can save us is Christ, Paul showed a rare depth of love. Like Jesus, he was willing to sacrifice so others would be saved. How concerned are you for those who don't know Christ? Are you willing to sacrifice your time, money, energy, comfort, and safety to see them come to faith in Jesus?

**9:4** The Jews viewed God's choosing of Israel in the Old Testament as being like adoption. They were undeserving and without rights as natural children. Yet God adopted them and granted them the status of his sons and daughters.

**9:6** God's word in the form of beautiful covenant promises came to Abraham. Covenant people, the true children of Abraham, are not just his biological descendants. They are all those who trust in God and in what Jesus Christ has done for them (see also 2:29; Galatians 3:7).

**9:11** The Jews were proud of the fact that their lineage came from Isaac, whose mother was Sarah (Abraham's legitimate wife), rather than Ishmael, whose mother was Hagar (Sarah's servant). Paul asserts that no one can claim to be chosen by God because of his or her heritage or good deeds. God freely chooses to save whomever he wills. The doctrine of election teaches that it is God's sovereign choice to save us by his goodness and mercy, not by our own merit.

**9:12-14** Was it right for God to choose Jacob, the younger, to be over Esau? In Malachi 1:2, 3, the statement "This is how I showed my love for you: I loved your ancestor Jacob, but I rejected his brother Esau" refers to the nations of Israel and Edom rather than to the individual brothers. God chose Jacob to continue the family line of the faithful because he knew his heart was for God. But he did not exclude Esau from knowing and loving him. Keep in mind the kind of God we worship: He is sovereign; he is not arbitrary; in all things he works for our good; he is trustworthy; he will save all who believe in him. When we understand these qualities of God, we know that his choices are good even if we don't understand all his reasons.

**9:16** The fallacy of gaining salvation by human effort remains as strong as ever—people still think good intentions are the key to unlock the door to eternal life. By the time they get to try the lock, they will find that their key does not fit. Others imagine that their efforts are building an invisible ladder to heaven made up of service, family, position, reputation, good work, and desire, although none of these rungs will support a feather. People are so busy trying to reach God that they completely miss the truth

**9:17**
†Exod 9:16

**9:18**
Exod 4:21; 14:4
Josh 11:20
Rom 11:25

**9:20**
Isa 29:16; 45:9

**9:21**
Jer 18:6
2 Tim 2:20

**9:22**
Jer 50:25

**9:23**
Rom 8:30

**9:24**
Rom 3:29

**9:25**
†Hos 2:23

**9:26**
†Hos 1:10

¹⁷For the Scriptures say that God told Pharaoh, "I have appointed you for the very purpose of displaying my power in you and to spread my fame throughout the earth."* ¹⁸So you see, God chooses to show mercy to some, and he chooses to harden the hearts of others so they refuse to listen.

¹⁹Well then, you might say, "Why does God blame people for not responding? Haven't they simply done what he makes them do?"

²⁰No, don't say that. Who are you, a mere human being, to argue with God? Should the thing that was created say to the one who created it, "Why have you made me like this?" ²¹When a potter makes jars out of clay, doesn't he have a right to use the same lump of clay to make one jar for decoration and another to throw garbage into? ²²In the same way, even though God has the right to show his anger and his power, he is very patient with those on whom his anger falls, who are destined for destruction. ²³He does this to make the riches of his glory shine even brighter on those to whom he shows mercy, who were prepared in advance for glory. ²⁴And we are among those whom he selected, both from the Jews and from the Gentiles.

²⁵Concerning the Gentiles, God says in the prophecy of Hosea,

"Those who were not my people,
    I will now call my people.
And I will love those
    whom I did not love before."*

²⁶And,

"Then, at the place where they were told,
    'You are not my people,'
there they will be called
    'children of the living God.'"*

**9:17** Exod 9:16 (Greek version).   **9:25** Hos 2:23.   **9:26** Greek *sons of the living God.* Hos 1:10.

---

**WARNING
SIGNS OF
DEVELOPING
HARDNESS**

Hardening is like a callus or like the tough bone fibers that bridge a fracture. Spiritual hardening begins with self-sufficiency, security in one's self, and self-satisfaction. The real danger is that at some point, repeated resistance to God will yield an actual inability to respond, which the Bible describes as a hardened heart. Insensitivity indicates advanced hardening. Here are some of the warning signs:

| Warning Sign | Reference |
|---|---|
| Disobeying—Pharaoh's willful disobedience led to his hardened heart. | Exodus 4:21 |
| Having wealth and prosperity—Taking God's blessings for granted can cause us to feel as if they were owed to us. | Deuteronomy 8:6-14 |
| Rebelling and being discontented—Suffering or discomfort can create an attitude that blames God. | Psalm 95:8 |
| Rejecting a deserved rebuke—Rejecting God's gift makes our neck stiff and our heart hard. | Proverbs 29:1 |
| Refusing to listen—Refusing to listen leads to a loss of spiritual hearing. | Zechariah 7:11-13 |
| Failing to respond—Listening to God with no intention of obeying produces an inability to obey. | Matthew 13:11-15 |

---

that God has already reached down to them. We cannot earn God's mercy—if we could, it would not be mercy.

**9:17, 18** Paul quotes from Exodus 9:16, where God foretold how Pharaoh would be used to declare God's power. Paul uses this argument to show that salvation was God's work, not people's. God's judgment on Pharaoh's choice to resist God was to confirm that sin and harden his heart. The consequences of Pharaoh's rebellion would be his own punishment.

**9:21** With this illustration, Paul is not saying that some of us are worth more than others but that the Creator has control over the created object. The created object, therefore, has no right to demand anything from its Creator—its very existence depends

on him. Keeping this perspective removes any temptation to have pride in personal achievement.

**9:25, 26** About seven hundred years before Jesus' birth, Hosea told of God's intention to restore his people. Paul applies Hosea's message to God's intention to bring Gentiles into his family after the Jews rejected his plan. Verse 25 is a quotation from Hosea 2:23 and verse 26 is from Hosea 1:10.

²⁷And concerning Israel, Isaiah the prophet cried out,

"Though the people of Israel are as numerous as the sand of the seashore,
only a remnant will be saved.
²⁸ For the LORD will carry out his sentence upon the earth
quickly and with finality."*

²⁹And Isaiah said the same thing in another place:

"If the LORD of Heaven's Armies
had not spared a few of our children,
we would have been wiped out like Sodom,
destroyed like Gomorrah."*

### Israel's Unbelief

³⁰What does all this mean? Even though the Gentiles were not trying to follow God's standards, they were made right with God. And it was by faith that this took place. ³¹But the people of Israel, who tried so hard to get right with God by keeping the law, never succeeded. ³²Why not? Because they were trying to get right with God by keeping the law* instead of by trusting in him. They stumbled over the great rock in their path. ³³God warned them of this in the Scriptures when he said,

"I am placing a stone in Jerusalem* that makes people stumble,
a rock that makes them fall.
But anyone who trusts in him
will never be disgraced."*

**10** Dear brothers and sisters,* the longing of my heart and my prayer to God is for the people of Israel to be saved. ²I know what enthusiasm they have for God, but it is misdirected zeal. ³For they don't understand God's way of making people right with himself. Refusing to accept God's way, they cling to their own way of getting right with God by trying to keep the law. ⁴For Christ has already accomplished the purpose for which the law was given.* As a result, all who believe in him are made right with God.

**9:27** †Isa 10:22 †Hos 1:10

**9:28** †Isa 10:22-23; 28:22

**9:29** †Isa 1:9

**9:30** Gal 2:16 Heb 11:7

**9:31** Isa 51:1 Rom 10:2-3 Gal 5:4

**9:33** Rom 10:11 1 Pet 2:6, 8

**10:2** Acts 22:3

**10:3** Rom 9:31-32

**10:4** Gal 3:24

**9:27-28** Isa 10:22-23 (Greek version).  **9:29** Isa 1:9.  **9:32** Greek by works.  **9:33a** Greek in Zion.  **9:33b** Isa 8:14; 28:16 (Greek version).  **10:1** Greek Brothers.  **10:4** Or For Christ is the end of the law.

---

**9:27-29** Isaiah prophesied that only a small number of God's original people, the Jews, would be saved. Paul saw this happening in every city where he preached. Even though he went to the Jews first, relatively few ever accepted the message. Verses 27 and 28 are based on Isaiah 10:22, 23; and 9:29 is from Isaiah 1:9.

**9:31-33** Sometimes we are like these people, trying to get right with God by keeping his laws. We may think that attending church, doing church work, giving offerings, and being nice will be enough. After all, we've played by the rules, haven't we? But Paul's words sting—this approach never succeeds. Paul explains that God's plan is not for those who try to earn his favor by being good; it is for those who realize that they can never be good enough and so must depend on Christ. We can be saved only by putting our faith in what Jesus Christ has done. If we do that, we will never be disappointed.

**9:32** The Jews had a worthy goal—to honor God. But they tried to achieve it the wrong way—by rigid and painstaking obedience to the law. Thus, some of them became more dedicated to the law than to God. They thought that if they kept the law, God would have to accept them as his people. But God cannot be controlled. The Jews did not see that their Scriptures, the Old Testament, taught that salvation depended on faith, not on human effort (see Genesis 15:6).

**9:32** The "great rock" they stumbled over was Jesus. The Jews did not believe in him because he didn't meet their expectations for the Messiah. Some people still stumble over Christ because salvation by faith doesn't make sense to them. They think they

must earn their way to God, or perhaps God will simply overlook their sins. Others stumble over Christ because his values are the opposite of the world's. He asks for humility, and many are unwilling to humble themselves before him. He requires obedience, and many refuse to put their wills at his disposal. Have you stumbled over this rock, or have you chosen to build your life on it?

**10:1** What will happen to the Jewish people who believe in God but not in Christ? Since they believe in the same God, won't they be saved? If that were true, Paul would not have worked so hard and sacrificed so much to teach them about Christ. Because Jesus is the most complete revelation of God, we cannot fully know God apart from Christ; and because God appointed Jesus to bring God and people together, we cannot come to God by another way. The Jews, like everyone else, must find salvation through Jesus Christ (John 14:6; Acts 4:12). Like Paul, we should pray that all Jews might be saved and lovingly share the Good News with them.

**10:3-5** Rather than living by faith in God, the Jews established customs and traditions (in addition to God's law) to try to make themselves acceptable in God's sight. But human effort, no matter how sincere, can never substitute for the righteousness God offers us by faith. The only way to earn salvation is to be perfect—and that is impossible. We can only hold out our empty hands and receive salvation as a gift.

**10:4** Christ accomplished the purpose for which the law was given in two ways: He fulfills the purpose and goal of the law (Matthew 5:17) in that he perfectly exemplified God's desires on earth. But he is also the termination of the law because in comparison to Christ, the law is powerless to save.

## Salvation Is for Everyone

**10:5**
Lev 18:5
Ezek 20:11, 13, 21
Rom 7:10

**10:6-8**
†Deut 30:12-14

5For Moses writes that the law's way of making a person right with God requires obedience to all of its commands.* 6But faith's way of getting right with God says, "Don't say in your heart, 'Who will go up to heaven?' (to bring Christ down to earth). 7And don't say, 'Who will go down to the place of the dead?' (to bring Christ back to life again)." 8In fact, it says,

> "The message is very close at hand;
> it is on your lips and in your heart."*

**10:9**
Matt 10:32

**10:11**
†Isa 28:16
Rom 9:33

**10:12**
Acts 15:9
Eph 2:4-7

**10:13**
†Joel 2:32
Acts 2:21

**10:15**
†Isa 52:7
†Nah 1:15

And that message is the very message about faith that we preach: 9If you confess with your mouth that Jesus is Lord and believe in your heart that God raised him from the dead, you will be saved. 10For it is by believing in your heart that you are made right with God, and it is by confessing with your mouth that you are saved. 11As the Scriptures tell us, "Anyone who trusts in him will never be disgraced."* 12Jew and Gentile* are the same in this respect. They have the same Lord, who gives generously to all who call on him. 13For "Everyone who calls on the name of the LORD will be saved."*

14But how can they call on him to save them unless they believe in him? And how can they believe in him if they have never heard about him? And how can they hear about him unless someone tells them? 15And how will anyone go and tell them without being sent? That is why the Scriptures say, "How beautiful are the feet of messengers who bring good news!"*

**10:16**
†Isa 53:1
John 12:38
Heb 4:2

**10:17**
Gal 3:2, 5
Col 3:16

**10:18**
†Ps 19:4

16But not everyone welcomes the Good News, for Isaiah the prophet said, "LORD, who has believed our message?"* 17So faith comes from hearing, that is, hearing the Good News about Christ. 18But I ask, have the people of Israel actually heard the message? Yes, they have:

> "The message has gone throughout the earth,
> and the words to all the world."*

**10:19**
†Deut 32:21

19But I ask, did the people of Israel really understand? Yes, they did, for even in the time of Moses, God said,

> "I will rouse your jealousy through people who are not even a nation.
> I will provoke your anger through the foolish Gentiles."*

**10:20**
†Isa 65:1
Rom 9:30

20And later Isaiah spoke boldly for God, saying,

> "I was found by people who were not looking for me.
> I showed myself to those who were not asking for me."*

**10:5** See Lev 18:5.   **10:6-8** Deut 30:12-14.   **10:11** Isa 28:16 (Greek version).   **10:12** Greek *and Greek.*
**10:13** Joel 2:32.   **10:15** Isa 52:7.   **10:16** Isa 53:1.   **10:18** Ps 19:4.   **10:19** Deut 32:21.   **10:20** Isa 65:1
(Greek version).

---

**10:5** In order to be saved by the law, a person would have to live a perfect life, not sinning once. Then why did God give the law since he knew people couldn't keep it? According to Paul, one reason the law was given was to show people how guilty they are (Galatians 3:19). The law was a shadow of Christ—that is, the sacrificial system educated the people so that when the true sacrifice came, they would be able to understand his work (Hebrews 10:1-4). The system of ceremonial laws was to last until the coming of Christ. The law points to our need for a Savior.

**10:6-8** Paul adapts Moses' farewell challenge from Deuteronomy 30:11-14 to apply to Christ. Christ has provided our salvation through his incarnation (God in human form) and resurrection. God's salvation is right in front of us. He will come to us wherever we are. All we need to do is to respond and accept his gift of salvation.

**10:8-12** Have you ever been asked, "How do I become a Christian?" These verses give you the beautiful answer: Salvation is as close as your own lips and heart. People think it must be a complicated process, but it is not. If we believe in our heart and say with our mouth that Christ is the risen Lord, we will be saved.

**10:14** In telling others about Christ, an effective witness must include more than being a good example. Eventually, we will have to explain the content, the *what* and the *how* of the gospel. Modeling the Christian life is important, but we will need to

connect the mind of the unbeliever and the message of the gospel. There should never be a debate between those who favor life-style evangelism (one's living proclaims the gospel) and confrontational evangelism (declaring the message). Both should be used together in promoting the gospel.

**10:15** We must take God's great message of salvation to others so that they can respond to the Good News. How will your loved ones and neighbors hear it unless someone tells them? Is God calling you to take a part in making his message known in your community? Think of one person who needs to hear the Good News, and think of something you can do to help him or her hear it. Then take that step as soon as possible.

**10:18-20** Many Jews who looked for the Messiah refused to believe in him when he came. God offered his salvation to the Gentiles ("people who were not looking for me"); thus, many Gentiles who didn't even know about a Messiah found and believed in him. Some religious people are spiritually blind, while those who have never been in a church are sometimes the most responsive to God's message. Because appearances are deceiving, and we can't see into people's hearts, beware of judging beforehand who will respond to the Good News and who will not.

21But regarding Israel, God said,

"All day long I opened my arms to them,
    but they were disobedient and rebellious."*

10:21
†Isa 65:2

### God's Mercy on Israel

**11** I ask, then, has God rejected his own people, the nation of Israel? Of course not! I my-self am an Israelite, a descendant of Abraham and a member of the tribe of Benjamin.

11:1
Phil 3:5

2No, God has not rejected his own people, whom he chose from the very beginning. Do you realize what the Scriptures say about this? Elijah the prophet complained to God about the people of Israel and said, 3"LORD, they have killed your prophets and torn down your altars. I am the only one left, and now they are trying to kill me, too."*

11:2
1 Sam 12:22

11:3
†1 Kgs 19:10, 14

4And do you remember God's reply? He said, "No, I have 7,000 others who have never bowed down to Baal!"*

11:4
†1 Kgs 19:18

5It is the same today, for a few of the people of Israel* have remained faithful because of God's grace—his undeserved kindness in choosing them. 6And since it is through God's kindness, then it is not by their good works. For in that case, God's grace would not be what it really is—free and undeserved.

11:5
Rom 9:27

11:6
Rom 4:4

7So this is the situation: Most of the people of Israel have not found the favor of God they are looking for so earnestly. A few have—the ones God has chosen—but the hearts of the rest were hardened. 8As the Scriptures say,

11:7
Rom 9:31

11:8
†Deut 29:4
†Isa 29:10
Matt 13:14
John 12:40
Acts 28:26-27

"God has put them into a deep sleep.
To this day he has shut their eyes so they do not see,
    and closed their ears so they do not hear."*

9Likewise, David said,

11:9-10
†Ps 69:22-23

"Let their bountiful table become a snare,
    a trap that makes them think all is well.
Let their blessings cause them to stumble,
    and let them get what they deserve.
10 Let their eyes go blind so they cannot see,
    and let their backs be bent forever."*

11Did God's people stumble and fall beyond recovery? Of course not! They were disobedient, so God made salvation available to the Gentiles. But he wanted his own people to become jealous and claim it for themselves. 12Now if the Gentiles were enriched because the people of Israel turned down God's offer of salvation, think how much greater a blessing the world will share when they finally accept it.

11:11
Acts 13:46; 18:6

10:21 Isa 65:2 (Greek version).   11:3 1 Kgs 19:10, 14.   11:4 1 Kgs 19:18.   11:5 Greek *for a remnant.*   11:8 Isa 29:10; Deut 29:4.   11:9-10 Ps 69:22-23 (Greek version).

---

**11:1ff** In this chapter Paul points out that not *all* Jews have rejected God's message of salvation. There are still a faithful few (11:5). Paul himself, after all, was a Jew, and so were Jesus' disciples and nearly all of the early Christian missionaries.

**11:2** Elijah was a great reforming prophet who challenged the northern kingdom of Israel to repent. See his Profile in 1 Kings 17, p. 545 for more information.

**11:2** God chose the Jews ("his own people") to be the people through whom the rest of the world could find salvation. But this did not mean the entire Jewish nation would be saved; only those who were faithful to God were considered true Jews (11:5). We are saved through faith in Christ, not because we are part of a nation, religion, or family. On whom or on what are you depending for salvation?

**11:6** Do you think it's easier for God to love you when you're good? Do you secretly suspect that God chose you because you deserved it? Do you think some people's behavior is so bad that God couldn't possibly save them? If you ever think this way, you don't entirely understand that salvation is by grace, a free gift. It cannot be earned, in whole or in part; it can only be accepted with thankfulness and praise.

**11:7** "The hearts of the rest were hardened" was God's punishment for their sin. It was a confirmation of their own stubbornness.

In judging them, God removed their ability to see and hear and to turn from sin; thus, they would experience the consequences of their rebellion. Resisting God is like saying to him, "Leave me alone!" But because God is always and everywhere present, his answer to that prayer might be to agree and make that person less sensitive, more hardened to him. The very possibility of that happening ought to keep us asking God specifically for ears that really hear and eyes that really see—openness and responsiveness to him.

**11:8-10** These verses describe the punishment for unresponsive hearts predicted by the prophet Isaiah (Isaiah 6:9-13). If people refuse to hear God's Good News, they eventually will be unable to understand it. Paul saw this happening in the Jewish congregations he visited on his missionary journeys. (Verse 8 is based on Deuteronomy 29:4 and Isaiah 29:10. Verses 9 and 10 are from Psalm 69:22, 23.)

**11:11ff** Paul had a vision of a church where all Jewish and Gentile believers would be united in their love of God and in obedience to Christ. While respecting God's law, this ideal church would look to Christ alone for salvation. A person's ethnic background and social status would be irrelevant (see Galatians 3:28). What mattered would be his or her faith in Christ.

But Paul's vision has not yet been realized. For the most part, Jewish people have rejected the Good News. They have depended

<sup>13</sup>I am saying all this especially for you Gentiles. God has appointed me as the apostle to the Gentiles. I stress this, <sup>14</sup>for I want somehow to make the people of Israel jealous of what you Gentiles have, so I might save some of them. <sup>15</sup>For since their rejection meant that God offered salvation to the rest of the world, their acceptance will be even more wonderful. It will be life for those who were dead! <sup>16</sup>And since Abraham and the other patriarchs were holy, their descendants will also be holy—just as the entire batch of dough is holy because the portion given as an offering is holy. For if the roots of the tree are holy, the branches will be, too.

<sup>17</sup>But some of these branches from Abraham's tree—some of the people of Israel—have been broken off. And you Gentiles, who were branches from a wild olive tree, have been grafted in. So now you also receive the blessing God has promised Abraham and his children, sharing in the rich nourishment from the root of God's special olive tree. <sup>18</sup>But you must not brag about being grafted in to replace the branches that were broken off. You are just a branch, not the root.

<sup>19</sup>"Well," you may say, "those branches were broken off to make room for me." <sup>20</sup>Yes, but remember—those branches were broken off because they didn't believe in Christ, and you are there because you do believe. So don't think highly of yourself, but fear what could happen. <sup>21</sup>For if God did not spare the original branches, he won't* spare you either.

<sup>22</sup>Notice how God is both kind and severe. He is severe toward those who disobeyed, but kind to you if you continue to trust in his kindness. But if you stop trusting, you also will be cut off. <sup>23</sup>And if the people of Israel turn from their unbelief, they will be grafted in again, for God has the power to graft them back into the tree. <sup>24</sup>You, by nature, were a branch cut from a wild olive tree. So if God was willing to do something contrary to nature by grafting you into his cultivated tree, he will be far more eager to graft the original branches back into the tree where they belong.

### God's Mercy Is for Everyone

<sup>25</sup>I want you to understand this mystery, dear brothers and sisters,* so that you will not feel proud about yourselves. Some of the people of Israel have hard hearts, but this will last only until the full number of Gentiles comes to Christ. <sup>26</sup>And so all Israel will be saved. As the Scriptures say,

"The one who rescues will come from Jerusalem,*
and he will turn Israel* away from ungodliness.
<sup>27</sup> And this is my covenant with them,
that I will take away their sins."*

11:21 Some manuscripts read *perhaps he won't.*   **11:25** Greek *brothers.*   **11:26a** Greek *from Zion.*
**11:26b** Greek *Jacob.*   **11:26-27** Isa 59:20-21; 27:9 (Greek version).

**Cross-references:**
**11:14** 1 Cor 9:20; 2 Tim 1:9
**11:15** Luke 15:24, 32; Rom 5:10
**11:17** Jer 11:16; Eph 2:11-16
**11:18** John 4:22
**11:20** Rom 12:16
**11:22** John 15:2, 14; Heb 3:14
**11:23** 2 Cor 3:14-16
**11:25** Luke 21:24; Rom 12:16
**11:26-27** Ps 14:7; †Isa 59:20-21; Jer 31:31-34; Heb 8:8; 10:16

---

on their heritage for salvation, and they do not have the heart of obedience that was so important to the Old Testament prophets and to Paul. Once Gentiles became dominant in many of the Christian churches, they began rejecting Jews and even persecuting them. Unfortunately, this practice has recurred through the centuries.

True Christians should not persecute others. Both Gentiles and Jews have done so much to damage the cause of Christ, whom they claim to serve, that Paul's vision often seems impossible to fulfill. Yet God chose the Jews, just as he chose the Gentiles, and he is still working to unite all believers so they become a holy temple where God lives by his Spirit (see Ephesians 2:11-22).

**11:13-15** Paul was appointed as an apostle to the Gentiles. He reminded his Jewish brothers and sisters of this fact, hoping that they, too, would want to be saved. The Jews rejected God's offer, and, thus, Gentiles were being offered salvation. But when a Jew comes to Christ, there is great rejoicing, as if a dead person has come back to life.

**11:16-24** Speaking to Gentile Christians, Paul warns them not to feel superior because some Jews were rejected. Abraham's faith is like the root of a productive tree, and the Jewish people are the tree's natural branches. Because of faithlessness, some of the Jews have been broken off, and Gentile believers, who were branches from a wild olive tree, have been grafted in. Both Jews and Gentiles share the tree's nourishment based on faith in God; neither can rest on heritage or culture for salvation.

**11:22** "Continue to trust in his kindness" refers to steadfast perseverance in faith. Steadfastness is a proof of the reality of faith and a by-product of salvation, not a means to it.

**11:26** Some say the phrase "and so all Israel will be saved" means that the majority of Jews in the final generation before Christ's return will turn to Christ for salvation. Others say that Paul is using the term *Israel* to refer to the "spiritual" nation of Israel, which is comprised of Jews and Gentiles who have received salvation through faith in Christ. Thus, "all Israel" (or all believers) will receive God's promised gift of salvation. Still others say that "all Israel" means Israel as a whole will have a role in Christ's Kingdom. The Jews' identity as a people won't be discarded. God chose the nation of Israel, and he has never rejected it. He also chose the church, through Jesus Christ, and he will never reject it either. This does not mean, of course, that all Jews or all church members will be saved. It is possible to be Jewish or to belong to a church without ever responding in faith. But just because some people have rejected Christ does not mean that God stops working with either Israel or the church. He continues to offer salvation freely to all. Still others say that the phrase "and so" means "in this way" or "this is how," referring to the necessity of faith in Christ.

²⁸Many of the people of Israel are now enemies of the Good News, and this benefits you Gentiles. Yet they are still the people he loves because he chose their ancestors Abraham, Isaac, and Jacob. ²⁹For God's gifts and his call can never be withdrawn. ³⁰Once, you Gentiles were rebels against God, but when the people of Israel rebelled against him, God was merciful to you instead. ³¹Now they are the rebels, and God's mercy has come to you so that they, too, will share* in God's mercy. ³²For God has imprisoned everyone in disobedience so he could have mercy on everyone.

³³Oh, how great are God's riches and wisdom and knowledge! How impossible it is for us to understand his decisions and his ways!

³⁴ For who can know the LORD's thoughts?
    Who knows enough to give him advice?*
³⁵ And who has given him so much
    that he needs to pay it back?*

³⁶For everything comes from him and exists by his power and is intended for his glory. All glory to him forever! Amen.

**11:29**
Heb 7:21

**11:32**
Gal 3:22
1 Tim 2:4

**11:33**
Isa 45:15; 55:8

**11:34**
Job 15:8; 36:22
†Isa 40:13
Jer 23:18
1 Cor 2:16

**11:35**
Job 41:11

**11:36**
1 Cor 8:6

## B. HOW TO BEHAVE (12:1—16:27)
Moving from the theological to the practical, Paul gives guidelines for living as a redeemed people in a fallen world. We are to give ourselves to Christ as living sacrifices, obey the government, love our neighbors, and take special care of those who are weak in the faith. He closes with personal remarks. Throughout this section, we learn how to live our faith each day.

### 1. Personal responsibility
*A Living Sacrifice to God*

**12** And so, dear brothers and sisters,* I plead with you to give your bodies to God because of all he has done for you. Let them be a living and holy sacrifice—the kind he will find acceptable. This is truly the way to worship him.* ²Don't copy the behavior and customs of this world, but let God transform you into a new person by changing the way you think. Then you will learn to know God's will for you, which is good and pleasing and perfect.

³Because of the privilege and authority* God has given me, I give each of you this warning: Don't think you are better than you really are. Be honest in your evaluation of yourselves,

**12:1**
Rom 6:13
1 Pet 2:5

**12:2**
Gal 1:4
Eph 4:23
Col 3:10

**12:3**
1 Cor 12:11
Eph 4:7

**11:31** Other manuscripts read *will now share;* still others read *will someday share.*  **11:34** Isa 40:13 (Greek version). **11:35** See Job 41:11.  **12:1a** Greek *brothers.*  **12:1b** Or *This is your spiritual worship;* or *This is your reasonable service.*  **12:3a** Or *Because of the grace;* compare 1:5.

**11:28-32** In this passage Paul shows how the Jews and the Gentiles benefit each other. Whenever God shows mercy to one group, the other shares the blessing. In God's original plan, the Jews would be the source of God's blessing to the Gentiles (see Genesis 12:3). When the Jews neglected this mission, God blessed the Gentiles anyway through the Jewish Messiah. He still maintained his love for the Jews because of his promises to Abraham, Isaac, and Jacob. The privileges and invitation of God given to Israel will never be withdrawn. But someday all faithful Jews will share in God's mercy. God's plans will not be thwarted: He will "have mercy on everyone." For a beautiful picture of Jews and Gentiles experiencing rich blessings, see Isaiah 60.

**11:34-36** The implication of these questions is that no one has fully understood the mind of the Lord. No one has been his counselor. And God owes nothing to any one of us. Isaiah and Jeremiah asked similar questions to show that we are unable to give advice to God or criticize his ways (Isaiah 40:13; Jeremiah 23:18). God alone is the possessor of absolute power and absolute wisdom. In the final analysis, all of us are absolutely dependent on God. He is the source of all things, including ourselves. He is the power that sustains and rules the world that we live in. And God works out all things to bring glory to himself. The all-powerful God deserves our praise.

**12:1** When sacrificing an animal according to God's law, a priest would kill the animal, cut it in pieces, and place it on the altar. Sacrifice was important, but even in the Old Testament God made it clear that obedience from the heart was much more important (see 1 Samuel 15:22; Psalm 40:6; Amos 5:21-24). God wants us to offer ourselves, not animals, as *living* sacrifices—daily laying

aside our own desires to follow him, putting all our energy and resources at his disposal and trusting him to guide us. We do this out of gratitude that our sins have been forgiven.

**12:1, 2** God has good, pleasing, and perfect plans for his children. He wants us to be transformed people with renewed minds, living to honor and obey him. Because he wants only what is best for us, and because he gave his Son to make our new life possible, we should joyfully give ourselves as living sacrifices for his service.

**12:2** Paul warned Christians: "Don't copy the behavior and customs of this world" that are usually selfish and often corrupting. Wise Christians decide that much worldly behavior is off-limits for them. Our refusal to conform to this world's values, however, must go even deeper than just behavior and customs; it must be firmly planted in our mind: "Let God transform you into a new person by changing the way you think." It is possible to avoid most worldly customs and still be proud, covetous, selfish, stubborn, and arrogant. Only when the Holy Spirit renews, reeducates, and redirects our mind are we truly transformed (see 8:5).

**12:3** Healthy self-esteem is important because some of us think too little of ourselves; on the other hand, some of us overestimate ourselves. The key to an honest and accurate self-evaluation is knowing the basis of our self-worth—our identity in Christ. Apart from him, we aren't capable of very much by eternal standards; in him, we are valuable and capable of worthy service. Evaluating yourself by the worldly standards of success and achievement can cause you to think too much about your worth in the eyes of others and thus miss your true value in God's eyes.

**12:4**
1 Cor 12:12

**12:5**
Eph 4:25

**12:6-8**
1 Pet 4:10-11

**12:9**
Amos 5:15
1 Tim 1:5

**12:10**
John 13:34
Phil 2:3
1 Thes 4:9
2 Pet 1:7

**12:11**
Acts 18:25; 20:19
Rev 3:15

**12:13**
Heb 13:2

**12:14**
Matt 5:44

**12:15**
Job 30:25

**12:16**
Prov 3:7
Isa 5:21

measuring yourselves by the faith God has given us.* 4Just as our bodies have many parts and each part has a special function, 5so it is with Christ's body. We are many parts of one body, and we all belong to each other.

6In his grace, God has given us different gifts for doing certain things well. So if God has given you the ability to prophesy, speak out with as much faith as God has given you. 7If your gift is serving others, serve them well. If you are a teacher, teach well. 8If your gift is to encourage others, be encouraging. If it is giving, give generously. If God has given you leadership ability, take the responsibility seriously. And if you have a gift for showing kindness to others, do it gladly.

9Don't just pretend to love others. Really love them. Hate what is wrong. Hold tightly to what is good. 10Love each other with genuine affection,* and take delight in honoring each other. 11Never be lazy, but work hard and serve the Lord enthusiastically.* 12Rejoice in our confident hope. Be patient in trouble, and keep on praying. 13When God's people are in need, be ready to help them. Always be eager to practice hospitality.

14Bless those who persecute you. Don't curse them; pray that God will bless them. 15Be happy with those who are happy, and weep with those who weep. 16Live in harmony with each other. Don't be too proud to enjoy the company of ordinary people. And don't think you know it all!

**12:3b** Or *by the faith God has given you;* or *by the standard of our God-given faith.*   **12:10** Greek *with brotherly love.*
**12:11** Or *but serve the Lord with a zealous spirit;* or *but let the Spirit excite you as you serve the Lord.*

---

**12:4, 5** Paul uses the concept of the human body to teach how Christians should live and work together. Just as the parts of the body function under the direction of the brain, so Christians are to work together under the command and authority of Jesus Christ (see 1 Corinthians 12:12-31; Ephesians 4:1-16).

**12:6** God gives us gifts so we can build up his church. To use them effectively, we must (1) realize that all gifts and abilities come from God; (2) understand that not everyone has the same gifts; (3) know who we are and what we do best; (4) dedicate our gifts to God's service and not to our personal success; (5) be willing to utilize our gifts wholeheartedly, not holding back anything from God's service. God's gifts differ in nature, power, and effectiveness according to his wisdom and graciousness, not according to our faith. Our role is to be faithful and to seek ways to serve others with what Christ has given us.

**12:6** "Prophesying" in Scripture is not always predicting the future. Often it means preaching God's messages (1 Corinthians 14:1-3).

**12:6-8** Look at this list of gifts and imagine the kinds of people who would have each gift. Prophets are often bold and articulate. Servers (those in ministry) are faithful and loyal. Teachers are clear thinkers. Encouragers know how to motivate others. Givers are generous and trusting. Leaders are good organizers and managers. Those who show kindness are caring people who are happy to give their time to others. It would be difficult for one person to embody all these gifts. An assertive prophet would not usually make a good counselor, and a generous giver might fail as a leader. When you identify your own gifts (and this list is far from complete), ask how you can use them to build up God's family. At the same time, realize that your gifts can't do the work of the church all alone. Be thankful for people whose gifts are completely different from yours. Let your strengths balance their weaknesses, and be grateful that their abilities make up for your deficiencies. Together you can build Christ's church.

**12:9-10** Most of us have learned how to be courteous to others—how to speak kindly, avoid hurting their feelings, and appear to take an interest in them. We may even be skilled in pretending to show compassion when we hear of others' needs, or to become indignant when we learn of injustice. But God calls us to real and genuine love that goes far beyond being hypocritical and polite. Genuine love requires concentration and effort. It means helping others become better people. It demands our time, money, and personal involvement. No individual has the capacity to express love to a whole community,

but the body of Christ in your town does. Look for people who need your love, and look for ways you and your fellow believers can love your community for Christ.

**12:10** We can honor others in one of two ways. One involves ulterior motives. We honor our bosses so they will reward us, our employees so they will work harder, the wealthy so they will contribute to our cause, the powerful so they will use their power for us and not against us. God's way involves love. As Christians, we honor people because they have been created in God's image, because they are our brothers and sisters in Christ, and because they have a unique contribution to make to Christ's church. Does God's way of honoring others sound too difficult for your competitive nature? Why not try to outdo one another in showing honor? Put others first!

**12:13** Christian hospitality differs from social entertaining. Entertaining focuses on the host: The home must be spotless; the food must be well prepared and abundant; the host must appear relaxed and good-natured. Hospitality, by contrast, focuses on the guests' needs, such as a place to stay, nourishing food, a listening ear, or just acceptance. Hospitality can happen in a messy home. It can happen around a dinner table where the main dish is canned soup. It can even happen while the host and the guest are doing chores together. Don't hesitate to offer hospitality just because you are too tired, too busy, or not wealthy enough to entertain.

**12:16** Many people use their contacts and relationships for selfish ambition. They select those people who will help them climb the social ladder. Christ demonstrated and taught that we should treat all people with respect—those of a different race, the handicapped, the poor, young and old, male and female. We must never consider others as being beneath us. Paul says we need to live in harmony with others and not be too proud to enjoy the company of ordinary people. Are you able to do humble tasks with others? Do you welcome conversation with unattractive, non-prestigious people? Are you willing to befriend newcomers and entry-level people? Or do you relate only to those who will help you get ahead?

17Never pay back evil with more evil. Do things in such a way that everyone can see you are honorable. 18Do all that you can to live in peace with everyone.

19Dear friends, never take revenge. Leave that to the righteous anger of God. For the Scriptures say,

"I will take revenge;
    I will pay them back,"*
says the LORD.

20Instead,

"If your enemies are hungry, feed them.
    If they are thirsty, give them something to drink.
In doing this, you will heap
    burning coals of shame on their heads."*

21Don't let evil conquer you, but conquer evil by doing good.

## Respect for Authority

**13** Everyone must submit to governing authorities. For all authority comes from God, and those in positions of authority have been placed there by God. 2So anyone who rebels against authority is rebelling against what God has instituted, and they will be punished. 3For the authorities do not strike fear in people who are doing right, but in those who are doing wrong. Would you like to live without fear of the authorities? Do what is right, and they will honor you. 4The authorities are God's servants, sent for your good. But if you are doing wrong, of course you should be afraid, for they have the power to punish you. They are God's servants, sent for the very purpose of punishing those who do what is wrong. 5So you must submit to them, not only to avoid punishment, but also to keep a clear conscience.

6Pay your taxes, too, for these same reasons. For government workers need to be paid. They are serving God in what they do. 7Give to everyone what you owe them: Pay your taxes and government fees to those who collect them, and give respect and honor to those who are in authority.

**12:19** Deut 32:35.    **12:20** Prov 25:21-22.

**12:17**
Prov 3:4; 20:22
1 Thes 5:15

**12:19**
†Deut 32:35

**12:20**
†Prov 25:21-22
Matt 5:44

**13:1**
Dan 2:21
John 19:11
Titus 3:1

**13:3**
1 Pet 2:13-14

**13:5**
1 Pet 2:13

**13:7**
Matt 22:21
Mark 12:17
Luke 20:25

---

**12:17-21** These verses summarize the core of Christian living. If we love someone the way Christ loves us, we will be willing to forgive. If we have experienced God's grace, we will want to pass it on to others. And remember, grace is *undeserved* favor. By giving an enemy a drink, we're not excusing his misdeeds. We're recognizing him, forgiving him, and loving him in spite of his sins—just as Christ did for us.

**12:19-21** In this day of lawsuits and incessant demands for legal rights, Paul's command sounds almost impossible. When someone hurts you deeply, instead of giving him what he deserves, Paul says to befriend him. Why does Paul tell us to forgive our enemies? (1) Forgiveness may break a cycle of retaliation and lead to mutual reconciliation. (2) It may make the enemy feel ashamed and change his or her ways. (3) By contrast, repaying evil for evil hurts you just as much as it hurts your enemy. Even if your enemy never repents, forgiving him or her will free you of a heavy load of bitterness.

**12:19-21** Forgiveness involves both attitudes and actions. If you find it difficult to *feel* forgiving toward someone who has hurt you, try responding with kind actions. If appropriate, tell this person that you would like to heal your relationship. Lend a helping hand. Send him or her a gift. Smile at him or her. Many times you will discover that right actions lead to right feelings.

**13:1** Are there times when we should not obey the government? We should never allow government to force us to disobey God. Jesus and his apostles never disobeyed the government for personal reasons; when they disobeyed, it was in order to follow God's moral standards. Their disobedience was not cheap: They were threatened, beaten, thrown into jail, tortured, or executed for their convictions. Like them, if we are compelled to disobey, we must be ready to accept the consequences.

**13:1ff** Christians understand Romans 13 in different ways. All Christians agree that we are to live at peace with the state as long

as the state allows us to live by our religious convictions. For hundreds of years, however, there have been at least three interpretations of how we are to do this:

(1) Some Christians believe that the state is so corrupt that Christians should have as little to do with it as possible. Although they should be good citizens as long as they can do so without compromising their beliefs, they should not work for the government, vote in elections, or serve in the military.

(2) Others believe that God has given the state authority in certain areas and the church authority in others. Christians can be loyal to both and can work for either. They should not, however, confuse the two. In this view, church and state are concerned with two totally different spheres—the spiritual and the physical—and thus complement each other but do not work together.

(3) Still others believe that Christians have a responsibility to make the state better. They can do this politically, by electing Christian or other high-principled leaders. They can also do this morally, by serving as an influence for good in society. In this view, church and state ideally work together for the good of all.

None of these views advocate rebelling against or refusing to obey the government's laws or regulations unless those laws clearly require you to violate the moral standards revealed by God. Wherever we find ourselves, we must be responsible citizens, as well as responsible Christians.

**13:3, 4** Willingly or unwittingly, people in authority are God's servants. They are allowed their positions in order to do good. When authorities are unjust, however, upright people are afraid. When authorities are just, people who are doing right have nothing to fear. This provides our principal motivation to pray for our leaders. Praying for those in authority over us will also mean that we will watch them closely. If we pray diligently for our leaders, we will be functioning as God's sentinels.

## Love Fulfills God's Requirements

**13:8**
Matt 5:34
John 13:34

**13:9**
Exod 20:13-15, 17
†Lev 19:18
†Deut 5:17-19, 21

**13:11**
1 Cor 7:29-31
1 Thes 5:5-6
Jas 5:8
1 Pet 4:7

**13:12**
Eph 5:11; 6:13
1 Thes 5:8

**13:13**
Luke 21:34
Eph 5:18

⁸Owe nothing to anyone—except for your obligation to love one another. If you love your neighbor, you will fulfill the requirements of God's law. ⁹For the commandments say, "You must not commit adultery. You must not murder. You must not steal. You must not covet."* These—and other such commandments—are summed up in this one commandment: "Love your neighbor as yourself."* ¹⁰Love does no wrong to others, so love fulfills the requirements of God's law.

¹¹This is all the more urgent, for you know how late it is; time is running out. Wake up, for our salvation is nearer now than when we first believed. ¹²The night is almost gone; the day of salvation will soon be here. So remove your dark deeds like dirty clothes, and put on the shining armor of right living. ¹³Because we belong to the day, we must live decent lives for all to see. Don't participate in the darkness of wild parties and drunkenness, or in sexual promiscuity and immoral living, or in quarreling and jealousy. ¹⁴Instead, clothe yourself with the presence of the Lord Jesus Christ. And don't let yourself think about ways to indulge your evil desires.

## The Danger of Criticism

**14:1**
1 Cor 9:22

**14:2**
1 Cor 10:25-27

**14** Accept other believers who are weak in faith, and don't argue with them about what they think is right or wrong. ²For instance, one person believes it's all right to eat

**13:9a** Exod 20:13-15, 17.   **13:9b** Lev 19:18.

---

**13:8** Why is love for others called an obligation? We are permanently in debt to Christ for the lavish love he has poured out on us. The only way we can even begin to repay this debt is by fulfilling our obligation to love others in turn. Because Christ's love will always be infinitely greater than ours, we will always have the obligation to love our neighbors.

**13:9** Somehow many of us have gotten the idea that self-love is wrong. But if this were the case, it would be pointless to love our neighbors as ourselves. But Paul lists fighting what he means by self-love. Even if you have low self-esteem, you probably don't willingly let yourself go hungry. You take care of your body and may even exercise. You clothe yourself reasonably well. You make sure there's a roof over your head. You try not to let yourself be cheated or injured. This is the kind of love we need to have for our neighbors. Do we see that others are fed, clothed, and housed as well as they can be? Are we concerned about issues of social justice? Loving others as ourselves means actively working to see that their needs are met. Interestingly, people who focus on others rather than on themselves rarely suffer from low self-esteem.

**13:10** Christians must obey the law of love, which supersedes both religious and civil laws. How easy it is to excuse our indifference to others merely because we have no legal obligation to help them and even to justify harming them if our actions are technically legal! But Jesus does not leave loopholes in the law of love. Whenever love demands it, we are to go beyond human legal requirements and imitate the God of love. See James 2:8, 9; 4:11 and 1 Peter 2:16, 17 for more about this law of love.

**13:12-14** The "night" refers to the present evil time. The "day" refers to the time of Christ's return. Some people are surprised that Paul lists fighting and jealousy with the gross and obvious sins of drunkenness and immorality. Like Jesus in his Sermon on the Mount (Matthew 5–7), Paul considers attitudes as important as actions. Just as hatred leads to murder, so jealousy leads to strife and lust to adultery. When Christ returns, he wants to find his people clean on the inside as well as on the outside.

**13:14** How do we clothe ourselves with the presence of the Lord Jesus Christ? First, we identify with Christ by being baptized (Galatians 3:27). This shows our solidarity with other Christians and with the death, burial, and resurrection of Jesus Christ. Second, we exemplify the qualities Jesus showed while he was here on earth (love, humility, truth, service). In a sense, we role-play what Jesus would do in our situation (see Ephesians 4:24-32; Colossians 3:10-17). We also must avoid those situations that open the door to gratifying sinful desires.

**14:1** Who is weak in faith and who is strong? We are all weak in some areas and strong in others. Our faith is strong in an area if we can survive contact with worldly people without falling into their patterns. It is weak in an area if we must avoid certain activities, people, or places in order to protect our spiritual life. It is important to take self-inventory in order to find out our strengths and weaknesses. Whenever in doubt, we should ask, Can I do that without sinning? Can I influence others for good, rather than being influenced by them?

In areas of strength, we should not fear being defiled by the world; rather we should go and serve God. In areas of weakness, we need to be cautious. If we have a strong faith but shelter it, we are not doing Christ's work in the world. If we have a weak faith but expose it, we are being extremely foolish.

**14:1** This verse assumes there will be differences of opinion in the church about what is right or wrong. Paul says we are not to quarrel about issues that are matters of opinion. Differences should not be feared or avoided but accepted and handled with love. Don't expect everyone, even in the best possible church, to agree on every subject. Through sharing ideas we can come to a fuller understanding of what the Bible teaches. Accept, listen to, and respect others. Differences of opinion need not cause division. They can be a source of learning and richness in our relationships.

**14:1ff** What is weak faith? Paul is speaking about immature faith that has not yet developed the muscle it needs to stand against external pressures. For example, if a person who once worshiped idols became a Christian, he might understand perfectly well that Christ saved him through faith and that idols have no real power. Still, because of his past associations, he might be badly shaken if he unknowingly ate meat that had been used in idol worship. If a person who once worshiped God on the required Jewish holy days became a Christian, he might well know that Christ saved him through faith, not through his keeping of the law. Still, when the festival days came, he might feel empty and unfaithful if he didn't dedicate those days to God.

Paul responds to both weak brothers in love. Both are acting according to their consciences, but their honest convictions do not need to be made into rules for the church. Certainly some issues are central to the faith and worth fighting for, but many are based on individual differences and should not be legislated. Our principle should be: In essentials, unity; in nonessentials, liberty; in everything, love.

**14:2** Eating "anything" may refer to a strong Christian being free from dietary restrictions, or it may refer to his eating meat offered to idols. The person weaker in the faith, however, may eat only vegetables and refuse to eat meat that has been offered to anything. But another believer with a sensitive conscience will eat only vegetables. ³Those who feel free to eat anything must not look down on those who don't. And those who don't eat certain foods must not condemn those who do, for God has accepted them. ⁴Who are you to condemn someone else's servants? Their own master will judge whether they stand or fall. And with the Lord's help, they will stand and receive his approval.

⁵In the same way, some think one day is more holy than another day, while others think every day is alike. You should each be fully convinced that whichever day you choose is acceptable. ⁶Those who worship the Lord on a special day do it to honor him. Those who eat any kind of food do so to honor the Lord, since they give thanks to God before eating. And those who refuse to eat certain foods also want to please the Lord and give thanks to God. ⁷For we don't live for ourselves or die for ourselves. ⁸If we live, it's to honor the Lord. And if we die, it's to honor the Lord. So whether we live or die, we belong to the Lord. ⁹Christ died and rose again for this very purpose—to be Lord both of the living and of the dead.

¹⁰So why do you condemn another believer*? Why do you look down on another believer? Remember, we will all stand before the judgment seat of God. ¹¹For the Scriptures say,

"'As surely as I live,' says the LORD,
'every knee will bend to me,
    and every tongue will confess and give praise to God.*'"

¹²Yes, each of us will give a personal account to God. ¹³So let's stop condemning each other. Decide instead to live in such a way that you will not cause another believer to stumble and fall.

¹⁴I know and am convinced on the authority of the Lord Jesus that no food, in and of itself, is wrong to eat. But if someone believes it is wrong, then for that person it is wrong. ¹⁵And if another believer is distressed by what you eat, you are not acting in love if you eat it. Don't let your eating ruin someone for whom Christ died. ¹⁶Then you will not be criticized for doing something you believe is good. ¹⁷For the Kingdom of God is not a matter of what we eat or drink, but of living a life of goodness and peace and joy in the Holy Spirit. ¹⁸If you serve Christ with this attitude, you will please God, and others will approve of you, too. ¹⁹So then, let us aim for harmony in the church and try to build each other up.

14:10 Greek *your brother;* also in 14:10b, 13, 15, 21.   14:11 Or *confess allegiance to God.* Isa 49:18; 45:23 (Greek version).

**14:3** Col 2:16

**14:4** Matt 7:1

**14:5** Gal 4:10

**14:6** 1 Cor 10:30

**14:7** 2 Cor 5:15 Gal 2:20

**14:8** Phil 1:20 1 Thes 5:10

**14:9** Rev 1:18

**14:10** Matt 25:31-32 Acts 17:31 2 Cor 5:10

**14:11** †Isa 45:23; 49:18

**14:12** Gal 6:5

**14:13** Matt 7:1 2 Cor 6:3

**14:14** Acts 10:15 1 Cor 8:7

**14:15** 1 Cor 8:11-13

**14:16** 1 Cor 10:30 Titus 2:5

**14:17** Rom 15:13 Gal 5:22

**14:19** Rom 12:18; 15:2

---

idols. But how would Christians end up eating meat that had been offered to idols? The ancient system of sacrifice was at the center of the religious, social, and domestic life of the Roman world. After a sacrifice was presented to a god in a pagan temple, only part of it was burned. The remainder was often sent to the market to be sold. Thus, a Christian might easily—even unknowingly—buy such meat in the marketplace or eat it at the home of a friend. Should a Christian question the source of his meat? Some thought there was nothing wrong with eating meat that had been offered to idols because idols were worthless. Others carefully checked the source of their meat or gave up meat altogether, in order to avoid a guilty conscience. The problem was especially acute for Christians who had once been idol worshipers. For them, such a strong reminder of their pagan days might weaken their newfound faith. Paul also deals with this problem in 1 Corinthians 8.

**14:10-12** Each person is accountable to Christ, not to others. While the church must be uncompromising in its stand against activities that are expressly forbidden by Scripture (adultery, homosexuality, murder, theft), it should not create additional rules and regulations and give them equal standing with God's law. Many times Christians base their moral judgments on opinion, personal dislikes, or cultural bias rather than on the Word of God. When they do this, they show that their own faith is weak; they do not think that God is powerful enough to guide his children. When we stand before God and give a personal account of our life, we won't be worried about what our Christian neighbor has done (see 2 Corinthians 5:10).

**14:13** Both strong and weak Christians can cause their brothers and sisters to stumble. The strong but insensitive Christian may flaunt his or her freedom and intentionally offend others' con-

sciences. The scrupulous but weak Christian may try to fence others in with petty rules and regulations, thus causing dissension. Paul wants his readers to be both strong in the faith and sensitive to others' needs. Because we are all strong in some areas and weak in others, we need to constantly monitor the effects of our behavior on others.

**14:13ff** Some Christians use an invisible weaker brother to support their own opinions, prejudices, or standards. "You must live by these standards," they say, "or you will be offending the weaker brother." In truth, the person would often be offending no one but the speaker. While Paul urges us to be sensitive to those whose faith may be harmed by our actions, we should not sacrifice our liberty in Christ just to satisfy the selfish motives of those who are trying to force their opinions on us. Neither fear them nor criticize them, but follow Christ as closely as you can.

**14:14** At the Jerusalem council (Acts 15), the Jewish church in Jerusalem asked the Gentile church in Antioch not to eat meat that had been sacrificed to idols. Paul was at the Jerusalem council, and he accepted this request, not because he felt that eating such meat was wrong in itself, but because this practice would deeply offend many Jewish believers. Paul did not think the issue was worth dividing the church over; his desire was to promote unity. So he concludes, "if someone believes it is wrong, then for that person it is wrong." Paul's practice was to honor, as far as possible, the convictions of others.

Believers are called to accept one another without judging our varied opinions. However, when the situation has to be faced, how should we deal with those who disagree with us? Paul's response is that all believers should act in love so as to maintain peace in the church.

**14:20**
Acts 10:15
1 Cor 8:9-12

**14:21**
1 Cor 8:13

**14:22**
1 Jn 3:21

20Don't tear apart the work of God over what you eat. Remember, all foods are acceptable, but it is wrong to eat something if it makes another person stumble. 21It is better not to eat meat or drink wine or do anything else if it might cause another believer to stumble. 22You may believe there's nothing wrong with what you are doing, but keep it between yourself and God. Blessed are those who don't feel guilty for doing something they have decided is right. 23But if you have doubts about whether or not you should eat something, you are sinning if you go ahead and do it. For you are not following your convictions. If you do anything you believe is not right, you are sinning.

### Living to Please Others

**15:2**
Rom 14:19
1 Cor 9:19; 10:24
Gal 6:2

**15:3**
†Ps 69:9

**15:4**
Rom 4:23-24
2 Tim 3:16

**15:5**
1 Cor 1:10
2 Cor 1:3

**15:6**
Rev 1:6

**15:7**
Rom 14:1

**15:8**
Matt 15:24
Acts 3:25-26
2 Cor 1:20

**15:9**
†2 Sam 22:50
†Ps 18:49

**15:10**
†Deut 32:43

**15:11**
†Ps 117:1

**15:12**
†Isa 11:10
Rev 5:5; 22:16

**15** We who are strong must be considerate of those who are sensitive about things like this. We must not just please ourselves. 2We should help others do what is right and build them up in the Lord. 3For even Christ didn't live to please himself. As the Scriptures say, "The insults of those who insult you, O God, have fallen on me."* 4Such things were written in the Scriptures long ago to teach us. And the Scriptures give us hope and encouragement as we wait patiently for God's promises to be fulfilled.

5May God, who gives this patience and encouragement, help you live in complete harmony with each other, as is fitting for followers of Christ Jesus. 6Then all of you can join together with one voice, giving praise and glory to God, the Father of our Lord Jesus Christ.

7Therefore, accept each other just as Christ has accepted you so that God will be given glory. 8Remember that Christ came as a servant to the Jews* to show that God is true to the promises he made to their ancestors. 9He also came so that the Gentiles might give glory to God for his mercies to them. That is what the psalmist meant when he wrote:

"For this, I will praise you among the Gentiles;
    I will sing praises to your name."*

10And in another place it is written,

"Rejoice with his people,
    you Gentiles."*

11And yet again,

"Praise the Lord, all you Gentiles.
    Praise him, all you people of the earth."*

12And in another place Isaiah said,

"The heir to David's throne* will come,
    and he will rule over the Gentiles.
They will place their hope on him."*

13I pray that God, the source of hope, will fill you completely with joy and peace because you trust in him. Then you will overflow with confident hope through the power of the Holy Spirit.

**15:3** Greek *who insult you have fallen on me.* Ps 69:9.   **15:8** Greek *servant of circumcision.*   **15:9** Ps 18:49.
**15:10** Deut 32:43.   **15:11** Ps 117:1.   **15:12a** Greek *The root of Jesse.* David was the son of Jesse.
**15:12b** Isa 11:10 (Greek version).

---

**14:20, 21** Sin is not just a private matter. Everything we do affects others, and we have to think of them constantly. God created us to be interdependent, not independent. We who are strong in our faith must, without pride or condescension, treat others with love, patience, and self-restraint.

**14:23** We try to steer clear of actions forbidden by Scripture, of course, but sometimes Scripture is silent. Then we should follow our consciences. "If you do anything you believe is not right, you are sinning" means that to go against a conviction will leave a person with a guilty or uneasy conscience. When God shows us that something is wrong for us, we should avoid it. But we should not look down on other Christians who exercise their freedom in those areas.

**15:4** The knowledge of the Scriptures affects our attitude toward the present and the future. The more we know about what God has done in years past, the greater the confidence we have about

what he will do in the days ahead. We need to diligently read our Bibles so we may have confidence that God's will is best for us.

**15:5-7** The Roman church was a diverse community. It was made up of Jews and Gentiles, slaves and free people, rich and poor, strong and weak. So it was difficult for them to accept one another. Accepting means taking people into our homes as well as into our hearts, sharing meals and activities, and avoiding racial and economic discrimination. We must go out of our way to avoid favoritism. Consciously spend time greeting those you don't normally talk to, minimize differences, and seek common ground for fellowship. In this way you are accepting others as Christ has accepted you, and God is given glory.

## 2. Personal notes
*Paul's Reason for Writing*

¹⁴I am fully convinced, my dear brothers and sisters,* that you are full of goodness. You know these things so well you can teach each other all about them. ¹⁵Even so, I have been bold enough to write about some of these points, knowing that all you need is this reminder. For by God's grace, ¹⁶I am a special messenger from Christ Jesus to you Gentiles. I bring you the Good News so that I might present you as an acceptable offering to God, made holy by the Holy Spirit. ¹⁷So I have reason to be enthusiastic about all Christ Jesus has done through me in my service to God. ¹⁸Yet I dare not boast about anything except what Christ has done through me, bringing the Gentiles to God by my message and by the way I worked among them. ¹⁹They were convinced by the power of miraculous signs and wonders and by the power of God's Spirit.* In this way, I have fully presented the Good News of Christ from Jerusalem all the way to Illyricum.*

²⁰My ambition has always been to preach the Good News where the name of Christ has never been heard, rather than where a church has already been started by someone else. ²¹I have been following the plan spoken of in the Scriptures, where it says,

"Those who have never been told about him will see,
and those who have never heard of him will understand."*

²²In fact, my visit to you has been delayed so long because I have been preaching in these places.

*Paul's Travel Plans*

²³But now I have finished my work in these regions, and after all these long years of waiting, I am eager to visit you. ²⁴I am planning to go to Spain, and when I do, I will stop off in Rome. And after I have enjoyed your fellowship for a little while, you can provide for my journey.

²⁵But before I come, I must go to Jerusalem to take a gift to the believers* there. ²⁶For you see, the believers in Macedonia and Achaia* have eagerly taken up an offering for the poor among the believers in Jerusalem. ²⁷They were glad to do this because they feel they owe a real debt to them. Since the Gentiles received the spiritual blessings of the Good News from the believers in Jerusalem, they feel the least they can do in return is to help them financially. ²⁸As soon as I have delivered this money and completed this good deed of theirs, I will come to see you on my way to Spain. ²⁹And I am sure that when I come, Christ will richly bless our time together.

³⁰Dear brothers and sisters, I urge you in the name of our Lord Jesus Christ to join in my struggle by praying to God for me. Do this because of your love for me, given to you by the Holy Spirit. ³¹Pray that I will be rescued from those in Judea who refuse to obey God. Pray

**15:14** 2 Pet 1:12
**15:15** Rom 1:5; 12:3
**15:16** Phil 2:17
**15:17** Phil 3:3
**15:18** Rom 1:5
**15:19** Acts 19:11; 1 Cor 2:4; 1 Thes 1:5
**15:20** Rom 1:15; 1 Cor 3:10; 2 Cor 10:13, 15
**15:21** †Isa 52:15
**15:22** Rom 1:10-13; 1 Thes 2:18
**15:23** Acts 19:21; Rom 1:10-11
**15:24** 1 Cor 16:6
**15:25** Acts 19:21; 20:22
**15:26** 1 Cor 16:1; 2 Cor 8:1; 9:2
**15:27** 1 Cor 9:11
**15:29** Rom 1:10-11
**15:30** 2 Cor 1:11; Col 1:8; 4:12
**15:31** 2 Thes 3:2

**15:14** Greek *brothers;* also in 15:30. **15:19a** Other manuscripts read *the Spirit;* still others read *the Holy Spirit.* **15:19b** *Illyricum* was a region northeast of Italy. **15:21** Isa 52:15 (Greek version). **15:25** Greek *God's holy people;* also in 15:26, 31. **15:26** *Macedonia* and *Achaia* were the northern and southern regions of Greece.

**15:19** Illyricum was a Roman territory on the Adriatic Sea between present-day Italy and Greece. See the map in chapter 1, p. 1893.

**15:20** Paul says that he has "ambition." Ambition can be a difficult topic for Christians because we see so many bad examples of ambitious people who claw their way to the top. But certainly that isn't the kind of ambition one sees in Paul. Instead of looking out for himself and working hard for personal advancement, he was ambitious to serve God—for Paul that meant to "preach the Good News where the name of Christ has never been heard." Are you ambitious for God? Do you want, more than anything else, to please him and to do his will? Ask God for "holy ambition."

**15:22** Paul wanted to visit the church at Rome, but he had delayed his visit because he had heard many good reports about the believers there and knew they were doing well on their own. It was more important for him to preach in areas that had not yet heard the Good News.

**15:23, 24** Paul was referring to the completion of his work in Corinth, the city from which he most likely wrote this letter. Most of Paul's three-month stay in Achaia (see Acts 20:3) was probably spent in Corinth. He believed that he had accomplished

what God wanted him to do there, and he was looking forward to taking the Good News to new lands west of Rome. When Paul eventually went to Rome, however, it was as a prisoner (see Acts 28). Tradition says that Paul was released for a time and that he used this opportunity to go to Spain to preach the Good News. This journey is not mentioned in the book of Acts.

**15:28** Paul's future plan was to go to Spain because Spain was at the very western end of the civilized world. He wanted to bring Christianity there. Also, Spain had many great minds and influential leaders in the Roman world (Lucan, Martial, Hadrian), and perhaps Paul thought Christianity would advance greatly in such an atmosphere.

**15:30** Too often we see prayer as a time for comfort, reflection, or making requests to God. But here Paul urges believers to join in his *struggle* by means of prayer. Prayer is a weapon that all believers should use in interceding for others. Many of us know believers who are living in difficult places in order to communicate the gospel. Sending them funds is part of joining them in their struggles, but prayer is a crucial way of being with them. Missionaries strongly desire the prayers of those who have sent them out. Do your prayers reflect that struggle on their behalf?

15:32
Phlm 1:7

15:33
Rom 16:20
Heb 13:20

also that the believers there will be willing to accept the donation* I am taking to Jerusalem. ³²Then, by the will of God, I will be able to come to you with a joyful heart, and we will be an encouragement to each other.

³³And now may God, who gives us his peace, be with you all. Amen.*

## Paul Greets His Friends

16:1
Acts 18:18

16:2
Phil 2:29

**16** I commend to you our sister Phoebe, who is a deacon in the church in Cenchrea. ²Welcome her in the Lord as one who is worthy of honor among God's people. Help her in whatever she needs, for she has been helpful to many, and especially to me.

³Give my greetings to Priscilla and Aquila, my co-workers in the ministry of Christ Jesus.

16:5
1 Cor 16:15, 19
Col 4:15
Phlm 1:2

16:7
Rom 16:11, 21
Col 4:10
Phlm 1:23

⁴In fact, they once risked their lives for me. I am thankful to them, and so are all the Gentile churches. ⁵Also give my greetings to the church that meets in their home.

Greet my dear friend Epenetus. He was the first person from the province of Asia to become a follower of Christ. ⁶Give my greetings to Mary, who has worked so hard for your benefit. ⁷Greet Andronicus and Junia,* my fellow Jews,* who were in prison with me. They are highly respected among the apostles and became followers of Christ before I did. ⁸Greet Ampliatus, my dear friend in the Lord. ⁹Greet Urbanus, our co-worker in Christ, and my dear friend Stachys.

16:10
Acts 11:14

16:11
Rom 16:7, 21

16:13
Mark 15:21
2 Jn 1:1

¹⁰Greet Apelles, a good man whom Christ approves. And give my greetings to the believers from the household of Aristobulus. ¹¹Greet Herodion, my fellow Jew.* Greet the Lord's people from the household of Narcissus. ¹²Give my greetings to Tryphena and Tryphosa, the Lord's workers, and to dear Persis, who has worked so hard for the Lord. ¹³Greet Rufus, whom the Lord picked out to be his very own; and also his dear mother, who has been a mother to me.

16:16
1 Cor 16:20
1 Thes 5:26
1 Pet 5:14

¹⁴Give my greetings to Asyncritus, Phlegon, Hermes, Patrobas, Hermas, and the brothers and sisters* who meet with them. ¹⁵Give my greetings to Philologus, Julia, Nereus and his sister, and to Olympas and all the believers* who meet with them. ¹⁶Greet each other in Christian love.* All the churches of Christ send you their greetings.

## Paul's Final Instructions

16:17
1 Cor 5:9, 11
2 Thes 3:6
2 Tim 3:5
Titus 3:10
2 Jn 1:10

16:18
Phil 3:19
Col 2:4
2 Pet 2:3

16:19
Matt 10:16

¹⁷And now I make one more appeal, my dear brothers and sisters. Watch out for people who cause divisions and upset people's faith by teaching things contrary to what you have been taught. Stay away from them. ¹⁸Such people are not serving Christ our Lord; they are serving their own personal interests. By smooth talk and glowing words they deceive innocent people. ¹⁹But everyone knows that you are obedient to the Lord. This makes me very happy. I

**15:31** Greek *the ministry;* other manuscripts read *the gift.*    **15:33** Some manuscripts do not include *Amen.* One very early manuscript places 16:25-27 here.    **16:7a** *Junia* is a feminine name. Some late manuscripts accent the word so it reads *Junias,* a masculine name; still others read *Julia* (feminine).    **16:7b** Or *compatriots;* also in 16:21.    **16:11** Or *compatriot.*    **16:14** Greek *brothers;* also in 16:17.    **16:15** Greek *all of God's holy people.*    **16:16** Greek *with a sacred kiss.*

---

**15:33** This phrase sounds like it should signal the end of the letter, and it does pronounce the end of Paul's teaching. He concludes his letter, then, with personal greetings and remarks.

**16:1, 2** Phoebe was known as a "deacon," or servant and helper. Apparently she was a wealthy person who helped support Paul's ministry. Phoebe was highly regarded in the church, and she may have delivered this letter from Corinth to Rome. This provides evidence that women had important roles in the early church. Cenchrea, the town where Phoebe lived, was the eastern port of Corinth, six miles from the city center.

**16:3** Priscilla and Aquila were a married couple who had become Paul's close friends. They, along with all other Jews, had been expelled from Rome by the emperor (Acts 18:2, 3) and had moved to Corinth. There they met Paul and invited him to live with them. They were Christians before they met Paul and probably told him much about the Roman church. Like Paul, Priscilla and Aquila were missionaries. They helped believers in Ephesus (Acts 18:18-28), in Rome when they were allowed to return, and again at Ephesus (2 Timothy 4:19).

**16:3** Priscilla and Aquila ministered effectively behind the scenes. Their tools were hospitality, friendship, and person-to-person teaching. They were not public speakers, but private evangelists. For some of the Romans, their home was used for church meetings (16:5). Priscilla and Aquila challenge us with what a

couple can do together to serve Christ. Do we regard our families and homes as gifts through which God can accomplish his work? How might God want to use your home and family to serve him?

**16:5ff** Paul's personal greetings went to Romans and Greeks, Jews and Gentiles, men and women, prisoners and prominent citizens. The church's base was broad, crossing cultural, social, and economic lines. From this list we learn that the Christian community was mobile. Though Paul had not yet been to Rome, he had met these people in other places on his journeys.

**16:7** The fact that Andronicus and Junia were "highly respected among the apostles" could mean they had distinguished themselves as apostles. They may have been a husband and wife team. Paul notes that they were "fellow Jews" who at one time had been in prison with him.

**16:17-20** When we read books or listen to sermons, we should check the content of what is written or said so that we won't be fooled by smooth talk and glowing words. Christians who study God's Word, asking him to reveal the truth, will not be fooled, even though superficial Christians may easily be taken in. For an example of believers who carefully checked God's Word, see Acts 17:10-12.

want you to be wise in doing right and to stay innocent of any wrong. 20The God of peace will soon crush Satan under your feet. May the grace of our Lord Jesus* be with you.

21Timothy, my fellow worker, sends you his greetings, as do Lucius, Jason, and Sosipater, my fellow Jews.

22I, Tertius, the one writing this letter for Paul, send my greetings, too, as one of the Lord's followers.

23Gaius says hello to you. He is my host and also serves as host to the whole church. Erastus, the city treasurer, sends you his greetings, and so does our brother Quartus.*

25Now all glory to God, who is able to make you strong, just as my Good News says. This message about Jesus Christ has revealed his plan for you Gentiles, a plan kept secret from the beginning of time. 26But now as the prophets* foretold and as the eternal God has commanded, this message is made known to all Gentiles everywhere, so that they too might believe and obey him. 27All glory to the only wise God, through Jesus Christ, forever. Amen.

**16:20** Some manuscripts read *Lord Jesus Christ.*  **16:23** Some manuscripts add verse 24, *May the grace of our Lord Jesus Christ be with you all. Amen.* Still others add this sentence after verse 27.  **16:26** Greek *the prophetic writings.*

**16:20**
Gen 3:15

**16:21**
Acts 13:1; 16:1;
17:5

**16:25**
1 Cor 2:1
Eph 1:9; 3:3-5
Col 1:26-27; 2:2
2 Tim 1:9-10
1 Pet 1:20

**16:26**
Rom 1:2, 5

**16:27**
Rom 11:36

---

**16:21** Timothy was a key person in the growth of the early church, traveling with Paul on his second missionary journey (Acts 16:1-3). Later Paul wrote two letters to him as he worked to strengthen the churches in Ephesus—1 and 2 Timothy. See his Profile in the book of 1 Timothy 2, p. 2059.

**16:25-27** Paul exclaims that it is wonderful to be alive when the plan, God's secret—his way of saving the Gentiles—is becoming known throughout the world! All the Old Testament prophecies were coming true, and God was using Paul as his instrument to tell this Good News.

**16:25-27** As Jerusalem was the center of Jewish life, Rome was the world's political, religious, social, and economic center.

There the major governmental decisions were made, and from there the Good News spread to the ends of the earth. The church in Rome was a cosmopolitan mixture of Jews, Gentiles, slaves, free people, men, women, Roman citizens, and world travelers; therefore, it had potential for both great influence and great conflict.

Paul had not yet been to Rome to meet all the Christians there, and, of course, he has not yet met us. We, too, live in a cosmopolitan setting with the entire world open to us. We also have the potential for both widespread influence and wrenching conflict. Listen carefully to Paul's teachings about unity, service, and love so you may apply them.

ON A bed of grass, a chameleon's skin turns green. On the earth, it becomes brown. The animal changes to match the environment. Many creatures blend into nature with God-given camouflage suits to aid their survival. It's natural to fit in and adapt to the environment. But followers of Christ are *new creations,* born from above and changed from within, with values and lifestyles that confront the world and clash with accepted morals. True believers don't blend in very well.

The Christians in Corinth were struggling with their environment. Surrounded by corruption and every conceivable sin, they felt the pressure to adapt. They knew they were free in Christ, but what did this freedom mean? How should they view idols or sexuality? What should they do about marriage, women in the church, and the gifts of the Spirit? These were more than theoretical questions—the church was being undermined by immorality and spiritual immaturity. The believers' faith was being tried in the crucible of immoral Corinth, and some of them were failing the test.

Paul heard of their struggles and wrote this letter to address their problems, heal their divisions, and answer their questions. Paul confronted them with their sin and their need for corrective action and clear commitment to Christ.

After a brief introduction (1:1–9), Paul immediately turns to the question of unity (1:10—4:21). He emphasizes the clear and simple gospel message around which all believers should rally, he explains the role of church leaders, and he urges them to grow up in their faith.

Paul then deals with the immorality of certain church members and the issue of lawsuits among Christians (5:1—6:8). He tells the believers to exercise church discipline and to settle their internal matters themselves. Because so many of the problems in the Corinthian church involved sex, Paul denounces sexual sin in the strongest possible terms (6:9–20).

Next, Paul answers some of the Corinthians' questions. Because prostitution and immorality were pervasive, marriages in Corinth were in shambles, and Christians weren't sure how to react. Paul gives pointed and practical answers (7:1–40). Concerning the question of meat sacrificed to idols, Paul suggests that they show complete commitment to Christ and sensitivity to other believers, especially weaker brothers and sisters (8:1—11:1).

Paul goes on to talk about worship, and he carefully explains the role of women, the Lord's Supper, and spiritual gifts (11:2—14:40). Sandwiched in the middle of this section is his magnificent description of the greatest gift—love (chapter 13). Then Paul concludes with a discussion of the resurrection (15:1–58), some final thoughts, greetings, and a benediction (16:1–24).

This letter confronts the Corinthians about their sins and shortcomings. And 1 Corinthians calls all Christians to be careful not to blend in with the world and accept its values and life-styles. We must live Christ-centered, blameless, loving lives that make a difference for God. As you read 1 Corinthians, examine your values in light of complete commitment to Christ.

## VITAL STATISTICS

**PURPOSE:**
To identify problems in the Corinthian church, to offer solutions, and to teach the believers how to live for Christ in a corrupt society

**AUTHOR:**
Paul

**ORIGINAL AUDIENCE:**
The church in Corinth

**DATE WRITTEN:**
Approximately A.D. 55, near the end of Paul's three-year ministry in Ephesus, during his third missionary journey

**SETTING:**
Corinth was a major cosmopolitan city, a seaport and major trade center—the most important city in Achaia. It was also filled with idolatry and immorality. The church was largely made up of Gentiles. Paul had established this church on his second missionary journey.

**KEY VERSE:**
"I appeal to you, dear brothers and sisters, by the authority of our Lord Jesus Christ, to live in harmony with each other. Let there be no divisions in the church. Rather, be of one mind, united in thought and purpose" (1:10).

**KEY PEOPLE:**
Paul, Timothy, members of Chloe's household

**KEY PLACES:**
Worship meetings in Corinth

**SPECIAL FEATURES:**
This is a strong, straight-forward letter.

## THE BLUEPRINT

A. PAUL ADDRESSES CHURCH
   PROBLEMS
   (1:1—6:20)
   1. Divisions in the church
   2. Disorder in the church

B. PAUL ANSWERS CHURCH
   QUESTIONS
   (7:1—16:24)
   1. Instruction on Christian marriage
   2. Instruction on Christian freedom
   3. Instruction on public worship
   4. Instruction on resurrection

Without Paul's presence, the Corinthian church had fallen into divisiveness and disorder. This resulted in many problems, which Paul addressed squarely. We must be concerned for unity and order in our local churches, but we should not mistake inactivity for order and cordiality for unity. We, too, must squarely address problems in our churches.

The Corinthians had sent Paul a list of questions, and he answered them in a way meant to correct abuses in the church and to show how important it is that they live what they believe. Paul gives us a Christian approach to problem solving. He analyzed the problem thoroughly to uncover the underlying issue and then highlighted the biblical values that should guide our actions.

## MEGATHEMES

| THEME | EXPLANATION | IMPORTANCE |
|---|---|---|
| *Loyalties* | The Corinthians were rallying around various church leaders and teachers—Peter, Paul, and Apollos. These loyalties led to intellectual pride and created a spirit of division in the church. | Our loyalty to human leaders or human wisdom must never divide Christians into camps. We must care for our fellow believers, not fight with them. Your allegiance must be to Christ. Let him lead you. |
| *Immorality* | Paul received a report of uncorrected sexual sin in the church at Corinth. The people had grown indifferent to immorality. Others had misconceptions about marriage. We are to live morally, keeping our bodies for God's service at all times. | Christians must never compromise with sinful ideas and practices. We should not blend in with people around us. You must live up to God's standard of morality and not condone immoral behavior, even if society accepts it. |
| *Freedom* | Paul taught freedom of choice on practices not expressly forbidden in Scripture. Some believers felt certain actions—like eating the meat of animals used in pagan rituals—were corrupt by association. Others felt free to participate in such actions without feeling that they had sinned. | We are free in Christ, yet we must not abuse our Christian freedom by being inconsiderate and insensitive to others. We must never encourage others to do something they feel is wrong just because we have done it. Let love guide your behavior. |
| *Worship* | Paul addressed disorder in worship. People were taking the Lord's Supper without first confessing sin. There was misuse of spiritual gifts and confusion over women's roles in the church. | Worship must be carried out properly and in an orderly manner. Everything we do to worship God should be done in a manner worthy of his high honor. Make sure that worship is harmonious, useful, and edifying to all believers. |
| *Resurrection* | Some people denied that Christ rose from the dead. Others felt that people would not physically be resurrected. Christ's resurrection assures us that we will have new, living bodies after we die. The hope of the Resurrection forms the secret of Christian confidence. | Since we will be raised again to life after we die, our life is not in vain. We must stay faithful to God in our morality and our service. We are to live today knowing we will spend eternity with Christ. |

## A. PAUL ADDRESSES CHURCH PROBLEMS (1:1—6:20)
Through various sources, Paul had received reports of problems in the Corinthian church, including jealousy, divisiveness, sexual immorality, and failure to discipline members. Churches today must also address the problems they faced. We can learn a great deal by observing how Paul handled these delicate situations.

### Greetings from Paul

**1** This letter is from Paul, chosen by the will of God to be an apostle of Christ Jesus, and from our brother Sosthenes.

**1:1**
Acts 18:17
Rom 1:1

**1:1** Paul wrote this letter to the church in Corinth while he was visiting Ephesus during his third missionary journey (Acts 19:1–20:1). Corinth and Ephesus faced each other across the Aegean Sea. Paul knew the Corinthian church well because he had spent 18 months in Corinth during his second missionary journey (Acts 18:1-18). While in Ephesus, he had heard about problems in Corinth (1:11). About the same time, a delegation from the

Corinthian church had visited Paul to ask his advice about their conflicts (16:17). Paul's purpose for writing was to correct those problems and to answer questions church members had asked in a previous letter (7:1).

**1:1** Paul was given a special calling from God to preach about Jesus Christ. Each Christian has a job to do, a role to take, or a contribution to make. One assignment may seem more spectacular

**1:2**
Rom 8:28;
10:12-13
2 Tim 2:22

**1:3**
Rom 1:7

**1:5**
2 Cor 8:7; 9:11

²I am writing to God's church in Corinth,* to you who have been called by God to be his own holy people. He made you holy by means of Christ Jesus,* just as he did for all people everywhere who call on the name of our Lord Jesus Christ, their Lord and ours.

³May God our Father and the Lord Jesus Christ give you grace and peace.

### Paul Gives Thanks to God

⁴I always thank my God for you and for the gracious gifts he has given you, now that you belong to Christ Jesus. ⁵Through him, God has enriched your church in every way—with all of

**1:2a** *Corinth* was the capital city of Achaia, the southern region of the Greek peninsula. **1:2b** Or *because you belong to Christ Jesus.*

---

**CORINTH AND EPHESUS**
Paul wrote this letter to Corinth during his three-year visit in Ephesus on his third missionary journey. The two cities sat across from each other on the Aegean Sea—both were busy and important ports. Titus may have carried this letter from Ephesus to Corinth (2 Corinthians 12:18).

---

than another, but all are necessary to carry out God's greater plans for his church and for his world (12:12-27). Be available to God by placing your gifts at his service. Then as you discover what he calls you to do, be ready to do it.

**1:1** Sosthenes may have been Paul's secretary who wrote down this letter as Paul dictated it. He was probably the Jewish synagogue leader in Corinth (Acts 18:17) who had been beaten during an attack on Paul and then later became a believer. Sosthenes was well known to the members of the Corinthian church, and so Paul included his familiar name in the opening of the letter.

**1:2** Corinth, a giant cultural melting pot with a great diversity of wealth, religions, and moral standards, had a reputation for being fiercely independent and as decadent as any city in the world. The Romans had destroyed Corinth in 146 B.C. after a rebellion. But in 46 B.C., the Roman emperor Julius Caesar rebuilt it because of its strategic seaport. By Paul's day (A.D. 50), the Romans had made Corinth the capital of Achaia (present-day Greece). It was a large city, offering Rome great profits through trade as well as the military protection of its ports. But the city's prosperity made it ripe for all sorts of corruption. Idolatry flourished, and there were more than a dozen pagan temples employing at least a thousand prostitutes. Corinth's reputation was such that prostitutes in other cities began to be called "Corinthian girls."

**1:2** A personal invitation makes a person feel wanted and welcome. We are "called by God to be his own holy people." God personally invites us to be citizens of his eternal Kingdom. Jesus Christ, God's Son, is the only one who can bring us into this glorious Kingdom because he is the only one who removes our sins. "To be made holy" (or sanctified) means that we are chosen or set apart by Christ for his service. We accept God's invitation by accepting his Son, Jesus Christ, and by trusting in the work he did on the cross to forgive our sins.

**1:2** This was probably not meant to be a private letter; rather, it may have been circulated to other churches in nearby cities. Although it deals with specific issues facing the church at Corinth, all believers can learn from it. The Corinthian church included a great cross section of believers—wealthy merchants, common laborers, former temple prostitutes, and middle-class families. Because of the wide diversity of people and backgrounds, Paul takes great pains to stress the need for both spiritual unity and Christlike character.

**1:3** Grace is God's free gift of salvation given to us in Christ. Receiving it brings us peace (see Romans 5:1). In a world of noise, confusion, and relentless pressures, people long for peace. Many give up the search, thinking it impossible to find, but true peace of heart and mind is available to us through faith in Jesus Christ.

**1:4-6** Paul thanked God for the Corinthian believers. During the Thanksgiving holiday, we focus on our blessings and express our gratitude to God for them. But thanks should be expressed every day. We can never say thank you enough to parents, friends, leaders, and especially to God. When thanksgiving becomes an integral part of your life, you will find that your attitude toward life will change. You will become more positive, gracious, loving, and humble. Whom do you need to thank today?

your eloquent words and all of your knowledge. 6This confirms that what I told you about Christ is true. 7Now you have every spiritual gift you need as you eagerly wait for the return of our Lord Jesus Christ. 8He will keep you strong to the end so that you will be free from all blame on the day when our Lord Jesus Christ returns. 9God will do this, for he is faithful to do what he says, and he has invited you into partnership with his Son, Jesus Christ our Lord.

## 1. Divisions in the church

10I appeal to you, dear brothers and sisters,* by the authority of our Lord Jesus Christ, to live in harmony with each other. Let there be no divisions in the church. Rather, be of one mind, united in thought and purpose. 11For some members of Chloe's household have told me about your quarrels, my dear brothers and sisters. 12Some of you are saying, "I am a follower of Paul." Others are saying, "I follow Apollos," or "I follow Peter,*" or "I follow only Christ."

13Has Christ been divided into factions? Was I, Paul, crucified for you? Were any of you baptized in the name of Paul? Of course not! 14I thank God that I did not baptize any of you except Crispus and Gaius, 15for now no one can say they were baptized in my name. 16(Oh yes, I also baptized the household of Stephanas, but I don't remember baptizing anyone else.) 17For Christ didn't send me to baptize, but to preach the Good News—and not with clever speech, for fear that the cross of Christ would lose its power.

### The Wisdom of God

18The message of the cross is foolish to those who are headed for destruction! But we who are being saved know it is the very power of God. 19As the Scriptures say,

**1:10** Greek *brothers;* also in 1:11, 26.   **1:12** Greek *Cephas.*

---

**1:7**
Rom 8:19, 23
Phil 3:20
2 Thes 1:7
Titus 2:13
2 Pet 3:12

**1:8**
Phil 1:6
1 Thes 3:13; 5:23

**1:10**
Rom 15:5
1 Cor 11:18

**1:12**
John 1:42
Acts 18:24
1 Cor 3:4

**1:14**
Acts 18:8; 19:29
Rom 16:23

**1:17**
Matt 28:19
John 4:2
Acts 26:17
2 Cor 10:10; 11:16

**1:18**
Rom 1:16
1 Cor 2:14
2 Cor 2:15; 4:3

**1:19**
†Isa 29:14

---

**1:7** The Corinthian church members had all the spiritual gifts they needed to live the Christian life, to witness for Christ, and to stand against the paganism and immorality of Corinth. But instead of using what God had given them, they were arguing over which gifts were more important. Paul addresses this issue in depth in chapters 12–14.

**1:7-9** Before tackling the problems, Paul described his hope for the Corinthians. He guaranteed these believers that God would consider them "free from all blame" when Christ returns (see also Ephesians 1:7-10). This guarantee was not because of their great gifts or their shining performance, but because of what Jesus Christ accomplished for them through his death and resurrection. *All* who believe in the Lord Jesus will be considered blameless when Jesus Christ returns (see also 1 Thessalonians 3:13; Hebrews 9:28). Today's struggles, difficulties, and failures don't tell the whole story. Keep the big picture in mind. If you have faith in Christ, even if it is weak, you *are* and *will be* saved.

**1:10** Paul founded the church in Corinth on his second missionary journey. Eighteen months after he left, arguments and divisions arose, and some church members slipped back into an immoral life-style. Paul wrote this letter to address the problems and to clear up confusion about right and wrong so that they would remove the immorality from among them. The Corinthian people had a reputation for jumping from fad to fad; Paul wanted to keep Christianity from degenerating into just another fad.

**1:10** By saying "brothers and sisters," Paul is emphasizing that all Christians are part of God's family. Believers share a unity that runs even deeper than that of blood brothers and sisters.

**1:10, 11** Like a frustrated coach watching his team bicker on the court, Paul called for a time-out. He saw the danger of divisions and arguments. The Corinthian believers' lack of unity was obvious. They may have been playing in the same "uniform," but they were doing as much as the opposition to bring about their own defeat. The problems weren't so much differences of opinion as divided allegiances. They were arguing over which position on the team was most important in a way that made them ineffective as a unit. They were on the field, but out of the game.

Divisions between Christians work like brick walls and barbed-wire fences to undermine the effectiveness of the message that believers are to proclaim. Focus on your coach, Jesus Christ, and the purpose he has for you. Strive for harmony. Keep arguments about allegiances off the team.

**1:12ff** In this large and diverse Corinthian church, the believers favored different preachers. Because there was as yet no written New Testament, the believers depended heavily on preaching and teaching for spiritual insight into the meaning of the Old Testament. Some followed Paul, who had founded their church; some who had heard Peter in Jerusalem followed him; others listened only to Apollos, an eloquent and popular preacher who had had a dynamic ministry in Corinth (Acts 18:24; 19:1). Although these three preachers were united in their message, their personalities attracted different people. At this time the church was in danger of dividing. By mentioning Jesus Christ 10 times in the first 10 verses, Paul makes it clear who it is all preachers and teachers should emphasize. God's message is much more important than any human messenger.

**1:12, 13** Paul wondered whether the Corinthians' quarrels had "divided" Christ into factions. This is a graphic picture of what happens when the church (the body of Christ) is divided. With the many churches and styles of worship available today, we could get caught up in the same game of "my preacher is better than yours!" To do so would divide Christ again. But Christ is not divided, and his true followers should not allow anything to divide them. Don't let your appreciation for any teacher, preacher, or author lead you into pride. Our allegiance must be to Christ and to the unity that he desires.

**1:17** When Paul said that Christ didn't send him to baptize, he wasn't minimizing the importance of baptism. Baptism was commanded by Jesus himself (Matthew 28:19) and practiced by the early church (Acts 2:41). Paul was emphasizing that no one person should do everything. Paul's gift was preaching, and that's what he did. Christian ministry should be a team effort; no preacher or teacher is a complete link between God and people, and no individual can do all that the apostles did. We must be content to operate within the gifts God has given to us, and carry out his plan wholeheartedly. (For more on different gifts, see chapters 12 and 13.)

**1:17** Some speakers use impressive words, but they are weak on content. Paul stressed solid content and practical help for his listeners. He wanted them to be impressed with his *message,* not just his style (see 2:1-5). You don't need to be a great speaker with a large vocabulary to share the Good News effectively. The persuasive power is in the story, not the storyteller. Paul was not against those who carefully prepare what they say (see 2:6) but against those who try to impress others with their knowledge or speaking ability.

**1:19** Paul summarizes Isaiah 29:14 to emphasize a point Jesus often made: God's way of thinking is not like the world's way

**1:20**
Job 12:17
Isa 19:11-12; 44:25
1 Cor 2:6, 8

**1:21**
Matt 11:25

**1:22**
Matt 12:38

**1:23**
1 Cor 2:2

**1:24**
Col 2:3

**1:25**
2 Cor 13:4

**1:26**
Matt 11:25
John 7:48
Jas 2:1-5

**1:27**
1 Cor 3:18-19

**1:28**
Rom 4:17

**1:29**
Eph 2:9

**1:30**
Jer 23:5-6
Rom 3:24
2 Cor 5:21

**1:31**
†Jer 9:24
2 Cor 10:17

"I will destroy the wisdom of the wise
 and discard the intelligence of the intelligent."*

20So where does this leave the philosophers, the scholars, and the world's brilliant debaters? God has made the wisdom of this world look foolish. 21Since God in his wisdom saw to it that the world would never know him through human wisdom, he has used our foolish preaching to save those who believe. 22It is foolish to the Jews, who ask for signs from heaven. And it is foolish to the Greeks, who seek human wisdom. 23So when we preach that Christ was crucified, the Jews are offended and the Gentiles say it's all nonsense.

24But to those called by God to salvation, both Jews and Gentiles,* Christ is the power of God and the wisdom of God. 25This foolish plan of God is wiser than the wisest of human plans, and God's weakness is stronger than the greatest of human strength.

26Remember, dear brothers and sisters, that few of you were wise in the world's eyes or powerful or wealthy* when God called you. 27Instead, God chose things the world considers foolish in order to shame those who think they are wise. And he chose things that are powerless to shame those who are powerful. 28God chose things despised by the world,* things counted as nothing at all, and used them to bring to nothing what the world considers important. 29As a result, no one can ever boast in the presence of God.

30God has united you with Christ Jesus. For our benefit God made him to be wisdom itself. Christ made us right with God; he made us pure and holy, and he freed us from sin. 31Therefore, as the Scriptures say, "If you want to boast, boast only about the LORD."*

**1:19** Isa 29:14.   **1:24** Greek *and Greeks.*   **1:26** Or *high born.*   **1:28** Or *God chose those who are low born.*
**1:31** Jer 9:24.

---

**HIGHLIGHTS OF 1 CORINTHIANS**

| | | |
|---|---|---|
| The Meaning of the Cross 1:18–2:16 | Be considerate of one another because of what Christ has done for us. There is no place for pride or a know-it-all attitude. We are to have the mind of Christ. |
| The Story of the Last Supper 11:23-29 | The Last Supper is a time of reflection on Christ's final words to his disciples before he died on the cross; we must celebrate this in an orderly and correct manner. |
| The Poem of Love 13:1-13 | Love is to guide all we do. We have different gifts, abilities, likes, dislikes—but we are called, without exception, to love. |
| The Christian's Destiny 15:42-58 | We are promised by Christ, who died for us, that as he came back to life after death, so our perishable bodies will be exchanged for heavenly bodies. Then we will live and reign with Christ. |

---

(normal human wisdom). And God offers eternal life, which the world can never give. We can spend a lifetime accumulating wisdom and yet never learn how to have a personal relationship with God. We must come to the crucified and risen Christ to receive eternal life and the joy of a personal relationship with our Savior.

**1:22-24** Many Jews considered the Good News of Jesus Christ to be foolish, because they thought the Messiah would be a conquering king accompanied by signs and miracles. Jesus had not restored David's throne as they expected. Besides, he was executed as a criminal, and how could a criminal be a savior? Greeks, too, considered the Good News foolish: They did not believe in a bodily resurrection, they did not see in Jesus the powerful characteristics of their mythological gods, and they thought no reputable person would be crucified. To them, death was defeat, not victory.

The Good News of Jesus Christ still sounds foolish to many. Our society worships power, influence, and wealth. Jesus came as a humble, poor servant, and he offers his Kingdom to those who have faith, not to those who do all kinds of good deeds to try to earn salvation. This looks foolish to the world, but Christ is the mighty power of God, the only way we can be saved. Knowing Christ personally is the greatest wisdom anyone can have.

**1:25** The message of Christ's death for sins sounds foolish to those who don't believe. Death seems to be the end of the road, the ultimate weakness. But Jesus did not stay dead. His resurrection demonstrated his power even over death. And he will save us

from eternal death and give us everlasting life if we trust him as Savior and Lord. This sounds so simple that many people won't accept it. They try other ways to obtain eternal life (being good, being wise, etc.). But all their attempts are futile. The "foolish" people who simply accept Christ's offer are actually the wisest of all, because they alone will live eternally with God.

**1:27** Is Christianity against rational thinking? Christians clearly do believe in using their minds to weigh the evidence and make wise choices. Paul is declaring that no amount of human knowledge can replace or bypass Christ's work on the cross. If it could, Christ would be accessible only to the intellectually gifted and well educated and not to ordinary people or to children.

**1:28-31** Paul continues to emphasize that the way to receive salvation is so simple that *any* person who wants to can understand it. Skill and wisdom do not get a person into God's Kingdom—simple faith does. So no one can boast that personal achievements helped him or her secure eternal life. Salvation is totally from God through Jesus' death. There is *nothing* we can do to earn our salvation; we need only to accept what Jesus has already done for us.

**1:30** God is our source and the reason for our personal relationship with Christ. Our union and identification with Christ results in our having God's wisdom (Colossians 2:3), being acceptable to God (2 Corinthians 5:21), being pure (1 Thessalonians 4:3-7), and having the penalty for our sins paid by Jesus (Mark 10:45).

## Paul's Message of Wisdom

**2** When I first came to you, dear brothers and sisters,* I didn't use lofty words and impressive wisdom to tell you God's secret plan.* ²For I decided that while I was with you I would forget everything except Jesus Christ, the one who was crucified. ³I came to you in weakness—timid and trembling. ⁴And my message and my preaching were very plain. Rather than using clever and persuasive speeches, I relied only on the power of the Holy Spirit. ⁵I did this so you would trust not in human wisdom but in the power of God.

⁶Yet when I am among mature believers, I do speak with words of wisdom, but not the kind of wisdom that belongs to this world or to the rulers of this world, who are soon forgotten. ⁷No, the wisdom we speak of is the mystery of God*—his plan that was previously hidden, even though he made it for our ultimate glory before the world began. ⁸But the rulers of this world have not understood it; if they had, they would not have crucified our glorious Lord. ⁹That is what the Scriptures mean when they say,

"No eye has seen, no ear has heard,
   and no mind has imagined
what God has prepared
   for those who love him."*

¹⁰But* it was to us that God revealed these things by his Spirit. For his Spirit searches out everything and shows us God's deep secrets. ¹¹No one can know a person's thoughts except that person's own spirit, and no one can know God's thoughts except God's own Spirit. ¹²And we have received God's Spirit (not the world's spirit), so we can know the wonderful things God has freely given us.

¹³When we tell you these things, we do not use words that come from human wisdom. Instead, we speak words given to us by the Spirit, using the Spirit's words to explain spiritual truths.* ¹⁴But people who aren't spiritual* can't receive these truths from God's Spirit. It all

**2:1** 1 Cor 1:17
**2:3** 2 Cor 10:1; Gal 4:13
**2:4** 1 Cor 4:20
**2:5** 2 Cor 4:7; 6:7
**2:6** Eph 4:13; Phil 3:15; Heb 5:14
**2:7** Rom 16:25
**2:8** Jas 2:1
**2:9** †Isa 64:4; 65:17
**2:10** Matt 11:25; 13:11; John 14:26; 15:26; 16:13-15; 1 Jn 2:27
**2:11** Prov 20:27; Jer 17:9; Rom 11:33
**2:12** John 16:13-15; Rom 8:15; 1 Cor 1:27
**2:13** 1 Cor 1:17; 2:4; 2 Pet 1:20-21
**2:14** John 8:47; 14:17; Jude 1:19

**2:1a** Greek *brothers.*   **2:1b** Greek *God's mystery;* other manuscripts read *God's testimony.*   **2:7** Greek *But we speak God's wisdom in a mystery.*   **2:9** Isa 64:4.   **2:10** Some manuscripts read *For.*   **2:13** Or *explaining spiritual truths in spiritual language,* or *explaining spiritual truths to spiritual people.*   **2:14** Or *who don't have the Spirit;* or *who have only physical life.*

---

**2:1** Paul was referring to his first visit to Corinth during his second missionary journey (A.D. 51), when he founded the church (Acts 18:1ff).

**2:1-5** A brilliant scholar, Paul could have overwhelmed his listeners with intellectual arguments. Instead, he shared the simple message of Jesus Christ by allowing the Holy Spirit to guide his words. In sharing the Good News with others, we should follow Paul's example and keep our message simple and basic. The Holy Spirit will give power to our words and use them to bring glory to Jesus.

**2:4** Paul's confidence was not in his keen intellect or speaking ability but in his knowledge that the Holy Spirit was helping and guiding him. Paul is not denying the importance of study and preparation for preaching; he had a thorough education in the Scriptures. Effective preaching results from studious preparation and reliance on the work of the Holy Spirit. Don't use Paul's statement as an excuse for not studying or preparing.

**2:7** "The mystery of God . . . that was previously hidden" was his offer of salvation to all people. Originally unknown to humanity, this plan became crystal clear when Jesus rose from the dead. His resurrection proved that he had power over sin and death and could offer us this power as well (see also 1 Peter 1:10-12 and the first note on Romans 16:25-27). God's plan, however, is still hidden to unbelievers because they either refuse to accept it, choose to ignore it, or simply haven't heard about it.

**2:8** Jesus was misunderstood and rejected by those whom the world considered wise and great. He was put to death by the rulers in Palestine—the high priest, King Herod, Pilate, and the Pharisees and Sadducees. Jesus' rejection by these rulers had been predicted in Isaiah 53:3 and Zechariah 12:10, 11.

**2:9** We cannot imagine all that God has in store for us, both in this life and for eternity. He will create a new heaven and a new earth (Isaiah 65:17; Revelation 21:1), and we will live with him forever. Until then, his Holy Spirit comforts and guides us. Knowing the wonderful and eternal future that awaits us gives us hope and courage to press on in this life, to endure hardship, and to avoid giving in to temptation. This world is not all there is. The best is yet to come.

**2:10** "God's deep secrets" refers to God's unfathomable nature and his wonderful plan—Jesus' death and resurrection—and to the promise of salvation, revealed only to those who believe that what God says is true. Those who believe in Christ's death and resurrection and put their faith in him will know all they need to know to be saved. This knowledge, however, can't be grasped by even the wisest people unless they accept God's message. All who reject God's message are foolish, no matter how wise the world thinks they are.

**2:13** Everyone wants to be wise. Yet Paul taught the Corinthians that true wisdom or discernment requires the believer to be guided by the Holy Spirit. Because Satan's greatest impact on us occurs when he deceives us, we need the Holy Spirit's help. Spiritual discernment enables us to draw conclusions based on God's perspective, make wise decisions in difficult circumstances, recognize the activities of God's Spirit, distinguish the correct and incorrect use of Scripture, and identify and expose false teachers. Ask God to give you his discernment as you serve him. Let that discernment guide you in your daily walk.

**2:14, 15** Non-Christians cannot understand spiritual truths, and they cannot grasp the concept that God's Spirit lives in believers. Don't expect most people to approve of or understand your decision to follow Christ. It all seems so silly to them. Just as a tone-deaf person cannot appreciate fine music, the person who rejects Christ cannot understand truths from God's Spirit. With the lines of communication broken, he or she won't be able to hear what God is saying to him or her.

We must not remain silent, however, using others' difficulty sounds foolish to them and they can't understand it, for only those who are spiritual can understand what the Spirit means. 15Those who are spiritual can evaluate all things, but they themselves cannot be evaluated by others. 16For,

"Who can know the LORD's thoughts?
　　Who knows enough to teach him?"*

But we understand these things, for we have the mind of Christ.

### Paul and Apollos, Servants of Christ

**3** Dear brothers and sisters,* when I was with you I couldn't talk to you as I would to spiritual people.* I had to talk as though you belonged to this world or as though you were infants in the Christian life.* 2I had to feed you with milk, not with solid food, because you weren't ready for anything stronger. And you still aren't ready, 3for you are still controlled by your sinful nature. You are jealous of one another and quarrel with each other. Doesn't that prove you are controlled by your sinful nature? Aren't you living like people of the world? 4When one of you says, "I am a follower of Paul," and another says, "I follow Apollos," aren't you acting just like people of the world?

5After all, who is Apollos? Who is Paul? We are only God's servants through whom you believed the Good News. Each of us did the work the Lord gave us. 6I planted the seed in your hearts, and Apollos watered it, but it was God who made it grow. 7It's not important who does the planting, or who does the watering. What's important is that God makes the seed grow. 8The one who plants and the one who waters work together with the same purpose. And both will be rewarded for their own hard work. 9For we are both God's workers. And you are God's field. You are God's building.

10Because of God's grace to me, I have laid the foundation like an expert builder. Now others are building on it. But whoever is building on this foundation must be very careful. 11For no one can lay any foundation other than the one we already have—Jesus Christ. 12Anyone who builds on that foundation may use a variety of materials—gold, silver, jewels,

**2:15**
1 Cor 3:1
1 Jn 2:20

**2:16**
†Isa 40:13
Rom 11:34

**3:1**
Gal 6:1
Eph 4:14

**3:2**
Heb 5:12-13
1 Pet 2:2

**3:3**
Rom 13:13
1 Cor 1:10-11;
11:18

**3:4**
1 Cor 1:12

**3:5**
Acts 18:24
Rom 12:3, 6
2 Cor 6:4

**3:6**
Acts 18:4-11

**3:8**
Pss 18:20; 62:12

**3:9**
Isa 61:3
Eph 2:20-22
1 Pet 2:5

**3:10**
Rom 15:20

**3:11**
Isa 28:16
Eph 2:20
1 Pet 2:4-6

**2:16** Isa 40:13 (Greek version).　**3:1a** Greek *Brothers.*　**3:1b** Or *to people who have the Spirit.*
**3:1c** Greek *in Christ.*

---

in understanding as an excuse. We are still one of God's communication channels. We must be alert to opportunities. Another person's question may be evidence that God's Spirit is drawing him or her to the point of decision. How would you respond today if someone asked you about your faith?

**2:15, 16** No one can know what the Lord is thinking (Romans 11:34), but through the guidance of the Holy Spirit, believers have insight into some of God's plans, thoughts, and actions. They, in fact, have "the mind of Christ." Through the Holy Spirit, we can begin to know God's thoughts, talk with him, and expect his answers to our prayers. Are you spending enough time with Christ to have his very mind in you? An intimate relationship with Christ comes only from spending time consistently in his presence and in his Word. Read Philippians 2:5ff for more on the mind of Christ.

**3:1-3** Paul called the Corinthians infants in the Christian life because they were not yet spiritually healthy and mature. The proof was that they quarreled like children, allowing divisions to distract them. Immature Christians are "worldly," controlled by their own desires; mature believers are in tune with God's desires. How much influence do your desires have on your life? Your goal should be to let God's desires be yours. Being controlled by your own desires will stunt your growth.

**3:6** Paul planted the seed of the Good News message in people's hearts. He was a missionary pioneer; he brought the message of salvation. Apollos watered the seed. He helped the believers grow stronger in the faith. Paul founded the church in Corinth, and Apollos built on that foundation. Tragically, the believers in Corinth had split into factions, pledging loyalty to different teachers (see 1:11-13). After the preachers' work is completed, God is the one who makes Christians grow. Our leaders should certainly be respected, but we should never place

them on pedestals that create barriers between people or set them up as a substitute for Christ.

**3:7-9** God's work involves many different individuals with a variety of gifts and abilities. There are no superstars in this task, only team members performing their own special roles. We can become useful members of God's team by setting aside our desires to receive glory for what we do. Don't seek the praise that comes from people—it is comparatively worthless. Instead, seek approval from God.

**3:10, 11** The foundation of the church—of all believers—is Jesus Christ. Nothing and no one else will do, wrote Paul. A building with no foundation, or one poorly constructed, will not last. The finest materials used to construct a home quickly rot and fall apart if they are resting on the ground. And a building is only as solid as its foundation. The foundation of our life is Jesus Christ; he is our base, our reason for being. Everything we are and do must fit into the pattern provided by him. Are you building your life on the only real and lasting foundation, or are you building on a faulty foundation, such as wealth, security, success, or fame? Be careful how you build.

**3:10-17** While some have applied these verses to personal spiritual growth, Paul's teaching has to do with ministry to others. What do we do to build others up? Do we build on Christ as foundation? Do we build with perishable materials? The Corinthians could construct their church with lasting, eternal teaching or with the changing, temporary wisdom of the day.

Paul's words challenge our methods of discipleship. Do we attach others to ourselves as the foundation, or to Christ? Do we use our abilities and spiritual gifts to build up others in the church or keep them tied to us? Do we use Bible-based teaching or merely adaptations of worldly wisdom?

wood, hay, or straw. 13But on the judgment day, fire will reveal what kind of work each builder has done. The fire will show if a person's work has any value. 14If the work survives, that builder will receive a reward. 15But if the work is burned up, the builder will suffer great loss. The builder will be saved, but like someone barely escaping through a wall of flames.

16Don't you realize that all of you together are the temple of God and that the Spirit of God lives in* you? 17God will destroy anyone who destroys this temple. For God's temple is holy, and you are that temple.

18Stop deceiving yourselves. If you think you are wise by this world's standards, you need to become a fool to be truly wise. 19For the wisdom of this world is foolishness to God. As the Scriptures say,

"He traps the wise
    in the snare of their own cleverness."*

20And again,

"The Lord knows the thoughts of the wise;
    he knows they are worthless."*

21So don't boast about following a particular human leader. For everything belongs to you— 22whether Paul or Apollos or Peter,* or the world, or life and death, or the present and the future. Everything belongs to you, 23and you belong to Christ, and Christ belongs to God.

## Paul's Relationship with the Corinthians

**4** So look at Apollos and me as mere servants of Christ who have been put in charge of explaining God's mysteries. 2Now, a person who is put in charge as a manager must be faithful. 3As for me, it matters very little how I might be evaluated by you or by any human authority. I don't even trust my own judgment on this point. 4My conscience is clear, but that doesn't prove I'm right. It is the Lord himself who will examine me and decide.

5So don't make judgments about anyone ahead of time—before the Lord returns. For he will bring our darkest secrets to light and will reveal our private motives. Then God will give to each one whatever praise is due.

6Dear brothers and sisters,* I have used Apollos and myself to illustrate what I've been saying. If you pay attention to what I have quoted from the Scriptures,* you won't be proud of one of your leaders at the expense of another. 7For what gives you the right to make such a judgment? What do you have that God hasn't given you? And if everything you have is from God, why boast as though it were not a gift?

**3:13**
1 Cor 4:5
**3:14**
2 Tim 1:12, 18; 4:8
**3:15**
Jude 1:23
**3:16**
1 Cor 6:19
2 Cor 6:16
**3:17**
Eph 2:21-22
**3:18**
Isa 5:21
1 Cor 8:2
Gal 6:3
**3:19**
†Job 5:13
1 Cor 1:20, 27
**3:20**
†Ps 94:11
**3:21**
Rom 8:32
**3:22**
Rom 8:38
**3:23**
1 Cor 11:3
**4:1**
Rom 16:25
Titus 1:7
**4:2**
Luke 12:42
**4:4**
Ps 143:2
**4:5**
Matt 7:1
1 Cor 3:8
2 Cor 5:10
Rev 20:12
**4:6**
1 Cor 1:12, 31
**4:7**
John 3:27
Rom 12:3, 6

**3:16** Or *among.*   **3:19** Job 5:13.   **3:20** Ps 94:11.   **3:22** Greek *Cephas.*   **4:6a** Greek *Brothers.*   **4:6b** Or *If you learn not to go beyond "what is written."*

---

**3:13-15** Two sure ways to destroy a building are to tamper with the foundation and to build with inferior materials. The church must be built on Christ, not on any other person or principle. Christ will evaluate each person's contribution to the life of the church, and judgment day will reveal the sincerity of each person's work. God will determine whether or not a person has been faithful to Jesus' instructions. Good work will be rewarded; unfaithful or inferior work will be discounted. "The builder will be saved, but like someone barely escaping through a wall of flames" means that unfaithful workers will be saved, but only by the skin of their teeth. All their accomplishments will count for nothing.

**3:16, 17** Paul wanted the Corinthians to understand that they were a unified assembly ("all of you together are the temple of God" and "the Spirit of God lives in you"). They were not to see themselves as a collection of competing interests or independent individuals. Paul was emphasizing the intent of Jesus' prayer in John 17:21-23 that believers be unified in God. What actions could you take this week to strengthen your ties to fellow Christians in the church of Jesus Christ?

**3:18-21** Paul was not telling the Corinthian believers to neglect the pursuit of knowledge. He was warning them not to glory in the wisdom of this age. God's way of thinking is far above ours; he knows all the futile thoughts of the "wise." The Corinthians were boasting about the wisdom of their leaders and teachers.

Their pride made them value the messenger more than the message. We are not to put our trust in anyone but God.

**3:22** Paul says that both life and death are ours. While nonbelievers are victims of life, swept along by its current and wondering if there is meaning to it, believers can use life well because they understand its true purpose. Nonbelievers can only fear death. For believers, however, death holds no terrors because Christ has conquered all fears (see 1 John 4:18). Death is only the beginning of eternal life with God.

**4:1, 2** Paul urged the Corinthians to think of him, Peter, and Apollos as mere servants of Christ entrusted with the secret things of God (see the note on 2:7). A servant does what his master tells him to do. We must do what God tells us to do in the Bible and through his Holy Spirit. Each day God presents us with needs and opportunities that challenge us to do what we know is right.

**4:5** It is tempting to judge fellow Christians, evaluating whether or not they are good followers of Christ. But only God knows a person's heart, and he is the only one with the right to judge. Paul's warning to the Corinthians should also warn us. We are to confront those who are sinning (see 5:12, 13), but we must not judge who is a better servant for Christ. When you judge someone, you invariably consider yourself better—and that is arrogant.

**4:6, 7** How easy it is for us to become attached to a spiritual leader. When someone has helped us, it's natural to feel loyalty.

**4:8**
Rev 3:17, 21

**4:9**
Rom 8:36
Heb 10:33

**4:10**
1 Cor 1:18; 3:18
2 Cor 11:19

**4:11**
Acts 23:2
Rom 8:35
2 Cor 11:23-27

**4:12**
Matt 5:44
Acts 18:3
1 Pet 3:9

**4:14**
1 Cor 6:5; 15:34
2 Cor 6:13

**4:16**
1 Cor 11:1
Phil 3:17
1 Thes 1:6

⁸You think you already have everything you need. You think you are already rich. You have begun to reign in God's kingdom without us! I wish you really were reigning already, for then we would be reigning with you. ⁹Instead, I sometimes think God has put us apostles on display, like prisoners of war at the end of a victor's parade, condemned to die. We have become a spectacle to the entire world—to people and angels alike.

¹⁰Our dedication to Christ makes us look like fools, but you claim to be so wise in Christ! We are weak, but you are so powerful! You are honored, but we are ridiculed. ¹¹Even now we go hungry and thirsty, and we don't have enough clothes to keep warm. We are often beaten and have no home. ¹²We work wearily with our own hands to earn our living. We bless those who curse us. We are patient with those who abuse us. ¹³We appeal gently when evil things are said about us. Yet we are treated like the world's garbage, like everybody's trash—right up to the present moment.

¹⁴I am not writing these things to shame you, but to warn you as my beloved children. ¹⁵For even if you had ten thousand others to teach you about Christ, you have only one spiritual father. For I became your father in Christ Jesus when I preached the Good News to you. ¹⁶So I urge you to imitate me.

¹⁷That's why I have sent Timothy, my beloved and faithful child in the Lord. He will remind you of how I follow Christ Jesus, just as I teach in all the churches wherever I go.

---

**SET AN EXAMPLE FOR OTHERS**
Throughout Scripture, setting an example is stressed as an important element of discipleship.

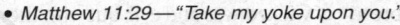

- *Matthew 11:29—"Take my yoke upon you."*
  Jesus told his followers to learn from his example of gentleness and humility.

- *Philippians 3:17—"Pattern your lives after mine."*
  Paul urged believers to follow his example of enthusiasm, perseverance, and maturity.

- *1 Thessalonians 1:6-7—"You imitated both us and the Lord. . . . You have become an example."*
  The new Christians at Thessalonica received training in discipleship from Paul, and even in suffering they expressed what they had learned.

- *1 Timothy 1:16—"But God had mercy on me so that Christ Jesus could use me as a prime example of his great patience with even the worst sinners."*
  Paul used his unworthiness to receive Christ as an example of grace so that no one would hold back from coming to Christ.

- *1 Peter 5:3—"Don't lord it over the people assigned to your care, but lead them by your own good example."*
  Peter taught Christian leaders to lead by example, not by commands.

Paul told the Corinthian believers to imitate him (4:16). As the body of Christ, believers must show Christ to the world by being examples. Nonbelievers should be able to see Christ in believers and be so drawn to what they see that they seek Christ and his salvation. What kind of example are you?

---

But Paul warns against having such pride in our favorite leaders that we cause divisions in the church. Any true spiritual leader is a representative of Christ and has nothing to offer that God hasn't given him or her. Don't let your loyalty cause strife, slander, or broken relationships. Make sure that your deepest loyalties are to Christ and not to his human agents. Those who spend more time in debating church leadership than in declaring Christ's message don't have the mind of Christ.

**4:6-13** The Corinthians had split into various cliques, each following its favorite preacher (Paul, Apollos, Peter, etc.). Each clique really believed it was the only one to have the whole truth and thus felt spiritually proud. But Paul told the groups not to boast about being tied to a particular preacher, because each preacher was simply a humble servant who had suffered for the same message of salvation in Jesus Christ. No preacher of God has more status than another.

**4:15** Paul was calling attention to his special role as the Corinthians' spiritual father. In an attempt to unify the church, Paul appealed to his relationship with them. By *father,* he meant he was the church's founder. Because he started the church, he could be trusted to have its best interests at heart. Paul's tough words were motivated by love—like the love a good father has for his children (see also 1 Thessalonians 2:11).

**4:16** Paul told the Corinthians to imitate him—to follow his example. He was able to make this statement because he walked close to God, spent time in God's Word and in prayer, and was aware of God's presence in his life at all times. God was Paul's example; therefore, Paul's life could be an example to other Christians. Paul wasn't expecting others to imitate everything he did, but they should imitate those aspects of his beliefs and conduct that were modeling Christ's way of living.

**4:17** Timothy had traveled with Paul on Paul's second missionary journey (see Acts 16:1-3) and was a key person in the growth of the early church. Timothy probably did not deliver this letter to Corinth but more likely arrived there shortly after the letter came (see 16:10). Timothy's role was to see that Paul's advice was read and implemented. Then he was to return to Paul and report on the church's progress.

<sup>18</sup>Some of you have become arrogant, thinking I will not visit you again. <sup>19</sup>But I will come— and soon—if the Lord lets me, and then I'll find out whether these arrogant people just give pretentious speeches or whether they really have God's power. <sup>20</sup>For the Kingdom of God is not just a lot of talk; it is living by God's power. <sup>21</sup>Which do you choose? Should I come with a rod to punish you, or should I come with love and a gentle spirit?

## 2. Disorder in the church

*Paul Condemns Spiritual Pride*

**5** I can hardly believe the report about the sexual immorality going on among you—something that even pagans don't do. I am told that a man in your church is living in sin with his stepmother.* <sup>2</sup>You are so proud of yourselves, but you should be mourning in sorrow and shame. And you should remove this man from your fellowship.

<sup>3</sup>Even though I am not with you in person, I am with you in the Spirit.* And as though I were there, I have already passed judgment on this man <sup>4</sup>in the name of the Lord Jesus. You must call a meeting of the church.* I will be present with you in spirit, and so will the power of our Lord Jesus. <sup>5</sup>Then you must throw this man out and hand him over to Satan so that his sinful nature will be destroyed* and he himself* will be saved on the day the Lord* returns.

<sup>6</sup>Your boasting about this is terrible. Don't you realize that this sin is like a little yeast that spreads through the whole batch of dough? <sup>7</sup>Get rid of the old "yeast" by removing this wicked person from among you. Then you will be like a fresh batch of dough made without yeast, which is what you really are. Christ, our Passover Lamb, has been sacrificed for us.* <sup>8</sup>So let us celebrate the festival, not with the old bread* of wickedness and evil, but with the new bread* of sincerity and truth.

<sup>9</sup>When I wrote to you before, I told you not to associate with people who indulge in sexual sin. <sup>10</sup>But I wasn't talking about unbelievers who indulge in sexual sin, or are greedy, or cheat people, or worship idols. You would have to leave this world to avoid people like that. <sup>11</sup>I meant that you are not to associate with anyone who claims to be a believer* yet indulges in sexual sin, or is greedy, or worships idols, or is abusive, or is a drunkard, or cheats people. Don't even eat with such people.

**5:1** Greek *his father's wife.*  **5:3** Or *in spirit.*  **5:4** Or *In the name of the Lord Jesus, you must call a meeting of the church.*  **5:5a** Or *so that his body will be destroyed;* Greek reads *for the destruction of the flesh.*  **5:5b** Greek *and the spirit.*  **5:5c** Other manuscripts read *the Lord Jesus;* still others read *our Lord Jesus Christ.*  **5:7** Greek *has been sacrificed.*  **5:8a** Greek *not with old leaven.*  **5:8b** Greek *but with unleavened [bread].*  **5:11** Greek *a brother.*

**4:19**
Acts 18:21
1 Cor 16:5
2 Cor 1:15-16

**4:20**
1 Cor 2:4

**4:21**
2 Cor 1:23; 2:1

**5:1**
Lev 18:7-8
Deut 22:30; 27:20
Eph 5:3

**5:3**
Col 2:5

**5:4**
2 Thes 3:6

**5:5**
1 Tim 1:20

**5:6**
Matt 16:6, 12
Gal 5:9

**5:7**
Exod 12:3-6, 21
Isa 53:7
1 Pet 1:19
Rev 5:6

**5:8**
Exod 12:15-19
Deut 16:3

**5:9**
2 Cor 6:14

**5:10**
John 17:15

**5:11**
Rom 16:17
2 Thes 3:6
2 Jn 1:10

**4:18-20** Some people talk a lot about faith, but that's all it is— talk. They may know all the right words to say, but their lives don't reflect God's power. Paul says that the Kingdom of God is to be *lived*, not just discussed. There is a big difference between knowing the right words and living them out. Don't be content to have the right answers about Christ. Let your life show that God's power is really working in you.

**4:19** It is not known whether Paul ever returned to Corinth, but it is likely. In 2 Corinthians 2:1, he writes that he decided not to make "another painful visit," implying that he had had a previous painful confrontation with the Corinthian believers (see 2 Corinthians 12:14; 13:1; and the note on 2 Corinthians 2:1).

**5:1ff** The church must discipline flagrant sin among its members. Such sins left unchecked can polarize and paralyze a church. The correction, however, should never be vengeful. Instead, it should be given to help bring about a cure. The Corinthian believers had refused to deal with a specific sin in the church: A man was having an affair with his mother (or stepmother). The church was ignoring the situation, and Paul was saying that it had a responsibility to maintain the standards of morality found in God's commandments. God tells us not to judge others. But he also tells us not to tolerate flagrant sin because allowing such sin to go undisciplined will have a dangerous effect on other believers (5:6).

**5:5** To hand this man "over to Satan" means to exclude him from the fellowship of believers. Without the spiritual support of Christians, this man would be left alone with his sin and Satan, and perhaps this would drive him to repentance. "So that his sinful nature will be destroyed" states the hope that the experience would bring this man to God to destroy his sinful nature through his turning from sin. *Sinful nature* could mean his body or flesh. This alternative translation would imply that Satan would afflict him physically

and thus bring him to God. Putting someone out of the church should be a last resort in disciplinary action. It should not be done out of vengeance but out of love, just as parents punish children to correct and restore them. The church's role should be to help, not hurt, offenders, motivating them to repent of their sins and to return to the fellowship of the church.

**5:6** Paul was writing to those who wanted to ignore this church problem. They didn't realize that allowing public sin to exist in the church affects all its members. Paul does not expect anyone to be sinless—all believers struggle with sin daily. Instead, he is speaking against those who deliberately sin, feel no guilt, and refuse to repent. This kind of sin cannot be tolerated in the church because it affects others. We have a responsibility to other believers. Blatant sins, left uncorrected, confuse and divide the congregation. While believers should encourage, pray for, and build up one another, they must also be intolerant of sin that jeopardizes the spiritual health of the church.

**5:7, 8** As the Hebrews prepared for their exodus from slavery in Egypt, they were commanded to prepare bread without yeast because they didn't have time to wait for it to rise. And because yeast also was a symbol of sin, they were commanded to sweep all of it out of the house (Exodus 12:15; 13:7). Christ is our Passover lamb, the perfect sacrifice for our sin. Because he has delivered us from the slavery of sin, we should have nothing to do with the sins of the past ("old bread").

**5:9** Paul is referring to an earlier letter to the Corinthian church, often called the lost letter because it has not been preserved.

**5:10, 11** Paul makes it clear that we should not disassociate ourselves from unbelievers—otherwise we could not carry out Christ's command to tell them about salvation (Matthew 28:18-20). But we are to distance ourselves from the person

5:12
Mark 4:11

5:13
†Deut 17:7; 19:19;
21:21, 24; 24:7

6:1
Matt 18:17

6:2
Dan 7:22
Luke 22:30
Rev 3:21

6:3
2 Pet 2:4
Jude 1:6

6:5
1 Cor 4:14

6:7
Matt 5:39
1 Thes 5:15
1 Pet 3:9

6:8
1 Thes 4:6

¹²It isn't my responsibility to judge outsiders, but it certainly is your responsibility to judge those inside the church who are sinning. ¹³God will judge those on the outside; but as the Scriptures say, "You must remove the evil person from among you."*

### Avoiding Lawsuits with Christians

**6** When one of you has a dispute with another believer, how dare you file a lawsuit and ask a secular court to decide the matter instead of taking it to other believers*! ²Don't you realize that someday we believers will judge the world? And since you are going to judge the world, can't you decide even these little things among yourselves? ³Don't you realize that we will judge angels? So you should surely be able to resolve ordinary disputes in this life. ⁴If you have legal disputes about such matters, why go to outside judges who are not respected by the church? ⁵I am saying this to shame you. Isn't there anyone in all the church who is wise enough to decide these issues? ⁶But instead, one believer* sues another—right in front of unbelievers!

⁷Even to have such lawsuits with one another is a defeat for you. Why not just accept the injustice and leave it at that? Why not let yourselves be cheated? ⁸Instead, you yourselves are the ones who do wrong and cheat even your fellow believers.*

**5:13** Deut 17:7.   **6:1** Greek *God's holy people;* also in 6:2.   **6:6** Greek *one brother.*   **6:8** Greek *even the brothers.*

---

**CHURCH DISCIPLINE**
The church, at times, must exercise discipline toward members who have sinned. But church discipline must be handled carefully, straightforwardly, and lovingly.

| Situations | Steps (Matthew 18:15-17) |
|---|---|
| Unintentional error and/or private sin | 1. Go to the brother or sister; show the fault to him or her in private. |
| Public sin and/or those done flagrantly and arrogantly | 2. If he/she does not listen, go with one or two witnesses. |
|  | 3. If he/she refuses to listen, take the matter before the church. |

*After these steps have been carried out, the next steps are*

1. Remove the one in error from the fellowship (1 Corinthians 5:2-13).

2. The church gives united disapproval, but forgiveness and comfort are in order if he/she chooses to repent (2 Corinthians 2:5-8).

3. Do not associate with the disobedient person; and if you must, speak to him/her as one who needs a warning (2 Thessalonians 3:14, 15).

4. After two warnings, reject the person from the fellowship (Titus 3:10).

---

who claims to be a Christian, yet indulges in sins explicitly forbidden in Scripture by rationalizing his or her actions. By rationalizing sin, a person harms others for whom Christ died and dims the image of God in himself or herself. A church that includes such a person is hardly fit to be the light of the world. To do so would distort the picture of Christ it presents to the world. Church leaders must be ready to correct, in love, for the sake of spiritual unity.

**5:12** The Bible consistently tells us not to criticize people by gossiping or making rash judgments. At the same time, however, we are to judge and deal with sin that can hurt others. Paul's instructions should not be used to handle trivial matters or to take revenge; nor should they be applied to individual problems between believers. These verses are instructions for dealing with open sin in the church by a person who claims to be a Christian and yet who sins without remorse. The church is to confront and discipline such a person in love. Also see the notes on 4:5 and 5:1ff.

**6:1-6** In chapter 5, Paul explained what to do with open immorality in the congregation. In chapter 6, he teaches how the congregation should handle smaller problems between believers. Society has set up a legal system in which disagreements can be resolved in courts. But Paul declares that Christians should not have to go to a secular court to resolve their differences. As Christians, we have the Holy Spirit and the mind of Christ, so why should we turn to those who lack God's wisdom? Because of all that we have been given as believers, and because of the authority that we will have in the future to judge the world and the angels, we should be

able to deal with disputes among ourselves. See John 5:22 and Revelation 3:21 for more on judging the world. Judging angels is mentioned in 2 Peter 2:4 and Jude 1:6.

**6:6-8** Why did Paul say that Christians should not take their disagreements to unbelievers in secular courts? (1) If the judge and jury are not Christians, they are not likely to be sensitive to Christian values. (2) The basis for going to court is often revenge; this should never be a Christian's motive. (3) Lawsuits harm the cause of Christ and make the church look bad, causing unbelievers to focus on its problems rather than on its purpose.

⁹Don't you realize that those who do wrong will not inherit the Kingdom of God? Don't fool yourselves. Those who indulge in sexual sin, or who worship idols, or commit adultery, or are male prostitutes, or practice homosexuality, ¹⁰or are thieves, or greedy people, or drunkards, or are abusive, or cheat people—none of these will inherit the Kingdom of God. ¹¹Some of you were once like that. But you were cleansed; you were made holy; you were made right with God by calling on the name of the Lord Jesus Christ and by the Spirit of our God.

**6:9-10**
Gal 5:19-21
Eph 5:5
Rev 22:15

**6:11**
Acts 22:16
Rom 8:30
1 Cor 1:2, 30

## Avoiding Sexual Sin

¹²You say, "I am allowed to do anything"—but not everything is good for you. And even though "I am allowed to do anything," I must not become a slave to anything. ¹³You say, "Food was made for the stomach, and the stomach for food." (This is true, though someday God will do away with both of them.) But you can't say that our bodies were made for sexual immorality. They were made for the Lord, and the Lord cares about our bodies. ¹⁴And God will raise us from the dead by his power, just as he raised our Lord from the dead.

¹⁵Don't you realize that your bodies are actually parts of Christ? Should a man take his body, which is part of Christ, and join it to a prostitute? Never! ¹⁶And don't you realize that if a man joins himself to a prostitute, he becomes one body with her? For the Scriptures say, "The two are united into one."* ¹⁷But the person who is joined to the Lord is one spirit with him.

**6:12**
1 Cor 10:23

**6:13**
Col 2:22
1 Thes 4:3-5

**6:14**
Acts 2:24
Rom 6:5
1 Cor 15:15, 20
Eph 1:19-20

**6:17**
John 17:21-23
Rom 8:9-11, 16
2 Cor 3:17
Gal 2:20

**6:16** Gen 2:24.

---

**6:9-11** Paul is describing characteristics of unbelievers. He doesn't mean that all those who have indulged in sexual sin or who have been idol worshipers, adulterers, male prostitutes, homosexuals, thieves, greedy people, drunkards, abusers, and swindlers are automatically and irrevocably excluded from heaven. Christians come out of all kinds of different backgrounds, including these. They may still struggle with evil desires, but they should not continue in these practices. In 6:11, Paul clearly states that even those who sin in these ways can have their lives changed by Christ. However, those who say that they are Christians but persist in these practices with no sign of remorse will not inherit the Kingdom of God. Such people need to reevaluate their lives to see if they truly believe in Christ.

**6:9-11** In a permissive society it is easy for Christians to overlook or tolerate some immoral behavior (greed, drunkenness, etc.) while remaining outraged at others (homosexuality, thievery). We must not participate in sin or condone it in any way; we cannot be selective about what we condemn or excuse. Staying away from more "acceptable" forms of sin is difficult, but it is no harder for us than it was for the Corinthians. God expects his followers in any age to have high standards.

**6:9** "Male prostitutes" refers to those who practice homosexuality. The temple of Apollo employed men whose job it was to fulfill the sexual desires of male and female worshipers.

Some attempt to legitimize homosexuality as an acceptable alternative lifestyle. Even some Christians say that people have a right to choose their sexual preference. But the Bible specifically calls homosexual behavior sin (see Leviticus 18:22-29; Romans 1:18-32, 1 Timothy 1:9-11). Christians must be careful, however, to condemn only the practice, not the people. Those who commit homosexual acts are not to be feared, ridiculed, or hated. They can be forgiven, and their lives can be transformed. The church should be a haven of forgiveness and healing for repentant homosexuals without compromising its stance against homosexual behavior.

**6:11** Paul emphasizes God's action in making believers new people. The three aspects of God's work are all part of our salvation: Our sins were washed away, we were set apart for special use (sanctified), and we have been made right with God (justified).

**6:12** Apparently the church had been quoting and misapplying the words "I am allowed to do anything." Some Christians in Corinth were excusing their sins by saying that (1) Christ had taken away all sin, and so they had complete freedom to live as they pleased, or (2) what they were doing was not strictly forbidden by Scripture. Paul answered both these excuses: (1) While Christ has taken away our sin, this does not give us freedom to go on doing what we know is wrong. The New Testament specifically

forbids many sins (see 6:9, 10) that were originally prohibited in the Old Testament (see Romans 12:9-21; 13:8-10). (2) Some actions are not sinful in themselves, but they are not appropriate because they can control our life and lead us away from God. (3) Some actions may hurt others. Anything we do that hurts rather than helps others is not right.

**6:12, 13** Many of the world's religions teach that the soul or spirit is important but the body is not; and Christianity has sometimes been influenced by these ideas. In truth, however, Christianity takes very seriously the realm of the physical. We worship a God who created a physical world and pronounced it good. He promises us a new earth, where real people will have transformed physical lives—not a pink cloud where disembodied souls listen to harp music. At the heart of Christianity is the story of God himself taking on flesh and blood and coming to live with us, offering both physical healing and spiritual restoration.

We humans, like Adam, are a combination of dust and spirit. Just as our spirits affect our bodies, so our physical bodies affect our spirits. We cannot commit sin with our bodies without damaging our souls because our bodies and souls are inseparably joined. In the new earth we will have resurrection bodies that are not corrupted by sin. Then we will enjoy the fullness of our salvation.

**6:12, 13** Freedom is a mark of the Christian faith—freedom from sin and guilt, and freedom to use and enjoy anything that comes from God. But Christians should not abuse this freedom and hurt themselves or others. Drinking too much leads to alcoholism; gluttony leads to obesity. Be careful that what God has allowed you to enjoy doesn't grow into a bad habit that controls you. For more about Christian freedom and everyday behavior, read chapter 8.

**6:13** Sexual immorality is a temptation that is always before us. In movies and on television, sex outside marriage is treated as a normal, even desirable, part of life, while marriage is often shown as confining and joyless. We can even be looked down on by others if we are suspected of being pure. But God does not forbid sexual sin just to be difficult. He knows its power to destroy us physically and spiritually. No one should underestimate the power of sexual immorality. It has devastated countless lives and destroyed families, churches, communities, and even nations. God wants to protect us from damaging ourselves and others, and so he offers to fill us—our loneliness, our desires—with himself.

**6:15-17** This teaching about sexual immorality and prostitutes was especially important for the Corinthian church because the temple of the love goddess Aphrodite was in Corinth. This temple employed more than a thousand prostitutes as priestesses, and sex was part of the worship ritual. Paul clearly stated that Chris-

**6:18**
1 Thes 4:3-4

**6:19**
Rom 14:7-8
1 Cor 3:16
2 Cor 6:16

**6:20**
Phil 1:20
1 Pet 1:18-19

**7:1**
1 Cor 7:8, 26

**7:3**
Exod 21:10
1 Pet 3:7

**7:5**
1 Thes 3:5

**7:6**
2 Cor 8:8

**7:7**
Matt 19:11-12
1 Cor 9:5; 12:11

¹⁸Run from sexual sin! No other sin so clearly affects the body as this one does. For sexual immorality is a sin against your own body. ¹⁹Don't you realize that your body is the temple of the Holy Spirit, who lives in you and was given to you by God? You do not belong to yourself, ²⁰for God bought you with a high price. So you must honor God with your body.

## B. PAUL ANSWERS CHURCH QUESTIONS (7:1—16:24)

After discussing disorder in the church, Paul moves to the list of questions that the Corinthians had sent him, including subjects of marriage, singleness, eating meat offered to idols, propriety in worship, orderliness in the Lord's Supper, spiritual gifts, and the resurrection. Questions that plague churches today are remarkably similar to these, so we can receive specific guidance in these areas from this letter.

### 1. Instruction on Christian marriage

**7** Now regarding the questions you asked in your letter. Yes, it is good to abstain from sexual relations.* ²But because there is so much sexual immorality, each man should have his own wife, and each woman should have her own husband.

³The husband should fulfill his wife's sexual needs, and the wife should fulfill her husband's needs. ⁴The wife gives authority over her body to her husband, and the husband gives authority over his body to his wife.

⁵Do not deprive each other of sexual relations, unless you both agree to refrain from sexual intimacy for a limited time so you can give yourselves more completely to prayer. Afterward, you should come together again so that Satan won't be able to tempt you because of your lack of self-control. ⁶I say this as a concession, not as a command. ⁷But I wish everyone were single, just as I am. Yet each person has a special gift from God, of one kind or another.

⁸So I say to those who aren't married and to widows—it's better to stay unmarried, just as

**7:1** Or *to live a celibate life;* Greek reads *It is good for a man not to touch a woman.*

---

tians are to have no part in sexual immorality, even if it is acceptable and popular in our culture.

**6:18** Christians are free to be all they can be for God, but they are not free *from* God. God created sex to be a beautiful and essential ingredient of marriage, but sexual sin—sex outside the marriage relationship—*always* hurts someone. It hurts God because it shows that we prefer following our own desires instead of the leading of the Holy Spirit. It hurts others because it violates the commitment so necessary to a relationship. It often brings disease to our bodies. And it deeply affects our personality, which responds in anguish when we harm ourselves physically and spiritually.

**6:19, 20** What did Paul mean when he said that our body belongs to God? Many people say they have the right to do whatever they want with their own bodies. Although they think that this is freedom, they are really enslaved to their own desires. When we become Christians, the Holy Spirit comes to live in us. Therefore, we no longer own our bodies. That God bought us "with a high price" refers to slaves purchased at an auction. Christ's death freed us from sin but also obligates us to his service. If you live in a building owned by someone else, you try not to violate the building's rules. Because your body belongs to God, you must not violate his standards for living.

**7:1** The Corinthians had written to Paul, asking him several questions relating to the Christian life and problems in the church. The first question was whether it was good to be married. Paul answers this and other questions in the remainder of this letter.

**7:1ff** Christians in Corinth were surrounded by sexual temptation. The city had a reputation even among pagans for sexual immorality and religious prostitution. It was to this kind of society that Paul delivered these instructions on sex and marriage. The Corinthians needed special, specific instructions because of their culture's immoral standards. For more on Paul's teaching about marriage, see Ephesians 5.

**7:3-5** Sexual temptations are difficult to withstand because they appeal to the normal and natural desires that God has given us. Marriage provides God's way to satisfy these natural sexual

desires and to strengthen the partners against temptation. Married couples have the responsibility to care for each other; therefore, husbands and wives should not withhold themselves sexually from one another but should fulfill each other's needs and desires. (See also the note on 10:13.)

**7:3-11** The Corinthian church was in turmoil because of the immorality of the culture around them. Some Greeks, in rejecting immorality, rejected sex and marriage altogether. The Corinthian Christians wondered if this was what they should do also, so they asked Paul several questions: "Because sex is perverted, shouldn't we also abstain in marriage?" "If my spouse is unsaved, should I seek a divorce?" "Should unmarried people and widows remain unmarried?" Paul answered many of these questions by saying, "For now, stay put. Be content in the situation where God has placed you. If you're married, don't seek to be single. If you're single, don't seek to be married (see 6:19, 20). Live God's way, one day at a time, and he will show you what to do."

**7:4** Spiritually, our bodies belong to God when we become Christians because Jesus Christ bought us by paying the price to release us from sin (see 6:19, 20). Physically, our bodies belong to our spouses because God designed marriage so that, through the union of husband and wife, the two become one (Genesis 2:24). Paul stressed complete equality in sexual relationships. Neither male nor female should seek dominance or autonomy.

**7:7** Both marriage and singleness are gifts from God. One is not morally better than the other, and both are valuable to accomplishing God's purposes. It is important for us, therefore, to accept our present situation. When Paul said he wished that all people were like him (unmarried), he was expressing his desire that more people would devote themselves *completely* to the ministry without the added concerns of a spouse and family, as he had done. He was not criticizing marriage—after all, it is God's created way of providing companionship and populating the earth.

I am. 9But if they can't control themselves, they should go ahead and marry. It's better to marry than to burn with lust.

7:9
1 Tim 5:14

10But for those who are married, I have a command that comes not from me, but from the Lord.* A wife must not leave her husband. 11But if she does leave him, let her remain single or else be reconciled to him. And the husband must not leave his wife.

7:10
Mal 2:14-16
Matt 5:32; 19:9
Mark 10:10-12
Luke 16:18

12Now, I will speak to the rest of you, though I do not have a direct command from the Lord. If a Christian man* has a wife who is not a believer and she is willing to continue living with him, he must not leave her. 13And if a Christian woman has a husband who is not a believer and he is willing to continue living with her, she must not leave him. 14For the Christian wife brings holiness to her marriage, and the Christian husband* brings holiness to his marriage. Otherwise, your children would not be holy, but now they are holy. 15(But if the husband or wife who isn't a believer insists on leaving, let them go. In such cases the Christian husband or wife* is no longer bound to the other, for God has called you* to live in peace.) 16Don't you wives realize that your husbands might be saved because of you? And don't you husbands realize that your wives might be saved because of you?

7:14
Mal 2:15

7:15
Rom 14:19

7:16
Rom 11:14
1 Pet 3:1

17Each of you should continue to live in whatever situation the Lord has placed you, and remain as you were when God first called you. This is my rule for all the churches. 18For instance, a man who was circumcised before he became a believer should not try to reverse it. And the man who was uncircumcised when he became a believer should not be circumcised now. 19For it makes no difference whether or not a man has been circumcised. The important thing is to keep God's commandments.

7:17
1 Cor 4:17; 14:33

7:18
Acts 15:1-19
Gal 5:2

7:19
Rom 2:25-27
Gal 5:6; 6:15
Col 3:11

20Yes, each of you should remain as you were when God called you. 21Are you a slave? Don't let that worry you—but if you get a chance to be free, take it. 22And remember, if you were a slave when the Lord called you, you are now free in the Lord. And if you were free

7:22
John 8:36
Eph 6:6
1 Pet 2:16

**7:10** See Matt 5:32; 19:9; Mark 10:11-12; Luke 16:18.   **7:12** Greek *a brother.*   **7:14** Greek *the brother.*
**7:15a** Greek *the brother or sister.*   **7:15b** Some manuscripts read *us.*

---

**7:9** Sexual pressure is not the best motive for getting married, but it is better to marry the right person than to "burn with lust." Many new believers in Corinth thought that all sex was wrong, and so engaged couples were deciding not to get married. In this passage, Paul was telling couples who wanted to marry that they should not frustrate their normal sexual drives by avoiding marriage. This does not mean, however, that people who have trouble controlling themselves should marry the first person who comes along. It is better to deal with the pressure of desire than to deal with an unhappy marriage.

**7:12** Paul's "command" about the permanence of marriage (7:10) comes from the Old Testament (Genesis 2:24) and from Jesus (Mark 10:2-12). His *suggestion* in this verse is based on God's command, and Paul applies it to the situation the Corinthians were facing. Paul ranked the command above the suggestion because one is an eternal principle while the other is a specific application. Nevertheless, for people in similar situations, Paul's suggestion is the best advice they will get. Paul was a man of God, an apostle, and he had the mind of Christ.

**7:12-14** Because of their desire to serve Christ, some people in the Corinthian church thought they ought to divorce their pagan spouses and marry Christians. But Paul affirmed the marriage commitment. God's ideal is for husbands and wives to stay together—even when one spouse is not a believer. The Christian spouse should try to win the other to Christ. It would be easy to rationalize leaving; however, Paul makes a strong case for staying with the unbelieving spouse and being a positive influence on the marriage. Paul, like Jesus, believed that marriage is permanent (see Mark 10:1-9).

**7:14** The blessings that flow to believers don't stop there but extend to others. God regards the marriage as set apart for his use by the presence of one Christian spouse. The other does not receive salvation automatically but is blessed by this relationship. The children of such a marriage have a godly influence and are set apart (because of God's blessing on the family unit) until they are old enough to make their own decision for Christ.

**7:15, 16** This verse is misused by some as a loophole to get out of marriage. But Paul's statements were given to encourage the Christian spouse to try to get along with the unbeliever and make the marriage work. If, however, the unbelieving spouse insists on leaving, Paul said to let him or her go. The only alternative would be for the Christian to deny his or her faith to preserve the marriage, and that would be worse than dissolving the marriage. Paul's chief purpose in writing this was to urge the married couples to seek unity, not separation (see 7:17; 1 Peter 3:1, 2).

**7:17** Apparently the Corinthians were ready to make wholesale changes without thinking through the ramifications. Paul was writing to say that people should be Christians where they are. You can do God's work and demonstrate your faith *anywhere.* If you became a Christian after marriage, and your spouse is not a believer, remember that you don't have to be married to a Christian to live for Christ. Don't assume that you are in the wrong place or stuck with the wrong person. You may be just where God wants you (see 7:20).

**7:18, 19** The ceremony of circumcision was an important part of the Jews' relationship with God. In fact, before Christ came, circumcision was commanded by God for those who claimed to follow him (Genesis 17:9-14). But after Christ's death, circumcision was no longer necessary (Acts 15; Romans 4:9-11; Galatians 5:2-4; Colossians 2:11). Pleasing God and obeying him are more important than observing traditional ceremonies.

**7:20** We may become so concerned about what we *could* be doing for God somewhere else that we miss great opportunities right where we are. Paul says that when you become a Christian, you should continue on with the work you have previously been doing—provided it isn't immoral or unethical. Every job can become Christian work when you realize that it can be an opportunity to honor, serve, and speak out for Christ. Because God has placed you where you are, take advantage of every opportunity to serve him there.

**7:22** Slavery was common throughout the Roman Empire. Some Christians in the Corinthian church were undoubtedly slaves. Paul said that although they were slaves to other human beings, they were free from the power of sin in their lives. People today are slaves to sin until they commit their lives to Christ, who alone can conquer sin's power. Sin, pride, and fear

**7:23**
1 Cor 6:20
1 Pet 1:18

when the Lord called you, you are now a slave of Christ. 23God paid a high price for you, so don't be enslaved by the world.* 24Each of you, dear brothers and sisters,* should remain as you were when God first called you.

**7:25**
2 Cor 4:1
1 Tim 1:12-13

25Now regarding your question about the young women who are not yet married. I do not have a command from the Lord for them. But the Lord in his mercy has given me wisdom that can be trusted, and I will share it with you. 26Because of the present crisis,* I think it is best to remain as you are. 27If you have a wife, do not seek to end the marriage. If you do not have a wife, do not seek to get married. 28But if you do get married, it is not a sin. And if a young woman gets married, it is not a sin. However, those who get married at this time will have troubles, and I am trying to spare you those problems.

**7:29**
Rom 13:11

29But let me say this, dear brothers and sisters: The time that remains is very short. So from now on, those with wives should not focus only on their marriage. 30Those who weep or who rejoice or who buy things should not be absorbed by their weeping or their joy or their possessions. 31Those who use the things of the world should not become attached to them. For this world as we know it will soon pass away.

**7:31**
1 Jn 2:17

32I want you to be free from the concerns of this life. An unmarried man can spend his time doing the Lord's work and thinking how to please him. 33But a married man has to think about his earthly responsibilities and how to please his wife. 34His interests are divided. In the same way, a woman who is no longer married or has never been married can be devoted to the Lord and holy in body and in spirit. But a married woman has to think about her earthly responsibilities and how to please her husband. 35I am saying this for your benefit, not to place restrictions on you. I want you to do whatever will help you serve the Lord best, with as few distractions as possible.

**7:34**
1 Tim 5:5

36But if a man thinks that he's treating his fiancée improperly and will inevitably give in to his passion, let him marry her as he wishes. It is not a sin. 37But if he has decided firmly not to marry and there is no urgency and he can control his passion, he does well not to marry. 38So the person who marries his fiancée does well, and the person who doesn't marry does even better.

**7:38**
Heb 13:4

39A wife is bound to her husband as long as he lives. If her husband dies, she is free to marry anyone she wishes, but only if he loves the Lord.* 40But in my opinion it would be better for her to stay single, and I think I am giving you counsel from God's Spirit when I say this.

**7:39**
Rom 7:2
2 Cor 6:14

**7:40**
1 Cor 7:6, 25

**7:23** Greek *don't become slaves of people.*  **7:24** Greek *brothers;* also in 7:29.  **7:26** Or *the pressures of life.*
**7:39** Greek *but only in the Lord.*

---

no longer have any claim over us, just as a slave owner no longer has power over the slaves he has sold. The Bible says we become Christ's slaves when we become Christians (Romans 6:18), but this actually means we gain our freedom, because sin no longer controls us.

**7:26** Paul probably foresaw the impending persecution that the Roman government would soon bring upon Christians. He gave this practical advice because being unmarried would mean less suffering and more freedom to throw one's life into the cause of Christ (7:29), even to the point of fearlessly dying for him. Paul's advice reveals his single-minded devotion to spreading the Good News.

**7:28** Many people naively think that marriage will solve all their problems. Here are some problems marriage won't solve: (1) loneliness, (2) sexual temptation, (3) one's deepest emotional needs, (4) life's difficulties. Marriage alone does not hold two people together but commitment does—commitment to Christ and to each other despite conflicts and problems. As wonderful as it is, marriage does not automatically solve every problem. Whether married or single, we must be content with our situation and focus on Christ, not on loved ones, to help address our problems.

**7:29** Paul urges all believers to make the most of their time before Christ's return. Every person in every generation should have this sense of urgency about telling the Good News to others. Life is short—there's not much time!

**7:29-31** Paul urges believers not to regard marriage, home, or financial security as the ultimate goals of life. As much as

possible, we should live unhindered by the cares of this world, not getting involved with burdensome mortgages, budgets, investments, or debts that might keep us from doing God's work. A married man or woman, as Paul points out (7:33, 34), must take care of earthly responsibilities but make every effort to keep them modest and manageable.

**7:32-34** Some single people feel tremendous pressure to be married. They think their lives can be complete only with a spouse. But Paul underlines one advantage of being single— the potential of a greater focus on Christ and his work. If you are unmarried, use your special opportunity to serve Christ wholeheartedly.

**7:38** When Paul says the unmarried person does even better, he is talking about the potential time available for service to God. The single person does not have the responsibility of caring for a spouse and raising a family. Singleness, however, does not ensure service to God; involvement in service depends on the commitment of the individual.

**7:40** Paul's advice comes from the Holy Spirit, who guides and equips both single and married people to fulfill their roles.

## 2. Instruction on Christian freedom
*Food Sacrificed to Idols*

**8** Now regarding your question about food that has been offered to idols. Yes, we know that "we all have knowledge" about this issue. But while knowledge makes us feel important, it is love that strengthens the church. ²Anyone who claims to know all the answers doesn't really know very much. ³But the person who loves God is the one whom God recognizes.*

⁴So, what about eating meat that has been offered to idols? Well, we all know that an idol is not really a god and that there is only one God. ⁵There may be so-called gods both in heaven and on earth, and some people actually worship many gods and many lords. ⁶But we know that there is only one God, the Father, who created everything, and we live for him. And there is only one Lord, Jesus Christ, through whom God made everything and through whom we have been given life.

⁷However, not all believers know this. Some are accustomed to thinking of idols as being real, so when they eat food that has been offered to idols, they think of it as the worship of real gods, and their weak consciences are violated. ⁸It's true that we can't win God's approval by what we eat. We don't lose anything if we don't eat it, and we don't gain anything if we do.

⁹But you must be careful so that your freedom does not cause others with a weaker conscience to stumble. ¹⁰For if others see you—with your "superior knowledge"—eating in the temple of an idol, won't they be encouraged to violate their conscience by eating food that has been offered to an idol? ¹¹So because of your superior knowledge, a weak believer* for whom Christ died will be destroyed. ¹²And when you sin against other believers* by encouraging them to do something they believe is wrong, you are sinning against Christ. ¹³So if what I eat causes another believer to sin, I will never eat meat again as long as I live—for I don't want to cause another believer to stumble.

*Paul Gives Up His Rights*

**9** Am I not as free as anyone else? Am I not an apostle? Haven't I seen Jesus our Lord with my own eyes? Isn't it because of my work that you belong to the Lord? ²Even if others think I am not an apostle, I certainly am to you. You yourselves are proof that I am the Lord's apostle.

³This is my answer to those who question my authority.* ⁴Don't we have the right to live

---

**8:1** Acts 15:20, 29

**8:2** 1 Cor 3:18; 13:8-9 Gal 6:3

**8:4** Deut 4:35, 39; 6:4 1 Cor 10:19

**8:6** John 1:3 Acts 17:28 1 Cor 12:5 Eph 4:5-6 Col 1:16

**8:7** Rom 14:14 1 Cor 10:18

**8:8** Rom 14:17

**8:9** Rom 14:1, 13, 21 2 Cor 6:3 Gal 5:13

**8:11** Rom 14:15, 20

**8:12** Matt 18:6

**8:13** Rom 14:21

**9:1** Acts 9:3; 18:9 1 Cor 15:8 1 Tim 2:7 2 Tim 1:11

**9:2** 2 Cor 3:2-3

**9:4** Luke 10:8 1 Cor 9:13-14

---

**8:3** Some manuscripts read *the person who loves has full knowledge.* **8:11** Greek *brother;* also in 8:13. **8:12** Greek *brothers.* **9:3** Greek *those who examine me.*

---

**8:1** Meat bought in the marketplace was likely to have been offered to an idol in one of the many pagan temples. Animals were brought to a temple, killed before an idol as part of a pagan religious ceremony, and eaten at a feast in the pagan temple or taken to butchers who sold the meat in the marketplace. The believers wondered if, by eating such meat, they were somehow participating in the worship of idols.

**8:1-3** Love is more important than knowledge. Knowledge can make us look good and feel important, but we can all too easily develop an arrogant, know-it-all attitude. Many people with strong opinions are unwilling to listen to and learn from God and others. We can obtain God's knowledge only by loving him (see James 3:17, 18). And we can know and be known by God only when we model him by showing love (1 John 4:7, 8).

**8:4-9** Paul addressed these words to believers who weren't bothered by eating meat that had been offered to idols. Although idols were phony, and the pagan ritual of sacrificing to them was meaningless, eating such meat offended some Christians with sensitive consciences. Paul said, therefore, that mature believers should avoid eating meat offered to idols if it would violate the conscience of weak Christians.

**8:10-13** Christian freedom does not mean that anything goes. It means that our salvation is not obtained by good deeds or legalistic rules; it is the free gift of God (Ephesians 2:8, 9). Christian freedom, then, is inseparably tied to Christian responsibility. New believers are often very sensitive to what is right or wrong, what they should or shouldn't do. Some actions may be perfectly all

right for us to do but may harm a Christian brother or sister who is still young in the faith and learning what the Christian life is all about. We must be careful not to offend a sensitive or younger Christian or, by our example, cause him or her to sin. When we love others, our freedom should be less important to us than strengthening the faith of a brother or sister in Christ.

**9:1** Some Corinthians were questioning Paul's authority and rights as an apostle, so Paul gave his credentials: He actually had seen and talked with the resurrected Christ, who had called him to be an apostle (see Acts 9:3-18). Such credentials make the advice he gives in this letter more persuasive. In 2 Corinthians 10-13, Paul defends his apostleship in greater detail.

**9:1** Changed lives were the evidence that God was using Paul. Does your faith have an impact on others? You can be a life-changer, helping others grow spiritually, if you dedicate yourself to being used by God and letting him make you effective.

**9:4ff** Paul uses himself as an illustration of giving up personal rights. Paul had the right to hospitality, to be married, and to be paid for his work. But he willingly gave up these rights to win people to Christ. When your focus is on living for Christ, your rights become comparatively unimportant.

**9:4-10** Jesus said that workers deserve their wages (Luke 10:7). Paul echoes this thought and urges the church to be sure to pay their Christian workers. We have the responsibility to care for our pastors, teachers, and other spiritual leaders. It is our duty to see that those who serve us in the ministry are fairly and adequately compensated. When the annual budget of your church comes up for review, support a proper salary for your ministers and staff.

**9:5**
Matt 8:14; 12:46
Mark 6:2-3
Luke 6:14

in your homes and share your meals? 5Don't we have the right to bring a Christian wife with us as the other apostles and the Lord's brothers do, and as Peter* does? 6Or is it only Barnabas and I who have to work to support ourselves?

**9:6**
2 Thes 3:8-9

7What soldier has to pay his own expenses? What farmer plants a vineyard and doesn't

**9:7**
Deut 20:6
Prov 27:18
1 Cor 3:6, 8
2 Tim 2:4

have the right to eat some of its fruit? What shepherd cares for a flock of sheep and isn't allowed to drink some of the milk? 8Am I expressing merely a human opinion, or does the law say the same thing? 9For the law of Moses says, "You must not muzzle an ox to keep it from eating as it treads out the grain."* Was God thinking only about oxen when he said

**9:9**
†Deut 25:4
1 Tim 5:18

this? 10Wasn't he actually speaking to us? Yes, it was written for us, so that the one who plows and the one who threshes the grain might both expect a share of the harvest.

**9:10**
2 Tim 2:6

11Since we have planted spiritual seed among you, aren't we entitled to a harvest of physi-

**9:11**
Rom 15:27

cal food and drink? 12If you support others who preach to you, shouldn't we have an even greater right to be supported? But we have never used this right. We would rather put up

**9:12**
2 Cor 6:3; 11:7-12

with anything than be an obstacle to the Good News about Christ.

**9:13**
Lev 6:16, 26
Num 18:8, 31

13Don't you realize that those who work in the temple get their meals from the offerings brought to the temple? And those who serve at the altar get a share of the sacrificial offer-ings. 14In the same way, the Lord ordered that those who preach the Good News should be

**9:14**
Matt 10:10
Luke 10:7
Gal 6:6
1 Tim 5:18

supported by those who benefit from it. 15Yet I have never used any of these rights. And I am not writing this to suggest that I want to start now. In fact, I would rather die than lose my

**9:15**
Acts 18:3
2 Cor 11:9-10

right to boast about preaching without charge. 16Yet preaching the Good News is not some-thing I can boast about. I am compelled by God to do it. How terrible for me if I didn't preach the Good News!

**9:16**
Acts 9:15
Rom 1:14

17If I were doing this on my own initiative, I would deserve payment. But I have no choice, for God has given me this sacred trust. 18What then is my pay? It is the opportunity to

**9:17**
Gal 2:7
Eph 3:1-8
Phil 1:16, 17
Col 1:25

preach the Good News without charging anyone. That's why I never demand my rights when I preach the Good News.

**9:5** Greek *Cephas.*   **9:9** Deut 25:4.

---

**STRONGER, WEAKER BELIEVERS**

*Advice to*

| | |
|---|---|
| Stronger believers . . . . . . . | Don't be proud of your maturity; don't flaunt your freedom. Act in love so you do not cause a weaker believer to stumble. |
| Weaker believers . . . . . . . . | Although you may not feel the same freedom in some areas as in others, take your time, pray to God, but do not force others to adhere to your stipulations. You would hinder other believers by making up rules and standards for how everyone ought to behave. Make sure your convictions are based on God's Word and are not simply an expression of your opinions. |
| Pastors and leaders . . . . . . | Teach correctly from God's Word, helping Christians to under-stand what is right and wrong in God's eyes and to see that they can have varied opinions on other issues and still be unified. Don't allow potential problems to get out of hand, causing splits and divisions. |

Paul advises those who are more mature in the faith about how they must care about their brothers and sisters in Christ who have more tender consciences; those "weaker" brothers and sisters are advised concerning their growth; and pastors and leaders are instructed on how to deal with the conflicts that easily could arise between these groups.

---

**9:5** The Lord's brothers attained leadership status in the church at Jerusalem. James (one of Jesus' brothers), for example, led the way to an agreement at the Jerusalem council (Acts 15) and wrote the book of James.

**9:13-15** As part of their pay, priests in the temple would receive a portion of the offerings as their food (see Numbers 18:8-24). These verses concerning Paul's rights and the church's responsi-bility have a two-part challenge for the church today. First, the church must support its workers in a fair and equitable way. That is the church's responsibility. It can research pay scales, examine the standard of living in its community, and do what is right and fair. Second, Christian workers must not let their attitude about pay and benefits hinder the gospel. It is too easy

for desire for more pay to enter into a person's mind and distract from serving. Ministers need Paul's attitude: a willingness not to demand their rights if to do so would hinder the gospel.

**9:16** Preaching the Good News was Paul's gift and calling, and he said he couldn't stop preaching even if he wanted to. Paul was driven by the desire to do what God wanted, using his gifts for God's glory. What special gifts has God given you? Are you motivated, like Paul, to honor God with your gifts?

¹⁹Even though I am a free man with no master, I have become a slave to all people to bring many to Christ. ²⁰When I was with the Jews, I lived like a Jew to bring the Jews to Christ. When I was with those who follow the Jewish law, I too lived under that law. Even though I am not subject to the law, I did this so I could bring to Christ those who are under the law. ²¹When I am with the Gentiles who do not follow the Jewish law,* I too live apart from that law so I can bring them to Christ. But I do not ignore the law of God; I obey the law of Christ.

²²When I am with those who are weak, I share their weakness, for I want to bring the weak to Christ. Yes, I try to find common ground with everyone, doing everything I can to save some. ²³I do everything to spread the Good News and share in its blessings.

²⁴Don't you realize that in a race everyone runs, but only one person gets the prize? So run to win! ²⁵All athletes are disciplined in their training. They do it to win a prize that will fade away, but we do it for an eternal prize. ²⁶So I run with purpose in every step. I am not just shadowboxing. ²⁷I discipline my body like an athlete, training it to do what it should. Otherwise, I fear that after preaching to others I myself might be disqualified.

## Lessons from Israel's Idolatry

**10** I don't want you to forget, dear brothers and sisters,* about our ancestors in the wilderness long ago. All of them were guided by a cloud that moved ahead of them, and all of them walked through the sea on dry ground. ²In the cloud and in the sea, all of them were baptized as followers of Moses. ³All of them ate the same spiritual food, ⁴and all of them drank the same spiritual water. For they drank from the spiritual rock that traveled with them, and that rock was Christ. ⁵Yet God was not pleased with most of them, and their bodies were scattered in the wilderness.

⁶These things happened as a warning to us, so that we would not crave evil things as they did, ⁷or worship idols as some of them did. As the Scriptures say, "The people celebrated with feasting and drinking, and they indulged in pagan revelry."* ⁸And we must not engage in sexual immorality as some of them did, causing 23,000 of them to die in one day.

⁹Nor should we put Christ* to the test, as some of them did and then died from snakebites. ¹⁰And don't grumble as some of them did, and then were destroyed by the angel of

**9:21** Greek *those without the law.*   **10:1** Greek *brothers.*   **10:7** Exod 32:6.   **10:9** Some manuscripts read *the Lord.*

**9:19**
Gal 5:13
**9:20**
Acts 16:3; 21:20-26
Rom 11:14
**9:21**
Rom 2:12, 14
Gal 6:2
**9:24**
Phil 3:14
2 Tim 4:7
**9:25**
2 Tim 2:5; 4:8
1 Pet 5:4
**9:26**
1 Tim 6:12
**9:27**
Rom 8:13; 13:14
2 Cor 13:5
**10:1**
Exod 13:21-22;
14:15-22
**10:3**
Exod 16:4, 35
John 6:31-58
**10:4**
Exod 17:6
Num 20:11
John 6:31-58; 7:37
**10:5**
Num 14:16, 23
**10:6**
Num 11:4, 34
Ps 106:14
**10:8**
Num 25:1-9
**10:9**
Exod 17:2
Num 21:5-6
**10:10**
Num 14:2, 36

---

**9:19-27** In 9:19-22 Paul asserts that he has freedom to do anything; in 9:24-27 he emphasizes a life of strict discipline. The Christian life involves both freedom and discipline. The goals of Paul's life were to glorify God and bring people to Christ. Thus, he stayed free of any philosophical position or material entanglement that might sidetrack him, while he strictly disciplined himself to carry out his goal. For Paul, both freedom and discipline were important tools to be used in God's service.

**9:22, 23** Paul gives several important principles for ministry: (1) Find common ground with those you contact; (2) avoid a know-it-all attitude; (3) make others feel accepted; (4) be sensitive to their needs and concerns; and (5) look for opportunities to tell them about Christ. These principles are just as valid for us as they were for Paul.

**9:24-27** Winning a race requires purpose and discipline. Paul uses this illustration to explain that the Christian life takes hard work, self-denial, and grueling preparation. As Christians, we are running toward our heavenly reward. The essential disciplines of prayer, Bible study, and worship equip us to run with vigor and stamina. Don't merely observe from the grandstand; don't just turn out to jog a couple of laps each morning. Train diligently— your spiritual progress depends upon it.

**9:25** Whatever happened to self-discipline? Many books and speakers guide wandering souls to self-fulfillment, self-satisfaction, and self-awareness. Not many tackle self-discipline.

Self-discipline requires an honest look at your strengths and weaknesses, with emphasis on the latter. It means building the will to say no when a powerful appetite inside you screams yes. For example, when you have self-discipline, you can (1) say no to friends or situations that will lead you away from Christ, (2) say no to casual sex, saving intimacy for marriage, and (3) say no to laziness in favor of "can do" and "will do." Self-discipline is a long, steady course in learning attitudes that do not come naturally, and

channeling natural appetites toward God's purposes. Where are your weak points? Pray with a friend for God's help to redirect weakness into strength.

**9:27** When Paul says he might be disqualified, he does not mean that he could lose his salvation but rather that he could lose his privilege of telling others about Christ. It is easy to tell others how to live and then not to take our own advice. We must be careful to practice what we preach.

**10:1ff** In chapter 9, Paul used himself as an example of a mature Christian who disciplines himself to better serve God. In chapter 10, he uses Israel as an example of spiritual immaturity, shown in their overconfidence and lack of self-discipline.

**10:1-5** The cloud and the sea mentioned here refer to Israel's escape from slavery in Egypt when God led them by a cloud and brought them safely through the Red Sea (Exodus 14). The spiritual food and water are the provisions God gave as they traveled through the wilderness (Exodus 15–16).

**10:2** "All of them were baptized" means that just as we are united in Christ by baptism, so the Israelites were united under Moses' leadership and through the events of the Exodus.

**10:7-10** The incident referred to in 10:7 took place when the Israelites made a gold calf and worshiped it in the wilderness (Exodus 32). The incident in 10:8 is recorded in Numbers 25:1-9 when the Israelites worshiped Baal of Peor and engaged in sexual immorality with Moabite women. The reference in 10:9 is to the Israelites' complaint about their food (Numbers 21:5, 6). They put the Lord to the test by seeing how far they could go. In 10:10, Paul refers to when the people complained against Moses and Aaron, and the plague that resulted (Numbers 14:2, 36; 16:41-50). The angel of death is also referred to in Exodus 12:23.

**10:10** Paul warned the Corinthian believers not to grumble. We start to grumble when our attention shifts from what we have to what we don't have. The people of Israel didn't seem to notice what

**10:13**
1 Cor 1:9
2 Pet 2:9

**10:14**
1 Jn 5:21

**10:16**
Matt 26:26-28
Acts 2:42
1 Cor 11:23-26

**10:17**
Rom 12:5
1 Cor 12:27
Eph 4:16
Col 3:15

**10:18**
Lev 7:6, 14-15

death. ¹¹These things happened to them as examples for us. They were written down to warn us who live at the end of the age.

¹²If you think you are standing strong, be careful not to fall. ¹³The temptations in your life are no different from what others experience. And God is faithful. He will not allow the temptation to be more than you can stand. When you are tempted, he will show you a way out so that you can endure.

¹⁴So, my dear friends, flee from the worship of idols. ¹⁵You are reasonable people. Decide for yourselves if what I am saying is true. ¹⁶When we bless the cup at the Lord's Table, aren't we sharing in the blood of Christ? And when we break the bread, aren't we sharing in the body of Christ? ¹⁷And though we are many, we all eat from one loaf of bread, showing that we are one body. ¹⁸Think about the people of Israel. Weren't they united by eating the sacrifices at the altar?

¹⁹What am I trying to say? Am I saying that food offered to idols has some significance, or

---

| WHY WE DON'T GIVE UP | Reference | The Purpose | The Plan | The Prize |
|---|---|---|---|---|
| Perseverance, persistence, the prize!! The Christian life was never promised as an easy way to live; instead, Paul constantly reminds us that we must have a purpose and a plan because times will be difficult and Satan will attack. But we never persevere without the promise of a prize— a promise God will keep. | 1 Corinthians 9:24-27 | • Run to get the prize<br>• Run with purpose in every step | • Discipline your body, training it | • An eternal prize |
| | Galatians 6:7-10 | • Don't get tired of doing good<br>• Don't give up<br>• Do good to everyone | • Live to please the Spirit | • Everlasting life |
| | Ephesians 6:10-20 | • Put on all of God's armor<br>• Pray on every occasion | • Use every piece of God's armor to resist the enemy | • Taking your stand against the devil's strategies |
| | Philippians 3:12-14 | • Press on to possess that perfection for which Christ possessed you | • Forget the past; press on to reach the end of the race | • The heavenly prize for which God calls you |
| | 2 Timothy 2:1-13 | • Teach these great truths to people who are able to pass them on to others<br>• Be strong in Christ's grace, even when your faith is faltering | • Endure suffering as a soldier, and don't get tied up in worldly affairs<br>• Follow the Lord's rules, as an athlete must do in order to win<br>• Work hard, like a farmer who enjoys the fruit of his labor | • We will live with Christ; we will reign with him<br>• He remains faithful |

---

God was doing for them—setting them free, making them a nation, giving them a new land—because they were so wrapped up in what God wasn't doing for them. They could think of nothing but the delicious Egyptian food they had left behind (Numbers 11:5).

Before we judge the Israelites too harshly, it's helpful to think about what occupies our attention most of the time. Are we grateful for what God has given us, or are we always thinking about what we would like to have? Don't allow your unfulfilled desires to cause you to forget God's gifts of life, family, friends, food, health, and work.

**10:11** Today's pressures make it easy to ignore or forget the lessons of the past. But Paul cautions us to remember the lessons the Israelites learned about God so we can avoid repeating their errors. The key to remembering is to study the Bible regularly so that these lessons remind us of how God wants us to live. We need not repeat their mistakes!

**10:13** In a culture filled with moral depravity and sin-inducing pressures, Paul encouraged the Corinthians about temptation. He said that (1) temptations happen to everyone, so don't feel you've been singled out; (2) others have resisted temptation, and so can you; (3) any temptation can be resisted because God will show you a way out. God will aid you in resisting temptation by helping you (1) recognize those people and situations that give you trouble, (2) run from anything you know is wrong, (3) choose to do only what is right, (4) pray for God's help, and (5) seek

friends who love God and can offer help when you are tempted. Running from a tempting situation is your first step on the way to victory (see 2 Timothy 2:22).

**10:14** Idol worship was the major expression of religion in Corinth. There were several pagan temples in the city, and they were very popular. The statues of wood or stone were not evil in themselves, but people gave them credit for what only God could do, such as provide good weather, crops, and children. Idolatry is still a serious problem today, but it takes a different form. We don't put our trust in statues of wood and stone but in paper money and plastic cards. Putting our trust in anything but God is idolatry. Our modern idols are those symbols of power, pleasure, or prestige that we so highly regard. When we understand contemporary parallels to idolatry, Paul's words to "flee from the worship of idols" become much more meaningful.

**10:16-21** The idea of unity and fellowship with God through eating a sacrifice was strong in Judaism and Christianity as well as in paganism. In Old Testament days, when a Jew offered a sacrifice, he ate a part of that sacrifice as a way of restoring his unity with God, against whom he had sinned (Deuteronomy 12:17, 18). Similarly, Christians participate in Christ's once-for-all sacrifice at the Lord's Table when they eat the bread and drink from the cup, symbolizing his body and blood. Recent converts from paganism could not help being affected if they knowingly ate with pagans in their feasts the meat offered to idols.

that idols are real gods? 20No, not at all. I am saying that these sacrifices are offered to demons, not to God. And I don't want you to participate with demons. 21You cannot drink from the cup of the Lord and from the cup of demons, too. You cannot eat at the Lord's Table and at the table of demons, too. 22What? Do we dare to rouse the Lord's jealousy? Do you think we are stronger than he is?

23You say, "I am allowed to do anything"\*—but not everything is good for you. You say, "I am allowed to do anything"—but not everything is beneficial. 24Don't be concerned for your own good but for the good of others.

25So you may eat any meat that is sold in the marketplace without raising questions of conscience. 26For "the earth is the Lord's, and everything in it."\*

27If someone who isn't a believer asks you home for dinner, accept the invitation if you want to. Eat whatever is offered to you without raising questions of conscience. 28(But suppose someone tells you, "This meat was offered to an idol." Don't eat it, out of consideration for the conscience of the one who told you. 29It might not be a matter of conscience for you, but it is for the other person.) For why should my freedom be limited by what someone else thinks? 30If I can thank God for the food and enjoy it, why should I be condemned for eating it?

31So whether you eat or drink, or whatever you do, do it all for the glory of God. 32Don't give offense to Jews or Gentiles\* or the church of God. 33I, too, try to please everyone in everything I do. I don't just do what is best for me; I do what is best for others so that many may be saved. 11:1And you should imitate me, just as I imitate Christ.

### 3. Instruction on public worship
*Proper Worship*

**11** 2I am so glad that you always keep me in your thoughts, and that you are following the teachings I passed on to you. 3But there is one thing I want you to know: The head of

**10:23** Greek *All things are lawful;* also in 10:23b.    **10:26** Ps 24:1.    **10:32** Greek *or Greeks.*

| | |
|---|---|
| **10:20** | Deut 32:17 |
| | Rev 9:20 |
| **10:21** | 2 Cor 6:15-16 |
| **10:22** | Deut 32:16, 21 |
| **10:23** | 1 Cor 6:12 |
| **10:24** | Rom 15:1-2 |
| **10:25** | Acts 10:15 |
| | 1 Cor 8:7 |
| **10:27** | Luke 10:8 |
| **10:28** | Rom 14:16 |
| | 1 Cor 8:7, 10-12 |
| **10:29** | 1 Cor 9:1, 19 |
| **10:31** | Col 3:17 |
| **10:32** | Matt 5:29 |
| | Acts 24:16 |
| | Rom 14:13 |
| | 1 Cor 8:13 |
| **10:33** | 1 Cor 9:20-22 |
| **11:1** | 1 Cor 4:16 |
| **11:2** | 1 Cor 15:2-3 |
| | 2 Thes 2:15; 3:6 |

**10:21** As followers of Christ we must give him our total allegiance. We cannot, as Paul explains, have a part in "the cup of the Lord and . . . the cup of demons." Eating at the Lord's Table means communing with Christ and identifying with his death. Drinking from the cup of demons means identifying with Satan by worshiping or promoting pagan (or evil) activities. Are you leading two lives, trying to follow both Christ and the crowd? The Bible says that you can't do both at the same time.

**10:23, 24** Sometimes it's hard to know when to defer to weaker believers. Paul gives a simple rule of thumb to help in making the decision: We should be sensitive and gracious. The goal here is not a general hypersensitivity that worries about what others might possibly think. Rather, it is a genuine awareness of others and a willingness to limit what we do when there is a real possibility of misunderstanding and offense. Some actions may not be wrong, but they may not be in the best interest of others. We have freedom in Christ, but we shouldn't exercise our freedom at the cost of hurting a Christian brother or sister. We are not to consider only ourselves; we must also consider the needs and perspective of others. For more on the proper attitude toward a weak believer, see the notes on 8:10-13 and Romans 14.

**10:25-27** Paul gave one answer to the dilemma: Buy whatever meat is sold at the market without asking whether or not it was offered to idols. It doesn't matter anyway, and no one's conscience would be bothered. When we become too worried about our every action, we become legalistic and cannot enjoy life. Everything belongs to God, and he has given us all things to enjoy. If we know something is a problem, then we can deal with it, but we don't need to go looking for problems.

**10:28-33** Why should we be limited by another person's conscience? Simply because we are to do all things for God's glory, even our eating and drinking. Nothing we do should cause another believer to stumble. We do what is best for others, so that they might be saved. We should also be sensitive to the meaning of our actions to new Christians who are sorting out how to renounce sinful ways from the past and live for Christ.

However, Christians should not make a career out of being the offended people with oversensitive consciences. Believers must not project their standards onto others. Many believers who have been Christians for years are still oversensitive and judgmental of others. Instead of being the offended weaker brothers and sisters, they are no more than offended "Pharisees."

Christian leaders and teachers should carefully teach about the freedom Christians have in matters not expressly forbidden by Scripture. New or weak Christians should not remain in a weak or sensitive state but should grow into maturity and discernment lest they prove to be an unnecessary burden on others' freedom in Christ.

**10:31** Our actions must be motivated by God's love so that all we do will be for his glory. Keep this as a guiding principle by asking, "Is this action glorifying God?" or "How can I honor God through this action?"

**10:33** Paul's criterion for all his actions was not what he liked best but what was best for those around him. The opposite approach would be (1) being insensitive and doing what we want, no matter who is hurt by it; (2) being oversensitive and doing nothing, for fear that someone may be displeased; (3) being a "yes person" by going along with everything, trying to gain approval from people rather than from God. In this age of "me first" and "looking out for number one," Paul's startling statement is a good standard. If we make the good of others one of our primary goals, we will develop a serving attitude that pleases God.

**11:1** Why did Paul say, "Imitate me"? Paul wasn't being arrogant—he did not think of himself as sinless. At this time, however, the Corinthian believers did not know much about the life and ministry of Christ. Paul could not tell them to imitate Jesus because the Gospels had not yet been written, so they did not know what Jesus was like. The best way to point these new Christians to Christ was to point them to a Christian whom they trusted (see also Galatians 4:12; Philippians 3:17; 1 Thessalonians 1:6; 2:14; 2 Thessalonians 3:7, 9). Paul had been in Corinth almost two years and had built a relationship of trust with many of these new believers.

**11:2ff** In this section Paul's main concern is irreverence in worship. We need to read it in the context of the situation in Corinth.

**11:3**
Gen 3:16
1 Cor 3:23
Eph 5:23

**11:5**
Acts 21:9

**11:7**
Gen 1:26; 5:1; 9:6
Jas 3:9

**11:8**
Gen 2:21-23
1 Tim 2:13

**11:9**
Gen 2:18

every man is Christ, the head of woman is man, and the head of Christ is God.* 4A man dishonors his head* if he covers his head while praying or prophesying. 5But a woman dishonors her head* if she prays or prophesies without a covering on her head, for this is the same as shaving her head. 6Yes, if she refuses to wear a head covering, she should cut off all her hair! But since it is shameful for a woman to have her hair cut or her head shaved, she should wear a covering.*

7A man should not wear anything on his head when worshiping, for man is made in God's image and reflects God's glory. And woman reflects man's glory. 8For the first man didn't come from woman, but the first woman came from man. 9And man was not made for

**11:3** Or to know: The source of every man is Christ, the source of woman is man, and the source of Christ is God. Or to know: Every man is responsible to Christ, a woman is responsible to her husband, and Christ is responsible to God.   **11:4** Or dishonors Christ.   **11:5** Or dishonors her husband.   **11:6** Or should have long hair.

---

**MAKING CHOICES ON SENSITIVE ISSUES**

All of us make hundreds of choices every day. Most choices have no right or wrong attached to them—like what you wear or what you eat. But we always face decisions that carry a little more weight. We don't want to do wrong, and we don't want to cause others to do wrong, so how can we make such decisions?

If I choose one course of action:

   . . . does it help my witness for Christ? (9:19-22)

   . . . am I motivated by a desire to help others know Christ? (9:23; 10:33)

   . . . does it help me do my best? (9:25)

   . . . is it against a specific command in Scripture and would thus cause me to sin? (10:12)

   . . . is it the best and most beneficial course of action? (10:23, 33)

   . . . am I thinking only of myself, or do I truly care about the other person? (10:24)

   . . . am I acting lovingly or selfishly? (10:28-31)

   . . . does it glorify God? (10:31)

   . . . will it cause someone else to sin? (10:32)

---

The matter of wearing hats or head coverings, although seemingly insignificant, had become a big problem because two cultural backgrounds were colliding. Jewish women always covered their heads in worship. For a woman to uncover her head in public was a sign of loose morals. On the other hand, Greek women may have been used to worshiping without head coverings.

In this letter Paul had already spoken about divisions and disorder in the church. Both are involved in this issue. Paul's solution came from his desire for unity among church members and for appropriateness in the worship service. He accepted God's sovereignty in creating the rules for relationships.

**11:2-16** This section focuses primarily on proper attitudes and conduct in worship, not on the marriage relationship or on the role of women in the church. While Paul's specific instructions may be cultural (women covering their heads in worship), the principles behind them are timeless: respect for spouse, reverence and appropriateness in worship, and focus of all of life on God. If you are doing something that might easily offend members and divide the church, then change your ways to promote church unity. Paul told the women who were not wearing head coverings to wear them, not because it was a scriptural command, but because it kept the congregation from dividing over a petty issue that served only to take people's minds off Christ.

**11:3** The phrase, "the head of every man is Christ," could mean that: (1) because Christ was present at Creation, he is the Creator of every man; and (2) Christ is every believer's source of life in the new creation.

The phrase "the head of woman is man" does not indicate the man's control or supremacy but rather his being her source. Because man was created first, the woman derives her existence from man, as man does from Christ and Christ from God. Evidently Paul was correcting some excesses in worship in which the emancipated Corinthian women were engaging.

The phrase, "the head of Christ is God," does not mean that Christ was inferior to God in any way. Paul was referring to the incarnation of Christ. Through Christ's coming to earth, believers receive forgiveness and are united with God and with one another. From this theological base, then, Paul began to address the issue of head coverings.

**11:3** The principle behind Paul's words is *submission*, which is a key element in the smooth functioning of any business, government, or family. God ordained submission in certain relationships to prevent chaos. It is essential to understand that submission is not surrender, withdrawal, or apathy. It does not mean inferiority, because God created all people in his image and all have equal value. Submission is mutual commitment and cooperation.

Thus, God calls for submission among *equals*. He did not make the man superior; he made a way for a husband and wife to work together. Jesus Christ, although equal with God the Father, submitted to him to carry out the plan for salvation. Likewise, although equal to man under God, the wife should submit to her husband for the sake of their marriage and family. Submission between equals is submission by choice, not by force. We serve God in these relationships by willingly submitting to others in our church, to our spouses, and to our government leaders.

**11:9-11** God created lines of authority in order for his created world to function smoothly. Although there must be lines of authority even in marriage, there should *not* be lines of superiority. God created men and women with unique and complementary characteristics. One sex is not better than the other. We must not let the issue of authority and submission become a wedge to destroy oneness in marriage. Instead, we should use our unique gifts to strengthen our marriages and to glorify God.

woman, but woman was made for man. 10For this reason, and because the angels are watching, a woman should wear a covering on her head to show she is under authority.*

11But among the Lord's people, women are not independent of men, and men are not independent of women. 12For although the first woman came from man, every other man was born from a woman, and everything comes from God.

13Judge for yourselves. Is it right for a woman to pray to God in public without covering her head? 14Isn't it obvious that it's disgraceful for a man to have long hair? 15And isn't long hair a woman's pride and joy? For it has been given to her as a covering. 16But if anyone wants to argue about this, I simply say that we have no other custom than this, and neither do God's other churches.

### Order at the Lord's Supper

17But in the following instructions, I cannot praise you. For it sounds as if more harm than good is done when you meet together. 18First, I hear that there are divisions among you when you meet as a church, and to some extent I believe it. 19But, of course, there must be divisions among you so that you who have God's approval will be recognized!

20When you meet together, you are not really interested in the Lord's Supper. 21For some of you hurry to eat your own meal without sharing with others. As a result, some go hungry while others get drunk. 22What? Don't you have your own homes for eating and drinking? Or do you really want to disgrace God's church and shame the poor? What am I supposed to say? Do you want me to praise you? Well, I certainly will not praise you for this!

23For I pass on to you what I received from the Lord himself. On the night when he was betrayed, the Lord Jesus took some bread 24and gave thanks to God for it. Then he broke it in pieces and said, "This is my body, which is given for you.* Do this to remember me." 25In the same way, he took the cup of wine after supper, saying, "This cup is the new covenant between God and his people—an agreement confirmed with my blood. Do this to remember me as often as you drink it." 26For every time you eat this bread and drink this cup, you are announcing the Lord's death until he comes again.

**11:12**
Rom 11:36

**11:16**
1 Cor 7:17; 10:32

**11:18**
1 Cor 1:10-12; 3:3
**11:19**
1 Jn 2:19

**11:21**
2 Pet 2:13
Jude 1:12
**11:22**
1 Cor 10:32
Jas 2:6
**11:23-25**
†Matt 26:26-28
†Mark 14:22-24
†Luke 22:17-20
**11:25**
Luke 22:20
1 Cor 10:16
2 Cor 3:6
**11:26**
Luke 22:19

**11:10** Greek *should have an authority on her head.* **11:24** Greek *which is for you;* other manuscripts read *which is broken for you.*

---

**11:10** This verse may mean that the woman should wear a covering on her head as a sign that she is under the man's authority. This is a fact even the angels understand as they observe Christians in worship. See the note on 11:2ff for an explanation of head coverings.

**11:14, 15** In talking about head coverings and length of hair, Paul is saying that believers should look and behave in ways that are honorable in their own culture. In many cultures long hair on men is considered appropriate and masculine. In Corinth, it was thought to be a sign of male prostitution in the pagan temples. And women with short hair were labeled prostitutes. Paul was saying that in the Corinthian culture, Christian women should keep their hair long. If short hair on women was a sign of prostitution, then a Christian woman with short hair would find it difficult to be a believable witness for Jesus Christ. Paul wasn't saying we should adopt all the practices of our culture but that we should avoid appearances and behavior that detract from our ultimate goal of being witnesses for Jesus Christ.

**11:17-34** The Lord's Supper (11:20) is a visible representation symbolizing the death of Christ for our sins. It reminds us of Christ's death and the glorious hope of his return. Our participation in it strengthens our faith through fellowship with Christ and with other believers.

**11:18, 19** Paul acknowledges that there are differences among church members. When they develop into self-willed divisions, however, they are destructive to the congregation. Those who cause division only serve to highlight those who are genuine believers.

**11:21, 22** When the Lord's Supper was celebrated in the early church, it included a feast or fellowship meal followed by the celebration of Communion. In the church in Corinth, the fellowship meal had become a time when some ate and drank excessively while others went hungry. There was little s[...]

caring. This certainly did not demonstrate the unity and love that should characterize the church, nor was it a preparation for Communion. Paul condemned these actions and reminded the church of the real purpose of the Lord's Supper.

**11:24, 25** What does the Lord's Supper mean? The early church remembered that Jesus instituted the Lord's Supper on the night of the Passover meal (Luke 22:13-20). Just as Passover celebrated deliverance from slavery in Egypt, so the Lord's Supper celebrates deliverance from sin by Christ's death.

Christians pose several different possibilities for what Christ meant when he said, "This is my body." (1) Some believe that the bread and wine actually become Christ's physical blood and body. (2) Others believe that the bread and wine remain unchanged, but Christ is spiritually present with the bread and wine. (3) Still others believe that the bread and wine symbolize Christ's body and blood. Christians generally agree, however, that participating in the Lord's Supper is an important element in the Christian faith and that Christ's presence, however we understand it, strengthens us spiritually.

**11:25** What is this new covenant? In the old covenant, people could approach God only through the priests and the sacrificial system. Jesus' death on the cross ushered in the new covenant or agreement between God and us. Now all people can personally approach God and communicate with him. The people of Israel first entered into this agreement after their exodus from Egypt (Exodus 24), and it was designed to point to the day when Jesus Christ would come. The new covenant completes, rather than replaces, the old covenant, fulfilling everything the old covenant looked forward to (see Jeremiah 31:31-34). Eating the bread and drinking the cup shows that we are remembering Christ's death for us and renewing our commitment to serve him.

**11:25** Jesus said, "Do this to remember me as often as you drink it." How do we remember Christ in the Lord's Supper? By thinking about what he did and why he did it. Further, the

**11:27**
Heb 10:29

**11:28**
2 Cor 13:5

27So anyone who eats this bread or drinks this cup of the Lord unworthily is guilty of sinning against* the body and blood of the Lord. 28That is why you should examine yourself before eating the bread and drinking the cup. 29For if you eat the bread or drink the cup without honoring the body of Christ,* you are eating and drinking God's judgment upon yourself. 30That is why many of you are weak and sick and some have even died.

**11:31**
1 Jn 1:9

**11:32**
Ps 94:12
Heb 12:5-6

**11:34**
1 Cor 4:19

31But if we would examine ourselves, we would not be judged by God in this way. 32Yet when we are judged by the Lord, we are being disciplined so that we will not be condemned along with the world.

33So, my dear brothers and sisters,* when you gather for the Lord's Supper, wait for each other. 34If you are really hungry, eat at home so you won't bring judgment upon yourselves when you meet together. I'll give you instructions about the other matters after I arrive.

## Spiritual Gifts

**12:1**
1 Cor 14:1

**12:2**
Hab 2:18-19
1 Thes 1:9

**12:3**
John 13:13
1 Jn 4:2-3

**12:4**
Rom 12:6
Eph 4:4
Heb 2:4

**12:6**
Eph 4:6

**12:8**
1 Cor 2:6

**12** Now, dear brothers and sisters,* regarding your question about the special abilities the Spirit gives us. I don't want you to misunderstand this. 2You know that when you were still pagans, you were led astray and swept along in worshiping speechless idols. 3So I want you to know that no one speaking by the Spirit of God will curse Jesus, and no one can say Jesus is Lord, except by the Holy Spirit.

4There are different kinds of spiritual gifts, but the same Spirit is the source of them all. 5There are different kinds of service, but we serve the same Lord. 6God works in different ways, but it is the same God who does the work in all of us.

7A spiritual gift is given to each of us so we can help each other. 8To one person the Spirit gives the ability to give wise advice*; to another the same Spirit gives a message of special

**11:27** Or *is responsible for.*   **11:29** Greek *the body;* other manuscripts read *the Lord's body.*   **11:33** Greek *brothers.*
**12:1** Greek *brothers.*   **12:8a** Or *gives a word of wisdom.*

---

remembering has both a backward and forward look. We remember Christ's death, and we remember that he is coming! If the Lord's Supper becomes just a ritual or a pious habit, it loses its significance. But when we appreciate what Christ has done and anticipate what he will do when he returns, the Lord's Supper takes on a profound sense of purpose. Take time to prepare yourself spiritually for Communion. Gratefully recall Christ's loving sacrifice for you. Let the reality that your sins are forgiven motivate you to love and serve him better.

**11:27ff** Paul gives specific instructions on how the Lord's Supper should be observed. (1) We should take the Lord's Supper thoughtfully because we are proclaiming that Christ died for our sins (11:26). (2) We should take it worthily, with due reverence and respect (11:27). (3) We should examine ourselves for any unconfessed sin or resentful attitude and be properly prepared (11:28). (4) We should be considerate of others, waiting until everyone is there and then eating in an orderly and unified manner (11:33).

**11:27-34** When Paul said that no one should take the Lord's Supper unworthily, he was speaking to the church members who were participating in it without thinking of its meaning. To not honor the "body of Christ" means not understanding what the Lord's Supper means and not distinguishing it from a normal meal. Those who did so were "guilty of sinning against the body and blood of the Lord." Instead of honoring his sacrifice, they were sharing in the guilt of those who crucified Christ. In reality, *no one* is worthy to take the Lord's Supper. We are all sinners saved by grace. This is why we should prepare ourselves for Communion through healthy introspection, confession of sin, and resolution of differences with others. These actions remove the barriers that affect our relationship with Christ and with other believers. Awareness of your sin should not keep you away from Communion but drive you to participate in it.

**11:30** That some of the people had died may have been a special supernatural judgment on the Corinthian church. This type of disciplinary judgment highlights the seriousness of the Communion service. The Lord's Supper is not to be taken lightly; this new covenant cost Jesus his life. It is not a meaningless ritual, but a sacrament given by Christ to help strengthen our faith.

**11:34** People should come to this meal desiring to fellowship with other believers and prepare for the Lord's Supper to follow, not to fill up on a big dinner. "If you are really hungry, eat at home" means that they should eat dinner beforehand so as to come to the fellowship meal in the right frame of mind.

**12:1ff** The spiritual gifts given to each person by the Holy Spirit are special abilities that are to be used to minister to the needs of the body of believers. This chapter is not an exhaustive list of spiritual gifts (see Romans 12; Ephesians 4; 1 Peter 4:10, 11 for more examples). There are many gifts; people have different gifts; some people have more than one gift, and one gift is not superior to another. All spiritual gifts come from the Holy Spirit, and their purpose is to build up Christ's body, the church.

**12:1ff** Instead of building up and unifying the Corinthian church, the issue of spiritual gifts was splitting it. Spiritual gifts had become symbols of spiritual power, causing rivalries. Some people thought they were more "spiritual" than others because of their gifts. This was a terrible misuse of spiritual gifts because their purpose is always to help the church function more effectively, not to divide it. We can be divisive if we insist on using our gifts our own way without being sensitive to others. We must never use our gifts as a means of manipulating others or serving our own self-interests.

**12:3** Anyone can claim to speak for God, and the world is full of false teachers. Paul gives us a test to help us discern whether or not a messenger is really from God: Does he or she confess Christ as Lord? Don't naively accept the words of all who claim to speak for God; test their credentials by finding out what they teach about Christ.

**12:6** God is completely involved in the giving, using, and empowering of gifts. Specific gifts, places of service, and activities vary, but they all have their best effects when they build up the body of Christ—the church. God creates a unique place in the body for every believer. Gifts and ministries may overlap, but each believer has a specialized, God-designed role. Part of the exciting adventure of following Christ involves discovering one's service contribution and then making it available to God. Make serving God and his people your motive as you utilize your gifts.

knowledge.* ⁹The same Spirit gives great faith to another, and to someone else the one Spirit gives the gift of healing. ¹⁰He gives one person the power to perform miracles, and another the ability to prophesy. He gives someone else the ability to discern whether a message is from the Spirit of God or from another spirit. Still another person is given the ability to speak in unknown languages,* while another is given the ability to interpret what is being said. ¹¹It is the one and only Spirit who distributes all these gifts. He alone decides which gift each person should have.

**12:9**
Matt 17:19-20
**12:10**
Acts 2:4
Rom 12:6
1 Cor 14:26-32
Gal 3:5
1 Jn 4:1
**12:11**
Rom 12:6-8
Eph 4:5, 7

### One Body with Many Parts

¹²The human body has many parts, but the many parts make up one whole body. So it is with the body of Christ. ¹³Some of us are Jews, some are Gentiles,* some are slaves, and some are free. But we have all been baptized into one body by one Spirit, and we all share the same Spirit.*

**12:12**
Rom 12:4-5
1 Cor 10:17; 12:27
**12:13**
John 7:37-39
Gal 3:28
Eph 2:18
Col 3:11

¹⁴Yes, the body has many different parts, not just one part. ¹⁵If the foot says, "I am not a part of the body because I am not a hand," that does not make it any less a part of the body. ¹⁶And if the ear says, "I am not part of the body because I am not an eye," would that make it any less a part of the body? ¹⁷If the whole body were an eye, how would you hear? Or if your whole body were an ear, how would you smell anything?

¹⁸But our bodies have many parts, and God has put each part just where he wants it. ¹⁹How strange a body would be if it had only one part! ²⁰Yes, there are many parts, but only one body. ²¹The eye can never say to the hand, "I don't need you." The head can't say to the feet, "I don't need you."

**12:18**
1 Cor 12:28

²²In fact, some parts of the body that seem weakest and least important are actually the most necessary. ²³And the parts we regard as less honorable are those we clothe with the greatest care. So we carefully protect those parts that should not be seen, ²⁴while the more

**12:8b** Or *gives a word of knowledge.*   **12:10** Or *in various tongues;* also in 12:28, 30.   **12:13a** Greek *some are Greeks.*   **12:13b** Greek *we were all given one Spirit to drink.*

---

**12:9** All Christians have faith. Some, however, have the spiritual gift of faith, which is an unusual measure of trust in the power of God.

**12:10** "The ability to prophesy" does not just refer to predicting the future; it can also mean giving a message received from God to the community of believers: "One who prophesies strengthens others, encourages them, and comforts them" (14:3). The prophet Joel had written the words of the Lord, "I will pour out my Spirit upon all people. Your sons and daughters will prophesy" (Joel 2:28). As with the gift of faith, the ability to share one's faith with power is available to everyone (see 14:1-5), but to some the Spirit gives a special measure of this gift. Paul wrote in Romans, "In his grace, God has given us different gifts for doing certain things well. So if God has given you the ability to prophesy, speak out with as much faith as God has given you" (Romans 12:6). Some have interpreted "prophecy" to be fulfilled in various sermons throughout church history. Others, however, say that prophecy is not a sermon, but a spontaneous, Spirit-inspired message that is orally delivered in the congregation for the edification and encouragement of the body of Christ.

**12:10** Opinions differ over exactly what Paul meant by "unknown languages." Some believe that this refers to earthly languages that a person did not know before (the same as the gift described in Acts 2:4-8). Other scholars say that this refers to an "ecstatic" language, a "heavenly" language. Most likely the second view is correct. Probably the only time that the word "tongues" refers to other earthly languages is when describing Pentecost. The rest of the time in the New Testament, the word refers to ecstatic languages unknown to anyone—languages of angels (13:1).

Speaking in tongues *is* a legitimate gift of the Spirit. The exercise of the gift demands some guidelines (as noted in chapter 14) so that the *purpose* of the gift—to help the body of Christ—is not lost. Those who speak in tongues should follow the guidelines; those who do not speak in tongues ought *not* seek the gift as a sign of salvation or of special closeness with God, for it is neither. It is a gift of God, given only to whomever God chooses. If a person has not experienced the gift of tongues, he or she ought

not seek it but seek what gifts God *has* given. For more, see the notes in chapter 14.

**12:11** No matter what gift(s) a person has, all spiritual gifts are distributed by the Holy Spirit. The Holy Spirit decides which gifts each believer should have. We are responsible to use and sharpen our gifts, but we can take no credit for what God has freely given us.

Note that discussions about spiritual gifts usually create difficulties when two central points are overlooked: (1) Properly used, spiritual gifts are not self-serving but serve the whole body of Christ (12:7); (2) each gift becomes practically useless when used without love (chapter 13). As you seek to identify and utilize the gifts God has given you, make loving God and loving fellow Christians your highest motives.

**12:12** Paul compares the body of Christ to a human body. Each part has a specific function that is necessary to the body as a whole. The parts are different for a purpose, and in their differences they must work together. Christians must avoid two common errors: (1) being proud of their abilities, or (2) thinking they have nothing to give to the body of believers. Instead of comparing ourselves to one another, we should use our different gifts, together, to spread the Good News of salvation.

**12:13** The church is composed of many types of people from a variety of backgrounds with a multitude of gifts and abilities. It is easy for these differences to divide people, as was the case in Corinth. But despite the differences, all believers have one thing in common—faith in Christ. On this essential truth the church finds unity. All believers are baptized by one Holy Spirit into one body of believers, the church. We don't lose our individual identities, but we have an overriding oneness in Christ. When we become a Christian, the Holy Spirit takes up residence in us, and we are born into God's family. "We all share the same Spirit" means that each of us has received the same Holy Spirit. As members of God's family, we may have different interests and gifts, but we are united by the Spirit into one spiritual body.

**12:23, 24** Paul argued for diversity of gifts and acceptance of the full range of gifts that God gives to his people. No one should feel honorable parts do not require this special care. So God has put the body together such that extra honor and care are given to those parts that have less dignity. 25This makes for harmony among the members, so that all the members care for each other. 26If one part suffers, all the parts suffer with it, and if one part is honored, all the parts are glad.

27All of you together are Christ's body, and each of you is a part of it. 28Here are some of the parts God has appointed for the church:

first are apostles,
second are prophets,
third are teachers,
then those who do miracles,
those who have the gift of healing,
those who can help others,
those who have the gift of leadership,
those who speak in unknown languages.

29Are we all apostles? Are we all prophets? Are we all teachers? Do we all have the power to do miracles? 30Do we all have the gift of healing? Do we all have the ability to speak in unknown languages? Do we all have the ability to interpret unknown languages? Of course not! 31So you should earnestly desire the most helpful gifts.

But now let me show you a way of life that is best of all.

### Love Is the Greatest

**13** If I could speak all the languages of earth and of angels, but didn't love others, I would only be a noisy gong or a clanging cymbal. 2If I had the gift of prophecy, and if I understood all of God's secret plans and possessed all knowledge, and if I had such faith that I could move mountains, but didn't love others, I would be nothing. 3If I gave everything I have to the poor and even sacrificed my body, I could boast about it;* but if I didn't love others, I would have gained nothing.

4Love is patient and kind. Love is not jealous or boastful or proud 5or rude. It does not demand its own way. It is not irritable, and it keeps no record of being wronged. 6It does not rejoice about injustice but rejoices whenever the truth wins out. 7Love never gives up, never loses faith, is always hopeful, and endures through every circumstance.

8Prophecy and speaking in unknown languages* and special knowledge will become useless. But love will last forever! 9Now our knowledge is partial and incomplete, and even

**13:3** Some manuscripts read *sacrificed my body to be burned.*   **13:8** Or *in tongues.*

---

**12:27**
Rom 12:5
Eph 1:23; 4:12
Col 1:18, 24

**12:28**
Rom 12:6-8
Eph 4:11-12

**12:31**
1 Cor 14:1, 39

**13:1**
1 Tim 1:5

**13:2**
Matt 17:20; 21:21
Mark 11:23
1 Cor 12:9

**13:3**
Matt 6:2

**13:4**
1 Pet 4:8

**13:5**
1 Cor 10:24
Phil 2:4

**13:6**
2 Thes 2:12
2 Jn 1:4
3 Jn 1:3-4

**13:7**
Prov 10:12
1 Pet 4:8

---

superior about his or her gift; instead, all should use their gifts to willingly serve. Too often the "up-front" gifts, like speaking or teaching, are more highly regarded than the "behind-the-scenes" gifts, like helping and serving. No one should discount the contribution of another person, no matter how insignificant it may seem. We should not be dissatisfied with the gift God has given us but be eager to serve. Nor should we envy those who seem to have more gifts than we do. In love, treat everyone's gift, yours included, as valuable to God.

**12:25, 26** What is your response when a fellow Christian is honored? How do you respond when someone is suffering? We are to be happy with those who are happy, and if they are sad, share their sorrow (Romans 12:15). Too often, unfortunately, we are jealous of those who rejoice and apathetic toward those who weep. Believers are in the world together—there is no such thing as private or individualistic Christianity. We need to get involved in the lives of others and not just enjoy our own relationship with God.

**12:30** Paul discusses the subject of speaking in and interpreting unknown languages in more detail in chapter 14. See also the second note at 12:10.

**12:31** The most helpful gifts are those that are beneficial to the body of Christ. Paul has already made it clear that one gift is not superior to another, but he urges the believers to discover how they can serve Christ's body with the gifts God has given them. Your spiritual gifts are not for your own self-advancement. They were given to you for serving God and enhancing the spiritual growth of the body of believers.

**13:1ff** In chapter 12 Paul gave evidence of the Corinthians' lack of love in the utilization of spiritual gifts; chapter 13 defines real love; and chapter 14 shows how love works. Love is more important than all the spiritual gifts exercised in the church body. Great faith, acts of dedication or sacrifice, and miracle-working power have little effect without love. Love makes our actions and gifts useful. Although people have different gifts, love is available to everyone.

**13:4-7** Our society confuses love and lust. Unlike lust, God's kind of love is directed outward toward others, not inward toward ourselves. It is utterly unselfish. This kind of love goes against our natural inclinations. It is impossible to have this love unless God helps us set aside our own natural desires so that we can love and not expect anything in return. Thus, the more we become like Christ, the more love we will show to others.

**13:5** Paul says that love "is not irritable." Sometimes we're irritated or angered by others, and we don't know why. Not all irritability stems from sinful or selfish motives, although the irritable treatment of others surely is wrong. Much irritability comes from a love of perfection, a deep desire that programs, meetings, and structures be run perfectly. A desire to run things perfectly can erupt into anger at events or people who get in the way or ruin that desire. Those who are easily irritated need to remember that perfection exists only in God. We need to love him and our fellow Christians, not the visions we have for perfection here on earth.

the gift of prophecy reveals only part of the whole picture! ¹⁰But when the time of perfection comes, these partial things will become useless.

¹¹When I was a child, I spoke and thought and reasoned as a child. But when I grew up, I put away childish things. ¹²Now we see things imperfectly, like puzzling reflections in a mirror, but then we will see everything with perfect clarity.* All that I know now is partial and incomplete, but then I will know everything completely, just as God now knows me completely.

¹³Three things will last forever—faith, hope, and love—and the greatest of these is love.

### The Gifts of Tongues and Prophecy

**14** Let love be your highest goal! But you should also desire the special abilities the Spirit gives—especially the ability to prophesy. ²For if you have the ability to speak in tongues,* you will be talking only to God, since people won't be able to understand you. You will be speaking by the power of the Spirit,* but it will all be mysterious. ³But one who prophesies strengthens others, encourages them, and comforts them. ⁴A person who speaks in tongues is strengthened personally, but one who speaks a word of prophecy strengthens the entire church.

⁵I wish you could all speak in tongues, but even more I wish you could all prophesy. For prophecy is greater than speaking in tongues, unless someone interprets what you are saying so that the whole church will be strengthened.

⁶Dear brothers and sisters,* if I should come to you speaking in an unknown language,* how would that help you? But if I bring you a revelation or some special knowledge or prophecy or teaching, that will be helpful. ⁷Even lifeless instruments like the flute or the harp must play the notes clearly, or no one will recognize the melody. ⁸And if the bugler doesn't sound a clear call, how will the soldiers know they are being called to battle? ⁹It's the same for you. If you speak to people in words they don't understand, how will they know what you are saying? You might as well be talking into empty space.

**13:12** Greek *see face to face.*  **14:2a** Or *in unknown languages;* also in 14:4, 5, 13, 14, 18, 22, 26, 27, 28, 39.  **14:2b** Or *speaking in your spirit.*  **14:6a** Greek *brothers;* also in 14:20, 26, 39.  **14:6b** Or *in tongues;* also in 14:19, 23.

**13:10**
Phil 3:12
**13:11**
Ps 131:2
**13:12**
2 Cor 5:7
1 Jn 3:2
**13:13**
Matt 22:37-40
Gal 5:5-6
1 Thes 1:3
1 Jn 4:16
**14:1**
Matt 22:37-40
Rom 12:6
1 Cor 12:1, 31;
14:39; 16:14
Eph 5:2
Col 3:14
1 Tim 1:5
Jas 2:8
**14:2**
Mark 16:17
Acts 2:4; 10:46-47;
19:6
**14:3**
Rom 14:19
**14:4**
1 Cor 14:18-19,
26-28
**14:5**
Num 11:29
**14:6**
Rom 6:17
Eph 1:17
**14:8**
Num 10:9
Jer 4:19

---

**13:10-12** When Paul wrote of "full understanding," he was referring to when we must see Christ face to face. God gives believers spiritual gifts for their lives on earth in order to build up, serve, and strengthen fellow Christians. The spiritual gifts are for the church. In eternity, we will be made perfect and complete and will be in the very presence of God. We will no longer need the spiritual gifts, so they will come to an end. Then, we will have a full understanding and appreciation for one another as unique expressions of God's infinite creativity. We will use our differences as a reason to praise God! Based on that perspective, let us treat each other with the same love and unity that we will one day share.

**13:13** Paul wrote that love endures forever. In morally corrupt Corinth, love had become a mixed-up term with little meaning. Today, people are still confused about love. Love is the greatest of all human qualities and is an attribute of God himself (1 John 4:8). Love involves unselfish service to others. *Faith* is the foundation and content of God's message; *hope* is the attitude and focus; *love* is action. When faith and hope are in line, you are free to love completely because you understand how God loves. Does your faith fully express itself in loving others?

**14:1** The ability to prophesy may involve predicting future events, but its main purpose is to communicate God's message to people, providing insight, warning, correction, and encouragement. See also the first note on 12:10.

**14:2** The gift of speaking in tongues (unknown languages) was a concern of the Corinthian church because the use of the gift had caused disorder in worship. Speaking in tongues is a legitimate gift of the Holy Spirit, but the Corinthian believers were using it as a sign of spiritual superiority rather than as a means to spiritual unity. Spiritual gifts are beneficial only when they are properly used to help everyone in the church. We should not exercise them only to make *ourselves* feel good. See also the second note at 12:10.

**14:2-5** Paul's words to the Corinthians about tongues and prophecy have much to say to our generation. Many Christians struggle with the discussion of tongues. Paul would clearly say that no one should put down those Christians who speak in tongues, and those who speak in tongues should not disparage those who do not. Paul makes several points about speaking in tongues: (1) It is a spiritual gift from God (14:2); (2) it is a desirable gift even though it isn't a requirement of faith (12:28-31); (3) it is less important than prophecy and teaching (14:4). Believers need unity and love. The enemy is not each other but the sinful world, Satan, and our selfish, sinful desires. But Paul would have another word for today: "I wish you could all prophesy." Although Paul himself spoke in tongues, he stresses prophecy (preaching) because it benefits the whole church, while speaking in tongues primarily benefits the speaker. Paul would encourage us to be so in tune with the Spirit that his messages of comfort, encouragement, and edification would be heard in our congregations today. Make sure your actions are encouraging and edifying.

**14:7-12** As musical instruments must clearly play each note in order for the music to be recognized, so Paul says words must be preached in the hearers' language in order to be helpful. Because there are many languages in the world (14:10), people sometimes can't understand each other. It is the same with speaking in tongues. Although this gift is helpful to many people in private worship as well as in public worship (with interpretation), Paul says that he would rather speak 5 words that his hearers can understand than 10,000 that they cannot (14:19).

**14:9** Paul confronted the self-oriented use of the gift of tongues. Spiritual people must be careful not to pursue self-development at the expense of broken, lost people. When we give too much attention to our own needs, ideas, and spiritual expression, we may push aside the Spirit's true desire and abandon those who need encouragement. Follow Paul's advice and make encouraging and edifying others the highest goal.

<sup>10</sup>There are many different languages in the world, and every language has meaning. <sup>11</sup>But if I don't understand a language, I will be a foreigner to someone who speaks it, and the one who speaks it will be a foreigner to me. <sup>12</sup>And the same is true for you. Since you are so eager to have the special abilities the Spirit gives, seek those that will strengthen the whole church.

**14:12**
Rom 14:19
1 Cor 12:1

<sup>13</sup>So anyone who speaks in tongues should pray also for the ability to interpret what has been said. <sup>14</sup>For if I pray in tongues, my spirit is praying, but I don't understand what I am saying.

**14:13**
1 Cor 12:10

<sup>15</sup>Well then, what shall I do? I will pray in the spirit,* and I will also pray in words I understand. I will sing in the spirit, and I will also sing in words I understand. <sup>16</sup>For if you praise God only in the spirit, how can those who don't understand you praise God along with you? How can they join you in giving thanks when they don't understand what you are saying? <sup>17</sup>You will be giving thanks very well, but it won't strengthen the people who hear you.

**14:15**
Eph 5:19
Col 3:16

**14:16**
1 Chr 16:36
Neh 8:6
Ps 106:48
Rev 5:14; 7:12

**14:17**
Rom 14:19

<sup>18</sup>I thank God that I speak in tongues more than any of you. <sup>19</sup>But in a church meeting I would rather speak five understandable words to help others than ten thousand words in an unknown language.

<sup>20</sup>Dear brothers and sisters, don't be childish in your understanding of these things. Be innocent as babies when it comes to evil, but be mature in understanding matters of this kind. <sup>21</sup>It is written in the Scriptures*:

**14:20**
Eph 4:14
Heb 5:12

**14:21**
Deut 28:49
†Isa 28:11-12

> "I will speak to my own people
>    through strange languages
>    and through the lips of foreigners.
> But even then, they will not listen to me,"*
>    says the LORD.

<sup>22</sup>So you see that speaking in tongues is a sign, not for believers, but for unbelievers. Prophecy, however, is for the benefit of believers, not unbelievers. <sup>23</sup>Even so, if unbelievers or people who don't understand these things come into your church meeting and hear everyone speaking in an unknown language, they will think you are crazy. <sup>24</sup>But if all of you are prophesying, and unbelievers or people who don't understand these things come into your meeting, they will be convicted of sin and judged by what you say. <sup>25</sup>As they listen, their secret thoughts will be exposed, and they will fall to their knees and worship God, declaring, "God is truly here among you."

**14:22**
1 Cor 14:1

**14:23**
Acts 2:13

**14:24**
John 16:8

**14:25**
Isa 45:14
Zech 8:23

## A Call to Orderly Worship

<sup>26</sup>Well, my brothers and sisters, let's summarize. When you meet together, one will sing, another will teach, another will tell some special revelation God has given, one will speak in tongues, and another will interpret what is said. But everything that is done must strengthen all of you.

**14:26**
Rom 14:19
1 Cor 12:7-10
Eph 4:12; 5:19

<sup>27</sup>No more than two or three should speak in tongues. They must speak one at a time, and someone must interpret what they say. <sup>28</sup>But if no one is present who can interpret, they must be silent in your church meeting and speak in tongues to God privately.

**14:27**
1 Cor 14:2, 5, 13

**14:15** Or *in the Spirit;* also in 14:15b, 16.   **14:21a** Greek *in the law.*   **14:21b** Isa 28:11-12.

---

**14:13-20** Up to this point, Paul has been explaining that the gift of speaking in tongues was of no value to the congregation as a whole, only to the person who speaks to God in the unknown language. But if the person also has the gift of interpretation, the tongue could be used in public worship if the one praying (or someone else with the gift of interpretation) would then "interpret what has been said." That way, the entire church would be edified by this gift.

**14:15** There is a proper place for the intellect in Christianity. In praying and singing, both the mind and the spirit are to be fully engaged. When we sing, we should also think about the meaning of the words. When we pour out our feelings to God in prayer, we should not turn off our capacity to think. True Christianity is neither barren intellectualism nor thoughtless emotionalism. See also Ephesians 1:17, 18; Philippians 1:9-11; Colossians 1:9.

**14:22-25** The way the Corinthians were speaking in tongues was helping no one because believers did not understand what was being said, and unbelievers thought that the people speaking in tongues were crazy. Speaking in tongues was supposed to be a *sign* to unbelievers (as it was in Acts 2). After speaking in tongues, believers were supposed to explain what was said and give the credit to God. The unsaved people would then be convinced of a spiritual reality and motivated to look further into the Christian faith. While this is one way to reach unbelievers, Paul says that clear preaching is usually better (14:5).

**14:26ff** Everything done in worship services must be beneficial to the worshipers. Every worshiper ought to consider himself or herself a contributor. These principles touch every aspect—singing, preaching, and the exercise of spiritual gifts. Contributions to the service (by singing, speaking, reading, praying, playing instruments, giving) must have love as their chief motivation. As you prepare to lead or participate in worship, seek to strengthen the faith of other believers.

29Let two or three people prophesy, and let the others evaluate what is said. 30But if someone is prophesying and another person receives a revelation from the Lord, the one who is speaking must stop. 31In this way, all who prophesy will have a turn to speak, one after the other, so that everyone will learn and be encouraged. 32Remember that people who prophesy are in control of their spirit and can take turns. 33For God is not a God of disorder but of peace, as in all the meetings of God's holy people.*

34Women should be silent during the church meetings. It is not proper for them to speak. They should be submissive, just as the law says. 35If they have any questions, they should ask their husbands at home, for it is improper for women to speak in church meetings.*

36Or do you think God's word originated with you Corinthians? Are you the only ones to whom it was given? 37If you claim to be a prophet or think you are spiritual, you should recognize that what I am saying is a command from the Lord himself. 38But if you do not recognize this, you yourself will not be recognized.*

39So, my dear brothers and sisters, be eager to prophesy, and don't forbid speaking in tongues. 40But be sure that everything is done properly and in order.

## 4. Instruction on resurrection

*The Resurrection of Christ*

**15** Let me now remind you, dear brothers and sisters,* of the Good News I preached to you before. You welcomed it then, and you still stand firm in it. 2It is this Good News that saves you if you continue to believe the message I told you—unless, of course, you believed something that was never true in the first place.*

3I passed on to you what was most important and what had also been passed on to me. Christ died for our sins, just as the Scriptures said. 4He was buried, and he was raised from the dead on the third day, just as the Scriptures said. 5He was seen by Peter* and then by the Twelve. 6After that, he was seen by more than 500 of his followers* at one time, most of whom are still alive, though some have died. 7Then he was seen by James and later by all

**14:29**
1 Cor 12:10
1 Thes 5:19-21

**14:32**
1 Jn 4:1

**14:33**
1 Cor 7:17

**14:34**
Gen 3:16
Eph 5:22
Col 3:18
1 Tim 2:11-12
Titus 2:5

**14:37**
2 Cor 10:7
1 Jn 4:6

**14:39**
1 Cor 12:31
1 Thes 5:20

**14:40**
1 Cor 14:33
Col 2:5

**15:3**
Isa 53:5-9
Luke 24:25-27
1 Pet 2:24

**15:4**
Ps 16:10
Hos 6:2
Jon 1:17
Luke 24:25-27
John 2:21-22
Acts 2:24-32

**15:5**
Matt 28:16-17
Mark 16:14
Luke 24:34, 36-43
John 20:19

**14:33** The phrase *as in all the meetings of God's holy people* could instead be joined to the beginning of 14:34. **14:35** Some manuscripts place verses 34-35 after 14:40. **14:38** Some manuscripts read *If you are ignorant of this, stay in your ignorance.* **15:1** Greek *brothers;* also in 15:31, 50, 58. **15:2** Or *unless you never believed it in the first place.* **15:5** Greek *Cephas.* **15:6** Greek *the brothers.*

**14:34, 35** Does this mean that women should not speak in church services today? It is clear from 11:5 that women prayed and prophesied in public worship. It is also clear in chapters 12–14 that women are given spiritual gifts and are encouraged to exercise them in the body of Christ. Women have much to contribute and can participate in worship services.

In the Corinthian culture, women were not allowed to confront men in public. Apparently some of the women who had become Christians thought that their Christian freedom gave them the right to question the men in public worship. This was causing division in the church. In addition, women of that day did not receive formal religious education as did the men. Women may have been raising questions in the worship services that could have been answered at home without disrupting the services. Paul was asking the women not to flaunt their Christian freedom during worship. The purpose of Paul's words was to promote unity, not to teach about women's roles in the church.

**14:40** Paul stated that God is not a God of disorder but of peace (14:33). Note that the preferred alternative to disorder is "peace." Too often, in resisting disorder, Christians have opted for rigid, predictable, and unvarying forms of worship in which God's presence is difficult to find as in disorderly gatherings. When there is chaos, the church is not allowing God to work among believers as he would like. Worship that "is done properly and in order" should not, however, rule out God's creativity, joy, and unpredictability. Do your part to have worship be a joyful, peaceful, winsome experience that draws people into it.

**15:2** Most churches contain people who do not yet believe. Some are moving in the direction of belief, and others are simply pretending. Imposters, however, are not to be removed (see Matthew 13:28, 29), for that is the Lord's work alone. The Good News about Jesus Christ will save us *if* we continue to believe it and faithfully follow it.

**15:3, 4** The central theme of the gospel is given in these verses, a key text for the defense of Christianity. The three most important points are: (1) *Christ died for our sins, just as the Scriptures said.* Without the truth of this message, Christ's death was worthless, and those who believe in him are still in their sins and without hope. However, Christ as the sinless Son of God took the punishment of sin so that those who believe can have their sins removed. "The Scriptures" refers to Old Testament prophecies such as Psalm 16:8-11 and Isaiah 53:5, 6. Christ's death on the cross was no accident or afterthought. It had been part of God's plan from all eternity in order to bring about the salvation of all who believe.

(2) *He was buried.* The fact of Christ's death is revealed in the fact of his burial. Many have tried to discount the actual death of Christ, but Jesus did in fact die and was buried in a tomb.

(3) *He was raised from the dead on the third day, as the Scriptures said.* Christ was raised permanently, forever; his Father raised him from the dead "on the third day" as noted in the Gospels (Friday afternoon to Sunday morning—three days in Jewish reckoning of time). This also occurred "as the Scriptures said." Jesus quoted the prophet Jonah in Matthew 12:40 (see Jonah 1:17) to show the connection to "three days" as prophesied in the Old Testament. Psalm 16:8-11 and Psalm 110 also foretell the resurrection of the Messiah.

**15:5-8** There will always be people who say that Jesus didn't rise from the dead. Paul assures us that many people saw Jesus after his resurrection: Peter; the twelve apostles; more than 500 Christian believers (most of whom were still alive when Paul wrote this, although some had died); James (Jesus' half brother); all the apostles; and finally Paul himself. The Resurrection is a historical fact. Don't be discouraged by doubters who deny the Resurrection. Be filled with hope because of the knowledge that one day you, and they, will see the living proof when Christ returns. (For more evidence on the Resurrection, see the chart in Mark 15, p. 1663.)

**15:7** This James is Jesus' half brother, who at first did not believe that Jesus was the Messiah (John 7:5). After seeing the

**15:8**
Acts 9:3-6
Gal 1:16

**15:9**
Acts 8:3
2 Cor 12:11
Eph 3:8

**15:10**
2 Cor 6:1; 11:5, 23

the apostles. ⁸Last of all, as though I had been born at the wrong time, I also saw him. ⁹For I am the least of all the apostles. In fact, I'm not even worthy to be called an apostle after the way I persecuted God's church.

¹⁰But whatever I am now, it is all because God poured out his special favor on me—and not without results. For I have worked harder than any of the other apostles; yet it was not I but God who was working through me by his grace. ¹¹So it makes no difference whether I preach or they preach, for we all preach the same message you have already believed.

### The Resurrection of the Dead

**15:12**
Acts 17:32; 23:8
2 Tim 2:18

¹²But tell me this—since we preach that Christ rose from the dead, why are some of you saying there will be no resurrection of the dead? ¹³For if there is no resurrection of the dead, then Christ has not been raised either. ¹⁴And if Christ has not been raised, then all our preaching is useless, and your faith is useless. ¹⁵And we apostles would all be lying about God—for we have said that God raised Christ from the grave. But that can't be true if there is no resurrection of the dead. ¹⁶And if there is no resurrection of the dead, then Christ has not been raised. ¹⁷And if Christ has not been raised, then your faith is useless and you are still guilty of your sins. ¹⁸In that case, all who have died believing in Christ are lost! ¹⁹And if our hope in Christ is only for this life, we are more to be pitied than anyone in the world.

**15:17**
Rom 4:25

**15:20**
Col 1:18
1 Pet 1:3
Rev 1:5

²⁰But in fact, Christ has been raised from the dead. He is the first of a great harvest of all who have died.

---

**PHYSICAL AND RESURRECTION BODIES**

| Physical Bodies | Resurrection Bodies |
| --- | --- |
| Perishable | Imperishable |
| Sown in dishonor | Raised in glory |
| Sown in weakness | Raised in power |
| Natural | Spiritual |
| From the dust | From heaven |

We all have a body—each looks different; each has different strengths and weaknesses. But as physical, earthly bodies, they are all alike. All believers are promised life after death and a body like Christ's (15:49), a resurrection body.

---

resurrected Christ, he became a believer and ultimately a leader of the church in Jerusalem (Acts 15:13). James wrote the New Testament book of James.

**15:8, 9** Paul's most important credential of his apostleship was that he was an eyewitness of the risen Christ (see Acts 9:3-6). The other apostles saw Christ in the flesh. Paul was in the next generation of believers—yet Christ appeared to him.

**15:9, 10** As a zealous Pharisee, Paul had been an enemy of the Christian church—even to the point of capturing and persecuting believers (see Acts 9:1-3). Thus, he felt unworthy to be called an apostle of Christ. Though undoubtedly the most influential of the apostles, Paul was deeply humble. He knew that he had worked hard and accomplished much but only because God had poured kindness and grace upon him. True humility is not convincing yourself that you are worthless but recognizing God's work in you. It is having God's perspective on who you are and acknowledging his grace in developing your abilities.

**15:10** Paul wrote of working harder than the other apostles. This was not an arrogant boast, because he knew that his power came from God and that it really didn't matter who worked hardest. Because of his prominent position as a Pharisee, Paul's conversion made him the object of even greater persecution than the other apostles; thus, he had to work harder to preach the same message.

**15:12ff** Most Greeks did not believe that people's bodies would be resurrected after death. They saw the afterlife as something that happened only to the soul. According to Greek philosophers, the soul was the real person, imprisoned in a physical body, and at death the soul was released. There was no immortality for the body, but the soul entered an eternal state. Christianity, by contrast, affirms that the body and soul will be united after resurrec-

tion. The church at Corinth was in the heart of Greek culture. Thus, many believers had a difficult time believing in a bodily resurrection. Paul wrote this part of his letter to clear up this confusion about the resurrection.

**15:13-18** The bodily resurrection of Christ is the center of the Christian faith. Because Christ rose from the dead, as he promised, we know that what he said is true and that he is God. The Resurrection affirms the truthfulness of Jesus' life and words. The Resurrection confirms Jesus' unique authority to say, "I am the resurrection and the life" (John 11:25). Because he rose, we have certainty that our sins are forgiven. Because he rose, he lives and represents us before God. Because he rose and defeated death, we know we also will be raised. Christ's resurrection guaranteed both his promise to us and his authority to make that promise. We must take him at his word and believe.

**15:19** Why does Paul say believers would be "more to be pitied than anyone in the world" if there were only earthly value to Christianity? In Paul's day, Christianity often brought a person persecution, ostracism from family, and, in many cases, poverty. There were few tangible benefits from being a Christian in that society. It was certainly not a step up the social or career ladder. More important is the fact that if Christ had not been resurrected from the dead, Christians would not be forgiven of their sins or have any hope of eternal life. If what Christians believe is a lie, we would be pitiful because we would be going through such suffering for no purpose. Fortunately, that is not the case!

**15:20** Just as the first part of the harvest was brought to the Temple as an offering (Leviticus 23:10ff) so Christ was the first to rise from the dead and never die again. He is our forerunner, the guarantee of our eventual resurrection to eternal life.

²¹So you see, just as death came into the world through a man, now the resurrection from the dead has begun through another man. ²²Just as everyone dies because we all belong to Adam, everyone who belongs to Christ will be given new life. ²³But there is an order to this resurrection: Christ was raised as the first of the harvest; then all who belong to Christ will be raised when he comes back.

²⁴After that the end will come, when he will turn the Kingdom over to God the Father, having destroyed every ruler and authority and power. ²⁵For Christ must reign until he humbles all his enemies beneath his feet. ²⁶And the last enemy to be destroyed is death. ²⁷For the Scriptures say, "God has put all things under his authority."* (Of course, when it says "all things are under his authority," that does not include God himself, who gave Christ his authority.) ²⁸Then, when all things are under his authority, the Son will put himself under God's authority, so that God, who gave his Son authority over all things, will be utterly supreme over everything everywhere.

²⁹If the dead will not be raised, what point is there in people being baptized for those who are dead? Why do it unless the dead will someday rise again?

³⁰And why should we ourselves risk our lives hour by hour? ³¹For I swear, dear brothers and sisters, that I face death daily. This is as certain as my pride in what Christ Jesus our Lord has done in you. ³²And what value was there in fighting wild beasts—those people of Ephesus*—if there will be no resurrection from the dead? And if there is no resurrection, "Let's feast and drink, for tomorrow we die!"* ³³Don't be fooled by those who say such things, for "bad company corrupts good character." ³⁴Think carefully about what is right, and stop sinning. For to your shame I say that some of you don't know God at all.

### The Resurrection Body

³⁵But someone may ask, "How will the dead be raised? What kind of bodies will they have?" ³⁶What a foolish question! When you put a seed into the ground, it doesn't grow into a plant unless it dies first. ³⁷And what you put in the ground is not the plant that will grow, but only a bare seed of wheat or whatever you are planting. ³⁸Then God gives it the new body he wants it to have. A different plant grows from each kind of seed. ³⁹Similarly there are different kinds of flesh—one kind for humans, another for animals, another for birds, and another for fish.

⁴⁰There are also bodies in the heavens and bodies on the earth. The glory of the heavenly bodies is different from the glory of the earthly bodies. ⁴¹The sun has one kind of glory, while the moon and stars each have another kind. And even the stars differ from each other in their glory.

**15:27** Ps 8:6.   **15:32a** Greek *fighting wild beasts in Ephesus.*   **15:32b** Isa 22:13.

**15:21**
Rom 5:12, 18
**15:22**
Rom 5:14-18
**15:23**
1 Thes 4:16
**15:24**
Dan 2:44; 7:14
**15:25**
Ps 110:1
Isa 9:7
Matt 22:44
**15:26**
2 Tim 1:10
Rev 20:14; 21:4
**15:27**
†Ps 8:6
Matt 28:18
Eph 1:22
Heb 2:8
1 Pet 3:22
**15:28**
1 Cor 3:23
Phil 3:21
**15:30**
Rom 8:36
2 Cor 11:26
**15:31**
2 Cor 4:10-11
**15:32**
†Isa 22:13
Luke 12:19-21
2 Cor 1:8
**15:34**
1 Cor 6:5
Eph 5:14
**15:35**
Ezek 37:3
**15:36**
John 12:24
**15:38**
Gen 1:11

---

**15:21** Death came into the world as a result of Adam and Eve's sin. In Romans 5:12-21, Paul explained why Adam's sin brought sin to all people, how death and sin spread to all humans because of this first sin, and the parallel between Adam's death and Christ's death.

**15:24-28** This is not a chronological sequence of events, and no specific time for these events is given. Paul's point is that the resurrected Christ will conquer all evil, including death. See Revelation 20:14 for words about the final destruction of death.

**15:25-28** Although God the Father and God the Son are equal, each has a special work to do and an area of sovereign control (15:28). Christ is not inferior to the Father, but his work is to defeat all evil on earth. First, he defeated sin and death on the cross, and in the end he will defeat Satan and all evil. World events may seem out of control, and justice may seem to have vanished. But God is in control, allowing evil to remain for a time until he sends Jesus to earth again. Then he will present to God a perfect new world.

**15:29** Some believers were baptized on behalf of others who had died unbaptized. Nothing more is known about this practice, but it obviously affirms a belief in the resurrection. Paul is not promoting baptism for the dead; he is illustrating his argument that the resurrection is a reality.

**15:30-34** If death ends it all, enjoying the moment would be all that matters. But Christians know that life continues beyond the grave and that life on earth is only a preparation for our life that will never end. What you do today matters for eternity. In light of eternity, sin is a foolish gamble. Your belief in the resurrection will affect your view of the future. It also ought to affect how you live today.

**15:31, 32** "I face death daily" refers to the dangers Paul encountered daily. The "wild beasts" in Ephesus referred to the savage opposition he had faced there.

**15:33** Keeping company with those who deny the resurrection can corrupt good Christian character. Don't let your relationships with unbelievers lead you away from Christ or cause your faith to waver.

**15:35ff** Paul launches into a discussion about what our resurrected bodies will be like. If you could select your own body, what kind would you choose—strong, athletic, beautiful? Paul explains that we will be recognizable in our resurrected body, yet it will be better than we can imagine, for it will be made to live forever. We will still have our own personality and individuality, but these will be perfected through Christ's work. The Bible does not reveal everything that our resurrected body will be able to do, but we know it will be perfect, without any infirmities (see Philippians 3:21).

**15:35ff** Paul compares the resurrection with the growth of a seed in a garden. Seeds placed in the ground don't grow unless they "die" first. The plant that grows looks very different from the seed because God gives it a new "body." There are different kinds of bodies—people, animals, fish, birds. Even the angels in heaven have bodies that are different in beauty and glory. Our resurrected body will be very different from our earthly body. It will be a spiritual body full of glory.

**15:42**
Dan 12:2-3
Matt 13:43
1 Cor 15:50

**15:43**
Phil 3:20-21
Col 3:4

**15:45**
†Gen 2:7
John 5:21; 6:63
Rom 8:2
2 Cor 3:17

**15:47**
Gen 2:7; 3:19
John 3:13, 31

**15:48**
Phil 3:20-21

**15:49**
Gen 5:3
Rom 8:29

**15:50**
John 3:3, 5

**15:51**
2 Cor 5:2-4
Phil 3:21
1 Thes 4:15-17

**15:52**
Matt 24:31

**15:53**
2 Cor 5:4

**15:54**
†Isa 25:8

**15:55**
†Hos 13:14

**15:56**
Rom 4:15; 5:12

**15:57**
Rom 8:37
1 Jn 5:4

**16:1**
Acts 11:29; 24:17
Rom 15:25-26

**16:2**
Acts 20:7

**16:3**
2 Cor 3:1; 8:18-19

⁴²It is the same way with the resurrection of the dead. Our earthly bodies are planted in the ground when we die, but they will be raised to live forever. ⁴³Our bodies are buried in brokenness, but they will be raised in glory. They are buried in weakness, but they will be raised in strength. ⁴⁴They are buried as natural human bodies, but they will be raised as spiritual bodies. For just as there are natural bodies, there are also spiritual bodies.

⁴⁵The Scriptures tell us, "The first man, Adam, became a living person."* But the last Adam—that is, Christ—is a life-giving Spirit. ⁴⁶What comes first is the natural body, then the spiritual body comes later. ⁴⁷Adam, the first man, was made from the dust of the earth, while Christ, the second man, came from heaven. ⁴⁸Earthly people are like the earthly man, and heavenly people are like the heavenly man. ⁴⁹Just as we are now like the earthly man, we will someday be like* the heavenly man.

⁵⁰What I am saying, dear brothers and sisters, is that our physical bodies cannot inherit the Kingdom of God. These dying bodies cannot inherit what will last forever.

⁵¹But let me reveal to you a wonderful secret. We will not all die, but we will all be transformed! ⁵²It will happen in a moment, in the blink of an eye, when the last trumpet is blown. For when the trumpet sounds, those who have died will be raised to live forever. And we who are living will also be transformed. ⁵³For our dying bodies must be transformed into bodies that will never die; our mortal bodies must be transformed into immortal bodies.

⁵⁴Then, when our dying bodies have been transformed into bodies that will never die,* this Scripture will be fulfilled:

"Death is swallowed up in victory.*
⁵⁵ O death, where is your victory?
　　O death, where is your sting?*"

⁵⁶For sin is the sting that results in death, and the law gives sin its power. ⁵⁷But thank God! He gives us victory over sin and death through our Lord Jesus Christ.

⁵⁸So, my dear brothers and sisters, be strong and immovable. Always work enthusiastically for the Lord, for you know that nothing you do for the Lord is ever useless.

### The Collection for Jerusalem

**16** Now regarding your question about the money being collected for God's people in Jerusalem. You should follow the same procedure I gave to the churches in Galatia. ²On the first day of each week, you should each put aside a portion of the money you have earned. Don't wait until I get there and then try to collect it all at once. ³When I come, I will

**15:45** Gen 2:7.　　**15:49** Some manuscripts read *let us be like.*　　**15:54a** Some manuscripts add *and our mortal bodies have been transformed into immortal bodies.*　　**15:54b** Isa 25:8.　　**15:55** Hos 13:14 (Greek version).

---

**15:42-44** Our present body is perishable and prone to decay. Our resurrection body will be transformed. The spiritual body will not be limited by the laws of nature. This does not necessarily mean we'll be superpeople, but our body will be different from and more capable than our present earthly body. Our spiritual body will not be weak, will never get sick, and will never die.

**15:45** Because Christ rose from the dead, he is a life-giving Spirit. This means that he entered into a new form of existence. He is the source of the spiritual life that will result in our resurrection. Christ's new glorified human body now suits his new glorified existence—just as Adam's human body was suitable to his natural life. When we are resurrected, God will give us a transformed, eternal body suited to our new eternal life.

**15:50-53** We all face limitations. Some may have physical, mental, or emotional disabilities. Some may be blind, but they can see a new way to live. Some may be deaf, but they can hear God's Good News. Some may be lame, but they can walk in God's love. In addition, they have the encouragement that those disabilities are only temporary. Paul tells us that we all will be given new bodies when Christ returns and that these bodies will be without disabilities, never to die or become sick. This can give us hope in our suffering.

**15:51, 52** Christians alive at that day will not have to die but will be transformed immediately. A trumpet blast will usher in the new heaven and earth. The Jews would understand the significance of this because trumpets were always blown to signal the start of great festivals and other extraordinary events (Numbers 10:10).

**15:54-56** Satan seemed to be victorious in the Garden of Eden (Genesis 3) and at the cross of Jesus. But God turned Satan's apparent victory into defeat when Jesus Christ rose from the dead (Colossians 2:15; Hebrews 2:14, 15). Thus, death is no longer a source of dread or fear. Christ overcame it, and one day we will also. The law will no longer make sinners out of us just because we cannot keep it. Death has been defeated, and we have hope beyond the grave.

**15:58** Paul says that because of the resurrection, nothing we do is useless. Sometimes we become apathetic about serving the Lord because we don't see any results. Knowing that Christ has won the ultimate victory should affect the way we live right now. Don't let discouragement over an apparent lack of results keep you from doing the work of the Lord enthusiastically as you have opportunity.

**16:1ff** Paul had just said that no good deed is ever useless (15:58). In this chapter he mentions some practical deeds that have value for all Christians.

**16:1-4** The Christians in Jerusalem were suffering from poverty and famine, so Paul was collecting money for them (Romans 15:25-31; 2 Corinthians 8:4; 9:1ff). He suggested that believers set aside a certain amount each week and give it to the church until he arrived to take it on to Jerusalem. Paul had planned to go straight to Corinth from Ephesus, but he changed his mind (2 Corinthians 1–2). When he finally arrived, he took the gift and delivered it to the Jerusalem church (Acts 21:18; 24:17).

write letters of recommendation for the messengers you choose to deliver your gift to Jerusalem. ⁴And if it seems appropriate for me to go along, they can travel with me.

## Paul's Final Instructions

⁵I am coming to visit you after I have been to Macedonia,* for I am planning to travel through Macedonia. ⁶Perhaps I will stay awhile with you, possibly all winter, and then you can send me on my way to my next destination. ⁷This time I don't want to make just a short visit and then go right on. I want to come and stay awhile, if the Lord will let me. ⁸In the meantime, I will be staying here at Ephesus until the Festival of Pentecost. ⁹There is a wide-open door for a great work here, although many oppose me.

¹⁰When Timothy comes, don't intimidate him. He is doing the Lord's work, just as I am. ¹¹Don't let anyone treat him with contempt. Send him on his way with your blessing when he returns to me. I expect him to come with the other believers.*

¹²Now about our brother Apollos—I urged him to visit you with the other believers, but he was not willing to go right now. He will see you later when he has the opportunity.

¹³Be on guard. Stand firm in the faith. Be courageous.* Be strong. ¹⁴And do everything with love.

¹⁵You know that Stephanas and his household were the first of the harvest of believers in Greece,* and they are spending their lives in service to God's people. I urge you, dear brothers and sisters,* ¹⁶to submit to them and others like them who serve with such devotion. ¹⁷I am very glad that Stephanas, Fortunatus, and Achaicus have come here. They have been providing the help you weren't here to give me. ¹⁸They have been a wonderful encouragement to me, as they have been to you. You must show your appreciation to all who serve so well.

## Paul's Final Greetings

¹⁹The churches here in the province of Asia* send greetings in the Lord, as do Aquila and Priscilla* and all the others who gather in their home for church meetings. ²⁰All the brothers and sisters here send greetings to you. Greet each other with Christian love.*

²¹HERE IS MY GREETING IN MY OWN HANDWRITING—PAUL.

²²If anyone does not love the Lord, that person is cursed. Our Lord, come!*

²³May the grace of the Lord Jesus be with you.

²⁴My love to all of you in Christ Jesus.*

16:5 *Macedonia* was in the northern region of Greece. 16:11 Greek *with the brothers;* also in 16:12. 16:13 Greek *Be men.* 16:15a Greek *in Achaia,* the southern region of the Greek peninsula. 16:15b Greek *brothers;* also in 16:20. 16:19a *Asia* was a Roman province in what is now western Turkey. 16:19b Greek *Prisca.* 16:20 Greek *with a sacred kiss.* 16:22 From Aramaic, *Marana tha.* Some manuscripts read *Maran atha, "Our Lord has come."* 16:24 Some manuscripts add *Amen.*

**16:5**
Acts 19:21
1 Cor 4:19
**16:6**
Rom 15:24
Titus 3:13
**16:7**
Acts 18:21
**16:8**
Acts 2:1; 18:19
**16:9**
Acts 14:27; 19:8-10
2 Cor 2:12
**16:10**
Acts 16:1
**16:11**
1 Tim 4:12
**16:12**
Acts 18:24
1 Cor 1:12
**16:13**
Eph 6:10
Phil 1:27; 4:1
1 Thes 3:8
**16:14**
1 Cor 14:1
**16:15**
1 Cor 1:16
**16:16**
1 Thes 5:12
**16:19**
Rom 16:5
**16:20**
Rom 16:16
**16:21**
Gal 6:11
Col 4:18
2 Thes 3:17
Phlm 1:19
**16:22**
Gal 1:8-9

---

**16:10, 11** Paul was sending Timothy ahead to Corinth. Paul respected Timothy and had worked closely with him (Philippians 2:22; 1 Timothy 1:2). Although Timothy was young, Paul encouraged the Corinthian church to welcome him because he was doing the Lord's work. God's work is not limited by age. Paul wrote two personal letters to Timothy that have been preserved in the Bible (1 and 2 Timothy).

**16:12** Apollos, who had preached in Corinth, was doing evangelistic work in Greece (see Acts 18:24-28; 1 Corinthians 3:3ff). Apollos didn't go to Corinth right away, partly because he knew of the factions there and didn't want to cause any more divisions.

**16:13, 14** As the Corinthians awaited Paul's next visit, they were directed to: (1) *be on guard.* They were to be constantly watchful or alert for spiritual enemies that might slip in and threaten to destroy them whether it be divisions, pride, sin, disorder, or erroneous theology; (2) *stand firm* in what they believed—that is, the gospel that they had been taught in the beginning, the gospel that had brought them salvation; (3) *be courageous* so that they could stand against false teachers, deal with sin in the congregation, and straighten out other problems; (4) *be strong,* with the strength given by the Holy Spirit; and (5) *do everything with love* because without love, they would be no more than prideful noisemakers. Today, as we wait for the return of Christ, we should follow the same instructions.

**16:19** Aquila and Priscilla were tentmakers (or leatherworkers) whom Paul had met in Corinth (Acts 18:1-3). They followed Paul to Ephesus and lived there with him, helping to teach others about

Jesus (Romans 16:3-5). Many in the Corinthian church would have known this Christian couple. They are also mentioned in Acts 18:18, 26; Romans 16:3; and 2 Timothy 4:19.

**16:21** Paul had a helper, or secretary, who wrote down this letter while he dictated. Paul wrote the final words, however, in his own handwriting. This is similar to adding a handwritten postscript (P.S.) to a typewritten letter. It also served to verify that this was a genuine letter from the apostle and not a forgery.

**16:22** The Lord Jesus Christ is coming back to earth again. To Paul, this was a wonderful hope, the very best he could look forward to. He was not afraid of seeing Christ—he could hardly wait! Do you share Paul's eager anticipation? Those who love Christ are looking forward to that glorious time of his return (Titus 2:13). To those who do not love the Lord, however, Paul says, let them be cursed.

**16:24** The church at Corinth was a church in trouble. Paul lovingly and forcefully confronted them and pointed them back to Christ. He dealt with divisions and conflicts, selfishness, inconsiderate use of freedom, disorder in worship, misuse of spiritual gifts, and wrong attitudes about the resurrection.

In every church, there are problems that create tensions and divisions. We should not ignore or gloss over problems in our churches or in our life. Instead, like Paul, we should deal with problems head-on as they arise. The lesson for us in 1 Corinthians is that unity and love in a church are far more important than leaders and labels.

## WHAT THE BIBLE TEACHES ABOUT WORSHIP

Worship is first and foremost an encounter with the living and holy God.

"'Do not come any closer,' the LORD warned. 'Take off your sandals, for you are standing on holy ground'" (Exodus 3:5).

God is our friend, but he is also our sovereign Lord. To approach him frivolously shows a lack of respect and sincerity. When you come to God in worship, do you approach him casually, or do you come as though you were an invited guest before a king?

Worship is only as real as the involvement of those participating.

"The LORD gave these instructions to Moses on Mount Sinai when he commanded the Israelites to present their offerings to the LORD in the wilderness of Sinai" (Leviticus 7:38).

All the rituals in Leviticus were meant to teach the people valuable lessons. But over time, the people became indifferent. When your church appears to be conducting dry, meaningless rituals, try rediscovering the meaning and purpose behind them. Your worship will be revitalized.

A true worship experience is often a direct result of preparation for worship.

"The LORD said to Moses, 'Give these instructions to the people of Israel: The offerings you present as special gifts are a pleasing aroma to me; they are my food. See to it that they are brought at the appointed times and offered according to my instructions'" (Numbers 28:1-2).

Following these rituals took time, and this gave the people the opportunity to prepare their hearts for worship. Unless your heart is ready, worship is meaningless. God is delighted when you are prepared to come before him in a spirit of thankfulness.

Believers should take advantage of every opportunity and praise God.

"Sing praises to God, our strength. Sing to the God of Jacob. Sing! Beat the tambourine. Play the sweet lyre and the harp. Blow the ram's horn at new moon, and again at full moon to call a festival!" (Psalm 81:1-3).

Israel's holidays reminded the nation of God's great miracles. Remember the spiritual origin of the holidays you celebrate, and use them as opportunities to worship God for his goodness to you, your family, and your nation.

Worship and music go hand in hand.

"David and the army commanders then appointed men from the families of Asaph, Heman, and Jeduthun to proclaim God's messages to the accompaniment of lyres, harps and cymbals" (1 Chronicles 25:1).

David instituted music for the temple worship services. Worship should involve the whole person, and music helps lift a person's thoughts and emotions to God. Through music you can celebrate God's greatness.

Worship is bringing the best believers have to Christ.

"They entered the house and saw the child with his mother, Mary, and they bowed down and worshiped him. Then they opened their treasure chests and gave him gifts of gold, frankincense, and myrrh" (Matthew 2:11).

The wise men brought gifts and worshiped Jesus for who he was. This is the essence of true worship—honoring Christ for who he is and being willing to give to him what is valuable to you. Worship God because he is worthy of the best you have to give.

Genuine worship results in submission and obedience to Jesus.

"Since you are so eager to have the special abilities the Spirit gives, seek those that will strengthen the whole church" (1 Corinthians 14:12).

Jesus is more than just a great leader. He is the Son of God. When you understand this profound truth, the only adequate response is worship. When you have a correct understanding of Christ, you will obey him.

Everything done in corporate worship must be beneficial to the worshipers.

"But even as he spoke, a bright cloud came over them, and a voice from the cloud said, 'This is my dearly loved Son, who brings me great joy. Listen to him'" (Matthew 17:5).

This principle touches every aspect of worship. Those contributing to a worship service must speak useful words or participate in a way that will strengthen the faith of other believers.

In worship, everything must be done in harmony and with order.

"Be sure that everything is done properly and in order" (1 Corinthians 14:40).

Even when the gifts of the Holy Spirit are being exercised, there is no excuse for disorder. When there is chaos, the church is not allowing God to work among believers as he would like. Make sure that what you bring to worship is appropriate, but also make sure that you participate.

## VITAL STATISTICS

**PURPOSE:**
To affirm Paul's ministry, defend his authority as an apostle, and refute the false teachers in Corinth

**AUTHOR:**
Paul

**ORIGINAL AUDIENCE:**
The church in Corinth

**DATE WRITTEN:**
Approximately A.D. 55–57, from Macedonia

**SETTING:**
Paul had already written three letters to the Corinthians (two are now lost). In 1 Corinthians (the second of these letters), he used strong words to correct and teach. Most of the church had responded in the right spirit; there were, however, those who were denying Paul's authority and questioning his motives.

**KEY VERSE:**
"So we are Christ's ambassadors; God is making his appeal through us. We speak for Christ when we plead 'Come back to God!'" (5:20)

**KEY PEOPLE:**
Paul, Timothy, Titus, false teachers

**KEY PLACES:**
Corinth, Jerusalem

**SPECIAL FEATURES:**
This is an intensely personal and autobiographical letter.

SLITHERING through the centuries, the serpent whispers his smooth-tongued promises, beguiling, deceiving, and tempting—urging men and women to reject God and to follow Satan. Satan's emissaries have been many—false prophets contradicting God's ancient spokesmen, "pious" leaders hurling blasphemous accusations, and heretical teachers infiltrating churches. And the deception continues. Our world is filled with cults, "isms," and ideologies, all claiming to provide the way to God.

Paul constantly struggled with those who would mislead God's people, and he poured his life into spreading the Good News to the uttermost parts of the world. During three missionary trips and other travels, he proclaimed Christ, made converts, and established churches. But often young believers were easy prey for false teachers, who were a constant threat to the gospel and the early church. So Paul had to spend much time warning and correcting these new Christians.

The church at Corinth was weak. Surrounded by idolatry and immorality, they struggled with their Christian faith and life-style. Through personal visits and letters, Paul tried to instruct them in the faith, resolve their conflicts, and solve some of their problems. First Corinthians was sent to deal with specific moral issues in the church and to answer questions about sex, marriage, and tender consciences. That letter confronted the issues directly and was well received by most. But there were false teachers who denied Paul's authority and slandered him. Paul then wrote 2 Corinthians to defend his position and to denounce those who were twisting the truth.

Second Corinthians must have been a difficult letter for Paul to write because he had to list his credentials as an apostle. Paul was reluctant to do so as a humble servant of Christ, but he knew it was necessary. Paul also knew that most of the believers in Corinth had taken his previous words to heart and were beginning to mature in their faith. He affirmed their commitment to Christ.

Second Corinthians begins with Paul reminding his readers of (1) his relationship to them—Paul had always been honest and straightforward with them (1:12–14), (2) his itinerary—he was planning to visit them again (1:15—2:2), and (3) his previous letter (2:3–11). Paul then moves directly to the subject of false teachers (2:17), and he reviews his ministry among the Corinthians to demonstrate the validity of his message and to urge them not to turn away from the truth (3:1—7:16).

Paul next turns to the issue of collecting money for the poor Christians in Jerusalem. He tells them how others have given, and he urges them to show their love in a tangible way as well (8:1—9:15). Paul then gives a strong defense of his authority as a genuine apostle while pointing out the deceptive influence of the false apostles (10:1—13:10).

As you read this intensely personal letter, listen to Paul's words of love and exhortation, and be committed to the truth of God's Word and prepared to reject all false teaching.

## THE BLUEPRINT

1. Paul explains his actions
   (1:1—2:11)
2. Paul defends his ministry
   (2:12—7:16)
3. Paul defends the collection
   (8:1—9:15)
4. Paul defends his authority
   (10:1—13:14)

In responding to the attacks on his character and authority, Paul explains the nature of Christian ministry and, as an example, openly shares about his ministry. This is an important letter for all who wish to be involved in any kind of Christian ministry, because it has much to teach us about how we should handle our ministries today. Like Paul, those involved in ministry should be blameless, sincere, confident, caring, open, and willing to suffer for the sake of Christ.

## MEGATHEMES

| THEME | EXPLANATION | IMPORTANCE |
|-------|-------------|------------|
| Trials | Paul experienced great suffering, persecution, and opposition in his ministry. He even struggled with a personal weakness—a "thorn" in the flesh. Through it all, Paul affirmed God's faithfulness. | God is faithful. His strength is sufficient for any trial. When trials come, they keep us from pride and teach us dependence on God. He comforts us so we can comfort others. |
| Church Discipline | Paul defends his role in church discipline. Neither immorality nor false teaching could be ignored. The church was to be neither too lax nor too severe in administering discipline. The church was to restore the corrected person when he or she repented. | The goal of all discipline in the church should be correction, not vengeance. For churches to be effective, they must confront and solve problems, not ignore them. In everything, we must act in love. |
| Hope | To encourage the Corinthians as they faced trials, Paul reminded them that they would receive new bodies in heaven. This would be a great victory in contrast to their present suffering. | To know we will receive new bodies offers us hope. No matter what adversity we face, we can keep going. Our faithful service will result in triumph. |
| Giving | Paul organized a collection of funds for the poor in the Jerusalem church. Many of the Asian churches gave money. Paul explains and defends his beliefs about giving, and he urges the Corinthians to follow through on their previous commitment. | Like the Corinthians, we should follow through on our financial commitments. Our giving must be generous, sacrificial, well planned, and based on need. Our generosity not only helps those in need but enables them to thank God. |
| Sound Doctrine | False teachers were challenging Paul's ministry and authority as an apostle. Paul asserts his authority in order to preserve correct Christian doctrine. His sincerity, his love for Christ, and his concern for the people were his defense. | We should share Paul's concern for correct teaching in our churches. But in so doing, we must share his motivation—love for Christ and people—and his sincerity. |

## 1. Paul explains his actions

*Greetings from Paul*

**1** This letter is from Paul, chosen by the will of God to be an apostle of Christ Jesus, and from our brother Timothy.

I am writing to God's church in Corinth and to all of his holy people throughout Greece.*  ²May God our Father and the Lord Jesus Christ give you grace and peace.

*God Offers Comfort to All*

³All praise to God, the Father of our Lord Jesus Christ. God is our merciful Father and the source of all comfort. ⁴He comforts us in all our troubles so that we can comfort others. When they are troubled, we will be able to give them the same comfort God has given us. ⁵For the more we suffer for Christ, the more God will shower us with his comfort through Christ. ⁶Even when we are weighed down with troubles, it is for your comfort and salvation! For when we ourselves are comforted, we will certainly comfort you. Then you can patiently endure the same things we suffer. ⁷We are confident that as you share in our sufferings, you will also share in the comfort God gives us.

⁸We think you ought to know, dear brothers and sisters,* about the trouble we went through in the province of Asia. We were crushed and overwhelmed beyond our ability to endure, and we thought we would never live through it. ⁹In fact, we expected to die. But as a result, we stopped relying on ourselves and learned to rely only on God, who raises the dead. ¹⁰And he did rescue us from mortal danger, and he will rescue us again. We have placed our

1:1
1 Cor 1:1
2 Cor 1:19
Eph 1:1

1:2
Rom 1:7

1:3
Eph 1:3
1 Pet 1:3

1:4
Isa 51:12; 66:13
2 Cor 7:6

1:5
2 Cor 4:10
Phil 3:10
Col 1:24

1:6
2 Cor 4:15

1:9
Jer 17:5, 7

1:10
2 Tim 4:18
2 Pet 2:9

**1:1** Greek *Achaia*, the southern region of the Greek peninsula.  **1:8** Greek *brothers*.

---

**1:1** Paul visited Corinth on his second missionary journey and founded a church there (Acts 18:1ff). He later wrote several letters to the believers in Corinth, two of which are included in the Bible. Paul's first letter to the Corinthians is lost (1 Corinthians 5:9-11), his second letter to them is our book of 1 Corinthians, his third letter is lost (2:6-9; 7:12), and his fourth letter is our book of 2 Corinthians. Second Corinthians was written less than a year after 1 Corinthians.

Paul wrote 1 Corinthians to deal with divisions in the church. When his advice was not taken and their problems weren't solved, Paul visited Corinth a second time. That visit was painful both for Paul and for the church (2:1). He then planned a third visit but delayed it and wrote 2 Corinthians instead. After writing 2 Corinthians, Paul visited Corinth once more (Acts 20:2, 3).

**1:1** Paul had great respect for Timothy (see also Philippians 2:19, 20; 1 Timothy 1:2), one of his traveling companions (Acts 16:1-3). Timothy had accompanied Paul to Corinth on his second missionary journey, and Paul had recently sent him there to minister (1 Corinthians 4:17; 16:10). Timothy's report to Paul about the crisis in the Corinthian church prompted Paul to make an unplanned visit to the church to deal with the problem in person (see 2:1). For more information on Timothy, see his Profile in 1 Timothy 2, p. 2059.

**1:1** The Romans had made Corinth the capital of Achaia (the southern half of present-day Greece). The city was a flourishing trade center because of its seaport. With the thousands of merchants and sailors who disembarked there each year, it had developed a reputation as one of the most immoral cities in the ancient world; its many pagan temples encouraged the practice of sexual immorality along with idol worship. In fact, the Greek word "to Corinthianize" came to mean "to practice sexual immorality." A Christian church in the city would face many pressures and conflicts. For more information on Corinth, see the first note on 1 Corinthians 1:2.

**1:3-5** Many think that when God comforts us, our troubles should go away. But if that were always so, people would turn to God only out of a desire to be relieved of pain and not out of love for him. We must understand that being "comforted" can

also mean receiving strength, encouragement, and hope to deal with our troubles. The more we suffer, the more comfort God gives us. If you are feeling overwhelmed, allow God to comfort you. Remember that every trial you endure will help you comfort other people who are suffering similar troubles.

**1:5** Suffering for Christ refers to those afflictions we experience as we serve Christ. At the same time, Christ suffers with his people, since they are united with him. In Acts 9:4, 5 Christ asked Paul why he was persecuting him. This implies that Christ suffered with the early Christians when they were persecuted.

**1:6, 7** Paul had a radically different view of suffering. Suffering—especially trials and discomfort associated with the advancement of Christ's Kingdom—is God's way of allowing Christians to become more like Jesus, to suffer for the gospel just as Jesus suffered for it (Philippians 1:29; 3:10). Peter agreed with Paul: Christians should rejoice when they suffer, for in their own suffering they will in some small way experience what it meant for Jesus to suffer for their sins (1 Peter 4:12, 13).

In addition to drawing people closer to Christ, suffering can also help them grow in their faith. God uses suffering to improve his people and shape them into better Christians. In fact, suffering should be thought of as the necessary pain that accompanies spiritual growth. In Romans, Paul noted that suffering produces perseverance, which, in turn, produces Christian character (Romans 5:3, 4; see also James 1:3, 4; 2 Peter 1:6; Revelation 2:2, 19). This passage highlights another benefit to suffering: It teaches the sufferer how to encourage others who are also suffering.

**1:8-10** Paul does not give details about their hardships in Asia, although his accounts of all three missionary journeys record many difficult trials he faced (Acts 13:2–14:28; Acts 15:40–21:17). He does write that they felt that they were going to die and realized that they could do nothing to help themselves—they simply had to rely on God.

**1:8-10** We often depend on our own skills and abilities when life seems easy and only turn to God when we feel unable to help ourselves. But as we realize our own powerlessness without him and our need for his constant help in our lives, we come to depend on him more and more. God is our source of power, and we receive his help by keeping in touch with him. With this attitude of dependence, problems will drive us to God rather than away from him. Learn how to rely on God daily.

**1:11**
Rom 15:30
2 Cor 4:15
Phil 1:19

confidence in him, and he will continue to rescue us. ¹¹And you are helping us by praying for us. Then many people will give thanks because God has graciously answered so many prayers for our safety.

### Paul's Change of Plans

**1:12**
Acts 23:1
1 Cor 1:17
2 Cor 2:17; 4:15

¹²We can say with confidence and a clear conscience that we have lived with a God-given holiness* and sincerity in all our dealings. We have depended on God's grace, not on our own human wisdom. That is how we have conducted ourselves before the world, and especially toward you. ¹³Our letters have been straightforward, and there is nothing written between the lines and nothing you can't understand. I hope someday you will fully understand

**1:14**
2 Cor 5:12
Phil 2:16

us, ¹⁴even if you don't understand us now. Then on the day when the Lord Jesus* returns, you will be proud of us in the same way we are proud of you.

**1:15**
Rom 1:11-13

¹⁵Since I was so sure of your understanding and trust, I wanted to give you a double blessing by visiting you twice—¹⁶first on my way to Macedonia and again when I returned from Macedonia.* Then you could send me on my way to Judea.

**1:16**
Acts 19:21
1 Cor 16:5-6

**1:17**
2 Cor 5:16

¹⁷You may be asking why I changed my plan. Do you think I make my plans carelessly? Do you think I am like people of the world who say "Yes" when they really mean "No"? ¹⁸As surely as God is faithful, our word to you does not waver between "Yes" and "No." ¹⁹For Jesus Christ, the Son of God, does not waver between "Yes" and "No." He is the one whom Silas,* Timothy, and I preached to you, and as God's ultimate "Yes," he always does what he says.

**1:19**
Acts 18:5
Heb 13:8

**1:20**
Rom 15:8-9
Rev 3:14

²⁰For all of God's promises have been fulfilled in Christ with a resounding "Yes!" And through Christ, our "Amen" (which means "Yes") ascends to God for his glory.

**1:12** Some manuscripts read *honesty.*   **1:14** Some manuscripts read *our Lord Jesus.*   **1:16** *Macedonia* was in the northern region of Greece.   **1:19** Greek *Silvanus.*

---

**DIFFERENCES BETWEEN 1 AND 2 CORINTHIANS**

The two letters to the Corinthian church that we find in the Bible are very different, with different tones and focuses.

| *1 Corinthians*/Practical | *2 Corinthians*/Personal |
|---|---|
| Focuses on the character of the Corinthian church | Focuses on Paul as he bares his soul and tells of his love for the Corinthian church |
| Deals with questions on marriage, freedom, spiritual gifts, and order in the church | Deals with the problem of false teachers, whereby Paul defends his authority and the truth of his message |
| Paul instructs in matters concerning the church's well-being | Paul gives his testimony because he knows that acceptance of his advice is vital to the church's well-being |
| Contains advice to help the church combat the pagan influences in the wicked city of Corinth | Contains testimony to help the church combat the havoc caused by false teachers |

---

**1:11** Paul requested prayer for himself and his companions as they traveled to spread God's message. Pray for pastors, teachers, missionaries, and others who are spreading the Good News. Satan will challenge anyone making a real difference for God.

**1:12-14** Paul knew the importance of honesty and sincerity in word and action, especially in a situation as in Corinth, where constructive criticism was necessary. So Paul did not come with impressive human wisdom. God wants us to be real and transparent in all our relationships. If we aren't, we may end up lowering ourselves to spreading rumors, gossiping, and second-guessing.

**1:15-17** Paul had recently made a brief, unscheduled visit to Corinth that was very painful for him and the church (see 2:1). After that visit, he told the church when he would return. But Paul changed his original travel plans. Instead of sailing from Ephesus to Corinth before going to Macedonia, he traveled from Ephesus directly to Macedonia, where he wrote a letter to the Corinthians that caused him much anguish and them much sorrow (7:8, 9). He had made his original plans, thinking that the church would have solved its problems. When the time came for Paul's scheduled trip to Corinth, however, the crisis had not been fully resolved (although progress was being made in some areas; 7:11-16). So he wrote a letter instead (2:3, 4; 7:8) because another visit might

have only made matters worse. Thus, Paul stayed away from Corinth because he was concerned over the church's unity, not because he was fickle.

**1:17-20** Paul's change of plans caused some of his accusers to say that he couldn't be trusted, hoping to undermine his authority. Paul said that he was not the type of person to say yes when he meant no. Paul explained that it was not indecision but concern for their feelings that forced him to change his plans. The reason for his trip—to bring joy (1:24)—could not be accomplished with the present crisis. Paul didn't want to visit them only to rebuke them severely (1:23). Just as the Corinthians could trust God to keep his promises, they could trust Paul as God's representative to keep his. He would still visit them, but at a better time.

**1:19, 20** Instead of defending himself, Paul reminded the Corinthians of God's faithfulness. There was no duplicity in God. His promises would be fulfilled. There would be no wavering between "yes" and "no." Jesus Christ was the premier example of this. "All of God's promises have been fulfilled in Christ with a resounding 'yes!'" Jesus is the embodiment of God's faithfulness. Because Jesus Christ is faithful, Paul (a messenger appointed by Jesus) would also be faithful in his ministry.

²¹It is God who enables us, along with you, to stand firm for Christ. He has commissioned us, ²²and he has identified us as his own by placing the Holy Spirit in our hearts as the first installment that guarantees everything he has promised us.

²³Now I call upon God as my witness that I am telling the truth. The reason I didn't return to Corinth was to spare you from a severe rebuke. ²⁴But that does not mean we want to dominate you by telling you how to put your faith into practice. We want to work together with you so you will be full of joy, for it is by your own faith that you stand firm.

**2** So I decided that I would not bring you grief with another painful visit. ²For if I cause you grief, who will make me glad? Certainly not someone I have grieved. ³That is why I wrote to you as I did, so that when I do come, I won't be grieved by the very ones who ought to give me the greatest joy. Surely you all know that my joy comes from your being joyful. ⁴I wrote that letter in great anguish, with a troubled heart and many tears. I didn't want to grieve you, but I wanted to let you know how much love I have for you.

*Forgiveness for the Sinner*

⁵I am not overstating it when I say that the man who caused all the trouble hurt all of you more than he hurt me. ⁶Most of you opposed him, and that was punishment enough. ⁷Now, however, it is time to forgive and comfort him. Otherwise he may be overcome by discouragement. ⁸So I urge you now to reaffirm your love for him.

⁹I wrote to you as I did to test you and see if you would fully comply with my instructions. ¹⁰When you forgive this man, I forgive him, too. And when I forgive whatever needs to be forgiven, I do so with Christ's authority for your benefit, ¹¹so that Satan will not outsmart us. For we are familiar with his evil schemes.

¹²When I came to the city of Troas to preach the Good News of Christ, the Lord opened a door of opportunity for me. ¹³But I had no peace of mind because my dear brother Titus hadn't yet arrived with a report from you. So I said good-bye and went on to Macedonia to find him.

**1:21**
1 Jn 2:20, 27
**1:22**
2 Cor 5:5
Eph 1:13-14; 4:30
**1:23**
1 Cor 4:21
**1:24**
1 Cor 15:1

**2:1**
1 Cor 4:21
2 Cor 12:21
**2:2**
2 Cor 7:8
**2:4**
2 Cor 2:9; 7:8, 12

**2:5**
1 Cor 5:1-2
2 Cor 7:11
**2:7**
Gal 6:1
Eph 4:32
**2:11**
2 Cor 4:4
1 Pet 5:8
**2:12**
Acts 14:27
2 Cor 4:3
**2:13**
2 Cor 7:5-6

---

**1:21, 22** The Holy Spirit guarantees that we belong to God and will receive all his benefits (Ephesians 1:13, 14). The Holy Spirit guarantees that salvation is ours now, and that we will receive so much more when Christ returns. The great comfort and power the Holy Spirit gives in this life is a foretaste or down payment ("first installment") of the benefits of our eternal life in God's presence. With the privilege of belonging to God comes the responsibility of identifying ourselves as his faithful servants. Don't be ashamed to let others know that you are his.

**1:23** The Corinthian church had written to Paul with questions about their faith (see 1 Corinthians 7:1). In response, Paul had written 1 Corinthians. But the church did not follow his instructions.

Paul had planned to visit them again, but instead, he wrote a letter that caused sorrow (7:8, 9) but also caused them to change their ways. He had not wanted to visit and repeat the same advice for the same problems. He wrote the emotional letter to encourage them to follow the advice that he had already given in previous letters and visits.

**1:24** Standing firm is not a way to be saved but the evidence that a person is really committed to Jesus. Endurance is not a means to earn salvation; it is the by-product of a truly devoted life. Endurance grows out of commitment to Jesus Christ. In Matthew 10:22, Jesus predicted that his followers would be severely persecuted by those who hated what he stood for. In the midst of terrible persecutions, however, they could have hope, knowing that salvation was theirs. Times of trial serve to sift true Christians from false or fair-weather Christians. When you are pressured to give up and turn your back on Christ, don't do it. Remember the benefits of standing firm and continue to live for Christ.

**2:1** Paul's phrase "another painful visit" indicates that he had already made one difficult trip to Corinth (see the notes on 1:1; 1:15-17) since founding the church. Paul had gone there to deal with those in the church who had been attacking and undermining his authority as an apostle of Jesus Christ, thus confusing other believers.

**2:3** Paul's last letter, referred to here, was not the book of 1 Corinthians, but a letter written between 1 and 2 Corinthians,

just after his unplanned, painful visit (2:1). Paul refers to this letter again in 7:8.

**2:4** Paul did not enjoy reprimanding his friends and fellow believers, but he cared enough about the Corinthians to confront them with their wrongdoing. Proverbs 27:6 says: "Wounds from a sincere friend are better than many kisses from an enemy." Sometimes our friends make choices that we know are wrong. If we ignore their behavior and let them continue in it, we won't be showing love to them. We show love by honestly sharing our concerns in order to help these friends be their very best for God. When we don't make any move to help, we show that we are more concerned about being well liked than about what will happen to them.

**2:5-11** Paul explained that it was time to forgive the man who had been punished by the church and had subsequently repented. He needed forgiveness, acceptance, and comfort. Satan would gain an advantage if they permanently separated this man from the congregation rather than forgiving and restoring him. This may have been the man who had required the disciplinary action described in 1 Corinthians 5, or he may have been the chief opponent of Paul who had caused him anguish (2:1-11). The sorrowful letter had finally brought about the repentance of the Corinthians (7:8-14), and their discipline of the man had led to his repentance. Church discipline should seek restoration. Two mistakes in church discipline should be avoided: being too lenient and not correcting mistakes, or being too harsh and not forgiving the sinner. There is a time to confront and a time to comfort.

**2:11** We use church discipline to help keep the church pure and to help wayward people repent. But Satan tries to harm the church by tempting it to use discipline in an unforgiving way. This causes those exercising discipline to become proud of their purity, and it causes the person who is being disciplined to become bitter and perhaps leave the church. We must remember that our purpose in discipline is to *restore* a person to the fellowship, not to destroy him or her. We must be cautious that personal anger is not vented under the guise of church discipline.

**2:13** Titus was a Greek convert whom Paul greatly loved and trusted (the book of Titus is a letter that Paul wrote to him). Titus

## 2. Paul defends his ministry

### Ministers of the New Covenant

**2:15**
1 Cor 1:18

**2:16**
Luke 2:34
2 Cor 3:5-6

**2:17**
2 Cor 1:12; 12:19

14But thank God! He has made us his captives and continues to lead us along in Christ's triumphal procession. Now he uses us to spread the knowledge of Christ everywhere, like a sweet perfume. 15Our lives are a Christ-like fragrance rising up to God. But this fragrance is perceived differently by those who are being saved and by those who are perishing. 16To those who are perishing, we are a dreadful smell of death and doom. But to those who are being saved, we are a life-giving perfume. And who is adequate for such a task as this?

17You see, we are not like the many hucksters* who preach for personal profit. We preach the word of God with sincerity and with Christ's authority, knowing that God is watching us.

**2:17** Some manuscripts read *the rest of the hucksters.*

---

**PAUL SEARCHES FOR TITUS**
Paul had searched for Titus, hoping to meet him in Troas and receive news about the Corinthian church. When he did not find Titus in Troas, he went on to Macedonia (2:13), most likely to Philippi, where he found Titus.

**Paul's journey** ———
**Titus's journey** - - - - -

0   300 Mi.
0   300 Km.

---

was one of the men responsible for collecting the money for the poverty-stricken Jerusalem church (8:6). Paul may also have sent Titus with the sorrowful letter. On his way to Macedonia, Paul was supposed to meet Titus in Troas. When Paul didn't find him there, he was worried for Titus's safety and left Troas to search for him in Macedonia. There Paul found him (7:6), and the good news that Paul received (7:8-16) led to this letter. Paul would send Titus back to Corinth with this letter (8:16, 17).

**2:14ff** In the middle of discussing his unscheduled trip to Macedonia, Paul thanked God for his ministry, his relationship with the Corinthian believers, and the way God had used him to help others wherever he went, despite difficulties (2:14–7:4). In 7:5, Paul resumed his story of his trip to Macedonia.

**2:14-16** In a Roman triumphal procession, the Roman general would display his treasures and captives amidst a cloud of incense burned for the gods. To the victors, the aroma was sweet; to the captives in the parade, it was the smell of slavery and death. When Christians preach the Good News, it is good news to some and repulsive news to others. Believers recognize the life-giving fragrance of the message. To nonbelievers, however, it smells foul, like death—their own.

**2:16, 17** Paul asks "who is adequate" for the task of representing Christ? Our adequacy is always from God (1 Corinthians

15:10; 2 Corinthians 3:5). He has already commissioned and sent us (see Matthew 28:18-20). He has given us the Holy Spirit to enable us to speak with Christ's power. He keeps his eye on us, protecting us as we work for him. As we realize that God has equipped us, we can overcome our feelings of inadequacy. Serving Christ, therefore, requires that we focus on what he can do through us, not on what we can't do by ourselves.

**2:17** Some preachers in Paul's day were "hucksters," preaching without understanding God's message or caring about what happened to their listeners. They weren't concerned about furthering God's Kingdom—they just wanted money. Today there are still preachers and teachers who care only about money and not about truth. Those who truly speak for God should teach God's Word with sincerity and integrity and should never preach for selfish reasons (1 Timothy 6:5-10).

**3** Are we beginning to praise ourselves again? Are we like others, who need to bring you letters of recommendation, or who ask you to write such letters on their behalf? Surely not! ²The only letter of recommendation we need is you yourselves. Your lives are a letter written in our* hearts; everyone can read it and recognize our good work among you. ³Clearly, you are a letter from Christ showing the result of our ministry among you. This "letter" is written not with pen and ink, but with the Spirit of the living God. It is carved not on tablets of stone, but on human hearts.

⁴We are confident of all this because of our great trust in God through Christ. ⁵It is not that we think we are qualified to do anything on our own. Our qualification comes from God. ⁶He has enabled us to be ministers of his new covenant. This is a covenant not of written laws, but of the Spirit. The old written covenant ends in death; but under the new covenant, the Spirit gives life.

### The Glory of the New Covenant

⁷The old way,* with laws etched in stone, led to death, though it began with such glory that the people of Israel could not bear to look at Moses' face. For his face shone with the glory of God, even though the brightness was already fading away. ⁸Shouldn't we expect far greater glory under the new way, now that the Holy Spirit is giving life? ⁹If the old way, which brings condemnation, was glorious, how much more glorious is the new way, which makes us right with God! ¹⁰In fact, that first glory was not glorious at all compared with the overwhelming glory of the new way. ¹¹So if the old way, which has been replaced, was glorious, how much more glorious is the new, which remains forever!

¹²Since this new way gives us such confidence, we can be very bold. ¹³We are not like Moses, who put a veil over his face so the people of Israel would not see the glory, even though it was destined to fade away. ¹⁴But the people's minds were hardened, and to this day whenever the old covenant is being read, the same veil covers their minds so they cannot understand the truth. And this veil can be removed only by believing in Christ. ¹⁵Yes, even today when they read Moses' writings, their hearts are covered with that veil, and they do not understand.

¹⁶But whenever someone turns to the Lord, the veil is taken away. ¹⁷For the Lord is the

**3:2** Some manuscripts read *your.*   **3:7** Or *ministry;* also in 3:8, 9, 10, 11, 12.

**3:1**
Acts 18:27
2 Cor 5:12; 10:12

**3:2**
1 Cor 9:2

**3:3**
Exod 24:12; 31:18;
32:15-16
Prov 3:3
Jer 31:33
Ezek 36:26

**3:5**
1 Cor 15:10
2 Cor 2:16

**3:6**
Jer 31:31
Luke 22:20
Rom 2:27; 7:6; 8:2
Heb 8:8-13

**3:7**
Exod 34:29-35

**3:9**
Deut 27:26
Rom 1:17; 3:21

**3:10-11**
Exod 34:29-30
John 17:10, 22

**3:13**
Exod 34:33-35

**3:14**
Acts 13:15
Rom 11:7-8
2 Cor 4:4

**3:16**
Isa 25:7
Rom 11:23

**3:17**
Gal 4:6-7

---

**3:1-3** Some false teachers had started carrying forged letters of recommendation to authenticate their authority. In no uncertain terms, Paul stated that he needed no such letters. The believers to whom Paul and his companions had preached were enough of a recommendation. Paul did use letters of introduction, however, many times. He wrote them on behalf of Phoebe (Romans 16:1, 2) and Timothy (1 Corinthians 16:10, 11). These letters helped Paul's trusted companions and friends find a welcome in various churches.

**3:3** Paul uses powerful imagery from famous Old Testament passages predicting the promised day of new hearts and new beginnings for God's people (see Jeremiah 31:33; Ezekiel 11:19; 36:26). No human being can take credit for this process of conversion. It is the work of God's Spirit. We do not become believers by following some manual or using some technique. Our conversion is a result of God's implanting his Spirit in our heart, giving us new power to live for him.

**3:4, 5** Paul was not boasting; he gave God the credit for all his accomplishments. While the false teachers boasted of their own power and success, Paul expressed his humility before God. No one can claim to be adequate without God's help. No one is competent to carry out the responsibilities of God's calling in his or her own strength. Without the Holy Spirit's enabling, our natural talent can carry us only so far. As Christ's witnesses, we need the character and special strength that only God gives.

**3:6** "The old written covenant ends in death; but under the new covenant, the Spirit gives life" means that trying to be saved by keeping the Old Testament laws will end in death. Only by believing in the Lord Jesus Christ can a person receive eternal life through the Holy Spirit. No one but Jesus has ever fulfilled the law perfectly; thus, the whole world is condemned to death. The law makes people realize their sin, but it cannot give life. Under the new covenant, which means promise or agreement, eternal life comes from

the Holy Spirit. The Spirit gives new life to all who believe in Christ. The moral law (Ten Commandments) still points out sin and shows us how to obey God, but forgiveness comes only through the grace and mercy of Christ (see Romans 7:10–8:2).

**3:7-11** Paul recalled the stone tablets on which God had written the old covenant—calling it "the old way." He identified the law, although leading to death, as nonetheless glorious because it was God's provision and proof of his intervention in the life of his people. But that which was summarized on stone is nowhere near as glorious as what came with "the new way"—life in the Holy Spirit. The Holy Spirit was present at the creation of the world as one of the agents in the origin of life itself (Genesis 1:2). He is the power behind the rebirth of every Christian and the one who helps us live the Christian life. By his power, we will be transformed into Christ's perfect likeness when he returns. Thank God for the fact that the best is yet to be.

**3:13-18** When Moses came down Mount Sinai with the Ten Commandments, his face glowed from being in God's presence (Exodus 34:29-35). Moses had to put on a veil to keep the people from being terrified by the brightness of his face and from seeing the radiance fade away. This veil illustrates the fading of the old system and the veiling of the people's minds because of their pride, hardness of heart, and refusal to repent. The veil kept them from understanding references to Christ in the Scriptures. When anyone becomes a Christian, the veil is taken away (3:16), giving eternal life and freedom from bondage. That person can then be like a mirror reflecting God's glory.

**3:17** Those who were trying to be saved by keeping the Old Testament law were soon tied up in rules and ceremonies. But now, through the Holy Spirit, God provides freedom from sin and condemnation (Romans 8:1). When we trust Christ to save us, he removes our heavy burden of trying to please him and

**3:18**
Rom 8:29
2 Cor 4:4, 6

**4:2**
2 Cor 2:17
1 Thes 2:5

**4:3**
1 Cor 1:18
2 Cor 3:14

**4:4**
John 12:39-41
2 Cor 3:14
Col 1:15
Heb 1:3

**4:5**
1 Cor 9:19
2 Cor 1:24

**4:6**
Gen 1:3
Ps 36:9
John 8:12; 12:46
Eph 5:8, 14
1 Pet 2:9
2 Pet 1:19

**4:7**
2 Cor 5:1
2 Tim 2:20

**4:8**
2 Cor 7:5

**4:9**
Rom 8:35

**4:10**
Rom 8:17
1 Cor 15:31
Gal 6:17
Phil 3:10
Col 1:24
2 Tim 2:11
1 Pet 4:13

**4:14**
Acts 2:24
1 Thes 2:19

Spirit, and wherever the Spirit of the Lord is, there is freedom. ¹⁸So all of us who have had that veil removed can see and reflect the glory of the Lord. And the Lord—who is the Spirit—makes us more and more like him as we are changed into his glorious image.

### Treasure in Fragile Clay Jars

**4** Therefore, since God in his mercy has given us this new way,* we never give up. ²We reject all shameful deeds and underhanded methods. We don't try to trick anyone or distort the word of God. We tell the truth before God, and all who are honest know this.

³If the Good News we preach is hidden behind a veil, it is hidden only from people who are perishing. ⁴Satan, who is the god of this world, has blinded the minds of those who don't believe. They are unable to see the glorious light of the Good News. They don't understand this message about the glory of Christ, who is the exact likeness of God.

⁵You see, we don't go around preaching about ourselves. We preach that Jesus Christ is Lord, and we ourselves are your servants for Jesus' sake. ⁶For God, who said, "Let there be light in the darkness," has made this light shine in our hearts so we could know the glory of God that is seen in the face of Jesus Christ.

⁷We now have this light shining in our hearts, but we ourselves are like fragile clay jars containing this great treasure.* This makes it clear that our great power is from God, not from ourselves.

⁸We are pressed on every side by troubles, but we are not crushed. We are perplexed, but not driven to despair. ⁹We are hunted down, but never abandoned by God. We get knocked down, but we are not destroyed. ¹⁰Through suffering, our bodies continue to share in the death of Jesus so that the life of Jesus may also be seen in our bodies.

¹¹Yes, we live under constant danger of death because we serve Jesus, so that the life of Jesus will be evident in our dying bodies. ¹²So we live in the face of death, but this has resulted in eternal life for you.

¹³But we continue to preach because we have the same kind of faith the psalmist had when he said, "I believed in God, so I spoke."* ¹⁴We know that God, who raised the Lord Jesus,* will

**4:1** Or ministry.   **4:7** Greek We now have this treasure in clay jars.   **4:13** Ps 116:10.   **4:14** Some manuscripts read who raised Jesus.

our guilt for failing to do so. By trusting Christ we are loved, accepted, forgiven, and freed to live for him. "Wherever the Spirit of the Lord is, there is freedom."

**3:18** The glory that the Spirit imparts to the believer is more excellent and lasts longer than the glory that Moses experienced. By gazing at the nature of God with unveiled minds, we can be more like him. In the Good News, we see the truth about Christ, and it transforms us morally as we understand and apply it. Through learning about Christ's life, we can understand how wonderful God is and what he is really like. As our knowledge deepens, the Holy Spirit helps us to change. Becoming Christlike is a progressive experience (see Romans 8:29; Galatians 4:19; Philippians 3:21; 1 John 3:2). The more closely we follow Christ, the more we will be like him.

**4:2** Paul condemned those who twist God's Word. Preachers, teachers, and anyone else who talks about Jesus Christ must remember that they stand in God's presence—he hears every word. Many Christian ministers and leaders twist Scripture in their attempt to motivate audiences. Others take Scripture out of context to promote their own views. When you tell people about Christ, be careful not to distort the message to please your audience. Proclaim the truth of God's Word.

**4:3, 4** The Good News is revealed to everyone, except to those who refuse to believe. Satan is "the god of this world." His work is to deceive, and he has blinded those who don't believe in Christ (see 11:14, 15). The allure of money, power, and pleasure blinds people to the light of Christ's Good News. Those who reject Christ and prefer their own pursuits have unknowingly made Satan their god.

**4:5** The focus of Paul's preaching was Christ and not himself. When you witness, tell people about what Christ has done and not about your abilities and accomplishments. People must be introduced to Christ, not to you. And if you hear someone

preaching about himself or his own ideas rather than about Christ, beware—he is a false teacher.

**4:5** Paul willingly served the Corinthian church even though the people must have deeply disappointed him. Serving people requires a sacrifice of time and personal desires. Being Christ's follower means serving others, even when they do not measure up to our expectations.

**4:7** The supremely valuable message of salvation in Jesus Christ has been entrusted by God to frail and fallible human beings. Paul's focus, however, was not on the perishable container but on its priceless contents—God's power dwelling in us. Though we are "fragile, clay jars," God uses us to spread his Good News, and he gives us power to do his work. Knowing that the power is his, not ours, should keep us from pride and motivate us to keep daily contact with God, our power source. Our responsibility is to let people see God through us.

**4:8-12** Paul reminds us that though we may think we are at the end of our rope, we are never at the end of our hope. Our perishable bodies are subject to sin and suffering, but God never abandons us. Because Christ has won the victory over death, we have eternal life. All our risks, humiliations, and trials are opportunities for Christ to demonstrate his power and presence in and through us. We must ask ourselves, "Could I handle the suffering and opposition that Paul did?" The success syndrome is a great enemy of effective ministry. From an earthly perspective, Paul was not very successful. Like Paul, we must carry out our ministry, looking to God for strength. When opposition, slander, or disappointment threaten to rob you of the victory, remember that no one can destroy what God has accomplished through you.

also raise us with Jesus and present us to himself together with you. ¹⁵All of this is for your benefit. And as God's grace reaches more and more people, there will be great thanksgiving, and God will receive more and more glory.

¹⁶That is why we never give up. Though our bodies are dying, our spirits are* being renewed every day. ¹⁷For our present troubles are small and won't last very long. Yet they produce for us a glory that vastly outweighs them and will last forever! ¹⁸So we don't look at the troubles we can see now; rather, we fix our gaze on things that cannot be seen. For the things we see now will soon be gone, but the things we cannot see will last forever.

### New Bodies

**5** For we know that when this earthly tent we live in is taken down (that is, when we die and leave this earthly body), we will have a house in heaven, an eternal body made for us by God himself and not by human hands. ²We grow weary in our present bodies, and we long to put on our heavenly bodies like new clothing. ³For we will put on heavenly bodies; we will not be spirits without bodies.* ⁴While we live in these earthly bodies, we groan and sigh, but it's not that we want to die and get rid of these bodies that clothe us. Rather, we want to put on our new bodies so that these dying bodies will be swallowed up by life. ⁵God himself has prepared us for this, and as a guarantee he has given us his Holy Spirit.

⁶So we are always confident, even though we know that as long as we live in these bodies we are not at home with the Lord. ⁷For we live by believing and not by seeing. ⁸Yes, we are fully confident, and we would rather be away from these earthly bodies, for then we will be at home with the Lord. ⁹So whether we are here in this body or away from this body, our goal is to please him. ¹⁰For we must all stand before Christ to be judged. We will each receive whatever we deserve for the good or evil we have done in this earthly body.

**4:15**
2 Cor 1:3-6
**4:16**
Eph 3:16
Col 3:10
**4:17**
Rom 8:17-18
1 Pet 1:6-7
**4:18**
Rom 8:24
2 Cor 5:7

**5:1**
1 Cor 15:47
2 Cor 4:7
2 Pet 1:13-14
**5:2**
Rom 8:23
1 Cor 15:53-54
**5:4**
1 Cor 15:53-54
**5:5**
Rom 8:23
2 Cor 1:22
Eph 1:13-14
**5:7**
1 Cor 13:12
**5:8**
Phil 1:23
**5:10**
Matt 16:27
Acts 10:42

**4:16** Greek *our inner being is.*    **5:3** Greek *we will not be naked.*

---

**4:15-18** Paul had faced suffering, trials, and distress as he preached the Good News. But he knew that they would one day be over, and he would obtain God's rest and rewards. As we face great troubles, it's easy to focus on the pain rather than on our ultimate goal. Just as athletes concentrate on the finish line and ignore their discomfort, we, too, must focus on the reward for our faith and the joy that lasts forever. No matter what happens to us in this life, we have the assurance of eternal life, when all suffering will end and all sorrow will flee away (Isaiah 35:10).

**4:16** It is easy to lose heart and quit. We all have faced problems in our relationships or in our work that have caused us to think about giving up. Rather than quitting when persecution wore him down, Paul concentrated on the inner strength that came from the Holy Spirit (Ephesians 3:16). Don't let fatigue, pain, or criticism force you off the job. Renew your commitment to serving Christ. Don't forsake your eternal reward because of the intensity of today's pain. Your very weakness allows the resurrection power of Christ to strengthen you moment by moment.

**4:17** Our troubles should not diminish our faith or disillusion us. We should realize that there is a purpose in our suffering. Problems and human limitations have several benefits: (1) They remind us of Christ's suffering for us; (2) they keep us from pride; (3) they cause us to look beyond this brief life; (4) they give us opportunities to prove our faith to others; and (5) they give God the opportunity to demonstrate his power. See your troubles as opportunities!

**4:18** Our ultimate hope when we are experiencing terrible illness, persecution, or pain is the realization that this life is not all there is—there is life after death! Knowing that we will live forever with God in a place without sin and suffering can help us live above the pain that we face in this life.

**5:1-10** Paul contrasts our earthly body and our future resurrection body. Paul clearly states that our present body makes us groan, but when we die we will not be spirits without bodies. We will have new bodies that will be perfect for our everlasting life.

Paul wrote as he did because the church at Corinth was surrounded by Greek culture, and many believers had difficulty with the concept of bodily resurrection because the Greeks did not believe in it. Most saw the afterlife as something that happened only to the soul, with the real person imprisoned in a physical body. They

believed that at death the soul was released; there was no immortality for the body, and the soul enters an eternal state. But the Bible teaches that the body and soul are not permanently separated.

Paul describes our resurrected body in more detail in 1 Corinthians 15:46-58. We will still have personalities and recognizable characteristics in our resurrected body, but through Christ's work, our body will be better than we can imagine. The Bible does not tell us everything about our resurrected body, but we know that it will be perfect, without sickness, disease, or pain (see Philippians 3:21; Revelation 21:4).

**5:4** Paul's knowledge that his dying body would be swallowed up by eternal life, is a universal hope. According to the writer of Ecclesiastes, God "has planted eternity in the human heart" (Ecclesiastes 3:11). Human beings have an innate sense of transcendence and longing for ultimate reality experienced only in the eternal presence of God. This spiritual desire is addressed by every world religion and cult and (at least secretly) desired by every person. What occurrences in daily life can provide you an opportunity to witness God's solution to this universal spiritual search? A baby's birth, a parent's death, or the death of a dream all can be springboards for sharing the hope you have in Christ. Spread the Good News!

**5:5** The Holy Spirit is God's "guarantee" of what will come. His work in our lives today assures us that the healing process will be thoroughly completed in Christ's presence. Each time the Holy Spirit reminds you of Scripture, convicts you of sin, restrains you from selfish behavior, or prompts you to love, you have evidence that he is present. You have the Spirit within you beginning the transformation process. Whether you deal with aches and pains or even disabling limitations, trust God that his total renovation of your body and soul is in process.

**5:6-8** Paul was not afraid to die because he was confident of spending eternity with Christ. Of course, facing the unknown may cause us anxiety, and leaving loved ones hurts deeply, but if we believe in Jesus Christ, we can share Paul's hope and confidence of eternal life with Christ. Death is only a prelude to eternal life with God. We will continue to live. Let this hope give you confidence and inspire you to faithful service.

**5:9, 10** While eternal life is a free gift given on the basis of God's grace (Ephesians 2:8, 9), each of us will still be judged by Christ.

## We Are God's Ambassadors

**5:12**
2 Cor 1:14; 3:1

**5:14**
Rom 6:6-7
Gal 2:20
Col 3:3

**5:15**
Rom 14:7-9

**5:16**
2 Cor 10:4

**5:17**
Isa 65:17
Gal 6:15
Rev 21:5

**5:18**
Rom 5:10

**5:19**
Rom 3:24; 4:8

**5:20**
Eph 6:20

**5:21**
Isa 53:6, 9
Jer 23:6
Gal 3:13
Heb 4:15; 7:26
1 Pet 2:22

**6:1**
1 Cor 3:9
2 Cor 5:20

**6:2**
†Isa 49:8

¹¹Because we understand our fearful responsibility to the Lord, we work hard to persuade others. God knows we are sincere, and I hope you know this, too. ¹²Are we commending ourselves to you again? No, we are giving you a reason to be proud of us,* so you can answer those who brag about having a spectacular ministry rather than having a sincere heart. ¹³If it seems we are crazy, it is to bring glory to God. And if we are in our right minds, it is for your benefit. ¹⁴Either way, Christ's love controls us.* Since we believe that Christ died for all, we also believe that we have all died to our old life.* ¹⁵He died for everyone so that those who receive his new life will no longer live for themselves. Instead, they will live for Christ, who died and was raised for them.

¹⁶So we have stopped evaluating others from a human point of view. At one time we thought of Christ merely from a human point of view. How differently we know him now! ¹⁷This means that anyone who belongs to Christ has become a new person. The old life is gone; a new life has begun!

¹⁸And all of this is a gift from God, who brought us back to himself through Christ. And God has given us this task of reconciling people to him. ¹⁹For God was in Christ, reconciling the world to himself, no longer counting people's sins against them. And he gave us this wonderful message of reconciliation. ²⁰So we are Christ's ambassadors; God is making his appeal through us. We speak for Christ when we plead, "Come back to God!" ²¹For God made Christ, who never sinned, to be the offering for our sin,* so that we could be made right with God through Christ.

**6** As God's partners,* we beg you not to accept this marvelous gift of God's kindness and then ignore it. ²For God says,

**5:12** Some manuscripts read *proud of yourselves.*   **5:14a** Or *urges us on.*   **5:14b** Greek *Since one died for all, then all died.*   **5:21** Or *to become sin itself.*   **6:1** Or *As we work together.*

---

He will reward us for how we have lived. God's gracious gift of salvation does not free us from the requirement of faithful obedience. All Christians must give account on the day of judgment of how they have lived (see Matthew 16:27; Romans 14:10-12; 1 Corinthians 3:10-15).

**5:11** Having a "fearful responsibility to the Lord" does not mean that believers become paralyzed. On the contrary, knowing God's perfection and that he will judge everyone's actions (5:10) should spur Christians to good deeds, to what pleases our God. The fear of the Lord also frees believers from all of life's anxieties and worries. Knowing that God is "for us" (Romans 8:31) can keep believers unafraid of earthly powers—people, governments, or the forces of nature (Proverbs 3:25, 26). God takes care of his own. The fear of God gives us uncommon courage in the face of life's troubles.

**5:12** Those who "brag about having a spectacular ministry rather than having a sincere heart" are the false preachers (see 2:17), who were concerned only about getting ahead in this world. They were preaching the Good News for money and popularity, while Paul and his companions were preaching out of concern for eternity. You can identify false preachers by finding out what really motivates them. If they are more concerned about themselves than about Christ, avoid them and their message.

**5:13-15** Everything that Paul and his companions did was to honor God. Not only did fear of God motivate them (5:11), but Christ's love controlled their actions. The word for "controls" means "to hold fast." In other words, the love of Christ was constraining them to certain courses of action. They knew that Jesus, out of his great love, had given up his life for their sakes. He had not acted out of his own self-interest, selfishly holding on to the glory of heaven that he already possessed (Philippians 2:6). Instead, Jesus had willingly "died for everyone." Because Christ died for us, we also are dead to our old life. Like Paul, we should no longer live to please ourselves; we should spend our life pleasing Christ.

**5:17** Christians are brand-new people on the *inside.* The Holy Spirit gives them new life, and they are not the same anymore. We are not reformed, rehabilitated, or reeducated—we are re-created (new creations), living in vital union with Christ (Colossians 2:6, 7).

At conversion we do not merely turn over a new leaf; we begin a new life under a new Master.

While this newness is true individually, Paul is saying much more. Not only are believers changed from within, but a whole new order of creative energy began with Christ. There is a new covenant, a new perspective, a new body, a new church. All of creation is being renewed. So take notice. This is not a superficial change that will be quickly superseded by another novelty. This is an entirely new order of all creation under Christ's authority. It requires a new way of looking at all people and all of creation. Does your life reflect this new perspective?

**5:18, 19** God brings us back to himself (reconciles us) by blotting out our sins (see also Ephesians 2:13-18) and making us right with him. When we trust in Christ, we are no longer God's enemies, or strangers or foreigners to him. Because we have been reconciled to God, we have the privilege of encouraging others to do the same, and thus we are those who have the "task of reconciling people to him."

**5:20** An ambassador is an official representative of one country to another. As believers, we are Christ's ambassadors, sent with his message of reconciliation to the world. An ambassador of reconciliation has an important responsibility. We dare not take this responsibility lightly. How well are you fulfilling your commission as Christ's ambassador?

**5:21** When we trust in Christ, we make an exchange: He takes our sin and makes us right with God. Our sin was laid on Christ at his crucifixion. His righteousness is given to us at our conversion. This is what Christians mean by Christ's atonement for sin. In the world, bartering works only when two people exchange goods of relatively equal value. But God offers to trade his righteousness for our sin—something of immeasurable worth for something completely worthless. How grateful we should be for his kindness to us.

**6:1** How could the Corinthian believers ignore God's message? Perhaps they were doubting Paul and his words, confused by the false teachers, who taught a different message. The people heard God's message but did not let it affect what they said and did. How often do you ignore God's message?

**6:2** God offers salvation to all people. Many people put off a

"At just the right time, I heard you.
    On the day of salvation, I helped you."*

Indeed, the "right time" is now. Today is the day of salvation.

## Paul's Hardships

3 We live in such a way that no one will stumble because of us, and no one will find fault with our ministry. 4 In everything we do, we show that we are true ministers of God. We patiently endure troubles and hardships and calamities of every kind. 5 We have been beaten, been put in prison, faced angry mobs, worked to exhaustion, endured sleepless nights, and gone without food. 6 We prove ourselves by our purity, our understanding, our patience, our kindness, by the Holy Spirit within us,* and by our sincere love. 7 We faithfully preach the truth. God's power is working in us. We use the weapons of righteousness in the right hand for attack and the left hand for defense. 8 We serve God whether people honor us or despise us, whether they slander us or praise us. We are honest, but they call us impostors. 9 We are ignored, even though we are well known. We live close to death, but we are still alive. We have been beaten, but we have not been killed. 10 Our hearts ache, but we always have joy. We are poor, but we give spiritual riches to others. We own nothing, and yet we have everything.

11 Oh, dear Corinthian friends! We have spoken honestly with you, and our hearts are open to you. 12 There is no lack of love on our part, but you have withheld your love from us. 13 I am asking you to respond as if you were my own children. Open your hearts to us!

## The Temple of the Living God

14 Don't team up with those who are unbelievers. How can righteousness be a partner with wickedness? How can light live with darkness? 15 What harmony can there be between Christ and the devil*? How can a believer be a partner with an unbeliever? 16 And what union can there be between God's temple and idols? For we are the temple of the living God. As God said:

**6:3**
1 Cor 8:9; 9:12

**6:4**
2 Cor 4:2

**6:5**
2 Cor 11:23-27

**6:6**
1 Tim 4:12

**6:7**
1 Cor 2:4
2 Cor 10:4

**6:8**
Matt 27:63
1 Cor 4:10, 13

**6:9**
Ps 118:18
2 Cor 1:8-10;
4:10-11

**6:10**
Acts 3:6
Rom 8:32
1 Cor 3:21
2 Cor 8:9

**6:11**
2 Cor 7:3

**6:14**
Eph 5:7, 11
1 Jn 1:6

**6:16**
†Lev 26:12
†Jer 32:38
Ezek 37:27

6:2 Isa 49:8 (Greek version).   6:6 Or *by our holiness of spirit.*   6:15 Greek *Beliar;* various other manuscripts render this proper name of the devil as *Belian, Beliab,* or *Belial.*

---

decision for Christ, thinking that there will be a better time—but they could easily miss their opportunity altogether. There is no time like the present to receive God's forgiveness. Don't let anything hold you back from coming to Christ. The right time is now!

**6:3** In everything he did, Paul always considered what his actions communicated about Jesus Christ. If you are a believer, you are a minister for God. In the course of each day, unbelievers observe you. Don't let your careless or undisciplined actions be some person's excuse for rejecting Christ.

**6:5** Being put in jail would cause many people to become bitter or to give up, but Paul saw jail time as one more opportunity to spread the Good News of Christ. Paul realized that his current circumstances weren't as important as what he did with them. Turning a bad situation into a good one, he reached out to the Roman soldiers who made up the palace guard and encouraged Christians who were afraid of persecution. We may not be in prison, but we still have plenty of opportunities to be discouraged—times of indecision, financial burdens, family conflict, church conflict, or the loss of our jobs. How we act in such situations will reflect what we believe. Like Paul, look for ways to demonstrate your faith even in bad situations. Whether or not the situation improves, your faith will grow stronger.

**6:8-10** What a difference it makes to know Jesus! He cares for us in spite of what the world thinks. Christians don't have to give in to public opinion and pressure. Paul stood faithful to God whether people praised him or slandered him. He remained joyous and content in the most difficult hardships. Don't let circumstances or people's expectations control you. Be firm as you stand true to God, and refuse to compromise his standards for living.

**6:11-13** "Our hearts are open to you" means that Paul had told the Corinthian believers his true feelings for them, clearly revealing how much he loved them. The Corinthians were reacting coldly to Paul's words, but Paul explained that his harsh words came from his love for them. It is easy to react against those

whom God has placed over us in leadership, rather than to accept their exhortations as a sign of their love for us. We need an open rather than a closed heart toward God's messengers.

**6:14-18** Paul urges believers to not "team up," that is, form partnerships with unbelievers because this might weaken their Christian commitment, integrity, or standards. It would be a mismatch. Earlier, Paul had explained that this did not mean isolating oneself from unbelievers (see 1 Corinthians 5:9, 10). Paul even urges Christians to stay with their unbelieving spouses (1 Corinthians 7:12, 13). He wanted believers to be active in their witness for Christ to unbelievers but not lock themselves into personal or business relationships that could cause them to compromise their faith. Believers should do everything in their power to avoid situations that could force them to divide their loyalties.

These verses also have strong application to marriage. Paul did not want single believers to enter into marriage with unbelievers. Such marriages cannot have unity in the most important issue in life—commitment and obedience to God. Because marriage involves two people becoming one, faith may become an issue, and one spouse may have to compromise beliefs for the sake of unity. Many people discount this problem only to regret it later. Don't allow emotion or passion to bind you with someone who will not be your spiritual partner. For those who have discovered God's light, there can be no fellowship or compromise with darkness (1 Corinthians 10:20, 21).

**6:16** Quoting from the prophet Isaiah, Paul asserted that the church is the temple of the living God. Corinth had an abundance of temples of pagan deities, so the recipients of his letter were able to visualize the contrast the apostle intended. Those who follow Christ are not known by a building; they are known as those in whom the Spirit of God lives. The church is not where believers go, it is who they are. God is not waiting for his people in some stained-glass setting. He is always with them. That is a sobering and yet a comforting thought. How does your behavior reflect on the God you represent?

"I will live in them
and walk among them.
I will be their God,
and they will be my people.*
¹⁷ Therefore, come out from among unbelievers,
and separate yourselves from them, says the LORD.
Don't touch their filthy things,
and I will welcome you.*
¹⁸ And I will be your Father,
and you will be my sons and daughters,
says the LORD Almighty.*"

**6:17**
†Isa 52:11
Ezek 20:34

**6:18**
†2 Sam 7:8, 14
Isa 43:6
Jer 31:9

**7:1**
1 Pet 1:15-16

**7** Because we have these promises, dear friends, let us cleanse ourselves from everything that can defile our body or spirit. And let us work toward complete holiness because we fear God. ²Please open your hearts to us. We have not done wrong to anyone, nor led anyone astray, nor taken advantage of anyone. ³I'm not saying this to condemn you. I said before that you are in our hearts, and we live or die together with you. ⁴I have the highest confidence in you, and I take great pride in you. You have greatly encouraged me and made me happy despite all our troubles.

**7:2**
2 Cor 6:12-13
**7:3**
2 Cor 6:11-12
Phil 1:7
**7:4**
2 Cor 8:24

*Paul's Joy at the Church's Repentance*
⁵When we arrived in Macedonia, there was no rest for us. We faced conflict from every direction, with battles on the outside and fear on the inside. ⁶But God, who encourages those who are discouraged, encouraged us by the arrival of Titus. ⁷His presence was a joy, but so was the news he brought of the encouragement he received from you. When he told us how much you long to see me, and how sorry you are for what happened, and how loyal you are to me, I was filled with joy!

**7:5**
2 Cor 2:13; 4:8
**7:6**
Isa 49:13
2 Cor 1:3-4; 2:13

⁸I am not sorry that I sent that severe letter to you, though I was sorry at first, for I know it was painful to you for a little while. ⁹Now I am glad I sent it, not because it hurt you, but because the pain caused you to repent and change your ways. It was the kind of sorrow God wants his people to have, so you were not harmed by us in any way. ¹⁰For the kind of sorrow God wants us to experience leads us away from sin and results in salvation. There's no regret for that kind of sorrow. But worldly sorrow, which lacks repentance, results in spiritual death.

**7:8**
2 Cor 2:2-4

**7:10**
Matt 27:3-5

**6:16** Lev 26:12; Ezek 37:27.   **6:17** Isa 52:11; Ezek 20:34 (Greek version).   **6:18** 2 Sam 7:14.

**6:17** Separation from the world involves more than keeping our distance from sinful practices; it means staying close to God. It involves more than avoiding worldly entertainment; it extends to how we spend our time and money. There is no way to separate ourselves totally from all sinful influences. Nevertheless, we are to resist the sin around us, without either giving up or giving in. When you know what God wants you to do, make a clean break with sinful practices.

**7:1** Cleansing is a twofold action: turning *away* from sin, and turning *toward* God. The Corinthians were to have nothing to do with paganism. They were to make a clean break with their past and give themselves to God alone. "Work toward complete holiness" literally means "perfecting holiness." It connotes becoming mature or complete. Thus, Paul wasn't suggesting that the Corinthians could become sinless in this life. Instead, he was prodding them to work at maturing in their faith. God had provided them with all the resources they needed, and Christ's Spirit would empower them to become Christlike (Romans 8:2).

**7:2** Paul insisted that the Corinthians should open their hearts for him. He knew how much those in the church need one another. If fellowship was necessary in Paul's day, it is all the more crucial today, when time is more valuable than money. Each day holds barely enough time to care for personal and family needs, let alone to meet the needs of others. Yet the activities that occupy our time are not as important as the community described in these verses. Paul's intention is not "coffee and donuts between church" fellow-

ship. Believers need accountability that comes from lives intertwined by the cords of commitment and love. If you are not in a small group Bible study, take the first steps. Offer hospitality to fellow believers; when others extend the hand of fellowship to you, grasp it enthusiastically.

**7:5** Here Paul resumed the story that he left in 2:13, where he said he went to Macedonia to look for Titus. Though Paul still had many problems and hardships to face, he still found comfort and joy in the progress of the ministry.

**7:8ff** "That severe letter" refers to the third letter (now lost) that Paul had written to the Corinthians. Apparently it had caused the people to begin to change. For an explanation of the chronology of Paul's letters to Corinth, see the first note on 1:1.

**7:10** Sorrow for our sins can result in changed behavior. Many people are sorry only for the effects of their sins or for being caught (sorrow "which lacks repentance"). Compare Peter's remorse and repentance with Judas's bitterness and act of suicide. Both denied Christ. One repented and was restored to faith and service; the other took his own life.

¹¹Just see what this godly sorrow produced in you! Such earnestness, such concern to clear yourselves, such indignation, such alarm, such longing to see me, such zeal, and such a readiness to punish wrong. You showed that you have done everything necessary to make things right. ¹²My purpose, then, was not to write about who did the wrong or who was wronged. I wrote to you so that in the sight of God you could see for yourselves how loyal you are to us. ¹³We have been greatly encouraged by this.

In addition to our own encouragement, we were especially delighted to see how happy Titus was about the way all of you welcomed him and set his mind* at ease. ¹⁴I had told him how proud I was of you—and you didn't disappoint me. I have always told you the truth, and now my boasting to Titus has also proved true! ¹⁵Now he cares for you more than ever when he remembers the way all of you obeyed him and welcomed him with such fear and deep respect. ¹⁶I am very happy now because I have complete confidence in you.

**7:12**
1 Cor 5:1-2
2 Cor 2:3, 9
**7:13**
2 Cor 2:13
**7:15**
Phil 2:12
**7:16**
2 Cor 2:3
2 Thes 3:4
Phlm 1:21

### 3. Paul defends the collection
*A Call to Generous Giving*

**8** Now I want you to know, dear brothers and sisters,* what God in his kindness has done through the churches in Macedonia. ²They are being tested by many troubles, and they are very poor. But they are also filled with abundant joy, which has overflowed in rich generosity.

³For I can testify that they gave not only what they could afford, but far more. And they did it of their own free will. ⁴They begged us again and again for the privilege of sharing in the gift for the believers* in Jerusalem. ⁵They even did more than we had hoped, for their first action was to give themselves to the Lord and to us, just as God wanted them to do.

⁶So we have urged Titus, who encouraged your giving in the first place, to return to you and encourage you to finish this ministry of giving. ⁷Since you excel in so many ways—in your faith, your gifted speakers, your knowledge, your enthusiasm, and your love from us*—I want you to excel also in this gracious act of giving.

⁸I am not commanding you to do this. But I am testing how genuine your love is by comparing it with the eagerness of the other churches.

⁹You know the generous grace of our Lord Jesus Christ. Though he was rich, yet for your sakes he became poor, so that by his poverty he could make you rich.

**8:1**
Acts 16:9
**8:2**
2 Cor 9:11
**8:4**
Acts 24:17
Rom 15:26
1 Cor 16:1, 3
**8:6**
2 Cor 12:13, 18
**8:7**
1 Cor 1:5; 16:1-2
2 Cor 9:8
**8:9**
Matt 8:20
Phil 2:6-7

**7:13** Greek *his spirit.* **8:1** Greek *brothers.* **8:4** Greek *for God's holy people.* **8:7** Some manuscripts read *your love for us.*

---

**7:11** Paul affirmed the Corinthians for their right response to the correction he had given them. It's difficult to accept criticism, correction, or rebuke with poise and grace. It is much more natural to be defensive and then counterattack. We can accept criticism with self-pity, thinking we don't really deserve it. We can be angry and resentful. But a mature Christian should graciously accept constructive criticism, sincerely evaluate it, and grow from it.

**8:1ff** Paul, writing from Macedonia, hoped that news of the generosity of these churches would encourage the Corinthian believers and motivate them to solve their problems and unite in fellowship.

**8:2-5** During his third missionary journey, Paul had collected money for the impoverished believers in Jerusalem. The churches in Macedonia—Philippi, Thessalonica, and Berea—had given money even though they were poor, and they had sacrificially given more than Paul expected. Although they were poor themselves, they wanted to help. The amount we give is not as important as why and how we give. God does not want us to give grudgingly. Instead, he wants us to give as these churches did—out of dedication to Christ, love for fellow believers, the joy of helping those in need, as well as the fact that it was simply the good and right thing to do. How well does your giving measure up to the standards set by the Macedonian churches?

**8:3-6** The Kingdom of God spreads through believers' concern and eagerness to help others. Here we see several churches joining to help others beyond their own circle of friends and their own city. Explore ways that you might link up with a ministry

outside your city, either through your church or through a Christian organization. By joining with other believers to do God's work, you increase Christian unity and help the Kingdom grow.

**8:7, 8** The Corinthian believers excelled in everything—they had faith, gifted speakers, knowledge, enthusiasm, and love. Paul encouraged them to also excel in the grace of giving. Too often, stewardship of money is given a different status than other aspects of discipleship. Most believers would not want growth in faith, knowledge, or love to stop at a certain level. Yet many decide a fixed percentage of their money to give and stay there for life. True discipleship includes growing in the mature use of all resources, so giving should expand as well. God can give you the desire and enable you to increase your capacity to give. Don't miss this opportunity for growth.

**8:9** There is no evidence that Jesus was any poorer than most first-century Palestinians; rather, Jesus became poor by giving up his rights as God and becoming human. In his incarnation, God voluntarily became man—the person Jesus of Nazareth. As a man, Jesus was subject to place, time, and other human limitations. He did not give up his eternal power when he became human, but he did set aside his glory and his rights (see the note on Philippians 2:5-7). In response to the Father's will, he limited his power and knowledge. Christ became "poor" when he became human because he set aside so much. Yet by doing so, he made us "rich" because we received salvation and eternal life.

What made Jesus' humanity unique was his freedom from sin. In Jesus we can see every attribute of God's character. The Incarnation is explained further in these Bible passages: John 1:1-14; Romans 1:2-5; Philippians 2:6-11; 1 Timothy 3:16; Hebrews 2:14; 1 John 1:1-3.

**8:10**
2 Cor 9:2

**8:12**
Prov 3:27-28
Mark 12:43-44
2 Cor 9:7

**8:14**
Acts 4:34
2 Cor 9:12

**8:15**
†Exod 16:18

10Here is my advice: It would be good for you to finish what you started a year ago. Last year you were the first who wanted to give, and you were the first to begin doing it. 11Now you should finish what you started. Let the eagerness you showed in the beginning be matched now by your giving. Give in proportion to what you have. 12Whatever you give is acceptable if you give it eagerly. And give according to what you have, not what you don't have. 13Of course, I don't mean your giving should make life easy for others and hard for yourselves. I only mean that there should be some equality. 14Right now you have plenty and can help those who are in need. Later, they will have plenty and can share with you when you need it. In this way, things will be equal. 15As the Scriptures say,

"Those who gathered a lot had nothing left over,
 and those who gathered only a little had enough."*

### Titus and His Companions

**8:16**
2 Cor 2:14

**8:18**
2 Cor 12:18

**8:19**
Acts 14:23
1 Cor 16:3-4

16But thank God! He has given Titus the same enthusiasm for you that I have. 17Titus welcomed our request that he visit you again. In fact, he himself was very eager to go and see you. 18We are also sending another brother with Titus. All the churches praise him as a preacher of the Good News. 19He was appointed by the churches to accompany us as we take the offering to Jerusalem*—a service that glorifies the Lord and shows our eagerness to help.

**8:21**
Prov 3:4
Rom 12:17

20We are traveling together to guard against any criticism for the way we are handling this generous gift. 21We are careful to be honorable before the Lord, but we also want everyone else to see that we are honorable.

22We are also sending with them another of our brothers who has proven himself many

**8:15** Exod 16:18. **8:19** See 1 Cor 16:3-4.

---

| **PRINCIPLES OF CONFRONTATION IN 2 CORINTHIANS** | Method | Reference |
|---|---|---|
| | Be firm and bold . . . . . . . . . . . . . . . . . . . . . . . . . . . . . . . . . . . . . . . . . . . . | 7:9; 10:2 |
| | Affirm all you see that is good . . . . . . . . . . . . . . . . . . . . . . . . . . . . . . | 7:4 |
| | Be accurate and honest . . . . . . . . . . . . . . . . . . . . . . . . . . . . . . . . . . . . | 7:14; 8:21 |
| | Know the facts . . . . . . . . . . . . . . . . . . . . . . . . . . . . . . . . . . . . . . . . . . . . | 11:22-27 |
| | Follow up after the confrontation . . . . . . . . . . . . . . . . . . . . . . . . . . . . | 7:13; 12:14 |
| | Be gentle after being firm . . . . . . . . . . . . . . . . . . . . . . . . . . . . . . . . . . | 7:15; 13:11-13 |
| | Speak words that reflect Christ's message, not your own ideas . . . . . . . | 10:3; 10:12, 13; 12:19 |
| | Use discipline only when all else fails. . . . . . . . . . . . . . . . . . . . . . . . . . | 13:2 |

Sometimes rebuke is necessary, but it must be used with caution. The purpose of any rebuke, confrontation, or discipline is to help people, not hurt them.

---

**8:10-15** The Christians in the Corinthian church had money, and apparently they had planned to collect money for the Jerusalem church a year previously (see also 9:2). Paul challenges them to act on their plans. Four principles of giving emerge here: (1) Your willingness to give enthusiastically is more important than the amount you give; (2) you should strive to fulfill your financial commitments; (3) if you give to others in need, they will, in turn, help you when you are in need; (4) you should give as a response to Christ, not for anything you can get out of it. How you give reflects your devotion to Christ.

**8:12** How do you decide how much to give? What about differences in the financial resources Christians have? Paul gives the Corinthian church several principles to follow: (1) Each person should follow through on previous promises (8:10, 11; 9:3); (2) each person should give as much as he or she is able (8:12; 9:6); (3) each person must make up his or her own mind how much to give (9:7); and (4) each person should give in proportion to what God has given him or her (9:10). God gives to us so that we can give to others.

**8:12** Paul says that we should give of what we have, not what we don't have. Sacrificial giving must be responsible. Paul wants believers to give generously, but not to the extent that those who

depend on the givers (their families, for example) must go without having their basic needs met. Give until it hurts, but don't give so that it hurts your family and/or relatives who need your financial support.

**8:18-21** "Another brother" was traveling with Paul and Titus, a man who was elected by the churches to also take the large financial gift to Jerusalem. Paul explained that by traveling together there could be no suspicion and people would know that the gift was being handled honestly. The church did not need to worry that the bearers of the collection would misuse the money.

Paul used every safeguard to maintain integrity in the collection of money for the Jerusalem church. Those outside the church can view skeptically the way believers handle money in the church. Financial scandals among high-profile ministries have alerted the non-believing world to the unethical gimmicks that some Christians use. It is possible to avoid mismanagement of God's resources. Does your church or organization have a system of checks and balances that prevent wrongful behavior? Are there financial practices in your ministry that need to be reviewed? Christians must have the highest standard of financial responsibility.

times and has shown on many occasions how eager he is. He is now even more enthusiastic because of his great confidence in you. 23If anyone asks about Titus, say that he is my partner who works with me to help you. And the brothers with him have been sent by the churches,* and they bring honor to Christ. 24So show them your love, and prove to all the churches that our boasting about you is justified.

**8:23**
Phil 2:25
**8:24**
2 Cor 7:4

### The Collection for Christians in Jerusalem

**9** I really don't need to write to you about this ministry of giving for the believers in Jerusalem.* 2For I know how eager you are to help, and I have been boasting to the churches in Macedonia that you in Greece* were ready to send an offering a year ago. In fact, it was your enthusiasm that stirred up many of the Macedonian believers to begin giving.

**9:1**
Acts 24:17
2 Cor 8:4, 20
**9:2**
2 Cor 8:11-12, 19

3But I am sending these brothers to be sure you really are ready, as I have been telling them, and that your money is all collected. I don't want to be wrong in my boasting about you. 4We would be embarrassed—not to mention your own embarrassment—if some Macedonian believers came with me and found that you weren't ready after all I had told them! 5So I thought I should send these brothers ahead of me to make sure the gift you promised is ready. But I want it to be a willing gift, not one given grudgingly.

**9:3**
1 Cor 16:2
2 Cor 8:23

**9:5**
Phil 4:17

6Remember this—a farmer who plants only a few seeds will get a small crop. But the one who plants generously will get a generous crop. 7You must each decide in your heart how much to give. And don't give reluctantly or in response to pressure. "For God loves a person who gives cheerfully."* 8And God will generously provide all you need. Then you will always have everything you need and plenty left over to share with others. 9As the Scriptures say,

**9:6**
Prov 11:24-25; 22:9
Gal 6:7, 9
**9:7**
Exod 25:2
Deut 15:7-10
2 Cor 8:12
**9:8**
Phil 4:19

"They share freely and give generously to the poor.
    Their good deeds will be remembered forever."*

**9:9**
†Ps 112:9

10For God is the one who provides seed for the farmer and then bread to eat. In the same way, he will provide and increase your resources and then produce a great harvest of generosity* in you.

**9:10**
Isa 55:10
Hos 10:12

11Yes, you will be enriched in every way so that you can always be generous. And when we take your gifts to those who need them, they will thank God. 12So two good things will result from this ministry of giving—the needs of the believers in Jerusalem* will be met, and they will joyfully express their thanks to God.

**9:11**
2 Cor 1:11; 4:15
**9:12**
2 Cor 8:14

13As a result of your ministry, they will give glory to God. For your generosity to them and to all believers will prove that you are obedient to the Good News of Christ. 14And they will pray for you with deep affection because of the overflowing grace God has given to you. 15Thank God for this gift* too wonderful for words!

**8:23** Greek *are apostles of the churches.*  **9:1** Greek *about the offering for God's holy people.*  **9:2** Greek *in Achaia, the southern region of the Greek peninsula. Macedonia was in the northern region of Greece.*  **9:7** See footnote on Prov 22:8.  **9:9** Ps 112:9.  **9:10** Greek *righteousness.*  **9:12** Greek *of God's holy people.*  **9:15** Greek *his gift.*

---

**9:1, 2** By describing how their own "enthusiasm" had incited the Macedonians to give, Paul was, in effect, prodding the Corinthians to rekindle their initial enthusiasm for giving. Paul wasn't naive about human behavior. The start and end of a marathon are much more thrilling than the miles in between. It takes stubborn determination to keep going. Paul also knew that it took a community to persevere. Just as teammates will cheer their runner on in a race, so Paul was sending Titus and two other believers to the Corinthians to cheer them on.

**9:3-5** Paul reminded the Corinthians to fulfill the commitment that they had already made (see also 8:10-12). They had said that they would collect a financial gift to send to the church in Jerusalem. Paul was sending a few men ahead of him to make sure their gift was ready, so it would be a real gift and not look like people had to give under pressure at the last minute. He was holding them accountable to keep their promise, so that neither Paul nor the Corinthians would be embarrassed.

**9:6-8** People may hesitate to give generously to God because they worry about having enough money left over to meet their own needs. Paul assured the Corinthians that God was able to meet their needs. The person who gives only a little will receive only a little in return. Don't let a lack of faith keep you from giving cheerfully and generously.

**9:7** A giving attitude is more important than the amount given. The person who can give only a small gift shouldn't be embarrassed. God is concerned about *how* a person gives from his or her resources (see Mark 12:41-44). According to that standard, the giving of the Macedonian churches would be difficult to match (8:3). God himself is a cheerful giver. Consider all he has done for us. He is pleased when we who are created in his image give generously and joyfully. Do you have a difficult time letting go of your money? It may reflect ungratefulness to God.

**9:10** God gives us resources to use and invest for him. Paul uses the illustration of seed to explain that the resources God gives us are not to be hidden, foolishly devoured, or thrown away. Instead, they should be cultivated in order to produce more crops. When we invest what God has given us in his work, he will provide us with even more to give in his service.

**9:13** Paul wanted his readers to be generous on every occasion. As he appealed to the Corinthians to give sacrificially to aid the Jerusalem congregation, he reminded them that God is the source of everything good (9:10). Believers are called to be generous because of the example of the Lord of life. A stingy Christian

## 4. Paul defends his authority

**10** Now I, Paul, appeal to you with the gentleness and kindness of Christ—though I realize you think I am timid in person and bold only when I write from far away. 2 Well, I am begging you now so that when I come I won't have to be bold with those who think we act from human motives.

3 We are human, but we don't wage war as humans do. 4*We use God's mighty weapons, not worldly weapons, to knock down the strongholds of human reasoning and to destroy false arguments. 5 We destroy every proud obstacle that keeps people from knowing God. We capture their rebellious thoughts and teach them to obey Christ. 6 And after you have become fully obedient, we will punish everyone who remains disobedient.

7 Look at the obvious facts.* Those who say they belong to Christ must recognize that we belong to Christ as much as they do. 8 I may seem to be boasting too much about the authority given to us by the Lord. But our authority builds you up; it doesn't tear you down. So I will not be ashamed of using my authority.

9 I'm not trying to frighten you by my letters. 10 For some say, "Paul's letters are demanding and forceful, but in person he is weak, and his speeches are worthless!" 11 Those people should realize that our actions when we arrive in person will be as forceful as what we say in our letters from far away.

12 Oh, don't worry; we wouldn't dare say that we are as wonderful as these other men who tell you how important they are! But they are only comparing themselves with each other, using themselves as the standard of measurement. How ignorant!

**10:4** English translations divide verses 4 and 5 in various ways.    **10:7** Or *You look at things only on the basis of appearance.*

---

**RAISING FUNDS HONORABLY**

| | | |
|---|---|---|
| Be dedicated to God . . . . . . . . . . 8:5 | Be accountable . . . . . . . . . . . . . . . . . 9:3 |
| Provide information . . . . . . . . . . . . 8:4 | Let people give willingly . . . . . . . . . . . 9:7 |
| Show definite purpose and goal . . 8:4 | Be generous yourselves. . . . . . . . . . . 8:7 |
| Be enthusiastic . . . . . . . . . . . . . . 8:7, 8, 11 | Have someone to keep it moving . . . . . 8:18-22 |
| Reveal honesty and integrity . . . . . 8:21 | Be persistent, trusting God to provide . . 8:2ff |

The topic of fund-raising is not one to be avoided or one that should embarrass us, but all fund-raising efforts should be planned and conducted responsibly.

---

should be an extinct species. Generosity proves that a person's heart has been cleansed of self-interest and filled with the servant spirit of Jesus himself. That is why acts of generosity result in God being praised. Do neighbors see generosity in your actions?

**10:1, 2** Paul's opponents questioned his authority. From 7:8-16 we know that the majority of Corinthian believers sided with Paul. However, a minority continued to slander him, saying that he was bold in his letters but had no authority in person. Chapters 10–13 are Paul's response to this charge.

**10:3-6** We, like Paul, are merely weak humans, but we don't need to use human plans and methods to win our battles. God's mighty weapons are available to us as we fight against the devil's "strongholds." The Christian must choose whose methods to use—God's or the world's. Paul assures us that God's mighty weapons—prayer, faith, hope, love, God's Word, the Holy Spirit—are powerful and effective (see Ephesians 6:13-18)! These weapons can break down the proud human arguments against God and the walls that Satan builds to keep people from finding God. When dealing with people's proud arguments that keep them from a relationship with Christ, we may be tempted to use our own methods. But nothing can break down these barriers like God's weapons.

**10:5** Paul uses military terminology to describe this warfare against sin and Satan. God must be the commander in chief—even our thoughts must be submitted to his control as we live for him. Spirit-empowered believers must capture every thought and yield it to Christ. When exposed to ideas or opportunities that might lead to wrong desires, you have a choice. You can recognize the danger and turn away, or you can allow unhealthy thoughts to take you captive. You capture your fantasies and

desires when you honestly admit them to the Lord and ask him to redirect your thinking. Ask God to give you the spirit of discernment to keep your thoughts focused on his truth.

**10:7-10** Those who opposed Paul portrayed him as weak and powerless, but Paul reminded the Corinthians that he had been given authority by the Lord. False teachers were encouraging the believers to ignore Paul, but Paul explained that the advice in his letters was to be taken seriously. He had authority because he and his companions had been the first to bring the Good News to Corinth (10:14). Everyone knew that because of this service, their faith had been built up.

**10:10** Some said that Paul's speaking amounted to nothing. Greece was known for its eloquent and persuasive orators. Evidently, some were judging Paul by comparing him to other speakers they had heard, and Paul was perhaps not the most powerful preacher (although he was an excellent debater). But Paul responded obediently to God's call and thus introduced Christianity to the Roman Empire. Moses and Jeremiah also had problems with speaking (see Exodus 4:10-12; Jeremiah 1:6). Preaching ability is not the first prerequisite of a great leader!

**10:12, 13** Paul criticized the false teachers who were trying to prove their goodness by comparing themselves with others rather than with God's standards. When we compare ourselves with others, we may feel proud because we think we're better. But when we measure ourselves against God's standards, it becomes obvious that we have no basis for pride. Don't worry about other people's accomplishments. Instead, ask yourself: How does my life measure up to what God wants? How does my life compare to that of Jesus Christ?

13 We will not boast about things done outside our area of authority. We will boast only about what has happened within the boundaries of the work God has given us, which includes our working with you. 14 We are not reaching beyond these boundaries when we claim authority over you, as if we had never visited you. For we were the first to travel all the way to Corinth with the Good News of Christ.

15 Nor do we boast and claim credit for the work someone else has done. Instead, we hope that your faith will grow so that the boundaries of our work among you will be extended. 16 Then we will be able to go and preach the Good News in other places far beyond you, where no one else is working. Then there will be no question of our boasting about work done in someone else's territory. 17 As the Scriptures say, "If you want to boast, boast only about the LORD."*

18 When people commend themselves, it doesn't count for much. The important thing is for the Lord to commend them.

### Paul and the False Apostles

**11** I hope you will put up with a little more of my foolishness. Please bear with me. 2 For I am jealous for you with the jealousy of God himself. I promised you as a pure bride* to one husband—Christ. 3 But I fear that somehow your pure and undivided devotion to Christ will be corrupted, just as Eve was deceived by the cunning ways of the serpent. 4 You happily put up with whatever anyone tells you, even if they preach a different Jesus than the one we preach, or a different kind of Spirit than the one you received, or a different kind of gospel than the one you believed.

5 But I don't consider myself inferior in any way to these "super apostles" who teach such things. 6 I may be unskilled as a speaker, but I'm not lacking in knowledge. We have made this clear to you in every possible way.

7 Was I wrong when I humbled myself and honored you by preaching God's Good News to you without expecting anything in return? 8 I "robbed" other churches by accepting their contributions so I could serve you at no cost. 9 And when I was with you and didn't have enough to live on, I did not become a financial burden to anyone. For the brothers who came

10:13 Rom 12:3
10:14 1 Cor 9:1
10:15 Rom 15:20; 2 Thes 1:3
10:16 Acts 19:21
10:17 †Jer 9:24; 1 Cor 1:31
10:18 Prov 27:2
11:2 Hos 2:19; Eph 5:26-27
11:3 Gen 3:1-6, 13; John 8:44; 1 Tim 2:14
11:4 Rom 8:15; Gal 1:6-8
11:5 Gal 2:6
11:6 1 Cor 1:17; Eph 3:4
11:7 1 Cor 9:12, 18; 2 Cor 12:13
11:9 2 Cor 12:13

10:17 Jer 9:24.   11:2 Greek *a virgin.*

---

**10:17, 18** When we do something well, we want to tell others and be recognized. But recognition is dangerous—it can lead to inflated pride. How much better it is to seek the praise of God rather than the praise of people. Then, when we receive praise, we will be free to give God the credit. What should you change about the way you live in order to receive God's commendation?

**11:1** Paul asked the Corinthian believers to bear with him as he talked more "foolishness." In other words, Paul felt foolish rehearsing his credentials as a preacher of the Good News (11:16-21). But he thought that he had to do this in order to silence the false teachers (11:13).

**11:2** Paul was anxious that the church's love should be for Christ alone, just as a pure bride saves her love for one man only. By "pure bride" he meant one who was unaffected by false doctrine.

**11:3** The Corinthians' pure and simple devotion to Christ was being threatened by false teaching. Paul did not want the believers to lose their single-minded love for Christ. Keeping Christ first in your life can be very difficult when you have so many distractions threatening to sidetrack your faith. Just as Eve lost her focus by listening to the serpent, you, too, can lose your focus by letting your life become overcrowded and confused. Is there anything that weakens your commitment to keep Christ first in your life? How can you minimize the distractions that threaten your devotion to him?

**11:4** The Corinthian believers were falling for smooth talk and messages that sounded good and seemed to make sense. Today there are many false teachings that seem to make sense. Don't believe someone simply because he or she sounds like an authority or says words you like to hear. Search the Bible and check his or her teachings against God's Word. The Bible should be your authoritative guide. The false teachers distorted the truth about Jesus and ended up preaching a different Jesus, a different spirit than the Holy Spirit, and a different way of salvation. Those who

teach anything different from what God's infallible Word says are both mistaken and misleading.

**11:5** Paul was saying that these marvelous teachers ("super apostles") were no better than he was. They may have been more eloquent speakers, but they spoke lies and were servants of Satan.

**11:6** Paul, a brilliant thinker, was not a trained, eloquent speaker. Although his ministry was effective (see Acts 17), he had not been trained in the Greek schools of oratory and speechmaking, as many of the false teachers probably had been. Paul believed in a simple presentation of the Good News (see 1 Corinthians 1:17), and some people thought this showed simple-mindedness. Thus, Paul's speaking performance was often used against him by false teachers.

Content is far more important than the presentation. A simple, clear presentation that helps listeners understand will be of great value. God's Word stands on its own merit and is not dependent on imperfect human beings to create its own hearing. Many people feel that if they can't sing, speak, teach, or preach as well as their idolized heroes, they are insecure about saying or doing anything. Don't apologize for your inadequacies. Accept your limitations with the same humility that you accept the strengths God has given you.

**11:7** The Corinthians may have thought that preachers could be judged by how much money they demanded. A good speaker would charge a large sum, a fair speaker would be a little cheaper, and a poor speaker would speak for free. The false teachers may have argued that because Paul asked no fee for his preaching, he must have been an amateur, with little authority or competence. Believers today must be careful not to assume that every preacher or evangelist who is well known or who demands a large honorarium necessarily teaches the truth.

**11:7-12** Paul could have asked the Corinthian church for financial support. Jesus himself taught that those who minister for God should be supported by the people to whom they minister (Matthew 10:10). But Paul thought that asking for support in Corinth might from Macedonia brought me all that I needed. I have never been a burden to you, and I never will be. 10As surely as the truth of Christ is in me, no one in all of Greece* will ever stop me from boasting about this. 11Why? Because I don't love you? God knows that I do.

12But I will continue doing what I have always done. This will undercut those who are looking for an opportunity to boast that their work is just like ours. 13These people are false apostles. They are deceitful workers who disguise themselves as apostles of Christ. 14But I

**11:11**
2 Cor 7:3; 12:15
**11:12**
1 Cor 9:12
**11:13**
Rev 2:2

11:10 Greek *Achaia*, the southern region of the Greek peninsula.

---

**PAUL'S CREDENTIALS**
One of Paul's biggest problems with the church in Corinth was his concern that they viewed him as no more than a blustering preacher; thus, they were not taking seriously his advice in his letters and on his visits. Paul addressed this attitude in the letter of 2 Corinthians, pointing out his credentials as an apostle of Christ and why the Corinthians should take his advice.

| | |
|---|---|
| 1:1, 21; 4:1 | Commissioned by God |
| 1:12 | Acted in holiness, sincerity, and dependence on God alone in his dealings with them |
| 1:13, 14 | Was straightforward and sincere in his letters |
| 1:18; 4:2 | Spoke truthfully |
| 1:22 | Had God's Holy Spirit |
| 2:4; 6:11; 11:11 | Loved the Corinthian believers |
| 2:17 | Spoke with sincerity and Christ's authority |
| 3:2, 3 | Worked among them and changed their lives |
| 4:1, 16 | Did not give up |
| 4:2 | Taught the Bible with integrity |
| 4:5 | Had Christ as the center of his message |
| 4:8-12; 6:4, 5, 9, 10 | Endured persecution as he taught the Good News |
| 5:18-20 | Was Christ's ambassador, called to tell the Good News |
| 6:3, 4 | Tried to live an exemplary life so others would not be kept from God |
| 6:6 | Led a pure life, understood the gospel, and displayed patience with the Corinthians |
| 6:7 | Was truthful and filled with God's power |
| 6:8 | Stood true to God first and always |
| 7:2; 11:7-9 | Never led anyone astray or took advantage of anyone |
| 8:20, 21 | Handled their offering for the Jerusalem believers in a responsible, blameless manner |
| 10:1-6 | Used God's weapons, not his own, for God's work |
| 10:7, 8 | Was confident that he belonged to Christ |
| 10:12, 13 | Would boast not in himself but in the Lord |
| 10:14, 15 | Had authority because he taught them the Good News |
| 11:23-33 | Endured pain and danger as he fulfilled his calling |
| 12:2-4 | Was blessed with an astounding vision |
| 12:6 | Lived as an example to the believers |
| 12:7-10 | Was constantly humbled by a "thorn" in the flesh that God refused to take away |
| 12:12 | Did miracles among them |
| 12:19 | Was always motivated to strengthen others spiritually |
| 13:4 | Was filled with God's power |
| 13:5, 6 | Passed the test |
| 13:9 | Was always concerned that his spiritual children become mature believers |

---

be misunderstood. There were many false teachers who hoped to make a good profit from preaching (2:17), and Paul might look like one of them. Paul separated himself completely from those false teachers in order to silence those who only claimed to do God's work.

**11:14, 15** One Jewish writing (the Apocalypse of Moses) says that the story of Eve's temptation includes Satan masquerading as an angel. Paul may have been thinking of this story, or he could have been referring to Satan's typical devices. In either case, nothing could be more deceitful than Satan, the prince of darkness (Ephesians 6:12; Colossians 1:13), disguising himself as an angel of light. In the same way, these false apostles were pretending to be apostles of Christ, while in reality they were agents of Satan.

**11:14, 15** Satan and his servants can deceive us by appearing to be attractive, good, and moral. Many unsuspecting people follow smooth-talking, Bible-quoting leaders into cults that alienate them from their families and lead them into the practice of immorality and deceit. Don't be fooled by external appearances. Our impressions alone are not an accurate indicator of who is or isn't a true follower of Christ; so it helps to ask these questions: (1) Do the teachings confirm Scripture (Acts 17:11)? (2) Does the teacher affirm and proclaim that Jesus Christ is God, who came into the world as a man to save people from their sins (1 John 4:1-3)? (3) Is the teacher's lifestyle consistent with biblical morality (Matthew 12:33-37)?

am not surprised! Even Satan disguises himself as an angel of light. 15So it is no wonder that his servants also disguise themselves as servants of righteousness. In the end they will get the punishment their wicked deeds deserve.

### Paul's Many Trials

16Again I say, don't think that I am a fool to talk like this. But even if you do, listen to me, as you would to a foolish person, while I also boast a little. 17Such boasting is not from the Lord, but I am acting like a fool. 18And since others boast about their human achievements, I will, too. 19After all, you think you are so wise, but you enjoy putting up with fools! 20You put up with it when someone enslaves you, takes everything you have, takes advantage of you, takes control of everything, and slaps you in the face. 21I'm ashamed to say that we've been too "weak" to do that!

But whatever they dare to boast about—I'm talking like a fool again—I dare to boast about it, too. 22Are they Hebrews? So am I. Are they Israelites? So am I. Are they descendants of Abraham? So am I. 23Are they servants of Christ? I know I sound like a madman, but I have served him far more! I have worked harder, been put in prison more often, been whipped times without number, and faced death again and again. 24Five different times the Jewish leaders gave me thirty-nine lashes. 25Three times I was beaten with rods. Once I was stoned. Three times I was shipwrecked. Once I spent a whole night and a day adrift at sea. 26I have traveled on many long journeys. I have faced danger from rivers and from robbers. I have faced danger from my own people, the Jews, as well as from the Gentiles. I have faced danger in the cities, in the deserts, and on the seas. And I have faced danger from men who claim to be believers but are not.* 27I have worked hard and long, enduring many sleepless nights. I have been hungry and thirsty and have often gone without food. I have shivered in the cold, without enough clothing to keep me warm.

28Then, besides all this, I have the daily burden of my concern for all the churches. 29Who is weak without my feeling that weakness? Who is led astray, and I do not burn with anger?

30If I must boast, I would rather boast about the things that show how weak I am. 31God, the Father of our Lord Jesus, who is worthy of eternal praise, knows I am not lying. 32When I was in Damascus, the governor under King Aretas kept guards at the city gates to catch me. 33I had to be lowered in a basket through a window in the city wall to escape from him.

### Paul's Vision and His Thorn in the Flesh

**12** This boasting will do no good, but I must go on. I will reluctantly tell about visions and revelations from the Lord. 2I* was caught up to the third heaven fourteen years ago. Whether I was in my body or out of my body, I don't know—only God knows. 3Yes, only

11:15 Phil 3:19
11:16 2 Cor 12:6
11:18 Phil 3:3-4
11:20 Gal 2:4; 4:9
11:21 2 Cor 10:10
11:22 Rom 11:1; Phil 3:5
11:23 Rom 8:36; 1 Cor 15:10; 2 Cor 6:4-5
11:24 Deut 25:3
11:25 Acts 14:19; 16:22; 27:41
11:26 Acts 9:23; 14:5; 20:3; 21:31; Gal 2:4
11:27 1 Cor 4:11; 2 Cor 6:5
11:29 1 Cor 9:22
11:30 2 Cor 12:5
11:31 2 Cor 1:23
11:32-33 Acts 9:24-25
12:1 Gal 1:12

11:26 Greek *from false brothers.* 12:2 Greek *I know a man in Christ who.*

---

**11:15** Paul reminds the Corinthians that the false teachers and hypocritical leaders will one day "get the punishment their wicked deeds deserve." The principle of judgment applies to all who speak on God's behalf. The apostle James said that teachers will be judged by the Lord with closer scrutiny than will those who sit under their teaching (James 3:1). If it is not already your practice, each time you sit down with the Scriptures to prepare a lesson or a sermon, spend some quiet moments in prayer asking the Holy Spirit to guide your preparation.

**11:22, 23** Paul presented his credentials to counteract the charges that the false teachers were making against him. He felt foolish boasting like this, but his list of credentials would silence any doubts about his authority. Paul wanted to keep the Corinthians from slipping under the spell of the false teachers and turning away from the Good News. Paul also gave a list of his credentials in his letter to the Philippians (see Philippians 3:4-8).

**11:23-29** Paul was angry that the false teachers had impressed and deceived the Corinthians (11:13-15). Therefore, he had reestablished his credibility and authority by listing the trials he had endured in his service for Christ. Some of these trials are recorded in the book of Acts (Acts 14:19; 16:22-24). Because Paul wrote this letter during his third missionary journey (Acts 18:23–21:17), his trials weren't over. He would experience yet further difficulties and humiliations for the cause of Christ (see Acts 21:30-33; 22:24-30). Paul was sacrificing his life for the Good

News, something the false teachers would never do. The trials and hurts we experience for Christ's sake build our character, demonstrate our faith, and prepare us for further service to the Lord.

**11:25** Sea travel was not as safe as it is today. Paul had been shipwrecked three times, and he would face another accident on his voyage to Rome (see Acts 27). By this time, Paul had probably made at least eight or nine voyages.

**11:28, 29** Not only did Paul face beatings and dangers, he also carried the daily concern for the young churches, worrying that they were staying true to the Good News and free from false teachings and inner strife. Paul was concerned for individuals in the churches he served. If God has placed you in a position of leadership and authority, treat people with Paul's kind of empathy and concern.

**11:32, 33** King Aretas, king of the Nabateans (Edomites) from 9 B.C. to A.D. 40, had appointed a governor to oversee the Nabatean segment of the population in Damascus. Somehow the Jews in Damascus had been able to enlist this governor to help them try to capture Paul (see Acts 9:22-25). Paul gave a "for instance" here, describing his escape from Damascus in a basket lowered from a window in the city wall. Paul recounted this incident to show what he had endured for Christ. The false teachers couldn't make such claims.

**12:2, 3** Paul continued his "boasting" by telling about visions and revelations he had received from the Lord. Paul explained that

**12:4**
Luke 23:43
Rev 2:7

God knows whether I was in my body or outside my body. But I do know ⁴that I was caught up* to paradise and heard things so astounding that they cannot be expressed in words, things no human is allowed to tell.

**12:5**
2 Cor 11:30

**12:6**
2 Cor 10:8

**12:7**
Job 2:6

⁵That experience is worth boasting about, but I'm not going to do it. I will boast only about my weaknesses. ⁶If I wanted to boast, I would be no fool in doing so, because I would be telling the truth. But I won't do it, because I don't want anyone to give me credit beyond what they can see in my life or hear in my message, ⁷even though I have received such wonderful revelations from God. So to keep me from becoming proud, I was given a thorn in my flesh, a messenger from Satan to torment me and keep me from becoming proud.

**12:8**
Matt 26:39, 44

**12:9**
Phil 4:13

**12:10**
2 Cor 6:4; 13:4

⁸Three different times I begged the Lord to take it away. ⁹Each time he said, "My grace is all you need. My power works best in weakness." So now I am glad to boast about my weaknesses, so that the power of Christ can work through me. ¹⁰That's why I take pleasure in my weaknesses, and in the insults, hardships, persecutions, and troubles that I suffer for Christ. For when I am weak, then I am strong.

### Paul's Concern for the Corinthians

**12:11**
2 Cor 11:1, 5

**12:12**
Rom 15:19

**12:13**
1 Cor 9:12, 18
2 Cor 11:7

**12:14**
1 Cor 4:14-15
2 Cor 13:1

**12:15**
2 Cor 11:11
Phil 2:17
1 Thes 2:8

¹¹You have made me act like a fool—boasting like this.* You ought to be writing commendations for me, for I am not at all inferior to these "super apostles," even though I am nothing at all. ¹²When I was with you, I certainly gave you proof that I am an apostle. For I patiently did many signs and wonders and miracles among you. ¹³The only thing I failed to do, which I do in the other churches, was to become a financial burden to you. Please forgive me for this wrong!

¹⁴Now I am coming to you for the third time, and I will not be a burden to you. I don't want what you have—I want you. After all, children don't provide for their parents. Rather, parents provide for their children. ¹⁵I will gladly spend myself and all I have for you, even though it seems that the more I love you, the less you love me.

**12:16**
2 Cor 11:9

¹⁶Some of you admit I was not a burden to you. But others still think I was sneaky and

**12:3-4** Greek *But I know such a man,* ⁴*that he was caught up.*   **12:11** Some manuscripts do not include *boasting like this.*

---

**12:10** When we are strong in abilities or resources, we are tempted to do God's work on our own, and that can lead to pride. When we are weak, allowing God to fill us with *his* power, then we are stronger than we could ever be on our own. God does not intend for us to be weak, passive, or ineffective—life provides enough hindrances and setbacks without us creating them. When those obstacles come, we must depend on God. Only his power will make us effective for him and will help us do work that has lasting value.

he didn't know if he was taken up in his body or in his spirit, but he had been in paradise ("the third heaven," perhaps referring to the highest part of the heavens, beyond the atmosphere and the stars, where God himself lives). This incident cannot be positively identified with a recorded event in Paul's career, although some think this may have been when he was stoned and left for dead (Acts 14:19, 20). Paul told about this incident to show that he had been uniquely touched by God.

**12:7, 8** We don't know what Paul's thorn in the flesh was because he doesn't tell us. Some have suggested that it was malaria, epilepsy, or a disease of the eyes (see Galatians 4:13-15). Whatever the case, it was a chronic and debilitating problem, which at times kept him from working. This thorn was a hindrance to his ministry, and he prayed for its removal; but God refused. Paul was a very self-sufficient person, so this thorn must have been difficult for him.

Three times Paul prayed for healing and did not receive it. He received, however, things far greater because he received greater grace from God, a stronger character, humility, and an ability to empathize with others. In addition, it benefited those around him as they saw God at work in his life. God, according to his sovereign plan, doesn't heal some believers of their physical ailments. We don't know why some are spared and others aren't. God chooses according to his divine purposes. Our task is to pray, to believe, and to trust. Paul is living proof that holy living and courageous faith do not ensure instant physical healing. When we pray for healing, we must trust our bodies to God's care. We must recognize that nothing separates us from his love (Romans 8:35-39) and that our spiritual condition is always more important than our physical condition.

**12:9** Although God did not remove Paul's affliction, he promised to demonstrate his power in Paul. The fact that God's power is displayed in our weaknesses should give us courage and hope. As we recognize our limitations, we will depend more on God for our effectiveness rather than on our own energy, effort, or talent. Our limitations not only help develop Christian character but also deepen our worship, because in admitting them, we affirm God's strength.

**12:11-15** Paul was not merely revealing his feelings; he was defending his authority as an apostle of Jesus Christ. Paul was hurt that the church in Corinth doubted and questioned him, so he defended himself for the cause of the Good News, not to satisfy his ego. When you are "put on trial," do you think only about saving your reputation or are you more concerned about what people will think about Christ?

**12:13** Paul explained that the only thing he did in the other churches that he didn't do in Corinth was to become a burden—to ask the believers to feed and house him. When he said, "Forgive me for this wrong," he was clearly being sarcastic. He actually did more for the Corinthians than for any other church, but still they misunderstood him.

**12:14** Paul had founded the church in Corinth on his first visit there (Acts 18:1). He subsequently made a second visit (2:1). He was planning what would be his third visit (see also 13:1). Paul explained that, as before, he didn't want to be paid, fed, or housed; he only wanted the believers to be nourished with the spiritual food he would feed them.

**12:16-19** Although Paul asked nothing of the Corinthian believers, some doubters were still saying that Paul must have been sneaky and made money from them somehow. But Paul again explained that everything he did for the believers was for their edification, not to enrich himself.

took advantage of you by trickery. [17]But how? Did any of the men I sent to you take advantage of you? [18]When I urged Titus to visit you and sent our other brother with him, did Titus take advantage of you? No! For we have the same spirit and walk in each other's steps, doing things the same way.

[19]Perhaps you think we're saying these things just to defend ourselves. No, we tell you this as Christ's servants, and with God as our witness. Everything we do, dear friends, is to strengthen you. [20]For I am afraid that when I come I won't like what I find, and you won't like my response. I am afraid that I will find quarreling, jealousy, anger, selfishness, slander, gossip, arrogance, and disorderly behavior. [21]Yes, I am afraid that when I come again, God will humble me in your presence. And I will be grieved because many of you have not given up your old sins. You have not repented of your impurity, sexual immorality, and eagerness for lustful pleasure.

## Paul's Final Advice

**13** This is the third time I am coming to visit you (and as the Scriptures say, "The facts of every case must be established by the testimony of two or three witnesses"*). [2]I have already warned those who had been sinning when I was there on my second visit. Now I again warn them and all others, just as I did before, that next time I will not spare them.

[3]I will give you all the proof you want that Christ speaks through me. Christ is not weak when he deals with you; he is powerful among you. [4]Although he was crucified in weakness, he now lives by the power of God. We, too, are weak, just as Christ was, but when we deal with you we will be alive with him and will have God's power.

[5]Examine yourselves to see if your faith is genuine. Test yourselves. Surely you know that Jesus Christ is among you*; if not, you have failed the test of genuine faith. [6]As you test yourselves, I hope you will recognize that we have not failed the test of apostolic authority.

[7]We pray to God that you will not do what is wrong by refusing our correction. I hope we won't need to demonstrate our authority when we arrive. Do the right thing before we come—even if that makes it look like we have failed to demonstrate our authority. [8]For we cannot oppose the truth, but must always stand for the truth. [9]We are glad to seem weak if it helps show that you are actually strong. We pray that you will become mature.

[10]I am writing this to you before I come, hoping that I won't need to deal severely with you when I do come. For I want to use the authority the Lord has given me to strengthen you, not to tear you down.

**13:1** Deut 19:15.   **13:5** Or *in you.*

### Cross references

**12:18** 2 Cor 8:6, 16-18
**12:19** Rom 9:1
**12:20** 1 Cor 4:21; 2 Cor 2:1-4
**12:21** 2 Cor 13:2
**13:1** †Deut 19:15; Matt 18:16; 2 Cor 12:14; 1 Tim 5:19
**13:2** 2 Cor 1:23; 12:21
**13:3** Matt 10:20; 1 Cor 5:4
**13:4** Rom 1:4; 6:4; Phil 2:7-8; 1 Pet 3:18
**13:5** John 14:20; 17:23, 26; Rom 8:10; 1 Cor 11:28; Gal 4:19; Col 1:27
**13:8** 1 Cor 13:6
**13:9** 1 Cor 2:3; 4:10
**13:10** 2 Cor 10:8, 11

---

**12:20, 21** After reading this catalog of sins, it is hard to believe that these are the people that Paul said possessed great gifts and excelled as leaders (8:7). Paul feared that the practices of wicked Corinth had invaded the congregation. He wrote sternly, hoping that they would straighten out their lives before he arrived. We must live differently from unbelievers, not letting secular society dictate how we are to treat others. Don't let culture influence your behavior.

**13:2** When Paul arrived the third time in Corinth, he would not be lenient toward unrepentant sinners. His actions could include (1) confronting and publicly denouncing their behavior, (2) exercising church discipline by calling them before the church leaders, or (3) excommunicating them from the church.

**13:4** That we "will be alive with him and will have God's power" should be a comfort to all believers. Christians are not just playing church. We are not in this angry ocean of a world in

a rubber raft with a plastic paddle. We are passengers on his Majesty's finest vessel, driven by the indwelling power of the Holy Spirit. We may be tempted to underestimate our ability to accomplish what Christ desires. We forget that Christ is on the bridge, directing the ship safely through the rough seas and finally into its eternal port.

**13:5** The Corinthians were called to examine and test themselves to see if they really were Christians. Just as we get physical checkups, Paul urges us to give ourselves spiritual checkups. We should look for a growing awareness of Christ's presence and power in our life. Then will we know if we are true Christians or merely impostors. If we're not actively seeking to grow closer to God, we are drawing farther away from him.

**13:8, 9** Just as parents want their children to grow into mature adults, so Paul wanted the Corinthians to grow into mature believers. As we share the Good News, our goal should be not merely to see others profess faith or begin attending church but to see them become mature in their faith. Don't set your sights too low.

**13:10** The authority Paul had received from the Lord was to strengthen the believers, not to tear them down. Paul gives good advice for our day. Fellow believers are the temple of the Holy Spirit. There is no room in the household of faith for the deprecation of a fellow worker. Before the week is over, write a note of encouragement to several people in your sphere of influence who probably aren't being built up by others in the church. Remind them how much their presence and abilities are needed in your congregation. Express how much you appreciate them.

### Paul's Final Greetings

**13:11**
Rom 15:33
Phil 4:4

¹¹Dear brothers and sisters,* I close my letter with these last words: Be joyful. Grow to maturity. Encourage each other. Live in harmony and peace. Then the God of love and peace will be with you.

**13:12**
Rom 16:16
1 Cor 16:20
1 Pet 5:14

¹²Greet each other with Christian love.* ¹³All of God's people here send you their greetings.

**13:13**
Rom 16:20
Phil 2:1

¹⁴*May the grace of the Lord Jesus Christ, the love of God, and the fellowship of the Holy Spirit be with you all.

**13:11** Greek *Brothers.*   **13:12** Greek *with a sacred kiss.*   **13:14** Some English translations include verse 13 as part of verse 12, and then verse 14 becomes verse 13.

**13:11** Paul's closing words—what he wanted the Corinthians to remember about the needs facing their church—are still fitting for the church today. When these qualities are not present, there are problems that must be dealt with. These traits do not come to a church by glossing over problems, conflicts, and difficulties. They are not produced by neglect, denial, withdrawal, or bitterness. They are the by-products of the extremely hard work of solving problems. Just as Paul and the Corinthians had to hammer out difficulties to bring peace, so we must *apply* the principles of God's Word and not just hear them.

**13:13** Paul's farewell blessing invokes all three members of the Trinity: Father (God), Son (Lord Jesus Christ), and Holy Spirit. Although the term *Trinity* is not explicitly used in Scripture, verses such as this one show that it was believed and experienced through knowing God's grace, love, and fellowship. See Luke 1:35—the angel Gabriel's announcement of Jesus' birth to Mary; Matthew 3:17—the Father's voice was heard at the baptism of Jesus; and Matthew 28:19—Jesus' commission to the disciples.

**13:13** Paul was dealing with an ongoing problem in the Corinthian church. He could have refused to communicate until they cleared up their situation, but he loved them and reached out to them again with the love of Christ. Love, however, means that sometimes we must confront those we care about. Both authority and personal concern are needed in dealing with people who are ruining their lives with sin. But there are several wrong approaches in confronting others, and these can further break relationships rather than heal them. We can be legalistic and blast people away with the laws they should be obeying. We can turn away from them because we don't want to face the situation. We can isolate them by gossiping about their problem and turning others against them as well. Or, like Paul, we can seek to build relationships by taking a better approach—sharing, communicating, and caring. This is a difficult approach that can drain us emotionally, but it is the best way for other people, and it is the only Christlike way to deal with others' sin.

# GALATIANS

## VITAL STATISTICS

**PURPOSE:**
To refute the Judaizers (who taught that Gentile believers must obey the Jewish law in order to be saved), and to call Christians to faith and freedom in Christ

**AUTHOR:**
Paul

**ORIGINAL AUDIENCE:**
The churches in southern Galatia, founded on Paul's first missionary journey (including Iconium, Lystra, Derbe)

**DATE WRITTEN:**
Approximately A.D. 49, from Antioch, prior to the Jerusalem council (A.D. 50)

**SETTING:**
The most pressing controversy in the early church was the relationship of new believers, particularly Gentiles, to the Jewish laws. This was especially a problem for the converts and for the young churches that Paul had founded on his first missionary journey. Paul wrote to correct this problem. Later, at the council in Jerusalem, the conflict was officially resolved by the church leaders.

**KEY VERSE:**
"So Christ has truly set us free. Now make sure that you stay free, and don't get tied up again in slavery to the law" (5:1).

**KEY PEOPLE:**
Paul, Peter, Barnabas, Titus, Abraham, false teachers

**KEY PLACES:**
Galatia, Jerusalem

**SPECIAL FEATURES:**
This letter is not addressed to any specific body of believers and was probably circulated to several churches in Galatia.

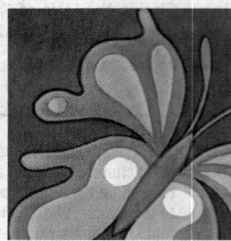

A FAMILY, executing their carefully planned escape at midnight, dashing for the border . . . a man standing outside prison walls, gulping fresh air, awash in the new sun . . . a young woman with every trace of the ravaging drug gone from her system . . . they are FREE! With fresh anticipation, they can begin life anew.

Whether fleeing oppression, stepping out of prison, or breaking a strangling habit, freedom means life. There is nothing so exhilarating as knowing that the past is forgotten and that new options await. People yearn to be free.

The book of Galatians is the charter of Christian freedom. In this profound letter, Paul proclaims the reality of our liberty in Christ—freedom from the law and the power of sin, and freedom to serve our living Lord.

Most of the first converts and early leaders in the church were Jewish Christians who proclaimed Jesus as their Messiah. As Jewish Christians, they struggled with a dual identity: Their Jewishness constrained them to be strict followers of the law; their newfound faith in Christ invited them to celebrate a holy liberty. They wondered how Gentiles (non-Jews) could be part of the Kingdom of Heaven.

This controversy tore the early church. Judaizers—an extremist Jewish faction within the church—taught that Gentile Christians had to submit to Jewish laws and traditions *in addition to* believing in Christ. As a missionary to the Gentiles, Paul had to confront this issue many times.

Galatians was written, therefore, to refute the Judaizers and to call believers back to the pure gospel. The Good News is for all people—Jews and Gentiles alike. Salvation is by God's grace through faith in Christ Jesus *and nothing else.* Faith in Christ means true freedom.

After a brief introduction (1:1–5), Paul addresses those who were accepting the Judaizers' perverted gospel (1:6–9). He summarizes the controversy, including his personal confrontation with Peter and other church leaders (1:10—2:16). He then demonstrates that salvation is by faith alone by alluding to his conversion (2:17–21), appealing to his readers' own experience of the gospel (3:1–5), and showing how the Old Testament teaches about grace (3:6–20). Next, he explains the purpose of God's laws and the relationship between law, God's promises, and Christ (3:21—4:31).

Having laid the foundation, Paul builds his case for Christian liberty. We are saved by faith, not by keeping the law (5:1–12); our freedom means that we are free to love and serve one another, not to do wrong (5:13–26); and Christians should carry each other's burdens and be kind to each other (6:1–10). In 6:11–18, Paul takes the pen into his own hand and shares his final thoughts.

As you read Galatians, try to understand this first-century conflict between grace and law, or faith and deeds, but also be aware of modern parallels. Like Paul, defend the truth of the gospel and reject all those who would add to or twist this truth. You are *free* in Christ—step into the light and celebrate!

## THE BLUEPRINT

1. Authenticity of the gospel
   (1:1—2:21)
2. Superiority of the gospel
   (3:1—4:31)
3. Freedom of the gospel
   (5:1—6:18)

In response to attacks from false teachers, Paul wrote to defend his apostleship and the authority of the gospel. The Galatians were beginning to turn from faith to legalism. The struggle between the gospel and legalism is still a relevant issue. Many today would have us return to trying to earn God's favor through following rituals or obeying a set of rules. As Christians, we are not boxed in but set free. To preserve our freedom, we must stay close to Christ and resist any who promote subtle ways for us to earn our salvation.

## MEGATHEMES

| THEME | EXPLANATION | IMPORTANCE |
|---|---|---|
| Law | A group of Jewish teachers insisted that non-Jewish believers must obey Jewish law and traditional rules. They believed a person was saved by following the law of Moses (with emphasis on circumcision, the sign of the covenant), in addition to faith in Christ. Paul opposed them by showing that the law can't save anyone. | We can't be saved by keeping the Old Testament law, even the Ten Commandments. The law served as a guide to point out our need to be forgiven. Christ fulfilled the obligations of the law for us. We must turn to him to be saved. He alone can make us right with God. |
| Faith | We are saved from God's judgment and penalty for sin by God's gracious gift to us. We receive salvation by faith—trusting in him—not in anything else. Becoming a Christian is in no way based on our initiative, wise choice, or good character. We can be right with God only by believing in him. | Your acceptance with God comes by believing in Christ alone. You must never add to or twist this truth. We are saved by faith, not by the good that we do. Have you placed your whole trust and confidence in Christ? He alone can forgive you and bring you into a relationship with God. |
| Freedom | Galatians is our charter of Christian freedom. We are not under the jurisdiction of Jewish laws and traditions nor under the authority of Jerusalem. Faith in Christ brings true freedom from sin and from the futile attempt to be right with God by keeping the law. | We are free in Christ, and yet freedom is a privilege. We are not free to disobey Christ or practice immorality, but we are free to serve the risen Christ. Let us use our freedom to love and to serve, not to do wrong. |
| Holy Spirit | We become Christians through the work of the Holy Spirit. He brings new life; even our faith to believe is a gift from him. The Holy Spirit instructs, guides, leads, and gives us power. He ends our bondage to evil desires, and he creates in us love, joy, peace, and many other wonderful changes. | When the Holy Spirit leads us, he produces his fruit in us. Just as we are saved by faith, not deeds, we also grow by faith. By believing, we can have the Holy Spirit within us, helping us live for Christ. Obey Christ by following the Holy Spirit's leading. |

# 1. Authenticity of the gospel

*Greetings from Paul*

**1** This letter is from Paul, an apostle. I was not appointed by any group of people or any human authority, but by Jesus Christ himself and by God the Father, who raised Jesus from the dead.

2All the brothers and sisters* here join me in sending this letter to the churches of Galatia. 3May God our Father and the Lord Jesus Christ* give you grace and peace. 4Jesus gave his life for our sins, just as God our Father planned, in order to rescue us from this evil world in which we live. 5All glory to God forever and ever! Amen.

**1:1** Acts 20:24
**1:3** Rom 1:7 / Phil 1:2 / Phlm 1:3
**1:4** Rom 4:25 / Gal 2:20 / 1 Tim 2:6 / Titus 2:14
**1:5** Rom 11:36

**1:2** Greek *brothers;* also in 1:11.　　**1:3** Some manuscripts read *God the Father and our Lord Jesus Christ.*

---

Rome

N

ASIA

Ephesus　Antioch　LYCAONIA
Athens　PISIDIA　Iconium
　　　　　　　　•Derbe
　　　　　Lystra
　　　　　　　　•Antioch

Mediterranean Sea

SYRIA

•Jerusalem

0　　　300 Mi.
0　　　300 Km.

**CITIES IN GALATIA**
Paul visited several cities in Galatia on each of his three missionary journeys. On his first journey he went through Antioch in Pisidia, Iconium, Lystra, and Derbe, and then retraced his steps; on his second journey he went by land from Antioch of Syria through the four cities in Galatia; on his third journey he also went through those cities on the main route to Ephesus.

---

**1:1** Paul and Barnabas had just completed their first missionary journey (Acts 13:2–14:28). They had visited Iconium, Lystra, and Derbe, cities in the Roman province of Galatia (present-day Turkey). Upon returning to Antioch, Paul was accused by some Jewish Christians of diluting Christianity to make it more appealing to Gentiles. These Jewish Christians disagreed with Paul's statements that Gentiles did not have to follow many of the religious laws that the Jews had obeyed for centuries. Some of Paul's accusers had even followed him to those Galatian cities and had told the Gentile converts they had to be circumcised and follow all the Jewish laws and customs in order to be saved. According to these people, Gentiles had to first become Jews in order to become Christians.

In response to this threat, Paul wrote this letter to the Galatian churches. In it, he explains that following the Old Testament laws, or the Jewish laws, will not bring salvation. A person is saved by grace through faith. Paul wrote this letter about A.D. 49, shortly before the meeting of the Jerusalem council, which settled the law-versus-grace controversy (Acts 15).

**1:1** Paul explained his apostleship in these words, not to separate himself from the original Twelve, but to show that his apostleship rested on the same basis as theirs. If the believers in Galatia questioned Paul's apostleship, then they also should question the apostleship of Peter, John, James, and all the others—and such questioning would be absurd. All the apostles were called by Jesus Christ and God the Father, and they answered to God as their final authority.

**1:1** For more information about Paul's life, see his Profile in Acts 9, p. 1837. Paul had been a Christian for about 15 years at this time.

**1:2** In Paul's time, Galatia was the Roman province located in the center section of present-day Turkey. Much of the region rests on a large and fertile plateau, and large numbers of people had moved to the region because of its favorable agriculture. One of Paul's goals during his missionary journeys was to visit regions with large population centers in order to reach as many people as possible.

**1:3-5** God's plan all along was to save us by Jesus' death. We have been rescued from the power of this present evil world— a world ruled by Satan and full of cruelty, tragedy, temptation, and deception. Being rescued from this evil world doesn't mean that we are taken out of it but that we are no longer enslaved to it. You were saved to live for God. Does your life reflect your gratitude for being rescued? Have you transferred your loyalty from this world to Christ?

## There Is Only One Good News

**1:6**
2 Cor 11:4

**1:7**
Acts 15:1, 24
Gal 5:10

**1:8**
2 Cor 11:14

**1:9**
Deut 4:2; 12:32
1 Cor 16:22
Rev 22:18

[6]I am shocked that you are turning away so soon from God, who called you to himself through the loving mercy of Christ.* You are following a different way that pretends to be the Good News [7]but is not the Good News at all. You are being fooled by those who deliberately twist the truth concerning Christ.

[8]Let God's curse fall on anyone, including us or even an angel from heaven, who preaches a different kind of Good News than the one we preached to you. [9]I say again what we have said before: If anyone preaches any other Good News than the one you welcomed, let that person be cursed.

**1:6** Some manuscripts read *through loving mercy.*

---

**THE MARKS OF THE TRUE GOSPEL AND OF FALSE GOSPELS**

| Marks of a false gospel | Marks of the true gospel |
|---|---|
| 2:21 . . . . . . . Treats Christ's death as meaningless | 1:11, 12 . . . . Teaches that the source of the gospel is God |
| 3:12 . . . . . . . Says people must obey the law in order to be saved | 2:20 . . . . . . . Knows that life is obtained through death; we trust in the Son of God who loved us and died for us so that we might die to sin and live for him |
| 4:10 . . . . . . . Tries to find favor with God by observing certain rituals | 3:14 . . . . . . . Explains that all believers have the Holy Spirit through faith |
| 5:4 . . . . . . . . Counts on keeping laws to be right with God | 3:21, 22 . . . . Declares that we cannot be saved by keeping laws; the only way of salvation is through faith in Christ, which is available to all |
| | 3:26-28 . . . . Says that all believers are one in Christ, so there is no basis for discrimination of any kind |
| | 5:24, 25 . . . . Proclaims that we are free from the grip of sin and that the Holy Spirit's power fills and guides us |

---

**1:6** Some people were preaching "a different way." They were teaching that to be saved, Gentile believers had to follow Jewish laws and customs, especially the rite of circumcision. Faith in Christ was not enough. This message undermined the truth that salvation is a gift, not a reward for certain deeds. Jesus Christ has made this gift available to all people, not just to Jews. Beware of people who say that we need more than simple faith in Christ to be saved. When people set up additional requirements for salvation, they deny the power of Christ's death on the cross (see 3:1-5).

**1:7** The Bible says there is only one way to be forgiven of sin: by believing in Jesus Christ as Savior and Lord. No other person, method, or ritual can give eternal life. Attempting to be open-minded and tolerant, some people assert that all religions are equally valid paths to God. In a free society, people have the right to their religious opinions, but this doesn't guarantee that their ideas are right. God does not accept man-made religion as a substitute for faith in Jesus Christ. He has provided just one way—Jesus Christ (John 14:6).

**1:7** Those who had confused the Galatian believers and perverted the Good News were zealous Jewish Christians who believed that the Old Testament practices, such as circumcision and dietary restrictions, were required of all believers. Because these teachers wanted to turn the Gentile Christians into Jews, they were called "Judaizers."

Most of the Galatian Christians were Greeks who were unfamiliar with Jewish laws and customs. The Judaizers were an extreme faction of Jewish Christians. Both groups believed in Christ, but their life-styles differed considerably. We do not know why the Judaizers may have traveled no small distance to teach their mistaken notions to the new Gentile converts. They may have been motivated by (1) a sincere wish to integrate Judaism with the new Christian faith, (2) a sincere love for their Jewish heritage, or (3) a jealous desire to destroy Paul's authority. Whether or not these Judaizers were sincere, their teaching threatened these new churches and had to be countered. When Paul said that their teaching twisted and changed the Good News, he was not rejecting everything Jewish. He himself was a Jew who worshiped in the Temple and attended the religious festivals. But he was concerned that *nothing* get in the way of the simple truth of his message—that salvation, for Jews and Gentiles alike, is through faith in Jesus Christ alone. Some time after the letter to the Galatians was sent, Paul met with the apostles in Jerusalem to discuss this matter further (see Acts 15).

**1:7** A twisting of the truth is more difficult to spot than an outright lie. The Judaizers were twisting the truth about Christ. They claimed to follow him, but they denied that Jesus' work on the cross was sufficient for salvation. There will always be people who twist the Good News. Either they do not understand what the Bible teaches, or they are uncomfortable with the truth as it stands. How can we tell when people are twisting the truth? Before accepting the teachings of any group, find out what the group teaches about Jesus Christ. If their teaching does not match the truth in God's Word, then it is not true.

**1:8, 9** Paul strongly denounced the Judaizers' twisting of the Good News of Christ. He said that God's curse should fall on anyone, even an angel from heaven, who came preaching a different kind of Good News. If an angel came preaching another message, he would not be from heaven, no matter how he looked. In 2 Corinthians 11:14, 15, Paul warned that Satan disguises himself as an angel of light. Here he invoked a curse on any angel who spreads a false teaching—a fitting response to an emissary of hell. Paul extended that curse to include himself if he should twist the Good News. His message must never change, for the truth of the Good News never changes. Paul used strong language because he was dealing with a life-and-death issue.

¹⁰Obviously, I'm not trying to win the approval of people, but of God. If pleasing people were my goal, I would not be Christ's servant.

**1:10**
1 Thes 2:4

### Paul's Message Comes from Christ

¹¹Dear brothers and sisters, I want you to understand that the gospel message I preach is not based on mere human reasoning. ¹²I received my message from no human source, and no one taught me. Instead, I received it by direct revelation from Jesus Christ.*

¹³You know what I was like when I followed the Jewish religion—how I violently persecuted God's church. I did my best to destroy it. ¹⁴I was far ahead of my fellow Jews in my zeal for the traditions of my ancestors.

¹⁵But even before I was born, God chose me and called me by his marvelous grace. Then it pleased him ¹⁶to reveal his Son to me* so that I would proclaim the Good News about Jesus to the Gentiles.

When this happened, I did not rush out to consult with any human being.* ¹⁷Nor did I go up to Jerusalem to consult with those who were apostles before I was. Instead, I went away into Arabia, and later I returned to the city of Damascus.

¹⁸Then three years later I went to Jerusalem to get to know Peter,* and I stayed with him for fifteen days. ¹⁹The only other apostle I met at that time was James, the Lord's brother. ²⁰I declare before God that what I am writing to you is not a lie.

²¹After that visit I went north into the provinces of Syria and Cilicia. ²²And still the Christians in the churches in Judea didn't know me personally. ²³All they knew was that people were saying, "The one who used to persecute us is now preaching the very faith he tried to destroy!" ²⁴And they praised God because of me.

**1:12**
1 Cor 2:10
Gal 1:1, 15-16
Eph 3:3
**1:13**
Acts 8:3; 9:21;
22:4-5; 26:4-11
**1:14**
Acts 22:3
**1:15**
Acts 9:15
**1:16**
Rom 1:17; 8:3, 10
Gal 2:9, 20
Col 1:27
**1:18**
Acts 9:22-23, 26-27
**1:19**
Matt 13:55
Acts 15:13
Gal 2:9, 12
**1:23**
Acts 9:20

**1:12** Or by the revelation of Jesus Christ.   **1:16a** Or in me.   **1:16b** Greek with flesh and blood.   **1:18** Greek Cephas.

**1:10** Do you spend your life trying to please everybody? Paul had to speak harshly to the Christians in Galatia because they were in serious danger. He did not apologize for his straightforward words, knowing that he could not serve Christ faithfully if he allowed the Galatian Christians to remain on the wrong track. Whose approval are you seeking—others' or God's? Pray for the courage to seek God's approval above anyone else's.

**1:11ff** Why should the Galatians have listened to Paul instead of the Judaizers? Paul answered this implicit question by furnishing his credentials: His message was received directly from Christ (1:12); he had been an exemplary Jew (1:13, 14); he had had a special conversion experience (1:15, 16; see also Acts 9:1-9); he had been confirmed and accepted in his ministry by the other apostles (1:18, 19; 2:1-9). Paul also presented his credentials to the Corinthian and Philippian churches (2 Corinthians 11–12; Philippians 3:4-9).

**1:12** There are two possible meanings consistent with the grammar of the phrase, "direct revelation from Jesus Christ." (1) This was a revelation by Christ to Paul that spelled out the gospel message, or (2) it was a personal revelation by Christ of his true identity that suddenly confirmed the gospel message against which Paul had been in bitter conflict. Within each meaning the fact remains that God provided the revelation and its content was the gospel.

**1:13, 14** Paul had been one of the most religious Jews of his day, scrupulously keeping the law and relentlessly persecuting Christians (see Acts 9:1, 2). Before his conversion Paul had been even more zealous for the law than the Judaizers. He had surpassed his contemporaries in religious knowledge and practice. Paul had been sincere in his zeal—but wrong. When he met Jesus Christ, his life changed. He then directed all his energies toward building up the Christian church.

**1:14** To be fully Jewish, a person must have descended from Abraham. In addition, a faithful Jew adhered to the Jewish laws and traditions. Gentiles (1:16) are non-Jews, whether in nationality or religion. In Paul's day, Jews thought of all Gentiles as pagans. Jews avoided Gentiles, believing that contact with Gentiles brought spiritual corruption. Although Gentiles could become Jews in reli-

gion by undergoing circumcision and by following Jewish laws and customs, they were never fully accepted.

Many Jews had difficulty understanding that God's message is for Jews and Gentiles alike. Some Jews thought that Gentiles had to become Jews before they could become Christians. But God planned to save both Jews and Gentiles. He had revealed this plan through Old Testament prophets (see, for example, Genesis 12:3; Isaiah 42:6; 66:19), and he had fulfilled it through Jesus Christ; he was proclaiming it to the Gentiles through Paul.

**1:15, 16** Because God was guiding his ministry, Paul wasn't doing anything that God hadn't already planned and given him power to do. Similarly, God appointed Jeremiah to be his spokesman even before Jeremiah was born (Jeremiah 1:5). God knows you intimately as well, and he chose you to be his even before you were born (see Psalm 139). He wants you to draw close to him and to fulfill the purpose he has for your life.

**1:15-24** Paul tells of his conversion to show that his message came directly from God. God commissioned him to preach the Good News to the Gentiles. After his call, Paul did not consult with anyone; instead, he spent three years in Arabia. Then he spoke with Peter and James, but he had no other contact with Jewish Christians for several more years. During those years, Paul preached to the Gentiles the message God had given him. His message did not come from human insight; it came from God.

**1:18** This was Paul's first visit to Jerusalem as a Christian, as recorded in Acts 9:26-30.

**1:21** Because of opposition in Jerusalem (see Acts 9:29, 30), Paul had gone to Syria and Cilicia. In those remote areas, he had no opportunity to receive instruction from the apostles.

**1:23** Paul was making the point that his authority and ministry were recognized by people who had never even seen him; yet the Galatians had met him, listened to him, and believed his message, only to turn around and doubt him! The Judean Christians only knew what people were saying: that the one who had persecuted believers was now preaching the faith he had tried to destroy. Instead of doubting Paul's credibility, the churches in Judea had believed and glorified God.

**1:24** Paul's changed life had brought praise from those who saw him or heard about him. His new life had astonished them. They

## The Apostles Accept Paul

2:1
Acts 15:2

2:2
Gal 1:6

2:3
Acts 16:3

2:4
Gal 1:7; 5:1, 13

**2** Then fourteen years later I went back to Jerusalem again, this time with Barnabas; and Titus came along, too. ²I went there because God revealed to me that I should go. While I was there I met privately with those considered to be leaders of the church and shared with them the message I had been preaching to the Gentiles. I wanted to make sure that we were in agreement, for fear that all my efforts had been wasted and I was running the race for nothing. ³And they supported me and did not even demand that my companion Titus be circumcised, though he was a Gentile.*

⁴Even that question came up only because of some so-called Christians there—false ones,

2:3 Greek *a Greek.*

---

**JUDAIZERS VERSUS PAUL**

| What the Judaizers said about Paul | Paul's defense |
|---|---|
| They said he was perverting the truth. | He received his message from Christ himself (1:11, 12). |
| They said he was a traitor to the Jewish faith. | Paul had been one of the most dedicated Jews of his time. Yet, in the midst of one of his most zealous acts, God transformed him through a revelation of the Good News about Jesus (1:13-16; Acts 9:1-30). |
| They said he compromised and watered down his message for the Gentiles. | The other apostles declared that the message Paul preached was the true gospel (2:1-10). |
| They said he was disregarding the law of Moses. | Far from degrading the law, Paul puts the law in its proper place. He says it shows people where they have sinned, and it points them to Christ (3:19-29). |

As the debate raged between the Gentile Christians and the Judaizers, Paul found it necessary to write to the churches in Galatia. The Judaizers were trying to undermine Paul's authority, and they taught a false gospel. In reply, Paul defended his authority as an apostle and the truth of his message. The debate over Jewish laws and Gentile Christians was officially resolved at the Jerusalem council (Acts 15), yet it continued to be a point of contention after that time.

---

had praised God because only God could have turned this zealous persecutor of Christians into a Christian himself. We may not have had as dramatic a change as Paul, but still our new life should honor God in every way. When people look at you, do they recognize that God has made changes in you? If not, perhaps you are not living as you should.

**2:1** Paul was converted around A.D. 35. The 14 years he mentions are probably calculated from the time of his conversion. Therefore, this trip to Jerusalem was not his first. Most likely, he made his first trip to Jerusalem around A.D. 38 (see Acts 9:26-30), and other trips to Jerusalem in approximately A.D. 44 (Acts 11:29, 30; Galatians 2:1-10), A.D. 49/50 (Acts 15), A.D. 52 (Acts 18:22), and A.D. 57 (Acts 21:15ff). Paul probably visited Jerusalem on several other occasions as well.

**2:1** Barnabas and Titus were two of Paul's close friends. Barnabas and Paul visited Galatia together on their first missionary journey. Paul wrote a personal letter to Titus, a faithful believer and church leader serving on the island of Crete (see the book of Titus). For more information on Barnabas, see his Profile in Acts 13, p. 1849. For more information on Titus, see the letter Paul wrote to him in the New Testament.

**2:1** After his conversion, Paul spent many years preparing for the ministry to which God had called him. This preparation period included time alone with God (1:16, 17), as well as time conferring with other Christians. Often new Christians, in their zeal, want to begin a full-time ministry without investing the necessary time studying the Bible and learning from qualified teachers. We need not wait to share Christ with our friends, but we may need more preparation before embarking on a special ministry, whether volunteer or paid. While we wait for God's timing, we should continue to study, learn, and grow.

**2:2** God told Paul, through a revelation, to confer with the church

leaders in Jerusalem about the message he was preaching to the Gentiles, so they would understand and approve of what he was doing. The essence of Paul's message to both Jews and Gentiles was that God's salvation is offered to all people regardless of race, sex, nationality, wealth, social standing, educational level, or anything else. Anyone can be forgiven by trusting in Christ (see Romans 10:8-13).

**2:2, 3** Even though God had specifically sent him to the Gentiles (Acts 9:15, 16), Paul needed to discuss his message with the leaders of the Jerusalem church (Acts 15). This meeting prevented a major split in the church, and it formally acknowledged the apostles' approval of Paul's preaching. Sometimes we avoid conferring with others because we fear that problems or arguments may develop. Instead, we should openly discuss our plans and actions with friends, counselors, and advisers. Good communication helps everyone understand the situation better, it reduces gossip, and it builds unity in the church.

**2:3-5** When Paul took Titus, a Greek Christian, to Jerusalem, the Judaizers ("false" Christians) said that Titus should be circumcised. Paul adamantly refused to give in to their demands. The apostles agreed that circumcision was an unnecessary rite for Gentile converts. Several years later, Paul circumcised Timothy, another Greek Christian (Acts 16:3). Unlike Titus, however, Timothy was half Jewish. Paul did not deny Jews the right to be circumcised; he was simply saying that Gentiles should not be asked to become Jews before becoming Christians.

**2:4** These false Christians were most likely from the party of the Pharisees (Acts 15:5). These were the strictest religious leaders of Judaism, some of whom had been converted. We don't know if these were representatives of well-meaning converts or of those trying to pervert Christianity. Most commentators agree that neither Peter nor James had any part in this conspiracy.

really*—who were secretly brought in. They sneaked in to spy on us and take away the freedom we have in Christ Jesus. They wanted to enslave us and force us to follow their Jewish regulations. 5 But we refused to give in to them for a single moment. We wanted to preserve the truth of the gospel message for you.

**2:5**
Gal 1:6; 2:14

6 And the leaders of the church had nothing to add to what I was preaching. (By the way, their reputation as great leaders made no difference to me, for God has no favorites.) 7 Instead, they saw that God had given me the responsibility of preaching the gospel to the Gentiles, just as he had given Peter the responsibility of preaching to the Jews. 8 For the same God who worked through Peter as the apostle to the Jews also worked through me as the apostle to the Gentiles.

**2:6**
Deut 10:17
Acts 10:34
Rom 2:11
2 Cor 12:11

**2:7**
Acts 9:15; 22:21
1 Thes 2:4

9 In fact, James, Peter,* and John, who were known as pillars of the church, recognized the gift God had given me, and they accepted Barnabas and me as their co-workers. They encouraged us to keep preaching to the Gentiles, while they continued their work with the Jews. 10 Their only suggestion was that we keep on helping the poor, which I have always been eager to do.

**2:9**
Rom 1:5

**2:10**
Acts 11:29-30;
24:17

### Paul Confronts Peter

11 But when Peter came to Antioch, I had to oppose him to his face, for what he did was very wrong. 12 When he first arrived, he ate with the Gentile Christians, who were not circumcised. But afterward, when some friends of James came, Peter wouldn't eat with the Gentiles anymore. He was afraid of criticism from these people who insisted on the necessity of circumcision. 13 As a result, other Jewish Christians followed Peter's hypocrisy, and even Barnabas was led astray by their hypocrisy.

**2:12**
Acts 11:2-3

**2:14**
Acts 10:28

**2:15**
Phil 3:4-5

14 When I saw that they were not following the truth of the gospel message, I said to Peter in front of all the others, "Since you, a Jew by birth, have discarded the Jewish laws and are living like a Gentile, why are you now trying to make these Gentiles follow the Jewish traditions?

**2:16**
Acts 15:10-11
Rom 1:17; 3:20, 28;
8:3
Gal 3:11
Eph 2:8

15 "You and I are Jews by birth, not 'sinners' like the Gentiles. 16 Yet we know that a person is

**2:4** Greek *some false brothers.*   **2:9** Greek *Cephas;* also in 2:11, 14.

---

**2:5** We normally think of taking a stand against those who might lead us into immoral behavior, but Paul had to take a hard line against the most moral of people. We must not give in to those who make the keeping of man-made standards a condition for salvation, even when such people are morally upright or in respected positions.

**2:6** It's easy to rate people on the basis of their official status and to be intimidated by powerful people. But Paul was not intimidated by these "great leaders" because all believers are equal in Christ. We should show respect for our spiritual leaders, but our ultimate allegiance must be to Christ. We are to serve him with our whole being. God doesn't rate us according to our status; he looks at the attitude of our hearts (1 Samuel 16:7). We should encourage leaders who show humility and a heartfelt desire to please God.

**2:7-9** The church leaders ("pillars")—James (the half-brother of Jesus, not the apostle), Peter, and John—realized that God was using Paul to reach the Gentiles, just as Peter was being used so greatly to reach the Jews. After hearing Paul's message, they gave Paul and Barnabas their approval to continue working among the Gentiles.

**2:10** The apostles were referring to the poor of Jerusalem. While many Gentile converts were financially comfortable, the Jerusalem church had suffered from the effects of a severe famine in Palestine (see Acts 11:28-30) and was struggling. So on his journeys, Paul had gathered funds for the Jewish Christians (Acts 24:17; Romans 15:25-29; 1 Corinthians 16:1-4; 2 Corinthians 8). The need for believers to care for the poor is a constant theme in Scripture. But often we do nothing, caught up in meeting our own needs and desires. Perhaps we don't see enough poverty to remember the needs of the poor. The world is filled with poor people, here and in other countries. What can you do to help?

**2:11** This was Antioch of Syria (distinguished from Antioch in Pisidia), a major trade center in the ancient world. Heavily populated by Greeks, it eventually became a strong Christian center. In Antioch the believers were first called Christians (Acts 11:26).

Antioch of Syria became the headquarters for the Gentile church and was Paul's base of operations.

**2:11ff** The Judaizers accused Paul of watering down the Good News to make it easier for Gentiles to accept, while Paul accused the Judaizers of nullifying the truth of the Good News by adding conditions to it. The basis of salvation was the issue: Is salvation through Christ alone, or does it come through Christ *and* adherence to the law? The argument came to a climax when Peter, Paul, the Judaizers, and some Gentile Christians all gathered together in Antioch to share a meal. Peter probably thought that by staying away from the Gentiles, he was promoting harmony—he did not want to offend James and the Jewish Christians. James had a very prominent position and presided over the Jerusalem council (Acts 15). But Paul charged that Peter's action violated the Good News. By joining the Judaizers, Peter implicitly was supporting their claim that Christ was not sufficient for salvation. Compromise is an important element in getting along with others, but we should never compromise the truth of God's Word. If we feel we have to change our Christian beliefs to match those of our companions, we are on dangerous ground.

**2:11, 12** Although Peter was a leader of the church, he was acting like a hypocrite. He knew better, yet he was driven by fear of what James and the others would think. Proverbs 29:25 says, "Fearing people is a dangerous trap." Paul knew that he had to confront Peter before his actions damaged the church. So, Paul publicly opposed Peter. Note, however, that Paul did not go to the other leaders, nor did he write letters to the churches telling them not to follow Peter's example. Instead, he opposed Peter face to face. Sometimes sincere Christians, even Christian leaders, make mistakes. And it may take other sincere Christians to get them back on track. If you are convinced that someone is doing harm to himself/herself or the church, try the direct approach. There is no place for backstabbing in the body of Christ.

**2:15, 16** If observing the Jewish laws cannot justify us, why should we still obey the Ten Commandments and other Old Testamade right with God by faith in Jesus Christ, not by obeying the law. And we have believed in Christ Jesus, so that we might be made right with God because of our faith in Christ, not because we have obeyed the law. For no one will ever be made right with God by obeying the law."*

17But suppose we seek to be made right with God through faith in Christ and then we are found guilty because we have abandoned the law. Would that mean Christ has led us into sin? Absolutely not! 18Rather, I am a sinner if I rebuild the old system of law I already tore down. 19For when I tried to keep the law, it condemned me. So I died to the law—I stopped trying to meet all its requirements—so that I might live for God. 20My old self has been crucified with Christ.* It is no longer I who live, but Christ lives in me. So I live in this earthly body by trusting in the Son of God, who loved me and gave himself for me. 21I do not treat the grace of God as meaningless. For if keeping the law could make us right with God, then there was no need for Christ to die.

**2:19**
Rom 6:10-14; 7:4
2 Cor 5:15

**2:20**
Rom 6:6; 8:37
Gal 1:4
1 Tim 2:6
Titus 2:14

## 2. Superiority of the gospel
### The Law and Faith in Christ

**3:1**
1 Cor 1:23
Gal 5:7

**3:2**
Rom 10:17

**3:3**
Gal 4:9

**3:4**
2 Jn 1:8

**3:5**
1 Cor 12:10

**3** Oh, foolish Galatians! Who has cast an evil spell on you? For the meaning of Jesus Christ's death was made as clear to you as if you had seen a picture of his death on the cross. 2Let me ask you this one question: Did you receive the Holy Spirit by obeying the law of Moses? Of course not! You received the Spirit because you believed the message you heard about Christ. 3How foolish can you be? After starting your Christian lives in the Spirit, why are you now trying to become perfect by your own human effort? 4Have you experienced* so much for nothing? Surely it was not in vain, was it?

5I ask you again, does God give you the Holy Spirit and work miracles among you because you obey the law? Of course not! It is because you believe the message you heard about Christ.

**2:16** Some translators hold that the quotation extends through verse 14; others through verse 16; and still others through verse 21. **2:20** Some English translations put this sentence in verse 19. **3:4** Or *Have you suffered.*

---

ment laws? We know that Paul was not saying the law is bad, because in another letter he wrote, "The law itself is holy, and its commands are holy and right and good" (Romans 7:12). Instead, he is saying that the law can never make us acceptable to God. The law still has an important role to play in the life of a Christian. The law (1) guards us from sin by giving us standards for behavior; (2) convicts us of sin, leaving us the opportunity to ask for God's forgiveness; and (3) drives us to trust in the sufficiency of Christ, because we can never keep the Ten Commandments perfectly. The law cannot possibly save us. But after we become Christians, it can guide us to live as God requires.

**2:17-19** Through studying the Old Testament Scriptures, Paul realized that he could not be saved by obeying God's laws. The prophets knew that God's plan of salvation did not rest on keeping the law (see the chart in chapter 3, p. 1989 for references). Because we have all been infected by sin, we cannot keep God's laws perfectly. Fortunately, God has provided a way of salvation that depends on Jesus Christ, not on our own efforts. Even though we know this truth, we must guard against the temptation of using service, good deeds, charitable giving, or any other effort as a substitute for faith.

**2:19, 20** How have our old selves been crucified with Christ? *Legally,* God looks at us as if we had died with Christ. Because our sins died with him, we are no longer condemned (Colossians 2:13-15). *Relationally,* we have become one with Christ, and his experiences are ours. Our Christian life began when, in unity with him, we died to our old life (see Romans 6:5-11). *In our daily life,* we must regularly crucify sinful desires that keep us from following Christ. This, too, is a kind of dying with him (Luke 9:23-25).

And yet the focus of Christianity is not on dying but on living. Because we have been crucified with Christ, we have also been raised with him (Romans 6:5). *Legally,* we have been reconciled with God (2 Corinthians 5:19) and are free to grow into Christ's likeness (Romans 8:29). And *in our daily life,* we have Christ's resurrection power as we continue to fight sin (Ephesians 1:19, 20). We are no longer alone, for Christ lives in us—he is our power for living and our hope for the future (Colossians 1:27).

**2:21** Believers today may still be in danger of acting as if there was no need for Christ to die. How? By replacing Jewish legalism with their own brand of Christian legalism, they are giving people

extra laws to obey. By believing they can earn God's favor by what they do, they are not trusting completely in Christ's work on the cross. By struggling to appropriate God's power to change them (sanctification), they are not resting in God's power to save them (justification). If we could be saved by being good, then Christ would not have had to die. But the cross is the only way to salvation.

**3:1** The Galatian believers had become fascinated by the false teachers' arguments, almost as though an evil spell had been cast on them. Magic was common in Paul's day (Acts 8:9-11; 13:6, 7). Magicians used both optical illusions and Satan's power to perform miracles, and people were drawn into the magicians' mysterious rites without recognizing their dangerous source.

**3:2, 3** Some of the believers in Galatia may have been in Jerusalem at Pentecost and received the Holy Spirit there. They knew that they hadn't received God's Spirit by obeying the Jewish laws. Paul stressed that just as they began their Christian lives in the power of the Spirit, so they should grow by the Spirit's power. The Galatians had taken a step backward when they had decided to insist on keeping the Jewish laws. We must realize that we grow spiritually because of God's work in us by his Spirit, not by following special rules.

**3:5** The Galatians knew that they had received the Holy Spirit when they believed, not when they obeyed the law. People still feel insecure in their faith because faith alone seems too easy. People still try to get closer to God by following rules. While certain disciplines (Bible study, prayer) and service may help us grow, they must not take the place of the Holy Spirit in us or become ends in themselves. By asking these questions, Paul hoped to get the Galatians to focus again on Christ as the foundation of their faith.

**3:5** The Holy Spirit gives Christians great power to live for God. Some Christians want more than this. They want to live in a state of perpetual excitement. The tedium of everyday living leads them to conclude that something is wrong spiritually. Often the Holy Spirit's greatest work is teaching us to persist, to keep on doing what is right even when it no longer seems interesting or exciting. The Galatians quickly turned from Paul's Good News to the teachings of the newest teachers in town; what they needed was the Holy Spirit's gift of persistence. If the Christian life seems ordinary, you may need the Spirit to stir you up. Every day offers a challenge to live for Christ.

⁶In the same way, "Abraham believed God, and God counted him as righteous because of his faith."* ⁷The real children of Abraham, then, are those who put their faith in God.

⁸What's more, the Scriptures looked forward to this time when God would declare the Gentiles to be righteous because of their faith. God proclaimed this good news to Abraham long ago when he said, "All nations will be blessed through you."* ⁹So all who put their faith in Christ share the same blessing Abraham received because of his faith.

¹⁰But those who depend on the law to make them right with God are under his curse, for the Scriptures say, "Cursed is everyone who does not observe and obey all the commands that are written in God's Book of the Law."* ¹¹So it is clear that no one can be made right with God by trying to keep the law. For the Scriptures say, "It is through faith that a righteous person has life."* ¹²This way of faith is very different from the way of law, which says, "It is through obeying the law that a person has life."*

¹³But Christ has rescued us from the curse pronounced by the law. When he was hung on the cross, he took upon himself the curse for our wrongdoing. For it is written in the Scriptures, "Cursed is everyone who is hung on a tree."* ¹⁴Through Christ Jesus, God has blessed the Gentiles with the same blessing he promised to Abraham, so that we who are believers might receive the promised* Holy Spirit through faith.

### The Law and God's Promise

¹⁵Dear brothers and sisters,* here's an example from everyday life. Just as no one can set aside or amend an irrevocable agreement, so it is in this case. ¹⁶God gave the promises to Abraham and his child.* And notice that the Scripture doesn't say "to his children,*" as if it meant many descendants. Rather, it says "to his child"—and that, of course, means Christ. ¹⁷This is what I am trying to say: The agreement God made with Abraham could not be canceled 430 years later when God gave the law to Moses. God would be breaking his promise. ¹⁸For if the inheritance could be received by keeping the law, then it would not be the result of accepting God's promise. But God graciously gave it to Abraham as a promise.

¹⁹Why, then, was the law given? It was given alongside the promise to show people their sins. But the law was designed to last only until the coming of the child who was promised. God gave his law through angels to Moses, who was the mediator between God and the people. ²⁰Now a mediator is helpful if more than one party must reach an agreement. But God, who is one, did not use a mediator when he gave his promise to Abraham.

**3:6** †Gen 15:6 / Rom 4:3
**3:8** †Gen 12:3 / Acts 3:25
**3:10** †Deut 27:26 / Jer 11:3
**3:11** †Hab 2:4 / Rom 1:17 / Heb 10:38
**3:12** †Lev 18:5 / Rom 10:5
**3:13** †Deut 21:23 / Gal 4:5
**3:14** Joel 2:28 / Acts 2:33
**3:15** Heb 9:17
**3:16** †Gen 12:7; 13:15; 17:7; 24:7
**3:17** Exod 12:40
**3:18** Rom 4:14; 11:6
**3:19** Exod 20:19 / Deut 5:5 / Acts 7:53 / Heb 2:2
**3:20** 1 Tim 2:5

**3:6** Gen 15:6.   **3:8** Gen 12:3; 18:18; 22:18.   **3:10** Deut 27:26.   **3:11** Hab 2:4.   **3:12** Lev 18:5.   **3:13** Deut 21:23 (Greek version).   **3:14** Some manuscripts read *the blessing of the.*   **3:15** Greek *Brothers.*   **3:16a** Greek *seed;* also in 3:16c, 19. See notes on Gen 12:7 and 13:15.   **3:16b** Greek *seeds.*

---

**3:6-9** The main argument of the Judaizers was that Gentiles had to become Jews in order to become Christians. Paul exposed the flaw in this argument by showing that real children of Abraham are those who have faith, not those who keep the law. Abraham himself was saved by his faith (Genesis 15:6). All believers in every age and from every nation share Abraham's blessing. This is a comforting promise, a great heritage for us, and a solid foundation for living.

**3:10** Paul quoted Deuteronomy 27:26 to prove that, contrary to what the Judaizers claimed, the law cannot justify and save—it can only condemn. Breaking even one commandment brings a person under condemnation. And because everyone has broken the commandments, everyone stands condemned. The law can do nothing to reverse the condemnation (Romans 3:20-24). But Christ took the curse of the law upon himself when he hung on the cross. He did this so we wouldn't have to bear our own punishment. The only condition is that we accept Christ's death on our behalf as the means to be saved (Colossians 1:20-23).

**3:11** Trying to be right with God by our own effort doesn't work. Good intentions such as "I'll do better next time" or "I'll never do that again" usually end in failure. Paul points to Habakkuk's declaration (Habakkuk 2:4) that by trusting God—believing in his provision for our sins and living each day in his power—we can break this cycle of failure.

**3:17** In the same way that we claim Jesus' death as God's provision for our salvation, Abraham believed in God and his promises, although they would not be made fully evident until centuries later on the cross. God promised, and Abraham answered in faith, even during the trial of God asking him to sacrifice his son. This is the heart of Christian faith. God promises to save us when we trust in Christ and take him at his word, just as Abraham did. We *know* in greater detail how God worked out his plan of grace in Christ. We have much less excuse for our unbelief!

**3:18, 19** The law has two functions. On the positive side, it reveals the nature and will of God and shows people how to live. On the negative side, it points out people's sins and shows them that it is impossible to please God by trying to obey all his laws completely. God's promise to Abraham dealt with Abraham's faith; the law focuses on actions. The covenant with Abraham shows that faith is the only way to be saved; the law shows how to obey God in grateful response. Faith does not annul the law; but the more we know God, the more we see how sinful we are. Then we are driven to depend on our faith in Christ alone for our salvation.

**3:19, 20** When God gave his promise to Abraham, he did it by himself alone, without angels or Moses as mediators. Although it is not mentioned in Exodus, Jews believed that the Ten Commandments had been given to Moses by angels (Stephen referred to this in his speech, see Acts 7:38, 53). Paul was showing the superiority of salvation and growth by faith over trying to be saved by keeping the Jewish laws. Christ is the best and only way given by God for us to come to him (1 Timothy 2:5).

**3:21**
Rom 8:2-4

**3:22**
Rom 3:11-19;
11:32

²¹Is there a conflict, then, between God's law and God's promises?* Absolutely not! If the law could give us new life, we could be made right with God by obeying it. ²²But the Scriptures declare that we are all prisoners of sin, so we receive God's promise of freedom only by believing in Jesus Christ.

### God's Children through Faith

²³Before the way of faith in Christ was available to us, we were placed under guard by the law. We were kept in protective custody, so to speak, until the way of faith was revealed.

**3:24**
Rom 10:4

**3:27**
Rom 6:3; 13:14

**3:28**
John 10:16; 17:21
1 Cor 12:13
Eph 2:14-15
Col 3:11

**3:29**
Rom 8:17
Gal 3:16

²⁴Let me put it another way. The law was our guardian until Christ came; it protected us until we could be made right with God through faith. ²⁵And now that the way of faith has come, we no longer need the law as our guardian.

²⁶For you are all children* of God through faith in Christ Jesus. ²⁷And all who have been united with Christ in baptism have put on Christ, like putting on new clothes.* ²⁸There is no longer Jew or Gentile,* slave or free, male and female. For you are all one in Christ Jesus. ²⁹And now that you belong to Christ, you are the true children* of Abraham. You are his heirs, and God's promise to Abraham belongs to you.

**3:21** Some manuscripts read *and the promises?*   **3:26** Greek *sons.*   **3:27** Greek *have put on Christ.*   **3:28** Greek *Jew or Greek.*   **3:29** Greek *seed.*

---

**DO WE STILL HAVE TO OBEY THE OLD TESTAMENT LAWS?**

When Paul says that non-Jews (Gentiles) are no longer bound by these laws, he is not saying that the Old Testament laws do not apply to us today. He is saying certain types of laws may not apply to us. In the Old Testament there were three categories of laws:

| | |
|---|---|
| Ceremonial law | This kind of law relates specifically to Israel's worship (see, for example, Leviticus 1:1-13). Its primary purpose was to point forward to Jesus Christ. Therefore, these laws were no longer necessary after Jesus' death and resurrection. While we are no longer bound by ceremonial laws, the principles behind them—to worship and love a holy God—still apply. The Jewish Christians often accused the Gentile Christians of violating the ceremonial law. |
| Civil law | This type of law dictated Israel's daily living (see Deuteronomy 24:10, 11, for example). Because modern society and culture are so radically different, some of these guidelines cannot be followed specifically. But the principles behind the commands should guide our conduct. At times, Paul asked Gentile Christians to follow some of these laws, not because they had to, but in order to promote unity. |
| Moral law | This sort of law is the direct command of God—for example, the Ten Commandments (Exodus 20:1-17). It requires strict obedience. It reveals the nature and will of God, and it still applies to us today. We are to obey this moral law, not to obtain salvation, but to live in ways pleasing to God. |

---

**3:21, 22** Before faith in Christ delivered us, we were imprisoned by sin, beaten down by past mistakes, and choked by desires that we knew were wrong. God knew we were sin's prisoners, but he provided a way of escape—faith in Jesus Christ. Without Christ, everyone is held in sin's grasp, and only those who place their faith in Christ ever get out of it. Look to Christ—he is reaching out to set you free.

**3:24, 25** The picture of the law as a guardian is similar to a tutor giving a young child supervision. We no longer need that kind of supervision. The law teaches us the *need* for salvation; God's grace *gives* us that salvation. The Old Testament still applies today. In it, God reveals his nature, his will for humanity, his moral laws, and his guidelines for living. But we cannot be saved by keeping that law; we must trust in Christ.

**3:28** Some Jewish males greeted each new day by praying, "Lord, I thank you that I am not a Gentile, a slave, or a woman." The role of women was enhanced by Christianity. Faith in Christ transcends these differences and makes all believers one in Christ. Make sure you do not impose distinctions that Christ has removed. Because all believers are his heirs, no one is more privileged than or superior to anyone else.

**3:28** It's our natural inclination to feel uncomfortable around people who are different from us and to gravitate toward those who are similar to us. But when we allow our differences to separate us from our fellow believers, we are disregarding clear biblical teaching. Make a point to seek out and appreciate people who are not just like you and your friends. You may find that you have a lot in common with them.

**3:29** The original promise to Abraham was intended for the whole world, not just for Abraham's physical descendants (see Genesis 12:3). All believers participate in this promise and are blessed as children of Abraham.

**4** Think of it this way. If a father dies and leaves an inheritance for his young children, those children are not much better off than slaves until they grow up, even though they actually own everything their father had. ²They have to obey their guardians until they reach whatever age their father set. ³And that's the way it was with us before Christ came. We were like children; we were slaves to the basic spiritual principles* of this world.

⁴But when the right time came, God sent his Son, born of a woman, subject to the law. ⁵God sent him to buy freedom for us who were slaves to the law, so that he could adopt us as his very own children.* ⁶And because we* are his children, God has sent the Spirit of his Son into our hearts, prompting us to call out, "Abba, Father."* ⁷Now you are no longer a slave but God's own child.* And since you are his child, God has made you his heir.

### Paul's Concern for the Galatians

⁸Before you Gentiles knew God, you were slaves to so-called gods that do not even exist. ⁹So now that you know God (or should I say, now that God knows you), why do you want to go back again and become slaves once more to the weak and useless spiritual principles of this world? ¹⁰You are trying to earn favor with God by observing certain days or months or seasons or years. ¹¹I fear for you. Perhaps all my hard work with you was for nothing. ¹²Dear brothers and sisters,* I plead with you to live as I do in freedom from these things, for I have become like you Gentiles—free from those laws.

You did not mistreat me when I first preached to you. ¹³Surely you remember that I was sick when I first brought you the Good News. ¹⁴But even though my condition tempted you to reject me, you did not despise me or turn me away. No, you took me in and cared for me as though I were an angel from God or even Christ Jesus himself. ¹⁵Where is that joyful and grateful spirit you felt then? I am sure you would have taken out your own eyes and given them to me if it had been possible. ¹⁶Have I now become your enemy because I am telling you the truth?

**4:3** Gal 3:23; Col 2:8, 20 **4:4** Mark 1:15; John 1:14; Eph 1:10; Heb 2:14 **4:5** Rom 8:15; Eph 1:5 **4:6** Rom 8:15-16 **4:7** Rom 8:17 **4:8** 2 Chr 13:9; Isa 37:19; Jer 2:11; 1 Cor 8:4-6; 1 Thes 1:9 **4:9** Col 2:20 **4:10** Rom 14:5; Col 2:16 **4:13** 1 Cor 2:3 **4:14** Matt 10:40 **4:16** Amos 5:10

**4:3** Or *powers;* also in 4:9. **4:5** Greek *sons;* also in 4:6. **4:6a** Greek *you.* **4:6b** *Abba* is an Aramaic term for "father." **4:7** Greek *son;* also in 4:7b. **4:12** Greek *brothers;* also in 4:28, 31.

---

**4:3-7** Paul uses the illustration of slavery to show that before Christ came and died for sins, people were in bondage to the law. Thinking they could be saved by it, they became enslaved to trying—and failing—to keep it. But we who were once slaves are now God's very own children who have an intimate relationship with him. Because of Christ, there is no reason to be afraid of God. We can come boldly into his presence, knowing that he will welcome us as his family members.

**4:4** "When the right time came," God sent Jesus to earth to die for our sins. For centuries the Jews had been wondering when their Messiah would come—but God's timing was perfect. We may sometimes wonder if God will ever respond to our prayers. But we must never doubt him or give up hope. At the right time he will respond. Are you waiting for God's timing? Trust his judgment and trust that he has your best interests in mind.

**4:4, 5** Jesus was born of a woman—he was human. He was born as a Jew—he was subject to God's law and fulfilled it perfectly. Thus, Jesus was the perfect sacrifice because, although he was fully human, he never sinned. His death bought freedom for us who were enslaved to sin so that we could be adopted into God's family.

**4:5-7** Under Roman law, an adopted child was guaranteed all legal rights to his father's property, even if he was formerly a slave. He was not a second-class son; he was equal to all other sons, biological or adopted, in his father's family. As adopted children of God, we share with Jesus all rights to God's resources. As God's heirs, we can claim what he has provided for us—our full identity as his children (see Romans 8:15-17).

**4:13, 14** Paul's illness was a sickness that he was enduring while he visited the Galatian churches. The world is often callous to people's pain and misery. Paul commended the Galatians for not scorning him, even though his condition was a trial to them (he didn't explain what was wrong with him). Such caring was what Jesus meant when he called us to serve the homeless, hungry, sick, and imprisoned as if they were Jesus himself (Matthew 25:34-40). Do you avoid those in pain or those facing difficulty—or are you willing to care for them as if they were Jesus Christ himself?

**4:15** Have you lost your joy? Paul sensed that the Galatians had lost the joy of their salvation because of legalism. Legalism can take away joy because (1) it makes people feel guilty rather than loved; (2) it produces self-hatred rather than humility; (3) it stresses performance over relationship; (4) it points out how far short we fall rather than how far we've come because of what Christ did for us. If you feel guilty and inadequate, check your focus. Are you living by faith in Christ or by trying to live up to the demands and expectations of others?

**4:16** Paul did not gain great popularity when he rebuked the Galatians for turning away from their first faith in Christ. Human nature hasn't changed much—we still get angry when we're scolded. But don't write off someone who challenges you. There may be truth in what he or she says. Receive his or her words with humility; carefully think them over. If you discover that you need to change an attitude or action, take steps to do it.

**4:17**
Gal 2:4, 12

¹⁷Those false teachers are so eager to win your favor, but their intentions are not good. They are trying to shut you off from me so that you will pay attention only to them. ¹⁸If someone is eager to do good things for you, that's all right; but let them do it all the time, not just when I'm with you.

**4:19**
Eph 4:13

¹⁹Oh, my dear children! I feel as if I'm going through labor pains for you again, and they will continue until Christ is fully developed in your lives. ²⁰I wish I were with you right now so I could change my tone. But at this distance I don't know how else to help you.

| THREE DISTORTIONS OF CHRISTIANITY | Group | Their definition of a Christian | Their genuine concern | The danger | Application question |
|---|---|---|---|---|---|
| Almost from the beginning there were forces at work within Christianity that would have destroyed or sidetracked the movement. Of these, three created many problems then and have continued to reappear in other forms even today. The three aberrations are contrasted to true Christianity. | Judaized Christianity | Christians are Jews who have recognized Jesus as the promised Savior. Therefore, any Gentile desiring to become a Christian must first become a Jew. | Having a high regard for the Scriptures and God's choice of Jews as his people, they did not want to see God's commands overlooked or broken. | Tends to add human traditions and standards to God's law. Also subtracts from the Scriptures God's clear concern for all nations. | Do you appreciate God's choice of a unique people through whom he offered forgiveness and eternal life to all peoples? |
| | Legalized Christianity | Christians are those who live by a long list of "don'ts." God's favor is earned by good behavior. | Recognized that real change brought about by God should lead to changes in behavior. | Tends to make God's love something to earn rather than to accept freely. Would reduce Christianity to a set of impossible rules and transform the Good News into bad news. | As important as change in action is, can you see that God may be desiring different changes in you than in others? |
| | Lawless Christianity | Christians live above the law. They need no guidelines. God's Word is not as important as our personal sense of God's guidance. | Recognized that forgiveness from God cannot be based on our ability to live up to his perfect standards. It must be received by faith as a gift made possible by Christ's death on the cross. | Forgets that Christians are still human and fail consistently when trying to live only by what they "feel" God wants. | Do you recognize the ongoing need for God's expressed commands as you live out your gratitude for his great salvation? |
| | True Christianity | Christians are those who believe inwardly and outwardly that Jesus' death has allowed God to offer them forgiveness and eternal life as a gift. They have accepted that gift through faith and are seeking to live a life of obedient gratitude for what God has done for them. | Christianity is both private and public, with heart-belief and mouth-confession. Our relationship to God and the power he provides result in obedience. Having received forgiveness and eternal life, we are now daily challenged to live that life with his help. | Avoids the above dangers. | How would those closest to you describe your Christianity? Do they think you live *so* that God will accept you, or do they know that you live *because* God has accepted you in Christ? |

**4:17** The false teachers claimed to be religious authorities and experts in Judaism and Christianity. Appealing to the believers' desire to do what was right, they drew quite a following. Paul said, however, that they were wrong and that their motives were selfish. False teachers are often respectable and persuasive. That is why all teachings should be checked against the Bible.

**4:19** Paul led many people to Christ and helped them mature spiritually. Perhaps one reason for his success as a spiritual

father was the deep concern he felt for his spiritual children; he compared his pain over their faithlessness to the pain of childbirth. We should have the same intense care for those to whom we are spiritual parents. When you lead people to Christ, remember to stand by them to help them grow.

## Abraham's Two Children

21 Tell me, you who want to live under the law, do you know what the law actually says? 22 The Scriptures say that Abraham had two sons, one from his slave wife and one from his freeborn wife.* 23 The son of the slave wife was born in a human attempt to bring about the fulfillment of God's promise. But the son of the freeborn wife was born as God's own fulfillment of his promise.

24 These two women serve as an illustration of God's two covenants. The first woman, Hagar, represents Mount Sinai where people received the law that enslaved them. 25 And now Jerusalem is just like Mount Sinai in Arabia,* because she and her children live in slavery to the law. 26 But the other woman, Sarah, represents the heavenly Jerusalem. She is the free woman, and she is our mother. 27 As Isaiah said,

"Rejoice, O childless woman,
   you who have never given birth!
Break into a joyful shout,
   you who have never been in labor!
For the desolate woman now has more children
   than the woman who lives with her husband!"*

28 And you, dear brothers and sisters, are children of the promise, just like Isaac. 29 But you are now being persecuted by those who want you to keep the law, just as Ishmael, the child born by human effort, persecuted Isaac, the child born by the power of the Spirit.

30 But what do the Scriptures say about that? "Get rid of the slave and her son, for the son of the slave woman will not share the inheritance with the free woman's son."* 31 So, dear brothers and sisters, we are not children of the slave woman; we are children of the free woman.

## 3. Freedom of the gospel

### Freedom in Christ

**5** So Christ has truly set us free. Now make sure that you stay free, and don't get tied up again in slavery to the law.

2 Listen! I, Paul, tell you this: If you are counting on circumcision to make you right with God, then Christ will be of no benefit to you. 3 I'll say it again. If you are trying to find favor with God by being circumcised, you must obey every regulation in the whole law of Moses. 4 For if you are trying to make yourselves right with God by keeping the law, you have been cut off from Christ! You have fallen away from God's grace.

5 But we who live by the Spirit eagerly wait to receive by faith the righteousness God has promised to us. 6 For when we place our faith in Christ Jesus, there is no benefit in being circumcised or being uncircumcised. What is important is faith expressing itself in love.

**4:22** See Gen 16:15; 21:2-3. **4:25** Greek *And Hagar, which is Mount Sinai in Arabia, is now like Jerusalem;* other manuscripts read *And Mount Sinai in Arabia is now like Jerusalem.* **4:27** Isa 54:1. **4:30** Gen 21:10.

**4:22** Gen 16:15; 21:2
**4:23** Rom 9:7-9
**4:26** Heb 12:22; Rev 3:12; 21:2, 10
**4:27** †Isa 54:1
**4:28** Gal 3:29
**4:29** Gen 21:9
**4:30** Gen 21:10; John 8:35
**4:31** Gal 3:29
**5:1** John 8:32, 36; Acts 15:10; Gal 2:4
**5:2** Acts 15:1
**5:3** Gal 3:10
**5:5** Rom 8:23-24
**5:6** 1 Cor 7:19; 1 Thes 1:3

**4:21ff** People are saved because of their faith in Christ, not because of what they do. Paul contrasted those who are enslaved to the law (represented by Hagar, the slave wife) with those who are free from the law (represented by Sarah, the freeborn wife). Hagar's abuse of Sarah (Genesis 16:4) was like the persecution that the Gentile Christians were getting from the Judaizers, who insisted on keeping the law in order to be saved. Eventually Sarah triumphed because God kept his promise to give her a son, just as those who worship Christ in faith will also triumph.

**4:24** Paul explained that what happened to Sarah and Hagar is an allegory or picture of the relationship between God and people. Paul was using a type of argument that was common in his day and that was probably being used against him by his opponents.

**5:1** Christ died to set us free from sin and from a long list of laws and regulations. Christ came to set us free—not free to do whatever we want because that would lead us back into slavery to our selfish desires. Rather, thanks to Christ, we are now free and able to do what was impossible before—to live unselfishly. Those who appeal to their freedom so that they can have their own way or indulge their own desires are falling back into sin. But it is also wrong to put a burden of law-keeping on Christians. We must stand against those who would enslave us with rules, methods, or special conditions for being saved or growing in Christ.

**5:2-4** Trying to be saved by keeping the law and being saved by grace are two entirely different approaches. "Christ will be of no benefit to you" means that Christ's provision for our salvation will not help us if we are trying to save ourselves. Obeying the law does not make it any easier for God to save us. All we can do is accept his gracious gift through faith. Our deeds of service must never be used to try to earn God's love or favor.

**5:3, 4** Circumcision was a symbol of having the right background and doing everything required by religion. No amount of work, discipline, or moral behavior can save us. If a person were counting on finding favor with God by being circumcised, he would also have to obey the rest of God's law completely. Trying to save ourselves by keeping all God's laws only separates us from God.

**5:6** We are saved by faith, not by deeds. But love for others and for God is the response of those whom God has forgiven. God's forgiveness is complete, and Jesus said that those who are forgiven much love much (Luke 7:47). Because faith expresses itself through love, you can check your love for others as a way to monitor your faith.

**5:7**
1 Cor 9:24

**5:8**
Rom 8:28

**5:9**
1 Cor 5:6

**5:10**
Gal 1:7

**5:11**
1 Cor 1:23

**5:13**
1 Pet 2:16

**5:14**
†Lev 19:18
Rom 13:9

7 You were running the race so well. Who has held you back from following the truth? 8 It certainly isn't God, for he is the one who called you to freedom. 9 This false teaching is like a little yeast that spreads through the whole batch of dough! 10 I am trusting the Lord to keep you from believing false teachings. God will judge that person, whoever he is, who has been confusing you.

11 Dear brothers and sisters,* if I were still preaching that you must be circumcised—as some say I do—why am I still being persecuted? If I were no longer preaching salvation through the cross of Christ, no one would be offended. 12 I just wish that those trouble-makers who want to mutilate you by circumcision would mutilate themselves.*

13 For you have been called to live in freedom, my brothers and sisters. But don't use your freedom to satisfy your sinful nature. Instead, use your freedom to serve one another in love. 14 For the whole law can be summed up in this one command: "Love your neighbor as yourself."* 15 But if you are always biting and devouring one another, watch out! Beware of destroying one another.

**5:11** Greek *Brothers;* similarly in 5:13.   **5:12** Or *castrate themselves,* or *cut themselves off from you;* Greek reads *cut themselves off.*   **5:14** Lev 19:18.

---

**VICES AND VIRTUES**
The Bible mentions many specific actions and attitudes that are either right or wrong. Look at the list included here. Are there a number of characteristics from the wrong column that are influencing you?

**VICES**
*(Neglecting God and others)*
Sexual immorality *(Galatians 5:19)*
Impurity *(Galatians 5:19)*
Lust *(Colossians 3:5)*
Hostility *(Galatians 5:20)*
Quarreling *(Galatians 5:20)*
Jealousy *(Galatians 5:20)*
Anger *(Galatians 5:20)*
Selfish ambition *(Galatians 5:20)*
Dissension *(Galatians 5:20)*
Arrogance *(2 Corinthians 12:20)*
Envy *(Galatians 5:21)*
Murder *(Revelation 22:12-16)*
Idolatry *(Galatians 5:20; Ephesians 5:5)*
Sorcery *(Galatians 5:20)*
Drunkenness *(Galatians 5:21)*
Wild parties *(Luke 15:13; Galatians 5:21)*
Cheating *(1 Corinthians 6:8)*
Adultery *(1 Corinthians 6:9, 10)*
Homosexuality *(1 Corinthians 6:9, 10)*
Greed *(1 Corinthians 6:9, 10; Ephesians 5:5)*
Stealing *(1 Corinthians 6:9, 10)*
Lying *(Revelation 22:12-16)*

**VIRTUES**
*(The by-products of living for God)*
Love *(Galatians 5:22)*
Joy *(Galatians 5:22)*
Peace *(Galatians 5:22)*
Patience *(Galatians 5:22)*
Kindness *(Galatians 5:22)*
Goodness *(Galatians 5:22)*
Faithfulness *(Galatians 5:22)*
Gentleness *(Galatians 5:23)*
Self-control *(Galatians 5:23)*

---

**5:9** A little yeast causes a whole lump of dough to rise. It only takes one wrong person to infect all the others.

**5:11** Persecution proved that Paul was preaching the true Good News. If he had taught what the false teachers were teaching, no one would be offended. But because he was teaching the truth, he was persecuted by both Jews and Judaizers. Have friends or loved ones rejected you because you have taken a stand for Christ? Jesus said not to be surprised if the world hates you, because it hated him (John 15:18, 19). Just as Paul continued to faithfully proclaim the message about Christ, you should continue doing the ministry God has given you—in spite of the obstacles others may put in your way.

**5:13** Paul distinguishes between freedom to sin and freedom to serve. Freedom or license to sin is no freedom at all, because it enslaves you to Satan, others, or your own sinful nature. Christians, by contrast, should not be slaves to sin, because they are free to do right and to glorify God through loving service to others.

**5:14, 15** When we believers lose the motivation of love, we become critical of others. We stop looking for good in them

and see only their faults. Soon we lose our unity. Have you talked behind someone's back? Have you focused on others' shortcomings instead of their strengths? Remind yourself of Jesus' command to love others as you love yourself (Matthew 22:39). When you begin to feel critical of someone, make a list of that person's positive qualities. When problems need to be addressed, confront in love rather than gossip.

## Living by the Spirit's Power

16So I say, let the Holy Spirit guide your lives. Then you won't be doing what your sinful nature craves. 17The sinful nature wants to do evil, which is just the opposite of what the Spirit wants. And the Spirit gives us desires that are the opposite of what the sinful nature desires. These two forces are constantly fighting each other, so you are not free to carry out your good intentions. 18But when you are directed by the Spirit, you are not under obligation to the law of Moses.

19When you follow the desires of your sinful nature, the results are very clear: sexual immorality, impurity, lustful pleasures, 20idolatry, sorcery, hostility, quarreling, jealousy, outbursts of anger, selfish ambition, dissension, division, 21envy, drunkenness, wild parties, and other sins like these. Let me tell you again, as I have before, that anyone living that sort of life will not inherit the Kingdom of God.

22But the Holy Spirit produces this kind of fruit in our lives: love, joy, peace, patience, kindness, goodness, faithfulness, 23gentleness, and self-control. There is no law against these things!

24Those who belong to Christ Jesus have nailed the passions and desires of their sinful nature to his cross and crucified them there. 25Since we are living by the Spirit, let us follow the Spirit's leading in every part of our lives. 26Let us not become conceited, or provoke one another, or be jealous of one another.

## We Harvest What We Plant

6 Dear brothers and sisters, if another believer* is overcome by some sin, you who are godly* should gently and humbly help that person back onto the right path. And be careful not to fall into the same temptation yourself. 2Share each other's burdens, and in this way obey the law of Christ. 3If you think you are too important to help someone, you are only fooling yourself. You are not that important.

6:1a Greek *Brothers, if a man.*   6:1b Greek *spiritual.*

**5:16**
Rom 8:4-6
**5:17**
Rom 7:15-23
**5:18**
Rom 6:14; 8:14
**5:19-21**
Rom 13:12-13
1 Cor 6:9-10
Eph 5:5
Rev 22:15
**5:22**
Eph 5:9
**5:24**
Rom 6:6
Col 3:5
**5:25**
Rom 8:4
Gal 5:16
**5:26**
Phil 2:3
**6:1**
1 Cor 2:15
Jas 5:19-20
1 Jn 5:16
**6:2**
Rom 15:1
**6:3**
Rom 12:3
1 Cor 3:18

---

**5:16-18** If your desire is to have the qualities listed in 5:22, 23, then you know that the Holy Spirit is leading you. At the same time, be careful not to confuse your subjective feelings with the Spirit's leading. Being led by the Holy Spirit involves the desire to hear, the readiness to obey God's Word, and the sensitivity to discern between your feelings and his promptings. Live each day controlled and guided by the Holy Spirit. Then the words of Christ will be in your mind, the love of Christ will be behind your actions, and the power of Christ will help you control your selfish desires.

**5:17** Paul describes the two forces fighting within us—the Holy Spirit and the sinful nature (our evil desires or inclinations that stem from our body; see also 5:16, 19, 24). Paul is not saying that these forces are equal—the Holy Spirit is infinitely stronger. But if we rely on our own wisdom, we will make wrong choices. If we try to follow the Spirit by our own human effort, we will fail. Our only way to freedom from our evil desires is through the empowering of the Holy Spirit (see Romans 8:9; Ephesians 4:23, 24; Colossians 3:3-8).

**5:19-21** We all have evil desires, and we can't ignore them. In order for us to follow the Holy Spirit's guidance, we must deal with them decisively (crucify them—5:24). These desires include obvious sins, such as sexual immorality and demonic activities. They also include less obvious sins, such as hostility, jealousy, and selfish ambition. Those who ignore such sins or refuse to deal with them reveal that they have not received the gift of the Spirit that leads to a transformed life.

**5:22, 23** The fruit of the Spirit is the spontaneous work of the Holy Spirit in us. The Spirit produces these character traits that are found in the nature of Christ. They are the by-products of Christ's control—we can't obtain them by *trying* to get them without his help. If we want the fruit of the Spirit to grow in us, we must join our life to his (see John 15:4, 5). We must know him, love him, remember him, and imitate him. As a result, we will fulfill the intended purpose of the law—to love God and our neighbors. Which of these qualities do you want the Spirit to produce in you?

**5:23** Because the God who sent the law also sent the Spirit, the by-products of the Spirit-filled life are in perfect harmony with the intent of God's law. A person who exhibits the fruit of the Spirit fulfills the law far better than a person who observes the rituals but has little love in his or her heart.

**5:24** In order to accept Christ as Savior, we need to turn from our sins and willingly nail our sinful nature to the cross. This doesn't mean, however, that we will never see traces of its evil desires again. As Christians we still have the capacity to sin, but we have been set free from sin's power over us and no longer have to give in to it. We must daily commit our sinful tendencies to God's control, daily crucify them, and moment by moment draw on the Spirit's power to overcome them (see 2:20; 6:14).

**5:25** God is interested in every part of our life, not just the spiritual part. As we live by the Holy Spirit's power, we need to submit every aspect of our life to God: emotional, physical, social, intellectual, vocational. Paul says that because we're saved, we should live like it! The Holy Spirit is the source of your new life, so keep in step with his leading. Don't let anything or anyone else determine your values and standards in any area of your life.

**5:26** Everyone needs a certain amount of approval from others. But those who go out of their way to secure honors or to win popularity become conceited and show they are not following the Holy Spirit's leading. Those who look to God for approval won't need to envy others. Because we are God's sons and daughters, we have his Holy Spirit as the loving guarantee of his approval. Seek to please God, and the approval of others won't seem so important.

**6:1-3** No Christian should ever think that he or she is totally independent and doesn't need help from others, and no one should feel excused from the task of helping others. The body of Christ—the church—functions only when the members work together for the common good. Do you know someone who needs help? Is there a Christian brother or sister who needs correction or encouragement? Humbly and gently reach out to that person offering to lift his or her load (John 13:34, 35).

6:4
2 Cor 13:5

6:6
1 Cor 9:11, 14

6:7
1 Cor 6:9
2 Cor 9:6

6:8
Job 4:8
Rom 8:13

6:9
2 Thes 3:13

6:10
Eph 2:19

6:11
1 Cor 16:21

6:13
Rom 2:25

6:14
Rom 6:2, 6
1 Cor 2:2
Gal 2:20

⁴Pay careful attention to your own work, for then you will get the satisfaction of a job well done, and you won't need to compare yourself to anyone else. ⁵For we are each responsible for our own conduct.

⁶Those who are taught the word of God should provide for their teachers, sharing all good things with them.

⁷Don't be misled—you cannot mock the justice of God. You will always harvest what you plant. ⁸Those who live only to satisfy their own sinful nature will harvest decay and death from that sinful nature. But those who live to please the Spirit will harvest everlasting life from the Spirit. ⁹So let's not get tired of doing what is good. At just the right time we will reap a harvest of blessing if we don't give up. ¹⁰Therefore, whenever we have the opportunity, we should do good to everyone—especially to those in the family of faith.

### Paul's Final Advice

¹¹NOTICE WHAT LARGE LETTERS I USE AS I WRITE THESE CLOSING WORDS IN MY OWN HANDWRITING.

¹²Those who are trying to force you to be circumcised want to look good to others. They don't want to be persecuted for teaching that the cross of Christ alone can save. ¹³And even those who advocate circumcision don't keep the whole law themselves. They only want you to be circumcised so they can boast about it and claim you as their disciples.

¹⁴As for me, may I never boast about anything except the cross of our Lord Jesus Christ. Because of that cross,* my interest in this world has been crucified, and the world's interest

**6:14** Or *Because of him.*

---

**OUR WRONG DESIRES VERSUS THE FRUIT OF THE SPIRIT**
The will of the Holy Spirit is in constant opposition to our sinful desires. The two are on opposite sides of the spiritual battle.

| Our wrong desires are | The fruit of the Spirit is |
| --- | --- |
| Evil | Good |
| Destructive | Productive |
| Easy to ignite | Difficult to ignite |
| Difficult to stifle | Easy to stifle |
| Self-centered | Self-giving |
| Oppressive and possessive | Liberating and nurturing |
| Decadent | Uplifting |
| Sinful | Holy |
| Deadly | Abundant life |

---

**6:4** When you do your very best, you feel good about the results. There is no need to compare yourself with others. People make comparisons for many reasons. Some point out others' flaws in order to feel better about themselves. Others simply want reassurance that they are doing well. When you are tempted to compare, look at Jesus Christ. His example will inspire you to do your very best, and his loving acceptance will comfort you when you fall short of your expectations.

**6:6** Paul says that students should take care of the material needs of their teachers (1 Corinthians 9:7-12). It is easy to receive the benefit of good Bible teaching and then to take our spiritual leaders for granted, ignoring their financial and physical needs. We should care for our teachers, not grudgingly or reluctantly, but with a generous spirit, showing honor and appreciation for all they have done (1 Timothy 5:17, 18).

**6:7, 8** It would certainly be a surprise if you planted corn and pumpkins came up. It's a natural law to harvest what we plant. It's true in other areas, too. If you gossip about your friends, you will lose their friendship. Every action has results. If you plant to please your own desires, you'll harvest a crop of sorrow and evil. If you plant to please God, you'll harvest joy and everlasting life. What kind of seeds are you planting?

**6:9, 10** It is discouraging to continue to do right and receive no word of thanks or see no tangible results. But Paul challenged the Galatians, and he challenges us to keep on doing good and to trust God for the results. In due time, we will reap a harvest of blessing.

**6:11** Up to this point, Paul had probably dictated the letter to a secretary. Here he takes the pen into his own hand to write his final, personal greetings. Paul did this in other letters as well, to add emphasis to his words and to validate that the letter was genuine.

**6:13** Some of the Judaizers were emphasizing circumcision as proof of holiness, but were ignoring the other Jewish laws. People often choose a certain principle or prohibition and make it the measure of faith. Some may condemn drunkenness but ignore gluttony. Others may despise promiscuity but tolerate prejudice. Some who are adamant against homosexuality ignore child abuse. The Bible in its entirety is our rule of faith and practice. We cannot pick and choose the mandates we will follow.

**6:14** The world is full of enticements. Daily we are confronted with subtle cultural pressures and overt propaganda. The only way to escape these destructive influences is to ask God to help crucify our interest in them, just as Paul did. How much do the interests of this world matter to you? (See 2:20 and 5:24 for more on this concept.)

in me has also died. <sup>15</sup>It doesn't matter whether we have been circumcised or not. What counts is whether we have been transformed into a new creation. <sup>16</sup>May God's peace and mercy be upon all who live by this principle; they are the new people of God.*

<sup>17</sup>From now on, don't let anyone trouble me with these things. For I bear on my body the scars that show I belong to Jesus.

<sup>18</sup>Dear brothers and sisters,* may the grace of our Lord Jesus Christ be with your spirit. Amen.

**6:15**
1 Cor 7:19
2 Cor 5:17
Gal 5:6

**6:17**
2 Cor 1:5; 4:10

**6:18**
Rom 16:20
2 Tim 4:22

6:16 Greek *this principle, and upon the Israel of God.*    6:18 Greek *Brothers.*

---

**6:15** It is easy to get caught up with the externals. Beware of those who emphasize actions that we should or shouldn't do, with no concern for the inward condition of the heart. Living a good life without an inward change leads to a shallow or empty spiritual walk. What matters to God is that we be completely changed from the inside out (2 Corinthians 5:17).

**6:18** Paul's letter to the Galatians boldly declares the freedom of the Christian. Doubtless these early Christians in Galatia wanted to grow in the Christian life, but they were being misled by those who said this could be done only by keeping certain Jewish laws.

How strange it would be for a prisoner who had been set free to walk back into his or her cell and refuse to leave! How strange for an animal, released from a trap, to go back inside it! How sad for a believer to be freed from the bondage of sin, only to return to rigid conformity to a set of rules and regulations!

If you believe in Jesus Christ, you have been set free. Instead of going back into some form of slavery, whether to legalism or to sin, use your freedom to live for Christ and serve him as he desires.

OUR churches come in all styles and shapes—secret meetings in homes; wide-open gatherings in amphitheaters; worship services packing thousands into a sanctuary while an overflow crowd watches on closed-circuit television; handfuls who kneel in urban storefronts. Buildings will vary, but the church is not confined to four walls. The church of Jesus Christ is *people,* his people, of every race and nation, who love Christ and are committed to serving him.

The "church age" began at Pentecost (Acts 2). Born in Jerusalem, the church spread rapidly through the ministry of the apostles and the early believers. Fanned by persecution, the gospel flame then spread to other cities and nations. On three courageous journeys, Paul and his associates established local assemblies in scores of Gentile cities.

One of the most prominent of those churches was at Ephesus. It was established in A.D. 53 on Paul's homeward journey to Jerusalem. But Paul returned a year later, on his third missionary trip, and stayed there for three years, preaching and teaching with great effectiveness (Acts 19:1–20). At another time, Paul met with the Ephesian elders, and he sent Timothy to serve as their leader (1 Timothy 1:3). Just a few years later, Paul was sent as a prisoner to Rome. There, he was visited by messengers from various churches, including Tychicus of Ephesus. Paul wrote this letter to the church and sent it with Tychicus. Not written to counteract heresy or to confront any specific problem, Ephesians is a letter of encouragement. In it Paul describes the nature and appearance of the church, and he challenges believers to function as the living body of Christ on earth.

After a warm greeting (1:1, 2), Paul affirms the nature of the church—the glorious fact that believers in Christ have been showered with God's kindness (1:3–8), chosen for greatness (1:9–12), marked with the Holy Spirit (1:13, 14), filled with the Spirit's power (1:15–23), freed from sin's curse and bondage (2:1–10), and brought near to God (2:11–18). As part of God's "house," we stand with the prophets, apostles, Jews, Gentiles, and Christ himself (2:19—3:13). Then, as though overcome with emotion by remembering all that God has done, Paul challenges the Ephesians to live close to Christ, and he breaks into spontaneous praise (3:14–21).

Paul then turns his attention to the implications of being in the body of Christ, the church. Believers should have unity in their commitment to Christ and their use of spiritual gifts (4:1–16). They should have the highest moral standards (4:17—6:9). For the individual, this means rejecting pagan practices (4:17—5:20), and for the family, this means mutual submission and love (5:21—6:9).

Paul then reminds believers that the church is in a constant battle with the forces of darkness and that they should use every spiritual weapon at their disposal (6:10–17). He concludes by asking for their prayers, commissioning Tychicus, and giving a benediction (6:18–24).

As you read this masterful description of the church, thank God for the diversity and unity in his family, pray for your brothers and sisters across the world, and draw close to those in your local church.

## VITAL STATISTICS

**PURPOSE:**
To strengthen the believers in Ephesus in their Christian faith by explaining the nature and purpose of the church, the body of Christ

**AUTHOR:**
Paul

**ORIGINAL AUDIENCE:**
The church at Ephesus, then circulated to neighboring local churches

**DATE WRITTEN:**
Approximately A.D. 60, from Rome, during Paul's imprisonment there

**SETTING:**
The letter was not written to confront any heresy or problem in the churches. It was sent with Tychicus to strengthen and encourage the churches in the area. Paul had spent over three years with the Ephesian church. As a result, he was very close to them. Paul met with the elders of the Ephesian church at Miletus (Acts 20:17–38)—a meeting that was filled with great sadness because he was leaving them for what he thought would be the last time. Because the letter contains no specific references to people or problems in the Ephesian church and because the words "in Ephesus" (1:1) are not present in some early manuscripts, Paul may have intended this to be a circular letter to be read to all the churches in the area.

**KEY VERSES:**
"For there is one body and one Spirit, just as you have been called to one glorious hope for the future. There is one Lord, one faith, one baptism, and one God and Father, who is over all and in all and living through all" (4:4–6).

**KEY PEOPLE:**
Paul, Tychicus

## THE BLUEPRINT

1. Unity in Christ
   (1:1—3:21)
2. Unity in the body of Christ
   (4:1— 6:24)

In this letter, Paul explains the wonderful things that we have received through Christ and refers to the church as a body to illustrate unity of purpose and show how each individual member is a part that must work together with all the other parts. In our own life, we should work to eradicate all backbiting, gossip, criticism, jealousy, anger, and bitterness, because these are barriers to unity in the church.

## MEGATHEMES

| THEME | EXPLANATION | IMPORTANCE |
|---|---|---|
| *God's Purpose* | According to God's eternal, loving plan, he directs, carries out, and sustains our salvation. | When we respond to Christ's love by trusting in him, his purpose becomes our mission. Have you committed yourself to fulfilling God's purpose? |
| *Christ the Center* | Christ is exalted as the center of the universe and the focus of history. He is the head of the body, the church. He is the Creator and sustainer of all creation. | Because Christ is central to everything, his power must be central in us. Begin by placing all your priorities under his control. |
| *Living Church* | Paul describes the nature of the church. The church, under Christ's control, is a living body, a family, a dwelling. God gives believers special abilities by his Holy Spirit to build the church. | We are part of Christ's body, and we must live in vital union with him. Our conduct must be consistent with this living relationship. Use your God-given abilities to equip believers for service. Fulfill your role in the living church. |
| *New Family* | Because God through Christ paid our penalty for sin and forgave us, we have been reconciled—brought near to him. We are a new society, a new family. Being united with Christ means we are to treat one another as family members. | We are one family in Christ, so there should be no barriers, no divisions, no basis for discrimination. We all belong to him, so we should live in harmony with one another. |
| *Christian Conduct* | Paul encourages all Christians to wise, dynamic Christian living, for with privileges goes family responsibility. As a new community, we are to live by Christ's new standards. | God provides his Holy Spirit to enable us to live his way. To utilize the Spirit's power, we must lay aside our evil desires and draw on the power of his new life. Submit your will to Christ, and seek to love others. |

## 1. Unity in Christ
*Greetings from Paul*

**1** This letter is from Paul, chosen by the will of God to be an apostle of Christ Jesus. I am writing to God's holy people in Ephesus,* who are faithful followers of Christ Jesus. ²May God our Father and the Lord Jesus Christ give you grace and peace.

1:2
Rom 1:7
Titus 1:4

**1:1** The most ancient manuscripts do not include *in Ephesus.*

**1:1** Paul wrote this letter to the Ephesian believers and all other believers to give them in-depth teaching about how to nurture and maintain the unity of the church. He wanted to put this important information in written form because he was in prison for preaching the Good News and could not visit the churches himself. The words "in Ephesus" are not present in some early manuscripts. Therefore, this was very likely a circular letter. It was first sent to Ephesus and then circulated to neighboring local churches. Paul mentions no particular problems or local situations, and he offers no personal greetings.

**1:1** Paul had been a Christian for nearly 30 years. He had taken three missionary trips and established churches all around the Mediterranean Sea. When he wrote Ephesians, Paul was under house arrest in Rome (see Acts 28:16ff). Though a prisoner, he

was free to have visitors and write letters. For more information on Paul, see his Profile in Acts 9, p. 1837.

**1:1** Ephesus was one of the five major cities in the Roman Empire, along with Rome, Corinth, Antioch, and Alexandria. Paul first visited Ephesus on his second missionary journey (Acts 18:19-21). During his third missionary journey, he stayed there for almost three years (Acts 19). Paul later met again with the elders of the Ephesian church at Miletus (Acts 20:16-38). Ephesus was a commercial, political, and religious center for all of Asia Minor. The temple to the Greek goddess Artemis (Diana is her Roman equivalent) was located there.

**1:1** "Faithful followers of Christ Jesus"—what an excellent reputation! Such a label would be an honor for any believer. What would it take for others to characterize you as a faithful follower of Christ Jesus? Hold fast to your faith, one day at a time; faithfully obey God, even in the details of life. Then, like the Ephesians, you will be known as a person who is faithful to the Lord.

1:4
2 Thes 2:13
1 Pet 1:2, 20
1:5
Rom 8:15, 29
1:6
Rom 3:24
Col 1:13
1:7
Col 1:14
Heb 9:12

...he Father of our Lord Jesus Christ, who has blessed us with every spiri-
... heavenly realms because we are united with Christ. 4Even before he
...d loved us and chose us in Christ to be holy and without fault in his eyes.
...dvance to adopt us into his own family by bringing us to himself through
...s what he wanted to do, and it gave him great pleasure. 6So we praise God
...ace he has poured out on us who belong to his dear Son.* 7He is so rich in

...eloved.

**LOCATION OF EPHESUS**

Ephesus was a strategic city, ranking in importance with Alexandria in Egypt and Antioch of Syria as a port. It lay on the most western edge of Asia Minor (modern-day Turkey), the most important port on the Aegean Sea on the main route from Rome to the east.

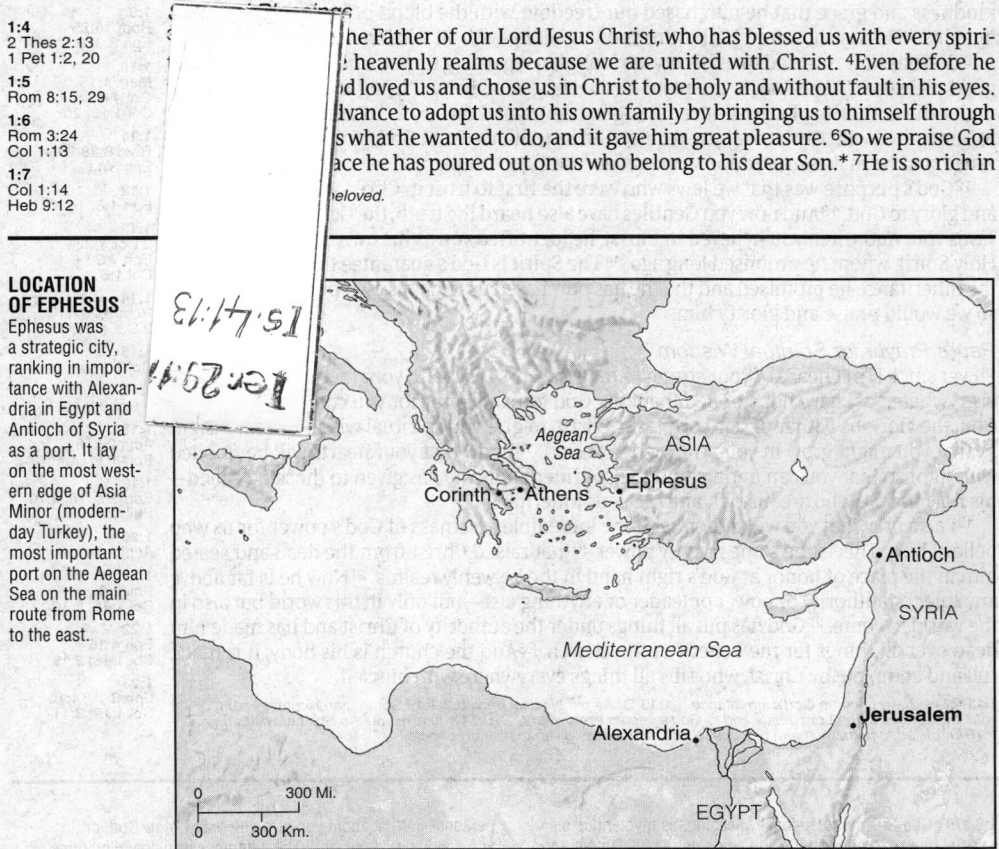

Aegean Sea
ASIA
Corinth • Athens • Ephesus
Antioch
SYRIA
Mediterranean Sea
Jerusalem
Alexandria
EGYPT

0    300 Mi.
0    300 Km.

**1:3** "Who has blessed us with every spiritual blessing in the heavenly realms" means that in Christ we have all the benefits of knowing God—being chosen for salvation, being adopted as his children, forgiveness, insight, the gifts of the Spirit, power to do God's will, the hope of living forever with Christ. Because we have an intimate relationship with Christ, we can enjoy these blessings now. The "heavenly realms" means that these blessings are eternal, not temporal. The blessings come from Christ's spiritual realm, not the earthly realm of the goddess Artemis. Other references to the heavenly realms in this letter include 1:20; 2:6; 3:10. Such passages reveal Christ in his victorious, exalted role as ruler of all.

**1:4** Paul says that God "chose us" to emphasize that salvation depends totally on God. We are not saved because we deserve it but because God is gracious and freely gives salvation. We did not influence God's decision to save us; he saved us according to his plan. Thus, there is no way to take credit for our salvation or to allow room for pride. The mystery of salvation originated in the timeless mind of God long before we existed. It is hard to understand how God could accept us. But because of Christ, we are holy and blameless in his sight. God chose us, and when we belong to him through Jesus Christ, God looks at us as if we had never sinned. All we can do is express our thanks for his wonderful love.

**1:5** That God "decided in advance to adopt us" is another way of saying that salvation is God's work and not our own doing. In his infinite love, God has adopted us as his own children. Through

Jesus' sacrifice, he has brought us into his family and made us heirs along with Jesus (Romans 8:17). In Roman law, adopted children had the same rights and privileges as biological children, even if they had been slaves. Paul uses this term to show how strong our relationship to God is. Have you entered into this loving relationship with God? For more on the meaning of adoption, see Galatians 4:5-7.

**1:7** To speak of Jesus' blood was an important first-century way of speaking of Christ's death. His death points to two wonderful truths—redemption and forgiveness. *Redemption* was the price paid to gain freedom for a slave (Leviticus 25:47-54). Through his death, Jesus paid the price to release us from slavery to sin. *Forgiveness* was granted in Old Testament times on the basis of the shedding of animals' blood (Leviticus 17:11). Now we are forgiven on the basis of the shedding of Jesus' blood—he died as the perfect and final sacrifice (see also Romans 5:9; Ephesians 2:13; Colossians 1:20; Hebrews 9:22; 1 Peter 1:19).

**1:7, 8** God showered his kindness on us—this is also called God's "grace." This is his voluntary and loving favor given to those he saves. We can't earn salvation, nor do we deserve it. No religious, intellectual, or moral effort can gain it, because it comes only from God's mercy and love. Without God's grace, no person can be saved. To receive it, we must acknowledge that we cannot save ourselves, that only God can save us, and that our only way to receive this loving favor is through faith in Christ.

kindness and grace that he purchased our freedom with the blood of his Son and forgave our sins. [8]He has showered his kindness on us, along with all wisdom and understanding.

[9]God has now revealed to us his mysterious plan regarding Christ, a plan to fulfill his own good pleasure. [10]And this is the plan: At the right time he will bring everything together under the authority of Christ—everything in heaven and on earth. [11]Furthermore, because we are united with Christ, we have received an inheritance from God,* for he chose us in advance, and he makes everything work out according to his plan.

[12]God's purpose was that we Jews who were the first to trust in Christ would bring praise and glory to God. [13]And now you Gentiles have also heard the truth, the Good News that God saves you. And when you believed in Christ, he identified you as his own* by giving you the Holy Spirit, whom he promised long ago. [14]The Spirit is God's guarantee that he will give us the inheritance he promised and that he has purchased us to be his own people. He did this so we would praise and glorify him.

### Paul's Prayer for Spiritual Wisdom

[15]Ever since I first heard of your strong faith in the Lord Jesus and your love for God's people everywhere,* [16]I have not stopped thanking God for you. I pray for you constantly, [17]asking God, the glorious Father of our Lord Jesus Christ, to give you spiritual wisdom* and insight so that you might grow in your knowledge of God. [18]I pray that your hearts will be flooded with light so that you can understand the confident hope he has given to those he called— his holy people who are his rich and glorious inheritance.*

[19]I also pray that you will understand the incredible greatness of God's power for us who believe him. This is the same mighty power [20]that raised Christ from the dead and seated him in the place of honor at God's right hand in the heavenly realms. [21]Now he is far above any ruler or authority or power or leader or anything else—not only in this world but also in the world to come. [22]God has put all things under the authority of Christ and has made him head over all things for the benefit of the church. [23]And the church is his body; it is made full and complete by Christ, who fills all things everywhere with himself.

1:11 Or *we have become God's inheritance.*   1:13 Or *he put his seal on you.*   1:15 Some manuscripts read *your faithfulness to the Lord Jesus and to God's people everywhere.*   1:17 Or *to give you the Spirit of wisdom.*
1:18 Or *called, and the rich and glorious inheritance he has given to his holy people.*

**1:9** Rom 16:25; Eph 3:3, 9
**1:10** Mark 1:15; Gal 4:4; Col 1:16, 20
**1:11** Rom 8:28-29; Eph 3:11
**1:12** Eph 1:6, 14
**1:13** 2 Cor 1:22; Eph 4:30; Col 1:5
**1:14** Rom 8:23; 2 Cor 1:22; 5:5
**1:16** Col 1:9
**1:17** 1 Cor 2:9-12
**1:18** Acts 26:18; Eph 1:11; 4:4
**1:19** Eph 3:7, 16; 6:10; Phil 3:21
**1:20** Acts 2:24
**1:21** Phil 2:9; Col 1:16; 2:10
**1:22** Eph 4:15; Col 1:18; 2:19
**1:23** Eph 3:19; 4:10; Col 1:19; 3:11

**1:9, 10** God was not intentionally keeping his mysterious plan a secret, but his plan for the world could not be fully understood until Christ rose from the dead. His purpose for sending Christ was to unite Jews and Gentiles in one body with Christ as the head. Many people still do not understand God's plan; but at the right time, he will bring us together to be with him forever. Then everyone will understand. On that day, all people will bow to Jesus as Lord, either because they love him or because they fear his power (see Philippians 2:10, 11).

**1:11** God's purpose is to offer salvation to the world, just as he planned to do long ago. God is sovereign; he is in charge. When your life seems chaotic, rest in this truth: Jesus is Lord, and God is in control. God's purpose to save you cannot be thwarted, no matter what evil Satan may bring.

**1:13, 14** The Holy Spirit is God's guarantee that we belong to him and that he will do what he has promised. The Holy Spirit is like a down payment, a deposit, a validating signature on the contract. The presence of the Holy Spirit in us demonstrates the genuineness of our faith, proves that we are God's children, and secures eternal life for us. His power works in us to transform us now, and what we experience now is a taste of the total change we will experience in eternity.

**1:16, 17** Paul prayed for the believers to know God better. How do you get to know someone? By reading biographical information or historical data about him? That will help you know a lot *about* that person, but it won't enable you to actually *know* him. If you want to get to know someone, you have to spend time with that person; there is no shortcut. The same holds true with God. Reading the Bible, great works of theology, and devotional material is wonderful, but there is no substitute for knowing God

personally. What about you? Do you really *know* God, or do you just know *about* him? The difference is in spending time with him. Study Jesus' life in the Gospels to see what he was like on earth two thousand years ago, and get to know him in prayer now. Personal knowledge of Christ will change your life.

**1:19, 20** The world fears the power of the atom, yet we belong to the God of the universe, who not only created that atomic power but also raised Jesus Christ from the dead. God's incomparably great power is available to help you. There is nothing too difficult for him.

**1:20-22** Having been raised from the dead, Christ is now the head of the church, the ultimate authority over the world. Jesus is the Messiah, God's anointed one, the one Israel longed for, the one who would set their broken world right. As Christians we can be confident that God has won the final victory and is in control of everything. We need not fear any dictator or nation or even death or Satan himself. The contract has been signed and sealed; we are waiting just a short while for delivery. Paul says, in Romans 8:37-39, that nothing can separate us from God and his love.

**1:22, 23** Christ fills the church with gifts and blessings. The church should be the full expression of Christ, who himself fills everything (see 3:19). When reading Ephesians, it is important to remember that it was written primarily to the entire church, not merely to an individual. Christ is the head, and we are the body of his church (Paul uses this metaphor in Romans 12:4, 5; 1 Corinthians 12:12-27; and Colossians 3:15 as well as throughout the book of Ephesians). The image of the body shows the church's unity. Each member is involved with all the others as they go about doing Christ's work on earth. We should not attempt to work, serve, or worship merely on our own. We need the entire body.

## Made Alive with Christ

**2:1**
Eph 2:5
Col 2:13

**2:3**
Gal 5:24
Col 3:6

**2:5**
Rom 5:6; 6:4
Eph 2:1
Col 2:13

**2** Once you were dead because of your disobedience and your many sins. ²You used to live in sin, just like the rest of the world, obeying the devil—the commander of the powers in the unseen world.* He is the spirit at work in the hearts of those who refuse to obey God. ³All of us used to live that way, following the passionate desires and inclinations of our sinful nature. By our very nature we were subject to God's anger, just like everyone else.

⁴But God is so rich in mercy, and he loved us so much, ⁵that even though we were dead

**2:2** Greek *obeying the commander of the power of the air.*

---

**OUR TRUE
IDENTITY
IN CHRIST**

| | |
|---|---|
| Romans 3:24 . . . . . . . . . | We are justified (declared "righteous"). |
| Romans 8:1 . . . . . . . . . . | No condemnation awaits us. |
| Romans 8:2 . . . . . . . . . | We are set free from the power of sin that leads to death. |
| 1 Corinthians 1:2 . . . . . . | We are sanctified (made holy) in Jesus Christ. |
| 1 Corinthians 1:30 . . . . . | We are pure and holy in Christ. |
| 1 Corinthians 15:22 . . . . | We will be given new life at the resurrection. |
| 2 Corinthians 5:17 . . . . . | We are new persons. |
| 2 Corinthians 5:21 . . . . . | We are made right with God. |
| Galatians 3:28 . . . . . . . | We are one in Christ with all other believers. |
| Ephesians 1:3 . . . . . . . . | We are blessed with every spiritual blessing in Christ. |
| Ephesians 1:4 . . . . . . . . | We are holy and without fault. |
| Ephesians 1:5, 6 . . . . . . | We are adopted as God's children. |
| Ephesians 1:7 . . . . . . . . | Our sins are taken away, and we are forgiven. |
| Ephesians 1:10, 11 . . . . . | We will be brought under Christ's authority. |
| Ephesians 1:13 . . . . . . . | We are identified as belonging to God by the Holy Spirit. |
| Ephesians 2:6 . . . . . . . . | We have been raised up to sit with Christ in the heavenly realms. |
| Ephesians 2:10 . . . . . . . | We are God's masterpiece. |
| Ephesians 2:13 . . . . . . . | We have been brought near to God. |
| Ephesians 3:6 . . . . . . . . | We share in the promise of blessings through Christ. |
| Ephesians 3:12 . . . . . . . | We can come boldly and confidently into God's presence. |
| Ephesians 5:29, 30 . . . . . | We are members of Christ's body, the church. |
| Colossians 2:10 . . . . . . . | We are made complete in Christ. |
| Colossians 2:11 . . . . . . . | We are set free from our sinful nature. |
| 2 Timothy 2:10 . . . . . . . | We will have eternal glory. |

---

**2:1, 2** Immediately after his prayer, Paul reminds the Ephesians of the reality of personal sin. Like them, we must never forget our past, the condition from which Jesus saved us. Those memories are the best fuel for our gratitude to Christ for all he has done in our behalf.

**2:2** Paul describes Satan, the devil, as "the commander of the powers in the unseen world." Paul's readers believed that Satan and the evil spiritual forces inhabited the region between earth and sky. Satan is thus pictured as ruling an evil spiritual kingdom—the demons and those who are against Christ. In the resurrection, Christ was victorious over the devil and his power. Therefore, Jesus Christ is the permanent ruler of the whole world; the devil is only the temporary ruler of the part of the world that chooses to follow him.

**2:3** The fact that all people, without exception, commit sin proves that without Christ we have a sinful nature. We are lost in sin and cannot save ourselves. Does this mean only Christians do good? Of course not—many people do good to others. On a relative scale, many are moral, kind, and law abiding. Comparing these people to criminals, we would say that they are very good indeed. But on God's absolute scale, *no one* is good enough to earn salvation ("dead because of your disobedience and your many sins," 2:1). Only through being united with Christ's perfect life can we become good in God's sight. "Subject to God's anger"

refers to those who are to receive God's wrath because of their rejection of Christ.

**2:4** We were dead in our sins, *but God* . . . We were rebels against him, *but God* . . . We were enslaved by the devil and our sinful natures, *but God* . . . These may be the two most welcome words in all of Scripture: "but God." God could have left us spiritually dead, in rebellion against him and in bondage to our sins. *But he didn't.* He did not save us because of, but rather in spite of, what he saw in us. In addition to thanking him for what he has done for us, we should also show humble patience and tolerance for others who seem unworthy or undeserving of our love and compassion. They may be spiritually dull, rebellious, and even antagonistic toward God. So were we; *but God loved us anyway.* Can we do less for fellow sinners?

**2:4, 5** In the previous verses Paul wrote about our old sinful nature (2:1-3). Here Paul emphasizes that we do not need to live any longer under sin's power. The penalty of sin and its power over us were miraculously destroyed by Christ on the cross. Through faith in Christ we stand acquitted, or not guilty, before God (Romans 3:21, 22). God does not take us out of the world or make us robots—we will still feel like sinning, and sometimes we will sin. The difference is that before we became Christians, we were dead in sin and were slaves to our sinful nature. But now we are alive with Christ (see also Galatians 2:20).

because of our sins, he gave us life when he raised Christ from the dead. (It is only by God's grace that you have been saved!) 6For he raised us from the dead along with Christ and seated us with him in the heavenly realms because we are united with Christ Jesus. 7So God can point to us in all future ages as examples of the incredible wealth of his grace and kindness toward us, as shown in all he has done for us who are united with Christ Jesus.

2:7
Titus 3:4

8God saved you by his grace when you believed. And you can't take credit for this; it is a gift from God. 9Salvation is not a reward for the good things we have done, so none of us can boast about it. 10For we are God's masterpiece. He has created us anew in Christ Jesus, so we can do the good things he planned for us long ago.

2:8
John 4:10
2:9
Rom 3:28
2 Tim 1:9
Titus 3:5

## Oneness and Peace in Christ

11Don't forget that you Gentiles used to be outsiders. You were called "uncircumcised heathens" by the Jews, who were proud of their circumcision, even though it affected only their bodies and not their hearts. 12In those days you were living apart from Christ. You were excluded from citizenship among the people of Israel, and you did not know the covenant promises God had made to them. You lived in this world without God and without hope. 13But now you have been united with Christ Jesus. Once you were far away from God, but now you have been brought near to him through the blood of Christ.

2:11
Col 2:11
2:12
Rom 9:4
1 Thes 4:13
2:13
Col 1:20
2:14
1 Cor 12:13

14For Christ himself has brought peace to us. He united Jews and Gentiles into one people when, in his own body on the cross, he broke down the wall of hostility that separated us. 15He did this by ending the system of law with its commandments and regulations. He made peace between Jews and Gentiles by creating in himself one new people from the two groups. 16Together as one body, Christ reconciled both groups to God by means of his death on the cross, and our hostility toward each other was put to death.

2:15
2 Cor 5:17
Gal 3:28
Col 1:21-22; 2:14
2:16
Col 1:20
2:17
Isa 57:19
Zech 9:10

17He brought this Good News of peace to you Gentiles who were far away from him, and peace to the Jews who were near. 18Now all of us can come to the Father through the same Holy Spirit because of what Christ has done for us.

2:18
Eph 3:12; 4:4

---

**2:6** Because of Christ's resurrection, we know that our body will also be raised from the dead (1 Corinthians 15:2-23) and that we have been given the power to live as Christians now (1:19). These ideas are combined in Paul's image of sitting with Christ in "the heavenly realms" (see the note on 1:3). Our eternal life with Christ is certain because we are united in his powerful victory.

**2:8, 9** When someone gives you a gift, do you say, "That's very nice—now how much do I owe you?" No, the appropriate response to a gift is "Thank you." Yet how often Christians, even after they have been given the gift of salvation, feel obligated to try to work their way to God. Because our salvation and even our faith are gifts, we should respond with gratitude, praise, and joy.

**2:8-10** We become Christians through God's unmerited favor, not as the result of any effort, ability, intelligent choice, or act of service on our part. However, out of gratitude for this free gift, we will seek to help and serve others with kindness, love, and gentleness, and not merely to please ourselves. While no action or work we do can help us obtain salvation, God's intention is that our salvation will result in acts of service. We are not saved merely for our own benefit but to serve Christ and build up the church (4:12).

**2:10** We are God's masterpiece (work of art, workmanship). Our salvation is something only God can do. It is his powerful, creative work in us. If God considers us his masterpieces, we dare not treat ourselves or others with disrespect or as inferior work.

**2:11-13** Pious Jews considered all non-Jews (Gentiles) ceremonially unclean. They thought of themselves as pure and clean because of their national heritage and religious ceremonies. Paul pointed out that Jews and Gentiles alike were unclean before God and needed to be cleansed by Christ. In order to realize how great a gift salvation is, we need to remember our former natural, unclean condition. Have you ever felt separate, excluded, hopeless? These verses are for you. No one is alienated from Christ's love or from the body of believers.

**2:11-13** Jews and Gentiles alike could be guilty of spiritual pride—Jews for thinking their faith and traditions elevated them above everyone else, Gentiles for trusting in their achievements,

power, or position. Spiritual pride blinds us to our own faults and magnifies the faults of others. Be careful not to become proud of your salvation. Instead, humbly thank God for what he has done, and encourage others who might be struggling in their faith.

**2:11-16** Before Christ's coming, Gentiles and Jews kept apart from one another. Jews considered Gentiles beyond God's saving power and therefore without hope. Gentiles resented Jewish claims. Christ revealed the total sinfulness of both Jews and Gentiles, and then he offered his salvation to both. Only Christ breaks down the walls of prejudice, reconciles all believers to God, and unifies us in one body.

**2:14ff** Christ has destroyed the barriers people build between themselves. Because these walls have been removed, we can have real unity with people who are not like us. This is true reconciliation. Because of Christ's death, we are all one (2:14); our hostility against each other has been put to death (2:16); we can all have access to the Father by the Holy Spirit (2:18); we are no longer strangers or foreigners to God (2:19); and we are all being built into a holy temple with Christ as our chief cornerstone (2:20, 21).

**2:14-22** There are many barriers that can divide us from other Christians: age, appearance, intelligence, political persuasion, economic status, race, theological perspective. One of the best ways to stifle Christ's love is to be friendly with only those people that we like. Fortunately, Christ has knocked down the barriers and has unified all believers in one family. His cross should be the focus of our unity. The Holy Spirit helps us look beyond the barriers to the unity we are called to enjoy.

**2:15** By his death, Christ ended the angry resentment between Jews and Gentiles, caused by the Jewish laws that favored the Jews and excluded the Gentiles. Christ died to abolish that whole system of Jewish laws. Then he took the two groups that had been opposed to each other and made them parts of himself. "One new people" means that Christ made a single entity out of the two. Thus, he fused all believers together to become one in himself.

**2:17, 18** The Jews were near to God because they already knew of him through the Scriptures and worshiped him in their religious

**2:20**
Isa 28:16
Matt 16:18
Acts 4:11
1 Cor 3:11
1 Pet 2:4-8
Rev 21:14

**2:21**
1 Cor 3:16
Eph 4:15-16

**3:1**
Eph 4:1
2 Tim 1:8

**3:2**
Col 1:25

**3:3**
Eph 1:9-10
Col 1:26

**3:5**
Eph 1:17

**3:6**
Eph 2:14-16

**3:7**
Rom 15:18
Col 1:23, 25

**3:8**
1 Cor 15:9-10

**3:9**
Rom 16:25

### A Temple for the Lord

19So now you Gentiles are no longer strangers and foreigners. You are citizens along with all of God's holy people. You are members of God's family. 20Together, we are his house, built on the foundation of the apostles and the prophets. And the cornerstone is Christ Jesus himself. 21We are carefully joined together in him, becoming a holy temple for the Lord. 22Through him you Gentiles are also being made part of this dwelling where God lives by his Spirit.

### God's Mysterious Plan Revealed

**3** When I think of all this, I, Paul, a prisoner of Christ Jesus for the benefit of you Gentiles*... 2assuming, by the way, that you know God gave me the special responsibility of extending his grace to you Gentiles. 3As I briefly wrote earlier, God himself revealed his mysterious plan to me. 4As you read what I have written, you will understand my insight into this plan regarding Christ. 5God did not reveal it to previous generations, but now by his Spirit he has revealed it to his holy apostles and prophets.

6And this is God's plan: Both Gentiles and Jews who believe the Good News share equally in the riches inherited by God's children. Both are part of the same body, and both enjoy the promise of blessings because they belong to Christ Jesus.* 7By God's grace and mighty power, I have been given the privilege of serving him by spreading this Good News.

8Though I am the least deserving of all God's people, he graciously gave me the privilege of telling the Gentiles about the endless treasures available to them in Christ. 9I was chosen

**3:1** Paul resumes this thought in verse 14: "When I think of all this, I fall to my knees and pray to the Father."
**3:6** Or *because they are united with Christ Jesus.*

---

**OUR LIVES BEFORE AND AFTER CHRIST**

| Before | After |
|---|---|
| Dead because of sin | Made alive with Christ |
| Under God's anger | Shown God's mercy and given salvation |
| Followed the ways of the world | Stand for Christ and truth |
| God's enemies | God's children |
| Enslaved to the devil | Free in Christ to love, serve, and sit with him |
| Followed our evil thoughts and desires | Raised up with Christ to glory |

---

ceremonies. The Gentiles were far away because they knew little or nothing about God. Because neither group could be saved by good deeds, knowledge, or sincerity, both needed to hear about the salvation available through Jesus Christ. Both Jews and Gentiles are now free to come to God through Christ. You have been brought near to him (2:13).

**2:19-22** A church building is sometimes called God's house. In reality, God's household is not a building but a group of people. He lives in us and shows himself to a watching world through us. People can see that God is love and that Christ is Lord as we live in harmony with each other and in accordance with what God says in his Word. We are citizens of God's Kingdom and members of his household.

**2:20** What does it mean to be built on the foundation of the apostles and prophets? It means that the church is not built on modern ideas but rather on the spiritual heritage given to us by the early apostles and prophets of the Christian church.

**3:1** Paul was under house arrest in Rome for preaching about Christ. The religious leaders in Jerusalem, who felt threatened by Christ's teachings and didn't believe he was the Messiah, pressured the Romans to arrest Paul and bring him to trial for treason and for causing rebellion among the Jews. Paul had appealed for his case to be heard by the emperor, and he was awaiting trial (see Acts 28:16-31). Even though he was under arrest, Paul maintained his firm belief that God was in control of all that happened to him. Do circumstances make you wonder if God has lost control of this world? Like Paul, remember that no matter what happens, God directs the world's affairs.

**3:2, 3** Paul's "special responsibility" refers to the special stewardship, trust, or commitment that Paul had been given. He had

been assigned the special work of preaching the Good News to the Gentiles, God's great plan shown to Paul in a revelation.

**3:5, 6** God's plan was not revealed to previous generations, not because God wanted to keep something from his people, but because he would reveal it to everyone in his perfect timing. God planned to have Jews and Gentiles comprise one body, the church. It was known in the Old Testament that the Gentiles would receive salvation (Isaiah 49:6); but it was never revealed in the Old Testament that all Gentile and Jewish believers would become equal in the body of Christ. Yet this equality was accomplished when Jesus destroyed the "wall of hostility" and created "one new people" (2:14, 15).

**3:7** When Paul became a servant of the gospel, God gave him the ability to share the gospel of Christ effectively. You are not an apostle, and you may not be an evangelist, but God will give you opportunities to tell others about Christ. And with the opportunities he will provide the ability, courage, and power. Make yourself available to God as his servant whenever an opportunity presents itself. As you focus on the other person and his or her needs, God will communicate your caring attitude. Your words will be natural, loving, and compelling.

**3:8** When Paul describes himself as "the least deserving of all God's people," he means that without God's help, he would never be able to do God's work. Yet God chose him to share the Good News with the Gentiles and gave him the power to do it. If we feel that our role is minor, we may be right—except that we have forgotten what a difference God makes. How does God want to use you? Draw on his power, do your part, and faithfully perform the special role God has called you to play in his plan.

to explain to everyone* this mysterious plan that God, the Creator of all things, had kept secret from the beginning. [10]God's purpose in all this was to use the church to display his wisdom in its rich variety to all the unseen rulers and authorities in the heavenly places. [11]This was his eternal plan, which he carried out through Christ Jesus our Lord.

[12]Because of Christ and our faith in him,* we can now come boldly and confidently into God's presence. [13]So please don't lose heart because of my trials here. I am suffering for you, so you should feel honored.

### Paul's Prayer for Spiritual Growth

[14]When I think of all this, I fall to my knees and pray to the Father,* [15]the Creator of everything in heaven and on earth.* [16]I pray that from his glorious, unlimited resources he will empower you with inner strength through his Spirit. [17]Then Christ will make his home in your hearts as you trust in him. Your roots will grow down into God's love and keep you strong. [18]And may you have the power to understand, as all God's people should, how wide, how long, how high, and how deep his love is. [19]May you experience the love of Christ, though it is too great to understand fully. Then you will be made complete with all the fullness of life and power that comes from God.

[20]Now all glory to God, who is able, through his mighty power at work within us, to accomplish infinitely more than we might ask or think. [21]Glory to him in the church and in Christ Jesus through all generations forever and ever! Amen.

## 2. Unity in the body of Christ

**4** Therefore I, a prisoner for serving the Lord, beg you to lead a life worthy of your calling, for you have been called by God. [2]Always be humble and gentle. Be patient with each

**3:10**
Rom 11:33
1 Cor 2:7
Eph 1:21; 6:12
1 Pet 1:12

**3:11**
Eph 1:11

**3:12**
Eph 2:18
Heb 4:16

**3:14**
Phil 2:10

**3:16**
Phil 4:13, 19
Col 1:11

**3:17**
John 14:23
Col 2:7

**3:18**
John 1:16
Col 2:9-10

**3:19**
Col 2:10

**3:20**
Eph 1:19-20
Col 1:29

**4:1**
Eph 3:1
Phil 1:7, 13

**4:2**
Col 3:12-13

**3:9** Some manuscripts do not include *to everyone.*   **3:12** Or *Because of Christ's faithfulness.*   **3:14** Some manuscripts read *the Father of our Lord Jesus Christ.*   **3:15** Or *from whom every family in heaven and on earth takes its name.*

---

**3:10** The "rulers and authorities in the heavenly places" are either angels who are witnesses to these events (see 1 Peter 1:12), or hostile spiritual forces opposed to God (2:2; 6:12).

**3:12** It is an awesome privilege to be able to approach God with freedom and confidence. Most of us would be apprehensive in the presence of a powerful ruler. But thanks to Christ, by faith we can enter directly into God's presence through prayer. We know we'll be welcomed with open arms because we are God's children through our union with Christ. Don't be afraid of God. Talk with him about everything. He is waiting to hear from you.

**3:13** Why should Paul's suffering make the Ephesians feel honored? If Paul had not preached the Good News, he would not be in jail—but then the Ephesians would not have heard the Good News and been converted either. Just as a mother endures the pain of childbirth in order to bring new life into the world, Paul endured the pain of persecution in order to bring new believers to Christ. Obeying Christ is never easy. He calls you to take your cross and follow him (Matthew 16:24)—that is, to be willing to endure pain so that God's message of salvation can reach the entire world. We should feel honored that others have suffered and sacrificed for us so that we might reap the benefit.

**3:14, 15** The family of God includes all who have believed in him in the past, all who believe in the present, and all who will believe in the future. We are all a family because we have the same Father. He is the source of all creation, the rightful owner of everything. God promises his love and power to his family, the church (3:16-21). If we want to receive God's blessings, it is important that we stay in contact with other believers in the body of Christ. Those who isolate themselves from God's family and try to go it alone cut themselves off from God's power.

**3:17-19** God's love is total, says Paul. It reaches every corner of our experience. It is *wide*—it covers the breadth of our own experience, and it reaches out to the whole world. God's love is *long*—it continues the length of our lives. It is *high*—it rises to the heights of our celebration and elation. His love is *deep*—it reaches to the depths of discouragement, despair, and even death. When you feel shut out or isolated, remember that you can never be lost

to God's love. For another prayer about God's immeasurable and inexhaustible love, see Paul's words in Romans 8:38, 39.

**3:19** This "fullness" is expressed only in Christ (Colossians 2:9, 10). In union with Christ and through his empowering Spirit, we are complete. We have all the fullness of God available to us. But we must appropriate that fullness through faith and through prayer as we daily live for him. Paul's prayer for the Ephesians is also for you. You can ask the Holy Spirit to fill every aspect of your life to the fullest.

**3:20, 21** This doxology—prayer of praise to God—ends part 1 of Ephesians. In the first section, Paul described the timeless role of the church. In part 2 (chapters 4–6), he will explain how church members should live in order to bring about the unity God wants. As in most of his books, Paul first lays a doctrinal foundation and then makes practical applications of the truths he has presented.

**4:1, 2** God has chosen us to be Christ's representatives on earth. In light of this truth, Paul challenges us to live lives worthy of the calling we have received—the awesome privilege of being called Christ's very own. This includes being humble, gentle, patient, understanding, and peaceful. People are watching your life. Can they see Christ in you? How well are you doing as his representative?

**4:1-6** "There is one body," says Paul. Unity does not just happen; we have to work at it. Often differences among people can lead to division, but this should not be true in the church. Instead of concentrating on what divides us, we should remember what unites us: *one* body, *one* Spirit, *one* future, *one* Lord, *one* faith, *one* baptism, *one* God! Have you learned to appreciate people who are different from you? Can you see how their differing gifts and viewpoints can help the church as it does God's work? Learn to enjoy the way we members of Christ's body complement one another. (See 1 Corinthians 12:12, 13 for more on this thought.)

**4:2** No one is ever going to be perfect here on earth, so we must accept and love other Christians in spite of their faults. When we see faults in fellow believers, we should be patient and gentle. Is there someone whose actions or personality really annoys you? Rather than dwelling on that person's weaknesses or looking for

**4:3**
Col 3:14-15

**4:4**
Rom 12:5
1 Cor 12:12-13
Eph 2:16, 18

**4:7**
Rom 12:3
1 Cor 12:7

**4:9**
John 3:13
Acts 2:27
1 Pet 3:18

**4:10**
Eph 1:23

**4:11**
1 Cor 12:28

**4:12**
1 Cor 12:27

**4:13**
Eph 1:23
Col 1:28

other, making allowance for each other's faults because of your love. ³Make every effort to keep yourselves united in the Spirit, binding yourselves together with peace. ⁴For there is one body and one Spirit, just as you have been called to one glorious hope for the future. ⁵There is one Lord, one faith, one baptism, ⁶and one God and Father, who is over all and in all and living through all.

⁷However, he has given each one of us a special gift* through the generosity of Christ. ⁸That is why the Scriptures say,

"When he ascended to the heights,
   he led a crowd of captives
   and gave gifts to his people."*

⁹Notice that it says "he ascended." This clearly means that Christ also descended to our lowly world.* ¹⁰And the same one who descended is the one who ascended higher than all the heavens, so that he might fill the entire universe with himself.

¹¹Now these are the gifts Christ gave to the church: the apostles, the prophets, the evangelists, and the pastors and teachers. ¹²Their responsibility is to equip God's people to do his work and build up the church, the body of Christ. ¹³This will continue until we all come to such unity in our faith and knowledge of God's Son that we will be mature in the Lord, measuring up to the full and complete standard of Christ.

**4:7** Greek *a grace.*  **4:8** Ps 68:18.  **4:9** Or *to the lowest parts of the earth.*

---

**THE ONENESS OF ALL BELIEVERS**

| Believers are one in | Our unity is experienced in |
| --- | --- |
| Body . . . . . . . . . . . . . . . . . . . . . . . . . | The fellowship of believers—the church |
| Spirit . . . . . . . . . . . . . . . . . . . . . . . . . | The Holy Spirit, who activates the fellowship |
| Hope . . . . . . . . . . . . . . . . . . . . . . . . . | That glorious future to which we are all called |
| Lord . . . . . . . . . . . . . . . . . . . . . . . . . | Christ, to whom we all belong |
| Faith . . . . . . . . . . . . . . . . . . . . . . . . . | Our singular commitment to Christ |
| Baptism . . . . . . . . . . . . . . . . . . . . . . . | Baptism—the sign of entry into the church |
| God . . . . . . . . . . . . . . . . . . . . . . . . . | God, who is our Father who keeps us for eternity |

Too often believers are separated because of minor differences in doctrine. But Paul here shows those areas where Christians must agree to attain true unity. When believers have this unity of spirit, petty differences should never be allowed to dissolve that unity.

---

faults, pray for him or her. Then do even more—spend time together and see if you can learn to like him or her.

**4:3** To build unity is one of the Holy Spirit's important roles. He leads, but we have to be willing to be led and to do our part to keep the peace. We do that by focusing on God, not on ourselves. For more about who the Holy Spirit is and what he does, see the notes on John 3:6; Acts 1:5; and Ephesians 1:13, 14.

**4:4-7** All believers in Christ belong to one body; all are united under one head, Christ himself (see 1 Corinthians 12:12-27). Each believer has God-given abilities that can strengthen the whole body. Your special ability may seem small or large, but it is yours to use in God's service. Ask God to use your unique gifts to contribute to the strength and health of the body of believers.

**4:6** God is "over all"—this shows his overruling care (transcendence). He is "in all" and "living through all"—this shows his active presence in the world and in the lives of believers (immanence). Any view of God that violates either his transcendence or his immanence does not paint a true picture of God.

**4:8** In Psalm 68:18, God is pictured as a conqueror marching to the gates and taking tribute from the fallen city. Paul uses that picture to teach that Christ, in his crucifixion and resurrection, was victorious over Satan. When Christ ascended to heaven, he gave gifts to the church, some of which Paul discusses in 4:11-13.

**4:9** The "lowly world" may be (1) the earth itself (lowly by comparison to heaven), (2) the grave, or (3) Hades (many believe Hades is the resting place of souls between death and resurrec-

tion). However we understand it, Christ is Lord of the whole universe, past, present, and future. Nothing or no one is hidden from him. The Lord of all came to earth and faced death to rescue all people. No one is beyond his reach.

**4:11, 12** Our oneness in Christ does not destroy our individuality. The Holy Spirit has given each Christian special gifts for building up the church. Now that we have these gifts, it is crucial to use them. Are you spiritually mature, exercising the gifts God has given you? If you know what your gifts are, look for opportunities to serve. If you don't know, ask God to show you, perhaps with the help of your minister or Christian friends. Then, as you begin to recognize your special area of service, use your gifts to strengthen and encourage the church.

**4:12, 13** God has given his church an enormous responsibility—to make disciples in every nation (Matthew 28:18-20). This involves preaching, teaching, healing, nurturing, giving, administering, building, and many other tasks. If we had to fulfill this command as individuals, we might as well give up without trying—it would be impossible. But God calls us as members of his body. Some of us can do one task; some can do another. Together we can obey God more fully than any of us could alone. It is a human tendency to overestimate what we can do by ourselves and to underestimate what we can do as a group. But as the body of Christ, we can accomplish more together than we would dream possible working by ourselves. Working together, the church can express the fullness of Christ (see the note on 3:19).

14Then we will no longer be immature like children. We won't be tossed and blown about by every wind of new teaching. We will not be influenced when people try to trick us with lies so clever they sound like the truth. 15Instead, we will speak the truth in love, growing in every way more and more like Christ, who is the head of his body, the church. 16He makes the whole body fit together perfectly. As each part does its own special work, it helps the other parts grow, so that the whole body is healthy and growing and full of love.

### Living as Children of Light

17With the Lord's authority I say this: Live no longer as the Gentiles do, for they are hopelessly confused. 18Their minds are full of darkness; they wander far from the life God gives because they have closed their minds and hardened their hearts against him. 19They have no sense of shame. They live for lustful pleasure and eagerly practice every kind of impurity.

20But that isn't what you learned about Christ. 21Since you have heard about Jesus and have learned the truth that comes from him, 22throw off your old sinful nature and your former way of life, which is corrupted by lust and deception. 23Instead, let the Spirit renew your thoughts and attitudes. 24Put on your new nature, created to be like God—truly righteous and holy.

25So stop telling lies. Let us tell our neighbors the truth, for we are all parts of the same body. 26And "don't sin by letting anger control you."* Don't let the sun go down while you are still angry, 27for anger gives a foothold to the devil.

28If you are a thief, quit stealing. Instead, use your hands for good hard work, and then give generously to others in need. 29Don't use foul or abusive language. Let everything you say be good and helpful, so that your words will be an encouragement to those who hear them.

4:26 Ps 4:4.

**4:14**
1 Cor 14:20
Eph 6:11

**4:15**
Eph 1:22

**4:16**
Col 2:19

**4:17**
Rom 1:21
Eph 2:2

**4:19**
Rom 1:24
Col 3:5

**4:22**
Rom 6:6
Col 3:5, 8-9
Jas 1:21

**4:23**
Rom 12:2

**4:24**
2 Cor 5:17
Col 3:10

**4:25**
†Zech 8:16
Col 3:8-9

**4:28**
1 Thes 4:11

**4:29**
Matt 12:36
Rom 14:19
Col 3:8

---

**4:14-16** Christ is the truth (John 14:6), and the Holy Spirit, who guides the church, is the Spirit of truth (John 16:13). Satan, by contrast, is the father of lies (John 8:44). As followers of Christ, we must be committed to the truth. This means both that our words should be honest and that our actions should reflect Christ's integrity. Speaking the truth in love is not always easy, convenient, or pleasant, but it is necessary if the church is going to do Christ's work in the world.

**4:15** In describing the mature Christian, Paul says that one of the marks is the ability to "speak the truth in love." This sounds so simple, but it seems so hard for us to do. Some of us are fairly good at speaking the truth, but we forget to be loving. Some of us are good at being loving, but we don't have it in us to level with others if the truth is painful. The instruction here is to do both: Speak the truth, but do it in a loving manner. Think of the trouble we would spare ourselves if we followed this practice, especially in the church! When you have a problem with another believer, don't go to someone else with it. Go directly to that person, and speak the truth in love.

**4:15, 16** Some Christians fear that any mistake will destroy their witness for the Lord. They see their own weaknesses, and they know that many non-Christians seem to have stronger character than they do. How can we grow more and more like Christ? The answer is that Christ forms us into a body—into a group of individuals who are united in their purpose and in their love for one another and for the Lord. If an individual stumbles, the rest of the group is there to pick that person up and help him or her walk with God again. If a person sins, he or she can find restoration through the church (Galatians 6:1) even as the rest of the body continues to witness to God's truth. As part of Christ's body, do you reflect part of Christ's character and carry out your special role in his work?

**4:17** The natural tendency of human beings is to think their way away from God—leaving them "hopelessly confused." Intellectual pride, rationalizations, and excuses all keep people from God. Don't be surprised if people can't grasp the Good News. The Good News will seem foolish to those who forsake faith and rely on their own understanding.

**4:17-24** People should be able to see a difference between Christians and non-Christians because of the way Christians live. We are to live full of light (5:8). Paul told the Ephesians to leave behind the old life of sin, since they were followers of Christ. Living the Christian life is a process. Although we have a new nature, we don't automatically think all good thoughts and express all right attitudes when we become new people in Christ. But if we keep listening to God, we will be changing all the time. As you look back over last year, do you see a process of change for the better in your thoughts, attitudes, and actions? Although change may be slow, it comes as you trust God to change you. For more about our new nature as believers, see Romans 6:6; 8:9; Galatians 5:16-26; Colossians 3:3-8.

**4:22-24** Our old way of life before we believed in Christ is completely in the past. We should put it behind us like old clothes to be thrown away. When we decide to accept Christ's gift of salvation (2:8-10), it is both a one time decision, as well as a daily conscious commitment. We are not to be driven by desire and impulse. We must put on the new nature, head in the new direction, and have the new way of thinking that the Holy Spirit gives.

**4:25** Lying to each other disrupts unity by creating conflicts and destroying trust. It tears down relationships and leads to open warfare in a church.

**4:26, 27** The Bible doesn't tell us that we shouldn't feel angry, but it points out that it is important to handle our anger properly. If vented thoughtlessly, anger can hurt others and destroy relationships. If bottled up inside, it can cause us to become bitter and destroy us from within. Paul tells us to deal with our anger immediately in a way that builds relationships rather than destroys them. If we nurse our anger, we will give the devil an opportunity to divide us. Are you angry with someone right now? What can you do to resolve your differences? Don't let the day end before you begin to work on mending your relationship.

**4:28-32** We can bring sorrow to the Holy Spirit by the way we live. Paul warns us against unwholesome language, bitterness, improper use of anger, harsh words, slander, and bad attitudes toward others. Instead of acting that way, we should be forgiving, just as God has forgiven us. Are you bringing sorrow or pleasing God with your attitudes and actions? Act in love toward your

**4:30**
Isa 63:10
Eph 1:13-14
1 Thes 5:19

**4:31**
Col 3:8
1 Pet 2:1

**4:32**
Col 3:12-13

**5:1**
Matt 5:48

**5:2**
John 13:34
Gal 1:14; 2:20

**5:3**
Col 3:5

**5:4**
Eph 4:29
Col 3:8

**5:5**
1 Cor 6:9-10
Col 3:5

**5:6**
Rom 1:18
Col 2:4, 8; 3:6

**5:8**
John 8:12
Eph 2:2

**5:11**
Rom 13:12

**5:13**
John 3:20-21

**5:14**
Isa 26:19; 51:17;
52:1; 60:1
John 5:25
Rom 13:11

**5:16**
Col 4:5

**5:17**
1 Thes 4:3

30And do not bring sorrow to God's Holy Spirit by the way you live. Remember, he has identified you as his own,* guaranteeing that you will be saved on the day of redemption.

31Get rid of all bitterness, rage, anger, harsh words, and slander, as well as all types of evil behavior. 32Instead, be kind to each other, tenderhearted, forgiving one another, just as God through Christ has forgiven you.

### Living in the Light

**5** Imitate God, therefore, in everything you do, because you are his dear children. 2Live a life filled with love, following the example of Christ. He loved us* and offered himself as a sacrifice for us, a pleasing aroma to God.

3Let there be no sexual immorality, impurity, or greed among you. Such sins have no place among God's people. 4Obscene stories, foolish talk, and coarse jokes—these are not for you. Instead, let there be thankfulness to God. 5You can be sure that no immoral, impure, or greedy person will inherit the Kingdom of Christ and of God. For a greedy person is an idolater, worshiping the things of this world.

6Don't be fooled by those who try to excuse these sins, for the anger of God will fall on all who disobey him. 7Don't participate in the things these people do. 8For once you were full of darkness, but now you have light from the Lord. So live as people of light! 9For this light within you produces only what is good and right and true.

10Carefully determine what pleases the Lord. 11Take no part in the worthless deeds of evil and darkness; instead, expose them. 12It is shameful even to talk about the things that ungodly people do in secret. 13But their evil intentions will be exposed when the light shines on them, 14for the light makes everything visible. This is why it is said,

"Awake, O sleeper,
  rise up from the dead,
  and Christ will give you light."

### Living by the Spirit's Power

15So be careful how you live. Don't live like fools, but like those who are wise. 16Make the most of every opportunity in these evil days. 17Don't act thoughtlessly, but understand what

**4:30** Or has put his seal on you.   **5:2** Some manuscripts read loved you.

---

brothers and sisters in Christ, just as God acted in love by sending his Son to die for your sins.

**4:30** The Holy Spirit within us is a guarantee that we belong to God. For more on this thought, see the note on 1:13, 14.

**4:32** This is Christ's law of forgiveness as taught in the Gospels (Matthew 6:14, 15; 18:35; Mark 11:25). We also see it in the Lord's Prayer—"Forgive us our sins, as we forgive those who sin against us" (Luke 11:4). God forgives us, not because we forgive others, but solely because of his great mercy. As we come to understand his mercy, however, we will want to pass it on to him. Having received forgiveness, we will pass it on to others. Those who are unwilling to forgive have not become one with Christ, who was willing to forgive even those who crucified him (Luke 23:34).

**5:1, 2** Just as children imitate their parents, we should follow God's example. His great love for us led him to sacrifice himself so that we might live. Our love for others should be of the same kind—a love that goes beyond affection to self-sacrificing service.

**5:4** Obscene stories and coarse jokes are so common that we begin to take them for granted. Paul cautions, however, that improper language should have no place in the Christian's conversation because it does not reflect God's gracious presence in us. How can we praise God and remind others of his goodness when we are speaking coarsely?

**5:5-7** Paul does not forbid all contact with unbelievers. Jesus taught his followers to befriend sinners and lead them to him (Luke 5:30-32). Instead, Paul writes against the lifestyle of people who make excuses for bad behavior and recommend its practice to others—whether they are in the church or outside of it. Such people quickly pollute the church and endanger its

unity and purpose. We must befriend unbelievers if we are to lead them to Christ, but we must be wary of those who are viciously evil, immoral, or opposed to all that Christianity stands for. Such people are more likely to influence us for evil than we are to influence them for good.

**5:8** As people who have light from the Lord, our actions should reflect our faith. We should live above reproach morally so that we will reflect God's goodness to others. Jesus stressed this truth in the Sermon on the Mount (Matthew 5:15, 16).

**5:10-14** It is important to avoid the "worthless deeds of evil and darkness" (any pleasure or activity that results in sin), but we must go even further. Paul instructs us to expose these deeds, because our silence may be interpreted as approval. God needs people who will take a stand for what is right. Christians must lovingly speak out for what is true and right.

**5:14** This is not a direct quote from Scripture but was probably taken from a hymn well known to the Ephesians. The hymn seems to have been based on Isaiah 26:19; 51:17; 52:1; 60:1; and Malachi 4:2. Paul was appealing to the Ephesians to wake up and realize the dangerous condition into which some of them had been slipping.

**5:15, 16** By referring to these days as evil, Paul was communicating his sense of urgency because of evil's pervasiveness. We need the same sense of urgency because our days are also difficult. We must keep our standards high, act wisely, and do good whenever we can.

the Lord wants you to do. ¹⁸Don't be drunk with wine, because that will ruin your life. Instead, be filled with the Holy Spirit, ¹⁹singing psalms and hymns and spiritual songs among yourselves, and making music to the Lord in your hearts. ²⁰And give thanks for everything to God the Father in the name of our Lord Jesus Christ.

### Spirit-Guided Relationships: Wives and Husbands

²¹And further, submit to one another out of reverence for Christ.

²²For wives, this means submit to your husbands as to the Lord. ²³For a husband is the head of his wife as Christ is the head of the church. He is the Savior of his body, the church. ²⁴As the church submits to Christ, so you wives should submit to your husbands in everything.

²⁵For husbands, this means love your wives, just as Christ loved the church. He gave up his life for her ²⁶to make her holy and clean, washed by the cleansing of God's word.* ²⁷He did this to present her to himself as a glorious church without a spot or wrinkle or any other blemish. Instead, she will be holy and without fault. ²⁸In the same way, husbands ought to love their wives as they love their own bodies. For a man who loves his wife actually shows love for himself. ²⁹No one hates his own body but feeds and cares for it, just as Christ cares for the church. ³⁰And we are members of his body.

**5:18** Prov 20:1; 23:31
**5:19** Col 3:16
**5:21** 1 Pet 5:5
**5:22** Gen 3:16
**5:23** 1 Cor 11:3
**5:26** John 15:3; 17:17 Heb 10:22
**5:27** Eph 1:4 Col 1:22
**5:29** 1 Cor 12:27
**5:30** 1 Cor 6:15; 12:27

**5:26** Greek *washed by water with the word.*

---

**5:18** Paul contrasts getting drunk with wine, which produces a temporary "high," to being filled with the Spirit, which produces lasting joy. Getting drunk with wine is associated with the old way of life and its selfish desires. In Christ, we have a better joy, higher and longer lasting, to cure our depression, monotony, or tension. We should not be concerned with how much of the Holy Spirit we have but with how much of us the Holy Spirit has. Submit yourself daily to his leading and draw constantly on his power.

**5:18, 19** The effects of alcohol are obvious, but what happens when we are under the influence of the Holy Spirit? In these verses, Paul lists three by-products of the Spirit's influence in our lives: singing, making music, and giving thanks. Paul did not intend to suggest that believers only discuss religious matters, but that whatever we do or say should be permeated with an attitude of joy, thankfulness to God, and encouragement of others. Instead of whining and complaining—which our culture has raised to an art form—we are to focus on the goodness of God and his mercies toward us. How would others characterize your words and attitudes?

**5:20** When you feel down, you may find it difficult to give thanks. Take heart—in all things God works for our good if we love him and are called by him (Romans 8:28). Thank God, not for your problems but for the strength he is building in you through the difficult experiences of your life. You can be sure that God's perfect love will see you through.

**5:21, 22** Submitting to another person is an often misunderstood concept. It does not mean becoming a doormat. Christ—at whose name "every knee should bow, in heaven and on earth and under the earth" (Philippians 2:10)—submitted his will to the Father, and we honor Christ by following his example. When we submit to God, we become more willing to obey his command to submit to others, that is, to subordinate our rights to theirs. In a marriage relationship, both husband and wife are called to submit. For the wife, this means willingly following her husband's leadership in Christ. For the husband, it means putting aside his own interests in order to care for his wife. Submission is rarely a problem in homes where both partners have a strong relationship with Christ and where each is concerned for the happiness of the other.

**5:22-24** In Paul's day, women, children, and slaves were to submit to the head of the family: Slaves would submit until they were freed, male children until they grew up, and women and girls their whole lives. Paul emphasized the equality of all believers in Christ (Galatians 3:28), but he did not suggest overthrowing Roman society to achieve it. Instead, he counseled all believers to submit to one another by choice—wives to husbands and also husbands to wives; slaves to masters and also masters to slaves;

children to parents and also parents to children. This kind of mutual submission preserves order and harmony in the family, while it increases love and respect among family members.

**5:22-24** Although some people have distorted Paul's teaching on submission by giving unlimited authority to husbands, we cannot get around it: Paul told wives to submit to their husbands. The fact that a teaching is not popular is no reason to discard it. One way to disarm the antagonism that the external culture may inject into the marriage relationship is to remember that the wife gets to submit and the husband gets to die. According to the Bible, the man is the spiritual head of the family, and his wife should acknowledge his leadership. But real spiritual leadership involves loving service (a form of dying). Just as Christ served the disciples, even to the point of washing their feet, so the husband is to serve his wife. A wise and Christ-honoring husband will not take advantage of his leadership role, and a wise and Christ-honoring wife will not try to undermine her husband's leadership. Either approach causes disunity and friction in marriage.

**5:22-28** Why did Paul tell wives to submit and husbands to love? Perhaps Christian women, newly freed in Christ, found submission difficult; perhaps Christian men, used to the Roman custom of giving unlimited power to the head of the family, were not used to treating their wives with respect and love. Of course both husbands and wives should submit to each other (5:21), just as both should love each other.

**5:25ff** Some Christians have thought that Paul was negative about marriage because of the counsel he gave in 1 Corinthians 7:32-38. These verses in Ephesians, however, show a high view of marriage. Here marriage is not a practical necessity or a cure for lust, but a picture of the relationship between Christ and his church! Why the apparent difference? Paul's counsel in 1 Corinthians was designed for a state of emergency during a time of persecution and crisis. Paul's counsel to the Ephesians is more the biblical ideal for marriage. Marriage, for Paul, is a holy union, a living symbol, a precious relationship that needs tender, self-sacrificing care.

**5:25-30** Paul devotes twice as many words to telling husbands to love their wives as to telling wives to submit to their husbands. How should a man love his wife? (1) He should be willing to sacrifice everything for her, (2) make her well being of primary importance, and (3) care for her as he cares for his own body. No wife needs to fear submitting to a man who treats her in this way.

**5:26, 27** Christ's death makes the church holy and clean. He cleanses us from the old ways of sin and sets us apart for his special sacred service (Hebrews 10:29; 13:12). Christ cleansed the church by the washing of baptism. Through baptism we are prepared for entrance into the church just as ancient Near Eastern

**5:31**
†Gen 2:24
Matt 19:5

**5:33**
1 Pet 3:1-2, 5

31As the Scriptures say, "A man leaves his father and mother and is joined to his wife, and the two are united into one."* 32This is a great mystery, but it is an illustration of the way Christ and the church are one. 33So again I say, each man must love his wife as he loves himself, and the wife must respect her husband.

### Children and Parents

**6:1**
Col 3:20

**6:2-3**
†Exod 20:12
†Deut 5:16
Matt 15:4

**6:4**
Col 3:21

**6** Children, obey your parents because you belong to the Lord,* for this is the right thing to do. 2"Honor your father and mother." This is the first commandment with a promise: 3If you honor your father and mother, "things will go well for you, and you will have a long life on the earth."*

4Fathers, do not provoke your children to anger by the way you treat them. Rather, bring them up with the discipline and instruction that comes from the Lord.

**5:31** Gen 2:24.   **6:1** Or *Children, obey your parents who belong to the Lord;* some manuscripts read simply *Children, obey your parents.*   **6:2-3** Exod 20:12; Deut 5:16.

| GOD'S ARMOR FOR US | Piece of Armor | Use | Application |
|---|---|---|---|
| We are engaged in a spiritual battle—all believers find themselves subject to the devil's attacks because they are no longer on the devil's side. Thus, Paul tells us to use *every piece* of God's armor to resist the devil's attacks and to stand true to God in the midst of those attacks. | Belt | Truth | The devil fights with lies, and sometimes his lies *sound* like truth; but only believers have God's truth, which can defeat the devil's lies. |
| | Body armor | Righteousness | The devil often attacks our heart—the seat of our emotions, self-worth, and trust. God's righteousness is the body armor that protects our heart and ensures his approval. He approves of us because he loves us and sent his Son to die for us. |
| | Shoes | Peace that comes from the Good News | The devil wants us to think that telling others the Good News is a worthless and hopeless task—the size of the task is too big and the negative responses are too much to handle. But the shoes God gives us are the motivation to continue to proclaim the true peace that is available in God—news everyone needs to hear. |
| | Shield | Faith | What *we* see are the devil's attacks in the form of insults, setbacks, and temptations. But the shield of faith protects us from the devil's fiery arrows. With God's perspective, we can see beyond our circumstances and know that ultimate victory is ours. |
| | Helmet | Salvation | The devil wants to make us doubt God, Jesus, and our salvation. The helmet protects our mind from doubting God's saving work for us. |
| | Sword | Word of God | The sword is the only weapon of *offense* in this list of armor. There are times when we need to take the offensive against the devil. When we are tempted, we need to trust in the truth of God's Word. |

brides were prepared for marriage by a ceremonial bath. It is God's Word that cleanses us (John 17:17; Titus 3:5).

**5:31-33** The union of husband and wife merges two persons in such a way that little can affect one without also affecting the other. Oneness in marriage does not mean losing your personality in the personality of the other. Instead, it means caring for your spouse as you care for yourself, learning to anticipate his or her needs, helping the other person become all he or she can be. The creation story tells of God's plan that husband and wife should be one (Genesis 2:24), and Jesus also referred to this plan (Matthew 19:4-6).

**6:1, 2** There is a difference between obeying and honoring. To obey means to do as one is told; to honor means to respect and love. Children are not commanded to disobey God in obeying their parents. Adult children are not asked to be subservient to domineering parents. Children are to obey while under their parents' care, but the responsibility to honor parents is for life.

**6:1-4** If our faith in Christ is real, it will usually prove itself in our relationships at home with those who know us best. Children and parents have a responsibility to each other. Children should

honor their parents even if the parents are demanding and unfair. Parents should care gently for their children, even if the children are disobedient and unpleasant. Ideally, of course, Christian parents and Christian children will relate to each other with thoughtfulness and love. This will happen if both parents and children put the others' interests above their own—that is, if they submit to one another.

**6:3** Some societies honor their elders. They respect their wisdom, defer to their authority, and pay attention to their comfort and happiness. This is how Christians should act. Where elders are respected, long life is a blessing, not a burden to them.

**6:4** The purpose of parental discipline is to help children grow, not to exasperate and provoke them to anger or discouragement (see also Colossians 3:21). Parenting is not easy—it takes lots of patience to raise children in a loving, Christ-honoring manner. But frustration and anger should not be causes for discipline. Instead, parents should act in love, treating their children as Jesus treats the people he loves. This is vital to children's development and to their understanding of what Christ is like.

## Slaves and Masters

[5] Slaves, obey your earthly masters with deep respect and fear. Serve them sincerely as you would serve Christ. [6] Try to please them all the time, not just when they are watching you. As slaves of Christ, do the will of God with all your heart. [7] Work with enthusiasm, as though you were working for the Lord rather than for people. [8] Remember that the Lord will reward each one of us for the good we do, whether we are slaves or free.

[9] Masters, treat your slaves in the same way. Don't threaten them; remember, you both have the same Master in heaven, and he has no favorites.

## The Whole Armor of God

[10] A final word: Be strong in the Lord and in his mighty power. [11] Put on all of God's armor so that you will be able to stand firm against all strategies of the devil. [12] For we* are not fighting against flesh-and-blood enemies, but against evil rulers and authorities of the unseen world, against mighty powers in this dark world, and against evil spirits in the heavenly places.

[13] Therefore, put on every piece of God's armor so you will be able to resist the enemy in the time of evil. Then after the battle you will still be standing firm. [14] Stand your ground, putting on the belt of truth and the body armor of God's righteousness. [15] For shoes, put on the peace that comes from the Good News so that you will be fully prepared.* [16] In addition to all of these, hold up the shield of faith to stop the fiery arrows of the devil.* [17] Put on salvation as your helmet, and take the sword of the Spirit, which is the word of God.

[18] Pray in the Spirit at all times and on every occasion. Stay alert and be persistent in your prayers for all believers everywhere.*

[19] And pray for me, too. Ask God to give me the right words so I can boldly explain God's mysterious plan that the Good News is for Jews and Gentiles alike.* [20] I am in chains now, still preaching this message as God's ambassador. So pray that I will keep on speaking boldly for him, as I should.

**6:5-7**
//Col 3:22-23
Titus 2:9-10

**6:8**
Col 3:24-25

**6:9**
Job 31:13-14
Col 4:1

**6:11**
Rom 13:12
1 Thes 5:8

**6:12**
Eph 3:10

**6:14**
Isa 11:5; 59:17
1 Thes 5:8

**6:15**
Isa 52:7

**6:16**
1 Jn 5:4

**6:17**
Isa 59:17
1 Thes 5:8
Heb 4:12

**6:18**
Rom 8:26-27
Phil 4:6
Col 4:2-3

**6:19**
Col 4:3-4

**6:12** Some manuscripts read *you.* **6:15** Or *For shoes, put on the readiness to preach the Good News of peace with God.* **6:16** Greek *the evil one.* **6:18** Greek *all of God's holy people.* **6:19** Greek *explain the mystery of the Good News;* some manuscripts read simply *explain the mystery.*

**6:5** Slaves played a significant part in this society. There were several million of them in the Roman Empire at this time. Because many slaves and owners had become Christians, the early church had to deal straightforwardly with the question of master/slave relations. Paul's statement neither condemns nor condones slavery. Instead, it tells masters and slaves how to live together in Christian households. In Paul's day, women, children, and slaves had few rights. In the church, however, they had freedoms that society denied them. Paul tells husbands, parents, and masters to be caring.

**6:6-8** Paul's instructions encourage responsibility and integrity on the job. Christian employees should do their jobs as if Jesus Christ were their supervisor. And Christian employers should treat their employees fairly and with respect. Can you be trusted to do your best, even when the boss is not around? Do you work hard and with enthusiasm? Do you treat your employees as people, not machines? Remember that no matter whom you work for, and no matter who works for you, the one you ultimately should want to please is your Father in heaven.

**6:9** Although Christians may be at different levels in earthly society, we are all equal before God. He does not play favorites; no one is more important than anyone else. Paul's letter to Philemon stresses the same point: Philemon, the master, and Onesimus, his slave, were brothers in Christ.

**6:10-17** In the Christian life we battle against rulers and authorities (the powerful evil forces of fallen angels headed by the devil, who is a vicious fighter, see 1 Peter 5:8). To withstand their attacks, we must depend on God's strength and use every piece of his armor. Paul is not only giving this counsel to the church, the body of Christ, but to all individuals within the church. The whole body needs to be armed. As you do battle against the "mighty

powers in this dark world," fight in the strength of the church, whose power comes from the Holy Spirit.

**6:12** These who are not "flesh-and-blood enemies" are demons over whom the devil has control. They are not mere fantasies—they are very real. We face a powerful army whose goal is to defeat Christ's church. When we believe in Christ, these beings become our enemies, and they try every device to turn us away from him and back to sin. Although we are assured of victory, we must engage in the struggle until Christ returns, because Satan is constantly battling against all who are on the Lord's side. We need supernatural power to defeat Satan, and God has provided this by giving us his Holy Spirit within us and his armor surrounding us. If you feel discouraged, remember Jesus' words to Peter: "Upon this rock I will build my church, and all the powers of hell will not conquer it" (Matthew 16:18).

**6:18** How can anyone pray at all times? One way is to make quick, brief prayers your habitual response to every situation you meet throughout the day. Another way is to order your life around God's desires and teachings so that your very life becomes a prayer. You don't have to isolate yourself from other people and from daily work in order to pray constantly. You can make prayer your life and your life a prayer while living in a world that needs God's powerful influence. We also should pray for all believers in Christ; so pray for the Christians you know and for the church around the world.

**6:19, 20** Undiscouraged and undefeated, Paul wrote powerful letters of encouragement from prison. Paul did not ask the Ephesians to pray that his chains would be removed but that he would continue to speak fearlessly for Christ in spite of them. God can use us in any circumstance to do his will. Even as we pray for a change in our circumstances, we should also pray that God will accomplish his plan through us right where we are. Knowing God's eternal purpose for us will help us through the difficult times.

## Final Greetings

**6:21**
Acts 20:4
2 Tim 4:12
Titus 3:12

**6:22**
Col 4:7-9

**6:23**
Gal 6:16
2 Thes 3:16

²¹ To bring you up to date, Tychicus will give you a full report about what I am doing and how I am getting along. He is a beloved brother and faithful helper in the Lord's work. ²²I have sent him to you for this very purpose—to let you know how we are doing and to encourage you.

²³Peace be with you, dear brothers and sisters,* and may God the Father and the Lord Jesus Christ give you love with faithfulness. ²⁴May God's grace be eternally upon all who love our Lord Jesus Christ.

**6:23** Greek *brothers.*

---

**6:21** Tychicus is also mentioned in Acts 20:4, Colossians 4:7, 2 Timothy 4:12, and Titus 3:12.

**6:24** This letter was written to the church at Ephesus, but it was also meant for circulation among other churches. In this letter, Paul highlights the supremacy of Christ, gives information on both the nature of the church and on how church members should live, and stresses the unity of all believers—male, female, parent, child, master, slave—regardless of sex, nationality, or social rank. The home and the church are difficult places to live the Christian life, because our real self comes through to those who know us well. Close relationships between imperfect people can lead to trouble—or to increased faith and deepened dependence on God. We can build unity in our churches through willing submission to Christ's leadership and humble service to one another.

# PHILIPPIANS

## VITAL STATISTICS

**PURPOSE:**
To thank the Philippians for the gift they had sent Paul and to strengthen these believers by showing them that true joy comes from Jesus Christ alone

**AUTHOR:**
Paul

**ORIGINAL AUDIENCE:**
The Christians at Philippi

**DATE WRITTEN:**
Approximately A.D. 61, from Rome during Paul's imprisonment there

**SETTING:**
Paul and his companions began the church at Philippi on his second missionary journey (Acts 16:11–40). This was the first church established on the European continent. The Philippian church had sent a gift with Epaphroditus (one of their members) to be delivered to Paul (4:18). Paul was in a Roman prison at the time. He wrote this letter to thank them for their gift and to encourage them in their faith.

**KEY VERSE:**
"Always be full of joy in the Lord. I say it again—rejoice!" (4:4)

**KEY PEOPLE:**
Paul, Timothy, Epaphroditus, Euodia, and Syntyche

**KEY PLACE:**
Philippi

THE WORD *happiness* evokes visions of unwrapping gifts on Christmas morning, strolling hand in hand with the one you love, being surprised on your birthday, responding with unbridled laughter to a comedian, or vacationing in an exotic locale. Everyone wants to be happy; we make chasing this elusive ideal a lifelong pursuit: spending money, collecting things, and searching for new experiences. But if happiness depends on our circumstances, what happens when the toys rust, loved ones die, health deteriorates, money is stolen, and the party's over? Often happiness flees and despair sets in.

In contrast to *happiness* stands *joy.* Running deeper and stronger, joy is the quiet, confident assurance of God's love and work in our lives—that he will be there no matter what! Happiness depends on happenings, but joy depends on Christ.

Philippians is Paul's joy letter. The church in that Macedonian city had been a great encouragement to Paul. The Philippian believers had enjoyed a very special relationship with him, so he wrote them a personal expression of his love and affection. They had brought him great joy (4:1). Philippians is also a joyful book because it emphasizes the real joy of the Christian life. The concept of *rejoicing* or *joy* appears sixteen times in four chapters, and the pages radiate this positive message, culminating in the exhortation to "always be full of joy in the Lord. I say it again—rejoice!" (4:4).

In a life dedicated to serving Christ, Paul had faced excruciating poverty, abundant wealth, and everything in between. He even wrote this joyful letter from prison. Whatever the circumstances, Paul had learned to be content (4:11, 12), finding real joy as he focused all of his attention and energy on knowing Christ (3:8) and obeying him (3:12, 13).

Paul's desire to know Christ above all else is wonderfully expressed in the following words: "Yes, everything else is worthless when compared with the infinite value of knowing Christ Jesus my Lord. For his sake I have discarded everything else, counting it all as garbage, so that I could gain Christ and become one with him. . . . I want to know Christ and experience the mighty power that raised him from the dead. I want to suffer with him, sharing in his death" (3:8–10). May we share Paul's aspiration and seek to know Jesus Christ more and more. Rejoice with Paul in Philippians, and rededicate yourself to finding joy in Christ.

## THE BLUEPRINT

1. Joy in suffering
   (1:1–30)
2. Joy in serving
   (2:1–30)
3. Joy in believing
   (3:1—4:1)
4. Joy in giving
   (4:2–23)

Although Paul was writing from prison, joy is a dominant theme in this letter. The secret of his joy is grounded in his relationship with Christ. People today desperately want to be happy but are tossed and turned by daily successes, failures, and inconveniences. Christians are to be joyful in every circumstance, even when things are going badly, even when we feel like complaining, even when no one else is joyful. Christ still reigns, and we still know him, so we can rejoice at all times.

## MEGATHEMES

| THEME | EXPLANATION | IMPORTANCE |
|---|---|---|
| *Humility* | Christ showed true humility when he laid aside his rights and privileges as God to become human. He poured out his life to pay the penalty we deserve. Laying aside self-interest is essential to all our relationships. | We are to take Christ's attitude in serving others. We must renounce personal recognition and merit. When we give up our self-interest, we can serve with joy, love, and kindness. |
| *Self-Sacrifice* | Christ suffered and died so we might have eternal life. With courage and faithfulness, Paul sacrificed himself for the ministry. He preached the gospel even while he was in prison. | Christ gives us power to lay aside our personal needs and concerns. To utilize his power, we must imitate those leaders who show self-denying concern for others. We dare not be self-centered. |
| *Unity* | In every church, in every generation, there are divisive influences (issues, loyalties, and conflicts). In the midst of hardships, it is easy to turn on one another. Paul encouraged the Philippians to agree with one another, stop complaining, and work together. | As believers, we should not contend with one another but unite against a mutual enemy. When we are unified in love, Christ's strength is most abundant. Keep before you the ideals of teamwork, consideration of others, and unselfishness. |
| *Christian Living* | Paul shows us how to live successful Christian lives. We can become mature by being so identi-fied with Christ that his attitude of humility and self-sacrifice becomes ours. Christ is both our source of power and our guide. | Developing our character begins with God's work in us. But growth also requires self-discipline, obedience to God's Word, and concentration on our part. |
| *Joy* | Believers can have profound contentment, serenity, and peace no matter what happens. This joy comes from knowing Christ personally and from depending on his strength rather than our own. | We can have joy, even in hardship. Joy does not come from outward circumstances but from inward strength. As Christians, we must not rely on what we have or what we experience to give us joy but on Christ within us. |

## 1. Joy in suffering
### Greetings from Paul

**1:1**
Acts 16:1
2 Cor 1:1

**1** This letter is from Paul and Timothy, slaves of Christ Jesus.
I am writing to all of God's holy people in Philippi who belong to Christ Jesus, includ-ing the elders* and deacons.

**1:2-3**
Rom 1:7-8

²May God our Father and the Lord Jesus Christ give you grace and peace.

**1:1** Or *overseers;* or *bishops.*

---

**1:1** This is a personal letter to the Philippians, not intended for general circulation to all the churches, as was the letter to the Ephesians. Paul wanted to thank the believers for helping him when he had a need. He also wanted to tell them why he could be full of joy despite his imprisonment and upcoming trial. In this uplifting letter, Paul counseled the Philippians about humility and unity and warned them about potential problems.

**1:1** On Paul's first missionary journey, he visited towns close to his headquarters in Antioch of Syria. On his second and third jour-neys, he traveled farther away. Because of the great distances between the congregations that Paul had founded, he could no longer personally oversee them all. Thus, he was compelled to write letters to teach and encourage the believers. Fortunately, Paul had a staff of volunteers (including Timothy, Mark, and Epaphras) who personally delivered these letters and often remained with the congregations for a while to teach and encourage them.

**1:1** For more information on Paul, see his Profile in Acts 9, p. 1837. Timothy's Profile is found in 1 Timothy 2, p. 2059.

**1:1** The Roman colony of Philippi was located in northern Greece (called Macedonia in Paul's day). Philip II of Macedon (the father of Alexander the Great) took the town from ancient Thrace in about 357 B.C., enlarged and strengthened it, and gave it his name. This thriving commercial center sat at the crossroads between Europe and Asia. In about A.D. 50, Paul, Silas, Timothy, and Luke crossed the Aegean Sea from Asia Minor and landed at Philippi (Acts 16:11-40). The church in Philippi consisted mostly of Gentile (non-Jewish) believers. Because they were not familiar with the Old Testament, Paul did not specifically quote any Old Testament passages in this letter.

**1:1** Elders (bishops or pastors) and deacons led the early Chris-tian churches. The qualifications and duties of the elders are explained in detail in 1 Timothy 3:1-7 and Titus 1:5-9. The qualifi-cations and duties of deacons are spelled out in 1 Timothy 3:8-13.

**1:2** We get upset at children who fail to appreciate small gifts, yet we undervalue God's immeasurable gifts of grace and peace. Instead, we seek the possessions and shallow experiences the

## Paul's Thanksgiving and Prayer

³Every time I think of you, I give thanks to my God. ⁴Whenever I pray, I make my requests for all of you with joy, ⁵for you have been my partners in spreading the Good News about Christ from the time you first heard it until now. ⁶And I am certain that God, who began the good work within you, will continue his work until it is finally finished on the day when Christ Jesus returns.

⁷So it is right that I should feel as I do about all of you, for you have a special place in my heart. You share with me the special favor of God, both in my imprisonment and in defending and confirming the truth of the Good News. ⁸God knows how much I love you and long for you with the tender compassion of Christ Jesus.

**1:6**
1 Cor 1:8

**1:7**
2 Cor 7:3

**1:8**
Rom 1:9

**LOCATION OF PHILIPPI**
Philippi sat on the Egnatian Way, the main transportation route in Macedonia, an extension of the Appian Way, which joined the eastern empire with Italy.

world offers. Compared to the big and bright "packages" of our culture, grace and peace appear insignificant. But when we unwrap them, we discover God's wonderful personal dealings with us. Inside the tiny package marked "grace and peace," we find an inexhaustible treasure of God's daily presence in our lives. Using these two words in his greetings to all the churches to whom he wrote, Paul wasn't offering something new. He was reminding his readers of what they already possessed in Christ. Thank God for his grace, and live in his peace.

**1:4** This is the first of many times Paul used the word *joy* in this letter. The Philippians were remembered with joy and thanksgiving whenever Paul prayed. By helping Paul, they were helping Christ's cause. The Philippians were willing to be used by God for whatever he wanted them to do. When others think about you, what comes to their minds? Are you remembered with joy by them? Do your acts of kindness lift up others?

**1:4, 5** The Philippians first heard the Good News about 10 years earlier when Paul and his companions visited Philippi (during Paul's second missionary journey) and founded the church there.

**1:5** When Paul said that the Philippians were partners in spreading the Good News, he was remembering how they contributed through their practical help when Paul was in Philippi and through their financial support when he was in prison. As we help our ministers, missionaries, and evangelists through prayer, hospitality, and financial gifts, we become partners with them in spreading the gospel message.

**1:6** The God who began a good work within us continues it throughout our lifetime and will finish it when we meet him face to face. God's work *for* us began when Christ died on the cross in our place. His work *within* us began when we first believed. Now the Holy Spirit lives in us, enabling us to be more like Christ every day. Paul is describing the process of Christian growth and maturity that began when we accepted Jesus and continues until Christ returns.

**1:6** Do you sometimes feel as though you aren't making progress in your spiritual life? When God starts a project, he completes it! As with the Philippians, God will help you grow in grace until he has completed his work in your life. When you are discouraged, remember that God won't give up on you. He promises to finish the work he has begun. When you feel incomplete, unfinished, or distressed by your shortcomings, remember God's promise and provision. Don't let your present condition rob you of the joy of knowing Christ or keep you from growing closer to him.

**1:7** When he mentions his imprisonment, Paul was probably referring to his imprisonment in Philippi (see Acts 16:22-36). In verses 13 and 14, Paul speaks of his Roman imprisonment. Wherever Paul was, even in prison, he faithfully preached the Good News. Remember Paul's inspiring example when hindrances, small or large, slow down your work for God.

**1:7, 8** Have you ever longed to see a friend with whom you share fond memories? Paul had such a longing to see the Christians at Philippi. His love and affection for them was based not

**1:9**
1 Thes 3:12

**1:10**
Rom 12:2
1 Cor 1:8

**1:11**
John 15:4

<sup>9</sup>I pray that your love will overflow more and more, and that you will keep on growing in knowledge and understanding. <sup>10</sup>For I want you to understand what really matters, so that you may live pure and blameless lives until the day of Christ's return. <sup>11</sup>May you always be filled with the fruit of your salvation—the righteous character produced in your life by Jesus Christ*—for this will bring much glory and praise to God.

### Paul's Joy That Christ Is Preached

**1:12**
2 Tim 2:9

**1:13**
Acts 28:30-31
Eph 3:1; 4:1

**1:14**
Phil 1:20

**1:15**
Phil 2:3

**1:17**
Acts 21:33

<sup>12</sup>And I want you to know, my dear brothers and sisters,* that everything that has happened to me here has helped to spread the Good News. <sup>13</sup>For everyone here, including the whole palace guard,* knows that I am in chains because of Christ. <sup>14</sup>And because of my imprisonment, most of the believers* here have gained confidence and boldly speak God's message* without fear.

<sup>15</sup>It's true that some are preaching out of jealousy and rivalry. But others preach about Christ with pure motives. <sup>16</sup>They preach because they love me, for they know I have been appointed to defend the Good News. <sup>17</sup>Those others do not have pure motives as they preach about Christ. They preach with selfish ambition, not sincerely, intending to make my chains more painful to me. <sup>18</sup>But that doesn't matter. Whether their motives are false or

**1:11** Greek *with the fruit of righteousness through Jesus Christ.*  **1:12** Greek *brothers.*  **1:13** Greek *including all the Praetorium.*  **1:14a** Greek *brothers in the Lord.*  **1:14b** Some manuscripts read *speak the message.*

---

merely on past experiences but also on the unity that comes when believers draw upon Christ's love. All Christians are part of God's family and thus share equally in the transforming power of his love. Do you feel a deep love for fellow Christians, friends and strangers alike? Let Christ's love motivate you to love other Christians and to express that love in your actions toward them.

**1:9** Often the best way to influence someone is to pray for him or her. Paul's prayer for the Philippians was that they would be unified in love. Their love was to result in greater knowledge of Christ and deeper understanding (moral discernment). Their love was not based on feelings but on what Christ had done for them. As you grow in Christ's love, your heart and mind must grow together. Are your love and insight growing?

**1:10** Paul prayed that the Philippian believers would have the ability to differentiate between right and wrong, good and bad, vital and trivial. We ought to pray for moral discernment so we can maintain our Christian morals and values. Hebrews 5:14 emphasizes the need for discernment.

**1:10** "The day of Christ's return" refers to the time when God will judge the world through Jesus Christ. We should live each day as though he might return at any moment.

**1:11** The "fruit of your salvation" includes all of the character traits flowing from a right relationship with God. There is no other way for us to gain this fruit of righteousness than through Christ. See Galatians 5:22, 23 for the "fruit of the Spirit."

**1:12** In the past, missionaries—those who spread the Good News—boarded ships to go to foreign lands and did not expect to see their homeland shores again. Their good-byes were final, in terms of earth time. There was no turning back. While air travel, e-mail, and other technologies have made worldwide separation much easier, pioneering with the Good News still requires a high sacrifice. Paul's passion was for others to discover the Good News of eternal life through Jesus Christ, no matter what the cost would be. Pressing through frontiers of spiritual darkness still requires pioneers today—people who will reach neglected people or new people groups. Pray for missionaries, support them, join them.

**1:12-14** Being imprisoned would cause many people to become bitter or to give up, but Paul saw it as one more opportunity to spread the Good News of Christ. Paul realized that his current circumstances weren't as important as what he did with them. Turning a bad situation into a good one, he reached out to the Roman soldiers who made up the palace guard and encouraged those Christians who were afraid of persecution. We may not be in prison, but we still have plenty of opportunities to be discouraged—times of indecision, financial burdens, family conflict,

church conflict, or the loss of our jobs. How we act in such situations will reflect what we believe. Like Paul, look for ways to demonstrate your faith even in bad situations. Whether or not the situation improves, your faith will grow stronger.

**1:13** How did Paul end up in chains in a Roman prison? While he was visiting Jerusalem, some Jews had him arrested for preaching the Good News, but he appealed to Caesar to hear his case (Acts 21:15–25:12). He was then escorted by soldiers to Rome, where he was placed under house arrest while awaiting trial—not a trial for breaking civil law, but for proclaiming the Good News of Christ. At that time, the Roman authorities did not consider this to be a serious charge. A few years later, however, Rome would take a different view of Christianity and make every effort to stamp it out of existence. Paul's house arrest allowed him some degree of freedom. He could have visitors, continue to preach, and write letters such as this one. A brief record of Paul's time in Rome is found in Acts 28:11-31. The "palace guard" refers to the elite troops housed in the emperor's palace.

**1:14** When we speak fearlessly for Christ or live faithfully for him during difficult situations, we encourage others to do the same. Be an encouragement by the way that you live.

**1:15-18** Paul had an amazingly selfless attitude. He knew that some were preaching to build their own reputations, taking advantage of his imprisonment to try to make a name for themselves. Regardless of the motives of these preachers, Paul rejoiced that the Good News was being preached. Some Christians serve for the wrong reasons. Paul wouldn't condone, nor does God excuse, their motives, but we should be glad if God uses their message, regardless of their motives.

**1:16** Paul could have become depressed, discouraged, or disillusioned. He could have wallowed in self-pity and despair. Instead, he regarded his imprisonment as being appointed by God. In fact, God had used Paul's imprisonment in Rome to bring the gospel to the center of the empire, as well as to give Paul lots of time to write letters that would one day end up in the New Testament and give us much teaching and encouragement. Do you have difficulty accepting your station in life? Do you resent where God has placed you? Although education and focused effort may enable us to take a new role or get a new job, often God puts us in a place to serve. Whether it is an actual prison or a place that feels like one, God wants you to serve him faithfully and joyfully.

genuine, the message about Christ is being preached either way, so I rejoice. And I will continue to rejoice. ¹⁹For I know that as you pray for me and the Spirit of Jesus Christ helps me, this will lead to my deliverance.

1:19
2 Cor 1:11

### Paul's Life for Christ

²⁰For I fully expect and hope that I will never be ashamed, but that I will continue to be bold for Christ, as I have been in the past. And I trust that my life will bring honor to Christ, whether I live or die. ²¹For to me, living means living for Christ, and dying is even better. ²²But if I live, I can do more fruitful work for Christ. So I really don't know which is better. ²³I'm torn between two desires: I long to go and be with Christ, which would be far better for me. ²⁴But for your sakes, it is better that I continue to live.

1:20
Rom 5:5; 14:8
1 Cor 6:20
Eph 6:19

1:21
Gal 2:20
Col 1:27

1:22
Rom 1:13

²⁵Knowing this, I am convinced that I will remain alive so I can continue to help all of you grow and experience the joy of your faith. ²⁶And when I come to you again, you will have even more reason to take pride in Christ Jesus because of what he is doing through me.

1:23
2 Cor 5:8
2 Tim 4:6

1:26
Phil 2:24

### Live as Citizens of Heaven

²⁷Above all, you must live as citizens of heaven, conducting yourselves in a manner worthy of the Good News about Christ. Then, whether I come and see you again or only hear about you, I will know that you are standing together with one spirit and one purpose, fighting together for the faith, which is the Good News. ²⁸Don't be intimidated in any way by your enemies. This will be a sign to them that they are going to be destroyed, but that you are going to be saved, even by God himself. ²⁹For you have been given not only the privilege of trusting in Christ but also the privilege of suffering for him. ³⁰We are in this struggle together. You have seen my struggle in the past, and you know that I am still in the midst of it.

1:27
Eph 4:1
Phil 4:1-2

1:28
2 Tim 2:11
Heb 13:6

1:29
Matt 5:11-12

1:30
Acts 16:19-40
1 Thes 2:2

## 2. Joy in serving
### Have the Attitude of Christ

**2** Is there any encouragement from belonging to Christ? Any comfort from his love? Any fellowship together in the Spirit? Are your hearts tender and compassionate? ²Then make me truly happy by agreeing wholeheartedly with each other, loving one another, and working together with one mind and purpose.

2:1
2 Cor 13:13
Col 3:12

2:2
1 Pet 3:8

---

**1:19-21** This was not Paul's final imprisonment in Rome. But he didn't know that. Awaiting trial, he knew he could either be released or executed. However, he trusted Christ to work it out for his deliverance. Paul's prayer was that when he stood trial, he would speak courageously for Christ and not be timid or ashamed. Whether he lived or died, he wanted to exalt Christ. As it turned out, he was released from this imprisonment but arrested again two or three years later. Only faith in Christ could sustain Paul in such adversity.

**1:20, 21** To those who don't believe in God, life on earth is all there is, and so it is natural for them to strive for this world's values: money, popularity, power, pleasure, and prestige. For Paul, however, to live meant to develop eternal values and to tell others about Christ, who alone could help them see life from an eternal perspective. Paul's whole purpose in life was to speak out boldly for Christ and to become more like him. Thus, Paul could confidently say that dying would be even better than living, because in death he would be removed from worldly troubles, and he would see Christ face to face (1 John 3:2, 3). If you're not ready to die, then you're not ready to live. Make certain of your eternal destiny; then you will be free to serve—devoting your life to what really counts, without fear of death.

**1:24** Paul had a purpose for living when he served the Philippians and others. We also need a purpose for living that goes beyond providing for our own physical needs. Whom can you serve or help? What is your purpose for living?

**1:27** Paul encouraged the believers to be unified, as they stood "side by side, fighting together for the faith, which is the Good News." How sad that much time and effort are lost in some churches by fighting against one another instead of uniting against the real opposition! It takes a courageous church to resist infighting and to maintain the common purpose of serving Christ.

**1:29** Paul considered it a privilege to suffer for Christ. We do not by nature consider suffering a privilege. Yet when we suffer, if we faithfully represent Christ, our message and example affect us and others for good (see Acts 5:41). Suffering has these additional benefits: (1) It takes our eyes off of earthly comforts; (2) it weeds out superficial believers; (3) it strengthens the faith of those who endure; (4) it serves as an example to others who may follow us. When we suffer for our faith, it doesn't mean that we have done something wrong. In fact, the opposite is often true—it verifies that we have been faithful. Use suffering to build your character. Don't resent it or let it tear you down.

**1:30** Throughout his life, Paul suffered for spreading the Good News. Like the Philippians, we are in conflict with anyone who would discredit the saving message of Christ. All true believers are in this fight together, uniting against the same enemy for a common cause.

Paul never urges Christians to seek suffering, as if there were virtue in pain. But we should not forget those who suffer. If your cupboard is full, share your food. If you control the wheels of power, work for justice and mercy. If you are wealthy, give generously to the poor. When life is comfortable, willingly take a share of someone else's pain, and so tell the world that the gospel is true.

**2:1-5** Many people—even Christians—live only to make a good impression on others or to please themselves. But selfishness brings discord. Paul therefore stressed spiritual unity, asking the Philippians to love one another and to be one in spirit and purpose. When we work together, caring for the problems of others as if they were our problems, we demonstrate Christ's example of putting others first, and we experience unity. Don't be so concerned about making a good impression or meeting your own needs that you strain relationships in God's family.

**2:3**
Rom 12:10
Gal 5:26
1 Pet 5:5

**2:4**
1 Cor 10:24

**2:6**
John 1:1-2; 5:18

**2:7**
John 1:14
Rom 8:3

**2:9**
Eph 1:20-21
Heb 1:3-4

**2:10**
Isa 45:23
Rom 14:11

**2:11**
John 13:13

³Don't be selfish; don't try to impress others. Be humble, thinking of others as better than yourselves. ⁴Don't look out only for your own interests, but take an interest in others, too.
⁵ You must have the same attitude that Christ Jesus had.

6 Though he was God,*
    he did not think of equality with God
        as something to cling to.
7 Instead, he gave up his divine privileges*;
    he took the humble position of a slave*
        and was born as a human being.
    When he appeared in human form,*
8   he humbled himself in obedience to God
        and died a criminal's death on a cross.

9 Therefore, God elevated him to the place of highest honor
        and gave him the name above all other names,
10 that at the name of Jesus every knee should bow,
        in heaven and on earth and under the earth,
11 and every tongue confess that Jesus Christ is Lord,
        to the glory of God the Father.

**2:6** Or *Being in the form of God.*   **2:7a** Greek *he emptied himself.*   **2:7b** Or *the form of a slave.*   **2:7c** Some English translations put this phrase in verse 8.

**2:3** Selfishness can ruin a church, but genuine humility can build it. Being humble involves having a true perspective about ourselves (see Romans 12:3). It does not mean that we should put ourselves down. Before God, we are sinners, saved only by God's grace, but we *are* saved and therefore have great worth in God's Kingdom. We are to lay aside selfishness and treat others with respect and common courtesy. Considering others' interests as more important than our own links us with Christ, who was a true example of humility.

**2:4** Philippi was a cosmopolitan city. The composition of the church reflected great diversity, with people from a variety of backgrounds and walks of life. Acts 16 gives us some indication of the diverse makeup of this church. The church included Lydia, a Jewish convert from Asia and a wealthy businesswoman (Acts 16:14); the slave girl (Acts 16:16, 17), probably a native Greek; and the jailer serving this colony of the empire, probably a Roman (Acts 16:25-36). With so many different backgrounds among the members, unity must have been difficult to maintain. Although there is no evidence of division in the church, its unity had to be safeguarded (3:2; 4:2). Paul encourages us to guard against any selfishness, prejudice, or jealousy that might lead to dissension. Showing genuine interest in others is a positive step forward in maintaining unity among believers.

**2:5** Jesus Christ was humble, willing to give up his rights in order to obey God and serve people. Like Christ, we should have a servant's attitude, serving out of love for God and for others, not out of guilt or fear. Remember, you can choose your attitude. You can approach life expecting to be served, or you can look for opportunities to serve others. See Mark 10:45 for more on Christ's attitude of servanthood.

**2:5-7** The Incarnation was the act of the preexistent Son of God voluntarily assuming a human body and human nature. Without ceasing to be God, he became a human being, the man called Jesus. He did not give up his deity to become human, but he set aside the right to his glory and power. In submission to the Father's will, Christ limited his power and knowledge. Jesus of Nazareth was subject to place, time, and many other human limitations. What made his humanity unique was his freedom from sin. In his full humanity, Jesus showed us everything about God's character that can be conveyed in human terms. The Incarnation is explained further in these passages: John 1:1-14; Romans 1:2-5; 2 Corinthians 8:9; 1 Timothy 3:16; Hebrews 2:14; and 1 John 1:1-3.

**2:5-11** These verses are probably from a hymn sung by the early Christian church. The passage holds many parallels to the prophecy of the suffering servant in Isaiah 53. As a hymn, it was not meant to be a complete statement about the nature and work of Christ. Several key characteristics of Jesus Christ, however, are praised in this passage: (1) Christ has always existed with God; (2) Christ is equal to God because he *is* God (John 1:1ff; Colossians 1:15-19); (3) though Christ is God, he became a man in order to fulfill God's plan of salvation for all people; (4) Christ did not just have the appearance of being a man—he actually became human to identify with our sins; (5) Christ voluntarily laid aside his divine rights and privileges out of love for his Father; (6) Christ died on the cross for our sins so we wouldn't have to face eternal death; (7) God glorified Christ because of his obedience; (8) God raised Christ to his original position at the Father's right hand, where he will reign forever as our Lord and Judge. How can we do anything less than praise Christ as our Lord and dedicate ourselves to his service!

**2:5-11** Often people excuse selfishness, pride, or evil by claiming their rights. They think, "I can cheat on this test; after all, I deserve to pass this class," or "I can spend all this money on myself—I worked hard for it," or "I can get an abortion; I have a right to control my own body." But as believers, we should have a different attitude, one that enables us to lay aside our rights in order to serve others. If we say we follow Christ, we must also say we want to live as he lived. We should develop his attitude of humility as we serve, even when we are not likely to get recognition for our efforts. Are you selfishly clinging to your rights, or are you willing to serve?

**2:8** Death on a cross (crucifixion) was the form of capital punishment that Romans used for notorious criminals. It was excruciatingly painful and humiliating. Prisoners were nailed or tied to a cross and left to die. Death might not come for several days, and it usually came by suffocation when the weight of the weakened body made breathing more and more difficult. Jesus died as one who was cursed (Galatians 3:13). How amazing that the perfect man should die this most shameful death so that we would not have to face eternal punishment!

**2:9-11** At the Last Judgment, even those who are condemned will recognize Jesus' authority and right to rule. People can choose now to commit their lives to Jesus as Lord or be forced to acknowledge him as Lord when he returns. Christ may return at any moment. Are you prepared to meet him?

### Shine Brightly for Christ

¹²Dear friends, you always followed my instructions when I was with you. And now that I am away, it is even more important. Work hard to show the results of your salvation, obeying God with deep reverence and fear. ¹³For God is working in you, giving you the desire and the power to do what pleases him.

¹⁴Do everything without complaining and arguing, ¹⁵so that no one can criticize you. Live clean, innocent lives as children of God, shining like bright lights in a world full of crooked and perverse people. ¹⁶Hold firmly to the word of life; then, on the day of Christ's return, I will be proud that I did not run the race in vain and that my work was not useless. ¹⁷But I will rejoice even if I lose my life, pouring it out like a liquid offering to God,* just like your faithful service is an offering to God. And I want all of you to share that joy. ¹⁸Yes, you should rejoice, and I will share your joy.

### Paul Commends Timothy

¹⁹If the Lord Jesus is willing, I hope to send Timothy to you soon for a visit. Then he can cheer me up by telling me how you are getting along. ²⁰I have no one else like Timothy, who genuinely cares about your welfare. ²¹All the others care only for themselves and not for what matters to Jesus Christ. ²²But you know how Timothy has proved himself. Like a son with his father, he has served with me in preaching the Good News. ²³I hope to send him to you just as soon as I find out what is going to happen to me here. ²⁴And I have confidence from the Lord that I myself will come to see you soon.

### Paul Commends Epaphroditus

²⁵Meanwhile, I thought I should send Epaphroditus back to you. He is a true brother, co-worker, and fellow soldier. And he was your messenger to help me in my need. ²⁶I am sending him because he has been longing to see you, and he was very distressed that you heard

**2:13**
Rom 8:28
1 Cor 12:6
Heb 13:21
**2:14**
1 Cor 10:10
**2:15**
Matt 5:45
John 12:36
Eph 5:1
**2:16**
1 Thes 2:19
**2:17**
Rom 15:16
2 Tim 4:6
**2:20**
1 Cor 16:10
**2:21**
1 Cor 10:24
**2:22**
1 Cor 4:17
1 Tim 1:2
**2:24**
Phil 1:25
**2:25**
Phil 4:18
**2:26**
Phil 1:8

**2:17** Greek *I will rejoice even if I am to be poured out as a liquid offering.*

**2:12** "Work hard to show the results of your salvation," in light of the preceding exhortation to unity, may mean that the entire church was to work together to rid themselves of divisions and discord. The Philippian Christians needed to be especially careful to obey Christ, now that Paul wasn't there to continually remind them about what was right. We, too, must be careful about what we believe and how we live, especially when we are on our own. In the absence of cherished Christian leaders, we must focus our attention and devotion even more on Christ so that we won't be sidetracked.

**2:13** What do we do when we don't feel like obeying? God has not left us alone in our struggles to do his will. He wants to come alongside us and be within us to help. God gives us the *desire* and the *power* to do what pleases him. The secret to a changed life is to submit to God's control and let him work. Next time ask God to help you *desire* to do his will.

**2:13** To be like Christ, we must train ourselves to think like Christ. To change our desires to be more like Christ's, we need the power of the indwelling Spirit (1:19), the influence of faithful Christians, obedience to God's Word (not just exposure to it), and sacrificial service. Often it is in *doing* God's will that we gain the *desire* to do it (see 4:8, 9). Do what he wants and trust him to change your desires.

**2:14-16** Why are complaining and arguing so harmful? If all that people know about a church is that its members constantly argue, complain, and gossip, they get a false impression of Christ and the Good News. Belief in Christ should unite those who trust him. If your church is always complaining and arguing, it lacks the unifying power of Jesus Christ. Stop arguing with other Christians or complaining about people and conditions within the church; instead, let the world see Christ.

**2:14-16** Our lives should be characterized by moral purity, patience, and peacefulness, so that we will "shine brightly" in a dark and depraved world. A transformed life is an effective witness to the power of God's Word. Are you shining brightly, or are you clouded by complaining and arguing? Don't let dissensions snuff out your light. Shine out for God. Your role is to shine until Jesus returns and bathes the world in his radiant glory.

**2:17** The drink offering was an important part of the sacrificial system of the Jews (for an explanation, see Numbers 28:7). Because this church had little Jewish background, the liquid offering may refer to the wine poured out to pagan deities prior to important public events. Paul regarded his life as a sacrifice.

**2:17** Even if he had to die, Paul was content, knowing that he had helped the Philippians live for Christ. When you're totally committed to serving Christ, sacrificing to build the faith of others brings a joyous reward.

**2:19, 22** When Paul wrote these words, most vocational training was done by fathers, and sons stayed loyal to the family business. Timothy displayed that same loyalty in his spiritual apprenticeship with Paul. Timothy was with Paul in Rome when Paul wrote this letter. He traveled with Paul on his second missionary journey when the church at Philippi was begun. (For more information on Timothy, see his Profile in 1 Timothy 2, p. 2059.)

Just as a skilled workman trains an apprentice, Paul was preparing Timothy to carry on the ministry in his absence. Paul encouraged younger Christians to learn, to observe, to help, and then to lead. Paul expected older Christians to teach, to model, to mentor, and then to turn over leadership. The benefits of such a process are new enthusiasm and vision, new methods and energy. Are you a teacher? Whom are you apprenticing for God's work? Are you a learner? How are you showing your eagerness to fulfill the call God has on your life?

**2:21** Paul observed that most believers are too preoccupied with their own needs to spend time working for Christ. Don't let your schedule and concerns crowd out your love and Christian service to others.

**2:23** Paul was in prison (either awaiting his trial or its verdict) for preaching about Christ. He was telling the Philippians that when he learned of the court's decision, he would send Timothy to them with the news. Paul wanted them to know that he was ready to accept whatever came (1:21-26).

**2:25** Epaphroditus delivered money from the Philippians to Paul; then he returned with this thank-you letter to Philippi. Epaphroditus may have been an elder in Philippi (2:25-30; 4:18) who, he was ill. 27And he certainly was ill; in fact, he almost died. But God had mercy on him—and also on me, so that I would not have one sorrow after another.

28So I am all the more anxious to send him back to you, for I know you will be glad to see him, and then I will not be so worried about you. 29Welcome him with Christian love* and with great joy, and give him the honor that people like him deserve. 30For he risked his life for the work of Christ, and he was at the point of death while doing for me what you couldn't do from far away.

## 3. Joy in believing
### The Priceless Value of Knowing Christ

**3** Whatever happens, my dear brothers and sisters,* rejoice in the Lord. I never get tired of telling you these things, and I do it to safeguard your faith.

2Watch out for those dogs, those people who do evil, those mutilators who say you must be circumcised to be saved. 3For we who worship by the Spirit of God* are the ones who are truly circumcised. We rely on what Christ Jesus has done for us. We put no confidence in human effort, 4though I could have confidence in my own effort if anyone could. Indeed, if others have reason for confidence in their own efforts, I have even more!

5I was circumcised when I was eight days old. I am a pure-blooded citizen of Israel and a member of the tribe of Benjamin—a real Hebrew if there ever was one! I was a member of the Pharisees, who demand the strictest obedience to the Jewish law. 6I was so zealous that I harshly persecuted the church. And as for righteousness, I obeyed the law without fault.

7I once thought these things were valuable, but now I consider them worthless because

**2:29** 1 Cor 16:16, 18; 1 Tim 5:17
**2:30** 1 Cor 16:17
**3:1** Phil 2:18; 4:4
**3:2** Ps 22:16, 20; Rev 22:15
**3:3** John 4:21-24; Rom 2:29; Gal 6:15; Col 2:11
**3:5** Luke 1:59; 2:21; Acts 23:6; Rom 11:1; 2 Cor 11:22
**3:6** Acts 8:3; 22:4; 26:9-11; Gal 1:13

**2:29** Greek *in the Lord.*  **3:1** Greek *brothers;* also in 3:13, 17.  **3:3** Some manuscripts read *worship God in spirit;* one early manuscript reads *worship in spirit.*

---

while staying with Paul, became ill (2:27, 30). After Epaphroditus recovered, he returned home. He is mentioned only in Philippians.

**2:29, 30** The world honors those who are intelligent, beautiful, rich, and powerful. What kind of people should the church honor? Paul indicates that we should honor those who give their lives for the sake of Christ, going where we cannot go ourselves. Our missionaries do that for us today by providing ministry where we are not able to go.

**3:1** As a safeguard, Paul reviewed the basics with these believers. The Bible is our safeguard both morally and theologically. When we read it individually and publicly in church, it alerts us to corrections we need to make in our thoughts, attitudes, and actions.

**3:2, 3** These "dogs" and "mutilators" were very likely Judaizers—Jewish Christians who wrongly believed that it was essential for Gentiles to follow all the Old Testament Jewish laws, especially submission to the rite of circumcision, in order to receive salvation. Many Judaizers were motivated by spiritual pride. Because they had invested so much time and effort in keeping their laws, they couldn't accept the fact that all their efforts couldn't bring them a step closer to salvation.

Paul criticized the Judaizers because they looked at Christianity backward—thinking that what they *did* (circumcision—cutting or mutilating the flesh) made them believers rather than the free gift of grace given by Christ. What believers do is a *result* of faith, not a *prerequisite* to faith. This had been confirmed by the early church leaders at the Jerusalem council 11 years earlier (Acts 15). Who are the Judaizers of our day? They are those who say that people must add something else to simple faith. No person should add anything to Christ's offer of salvation by grace through faith.

**3:2, 3** It is easy to place more emphasis on human effort than on internal faith, but God values the attitude of our heart above all else. Don't judge people's spirituality by their fulfillment of duties or by their level of human activity. And don't think that you will satisfy God by feverishly doing his work. God notices all you do for him and will reward you for it, but only if it comes as a loving response to his free gift of salvation.

**3:4-6** At first glance, it looks like Paul is boasting about his achievements. But he is actually doing the opposite, showing that human achievements, no matter how impressive, cannot

earn a person salvation and eternal life with God. Paul had impressive credentials: upbringing, nationality, family background, inheritance, orthodoxy, activity, and morality (see 2 Corinthians 11; Galatians 1:13-24, for more of his credentials). However, his conversion to faith in Christ (Acts 9) wasn't based on what he had done but on God's grace. Paul did not depend on his deeds to please God, because even the most impressive credentials fall short of God's holy standards. Are you depending on Christian parents, church affiliation, or just being good to make you right with God? Credentials, accomplishments, or reputation cannot earn salvation. Salvation comes only through faith in Christ.

**3:5** Paul belonged to the tribe of Benjamin, a heritage greatly esteemed among the Jews. From this tribe had come Israel's first king, Saul (1 Samuel 10:20-24). The tribes of Benjamin and Judah were the only two tribes to return to Israel after the Exile (Ezra 4:1). Paul was also a Pharisee, a member of a very devout Jewish sect that scrupulously kept its own numerous rules in addition to the laws of Moses. Paul explains for these mostly Gentile believers that his Jewish credentials are impeccable.

**3:6** Why had Paul, a devout Jewish leader, persecuted the church? Agreeing with the leaders of the religious establishment, Paul had thought that Christianity was heretical and blasphemous. Because Jesus did not meet his expectations of what the Messiah would be like, Paul had assumed that Jesus' claims were false—and therefore wicked. In addition, he had seen Christianity as a political menace because it threatened to disrupt the fragile harmony between the Jews and the Roman government.

**3:7** When Paul spoke of "these things," he was referring to his credentials, credits, and successes. After showing that he could beat the Judaizers at their own game (being proud of who they were and what they had done), Paul showed that it was the wrong game. Be careful of considering past achievements so important that they get in the way of your relationship with Christ.

of what Christ has done. ⁸Yes, everything else is worthless when compared with the infinite value of knowing Christ Jesus my Lord. For his sake I have discarded everything else, counting it all as garbage, so that I could gain Christ ⁹and become one with him. I no longer count on my own righteousness through obeying the law; rather, I become righteous through faith in Christ.* For God's way of making us right with himself depends on faith. ¹⁰I want to know Christ and experience the mighty power that raised him from the dead. I want to suffer with him, sharing in his death, ¹¹so that one way or another I will experience the resurrection from the dead!

### Pressing toward the Goal

¹²I don't mean to say that I have already achieved these things or that I have already reached perfection. But I press on to possess that perfection for which Christ Jesus first possessed me. ¹³No, dear brothers and sisters, I have not achieved it,* but I focus on this one thing: Forgetting the past and looking forward to what lies ahead, ¹⁴I press on to reach the end of the race and receive the heavenly prize for which God, through Christ Jesus, is calling us.

¹⁵Let all who are spiritually mature agree on these things. If you disagree on some point, I believe God will make it plain to you. ¹⁶But we must hold on to the progress we have already made.

**3:9** Or *through the faithfulness of Christ.*    **3:13** Some manuscripts read *not yet achieved it.*

**3:8**
John 17:3
Eph 4:13
2 Pet 3:18

**3:9**
Rom 1:17; 3:21-22;
9:30; 10:3
Gal 2:16

**3:10**
Rom 6:3-5; 8:17, 29
Gal 6:17

**3:11**
Acts 26:8
1 Cor 15:23
Rev 20:5-6

**3:12**
1 Tim 6:12, 19

**3:13**
Luke 9:62

**3:14**
1 Cor 9:24
2 Tim 4:7-8
Heb 12:1

**3:15**
1 Cor 2:6
Phil 1:9-10

---

**3:8** After Paul considered everything he had accomplished in his life, he decided to write it all off as "worthless" when compared with the greatness of knowing Christ. We should value our relationship with Christ as more important than anything else. To know Christ should be our ultimate goal. Yet how do we know him better? (1) Study the life of Christ in the Gospels. See how Christ lived and responded to people (Matthew 11:29). (2) Study all the New Testament references to Christ (Colossians 1:15–2:15). (3) As you worship and pray, let the Holy Spirit remind you of Christ's words (John 14:26). (4) Take up Christ's mission to preach the gospel and learn from his sufferings (Matthew 28:19; Philippians 3:10).

To do these things, however, may mean that you must make major changes in your thinking and in your lifestyle. Are you willing to change your values in order to know Christ better? Will you fix or rearrange your crowded schedule in order to set aside a few minutes each day for prayer and Bible study? Will you change some of your plans, goals, and desires in order to conform with what you learn about Christ? Whatever you must change or give up, having Christ and becoming one with him will be more than worth the sacrifice.

**3:9** No amount of law keeping, self-improvement, discipline, or religious effort can make us right with God. Righteousness comes only from God, and we are made righteous (receive right standing with him) by trusting in Christ. He exchanges our sin and shortcomings for his complete righteousness. See 2 Corinthians 5:21 for more on Christ's gift of righteousness.

**3:9, 10** Paul gave up everything—family, friendship, and freedom—in order to know Christ and his resurrection power. We, too, have access to this knowledge and this power, but we may have to make sacrifices to enjoy it fully. What are you willing to give up in order to know Christ? A crowded schedule in order to set aside a few minutes each day for prayer and Bible study? Your friend's approval? Some of your plans or pleasures? Whatever it is, knowing Christ is more than worth the sacrifice.

**3:10** When we become one with Christ by trusting in him, we experience the power that raised him from the dead. That same mighty power will help us live morally renewed and regenerated lives. But before we can walk in newness of life, we must die to sin. Just as the Resurrection gives us Christ's power to live for him, his crucifixion marks the death of our old sinful nature. We can't know the victory of the Resurrection without personally applying the Crucifixion.

**3:11** When Paul wrote, "so that one way or another I will experience the resurrection from the dead," he was not implying uncertainty or doubt. He was unsure of the way that he would meet God, whether by execution or by natural death. He did not doubt that he would be raised, but attainment of it was within God's power and not his own.

**3:11** Just as Christ was exalted after his resurrection, so we will one day share Christ's glory (Revelation 22:1-7). Paul knew that he might die soon, but he had faith that he would be raised to life again.

**3:12-14** Paul said that his goal was to know Christ, to be like Christ, and to be all Christ had in mind for him. This goal took all of Paul's energies. This is a helpful example for us. We should not let anything take our eyes off our goal—knowing Christ. With the single-mindedness of an athlete in training, we must lay aside everything harmful and forsake anything that may distract us from being effective Christians. What is holding you back?

**3:13, 14** Paul had reason to forget the past—he had held the coats of those who had stoned Stephen, the first Christian martyr (Acts 7:57, 58, Paul is called Saul here). We have all done things for which we are ashamed, and we live in the tension of what we have been and what we want to be. Because our hope is in Christ, however, we can let go of past guilt and look forward to what God will help us become. Don't dwell on your past. Instead, grow in the knowledge of God by concentrating on your relationship with him *now.* Realize that you are forgiven, and then move on to a life of faith and obedience. Look forward to a fuller and more meaningful life because of your hope in Christ.

**3:15, 16** Sometimes trying to live a perfect Christian life can be so difficult that it leaves us drained and discouraged. We may feel so far from perfect that we think we can never please God with our life. Paul used *perfection* (3:12) to mean mature or complete, not flawless in every detail. Those who are mature should press on in the Holy Spirit's power, knowing that Christ will reveal and fill in any discrepancy between what we are and what we should be. Christ's provision is no excuse for lagging devotion, but it provides relief and assurance for those who feel driven.

**3:16** Christian maturity involves acting on the guidance that you have already received. We can always make excuses that we still have so much to learn. The instruction for us is to live up to what we already know and live out what we have already learned. We do not have to be sidetracked by an unending search for truth.

**3:17**
1 Cor 4:16
1 Pet 5:3

**3:18**
Gal 6:12

**3:20**
Eph 2:19
Heb 12:22-23

**3:21**
Rom 8:29
1 Cor 15:28, 43-53

17Dear brothers and sisters, pattern your lives after mine, and learn from those who follow our example. 18For I have told you often before, and I say it again with tears in my eyes, that there are many whose conduct shows they are really enemies of the cross of Christ. 19They are headed for destruction. Their god is their appetite, they brag about shameful things, and they think only about this life here on earth. 20But we are citizens of heaven, where the Lord Jesus Christ lives. And we are eagerly waiting for him to return as our Savior. 21He will take our weak mortal bodies and change them into glorious bodies like his own, using the same power with which he will bring everything under his control.

**4:1**
Phil 1:8

**4** Therefore, my dear brothers and sisters,* stay true to the Lord. I love you and long to see you, dear friends, for you are my joy and the crown I receive for my work.

4:1 Greek *brothers;* also in 4:8.

---

**THREE STAGES OF PERFECTION**

*1. Perfect Relationship*

We are perfect because of our eternal union with the infinitely perfect Christ. When we become his children, we are declared "not guilty" and thus righteous because of what Christ, God's beloved Son, has done for us. This perfection is absolute and unchangeable, and it is this perfect relationship that guarantees that we will one day be "completely perfect" (below). See Colossians 2:8-10; Hebrews 10:8-14.

*2. Perfect Progress*

We can grow and mature spiritually as we continue to trust Christ, learn more about him, draw closer to him, and obey him. Our progress is changeable (in contrast to our relationship, above) because it depends on our daily walk—at times in life we mature more than at other times. But we are growing toward perfection if we "press on" (Philippians 3:12). These good deeds do not perfect us; rather, as God perfects us, we do good deeds for him. See Philippians 3:1-15.

*3. Completely Perfect*

When Christ returns to take us into his eternal Kingdom, we will be glorified and made completely perfect. See Philippians 3:20, 21.

All phases of perfection are grounded in faith in Christ and what he has done, not what we can do for him. We cannot perfect ourselves; only God can work in and through us to "continue his work until it is finally finished on the day when Christ Jesus returns" (1:6).

---

**3:17** Paul challenged the Philippians to pursue Christlikeness by following Paul's own pattern or example. This did not mean, of course, that they should copy everything he did; he had just stated that he was not perfect (3:12). But as he focused his life on being like Christ, so should they. The Gospels may not yet have been in circulation, so Paul could not tell them to read the Bible to see what Christ was like. Therefore, he urged them to imitate him. That Paul could tell people to follow his example is a testimony to his character. Can you do the same? What kind of follower would a new Christian become if he or she imitated you?

**3:17-21** Paul criticized not only the Judaizers (see the first note on 3:2, 3) but also self-indulgent Christians, people who claimed to be Christians but didn't live up to Christ's model of servanthood and self-sacrifice. Such people satisfy their own desires before even thinking about the needs of others. Freedom in Christ does not mean freedom to be selfish. It means taking every opportunity to serve and to become the best person you can be.

**3:19** Paul gets tough with people who live to appease their appetites, who believe so strongly in their greatness that they become slaves to pride. What horrible people these must be—so concerned with earthly trivia that during worship their minds wander; so consumed with work that worship is inconvenient; so busy planning the next party that there is no time for prayer. Paul says they are headed for destruction because all they can think about is this life here on earth.

But then we must ask ourselves: Is too much of our time spent on efforts that will not endure in eternity, seeking earthly pleasures, or satisfying our physical desires? We must set our minds on knowing Christ, not on the pursuits of this world.

**3:20** Citizens of a Roman colony were expected to promote the interests of Rome and maintain the dignity of the city. In the same way, citizens of heaven ought to promote heaven's interests on earth and lead lives worthy of heavenly citizenship. Too many Christians have failed to transfer their citizenship to heaven. They still seek earthly pleasures and treasures instead of heavenly ones. Paul told the Colossians to remember that they are citizens of heaven, where the Lord Jesus Christ lives. Have you transferred your citizenship? How are you promoting heaven's interests?

**3:21** The phrase "weak mortal bodies" does not imply any negative attitude toward the human body. However, the bodies we will receive when we are raised from the dead will be glorious, like Christ's resurrected body. Those who struggle with pain, physical limitations, or disabilities can have wonderful hope in the resurrection. For a more detailed discussion of our new bodies, see 1 Corinthians 15:35ff and 2 Corinthians 5:1-10.

**4:1** How do we "stay true to the Lord"? This refers to what Paul has just taught in 3:20, 21. The way to stay true is to keep our eyes on Christ, to remember that this world is not our home, and to focus on the fact that Christ will bring everything under his control. Staying true means steadfastly resisting the negative influences of temptation, false teaching, or persecution. It requires perseverance when we are challenged or opposed. Don't lose heart or give up. God promises to give us strength of character. With the Holy Spirit's help and with the help of fellow believers, you can stay true to the Lord.

## 4. Joy in giving

*Words of Encouragement*

²Now I appeal to Euodia and Syntyche. Please, because you belong to the Lord, settle your disagreement. ³And I ask you, my true partner,* to help these two women, for they worked hard with me in telling others the Good News. They worked along with Clement and the rest of my co-workers, whose names are written in the Book of Life.

⁴Always be full of joy in the Lord. I say it again—rejoice! ⁵Let everyone see that you are considerate in all you do. Remember, the Lord is coming soon.

⁶Don't worry about anything; instead, pray about everything. Tell God what you need, and thank him for all he has done. ⁷Then you will experience God's peace, which exceeds anything we can understand. His peace will guard your hearts and minds as you live in Christ Jesus.

⁸And now, dear brothers and sisters, one final thing. Fix your thoughts on what is true, and honorable, and right, and pure, and lovely, and admirable. Think about things that are excellent and worthy of praise. ⁹Keep putting into practice all you learned and received from me—everything you heard from me and saw me doing. Then the God of peace will be with you.

*Paul's Thanks for Their Gifts*

¹⁰How I praise the Lord that you are concerned about me again. I know you have always been concerned for me, but you didn't have the chance to help me. ¹¹Not that I was ever in

**4:3** Or *loyal Syzygus.*

**4:2**
Phil 2:2

**4:4**
Phil 3:1

**4:5**
Heb 10:37
Jas 5:8-9

**4:6**
Matt 6:25
1 Pet 5:7

**4:7**
Isa 26:3
John 14:27

**4:9**
Rom 15:33; 16:20
1 Cor 14:33
1 Thes 5:23

**4:11**
1 Tim 6:6

---

**4:2, 3** Paul did not warn the Philippian church of doctrinal errors, but he did address some relational problems. These two women had been workers for Christ in the church. Their broken relationship was no small matter, because many had become believers through their efforts. It is possible to believe in Christ, work hard for his Kingdom, and yet have broken relationships with others who are committed to the same cause. But there is no excuse for remaining unreconciled. Do you need to be reconciled to someone today? If you're facing a conflict you can't resolve, don't let the tension build into an explosion. Don't withdraw or resort to cruel power plays. Don't stand idly by and wait for the dispute to resolve itself. Instead, seek the help of those known for peacemaking.

**4:3** The identity of this "true partner" remains a mystery. It could be Epaphroditus, the bearer of this letter, or a comrade of Paul in prison. It could also be someone named Syzygus, another way to understand the word for "partner."

**4:3** Those "whose names are written in the Book of Life" are all who are marked for salvation through their faith in Christ (see also Luke 10:17-20; Revelation 20:11-15).

**4:4** It seems strange that a man in prison would be telling a church to rejoice. But Paul's attitude teaches us an important lesson: Our inner attitudes do not have to reflect our outward circumstances. Paul was full of joy because he knew that no matter what happened to him, Jesus Christ was with him. Several times in this letter Paul urged the Philippians to be joyful, probably because they needed to hear this. It's easy to get discouraged about unpleasant circumstances or to take unimportant events too seriously. If you haven't been joyful lately, you may not be looking at life from the right perspective.

**4:4, 5** Ultimate joy comes from Christ dwelling within us. Christ is near, and at his second coming we will fully realize this ultimate joy. He who lives within us will fulfill his final purposes for us.

**4:5** We are to be considerate (reasonable, fair minded, and charitable) to those outside the church, and not just to fellow believers. This means we are not to seek revenge against those who treat us unfairly, nor are we to be overly vocal about our personal rights.

**4:6, 7** Imagine never worrying about anything! It seems like an impossibility; we all have worries on the job, in our homes, at school. But Paul's advice is to turn our worries into prayers.

Do you want to worry less? Then pray more! Whenever you start to worry, stop and pray.

**4:7** God's peace is different from the world's peace (see John 14:27). True peace is not found in positive thinking, in absence of conflict, or in good feelings. It comes from knowing that God is in control. Our citizenship in Christ's Kingdom is sure, our destiny is set, and we can have victory over sin. Let God's peace guard your heart against anxiety.

**4:8** What we put into our mind determines what comes out in our words and actions. Paul tells us to program our mind with thoughts that are true, honorable, right, pure, lovely, admirable, excellent, and worthy of praise. Do you have problems with impure thoughts and daydreams? Examine what you are putting into your mind through television, Internet, books, conversations, movies, and magazines. Replace harmful input with wholesome material. Above all, read God's Word and pray. Ask God to help you focus your mind on what is good and pure. It takes practice, but it can be done.

**4:9** It's not enough to hear or read the Word of God or even to know it well. We must also put it into practice. How easy it is to listen to a sermon and forget what the preacher said. How easy it is to read the Bible and not think about how to live differently. How easy it is to debate what a passage means and not live out that meaning. Exposure to God's Word is not enough. It must lead to obedience.

**4:10** In 1 Corinthians 9:11-18, Paul wrote that he didn't accept gifts from the Corinthian church because he didn't want to be accused of preaching only to get money. But Paul maintained that it was a church's responsibility to support God's ministers (1 Corinthians 9:14). He accepted the Philippians' gift because they gave it willingly and because he was in need.

**4:10-14** Are you able to get along happily (be content) in any circumstances you face? Paul knew how to be satisfied whether he had plenty or whether he was in need. The secret was drawing on Christ's power for strength. Do you have great needs, or are you dissatisfied because you don't have what you want? Learn to rely on God's promises and Christ's power to help you be content. If you always want more, ask God to remove that desire and teach you how to be satisfied in every circumstance. He will supply all your needs, but in a way that he knows is best for you. (See the note on 4:19 for more on God supplying our needs.)

**4:12**
1 Cor 4:11
2 Cor 11:9

**4:13**
2 Cor 12:9-10

**4:15**
2 Cor 11:8-9
Phil 1:5

**4:16**
Acts 17:1
1 Thes 2:9

**4:17**
1 Cor 9:11

**4:18**
2 Cor 9:12
Phil 2:25

need, for I have learned how to be content with whatever I have. ¹²I know how to live on almost nothing or with everything. I have learned the secret of living in every situation, whether it is with a full stomach or empty, with plenty or little. ¹³For I can do everything through Christ,* who gives me strength. ¹⁴Even so, you have done well to share with me in my present difficulty.

¹⁵As you know, you Philippians were the only ones who gave me financial help when I first brought you the Good News and then traveled on from Macedonia. No other church did this. ¹⁶Even when I was in Thessalonica you sent help more than once. ¹⁷I don't say this because I want a gift from you. Rather, I want you to receive a reward for your kindness.

¹⁸At the moment I have all I need—and more! I am generously supplied with the gifts you sent me with Epaphroditus. They are a sweet-smelling sacrifice that is acceptable and

**4:13** Greek *through the one.*

| TRAINING FOR THE CHRISTIAN LIFE | Reference | Metaphors | Training | Our Goal as Believers |
|---|---|---|---|---|
| As a great amount of training is needed for athletic activities, so we must train diligently for the Christian life. Such training takes time, dedication, energy, continued practice, and vision. We must all commit ourselves to the Christian life, but we must first know the rules as prescribed in God's Word (2 Timothy 2:5). | 1 Corinthians 9:24-27 | Race | Go into strict training in order to get the prize. | We train ourselves to run the race of life. So we keep our eyes on Christ—the goal—and don't get sidetracked or slowed down. When we do this, we will win a reward in Christ's Kingdom. |
| | Philippians 3:13, 14 | Race | Focus all your energies toward winning the race. | Living the Christian life demands all of our energies. We can forget the past and strain to reach the goal because we know Christ promises eternity with him at the race's end. |
| | 1 Timothy 4:7-10 | Training | Training for godliness will help you grow in faith and character. | Just as we exercise to keep physically fit, we must also train ourselves to be spiritually fit. As our faith develops, we become better Christians, living in accordance with God's will. Such a life will attract others to Christ and pay dividends in both this life and the next. |
| | 2 Timothy 4:7, 8 | Fight, Race | Fighting the good fight and persevering to the end. | The Christian life is a fight against evil forces from without and temptation from within. If we stay true to God through it all, he promises an end, a rest, and a crown. |

**4:12, 13** Paul could get along happily because he could see life from God's point of view. He focused on what he was supposed to *do,* not what he felt he should *have.* Paul had his priorities straight, and he was grateful for everything God had given him. Paul had detached himself from the nonessentials so that he could concentrate on the eternal. Often the desire for more or better possessions is really a longing to fill an empty place in a person's life. To what are you drawn when you feel empty inside? How can you find true contentment? The answer lies in your perspective, your priorities, and your source of power.

**4:13** Can we really do everything? The power we receive in union with Christ is sufficient to do his will and to face the challenges that arise from our commitment to doing it. He does not grant us superhuman ability to accomplish anything we can imagine without regard to his interests. As we contend for the faith, we will face troubles, pressures, and trials. As they come, ask Christ to strengthen you.

**4:14** The Philippians shared in Paul's financial support while he was in prison.

**4:15** What makes money so magnetic and giving it away so stressful? Money measures our energy; it represents our day-to-day security. Giving money away puts our work and our futures at risk. Not every charity deserves your attention, and you're wise to scrutinize missionary appeals as well. But

once you've determined that a project honors the Lord, don't hold back—give generously and joyfully. Like the Philippians, you'll be establishing an eternal partnership.

**4:17** When we give to those in need, it not only benefits the receiver but it benefits us as well. It was not the Philippians' gift but their spirit of love and devotion that Paul appreciated most.

**4:18** Paul was not referring to a sin offering but to a peace offering, "a sweet-smelling sacrifice that is acceptable and pleasing to God" (Leviticus 7:12-15 contains the instructions for such offerings of thanksgiving). Although the Greek and Roman Christians were not Jews and they had not offered sacrifices according to the Old Testament laws, they were well acquainted with the pagan rituals of offering sacrifices.

pleasing to God. ¹⁹And this same God who takes care of me will supply all your needs from his glorious riches, which have been given to us in Christ Jesus.

²⁰Now all glory to God our Father forever and ever! Amen.

## Paul's Final Greetings

²¹Give my greetings to each of God's holy people—all who belong to Christ Jesus. The brothers who are with me send you their greetings. ²²And all the rest of God's people send you greetings, too, especially those in Caesar's household.

²³May the grace of the Lord Jesus Christ be with your spirit.

**4:19**
Ps 23:1
2 Cor 9:8

**4:20**
Rom 11:36

**4:22**
Phil 1:13

**4:23**
Rom 16:20
Gal 6:18
2 Tim 4:22

---

**4:19** We can trust that God will always meet our needs. Whatever we need on earth he will always supply, even if it is the courage to face death as Paul did. Whatever we need in heaven he will supply. We must remember, however, the difference between our wants and our needs. Most people want to feel good and avoid discomfort or pain. We may not get all that we want. By trusting in Christ, our attitudes and appetites can change from wanting everything to accepting his provision and power to live for him.

**4:22** There were many Christians in Rome; some were even in Caesar's household. Perhaps Paul, while awaiting trial, was making converts of the Roman civil service! Paul sent greetings from these Roman Christians to the believers at Philippi. The Good News had spread to all strata of society, linking people who had no other bond but Christ. The Roman Christians and the Philippian Christians were brothers and sisters because of their unity in Christ. Believers today are also linked to others across cultural, economic, and social barriers. Because all believers are brothers and sisters in Christ, let us live like God's true family.

**4:23** In many ways the Philippian church was a model congregation. It was made up of many different kinds of people who were learning to work together. But Paul recognized that problems could arise, so in his thank-you letter he prepared the Philippians for difficulties that could crop up within a body of believers. Although a prisoner in Rome, Paul had learned the true secret of joy and peace—imitating Christ and serving others. By focusing our mind on Christ, we will learn unity, humility, joy, and peace. We will also be motivated to live for him. We can live confidently for him because we have "the grace of the Lord Jesus Christ" with us.

REMOVE the head coach, and the team flounders; break the fuel line, and the car won't run; unplug the electrical appliance, and it has no power. Whether for leadership, power, or life, connections are vital!

Colossians is a book of connections. Writing from prison in Rome, Paul combatted false teachings, which had infiltrated the Colossian church. The problem was "syncretism," combining ideas from other philosophies and religions (such as paganism, strains of Judaism, and Greek thought) with Christian truth. The resulting heresy later became known as "Gnosticism," emphasizing special knowledge (*gnosis* in Greek) and denying Christ as God and Savior. To combat this devious error, Paul stressed Christ's deity—his connection with the Father—and his sacrificial death on the cross for sin. Only by being connected with Christ through faith can anyone have eternal life, and only through a continuing connection with him can anyone have power for living. Christ is God incarnate and the *only* way to forgiveness and peace with God the Father. Paul also emphasized believers' connections with each other as Christ's body on earth.

Paul's introduction to the Colossians includes a greeting, a note of thanksgiving, and a prayer for spiritual wisdom and strength for these brothers and sisters in Christ (1:1–12). He then moves into a doctrinal discussion of the person and work of Christ (1:13–23), stating that Christ is "the visible image of the invisible God" (1:15), the Creator (1:16), "the head of the church, which is his body" (1:18), and "supreme over all who rise from the dead" (1:18). His death on the cross makes it possible for us to stand in the presence of God (1:22).

Paul then explains how the world's teachings are totally empty when compared with God's plan, and he challenges the Colossians to reject shallow answers and to live in union with Christ (1:24—2:23).

Against this theological backdrop, Paul turns to practical considerations—what the divinity, death, and resurrection of Jesus should mean to all believers (3:1—4:6). Because our eternal destiny is sure, heaven should fill our thoughts (3:1–4), sexual impurity and other worldly lusts should not be named among us (3:5–8), and truth, love, and peace should mark our lives (3:9–15). Our love for Christ should also translate into love for others—friends, fellow believers, spouses, children, parents, slaves, and masters (3:16—4:1). We should constantly communicate with God through prayer (4:2–4), and we should take every opportunity to tell others the Good News (4:5, 6). In Christ we have everything we need for salvation and for living the Christian life.

Paul had probably never visited Colosse, so he concludes this letter with personal comments about their common Christian associations, providing a living lesson of the connectedness of the body of Christ.

Read Colossians as a book for an embattled church in the first century, but read it also for its timeless truths. Gain a fresh appreciation for Christ as the *fullness* of God and the *only* source for living the Christian life. Know that he is your leader, head, and power source, and make sure of your connection to him.

## VITAL STATISTICS

**PURPOSE:**
To combat errors in the church and to show that believers have everything they need in Christ

**AUTHOR:**
Paul

**ORIGINAL AUDIENCE:**
The church at Colosse, a city in Asia Minor

**DATE WRITTEN:**
Approximately A.D. 60, during Paul's imprisonment in Rome

**SETTING:**
Paul had never visited Colosse. Evidently the church had been founded by Epaphras and other converts from Paul's missionary travels. The church, however, had been infiltrated by religious relativism, with some believers attempting to combine elements of paganism and secular philosophy with Christian doctrine. Paul confronts these false teachings and affirms the sufficiency of Christ.

**KEY VERSES:**
"For in Christ lives all the fullness of God in a human body. So you also are complete through your union with Christ, who is the head over every ruler and authority" (2:9, 10).

**KEY PEOPLE:**
Paul, Timothy, Tychicus, Onesimus, Aristarchus, Mark, Epaphras

**KEY PLACES:**
Colosse, Laodicea (4:15, 16)

**SPECIAL FEATURES:**
Christ is presented as having absolute supremacy and sole sufficiency. Colossians has similarities to Ephesians, probably because it was written at about the same time, but it has a different emphasis.

## THE BLUEPRINT

1. What Christ has done
   (1:1—2:23)
2. What Christians should do
   (3:1—4:18)

In this letter Paul clearly teaches that Christ has paid for sin, that Christ has reconciled us to God, and that Christ gives us the pattern and the power to grow spiritually. Because in Christ lives all the fullness of God, when we learn what he is like, we see what we need to become. Since Christ is Lord over all creation, we should crown him Lord over our lives. Since Christ is the head of the body, his church, we should nurture our vital connection to him.

## MEGATHEMES

| THEME | EXPLANATION | IMPORTANCE |
|---|---|---|
| Christ Is God | Jesus Christ is God in the flesh, Lord of all creation, and Lord of the new creation. He is the visible image of the invisible God. He is eternal, preexistent, omnipotent, equal with the Father. He is supreme and complete. | Because Christ is supreme, our lives must be Christ-centered. To recognize him as God means to regard our relationship with him as most vital and to make his interests our top priority. |
| Christ Is Head of the Church | Because Christ is God, he is the head of the church, his true believers. Christ is the founder, the leader, and the highest authority on earth. He requires first place in all our thoughts and activities. | To acknowledge Christ as our head, we must welcome his leadership in all we do or think. No person, group, or church can regard any loyalty as more critical than that of loyalty to Christ. |
| Union with Christ | Because our sin has been forgiven and we have been reconciled to God, we have a union with Christ that can never be broken. In our faith connection with him, we identify with his death, burial, and resurrection. | We should live in constant contact and communication with God. When we do, we all will be unified with Christ and with one another. |
| Heresy | False teachers were promoting a heresy that stressed self-made rules (legalism). They also sought spiritual growth by discipline of the body (asceticism) and visions (mysticism). This search created pride in their self-centered efforts. | We must not cling to our own ideas and try to blend them into Christianity. Nor should we let our hunger for a more fulfilling Christian experience cause us to trust in a teacher, a group, or a system of thought more than in Christ himself. Christ is our hope and our true source of wisdom. |

### LOCATION OF COLOSSE

Paul had no doubt been through Laodicea on his third missionary journey, as it lay on the main route to Ephesus, but he had never been to Colosse. Though a large city with a significant population, Colosse was smaller and less important than the nearby cities of Laodicea and Hierapolis.

## 1. What Christ has done

### Greetings from Paul

1:1
1 Cor 1:1
Eph 1:1

**1** This letter is from Paul, chosen by the will of God to be an apostle of Christ Jesus, and from our brother Timothy.

1:2
Rom 1:7

² We are writing to God's holy people in the city of Colosse, who are faithful brothers and sisters* in Christ.

May God our Father give you grace and peace.

### Paul's Thanksgiving and Prayer

³ We always pray for you, and we give thanks to God, the Father of our Lord Jesus Christ. ⁴ For we have heard of your faith in Christ Jesus and your love for all of God's people,

1:4
Eph 1:15

**1:2** Greek *faithful brothers.*

---

**THE COLOSSIAN HERESY**
Paul answered the various tenets of the Colossian heresy that threatened the church. This heresy was a "mixed bag," containing elements from several different heresies, some of which contradicted each other (as the chart shows).

| The Heresy | Reference | Paul's Answer |
|---|---|---|
| Spirit is good; matter is evil. | 1:15-20 | God created heaven and earth for his glory. |
| One must follow ceremonies, rituals, and restrictions in order to be saved or perfected. | 2:11, 16-23; 3:11 | These were only shadows that ended when Christ came. He is all you need to be saved. |
| One must deny the body and live in strict asceticism. | 2:18-23 | Asceticism is no help in conquering evil thoughts and desires; instead, it leads to pride. |
| Angels must be worshiped. | 2:18 | Angels are not to be worshiped; Christ alone is worthy of worship. |
| Christ could not be both human and divine. | 1:15-20; 2:2, 3 | Christ is God in the flesh; he is the eternal one, head of the body, first in everything, supreme. |
| One must obtain "secret knowledge" in order to be saved or perfected—and this was not available to everyone. | 2:2, 18 | God's mysterious plan is Christ himself, and he has been revealed to all. |
| One must adhere to human wisdom, tradition, and philosophies. | 2:4, 8-10; 3:15-17 | By themselves, these can be misleading and shallow because they have human origin; instead, we should remember what Christ taught and follow his words as our ultimate authority. |
| It is even better to combine aspects of several religions. | 2:10 | You are complete through your union with Christ; he is all-sufficient. |
| There is nothing wrong with immorality. | 3:1-11 | Get rid of sin and evil because you have been chosen by God to live a new life as a representative of the Lord Jesus. |

---

**1:1** Colossians, along with Philippians, Ephesians, and Philemon, is called a "Prison Letter" because Paul wrote it from prison in Rome. This prison was actually a house where Paul was kept under close guard at all times (probably chained to a soldier) but given certain freedoms not offered to most prisoners. He was allowed to write letters and to see any visitors he wanted to see.

**1:1** Paul was an apostle "chosen by the will of God." Paul often would establish his credentials as chosen and sent by God because he had not been one of the original 12 disciples. *Apostle* means "one sent out by God to preach the gospel." "Chosen by the will of God" means that he was appointed; this was not just a matter of his own personal aspirations.

**1:1** Paul mentions Timothy in other New Testament letters as well: 2 Corinthians, Philippians, 1 and 2 Thessalonians, and Philemon. Paul also wrote two letters to Timothy (1 and 2 Timothy). For more information on these men, two of the greatest missionaries of the early church, see Paul's Profile in Acts 9, p. 1837 and Timothy's Profile in 1 Timothy 2, p. 2059.

**1:2** The city of Colosse was 100 miles east of Ephesus on the Lycus River. It was not as influential as the nearby city of Laodicea, but as a trading center, it was a crossroads for ideas and religions. Colosse had a large Jewish population—many Jews had fled there

when they were forced out of Jerusalem under the persecutions of Antiochus III and IV, almost 200 years before Christ. The church in Colosse had been founded by Epaphras (1:7), one of Paul's converts. Paul had not yet visited this church. His purpose in writing was to refute heretical teachings about Christ that had been causing confusion among the Christians there.

**1:2, 3** Letters in Paul's day frequently would begin with identifying the writer and the readers, followed by a greeting of peace. Paul usually would add Christian elements to his greetings, reminding his readers of his call by God to spread the Good News, emphasizing that the authority for his words came from God, and giving thanks for God's blessings.

**1:4, 5** Throughout this letter Paul combats a heresy similar to Gnosticism (see the notes on 1:9-14; 1:15-23; 2:4ff). Gnostics believed that it took special knowledge to be accepted by God; for them, even for those who claimed to be Christians, Christ alone was not the way of salvation (1:20). In his introductory comments, therefore, Paul commended the Colossians for their faith, love, and hope as they looked forward to heaven (see 1 Corinthians 13:13). He deliberately omitted the word *knowledge* because of the "special knowledge" aspect of the heresy. It is not *what* we know that brings salvation but *whom* we know. Knowing Christ is knowing God.

⁵which come from your confident hope of what God has reserved for you in heaven. You have had this expectation ever since you first heard the truth of the Good News.

⁶This same Good News that came to you is going out all over the world. It is bearing fruit everywhere by changing lives, just as it changed your lives from the day you first heard and understood the truth about God's wonderful grace.

⁷You learned about the Good News from Epaphras, our beloved co-worker. He is Christ's faithful servant, and he is helping us on your behalf.* ⁸He has told us about the love for others that the Holy Spirit has given you.

⁹So we have not stopped praying for you since we first heard about you. We ask God to give you complete knowledge of his will and to give you spiritual wisdom and understanding. ¹⁰Then the way you live will always honor and please the Lord, and your lives will produce every kind of good fruit. All the while, you will grow as you learn to know God better and better.

¹¹We also pray that you will be strengthened with all his glorious power so you will have all the endurance and patience you need. May you be filled with joy,* ¹²always thanking the Father. He has enabled you to share in the inheritance that belongs to his people, who live in the light. ¹³For he has rescued us from the kingdom of darkness and transferred us into the Kingdom of his dear Son, ¹⁴who purchased our freedom* and forgave our sins.

### Christ Is Supreme

¹⁵ Christ is the visible image of the invisible God.
He existed before anything was created and is supreme over all creation,*

**1:5**
Eph 1:13
1 Pet 1:4
**1:6**
Rom 1:13
**1:7**
Col 4:12
Phlm 1:23
**1:9**
Eph 1:15-17
**1:10**
Eph 4:1
Phil 1:27
1 Thes 2:12
**1:11**
Eph 3:16
**1:12**
Acts 26:18
Eph 5:20
**1:13**
Matt 3:17
Acts 26:18
Eph 1:6; 2:2; 6:12
**1:14**
Eph 1:7
**1:15**
John 1:1, 18; 14:9
2 Cor 4:4
Heb 1:3
Rev 3:14

**1:7** Or *he is ministering on your behalf;* some manuscripts read *he is ministering on our behalf.* **1:11** Or *all the patience and endurance you need with joy.* **1:14** Some manuscripts add *with his blood.* **1:15** Or *He is the firstborn of all creation.*

---

**1:5** We can have "confident hope" of what God has for us in heaven because we know that our future destination and salvation are sure (1 Peter 1:3, 4). We are free to live for Christ and love others. When you find yourself doubting or wavering in your faith or love, remember your destination—heaven.

**1:6** Wherever Paul went, he preached the Good News—to Gentile audiences, to hostile Jewish leaders, and even to his Roman guards. Whenever people believed in the message that Paul spoke, they were changed. God's Word is not just for our information, it is for our transformation! Becoming a Christian means beginning a whole new relationship with God, not just turning over a new leaf or determining to do right. New believers have a changed purpose, direction, attitude, and behavior. They are no longer seeking to serve themselves, but they are bearing fruit for God. How is the Good News reaching others through your life?

**1:7** Epaphras had founded the church at Colosse while Paul was living in Ephesus (Acts 19:10). Epaphras may have been converted in Ephesus, and then he returned to Colosse, his hometown. For some reason, he visited Rome and, while there, told Paul about the problem of the Colossian heresy. This prompted Paul to write this letter. Epaphras is also mentioned in Philemon 1:23 (the Colossian church met in Philemon's house).

**1:8** Because of their love for one another, Christians can have an impact that goes far beyond their neighborhoods and communities. Christian love comes from the Holy Spirit (see Galatians 5:22). The Bible speaks of it as an action and attitude, not just an emotion. Love is a by-product of our new life in Christ (see Romans 5:5; 1 Corinthians 13). Christians have no excuse for not loving, because Christian love is a decision to *act* in the best interests of others.

**1:9-14** Paul was exposing a heresy in the Colossian church that was similar to Gnosticism (see the note on 2:4ff for more information). Gnostics valued the accumulation of knowledge, but Paul pointed out that knowledge in itself is empty. To be worth anything, it must lead to a changed life and right living. His prayer for the Colossians has two dimensions: (1) that they might have complete knowledge of God's will and have spiritual wisdom and understanding; (2) that their lives would produce every kind of good fruit, even as they learned to know God better and better. Knowledge is not merely to be accumulated; it should give us

direction for living. Paul wanted the Colossians to be wise, but he also wanted them to *use* their knowledge. Knowledge of God is not a secret that only a few can discover; it is open to everyone. God wants us to learn more about him, and also to put belief into practice by helping others.

**1:9-14** Sometimes we wonder how to pray for missionaries and other leaders we have never met. Paul had never met the Colossians, but he faithfully prayed for them. His prayers teach us how to pray for others, whether we know them or not. We can request that they (1) understand what God wants them to do, (2) gain spiritual wisdom, (3) honor and please God, (4) produce every kind of good fruit, (5) learn to know God better and better, (6) be strengthened with God's glorious power, (7) have great endurance and patience, (8) be filled with joy, and (9) give thanks always. All believers have these same basic needs. When you don't know how to pray for someone, use Paul's prayer pattern for the Colossians.

**1:12-14** Paul lists five benefits God gives all believers through Christ: (1) He has enabled us to share in his inheritance (see also 2 Corinthians 5:21); (2) he has rescued us from Satan's kingdom of darkness and made us his children (see also 2:15); (3) he has brought us into his eternal Kingdom (see also Ephesians 1:5, 6); (4) he has purchased our freedom from sin and judgment with his blood (see also Hebrews 9:12); and (5) he has forgiven all our sins (see also Ephesians 1:7). Thank God for what you have received in Christ.

**1:13** The Colossians feared the unseen forces of darkness, but Paul says that true believers have been transferred from darkness to light, from slavery to freedom, from guilt to forgiveness, and from the power of Satan to the power of God. We have been rescued from a rebel kingdom to serve the rightful King. Our conduct should reflect our new allegiance.

**1:15, 16** This is one of the strongest statements about the divine nature of Christ found anywhere in the Bible. Jesus is not only equal to God (Philippians 2:6), he *is* God (John 10:30, 38; 12:45; 14:1-11); as the visible image of the invisible God, he is the exact representation of God. He not only reflects God, but he reveals God to us (John 1:18; 14:9); as supreme over all creation, he has all the priority and authority. He came from heaven, not from the dust of the earth (1 Corinthians 15:47), and he is Lord of all

<sup>16</sup> for through him God created everything
    in the heavenly realms and on earth.
He made the things we can see
    and the things we can't see—
such as thrones, kingdoms, rulers, and authorities in the unseen world.
    Everything was created through him and for him.
<sup>17</sup> He existed before anything else,
    and he holds all creation together.

<sup>18</sup> Christ is also the head of the church,
    which is his body.
He is the beginning,
    supreme over all who rise from the dead.*
    So he is first in everything.
<sup>19</sup> For God in all his fullness
    was pleased to live in Christ,
<sup>20</sup> and through him God reconciled
    everything to himself.

**1:18** Or *the firstborn from the dead.*

---

**HOW TO PRAY FOR OTHER CHRISTIANS**

1. Be thankful for their faith and changed lives (1:3).
2. Ask God to help them know his will (1:9).
3. Ask God to give them spiritual wisdom and understanding (1:9).
4. Ask God to help them live to honor and please him (1:10).
5. Ask God to give them more knowledge of himself (1:10).
6. Ask God to give them strength for endurance and patience (1:11).
7. Ask God to fill them with joy and thankfulness (1:11, 12).

How many people in your life could be touched if you prayed in this way?

---

(Romans 9:5; 10:11-13; Revelation 1:5; 17:14). He is completely holy (Hebrews 7:26-28; 1 Peter 1:19; 2:22; 1 John 3:5), and he has authority to judge the world (Romans 2:16; 2 Corinthians 5:10; 2 Timothy 4:1). Therefore, Christ is supreme over all creation, including the spirit world. We, like the Colossian believers, must believe in the deity of Jesus Christ (that Jesus is God) or our Christian faith is hollow, misdirected, and meaningless. This is a central truth of Christianity. We must oppose those who say that Jesus was merely a prophet or a good teacher.

**1:15-23** In the Colossian church there were several misconceptions about Christ that Paul directly refuted: (1) Believing that matter is evil, false teachers argued that God would not have come to earth as a true human being in bodily form. Paul stated that Christ is the image—the exact likeness—of God and is himself God, and yet he died on the cross as a human being. (2) They believed that God did not create the world because he would not have created evil. Paul proclaimed that Jesus Christ, who was also God in the flesh, is the Creator of both heaven and earth. (3) They said that Christ was not the unique Son of God but rather one of many intermediaries between God and people. Paul explained that Christ existed before anything else and is the firstborn of those resurrected. (4) They refused to see Christ as the source of salvation, insisting that people could find God only through special and secret knowledge. In contrast, Paul openly proclaimed the way of salvation to be through Christ alone. Paul continued to bring the argument back to Christ. When we share the Good News, we, too, must keep the focus on Christ.

**1:16** Because the false teachers believed that the physical world was evil, they thought that God himself could not have created it. If Christ were God, they reasoned, he would be in charge only of the spiritual world. But Paul explained that all the thrones, kingdoms, rulers, and authorities of both the spiritual and physical worlds were created by and are under the authority of Christ himself. This includes not only the government but also the spiritual

world that the heretics were so concerned about. Christ has no equal and no rival. He is the Lord of all.

**1:17** God is not only the creator of the world but he is also its sustainer. In him, everything is held together, protected, and prevented from disintegrating into chaos. Because Christ is the sustainer of all life, none of us is independent from him. We are all his servants who must daily trust him to protect us, care for us, and sustain us.

**1:18** Christ is "supreme over all who rise from the dead." Jesus was raised from death, and his resurrection proves his lordship over the material world. All who trust in Christ will also defeat death and rise again to live eternally with him (1 Corinthians 15:20; 1 Thessalonians 4:14). Because of Christ's death on the cross, he has been exalted and elevated to the status that was rightfully his (see Philippians 2:5-11). Because Christ is spiritually supreme in the universe, surely we should give him first place in all our thoughts and activities. See the second note on Luke 24:6, 7 for more about the significance of Christ's resurrection.

**1:19** By this statement, Paul was refuting the Greek idea that Jesus could not be human and divine at the same time. Christ was fully human; he was also fully divine. Christ has always been God and always will be God. When we have Christ, we have all of God in human form. Don't diminish any aspect of Christ—either his humanity or his divinity.

**1:20** Christ's death provided a way for all people to come to God. It cleared away the sin that keeps us from having a right relationship with our creator. This does not mean that everyone has been saved but that the way has been cleared for anyone who will trust Christ to be saved. We can have peace with God and be reconciled to him by accepting Christ, who died in our place. Is there a distance between you and the Creator? Be reconciled to God. Come to him through Christ.

He made peace with everything in heaven and on earth
   by means of Christ's blood on the cross.

21 This includes you who were once far away from God. You were his enemies, separated from him by your evil thoughts and actions. 22 Yet now he has reconciled you to himself through the death of Christ in his physical body. As a result, he has brought you into his own presence, and you are holy and blameless as you stand before him without a single fault. 23 But you must continue to believe this truth and stand firmly in it. Don't drift away from the assurance you received when you heard the Good News. The Good News has been preached all over the world, and I, Paul, have been appointed as God's servant to proclaim it.

### Paul's Work for the Church
24 I am glad when I suffer for you in my body, for I am participating in the sufferings of Christ that continue for his body, the church. 25 God has given me the responsibility of serving his church by proclaiming his entire message to you. 26 This message was kept secret for centuries and generations past, but now it has been revealed to God's people. 27 For God wanted them to know that the riches and glory of Christ are for you Gentiles, too. And this is the secret: Christ lives in you. This gives you assurance of sharing his glory.

28 So we tell others about Christ, warning everyone and teaching everyone with all the wisdom God has given us. We want to present them to God, perfect* in their relationship to Christ. 29 That's why I work and struggle so hard, depending on Christ's mighty power that works within me.

**2** I want you to know how much I have agonized for you and for the church at Laodicea, and for many other believers who have never met me personally. 2 I want them to be encouraged and knit together by strong ties of love. I want them to have complete confidence that they understand God's mysterious plan, which is Christ himself. 3 In him lie hidden all the treasures of wisdom and knowledge.

**1:28** Or *mature*.

| | |
|---|---|
| **1:21** | Rom 5:10 / Eph 2:3, 12 |
| **1:22** | Rom 7:4 / Eph 1:4; 5:27 |
| **1:23** | Eph 3:17 / Col 1:5-6 |
| **1:24** | Phil 2:17; 3:10 / 2 Tim 1:8 |
| **1:26** | Rom 16:25-26 / Eph 3:3, 5, 9-10 |
| **1:27** | Rom 8:10 / Eph 3:9-11 |
| **1:28** | Eph 4:13 |
| **1:29** | Eph 1:19; 3:7 / Phil 4:13 |
| **2:1** | Col 4:12-13 |
| **2:2** | Matt 11:25-27 / Eph 1:18-19 / Col 2:19 |
| **2:3** | Isa 11:2 / Rom 11:33 / Eph 3:8, 19 |

---

**1:21** Because we were alienated from God, we were strangers to his way of thinking and were "enemies." Sin corrupted our way of thinking about God. Wrong thinking leads to sin, which further perverts and destroys our thoughts about him. When we were out of harmony with God, our natural condition was to be totally hostile to his standards. See Romans 1:21-32 for more on the perverted thinking of unbelievers.

**1:21, 22** *No one* is good enough to save himself or herself. If we want to live eternally with Christ, we must depend totally on God's grace. This is true whether we have been murderers or honest, hardworking citizens. We have all sinned repeatedly, and *any* sin is enough to cause us to need to come to Jesus Christ for salvation and eternal life. Apart from Christ, there is no way for our sin to be forgiven and removed.

**1:22** In order to answer the accusation that Jesus was only a spirit and not a true human being, Paul explained that Jesus' physical body actually died. Jesus suffered death fully as a human so that we could be assured that he died in our place. Jesus faced death as God so we can be assured that his sacrifice was complete and that he truly removed our sin.

**1:22, 23** The way to be free from sin is to trust Jesus Christ to take it away. We must stand firmly in the truth of the Good News, putting our confidence in Jesus alone to forgive our sins, to make us right with God, and to empower us to live the way he desires. When a judge in a court of law declares the defendant not guilty, the person is acquitted of all the accusations or charges. Legally, it is as if he or she had never been accused. When God forgives our sins, our record is wiped clean. From his perspective, it is as though we had never sinned. God's solution is available to you. No matter what you have done or what you have been like, God's forgiveness is for you.

**1:24** Paul's, statement, "I am participating in the sufferings of Christ that continue for his body, the church," may mean that suffering is unavoidable in bringing the Good News of Christ to the world. When we suffer, Christ feels it with us. But this suffer-

ing can be endured joyfully because it changes lives and brings people into God's Kingdom (see 1 Peter 4:1, 2, 12-19). For more about how Paul could rejoice despite his suffering, see the note on Philippians 1:29.

**1:26, 27** The false teachers in the Colossian church believed that spiritual perfection was a secret and hidden plan that only a few privileged people could discover. Their secret plan was meant to be exclusive. Paul said that he was proclaiming the entire message of God, not just a part of the plan. He also called God's plan a "message . . . kept secret for centuries and generations past," not in the sense that only a few would understand, but because it was hidden until Christ came. Through Christ it was made open to all. God's secret plan is "Christ lives in you"—God planned to have his Son, Jesus Christ, live in the hearts of all who believe in him—even Gentiles like the Colossians. Do you know Christ? He is not hidden if you will come to him.

**1:28, 29** The word *perfect* means "mature or complete," not "flawless." Paul wanted to see each believer mature spiritually. Like Paul, we must work wholeheartedly like an athlete, but we should not strive in our own strength alone. We have the power of God's Spirit working in us. We can learn and grow daily, motivated by love and not by fear or pride, knowing that God gives the energy to become mature.

**1:28, 29** Christ's message is for everyone; so everywhere Paul and Timothy went, they brought the Good News to all who would listen. An effective presentation of the Good News includes warning and teaching. The warning is that without Christ, people are doomed to eternal separation from God. The teaching is that salvation is available through faith in Christ. As Christ works in you, tell others about him, warning and teaching them in love. Whom do you know that needs to hear this message?

**2:1** Laodicea was located a few miles northwest of Colosse. Like the church at Colosse, the Laodicean church was probably founded by one of Paul's converts while Paul was staying in Ephesus (Acts 19:10). The city was a wealthy center of trade

**2:5**
1 Cor 5:3-4

4I am telling you this so no one will deceive you with well-crafted arguments. 5For though I am far away from you, my heart is with you. And I rejoice that you are living as you should and that your faith in Christ is strong.

### Freedom from Rules and New Life in Christ

**2:6**
Col 1:10

6And now, just as you accepted Christ Jesus as your Lord, you must continue to follow him. 7Let your roots grow down into him, and let your lives be built on him. Then your faith will grow strong in the truth you were taught, and you will overflow with thankfulness.

**2:7**
Eph 3:17

**2:8**
Col 2:4
1 Tim 6:20

8Don't let anyone capture you with empty philosophies and high-sounding nonsense that come from human thinking and from the spiritual powers* of this world, rather than

**2:8** Or *the spiritual principles;* also in 2:20.

---

| **SALVATION THROUGH FAITH** | | Religion by Self-Effort | Salvation by Faith |
|---|---|---|---|
| | Goal | Please God by our own good deeds | Trust in Christ and then live to please God |
| | Means | Practice, diligent service, discipline, and obedience, in hope of reward | Confess, submit, and commit ourselves to Christ's control |
| | Power | Good, honest effort through self-determination | The Holy Spirit in us helps us do good work for Christ's Kingdom |
| | Control | Self-motivation; self-control | Christ is in us; we are in Christ |
| | Results | Chronic guilt, apathy, depression, failure, constant desire for approval | Joy, thankfulness, love, guidance, service, forgiveness |

Salvation by faith in Christ sounds too easy for many people. They would rather think that they have done something to save themselves. Their religion becomes one of self-effort that leads either to disappointment or pride, but finally to eternal death. Christ's simple way is the only way, and it alone leads to eternal life.

---

and commerce, but later Christ would criticize the believers at Laodicea for their lukewarm commitment (Revelation 3:14-22). The fact that Paul wanted this letter to be passed on to the Laodicean church (4:16) indicates that false teaching may have spread there as well. Paul was counting on ties of love to bring the churches together to stand against this heresy and to encourage each other to remain true to God's plan of salvation in Christ. Our churches should be encouraging, unified communities, committed to carrying out Christ's work.

**2:4ff** The problem that Paul was combating in the Colossian church was similar to Gnosticism (from the Greek word for *knowledge*). This *heresy* (a teaching contrary to biblical doctrine) undermined Christianity in several basic ways: (1) It insisted that important secret knowledge was hidden from most believers; Paul, however, said that Christ provides all the knowledge we need. (2) It taught that the body was evil; Paul countered that God himself lived in a body—that is, he was embodied in Jesus Christ. (3) It contended that Christ only seemed to be human but was not; Paul insisted that Jesus was fully human and fully God.

Gnosticism became fashionable in the second century. Even in Paul's day, these ideas sounded attractive to many, and exposure to such teachings could easily seduce a church that didn't know Christian doctrine well. Similar teachings still pose significant problems for many in the church today. We combat heresy by becoming thoroughly acquainted with God's Word through personal study and sound Bible teaching.

**2:4** Christian faith provides a growth track into knowledge of the truth, but along the way, how do we guard against being deceived by lies that are masquerading as "well-crafted arguments"?

If your growth track is too narrow, you become thickheaded and insular—no one can teach you a thing. Before long, you can't teach anyone around you, for no one is listening. You are isolated. Love disappears from your life.

If your track is too wide and every idea is an exciting new

possibility, you'll waste a lot of time just keeping on track and risk some dangerous detours.

The key is centering on Christ and grounding yourself in his Word. Learn daily about the Savior. Study the Bible. Develop your theological knowledge. Stay humble and curious about the amazing complexity of the world God has made. Ask lots of questions about the assumptions behind ideas new to you. Press toward wisdom. Pray for understanding. God has given us minds for learning—never quit using yours.

**2:6, 7** Receiving Christ as Lord of your life is the beginning of life with Christ. But you must continue to follow his leadership by being rooted, built up, and strengthened in the faith. Christ wants to guide you and help you with your daily problems. You can live for Christ by (1) committing your life and submitting your will to him (Romans 12:1, 2); (2) seeking to learn from him, his life, and his teachings (Colossians 3:16); and (3) recognizing the Holy Spirit's power in you (Acts 1:8; Galatians 5:22).

**2:7** Paul uses the illustration of our being rooted in Christ. Just as plants draw nourishment from the soil through their roots, so we draw our life-giving strength from Christ. The more we draw our strength from him, the less we will be fooled by those who falsely claim to have life's answers. If Christ is our strength, we will be free from human regulations.

**2:8** Paul writes against any philosophy of life based only on human ideas and experiences. Paul himself was a gifted philosopher, so he is not condemning philosophy. He is condemning teaching that credits humanity, not Christ, with being the answer to life's problems. That approach becomes a false religion. There are many man-made approaches to life's problems that totally disregard God. To resist heresy you must use your mind, keep your eyes on Christ, and study God's Word.

from Christ. 9For in Christ lives all the fullness of God in a human body.* 10So you also are complete through your union with Christ, who is the head over every ruler and authority.

11When you came to Christ, you were "circumcised," but not by a physical procedure. Christ performed a spiritual circumcision—the cutting away of your sinful nature.* 12For you were buried with Christ when you were baptized. And with him you were raised to new life because you trusted the mighty power of God, who raised Christ from the dead.

13You were dead because of your sins and because your sinful nature was not yet cut away. Then God made you alive with Christ, for he forgave all our sins. 14He canceled the record of the charges against us and took it away by nailing it to the cross. 15In this way, he disarmed* the spiritual rulers and authorities. He shamed them publicly by his victory over them on the cross.

16So don't let anyone condemn you for what you eat or drink, or for not celebrating certain holy days or new moon ceremonies or Sabbaths. 17For these rules are only shadows of

**2:9**
John 1:14, 16
**2:10**
Eph 1:21-22; 3:19
**2:12**
Rom 6:5
Eph 1:19-20; 2:6
**2:13**
Eph 2:1, 5
**2:14**
Eph 2:15
1 Pet 2:24
**2:15**
John 12:31
2 Cor 2:14
Eph 4:8
**2:16**
1 Chr 23:31
Rom 14:3, 5

2:9 Or *in him dwells all the completeness of the Godhead bodily.*   2:11 Greek *the cutting away of the body of the flesh.*   2:15 Or *he stripped off.*

---

**2:9** Again Paul asserts Christ's deity. "In Christ lives all the fullness of God in a human body" means that all of God was in Christ's human body. When we have Christ, we have everything we need for salvation and right living. See the note on 1:15, 16 for more on the divine nature of Christ.

**2:10** Look around you. People are searching for something to give their lives a boost. Few people seem content within themselves. A strange and often hard-to-identify inner vacuum gives most people an uneasy sense of incompleteness. Christ fills that vacuum! As Jesus' person is fully divine, so we, united by faith to Jesus, find personal fulfillment in him: "You also are complete through your union with Christ."

When you know Jesus Christ, you don't need to seek God by means of other religions, cults, or unbiblical philosophies as the Colossians were doing. Christ alone holds the answers to the true meaning of life because he *is* life. Christ is the unique source of knowledge and power for the Christian life. No Christian needs anything in addition to what Christ has provided to be saved. Some days may not feel like it, but in Jesus, the vacuum is gone; the full power and presence of God have taken up residence in your mind and heart. You are a new person, equipped for life and satisfied in God. Take some risks—God will guide you. Give more generously—God will supply. Love more freely—God will energize you. Say "can do" more often—God will amaze you.

**2:11** Jewish males were circumcised as a sign of the Jews' covenant with God (Genesis 17:9-14). With the death of Christ, circumcision was no longer necessary. So now our commitment to God is written on our heart, not our body. Christ sets us free from our evil desires by a spiritual operation, not a bodily one. God removes the old nature and gives us a new nature.

**2:11, 12** In this passage, circumcision is related to baptism; therefore, some see baptism as the New Testament sign of the covenant, identifying the person with the covenant community. Baptism parallels the death, burial, and resurrection of Christ, and it also portrays the death and burial of our sinful old way of life followed by resurrection to new life in Christ. Remembering that our old sinful life is dead and buried with Christ gives us a powerful motive to resist sin. Not wanting the desires of our past to come back to power again, we can consciously choose to treat our desires as if they were dead. Then we can continue to enjoy our wonderful new life with Christ (see Galatians 3:27 and Colossians 3:1-4).

**2:13-15** Before we believed in Christ, our nature was evil. We disobeyed, rebelled, and ignored God (even at our best, we did not love him with all our heart, soul, and mind). The Christian, however, has a new nature. God has crucified the old rebellious nature (Romans 6:6) and replaced it with a new loving nature (Colossians 3:9, 10). The penalty of sin died with Christ on the cross. God has declared us not guilty, and we need no longer live under sin's power. God does not take us out of the world or make us robots—we will still feel like sinning, and sometimes we will

sin. The difference is that before we were saved, we were slaves to our sinful nature; but now we are free to live for Christ (see Galatians 2:20).

**2:14** The record that was canceled contained the legal demands of the Old Testament law. The law opposed us by its demands for payment for our sin. Although no one can be saved by merely keeping that record, the moral truths and principles in the Old Testament still teach and guide today.

**2:14** We can enjoy our new lives in Christ because we have joined him in his death and resurrection. Our evil desires, our bondage to sin, and our love of sin died with him. Now, joining him in his resurrection life, we may have unbroken fellowship with God and freedom from sin. Our debt for sin has been paid in full; our sins are swept away and forgotten by God; and we can be clean and new. For more on the difference between our new life in Christ and our old sinful nature, read Ephesians 4:23, 24 and Colossians 3:3-15.

**2:15** Who are these spiritual rulers and authorities? Several suggestions have been made, including (1) demonic powers, (2) the gods of the powerful nations, (3) angels (highly regarded by the heretical teachers), or (4) the government of Rome. Since Paul did not identify who these rulers and authorities were, it could be any one of them, or all four. What Christ "disarmed" on the cross was any embodiment of rebellion in the world—whether that be Satan and his demons, false idols of pagan religious, evil world governments, or even God's good angels when they become objects of worship (as in the Colossian heresy). This "disarming" occurred when Jesus died on the cross, like stripping a defeated enemy of armor on the battlefield. Evil no longer has any power over believers because Christ has disarmed it. Paul already had told the Colossians, "He has rescued us from the kingdom of darkness and transferred us into the Kingdom of his dear Son" (1:13).

**2:16** "What you eat or drink" probably refers to the Jewish dietary laws. The festivals mentioned are Jewish holy days celebrated annually, monthly (new moon), and weekly (the Sabbath). These rituals distinguished the Jews from their pagan neighbors. Failure to observe them could be easily noticed by those who were keeping track of what others did. But we should not let ourselves be judged by the opinions of others because Christ has set us free.

**2:16, 17** Paul told the Colossian Christians not to let others criticize their diet or their religious ceremonies. Instead of outward observance, believers should focus on faith in Christ alone. Our worship, traditions, and ceremonies can help bring us close to God, but we should never criticize fellow Christians whose traditions and ceremonies differ from ours. More important than how we worship is that we worship Christ. Don't let anyone judge you. You are responsible to Christ.

**2:17** Old Testament laws, holidays, and festivals pointed toward Christ. Paul calls them "shadows" of the reality that was to come—Christ himself. When Christ came, he dispelled the shadows. If we have Christ, we have what we need to know and please God.

**2:17**
Heb 8:5; 10:1

**2:19**
Eph 1:22;
4:15-16

**2:20**
Rom 6:6
Gal 4:3, 9

**2:22**
1 Cor 6:13

**2:23**
1 Tim 4:3

the reality yet to come. And Christ himself is that reality. ¹⁸Don't let anyone condemn you by insisting on pious self-denial or the worship of angels,* saying they have had visions about these things. Their sinful minds have made them proud, ¹⁹and they are not connected to Christ, the head of the body. For he holds the whole body together with its joints and ligaments, and it grows as God nourishes it.

²⁰You have died with Christ, and he has set you free from the spiritual powers of this world. So why do you keep on following the rules of the world, such as, ²¹"Don't handle! Don't taste! Don't touch!"? ²²Such rules are mere human teachings about things that deteriorate as we use them. ²³These rules may seem wise because they require strong devotion, pious self-denial, and severe bodily discipline. But they provide no help in conquering a person's evil desires.

**2:18** Or *or worshiping with angels.*

---

**FROM DEATH TO LIFE**
What happens when we accept Christ

The Bible uses many illustrations to teach what happens when we choose to let Jesus be Lord of our lives. Following are some of the most vivid pictures:

1. Because Christ died for us, we have been crucified with him.

Romans 6:2-13; 7:4-6
2 Corinthians 5:14
Galatians 2:20; 5:24; 6:14
Colossians 2:20; 3:3-5
1 Peter 2:24

2. Our old, rebellious nature died with Christ.

Romans 6:6; 7:4-6
Colossians 3:9, 10

3. Christ's resurrection guarantees our new life now and eternal life with him later.

Romans 6:4, 11
Colossians 2:12, 13; 3:1, 3

This process is acted out in baptism (Colossians 2:12), based on our faith in Christ: (1) The old sinful nature dies (crucified). (2) We are ready to receive a new life (buried). (3) Christ gives us new life (resurrected).

---

**2:18** The false teachers were claiming that God was far away and could be approached only through various levels of angels. They taught that people had to worship angels in order, eventually, to reach God. This is unscriptural; the Bible teaches that angels are God's servants, and it forbids worshiping them (Exodus 20:3, 4; Revelation 22:8, 9). As you grow in your Christian faith, let God's Word be your guide, not the opinions of other people.

**2:19** The fundamental problem with the false teachers was that they were not connected to Christ, the head of the body of believers. If they had been joined to him, they could not have taught false doctrine or lived immorally. Anyone who teaches about God without being connected to him by faith should not be trusted.

**2:20** The "rules of the world" are the beliefs of pagans. See 2:8 for more on Paul's view of non-Christian philosophy.

**2:20; 3:1** How do we die with Christ, and how are we raised with him? When a person becomes a Christian, he or she is given new life through the power of the Holy Spirit. See the notes on 2:11, 12 and 2:13-15 for further information.

**2:20-23** People should be able to see a difference between the way Christians and non-Christians live. Still, we should not expect instant maturity in new Christians. Christian growth is a lifelong process. Although we have a new nature, we don't automatically think all good thoughts and have all pure attitudes when we become new people in Christ. But if we keep listening to God, we will be changing all the time. As you look over the last year, what changes for the better have you seen in your thoughts and attitudes? Change may be slow, but your life will change significantly if you trust God to change you.

**2:20-23** We cannot reach up to God by following rules of pious self-denial, by observing rituals, or by practicing religion. Paul isn't saying all rules are bad (see the note on Galatians 2:15, 16). But keeping laws or rules will not earn salvation. The Good News

is that God reaches down to human beings, and he asks for our response. Man-made religions focus on human effort; Christianity focuses on Christ's work. Believers must put aside sinful desires, but doing so is the by-product of our new life in Christ, not the reason for our new life. Our salvation does not depend on our own discipline and rule keeping but on the power of Christ's death and resurrection.

**2:22, 23** We can guard against man-made religions by asking these questions about any religious group: (1) Does it stress man-made rules and taboos rather than God's grace? (2) Does it foster a critical spirit toward others, or does it exercise discipline discreetly and lovingly? (3) Does it stress formulas, secret knowledge, or special visions more than the Word of God? (4) Does it elevate self-righteousness, honoring those who keep the rules, rather than elevating Christ? (5) Does it neglect Christ's universal church, claiming to be an elite group? (6) Does it teach humiliation of the body as a means to spiritual growth rather than focus on the growth of the whole person? (7) Does it disregard the family rather than hold it in high regard as the Bible does?

**2:23** To the Colossians, the discipline demanded by the false teachers seemed good, and legalism still attracts many people today. Following a long list of religious rules requires strong self-discipline and can make a person appear moral, but religious rules cannot change a person's heart. Only the Holy Spirit can do that.

## 2. What Christians should do

*Living the New Life*

**3** Since you have been raised to new life with Christ, set your sights on the realities of heaven, where Christ sits in the place of honor at God's right hand. 2 Think about the things of heaven, not the things of earth. 3 For you died to this life, and your real life is hidden with Christ in God. 4 And when Christ, who is your* life, is revealed to the whole world, you will share in all his glory.

5 So put to death the sinful, earthly things lurking within you. Have nothing to do with sexual immorality, impurity, lust, and evil desires. Don't be greedy, for a greedy person is an idolater, worshiping the things of this world. 6 Because of these sins, the anger of God is coming.* 7 You used to do these things when your life was still part of this world. 8 But now is the time to get rid of anger, rage, malicious behavior, slander, and dirty language. 9 Don't lie to each other, for you have stripped off your old sinful nature and all its wicked deeds. 10 Put on your new nature, and be renewed as you learn to know your Creator and become like him. 11 In this new life, it doesn't matter if you are a Jew or a Gentile,* circumcised or uncircumcised, barbaric, uncivilized,* slave, or free. Christ is all that matters, and he lives in all of us.

**3:1**
Matt 6:33
Eph 2:6

**3:3**
Rom 6:2
2 Cor 5:14

**3:5**
Rom 6:6; 8:13
Gal 5:19-21
Eph 4:19; 5:3, 5

**3:7**
Eph 2:2

**3:8**
Eph 4:25-31; 5:4

**3:9**
Eph 4:25

**3:10**
Rom 12:2
Eph 2:10; 4:24

**3:11**
Rom 10:12
1 Cor 12:13
Gal 3:28

**3:4** Some manuscripts read *our.* **3:6** Some manuscripts read *is coming on all who disobey him.* **3:11a** Greek *a Greek.* **3:11b** Greek *Barbarian, Scythian.*

---

**3:1ff** In chapter 2, Paul exposed the wrong reasons for self-denial. In chapter 3, he explains true Christian behavior—putting on the new nature by accepting Christ and regarding the earthly nature as dead. We change our moral and ethical behavior by letting Christ live within us, so that he can shape us into what we *should* be.

**3:1, 2** Setting our sights on the realities of heaven means striving to put heaven's priorities into daily practice. Letting heaven fill our thoughts means concentrating on the eternal rather than the temporal. See Philippians 4:7 and Colossians 3:15 for more on Christ's rule in our hearts and minds.

**3:2, 3** "For you died to this life" means that we should have as little desire for improper worldly pleasures as a dead person would have. The Christian's real home is where Christ lives (John 14:2, 3). This truth provides a different perspective on our lives here on earth. To "think about the things of heaven" means to look at life from God's perspective and to seek what he desires. This provides the antidote to materialism; we gain the proper perspective on material goods when we take God's view of them. It also provides the antidote to sensuality. By seeking what Christ desires, we have the power to break our obsession with pleasure and leisure activities. But it also provides the antidote to empty religiosity because following Christ means loving and serving in this world. Regard the world around you as God does; then you will live in harmony with him.

**3:3** What does it mean that a believer's life is "hidden with Christ"? *Hidden* means "concealed and safe." This is not only a future hope but an accomplished fact right now. Our service and conduct do not earn our salvation, but they are results of our salvation. Take heart that your salvation is sure, and live each day for Christ.

**3:4** Christ gives us power to live for him now, and he gives us hope for the future—he will return. In the rest of this chapter Paul explains how Christians should act *now* in order to be prepared for Christ's return.

**3:5** We should consider ourselves dead and unresponsive to sexual immorality, impurity, lust, and evil desires. The warning in this verse is not against sex, but against sexual perversion. Where is the line between the two?

The Bible everywhere celebrates heterosexual, monogamous marriage as the proper situation for sexual fulfillment. Christian men and women should be open to true love—and to sexual intimacy—within the commitment to lifelong fidelity. That is God's way. The rest is dangerous and futile. Stay away. Sexual

sin and perversion will drain your energies and turn your heart away from God.

**3:6** "The anger of God" refers to God's judgment on these kinds of behavior, culminating with future and final punishment of evil. When tempted to sin, remember that you must one day stand before God.

**3:8-10** We must rid ourselves of all evil practices and immorality. Then we can commit ourselves to what Christ teaches. Paul was urging the believers to remain true to their confession of faith. They were to rid themselves of the old life and put on the new nature given by Christ. If you have made such a commitment to Christ, are you remaining true to it?

**3:9** Lying to one another disrupts unity by destroying trust. It tears down relationships and may lead to serious conflict in a church. So don't exaggerate statistics, pass on rumors and gossip, or say things to build up your own image. Be committed to telling the truth.

Jesus wants to clean your life and your church of sexual sin and verbal sin. There is no place in the Kingdom of God for hedonistic sexual experimentation or for gossip, rage, and backbiting. In their place, witness to the world like a lighthouse on a stormy night by displaying love, faith, and hope.

**3:10** What does it mean to put on your new nature? It means that your conduct should match your faith. If you are a Christian, you should act like it. To be a Christian means more than just making good resolutions and having good intentions; it means taking the right actions. This is a straightforward step that is as simple as putting on your clothes. You must rid yourself of all evil practices and immorality. Then you can commit yourself to what Christ teaches. If you have made such a commitment to Christ, are you remaining true to it? What old clothes do you need to strip off?

**3:10** Every Christian is in a continuing education program. The more we know of Christ and his work, the more we are being changed to be like him. Because this process is lifelong, we must never stop learning and obeying. There is no justification for drifting along, but there is an incentive to find the rich treasures of growing in him. It takes practice, ongoing review, patience, and concentration to keep in line with his will.

**3:11** The Christian church should have no barriers of nationality, race, educational level, social standing, wealth, gender, religion, or power. Christ breaks down all barriers and accepts all people who come to him. Nothing should keep us from telling others about Christ or accepting into our fellowship any and all believers (Ephesians 2:14, 15). Christians should be building bridges, not walls.

**3:12**
Eph 4:2, 32
1 Pet 1:2

**3:13**
Eph 4:32; 5:2

**3:14**
Rom 13:8

**3:15**
John 14:27
Eph 2:14-16
Phil 4:7

**3:17**
1 Cor 10:31
Eph 5:20

¹²Since God chose you to be the holy people he loves, you must clothe yourselves with tenderhearted mercy, kindness, humility, gentleness, and patience. ¹³Make allowance for each other's faults, and forgive anyone who offends you. Remember, the Lord forgave you, so you must forgive others. ¹⁴Above all, clothe yourselves with love, which binds us all together in perfect harmony. ¹⁵And let the peace that comes from Christ rule in your hearts. For as members of one body you are called to live in peace. And always be thankful.

¹⁶Let the message about Christ, in all its richness, fill your lives. Teach and counsel each other with all the wisdom he gives. Sing psalms and hymns and spiritual songs to God with thankful hearts. ¹⁷And whatever you do or say, do it as a representative of the Lord Jesus, giving thanks through him to God the Father.

---

| SINS VS. SIGNS OF LOVE | Sins of Sexual Attitude and Behavior | Sins of Speech | Signs of Love |
|---|---|---|---|
| | Sexual immorality | Anger/Rage | Mercy |
| | Impurity | Malicious behavior | Kindness |
| | Lust | Slander | Humility |
| | Evil desires | Dirty language | Gentleness |
| | Greed | Lying | Patience |
| | | | Forgiveness |

In Colossians 3:5 Paul tells us to put to death the things found in list 1. In 3:8, 9 he tells us to rid ourselves of the things found in list 2. In 3:12, 13 we're told to clothe ourselves with the things found in list 3. List 1 deals with sins of sexual attitudes and behavior—they are particularly destructive because of what they do to destroy any group or church. List 2 deals with sins of speech—these are the relationship breakers. List 3 contains the relationship builders, which we are to express as members of Christ's body.

---

**3:12-17** Paul offers a strategy to help us live for God day by day: (1) Imitate Christ's compassionate, forgiving attitude (3:12, 13); (2) let love guide your life (3:14); (3) let the peace of Christ rule in your heart (3:15); (4) always be thankful (3:15); (5) keep God's Word in you at all times (3:16); (6) live as Jesus Christ's representative (3:17).

**3:13** The key to forgiving others is remembering how much God has forgiven you. Is it difficult for you to forgive someone who has wronged you a little when God has forgiven you so much? Realizing God's infinite love and forgiveness can help you love and forgive others. Let God worry about the wrongs you've suffered. Don't quench your life in bitter feuding; live renewed in love and joy.

**3:14** All the virtues that Paul encourages us to develop are perfectly bound together by love. As we clothe ourselves with these virtues, the last garment we are to put on is love, which holds all of the others in place. To practice any list of virtues without practicing love will lead to distortion, fragmentation, and stagnation (1 Corinthians 13:3).

**3:14, 15** Christians should live in peace. To live in peace does not mean that suddenly all differences of opinion are eliminated, but it does require that loving Christians work together despite their differences. Such love is not a feeling but a decision to meet others' needs (see 1 Corinthians 13). To clothe ourselves with love leads to peace between individuals and among the members of the body of believers. Do problems in your relationships with other Christians cause open conflicts or mutual silence? Consider what you can do to heal those relationships with love.

**3:15** The word *rule* comes from the language of athletics: Paul tells us to let Christ's peace be umpire or referee in our heart. Our heart is the center of conflict because there our feelings and desires clash—our fears and hopes, distrust and trust, jealousy and love. How can we deal with these constant conflicts and live as God wants? Paul explains that we must decide between conflicting elements by using the rule of peace. Which choice will promote peace in our souls and in our churches? For more on the peace of Christ, see Philippians 4:7.

**3:16** Although the early Christians had access to the Old Testament and freely used it, they did not yet have the New Testament or any other Christian books to study. Their stories and teachings about Christ were memorized and passed on from person to person. Sometimes the teachings were set to music, and so music became an important part of Christian worship and education.

**3:16** Thankful people can worship wholeheartedly. Gratitude opens our hearts to God's peace and enables us to put on love. Discontented people constantly calculate what's wrong with their lot in life.

To increase your thankfulness, take an inventory of all you have (including your relationships, memories, abilities, and family, as well as material possessions). Use the inventory for prayers of gratitude. On Sunday, before worship, quit rushing around; instead, take time to reflect on reasons for thanks. Declare Sunday as your "thanks, faith, and hope" day. Celebrate God's goodness to you, and ask in prayer for all your needs for the week ahead.

**3:17** "Whatever you do or say, do it as a representative of the Lord Jesus" means bringing honor to Christ in every aspect and activity of daily living. As a Christian, you represent Christ at all times—wherever you go and whatever you say. What impression do people have of Christ when they see or talk with you? What changes would you make in your life in order to honor Christ?

## Instructions for Christian Households

¹⁸Wives, submit to your husbands, as is fitting for those who belong to the Lord.
  ¹⁹Husbands, love your wives and never treat them harshly.
  ²⁰Children, always obey your parents, for this pleases the Lord. ²¹Fathers, do not aggravate your children, or they will become discouraged.
  ²²Slaves, obey your earthly masters in everything you do. Try to please them all the time, not just when they are watching you. Serve them sincerely because of your reverent fear of the Lord. ²³Work willingly at whatever you do, as though you were working for the Lord rather than for people. ²⁴Remember that the Lord will give you an inheritance as your reward, and that the Master you are serving is Christ.* ²⁵But if you do what is wrong, you will be paid back for the wrong you have done. For God has no favorites.

**4** Masters, be just and fair to your slaves. Remember that you also have a Master—in heaven.

## An Encouragement for Prayer

²Devote yourselves to prayer with an alert mind and a thankful heart. ³Pray for us, too, that God will give us many opportunities to speak about his mysterious plan concerning Christ. That is why I am here in chains. ⁴Pray that I will proclaim this message as clearly as I should.

3:24 Or *and serve Christ as your Master.*

| | |
|---|---|
| **3:18** | Eph 5:22 |
| **3:19** | Eph 5:25 / 1 Pet 3:7 |
| **3:20** | Eph 6:1 |
| **3:21-25** | //Eph 6:4-8 |
| **3:25** | Acts 10:34 |
| **4:1** | Lev 25:43 / Eph 6:9 |
| **4:2** | Luke 18:1 / Eph 6:18 / 1 Thes 5:17 |
| **4:4** | Eph 6:20 |

---

**3:18—4:1** Paul gives rules for three sets of household relationships: (1) husbands and wives, (2) parents and children, and (3) slave owners and slaves. In each case there is mutual responsibility to submit and love, to obey and encourage, to work hard and be fair. Examine your family and work relationships. Do you relate to others as God intended? See Ephesians 5:21—6:9 for similar instructions.

**3:18, 19** Why is submission of wives to husbands "fitting for those who belong to the Lord"? This may have been good advice for Christian women, newly freed in Christ, who found submission difficult. Paul told them that they should willingly follow their husbands' leadership in Christ. But Paul had words for husbands as well: "Husbands, love your wives and never treat them harshly." It may also have been true that Christian men, used to the Roman custom of giving unlimited power to the head of the family, were not used to treating their wives with respect and love. Real spiritual leadership involves service. Just as Christ served the disciples, even to the point of washing their feet, so the husband is to serve his wife. This means putting aside his own interests in order to care for his wife. A wise and Christ-honoring husband will not abuse his leadership role. At the same time, a wise and Christ-honoring wife will not try to undermine her husband's leadership. Either approach causes disunity and friction in marriage. For more on submission, see the notes on Ephesians 5:21-33.

**3:20, 21** Children must be handled with care. They need firm discipline administered in love. Parents should not aggravate them by nagging, deriding, or destroying their self-respect so that they quit trying.

However, the opposite problem occurs when parents are afraid to correct a child for fear of stifling some aspect of his or her personality or losing his or her love. Single parents or parents who cannot spend much time with a child may be prone to indulgence. But such children, especially, need the security of guidance and structure. Boundaries and guidelines will not embitter a child. Instead, they will set the child free to live securely within the boundaries.

**3:22—4:1** Paul does not condemn or condone slavery but explains that Christ transcends all divisions between people.

Slaves are told to work hard as though their owner were Christ himself (3:23); but owners should be just and fair (4:1). Perhaps Paul was thinking specifically of Onesimus and Philemon—the slave and master whose conflict lay behind the letter to Philemon (see the book of Philemon). Philemon was a slave owner in the Colossian church, and Onesimus had been his slave (4:9).

**3:23** Since the Creation, God has given us work to do. If we could regard our work as an act of worship or service to God, such an attitude would take some of the drudgery and boredom out of it. We could work without complaining or resentment if we would treat our job problems as the cost of discipleship.

**4:1** Slave owners were to provide what was just and fair. Similarly today, employers should pay fair wages and treat their employees justly. Paul's instructions encourage responsibility and integrity on the job. Christian employees should do their jobs as if Jesus Christ were their supervisor. And Christian employers should treat their employees fairly and with respect. Can you be trusted to do your best, even when the boss is not around? Do you work hard and with enthusiasm? Do you treat your employees as people, not machines? Employers should pay fair wages and treat their employees justly. Leaders should take care of their volunteers and not abuse them. If you have responsibility over others, make sure you do what is just and fair. Remember that no matter whom you work for, and no matter who works for you, the One you ultimately should want to please is your Father in heaven. You are accountable to him.

**4:2** Have you ever grown tired of praying for something or someone? Paul says we should "devote" ourselves to prayer and be "alert" in prayer. Our persistence is an expression of our faith that God answers our prayers. Faith shouldn't die if the answers come slowly, for the delay may be God's way of working his will in our life. When you feel tired of praying, know that God is present, always listening, always answering—maybe not in ways you had hoped, but in ways that he knows are best.

**4:3** The "mysterious plan" is Christ's Good News of salvation. The whole focus of Paul's life was to tell others about Christ, explaining and preaching this wonderful mystery.

**4:4** Paul asked for prayer that he could proclaim the Good News about Christ clearly, and we can request prayer to do the same. No matter what approach to evangelism we use, whether emphasizing lifestyle and example or whether building relationships, we should never obscure the message of the Good News.

**4:5**
Eph 5:15-16
**4:6**
Eph 4:29
1 Pet 3:15

5Live wisely among those who are not believers, and make the most of every opportunity. 6Let your conversation be gracious and attractive* so that you will have the right response for everyone.

### Paul's Final Instructions and Greetings

**4:7-8**
Acts 20:4
Eph 6:21-22
**4:9**
Phlm 1:10

7Tychicus will give you a full report about how I am getting along. He is a beloved brother and faithful helper who serves with me in the Lord's work. 8I have sent him to you for this very purpose—to let you know how we are doing and to encourage you. 9I am also sending Onesimus, a faithful and beloved brother, one of your own people. He and Tychicus will tell you everything that's happening here.

**4:10**
Acts 12:12; 15:37;
19:29; 20:4; 27:2

10Aristarchus, who is in prison with me, sends you his greetings, and so does Mark, Barnabas's cousin. As you were instructed before, make Mark welcome if he comes your way. 11Jesus (the one we call Justus) also sends his greetings. These are the only Jewish believers among my co-workers; they are working with me here for the Kingdom of God. And what a comfort they have been!

**4:12**
Col 1:7
Phlm 1:23
**4:13**
Col 2:1
**4:14**
2 Tim 4:10-11
Phlm 1:24
**4:15**
Rom 16:5

12Epaphras, a member of your own fellowship and a servant of Christ Jesus, sends you his greetings. He always prays earnestly for you, asking God to make you strong and perfect, fully confident that you are following the whole will of God. 13I can assure you that he prays hard for you and also for the believers in Laodicea and Hierapolis.

14Luke, the beloved doctor, sends his greetings, and so does Demas. 15Please give my greetings to our brothers and sisters* at Laodicea, and to Nympha and the church that meets in her house.

**4:6** Greek *and seasoned with salt.*   **4:15** Greek *brothers.*

---

**RULES OF SUBMISSION**

*Wives*, submit to your husbands (3:18).

*Children*, always obey your parents (3:20).

*Slaves*, obey your earthly masters (3:22).

(*Employees*, work hard for your employers.)

*Husbands*, love your wives and never treat them harshly (3:19).

*Fathers*, do not aggravate your children, or they will become discouraged (3:21).

*Masters*, be just and fair to your slaves (4:1).

(*Employers*, be just and fair with your employees.)

The New Testament includes many instructions concerning relationships. Most people read these instructions for the other person and ignore the ones that apply to themselves. But you can't control another person's behavior, only your own. Start by following your own instructions and not insisting on the obedience of others first.

---

**4:5** We should be wise in our contacts with non-believers, making the most of our opportunities to tell them the Good News of salvation. What opportunities do you have?

**4:6** When we tell others about Christ, it is important always to be gracious in what we say. No matter how much sense the message makes, we lose our effectiveness if we are not courteous. Just as we like to be respected, we must respect others if we want them to listen to what we have to say.

**4:7** Tychicus was one of Paul's personal representatives and probably the bearer of the letters to the Colossians and Ephesians (see also Ephesians 6:21, 22). He accompanied Paul to Jerusalem with the collection for the church (Acts 20:4).

**4:10** Aristarchus was a Thessalonian who accompanied Paul on his third missionary journey. He was with Paul in the riot at Ephesus (Acts 19:29). He and Tychicus were with Paul in Greece (Acts 20:4). Aristarchus went to Rome with Paul (Acts 27:2). Mark started out with Paul and Barnabas on their first missionary journey (Acts 12:25), but he left in the middle of the trip for unknown reasons (Acts 13:13). Barnabas and Mark were relatives, and when Paul refused to take Mark on another journey, Barnabas and Mark journeyed together to preach the Good News (Acts 15:37-41). Mark also worked with Peter (Acts 12:12, 13; 1 Peter 5:13). Later, Mark and Paul were reconciled (Philemon 1:24). Mark wrote the Gospel of Mark. His Profile is in Acts 13, p. 1847.

**4:12** Epaphras founded the Colossian church (see the note on 1:7), and his report to Paul in Rome caused Paul to write this letter. Epaphras was a hero of the Colossian church, one of the believers who helped keep the church together despite growing troubles. His earnest prayers for the believers show his deep love and concern for them.

**4:13** Laodicea was located a few miles northwest of Colosse; Hierapolis was about five miles north of Laodicea. See the note on 2:1 for more about Laodicea.

**4:14** Luke spent much time with Paul, not only accompanying him on most of his third missionary journey but sitting with him in the prison at Rome. Luke wrote the Gospel of Luke and the book of Acts. His Profile is in Acts 17, p. 1865. Demas was faithful for a while, but then he deserted Paul because he loved "the things of this life" (2 Timothy 4:10).

**4:15** The early Christians often met in homes. Church buildings were not common until the third century.

16After you have read this letter, pass it on to the church at Laodicea so they can read it, too. And you should read the letter I wrote to them.

17And say to Archippus, "Be sure to carry out the ministry the Lord gave you."

18HERE IS MY GREETING IN MY OWN HANDWRITING—PAUL.
Remember my chains.
May God's grace be with you.

**4:16**
1 Thes 5:27
2 Thes 3:14

**4:17**
2 Tim 4:5
Phlm 1:2

**4:18**
1 Cor 16:21
2 Thes 3:17

**4:16** Some suggest that the letter from Laodicea may be the book of Ephesians, because the letter to the Ephesians was circulated to all the churches in Asia Minor. It is also possible that there was a special letter to the Laodiceans, of which we have no record today. Paul wrote several letters that have been lost (see, for example, 2 Corinthians 2:3 and note).

**4:17** Paul's letter to Philemon is also addressed to Archippus (Philemon 1:2). Paul called him a "fellow soldier." He may have been a Roman soldier who had become a member of the Colossian church, or he may have been Philemon's son.

**4:17** Paul encouraged Archippus to make sure that he carried out the ministry he had received in the Lord. There are many ways for us to leave our ministries unfinished. We can easily get side-tracked morally, we can become exhausted and stop, we can get mad and quit, or we can let it slide and leave it up to others. We should see to it that we finish God's assignments, completing the work we have received.

**4:18** Paul usually dictated his letters to a secretary and then often ended with a short note in his own handwriting (see also 1 Corinthians 16:21; Galatians 6:11). This assured the recipients that false teachers were not writing letters in Paul's name. It also gave the letters a personal touch.

**4:18** To understand the letter to the Colossians, we need to know that the church was facing pressure from a heresy that promised deeper spiritual life through secret knowledge (an early form of Gnosticism). The false teachers were destroying faith in Christ by undermining Christ's humanity and divinity.

Paul makes it clear in Colossians that Christ alone is the source of our spiritual life, the head of the body of believers. Christ is Lord of both the physical and spiritual worlds. The path to deeper spiritual life is not through religious duties, special knowledge, or secrets; it is only through a clear connection with the Lord Jesus Christ. We must never let anything come between us and our Savior.

SLOWLY they walk, one by one, scattering the leaves and trampling the grass under measured and heavy steps. The minister's words still echoing in their minds, they hear workmen moving toward the terrible place, preparing to cover the casket of their loved one. Death, the enemy, has torn the bonded relationships of family and friends, leaving only memories . . . and tears . . . and loneliness.

But like a golden shaft of sun piercing the winter sky, a singular truth shatters the oppressive gloom: Death is not the end! Christ is the victor over death, and there is the hope of resurrection through him.

As with every member of the human family, first-century Christians came face to face with their mortality. Many of them met early deaths at the hands of those who hated Christ and all allied with him. Whether at the hands of zealous Jews (like Paul before his conversion), angry Greeks, or ruthless Roman authorities, persecution included stonings, beatings, crucifixions, torture, and death. To be a follower of Christ meant to give up everything.

Paul established the church in Thessalonica during his second missionary journey (about A.D. 51). He wrote this letter a short time later to encourage the young believers there. He wanted to assure them of his love, to praise them for their faithfulness during persecution, and to remind them of their hope—the sure return of their Lord and Savior.

Paul begins this letter with a note of affirmation, thanking God for the strong faith and good reputation of the Thessalonians (1:1–10). Then Paul reviews their relationship—how he and his companions brought the gospel to them (2:1–12), how they accepted the message (2:13–16), and how he longed to be with them again (2:17–20). Because of his concern, he had sent Timothy to encourage them in their faith (3:1–13).

Paul then presents the core of his message—exhortation and comfort. He challenges them to please God in their daily living by avoiding sexual immorality (4:1–8), loving each other (4:9, 10), and living as good citizens in a sinful world (4:11, 12).

Paul comforts the Thessalonians by reminding them of the hope of resurrection (4:13–18). Then he warns them to be prepared at all times, for Jesus Christ could return at any moment. When Christ returns, those Christians who are alive and those who have died will be raised to new life (5:1–11).

Paul then gives the Thessalonians a handful of reminders on how to prepare themselves for the Second Coming: Warn the lazy (5:14), encourage the timid (5:14), help the weak (5:14), be patient with everyone (5:14), be kind to everyone (5:15), be joyful always (5:16), pray continually (5:17), give thanks (5:18), test everything that is taught (5:20, 21), and avoid evil (5:22). Paul concludes his letter with two benedictions and a request for prayer.

As you read this letter, listen carefully to Paul's practical advice for Christian living. And when burdened by grief and overwhelmed by sorrow, take hope in the reality of Christ's return, resurrection, and eternal life!

## VITAL STATISTICS

**PURPOSE:**
To strengthen the Thessalonian Christians in their faith and give them the assurance of Christ's return

**AUTHOR:**
Paul

**ORIGINAL AUDIENCE:**
The church at Thessalonica

**DATE WRITTEN:**
Approximately A.D. 51 from Corinth; one of Paul's earliest letters

**SETTING:**
The church at Thessalonica was very young, having been established only two or three years before this letter was written. The Thessalonian Christians needed to mature in their faith. In addition, there was a misunderstanding concerning Christ's second coming—some thought Christ would return immediately; thus, they were confused when their loved ones died because they expected Christ to return beforehand. Also, believers were being persecuted.

**KEY VERSE:**
"For since we believe that Jesus died and was raised to life again, we also believe that when Jesus returns, God will bring back with him the believers who have died" (4:14).

**KEY PEOPLE:**
Paul, Timothy, Silas

**KEY PLACE:**
Thessalonica

**SPECIAL FEATURES:**
Paul received from Timothy a favorable report about the Thessalonians. However, Paul wrote this letter to correct their misconceptions about the resurrection and the second coming of Christ.

## THE BLUEPRINT

1. Faithfulness to the Lord
   (1:1—3:13)
2. Watchfulness for the Lord
   (4:1—5:28)

Paul and his companions were faithful to bring the gospel to the Thessalonians in the midst of persecution. The Thessalonians had only recently become Christians, and yet they had remained faithful to the Lord, despite the fact that the apostles were not with them. Others have been faithful in bringing God's Word to us. We must remain faithful and live in the expectation that Christ will return at any time.

## MEGATHEMES

| THEME | EXPLANATION | IMPORTANCE |
| --- | --- | --- |
| *Persecution* | Paul and the new Christians at Thessalonica experienced persecution because of their faith in Christ. We can expect trials and troubles as well. We need to stand firm in our faith in the midst of trials, being strengthened by the Holy Spirit. | The Holy Spirit helps us to remain strong in faith, able to show genuine love to others and maintain our moral character even when we are being persecuted, slandered, or oppressed. |
| *Paul's Ministry* | Paul expressed his concern for this church even while he was being slandered. Paul's commitment to share the gospel in spite of difficult circumstances is a model we should follow. | Paul not only delivered his message, but gave of himself. In our ministries, we must become like Paul—faithful and bold, yet sensitive and self-sacrificing. |
| *Hope* | One day all believers, both those who are alive and those who have died, will be united with Christ. To those Christians who die before Christ's return, there is hope—the hope of the resurrection of the body. | If we believe in Christ, we will live with him forever. All those who belong to Jesus Christ—from throughout history—will be present with him at his second coming. We can be confident that we will be with loved ones who have trusted in Christ. |
| *Being Prepared* | No one knows the time of Christ's return. We are to live moral and holy lives, ever watchful for his coming. Believers must not neglect daily responsibilities, but always work and live to please the Lord. | The gospel is not only what we believe but also what we must live. The Holy Spirit leads us in faithfulness, so we can avoid lust and fraud. Live as though you expect Christ's return at any time. Don't be caught unprepared. |

### LOCATION OF THESSALONICA

Paul visited Thessalonica on his second and third missionary journeys. It was a seaport and trade center located on the Egnatian Way, a busy international highway. Paul probably wrote his two letters to the Thessalonians from Corinth.

## 1. Faithfulness to the Lord
### Greetings from Paul

**1:1**
Acts 17:1
2 Thes 1:1

**1** This letter is from Paul, Silas,* and Timothy.

We are writing to the church in Thessalonica, to you who belong to God the Father and the Lord Jesus Christ.

May God give you grace and peace.

### The Faith of the Thessalonian Believers

**1:3**
1 Cor 13:13
2 Thes 1:11

**1:4**
2 Thes 2:13
2 Pet 1:10

**1:5**
1 Cor 2:4-5; 4:20
2 Thes 3:7

**1:6**
Acts 17:1-9
1 Cor 4:16

2 We always thank God for all of you and pray for you constantly. 3 As we pray to our God and Father about you, we think of your faithful work, your loving deeds, and the enduring hope you have because of our Lord Jesus Christ.

4 We know, dear brothers and sisters,* that God loves you and has chosen you to be his own people. 5 For when we brought you the Good News, it was not only with words but also with power, for the Holy Spirit gave you full assurance* that what we said was true. And you know of our concern for you from the way we lived when we were with you. 6 So you received the message with joy from the Holy Spirit in spite of the severe suffering it brought you. In this way, you imitated both us and the Lord. 7 As a result, you have become an example to all the believers in Greece—throughout both Macedonia and Achaia.*

**1:1** Greek *Silvanus*, the Greek form of the name.  **1:4** Greek *brothers.*  **1:5** Or *with the power of the Holy Spirit, so you can have full assurance.*  **1:7** *Macedonia* and *Achaia* were the northern and southern regions of Greece.

---

**1:1** Paul and his companions probably arrived in Thessalonica in the early summer of A.D. 50. They planted the first Christian church in that city, but had to leave in a hurry because their lives were threatened (Acts 17:1-10). At the first opportunity, probably when he stopped at Corinth, Paul sent Timothy back to Thessalonica to see how the new believers were doing. Timothy returned to Paul with good news: The Christians in Thessalonica were remaining firm in the faith and were unified. But the Thessalonians did have some questions about their new faith. Paul had not had time to answer all their questions during his brief visit, and in the meantime, other questions had arisen. So Paul wrote this letter to answer their questions and to commend them on their faithfulness to Christ.

**1:1** For more information on Paul, see his Profile in Acts 9, p. 1837. Silas accompanied Paul on his second missionary journey (Acts 15:36–17:15). He helped Paul establish the church in Thessalonica (Acts 17:1-9). He is also mentioned in 2 Corinthians 1:19, 2 Thessalonians 1:1, and in 1 Peter 5:12. Silas's Profile is found in Acts 16, p. 1859. Timothy's Profile is in 1 Timothy 2, p. 2059.

**1:1** Thessalonica was the capital and largest city (about 200,000 population) of the Roman province of Macedonia. The most important Roman highway (the Egnatian Way)—extending from Rome all the way to the Orient—went through Thessalonica. This highway, along with the city's thriving seaport, made Thessalonica one of the wealthiest and most flourishing trade centers in the Roman Empire. Recognized as a free city, Thessalonica was allowed self-rule and was exempt from most of the restrictions placed by Rome on other cities in the empire. With its international flavor, however, came many pagan religions and cultural influences that challenged the faith of the young Christians there.

**1:3** The Thessalonians had stood firm when they were persecuted (1:6; 3:1-4, 7, 8). Paul commended these young Christians for their faithful work, loving deeds, and anticipation of the Lord's return. These characteristics are the marks of effective Christians in any age.

**1:4** Paul reminded the Thessalonians of their status as God's "chosen" ones. Very few issues cause more confusion and even arguments among Christians than the issue of election (being chosen by God). It is difficult to simultaneously embrace God's sovereignty in choosing us and our human responsibility in choosing to follow him. Even though we may not be able to completely comprehend how these two truths can coexist, we can say the following: *Being chosen* comes from the heart of God (not our

minds), should be an incentive to please God (not ignore him), and should give birth to gratitude (not complacency). *Human responsibility* requires that we actively confess Christ as Lord, focus on living to please him, and share the gospel with others.

God's choice of us energizes us to obey and to serve. Our choice of God challenges us to build lives worthy of him. As you consider God's divine selection of you, how do you respond?

**1:5** The Good News came "with power"; it had a powerful effect on the Thessalonians. Whenever the Bible is heard and obeyed, lives are changed! Christianity is more than a collection of interesting facts; it is the power of God to everyone who believes. What has God's power done in your life since you first believed?

**1:5** The Holy Spirit changes people when they believe the Good News. When we tell others about Christ, we must depend on the Holy Spirit to open their eyes and convince them that they need salvation. God's power—not our cleverness or persuasion—changes people. Without the work of the Holy Spirit, our words are meaningless. The Holy Spirit not only convicts people of sin but also assures them of the truth of the Good News. (For more information on the Holy Spirit, see John 14:23-26; 15:26, 27; and the notes on John 3:6 and Acts 1:5.)

**1:5** Paul wrote, "And you know of our concern for you from the way we lived when we were with you." The Thessalonians had seen that what Paul, Silas, and Timothy were preaching was true because these men had lived it. Does your life confirm or contradict what you say you believe?

**1:6** The message of salvation, though welcomed with great joy, brought the Thessalonians severe suffering because it led to persecution from both Jews and Gentiles (3:2-4; Acts 17:5). Many believers today think that pain is the exception in the Christian life. When suffering occurs, they say, "Why me?" They feel as though God deserted them, or perhaps they accuse him of not being as dependable as they thought he should be. In reality, the world is sinful, so even believers suffer. God allows some Christians to become martyrs for the faith, and he allows others to survive persecution. Rather than asking, "Why me?" we should ask, "Why not me?" Our faith and the values of this world are on a collision course. If we expect pain and suffering to come, we will not be shocked when they occur. We can take comfort in knowing that Jesus also suffered. He understands our fears, our weaknesses, and our disappointments (Hebrews 2:16-18; 4:14-16). He promised never to leave us (Matthew 28:18-20), and he intercedes on our behalf (Hebrews 7:24, 25). In times of pain, persecution, or suffering, trust confidently in Christ.

8And now the word of the Lord is ringing out from you to people everywhere, even beyond Macedonia and Achaia, for wherever we go we find people telling us about your faith in God. We don't need to tell them about it, 9for they keep talking about the wonderful welcome you gave us and how you turned away from idols to serve the living and true God. 10And they speak of how you are looking forward to the coming of God's Son from heaven—Jesus, whom God raised from the dead. He is the one who has rescued us from the terrors of the coming judgment.

### Paul Remembers His Visit

**2** You yourselves know, dear brothers and sisters,* that our visit to you was not a failure. 2You know how badly we had been treated at Philippi just before we came to you and how much we suffered there. Yet our God gave us the courage to declare his Good News to you boldly, in spite of great opposition. 3So you can see we were not preaching with any deceit or impure motives or trickery.

4For we speak as messengers approved by God to be entrusted with the Good News. Our purpose is to please God, not people. He alone examines the motives of our hearts. 5Never once did we try to win you with flattery, as you well know. And God is our witness that we were not pretending to be your friends just to get your money! 6As for human praise, we have never sought it from you or anyone else.

7As apostles of Christ we certainly had a right to make some demands of you, but instead we were like children* among you. Or we were like a mother feeding and caring for her own children. 8We loved you so much that we shared with you not only God's Good News but our own lives, too.

9Don't you remember, dear brothers and sisters, how hard we worked among you? Night and day we toiled to earn a living so that we would not be a burden to any of you as we preached God's Good News to you. 10You yourselves are our witnesses—and so is God—that we were devout and honest and faultless toward all of you believers. 11And you know that we

1:8
Rom 1:8
2 Thes 3:1

1:9
Acts 14:15
1 Cor 12:2

1:10
Phil 3:20
1 Thes 5:9
Titus 2:13
Heb 9:28
Rev 1:7

2:1
1 Thes 1:5, 9

2:2
Acts 16:22; 17:2
Phil 1:30

2:3
2 Cor 4:2
2 Pet 1:16

2:4
Gal 1:10
1 Tim 1:11

2:5
Acts 20:33

2:7
2 Tim 2:24

2:8
2 Cor 12:15

2:9
Acts 18:3
2 Cor 11:9
2 Thes 3:8

2:10
1 Thes 1:5

2:11
1 Cor 4:14

**2:1** Greek *brothers;* also in 2:9, 14, 17.   **2:7** Some manuscripts read *we were gentle.*

---

**1:9, 10** All of us should respond to the Good News as the Thessalonians did: *Turn* to God, *serve* God, and *look forward* to the return of his Son, Christ, from heaven. We should turn from sin to God because Christ is coming to judge the earth. We should be fervent in our service because we have little time before Christ returns. We should be prepared for Christ to return because we don't know when he will come.

**1:10** Paul emphasized Christ's second coming throughout this book. Because the Thessalonian church was being persecuted, Paul encouraged them to look forward to the deliverance that Christ would bring. A believer's hope is in the return of Jesus (Titus 2:13). Our perspective on life remains incomplete without this hope. Just as surely as Christ was raised from the dead and ascended into heaven, he will return (Acts 1:11).

**2:1, 2** "Our visit to you" refers to Paul's first visit to Thessalonica recorded in Acts 17:1-9. The Thessalonians knew that Paul had been imprisoned in Philippi just prior to coming to Thessalonica (see Acts 16:11–17:1). Fear of imprisonment did not keep Paul from preaching the Good News. If God wants us to do something, he will give us the strength and courage to boldly speak out for him despite any obstacles that may come our way. Boldness is not reckless impulsiveness. Boldness requires courage to press through fears and do what is right. How can we be more bold? Like the apostles, we need to pray for that kind of courage. To gain boldness, you can pray for the Holy Spirit's power, look for opportunities to talk about Christ, and start right where you are being bolder in even small ways.

**2:3** This pointed statement may be a response to accusations from the Jewish leaders who had stirred up the crowds (Acts 17:5). Paul did not seek money, fame, or popularity by sharing the Good News. He demonstrated the sincerity of his motives by showing that he and Silas had suffered for sharing the Good News in Philippi. People become involved in ministry for a variety of reasons, not all of them good or pure. When their bad motives are exposed, all of Christ's work suffers. When you get involved in ministry, do so out of love for Christ and others.

**2:4-8** In trying to persuade people, we may be tempted to alter our position just enough to make our message more palatable or to use flattery or praise. Paul never changed his *message* to make it more acceptable, but he did tailor his *methods* to each audience. Although our presentation must be altered to be appropriate to the situation, the truth of the Good News must never be compromised.

**2:5** It's disgusting to hear a person butter up someone. Flattery is phony, and it covers up a person's real intentions. Christians should not be flatterers. Those who proclaim God's truth have a special responsibility to be honest. Are you honest and straightforward in your words and actions? Or do you tell people what they want to hear in order to get what you want or to get ahead?

**2:6-8** When Paul was with the Thessalonians, he didn't flatter them, seek their praise, or become a burden to them. He and Silas completely focused their efforts on presenting God's message of salvation to the Thessalonians. This was important! The Thessalonian believers had their lives changed by God, not Paul; it was Christ's message they believed, not Paul's. When we witness for Christ, our focus should not be on the impression we make. As true ministers of Christ, we should point to him, not to ourselves.

**2:7** That Paul and his companions "were like children" among the Thessalonians does not mean they were immature or untrained. Rather, Paul was making the point that, like children, they were honest, straightforward, and without guile in their presentation of the gospel and of their lives.

**2:9** Although Paul had the right to receive financial support from the people he taught, he supported himself as a tentmaker (Acts 18:3) so that he wouldn't be a burden to the new Thessalonian believers.

**2:11** No loving father would neglect the safety of his children, allowing them to walk into circumstances that might be harmful or fatal. In the same way, we must take new believers under our wing until they are mature enough to stand firm in their faith. We must help new Christians become strong enough to influence others for the sake of the Good News.

**2:12**
Eph 4:1
Col 1:10
1 Pet 1:15

**2:13**
1 Thes 1:2
2 Thes 2:13

**2:14**
Acts 17:5
1 Thes 1:6

**2:15**
Luke 24:20
Acts 2:23; 7:52

**2:16**
Matt 23:32-33
Acts 13:45, 50;
17:5; 20:3; 21:27;
24:9

**2:17**
1 Cor 5:3
1 Thes 3:10

**2:18**
Rom 1:13; 15:22

**2:19**
Phil 2:16

**2:20**
2 Cor 1:14

treated each of you as a father treats his own children. ¹²We pleaded with you, encouraged you, and urged you to live your lives in a way that God would consider worthy. For he called you to share in his Kingdom and glory.

¹³Therefore, we never stop thanking God that when you received his message from us, you didn't think of our words as mere human ideas. You accepted what we said as the very word of God—which, of course, it is. And this word continues to work in you who believe.

¹⁴And then, dear brothers and sisters, you suffered persecution from your own countrymen. In this way, you imitated the believers in God's churches in Judea who, because of their belief in Christ Jesus, suffered from their own people, the Jews. ¹⁵For some of the Jews killed the prophets, and some even killed the Lord Jesus. Now they have persecuted us, too. They fail to please God and work against all humanity ¹⁶as they try to keep us from preaching the Good News of salvation to the Gentiles. By doing this, they continue to pile up their sins. But the anger of God has caught up with them at last.

### Timothy's Good Report about the Church

¹⁷Dear brothers and sisters, after we were separated from you for a little while (though our hearts never left you), we tried very hard to come back because of our intense longing to see you again. ¹⁸We wanted very much to come to you, and I, Paul, tried again and again, but Satan prevented us. ¹⁹After all, what gives us hope and joy, and what will be our proud reward and crown as we stand before our Lord Jesus when he returns? It is you! ²⁰Yes, you are our pride and joy.

---

**THE EVENTS OF CHRIST'S RETURN**

1. Christ will return visibly, with a commanding shout.
2. There will be an unmistakable call from an angel.
3. There will be a trumpet fanfare such as has never been heard.
4. Believers in Christ who are dead will rise from their graves.
5. Believers who are alive will be caught up in the clouds to meet the Lord.

While Christians have often disagreed about what events will lead up to the return of Christ, there has been less disagreement about what will happen once Christ does return.

---

**2:12** By his words and example, Paul encouraged the Thessalonians to live in a way God would consider worthy. Is there anything about your daily life that would embarrass God? What do people think of God from watching you?

**2:13** Paul said that the word of God continued to work in the believers' lives. Paul knew that God's words are not mere sermons or documents but a real source of transforming power. This Bible you hold in your hands is full of real and living power. Its words are transforming lives all over the world every day. Read it. Encourage fellow believers to read it. Encourage non-Christian friends to read it. All who do so, truly seeking to learn, will be touched by its power. They will never be the same.

**2:14** Just as the Jewish Christians in Jerusalem were persecuted by other Jews, so the Gentile Christians in Thessalonica were persecuted by their fellow Gentiles. Persecution is discouraging, especially when it comes from your own people. When you take a stand for Christ, you may face opposition, disapproval, and ridicule from your neighbors, friends, and even family members.

**2:14** When Paul refers to the Jews, he is talking about certain Jews who opposed his preaching of the Good News. He does not mean all Jews. Many of Paul's converts were Jewish. Paul himself was a Jew (2 Corinthians 11:22).

**2:15** Having believed the Good News and accepted new life in Christ, apparently many Thessalonians thought that they would be protected from death until Christ returned. Then, when believers began to die under persecution, some Thessalonian Christians started to question their faith. Many of Paul's comments throughout this letter were addressed to these people, as he explained what happens when believers die (see 4:13ff).

**2:15, 16** Why were so many Jews opposed to Christianity? (1) Although the Jewish religion had been declared legal by the Roman government, it still had a tenuous relationship with the government. At this time, Christianity was viewed as a sect of Judaism. The Jews were afraid that reprisals leveled against the Christians might be expanded to include them. (2) The Jewish leaders thought Jesus was a false prophet, and they didn't want his teachings to spread. (3) The leaders feared that if many Jews were drawn away, their own political position might be weakened. (4) Jews were proud of their special status as God's chosen people and resented the fact that Gentiles could be full members within the Christian church.

**2:18** Satan is real. He is called "the god of this world" (2 Corinthians 4:4) and "the commander of the powers in the unseen world" (Ephesians 2:2). We don't know exactly what hindered Paul from returning to Thessalonica—opposition, illness, travel complications, or a direct attack by Satan—but Satan worked in some way to keep him away. Many of the difficulties that prevent us from accomplishing God's work can be attributed to Satan (see Ephesians 6:12).

**2:20** The ultimate reward for Paul's ministry was not money, prestige, or fame, but new believers whose lives had been changed by God through the preaching of the Good News. This was why he longed to see them. No matter what ministry God has given to you, your highest reward and greatest joy should be those who come to believe in Christ and are growing in him.

**3** Finally, when we could stand it no longer, we decided to stay alone in Athens, ²and we sent Timothy to visit you. He is our brother and God's co-worker\* in proclaiming the Good News of Christ. We sent him to strengthen you, to encourage you in your faith, ³and to keep you from being shaken by the troubles you were going through. But you know that we are destined for such troubles. ⁴Even while we were with you, we warned you that troubles would soon come—and they did, as you well know. ⁵That is why, when I could bear it no longer, I sent Timothy to find out whether your faith was still strong. I was afraid that the tempter had gotten the best of you and that our work had been useless.

⁶But now Timothy has just returned, bringing us good news about your faith and love. He reports that you always remember our visit with joy and that you want to see us as much as we want to see you. ⁷So we have been greatly encouraged in the midst of our troubles and suffering, dear brothers and sisters,\* because you have remained strong in your faith. ⁸It gives us new life to know that you are standing firm in the Lord.

⁹How we thank God for you! Because of you we have great joy as we enter God's presence. ¹⁰Night and day we pray earnestly for you, asking God to let us see you again to fill the gaps in your faith.

¹¹May God our Father and our Lord Jesus bring us to you very soon. ¹²And may the Lord make your love for one another and for all people grow and overflow, just as our love for you overflows. ¹³May he, as a result, make your hearts strong, blameless, and holy as you stand before God our Father when our Lord Jesus comes again with all his holy people. Amen.

## 2. Watchfulness for the Lord
*Live to Please God*

**4** Finally, dear brothers and sisters,\* we urge you in the name of the Lord Jesus to live in a way that pleases God, as we have taught you. You live this way already, and we encourage you to do so even more. ²For you remember what we taught you by the authority of the Lord Jesus.

**3:1** Acts 17:15
**3:2** Acts 16:1-3
**3:3** 2 Tim 3:12
**3:4** 1 Thes 2:14
**3:5** Matt 4:3; Phil 2:16
**3:6** Acts 18:5
**3:7** 2 Thes 1:4
**3:8** 1 Cor 16:13
**3:10** 1 Thes 2:16-17; 2 Tim 1:3
**3:12** Phil 1:9
**3:13** Zech 14:5; 1 Cor 1:8; 1 Thes 1:7, 10; 2:19
**4:1** Eph 4:1; 2 Thes 3:6
**4:2** 2 Thes 3:4

**3:2** Other manuscripts read *and God's servant*; still others read *and a co-worker*, or *and a servant and co-worker for God*, or *and God's servant and our co-worker*.   **3:7** Greek *brothers*.   **4:1** Greek *brothers*; also in 4:10, 13.

---

**3:1-3** Some think that troubles are always caused by sin or a lack of faith. Trials may be a part of God's plan for believers. Experiencing problems and persecutions can build character (James 1:2-4), perseverance (Romans 5:3-5), and sensitivity toward others who also face trouble (2 Corinthians 1:3-7). Problems are unavoidable for God's people. Your troubles may be a sign of effective Christian living.

**3:2-5** Because Paul could not return to Thessalonica (2:18), he sent Timothy as his representative. According to Acts 17:10, Paul left Thessalonica and went to Berea. When trouble broke out in Berea, some Christians took Paul to Athens, while Silas and Timothy stayed behind (Acts 17:13-15). Then Paul directed Silas and Timothy to join him in Athens. Later, Paul sent Timothy to encourage the Thessalonian Christians to be strong in their faith in the face of persecution and other troubles.

**3:4** Some people turn to God with the hope of escaping suffering on earth. But God doesn't promise that. Instead, he gives us power to grow through our sufferings. The Christian life involves obedience to Christ despite temptations and hardships.

**3:5** Satan ("the tempter") is the most powerful of the evil spirits. His power can affect both the spiritual world (Ephesians 2:1-3; 6:10-12) and the physical world (2 Corinthians 12:7-10). Satan even tempted Jesus (Matthew 4:1-11). But Jesus defeated Satan when he died on the cross for our sins and rose again to bring us new life. At the proper time God will overthrow Satan forever (Revelation 20:7-10).

**3:7, 8** During persecution or pressure, believers should encourage one another. Christians who stand firm in the Lord are an encouragement to ministers and teachers (who can see the benefit of their work in those who remain faithful) and also an encouragement to those who are new in their faith (who can learn from the steadfastness of the mature).

**3:9, 10** It brings great joy to a Christian to see another person come to faith in Christ and mature in that faith. Paul experienced

this joy countless times. He thanked God for those who had come to know Christ and for their strong faith. He also prayed for their continued growth. If new Christians have brought you joy, thank God for them and support them as they continue to grow in the faith. Likewise, have you benefited from the ministry of others? Has someone's guidance and faithfulness stimulated you to grow in Christ? Consider how you may bring some word of encouragement or some thoughtful gift. Let that important person know that you have followed his or her example by being faithful to Christ.

**3:11** Paul wanted to return to Thessalonica. We have no record that he was able to do so; but when he was traveling through Asia on his third journey, he was joined by Aristarchus and Secundus, who were from Thessalonica (Acts 20:4, 5).

**3:12** If we are full of God's love, it will overflow to others. It's not enough merely to be courteous to others; we must actively and persistently show love to them. Our love should be growing continually. If your capacity to love has remained unchanged for some time, ask God to fill you again with his never-ending supply. Then look for opportunities to let his love spill over in refreshment to others.

**3:13** "When our Lord Jesus comes again with all his holy people" refers to the second coming of Christ when he will establish his eternal Kingdom. At that time, Christ will gather all believers, those who have died and those who are alive, into one united family under his rule. All believers from all times, including these Thessalonian believers, will be with Christ in his Kingdom.

**4:1-8** Sexual standards were very low in the Roman Empire, and in many societies today, they are not any higher. The temptation to engage in sexual intercourse outside the marriage relationship has always been powerful. Giving in to that temptation can have disastrous results. Sexual sins always hurt someone: individuals, families, businesses, churches. Sexual desires and activities must be placed under Christ's control. God created sex for procreation and pleasure and as an expression of love between a husband

**4:3**
Heb 10:10
1 Pet 1:16
**4:4**
1 Cor 7:2
**4:7**
Lev 11:44
2 Thes 2:13-14
1 Pet 1:15
**4:8**
Rom 5:5
1 Jn 3:24
**4:9**
1 Jn 2:20, 27
**4:10**
1 Thes 3:12
2 Thes 3:4

³God's will is for you to be holy, so stay away from all sexual sin. ⁴Then each of you will control his own body* and live in holiness and honor—⁵not in lustful passion like the pagans who do not know God and his ways. ⁶Never harm or cheat a Christian brother in this matter by violating his wife,* for the Lord avenges all such sins, as we have solemnly warned you before. ⁷God has called us to live holy lives, not impure lives. ⁸Therefore, anyone who refuses to live by these rules is not disobeying human teaching but is rejecting God, who gives his Holy Spirit to you.

⁹But we don't need to write to you about the importance of loving each other,* for God himself has taught you to love one another. ¹⁰Indeed, you already show your love for all the believers* throughout Macedonia. Even so, dear brothers and sisters, we urge you to love them even more.

**4:4** Or *will know how to take a wife for himself;* or *will learn to live with his own wife;* Greek reads *will know how to possess his own vessel.* **4:6** Greek *Never harm or cheat a brother in this matter.* **4:9** Greek *about brotherly love.* **4:10** Greek *the brothers.*

---

**CHECKLIST FOR ENCOURAGERS**
The command to "encourage" others is found throughout the Bible. In 5:11-23, Paul gives many specific examples of how we can encourage others.

| Reference | Example | Suggested Application |
|---|---|---|
| 5:11 | Build each other up. | Point out to someone a quality you appreciate in him or her. |
| 5:12 | Honor leaders. | Look for ways to cooperate. |
| 5:13 | Show leaders great respect. | Hold back your next critical comments about those in positions of responsibility. Say "thank you" to your leaders for their efforts. |
| 5:13 | Live in peace. | Search for ways to get along with others. |
| 5:14 | Warn the lazy. | Challenge someone to join you in a project. |
| 5:14 | Encourage the timid. | Encourage those who are timid by reminding them of God's promises. |
| 5:14 | Help the weak. | Support those who are weak by loving them and praying for them. |
| 5:14 | Be patient. | Think of a situation that tries your patience, and plan ahead of time how you can stay calm. |
| 5:15 | Resist revenge. | Instead of planning to get even with those who mistreat you, do good to them. |
| 5:16 | Be joyful. | Remember that even in the midst of turmoil, God is in control. |
| 5:17 | Pray continually. | God is always with you—talk to him. |
| 5:18 | Give thanks. | Make a list of all the gifts God has given you, giving thanks to God for each one. |
| 5:19 | Do not stifle the Holy Spirit. | Cooperate with the Spirit the next time he prompts you to participate in a Christian meeting. |
| 5:20 | Do not scoff at prophecies. | Receive God's word from those who speak for him. |
| 5:22 | Avoid every kind of evil. | Avoid situations where you will be drawn into temptation. |
| 5:23 | Count on God's constant help. | Realize that the Christian life is to be lived not in our own strength but through God's power. |

---

and wife. Therefore, the sexual experience must be limited to the marriage. Besides the physical consequences of sexual sin, there are also spiritual consequences. For more on why sexual sin is so harmful, see the note on 1 Corinthians 6:18.

**4:3** It is God's will for you to be holy, but how can you go about doing that? The Bible teaches that holiness is not a state of being that you must manufacture on your own with hard work and good deeds and constant fear of failure. Instead, being made holy occurs in the process of living the Christian life. If you have accepted Christ's sacrifice on your behalf, then you are considered holy and complete in God's eyes. Yet you must continue to learn and grow during your time on earth. The Holy Spirit works in you, conforming you to the image of Christ (Romans 8:29).

**4:4, 5** Paul said that lustful passions should not control God's people. Some argue that if they've already sinned by having lustful thoughts, they might as well go ahead with lustful actions too. Acting out sinful desires is harmful in several ways: (1) It causes people to excuse sin rather than to stop sinning; (2) it destroys marriages; (3) it is deliberate rebellion against God's Word; and (4) it always hurts someone else in addition to the sinner. Sinful action is more dangerous than sinful desire, so desires should not be acted out. Nevertheless, sinful desire is just as damaging to righteousness. Left unchecked, wrong desires will result in wrong actions and will turn people away from God.

<sup>11</sup>Make it your goal to live a quiet life, minding your own business and working with your hands, just as we instructed you before. <sup>12</sup>Then people who are not Christians will respect the way you live, and you will not need to depend on others.

### The Hope of the Resurrection

<sup>13</sup>And now, dear brothers and sisters, we want you to know what will happen to the believers who have died* so you will not grieve like people who have no hope. <sup>14</sup>For since we believe that Jesus died and was raised to life again, we also believe that when Jesus returns, God will bring back with him the believers who have died.

<sup>15</sup>We tell you this directly from the Lord: We who are still living when the Lord returns will not meet him ahead of those who have died.* <sup>16</sup>For the Lord himself will come down from heaven with a commanding shout, with the voice of the archangel, and with the trumpet call of God. First, the Christians who have died* will rise from their graves. <sup>17</sup>Then, together with them, we who are still alive and remain on the earth will be caught up in the clouds to meet the Lord in the air. Then we will be with the Lord forever. <sup>18</sup>So encourage each other with these words.

**5** Now concerning how and when all this will happen, dear brothers and sisters,* we don't really need to write you. <sup>2</sup>For you know quite well that the day of the Lord's return will come unexpectedly, like a thief in the night. <sup>3</sup>When people are saying, "Everything is peaceful and secure," then disaster will fall on them as suddenly as a pregnant woman's labor pains begin. And there will be no escape.

<sup>4</sup>But you aren't in the dark about these things, dear brothers and sisters, and you won't be surprised when the day of the Lord comes like a thief.* <sup>5</sup>For you are all children of the light and of the day; we don't belong to darkness and night. <sup>6</sup>So be on your guard, not asleep like the others. Stay alert and be clearheaded. <sup>7</sup>Night is the time when people sleep and drinkers get drunk. <sup>8</sup>But let us who live in the light be clearheaded, protected by the armor of faith and love, and wearing as our helmet the confidence of our salvation.

<sup>9</sup>For God chose to save us through our Lord Jesus Christ, not to pour out his anger on us. <sup>10</sup>Christ died for us so that, whether we are dead or alive when he returns, we can live with him forever. <sup>11</sup>So encourage each other and build each other up, just as you are already doing.

**4:11**
Eph 4:28
**2** Thes 3:10-12

**4:14**
Rom 14:9
1 Cor 15:3-4, 12

**4:15**
1 Cor 7:10, 25;
15:52

**4:16**
Matt 24:30
1 Cor 15:52
1 Thes 1:10
2 Thes 1:7

**4:17**
Acts 1:9
Rev 11:12

**5:2**
Matt 24:42-44

**5:3**
Jer 4:10; 6:14
Matt 24:39

**5:4**
1 Jn 2:8

**5:5**
John 12:36
Eph 5:9

**5:7**
Acts 2:15

**5:8**
Isa 59:17
Eph 6:14, 17
1 Pet 1:13

**5:9**
1 Thes 1:10
2 Thes 2:13-14

**5:10**
Rom 14:8-9

**4:13** Greek *those who have fallen asleep;* also in 4:14. **4:15** Greek *those who have fallen asleep.* **4:16** Greek *the dead in Christ.* **5:1** Greek *brothers;* also in 5:4, 12, 14, 25, 26, 27. **5:4** Some manuscripts read *comes upon you as if you were thieves.*

---

**4:11, 12** Christian living is more than simply loving other Christians. We must be responsible in all areas of life. Some of the Thessalonian Christians had adopted a life of idleness, depending on others for handouts. Some Greeks looked down on manual labor. So Paul told the Thessalonians to work hard and live quiet lives. You can't be effective in sharing your faith with others if they don't respect you. Whatever you do, do it faithfully and be a positive force in society.

**4:13ff** The Thessalonians were wondering why many of their fellow believers had died and what would happen to them when Christ returned. Paul wanted the Thessalonians to understand that death is not the end of the story. The great hope for all believers is in the Resurrection. Because Jesus Christ came back to life, so will all believers, including those who have already died. Therefore, we need not despair when loved ones die or world events take a tragic turn. God will turn tragedy to triumph, poverty to riches, pain to glory, and defeat to victory. All believers throughout history will stand reunited in God's very presence, safe and secure. As Paul comforted the Thessalonians with the promise of the Resurrection, so we should comfort and reassure each other with this great hope.

**4:15** What did Paul mean when he wrote, "We tell you this directly from the Lord"? Either this was something that the Lord had revealed directly to Paul, or it was a teaching of Jesus that had been passed along orally by the apostles and other Christians.

**4:15-18** Knowing exactly *when* the dead will be raised, in relation to the other events at the Second Coming, is not as important as knowing *why* Paul wrote these words: to challenge believers to comfort and encourage one another. This passage can be a great comfort when any believer dies. The same love that should unite believers in this life (4:9) will unite believers when Christ returns and reigns for eternity.

**4:16** An "archangel" is an angel with a position of authority and leadership. Michael is the only archangel mentioned in the New Testament (see Jude 1:9; Daniel 10:13; 12:1).

**5:1-3** "How and when all this will happen" refers to the knowledge of what will happen in the future, specifically at the return of Christ. Efforts to determine the date of Christ's return are foolish. Don't be misled by anyone who claims to know. We are told here that no one knows and that even believers will be surprised. The Lord will return suddenly and unexpectedly, warns Paul, so be ready! Because no one knows when Jesus will come back to earth, we should be prepared at all times. Suppose he were to return today. How would he find you living? Are you ready to meet him? Live each day prepared to welcome Christ.

**5:2** The "day of the Lord's return" is a future time when God will intervene directly and dramatically in world affairs. Predicted and discussed often in the Old Testament (Isaiah 13:6-12; Joel 2:28-32; Zephaniah 1:14-18), the day of the Lord will include both punishment and blessing. Christ will judge sin and set up his eternal Kingdom.

**5:4, 5** It is good that we don't know exactly when Christ will return. If we knew the precise date, we might be tempted to be lazy in our work for Christ. Worse yet, we might plan to keep sinning and then turn to God right at the end. Heaven is not our only goal; we have work to do here. Christians must keep on doing God's work until death or until we see the unmistakable return of our Savior.

**5:8** For more about the Christian's armor, see Ephesians 6:13-17.

**5:9-11** As you near the end of a long race, your legs ache, your throat burns, and your whole body cries out for you to stop. This is when friends and fans are most valuable. Their encouragement helps you push through the pain to the finish line. In the same way,

5:12
1 Tim 5:17

5:15
Prov 20:22
Rom 12:17
1 Pet 3:9

5:16
Phil 4:4

5:17
Luke 18:1

5:18
Eph 5:20

5:19
Eph 4:30

5:20
1 Cor 14:1, 39

5:23
Rom 15:33

5:24
1 Cor 1:9

5:27
Col 4:16

5:28
Rom 16:20

## Paul's Final Advice

12Dear brothers and sisters, honor those who are your leaders in the Lord's work. They work hard among you and give you spiritual guidance. 13Show them great respect and whole-hearted love because of their work. And live peacefully with each other.

14Brothers and sisters, we urge you to warn those who are lazy. Encourage those who are timid. Take tender care of those who are weak. Be patient with everyone.

15See that no one pays back evil for evil, but always try to do good to each other and to all people.

16Always be joyful. 17Never stop praying. 18Be thankful in all circumstances, for this is God's will for you who belong to Christ Jesus.

19Do not stifle the Holy Spirit. 20Do not scoff at prophecies, 21but test everything that is said. Hold on to what is good. 22Stay away from every kind of evil.

## Paul's Final Greetings

23Now may the God of peace make you holy in every way, and may your whole spirit and soul and body be kept blameless until our Lord Jesus Christ comes again. 24God will make this happen, for he who calls you is faithful.

25Dear brothers and sisters, pray for us.

26Greet all the brothers and sisters with Christian love.*

27I command you in the name of the Lord to read this letter to all the brothers and sisters.

28May the grace of our Lord Jesus Christ be with you.

**5:26** Greek *with a holy kiss.*

---

Christians are to encourage one another. Be sensitive to others' need for encouragement, and offer supportive words or actions.

**5:12, 13** "Those who are your leaders in the Lord's work" probably refers to elders and deacons in the church. How can you honor your pastor and other church leaders? Express your appreciation, tell them how you have been helped by their leadership and teaching, and thank them for their ministry in your life. If you say nothing, how will they know where you stand? Remember, they need and deserve your support and love.

**5:14** Don't loaf around with the lazy; warn them. Don't yell at the timid and weak; encourage and help them. At times it can be difficult to distinguish between idleness and timidity. Two people may be doing nothing—one out of laziness and the other out of shyness or fear of doing something wrong. The key to ministry is sensitivity: sensing the condition of each person and offering the appropriate remedy for each situation. You can't effectively help until you know the problem. You can't apply the medicine until you know where the wound is.

**5:16-18** Our joy, prayers, and thankfulness should not fluctuate with our circumstances or feelings. Obeying these three commands—be joyful, never stop praying, and be thankful—often goes against our natural inclinations. When we make a conscious decision to do what God says, however, we will begin to see people in a new perspective. When we do God's will, we will find it easier to be joyful and thankful.

**5:17** We cannot spend all our time on our knees, but it is possible to have a prayerful attitude at all times. This attitude is built upon acknowledging our dependence on God, realizing his presence within us, and determining to obey him fully. Then we will find it natural to pray frequent, spontaneous, short prayers. A prayerful attitude is not a substitute for regular times of prayer but should be an outgrowth of those times.

**5:17** Have you ever grown tired of praying for something or someone? Paul said that believers should never stop praying. A Christian's persistence is an expression of faith that God answers prayer. Faith shouldn't die if the answers come slowly, for the delay may be God's way of working his will. When you feel tired of praying, know that God is present, always listening, always answering—in ways that he knows are best.

**5:18** Paul was not teaching us that we should thank God *for* everything that happens to us, but *in* everything. Evil does not come from God, so we should not thank him for it. But when evil

strikes, we can still be thankful for God's presence and for the good that he will accomplish through the distress.

**5:19** By warning us not to "stifle the Holy Spirit," Paul means that we should not ignore or toss aside the gifts the Holy Spirit gives. Here, he mentions prophecy (5:20); in 1 Corinthians 14:39, he mentions speaking in tongues. Sometimes spiritual gifts are controversial, and they may cause division in a church. Rather than trying to solve the problems, some Christians prefer to smother the gifts. This impoverishes the church. We should not stifle the Holy Spirit's work in anyone's life but encourage the full expression of these gifts to benefit the whole body of Christ.

**5:20, 21** We shouldn't make fun of those who are called to speak for God ("scoff at prophecies"), but we should always "test everything that is said," checking their words against the Bible. We are on dangerous ground if we laugh at a person who speaks the truth. Instead, we should carefully check out what people say, accepting what is true and rejecting what is false.

**5:22-24** Christians cannot avoid every kind of evil because we live in a sinful world. We can, however, make sure that we don't give evil a foothold by avoiding tempting situations and concentrating on obeying God.

**5:23** The spirit, soul, and body refer not so much to the distinct parts of a person as to the entire being of a person. This expression is Paul's way of saying that God must be involved in *every* aspect of life. It is wrong to think that we can separate the spiritual life from everything else, obeying God only in some ethereal sense or living for him only one day each week. Christ must control *all* of us, not just a "religious" part.

**5:27** For all the Christians to hear this letter, it had to be read in a public meeting—there were not enough copies to circulate. Paul wanted to make sure that everyone had the opportunity to hear his message because he was answering important questions and offering needed encouragement.

**5:28** The Thessalonian church was young, and they needed help and encouragement. Both the persecution they faced and the temptations of their pagan culture were potential problems for these new Christians. Paul wrote to strengthen their faith and bolster their resistance to persecution and temptation. We, too, have a responsibility to help new believers—to make sure that they continue in their faith and don't become sidetracked by wrong beliefs or practices. First Thessalonians can better equip us to help our brothers and sisters in Christ.

## VITAL STATISTICS

**PURPOSE:**
To clear up the confusion about the second coming of Christ

**AUTHOR:**
Paul

**ORIGINAL AUDIENCE:**
The church at Thessalonica

**DATE WRITTEN:**
Approximately A.D. 51 or 52, a few months after 1 Thessalonians, from Corinth

**SETTING:**
Many in the church were confused about the timing of Christ's return. Because of mounting persecution, they thought the day of the Lord must be imminent, and they interpreted Paul's first letter to say that the Second Coming would be at any moment. In light of this misunderstanding, many persisted in being idle and disorderly, with the excuse of waiting for Christ's return.

**KEY VERSE:**
"May the Lord lead your hearts into a full understanding and expression of the love of God and the patient endurance that comes from Christ" (3:5).

**KEY PEOPLE:**
Paul, Silas, Timothy

**KEY PLACE:**
Thessalonica

**SPECIAL FEATURES:**
This is a follow-up letter to 1 Thessalonians. In this letter, Paul indicates various events that must precede the second coming of Christ.

"BUT I thought he said . . . ," "I'm sure he meant . . . ," "It is clear to me that we should . . . ," "I disagree. I think we must . . ."

Effective communication is difficult; often the message sent is *not* the message received in the home, marketplace, neighborhood, or church. Even when clearly stated or written, words can be misinterpreted and misunderstood, especially when filtered through the sieve of prejudices and preconceptions.

Paul faced this problem with the Thessalonians. He had written them earlier to help them grow in the faith, comforting and encouraging them by affirming the reality of Christ's return. Just a few months later, however, word came from Thessalonica that some had misunderstood Paul's teaching about the Second Coming. His announcement that Christ could come at any moment had caused some to stop working and just wait, rationalizing their idleness by pointing to Paul's teaching. Adding fuel to this fire was the continued persecution of the church. Many felt that indeed this must be the "day of the Lord."

Responding quickly, Paul sent a second letter to this young church. In it he gave further instruction concerning the Second Coming and the day of the Lord (2:1, 2). Second Thessalonians, therefore, continues the subject of 1 Thessalonians and is a call to continued courage and consistent conduct.

The letter begins with Paul's trademark—a personal greeting and a statement of thanksgiving for their faith (1:1–3). He mentions their perseverance in spite of their persecution and trials (1:4) and uses this situation to broach the subject of Christ's return. At that time, Christ will vindicate the righteous who endure and will punish the wicked (1:5–12).

Paul then directly answers the misunderstanding concerning the timing of the events of the end times. He tells them not to listen to rumors and reports that the day of the Lord has already begun (2:1, 2) because a number of events must occur before Christ returns (2:3–12). Meanwhile, they should stand firm for Christ's truth (2:13–15), receive God's encouragement and hope (2:16, 17), pray for strength and for the spread of the Lord's message (3:1–5), and warn those who are idle (3:6–15). Paul ends with personal greetings and a benediction (3:16–18).

Almost 2,000 years later, we stand much closer to the time of Christ's return; but we also would be wrong to see his imminent appearance as an excuse for idle waiting and heavenward gazing. Being prepared for his coming means spreading the gospel, reaching out to those in need, and building the church, his body. As you read 2 Thessalonians, then, see clearly the reality of his return and your responsibility to live for him until that day.

## THE BLUEPRINT

1. The bright hope of Christ's return (1:1—2:17)
2. Living in the light of Christ's return (3:1–18)

Paul wrote to encourage those who were facing persecution and to correct a misunderstanding about the timing of Christ's return. The teaching about the Lord's return promoted idleness in this young church. The imminent coming of Christ should never make us idle; we should be even more busy—living purely, using our time well, and working for his Kingdom. We must work not only during easy times when it is convenient but also during difficult times. Christians must patiently watch for Christ's return and work for him while they wait.

## MEGATHEMES

| THEME | EXPLANATION | IMPORTANCE |
| --- | --- | --- |
| Persecution | Paul encouraged the church to persevere in spite of troubles and trials. God will bring victory to his faithful followers and judge those who persecute them. | God promises to reward our faith by giving us his power and helping us bear persecution. Suffering for our faith will strengthen us to serve Christ. We must be faithful to him. |
| Christ's Return | Since Paul had said that the Lord could come at any moment, some of the Thessalonian believers had stopped working in order to wait for Christ. | Christ will return and bring total victory to all who trust in him. If we are ready, we need not be concerned about *when* he will return. We should stand firm, keep working, and wait for Christ. |
| Great Rebellion | Before Christ's return, there will be a great rebellion against God led by the man of lawlessness (the Antichrist). God will remove all the restraints on evil before he brings judgment on the rebels. The Antichrist will attempt to deceive many. | We should not be afraid when we see evil increase. God is in control, no matter how evil the world becomes. God guards us during Satan's attacks. We can have victory over evil by remaining faithful to God. |
| Persistence | Because church members had quit working and become disorderly and disobedient, Paul chastised them for their idleness. He called on them to show courage and true Christian conduct. | We must never get so tired of doing right that we quit. We can be persistent by making the most of our time and talents. Our endurance will be rewarded. |

## 1. The bright hope of Christ's return
*Greetings from Paul*

**1:1**
1 Thes 1:1

**1** This letter is from Paul, Silas,* and Timothy.

We are writing to the church in Thessalonica, to you who belong to God our Father and the Lord Jesus Christ.

**1:2**
Rom 1:7

²May God our Father* and the Lord Jesus Christ give you grace and peace.

**1:1** Greek *Silvanus*, the Greek form of the name.    **1:2** Some manuscripts read *God the Father*.

**1:1** Paul wrote this letter from Corinth less than a year after he had written 1 Thessalonians. He and his companions, Timothy and Silas, had visited Thessalonica on Paul's second missionary journey (Acts 17:1-10). They established the church there, but Paul had to leave suddenly because of persecution. This prompted him to write his first letter (1 Thessalonians), which contains words of comfort and encouragement. Paul then heard how the Thessalonians had responded to this letter. The good news was that they were continuing to grow in their faith. But the bad news was that false teachings about Christ's return were spreading, leading many to quit their jobs and wait for the end of the world. So Paul wrote to them again. While the purpose of Paul's first letter was to comfort the Thessalonians with the assurance of Christ's second coming, the purpose of his second letter is to correct false teaching about the Second Coming.

**1:1** Paul, Silas, and Timothy were together in Corinth (Acts 18:5).

Paul wrote this letter on behalf of all three of them. Paul often included Timothy as a co-sender of his letters (see Philippians 1:1; Colossians 1:1; 1 Thessalonians 1:1). For more information about Paul, see his Profile in Acts 9, p. 1837. Silas's Profile is in Acts 16, p. 1859, and Timothy's Profile is found in 1 Timothy 2, p. 2059.

**1:1** Thessalonica was the capital and largest city of the Roman province of Macedonia. The most important Roman highway—extending from Rome to the Orient—went through Thessalonica. This highway, along with the city's thriving seaport, made Thessalonica one of the wealthiest and most flourishing trade centers in the Roman Empire. Recognized as a free city, Thessalonica was allowed self-rule and was exempt from most of the restrictions placed by Rome on other cities. Because of this open climate, however, the city had many pagan religions and cultural influences that challenged the Christians' faith.

### Encouragement during Persecution

3Dear brothers and sisters,* we can't help but thank God for you, because your faith is flourishing and your love for one another is growing. 4We proudly tell God's other churches about your endurance and faithfulness in all the persecutions and hardships you are suffering. 5And God will use this persecution to show his justice and to make you worthy of his Kingdom, for which you are suffering. 6In his justice he will pay back those who persecute you.

7And God will provide rest for you who are being persecuted and also for us when the Lord Jesus appears from heaven. He will come with his mighty angels, 8in flaming fire, bringing judgment on those who don't know God and on those who refuse to obey the Good News of our Lord Jesus. 9They will be punished with eternal destruction, forever separated from the Lord and from his glorious power. 10When he comes on that day, he will receive glory from his holy people—praise from all who believe. And this includes you, for you believed what we told you about him.

11So we keep on praying for you, asking our God to enable you to live a life worthy of his call. May he give you the power to accomplish all the good things your faith prompts you to do. 12Then the name of our Lord Jesus will be honored because of the way you live, and you will be honored along with him. This is all made possible because of the grace of our God and Lord, Jesus Christ.*

### Events prior to the Lord's Second Coming

**2** Now, dear brothers and sisters,* let us clarify some things about the coming of our Lord Jesus Christ and how we will be gathered to meet him. 2Don't be so easily shaken or alarmed by those who say that the day of the Lord has already begun. Don't believe them, even if they claim to have had a spiritual vision, a revelation, or a letter supposedly from us.

**1:5** Phil 1:28; 1 Thes 2:12
**1:6** Rev 6:10
**1:7** Matt 25:31; 1 Thes 4:16
**1:8** Ps 79:6; Isa 66:15
**1:9** Isa 2:10, 19, 21; 1 Thes 5:3; 2 Thes 2:8
**1:10** John 17:10; 1 Thes 3:13
**1:12** Isa 66:5; Mal 1:11
**2:1** 1 Thes 4:13-17
**2:2** 2 Thes 2:15; 3:17

**1:3** Greek *Brothers.*   **1:12** Or *of our God and our Lord Jesus Christ.*   **2:1** Greek *brothers;* also in 2:13, 15.

**1:3ff** Regardless of the contents of Paul's letters, his style was affirming. Paul began most of his letters by stating what he most appreciated about his readers and the joy he felt because of their faith in God. We also should look for ways to encourage and build up other believers. For more on encouragement, see the note in 1 Timothy 4:12-16.

**1:4** The keys to surviving persecution and trials are endurance and faithfulness. When faced with crushing troubles, we can have faith that God is using our trials for our good and for his glory. Knowing that God is fair and just will give us patience in our suffering because we know that he has not forgotten us. In God's perfect timing, he will relieve our suffering and punish those who persecute us. Do you trust God's timing? That is the first step toward growing in endurance and faithfulness.

**1:4-6** Paul had been persecuted during his first visit to Thessalonica (Acts 17:5-9). No doubt those who had responded to his message and had become Christians were continuing to be persecuted by both Jews and Gentiles. In Paul's first letter to the Thessalonians, he had said that Christ's return would bring deliverance from persecution for the believers and judgment on the persecutors. But this caused the people to expect Christ's return right away to rescue and vindicate them. So Paul had to point out that while waiting for God's Kingdom, believers could and should grow in their endurance and faithfulness through the hardships they were suffering.

**1:5** As we live for Christ, we will experience troubles because we are trying to be God's people in a perverse world. Some people say that troubles are the result of sin or lack of faith, but Paul teaches that they may be a part of God's plan for believers. Our problems can help us look upward and forward, instead of inward (Mark 13:35, 36; Philippians 3:13, 14), they can build strong character (Romans 5:3, 4), and they can provide us with opportunities to comfort others who also are struggling (2 Corinthians 1:3-5). Your troubles may be an indication that you are taking a stand for Christ. When you do so, you are experiencing the privilege of showing that you are worthy of God's Kingdom (see also 1:11).

**1:7** The "rest" mentioned by Paul has two dimensions. We can rest in knowing that our sufferings are strengthening us, making us ready for Christ's Kingdom. We can also rest in the fact that one day everyone will stand before God. At that time, wrongs will be righted, judgment will be pronounced, and evil will be terminated.

**1:9** The "eternal destruction" that Paul describes is the lake of fire (see Revelation 20:14)—the place of eternal separation from God. Those people who will be separated from God in eternity will no longer have any hope for salvation.

**1:11, 12** As Christians, our calling from God is to become like Christ (Romans 8:29). This is a gradual, lifelong process that will be completed when we see Christ face to face (1 John 3:2). To be "worthy" of this calling means to *want* to do what is right and good (as Christ would). We aren't perfect yet, but we're moving in that direction as God works in us.

**2:1ff** Paul describes the end of the world and Christ's second coming. He says that great suffering and trouble lie ahead, but evil will not prevail because Christ will return to judge all people. Although Paul presents a few signs of the end times, his emphasis, like Jesus' (Mark 13), is the need for each person to prepare for Christ's return by living rightly day by day. If we are ready, we won't have to be concerned about the preceding events or the timing of Christ's return. God controls all events. (See 1 Thessalonians 4 and 5 for Paul's earlier teaching on this subject.)

**2:1, 2** In the Bible, "the day of the Lord" is used in two ways: It can mean the end times (beginning with Christ's birth and continuing until today), and it can mean the final judgment day (in the future). Because some false teachers were saying that judgment day had come, many believers were waiting expectantly for their vindication and for relief from suffering. But judgment day had not yet come; other events would have to happen first.

**2:2** "A spiritual vision, a revelation, or a letter" could refer to the fact that false teaching had come from (1) someone claiming to have had a divine revelation, (2) someone passing on a teaching as though it were from Paul, or (3) someone distributing a letter supposedly written by Paul.

**2:3**
1 Tim 4:1
**2:4**
Isa 14:13-14
1 Cor 8:5

³Don't be fooled by what they say. For that day will not come until there is a great rebellion against God and the man of lawlessness* is revealed—the one who brings destruction.* ⁴He will exalt himself and defy everything that people call god and every object of worship. He will even sit in the temple of God, claiming that he himself is God.

**2:7**
1 Jn 4:3
**2:8**
Job 4:9
Isa 11:4
Rev 19:15

⁵Don't you remember that I told you about all this when I was with you? ⁶And you know what is holding him back, for he can be revealed only when his time comes. ⁷For this lawlessness is already at work secretly, and it will remain secret until the one who is holding it back steps out of the way. ⁸Then the man of lawlessness will be revealed, but the Lord Jesus will kill him with the breath of his mouth and destroy him by the splendor of his coming.

**2:3a** Some manuscripts read *the man of sin.*   **2:3b** Greek *the son of destruction.*

## LOCATION OF THESSALONICA

After Paul visited Thessalonica on his second missionary journey, he went on to Berea, Athens, and Corinth (Acts 17—18). From Corinth, Paul wrote his two letters to the Thessalonian church.

**2:3** Throughout history there have been individuals who epitomized evil and who were hostile to everything Christ stands for (see 1 John 2:18; 4:3; 2 John 1:7). These antichrists have lived in every generation and will continue to work their evil. Then just before Christ's second coming, "the man of lawlessness . . . the one who brings destruction," a completely evil man, will arise. He will be Satan's tool, equipped with Satan's power (2:9). This lawless man will be *the* Antichrist.

It is dangerous, however, to label any person as the Antichrist and to try to predict Christ's coming based on that assumption. Paul mentions a man of lawlessness, not so we might attempt to identify him, but so we might be ready for anything that threatens our faith. If our faith is strong, we don't need to be afraid of what lies ahead, because we know that this lawless man has already been defeated by God, no matter how powerful he becomes or how terrible our situation seems. God is in control, and he will be victorious. Our task is to be prepared for Christ's return and to spread the Good News so that even more people will also be prepared.

**2:3ff** When Paul first wrote to the Thessalonians, they were in danger of losing hope in the Second Coming. Then they shifted to the opposite extreme—some of them thought that Jesus would be coming at any minute and so they stopped being productive for God. Paul tried to restore the balance by describing certain events that would happen before Christ's return.

**2:6, 7** What holds back the lawless one? We do not know for certain. Three possibilities have been suggested: (1) government and law, which help to curb evil; (2) the ministry and activity of the church and the effects of the Good News; or (3) the Holy Spirit. The Bible is not clear on who this restrainer is, only that he will not restrain forever. But we should not fear this time when the restraint is removed—God is far stronger than the man of lawlessness, and God will save his people.

**2:7** "This lawlessness is already at work secretly" means that the work that this Antichrist will do is already going on. *Secretly* means something no one can discover but something God will reveal. *Lawlessness* is the hidden, subtle, underlying force from which all sin springs. Civilization still has a veneer of decency through law enforcement, education, science, and reason. Although we are horrified by criminal acts, we have yet to see the real horror of complete lawlessness. This will happen when "the one who is holding it back steps out of the way." Why will God allow this to happen? To show people and nations their own sinfulness, and to show them by bitter experience the true alternative to the lordship of Christ. People totally without God can act no better than vicious animals. Lawlessness, to a certain extent, is already going on, but the man of lawlessness has not yet been revealed.

⁹This man will come to do the work of Satan with counterfeit power and signs and miracles. ¹⁰He will use every kind of evil deception to fool those on their way to destruction, because they refuse to love and accept the truth that would save them. ¹¹So God will cause them to be greatly deceived, and they will believe these lies. ¹²Then they will be condemned for enjoying evil rather than believing the truth.

### Believers Should Stand Firm

¹³As for us, we can't help but thank God for you, dear brothers and sisters loved by the Lord. We are always thankful that God chose you to be among the first* to experience salvation—a salvation that came through the Spirit who makes you holy and through your belief in the truth. ¹⁴He called you to salvation when we told you the Good News; now you can share in the glory of our Lord Jesus Christ.

¹⁵With all these things in mind, dear brothers and sisters, stand firm and keep a strong grip on the teaching we passed on to you both in person and by letter.

¹⁶Now may our Lord Jesus Christ himself and God our Father, who loved us and by his grace gave us eternal comfort and a wonderful hope, ¹⁷comfort you and strengthen you in every good thing you do and say.

## 2. Living in the light of Christ's return
### Paul's Request for Prayer

**3** Finally, dear brothers and sisters,* we ask you to pray for us. Pray that the Lord's message will spread rapidly and be honored wherever it goes, just as when it came to you. ²Pray, too, that we will be rescued from wicked and evil people, for not everyone is a believer. ³But the Lord is faithful; he will strengthen you and guard you from the evil one.* ⁴And we are confident in the Lord that you are doing and will continue to do the things we commanded you. ⁵May the Lord lead your hearts into a full understanding and expression of the love of God and the patient endurance that comes from Christ.

**2:13** Some manuscripts read *chose you from the very beginning.*   **3:1** Greek *brothers;* also in 3:6, 13.
**3:3** Or *from evil.*

---

**2:9**
Matt 24:24
Rev 13:13
**2:10**
1 Cor 1:18
**2:11**
Rom 1:24, 28
2 Tim 4:4
**2:12**
Rom 1:18, 32; 2:8
**2:13**
Deut 33:12
Eph 1:4
**2:14**
1 Thes 4:7; 5:9
**2:15**
1 Cor 11:2; 16:13
**2:16**
John 3:16
**2:17**
1 Thes 3:2; 5:11

**3:1**
1 Thes 1:8; 5:25
**3:2**
Rom 15:31
**3:3**
1 Cor 1:9
**3:4**
1 Thes 4:10
**3:5**
1 Chr 29:18

---

**2:9** This evil man will use "counterfeit power and signs and miracles" to deceive and draw a following. Miracles from God can help strengthen our faith and lead people to Christ, but all miracles are not necessarily from God. Christ's miracles were significant, not just because of their power, but because of their purpose—to help, to heal, and to point us to God. The man of lawlessness will have power to do amazing things, but his power will be from Satan. He will use this power to destroy and to lead people away from God and toward himself. If any so-called religious personality draws attention only to himself or herself, his or her work is not from God.

**2:10-12** Does God cause people to be deceived? To understand God's allowing such deception, we must first understand God's nature. (1) God himself is good (Psalm 11:7). (2) God created a good world that fell because of humanity's sin (Romans 5:12). (3) Someday God will re-create the world and it will be good again (Revelation 21:1). (4) God is stronger than evil (Matthew 13:41-43; Revelation 19:11-21). (5) God allows evil and thus has control over it. God did not create evil, and he offers help to those who wish to overcome it (Matthew 11:28-30). (6) God uses everything—both good and evil—for his good purposes (Genesis 50:20; Romans 8:28).

The Bible reveals a God who hates all evil and will one day do away with it completely and forever (Revelation 20:10-15). God does not entice anyone to become evil. Those committed to evil, however, may be used by God to sin even more in order to hasten their deserved judgment (see Exodus 11:10). We don't need to understand every detail of how God works in order to have perfect confidence in his absolute power over evil and his total goodness toward us.

**2:13** Paul consistently taught that salvation begins and ends with God. We can do nothing to be saved on our own merit—we must accept God's gift of salvation (see the note on Ephesians 1:4). There is no other way to receive forgiveness from sin. Paul is encouraging the Thessalonian believers by reminding them that they were chosen by God from the beginning. Being made holy is the process of Christian growth through which the Holy Spirit makes us like Christ (Romans 8:29). See the note on 1:11, 12.

**2:14** God worked through Paul and his companions to tell the Good News so that people could share in Christ's glory. It may seem strange that God works through us—fallible, unfaithful, untrustworthy human creatures. But he has given us the fantastic privilege of accomplishing his great mission—telling the world how to find salvation.

**2:15** Paul knew that the Thessalonians would face pressure from persecutions, false teachers, worldliness, and apathy to waver from the truth and to leave the faith. So he urged them to "stand firm" and hold on to the truth they had been taught both through his letters and in person. We also may face persecution, false teachings, worldliness, and apathy. We should hold on to the truth of Christ's teachings because our life depends on it. Never forget the reality of Christ's life and love!

**3:1-3** Beneath the surface of the routine of daily life, a fierce struggle among invisible spiritual powers is being waged. Our main defense is prayer that God will protect us from the evil one and that he will strengthen us. (See also comments on Ephesians 6:10-19 concerning our armor for spiritual warfare.) The following guidelines can help you prepare for and survive satanic attacks: (1) Take the threat of spiritual attack seriously; (2) pray for strength and help from God; (3) study the Bible to recognize Satan's style and tactics; (4) memorize Scripture so it will be a source of help no matter where you are; (5) associate with those who speak the truth; and (6) practice what you are taught by sound spiritual leaders.

## An Exhortation to Proper Living

**3:6**
Rom 16:17
1 Cor 11:2

6And now, dear brothers and sisters, we give you this command in the name of our Lord Jesus Christ: Stay away from all believers* who live idle lives and don't follow the tradition they received* from us. 7For you know that you ought to imitate us. We were not idle when we were with you. 8We never accepted food from anyone without paying for it. We worked hard day and night so we would not be a burden to any of you. 9We certainly had the right to ask you to feed us, but we wanted to give you an example to follow. 10Even while we were with you, we gave you this command: "Those unwilling to work will not get to eat."

**3:8**
Acts 18:3
1 Thes 2:9

**3:9**
Matt 10:10
1 Cor 9:4, 6

11Yet we hear that some of you are living idle lives, refusing to work and meddling in other people's business. 12We command such people and urge them in the name of the Lord Jesus Christ to settle down and work to earn their own living. 13As for the rest of you, dear brothers and sisters, never get tired of doing good.

**3:10**
1 Thes 4:11

**3:11**
1 Tim 5:13

14Take note of those who refuse to obey what we say in this letter. Stay away from them so they will be ashamed. 15Don't think of them as enemies, but warn them as you would a brother or sister.*

**3:12**
1 Thes 4:11

**3:15**
Gal 6:1
1 Thes 5:14

## Paul's Final Greetings

**3:16**
Rom 15:33

16Now may the Lord of peace himself give you his peace at all times and in every situation. The Lord be with you all.

**3:17**
1 Cor 16:21
Gal 6:11
Col 4:18
Phlm 1:19

17HERE IS MY GREETING IN MY OWN HANDWRITING—PAUL. I DO THIS IN ALL MY LETTERS TO PROVE THEY ARE FROM ME.

18May the grace of our Lord Jesus Christ be with you all.

**3:6a** Greek *from every brother.*   **3:6b** Some manuscripts read *you received.*   **3:15** Greek *as a brother.*

---

**3:6-10** Paul was writing here about the person who is lazy. Paul explained that when he and his companions were in Thessalonica, they worked hard, buying what they needed rather than becoming a burden to any of the believers. The rule they followed was, "Those unwilling to work will not get to eat." There's a difference between leisure and laziness. Relaxation and recreation provide a necessary and much needed balance to our lives; when it is time to work, however, Christians should jump right in. We should make the most of our talent and time, doing all we can to provide for ourselves and our dependents. Rest when you should be resting, and work when you should be working.

**3:6-15** Some people in the Thessalonian church were falsely teaching that because Christ would return any day, people should set aside their responsibilities, quit work, do no future planning, and just wait for the Lord. But their lack of activity only led them into sin. They became a burden to the church which was supporting them, they wasted time that could have been used for helping others, and they became meddlers (3:11). These church members may have thought that they were being more spiritual by not working, but Paul tells them to be responsible and get back to work. Being ready for Christ means obeying him in every area of life. Because we know that Christ is coming, we must live in such a way that our faith and our daily practice will please him when he arrives.

**3:11, 12** An idle person who doesn't work ends up filling his or her time with less than helpful activities, like gossip. Rumors and hearsay are tantalizing, exciting to hear, and make us feel like insiders. But they tear people down. If you often find your nose in other people's business, you may be underemployed. Look for a task to do for Christ or for your family, and get to work.

**3:14, 15** Paul counseled the church to stop supporting financially and associating with those who persisted in idleness. Hunger and loneliness can be very effective ways to make the idle person become productive. Paul was not advising coldness or cruelty, but tough love to help a person become responsible.

**3:18** The book of 2 Thessalonians is especially meaningful for those who are being persecuted or are under pressure because of their faith. In chapter 1 we are told what suffering can do for us. In chapter 2 we are assured of final victory. In chapter 3 we are encouraged to continue living responsibly in spite of difficult circumstances. Christ's return is more than a doctrine; it is a promise. It is not just for the future; it has a vital impact on how we live now.

# 1 TIMOTHY

## VITAL STATISTICS

PURPOSE:
To give encouragement and instruction to Timothy, a young leader

AUTHOR:
Paul

ORIGINAL AUDIENCE:
Timothy, Paul's son in the faith

DATE WRITTEN:
Approximately A.D. 64, from Rome or Macedonia (possibly Philippi), probably just prior to Paul's final imprisonment in Rome

SETTING:
Timothy was one of Paul's closest companions. Paul had sent Timothy to the church at Ephesus to counter the false teaching that had arisen there (1:3, 4). Timothy probably served for a time as a leader in the church at Ephesus. Paul hoped to visit Timothy (3:14, 15; 4:13), but in the meantime, he wrote this letter to give Timothy practical advice about the ministry.

KEY VERSE:
"Don't let anyone think less of you because you are young. Be an example to all believers in what you say, in the way you live, in your love, your faith, and your purity" (4:12).

KEY PEOPLE:
Paul, Timothy

KEY PLACE:
Ephesus

SPECIAL FEATURES:
First Timothy is a personal letter and a handbook of church administration and discipline.

WITHOUT trying, we model our values. Parents in particular demonstrate to their children what they consider important and valuable. "Like father, like son" is not just a well-worn cliché; it is a truth repeated in our homes. And experience proves that children often follow the life-styles of their parents, repeating their successes and mistakes.

Timothy is a prime example of one who was influenced by godly relatives. His mother, Eunice, and grandmother, Lois, were Jewish believers who helped shape his life and promote his spiritual growth (2 Timothy 1:5; 3:15). The first "second generation" Christian mentioned in the New Testament, Timothy became Paul's protégé and pastor of the church at Ephesus. As a young minister, Timothy faced all sorts of pressures, conflicts, and challenges from the church and his surrounding culture. To counsel and encourage Timothy, Paul sent this very personal letter.

Paul wrote 1 Timothy in about A.D. 64, probably just prior to his final Roman imprisonment. Because he had appealed to Caesar, Paul had been sent as a prisoner to Rome (see Acts 25—28). Most scholars believe that Paul was released about A.D. 62 (possibly because the "statute of limitations" had expired), and that during the next few years he was able to travel. During this time, he wrote 1 Timothy and Titus. Soon, however, Emperor Nero began his campaign to eliminate Christianity. It is believed that during this time Paul was imprisoned again and eventually executed. During this second Roman imprisonment, Paul wrote 2 Timothy. Titus and the two letters to Timothy comprise what are called the "Pastoral Letters."

Paul's first letter to Timothy affirms their relationship (1:2). Paul begins his fatherly advice, warning Timothy about false teachers (1:3–11) and urging him to hold on to his faith in Christ (1:12–20). Next, Paul considers public worship, emphasizing the importance of prayer (2:1–7) and order in church meetings (2:8–15). This leads to a discussion of the qualifications of church leaders—elders and deacons. Here Paul lists specific criteria for each office (3:1–16).

Paul speaks again about false teachers, telling Timothy how to recognize them and respond to them (4:1–16). Next, he gives practical advice on pastoral care to the young and old (5:1, 2), widows (5:3–16), elders (5:17–25), and slaves (6:1, 2). Paul concludes by exhorting Timothy to guard his motives (6:3–10), to stand firm in his faith (6:11, 12), to live above reproach (6:13–16), and to minister faithfully (6:17–21).

First Timothy holds many lessons. If you are a church leader, take note of Paul's relationship with this young disciple—his careful counsel and guidance. Measure yourself against the qualifications that Paul gives for elders and deacons. If you are young in the faith, follow the example of godly Christian leaders like Timothy, who imitated Paul's life. If you are a parent, remind yourself of the profound effect a Christian home can have on family members. A faithful mother and grandmother led Timothy to Christ, and Timothy's ministry helped change the world.

## THE BLUEPRINT

1. Instructions on right belief
   (1:1–20)
2. Instructions for the church
   (2:1–3:16)
3. Instructions for elders
   (4:1–6:21)

Paul advised Timothy on such practical topics as qualifications for church leaders, public worship, confronting false teaching, and how to treat various groups of people within the church. Right belief and right behavior are critical for anyone who desires to lead or serve effectively in the church. We should all believe rightly, participate in church actively, and minister to one another lovingly.

## MEGATHEMES

| THEME | EXPLANATION | IMPORTANCE |
|---|---|---|
| Sound Doctrine | Paul instructed Timothy to preserve the Christian faith by teaching sound doctrine and modeling right living. Timothy had to oppose false teachers, who were leading church members away from belief in salvation by faith in Jesus Christ alone. | We must know the truth in order to defend it. We must cling to the belief that Christ came to save us. We should stay away from those who twist the words of the Bible for their own purposes. |
| Public Worship | Prayer in public worship must be done with a proper attitude toward God and fellow believers. | Christian character must be evident in every aspect of worship. We must rid ourselves of any anger, resentment, or offensive behavior that might disrupt worship or damage church unity. |
| Church Leadership | Paul gives specific instructions concerning the qualifications for church leaders so that the church might honor God and operate smoothly. | Church leaders must be wholly committed to Christ. If you are a new or young Christian, don't be anxious to become a leader in the church. Seek to develop your Christian character first. Be sure to seek God, not your own ambition. |
| Personal Discipline | It takes discipline to be a leader in the church. Timothy, like all pastors, had to guard his motives, minister faithfully, and live above reproach. Any pastor must keep morally and spiritually fit. | To stay in good spiritual shape, you must discipline yourself to study God's Word and to obey it. Put your spiritual abilities to work! |
| Caring Church | The church has a responsibility to care for the needs of all its members, especially the sick, the poor, and the widowed. Caring must go beyond good intentions. | Caring for the family of believers demonstrates our Christlike attitude and exhibits genuine love to non-believers. |

## 1. Instructions on right belief

*Greetings from Paul*

**1:1**
Col 1:27
Titus 1:3; 3:4

**1** This letter is from Paul, an apostle of Christ Jesus, appointed by the command of God our Savior and Christ Jesus, who gives us hope.

**1:2**
Acts 16:1
2 Tim 1:2
Titus 1:4

²I am writing to Timothy, my true son in the faith.

May God the Father and Christ Jesus our Lord give you grace, mercy, and peace.

---

**1:1** This letter was written to Timothy in A.D. 64 or 65, after Paul's first imprisonment in Rome (Acts 28:16-31). Apparently Paul had been out of prison for several years, and during that time he had revisited many churches in Asia and Macedonia. When he and Timothy returned to Ephesus, they found widespread false teaching in the church. Paul had warned the Ephesian elders to be on guard against the false teachers who inevitably would come after he had left (Acts 20:17-31). Paul sent Timothy to lead the Ephesian church while he moved on to Macedonia. From there Paul wrote this letter of encouragement and instruction to help Timothy deal with the difficult situation in the Ephesian church.

Later, Paul was arrested again and brought back to a Roman prison.

**1:1** Paul calls himself an *apostle*, meaning "one who is sent." Paul was sent by Jesus Christ to bring the message of salvation to the Gentiles (Acts 9:1-20). He was an apostle "by the command of God" because in Acts 13:2, the Holy Spirit, through the prophets, said, "Dedicate Barnabas and Saul [Paul] for the special work to which I have called them." From Romans 16:25, 26 and Titus 1:3, it is obvious that Paul regarded his commission as direct from God. For more information on Paul, see his Profile in Acts 9, p. 1837.

## Warnings against False Teachings

3 When I left for Macedonia, I urged you to stay there in Ephesus and stop those whose teaching is contrary to the truth. 4 Don't let them waste their time in endless discussion of myths and spiritual pedigrees. These things only lead to meaningless speculations,* which don't help people live a life of faith in God.*

5 The purpose of my instruction is that all believers would be filled with love that comes from a pure heart, a clear conscience, and genuine faith. 6 But some people have missed this whole point. They have turned away from these things and spend their time in meaningless discussions. 7 They want to be known as teachers of the law of Moses, but they don't know what they are talking about, even though they speak so confidently.

8 We know that the law is good when used correctly. 9 For the law was not intended for people who do what is right. It is for people who are lawless and rebellious, who are ungodly and sinful, who consider nothing sacred and defile what is holy, who kill their father or mother or commit other murders. 10 The law is for people who are sexually immoral, or who practice homosexuality, or are slave traders,* liars, promise breakers, or who do anything else that contradicts the wholesome teaching 11 that comes from the glorious Good News entrusted to me by our blessed God.

## Paul's Gratitude for God's Mercy

12 I thank Christ Jesus our Lord, who has given me strength to do his work. He considered me trustworthy and appointed me to serve him, 13 even though I used to blaspheme the name of Christ. In my insolence, I persecuted his people. But God had mercy on me because I did it in ignorance and unbelief. 14 Oh, how generous and gracious our Lord was! He filled me with the faith and love that come from Christ Jesus.

**1:4a** Greek *in myths and endless genealogies, which cause speculation.*   **1:4b** Greek *a stewardship of God in faith.*   **1:10** Or *kidnappers.*

**1:3**
Acts 20:1
Gal 1:6-7
1 Tim 6:3

**1:4**
1 Tim 4:7
Titus 3:9

**1:5**
Rom 13:10
Gal 5:14
2 Tim 1:5

**1:6**
2 Tim 2:23
Titus 1:10

**1:9**
Gal 3:19; 5:23

**1:10**
1 Tim 6:3
2 Tim 4:3
Titus 1:9; 2:1

**1:11**
Gal 2:7

**1:12**
Acts 9:15
Gal 1:15-16
Phil 4:13

**1:13**
Acts 8:3; 26:9
1 Cor 15:9

**1:14**
Rom 5:20
2 Tim 1:13

---

**1:3, 4** Paul first visited Ephesus on his second missionary journey (Acts 18:19-21). Later, on his third missionary journey, he stayed there for almost three years (Acts 19–20). Ephesus, along with Rome, Corinth, Antioch, and Alexandria, was one of the major cities in the Roman Empire. It was a center for the commerce, politics, and religions of Asia Minor, and the location of the temple dedicated to the goddess Artemis (Diana).

**1:3, 4** The church at Ephesus may have been plagued by the same heresy that was threatening the church at Colosse—the teaching that to be acceptable to God, a person had to discover certain hidden knowledge and had to worship angels (Colossians 2:8, 18). The false teachers were motivated by their own interests rather than Christ's. They embroiled the church in endless and irrelevant questions and controversies, taking precious time away from the study of the truth. Stay away from religious speculation and pointless theological arguments. Such exercises may seem harmless at first, but they have a way of sidetracking us from the central message of the Good News—the person and work of Jesus Christ. They expend time we should use to share the Good News with others, and they don't help people grow in the faith. Avoid anything that keeps you from doing God's work.

**1:3-7** Many leaders and authorities today demand allegiance, some of whom would even have us turn from Christ to follow them. When they seem to know the Bible, their influence can be dangerously subtle. They are modern-day false teachers. How can you recognize false teachers? (1) They teach what is contrary to the truth found in Scripture (1:3; 1:6, 7; 4:1-3). (2) They promote trivial and divisive controversies instead of helping people come to Jesus (1:4). (3) They aren't concerned about personal evidence of God's presence in their lives, spending their time on "meaningless discussions" instead (1:6). (4) Their motivation is to make a name for themselves (1:7). To protect yourself from the deception of false teachers, learn what the Bible teaches and remain steadfast in your faith in Christ alone.

**1:6** Arguing about details of the Bible can send us off on interesting but irrelevant tangents and cause us to miss the intent of God's message. The false teachers at Ephesus constructed vast speculative systems and then argued about the minor

details of their wholly imaginary ideas. We should allow nothing to distract us from the Good News of salvation in Jesus Christ, the main point of Scripture. We should know what the Bible says, apply it to our lives daily, and teach it to others. When we do this, we will be able to evaluate all teachings in light of the central truth about Jesus.

**1:7-11** The false teachers wanted to become famous as teachers of God's law, but they didn't even understand the law's purpose. The law was not meant to give believers a list of commands for every occasion but to show unbelievers their sin and bring them to God. For more of what Paul taught about our relationship to law, see Romans 5:20, 21; 13:9, 10; Galatians 3:24-29.

**1:10** Some attempt to legitimize homosexuality as an acceptable alternative lifestyle. Even some Christians say people have a right to choose their sexual preference. But the entire Bible (both in the Old and New Testaments) calls homosexual behavior sin (see Leviticus 18:22; Romans 1:18-32; 1 Corinthians 6:9-11). We must be careful, however, to condemn only the practice and not the people. People who live this lifestyle can be forgiven, and their lives can be transformed. The church should be a haven of forgiveness and healing for repentant homosexuals without compromising its stance against homosexual behavior. For more on this subject see the notes on Romans 1:26, 27.

**1:12-17** People can feel so guilt-ridden by their past that they think God could never forgive and accept them. But consider Paul's past. He had scoffed at the teachings of Jesus and had hunted down and murdered God's people before coming to faith in Christ (Acts 9:1-9). God forgave Paul and used him mightily for his Kingdom. No matter how shameful your past, God also can forgive and use you.

**1:14** Paul's boldness in Christ can be intimidating. We may feel that our faith in God and our love for Christ and for others will always be inadequate. We will experience times of failure. But we can remain confident that Christ will help our faith and love grow as our relationship with him deepens. Paul's prayer for the Philippians applies to us also: "I am certain that God, who began the good work within you, will continue his work until it is finally finished on the day when Christ Jesus returns" (Philippians 1:6).

**1:15**
Luke 15:2; 19:10
Rom 5:8

15This is a trustworthy saying, and everyone should accept it: "Christ Jesus came into the world to save sinners"—and I am the worst of them all. 16But God had mercy on me so that Christ Jesus could use me as a prime example of his great patience with even the worst sinners. Then others will realize that they, too, can believe in him and receive eternal life. 17All honor and glory to God forever and ever! He is the eternal King, the unseen one who never dies; he alone is God. Amen.

**1:17**
Rom 16:27
1 Tim 6:15

### Timothy's Responsibility

**1:18**
1 Tim 6:12

18Timothy, my son, here are my instructions for you, based on the prophetic words spoken about you earlier. May they help you fight well in the Lord's battles. 19Cling to your faith in Christ, and keep your conscience clear. For some people have deliberately violated their consciences; as a result, their faith has been shipwrecked. 20Hymenaeus and Alexander are two examples. I threw them out and handed them over to Satan so they might learn not to blaspheme God.

**1:19**
2 Tim 4:7

**1:20**
1 Cor 5:5
2 Tim 2:17; 4:14

## 2. Instructions for the church
### Instructions about Worship

**2:2**
Rom 13:1

**2:4**
1 Tim 4:10
2 Tim 2:25

**2** I urge you, first of all, to pray for all people. Ask God to help them; intercede on their behalf, and give thanks for them. 2Pray this way for kings and all who are in authority so that we can live peaceful and quiet lives marked by godliness and dignity. 3This is good and pleases God our Savior, 4who wants everyone to be saved and to understand the truth.

---

**1:15** Here Paul summarizes the Good News: Jesus came into the world to save sinners, and no sinner is beyond his saving power. (See Luke 5:32 for Jesus' purpose for being on earth.) Jesus didn't come merely to show us how to live better lives or challenge us to be better people. He came to offer us salvation that leads to eternal life. Have you accepted his offer?

**1:15** Paul was not nearly as interested in creating an image as he was in being an example. He did not hesitate to share his past, because he knew his failures would allow others to have hope. At times we hesitate to share our past struggles with others because we are afraid it will tarnish our image. Paul demonstrated that lowering our guard can be an important step in communicating the gospel. People will not believe the gospel is important if they can't see that it is crucial in your life. How has Christ shown patience with you? Did he stay with you when you doubted and rebelled? Did he remain faithful when you ignored his prior claim on your life? Did he love you when you disregarded his Word and his church? Remember that his patience is unlimited for those who love him. Don't be afraid to let others know what Christ has done for you.

**1:18** Paul highly valued the gift of prophecy (1 Corinthians 14:1). Through prophecy important messages of warning and encouragement came to the church. Just as pastors are ordained and set apart for ministry in church today, Timothy had been set apart for ministry when elders laid their hands on him (see 4:14). Apparently at this ceremony, several believers had prophesied about Timothy's gifts and strengths. These words from the Lord must have encouraged Timothy throughout his ministry.

**1:19** How can you keep your conscience clear? Treasure your faith in Christ more than anything else and do what you know is right. Each time you deliberately ignore your conscience, you are hardening your heart. Over a period of time your capacity to tell right from wrong will diminish. As you walk with God, he will speak to you through your conscience, letting you know the difference between right and wrong. Be sure to act on those inner tugs so that you do what is right—then your conscience will remain clear.

**1:20** We don't know who Alexander was—he may have been an associate of Hymenaeus. Hymenaeus's error is explained in 2 Timothy 2:17, 18. He weakened people's faith by teaching that the resurrection had already occurred. Paul says that he handed both of these men over to Satan, meaning that Paul had removed them from the fellowship of the church. Paul did this so that they would see their error and repent. The ultimate purpose of this punishment was correction. The church today is too often lax in disciplining Christians who deliberately sin. Deliberate disobedience should be responded to quickly and sternly to prevent the entire congregation from being affected. But discipline must be done in a way that tries to bring the offender back to Christ and into the loving embrace of the church. The definition of discipline includes these words: strengthening, purifying, training, correcting, perfecting. Condemnation, suspicion, withholding of forgiveness, or permanent exile should not be a part of church discipline.

**2:1-4** Although God is all-powerful and all-knowing, he has chosen to let us help him change the world through our prayers. How this works is a mystery to us because of our limited understanding, but it is a reality. Paul based his instruction about prayer for *everyone* on his conviction that God's invitation for salvation extends equally to all people. The word *everyone* captures the nature of the gospel. The world that God loves includes every person (John 3:16). He loves us as individuals whom he knows intimately (Psalm 139:13-18). Paul urges us to pray for "all people." Our earnest prayers will have powerful results (James 5:16).

**2:2** We should pray for those in authority around the world so that their societies will be conducive to the spread of the Good News. Paul's command to pray for kings is remarkable considering that Nero, a notoriously cruel ruler, was emperor at this time (A.D. 54–68). When Paul wrote this letter, persecution was a growing threat to believers. Later, when Nero needed a scapegoat for the great fire that destroyed much of Rome in A.D. 64, he blamed the Roman Christians so as to take the focus off himself. Then persecution erupted throughout the Roman Empire. Not only were Christians denied certain privileges in society, some were even publicly butchered, burned, or fed to animals.

**2:4** Both Peter and Paul said that God wants everyone to be saved (see 2 Peter 3:9). This does not mean that all *will* be saved, because the Bible makes it clear that many reject Christ (Matthew 25:31-46; John 12:44-50; Hebrews 10:26-29). The Good News has a universal scope; it is not directed only to people of one race, one sex, or one national background. God loves the whole world and sent his Son to save sinners. No one is outside God's mercy or beyond the reach of his offer of salvation.

⁵For there is only one God and one Mediator who can reconcile God and humanity—the man Christ Jesus. ⁶He gave his life to purchase freedom for everyone. This is the message God gave to the world at just the right time. ⁷And I have been chosen as a preacher and apostle to teach the Gentiles this message about faith and truth. I'm not exaggerating—just telling the truth.

⁸In every place of worship, I want men to pray with holy hands lifted up to God, free from anger and controversy.

⁹And I want women to be modest in their appearance.* They should wear decent and appropriate clothing and not draw attention to themselves by the way they fix their hair or by wearing gold or pearls or expensive clothes. ¹⁰For women who claim to be devoted to God should make themselves attractive by the good things they do.

¹¹Women should learn quietly and submissively. ¹²I do not let women teach men or have authority over them.* Let them listen quietly. ¹³For God made Adam first, and afterward he made Eve. ¹⁴And it was not Adam who was deceived by Satan. The woman was deceived, and sin was the result. ¹⁵But women will be saved through childbearing,* assuming they continue to live in faith, love, holiness, and modesty.

2:9 Or to pray in modest apparel.   2:12 Or teach men or usurp their authority.   2:15 Or will be saved by accepting their role as mothers, or will be saved by the birth of the Child.

**2:5**
Rom 3:29-30
**2:6**
Gal 1:4; 2:20
**2:7**
Acts 9:15
2 Tim 1:1
**2:8**
Pss 24:4; 63:4
**2:9**
1 Pet 3:3-5

**2:11**
1 Cor 14:34
**2:12**
Eph 5:22
**2:13**
Gen 1:27; 2:7, 22
**2:14**
Gen 3:1-6, 13

---

**2:5, 6** Though some people think there are many ways to God, in practice, each person must choose a single way. We can stand on one side of a gorge and discuss the possibility of many bridges across the abyss, but if we are determined to cross, we will have to commit to one bridge. Those who insist that there are many bridges to God usually fit one of the following categories: (1) They have not personally committed to any "bridge." They are surprised that their belief in multiple ways does not exempt them from having to choose one. (2) Their belief in "many ways to God" hides their true belief that finding God doesn't really matter at all. (3) They are convinced that arguing for "many ways to God" will insure that they won't be wrong. If there is only one way, their generalized belief will presumably have included it. (4) They have decided that believing in "many ways to God" requires less work than going to the trouble of actually considering the claims of various religious systems.

The facts remain: We human beings are separated from God by sin and we need a Savior—a way across the abyss of sin and back to God. Only one person in the universe is our Mediator and can stand between us and God and bring us together again—Jesus, who is both God and man. Jesus' sacrifice brought new life to all people. Have you let him bridge the gap between you and God?

**2:7** Paul describes himself as a preacher and apostle. He was given the special privilege of announcing the Good News to the Gentiles. He gives his credentials as an apostle in 1 Corinthians 15:7-11.

**2:8** Besides displeasing God, anger and controversy make prayer difficult. That is why Jesus said that we should interrupt our prayers, if necessary, to make peace with others (Matthew 5:23, 24). God wants us to obey him immediately and thoroughly. Our goal should be to have a right relationship with God and also with others.

**2:9, 10** It is not unscriptural for a woman to want to be attractive. Today, however, to what degree should women take this advice about fixing their hair or wearing gold, pearls, or expensive clothes? Paul was not prohibiting these things; he was simply saying that women should not be drawing attention to themselves through these things. Modesty and decency are the key words. All women would do well to remember that beauty begins on the inside. A gentle, modest, loving character gives a light to the face that cannot be duplicated by even the best cosmetics. A carefully groomed and well-decorated exterior is artificial and cold unless inner beauty is present. The general rule for both women and men emphasizes that both behavior and dress must express submission to and respect for Jesus Christ.

**2:9-15** To understand these verses, we must understand the situation in which Paul and Timothy worked. In first-century Jewish culture, women were not allowed to study. When Paul said that

women should "learn quietly and submissively," he was offering them an amazing new opportunity to learn God's Word. That they were to listen and learn quietly and submissively referred to an attitude of quietness and composure (not total silence). In addition, Paul himself acknowledges that women publicly prayed and prophesied (1 Corinthians 11:5). Apparently, however, the women in the Ephesian church were abusing their newly acquired Christian freedom. Because these women were new converts, they did not yet have the necessary experience, knowledge, or Christian maturity to teach those who already had extensive scriptural education.

**2:12** Some interpret this passage to mean that women should never teach in the assembled church; however, commentators point out that Paul did not forbid women from ever teaching. Paul's commended co-worker, Priscilla, taught Apollos, the great preacher (Acts 18:24-26). Paul frequently mentioned other women who held positions of responsibility in the church. Phoebe worked in the church (Romans 16:1). Mary, Tryphena, Tryphosa and Persis were the Lord's workers (Romans 16:6, 12), as were Euodia and Syntyche (Philippians 4:2). Paul was very likely prohibiting the Ephesian women, not all women, from teaching (see the note on 2:9-15).

Paul did not want the Ephesian women to teach because they didn't yet have enough knowledge or experience. The Ephesian church had a particular problem with false teachers. Evidently the women were especially susceptible to the false teachings (2 Timothy 3:1-9) because they did not yet have enough biblical knowledge to discern the truth. In addition, some of the women were apparently flaunting their newfound Christian freedom by wearing inappropriate clothing (2:9). Paul was telling Timothy not to put anyone (in this case, women) into a position of leadership who was not yet mature in the faith (see 3:6; 5:22). The same principle applies to churches today (see the note on 3:6).

**2:13, 14** In previous letters Paul had discussed male/female roles in marriage (Ephesians 5:21-33; Colossians 3:18, 19). Here he talks about male/female roles within the church. Some scholars see these verses about Adam and Eve as an illustration of what was happening in the Ephesian church. Just as Eve had been deceived in the Garden of Eden, so the women in the church were being deceived by false teachers. And just as Adam was the first human created by God, so the men in the church in Ephesus should be the first to speak and teach, because they had more training. This view, then, stresses that Paul's teaching here is not universal but applies to churches with similar problems. Other scholars, however, contend that the roles Paul points out are God's design for his created order—God established these roles to maintain harmony in both the family and the church.

**2:14** Paul is not excusing Adam for his part in the Fall (Genesis 3:6, 7, 17-19). On the contrary, in his letter to the Romans Paul

TIMOTHY

Painful lessons are usually doorways to new opportunities. Even the apostle Paul had much to learn. Shortly after his disappointing experience with John Mark, Paul recruited another eager young man, Timothy, to be his assistant. Paul's intense personality may have been too much for John Mark to handle. It could easily have created the same problem for Timothy. But Paul seems to have learned a lesson in patience from his old friend Barnabas. As a result, Timothy became a "son" to Paul.

Timothy probably became a Christian after Paul's first missionary visit to Lystra (Acts 16:1-5). Timothy already had solid Jewish training in the Scriptures from his mother and grandmother. By Paul's second visit, Timothy had grown into a respected disciple of Jesus. He did not hesitate to join Paul and Silas on their journey. His willingness to be circumcised as an adult is clearly a mark of his commitment. (Timothy's mixed Greek/Jewish background could have created problems on their missionary journeys, because many of their audiences would be made up of Jews who were concerned about the strict keeping of this tradition. Timothy's submission to the rite of circumcision helped to avoid that potential problem.)

Beyond the tensions created by his mixed racial background, Timothy seemed to struggle with a naturally timid character and a sensitivity to his youthfulness. Unfortunately, many who share Timothy's character traits are quickly written off as too great a risk to deserve much responsibility. By God's grace, Paul saw great potential in Timothy. Paul demonstrated his confidence in Timothy by entrusting him with important responsibilities. Paul sent Timothy as his personal representative to Corinth during a particularly tense time (1 Corinthians 4:14-17). Although Timothy was apparently ineffective in that difficult mission, Paul did not give up on him. Timothy continued to travel with Paul.

Our last pictures of Timothy come from the most personal letters in the New Testament: 1 and 2 Timothy. The aging apostle Paul was near the end of his life, but his burning desire to continue his mission had not dimmed. Paul was writing to one of his closest friends—they had traveled, suffered, cried, and laughed together. They shared the intense joy of seeing people respond to the Good News and the agonies of seeing the gospel rejected and distorted. Paul left Timothy in Ephesus to oversee the young church there (1 Timothy 1:3-4). He wrote to encourage Timothy and give him needed direction. These letters have provided comfort and help to countless other "Timothys" through the years. When you face a challenge that seems beyond your abilities, read 1 and 2 Timothy, and remember that others have shared your experience.

| | |
|---|---|
| **Strengths and accomplishments** | • Became a believer during Paul's first missionary journey and joined him for his other two journeys<br>• Was a respected Christian in his hometown<br>• Was Paul's special representative on several occasions<br>• Received two personal letters from Paul<br>• Probably knew Paul better than any other person, becoming like a son to Paul |
| **Weaknesses and mistakes** | • Struggled with a timid and reserved nature<br>• Allowed others to look down on his youthfulness<br>• Was apparently unable to correct some of the problems in the church at Corinth when Paul sent him there |
| **Lessons from his life** | • Youthfulness should not be an excuse for ineffectiveness<br>• Our inadequacies and inabilities should not keep us from being available to God |
| **Vital statistics** | • Where: Lystra<br>• Occupations: Missionary, pastor<br>• Relatives: Mother: Eunice. Grandmother: Lois. Father: a Greek.<br>• Contemporaries: Paul, Silas, Luke, Mark, Peter, Barnabas |
| **Key verses** | "I have no one else like Timothy, who genuinely cares about your welfare. All the others care only for themselves and not for what matters to Jesus Christ. But you know how Timothy has proved himself. Like a son with his father, he has served with me in preaching the Good News" (Philippians 2:20-22). |

Timothy's story is told in Acts, starting in chapter 16. He is also mentioned in Romans 16:21; 1 Corinthians 4:17; 16:10-11; 2 Corinthians 1:1, 19; Philippians 1:1; 2:19-23; Colossians 1:1; 1 Thessalonians 1:1-10; 2:3-4; 3:2-6; 1 and 2 Timothy; Philemon; Hebrews 13:23.

---

places the primary blame for humanity's sinful nature on Adam (Romans 5:12-21).

**2:15** The phrase "saved through childbearing" can be understood several ways: (1) Man sinned, so men were condemned to painful labor. Woman sinned, so women were condemned to pain in childbearing. Both men and women, however, can be saved through trusting Christ and obeying him. (2) Women who fulfill their God-given roles are demonstrating true commitment and

obedience to Christ. One of the most important roles for a wife and mother is to care for her family. (3) The childbearing mentioned here refers to the birth of Jesus Christ. Women (and men) are saved spiritually because of the most important birth, that of Christ himself. (4) From the lessons learned through the trials of childbearing, women can develop qualities that teach them about love, trust, submission, and service.

## Leaders in the Church

**3** This is a trustworthy saying: "If someone aspires to be an elder,* he desires an honorable position." ²So an elder must be a man whose life is above reproach. He must be faithful to his wife.* He must exercise self-control, live wisely, and have a good reputation. He must enjoy having guests in his home, and he must be able to teach. ³He must not be a heavy drinker* or be violent. He must be gentle, not quarrelsome, and not love money. ⁴He must manage his own family well, having children who respect and obey him. ⁵For if a man cannot manage his own household, how can he take care of God's church?

⁶An elder must not be a new believer, because he might become proud, and the devil would cause him to fall.* ⁷Also, people outside the church must speak well of him so that he will not be disgraced and fall into the devil's trap.

⁸In the same way, deacons must be well respected and have integrity. They must not be heavy drinkers or dishonest with money. ⁹They must be committed to the mystery of the faith now revealed and must live with a clear conscience. ¹⁰Before they are appointed as deacons, let them be closely examined. If they pass the test, then let them serve as deacons.

¹¹In the same way, their wives* must be respected and must not slander others. They must exercise self-control and be faithful in everything they do.

¹²A deacon must be faithful to his wife, and he must manage his children and household well. ¹³Those who do well as deacons will be rewarded with respect from others and will have increased confidence in their faith in Christ Jesus.

**3:1**
Acts 20:28
**3:2-7**
Titus 1:6-9

**3:7**
2 Cor 8:21
2 Tim 2:26

**3:9**
1 Tim 1:19

---

**3:1** Or *an overseer,* or *a bishop;* also in 3:2, 6.  **3:2** Or *must have only one wife,* or *must be married only once;* Greek reads *must be the husband of one wife;* also in 3:12.  **3:3** Greek *must not drink too much wine;* similarly in 3:8. **3:6** Or *he might fall into the same judgment as the devil.*  **3:11** Or *the women deacons.* The Greek word can be translated *women* or *wives.*

---

**3:1** To be a church leader ("elder") is a heavy responsibility because the church belongs to the living God. The word *elder* can refer to a pastor, church leader, or presiding overseer. It is good to want to be a spiritual leader, but the standards are high. Paul enumerates some of the qualifications here. Church leaders should not be elected because they are popular, nor should they be allowed to push their way to the top. Instead, they should be chosen by the church because of their respect for the truth, both in what they believe and in how they live. Do you hold a position of spiritual leadership, or would you like to be a leader someday? Check yourself against Paul's standard of excellence. Those with great responsibility must meet high expectations.

**3:1-13** All believers, even if they never plan to be church leaders, should strive to follow these guidelines because they are consistent with what God says is true and right. For example, some people are effectively "able to teach" who never teach or lead formally at church. Their lessons are passed on to one or two others. They become mentors of spiritual truth. Paul described this intimate kind of teaching in 2 Timothy 2:2, "You have heard me teach things that have been confirmed by many reliable witnesses. Now teach these truths to other trustworthy people who are able to pass them on to others." More is learned through living than through lectures. If you have been able to communicate your faith clearly to another person, you have demonstrated teaching at its best. In measuring your ability to teach, don't consider how many students you have had; instead, ask how much truth you have passed on to even one student whom God has brought your way.

**3:2** Paul's statement that each elder should be faithful to his wife prohibits both polygamy and promiscuity. This does not prohibit an unmarried person from becoming an elder or a widowed elder from remarrying.

**3:4, 5** Christian workers and volunteers sometimes make the mistake of being so involved in their work that they neglect their families, and especially the firm discipline of their children. Spiritual leadership, however, must begin at home. If a man is not willing to care for, discipline, and teach his children, he is not qualified to lead the church. Don't allow your volunteer activities to detract from your family responsibilities.

**3:6** New believers should become secure and strong in the faith before taking leadership roles in the church. Too often, in a church desperate for workers, new believers are placed in positions of responsibility prematurely. New faith needs time to mature. New believers should have a place of service, but they should not be put into leadership positions until they are firmly grounded in their faith, with a solid Christian lifestyle and a knowledge of the Word of God.

**3:6** Younger believers who are selected for office need to beware of the damaging effects of pride. Pride can seduce emotions and cloud reason. It can make those who are immature susceptible to the influence of unscrupulous people. Pride and conceit were the devil's downfall, and he uses pride to trap others.

**3:7** People outside the church should speak well of those who would lead in the church. The good reputation with outsiders that Paul required is realized when Christians act as dependable friends and good neighbors. How we carry out our duties as citizens, neighbors, and friends facilitates or frustrates our ability to communicate the gospel. Do you have friends who are not believers? Does your conduct help or hinder the cause of Christ? As the church carries out its mission in an increasingly secular world, the church needs those who build bridges with unbelievers in order to bring them the gospel.

**3:8-13** *Deacon* means "one who serves." This position was possibly begun by the apostles in the Jerusalem church (Acts 6:1-6) to care for the physical needs of the congregation—at that time, the needs of the Greek-speaking widows. Deacons were leaders in the church, and their qualifications resemble those of the elders. In some churches today, the office of deacon has lost its importance. New Christians are often asked to serve in this position, but that is not the New Testament pattern. Paul says that potential deacons should have high qualifications and be very carefully chosen.

**3:11** "Wives" can refer to women helpers or deaconesses. It could also mean wives of deacons or female leaders of the church (such as Phoebe, the deaconess mentioned in Romans 16:1). In either case, Paul expected the behavior of prominent women in the church to be just as responsible and blameless as that of prominent men.

## The Truths of Our Faith

**3:15**
Matt 16:16-18
Eph 2:19-21

14I am writing these things to you now, even though I hope to be with you soon, 15so that if I am delayed, you will know how people must conduct themselves in the household of God. This is the church of the living God, which is the pillar and foundation of the truth.

**3:16**
Isa 7:14
Matt 4:11
John 1:14
Rom 1:3-4
Acts 1:9
1 Jn 4:2-3; 5:6

16Without question, this is the great mystery of our faith*:

> Christ* was revealed in a human body
>    and vindicated by the Spirit.*
> He was seen by angels
>    and announced to the nations.
> He was believed in throughout the world
>    and taken to heaven in glory.

## 3. Instructions for elders

### Warnings against False Teachers

**4:1**
John 16:13
2 Tim 3:1
2 Pet 3:3

**4** Now the Holy Spirit tells us clearly that in the last times some will turn away from the true faith; they will follow deceptive spirits and teachings that come from demons.

**4:2**
Eph 4:19

2These people are hypocrites and liars, and their consciences are dead.*

**4:3**
Gen 9:3
Rom 14:6
1 Cor 10:30-31

3They will say it is wrong to be married and wrong to eat certain foods. But God created those foods to be eaten with thanks by faithful people who know the truth. 4Since everything God created is good, we should not reject any of it but receive it with thanks. 5For we know it is made acceptable* by the word of God and prayer.

**4:4**
Gen 1:31
Acts 10:15

### A Good Servant of Christ Jesus

**4:6**
2 Tim 3:15

6If you explain these things to the brothers and sisters,* Timothy, you will be a worthy servant of Christ Jesus, one who is nourished by the message of faith and the good teaching you

**3:16a** Or of godliness. **3:16b** Greek He who; other manuscripts read God. **3:16c** Or in his spirit. **4:2** Greek are seared. **4:5** Or made holy. **4:6** Greek brothers.

---

**3:14, 15** The Bible is the written form of what God expects us to know and do. God chose Paul to carry out one phase of the plan. Through Paul, the inspired teaching was written down. As such, it was passed on to Timothy. Then, it was passed on to others. Later, it was passed on to us. Times have changed, but the original authority remains. Because the Bible is from God, it must be studied seriously, understood thoroughly, and applied faithfully. Paul intended this letter to teach believers how to conduct themselves. We would do well to read carefully.

**3:16** In this short hymn, Paul affirms the humanity and divinity of Christ. By so doing he reveals the heart of the Good News, "the great mystery of our faith" (the secret of how we become godly). "Revealed in a human body"—Jesus was a man; Jesus' incarnation is the basis of our being right with God. "Vindicated by the Spirit"—Jesus' resurrection showed that the Holy Spirit's power was in him (Romans 8:11). "Seen by angels" and "taken to heaven"—Jesus is divine. We can't please God on our own; we must depend on Christ. As a man, Jesus lived a perfect life, and so he is a perfect example of how to live. As God, Jesus gives us the power to do what is right. It is possible to live a godly life—through following Christ.

**4:1** The "last times" began with Christ's resurrection and will continue until his return when he will set up his Kingdom and judge all humanity.

**4:1, 2** False teachers were and still are a threat to the church. Jesus and the apostles repeatedly warned against them (see, for example, Mark 13:21-23; Acts 20:28-31; 2 Thessalonians 2:1-12; 2 Peter 3:3-7). It is not enough that a teacher appears to know what he is talking about, is disciplined and moral, or says that he is speaking for God. If his words contradict the Bible, his teaching is false. Like Timothy, we must guard against any teaching that causes believers to dilute or reject any aspect of their faith. Such false teaching can be very direct or extremely subtle. Believers ought to respond quickly when they sense false teaching being promoted. The truth does not mind honest questions. Sometimes the source may prove to be ignorant of the error and appreciate the correction. But a firm warning may at least keep potential

victims from the disastrous results of apostasy that Paul described. For how to spot false teaching, see the note on 1:3-7.

**4:1-5** Paul said the false teachers were hypocrites and liars who encouraged people to follow "deceptive spirits and teachings that come from demons." The danger that Timothy faced in Ephesus seems to have come from certain people in the church who were following some Greek philosophers who taught that the body was evil and that only the soul mattered. The false teachers refused to believe that the God of creation was good, because his very contact with the physical world would have soiled him. Though these Greek-influenced church members honored Jesus, they could not believe he was truly human. Paul knew that their teachings, if left unchecked, would greatly distort Christian truth.

Satan deceives people by offering a clever imitation of the real thing. The false teachers gave stringent rules (such as forbidding people to marry or to eat certain foods). This made them appear self-disciplined and righteous. Their strict disciplines for the body, however, could not remove sin (see Colossians 2:20-23). We must not be unduly impressed by a teacher's style or credentials; we must look to his teaching about Jesus Christ. His conclusions about Christ show the source of his message.

**4:4, 5** In opposition to the false teachers, Paul affirmed that everything God created is good (see Genesis 1). We should ask for God's blessing on his created gifts that give us pleasure and thank him for them. This doesn't mean that we should abuse what God has made (for example, gluttony abuses God's gift of good food, lust abuses God's gift of love, and murder abuses God's gift of life). Instead of abusing, we should enjoy these gifts by using them to serve and honor God. Have you thanked God for the good gifts he has given? Are you using the gifts in ways pleasing to you *and* to God?

have followed. 7Do not waste time arguing over godless ideas and old wives' tales. Instead, train yourself to be godly. 8"Physical training is good, but training for godliness is much better, promising benefits in this life and in the life to come." 9This is a trustworthy saying, and everyone should accept it. 10This is why we work hard and continue to struggle,* for our hope is in the living God, who is the Savior of all people and particularly of all believers.

11Teach these things and insist that everyone learn them. 12Don't let anyone think less of you because you are young. Be an example to all believers in what you say, in the way you live, in your love, your faith, and your purity. 13Until I get there, focus on reading the Scriptures to the church, encouraging the believers, and teaching them.

14Do not neglect the spiritual gift you received through the prophecy spoken over you when the elders of the church laid their hands on you. 15Give your complete attention to these matters. Throw yourself into your tasks so that everyone will see your progress. 16Keep a close watch on how you live and on your teaching. Stay true to what is right for the sake of your own salvation and the salvation of those who hear you.

### Advice about Widows, Elders, and Slaves

**5** Never speak harshly to an older man,* but appeal to him respectfully as you would to your own father. Talk to younger men as you would to your own brothers. 2Treat older women as you would your mother, and treat younger women with all purity as you would your own sisters.

3Take care of* any widow who has no one else to care for her. 4But if she has children or grandchildren, their first responsibility is to show godliness at home and repay their parents by taking care of them. This is something that pleases God.

**4:7**
1 Tim 1:4
2 Tim 2:16
Titus 1:14

**4:8**
1 Tim 6:6

**4:9**
1 Tim 1:15

**4:10**
1 Tim 2:3-4

**4:11**
1 Tim 5:7; 6:2

**4:12**
Titus 2:15

**4:13**
1 Tim 3:14

**4:14**
Acts 6:6; 8:17
2 Tim 1:6

**5:1**
Lev 19:32
Titus 2:2, 6

**5:4**
Eph 6:2
1 Tim 2:3

4:10 Some manuscripts read *continue to suffer.*   5:1 Or *an elder.*   5:3 Or *Honor.*

---

**4:7-10** Are you in shape both physically and spiritually? In our society, much emphasis is placed on physical fitness, but spiritual health is even more important. Our physical health is susceptible to disease and injury, but faith can sustain us through any tragedy. To train ourselves to be godly, we must develop our faith by using our God-given abilities in the service of the church (see 4:14-16). Are you developing your spiritual muscles?

**4:10** Christ is the Savior for all, but his salvation becomes effective only for those who trust him.

**4:12** Timothy was a young pastor. It would have been easy for older Christians to look down on him because of his youth. He had to earn the respect of his elders by setting an example in his speech, life, love, faith, and purity. Regardless of your age, God can use you. Whether you are young or old, don't think of your age as a handicap. Live so others can see Christ in you.

**4:12-16** Apparently Timothy needed some encouragement. Most likely, so do many people around us. Each day we have many opportunities to support and inspire family members, fellow workers, and even total strangers. People need help and affirmation all along the way. Paul modeled six important principles to help us encourage others: (1) Begin with encouragement. People who know we will encourage them will be happy to work with us. (2) Expect of others only what you expect of yourself. People will resist being held to unfair standards. (3) Develop expectations of others with consideration for their skills, maturity, and experience. People will reject or fail to meet expectations that do not fit them. Be patient with distracted or slow learners. (4) Monitor your expectations of others. Changing circumstances sometimes require revised or reduced expectations. (5) Clarify your expectations with others. People are not likely to hit a target that no one has identified. (6) End with encouragement. People love to be thanked for a job well done.

**4:13** The "Scriptures" referred to here are, in fact, the Old Testament. We must make sure to emphasize the entire Bible, both the Old and the New Testaments. There are rich rewards in studying the people, events, prophecies, and principles of the Old Testament.

**4:14** Highly skilled and talented athletes lose their abilities if their muscles aren't toned by constant use. Likewise, we will lose our spiritual gifts if we don't put them to work. Our talents are

improved by exercise, but failing to use them causes them to waste away from lack of practice and nourishment. What gifts and abilities has God given you? Use them regularly in serving God and others. (See Romans 12:1-8; 2 Timothy 1:6-8 for more on using well the abilities God has given us.)

**4:16** We must be on constant guard against falling into sin that can so easily destroy us. Yet we must watch what we believe ("teaching") just as closely. Wrong beliefs can quickly lead us into sin and heresy. We should be on guard against those who would persuade us that how we live is more important than what we believe. We should keep a close watch on both, staying true to the faith.

**5:2** Men in the ministry can avoid improper attitudes toward women by treating them as family members. If men see women as fellow members in God's family, they will protect them and help them grow spiritually.

**5:3ff** Paul wanted Christian families to be as self-supporting as possible. He insisted that children and grandchildren take care of the widows in their families (5:4); he suggested that younger widows remarry and start new families (5:14); he ordered the church not to support lazy members who refused to work (2 Thessalonians 3:10). Nevertheless, when necessary, the believers pooled their resources (Acts 2:44-47); they gave generously to help disaster-ridden churches (1 Corinthians 16:1-4); they took care of a large number of widows (Acts 6:1-6). The church has always had limited resources and has always had to balance financial responsibility with generosity. It only makes sense for members to work as hard as they can and to be as independent as possible, so they can adequately care for themselves and for less fortunate members. When church members are both responsible and generous, everyone's needs will be met.

**5:3-5** Because there were no pensions, no social security, no life insurance, and few honorable jobs for women, widows were usually unable to support themselves. The responsibility for caring for the helpless naturally falls first on their families—the people whose lives are most closely linked with theirs. Paul stresses the importance of each family caring for the needs of its widows and not leaving it for the church. The church can then care for those widows who have no families. A widow who had no children or

5:5
Luke 2:36-37
1 Pet 3:5

5:6
Luke 15:24
Jas 5:5

5:10
Gen 18:3-5
Acts 9:36

5:13
2 Thes 3:11

5:14
1 Cor 7:9

5:15
1 Tim 1:19-20

5:17
Phil 2:29
1 Thes 5:12

5:18
†Deut 25:4
Matt 10:10
†Luke 10:7
1 Cor 9:9

5:19
Matt 18:16

⁵Now a true widow, a woman who is truly alone in this world, has placed her hope in God. She prays night and day, asking God for his help. ⁶But the widow who lives only for pleasure is spiritually dead even while she lives. ⁷Give these instructions to the church so that no one will be open to criticism.

⁸But those who won't care for their relatives, especially those in their own household, have denied the true faith. Such people are worse than unbelievers.

⁹A widow who is put on the list for support must be a woman who is at least sixty years old and was faithful to her husband.* ¹⁰She must be well respected by everyone because of the good she has done. Has she brought up her children well? Has she been kind to strangers and served other believers humbly?* Has she helped those who are in trouble? Has she always been ready to do good?

¹¹The younger widows should not be on the list, because their physical desires will overpower their devotion to Christ and they will want to remarry. ¹²Then they would be guilty of breaking their previous pledge. ¹³And if they are on the list, they will learn to be lazy and will spend their time gossiping from house to house, meddling in other people's business and talking about things they shouldn't. ¹⁴So I advise these younger widows to marry again, have children, and take care of their own homes. Then the enemy will not be able to say anything against them. ¹⁵For I am afraid that some of them have already gone astray and now follow Satan.

¹⁶If a woman who is a believer has relatives who are widows, she must take care of them and not put the responsibility on the church. Then the church can care for the widows who are truly alone.

¹⁷Elders who do their work well should be respected and paid well,* especially those who work hard at both preaching and teaching. ¹⁸For the Scripture says, "You must not muzzle an ox to keep it from eating as it treads out the grain." And in another place, "Those who work deserve their pay!"*

¹⁹Do not listen to an accusation against an elder unless it is confirmed by two or three

**5:9** Greek *was the wife of one husband.* **5:10** Greek *and washed the feet of God's holy people?* **5:17** Greek *should be worthy of double honor.* **5:18** Deut 25:4; Luke 10:7.

---

other family members to support her was doomed to poverty. From the beginning, the church took care of its widows, who in turn gave valuable service to the church.

The church should support those who have no families and should also help the elderly, young, disabled, ill, or poverty-stricken with their emotional and spiritual needs. Often families who are caring for their own helpless members have heavy burdens. They may need extra money, a listening ear, a helping hand, or a word of encouragement. Interestingly, those who are helped often turn around and help others, turning the church into more of a caring community. Don't wait for people to ask. Take the initiative and look for ways to serve them.

**5:8** Healthy homes remain the best possible training environment for children. When it comes to caring for relatives and honoring parents, children take most of their cues by watching how Mom and Dad honor the grandparents. If our children see the way we, as parents, care for our parents, they will understand the importance of such honor for us in the future. Healthy, practical honor becomes a priceless gift that one generation gives to another. Disrespect and lack of care provide harmful examples that will eventually turn on us. The warning in the verse is ominous indeed.

**5:9-16** Apparently some older widows had been "put on the list for support," meaning that they had taken a vow committing themselves to work for the church in exchange for financial support. Paul lists a few qualifications for these church workers: These widows should be at least 60 years old, should have been faithful to their husbands, and should be well known for their kind deeds. Younger widows should not be included in this group because they might desire to marry again and thus have to break their pledge (5:11, 12).

Three out of four wives today eventually are widowed, so many of the older women in our churches have lost their husbands. Does your church provide an avenue of service for these women?

Could you help match their gifts and abilities with your church's needs? Often their maturity and wisdom can be of great service in the church.

**5:15** "Gone astray and now follow Satan" refers to the immoral conduct that identified these women with their pagan neighbors.

**5:17** Preaching and teaching are closely related. Preaching is proclaiming the Word of God and confronting listeners with the truth of Scripture. Teaching is explaining the truth in Scripture, helping learners understand difficult passages, and helping them apply God's Word to daily life. Paul says that these elders are worthy of double honor. Unfortunately, however, we often take them for granted by not providing adequately for their needs or by subjecting them to heavy criticism. Think of how you can honor your leaders who work hard at preaching and teaching.

**5:17, 18** Faithful church leaders should be supported and appreciated. Too often they are targets for criticism because the congregation has unrealistic expectations. How do you treat your church leaders? Do you enjoy finding fault, or do you show your appreciation? Do they receive enough financial support to allow them to live without worry and to provide for the needs of their families? Jesus and Paul emphasized the importance of supporting those who lead and teach us (see Galatians 6:6 and the notes on Luke 10:7 and 1 Corinthians 9:4-10). Our ministers deserve to know that we are giving to them cheerfully, gratefully, and generously.

**5:19-21** Church leaders are not exempt from sin, faults, and mistakes. But they are often criticized for the wrong reasons—minor imperfections, failure to meet someone's expectations, personality clashes. Thus, Paul said that accusations should not even be heard unless two or three witnesses confirm them. Sometimes church leaders should be confronted about their behavior, and sometimes they should be rebuked. But all rebuking must be done fairly and lovingly and for the purpose of restoration.

witnesses. 20Those who sin should be reprimanded in front of the whole church; this will serve as a strong warning to others.

21I solemnly command you in the presence of God and Christ Jesus and the highest angels to obey these instructions without taking sides or showing favoritism to anyone.

22Never be in a hurry about appointing a church leader.* Do not share in the sins of others. Keep yourself pure.

23Don't drink only water. You ought to drink a little wine for the sake of your stomach because you are sick so often.

24Remember, the sins of some people are obvious, leading them to certain judgment. But there are others whose sins will not be revealed until later. 25In the same way, the good deeds of some people are obvious. And the good deeds done in secret will someday come to light.

**6** All slaves should show full respect for their masters so they will not bring shame on the name of God and his teaching. 2If the masters are believers, that is no excuse for being disrespectful. Those slaves should work all the harder because their efforts are helping other believers* who are well loved.

### False Teaching and True Riches

Teach these things, Timothy, and encourage everyone to obey them. 3Some people may contradict our teaching, but these are the wholesome teachings of the Lord Jesus Christ. These teachings promote a godly life. 4Anyone who teaches something different is arrogant and lacks understanding. Such a person has an unhealthy desire to quibble over the meaning of words. This stirs up arguments ending in jealousy, division, slander, and evil suspicions. 5These people always cause trouble. Their minds are corrupt, and they have turned their backs on the truth. To them, a show of godliness is just a way to become wealthy.

6Yet true godliness with contentment is itself great wealth. 7After all, we brought nothing with us when we came into the world, and we can't take anything with us when we leave it. 8So if we have enough food and clothing, let us be content.

**5:22** Greek *about the laying on of hands.*   **6:2** Greek *brothers.*

| | |
|---|---|
| 5:20 | Deut 13:11<br>Eph 5:11 |
| 5:21 | 1 Tim 6:13 |
| 5:22 | 1 Tim 4:14 |
| 5:23 | 1 Tim 3:8 |
| 5:24-25 | Rev 14:13 |
| 6:1 | Eph 6:5<br>Titus 2:9-10 |
| 6:2 | Phlm 1:16 |
| 6:3 | 1 Tim 1:3, 10 |
| 6:4 | 2 Tim 2:14 |
| 6:5 | 2 Tim 3:8; 4:4<br>Titus 1:14 |
| 6:6 | Phil 4:11-12<br>Heb 13:5 |
| 6:7 | Eccl 5:15<br>Job 1:21 |
| 6:8 | Prov 30:8<br>Heb 13:5 |

---

**5:21** Church leadership is a heavy responsibility. As difficult as it might be, Timothy was not to waver on any of Paul's instructions (and particularly the instructions about rebuking elders). Any needed discipline or rebuke must be administered without regard to Timothy's personal inclinations or favoritism. Likewise, leadership in the church today must be handled with maturity, faithfulness, godliness, and lack of favoritism. The health of a body of believers is far more important than playing favorites with someone who is not meeting the standards set forth here.

**5:22, 24, 25** Paul says that a church should never be in a hurry about choosing its leaders, especially the pastor, because major problems or sins might be overlooked. It is a serious responsibility to choose church leaders. They must have strong faith and be morally upright, having the qualities described in 3:1-13 and Titus 1:5-9. Not everyone who wants to be a church leader is eligible. Be certain of an applicant's qualifications before asking him or her to take a leadership position.

**5:23** It is unclear why Paul gave this advice to Timothy. Perhaps contaminated water had led to Timothy's indigestion, and so he should stop drinking only water. Whatever the reason, this statement is not an invitation to overindulgence or alcoholism.

**6:1, 2** In Paul's culture there was a great social and legal gulf separating masters and slaves. But as Christians, masters and slaves became spiritual equals, brothers and sisters in Christ Jesus (Galatians 3:28). Paul did not speak against the institution of slavery, but he gave guidelines for Christian slaves and Christian masters. His counsel for the master/slave relationship can be applied to the employer/employee relationship today. Employees should work hard, showing respect for their employers. In turn, employers should be fair (Ephesians 6:5-9;

Colossians 3:22–4:15). Our work should reflect our faithfulness to and love for Christ.

**6:3-5** Paul told Timothy to stay away from those who just wanted to make money from preaching and from those who strayed from the sound teachings of the Good News into quarrels that caused strife in the church. A person's understanding of the finer points of theology should not become the basis for lording it over others or for making money. Stay away from people who just want to argue.

**6:6** This statement is the key to spiritual growth and personal fulfillment. We should honor God and center our desires on him (Matthew 6:33), and we should be content with what God is doing in our lives (Philippians 4:11-13).

**6:6-10** Despite overwhelming evidence to the contrary, most people still believe that money brings happiness. Rich people craving greater riches can be caught in an endless cycle that only ends in ruin and destruction. How can you keep away from the love of money? Paul gives us some guidelines: (1) Realize that one day riches will all be gone (6:7, 17); (2) be content with what you have (6:8); (3) monitor what you are willing to do to get more money (6:9, 10); (4) love people more than money (6:11); (5) love God's work more than money (6:11); (6) freely share what you have with others (6:18). (See Proverbs 30:7-9 for more on avoiding the love of money.)

**6:8, 9** "If we have enough . . . let us be content." But when is *enough* enough? How can we truly be content? There is a difference between what we *need* and what we *want*. We may have all we need to live (that is, we have *enough*), but we let ourselves become anxious and discontent over what we merely want. Like Paul, we can choose to be content without having all that we want. The only alternative is to be "trapped by many foolish and harmful desires" that ultimately lead only to "ruin and destruction."

6:9
Prov 23:4; 28:22

9 But people who long to be rich fall into temptation and are trapped by many foolish and harmful desires that plunge them into ruin and destruction. 10 For the love of money is the root of all kinds of evil. And some people, craving money, have wandered from the true faith and pierced themselves with many sorrows.

## Paul's Final Instructions

6:11
2 Tim 2:22

6:12
1 Cor 9:25-26
2 Tim 4:7

6:13
John 18:33-37

6:14
1 Thes 3:13

6:15
Deut 10:17
1 Tim 1:17
Rev 17:14

6:16
Exod 33:20
Ps 104:2
John 1:18; 5:26
1 Tim 1:17

6:17
Luke 12:20-21

6:19
Matt 6:20
1 Tim 6:12

6:20
2 Tim 1:14; 2:16

6:21
2 Tim 2:18

11 But you, Timothy, are a man of God; so run from all these evil things. Pursue righteousness and a godly life, along with faith, love, perseverance, and gentleness. 12 Fight the good fight for the true faith. Hold tightly to the eternal life to which God has called you, which you have confessed so well before many witnesses. 13 And I charge you before God, who gives life to all, and before Christ Jesus, who gave a good testimony before Pontius Pilate, 14 that you obey this command without wavering. Then no one can find fault with you from now until our Lord Jesus Christ comes again. 15 For at just the right time Christ will be revealed from heaven by the blessed and only almighty God, the King of all kings and Lord of all lords. 16 He alone can never die, and he lives in light so brilliant that no human can approach him. No human eye has ever seen him, nor ever will. All honor and power to him forever! Amen.

17 Teach those who are rich in this world not to be proud and not to trust in their money, which is so unreliable. Their trust should be in God, who richly gives us all we need for our enjoyment. 18 Tell them to use their money to do good. They should be rich in good works and generous to those in need, always being ready to share with others. 19 By doing this they will be storing up their treasure as a good foundation for the future so that they may experience true life.

20 Timothy, guard what God has entrusted to you. Avoid godless, foolish discussions with those who oppose you with their so-called knowledge. 21 Some people have wandered from the faith by following such foolishness.

May God's grace be with you all.

---

**6:11, 12** Paul uses active and forceful verbs to describe the Christian life: run, pursue, fight, hold tightly. Some think Christianity is a passive religion that advocates waiting for God to act. On the contrary, we must have an *active* faith, training, working hard, sacrificing, and doing what we know is right. Is it time for action on your part? Christian service, like athletics, requires training and sacrifice. Our discipline and obedience largely define whether or not we will be contributors or merely spectators. How would other believers rank your contributing role on Christ's team?

**6:13** Jesus' trial before Pilate is recorded in the Gospels: Matthew 27:11-26; Mark 15:1-15; Luke 23:1-25; John 18:28–19:16.

**6:17-19** Ephesus was a wealthy city, and the Ephesian church probably had many wealthy members. Paul advised Timothy to deal with any potential problems by teaching that having riches carries great responsibility. If you have been blessed with wealth,

then thank the Lord. Don't be proud and don't trust in your money. Use your money to do good. Be rich in good works, generous, and ready to share. No matter how much money you have, your life should demonstrate that God controls the wealth that he has placed under your care.

**6:21** The book of 1 Timothy provides guiding principles for local churches, including rules for public worship and qualifications for elders (overseers, pastors), deacons, and special church workers (widows). Paul tells the church leaders to correct incorrect doctrine and to deal lovingly and fairly with all people in the church. The church is not organized simply for the sake of organization but so that Christ can be honored and glorified. While studying these guidelines, don't lose sight of what is most important in the life of the church—knowing God, working together in loving harmony, and taking God's Good News to the world.

# 2 TIMOTHY

## VITAL STATISTICS

**PURPOSE:**
To give final instructions and encouragement to Timothy, pastor of the church at Ephesus

**AUTHOR:**
Paul

**ORIGINAL AUDIENCE:**
Timothy

**DATE WRITTEN:**
Approximately A.D. 66 or 67, from prison in Rome. After a year or two of freedom, Paul was arrested again and executed under Emperor Nero.

**SETTING:**
Paul was virtually alone in prison; only Luke was with him. Paul wrote this letter to pass the torch to the new generation of church leaders. He also asked for visits from his friends and for his books, especially the papers—possibly parts of the Old Testament, the Gospels, and other biblical manuscripts.

**KEY VERSE:**
"Work hard so you can present yourself to God and receive his approval. Be a good worker, one who does not need to be ashamed and who correctly explains the word of truth" (2:15).

**KEY PEOPLE:**
Paul, Timothy, Luke, Mark, and others

**KEY PLACES:**
Rome, Ephesus

**SPECIAL FEATURES:**
Because this is Paul's last letter, it reveals his heart and his priorities—sound doctrine, steadfast faith, confident endurance, and lasting love.

"FAMOUS last words" is more than a cliché. When notable men and women of influence are about to die, the world waits to hear their final words of insight and wisdom. Then those quotes are repeated worldwide. This is also true with a dying loved one. Gathered at his or her side, the family strains to hear every whispered syllable of blessing, encouragement, and advice, knowing that this will be the final message.

One of the most knowledgeable, influential, and beloved men of history is the apostle Paul. And we have his famous last words.

Paul was facing death. He was not dying of a disease in a sterile hospital with loved ones gathered nearby. He was very much alive, but his condition was terminal. Convicted as a follower of Jesus of Nazareth, Paul sat in a cold Roman prison, cut off from the world, with just a visitor or two and his writing materials. Paul knew that soon he would be executed (4:6), so he wrote his final thoughts to his "son" Timothy, passing to him the torch of leadership, reminding him of what was truly important, and encouraging him in the faith. Imagine how Timothy must have read and reread every word; this was the last message from his beloved mentor, Paul. Because of the situation and the recipient, this is the most intimate and moving of all Paul's letters and his last.

Paul's introduction is tender, and every phrase exudes the love he has for Timothy (1:1–5). He then reminds Timothy of the qualities necessary for a faithful minister of Jesus Christ (1:6—2:13). Timothy should remember his call and use his gifts with boldness (1:6–12), keep to the truth (1:13–18), prepare others to follow him in the ministry (2:1, 2), be disciplined and ready to endure suffering (2:3–7), and keep his eyes and mind focused on Christ (2:8–13). Paul challenges Timothy to hold to sound doctrine, reject error and avoid foolish talk, correctly explain the word of truth (2:14–19), and keep his life pure (2:20–26).

Next, Paul warns Timothy of the opposition that he and other believers would face in the last days from self-centered people who use the church for their own gain and teach false doctrines (3:1–9). Paul tells Timothy to be prepared for these unfaithful people by remembering his example (3:10, 11), understanding the real source of the opposition (3:12, 13), and finding strength and power in the Word of God (3:14–17). Then Paul gives Timothy a stirring charge: to preach the Word (4:1–4) and to fulfill his ministry until the end (4:5–8).

Paul concludes with personal requests and items of information. In these final words, he reveals his loneliness and his strong love for his brothers and sisters in Christ (4:9–22).

There has never been another person like Paul, the missionary apostle. He was a man of deep faith, undying love, constant hope, tenacious conviction, and profound insight. And he was inspired by the Holy Spirit to give us God's message. As you read 2 Timothy, know that you are reading the last words of this great man of God—his last words to Timothy and to all who would claim to follow Christ. Recommit yourself to stand courageously for the truth, knowing the Word and being empowered by the Holy Spirit.

## THE BLUEPRINT

1. Foundations of Christian service (1:1—2:26)
2. Difficult times for Christian service (3:1—4:22)

Paul gives helpful advice to Timothy to remain solidly grounded in Christian service and to endure suffering during the difficult days to come. It is easy for us to serve Christ for the wrong reasons: because it is exciting, rewarding, or personally enriching. Without a proper foundation, however, we will find it easy to quit during difficult times. All believers need a strong foundation for their service, because Christian service does not get easier as we grow older, and it will become no easier as the time of Christ's return grows closer.

## MEGATHEMES

| THEME | EXPLANATION | IMPORTANCE |
|---|---|---|
| Boldness | In the face of opposition and persecution, Timothy was to carry out his ministry without fear or shame. Paul urged him to utilize boldly the gifts of preaching and teaching that the Holy Spirit had given him. | The Holy Spirit helps us to be wise and strong. God honors our confident testimony even when we suffer. To get over our fear of what people might say or do, we must take our eyes off of people and look only to God. |
| Faithfulness | Christ was faithful to all of us in dying for our sin. Paul was a faithful minister even when he was in prison. Paul urged Timothy to maintain not only sound doctrine but also loyalty, diligence, and endurance. | We can count on opposition, suffering, and hardship as we serve Christ. But this shows that our faithfulness is having an effect on others. As we trust Christ, he counts us worthy to suffer, and he will give us the strength we need to be steadfast. |
| Preaching and Teaching | Paul and Timothy were active in preaching and teaching the Good News about Jesus Christ. Paul encouraged Timothy not only to carry the torch of truth but also to train others, passing on to them sound doctrine and enthusiasm for Christ's mission. | We must prepare people to transmit God's Word to others so that they in turn might pass it on. Does your church carefully train others to teach? |
| Error | In the final days before Christ returns, there will be false teachers, spiritual dropouts, and heretics. The remedy for error is to have a solid program for teaching Christians. | Because of deception and false teaching, we must be disciplined and ready to reject error. Know the Word of God as your sure defense against error and confusion. |

## 1. Foundations of Christian service
### Greetings from Paul

**1:1**
John 5:24
Titus 1:1
1 Jn 5:10-11, 20

**1** This letter is from Paul, chosen by the will of God to be an apostle of Christ Jesus. I have been sent out to tell others about the life he has promised through faith in Christ Jesus. ²I am writing to Timothy, my dear son.

**1:2**
1 Tim 1:2

May God the Father and Christ Jesus our Lord give you grace, mercy, and peace.

---

**1:1** This letter has a somber tone. Paul had been imprisoned for the last time, and he knew he would soon die. Unlike Paul's first imprisonment in Rome, when he was in a house (Acts 28:16, 23, 30) where he continued to teach, this time he was probably confined to a cold dungeon, awaiting his death (4:6-8). Emperor Nero had begun a major persecution in A.D. 64 as part of his plan to pass the blame for the great fire of Rome from himself to the Christians. This persecution spread across the empire and included social ostracism, public torture, and murder. As Paul was waiting to die, he wrote a letter to his dear friend Timothy, a younger man who was like a son to him (1:2). Written in approximately A.D. 66/67, these are the last words we have from Paul.

**1:1** When we are united with Christ, life takes on both immediate and eternal dimensions. Paul's use of the phrase, "life he has promised," can apply to the life that Jesus gives immediately to those who trust him, as well as to the life fully realized in eternity.

On one hand, Paul said, "Anyone who belongs to Christ has become a new person" (2 Corinthians 5:17). So new life begins at conversion. Yet on the other hand, we "wait with eager hope for the day when God will give us our full rights as his adopted children, including the new bodies he has promised us" (Romans 8:23). The present experience we enjoy provides a foretaste of our complete redemption at Christ's return. When we struggle with difficulties in this life, remember that the best is yet to come.

**1:2** Paul's second letter to Timothy was written about two to four years after his first letter. Timothy had been Paul's traveling companion on the second and third missionary journeys, and Paul had left him in Ephesus to help the church there (1 Timothy 1:3, 4). For more information on Timothy, see his Profile in 1 Timothy 2, p. 2059. For more information on the great missionary Paul, see his Profile in Acts 9, p. 1837.

## Encouragement to Be Faithful

<sup>3</sup> Timothy, I thank God for you—the God I serve with a clear conscience, just as my ancestors did. Night and day I constantly remember you in my prayers. <sup>4</sup> I long to see you again, for I remember your tears as we parted. And I will be filled with joy when we are together again.

<sup>5</sup> I remember your genuine faith, for you share the faith that first filled your grandmother Lois and your mother, Eunice. And I know that same faith continues strong in you. <sup>6</sup> This is why I remind you to fan into flames the spiritual gift God gave you when I laid my hands on you. <sup>7</sup> For God has not given us a spirit of fear and timidity, but of power, love, and self-discipline.

<sup>8</sup> So never be ashamed to tell others about our Lord. And don't be ashamed of me, either, even though I'm in prison for him. With the strength God gives you, be ready to suffer with me for the sake of the Good News. <sup>9</sup> For God saved us and called us to live a holy life. He did this, not because we deserved it, but because that was his plan from before the beginning of time—to show us his grace through Christ Jesus. <sup>10</sup> And now he has made all of this plain to us by the appearing of Christ Jesus, our Savior. He broke the power of death and illuminated the way to life and immortality through the Good News. <sup>11</sup> And God chose me to be a preacher, an apostle, and a teacher of this Good News.

<sup>12</sup> That is why I am suffering here in prison. But I am not ashamed of it, for I know the one in whom I trust, and I am sure that he is able to guard what I have entrusted to him* until the day of his return.

1:12 Or *what has been entrusted to me.*

| | |
|---|---|
| **1:4** | Acts 20:37<br>2 Tim 4:9 |
| **1:5** | Acts 16:1 |
| **1:6** | 1 Tim 4:14 |
| **1:7** | Rom 8:15 |
| **1:8** | Rom 1:16<br>Eph 3:1<br>2 Tim 2:3 |
| **1:9** | Rom 8:28; 11:14<br>Eph 2:8-9<br>Titus 3:5 |
| **1:10** | 1 Cor 15:54 |
| **1:11** | 1 Tim 2:7 |
| **1:12** | 1 Tim 6:20 |

---

**1:3** Paul consistently prayed for Timothy, his friend, his fellow traveler, his son in the faith, and a strong leader in the Christian church. Although the two men were separated from each other, their prayers provided a source of mutual encouragement. We, too, should pray consistently for others, especially for those who do God's work. On your prayer list, include your pastor, other church leaders, and missionaries around the world. They need your prayers.

**1:4** We don't know when Paul and Timothy last parted, but it was probably when Paul was arrested and taken to Rome for his second imprisonment. The tears they shed at parting revealed the depth of their relationship.

**1:5** Timothy's mother and grandmother, Eunice and Lois, were early Christian converts, possibly through Paul's ministry in their home city, Lystra (Acts 16:1). They had communicated their strong Christian faith to Timothy, even though his father was probably not a believer. Don't hide your light at home; our families are fertile fields for planting seeds of the Good News. Let your parents, children, spouse, brothers, and sisters know of your faith in Jesus, and be sure they see Christ's love, helpfulness, and joy in you.

**1:6** At the time of his ordination, Timothy had received special gifts of the Spirit to enable him to serve the church (see 1 Timothy 4:14). In telling Timothy to "fan into flames the spiritual gift God gave you," Paul was encouraging him to persevere. Timothy did not need new revelations or new gifts; he needed the courage and self-discipline to hang on to the truth and to use the gifts he had already received (see 1:13, 14). If Timothy would step out boldly in faith and proclaim the Good News once again, the Holy Spirit would go with him and give him power. When you use the gifts God has given you, you will find that God will give you the power you need to accomplish whatever task he gives you.

**1:6** Clearly Timothy's spiritual gift had been given to him when Paul and the elders had laid their hands on him and set him apart for ministry (see 1 Timothy 4:14). God gives all Christians gifts to use to build up the body of Christ (see 1 Corinthians 12:4-31), and he gives special gifts to some through church leaders, who serve as God's instruments.

**1:6, 7** Timothy was experiencing great opposition to his message and to himself as a leader. His youth, his association with Paul, and his leadership had come under fire from believers and nonbelievers alike. Paul urged him to be bold. When we allow people to intimidate us, we neutralize our effectiveness for God. The power of the Holy Spirit can help us overcome our fear of

what some might say or do to us so that we can continue to do God's work.

**1:7** Paul mentions three characteristics of the effective Christian leader: power, love, and self-discipline. These are available to us because the Holy Spirit lives in us. Follow his leading each day so that your life will more fully exhibit these characteristics. See Galatians 5:22, 23 for a list of the by-products of the Holy Spirit living in us.

**1:8** In this time of mounting persecution, Timothy may have been afraid to continue preaching the Good News. His fears were based on fact because believers were being arrested and executed. Paul told Timothy to expect suffering—Timothy, like Paul, would be jailed for preaching the Good News (Hebrews 13:23). But Paul promised Timothy that God would give him strength and that he would be ready when it was his turn to suffer. Even when there is no persecution, sharing our faith in Christ can be difficult. Fortunately we, like Paul and Timothy, can rely on the Holy Spirit to give us courage. Don't be ashamed to testify of your personal faith in Jesus Christ.

**1:9, 10** In these verses Paul gives a brief summary of the Good News. God loves us, chose us, and sent Christ to die for us. We can have eternal life through faith in him because he broke the power of death with his resurrection. We do not deserve to be saved, but God offers us salvation anyway. What we must do is believe in him and accept his offer.

**1:12** In spite of the suffering that might have caused Paul to despair, he affirmed his confidence in God's protection. This was not a claim to strong faith; rather, it was a trust in one so powerful that even a weak faith was sufficient. Paul based his confidence in Christ on his intimate relationship with him. Paul's knew the one in whom he trusted with personal knowledge; he knew Christ so well that no earthly experience could break the bond of love by which Christ held him. If your situation looks bleak, give your concerns to Christ because you know him and love him. Realize that he will guard all you have entrusted to him until the day of his return. For more on our security in Christ, see Romans 8:38, 39.

**1:12** The phrase "guard what I have entrusted to him" could mean: (1) Paul knew that God would protect the souls of those converted through his preaching; (2) Paul trusted God to guard his own soul until Christ's second coming; or (3) Paul was confident that, though he was in prison and facing death, God would carry out the Good News ministry through others such as Timothy. Paul may have expressed his confidence to encourage Timothy, who

**1:13**
Rom 6:17
1 Tim 1:14

**1:14**
Rom 8:9, 11, 16
Gal 4:6

**1:15**
2 Tim 4:10, 16

**1:16**
2 Tim 4:19

**1:18**
Heb 6:10

**2:1**
Eph 6:10

**2:2**
2 Tim 1:13

**2:3**
2 Tim 1:8; 4:5

**2:5**
1 Cor 9:25

**2:6**
1 Cor 9:7, 10

**2:8**
Acts 2:24
Rom 1:3

**2:9**
Eph 3:1
Phil 1:12-14

[13]Hold on to the pattern of wholesome teaching you learned from me—a pattern shaped by the faith and love that you have in Christ Jesus. [14]Through the power of the Holy Spirit who lives within us, carefully guard the precious truth that has been entrusted to you.

[15]As you know, everyone from the province of Asia has deserted me—even Phygelus and Hermogenes.

[16]May the Lord show special kindness to Onesiphorus and all his family because he often visited and encouraged me. He was never ashamed of me because I was in chains. [17]When he came to Rome, he searched everywhere until he found me. [18]May the Lord show him special kindness on the day of Christ's return. And you know very well how helpful he was in Ephesus.

### A Good Soldier of Christ Jesus

**2** Timothy, my dear son, be strong through the grace that God gives you in Christ Jesus. [2]You have heard me teach things that have been confirmed by many reliable witnesses. Now teach these truths to other trustworthy people who will be able to pass them on to others.

[3]Endure suffering along with me, as a good soldier of Christ Jesus. [4]Soldiers don't get tied up in the affairs of civilian life, for then they cannot please the officer who enlisted them. [5]And athletes cannot win the prize unless they follow the rules. [6]And hardworking farmers should be the first to enjoy the fruit of their labor. [7]Think about what I am saying. The Lord will help you understand all these things.

[8]Always remember that Jesus Christ, a descendant of King David, was raised from the dead. This is the Good News I preach. [9]And because I preach this Good News, I am suffering

was undoubtedly discouraged by the problems in Ephesus and fearful of persecution. Even in prison, Paul knew that God was still in control. No matter what setbacks or problems we face, we can trust fully in God.

**1:13, 14** Timothy was in a time of transition. He had been Paul's bright young helper; soon he would be on his own as leader of a church in a difficult environment. Although his responsibilities were changing, Timothy was not without help. He had everything he needed to face the future if he would hold on tightly to the Lord's resources. When you are facing difficult transitions, follow Paul's advice to Timothy and look back at your experience. Who is the foundation of your faith? How can you build on that foundation? What gifts has the Holy Spirit given you? Use the gifts you have been given.

**1:15, 16** Nothing more is known about Phygelus and Hermogenes, who evidently opposed Paul's ministry. These men serve as a warning that even leaders can fall. Onesiphorus was mentioned as a positive example in contrast to these men.

**2:1** How can someone be strong through grace? Grace is God's undeserved favor on our behalf. Just as we are saved by God's grace (Ephesians 2:8, 9), we should live by it (Colossians 2:6). This means trusting completely in Christ and *his* power, and not trying to live for Christ in our strength alone. Receive and utilize Christ's power. He will give you the strength to do his work.

**2:2** If the church were to consistently follow this advice, it would expand geometrically as well-taught believers would teach others and commission them, in turn, to teach still others. Disciples need to be equipped to pass on their faith; our work is not done until new believers are able to make disciples of others (see Ephesians 4:12, 13).

**2:3** The body of Christ contains all believers who have ever lived, not just those who are alive now. When we suffer, we share in a common experience, not just with those alive today, but with all those who have ever suffered for the sake of the gospel. All the martyrs, missionaries, and pioneers of the faith had to face what we face. Let us have the same courage, commitment, and willingness to renounce worldly pleasure in order to serve God. Can you face the challenge? "Therefore, since we are surrounded by such a huge crowd of witnesses to the life of faith, let us strip off every weight that slows us down, especially the sin that so easily trips us up. And let us run with endurance the race God has set before us" (Hebrews 12:1).

**2:3-7** As Timothy preached and taught, he would face suffering, but he should be able to endure. Paul used comparisons with soldiers, athletes, and farmers who must discipline themselves and be willing to sacrifice to achieve the results they want. Like soldiers, we have to give up worldly security and endure rigorous discipline. Like athletes, we must train hard and follow the rules. Like farmers, we must work extremely hard and be patient. But we keep going despite suffering because of the thought of victory, the vision of winning, and the hope of harvest. We will see that our suffering is worthwhile when we achieve our goal of glorifying God, winning people to Christ, and one day living eternally with him.

**2:7** Paul told Timothy to think about his words, and God would give him understanding. God speaks through the Bible, his Word, but we need to be open and receptive to him. As you read the Bible, ask God to show you his timeless truths and their application to your life. Then consider what you have read by thinking it through and meditating on it. God will give you understanding.

**2:8** False teachers were a problem in Ephesus (see Acts 20:29, 30; 1 Timothy 1:3-11). At the heart of false teaching is an incorrect view of Christ. In Timothy's day many asserted that Christ was divine but not human—God but not man. These days we often hear that Jesus was human but not divine—man but not God. Either view destroys the good news that Jesus Christ has taken our sins on himself and has reconciled us to God. In this verse, Paul firmly states that Jesus is fully man ("a descendant of King David") and fully God ("raised from the dead"). This is an important doctrine for all Christians. For more on this key concept, see the note on Philippians 2:5-7.

**2:9** Paul was in chains in prison because of the Good News he preached. The truth about Jesus is no more popular in our day than in Paul's, but it still reaches receptive hearts. When Paul said that Jesus was God, he angered the Jews who had condemned Jesus for blasphemy; many Jews, however, became followers of Christ (1 Corinthians 1:24). He angered the Romans who worshiped the emperor as god, but even some in Caesar's household turned to Jesus (Philippians 4:22). When Paul said Jesus was human, he angered the Greeks, who thought divinity was soiled if it had any contact with humanity; still, many Greeks accepted the faith (Acts 11:20, 21). The truth that Jesus is one person with two united natures has never been easy to understand, but that doesn't make it untrue. The truth of God's Word is being believed by people every day and changing their lives for eternity. Despite the opposition, continue to proclaim Christ. Some will listen and believe.

and have been chained like a criminal. But the word of God cannot be chained. ¹⁰So I am willing to endure anything if it will bring salvation and eternal glory in Christ Jesus to those God has chosen.

2:10
Col 1:24

¹¹This is a trustworthy saying:

If we die with him,
    we will also live with him.
¹² If we endure hardship,
    we will reign with him.
If we deny him,
    he will deny us.
¹³ If we are unfaithful,
    he remains faithful,
    for he cannot deny who he is.

2:11
Rom 6:2-11
1 Thes 5:10

2:12
Matt 10:33
Rom 8:17
1 Pet 4:13

2:13
Num 23:19
Rom 3:3
1 Cor 1:9

¹⁴Remind everyone about these things, and command them in God's presence to stop fighting over words. Such arguments are useless, and they can ruin those who hear them.

2:14
1 Tim 1:4; 6:4
Titus 3:9

## An Approved Worker

¹⁵Work hard so you can present yourself to God and receive his approval. Be a good worker, one who does not need to be ashamed and who correctly explains the word of truth. ¹⁶Avoid worthless, foolish talk that only leads to more godless behavior. ¹⁷This kind of talk spreads like cancer,* as in the case of Hymenaeus and Philetus. ¹⁸They have left the path of truth, claiming that the resurrection of the dead has already occurred; in this way, they have turned some people away from the faith.

¹⁹But God's truth stands firm like a foundation stone with this inscription: "The LORD knows those who are his,"* and "All who belong to the LORD must turn away from evil."*

²⁰In a wealthy home some utensils are made of gold and silver, and some are made of

2:17
1 Tim 1:20

2:18
1 Tim 1:19; 6:21

2:19
†Num 16:5
Isa 52:11
John 10:14

2:20
Rom 9:21

2:17 Greek *gangrene.*   2:19a Num 16:5.   2:19b See Isa 52:11.

---

**2:11-13** This is probably an early Christian hymn. God is faithful to his children. Although we may suffer great hardships here, God promises that someday we will live eternally with him. What will this involve? It means believers will live in Christ's Kingdom, and that we will share in the administration of that Kingdom. This truth comforted Paul as he went through suffering and death. Are you facing hardships? Don't turn away from God—he promises you a wonderful future with him. For more information about living eternally with God, see Matthew 16:24-27; 19:28-30; Luke 22:28-30; Romans 5:17; 6:8; 8:10, 11, 17; 1 Corinthians 15:42-58; Colossians 3:3, 4; 1 Thessalonians 4:13-18; Revelation 3:21; 21:1–22:21.

**2:13** Jesus is faithful. He will stay by our side even when we have endured so much that we seem to have no faith left. We may be faithless at times, but Jesus is faithful to his promise to be with us "to the end of the age" (Matthew 28:20). Refusing Christ's help will break our communication with God, but he will never turn his back on us even though we may turn our back on him.

**2:14-16** Paul urged Timothy to remind the believers not to argue over unimportant details ("fighting over words") or have foolish discussions because such arguments are confusing, useless, and even harmful. False teachers loved to cause strife and divisions by their meaningless quibbling over unimportant details (see 1 Timothy 6:3-5). To explain the word of truth correctly, we must study what the Word of God says so we can understand what it means.

**2:15** Because God will examine what kind of workers we have been for him, we should build our lives on his Word and build his Word into our lives. It alone tells us how to live for him and serve him. Believers who ignore the Bible will certainly be ashamed at the judgment. Consistent and diligent study of God's Word is vital; otherwise we will be lulled into neglecting God and our true purpose for living.

**2:16** In important areas of Christian teaching, we must carefully work through our disagreements. But when we bicker long hours

over words and theories that are not central to the Christian faith and life, we only provoke anger and hurt feelings. Even if "foolish talk" reaches a resolution, it gains little ground for the Kingdom. Learning and discussing are not bad unless they keep believers constantly focusing on false doctrine or unhelpful trivialities. Don't let anything keep you from your work for and service to God.

**2:17, 18** Hymenaeus was also mentioned in 1 Timothy 1:20. Paul had turned Hymenaeus over to Satan because his false teaching concerning the resurrection was destroying some people's faith.

**2:18** The false teachers were denying the resurrection of the body. They believed that when a person became a Christian, he or she was spiritually reborn, and that was the only resurrection there would ever be. To them, resurrection was symbolic and spiritual, not physical. Paul clearly taught, however, that believers will be resurrected after they die, and that their bodies as well as their souls will live eternally with Christ (1 Corinthians 15:35ff; 2 Corinthians 5:1-10; 1 Thessalonians 4:15-18). We should not try to shape the doctrines of Scripture to match our opinions. If we do, we are putting ourselves above God. Instead, our beliefs should be consistent with God's Word.

**2:19** False teachers still spout lies. Some distort the truth, some dilute it, and some simply delete it by saying that God's truth no longer applies. But no matter how many people follow the liars, the solid foundation of God's truth never changes, is never shaken, and will never fade. When we follow God's truth, we will live God's way.

**2:20, 21** Here Paul urged Timothy to be the kind of person Christ could use for his noblest purposes. Don't settle for less than God's highest and best. Allow him to use you as an instrument of his will. You do this by staying close to him and keeping yourself pure so that sin and its consequences do not get in the way of what God could do in your life. While God can redeem any situation, how much better it is to stay close to Christ and ready to be used by him at a moment's notice.

**2:21**
2 Tim 3:17

wood and clay. The expensive utensils are used for special occasions, and the cheap ones are for everyday use. 21If you keep yourself pure, you will be a special utensil for honorable use. Your life will be clean, and you will be ready for the Master to use you for every good work.

**2:22**
1 Tim 6:11

22Run from anything that stimulates youthful lusts. Instead, pursue righteous living, faithfulness, love, and peace. Enjoy the companionship of those who call on the Lord with pure hearts.

**2:23**
1 Tim 4:7

**2:24**
1 Tim 3:2-3
Titus 1:7

**2:26**
1 Tim 3:7

23Again I say, don't get involved in foolish, ignorant arguments that only start fights. 24A servant of the Lord must not quarrel but must be kind to everyone, be able to teach, and be patient with difficult people. 25Gently instruct those who oppose the truth. Perhaps God will change those people's hearts, and they will learn the truth. 26Then they will come to their senses and escape from the devil's trap. For they have been held captive by him to do whatever he wants.

## 2. Difficult times for Christian service
### The Dangers of the Last Days

**3:1**
1 Tim 4:1
Jude 1:18

**3:2-3**
Rom 1:29-31

**3** You should know this, Timothy, that in the last days there will be very difficult times. 2For people will love only themselves and their money. They will be boastful and proud, scoffing at God, disobedient to their parents, and ungrateful. They will consider nothing sacred. 3They will be unloving and unforgiving; they will slander others and have no self-control. They will be cruel and hate what is good. 4They will betray their friends, be reckless, be puffed up with pride, and love pleasure rather than God. 5They will act religious, but they will reject the power that could make them godly. Stay away from people like that!

**3:6**
Jude 1:4

6They are the kind who work their way into people's homes and win the confidence of* vulnerable women who are burdened with the guilt of sin and controlled by various desires. 7(Such women are forever following new teachings, but they are never able to understand

**3:6** Greek *and take captive.*

---

**2:22** Running away is sometimes considered cowardly. But wise people realize that removing themselves physically from temptation often can be the most courageous action to take. Timothy, a young man, was warned to run from anything that produced evil thoughts. Do you have a recurring temptation that you find difficult to resist? Remove yourself physically from any situation that stimulates your desire to sin. Knowing when to run is as important in spiritual battle as knowing when and how to fight. (See also 1 Timothy 6:11.)

**2:23-26** As a teacher, Timothy helped those who were confused about the truth. Paul's advice to Timothy, and to all who teach God's truth, is to be kind and gentle, patiently and courteously explaining the truth. Good teaching never promotes quarrels or foolish arguments. Whether you are teaching Sunday school, leading a Bible study, or preaching in church, remember to listen to people's questions and treat them respectfully, while avoiding foolish debates. If you do this, those who oppose you will be more willing to hear what you have to say and perhaps turn from their error.

**3:1** Paul's reference to the "last days" reveals his sense of urgency. The last days began after Jesus' resurrection when the Holy Spirit came upon the believers at Pentecost. The "last days" will continue until Christ's second coming. This means that *we* are living in the last days. So we should make the most of the time that God has given us (Ephesians 5:16; Colossians 4:5).

**3:1ff** In many parts of the world today, being a Christian is not especially difficult—people aren't jailed for reading the Bible or executed for preaching Christ. (However, this kind of persecution is very real for many believers.) Paul's descriptive list of behavior in the last days describes our society—even, unfortunately, the behavior of many Christians. Check your life against Paul's list. Don't give in to society's pressures. Don't settle for comfort without commitment. Stand up against evil by living as God would have his people live.

**3:4** Why is it so tempting to "love pleasure rather than God"? Pleasure is something we can control; God cannot be controlled.

Most pleasures can be obtained easily; love for God requires effort and sometimes sacrifice. Pleasure benefits us now; the benefits of loving God are often in the future. Pleasure has a narcotic effect; it takes our minds off ourselves and our problems. Love for God reminds us of our needs and our responsibilities. Pleasure cooperates with pride. It makes us feel good when we look good in the eyes of others. To love God we must lay aside our pride and our accomplishments. Have you chosen to love pleasure, or to love God? How do you know?

**3:5** The "act" or appearance of being religious includes going to church, knowing Christian doctrine, using Christian clichés, and following a community's Christian traditions. Such practices can make a person look good, but if the inner attitudes of belief, love, and worship are lacking, the outer appearance is meaningless. Paul warns us not to be deceived by people who only appear to be Christians. It may be difficult to distinguish them from true Christians at first, but their daily behavior will give them away. The characteristics described in 3:2-4 are unmistakable.

**3:6, 7** Because of their cultural background, women in the Ephesian church had received no formal religious training. They enjoyed their new freedom to study Christian truths, but their eagerness to learn made them a target for false teachers. Paul warned Timothy to watch out for men who would take advantage of these women. New believers need to grow in their knowledge of the Word because ignorance can make them vulnerable to deception.

**3:7** This verse is not opposing study and learning; it is warning about ineffective learning. It is possible to be a perpetual student and never graduate to putting theory into practice. But honest seekers and true students look for answers. Remember this as you study God's Word. Seek to find God's truth and will for your life. Then do as he says.

the truth.) ⁸These teachers oppose the truth just as Jannes and Jambres opposed Moses. They have depraved minds and a counterfeit faith. ⁹But they won't get away with this for long. Someday everyone will recognize what fools they are, just as with Jannes and Jambres.

### Paul's Charge to Timothy

¹⁰But you, Timothy, certainly know what I teach, and how I live, and what my purpose in life is. You know my faith, my patience, my love, and my endurance. ¹¹You know how much persecution and suffering I have endured. You know all about how I was persecuted in Antioch, Iconium, and Lystra—but the Lord rescued me from all of it. ¹²Yes, and everyone who wants to live a godly life in Christ Jesus will suffer persecution. ¹³But evil people and impostors will flourish. They will deceive others and will themselves be deceived.

¹⁴But you must remain faithful to the things you have been taught. You know they are true, for you know you can trust those who taught you. ¹⁵You have been taught the holy Scriptures from childhood, and they have given you the wisdom to receive the salvation that comes by trusting in Christ Jesus. ¹⁶All Scripture is inspired by God and is useful to teach us what is true and to make us realize what is wrong in our lives. It corrects us when we are wrong and teaches us to do what is right. ¹⁷God uses it to prepare and equip his people to do every good work.

**4** I solemnly urge you in the presence of God and Christ Jesus, who will someday judge the living and the dead when he appears to set up his Kingdom: ²Preach the word of God. Be prepared, whether the time is favorable or not. Patiently correct, rebuke, and encourage your people with good teaching.

**3:8**
1 Tim 6:5

**3:10**
1 Tim 4:6
**3:11**
Ps 34:19
Acts 13:14, 50-51;
14:5, 19
**3:12**
John 15:20
Acts 14:22
**3:14**
2 Tim 1:13; 2:2
**3:15**
John 5:39
**3:16**
Rom 15:4
2 Pet 1:20-21
**3:17**
1 Tim 6:11
2 Tim 2:21

**4:1**
Acts 10:42
**4:2**
1 Tim 5:20
Titus 1:13

---

**3:8, 9** According to tradition, Jannes and Jambres were two of the magicians who had counterfeited Moses' miracles before Pharaoh (Exodus 7:11, 12). Paul explained that just as Moses had exposed and defeated them (Exodus 8:18, 19), God would overthrow the false teachers who were plaguing the Ephesian church.

**3:9** We can hide our sin for a while, but eventually the truth will be revealed. Sooner or later, distraction, opposition, anger, or fatigue will wear us down, and our true hearts will be exposed. The trials of life will conspire against our efforts to maintain a religious front. We can't pick when and where we will be tested by adversity. Build your character carefully because it will come out under stress. Live each day as if your actions will one day be known to everyone. It is useless, in the middle of a test, to acknowledge that you should have prepared. Now is the time to change anything you wouldn't want revealed later.

**3:11** In Lystra, Timothy's hometown, Paul had been stoned and left for dead (Acts 14:19); and this was only one incident among many. In 2 Corinthians 11:23-33 Paul summarized his lifetime of suffering for the sake of the Good News. Paul mentioned his suffering here to contrast his experience with that of the pleasure-seeking false teachers.

**3:12** In this charge, Paul told Timothy that people who obey God and live for Christ will be persecuted. Don't be surprised when people misunderstand, criticize, and even try to hurt you because of what you believe and how you live. Don't give up. Continue to live as you know you should. God is the only one you need to please.

**3:13** Don't expect false teachers and evil people to reform and change on their own. Left alone, they will go from bad to worse. If you have the opportunity, correct them so as to bring them back to faith in Christ. Fight for the truth, especially to protect younger Christians.

**3:14** Besieged by false teachers and the inevitable pressures of a growing ministry, Timothy could easily have abandoned his faith or modified his doctrine. Once again Paul counseled Timothy to look to his past and to hold to the basic teachings about Jesus that are eternally true. Like Timothy, we are surrounded by false teachings. But we must not allow our society to distort or crowd out God's eternal truth. Spend time every day reflecting on the foundation of your Christian faith found in God's Word, the great truths that build up your life.

**3:15** Timothy was one of the first second-generation Christians: He became a Christian, not because an evangelist preached a

powerful sermon, but because his mother and grandmother had taught him the holy Scriptures when he was a small child (1:5). A parent's work is vitally important. At home and in church, we should realize that teaching small children is both an opportunity and a responsibility. Jesus wanted little children to come to him (Matthew 19:13-15). Like Timothy's mother and grandmother, Eunice and Lois, do your part in leading children to Christ.

**3:15** For Timothy, the "holy Scriptures" were the books of the Old Testament. The Old Testament is important because it points to Jesus Christ. At the same time, faith in Christ makes the whole Bible intelligible.

**3:16** The Bible is not a collection of stories, fables, myths, or merely human ideas about God. It is not a human book. Through the Holy Spirit, God revealed his person and plan to certain believers, who wrote down his message for his people (2 Peter 1:20, 21). This process is known as *inspiration*. The writers wrote from their own personal, historical, and cultural contexts. Although they used their own minds, talents, language, and style, they wrote what God wanted them to write. Scripture is completely trustworthy because God was in control of its writing. Its words are entirely authoritative for our faith and life. The Bible is "God-breathed." Read it, and use its teachings to guide your conduct.

**3:16, 17** The whole Bible is God's inspired Word. Because it is inspired and trustworthy, we should *read* it and *apply* it to our life. The Bible is our standard for testing everything else that claims to be true. It is our safeguard against false teaching and our source of guidance for how we should live. It is our only source of knowledge about how we can be saved. God wants to show you what is true and equip you to live for him. How much time do you spend in God's Word? Read it regularly to discover God's truth and to become confident in your life and faith. Develop a plan for reading the whole Bible, not just the familiar passages.

**3:17** In our zeal for the *truth* of Scripture, we must never forget its *purpose*—to equip us to do good. We should not study God's Word simply to increase our knowledge or to prepare us to win arguments. We should study the Bible so that we will know how to do Christ's work in the world. Our knowledge of God's Word is not useful unless it strengthens our faith and leads us to do good.

**4:1, 2** It was important for Timothy to preach the Good News so that the Christian faith could spread throughout the world. We believe in Christ today because people like Timothy were faithful to their mission. It is still vitally important for believers to spread

4:3
2 Tim 3:1-2
4:4
1 Tim 1:4
4:5
2 Tim 1:8
4:7
1 Cor 9:24-27
Phil 3:12-14
1 Tim 6:12
4:8
1 Cor 9:25
Phil 3:14
Col 1:5
Rev 2:10

³For a time is coming when people will no longer listen to sound and wholesome teaching. They will follow their own desires and will look for teachers who will tell them whatever their itching ears want to hear. ⁴They will reject the truth and chase after myths.

⁵But you should keep a clear mind in every situation. Don't be afraid of suffering for the Lord. Work at telling others the Good News, and fully carry out the ministry God has given you.

⁶As for me, my life has already been poured out as an offering to God. The time of my death is near. ⁷I have fought the good fight, I have finished the race, and I have remained faithful. ⁸And now the prize awaits me—the crown of righteousness, which the Lord, the righteous Judge, will give me on the day of his return. And the prize is not just for me but for all who eagerly look forward to his appearing.

## Paul's Final Words

⁹Timothy, please come as soon as you can. ¹⁰Demas has deserted me because he loves the things of this life and has gone to Thessalonica. Crescens has gone to Galatia, and Titus has gone to Dalmatia. ¹¹Only Luke is with me. Bring Mark with you when you come, for he will

4:11
Col 4:10, 14
Phlm 1:24

the Good News. Half the people who have ever lived are alive today, and most of them do not know Christ. He is coming soon, and he wants to find his faithful believers ready for him. It may be inconvenient to take a stand for Christ or to tell others about his love, but preaching the Word of God is the most important responsibility the church and its members have been given. Be prepared for, courageous in, and sensitive to God-given opportunities to tell the Good News.

**4:2** We should always be ready to serve God in any situation, whether or not it is convenient. Be sensitive to the opportunities God gives you.

**4:2** Paul told Timothy to "correct, rebuke, and encourage." It is difficult to accept correction, to be told we have to change. But no matter how much the truth hurts, we must be willing to listen to it so we can more fully obey God.

**4:3-5** Many speakers, teachers, and writers talk about the pursuit of knowledge. But often they don't want knowledge; they want power. Such people won't listen to "sound and wholesome teaching." Instead, they "reject the truth and chase after myths." You can see this everywhere—from liberal churches to university campuses. People claiming to have a bit more enlightenment than what the dusty Bible has to say; people claiming to improve on God's words. Such people have several things in common: (1) *They do not tolerate the truth.* They have no interest or respect for absolute truth or any standard for judgment. (2) *They reject truth for sensationalism.* They want truth that fits their situation and makes sense for them. What they feel, what works for them, what seems compelling—that is their truth and they claim an absolute right to it. No one should even attempt to tell them differently. (3) *They gather viewpoints to suit their selfish desires.* Although they profess objectivity, their only defense for their viewpoints is that those viewpoints suit their desires.

Such teachers have a following because they are telling people "whatever their itching ears want to hear." These people are following myths. Be careful. False teaching can be found in many places—even inside the doors of some churches. Like Timothy, you must "keep a clear mind in every situation" and seek God's Word for the truth.

**4:5** To keep cool when you are jarred and jolted by people or circumstances, don't react quickly. In any work of ministry that you undertake, keeping a clear mind in every situation makes you morally alert to temptation, resistant to pressure, and vigilant when facing heavy responsibility.

**4:6-8** As he neared the end of his life, Paul could confidently say that he had been faithful to his call. Thus, he faced death calmly, knowing that he would be rewarded by Christ. Is your life preparing you for death? Do you share Paul's confident expectation of meeting Christ? The good news is that the heavenly reward is not just for giants of the faith like Paul, but for all who are eagerly looking forward to Christ's second coming. Paul gave these words

to encourage Timothy and us, so that no matter how difficult the fight seems, we can keep fighting. When we are with Jesus Christ, we will discover that it was all worth it.

**4:8** In Roman athletic games, a laurel wreath would be given to each winner. A symbol of triumph and honor, it was the most coveted prize in ancient Rome. This is probably what Paul was referring to when he spoke of a "crown." But his would be a crown of righteousness. See 2 Corinthians 5:10 and the note on Matthew 19:27 for more on the rewards awaiting us for our faith and deeds. Although Paul would not receive an earthly reward, he would be rewarded in heaven. Whatever we may face— discouragement, persecution, or death—we know we will receive reward with Christ in heaven.

**4:9, 10** Paul was virtually alone and probably lonely. No one had come to his trial to speak in his defense (4:16), and Demas had left the faith (4:10). Crescens and Titus had left, but not for the same reasons as Demas. Paul did not criticize or condemn them. Demas had been one of Paul's coworkers (Colossians 4:14; Philemon 1:24), but he had deserted Paul because he loved "the things of this life." In other words, Demas loved worldly values and worldly pleasures. There are two ways to love the world. God loves the world as he created it and as it could be if it were rescued from evil. Others, like Demas, love the world as it is, sin and all. Do you love the world as it could be if justice were done, the hungry were fed, and people loved one another? Or do you love what the world has to offer—wealth, power, pleasure—even if gaining it means hurting people and neglecting the work God has given you to do?

**4:11, 12** Mentioning Demas reminded Paul of more faithful coworkers. Luke had traveled much with Paul, writing both the Gospel of Luke and the book of Acts (much of which is a firsthand account). Tychicus, one of his most trusted companions (Acts 20:4; Ephesians 6:21; Colossians 4:7; Titus 3:12), had already left for Ephesus.

That Paul requested for Timothy to bring Mark might give us pause. Mark had left Paul and Barnabas on the first missionary journey, and this had greatly upset Paul (Acts 13:13; 15:36-41), causing a rift between Paul and Barnabas that was so severe that they parted company. Somewhere along the line, Paul had given Mark a second chance, and Mark had proven to be a worthy helper. We don't have all the details in Mark's changed life or Paul's change of heart, but Paul realized that people can change.

There's a lesson in these few words. We should allow people to grow up and not hold them back from ministry or leadership for faults in the past that have now been corrected. When we encourage someone and open our minds to the possibility that he or she has changed and matured, we may be salvaging a significant ministry. Mark went on not only to be Paul's good friend and a trusted Christian leader (Colossians 4:10; Philemon 1:24), but he also wrote the Gospel of Mark.

be helpful to me in my ministry. [12] I sent Tychicus to Ephesus. [13] When you come, be sure to bring the coat I left with Carpus at Troas. Also bring my books, and especially my papers.*

[14] Alexander the coppersmith did me much harm, but the Lord will judge him for what he has done. [15] Be careful of him, for he fought against everything we said.

[16] The first time I was brought before the judge, no one came with me. Everyone abandoned me. May it not be counted against them. [17] But the Lord stood with me and gave me strength so that I might preach the Good News in its entirety for all the Gentiles to hear. And he rescued me from certain death.* [18] Yes, and the Lord will deliver me from every evil attack and will bring me safely into his heavenly Kingdom. All glory to God forever and ever! Amen.

## Paul's Final Greetings

[19] Give my greetings to Priscilla and Aquila and those living in the household of Onesiphorus. [20] Erastus stayed at Corinth, and I left Trophimus sick at Miletus.

[21] Do your best to get here before winter. Eubulus sends you greetings, and so do Pudens, Linus, Claudia, and all the brothers and sisters.*

[22] May the Lord be with your spirit. And may his grace be with all of you.

**4:12**
Acts 20:4
Eph 6:21-22
Col 4:7-8
**4:14**
1 Tim 1:20
**4:17**
Ps 22:21
Dan 6:22
Acts 9:15
**4:18**
Ps 121:7
Rom 11:36
**4:19**
Acts 18:2
2 Tim 1:16
**4:20**
Acts 19:22; 20:4
Rom 16:23

**4:13** Greek *especially the parchments.* **4:17** Greek *from the mouth of a lion.* **4:21** Greek *brothers.*

---

**4:13** Paul's arrest probably had occurred so suddenly that he had not been allowed to return home to gather his personal belongings. Because he was a prisoner in a damp and chilly dungeon, Paul asked Timothy to bring him his coat. Even more than the coat, Paul wanted his papers (or parchments). These may have included parts of the Old Testament, the Gospels, copies of his own letters, or other important documents.

**4:14, 15** Alexander may have been a witness against Paul at his trial. He may have been the Alexander mentioned in 1 Timothy 1:20.

**4:17** With his mentor in prison and his church in turmoil, Timothy was probably not feeling very brave. Paul may have been subtly telling Timothy that the Lord had called Timothy to preach and would give him the courage to continue to do so. God always gives us the strength to do what he has commanded. This strength may not be evident, however, until we step out in faith and actually begin doing the task.

**4:18** Here Paul was affirming his belief in eternal life after death. Paul knew the end was near, and he was ready for it. Paul was confident in God's power even as he faced death. Anyone facing a life-and-death struggle can be comforted knowing that God will bring each believer safely through death to his heavenly Kingdom.

**4:19, 20** Priscilla and Aquila were fellow Christian leaders with whom Paul had lived and worked (Acts 18:2, 3). Onesiphorus visited and encouraged Paul in jail. Erastus was one of Paul's

trusted companions (Acts 19:22), as was Trophimus (Acts 20:4; 21:29).

**4:19-22** Paul ended the final chapter in his book and in his life by greeting those who were closest to him. Although Paul had spent most of his life traveling, he had developed close and lasting friendships. Too often we rush through our days, barely touching anyone's life. Do you have a Paul—a mentor or teacher who provides leadership, accountability, and encouragement? Do you have a Priscilla or Aquila—a coworker or peer who prays with you in times of stress, loves you, and supports you? Do you have a Timothy—a younger leader whom you are helping, encouraging, and discipling? Like Paul, we should take time to weave our lives into others' through close personal relationships.

**4:22** As Paul reached the end of his life, he could look back and know he had been faithful to God's call. Now it was time to pass the torch to the next generation, preparing leaders to take his place so that the world would continue to hear the life-changing message of Jesus Christ. Timothy was Paul's living legacy, a product of Paul's faithful teaching, discipleship, and example. Because of Paul's work with many believers, including Timothy, the world is filled with believers today who are also carrying on the work. What legacy will you leave behind? Whom are you training to carry on your work? It is our responsibility to do all we can to keep God's Good News alive for the next generation.

# TITUS

THE VACUUM produced when a strong leader departs can devastate a movement, organization, or institution. Having been dependent on his or her skill, style, and personality, associates and subordinates flounder or vie for control. Soon efficiency and vitality are lost, and decline and demise follow. Often this pattern is repeated in churches. A great speaker or teacher gathers a following, and soon a church is flourishing. It is alive, vital, and effective. Lives are being changed and people led into the Kingdom. But when this person leaves or dies, with him or her goes the drive and the heart of the organization.

People flocked to hear Paul's teaching. Educated, articulate, motivated, and filled with the Holy Spirit, this man of God faithfully proclaimed the Good News throughout the Roman Empire; lives were changed and churches begun. But Paul knew that the church must be built on Christ, not on a person. And he knew that eventually he would not be there to build, encourage, discipline, and teach. So he trained young pastors to assume leadership in the churches after he was gone. Paul urged them to center their lives and preaching on the Word of God (2 Timothy 3:16, 17) and to train others to carry on the ministry (2 Timothy 2:2).

Titus was a Greek believer. Taught and nurtured by Paul, he stood before the leaders of the church in Jerusalem as a living example of what Christ was doing among the Gentiles (Galatians 2:1–3). Like Timothy, he was one of Paul's trusted traveling companions and closest friends. Later he became Paul's special ambassador (2 Corinthians 7:5–16) and eventually the overseer of the churches on Crete (Titus 1:5). Slowly and carefully, Paul developed Titus into a mature Christian and a responsible leader. The letter to Titus was a step in this discipleship process. As with Timothy, Paul told Titus how to organize and lead the churches.

Paul begins his letter with a longer than usual greeting and introduction, outlining the leadership progression: Paul's ministry (1:1–3), Titus's responsibilities (1:4, 5), and those leaders whom Titus would appoint and train (1:5). Paul then lists pastoral qualifications (1:6–9) and contrasts faithful elders with the false leaders and teachers (1:10–16).

Next, Paul emphasizes the importance of good deeds in the life of the Christian, telling Titus how to relate to the various age groups in the church (2:2–6). He urges Titus to be a good example of a mature believer (2:7, 8) and to teach with courage and conviction (2:9–15). He then discusses the general responsibilities of Christians in society: Titus should remind the people of these (3:1–8), and he should avoid divisive arguments (3:9–11). Paul concludes with a few matters of itinerary and personal greetings (3:12–15).

Paul's letter to Titus is brief, but it is an important link in the discipleship process, helping a young man grow into leadership in the church. As you read this pastoral letter, you will gain insight into the organization and life of the early church, and you will find principles for structuring contemporary churches. But you should also see how to be a responsible Christian leader. Read the letter to Titus and determine, like Paul, to train men and women to lead and teach others.

## VITAL STATISTICS

**PURPOSE:**
To advise Titus in his responsibility of supervising the churches on the island of Crete

**AUTHOR:**
Paul

**ORIGINAL AUDIENCE:**
Titus, a Greek, probably converted to Christ through Paul's ministry (he had become Paul's special representative to the island of Crete)

**DATE WRITTEN:**
Approximately A.D. 64, around the same time 1 Timothy was written; probably from Macedonia when Paul traveled between his Roman imprisonments

**SETTING:**
Paul sent Titus to organize and oversee the churches on Crete. This letter tells Titus how to do this job.

**KEY VERSE:**
"I left you on the island of Crete so you could complete our work there and appoint elders in each town as I instructed you" (1:5).

**KEY PEOPLE:**
Paul, Titus

**KEY PLACES:**
Crete, Nicopolis

**SPECIAL FEATURES:**
Titus is very similar to 1 Timothy with its instructions to church leaders.

## THE BLUEPRINT

1. Leadership in the church
   (1:1–16)
2. Right living in the church
   (2:1–15)
3. Right living in society
   (3:1–15)

Paul calls for church order and right living on an island known for laziness, gluttony, lying, and evil. The Christians are to be self-disciplined as individuals, and they must be orderly as people who form one body, the church. We need to obey this message in our day when discipline is not respected or rewarded by our society. Although others may not appreciate our efforts, we must live upright lives, obey the government, and control our speech. We should live together peacefully in the church and be living examples of our faith to contemporary society.

## MEGATHEMES

| THEME | EXPLANATION | IMPORTANCE |
|---|---|---|
| A Good Life | The Good News of salvation is that we can't be saved by living a good life; we are saved only by faith in Jesus Christ. But the gospel transforms people's lives, so that they eventually perform good deeds. Our service won't save us, but we are saved to serve. | A good life is a witness to the gospel's power. As Christians, we must have commitment and discipline to serve. Are you putting your faith into action by serving others? |
| Character | Titus's responsibility in Crete was to appoint elders to maintain proper organization and discipline, so Paul listed the qualities needed for the eldership. Their conduct in their homes revealed their fitness for service in the church. | It's not enough to be educated or to have a loyal following to be Christ's kind of leader. You must have self-control, spiritual and moral fitness, and Christian character. Who you are is just as important as what you can do. |
| Church Relationships | Church teaching must relate to various groups. Older Christians were to teach and to be examples to younger men and women. People of every age and group have a lesson to learn and a role to play. | Right living and right relationships go along with right doctrine. Treat relationships with other believers as an outgrowth of your faith. |
| Citizenship | Christians must be good citizens in society, not just in church. Believers must obey the government and work honestly. | How you fulfill your civic duties is a witness to the watching world. Your community life should reflect Christ's love as much as your church life does. |

## 1. Leadership in the church

*Greetings from Paul*

**1** This letter is from Paul, a slave of God and an apostle of Jesus Christ. I have been sent to proclaim faith to* those God has chosen and to teach them to know the truth that shows them how to live godly lives. ²This truth gives them confidence that they have eternal life, which God—who does not lie—promised them before the world began. ³And now at just the right time he has revealed this message, which we announce to everyone. It is by the command of God our Savior that I have been entrusted with this work for him.

**1:1** Or *to strengthen the faith of.*

**1:1**
1 Tim 2:4
**1:2**
2 Tim 1:1, 9
Titus 3:7
**1:3**
1 Tim 1:1, 11
Titus 2:10

**1:1** Paul wrote this letter between his first and second imprisonments in Rome (before he wrote 2 Timothy) to guide Titus in working with the churches on the island of Crete. Paul had visited Crete with Titus and had left him there to minister (1:5). Crete had a strong pagan influence because this small island may have been a training center for Roman soldiers. Therefore, the church in Crete needed strong Christian leadership.

**1:1** Paul calls himself "a slave of God"—that is, one who was committed to obeying God. This obedience led Paul to spend his life telling others about Christ. He also calls himself "an apostle." Even though Paul was not one of the original 12, he was specially called by God to bring the Good News to the Gentiles (see Acts 9:1-16 for an account of his call). The word *apostle* means "messenger or missionary." "Those God has chosen" refers to God's choice of his people, the church. For more information on Paul, see his Profile in Acts 9, p. 1837.

**1:1** In one short phrase, Paul gives insight into his reason for living. The process begins with the proclamation of *faith*, continues with *knowledge* of the truth, which is then shown by people living *godly lives.* Paul wanted men and women to be mature in

Jesus Christ. This was his ultimate objective by which he evaluated all he did.

How would your church evaluate its ultimate objectives? What specific goals, ministries, and service opportunities bring believers to faith, spiritual maturity, and godly living? Do established members reflect good Christian conduct and desire for Christian service?

How would you describe your purpose in life? To what are you devoted? Are you willing to share your faith, teach the truth, and live a godly life for all to see?

**1:2** Apparently lying was commonplace in Crete (1:12). Paul made it clear at the start that God does not lie. The foundation of our faith is trust in God's character. Because God *is* truth, he is the *source* of all truth, and he cannot lie. Believing in him leads to living a God-honoring lifestyle (1:1). The eternal life that God has promised will be ours because he keeps his promises. Build your faith on the foundation of a trustworthy God who never lies.

**1:3** God is called "our Savior," as is Christ Jesus (1:4). "God" here refers to the Father. Jesus did the work of salvation by dying for our sins, and, therefore, he is our Savior. God planned the

**1:4**
2 Cor 2:13
2 Tim 4:10

⁴I am writing to Titus, my true son in the faith that we share. May God the Father and Christ Jesus our Savior give you grace and peace.

### Titus's Work in Crete

**1:5**
Acts 14:23

**1:6-9**
//1 Tim 3:2-7
2 Tim 2:24-26

**1:7**
1 Cor 4:1

⁵I left you on the island of Crete so you could complete our work there and appoint elders in each town as I instructed you. ⁶An elder must live a blameless life. He must be faithful to his wife,* and his children must be believers who don't have a reputation for being wild or rebellious. ⁷An elder* is a manager of God's household, so he must live a blameless life. He must not be arrogant or quick-tempered; he must not be a heavy drinker,* violent, or dishonest with money.

⁸Rather, he must enjoy having guests in his home, and he must love what is good. He must

**1:6** Or *must have only one wife,* or *must be married only once;* Greek reads *must be the husband of one wife.* **1:7a** Or *An overseer,* or *A bishop.* **1:7b** Greek *must not drink too much wine.*

**TITUS GOES TO CRETE**
Tradition says that after Paul was released from prison in Rome (before his second and final Roman imprisonment), he and Titus traveled together for a while. They stopped in Crete, and when it was time for Paul to go, he left Titus behind to help the churches there.

work of salvation, and he forgives our sins. Both the Father and the Son acted to save us from our sins.

**1:4** Titus, a Greek, was one of Paul's most trusted and dependable coworkers. Paul had sent Titus to Corinth on several special missions to help the church in its troubles (2 Corinthians 7–8). Paul and Titus also had traveled together to Jerusalem (Galatians 2:3) and Crete (1:5). Paul left Titus in Crete to lead the new churches that were springing up on the island. Titus is last mentioned by Paul in 2 Timothy 4:10, Paul's final recorded letter. Titus had leadership ability, so Paul gave him leadership responsibility, urging him to use his abilities well.

**1:5** Crete, a small island in the Mediterranean Sea, had a large population of Jews. The churches there were probably founded by Cretan Jews who had been in Jerusalem at Pentecost (Acts 2:11) more than 30 years before Paul wrote this letter. The work that needed completion refers to establishing correct teaching and appointing elders in every town. Paul had appointed elders in various churches during his journeys (Acts 14:23). He could not stay in each church, but he knew that these new churches needed strong spiritual leadership. The men chosen were to lead the churches by teaching sound doctrine, helping believers mature spiritually, and equipping them to live for Jesus Christ despite opposition.

**1:5-9** Paul briefly describes some qualifications that the elders should have. Paul had given Timothy a similar set of instructions for the church in Ephesus (see 1 Timothy 3:1-7; 5:22). Notice that most of the qualifications involve character, not knowledge or skill. A person's lifestyle and relationships provide a window into his or her character. Consider these qualifications as you evaluate a person for a position of leadership in your church. It is important to have leaders who can effectively preach God's Word; it is even more important to have those who can live out God's Word and be examples for others to follow.

**1:8** One qualification for an elder was that he must "enjoy having guests in his home." Christian leaders must be known for their hospitality. In the early days of Christianity, traveling evangelists and teachers were helped by Christians who housed and fed them. We would benefit from inviting people to eat with us—visitors, fellow church members, young people, those in need. Giving hospitality is very important today because so many people struggle with loneliness. In our self-centered society, we can show that we care by being hospitable. Christians were not to entertain false teachers (2 John 1:10), but this prohibition did not apply to non-Christians in general. God wants us to be generous, courteous, and hospitable with non-Christians; through our friendship, some may be won to Christ.

live wisely and be just. He must live a devout and disciplined life. ⁹He must have a strong belief in the trustworthy message he was taught; then he will be able to encourage others with wholesome teaching and show those who oppose it where they are wrong.

¹⁰For there are many rebellious people who engage in useless talk and deceive others. This is especially true of those who insist on circumcision for salvation. ¹¹They must be silenced, because they are turning whole families away from the truth by their false teaching. And they do it only for money. ¹²Even one of their own men, a prophet from Crete, has said about them, "The people of Crete are all liars, cruel animals, and lazy gluttons."* ¹³This is true. So reprimand them sternly to make them strong in the faith. ¹⁴They must stop listening to Jewish myths and the commands of people who have turned away from the truth.

¹⁵Everything is pure to those whose hearts are pure. But nothing is pure to those who are corrupt and unbelieving, because their minds and consciences are corrupted. ¹⁶Such people claim they know God, but they deny him by the way they live. They are detestable and disobedient, worthless for doing anything good.

## 2. Right living in the church
*Promote Right Teaching*

**2** As for you, Titus, promote the kind of living that reflects wholesome teaching. ²Teach the older men to exercise self-control, to be worthy of respect, and to live wisely. They must have sound faith and be filled with love and patience.

³Similarly, teach the older women to live in a way that honors God. They must not slander

| | |
|---|---|
| **1:9** | 1 Tim 1:10 |
| | 2 Tim 4:3 |
| | Titus 2:1 |
| **1:10** | 1 Tim 1:6 |
| **1:11** | 1 Tim 5:13 |
| **1:13** | 1 Tim 5:20 |
| **1:14** | Col 2:22 |
| | 1 Tim 1:4; 4:7 |
| | 2 Tim 4:4 |
| **1:15** | Matt 15:10-11 |
| | Rom 14:14-20 |
| **1:16** | 1 Jn 1:6; 2:4 |
| **2:1** | 1 Tim 1:10 |
| | Titus 1:9 |
| **2:3** | 1 Tim 3:8, 11 |

1:12 This quotation is from Epimenides of Knossos.

---

**1:10** "Those who insist on circumcision for salvation" were the Judaizers, Jews who taught that the Gentiles had to obey all the Jewish laws before they could become Christians. This regulation confused new Christians and caused problems in many churches where Paul had preached the Good News. Paul wrote letters to several churches to help them understand that Gentile believers did not have to become Jews first in order to be Christians; God accepts anyone who comes to him in faith (see Romans 1:17; Galatians 3:2-7). Although the Jerusalem council had dealt with this issue (see Acts 15), devout Jews who refused to believe in Jesus still tried to cause problems in the Christian churches. Church leaders must be alert and take action on anything that divides Christians.

**1:10-14** Paul warns Titus to be on the lookout for people who teach wrong doctrines and lead others into error. Some false teachers are simply confused: They speak their misguided opinions without checking them against the Bible. Others have evil motives: They pretend to be Christians only because they can get more money, additional business, or a feeling of power from being a leader in the church. Jesus and the apostles repeatedly warned against false teachers (see Mark 13:22; Acts 20:29; 2 Thessalonians 2:3-12; 2 Peter 3:3-7) because their teachings attack the foundations of truth and integrity upon which the Christian faith is built. You can recognize false teachers because they will (1) focus more attention on themselves than on Christ, (2) ask you to do something that will compromise or dilute your faith, (3) de-emphasize the divine nature of Christ or the inspiration of the Bible, or (4) urge believers to make decisions based more on human judgment than on prayer and biblical guidelines.

**1:12** Paul is quoting a line from a poem by Epimenides, a poet and philosopher who had lived in Crete 600 years earlier. Some Cretans had a bad reputation and were known for lying. Paul used this familiar phrase to make the point that Titus's ministry and leadership were very much needed.

**1:15** Some people see good all around them, while others see nothing but evil. What is the difference? Our souls become filters through which we perceive goodness or evil. The pure (those who have Christ in control of their lives) learn to see goodness and purity even in this evil world. But corrupt and unbelieving people find evil in everything because their evil minds and hearts color even the good they see and hear. Whatever you choose to fill your mind with will affect the way you think and act. Turn your

thoughts to God and his Word, and you will discover more and more goodness, even in this evil world. A mind filled with good has little room for what is evil (see Philippians 4:8).

**1:16** Many people claim to know God. How can we know if they really do? We will not know for certain in this life, but a glance at their lifestyles will quickly tell us what they value and whether they have ordered their lives around Kingdom priorities. Our conduct speaks volumes about what we believe (see 1 John 2:4-6). What do people know about God and about your faith by watching your life?

**2:1** Notice the emphasis on "wholesome teaching" in Paul's instructions to Titus. This is the *content* of our faith. But how can you recognize wholesome teaching? When a teaching is sound, it combines correct knowledge and understanding with consistent practice. It must be found in the Bible, keep Jesus Christ central, result in consistently good behavior and actions, and promote spiritual health in ourselves and others.

Believers must be grounded in the truths of the Bible so they won't be swayed by the powerful oratory of false teachers, the possible devastation of tragic circumstances, or the pull of emotions. Those responsible for preaching and teaching must challenge people to understand sound doctrine. Learn the Bible, study theology, apply biblical principles, and *live* what you learn.

**2:2-8** Having people of all ages in the church makes it strong, but it also brings potential for problems. Paul gave Titus counsel on how to help various groups of people. The older people should teach the younger by words *and* by example. This is how values are passed on from generation to generation. Does your church carry out this basic function?

**2:2, 5** Self-control is an important aspect of living the Christian life. The Christian community, then and now, is made up of people from differing backgrounds and viewpoints, making conflict inevitable. We live in a pagan and often hostile world. To stay above reproach, believers need wisdom and discernment to be discreet and to master their wills, tongues, and passions so that Christ is not dishonored. How is your self-control?

**2:3-5** Women who were new Christians were to learn how to have harmony in the homes by watching older women who had been Christians for some time. We have the same need today. Young wives and mothers should learn to live in a Christian manner—loving their husbands and caring for their children—through observing exemplary women of God. If you are of an age or in others or be heavy drinkers.* Instead, they should teach others what is good. ⁴These older women must train the younger women to love their husbands and their children, ⁵to live wisely and be pure, to work in their homes,* to do good, and to be submissive to their husbands. Then they will not bring shame on the word of God.

⁶In the same way, encourage the young men to live wisely. ⁷And you yourself must be an example to them by doing good works of every kind. Let everything you do reflect the integrity and seriousness of your teaching. ⁸Teach the truth so that your teaching can't be criticized. Then those who oppose us will be ashamed and have nothing bad to say about us.

⁹Slaves must always obey their masters and do their best to please them. They must not talk back ¹⁰or steal, but must show themselves to be entirely trustworthy and good. Then they will make the teaching about God our Savior attractive in every way.

¹¹For the grace of God has been revealed, bringing salvation to all people. ¹²And we are instructed to turn from godless living and sinful pleasures. We should live in this evil world with wisdom, righteousness, and devotion to God, ¹³while we look forward with hope to that wonderful day when the glory of our great God and Savior, Jesus Christ, will be revealed. ¹⁴He gave his life to free us from every kind of sin, to cleanse us, and to make us his very own people, totally committed to doing good deeds.

¹⁵You must teach these things and encourage the believers to do them. You have the authority to correct them when necessary, so don't let anyone disregard what you say.

### 3. Right living in society
*Do What Is Good*

**3** Remind the believers to submit to the government and its officers. They should be obedient, always ready to do what is good. ²They must not slander anyone and must avoid quarreling. Instead, they should be gentle and show true humility to everyone.

**2:3** Greek *be enslaved to much wine.*    **2:5** Some manuscripts read *to care for their homes.*

**2:5**
Eph 5:22
1 Tim 5:14

**2:7**
1 Tim 4:12
1 Pet 5:3

**2:8**
1 Pet 2:12

**2:9**
Eph 6:5

**2:11**
1 Tim 2:4
2 Tim 1:10

**2:13**
John 1:1; 20:28
Rom 9:5
1 Cor 1:7
Phil 3:20
2 Pet 1:1
1 Jn 5:20

**2:14**
Eph 2:10
1 Pet 2:9
1 Jn 1:7

**2:15**
1 Tim 4:12

**3:1**
Rom 13:1
1 Pet 2:13

**3:2**
Eph 4:31

---

a position where people look up to you, make sure that your example is motivating younger believers to live in a way that honors God.

**2:6** This advice given to young men was very important. In ancient Greek society, the role of the husband/father was not viewed as a nurturing role but merely as a functional one. Many young men today have been raised in families where fathers have neglected their responsibilities to their wives and children. Husbands and fathers who are good examples of Christian living are important role models for young men who need to *see* how it is done.

**2:7, 8** Paul urges Titus to be a good example to those around him so that others might see Titus's good deeds and imitate him. Paul's life would give his words greater impact. If you want someone to act a certain way, be sure that you live that way yourself. Then you will earn the right to be heard, and your life will reinforce what you teach.

**2:8** Paul counsels Titus to be above criticism in how he taught. This quality of integrity comes from careful Bible study and listening before speaking. This is especially important when teaching or confronting others about spiritual or moral issues. If we are impulsive, unreasonable, and confusing, we are likely to start arguments rather than to convince people of the truth.

**2:9, 10** Slavery was common in Paul's day. Paul did not condemn slavery in any of his letters, but he advised slaves and masters to be loving and responsible in their conduct (see also Ephesians 6:5-9). The standards set by Paul can help any employee/employer relationship. Employees should always do their best work and be trustworthy, not just when the employer is watching. Businesses lose millions of dollars a year to employee theft and time-wasting. If all Christian employees would follow Paul's advice at work, what a transformation it would make!

**2:12, 13** Paul brings out two aspects of Christian living that must be stressed today. "We should live in this evil world . . . while we look forward with hope." Both aspects of *living* and *looking forward* are essential to our Christian sanity in this present evil age. The living is made bearable because we live for God—seeking to build his Kingdom with whatever gifts he has given us. And it is that very Kingdom to which we are looking forward. As we live and look

forward, we anticipate three great benefits of Christ's return: (1) Christ's personal presence—we look forward to being with him. (2) Redemption from our sinful nature—we long for the end of the battle with sin and our perfection in Christ. (3) Restoration of creation—we anticipate the complete rule of grace when the image of God will be fully realized in people and when the created order will be restored.

**2:14** Christ's freeing us from sin opens the way for him to "cleanse" us. He freed us from sin (redeemed us) by purchasing our release from the captivity of sin with a ransom (see Mark 10:45 for more on Christ as our ransom). We are not only free from the sentence of death for our sin, but we are also purified from sin's influence as we grow in Christ.

**2:15** Paul tells Titus to teach the Scriptures as well as to live them. We must also teach, encourage, and correct others, when necessary. We can easily feel afraid when others are older, more influential in the community, or wealthier. Like Titus, we should not let ourselves be threatened when we are trying to minister to others or provide leadership in the church.

**3:1** As Christians, our first allegiance is to Jesus as Lord, but we must obey our government and its leaders as well. Christians are not above the law. Obeying the civil law is only the beginning of our Christian responsibility; we must do what we can to be good citizens. (See Acts 5:29 and Romans 13:1ff for more on the Christian's attitude toward government.)

**3:2** How does one "show true humility"? Humility is a very elusive character trait, yet the Bible regards it as a highly important quality. Jesus referred to himself as "humble and gentle at heart" (Matthew 11:29). In Romans 12:3, Paul wrote the clearest definition of humility apart from Jesus' own example: "Don't think you are better than you really are. Be honest in your evaluation of yourselves, measuring yourselves by the faith God has given us."

Humility, then, boils down to having an honest estimate of ourselves before God. We show false humility when we project negative worth on our abilities and efforts. We show pride when we inflate the value of our efforts or look down on others. True humility seeks to view our character and accomplishments honestly. Recognizing that we have succeeded in an effort need not be pride.

³Once we, too, were foolish and disobedient. We were misled and became slaves to many lusts and pleasures. Our lives were full of evil and envy, and we hated each other.

⁴But—"When God our Savior revealed his kindness and love, ⁵he saved us, not because of the righteous things we had done, but because of his mercy. He washed away our sins, giving us a new birth and new life through the Holy Spirit.* ⁶He generously poured out the Spirit upon us through Jesus Christ our Savior. ⁷Because of his grace he declared us righteous and gave us confidence that we will inherit eternal life." ⁸This is a trustworthy saying, and I want you to insist on these teachings so that all who trust in God will devote themselves to doing good. These teachings are good and beneficial for everyone.

⁹Do not get involved in foolish discussions about spiritual pedigrees* or in quarrels and fights about obedience to Jewish laws. These things are useless and a waste of time. ¹⁰If people are causing divisions among you, give a first and second warning. After that, have nothing more to do with them. ¹¹For people like that have turned away from the truth, and their own sins condemn them.

## Paul's Final Remarks and Greetings

¹²I am planning to send either Artemas or Tychicus to you. As soon as one of them arrives, do your best to meet me at Nicopolis, for I have decided to stay there for the winter. ¹³Do everything you can to help Zenas the lawyer and Apollos with their trip. See that they are given everything they need. ¹⁴Our people must learn to do good by meeting the urgent needs of others; then they will not be unproductive.

¹⁵Everybody here sends greetings. Please give my greetings to the believers—all who love us.

May God's grace be with you all.

**3:5** Greek *He saved us through the washing of regeneration and renewing of the Holy Spirit.*   **3:9** Or *spiritual genealogies.*

| | |
|---|---|
| **3:3** | 1 Cor 6:11 / Eph 5:8 |
| **3:5** | John 3:5 / Eph 2:4, 8 / 1 Pet 1:3 |
| **3:6** | Joel 2:28 / Rom 5:5 |
| **3:7** | Rom 3:24 |
| **3:8** | Titus 2:14; 3:14 |
| **3:9** | 2 Tim 2:14, 16, 23 |
| **3:10** | Matt 18:15-17 / Rom 16:17 |
| **3:12** | Acts 20:4 / Eph 6:21-22 / 2 Tim 4:9, 21 |
| **3:13** | Acts 18:24 |
| **3:14** | Eph 4:28 / Titus 2:14; 3:8 |
| **3:15** | Col 4:18 |

---

**3:3** Following a life of pleasure and giving in to every sensual desire leads to slavery. Many think freedom consists of doing anything they want. But this path leads to a slavish addiction to sensual gratification. A person is no longer free but is a slave to what his or her body dictates (2 Peter 2:19). Christ frees us from the desires and control of sin. Have you been released?

**3:4-8** Paul summarizes what Christ does for us when he saves us. We move from a life full of sin to one where we are led by God's Holy Spirit. *All* our sins, not merely some, are washed away. Washing refers to the water of baptism, which is a sign of salvation. In becoming a Christian, the believer acknowledges Christ as Lord and recognizes Christ's saving work. We gain eternal life with *all* its treasures. We have a new life through the Holy Spirit, and he continually renews our hearts. None of this occurs because we earned or deserved it; it is all God's gift.

**3:4-6** All three persons of the Trinity are mentioned in these verses because all three participate in the work of salvation. Based upon the redemptive work of his Son, the Father forgives us and sends the Holy Spirit to wash away our sins and continually renew us.

**3:8** In this chapter, Paul stressed that believers must devote themselves to doing good. Paul understood good works as faithful service, acts of charity, and involvement in civil affairs. While good works can't save us or even increase God's love for us, they are true indications of our faith and love for Christ. Paul did not make this aspect of discipleship optional. Service to others is a requirement. Everyone who is a Christian should be involved. Does your church encourage everyone's involvement and service? What can your church do to help every member identify the good works he or she should be doing?

**3:9** Paul warns Titus, as he warned Timothy, not to get involved in foolish and unprofitable arguments (2 Timothy 2:14). This does not mean we should refuse to study, discuss, and examine different interpretations of difficult Bible passages. Paul is warning against petty quarrels, not honest discussion that leads to wisdom. If foolish arguments develop, it is best to turn the discussion back to a helpful direction or politely excuse yourself.

**3:9** The false teachers were basing their heresies on spiritual pedigrees and speculations about the Jewish laws (see 1 Timothy 1:3, 4). Similar to the methods used by false teachers in Ephesus and Colosse, they were building their case on genealogies of angels. We should avoid false teachers, not even bothering to get involved in their foolish discussions. Overreaction sometimes gives more attention to their points of view.

**3:10, 11** A person must be warned when he or she is causing division that threatens the unity of the church. This should not be a heavy-handed action but a warning to correct the individual's divisive nature and restore him or her to fellowship. A person who refuses to be corrected should be put outside the fellowship. As Paul said, that person is self-condemned—he or she is sinning and knows it. (See also Matthew 18:15-18 and 2 Thessalonians 3:14, 15 for help in handling such problems in the church.)

**3:12** The city of Nicopolis was on the western coast of Greece. Artemas or Tychicus would take over Titus's work on the island of Crete so Titus could meet Paul in Nicopolis. Tychicus was another of Paul's trusted companions (Acts 20:4; Ephesians 6:21; Colossians 4:7). Titus would have to leave soon because sea travel was dangerous in the winter months.

**3:13** Apollos was a famous Christian preacher. A native of Alexandria in North Africa, he became a Christian in Ephesus and was trained by Aquila and Priscilla (Acts 18:24-28; 1 Corinthians 1:12).

**3:15** The letters of Paul to Titus and Timothy are his last writings and mark the end of his life and ministry. These letters are rich treasures for us today because they give vital information for church leadership. They provide a strong model for elders, pastors, and other Christian leaders as they develop younger leaders to carry on the work, following Paul's example of preparing Timothy and Titus to carry on his ministry. For practical guidelines on church leadership and problem solving, carefully study the principles found in these letters.

# PHILEMON

AT THE foreman's signal, the giant ball is released, and with dynamite force and a reverberating crash, it meets the wall, snapping bricks like twigs and scattering pieces of mortar. Repeatedly, the powerful pendulum works, and soon the barrier has been reduced to rubble. Then it is carted away so that construction can begin.

Life has many walls and fences that divide, separate, and compartmentalize. Not made of wood or stone, they are personal obstructions, blocking people from each other and from God. But Christ came as the great wall remover, tearing down the sin partition that separates us from God and blasting the barriers that keep us from each other. His death and resurrection opened the way to eternal life to bring all who believe into the family of God (see Ephesians 2:14–18).

Roman, Greek, and Jewish cultures were littered with barriers, as society assigned people to classes and expected them to stay in their place—men and women, slave and free, rich and poor, Jews and Gentiles, Greeks and barbarians, pious and pagan. But with the message of Christ, the walls came down, and Paul could declare, "In this new life, it doesn't matter if you are a Jew or a Gentile, circumcised or uncircumcised, barbaric, uncivilized, slave, or free. Christ is all that matters, and he lives in all of us" (Colossians 3:11).

This life-changing truth forms the backdrop for the letter to Philemon. One of three personal letters in the Bible, the letter to Philemon is Paul's personal plea for a slave. Onesimus "belonged" to Philemon, a member of the Colossian church and Paul's friend. But Onesimus, the slave, had stolen from his master and had run away. He had run to Rome, where he had met Paul, and there he had responded to the Good News and had come to faith in Christ (1:10). So Paul wrote to Philemon and reintroduced Onesimus to him, explaining that he was sending him back, not just as a slave but as a brother (1:11, 12, 16). Tactfully he asked Philemon to accept and forgive his brother (1:10, 14, 15, 20). The barriers of the past and the new ones erected by Onesimus's desertion and theft should divide them no longer—they are one in Christ.

This small book is a masterpiece of grace and tact and a profound demonstration of the power of Christ and of true Christian fellowship in action. What barriers stand in your home, neighborhood, and church? What separates you from fellow believers? Race? Status? Wealth? Education? Personality? As with Philemon, God calls you to seek unity, breaking down those walls and embracing your brothers and sisters in Christ.

## VITAL STATISTICS

**PURPOSE:**
To convince Philemon to forgive his runaway slave, Onesimus, and to accept him as a brother in the faith

**AUTHOR:**
Paul

**ORIGINAL AUDIENCE:**
Philemon, who was probably a wealthy member of the Colossian church

**DATE WRITTEN:**
Approximately A.D. 60, during Paul's first imprisonment in Rome, at about the same time Ephesians and Colossians were written

**SETTING:**
Slavery was very common in the Roman Empire, and evidently some Christians had slaves. Paul does not condemn the institution of slavery in his writings, but he makes a radical statement by calling this slave Philemon's brother in Christ.

**KEY VERSES:**
"It seems Onesimus ran away for a little while so that you could have him back forever. He is no longer like a slave to you. He is more than a slave, for he is a beloved brother, especially to me. Now he will mean much more to you, both as a man and as a brother in the Lord" (1:15, 16).

**KEY PEOPLE:**
Paul, Philemon, Onesimus

**KEY PLACES:**
Colosse, Rome

**SPECIAL FEATURES:**
This is a private, personal letter to a friend.

## THE BLUEPRINT

1. Paul's appreciation of Philemon
   (1:1–7)
2. Paul's appeal for Onesimus
   (1:8–25)

Paul pleads on behalf of Onesimus, a runaway slave. Paul's intercession for him illustrates what Christ has done for us. As Paul interceded for a slave, so Christ intercedes for us, slaves to sin. As Onesimus was reconciled to Philemon, so we are reconciled to God through Christ. As Paul offered to pay the debts of a slave, so Christ paid our debt of sin. Like Onesimus, we must return to God our Master and serve him.

## MEGATHEMES

| THEME | EXPLANATION | IMPORTANCE |
|-------|-------------|------------|
| Forgiveness | Philemon was Paul's friend and the legal owner of the slave Onesimus. Paul asked Philemon not to punish Onesimus but to forgive and restore him as a new Christian brother. | Christian relationships must be full of forgiveness and acceptance. Can you forgive those who have wronged you? |
| Barriers | Slavery was widespread in the Roman Empire, but no one is lost to God or beyond his love. Slavery was a barrier between people, but Christian love and fellowship are to overcome such barriers. | In Christ we are one family. No walls of racial, economic, or political differences should separate us. Let Christ work through you to remove barriers between Christian brothers and sisters. |
| Respect | Paul was a friend of both Philemon and Onesimus. He had the authority as an apostle to tell Philemon what to do. Yet Paul chose to appeal to his friend in Christian love rather than to order him what to do. | Tactful persuasion accomplishes a great deal more than commands when dealing with people. Remember to exhibit courtesy and respect in your relationships. |

## 1. Paul's appreciation of Philemon

### Greetings from Paul

This letter is from Paul, a prisoner for preaching the Good News about Christ Jesus, and from our brother Timothy.

    I am writing to Philemon, our beloved co-worker, 2and to our sister Apphia, and to our fellow soldier Archippus, and to the church that meets in your* house.

    3May God our Father and the Lord Jesus Christ give you grace and peace.

**1:1**
Eph 4:1
Phil 1:7
Phlm 1:9, 23

**1:2**
Rom 16:5
Phil 2:25
Col 4:17

### Paul's Thanksgiving and Prayer

4I always thank my God when I pray for you, Philemon, 5because I keep hearing about your faith in the Lord Jesus and your love for all of God's people. 6And I am praying that you will put into action the generosity that comes from your faith as you understand and experience

**1:4**
Rom 1:8-9

**1:6**
Phil 1:9

2 Throughout this letter, *you* and *your* are singular except in verses 3, 22, and 25.

---

**1:1** Paul wrote this letter from Rome in about A.D. 60, when he was under house arrest (see Acts 28:30, 31). Onesimus was a domestic slave who belonged to Philemon, a wealthy man and a member of the church in Colosse. Onesimus had run away from Philemon and had made his way to Rome, where he met Paul, who apparently led him to Christ (1:10). Paul convinced Onesimus that running from his problems wouldn't solve them, and he persuaded Onesimus to return to his master. Paul wrote this letter to Philemon to ask him to be reconciled to his runaway slave.

**1:1** For more information on Paul's life, see his Profile in Acts 9, p. 1837. Timothy's name is included with Paul's in 2 Corinthians, 1 Thessalonians, 2 Thessalonians, Philippians, Colossians, and Philemon—the last three of these letters are from a group known as the "Prison Letters." Timothy was one of Paul's trusted companions; Paul wrote two letters to him—1 and 2 Timothy. See Timothy's Profile in 1 Timothy 2, p. 2059.

**1:1** Philemon was a Greek landowner living in Colosse. He had been converted under Paul's ministry, and the Colossian church met in his home. Onesimus was one of Philemon's slaves.

**1:2** Apphia may have been Philemon's wife. Archippus may have been Philemon's son or perhaps an elder in the Colossian church. In either case, Paul included him as a recipient of the

letter, possibly so Archippus could read the letter with Philemon and encourage him to take Paul's advice.

**1:2** The early churches often would meet in people's homes. Because of sporadic persecutions and the great expense involved, church buildings were typically not constructed at this time.

**1:4-7** Like cold water on a long hike, this Christian brother Philemon knew how to be refreshing. He was able to revive and restore his brothers and sisters in the faith. His love and generosity had replenished and stimulated them. Philemon also encouraged Paul by his love and loyalty. Are you a refreshing influence on others, or do your attitude and temperament add to the burden they carry? Instead of draining others' energy and motivation with complaints and problems, replenish their spirits by encouragement, love, and a helpful attitude.

**1:6** Paul's prayer for Philemon was setting the stage for the request Paul would make in this letter. Philemon was active in his faith and generous in sharing its blessings. As he gained fuller understanding of all that Christ had done on his behalf, this knowledge should cause him to respond appropriately to Paul's request regarding Onesimus. Are you active and effective in sharing with others your faith, your resources, and your love?

1:7
2 Cor 7:4, 13

all the good things we have in Christ. 7 Your love has given me much joy and comfort, my brother, for your kindness has often refreshed the hearts of God's people.

## 2. Paul's appeal for Onesimus

1:9
Eph 3:1; 4:1
Phil 1:7

8 That is why I am boldly asking a favor of you. I could demand it in the name of Christ because it is the right thing for you to do. 9 But because of our love, I prefer simply to ask you. Consider this as a request from me—Paul, an old man and now also a prisoner for the sake of Christ Jesus.*

9 Or *a prisoner of Christ Jesus.*

**ONESIMUS**

God must have a special love for runaways. The pages of Scripture record dozens of people who were prone to flight. From Adam and Eve's attempt to elude God, through Jacob's escape from his brother, past generations of God's people on the run, to that inner circle of disciples who fled from the garden when Jesus was captured, the Bible is a collection of runaway lives. God's special love for runaways is beautifully illustrated in the life of a slave named Onesimus.

We are not told why Onesimus ran away from Philemon's house in Colosse. Eventually, he and Paul were reunited in Rome. Though we might crave details, Paul simply wrote that Onesimus became a follower of Jesus. Later, his spiritual growth caused Paul to call him a "faithful and beloved brother" (Colossians 4:9).

Eventually, Paul and Onesimus decided it was time for the runaway slave to return home. Paul wrote a letter of explanation to his friend Philemon, assuring him that Onesimus would now serve him wholeheartedly. Although the culture of the day gave masters complete control over their slaves and although severe punishment usually faced a runaway, Paul challenged Philemon to think of Onesimus more as a brother than as a slave. Paul took responsibility for any restitution Philemon might require of Onesimus. As difficult as it might be for him, Onesimus, the runaway slave turned believer, had to return and face his old life as a new person.

When God finds runaways, he often sends them back to the very places and people from which they ran in the first place. As God has become real in your life, how has your past come into new perspective? Are there still situations from your past that need to be resolved? In what ways has your relationship with Christ given you new opportunities and resources to face what you used to run away from?

| | |
|---|---|
| **Strengths and accomplishments** | • Tracked down and listened to the apostle Paul's message<br>• Grew into an able believer and assistant to Paul while in Rome<br>• Returned to his previous master as a willing slave |
| **Weakness and mistake** | • Ran away from his master, Philemon |
| **Lessons from his life** | • God is in the radical forgiveness business<br>• We cannot run from God and hope to escape |
| **Vital statistics** | • Where: Colosse<br>• Occupation: Slave |
| **Key verses** | "It seems Onesimus ran away for a little while so that you could have him back forever. He is no longer like a slave to you. He is more than a slave, for he is a beloved brother, especially to me. Now he will mean much more to you, both as a man and as a brother in the Lord" (Philemon 1:15-16). |

Onesimus is mentioned in Colossians 4:9 and is the subject of Paul's letter to Philemon.

**1:8, 9** Because Paul was an elder and an apostle, he could have used his authority with Philemon, commanding him to deal kindly with his runaway slave. But Paul based his request not on his own authority but on Philemon's Christian commitment. Paul wanted Philemon's heartfelt, not grudging, obedience. When you know something is right and you have the power to demand it, do you appeal to your authority or to the other person's commitment?

Paul provides a good example of how to deal with conflict between Christians. When reconciling a separation or mediating a dispute, trust must be rebuilt between the conflicting parties. Notice the steps that Paul used to help rebuild the trust: (1) He identified with those involved, calling Philemon "brother" and Onesimus "my child." (2) He requested, not ordered, Philemon

to do the right thing. (3) He sought Philemon's voluntary consent, not his submission to rules or authority. (4) He appealed to Christian love, not to power or authority. (5) He agreed to absorb the loss and pay any cost for restoration. Instead of overusing power or position, use Paul's approach to rebuild a trusting relationship.

¹⁰I appeal to you to show kindness to my child, Onesimus. I became his father in the faith while here in prison. ¹¹Onesimus* hasn't been of much use to you in the past, but now he is very useful to both of us. ¹²I am sending him back to you, and with him comes my own heart.

¹³I wanted to keep him here with me while I am in these chains for preaching the Good News, and he would have helped me on your behalf. ¹⁴But I didn't want to do anything without your consent. I wanted to help because you were willing, not because you were forced. ¹⁵It seems you lost Onesimus for a little while so that you could have him back forever. ¹⁶He is no longer like a slave to you. He is more than a slave, for he is a beloved brother, especially to me. Now he will mean much more to you, both as a man and as a brother in the Lord.

¹⁷So if you consider me your partner, welcome him as you would welcome me. ¹⁸If he has wronged you in any way or owes you anything, charge it to me. ¹⁹I, PAUL, WRITE THIS WITH MY OWN HAND: I WILL REPAY IT. AND I WON'T MENTION THAT YOU OWE ME YOUR VERY SOUL!

²⁰Yes, my brother, please do me this favor* for the Lord's sake. Give me this encouragement in Christ.

²¹I am confident as I write this letter that you will do what I ask and even more! ²²One more thing—please prepare a guest room for me, for I am hoping that God will answer your prayers and let me return to you soon.

## Paul's Final Greetings

²³Epaphras, my fellow prisoner in Christ Jesus, sends you his greetings. ²⁴So do Mark, Aristarchus, Demas, and Luke, my co-workers.

²⁵May the grace of the Lord Jesus Christ be with your spirit.

**1:10**
1 Cor 4:14
Col 4:9

**1:13**
Phil 2:30

**1:14**
2 Cor 9:7
1 Pet 5:2

**1:15**
Gen 45:5, 8

**1:16**
Matt 23:8
1 Cor 7:22
Eph 6:9

**1:17**
2 Cor 8:23

**1:19**
1 Cor 16:21

**1:22**
Phil 1:25-26; 2:24

**1:23**
Col 1:7; 4:10

**1:25**
Gal 6:18

**11** *Onesimus* means "useful." **20** Greek *onaimen,* a play on the name Onesimus.

---

**1:10** A master had the legal right to kill a runaway slave, so Onesimus feared for his life. Paul wrote this letter to Philemon to help him understand his new relationship with Onesimus, who was now a Christian brother, not a mere possession.

**1:10ff** From his prison cell, Paul had led Onesimus to the Lord. Paul asked Philemon to forgive his runaway slave who had become a Christian and, even going beyond forgiveness, to accept Onesimus as a brother. As Christians, we should forgive as we have been forgiven (Matthew 6:12; Ephesians 4:31, 32). True forgiveness means that we treat the one we've forgiven as we would want to be treated. Is there someone you say you have forgiven but who still needs your kindness?

**1:11-15** *Onesimus* means "useful." Paul used a play on words, saying that Onesimus had not been much use to Philemon in the past but now had become very useful to both Philemon and Paul. Although Paul wanted to keep Onesimus with him, he was sending Onesimus back, requesting that Philemon accept him not only as a forgiven runaway servant but also as a brother in Christ.

**1:15, 16** Slavery was widespread throughout the Roman Empire. In these early days, Christians did not have the political power to change the slavery system. Paul didn't condemn or condone slavery, but he worked to transform relationships. The Good News begins to change social structures by changing the *people* within those structures. (See also 1 Corinthians 7:20-24; Ephesians 6:5-9; Colossians 3:22–4:1 for more on master/slave relationships.)

**1:16** What a difference Onesimus's status as a Christian made in his relationship to Philemon. He was no longer merely a slave, but he was also a brother. That meant that both Onesimus and Philemon were members of God's family—equals in Christ. A Christian's status as a member of God's family transcends all other distinctions among believers. Do you look down on any fellow Christians? Remember, they are your equals before Christ (Galatians 3:28). How you treat your brothers and sisters in Christ's family reflects your true Christian commitment.

**1:17** Paul called Philemon his "partner," but he did not mean a partner in the business sense of the word. Philemon was a partner in grace. Paul and Philemon shared the same experience in Jesus Christ of being saved; in that sense, they were equals. Too often our relationships in the church don't possess true partnership but reflect merely tolerance of one another. Do you have room in your heart to welcome other believers warmly? Treat them as partners in God's grace and love, not just fellow workers. Let your common interests in Christ and your common feeling of gratitude for Christ's love knit you together with others.

**1:17-19** Paul genuinely loved Onesimus. Paul showed his love by personally guaranteeing payment for any stolen goods or wrongs for which Onesimus might be responsible. Paul's investment in the life of this new believer certainly encouraged and strengthened Onesimus's faith. Are there young believers who need you to demonstrate such self-sacrifice toward them? Be grateful when you can invest in the lives of others, helping them with Bible study, prayer, encouragement, support, and friendship.

**1:19** Philemon owed his soul to Paul, meaning that Paul had led Philemon to Christ. Because Paul was Philemon's spiritual father, he was hoping that Philemon would feel a debt of gratitude that he would repay by accepting Onesimus with a spirit of forgiveness.

**1:22** Paul was released from prison soon after writing this letter, but the Bible doesn't say whether or not he returned to Colosse.

**1:23** Epaphras was well known to the Colossians because he had founded the church there (Colossians 1:7). He was a hero to this church, helping to hold it together in spite of growing persecution and struggles with false doctrine. His report to Paul about the problems in Colosse had prompted Paul to write his letter to the Colossians. Epaphras's greetings to the Colossian Christians reveal his deep love for them (Colossians 4:12, 13). He may have been in prison with Paul for preaching the Good News.

**1:24** Mark, Aristarchus, Demas, and Luke are also mentioned in Colossians 4:10, 14. Mark had accompanied Paul and Barnabas on their first missionary journey (Acts 12:25ff). Mark also wrote the Gospel of Mark. Luke had accompanied Paul on his third missionary journey and was the writer of the Gospel of Luke and the book of Acts. Demas had been faithful to Paul for a while but later deserted him (see 2 Timothy 4:10).

**1:25** Paul urged Philemon to be reconciled to his slave, receiving him as a brother and fellow member of God's family. *Reconciliation* means reestablishing relationship. Christ has reconciled us to God and to others. Many barriers come between people—race, social status, sex, personality differences—but Christ can break down these barriers. Jesus Christ changed Onesimus's relationship to Philemon from slave to brother. Christ can transform our most hopeless relationships into deep and loving friendships.

# HEBREWS

CONSCIENTIOUS consumers shop for value, the best products for the money. Wise parents desire only the best for their children, nourishing their growing bodies, minds, and spirits. Individuals with integrity seek the best investment of time, talents, and treasures. In every area, to settle for less would be wasteful, foolish, and irresponsible. Yet it is a natural pull to move toward what is convenient and comfortable.

Judaism was not second-rate or easy. Divinely designed, it was the best religion, expressing true worship and devotion to God. The commandments, the rituals, and the prophets described God's promises and revealed the way to forgiveness and salvation. But Christ came, fulfilling the Law and the Prophets, conquering sin, shattering all barriers to God, freely providing eternal life.

This message was difficult for Jews to accept. Although they had sought the Messiah for centuries, they were entrenched in thinking and worshiping in traditional forms. Following Jesus seemed to repudiate their marvelous heritage and Scriptures. With caution and questions they listened to the gospel, but many rejected it and sought to eliminate this "heresy." Those who did accept Jesus as the Messiah often found themselves slipping back into familiar routines, trying to live a hybrid faith.

Hebrews is a masterful document written to Jews who were evaluating Jesus or struggling with this new faith. The message of Hebrews is that Jesus is better, Christianity is superior, Christ is supreme and completely sufficient for salvation.

Hebrews begins by emphasizing that the old (Judaism) and the new (Christianity) are both religions revealed by God (1:1–3). In the doctrinal section that follows (1:4—10:18), the writer shows how Jesus is superior to angels (1:4—2:18), superior to their leaders (3:1—4:13), and superior to their priests (4:14—7:28). Christianity surpasses Judaism because it has a better covenant (8:1–13), a better sanctuary (9:1–10), and a more sufficient sacrifice for sins (9:11—10:18).

Having established the superiority of Christianity, the writer moves on to the practical implications of following Christ. The readers are exhorted to hold on to their new faith, encourage each other, and look forward to Christ's return (10:19–25). They are warned about the consequences of rejecting Christ's sacrifice (10:26–31) and reminded of the rewards for faithfulness (10:32–39). Then the author explains how to live by faith, giving illustrations of the faithful men and women in Israel's history (11:1–40) and giving encouragement and exhortation for daily living (12:1–17). This section ends by comparing the old covenant with the new (12:18–29). The writer concludes with moral exhortations (13:1–17), a request for prayer (13:18, 19), and a benediction and greetings (13:20–25).

Whatever you are considering as the focus of life, Christ is better. He is the perfect revelation of God, the final and complete sacrifice for sin, the compassionate and understanding mediator, and the *only* way to eternal life. Read Hebrews and begin to see history and life from God's perspective. Then give yourself unreservedly and completely to Christ.

## VITAL STATISTICS

**PURPOSE:**
To present the sufficiency and superiority of Christ

**AUTHOR:**
Paul, Luke, Barnabas, Apollos, Silas, Philip, Priscilla, and others have been suggested because the name of the author is not given in the biblical text itself. Whoever it was speaks of Timothy as "brother" (13:23).

**ORIGINAL AUDIENCE:**
Hebrew Christians (perhaps second-generation Christians, see 2:3) who may have been considering a return to Judaism, perhaps because of immaturity, stemming from a lack of understanding of biblical truths

**DATE WRITTEN:**
Probably before the destruction of the Temple in Jerusalem in A.D. 70 because the religious sacrifices and ceremonies are referred to in the book, but no mention is made of the Temple's destruction

**SETTING:**
These Jewish Christians were probably undergoing fierce persecution, socially and physically, both from Jews and from Romans. Christ had not returned to establish his Kingdom, and the people needed to be reassured that Christianity was true and that Jesus was indeed the Messiah.

**KEY VERSE:**
"The Son radiates God's own glory and expresses the very character of God, and he sustains everything by the mighty power of his command. When he had cleansed us from our sins, he sat down in the place of honor at the right hand of the majestic God in heaven" (1:3).

**KEY PEOPLE:**
Old Testament men and women of faith (chapter 11)

## THE BLUEPRINT

A. THE SUPERIORITY OF CHRIST
   (1:1—10:18)
   1. Christ is greater than the angels
   2. Christ is greater than Moses
   3. Christ is greater than the Old
      Testament priesthood
   4. The new covenant is greater than
      the old

B. THE SUPERIORITY OF FAITH
   (10:19—13:25)

The superiority of Christ over everyone and everything is clearly demonstrated by the author. Christianity supersedes all other religions and can never be surpassed. Where can one find anything better than Christ? Living in Christ is having the best there is in life. All competing religions are deceptions or cheap imitations.

Jews who had become Christians in the first century were tempted to fall back into Judaism because of uncertainty, the security of custom, and persecution. Today believers are also tempted to fall back into legalism, fulfilling minimum religious requirements rather than pressing on in genuine faith. We must strive to live by faith each day.

## MEGATHEMES

| THEME | EXPLANATION | IMPORTANCE |
|---|---|---|
| Christ Is Superior | Hebrews reveals Jesus' true identity as God. Jesus is the ultimate authority. He is greater than any religion or any angel. He is superior to any Jewish leader (such as Abraham, Moses, or Joshua) and superior to any priest. He is the complete revelation of God. | Jesus alone can forgive our sin. He has secured our forgiveness and salvation by his death on the cross. We can find peace with God and real meaning for life by believing in Christ. We should not accept any alternative to or substitute for him. |
| High Priest | In the Old Testament, the high priest represented the Jews before God. Jesus Christ links us with God. There is no other way to reach God. Because Jesus Christ lived a sinless life, he is the perfect substitute to die for our sin. He is our perfect representative with God. | Jesus guarantees our access to God the Father. He intercedes for us so we can boldly come to the Father with our needs. When we are weak, we can come confidently to God for forgiveness and ask for his help. |
| Sacrifice | Christ's sacrifice was the ultimate fulfillment of all that the Old Testament sacrifices represented— God's forgiveness for sin. Because Christ is the perfect sacrifice for our sin, our sins are completely forgiven—past, present, and future. | Christ removed sin, which barred us from God's presence and fellowship. But we must accept his sacrifice for us. By believing in him, we are no longer guilty but cleansed and made whole. His sacrifice clears the way for us to have eternal life. |
| Maturity | Though we are saved from sin when we believe in Christ, we are given the task of going on and growing in our faith. Through our relationship with Christ, we can live blameless lives, be set aside for his special use, and develop maturity. | The process of maturing in our faith takes time. Daily commitment and service produce maturity. When we are mature in our faith, we are not easily swayed or shaken by temptations or worldly concerns. |
| Faith | Faith is confident trust in God's promises. God's greatest promise is that we can be saved through Jesus. | If we trust in Jesus Christ for our complete salvation, he will transform us completely. A life of obedience and complete trust is pleasing to God. |
| Endurance | Faith enables Christians to face trials. Genuine faith includes the commitment to stay true to God when we are under fire. Endurance builds character and leads to victory. | We can have victory in our trials if we don't give up or turn our back on Christ. Stay true to Christ and pray for endurance. |

## A. THE SUPERIORITY OF CHRIST (1:1—10:18)

The relationship of Christianity to Judaism was a critical issue in the early church. The author clears up confusion by carefully explaining how Christ is superior to angels, Moses, and high priests. The new covenant is shown to be far superior to the old. This can be a great encouragement to us and help us avoid drifting away from our faith in Christ.

### 1. Christ is greater than the angels

*Jesus Christ Is God's Son*

**1:1**
Num 12:6-8
**1:2**
Matt 21:38
John 1:3
1 Pet 1:20
**1:3**
Ps 110:1
John 14:9
2 Cor 4:4
Col 1:15

**1** Long ago God spoke many times and in many ways to our ancestors through the prophets. 2And now in these final days, he has spoken to us through his Son. God promised everything to the Son as an inheritance, and through the Son he created the universe. 3The Son radiates God's own glory and expresses the very character of God, and he sustains everything by the mighty power of his command. When he had cleansed us from our sins, he sat down in the place of honor at the right hand of the majestic God in heaven. 4This shows that the Son is far greater than the angels, just as the name God gave him is greater than their names.

---

**CHRIST AND THE ANGELS**

| Hebrews passage | Old Testament passage | How Christ is superior to angels |
|---|---|---|
| 1:5, 6 | Psalm 2:7 | Christ is called "Son" of God, a title never given to an angel. |
| 1:7, 14 | Psalm 104:4 | Angels are important but are still only servants under God. |
| 1:8, 9 | Psalm 45:6 | Christ's Kingdom is forever. |
| 1:10 | Psalm 102:25 | Christ is the Creator of the world. |
| 1:13 | Psalm 110:1 | Christ is given unique honor by God. |

The writer of Hebrews quotes from the Old Testament repeatedly in demonstrating Christ's greatness in comparison to the angels. This audience of first-century Jewish Christians had developed an imbalanced belief in angels and their role. Christ's lordship is affirmed without disrespect to God's valued angelic messengers.

---

**1:1** The book of Hebrews describes in detail how Jesus Christ not only fulfills the promises and prophecies of the Old Testament but is better than everything in the Jewish system of thought. The Jews accepted the Old Testament, but most of them rejected Jesus as the long-awaited Messiah. The recipients of this letter seem to have been Jewish Christians. They were well versed in Scripture, and they had professed faith in Christ. Whether through doubt, persecution, or false teaching, however, they may have been in danger of giving up their Christian faith and returning to Judaism.

The authorship of this book is uncertain. Several names have been suggested, including Luke, Barnabas, Apollos, Priscilla, and Paul. Most scholars do not believe that Paul was the author, because the writing style of Hebrews is quite different from that of his letters. In addition, Paul identified himself in his other letters and appealed to his authority as an apostle, whereas this writer of Hebrews, who never gives his or her name, appeals to eyewitnesses of Jesus' ministry for authority. Nevertheless, the author of Hebrews evidently knew Paul well. Hebrews was probably written by one of Paul's close associates who often heard him preach.

**1:1, 2** God used many approaches to send his messages to people in Old Testament times. He spoke to Isaiah in visions (Isaiah 6), to Jacob in a dream (Genesis 28:10-22), and to Abraham and Moses personally (Genesis 18; Exodus 31:18). Jewish people familiar with these stories would not have found it hard to believe that God was still revealing his will, but it was astonishing for them to think that God had revealed *himself* by speaking through his Son, Jesus Christ. Jesus is the fulfillment and culmination of God's revelation through the centuries. When we know him, we have all we need to be saved from our sin and to have a perfect relationship with God.

**1:2** Jesus was God's agent in creating the world: "For through him God created everything" (Colossians 1:16). As followers of Christ, we may give easy assent to this truth but deny it in practice. We may believe that Christ knows and controls the laws of heaven (pertaining to salvation and spiritual growth), but we may act each day as though our financial, family, or medical problems

are beyond his reach. If Jesus could create the universe, then no part of life is out of his control. Do not exclude Jesus' wisdom and the Bible's guidance in your complex problems of life. No expert, professor, doctor, lawyer, or financial adviser knows more about your ultimate security and well being than Jesus does. Go first to God for advice. Talk to him in prayer and listen to him in his Word. He can sustain you in times of stress. From that perspective you can evaluate all the other wisdom and help made available to you.

**1:3** Not only is Jesus the exact representation of God, but he is God himself—the very God who spoke in Old Testament times. He is eternal; he worked with the Father in creating the world (John 1:3; Colossians 1:16). He is the full revelation of God. You can have no clearer view of God than by looking at Christ. Jesus Christ is the complete expression of God in a human body.

**1:3** The book of Hebrews links God's saving power with his creative power. In other words, the power that brought the universe into being and that keeps it operating is the very power that cleanses our sins. How mistaken we would be to ever think that God couldn't forgive us. No sin is too big for the Ruler of the universe to handle. He can and will forgive us when we come to him through his Son. That Jesus *sat down* means that the work was complete. Christ's sacrifice was final.

**1:4** The "far greater" name that was given to Jesus is "Son." This name given to him by his Father is greater than the names and titles of the angels.

**1:4ff** False teachers in many of the early churches taught that God could be approached only through angels. Instead of worshiping God directly, followers of these heretics revered angels. Hebrews clearly denounces such teaching as false. Some thought of Jesus as the highest angel of God. But Jesus is not a superior angel, and in any case, angels are not to be worshiped (see Colossians 2:18; Revelation 19:1-10). We should not regard any intermediaries or authorities as greater than Christ. Jesus is God. He alone deserves our worship.

## The Son Is Greater Than the Angels

⁵For God never said to any angel what he said to Jesus:

"You are my Son.
Today I have become your Father.*"

God also said,

"I will be his Father,
and he will be my Son."*

⁶And when he brought his supreme* Son into the world, God said,*

"Let all of God's angels worship him."*

⁷Regarding the angels, he says,

"He sends his angels like the winds,
his servants like flames of fire."*

⁸But to the Son he says,

"Your throne, O God, endures forever and ever.
You rule with a scepter of justice.
⁹ You love justice and hate evil.
Therefore, O God, your God has anointed you,
pouring out the oil of joy on you more than on anyone else."*

¹⁰He also says to the Son,

"In the beginning, Lord, you laid the foundation of the earth
and made the heavens with your hands.
¹¹ They will perish, but you remain forever.
They will wear out like old clothing.
¹² You will fold them up like a cloak
and discard them like old clothing.
But you are always the same;
you will live forever."*

¹³And God never said to any of the angels,

"Sit in the place of honor at my right hand
until I humble your enemies,
making them a footstool under your feet."*

¹⁴Therefore, angels are only servants—spirits sent to care for people who will inherit salvation.

| Reference | |
|---|---|
| 1:5 | †Ps 2:7 †2 Sam 7:14 |
| 1:6 | †Deut 32:43 †Ps 8:4 |
| 1:7 | †Pss 8:5; 104:4 |
| 1:8-9 | †Ps 45:6-7 |
| 1:10-12 | †Ps 102:25-27 |
| 1:13 | Ps 110:1 Matt 22:44 |
| 1:14 | Pss 34:7; 91:11 |

1:5a Or Today I reveal you as my Son. Ps 2:7.   1:5b 2 Sam 7:14.   1:6a Or firstborn.   1:6b Or when he again brings his supreme Son [or firstborn Son] into the world, God will say.   1:6c Deut 32:43.   1:7 Ps 104:4 (Greek version). 1:8-9 Ps 45:6-7.   1:10-12 Ps 102:25-27.   1:13 Ps 110:1.

---

**1:5, 6** Jesus is God's honored, firstborn Son. In Jewish families the firstborn son held the place of highest privilege and responsibility. The Jewish Christians reading this message would understand that as God's firstborn, Jesus was superior to any created being.

**1:10-12** The author of Hebrews quotes Psalm 102:25-27. In the quotation, he regards God as the speaker and applies the words to the Son, Jesus. The earth and the heavens folded up like a cloak reveals that the earth is not permanent or indestructible (a position held by many Greek and Roman philosophies). Jesus' authority is established over all of creation, so we dare not treat any created object or earthly resource as more important than he is. When we spend more time on ourselves than on serving Christ, we treat ourselves (his creation) as being more important than our Creator. When we regard our finances, rather than our faith in Christ, as the basis for security, we give higher status to an earthly resource than we do to God. Rather than trusting in changeable and temporary resources, trust in God, who is eternal.

**1:11, 12** Because the readers of Hebrews (Jewish Christians) had experienced the rejection of their fellow Jews, they often felt isolated. Many were tempted to exchange the changeless Christ for their familiar old faith. The writer of Hebrews warned them not to do this: Christ is our only security in a changing world. Whatever may happen in this world, Christ remains forever changeless. If we trust him, we are absolutely secure, because we stand on the firmest foundation in the universe—Jesus Christ. A famous hymn captures this truth: "On Christ the solid rock I stand, all other ground is sinking sand."

**1:12** What does it mean that Christ is changeless ("you are always the same")? It means that Christ's character will never change. He persistently shows his love to us. He is always fair, just, and merciful to us who are so undeserving. Be thankful that Christ is changeless; he will always help you when you need it and offer forgiveness when you call.

**1:14** Angels are God's messengers, spiritual beings created by God and under his authority (Colossians 1:16). They have several functions: serving believers (1:14), protecting the helpless (Matthew 18:10), proclaiming God's messages (Revelation 14:6-12), and executing God's judgment (Acts 12:1-23; Revelation 20:1-3).

## A Warning against Drifting Away

**2** So we must listen very carefully to the truth we have heard, or we may drift away from it. ²For the message God delivered through angels has always stood firm, and every violation of the law and every act of disobedience was punished. ³So what makes us think we can escape if we ignore this great salvation that was first announced by the Lord Jesus himself and then delivered to us by those who heard him speak? ⁴And God confirmed the message by giving signs and wonders and various miracles and gifts of the Holy Spirit whenever he chose.

## Jesus, the Man

⁵And furthermore, it is not angels who will control the future world we are talking about. ⁶For in one place the Scriptures say,

> "What are mere mortals that you should think about them,
>     or a son of man* that you should care for him?
> ⁷ Yet you made them only a little lower than the angels
>     and crowned them with glory and honor.*
> ⁸ You gave them authority over all things."*

Now when it says "all things," it means nothing is left out. But we have not yet seen all things put under their authority. ⁹What we do see is Jesus, who was given a position "a little lower than the angels"; and because he suffered death for us, he is now "crowned with glory and

**2:2**
Deut 33:2
Acts 7:38, 53
Gal 3:19

**2:3**
Heb 1:2; 10:29

**2:4**
Mark 16:20

**2:6-8**
Ps 8:4-6

**2:8**
1 Cor 15:27

**2:9**
Phil 2:6-9

**2:6** Or *the Son of Man.*   **2:7** Some manuscripts add *You gave them charge of everything you made.*
**2:6-8** Ps 8:4-6 (Greek version).

---

**LESSONS FROM
CHRIST'S
HUMANITY**

Christ is the perfect human leader . . . . . . . . and he wants to lead you

model . . . . . . . . and he is worth imitating

sacrifice. . . . . . . . and he died for you

conqueror . . . . . and he conquered death to give you eternal life

High Priest . . . . and he is merciful, loving, and understanding

God, in Christ, became a living, breathing human being. Hebrews points out many reasons why this is so important.

---

**2:1-3** The author called his readers to pay attention to the truth they had heard so that they wouldn't drift away into false teachings. Paying careful attention is hard work. It involves focusing our mind, body, and senses. Listening to Christ means not merely hearing but also obeying (see James 1:22-25). We must listen carefully and be ready to carry out his instructions.

**2:1** These early believers were in danger of falling away from following Jesus. They had heard the words of the gospel, but those words had not sunk in. People raised in believing families and churches risk the same danger today. They hear the words and more or less agree, but mental assent to Christ's leadership is insufficient to be Christ's disciple. Are you a Sunday school teacher, a small group leader, or a club leader? Don't assume that people who comply and conform are truly committed to Christ. Get to know each person who attends your group and challenge each with the truth and implications of commitment to Christ. Don't surrender anyone to casual belief.

**2:2, 3** "The message God delivered through angels" refers to the teaching that angels, as messengers for God, had brought the law to Moses (see Galatians 3:19). A central theme of Hebrews is that Christ is infinitely greater than all other proposed ways to God. The author was saying that the faith of his Jewish readers was good, but faith must point to Christ. Just as Christ is greater than angels, so Christ's message is more important than theirs. No one will escape God's punishment if he or she is indifferent to the salvation offered by Christ.

**2:3** Eyewitnesses to Jesus' ministry had handed down his teachings to the readers of this book. These readers were second-generation believers who had not seen Christ in the flesh. They are like us; we have not seen Jesus personally. We base our belief

in Jesus on the eyewitness accounts recorded in the Bible. See John 20:29 for Jesus' encouragement to those who believe without ever having seen him.

**2:4** "God confirmed the message" continues the thought from 2:3. Those who had heard Jesus speak and then had passed on his words also had the truth of their words confirmed by "signs and wonders and various miracles and gifts of the Holy Spirit." In the book of Acts, miracles and gifts of the Spirit authenticated the Good News wherever it was preached (see Acts 9:31-42; 14:1-20). Paul, who discussed spiritual gifts in Romans 12, 1 Corinthians 12–14, and Ephesians 4, taught that their purpose is to build up the church, making it strong and mature. When we see the gifts of the Spirit in an individual or congregation, we know that God is truly present. As we receive God's gifts, we should thank him for them and put them to use in the church.

**2:8, 9** God put Jesus in charge of everything, and Jesus revealed himself to us. We do not yet see Jesus reigning on earth, but we can picture him in his heavenly glory. When you are confused by present events and anxious about the future, remember Jesus' true position and authority. He is Lord of all, and one day he will rule on earth as he does now in heaven. This truth can give stability to your decisions day by day.

**2:9, 10** God's grace to us led Christ to his death. Jesus did not come into the world to gain status or political power, but to suffer and die so that we could have eternal life ("bring many children into glory"). If it is difficult for us to identify with Christ's servant attitude, perhaps we need to evaluate our own motives. Are we more interested in power or participation, domination or service, getting or giving?

honor." Yes, by God's grace, Jesus tasted death for everyone. [10]God, for whom and through whom everything was made, chose to bring many children into glory. And it was only right that he should make Jesus, through his suffering, a perfect leader, fit to bring them into their salvation.

[11]So now Jesus and the ones he makes holy have the same Father. That is why Jesus is not ashamed to call them his brothers and sisters.* [12]For he said to God,

"I will proclaim your name to my brothers and sisters.
    I will praise you among your assembled people."*

[13]He also said,

"I will put my trust in him,"
    that is, "I and the children God has given me."*

[14]Because God's children are human beings—made of flesh and blood—the Son also became flesh and blood. For only as a human being could he die, and only by dying could he break the power of the devil, who had* the power of death. [15]Only in this way could he set free all who have lived their lives as slaves to the fear of dying.

[16]We also know that the Son did not come to help angels; he came to help the descendants of Abraham. [17]Therefore, it was necessary for him to be made in every respect like us, his brothers and sisters,* so that he could be our merciful and faithful High Priest before God. Then he could offer a sacrifice that would take away the sins of the people. [18]Since he himself has gone through suffering and testing, he is able to help us when we are being tested.

## 2. Christ is greater than Moses

**3** And so, dear brothers and sisters who belong to God and* are partners with those called to heaven, think carefully about this Jesus whom we declare to be God's messenger* and High Priest. [2]For he was faithful to God, who appointed him, just as Moses served faithfully when he was entrusted with God's entire* house.

**2:10**
Luke 13:32; 24:46
Rom 11:36
Heb 5:9

**2:11**
Matt 28:10
John 20:17
Rom 8:29
Heb 10:10; 13:12

**2:12**
†Ps 22:22

**2:13**
†Isa 8:17-18
John 17:11-12

**2:14**
John 1:14
Rom 8:3
1 Cor 15:54-57
2 Tim 1:10
1 Jn 3:8

**2:17**
Phil 2:7
Heb 3:1; 4:15; 5:1
1 Jn 2:2; 4:10

**2:18**
Heb 4:15; 5:2

**3:1**
Heb 2:17; 4:14

**3:2**
Num 12:7-8

2:11 Greek *brothers;* also in 2:12.  2:12 Ps 22:22.  2:13 Isa 8:17-18.  2:14 Or *has.*  2:17 Greek *like the brothers.*
3:1a Greek *And so, holy brothers who.*  3:1b Greek *God's apostle.*  3:2 Some manuscripts do not include *entire.*

---

**2:10** How was Jesus made a perfect leader through suffering? Jesus' suffering made him a perfect leader, or pioneer, of our salvation (see the note on 5:8 and 5:9). Jesus did not need to suffer for his own salvation, because he was God in human form. His perfect obedience (which led him down the road of suffering) demonstrates that he was the complete sacrifice for us. Through suffering, Jesus completed the work necessary for our own salvation. Our suffering can make us more sensitive servants of God. People who have known pain are able to reach out with compassion to others who hurt. If you have suffered, ask God how your experience can be used to help others.

**2:11-13** We who have been set apart for God's service, cleansed, and made holy (sanctified) by Jesus now have the same Father he has, so he has made us his brothers and sisters. Various psalms look forward to Christ and his work in the world. Here the writer quotes a portion of Psalm 22, a messianic psalm. Because God has adopted all believers as his children, Jesus calls them his brothers and sisters.

**2:14, 15** Jesus had to become human so that he could die and rise again in order to destroy the devil's power over death (Romans 6:5-11). Only then could Christ deliver those who had lived in constant fear of death and free them to live for him. When we belong to God, we need not fear death, because we know that death is only the doorway into eternal life (1 Corinthians 15).

**2:14, 15** Christ's death and resurrection set us free from the fear of death because death has been defeated. Every person must die, but death is not the end; instead, it is the doorway to a new life. All who dread death should have the opportunity to know the hope that Christ's victory brings. How can you share this truth with those close to you?

**2:16, 17** In the Old Testament, the high priest was the mediator between God and his people. His job was to regularly offer animal sacrifices according to the law and to intercede with God for

forgiveness of the people's sins. Jesus Christ is now our High Priest. He came to earth as a human being; therefore, he understands our weaknesses and shows mercy to us. He has *once and for all* paid the penalty for our sins by his own sacrificial death (atonement), and he can be depended on to restore our broken relationship with God. We are released from sin's domination over us when we commit ourselves fully to Christ, trusting completely in what he has done for us (see the note on 4:14 for more about Jesus as the great High Priest).

**2:18** Knowing that Christ suffered pain and faced temptation helps us face our trials. Jesus understands our struggles because he faced them as a human being. We can trust Christ to help us survive suffering and overcome temptation. When you face trials, go to Jesus for strength and patience. He understands your needs and is able to help (see 4:14-16).

**3:1** This verse would have been especially meaningful to Jewish Christians. For Jews, the highest human authority was the high priest. For Christians, the highest human authorities were God's messengers, the apostles. Jesus, God's messenger and High Priest, is the ultimate authority in the church.

**3:1** The writer says to "think carefully about this Jesus," to fix our minds, ponder carefully, and focus on the true significance of Jesus. How much do we do that? In our age of sound bites, fast food, and quick-fix solutions, very few people take time to think about anything or anyone. In Jesus we have one to whom we should listen (God's messenger), through whom we come to the Father (High Priest), and to whom we give obedience (he is entrusted with God's entire house). When you think about the significance and superiority of Jesus, how does it affect your life today? Your decisions? Your actions?

**3:2, 3** To the Jewish people, Moses was a great hero; he had led their ancestors, the Israelites, from Egyptian bondage to the border of the Promised Land. He also had written the first five

**3:3**
2 Cor 3:7-11

**3:5**
Exod 14:31
Num 12:7

**3:6**
Eph 2:19-22
1 Tim 3:15
1 Pet 2:5

**3:7-11**
†Ps 95:7-11

**3:8**
Exod 17:7

**3:11**
Num 14:21-23

**3:13**
Eph 4:22

**3:14**
Heb 3:6

**3:15**
†Ps 95:7-8

³But Jesus deserves far more glory than Moses, just as a person who builds a house deserves more praise than the house itself. ⁴For every house has a builder, but the one who built everything is God.

⁵Moses was certainly faithful in God's house as a servant. His work was an illustration of the truths God would reveal later. ⁶But Christ, as the Son, is in charge of God's entire house. And we are God's house, if we keep our courage and remain confident in our hope in Christ.*

⁷That is why the Holy Spirit says,

"Today when you hear his voice,
8    don't harden your hearts
    as Israel did when they rebelled,
    when they tested me in the wilderness.
⁹ There your ancestors tested and tried my patience,
    even though they saw my miracles for forty years.
¹⁰ So I was angry with them, and I said,
    'Their hearts always turn away from me.
    They refuse to do what I tell them.'
¹¹ So in my anger I took an oath:
    'They will never enter my place of rest.'"*

¹²Be careful then, dear brothers and sisters.* Make sure that your own hearts are not evil and unbelieving, turning you away from the living God. ¹³You must warn each other every day, while it is still "today," so that none of you will be deceived by sin and hardened against God. ¹⁴For if we are faithful to the end, trusting God just as firmly as when we first believed, we will share in all that belongs to Christ. ¹⁵Remember what it says:

"Today when you hear his voice,
    don't harden your hearts
    as Israel did when they rebelled."*

**3:6** Some manuscripts add *faithful to the end.*    **3:7-11** Ps 95:7-11.    **3:12** Greek *brothers.*    **3:15** Ps 95:7-8.

---

books of the Old Testament, and he was the prophet through whom God had given the law; therefore, Moses was the greatest prophet in the Scriptures. But Jesus is worthy of greater honor as the central figure of faith than Moses, who was merely a human servant. Jesus is more than human; he is God himself (1:3). As Moses led the people of Israel out of Egyptian bondage, so Christ leads us out of sin's slavery. Why settle for Moses, the author of Hebrews asks, when you can have Jesus Christ, who appointed Moses?

**3:5** Moses was faithful to God's calling not only to deliver Israel but also to prepare the way for the Messiah ("his work was an illustration of the truths God would reveal later"). All the Old Testament believers also served to prepare the way. Thus, knowing the Old Testament is the best foundation for understanding the New Testament. In reading the Old Testament, we see (1) how God used people to accomplish his purposes, (2) how God used events and personalities to illustrate important truths, (3) how, through prophets, God announced the Messiah, and (4) how, through the system of sacrifices, God prepared people to understand the Messiah's work. If you include the Old Testament in your regular Bible reading, the New Testament will grow clearer and more meaningful to you.

**3:6** Because Christ lives in us as believers, we can remain courageous and hopeful to the end. We are not saved by being steadfast and firm in our faith, but our courage and hope do reveal that our faith is real. Without this enduring faithfulness, we could easily be blown away by the winds of temptation, false teaching, or persecution (see also 3:14).

**3:7-15** This passage refers to the Israelites who had hardened their hearts in the wilderness. A hardened heart is as useless as a hardened lump of clay or a hardened loaf of bread. Nothing can restore it and make it useful. The writer of Psalm 95 warns against hardening our hearts as Israel did in the wilderness by continuing to resist God's will (Exodus 17:7; Numbers 13; 14; 20). The people

were so convinced that God couldn't deliver them that they simply lost their faith in him. People with hardened hearts are so stubbornly set in their ways that they cannot turn to God. This does not happen suddenly or all at once; it is the result of a series of choices to disregard God's will. Let people know that those who resist God long enough, God will toss aside like hardened bread, useless and worthless.

**3:11** God's *rest* has several meanings in Scripture: (1) the seventh day of creation and the weekly Sabbath commemorating it (Genesis 2:2; Hebrews 4:4-9); (2) the Promised Land of Canaan (Deuteronomy 12:8-12; Psalm 95); (3) peace with God now because of our relationship with Christ through faith (Matthew 11:28; Hebrews 4:1, 3, 8-11); and (4) our future eternal life with Christ (Hebrews 4:8-11). All of these meanings were probably familiar to the Jewish Christian readers of Hebrews. We can apply the verses as a warning about God's anger in the face of human rebellion against his Kingdom. By rejecting God's provision (Christ) and not enduring in our faith, we miss the opportunity for spiritual rest.

**3:12-14** Our hearts turn away from the living God when we stubbornly refuse to believe him. If we persist in our unbelief, God will eventually leave us alone in our sin. But God can give us new hearts, new desires, and new spirits (Ezekiel 36:22-27). To prevent having an unbelieving heart, stay in fellowship with other believers, talk daily about your mutual faith, be aware of the deceitfulness of sin (it attracts but also destroys), and encourage each other with love and concern.

**3:15-19** The Israelites failed to enter the Promised Land because they did not believe in God's protection, and they did not believe that God would help them conquer the giants in the land (see Numbers 14–15). So God sent them into the wilderness to wander for 40 years. This was an unhappy alternative to the wonderful gift he had planned for them. Lack of trust in God always prevents us from receiving his best.

16And who was it who rebelled against God, even though they heard his voice? Wasn't it the people Moses led out of Egypt? 17And who made God angry for forty years? Wasn't it the people who sinned, whose corpses lay in the wilderness? 18And to whom was God speaking when he took an oath that they would never enter his rest? Wasn't it the people who disobeyed him? 19So we see that because of their unbelief they were not able to enter his rest.

**3:16-18**
Num 14:1-35
**3:17**
Num 14:29
1 Cor 10:5
**3:18**
Num 14:22-23

### Promised Rest for God's People

**4** God's promise of entering his rest still stands, so we ought to tremble with fear that some of you might fail to experience it. 2For this good news—that God has prepared this rest—has been announced to us just as it was to them. But it did them no good because they didn't share the faith of those who listened to God.* 3For only we who believe can enter his rest. As for the others, God said,

**4:2**
1 Thes 2:13
**4:3**
†Ps 95:11

"In my anger I took an oath:
 'They will never enter my place of rest,'"*

even though this rest has been ready since he made the world. 4We know it is ready because of the place in the Scriptures where it mentions the seventh day: "On the seventh day God rested from all his work."* 5But in the other passage God said, "They will never enter my place of rest."*

6So God's rest is there for people to enter, but those who first heard this good news failed to enter because they disobeyed God. 7So God set another time for entering his rest, and that time is today. God announced this through David much later in the words already quoted:

**4:4**
†Gen 2:2
**4:5**
†Ps 95:11
**4:6**
Heb 3:18
**4:7**
†Ps 95:7-8

"Today when you hear his voice,
 don't harden your hearts."*

8Now if Joshua had succeeded in giving them this rest, God would not have spoken about another day of rest still to come. 9So there is a special rest* still waiting for the people of God. 10For all who have entered into God's rest have rested from their labors, just as God did after creating the world. 11So let us do our best to enter that rest. But if we disobey God, as the people of Israel did, we will fall.

**4:8**
Josh 22:4
**4:10**
Gen 2:2
Rev 14:13

**4:2** Some manuscripts read *they didn't combine what they heard with faith.*   **4:3** Ps 95:11.   **4:4** Gen 2:2.
**4:5** Ps 95:11.   **4:7** Ps 95:7-8.   **4:9** Or *a Sabbath rest.*

---

**4:1-3** Some of the Jewish Christians who received this letter may have been on the verge of turning back from their promised rest in Christ, just as the people in Moses' day had turned back from the Promised Land. In both cases, the difficulties of the present moment overshadowed the reality of God's promise, and the people doubted that God would fulfill his promises. When we trust our own efforts instead of Christ's power, we, too, are in danger of turning back. Our own efforts are never adequate; only Christ can see us through.

**4:2** The Israelites of Moses' day illustrate a problem facing many who fill our churches today. They know a great deal about Christ, but they do not know him personally—they don't combine their knowledge with faith. Let the Good News about Christ benefit your life. Believe in him and then act on what you know. Trust in Christ and do what he says.

**4:4** God rested on the seventh day, not because he was tired, but to indicate the completion of creation. The world was perfect, and God was well satisfied with it. This rest is a foretaste of our eternal joy when creation will be renewed and restored, every mark of sin will be removed, and the world will be made perfect again. Our Sabbath-rest in Christ begins when we trust him to complete his good and perfect work in us (see the note on 3:11).

**4:6, 7** God had given the Israelites the opportunity to enter Canaan, but they disobeyed and failed to enter (Numbers 13–14). Now God offers us the opportunity to enter his ultimate place of rest—he invites us to come to Christ. To enter his rest, you must believe that God has this relationship in mind for you; you must stop trying to create it; you must trust in Christ for it; and you must determine to obey him. *Today* is the best time to find peace with God. Tomorrow may be too late.

**4:8-11** God wants us to enter his rest. For the Israelites of Moses' time, this rest was the earthly rest to be found in the Promised Land. For Christians, it is peace with God now and eternal life on a new earth later. We do not need to wait for the next life to enjoy God's rest and peace; we may have it daily now! Our daily rest in the Lord will not end with death but will become an eternal rest in the place that Christ is preparing for us (John 14:1-4).

**4:10** Busy people often work especially hard the week before vacation, tying up loose ends so they can relax. Students usually have their final exams right before semester breaks. When we know a rest is coming, we put extra effort into finishing our work.

Healthy Christians love the work God has given them, doing it with passion and gusto, putting all their strength and care into it. But Christians love God's promise of heaven's rest even more and look forward to God's rest with great joy. Today, renew your effort to work hard for God. Rest is coming. Relish the thought.

**4:11** If Jesus has provided for our rest through faith, why must we "do our best to enter that rest"? This is not the struggle of doing good in order to obtain salvation, nor is it a mystical struggle to overcome selfishness. It refers to making every effort to appreciate and benefit from what God has already provided. Salvation is not to be taken for granted; to appropriate the gift God offers requires decision and commitment.

**4:12**
Isa 49:2
Jer 23:29
1 Cor 14:24-25
Eph 6:17
1 Pet 1:23

**4:13**
2 Chr 16:9
Ps 33:13-15

**4:14**
Heb 2:17; 3:1

**4:15**
2 Cor 5:21
Heb 2:17-18

**4:16**
Heb 7:19

**5:1**
Heb 2:17; 7:27; 8:3

**5:2**
Heb 2:17; 4:15

**5:3**
Lev 9:7; 16:6
Heb 7:27; 9:7

**5:4**
Exod 28:1

**5:5**
Acts 13:33

¹²For the word of God is alive and powerful. It is sharper than the sharpest two-edged sword, cutting between soul and spirit, between joint and marrow. It exposes our innermost thoughts and desires. ¹³Nothing in all creation is hidden from God. Everything is naked and exposed before his eyes, and he is the one to whom we are accountable.

### 3. Christ is greater than the Old Testament priesthood
*Christ Is Our High Priest*

¹⁴So then, since we have a great High Priest who has entered heaven, Jesus the Son of God, let us hold firmly to what we believe. ¹⁵This High Priest of ours understands our weaknesses, for he faced all of the same testings we do, yet he did not sin. ¹⁶So let us come boldly to the throne of our gracious God. There we will receive his mercy, and we will find grace to help us when we need it most.

**5** Every high priest is a man chosen to represent other people in their dealings with God. He presents their gifts to God and offers sacrifices for their sins. ²And he is able to deal gently with ignorant and wayward people because he himself is subject to the same weaknesses. ³That is why he must offer sacrifices for his own sins as well as theirs.

⁴And no one can become a high priest simply because he wants such an honor. He must be called by God for this work, just as Aaron was. ⁵That is why Christ did not honor himself by assuming he could become High Priest. No, he was chosen by God, who said to him,

---

**THE CHOICES OF MATURITY**

| Mature Choices | | Versus | Immature Choices |
|---|---|---|---|
| Teaching others . . . . . . . . . . . . . . . . . | | rather than . . . . | just being taught |
| Developing depth of understanding . . . | | rather than . . . . | struggling with the basics |
| Self-evaluation . . . . . . . . . . . . . . . . . | | rather than . . . . | self-criticism |
| Seeking unity . . . . . . . . . . . . . . . . . . | | rather than . . . . | promoting disunity |
| Desiring spiritual challenges . . . . . . . . | | rather than . . . . | desiring entertainment |
| Careful study and observation . . . . . . . | | rather than . . . . | opinions and halfhearted efforts |
| Active faith . . . . . . . . . . . . . . . . . . . . | | rather than . . . . | cautious apathy and doubt |
| Confidence . . . . . . . . . . . . . . . . . . . . | | rather than . . . . | fear |
| Feelings and experiences evaluated in the light of God's Word . . . . . . . . . . | | rather than . . . . | experiences evaluated according to feelings |

One way to evaluate spiritual maturity is by looking at the choices we make. The writer of Hebrews notes many of the ways these choices change with personal growth.

---

**4:12** The Word of God is not simply a collection of words from God, a vehicle for communicating ideas; it is living, life-changing, and dynamic as it works in us. With the incisiveness of a surgeon's knife, God's Word reveals who we are and what we are not. It penetrates the core of our moral and spiritual life. It discerns what is within us, both good and evil. The demands of God's Word require decisions. We must not only listen to the Word; we must also let it shape our lives.

**4:13** Nothing can be hidden from God. He knows about everyone everywhere, and everything about us is wide open to his all-seeing eyes. God sees all we do and knows all we think. Even when we are unaware of his presence, he is there. When we try to hide from him, he sees us. We can have no secrets from God. It is comforting to realize that although God knows us intimately, he still loves us.

**4:14** Christ is superior to the priests, and his priesthood is superior to their priesthood. To the Jews, the high priest was the highest religious authority in the land. He alone entered the Most Holy Place in the Temple once a year to make atonement for the sins of the whole nation (Leviticus 16). Like the high priest, Jesus mediates between God and us. As humanity's representative, he intercedes for us before God. As God's representative, he assures us of God's forgiveness. Jesus has more authority than the Jewish high priests because he is truly God and truly man. Unlike the high priest, who could go before God only once a year, Christ is

always at God's right hand, interceding for us. He is always available to hear us when we pray.

**4:15** Jesus is like us because he experienced a full range of temptations throughout his life as a human being. We can be comforted knowing that Jesus faced temptation—he can sympathize with us. We can be encouraged knowing that Jesus faced temptation without giving in to sin. He shows us that we do not have to sin when facing the seductive lure of temptation. Jesus is the only perfect human being who has ever lived.

**4:16** Prayer is our approach to God, and we are to come "boldly." Some Christians approach God meekly with heads hung low, afraid to ask him to meet their needs. Others pray flippantly, giving little thought to what they say. Come with reverence because he is your King. But also come with bold assurance because he is your Friend and Counselor.

**5:4-6** This chapter stresses both Christ's divine appointment and his humanity. The writer uses two Old Testament verses to show Christ's divine appointment: Psalms 2:7 and 110:4. At the time this book was written, the Romans selected the high priest in Jerusalem. In the Old Testament, however, God chose Aaron, and only Aaron's descendants could be high priests. Christ, like Aaron, was chosen and called by God.

"You are my Son.
    Today I have become your Father.*"

6And in another passage God said to him,

"You are a priest forever in the order of Melchizedek."*

7While Jesus was here on earth, he offered prayers and pleadings, with a loud cry and tears, to the one who could rescue him from death. And God heard his prayers because of his deep reverence for God. 8Even though Jesus was God's Son, he learned obedience from the things he suffered. 9In this way, God qualified him as a perfect High Priest, and he became the source of eternal salvation for all those who obey him. 10And God designated him to be a High Priest in the order of Melchizedek.

### A Call to Spiritual Growth

11There is much more we would like to say about this, but it is difficult to explain, especially since you are spiritually dull and don't seem to listen. 12You have been believers so long now that you ought to be teaching others. Instead, you need someone to teach you again the basic things about God's word.* You are like babies who need milk and cannot eat solid food. 13For someone who lives on milk is still an infant and doesn't know how to do what is right. 14Solid food is for those who are mature, who through training have the skill to recognize the difference between right and wrong.

6 So let us stop going over the basic teachings about Christ again and again. Let us go on instead and become mature in our understanding. Surely we don't need to start again with the fundamental importance of repenting from evil deeds* and placing our faith in God. 2You don't need further instruction about baptisms, the laying on of hands, the resurrection of the dead, and eternal judgment. 3And so, God willing, we will move forward to further understanding.

**5:5** Or Today I reveal you as my Son. Ps 2:7.    **5:6** Ps 110:4.    **5:12** Or about the oracles of God.    **6:1** Greek from dead works.

| Ref | Cross-ref |
|---|---|
| 5:6 | †Ps 110:4 |
| 5:7 | Matt 26:38-46 / Mark 14:32-42 / Luke 22:39-46 |
| 5:8 | Phil 2:8 / Heb 1:2 |
| 5:10 | Ps 110:4 / Heb 5:6 |
| 5:12 | 1 Cor 3:2 / 1 Pet 2:2 |
| 5:13 | 1 Cor 14:20 / Eph 4:14 |
| 5:14 | Rom 16:19 / 1 Cor 2:6 |
| 6:1 | Phil 3:12-14 / Heb 5:12; 9:14 |
| 6:2 | Acts 2:4; 6:6; 17:18, 32 |

**5:6** Melchizedek was a priest of Salem (now called Jerusalem). His Profile is found in Genesis 15, p. 29. Melchizedek's position is explained in Hebrews 7.

**5:7** Jesus was in great agony as he prepared to face death (Luke 22:41-44). Although Jesus cried out to God, asking to be delivered, he was prepared to suffer humiliation, separation from his Father, and death in order to do God's will. At times we will undergo trials, not because we want to suffer, but because we want to obey God. Let Jesus' obedience sustain and encourage you in times of trial. You will be able to face anything if you know that Jesus Christ is with you.

**5:7** Have you ever felt that God didn't hear your prayers? Be sure you are praying with reverent submission, willing to do what God wants. God responds to his obedient children.

**5:8** Jesus' human life was not a script that he passively followed. It was a life that he chose freely (John 10:17, 18). It was a continuous process of making the will of God the Father his own. Jesus chose to obey, even though obedience led to suffering and death. Because Jesus obeyed perfectly, even under great trial, he can help us obey, no matter how difficult obedience seems to be.

**5:9** Christ was always morally perfect. By obeying, he demonstrated his perfection to us, not to God or to himself. In the Bible, perfect usually means completeness or maturity. By sharing our experience of suffering, Christ shared our human experience completely. He is now able to offer eternal salvation to those who obey him. See Philippians 2:5-11 for Christ's attitude as he took on human form.

**5:9** The "eternal salvation" we have been offered means the elimination of a verdict on our sin, the setting aside of judgment, and the award of undeserved membership in God's family. It is a change in destiny, an awakening of hope, an overcoming of death. Salvation turns a person toward heaven and inaugurates a life of discipleship with the living Christ. It is God's vote for you, God's invitation to you, God's energy invested in you. Salvation is the reason you can smile in the morning and rest in the evening. God loves you, and you belong to him.

**5:12, 13** These Jewish Christians were immature. Some of them should have been teaching others, but they had not even applied the basics to their own lives. They were reluctant to move beyond age-old traditions, established doctrines, and discussion of the basics. They wouldn't be able to understand the high-priestly role of Christ unless they moved out of their comfortable position, cut some of their Jewish ties, and stopped trying to blend in with their culture. Commitment to Christ moves people out of their comfort zones.

**5:12-14** In order to grow from infant Christians to mature Christians, we must learn discernment. We must train our conscience, our senses, our mind, and our body to distinguish good from evil. Can you recognize temptation before it traps you? Can you tell the difference between a correct use of Scripture and a mistaken one?

**5:14** Our capacity to feast on deeper knowledge of God ("solid food") is determined by our spiritual growth. Too often we want God's banquet before we are spiritually capable of digesting it. As you grow in the Lord and put into practice what you have learned, your capacity to understand will also grow.

**6:1, 2** Certain basic teachings are essential for all believers to understand. Those basics include the importance of faith, the foolishness of trying to be saved by good deeds, the meaning of baptism and spiritual gifts, and the facts of resurrection and eternal life. To go on to maturity in our understanding, we need to move beyond (but not away from) the basic teachings to a more complete understanding of the faith. And this is what the author intends for his readers to do (6:3). Mature Christians should be teaching new Christians the basics. Then, acting on what they know, the mature will learn even more from God's Word.

**6:3** These Christians needed to move beyond the basics of their faith to an understanding of Christ as the perfect High

**6:4**
John 4:10
Eph 2:8

**6:5**
Ps 34:8
1 Pet 2:3

**6:6**
2 Pet 2:21
1 Jn 5:16

⁴For it is impossible to bring back to repentance those who were once enlightened—those who have experienced the good things of heaven and shared in the Holy Spirit, ⁵ who have tasted the goodness of the word of God and the power of the age to come—⁶ and who then turn away from God. It is impossible to bring such people back to repentance; by rejecting the Son of God, they themselves are nailing him to the cross once again and holding him up to public shame.

| ABRAHAM IN THE NEW TESTAMENT | | | |
|---|---|---|---|
| Abraham was an ancestor of Jesus Christ. | Matthew 1:1, 2, 17; Luke 3:23, 34 | Jesus Christ was human; he was born into the line of Abraham, whom God had chosen to be the father of a great nation through which the whole world would be blessed. We are blessed because of what Jesus Christ, Abraham's descendant, did for us. |
| Abraham was the father of the Jewish nation. | Matthew 3:9; Luke 3:8; Acts 13:26; Romans 4:1; 11:1; 2 Corinthians 11:22; Hebrews 6:13, 14 | God wanted to set apart a nation for himself, a nation that would tell the world about him. He began with a man of faith who, though old and childless, believed God's promise of innumerable descendants. We can trust God to do the impossible when we have faith. |
| Abraham, because of his faith, now sits in the Kingdom with Christ. | Matthew 8:11; Luke 13:28; 16:23-31 | Abraham followed God, and now he is enjoying his reward—eternity with God. We will one day meet Abraham because we have been promised eternity as well. |
| God *is* Abraham's God; thus, Abraham is alive with God. | Matthew 22:32; Mark 12:26; Luke 20:37; Acts 7:32 | As Abraham lives forever, we will live forever, because we, like Abraham, have chosen the life of faith. |
| Abraham received great promises from God. | Luke 1:55, 72, 73; Acts 3:25; 7:17, 18; Galatians 3:6, 14-16; Hebrews 6:13-15 | Many of the promises God made to Abraham seemed impossible to be realized, but Abraham trusted God. The promises to believers in God's Word also seem too incredible to believe, but we can trust God to keep all his promises. |
| Abraham followed God. | Acts 7:2-8; Hebrews 11:8, 17-19 | Abraham followed God's leading from his homeland to an unknown territory, which became the Jews' Promised Land. When we follow God, even before he makes all his plans clear to us, we will never be disappointed. |
| God blessed Abraham because of his faith. | Romans 4; Galatians 3:6-9, 14-19; Hebrews 11:8, 17-19; James 2:21-24 | Abraham showed faith in times of disappointment, trial, and testing. Because of Abraham's faith, God counted him righteous and called him his "friend." God accepts us because of our faith. |
| Abraham is the father of all those who come to God by faith. | Romans 9:6-8; Galatians 3:6-9, 14-29 | The Jews are Abraham's children, and Christ was his descendant. We are Christ's brothers and sisters; thus, all believers are Abraham's children and God's children. Abraham was righteous because of his faith; we are made righteous through faith in Christ. The promises made to Abraham apply to us because of Christ. |

Priest and the fulfillment of all the Old Testament prophecies. Rather than arguing about the respective merits of Judaism and Christianity, they needed to depend on Christ and live effectively for him.

**6:4-6** In the first century, a pagan who investigated Christianity and then went back to paganism made a clean break with the church. But for Jewish Christians who decided to return to Judaism, the break was less obvious. Their lifestyle remained relatively unchanged. But by deliberately turning away from Christ, they were cutting themselves off from God's forgiveness. Those who persevere in believing are true saints; those who continue to reject Christ are unbelievers, no matter how well they behave.

**6:6** This verse points to the danger of the Hebrew Christians' returning to Judaism and thus committing apostasy. Some apply

this verse today to superficial believers who renounce their Christianity or to unbelievers who come close to salvation and then turn away. Either way, those who reject Christ will not be saved. Christ died once for all. He will not be crucified again. Apart from his cross, there is no other possible way of salvation. However, the author does not indicate that his readers were in danger of renouncing Christ (see 6:9). He is warning against hardness of heart that would make repentance inconceivable for the sinner.

7 When the ground soaks up the falling rain and bears a good crop for the farmer, it has God's blessing. 8 But if a field bears thorns and thistles, it is useless. The farmer will soon condemn that field and burn it.

6:8
Gen 3:17-18

9 Dear friends, even though we are talking this way, we really don't believe it applies to you. We are confident that you are meant for better things, things that come with salvation. 10 For God is not unjust. He will not forget how hard you have worked for him and how you have shown your love to him by caring for other believers,* as you still do. 11 Our great desire is that you will keep on loving others as long as life lasts, in order to make certain that what you hope for will come true. 12 Then you will not become spiritually dull and indifferent. Instead, you will follow the example of those who are going to inherit God's promises because of their faith and endurance.

6:10
Matt 10:40, 42
1 Thes 1:3

6:11
Heb 3:6; 10:22

6:12
Heb 10:36; 13:7

## God's Promises Bring Hope

13 For example, there was God's promise to Abraham. Since there was no one greater to swear by, God took an oath in his own name, saying:

6:13
Gen 22:16

6:14
†Gen 22:17

14 "I will certainly bless you,
    and I will multiply your descendants beyond number."*

6:15
Gen 21:15

15 Then Abraham waited patiently, and he received what God had promised.

6:17
Ps 110:4
Heb 11:9

16 Now when people take an oath, they call on someone greater than themselves to hold them to it. And without any question that oath is binding. 17 God also bound himself with an oath, so that those who received the promise could be perfectly sure that he would never change his mind. 18 So God has given both his promise and his oath. These two things are unchangeable because it is impossible for God to lie. Therefore, we who have fled to him for refuge can have great confidence as we hold to the hope that lies before us. 19 This hope is a strong and trustworthy anchor for our souls. It leads us through the curtain into God's inner sanctuary. 20 Jesus has already gone in there for us. He has become our eternal High Priest in the order of Melchizedek.

6:18
Num 23:19
1 Sam 15:29
Titus 1:2
Heb 3:6

6:19
Lev 16:2-3, 12, 15
Heb 9:2-3, 7

6:20
Ps 110:4
Heb 4:14; 5:6

## Melchizedek Is Greater Than Abraham

7 This Melchizedek was king of the city of Salem and also a priest of God Most High. When Abraham was returning home after winning a great battle against the kings, Melchizedek met him and blessed him. 2 Then Abraham took a tenth of all he had captured in battle

7:1-2
Gen 14:17-20

6:10 Greek for God's holy people.    6:14 Gen 22:17.

---

**6:7, 8** The writer uses an analogy from agriculture to make a simple point. Real seeds (the gospel) given genuine care by the farmer (God) and planted in a fertile field (your heart and life) will produce a bountiful crop (spiritual maturity). Weeds (temptations) threaten to overwhelm the crop. If the field produces only weeds, then the seeds are lost and the field ruined.

An unproductive Christian life falls under God's condemnation. You have been watered by God's grace with clear and abundant teaching and preaching. What excuse do you have for a useless or unproductive life? Don't be a Christian in name only. Make sure your life bears fruit.

**6:10** It's easy to get discouraged, thinking that God has forgotten us. But God is never unjust. He never forgets or overlooks our hard work for him. Presently you may not be receiving rewards and acclaim, but God knows your efforts of love and ministry. Let God's love for you and his intimate knowledge of your service for him bolster you as you face disappointment and rejection here on earth.

**6:11, 12** Hope keeps the Christian from becoming lazy or feeling bored. Like an athlete, train hard and run well, remembering the reward that lies ahead (Philippians 3:14).

**6:15** Abraham waited patiently; it was 25 years from the time God had promised him a son (Genesis 12:7; 13:14-16; 15:4, 5; 17:16) to Isaac's birth (Genesis 21:1-3). Because our trials and temptations are often so intense, they seem to last for an eternity. Both the Bible and the testimony of mature Christians encourage us to wait for God to act in his timing, even when our needs seem too great to wait any longer.

**6:17** God's promises are unchanging and trustworthy because God is unchanging and trustworthy. When promising Abraham a son, God took an oath in his own name. The oath was as good as God's name, and God's name was as good as his divine nature.

**6:18, 19** These two unchangeable things are God's promise and his oath. God embodies all truth; therefore, he cannot lie. Because God is truth, you can be secure in his promises; you don't need to wonder if he will change his plans. Our hope is secure and immovable, anchored in God, just as a ship's anchor holds firmly to the seabed. To the true seeker who comes to God in belief, God gives an unconditional promise of acceptance. When you ask God with openness, honesty, and sincerity to save you from your sins, *he will do it*. This truth should give you encouragement, assurance, and confidence.

**6:19, 20** A curtain hung between the Holy Place and the Most Holy Place, "God's inner sanctuary." This curtain prevented anyone from entering, gazing into, or even getting a fleeting glimpse of the interior of the Most Holy Place (see also 9:1-8). The high priest could enter there only once a year to stand in God's presence and atone for the sins of the entire nation. But Christ is in God's presence at all times, not just once a year, as the High Priest who can continually intercede for us.

**7:2ff** The writer uses this story from Genesis 14:18-20 to show that Christ is even greater than Abraham, father of the Jewish nation, and Levi (Abraham's descendant). Therefore, the Jewish priesthood (made up of Levi's descendants) was inferior to Melchizedek's priesthood (a type of Christ's priesthood).

and gave it to Melchizedek. The name Melchizedek means "king of justice," and king of Salem means "king of peace." ³There is no record of his father or mother or any of his ancestors—no beginning or end to his life. He remains a priest forever, resembling the Son of God.

⁴Consider then how great this Melchizedek was. Even Abraham, the great patriarch of Israel, recognized this by giving him a tenth of what he had taken in battle. ⁵Now the law of Moses required that the priests, who are descendants of Levi, must collect a tithe from the rest of the people of Israel,* who are also descendants of Abraham. ⁶But Melchizedek, who was not a descendant of Levi, collected a tenth from Abraham. And Melchizedek placed a blessing upon Abraham, the one who had already received the promises of God. ⁷And without question, the person who has the power to give a blessing is greater than the one who is blessed.

⁸The priests who collect tithes are men who die, so Melchizedek is greater than they are, because we are told that he lives on. ⁹In addition, we might even say that these Levites—the ones who collect the tithe—paid a tithe to Melchizedek when their ancestor Abraham paid a tithe to him. ¹⁰For although Levi wasn't born yet, the seed from which he came was in Abraham's body when Melchizedek collected the tithe from him.

¹¹So if the priesthood of Levi, on which the law was based, could have achieved the perfection God intended, why did God need to establish a different priesthood, with a priest in the order of Melchizedek instead of the order of Levi and Aaron?*

¹²And if the priesthood is changed, the law must also be changed to permit it. ¹³For the priest we are talking about belongs to a different tribe, whose members have never served at the altar as priests. ¹⁴What I mean is, our Lord came from the tribe of Judah, and Moses never mentioned priests coming from that tribe.

### Jesus Is like Melchizedek

¹⁵This change has been made very clear since a different priest, who is like Melchizedek, has appeared. ¹⁶Jesus became a priest, not by meeting the physical requirement of belonging to the tribe of Levi, but by the power of a life that cannot be destroyed. ¹⁷And the psalmist pointed this out when he prophesied,

"You are a priest forever in the order of Melchizedek."*

¹⁸Yes, the old requirement about the priesthood was set aside because it was weak and useless. ¹⁹For the law never made anything perfect. But now we have confidence in a better hope, through which we draw near to God.

²⁰This new system was established with a solemn oath. Aaron's descendants became priests without such an oath, ²¹but there was an oath regarding Jesus. For God said to him,

"The LORD has taken an oath and will not break his vow:
    'You are a priest forever.'"*

**7:5** Greek *from their brothers.*   **7:11** Greek *the order of Aaron?*   **7:17** Ps 110:4.   **7:21** Ps 110:4.

---

**7:3** Ps 110:4

**7:4** Gen 14:20

**7:5** Num 18:21, 26

**7:6** Rom 4:13

**7:7** Gen 14:19

**7:8** Heb 5:6; 6:20

**7:11** Ps 110:4 Heb 5:6; 7:17

**7:14** Gen 49:10 Isa 11:1 Matt 1:3; 2:6 Luke 3:33 Rom 1:3 Rev 5:5

**7:17** †Ps 110:4 Heb 5:6; 6:20

**7:18** Rom 8:3

**7:19** Rom 3:20 Heb 9:9; 10:19-22

**7:21** †Ps 110:4 Heb 5:6; 6:20; 7:17

---

**7:3-10** Melchizedek was a priest of God Most High (see the note on Genesis 14:18 and his Profile in Genesis 15, p. 29). He is said to remain a priest forever (see also Psalm 110:4), because his priesthood has no record of beginning or ending. He was a priest of God in Salem (Jerusalem) long before the nation of Israel and the regular priesthood began.

**7:11-17** Jesus' high-priestly role was superior to that of any priest of Levi, because the Messiah was a priest of a higher order (Psalm 110:4). If the Jewish priests and their laws had been able to save people, why would God need to send Christ as a priest, who came not from the tribe of Levi (the priestly tribe) but from the tribe of Judah? The animal sacrifices had to be repeated, and they offered only temporary forgiveness; but Christ's sacrifice was offered once, and it offers total and permanent forgiveness. Under the new covenant, the Levitical priesthood was canceled in favor of Christ's role as High Priest. Because Christ is our High Priest, we need to pay attention to him. No minister, leader, or Christian friend can substitute for Christ's work and for his role in our salvation.

**7:18, 19** The law was not intended to save people or to make them perfect, but to point out sin (see Romans 3:20; 5:20) and to point toward Christ (see Galatians 3:24, 25). Salvation comes through Christ, whose sacrifice brings forgiveness for our sins. Being ethical, working diligently to help others, and giving to charitable causes are all commendable, but all of our good deeds cannot save us or make us right with God.

**7:19** How can you draw near to God? The Bible makes it clear that your own body is God's temple. Your spirit needs and wants closeness with God. You want to know the living God personally, not as an idea or concept, not as a distant monarch. You can draw near to God through prayer, worship, and Bible meditation. You need not live like a monk, but you probably need more prayer in your life. The habit of worship has become a convenience to be wedged between sports and other recreations. Instead, make worship your top priority. Bible meditation may include verse memory, songs, and quiet personal reading. The Bible is the word of God for you. Use it every day and you will draw nearer and nearer to God.

²²Because of this oath, Jesus is the one who guarantees this better covenant with God.

²³There were many priests under the old system, for death prevented them from remaining in office. ²⁴But because Jesus lives forever, his priesthood lasts forever. ²⁵Therefore he is able, once and forever, to save* those who come to God through him. He lives forever to intercede with God on their behalf.

²⁶He is the kind of high priest we need because he is holy and blameless, unstained by sin. He has been set apart from sinners and has been given the highest place of honor in heaven.* ²⁷Unlike those other high priests, he does not need to offer sacrifices every day. They did this for their own sins first and then for the sins of the people. But Jesus did this once for all when he offered himself as the sacrifice for the people's sins. ²⁸The law appointed high priests who were limited by human weakness. But after the law was given, God appointed his Son with an oath, and his Son has been made the perfect High Priest forever.

## 4. The new covenant is greater than the old
### Christ Is Our High Priest

**8** Here is the main point: We have a High Priest who sat down in the place of honor beside the throne of the majestic God in heaven. ²There he ministers in the heavenly Tabernacle,* the true place of worship that was built by the Lord and not by human hands.

³And since every high priest is required to offer gifts and sacrifices, our High Priest must make an offering, too. ⁴If he were here on earth, he would not even be a priest, since there already are priests who offer the gifts required by the law. ⁵They serve in a system of worship that is only a copy, a shadow of the real one in heaven. For when Moses was getting ready to build the Tabernacle, God gave him this warning: "Be sure that you make everything according to the pattern I have shown you here on the mountain."*

⁶But now Jesus, our High Priest, has been given a ministry that is far superior to the old priesthood, for he is the one who mediates for us a far better covenant with God, based on better promises.

7:25 Or *is able to save completely.*   7:26 Or *has been exalted higher than the heavens.*   8:2 Or *tent;* also in 8:5.
8:5 Exod 25:40; 26:30.

**Marginal references:**
7:22 Heb 8:6; 12:24
7:24 Isa 9:6-7; Rev 1:18
7:25 Rom 8:34; 1 Jn 2:1
7:26 2 Cor 5:21; Heb 4:14
7:27 Lev 9:7; 16:6, 11, 15; Eph 5:2; Heb 9:12
7:28 Heb 2:10; 5:1-2
8:1 Heb 1:3; 2:17; 4:14; 6:20; 7:26; 9:11
8:2 Heb 9:11
8:3 Heb 5:1
8:5 †Exod 25:40; 26:30; Col 2:17; Heb 9:23
8:6 Heb 7:22; 9:15; 12:24

---

**7:22-24** Jesus has a permanent priesthood. He should be everyone's ultimate authority for spiritual life. In our culture today, however, many people have advisers and counselors whom they elevate almost to the role of priest. People look to political leaders, lawyers, physicians, insurance agents, and financial advisers to provide hope, long life, and security against all disasters. Many Christians regard the advice of priests and ministers, Christian friends, and even pop musicians before they consider the words of Jesus written in the Bible. Make sure your first allegiance and priority is to know and follow the advice given by Jesus.

**7:25** No one can add to what Jesus did to save us; our past, present, and future sins are all forgiven, and Jesus is with the Father as a sign that our sins are forgiven. As our High Priest, Christ is our Advocate, the mediator between us and God. He looks after our interests and intercedes for us with God. The Old Testament high priest went before God once a year to plead for the forgiveness of the nation's sins; Christ makes perpetual intercession before God for us. Christ's continuous presence in heaven with the Father assures us that our sins have been paid for and forgiven (see Romans 8:33, 34; Hebrews 2:17, 18; 4:15, 16; 9:24). This wonderful assurance frees us from guilt and from fear of failure. If you are a Christian, remember that Christ has paid the price for your sins once and for all (see also 9:24-28).

**7:27** In Old Testament times when animals were sacrificed, they were cut into pieces, the parts were washed, the fat was burned, the blood was sprinkled, and the meat was boiled. Blood was demanded as atonement for sin, and God accepted animal blood to cover the people's sin (Leviticus 17:11). Because of the sacrificial system, the Israelites were generally aware that sin costs someone something and that they themselves were sinful. Many people take Christ's work on the cross for granted. They don't realize how costly it was for Jesus to secure our forgiveness—

it cost him his life and painful, temporary separation from his Father (Matthew 27:46; 1 Peter 1:18, 19).

Because Jesus died *once for all,* he brought the sacrificial system to an end. He forgave sins—past, present, and future. The Jews did not need to go back to the old system because Christ, the perfect sacrifice, completed the work of redemption. You don't have to look for another way to have your sins forgiven—Christ was the final sacrifice for you.

**7:28** So much is attributed to Jesus in this chapter that it might appear that there is nothing you need to do, or can do, to make salvation a reality for you. And that is true. Jesus has done it all. Nothing you do can improve his work. Nothing you do adds to God's acceptance of Jesus' sacrifice.

So how do the benefits of Jesus' sacrifice become yours? You accept the gift of salvation by faith, trusting entirely in Jesus for salvation. You can do that now through a simple prayer: "Dear God, I trust in Jesus alone. Please forgive my sins through him, and give me the eternal life secured by him. Amen."

**8:4** Under the old Jewish system, priests were chosen only from the tribe of Levi, and sacrifices were offered daily on the altar for forgiveness of sins (see 7:12-14). This system would not have allowed Jesus to be a priest, because he was from the tribe of Judah. But his perfect sacrifice ended all need for further priests and sacrifices.

The use of the present tense, "there already are priests who offer the gifts," indicates that this book was written before A.D. 70 when the Temple in Jerusalem was destroyed, ending the sacrifices.

**8:5** The pattern for the Tabernacle built by Moses was given by God. It was a pattern of the spiritual reality of Christ's sacrifice, and thus it looked forward to the future reality. There is no Tabernacle in heaven of which the earthly one is a copy, but rather the earthly Tabernacle was an expression of eternal, theological principles. Because the Temple at Jerusalem had not yet been destroyed, using the worship system there as an example would have had a great impact on this original audience.

**8:7**
Heb 7:11
**8:8-12**
†Jer 31:31-34

7 If the first covenant had been faultless, there would have been no need for a second covenant to replace it. 8 But when God found fault with the people, he said:

"The day is coming, says the LORD,
  when I will make a new covenant
  with the people of Israel and Judah.
9 This covenant will not be like the one
  I made with their ancestors
  when I took them by the hand
  and led them out of the land of Egypt.
They did not remain faithful to my covenant,
  so I turned my back on them, says the LORD.

**8:10**
Heb 10:16

10 But this is the new covenant I will make
  with the people of Israel on that day,* says the LORD:
I will put my laws in their minds,
  and I will write them on their hearts.
I will be their God,
  and they will be my people.

**8:11**
John 6:45

11 And they will not need to teach their neighbors,
  nor will they need to teach their relatives,*
  saying, 'You should know the LORD.'

**8:10** Greek *after those days.*   **8:11** Greek *their brother.*

---

| THE OLD AND NEW COVENANTS | Reference | The Old Covenant under Moses | The New Covenant in Christ | Application |
|---|---|---|---|---|
| Like pointing out the similarities and differences between the photograph of a person and the actual person, the writer of Hebrews shows the connection between the old Mosaic covenant and the new Messianic covenant. He proves that the old covenant was a shadow of the real Christ. | 8:3-4 | Gifts and sacrifices by those guilty of sin | Self-sacrifice by the guiltless Christ | Christ died for you |
| | 8:5-6, 10-12 | Focused on a physical building where one goes to worship | Focuses on the reign of Christ in believers' hearts | God is directly involved in your life |
| | 8:5-6, 10-12 | A shadow | A reality | Not temporal, but eternal |
| | 8:6 | Limited promises | Limitless promises | We can trust God's promises to us |
| | 8:8-9 | Failed agreement by people | Faithful agreement by Christ | Christ has kept the agreement where people couldn't |
| | 9:1 | External standards and rules | Internal standards—a new heart | God sees both actions and motives—we are accountable to God, not rules |
| | 9:7 | Limited access to God | Unlimited access to God | God is personally available |
| | 9:9-10 | Legal cleansing | Personal cleansing | God's cleansing is complete |
| | 9:11-14; 24-28 | Continual sacrifice | Conclusive sacrifice | Christ's sacrifice was perfect and final |
| | 9:22 | Forgiveness earned | Forgiveness freely given | We have true and complete forgiveness |
| | 9:24-28 | Repeated yearly | Completed by Christ's death | Christ's death can be applied to our sin |
| | 9:26 | Available to some | Available to all | Available to you |

---

**8:8-12** This passage is a quotation of Jeremiah 31:31-34, which compares the new covenant with the old. The old covenant was the covenant of law between God and Israel. The new and better way is the covenant of grace—Christ's offer to forgive our sins and bring us to God through his sacrificial death. This covenant is new in extent—it goes beyond Israel and Judah to include all the Gentile nations. It is new in application because it is written on our heart and in our mind. It offers a new way to forgiveness, not through animal sacrifice but through faith. Have you entered into this new covenant and begun walking in the better way?

**8:10** If our heart is not changed, following God's rules will be unpleasant and difficult. We will rebel against being told how to live. The Holy Spirit, however, gives us new desires, helping us *want* to obey God (see Philippians 2:12, 13). With a new heart, we find that serving God is our greatest joy.

**8:10, 11** Under God's new covenant, God's law is inside us. It is no longer an external set of rules and principles. The Holy Spirit reminds us of Christ's words, activates our conscience, influences our motives and desires, and makes us want to obey. Now doing God's will is something we desire with all our heart and mind.

For everyone, from the least to the greatest,
　　will know me already.
12 And I will forgive their wickedness,
　　and I will never again remember their sins."*

**8:12**
Heb 10:17

13 When God speaks of a "new" covenant, it means he has made the first one obsolete. It is now out of date and will soon disappear.

**8:13**
Heb 12:24

## Old Rules about Worship

**9** That first covenant between God and Israel had regulations for worship and a place of worship here on earth. ²There were two rooms in that Tabernacle.* In the first room were a lampstand, a table, and sacred loaves of bread on the table. This room was called the Holy Place. ³Then there was a curtain, and behind the curtain was the second room* called the Most Holy Place. ⁴In that room were a gold incense altar and a wooden chest called the Ark of the Covenant, which was covered with gold on all sides. Inside the Ark were a gold jar containing manna, Aaron's staff that sprouted leaves, and the stone tablets of the covenant. ⁵Above the Ark were the cherubim of divine glory, whose wings stretched out over the Ark's cover, the place of atonement. But we cannot explain these things in detail now.

**9:2**
Exod 25:23-40;
26:1-30
Lev 24:5
**9:3**
Exod 26:31-33
**9:4**
Exod 16:33;
25:10-16; 30:1-6
Num 17:8-10
Deut 10:3-5
**9:5**
Exod 25:17-22

⁶When these things were all in place, the priests regularly entered the first room* as they performed their religious duties. ⁷But only the high priest ever entered the Most Holy Place, and only once a year. And he always offered blood for his own sins and for the sins the people had committed in ignorance. ⁸By these regulations the Holy Spirit revealed that the entrance to the Most Holy Place was not freely open as long as the Tabernacle* and the system it represented were still in use.

**9:6**
Num 18:2-6
**9:7**
Exod 30:10
Lev 16:2, 14-15
Heb 5:2-3
**9:8**
John 14:6
Heb 10:19-20

⁹This is an illustration pointing to the present time. For the gifts and sacrifices that the priests offer are not able to cleanse the consciences of the people who bring them. ¹⁰For that old system deals only with food and drink and various cleansing ceremonies—physical regulations that were in effect only until a better system could be established.

**9:9**
Heb 5:1; 10:1-2
**9:10**
Lev 11:2, 25; 15:8
Num 6:3; 19:13

## Christ Is the Perfect Sacrifice

¹¹So Christ has now become the High Priest over all the good things that have come.* He has entered that greater, more perfect Tabernacle in heaven, which was not made by human hands and is not part of this created world. ¹²With his own blood—not the blood of goats and calves—he entered the Most Holy Place once for all time and secured our redemption forever.

**9:11**
Heb 8:2; 10:1
**9:12**
Heb 7:27

**8:8-12** Jer 31:31-34.　**9:2** Or *tent;* also in 9:11, 21.　**9:3** Greek *second tent.*　**9:6** Greek *first tent.*　**9:8** Or *the first room;* Greek reads *the first tent.*　**9:11** Some manuscripts read *that are about to come.*

---

**8:13** Some of the Jewish believers were clinging to the obsolete old ways instead of embracing Christ's new covenant. All the joy of newfound faith and all the relief of fresh forgiveness had given way to a kind of boredom that was never supposed to be. Growth had stopped. What should be done if this happens to you?

Realize that life in Christ is never complete. Heaven promises completeness; until then, growth is the normal pattern. Growth often endures seasons of drought and drabness. That's also normal. Think about what you are doing that might be spiritually ineffective or obsolete. The key to growth includes daily devotion to Christ through Bible study and prayer. Perhaps you need to intensify your study and find helps that provide more substance. Perhaps you need to grow by engaging in new areas of service that express your faith. Seek God for how he would have you keep growing in your faith.

**9:5** "Cherubim" are mighty angels. One of the functions of the cherubim was to serve as guardians. These angels guarded the entrances to both the tree of life (Genesis 3:24) and the Most Holy Place (Exodus 26:31-33). With their wings "stretched out over the Ark's cover, the place of atonement," these two gold statues were believed to support God's invisible presence (Ezekiel 9:3; 10:4, 18). Here they are called "the cherubim of divine glory," referring to God's glory which hovered over the Ark of the Covenant (Exodus 40:34-36; Leviticus 16:2).

**9:6-8** The high priest could enter the Most Holy Place (9:3), the innermost room of the Tabernacle, one day each year to atone for the nation's sins. The Most Holy Place was a small room that contained the Ark of the Covenant (a gold-covered chest containing the original stone tablets on which the Ten Commandments were written, a jar of manna, and Aaron's staff). The top of the chest served as the "atonement cover" (the altar) on which the blood would be sprinkled by the high priest on the Day of Atonement. The Most Holy Place was the most sacred spot on earth for the Jews and only the high priest could enter it. The other priests and the common people were forbidden to come into the room. Their only access to God was through the high priest, who would offer a sacrifice and use the animal's blood to atone first for his own sins and then for the people's sins (see also 10:19).

**9:10** The people had to keep the Old Testament dietary laws and ceremonial cleansing laws until Christ came with God's new and better way.

**9:12** This imagery comes from the Day of Atonement rituals described in Leviticus 16. Through his own death, Christ freed us from the slavery of sin forever.

**9:12-14** Though you know Christ, you may believe that you have to work hard to make yourself good enough for God. But rules and rituals have never cleansed people's hearts. By Jesus' blood alone (1) we have our conscience cleansed, (2) we are freed from death's sting and can live to serve God, and (3) we are freed from sin's power. If you are carrying a load of guilt because you are finding that you can't be good enough for God, take another look at Jesus' death and what it means for you. Christ can heal your

**9:13**
Lev 16:3, 14-15
Num 19:9, 17

**9:14**
Heb 6:1
1 Pet 3:18
1 Jn 1:7

**9:15**
1 Tim 2:5
Heb 7:22

¹³Under the old system, the blood of goats and bulls and the ashes of a young cow could cleanse people's bodies from ceremonial impurity. ¹⁴Just think how much more the blood of Christ will purify our consciences from sinful deeds* so that we can worship the living God. For by the power of the eternal Spirit, Christ offered himself to God as a perfect sacrifice for our sins. ¹⁵That is why he is the one who mediates a new covenant between God and people, so that all who are called can receive the eternal inheritance God has promised them. For Christ died to set them free from the penalty of the sins they had committed under that first covenant.

¹⁶Now when someone leaves a will,* it is necessary to prove that the person who made it is dead.* ¹⁷The will goes into effect only after the person's death. While the person who made it is still alive, the will cannot be put into effect.

**9:18-19**
Exod 24:6-8
Lev 14:4
Num 19:6

**9:20**
†Exod 24:8
Matt 26:28

**9:21**
Lev 8:15, 19

**9:22**
Lev 17:11

**9:23**
Heb 8:5

¹⁸That is why even the first covenant was put into effect with the blood of an animal. ¹⁹For after Moses had read each of God's commandments to all the people, he took the blood of calves and goats,* along with water, and sprinkled both the book of God's law and all the people, using hyssop branches and scarlet wool. ²⁰Then he said, "This blood confirms the covenant God has made with you."* ²¹And in the same way, he sprinkled blood on the Tabernacle and on everything used for worship. ²²In fact, according to the law of Moses, nearly everything was purified with blood. For without the shedding of blood, there is no forgiveness.

²³That is why the Tabernacle and everything in it, which were copies of things in heaven, had to be purified by the blood of animals. But the real things in heaven had to be purified with far better sacrifices than the blood of animals.

**9:24**
Rom 8:34
Heb 8:2; 9:12
1 Jn 2:1

**9:25**
Heb 9:7; 10:19

**9:26**
1 Cor 10:11
Heb 7:27
1 Pet 3:18

²⁴For Christ did not enter into a holy place made with human hands, which was only a copy of the true one in heaven. He entered into heaven itself to appear now before God on our behalf. ²⁵And he did not enter heaven to offer himself again and again, like the high priest here on earth who enters the Most Holy Place year after year with the blood of an animal. ²⁶If that had been necessary, Christ would have had to die again and again, ever since the world began. But now, once for all time, he has appeared at the end of the age* to remove sin by his own death as a sacrifice.

**9:14** Greek *from dead works.*  **9:16a** Or *covenant;* also in 9:17.  **9:16b** Or *Now when someone makes a covenant, it is necessary to ratify it with the death of a sacrifice.*  **9:19** Some manuscripts do not include *and goats.*  **9:20** Exod 24:8.  **9:26** Greek *the ages.*

---

conscience and deliver you from the frustration of trying to earn God's favor. Bring your guilt-ridden life to Christ, confess your inability to clean up your own conscience, ask him to forgive you. Thank him for his deliverance. God can forgive you and clear your record.

**9:13, 14** When the people sacrificed animals, God considered the people's faith and obedience, cleansed them from sin, and made them *ceremonially* acceptable according to Old Testament law. But Christ's sacrifice transforms our lives and hearts and makes us clean on the inside. His sacrifice is infinitely more effective than animal sacrifices. No barrier of sin or weakness on our part can stifle his forgiveness.

**9:14** Sinful deeds are more than just wrong actions; ironically, these also include our attempts to reach God by being good enough! Our culture glorifies self-effort and personal achievement. It defines a successful person as one who obtains certain goals: financial security, health and fitness, and the respect of others. But here the Bible gives us a different picture of successful living: accept Jesus' sacrifice for your sin, abandon the futility of sinful deeds, and let the blood of Christ purify your conscience (see 10:19-22).

**9:15** People in Old Testament times were saved through Christ's sacrifice, although that sacrifice had not yet happened. In offering unblemished animal sacrifices, they were anticipating Christ's coming and his death for sin. There was no point in returning to the sacrificial system now that Christ had come and had become the final, perfect sacrifice.

**9:22** Why does forgiveness require the shedding of blood? This is no arbitrary decree on the part of a bloodthirsty God, as some have suggested. There is no greater symbol of life than blood; blood keeps us alive. Jesus shed his blood—gave his life—for our

sins so that we wouldn't have to experience spiritual death, eternal separation from God. Jesus is the source of life, not death. He gave his own life to pay our penalty for us so that we might live. After shedding his blood for us, Christ rose from the grave and proclaimed victory over sin and death.

**9:23** In a way that we don't fully understand, the earthly Tabernacle was a copy and symbol of heavenly realities. This purification of the heavenly things can best be understood as referring to Christ's spiritual work for us in heaven (see the note on 8:5).

**9:24** Among references to priests, Tabernacles, sacrifices, and other ideas unfamiliar to us, we come to this description of Christ appearing in God's presence on our behalf. We can relate to this role and be encouraged by it. Christ is on our side at God's side. He is our Lord and Savior. He is not there to convince or remind God that our sins are forgiven but to present both our needs and our service for him as an offering (see 7:25).

**9:24-28** All people die physically, but Christ died so that we would not have to die spiritually. We can have wonderful confidence in his saving work for us, doing away with sin—past, present, and future. He has forgiven our past sin—when he died on the cross, he sacrificed himself once for all (9:26); he has given us the Holy Spirit to help us deal with present sin; he appears before God for us now in heaven (9:24); and he promises to return (9:28) and raise us to eternal life in a world where sin will be banished.

**9:26** The "end of the age" refers to the time of Christ's coming to earth in fulfillment of the Old Testament prophecies. Christ ushered in the new era of grace and forgiveness. We are still living in the "end of the age." The day of the Lord has begun and will be completed at Christ's return.

27And just as each person is destined to die once and after that comes judgment, 28so also Christ died once for all time as a sacrifice to take away the sins of many people. He will come again, not to deal with our sins, but to bring salvation to all who are eagerly waiting for him.

### Christ's Sacrifice Once for All

**10** The old system under the law of Moses was only a shadow, a dim preview of the good things to come, not the good things themselves. The sacrifices under that system were repeated again and again, year after year, but they were never able to provide perfect cleansing for those who came to worship. 2If they could have provided perfect cleansing, the sacrifices would have stopped, for the worshipers would have been purified once for all time, and their feelings of guilt would have disappeared.

3But instead, those sacrifices actually reminded them of their sins year after year. 4For it is not possible for the blood of bulls and goats to take away sins. 5That is why, when Christ* came into the world, he said to God,

"You did not want animal sacrifices or sin offerings.
But you have given me a body to offer.
6 You were not pleased with burnt offerings
or other offerings for sin.
7 Then I said, 'Look, I have come to do your will, O God—
as is written about me in the Scriptures.'"*

8First, Christ said, "You did not want animal sacrifices or sin offerings or burnt offerings or other offerings for sin, nor were you pleased with them" (though they are required by the law of Moses). 9 Then he said, "Look, I have come to do your will." He cancels the first covenant in order to put the second into effect. 10For God's will was for us to be made holy by the sacrifice of the body of Jesus Christ, once for all time.

11Under the old covenant, the priest stands and ministers before the altar day after day, offering the same sacrifices again and again, which can never take away sins. 12But our High

**9:27**
Gen 3:19

**9:28**
Isa 53:12
Phil 3:20
Heb 7:27
1 Pet 2:24

**10:1**
Col 2:17
Heb 7:19; 8:5; 9:11

**10:3**
Lev 16:34
Heb 9:7

**10:4**
Lev 16:15, 21
Heb 9:13

**10:5-7**
†Ps 40:6-8

**10:8**
†Ps 40:6

**10:10**
Eph 5:2
Heb 7:27; 9:12, 28
1 Pet 2:24

**10:11**
Heb 5:1

**10:12**
Ps 110:1
Matt 22:44
Col 3:1
Heb 1:3

**10:5** Greek *he*; also in 10:8.    **10:5-7** Ps 40:6-8 (Greek version).

---

**9:27** Judgment is not a popular theme today, but the Bible teaches that judgment is coming. Do you look forward to Christ's return, or do you see it as a threat? As sure as death itself, judgment awaits. At God's judgment there will be no higher court of appeal should the verdict not be to your liking. If you hope for a favorable verdict in this court, put your hope entirely on Jesus. Pray today—now if you haven't before—for the freedom and pardon Jesus has won for you. Then rejoice that God's judgment of you will be based on the perfect life of his Son, Jesus. After that, tell others, for many will face an unfavorable judgment without Jesus.

**10:3** When people gathered for the offering of sacrifices on the Day of Atonement, they were reminded of their sins, and they undoubtedly felt guilty all over again. What they needed most was forgiveness—the permanent, powerful, sin-destroying forgiveness we have from Christ. When we confess a sin to him, we need never think of it again. Christ has forgiven us, and the sin no longer exists. See 1 John 1:9.

**10:4** Animal sacrifices could not take away sins; they provided only a temporary way to deal with sin until Jesus came to deal with sin permanently. How, then, were people forgiven in Old Testament times? Because Old Testament believers were following God's command to offer sacrifices, he graciously forgave them when, by faith, they made their sacrifices. But that practice looked forward to Christ's perfect sacrifice. Christ's way was superior to the Old Testament way because the old way only pointed to what Christ would do to take away sins.

**10:5-10** This quotation is not cited in any other New Testament book. However, it is a central teaching of the Old Testament that God desires obedience and a right heart, not empty compliance with the sacrifice system (see the chart in Hosea 7, p. 1413). The writer of Hebrews applies to Christ the words of the psalmist in Psalm 40:6-8. Christ came to offer his body on the cross for us as a sacrifice that is completely acceptable to God. God's new and living way for us to please him is not by keeping laws or even by abstain-

ing from sin. It is by coming to him in faith to be forgiven, and then following him in loving obedience.

**10:5-10** The costly sacrifice of an animal's life impressed upon the sinner the seriousness of his or her own sin before God. Because Jesus shed his own blood for us, his sacrifice is infinitely greater than any Old Testament offering. Considering the immeasurable gift he gave us, we should respond by giving him our devotion and service.

**10:9** Canceling the first covenant in order to put into effect a far better one meant doing away with the system of sacrifices contained in the ceremonial law. It didn't mean eliminating God's *moral* law (the Ten Commandments). The ceremonial law prepared people for Christ's coming. With Christ's death and resurrection, that system was no longer needed. And through Christ we can fulfill the moral law as we let him live in us.

**10:11, 12** Christ's work is contrasted with the work of the Jewish priests. The priests' work was never finished, so they had to stand day after day and offer sacrifices; Christ's sacrifice (dying in our place) is finished, so he is seated. The priests repeated the sacrifices often; Christ sacrificed once for all. The sacrifice system couldn't completely remove sin; Christ's sacrifice effectively cleansed us.

**10:12** If the Jewish readers of this book were to return to the old Jewish system, they would be implying that Christ's sacrifice wasn't enough to forgive their sins. Adding anything to his sacrifice or taking anything from it denies its validity. Any system to gain salvation through good deeds is essentially rejecting the significance of Christ's death and spurning the Holy Spirit's work. Beware of anyone who tells you that Christ's sacrifice still leaves you incomplete or that something else is needed to make you acceptable to God. When we believe in Christ, he makes us completely right with God. Our loving relationship leads us to follow him in willing obedience and service. He is pleased with our service, but we cannot be saved by our good deeds.

10:13
Ps 110:1

10:15
Heb 3:7

10:16-17
†Jer 31:33-34

Priest offered himself to God as a single sacrifice for sins, good for all time. Then he sat down in the place of honor at God's right hand. 13 There he waits until his enemies are humbled and made a footstool under his feet. 14 For by that one offering he forever made perfect those who are being made holy.

15 And the Holy Spirit also testifies that this is so. For he says,

16 "This is the new covenant I will make
　　with my people on that day,* says the LORD:
I will put my laws in their hearts,
　　and I will write them on their minds."*

17 Then he says,

"I will never again remember
　　their sins and lawless deeds."*

18 And when sins have been forgiven, there is no need to offer any more sacrifices.

## B. THE SUPERIORITY OF FAITH (10:19—13:25)

Moving from argument to instruction, the author cites many examples of those who have demonstrated faith throughout history. Living by faith is far better than merely fulfilling rituals and rules. This can challenge us to grow in faith and to live in obedience to God each day.

### A Call to Persevere

10:19
Eph 3:12

10:20
John 4:6
Heb 6:19; 9:8

10:21
Heb 2:17; 3:6

10:22
Ezek 36:25
Eph 5:26

10:23
1 Cor 1:9; 10:13
Heb 3:6

10:25
Acts 2:42
Heb 3:13

19 And so, dear brothers and sisters,* we can boldly enter heaven's Most Holy Place because of the blood of Jesus. 20 By his death,* Jesus opened a new and life-giving way through the curtain into the Most Holy Place. 21 And since we have a great High Priest who rules over God's house, 22 let us go right into the presence of God with sincere hearts fully trusting him. For our guilty consciences have been sprinkled with Christ's blood to make us clean, and our bodies have been washed with pure water.

23 Let us hold tightly without wavering to the hope we affirm, for God can be trusted to keep his promise. 24 Let us think of ways to motivate one another to acts of love and good works. 25 And let us not neglect our meeting together, as some people do, but encourage one another, especially now that the day of his return is drawing near.

10:16a Greek *after those days.* 10:16b Jer 31:33a. 10:17 Jer 31:34b. 10:19 Greek *brothers.* 10:20 Greek *Through his flesh.*

---

**10:14** We have been made perfect, yet we are being made holy. Through his death and resurrection, Christ, once for all, made his believers perfect in God's sight. At the same time, he is making them holy (progressively cleansed and set apart for his special use) in their daily pilgrimage here. We should not be surprised, ashamed, or shocked that we still need to grow. God is not finished with us. We can encourage this growth process by deliberately applying Scripture to all areas of our life, by accepting the discipline and guidance Christ provides, and by giving him control of our desires and goals.

**10:17** The writer concludes his argument with this powerful statement that God will never again remember our sins. Christ forgives completely, so there is no need to confess our past sins repeatedly. As believers, we can be confident that the sins we confess and renounce are forgiven and forgotten.

**10:19** The Most Holy Place in the Temple was sealed from view by a curtain (10:20). Only the high priest could enter this holy room, and he did so only once a year on the Day of Atonement when he offered the sacrifice for the nation's sins. But Jesus' death removed the curtain, and all believers may walk into God's presence at any time (see also 6:19, 20).

**10:21, 22** How is it possible for us to go right into the presence of God? We come not halfheartedly or with improper motives or pretense, but with pure, individual, and sincere worship. We can know that we have "sincere hearts" if we evaluate our thoughts and motives according to his Word (see 4:12). Christians can approach God boldly, free from our "guilty consciences" and in full assurance because of the work of Jesus Christ. We can go to God without doubting, knowing that he will hear and answer

us. Under the new covenant, our hearts and consciences are cleansed completely, not partially or temporarily (see 9:14). Our clean consciences allow us to enter God's presence with boldness. Finally, the imagery of our bodies having been "washed with pure water" actually pictures an inward cleansing. Just as baptism is an outward sign that represents the purification that Christ does inside us, so this washing speaks of an internal cleansing from sin. Once cleansed, we can approach God.

**10:22-25** We have significant privileges associated with our new life in Christ: (1) We have personal access to God through Christ and can draw near to him without an elaborate system (10:22); (2) we may grow in faith, overcome doubts and questions, and deepen our relationship with God (10:23); (3) we may enjoy motivation from one another (10:24); (4) we may worship together (10:25).

**10:25** To neglect Christian meetings is to give up the encouragement and help of other Christians. We gather together to share our faith and to strengthen one another in the Lord. As we get closer to the day when Christ will return, we will face many spiritual struggles, and even times of persecution. Anti-Christian forces will grow in strength. Difficulties should never be excuses for missing church services. Rather, as difficulties arise, we should make an even greater effort to be faithful in attendance.

26 Dear friends, if we deliberately continue sinning after we have received knowledge of the truth, there is no longer any sacrifice that will cover these sins. 27 There is only the terrible expectation of God's judgment and the raging fire that will consume his enemies. 28 For anyone who refused to obey the law of Moses was put to death without mercy on the testimony of two or three witnesses. 29 Just think how much worse the punishment will be for those who have trampled on the Son of God, and have treated the blood of the covenant, which made us holy, as if it were common and unholy, and have insulted and disdained the Holy Spirit who brings God's mercy to us. 30 For we know the one who said,

> "I will take revenge.
>     I will pay them back."*

He also said,

> "The LORD will judge his own people."*

31 It is a terrible thing to fall into the hands of the living God.

32 Think back on those early days when you first learned about Christ.* Remember how you remained faithful even though it meant terrible suffering. 33 Sometimes you were exposed to public ridicule and were beaten, and sometimes you helped others who were suffering the same things. 34 You suffered along with those who were thrown into jail, and when all you owned was taken from you, you accepted it with joy. You knew there were better things waiting for you that will last forever.

35 So do not throw away this confident trust in the Lord. Remember the great reward it brings you! 36 Patient endurance is what you need now, so that you will continue to do God's will. Then you will receive all that he has promised.

37 "For in just a little while,
    the Coming One will come and not delay.
38 And my righteous ones will live by faith.*
    But I will take no pleasure in anyone who turns away."*

39 But we are not like those who turn away from God to their own destruction. We are the faithful ones, whose souls will be saved.

10:30a Deut 32:35.   10:30b Deut 32:36.   10:32 Greek *when you were first enlightened.*   10:38 Or *my righteous ones will live by their faithfulness;* Greek reads *my righteous one will live by faith.*   10:37-38 Hab 2:3-4.

**Cross-references (margin):**

10:26 Heb 6:4-8; 2 Pet 2:20
10:27 Isa 26:11
10:28 Deut 17:6
10:30 †Deut 32:35-36; Ps 135:14
10:31 2 Cor 5:11
10:33 1 Cor 4:9; 1 Thes 2:14
10:34 Heb 13:3
10:36 Heb 9:15
10:37-38 †Hab 2:3-4; Rom 1:17; Gal 3:11

---

**10:26** When people deliberately reject Christ's offer of salvation, they reject God's most precious gift. They ignore the leading of the Holy Spirit, the one who communicates to us God's saving love. This warning was given to Jewish Christians who were tempted to reject Christ for Judaism, but it applies to anyone who rejects Christ for another religion or, having understood Christ's atoning work, deliberately turns away from it (see also Numbers 15:30, 31 and Mark 3:28-30). The point is that there is no other acceptable sacrifice for sin than the death of Christ on the cross. If someone deliberately rejects the sacrifice of Christ after clearly understanding the Good News teaching about it, then there is no way for that person to be saved, because God has not provided any other name in all of heaven for people to call on to save them (see Acts 4:12).

**10:29** How have people insulted and disdained the Holy Spirit? The sacrifice of Christ is tied with the Holy Spirit; therefore, to scorn Christ's sacrifice is to insult and disdain the Holy Spirit by arrogantly rejecting him. The Holy Spirit is a person, not just a force or influence. To reject him is to cut off the means of God's acceptance. This is equivalent to blasphemy against the Holy Spirit (see Matthew 12:31, 32). Deserving of great punishment are those who insult the Holy Spirit who brings God's mercy.

**10:31** God's power is awesome, and his punishment terrible. These words give us a glimpse into the holiness of God. He is sovereign; his power is unlimited; he will do as he promises. This judgment is for those who have rejected God's mercy. For them, falling into God's hands will be a dreadful experience. They will have no more excuses. They will discover that they were wrong, but it will be too late. For those who accept Christ's love and his salvation, however, the coming judgment is no cause for worry. Being saved through his grace, they have nothing to fear (see 1 John 4:18).

**10:32-36** Hebrews encourages believers to persevere in their Christian faith and conduct when facing persecution and pressure. We don't usually think of suffering as good for us, but it can build our character and our patience. During times of great stress, we may feel God's presence more clearly and find help from Christians we never thought would care. Knowing that Jesus is with us in our suffering and that he will return one day to put an end to all pain helps us grow in our faith and our relationship with him (see Romans 5:3-5).

**10:35-38** The Bible gives us a clear choice between two life directions. Because life often forks off in two directions, you must take the higher road, even though it looks more difficult and treacherous. The climb gets steep in places. The climb takes a toll on your energy. It gets lonely. Not many are on it, but more than you imagined, and some because of your example. It gets slippery; the devil blows ice on the narrow passages. Despite its dangers, the higher road is bound for the peak, and you'll make it—God has a lifeline around you. When you are tempted to falter in your faith or to turn back from following Christ, keep focused on what he has done for you and what he offers in the future (see Romans 8:12-25; Galatians 3:10-13). Then keep climbing.

**10:36** For the time being, these believers needed patient endurance, that is, to remain steadfast, to hold firm. Because Christ lives in us, we can have that kind of endurance. Jesus predicted that his followers would be severely persecuted by those who hated him (Matthew 10:22). In the midst of terrible persecution,

### Great Examples of Faith

11:1
Rom 8:24
Heb 3:6, 14

**11** Faith is the confidence that what we hope for will actually happen; it gives us assurance about things we cannot see. 2Through their faith, the people in days of old earned a good reputation.

11:3
Gen 1:1-31
Ps 33:6, 9
John 1:3
Rom 1:19-20
Heb 1:2

3By faith we understand that the entire universe was formed at God's command, that what we now see did not come from anything that can be seen.

4It was by faith that Abel brought a more acceptable offering to God than Cain did. Abel's offering gave evidence that he was a righteous man, and God showed his approval of his gifts. Although Abel is long dead, he still speaks to us by his example of faith.

11:4
Gen 4:3-10

11:5
Gen 5:22-24

5It was by faith that Enoch was taken up to heaven without dying—"he disappeared, because God took him."* For before he was taken up, he was known as a person who pleased God. 6And it is impossible to please God without faith. Anyone who wants to come to him must believe that God exists and that he rewards those who sincerely seek him.

11:6
Heb 7:19

11:7
Gen 6:13-22
Rom 3:22
1 Pet 3:20

7It was by faith that Noah built a large boat to save his family from the flood. He obeyed God, who warned him about things that had never happened before. By his faith Noah condemned the rest of the world, and he received the righteousness that comes by faith.

11:8
Gen 12:1-5
Acts 7:2-4

8It was by faith that Abraham obeyed when God called him to leave home and go to another land that God would give him as his inheritance. He went without knowing where he was going. 9And even when he reached the land God promised him, he lived there by faith—for he was like a foreigner, living in tents. And so did Isaac and Jacob, who inherited the same promise. 10Abraham was confidently looking forward to a city with eternal foundations, a city designed and built by God.

11:9
Gen 12:8

11:10
Heb 12:22
Rev 21:2

**11:5** Gen 5:24.

---

they could have hope, however, knowing that salvation was theirs. Times of trial serve to sift true Christians from false or fair-weather Christians. When you are pressured to give up and turn your back on Christ, remember the benefits of standing firm and continue to live for Christ. Patient endurance is not a way to be saved but the evidence that you are really committed to Jesus.

**11:1** Do you remember how you felt when you were very young and your birthday approached? You were excited and anxious. You knew you would certainly receive gifts and other special treats. But some things would be a surprise. Birthdays combine assurance and anticipation, and so does faith! Faith is the confidence based on past experience that God's new and fresh surprises will surely be ours.

**11:1** The beginning point of faith is believing in God's character: He *is* who he says. The end point is believing in God's promises: He will *do* what he says. When we believe that God will fulfill his promises even though we don't see those promises materializing yet, we demonstrate true faith (see John 20:24-31).

**11:3** God called the universe into existence out of nothing; he declared that it was to be, and it was. Our faith is in the God who created the entire universe by his word. God's word has awesome power. When he speaks, do you listen and respond? How can you better prepare yourself to respond to God's word?

**11:4** Cain and Abel were Adam and Eve's first two sons. Abel offered a sacrifice that pleased God, while Cain's sacrifice was unacceptable. Abel's Profile is found in Genesis 5, p. 15. Cain's Profile is in Genesis 6, p. 17. Abel's sacrifice (an animal substitute) was more acceptable to God, both because it was a blood sacrifice and, most important, because of Abel's attitude when he offered it.

**11:6** Believing that God exists is only the beginning; even the demons believe that much (James 2:19, 20). God will not settle for mere acknowledgment of his existence. He wants your faith that leads to a personal, dynamic relationship.

But does faith make sense, really? Do you believe because faith makes sense, or because faith doesn't need to make sense? Some Christians think people cannot understand God and should not try. Others believe that nothing true is irrational, including true faith. The truth is, God gave us minds that should be devel-

oped and used. To ignore intellectual growth is to live a stunted and naive life. God wants our trust and faith, even while we ponder and wonder about so many matters mysterious to us. Even so, we do not believe in a void nor leap into the dark. Faith is reasonable, though reason alone cannot explain the whole of it. So use your mind to think things through. But leave room for the unexplainable works of God.

**11:6** Sometimes we wonder about the fate of those who haven't heard of Christ and have not even had a Bible to read. God assures us that all who honestly seek him—who act in faith on the knowledge of God that they possess—will be rewarded. When you tell others the Good News, encourage them to be honest and diligent in their search for truth. Those who hear the Good News are responsible for what they have heard (see 2 Corinthians 6:1, 2).

**11:7** Noah experienced rejection because he was different from his neighbors. God commanded him to build a huge boat in the middle of dry land, and although God's command seemed foolish, Noah obeyed. Noah's obedience made him appear strange to his neighbors, just as the new beliefs of Jewish Christians undoubtedly made them stand out. As you obey God, don't be surprised if others regard you as "different." Your obedience makes their disobedience stand out. Remember, if God asks you to do something, he will give you the necessary strength to carry out that task. For more information on Noah, see his Profile in Genesis 8, p. 19.

**11:8-10** Abraham's life was filled with faith. At God's command, he left home and went to another land—obeying without question (Genesis 12:1ff). He believed the covenant that God made with him (Genesis 12:2, 3; 13:14-16; 15:1-6). In obedience to God, Abraham was even willing to sacrifice his son Isaac (Genesis 22:1-19). Do not be surprised if God asks you to give up secure, familiar surroundings in order to carry out his will. For further information on Abraham, see his Profile in Genesis 18, p. 33.

11It was by faith that even Sarah was able to have a child, though she was barren and was too old. She believed* that God would keep his promise. 12And so a whole nation came from this one man who was as good as dead—a nation with so many people that, like the stars in the sky and the sand on the seashore, there is no way to count them.

13All these people died still believing what God had promised them. They did not receive what was promised, but they saw it all from a distance and welcomed it. They agreed that they were foreigners and nomads here on earth. 14Obviously people who say such things are looking forward to a country they can call their own. 15If they had longed for the country they came from, they could have gone back. 16But they were looking for a better place, a heavenly homeland. That is why God is not ashamed to be called their God, for he has prepared a city for them.

17It was by faith that Abraham offered Isaac as a sacrifice when God was testing him. Abraham, who had received God's promises, was ready to sacrifice his only son, Isaac, 18even though God had told him, "Isaac is the son through whom your descendants will be counted."* 19Abraham reasoned that if Isaac died, God was able to bring him back to life again. And in a sense, Abraham did receive his son back from the dead.

20It was by faith that Isaac promised blessings for the future to his sons, Jacob and Esau.

21It was by faith that Jacob, when he was old and dying, blessed each of Joseph's sons and bowed in worship as he leaned on his staff.

22It was by faith that Joseph, when he was about to die, said confidently that the people of Israel would leave Egypt. He even commanded them to take his bones with them when they left.

23It was by faith that Moses' parents hid him for three months when he was born. They saw that God had given them an unusual child, and they were not afraid to disobey the king's command.

11:11 Or It was by faith that he [Abraham] was able to have a child, even though Sarah was barren and he was too old. He believed.    11:18 Gen 21:12.

11:11 Gen 17:19; 21:1-3
11:12 Gen 15:5-6; 22:17; Rom 4:19
11:13 Gen 23:4; Matt 13:17; Heb 11:39
11:14 Heb 13:14
11:15 Gen 24:6-8
11:16 Gen 26:24; Exod 3:6, 15
11:17 Gen 22:1-10; Jas 2:21
11:18 †Gen 21:12
11:19 Rom 4:21
11:20 Gen 27:27-29
11:21 Gen 47:31; 48:15-16
11:22 Gen 50:24-25; Exod 13:19
11:23 Exod 1:16, 22; 2:2

**11:11, 12** Sarah was Abraham's wife. They were unable to have children through many years of their marriage. God promised Abraham a son, but Sarah doubted that she could become pregnant in her old age. At first she laughed, but afterward, she believed (Genesis 18). For more information on Sarah, see her Profile in Genesis 19, p. 35.

**11:13** That we are "foreigners and nomads" on earth may be an awareness forced on us by circumstances. It may come late in life or as the result of difficult times. But this world is not our home. We cannot live here forever (see also 1 Peter 1:1). It is best for us not to be so attached to this world's desires and possessions that we can't move out at God's command.

**11:13-16** These people of faith died without receiving all that God had promised, but they never lost their vision of heaven ("a better place, a heavenly homeland"). Many Christians become frustrated and defeated because their needs, wants, expectations, and demands are not immediately met when they accept Christ as Savior. They become impatient and want to quit. Are you discouraged because the achievement of your goal seems far away? Take courage from these heroes of faith, who lived and died without seeing the fruit of their faith on earth and yet continued to believe (see 11:36-39).

**11:17-19** Abraham was willing to give up his son when God commanded him to do so (Genesis 22:1-19). God did not let Abraham take Isaac's life, because God had given the command in order to test Abraham's faith. Instead of taking Abraham's son, God gave Abraham a whole nation of descendants through Isaac. If you are afraid to trust God with the possession, dream, or person you treasure most, pay attention to Abraham's example. Because Abraham was willing to give up everything for God, he received back more than he could have imagined. What we receive, however, is not always immediate or in the form of material possessions. Material things should be among the least satisfying of rewards. Our best and greatest rewards await us in eternity.

**11:20** Isaac was the son who had been promised to Abraham and Sarah in their old age. It was through Isaac that God fulfilled his promise to eventually give Abraham countless descendants. Isaac had twin sons, Jacob and Esau. God chose the younger son, Jacob, through whom to continue the fulfillment of his promise to Abraham. For more information on Isaac, see his Profile in Genesis 19, p. 37.

**11:21** Jacob was Isaac's son and Abraham's grandson. Jacob's sons became the fathers of Israel's 12 tribes. Even when Jacob (also called "Israel") was dying in a strange land, he believed the promise that Abraham's descendants would be like the sand on the seashore and that Israel would become a great nation (Genesis 48:1-22). True faith helps us see beyond the grave. For more information on Jacob and Esau, see their Profiles in Genesis 25, pp. 47 and 49.

**11:22** Joseph, one of Jacob's sons, was sold into slavery by his jealous brothers (Genesis 37). Eventually, Joseph was sold again, this time to an official of the Pharaoh of Egypt. Because of Joseph's faithfulness to God, however, he was given a top-ranking position in Egypt. Although Joseph could have used that position to build a personal empire, he remembered God's promise to Abraham. After he had been reconciled to his brothers, Joseph brought his family to be near him and requested that his bones be taken to the Promised Land when the Jews eventually left Egypt (Genesis 50:24, 25). Faith means trusting in God and doing what he wants, regardless of the circumstances or consequences. For more information on Joseph, see his Profile in Genesis 37, p. 71.

**11:23** Moses' parents trusted God to protect their son's life. They were not merely proud parents; they were believers who had faith that God would care for him. As a parent, have you trusted God enough to take care of your children? God has a plan for every person, and your important task is to pray for your children and prepare them to do the work God has planned for them to do. Faith allows us to entrust even our children to God.

**11:24**
Exod 2:10-12

**11:26**
Heb 13:13

**11:27**
Exod 12:50-51

**11:28**
Exod 12:21-30

**11:29**
Exod 14:21-31

**11:30**
Josh 6:12-21

**11:31**
Josh 2:11-12;
6:20-25
Jas 2:25

**11:32**
Judg 4–13
1 Sam 1:20;
16:1, 13

**11:33**
1 Sam 17:34-36
Dan 6:1-27

**11:34**
2 Kgs 20:7
Dan 3:19-27

**11:35**
1 Kgs 17:17-24
2 Kgs 4:25-37

**11:36**
Gen 39:20
Jer 20:2; 37:15

**11:37**
1 Kgs 19:10
2 Chr 24:20-22

**11:38**
1 Kgs 18:4; 19:9

24It was by faith that Moses, when he grew up, refused to be called the son of Pharaoh's daughter. 25He chose to share the oppression of God's people instead of enjoying the fleeting pleasures of sin. 26He thought it was better to suffer for the sake of Christ than to own the treasures of Egypt, for he was looking ahead to his great reward. 27It was by faith that Moses left the land of Egypt, not fearing the king's anger. He kept right on going because he kept his eyes on the one who is invisible. 28It was by faith that Moses commanded the people of Israel to keep the Passover and to sprinkle blood on the doorposts so that the angel of death would not kill their firstborn sons.

29It was by faith that the people of Israel went right through the Red Sea as though they were on dry ground. But when the Egyptians tried to follow, they were all drowned.

30It was by faith that the people of Israel marched around Jericho for seven days, and the walls came crashing down.

31It was by faith that Rahab the prostitute was not destroyed with the people in her city who refused to obey God. For she had given a friendly welcome to the spies.

32How much more do I need to say? It would take too long to recount the stories of the faith of Gideon, Barak, Samson, Jephthah, David, Samuel, and all the prophets. 33By faith these people overthrew kingdoms, ruled with justice, and received what God had promised them. They shut the mouths of lions, 34quenched the flames of fire, and escaped death by the edge of the sword. Their weakness was turned to strength. They became strong in battle and put whole armies to flight. 35Women received their loved ones back again from death.

But others were tortured, refusing to turn from God in order to be set free. They placed their hope in a better life after the resurrection. 36Some were jeered at, and their backs were cut open with whips. Others were chained in prisons. 37Some died by stoning, some were sawed in half,* and others were killed with the sword. Some went about wearing skins of sheep and goats, destitute and oppressed and mistreated. 38They were too good for this world, wandering over deserts and mountains, hiding in caves and holes in the ground.

**11:37** Some manuscripts add *some were tested.*

---

**11:24-28** Moses became one of Israel's greatest leaders, a prophet and a lawgiver. But when he was born, his people were slaves in Egypt, and the Egyptian officials had ordered that all Hebrew baby boys were to be killed. Moses was spared, however, and Pharaoh's daughter raised Moses in Pharaoh's own household (Exodus 1–2)! It took faith for Moses to give up his place in the palace, but he could do it because he saw the fleeting nature of great wealth and prestige. It is easy to be deceived by the temporary benefits of wealth, popularity, status, and achievement, and to be blind to the long-range benefits of God's Kingdom. Faith helps us look beyond the world's value system to see the eternal values of God's Kingdom. For more information on Moses, see his Profile in Exodus 14, p. 117.

**11:26** True wealth is eternal. Consider the most powerful or well-known people in our world—how many got where they are by being humble, self-effacing, and gentle? Not many! But in the life to come, the last will be first—if they got in last place by choosing to follow Jesus. Hebrews has a critical message for earth-loving Christians. Don't forfeit eternal rewards for temporary benefits. Like Moses, be willing to make sacrifices now for greater rewards later (Matthew 6:19-21).

**11:31** When Joshua planned the conquest of Jericho, he sent spies to investigate the fortifications of the city. The spies met Rahab, who had two strikes against her—she was a Gentile and a prostitute. But she showed that she had faith in God by welcoming the spies and by trusting God to spare her and her family when the city was destroyed. Faith helps us turn around and do what is right regardless of our past or the disapproval of others. For more information on Rahab, see her Profile in Joshua 6, p. 321.

**11:32-35** The Old Testament records the lives of the various people who experienced these great victories. Joshua and Deborah overthrew kingdoms (the book of Joshua; Judges 4–5). Nehemiah ruled with justice (the book of Nehemiah). Daniel was saved from the mouths of lions (Daniel 6). Shadrach, Meshach, and Abednego were kept from harm in the flames of a blazing furnace (Daniel 3). Elijah escaped the edge of the swords of evil Queen Jezebel's

henchmen (1 Kings 19:2ff). Hezekiah regained strength after sickness (2 Kings 20). Gideon was strong in battle (Judges 7). A widow's son was brought back to life by the prophet Elisha (2 Kings 4:8-37).

We, too, can experience victory through faith in Christ. Our victories over oppressors may be like those of the Old Testament saints, but more likely, our victories will be directly related to the role God wants us to play. Even though our body deteriorates and dies, we will live forever because of Christ. In the promised resurrection, even death will be defeated, and Christ's victory will be made complete.

**11:32-40** These verses summarize the lives of other great men and women of faith. Some experienced outstanding victories, even over the threat of death. But others were severely mistreated, tortured, and even killed. Having a steadfast faith in God does not guarantee a happy, carefree life. On the contrary, our faith almost guarantees us some form of abuse from the world. While we are on earth, we may never see the purpose of our suffering. But we know that God will keep his promises to us. Do you believe that God will keep his promises to you?

**11:35-39** Many think that pain is the exception in the Christian life. When suffering occurs, they say, "Why me?" They feel as though God deserted them, or perhaps they accuse him of not being as dependable as they thought. In reality, however, we live in an evil world filled with suffering, even for believers. But God is still in control. He allows some Christians to become martyrs for the faith, and he allows others to survive persecution. Rather than asking, "Why me?" it is much more helpful to ask, "Why not me?" Our faith and the values of this world are on a collision course. If we expect pain and suffering to come, we will not be shocked when they hit. But we can also take comfort in knowing that Jesus also suffered. He understands our fears, our weaknesses, and our disappointments (see 2:16-18; 4:14-16). He promised never to leave us (Matthew 28:18-20), and he intercedes on our behalf (7:24, 25). In times of pain, persecution, or suffering, we should trust confidently in Christ.

<sup>39</sup>All these people earned a good reputation because of their faith, yet none of them received all that God had promised. <sup>40</sup>For God had something better in mind for us, so that they would not reach perfection without us.

**11:40**
Rom 11:26
Rev 6:11

## God's Discipline Proves His Love

**12** Therefore, since we are surrounded by such a huge crowd of witnesses to the life of faith, let us strip off every weight that slows us down, especially the sin that so easily trips us up. And let us run with endurance the race God has set before us. <sup>2</sup>We do this by keeping our eyes on Jesus, the champion who initiates and perfects our faith.* Because of the joy* awaiting him, he endured the cross, disregarding its shame. Now he is seated in the place of honor beside God's throne. <sup>3</sup>Think of all the hostility he endured from sinful people;* then you won't become weary and give up. <sup>4</sup>After all, you have not yet given your lives in your struggle against sin.

**12:1**
1 Cor 9:24
Phil 3:12-14
**12:2**
Ps 110:1
Phil 2:8-9
Heb 2:9-10
1 Pet 1:11
**12:4**
Heb 10:32-34

<sup>5</sup>And have you forgotten the encouraging words God spoke to you as his children?* He said,

**12:5-6**
†Prov 3:11-12

"My child,* don't make light of the Lord's discipline,
   and don't give up when he corrects you.
<sup>6</sup> For the Lord disciplines those he loves,
   and he punishes each one he accepts as his child."*

**12:6**
Rev 3:19

<sup>7</sup>As you endure this divine discipline, remember that God is treating you as his own children. Who ever heard of a child who is never disciplined by its father? <sup>8</sup>If God doesn't discipline you as he does all of his children, it means that you are illegitimate and are not really his children at all. <sup>9</sup>Since we respected our earthly fathers who disciplined us, shouldn't we submit even more to the discipline of the Father of our spirits, and live forever?*

**12:7**
Deut 8:5
2 Sam 7:14
**12:8**
1 Pet 5:9
**12:9**
Isa 38:16

<sup>10</sup>For our earthly fathers disciplined us for a few years, doing the best they knew how. But God's discipline is always good for us, so that we might share in his holiness. <sup>11</sup>No discipline is enjoyable while it is happening—it's painful! But afterward there will be a peaceful harvest of right living for those who are trained in this way.

**12:10**
2 Pet 1:4
**12:11**
Jas 3:17-18

**12:2a** Or *Jesus, the originator and perfecter of our faith.*   **12:2b** Or *Instead of the joy.*   **12:3** Some manuscripts read *Think of how people hurt themselves by opposing him.*   **12:5a** Greek *sons;* also in 12:7, 8.   **12:5b** Greek *son;* also in 12:6, 7.   **12:5-6** Prov 3:11-12 (Greek version).   **12:9** Or *and really live?*

---

**11:39, 40** Hebrews 11 has been called faith's hall of fame. No doubt the author surprised his readers by this conclusion: These mighty Jewish heroes did not receive all that God had promised because they died before Christ came. In God's plan, they and the Christian believers (who were also enduring much testing) would be rewarded together. Once again Hebrews shows that Christianity offers a better way than Judaism.

**11:40** There is a solidarity among believers (see 12:23). Old and New Testament believers will be glorified together. Not only are we one in the body of Christ with all those alive, but we are also one with all those who ever lived. It takes all of us to be perfect in him.

**12:1** This "huge crowd of witnesses" is composed of the people described in chapter 11. Their faithfulness is a constant encouragement to us. We do not struggle alone, and we are not the first to struggle with the problems we face. Others have run the race and won, and their witness stirs us to run and win also. What an inspiring heritage we have!

**12:1** Long-distance runners work hard to build endurance and strength. On race day, their clothes are lightweight and their bodies lean. To run the race that God has set before us, we must also strip off the excess weight that slows us down. How can we do that? (1) Choose friends who are also committed to the race. Wrong friends will have values and activities that may deter you from the course. Much of your own weight may result from the crowd you run with. Make wise choices. (2) Drop certain activities. That is, for you at this time these may be weight. Try dropping them for a while; then check the results in your life. (3) Get help for addictions that disable you. If you have a secret "weight" such as pornography, gambling, or alcohol, admit your need and get help today.

**12:1-4** The Christian life involves hard work. It requires us to give up whatever endangers our relationship with God, to run with endurance, and to struggle against sin with the power of the Holy Spirit. To live effectively, we must keep our eyes on Jesus. We will stumble if we look away from him to stare at ourselves or at the circumstances surrounding us. We should be running for Christ, not ourselves, and we must always keep him in sight.

**12:3** When we face hardship and discouragement, it is easy to lose sight of the big picture. But we're not alone; there is help. Many have already made it through life, enduring far more difficult circumstances than we have experienced. Suffering is the training ground for Christian maturity. It develops our patience and makes our final victory sweet.

**12:4** These readers were facing difficult times of persecution, but none of them had yet died for their faith. Because they were still alive, the writer urged them to continue to run their race. Just as Christ did not give up, neither should they.

**12:5-11** Who loves his child more—the father who allows the child to do what will harm him, or the one who corrects, trains, and even punishes the child to help him learn what is right? It's never pleasant to be corrected and disciplined by God, but his discipline is a sign of his deep love for us. When God corrects you, see it as proof of his love, and ask him what he is trying to teach you.

**12:11** We may respond to discipline in several ways: (1) We can accept it with resignation; (2) we can accept it with self-pity, thinking we really don't deserve it; (3) we can be angry and resentful toward God; or (4) we can accept it gratefully, as the appropriate response we owe a loving Father.

[12]So take a new grip with your tired hands and strengthen your weak knees. [13]Mark out a straight path for your feet so that those who are weak and lame will not fall but become strong.

### A Call to Listen to God

[14]Work at living in peace with everyone, and work at living a holy life, for those who are not holy will not see the Lord. [15]Look after each other so that none of you fails to receive the grace of God. Watch out that no poisonous root of bitterness grows up to trouble you, corrupting many. [16]Make sure that no one is immoral or godless like Esau, who traded his birthright as the firstborn son for a single meal. [17]You know that afterward, when he wanted his father's blessing, he was rejected. It was too late for repentance, even though he begged with bitter tears.

[18]You have not come to a physical mountain,* to a place of flaming fire, darkness, gloom, and whirlwind, as the Israelites did at Mount Sinai. [19]For they heard an awesome trumpet blast and a voice so terrible that they begged God to stop speaking. [20]They staggered back under God's command: "If even an animal touches the mountain, it must be stoned to death."* [21]Moses himself was so frightened at the sight that he said, "I am terrified and trembling."*

[22]No, you have come to Mount Zion, to the city of the living God, the heavenly Jerusalem, and to countless thousands of angels in a joyful gathering. [23]You have come to the assembly of God's firstborn children, whose names are written in heaven. You have come to God himself, who is the judge over all things. You have come to the spirits of the righteous ones in heaven who have now been made perfect. [24]You have come to Jesus, the one who mediates the new covenant between God and people, and to the sprinkled blood, which speaks of forgiveness instead of crying out for vengeance like the blood of Abel.

[25]Be careful that you do not refuse to listen to the One who is speaking. For if the people of Israel did not escape when they refused to listen to Moses, the earthly messenger, we will certainly not escape if we reject the One who speaks to us from heaven! [26]When God spoke from Mount Sinai his voice shook the earth, but now he makes another promise: "Once again I will shake not only the earth but the heavens also."* [27]This means that all of creation will be shaken and removed, so that only unshakable things will remain.

**12:18** Greek *to something that can be touched.*   **12:20** Exod 19:13.   **12:21** Deut 9:19.   **12:26** Hag 2:6.

---

**12:12, 13** God is not only a disciplining parent but also a demanding coach who pushes us to our limits and requires our lives to be disciplined. Although we may not feel strong enough to push on to victory, we will be able to accomplish it as we follow Christ and draw on his strength. Then we can use our growing strength to help those around us who are weak and struggling.

**12:12, 13** We must not live with only our own survival in mind. Others will follow our example, and we have a responsibility to them if we are living for Christ, as we claim to be. Does your example make it easier for others to believe in and follow Christ, and to mature in him? Or would those who follow you end up confused and misled?

**12:14** The readers were familiar with the ceremonial cleansing ritual that prepared them for worship, and they knew that they had to be holy or clean in order to enter the Temple. Sin always blocks our vision of God; so if we want to see God, we must renounce sin and obey him (see Psalm 24:3, 4). Holiness is coupled with living in peace. A right relationship with God leads to right relationships with fellow believers. Although we will not always feel loving toward all other believers, we must pursue peace as we become more Christlike.

**12:15** Like a small root that grows into a great tree, bitterness springs up in our hearts and overshadows even our deepest Christian relationships. A "poisonous root of bitterness" comes when we allow disappointment to grow into resentment, or when we nurse grudges over past hurts. Bitterness brings with it jealousy, dissension, and immorality. When the Holy Spirit fills us, however, he can heal the hurt that causes bitterness.

**12:16, 17** Esau's story shows us that mistakes and sins sometimes have lasting consequences (Genesis 25:29-34; 27:36). Even repentance and forgiveness do not always eliminate sin's consequences. How often do you make decisions based on what you want now, rather than on what you need in the long run? Evaluate the long-range effects of your decisions and actions.

**12:18-24** What a contrast between the people's terrified approach to God at Mount Sinai and their joyful approach at Mount Zion! What a difference Jesus has made! Before Jesus came, God seemed distant and threatening. After Jesus came, God welcomes us through Christ into his presence. Accept God's invitation!

**12:22** As Christians, we are citizens of the heavenly Jerusalem right now; because Christ rules our lives, the Holy Spirit is always with us, and we experience close fellowship with other believers. The full and ultimate rewards and reality of the heavenly Jerusalem are depicted in Revelation 21.

**12:27-29** Eventually the world will crumble, and only God's Kingdom will last. Those who follow Christ are part of this unshakable Kingdom, and they will withstand the shaking, sifting, and burning. When we feel unsure about the future, we can take confidence from these verses. No matter what happens here, our future is built on a solid foundation that cannot be destroyed. Don't put your confidence in what will be destroyed; instead, build your life on Christ and his unshakable Kingdom. (See Matthew 7:24-27 for the importance of building on a solid foundation.)

28Since we are receiving a Kingdom that is unshakable, let us be thankful and please God by worshiping him with holy fear and awe. 29For our God is a devouring fire.

## Concluding Words

**13** Keep on loving each other as brothers and sisters.* 2Don't forget to show hospitality to strangers, for some who have done this have entertained angels without realizing it! 3Remember those in prison, as if you were there yourself. Remember also those being mistreated, as if you felt their pain in your own bodies.

4Give honor to marriage, and remain faithful to one another in marriage. God will surely judge people who are immoral and those who commit adultery.

5Don't love money; be satisfied with what you have. For God has said,

"I will never fail you.
      I will never abandon you."*

6So we can say with confidence,

"The LORD is my helper,
      so I will have no fear.
   What can mere people do to me?"*

7Remember your leaders who taught you the word of God. Think of all the good that has come from their lives, and follow the example of their faith.

**13:1** Greek *Continue in brotherly love.*    **13:5** Deut 31:6, 8.    **13:6** Ps 118:6.

**12:28**
Dan 2:44

**13:1**
Rom 12:10

**13:2**
Gen 18:1-8; 19:1-3

**13:3**
Matt 25:36
Col 4:18
Heb 10:34

**13:4**
1 Cor 7:38

**13:5**
Gen 28:15
†Deut 31:5
Josh 1:5

**13:6**
†Ps 118:6

**13:7**
Heb 6:12

---

**12:28** Here are five ways we can be thankful: (1) We can be thankful that God answers our prayers (Isaiah 65:24; John 11:41). (2) We can be thankful for God's provision for our needs (1 Thessalonians 5:17, 18; 1 Timothy 4:4, 5). (3) We can be thankful for God's blessings (1 Chronicles 16:34; Philippians 4:6). (4) We can be thankful for God's character and wondrous works (Psalm 7:17; 2 Corinthians 9:15; Revelation 11:17). (5) We can be thankful for our brothers and sisters in Christ (1 Corinthians 1:4; Ephesians 1:16; Philippians 1:3-5).

**12:29** There is a big difference between the flame of a candle and the roaring blast of a forest fire. We cannot even stand near a raging fire. Even with sophisticated firefighting equipment, a devouring fire is often beyond human control. God is not within our control either. We cannot force him to do anything for us through our prayers. He cannot be contained. Yet, he is a God of compassion. He has saved us from sin, and he will save us from death. But everything that is worthless and sinful will be devoured by the fire of his wrath. Only what is good, dedicated to God, and righteous will remain.

**13:1-5** Real love for others produces tangible actions: (1) hospitality to strangers (13:2); (2) empathy for those who are in prison and those who have been mistreated (13:3); (3) respect for your marriage vows (13:4); and (4) contentment with what you have (13:5). Make sure that your love runs deep enough to affect your hospitality, empathy, fidelity, and contentment.

**13:2** Three Old Testament people "entertained angels without realizing it": (1) Abraham (Genesis 18:1ff), (2) Gideon (Judges 6:11ff), and (3) Manoah (Judges 13:2ff). Some people say they cannot be hospitable because their homes are not large enough or nice enough. But even if you have no more than a table and two chairs in a rented room, there are people who would be grateful to spend time in your home. Are there visitors to your church with whom you could share a meal? Do you know single people who would enjoy an evening of conversation? Is there any way your home could meet the needs of traveling missionaries? Hospitality simply means making other people feel comfortable and at home.

**13:3** We are to have empathy for those in prison, especially for (but not limited to) Christians imprisoned for their faith. Jesus said that his true followers would represent him as they visit those in prison (Matthew 25:36). Prisons are a mission field—believers can send in evangelists and Bible teachers. Prison systems are political projects—Christian voices are needed regarding justice and mercy in funding, staff training, and rehabilitative programs. Prisons are an international problem—through multi-national Christian agencies, believers can help victims in other countries. Compassion for suffering people demands no less. There is a wide open field of ways to obey this command to "remember those in prison."

**13:4** Giving honor to marriage will require the utmost in Christian conviction and sensitivity. Modern social theory may redefine the family, and the definitions may be far from its biblical foundation. What can you do? Witness to the depth of God's love for you by keeping your marriage happy and strong. Remain faithful—in body and in mind. Pray for your spouse. Honor biblical marriage (consenting man-woman unions) by resisting political pressure to recognize and legalize other sexual preferences. Teach children the biblical meaning of marriage. Pray early for their own eventual spouses and families. Make marriage enrichment the goal of your small group discussions and study. Encourage the marriages around you to stay strong as well.

**13:5, 6** How can we learn to be satisfied with what we have? Strive to live with less rather than desiring more; give away out of your abundance rather than accumulating more; relish what you have rather than resent what you're missing. We become satisfied when we realize God's sufficiency for our needs. Christians who become materialistic are saying by their actions that God can't take care of them—or at least that he won't take care of them the way they want. Insecurity can lead to the love of money, whether we are rich or poor. The only antidote is to trust God to meet all our needs. See God's love expressed in what he has provided, and remember that money and possessions will all pass away. (See Philippians 4:11 for more on contentment, and 1 John 2:17 for the futility of earthly desires.)

**13:7** If you are a Christian, you owe much to others who have taught you and modeled for you what you needed to know about the Good News and Christian living. Continue following the good examples of those who have invested themselves in you by investing in your life through evangelism, service, and Christian education.

**13:8**
Heb 1:12

**13:9**
Eph 4:14
Col 2:7, 16

**13:11**
Lev 4:12, 21; 16:27

**13:12**
John 19:17
Heb 9:12

**13:13**
Heb 11:26

**13:14**
Heb 11:10; 12:22

**13:15**
Ps 50:14
Hos 14:2
1 Pet 2:5

**13:16**
Phil 4:18

**13:17**
Isa 62:6
Ezek 3:17
Acts 20:28

**13:19**
Phlm 1:22

**13:20**
Isa 55:3
Jer 32:40; 50:5
Ezek 37:26
Zech 9:11
John 10:11

**13:21**
Rom 11:36
Phil 2:13

8 Jesus Christ is the same yesterday, today, and forever. 9 So do not be attracted by strange, new ideas. Your strength comes from God's grace, not from rules about food, which don't help those who follow them.

10 We have an altar from which the priests in the Tabernacle* have no right to eat. 11 Under the old system, the high priest brought the blood of animals into the Holy Place as a sacrifice for sin, and the bodies of the animals were burned outside the camp. 12 So also Jesus suffered and died outside the city gates to make his people holy by means of his own blood. 13 So let us go out to him, outside the camp, and bear the disgrace he bore. 14 For this world is not our permanent home; we are looking forward to a home yet to come.

15 Therefore, let us offer through Jesus a continual sacrifice of praise to God, proclaiming our allegiance to his name. 16 And don't forget to do good and to share with those in need. These are the sacrifices that please God.

17 Obey your spiritual leaders, and do what they say. Their work is to watch over your souls, and they are accountable to God. Give them reason to do this with joy and not with sorrow. That would certainly not be for your benefit.

18 Pray for us, for our conscience is clear and we want to live honorably in everything we do. 19 And especially pray that I will be able to come back to you soon.

20 Now may the God of peace—
   who brought up from the dead our Lord Jesus,
the great Shepherd of the sheep,
   and ratified an eternal covenant with his blood—
21 may he equip you with all you need
   for doing his will.
May he produce in you,*
   through the power of Jesus Christ,

**13:10** Or *tent.* **13:21** Some manuscripts read *in us.*

---

**13:8** Though human leaders have much to offer, we must keep our eyes on Christ, our ultimate leader. Unlike any human leaders, he will never change. Christ has been and will be the same forever. In a changing world we can trust our unchanging Lord.

**13:9** Apparently some were teaching that keeping the Old Testament ceremonial laws and rituals (such as not eating certain foods) was important for salvation. But these laws were useless for conquering a person's evil thoughts and desires (Colossians 2:23). The laws could influence conduct, but they could not change the heart. Lasting changes in conduct begin when the Holy Spirit lives in each person.

**13:13** The Jewish Christians were being ridiculed and persecuted by Jews who didn't believe in Jesus the Messiah. Most of the book of Hebrews tells them how Christ is greater than the sacrificial system. Here the writer drives home the point of his lengthy argument: It may be necessary to leave the "camp" and suffer with Christ. To be outside the camp meant to be unclean—in the days of the Exodus, those who were ceremonially unclean had to stay outside the camp. But Jesus suffered humiliation and uncleanness outside the Jerusalem gates on their behalf. The time had come for Jewish Christians to declare their loyalty to Christ above any other loyalty, to choose to follow the Messiah whatever suffering that might entail. They needed to move outside the safe confinement of their past, their traditions, and their ceremonies to live for Christ. What holds you back from complete loyalty to Jesus Christ?

**13:14** Christians love their families, spouses, jobs, and churches—but their sights should be set ahead beyond the horizon. Christians are activists, invested in witnessing to a needy world—but they take frequent glances toward a promised community still to come. Christians are gardeners and builders, shaping environments, turning weed pits into floral splendor, painting and patching and clearing—but they know God is building something far more beautiful and breathtaking just for them. Christians should be characterized by looking forward to the future. We should not be attached to this world, because all that we are and have here is temporary. We should not love our present home so much that we lose sight of God's future blessing. Don't store up your treasures here; store them in heaven (Matthew 6:19-21).

**13:15** Our lips should confess God's name in praise. Yet, in your typical day, how many times do you hear God's name used profanely? Christians should turn their frequency toward praise! Praise God early in the day before the rush, then again in the hurried middle, and at the end as business winds down. Offer Jesus a continual sacrifice of praise.

**13:15, 16** Since these Jewish Christians, because of their witness to the Messiah, no longer worshiped with other Jews, they should consider praise and acts of service their sacrifices— ones they could offer anywhere, anytime. This must have reminded them of the prophet Hosea's words, "Forgive all our sins and graciously receive us, so that we may offer you our praises" (Hosea 14:2). A "sacrifice of praise" today would include thanking Christ for his sacrifice on the cross and telling others about it. Acts of kindness and sharing are particularly pleasing to God, even when they go unnoticed by others.

**13:17** The task of church leaders is to help people mature in Christ. Cooperative followers greatly ease the burden of leadership. Does your conduct give your leaders reason to report joyfully about you?

**13:18, 19** The writer recognizes the need for prayer. Christian leaders are especially vulnerable to criticism from others, pride (if they succeed), depression (if they fail), and Satan's constant efforts to destroy their work for God. The leaders in your church have been placed in that position by a loving God who has entrusted them with the responsibility of caring for you. Your leaders need your prayers! For whom should you regularly pray?

**13:20, 21** These verses include two significant results of Christ's death and resurrection. God works in us to make us the kind of people that would please him, and he equips us to do the kind of *work* that would please him. Let God change you from within and then use you to help others.

every good thing that is pleasing to him.
All glory to him forever and ever! Amen.

²²I urge you, dear brothers and sisters,* to pay attention to what I have written in this brief exhortation.

²³I want you to know that our brother Timothy has been released from jail. If he comes here soon, I will bring him with me to see you.

²⁴Greet all your leaders and all the believers there.* The believers from Italy send you their greetings.

²⁵May God's grace be with you all.

**13:22** Greek *brothers*.   **13:24** Greek *all of God's holy people*.

**13:22**
1 Pet 5:12

**13:23**
Acts 16:1

---

**13:23**  We have no record of Timothy's imprisonment, but we know that he had been in prison because it states here that he had been released. For more about Timothy, see his Profile in 1 Timothy 2, p. 2059.

**13:24, 25**  Hebrews is a call to Christian maturity. It was addressed to first-century Jewish Christians, but it applies to Christians of any age or background. Christian maturity means making Christ the beginning and end of our faith. To grow in maturity, we must center our life on him, not depending on religious ritual, not falling back into sin, not trusting in ourselves, and not letting anything come between us and Christ. Christ is sufficient and superior.

# JAMES

"MIRACULOUS!" . . . "Revolutionary!" . . . "Greatest ever!" We are inundated by a flood of extravagant claims as we channel surf the television or flip magazine pages. The messages leap out at us. The products assure that they are new, improved, fantastic, and capable of changing our lives. For only a few dollars, we can have "cleaner clothes," "whiter teeth," "glamorous hair," and "tastier food." Automobiles, perfume, diet drinks, and mouthwash are guaranteed to bring happiness, friends, and the good life. And just before an election, no one can match the politicians' promises. But talk is cheap, and too often we soon realize that the boasts were hollow, quite far from the truth.

"Jesus is the answer!" . . . "Believe in God!" . . . "Follow me to church!" Christians also make great claims but are often guilty of belying them with their actions. Professing to trust God and to be his people, they cling tightly to the world and its values. Possessing all the right answers, they contradict the gospel with their lives.

With energetic style and crisp, well-chosen words, James confronts this conflict head-on. It is not enough to talk the Christian faith, he says; we must live it. "What good is it, dear brothers and sisters, if you say you have faith but don't show it by your actions? Can that kind of faith save anyone?" (2:14). The proof of the reality of our faith is a changed life.

Genuine faith will inevitably produce good deeds. This is the central theme of James' letter, around which he supplies practical advice on living the Christian life.

James begins his letter by outlining some general characteristics of the Christian life (1:1–27). Next, he exhorts Christians to act justly in society (2:1–13). He follows this practical advice with a theological discourse on the relationship between faith and action (2:14–26). Then James shows the importance of controlling one's speech (3:1–12). In 3:13–18, James distinguishes two kinds of wisdom—earthly and heavenly. Then he encourages his readers to turn from evil desires and obey God (4:1–12). James reproves those who trust in their own plans and possessions (4:13—5:6). Finally, he exhorts his readers to be patient with each other (5:7–11), to be straightforward in their promises (5:12), to pray for each other (5:13–18), and to help each other remain faithful to God (5:19, 20).

This letter could be considered a how-to book on Christian living. Confrontation, challenges, and a call to commitment await you in its pages. Read James and become a *doer* of the Word (1:22–25).

## VITAL STATISTICS

**PURPOSE:**
To expose hypocritical practices and to teach right Christian behavior

**AUTHOR:**
James, Jesus' brother, a leader in the Jerusalem church

**ORIGINAL AUDIENCE:**
First-century Jewish Christians residing in Gentile communities outside Palestine

**DATE WRITTEN:**
Probably A.D. 49, prior to the Jerusalem council held in A.D. 50

**SETTING:**
This letter expresses James' concern for persecuted Christians who were once part of the Jerusalem church.

**KEY VERSE:**
"Now someone may argue, 'Some people have faith; others have good deeds.' But I say, 'How can you show me your faith if you don't have good deeds? I will show you my faith by my good deeds'" (2:18).

## THE BLUEPRINT

1. Genuine religion (1:1–27)
2. Genuine faith (2:1—3:12)
3. Genuine wisdom (3:13—5:20)

James wrote to Jewish Christians who had been scattered throughout the Mediterranean world because of persecution. In their hostile surroundings they were tempted to let intellectual agreement pass for true faith. This letter can have rich meaning for us as we are reminded that genuine faith transforms lives. We are encouraged to put our faith into action. It is easy to say we have faith, but true faith will produce loving actions toward others.

## MEGATHEMES

| THEME | EXPLANATION | IMPORTANCE |
|---|---|---|
| *Living Faith* | James wants believers not only to hear the truth but also to put it into action. He contrasts empty faith (claims without conduct) with faith that works. Commitment to love and to serve others is evidence of true faith. | Living faith makes a difference. Make sure your faith is more than just a statement; it should also result in action. Seek ways of putting your faith to work. |
| *Trials* | In the Christian life there are trials and temptations. Successfully overcoming these adversities produces maturity and strong character. | Don't resent troubles when they come. Pray for wisdom; God will supply all you need to face persecution or adversity. He will give you patience and keep you strong in times of trial. |
| *Law of Love* | We are saved by God's gracious mercy, not by keeping the law. But Christ gave us a special command: "Love your neighbor as yourself" (Matthew 19:19). We are to love and serve those around us. | Keeping the law of love shows that our faith is vital and real. When we show love to others, we are overcoming our own selfishness. |
| *Wise Speech* | Wisdom shows itself in wise speech. God holds us responsible for the results of our destructive words. The wisdom of God that helps control the tongue can help control all our actions. | Accepting God's wisdom will affect your speech. Your words will convey true humility and lead to peace. Think before you speak and allow God to give you self-control. |
| *Wealth* | James taught Christians not to compromise with worldly attitudes about wealth. Because the glory of wealth fades, Christians should store up God's treasures through sincere service. Christians must not show partiality to the wealthy or be prejudiced against the poor. | All of us are accountable for how we use what we have. We should not hoard wealth but be generous toward others. In addition, we should not be impressed by the wealthy nor look down on those who are poor. |

## 1. Genuine religion

### Greetings from James

**1** This letter is from James, a slave of God and of the Lord Jesus Christ. I am writing to the "twelve tribes"—Jewish believers scattered abroad. Greetings!

**1:1**
1 Pet 1:1

### Faith and Endurance

²Dear brothers and sisters,* when troubles come your way, consider it an opportunity for great joy. ³For you know that when your faith is tested, your endurance has a chance to grow. ⁴So let it grow, for when your endurance is fully developed, you will be perfect and complete, needing nothing.

**1:2**
1 Pet 1:6
**1:3**
1 Pet 1:7

⁵If you need wisdom, ask our generous God, and he will give it to you. He will not rebuke

**1:5**
Prov 2:3-6
Matt 7:7

**1:2** Greek *brothers;* also in 1:16, 19.

---

**1:1** The writer of this letter, a leader of the church in Jerusalem (see Acts 12:17; 15:13), was James, Jesus' half brother, not James the apostle. The book of James was one of the earliest letters, probably written before A.D. 50. After Stephen was martyred (Acts 7:55–8:3), persecution increased, and Christians in Jerusalem were scattered throughout the Roman world. There were thriving Jewish-Christian communities in Rome, Alexandria, Cyprus, and cities in Greece and Asia Minor. Because these early believers did not have the support of established Christian churches, James wrote to them as a concerned leader, to encourage them in their faith during those difficult times.

**1:2, 3** James doesn't say *if* trouble comes your way but *when* it does. He assumes that we will have troubles and that it is possible to profit from them. The point is not to pretend to be happy when we face pain but to have a positive outlook ("consider it an opportunity for great joy") because of what troubles can produce in our life. James tells us to turn our hardships into times of learning. Tough times can teach us perseverance. For other passages dealing with perseverance (also called patience and steadfastness), see Romans 2:7; 5:3-5; 8:24, 25; 2 Corinthians 6:3-7; 2 Peter 1:2-9.

**1:2-4** We can't really know the depth of our character until we see how we react under pressure. It is easy to be kind to others when everything is going well, but can we still be kind when others are treating us unfairly? God wants to make us mature and complete, not to keep us from all pain. Instead of complaining about our struggles, we should see them as opportunities for growth. Thank God for promising to be with you in rough times. Ask him to help you solve your problems or to give you the strength to endure them. Then be patient. God will not leave you alone with your problems; he will stay close and help you grow.

**1:5** By "wisdom," James is talking not only about knowledge but about the ability to make wise decisions in difficult circumstances. Whenever we need wisdom, we can pray to God, and he will generously supply what we need. Christians don't have to grope around in the dark, hoping to stumble upon answers. We can ask for God's wisdom to guide our choices.

**1:5** The wisdom that we need has three distinct characteristics:
(1) *It is practical.* The wisdom from God relates to life even during the most trying times. It is not a wisdom isolated from suffering and trials. This wisdom is the tool by which trials are overcome. An intelligent person may have profound ideas, but a wise person puts profound ideas into action. Intelligence will allow someone to describe several reasons why the car broke down. The wise person chooses the most likely reason and proceeds to take action.
(2) *It is divine.* God's wisdom goes beyond common sense.

**1:6**
Matt 21:22
Mark 11:24

you for asking. 6 But when you ask him, be sure that your faith is in God alone. Do not waver, for a person with divided loyalty is as unsettled as a wave of the sea that is blown and tossed by the wind. 7 Such people should not expect to receive anything from the Lord. 8 Their loyalty is divided between God and the world, and they are unstable in everything they do.

**1:10-11**
Ps 102:4, 11
Isa 40:6-7
1 Pet 1:24

9 Believers who are* poor have something to boast about, for God has honored them. 10 And those who are rich should boast that God has humbled them. They will fade away like a little flower in the field. 11 The hot sun rises and the grass withers; the little flower droops and falls, and its beauty fades away. In the same way, the rich will fade away with all of their achievements.

**1:12**
1 Cor 9:25
2 Tim 4:8
Jas 5:11
Rev 2:10; 3:11

12 God blesses those who patiently endure testing and temptation. Afterward they will receive the crown of life that God has promised to those who love him. 13 And remember,

**1:9** Greek *The brother who is.*

---

**CHAPTER SUMMARY**

---

Common sense does not lead us to choose joy in the middle of trials. This wisdom begins with respect for God, leads to living by God's direction, and results in the ability to tell right from wrong. It is a wisdom that James will describe at length in chapter 3.

(3) *It is Christlike.* Asking for wisdom is ultimately asking to be like Christ. The Bible identifies Christ as the "wisdom of God" (1 Corinthians 1:24; 2:1-7).

**1:6** We must believe not only in the existence of God but also in his loving care. This includes relying on God and expecting that he will hear and answer when we pray. We must put away our critical attitude when we come to him. God does not grant every thoughtless or selfish request. We must have confidence that God will align our desires with his purposes. For more on this concept, read the note on Matthew 21:22.

**1:6** A person with divided loyalty is not completely convinced that God's way is best. He treats God's Word like any human advice and retains the option to disobey. He vacillates between allegiance to subjective feelings, the world's ideas, and God's commands. If your faith is new, weak, or struggling, remember that you can trust God. Then be loyal by committing yourself wholeheartedly to God.

**1:6-8** If you have ever seen the constant rolling of huge waves at sea, you know how restless they are—subject to the forces of wind, gravity, and tide. Divided loyalty leaves a person as unsettled as the restless waves. If you want to stop being tossed about, rely on God to show you what is best for you. Ask him for wisdom, and trust that he will give it to you. Then your decisions will be sure and solid.

**1:9** Christianity brings a new dignity to the poor and not-so-influential people of this world. That dignity is most apparent in the church, where there are not (or should not be) any class distinctions. All believers share the distinction and dignity of being changed by the gospel and being charged with the mission of taking that same Good News to the rest of the world. Believers know they have dignity before God because Christ died for them. Mary, the mother of Jesus, is a great example of this truth. The dignity that she displayed when she realized what God had done for her is seen in her prayer of praise, called the *Magnificat* (Luke 1:46-55). Whatever our social or economic situation, James challenges us to see beyond it to our eternal advantages. What we can have in Jesus Christ outweighs anything in this life. Knowing him gives us our high position, where we find our true dignity.

**1:9-11** The poor should be glad that riches mean nothing to God; otherwise these people would be considered unworthy. The rich

should be glad that money means nothing to God because money is easily lost. We find true wealth by developing our spiritual life, not by developing our financial assets. God is interested in what is lasting (our souls), not in what is temporary (our money and possessions). See Mark 4:18, 19 for Jesus' words on this subject. Strive to treat each person as Christ would treat him or her.

**1:10, 11** If wealth, power, and status mean nothing to God, why do we attribute so much importance to them and so much honor to those who possess them? Do your material possessions give you goals and your only reason for living? If they were gone, what would be left? What you have in your heart, not your bank account, matters to God and endures for eternity.

**1:12** The crown of life is like the victory wreath given to winning athletes (see 1 Corinthians 9:25). God's crown of life is not glory and honor here on earth but the reward of eternal life—living with God forever. The way to be in God's winners' circle is by loving him and staying faithful even under pressure.

**1:12-15** Temptation comes from evil desires inside us, not from God. It begins with an evil thought and becomes sin when we dwell on the thought and allow it to become an action. Like a snowball rolling downhill, sin grows more destructive the more we let it have its way. The best time to stop a temptation is before it is too strong or moving too fast to control. See Matthew 4:1-11; 1 Corinthians 10:13; and 2 Timothy 2:22 for more about escaping temptation.

**1:13, 14** People who live for God often wonder why they still have temptations. Does God tempt them? God *tests* people, but he does not *tempt* them by trying to seduce them to sin. God allows Satan to tempt people, however, in order to refine their faith and to help them grow in their dependence on Christ. We can resist the temptation to sin by turning to God for strength and choosing to obey his Word.

**1:13-15** It is easy to blame others and make excuses for evil thoughts and wrong actions. We use excuses such as: (1) It's the other person's fault; (2) I couldn't help it; (3) everybody's doing it; (4) it was just a mistake; (5) nobody's perfect; (6) the devil made me do it; (7) I was pressured into it; (8) I didn't know it was wrong; or (9) God is tempting me. A person who makes excuses is trying to shift the blame from himself or herself to something or someone else. A Christian, on the other hand, accepts responsibility for his or her wrongs, confesses them, and asks God for forgiveness.

when you are being tempted, do not say, "God is tempting me." God is never tempted to do wrong,* and he never tempts anyone else. ¹⁴Temptation comes from our own desires, which entice us and drag us away. ¹⁵These desires give birth to sinful actions. And when sin is allowed to grow, it gives birth to death.

¹⁶So don't be misled, my dear brothers and sisters. ¹⁷Whatever is good and perfect comes down to us from God our Father, who created all the lights in the heavens.* He never changes or casts a shifting shadow.* ¹⁸He chose to give birth to us by giving us his true word. And we, out of all creation, became his prized possession.*

### Listening and Doing

¹⁹Understand this, my dear brothers and sisters: You must all be quick to listen, slow to speak, and slow to get angry. ²⁰Human anger* does not produce the righteousness* God desires. ²¹So get rid of all the filth and evil in your lives, and humbly accept the word God has planted in your hearts, for it has the power to save your souls.

²²But don't just listen to God's word. You must do what it says. Otherwise, you are only fooling yourselves. ²³For if you listen to the word and don't obey, it is like glancing at your face in a mirror. ²⁴You see yourself, walk away, and forget what you look like. ²⁵But if you look carefully into the perfect law that sets you free, and if you do what it says and don't forget what you heard, then God will bless you for doing it.

²⁶If you claim to be religious but don't control your tongue, you are fooling yourself, and your religion is worthless. ²⁷Pure and genuine religion in the sight of God the Father means caring for orphans and widows in their distress and refusing to let the world corrupt you.

## 2. Genuine faith
### A Warning against Prejudice

**2** My dear brothers and sisters,* how can you claim to have faith in our glorious Lord Jesus Christ if you favor some people over others?

| | |
|---|---|
| **1:14** | Prov 19:3 |
| **1:16** | 1 Cor 6:9 |
| **1:17** | Gen 1:16 / Ps 136:7 / Matt 7:11 |
| **1:18** | John 1:13 / 1 Pet 1:23 |
| **1:19** | Prov 10:19; 15:1 / Eccl 7:9 |
| **1:21** | Eph 1:13; 4:22 / 1 Pet 2:1 |
| **1:22** | Matt 7:21, 26 / Rom 2:13 |
| **1:25** | John 13:17 / Rom 8:2 / Gal 6:2 / Jas 2:12 / 1 Pet 2:16 |
| **1:26** | Ps 34:13 |
| **1:27** | Deut 14:29 / 1 Jn 2:15-17 |
| **2:1** | Prov 24:23 / Acts 10:34 / 1 Cor 2:8 |

**1:13** Or *God should not be put to a test by evil people.* **1:17a** Greek *from above, from the Father of lights.* **1:17b** Some manuscripts read *He never changes, as a shifting shadow does.* **1:18** Greek *we became a kind of firstfruit of his creatures.* **1:20a** Greek *A man's anger.* **1:20b** Or *the justice.* **2:1** Greek *brothers;* also in 2:5, 14.

---

**1:17** The Bible often compares goodness with light and evil with shadow and darkness. For other passages where God is pictured as light, see Psalm 27:1, Isaiah 60:19-22, and John 1:1-14.

**1:19** When we talk too much and listen too little, we communicate to others that we think our ideas are much more important than theirs. James wisely advises us to reverse this process. Put a mental stopwatch on your conversations, and keep track of how much you talk and how much you listen. When people talk with you, do they feel that their viewpoints and ideas have value?

**1:19, 20** These verses speak of anger that erupts when our ego is bruised: *"I* am hurt;" *"My* opinions are not being heard." When injustice and sin occur, we *should* become angry because others are being hurt. But we should not become angry when we fail to win an argument or when we feel offended or neglected. Selfish anger never helps anybody.

**1:21** James advises us to get rid of all that is wrong in our lives and "humbly accept" the salvation message we have received, because it alone can save us.

**1:22-25** It is important to listen to what God's Word says, but it is much more important to obey it and to *do* what it says. We can measure the effectiveness of our Bible study time by the effect it has on our behavior and attitudes. Do you put into action what you have studied?

**1:25** It seems paradoxical that a law could give us freedom, but God's law offers us a true reflection of our sinful condition and gives us the opportunity to ask for God's forgiveness (see Romans 7:7, 8). As Christians, we are saved by God's grace, and salvation frees us from sin's control. As believers, we are free to live as God created us to live. Of course, this does not mean that we are free to do as we please (see 1 Peter 2:16). We are now free to obey God.

**1:26** See the notes in chapter 3 for more on controlling the tongue. No matter how spiritual we may think we are, we all could control our speech more effectively.

**1:27** In the first century, orphans and widows had very little means of economic support. Unless a family member was willing to care for them, they were reduced to begging, selling themselves as slaves, or starving. By caring for these people, the church put God's Word into practice. When we give with no thought of receiving, we show what it means to truly serve others.

**1:27** To keep ourselves from letting the world corrupt us, we need to commit ourselves to Christ's ethical and moral system, not the world's. We are not to adapt to the world's value system, which is based on money, power, and pleasure. True faith means nothing if we are contaminated with such values.

**2:1ff** In this chapter James argues against favoritism and for the necessity of good deeds. He presents three principles of faith: (1) Commitment is an essential part of faith. You cannot be a Christian simply by affirming the right doctrines or agreeing with biblical facts (2:19). You must commit your mind and heart to Christ. (2) Right actions are the natural by-products of true faith. A genuine Christian will have a changed life (2:18). (3) Faith without good deeds doesn't do anybody any good—it is useless (2:14-17). James's teachings are consistent with Paul's teaching that we receive salvation by faith alone. Paul emphasizes the purpose of faith: to bring salvation. James emphasizes the results of faith: a changed life.

**2:1-7** James condemns acts of favoritism. Often we treat a well-dressed, impressive-looking person better than someone who looks shabby. We do this because we would rather identify with successful people than with apparent failures. The irony, as James reminds us, is that the supposed winners may have gained their impressive lifestyle at our expense. In addition, the rich find it difficult to identify with the Lord Jesus, who came as a humble servant. Are you easily impressed by status, wealth, or fame? Are you partial to the "haves" while ignoring the "have nots"? This attitude is sinful. God views all people as equals, and if he favors anyone, it is the poor and the powerless. We should follow his example.

2For example, suppose someone comes into your meeting* dressed in fancy clothes and expensive jewelry, and another comes in who is poor and dressed in dirty clothes. 3If you give special attention and a good seat to the rich person, but you say to the poor one, "You can stand over there, or else sit on the floor"—well, 4doesn't this discrimination show that your judgments are guided by evil motives?

5Listen to me, dear brothers and sisters. Hasn't God chosen the poor in this world to be rich in faith? Aren't they the ones who will inherit the Kingdom he promised to those who love him? 6But you dishonor the poor! Isn't it the rich who oppress you and drag you into court? 7Aren't they the ones who slander Jesus Christ, whose noble name* you bear?

8Yes indeed, it is good when you obey the royal law as found in the Scriptures: "Love your neighbor as yourself."* 9But if you favor some people over others, you are committing a sin. You are guilty of breaking the law.

10For the person who keeps all of the laws except one is as guilty as a person who has broken all of God's laws. 11For the same God who said, "You must not commit adultery," also said, "You must not murder."* So if you murder someone but do not commit adultery, you have still broken the law.

12So whatever you say or whatever you do, remember that you will be judged by the law

**2:4** John 7:23-24
**2:5** Luke 6:20; 1 Cor 1:26-28
**2:7** Acts 11:26; 1 Pet 4:16
**2:8** †Lev 19:18; Matt 7:12; Rom 13:8
**2:10** Matt 5:19; Gal 5:3
**2:11** †Exod 20:13-14; †Deut 5:17-18; Matt 19:18
**2:12** Jas 1:25

**2:2** Greek *your synagogue.* **2:7** Greek *slander the noble name.* **2:8** Lev 19:18. **2:11** Exod 20:13-14; Deut 5:17-18.

---

**SHOWING FAVORITISM**
Why it is wrong to show favoritism to the wealthy:

1. It is inconsistent with Christ's teachings.
2. It results from evil thoughts.
3. It insults people made in God's image.
4. It is a by-product of selfish motives.
5. It goes against the biblical definition of love.
6. It shows a lack of mercy to those less fortunate.
7. It is hypocritical.
8. It is a sin.

---

**2:2-4** Why is it wrong to judge a person by his or her economic status? Wealth may indicate intelligence, wise decisions, and hard work. On the other hand, it may only mean that a person had the good fortune of being born into a wealthy family. Or it may be the sign of greed, dishonesty, or selfishness. By honoring someone just because he or she dresses well, we are making appearance more important than character. Sometimes we do this because: (1) poverty makes us uncomfortable; we don't want to face our responsibilities to those who have less than we do; (2) we want to be wealthy, too, and hope to use the rich person as a means to that end; (3) we want the rich person to join our church and help support it financially. All these motives are selfish, stemming from the view that we are superior to the poor person. If we say that Christ is our Lord, then we must live as he requires, showing no favoritism and loving all people regardless of whether they are rich or poor.

**2:2-4** We are often partial to the rich because we mistakenly assume that riches are a sign of God's blessing and approval. But God does not promise us earthly rewards or riches; in fact, Christ calls us to be ready to suffer for him and give up everything in order to hold on to eternal life (Matthew 6:19-21; 19:28-30; Luke 12:14-34; Romans 8:15-21; 1 Timothy 6:17-19). We will have untold riches in eternity if we are faithful in our present life (Luke 6:35; John 12:23-25; Galatians 6:7-10; Titus 3:4-8).

**2:5** When James speaks about the poor, he is talking about those who have no money and also about those whose simple values are despised by much of our affluent society. Perhaps the "poor" people prefer serving to managing, human relationships to financial security, peace to power. This does not mean that the poor will automatically go to heaven and the rich to hell. Poor people, however, are usually more aware of their powerlessness. Thus, it is often easier for them to acknowledge their need for

salvation. One of the greatest barriers to salvation for the rich is pride. For the poor, bitterness can often bar the way to acceptance of salvation.

**2:8** The "royal law" was given by our great King Jesus Christ, who said, "Love each other in the same way that I have loved you" (John 15:12). This law, originally summarized in Leviticus 19:18, is the basis for all the laws of how people should relate to one another. Christ reinforced this truth in Matthew 22:37-40, and Paul taught it in Romans 13:8 and Galatians 5:14.

**2:8, 9** We must treat all people as we would want to be treated. We should not ignore the rich, because then we would be withholding our love. But we must not favor them for what they can do for us, while ignoring the poor who can offer us seemingly so little in return.

**2:10** Christians must not use this verse to justify sinning. We dare not say, "Because I can't keep every demand of God, why even try?" James reminds us that if we've broken just one law, we are sinners. We can't decide to keep part of God's law and ignore the rest. You can't break the law a little bit; if you have broken it at all, you need Christ to pay for your sin. Measure yourself, not someone else, against God's standards. Ask for forgiveness where you need it, and then renew your effort to put your faith into practice.

**2:12** As Christians, we are saved by God's free gift (grace) through faith, not by keeping the law. But as Christians, we are also required to obey Christ. The apostle Paul taught that "we must all stand before Christ to be judged" (2 Corinthians 5:10) for our conduct. God's grace does not cancel our duty to obey him; it gives our obedience a new basis. The law is no longer an external set of rules, but it is a "law that sets you free"—one we joyfully and willingly carry out, because we love God and have the power of his Holy Spirit (see 1:25).

that sets you free. ¹³There will be no mercy for those who have not shown mercy to others. But if you have been merciful, God will be merciful when he judges you.

**2:13**
Matt 18:32-35

### Faith without Good Deeds Is Dead

¹⁴What good is it, dear brothers and sisters, if you say you have faith but don't show it by your actions? Can that kind of faith save anyone? ¹⁵Suppose you see a brother or sister who has no food or clothing, ¹⁶and you say, "Good-bye and have a good day; stay warm and eat well"—but then you don't give that person any food or clothing. What good does that do?

**2:15**
Matt 25:35-36
**2:16**
1 Jn 3:17-18
**2:17**
Gal 5:6
Jas 2:20, 26

¹⁷So you see, faith by itself isn't enough. Unless it produces good deeds, it is dead and useless.

**2:18**
Matt 7:16-17
Rom 3:28

¹⁸Now someone may argue, "Some people have faith; others have good deeds." But I say, "How can you show me your faith if you don't have good deeds? I will show you my faith by my good deeds."

**2:19**
Deut 6:4
Matt 8:29

¹⁹You say you have faith, for you believe that there is one God.* Good for you! Even the demons believe this, and they tremble in terror. ²⁰How foolish! Can't you see that faith without good deeds is useless?

**2:20**
Gal 5:6
Jas 2:14, 17, 26

²¹Don't you remember that our ancestor Abraham was shown to be right with God by his actions when he offered his son Isaac on the altar? ²²You see, his faith and his actions worked together. His actions made his faith complete. ²³And so it happened just as the Scriptures say: "Abraham believed God, and God counted him as righteous because of his faith."* He was even called the friend of God.* ²⁴So you see, we are shown to be right with God by what we do, not by faith alone.

**2:21**
Gen 22:9, 12
**2:22**
Heb 11:17
**2:23**
†Gen 15:6
Isa 41:8
Rom 4:3-5

²⁵Rahab the prostitute is another example. She was shown to be right with God by her actions when she hid those messengers and sent them safely away by a different road. ²⁶Just as the body is dead without breath,* so also faith is dead without good works.

**2:25**
Josh 2:4, 6, 15
Heb 11:31
**2:26**
Gal 5:6
Jas 2:14, 17, 20

### Controlling the Tongue

**3** Dear brothers and sisters,* not many of you should become teachers in the church, for we who teach will be judged more strictly. ²Indeed, we all make many mistakes. For if we could control our tongues, we would be perfect and could also control ourselves in every other way.

**3:1**
Rom 2:21
**3:2**
Jas 1:4, 26

³We can make a large horse go wherever we want by means of a small bit in its mouth. ⁴And a small rudder makes a huge ship turn wherever the pilot chooses to go, even though the winds are strong. ⁵In the same way, the tongue is a small thing that makes grand speeches.

**3:3**
Ps 32:9
**3:5**
Prov 26:20

**2:19** Some manuscripts read *that God is one;* see Deut 6:4.   **2:23a** Gen 15:6.   **2:23b** See Isa 41:8.
**2:26** Or *without spirit.*   **3:1** Greek *brothers;* also in 3:10.

---

**2:13** Only God in his mercy can forgive our sins. We can't earn forgiveness by forgiving others. But when we withhold forgiveness from others after having received it ourselves, we show that we don't understand or appreciate God's mercy toward us (see Matthew 6:14, 15; 18:21ff; Ephesians 4:31, 32).

**2:14** When someone claims to have faith, what he or she may have is intellectual assent—agreement with a set of Christian teachings—and as such it would be incomplete faith. True faith transforms our conduct as well as our thoughts. If our life remains unchanged, we don't truly believe the truths we claim to believe.

**2:17** We cannot earn our salvation by serving and obeying God. But such actions show that our commitment to God is real. Deeds of loving service are not a substitute for, but rather a verification of, our faith in Christ.

**2:18** At first glance, this verse seems to contradict Romans 3:28, "We are made right with God through faith and not by obeying the law." Deeper investigation, however, shows that the teachings of James and Paul are not at odds. While it is true that our good deeds can never earn salvation, true faith always results in a changed life and good deeds. Paul speaks against those who try to be saved by deeds instead of true faith; James speaks against those who confuse mere intellectual assent with true faith. After all, even demons know who Jesus is, but they don't obey him (2:19). True faith involves a commitment of your whole self to God.

**2:21-24** James says that Abraham was "shown to be right with God" for what he *did* because he *believed* God (Romans 4:1-5). James and Paul are not contradicting but complementing each other. Let's not conclude that the truth is a blending of these two statements. We are not justified by what we do in any way. True faith always results in good deeds, but the deeds do not justify us. Faith brings us salvation; active obedience demonstrates that our faith is genuine.

**2:25** Rahab lived in Jericho, a city the Israelites conquered as they entered the Promised Land (Joshua 2). When Israel's spies came to the city, she hid them and helped them escape. In this way she demonstrated faith in God's purpose for Israel. As a result, she and her family were saved when the city was destroyed. Hebrews 11:31 lists Rahab among the heroes of faith.

**3:1** Teaching was a highly valued and respected profession in Jewish culture, and many Jews who embraced Christianity wanted to become teachers. James warned that although it is good to aspire to teach, teachers' responsibility is great because their words and example affect others' spiritual lives. If you are in a teaching or leadership role, how are you affecting those you lead?

**3:2, 3** What you say and what you *don't* say are both important. To use proper speech you must not only say the right words at the right time but also not say what you shouldn't. Examples of an untamed tongue include gossiping, putting others down, bragging, manipulating, false teaching, exaggerating, complaining, flattering, and lying. Before you speak, ask, Is what I want to say true? Is it necessary? Is it kind?

**3:6**
Prov 16:27
Matt 12:36-37;
15:11, 18-19

But a tiny spark can set a great forest on fire. ⁶And the tongue is a flame of fire. It is a whole world of wickedness, corrupting your entire body. It can set your whole life on fire, for it is set on fire by hell itself.*

**3:8**
Ps 140:3
Rom 3:13

⁷People can tame all kinds of animals, birds, reptiles, and fish, ⁸but no one can tame the tongue. It is restless and evil, full of deadly poison. ⁹Sometimes it praises our Lord and Father, and sometimes it curses those who have been made in the image of God. ¹⁰And so blessing and cursing come pouring out of the same mouth. Surely, my brothers and sisters, this is not right! ¹¹Does a spring of water bubble out with both fresh water and bitter water? ¹²Does a fig tree produce olives, or a grapevine produce figs? No, and you can't draw fresh water from a salty spring.*

**3:9**
Gen 1:26-27; 5:1
1 Cor 11:7

**3:12**
Matt 7:16

### 3. Genuine wisdom
#### True Wisdom Comes from God

**3:13**
Jas 2:18

**3:14**
2 Cor 12:20

**3:15**
Jas 1:5, 17

**3:16**
1 Cor 3:3
Gal 5:20-21

**3:17**
Rom 12:9
Heb 12:11

**3:18**
Matt 5:9
Phil 1:11

¹³If you are wise and understand God's ways, prove it by living an honorable life, doing good works with the humility that comes from wisdom. ¹⁴But if you are bitterly jealous and there is selfish ambition in your heart, don't cover up the truth with boasting and lying. ¹⁵For jealousy and selfishness are not God's kind of wisdom. Such things are earthly, unspiritual, and demonic. ¹⁶For wherever there is jealousy and selfish ambition, there you will find disorder and evil of every kind.

¹⁷But the wisdom from above is first of all pure. It is also peace loving, gentle at all times, and willing to yield to others. It is full of mercy and good deeds. It shows no favoritism and is always sincere. ¹⁸And those who are peacemakers will plant seeds of peace and reap a harvest of righteousness.*

**3:6** Or *for it will burn in hell* (Greek *Gehenna*).   **3:12** Greek *from salt.*   **3:18** Or *of good things, or of justice.*

| SPEECH | When our speech is motivated by | It is full of |
|---|---|---|
| | Satan . . . . . . . . . . . . . . . . . . . . . . . . . . . . . | Bitter jealousy |
| | | Selfish ambition |
| | | Earthly concerns and desires |
| | | Unspiritual thoughts and ideas |
| | | Disorder |
| | | Evil |
| | God and his wisdom . . . . . . . . . . . . . . . | Purity |
| | | Peace |
| | | Consideration for others |
| | | Submission |
| | | Mercy |
| | | Sincerity, impartiality |
| | | Goodness |

**3:6** James compares the damage the tongue can do to a raging fire—the tongue's wickedness has its source in hell itself. The uncontrolled tongue can do terrible damage. Satan uses the tongue to divide people and pit them against one another. Idle and hateful words are damaging because they spread destruction quickly, and no one can stop the results once they are spoken. We dare not be careless with what we say, thinking we can apologize later, because even if we do, the scars remain. A few words spoken in anger can destroy a relationship that took years to build. Before you speak, remember that words are like fire— you can neither control nor reverse the damage they can do.

**3:8** If no human being can tame the tongue, why bother trying? Even though we may not achieve perfect control of our tongues, the Holy Spirit will help us learn self-control. Remember that we are not fighting the tongue's fire in our own strength. The Holy Spirit will give us increasing power to monitor and control what we say, so that when we are offended, the Spirit will remind us of God's love, and we won't react in a hateful manner. When we are criticized, the Spirit will heal the hurt and help us to not lash out.

**3:9-12** Our contradictory speech often puzzles us. At times our words are right and pleasing to God, but at other times they are violent and destructive. Which of these speech patterns reflects our true identity? We were made in God's image, but the tongue gives us a picture of our basic sinful nature. God works to change us from the inside out. When the Holy Spirit purifies a heart, he gives self-control so that the person will speak words that please God.

**3:13-18** Have you ever known anyone who claimed to be wise but who acted foolishly? True wisdom can be measured by a person's character. Just as you can identify a tree by the type of fruit it produces, you can evaluate your wisdom by the way you act. Foolishness leads to disorder, but wisdom leads to peace and goodness. Are you tempted to escalate the conflict, pass on the gossip, or fan the fire of discord? Careful, winsome speech and wise, loving words are the seeds of peace. God loves peacemakers (Matthew 5:9).

**3:14, 15** Bitter jealousy and selfish ambition are inspired by the devil. It is easy for us to be drawn into wrong desires by the pressures of society and sometimes even by well-meaning Christians. By listening to the advice: "Assert yourself," "Go for it," "Set high goals," we can be drawn into greed and destructive competitiveness. Seeking God's wisdom delivers us from the need to compare ourselves to others and to want what they have.

## Drawing Close to God

**4** What is causing the quarrels and fights among you? Don't they come from the evil desires at war within you? ² You want what you don't have, so you scheme and kill to get it. You are jealous of what others have, but you can't get it, so you fight and wage war to take it away from them. Yet you don't have what you want because you don't ask God for it. ³And even when you ask, you don't get it because your motives are all wrong—you want only what will give you pleasure.

⁴You adulterers!* Don't you realize that friendship with the world makes you an enemy of God? I say it again: If you want to be a friend of the world, you make yourself an enemy of God. ⁵ What do you think the Scriptures mean when they say that the spirit God has placed within us is filled with envy?* ⁶ But he gives us even more grace to stand against such evil desires. As the Scriptures say,

"God opposes the proud
but favors the humble."*

⁷So humble yourselves before God. Resist the devil, and he will flee from you. ⁸Come close to God, and God will come close to you. Wash your hands, you sinners; purify your hearts, for your loyalty is divided between God and the world. ⁹Let there be tears for what you have done. Let there be sorrow and deep grief. Let there be sadness instead of laughter, and gloom instead of joy. ¹⁰Humble yourselves before the Lord, and he will lift you up in honor.

## Warning against Judging Others

¹¹Don't speak evil against each other, dear brothers and sisters.* If you criticize and judge each other, then you are criticizing and judging God's law. But your job is to obey the law, not to judge whether it applies to you. ¹²God alone, who gave the law, is the Judge. He alone has the power to save or to destroy. So what right do you have to judge your neighbor?

**4:4** Greek *You adulteresses!*  **4:5** Or *that God longs jealously for the human spirit he has placed within us?* or *that the Holy Spirit, whom God has placed within us, opposes our envy?*  **4:6** Prov 3:34 (Greek version).
**4:11** Greek *brothers.*

| Cross-references |
|---|
| **4:2** 1 Jn 3:15 |
| **4:3** 1 Jn 3:22; 5:14 |
| **4:4** John 15:19; 1 Jn 2:15 |
| **4:5** 1 Cor 6:19; 2 Cor 6:16 |
| **4:6** †Prov 3:34; Matt 23:12; 1 Pet 5:5 |
| **4:7** Eph 6:12; 1 Pet 5:6-9 |
| **4:8** Ps 73:28; Isa 1:16; Zech 1:3; Mal 3:7 |
| **4:9** Luke 6:25 |
| **4:10** Job 5:11; 1 Pet 5:6 |
| **4:11** Matt 7:1; 2 Cor 12:20; 1 Pet 2:1 |
| **4:12** Matt 10:28; Rom 2:1; 14:4; Jas 5:9 |

---

**4:1-3** Quarrels and fights among believers are always harmful. James explains that these conflicts result from evil desires battling within us: We want more possessions, more money, higher status, more recognition. When we don't get what we want, we fight in order to have it. Instead of aggressively grabbing what we want, we should submit ourselves to God, ask God to help us get rid of our selfish desires, and trust him to give us what we really need.

**4:2, 3** James mentions the most common problems in prayer: not asking, asking for the wrong things, or asking for the wrong reasons. Do you talk to God at all? When you do, what do you talk about? Do you ask only to satisfy your desires? Do you seek God's approval for what you already plan to do? Your prayers will become powerful when you allow God to change your desires so that they perfectly correspond to his will for you (1 John 3:21, 22).

**4:3, 4** There is nothing wrong with wanting a pleasurable life. God gives us good gifts that he wants us to enjoy (1:17; Ephesians 4:7; 1 Timothy 4:4, 5). But having friendship with the world involves seeking pleasure at others' expense or at the expense of obeying God. Pleasure that keeps us from pleasing God is sinful; pleasure from God's rich bounty is good.

**4:4-6** The cure for evil desires is humility (see Proverbs 16:18, 19; 1 Peter 5:5, 6). Pride makes us self-centered and leads us to conclude that we deserve all we can see, touch, or imagine. It creates greedy appetites for far more than we need. We can be released from our self-centered desires by humbling ourselves before God, realizing that all we really need is his approval. When the Holy Spirit fills us, we see that this world's seductive attractions are only cheap substitutes for what God has to offer.

**4:5** This verse may mean that because of our fallen nature, we have a tendency toward envy. James is not quoting a specific verse or passage—he is summing up a teaching of Scripture.

See Romans 6:6-8 and Galatians 5:17-21 for more on the human tendency toward envy and discontent.

**4:7** Although God and the devil are at war, we don't have to wait until the end to see who will win. God has *already* defeated Satan (Revelation 12:10-12), and when Christ returns, the devil and all he stands for will be eliminated forever (Revelation 20:10-15). Satan is here now, however, and he is trying to win us over to his evil cause. With the Holy Spirit's power, we can resist the devil, and he will flee from us.

**4:7-10** How can you come close to God? James gives five ways: (1) *Humble yourselves before God* (4:7). Yield to his authority and will, commit your life to him and his control, and be willing to follow him. (2) *Resist the devil* (4:7). Don't allow Satan to entice and tempt you. (3) *Wash your hands . . . and purify your hearts* (that is, lead a pure life) (4:8). Be cleansed from sin, replacing your desire to sin with your desire to experience God's purity. (4) *Let there be sorrow and deep grief* for your sins (4:9). Don't be afraid to express deep heartfelt sorrow for what you have done. (5) *Humble yourselves before the Lord,* and he will lift you up in honor (4:10; 1 Peter 5:6).

**4:10** Bowing in humility before the Lord means recognizing that our worth comes from God alone. To be humble involves leaning on his power and his guidance, and not going our own independent way. Although we do not deserve God's favor, he wants to lift us up and give us worth and dignity, despite our human shortcomings.

**4:11, 12** Jesus summarized the law as love for God and neighbor (Matthew 22:37-40), and Paul said that love demonstrated toward a neighbor would fully satisfy the law (Romans 13:6-10). When we fail to love, we are actually breaking God's law. Examine your attitude and actions toward others. Do you build people up or tear them down? When you're ready to criticize someone, remember God's law of love and say something good instead. Saying something beneficial to others will cure you of finding fault and increase your ability to obey God's law of love.

**4:13-14**
Prov 27:1
Luke 12:18-20
**4:15**
Acts 18:21
**4:16**
1 Cor 5:6
**4:17**
Luke 12:47

### Warning about Self-Confidence

13Look here, you who say, "Today or tomorrow we are going to a certain town and will stay there a year. We will do business there and make a profit." 14How do you know what your life will be like tomorrow? Your life is like the morning fog—it's here a little while, then it's gone. 15What you ought to say is, "If the Lord wants us to, we will live and do this or that." 16Otherwise you are boasting about your own plans, and all such boasting is evil.

17Remember, it is sin to know what you ought to do and then not do it.

**5:1**
Prov 11:4, 28
Isa 13:6
**5:2**
Matt 6:19

### Warning to the Rich

**5** Look here, you rich people: Weep and groan with anguish because of all the terrible troubles ahead of you. 2Your wealth is rotting away, and your fine clothes are moth-eaten rags. 3Your gold and silver have become worthless. The very wealth you were counting

---

**FAITH THAT WORKS**
James offers a larger number of similarities to the Sermon on the Mount than any other book in the New Testament. James relied heavily on Jesus' teachings.

| Lesson | Reference |
|---|---|
| When troubles come your way, consider it an opportunity for great joy. | James 1:2 Matthew 5:10-12 |
| When your endurance is fully developed, you will be perfect and complete, needing nothing. | James 1:4 Matthew 5:48 |
| Ask God, and he will answer. | James 1:5; 5:15 Matthew 7:7-12 |
| Believers who are poor (who don't amount to much by the world's standards) should be glad, for God has honored them. | James 1:9 Matthew 5:3 |
| Watch out for your anger. . . . It can be dangerous. | James 1:19, 20 Matthew 5:22 |
| Be merciful to others, as God is merciful to you. | James 2:13 Matthew 5:7; 6:14 |
| Your faith must express itself in your actions. | James 2:14-16 Matthew 7:21-23 |
| Blessed are the peacemakers; they plant seeds of peace and reap a harvest of righteousness. | James 3:17, 18 Matthew 5:9 |
| Friendship with the world makes you an enemy of God. | James 4:4 Matthew 6:24 |
| When you humble yourself and realize your dependence on God, he will lift you up. | James 4:10 Matthew 5:3, 4 |
| Don't speak evil against each other. If you do, you are criticizing and judging God's law. | James 4:11 Matthew 7:1, 2 |
| Treasures on earth will only rot away and be eaten by moths. Store up eternal treasures in heaven. | James 5:2, 3 Matthew 6:19 |
| Be patient in suffering, as God's prophets were patient. | James 5:10 Matthew 5:12 |
| Be honest in your speech; just say a simple yes or no so that you will not sin. | James 5:12 Matthew 5:33-37 |

---

**4:13-16** It is good to have goals, but goals can disappoint us if we leave God out of them. There is no point in making plans as though God does not exist because the future is in his hands. The beginning of good planning is to ask: "What would I like to be doing ten years from now? One year from now? Tomorrow? How will I react if God steps in and rearranges my plans?" We can plan ahead, but we must hold on to our plans loosely. If we put God's desires at the center of our planning, he will never disappoint us.

**4:14** Life is short no matter how many years we live. Don't be deceived into thinking that you have lots of remaining time to live for Christ, to enjoy your loved ones, or to do what you know you should. Live for God today! Then, no matter when your life ends, you will have fulfilled God's plan for you.

**4:17** We tend to think that *doing* wrong is sin. But James tells us that sin is also *not* doing right. (These two kinds of sin are sometimes called sins of commission and sins of omission.) It is a sin to lie; it can also be a sin to know the truth and not tell it. It is a sin to speak evil of someone; it is also a sin to avoid that person

when you know he or she needs your friendship. You should be willing to help as the Holy Spirit guides you. If God has directed you to do a kind act, to render a service, or to restore a relationship, do it. You will experience a renewed and refreshed vitality to your Christian faith.

**5:1-6** James proclaims the worthlessness of riches, not the worthlessness of the rich. Today's money will be worthless when Christ returns, so we should spend our time accumulating the kind of treasures that will be worthwhile in God's eternal Kingdom. Money is not the problem; Christian leaders need money to live and to support their families; missionaries need money to help them spread the Good News; churches need money to do their work effectively. It is the *love* of money that leads to evil (1 Timothy 6:10) and causes some people to oppress others in order to get more. This is a warning to all Christians who are tempted to adopt worldly standards rather than God's standards (Romans 12:1, 2) as well as an encouragement to all those who are oppressed by the rich. Also read Matthew 6:19-21 to see what Jesus says about riches.

on will eat away your flesh like fire. This treasure you have accumulated will stand as evidence against you on the day of judgment. 4For listen! Hear the cries of the field workers whom you have cheated of their pay. The wages you held back cry out against you. The cries of those who harvest your fields have reached the ears of the LORD of Heaven's Armies.

**5:4**
Lev 19:13
Deut 24:14-15
Ps 18:6
Isa 5:9

5You have spent your years on earth in luxury, satisfying your every desire. You have fattened yourselves for the day of slaughter. 6You have condemned and killed innocent people,* who do not resist you.*

**5:5**
Jer 12:3; 25:34
Luke 16:19-23

### Patience and Endurance

7Dear brothers and sisters,* be patient as you wait for the Lord's return. Consider the farmers who patiently wait for the rains in the fall and in the spring. They eagerly look for the valuable harvest to ripen. 8You, too, must be patient. Take courage, for the coming of the Lord is near.

**5:7**
Deut 11:14
Jer 5:24
Joel 2:23

**5:8**
Rom 13:11-12
Heb 10:37

9Don't grumble about each other, brothers and sisters, or you will be judged. For look—the Judge is standing at the door!

**5:9**
Matt 24:33
1 Cor 4:5
Jas 4:12

10For examples of patience in suffering, dear brothers and sisters, look at the prophets who spoke in the name of the Lord. 11We give great honor to those who endure under suffering. For instance, you know about Job, a man of great endurance. You can see how the Lord was kind to him at the end, for the Lord is full of tenderness and mercy.

**5:11**
Job 1:20-22;
2:7-10; 42:10-17
Ps 103:8

12But most of all, my brothers and sisters, never take an oath, by heaven or earth or anything else. Just say a simple yes or no, so that you will not sin and be condemned.

**5:12**
Matt 5:34-37

### The Power of Prayer

13Are any of you suffering hardships? You should pray. Are any of you happy? You should sing praises. 14Are any of you sick? You should call for the elders of the church to come and pray over you, anointing you with oil in the name of the Lord. 15Such a prayer offered in faith will heal the sick, and the Lord will make you well. And if you have committed any sins, you will be forgiven.

**5:13**
Col 3:16

**5:14**
Mark 6:13

**5:15**
Mark 16:18
Jas 1:6

16Confess your sins to each other and pray for each other so that you may be healed. The

**5:16**
Matt 18:15-18
1 Jn 1:9

**5:6a** Or *killed the Righteous One.*   **5:6b** Or *Don't they resist you?* or *Doesn't God oppose you?* or *Aren't they now accusing you before God?*   **5:7** Greek *brothers;* also in 5:9, 10, 12, 19.

---

**5:6** "Innocent people" refers to defenseless persons, probably poor laborers. Poor people who could not pay their debts were thrown in prison or forced to sell all their possessions. At times, they were even forced to sell their family members into slavery. With no opportunity to work off their debts, poor people often died of starvation. God called this murder. Hoarding money, exploiting employees, and living self-indulgently will not escape God's notice.

**5:7, 8** The farmer must wait patiently for his crops to grow; he cannot hurry the process. But he does not take the summer off and hope that all goes well in the fields. There is much work to do to ensure a good harvest. In the same way, we must wait patiently for Christ's return. We cannot make him come back any sooner. But while we wait, there is much work that we can do to advance God's Kingdom. Both the farmer and the Christian must live by faith, looking toward the future reward for their labors. Don't live as if Christ will never come. Work faithfully to build his Kingdom. The King *will* come when the time is right.

**5:9** When things go wrong, we tend to grumble against and blame others for our miseries (see the second note on Genesis 3:11-13). Blaming others is easier than owning our share of the responsibility, but it can be both destructive and sinful. Before you judge others for their shortcomings, remember that Christ the Judge will come to evaluate each of us (Matthew 7:1-5; 25:31-46). He will not let us get away with shifting the blame to others.

**5:10, 11** Many prophets suffered and were persecuted, such as Moses, Elijah, and Jeremiah. For a complete list of those persecuted, see the chart in 2 Chronicles 18, pp. 690-691. For more on the topic of suffering, see the notes on Job 1:1ff; 2:10; 3:23-26; 4:7, 8; 42:17; and Job's Profile in Job 3, p. 789.

**5:12** A person with a reputation for exaggeration or lying often can't get anyone to believe him on his word alone. Christians should never become like that. Always be honest so that others will believe your simple yes or no. By avoiding lies, half-truths, and omissions of the truth, you will become known as a trustworthy person.

**5:14, 15** James is referring to someone who is physically ill. In Scripture, oil was both a medicine (see the parable of the Good Samaritan in Luke 10:30-37) and a symbol of the Spirit of God (as used in anointing kings, see 1 Samuel 16:1-13). Thus, oil can represent both the medical and the spiritual spheres of life. Christians should not separate the physical and the spiritual. Jesus Christ is Lord over both the body and the spirit.

**5:14, 15** People in the church are not alone. Members of Christ's body should be able to count on others for support and prayer, especially when they are sick or suffering. The elders should be on call to respond to the illness of any member, and the church should be sensitive to the needs of all its members.

**5:15** The "prayer offered in faith" does not refer to the faith of the sick person but to the faith of the people praying. God heals, faith doesn't, and all prayers are subject to God's will. But prayer is part of God's healing process.

**5:16** Christ has made it possible for us to go directly to God for forgiveness. But confessing our sins to each other still has an important place in the life of the church. (1) If we have sinned against an individual, we must ask him or her to forgive us. (2) If our sin has affected the church, we must confess it publicly. (3) If we need loving support as we struggle with a sin, we should confess that sin to those who are able to provide that support. (4) If we doubt God's forgiveness, after confessing a sin to him, we may wish to confess that sin to a fellow believer for assurance of God's pardon. In Christ's Kingdom, every believer is a priest to other believers (1 Peter 2:9).

**5:17**
1 Kgs 17:1-7
Luke 4:25

earnest prayer of a righteous person has great power and produces wonderful results. [17]Elijah was as human as we are, and yet when he prayed earnestly that no rain would fall,

**5:18**
1 Kgs 18:42-45

none fell for three and a half years! [18]Then, when he prayed again, the sky sent down rain and the earth began to yield its crops.

*Restore Wandering Believers*

**5:19**
Matt 18:15

[19]My dear brothers and sisters, if someone among you wanders away from the truth and is

**5:20**
Prov 10:12
1 Pet 4:8

brought back, [20]you can be sure that whoever brings the sinner back will save that person from death and bring about the forgiveness of many sins.

---

**5:16-18** The Christian's most powerful resource is communion with God through prayer. The results are often greater than we thought were possible. Some people see prayer as a last resort to be tried when all else fails. This approach is backward. Prayer should come first. Because God's power is infinitely greater than ours, it only makes sense to rely on it—especially because God encourages us to do so.

**5:17** For more about the great prophet Elijah, read his Profile in 1 Kings 17, p. 545.

**5:19, 20** Clearly this person who has wandered from the truth is a believer who has fallen into sin—one who is no longer living a life consistent with his or her beliefs. Christians disagree over whether or not it is possible for people to lose their salvation, but all agree that those who fall away from their faith are in serious

trouble and need to repent. James urges Christians to help backsliders return to God. By taking the initiative, praying for the person, and acting in love, we can meet the person where he or she is and bring him or her back to God and his forgiveness.

**5:20** The book of James emphasizes faith in action. Right living is the evidence and result of faith. The church must serve with compassion, speak lovingly and truthfully, live in obedience to God's commands, and love one another. The body of believers ought to be an example of heaven on earth, drawing people to Christ through love for God and each other. If we truly believe God's Word, we will *live* it day by day. God's Word is not merely something we read or think about, but something we do. Belief, faith, and trust must have hands and feet—ours!

# 1 PETER

CRUSHED, overwhelmed, devastated, torn—these waves of feelings wash over those who suffer, obliterating hope and threatening to destroy them. Suffering has many forms—physical abuse, debilitating disease, social ostracism, persecution. The pain and anguish tempt a person to turn back, to surrender, to give in.

Many first-century followers of Christ were suffering and being abused and persecuted for believing in and obeying Jesus. Beginning in Jerusalem at the hands of their Jewish brothers, the persecution spread to the rest of the world—wherever Christians gathered. It climaxed when Rome determined to rid the empire of the "Christ-ones"—those who would not bow to Caesar.

Peter knew persecution firsthand. Beaten and jailed, he had been threatened often. He had seen fellow Christians die and the church scattered. But he knew Christ, and nothing could shake his confidence in his risen Lord. So Peter wrote to the church scattered and suffering for the faith, giving comfort and hope, and urging continued loyalty to Christ.

Peter begins by thanking God for salvation (1:2–6). He explains to his readers that trials will refine their faith (1:7–9). They should believe in spite of their circumstances; for many in past ages believed in God's plan of salvation, even the prophets of old who wrote about it but didn't understand it. But now salvation has been revealed in Christ (1:10–13).

In response to such a great salvation, Peter commands them to live holy lives (1:14–16), to reverently fear and trust God (1:17–21), to be honest and loving (1:22—2:1), and to become like Christ (2:1–3).

Jesus Christ, as "the living cornerstone" upon whom the church is to be built (2:4, 6), is also the stone that was rejected, causing those who are disobedient to stumble and fall (2:7, 8). But the church, built upon this stone, is to be God's royal priesthood (2:9, 10).

Next, Peter explains how believers should live during difficult times (2:11—4:11). Christians should be above reproach (2:12–17), imitating Christ in all their social roles—masters and servants, husbands and wives, church members and neighbors (2:18—3:17). Christ should be our model for obedience to God in the midst of great suffering (3:18—4:11).

Peter then outlines the right attitude to have about persecution: Expect it (4:12), be thankful for the privilege of suffering for Christ (4:13–18), and trust God for deliverance (4:19).

Next, Peter gives some special instructions: Elders should care for God's flock (5:1–4), younger men should be submissive to those who are older (5:5, 6), and everyone should trust God and resist Satan (5:7–11).

Peter concludes by introducing Silas and by sending personal greetings, possibly from the church in Rome, and from Mark (5:12–14).

When you suffer for doing what is right, remember that following Christ is a costly commitment. When persecuted for your faith, rejoice that you have been counted worthy to suffer for your Lord. He suffered for us; as his followers, we should expect nothing less. As you read 1 Peter, remember that trials will come to refine your faith. When they come, remain faithful to God.

## THE BLUEPRINT

1. God's great blessings to his people (1:1—2:10)
2. The conduct of God's people in the midst of suffering (2:11—4:19)
3. The shepherding of God's people in the midst of suffering (5:1—14)

Peter wrote to Jewish Christians who were experiencing persecution for their faith. He wrote to comfort them with the hope of eternal life and to challenge them to continue living holy lives. Those who suffer for being Christians become partners with Christ in his suffering. As we suffer, we must remember that Christ is both our hope in the midst of suffering and our example of how to endure suffering faithfully.

## MEGATHEMES

| THEME | EXPLANATION | IMPORTANCE |
|---|---|---|
| Salvation | Our salvation is a gracious gift from God. God chose us out of his love for us, Jesus died to pay the penalty for our sin, and the Holy Spirit cleansed us from sin when we believed. Eternal life is a wonderful gift for those who trust in Christ. | Our safety and security are in God. If we experience joy in relationship with Christ now, how much greater will our joy be when he returns and we see him face to face. Such a hope should motivate us to serve Christ with greater commitment. |
| Persecution | Peter offers faithful believers comfort and hope. We should expect ridicule, rejection, and suffering because we are Christians. Persecution makes us stronger because it refines our faith. We can face persecution victoriously, as Christ did, if we rely on him. | Christians still suffer for what they believe. We should expect persecution, but we don't have to be terrified by it. The fact that we will live eternally with Christ should give us the confidence, patience, and hope to stand firm even when we are persecuted. |
| God's Family | We are privileged to belong to God's family, a community with Christ as the founder and foundation. Everyone in this community is related—we are all brothers and sisters, loved equally by God. | Because Christ is the foundation of our family, we must be devoted, loyal, and faithful to him. By obeying him, we show that we are his children. We must accept the challenge to live differently from the society around us. |
| Family Life | Peter encouraged the wives of unbelievers to submit to their husbands' authority as a means of winning them to Christ. He urged all family members to treat others with sympathy, love, compassion, and humility. | We must treat our families lovingly. Though it's never easy, willing service is the best way to influence loved ones. To gain the strength we need for self-discipline and submission, we need to pray for God's help. |
| Judgment | God will judge everyone with perfect justice. We all will face God. He will punish evildoers and those who persecute God's people. Those who love him will be rewarded with life forever in his presence. | Because all are accountable to God, we can leave judgment of others to him. We must not hate or resent those who persecute us. We should realize that we will be held responsible for how we live each day. |

# 1. God's great blessings to his people
## Greetings from Peter

**1** This letter is from Peter, an apostle of Jesus Christ.

I am writing to God's chosen people who are living as foreigners in the provinces of Pontus, Galatia, Cappadocia, Asia, and Bithynia.* ²God the Father knew you and chose you long ago, and his Spirit has made you holy. As a result, you have obeyed him and have been cleansed by the blood of Jesus Christ.

May God give you more and more grace and peace.

**1:2**
Rom 8:29
2 Thes 2:13
Heb 12:24

## The Hope of Eternal Life

³All praise to God, the Father of our Lord Jesus Christ. It is by his great mercy that we have been born again, because God raised Jesus Christ from the dead. Now we live with great

1:1 *Pontus, Galatia, Cappadocia, Asia,* and *Bithynia* were Roman provinces in what is now Turkey.

---

**1:1** The apostle Peter wrote this letter to encourage believers who would likely face trials and persecution under Emperor Nero. During most of the first century, Christians were not hunted down and killed throughout the Roman Empire. They could, however, expect social and economic persecution from three main sources: the Romans, the Jews, and their own families. All would very likely be misunderstood; some would be harassed; a few would be tortured and even put to death.

The legal status of Christians in the Roman Empire was unclear. Many Romans still thought of Christians as members of a Jewish sect, and because the Jewish religion was legal, they considered Christianity legal also—as long as Christians complied with the empire's laws. However, they became the target of persecution when they refused to worship the emperor as a god, refused to worship at pagan temples (so business for these moneymaking enterprises dropped wherever Christianity took hold), or exposed and rejected the horrible immorality of pagan culture.

Many Jews did not appreciate being legally associated with Christians. As the book of Acts frequently records, Jews occasionally harmed Christians physically, drove them out of town, or attempted to turn Roman officials against them. Saul, later the great apostle Paul, was an early Jewish persecutor of Christians.

Another source of persecution was the Christian's own family. Under Roman law, the head of the household had absolute authority over all its members. Unless the ruling male became a Christian, the wife, children, and servants who were believers might well face extreme hardship. If they were sent away, they would have no place to turn but the church; if they were beaten, no court of law would uphold their interests.

Peter may have been writing especially for new Christians and those planning to be baptized. Peter wanted to warn them about what lay ahead, and they needed his encouraging words to help them face opposition. This letter is still helpful for any Christians facing trials. Many Christians around the world are living under governments more repressive than the Roman Empire of the first century. Christians everywhere are subject to misunderstanding, ridicule, and even harassment by unbelieving friends, employers, and family members. None of us is exempt from catastrophe, pain, illness, and death—trials that, like persecution, make us lean heavily on God's grace. For today's readers, as well as for Peter's original audience, the theme of this letter is *hope.*

**1:1** Peter (also called Simon and Cephas) was one of the 12 disciples chosen by Jesus (Mark 1:16-18; John 1:42) and, with James and John, was part of the inner group that Jesus singled out for special training and fellowship. Peter was one of the first to recognize Jesus as the Messiah, God's Son, and Jesus gave him a special leadership role in the church (Matthew 16:16-19; Luke 22:31, 32; John 21:15-19). Although during Jesus' trial Peter denied knowing Jesus, Peter repented and became a great apostle. For more information on Peter, see his Profile in Matthew 27, p. 1603.

**1:1** This letter is addressed to "God's chosen people who are living as foreigners" in various parts of the world—the Jewish

Christians scattered throughout the world as a result of persecution against believers in and around Jerusalem. The first believers and leaders of the early church were Jews. When they became Christians, they didn't give up their Jewish heritage, just as you didn't give up your nationality when you became a follower of Christ. Because of persecution, these believers had been scattered throughout the Roman world (this scattering is described in Acts 8:1-4). Persecution didn't stop the spread of the Good News; instead, persecution served as a way to introduce the Good News to the whole empire. Thus, the churches to whom Peter wrote also included Gentile Christians.

**1:2** Peter encouraged his readers by this strong declaration that they were *chosen* by God the Father. At one time, only the nation of Israel could claim to be God's chosen people; but through Christ, all believers—Jews and Gentiles—belong to God. Our salvation and security rest in God's merciful choice; no trials or persecutions can take away the eternal life he gives to those who believe in him.

**1:2** This verse mentions all three members of the Trinity: God the Father, God the Son (Jesus Christ), and God the Holy Spirit. All members of the Trinity work to bring about our salvation. The Father chose us before we chose him (Ephesians 1:4). Jesus Christ, the Son, died for us while we were still sinners (Romans 5:6-10). The Holy Spirit brings us the benefits of salvation and sets us apart (makes us holy, sanctifies us) for God's service (2 Thessalonians 2:13).

**1:2** How did God "choose" us? Don't we make our own choices? God alone originates and accomplishes our salvation because of his grace; we do nothing to earn it. Being "chosen" in no way removes the necessity for people to choose to follow. The fact that God knows all events and decisions beforehand, even ordains them beforehand, does not mean that he forces the actions of his creatures or leaves them with no choice. Instead, God's foreknowledge means that he took the initiative and chose people before they had done anything to deserve it. God had intimate knowledge of these future believers; he knew who would believe, and he knew them personally. Those chosen ones were known by God the Father as a father knows his children, except that God knew about them from eternity past. God is not trapped in time—what he knows is from eternity past into eternity future. Believers are chosen, but not against their will. When the time comes, they accept the gospel message.

**1:3** The term *born again* refers to spiritual birth (regeneration)—the Holy Spirit's act of bringing believers into God's family. Jesus used this concept of new birth when he explained salvation to Nicodemus (see John 3). This term is a wonderful metaphor of new life from God. You cannot be a Christian without a fresh beginning based on the salvation Christ brings. To be born again is a magnificent gift from God.

**1:3-5** Do you need encouragement? Peter's words offer joy and hope in times of trouble, and he bases his confidence on what God has done for us in Christ Jesus. We live with the wonderful expectation of eternal life (1:3). Our hope is not only for the expectation, 4 and we have a priceless inheritance—an inheritance that is kept in heaven for you, pure and undefiled, beyond the reach of change and decay. 5And through your faith, God is protecting you by his power until you receive this salvation, which is ready to be revealed on the last day for all to see.

6So be truly glad.* There is wonderful joy ahead, even though you have to endure many trials for a little while. 7These trials will show that your faith is genuine. It is being tested as fire tests and purifies gold—though your faith is far more precious than mere gold. So when your faith remains strong through many trials, it will bring you much praise and glory and honor on the day when Jesus Christ is revealed to the whole world.

1:6 Or So you are truly glad.

**THE CHURCHES OF PETER'S LETTER**

Peter addressed his letter to the churches located throughout Bithynia, Pontus, Asia, Galatia, and Cappadocia. Paul had evangelized many of these areas; other areas had churches that were begun by the Jews who were in Jerusalem on the day of Pentecost and heard Peter's powerful sermon (see Acts 2:9-11).

future; eternal life begins when we trust Christ and join God's family. God will help us remain true to our faith through whatever difficult times we must face. The "last day" is the judgment day of Christ described in Romans 14:10 and Revelation 20:11-15. No matter what trials or persecution you may face, your soul cannot be harmed if you have accepted Christ's gift of salvation. You will receive the promised rewards.

**1:4** The Jews had looked forward to an inheritance in the Promised Land of Canaan (Numbers 32:19; Deuteronomy 2:12; 19:8). Although the nation had received that right of inheritance, eventually they defiled their faith through the influence of foreign nations. The people's sins had caused the promise to become only a fading memory. Christians now look forward to another inheritance, a "priceless" inheritance—eternal life in the eternal city of God. God has reserved the inheritance; it will never fade or decay; it will be unstained by sin. The best part is that *you* have an inheritance if you have trusted Christ as your Savior.

**1:6** Why were Christians the target of persecution? (1) They refused to worship the emperor as a god and thus were viewed as atheists and traitors. (2) They refused to worship at pagan temples, so business for these moneymaking enterprises dropped wherever Christianity took hold. (3) They didn't support the Roman ideals of self, power, and conquest; and the Romans scorned the Christian ideal of self-sacrificing service. (4) They exposed and rejected the horrible immorality of pagan culture.

**1:6, 7** Peter mentions trials and suffering several times in this letter: 1:6, 7; 3:13-17; 4:12-19; 5:9. All believers face such trials when they let their light shine into the darkness. We must accept trials as part of the refining process that burns away impurities and prepares us to meet Christ. As gold is heated, impurities float to the top and can be skimmed off. Likewise, our trials, struggles, and persecutions refine and strengthen our faith, making us useful to God. Instead of asking, "Why me?" we should respond to suffering with a new set of responses: (1) *Confidence* that God knows, plans, and directs our lives for the good. It's hard to calculate sometimes, but God always provides his love and strength for us. God leads us toward a better future. (2) *Perseverance* when facing grief, anger, sorrow, and pain. We express our grief, but we don't give in to bitterness and despair. (3) *Courage* because with Jesus as Brother and Savior, we need not be afraid. He who suffered for us will not abandon us. Jesus carries us through everything.

8You love him even though you have never seen him. Though you do not see him now, you trust him; and you rejoice with a glorious, inexpressible joy. 9The reward for trusting him will be the salvation of your souls.

10This salvation was something even the prophets wanted to know more about when they prophesied about this gracious salvation prepared for you. 11They wondered what time or situation the Spirit of Christ within them was talking about when he told them in advance about Christ's suffering and his great glory afterward.

12They were told that their messages were not for themselves, but for you. And now this Good News has been announced to you by those who preached in the power of the Holy Spirit sent from heaven. It is all so wonderful that even the angels are eagerly watching these things happen.

## A Call to Holy Living

13So think clearly and exercise self-control. Look forward to the gracious salvation that will come to you when Jesus Christ is revealed to the world. 14So you must live as God's obedient children. Don't slip back into your old ways of living to satisfy your own desires. You didn't know any better then. 15But now you must be holy in everything you do, just as God who chose you is holy. 16For the Scriptures say, "You must be holy because I am holy."*

17And remember that the heavenly Father to whom you pray has no favorites. He will judge or reward you according to what you do. So you must live in reverent fear of him during your time as "foreigners in the land." 18For you know that God paid a ransom to save you from the empty life you inherited from your ancestors. And the ransom he paid was not mere gold or silver. 19It was the precious blood of Christ, the sinless, spotless Lamb of God. 20God chose him as your ransom long before the world began, but he has now revealed him to you in these last days.

1:16 Lev 11:44-45; 19:2; 20:7.

### Cross-references

**1:8**
John 20:29
2 Cor 5:7

**1:9**
Rom 6:22

**1:10**
Matt 13:17; 26:24

**1:11**
Isa 53
Luke 24:26
Acts 16:7
2 Pet 1:21

**1:12**
Acts 2:2-4
Eph 3:10

**1:14**
Rom 12:2
Eph 2:3; 4:17-18
1 Pet 1:2; 4:2

**1:15**
2 Cor 7:1
1 Thes 4:7
1 Jn 3:3

**1:16**
†Lev 11:44-45;
19:2; 20:7

**1:17**
Ps 89:26
Jer 3:19

**1:19**
Exod 12:5
John 1:29
Heb 9:14

**1:20**
Acts 2:23
Eph 1:4

---

**1:8, 9** Jesus had said to his disciple Thomas, who came to believe after touching the resurrected Christ: "You believe because you have seen me. Blessed are those who believe without seeing me" (John 20:29). Peter, having heard those words, repeats them here: "You love him even though you have never seen him." That faith brings both salvation and the promise of a day when pain will end and perfect justice begin. Faith will be rewarded and evil will be punished. But what should we do until then? The Bible's answer is simple but not easy: Because we know the future, we must faithfully serve God here and now. If today that means resolving a conflict, mending a hurt, working a dull job, confronting a belligerent child, rebuilding a marriage, or just waiting for guidance—do it all with the joy of God, who will return with his reward!

**1:11** The Spirit of Christ is another name for the Holy Spirit. Before Jesus left his ministry on earth to return to heaven, he promised to send the Holy Spirit, the Counselor, to teach, help, and guide his followers (John 14:15-17, 26; 16:7). The Holy Spirit would tell them all about Jesus and would reveal his glory (John 15:26; 16:14). The Old Testament prophets, writing under the Holy Spirit's inspiration (2 Peter 1:20, 21), described the coming of the Messiah. The New Testament apostles, through the inspiration of the same Spirit, preached the crucified and risen Lord.

**1:13, 14** The imminent return of Christ should motivate us to live for him. This means being mentally alert ("think clearly"), disciplined ("exercise self-control"), and focused ("look forward"). Are you ready to meet Christ, living as God's obedient child?

**1:14-16** The God of Israel and of the Christian church is holy—he sets the standard for morality. Unlike the Roman gods, he is not warlike, adulterous, or spiteful. Unlike the gods of the pagan cults popular in the first century, he is not bloodthirsty or promiscuous. He is a God of mercy and justice who cares personally for each of his followers. Our holy God expects us to imitate him by following his high moral standards and by being both merciful and just.

**1:14-16** Peter's words mean that all parts of our lives and character should be in the process of becoming conformed, both inwardly and outwardly, to God's standards. After people commit their lives to Christ, they sometimes still feel a pull back to their old ways. Peter tells us to be like our heavenly Father—holy in everything we do. Holiness means being totally devoted or dedicated to God, set aside for his special use and set apart from sin and its influence. We're to be set apart and different, not blending in with the crowd, yet not being different just for the sake of being different. God's qualities in our lives make us different. Our focus and priorities must be his. All this is in direct contrast to our old ways (1:14). We cannot become holy on our own, but God gives us his Holy Spirit to help us obey and to give us power to overcome sin. Don't use the excuse that you can't help slipping into sin. Rely on God's power to free you from sin's grip.

**1:17** "Reverent fear" is the healthy respect of a believer for the all-powerful God. Because God is the Judge of all the earth, we dare not ignore him or treat him casually. We should not assume that our privileged status as God's children gives us freedom to do whatever we want. We should not be spoiled children but grateful children who love to show respect for our heavenly Father.

**1:18, 19** A slave was "ransomed" when someone paid money to buy his or her freedom. God ransomed us from the tyranny of sin, not with money, but with the precious blood of his own Son (Romans 6:6, 7; 1 Corinthians 6:20; Colossians 2:13, 14; Hebrews 9:12). We cannot escape from sin on our own; only the life of God's Son can free us.

**1:20** Christ's sacrifice for our sins was not an afterthought, not something God decided to do when the world spun out of control. This plan was set in motion by the all-knowing, eternal God long before the world was created. What a comfort it must have been to Jewish believers to know that Christ's coming and his work of salvation were planned by God long before the world began. This assured them that the law was not being scrapped because it didn't work but that both the law *and* the coming of Christ were part of God's eternal plan.

**1:21**
John 14:6
Rom 4:24

**1:22**
John 13:34
Rom 12:10

**1:23**
John 1:13; 3:3
Heb 4:12

21 Through Christ you have come to trust in God. And you have placed your faith and hope in God because he raised Christ from the dead and gave him great glory. 22 You were cleansed from your sins when you obeyed the truth, so now you must show sincere love to each other as brothers and sisters.* Love each other deeply with all your heart.* 23 For you have been born again, but not to a life that will quickly end. Your new life will last forever because it comes from the eternal, living word of God. 24 As the Scriptures say,

"People are like grass;
    their beauty is like a flower in the field.
The grass withers and the flower fades.
25    But the word of the Lord remains forever."*

And that word is the Good News that was preached to you.

**2:1**
Eph 4:22, 31

**2:2**
1 Cor 3:2
Heb 5:12-13

**2:3**
†Ps 34:8

**2:4**
Ps 118:22
Isa 28:16
1 Pet 2:7

**2:5**
Exod 19:6
Isa 61:6
Eph 2:21-22
1 Tim 3:15
Heb 13:15
Rev 1:6

**2:6**
†Isa 28:16
Rom 9:32-33
Eph 2:20

**2** So get rid of all evil behavior. Be done with all deceit, hypocrisy, jealousy, and all unkind speech. 2 Like newborn babies, you must crave pure spiritual milk so that you will grow into a full experience of salvation. Cry out for this nourishment, 3 now that you have had a taste of the Lord's kindness.

### Living Stones for God's House

4 You are coming to Christ, who is the living cornerstone of God's temple. He was rejected by people, but he was chosen by God for great honor.

5 And you are living stones that God is building into his spiritual temple. What's more, you are his holy priests.* Through the mediation of Jesus Christ, you offer spiritual sacrifices that please God. 6 As the Scriptures say,

"I am placing a cornerstone in Jerusalem,*
    chosen for great honor,
and anyone who trusts in him
    will never be disgraced."*

**1:22a** Greek *must have brotherly love.*   **1:22b** Some manuscripts read *with a pure heart.*   **1:24-25** Isa 40:6-8.
**2:5** Greek *holy priesthood.*   **2:6a** Greek *in Zion.*   **2:6b** Isa 28:16 (Greek version).

---

**1:22** "Sincere love" involves selfless giving; a self-centered person can't truly love. God's love and forgiveness free you to take your eyes off yourselves and to meet others' needs. By sacrificing his life, Christ showed that he truly loves you. Now you can love others by following his example and giving of yourself sacrificially.

**1:24, 25** Quoting Isaiah 40:6-8, Peter reminds believers that everything in this life—possessions, accomplishments, people—will eventually fade away and disappear. Only God's will, word, and work are permanent. We must stop grasping the temporary and begin focusing our time, money, and energy on the permanent: the Word of God and our eternal life in Christ.

**2:2, 3** One characteristic all children share is that they want to grow up—to be like big brother or sister or like their parents. When we are born again, we become spiritual newborn babies. If we are healthy, we will yearn to grow. How sad it is that some people never grow up. The need for milk is a natural instinct for a baby, and it signals the desire for nourishment that will lead to growth. Once we see our need for God's Word and begin to find nourishment in Christ, our spiritual appetite will increase, and we will start to mature. How strong is your desire for God's Word?

**2:4-8** In describing the church as God's spiritual temple, Peter drew on several Old Testament texts familiar to his Jewish Christian readers: Psalm 118:22; Isaiah 8:14; 28:16. Peter's readers would have understood the living stones to be Israel; then Peter applied the image of "cornerstone" to Christ. Once again Peter showed that the church does not cancel the Jewish heritage but fulfills it.

**2:4-8** Peter portrays the church as a living, spiritual temple, with Christ as the foundation and cornerstone and each believer as a stone. Paul portrays the church as a body, with Christ as the head and each believer as a member (see, for example, Ephesians 4:15, 16). Both pictures emphasize *community.* One stone is not a temple or even a wall; one body part is useless without the others. In our individualistic society, it is easy to forget our interdependence with other Christians. When God calls you to a task, remember that he is also calling others to work with you. Together your individual efforts will be multiplied. Look for those people and join with them to build a beautiful house for God.

**2:5** What are the "spiritual sacrifices" that we offer to God? When sacrificing an animal according to God's law, a priest would kill the animal, cut it in pieces, and place it on the altar. Sacrifice was important, but even in the Old Testament God made it clear that obedience from the heart was much more important (see 1 Samuel 15:22; Psalm 40:6; Amos 5:21-24). God wants us, his "holy priests," to offer ourselves as living and spiritual sacrifices—daily laying aside our own desires and following him, putting all our energy and resources at his disposal, and trusting him to guide us.

**2:6-8** No doubt Peter often thought of Jesus' words to him right after he confessed that Jesus was "the Messiah, the Son of the living God": "You are Peter . . . and upon this rock I will build my church, and all the powers of hell will not conquer it" (Matthew 16:16, 18). What is the stone that really counts in the building of the church? Peter answers: Christ himself. Jesus Christ is called "the stone that makes people stumble, the rock that makes them fall." Some will stumble over Christ because they reject him or refuse to believe that he is who he says he is. But Psalm 118:22 says that "the stone that the builders rejected has now become the cornerstone," the most important part of God's building, the church. What are the characteristics of Christ, the cornerstone? (1) He is completely trustworthy; (2) he is precious to believers; (3) and, though rejected by some, he is the most important part of the church. People who refuse to believe in Christ have made the greatest mistake of their lives. They have stumbled over the one person who could save them and give meaning to their lives, and they have fallen into God's hands for judgment.

7 Yes, you who trust him recognize the honor God has given him. But for those who reject him,

> "The stone that the builders rejected
> has now become the cornerstone."*

8 And,

> "He is the stone that makes people stumble,
> the rock that makes them fall."*

They stumble because they do not obey God's word, and so they meet the fate that was planned for them.

9 But you are not like that, for you are a chosen people. You are royal priests,* a holy nation, God's very own possession. As a result, you can show others the goodness of God, for he called you out of the darkness into his wonderful light.

10 "Once you had no identity as a people;
   now you are God's people.
Once you received no mercy;
   now you have received God's mercy."*

## 2. The conduct of God's people in the midst of suffering

11 Dear friends, I warn you as "temporary residents and foreigners" to keep away from worldly desires that wage war against your very souls. 12 Be careful to live properly among your unbelieving neighbors. Then even if they accuse you of doing wrong, they will see your honorable behavior, and they will give honor to God when he judges the world.*

### Respecting People in Authority

13 For the Lord's sake, respect all human authority—whether the king as head of state, 14 or the officials he has appointed. For the king has sent them to punish those who do wrong and to honor those who do right.

15 It is God's will that your honorable lives should silence those ignorant people who make foolish accusations against you. 16 For you are free, yet you are God's slaves, so don't use your

**2:7** †Ps 118:22
Matt 21:42
Acts 4:11

**2:8** †Isa 8:14
Luke 2:34
Rom 9:22

**2:9** †Exod 19:5-6
Deut 7:6; 10:15
†Isa 43:20-21
Acts 26:18
1 Pet 2:5
Rev 1:6

**2:10** †Hos 1:6, 9; 2:23
Rom 9:25; 10:19

**2:11** Rom 13:14
Gal 5:16
Jas 4:1

**2:12** Phil 2:15
Titus 2:14

**2:13-14** Rom 13:1-7
Titus 3:1

**2:15** 1 Pet 2:12; 3:17

**2:16** Gal 5:13

**2:7** Ps 118:22.  **2:8** Isa 8:14.  **2:9** Greek *a royal priesthood.*  **2:10** Hos 1:6, 9; 2:23.  **2:12** Or *on the day of visitation.*

---

**2:9** Christians sometimes speak of "the priesthood of all believers." In Old Testament times, people did not approach God directly. A priest acted as intermediary between God and sinful human beings. With Christ's victory on the cross, that pattern changed. Now we can come directly into God's presence without fear (Hebrews 4:16), and we are given the responsibility of bringing others to him also (2 Corinthians 5:18-21). When we are united with Christ as members of his body, we join in his priestly work of reconciling God and people.

**2:9, 10** People often base their self-concept on their accomplishments. But our relationship with Christ is far more important than our jobs, successes, wealth, or knowledge. We have been chosen by God as his very own, and we have been called to represent him to others. Remember that your value comes from being one of God's children, not from what you can achieve. You have worth because of what *God does,* not because of what you do.

**2:11** As believers, we are "temporary residents and foreigners" in this world because our real home is with God. Heaven is not the pink-cloud-and-harp existence popular in cartoons. Heaven is where God lives. Life in heaven operates according to God's principles and values, and it is eternal and unshakable. The Kingdom of Heaven came to earth in the symbolism of the Jewish sanctuary (the Tabernacle and Temple), where God's presence dwelt. It came in a fuller way in the person of Jesus Christ: "God with us." It spread through the entire world as the Holy Spirit came to live in every believer.

Someday, after God judges and destroys all sin, the Kingdom of Heaven will rule every corner of this earth. John saw this day in a vision, and he cried out, "Look, God's home is now among his people! He will live with them, and they will be his people. God himself will be with them" (Revelation 21:3). Our true loyalty

should be to our citizenship in heaven, not to our citizenship here, because the earth will be destroyed. Our loyalty should be to God's truth, his way of life, and his dedicated people. Because we are loyal to God, we often will feel like strangers in a world that would prefer to ignore God.

**2:12** Peter's advice sounds like Jesus' in Matthew 5:16: If your actions are above reproach, even hostile people will end up praising God. Peter's readers were scattered among unbelieving Gentiles who were inclined to believe and spread vicious lies about Christians. Gracious, godly, and winsome behavior on the part of Christians could show these rumors to be false and might even win some of the unsaved critics to the Lord. Don't write off people because they misunderstand Christianity; instead, show them Christ by your life. The day may come when those who criticize you will praise God with you.

**2:13-17** When Peter told his readers to respect all human authority, he was speaking of the Roman Empire under Nero, a notoriously cruel tyrant. Obviously he was not telling believers to compromise their consciences; as Peter had told the high priest years earlier, "We must obey God rather than any human authority" (Acts 5:29). But in most aspects of daily life, it was possible and desirable for Christians to live according to the law of their land. Today, some Christians live in freedom while others live under repressive governments. All are commanded to cooperate with the rulers as far as conscience will allow. We are to do this "for the Lord's sake"—so that his Good News and his people will be respected. If we are to be persecuted, it should be for obeying God, not for breaking moral or civil laws. For more about the Christian's relationship to government, see the note on Romans 13:1ff.

**2:16** Christians have freedom in Christ, but the apostles defined freedom more narrowly than the normal use of the word in

**2:17**
Prov 24:21
Rom 12:10; 13:7

freedom as an excuse to do evil. [17]Respect everyone, and love your Christian brothers and sisters.* Fear God, and respect the king.

### Slaves

**2:18**
Eph 6:5
Jas 3:17

[18]You who are slaves must accept the authority of your masters with all respect.* Do what they tell you—not only if they are kind and reasonable, but even if they are cruel. [19]For God is pleased with you when you do what you know is right and patiently endure unfair treat-

**2:20**
1 Pet 3:14, 17

ment. [20]Of course, you get no credit for being patient if you are beaten for doing wrong. But if you suffer for doing good and endure it patiently, God is pleased with you.

**2:21**
Acts 14:22
1 Pet 3:9, 18

[21]For God called you to do good, even if it means suffering, just as Christ suffered* for you. He is your example, and you must follow in his steps.

[22] He never sinned,
nor ever deceived anyone.*

**2:23**
Isa 53:7
1 Pet 3:9

[23] He did not retaliate when he was insulted,
nor threaten revenge when he suffered.
He left his case in the hands of God,
who always judges fairly.

**2:24**
†Isa 53:4, 12

[24] He personally carried our sins
in his body on the cross
so that we can be dead to sin
and live for what is right.
By his wounds
you are healed.

**2:25**
†Isa 53:6
Heb 13:20
1 Pet 5:4

[25] Once you were like sheep
who wandered away.
But now you have turned to your Shepherd,
the Guardian of your souls.

### Wives

**3:1**
1 Cor 7:16; 9:19
1 Pet 2:18

**3** In the same way, you wives must accept the authority of your husbands. Then, even if some refuse to obey the Good News, your godly lives will speak to them without any words. They will be won over [2]by observing your pure and reverent lives.

**2:17** Greek *love the brotherhood.*   **2:18** Or *because you fear God.*   **2:21** Some manuscripts read *died.*   **2:22** Isa 53:9.

---

common language. Christians use freedom as a tool for a life of exuberant service. It's the foundation that God gives to us to reach our highest potential. Because God gives us freedom from religious rules and eternal guilt, we must not seek to indulge our own desires; instead, we should reach for the best God has for us. Let your freedom sing of power, joy, and love—accountable to God, devoted to others.

**2:18-21** Many Christians were household slaves. It would be easy for them to submit to masters who were gentle and kind, but Peter encouraged loyalty and perseverance even in the face of unjust treatment. In the same way, we should submit to our employers, whether they are considerate or harsh. By so doing, we may win them to Christ by our good example. Paul gave similar advice in his letters (see Ephesians 6:5-9; Colossians 3:22–4:15), as did Jesus (Matthew 5:46; Luke 6:32-36).

**2:21, 22** We may suffer for many reasons. Some suffering is the direct result of our own sin; some happens because of our foolishness; some is the result of living in a fallen world. Peter is writing about suffering that comes as a result of doing good. Christ never sinned, and yet he suffered so that we could be set free. Jesus' suffering was part of God's plan (Matthew 16:21-23; Luke 24:25-27, 44-47) and was intended to save us (Matthew 20:28; 26:28). All who follow Jesus must be prepared to suffer (Mark 8:34, 35). Our goal should be to face suffering as he did—with patience, calmness, and confidence that God is in control of the future.

**2:24** Christ died for *our* sins, in *our* place, so we would not have to suffer the punishment we deserve. This is called "substitutionary atonement."

**3:1ff** When a man became a Christian, he usually would bring his whole family into the church with him (see, for example, the story of the conversion of the Philippian jailer in Acts 16:29-34). By contrast, a woman who became a Christian usually came into the church alone. Under Roman law, the husband and father had absolute authority over all members of his household, including his wife. Demanding her rights as a free woman in Christ could endanger her marriage if her husband disapproved. Peter reassured Christian women who were married to unbelievers that they did not need to preach to their husbands. Under the circumstances, their best approach would be one of godly behavior: They should show their husbands the kind of self-giving love that Christ showed the church. By being exemplary wives, they would please their husbands. At the very least, the men might then allow them to continue practicing their faith. At best, their husbands would join them and become Christians, too.

**3:1-7** A changed life speaks loudly and clearly, and it is often the most effective way to influence a family member. Peter instructs Christian wives to develop inner beauty rather than being overly concerned about their outward appearance. Their husbands will be won over by their love. This does not mean that Christian women should be dowdy and frumpy; it is good to take care of oneself and look one's best. But far more important is the developing of an inner spirit of godliness. Live your Christian faith quietly and consistently in your home, so that your family will see Christ in you. True beauty begins inside (Proverbs 31:30).

³Don't be concerned about the outward beauty of fancy hairstyles, expensive jewelry, or beautiful clothes. ⁴You should clothe yourselves instead with the beauty that comes from within, the unfading beauty of a gentle and quiet spirit, which is so precious to God. ⁵This is how the holy women of old made themselves beautiful. They trusted God and accepted the authority of their husbands. ⁶For instance, Sarah obeyed her husband, Abraham, and called him her master. You are her daughters when you do what is right without fear of what your husbands might do.

**Husbands**

⁷In the same way, you husbands must give honor to your wives. Treat your wife with understanding as you live together. She may be weaker than you are, but she is your equal partner in God's gift of new life. Treat her as you should so your prayers will not be hindered.

**All Christians**

⁸Finally, all of you should be of one mind. Sympathize with each other. Love each other as brothers and sisters.* Be tenderhearted, and keep a humble attitude. ⁹Don't repay evil for evil. Don't retaliate with insults when people insult you. Instead, pay them back with a blessing. That is what God has called you to do, and he will bless you for it. ¹⁰For the Scriptures say,

"If you want to enjoy life
      and see many happy days,
keep your tongue from speaking evil
      and your lips from telling lies.
¹¹ Turn away from evil and do good.
      Search for peace, and work to maintain it.

**3:8** Greek *Show brotherly love.*

**3:3**
Isa 3:18-23
1 Tim 2:9

**3:4**
Rom 2:29

**3:5**
1 Tim 5:5

**3:6**
Gen 18:12

**3:7**
Eph 5:25
Col 3:19

**3:8**
Rom 15:5
Eph 4:2, 32

**3:9**
Matt 5:44
Rom 12:17
1 Thes 5:15
Heb 6:14

**3:10-12**
†Ps 34:12-16

**3:5** To be submissive to another's authority means to cooperate voluntarily out of love and respect for God and for that person. Ideally, submission is mutual ("Submit to one another out of reverence for Christ"—Ephesians 5:21). Even when it is one-sided, however, the expression of submission can be an effective Christian witness. Jesus Christ submitted to death so that we could be saved; we may sometimes have to submit to unpleasant circumstances so that others will see Christ in us. (Christian submission never requires us to disobey God, remain in an unsafe situation, or participate in what our conscience forbids.) One-sided submission requires tremendous strength. We could not do it without the power of the Holy Spirit working in us.

**3:7** When Peter says that women may be "weaker" than men, he was not implying moral or intellectual inferiority, but was recognizing women's physical limitations. Women in his day, if unprotected by men, were vulnerable to attack, abuse, and financial disaster. Women's lives may be easier today, but women are still vulnerable to criminal attack and family abuse. And in spite of increased opportunities in the workplace, many women still earn less than men, and the vast majority of the nations' poor are single mothers and their children. A man who honors his wife as a member of the weaker sex will protect, respect, help, and stay with her. He will not expect her to work full-time outside the home and full-time at home; he will lighten her load wherever he can. He will be sensitive to her needs, and he will relate to her with courtesy, consideration, insight, and tact.

**3:7** If a man is not considerate and respectful of his wife, his prayers will not be heard, because a living relationship with God depends on right relationships with others. Jesus said that if you have a problem with a fellow believer, you must make it right with that person before coming to worship (Matthew 5:23, 24). This principle carries over into family relationships. If men use their position to mistreat their wives, their prayers will be hindered.

**3:8** Peter lists five key elements that should characterize any group of believers: (1) one mind—pursuing the same goals; (2) sympathy—being responsive to others' needs; (3) love—seeing and treating each other as brothers and sisters; (4) tenderness—being affectionately sensitive and caring; and (5) humility—being willing to encourage one another and rejoice in each other's successes. These five qualities go a long way toward helping believers serve God effectively.

**3:8, 9** Where is God? How can we know God is real? Who says the Bible is any better than other holy books? To answer these questions, God sent his Son, Jesus Christ, as living evidence. God also chose Peter and others to show what a difference true faith makes in the real world. So here the once rash, belligerent, domineering, and arrogant Peter bears witness to a life of harmony, compassion, love, and humility. What a difference God makes! You, too, are God's witness to skeptical people. Let your life be evidence of God's truth. Let your pride become humility and your insensitivity give way to genuine affection for others.

**3:9** In our fallen world, it is often deemed acceptable by some to tear people down verbally or to get back at them if we feel hurt. Peter, remembering Jesus' teaching to turn the other cheek (Matthew 5:39), encourages his readers to pay back wrongs with a blessing, such as praying for the offenders. In God's Kingdom, revenge is unacceptable behavior, as is insulting a person, no matter how indirectly it is done. Rise above getting back at those who hurt you. Instead of reacting angrily to these people, pray for them.

**3:10** For more about controlling your tongue, see the notes in James 3:2-18.

**3:11** Too often we see peace as merely the absence of conflict, and we think of peacemaking as a passive role. But an effective peacemaker actively pursues peace by building good relationships, knowing that peace is a by-product of commitment. The peacemaker anticipates problems and deals with them before they occur. When conflicts arise, they are brought into the open and dealt with before they grow unmanageable. Making peace is hard work—you have to search for it and work to maintain it—but it results in God's blessing.

12 The eyes of the Lord watch over those who do right,
> and his ears are open to their prayers.
> But the Lord turns his face
> against those who do evil."*

### Suffering for Doing Good

13Now, who will want to harm you if you are eager to do good? 14But even if you suffer for doing what is right, God will reward you for it. So don't worry or be afraid of their threats. 15Instead, you must worship Christ as Lord of your life. And if someone asks about your Christian hope, always be ready to explain it. 16But do this in a gentle and respectful way.* Keep your conscience clear. Then if people speak against you, they will be ashamed when they see what a good life you live because you belong to Christ. 17Remember, it is better to suffer for doing good, if that is what God wants, than to suffer for doing wrong!

18Christ suffered* for our sins once for all time. He never sinned, but he died for sinners to bring you safely home to God. He suffered physical death, but he was raised to life in the Spirit.*

19So he went and preached to the spirits in prison—20those who disobeyed God long ago when God waited patiently while Noah was building his boat. Only eight people were saved from drowning in that terrible flood.* 21And that water is a picture of baptism, which now saves you, not by removing dirt from your body, but as a response to God from* a clean conscience. It is effective because of the resurrection of Jesus Christ.

22Now Christ has gone to heaven. He is seated in the place of honor next to God, and all the angels and authorities and powers accept his authority.

**3:13** Titus 2:14
**3:14-15** Isa 8:12-13
**3:15** Col 4:6
**3:16** 1 Pet 2:12
**3:17** 1 Pet 2:20; 4:15-16
**3:18** Eph 2:18 Heb 9:26, 28
**3:19** 1 Pet 4:6
**3:20** Gen 6:1–7:24
**3:21** Heb 9:13; 10:22
**3:22** Matt 28:18 Mark 16:19 Rom 8:38 Heb 1:4, 6; 4:14

**3:10-12** Ps 34:12-16.   **3:16** Some English translations put this sentence in verse 15.   **3:18a** Some manuscripts read *died*.   **3:18b** Or *in spirit*.   **3:20** Greek *saved through water*.   **3:21** Or *as an appeal to God for*.

---

**SUBMISSION**
Submission is:

Functional . . . . . . . . . . . . . . a distinguishing of our roles and the work we are called to do

Relational. . . . . . . . . . . . . . a loving acknowledgment of another's value as a person

Reciprocal . . . . . . . . . . . . . . a mutual, humble cooperation with one another

Universal . . . . . . . . . . . . . . an acknowledgment by the church of the all-encompassing lordship of Jesus Christ

Submission is voluntarily cooperating with someone, first out of love and respect for God and then out of love and respect for that person. Submitting to unbelievers is difficult, but it is a vital part of leading them to Jesus Christ. We are not called to submit to nonbelievers to the point that we compromise our relationship with God, but we must look for every opportunity to humbly serve in the power of God's Spirit.

---

**3:15** Some Christians believe that faith is a personal matter that should be kept to oneself. It is true that we shouldn't be boisterous or obnoxious in sharing our faith, but we should always be ready to give an answer, gently and respectfully, when asked about our faith, our lifestyle, or our Christian perspective. Can others see your hope in Christ? Are you prepared to tell them what Christ has done in your life?

**3:16** You may not be able to keep people from speaking evil against you, but you can at least stop supplying them with ammunition. As long as you do what is right, their accusations will be empty and only embarrass them. Keep your conduct above criticism!

**3:18-20** The meaning of preaching "to the spirits in prison" is not completely clear, and commentators have explained it in different ways. The traditional interpretation is that between his death and resurrection, Christ announced salvation to God's faithful followers who had been waiting for their salvation during the whole Old Testament era. Some think that this passage says that Christ's Spirit was in Noah as Noah preached to those imprisoned by sin (but now in hell). Still others say that Christ went to Hades to proclaim his victory and final condemnation to the fallen angels imprisoned there since Noah's day (see 2 Peter 2:4).

In any case, the passage shows that Christ's Good News of salvation and victory is not limited. While some Bible passages, such as this one, may remain unclear, we can discover certain truths from them along with the context of the rest of Scripture. In this passage, we discover that: (1) God speaks. While we puzzle over what, where, and how, we can see that God is communicating to the world. (2) God triumphs. Christ victoriously preached, indicating his power, control, and transcendence over all creation. (3) God saves. God exerts himself to rescue those who desire him. This mysterious passage tells us at least this much—and that is much indeed.

**3:21** Peter says that Noah's salvation from the Flood symbolized baptism, a ceremony involving water. In baptism we identify with Jesus Christ, who separates us from the lost and gives us new life. It is not the ceremony that saves us; instead, the ceremony is evidence of our faith in Christ's death and resurrection. Baptism is a symbol of the cleansing that happens in the hearts of those who believe (Romans 6:3-5; Galatians 3:27; Colossians 2:12). By identifying themselves with Christ through baptism, Peter's readers could resist turning back, even under the pressure of persecution. Public baptism would keep them from the temptation to renounce their faith.

## Living for God

**4** So then, since Christ suffered physical pain, you must arm yourselves with the same attitude he had, and be ready to suffer, too. For if you have suffered physically for Christ, you have finished with sin.* ²You won't spend the rest of your lives chasing your own desires, but you will be anxious to do the will of God. ³You have had enough in the past of the evil things that godless people enjoy—their immorality and lust, their feasting and drunkenness and wild parties, and their terrible worship of idols.

⁴Of course, your former friends are surprised when you no longer plunge into the flood of wild and destructive things they do. So they slander you. ⁵But remember that they will have to face God, who will judge everyone, both the living and the dead. ⁶That is why the Good News was preached to those who are now dead*—so although they were destined to die like all people,* they now live forever with God in the Spirit.*

⁷The end of the world is coming soon. Therefore, be earnest and disciplined in your prayers. ⁸Most important of all, continue to show deep love for each other, for love covers a multitude of sins. ⁹Cheerfully share your home with those who need a meal or a place to stay.

¹⁰God has given each of you a gift from his great variety of spiritual gifts. Use them well to serve one another. ¹¹Do you have the gift of speaking? Then speak as though God himself were speaking through you. Do you have the gift of helping others? Do it with all the strength and energy that God supplies. Then everything you do will bring glory to God through Jesus Christ. All glory and power to him forever and ever! Amen.

## Suffering for Being a Christian

¹²Dear friends, don't be surprised at the fiery trials you are going through, as if something strange were happening to you. ¹³Instead, be very glad—for these trials make you partners with Christ in his suffering, so that you will have the wonderful joy of seeing his glory when it is revealed to all the world.

| | |
|---|---|
| **4:1** | Rom 6:7 Gal 2:20 Col 3:5 1 Pet 2:21 |
| **4:2** | Rom 6:2 1 Pet 1:14 |
| **4:3** | Rom 13:13 Eph 2:2 |
| **4:5** | Acts 10:42 |
| **4:6** | 1 Pet 3:19 |
| **4:7** | Rom 13:11-12 |
| **4:8** | Prov 10:12 Jas 5:20 1 Pet 1:22 |
| **4:10** | Rom 12:6-8 |
| **4:11** | 1 Cor 10:31 |
| **4:12** | 1 Pet 1:6-7 |
| **4:13** | Rom 8:17 2 Cor 1:5 |

4:1 Or *For the one [or One] who has suffered physically has finished with sin.*   **4:6a** Greek *preached even to the dead.*   **4:6b** Or *so although people had judged them worthy of death.*   **4:6c** Or *in spirit.*

---

**4:1, 2** Suffering helps us be like Christ, yet people will do anything to avoid pain. Followers of Christ, however, should be willing and prepared to do God's will and to suffer for it if necessary. We can overcome sin when we focus on Christ and what he wants us to do. Pain and danger reveal our true values. Anyone who suffers for doing good and still faithfully obeys in spite of suffering has made a clean break with sin.

**4:3, 4** People whose lives change radically at conversion may experience contempt from old friends. They may be scorned not only because they refuse to participate in certain activities but also because their priorities have changed and they are now heading in the opposite direction. Their lives incriminate their friends' sinful activities. Mature Christians should help new believers resist such pressures of opposition by helping them to be faithful to Christ, surrounding them as new friends, and encouraging them to develop new habits and activities that are not only enjoyable but positive for their spiritual growth.

**4:5** The basis of salvation is our belief in Jesus (Acts 16:31), but the basis for judgment is how we have lived. All people will be judged: believers for the rewards they will receive; unbelievers for punishment. Those who inflict persecution are marked for punishment when they stand before God. All will give an account to God, so we must be ready. This may give you a new perspective on your activities and actions today. Are you prepared to explain them to God?

**4:5, 6** Many people in the early church had concerns about life after death. In Thessalonica, Christians worried that loved ones who died before Christ's return might never see Christ

(1 Thessalonians 4:13-18). Peter's readers needed to be reminded that the dead (both the faithful and their oppressors) would be judged. The judgment will be perfectly fair, he pointed out, because even the dead have heard the Good News (see also 3:18, 19). The Good News was first announced when Jesus Christ preached on the earth, but it has been operating since before the creation of the world (Ephesians 1:4), and it affects all people, the dead as well as the living.

**4:7-9** We should live expectantly because Christ is coming soon. Getting ready to meet Christ involves continually growing in love for God and for others (see Jesus' summary of the law in Matthew 22:37-40). It is important to pray regularly and to reach out to needy people. Your possessions, status, and power will mean nothing in God's Kingdom, but you will spend eternity with other people. Invest your time and talents where they will make an eternal difference.

**4:9** For more about hospitality, see the note on Romans 12:13.

**4:10, 11** Our abilities should be faithfully used in serving others; none are for our own exclusive enjoyment. Some people, well aware of their abilities, believe that they have the right to use their abilities as they please. Others feel that they have no special talents at all. Peter addresses both groups in these verses. Everyone has some gifts; find yours and use them. Peter mentions speaking and serving. Paul lists these and other abilities in Romans 12:6-8, 1 Corinthians 12:8-11, and Ephesians 4:11. Even as you seek to discover your gifts, if you see a need in the church, seek to meet it. You may find gifts in areas you might not have guessed!

**4:11** How is God glorified when we use our abilities? When we use them as he directs, to help others, they will see Jesus in us and glorify him for the help they have received. Peter may have been thinking of Jesus' words, "Let your good deeds shine out for all to see, so that everyone will praise your heavenly Father" (Matthew 5:16).

**4:14**
Matt 5:11
John 15:21

**4:15**
1 Thes 4:11
2 Thes 3:11
1 Tim 5:13

**4:17**
2 Thes 1:8

**4:18**
†Prov 11:31

**4:19**
Ps 31:5
1 Pet 2:20

¹⁴So be happy when you are insulted for being a Christian,* for then the glorious Spirit of God* rests upon you.* ¹⁵If you suffer, however, it must not be for murder, stealing, making trouble, or prying into other people's affairs. ¹⁶But it is no shame to suffer for being a Christian. Praise God for the privilege of being called by his name! ¹⁷For the time has come for judgment, and it must begin with God's household. And if judgment begins with us, what terrible fate awaits those who have never obeyed God's Good News? ¹⁸And also,

"If the righteous are barely saved,
    what will happen to godless sinners?"*

¹⁹So if you are suffering in a manner that pleases God, keep on doing what is right, and trust your lives to the God who created you, for he will never fail you.

## 3. The shepherding of God's people in the midst of suffering
### Advice for Elders and Young Men

**5:1**
Luke 24:48
Rev 1:9

**5:2**
John 21:16
Acts 20:28

**5:3**
2 Cor 1:24
Phil 3:17
Titus 2:7

**5:4**
1 Cor 9:25
Heb 13:20-21

**5** And now, a word to you who are elders in the churches. I, too, am an elder and a witness to the sufferings of Christ. And I, too, will share in his glory when he is revealed to the whole world. As a fellow elder, I appeal to you: ²Care for the flock that God has entrusted to you. Watch over it willingly, not grudgingly—not for what you will get out of it, but because you are eager to serve God. ³Don't lord it over the people assigned to your care, but lead them by your own good example. ⁴And when the Great Shepherd appears, you will receive a crown of never-ending glory and honor.

**4:14a** Greek *for the name of Christ.*   **4:14b** Or *for the glory of God, which is his Spirit.*   **4:14c** Some manuscripts add *On their part he is blasphemed, but on your part he is glorified.*   **4:18** Prov 11:31 (Greek version).

---

**4:14-16**  Again Peter brings to mind Jesus' words: "God blesses you when people mock you and persecute you and lie about you and say all sorts of evil things against you because you are my followers" (Matthew 5:11). Christ will send his Spirit to strengthen those who are persecuted for their faith. Peter creates no illusions; God's plan for your life may include pain and hardship. When trouble comes, don't be surprised.

This does not mean that all suffering is the result of good Christian conduct. Peter says to distinguish between suffering for being a believer and suffering for doing wrong things. For example, a Christian may think he is being picked on for his faith when it is obvious to everyone else that his own unpleasant behavior is the cause of his problems. It may take careful thought or wise counsel to determine the real cause of our suffering. We can be assured, however, that whenever we suffer because of our loyalty to Christ, he will be with us all the way.

**4:16**  It is not shameful to suffer for being a Christian. When Peter and John were persecuted for preaching the Good News, they rejoiced because such persecution was a mark of God's approval of their work (Acts 5:41). Don't seek out suffering, and don't try to avoid it. Instead, keep on doing what is right whether or not it brings suffering.

**4:17, 18**  This refers not to final judgment but to God's refining discipline (Hebrews 12:7). God often allows believers to sin and then experience the consequences. He does this for several reasons: (1) to show us our potential for sinning, (2) to encourage us to turn from sin and more constantly depend on him, (3) to prepare us to face other, even stronger temptations in the future, and (4) to help us stay faithful and keep on trusting him. If believers need earthly discipline (judgment) from God, how much more will unbelievers receive it? If the righteous are barely saved (only because of God's mercy), what chance have those who reject Christ?

**4:19**  Everywhere the Bible counsels that we trust God—in good times and bad, during sunny skies and thunderclouds, when we have a pocket full of change and a pocket full of sawdust. How does trust work? (1) *Trust overcomes fear.* Genuine trust in God says, "Whatever mess I'm in, my heavenly Father will lead me." (2) *Trust overcomes depression.* No matter how overwhelming the situation or how low it makes you feel, God can draw you back to the light. (3) *Trust overcomes hate.* When careless or cruel people hurt you, sometimes irreparably, you can hate forever or

you can trust God, but you can't do both. God is there to steady even the worst situation—always with a promise, always with hope. Commit your life to him for safekeeping. Rely on him when you face your worst circumstances.

**5:1**  Elders were church officers providing supervision, protection, discipline, instruction, and direction for the other believers. *Elder* simply means "older." Both Greeks and Jews gave positions of great honor to wise older men, and the Christian church continued this pattern of leadership. Elders carried great responsibility, and they were expected to be good examples.

**5:1, 2**  Peter, one of Jesus' 12 disciples, was one of the three who saw Christ's glory at the Transfiguration (Mark 9:1-13; 2 Peter 1:16-18). Often the spokesman for the apostles, Peter witnessed Jesus' death and resurrection, preached at Pentecost, and became a pillar of the Jerusalem church. But writing to the elders, he identified himself as a fellow elder, not a superior. He asked them to "care for the flock," exactly what Jesus had told him to do (John 21:15-17). Peter was taking his own advice as he worked along with the other elders in caring for God's faithful people. His identification with the elders is a good example of Christian leadership, showing that authority is based on service, not power (Mark 10:42-45).

**5:2-5**  Peter describes several characteristics of good leaders in the church: (1) They realize they are caring for God's flock, not their own; (2) they lead out of eagerness to serve, not out of obligation; (3) they are concerned for what they can give, not for what they can get; (4) they lead by example, not force. All of us lead others in some way. Whatever our role, our leadership should be in line with these characteristics.

**5:4**  The Great Shepherd is Jesus Christ. This refers to his second coming, when he will judge all people and give rewards to his faithful followers. The "crown," while metaphorical, pictures the glory believers will receive that is eternal and unchanging. What better motivation for selfless service! What better motivation for keeping the faith in the face of suffering and temptation!

<sup>5</sup> In the same way, you younger men must accept the authority of the elders. And all of you, serve each other in humility, for

> "God opposes the proud
> but favors the humble."*

<sup>6</sup> So humble yourselves under the mighty power of God, and at the right time he will lift you up in honor. <sup>7</sup> Give all your worries and cares to God, for he cares about you.

<sup>8</sup> Stay alert! Watch out for your great enemy, the devil. He prowls around like a roaring lion, looking for someone to devour. <sup>9</sup> Stand firm against him, and be strong in your faith. Remember that your Christian brothers and sisters* all over the world are going through the same kind of suffering you are.

<sup>10</sup> In his kindness God called you to share in his eternal glory by means of Christ Jesus. So after you have suffered a little while, he will restore, support, and strengthen you, and he will place you on a firm foundation. <sup>11</sup> All power to him forever! Amen.

## Peter's Final Greetings

<sup>12</sup> I have written and sent this short letter to you with the help of Silas,* whom I commend to you as a faithful brother. My purpose in writing is to encourage you and assure you that what you are experiencing is truly part of God's grace for you. Stand firm in this grace.

<sup>13</sup> Your sister church here in Babylon* sends you greetings, and so does my son Mark. <sup>14</sup> Greet each other with Christian love.*

Peace be with all of you who are in Christ.

**5:5** Prov 3:34 (Greek version). **5:9** Greek *your brothers.* **5:12** Greek *Silvanus.* **5:13** Greek *The elect one in Babylon.* Babylon was probably symbolic for Rome. **5:14** Greek *with a kiss of love.*

| | |
|---|---|
| **5:5**<br>†Prov 3:34<br>Jas 4:6 | |
| **5:6**<br>Jas 4:10 | |
| **5:7**<br>Ps 55:22<br>Matt 6:25<br>Heb 13:5 | |
| **5:8**<br>Job 1:7<br>Jas 4:7 | |
| **5:9**<br>Eph 6:11-13<br>Jas 4:7 | |
| **5:10**<br>1 Thes 2:12<br>2 Tim 2:10<br>1 Pet 1:6 | |
| **5:12**<br>Acts 15:22<br>Heb 13:22 | |
| **5:13**<br>Acts 12:12 | |
| **5:14**<br>Rom 16:16<br>Eph 6:23 | |

---

**5:5** Both young and old can benefit from Peter's instructions. Pride often keeps older people from trying to understand young people and keeps young people from listening to those who are older. Peter told both young and old to be humble and to serve each other. Young men should follow the leadership of older men, who should lead by example. Respect those who are older than you, listen to those younger than you, and be humble enough to admit that you can learn from others.

**5:6** We often worry about our position and status, hoping to get proper recognition for what we do. But Peter advises us to remember that God's recognition counts more than human praise. God is able and willing to bless us according to his timing. Humbly obey God regardless of present circumstances, and in his good time—either in this life or in the next—he will honor you.

**5:7** Carrying your worries, stresses, and daily struggles by yourself shows that you have not trusted God fully with your life. It takes humility, however, to recognize that God cares, to admit your need, and to let others in God's family help you. Sometimes we think that struggles caused by our own sin and foolishness are not God's concern. But when we turn to God in repentance, he will bear the weight even of those struggles. Letting God have your anxieties calls for action, not passivity. Don't submit to circumstances but to the Lord, who controls circumstances.

**5:8, 9** Lions attack sick, young, or straggling animals; they choose victims who are alone or not alert. Peter warns us to watch out for Satan when we are suffering or being persecuted. If you are feeling alone, weak, helpless, and cut off from other believers, or if you are so focused on your troubles that you forget to watch for danger, those are the times when you are especially vulnerable to Satan's attacks. During times of suffering, seek other Christians for support. Keep your eyes on Christ, and resist the devil. Then, says James, "he will flee from you" (James 4:7).

**5:10** When we are suffering, we often feel as though our pain will never end. Peter gave these faithful Christians a broader perspec-

tive. In comparison with eternity, their suffering would last only "a little while." Some of Peter's readers would be strengthened and delivered in their own lifetimes. Others would be released from their suffering through death. All of God's faithful followers are assured of an eternal life with Christ, where there will be no suffering (Revelation 21:4).

**5:12** Silas was one of the men chosen to deliver the letter from the Jerusalem council to the church in Antioch (Acts 15:22). He accompanied Paul on his second missionary journey (Acts 15:40–18:11), is mentioned by Paul in the salutation of Paul's letters to the Thessalonians (1 Thessalonians 1:1; 2 Thessalonians 1:1), and ministered with Timothy in Corinth (2 Corinthians 1:19).

**5:13** Mark, also called John Mark, was known to many of this letter's readers because he had traveled widely (Acts 12:25–13:13; 15:36-41) and was recognized as a leader in the church (Colossians 4:10; Philemon 1:24). Mark was probably with the disciples at the time of Jesus' arrest (Mark 14:51, 52). Tradition says that Peter was Mark's main source of information when Mark wrote his Gospel.

**5:14** Peter wrote this letter just before the cruel emperor Nero began persecuting Christians in Rome and throughout the empire. Afraid for his life, Peter had three times denied even knowing Jesus (John 18:15-27). But here, having learned how to stand firm in an evil world, he encouraged other Christians who were facing persecution for their faith. Peter was martyred for his faith because he lived by the words he wrote. Those who stand for Christ will be persecuted because the world is ruled by Christ's greatest enemy. But just as the small group of early believers stood against persecution, so we must be willing to stand for our faith with the patience, endurance, and courage that Peter exhibited.

# 2 PETER

WARNINGS have many forms: lights, signs, sights, sounds, smells, feelings, and written words. With varied focus, their purpose is the same—to advise alertness and give notice of imminent danger. Responses to these warnings will also vary—from disregard and neglect to evasive or corrective action. How a person reacts to a warning is usually determined by the situation and the source. One reacts differently to an impending storm than to an onrushing automobile, and the counsel of a trusted friend is heeded more than advice from a stranger or the fearful imaginings of a child.

Second Peter is a letter of warning—from an authority none other than the courageous, experienced, and faithful apostle. And it is the last communication from this great warrior of Christ. Soon thereafter he would die, martyred for his faith.

Previously Peter had written to comfort and encourage believers in the midst of suffering and persecution—an external onslaught. But three years later, in this letter containing his last words, he wrote to warn them of an internal attack—complacency and heresy. He spoke of holding fast to the nonnegotiable facts of the faith, of growing and maturing in the faith, and of rejecting all who would distort the truth. To follow this advice would ensure Christ-honoring individuals and Christ-centered churches.

After a brief greeting (1:1), Peter gives the antidote for stagnancy and shortsightedness in the Christian life (1:2–11). Then he explains that his days are numbered (1:12–15) and that the believers should listen to his messages and the words of Scripture (1:16–21).

Next, Peter gives a blunt warning about false teachers (2:1–22). They will become prevalent in the last days (2:1, 2); they will do or say anything for money (2:3); they will despise the things of God (2:2, 10, 11); they will do whatever they feel like doing (2:12–17); they will be proud and boastful (2:18, 19); they will be judged and punished by God (2:3–10, 20–22).

Peter concludes his brief letter by explaining why he has written it (3:1–18): to remind them of the words of the prophets and apostles that predicted the coming of false teachers, to give the reasons for the delay in Christ's return (3:1–13), and to encourage them to beware of heresies and to grow in their faith (3:14–18).

Addressed to those who "share the same precious faith," 2 Peter could have been written to us. Our world is filled with false prophets and teachers, who claim to have the truth and who clamor for attention and allegiance. Listen carefully to Peter's message and heed his warning. Determine to grow in your knowledge of Christ and to reject all those who preach anything inconsistent with God's Word.

## VITAL STATISTICS

**PURPOSE:**
To warn Christians about false teachers and to exhort them to grow in their faith in and knowledge of Christ

**AUTHOR:**
Peter

**ORIGINAL AUDIENCE:**
The church at large

**DATE WRITTEN:**
Approximately A.D. 67, three years after 1 Peter was written, possibly from Rome

**SETTING:**
Peter knew that his time on earth was limited (1:13, 14), so he wrote about what was on his heart, warning believers of what would happen when he was gone—especially about the presence of false teachers. He reminded his readers of the unchanging truth of the gospel.

**KEY VERSE:**
"By his divine power, God has given us everything we need for living a godly life. We have received all of this by coming to know him, the one who called us to himself by means of his marvelous glory and excellence" (1:3).

**KEY PEOPLE:**
Peter, Paul

**SPECIAL FEATURES:**
The date and destination are uncertain, and the authorship has been disputed. Because of this, 2 Peter was the last book admitted to the canon of the New Testament Scripture. Also, there are similarities between 2 Peter and Jude.

## THE BLUEPRINT

1. Guidance for growing Christians (1:1–21)
2. Danger to growing Christians (2:1–22)
3. Hope for growing Christians (3:1–18)

While Peter wrote his first letter to teach about handling persecution (trials from without), he wrote this letter to teach about handling heresy (trials from within). False teachers are often subtly deceitful. Believers today must still be vigilant against falling into false doctrine, heresy, and cult activity. This letter gives us clues to help detect false teaching.

## MEGATHEMES

| THEME | EXPLANATION | IMPORTANCE |
|---|---|---|
| *Diligence* | If our faith is real, it will be evident in our godly behavior. If people are diligent in Christian growth, they won't backslide or be deceived by false teachers. | Growth is essential. It begins with faith and culminates in love for others. To keep growing we need to know God, keep on following him, and remember what he taught us. We must remain diligent in faithful obedience and Christian growth. |
| *False Teachers* | Peter warns the church to beware of false teachers. These teachers were proud of their position, promoted sexual sin, and advised against keeping the Ten Commandments. Peter countered them by pointing to the Spirit-inspired Scriptures as our authority. | Christians need discernment to be able to resist false teachers. God can rescue us from their lies if we stay true to his Word, the Bible, and reject those who distort the truth. |
| *Christ's Return* | One day Christ will create a new heaven and earth, where we will live forever. As Christians, our hope is in this promise. But with Christ's return comes his judgment on all who refuse to believe. | The cure for complacency, lawlessness, and heresy is found in the confident assurance that Christ will return. God is still giving unbelievers time to repent. To be ready, Christians must keep on trusting and resist the pressure to give up waiting for Christ's return. |

## 1. Guidance for growing Christians

### Greetings from Peter

**1** This letter is from Simon* Peter, a slave and apostle of Jesus Christ.

I am writing to you who share the same precious faith we have. This faith was given to you because of the justice and fairness* of Jesus Christ, our God and Savior.

**1:1** Rom 1:1, 12 Titus 2:13 1 Pet 1:1

²May God give you more and more grace and peace as you grow in your knowledge of God and Jesus our Lord.

**1:2** 2 Pet 3:18 Jude 1:2

### Growing in Faith

³By his divine power, God has given us everything we need for living a godly life. We have received all of this by coming to know him, the one who called us to himself by means of his marvelous glory and excellence. ⁴And because of his glory and excellence, he has given us great and precious promises. These are the promises that enable you to share his divine nature and escape the world's corruption caused by human desires.

**1:3** 1 Pet 2:9
**1:4** 2 Cor 7:1 Jas 1:27

⁵In view of all this, make every effort to respond to God's promises. Supplement your faith with a generous provision of moral excellence, and moral excellence with knowledge, ⁶and knowledge with self-control, and self-control with patient endurance, and patient endurance with godliness, ⁷and godliness with brotherly affection, and brotherly affection with love for everyone.

**1:5** Col 2:3
**1:6** Acts 24:25 1 Cor 9:25 Gal 5:22
**1:7** John 13:34-35 Rom 12:10 1 Pet 1:22

**1:1a** Greek *Symeon.*   **1:1b** Or *to you in the righteousness.*

**1:1** First Peter was written just before the time that the Roman emperor Nero began his persecution of Christians. Second Peter was written two or three years later (between A.D. 66 and 68), after persecution had intensified. First Peter was a letter of encouragement to the Christians who suffered, but 2 Peter focuses on the church's internal problems, especially on the false teachers who were causing people to doubt their faith and turn away from Christianity. Second Peter combats their heresies by denouncing the evil motives of the false teachers and reaffirming Christianity's truths—the authority of Scripture, the primacy of faith, and the certainty of Christ's return.

**1:2** Many believers want an abundance of God's grace and peace, but they are unwilling to put forth the effort to get to know him better through Bible study and prayer. To enjoy the privileges God offers us freely, we must grow in our knowledge of God and Jesus our Lord.

**1:3, 4** The power to lead a godly life comes from God. Because we don't have the resources to be truly godly, God allows us to "share his divine nature" in order to keep us from sin and help us live for him. When we are born again, God by his Spirit empowers us with his own goodness. See John 3:6; 14:17-23; 2 Corinthians 5:21; and 1 Peter 1:22, 23.

**1:5-9** Faith must be more than belief in certain facts; it must result in action, growth in Christian character, and the practice of moral discipline, or it will die away (James 2:14-17). Peter lists several of faith's actions: learning to know God better, developing perseverance, doing God's will, loving others. These actions do not come automatically; they require hard work. They are not optional; all of them must be a continual part of the Christian life. We don't finish one and start on the next, but we work on them all together. God empowers and enables us, but he also gives us the responsibility to learn and to grow.

**1:6** False teachers were saying that self-control was not needed because deeds do not help the believer anyway (2:19). It is true that deeds cannot save us, but it is absolutely false to think they are unimportant. We are saved so that we can grow to resemble

**1:8**
John 15:2
Col 1:10
2 Pet 1:2-3

**1:10**
Rom 8:28
Jude 1:24

**1:13-14**
John 13:36;
21:18-19
2 Cor 5:1, 4
2 Pet 3:1

**1:16-18**
Matt 17:1-6
Mark 13:26
Luke 9:28-32

**1:19**
Ps 119:105
Luke 1:78
2 Cor 4:6
1 Pet 1:10-12
Rev 22:16

**1:21**
1 Cor 2:13
2 Tim 3:16

⁸The more you grow like this, the more productive and useful you will be in your knowledge of our Lord Jesus Christ. ⁹But those who fail to develop in this way are shortsighted or blind, forgetting that they have been cleansed from their old sins.

¹⁰So, dear brothers and sisters,* work hard to prove that you really are among those God has called and chosen. Do these things, and you will never fall away. ¹¹Then God will give you a grand entrance into the eternal Kingdom of our Lord and Savior Jesus Christ.

### Paying Attention to Scripture

¹²Therefore, I will always remind you about these things—even though you already know them and are standing firm in the truth you have been taught. ¹³And it is only right that I should keep on reminding you as long as I live.* ¹⁴For our Lord Jesus Christ has shown me that I must soon leave this earthly life,* ¹⁵so I will work hard to make sure you always remember these things after I am gone.

¹⁶For we were not making up clever stories when we told you about the powerful coming of our Lord Jesus Christ. We saw his majestic splendor with our own eyes ¹⁷when he received honor and glory from God the Father. The voice from the majestic glory of God said to him, "This is my dearly loved Son, who brings me great joy."* ¹⁸We ourselves heard that voice from heaven when we were with him on the holy mountain.

¹⁹Because of that experience, we have even greater confidence in the message proclaimed by the prophets. You must pay close attention to what they wrote, for their words are like a lamp shining in a dark place—until the Day dawns, and Christ the Morning Star shines* in your hearts. ²⁰Above all, you must realize that no prophecy in Scripture ever came from the prophet's own understanding,* ²¹or from human initiative. No, those prophets were moved by the Holy Spirit, and they spoke from God.

**1:10** Greek *brothers.* **1:13** Greek *as long as I am in this tent* [or *tabernacle*]. **1:14** Greek *I must soon put off my tent* [or *tabernacle*]. **1:17** Matt 17:5; Mark 9:7; Luke 9:35. **1:19** Or *rises.* **1:20** Or *is a matter of one's own interpretation.*

---

Christ and serve others. God wants to produce his character in us. But to do this, he demands our discipline and effort. As we obey Christ, who guides us by his Spirit, we will develop self-control not only with respect to food and drink but also with respect to our emotions.

**1:9** Our faith must go beyond what we believe; it must become a dynamic part of all we do, resulting in good fruit and spiritual maturity. Salvation does not depend on good deeds, but it results in good deeds. A person who claims to be saved while remaining unchanged does not understand faith or what God has done for him or her.

**1:10** Peter wanted to rouse the complacent believers who had listened to the false teachers and believed that because salvation is not based on good deeds they could live any way they wanted. If you truly belong to the Lord, Peter wrote, your hard work will prove it. If you're not working to develop the qualities listed in 1:5-7, you may not belong to him. If you are the Lord's— and your hard work backs up your claim to be chosen by God— you will be able to resist the lure of false teaching or glamorous sin. What does your life say about your faith?

**1:12-15** Outstanding coaches constantly review the basics of the sport with their teams, and good athletes can execute the fundamentals consistently well. Believers must not neglect the basics of their faith, even as they go on to study deeper truths. Just as an athlete needs constant practice, Christians need constant reminders of the fundamentals of our faith and of how we came to believe in the first place. Don't allow yourself to be bored or impatient with messages on the basics of the Christian life. Instead, take the attitude of an athlete who continues to practice and refine the basics.

**1:13, 14** Peter knew that he would die soon. Many years before, Christ had prepared Peter for the kind of death he would face (see John 21:18, 19). At this time, Peter knew that his death was at hand. Peter was martyred for the faith about A.D. 68. According to one tradition, he was crucified upside down, at his own request, because he did not feel worthy to die in the same manner as his Master.

**1:16-18** Peter is referring to the Transfiguration where Jesus' divine identity was revealed to him and two other disciples, James and John (see Matthew 17:1-8; Mark 9:2-8; Luke 9:28-36).

**1:16-21** This section is a strong statement on the inspiration of Scripture. Peter affirms that the Old Testament prophets wrote God's messages. He puts himself and the other apostles in the same category because they also proclaim God's truth. The Bible is not a collection of fables or human ideas about God. It is God's very words given *through* people *to* people. Peter emphasized his authority as an eyewitness as well as the God-inspired authority of Scripture to prepare the way for his harsh words against the false teachers. If these wicked men were contradicting the apostles and the Bible, their message could not be from God.

**1:19** Christ is the "Morning Star," and when he returns, he will shine in his full glory. Until that day we have Scripture and the Holy Spirit to illuminate it for us and guide us as we seek the truth (see also Luke 1:78; Ephesians 5:14; Revelation 2:28; 22:16).

**1:20, 21** "Those prophets were moved by the Holy Spirit, and they spoke from God" means that Scripture did not come from the creative work of the prophets' own invention or interpretation. God inspired the writers, so their message is authentic and reliable. God used the talents, education, and cultural background of each writer (they were not mindless robots); and God cooperated with the writers in such a way as to ensure that the message he intended was faithfully communicated in the very words they wrote.

## 2. Danger to growing Christians
*False Teachers*

**2** But there were also false prophets in Israel, just as there will be false teachers among you. They will cleverly teach destructive heresies and even deny the Master who bought them. In this way, they will bring sudden destruction on themselves. ²Many will follow their evil teaching and shameful immorality. And because of these teachers, the way of truth will be slandered. ³In their greed they will make up clever lies to get hold of your money. But God condemned them long ago, and their destruction will not be delayed.

⁴For God did not spare even the angels who sinned. He threw them into hell,* in gloomy pits of darkness,* where they are being held until the day of judgment. ⁵And God did not spare the ancient world—except for Noah and the seven others in his family. Noah warned the world of God's righteous judgment. So God protected Noah when he destroyed the world of ungodly people with a vast flood. ⁶Later, God condemned the cities of Sodom and Gomorrah and turned them into heaps of ashes. He made them an example of what will happen to ungodly people. ⁷But God also rescued Lot out of Sodom because he was a righteous man who was sick of the shameful immorality of the wicked people around him. ⁸Yes, Lot was a righteous man who was tormented in his soul by the wickedness he saw and heard day after day. ⁹So you see, the Lord knows how to rescue godly people from their trials, even while keeping the wicked under punishment until the day of final judgment. ¹⁰He is especially hard on those who follow their own twisted sexual desire, and who despise authority.

These people are proud and arrogant, daring even to scoff at supernatural beings* without so much as trembling. ¹¹But the angels, who are far greater in power and strength, do not dare to bring from the Lord* a charge of blasphemy against those supernatural beings.

¹²These false teachers are like unthinking animals, creatures of instinct, born to be caught and destroyed. They scoff at things they do not understand, and like animals, they will be destroyed. ¹³Their destruction is their reward for the harm they have done. They

**2:1** Deut 13:1-3 / Matt 7:15 / 1 Tim 4:1 / Jude 1:4
**2:3** Rom 16:18 / 1 Thes 2:5
**2:4** Gen 6:1-4 / //Jude 1:6 / Rev 20:1-2
**2:5** Gen 6:5–8:18 / 1 Pet 3:20 / 2 Pet 3:6
**2:6** Gen 19:24 / Matt 10:15 / Rom 9:29 / //Jude 1:7
**2:7** Gen 19:1-16 / 2 Pet 3:17
**2:9** //Jude 1:6
**2:10** 2 Pet 3:3 / //Jude 1:7-8, 16, 18
**2:11** //Jude 1:9
**2:12** //Jude 1:10
**2:13** Rom 13:13 / 1 Cor 11:20-21 / //Jude 1:12

**2:4a** Greek *Tartarus.* **2:4b** Some manuscripts read *in chains of gloom.* **2:10** Greek *at glorious ones,* which are probably evil angels. **2:11** Other manuscripts read *to the Lord;* still others do not include this phrase at all.

**2:1** Jesus had told the disciples that false teachers would come (Matthew 24:11; Mark 13:22, 23). Peter had heard these words, and at this time he was seeing them come true. Just as false prophets had contradicted the true prophets in Old Testament times (see, for example, Jeremiah 23:16-40; 28:1-17), telling people only what they wanted to hear, so false teachers were twisting Christ's teachings and the words of his apostles. These teachers were belittling the significance of Jesus' life, death, and resurrection. Some claimed that Jesus couldn't be God; others claimed that he couldn't have been a real man. These teachers allowed and even encouraged all kinds of immorality, especially sexual sin. We must be careful to avoid false teachers today. Any book, tape series, or TV message must be evaluated in the light of God's Word. Beware of special meanings or interpretations that belittle Christ or his work.

**2:3** Peter gives three warning signs for identifying false teachers:
(1) *Immorality.* Do their lives contain or condone immoral practices? Does the group listening to the false teachers have a lot of immoral sexual relationships?
(2) *Greed.* Teachers have a right to financial support (1 Corinthians 9:1-14; Galatians 6:6; 1 Timothy 5:17, 18), but is money the teacher's or group's prime motivation? Before you send money to any cause, evaluate it carefully. Is the teacher or preacher clearly serving God or merely promoting his/her own interests? Will the person or organization use the money to promote valid ministry, or will it merely finance further promotions or extravagant lifestyles?
(3) *Lying.* Is the leader offended when you ask for the scriptural backing behind his/her statements? Does he/she fudge on the facts when asked for evidence?
Believers today would do well to heed Peter's warnings against false teachers; the danger is great.

**2:4-6** If God did not spare angels, or people who lived before the Flood, or the citizens of Sodom and Gomorrah, he would not spare these false teachers. These words that promised justice were a great comfort to those who were oppressed. God will

punish all evildoers. These words also served as a warning to wanderers to not stray away from the truth. Some people would have us believe that God will save all people because he is so loving. But it is foolish to think that God will cancel the last judgment. Don't ever minimize the certainty of God's judgment on those who rebel against him.

**2:7-9** Just as God rescued Lot from Sodom, so he is able to rescue us from the temptations and trials we face in a wicked world. Lot was not sinless, but he put his trust in God and was spared when Sodom was destroyed. For more information on Lot, see his Profile in Genesis 13, p. 25. God also will judge those who cause the temptations and trials, so we need never worry about justice being done.

**2:10-12** The "supernatural beings" may be angels, all the glories of the unseen world, or more probably, fallen angels. A similar passage is found in Jude 1:8-10. Whoever they are, the false teachers slandered the spiritual realities they did not understand, taking Satan's power lightly and claiming to have the ability to judge evil. Many in our world today mock the supernatural. They deny the reality of the spiritual world and claim that only what can be seen and felt is real. Like the false teachers of Peter's day, they are fools who will be proven wrong in the end. Don't take Satan and his supernatural powers of evil lightly, and don't become arrogant about how defeated he will be. Although Satan will be destroyed completely, he is at work now trying to render Christians complacent and ineffective.

**2:13, 14** The fellowship meal may have been part of the celebration of the Lord's Supper—a full meal that ended with Communion. The false teachers, although they were sinning openly, took part in these meals with everyone else in the church. In one of the greatest of hypocritical acts, they attended a sacred meal designed to promote love and unity among believers, while at the same time they gossiped and slandered those who disagreed with their opinions. Paul told the Corinthians, "So anyone who eats this bread or drinks this cup of the Lord unworthily is guilty of sinning against the body and blood of the love to indulge in evil pleasures in broad daylight. They are a disgrace and a stain among you. They delight in deception* even as they eat with you in your fellowship meals. [14]They commit adultery with their eyes, and their desire for sin is never satisfied. They lure unstable people into sin, and they are well trained in greed. They live under God's curse. [15]They have wandered off the right road and followed the footsteps of Balaam son of Beor,* who loved to earn money by doing wrong. [16]But Balaam was stopped from his mad course when his donkey rebuked him with a human voice.

[17]These people are as useless as dried-up springs or as mist blown away by the wind. They are doomed to blackest darkness. [18]They brag about themselves with empty, foolish boasting. With an appeal to twisted sexual desires, they lure back into sin those who have barely escaped from a lifestyle of deception. [19]They promise freedom, but they themselves are slaves of sin and corruption. For you are a slave to whatever controls you. [20]And when people escape from the wickedness of the world by knowing our Lord and Savior Jesus Christ and then get tangled up and enslaved by sin again, they are worse off than before. [21]It would be better if they had never known the way to righteousness than to know it and then reject the command they were given to live a holy life. [22]They prove the truth of this proverb: "A dog returns to its vomit."* And another says, "A washed pig returns to the mud."

## 3. Hope for growing Christians
### The Day of the Lord Is Coming

**3** This is my second letter to you, dear friends, and in both of them I have tried to stimulate your wholesome thinking and refresh your memory. [2]I want you to remember what the holy prophets said long ago and what our Lord and Savior commanded through your apostles.

[3]Most importantly, I want to remind you that in the last days scoffers will come, mocking the truth and following their own desires. [4]They will say, "What happened to the promise that Jesus is coming again? From before the times of our ancestors, everything has remained the same since the world was first created."

[5]They deliberately forget that God made the heavens by the word of his command, and he brought the earth out from the water and surrounded it with water. [6]Then he used the water to destroy the ancient world with a mighty flood. [7]And by the same word, the present heavens and earth have been stored up for fire. They are being kept for the day of judgment, when ungodly people will be destroyed.

[8]But you must not forget this one thing, dear friends: A day is like a thousand years to the Lord, and a thousand years is like a day. [9]The Lord isn't really being slow about his promise, as some people think. No, he is being patient for your sake. He does not want anyone to be

---

**2:14**
Eph 2:3
2 Pet 2:18; 3:16
**2:15**
Num 22:5-7, 17
Deut 23:5
//Jude 1:11
Rev 2:14
**2:16**
Num 22:21-28
**2:17**
//Jude 1:12-13
**2:18**
2 Pet 1:4
//Jude 1:16
**2:20**
Matt 12:45
**2:21**
Ezek 18:24
Heb 6:4; 10:26

**3:2**
//Jude 1:17
**3:3**
1 Tim 4:1
2 Pet 2:10
//Jude 1:18
**3:4**
Isa 5:19
Jer 17:15
**3:5**
Gen 1:6-9
Heb 11:3
**3:6**
Gen 7:11-21
**3:7**
Matt 10:15
2 Thes 1:7
**3:8**
Ps 90:4
**3:9**
Hab 2:3
Rom 2:4
1 Tim 2:4
Rev 2:21

---

**2:13** Some manuscripts read *in fellowship meals.*   **2:15** Some manuscripts read *Bosor.*   **2:22** Prov 26:11.

---

Lord" (1 Corinthians 11:27). These men were guilty of more than false teaching and promoting evil pleasures; they were guilty of leading others away from God's Son, Jesus.

**2:15** Balaam was hired by a pagan king to curse Israel. He did what God told him to do for a time (Numbers 22–24), but eventually his evil motives and desire for money won out (Numbers 25:1-3; 31:16). Like the false teachers of Peter's day, Balaam used religion for personal advancement, a sin that God does not take lightly.

**2:19** A person is a slave to whatever controls him or her. Many believe that freedom means doing anything we want. But no one is ever completely free in that sense. If we refuse to follow God, we will follow our own sinful desires and become enslaved to what our body wants. If we submit our lives to Christ, he will free us from slavery to sin. Christ frees us to serve him, a freedom that results in our ultimate good.

**2:20-22** Peter is speaking of people who have learned about Christ and how to be saved but then reject the truth and return to their sin. These people are worse off than before because they have rejected the only way out of sin, the only way of salvation. Like someone sinking in quicksand who refuses to grab the rope thrown to him or her, the person who turns away from Christ rejects the only means of escape (see the note on Luke 11:24-26).

**3:3, 4** "In the last days" scoffers will say that Jesus is never coming back, but Peter refutes their argument by explaining God's mastery over time. The "last days" is the time between Christ's first and second comings; thus, we, like Peter, live in the last days. We must do the work to which God has called us and believe that he will return as he promised.

**3:7** In Noah's day the earth was judged by water; at the Second Coming it will be judged by fire. This fire is described in Revelation 19:20; 20:10-15.

**3:8, 9** God may have seemed slow to these believers as they faced persecution every day and longed to be delivered. But God is not slow; he just is not on *our* timetable (Psalm 90:4). Jesus is waiting so that more sinners will repent and turn to him. We must not sit and wait for Christ to return, but we should realize that time is short and we have important work to do. Be ready to meet Christ anytime, even today; yet plan your course of service as though he may not return for many years.

destroyed, but wants everyone to repent. ¹⁰But the day of the Lord will come as unexpectedly as a thief. Then the heavens will pass away with a terrible noise, and the very elements themselves will disappear in fire, and the earth and everything on it will be found to deserve judgment.*

¹¹Since everything around us is going to be destroyed like this, what holy and godly lives you should live, ¹²looking forward to the day of God and hurrying it along. On that day, he will set the heavens on fire, and the elements will melt away in the flames. ¹³But we are looking forward to the new heavens and new earth he has promised, a world filled with God's righteousness.

¹⁴And so, dear friends, while you are waiting for these things to happen, make every effort to be found living peaceful lives that are pure and blameless in his sight.

¹⁵And remember, our Lord's patience gives people time to be saved. This is what our beloved brother Paul also wrote to you with the wisdom God gave him—¹⁶speaking of these things in all of his letters. Some of his comments are hard to understand, and those who are ignorant and unstable have twisted his letters to mean something quite different, just as they do with other parts of Scripture. And this will result in their destruction.

## Peter's Final Words

¹⁷I am warning you ahead of time, dear friends. Be on guard so that you will not be carried away by the errors of these wicked people and lose your own secure footing. ¹⁸Rather, you must grow in the grace and knowledge of our Lord and Savior Jesus Christ.

All glory to him, both now and forever! Amen.

3:10 Other manuscripts read *will be burned up;* still others read *will be found destroyed.*

**3:10** Matt 24:43-44 / 1 Thes 5:2 / Rev 3:3; 16:5
**3:12** Ps 50:3 / 1 Cor 1:7
**3:13** Isa 60:21; 65:17; 66:22 / Rev 21:1, 27; 22:15
**3:14** 1 Thes 3:13 / 1 Pet 1:7
**3:15** Rom 2:4 / Eph 3:3 / Col 1:25-27
**3:16** 2 Pet 2:14
**3:17** 1 Cor 10:12 / 2 Pet 2:18 / Rev 2:5
**3:18** Rom 11:36 / 2 Tim 4:18 / 2 Pet 1:2, 11; 2:20

---

**3:10, 11** The day of the Lord is the day of God's judgment on the earth. Here it is used in reference to Christ's return. Christ's second coming will be sudden and terrible for those who do not believe in him. But if we are morally clean and spiritually alert, it won't come as a surprise. For other prophetic pictures of the day of the Lord, see Isaiah 34:4; Joel 3:15, 16; Matthew 24; Mark 13; Luke 21; Revelation 6:12-17. Realizing that the earth is going to be burned up, we should put our confidence in what is lasting and eternal and not be bound to earth and its treasures or pursuits. Do you spend more of your time piling up possessions or striving to develop Christlike character?

**3:13** God's purpose for people is not destruction but re-creation (see Isaiah 66:22; Revelation 21–22). God will purify the heavens and earth with fire; then he will create them anew. We can joyously look forward to the restoration of God's good world.

**3:14** We should not become lazy and complacent because Christ has not yet returned. Instead, we should live in eager expectation of his coming. What would you like to be doing when Christ returns? That is how you should be living each day.

**3:15, 16** By the time of Peter's writing, Paul's letters already had a widespread reputation. Notice that Peter spoke of Paul's letters as if they were on a level with "other parts of Scripture." Already the early church was thinking of Paul's letters as inspired by God.

**3:15-18** Peter and Paul had very different backgrounds and personalities, and they preached from different viewpoints. Paul

emphasized salvation by grace, not law, while Peter preferred to talk about Christian life and service. The two men did not contradict each other, however, and they always held each other in high esteem. The false teachers intentionally misused Paul's writings by distorting them to condone lawlessness. No doubt this made the teachers popular, because people always like to have their favorite sins justified, but the net effect was to totally destroy Paul's message. Paul may have been thinking of teachers like these when he wrote in Romans 6:15: "Since God's grace has set us free from the law, does that mean we can go on sinning? Of course not!" Peter warned his readers to avoid the mistakes of those wicked teachers by growing in the special favor and knowledge of Jesus. The better we know Jesus, the less attractive false teaching will be.

**3:18** Peter concludes this brief letter as he began, urging his readers to grow in the grace and knowledge of the Lord and Savior Jesus Christ; that is, they were to get to know him better and better. This is the best way to discern false teaching. No matter where we are in our spiritual journey, no matter how mature we are in our faith, the sinful world will always challenge our faith. We still have much room for growth. Every day we need to draw closer to Christ so that we will be prepared to stand for truth in any and all circumstances.

# 1 JOHN

"A GOOD man . . . yes . . . perhaps one of the best who ever lived . . . but just a man," say many. Others disagree, claiming that he suffered from delusions of grandeur—a "messiah complex." And the argument rages over the true identity of this man called Jesus. Suggestions have ranged from "simple teacher" to "egomaniac" and "misguided fool." Whoever he was, all would agree that Jesus left his mark on history.

Hearing these discussions, even Christians can begin to wonder and doubt. Is Jesus really God? Did he come to save sinners like us? Does God care about me?

First John was written to dispel doubts and to build assurance by presenting a clear picture of Christ. Entering history, Jesus was and is God in the flesh and God in focus—seen, heard, and touched by the author of this letter, John the apostle. John walked and talked with Jesus, saw him heal, heard him teach, watched him die, met him arisen, and saw him ascend. John knew God—he had lived with him and had seen him work. And John enjoyed fellowship with the Father and the Son all the days of his life.

The elder statesman in the church, John wrote this letter to his "dear children." In it he presented God as light, as love, and as life. He explained in simple and practical terms what it means to have fellowship with God.

At the same time, false teachers had entered the church, denying the incarnation of Christ. John wrote to correct their serious errors. So John's letter is a model for us to follow as we combat modern heresies.

John opens this letter by presenting his credentials as an eyewitness of the Incarnation and by stating his reason for writing (1:1–4). He then presents God as "light," symbolizing absolute purity and holiness (1:5–7), and he explains how believers can walk in the light and have fellowship with God (1:8–10). If they do sin, Christ is their advocate (2:1, 2). John urges them to obey Christ fully and to love all the members of God's family (2:3–17). He warns his readers of "antichrists" and the Antichrist who will try to lead them away from the truth (2:18–29).

In the next section, John presents God as "love"—giving, dying, forgiving, and blessing (3:1—4:21). God *is* love, and because God loves us, he calls us his children and makes us like Christ (3:1, 2). This truth should motivate us to live close to him (3:3–6). We can be sure of our family relationship with God when our lives are filled with good deeds and love for others (3:7–24). Again, John warns of false teachers who twist the truth. We should reject these false teachers (4:1–6) as we continue to live in God's love (4:7–21).

In the last section, John presents God as "life" (5:1–21). God's life is in his Son. To have his Son is to have eternal life.

Do you know God? Do you know Christ? Do you know that you have eternal life? First John was written to help you know the reality of God in your life through faith in Christ, to assure you that you have eternal life, and to encourage you to remain in fellowship with the God who is light and love. Read this letter written by one overwhelmed by God's love, and with renewed confidence, pass on his love to others.

## VITAL STATISTICS

**PURPOSE:**
To reassure Christians in their faith and to counter false teachings

**AUTHOR:**
The apostle John

**ORIGINAL AUDIENCE:**
The letter is untitled and was written to no particular church. It was sent as a pastoral letter to several Gentile congregations.

**DATE WRITTEN:**
Probably between A.D. 85 and 90 from Ephesus

**SETTING:**
John was an older man and perhaps the only surviving apostle at this time. He had not yet been banished to the island of Patmos, where he would live in exile. As an eyewitness of Christ, he wrote authoritatively to give this new generation of believers assurance and confidence in God and in their faith.

**KEY VERSE:**
"I have written this to you who believe in the name of the Son of God, so that you may know you have eternal life" (5:13).

**KEY PEOPLE:**
John, Jesus

**SPECIAL FEATURES:**
John is the apostle of love, and love is mentioned throughout this letter. There are a number of similarities between this letter and John's Gospel—in vocabulary, style, and main ideas. John uses brief statements and simple words, and he features sharp contrasts—light and darkness, truth and error, God and Satan, life and death, and love and hate.

## THE BLUEPRINT

1. God is light
   (1:1—2:29)
2. God is love
   (3:1—4:21)
3. God is life
   (5:1—21)

John wrote about the most vital aspects of faith so that his readers would know Christian truth from error. He emphasizes the basics of faith so that we can be confident in our faith. In our dark world, God is light. In our cold world, God brings the warmth of love. In our dying world, God brings life. When we lack confidence, these truths bring us certainty.

## MEGATHEMES

| THEME | EXPLANATION | IMPORTANCE |
|---|---|---|
| Sin | Even Christians sin. Sin requires God's forgiveness, and Christ's death provides it for us. Determining to live according to God's standards in the Bible shows that our life is being transformed. | We cannot deny our sin nature, maintain that we are "above" sinning, or minimize the consequences of sin in our relationship with God. We must resist the attraction of sin, yet we must confess when we do sin. |
| Love | Christ commands us to love others as he loved us. This love is evidence that we are truly saved. God is the Creator of love; he cares that his children love each other. | Love means putting others first and being unselfish. Love is action—showing others we care—not just saying it. To show love we must give sacrificially of our time and money to meet the needs of others. |
| Family of God | We become God's children by believing in Christ. God's life in us enables us to love our fellow family members. | How we treat others shows who our Father is. Live as a faithful, loving family member. |
| Truth and Error | Teaching that the physical body does not matter, false teachers encouraged believers to throw off moral restraints. They also taught that Christ wasn't really a man and that we must be saved by having some special mystical knowledge. The result was that people became indifferent to sin. | God is truth and light, so the more we get to know him, the better we can keep focused on the truth. Don't be led astray by any teaching that denies Christ's deity or humanity. Check the message; test the claims. |
| Assurance | God is in control of heaven and earth. Because his word is true, we can have assurance of eternal life and victory over sin. By faith we can be certain of our eternal destiny with him. | Assurance of our relationship with God is a promise, but it is also a way of life. We build our confidence by trusting in God's Word and in Christ's provision for our sin. |

## 1. God is light
### Introduction

**1** We proclaim to you the one who existed from the beginning,* whom we have heard and seen. We saw him with our own eyes and touched him with our own hands. He is the Word of life. ²This one who is life itself was revealed to us, and we have seen him. And now we testify and proclaim to you that he is the one who is eternal life. He was with the Father, and then he was revealed to us. ³We proclaim to you what we ourselves have actually seen

**1:1** Greek *What was from the beginning.*

**1:1**
John 1:1, 4, 14
1 Jn 4:14

**1:2**
John 1:1-4; 19:35;
20:30-31
1 Jn 5:11, 13, 20

**1:1** First John was written by John, one of Jesus' original 12 disciples. He was probably "the disciple Jesus loved" (John 21:20), and along with Peter and James, he had a special relationship with Jesus. This letter was written between A.D. 85 and 90 from Ephesus, before John's exile to the island of Patmos (see Revelation 1:9). Jerusalem had been destroyed in A.D. 70, and Christians were scattered throughout the empire. By the time John wrote this letter, Christianity had been around for more than a generation. It had faced and survived severe persecution. The main problem confronting the church at this time was declining commitment: Many believers were conforming to the world's standards, failing to stand up for Christ and compromising their faith. False teachers were plentiful, and they were accelerating the church's downward slide away from the Christian faith.

    John wrote this letter to put believers back on track, to show the difference between light and darkness (truth and error), and to encourage the church to grow in genuine love for God and for one another. He also wrote to assure true believers that they possessed eternal life and to help them know that their faith was

genuine—so they could enjoy all the benefits of being God's children. For more about John, see his Profile in John 13, p. 1783.

**1:1-5** John opens his first letter to the churches similarly to the way he began his Gospel, emphasizing that Christ ("the Word of life") is eternal, that God came into the world as a human, that he, John, was an eyewitness to Jesus' life. John had lived with Jesus, having personal, physical contact with Jesus. He knew beyond any doubt that Jesus brings light and life.

**1:3** As an eyewitness to Jesus' ministry, John was qualified to teach the truth about him. The readers of this letter had not seen and heard Jesus themselves, but they could trust that what John wrote was accurate. We are like those second- and third-generation Christians. Though we have not personally seen, heard, or touched Jesus, we have the New Testament record of his eyewitnesses, and we can trust that they spoke the truth about him. See John 20:29.

**1:3, 4** John writes about having fellowship with other believers. There are three principles behind true Christian fellowship:

**1:4**
John 15:11; 16:24

and heard so that you may have fellowship with us. And our fellowship is with the Father and with his Son, Jesus Christ. ⁴We are writing these things so that you may fully share our joy.*

### Living in the Light

**1:5**
John 1:9; 8:12
1 Tim 6:16

**1:6**
John 3:19-21
2 Cor 6:14

**1:7**
Heb 9:14

⁵This is the message we heard from Jesus* and now declare to you: God is light, and there is no darkness in him at all. ⁶So we are lying if we say we have fellowship with God but go on living in spiritual darkness; we are not practicing the truth. ⁷But if we are living in the light, as God is in the light, then we have fellowship with each other, and the blood of Jesus, his Son, cleanses us from all sin.

⁸If we claim we have no sin, we are only fooling ourselves and not living in the truth.

**1:4** Or *so that our joy may be complete;* some manuscripts read *your joy.*    **1:5** Greek *from him.*

---

**JOHN COUNTERS FALSE TEACHINGS**

John counters two major threads in the false teachings of the heretics in this letter:

1:6, 8, 10 . . . . . . . . . They denied the reality of sin. John says that if we continue in sin, we can't claim to belong to God. If we say we have no sin, we are only fooling ourselves and refusing to live according to the truth.

2:22; 4:1-3 . . . . . . . . They denied that Jesus was the Messiah—God in the flesh. John said that if we believe that Jesus was God incarnate and trust him for our salvation, we are children of God.

---

First, our fellowship is grounded in the testimony of God's Word. Without this underlying strength, togetherness is impossible. Second, it is mutual, depending on the unity of believers. Third, it is renewed daily through the Holy Spirit. True fellowship combines social and spiritual interaction, and it is made possible only through a living relationship with Christ.

**1:5, 6**  Light represents what is good, pure, true, holy, and reliable. Darkness represents what is sinful and evil. The statement "God is light" means that God is perfectly holy and true and that he alone can guide us out of the darkness of sin. Light is also related to truth in that light exposes whatever exists, whether it is good or bad. In the dark, good and evil look alike; in the light, they can be clearly distinguished. Just as darkness cannot exist in the presence of light, sin cannot exist in the presence of a holy God. If we want to have a relationship with God, we must put aside our sinful ways of living. To claim that we belong to him but then to go out and live for ourselves is hypocrisy. Christ will expose and judge such deceit.

**1:6**  Here John was confronting the first of three claims of the false teachers: that we can have fellowship with God and go on living in spiritual darkness. False teachers who thought that the physical body was evil or worthless taught one of two approaches to behavior: They insisted on denying bodily desires through rigid discipline, or they approved of gratifying every physical lust because the body was going to be destroyed anyway. Obviously the second approach was more popular! Here John is saying that no one can claim to be a Christian and still live in evil and immorality. We can't love God and court sin at the same time.

**1:7**  How does Jesus' blood cleanse us from all sin? In Old Testament times, believers symbolically transferred their sins to an animal, which they then sacrificed (see a description of this ceremony in Leviticus 4). The animal died in their place to pay for their sin and to allow them to continue living in God's favor. God graciously forgave them because of their faith in him and because they obeyed his commandments concerning the sacrifice. Those sacrifices anticipated the day when Christ would completely remove sin. Real cleansing from sin came with Jesus, "the Lamb of God who takes away the sin of the world" (John 1:29). Sin, by its very nature, brings death—that is a fact as certain as the law of gravity. Jesus did not die for his own sins; he had none. Instead, by a transaction that we may never fully understand, he died for the sins of the world. When we commit our life to Christ and thus identify

ourselves with him, his death becomes ours. He has paid the penalty for our sins, and his blood has purified us. Just as Christ rose from the grave, we rise to a new life of fellowship with him (Romans 6:4).

**1:8**  Here John was attacking the second claim of the false teachers: that people had no natural tendency toward sin, that they had "no sin," and that they were then incapable of sinning. This is a lie. The false teachers refused to take sin seriously. They wanted to be considered Christians, but they saw no need to confess and repent. The death of Christ did not mean much to them because they didn't think they needed it. Instead of repenting and being purified by Christ's blood, they were encouraging sin among believers. In this life we are always capable of sinning, so we should never let down our guard.

**1:8-10**  The false teachers not only denied that sin breaks fellowship with God (1:6) and that they had a sinful nature (1:8), but they also denied that their conduct involved any sin at all (1:10). That was a lie that ignored one basic truth: All people are sinners by nature and by practice. At conversion all our sins are forgiven—past, present, and future. Yet even after we become Christians, we still sin and still need to confess. This kind of confession is not offered to gain God's acceptance but to remove the barrier to fellowship that our sin has put between us and him. It is difficult, however, for many people to admit their faults and shortcomings, even to God. It takes humility and honesty to recognize our weaknesses, and most of us would rather pretend that we are strong. But we need not fear revealing our sins to God—he knows them already. He will not push us away, no matter what we've done. Instead, he will draw us to himself.

⁹But if we confess our sins to him, he is faithful and just to forgive us our sins and to cleanse us from all wickedness. ¹⁰If we claim we have not sinned, we are calling God a liar and showing that his word has no place in our hearts.

**2** My dear children, I am writing this to you so that you will not sin. But if anyone does sin, we have an advocate who pleads our case before the Father. He is Jesus Christ, the one who is truly righteous. ²He himself is the sacrifice that atones for our sins—and not only our sins but the sins of all the world.

³And we can be sure that we know him if we obey his commandments. ⁴If someone claims, "I know God," but doesn't obey God's commandments, that person is a liar and is not living in the truth. ⁵But those who obey God's word truly show how completely they love him. That is how we know we are living in him. ⁶Those who say they live in God should live their lives as Jesus did.

### A New Commandment

⁷Dear friends, I am not writing a new commandment for you; rather it is an old one you have had from the very beginning. This old commandment—to love one another—is the same message you heard before. ⁸Yet it is also new. Jesus lived the truth of this commandment, and you also are living it. For the darkness is disappearing, and the true light is already shining.

⁹If anyone claims, "I am living in the light," but hates a Christian brother or sister,* that

**2:9** Greek *hates his brother;* similarly in 2:11.

**1:9** Heb 9:14
**1:10** 1 Jn 5:10
**2:1** 1 Tim 2:5; Heb 7:25; 9:24
**2:2** John 1:29; Rom 3:25; Heb 2:17; 1 Jn 4:10
**2:5** John 14:21, 23
**2:6** Matt 11:29; John 13:15; 1 Pet 2:21
**2:7** John 13:34; 2 Jn 1:5-6
**2:8** John 1:9; 13:34; Rom 13:12
Eph 5:8; 1 Thes 5:5

---

**1:9** Confession is supposed to free us to enjoy fellowship with Christ. It should ease our consciences and lighten our cares. But some Christians do not understand how it works. They feel so guilty that they confess the same sins over and over; then they wonder if they might have forgotten something. Other Christians believe that God forgives them when they confess, but if they died with unconfessed sins, they would be forever lost. These Christians do not understand that God *wants* to forgive us. He allowed his beloved Son to die just so he could offer us pardon. When we come to Christ, he forgives all the sins we have committed or will ever commit. We don't need to confess the sins of the past all over again, and we don't need to fear that God will reject us if we don't keep our slate perfectly clean. Of course we should continue to confess our sins, but not because failure to do so will make us lose our salvation. Our relationship with Christ is secure. Instead, we should confess so that we can enjoy maximum fellowship and joy with him.

True confession also involves a commitment not to continue in sin. We wouldn't be genuinely confessing our sins to God if we planned to commit them again and just wanted temporary forgiveness. We should also pray for strength to defeat temptation the next time we face it.

**1:9** If God has forgiven us for our sins because of Christ's death, why must we confess our sins? In admitting our sins and receiving Christ's cleansing, we are (1) agreeing with God that our sin truly is sin and that we are willing to turn from it, (2) ensuring that we don't conceal our sins from him and consequently from ourselves, and (3) recognizing our tendency to sin and relying on his power to overcome it.

**2:1** John uses "dear children" in a warm, fatherly way. He is not talking down to his readers but is showing affection for them. At this writing, John was a very old man. He had spent almost all his life in ministry, and many of his readers were indeed his spiritual children.

**2:1, 2** To people who are feeling guilty and condemned, John offers reassurance. They know they have sinned, and Satan (called "the accuser" in Revelation 12:10) is demanding the death penalty. When you feel this way, don't give up hope—the best defense attorney in the universe is pleading your case. Jesus Christ, your advocate, your defender, is the Judge's Son. He has already suffered your penalty in your place. You can't be tried for a case that is no longer on the docket. United with Christ, you are as safe as he is. Don't be afraid to ask Christ to plead your case—he has already won it (see Romans 8:33, 34; Hebrews 7:24, 25).

**2:2** Jesus Christ is the atoning sacrifice for our sins (see also 4:10). He is our defense attorney. He can stand before God as our mediator because his death satisfied the wrath of God against sin and paid the death penalty for our sin. Thus, Christ both satisfies God's requirement and removes our sin. In him we are forgiven and purified.

**2:2** Sometimes it is difficult to forgive those who wrong us. Imagine how hard it would be to forgive all people, no matter what they had done! This is what God has done in Jesus. No one, no matter what sin has been committed, is beyond forgiveness. All a person has to do is turn from sin, receive Christ's forgiveness, and commit his or her life to him.

**2:3-6** How can you be sure that you belong to Christ? This passage gives two ways to know: if you do what Christ says and live as Christ wants. What does Christ tell us to do? John answers in 3:23: "Believe in the name of his Son, Jesus Christ, and love one another." True Christian faith results in loving behavior; that is why John says that the way we act can give us assurance that we belong to Christ.

**2:6** To live as Jesus lived doesn't mean choosing 12 disciples, performing great miracles, and being crucified. We cannot merely copy Christ's life; much of what Jesus did had to do with his identity as God's Son, the fulfillment of his special role in dying for sin, and the cultural context of the first-century Roman world. To walk today as Christ did, we must obey his teachings and follow his example of complete obedience to God and loving service to people.

**2:7, 8** The commandment to love others is both old and new. It is old because it comes from the Old Testament (Leviticus 19:18). It is new because Jesus interpreted it in a radically new way (John 13:34, 35). In the Christian church, love is not only expressed by showing respect; it is also expressed through self-sacrifice and servanthood (John 15:13). In fact, it can be defined as "selfless giving," reaching beyond friends to enemies and persecutors (Matthew 5:43-48). Love should be the unifying force and the identifying mark of the Christian community. Love is the key to walking in the light, because we cannot grow spiritually while we hate others. Our growing relationship with God will result in growing relationships with others.

**2:9-11** Does this mean that if you dislike someone you aren't a Christian? These verses are not talking about disliking a disagreeable Christian brother or sister. There will always be people we will not like as well as others. John's words focus on the attitude that causes us to ignore or despise others, to treat them as

**2:10**
Rom 14:13

**2:11**
John 12:35
2 Cor 4:4
2 Pet 1:9
1 Jn 2:9; 3:15

**2:12**
1 Cor 6:11

**2:13**
John 1:1; 16:33
1 Jn 1:1; 4:4; 5:18

**2:14**
John 1:1-2
Eph 6:10
1 Jn 1:1; 1:10

**2:15**
Rom 12:2
Jas 4:4

**2:16**
Rom 13:14
Eph 2:3

person is still living in darkness. ¹⁰Anyone who loves another brother or sister* is living in the light and does not cause others to stumble. ¹¹But anyone who hates another brother or sister is still living and walking in darkness. Such a person does not know the way to go, having been blinded by the darkness.

¹² I am writing to you who are God's children
    because your sins have been forgiven through Jesus.*

¹³ I am writing to you who are mature in the faith*
    because you know Christ, who existed from the beginning.
I am writing to you who are young in the faith
    because you have won your battle with the evil one.

¹⁴ I have written to you who are God's children
    because you know the Father.
I have written to you who are mature in the faith
    because you know Christ, who existed from the beginning.
I have written to you who are young in the faith
    because you are strong.
God's word lives in your hearts,
    and you have won your battle with the evil one.

### Do Not Love This World

¹⁵Do not love this world nor the things it offers you, for when you love the world, you do not have the love of the Father in you. ¹⁶For the world offers only a craving for physical

**2:10** Greek *loves his brother.*   **2:12** Greek *through his name.*   **2:13** Or *to you fathers;* also in 2:14.

---

**A BOOK OF CONTRASTS**

One of the distinct features of John's willing style was his habit of noting both sides of a conflict. He wrote to show the difference between real Christianity and anything else. Here are some of his favorite contrasts.

| Contrast between | Passage |
| --- | --- |
| Light and darkness | 1:5 |
| The new commandment and the old commandment | 2:7, 8 |
| Loving the Father and loving the world | 2:15, 16 |
| Christ and Antichrist | 2:18, 22 |
| Truth and lies | 2:20, 21 |
| Children of God and children of the devil | 3:1-10 |
| Eternal life and eternal death | 3:14 |
| Love and hatred | 3:15, 16 |
| True prophecy and false prophecy | 4:1-3 |
| Love and fear | 4:18, 19 |
| Having life and not having life | 5:11, 12 |

---

irritants, competitors, or enemies. Christian love is not a feeling but a choice. We can choose to be concerned with people's well being and treat them with respect, whether or not we feel affection toward them. If we choose to love others, God will help us express our love.

**2:12-14** John was writing to believers of all ages. The "children" had experienced forgiveness through Jesus. Those who were "mature in the faith" had a long-standing relationship with Christ. The "young in the faith" had battled with Satan's temptations and had won. Each stage of life in the Christian pilgrimage builds upon the other. As children learn about Christ, they grow in their ability to win battles with temptation. As young adults move from victory to victory, they grow in their relationship with Christ. Older adults, having known Christ for years, have developed the wisdom needed to teach young people and start the cycle all over again. Has your Christian growth reached the maturity level appropriate for your stage in life?

**2:15, 16** Some people think that worldliness is limited to external behavior—the people we associate with, the places we go,

the activities we enjoy. Worldliness is also internal because it begins in the heart and is characterized by three attitudes: (1) *craving for physical pleasure*—preoccupation with gratifying physical desires; (2) *craving for everything we see*—coveting and accumulating things, bowing to the god of materialism; and (3) *pride in our achievements and possessions*—obsession with one's status or importance. When the serpent tempted Eve (Genesis 3:6), he tempted her in these areas. Also, when the devil tempted Jesus in the wilderness, these were his three areas of attack (see Matthew 4:1-11).

By contrast, God values self-control, a spirit of generosity, and a commitment to humble service. It is possible to give the impression of avoiding worldly pleasures while still harboring worldly attitudes in one's heart. It is also possible, like Jesus, to love sinners and spend time with them while maintaining a commitment to the values of God's Kingdom. What values are most important to you? Do your actions reflect the world's values or God's values?

pleasure, a craving for everything we see, and pride in our achievements and possessions. These are not from the Father, but are from this world. [17]And this world is fading away, along with everything that people crave. But anyone who does what pleases God will live forever.

**2:17**
Matt 7:21
1 Cor 7:31

### Warning about Antichrists

[18]Dear children, the last hour is here. You have heard that the Antichrist is coming, and already many such antichrists have appeared. From this we know that the last hour has come. [19]These people left our churches, but they never really belonged with us; otherwise they would have stayed with us. When they left, it proved that they did not belong with us.

**2:18**
Matt 24:24

**2:19**
Acts 20:30
1 Cor 11:19

[20]But you are not like that, for the Holy One has given you his Spirit,* and all of you know the truth. [21]So I am writing to you not because you don't know the truth but because you know the difference between truth and lies. [22]And who is a liar? Anyone who says that Jesus is not the Christ.* Anyone who denies the Father and the Son is an antichrist.* [23]Anyone who denies the Son doesn't have the Father, either. But anyone who acknowledges the Son has the Father also.

**2:22**
1 Jn 4:3

**2:23**
John 8:19; 17:3
1 Jn 4:15; 5:1

[24]So you must remain faithful to what you have been taught from the beginning. If you do, you will remain in fellowship with the Son and with the Father. [25]And in this fellowship we enjoy the eternal life he promised us.

**2:24**
1 Jn 4:15; 5:1
2 Jn 1:9

**2:25**
John 3:15; 6:40;
17:3

[26]I am writing these things to warn you about those who want to lead you astray. [27]But you have received the Holy Spirit,* and he lives within you, so you don't need anyone to teach you what is true. For the Spirit* teaches you everything you need to know, and what he teaches is true—it is not a lie. So just as he has taught you, remain in fellowship with Christ.

**2:27**
John 14:16, 26;
16:13
1 Cor 2:10-12

**2:20** Greek *But you have an anointing from the Holy One.*   **2:22a** Or *not the Messiah.*   **2:22b** Or *the antichrist.*
**2:27a** Greek *the anointing from him.*   **2:27b** Greek *the anointing.*

---

**2:17** When the desire for possessions and sinful pleasures feels so intense, we probably doubt that these objects of desire will all one day pass away. It may be even more difficult to believe that the person who does the will of God will live forever. But this was John's conviction based on the facts of Jesus' life, death, resurrection, and promises. Knowing that this evil world will end can give you the courage to deny yourself temporary pleasures in this world in order to enjoy what God has promised for eternity.

**2:18-23** John is talking about the last days, the time between Christ's first and second comings. The first-century readers of 1 John lived in the last days, and so do we. During this time, antichrists (false teachers who pretend to be Christians and who lure weak members away from Christ) will appear. Finally, just before the world ends, one great Antichrist will arise (Revelation 13; 19:20; 20:10). We do not need to fear these evil people, however. The Holy Spirit shows us their errors, so we will not be deceived. However, we must teach God's Word clearly and carefully to the peripheral, weak members among us so that they won't fall prey to these teachers who "come disguised as harmless sheep but are really vicious wolves" (Matthew 7:15).

**2:19** The antichrists were not total strangers to the church; they once had been in the church, but they did not really belong to it. John does not say why they left; it is clear that their reasons for joining in the first place were wrong. Some people may call themselves Christians for less than the best reasons. Perhaps going to church is a family tradition. Maybe they like the social and business contacts that make there. Or possibly going to church is a long-standing habit, and they have never stopped to ask themselves why they do it. What is your main reason for being a Christian? Unless it is a Christ-centered reason, you may not really belong. You don't have to settle for less than the best. You can become personally acquainted with Jesus Christ and become a loyal, trustworthy follower.

**2:20** When a person becomes a Christian, he or she receives the Holy Spirit. One way the Holy Spirit helps the believer and the church is by communicating truth. Jesus is the truth (John 14:6), and the Holy Spirit guides believers to him (John 16:13). People who are opposed to Christ are also opposed to his truth, and the Holy Spirit is not working in their lives. When we are led

by the Spirit, we can stand against false teachers and the Antichrist. Ask the Spirit to guide you each day (see 2:27).

**2:22, 23** Apparently the antichrists in John's day were claiming faith in God while denying and opposing Christ. To do so, John firmly states, is impossible. Because Jesus is God's Son and the Messiah, to deny Christ is to reject God's way of revealing himself to the world. A person who accepts Christ as God's Son, however, accepts God the Father at the same time. The two are one and cannot be separated. Many cultists today call themselves Christians, but they deny that Jesus is divine. We must expose these heresies and oppose such teachings so that the weak believers among us do not succumb to their teachings.

**2:24** These Christians had heard the Good News, very likely from John himself. They knew that Christ was God's Son, that he died for their sins and was raised to give them new life, and that he would return and establish his Kingdom in its fullness. But their fellowship was being infiltrated by teachers who denied these basic doctrines of the Christian faith, and some of the believers were in danger of succumbing to false arguments. John encouraged them to hold on to the Christian truth they heard at the beginning of their walk with Christ. It is important to grow in our knowledge of the Lord, to deepen our understanding through careful study, and to teach these truths to others. But no matter how much we learn, we must never abandon the basic truths about Christ. Jesus will always be God's Son, and his sacrifice for our sins is permanent. No truth will ever contradict these teachings in the Bible.

**2:26, 27** Christ had promised to send the Holy Spirit to teach his followers and to remind them of all that Christ had taught (John 14:26). As a result, Christians have the Holy Spirit within them to keep them from going astray. In addition, they have the God-inspired Scriptures, against which they can test questionable teachings. To stay true to Christ, we must follow his Word and his Spirit. Let the Holy Spirit help you discern truth from error. For more about who the Holy Spirit is and what he does, see the notes on John 3:6, Acts 1:5, and Ephesians 1:13, 14.

**2:27** Christ lives in us through the Holy Spirit, and we also live in Christ. This means that we place our total trust in him, rely on him for guidance and strength, and live as he wants us to live.

**2:28**
Col 3:4
1 Thes 2:19
1 Jn 3:2, 21

**2:29**
1 Jn 3:7, 10; 4:7

28And now, dear children, remain in fellowship with Christ so that when he returns, you will be full of courage and not shrink back from him in shame.

29Since we know that Christ is righteous, we also know that all who do what is right are God's children.

## 2. God is love
### Living as Children of God

**3:1**
John 1:12-13; 16:3;
17:26
Rom 8:16
Eph 1:4-5

**3:2**
John 17:24
Rom 8:19, 29
2 Cor 3:18
Phil 3:21

**3:4**
Matt 7:23

**3:5**
Isa 53:1-12
John 1:29
2 Cor 5:21

**3:6**
Rom 6:14
1 Jn 3:9

**3:8**
John 8:44

**3:9**
Jas 1:18
1 Pet 1:3

**3:10**
John 1:12-13

**3** See how very much our Father loves us, for he calls us his children, and that is what we are! But the people who belong to this world don't recognize that we are God's children because they don't know him. 2Dear friends, we are already God's children, but he has not yet shown us what we will be like when Christ appears. But we do know that we will be like him, for we will see him as he really is. 3And all who have this eager expectation will keep themselves pure, just as he is pure.

4Everyone who sins is breaking God's law, for all sin is contrary to the law of God. 5And you know that Jesus came to take away our sins, and there is no sin in him. 6Anyone who continues to live in him will not sin. But anyone who keeps on sinning does not know him or understand who he is.

7Dear children, don't let anyone deceive you about this: When people do what is right, it shows that they are righteous, even as Christ is righteous. 8But when people keep on sinning, it shows that they belong to the devil, who has been sinning since the beginning. But the Son of God came to destroy the works of the devil. 9Those who have been born into God's family do not make a practice of sinning, because God's life* is in them. So they can't keep on sinning, because they are children of God. 10So now we can tell who are children of God and who are children of the devil. Anyone who does not live righteously and does not love other believers* does not belong to God.

**3:9** Greek *because his seed.*   **3:10** Greek *does not love his brother.*

---

It implies a personal, life-giving relationship. John uses the same idea in John 15:5, where he speaks of Christ as the vine and his followers as the branches (see also 3:24; 4:15).

**2:28, 29** The visible proof of being a Christian is right behavior. Many people do good deeds but don't have faith in Jesus Christ. Others claim to have faith but rarely produce good deeds. A deficit in either faith or right behavior will be a cause for shame when Christ returns. Because true faith always results in good deeds, those who claim to have faith *and* who consistently do what is right are true believers. Good deeds cannot produce salvation (see Ephesians 2:8, 9), but they are necessary proof that true faith is actually present (James 2:14-17).

**3:1** As believers, our self-worth is based on the fact that God loves us and calls us his children. We are his children *now*, not just sometime in the distant future. Knowing that we are his children should encourage us to live as Jesus did. For other references about being part of God's family, see Romans 8:14-17; Galatians 3:26, 27; 4:6, 7.

**3:1ff** Verse 1 tells us who we are—members of God's family, his children. Verse 2 tells us who we are becoming—reflections of God. The rest of the chapter tells us what we have as we grow to resemble God: (1) victory over sin (3:4-9); (2) love for others (3:10-18); and (3) confidence before God (3:19-24).

**3:2, 3** The Christian life is a process of becoming more and more like Christ (see Romans 8:29). This process will not be complete until we see Christ face to face (1 Corinthians 13:12; Philippians 3:21), but knowing that it is our ultimate destiny should motivate us to purify ourselves. To keep pure means to keep morally straight, free from the corruption of sin. God also purifies us, but there is action we must take to remain morally fit (see 1 Timothy 5:22; James 4:8; 1 Peter 1:22).

**3:4ff** There is a difference between committing a sin and continuing to sin. Even the most faithful believers sometimes commit sins, but they do not cherish a particular sin or continually choose to commit it. A believer who commits a sin can repent, confess it, and find forgiveness. A person who continues to sin, by contrast, is not sorry for what he or she is doing. Thus, this person never confesses and never receives forgiveness. Such a

person is in opposition to God, no matter what religious claims he or she makes.

**3:5** Under the Old Testament sacrifice system, a lamb without blemish was offered as a sacrifice for sin. Jesus is "the Lamb of God who takes away the sin of the world" (John 1:29). Because Jesus lived a perfect life and sacrificed himself for our sins, we can be completely forgiven (2:2). We can look back to his death for us and know that we need never suffer eternal death (1 Peter 1:18-20).

**3:8, 9** We all have areas where temptation is strong and habits are hard to conquer. These weaknesses give the devil a foothold, so we must deal with our areas of vulnerability. If we are struggling with a particular sin, however, these verses are not directed at us, even if for the time we seem to keep on sinning. John is not talking about people whose victories are still incomplete; he is talking about people who make a practice of sinning and look for ways to justify it.

Three steps are necessary to find victory over prevailing sin: (1) Seek the power of the Holy Spirit and God's Word; (2) stay away from tempting situations; and (3) seek the help of the body of Christ—be open to their willingness to hold you accountable and to pray for you.

**3:9** "They can't keep on sinning" means that true believers do not make a practice of sinning, nor do they become indifferent to God's moral law. All believers still sin, but they are working to gain victory over sin.

**3:9** We are "born into God's family" when the Holy Spirit lives in us and gives us Jesus' new life. Being born again is more than a fresh start; it is a rebirth, receiving a new family name based on Christ's death for us. When this happens, God forgives us and totally accepts us; the Holy Spirit gives us a new mind and heart, lives in us, and begins helping us to become like Christ. Our perspective changes, too, because we have a mind that is renewed day by day by the Holy Spirit (see Romans 12:2; Ephesians 4:22-24). So we must begin to think and act differently. See John 3:1-21 for more on being born again.

## Love One Another

[11] This is the message you have heard from the beginning: We should love one another. [12] We must not be like Cain, who belonged to the evil one and killed his brother. And why did he kill him? Because Cain had been doing what was evil, and his brother had been doing what was righteous. [13] So don't be surprised, dear brothers and sisters,* if the world hates you.

[14] If we love our Christian brothers and sisters,* it proves that we have passed from death to life. But a person who has no love is still dead. [15] Anyone who hates another brother or sister* is really a murderer at heart. And you know that murderers don't have eternal life within them.

[16] We know what real love is because Jesus gave up his life for us. So we also ought to give up our lives for our brothers and sisters. [17] If someone has enough money to live well and sees a brother or sister* in need but shows no compassion—how can God's love be in that person? [18] Dear children, let's not merely say that we love each other; let us show the truth by our actions. [19] Our actions will show that we belong to the truth, so we will be confident when we stand before God. [20] Even if we feel guilty, God is greater than our feelings, and he knows everything.

[21] Dear friends, if we don't feel guilty, we can come to God with bold confidence. [22] And we will receive from him whatever we ask because we obey him and do the things that please him.

[23] And this is his commandment: We must believe in the name of his Son, Jesus Christ, and love one another, just as he commanded us. [24] Those who obey God's commandments remain in fellowship with him, and he with them. And we know he lives in us because the Spirit he gave us lives in us.

## Discerning False Prophets

**4** Dear friends, do not believe everyone who claims to speak by the Spirit. You must test them to see if the spirit they have comes from God. For there are many false prophets in the world. [2] This is how we know if they have the Spirit of God: If a person claiming to be a prophet* acknowledges that Jesus Christ came in a real body, that person has the Spirit of

**3:11**
John 13:34; 15:12

**3:12**
Gen 4:3-8

**3:13**
John 15:18

**3:15**
Matt 5:21-22
John 8:44

**3:16**
John 13:1; 15:13
Phil 2:17

**3:17**
Deut 15:7-8
Jas 2:15

**3:18**
Rom 12:9
Jas 1:22

**3:19**
John 18:37

**3:21**
Rom 5:1

**3:22**
Matt 7:7
John 8:29; 14:13

**3:23**
John 6:29; 13:34

**3:24**
Rom 8:9

**4:1**
1 Thes 5:21
1 Jn 2:18

**4:2**
John 1:14
1 Cor 12:3

**3:13** Greek *brothers.*   **3:14** Greek *the brothers;* similarly in 3:16.   **3:15** Greek *hates his brother.*   **3:17** Greek *sees his brother.*   **4:2** Greek *If a spirit;* similarly in 4:3.

---

**3:12, 13** Cain killed his brother, Abel, when God accepted Abel's offering and not his (Genesis 4:1-16). Abel's offering showed that Cain was not giving his best to God, and Cain's jealous anger drove him to murder. People who are morally upright expose and shame those who aren't. If we live for God, the world will often hate us, because we make them painfully aware of their immoral way of living.

**3:15** John echoes Jesus' teaching that whoever hates another person is a murderer at heart (Matthew 5:21, 22). Christianity is a religion of the heart; outward compliance alone is not enough. Bitterness against someone who has wronged you is an evil cancer within you and will eventually destroy you. Don't let a "poisonous root of bitterness" (Hebrews 12:15) grow in you or your church.

**3:16** Real love is an action, not a feeling. It produces selfless, sacrificial giving. The greatest act of love is giving oneself for others. How can we "give up our lives"? By serving others with no thought of receiving anything in return. Sometimes it is easier to say we'll die for others than to truly live for them—this involves putting others' desires first. Jesus taught this same principle of love in John 15:13.

**3:17, 18** These verses give an example of how to give up our life for others—to help those in need. This is strikingly similar to James's teaching (James 2:14-17). How clearly do your actions say you really love others? Are you as generous as you should be with your money, possessions, and time?

**3:19, 20** Many are afraid that they don't love others as they should. They feel guilty because they think they are not doing enough to show proper love to Christ. Their consciences bother them. John has these people in mind in this letter. How do we escape the gnawing accusations of our consciences? Not by ignoring them or rationalizing our behavior but by setting our heart on God's love. When we feel guilty, we should remind ourselves that God knows our motives as well as our actions. His voice of assurance is stronger than the accusing voice of our conscience. If we are in Christ, he will not condemn us (Romans 8:1; Hebrews 9:14, 15). So if you are living for the Lord but feeling that you are not good enough, remind yourself that God is greater than your conscience.

**3:21, 22** If your conscience is clear, you can come to God without fear, confident that your requests will be heard. John reaffirms Jesus' promise that whatever we ask for will be given to us (Matthew 7:7; see also Matthew 21:22; John 9:31; 15:7). You will receive if you obey and do what pleases him because you will then be asking in line with God's will. Of course this does not mean that you can have anything you want, like instant riches. If you are truly seeking God's will, there are some requests you will not make.

**3:23** In the Bible, a person's name stands for his or her character. It represents who he or she really is. We are to believe not only in Jesus' words, but also in his very person as the Son of God. Moreover, to believe "in the name" means to pattern your life after Christ's, to become more like him by uniting yourself with him. And if we are living like Christ, we will "love one another."

**3:24** The mutual relationship, living in Christ as he lives in us, shows itself in Christians who keep these three essential commands: (1) Believe in Christ, (2) love the brothers and sisters, and (3) live morally upright lives. The Spirit's presence is not only spiritual and mystical, but it is also practical. Our conduct verifies his presence.

**4:1, 2** "Do not believe everyone who claims to speak by the Spirit. You must test them to see if the spirit they have comes from God" means that we shouldn't believe everything we hear just because someone says it is a message from God. There are many ways to test teachers to see if their message is truly from the Lord. One is to check to see if their words match what God

**4:3**
2 Jn 1:7
**4:4**
John 12:31
Rom 8:31
1 Jn 2:1
**4:5**
John 15:19;
17:14, 16
**4:6**
John 8:47; 14:17
1 Cor 14:37
1 Tim 4:1
**4:7**
1 Jn 2:29; 3:11; 4:9
John 3:16

God. ³But if someone claims to be a prophet and does not acknowledge the truth about Jesus, that person is not from God. Such a person has the spirit of the Antichrist, which you heard is coming into the world and indeed is already here.

⁴But you belong to God, my dear children. You have already won a victory over those people, because the Spirit who lives in you is greater than the spirit who lives in the world. ⁵Those people belong to this world, so they speak from the world's viewpoint, and the world listens to them. ⁶But we belong to God, and those who know God listen to us. If they do not belong to God, they do not listen to us. That is how we know if someone has the Spirit of truth or the spirit of deception.

## Loving One Another

⁷Dear friends, let us continue to love one another, for love comes from God. Anyone who loves is a child of God and knows God. ⁸But anyone who does not love does not know God, for God is love.

---

**HERESIES**  Most of the eyewitnesses to Jesus' ministry had died by the time John composed this letter. Some of the second- or third-generation Christians began to have doubts about what they had been taught about Jesus. Some Christians with a Greek background had a hard time believing that Jesus was human as well as divine, because in Platonic thought the spirit was all-important. The body was only a prison from which one desired to escape. Heresies developed from a uniting of this kind of Platonic thought and Christianity.

A particularly widespread false teaching, later called *Docetism* (from a Greek word meaning "to seem"), held that Jesus was actually a spirit who only appeared to have a body. In reality he cast no shadow and left no footprints; he was God but not man. Another heretical teaching, related to *Gnosticism* (from a Greek word meaning "knowledge", held that all physical matter was evil, the spirit was good, and only the intellectually enlightened could enjoy the benefits of religion. Both groups found it hard to believe in a Savior who was fully human.

John answers these false teachers as an eyewitness to Jesus' life on earth. He saw Jesus, talked with him, touched him—he knew that Jesus was more than a mere spirit. In the very first sentence of his letter, John establishes that Jesus had been alive before the world began and also that he lived as a man among men and women. In other words, he was both divine and human.

Through the centuries, many heretics have denied that Jesus was both God and man. In John's day people had trouble believing he was human; today more people have problems seeing him as God. But Jesus' divine-human nature is the pivotal issue of Christianity. Before you accept what religious teachers say about any topic, listen carefully to what they believe about Jesus. To deny either his divinity or his humanity is to consider him less than Christ, the Savior.

---

says in the Bible. Other tests include their commitment to the body of believers (2:19), their life-styles (3:23, 24), and the fruit of their ministries (4:6). But the most important test of all, says John, is what they believe about Christ. Do they teach that Jesus is fully God and fully man? Our world is filled with voices claiming to speak for God. Give them these tests to see if they are indeed speaking God's truth.

**4:3**  The Antichrist will be a person who epitomizes all that is evil, and he will be readily received by an evil world. He is more fully described in 2 Thessalonians 2:3-12 and Revelation 13. The "spirit of the Antichrist" is already here (see the note on 2:18-23). Those who reject Christ are unknowingly or consciously siding with the spirit of the Antichrist.

**4:4**  It is easy to be frightened by the wickedness we see all around us and to be overwhelmed by the problems we face. Evil is obviously much stronger than we are. John assures us, however, that God is even stronger. He will conquer all evil—and his Spirit and his Word live in our heart!

**4:6**  False teachers are popular with the world because, like the false prophets of the Old Testament, they tell people what they want to hear. John warns that Christians who faithfully teach God's Word will not win any popularity contests in the world. People don't want to hear their sins denounced; they don't want to listen to demands that they change their behavior. A false teacher will be well received by non-Christians.

**4:7ff**  Everyone believes that love is important, but love is usually thought of as a feeling. In reality, love is a choice and an

action, as 1 Corinthians 13:4-7 shows. God is the source of our love. He loved us enough to sacrifice his Son for us. Jesus is our example of what it means to love; everything he did in life and death was supremely loving. The Holy Spirit gives us the power to love; he lives in our heart and makes us more and more like Christ. God's love always involves a choice and an action, and our love should be like his. How well do you display your love for God in the choices you make and the actions you take?

**4:8**  John says, "God is love," not "Love is God." Our world, with its shallow and selfish view of love, has turned these words around and contaminated our understanding of love. The world thinks that love is what makes a person feel good and that it is all right to sacrifice moral principles and others' rights in order to obtain such "love." But that isn't real love; it is the exact opposite—selfishness. And God is not that kind of "love." Real love is like God, who is holy, just, and perfect. If we truly know God, we will love as he does.

⁹God showed how much he loved us by sending his one and only Son into the world so that we might have eternal life through him. ¹⁰This is real love—not that we loved God, but that he loved us and sent his Son as a sacrifice to take away our sins.

¹¹Dear friends, since God loved us that much, we surely ought to love each other. ¹²No one has ever seen God. But if we love each other, God lives in us, and his love is brought to full expression in us.

¹³And God has given us his Spirit as proof that we live in him and he in us. ¹⁴Furthermore, we have seen with our own eyes and now testify that the Father sent his Son to be the Savior of the world. ¹⁵All who confess that Jesus is the Son of God have God living in them, and they live in God. ¹⁶We know how much God loves us, and we have put our trust in his love.

God is love, and all who live in love live in God, and God lives in them. ¹⁷And as we live in God, our love grows more perfect. So we will not be afraid on the day of judgment, but we can face him with confidence because we live like Jesus here in this world.

¹⁸Such love has no fear, because perfect love expels all fear. If we are afraid, it is for fear of punishment, and this shows that we have not fully experienced his perfect love. ¹⁹We love each other* because he loved us first.

²⁰If someone says, "I love God," but hates a Christian brother or sister,* that person is a liar; for if we don't love people we can see, how can we love God, whom we cannot see? ²¹And he has given us this command: Those who love God must also love their Christian brothers and sisters.*

### 3. God is life

*Faith in the Son of God*

**5** Everyone who believes that Jesus is the Christ* has become a child of God. And everyone who loves the Father loves his children, too. ²We know we love God's children if we love God and obey his commandments. ³Loving God means keeping his commandments,

**Cross references (right margin):**
- 4:10 Rom 5:8, 10; 1 Jn 2:2
- 4:11 Matt 18:33
- 4:12 John 1:18; 14:23; 1 Tim 6:16
- 4:13 Rom 8:9; 1 Jn 3:24
- 4:14 John 1:14; 3:17; 4:42; 1 Jn 2:2
- 4:15 John 6:69; 1 Jn 5:5
- 4:17 1 Jn 2:5; 3:21
- 4:18 Rom 8:15
- 4:20 1 Jn 2:4; 3:17
- 4:21 Matt 5:43; 22:37-39
- 5:1 John 1:13; 3:3; 8:42
- 5:3 Matt 11:30; John 14:15

**4:19** Greek *We love.* Other manuscripts read *We love God;* still others read *We love him.* **4:20** Greek *hates his brother.* **4:21** Greek *The one who loves God must also love his brother.* **5:1** Or *the Messiah.*

---

**4:9** Jesus is God's *only* Son. While all believers are sons and daughters of God, only Jesus lives in this special unique relationship (see John 1:18; 3:16).

**4:9, 10** Love explains: (1) why God creates—because he loves, he creates people to love; (2) why God cares—because he loves them, he cares for sinful people; (3) why we are free to choose—God wants a loving response from us; (4) why Christ died—his love for us caused him to offer a solution to the problem of sin; and (5) why we receive eternal life—God's love expresses itself to us forever.

**4:10** Nothing sinful or evil can exist in God's presence. He is absolute goodness. He cannot overlook, condone, or excuse sin as though it never happened. He loves us, but his love does not make him morally lax. If we trust in Christ, however, we will not have to bear the penalty for our sins (1 Peter 2:24). We will be acquitted (Romans 5:18) by his atoning sacrifice.

**4:12** If no one has ever seen God, how can we ever know him? John in his Gospel said, "The unique One, who is himself God, is near to the Father's heart. He has revealed God to us" (John 1:18). Jesus is the complete expression of God in human form, and he has revealed God to us. When we love one another, the invisible God reveals himself to others through us, and his love is made complete.

**4:12** Some people simply enjoy being with others. They make friends with strangers easily and always are surrounded by friends. Other people are shy or reserved. They have a few friends and are frequently uncomfortable talking with people they don't know or mingling in crowds. Shy people don't need to become extroverts in order to love others. John isn't telling us *how many* people to love, but *how much* to love the people we already know. Our job is to love faithfully the people God has given us to love, whether there are two or two hundred of them. If God sees that we are ready to love others, he will bring them to us. No matter how shy we are, we don't need to be afraid of the love commandment. God provides us the strength to do what he asks.

**4:13** When we become Christians, we receive the Holy Spirit. God's presence in our life is proof that we really belong to him. He also gives us the power to love (Romans 5:5; 8:9; 2 Corinthians 1:22). Rely on that power as you reach out to others. As you do so, you will gain confidence. See also Romans 8:16.

**4:17** The day of judgment is that time when all people will appear before Christ and be held accountable for their actions. With God living in us through Christ, we have no reason to fear this day because we have been saved from punishment. Instead, we can look forward to the day of judgment because it will mean the end of sin and the beginning of a face-to-face relationship with Jesus Christ.

**4:18** If we ever are afraid of the future, eternity, or God's judgment, we can remind ourselves of God's love. We know that he loves us perfectly (Romans 8:38, 39). We can resolve our fears first by focusing on his immeasurable love for us, and then by allowing him to love others through us. His love will quiet your fears and give you confidence.

**4:19** God's love is the source of all human love, and it spreads like fire. In loving his children, God kindles a flame in their hearts. In turn, they love others, who are warmed by God's love through them.

**4:20, 21** It is easy to say we love God when that love doesn't cost us anything more than weekly attendance at religious services. But the real test of our love for God is how we treat the people right in front of us—our family members and fellow believers. We cannot truly love God while neglecting to love those who are created in his image.

**5:1, 2** When we become Christians, we become part of God's family, with fellow believers as our brothers and sisters. It is God who determines who the other family members are, not us. We are simply called to accept and love them. How well do you treat your fellow family members?

**5:3, 4** Jesus never promised that obeying him would be easy. But the hard work and self-discipline of serving Christ is no

5:5
Rom 8:37

5:6
John 1:31-34; 14:7;
19:34-35

5:9
Matt 3:16-17
John 5:32-37;
8:17-18

5:10
John 3:33
Rom 8:16
Gal 4:6

5:12
John 3:15-16, 36;
5:24; 14:6; 17:2-3
2 Jn 1:9

5:13
John 20:31

5:14
Matt 7:7
John 14:13; 15:7

5:16
Exod 23:21
Jer 7:16; 14:11
Matt 12:31
Heb 6:4-6; 10:26
Jas 5:15

5:18
John 10:28-29
1 Jn 2:13; 3:9

and his commandments are not burdensome. [4]For every child of God defeats this evil world, and we achieve this victory through our faith. [5]And who can win this battle against the world? Only those who believe that Jesus is the Son of God.

[6]And Jesus Christ was revealed as God's Son by his baptism in water and by shedding his blood on the cross*—not by water only, but by water and blood. And the Spirit, who is truth, confirms it with his testimony. [7]So we have these three witnesses*—[8]the Spirit, the water, and the blood—and all three agree. [9]Since we believe human testimony, surely we can believe the greater testimony that comes from God. And God has testified about his Son. [10]All who believe in the Son of God know in their hearts that this testimony is true. Those who don't believe this are actually calling God a liar because they don't believe what God has testified about his Son.

[11]And this is what God has testified: He has given us eternal life, and this life is in his Son. [12]Whoever has the Son has life; whoever does not have God's Son does not have life.

## Conclusion

[13]I have written this to you who believe in the name of the Son of God, so that you may know you have eternal life. [14]And we are confident that he hears us whenever we ask for anything that pleases him. [15]And since we know he hears us when we make our requests, we also know that he will give us what we ask for.

[16]If you see a Christian brother or sister* sinning in a way that does not lead to death, you should pray, and God will give that person life. But there is a sin that leads to death, and I am not saying you should pray for those who commit it. [17]All wicked actions are sin, but not every sin leads to death.

[18]We know that God's children do not make a practice of sinning, for God's Son holds them securely, and the evil one cannot touch them. [19]We know that we are children of God and that the world around us is under the control of the evil one.

5:6 Greek *This is he who came by water and blood.* 5:7 A few very late manuscripts add *in heaven—the Father, the Word, and the Holy Spirit, and these three are one. And we have three witnesses on earth.* 5:16 Greek *a brother.*

---

burden to those who love him. And if our load starts to feel heavy, we can always trust Christ to help us bear it (see Matthew 11:28-30).

**5:6-8** At this time, there was a false teaching in circulation that said Jesus was "the Christ" only between his baptism and his death—that is, he was merely human until he was baptized, at which time "the Christ" then descended upon him but then later left him before his death on the cross. But if Jesus died only as a man, he could not have taken upon himself the sins of the world, and Christianity would be an empty religion. Only an act of God could take away the punishment that we deserve for our sin.

**5:7-9** The Gospels twice record God's clear declaration that Jesus was his Son—at Jesus' baptism (Matthew 3:16, 17) and at his transfiguration (Matthew 17:5).

**5:12** Whoever believes in God's Son has eternal life. He is all you need. You don't need to *wait* for eternal life because it begins the moment you believe. You don't need to *work* for it because it is already yours. You don't need to *worry* about it because you have been given eternal life by God himself—and it is guaranteed.

**5:13** Some people *hope* that they will receive eternal life. John says we can *know* we have it. Our certainty is based on God's promise that he has given us eternal life through his Son. This is true whether you feel close to God or far away from him. Eternal life is not based on feelings but on facts. You can know that you have eternal life if you believe God's truth. If you aren't sure that you are a Christian, ask yourself: Have I honestly committed my life to him as my Savior and Lord? If so, you know by faith that you are indeed a child of God.

**5:14, 15** The emphasis here is on God's will, not our will. When we communicate with God, we don't demand what we want; rather we discuss with him what *he* wants for us. If we align our prayers to his will, he will listen; and we can be certain that if he listens, he will give us a definite answer. Start praying with confidence!

**5:16, 17** Commentators differ widely in their thoughts about what this sin that leads to death is and whether the death it causes is physical or spiritual. Paul wrote that some Christians had died because they took Communion unworthily (1 Corinthians 11:27-30), and Ananias and Sapphira were struck dead when they lied to God (Acts 5:1-11). Blasphemy against the Holy Spirit results in spiritual death (Mark 3:29), and the book of Hebrews describes the spiritual death of the person who turns against Christ (Hebrews 6:4-6). John was probably referring to the people who had left the Christian fellowship and joined the antichrists. By rejecting the only way of salvation, these people were putting themselves out of reach of prayer. In most cases, however, even if we knew what the terrible sin was, we would have no sure way of knowing whether a certain person had committed it. Therefore, we should continue praying for our loved ones and for our Christian brothers and sisters, leaving the judgment up to God. Note that John says, "I am not saying you should pray for those who commit it," rather than, "You cannot pray for them." He recognized the lack of certainty.

**5:18, 19** Christians commit sins, of course, but they ask God to forgive them, and then they continue serving him. God has freed believers from their slavery to Satan, and he keeps them safe from Satan's continued attacks. The rest of the world does not have the Christian's freedom to obey God. Unless they come to Christ in faith, they have no choice but to obey Satan. There is no middle ground; people either belong to God and obey him, or they live under Satan's control.

20And we know that the Son of God has come, and he has given us understanding so that we can know the true God.* And now we live in fellowship with the true God because we live in fellowship with his Son, Jesus Christ. He is the only true God, and he is eternal life.

21Dear children, keep away from anything that might take God's place in your hearts.*

**5:20** Greek *the one who is true.*    **5:21** Greek *keep yourselves from idols.*

**5:20**
Luke 24:45
John 1:1, 4; 17:3
Rom 9:5
Rev 3:7

**5:21**
1 Cor 10:14
1 Thes 1:9

---

**5:21**    Many things can take God's place in our lives. This includes anything that substitutes for the true faith, anything that denies Christ's full deity and humanity, any human idea that claims to be more authoritative than the Bible, any loyalty that replaces God at the center of our life.

**5:21**    John presents a clear picture of Christ. What we think about Jesus Christ is central to our teaching, preaching, and living. Jesus is the God-man, fully God and fully human at the same time. He came to earth to die in our place for our sins. Through faith in him, we are given eternal life and the power to do his will. What is your answer to the most important question you could ever ask: Who is Jesus Christ?

TRUTH and love are frequently discussed in our world but seldom practiced.

From politicians to marketers, people conveniently ignore or conceal facts and use words to enhance positions or sell products. Perjury is common, and integrity and credibility are endangered species. Words, twisted in meaning and torn from context, have become mere tools for ego building. It is not surprising that we have to "swear" to tell the truth.

And what about love? Our world is filled with its words: Popular songs, greeting cards, media counselors, and romantic novels shower us with notions and dreams of ethereal, idyllic relationships and feelings. Real love, however, is scarce—selfless giving, caring, sharing, and even dying. We yearn to love and be loved, but we see few living examples of real love. Plentiful are those who grasp, hoard, and watch out for "number one."

Christ is the antithesis of society's prevailing values, that is, falsehood and self-centeredness—for *he is truth and love* in person. Therefore, all who claim loyalty to him must be committed to these ideals—following the truth and living the truth, reflecting love and acting with love toward one another.

The apostle John had seen Truth and Love firsthand—he had been with Jesus. So affected was this disciple that all of his writings, from the Gospel to the book of Revelation, are filled with this theme: Truth and love are vital to the Christian and are inseparable in the Christian life. Second John, his brief letter to a dear friend, is no different. John says to live in the truth and obey God (1:4), watch out for deceivers (1:7), and love God and each other (1:6).

Second John will take just a few minutes to read, but its message should last a lifetime. As you reflect on these few paragraphs penned by the wise and aged follower of Christ, recommit yourself to being a person of truth, of love, and of obedience.

## VITAL STATISTICS

**PURPOSE:**
To emphasize the basics of following Christ—truth and love—and to warn against false teachers

**AUTHOR:**
The apostle John

**ORIGINAL AUDIENCE:**
To "the chosen lady" and her children—or possibly to a local church

**DATE WRITTEN:**
About the same time as 1 John, approximately A.D. 90 from Ephesus

**SETTING:**
Evidently this woman and her family were involved in one of the churches that John was overseeing—they had developed a strong friendship with John. John was warning her of the false teachers who were becoming prevalent in some of the churches.

**KEY VERSE:**
"Love means doing what God has commanded us, and he has commanded us to love one another, just as you heard from the beginning " (1:6).

**KEY PEOPLE:**
John, the chosen lady, and her children

## THE BLUEPRINT

1. Watch out for false teachers (1:1–11)
2. John's final words (1:12, 13)

False teachers were a dangerous problem for the church to which John was writing. His warning against showing hospitality to false teachers may sound harsh and unloving to many today. Yet these men were teaching heresy that could seriously harm many believers—for eternity.

## MEGATHEMES

| THEME | EXPLANATION | IMPORTANCE |
|---|---|---|
| Truth | Following God's Word, the Bible, is essential to Christian living because God is truth. Christ's true followers consistently obey his truth. | To be loyal to Christ's teaching, we must seek to know the Bible, but we may never twist its message to our own needs or purposes or encourage others who misuse it. |
| Love | Christ's command is for Christians to love one another. This is the basic ingredient of true Christianity. | To obey Christ fully, we must believe his command to love others. Helping, giving, and meeting needs put love into practice. |
| False Leaders | We must be wary of religious leaders who are not true to Christ's teaching. We should not give them a platform to spread false teaching. | Don't encourage those who are opposed to Christ. Politely remove yourself from association with false leaders. Be aware of what is being taught in your church. |

## 1. Watch out for false teachers

*Greetings*

This letter is from John, the elder.*

I am writing to the chosen lady and to her children,* whom I love in the truth—as does everyone else who knows the truth—²because the truth lives in us and will be with us forever.

³Grace, mercy, and peace, which come from God the Father and from Jesus Christ—the Son of the Father—will continue to be with us who live in truth and love.

*Live in the Truth*

⁴How happy I was to meet some of your children and find them living according to the truth, just as the Father commanded.

⁵I am writing to remind you, dear friends,* that we should love one another. This is not a new commandment, but one we have had from the beginning. ⁶Love means doing what God has commanded us, and he has commanded us to love one another, just as you heard from the beginning.

⁷I say this because many deceivers have gone out into the world. They deny that Jesus

**1:1**
1 Pet 5:13
1 Jn 3:18-19
3 Jn 1:1

**1:2**
John 8:32; 14:17
1 Jn 1:8; 3:19

**1:3**
1 Tim 1:2

**1:4**
3 Jn 1:3-4

**1:5**
John 13:34; 15:12
1 Jn 2:7

**1:6**
John 14:15, 23-24
1 Jn 2:5, 7; 4:7-12;
5:3

**1:7**
1 Tim 4:1-5
2 Pet 2:1-3
1 Jn 2:18, 26; 4:1-3

**1a** Greek *From the elder.*   **1b** Or *the church God has chosen and its members.*   **5** Greek *I urge you, lady.*

**1:1** The "elder" is John, one of Jesus' 12 disciples and the writer of the Gospel of John, three letters, and the book of Revelation. For more information about John, see his Profile in John 13, p. 1783. This letter was written shortly after 1 John to warn about false teachers. The salutation "to the chosen lady and to her children" could refer to a specific woman or to a church whose identity is no longer known. John may have written this from Ephesus.

**1:1, 2** John wrote this second letter (which probably fit on one sheet of papyrus) to warn believers against inadvertently supporting false teachers. The number of itinerant evangelists and teachers had grown by the end of the first century; mixed in with the legitimate missionaries were others who were promoting heretical ideas about Christ and the gospel. Little has changed in two thousand years. Advocates of unorthodox beliefs still exist and still attempt to confuse and deceive the people of God. This letter, 2 John, should serve as a wake-up call to believers to be alert, to be careful, and to be solidly grounded in the faith. Are you prepared to recognize false doctrine?

**1:3, 4** The "truth" is the truth about Jesus Christ, as opposed to the lies of the false teachers (see 1 John 2:21-23). John refers to truth five times in the first four verses of this brief letter. In contrast to so many in our culture who dogmatically deny truth ("There are no ultimate realities") or absurdly define it according to personal preference ("Your truth is your truth and my truth is my truth"), John declared the existence of an Absolute. God is that ultimate standard by which all else can be judged. God is true, his words and ways are true, and whatever or whoever contradicts or opposes him is false, deceptive,

and dangerous. Christian leaders, teachers, and parents must engage now in the difficult but critical battle for truth. To paraphrase a familiar saying: "All that is required for Deception to triumph is for the people of the Truth to do nothing." Begin an intentional campaign to teach those under your care how to distinguish between truth and error.

**1:5, 6** The statement that Christians should love one another is a recurrent New Testament theme. Yet love for one's neighbor is an old command, first appearing in the third book of Moses (Leviticus 19:18). We can show love in many ways: by avoiding prejudice and discrimination; by accepting people; by listening, helping, giving, serving, and refusing to judge. Knowing God's command is not enough. We must put it into practice, "doing what God has commanded us" (see also Matthew 22:37-39 and 1 John 2:7, 8).

**1:7** In John's day, many false teachers (deceivers) taught that spirit was good and matter was evil; therefore, they reasoned that Jesus could not have been both God and man. In strong terms, John warns against this kind of teaching. Many false teachers still promote an understanding of Jesus that is not biblical. These teachers are dangerous because they distort the truth and undermine the foundations of Christian faith. They may use the right words but change the meanings.

**1:7** The term translated "deceivers" can also be translated "impostors"; it carries the idea of leading another astray. Notice that the verse refers to "many" such charlatans and pretenders. The great danger of deceitful leaders is that they seem so sincere and believable. They are not easy to spot in a crowd. Usually they are winsome and attractive; otherwise, how would they gather people to themselves? We do not want to become paranoid and

**1:8**
1 Cor 3:8-9

**1:9**
John 8:31
1 Jn 2:23

**1:10**
Rom 16:17
Eph 5:11

**1:12**
Num 12:8
1 Jn 1:4
3 Jn 1:13-14

Christ came* in a real body. Such a person is a deceiver and an antichrist. ⁸Watch out that you do not lose what we* have worked so hard to achieve. Be diligent so that you receive your full reward. ⁹Anyone who wanders away from this teaching has no relationship with God. But anyone who remains in the teaching of Christ has a relationship with both the Father and the Son.

¹⁰If anyone comes to your meeting and does not teach the truth about Christ, don't invite that person into your home or give any kind of encouragement. ¹¹Anyone who encourages such people becomes a partner in their evil work.

## 2. John's final words

¹²I have much more to say to you, but I don't want to do it with paper and ink. For I hope to visit you soon and talk with you face to face. Then our joy will be complete.

¹³Greetings from the children of your sister,* chosen by God.

**7** Or *will come.*   **8** Some manuscripts read *you.*   **13** Or *from the members of your sister church.*

suspicious about everyone we meet, but we do need to be wise in evaluating the character and conduct of those who would seek to influence people. The way your teachers live shows a lot about what they believe about Christ. For more on testing teachers, see 1 John 4:1.

**1:8** To "receive your full reward" refers not to salvation but to the rewards of loyal service. All who value the truth and persistently hold to it will win their full reward. Those who live for themselves and justify their self-centeredness by teaching false doctrines will lose that reward (see Matthew 7:21-23).

**1:10** John instructs the believers not to show hospitality to false teachers. They were to do nothing that would encourage the heretics in their propagation of falsehoods. In addition, if believers

were to invite them in, such action would show that they were approving of what the false teachers said and did. John is condemning the support of those who are dedicated to opposing the true teachings of God, not condemning hospitality to unbelievers. John adds that a person who supports a false teacher in any way shares in the teacher's evil work.

**1:10** False teaching is serious business, and we dare not overlook it. It is so serious that John wrote this letter to warn against it. Because our world has so many false teachings, we might be tempted to take many of them lightly. Instead, we should realize the dangers they pose and actively refuse to give heresies any foothold.

## VITAL STATISTICS

**PURPOSE:**
To commend Gaius for his hospitality and to encourage him in his Christian life

**AUTHOR:**
The apostle John

**ORIGINAL AUDIENCE:**
Gaius, a prominent Christian in one of the churches known to John

**DATE WRITTEN:**
Approximately A.D. 90 from Ephesus

**SETTING:**
Church leaders traveled from town to town helping to establish new congregations. They depended on the hospitality of fellow believers. Gaius was one who welcomed these leaders into his home.

**KEY VERSE:**
"Dear friend, you are being faithful to God when you care for the traveling teachers who pass through, even though they are strangers to you" (1:5).

**KEY PEOPLE:**
John, Gaius, Diotrephes, Demetrius

BY SPECIAL invitation or with a surprise knock, company arrives and with them comes the promise of soiled floors, extra laundry, dirty dishes, altered schedules, personal expense, and inconvenience. From sharing a meal to providing a bed, *hospitality* costs . . . in time, energy, and money. But how we treat others reflects our true values—what is really important to us. Do we see people as objects or inconveniences, or as unique creations of a loving God? And which is more important to God, a person or a carpet? Perhaps the most effective way to demonstrate God's values and Christ's love to others is to invite and welcome guests into our homes.

For Gaius, hospitality was a habit, and his reputation for friendship and generosity, especially to traveling teachers and missionaries (1:5), had spread. To affirm and thank Gaius for his Christian lifestyle, and to encourage him in his faith, John wrote this personal note.

John's format for this letter centers around three men: Gaius, the example of one who follows Christ and loves others (1:1–8); Diotrephes, the self-proclaimed church leader who does not reflect God's values (1:9–11); and Demetrius, who also follows the truth (1:12). John encourages Gaius to practice hospitality, continue to walk in the truth, and do what is right.

Although this is a personal letter, we can look over the shoulder of Gaius and apply its lessons to our life. As you read 3 John, with which man do you identify? Are you a Gaius, generously giving to others? a Demetrius, loving the truth? or a Diotrephes, looking out for yourself and your things? Determine to reflect Christ's values in your relationships, opening your home and touching others with his love.

---

## THE BLUEPRINT

1. God's children live by the standards of the gospel (1:1–12)
2. John's final words (1:13–15)

John wrote to commend Gaius, who was taking care of traveling teachers and missionaries, and to warn against people like Diotrephes, who was proud and refused to listen to spiritual leaders in authority. If we are to live in the truth of the gospel, we must look for ways to support pastors, Christian workers, and missionaries today. All Christians should work together to support God's work both at home and around the world.

---

## MEGATHEMES

| THEME | EXPLANATION | IMPORTANCE |
|---|---|---|
| Hospitality | John wrote to encourage those who were kind to others. Genuine hospitality for traveling Christian workers was needed then and is still important today. | Faithful Christian teachers and missionaries need our support. Whenever you can extend hospitality to others, it will make you a partner in their ministry. |
| Pride | Diotrephes not only refused to offer hospitality but also set himself up as a church boss. Pride disqualified him from being a real leader. | Christian leaders must shun pride and its effects on them. Be careful not to misuse your position of leadership. |
| Faithfulness | Gaius and Demetrius were commended for their faithful work in the church. They were held up as examples of faithful, selfless servants. | Don't take for granted Christian workers who serve faithfully. Be sure to encourage them so they won't grow weary of serving. |

## 1. God's children live by the standards of the gospel

**1:1**
2 Jn 1:1

*Greetings*

This letter is from John, the elder.*

**1:3**
2 Jn 1:4

I am writing to Gaius, my dear friend, whom I love in the truth.

**1:4**
1 Cor 4:15
Gal 4:19
1 Jn 2:1

²Dear friend, I hope all is well with you and that you are as healthy in body as you are strong in spirit. ³Some of the traveling teachers* recently returned and made me very happy by telling me about your faithfulness and that you are living according to the truth. ⁴I could have no greater joy than to hear that my children are following the truth.

**1:5**
Rom 12:13
Heb 13:2
1 Pet 4:10

*Caring for the Lord's Workers*

**1:6**
Col 1:10
Titus 3:13

⁵Dear friend, you are being faithful to God when you care for the traveling teachers who pass through, even though they are strangers to you. ⁶They have told the church here of your loving friendship. Please continue providing for such teachers in a manner that pleases God. ⁷For they are traveling for the Lord,* and they accept nothing from people who are not

**1:7**
Matt 10:9-14
Mark 6:8-13
Luke 9:3-5; 10:4-11
Acts 20:33, 35

**1** Greek *From the elder.* **3** Greek *the brothers;* also in verses 5 and 10. **7a** Greek *They went out on behalf of the Name.*

---

**1:1** This letter provides us an important glimpse into the life of the early church. Third John, addressed to Gaius, highlights the need for showing hospitality to traveling preachers and other believers. It also warns against a would-be church dictator.

**1:1** The "elder," John, was one of Jesus' 12 disciples and the writer of the Gospel of John, three letters, and the book of Revelation. For more information about John, see his Profile in John 13, p. 1783. We have no further information about Gaius, but he is someone whom John loved dearly. Perhaps Gaius had shared his home and hospitality with John at some time during John's travels. If so, John would have appreciated his actions because traveling preachers depended on expressions of hospitality to survive (see Matthew 10:11-16).

**1:2** John was concerned for Gaius's physical *and* spiritual well-being. This was the opposite of the popular heresy that taught the separation of spirit and matter and despised the physical side of life. Today, many people still fall into this way of thinking. This non-Christian attitude logically leads to one of two responses: neglect of the body and physical health, or indulgence of the body's sinful desires. God is concerned for both your body and your soul. As a responsible Christian, you should neither neglect nor indulge yourself but care for your physical needs and discipline your body so that you are at your best for God's service.

**1:4** John writes about "my children" because, as a result of his preaching, he was the spiritual father of many, including Gaius.

**1:5, 6** In the church's early days, traveling prophets, evangelists, and teachers were helped on their way by people like Gaius, who housed and fed them. Hospitality is a lost art in many churches today. We would do well to invite more people for meals—fellow church members, young people, traveling missionaries, those in need, visitors. This is an active and much-appreciated way to show your love. In fact, it is probably more important today. Because of our individualistic, self-centered society, many lonely people wonder if anyone cares whether they live or die. If you find such a lonely person, show him or her that *you* care!

**1:7** The traveling missionaries neither asked for nor accepted anything from nonbelievers. This was not intended to be a criticism of unbelievers, but a statement of how things ought to be. Imagine the awkwardness of a Christian worker's requesting funds or lodging from the very people he or she was trying to reach! Instead, it is the responsibility of churches and Christian individuals to support those who are called by God to full-time vocational ministry. In that way, unbelievers will not be questioning the missionaries' motives for preaching. God's true preachers do not preach to make money but to fulfill their calling and express their love for God. It is the church's responsibility to care for Christian workers; this should never be left to nonbelievers. Don't just automatically discard the next missionary fund-raising letter you receive. That appeal may be God's invitation for you to become a partner in a new gospel venture.

believers.* [8]So we ourselves should support them so that we can be their partners as they teach the truth.

[9]I wrote to the church about this, but Diotrephes, who loves to be the leader, refuses to have anything to do with us. [10]When I come, I will report some of the things he is doing and the evil accusations he is making against us. Not only does he refuse to welcome the traveling teachers, he also tells others not to help them. And when they do help, he puts them out of the church.

[11]Dear friend, don't let this bad example influence you. Follow only what is good. Remember that those who do good prove that they are God's children, and those who do evil prove that they do not know God.*

[12]Everyone speaks highly of Demetrius, as does the truth itself. We ourselves can say the same for him, and you know we speak the truth.

## 2. John's final words

[13]I have much more to say to you, but I don't want to write it with pen and ink. [14]For I hope to see you soon, and then we will talk face to face.

[15]*Peace be with you.

Your friends here send you their greetings. Please give my personal greetings to each of our friends there.

**1:10**
John 9:22, 34
2 Jn 1:12
3 Jn 1:5

**1:11**
Ps 34:14
1 Jn 2:29; 3:6, 9-10

**1:12**
John 19:35; 21:24

**1:13**
Num 12:8
2 Jn 1:12

**1:14**
2 Jn 1:12

**7b** Greek *from Gentiles.*  **11** Greek *they have not seen God.*  **15** Some English translations combine verses 14 and 15 into verse 14.

---

**1:8** When you help someone who is spreading the Good News, you are in a very real way a partner in the ministry. This is the other side of the principle in 2 John 1:10 (see the note there). Not everyone should go to the mission field; those who work for Christ at home are vital to the ministry of those who go and who need support. We can support missionaries by praying for them and by giving our money, hospitality, and time.

**1:9** This letter to which John refers was neither 1 nor 2 John but another letter that no longer exists.

**1:9, 10** All we know about Diotrephes is that he wanted to control the church. John denounced: (1) his refusal to have anything to do with other spiritual leaders, (2) his slander of the leaders, (3) his bad example in refusing to welcome any teachers, and (4) his attempt to excommunicate those who opposed his leadership. Sins such as pride, jealousy, and slander are still present in the church, and when a leader makes a habit of encouraging sin and discouraging right actions, he or she must be stopped. If no one speaks up, great harm can come to the church. We must confront sin in the church; if we ignore it, it will continue to grow. A true Christian leader is a servant, not an autocrat!

**1:12** We know nothing about Demetrius except that he may have carried this letter from John to Gaius. The book of Acts mentions an Ephesian silversmith named Demetrius, who opposed Paul (Acts 19:24ff), but this is probably another man. In contrast to the corrupt Diotrephes, Demetrius had a high regard for truth. John personified truth as a witness to Demetrius's character and teaching. In other words, if truth could speak, it would speak on Demetrius's behalf. When Demetrius arrived, Gaius certainly opened his home to him.

**1:14** Whereas 2 John emphasizes the need to refuse hospitality to false teachers, 3 John urges continued hospitality to those who teach the truth. Hospitality is a strong sign of support for people and their work. It means giving of your resources to them so their stay will be comfortable and their work and travel easier. Actively look for creative ways to show hospitality to God's workers. It may be in the form of a letter of encouragement, a gift, financial support, an open home, or prayer.

# JUDE

TO PROTECT from harm, to guard from attack, to repulse enemies—for centuries rugged defenders have built walls, launched missiles, and waged wars, expending material and human resources in the battle to save nations and cities. And with total commitment and courageous abandon, individuals have fought for their families. It is a rule of life that we fight for survival, defending with all our strength what is most precious to us, from every real or imagined attack.

God's Word and the gift of eternal life have infinite value and have been entrusted to Christ's faithful followers. Many people live in opposition to God and his followers. They twist God's words, seeking to deceive and destroy the unwary. But God's truth must go forth, carried and defended by those who have committed their lives to his Son. It is an important task, an awesome responsibility, and a profound privilege to have this commission.

This was Jude's message to Christians everywhere. Opposition would come and godless teachers would arise, but Christians should "defend the faith" (1:3) by rejecting all falsehood and immorality (1:4–19), remembering God's mighty acts of rescue and punishment (1:5–11, 14–16) and the warnings of the apostles (1:17–19). His readers are to build up their own faith through prayer (1:20), keeping close to Christ (1:21), helping others (1:22, 23), and hating sin (1:23). Then Jude concludes with a glorious benediction of praise to God (1:24, 25).

How much do you value God's Word, the fellowship of the church, and obedience to Jesus Christ? Many false teachers are waiting to destroy your Christ-centered life, the credibility of God's Word, and the unity of the body of Christ. Read Jude and determine to stand firm in your faith and defend God's truth at all costs. *Nothing* is more valuable.

## VITAL STATISTICS

PURPOSE:
To remind the church of the need for constant vigilance—to keep strong in the faith and to oppose heresy

AUTHOR:
Jude, brother of Jesus and James

ORIGINAL AUDIENCE:
Jewish Christians

DATE WRITTEN:
Approximately A.D. 65

SETTING:
From the first century on, the church has been threatened by heresy and false teaching; we must always be on our guard.

KEY VERSE:
"Dear friends, I had been eagerly planning to write to you about the salvation we all share. But now I find that I must write about something else, urging you to defend the faith that God has entrusted once for all time to his holy people" (1:3).

KEY PEOPLE:
Jude, James, Jesus

## THE BLUEPRINT

1. The danger of false teachers (1:1–16)
2. The duty to fight for God's truth (1:17–25)

Jude wrote to motivate Christians everywhere to action. He wanted them to recognize the dangers of false teaching, to protect themselves and other believers, and to win back those who had already been deceived. Jude was writing against godless teachers who were saying that Christians could do as they pleased without fear of God's punishment. While few teach this heresy openly in the church today, many in the church act as though this were true. This letter contains a warning against living a nominal Christian life.

## MEGATHEMES

| THEME | EXPLANATION | IMPORTANCE |
|---|---|---|
| *False Teachers* | Jude warns against false teachers and leaders who reject the lordship of Christ, undermine the faith of others, and lead them astray. These leaders and any who follow them will be punished. | We must staunchly defend Christian truth. Make sure that you avoid leaders and teachers who distort the Bible to suit their own purposes. Genuine servants of God will faithfully portray Christ in their words and conduct. |
| *Apostasy* | Jude also warns against apostasy—turning away from Christ. We are to remember that God punishes rebellion against him. We must be careful not to drift away from a faithful commitment to Christ. | Those who do not seek to know the truth in God's Word are susceptible to apostasy. Christians must guard against any false teachings that would distract them from the truth preached by the apostles and written in God's Word. |

## 1. The danger of false teachers

### Greetings from Jude

This letter is from Jude, a slave of Jesus Christ and a brother of James.

I am writing to all who have been called by God the Father, who loves you and keeps you safe in the care of Jesus Christ.*

²May God give you more and more mercy, peace, and love.

1:1<br>Matt 13:55<br>Rom 1:1, 6-7<br>Jas 1:1<br>1:2<br>2 Pet 1:2

### The Danger of False Teachers

³Dear friends, I had been eagerly planning to write to you about the salvation we all share. But now I find that I must write about something else, urging you to defend the faith that God has entrusted once for all time to his holy people. ⁴I say this because some ungodly people have wormed their way into your churches, saying that God's marvelous grace allows us to live immoral lives. The condemnation of such people was recorded long ago, for they have denied our only Master and Lord, Jesus Christ.

⁵So I want to remind you, though you already know these things, that Jesus* first rescued the nation of Israel from Egypt, but later he destroyed those who did not remain faithful.

1:3<br>1 Tim 6:12<br>Titus 1:4<br>2 Pet 3:1-2<br>1:4<br>Gal 2:4<br>2 Pet 2:1-2<br>1 Jn 2:21<br>1:5<br>Exod 14:21-31<br>Num 14:29-37<br>Deut 2:15<br>1 Cor 10:5-10

1 Or *keeps you for Jesus Christ.*   5 As in the best manuscripts; various other manuscripts read *[the] Lord,* or *God,* or *Christ;* one reads *God Christ.*

**1:1** Jude's letter focuses on *apostasy*—when people turn away from God's truth and embrace false teachings. Jude reminded his readers of God's judgment on those who had left the faith. This letter warns against false teachers—in this case, probably Gnostic teachers (see the note on Colossians 2:4ff for a description of the Gnostic heresy). Gnostics opposed two of the basic tenets of Christianity—the incarnation of Christ and the call to Christian ethics. Jude wrote to combat these false teachings and to encourage true doctrine and right conduct.

**1:1** Jude was a brother of James, who was one of the leaders in the early church. Both of these men were Jesus' half brothers. Mary was their mother, and Joseph was their father. Although Mary was Jesus' true mother, God was Jesus' true Father.

**1:3** Jude emphasizes the important relationship between correct doctrine and true faith. The truth of the Bible must not be compromised because it gives us the real facts about Jesus and salvation. The Bible is inspired by God and should never be twisted or manipulated; when it is, we can become confused over right and wrong and lose sight of the only path that leads to eternal life. Before writing about salvation, then, Jude felt he had to set his readers back on the right track, calling them back to the basics of their faith. Then the way to salvation would be clearer. "His holy people" refers to all believers.

**1:3** How do ordinary Christians "defend the faith" today? Think about these ideas:

(1) We can defend the faith by knowing the truth. We do that by studying the Bible. Don't ever imagine that pastors and seminary professors hold a monopoly on this task. Without study, you cannot know what to defend. You must understand the basic doctrines of the faith so that you can recognize false doctrines and prevent wrong teaching from undermining your faith and hurting others.

(2) We can defend the faith as we grow personally with Christ. While knowledge is important, your personal relationship with Christ is essential. Through that relationship, God has given you the Holy Spirit as a teacher. Unattached to God, you may know everything, but understand nothing. Attached to Christ, you are given spiritual understanding as well as experiences with Christ that underscore your faith.

(3) We can defend the faith by remaining unified on the essentials. While Christians can certainly disagree on many non-essentials (music in worship, methods of worship, methods of outreach), we must always defend the truth of the basics of our faith as found in God's Word.

**1:4** Even some of our churches today have false ("ungodly") teachers who have "wormed" their way in and are twisting the Bible's teachings to justify their own opinions, lifestyle, or wrong behavior. In doing this, they may gain temporary freedom to do as they wish, but they will discover that in distorting Scripture they are playing with fire. God will judge them for excusing, tolerating, and promoting sin.

**1:4** Many first-century false teachers were teaching that Christians could do whatever they liked without fear of God's punishment. They had a light view of God's holiness and his justice. Paul refuted this same kind of false teaching in Romans 6:1-23. Even today, some Christians minimize the sinfulness of sin, believing that how they live has little to do with their faith. But what a person truly believes will show up in how he or she acts. Those who truly have faith will show it by their deep respect for God and their sincere desire to live according to the principles in his Word.

**1:5-7** Jude gives three examples of rebellion: (1) the nation of Israel—who, although they were delivered from Egypt, refused to trust God and enter the Promised Land (Numbers 14:26-39); (2) the angels—although they were once pure, holy, and living in

**1:6**
//2 Pet 2:4, 9

**1:7**
Gen 19:4-25
Matt 10:15
//2 Pet 2:6, 10

**1:8**
//2 Pet 2:10

**1:9**
Dan 10:13, 21;
12:1
Zech 3:2
//2 Pet 2:11
Rev 12:7

**1:10**
//2 Pet 2:12

**1:11**
Gen 4:3-8
Num 16:1-35; 22:7;
31:16
//2 Pet 2:15-16
1 Jn 3:12
Rev 2:14

**1:12**
Ezek 34:8
Matt 15:13
1 Cor 11:20-22
//2 Pet 2:13

**1:13**
Isa 57:20
Phil 3:19
//2 Pet 2:17

**1:14**
Gen 5:18-24
Deut 33:2
1 Chr 1:1-3
Zech 14:5
Matt 25:31

**1:15**
2 Pet 2:6-9

**1:16**
//2 Pet 2:10, 18

6And I remind you of the angels who did not stay within the limits of authority God gave them but left the place where they belonged. God has kept them securely chained in prisons of darkness, waiting for the great day of judgment. 7And don't forget Sodom and Gomorrah and their neighboring towns, which were filled with immorality and every kind of sexual perversion. Those cities were destroyed by fire and serve as a warning of the eternal fire of God's judgment.

8In the same way, these people—who claim authority from their dreams—live immoral lives, defy authority, and scoff at supernatural beings.* 9But even Michael, one of the mightiest of the angels,* did not dare accuse the devil of blasphemy, but simply said, "The Lord rebuke you!" (This took place when Michael was arguing with the devil about Moses' body.) 10But these people scoff at things they do not understand. Like unthinking animals, they do whatever their instincts tell them, and so they bring about their own destruction. 11What sorrow awaits them! For they follow in the footsteps of Cain, who killed his brother. Like Balaam, they deceive people for money. And like Korah, they perish in their rebellion.

12When these people eat with you in your fellowship meals commemorating the Lord's love, they are like dangerous reefs that can shipwreck you.* They are like shameless shepherds who care only for themselves. They are like clouds blowing over the land without giving any rain. They are like trees in autumn that are doubly dead, for they bear no fruit and have been pulled up by the roots. 13They are like wild waves of the sea, churning up the foam of their shameful deeds. They are like wandering stars, doomed forever to blackest darkness.

14Enoch, who lived in the seventh generation after Adam, prophesied about these people. He said, "Listen! The Lord is coming with countless thousands of his holy ones 15to execute judgment on the people of the world. He will convict every person of all the ungodly things they have done and for all the insults that ungodly sinners have spoken against him."* 16These people are grumblers and complainers, living only to satisfy their desires. They brag loudly about themselves, and they flatter others to get what they want.

**8** Greek *at glorious ones,* which are probably evil angels.  **9** Greek *Michael, the archangel.*  **12** Or *they are contaminants among you;* or *they are stains.*  **14-15** The quotation comes from intertestamental literature: Enoch 1:9.

---

God's presence, some gave in to pride and joined Satan to rebel against God (2 Peter 2:4); (3) the cities of Sodom and Gomorrah—the inhabitants were so full of sin that God wiped them off the face of the earth (Genesis 19:1-29). If the chosen people, angels, and sinful cities were punished, how much more would these false teachers be severely judged?

**1:7** Many people don't want to believe that God sentences people to "eternal fire" for rejecting him. But this is clearly taught in Scripture. Sinners who don't seek forgiveness from God will face eternal separation from him. Jude warns all who rebel against, ignore, or reject God.

**1:8** The "supernatural beings" here are probably evil angels. Just as the men of Sodom insulted angels (Genesis 19), these false teachers scoffed at any authority. For information on the danger of insulting even the fallen angels, see the note on 2 Peter 2:10-12.

**1:9** This incident is not recorded in any other place in Scripture. Moses' death is recorded in Deuteronomy 34. Here Jude may have been making use of an ancient book called *The Assumption of Moses.*

**1:10** False teachers claimed to possess secret knowledge that gave them authority. Their "knowledge" of God was esoteric—mystical and beyond human understanding. The nature of God *is* beyond our understanding, but God, in his grace, has chosen to reveal himself to us—in his Word and supremely in Jesus Christ. Therefore, we must seek to know all we can about what he has revealed, even though we cannot fully comprehend God with our finite human minds. Beware of those who claim to have all the answers and who belittle what they do not understand.

**1:11** Jude gives three examples of men who did whatever they wanted (1:10): Cain, who murdered his brother out of vengeful jealousy (Genesis 4:1-16); Balaam, who prophesied out of greed, not out of obedience to God's command (Numbers

22–24); Korah, who rebelled against God's divinely appointed leaders, wanting the power for himself (Numbers 16:1-35). These stories illustrate attitudes that are typical of false teachers—pride, selfishness, jealousy, greed, lust for power, and disregard of God's will.

**1:12** When the Lord's Supper was celebrated in the early church, believers would eat a full meal before taking part in Communion with the sharing of the bread and wine. The meal was called a "fellowship meal," and it was designed to be a sacred time of fellowship to prepare one's heart for Communion. In several of the churches, however, this meal had turned into a time of gluttony and drunken revelry. In Corinth, for example, some people hastily gobbled food while others went hungry (1 Corinthians 11:20-22). No church function should be an occasion for selfishness, gluttony, greed, disorder, or other sins that destroy unity or take one's mind away from the real purpose for gathering together.

**1:12** The false teachers were "doubly dead." They were useless "trees" because they weren't producing fruit. They weren't even believers, so they would be rooted up and burned.

**1:14** Enoch is mentioned briefly in Genesis 5:21-24. This quotation is from an apocryphal book called the book of Enoch.

**1:14** Jesus is also mentioned as coming with angels ("holy ones") in Matthew 16:27 and 24:31. Daniel 7:10 speaks of God judging humanity in the presence of ten thousand times ten thousand angels.

## 2. The duty to fight for God's truth

*A Call to Remain Faithful*

¹⁷But you, my dear friends, must remember what the apostles of our Lord Jesus Christ said. ¹⁸They told you that in the last times there would be scoffers whose purpose in life is to satisfy their ungodly desires. ¹⁹These people are the ones who are creating divisions among you. They follow their natural instincts because they do not have God's Spirit in them.

²⁰But you, dear friends, must build each other up in your most holy faith, pray in the power of the Holy Spirit,* ²¹and await the mercy of our Lord Jesus Christ, who will bring you eternal life. In this way, you will keep yourselves safe in God's love.

²²And you must show mercy to* those whose faith is wavering. ²³Rescue others by snatching them from the flames of judgment. Show mercy to still others,* but do so with great caution, hating the sins that contaminate their lives.*

*A Prayer of Praise*

²⁴Now all glory to God, who is able to keep you from falling away and will bring you with great joy into his glorious presence without a single fault. ²⁵All glory to him who alone is God, our Savior through Jesus Christ our Lord. All glory, majesty, power, and authority are his before all time, and in the present, and beyond all time! Amen.

**1:17**
Heb 2:3
2 Pet 3:2

**1:18**
//2 Pet 3:3
Jude 1:16

**1:20**
Eph 6:18
Col 2:7
1 Thes 5:11

**1:21**
2 Tim 1:18

**1:23**
Amos 4:11
Zech 3:2-5
Rev 3:4

**1:24**
Rom 16:25
2 Cor 4:14
Phil 1:10
1 Thes 5:23

**1:25**
Rom 16:27
2 Pet 3:18

**20** Greek *pray in the Holy Spirit.*　**22** Some manuscripts read *must reprove.*　**22-23a** Some manuscripts have only two categories of people: (1) those whose faith is wavering and therefore need to be snatched from the flames of judgment, and (2) those who need to be shown mercy.　**23b** Greek *with fear, hating even the clothing stained by the flesh.*

---

**1:17** Other apostles also warned about false teachers. See Acts 20:29; 1 Timothy 4:1, 2; 2 Timothy 3:1-5; 2 Peter 2:1-3; 2 John 7.

**1:18** The "last times" is a common phrase referring to the time between Jesus' first and second comings. We live in the last times.

**1:21** John warns his readers to live close to God and his people, not listening to false teachers who would try to pull you away from him (John 15:9, 10).

**1:22, 23** Bringing people to Jesus saves them from God's judgment. We can do this through compassion and kindness. We are to hate the sin, but we must witness to and love the sinner. Unbelievers, no matter how successful they seem by worldly standards, are lost and in need of salvation. We should not take witnessing lightly—it is a matter of life and death.

**1:23** In trying to find common ground with those to whom we witness, we must be careful not to fall into the quicksand of compromise. When reaching out to others, we must be sure that our own footing is safe and secure. Be careful not to become so much like non-Christians that no one can tell who you are or what you believe. Influence them for Christ—don't allow them to influence you to sin!

**1:24** As the letter begins, so it ends—with assurance. God keeps believers from falling prey to false teachers. Although false teach-

ers are widespread and dangerous, we don't have to be afraid if we trust God and are rooted and grounded in him.

**1:24** To be sinless and perfect ("without a single fault") will be the ultimate condition of the believer when he or she finally sees Christ face-to-face. When Christ appears and we are given our new bodies, we will be like Christ (1 John 3:2). Coming into Christ's presence will be more wonderful than we could ever imagine!

**1:25** The audience to whom Jude wrote was vulnerable to heresies and to temptations toward immoral living. Jude encouraged the believers to remain firm in their faith and trust in God's promises for their futures. This was all the more important because they were living in a time of increased apostasy. We, too, are living in the last days, much closer to the end than were the original readers of this letter. We, too, are vulnerable to doctrinal error. We, too, are tempted to give in to sin. Although much false teaching is around us, we need not be afraid or give up in despair—God can keep us from falling, and he guarantees that if we remain faithful, he will bring us into his presence and give us everlasting joy.

WITH tiny wrinkles and cries, he entered the world and, wrapped in strips of cloth, took his first nap on a bed of straw. Subject to time and to parents, he grew to manhood in Roman-occupied Judea, his gentle hands becoming strong and calloused in Joseph's woodworking shop. As a man, he walked through the countryside and city, touching individuals, preaching to crowds, and training 12 men to carry on his work. At every step he was hounded by those seeking to rid the world of his influence. Finally, falsely accused and tried, he was condemned to a disgraceful execution by foreign hands. And he died—spat upon, cursed, pierced by nails, and hung heavenward for all to deride. Jesus, the God-man, gave his life completely so that all might live.

At God's appointed time, the risen and ascended Lord Jesus will burst onto the world scene. Then everyone will know that Jesus is Lord of the universe! Those who love him will rejoice, greeting their Savior with hearts overflowing into songs of praise. But his enemies will be filled with fear. Allied with Satan, the enemies of Christ will marshal their legions against Christ and his armies. But who can withstand God's wrath? Christ will win the battle and reign victorious forever! Jesus, the humble suffering servant, is also the powerful, conquering King and Judge.

Revelation is a book of hope. John, the beloved apostle and eyewitness of Jesus, proclaimed that the victorious Lord would surely return to vindicate the righteous and judge the wicked. But Revelation is also a book of warning. Things were not as they should have been in the churches, so Christ called the members to commit themselves to live in righteousness.

Although Jesus gave this revelation of himself to John nearly 2,000 years ago, it still stands as a comfort and challenge to God's people today. We can take heart as we understand John's vision of hope: Christ will return to rescue his people and settle accounts with all who defy him.

John begins this book by explaining how he received this revelation from God (1:1–20). He then records specific messages from Jesus to the seven churches in Asia (2:1—3:22). Suddenly, the scene shifts as a mosaic of dramatic and majestic images bursts into view before John's eyes. This series of visions portrays the future rise of evil, culminating in the Antichrist (4:1—18:24). Then follows John's recounting of the triumph of the King over all kings, the wedding of the Lamb, the final judgment, and the coming of the new Jerusalem (19:1—22:5). Revelation concludes with the promise of Christ's soon return (22:6–21), and John breathes a prayer that has been echoed by Christians through the centuries: "Amen! Come, Lord Jesus!" (22:20).

As you read the book of Revelation, marvel with John at the wondrous panorama of God's revealed plan. Listen as Christ warns the churches, and root out any sin that blocks your relationship with him. Be full of hope, knowing that God is in control, Christ's victory is assured, and all who trust him will be saved.

## VITAL STATISTICS

**PURPOSE:**
To reveal the full identity of Christ and to give warning and hope to believers

**AUTHOR:**
The apostle John

**ORIGINAL AUDIENCE:**
The seven churches in Asia and all believers everywhere

**DATE WRITTEN:**
Approximately A.D. 95 from Patmos

**SETTING:**
Most scholars believe that the seven churches of Asia to whom John writes were experiencing the persecution that took place under Emperor Domitian (A.D. 90–95). It seems that the Roman authorities had exiled John to the island of Patmos (off the coast of Asia). John, who had been an eyewitness of the incarnate Christ, had a vision of the glorified Christ. God also revealed to John what would take place in the future—judgment and the ultimate triumph of God over evil.

**KEY VERSE:**
"God blesses the one who reads the words of this prophecy to the church, and he blesses all who listen to its message and obey what it says, for the time is near" (1:3).

**KEY PEOPLE:**
John, Jesus

**KEY PLACES:**
Patmos, the seven churches, the new Jerusalem

**SPECIAL FEATURES:**
Revelation is written in "apocalyptic" form—a type of Jewish literature that uses symbolic imagery to communicate hope (in the ultimate triumph of God) to those in the midst of persecution. The events are ordered according to literary, rather than strictly chronological, patterns.

## THE BLUEPRINT

A.  LETTERS TO THE CHURCHES
    (1:1—3:22)

The vision John received opens with instructions for him to write to seven churches. He both commends them for their strengths and warns them about their flaws. Each letter was directed to a church then in existence but also speaks to conditions in the church throughout history. Both in the church and in our individual lives, we must constantly fight against the temptation to become loveless, immoral, lenient, compromising, lifeless, or casual about our faith. The letters make it clear how our Lord feels about these qualities.

B.  MESSAGE FOR THE CHURCH
    (4:1—22:21)
    1.  Worshiping God in heaven
    2.  Opening the seven seals
    3.  Sounding the seven trumpets
    4.  Observing the great conflict
    5.  Pouring out the seven plagues
    6.  Seizing the final victory
    7.  Making all things new

This revelation is both a warning to Christians who have grown apathetic and an encouragement to those who are faithfully enduring the struggles in this world. It reassures us that good will triumph over evil, gives us hope as we face difficult times, and gives guidance when we are wavering in our faith. Christ's message to the church is a message of hope for all believers in every generation.

## MEGATHEMES

| THEME | EXPLANATION | IMPORTANCE |
|---|---|---|
| God's Sovereignty | God is sovereign. He is greater than any power in the universe. God is not to be compared with any leader, government, or religion. He controls history for the purpose of uniting true believers in loving fellowship with him. | Though Satan's power may temporarily increase, we are not to be led astray. God is all-powerful. He is in control. He will bring his true family safely into eternal life. Because he cares for us, we can trust him with our very life. |
| Christ's Return | Christ came to earth as a "Lamb," the symbol of his perfect sacrifice for our sin. He will return as the triumphant "Lion," the rightful ruler and conqueror. He will defeat Satan, settle accounts with all those who reject him, and bring his faithful people into eternity. | Assurance of Christ's return gives suffering Christians the strength to endure. We can look forward to his return as king and judge. Since no one knows the time when he will appear, we must be ready at all times by keeping our faith strong. |
| God's Faithful People | John wrote to encourage the church to resist the demands to worship the Roman emperor. He warns all God's faithful people to be devoted only to Christ. Revelation identifies who the faithful people are and what they should be doing until Christ returns. | You can take your place in the ranks of God's faithful people by believing in Christ. Victory is sure for those who resist temptation and make loyalty to Christ their top priority. |
| Judgment | One day God's anger toward sin will be fully and completely unleashed. Satan will be defeated with all of his agents. False religion will be destroyed. God will reward the faithful with eternal life, but all who refuse to believe in him will face eternal punishment. | Evil and injustice will not prevail forever. God's final judgment will put an end to these. We need to be certain of our commitment to Jesus if we want to escape this great final judgment. No one who rejects Christ will escape God's punishment. |
| Hope | One day God will create a new heaven and a new earth. All believers will live with him forever in perfect peace and security. Those who have already died will be raised to life. These promises for the future bring us hope. | Our great hope is that what Christ promises will come true. When we have confidence in our final destination, we can follow Christ with unwavering dedication no matter what we must face. We can be encouraged by hoping in Christ's return. |

## A. LETTERS TO THE CHURCHES (1:1—3:22)

Near the end of his life, John received a vision from Christ, which he recorded for the benefit of the seven churches in Asia and for Christians throughout history. This is the only book in the Bible that promises a blessing to those who listen to its words and do what it says.

### Prologue

**1:1**
Dan 2:28-29, 45
John 12:49; 17:8
Rev 1:19; 5:7; 17:1;
22:6, 8, 16
**1:2**
Rev 1:9; 6:9

**1** This is a revelation from* Jesus Christ, which God gave him to show his servants the events that must soon* take place. He sent an angel to present this revelation to his servant John, 2 who faithfully reported everything he saw. This is his report of the word of God and the testimony of Jesus Christ.

**1:1a** Or *of.* **1:1b** Or *suddenly,* or *quickly.*

| INTERPRETING THE BOOK OF REVELATION | Approach | Description | Challenge | Caution |
|---|---|---|---|---|
| | Preterist View | John is writing to encourage Christians in his own day who are experiencing persecution from the Roman Empire. | To gain the same kind of encouragement John's first readers gained from the vivid images of God's sovereignty | Do not forget that most biblical prophecy has both an immediate and a future application. |
| | Futurist View | Except for the first three chapters, John is describing events that will occur at the end of history. | To see in contemporary events many of the characteristics John describes and realize that the end could come at any time | Do not assume that we have "figured out" the future, since Jesus said that no one will know the day of his return before it happens. |
| | Historicist View | The book of Revelation is a presentation of history from John's day until the second coming of Christ and beyond. | To note the consistency of human evil throughout history and recognize that names may change but the rebellion against God has not | Be careful before identifying current events or leaders as fulfilling aspects of the book of Revelation. |
| | Idealist View | The book of Revelation is a symbolic representation of the continual struggle of good and evil. It does not refer to any particular historical events. It is applicable at any point in history. | To gain insight into the past, to prepare for the future, and to live obediently and confidently in the present | Do not avoid the book because it is difficult. Try to understand Revelation within its broader literary context. |

Over the centuries, four main approaches to interpreting the book of Revelation have developed. Each approach has had capable supporters, but none has proved itself the only way to read this book. However, the most basic application question for each approach can be summarized by asking yourself, Will this help me become a better follower of Jesus Christ today?

---

**1:1** Revelation is a book about the future *and* about the present. It offers future hope to all believers, especially those who have suffered for their faith, by proclaiming Christ's final victory over evil and the reality of eternal life with him. It also gives present guidance as it teaches us about Jesus Christ and how we should live for him now. Through graphic pictures we learn that (1) Jesus Christ is coming again, (2) evil will be judged, and (3) the dead will be raised to judgment, resulting in eternal life or eternal destruction.

**1:1** According to tradition, John, the author, was the only one of Jesus' original 12 disciples who was not killed for the faith. He also wrote the Gospel of John and the letters of 1, 2, and 3 John. When he wrote Revelation, John was in exile on the island of Patmos in the Aegean Sea, sent there by the Romans for his witness about Jesus Christ. For more information on John, see his Profile in John 13, p. 1783.

**1:1** This book is the revelation *from, concerning,* and *of* Jesus Christ. God gave the revelation of his plan to Jesus Christ, who, in turn, revealed it to John. The book of Revelation unveils Christ's full identity and God's plan for the end of the world, and it focuses on Jesus Christ, his second coming, his victory over evil, and the establishment of his Kingdom. As you read and study Revelation, don't focus so much on the timetable of the events or the details

of John's imagery that you miss the main message—the infinite love, power, and justice of the Lord Jesus Christ.

**1:1** The book of Revelation is *apocalyptic* (meaning uncovered, unveiled, or revealed) in style. This style of ancient literature usually featured spectacular and mysterious imagery, and such literature was written under the name of an ancient hero. John was acquainted with Jewish apocalyptic works, but his book is different in several ways: (1) He uses his own name rather than the name of an ancient hero; (2) he denounces evil and exhorts people to high Christian standards; (3) he offers hope rather than gloom. John was not a psychic attempting to predict the future; he was a prophet of God describing what God had shown him.

**1:1** For more about angels, see the note on 5:11.

**1:1** Jesus gave his message to John in a revelation (or vision), allowing John to see and record certain future events so they could be an encouragement to all believers. The vision includes many signs and symbols that convey the essence of what is to happen. What John saw, in most cases, was indescribable, so he used illustrations to show what it was *like.* When reading this symbolic language, we don't have to understand every detail—John himself didn't. Instead, realize that John's imagery shows us that Christ is indeed the glorious and victorious Lord of all.

³God blesses the one who reads the words of this prophecy to the church, and he blesses all who listen to its message and obey what it says, for the time is near.

*John's Greeting to the Seven Churches*

⁴This letter is from John to the seven churches in the province of Asia.*

Grace and peace to you from the one who is, who always was, and who is still to come; from the sevenfold Spirit* before his throne; ⁵ and from Jesus Christ. He is the faithful witness to these things, the first to rise from the dead, and the ruler of all the kings of the world.

1:4a *Asia* was a Roman province in what is now western Turkey.   1:4b Greek *the seven spirits.*

1:3
Rev 22:7, 10

1:4
Exod 3:14
Rev 1:8; 3:1; 4:5, 8;
5:6; 11:17; 16:5

1:5
Ps 89:27
Isa 40:2
Col 1:18
Rev 3:14; 19:11, 16

**THE SEVEN CHURCHES**
The seven churches were located on a major Roman road. A letter carrier would leave the island of Patmos (where John was exiled), arriving first at Ephesus. He would travel north to Smyrna and Pergamum, turn southeast to Thyatira, and continue on to Sardis, Philadelphia, and Laodicea—in the exact order in which the letters were dictated.

**1:1-3** The book of Revelation reveals future events, but there is not the gloomy pessimism we might expect. The drama of these unfolding events is spectacular, but there is nothing to fear if you are on the winning side. When you think about the future, walk with confidence because Christ, the Victor, walks with you.

**1:3** Revelation is a book of prophecy that is both *prediction* (foretelling future events) and *proclamation* (preaching about who God is and what he will do). Prophecy is more than telling the future. Behind the predictions are important principles about God's character and promises. As we read, we will get to know God better so that we can trust him completely.

**1:3** The typical news reports—filled with violence, scandal, and political haggling—are depressing, and we may wonder where the world is heading. God's plan for the future, however, provides inspiration and encouragement because we know he will intervene in history to conquer evil. John encourages churches to read this book aloud so everyone can hear it, apply it ("obey" it), and be assured of the fact that God will triumph.

**1:3** When John says that "the time is near," he is urging his readers to be ready at all times for the last judgment and the establishment of God's Kingdom. We do not know when these events will occur, but we must always be prepared. They will happen quickly, and there will be no second chance to change sides.

**1:4** Jesus told John to write to seven churches that knew and trusted him and had read his earlier letters (see 1:11). The letters were addressed so that they could be read and passed on in a

systematic fashion, following the main Roman road clockwise around the province of Asia (now called Turkey).

**1:4** The "sevenfold Spirit" is another name for the Holy Spirit. The number seven is used throughout Revelation to symbolize completeness and perfection. For more about the Holy Spirit, see the notes on John 3:6 and Acts 1:5.

**1:4-6** The Trinity—the Father ("the one who is, who always was, and who is still to come"), the Holy Spirit ("the sevenfold Spirit"), and the Son (Jesus Christ)—is the source of all truth (John 14:6, 17; 1 John 2:27; Revelation 19:11). Thus, we can be assured that John's message is reliable and is God's word to us.

**1:5** Others had risen from the dead—people whom the prophets, Jesus, and the apostles brought back to life during their ministries—but later those people died again. Jesus was the first who rose from the dead in an imperishable body (1 Corinthians 15:20), never to die again. He is the "first to rise from the dead."

**1:5, 6** Many hesitate to witness about their faith in Christ because they don't feel the change in their lives has been spectacular enough. But you qualify as a witness for Jesus because of what he has done for you, not because of what you have done for him. Christ demonstrated his great love by setting us free from our sins through his death on the cross ("freed us from our sins by shedding his blood for us"), guaranteeing us a place in his Kingdom, and making us priests to administer God's love to others. The fact that the all-powerful God has offered eternal life to you is nothing short of spectacular.

**1:5-7** Jesus is portrayed as the all-powerful King, victorious in

**1:6**
Isa 61:6
1 Pet 2:5, 9

All glory to him who loves us and has freed us from our sins by shedding his blood for us. <sup>6</sup>He has made us a Kingdom of priests for God his Father. All glory and power to him forever and ever! Amen.

**1:7**
Dan 7:13
Zech 12:10
Matt 24:30

<sup>7</sup> Look! He comes with the clouds of heaven.
    And everyone will see him—
    even those who pierced him.
And all the nations of the world
    will mourn for him.
Yes! Amen!

---

**A JOURNEY THROUGH THE BOOK OF REVELATION**
Revelation is a complex book, and it has baffled interpreters for centuries. We can avoid a great deal of confusion by understanding the literary structure of this book. This approach will allow us to understand the individual scenes within the overall structure of Revelation and keep us from getting unnecessarily bogged down in the details of each vision. John gives hints throughout the book to indicate a change of subject, or a flashback to an earlier scene.

In chapter 1, John relates the circumstances that led to the writing of this book (1:1-20). In chapters 2 and 3, Jesus gives special messages to the seven churches of Asia Minor (2:1–3:22).

Suddenly, John is caught up into heaven, where he sees a vision of God Almighty on his throne. All of Christ's followers and the heavenly angels are worshiping God (4:1-11). John watches as God gives a scroll with seven seals to the worthy Lamb, Jesus Christ (5:1-14). The Lamb begins to open the seals one by one. As each seal is opened, a new vision appears.

As the first four seals are opened, riders appear on horses of different colors: war, famine, disease, and death are in their path (6:1-8). As the fifth seal is opened, John sees those in heaven who have been martyred for their faith in Christ (6:9-11).

A set of contrasting images appears at the opening of the sixth seal. On one side, there is a great earthquake, stars fall from the sky, and the sky rolls up like a scroll (6:12-17). On the other side, multitudes are before the throne, worshiping and praising God and the Lamb (7:1-17).

Finally, the seventh seal is opened (8:1-5), unveiling a series of God's judgments announced by seven angels with seven trumpets. The first four angels bring hail, fire, a mountain of fire, and a falling star—the sun and moon are darkened (8:6-13). The fifth trumpet announces the coming of locusts with the power to sting (9:1-12). The sixth trumpet heralds the coming of an army of warriors on horses (9:13-21). In 10:1-11, John is given a small scroll to eat. Following this, John is commanded to measure the Temple of God (11:1, 2). He sees two witnesses, who proclaim God's judgment on the earth for three and a half years (11:3-14).

Finally, the seventh trumpet sounds, calling the rival forces of good and evil to the final battle. On one side is Satan and his forces; on the other side stands Jesus Christ with his forces (11:15–13:18). In the midst of this call to battle, John sees three angels announcing the final judgment (14:6-13). Two angels begin to reap this harvest of judgment on the earth (14:14-20). Following on the heels of these two angels are seven more angels, who pour out God's judgment on the earth from seven bowls (15:1–16:21). One of these angels from the group of seven reveals to John a vision of a "great prostitute" called Babylon (symbolizing the Roman Empire), riding a scarlet beast (17:1-18). After the defeat of Babylon (18:1-24), a great multitude in heaven shouts praise to God for his mighty victory (19:1-10).

The final three chapters of the book of Revelation catalog the events that finalize Christ's victory over the enemy: Satan's 1,000-year imprisonment (20:1-10), the final judgment (20:11-15), and the creation of a new earth and a new Jerusalem (21:1–22:6). An angel then gives John final instructions concerning the visions John has seen and what to do once he has written them all down (22:7-11).

Revelation concludes with the promise of Christ's soon return, an offer to drink of the water of life that flows through the great street of the new Jerusalem, and a warning to those who read the book (22:12-21). May we pray with John, "Amen! Come, Lord Jesus!" (22:20).

The Bible ends with a message of warning and hope for men and women of every generation. Christ is victorious, and all evil has been done away with. As you read the book of Revelation, marvel at God's grace in the salvation of the saints and his power over the evil forces of Satan, and remember the hope of this victory to come.

---

battle, glorious in peace. He is not just a humble earthly teacher, he is the glorious God. When you read John's description of the vision, keep in mind that his words are not just good advice; they are truth from the King of kings. Don't just read his words for their interesting and amazing portrayal of the future. Let the truth about Christ penetrate your life, deepen your faith in him, and strengthen your commitment to follow him no matter what the cost.

**1:7** John is announcing the return of Jesus to earth (see also Matthew 24; Mark 13; 1 Thessalonians 4:15-18). Jesus' second coming will be visible and victorious. All people will see him arrive (Mark 13:26), and they will *know* it is Jesus. When he

comes, he will conquer evil and judge all people according to their deeds (20:11-15).

**1:7** "Those who pierced him" could refer to the Roman soldiers who pierced Jesus' side as he hung on the cross or to the Jews who were responsible for his death. John saw Jesus' death with his own eyes, and he never forgot the horror of it (see John 19:34, 35; see also Zechariah 12:10).

8"I am the Alpha and the Omega—the beginning and the end,"* says the Lord God. "I am the one who is, who always was, and who is still to come—the Almighty One."

**1:8**
Amos 3:13; 4:13

### Vision of the Son of Man

9 I, John, am your brother and your partner in suffering and in God's Kingdom and in the patient endurance to which Jesus calls us. I was exiled to the island of Patmos for preaching the word of God and for my testimony about Jesus. 10 It was the Lord's Day, and I was worshiping in the Spirit.* Suddenly, I heard behind me a loud voice like a trumpet blast. 11 It said, "Write in a book* everything you see, and send it to the seven churches in the cities of Ephesus, Smyrna, Pergamum, Thyatira, Sardis, Philadelphia, and Laodicea."

**1:9**
Phil 4:14
2 Tim 2:12

**1:11**
Rev 1:2, 19; 2:1,
18, 24; 3:1, 7, 14

12 When I turned to see who was speaking to me, I saw seven gold lampstands. 13 And standing in the middle of the lampstands was someone like the Son of Man.* He was wearing a long robe with a gold sash across his chest. 14 His head and his hair were white like wool, as white as snow. And his eyes were like flames of fire. 15 His feet were like polished bronze refined in a furnace, and his voice thundered like mighty ocean waves. 16 He held seven stars in his right hand, and a sharp two-edged sword came from his mouth. And his face was like the sun in all its brilliance.

**1:12**
Zech 4:2

**1:13**
Dan 7:13; 10:5

**1:14**
Dan 7:9; 10:6

**1:15**
Ezek 1:24; 43:2

**1:16**
Isa 49:2

17 When I saw him, I fell at his feet as if I were dead. But he laid his right hand on me and said, "Don't be afraid! I am the First and the Last. 18 I am the living one. I died, but look—I am alive forever and ever! And I hold the keys of death and the grave.*

**1:17**
Isa 44:6; 48:12
Dan 8:18

19 "Write down what you have seen—both the things that are now happening and the things that will happen.* 20 This is the meaning of the mystery of the seven stars you saw in my right hand and the seven gold lampstands: The seven stars are the angels* of the seven churches, and the seven lampstands are the seven churches.

**1:19**
Isa 48:6
Rev 1:1

**1:20**
Rev 1:4, 12, 16;
2:1; 3:1

**1:8** Greek *I am the Alpha and the Omega*, referring to the first and last letters of the Greek alphabet. **1:10** Or *in spirit*. **1:11** Or *on a scroll*. **1:13** Or *like a son of man*. See Dan 7:13. "Son of Man" is a title Jesus used for himself. **1:18** Greek *and Hades*. **1:19** Or *what you have seen and what they mean—the things that have already begun to happen*. **1:20** Or *the messengers*.

---

**1:8** Alpha and omega are the first and last letters of the Greek alphabet. The Lord God is the beginning and the end. God the Father is the eternal Lord and Ruler of the past, present, and future (see also 4:8; Isaiah 44:6; 48:12-15). Without him you have nothing that is eternal, nothing that can change your life, nothing that can save you from sin. Is the Lord your reason for living, "the Alpha and the Omega" of your life? Honor the one who is the beginning and the end of all existence, wisdom, and power.

**1:9** Patmos was a small rocky island in the Aegean Sea, about 50 miles offshore from the city of Ephesus on the Asia Minor seacoast (see map).

**1:9** The Christian church was facing severe persecution. Almost all believers were socially, politically, or economically suffering because of this empire-wide persecution, and some were even being killed for their faith. John was exiled to Patmos because he refused to stop preaching the Good News. We may not face persecution for our faith as the early Christians did, but even with our freedom few of us have the courage to share God's Word with others. If we hesitate to share our faith during easy times, how will we do during times of persecution?

**1:12, 13** The seven gold lampstands are the seven churches in Asia (1:11, 20), and Jesus stands among them. No matter what the churches face, Jesus protects them with his all-encompassing love and reassuring power. Through his Spirit, Jesus Christ is still among the churches today. When a church faces persecution, it should remember Christ's deep love and compassion. When a church is troubled by internal strife and conflict, it should remember Christ's concern for purity and his intolerance of sin.

**1:13, 14** This "Son of Man" is Jesus himself. The title *Son of Man* occurs many times in the New Testament in reference to Jesus as the Messiah. John recognized Jesus because he lived with him for three years and had seen him both as the Galilean preacher and as the glorified Son of God at the Transfiguration (Matthew 17:1-8). Here Jesus appears as the mighty Son of Man. His white hair indicates his wisdom and divine nature (see also Daniel 7:9); his bright eyes symbolize judgment of all evil; the gold sash across his chest reveals him as the High Priest, who

goes into God's presence to obtain forgiveness of sin for those who have believed in him.

Revelation will challenge your mental picture of Jesus Christ. What forms your impression of him right now—famous paintings, movies, Sunday school art? Do you ever picture Jesus with a gold sash and snow white, woolly hair? Do his eyes flash fire and his feet glow like bronze? When you imagine Jesus speaking to you, does his voice thunder like mighty ocean waves? Reevaluate the way you think of Jesus as you read and study Revelation. Allow his powerful presence to transform your life.

**1:16** The sword in Jesus' mouth symbolizes the power and force of his message. His words of judgment are as sharp as swords (Isaiah 49:2; Hebrews 4:12).

**1:17, 18** As the Roman government stepped up its persecution of Christians, John must have wondered if the church could survive and stand against the opposition. But Jesus appeared in glory and splendor, reassuring John that he and his fellow believers had access to God's strength to face these trials. If you are facing difficult problems, remember that the power available to John and the early church is also available to you (see 1 John 4:4).

**1:17, 18** Our sins have convicted and sentenced us, but Jesus holds the keys of death and the grave. He alone can free us from eternal bondage to Satan. He alone has the power and authority to set us free from sin's control. Believers don't have to fear death or the grave because Christ holds the keys to both. All we must do is turn from sin and turn to him in faith. When we attempt to control our lives and disregard God, we set a course that leads directly to hell. But when we place our life in Christ's hands, he restores us now and resurrects us later to an eternal, peaceful relationship with him.

**1:20** Who are the "angels of the seven churches"? Some say that they are angels designated to guard the churches; others say that they are elders or pastors of the local churches. Because the seven letters in chapters 2 and 3 contain reprimands, it is doubtful that these angels are heavenly messengers. If these are earthly leaders or messengers, they are accountable to God for the churches they represent.

## The Message to the Church in Ephesus

**2:1**
Rev 1:12-16, 20;
3:1

**2** "Write this letter to the angel* of the church in Ephesus. This is the message from the one who holds the seven stars in his right hand, the one who walks among the seven gold lampstands:

**2:2**
2 Cor 11:13
1 Jn 4:1
Rev 2:19

2"I know all the things you do. I have seen your hard work and your patient endurance. I know you don't tolerate evil people. You have examined the claims of those who say they are apostles but are not. You have discovered they are liars. 3You have patiently

**2:3**
John 15:21

suffered for me without quitting.

**2:4**
Jer 2:2
Matt 24:12

4"But I have this complaint against you. You don't love me or each other as you did

**2:1** Or *the messenger;* also in 2:8, 12, 18.

---

**THE NAMES OF JESUS IN REVELATION**

| Reference | Jesus' Name | Reference | Jesus' Name |
|---|---|---|---|
| 1:13 | The Son of Man | 12:10 | Christ |
| 1:17 | The First and the Last | 19:11 | Faithful and True |
| 1:18 | The living one | 19:13 | The Word of God |
| 2:18 | The Son of God | 19:16 | King over all kings |
| 3:14 | The faithful and true witness | 19:16 | Lord over all lords |
| 5:5 | The Lion of the tribe of Judah | 22:13 | The Alpha and the Omega |
| 5:5 | The heir to David's throne | 22:13 | The Beginning and the End |
| 5:6 | Lamb | 22:16 | The bright morning star |
| 7:17 | Shepherd | | |

Scattered among the vivid images of the book of Revelation is a large collection of names for Jesus. Each one tells something of his character and highlights a particular aspect of his role within God's plan of redemption.

---

**2:1** Ephesus was the capital of Asia Minor, a center of land and sea trade, and, along with Alexandria and Antioch in Syria, one of the three most influential cities in the eastern part of the Roman Empire. The temple to Artemis, one of the ancient wonders of the world, was located in this city, and a major industry was the manufacture of images of this goddess (see Acts 19:21-41). Paul ministered in Ephesus for three years and warned the Ephesians that false teachers would come and try to draw people away from the faith (see Acts 20:29-31). False teachers did indeed cause problems in the Ephesian church, but the church resisted them, as we can see from Paul's letter to the Ephesians. John spent much of his ministry in this city and knew that they had resisted false teaching (2:2).

**2:1** The one who "walks among the seven gold lampstands" (the seven churches) is Jesus (1:11-13). He holds the "seven stars in his right hand" (messengers of the churches), indicating his power and authority over the churches and their leaders. Ephesus had become a large, proud church, and Jesus' message would remind them that he alone is the head of the body of believers.

**2:1ff** Does God care about your church? If you are tempted to doubt it, look more closely at these seven letters. The Lord of the universe knew each of these churches and its precise situation. In each letter, Jesus told John to write about specific people, places, and events. He praised believers for their successes and told them how to correct their failures. Just as Jesus cared for each of these churches, he cares for yours. He wants it to reach its greatest potential. The group of believers with whom you worship and serve is God's vehicle for changing the world. Take it seriously—God does.

**2:2** Over a long period of time, the church in Ephesus had steadfastly refused to tolerate sin among its members. This was not easy in a city noted for immoral sexual practices associated with the worship of the goddess Artemis. We also are living in times of widespread sin and sexual immorality. It is popular to be open-minded toward many types of sin, calling them personal choices

or alternative lifestyles. But when the body of believers begins to tolerate sin in the church, it is lowering the standards and compromising the church's witness. Remember that God's approval is infinitely more important than the world's. Use God's Word, not what people around you are willing to accept, to set the standards for what is right or wrong.

**2:2, 3** Christ commended the church at Ephesus for (1) working hard, (2) patiently enduring, (3) not tolerating evil people, (4) critically examining the claims of false apostles, and (5) suffering without quitting. Every church should have these characteristics. But these good efforts should spring from our love for Jesus Christ. Both Jesus and John stressed love for one another as an authentic proof of the Good News (John 13:34; 1 John 3:18, 19). In the battle to maintain sound teaching and moral and doctrinal purity, it is possible to lose a charitable spirit. Prolonged conflict can weaken or destroy our patience and affection. In defending the faith, guard against any structure or rigidity that weakens love.

**2:4** Paul had once commended the church at Ephesus for its love for God and others (Ephesians 1:15), but many of the church founders had died, and many of the second-generation believers had lost their zeal for God. They were a busy church—the members did much to benefit themselves and the community—but they were acting out of the wrong motives. Work for God must be motivated by love for God, or it will not last.

**2:4, 5** Just as when a man and woman fall in love, so also new believers rejoice at their newfound forgiveness. But when we lose sight of the seriousness of sin, we begin to lose the thrill of our forgiveness (see 2 Peter 1:9). In the first steps of your Christian life, you may have had enthusiasm without knowledge. Do you now have knowledge without enthusiasm? Both are necessary if we are to keep love for God intense and untarnished (see Hebrews 10:32, 35). Do you love God with the same fervor as when you were a new Christian?

at first!\*5 Look how far you have fallen! Turn back to me and do the works you did at first. If you don't repent, I will come and remove your lampstand from its place among the churches.6 But this is in your favor: You hate the evil deeds of the Nicolaitans, just as I do.

7 "Anyone with ears to hear must listen to the Spirit and understand what he is saying to the churches. To everyone who is victorious I will give fruit from the tree of life in the paradise of God.

**2:5**
Rev 2:16, 22;
3:3, 19
**2:6**
Ps 139:21
**2:7**
Gen 2:8-9; 3:22-24
Ezek 31:8-9

### The Message to the Church in Smyrna

8 "Write this letter to the angel of the church in Smyrna. This is the message from the one who is the First and the Last, who was dead but is now alive:

9 "I know about your suffering and your poverty—but you are rich! I know the blasphemy of those opposing you. They say they are Jews, but they are not, because their synagogue belongs to Satan. 10 Don't be afraid of what you are about to suffer. The devil will throw some of you into prison to test you. You will suffer for ten days. But if you remain faithful even when facing death, I will give you the crown of life.

11 "Anyone with ears to hear must listen to the Spirit and understand what he is saying to the churches. Whoever is victorious will not be harmed by the second death.

**2:8**
Rev 1:11, 17-18
**2:9**
2 Cor 6:10;
11:14-15
Rev 3:9
**2:10**
Dan 1:12, 14
Jas 1:12
Rev 3:9; 17:14
**2:11**
Rev 2:7; 20:6, 14

### The Message to the Church in Pergamum

12 "Write this letter to the angel of the church in Pergamum. This is the message from the one with the sharp two-edged sword:

**2:12**
Rev 1:16; 2:16

**2:4** Greek *You have lost your first love.*

---

**2:5** For Jesus to "remove your lampstand from its place" would mean the church would cease to be an effective church. Just as the seven-branched candlestick in the Temple gave light for the priests to see, the churches were to give light to their surrounding communities. But Jesus warned them that their lights could go out. In fact, Jesus himself would extinguish any light that did not fulfill its purpose. The church needed to repent of its sins.

**2:6** The Nicolaitans were believers who compromised their faith in order to enjoy some of the sinful practices of Ephesian society. The name *Nicolaitans* is held by some to be roughly the Greek equivalent of the Hebrew word for "Balaamites." Balaam was a prophet who had induced the Israelites to carry out their lustful desires (see 2:14 and Numbers 31:16). When we want to take part in an activity that we know is wrong, we may make excuses to justify our behavior, saying that it isn't as bad as it seems or that it won't hurt our faith. Christ has strong words for those who look for excuses to sin.

**2:6** Through John, Jesus commended the church at Ephesus for hating the wicked practices of the Nicolaitans. Note that they didn't hate the people, just their sinful actions. We should accept and love all people but refuse to tolerate any evil. God cannot tolerate sin, and he expects us to stand against it. The world needs Christians who will stand for God's truth and point people toward right living.

**2:7** Two trees had been in the Garden of Eden—the tree of life and the tree of the knowledge of good and evil (see Genesis 2:9). Eating from the tree of life brought eternal life with God; eating from the tree of knowledge brought realization of good and evil. When Adam and Eve ate from the tree of knowledge, they disobeyed God's command. So they were excluded from Eden and barred from eating from the tree of life. Eventually, evil will be destroyed and believers will be brought into a restored paradise. In the new earth, everyone will eat from the tree of life and live forever.

**2:8** The city of Smyrna was about 25 miles north of Ephesus. It was nicknamed "Port of Asia" because it had an excellent harbor on the Aegean Sea. The church in this city struggled against two hostile forces: a Jewish population strongly opposed to Christianity, and a non-Jewish population that was loyal to Rome and supported emperor worship. Persecution and suffering were inevitable in an environment like this.

**2:9, 10** Persecution comes from Satan, not from God. Satan, the devil, will cause believers to be thrown into prison and even killed.

But believers need not fear death, because it will only result in their receiving the crown of life. Satan may harm their earthly bodies, but he can do them no spiritual harm. That their "synagogue belongs to Satan" means that these Jews were serving Satan's purposes, not God's, when they gathered to worship. "Ten days" means that although persecution would be intense, it would be relatively short. It would have a definite beginning and end, and God would remain in complete control.

**2:9-11** Pain is part of life, but it is never easy to suffer, no matter what the cause. Jesus commended the church at Smyrna for its faith in suffering. He then encouraged the believers that they need not fear the future if they remained faithful. If you are experiencing difficult times, don't let them turn you away from God. Instead, let them draw you toward greater faithfulness. Trust God and remember your heavenly reward (see also 22:12-14).

**2:10** Smyrna was famous for its athletic games. A crown was the victory wreath, the trophy for the champion at the games. If we have been faithful, we will receive the prize of victory—eternal life (James 1:12). The message to the Smyrna church was to remain faithful during suffering because God is in control and his promises are reliable. Jesus never says that by being faithful to him we will avoid troubles, suffering, and persecution. Rather, we must be faithful to him *in* our sufferings. Only then will our faith prove to be genuine. We remain faithful by keeping our eyes on Christ and on what he promises us now and in the future (see Philippians 3:13, 14; 2 Timothy 4:8).

**2:11** Believers and unbelievers alike experience physical death. All people will be resurrected, but believers will be resurrected to eternal life with God while unbelievers will be resurrected to be punished with a second death, eternal separation from God (see also 20:14; 21:8, 27; 22:15).

**2:12** The city of Pergamum was built on a hill 1,000 feet above the surrounding countryside, creating a natural fortress. It was a sophisticated city, a center of Greek culture and education, with a 200,000-volume library. But it was also the center of four cults, and it rivaled Ephesus in its worship of idols. The city's chief god was Asclepius, whose symbol was a serpent and who was considered the god of healing. People came to Pergamum from all over the world to seek healing from this god.

**2:12** Just as the Romans used their swords for authority and judgment, Jesus' sharp two-edged sword represents God's ultimate authority and judgment. It may also represent God's future

**2:13**
Rev 14:12

13 "I know that you live in the city where Satan has his throne, yet you have remained loyal to me. You refused to deny me even when Antipas, my faithful witness, was martyred among you there in Satan's city.

**2:14**
Num 31:16
1 Cor 6:13
2 Pet 2:15
Jude 1:11

14 "But I have a few complaints against you. You tolerate some among you whose teaching is like that of Balaam, who showed Balak how to trip up the people of Israel. He taught them to sin by eating food offered to idols and by committing sexual sin. 15 In a similar way, you have some Nicolaitans among you who follow the same teaching. 16 Repent of your sin, or I will come to you suddenly and fight against them with the sword of my mouth.

**2:15**
Rev 2:6

**2:16**
2 Thes 2:8
Rev 1:16; 2:5;
22:7, 12, 20

17 "Anyone with ears to hear must listen to the Spirit and understand what he is saying to the churches. To everyone who is victorious I will give some of the manna that has been hidden away in heaven. And I will give to each one a white stone, and on the stone will be engraved a new name that no one understands except the one who receives it.

**2:17**
Ps 78:24
Isa 62:2; 65:15
John 6:49-58
Rev 3:12; 19:12

### The Message to the Church in Thyatira

**2:18**
Dan 10:6
Rev 1:14-15

18 "Write this letter to the angel of the church in Thyatira. This is the message from the Son of God, whose eyes are like flames of fire, whose feet are like polished bronze:

**THE LETTERS TO THE SEVEN CHURCHES**

| Church | Reference | Commendation | Rebuke | Action |
|---|---|---|---|---|
| Ephesus | 2:1-7 | Hard work, endurance | They do not love as at first | Remember and repent |
| Smyrna | 2:8-11 | Suffered persecution, poverty | None | Don't fear; be faithful |
| Pergamum | 2:12-17 | Remained loyal | Tolerate compromise | Repent |
| Thyatira | 2:18-29 | Love, faith, service, endurance | Tolerate immorality | Repent |
| Sardis | 3:1-6 | Effective | Superficial | Wake up; repent |
| Philadelphia | 3:7-13 | Faithful | None | Hold on |
| Laodicea | 3:14-22 | None | Lukewarm | Be diligent and repent |

This summary of the letters to the seven churches shows us the qualities our churches should seek and those we should avoid.

separation of believers from unbelievers. Unbelievers cannot experience the eternal rewards of living in God's Kingdom.

**2:13** As the center for four idolatrous cults (Zeus, Dionysius, Asclepius, and Athene), Pergamum was called the city "where Satan has his throne." Surrounded by worship of Satan and the Roman emperor as god, the church at Pergamum refused to renounce its faith, even when Satan's worshipers martyred one of its members. Standing firm against the strong pressures and temptations of society is never easy, but the alternative is deadly (2:11).

**2:13-15** It was not easy to be a Christian in Pergamum. Believers experienced great pressure to compromise or leave the faith. (For information on the Nicolaitans, see the first note on 2:6.) Nothing is known about Antipas except that he did *not* compromise. He was faithful, and he died for his faith. Apparently, however, some in the church were tolerating those who taught or practiced what Christ opposed. Compromise can be defined as a blending of the qualities of two different things or a concession of principles. Cooperate with people as much as you can, but avoid any alliance, partnership, or participation that could lead to immoral practices.

**2:14** There is room for differences of opinion among Christians in some areas, but there is no room for heresy and moral impurity. Your town might not participate in idol feasts, but it probably has pornography, sexual sin, cheating, gossiping, and lying. Don't tolerate sin by bowing to the pressure to be open-minded.

**2:14-16** Balak was a king who feared the large number of Israelites traveling through his country, so he hired Balaam to pronounce a curse on them. Balaam refused at first to do it, but an offer of

money made him willing (Numbers 22–24). Later Balaam influenced the Israelites to turn to idol worship (Numbers 31:16; also see 2 Peter 2:15; Jude 1:11). Here Christ rebuked the church for tolerating those who, like Balaam, lead people away from God.

**2:16** This sword is God's judgment against rebellious nations (19:15, 21) and all forms of sin. See also the note on 1:16 and the second note on 2:12.

**2:17** This "manna that has been hidden away in heaven" suggests the spiritual nourishment that the faithful believers will receive. As the Israelites traveled toward the Promised Land, God provided manna from heaven for their physical nourishment (Exodus 16:13-18). Jesus, as the bread of life (John 6:51), provides spiritual nourishment that satisfies our deepest hunger.

**2:17** It is unclear what the white stones are or exactly what the name on each will be. Because they relate to the hidden manna, they may be symbols of the believer's eternal nourishment or eternal life. The stones are significant because each will bear the new name of every person who truly believes in Christ. They are the evidence that a person has been accepted by God and declared worthy to receive eternal life. A person's name represented his or her character. God will give us a new name and a new heart.

**2:18** Thyatira was a working person's town, with many trade guilds for cloth making, dyeing, and pottery. Lydia, Paul's first convert in Philippi, was a merchant from Thyatira (Acts 16:14). The city was basically secular, with no focus on any particular religion.

19"I know all the things you do. I have seen your love, your faith, your service, and your patient endurance. And I can see your constant improvement in all these things.

20"But I have this complaint against you. You are permitting that woman—that Jezebel who calls herself a prophet—to lead my servants astray. She teaches them to commit sexual sin and to eat food offered to idols. 21I gave her time to repent, but she does not want to turn away from her immorality.

22"Therefore, I will throw her on a bed of suffering,* and those who commit adultery with her will suffer greatly unless they repent and turn away from her evil deeds. 23I will strike her children dead. Then all the churches will know that I am the one who searches out the thoughts and intentions of every person. And I will give to each of you whatever you deserve.

24"But I also have a message for the rest of you in Thyatira who have not followed this false teaching ('deeper truths,' as they call them—depths of Satan, actually). I will ask nothing more of you 25except that you hold tightly to what you have until I come. 26To all who are victorious, who obey me to the very end,

To them I will give authority over all the nations.
27 They will rule the nations with an iron rod
    and smash them like clay pots.*

28They will have the same authority I received from my Father, and I will also give them the morning star!

29"Anyone with ears to hear must listen to the Spirit and understand what he is saying to the churches.

### The Message to the Church in Sardis

**3** "Write this letter to the angel* of the church in Sardis. This is the message from the one who has the sevenfold Spirit* of God and the seven stars:

| | |
|---|---|
| **2:19** | Rev 2:2 |
| **2:20** | 1 Kgs 16:31 |
| | 2 Kgs 9:7, 22 |
| **2:21** | Rev 9:20 |
| **2:22** | Rev 17:2 |
| **2:23** | Prov 24:12 |
| | Jer 17:10 |
| | Matt 16:27 |
| | Luke 16:15 |
| | Rom 8:27 |
| **2:25** | Rev 3:11 |
| **2:26-27** | Ps 2:8-9 |
| | Matt 10:22 |
| | Rev 12:5 |
| **2:28** | Rev 22:16 |
| **2:29** | Rev 2:7 |
| **3:1** | Rev 1:4, 11, 16; 3:8, 15 |

**2:22** Greek *a bed.*   **2:26-27** Ps 2:8-9 (Greek Version).   **3:1a** Or *the messenger;* also in 3:7, 14.   **3:1b** Greek *the seven spirits.*

**2:19** The believers in Thyatira were commended for growing in good deeds. We should not only take comfort in gathering for worship or rejoice when people give their lives to Christ in our church. We should also seek to grow in love, faith, and acts of service. Because the times are critical, we must spend our days wisely and faithfully.

**2:20** A woman in the church in Thyatira was teaching that immorality was not a serious matter for believers. Her name may have been Jezebel, or John may have used the name Jezebel to symbolize the kind of evil she was promoting. Jezebel, a pagan queen of Israel, was considered the most evil woman who ever lived (see 1 Kings 19:1, 2; 21:1-15; 2 Kings 9:7-10, 30-37; and her Profile in 1 Kings 20, p. 553).

**2:20** Why is sexual immorality serious? Sex outside marriage always hurts someone. It hurts God because it shows that we prefer to satisfy our desires our own way instead of according to God's Word or to satisfy them immediately instead of waiting for his timing. It hurts others because it violates the commitment so necessary to a relationship. It hurts us because it often brings disease to our bodies and adversely affects our personalities. Sexual immorality has tremendous power to destroy families, churches, and communities because it destroys the integrity on which these relationships are built. God wants to protect us from hurting ourselves and others; thus, we are to have no part in sexual immorality, even if our culture accepts it.

**2:20** In pagan temples, meat was often offered to idols. Then the meat that wasn't burned was sold to shoppers in the temple marketplace. Eating food offered to idols wasn't wrong in itself, but it could violate the conscience of weaker Christian brothers and sisters who would be bothered by it (see 1 Corinthians 8 and the note on Romans 14:2). Jezebel was obviously more concerned about her own selfish pleasure and freedom than about the needs and concerns of fellow believers.

**2:21** Jezebel was unwilling to repent. *Repent* means "to change one's mind and to turn from sin" and its disastrous consequences

to God and eternal life. In his mercy, God has given us time to decide to follow him. Only our stubborn willfulness stands in the way.

**2:23** We cannot hide from Christ; he knows what is in our heart and mind, and still he loves us. The sins we try to hide from God need to be confessed to him.

**2:24, 25** The "deeper truths" of Satan were either false teachings advocated by heretics, or secret insights by so-called believers "guaranteed" to promote deeper spiritual life. What was the appeal of such teaching? It may have been appealing to hear that what happens in the body is inconsequential; therefore, it is not sinful to fulfill sexual desires outside of marriage. Another appeal to the "deep things" may have been the sense of pride that such knowledge stimulated in those seeking it. We should hold tightly to the basics of our Christian faith and view with extreme caution any new teaching that turns us away from the Bible, the fellowship of our church, or our basic confession of faith.

**2:26, 27** Christ says that those who are victorious (those who remain faithful until the end and continue to please God) will rule over Christ's enemies and reign with him as he judges evil (see also Psalm 2:8, 9; Isaiah 30:14; Jeremiah 19:11; 1 Corinthians 6:2, 3; Revelation 12:5; 19:15; 20:3, 4 for more about God's judgment).

**2:28** Christ is also called the morning star in 22:16. A morning star appears just before dawn, when the night is coldest and darkest. When the world is at its bleakest point, Christ will burst onto the scene, exposing evil with his light of truth and bringing his promised reward.

**3:1** The wealthy city of Sardis was actually in two locations. The older section of the city was on a mountain, and when its population outgrew the spot, a newer section was built in the valley below.

**3:1** The "sevenfold Spirit" is another name for the Holy Spirit. The seven stars are the messengers, or leaders, of the churches (see the note on 2:1).

**3:1** The problem in the Sardis church was not heresy but spiritual death. In spite of its reputation for being active, Sardis was infested

**3:3**
Matt 24:42-44
Luke 22:32
1 Thes 5:2-6
2 Pet 3:10
Rev 2:5; 16:15

**3:4**
Jude 1:23

**3:5**
Exod 32:32-33
Ps 69:28
Matt 10:32
Luke 12:8
Rev 13:8; 17:8;
20:12

**3:6**
Rev 2:7

**3:7**
Job 12:14
Isa 22:22
Matt 16:19

**3:8**
Acts 14:27
Rev 2:13

**3:9**
Isa 43:4; 49:23
2 Cor 11:14-15
Rev 2:9

**3:10**
2 Pet 2:9
Rev 2:10

**3:11**
Rev 2:25;
22:7,12, 20

**3:12**
Ezek 48:35
Gal 4:26
Rev 21:2, 10

"I know all the things you do, and that you have a reputation for being alive—but you are dead. 2Wake up! Strengthen what little remains, for even what is left is almost dead. I find that your actions do not meet the requirements of my God. 3Go back to what you heard and believed at first; hold to it firmly. Repent and turn to me again. If you don't wake up, I will come to you suddenly, as unexpected as a thief.

4"Yet there are some in the church in Sardis who have not soiled their clothes with evil. They will walk with me in white, for they are worthy. 5All who are victorious will be clothed in white. I will never erase their names from the Book of Life, but I will announce before my Father and his angels that they are mine.

6"Anyone with ears to hear must listen to the Spirit and understand what he is saying to the churches.

### The Message to the Church in Philadelphia

7"Write this letter to the angel of the church in Philadelphia.

This is the message from the one who is holy and true,
    the one who has the key of David.
What he opens, no one can close;
    and what he closes, no one can open:*

8"I know all the things you do, and I have opened a door for you that no one can close. You have little strength, yet you obeyed my word and did not deny me. 9Look, I will force those who belong to Satan's synagogue—those liars who say they are Jews but are not—to come and bow down at your feet. They will acknowledge that you are the ones I love.

10"Because you have obeyed my command to persevere, I will protect you from the great time of testing that will come upon the whole world to test those who belong to this world. 11I am coming soon.* Hold on to what you have, so that no one will take away your crown. 12All who are victorious will become pillars in the Temple of my God,

**3:7** Isa 22:22.   **3:11** Or *suddenly,* or *quickly.*

with sin. Its deeds were evil, and its clothes soiled. The Spirit has no words of commendation for this church that looked so good on the outside but was so corrupt on the inside.

Even though Christ called Sardis a dead church, he also affirmed the handful of people who were faithful believers. Christ loves to defeat death. If you find yourself in a dead church, make sure you preserve your own faithfulness. Ask God to intervene. Ask God to help you find other believers, and pray together for an awakening of your church.

**3:3** The church at Sardis was urged to go back to what they first heard and believed, to get back to the basics of the faith. It is important to grow in our knowledge of the Lord, to deepen our understanding through careful study. But no matter how much we learn, we must never abandon the basic truths. No new truth from God will ever contradict these fundamental biblical teachings.

The church was also told to wake up. Their wealth and comfort had lulled them to sleep. Their self-satisfaction caused them to die spiritually. Not only had they wandered from the apostles' teaching, but they were no longer growing in faith or evangelism. They lacked compassionate service to others and had no unity or love. Are you watchful and alert? If God has given you a place of responsibility to teach, lead, or serve, use that position to encourage those around you to be spiritually awake and morally prepared.

**3:5** To be "clothed in white" means to be set apart for God and made pure. Christ promises future honor and eternal life to those who stand firm in their faith. The names of all believers are registered in the Book of Life. This book symbolizes God's knowledge of who belongs to him. All such people are guaranteed a listing in the Book of Life and are introduced to the hosts of heaven as belonging to Christ (see Luke 12:8, 9).

**3:7** Philadelphia was founded by the citizens of Pergamum. The community was built in a frontier area as a gateway to the central plateau of Asia Minor. Philadelphia's residents kept barbarians out

of the region and brought in Greek culture and language. The city was destroyed by an earthquake in A.D. 17, and aftershocks kept the people so worried that most of them lived outside the city limits.

**3:7** The "key of David" represents Christ's authority to open the door into his future Kingdom. After the door is opened, no one can close it—salvation is assured. Once it is closed, no one can open it—judgment is certain.

**3:10** Some believe that "I will protect you from the great time of testing" means there will be a future time of great tribulation from which true believers will be spared. Others interpret this to mean that the church will go through the time of tribulation and that God will keep them strong in the midst of it. Still others believe this refers to times of great distress in general, the church's suffering through the ages. We cannot interpret from this verse when or for how long Christians will experience the "great time of testing." Today, millions of Christians are suffering and dying at the hands of godless tyrants throughout the world. To them, the time of testing has already begun. Whenever Christians suffer, Christ promises protection of their eternal souls (see Luke 21:17-19).

**3:11** Christians have differing gifts, abilities, experience, and maturity. God doesn't expect us all to be and act the same, but he does expect us to "hold on" to what we have, to persevere in using our resources for him. The Philadelphians are commended for their effort to obey (3:8) and encouraged to hold tightly to whatever strength they have. You may be a new believer and feel that your faith and spiritual strength are little. Use what you have to live for Christ, and God will commend you.

**3:12** The new Jerusalem is the future dwelling of the people of God (21:2). We will have a new citizenship in God's future Kingdom. Everything will be new, pure, and secure.

and they will never have to leave it. And I will write on them the name of my God, and they will be citizens in the city of my God—the new Jerusalem that comes down from heaven from my God. And I will also write on them my new name.

¹³ "Anyone with ears to hear must listen to the Spirit and understand what he is saying to the churches.

**3:13**
Rev 2:7

### The Message to the Church in Laodicea

¹⁴ "Write this letter to the angel of the church in Laodicea. This is the message from the one who is the Amen—the faithful and true witness, the beginning* of God's new creation:

**3:14**
John 1:3
2 Cor 1:20
Col 1:15-18
Rev 1:5

¹⁵ "I know all the things you do, that you are neither hot nor cold. I wish that you were one or the other!¹⁶ But since you are like lukewarm water, neither hot nor cold, I will spit you out of my mouth!¹⁷ You say, 'I am rich. I have everything I want. I don't need a thing!' And you don't realize that you are wretched and miserable and poor and blind and naked.¹⁸ So I advise you to buy gold from me—gold that has been purified by fire. Then you will be rich. Also buy white garments from me so you will not be shamed by your nakedness, and ointment for your eyes so you will be able to see.¹⁹ I correct and discipline everyone I love. So be diligent and turn from your indifference.

**3:15**
Rom 12:11

**3:17**
Hos 12:8
Zech 11:5
1 Cor 4:8

**3:19**
Prov 3:12
1 Cor 11:32
Heb 12:6
Rev 2:5

²⁰ "Look! I stand at the door and knock. If you hear my voice and open the door, I will come in, and we will share a meal together as friends.²¹ Those who are victorious will sit with me on my throne, just as I was victorious and sat with my Father on his throne.

**3:20**
John 14:23

**3:21**
Matt 19:28
Rev 5:5

²² "Anyone with ears to hear must listen to the Spirit and understand what he is saying to the churches."

**3:22**
Rev 2:7

**3:14** Or *the ruler,* or *the source.*

---

**3:15** Laodicea was the wealthiest of the seven cities, known for its banking industry, manufacture of wool, and a medical school that produced eye ointment. But the city had always had a problem with its water supply. At one time an aqueduct was built to bring water to the city from hot springs. But by the time the water reached the city, it was neither hot nor refreshingly cool—only lukewarm. The church had become as bland as the tepid water that came into the city.

**3:16** Lukewarm water makes a disgusting drink. The church in Laodicea had become lukewarm and thus distasteful and repugnant. The believers didn't take a stand for anything; indifference had led to idleness. By neglecting to do anything for Christ, the church had become hardened and self-satisfied, and it was destroying itself. There is nothing more disgusting than a half-hearted, nominal Christian who is self-sufficient. Don't settle for following God halfway. Let Christ fire up your faith and get you into the action.

**3:17** Some believers assume that numerous material possessions are a sign of God's spiritual blessing. Laodicea was a wealthy city, and the church was also wealthy. But what the Laodiceans could see and buy had become more valuable to them than what is unseen and eternal. Wealth, luxury, and ease can make people feel confident, satisfied, and complacent. But no matter how much you possess or how much money you make, you have nothing if you don't have a vital relationship with Christ. How does your current level of wealth affect your spiritual desire? Instead of centering your life primarily on comfort and luxury, find your true riches in Christ.

**3:18** Laodicea was known for its great wealth; Christ told the Laodiceans to buy their gold from him (real spiritual treasures). The city was proud of its cloth and dyeing industries; Christ told them to buy white garments from him (his righteousness). Laodicea prided itself on its precious eye ointment that healed

many eye problems; Christ told them to buy ointment for their eyes so they could see the truth (John 9:39). Christ was showing the Laodiceans that true value was not in material possessions but in a right relationship with God. Their possessions and achievements were valueless compared with the everlasting future of Christ's Kingdom.

**3:19** God would discipline this lukewarm church unless it turned from its indifference toward him. God's purpose in discipline is not to punish but to bring people back to him. Are you lukewarm in your devotion to God? God may discipline you to help you out of your uncaring attitude, but he uses only loving discipline. You can avoid God's discipline by drawing near to him again through confession, service, worship, and studying his Word. Just as the spark of love can be rekindled in marriage, so the Holy Spirit can re-ignite our zeal for God when we allow him to work in our heart.

**3:20** The Laodicean church was complacent and rich. They felt self-satisfied, but they didn't have Christ's presence among them. Christ knocked at the door of their hearts, but they were so busy enjoying worldly pleasures that they didn't notice that he was trying to enter. The pleasures of this world—money, security, material possessions—can be dangerous, because their temporary satisfaction makes us indifferent to God's offer of lasting satisfaction. If you find yourself feeling indifferent to church, to God, or to the Bible, you have begun to shut God out of your life. Leave the door of your heart constantly open to God, and you won't need to worry about hearing his knock. Letting him in is your only hope for lasting fulfillment.

**3:20** Jesus knocks at the door of our heart because he wants to save us and have fellowship with us. He is patient and persistent in trying to get through to us—not breaking and entering, but knocking. He allows us to decide whether or not to open our life to him. Do you intentionally keep his life-changing presence and power on the other side of the door?

**3:22** At the end of each letter to these churches, the believers were urged to listen and understand what was written to them. Although a different message was addressed to each church, all the messages contain warnings and principles for everyone. Which letter speaks most directly to your church? Which has the greatest bearing on your own spiritual condition at this time? How will you respond?

## B. MESSAGE FOR THE CHURCH (4:1—22:21)

Moving from the conditions within the churches in Asia to the future of the universal church, John sees the course of coming events in a way similar to Daniel and Ezekiel. Many of these passages contain clear spiritual teachings, but others seem beyond our ability to understand. The clear teaching of this book is that God will defeat all evil in the end. We must live in obedience to Jesus Christ, the coming Conqueror and Judge.

### 1. Worshiping God in heaven

**4** Then as I looked, I saw a door standing open in heaven, and the same voice I had heard before spoke to me like a trumpet blast. The voice said, "Come up here, and I will show you what must happen after this." ²And instantly I was in the Spirit,* and I saw a throne in heaven and someone sitting on it. ³The one sitting on the throne was as brilliant as gemstones—like jasper and carnelian. And the glow of an emerald circled his throne like a rainbow. ⁴Twenty-four thrones surrounded him, and twenty-four elders sat on them. They were all clothed in white and had gold crowns on their heads. ⁵From the throne came flashes of lightning and the rumble of thunder. And in front of the throne were seven torches with burning flames. This is the sevenfold Spirit* of God. ⁶In front of the throne was a shiny sea of glass, sparkling like crystal.

In the center and around the throne were four living beings, each covered with eyes, front and back. ⁷The first of these living beings was like a lion; the second was like an ox; the third had a human face; and the fourth was like an eagle in flight. ⁸Each of these living beings had six wings, and their wings were covered all over with eyes, inside and out. Day after day and night after night they keep on saying,

"Holy, holy, holy is the Lord God, the Almighty—
the one who always was, who is, and who is still to come."

⁹Whenever the living beings give glory and honor and thanks to the one sitting on the throne (the one who lives forever and ever), ¹⁰the twenty-four elders fall down and worship the one sitting on the throne (the one who lives forever and ever). And they lay their crowns before the throne and say,

¹¹ "You are worthy, O Lord our God,
to receive glory and honor and power.
For you created all things,
and they exist because you created what you pleased."

**4:2** Or *in spirit.*   **4:5** Greek *They are the seven spirits.*

**Cross-references (margin):**

**4:1** Exod 19:20, 24; Ezek 1:1; Dan 2:28-29, 45
**4:2** Isa 6:1; Ezek 1:26-27
**4:3** Ezek 1:26-28
**4:4** Isa 24:23; Rev 11:16; 19:4
**4:5** Exod 19:16; Ezek 1:13; Zech 4:2; Rev 1:4; 5:6
**4:6-7** Ezek 1:5-22; 10:12, 14; Rev 15:7; 19:4
**4:8** Isa 6:2; Ezek 1:18; 10:12; Amos 3:13
**4:9** Dan 4:34; Rev 4:2; 5:1
**4:10** Rev 4:4; 5:8, 14
**4:11** Rev 10:6

---

**4:1** Chapters 4 and 5 record glimpses into Christ's glory. Here we see into the throne room of heaven. God is on the throne and orchestrating all the events that John will record. The world is not spinning out of control; the God of creation will carry out his plans as Christ initiates the final battle with the forces of evil. John shows us heaven before showing us earth so that we will not be frightened by future events.

**4:1** The voice John had first heard that sounded like a trumpet blast was the voice of Christ (see 1:10, 11).

**4:2** Four times in the book of Revelation John says he was "in the Spirit" (1:10; 4:2; 17:3; 21:10). This expression means that the Holy Spirit was giving him a vision—showing him situations and events he could not have seen with mere human eyesight. All true prophecy comes from God through the Holy Spirit (2 Peter 1:20, 21).

**4:4** Who are these 24 elders? Because there were 12 tribes of Israel in the Old Testament and 12 apostles in the New Testament, the 24 elders in this vision probably represent all the redeemed of God for all time (both before and after Christ's death and resurrection). They symbolize all those—both Jews and Gentiles—who are now part of God's family. The 24 elders show us that *all* the redeemed of the Lord are worshiping him.

**4:5** In Revelation, lightning and thunder are connected with significant events in heaven. They remind us of the lightning and thunder at Mount Sinai when God gave the people his laws (Exodus 19:16). The Old Testament often uses such imagery to reflect God's power and majesty (Psalm 77:18).

**4:5** The "sevenfold Spirit of God" is another name for the Holy Spirit. See also Zechariah 4:2-6, where seven lamps (like the seven torches here) are equated with the one Spirit.

**4:6** Glass was very rare in New Testament times, and crystal-clear glass was virtually impossible to find (see 1 Corinthians 13:12). The "sea of glass" highlights both the magnificence and holiness of God.

**4:6, 7** Just as the Holy Spirit is seen symbolically in the seven lighted lamps, so the "four living beings" represent the attributes (the qualities and character) of God. These creatures were not real animals. Like the cherubim (the highest order of the angels), they guard God's throne, lead others in worship, and proclaim God's holiness. God's attributes symbolized in the animal-like appearance of these four creatures are majesty and power (the lion), faithfulness (the ox), intelligence (the human), and sovereignty (the eagle). The Old Testament prophet Ezekiel saw four similar creatures in one of his visions (Ezekiel 1:5-10).

**4:9** John describes these scenes in such detail because Christians in the first century came from many backgrounds. Not all of them understood Jewish history or knew the glory of the Temple. Revelation instructs us in worship. It shows us where, why, and how to praise God. Worship takes our minds off our problems and focuses them on God. Worship leads us from individual meditation to corporate worship. Worship causes us to consider and appreciate God's character. Worship lifts our perspective from the earthly to the heavenly.

**4:11** The point of this chapter is summed up in this verse: All creatures in heaven and earth will praise and honor God because he is the creator and sustainer of everything.

## The Lamb Opens the Scroll

**5** Then I saw a scroll* in the right hand of the one who was sitting on the throne. There was writing on the inside and the outside of the scroll, and it was sealed with seven seals. ²And I saw a strong angel, who shouted with a loud voice: "Who is worthy to break the seals on this scroll and open it?" ³But no one in heaven or on earth or under the earth was able to open the scroll and read it.

⁴Then I began to weep bitterly because no one was found worthy to open the scroll and read it. ⁵But one of the twenty-four elders said to me, "Stop weeping! Look, the Lion of the tribe of Judah, the heir to David's throne,* has won the victory. He is worthy to open the scroll and its seven seals."

⁶Then I saw a Lamb that looked as if it had been slaughtered, but it was now standing between the throne and the four living beings and among the twenty-four elders. He had seven horns and seven eyes, which represent the sevenfold Spirit* of God that is sent out into every part of the earth. ⁷He stepped forward and took the scroll from the right hand of the one sitting on the throne. ⁸And when he took the scroll, the four living beings and the twenty-four elders fell down before the Lamb. Each one had a harp, and they held gold bowls filled with incense, which are the prayers of God's people. ⁹And they sang a new song with these words:

"You are worthy to take the scroll
    and break its seals and open it.
For you were slaughtered, and your blood has ransomed people for God
    from every tribe and language and people and nation.
¹⁰ And you have caused them to become
    a Kingdom of priests for our God.
    And they will reign* on the earth."

¹¹Then I looked again, and I heard the voices of thousands and millions of angels around the throne and of the living beings and the elders. ¹²And they sang in a mighty chorus:

**5:1**
Isa 29:11
Ezek 2:9-10
Dan 12:4

**5:3**
Phil 2:10

**5:5**
Gen 49:9
Isa 11:1, 10
Heb 7:14

**5:6**
Isa 53:7
Zech 4:10
John 1:29, 36
Rev 1:4; 4:5

**5:7**
Rev 5:1

**5:8**
Rev 4:4, 6; 8:3-4;
14:2; 15:2

**5:9**
Ps 144:9
Rev 14:3

**5:10**
Exod 19:6
1 Pet 2:5-9
Rev 1:6; 20:4

**5:11**
Dan 7:10
Heb 12:22
Rev 4:4, 6

**5:12**
1 Chr 29:11
Isa 53:7
John 1:29, 36
Rev 4:11

**5:1** Or *book;* also in 5:2, 3, 4, 5, 7, 8, 9.   **5:5** Greek *the root of David.* See Isa 11:10.   **5:6** Greek *which are the seven spirits.*   **5:10** Some manuscripts read *they are reigning.*

---

**5:1ff** Chapter 5 continues the glimpse into heaven begun in chapter 4.

**5:1** In John's day, books were written on scrolls—pieces of papyrus or vellum up to 30 feet long, rolled up and sealed with clay or wax. The scroll that John sees contains the full account of what God has in store for the world. The seven seals indicate the importance of its contents. The seals are located throughout the scroll so that as each one is broken, more of the scroll can be read to reveal another phase of God's plan for the end of the world. Only Christ is worthy to break the seals and open the scroll (5:3-5).

**5:5** The Lion, Jesus, proved himself worthy to break the seals and open the scroll by living a perfect life of obedience to God, dying on the cross for the sins of the world, and rising from the dead to show his power and authority over evil and death. Only Christ conquered sin, death, hell, and Satan himself; so only he can be trusted with the world's future. "Heir to David's throne" refers to Jesus being from David's family line, thus fulfilling the promise of the Messiah in the Old Testament.

**5:5, 6** Jesus Christ is pictured as both a Lion (symbolizing his authority and power) and a Lamb (symbolizing his submission to God's will). One of the elders calls John to look at the Lion, but when John looks he sees a Lamb. Christ the Lamb was the perfect sacrifice for the sins of all; therefore, only he can save us from the terrible events revealed by the scroll. Christ the Lamb won the greatest battle of all. He defeated all the forces of evil by dying on the cross. The role of Christ the Lion will be to lead the battle where Satan is finally defeated (19:19-21). Christ the Lion is victorious because of what Christ the Lamb has already done. We will participate in his victory, not because of our effort or goodness, but because he has promised eternal life to all who believe in him.

**5:6** John says the Lamb "had been slaughtered"; the wounds inflicted on Jesus' body during his trial and crucifixion could still be seen (see John 20:24-31). Jesus was called the Lamb of God by John the Baptist (John 1:29). In the Old Testament, lambs were sacrificed to atone for sins; the Lamb of God died as the final sacrifice for all sins (see Isaiah 53:7; Hebrews 10:1-12, 18).

**5:6** The horns symbolize strength and power (see 1 Kings 22:11; Zechariah 1:18). Although Christ is a sacrificial lamb, he is in no way weak. He was killed, but now he lives in God's strength and power. In Zechariah 4:2-10, the eyes are equated with the seven lamps and the one Spirit.

**5:9, 10** People from every nation are praising God before his throne. God's message of salvation and eternal life is not limited to a specific culture, race, or country. Anyone who comes to God in repentance and faith is accepted by him and will be part of his Kingdom. Don't allow prejudice or bias to keep you from sharing Christ with others. Christ welcomes all people into his Kingdom.

**5:9, 10** The song of God's people praises Christ's work. He (1) was killed, (2) ransomed them with his blood, (3) gathered them into a Kingdom, (4) made them priests, and (5) appointed them to reign on the earth. Jesus has already died and paid the penalty for sin. He is now gathering us into his Kingdom and making us priests. In the future we will reign with him. Worship God and praise him for what he has done, what he is doing, and what he will do for all who trust in him. When we realize the glorious future that awaits us, we will find the strength to face our present difficulties.

**5:10** The believers' song praises Christ for bringing them into the Kingdom and making them kings and priests. While now we are sometimes despised and mocked for our faith (John 15:17-27), in the future we will reign over all the earth (Luke 22:29, 30). Christ's death made all believers priests of God—the channels of blessing between God and people (1 Peter 2:5-9).

**5:11** Angels are spiritual beings created by God who help carry out his work on earth. They bring messages (Luke 1:26-28),

"Worthy is the Lamb who was slaughtered—
    to receive power and riches
and wisdom and strength
    and honor and glory and blessing."

**5:13**
Phil 2:10
Rev 4:11; 5:7

¹³And then I heard every creature in heaven and on earth and under the earth and in the sea. They sang:

"Blessing and honor and glory and power
    belong to the one sitting on the throne
    and to the Lamb forever and ever."

**5:14**
Rev 4:6, 9-10

¹⁴And the four living beings said, "Amen!" And the twenty-four elders fell down and worshiped the Lamb.

---

| **EVENTS IN REVELATION DESCRIBED ELSEWHERE IN THE BIBLE** | Other Reference | Revelation Reference | Event |
|---|---|---|---|
| | Ezekiel 1:22-28 | 4:2, 3; 10:1-3 | Glowing rainbow around God's throne |
| | Isaiah 53:7 | 5:6-8 | Christ is pictured as a Lamb |
| | Psalm 96 | 5:9-14 | New song |
| | Zechariah 1:7-11; 6:1-8 | 6:1-8 | Horses and riders |
| | Isaiah 2:19-22 | 6:12; 8:5; 11:13 | Earthquake |
| | Joel 2:28-32; Acts 2:14-21 | 6:12 | Moon turns red as blood |
| | Mark 13:21-25 | 6:13 | Stars falling from the sky |
| | Isaiah 34:1-4 | 6:14 | Sky rolled up like a scroll |
| | Zephaniah 1:14-18; 1 Thessalonians 5:1-3 | 6:15-17 | God's inescapable wrath |
| | Jeremiah 49:35-39 | 7:1 | Four winds of judgment |
| | Luke 8:26-34 | 9:1, 2; 17:3-8 | Bottomless pit |
| | Joel 1:2—2:11 | 9:3-11 | Plague of locusts |
| | Luke 21:20-24 | 11:1, 2 | Trampling of the holy city of Jerusalem |
| | Zechariah 4 | 11:3-6 | Two olive trees as witnesses |
| | Daniel 7 | 13:1-10 | A beast coming out of the sea |
| | 2 Thessalonians 2:7-14 | 13:11-15 | Astounding signs and miracles done by the evil beast |
| | Jeremiah 25:15-29 | 14:9-12 | Drinking the cup of God's wrath |
| | Isaiah 21:1-10 | 18:2, 3 | "Babylon" falls |
| | Matthew 22:1-14 | 19:5-8 | Wedding feast of the Lamb |
| | Ezekiel 38, 39 | 20:7-10 | Conflict with Gog and Magog |
| | John 5:19-30 | 20:11-15 | Judging of all people |
| | Ezekiel 37:21-28 | 21:3 | God lives among his people |
| | Isaiah 25:1-8 | 21:4 | Our tears will be wiped away forever |
| | Genesis 2:8-14 | 22:1, 2 | Tree of life |
| | 1 Corinthians 13:11, 12 | 22:3-5 | We will see God face to face |
| | Daniel 7:18-28 | 22:5 | Believers will reign with God forever |

---

protect God's people (Daniel 6:22), offer encouragement (Genesis 16:7ff), give guidance (Exodus 14:19), bring punishment (2 Samuel 24:16), patrol the earth (Ezekiel 1:9-14), and fight the forces of evil (2 Kings 6:16-18; Revelation 20:1). There are both good and evil angels (12:7), but because evil angels are allied with Satan, they have considerably less power and authority than good angels. Eventually, the main role of the good angels will be to offer continuous praise to God (see also 19:1-3).

**5:14** The scene in chapter 5 shows us that only the Lamb, Jesus Christ, is worthy to open the scroll (the events of history). Jesus,

not Satan, holds the future. Jesus Christ is in control, and he alone is worthy to set into motion the events of the last days of history.

## 2. Opening the seven seals

*The Lamb Breaks the First Six Seals*

**6** As I watched, the Lamb broke the first of the seven seals on the scroll.* Then I heard one of the four living beings say with a voice like thunder, "Come!" 2I looked up and saw a white horse standing there. Its rider carried a bow, and a crown was placed on his head. He rode out to win many battles and gain the victory.

3When the Lamb broke the second seal, I heard the second living being say, "Come!" 4Then another horse appeared, a red one. Its rider was given a mighty sword and the author-ity to take peace from the earth. And there was war and slaughter everywhere.

5When the Lamb broke the third seal, I heard the third living being say, "Come!" I looked up and saw a black horse, and its rider was holding a pair of scales in his hand. 6And I heard a voice from among the four living beings say, "A loaf of wheat bread or three loaves of barley will cost a day's pay.* And don't waste* the olive oil and wine."

7When the Lamb broke the fourth seal, I heard the fourth living being say, "Come!" 8I looked up and saw a horse whose color was pale green. Its rider was named Death, and his companion was the Grave.* These two were given authority over one-fourth of the earth, to kill with the sword and famine and disease* and wild animals.

9When the Lamb broke the fifth seal, I saw under the altar the souls of all who had been martyred for the word of God and for being faithful in their testimony. 10They shouted to the Lord and said, "O Sovereign Lord, holy and true, how long before you judge the people who belong to this world and avenge our blood for what they have done to us?" 11Then a white robe was given to each of them. And they were told to rest a little longer until the full number of their brothers and sisters*—their fellow servants of Jesus who were to be mar-tyred—had joined them.

**6:1**
Rev 5:1, 6

**6:2**
Zech 1:8; 6:1-3
Rev 14:14;
19:11-12

**6:4**
Zech 1:8; 6:2
Matt 10:34

**6:5**
Zech 6:2, 6-8

**6:8**
Jer 14:12; 15:2-3
Hos 13:14
Rev 1:18; 20:13

**6:9**
Exod 29:12
Lev 4:7
Rev 20:4

**6:10**
Ps 79:10
Zech 1:12
Luke 18:7
Rev 3:7, 10; 19:2

**6:11**
Heb 11:40
Rev 3:4

**6:1** Or *book.*   **6:6a** Greek *A choinix* [1 quart or 1 liter] *of wheat for a denarius, and 3 choinix of barley for a denarius.* A denarius was equivalent to a laborer's full day's wage.   **6:6b** Or *harm.*   **6:8a** Greek *was Hades.*   **6:8b** Greek *death.*   **6:11** Greek *their brothers.*

---

**6:1ff** This is the first of three seven-part judgments. The trum-pets (chapters 8–9) and the bowls (chapter 16) are the other two. As each seal is opened, Christ the Lamb sets in motion events that will bring about the end of human history. This scroll is not completely opened until the seventh seal is broken (8:1). The contents of the scroll reveal humanity's depravity and portray God's authority over the events of human history.

**6:2ff** Four horses appear as the first four seals are opened. The horses represent God's judgment of people's sin and rebellion. God is directing human history—even using his enemies to accomplish his purposes. The four horses are a foretaste of the final judgments yet to come. Some view this chapter as a parallel to the Olivet Discourse (see Matthew 24). The imagery of four horses is also found in Zechariah 6:1-8.

**6:2-8** Each of the four horses is a different color. Some assume that the white horse represents victory and that its rider must be Christ (because Christ later rides to victory on a white horse— 19:11). But because the other three horses relate to judgment and destruction, this rider on a white horse would most likely not be Christ. The four are part of the unfolding judgment of God, and it would be premature for Christ to ride forth as conqueror. The other horses represent different kinds of judgment: red for warfare and bloodshed; black for famine; pale green for death. The high prices of wheat and barley illustrate famine conditions. But the worst is yet to come.

**6:4** Complete peace will only come when Christ returns. The picture in Revelation of the coming persecutions and natural disasters is gloomy, but ultimately it is cause for great joy. When believers see these events happening, they will know that their Messiah's return is coming soon, and they can look forward to his reign of justice and peace. Rather than being terrified by what is happening in our world, we should confidently await Christ's return to bring justice and restoration to his people.

**6:8** It is not clear whether "the Grave" was on a separate horse than Death or merely rode along with Death, but the riders described in verses 2-8 are commonly referred to as the four

horsemen of the Apocalypse. The four riders are given power over one-fourth of the earth, indicating that God is still limiting his judgment—it is not yet complete. With these judgments there is still time for unbelievers to turn to Christ and away from their sin. In this case, the limited punishment not only demonstrates God's wrath on sin but also his merciful love in giving people yet another opportunity to turn to him before he brings final judg-ment. We must not presume upon God's patience. Our repen-tance must be visible and authentic. In what ways does your life reflect new and different behavior?

**6:9** The altar represents the altar of sacrifice in the Temple, where animals were sacrificed to atone for sins. Instead of the animals' blood at the base of the altar, John saw the souls of martyrs who had died for preaching the Good News. These martyrs were told that still more would lose their lives for their belief in Christ (6:11). In the face of warfare, famine, persecution, and death, Christians will be called on to stand firmly for what they believe. Only those who endure to the end will be rewarded by God (Mark 13:13).

**6:9-11** The martyrs are eager for God to bring justice to the earth, but they are told to wait. God is not waiting until a certain number is reached, but he is promising that those who suffer and die for their faith will not be forgotten. Rather, they will be singled out by God for special honor. We may wish for justice immediately, as these martyrs did, but we must be patient. God works according to his own timetable, and he promises justice. No suffering for the sake of God's Kingdom, however, is wasted.

**6:10** The martyrs call out to God, "How long will it be before you judge the people who belong to this world and avenge our blood for what they have done to us?" As we see the world's wickedness, we, too, may cry out to God, "How long?" In the following chapters, the judgment comes at last. We may be distressed and impatient, but God has his plan and his timing, and we must learn to trust him to know what is best. Judgment is coming—be sure of that. Thank God for the time he has given you to turn from sin. Use the available time to work to help others turn to him.

**6:12**
Joel 2:10
Matt 24:29
Rev 16:18

**6:13**
Isa 34:4
Rev 8:10; 9:1

**6:14**
Ps 46:2
2 Pet 3:10
Rev 16:20; 20:11;
21:1

**6:15**
Isa 2:10, 19, 21
Jer 4:29

**6:16**
Hos 10:8
Luke 23:30

**6:17**
Joel 2:11
Zeph 1:14-15
Mal 3:2

**7:1**
Jer 49:36
Ezek 37:9
Dan 7:2
Zech 6:5
Matt 24:31

**7:2**
Rev 9:4

**7:3**
Ezek 9:4, 6
Rev 6:6; 9:4; 14:1;
22:4

**7:4**
Rev 14:1, 3

¹²I watched as the Lamb broke the sixth seal, and there was a great earthquake. The sun became as dark as black cloth, and the moon became as red as blood. ¹³Then the stars of the sky fell to the earth like green figs falling from a tree shaken by a strong wind. ¹⁴The sky was rolled up like a scroll, and all of the mountains and islands were moved from their places.

¹⁵Then everyone—the kings of the earth, the rulers, the generals, the wealthy, the powerful, and every slave and free person—all hid themselves in the caves and among the rocks of the mountains. ¹⁶And they cried to the mountains and the rocks, "Fall on us and hide us from the face of the one who sits on the throne and from the wrath of the Lamb. ¹⁷For the great day of their wrath has come, and who is able to survive?"

### God's People Will Be Preserved

**7** Then I saw four angels standing at the four corners of the earth, holding back the four winds so they did not blow on the earth or the sea, or even on any tree. ²And I saw another angel coming up from the east, carrying the seal of the living God. And he shouted to those four angels, who had been given power to harm land and sea, ³"Wait! Don't harm the land or the sea or the trees until we have placed the seal of God on the foreheads of his servants."

⁴And I heard how many were marked with the seal of God—144,000 were sealed from all the tribes of Israel:

⁵ from Judah ............................................................ 12,000
　 from Reuben ......................................................... 12,000
　 from Gad .............................................................. 12,000
⁶ from Asher ............................................................ 12,000
　 from Naphtali......................................................... 12,000
　 from Manasseh ...................................................... 12,000
⁷ from Simeon........................................................... 12,000
　 from Levi............................................................... 12,000
　 from Issachar ......................................................... 12,000
⁸ from Zebulun.......................................................... 12,000
　 from Joseph .......................................................... 12,000
　 from Benjamin........................................................ 12,000

---

**6:12** The sixth seal changes the scene back to the physical world. The first five judgments were directed toward specific areas, but this judgment is universal. Everyone will be afraid when the earth itself trembles.

**6:15-17** At the sight of God sitting on the throne, all human beings, great and small, will be terrified, calling for the mountains to fall on them so that they will not have to face the judgment of the Lamb. This vivid picture was not intended to frighten believers. For them, the Lamb is a gentle Savior. But those kings, rulers, and generals and other powerful people who previously showed no fear of God and arrogantly flaunted their unbelief will find that they were wrong, and in that day they will have to face God's wrath. No one who has rejected God can survive the day of his wrath, but those who belong to Christ will receive a reward rather than punishment. Do you belong to Christ? If so, you need not fear these final days.

**7:1ff** The sixth seal has been opened, and the people of the earth have tried to hide from God, saying, "Who is able to survive?" (6:12-17). Just when all hope seems lost, four angels hold back the four winds of judgment until God's people are sealed as his own. Only then will God open the seventh seal (8:1).

**7:2** A seal on a scroll or document identified and protected its contents. God places his own seal on his followers, identifying them as his own and guaranteeing his protection over their souls. This shows how valuable we are to him. Our physical bodies may be beaten, maimed, or even destroyed, but *nothing* can harm our souls when we have been sealed by God. See Ephesians 1:13 for the seal of the Holy Spirit.

**7:3** God's seal is placed on the foreheads of his servants. This seal is the exact opposite of the mark of the beast explained in

13:16. These two marks place the people in two distinct categories—those owned by God and those owned by Satan.

**7:4-8** The number 144,000 is 12 x 12 x 1,000, symbolizing completeness—*all* God's followers will be brought safely to him; not one will be overlooked or forgotten. God seals these believers either by withdrawing them from the earth (this is called the Rapture) or by giving them special strength and courage to make it through this time of great persecution. Even though many believers have to undergo persecution, the seal does not necessarily guarantee protection from physical harm—many will die (see 6:11)—but God will protect them from spiritual harm. No matter what happens, they will be brought to their reward of eternal life. Their destiny is secure. These believers will not fall away from God even though they may undergo intense persecution.

This is not saying that 144,000 individuals must be sealed before the persecution comes, but that when persecution begins, the faithful will have already been sealed (marked by God), and they will remain true to him until the end.

**7:4-8** This is a different list from the usual listing of the 12 tribes in the Old Testament, because it is a symbolic list of God's true followers. (1) Judah is mentioned first because Judah is both the tribe of David and of Jesus the Messiah (Genesis 49:8-12; Matthew 1:1). (2) Levi had no tribal allotment because of the Levites' work for God in the Temple (Deuteronomy 18:1), but here the tribe is given a place as a reward for faithfulness. (3) Dan is not mentioned because it was known for rebellion and idolatry, traits unacceptable for God's followers (Genesis 49:17). (4) The two tribes representing Joseph (usually called Ephraim and Manasseh, after Joseph's sons) are here called Joseph and Manasseh because of Ephraim's rebellion. See Genesis 49 for the story of the beginning of these 12 tribes.

## Praise from the Great Crowd

⁹After this I saw a vast crowd, too great to count, from every nation and tribe and people and language, standing in front of the throne and before the Lamb. They were clothed in white robes and held palm branches in their hands. ¹⁰And they were shouting with a great roar,

"Salvation comes from our God who sits on the throne
    and from the Lamb!"

¹¹And all the angels were standing around the throne and around the elders and the four living beings. And they fell before the throne with their faces to the ground and worshiped God. ¹²They sang,

"Amen! Blessing and glory and wisdom
    and thanksgiving and honor
and power and strength belong to our God
    forever and ever! Amen."

¹³Then one of the twenty-four elders asked me, "Who are these who are clothed in white? Where did they come from?"

¹⁴And I said to him, "Sir, you are the one who knows."

Then he said to me, "These are the ones who died in* the great tribulation.* They have washed their robes in the blood of the Lamb and made them white.

¹⁵ "That is why they stand in front of God's throne
    and serve him day and night in his Temple.
And he who sits on the throne
    will give them shelter.
¹⁶ They will never again be hungry or thirsty;
    they will never be scorched by the heat of the sun.
¹⁷ For the Lamb on the throne*
    will be their Shepherd.
He will lead them to springs of life-giving water.
    And God will wipe every tear from their eyes."

## The Lamb Breaks the Seventh Seal

**8** When the Lamb broke the seventh seal on the scroll,* there was silence throughout heaven for about half an hour. ²I saw the seven angels who stand before God, and they were given seven trumpets.

---

7:14a Greek who came out of.   7:14b Or the great suffering.   7:17 Greek on the center of the throne.   8:1 Or book.

**Cross-references (margin):**

7:9 Rev 3:5; 5:9
7:10 Rev 5:13; 12:10; 19:1; 22:3
7:11 Rev 4:4, 6, 10
7:12 Rev 5:12-14
7:13 Rev 6:11; 7:9
7:14 Dan 12:1; Rev 6:11; 22:14
7:15 Rev 4:9; 11:19; 22:3
7:16 Isa 49:10
7:17 Ps 23:1-5; Isa 25:8; 49:10; John 10:11, 14; Rev 21:4, 6; 22:1
8:1 Rev 6:1-17
8:2 Rev 9:1, 13; 11:15

---

**7:9** Who is this vast crowd? While some interpreters identify it as the martyrs described in 6:9, it may also be the same group as the 144,000 just mentioned (7:4-8). The 144,000 were sealed by God before the great time of persecution; the vast crowd was brought to eternal life, as God had promised. Before, they were being prepared; now, they are victorious. This crowd in heaven is composed of all those who remained faithful to God throughout the generations. No true believer ever need worry about which group he or she will be in. God includes and protects each of us, and we are guaranteed a place in his presence.

**7:10** People try many methods to remove the guilt of sin— good deeds, intellectual pursuits, and even casting blame on others. The crowd in heaven, however, praises God, saying that salvation comes from him and from the Lamb. Salvation from sin's penalty can come only through Jesus Christ. Have you had the guilt of sin removed in the only way possible?

**7:11** More information about the elders is found in the note on 4:4. The four living beings are explained further in the note on 4:6, 7.

**7:14** "The great tribulation" has been explained in several ways. Some believe it refers to the suffering of believers through the ages; others believe that there is a specific time of intense tribulation yet to come. In either case, these believers come through their times of suffering by remaining loyal to God. Because they remain faithful, God will give them eternal life with him (7:17).

**7:14** It is difficult to imagine how blood could make any cloth

white, but the blood of Jesus Christ is the world's greatest purifier because it removes the stain of sin. White symbolizes sinless perfection or holiness, which can be given to people only by the death of the sinless Lamb of God on our behalf. This is a picture of how we are saved through faith (see Isaiah 1:18; Romans 3:21-26).

**7:16, 17** God will provide for his children's needs in their eternal home where there will be no hunger, thirst, or pain, and he will wipe away all tears. When you are suffering or torn apart by sorrow, take comfort in this promise of complete protection and relief.

**7:17** In verses 1-8 we see the believers receiving a seal to protect them through a time of great tribulation and suffering; in verses 9-17 we see the believers finally with God in heaven. All who have been faithful through the ages are singing before God's throne. Their tribulations and sorrows are over: no more tears for sin, for all sins are forgiven; no more tears for suffering, for all suffering is over; no more tears for death, for all believers have been resurrected to die no more.

**8:1** There was silence in heaven for about half an hour. With all the activity, this dramatic pause must have seemed to last for an eternity. During this time, the only activity was the prayers of the saints (8:3, 4). We must seek God in times of silence. How proper for us to be quiet and honor God for his power and might. Take time each day to be silent and exalt God. Silence also conveys trust and confidence in God (see Isaiah 30:15). We can trust God that he will give us strength and provide the justice against oppressors that we seek.

8:3
Exod 30:1-3
Rev 9:13

8:4
Ps 141:2
Rev 5:8; 8:3

8:5
Exod 19:16-19
Lev 16:12
Rev 4:5; 11:19;
16:18

8:7
Ezek 38:22

8:8
Jer 51:25

8:10
Isa 14:12
Rev 6:13; 9:1; 16:4

8:11
Jer 9:15

8:12
Exod 10:21
Ezek 32:7-8
Rev 6:12-13

8:13
Rev 3:10; 9:12

9:1
Isa 14:12
Luke 8:31; 10:18

9:3
Rev 9:5, 10

³Then another angel with a gold incense burner came and stood at the altar. And a great amount of incense was given to him to mix with the prayers of God's people as an offering on the gold altar before the throne. ⁴The smoke of the incense, mixed with the prayers of God's holy people, ascended up to God from the altar where the angel had poured them out. ⁵Then the angel filled the incense burner with fire from the altar and threw it down upon the earth; and thunder crashed, lightning flashed, and there was a terrible earthquake.

## 3. Sounding the seven trumpets
### The First Four Trumpets
⁶Then the seven angels with the seven trumpets prepared to blow their mighty blasts.

⁷The first angel blew his trumpet, and hail and fire mixed with blood were thrown down on the earth. One-third of the earth was set on fire, one-third of the trees were burned, and all the green grass was burned.

⁸Then the second angel blew his trumpet, and a great mountain of fire was thrown into the sea. One-third of the water in the sea became blood, ⁹one-third of all things living in the sea died, and one-third of all the ships on the sea were destroyed.

¹⁰Then the third angel blew his trumpet, and a great star fell from the sky, burning like a torch. It fell on one-third of the rivers and on the springs of water. ¹¹The name of the star was Bitterness.* It made one-third of the water bitter, and many people died from drinking the bitter water.

¹²Then the fourth angel blew his trumpet, and one-third of the sun was struck, and one-third of the moon, and one-third of the stars, and they became dark. And one-third of the day was dark, and also one-third of the night.

¹³Then I looked, and I heard a single eagle crying loudly as it flew through the air, "Terror, terror, terror to all who belong to this world because of what will happen when the last three angels blow their trumpets."

### The Fifth Trumpet Brings the First Terror
**9** Then the fifth angel blew his trumpet, and I saw a star that had fallen to earth from the sky, and he was given the key to the shaft of the bottomless pit.* ²When he opened it, smoke poured out as though from a huge furnace, and the sunlight and air turned dark from the smoke.

³Then locusts came from the smoke and descended on the earth, and they were given

**8:11** Greek *Wormwood.*    **9:1** Or *the abyss,* or *the underworld;* also in 9:11.

---

**8:1, 2** When the seventh seal is opened, the seven trumpet judgments are revealed. In the same way, the seventh trumpet will announce the seven bowl judgments in 11:15 and 16:1-21. The trumpet judgments, like the seal judgments, are only partial. God's final and complete judgment has not yet come.

**8:3-5** An incense burner filled with live coals was used in Temple worship. Incense was poured on the coals, and the sweet-smelling smoke drifted upward, symbolizing believers' prayers ascending to God (see Exodus 30:7-9).

The angel then threw the incense burner down upon the earth. This symbolizes the judgment of God released on earth in answer to the prayers of the saints for justice for those who had oppressed and killed them. This shows that judgment, vindication, and revenge are in God's hands, not ours (see Matthew 5:38; Romans 12:9; 1 Peter 3:9). No matter how strong the desire to exact revenge and retaliate at our enemies, our work is to pray to God for his justice.

**8:6** The trumpet blasts have three purposes: (1) to warn that judgment is certain, (2) to call the forces of good and evil to battle, and (3) to announce the return of the King, the Messiah. These warnings urge us to make sure our faith is firmly fixed on Christ.

**8:7-12** Since only one-third of the earth is destroyed by these trumpet judgments, this is only a partial judgment from God. His full wrath is yet to be unleashed.

**8:13** Habakkuk used the image of an eagle to symbolize swiftness and destruction (see Habakkuk 1:8). The picture here is also of an eagle flying over all the earth, warning of the terrors yet to come. While both believers and unbelievers experience the terrors described in verses 7-12, those "who belong to this world" are the unbelievers who will meet spiritual harm through the next three

trumpet judgments. God has guaranteed believers protection from spiritual harm (7:2, 3).

**9:1** It is not known whether this "star" that fell from the sky is Satan, a fallen angel, Christ, or a good angel. Most likely it is a good angel, because the key to the shaft of the bottomless pit is normally held by Christ (1:17, 18), and it was temporarily given to this other being from heaven (see also 20:1). This being, whoever he may be, is still under God's control and authority. The bottomless pit represents the place of the demons and of Satan, the king of demons (9:11). See also Luke 8:31 for another reference to the bottomless pit.

**9:3** The prophet Joel described a locust plague as a foreshadowing of the "day of the LORD," meaning God's coming judgment (Joel 2:1-10). In the Old Testament, locusts were symbols of destruction because they destroyed vegetation. Here, however, they symbolize an invasion of demons called to torture people who do not believe in God. The limitations placed on the demons (they could only torment people for five months) show that they are under God's authority.

**9:3ff** Most likely these locusts are demons—evil spirits ruled by Satan who tempt people to sin. They were not created by Satan, because God is the Creator of all; rather, they are fallen angels who joined Satan in his rebellion. God limits what they can do; they can do nothing without his permission. Their main purpose on earth is to prevent, distort, or destroy people's relationship with God. Because they are corrupt and degenerate, their appearance reflects the distortion of their spirits. While it is important to recognize their evil activity so we can stay away from them, we must avoid any curiosity about or involvement with demonic forces or with the occult.

power to sting like scorpions. ⁴They were told not to harm the grass or plants or trees, but only the people who did not have the seal of God on their foreheads. ⁵They were told not to kill them but to torture them for five months with pain like the pain of a scorpion sting. ⁶In those days people will seek death but will not find it. They will long to die, but death will flee from them!

⁷The locusts looked like horses prepared for battle. They had what looked like gold crowns on their heads, and their faces looked like human faces. ⁸They had hair like women's hair and teeth like the teeth of a lion. ⁹They wore armor made of iron, and their wings roared like an army of chariots rushing into battle. ¹⁰They had tails that stung like scorpions, and for five months they had the power to torment people. ¹¹Their king is the angel from the bottomless pit; his name in Hebrew is *Abaddon,* and in Greek, *Apollyon*—the Destroyer.

¹²The first terror is past, but look, two more terrors are coming!

### The Sixth Trumpet Brings the Second Terror

¹³Then the sixth angel blew his trumpet, and I heard a voice speaking from the four horns of the gold altar that stands in the presence of God. ¹⁴And the voice said to the sixth angel who held the trumpet, "Release the four angels who are bound at the great Euphrates River." ¹⁵Then the four angels who had been prepared for this hour and day and month and year were turned loose to kill one-third of all the people on earth. ¹⁶I heard the size of their army, which was 200 million mounted troops.

¹⁷And in my vision, I saw the horses and the riders sitting on them. The riders wore armor that was fiery red and dark blue and yellow. The horses had heads like lions, and fire and smoke and burning sulfur billowed from their mouths. ¹⁸One-third of all the people on earth were killed by these three plagues—by the fire and smoke and burning sulfur that came from the mouths of the horses. ¹⁹Their power was in their mouths and in their tails. For their tails had heads like snakes, with the power to injure people.

²⁰But the people who did not die in these plagues still refused to repent of their evil deeds and turn to God. They continued to worship demons and idols made of gold, silver, bronze, stone, and wood—idols that can neither see nor hear nor walk! ²¹And they did not repent of their murders or their witchcraft or their sexual immorality or their thefts.

### The Angel and the Small Scroll

**10** Then I saw another mighty angel coming down from heaven, surrounded by a cloud, with a rainbow over his head. His face shone like the sun, and his feet were like pillars of fire. ²And in his hand was a small scroll* that had been opened. He stood with his right foot on the sea and his left foot on the land. ³And he gave a great shout like the roar of a lion. And when he shouted, the seven thunders answered.

**10:2** Or *book;* also in 10:8, 9, 10.

---

**9:11** The locust-demons have a leader whose name in Hebrew and in Greek means "Destroyer." It may be a play on words by John to show that those who worshiped the great god Apollo worshiped only a demon.

**9:13** The altar in the Temple had four projections, one at each corner, and these were called the horns of the altar (see Exodus 27:2).

**9:14** The word *angels* here means fallen angels or demons. These four unidentified demons will be exceedingly evil and destructive. But note that they do not have the power to release themselves and do their evil work on earth. Instead, they are held back by God and will be released at a specific time, doing only what he allows them to do.

**9:15** Here one-third of all people are killed. In 6:7, 8, one-fourth of all people were killed. Thus, over one-half of the people in the world will have been killed by God's great judgments. Even more would have been killed if God had not set limits on the destruction.

**9:16** In John's day, this number of mounted troops in an army was inconceivable, but today there are countries and alliances that could easily amass this many soldiers. This huge army, led by the four demons, will be sent out to destroy one-third of the earth's population. But the judgment is still not complete.

**9:20, 21** These people were so hard-hearted that even plagues did not drive them to God. People don't usually fall into immoral-

ity and evil suddenly—they slip into it a little bit at a time until, hardly realizing what has happened, they are irrevocably mired in their wicked ways. Any person who allows sin to take root in his or her life will end up in this predicament. Temptation entertained today becomes sin tomorrow, a habit the next day, then death and separation from God forever (see James 1:15). To think you could never become this evil is the first step toward a hard heart. Acknowledge your need to confess your sin before God.

**10:1-6** The purpose of this mighty angel is clear—to announce the final judgments on the earth. His right foot on the sea and left foot on the land (10:2) indicate that his words deal with all creation, not just a limited part as did the seal and trumpet judgments. The seventh trumpet (11:15) will usher in the seven bowl judgments, which will bring an end to the present world. When this universal judgment comes, God's truth will prevail.

**10:2** We see two scrolls in Revelation. The first contains a revelation of judgments against evil (5:1ff). The contents of the second small scroll are not indicated, but it also may contain a revelation of judgment.

**10:2** This powerful angel conveyed his high rank and his authority from God by straddling the land and the sea. His huge size contrasts with the smallness of God's enemies. When things are going badly in your life, remember that this angel represents the kind of power that is on your side. God's angelic forces are with

---

*Cross-references (right margin):*

**9:4**
Ezek 9:4, 6
Rev 7:3

**9:6**
Job 3:21
Rev 6:16

**9:7**
Joel 2:4-5

**9:8**
Joel 1:6

**9:9**
Joel 2:5

**9:11**
Job 26:6; 28:22

**9:14**
Gen 15:18

**9:15**
Rev 8:7-12; 9:18;
20:7

**9:17**
Job 41:10-12

**9:20**
Deut 4:28; 32:17
Ps 115:4-7
Dan 5:23
Mic 5:13
Acts 7:41
1 Cor 10:19-20
Rev 2:21

**9:21**
Rev 16:9, 11, 21

**10:1**
Matt 17:2

**10:3**
Ps 29:3-9

**10:4**
Dan 8:26; 12:4, 9
Rev 22:10

**10:5**
Deut 32:40
Dan 12:7

**10:6**
Gen 14:19, 22
Exod 20:11
Neh 9:6
Ps 146:6

**10:7**
Dan 9:6, 10
Amos 3:7
Rev 11:15

**10:9**
Jer 15:16
Ezek 2:8–3:3

**10:11**
Jer 1:9-10; 25:30
Rev 5:9

**11:1**
Ezek 40:3
Rev 21:15

**11:2**
Ezek 40:17-20
Luke 21:24
Rev 12:6; 13:5

**11:3**
Rev 2:13

**11:4**
Zech 4:3, 11, 14

**11:5**
2 Sam 22:9
2 Kgs 1:10
Jer 5:14

**11:6**
Exod 7:17-20
1 Kgs 17:1

⁴When the seven thunders spoke, I was about to write. But I heard a voice from heaven saying, "Keep secret* what the seven thunders said, and do not write it down."

⁵Then the angel I saw standing on the sea and on the land raised his right hand toward heaven. ⁶He swore an oath in the name of the one who lives forever and ever, who created the heavens and everything in them, the earth and everything in it, and the sea and everything in it. He said, "There will be no more delay. ⁷When the seventh angel blows his trumpet, God's mysterious plan will be fulfilled. It will happen just as he announced it to his servants the prophets."

⁸Then the voice from heaven spoke to me again: "Go and take the open scroll from the hand of the angel who is standing on the sea and on the land."

⁹So I went to the angel and told him to give me the small scroll. "Yes, take it and eat it," he said. "It will be sweet as honey in your mouth, but it will turn sour in your stomach!" ¹⁰So I took the small scroll from the hand of the angel, and I ate it! It was sweet in my mouth, but when I swallowed it, it turned sour in my stomach.

¹¹Then I was told, "You must prophesy again about many peoples, nations, languages, and kings."

### The Two Witnesses

**11** Then I was given a measuring stick, and I was told, "Go and measure the Temple of God and the altar, and count the number of worshipers. ²But do not measure the outer courtyard, for it has been turned over to the nations. They will trample the holy city for 42 months. ³And I will give power to my two witnesses, and they will be clothed in burlap and will prophesy during those 1,260 days."

⁴These two prophets are the two olive trees and the two lampstands that stand before the Lord of all the earth. ⁵If anyone tries to harm them, fire flashes from their mouths and consumes their enemies. This is how anyone who tries to harm them must die. ⁶They have power to shut the sky so that no rain will fall for as long as they prophesy. And they have the power to turn the rivers and oceans into blood, and to strike the earth with every kind of plague as often as they wish.

**10:4** Greek *Seal up.*

---

you (Matthew 18:10; Hebrews 1:14). Keep your problems in their proper perspective by remembering that God's power is available to you to deal with your problems.

**10:4** Throughout history people have wanted to know what would happen in the future, and God reveals some of it in this book. But John was stopped from revealing certain parts of his vision. An angel also told the prophet Daniel that some visions he saw were not to be revealed yet to everyone (Daniel 12:9), and Jesus told his disciples that the time of the end is known by no one but God (Mark 13:32, 33). God has revealed all we need to know to live for him now. In our desire to be ready for the end, we must not place more emphasis on speculation about the last days than on living for God while we wait.

**10:7** By saying that "God's mysterious plan will be fulfilled," John was pointing to God's removal of all evil and the final exaltation of Christ as Lord. This pronouncement would bring fear to God's enemies. For God's chosen ones, however, it would bring hope and peace. Do you really long for Christ's return? Do you long for God and his people to be vindicated? Believers ought to pray for God's justice to be carried out and his plan fulfilled. We should want Christ to come because of the triumph of his Kingdom—not because things are bad or because we want out of our struggles. Pray expectantly for the fulfillment of God's plan.

**10:9, 10** The prophet Ezekiel also had a vision in which he was told to eat a scroll filled with judgments against the nation of Israel (Ezekiel 3:1ff). The taste was sweet in his mouth, but the scroll's contents brought destruction—just like the scroll John was told to eat. God's Word is sweet to us as believers because it brings encouragement, but it sours our stomach because of the coming judgment we must pronounce on unbelievers.

**11:1ff** This Temple is most likely a symbol of the church (all true believers), because there will be no Temple in the new Jerusalem (21:22). John measured the Temple to show that God is building

walls of protection around his people to spare them from spiritual harm, and that there is a place reserved for all believers who remain faithful to God.

**11:1, 2** Those worshiping inside the Temple will be protected spiritually, but those outside will face great suffering. This is a way of saying that true believers will be protected through persecution, but those who refuse to believe will be destroyed.

**11:3** These two witnesses bear strong resemblance to Moses and Elijah, two of God's mighty prophets. With God's power, Moses called plagues down upon the nation of Egypt (see Exodus 7–11). Elijah defeated the prophets of Baal (1 Kings 18). Both of these men appeared with Christ at his transfiguration (see Matthew 17:1-7).

**11:3** In the book of Revelation, numbers are likely to have symbolic rather than literal meanings. The 42 months or 1,260 days equal 3½ years. As half of the perfect number 7, 3½ can indicate incompletion, imperfection, or even evil. Notice the events predicted for this time period: there is trouble (Daniel 12:7), the holy city is trampled (11:2), the woman takes refuge in the wilderness (12:6), and the devil-inspired beast exercises his authority (13:5). Some commentators link the 3½ years with the period of famine in the days of Elijah (Luke 4:25; James 5:17). Since Malachi predicted the return of Elijah before the Last Judgment (Malachi 4:5), and since the events in Daniel and Revelation pave the way for the Second Coming, perhaps John was making this connection. It is possible, of course, that the 3½ years are literal. If so, we will clearly recognize when the 3½ years are over! Whether symbolic or literal, however, they indicate that evil's reign will have a definite end.

⁷When they complete their testimony, the beast that comes up out of the bottomless pit* will declare war against them, and he will conquer them and kill them. ⁸And their bodies will lie in the main street of Jerusalem,* the city that is figuratively called "Sodom" and "Egypt," the city where their Lord was crucified. ⁹And for three and a half days, all peoples, tribes, languages, and nations will stare at their bodies. No one will be allowed to bury them. ¹⁰All the people who belong to this world will gloat over them and give presents to each other to celebrate the death of the two prophets who had tormented them.

¹¹But after three and a half days, God breathed life into them, and they stood up! Terror struck all who were staring at them. ¹²Then a loud voice from heaven called to the two prophets, "Come up here!" And they rose to heaven in a cloud as their enemies watched.

¹³At the same time there was a terrible earthquake that destroyed a tenth of the city. Seven thousand people died in that earthquake, and everyone else was terrified and gave glory to the God of heaven.

¹⁴The second terror is past, but look, the third terror is coming quickly.

### The Seventh Trumpet Brings the Third Terror

¹⁵Then the seventh angel blew his trumpet, and there were loud voices shouting in heaven:

"The world has now become the Kingdom of our Lord and of his Christ,*
    and he will reign forever and ever."

¹⁶The twenty-four elders sitting on their thrones before God fell with their faces to the ground and worshiped him. ¹⁷And they said,

"We give thanks to you, Lord God, the Almighty,
    the one who is and who always was,
for now you have assumed your great power
    and have begun to reign.
¹⁸ The nations were filled with wrath,
    but now the time of your wrath has come.
It is time to judge the dead
    and reward your servants the prophets,
        as well as your holy people,
    and all who fear your name,
        from the least to the greatest.
It is time to destroy
    all who have caused destruction on the earth."

11:7 Or *the abyss,* or *the underworld.*   11:8 Greek *the great city.*   11:15 Or *his Messiah.*

**Cross-references:**
11:7 Dan 7:21; Rev 13:1, 7
11:8 Isa 1:9-10
11:9 Ps 79:2-3
11:11 Ezek 37:5, 10
11:12 2 Kgs 2:11; Acts 1:9; Rev 4:1
11:13 Ezek 38:19-20; Rev 16:9, 11
11:15 Ps 10:16; Dan 2:44; 7:14, 27; Rev 10:7; 12:10; 16:17
11:16 Rev 4:4, 10
11:17 Amos 3:13; 4:13; Rev 1:8; 19:6
11:18 Ps 2:1; Rev 10:7; 19:5; 20:12

---

**11:7** This beast could be Satan or an agent of Satan.

**11:8, 9** Jerusalem, once the great city and the capital of Israel, is now enemy territory. It is compared with Sodom and with Egypt, both well known for their evil. By the time of John's writing, Jerusalem had been destroyed by the Romans in 70 A.D., nearly a million Jews had been slaughtered, and the Temple treasures had been carried off to Rome.

**11:10** As representatives of every believer who has witnessed for Jesus Christ, the two final, faithful witnesses are a picture of both invincibility and vulnerability. They win, they lose, they win again. Truth remains victorious, even though human channels fall. Their message—and God's plan—march on in spite of death, for even death proves to be a defeated foe.

Seldom do we face the possibility of death when we share our faith. Why should Satan threaten our lives when fear of embarrassment or rejection is enough to keep us silent? But if Jesus has truly changed our lives, we will find a way to let others know. Not to witness represents more than just fear; it also reveals selfishness. Have those near you heard what Jesus has done for you?

**11:13** The ultimate goal of God's saving plan is that everything in creation will glorify him. "Glory" refers to the splendor, radiance, and magnificence of God. It refers not only to God in his essential nature but to the praiseworthy effects of what God has accomplished. We glorify God because his glory is true and real, and we acknowledge his greatness. In so doing, we see our rightful position as his servants. When we glorify him in our singing, our speaking, and our living, we experience some of his transcendence and thus edify and uplift our own spirits. Glorifying God prompts us to moral action and loving service.

**11:15** The seventh trumpet is sounded, announcing the arrival of the King. There is now no turning back. The coming judgments are no longer partial but complete in their destruction. God is in control, and he unleashes his full wrath on the evil world that refuses to turn to him (9:20, 21). When his wrath begins, there will be no escape.

**11:16** For more on the 24 elders, see the note on 4:4.

**11:18** In the Bible, God gives rewards to his people according to what they deserve. Throughout the Old Testament, obedience often brought reward in this life (Deuteronomy 28), but obedience and immediate reward are not always linked. If they were, good people would always be rich, and suffering would always be a sign of sin. If we were quickly rewarded for every faithful deed, we would soon think we were pretty good. Before long, we would be doing many good deeds for purely selfish reasons. While it is true that God will reward us for our earthly deeds (see 20:12), our greatest reward will be eternal life in his presence.

11:19
2 Chr 5:7
Rev 4:5; 15:5

¹⁹Then, in heaven, the Temple of God was opened and the Ark of his covenant could be seen inside the Temple. Lightning flashed, thunder crashed and roared, and there was an earthquake and a terrible hailstorm.

## 4. Observing the great conflict
*The Woman and the Dragon*

12:2
Isa 26:17; 66:6-9
Mic 4:10
12:3
Dan 7:7, 24
Rev 13:1; 17:3, 7, 12, 16
12:4
Dan 8:10
12:5
Ps 2:9
Rev 2:27; 19:15
12:6
Rev 11:2; 13:5
12:7
Dan 10:13; 12:1
Jude 1:9
Rev 12:3
12:9
Gen 3:1
Zech 3:1-2
Matt 4:10
Luke 10:18
Rev 12:3; 20:2-10
12:10
Job 1:9-11
Zech 3:1
Rev 7:10; 11:15

**12** Then I witnessed in heaven an event of great significance. I saw a woman clothed with the sun, with the moon beneath her feet, and a crown of twelve stars on her head. ²She was pregnant, and she cried out because of her labor pains and the agony of giving birth.

³Then I witnessed in heaven another significant event. I saw a large red dragon with seven heads and ten horns, with seven crowns on his heads. ⁴His tail swept away one-third of the stars in the sky, and he threw them to the earth. He stood in front of the woman as she was about to give birth, ready to devour her baby as soon as it was born.

⁵She gave birth to a son who was to rule all nations with an iron rod. And her child was snatched away from the dragon and was caught up to God and to his throne. ⁶And the woman fled into the wilderness, where God had prepared a place to care for her for 1,260 days.

⁷Then there was war in heaven. Michael and his angels fought against the dragon and his angels. ⁸And the dragon lost the battle, and he and his angels were forced out of heaven. ⁹This great dragon—the ancient serpent called the devil, or Satan, the one deceiving the whole world—was thrown down to the earth with all his angels.

¹⁰Then I heard a loud voice shouting across the heavens,

"It has come at last—
  salvation and power

---

**11:19** In Old Testament days, the Ark of the Covenant was the most sacred treasure of the Israelite nation. For more information about the Ark, see the note on Exodus 37:1.

**12:1–14:20** The seventh trumpet (11:15) ushers in the bowl judgments (15:1–16:21), but in the intervening chapters (12–14), John sees the conflict between God and Satan. He sees the source of all sin, evil, persecution, and suffering on the earth, and he understands why the great battle between the forces of God and Satan must soon take place. In these chapters the nature of evil is exposed, and Satan is seen in all his wickedness.

**12:1-6** The woman represents God's faithful people who have been waiting for the Messiah; the crown of 12 stars represents the 12 tribes of Israel. God set apart the Jews for himself (Romans 9:4, 5), and that nation gave birth to the Messiah. The son (12:5) is Jesus, born to a devout Jewish girl named Mary (Luke 1:26-33). Evil King Herod immediately tried to destroy the infant Jesus (Matthew 2:13-20). Herod's desire to kill this newborn king, whom he saw as a threat to his throne, was motivated by Satan (the red dragon), who wanted to kill the world's Savior. The heavenly pageant of Revelation 12 shows that Christ's lowly birth in the town of Bethlehem had cosmic significance.

**12:3, 4** The large red dragon, Satan, has seven heads, ten horns, and seven crowns, representing his power and the kingdoms of the world over which he rules. The stars that plunged to earth with him are usually considered to be the angels who fell with Satan and became his demons. According to Hebrew tradition, one-third of all the angels in heaven fell with Satan. For more on demons, see the notes on 9:3ff and Mark 5:1-20.

**12:6** The wilderness represents a place of spiritual refuge and protection from Satan. Because God aided the woman's escape into the wilderness, we can be sure that he offers security to all true believers. Satan always attacks God's people, but God keeps them spiritually secure. Some will experience physical harm, but all will be protected from spiritual harm. God will not let Satan take the souls of God's true followers. When Satan's attacks seem overpowering, remember that God is ruler over all. Trust him.

**12:6** The 1,260 days (3½ years) is the same length of time that the dragon is allowed to exercise his authority (13:5) and that the holy city is trampled (see the second note on 11:3).

**12:7** This event fulfills Daniel 12:1ff. Michael is a high-ranking angel. One of his responsibilities is to guard God's community of believers.

**12:7ff** Much more happened at Christ's birth, death, and resurrection than most people realize. A war between the forces of good and evil was under way. With Christ's resurrection, Satan's ultimate defeat was assured. Some believe that Satan's fall to earth took place at Jesus' resurrection or ascension and that the 1,260 days (3½ years) is a symbolic way of referring to the time between Christ's first and second comings. Others say that Satan's defeat will occur in the middle of a literal seven-year tribulation period, following the rapture of the church and preceding the second coming of Christ and the beginning of Christ's 1,000-year reign. Whatever the case, we must remember that Christ is victorious—Satan has already been defeated because of Christ's death on the cross (12:10-12).

**12:9** The devil is not a symbol or legend; he is very real. Originally Satan was an angel of God, but through his own pride, he became corrupt. Satan is God's enemy, and he constantly tries to hinder God's work, but he is limited by God's power and can do only what he is permitted to do (Job 1:6–2:8). The name *Satan* means "accuser" (12:10). He actively looks for people to attack (1 Peter 5:8, 9). Satan likes to pursue believers who are vulnerable in their faith, who are spiritually weak, or who are isolated from other believers.

Even though God permits the devil to do his work in this world, God is still in control. And Jesus has complete power over Satan—he defeated Satan when he died and rose again for the sins of everyone. One day Satan will be bound forever, never again to do his evil work (see 20:10).

**12:10** Many believe that until this time, Satan still had access to God (see the note on Job 1:7ff). But here his access is forever barred (see also 9:1). He can no longer accuse people before God (see how Satan made accusations about Job before God in Job 1:6ff).

and the Kingdom of our God,
  and the authority of his Christ.*
For the accuser of our brothers and sisters*
  has been thrown down to earth—
the one who accuses them
  before our God day and night.

<sup>11</sup> And they have defeated him by the blood of the Lamb
  and by their testimony.
And they did not love their lives so much
  that they were afraid to die.
<sup>12</sup> Therefore, rejoice, O heavens!
  And you who live in the heavens, rejoice!
But terror will come on the earth and the sea,
  for the devil has come down to you in great anger,
  knowing that he has little time."

<sup>13</sup>When the dragon realized that he had been thrown down to the earth, he pursued the woman who had given birth to the male child. <sup>14</sup>But she was given two wings like those of a great eagle so she could fly to the place prepared for her in the wilderness. There she would be cared for and protected from the dragon* for a time, times, and half a time.

<sup>15</sup>Then the dragon tried to drown the woman with a flood of water that flowed from his mouth. <sup>16</sup>But the earth helped her by opening its mouth and swallowing the river that gushed out from the mouth of the dragon. <sup>17</sup>And the dragon was angry at the woman and declared war against the rest of her children—all who keep God's commandments and maintain their testimony for Jesus.

<sup>18</sup>Then the dragon took his stand* on the shore beside the sea.

### The Beast out of the Sea

**13** Then I saw a beast rising up out of the sea. It had seven heads and ten horns, with ten crowns on its horns. And written on each head were names that blasphemed God. <sup>2</sup>This beast looked like a leopard, but it had the feet of a bear and the mouth of a lion! And the dragon gave the beast his own power and throne and great authority.

**12:10a** Or *his Messiah.*   **12:10b** Greek *brothers.*   **12:14** Greek *the serpent;* also in 12:15. See 12:9.   **12:18** Greek *Then he took his stand;* some manuscripts read *Then I took my stand.* Some translations put this entire sentence into 13:1.

**12:11** Rev 2:10; 6:9; 7:14; 15:2

**12:12** Rev 8:13; 18:20

**12:14** Exod 19:4; Dan 7:25; 12:7; Rev 17:3, 18

**12:17** Rev 1:2; 11:7; 13:7

**13:1** Dan 7:2-8; Rev 17:12

**13:2** Dan 7:4-6; Rev 2:13; 12:3

**12:11** The critical blow to Satan came when the Lamb, Jesus Christ, shed his blood for our sins. The victory is won by sacrifice—Christ's death in our place to pay the penalty for our sin, and the sacrifices we make because of our faith in him. As we face the battle with Satan, we should not fear it or try to escape from it, but we should loyally serve Christ, who alone brings victory (see Romans 8:34-39).

**12:12** The devil begins to step up his persecution because he knows that "he has little time." We are living in the last days, and Satan's work has become more intense. Even though the devil is very powerful, as we can see by the condition of our world, he is always under God's control. One of the reasons God allows Satan to work evil and bring temptation is so that those who pretend to be Christ's followers will be weeded out from Christ's true believers. Knowing that the last great confrontation with Jesus is near, Satan is desperately trying to recruit as great an enemy force as possible for this final battle.

**12:17** While the woman (12:1) represents faithful Jews and the son (12:5) represents Christ, the rest of her children could be either Jewish believers or, most likely, all believers.

**12:17** The apostle Paul tells us that we are in a spiritual battle (Ephesians 6:10-12). John says that the war is still being waged, but the outcome has already been determined. Satan and his followers have been defeated and will be destroyed. Nevertheless Satan is battling daily to bring more into his ranks and to keep his own from defecting to God's side. Those who belong to Christ have gone into battle on God's side, and he has guaranteed them victory. God will not lose the war, but we must make certain not to lose the battle for our own souls. Don't waver in your commit-

ment to Christ. A great spiritual battle is being fought, and there is no time for indecision.

**13:1** This beast was initially identified with Rome because the Roman Empire, in its early days, encouraged an evil lifestyle, persecuted believers, and opposed God and his followers. But the beast also symbolizes the Antichrist—not Satan, but someone under Satan's power and control. This Antichrist looks like a combination of the four beasts that Daniel saw centuries earlier in a vision (Daniel 7). As the dragon (12:17) is in opposition to God, so the beast from the sea is against Christ and may be seen as Satan's false messiah. The early Roman Empire was strong and also anti-Christ (or against Christ's standards); many other individual powers throughout history have been anti-Christ. Many Christians believe that Satan's evil will culminate in a final Antichrist who will focus all the powers of evil against Jesus Christ and his followers.

**13:1ff** Chapter 13 introduces Satan's (the dragon's) two evil accomplices: (1) the beast out of the sea (13:1ff) and (2) the beast out of the earth (13:11ff). Together, the three evil beings form an unholy trinity in direct opposition to the Holy Trinity of God the Father, God the Son, and God the Holy Spirit.

When Satan tempted Jesus in the wilderness, he wanted Jesus to show his power by turning stones into bread, to do miracles by jumping from a high place, and to gain political power by worshiping him (see Matthew 4:1-11). Satan's plan was to rule the world through Jesus, but Jesus refused to do Satan's bidding. Thus, Satan turns to the fearsome beasts described in Revelation. To the beast out of the sea he gives political power. To the beast out of the earth he gives power to do miracles. Both beasts work together to capture the control of the whole world. This unholy trinity—the dragon, the beast out of the sea, and the false

**13:3**
2 Thes 2:9-12
Rev 17:8

³I saw that one of the heads of the beast seemed wounded beyond recovery—but the fatal wound was healed! The whole world marveled at this miracle and gave allegiance to the beast. ⁴They worshiped the dragon for giving the beast such power, and they also worshiped the beast. "Who is as great as the beast?" they exclaimed. "Who is able to fight against him?"

**13:5**
Dan 7:8, 11, 20, 25; 11:36
2 Thes 2:4
Rev 11:2

**13:7**
Rev 5:9; 11:7

**13:8**
Dan 12:1

⁵Then the beast was allowed to speak great blasphemies against God. And he was given authority to do whatever he wanted for forty-two months. ⁶And he spoke terrible words of blasphemy against God, slandering his name and his dwelling—that is, those who dwell in heaven.* ⁷And the beast was allowed to wage war against God's holy people and to conquer them. And he was given authority to rule over every tribe and people and language and nation. ⁸And all the people who belong to this world worshiped the beast. They are the ones whose names were not written in the Book of Life before the world was made—the Book that belongs to the Lamb who was slaughtered.*

⁹ Anyone with ears to hear
　　should listen and understand.

**13:10**
Jer 15:2; 43:11
Matt 26:52
Heb 6:12

¹⁰ Anyone who is destined for prison
　　will be taken to prison.
Anyone destined to die by the sword
　　will die by the sword.

This means that God's holy people must endure persecution patiently and remain faithful.

### The Beast out of the Earth

**13:11**
Rev 13:1, 4

**13:12**
Rev 14:9-10; 19:20

¹¹Then I saw another beast come up out of the earth. He had two horns like those of a lamb, but he spoke with the voice of a dragon. ¹²He exercised all the authority of the first beast. And he required all the earth and its people to worship the first beast, whose fatal wound

**13:6** Some manuscripts read *and his dwelling and all who dwell in heaven.*　　**13:8** Or *not written in the Book of Life that belongs to the Lamb who was slaughtered before the world was made.*

---

| SATAN'S WORK IN THE WORLD | | |
|---|---|---|
| His hatred for Christ | 12:13-15 |
| His hatred for God's people | 12:17 |
| His power and authority | 13:2 |
| His popularity among unbelievers | 13:3, 4 |
| His blasphemy against God | 13:6 |
| His war against believers | 13:7 |
| His ability to deceive | 13:14 |

---

prophet (see 16:13)—unite in a desperate attempt to overthrow God, but their efforts are doomed to failure. See what becomes of them in 19:19-21 and 20:10.

**13:3ff** Because the beast, the Antichrist, is a false messiah, he will be a counterfeit of Christ and will even stage a false resurrection (13:14). People will follow and worship him because they will be awed by his power and miracles (13:3, 4). He will unite the world under his leadership (13:7, 8), and he will control the world economy (13:16, 17). People are impressed by power and will follow those who display it forcefully or offer it to their followers. But those who follow the beast will only be fooling themselves: He will use his power to manipulate others, to point to himself, and to promote evil plans. God, by contrast, uses his infinitely greater power to love and to build up. Don't be misled by claims of great miracles or reports about a resurrection or reincarnation of someone claiming to be Christ. When Jesus returns, he will reveal himself to everyone (Matthew 24:23-28).

**13:5** The power given to the beast will be limited by God. He will allow the beast to exercise authority only for a short time. Even while the beast is in power, God will still be in control (11:15; 12:10-12).

**13:7** The beast will conquer God's people and rule over them, but he will not be able to harm them spiritually. He will establish worldwide dominance and demand that everyone worship him.

And many *will* worship him—everyone except true believers. Refusal to worship the beast will result in temporary suffering for God's people, but they will be rewarded with eternal life in the end.

**13:8** See the note on 3:5 for more information on the Book of Life.

**13:10** In this time of persecution, being faithful to Christ could bring imprisonment and even execution. Some believers will be hurt or killed. But all that the beast and his followers will be able to do to believers is harm them physically; no spiritual harm will come to those whose faith in God is sincere. All believers will enter God's presence perfected and purified by the blood of the Lamb (7:9-17).

**13:10** The times of great persecution that John saw will provide an opportunity for believers to exercise patient endurance and faithfulness. The tough times we face right now are also opportunities for spiritual growth. Don't fall into Satan's trap and turn away from God when hard times come. Instead, use those tough times as opportunities for testifying for God (see Philippians 1:28, 29).

**13:11ff** The first beast came out of the sea (13:1), but this second beast comes out of the earth. Later identified as the false prophet (16:13; 19:20), he is a counterfeit of the Holy Spirit. He seems to do good, but the purpose of his miracles is to deceive.

had been healed. <sup>13</sup>He did astounding miracles, even making fire flash down to earth from the sky while everyone was watching. <sup>14</sup>And with all the miracles he was allowed to perform on behalf of the first beast, he deceived all the people who belong to this world. He ordered the people to make a great statue of the first beast, who was fatally wounded and then came back to life. <sup>15</sup>He was then permitted to give life to this statue so that it could speak. Then the statue of the beast commanded that anyone refusing to worship it must die.

<sup>16</sup>He required everyone—small and great, rich and poor, free and slave—to be given a mark on the right hand or on the forehead. <sup>17</sup>And no one could buy or sell anything without that mark, which was either the name of the beast or the number representing his name. <sup>18</sup>Wisdom is needed here. Let the one with understanding solve the meaning of the number of the beast, for it is the number of a man.* His number is 666.*

### The Lamb and the 144,000

**14** Then I saw the Lamb standing on Mount Zion, and with him were 144,000 who had his name and his Father's name written on their foreheads. <sup>2</sup>And I heard a sound from heaven like the roar of mighty ocean waves or the rolling of loud thunder. It was like the sound of many harpists playing together.

<sup>3</sup>This great choir sang a wonderful new song in front of the throne of God and before the four living beings and the twenty-four elders. No one could learn this song except the 144,000 who had been redeemed from the earth. <sup>4</sup>They have kept themselves as pure as virgins,* following the Lamb wherever he goes. They have been purchased from among the people on the earth as a special offering* to God and to the Lamb. <sup>5</sup>They have told no lies; they are without blame.

13:13
1 Kgs 18:24-39
Matt 24:24
2 Thes 2:9
Rev 19:20
13:14
2 Thes 2:9
Rev 12:9; 13:3, 12
13:15
Dan 3:3-6
Rev 20:4
13:16
Rev 14:9; 19:18
13:17
Rev 14:9, 11; 16:2;
19:20; 20:4
13:18
Rev 17:9
14:1
Rev 3:12; 7:4
14:2
Rev 1:15; 19:6
14:3
Rev 4:4, 6
14:4
2 Cor 11:2
14:5
Isa 53:9
Zeph 3:13
1 Pet 2:22

**13:18a** Or *of humanity.*   **13:18b** Some manuscripts read *616.*   **14:4a** Greek *They are virgins who have not defiled themselves with women.*   **14:4b** Greek *as firstfruits.*

**13:14** Throughout the Bible we see miracles performed as proofs of God's power, love, and authority. But here we see counterfeit miracles performed to deceive. This is a reminder of Pharaoh's magicians, who duplicated Moses' signs in Egypt. True signs and miracles point us to Jesus Christ, but miracles alone can be deceptive. That is why we must ask with respect to each miracle we see: Is this consistent with what God says in the Bible? The second beast here gains influence through the signs and wonders that he can perform on behalf of the first beast. The second beast orders the people to worship a statue in honor of the first beast—a direct flouting of the second commandment (Exodus 20:4-6). Allowing the Bible to guide our faith and practice will keep us from being deceived by false signs, however convincing they appear to be. Any teaching that contradicts God's Word is false.

**13:16, 17** In every generation, Christians need to maintain a healthy skepticism about society's pleasures and rewards. In our educational, economic, and civic structures, there are incentives and rewards. Cooperating Christians must always support what is good and healthy about our society, but we must stand against sin. In some cases, such as Satan's system described here, the system or structure becomes so evil that there is no way to cooperate with it.

**13:16-18** This mark of the beast is designed to mock the seal that God places on his followers (7:2, 3). Just as God marks his people to save them, so Satan's beast marks his people to save them from the persecution that Satan will inflict upon God's followers. Identifying this particular mark is not as important as identifying the purpose of the mark. Those who accept it show their allegiance to Satan, their willingness to operate within the economic system he promotes, and their rebellion against God. To refuse the mark means to commit oneself entirely to God, preferring death to compromising one's faith in Christ.

**13:18** The meaning of this number has been discussed more than that of any other part of the book of Revelation. The three sixes have been said to represent many things, including the number of a man or the unholy trinity of Satan, the first beast, and the false prophet (16:13). If the number seven is considered to be the perfect number in the Bible, and if three sevens represent complete perfection, then the number 666 falls completely short of perfection. The first readers of this book probably applied the number to the emperor Nero, who symbolized all the evils of the Roman Empire. (The Greek letters of Nero's name represent numbers that total 666.) Whatever specific application the number is given, the number symbolizes the worldwide dominion and complete evil of this unholy trinity designed to undo Christ's work and overthrow him.

**14:1ff** Chapter 13 described the onslaught of evil that will occur when Satan and his helpers control the world. Chapter 14 gives a glimpse into eternity to show believers what awaits them if they endure. The Lamb is the Messiah. Mount Zion, often another name for Jerusalem, the capital of Israel, is contrasted with the worldly empire. The 144,000 represent believers who have endured persecutions on earth and now are ready to enjoy the eternal benefits and blessings of life with God forever. The three angels contrast the destiny of believers with that of unbelievers.

**14:4** These people are true believers whose robes have been washed and made white in Christ's blood (7:14) through his death ("purchased from among the people on the earth"). In the Old Testament, idolatry was often portrayed as spiritual adultery (see the book of Hosea). Their being "pure as virgins" is best understood symbolically, meaning that they are free from involvement with the pagan world system. To remain spiritually pure means resisting the seductions and idolatries of the present world—power, wealth, and sexual immorality. To do so requires daily application of God's Word, for it has a purifying effect on the mind and heart. It requires great resolution not to give in to these temptations.

Following Christ, the Lamb, "wherever he goes" requires heroic effort to carry out Christ's commission to face oppression and even death if required. Too many shrink back when the work is difficult or the future looks bleak. Join those who take their stand with Christ and against sin.

The "special offering" refers to the act of dedicating the first part of the harvest as holy to God (Exodus 23:19; see also James 1:18).

**14:6**
Rev 5:9

**14:7**
Acts 4:24
Rev 15:4

**14:8**
Isa 21:9
Jer 51:8
Rev 16:19; 17:5;
18:2, 10

**14:9**
Rev 13:12-17

**14:10**
Ps 75:8
Isa 51:17, 22-23
Jer 25:15
Rev 16:19; 19:20;
20:10; 21:8

**14:11**
Isa 34:10
Rev 13:12-17

**14:12**
Rev 2:13; 12:17;
13:10

**14:13**
Heb 4:10

**14:14**
Dan 7:13
Rev 1:13

**14:15**
Joel 3:13
Matt 13:39-40
Mark 4:29

**14:18**
Joel 3:13
Rev 6:9; 14:15

## The Three Angels

⁶And I saw another angel flying through the sky, carrying the eternal Good News to proclaim to the people who belong to this world—to every nation, tribe, language, and people. ⁷"Fear God," he shouted. "Give glory to him. For the time has come when he will sit as judge. Worship him who made the heavens, the earth, the sea, and all the springs of water."

⁸Then another angel followed him through the sky, shouting, "Babylon is fallen—that great city is fallen—because she made all the nations of the world drink the wine of her passionate immorality."

⁹Then a third angel followed them, shouting, "Anyone who worships the beast and his statue or who accepts his mark on the forehead or on the hand ¹⁰must drink the wine of God's anger. It has been poured full strength into God's cup of wrath. And they will be tormented with fire and burning sulfur in the presence of the holy angels and the Lamb. ¹¹The smoke of their torment will rise forever and ever, and they will have no relief day or night, for they have worshiped the beast and his statue and have accepted the mark of his name."

¹²This means that God's holy people must endure persecution patiently, obeying his commands and maintaining their faith in Jesus.

¹³And I heard a voice from heaven saying, "Write this down: Blessed are those who die in the Lord from now on. Yes, says the Spirit, they are blessed indeed, for they will rest from their hard work; for their good deeds follow them!"

## The Harvest of the Earth

¹⁴Then I saw a white cloud, and seated on the cloud was someone like the Son of Man.* He had a gold crown on his head and a sharp sickle in his hand.

¹⁵Then another angel came from the Temple and shouted to the one sitting on the cloud, "Swing the sickle, for the time of harvest has come; the crop on earth is ripe." ¹⁶So the one sitting on the cloud swung his sickle over the earth, and the whole earth was harvested.

¹⁷After that, another angel came from the Temple in heaven, and he also had a sharp sickle. ¹⁸Then another angel, who had power to destroy with fire, came from the altar. He shouted to the angel with the sharp sickle, "Swing your sickle now to gather the clusters of

**14:14** Or *like a son of man*. See Dan 7:13. "Son of Man" is a title Jesus used for himself.

---

**14:6, 7** Some believe that this is a final, worldwide appeal to all people to recognize the one true God. No one will have the excuse of never hearing God's truth. Others, however, see this as an announcement of judgment rather than as an appeal. The people of the world have had their chance to proclaim their allegiance to God, and now God's great judgment is about to begin. If you are reading this, you have already heard God's truth. You know that God's final judgment will not be put off forever. Have you joyfully received the everlasting Good News? Have you confessed your sins and trusted in Christ to save you? If so, you have nothing to fear from God's judgment. The Judge of all the earth is your Savior!

**14:8** Babylon was the name of both an evil city and an immoral empire, a world center for idol worship. Babylon ransacked Jerusalem and carried the people of Judah into captivity (see 2 Kings 25 and 2 Chronicles 36). Just as Babylon was the Jews' worst enemy, the Roman Empire was the worst enemy of the early Christians. John, who probably did not dare speak against Rome openly, applied the name *Babylon* to this enemy of God's people (Rome)—and, by extension, to all God's enemies of all times.

**14:9-11** Those who worship the beast, accept his mark, and operate according to his world economic system will ultimately face God's judgment. Our world values money, power, and pleasure over God's leadership. To get what the world values, many people deny God and violate Christian principles. Thus, they must drink of the wine of God's anger (see Psalm 75; Isaiah 51:17).

**14:11** The ultimate result of sin is unending separation from God. Because human beings are created in God's image with an inborn thirst for fellowship with him, separation from God will be the ultimate torment and misery. Sin always brings misery, but in this life we can choose to repent and restore our relationship with God. In eternity there will no longer be opportunity for repen-

tance. If in this life we choose to be independent of God, in the next life we will be separated from him forever. Nobody is forced to choose eternal separation from God, and nobody suffers this fate by accident. Jesus invites all of us to open the door of our heart to him (3:20). If we do this, we will enjoy everlasting fellowship with him.

**14:12** This news about God's ultimate triumph should encourage God's people to remain faithful through every trial and persecution. They can do this, God promises, by trusting in Jesus and obeying the commands found in his Word. The secret to enduring, therefore, is trust and obedience. Trust God to give you patience to endure even the small trials you face daily; obey him even when obedience is unattractive or dangerous.

**14:13** While it is true that money, fame, and belongings can't be taken with us from this life, God's people *can* produce fruit that survives even death. God will remember our love, kindness, and faithfulness, and those who accept Christ through our witness will join us in the new earth. Be sure that your values are in line with God's values, and decide today to produce fruit that lasts forever.

**14:14-16** This is an image of judgment: Christ is separating the faithful from the unfaithful like a farmer harvesting his crops. This is a time of joy for the Christians who have been persecuted and martyred—they will receive their long-awaited reward. Christians should not fear the Last Judgment. Jesus said, "I tell you the truth, those who listen to my message and believe in God who sent me have eternal life. They will never be condemned for their sins, but they have already passed from death into life" (John 5:24).

grapes from the vines of the earth, for they are ripe for judgment." ¹⁹So the angel swung his sickle over the earth and loaded the grapes into the great winepress of God's wrath. ²⁰The grapes were trampled in the winepress outside the city, and blood flowed from the winepress in a stream about 180 miles* long and as high as a horse's bridle.

14:19
Isa 63:2-6
Rev 19:15

14:20
Gen 49:11
Isa 63:3
Lam 1:15
Rev 19:15

## 5. Pouring out the seven plagues
### The Song of Moses and of the Lamb

**15** Then I saw in heaven another marvelous event of great significance. Seven angels were holding the seven last plagues, which would bring God's wrath to completion. ²I saw before me what seemed to be a glass sea mixed with fire. And on it stood all the people who had been victorious over the beast and his statue and the number representing his name. They were all holding harps that God had given them. ³And they were singing the song of Moses, the servant of God, and the song of the Lamb:

15:1
Lev 26:21
Rev 15:6; 16:1;
21:9

15:2
Rev 4:6

15:3
Exod 15:1
Deut 32:14
Ps 145:17
Jer 10:7
Amos 3:13; 4:13
Rev 1:8; 4:8

> "Great and marvelous are your works,
>     O Lord God, the Almighty.
> Just and true are your ways,
>     O King of the nations.*
> ⁴ Who will not fear you, Lord,
>     and glorify your name?
> For you alone are holy.
> All nations will come and worship before you,
>     for your righteous deeds have been revealed."

15:4
Ps 86:9
Jer 10:6-7
Mal 1:11

### The Seven Bowls of the Seven Plagues

⁵ Then I looked and saw that the Temple in heaven, God's Tabernacle, was thrown wide open. ⁶The seven angels who were holding the seven plagues came out of the Temple. They were clothed in spotless white linen* with gold sashes across their chests. ⁷Then one of the four living beings handed each of the seven angels a gold bowl filled with the wrath of God, who lives forever and ever. ⁸The Temple was filled with smoke from God's glory and power. No one could enter the Temple until the seven angels had completed pouring out the seven plagues.

15:5
Rev 11:19

15:6
Lev 26:21

15:8
Exod 40:34
1 Kgs 8:10-11
2 Chr 5:13-14
Isa 6:4

**16** Then I heard a mighty voice from the Temple say to the seven angels, "Go your ways and pour out on the earth the seven bowls containing God's wrath." ²So the first angel left the Temple and poured out his bowl on the earth, and horrible, malignant sores broke out on everyone who had the mark of the beast and who worshiped his statue.

16:1
Isa 66:6
Zeph 3:8

16:2
Exod 9:9-11

**14:20** Greek *1,600 stadia* [296 kilometers].    **15:3** Some manuscripts read *King of the ages.*    **15:6** Other manuscripts read *white stone;* still others read *white [garments] made of linen.*

---

**14:19** A winepress was a large vat or trough where grapes were collected and then crushed. The juice flowed out of a duct that led into a large holding vat. The winepress is often used in the Bible as a symbol of God's wrath and judgment against sin (Isaiah 63:3-6; Lamentations 1:15; Joel 3:12, 13). The distance of 180 miles is approximately the north-south length of Palestine.

To those unaccustomed to vivid descriptions of God's anger in judgement, these are disturbing images. People dislike the idea of other people, even evil ones, being trampled like grapes. The depth and length of the blood flow provides a sickening scene of the immensity of God's judgment. But unless we face the necessity of God's judgment, we will never see our desperate need for his mercy. A god with only a grandfatherly kindness would not inspire our repentance, obedience, or worship. God has promised a harsh harvest for those who reject him. Those who know God well enough to fear his wrath know God well enough to desire his grace. The crushing wrath of God is coming. Blessed are those who have had their sins forgiven, and blessed are those who lead others to God's mercy.

**15:1** The seven last plagues are also called the seven bowl judgments. They actually begin in chapter 16. Unlike the previous plagues, these are universal, and they will culminate in the abolition of all evil and the end of the world.

**15:3, 4** The song of Moses celebrated Israel's deliverance from Egypt (Exodus 15). The song of the Lamb celebrates the ultimate deliverance of God's people from the power of Satan.

**15:5-8** This imagery brings us back to the time of the Exodus in the wilderness when the Ark of the Covenant (the symbol of God's presence among his people) resided in the Tabernacle. The angels' garments are reminiscent of the high priest's clothing, showing that they are free from corruption, immorality, and injustice. The smoke that fills the Temple is the manifestation of God's glory and power. There is no escape from this judgment.

**15:8** John saw the Temple filled with the glory and power of God. The key to God's eternal glory and power is his holiness (4:8). God's glory is not only his strength but also his perfect moral character. God will never do anything that is not morally perfect. This reassures us that we can trust him, yet it places a demand on us. Our desire to be holy (dedicated to God and morally pure) is our only suitable response. Our eternal reign with Christ won't begin until all evil is destroyed by his judgment. We must wait for his timetable to be revealed.

**16:1ff** The bowl judgments are God's final and complete judgments on the earth. The end has come. There are many similarities between the bowl judgments and the trumpet judgments

**16:3**
Exod 7:17-21

3 Then the second angel poured out his bowl on the sea, and it became like the blood of a corpse. And everything in the sea died.

**16:4**
Exod 7:17-21
Ps 78:44

4 Then the third angel poured out his bowl on the rivers and springs, and they became blood. 5 And I heard the angel who had authority over all water saying,

**16:5**
Rev 1:4, 8; 4:8;
11:17

"You are just, O Holy One, who is and who always was,
    because you have sent these judgments.

**16:6**
Ps 79:3
Isa 49:26

6 Since they shed the blood
    of your holy people and your prophets,
you have given them blood to drink.
    It is their just reward."

**16:7**
Rev 1:8; 6:9; 14:18;
15:3; 19:2

7 And I heard a voice from the altar,* saying,

"Yes, O Lord God, the Almighty,
    your judgments are true and just."

8 Then the fourth angel poured out his bowl on the sun, causing it to scorch everyone with its fire. 9 Everyone was burned by this blast of heat, and they cursed the name of God, who had control over all these plagues. They did not repent of their sins and turn to God and give

**16:10**
Exod 10:21
Isa 8:22
Rev 8:12; 9:2; 13:2

him glory.
10 Then the fifth angel poured out his bowl on the throne of the beast, and his kingdom was plunged into darkness. His subjects ground their teeth in anguish, 11 and they cursed the

**16:11**
Rev 9:20-21

God of heaven for their pains and sores. But they did not repent of their evil deeds and turn to God.

**16:12**
Isa 11:15-16; 44:27
Jer 50:38; 51:36

12 Then the sixth angel poured out his bowl on the great Euphrates River, and it dried up

**16:7** Greek *I heard the altar.*

---

**BLESSINGS IN REVELATION**
Seven times in Revelation, God promises blessings upon the believers.

| Reference | Verse |
|---|---|
| 1:3 . . . . . . . | "God blesses the one who reads the words of this prophecy to the church, and he blesses all who listen to its message and obey what it says." |
| 14:13 . . . . . | "Blessed are those who die in the Lord from now on. Yes, says the Spirit, they are blessed indeed, for they will rest from their hard work; for their good deeds follow them!" |
| 16:15 . . . . . | "Blessed are all who are watching for me, who keep their clothing ready so they will not have to walk around naked and ashamed." |
| 19:9 . . . . . . | "Blessed are those who are invited to the wedding feast of the Lamb." |
| 20:6 . . . . . . | "Blessed and holy are those who share in the first resurrection. For them the second death holds no power, but they will be priests of God and of Christ and will reign with him a thousand years." |
| 22:7 . . . . . . | "Blessed are those who obey the words of prophecy written in this book." |
| 22:14 . . . . . | "Blessed are those who wash their robes. They will be permitted to enter through the gates of the city and eat the fruit from the tree of life." |

---

(8:6–11:19), but there are three main differences: (1) These judgments are complete whereas the trumpet judgments are partial; (2) the trumpet judgments still give unbelievers the opportunity to repent, but the bowl judgments do not; and (3) people are indirectly affected by several of the trumpet judgments but directly attacked by all the bowl judgments.

**16:6** The angel acclaimed God for his justice in dealing with those who had killed the martyrs. God's wrath may be hard for us to accept. In a moral universe, however, God must ultimately oppose and destroy evil. Those who join the revolt against God suffer with their leaders.

We must avoid the misconception that God must be fair and kind in his dealings with humanity. This view of justice is merely a projection of a human idea. People who believe this notion appeal to tolerance and forgiveness and assume that God must play by our rules. In reality, God sets his own standard of justice. He uses his power according to his own moral perfection. Thus, whatever he chooses or decrees is fair, even if we don't understand it or like it. Those who rebel and reject God are

not rejecting a "lifestyle option"; they are rejecting truth and justice itself.

**16:7** The significance of the altar itself responding is that *everyone and everything* will be praising God, acknowledging his righteousness and perfect justice.

**16:9-21** We know that the people realize that these judgments come from God because they curse him for sending them. But they still refuse to recognize God's authority and repent of their sins. Christians should not be surprised at the hostility and hardness of heart of unbelievers. Even when the power of God is fully and completely revealed, many will still refuse to repent. Don't wait until "just the right time" before turning to God. Do it now while you still have the chance. If you continually ignore God's warnings, you will eventually be unable to hear him at all.

**16:12** The Euphrates River was a natural protective boundary against the empires to the east (Babylon, Assyria, Persia). If it dried up, nothing could hold back invading armies. The armies from the east symbolize unhindered judgment.

so that the kings from the east could march their armies toward the west without hindrance. <sup>13</sup>And I saw three evil* spirits that looked like frogs leap from the mouths of the dragon, the beast, and the false prophet. <sup>14</sup>They are demonic spirits who work miracles and go out to all the rulers of the world to gather them for battle against the Lord on that great judgment day of God the Almighty.

<sup>15</sup>"Look, I will come as unexpectedly as a thief! Blessed are all who are watching for me, who keep their clothing ready so they will not have to walk around naked and ashamed."

<sup>16</sup>And the demonic spirits gathered all the rulers and their armies to a place with the Hebrew name *Armageddon*.*

<sup>17</sup>Then the seventh angel poured out his bowl into the air. And a mighty shout came from the throne in the Temple, saying, "It is finished!" <sup>18</sup>Then the thunder crashed and rolled, and lightning flashed. And a great earthquake struck—the worst since people were placed on the earth. <sup>19</sup>The great city of Babylon split into three sections, and the cities of many nations fell into heaps of rubble. So God remembered all of Babylon's sins, and he made her drink the cup that was filled with the wine of his fierce wrath. <sup>20</sup>And every island disappeared, and all the mountains were leveled. <sup>21</sup>There was a terrible hailstorm, and hailstones weighing as much as seventy-five pounds* fell from the sky onto the people below. They cursed God because of the terrible plague of the hailstorm.

## 6. Seizing the final victory
### The Great Prostitute

**17** One of the seven angels who had poured out the seven bowls came over and spoke to me. "Come with me," he said, "and I will show you the judgment that is going to come on the great prostitute, who rules over many waters. <sup>2</sup>The kings of the world have committed adultery with her, and the people who belong to this world have been made drunk by the wine of her immorality."

<sup>3</sup>So the angel took me in the Spirit* into the wilderness. There I saw a woman sitting on a scarlet beast that had seven heads and ten horns, and blasphemies against God were written all over it. <sup>4</sup>The woman wore purple and scarlet clothing and beautiful jewelry made of gold and precious gems and pearls. In her hand she held a gold goblet full of obscenities and the impurities of her immorality. <sup>5</sup>A mysterious name was written on her forehead: "Babylon the Great, Mother of All Prostitutes and Obscenities in the World." <sup>6</sup>I could see that she was

**16:13** Greek *unclean*.   **16:16** Or *Harmagedon*.   **16:21** Greek *1 talent* [34 kilograms].   **17:3** Or *in spirit*.

**16:13**
Rev 12:3;
13:1, 11-17

**16:14**
Rev 6:17; 17:14;
19:19

**16:15**
1 Thes 5:2
Rev 3:3, 18

**16:16**
Judg 5:19
2 Kgs 9:27; 23:29
Zech 12:11

**16:17**
Isa 66:6
Rev 11:15; 21:6

**16:18**
Dan 12:1
Matt 24:21
Rev 4:5; 6:12

**16:19**
Rev 14:8, 10

**16:20**
Rev 6:14; 20:11

**16:21**
Exod 9:23-25
Rev 11:19; 16:9, 11

**17:1**
Jer 51:13
Rev 17:15; 19:2

**17:2**
Jer 51:7
Rev 14:8; 18:3

**17:3**
Rev 1:10; 12:6;
13:1

**17:4**
Jer 51:7
Ezek 28:13

**17:5**
2 Thes 2:7
Rev 17:2, 7

**17:6**
Rev 16:6; 18:24

**16:13, 14** These evil spirits performing miraculous signs, who come out of the mouths of the unholy trinity, unite the rulers of the world for battle against God. The imagery of the demons coming out of the mouths of the three evil rulers signifies the verbal enticements and propaganda that will draw many people to their evil cause. For more about demons, see the note on 9:3ff.

**16:15** Christ will return unexpectedly (1 Thessalonians 5:1-6), so we must be ready when he returns. We can prepare ourselves by standing firm in temptation and by being committed to God's moral standards. In what ways does your life show either your readiness or your lack of preparation for Christ's return?

**16:16** This battlefield called Armageddon is near the city of Megiddo (southeast of the modern port of Haifa), which guarded a large plain in northern Israel. It is a strategic location near a prominent international highway leading north from Egypt through Israel, along the coast, and on to Babylon. Megiddo overlooked the entire plain southward toward Galilee and westward toward the mountains of Gilboa.

**16:16** Sinful people will unite to fight against God in a final display of rebellion. Many are already united against Christ and his people—those who stand for truth, peace, justice, and morality. Your personal battle with evil foreshadows the great battle pictured here, where God will meet evil and destroy it once and for all. Be strong and courageous as you battle against sin and evil: You are fighting on the winning side.

**16:17-21** For more information on Babylon and what it represents in Revelation, see the note on 14:8. The city's division into three sections is a symbol of its complete destruction.

**17:1ff** The destruction of Babylon mentioned in 16:17-21 is now described in greater detail. The "great prostitute," called Babylon, represents the early Roman Empire with its many gods and the blood of Christian martyrs on its hands. The water stands for either sea commerce or a well-watered (well-provisioned) city. The great prostitute represents the seductiveness of the governmental system that uses immoral means to gain its own pleasure, prosperity, and advantage. In contrast to the prostitute, Christ's bride, the church, is pure and obedient (19:6-9). The wicked city of Babylon contrasts with the heavenly city of Jerusalem (21:10–22:5). The original readers probably rather quickly identified Babylon with Rome, but Babylon also symbolizes any system that is hostile to God (see 17:5).

**17:3** The angel took John into the wilderness to see the prostitute in her reality. (The scarlet beast is either the dragon of 12:3 or the beast out of the sea described in 13:1.) Sometimes we can only get a clear view of reality when we step back from our daily lives and see the patterns of evil and sin around us. Retreats, conferences, and days of prayer and fasting can help us extricate ourselves from jobs, newspapers, and television and bring us to new spiritual heights. Take time to view the reality of your life and evaluate its direction and activities. Do these glorify God and renew you to serve others?

**17:6** Throughout history, people have been killed for their faith. Over the last century, millions have been killed by oppressive governments, and many of those victims were believers. The woman's drunkenness shows her pleasure in her evil accomplishments and her false feeling of triumph over the church. But drunk—drunk with the blood of God's holy people who were witnesses for Jesus. I stared at her in complete amazement.

7"Why are you so amazed?" the angel asked. "I will tell you the mystery of this woman and of the beast with seven heads and ten horns on which she sits. 8The beast you saw was once alive but isn't now. And yet he will soon come up out of the bottomless pit* and go to eternal destruction. And the people who belong to this world, whose names were not written in the Book of Life before the world was made, will be amazed at the reappearance of this beast who had died.

9"This calls for a mind with understanding: The seven heads of the beast represent the seven hills where the woman rules. They also represent seven kings. 10Five kings have already fallen, the sixth now reigns, and the seventh is yet to come, but his reign will be brief.

11"The scarlet beast that was, but is no longer, is the eighth king. He is like the other seven, and he, too, is headed for destruction. 12The ten horns of the beast are ten kings who have not yet risen to power. They will be appointed to their kingdoms for one brief moment to reign with the beast. 13They will all agree to give him their power and authority. 14Together they will go to war against the Lamb, but the Lamb will defeat them because he is Lord of all lords and King of all kings. And his called and chosen and faithful ones will be with him."

15Then the angel said to me, "The waters where the prostitute is ruling represent masses of people of every nation and language. 16The scarlet beast and his ten horns all hate the prostitute. They will strip her naked, eat her flesh, and burn her remains with fire. 17For God has put a plan into their minds, a plan that will carry out his purposes. They will agree to give their authority to the scarlet beast, and so the words of God will be fulfilled. 18And this woman you saw in your vision represents the great city that rules over the kings of the world."

### The Fall of Babylon

**18** After all this I saw another angel come down from heaven with great authority, and the earth grew bright with his splendor. 2He gave a mighty shout:

"Babylon is fallen—that great city is fallen!
  She has become a home for demons.

17:8 Or *the abyss,* or *the underworld.*

---

**17:8**
Dan 12:1
Rev 11:7; 13:1, 3

**17:9**
Rev 13:18

**17:12**
Dan 7:20, 24
Rev 18:10, 17, 19

**17:14**
Matt 22:14
1 Tim 6:15

**17:15**
Rev 13:7; 17:1

**17:16**
Lev 21:9
Ezek 16:37, 39
Rev 18:8, 19

**17:17**
Rev 10:7; 17:13

**17:18**
Rev 16:19

**18:2**
Isa 13:19-22; 21:9
Jer 50:39

---

every martyr who has fallen before her sword has only served to strengthen the faith of the church. Persecution is by no means a thing of the past. Christians in many parts of the world know that faith in Christ amounts to a death sentence. Believers who live in places free of such persecution must not forget to pray for their brothers and sisters in Christ in those difficult parts of the world.

**17:8** In chapter 12 we met the dragon (Satan). In chapter 13 we saw the beast from the sea and the power he received from Satan. In chapters 14–16 we see God's great judgments. In this chapter, a scarlet beast similar to the beast and the dragon appears as an ally of the great prostitute. The beast was alive, died, and then came back to life. The beast's resurrection symbolizes the persistence of evil. This resurgence of evil power will convince many to join forces with the beast, but those who choose the side of evil condemn themselves to the devil's fate—eternal torment.

**17:8** For more information on the Book of Life, see the note on 3:5.

**17:9-11** Here John is referring to Rome, the city famous for its seven hills. Many say that this city also symbolized all evil in the world—any person, religion, group, government, or structure that opposed Christ. Whatever view is taken of the seven hills and seven kings, this section indicates the climax of Satan's struggle against God. Evil's power is limited, and its destruction is on the horizon.

**17:12** As we ponder the identity of the seven kings and the emergence of the ten kings, we must see John's theme of worldly power and its ultimate ineffectiveness against God and his people. Their authority only lasts "for one brief moment," symbolizing its brevity and ultimate destruction. As Christians, have we become infatuated with the worldly power of movie stars, sports celebrities, political coalitions, and world economic forces? Are you

craving the power and prestige that position, wealth, and connections offer? If so, you are an easy target for Satan's great deception. Worldly power is Satan's trap; the desire for it can turn us away from God. Worship only God and make it your strongest desire to serve him.

**17:16** In a dramatic turn of events, the prostitute's allies turn on her and destroy her. This is how evil operates. Destructive by its very nature, it discards its own adherents when they cease to serve its purposes. An unholy alliance is an uneasy alliance because each partner puts its own interests first.

**17:17** No matter what happens, we must trust that God is still in charge, that God overrules all the plans and intrigues of the evil one, and that God's plans will happen just as he says. God even uses people opposed to him as tools to execute his will. Although he allows evil to permeate this present world, the new earth will never know sin.

**18:1ff** This chapter shows the complete destruction of Babylon, John's metaphorical name for the evil world power and all it represents. Everything that tries to block God's purposes will come to a violent end. For more information on how the book of Revelation uses the name *Babylon,* see the note on 14:8.

**18:2, 3** Merchants in the Roman Empire grew rich by exploiting the sinful pleasures of their society. Many businesspeople today do the same thing. Businesses and governments are often based on greed, money, and power. Many bright individuals are tempted to take advantage of an evil system to enrich themselves. Christians are warned to stay free from the lure of money, status, and the good life. We are to live according to the values Christ exemplified: service, giving, self-sacrifice, obedience, and truth.

She is a hideout for every foul* spirit,
    a hideout for every foul vulture
    and every foul and dreadful animal.*
3 For all the nations have fallen*
    because of the wine of her passionate immorality.
The kings of the world
    have committed adultery with her.
Because of her desires for extravagant luxury,
    the merchants of the world have grown rich."

4Then I heard another voice calling from heaven,

    **18:4**
    Isa 48:20; 52:11
    Jer 51:6, 9, 45

"Come away from her, my people.
    Do not take part in her sins,
    or you will be punished with her.
5 For her sins are piled as high as heaven,
    and God remembers her evil deeds.

    **18:5**
    Jer 51:9

6 Do to her as she has done to others.
    Double her penalty* for all her evil deeds.
She brewed a cup of terror for others,
    so brew twice as much* for her.

    **18:6**
    Jer 50:15, 29

7 She glorified herself and lived in luxury,
    so match it now with torment and sorrow.
She boasted in her heart,
    'I am queen on my throne.
I am no helpless widow,
    and I have no reason to mourn.'

    **18:7**
    Isa 47:8

8 Therefore, these plagues will overtake her in a single day—
    death and mourning and famine.
She will be completely consumed by fire,
    for the Lord God who judges her is mighty."

    **18:8**
    Isa 47:9
    Jer 50:31-34

9And the kings of the world who committed adultery with her and enjoyed her great luxury will mourn for her as they see the smoke rising from her charred remains. 10They will stand at a distance, terrified by her great torment. They will cry out,

    **18:9**
    Ezek 26:16
    Rev 17:2
    **18:10**
    Ezek 26:17
    Rev 14:8

"How terrible, how terrible for you,
    O Babylon, you great city!
In a single moment
    God's judgment came on you."

11The merchants of the world will weep and mourn for her, for there is no one left to buy their goods. 12She bought great quantities of gold, silver, jewels, and pearls; fine linen,

    **18:11**
    Ezek 27:27, 36
    Rev 18:3
    **18:12-13**
    Ezek 27:12-22

**18:2a** Greek *unclean;* also in each of the two following phrases.  **18:2b** Some manuscripts condense the last two lines to read *a hideout for every foul [unclean] and dreadful vulture.*  **18:3** Some manuscripts read *have drunk.*  **18:6a** Or *Give her an equal penalty.*  **18:6b** Or *brew just as much.*

---

**18:4-8** The people of Babylon had lived in luxury and pleasure. The city boasted, "I am queen on my throne. . . . I have no reason to mourn." The powerful, wealthy people of this world are susceptible to this same attitude. A person who is financially comfortable often feels invulnerable, secure, and in control, feeling no need for God or anyone else. This kind of attitude defies God, and his judgment against it is harsh. We are told to avoid Babylon's sins. If you are financially secure, don't become complacent and deluded by the myth of self-sufficiency. Use your resources to help others and advance God's Kingdom.

**18:9, 10** Those who are tied to the world's system will lose everything when it collapses. What they have worked for a lifetime to build up will be destroyed in one hour. Those who work only for material rewards will have nothing when they die or when their possessions are destroyed. What can we take with us to the new earth? Our faith, our Christian character, and our relationships with other believers. These are more important than any amount of money, power, or pleasure.

**18:9-19** Those who are in control of various parts of the eco-

nomic system will mourn at Babylon's fall. The political leaders will mourn because they were the overseers of Babylon's wealth and were in a position to enrich themselves greatly. The merchants will mourn because Babylon, the greatest customer for their goods, will be gone. The sea captains will no longer have anywhere to bring their goods because the merchants will have nowhere to sell them. The fall of the evil world system affects all who enjoyed and depended on it. No one will remain unaffected by Babylon's fall.

**18:11-14** The voice from heaven (18:4) continued to prophesy against the greedy merchants. "The fancy things you loved" and the "luxuries and splendor" were gone. This list of merchandise illustrates the extreme materialism of this society. Few of these goods were necessities—most are luxuries. Even people had become commodities—sold as slaves to Babylon. The desire for nonessential luxuries had driven these merchants. Yet, how many of these luxuries listed are in *your* home? Most people will find that they own almost everything on this list. We are people who truly live in great luxury. We, too, are in danger of being absorbed purple, silk, and scarlet cloth; things made of fragrant thyine wood, ivory goods, and objects made of expensive wood; and bronze, iron, and marble. [13] She also bought cinnamon, spice, incense, myrrh, frankincense, wine, olive oil, fine flour, wheat, cattle, sheep, horses, chariots, and bodies—that is, human slaves.

[14] "The fancy things you loved so much
    are gone," they cry.
"All your luxuries and splendor
    are gone forever,
    never to be yours again."

**18:15**
Ezek 27:36

[15] The merchants who became wealthy by selling her these things will stand at a distance, terrified by her great torment. They will weep and cry out,

**18:16**
Rev 17:4

[16] "How terrible, how terrible for that great city!
    She was clothed in finest purple and scarlet linens,
    decked out with gold and precious stones and pearls!

**18:17**
Ezek 27:27-29
Rev 17:16

[17] In a single moment
    all the wealth of the city is gone!"

And all the captains of the merchant ships and their passengers and sailors and crews will stand at a distance. [18] They will cry out as they watch the smoke ascend, and they will say, "Where is there another city as great as this?" [19] And they will weep and throw dust on their heads to show their grief. And they will cry out,

**18:18**
Ezek 27:32
Rev 18:4

**18:19**
Ezek 27:30-34

"How terrible, how terrible for that great city!
    The shipowners became wealthy
    by transporting her great wealth on the seas.
In a single moment it is all gone."

**18:20**
Jer 51:48
Rev 12:12; 19:2

[20] Rejoice over her fate, O heaven
    and people of God and apostles and prophets!
For at last God has judged her
    for your sakes.

**18:21**
Jer 51:63

[21] Then a mighty angel picked up a boulder the size of a huge millstone. He threw it into the ocean and shouted,

"Just like this, the great city Babylon
    will be thrown down with violence
    and will never be found again.

**18:22**
Ezek 26:13

[22] The sound of harps, singers, flutes, and trumpets
    will never be heard in you again.
No craftsmen and no trades
    will ever be found in you again.
The sound of the mill
    will never be heard in you again.

---

**HOW CAN
A PERSON
KEEP AWAY
FROM THE EVIL
SYSTEM?**
Here are some
suggestions:

1. People must always be more important than products.
2. Keep away from pride in your own programs, plans, and successes.
3. Remember that God's will and Word must never be compromised.
4. People must always be considered above the making of money.
5. Do what is right, no matter what the cost.
6. Be involved in businesses that provide worthwhile products or services—
    not just things that feed the world's desires.

---

in possessions and pleasure. Make sure that your desires lead you in the right direction. Put boundaries on them. Don't go after everything you see. Keep your desires on serving God and building his Kingdom by helping others.

**18:11-19** God's people should not live for money, because money will be worthless in eternity. And they should keep on

guard constantly against greed, a sin that is always ready to take over their lives. God wants us to work and to provide for our families, and he commands the proper use of money. But when the desire for money fills our lives, it becomes a false god. Don't be enslaved by the desire for wealth.

23 The light of a lamp
     will never shine in you again.
The happy voices of brides and grooms
     will never be heard in you again.
For your merchants were the greatest in the world,
     and you deceived the nations with your sorceries.
24 In your* streets flowed the blood of the prophets and of God's holy people
     and the blood of people slaughtered all over the world."

*Songs of Victory in Heaven*

**19** After this, I heard what sounded like a vast crowd in heaven shouting,

"Praise the LORD!*
     Salvation and glory and power belong to our God.
2 His judgments are true and just.
     He has punished the great prostitute
who corrupted the earth with her immorality.
     He has avenged the murder of his servants."

3And again their voices rang out:

"Praise the LORD!
     The smoke from that city ascends forever and ever!"

4Then the twenty-four elders and the four living beings fell down and worshiped God,
who was sitting on the throne. They cried out, "Amen! Praise the LORD!"
5And from the throne came a voice that said,

"Praise our God,
     all his servants,
all who fear him,
     from the least to the greatest."

6Then I heard again what sounded like the shout of a vast crowd or the roar of mighty
ocean waves or the crash of loud thunder:

"Praise the LORD!
     For the Lord our God,* the Almighty, reigns.
7 Let us be glad and rejoice,
     and let us give honor to him.
For the time has come for the wedding feast of the Lamb,
     and his bride has prepared herself.
8 She has been given the finest of pure white linen to wear."
     For the fine linen represents the good deeds of God's holy people.

9And the angel said to me, "Write this: Blessed are those who are invited to the wedding
feast of the Lamb." And he added, "These are true words that come from God."
10Then I fell down at his feet to worship him, but he said, "No, don't worship me. I am a
servant of God, just like you and your brothers and sisters* who testify about their faith in
Jesus. Worship only God. For the essence of prophecy is to give a clear witness for Jesus.*"

**Cross-references:**
18:23 Jer 7:34; 16:9; 25:10 Nah 3:4
18:24 Jer 51:49 Matt 23:35-37 Rev 16:6; 17:6
19:1 Rev 4:11; 7:10; 12:10
19:3 Isa 34:10 Rev 14:11
19:4 Rev 4:4, 6, 10
19:5 Pss 115:13; 134:1; 135:1 Rev 11:18
19:6 Rev 11:15
19:7 Matt 22:2; 25:10 Eph 5:32 Rev 21:2, 9
19:9 Luke 14:15 Rev 21:5; 22:6
19:10 Acts 10:25-26 Rev 22:8-9

18:24 Greek *her.*   19:1 Greek *Hallelujah;* also in 19:3, 4, 6. *Hallelujah* is the transliteration of a Hebrew term that means "Praise the LORD."   19:6 Some manuscripts read *the Lord God.*   19:10a Greek *brothers.*   19:10b Or *is the message confirmed by Jesus.*

**19:1ff** Praise is the heartfelt response to God by those who love him. The more you get to know God and realize what he has done, the more you will respond with praise. Praise is at the heart of true worship. Let your praise of God flow out of your realization of who he is and how much he loves you.

**19:1-8** A vast crowd in heaven initiates the chorus of praise to God for his victory (19:1-3). Then the 24 elders (identified in the note on 4:4) join the chorus (19:4). Finally, the great choir of heaven once again praises God—the wedding of the Lamb has come (19:6-8). See Matthew 25:1-13 where Christ compares the coming of his Kingdom to a wedding for which we must be prepared.

**19:2** The identity of this great prostitute is explained in the note on 17:1ff.

**19:7, 8** This is the culmination of human history—the judgment of the wicked and the wedding of the Lamb and his bride, the church. The church consists of all faithful believers from all time. The bride's clothing stands in sharp contrast to the gaudy clothing of the great prostitute of 17:4 and 18:16. The bride's clothing represents the good deeds of the believers. These good deeds are not done by believers to their merit, but they reflect the work of Christ to save us (7:9, 14).

**19:10** The angel did not accept John's homage and worship because only God is worthy of worship. Like John, it would be

## The Rider on the White Horse

19:11
Isa 11:4
Rev 3:14

19:12
Rev 1:14; 2:17

19:13
Isa 63:1-3
John 1:1, 14
1 Jn 1:1-2

19:14
Rev 3:4

19:15
Isa 11:4; 63:3
2 Thes 2:8
Rev 2:27; 14:20

19:16
Rev 17:14

19:17-18
Ezek 39:17-20

19:20
Isa 30:33
Dan 7:11
Rev 13:12-16;
20:10, 14-15; 21:8

¹¹Then I saw heaven opened, and a white horse was standing there. Its rider was named Faithful and True, for he judges fairly and wages a righteous war. ¹²His eyes were like flames of fire, and on his head were many crowns. A name was written on him that no one understood except himself. ¹³He wore a robe dipped in blood, and his title was the Word of God. ¹⁴The armies of heaven, dressed in the finest of pure white linen, followed him on white horses. ¹⁵From his mouth came a sharp sword to strike down the nations. He will rule them with an iron rod. He will release the fierce wrath of God, the Almighty, like juice flowing from a winepress. ¹⁶On his robe at his thigh* was written this title: King of all kings and Lord of all lords.

¹⁷Then I saw an angel standing in the sun, shouting to the vultures flying high in the sky: "Come! Gather together for the great banquet God has prepared. ¹⁸Come and eat the flesh of kings, generals, and strong warriors; of horses and their riders; and of all humanity, both free and slave, small and great."

¹⁹Then I saw the beast and the kings of the world and their armies gathered together to fight against the one sitting on the horse and his army. ²⁰And the beast was captured, and with him the false prophet who did mighty miracles on behalf of the beast—miracles that deceived all who had accepted the mark of the beast and who worshiped his statue. Both the beast and his false prophet were thrown alive into the fiery lake of burning sulfur. ²¹Their entire army was killed by the sharp sword that came from the mouth of the one riding the white horse. And the vultures all gorged themselves on the dead bodies.

## The Thousand Years

20:1
Rev 1:18; 10:1

20:2
Rev 12:9

**20** Then I saw an angel coming down from heaven with the key to the bottomless pit* and a heavy chain in his hand. ²He seized the dragon—that old serpent, who is the

19:16 Or *On his robe and thigh.*   20:1 Or *the abyss,* or *the underworld;* also in 20:3.

---

easy for us to become overwhelmed by this prophetic pageant. But Jesus is the central focus of God's revelation and his redemptive plan (as announced by the prophets). As you read the book of Revelation, don't get bogged down in all the details of the awesome visions; remember that the overarching theme in all the visions is the ultimate victory of Jesus Christ over evil.

**19:11** The name "Faithful and True" contrasts with the faithless and deceitful Babylon described in chapter 18.

**19:11-21** John's vision shifts again. Heaven opens, and Jesus appears—this time not as a Lamb but as a warrior on a white horse (symbolizing victory). Jesus came first as a Lamb to be a sacrifice for sin, but he will return as a conqueror and king to execute judgment (2 Thessalonians 1:7-10). Jesus' first coming brought forgiveness; his second will bring judgment. The battle lines have been drawn between God and evil, and the world is waiting for the King to ride onto the field.

**19:12** Although Jesus is called "Faithful and True" (19:11), "Word of God" (19:13), and "King of all kings and Lord of all lords" (19:16), this verse implies that no name can do him justice. He is greater than any description or expression the human mind can devise.

**19:13** For more about the symbolism of Jesus' robe being dipped in blood, see the second note on 7:14.

**19:15** This scene provides a graphic display of the wrath of God. It shows God's anger and judgment against sin and against those who have constantly rejected Christ as the means of forgiveness and reconciliation. God's wrath exists alongside his mercy. In each generation, there must be balanced preaching and teaching about God's grace and his anger against sin.

In our day, however, teaching about God's love and tolerance have become so predominant that God's anger seems to be mythical. Such a portrayal of God hardly warns people away from sin. Teaching about God's wrath may be watered down by some, but it is nevertheless real and will be terrible for those who have steadfastly refused him (1 Thessalonians 1:10). In your study and teaching, do not emphasize God's mercy to the exclusion of his wrath.

**19:16** This title indicates our God's sovereignty. Most of the world is worshiping the beast, the Antichrist, whom they believe

has all power and authority. Then suddenly out of heaven ride Christ and his army of angels—the "King of all kings and Lord of all lords." His entrance signals the end of the false powers.

**19:17** This "great banquet" is a grim contrast to the wedding feast of the Lamb (19:9). One is a celebration; the other is devastation.

**19:19** The beast is identified in the note on 13:1.

**19:19-21** The battle lines have been drawn, and the greatest confrontation in the history of the world is about to begin. The beast (the Antichrist) and the false prophet have gathered the governments and armies of the earth under the Antichrist's rule. The enemy armies believe they have come of their own volition; in reality, God has summoned them to battle in order to defeat them. That they would even presume to fight against God shows how their pride and rebellion have distorted their thinking. There really is no fight, however, because the victory was won when Jesus died on the cross for sin and rose from the dead. Thus, the evil leaders are immediately captured and sent to their punishment, and the forces of evil are annihilated.

**19:20** The fiery lake of burning sulfur is the final destination of the wicked. This lake is different from the bottomless pit referred to in 9:1. The Antichrist and the false prophet are thrown into the fiery lake. Then their leader, Satan himself, will be thrown into that lake (20:10), and finally death and the grave (20:14). Afterward, everyone whose name is not recorded in the Book of Life will be thrown into the fiery lake (20:15).

**20:1** The angel and the bottomless pit are explained in the notes on 9:1 and 19:20.

**20:2** The dragon, Satan, is discussed in more detail in the notes on 12:3, 4 and 12:9. The dragon is not bound as punishment— that occurs in 20:10—but so that he cannot deceive the nations.

**20:2-4** The 1,000 years are often referred to as the *Millennium* (Latin for 1,000). Just how and when this 1,000 years takes place is understood differently among Christian scholars. The three major positions on this issue are called postmillennialism, premillennialism, and amillennialism.

(1) *Postmillennialism* looks for a literal 1,000-year period of peace on earth ushered in by the church. At the end of the 1,000

devil, Satan—and bound him in chains for a thousand years. ³The angel threw him into the bottomless pit, which he then shut and locked so Satan could not deceive the nations anymore until the thousand years were finished. Afterward he must be released for a little while.

⁴Then I saw thrones, and the people sitting on them had been given the authority to judge. And I saw the souls of those who had been beheaded for their testimony about Jesus and for proclaiming the word of God. They had not worshiped the beast or his statue, nor accepted his mark on their forehead or their hands. They all came to life again, and they reigned with Christ for a thousand years.

⁵This is the first resurrection. (The rest of the dead did not come back to life until the thousand years had ended.) ⁶Blessed and holy are those who share in the first resurrection. For them the second death holds no power, but they will be priests of God and of Christ and will reign with him a thousand years.

### The Defeat of Satan

⁷When the thousand years come to an end, Satan will be let out of his prison. ⁸He will go out to deceive the nations—called Gog and Magog—in every corner of the earth. He will gather them together for battle—a mighty army, as numberless as sand along the seashore. ⁹And I saw them as they went up on the broad plain of the earth and surrounded God's people and the beloved city. But fire from heaven came down on the attacking armies and consumed them.

¹⁰Then the devil, who had deceived them, was thrown into the fiery lake of burning sulfur, joining the beast and the false prophet. There they will be tormented day and night forever and ever.

### The Final Judgment

¹¹And I saw a great white throne and the one sitting on it. The earth and sky fled from his presence, but they found no place to hide. ¹²I saw the dead, both great and small, standing

**20:3**
2 Pet 2:4
Jude 1:6

**20:4**
Dan 7:9, 22, 27
Matt 19:28
Rev 13:12-16

**20:5**
Ezek 37:10
Luke 14:14

**20:6**
1 Pet 2:5, 9
Rev 1:6; 5:10;
20:14

**20:7**
Rev 20:2

**20:8**
Ezek 38:2

**20:9**
Ps 87:2
Ezek 38:22; 39:6

**20:10**
Rev 14:10; 19:20;
20:15

**20:11-12**
Dan 7:9-10
Matt 25:31-46

---

years, Satan will be unleashed once more, but then Christ will return to defeat him and reign forever. Christ's second coming will not occur until after the 1,000-year period.

(2) *Premillennialism* also views the 1,000 years as a literal time period but holds that Christ's second coming initiates his 1,000-year reign and that this reign occurs before the final removal of Satan.

(3) *Amillennialism* understands the 1,000-year period to be symbolic of the time between Christ's ascension and his return. This Millennium is the reign of Christ in the hearts of believers and in his church; thus, it is another way of referring to the church age. This period will end with the second coming of Christ.

These different views about the Millennium need not cause division and controversy in the church because each view acknowledges what is most crucial to Christianity: Christ will return, defeat Satan, and reign forever! Whatever and whenever the Millennium is, Jesus Christ will unite all believers; therefore, we should not let this issue divide us.

**20:3** John doesn't say why God releases Satan for a little while, but it is part of God's plan for judging the world. Perhaps it is to expose those who rebel against God in their hearts and confirm those who are truly faithful to God. Whatever the reason, Satan's release results in the final destruction of all evil (20:12-15).

**20:4** The beast's mark is explained in the note on 13:16-18.

**20:5, 6** Christians hold two basic views concerning this first resurrection: (1) Some believe that the first resurrection is spiritual (in our heart at salvation) and that the Millennium is our spiritual reign with Christ between his first and second comings. During this time, we are priests of God because Christ reigns in our hearts. In this view, the second resurrection is the bodily resurrection of all people for judgment. (2) Others believe that the first resurrection occurs after Satan has been set aside. It is a physical resurrection of believers, who then reign with Christ on the earth for a literal 1,000 years. The second resurrection occurs at the end of this Millennium in order to judge unbelievers who have died.

**20:6** The second death is spiritual death—everlasting separation from God (see 21:8).

**20:7-9** Gog and Magog symbolize all the forces of evil that band together to battle God. Noah's son Japheth had a son named Magog (Genesis 10:2). Ezekiel presents Gog as a leader of forces against Israel (Ezekiel 38–39).

**20:9** This is not a typical battle where the outcome is in doubt during the heat of the conflict. Here there is no contest. Two mighty forces of evil—those of the beast (19:19) and of Satan (20:8)—unite to do battle against God. The Bible uses just two verses to describe each battle: The evil beast and his forces are captured and thrown into the fiery lake (19:20, 21), and fire from heaven consumes Satan and his attacking armies (20:9, 10). For God, it is as easy as that. There will be no doubt, no worry, no second thoughts for believers about whether they have chosen the right side. If you are with God, you will experience this tremendous victory with Christ.

**20:10** Satan's power is not eternal—he will meet his doom. He began his evil work in people at the beginning (Genesis 3:1-6) and continues it today, but he will be destroyed when he is thrown into the fiery lake of burning sulfur. The devil will be released from the bottomless pit ("his prison," 20:7), but he will never be released from the fiery lake. He will never be a threat to anyone again.

**20:12-15** At the judgment, the books will be opened. The Book of Life contains the names of those who have put their trust in Christ to save them. These books also contain the recorded deeds of everyone, good or evil. Everyone's life will be reviewed and evaluated. No one is saved by deeds, but deeds are seen as clear evidence of a person's actual relationship with God. Jesus will look at how we have handled gifts, opportunities, and responsibilities. God's gracious gift of salvation does not free us from the requirement of faithful obedience and service. Each of us must serve Christ in the best way we know and live each day knowing the books will one day be opened.

**20:13**
Isa 26:19
Matt 16:27
John 5:28-29
Rev 1:18

**20:14**
1 Cor 15:26, 55
Rev 19:20

**21:1**
Isa 65:17; 66:22

**21:2**
Isa 52:1; 61:10

**21:3**
2 Chr 6:18
Ezek 37:27
Zech 2:10
2 Cor 6:16

**21:4**
Isa 25:8; 35:10;
43:18; 65:19

**21:5**
Isa 43:19
2 Cor 5:17

**21:6**
Rev 1:8; 22:13

before God's throne. And the books were opened, including the Book of Life. And the dead were judged according to what they had done, as recorded in the books. 13 The sea gave up its dead, and death and the grave* gave up their dead. And all were judged according to their deeds. 14 Then death and the grave were thrown into the lake of fire. This lake of fire is the second death. 15 And anyone whose name was not found recorded in the Book of Life was thrown into the lake of fire.

## 7. Making all things new
### The New Jerusalem

**21** Then I saw a new heaven and a new earth, for the old heaven and the old earth had disappeared. And the sea was also gone. 2 And I saw the holy city, the new Jerusalem, coming down from God out of heaven like a bride beautifully dressed for her husband.

3 I heard a loud shout from the throne, saying, "Look, God's home is now among his people! He will live with them, and they will be his people. God himself will be with them.* 4 He will wipe every tear from their eyes, and there will be no more death or sorrow or crying or pain. All these things are gone forever."

5 And the one sitting on the throne said, "Look, I am making everything new!" And then he said to me, "Write this down, for what I tell you is trustworthy and true." 6 And he also said, "It is finished! I am the Alpha and the Omega—the Beginning and the End. To all who are

20:13 Greek *and Hades;* also in 20:14.   21:3 Some manuscripts read *God himself will be with them, their God.*

---

**THE BEGINNING AND THE END**

| Genesis | Revelation |
|---|---|
| The sun is created. . . . . . . . . . . . . . . . . | The sun is not needed. |
| Satan is victorious. . . . . . . . . . . . . . . . . . | Satan is defeated. |
| Sin enters the human race. . . . . . . . . . . . | Sin is banished. |
| People run and hide from God. . . . . . . . . . | People are invited to live with God forever. |
| People are cursed. . . . . . . . . . . . . . . . . . . | The curse is removed. |
| Tears are shed, with sorrow for sin. . . . . . . | No more sin, no more tears or sorrow. |
| The garden and earth are cursed. . . . . . . . | God's city is glorified; the earth is made new. |
| Paradise is lost. . . . . . . . . . . . . . . . . . . . | Paradise is regained. |
| People are doomed to death. . . . . . . . . . . . | Death is defeated; believers live forever with God. |

The Bible records for us the beginning of the world and the end of the world. The story of mankind, from beginning to end—from the fall into sin to redemption and God's ultimate victory over evil—is found in the pages of the Bible.

---

**20:14** Death and the grave are thrown into the lake of fire. God's judgment is finished. The lake of fire is the ultimate destination of everything wicked—Satan, the beast, the false prophet, the demons, death, the grave, and all those whose names are not recorded in the Book of Life because they did not place their faith in Jesus Christ. John's vision does not permit any gray areas in God's judgment. If by faith we have not identified with Christ, confessing him as Lord, there will be no hope, no second chance, no other appeal.

**21:1** The earth as we know it will not last forever, but after God's great judgment, he will create a new earth (see Romans 8:18-21; 2 Peter 3:7-13). God had also promised Isaiah that he would create a new and eternal earth (Isaiah 65:17; 66:22). The sea is gone as well; in John's time, the sea was viewed as dangerous and changeable. It was also the source of the beast (13:1). We don't know how the new earth will look or where it will be, but God and his followers—those whose names are written in the Book of Life—will be united to live there forever. Will you be there?

**21:2, 3** The new Jerusalem is where God lives among his people. Instead of our going up to meet him, he comes down to be with us, just as God became man in Jesus Christ and lived among us (John 1:14). Wherever God reigns, there is peace, security, and love.

**21:3, 4** Have you ever wondered what eternity will be like? The "holy city, the new Jerusalem" is described as the place where

God will remove all sorrows. Forevermore, there will be no death, sorrow, crying, or pain. What a wonderful truth! No matter what you are going through, it's not the last word—God has written the final chapter, and it is about true fulfillment and eternal joy for those who love him. We do not know as much as we would like, but it is enough to know that eternity with God will be more wonderful than we could ever imagine.

**21:5** God is the Creator. The Bible begins with the majestic story of his creation of the universe, and it concludes with his creation of a new heaven and a new earth. This is a tremendous hope and encouragement for the believer. When we are with God, with our sins forgiven and our future secure, we will be like Christ. We will be made perfect like him.

**21:6** Just as God finished the work of creation (Genesis 2:1-3) and Jesus finished the work of redemption (John 19:30), so the Trinity will finish the entire plan of salvation by inviting the redeemed into a new creation.

**21:6** For more about the water of life, see the note on 22:1.

thirsty I will give freely from the springs of the water of life. ⁷All who are victorious will inherit all these blessings, and I will be their God, and they will be my children.

⁸"But cowards, unbelievers, the corrupt, murderers, the immoral, those who practice witchcraft, idol worshipers, and all liars—their fate is in the fiery lake of burning sulfur. This is the second death."

⁹Then one of the seven angels who held the seven bowls containing the seven last plagues came and said to me, "Come with me! I will show you the bride, the wife of the Lamb."

¹⁰So he took me in the Spirit* to a great, high mountain, and he showed me the holy city, Jerusalem, descending out of heaven from God. ¹¹It shone with the glory of God and sparkled like a precious stone—like jasper as clear as crystal. ¹²The city wall was broad and high, with twelve gates guarded by twelve angels. And the names of the twelve tribes of Israel were written on the gates. ¹³There were three gates on each side—east, north, south, and west. ¹⁴The wall of the city had twelve foundation stones, and on them were written the names of the twelve apostles of the Lamb.

¹⁵The angel who talked to me held in his hand a gold measuring stick to measure the city, its gates, and its wall. ¹⁶When he measured it, he found it was a square, as wide as it was long. In fact, its length and width and height were each 1,400 miles.* ¹⁷Then he measured the walls and found them to be 216 feet thick* (according to the human standard used by the angel).

¹⁸The wall was made of jasper, and the city was pure gold, as clear as glass. ¹⁹The wall of the city was built on foundation stones inlaid with twelve precious stones:* the first was jasper, the second sapphire, the third agate, the fourth emerald, ²⁰the fifth onyx, the sixth carnelian, the seventh chrysolite, the eighth beryl, the ninth topaz, the tenth chrysoprase, the eleventh jacinth, the twelfth amethyst.

²¹The twelve gates were made of pearls—each gate from a single pearl! And the main street was pure gold, as clear as glass.

²²I saw no temple in the city, for the Lord God Almighty and the Lamb are its temple. ²³And the city has no need of sun or moon, for the glory of God illuminates the city, and the Lamb is its light. ²⁴The nations will walk in its light, and the kings of the world will enter the city in all their glory. ²⁵Its gates will never be closed at the end of day because there is no night there. ²⁶And all the nations will bring their glory and honor into the city. ²⁷Nothing evil* will be allowed to enter, nor anyone who practices shameful idolatry and dishonesty—but only those whose names are written in the Lamb's Book of Life.

21:7
2 Sam 7:14
Rom 8:14
2 Cor 6:16
21:8
Ps 5:6
1 Cor 6:9
Eph 5:5
21:9
Rev 15:1, 7; 19:7
21:10
Ezek 40:1-2
Rev 1:10; 17:3
21:11
Isa 60:1-2, 19
Ezek 43:2
Rev 4:3
21:12
Exod 28:21
Ezek 48:30-34
Rev 22:14
21:14
Eph 2:20
Heb 11:10
21:15
Ezek 40:3, 5
21:16-17
Ezek 48:16-17
21:19
Exod 28:17-20
Isa 54:11-12
Ezek 28:13
21:21
Isa 54:12
21:22
John 4:21-24;
17:21-24
21:23
Isa 60:19-20
21:24
Isa 60:3, 5
21:25
Isa 60:11
Zech 14:7
21:27
Isa 52:1

21:10 Or *in spirit.*   21:16 Greek *12,000 stadia* [2,220 kilometers].   21:17 Greek *144 cubits* [65 meters].
21:19 The identification of some of these gemstones is uncertain.   21:27 Or *ceremonially unclean.*

---

**21:7, 8** The "cowards" are the fearful ones who abandon Christ at the threats of the beast. They fear persecution so badly that they choose temporary safety over eternal life. They are put in the same list as the unbelieving, the corrupt, the murderers, the immoral, the idolaters, the liars, and those practicing magic arts.

By contrast, people who are victorious "endure to the end" (Mark 13:13). They will receive the blessings that God promised: To follow Christ requires boldness and bravery to stand for him when oppression occurs. Pray for courage to do what is right no matter what pressure you face. Those who can endure the testing of evil and remain faithful will be rewarded by God.

**21:8** The lake is explained in the notes on 19:20 and 20:14. The second death is spiritual death, meaning either eternal torment or destruction. In either case, it is permanent separation from God.

**21:10ff** The rest of the chapter is a stunning description of the new city of God. The vision is symbolic and shows us that our new home with God will defy description. We will not be disappointed by it in any way.

**21:12-14** The new Jerusalem is a picture of God's future home for his people. The 12 tribes of Israel (21:12) probably represent all the faithful in the Old Testament; the 12 apostles (21:14) represent the church. Thus, both believing Gentiles and Jews who have been faithful to God will live together in the new earth.

**21:15-17** The city's measurements are symbolic of a place that will hold all God's people. These measurements are all multiples of 12, the number for God's people: There were 12 tribes in Israel, and 12 apostles who started the church. The walls are

144 (12 x 12) cubits (216 feet) thick. There are 12 layers in the walls, and 12 gates in the city; and the length, width, and height are all the same, 12,000 stadia (1,400 miles). The new Jerusalem is a perfect cube, the same shape as the Most Holy Place in the Temple (1 Kings 6:20). These measurements illustrate that this new home will be perfect for us.

**21:18-21** The picture of walls made of jewels reveals that the new Jerusalem will be a place of purity and durability—it will last forever.

**21:22-24** The Temple, the center of God's presence among his people, was the primary place of worship. No temple is needed in the new city, however, because God's presence will be everywhere. God will be the light in the new Jerusalem. Light represents what is good, pure, true, holy, and reliable. Darkness represents what is sinful and evil. That God's glory illuminates the city means that the city will be enveloped by him, who is perfectly holy and true. Light is also related to truth in that it exposes whatever exists. Just as darkness cannot exist in the presence of light, so sin cannot exist in the presence of a holy God. The city will be completely without sin and evil. We will be able to worship God throughout the city; nothing will hinder us from being with him.

**21:25-27** Not everyone will be allowed into the new Jerusalem, but "only those whose names are written in the Lamb's Book of Life." (The Book of Life is explained in the notes on 3:5 and 20:12-15.) Don't think that you will get in because of your background, personality, or good behavior. Eternal life is available to you only because of what Jesus, the Lamb, has done. Trust him today to secure your citizenship in his new creation.

**22:1**
Ezek 47:1
Joel 3:18
Zech 14:8
John 7:37-39

**22:2**
Gen 2:9
Ezek 47:12

**22:3**
Zech 14:11

**22:4**
Pss 17:15; 42:2
Matt 5:8

**22:5**
Isa 60:19-20
Dan 7:18, 27
Zech 14:7

**22** Then the angel showed me a river with the water of life, clear as crystal, flowing from the throne of God and of the Lamb. ²It flowed down the center of the main street. On each side of the river grew a tree of life, bearing twelve crops of fruit,* with a fresh crop each month. The leaves were used for medicine to heal the nations.

³No longer will there be a curse upon anything. For the throne of God and of the Lamb will be there, and his servants will worship him. ⁴And they will see his face, and his name will be written on their foreheads. ⁵And there will be no night there—no need for lamps or sun—for the Lord God will shine on them. And they will reign forever and ever.

⁶Then the angel said to me, "Everything you have heard and seen is trustworthy and true. The Lord God, who inspires his prophets,* has sent his angel to tell his servants what will happen soon.*"

### Jesus Is Coming

⁷"Look, I am coming soon! Blessed are those who obey the words of prophecy written in this book.*"

**22:8**
1 Jn 1:1-3

⁸I, John, am the one who heard and saw all these things. And when I heard and saw them, I fell down to worship at the feet of the angel who showed them to me. ⁹But he said, "No, don't worship me. I am a servant of God, just like you and your brothers the prophets, as well as all who obey what is written in this book. Worship only God!"

¹⁰Then he instructed me, "Do not seal up the prophetic words in this book, for the time is

**22:2** Or *twelve kinds of fruit.*    **22:6a** Or *The Lord, the God of the spirits of the prophets.*    **22:6b** Or *suddenly,* or *quickly;* also in 22:7, 12, 20.    **22:7** Or *scroll;* also in 22:9, 10, 18, 19.

---

**WHAT WE KNOW ABOUT ETERNITY**

| Description | Reference |
|---|---|
| A place prepared for us | John 14:2, 3 |
| Unlimited by physical properties (1 Corinthians 15:35-49) | John 20:19, 26 |
| Like Jesus | 1 John 3:2 |
| New bodies | 1 Corinthians 15 |
| A wonderful experience | 1 Corinthians 2:9 |
| A new environment | Revelation 21:1 |
| A new experience of God's presence (1 Corinthians 13:12) | Revelation 21:3 |
| New emotions | Revelation 21:4 |
| No more death | Revelation 21:4 |

The Bible devotes much less space to describing eternity than it does to convincing people that eternal life is available as a free gift from God. Most of the brief descriptions of eternity would be more accurately called hints, since they use terms and ideas from present experience to describe what we cannot fully grasp until we are there ourselves. These references hint at aspects of what our future will be like if we have accepted Christ's gift of eternal life.

---

**22:1** The water of life is a symbol of eternal life. Jesus used this same image with the Samaritan woman (John 4:7-14). It pictures the fullness of life with God and the eternal blessings that come when we believe in him and allow him to satisfy our spiritual thirst (see 22:17).

**22:2** This tree of life is like the tree of life in the Garden of Eden (Genesis 2:9). After Adam and Eve sinned, they were forbidden to eat from the tree of life because they could not have eternal life as long as they were under sin's control. But because of the forgiveness of sin through the blood of Jesus, there will be no evil or sin in this city. We will be able to eat freely from the tree of life when sin's control over us is destroyed and our eternity with God is secure.

**22:2** Why would the nations need to be healed if all evil is gone? John is quoting from Ezekiel 47:12, where water flowing from the Temple produces trees with healing leaves. He is not implying that there will be illness in the new earth; he is emphasizing that the water of life produces health and strength wherever it goes.

**22:3** "No longer will there be a curse upon anything" means that nothing accursed will be in God's presence. This fulfills Zechariah's prophecy (see Zechariah 14:11).

**22:8, 9** The first of the Ten Commandments is "You must not have any other god but me" (Exodus 20:3). Jesus said that the

greatest command of Moses' laws was "You must love the LORD your God with all your heart, all your soul, and all your mind" (Matthew 22:37). Here, at the end of the Bible, this truth is reiterated. The angel instructs John to worship God, and worship is a major emphasis in Revelation. The first step toward meaningful worship is a desire to know God. If we thirst for him, the Bible promises that he will provide for us and satisfy our needs. Would you like your worship to be completely transformed? Confess any sins that might be hindering your fellowship with God. Then ask God to stir your heart, to instill within you an unquenchable thirst to know him. Meditate upon how God has revealed himself in the Bible, and ask him to reveal himself to you again. When you see God in a new way, worship will be your only fitting response.

**22:10, 11** The angel tells John what to do after his vision is over. Instead of sealing up what he has written, as Daniel was commanded to do (Daniel 12:4-12), the book is to be left open so that all can read and understand. Daniel's message was sealed because it was not a message for Daniel's time. But the book of Revelation was a message for John's time, and it is relevant today. As Christ's return gets closer, there is a greater polarization between God's followers and Satan's followers. We must read the book of Revelation, hear its message, and be prepared for Christ's imminent return.

near. [11]Let the one who is doing harm continue to do harm; let the one who is vile continue to be vile; let the one who is righteous continue to live righteously; let the one who is holy continue to be holy."

[12]"Look, I am coming soon, bringing my reward with me to repay all people according to their deeds. [13]I am the Alpha and the Omega, the First and the Last, the Beginning and the End."

[14]Blessed are those who wash their robes. They will be permitted to enter through the gates of the city and eat the fruit from the tree of life. [15]Outside the city are the dogs—the sorcerers, the sexually immoral, the murderers, the idol worshipers, and all who love to live a lie.

[16]"I, Jesus, have sent my angel to give you this message for the churches. I am both the source of David and the heir to his throne.* I am the bright morning star."

[17]The Spirit and the bride say, "Come." Let anyone who hears this say, "Come." Let anyone who is thirsty come. Let anyone who desires drink freely from the water of life. [18]And I solemnly declare to everyone who hears the words of prophecy written in this book: If anyone adds anything to what is written here, God will add to that person the plagues described in this book. [19]And if anyone removes any of the words from this book of prophecy, God will remove that person's share in the tree of life and in the holy city that are described in this book.

[20]He who is the faithful witness to all these things says, "Yes, I am coming soon!" Amen! Come, Lord Jesus!
[21]May the grace of the Lord Jesus be with God's holy people.*

22:16 Greek *I am the root and offspring of David.* 22:21 Other manuscripts read *be with all;* still others read *be with all of God's holy people.* Some manuscripts add *Amen.*

**22:11**
Dan 12:10

**22:12**
Matt 16:27

**22:13**
Rev 1:8, 17; 21:6

**22:14**
Gen 2:9; 3:22
Ezek 47:12

**22:15**
1 Cor 6:9-10
Gal 5:19-21

**22:16**
Num 24:17
Isa 11:1, 10
Matt 1:1
Rom 1:3

**22:17**
Isa 55:1
John 7:37-39

**22:18**
Deut 4:2; 12:32
Prov 30:6
Rev 15:6–16:21

**22:19**
Gen 2:9; 3:22
Ezek 47:12

**22:20**
1 Cor 16:22

**22:21**
Rom 16:20
2 Thes 3:18

---

**22:12-14** Those who wash their robes are those who seek to purify themselves from a sinful way of life. They strive daily to remain faithful and ready for Christ's return. This concept is also explained in the second note on 7:14.

**22:14** In Eden, Adam and Eve were barred from any access to the tree of life because of their sin (Genesis 3:22-24). In the new earth, God's people will eat from the tree of life because their sins have been removed by Christ's death and resurrection. Those who eat the fruit of this tree will live forever. If Jesus has forgiven your sins, you will have the right to eat from this tree. For more on this concept, see the first note on 22:2.

**22:15** Jesus will exclude from the holy city those "who love to live a lie." These are people whose lives have gone so wrong that they resemble Satan, who deceived the whole world (12:9; 13:13-15; 16:14). They are hypocrites, trying to live one way while pretending to believe another. They are like the Nicolaitans, mentioned in 2:15, who were among the believers but compromised their faith in order to also include worship of the Roman emperor. John records Jesus' statement that Satan is the father of lies (John 8:44).

Today we see leaders who twist the truth to serve their purposes. Many people have lost the ability to distinguish what's true from what they wish was true. Dishonest people soon begin to believe the lies they construct around themselves. Then they lose the ability to tell the difference between truth and lies. By believing your own lies, you deceive yourself, you alienate yourself from God, and you lose credibility in all your relationships. In the long run, honesty wins out.

**22:16** Jesus is both David's "source" and "heir." As the Creator of all, Jesus existed long before David. As a human, however, he was one of David's direct descendants (see Isaiah 11:1-5; Matthew 1:1-17). As the Messiah, he is the "bright morning star," the light of salvation to all.

**22:17** Both the Holy Spirit and the bride, the church, extend the invitation to all the world to come to Jesus and experience the joys of salvation in Christ.

**22:17** When Jesus met the Samaritan woman at the well, he told her of the living water that he could supply (John 4:10-15). This image is used again as Christ invites anyone to come and drink of the water of life. The Good News is unlimited in scope—all people everywhere may come. Salvation cannot be earned, but God gives it freely. We live in a world desperately thirsty for living water, and many are dying of thirst. But it's still not too late. Let us invite everyone to come and drink.

**22:18, 19** This warning is given to those who might purposefully distort the message in this book. Moses gave a similar warning in Deuteronomy 4:1-4. We, too, must handle the Bible with care and great respect so that we do not distort its message, even unintentionally. We should be quick to put its principles into practice in our life. No human explanation or interpretation of God's Word should be elevated to the same authority as the text itself.

**22:20** We don't know the day or the hour, but Jesus is coming soon and unexpectedly. This is good news to those who trust him, but a terrible message for those who have rejected him and stand under judgment. *Soon* means "at any moment," and we must be ready for him, always prepared for his return. Would Jesus' sudden appearance catch you off guard?

**22:21** Revelation closes human history as Genesis opened it—in paradise. But there is one distinct difference in Revelation—evil is gone forever. Genesis describes Adam and Eve walking and talking with God; Revelation describes people worshiping God face to face. Genesis describes a garden with an evil serpent; Revelation describes a perfect city with no evil. The Garden of Eden was destroyed by sin; but paradise is re-created in the new Jerusalem.

The book of Revelation ends with an urgent plea: "Come, Lord Jesus!" In a world of problems, persecution, evil, and immorality, Christ calls us to endure in our faith. Our efforts to better our world are important, but their results cannot compare with the transformation that Jesus will bring about when he returns. He alone controls human history, forgives sin, and will re-create the earth and bring lasting peace.

Revelation is, above all, a book of hope. It shows that no matter what happens on earth, God is in control. It promises that evil will not last forever. And it depicts the wonderful reward that is waiting for all those who believe in Jesus Christ as Savior and Lord.

This section includes:
**How to Become a Christian**
**How to Follow Up with a New Believer**
**Mining the Treasures of the** *Life Application Study Bible*
**So You've Been Asked to Speak . . .**
**Taking the Step to Application**

## How to Become a Christian

As a believer, you will have the opportunity to talk to others about your faith. At times you will find a person who wants to know how he or she can become a Christian. Following is a guide you can use to help a person understand what it means to begin a relationship with Christ.

FACT: You were created by a loving God. You have great value. God loves you and wants to have a personal relationship with you.

SET-UP: Explain to the person that the world tells us that we are accidents of nature. We began as ooze in a pond, evolved into apes, and finally into humans. We live, we die, so we should grab for all we can get in this life—after all, that's the only way to fulfillment. In contrast, the Bible tells us that we are *not* accidents. We were created by a loving God who knew about us before we were born. We are here for a purpose, and we can find ultimate fulfillment by finding a relationship with him.

Read the following verses and make the following points:

### God created you.

Psalm 139:13-16. *You made all the delicate, inner parts of my body and knit me together in my mother's womb. Thank you for making me so wonderfully complex! Your workmanship is marvelous—how well I know it. You watched me as I was being formed in utter seclusion, as I was woven together in the dark of the womb. You saw me before I was born. Every day of my life was recorded in your book. Every moment was laid out before a single day had passed.*

God knew you before you were born—even while you were in your mother's womb. He knew all about your family and your life until now. [Be sensitive that some people have had difficult circumstances in their lives. Explain that God has not been absent, but has been drawing this person to himself.] He wants to give you a brand new start and a new way of living. He can do that when you give him your life. Why would you do that? Because . . .

### God wants to have a personal relationship with you.

John 17:3. *And this is the way to have eternal life—to know you, the only true God, and Jesus Christ, the one you sent to earth.*

God is not some "force," an unspeaking or unseeing idol, or merely another name for your own self-esteem. Instead, God is a person, your Creator, who created you to be in relationship with him. Why? Because . . .

### God loves you.

John 3:16. *For God loved the world so much that he gave his only Son, so that everyone who believes in him will not perish but have eternal life.*

You can turn your life over to God's control because he loves you and wants the very best for you. In fact, he loves you so much that he gave his Son, Jesus, to die on the cross for you. I'll explain more about that in a minute. I just want you to realize that when you trust God, you are actually trusting the One who created you. When you turn your life over to him, you are giving your life to the One who knows you inside out. Don't you think that's a good place to put your trust?

FACT: Your sin keeps you from having a personal relationship with God.

SET-UP: Most people don't understand the concept of sin. We live in a fairly amoral world that believes each person can decide what is right, what is true, and what is "moral"—whatever that might mean. Television and movies don't help with their portrayals of happy people blatantly living sinful lives. You will probably need to explain that God has set some standards about right and wrong, and that there is such a thing as "sin."

### What is sin?

James 4:17. *Remember, it is sin to know what you ought to do and then not do it.*

1 John 3:4. *Everyone who sins is breaking God's law, for all sin is contrary to the law of God.*

God is holy and perfect; people are sinful. You probably know that for yourself—if you tried to be perfect for a day, you'd quickly discover that you couldn't do it. [Here, you can draw a picture of a chasm, with a stick figure on one side and the word "God" on the other. Put the word "sin" in the chasm and explain further.] Sin means not understanding or even caring about what is "right." You defy God when you know what is right and then refuse to do it.

### Who has sinned?

Romans 3:23. *For everyone has sinned; we all fall short of God's glorious standard.*

Romans 5:17. *For the sin of this one man, Adam, caused death to rule over many.*

The Bible says "everyone has sinned." We simply cannot help it—we're human. When Adam sinned (way back in the Garden of Eden in the book of Genesis), sin entered the human race and sinfulness is part of our natures. You might be asking, "So what?"

### What's so bad about sin?

Romans 6:23. *For the wages of sin is death.*

Isaiah 59:2. *It's your sins that have cut you off from God.*

Sin leads to death. That's a big problem! Because God is perfect, he cannot have anything to do with us because we are sinners. He wants to have a personal relationship with us but he can't because of sin! So what did God do?

FACT: Only through Jesus Christ can you have a personal relationship with God.

SET-UP: Sometimes people don't understand the concept of having a "relationship" with a being they cannot see or touch. Yet it is a reality. That's why Jesus Christ came. He was a human being who lived on this earth so that we could understand what God is like. At this point you may discover that the person has lots of questions (for example, "How can God be God and also Jesus?"), the details of which can send you off the point. If that happens, explain that you don't have all of the answers to some of those kinds of questions—in fact, some questions are simply unanswerable because we humans cannot completely understand God and how he works. Explain that having a relationship with Christ is a spiritual reality that must be experienced, and that doing so will answer a lot of questions. The key questions to deal with at this point in the discussion include:

### Why Jesus Christ?

John 14:6—*Jesus told him, "I am the way, the truth, and the life. No one can come to the Father except through me."*

Remember how God can't have anything to do with us because of sin? Well, he decided to deal with our sin. Problem was, he had made it clear throughout the Old Testament that sin leads to death. In the Old Testament, people sacrificed animals as a way to show how sorry they were for their sins. And that was only temporary. God's plan all along was to send his Son, Jesus—a perfect human being—to be the final and ultimate sacrifice.

### Why did Jesus have to die?

1 Peter 3:18. *Christ suffered for our sins once for all time. He never sinned, but he died for sinners to bring you safely home to God. He suffered physical death, but he was raised to life in the Spirit.*

Jesus died to take the penalty our sins deserved. In essence, he took our punishment so that we wouldn't have to! Now, because of Jesus, the way is prepared for us to be able to have a personal relationship with a holy God. [At this point, you can draw a cross in the chasm, connecting the two sides. On the cross, write the word "Jesus." This visually shows that Jesus is the only way to God. Also add that Jesus did not stay dead. He rose from the dead, which is a promise to us that we will also rise from the dead and go to heaven to be with him.] So what do you need to do next?

**FACT:** You must personally respond by trusting Jesus Christ as Savior and Lord.

**SET-UP:** The fact of salvation means nothing unless a person accepts it for himself or herself. Emphasize that even if the person grew up in church, he or she still needs to accept Jesus personally. Also emphasize that even if the person has led a terrible life, no one is too bad for God— a person does not have to "clean up his act" before coming to Christ. In fact, Jesus died to take away all that sin and to help the person start anew. So emphasize that being good is not good enough, yet no one is too bad to be able to be forgiven—God wants all people to come to him. All people need to trust in Jesus in order to be saved. So what kind of response should a person have? Talk about the following:

### You respond with belief in Christ.

Romans 10:9-10. *If you confess with your mouth that Jesus is Lord and believe in your heart that God raised him from the dead, you will be saved. For it is by believing in your heart that you are made right with God, and it is by confessing with your mouth that you are saved.*

You simply need to believe. That doesn't mean that you don't have any questions or that you understand everything. It simply means recognizing that you are indeed a sinner in need of a Savior. You recognize that you cannot be good enough for a perfect God on your own. And you understand that God loved you so much that he sent Jesus to save you. If you believe that, say so.

### You respond by receiving Christ.

John 1:12. *But to all who believed him and accepted him, he gave the right to become children of God.*

"Receiving Christ" means acknowledging your belief in Christ, inviting him to come into your life, turning to God from your present way of living (repentance), and then beginning the adventure of letting God direct your life! And the moment you ask, it's done. Jesus has come in!

**QUESTION:** Would you like to accept Jesus as your Savior?

**SET-UP:** If the person is ready, explain that he or she can express belief and trust in Christ through prayer. Prayer is simply talking to God. He knows what a person means even when it is difficult to express. Tell the person that he or she may use their own words, or they can repeat the following prayer after you:

> *Dear God, I know that my sin has separated me from you. Thank you that Jesus Christ died in my place. I ask Jesus to forgive my sin and to come into my life. Please begin to direct my life. Thank you for giving me eternal life. In Jesus' name, Amen.*

That's it! You can officially welcome this person into God's family—your new brother or sister in Christ!

Just as a baby is not born and then left to fend for himself, so a newborn believer in God's family needs some guidance. As the one who introduced him or her to Christ, you should attempt to help this new believer grow. The following pages will show you how.

## How to Follow Up with a New Believer

*Helping a New Believer Take the Next Steps in the Christian Life*

If you have had the privilege of helping someone make the step of faith and accept Jesus as Savior, you want to continue that relationship if possible by offering some help to that new believer about the basics of the Christian faith. Your friend may wonder: "What does 'being a

Christian' mean? How does it make a difference in my life? What should I be doing differently from now on?" This section gives you fourteen discussion points to use with a new believer. You don't need to (and shouldn't) cover all of these points in one sitting. These are designed to be discussion points that you can use over the course of several weeks as part of discipling someone in understanding the basic tenets of the Christian faith and ways they can keep growing.

Tell your friend that you would like to get together regularly (in person, by phone, by e-mail, by instant messaging, whatever works) over the next few weeks to talk about the next steps in his or her walk with God. After you've worked out a schedule, give the person a first assignment—to get a Bible (if he or she doesn't already have one—or doesn't have one in an easy-to-read translation). You might offer to go with the person, as the first trip to a Christian bookstore and its wide array of Bibles can be a bit daunting. Or even better—purchase a Bible yourself and give it as a gift. Also ask the person to get a journal in which to record some of the material you will be sharing as well as some of his or her own thoughts.

You can use each numbered point below as a basis for each meeting, or divide up the material as you wish. Read the Bible verses. As you meet together, help your friend find the verses in the Bible and underline them. Encourage him or her to ask whatever questions come to mind. You may not know all the answers. If you don't, be honest and say, "I don't know the answer to that question, but I'll do some research and see what I can find out." Then do what you can to try to answer that question to the best of your ability.

Also realize that God will do his work in his timing. Don't expect a new believer to suddenly get rid of all vices (not swear anymore, quit smoking, and change his or her wardrobe the very next day after accepting Christ). Part of your discipleship process will be to help him or her learn how to be sensitive to God's leading. You will need to be sensitive as well—to know what to say and when to say it, and what not to say until the time is right. Commit yourself to praying daily for this new believer!

Here are the points to discuss:

### 1. You can be assured of your salvation.
You recently became a Christian, but you may have experienced doubts about what really happened to you. So I want to share with you some assurances that God gives in the Bible.

> **God assures you that Jesus Christ has come into your life.**
>
> John 14:20. *When I am raised to life again, you will know that I am in my Father, and you are in me, and I am in you.*
>
> **God assures you that your sins have been forgiven.**
>
> Colossians 2:13-14. *God made you alive with Christ, for he forgave all our sins. He canceled the record of the charges against us and took it away by nailing it to the cross.*
>
> **God assures you that you have eternal life.**
>
> 1 John 5:13. *I have written this to you who believe in the name of the Son of God, so that you may know you have eternal life.*

ASSIGNMENT: In your journal, write a description of when, where, and how you became a Christian. Make a note of the assurances that God has given you today.

### 2. You can know that you are loved unconditionally.
No matter what else may be going on in your life, no matter what acceptance or rejection you may be facing from others, you can know that God has completely accepted you and loves you unconditionally.

> **God loves you, chose you, and adopts you into his own family.**
>
> Ephesians 1:4-5. *Even before he made the world, God loved us and chose us in Christ to be holy and without fault in his eyes. God decided in advance to adopt us into his own family by bringing us to himself through Jesus Christ. This is what he wanted to do, and it gave him great pleasure.*

ASSIGNMENT: Write about what it means to you to be a part of God's family and to be loved unconditionally.

### 3. You have a new life in Christ.
What's next? God has given you a new life, but don't expect to be different all at once. Just as a new baby has to grow and learn, so God is going to work in you and help you to grow.

**You have begun a relationship that will continue the rest of your life.**

Colossians 2:6-7. *And now, just as you accepted Christ Jesus as your Lord, you must continue to follow him. Let your roots grow down into him, and let your lives be built on him. Then your faith will grow strong in the truth you were taught, and you will overflow with thankfulness.*

ASSIGNMENT: Write how it feels to know that God has given you a new life. What does that mean to you personally?

### 4. You have the privilege of prayer.
Just as good friends can talk to each other, so God, your heavenly Father, wants you to talk to him. And, while you may not understand it right now, you'll find that he "talks" to you as well.

**You can pray to God about anything and everything. He wants to hear from you.**

Philippians 4:6. *Don't worry about anything; instead, pray about everything. Tell God what you need, and thank him for all he has done.*

ASSIGNMENT: Commit yourself to getting used to talking to God. Start out with about three minutes a day of focused time talking to God. Talk to him as you would to a friend. In your journal, begin a list of the things you're talking to God about and the concerns that you're bringing to him.

### 5. You have the treasure of God's Word.
When you buy a new gadget, you usually get an instruction manual. With your new life in Christ, you need God's instruction manual, the Bible. In fact, the communication you "hear" from God will often come as you read his Word.

**You can trust God's Word.**

2 Timothy 3:16. *All Scripture is inspired by God and is useful to teach us what is true and to make us realize what is wrong in our lives. It corrects us when we are wrong and teaches us to do what is right.*

ASSIGNMENT: Commit yourself to spending five minutes a day reading the Bible. Begin in the book of Mark (in the New Testament) and read about Jesus. As a result of something you read, write in your journal something you learned or something you need to do.

### 6. You have a great friend in Jesus, so get to know him!
As you're reading in the book of Mark, you've been learning more about Jesus. In essence, Jesus is God put into focus for human eyes. Jesus came in order to show us God and then to take the punishment for our sins.

**Only because of Jesus do you have a personal relationship with God.**

Colossians 1:19-20. *For God in all his fullness was pleased to live in Christ, and through him God reconciled everything to himself. He made peace with everything in heaven and on earth by means of Christ's blood on the cross.*

ASSIGNMENT: Write a prayer to Jesus, thanking him for all he did for you.

### 7. You have a new lifestyle.
A good foundation is essential for a house to stand strong. Jesus wants you to know that obeying God will give your life a solid foundation.

**You show your love for Jesus by doing as he says.**

John 14:15. *If you love me, obey my commandments.*

Philippians 2:13. *For God is working in you, giving you the desire and the power to do what pleases him.*

ASSIGNMENT: In your journal, write one area of your life where you are obeying God and one where you think you are not. Ask God to show you what he wants you to do, and then to give you the strength to do it.

### 8. God will help you to follow and obey him.
As a Christian, you have been given the Holy Spirit. He will give you insight into what God is like and what he wants you to do.

**God gives you his Holy Spirit to enable you to live the Christian life.**

John 14:26. *But when the Father sends the Advocate as my representative—that is, the Holy Spirit—he will teach you everything and will remind you of everything I have told you.*

ASSIGNMENT: Write down one question that you'd like the Holy Spirit to help you with. Now take a couple of minutes and just talk to God about it.

### 9. You can resist temptation.

Becoming a Christian is like switching sides in a battle. You used to be on Satan's side and now you're on God's side—and Satan isn't happy about it! He wants to try to trip you up and tempt you to disobey God.

**You're not alone in temptation. God promises to show the way out.**

1 Corinthians 10:13. *The temptations in your life are no different from what others experience. And God is faithful. He will not allow the temptation to be more than you can stand. When you are tempted, he will show you a way out so that you can endure.*

ASSIGNMENT: List three temptations that Satan often uses on you. Now thank God ahead of time that he will show you how not to give in next time.

### 10. You can continue to receive forgiveness.

As a child in God's family, you'll still mess up. But God's love for you is so great that he will continue to forgive you.

**When you mess up, go to God and ask him to forgive you.**

1 John 1:9. *But if we confess our sins to him, he is faithful and just to forgive us our sins and to cleanse us from all wickedness.*

ASSIGNMENT: Write down ways that you have disobeyed God recently. Look at each one and confess it through prayer. Then cross out each sin. Let this remind you of God's loving forgiveness. Commit to obey him in the future.

### 11. You have the privilege of worship.

When you became a Christian, you joined a family—sometimes called "the body of Christ," which means you're now "related" to Christians all over the world! You need to join a portion of that family by beginning to attend a local church.

**You need the church to help you continue to grow.**

Hebrews 10:25. *And let us not neglect our meeting together, as some people do, but encourage one another, especially now that the day of his return is drawing near.*

ASSIGNMENT: Go with some friends or family to church this week. List two ways you worshiped God.

### 12. You can let others know about what Christ has done for you.

If you found a really great doctor, or a helpful mechanic, or even a terrific diet, you probably would tell your closest friend about it. Since you've found the One who forgives sin and gives you a new life, don't you think that's something you ought to share?

**The news you have to share is the best news anyone could hear!**

Romans 1:16. *For I am not ashamed of this Good News about Christ. It is the power of God at work, saving everyone who believes—the Jew first and also the Gentile.*

ASSIGNMENT: Write down the name of one person who needs to know Jesus Christ. Start praying for that person to become a Christian. Ask a Christian friend to pray with you for the person and to help you learn how to share your faith with him or her.

### 13. Take time to memorize Scripture.

To fight a battle you need powerful equipment. The Holy Spirit will use the power of God's Word like a sword to defeat Satan. A great strategy is to memorize Scripture so you always have it with you.

**Memorized verses will give you comfort and help you in temptation.**

Ephesians 6:17. *Take the sword of the Spirit, which is the word of God.*

ASSIGNMENT: Review the verses you've underlined in your Bible. Choose one or two favorites and begin to memorize them.

### 14. Realize your long-term goal—to be like Christ.
You've been a Christian for a short time now, and you're learning that you have a lifelong relationship with Christ. So what's your long-range goal? Becoming like Christ!

**Fortunately, you don't do this alone. God works in you to help you become more like his Son.**

Philippians 1:6. *And I am sure that God, who began the good work within you, will continue his work until it is finally finished on the day when Christ Jesus returns.*

Psalm 119:105. *Your word is a lamp to guide my feet and a light for my path.*

ASSIGNMENT: Make a list of at least five ways you want to become more like Jesus. Spend time asking God to help you. Remind yourself to read this part of your journal in one month to check on your spiritual growth.

## Mining the Treasures of the *Life Application Study Bible*

As a believer in Christ, you will often be asked questions about your faith—sometimes these are from honest seekers with tough questions that have bothered them; sometimes they're questions used by the questioners in hopes of tripping you up. In either case, it helps to be prepared with answers, or at least to know where to find the answers. The *Life Application Study Bible* notes were written not only to help explain the contents of the Bible and to get people started in thinking about application, but also to answer some of these key questions.

The treasures are here, and so we have mined them for you by guiding you to the notes that best answer questions in the following twenty-five categories. The references noted after each question are for the note(s) that will best help you to answer that question. (A number in parentheses indicates that there is more than one note on that particular Scripture.)

### BELIEF
Why should I believe? *See notes on Genesis 15:6; Exodus 9:12.*
What does it mean to "believe" in Jesus? *See note on John 3:16(3).*

### BIBLE
Why should I read the Bible? *See notes on 2 Chronicles 17:7-9; 34:31; Psalm 119:19.*
Why should I trust the Bible? *See notes on Psalm 33:4; Proverbs 16:22; 2 Peter 1:16-21.*
Why do you call the Bible God's Word? *See note on 2 Timothy 3:16-17.*
How is the Bible different from other religious literature? *See note on 2 Timothy 3:16.*

### CHURCH
How should I choose a church? *See notes on 1 Corinthians 3:10-11; 1 Peter 5:8-9.*
If eternal life is free, what's this 10 percent I keep hearing about? *See notes on Deuteronomy 14:22-23; 2 Corinthians 8:10-15; 8:12(1 and 2).*
Isn't participation in church optional? *See note on Luke 4:16.*

### DEATH
What happens when people die? *See notes on Hebrews 2:14-15(1 and 2); 1 Thessalonians 4:15-18.*
How can I be ready to die? *See notes on Genesis 50:24; Psalm 23:4.*

### DEVIL
Is the devil real? *See notes on Job 1:6-12; Matthew 4:1(2).*
What does the devil do? *See notes on Genesis 3:5; 3:6.*
How powerful is the devil? *See note on Joshua 6:2-5.*

**FAITH**

How strong does my faith have to be? *See notes on Matthew 17:17-20; Luke 17:6; Romans 14:1ff.*
Is faith enough? That seems too easy. *See notes on 2 Kings 5:12; Matthew 3:9-10; Philippians 3:2-3(2); James 2:1ff.*
How can I tell others about my faith? *See notes on Exodus 3:16-17; Revelation 1:5-6.*

**FORGIVENESS**

How can I know that God forgives me? *See notes on Psalm 32:1-2; Isaiah 1:18; Hebrews 10:17; 1 John 1:9(1).*

**FUTURE**

What can God tell me about the future? *See notes on Job 19:25-27; Matthew 24:3ff; John 14:19-21; Revelation 21:7-8; 22:20.*
How is the world going to end? *See notes on Mark 13:5-7; Luke 12:40; 1 John 2:18-23.*

**GOD**

What is God really like? *See notes on Genesis 1:1; 18:14; Numbers 14:17-20; Deuteronomy 27:15-26; Psalm 34:9-10; 36:5-8; 99:5; John 14:5-6; 2 Thessalonians 2:10-12.*
What are idols and what's wrong with them? *See notes on Exodus 20:1-6; 32:4-5; 1 Kings 18:29.*
Isn't God only all about rules? *See note on Isaiah 5:11-13.*

**GOSPEL**

What is the gospel? *See notes on Matthew 4:23-24; John 3:16(1); Romans 1:3-5; 1 Corinthians 15:3-4.*

**GRACE**

What is grace? *See note on Ephesians 1:7-8.*
How important it is to have God's grace? *See note on Nehemiah 9:28-31.*

**HEAVEN/HELL**

What does the Bible really say about heaven? *See notes on Mark 12:24; 1 Corinthians 2:9; 1 Peter 2:11.*
What does the Bible really say about hell? *See notes on Matthew 25:46; 2 Thessalonians 1:9; Jude 1:7; Revelation 20:14.*

**HOLY SPIRIT**

Who is the Holy Spirit? *See notes on Psalm 48:14; John 14:15-16; 14:17ff; Acts 1:5.*

**JESUS**

How do we know Jesus wasn't just a really great teacher? *See notes on Matthew 17:5; Luke 24:6-7(2); John 5:31ff; Philippians 2:5-11(1).*
What do you mean when you say Jesus is God? *See notes on Hebrews 1:1-2; 1:3(1).*
What did Jesus do for me? *See notes on Mark 15:31; 2 Corinthians 5:21; Colossians 1:12-14; Hebrews 9:22.*

**LIFE**

What does God really want from me? *See notes on Numbers 9:23; Judges 21:25; Proverbs 13:6; Ecclesiastes 1:8-11; 1 John 4:20-21.*
Doesn't God want me to be perfect? How can I do that? *See notes on Matthew 5:48; Romans 5:20; Hebrews 10:14.*
How can I "commit" my life to God? *See notes on Proverbs 16:3; 1 Peter 1:14-16(2).*
If I am a Christian, how am I supposed to live? *See notes on Exodus 23:24-25; Joshua 1:5; John 17:18; Romans 13:1ff; 1 Peter 1:8-9.*

**OLD TESTAMENT**

The Old Testament seems so—*old*. How much of it really applies to me today? *See notes on Deuteronomy 4:8; Matthew 5:17-20; Acts 21:23-24(2).*
How do the Old and New Testaments relate? *See notes on Leviticus 1:2(2); Matthew 13:52; Hebrews 3:5.*

**ONLY ONE WAY**

How can Christians insist that Jesus is the only way to God? *See notes on John 6:67-68; Acts 4:12; 1 Timothy 2:5-6; 2 Timothy 4:3-5; Hebrews 10:26.*
Why isn't just being "good" good enough? *See note on Colossians 1:21-22; Hebrews 7:28; 9:14.*

**OTHER RELIGIONS**

How can you say that devout people who follow other religions are wrong? *See notes on Colossians 2:20-23(2); 2:22-23; 2John 1:1-2; 1:3-4.*

What makes Christianity any different from the rest of religions? *See notes on Hebrews 7:25; 1John 5:12; 5:13.*

**PRAYER**

What good does prayer do? *See notes on 2Chronicles 6:19-42; Psalm 4:3; Mark 9:29.*

If God knows everything, why pray? *See notes on Isaiah 38:1-5; Acts 1:12-13.*

How should I pray? *See notes on Jonah 2:1ff; Mark 11:22-23; Hebrews 4:16; 1John 5:14-15.*

**REPENTANCE/CONFESSION**

Why are confession and repentance necessary? *See notes on Leviticus 5:5; 2Samuel 12:14(1); Matthew 3:1-2(1); 1John 1:9(1 and 2).*

**SIN**

What is sin? *See note on James 4:17.*

Why is sin dangerous? What's the big deal? *See notes on 2Samuel 11:1ff; 1Kings 11:9-10; 1Chronicles 21:13-14; 21:14; 1Corinthians 6:12-13(1); 1Thessalonians 4:4-5; Revelation 9:20-21.*

Why should I call myself a sinner when I can think of a lot of people who are *really* bad? *See note on Romans 3:23.*

How could a loving God send sincere people to hell? *See notes on Deuteronomy 7:2; Romans 1:18-20(1 and 2).*

Can someone be too sinful to be saved? *See notes on 2Chronicles 33:12-13; Psalm 51:1ff; 51:1-7.*

**SPIRITUAL GIFTS**

What are spiritual gifts? Does everyone have one? *See notes on Romans 12:6(1); 12:6-8; Ephesians 4:11-12.*

**SUFFERING**

Why do bad things happen to good people? *See notes on Job 1:1ff; 2:10; Acts 12:2-11; Romans 8:28.*

How does God help me deal with the problems in my life? *See notes on Exodus 5:22-23; Job 5:17-26; Psalm 106:40-42; Philippians 1:29; 1Thessalonians 3:1-3; Hebrews 11:35-39.*

**TEMPTATION**

How does the devil tempt me? *See notes on Luke 4:3(1 and 2).*

Why does the devil tempt me? *See note on Genesis 3:1-6.*

At what point does temptation become sin? *See note on Matthew 4:1ff(1).*

How do I handle temptation? *See notes on Matthew 26:40-41; Luke 4:1-13; 1Corinthians 10:13.*

**TRINITY**

Why isn't the Trinity like believing in three gods? *See notes on Matthew 3:16-17; Mark 1:10-11; Acts 1:4-5.*

## So You've Been Asked to Speak . . .

Chances are you're going to find yourself faced with the task of leading a Bible study, giving a devotional, offering a short talk, or teaching a Sunday school class. Or perhaps you will be given the responsibility for leading a small group study and you won't know where to begin.

The *Life Application Study Bible* is an inexhaustible resource of information. If you follow some of the steps and hints below, you'll be able to put together a talk that is both informative and challenging—to any audience, at any time.

### Ways to Use the Life Application Study Bible as a Research Tool
### Using the Master Index

If you need to cover a topic, take a quick trip to the Master Index and look up the topic. There you will find notes on that topic (with a phrase that gives you an idea of the content of the note) as well as any charts or personality profiles on that topic. (See the Sample Lesson on the next page to get an idea how this would work.)

## Focusing on a Book of the Bible
For studying a Bible book, the *Life Application Study Bible* has plenty of overview material to help. Simply start at the beginning of the book you're studying. For example, if you're working through Jonah with your Bible study group or preparing to speak about that book, use the introductory material to get a sense of the time frame, the author and reason for writing, and an introduction that places the book into a contemporary setting. Study the Blueprint to understand how the book is laid out. Read the Megathemes and discover the main themes of that book and their importance. Many books also include overview maps with key events noted to give you the geographical context and flow.

## Focusing on a Particular Passage
If you have been assigned a verse or passage of Scripture to discuss, use the life application notes, cross-references, and section headings to help you put the passage into context. If you don't find a note on that particular verse, consider the topic that you want to discuss and go to the index to look up the topic and other notes that will give further insight.

## Using the Cross-References
The cross-references are an often-missed resource. For example, if you're studying the life of David or of Solomon, you can use the cross-references in the inside column beside the text to send you to the same account recorded in 2 Samuel or in 1 Chronicles.

## Studying the Personality Profiles
The Personality Profiles are a nearly inexhaustible resource of study ideas. For instance, in a women's Bible study, you could work your way through the profiles of women. Or you could study the profiles ahead of time and do a topical study based on the life lessons for various women (using them like case studies). You can study all the people in a particular book, compare various kings or apostles, or even study the Bible characters by age (for example, choosing some of the more elderly faithful followers, such as Simeon and Anna, for an older group).

## Employing the Charts as Visual Aids
The charts are designed to be simple and to summarize Bible data and teachings. They will give you an overview of a topic either from a specific book or the Bible as a whole. You could do an entire study from one chart or series of charts. For example, the charts in Proverbs pull together scattered verses on similar topics. These would be helpful in discussing key topics covered in Proverbs. In addition, the Bible includes several large charts that give sweeping overviews on various topics.

## Seeing the Big Picture of Jesus by Using the Harmony of the Gospels
In studying a Gospel or the life of Christ, the Harmony of the Gospels presents his story in chronological order (the events are numbered, and the numbers also appear in the text) and will show you where the same stories appear in other Gospels. (The Harmony of the Gospels is located after the Gospel of John.) In addition, none of the footnotes have been repeated—so the notes you read in Matthew on the feeding of the five thousand will be different from the notes you read about that same story elsewhere. Use the Harmony to help you get a full picture of an event by seeing it from the different perspectives of all who wrote about the same event. Read the same accounts in different Gospels. Notice the differing details. Consider the point of view of the authors.

## Getting a Wider Perspective by Using the Harmony of Kings and Chronicles
In a study of the books of Kings or Chronicles, the Harmony of the Kings and Chronicles (located between the books of 1 and 2 Kings) will give you a visual timeline for when the various kings ruled, tell whether accounts of their reigns are recorded in other books, and show the prophet who was preaching at the time. Similarly, if you're studying any of the prophetic books, you can use the Harmony to learn about what was going on in the kingdom to which the prophet had been called to speak. This will give you great insight into why the prophet spoke as he did.

## Sampling the Maps
If your group is interested in maps, use the maps in the Gospels (in conjunction with the Harmony) to trace Jesus' steps throughout his ministry. Use the maps of Paul's journeys and follow his footsteps across Asia Minor and on to Rome. Use the maps in Genesis to help your readers visualize the whereabouts of the people they are studying.

Those are just a few suggestions for using the resources in the *Life Application Study Bible*. The following section takes you through steps for planning a topical talk using the Master Index.

### A Sample Lesson in Six Easy Steps
You've been given the assignment to give a talk to a group about the importance of prayer in a Christian's life.

STEP ONE: Pray.
Begin by asking God to guide you as you put together your talk. Ask him to give you insight and wisdom. Ask him to guide the process and give you the right words to say.

STEP TWO: Anticipate questions.
List questions your group might have about this topic, focusing on particular issues that may be important to them at this time. (For example, if a family is facing a difficult illness and God doesn't seem to be answering their request, you will need to be prepared to discuss the issue of unanswered prayer.)

STEP THREE: Prepare an outline.
Keeping in mind the questions from step two, begin an outline. Three points are usually good. Give an introduction (an anecdote, a question, an example). List the three points you want to make about prayer. Give an application-oriented conclusion (see the article, "Taking the Step to Application" on the following pages).

STEP FOUR: Go to the Master Index.
Look up "Prayer" in the Master Index. You'll find a long list of notes on various verses. Whittle it down by looking at the topic sentence for each note; then jot down the locations of notes you think might fit into your outline. Also notice that the Master Index lists three charts that focus on prayer and three Personality Profiles that include life lessons on the topic of prayer. Make a note of the page numbers for these.

STEP FIVE: Read the passages, notes, and other helpful materials.
Now refer to your jotted list and read the notes, charts, and profiles. When you find Bible verses and significant points in the notes that you want to use, write them on your three-point outline.

STEP SIX: Put it all together.
Now make your points flow together. Write transition sentences between points. Finally, add a conclusion that challenges your listeners to take the message to heart and let it make a difference in their lives.

## Taking the Step to Application
Whether you are studying the Bible for yourself or teaching it to others, moving toward application is the most important part of the studying and teaching process. You see, just having information about what is in the Bible is not enough (even Satan knew enough of the Bible to be able to quote it—Matthew 4:1–11). Understanding the context or the concepts is not enough. Even being able to see that it is relevant to today's world is not enough. For the Bible to really make a difference in our lives, we need to (1) receive the message personally, (2) reflect on our lives and identify what needs to change as a result of God's Word, and (3) lay out a plan to make that change. Taking the step to application means that we finish our Bible study or go away from a lesson asking:

Now that I know what God wants me to do, how am I going to start doing it?

Application is the step between *knowing* what the Bible says and *doing* what it says. While the truths of the Bible never change, people's life situations are different and are constantly changing. You must continue to study the Bible and learn the new things God wants you to learn. And when you teach, you may be able to tell your listeners how *you* are applying certain principles from God's Word, but at the same time you need to give them the tools and the opportunity to apply the Bible to *their own* life situations. So how do you do that? We have developed a Bible study system called the Pyramid. Using the nine sets of questions in the Pyramid, you will be able to study the Bible and then apply its principles more practically and thoroughly to your personal life situations.

PRINCIPLES

POINT     PRESENT

PLOT     PARALLELS

PLACE     PRIORITIES

PEOPLE     PLAN

## LIFE APPLICATION PYRAMID

Each step is described in detail below, followed by the questions you should ask yourself as you work your way over the Pyramid toward application. After point 5, at the top of the Pyramid, we offer an example of how your study might look. Then follow points 6 to 9 down the other side of the Pyramid. We have provided an example here as well although these points will vary greatly for each individual.

### 1. People
Begin by identifying the people in the passage, the characters who are actively involved. Sometimes no specific individuals or groups will be named (such as when you're reading Proverbs or Romans). But don't forget the author and the original audience. Note the people and learn something about them. (For example, if you're reading Isaiah's message to Moab, look up the "Moabites" in the Master Index and read the notes to better understand the people in this passage.) So you should ask,

- Who are all the people in this passage?
- How are these people like people in my world?
- What characteristics of these people do I see in myself?

### 2. Place
Next, consider Place. This step puts the passage in its original setting, the historical and cultural context. You can learn about Place by again using the Master Index and looking up the notes (and often the maps). The more you know about the culture, history, and problems of the people in the passage, the more you will be able to find parallels to your life today. Ask,

- What is the setting of this passage?
- What are the significant details in the history, culture, and geography?
- What are the similarities to my world?

### 3. Plot
This step answers "What's happening?" Usually you can discover this by the context of the passage and book. The notes in the section you're reading will also help you to unravel the plot of a particular passage. Ask,

- What is happening in this passage?
- What is the conflict or tension?
- What would I have done in this situation?
- How is this similar to what is happening in my life or in the world today?

### 4. Point
Before you can determine what something in the Bible means for you today, you must first ascertain the meaning for the original audience. The events recorded in the Bible happened to real people at specific times in history. Real audiences heard the parables, and real churches received the epistles. Therefore, carefully consider the cultural context (what you learned in the first three steps) to find the particular lessons that God wanted to teach these people. A clear understanding of the Point can prevent damaging misapplication and is invaluable for determining the timeless truths in the passage. To determine the Point, ask,

- What was the intended message for the original audience?
- What did the people in the passage learn?
- What did God want them to do?
- What was God's solution to the problem?

## 5. Principles

The next step is to determine what transferable principles are embedded in the passage. The Point and Principles may be exactly the same—or may be indirectly related. The Principles are the distilled essence of a passage. You should ask,

- What is the message for all of humankind?
- What are the timeless truths?
- What is the moral of the story?

Here are possible answers for Acts 27:27–44 for the first five steps up the Bible study Pyramid.

PEOPLE: Luke (the author, included in the "we" passage), Paul, the sailors, other prisoners, soldiers guarding the other prisoners, the army officer guarding Paul (Julius, see 27:1), God.

PLACE: on ship, sailing across the Adriatic Sea (27:27), near the island of Malta (28:1), during a terrible storm, as Paul and other Roman prisoners were being taken to Rome for trial; the journey was undertaken "late in the fall" (Acts 27:9), so it may have been October, a time when dangerous storms could arise suddenly.

PLOT: Paul had warned that the trip would be disastrous (27:9-10), but the pilot and officer didn't listen and determined to sail anyway. When the terrible storm arose, Paul encouraged everyone (27:22) and told them what to do; this time the Roman crew listened (27:31-38). Paul also thanked God in front of everyone (27:35). When the ship began to break up, the soldiers were about to kill their prisoners (so they wouldn't escape), but the officer guarding Paul stopped them (27:43).

POINT: Paul was confident of God's protection and care, even during a life-threatening storm. This confidence freed Paul to encourage others, even his captors, and to give a clear testimony of his faith in Christ.

PRINCIPLES: God is present and in control of all our "storms"; we can take courage and have hope because we know that God is with us and he cares for us. Even when we are going through difficult times, we should encourage and help others and give clear evidence of our faith.

Now you've made it up one side of the Pyramid. The path to the top of the Pyramid narrows to a single point and a few principles, but the paths going down the other side are diverse and varied for each person and for each situation. Points 6 to 9 are as follows:

## 6. Present

This step expands the areas of application for the Point and Principles that you have extracted so far. A different kind of thinking is required because you are expanding possibilities and adding your life to the Principles. Here you describe these significant implications of these timeless truths for life at home, school, job, and in your neighborhood. This step brings the truth into your context, into today's world, here and now. The meaning for the original audience may be clear, but the implications for the Present may be rich and varied. Ask,

- What do these Principles mean for my society and culture?
- How is this relevant?
- What back then is similar to today?
- How can I make the timeless truth timely?

## 7. Parallels

This step is similar to Present, except that it is very personal, addressing specific life situations, fears, hopes, and relationships. This is the time to explore all the areas of life where the truth might apply. Thus, you should ask,

- What does this truth mean for me?
- Where are my areas of need, conviction, and opportunity?
- Where in my life might this truth possibly apply?

## 8. Priorities

After surfacing application areas, select one that you consider to be most important—one that God is nudging you about. This is one of the more difficult steps—it can be easy to start rationalizing or to make excuses. But to truly get God's Word into your life and grow as a believer, you need to listen when God speaks. In taking this step, you are answering the question, "So what?";

that is, what does this passage say about how I should change? This involves asking these tough questions:

- How should I adjust my Priorities?
- What should I change about my values, beliefs, attitudes, or character?
- What about my thoughts and motives should change?
- What kind of person does God want me to become?

## 9. Plan

After pinpointing what needs to change, you need to take action. You need to answer the question, "Now what?" and put truth into practice by determining to change and then making plans to live differently. Planning involves selecting a goal, breaking it down into bite-size pieces, and getting moving! These questions will help:

- What does God want me to do about what I have learned?
- What steps will get me to that goal?
- What should be my first step? How should I get started?

Here are possible answers for Acts 27:27–44 for the last four steps down the Bible study Pyramid. While the answers in Steps 1 through 5 are pretty straightforward, the answers in Steps 6 through 9 will vary greatly from person to person, so these are merely suggestions:

PRESENT: I'm not a prisoner of a foreign government being taken to trial by ship in a terrible storm, but I do have rough seas in my life. I have a conflict with my daughter's teacher, a problem with one of my company's clients, and other difficult situations.

PARALLELS: The main parallel to my life is Paul's attitude in the middle of the crisis— he remained calm, gave instructions, encouraged everyone, and was a positive example of a follower of Christ. In both the problem at school and the one at work, I need to explain my case calmly and confidently. But in doing this, I should be positive and helpful, not negative, hateful, or divisive.

PRIORITIES: My natural tendency is to get angry and tell someone off when I think he or she is wrong, or to shout orders without being sensitive to the feelings of others. I think that God wants me to be more patient and understanding. Perhaps through the *way* I communicate, I can be a positive witness for Christ.

PLAN: With the conflict at school, I need to speak directly to the teacher (not write a letter) and explain my position carefully, calmly, and with concern for the feelings of the teacher. I will make an appointment, write out my points beforehand so I won't get off on tangents and get upset, and carefully explain my position while letting the teacher know that I respect him.

Remember, a big difference stands between *knowing* and *doing*, and another big difference between *teaching* and *doing*. So as you begin taking the steps to application in both your personal study and in your teaching, ask yourself:

Am I doing what God wants me to do?
Am I obeying him?

Be honest in your self-evaluation. Applying the Bible begins *now*, with *you*. James wrote:

> But don't just listen to God's word. You must do what it says. Otherwise, you are only fooling yourselves. For if you listen to the word and don't obey, it is like glancing at your face in a mirror. You see yourself, walk away, and forget what you look like. But if you look carefully into the perfect law that sets you free, and if you do what it says and don't forget what you heard, then God will bless you for doing it (James 1:22–25).

This article is adapted from Dave Veerman, *How to Apply the Bible* (Carol Stream, Ill.: Tyndale House Publishers, 1993). Books are available at www.lifeapplicationbible.com.

This 365-day reading plan leads you from Genesis to Revelation in just a year. Though it doesn't include every chapter and verse, it offers a complete view of Scripture and does so without being overwhelming. By skipping past material that appears more than once, it gives you a streamlined look at the entire Bible. Take this tour of God's Word to discover its life-changing wisdom and power.

| | | | | | |
|---|---|---|---|---|---|
| **JAN** | **1** | Day 1 | Genesis 1:1–2:3 | **14** | Day 45 | Exodus 19:1-25 |

JAN 1 ... Day 1 ....... Genesis 1:1–2:3
    2 ... Day 2 ....... Genesis 2:15–3:24
    3 ... Day 3 ....... Genesis 4:1-16
    4 ... Day 4 ....... Genesis 6:9-22
    5 ... Day 5 ....... Genesis 7:1-24
    6 ... Day 6 ....... Genesis 8:1-22
    7 ... Day 7 ....... Genesis 9:1-17
    8 ... Day 8 ....... Genesis 11:1-9
    9 ... Day 9 ....... Genesis 12:1-9; 17:1-8
   **10** ... Day 10 ....... Genesis 18:1-15
   **11** ... Day 11 ....... Genesis 19:15-29
   **12** ... Day 12 ....... Genesis 21:8-21
   **13** ... Day 13 ....... Genesis 22:1-19
   **14** ... Day 14 ....... Genesis 24:1-27
   **15** ... Day 15 ....... Genesis 24:28-67
   **16** ... Day 16 ....... Genesis 25:19-34
   **17** ... Day 17 ....... Genesis 27:1-40
   **18** ... Day 18 ....... Genesis 28:10-22
   **19** ... Day 19 ....... Genesis 29:14-30
   **20** ... Day 20 ....... Genesis 32:1–33:16
   **21** ... Day 21 ....... Genesis 37:1-36
   **22** ... Day 22 ....... Genesis 39:1-23
   **23** ... Day 23 ....... Genesis 40:1-23
   **24** ... Day 24 ....... Genesis 41:1-36
   **25** ... Day 25 ....... Genesis 41:37-57
   **26** ... Day 26 ....... Genesis 42:1-38
   **27** ... Day 27 ....... Genesis 43:1-34
   **28** ... Day 28 ....... Genesis 44:1-34
   **29** ... Day 29 ....... Genesis 45:1-28
   **30** ... Day 30 ....... Genesis 49:1-33
   **31** ... Day 31 ....... Exodus 1:8–2:10
**FEB**  **1** ... Day 32 ....... Exodus 2:11-25
    2 ... Day 33 ....... Exodus 3:1-22
    3 ... Day 34 ....... Exodus 4:1-17
    4 ... Day 35 ....... Exodus 5:1-23
    5 ... Day 36 ....... Exodus 6:1-13
    6 ... Day 37 ....... Exodus 7:1-14
    7 ... Day 38 ....... Exodus 7:15–9:7
    8 ... Day 39 ....... Exodus 9:8–10:29
    9 ... Day 40 ....... Exodus 11:1-10; 12:29-36
   **10** ... Day 41 ....... Exodus 13:17–14:31
   **11** ... Day 42 ....... Exodus 15:22-27; 17:1-7
   **12** ... Day 43 ....... Exodus 16:1-36
   **13** ... Day 44 ....... Exodus 18:1-27

   **14** ... Day 45 ....... Exodus 19:1-25
   **15** ... Day 46 ....... Exodus 20:1-22
   **16** ... Day 47 ....... Exodus 32:1-29
   **17** ... Day 48 ....... Exodus 40:1-38
   **18** ... Day 49 ....... Numbers 12:1-16
   **19** ... Day 50 ....... Numbers 13:1–14:4
   **20** ... Day 51 ....... Numbers 14:5-45
   **21** ... Day 52 ....... Numbers 21:4-9
   **22** ... Day 53 ....... Numbers 22:5-38
   **23** ... Day 54 ....... Deuteronomy 29:1-29
   **24** ... Day 55 ....... Deuteronomy 30:1-20
   **25** ... Day 56 ....... Deuteronomy 31:1-8
   **26** ... Day 57 ....... Deuteronomy 34:1-12
   **27** ... Day 58 ....... Joshua 1:1-18
   **28** ... Day 59 ....... Joshua 2:1-24
**MAR**  **1** ... Day 60 ....... Joshua 3:1-17
    2 ... Day 61 ....... Joshua 5:13–6:27
    3 ... Day 62 ....... Joshua 7:1-26
    4 ... Day 63 ....... Joshua 10:1-15
    5 ... Day 64 ....... Joshua 23:1-16
    6 ... Day 65 ....... Joshua 24:1-31
    7 ... Day 66 ....... Judges 4:4-24
    8 ... Day 67 ....... Judges 6:1-40
    9 ... Day 68 ....... Judges 7:1-25
   **10** ... Day 69 ....... Judges 13:1-25
   **11** ... Day 70 ....... Judges 14:1-20
   **12** ... Day 71 ....... Judges 15:1-20
   **13** ... Day 72 ....... Judges 16:1-21
   **14** ... Day 73 ....... Judges 16:22-31
   **15** ... Day 74 ....... Ruth 1:1-22
   **16** ... Day 75 ....... Ruth 2:1-23
   **17** ... Day 76 ....... Ruth 3:1-18
   **18** ... Day 77 ....... Ruth 4:1-22
   **19** ... Day 78 ....... 1 Samuel 1:1-28
   **20** ... Day 79 ....... 1 Samuel 3:1-21
   **21** ... Day 80 ....... 1 Samuel 8:1-5
   **22** ... Day 81 ....... 1 Samuel 8:6-22
   **23** ... Day 82 ....... 1 Samuel 9:1-21
   **24** ... Day 83 ....... 1 Samuel 10:1-27
   **25** ... Day 84 ....... 1 Samuel 14:1-23
   **26** ... Day 85 ....... 1 Samuel 16:1-13
   **27** ... Day 86 ....... 1 Samuel 17:1-31
   **28** ... Day 87 ....... 1 Samuel 17:32-58
   **29** ... Day 88 ....... 1 Samuel 18:1-30

Following is a list of abbreviations in the Master Index:

## BOOKS OF THE BIBLE

| | | |
|---|---|---|
| Genesis . . . . . . . . . . . . . . . . . Gn | Isaiah . . . . . . . . . . . . . . . . . . . . Is | Romans . . . . . . . . . . . . . . . Rom |
| Exodus . . . . . . . . . . . . . . . . . Ex | Jeremiah . . . . . . . . . . . . . . . . Jer | 1 Corinthians . . . . . . . . . . . 1 Cor |
| Leviticus . . . . . . . . . . . . . . . . Lv | Lamentations . . . . . . . . . . Lam | 2 Corinthians . . . . . . . . . . . 2 Cor |
| Numbers . . . . . . . . . . . . . . . Nm | Ezekiel . . . . . . . . . . . . . . . . . . Ez | Galatians . . . . . . . . . . . . . . . Gal |
| Deuteronomy . . . . . . . . . . . . Dt | Daniel . . . . . . . . . . . . . . . . . . Dn | Ephesians . . . . . . . . . . . . . Eph |
| Joshua . . . . . . . . . . . . . . . . . Jos | Hosea . . . . . . . . . . . . . . . . . Hos | Philippians . . . . . . . . . . . . . Phil |
| Judges . . . . . . . . . . . . . . . . . Jgs | Joel . . . . . . . . . . . . . . . . . . . . . Jl | Colossians . . . . . . . . . . . . . Col |
| Ruth . . . . . . . . . . . . . . . . . . . . Ru | Amos . . . . . . . . . . . . . . . . . . Am | 1 Thessalonians . . . . . . . 1 Thes |
| 1 Samuel . . . . . . . . . . . . . . 1 Sm | Obadiah . . . . . . . . . . . . . . . . Ob | 2 Thessalonians . . . . . . . 2 Thes |
| 2 Samuel . . . . . . . . . . . . . . 2 Sm | Jonah . . . . . . . . . . . . . . . . . Jon | 1 Timothy . . . . . . . . . . . . . . 1 Tm |
| 1 Kings . . . . . . . . . . . . . . . 1 Kgs | Micah . . . . . . . . . . . . . . . . . . Mi | 2 Timothy . . . . . . . . . . . . . . 2 Tm |
| 2 Kings . . . . . . . . . . . . . . . 2 Kgs | Nahum . . . . . . . . . . . . . . . . . Na | Titus . . . . . . . . . . . . . . . . . . . Ti |
| 1 Chronicles . . . . . . . . . . . 1 Chr | Habakkuk . . . . . . . . . . . . . . . Hb | Philemon . . . . . . . . . . . . . Phlm |
| 2 Chronicles . . . . . . . . . . . 2 Chr | Zephaniah . . . . . . . . . . . . . Zep | Hebrews . . . . . . . . . . . . . . Heb |
| Ezra . . . . . . . . . . . . . . . . . . . Ezr | Haggai . . . . . . . . . . . . . . . . . Hg | James . . . . . . . . . . . . . . . . . Jas |
| Nehemiah . . . . . . . . . . . . . Neh | Zechariah . . . . . . . . . . . . . . Zec | 1 Peter . . . . . . . . . . . . . . . . 1 Pt |
| Esther . . . . . . . . . . . . . . . . . Est | Malachi . . . . . . . . . . . . . . . Mal | 2 Peter . . . . . . . . . . . . . . . . 2 Pt |
| Job . . . . . . . . . . . . . . . . . . . . Jb | Matthew . . . . . . . . . . . . . . . . Mt | 1 John . . . . . . . . . . . . . . . . 1 Jn |
| Psalms . . . . . . . . . . . . . . . . . Ps | Mark . . . . . . . . . . . . . . . . . . Mk | 2 John . . . . . . . . . . . . . . . . 2 Jn |
| Proverbs . . . . . . . . . . . . . . . Prv | Luke . . . . . . . . . . . . . . . . . . . Lk | 3 John . . . . . . . . . . . . . . . . 3 Jn |
| Ecclesiastes . . . . . . . . . . . . Eccl | John . . . . . . . . . . . . . . . . . . . . Jn | Jude . . . . . . . . . . . . . . . . . Jude |
| Song of Songs . . . . . . . . . Song | Acts . . . . . . . . . . . . . . . . . . Acts | Revelation . . . . . . . . . . . . . . Rv |

This is an index to the notes, charts, maps, and personality profiles in the *Life Application Study Bible*. Every entry concerning a note has a Bible reference and a page number; every entry concerning a chart, map, or personality profile has a page number. In some instances, a Bible reference is followed by a number in parentheses to indicate that there is more than one note on that particular Scripture. For example, Rv 1:1(2) means that the reader should look up the second note with the heading of 1:1 in Revelation. In most cases, the entries follow in biblical/canonical order (i.e., from Genesis to Revelation). In some cases, however, the entries follow a chronological order—this is especially true with important people in the Bible. Following the general index are special indexes: Index to Charts, Index to Maps, and Index to Personality Profiles. Because of the emphasis on application in the *Life Application Study Bible,* these indexes are helpful guides for personal and group Bible study, sermon preparation, or teaching.

## ADVANTAGE
don't take advantage of your position . . . 1 Sm 2:12ff . . . . . . . 411
  Mi 2:1-2 . . . . . . . . 1477
seek places of service, not advantage . . . Mt 18:3-4 . . . . . . . 1580
money changers took advantage
  of others . . . . . . . . . . . . . . . . . . . . . . Mt 21:12 . . . . . . . . 1586

## ADVERSITY
see CONFLICT(S); PROBLEMS; TROUBLES

## ADVICE
of parents often helpful . . . . . . . . . . . . . . Gn 26:34-35 . . . . . . . 51
always seek God's . . . . . . . . . . . . . . . . . . . Gn 48:15 . . . . . . . . . 89
be careful about negativism in . . . . . . . . Nm 13:33–14:4 . . . 222
don't be too quick to reject it . . . . . . . . . Nm 14:6-10 . . . . . . 223
seek God's even in minor issues . . . . . . Jos 9:14-17 . . . . . . 327
how to carefully evaluate it . . . . . . . . . . 1 Kgs 12:6-14 . . . 534
  2 Chr 10:1-15 . . . . . 678
don't seek God's advice if you're
  going to ignore it . . . . . . . . . . . . . . . 2 Chr 18:3-8(2) . 688–89
test others' advice against God's Word . . 2 Chr 22:4-5 . . . . . . 695
understand a person's situation
  before giving it . . . . . . . . . . . . . . . . . . Jb 5:17 . . . . . . . . . . 793
some need compassion more
  than advice . . . . . . . . . . . . . . . . . . . . Jb 6:6-7 . . . . . . . . . 794
seek it from those with more wisdom
  and experience . . . . . . . . . . . . . . . . . Prv 6:20-23 . . . 1011–12
  10:20 . . . . . . . . . 1017
seeking it from everyone but God . . . . . Is 30:1 . . . . . . . . . 1136
love often means giving tough advice . . . Mk 10:21(2) . . . . 1642
of Gamaliel to Jewish council . . . . . . . . . Acts 5:39 . . . . . . . 1826
PROFILE: Absalom (in 2 Sm) . . . . . . . . . . . . . . . . . . . . . 487

## ADVISERS
good leaders need and use them . . . . . . . Prv 11:14 . . . . . . . 1019
seek out reliable ones . . . . . . . . . . . . . . . Prv 15:22 . . . . . . . 1027
Herod's faulty counsel about Jesus . . . . Mt 2:3 . . . . . . . . . 1536
PROFILE: Nebuchadnezzar (in Dn) . . . . . . . . . . . . . . . . . . 1385

## AFFECTIONS
control the way we live . . . . . . . . . . . . . . Prv 4:23-27 . . . . . . 1009

## AFFIRMATION
humility is realistic affirmation . . . . . . . . Lk 14:11 . . . . . . . 1718
be affirming when correcting others . . . . 1 Cor 1:4-6 . . . . . . 1927
Paul always had attitude of . . . . . . . . . . . 2 Thes 1:3ff . . . . . . 2050

## AFFLICTION
see SUFFERING

## AFRAID
see FEAR; WORRY

## AGE
how did Bible people live so long? . . . . . Gn 5:25-27 . . . . . . . . 15
our responsibility to honor the elderly . . . Lv 19:32 . . . . . . . . . 185
old age not a barrier to being used
  by God . . . . . . . . . . . . . . . . . . . . . . . . Jos 13:1 . . . . . . . . 333
young age not a barrier to being used
  by God . . . . . . . . . . . . . . . . . . . . . . . . Jn 6:8-9(2) . . . . . . 1763
  1 Tm 4:12 . . . . . . 2062
begin to obey God at a young age . . . . . . 2 Kgs 22:1-2 . . . . . . 608
not a criterion for wisdom . . . . . . . . . . . . 2 Chr 34:3 . . . . . . . 714
elderly have great value . . . . . . . . . . . . . . Ps 92:14 . . . . . . . . 943
  Lk 2:36 . . . . . . . . 1677
those older than you can give good
  advice . . . . . . . . . . . . . . . . . . . . . . . . . Prv 6:20-23 . . . . . . 1011
seek God while still young . . . . . . . . . . . . Eccl 11:9-10 . . . . . 1073
  12:1 . . . . . . . . . . . 1073
Jesus began his ministry at age 30 . . . . . Lk 3:23 . . . . . . . . 1682
respect of elders . . . . . . . . . . . . . . . . . . . Eph 6:3 . . . . . . . . 2009
dealing with a variety of ages
  in the church . . . . . . . . . . . . . . . . . . . Ti 2:2-8 . . . . . . . . 2078
Bible relevant to all ages . . . . . . . . . . . . . 1 Jn 2:12-14 . . . . . 2147
PROFILES: Timothy (in 1 Tm) . . . . . . . . . . . . . . . . . . . . 2059
  Simeon & Anna (in Lk) . . . . . . . . . . . . . . . . . . 1681

## AGREEMENTS
don't break the agreement you made
  to follow God . . . . . . . . . . . . . . . . . . . Dt 2:14-15 . . . . . . . 266
agreeing to God's plan for us . . . . . . . . . . Jos 1:16 . . . . . . . . 315

aided by the Holy Spirit . . . . . . . . . . . . . . Mt 18:19-20 . . . . . 1581
CHART: Covenants . . . . . . . . . . . . . . . . . . . . . . . . . . . . . 475

## AGRICULTURE
devastating effects of famine . . . . . . . . . . Gn 41:54 . . . . . . . . . 79

## AGRIPPA, HEROD
see HEROD AGRIPPA I or HEROD AGRIPPA II

## AHAB (king of Israel)
his strength no match for God . . . . . . . . . 1 Kgs 17:1(2) . . . . . 544
a pouter . . . . . . . . . . . . . . . . . . . . . . . . . . 1 Kgs 21:4 . . . . . . . 554
lessons from his repentance . . . . . . . . . . 1 Kgs 21:29 . . . . . . 555
couldn't escape God's judgment . . . . . . . 1 Kgs 22:34 . . . . . . 557
his death . . . . . . . . . . . . . . . . . . . . . . . . . . 1 Kgs 22:35 . . . . . . 557
MAPS: The Showdown at Carmel . . . . . . . . . . . . . . . . . . 546
  God Delivers Ahab . . . . . . . . . . . . . . . . . . . . . . . . . . . 551
PROFILE: Ahab (in 1 Kgs) . . . . . . . . . . . . . . . . . . . . . . . . 549

## AHAZ (king of Judah)
made wrong alliance with Assyria . . . . . . 2 Kgs 16:5 . . . . . . . 594
  Is 7:8 . . . . . . . . . . 1102
relied more on money than on God . . . . . 2 Kgs 16:10 . . . . . . 594
PROFILE: Ahaz (in 2 Chr) . . . . . . . . . . . . . . . . . . . . . . . . 703

## AHIJAH
predicted the divided kingdom . . . . . . . . 1 Kgs 11:29-39 . . . 533
  2 Chr 10:2-3 . . . . . 678

## AHIMELECH (high priest)
broke law to meet David's needs . . . . . . 1 Sm 21:1ff . . . . . . 445

## AHITHOPHEL (Absalom's adviser)
gave Absalom foolish advice . . . . . . . . . . 2 Sm 16:23 . . . . . . 490

## AI
lessons Joshua learned from
  unsuccessful attack on . . . . . . . . . . . Jos 8:1 . . . . . . . . . 325
MAP: The battle for Ai . . . . . . . . . . . . . . . . . . . . . . . . . . 325

## AIDS
fear of AIDS similar to fear of leprosy
  in Bible times . . . . . . . . . . . . . . . . . . . 2 Kgs 5:1 . . . . . . . . 574
  Lk 5:12 . . . . . . . . 1688

## ALCOHOL
see DRINKING

## ALLEGIANCE
see LOYALTY

## ALLIANCES
can lead to compromise . . . . . . . . . . . . . . Nm 25:1 . . . . . . . . 243
how enemy alliance benefited Joshua . . . Jos 10:5-8 . . . . . . . 328
with those who follow God . . . . . . . . . . . Jgs 8:5-9 . . . . . . . . 371
marital alliances brought Solomon's
  downfall . . . . . . . . . . . . . . . . . . . . . . . 1 Kgs 3:1 . . . . . . . . 517
dangerous with unbelievers . . . . . . . . . . . 2 Chr 18:1ff . . . . . . 688
Ahaz's alliance with Assyria . . . . . . . . . . 2 Kgs 16:5 . . . . . . . 594
what to ask before entering into . . . . . . . 2 Chr 20:37 . . . . . . 694
CHART: Alliances Today . . . . . . . . . . . . . . . . . . . . . . . . . 1119

## ALONE
when Jesus sought solitude . . . . . . . . . . Mt 14:13-14 . . . . . 1572
important priority of Jesus . . . . . . . . . . . . Mt 14:23 . . . . . . . 1572
  Lk 5:16 . . . . . . . . 1688

## ALTARS
explanation of . . . . . . . . . . . . . . . . . . . . . . Gn 12:7 . . . . . . . . . . 24
why Abraham built them to God . . . . . . . Gn 12:7 . . . . . . . . . . 24
why God gave specific directions
  for building them . . . . . . . . . . . . . . . . Ex 20:24-26 . . . . . . 128
significance of the holy fire . . . . . . . . . . . Lv 6:12-13 . . . . . . . 166
removing pagan "altars" from our lives . . Dt 12:2-3 . . . . . . . . 281
a priority for returned exiles . . . . . . . . . . Ezr 3:2-3 . . . . . . . . 725
  3:5 . . . . . . . . . . . . 725

## AMALEKITES
who they were . . . . . . . . . . . . . . . . . . . . . . Ex 17:8 . . . . . . . . . 123
  2 Sm 1:13(2) . . . . . 462
why God ordered destruction of . . . . . . . 1 Sm 15:2-3 . . . . . . 433

## AMBITION
was Korah's undoing . . . . . . . . . . . . . . . . Nm 16:8-10 . . . . . . 227

**GOD, KINGDOM OF**

**GODLINESS**

**GODS/GODDESSES**

**GOD'S LAW**

**GOD'S WILL**

**GOD'S WORD**

**GOG**

**GOLD**

**GOLD CALF**

**GOLDEN RULE**

**GOLGOTHA**

**GOLIATH**

**GOMER**

**GOOD, GOODNESS**

## RELUCTANCE

## REMEMBER, REMEMBERING

## REMINDERS

## REMNANT

## RENEWAL

## REPENTANCE

## REPETITION

## REPLACEMENT

## REPRESENTATIVES

## REPULSIVE

## REPUTATION

# INDEX TO MAPS

Maps in the Gospels concerning Jesus' ministry are given in chronological order—see Harmony of the Gospels.

# INDEX TO PERSONALITY PROFILES

The personality profiles are listed in alphabetical order. The name of the book where the profile appears is also noted.

**AARON** First high priest of Israel; elder brother and spokesman of Moses (Exod 4:14-31; 7:1-2); confronted Pharaoh with Moses (Exod 5–12); held up Moses' hands during battle (Exod 17:8-15); led Israel while Moses was absent (Exod 24:14); priestly clothing and accessories (Exod 28); his ordination (Exod 29; Lev 8); his failure with the gold calf (Exod 32; Acts 7:40); spoke against Moses, then interceded on behalf of sister, Miriam (Num 12:1-16); helped stop the plague (Num 16:45-48); priesthood confirmed (Num 17; Heb 5:1-4); failed at Meribah and was denied entry to Promised Land (Num 20:1-13); died (Num 20:22-29; 33:38-39).

**ABANDON, ABANDONED, ABANDONS (v)** to desert or forsake
Josh 1:5 . . . will not fail you or *a* you.
Josh 24:16 . . . We would never *a* the LORD
Ezra 9:9 . . . God did not *a* us in our slavery.
Neh 9:31 . . . completely or *a* them forever.
Ps 22:1 . . . why have you *a-ed* me?
Ps 37:25 . . . never seen the godly *a-ed*
Ps 37:28 . . . he will never *a* the godly.
Prov 15:10 . . . Whoever *a-s* the right path
Matt 27:46 . . . why have you *a-ed* me?
John 16:1 . . . you won't *a* your faith.
Rom 1:24 . . . So God *a-ed* them to do
Rom 1:28 . . . *a-ed* them to their foolish
2 Cor 4:9 . . . down, but never *a-ed* by God.
Heb 13:5 . . . I will never *a* you.

**ABASED (KJV)**
Ezek 21:26 . . . mighty will be *brought down.*
Matt 23:12 . . . themselves will be *humbled*
Phil 4:12 . . . how to *live on almost nothing*

**ABIDE(TH), ABIDING (KJV)**
Luke 2:8 . . . shepherds *staying* in the fields
John 12:46 . . . no longer *remain* in the dark
John 15:4 . . . be fruitful unless you *remain*

**ABOUND(ED) (KJV)**
Prov 28:20 . . . person will *get a rich reward*
Matt 24:12 . . . Sin will *be rampant everywhere*
Rom 5:15 . . . *even greater* is God's wonderful grace
Rom 5:20 . . . grace *became more abundant*
2 Cor 8:7 . . . *excel* also in this gracious act

**ABRAHAM (ABRAM)** Father of the nation of Israel (Isa 51:2; John 8:37-59); friend of God (Isa 41:8); father of all people of faith (Gen 12–25; Rom 4; Heb 11); made covenant with the LORD (Gen 12:1-3; 13:14-17; 15:12-21; 22:15-18; 50:24; Exod 2:24; 32:13; Lev 26:42; 2 Kgs 13:23; 1 Chr 13:23; 16:16; Neh 9:8; Ps 105:9; Luke 1:73; Acts 3:25; Gal 3:17-20; Heb 6:13);

descendant of Terah from Ur (Gen 11:27-31); husband of Sarah (Sarai) (Gen 11:29); called to leave home (Gen 12:1-9; Acts 7:2-4; Heb 11:8-10); went to Egypt and deceived the Pharaoh (Gen 12:10-20); chose Canaan over the Jordan Plain (Gen 13); rescued Lot from enemies (Gen 14:11-16); blessed by Melchizedek (Gen 14:18-24; Heb 7:1); covenant restated by God (Gen 15); faith counted as righteousness (Gen 15:6; Rom 4:3; Gal 3:6-9; Jas 2:21-23); given son (Ishmael) by Hagar (Gen 16); circumcision commanded (Gen 17; Rom 4:9-12); name changed to "Abraham" (Gen 17:5; Neh 9:7); son promised to Sarah (Gen 17:16; 18:10); welcomed heavenly visitor (Gen 18:1-15); bargained to save Sodom and Gomorrah (Gen 18:16-33); deceived Abimelech (Gen 20); named as a prophet (Gen 20:7); given son (Isaac) by Sarah (Gen 21:1-7; Heb 11:11-12); sent Hagar and Ishmael away (Gen 21:9-14; Gal 4:21-31); offered Issac as test (Gen 22:1-19; Heb 11:17-19; Jas 2:21); secured burial ground for Sarah (Gen 23); found a wife for Isaac (Gen 24); descendants through wife Keturah (Gen 25:1-6); died (Gen 25:7-11).

**ABUNDANCE (n)** great quantity, affluence; more than ample
Job 36:31 . . . giving them food in *a.*
Ps 66:12 . . . a place of great *a.*
Jer 31:14 . . . The priests will enjoy *a,*
Matt 13:12 . . . have an *a* of knowledge.
Matt 25:29 . . . they will have an *a.*
John 1:16 . . . From his *a* we have all

**ABUNDANT (adj)** marked by great plenty, abounding
Deut 28:11 . . . livestock, and *a* crops.
Ps 68:9 . . . You sent *a* rain, O God
Jer 31:12 . . . good gifts—the *a* crops
John 16:24 . . . you will have *a* joy.
2 Cor 8:2 . . . are also filled with *a* joy,

**ABUSIVE (adj)** using harsh, insulting language; characterized by wrong or improper use or action
1 Cor 5:11 . . . worships idols, or is *a,*
1 Cor 6:10 . . . drunkards, or are *a,* or
Eph 4:29 . . . use foul or *a* language.

**ABYSS (KJV)**
Luke 8:31 . . . send them into the *bottomless pit*
Rev 9:1 . . . the shaft of the *bottomless pit*
Rev 9:11 . . . the angel from the *bottomless pit*

**ACCEPT, ACCEPTED, ACCEPTS (v)** to receive willingly
Gen 4:4 . . . The LORD *a-ed* Abel

Gen 4:7 . . . be *a-ed* if you do what is right.
Deut 16:19 . . . Never *a* a bribe, for bribes
Job 42:8 . . . I will *a* his prayer
Job 42:9 . . . the LORD *a-ed* Job's prayer.
Eccl 5:18 . . . to *a* their lot in life.
Luke 4:24 . . . no prophet is *a-ed* in his
Luke 10:16 . . . who *a-s* your message
John 1:12 . . . believed him and *a-ed* him,
John 17:8 . . . They *a-ed* it and know that
Rom 11:12 . . . when they finally *a* it.
Gal 2:9 . . . they *a-ed* Barnabas and me
Col 2:6 . . . just as you *a-ed* Christ Jesus
1 Tim 1:15 . . . everyone should *a* it:
1 Tim 4:9 . . . everyone should *a* it.
Jas 1:21 . . . *a* the word God has planted

**ACCEPTABLE (adj)** capable or worthy of being accepted; welcome, pleasing, favorable
Mark 7:19 . . . every kind of food is *a*
Rom 4:2 . . . had made him *a* to God,
Rom 12:1 . . . the kind he will find *a.*
Rom 14:20 . . . all foods are *a,* but it is
2 Cor 8:12 . . . is *a* if you give it eagerly.
1 Tim 4:5 . . . made *a* by the word of God

**ACCURSED (KJV)**
Deut 21:23 . . . anyone who is hung is *cursed*
Josh 6:18 . . . things *set apart for destruction*
1 Cor 12:3 . . . will *curse* Jesus, and no one
Gal 1:9 . . . let that person be *cursed*

**ACCUSE, ACCUSED, ACCUSES, ACCUSING (v)** to charge with fault or offense; blame
Job 22:4 . . . he *a-s* you and brings judgment
Ps 27:12 . . . For they *a* me of things
Dan 6:5 . . . grounds for *a-ing* Daniel
Luke 23:14 . . . *a-ing* him of leading a revolt.
John 5:45 . . . it isn't I who will *a*
John 7:7 . . . because I *a* it of doing evil.
John 8:46 . . . can truthfully *a* me of sin?
Acts 18:13 . . . *a-d* Paul of "persuading
Rom 2:15 . . . and thoughts either *a* them
Rom 8:33 . . . Who dares *a* us whom God
Rev 12:10 . . . who *a-s* them before our God

**ACKNOWLEDGE, ACKNOWLEDGES (v)** to express a gratitude of debt; to recognize as valid; to confess (wrongdoing)
Jer 3:13 . . . Only *a* your guilt. Admit
Matt 10:32 . . . Everyone who *a-s* me
Luke 12:8 . . . Son of Man will also *a*
Rom 1:28 . . . thought it foolish to *a* God,
1 Jn 2:23 . . . anyone who *a-s* the Son
1 Jn 4:3 . . . and does not *a* the truth

**ADAM** First man (Gen 1:26–2:25; Rom 5:14; 1 Tim 2:13-14); son of God (Luke 3:38);

sinned (Gen 3:1-19; Hos 6:7; Rom 5:12-21); descendants of (Gen 5); died (Gen 5:5; 1 Cor 15:22-49).

**ADD, ADDED (v)** to make or serve as an addition
Deut 4:2 . . . Do not *a* to or subtract from
Deut 12:32 . . . You must not *a* anything to
Prov 30:6 . . . Do not *a* to his words,
Eccl 3:14 . . . Nothing can be *a-ed* to it
Matt 6:27 . . . worries *a* a single moment
Luke 12:25 . . . worries *a* a single moment
Acts 2:47 . . . each day the Lord *a-ed* to their
Rev 22:18 . . . God will *a* to that person

**ADMONISH(ED) (KJV)**
Eccl 12:12 . . . give you *some further advice*
Jer 42:19 . . . Don't forget this *warning* I
2 Thes 3:15 . . . *warn* them as you would
Heb 8:5 . . . God *gave* him this *warning*

**ADMONITION (KJV)**
1 Cor 10:11 . . . written down *to warn us*
Eph 6:4 . . . *instruction* that comes from the Lord
Titus 3:10 . . . a first and second *warning*

**ADOPT, ADOPTED (v)** to take another's child into one's own family
Rom 8:15 . . . when he *a-ed* you as his own
Rom 8:23 . . . rights as his *a-ed* children,
Rom 9:4 . . . to be God's *a-ed* children.
Gal 4:5 . . . so that he could *a* us as
Eph 1:5 . . . decided in advance to *a* us

**ADULTERY (n)** unlawful sexual relations between a married and an unmarried person; symbolic of idolatry
Exod 20:14 . . . You must not commit *a*.
Deut 5:18 . . . You must not commit *a*.
Prov 6:32 . . . who commits *a* is an utter fool,
Matt 5:27 . . . You must not commit *a*.
Matt 19:18 . . . You must not commit *a*.
Mark 10:11 . . . someone else commits *a*
Luke 18:20 . . . You must not commit *a*.
John 8:4 . . . caught in the act of *a*.
1 Cor 6:9 . . . *a*, or are male prostitutes,

**ADVICE (n)** recommendation regarding a decision or course of conduct; counsel
1 Kgs 12:8 . . . rejected the *a* of
2 Chr 10:8 . . . rejected the *a* of
Prov 12:5 . . . *a* of the wicked is
Prov 12:26 . . . godly give good *a* to their
Prov 15:22 . . . Plans go wrong for lack of *a*;
Isa 44:25 . . . I cause the wise to give bad *a*,
Rom 11:34 . . . enough to give him *a*?

**ADVISE (v)** to give advice; to counsel
Ps 32:8 . . . I will *a* you and watch over
1 Tim 5:14 . . . I *a* these younger widows
Rev 3:18 . . . I *a* you to buy gold from me—

**ADVISERS (n)** one who gives advice; counselor
1 Sam 28:23 . . . his *a* joined the woman in
1 Kgs 12:14 . . . counsel of his younger *a*.
Esth 1:13 . . . consulted with his wise *a*,
Prov 11:14 . . . safety in having many *a*.
Prov 29:12 . . . all his *a* will be wicked.

**ADVOCATE (n)** one who pleads the cause of another; defender
*see also* (HOLY) SPIRIT
Job 16:19 . . . My *a* is there on high.
John 14:16 . . . he will give you another *A*,

John 14:26 . . . the Father sends the *A*
John 15:26 . . . I will send you the *A*—
John 16:7 . . . if I don't, the *A* won't come.
1 Jn 2:1 . . . an *a* who pleads our case

**AFRAID (adj)** fearful or apprehensive about an unwanted or uncertain situation
Gen 3:10 . . . I was *a* because I was naked.
Gen 26:24 . . . Do not be *a*, for I am
Exod 3:6 . . . he was *a* to look at God.
Deut 1:21 . . . Don't be *a*!
Deut 20:1 . . . your own, do not be *a*.
Ps 23:4 . . . I will not be *a*, for you are
Isa 10:24 . . . do not be *a* of the Assyrians
Isa 41:10 . . . Don't be *a*, for I am
Isa 43:1 . . . Do not be *a*, for I have
Matt 8:26 . . . Why are you *a*?
Matt 10:31 . . . So don't be *a*;
Mark 5:36 . . . Don't be *a*.
John 14:27 . . . don't be troubled or *a*.
2 Tim 4:5 . . . Don't be *a* of suffering
1 Pet 3:14 . . . don't worry or be *a*

**AGREE, AGREED, AGREEING (v)** to admit, concede
Matt 18:19 . . . If two of you *a* here on
Luke 7:29 . . . *a-d* that God's way was right,
Rom 7:16 . . . that I *a* that the law is good.
Phil 2:2 . . . make me truly happy by *a-ing*

**ALCOHOL (n)** drink (as wine or beer) containing ethanol
Prov 20:1 . . . *a* leads to brawls.
Isa 5:22 . . . boast about all the *a* they

**ALCOHOLIC (adj)** containing alcohol
Num 6:3 . . . give up wine and other *a*

**ALIEN (KJV)**
Exod 18:3 . . . a *foreigner* in a foreign
Job 19:15 . . . I am like a *foreigner* to them
Eph 2:12 . . . You were *excluded from citizenship*

**ALIENATED (KJV)**
Ezek 48:14 . . . traded or *used by others*
Eph 4:18 . . . *wander far from* the life God
Col 1:21 . . . were *once far away from God*

**ALIVE (adj)** animate, having life; active; aware
Gen 45:7 . . . keep you and your families *a*
Ps 41:2 . . . them and keeps them *a*.
Luke 24:23 . . . Jesus is *a*!
Acts 1:3 . . . ways that he was actually *a*.
Rom 6:11 . . . the power of sin and *a* to God
Rev 2:8 . . . who was dead but is now *a*:

**ALLELUIA (KJV)**
Rev 19:1 . . . shouting, *"Praise the Lord!*
Rev 19:3 . . . rang out: *"Praise the Lord!*
Rev 19:4 . . . "Amen! *Praise the Lord!"*
Rev 19:6 . . . *"Praise the Lord!* For the Lord

**ALMIGHTY (n)** having absolute power over all; God
Gen 17:1 . . . I am El-Shaddai—'God *A*.'
Exod 6:3 . . . as El-Shaddai—'God *A*'—
Ruth 1:20 . . . *A* has made life very bitter
Job 6:14 . . . without any fear of the *A*.
Job 33:4 . . . breath of the *A* gives me life.
Ps 91:1 . . . rest in the shadow of the *A*.
Rev 4:8 . . . the *A*—the one who always was,
Rev 15:3 . . . O Lord God, the *A*.
Rev 19:6 . . . our God, the *A*, reigns.

**ALTAR, ALTARS (n)** high places of worship on which sacrifices are offered or incense is burned

Gen 8:20 . . . Noah built an *a* to the LORD,
Gen 12:7 . . . Abram built an *a* there
Gen 22:9 . . . Abraham built an *a* and
Gen 26:25 . . . Isaac built an *a* there
Exod 27:1 . . . construct a square *a* 7½ feet
Exod 30:1 . . . make another *a* of acacia
Exod 37:25 . . . incense *a* of acacia wood.
Josh 8:30 . . . Joshua built an *a* to the LORD,
Josh 22:10 . . . a large and imposing *a*.
1 Sam 7:17 . . . Samuel built an *a* to the
2 Chr 4:1 . . . made a bronze *a* 30 feet long,
2 Chr 4:19 . . . Temple of God: the gold *a*;
2 Chr 32:12 . . . only at the *a* at the Temple
2 Chr 33:16 . . . restored the *a* of the LORD
Ezra 3:2 . . . rebuilding the *a* of the God
Isa 6:6 . . . coal he had taken from the *a*
Matt 5:23 . . . presenting a sacrifice at the *a*
Acts 17:23 . . . your *a-s* had this inscription
Heb 13:10 . . . an *a* from which the priests
Rev 6:9 . . . I saw under the *a* the souls

**ALWAYS (adv)** at all times; forever, perpetually
1 Kgs 2:4 . . . will *a* sit on the throne
Ps 16:8 . . . the LORD is *a* with me.
Ps 52:8 . . . will *a* trust in God's unfailing
Ps 102:27 . . . But you are *a* the same;
Ps 106:3 . . . and *a* do what is right.
Prov 23:7 . . . They are *a* thinking about
Isa 16:5 . . . He will *a* do what is just
Matt 28:20 . . . I am with you *a*, even to
Mark 14:7 . . . You will *a* have the poor
John 12:8 . . . you will not *a* have me.
1 Pet 3:15 . . . *a* be ready to explain it.

**AMAZE, AMAZED (v)** to fill with wonder, astound
Matt 7:28 . . . were *a-d* at his teaching
Mark 7:37 . . . They were completely *a-d* and
Mark 10:24 . . . This *a-d* them. But Jesus
Luke 2:33 . . . Jesus' parents were *a-d* at
Acts 2:7 . . . They were completely *a-d*.

**AMAZING (adj)** causing amazement, great wonder, or surprise
1 Chr 16:24 . . . about the *a* things he does.
Ps 96:3 . . . about the *a* things he does.
Ps 126:2 . . . What *a* things the LORD has

**AMBASSADOR, AMBASSADORS (n)** an authorized representative or messenger
2 Cor 5:20 . . . So we are Christ's *a-s*;
Eph 6:20 . . . this message as God's *a*.

**AMBITION (n)** aspiration to achieve a particular goal, good or bad
Gal 5:20 . . . anger, selfish *a*, dissension,
Phil 1:17 . . . They preach with selfish *a*,
Jas 3:14 . . . there is selfish *a* in your heart,

**ANCESTOR, ANCESTORS (n)** one from whom a person is descended; forefather
Exod 3:15 . . . God of your *a-s*—the God of
Deut 19:14 . . . markers your *a-s* set up
Isa 9:7 . . . throne of his *a* David for all
Isa 43:27 . . . your first *a* sinned against me;
Mark 11:10 . . . Kingdom of our *a* David!
Luke 1:32 . . . the throne of his *a* David.
Rom 9:5 . . . Abraham, Isaac, and Jacob are their *a-s*,
Gal 1:14 . . . for the traditions of my *a-s*.
Heb 1:1 . . . to our *a-s* through the prophets.

**ANGEL, ANGELS (n)** human or superhuman agent or messenger of God
Exod 23:20 . . . I am sending an *a*

2 Sam 24:16 . . . and said to the death *a,*
Ps 91:11 . . . will order his *a-s* to protect
Matt 4:6 . . . will order his *a-s* to protect
Matt 28:2 . . . an *a* of the Lord came down
Luke 1:26 . . . God sent the *a* Gabriel
Luke 2:9 . . . an *a* of the Lord appeared
Luke 20:36 . . . they will be like *a-s.*
Acts 12:7 . . . The *a* struck him on the side
1 Cor 6:3 . . . we will judge *a-s?*
2 Cor 11:14 . . . disguises himself as an *a*
Gal 1:8 . . . or even an *a* from heaven,
Heb 1:6 . . . all of God's *a-s* worship him.
Heb 2:7 . . . a little lower than the *a-s*
Heb 13:2 . . . entertained *a-s* without
1 Pet 1:12 . . . the *a-s* are eagerly watching
2 Pet 2:4 . . . even the *a-s* who sinned.
Jude 1:6 . . . I remind you of the *a-s*

**ANGER (n)** a strong feeling of displeasure
Exod 34:6 . . . slow to *a* and filled with
Num 14:18 . . . slow to *a* and filled with
Deut 9:19 . . . furious *a* of the LORD,
Deut 29:28 . . . In great *a* and fury
2 Kgs 22:13 . . . LORD's great *a* is burning
Ps 30:5 . . . his *a* lasts only a moment,
Ps 78:38 . . . Many times he held back his *a*
Rom 1:18 . . . God shows his *a* from heaven
Rom 2:5 . . . a day of *a* is coming,
Eph 4:26 . . . by letting *a* control you.
1 Thes 5:9 . . . pour out his *a* on us.
Jas 1:20 . . . Human *a* does not produce
Rev 14:10 . . . the wine of God's *a.*

**ANGRY (adj)** feeling or showing anger; wrathful
Exod 32:11 . . . so *a* with your own people
Neh 9:17 . . . merciful, slow to become *a,*
Ps 103:8 . . . merciful, slow to get *a*
Prov 22:24 . . . Don't befriend *a* people
Jon 4:2 . . . slow to get *a* and filled
Matt 5:22 . . . if you are even *a* with
Mark 10:14 . . . he was *a* with his disciples.
John 3:36 . . . under God's *a* judgment.
Acts 4:25 . . . Why were the nations so *a?*
Jas 1:19 . . . to speak, and slow to get *a.*

**ANGUISH (n)** extreme pain, distress, or anxiety
Isa 53:11 . . . by his *a,* he will be satisfied.
Zeph 1:15 . . . of terrible distress and *a,*
Matt 24:21 . . . greater *a* than at any time
Luke 16:24 . . . I am in *a* in these flames.
Rev 16:10 . . . ground their teeth in *a,*

**ANOINT, ANOINTED, ANOINTING (v)** to smear
or rub with oil; used for healing or consecration
to sacred duty; used for grooming or burial;
figurative for divine appointment
*see also* ANOINTED ONE
Exod 30:26 . . . oil to *a* the Tabernacle,
Exod 30:30 . . . *A* Aaron and his sons
Lev 8:12 . . . *a-ing* him and making him holy
1 Sam 15:1 . . . told me to *a* you as king
2 Sam 2:4 . . . David and *a-ed* him king over
2 Sam 23:1 . . . man *a-ed* by the God of Jacob,
Ps 23:5 . . . honor me by *a-ing* my head
Ps 92:10 . . . You have *a-ed* me with
Isa 61:1 . . . the LORD has *a-ed* me
Dan 9:24 . . . and to *a* the Most Holy Place.
Acts 10:38 . . . you know that God *a-ed* Jesus
Heb 1:9 . . . your God has *a-ed* you,
Jas 5:14 . . . pray over you, *a-ing* you with oil

**ANOINTED ONE (n)** one chosen by divine
election
1 Sam 2:10 . . . the strength of his *a* one."

1 Sam 26:9 . . . the LORD's *a* one?
Ps 132:17 . . . my *a* one will be a light for
Dan 9:25 . . . a ruler—the *A* One—
Isa 45:1 . . . says to Cyrus, his *a* one,

**ANTICHRIST, ANTICHRISTS (n)** opponent of
Christ; the personification of evil
1 Jn 2:18 . . . heard that the *A* is coming,
1 Jn 2:18 . . . many such *a-s* have appeared.
1 Jn 4:3 . . . has the spirit of the *A,*
2 Jn 1:7 . . . deceiver and an *a.*

**ANXIETY, CARE(S) (KJV)**
Ps 139:23 . . . know my *anxious thoughts*
Phil 4:6 . . . Don't *worry* about anything
1 Pet 5:7 . . . your *worries and cares* to God,

**APPEAR, APPEARED, APPEARING, APPEARS
(v)** to come out of hiding and show up in public
view; to make one's presence known
Gen 1:9 . . . so dry ground may *a.*
Num 14:10 . . . presence of the LORD *a-ed*
Deut 33:16 . . . *a-ed* in the burning bush.
Mal 3:2 . . . and face him when he *a-s?*
Matt 1:20 . . . angel of the Lord *a-ed* to him
Matt 24:30 . . . will *a* in the heavens,
Luke 2:9 . . . angel of the Lord *a-ed* among
Luke 16:15 . . . You like to *a* righteous
Phil 2:7 . . . When he *a-ed* in human form,
2 Thes 1:7 . . . the Lord Jesus *a-s* from
2 Tim 1:10 . . . by the *a-ing* of Christ Jesus,
2 Tim 4:1 . . . *a-s* to set up his Kingdom:
Heb 9:24 . . . *a* now before God on our
Heb 9:26 . . . *a-ed* at the end of the age
1 Pet 5:4 . . . when the Great Shepherd *a-s,*
1 Jn 3:2 . . . will be like when Christ *a-s.*

**APPROVAL (n)** an act or instance of approving
Ps 90:17 . . . LORD our God show us his *a*
John 6:27 . . . the seal of his *a.*
Rom 14:4 . . . stand and receive his *a.*
1 Cor 11:19 . . . you who have God's *a*
2 Tim 2:15 . . . and receive his *a.*
Heb 11:4 . . . God showed his *a* of his gifts.

**APPROVE, APPROVED, APPROVES (v)** to
have or express a favorable opinion of; to attest
Gen 7:2 . . . animal I have *a-ed* for eating
Prov 12:2 . . . LORD *a-s* of those who
Rom 14:18 . . . and others will *a* of you,
Rom 16:10 . . . a good man whom Christ *a-s.*
1 Thes 2:4 . . . speak as messengers *a-ed*

**ARARAT (n)** a mountain on the far east border
of modern Turkey; the mountain Noah's ark
rested on after the Flood
Gen 8:4 . . . to rest on the mountains of *A.*

**ARCHANGEL, ARCHANGELS (n)** a leader and
chief angel; biblically designated as Michael
Dan 10:13 . . . one of the *a-s,* came to help
Dan 12:1 . . . At that time Michael, the *a*
1 Thes 4:16 . . . with the voice of the *a,*

**ARGUE, ARGUING (v)** to contend or disagree
in words; to dispute
Job 13:8 . . . Will you *a* God's case
Job 40:2 . . . to *a* with the Almighty?
Prov 25:9 . . . When *a-ing* with your neighbor,
Isa 45:9 . . . those who *a* with their Creator.
Rom 14:1 . . . and don't *a* with them
1 Cor 11:16 . . . anyone wants to *a*

**ARM, ARMS (n)** upper limb of the body;
extension or projection of; lineage; figurative of
power or might

Num 11:23 . . . Has my *a* lost its power?
Deut 4:34 . . . a powerful *a,* and terrifying
Deut 7:19 . . . strong hand and powerful *a*
Deut 33:27 . . . everlasting *a-s* are under
Ps 44:3 . . . it was not their own strong *a*
Ps 98:1 . . . his holy *a* has shown
Isa 40:11 . . . carry the lambs in his *a-s,*
Isa 65:2 . . . opened my *a-s* to a rebellious
Jer 27:5 . . . powerful *a* I made the earth
Mark 10:16 . . . took the children in his *a-s*
1 Pet 4:1 . . . you must *a* yourselves with

**ARMAGEDDON (n)** the gathering place for the
final battle between God's forces and Satan's
forces associated with Christ's second coming
Rev 16:16 . . . with the Hebrew name *A.*

**ARMOR (n)** weapons of war or self-defense;
figurative of spiritual resources
Ps 91:4 . . . are your *a* and protection.
Isa 59:17 . . . righteousness as his body *a*
Jer 46:4 . . . and prepare your *a.*
Rom 13:12 . . . put on the shining *a*
Eph 6:11 . . . Put on all of God's *a*
Eph 6:13 . . . put on every piece of God's *a*
1 Thes 5:8 . . . protected by the *a* of faith

**ARMY, ARMIES (n)** large band of men
organized and armed for war; any large
multitude devoted to a cause
Ps 33:16 . . . best-equipped *a* cannot save
Ps 84:12 . . . LORD of Heaven's *A-ies,*
Isa 6:3 . . . LORD of Heaven's *A-ies!*
Isa 45:13 . . . LORD of Heaven's *A-ies,*
Isa 51:15 . . . the LORD of Heaven's *A-ies.*
Joel 2:2 . . . great and mighty *a* appears.
Joel 2:5 . . . like a mighty *a* moving into
Joel 2:11 . . . This is his mighty *a,*
Hag 1:5 . . . LORD of Heaven's *A-ies* says:
Zech 8:6 . . . LORD of Heaven's *A-ies* says:
Rev 19:14 . . . The *a-ies* of heaven,
Rev 19:19 . . . the horse and his *a.*

**ARROGANCE (n)** a feeling or an impression of
superiority manifested in an overbearing
manner or presumptuous claims
1 Sam 2:3 . . . Don't speak with such *a!*
Prov 8:13 . . . I hate pride and *a,*
Isa 16:6 . . . its pride and *a* and rage.
2 Cor 12:20 . . . slander, gossip, *a,*

**ARROGANT (adj)** exaggerating or disposed to
exaggerate one's own worth or importance in an
overbearing manner
Ps 31:23 . . . harshly punishes the *a.*
Ps 119:78 . . . upon the *a* people who lied
1 Tim 6:4 . . . is *a* and lacks understanding.
Titus 1:7 . . . not be *a* or quick-tempered;

**ASHAMED (v)** feeling shame, guilt, or
disgrace
Ps 69:6 . . . be *a* because of me,
Jer 31:19 . . . I was thoroughly *a* of all I did
Jer 48:13 . . . were *a* of their gold calf
Mark 8:38 . . . If anyone is *a* of me
Luke 9:26 . . . If anyone is *a* of me
Rom 1:16 . . . I am not *a* of this Good News
2 Tim 1:8 . . . So never be *a* to tell others
2 Tim 2:15 . . . who does not need to be *a*

**ASLEEP (adj)** state of bodily rest; figurative for
physical death or spiritual dullness
*see also* DIE, SLEEP
Judg 4:21 . . . Sisera fell *a* from exhaustion,
1 Kgs 18:27 . . . away on a trip, or is *a* and

Matt 9:24 . . . isn't dead; she's only *a.* "
Matt 26:40 . . . disciples and found them *a.*
John 11:11 . . . Lazarus has fallen *a,* but
1 Thes 5:6 . . . be on your guard, not *a* like

**ASTRAY (adv)** off the right path or route; in error, away from what is desirable or proper
Prov 20:1 . . . Those led *a* by drink
Isa 47:10 . . . 'knowledge' have led you *a,*
Jer 50:6 . . . shepherds have led them *a*
1 Jn 2:26 . . . who want to lead you *a.*

**ASTROLOGERS (n)** one who studies the stars and planets to foresee or foretell future events by their positions and aspects
Isa 47:13 . . . all your *a,* those stargazers
Dan 2:2 . . . enchanters, sorcerers, and *a,*

**ATE (v)** *see also* EAT
Gen 3:6 . . . some of the fruit and *a* it.
Ezek 3:3 . . . And when I *a* it, it tasted as
Matt 15:37 . . . *a* as much as they wanted.
Rev 10:10 . . . I *a* it! It was sweet

**ATHLETE, ATHLETES (n)** a person who is trained or skilled in exercises, sports, or games requiring physical strength, agility, or stamina
Ps 19:5 . . . like a great *a* eager to run
1 Cor 9:25 . . . All *a-s* are disciplined
1 Cor 9:27 . . . body like an *a,* training it
2 Tim 2:5 . . . *a-s* cannot win the prize unless

**ATONE, ATONES (v)** to supply satisfaction for; to make amends; to reconcile
*see also* FORGIVE
Dan 9:24 . . . their sin, to *a* for their guilt,
1 Jn 2:2 . . . sacrifice that *a-s* for our sins—

**ATONEMENT (n)** reconciliation; reparation for an offense or injury; cleansing
*see also* FORGIVENESS
Exod 25:17 . . . cover—the place of *a*—
Lev 23:27 . . . Day of *A* on the tenth day
2 Chr 29:24 . . . to make *a* for the sins
Prov 16:6 . . . faithfulness make *a* for sin.

**ATTITUDE, ATTITUDES (n)** a mental position with regard to a fact or state; a feeling or emotion toward a fact or state
Eph 4:23 . . . your thoughts and *a-s.*
Phil 2:5 . . . have the same *a* that Christ
1 Pet 3:8 . . . keep a humble *a.*
1 Pet 4:1 . . . with the same *a* he had,

**AUTHORITY, AUTHORITIES (n)** the right to govern; the freedom or ability to act
Matt 28:18 . . . been given all *a* in heaven
Luke 10:19 . . . have given you *a* over
John 5:22 . . . absolute *a* to judge,
Acts 1:7 . . . *a* to set those dates and times,
Rom 13:1 . . . submit to governing *a-ies.*
Rom 13:1 . . . For all *a* comes from God,
Rom 13:2 . . . anyone who rebels against *a*
Rom 13:3 . . . without fear of the *a-ies?*
1 Cor 4:3 . . . by any human *a.*
1 Cor 15:24 . . . ruler and *a* and power.
Eph 1:22 . . . things under the *a* of Christ
Eph 3:10 . . . all the unseen rulers and *a-ies*
Eph 6:12 . . . against evil rulers and *a-ies*
Col 2:10 . . . every ruler and *a.*
Col 2:15 . . . the spiritual rulers and *a-ies.*
1 Tim 2:2 . . . all who are in *a* so that
Titus 2:15 . . . You have the *a* to correct
1 Pet 2:18 . . . accept the *a* of your masters
1 Pet 3:1 . . . accept the *a* of your husbands.

1 Pet 3:22 . . . the angels and *a-ies* and
1 Pet 5:5 . . . accept the *a* of the elders.
Jude 1:6 . . . the limits of *a* God gave them

**AVOID, AVOIDING (v)** to keep away from; to depart or withdraw from
Prov 4:24 . . . *A* all perverse talk;
Prov 14:16 . . . are cautious and *a* danger;
Prov 16:6 . . . By fearing the LORD, people *a*
Prov 20:3 . . . *A-ing* a fight is a mark
Eccl 7:18 . . . fears God will *a* both
Rom 2:3 . . . think you can *a* God's

**AWE (n)** an emotion variously combining dread, respect, and wonder that is inspired by authority or the sacred
*see also* FEAR, REVERENCE
1 Kgs 3:28 . . . people were in *a* of the king,
Ps 119:120 . . . I stand in *a* of your
Luke 5:26 . . . with great wonder and *a,*
Acts 2:43 . . . sense of *a* came over them
Heb 12:28 . . . holy fear and *a.*

**AWESOME (adj)** characterized by reverential fear; expressive of or inspiring awe
*see also* WONDERFUL
Exod 34:10 . . . the *a* power I will display
Deut 7:21 . . . a great and *a* God.
2 Sam 7:23 . . . You performed *a* miracles
Neh 1:5 . . . the great and *a* God
Job 10:16 . . . display your *a* power
Ps 47:2 . . . Most High is *a.*
Ps 65:5 . . . answer our prayers with *a*
Ps 99:3 . . . your great and *a* name.
Ps 106:22 . . . such *a* deeds at the Red Sea.
Ps 131:1 . . . too *a* for me to grasp.
Dan 9:4 . . . a great and *a* God!

**BABY, BABIES (n)** infant child; youngest of a group; figurative of new or immature Christians
Exod 2:7 . . . women to nurse the *b* for you?
Luke 1:44 . . . *b* in my womb jumped for
Luke 2:12 . . . find a *b* wrapped snugly
Luke 2:16 . . . the *b,* lying in the manger.
Acts 7:19 . . . abandon their newborn *b-ies*
1 Cor 14:20 . . . Be innocent as *b-ies* when
1 Pet 2:2 . . . Like newborn *b-ies,* you must

**BABYLON (n)** capital city of the Babylonian Empire; a city devoted to materialism and sensual pleasure; Biblical writers used as model of paganism and idolatry
Ps 137:1 . . . Beside the rivers of *B,* we sat
Jer 29:10 . . . will be in *B* for seventy years.
Jer 51:37 . . . *B* will become a heap of ruins,
Rev 14:8 . . . shouting, "*B* is fallen—

**BAPTISM, BAPTISMS (n)** a Christian ordinance; a washing with water to demonstrate cleansing from sin, linked with repentance and admission into the community of faith; figurative of an ordeal or initiation
Matt 3:16 . . . After his *b,* as Jesus came up
Luke 3:7 . . . crowds came to John for *b,*
Acts 19:3 . . . what *b* did you experience?
Rom 6:3 . . . joined with Christ Jesus in *b,*
Gal 3:27 . . . united with Christ in *b*
Eph 4:5 . . . one Lord, one faith, one *b,*
Heb 6:2 . . . further instruction about *b-s,*
1 Pet 3:21 . . . that water is a picture of *b,*

**BAPTIZE, BAPTIZED, BAPTIZING (v)** to engage in the ordinance of baptism (see above)
*see also* WASH
Matt 3:13 . . . River to be *b-d* by John.
Matt 28:19 . . . of all the nations, *b-ing*
Mark 1:4 . . . that people should be *b-d*
Mark 1:8 . . . will *b* you with the Holy Spirit!
Mark 10:38 . . . suffering I must be *b-d* with?
Luke 3:3 . . . that people should be *b-d*
Luke 3:16 . . . I *b* you with water;
Luke 3:21 . . . Jesus himself was *b-d.*
John 1:28 . . . where John was *b-ing.*
John 1:31 . . . I have been *b-ing* with water
John 1:33 . . . is the one who will *b* with
John 3:22 . . . with them there, *b-ing* people.
John 3:26 . . . is also *b-ing* people.
John 4:1 . . . was *b-ing* and making more
John 4:2 . . . Jesus himself didn't *b* them—
John 10:40 . . . where John was first *b-ing*
Acts 1:5 . . . will be *b-d* with the Holy Spirit.
Acts 1:22 . . . time he was *b-d* by John
Acts 2:41 . . . *b-d* and added to the church
Acts 8:12 . . . and women were *b.*
Acts 8:38 . . . water, and Philip *b-d* him.
Acts 11:16 . . . will be *b-d* with the Holy
Acts 16:15 . . . She was *b-d* along with
Acts 16:33 . . . were immediately *b-d.*
Acts 19:5 . . . *b-d* in the name of the Lord
1 Cor 1:13 . . . you *b-d* in the name of Paul?
1 Cor 1:14 . . . I did not *b* any of you
1 Cor 1:16 . . . *b-d* the household of
1 Cor 10:2 . . . were *b-d* as followers
1 Cor 15:29 . . . *b-d* for those who are dead?
Col 2:12 . . . when you were *b-d.*

**BEAST, BEASTS (n)** devilish creature(s) ravishing the earth during the Tribulation; animals, as distinguished from plants or humans; a contemptible person
Dan 7:3 . . . Then four huge *b-s* came up
Dan 7:6 . . . authority was given to this *b.*
1 Cor 15:32 . . . fighting wild *b-s*—those
Rev 13:18 . . . number of the *b,* for it is
Rev 16:2 . . . had the mark of the *b*
Rev 19:20 . . . accepted the mark of the *b*

**BEAUTIFUL (adj)** lovely, handsome, or pleasing to the eye; excellent
Gen 2:9 . . . trees that were *b*
Gen 6:2 . . . sons of God saw the *b*
Prov 11:22 . . . A *b* woman who lacks
Eccl 3:11 . . . everything *b* for its own time.
Isa 53:2 . . . was nothing *b* or majestic
Lam 2:15 . . . the city called 'Most *B*
Acts 3:2 . . . the one called the *B* Gate,
Rom 10:15 . . . How *b* are the feet of

**BEAUTY (n)** a particularly graceful, ornamental, or excellent quality; the quality in a person or thing that gives pleasure to the senses
2 Sam 11:2 . . . a woman of unusual *b*
Ps 50:2 . . . the perfection of *b,* God shines
Prov 31:30 . . . and *b* does not last;
Isa 28:1 . . . but its glorious *b* will fade
Jas 1:11 . . . and its *b* fades away.
1 Pet 1:24 . . . their *b* is like a flower
1 Pet 3:4 . . . *b* of a gentle and quiet spirit,

**BEGINNING (n)** the point at which something starts; the first part; the origin, source
Gen 1:1 . . . In the *b* God created
John 1:1 . . . In the *b* the Word already

Rom 16:25 . . . secret from the *b* of time.
1 Jn 1:1 . . . one who existed from the *b*,
Rev 21:6 . . . the *B* and the End.
Rev 22:13 . . . the *B* and the End.

**BELIEVE, BELIEVED, BELIEVES, BELIEVING (v)**
to trust in; to hold a firm conviction about; to
accept as true, genuine, or real
*see also* FAITH, TRUST
Gen 15:6 . . . Abram *b-d* the LORD,
Prov 14:15 . . . simpletons *b* everything
Isa 53:1 . . . Who has *b-d* our message?
Matt 27:42 . . . we will *b* in him!
Mark 9:23 . . . is possible if a person *b-s.*
Mark 9:24 . . . I do *b*, but help me
Mark 15:32 . . . we can see it and *b* him!
Luke 8:12 . . . prevent them from *b-ing*
Luke 24:25 . . . You find it so hard to *b*
John 1:7 . . . so that everyone might *b*
John 1:12 . . . all who *b-d* him and accepted
John 3:16 . . . everyone who *b-s* in him
John 4:41 . . . hear his message and *b.*
John 5:38 . . . because you do not *b* me—
John 6:69 . . . We *b*, and we know you are
John 7:5 . . . his brothers didn't *b* in him.
John 7:39 . . . to everyone *b-ing* in him.
John 9:35 . . . asked, "Do you *b* in the Son
John 9:38 . . . Yes, Lord, I *b!*
John 10:37 . . . Don't *b* me unless
John 11:25 . . . Anyone who *b-s* in me
John 11:27 . . . *b-d* you are the Messiah,
John 11:40 . . . see God's glory if you *b?*
John 12:37 . . . did not *b* in him.
John 12:38 . . . who has *b-d* our message?
John 13:19 . . . you will *b* that I AM
John 14:11 . . . Or at least *b* because of the
John 14:12 . . . anyone who *b-s* in me
John 16:30 . . . *b* that you came from God.
John 17:21 . . . world will *b* you sent me.
John 19:35 . . . so that you also can *b.*
John 20:8 . . . and he saw and *b-d*—
John 20:29 . . . *b* because you have seen
John 20:31 . . . and that by *b-ing* in him
Acts 10:43 . . . that everyone who *b-s* in him
Acts 13:8 . . . keep the governor from *b-ing.*
Acts 16:31 . . . *B* in the Lord Jesus and
Acts 19:4 . . . *b* in the one who would come
Acts 26:27 . . . do you *b* the prophets?
Acts 27:25 . . . For I *b* God.
Rom 1:16 . . . saving everyone who *b-s*—
Rom 3:22 . . . for everyone who *b-s*, no
Rom 3:25 . . . *b* that Jesus sacrificed his life,
Rom 4:3 . . . tell us, "Abraham *b-d* God,
Rom 4:20 . . . never wavered in *b-ing* God's
Rom 10:9 . . . *b* in your heart that God
Rom 10:10 . . . For it is by *b-ing* in your heart
Rom 10:14 . . . unless they *b* in him?
Rom 14:23 . . . anything you *b* is not right,
Rom 16:26 . . . they too might *b* and obey
1 Cor 1:21 . . . to save those who *b.*
1 Cor 15:2 . . . *b-d* something that was never
2 Cor 5:7 . . . by *b-ing* and not by seeing.
2 Cor 5:14 . . . Since we *b* that Christ
Gal 3:2 . . . because you *b-d* the message
Gal 3:6 . . . same way, "Abraham *b-d* God,
Eph 2:8 . . . his grace when you *b-d.*
Col 1:23 . . . continue to *b* this truth
1 Thes 4:14 . . . For since we *b* that Jesus
2 Thes 2:11 . . . and they will *b* these lies.
2 Thes 2:12 . . . enjoying evil rather than *b-ing*
1 Tim 3:16 . . . He was *b-d* in throughout the

Heb 3:14 . . . firmly as when we first *b-d,*
Heb 11:6 . . . must *b* that God exists
Heb 11:13 . . . still *b-ing* what God had
Jas 2:19 . . . you *b* that there is one God.
1 Jn 3:23 . . . We must *b* in the name
1 Jn 4:1 . . . friends, do not *b* everyone
1 Jn 5:1 . . . Everyone who *b-s* that Jesus is
1 Jn 5:10 . . . All who *b* in the Son

**BELONG, BELONGED, BELONGS (v)** to be the
property of a person or thing
Lev 25:55 . . . people of Israel *b* to me.
Lev 27:30 . . . *b-s* to the LORD and
Ps 22:28 . . . royal power *b-s* to the LORD.
John 8:47 . . . Anyone who *b-s* to God
John 15:19 . . . if you *b-ed* to it,
Rom 1:6 . . . called to *b* to Jesus
Rom 12:5 . . . we all *b* to each other.
2 Cor 10:7 . . . who say they *b* to Christ
Gal 5:24 . . . Those who *b* to Christ
1 Thes 5:5 . . . we don't *b* to darkness
2 Tim 2:19 . . . All who *b* to the LORD
1 Pet 3:16 . . . because you *b* to Christ.
1 Jn 4:6 . . . If they do not *b* to God,

**BENEFIT, BENEFITS (n)** advantages or
blessings; something that promotes well-being
Prov 12:14 . . . Wise words bring many *b-s,*
Acts 18:27 . . . he proved to be of great *b* to
2 Cor 4:15 . . . this is for your *b.*

**BENEFIT, BENEFITS (v)** to be useful or
profitable to; to favor (another) or gain (for
oneself)
Job 36:28 . . . and everyone *b-s.*
Prov 9:12 . . . you will be the one to *b.*
Luke 9:25 . . . what do you *b* if you gain
1 Cor 9:14 . . . by those who *b* from it.

**BESTOWED (KJV)**
Isa 63:7 . . . he has *granted* according

**BETHLEHEM (n)** a city about five miles south
of Jerusalem in the hill country of Judah; the
ancestral home of King David and the birthplace
of Jesus Christ
Ruth 1:19 . . . When they came to *B,*
1 Sam 16:1 . . . go to *B.*
2 Sam 23:15 . . . the well by the gate in *B.*
Mic 5:2 . . . *B* Ephrathah, are only a small
Matt 2:1 . . . Jesus was born in *B* in Judea,
Matt 2:6 . . . you, O *B* in the land of Judah,

**BETRAY, BETRAYED (v)** to turn your back on a
friend; to deliver to an enemy by treachery; to
lead astray, seduce
Num 5:6 . . . men or women—*b* the LORD
Deut 32:51 . . . both of you *b-ed* me
Jer 38:22 . . . They have *b-ed* and misled you.
Mal 2:10 . . . Then why do we *b* each other,
Matt 10:21 . . . A brother will *b* his brother
Matt 24:10 . . . and *b* and hate each other.
Matt 26:21 . . . one of you will *b* me.
Matt 27:4 . . . I have *b-ed* an innocent man.
Luke 6:16 . . . (who later *b-ed* him).
John 18:5 . . . Judas, who *b-ed* him,

**BIRTH (n)** the emergence of a new individual
from the body of its parent; beginning, start
Gen 25:24 . . . the time came to give *b,*
Ps 58:3 . . . even from *b* they have lied
Matt 24:8 . . . only the first of the *b* pains,
John 3:6 . . . Spirit gives *b* to spiritual life.
Titus 3:5 . . . giving us a new *b* and new life
Jas 1:15 . . . it gives *b* to death.

**BIRTHRIGHT (KJV)**
Gen 25:31 . . . me your *rights as the firstborn
son*
1 Chr 5:1 . . . *birthright* was given to the
Heb 12:16 . . . his *birthright as the firstborn son*

**BITTERNESS (n)** an intense or severe
expression or feeling of pain, grief, or regret;
exhibiting intense animosity
Prov 14:10 . . . Each heart knows its own *b,*
Prov 17:25 . . . *b* to the one who gave them
Rom 3:14 . . . full of cursing and *b.*
Eph 4:31 . . . Get rid of all *b*, rage,

**BLAME (n)** an expression of disapproval or
reproach; responsibility for something believed
to deserve censure
1 Cor 1:8 . . . free from all *b* on the day
Rev 14:5 . . . they are without *b.*

**BLAMELESS (adj)** characterized by being free
from sin and fault
*see also* INTEGRITY, RIGHTEOUS
Gen 6:9 . . . only *b* person living on earth
Job 1:8 . . . *b*—a man of complete integrity.
Ps 18:23 . . . I am *b* before God;
Prov 13:6 . . . guards the path of the *b,*
Prov 29:10 . . . The bloodthirsty hate *b*
Phil 1:10 . . . live pure and *b* lives
Col 1:22 . . . and you are holy and *b*
1 Thes 5:23 . . . kept *b* until our Lord
Titus 1:6 . . . must live a *b* life.
2 Pet 3:14 . . . are pure and *b* in his sight.

**BLASPHEME, BLASPHEMED, BLASPHEMES,
BLASPHEMING (v)** to dishonor or revile God;
to speak of or address with irreverence
Lev 24:11 . . . son of an Israelite woman *b-ed*
Lev 24:16 . . . Anyone who *b-s* the Name
Num 15:30 . . . have *b-ed* the LORD,
Isa 52:5 . . . My name is *b-ed* all day long.
Dan 11:36 . . . even *b-ing* the God of gods.
Mark 3:29 . . . who *b-s* the Holy Spirit
Luke 12:10 . . . who *b-s* the Holy Spirit
Acts 6:11 . . . We heard him *b* Moses,
Rom 2:24 . . . Gentiles *b* the name of God
1 Tim 1:13 . . . to *b* the name of Christ.
1 Tim 1:20 . . . learn not to *b* God.
Rev 13:1 . . . were names that *b-ed* God.

**BLASPHEMY, BLASPHEMIES (n)** the words or
actions that dishonor God; the act of insulting or
showing contempt or lack of reverence for God
Neh 9:18 . . . They committed terrible *b-ies.*
Mark 3:28 . . . all sin and *b* can be forgiven,
Mark 14:64 . . . You have all heard his *b.*
John 10:33 . . . for any good work, but for *b!*
2 Pet 2:11 . . . a charge of *b* against those
Rev 13:5 . . . to speak great *b-ies* against God.
Rev 13:6 . . . words of *b* against God,
Rev 17:3 . . . and *b-ies* against God were

**BLESS, BLESSED, BLESSES (v)** to confer
prosperity or happiness upon; to honor in
worship; to offer approval or encouragement;
to bring pleasure or divine favor
Gen 1:22 . . . Then God *b-ed* them,
Gen 12:3 . . . I will *b* those who *b* you
Gen 22:18 . . . of the earth will be *b-ed*—
Ps 16:7 . . . I will *b* the LORD who guides
Prov 31:28 . . . Her children stand and *b*
Matt 5:3 . . . God *b-es* those who are poor
Matt 5:7 . . . God *b-es* those who are merciful,
Matt 5:9 . . . God *b-es* those who work for

Matt 5:11 . . . God *b-es* you when people mock
Acts 20:35 . . . *b-ed* to give than to receive.
Jas 1:12 . . . God *b-es* those who patiently
Rev 22:7 . . . *B-ed* are those who obey
Rev 22:14 . . . *B-ed* are those who wash their robes.

**BLESSING, BLESSINGS (n)** happiness; praise; divine favor or heavenly reward; the antidote to cursings
Josh 8:34 . . . *b-s* and curses Moses
Prov 13:21 . . . *b-s* reward the righteous.
John 12:13 . . . *B-s* on the one who comes in
Acts 4:33 . . . God's great *b* was upon them
Acts 11:23 . . . evidence of God's *b*,
Rom 15:27 . . . spiritual *b-s* of the Good
Eph 3:6 . . . both enjoy the promise of *b-s*
Rev 7:12 . . . *B* and glory and wisdom

**BLIND (adj)** sightless; lacking spiritual discernment
Matt 11:5 . . . the *b* see, the lame walk,
Matt 15:14 . . . *b* guides leading the *b*,
Mark 10:46 . . . *b* beggar named
Luke 6:39 . . . Can one *b* person lead

**BLINDED (v)** to withhold light from or pull wool over; to be without sight; from God, given as a punishment
John 12:40 . . . The Lord has *b* their eyes
2 Cor 4:4 . . . god of this world, has *b* the

**BLOOD (n)** fluid in the circulatory system; signifies human life; kinfolk; of animals, used in priestly sacrifices; of Christ, effective for the forgiveness of sins; on hands or head, symbolic of guilt
Exod 12:13 . . . When I see the *b*, I will pass
Deut 12:23 . . . But never consume the *b*,
Isa 1:11 . . . no pleasure from the *b* of bulls
Mark 14:24 . . . my *b*, which confirms the
John 6:53 . . . and drink his *b*, you cannot
Acts 15:20 . . . and from consuming *b*.
1 Cor 11:25 . . . confirmed with my *b*.
Eph 1:7 . . . with the *b* of his Son
Eph 2:13 . . . through the *b* of Christ.
Heb 9:7 . . . offered *b* for his own sins
Heb 9:20 . . . This *b* confirms the covenant
1 Pet 1:2 . . . cleansed by the *b* of Jesus
1 Pet 1:19 . . . the precious *b* of Christ,
1 Jn 1:7 . . . the *b* of Jesus, his Son, cleanses
Rev 1:5 . . . by shedding his *b* for us.
Rev 5:9 . . . your *b* has ransomed people
Rev 7:14 . . . in the *b* of the Lamb
Rev 12:11 . . . by the *b* of the Lamb
Rev 19:13 . . . He wore a robe dipped in *b*,

**BLOT (v)** to wipeout, destroy; to erase or cover up
Ps 51:1 . . . *b* out the stain of my sins.
Isa 43:25 . . . I alone—will *b* out your sins

**BOAST, BOASTED, BOASTING (v)** to puff oneself up in speech, brag
Isa 20:5 . . . and *b-ed* of their allies in Egypt!
Jer 9:23 . . . the wise *b* in their wisdom,
Rom 2:17 . . . *b* about your special
1 Cor 1:31 . . . *b*, *b* only about the Lord.
2 Cor 8:24 . . . our *b-ing* about you is justified.
2 Cor 10:13 . . . We will *b* only about
Gal 6:14 . . . *b* about anything except
Eph 2:9 . . . none of us can *b* about it.
Jas 1:9 . . . poor have something to *b* about,

Jas 4:16 . . . *b-ing* about your own plans,
2 Pet 2:18 . . . empty, foolish *b-ing*.

**BODY, BODIES (n)** one's physical essence; a corpse; a group of people
Job 19:26 . . . in my *b* I will see God!
Ps 49:14 . . . Their *b-ies* will rot in the grave,
Isa 26:19 . . . their *b-ies* will rise again!
Matt 26:41 . . . willing, but the *b* is weak!
Mark 14:22 . . . Take it, for this is my *b*.
Rom 12:4 . . . our *b-ies* have many parts
1 Cor 6:15 . . . that your *b-ies* are actually
1 Cor 6:19 . . . that your *b* is the temple
1 Cor 6:20 . . . honor God with your *b*.
1 Cor 11:24 . . . my *b*, which is given for
1 Cor 12:13 . . . into one *b* by one Spirit,
1 Cor 15:44 . . . as spiritual *b-ies*.
2 Cor 5:1 . . . eternal *b* made for us by God
2 Cor 5:2 . . . to put on our heavenly *b-ies*
2 Cor 5:4 . . . so that these dying *b-ies* will
Eph 1:23 . . . the church is his *b*;
Eph 3:6 . . . Both are part of the same *b*,
Eph 5:28 . . . love their own *b-ies*.
Eph 5:30 . . . are members of his *b*.
Col 1:24 . . . for his *b*, the church.

**BOLD (adj)** fearless before danger; self-assured, confident; prominent
2 Sam 7:27 . . . been *b* enough to pray
1 Chr 17:25 . . . been *b* enough to pray
Phil 1:20 . . . continue to be *b* for Christ,

**BOLDLY (adv)** showing or requiring a fearless daring spirit
Acts 26:26 . . . I speak *b*, for I am sure
Eph 3:12 . . . *b* and confidently into God's
Heb 4:16 . . . let us come *b* to the throne
Heb 10:19 . . . *b* enter heaven's Most Holy

**BOLDNESS (n)** fearlessness before danger; self-assurance; confidence; prominence
Acts 4:13 . . . they saw the *b* of Peter
Acts 4:29 . . . give us, your servants, great *b*

**BONE, BONES (n)** one of the hard parts of the skeleton
Gen 2:23 . . . This one is *b* from my *b*,
Ps 22:14 . . . all my *b-s* are out of joint.
Ps 22:17 . . . I can count all my *b-s*.
Ezek 37:1 . . . a valley filled with *b-s*.
John 19:36 . . . Not one of his *b-s* will be

**BOOK, BOOKS (n)** a long written or printed literary composition; written records, register, or accounting
Josh 1:8 . . . Study this *B* of Instruction
Ps 69:28 . . . names from the *B* of Life;
Ps 139:16 . . . recorded in your *b*.
Eccl 12:12 . . . for writing *b-s* is endless,
Dan 7:10 . . . and the *b-s* were opened.
Dan 12:1 . . . name is written in the *b*
John 21:25 . . . could not contain the *b-s*
Phil 4:3 . . . are written in the *B* of Life.
Rev 3:5 . . . names from the *B* of Life.
Rev 20:12 . . . including the *B* of Life.
Rev 20:12 . . . as recorded in the *b-s*.
Rev 21:27 . . . in the Lamb's *B* of Life.

**BORN (v)** to give birth to or produce; to be productive; spiritually, to renew or confirm a commitment of faith
Ps 51:5 . . . For I was *b* a sinner—
Eccl 3:2 . . . A time to be *b* and a time to die.
Isa 9:6 . . . For a child is *b* to us,
Luke 2:11 . . . the Lord—has been *b* today

John 3:3 . . . unless you are *b* again,
John 3:7 . . . You must be *b* again.
1 Pet 1:3 . . . we have been *b* again,
1 Pet 1:23 . . . you have been *b* again,

**BOTTOMLESS (adj)** unfathomable; boundless, unlimited
Luke 8:31 . . . into the *b* pit.
Rev 9:1 . . . shaft of the *b* pit.
Rev 9:11 . . . the angel from the *b* pit;
Rev 11:7 . . . out of the *b* pit
Rev 17:8 . . . up out of the *b* pit
Rev 20:1 . . . the key to the *b* pit
Rev 20:3 . . . into the *b* pit,

**BRANCH, BRANCHES (n)** limb of a (family) tree; part of a complex body (of knowledge); figurative of offspring and of disciples (of Christ and his disciples)
Isa 4:2 . . . the *b* of the LORD will be beautiful
Dan 4:21 . . . nested in its *b-es*.
Zech 3:8 . . . bring my servant, the *B*.
John 15:2 . . . *b* of mine that doesn't
John 15:4 . . . a *b* cannot produce fruit if
John 15:5 . . . you are the *b-es*.
Rom 11:20 . . . those *b-es* were broken off
Rom 11:21 . . . not spare the original *b-es*,

**BREAD (n)** basic staple in diet of ancient Israel; signifies livelihood
Exod 23:15 . . . Festival of Unleavened *B*.
Prov 20:17 . . . Stolen *b* tastes sweet,
Mark 14:22 . . . Jesus took some *b* and
Luke 4:3 . . . this stone to become a loaf of *b*.
Luke 9:13 . . . only five loaves of *b*
John 6:48 . . . Yes, I am the *b* of life!
John 6:51 . . . I am the living *b*
1 Cor 10:16 . . . when we break the *b*,
1 Cor 11:23 . . . the Lord Jesus took some *b*
1 Cor 11:26 . . . eat this *b* and drink

**BREATH (n)** air inhaled and exhaled in breathing; a spoken sound, utterance; a slight indication, suggestion
Gen 2:7 . . . He breathed the *b* of life
Exod 15:8 . . . At the blast of your *b*,
Ps 18:15 . . . at the blast of your *b*,
Ps 144:4 . . . we are like a *b* of air;

**BREATHED (v)** to inhale and exhale freely; to blow softly
Gen 2:7 . . . He *b* the breath of life
Mark 15:37 . . . and *b* his last.
John 20:22 . . . Then he *b* on them

**BRIBE (n)** something that serves to induce or influence
Deut 16:19 . . . Never accept a *b*,

**BRIBERY (n)** the act or practice of giving or taking a bribe
Job 15:34 . . . homes, enriched through *b*,

**BRIDE (n)** a woman just married or about to be married
2 Cor 11:2 . . . as a pure *b* to one husband—
Rev 19:7 . . . *b* has prepared herself.
Rev 21:2 . . . like a *b* beautifully dressed
Rev 21:9 . . . the *b*, the wife of the Lamb.
Rev 22:17 . . . Spirit and the *b* say, "Come."

**BRIDEGROOM (n)** a man just married or about to be married
Ps 19:5 . . . like a radiant *b* after
Matt 25:1 . . . and went to meet the *b*.
Matt 25:5 . . . When the *b* was delayed,

**BRIDESMAIDS (n)** women attendants of a bride
Matt 25:1 . . . ten *b* who took their lamps

**BROTHER, BROTHERS (n)** male family
members with the same parents; kinsmen in the
extended family, church, or nation; co-workers
in ministry; fellow believers, followers, or
friends in Christ
Ps 133:1 . . . *b-s* live together in harmony!
Prov 18:24 . . . friend sticks closer than a *b.*
Prov 27:10 . . . to ask your *b* for assistance.
Mark 3:33 . . . Who are my *b-s?*
Mark 10:29 . . . given up house or *b-s* or
John 7:5 . . . even his *b-s* didn't believe
Heb 2:11 . . . ashamed to call them his *b-s*
Heb 13:1 . . . each other as *b-s* and sisters.
Jas 2:15 . . . you see a *b* or sister
Jas 4:11 . . . evil against each other, dear *b-s*
1 Pet 1:22 . . . each other as *b-s* and sisters.
1 Pet 3:8 . . . Love each other as *b-s* and
1 Jn 2:9 . . . a Christian *b* or sister,
1 Jn 3:16 . . . for our *b-s* and sisters.
1 Jn 3:17 . . . sees a *b* or sister in need
1 Jn 4:20 . . . hates a Christian *b* or sister,
1 Jn 4:21 . . . love their Christian *b-s* and
Rev 12:10 . . . the accuser of our *b-s* and

**BUILD, BUILDING, BUILDS, BUILT (v)** to erect
or construct; to edify or encourage; to increase,
enlarge
Gen 6:14 . . . *B* a large boat from cypress
1 Kgs 6:14 . . . Solomon finished *b-ing* the
Neh 4:17 . . . who were *b-ing* the wall.
Ps 127:1 . . . Unless the LORD *b-s* a house,
Prov 14:1 . . . A wise woman *b-s* her home,
Prov 16:12 . . . his rule is *b-t* on justice.
Hag 1:9 . . . busy *b-ing* your own fine houses.
Matt 7:24 . . . a person who *b-s* a house
Matt 16:18 . . . rock I will *b* my church,
Rom 14:19 . . . try to *b* each other up.
1 Cor 3:10 . . . Now others are *b-ing* on it.
1 Cor 3:12 . . . Anyone who *b-s* on that
2 Cor 10:8 . . . But our authority *b-s* you up;
Eph 2:20 . . . *b-t* on the foundation of the
Eph 4:12 . . . do his work and *b* up the church,
Col 2:7 . . . let your lives be *b-t* on him.
1 Thes 5:11 . . . and *b* each other up,
Heb 3:3 . . . as a person who *b-s* a house
1 Pet 2:5 . . . God is *b-ing* into his spiritual
Jude 1:20 . . . friends, must *b* each other up

**BUILDER, BUILDERS (n)** one who builds
Ps 118:22 . . . The stone that the *b-s* rejected
Mark 12:10 . . . stone that the *b-s* rejected
Acts 4:11 . . . The stone that you *b-s* rejected
1 Cor 3:10 . . . like an expert *b.*
1 Cor 3:14 . . . that *b* will receive a reward.
Heb 3:4 . . . For every home has a *b,*
1 Pet 2:7 . . . The stone that the *b-s* rejected

**BURDEN, BURDENS (n)** a (usually) heavy load
to be borne—physically, emotionally, or
spiritually
Ps 38:4 . . . a *b* too heavy to bear.
Matt 11:28 . . . weary and carry heavy *b-s,*
Matt 11:30 . . . the *b* I give you is light.
Acts 15:28 . . . to lay no greater *b* on you
2 Cor 11:9 . . . a financial *b* to anyone.
2 Cor 11:28 . . . the daily *b* of my concern
2 Cor 12:14 . . . I will not be a *b* to you.
Gal 6:2 . . . Share each other's *b-s,*
1 Thes 2:9 . . . so that we would not be a *b*
2 Thes 3:8 . . . so we would not be a *b*

**BURDENED (v)** to load; to oppress
Isa 43:23 . . . I have not *b* and wearied you
Isa 43:24 . . . Instead, you have *b* me
2 Tim 3:6 . . . are *b* with the guilt of sin

**BURN, BURNED, BURNING (v)** to consume by
fire; to be emotionally excited or agitated; to
produce or undergo discomfort or pain
*see also* BURNING
Exod 27:20 . . . keep the lamps *b-ing*
Lev 6:9 . . . must be kept *b-ing* all night.
Deut 7:5 . . . and *b* their idols.
Ps 79:5 . . . will your jealousy *b* like fire?
Isa 30:27 . . . far away, *b-ing* with anger,
Jer 23:29 . . . Does not my word *b* like fire?
Rom 1:27 . . . *b-ed* with lust for each other.
1 Cor 7:9 . . . to marry than to *b* with lust.

**BURNING (adj)** being on fire
*see also* BURN
Prov 25:22 . . . heap *b* coals of shame
Rom 12:20 . . . heap *b* coals of shame
Rev 19:20 . . . fiery lake of *b* sulfur.

**BURY, BURIED (v)** to deposit (a dead body)
in the earth or in a tomb; figurative of denying
oneself and submitting to Christ
Deut 34:6 . . . The LORD *b-ied* him
Ruth 1:17 . . . and there I will be *b-ied.*
Mark 6:29 . . . get his body and *b-ied* it in
Luke 9:60 . . . dead *b* their own dead!
Luke 23:30 . . . plead with the hills, '*B* us.'
Rom 6:4 . . . and were *b-ied* with Christ
1 Cor 15:4 . . . *b-ied,* and he was raised
Col 2:12 . . . For you were *b-ied* with Christ

**BUSH (n)** a low, densely branched shrub
Exod 3:2 . . . fire from the middle of a *b.*
Mark 12:26 . . . story of the burning *b?*
Luke 20:37 . . . wrote about the burning *b.*
Acts 7:35 . . . him in the burning *b,*

**CAESAR** a title applied to several emperors of
the Roman Empire
Matt 22:21 . . . to *C* what belongs to *C,*

**CALF (n)** the young of a domestic cow
Exod 32:4 . . . it into the shape of a *c.*
Luke 15:23 . . . kill the *c* we have been
Acts 7:41 . . . made an idol shaped like a *c,*

**CALL, CALLED, CALLING, CALLS (v)** to make
a request or demand; to designate or name
*see also* CHOSE, CHOSEN
Gen 2:23 . . . She will be *c-ed* 'woman,'
1 Kgs 18:24 . . . *c* on the name of your god,
2 Kgs 5:11 . . . leprosy and *c* on the name
2 Chr 7:14 . . . who are *c-ed* by my name
Ps 147:4 . . . stars and *c-s* them all by name.
Isa 40:26 . . . *c-ing* each by its name.
Isa 45:3 . . . the one who *c-s* you by name.
Isa 56:7 . . . Temple will be *c-ed* a house of
Hos 11:1 . . . I *c-ed* my son out of Egypt.
Joel 2:32 . . . everyone who *c-s* on the name
Matt 2:15 . . . I *c-ed* my Son out of Egypt.
Matt 9:13 . . . I have come to *c* not those
Matt 22:14 . . . many are *c-ed,* but few are
Matt 22:43 . . . *c* the Messiah 'my Lord'?
Mark 2:17 . . . I have come to *c* not those
Mark 10:49 . . . Come on, he's *c-ing* you!
Luke 1:32 . . . *c-ed* the Son of the Most High.
Luke 23:15 . . . this man has done *c-s*
Acts 2:21 . . . everyone who *c-s* on the name
Acts 2:39 . . . have been *c-ed* by the Lord

Acts 9:14 . . . arrest everyone who *c-s* upon
Acts 22:16 . . . sins washed away by *c-ing* on
Rom 1:6 . . . *c-ed* to belong to Jesus
Rom 8:28 . . . *c-ed* according to his purpose
Rom 10:12 . . . to all who *c* on him.
Rom 10:13 . . . Everyone who *c-s* on the
Rom 11:29 . . . *c* can never be withdrawn.
1 Cor 1:2 . . . who have been *c-ed* by God
1 Cor 1:2 . . . *c* on the name of our Lord
1 Cor 1:24 . . . *c-ed* by God to salvation,
1 Cor 7:17 . . . when God first *c-ed* you.
Gal 1:6 . . . so soon from God, who *c-ed* you
Gal 5:13 . . . been *c-ed* to live in freedom.
Eph 1:18 . . . to those he *c-ed*—his holy
Col 3:15 . . . you are *c-ed* to live in peace.
1 Thes 2:12 . . . *c-ed* you to share in his
1 Thes 4:7 . . . God has *c-ed* us to live holy
1 Thes 5:24 . . . he who *c-s* you is faithful.
2 Tim 2:22 . . . those who *c* on the Lord
Heb 9:15 . . . all who are *c-ed* can receive
1 Pet 2:9 . . . he *c-ed* you out of the darkness
1 Pet 3:9 . . . what God has *c-ed* you to do,
1 Pet 5:10 . . . God *c-ed* you to share in his
2 Pet 1:10 . . . are among those God has *c-ed*

**CALVARY (KJV)**
Luke 23:33 . . . place called *The Skull,*

**CAMEL (n)** either of two large ruminant
mammals used as draft and saddle animals in
desert regions especially of Africa and Asia
Matt 19:24 . . . easier for a *c* to go through
Matt 23:24 . . . but you swallow a *c!*

**CANDLE (n)** a usually molded or dipped mass
of wax or tallow containing a wick that may be
burned
Isa 42:3 . . . or put out a flickering *c.*
Matt 12:20 . . . or put out a flickering *c.*

**CANDLESTICK(S) (KJV)**
Exod 25:31 . . . Make a *lampstand* of pure,
Dan 5:5 . . . palace, near the *lampstand.*
Matt 5:15 . . . a lamp is placed on a *stand*
Heb 9:2 . . . a *lampstand,* a table, and sacred
Rev 1:12 . . . I saw seven gold *lampstands*

**CAPSTONE, HEADSTONE (KJV)**
Ps 118:22 . . . become the *cornerstone*
Zech 4:7 . . . the *final stone* of the Temple
Matt 21:42 . . . now become the *cornerstone.*
Luke 20:17 . . . now become the *cornerstone.*

**CAPTIVE (adj)** (people) taken and held against
their will
Prov 5:22 . . . is held *c* by his own sins;
Acts 8:23 . . . and are held *c* by sin.
2 Tim 2:26 . . . they have been held *c*

**CAPTIVES (n)** a prisoner
Ps 68:18 . . . you led a crowd of *c.*
Isa 60:11 . . . led as *c* in a victory
Isa 61:1 . . . that *c* will be released
Luke 4:18 . . . that *c* will be released,

**CARE, CARED, CARES, CARING (v)** to feel
interest or concern; to attend to or provide for
the needs, operation, or treatment of
Deut 1:31 . . . LORD your God *c-d* for you
Ps 8:4 . . . human beings that you should *c*
Ps 37:17 . . . LORD takes *c* of the godly.
Ps 65:9 . . . take *c* of the earth and
Ps 116:15 . . . *c-s* deeply when his loved ones
Ps 138:6 . . . is great, he *c-s* for the humble,
Prov 12:10 . . . godly *c* for their animals,

Prov 27:23 . . . into *c-ing* for your herds,
Isa 53:8 . . . No one *c-d* that he died without
Jer 23:2 . . . Instead of *c-ing* for my flock
Matt 6:30 . . . if God *c-s* so wonderfully for
Matt 25:36 . . . sick, and you *c-d* for me.
Luke 10:34 . . . an inn, where he took *c* of
John 10:13 . . . really *c* about the sheep.
John 12:25 . . . who *c* nothing for their life
John 21:16 . . . Then take *c* of my sheep,
Eph 5:29 . . . just as Christ *c-s* for the church.
Phil 2:21 . . . others *c* only for themselves
1 Thes 2:7 . . . *c-ing* for her own children.
1 Tim 5:14 . . . take *c* of their own homes.
1 Tim 5:16 . . . she must take *c* of them and
Heb 2:6 . . . that you should *c* for him?
1 Pet 5:2 . . . *C* for the flock that God
1 Pet 5:7 . . . and cares to God, for he *c-s*

**CAREFUL (adj)** marked by wary caution;
meticulous
Exod 34:12 . . . *c* never to make a treaty
Lev 18:4 . . . and be *c* to obey my decrees,
Lev 22:2 . . . be very *c* with the sacred gifts
Lev 26:3 . . . are *c* to obey my commands,
Deut 4:9 . . . But watch out! Be *c* never to
Deut 6:3 . . . and be *c* to obey.
Deut 8:1 . . . Be *c* to obey all the commands
Deut 12:1 . . . *c* to obey when you live in
Deut 12:28 . . . Be *c* to obey all my
Josh 1:7 . . . and very courageous. Be *c*
Josh 23:11 . . . be very *c* to love the LORD
2 Kgs 21:8 . . . Israelites will be *c* to obey
1 Cor 8:9 . . . be *c* so that your freedom
1 Cor 10:12 . . . strong, be *c* not to fall.
Eph 5:15 . . . So be *c* how you live.

**CARNAL(LY) (KJV)**
Rom 7:14 . . . *all too human,* a slave to sin
Rom 8:6 . . . letting your *sinful nature* control
1 Cor 3:3 . . . still *controlled by your sinful
nature*
2 Cor 10:4 . . . not *worldly* weapons

**CARPENTER (n)** a worker who builds or repairs
wooden structures or their structural parts
Matt 13:55 . . . He's just the *c*'s son,
Mark 6:3 . . . He's just a *c,* the son of Mary

**CARRY, CARRIED, CARRIES (v)** to transport or
convey; to sustain the weight of; to bring to a
successful end
Exod 19:4 . . . how I *c-ied* you on eagles'
Lev 16:22 . . . will *c* all the people's sins
Deut 32:11 . . . to take them up and *c-ied*
Ps 68:19 . . . For each day he *c-ies* us in his
Ps 103:20 . . . ones who *c* out his plans,
Isa 40:11 . . . *c* the lambs in his arms,
Isa 53:4 . . . it was our weaknesses he *c-ied;*
Isa 63:9 . . . He lifted them up and *c-ied* them
Luke 14:27 . . . do not *c* your own cross
Col 4:17 . . . Be sure to *c* out the ministry
1 Pet 2:24 . . . He personally *c-ied* our sins
2 Pet 3:17 . . . not be *c-ied* away by the errors

**CATTLE (n)** bovine animals on a farm or ranch
Ps 50:10 . . . I own the *c* on a thousand

**CELEBRATE, CELEBRATED, CELEBRATING (v)**
to perform (a sacrament or ceremony) publicly
and with appropriate rites; to observe a notable
occasion with festivities
Exod 10:9 . . . together in *c-ing* a festival
Exod 12:47 . . . Israel must *c* this Passover
Exod 13:5 . . . You must *c* this event in this

Exod 23:14 . . . *c* three festivals in my
Exod 34:18 . . . *c* the Festival of
Exod 34:22 . . . *c* the Festival of the Final
Num 9:2 . . . *c* the Passover at the
Deut 16:1 . . . your God, *c* the Passover
2 Sam 6:21 . . . so I *c* before the LORD.
2 Kgs 23:21 . . . *c* the Passover to the LORD
2 Chr 30:1 . . . to *c* the Passover.
2 Chr 30:13 . . . *c* the Festival of
2 Chr 30:23 . . . *c-d* joyfully for another
Neh 8:12 . . . to *c* with great joy
Esth 8:15 . . . people of Susa *c-d* the new
Esth 9:19 . . . villages *c* an annual festival
Esth 9:21 . . . to *c* an annual festival
Matt 25:21 . . . Let's *c* together!
Luke 15:23 . . . We must *c* with a feast,
Luke 15:32 . . . We had to *c* this happy day.
John 18:28 . . . to *c* the Passover.
Col 2:16 . . . for not *c-ing* certain holy days
Rev 11:10 . . . to *c* the death of the two prophets

**CELEBRATION, CELEBRATIONS (n)** a party or
festival in honor of a religious ceremony or
holiday; the observation of a notable occasion
with festivities
Num 9:3 . . . regulations concerning this *c.*
2 Sam 6:12 . . . City of David with a great *c.*
Esth 8:17 . . . had a great *c* and declared
Jer 31:13 . . . young—will join in the *c.*
Joel 1:16 . . . No joyful *c-s* are held in the
Zech 8:19 . . . *c* for the people of Judah.
John 11:55 . . . for the Jewish Passover *c,*

**CHAFF (n)** the seed coverings and other debris
separated from the seed in threshing grain;
something comparatively worthless
Ps 1:4 . . . worthless *c,* scattered by the wind.
Ps 35:5 . . . Blow them away like *c* in the
Dan 2:35 . . . like *c* on a threshing floor.
Matt 3:12 . . . separate the *c* from the

**CHANGE, CHANGED, CHANGES (v)** to make
different or transform; to shift, exchange, or
transfer
Exod 32:14 . . . the LORD *c-d* his mind about
1 Sam 10:6 . . . be *c-d* into a different person.
1 Sam 15:29 . . . human that he should *c*
Ps 93:5 . . . Your royal laws cannot be *c-d.*
Isa 14:27 . . . who can *c* his plans?
Jer 33:25 . . . than I would *c* my laws
Jon 3:9 . . . Perhaps even yet God will *c* his mind
Mal 3:6 . . . I am the LORD, and I do not *c.*
2 Cor 3:18 . . . we are *c-d* into his glorious
Heb 6:17 . . . he would never *c* his mind.
Jas 1:17 . . . never *c-s* or casts a shifting

**CHARACTER (n)** moral excellence and
firmness; main or essential nature
Rom 5:4 . . . develops strength of *c,*
1 Cor 15:33 . . . corrupts good *c.*
Heb 1:3 . . . expresses the very *c* of God,

**CHARITY (KJV)**
1 Cor 8:1 . . . *love* that strengthens the church
1 Cor 13:1 . . . but didn't *love* others, I would
Col 3:14 . . . clothe yourselves with *love,*
1 Tim 4:12 . . . in your *love,* your faith, and
2 Pet 1:7 . . . affection with *love* for everyone

**CHASTE (KJV)**
2 Cor 11:2 . . . as a *pure* bride to one
husband—
Titus 2:5 . . . to live wisely and be *pure*
1 Pet 3:2 . . . *pure* and reverent lives

**CHASTEN(ED) (KJV)**
Ps 6:1 . . . or *discipline* me in your rage
Prov 19:18 . . . *Discipline* your children
1 Cor 11:32 . . . *being disciplined* so that we
Heb 12:11 . . . No *discipline* is enjoyable
Rev 3:19 . . . I correct and *discipline*

**CHEAT, CHEATED, CHEATING, CHEATS (v)**
to deprive of something valuable by deceit or
fraud; to practice fraud or trickery
Gen 31:7 . . . he has *c-ed* me, changing my
1 Sam 12:3 . . . Have I ever *c-ed* any of you?
1 Sam 12:4 . . . have never *c-ed* or oppressed
Amos 8:5 . . . get back to *c-ing* the helpless.
Mal 3:8 . . . You have *c-ed* me of the tithes
Mark 10:19 . . . You must not *c* anyone.
Mark 12:40 . . . they shamelessly *c* widows
1 Cor 5:10 . . . are greedy, or *c* people,
1 Cor 5:11 . . . is a drunkard, or *c-s* people.
1 Cor 6:7 . . . not let yourselves be *c-ed?*
1 Cor 6:8 . . . who do wrong and *c* even
1 Cor 6:10 . . . abusive, or *c* people—

**CHEEK (n)** the fleshy side of the face below the
eye and above and to the side of the mouth
Matt 5:39 . . . slaps you on the right *c,*
Luke 6:29 . . . offer the other *c* also.

**CHEERFUL (adj)** full of good spirits; merry,
ungrudging
Prov 15:30 . . . A *c* look brings joy
Prov 17:22 . . . A *c* heart is good medicine,

**CHEERFULLY (adv)** marked by or suggestive of
lighthearted ease of mind and spirit; cheerily,
gladly
2 Cor 9:7 . . . loves a person who gives *c.*
1 Pet 4:9 . . . *C* share your home with those

**CHERUBIM (n)** winged angelic beings, often
associated with worship and praise of God
Gen 3:24 . . . God stationed mighty *c* to the
Exod 25:19 . . . Mold the *c* on each end
1 Sam 4:4 . . . enthroned between the *c.*
1 Kgs 6:23 . . . He made two *c* of wild olive
Isa 37:16 . . . between the mighty *c!*
Ezek 10:1 . . . over the heads of the *c.*

**CHILD, CHILDREN (n)** an unborn or recently
born person; a young person between infancy
and youth, not yet of age; offspring or
descendants
*see also* SON(S)
Exod 20:5 . . . family is affected—even *c-ren*
Deut 24:16 . . . sins of their *c-ren,* nor *c-ren*
Deut 32:46 . . . as a command to your *c-ren*
1 Kgs 3:26 . . . Give her the *c*—please do
Job 1:5 . . . Perhaps my *c-ren* have sinned
Ps 8:2 . . . You have taught *c-ren* and infants
Prov 20:7 . . . blessed are their *c-ren* who
Prov 23:13 . . . discipline your *c-ren.*
Prov 29:15 . . . To discipline a *c* produces
Prov 31:28 . . . Her *c-ren* stand and bless
Isa 7:14 . . . The virgin will conceive a *c!*
Isa 9:6 . . . For a *c* is born to us,
Isa 54:13 . . . I will teach all your *c-ren,*
Mal 4:6 . . . hearts of *c-ren* to their fathers.
Matt 1:23 . . . The virgin will conceive a *c!*
Matt 5:9 . . . will be called the *c-ren* of God.
Matt 18:3 . . . and become like little *c-ren,*
Mark 9:37 . . . welcomes a little *c* like this
Mark 10:14 . . . Let the *c-ren* come to me.
Mark 10:16 . . . took the *c-ren* in his arms
Luke 1:42 . . . and your *c* is blessed.

Luke 6:35 . . . as *c-ren* of the Most High,
Luke 18:15 . . . their little *c-ren* to Jesus
John 1:12 . . . to become *c-ren* of God.
John 12:36 . . . become *c-ren* of the light.
Acts 2:39 . . . to your *c-ren*, and even to the
Rom 9:26 . . . called '*c-ren* of the living God.'
1 Cor 13:11 . . . and reasoned as a *c*.
Gal 3:26 . . . you are all *c-ren* of God
Eph 3:6 . . . riches inherited by God's *c-ren.*
Eph 6:1 . . . *C-ren*, obey your parents
Eph 6:4 . . . not provoke your *c-ren* to anger
Col 3:21 . . . do not aggravate your *c-ren,*
1 Tim 3:4 . . . having *c-ren* who respect and
1 Tim 3:12 . . . manage his *c-ren* and
1 Tim 5:10 . . . brought up her *c-ren* well?
Heb 12:7 . . . treating you as his own *c-ren.*
1 Jn 4:7 . . . Anyone who loves is a *c* of God
1 Jn 5:4 . . . every *c* of God defeats this evil
1 Jn 5:18 . . . God's *c-ren* do not make a

**CHILDLESS (adj)** a person characterized by
lack of children; barren
Ps 113:9 . . . He gives the *c* woman a family,
Isa 54:1 . . . Sing, O *c* woman, you who
Gal 4:27 . . . Rejoice, O *c* woman, you who

**CHILDLIKE (adj)** resembling, suggesting, or
appropriate to a child; marked by innocence,
trust, and ingenuousness
Ps 116:6 . . . protects those of *c* faith;
Matt 11:25 . . . revealing them to the *c*.

**CHOOSE, CHOOSES (v)** to decide; to have a
preference for; to select freely and after
consideration
*see also* CALL, CHOSE
Deut 30:19 . . . Oh, that you would *c* life, so
Josh 24:15 . . . *c* today whom you will serve.
Eccl 10:2 . . . A wise person *c-s* the right road;
Jer 27:5 . . . things of mine to anyone I *c.*
Dan 4:25 . . . gives them to anyone he *c-s.*
John 15:16 . . . You didn't *c* me.
Rom 9:11 . . . God *c-s* people according to
Rom 9:18 . . . he *c-s* to harden the hearts of

**CHOSE, CHOSEN (v)** *see also* CALL, CHOOSE,
CHOSEN
Matt 22:14 . . . called, but few are *c-n.*
John 15:16 . . . You didn't choose me. I *c* you.
Rom 1:1 . . . *c-n* by God to be an apostle
Rom 8:29 . . . *c* them to become like his
1 Cor 1:1 . . . Paul, *c-n* by the will of God
1 Cor 1:27 . . . *c* things that are powerless
Eph 1:4 . . . loved us and *c* us in Christ
Eph 1:11 . . . God, for he *c* us in advance,
2 Thes 2:13 . . . thankful that God *c* you
1 Pet 1:15 . . . as God who *c* you is holy.
2 Pet 1:10 . . . God has called and *c-n.*

**CHOSEN (adj)** selected or marked for special
favor or privilege; elect
*see also* CALLED
1 Chr 16:22 . . . Do not touch my *c* people,
Isa 41:8 . . . my *c* one, descended from Abraham
Mark 13:20 . . . for the sake of his *c* ones
Luke 23:35 . . . God's Messiah, the *C* One.
John 1:34 . . . that he is the *C* One of God.
1 Pet 1:1 . . . writing to God's *c* people
1 Pet 2:9 . . . for you are a *C* people.

**CHRIST (n)** Son of God, Messiah, Anointed One
*see also* JESUS, MESSIAH
Rom 1:4 . . . He is Jesus *C* our Lord.
Rom 3:22 . . . by placing our faith in Jesus *C.*

Rom 5:1 . . . what Jesus *C* our Lord has done
Rom 5:6 . . . *C* came at just the right time
Rom 5:11 . . . *C* has made us friends of God.
Rom 6:4 . . . as *C* was raised from the dead
Rom 6:23 . . . eternal life through *C* Jesus
Rom 7:4 . . . when you died with *C*.
Rom 8:1 . . . who belong to *C* Jesus.
Rom 8:34 . . . *C* Jesus died for us and
Rom 8:35 . . . separate us from *C*'s love?
Rom 14:9 . . . *C* died and rose again for this
Rom 15:5 . . . fitting for followers of *C* Jesus.
Rom 15:20 . . . where the name of *C* has never
1 Cor 1:2 . . . the name of our Lord Jesus *C,*
1 Cor 1:13 . . . Has *C* been divided into
1 Cor 1:17 . . . cross of *C* would lose its power.
1 Cor 1:23 . . . preach that *C* was crucified,
1 Cor 1:30 . . . God has united you with *C*
1 Cor 5:7 . . . *C,* our Passover Lamb,
1 Cor 6:15 . . . his body, which is part of *C,*
1 Cor 8:12 . . . you are sinning against *C.*
1 Cor 9:19 . . . to bring many to *C.*
1 Cor 10:4 . . . that rock was *C.*
1 Cor 10:9 . . . Nor should we put *C* to the test,
1 Cor 11:3 . . . and the head of *C* is God.
1 Cor 12:27 . . . you together are *C*'s body,
1 Cor 15:3 . . . *C* died for our sins,
2 Cor 1:5 . . . the more we suffer for *C,* the
2 Cor 3:3 . . . you are a letter from *C*
2 Cor 3:14 . . . removed only by believing in *C.*
2 Cor 5:10 . . . stand before *C* to be judged.
2 Cor 5:14 . . . *C*'s love controls us.
2 Cor 5:20 . . . we are *C*'s ambassadors;
Gal 1:7 . . . twist the truth concerning *C.*
Gal 2:4 . . . the freedom we have in *C* Jesus.
Gal 2:21 . . . need for *C* to die.
Gal 3:13 . . . But *C* has rescued us
Gal 4:19 . . . continue until *C* is fully developed
Gal 5:4 . . . you have been cut off from *C!*
Gal 5:24 . . . Those who belong to *C* Jesus
have
Eph 1:3 . . . because we are united with *C.*
Eph 1:10 . . . under the authority of *C*—
Eph 1:20 . . . that raised *C* from the dead
Eph 2:10 . . . created us anew in *C* Jesus,
Eph 2:20 . . . the cornerstone is *C* Jesus
Eph 4:7 . . . through the generosity of *C.*
Eph 4:32 . . . God through *C* has forgiven you.
Eph 5:21 . . . out of reverence for *C.*
Eph 5:23 . . . head of his wife as *C* is the head
Eph 5:25 . . . wives, just as *C* loved the
Phil 1:21 . . . living means living for *C,*
Phil 1:23 . . . with *C,* which would be far better
Phil 1:29 . . . the privilege of trusting in *C*
Phil 2:5 . . . the same attitude that *C* Jesus had.
Phil 3:18 . . . enemies of the cross of *C.*
Col 1:22 . . . through the death of *C*
Col 2:2 . . . mysterious plan, which is *C*
Col 2:6 . . . accepted *C* Jesus as your Lord,
Col 2:13 . . . God made you alive with *C,*
Col 3:1 . . . raised to new life with *C,*
Col 3:3 . . . real life is hidden with *C* in God.
Col 3:15 . . . peace that comes from *C*
1 Thes 5:9 . . . through our Lord Jesus *C,*
1 Tim 1:15 . . . *C* Jesus came into the world
1 Tim 2:5 . . . humanity—the man *C* Jesus.
2 Tim 1:10 . . . by the appearing of *C* Jesus,
2 Tim 2:3 . . . as a good soldier of *C* Jesus.
2 Tim 2:10 . . . eternal glory in *C* Jesus
2 Tim 3:12 . . . a godly life in *C* Jesus will
2 Tim 3:15 . . . by trusting in *C* Jesus.

2 Tim 4:1 . . . of God and *C* Jesus, who will
Titus 2:13 . . . and Savior, Jesus *C,* will be
Heb 3:14 . . . share in all that belongs to *C.*
Heb 6:1 . . . teachings about *C* again and
Heb 9:14 . . . the blood of *C* will purify
Heb 9:28 . . . *C* died once for all time
Heb 10:10 . . . body of Jesus *C,* once for all
Heb 13:8 . . . Jesus *C* is the same yesterday,
1 Pet 1:11 . . . the Spirit of *C* within them
1 Pet 1:19 . . . blood of *C,* the sinless,
1 Pet 2:21 . . . just as *C* suffered for you.
1 Pet 3:15 . . . you must worship *C* as Lord
1 Pet 4:13 . . . partners with *C* in his suffering,
2 Pet 1:16 . . . coming of our Lord Jesus *C.*
1 Jn 2:1 . . . He is Jesus *C,* the one who is
1 Jn 2:22 . . . says that Jesus is not the *C.*
1 Jn 4:2 . . . that Jesus *C* came in a real
1 Jn 5:1 . . . Jesus is the *C* has become
1 Jn 5:20 . . . fellowship with his Son, Jesus *C.*
Rev 1:1 . . . from Jesus *C,* which God gave
Rev 1:5 . . . and from Jesus *C.*
Rev 20:4 . . . and they reigned with *C* for
Rev 20:6 . . . God and of *C* and will reign

**CHRISTIAN, CHRISTIANS (n)** one who
professes belief in and follows the teachings of
Jesus Christ; believer
Acts 11:26 . . . believers were first called *C-s.*
Acts 26:28 . . . persuade me to become a *C*
Gal 2:4 . . . some so-called *C-s*
1 Thes 4:12 . . . people who are not *C-s*
1 Pet 4:14 . . . insulted for being a *C,*
1 Pet 4:16 . . . to suffer for being a *C.*
1 Pet 5:9 . . . your *C* brothers and sisters

**CHURCH, CHURCHES (n)** "assembly" or
"called ones"; the body of believers gathered to
worship Jesus (not the building in which they
meet)
Matt 16:18 . . . this rock I will build my *c,*
Matt 18:17 . . . take your case to the *c.*
Acts 16:5 . . . the *c-es* were strengthened
Acts 20:28 . . . shepherd God's flock—his *c,*
1 Cor 15:9 . . . way I persecuted God's *c.*
Gal 1:13 . . . I violently persecuted God's *c.*
Eph 5:23 . . . Christ is the head of the *c.*
Col 1:18 . . . head of the *c,* which is his
Col 1:24 . . . continue for his body, the *c.*
2 Thes 1:4 . . . tell God's other *c-es* about your
Rev 1:20 . . . angels of the seven *c-es,*

**CIRCUMCISE, CIRCUMCISED, CIRCUMCISING
(v)** to cut off the foreskin of a male child
Gen 17:10 . . . among you must be *c-ed.*
Gen 17:12 . . . *c-d* on the eighth day after his
Josh 5:3 . . . Joshua made flint knives and *c*
John 7:23 . . . correct time for *c-ing* your son
Acts 21:21 . . . not to *c* their children
Rom 4:11 . . . even before he was *c-ed.*
1 Cor 7:19 . . . or not a man has been *c-ed.*

**CIRCUMCISION (n)** the condition of being
circumcised; the ceremony signifying Israel's
covenant with God; act symbolic of cleansing
Rom 2:25 . . . *c* has value only if you obey
Rom 2:29 . . . true *c* is not merely
Gal 5:2 . . . If you are counting on *c* to make

**CITIZEN, CITIZENS (n)** a person owing
allegiance to and deriving protection from a
sovereign state
Acts 22:28 . . . But I am a *c* by birth!
Eph 2:19 . . . You are *c-s* along with
Phil 3:20 . . . But we are *c-s* of heaven,

**CLAY (n)** an earthy material that is pliable when moist but hard when fired and is used for brick, tile, and pottery

Isa 45:9 . . . Does the *c* dispute with the one
Isa 64:8 . . . *c,* and you are the potter.
Lam 4:2 . . . are now treated like pots of *c*
Dan 2:33 . . . of iron and baked *c.*
Rom 9:21 . . . to use the same lump of *c*
2 Cor 4:7 . . . *c* jars containing this great
2 Tim 2:20 . . . are made of wood and *c.*

**CLEAN (adj)** unadulterated, pure; without guilt or moral corruption; without ceremonial defilement; fit for use or human consumption
*see also* PURE

Lev 10:10 . . . unclean and what is *c.*
Ps 51:2 . . . Wash me *c* from my guilt.
Ps 51:10 . . . Create in me a *c* heart, O God.
Acts 10:15 . . . if God has made it *c.*

**CLEAN (v)** to rid of impurities or corruption

Ps 51:7 . . . and I will be *c;* wash me,
John 13:10 . . . you disciples are *c,* but not all
2 Tim 2:21 . . . Your life will be *c,*

**CLEANSE, CLEANSED, CLEANSES (v)** to make clean, pure, holy
*see also* PURIFY, WASH

Ps 19:12 . . . *C* me from these hidden
Prov 20:9 . . . Who can say, "I have *c-d* my
Jer 4:14 . . . O Jerusalem, *c* your heart
Acts 15:9 . . . he *c-d* their hearts through
1 Cor 6:11 . . . were *c-d;* you were made holy;
2 Cor 7:1 . . . let us *c* ourselves from
Titus 2:14 . . . *c* us, and to make us his
Heb 1:3 . . . he had *c-d* us from our sins,
Heb 9:13 . . . of a young cow could *c*
1 Pet 1:2 . . . and have been *c-d* by the blood
1 Pet 1:22 . . . You were *c-d* from your sins
2 Pet 1:9 . . . that they have been *c-d*
1 Jn 1:7 . . . blood of Jesus, his Son, *c-s* us
1 Jn 1:9 . . . and to *c* us from all wickedness.

**CLING (v)** to adhere as if glued firmly; to hold or hold on tightly or tenaciously

Deut 10:20 . . . worship him and *c* to him.
Deut 13:4 . . . listen to his voice, and *c* to
Matt 10:39 . . . If you *c* to your life,
Luke 8:15 . . . who hear God's word, *c* to it,
John 20:17 . . . "Don't *c* to me," Jesus
Phil 2:6 . . . as something to *c* to.

**CLOSE, CLOSED, CLOSES (v)** to draw near; to contract, fold, swing, or slide so as to leave no opening

Gen 7:16 . . . Then the LORD *c-d* the door
Ps 34:18 . . . is *c* to the brokenhearted;
Ps 148:14 . . . of Israel who are *c* to him.
Prov 28:27 . . . who *c* their eyes to poverty
Isa 22:22 . . . no one will be able to *c* them;
Isa 40:11 . . . in his arms, holding them *c*
Acts 28:27 . . . and they have *c-d* their eyes—
Rev 3:7 . . . what he *c-s,* no one can open:
Rev 21:25 . . . Its gates will never be *c-d*

**CLOUD, CLOUDS (n)** a visible mass of particles of condensed vapor suspended in the atmosphere

1 Kgs 18:44 . . . I saw a little *c* about the
Ps 68:4 . . . praises to him who rides the *c-s.*
Ps 108:4 . . . faithfulness reaches to the *c-s.*
Isa 19:1 . . . Egypt, riding on a swift *c.*
Dan 7:13 . . . coming with the *c-s* of heaven.
Mark 13:26 . . . coming on the *c-s* with great

Luke 21:27 . . . Son of Man coming on a *c*
1 Thes 4:17 . . . up in the *c-s* to meet the Lord
Rev 1:7 . . . He comes with the *c-s* of heaven.
Rev 14:14 . . . I saw a white *c,* and seated on

**COALS (n)** a piece of glowing carbon or charred wood; ember

Prov 25:22 . . . heap burning *c* of shame
Rom 12:20 . . . heap burning *c* of shame

**COAT (n)** an outer garment worn on the upper body

Matt 5:40 . . . give your *c,* too.
Luke 6:29 . . . your *c,* offer your shirt

**COIN, COINS (n)** a usually flat piece of metal issued by governmental authority as money

Mark 12:15 . . . Show me a Roman *c,*
Mark 12:42 . . . dropped in two small *c-s.*
Luke 12:6 . . . sparrows—two copper *c-s?*
Luke 15:8 . . . woman has ten silver *c-s*

**COMFORT (n)** consolation in time of trouble or worry; solace

Gen 24:67 . . . she was a special *c* to him
Job 10:20 . . . I may have a moment of *c*
Ps 94:19 . . . your *c* gave me renewed hope
Zech 10:2 . . . falsehoods that give no *c.*
2 Cor 1:5 . . . shower us with his *c*
2 Cor 1:7 . . . share in the *c* God gives us.
Col 4:11 . . . And what a *c* they have been!

**COMFORT, COMFORTED, COMFORTS (v)** to give strength and hope to; to console

Gen 37:35 . . . he refused to be *c-ed.*
Ruth 2:13 . . . You have *c-ed* me by speaking
Job 2:11 . . . traveled from their homes to *c*
Job 42:11 . . . consoled him and *c-ed* him
Ps 69:20 . . . one would turn and *c* me.
Ps 86:17 . . . O LORD, help and *c* me.
Ps 119:50 . . . it *c-s* me in all my troubles
Ps 119:52 . . . O LORD, they *c* me.
Isa 40:1 . . . *C, c* my people,
Isa 49:13 . . . the LORD has *c-ed* his people
Isa 51:3 . . . The LORD will *c* Israel again
Isa 51:12 . . . I, am the one who *c-s* you.
Isa 51:19 . . . Who is left to *c* you?
Isa 52:9 . . . the LORD has *c-ed* his people.
Isa 61:1 . . . to *c* the brokenhearted
Isa 66:13 . . . as a mother *c-s* her child.
Lam 1:2 . . . there is no one left to *c* her.
Lam 1:17 . . . but no one *c-s* her.
Zech 1:17 . . . the LORD will again *c* Zion
Matt 5:4 . . . mourn, for they will be *c-ed.*
1 Cor 14:3 . . . encourages them, and *c-s*
2 Cor 1:4 . . . He *c-s* us in all our troubles
2 Cor 1:4 . . . so that we can *c* others.
2 Cor 1:6 . . . when we ourselves are *c-ed,*
2 Cor 1:6 . . . we will certainly *c* you.
2 Cor 2:7 . . . forgive and *c* him.

**COMFORTER (KJV)**

John 14:16 . . . another *Advocate,* who will
John 14:26 . . . sends the *Advocate* as my
John 15:26 . . . the *Advocate*—the Spirit of
John 16:7 . . . if I don't, the *Advocate* won't

**COMMAND, COMMANDS (n)** an order given; religious instruction
*see also* COMMANDMENT

Exod 20:6 . . . who love me and obey my *c-s.*
Exod 24:12 . . . the instructions and *c-s*
Lev 22:31 . . . keep all my *c-s*
Num 15:39 . . . and obey all the *c-s*
Deut 4:2 . . . or subtract from these *c-s*

Deut 6:6 . . . wholeheartedly to these *c-s*
Deut 7:9 . . . who love him and obey his *c-s.*
Deut 8:1 . . . Be careful to obey all the *c-s*
Deut 11:1 . . . decrees, regulations, and *c-s.*
Deut 11:27 . . . if you obey the *c-s* of the
Deut 28:1 . . . keep all his *c-s* that I am giving
Deut 32:46 . . . as a *c* to your children
Josh 1:9 . . . my *c*—be strong and
1 Kgs 8:58 . . . obey all the *c-s,* decrees,
1 Kgs 8:61 . . . obey his decrees and *c-s,*
1 Chr 28:7 . . . if he continues to obey my *c-s*
Neh 1:5 . . . who love him and obey his *c-s,*
Job 36:10 . . . *c-s* that they turn from evil.
Ps 33:9 . . . It appeared at his *c.*
Ps 78:7 . . . and obeying his *c-s.*
Ps 103:20 . . . listening for each of his *c-s.*
Ps 112:1 . . . and delight in obeying his *c-s.*
Ps 119:32 . . . I will pursue your *c-s,*
Ps 119:47 . . . How I delight in your *c-s!*
Ps 119:73 . . . the sense to follow your *c-s.*
Ps 119:96 . . . your *c-s* have no limit.
Ps 119:127 . . . I love your *c-s* more than
Ps 119:143 . . . I find joy in your *c-s.*
Ps 119:172 . . . all your *c-s* are right.
Ps 119:176 . . . I have not forgotten your *c-s.*
Prov 3:1 . . . Store my *c-s* in your heart.
Prov 6:23 . . . For their *c* is a lamp
Eccl 12:13 . . . Fear God and obey his *c-s,*
Isa 48:18 . . . you had listened to my *c-s!*
Dan 9:4 . . . who love you and obey your *c-s.*
Matt 28:20 . . . disciples to obey all the *c-s*
John 15:17 . . . my *c:* Love each other.
Acts 17:30 . . . he *c-s* everyone everywhere to
Rom 7:8 . . . sin used this *c* to arouse
Rom 7:9 . . . I learned the *c* not to covet,
Rom 7:12 . . . law itself is holy, and its *c-s* are
1 Cor 14:37 . . . saying is a *c* from the Lord
Gal 5:14 . . . summed up in this one *c:*
2 Thes 3:6 . . . we give you this *c*
2 Pet 2:21 . . . reject the *c* they were given

**COMMAND, COMMANDED, COMMANDING (v)** to issue a charge or directive

Gen 7:5 . . . everything as the LORD *c-ed*
Exod 7:6 . . . did just as the LORD had *c-ed*
Exod 19:7 . . . everything the LORD had *c-ed*
Deut 6:1 . . . LORD your God *c-ed* me to teach
Deut 6:24 . . . our God *c-ed* us to obey
Deut 15:11 . . . why I am *c-ing* you to share
John 15:14 . . . my friends if you do what I *c.*
2 Tim 2:14 . . . *c* them in God's presence
2 Pet 3:2 . . . Savior *c-ed* through your
1 Jn 3:23 . . . just as he *c-ed* us.
2 Jn 1:4 . . . just as the Father *c-ed.*

**COMMANDMENT, COMMANDMENTS (n)** a gracious provision of God's law or covenant, obeyed as an act of love and devotion
*see also* COMMAND

Exod 34:28 . . . Ten *C-s*—on the stone
Deut 4:13 . . . his covenant—the Ten *C-s*
Deut 10:4 . . . LORD wrote the Ten *C-s* on
Ps 103:18 . . . of those who obey his *c-s!*
Ps 111:7 . . . all his *c-s* are trustworthy.
Ps 111:10 . . . who obey his *c-s* will grow
Ps 119:93 . . . I will never forget your *c-s,*
Prov 19:16 . . . the *c-s* and keep your life;
Matt 5:19 . . . if you ignore the least *c*
Matt 19:17 . . . eternal life, keep the *c-s.*
Matt 22:36 . . . the most important *c*
Matt 22:38 . . . the first and greatest *c.*
Mark 10:19 . . . you know the *c-s:*

Mark 12:28 . . . *c-s,* which is the most
Luke 18:20 . . . you know the *c-s:*
John 13:34 . . . a new *c:* Love each other.
John 14:15 . . . If you love me, obey my *c-s.*
Rom 13:9 . . . in this one *c:* "Love your
1 Cor 7:19 . . . is to keep God's *c-s.*
Eph 2:15 . . . law with its *c-s* and regulations.
Eph 6:2 . . . the first *c* with a promise:
Heb 9:19 . . . had read each of God's *c-s*
1 Jn 2:3 . . . we know him if we obey his *c-s.*
1 Jn 3:24 . . . Those who obey God's *c-s*
1 Jn 5:3 . . . God means keeping his *c-s,*
Rev 12:17 . . . who keep God's *c-s* and

**COMMIT, COMMITS, COMMITTED, COMMITTING (v)** to carry into action deliberately, perpetrate; to obligate or pledge oneself
Deut 30:20 . . . *c-ting* yourself firmly to him.
2 Chr 16:9 . . . hearts are fully *c-ted* to him.
2 Chr 17:6 . . . deeply *c-ted* to the ways
Prov 6:32 . . . the man who *c-s* adultery
Prov 29:22 . . . a hot-tempered person *c-s*
Matt 5:28 . . . has already *c-ted* adultery
Matt 5:32 . . . causes her to *c* adultery.
Matt 19:9 . . . someone else *c-s* adultery—
Mark 10:11 . . . someone else *c-s* adultery
Mark 10:19 . . . You must not *c* adultery.
Luke 16:18 . . . her husband *c-s* adultery.
Rom 13:9 . . . You must not *c* adultery.
Titus 2:14 . . . totally *c-ted* to doing good
Jas 2:11 . . . You must not *c* adultery,
Rev 18:3 . . . world have *c-ted* adultery with
Rev 18:9 . . . the world who *c-ted* adultery

**COMPANY (n)** association with another, fellowship; companions, associates
Prov 21:16 . . . end up in the *c* of the dead.
Prov 24:1 . . . or desire their *c.*
Rom 12:16 . . . to enjoy the *c* of ordinary
1 Cor 15:33 . . . for "bad *c* corrupts good

**COMPASSION (n)** sympathy, usually granted because of unusual or distressing circumstances
Exod 34:6 . . . The God of *c* and mercy!
Ps 51:1 . . . Because of your great *c,*
Ps 86:15 . . . a God of *c* and mercy, slow to
Ps 145:9 . . . He showers *c* on all
Isa 49:13 . . . and will have *c* on them
Isa 63:15 . . . your mercy and *c* now?
Lam 3:32 . . . brings grief, he also shows *c*
Hos 2:19 . . . unfailing love and *c.*
Mic 7:19 . . . you will have *c* on us.
Zech 10:6 . . . because of my *c.*
Mark 1:41 . . . Moved with *c,* Jesus reached
Mark 6:34 . . . and he had *c* on them
Luke 15:20 . . . with love and *c,* he ran to
Rom 9:15 . . . show *c* to anyone I choose.

**COMPASSIONATE (adj)** having or showing compassion; sympathetic
Ps 103:13 . . . tender and *c* to those who
Ps 112:4 . . . They are generous, *c,*
Ps 145:8 . . . is merciful and *c,* slow to
Joel 2:13 . . . he is merciful and *c,* slow to
Luke 6:36 . . . You must be *c,* just as your
Phil 2:1 . . . Are your hearts tender and *c?*

**COMPLAINED, COMPLAINING (v)** to express grief, pain, or discontent; to make a formal accusation or charge
Exod 15:24 . . . the people *c* and turned
Num 14:2 . . . in the wilderness!" they *c.*
Num 14:29 . . . Because you *c* against me,

John 6:43 . . . Jesus replied, "Stop *c-ing*
Phil 2:14 . . . Do everything without *c-ing*

**CONCEIT (n)** excessive appreciation of one's own worth or virtue
Ps 36:2 . . . In their blind *c,* they cannot

**CONCEITED (adj)** having or showing an excessively high opinion of oneself
Gal 5:26 . . . us not become *c,* or provoke

**CONDEMN, CONDEMNED, CONDEMNING, CONDEMNS (v)** to declare guilty; to sentence or doom
Job 15:6 . . . Your own mouth *c-s* you, not I.
Job 40:8 . . . my justice and *c* me just to
Ps 37:33 . . . or let the godly be *c-ed*
Ps 102:20 . . . to release those *c-ed* to die.
Prov 12:2 . . . *c-s* those who plan wickedness.
Prov 17:15 . . . guilty and *c-ing* the innocent—
Isa 53:8 . . . Unjustly *c-ed,* he was led away.
Matt 12:7 . . . not have *c-ed* my innocent
Matt 12:37 . . . acquit you or *c* you.
Matt 12:41 . . . on judgment day and *c* it,
Matt 27:3 . . . Jesus had been *c-ed* to die,
Luke 11:31 . . . on judgment day and *c* it,
John 8:10 . . . even one of them *c* you?
Rom 2:1 . . . think you can *c* such people,
Rom 2:1 . . . you are *c-ing* yourself,
Rom 3:7 . . . how can God *c* me as a sinner
Rom 3:8 . . . deserve to be *c-ed.*
Rom 8:34 . . . Who then will *c* us? No one—
Rom 14:3 . . . foods must not *c* those who
Rom 14:13 . . . So let's stop *c-ing* each other.
1 Cor 4:9 . . . a victor's parade, *c-ed* to die.
2 Cor 7:3 . . . saying this to *c* you.
Col 2:16 . . . So don't let anyone *c* you
Jas 5:6 . . . You have *c-ed* and killed
Jas 5:12 . . . not sin and be *c-ed.*

**CONDEMNATION (n)** conviction of guilt; censure or blame
Rom 5:9 . . . save us from God's *c.*
Rom 5:18 . . . Adam's one sin brings *c*
Rom 7:13 . . . bring about my *c* to death.
Rom 8:1 . . . there is no *c* for those who
2 Cor 3:9 . . . which brings *c,* was glorious,

**CONFESS, CONFESSED, CONFESSES, CONFESSING (v)** to admit or acknowledge (sin or faith)
1 Sam 7:6 . . . *c-ed* that they had sinned
Ezra 10:11 . . . So now *c* your sin to
Ps 32:3 . . . I refused to *c* my sin,
Ps 32:5 . . . Finally, I *c-ed* all my sins
Ps 38:18 . . . But I *c* my sins;
Ps 66:18 . . . If I had not *c-ed* the sin in my
Dan 9:4 . . . to the LORD my God and *c-ed:*
Dan 9:20 . . . praying and *c-ing* my sin
Matt 18:15 . . . *c-es* it, you have won
Mark 1:5 . . . And when they *c-ed* their sins,
Rom 10:10 . . . by *c-ing* with your mouth
Rom 14:11 . . . every tongue will *c* and give
Phil 2:11 . . . and every tongue *c* that Jesus
1 Tim 6:12 . . . which you have *c-ed* so well
Jas 5:16 . . . *C* your sins to each other
1 Jn 1:9 . . . But if we *c* our sins to him,

**CONFIDENCE (n)** faith or belief that one will act in a right, proper, or effective way; a feeling or consciousness of one's powers; a quality or state of being certain
Ps 146:3 . . . Don't put your *c* in powerful
Isa 30:15 . . . In quietness and *c* is your

2 Cor 8:22 . . . of his great *c* in you.
Phil 1:14 . . . believers here have gained *c*
Phil 2:24 . . . And I have *c* from the Lord
Phil 3:4 . . . I could have *c* in my own
Col 2:2 . . . want them to have complete *c*
1 Thes 5:8 . . . as our helmet the *c* of our
Titus 1:2 . . . This truth gives them *c*
Heb 11:1 . . . Faith is the *c* that what we
2 Pet 1:19 . . . we have even greater *c*
1 Jn 4:17 . . . but we can face him with *c*

**CONFIDENT (adj)** full of conviction, certain; trustful
Ps 27:13 . . . Yet I am *c* I will see the
Ps 57:7 . . . My heart is *c* in you, O God;
2 Cor 3:4 . . . We are *c* of all this
Eph 1:18 . . . can understand the *c* hope
Col 1:5 . . . *c* hope of what God has reserved
Col 4:12 . . . fully *c* that you are following
2 Thes 3:4 . . . And we are *c* in the Lord
Heb 3:6 . . . keep our courage and remain *c*

**CONFIDENTLY (adv)** acting with confidence
Ps 112:7 . . . they *c* trust the LORD
Rom 5:2 . . . we *c* and joyfully look forward
Eph 3:12 . . . boldly and *c* into God's

**CONFLICT (n)** fight, battle, war
Prov 13:10 . . . Pride leads to *c;*
Prov 17:1 . . . filled with feasting—and *c.*
Gal 3:21 . . . Is there a *c,* then, between

**CONSCIENCE, CONSCIENCES (n)** one's moral sensitivity or scruples
2 Sam 24:10 . . . census, David's *c* began to
Acts 24:16 . . . maintain a clear *c* before God
Rom 14:2 . . . with a sensitive *c* will eat
1 Cor 8:7 . . . their weak *c-s* are violated.
1 Cor 8:10 . . . to violate their *c* by eating
1 Cor 10:25 . . . raising questions of *c.*
1 Tim 1:5 . . . a clear *c,* and genuine faith.
1 Tim 1:19 . . . and keep your *c* clear.
Titus 1:15 . . . minds and *c-s* are corrupted.
Heb 9:9 . . . are not able to cleanse the *c-s*
Heb 9:14 . . . will purify our *c-s* from sinful
Heb 10:22 . . . guilty *c-s* have been sprinkled
Heb 13:18 . . . for our *c* is clear
1 Pet 3:16 . . . Keep your *c* clear.
1 Pet 3:21 . . . to God from a clean *c.*

**CONSECRATE, CONSECRATED (v)** to devote irrevocably to God by a solemn ceremony; to make or declare sacred
*see also* DEDICATE, DEVOTE
Exod 40:9 . . . all its furnishings to *c* them
Lev 19:24 . . . the entire crop must be *c-d*
2 Chr 29:31 . . . you have *c-d* yourselves

**CONSIDERATE (adj)** thoughtful of the rights and feelings of others
Phil 4:5 . . . see that you are *c* in all you

**CONSTANT (adj)** marked by steadfast faithfulness; continually occurring or recurring
Ps 119:98 . . . they are my *c* guide.
Prov 27:15 . . . is as annoying as *c* dripping
Luke 18:5 . . . with her *c* requests!

**CONTAIN (v)** to keep within limits; to restrain or control
1 Kgs 8:27 . . . heavens cannot *c* you.
John 21:25 . . . world could not *c* the books

**CONTENT, CONTENTED (adj)** feeling or showing satisfaction with one's possessions, status, or situation; pleased

Josh 7:7 . . . If only we had been *c*
1 Kgs 4:20 . . . They were very *c-ed,*
Prov 13:25 . . . godly eat to their hearts' *c,*
Luke 3:14 . . . And be *c* with your pay.
Phil 4:11 . . . I have learned how to be *c*
1 Tim 6:8 . . . food and clothing, let us be *c.*

**CONTENTMENT (n)** the quality or state of being contented
1 Tim 6:6 . . . godliness with *c* is

**CONTROL, CONTROLS (v)** to exercise restraining or directing influence over; to rule
Job 37:15 . . . know how God *c-s* the storm
Rom 6:12 . . . Do not let sin *c*
Rom 8:6 . . . letting the Spirit *c* your mind
Rom 8:8 . . . still under the *c* of
1 Cor 7:9 . . . they can't *c* themselves.
1 Cor 7:37 . . . and he can *c* his passion,
2 Cor 5:14 . . . Christ's love *c-s* us.
Jas 1:26 . . . but don't *c* your tongue,
Jas 3:2 . . . could also *c* ourselves
2 Pet 2:19 . . . a slave to whatever *c-s* you.

**CONVICT, CONVICTED (v)** to find or prove guilty of an offense
Prov 24:25 . . . for those who *c* the guilty;
John 7:51 . . . Is it legal to *c* a man
John 16:8 . . . he will *c* the world of
1 Cor 14:24 . . . they will be *c-ed* of sin
Jude 1:15 . . . He will *c* every person

**CONVINCE, CONVINCED, CONVINCING (v)** to persuade to a belief, consent, or course of action
Exod 4:31 . . . people of Israel were *c-d*
Job 6:26 . . . your words are *c-ing*
Acts 18:4 . . . to *c* the Jews and Greeks
Rom 2:19 . . . are *c-d* that you are a guide
Rom 8:38 . . . I am *c-d* that nothing
Rom 14:14 . . . I know and am *c-d*
Rom 15:14 . . . I am fully *c-d,*
Phil 1:25 . . . I am *c-d* that I will

**CORNERSTONE (n)** a stone forming a corner or angle in a wall; foundation
Ps 118:22 . . . now become the *c.*
Mark 12:10 . . . now become the *c.*
Acts 4:11 . . . now become the *c.*
Eph 2:20 . . . And the *c* is Christ
1 Pet 2:7 . . . now become the *c.*

**CORRECT, CORRECTED, CORRECTING, CORRECTS (v)** to set right with remedies, revisions, or reforms
Job 5:17 . . . joy of those *c-ed* by God!
Ps 141:5 . . . If they *c* me,
Prov 3:12 . . . For the LORD *c-s* those
Prov 9:8 . . . don't bother *c-ing* mockers;
Prov 19:25 . . . if you *c* the wise,
Jer 5:3 . . . refused to be *c-ed.*
Jer 10:24 . . . Do not *c* me in anger,
2 Tim 3:16 . . . It *c-s* us when we
2 Tim 4:2 . . . Patiently *c,* rebuke,
Titus 2:15 . . . the authority to *c* them
Heb 12:5 . . . give up when he *c-s* you.

**CORRECTION (n)** a rebuke or punishment; the action of making right
Prov 10:17 . . . those who ignore *c*
Prov 12:1 . . . it is stupid to hate *c.*
Prov 15:5 . . . learns from *c* is wise.
Prov 15:10 . . . whoever hates *c* will die.
Prov 15:32 . . . if you listen to *c,*
Zeph 3:2 . . . it refuses all *c.*

**CORRUPT (adj)** morally degenerate and perverted; depraved
Gen 6:11 . . . the earth had become *c*
Ps 14:1 . . . They are *c,*
Ps 14:3 . . . all have become *c.*
Prov 19:28 . . . A *c* witness
Luke 9:41 . . . faithless and *c* people!

**CORRUPT, CORRUPTED, CORRUPTS (v)** to change from good to bad, physically or morally
Eccl 7:7 . . . and bribes *c* the heart.
1 Cor 15:33 . . . bad company *c-s* good
Jas 1:27 . . . let the world *c* you.
Titus 1:15 . . . and consciences are *c-ed.*

**COST (n)** loss or penalty incurred especially in gaining something; price
Num 16:38 . . . sinned at the *c* of their lives,
Luke 14:28 . . . calculating the *c*

**COST (v)** to require effort, suffering, or loss
Prov 7:23 . . . it would *c* him his life.
Rev 6:6 . . . barley will *c* a day's pay.

**COUNSEL (n)** advice; policy, plan, or action
Ps 37:30 . . . godly offer good *c;*
Ps 73:24 . . . guide me with your *c,*
Ps 107:11 . . . scorning the *c* of the
Prov 27:9 . . . The heartfelt *c* of a friend
1 Cor 7:40 . . . I am giving you *c*

**COUNSEL (v)** to advise
Col 3:16 . . . Teach and *c* each other

**COUNSELOR (n)** one who gives advice or wisdom
*see also* ADVOCATE, HOLY SPIRIT
Isa 9:6 . . . Wonderful *C,* Mighty God,

**COUNT, COUNTED, COUNTING, COUNTS (v)** to number; to consider
Gen 15:6 . . . and the LORD *c-ed* him as
Ps 22:17 . . . I can *c* all my bones.
Ps 130:5 . . . yes, I am *c-ing* on him.
Ps 147:4 . . . He *c-s* the stars
Prov 20:25 . . . and only later *c-ing* the cost.
Acts 5:41 . . . *c-ed* them worthy to suffer
Rom 4:9 . . . Abraham was *c-ed* as righteous
Rom 4:24 . . . that God will also *c* us
Rom 5:13 . . . it was not *c-ed* as sin
2 Cor 5:19 . . . no longer *c-ing* people's sins
Gal 3:6 . . . and God *c-ed* him as righteous
Jas 2:23 . . . and God *c-ed* him as righteous

**COUNTENANCE (KJV)**
Gen 4:6 . . . Why do you *look* so dejected
Num 6:26 . . . LORD *show you his favor*
1 Sam 16:7 . . . Don't judge by his *appearance*
Prov 15:13 . . . glad heart makes a happy *face*
Luke 9:29 . . . *appearance of his face* was transformed

**COURAGE (n)** mental or moral strength
Judg 5:21 . . . March on with *c,* my soul!
2 Chr 15:8 . . . he took *c*
Dan 11:25 . . . stir up his *c* and raise a
Mark 6:50 . . . Take *c!* I am here!
Acts 27:22 . . . But take *c!*
Heb 3:6 . . . if we keep our *c*
Jas 5:8 . . . Take *c,* for the coming
1 Jn 2:28 . . . be full of *c* and not shrink

**COURAGEOUS (adj)** having or characterized by courage; brave
Deut 31:6 . . . So be strong and *c!*
Josh 1:6 . . . Be strong and *c,*
2 Sam 10:12 . . . Be *c!*

2 Chr 32:7 . . . Be strong and *c!*
Ps 31:24 . . . be strong and *c,*
1 Cor 16:13 . . . Be *c.*

**COURT, COURTS (n)** a place for the administration of justice; an open space enclosed by buildings
Ps 82:1 . . . presides over heaven's *c;*
Ps 84:10 . . . single day in your *c-s*
Ps 96:8 . . . come into his *c-s.*
Ps 100:4 . . . go into his *c-s*
Prov 22:22 . . . exploit the needy in *c.*
Prov 25:8 . . . to go to *c.*
Isa 3:13 . . . takes his place in *c*
Amos 5:15 . . . *c-s* into true halls of justice.
Zech 8:16 . . . verdicts in your *c-s*
Matt 5:25 . . . are on the way to *c*

**COVENANT, COVENANTS (n)** a mutual agreement or contract (between persons, between nations, or between God and humanity) with conditions and consequences spelled out
*see also* PROMISE, VOW
Gen 9:9 . . . hereby confirm my *c*
Gen 17:2 . . . I will make a *c* with you,
Exod 19:5 . . . and keep my *c,*
Deut 4:13 . . . He proclaimed his *c—*
Judg 2:1 . . . never break my *c*
1 Kgs 8:21 . . . which contains the *c*
2 Kgs 23:2 . . . Book of the *C*
2 Chr 6:14 . . . You keep your *c*
Neh 1:5 . . . keeps his *c* of unfailing love
Ps 105:8 . . . stands by his *c—*
Prov 2:17 . . . and ignores the *c*
Isa 61:8 . . . an everlasting *c* with them.
Jer 31:31 . . . make a new *c* with the people
Hos 10:4 . . . make *c-s* they don't intend
Mal 3:1 . . . messenger of the *c,*
Mark 14:24 . . . confirms the *c*
Luke 22:20 . . . new *c* between God and his
Rom 9:4 . . . He made *c-s* with them
1 Cor 11:25 . . . new *c* between God and his
2 Cor 3:6 . . . under the new *c,*
Heb 8:6 . . . a far better *c* with God,
Heb 9:15 . . . mediates a new *c* between
Heb 12:24 . . . the new *c* between God and

**COVER (n)** something that is placed over or about another thing; lid or top piece
Exod 25:17 . . . make the Ark's *c—*
Exod 25:21 . . . put the atonement *c*
Lev 16:2 . . . the atonement *c.*

**COVER, COVERED, COVERS (v)** to hide from sight or knowledge; to lay or spread something over; to lie over
Gen 3:7 . . . to *c* themselves.
Exod 33:22 . . . and *c* you with my hand
Job 29:14 . . . Righteousness *c-ed* me
Ps 85:2 . . . you *c-ed* all their sins.
Ps 91:4 . . . He will *c* you with
Isa 6:2 . . . they *c-ed* their faces,
Matt 10:26 . . . everything that is *c-ed*
1 Cor 11:4 . . . if he *c-s* his head while
2 Cor 3:15 . . . their hearts are *c-ed*
Jas 3:14 . . . don't *c* up the truth
1 Pet 4:8 . . . love *c-s* a multitude of sins.

**COVET, COVETED, COVETING (v)** to inordinately desire unjust gain or another's property
*see also* DESIRE
Exod 20:17 . . . not *c* your neighbor's wife,
Exod 34:24 . . . so no one will *c*

Deut 7:25 . . . must not *c* the silver or gold
Acts 20:33 . . . *c-ed* anyone's silver or gold
Rom 7:7 . . . have known that *c-ing* is wrong
Rom 13:9 . . . You must not *c.*

**CREATE, CREATED, CREATING (v)** to bring
into being; to form, make, or produce
Gen 1:1 . . . God *c-d* the heavens
Gen 1:27 . . . male and female he *c-d* them;
Gen 6:7 . . . human race I have *c-d* from
Ps 51:10 . . . *C* in me a clean heart
Ps 104:30 . . . life is *c-d,* and you renew
Prov 8:22 . . . before he *c-d* anything else.
Isa 43:1 . . . the LORD who *c-d* you.
Isa 43:7 . . . I who *c-d* them.
Isa 45:8 . . . I, the LORD, *c-d* them.
Isa 54:16 . . . I have *c-d* the blacksmith
Isa 65:17 . . . I am *c-ing* new heavens and
John 1:3 . . . *c-d* everything through him,
Rom 1:20 . . . since the world was *c-d,*
Rom 1:25 . . . served the things God *c-d*
Rom 9:20 . . . the thing that was *c-d* say
Eph 2:10 . . . He has *c-d* us anew
Eph 2:15 . . . by *c-ing* in himself
Eph 4:24 . . . *c-d* to be like God—
Col 1:16 . . . Everything was *c-d* through
1 Tim 4:3 . . . But God *c-d* those foods
Heb 1:2 . . . through the Son he *c-d*
1 Pet 4:19 . . . to the God who *c-d* you,
Rev 4:11 . . . For you *c-d* all things,
Rev 10:6 . . . who *c-d* the heavens

**CREATION (n)** something that is created; the
world; the act of bringing the world into existence
Gen 2:3 . . . from all his work of *c.*
Mark 10:6 . . . from the beginning of *c.*
Rom 8:19 . . . For all *c* is waiting
Rom 8:39 . . . nothing in all *c* will ever
Gal 6:15 . . . into a new *c.*
Col 1:17 . . . holds all *c* together.
Heb 12:27 . . . all of *c* will be shaken
Jas 1:18 . . . we, out of all *c,*
Rev 3:14 . . . of God's new *c:*

**CREATOR (n)** maker; one who creates
*see also* MAKER
Gen 14:19 . . . God Most High, *C* of heaven
Job 40:19 . . . only its *C* can threaten
Eccl 12:1 . . . to forget your *C.*
Isa 40:28 . . . the *C* of all the earth.
Isa 45:9 . . . argue with their *C.*
Isa 51:13 . . . the LORD, your *C,*
Jer 51:19 . . . He is the *C* of everything
Rom 1:25 . . . instead of the *C* himself,
Eph 3:9 . . . the *C* of all things,
Eph 3:15 . . . the *C* of everything

**CRITICISM (n)** a critical observation or remark;
critique
Prov 15:31 . . . listen to constructive *c,*
Prov 25:12 . . . valid *c* is like a gold
Prov 28:23 . . . people appreciate honest *c*
Prov 29:1 . . . refuses to accept *c*
2 Cor 8:20 . . . guard against any *c*

**CRITICIZE, CRITICIZED, CRITICIZING (v)** to
find fault with; to point out the faults of
Job 34:29 . . . who can *c* him?
Eccl 7:5 . . . be *c-d* by a wise person
Rom 14:16 . . . not be *c-d* for doing
Phil 2:15 . . . no one can *c* you.
Titus 2:8 . . . teaching can't be *c-d.*
Jas 4:11 . . . *c-ing* and judging God's law.

**CROOKED (adj)** not straight, twisted;
dishonest, evil
Ps 125:5 . . . those who turn to *c* ways,
Prov 5:6 . . . staggers down a *c* trail
Prov 8:8 . . . nothing devious or *c* in it.
Prov 10:9 . . . those who follow *c* paths
Prov 21:8 . . . The guilty walk a *c* path;
Eccl 7:13 . . . what he has made *c?*
Isa 59:8 . . . have mapped out *c* roads,

**CROSS (n)** an upright post used as an instru-
ment of death in ancient times; the means by
which atonement was made between God and
humanity
Mark 8:34 . . . take up your *c,*
Luke 9:23 . . . take up your *c* daily,
Acts 2:23 . . . you nailed him to a *c*
Acts 5:30 . . . hanging him on a *c.*
1 Cor 1:18 . . . message of the *c* is
Gal 3:1 . . . death on the *c.*
Gal 6:12 . . . that the *c* of Christ alone
Phil 2:8 . . . criminal's death on a *c.*
Col 1:20 . . . Christ's blood on the *c.*
Heb 12:2 . . . he endured the *c,*
1 Pet 2:24 . . . his body on the *c*

**CROWN, CROWNS (n)** top of the head; a cap
or headdress worn by victors, priests, or
royalty
Prov 16:31 . . . Gray hair is a *c* of glory;
Song 3:11 . . . He wears the *c* his mother
Isa 61:3 . . . will give a *c* of beauty
Isa 62:3 . . . a splendid *c* in the hand
Zech 9:16 . . . like jewels in a *c.*
Matt 27:29 . . . thorn branches into a *c*
Mark 15:17 . . . thorn branches into a *c*
John 19:2 . . . wove a *c* of thorns
John 19:5 . . . wearing the *c* of thorns
Phil 4:1 . . . and the *c* I receive
1 Thes 2:19 . . . our proud reward and *c*
Jas 1:12 . . . will receive the *c* of life
Rev 2:10 . . . will give you the *c* of life.
Rev 3:11 . . . take away your *c.*
Rev 4:4 . . . had gold *c-s* on their heads.
Rev 4:10 . . . lay their *c-s* before the throne
Rev 12:3 . . . with seven *c-s* on his heads.
Rev 14:14 . . . He had a gold *c* on his head
Rev 19:12 . . . on his head were many *c-s.*

**CROWN, CROWNED, CROWNS (v)** to place a
crown on the head of; to bless or adorn
Ps 8:5 . . . and *c-ed* them with
Ps 149:4 . . . he *c-s* the humble
Prov 14:18 . . . are *c-ed* with knowledge.
Isa 51:11 . . . *c-ed* with everlasting joy.
Heb 2:7 . . . and *c-ed* them with
Heb 2:9 . . . *c-ed* with glory and honor.

**CRUCIFIXION (n)** the execution or death of a
person on a cross
Matt 23:34 . . . you will kill some by *c,*
John 19:41 . . . The place of *c* was near

**CRUCIFY, CRUCIFIED (v)** to execute or nail to
the cross; to put to death
Matt 26:2 . . . handed over to be *c-ied.*
Matt 27:22 . . . *C* him!
Matt 27:44 . . . who were *c-ied* with him
Mark 15:13 . . . *C* him!
Mark 15:27 . . . revolutionaries were *c-ied*
Mark 15:32 . . . who were *c-ied* with Jesus
Mark 16:6 . . . who was *c-ied.*
Luke 23:21 . . . *C* him! *C* him!
Luke 23:23 . . . that Jesus be *c-ied,*

Luke 23:33 . . . criminals were also *c-ied*—
Luke 24:20 . . . and they *c-ied* him.
John 19:6 . . . *C* him! *C* him!
John 19:10 . . . to release you or *c* you?
John 19:20 . . . where Jesus was *c-ied*
John 19:32 . . . the two men *c-ied* with
Jesus.
Acts 4:10 . . . the man you *c-ied*
Rom 6:6 . . . were *c-ied* with Christ
1 Cor 1:13 . . . Was I, Paul, *c-ied* for you?
1 Cor 1:23 . . . preach that Christ was *c-ied,*
1 Cor 2:8 . . . would not have *c-ied*
2 Cor 13:4 . . . he was *c-ied* in weakness,
Gal 5:24 . . . and *c-ied* them there.
Rev 11:8 . . . where their Lord was *c-ied.*

**CRY, CRIES (n)** entreaty, appeal; an inarticulate
utterance of distress, rage, or pain
Exod 2:23 . . . their *c* rose up to God.
Ps 5:2 . . . Listen to my *c* for help,
Ps 34:15 . . . open to their *c-ies* for help.
Ps 40:1 . . . and heard my *c.*
Ps 142:6 . . . Hear my *c,* for I am
Prov 21:13 . . . to the *c-ies* of the poor

**CRY, CRIED (v)** to shout; to beg or beseech;
to shed tears often noisily
Exod 14:10 . . . They *c-ied* out to the LORD,
Josh 24:7 . . . When your ancestors *c-ied* out
Judg 3:9 . . . people of Israel *c-ied* out
Judg 4:3 . . . people of Israel *c-ied* out
Judg 6:6 . . . Then the Israelites *c-ied* out
Judg 10:12 . . . you *c-ied* out to me
Ps 18:6 . . . in my distress I *c-ied* out
Eccl 3:4 . . . A time to *c* and a time
Lam 2:18 . . . *C* aloud before the LORD,
Hab 2:11 . . . walls *c* out against you,

**CUP (n)** a drinking vessel; figurative of
human vessel; token of tangible consolation,
salvation of Christ, wrath of God, drunkenness,
or fate
Ps 23:5 . . . My *c* overflows
Matt 26:39 . . . let this *c* of suffering
Matt 26:42 . . . If this *c* cannot be
Mark 10:39 . . . drink from my bitter *c*
Mark 14:23 . . . And he took a *c* of wine
Mark 14:36 . . . take this *c* of suffering
Luke 22:20 . . . This *c* is the new covenant
John 18:11 . . . from the *c* of suffering
1 Cor 10:16 . . . When we bless the *c*
1 Cor 10:21 . . . from the *c* of the Lord
1 Cor 11:25 . . . took the *c* of wine after
1 Cor 11:25 . . . This *c* is the new covenant

**CURE (n)** recovery or relief from a disease; a
complete or permanent solution
Jer 30:15 . . . wound that has no *c?*
Luke 8:43 . . . she could find no *c.*

**CURE, CURED (v)** to restore to health,
soundness, or normality
Isa 30:26 . . . and *c* the wounds
Matt 11:5 . . . the lepers are *c-d,*
John 5:10 . . . said to the man who was *c-d,*

**CURSE, CURSES, CURSING (n)**
a condemnation or judgment
Num 5:23 . . . priest will write these *c-s*
Josh 8:34 . . . blessings and *c-s* Moses had
Rom 3:14 . . . full of *c-ing* and bitterness.
Rom 8:20 . . . was subjected to God's *c.*
Gal 3:10 . . . right with God are under his *c,*
Gal 3:13 . . . the *c* for our wrongdoing.

Jas 3:10 . . . and *c-ing* come pouring out
Rev 22:3 . . . No longer will there be a *c*

**CURSE, CURSES (v)** to pronounce a sentence;
to afflict; to call upon a supernatural power to
bring injury upon; to utter profane language
against
Gen 8:21 . . . will never again *c* the ground
Gen 12:3 . . . *c* those who treat you
Prov 3:33 . . . *c-s* the house of the wicked,
Matt 5:22 . . . And if you *c* someone,
Rom 12:14 . . . Don't *c* them;
1 Cor 12:3 . . . will *c* Jesus, and no one
Jas 3:9 . . . and sometimes it *c-s* those who

**CURSED (adj)** being under or deserving a
curse
Gen 3:17 . . . the ground is *c* because
Deut 21:23 . . . anyone who is hung is *c*
Deut 27:16 . . . *C* is anyone who dishonors
Deut 27:18 . . . *C* is anyone who leads
Deut 27:20 . . . *C* is anyone who has sexual
Deut 27:24 . . . *C* is anyone who attacks a
Deut 27:26 . . . *C* is anyone who does not
Prov 28:27 . . . poverty will be *c.*
Gal 3:10 . . . *C* is everyone who does not
Gal 3:13 . . . *C* is everyone who is hung

**CURTAIN (n)** a hanging screen usually capable
of being drawn back or up
Isa 40:22 . . . the heavens like a *c*
Mark 15:38 . . . And the *c* in the sanctuary

**DANCE (n)** a series of rhythmic bodily
movements usually performed to music
Mark 6:22 . . . a *d* that greatly pleased

**DANCE, DANCED, DANCING (v)** to move up
and down or about in a quick or lively manner
2 Sam 6:14 . . . David *d-d* before the LORD
Ps 30:11 . . . into joyful *d-ing.*
Eccl 3:4 . . . and a time to *d.*
Matt 11:17 . . . and you didn't *d,*

**DANGER (n)** harm or damage
Ps 57:1 . . . until the *d* passes by.
Prov 22:3 . . . prudent person foresees *d*
Matt 5:22 . . . in *d* of being brought
Rom 8:35 . . . or in *d,* or threatened
2 Cor 1:10 . . . did rescue us from mortal *d,*
2 Cor 11:26 . . . I have faced *d* from rivers

**DANGEROUS (adj)** able or likely to inflict injury
or harm
Prov 29:25 . . . Fearing people is a *d* trap,

**DARK, DARKEST (adj)** devoid or partially
devoid of light; wholly or partially black
Exod 20:21 . . . approached the *d* cloud
Ps 23:4 . . . walk through the *d-est* valley,
Song 1:6 . . . because I am *d*—
Song 5:10 . . . My lover is *d* and dazzling,
Joel 2:31 . . . The sun will become *d,*
Acts 2:20 . . . The sun will become *d,*
2 Pet 1:19 . . . lamp shining in a *d* place—

**DARKENED (v)** to make dark
Matt 24:29 . . . the sun will be *d,*

**DARKNESS (n)** the state of being devoid of
light; nightfall; in spiritual terms, secret, closed,
blinded, or evil; place of punishment (hell)
Gen 1:2 . . . and *d* covered the deep waters.
Gen 1:4 . . . the light from the *d.*
Ps 18:28 . . . my God, lights up my *d.*
Matt 4:16 . . . people who sat in *d*

Luke 23:44 . . . it was about noon, and *d* fell
John 1:5 . . . light shines in the *d,*
John 3:19 . . . people loved the *d* more
John 12:35 . . . the *d* will not overtake
2 Cor 4:6 . . . Let there be light in the *d,*
2 Cor 6:14 . . . can light live with *d?*
Eph 5:8 . . . once you were full of *d,*
Eph 5:11 . . . deeds of evil and *d;*
1 Pet 2:9 . . . called you out of the *d*
1 Jn 1:5 . . . there is no *d* in him at all.
1 Jn 2:9 . . . is still living in *d.*
Jude 1:6 . . . chained in prisons of *d,*

**DAUGHTER, DAUGHTERS (n)** the female
offspring or adopted offspring of parents
Gen 19:36 . . . Lot's *d-s* became pregnant
Num 36:10 . . . The *d-s* of Zelophehad
Judg 11:40 . . . the fate of Jephthah's *d.*
Esth 2:7 . . . raised her as his own *d.*
Joel 2:28 . . . sons and *d-s* will prophesy.
Mark 5:34 . . . said to her, "*D,* your faith
Mark 7:29 . . . the demon has left your *d.*

**DAVID** King of Israel (United Kingdom); son
of Jesse, in the family line of Jesus (Ruth 4:17-
22; Matt 1:1; Luke 3:31); anointed king (1 Sam
16:1-13); skillful musician to Saul (1 Sam
16:14-23; 18:10); David and Goliath (1 Sam 17);
faithful friendship with Jonathan (1 Sam 18:1-
4); envied by Saul; loved by the people (1 Sam
18:5-16); married Michal (1 Sam 18:17-30);
wives and children (2 Sam 3:2-5; 5:13-16; 1 Chr
3:1-9); fled from Saul (1 Sam 19–23); ate used
"Bread of the Presence" (1 Sam 21:1-6; Matt
12:3-4); dealings with the Philistines (1 Sam
21:10-14; 27–30); spared Saul twice (1 Sam
22–24; 26); married widow Abigail (1 Sam 25:2-
42); lamented death of Saul and Jonathan
(2 Sam 1); contended with Saul's dynasty
(2 Sam 2–4); anointed king of Judah (2 Sam
2:1-7); lamented Abner's death (2 Sam 3:31-
39); made king over all Israel (2 Sam 5:1-5);
victories over the Philistines (2 Sam 5:17-25;
21:15-22; 1 Chr 14:8-17; 20:4-8); made
Jerusalem the royal city (2 Sam 5:6-16); moved
Ark to Jerusalem (2 Sam 6); eternal covenant
with God (2 Sam 7; 1 Chr 17); showed loyal
love to Mephibosheth (2 Sam 9); committed
adultery with Bathsheba (2 Sam 11–12; Pss 32;
51); plotted Uriah's death (2 Sam 11:14-25);
rebuked by Nathan (2 Sam 12:1-12); repented
of affair and intrigue (2 Sam 12:13); rebellion
and death of Absalom (2 Sam 14–18); lamented
Absalom's death (2 Sam 18:33–19:8); rebellion
and death of Sheba (2 Sam 20); judged for
taking census (2 Sam 24:1-25); made Solomon
next king (1 Kgs 1:28–2:9); final words to
Solomon (1 Kgs 2:1-9); died (1 Kgs 2:10-12);
preparations for the Temple (1 Chr 22–29).

**DAY, DAYS (n)** the time of light between one
night and the next; a specified time or period; a
24-hour time period
Gen 1:5 . . . called the light "*d*" and the
Gen 2:2 . . . On the seventh *d* God had
Exod 16:30 . . . the seventh *d.*
Lev 23:28 . . . it is the *D* of Atonement,
Josh 1:8 . . . Meditate on it *d* and night so
2 Kgs 7:9 . . . This is a *d* of good news,
Ps 23:6 . . . pursue me all the *d-s* of my life,
Ps 84:10 . . . A single *d* in your
Ps 118:24 . . . This is the *d* the LORD has

Isa 13:9 . . . coming—the terrible *d* of his
Jer 46:10 . . . this is the *d* of the LORD,
Jer 50:31 . . . Your *d* of reckoning
Hos 3:5 . . . In the last *d-s,* they will
Joel 1:15 . . . How terrible that *d* will be!
Joel 2:31 . . . great and terrible *d* of the
Amos 5:20 . . . Yes, the *d* of the LORD
Zeph 1:14 . . . That terrible *d* of the
Zech 14:1 . . . Watch, for the *d* of the LORD
Zech 14:7 . . . be continuous *d!*
Mal 4:5 . . . great and dreadful *d* of the
Matt 24:38 . . . In those *d-s* before the
Luke 11:3 . . . Give us each *d* the food we
Acts 2:17 . . . 'In the last *d-s,*' God says,
Rom 14:5 . . . some think one *d* is more holy
1 Cor 5:5 . . . be saved on the *d* the Lord
2 Cor 4:16 . . . renewed every *d.*
1 Thes 5:2 . . . the *d* of the Lord's return
1 Thes 5:4 . . . surprised when the *d* of the
2 Thes 2:2 . . . say that the *d* of the Lord
2 Tim 3:1 . . . in the last *d-s* there will be
Heb 1:2 . . . now in these final *d-s,* he has
2 Pet 3:3 . . . in the last *d-s* scoffers will
2 Pet 3:10 . . . But the *d* of the Lord
Rev 16:14 . . . that great judgment *d* of God

**DEAD (n)** the state of being dead (physically or
spiritually); (un)believers who have died
Matt 8:22 . . . the spiritually *d* bury their
Luke 24:46 . . . rise from the *d* on the third
1 Cor 15:29 . . . If the *d* will not
Rev 20:12 . . . I saw the *d,* both great and

**DEAD (adj)** without (physical or spiritual) life;
fatal; useless; unresponsive
Rom 6:11 . . . be *d* to the power of sin
Eph 2:1 . . . Once you were *d* because of
Jas 2:17 . . . good deeds, it is *d* and useless.
1 Pet 2:24 . . . that we can be *d* to sin and
Rev 2:8 . . . Last, who was *d* but is now

**DEATH (n)** the cessation of (physical or
spiritual) life; personification and consequence
of evil
Exod 21:12 . . . must be put to *d.*
Ruth 1:17 . . . anything but *d* to separate
Prov 11:19 . . . evil people find *d.*
Prov 14:12 . . . it ends in *d.*
Prov 23:14 . . . save them from *d.*
Isa 38:17 . . . have rescued me from *d*
Acts 2:24 . . . for *d* could not keep him
Rom 5:12 . . . brought *d,* so *d* spread to
Rom 6:23 . . . the wages of sin is *d,*
Rom 7:24 . . . dominated by sin and *d?*
1 Cor 15:21 . . . see, just as *d* came into the
1 Cor 15:26 . . . enemy to be destroyed is *d.*
2 Cor 3:6 . . . written covenant ends in *d;*
Gal 3:1 . . . the meaning of Jesus Christ's *d*
2 Tim 1:10 . . . power of *d* and illuminated
Heb 2:14 . . . the power of *d.*
Heb 9:17 . . . after the person's *d.*
1 Jn 5:16 . . . there is a sin that leads to *d,*
Rev 2:11 . . . by the second *d.*
Rev 20:6 . . . them the second *d* holds no
Rev 20:14 . . . is the second *d.*
Rev 21:4 . . . be no more *d* or sorrow or
Rev 21:8 . . . This is the second *d.*

**DEBAUCHERY (KJV)**
Rom 13:13 . . . promiscuity and *immoral living*
2 Cor 12:21 . . . eagerness for *lustful pleasure*
Gal 5:19 . . . impurity, *lustful pleasures*
1 Pet 4:3 . . . their *immorality* and lust, their

**DEBT, DEBTS (n)**  what is owing; sense of obligation
Deut 15:1 . . . cancel the *d-s* of everyone
Deut 15:3 . . . This release from *d*, however,
Deut 15:9 . . . year for canceling *d-s* is close
1 Sam 22:2 . . . trouble or in *d* or who were
2 Kgs 4:7 . . . pay your *d-s,* and
Prov 22:26 . . . another person's *d* or put up
Neh 10:31 . . . will cancel all *d-s* owed to us.
Matt 18:25 . . . to pay the *d.*
Matt 18:27 . . . and forgave his *d.*
Matt 18:30 . . . in prison until the *d* could
Matt 18:32 . . . you that tremendous *d*
Luke 7:42 . . . canceling their *d-s.*
Luke 7:43 . . . canceled the larger *d.*

**DECEIT (n)**  fraud; trickery; lying
Mark 7:22 . . . greed, wickedness, *d,* lustful
Acts 13:10 . . . of every sort of *d* and fraud,
1 Pet 2:1 . . . done with all *d,* hypocrisy,

**DECEITFUL (adj)**  not honest; misleading, deceptive
Isa 59:13 . . . planning our *d* lies.
2 Cor 11:13 . . . They are *d* workers who

**DECEIVE, DECEIVED, DECEIVES, DECEIVING (v)**  to lead astray; to cause to accept as true what is false
Gen 3:13 . . . "The serpent *d-d* me," she
Prov 10:31 . . . the tongue that *d-s* will be
Prov 14:8 . . . but fools *d* themselves.
Prov 26:24 . . . but they're *d-ing* you.
Matt 24:24 . . . so as to *d,* if possible, even
Mark 13:6 . . . They will *d* many.
Rom 7:11 . . . those commands and *d-d* me;
Rom 16:18 . . . they *d* innocent people.
Col 2:4 . . . so no one will *d* you with
1 Cor 3:18 . . . Stop *d-ing* yourselves.
2 Cor 11:3 . . . as Eve was *d-d* by the cunning
1 Tim 2:14 . . . The woman was *d-d,* and sin
2 Tim 3:13 . . . They will *d* others and will
2 Tim 3:13 . . . will themselves be *d-d.*
Heb 3:13 . . . you will be *d-d* by sin
Rev 20:3 . . . Satan could not *d* the nations
Rev 20:10 . . . devil, who had *d-d* them, was

**DECEPTION (n)**  something that deceives; trick; the act of deceiving
Isa 28:15 . . . refuge made of lies and *d.*
Dan 8:25 . . . He will be a master of *d*
Rom 1:29 . . . quarreling, *d,* malicious
Eph 4:22 . . . corrupted by lust and *d.*
2 Thes 2:10 . . . kind of evil *d* to fool those
1 Jn 4:6 . . . truth or spirit of *d.*

**DECIDE, DECIDED, DECIDES (v)**  to make a final choice or judgment about; to select as a course of action
1 Sam 14:7 . . . whatever you *d.*
Job 14:5 . . . You have *d-d* the length of
Ps 75:7 . . . he *d-s* who will rise and
Rom 14:13 . . . *D* instead to live
Rom 14:22 . . . they have *d-d* is right.
1 Cor 2:2 . . . For I *d-d* that while I
1 Cor 6:2 . . . can't you *d* even these
1 Cor 12:11 . . . He alone *d-s* which gift
2 Cor 9:7 . . . You must each *d* in your heart

**DECISION, DECISIONS (n)**  a determination arrived at after consideration; conclusion
Joel 3:14 . . . waiting in the valley of *d.*
Mic 3:11 . . . You rulers make *d-s* based on
Rom 11:33 . . . to understand his *d-s* and his

**DEDICATE, DEDICATED (v)**  to devote to the worship of a divine being; to set apart to a definite use
*see also* CONSECRATE, DEVOTE
Exod 13:2 . . . *D* to me every firstborn
Num 6:9 . . . the hair they have *d-d* will be
Num 6:18 . . . the hair that had been *d-d*
Num 18:6 . . . a gift to you, *d-d* to the LORD
1 Kgs 8:63 . . . Israel *d-d* the Temple
Neh 3:1 . . . which they *d-d,* and the Tower
Luke 2:23 . . . he must be *d-d* to the LORD.

**DEED, DEEDS (n)**  a signed instrument containing some legal transfer, bargain, or contract; a usually illustrious act or action; feat, exploit
Ps 45:4 . . . perform awe-inspiring *d-s!*
Ps 66:3 . . . awesome are your *d-s!*
Ps 71:24 . . . your righteous *d-s* all day
Ps 88:12 . . . your wonderful *d-s?*
Ps 96:3 . . . his glorious *d-s* among the
Ps 105:2 . . . his wonderful *d-s.*
Prov 31:31 . . . Let her *d-s* publicly declare
Isa 64:6 . . . our righteous *d-s,* they are
Jer 32:10 . . . and sealed the *d* of purchase
Matt 5:16 . . . let your good *d-s* shine out for
Rom 4:2 . . . If his good *d-s* had made him
2 Cor 9:9 . . . Their good *d-s* will be
Col 3:9 . . . all its wicked *d-s.*
Jas 2:18 . . . my faith by my good *d-s.*
Jas 2:20 . . . without good *d-s* is useless?

**DEFEND, DEFENDING, DEFENDS (v)**  to maintain or support in the face of argument or hostile criticism; to drive danger or attack away from
Deut 33:7 . . . strength to *d* their cause;
Ps 10:14 . . . You *d* the orphans.
Ps 34:7 . . . he surrounds and *d-s* all who
Ps 72:4 . . . Help him to *d* the poor,
Ps 106:8 . . . saved them—to *d* the honor of
Phil 1:7 . . . and in *d-ing* and confirming the
Phil 1:16 . . . been appointed to *d* the Good
Jude 1:3 . . . urging you to *d* the faith

**DEFENDER (n)**  one who guards and protects
Ps 68:5 . . . the fatherless, *d* of widows—
Prov 22:23 . . . the LORD is their *d.*
Isa 51:22 . . . your God and *D,* says:

**DEFILE, DEFILED, DEFILING (v)**  to make unclean—either physically, sexually, ethically, or ceremonially
Num 6:7 . . . must not *d* themselves,
Num 15:39 . . . desires and *d-ing* yourselves,
Ezek 23:7 . . . idols and *d-ing* herself.
Ezek 44:7 . . . In this way, you *d-d* my Temple
Matt 15:11 . . . you are *d-d* by the words
Mark 7:23 . . . they are what *d* you.
Acts 21:28 . . . even *d-s* this holy place
2 Cor 7:1 . . . that can *d* our body or

**DELIGHT, DELIGHTS (n)**  source of great pleasure; joy
Ps 36:8 . . . your river of *d-s.*
Ps 40:6 . . . You take no *d* in sacrifices
Ps 119:111 . . . they are my heart's *d.*
Prov 8:30 . . . I was his constant *d,*
Isa 58:13 . . . and speak of it with *d*
Jer 15:16 . . . my joy and my heart's *d,*
Mal 3:12 . . . your land will be such a *d,*
Mark 12:37 . . . to him with great *d.*

**DELIGHT, DELIGHTED, DELIGHTING, DELIGHTS (v)**  to enjoy
Exod 4:14 . . . He will be *d-ed* to see you.

2 Sam 22:20 . . . because he *d-s* in me.
Ps 1:2 . . . But they *d* in the law of
Ps 18:19 . . . he rescued me because he *d-s*
Ps 27:4 . . . *d-ing* in the LORD's
Ps 37:4 . . . Take *d* in the LORD,
Ps 119:70 . . . I *d* in your instructions.
Prov 3:12 . . . a child in whom he *d-s.*
Prov 11:1 . . . he *d-s* in accurate weights.
Prov 11:20 . . . he *d-s* in those with integrity.
Song 8:10 . . . he is *d-ed* with what he sees.
Isa 11:3 . . . He will *d* in obeying
Isa 65:19 . . . and *d* in my people.
Isa 66:3 . . . *d-ing* in their detestable sins—
Jer 9:24 . . . I *d* in these things.

**DEMON-POSSESSED (adj)**  characterized by the possession or control of demons
Matt 4:24 . . . if they were *d* or epileptic
Matt 8:16 . . . That evening many *d* people
Matt 8:33 . . . happened to the *d* men.
Matt 9:32 . . . When they left, a *d* man who
Matt 12:22 . . . Then a *d* man, who was
Mark 1:32 . . . many sick and *d* people were
Mark 5:16 . . . about the *d* man and
Luke 8:36 . . . others how the *d* man had

**DEMON, DEMONS (n)**  an agent of the Devil; an evil spirit
Deut 32:17 . . . They offered sacrifices to *d-s,*
Matt 8:31 . . . So the *d-s* begged, "If you cast
Matt 9:34 . . . by the prince of *d-s.*
Matt 11:18 . . . He's possessed by a *d.*
Matt 12:24 . . . he can cast out *d-s.*
Matt 12:28 . . . if I am casting out *d-s* by the
Matt 17:18 . . . Jesus rebuked the *d*
Mark 5:18 . . . been *d* possessed begged
Mark 1:34 . . . But because the *d-s* knew who
Mark 5:15 . . . by the legion of *d-s.*
Mark 7:29 . . . the *d* has left your daughter.
Mark 9:38 . . . to cast out *d-s,* but we told
Mark 16:9 . . . cast out seven *d-s.*
Mark 16:17 . . . will cast out *d-s* in my name,
Luke 4:33 . . . possessed by a *d*—an evil
Luke 7:33 . . . He's possessed by a *d.*
Luke 8:2 . . . he had cast out seven *d-s;*
Luke 8:30 . . . with many *d-s.*
Luke 8:33 . . . Then the *d-s* came out of the
Luke 8:38 . . . freed from the *d-s* begged
Luke 9:49 . . . to cast out *d-s,* but we told
Luke 10:17 . . . Lord, even the *d-s* obey us
Luke 11:14 . . . Jesus cast out a *d* from
Luke 11:19 . . . They cast out *d-s,* too, so they
Luke 11:20 . . . casting out *d-s* by the power
John 8:49 . . . Jesus said, "I have no *d* in me.
John 10:21 . . . possessed by a *d!*
Rom 8:38 . . . neither angels nor *d-s,*
1 Cor 10:20 . . . to participate with *d-s.*
1 Cor 10:21 . . . the cup of *d-s,* too.
1 Cor 10:21 . . . the table of *d-s,* too.
1 Tim 4:1 . . . teachings that come from *d-s.*
Rev 9:20 . . . to worship *d-s* and idols made
Rev 18:2 . . . become a home for *d-s.*

**DENY, DENIED, DENIES (v)**  to disavow or refuse to accept as true; to refuse to grant
Exod 23:6 . . . you must not *d* justice to the
Deut 27:19 . . . is anyone who *d-ies* justice
Prov 30:9 . . . I may *d* you and say,
Matt 10:33 . . . everyone who *d-ies* me
Matt 26:35 . . . I will never *d* you!
Matt 26:70 . . . But Peter *d-ied* it

Luke 12:9 . . . anyone who *d-ies* me
Luke 22:34 . . . you will *d* three times
John 18:25 . . . He *d-ied* it, saying,
Acts 4:16 . . . We can't *d* that they
1 Tim 5:8 . . . have *d-ied* the true faith.
2 Tim 2:12 . . . *d* him, he will *d* us.
Titus 1:16 . . . *d* him by the way they live.
2 Pet 2:1 . . . and even *d* the Master who
1 Jn 2:22 . . . Anyone who *d-ies* the Father
1 Jn 2:23 . . . Anyone who *d-ies* the Son
Jude 1:4 . . . they have *d-ied* our only
   Master
Rev 3:8 . . . and did not *d* me.

**DEPEND (v)** to place reliance or trust
Prov 3:5 . . . do not *d* on your own
Jer 49:11 . . . widows, too, can *d* on me
Gal 3:10 . . . But those who *d* on the law

**DEPRIVE (v)** to withhold something from; to
remove
Isa 10:2 . . . They *d* the poor
1 Cor 7:5 . . . Do not *d* each other of

**DESERT, DESERTS (n)** arid land with usually
sparse vegetation
*see also* WILDERNESS
Prov 21:19 . . . better to live alone in the *d*
Isa 32:2 . . . like streams of water in the *d*
Isa 43:20 . . . giving them water in the *d.*
2 Cor 11:26 . . . cities, in the *d-s,* and on the

**DESERVE, DESERVED, DESERVES (v)** to be
worthy, fit, or suitable for some reward or
requital; to merit
Judg 9:16 . . . the honor he *d-s* for all he
2 Sam 12:5 . . . do such a thing *d-s* to die!
Neh 9:33 . . . gave us only what we *d-d.*
Ps 103:10 . . . with us, as we *d.*
Prov 14:14 . . . Backsliders get what they *d;*
Dan 9:18 . . . not because we *d* help,
Zech 1:6 . . . received what we *d-d* from the
Luke 7:4 . . . If anyone *d-s* your help,
Acts 26:31 . . . done anything to *d* death or
Rom 3:8 . . . who say such things *d* to be
Rom 11:9 . . . get what they *d.*
2 Cor 11:15 . . . their wicked deeds *d.*
1 Tim 5:18 . . . Those who work *d* their pay!
Heb 3:3 . . . But Jesus *d-s* far more

**DESIRABLE (adj)** attractive; worth seeking or
doing
Ps 19:10 . . . They are more *d* than gold,

**DESIRE, DESIRES (n)** conscious impulse
toward something that promises enjoyment or
satisfaction in its attainment; longing, craving
Job 17:11 . . . My heart's *d-s* are broken.
Ps 10:3 . . . brag about their evil *d-s;*
Ps 37:4 . . . give you your heart's *d-s.*
Ps 145:19 . . . He grants the *d-s* of those who
Song 6:12 . . . my strong *d-s* had taken me
Mark 4:19 . . . wealth, and the *d* for other
Rom 1:26 . . . to their shameful *d-s.*
Rom 6:12 . . . not give in to sinful *d-s.*
Rom 7:5 . . . sinful *d-s* were at work
Rom 13:14 . . . indulge your evil *d-s.*
Gal 5:24 . . . the passions and *d-s* of their
Phil 2:13 . . . you the *d* and the power
Col 2:23 . . . a person's evil *d-s.*
Col 3:5 . . . lust, and evil *d-s.*
1 Tim 6:9 . . . and harmful *d-s* that plunge
2 Tim 4:3 . . . follow their own *d-s* and will
Jas 1:14 . . . from our own *d-s,* which entice

Jas 4:1 . . . from the evil *d-s* at war within
1 Pet 2:11 . . . from worldly *d-s* that wage
1 Pet 4:2 . . . chasing your own *d-s,*
2 Pet 2:10 . . . their own twisted sexual *d,*
2 Pet 2:18 . . . twisted sexual *d-s,* they lure
2 Pet 3:3 . . . following their own *d-s.*
Jude 1:18 . . . their ungodly *d-s.*

**DESIRE, DESIRED, DESIRES (v)** to long or
hope for; to wish or request
*see also* COVET
Gen 3:16 . . . And you will *d* to control
Ps 51:6 . . . But you *d* honesty from
Ps 51:16 . . . You do not *d* a sacrifice,
Prov 8:11 . . . Nothing you *d* can compare
Prov 21:10 . . . Evil people *d* evil;
Rom 1:24 . . . things their hearts *d-d.*
1 Cor 12:31 . . . earnestly *d* the most
1 Cor 14:1 . . . you should also *d* the special
1 Tim 3:1 . . . an elder, he *d-s* an honorable
Jas 1:20 . . . righteousness God *d-s.*
Rev 22:17 . . . Let anyone who *d-s* drink

**DESPAIR (n)** utter loss of hope
Ps 40:2 . . . out of the pit of *d,*
Ps 79:8 . . . on the brink of *d.*
Ps 130:1 . . . the depths of *d,* O LORD,
Isa 61:3 . . . praise instead of *d.*
2 Cor 4:8 . . . but not driven to *d.*

**DESPISE, DESPISED, DESPISES (n)** to scorn
or regard as unworthy, sometimes with malice
or outrage
2 Sam 12:9 . . . you *d-d* the word of the LORD
Job 5:17 . . . Do not *d* the discipline
Job 9:21 . . . to me—I *d* my life.
Ps 22:6 . . . I am scorned and *d-d* by all!
Prov 1:7 . . . but fools *d* wisdom and
Prov 12:8 . . . a warped mind is *d-d.*
Prov 15:5 . . . Only a fool *d-s* a parent's
Prov 15:20 . . . foolish children *d* their
Prov 29:27 . . . The righteous *d* the unjust;
Prov 30:17 . . . and *d-s* a mother's
Isa 53:3 . . . He was *d-d,* and we did not
Mic 7:6 . . . For the son *d-s* his father.
Luke 16:13 . . . to one and *d* the other.
Gal 4:14 . . . you did not *d* me or
2 Pet 2:10 . . . and who *d* authority.

**DESTINED (v)** to decree beforehand; to
predetermine
Luke 2:34 . . . This child is *d* to cause
Heb 9:27 . . . each person is *d* to die once

**DESTITUTE (adj)** lacking possessions and
resources; suffering extreme poverty
Ps 82:3 . . . of the oppressed and the *d.*
Ps 102:17 . . . prayers of the *d.*
Rom 8:35 . . . or hungry, or *d,* or in
Heb 11:37 . . . *d* and oppressed

**DESTROY, DESTROYED, DESTROYING,
DESTROYS (v)** to kill; to cause devastation or
ruin
*see also* PERISH
Gen 6:17 . . . that will *d* every living
Gen 9:11 . . . will a flood *d* the earth.
Num 32:15 . . . responsible for *d-ing* this
Deut 28:63 . . . find pleasure in *d-ing* you
Josh 10:40 . . . He completely *d-ed* everyone
Prov 6:32 . . . fool, for he *d-s* himself.
Prov 10:21 . . . fools are *d-ed* by their lack
Prov 10:29 . . . but it *d-s* the wicked.
Prov 11:3 . . . dishonesty *d-s* treacherous

Prov 11:9 . . . the godless *d* their friends,
Prov 18:9 . . . as someone who *d-s* things.
Prov 18:24 . . . "friends" who *d* each other,
Prov 29:1 . . . will suddenly be *d-ed* beyond
Isa 11:4 . . . his mouth will *d* the wicked.
Dan 2:44 . . . never be *d-ed* or conquered.
Jon 3:9 . . . fierce anger from *d-ing* us.
Jon 4:2 . . . turn back from *d-ing* people.
Matt 10:28 . . . God, who can *d* both soul
Luke 9:25 . . . but are yourself lost or *d-ed?*
John 10:10 . . . and kill and *d.*
Rom 2:12 . . . they will be *d-ed,* even though
1 Cor 3:17 . . . anyone who *d-s* this temple.
1 Cor 5:5 . . . nature will be *d-ed* and he
1 Cor 8:11 . . . died will be *d-ed.*
1 Cor 15:24 . . . *d-ed* every ruler and
1 Cor 15:26 . . . enemy to be *d-ed* is death.
2 Cor 4:9 . . . are not *d-ed.*
Gal 5:15 . . . Beware of *d-ing* one another.
Heb 7:16 . . . that cannot be *d-ed.*
2 Pet 2:12 . . . be caught and *d-ed.*
2 Pet 3:7 . . . people will be *d-ed.*
Jude 1:5 . . . but later he *d-ed* those who did
Rev 11:18 . . . It is time to *d* all who have

**DESTRUCTION (n)** the state or fact of being
destroyed, ruin; place of punishment (hell)
Ps 1:6 . . . leads to *d.*
Prov 16:18 . . . Pride goes before *d,*
1 Cor 1:18 . . . are headed for *d!*
2 Thes 1:9 . . . punished with eternal *d,*
2 Thes 2:3 . . . the one who brings *d.*
1 Tim 6:9 . . . into ruin and *d.*
2 Pet 2:3 . . . their *d* will not be delayed.
Rev 17:8 . . . and go to eternal *d.*

**DETERMINE, DETERMINED, DETERMINES (v)**
to decide; to resolve
Exod 28:30 . . . objects used to *d* the LORD's
Ezra 7:10 . . . because Ezra had *d-d* to study
Ps 17:3 . . . I am *d-d* not to sin in
Ps 119:30 . . . I have *d-d* to live by
Ps 119:112 . . . I am *d-d* to keep your
Prov 4:23 . . . it *d-s* the course of your life.
Prov 16:9 . . . but the LORD *d-s* our steps.
Dan 1:8 . . . But Daniel was *d-d* not to
Dan 11:36 . . . what has been *d-d* will surely
Matt 12:34 . . . heart *d-s* what you say.
Luke 22:22 . . . it has been *d-d* that the Son
Acts 4:28 . . . was *d-d* beforehand according

**DETEST, DETESTS (v)** to loathe; to denounce
Prov 8:7 . . . the truth and *d* every kind of
Prov 12:22 . . . The LORD *d-s* lying lips,
Prov 15:8 . . . The LORD *d-s* the sacrifice
Prov 15:26 . . . The LORD *d-s* evil plans,
Prov 16:5 . . . The LORD *d-s* the proud;
Prov 20:10 . . . the LORD *d-s* double
Prov 24:9 . . . everyone *d-s* a mocker.

**DETESTABLE (adj)** arousing or meriting
intense dislike; abominable
Lev 11:10 . . . They are *d* to you.
Prov 3:32 . . . wicked people are *d* to the
Prov 17:15 . . . both are *d* to the LORD.
Prov 21:27 . . . an evil person is *d,*
Luke 16:15 . . . What this world honors is *d*

**DEVIL (n)** Satan; enemy of God and of
everything good; destroyer, tempter, adversary
*see also* SATAN
Matt 4:1 . . . tempted there by the *d.*
Matt 4:11 . . . Then the *d* went away,

Matt 13:39 . . . among the wheat is the *d.*
Matt 25:41 . . . prepared for the *d* and his
Luke 4:2 . . . tempted by the *d* for forty
Luke 4:13 . . . When the *d* had finished
Luke 8:12 . . . to have the *d* come and take
John 6:70 . . . but one is a *d.*
John 13:2 . . . *d* had already prompted
Eph 4:27 . . . foothold to the *d.*
Eph 6:11 . . . strategies of the *d.*
Eph 6:16 . . . fiery arrows of the *d.*
2 Tim 2:26 . . . escape from the *d* 's trap.
Jas 4:7 . . . Resist the *d,* and he
1 Jn 3:8 . . . the works of the *d.*
1 Jn 3:10 . . . children of the *d.*
Jude 1:9 . . . accuse the *d* of blasphemy,
Rev 12:9 . . . called the *d,* or Satan,

**DEVOTE, DEVOTED (v)** to commit by a solemn act
*see also* CONSECRATE, DEDICATE
2 Chr 31:4 . . . could *d* themselves fully
Acts 2:42 . . . the believers *d-d* themselves to
Col 4:2 . . . *D* yourselves to prayer

**DEVOTED (adj)** characterized by loyalty and devotion
1 Kgs 18:3 . . . (Obadiah was a *d* follower of
Ps 86:2 . . . for I am *d* to you.
Matt 6:24 . . . you will be *d* to one and
1 Tim 2:10 . . . claim to be *d* to God should

**DICE (n)** a small cube marked on each face with numbers and used usually for games and gambling by being shaken and thrown
Ps 22:18 . . . throw *d* for my clothing
Matt 27:35 . . . his clothes by throwing *d.*

**DIE, DIED, DIES (v)** to pass from physical life; to cease from existence
*see also* PERISH
Gen 2:17 . . . you are sure to *d.*
Gen 3:3 . . . if you do, you will *d.*
Esth 4:16 . . . If I must *d,* I must *d.*
Job 2:9 . . . Curse God and *d.*
Prov 5:23 . . . He will *d* for lack of
Prov 11:7 . . . When the wicked *d,* their
Prov 11:10 . . . when the wicked *d.*
Prov 23:13 . . . They won't *d* if you
Eccl 7:2 . . . After all, everyone *d-s*—so the
Isa 22:13 . . . drink, for tomorrow we *d!*
Isa 66:24 . . . that devour them will never *d,*
Jer 31:30 . . . All people will *d* for their
Matt 26:52 . . . will *d* by the sword.
Mark 9:48 . . . the maggots never *d* and the
Luke 16:22 . . . The rich man also *d-d* and
John 13:37 . . . I'm ready to *d* for you.
Rom 4:25 . . . handed over to *d* because of
Rom 5:6 . . . the right time and *d-d* for us
Rom 5:7 . . . be willing to *d* for a person
Rom 5:8 . . . by sending Christ to *d* for us
Rom 5:14 . . . Still, everyone *d-d*—from the
Rom 6:7 . . . For when we *d-d* with Christ we
Rom 6:10 . . . When he *d-d,* he *d-d* once
Rom 7:2 . . . But if he *d-s,* the laws of
Rom 7:6 . . . the law, for we *d-d* to it and
Rom 14:8 . . . whether we live or *d,* we
1 Cor 7:39 . . . If her husband *d-s,* she is free
1 Cor 9:15 . . . I would rather *d* than lose
1 Cor 15:6 . . . though some have *d-d.*
1 Cor 15:18 . . . all who have *d-d* believing in
1 Cor 15:22 . . . Just as everyone *d-s* because
1 Cor 15:32 . . . for tomorrow we *d!*
1 Cor 15:36 . . . plant unless it *d-s* first.

1 Cor 15:42 . . . in the ground when we *d,*
1 Cor 15:51 . . . will not all *d,* but we will
2 Cor 5:15 . . . for Christ, who *d-d* and was
Col 2:20 . . . You have *d-d* with Christ,
1 Thes 4:16 . . . who have *d* will rise from
1 Thes 5:10 . . . Christ *d-d* for us so
1 Tim 6:16 . . . He alone can never *d,*
2 Tim 2:11 . . . saying: If we *d* with him,
Heb 9:27 . . . is destined to *d* once and
1 Pet 3:18 . . . sinned, but he *d-d* for sinners

**DILIGENT (adj)** characterized by steady, earnest, and energetic effort; painstaking
Ezra 4:22 . . . Be *d,* and don't
Prov 12:27 . . . but the *d* make use of

**DISAPPEAR, DISAPPEARED, DISAPPEARING (v)** to pass from view; to cease to be
1 Kgs 20:40 . . . the prisoner *d-ed!*
Job 17:11 . . . My hopes have *d-ed.*
Ps 37:20 . . . they will *d* like smoke.
Prov 26:20 . . . and quarrels *d* when gossip
Isa 29:14 . . . of the intelligent will *d.*
Isa 51:6 . . . the skies will *d* like smoke,
Matt 5:18 . . . until heaven and earth *d,*
Matt 24:35 . . . Heaven and earth will *d,*
Mark 13:31 . . . Heaven and earth will *d,*
Luke 16:17 . . . and earth to *d* than for the
John 5:13 . . . for Jesus had *d-ed* into the
Heb 8:13 . . . and will soon *d.*
1 Jn 2:8 . . . the darkness is *d-ing,* and the

**DISASTER, DISASTERS (n)** a sudden calamitous event bringing great damage, loss, or destruction; a sudden or great misfortune or failure
Exod 32:12 . . . this terrible *d* you have
Deut 31:17 . . . will say, 'These *d-s* have come
Deut 31:21 . . . when great *d-s* come down
Ps 91:6 . . . nor the *d* that strikes at
Prov 3:25 . . . not be afraid of sudden *d*
Prov 27:10 . . . When *d* strikes,
Jer 17:17 . . . the day of *d.*
Jer 29:11 . . . plans for good and not for *d,*
1 Thes 5:3 . . . then *d* will fall on them

**DISCERNMENT (n)** the quality of being able to grasp and comprehend what is obscure
Ps 119:125 . . . Give *d* to me,
Prov 1:4 . . . knowledge and *d* to the young.
Prov 5:2 . . . you will show *d,* and your
Prov 8:12 . . . knowledge and *d.*
Prov 28:11 . . . a poor person with *d* can see

**DISCIPLE, DISCIPLES (n)** student or follower of some doctrine or teacher
Matt 28:19 . . . go and make *d-s* of all the
Mark 16:20 . . . the *d-s* went everywhere and
Luke 6:13 . . . all of his *d-s* and chose twelve
Luke 14:26 . . . you cannot be my *d.*
Luke 14:33 . . . become my *d* without
John 6:66 . . . many of his *d-s* turned away
John 8:31 . . . are truly my *d-s* if you remain
John 13:5 . . . to wash the *d-s'* feet, drying
John 13:23 . . . The *d* Jesus loved
John 15:8 . . . fruit, you are my true *d-s.*
John 19:26 . . . there beside the *d* he loved,
John 21:7 . . . Then the *d* Jesus loved
John 21:20 . . . the *d* Jesus loved—

**DISCIPLINE (n)** punishment; instruction
Deut 11:2 . . . the *d* of the LORD
Prov 10:17 . . . People who accept *d* are on
Prov 13:1 . . . child accepts a parent's *d;*

Prov 13:24 . . . spare the rod of *d* hate their
Prov 15:32 . . . If you reject *d,* you only
Heb 12:5 . . . of the LORD's *d,* and don't
Heb 12:11 . . . No *d* is enjoyable

**DISCIPLINE, DISCIPLINED, DISCIPLINES (v)** to punish or correct with love; to exercise self-control
Deut 8:5 . . . as a parent *d-s* a child,
Deut 8:5 . . . LORD your God *d-s* you for your
Ps 38:1 . . . in your anger or *d* me in your
Ps 39:11 . . . When you *d* us for our
Ps 119:67 . . . wander off until you *d-d* me;
Ps 119:75 . . . you *d-d* me because I needed
Prov 15:10 . . . right path will be severely *d-d;*
Jer 30:11 . . . I will *d* you, but with
Jer 31:18 . . . saying, 'You *d-d* me severely,
1 Cor 9:25 . . . All athletes are *d-d* in their
1 Cor 9:27 . . . I *d* my body like
1 Cor 11:32 . . . we are being *d-d* so that we
Heb 12:6 . . . For the LORD *d-s* those he
Heb 12:7 . . . who is never *d-d* by its father?
Heb 12:9 . . . fathers who *d-d* us, shouldn't
1 Pet 4:7 . . . be earnest and *d-d* in your

**DISCOURAGED (v)** to dissuade or hinder; to deprive of courage or confidence
Deut 31:8 . . . be afraid or *d,* for the LORD
2 Sam 11:25 . . . not to be *d,* " David said.
1 Chr 28:20 . . . afraid or *d,* for the LORD
Isa 41:10 . . . Don't be *d,* for I am
2 Cor 7:6 . . . who are *d,* encouraged us by
Col 3:21 . . . will become *d.*

**DISCOURAGEMENT (n)** the state of being discouraged
2 Cor 2:7 . . . may be overcome by *d.*

**DISCRIMINATION (n)** prejudiced outlook, action, or treatment
Jas 2:4 . . . doesn't this *d* show that your

**DISEASE, DISEASES (n)** sickness, malady
Exod 4:6 . . . a severe skin *d.*
2 Chr 16:12 . . . a serious foot *d.*
Ps 91:6 . . . not dread the *d* that stalks
Ps 103:3 . . . heals all my *d-s.*
Matt 9:35 . . . every kind of *d* and illness.
Matt 10:1 . . . every kind of *d* and illness.
Luke 4:40 . . . matter what their *d-s* were,

**DISGRACE (n)** loss of grace, favor, or honor; source of shame
Prov 11:2 . . . Pride leads to *d,* but with
Prov 14:34 . . . but sin is a *d* to any people.
Acts 5:41 . . . worthy to suffer *d* for the
Heb 13:13 . . . and bear the *d* he bore.

**DISGRACE, DISGRACED (v)** to cause to lose favor or standing; to be a source of shame to
Ps 25:3 . . . trusts in you will ever be *d-d,*
Ps 37:19 . . . will not be *d-d* in hard times;
Prov 29:15 . . . but a mother is *d-d* by an
Matt 1:19 . . . did not want to *d* her
Rom 9:33 . . . in him will never be *d-d.*
Rom 10:11 . . . in him will never be *d-d.*
1 Tim 3:7 . . . will not be *d-d* and fall into

**DISHONEST (adj)** characterized by lack of truth, honesty, or trustworthiness
Lev 19:35 . . . Do not use *d* standards when
Prov 20:23 . . . not pleased by *d* scales.
Luke 16:8 . . . to admire the *d* rascal for
Luke 16:10 . . . But if you are *d* in little

**DISHONESTY (n)** lack of honesty or integrity
Jer 22:17 . . . eyes only for greed and *d!*
Jer 23:14 . . . commit adultery and love *d.*
Rom 3:7 . . . sinner if my *d* highlights his
Rev 21:27 . . . idolatry and *d*—but only

**DISHONOR, DISHONORED, DISHONORING, DISHONORS (v)** to degrade or bring shame upon
Exod 21:17 . . . Anyone who *d-s* father or
Exod 22:28 . . . You must not *d* God or
Lev 20:19 . . . This would *d* a close
Deut 27:16 . . . is anyone who *d-s* father or
Ezra 4:14 . . . see the king *d-ed* in this way,
Lam 2:2 . . . *d-ing* the kingdom and its
John 8:49 . . . my Father—and you *d* me.
Rom 2:23 . . . the law, but you *d* God by
1 Cor 11:4 . . . A man *d-s* his head if
1 Cor 11:5 . . . a woman *d-s* her head if
Jas 2:6 . . . But you *d* the poor!

**DISOBEY, DISOBEYED, DISOBEYING (v)** to fail to obey
Judg 2:2 . . . But you *d-ed* my command.
1 Kgs 13:26 . . . man of God who *d-ed* the
2 Chr 24:20 . . . says: Why do you *d* the
Neh 9:29 . . . and obstinate and *d-ed* your
Esth 3:3 . . . Why are you *d-ing* the king's
Dan 9:11 . . . Israel has *d-ed* your instruction
Acts 7:53 . . . You deliberately *d-ed* God's
Rom 1:30 . . . and they *d* their parents.
Rom 5:19 . . . Because one person *d-ed* God,
Eph 5:6 . . . fall on all who *d* him.
Heb 3:18 . . . the people who *d-ed* him?
Heb 4:6 . . . enter because they *d-ed* God.
Heb 4:11 . . . But if we *d* God, as the
1 Pet 3:20 . . . those who *d-ed* God long ago

**DISORDER (n)** lack of order; confusion
1 Cor 14:33 . . . not a God of *d* but of peace,
Jas 3:16 . . . you will find *d* and evil of

**DISORDERLY (adv)** in a manner that lacks order; turbulently
2 Cor 12:20 . . . arrogance, and *d* behavior.

**DISPUTE, DISPUTES (n)** verbal controversy; quarrel or debate
Prov 18:18 . . . it settles *d-s* between
1 Cor 6:1 . . . you has a *d* with another

**DISSENSION (n)** disagreement; discord
Gal 5:20 . . . selfish ambition, *d,* division,

**DISTRESS (n)** a troubling or painful situation; a state of danger or desperate need
Exod 3:7 . . . their cries of *d* because of
Job 36:16 . . . to a place free from *d.*
Ps 18:6 . . . But in my *d* I cried out
Ps 118:5 . . . In my *d* I prayed to
Ps 143:11 . . . bring me out of this *d.*
Jas 1:27 . . . and widows in their *d*

**DIVIDE, DIVIDED (v)** to separate into parts; to distribute; to make distinctions
Ps 22:18 . . . They *d* my garments
Luke 12:51 . . . have come to *d* people
1 Cor 1:13 . . . Has Christ been *d-d* into
Jas 4:8 . . . your loyalty is *d-d* between God

**DIVISION, DIVISIONS (n)** act or process of dividing, separating, distributing; a portion, part, grouping, or distinction
1 Cor 1:10 . . . there be no *d-s* in the church.
1 Cor 11:18 . . . that there are *d-s* among
Gal 5:20 . . . selfish ambition, dissension, *d,*
Titus 3:10 . . . are causing *d-s* among you,

**DIVORCE (n)** the action or an instance of legally dissolving a marriage
Deut 24:1 . . . a letter of *d,* hands it to
Mal 2:16 . . . "For I hate *d!*" says the
Matt 19:8 . . . Moses permitted *d* only as a

**DIVORCE, DIVORCED, DIVORCES (v)** to dissolve a marriage; to end a relationship
Lev 21:7 . . . a woman who is *d-d* from her
Lev 21:14 . . . who is *d-d,* or a woman
Lev 22:13 . . . a widow or is *d-d* and has no
Num 30:9 . . . is a widow or is *d-d,* she must
Deut 22:19 . . . and he may never *d* her.
1 Chr 8:8 . . . After Shaharaim *d-d* his wives
Jer 3:1 . . . If a man *d-s* a woman and
Jer 3:8 . . . saw that I *d-d* faithless Israel
Matt 5:31 . . . A man can *d* his wife by
Matt 5:32 . . . a man who *d-s* his wife, unless
Matt 5:32 . . . who marries a *d-d* woman also
Mark 10:2 . . . be allowed to *d* his wife?
Mark 10:11 . . . Whoever *d-s* his wife and
Mark 10:12 . . . if a woman *d-s* her husband
Luke 16:18 . . . a man who *d-s* his wife and
Luke 16:18 . . . marries a woman *d-d* from

**DOG, DOGS (n)** a carnivorous (usually domestic) mammal similar to wolves and coyotes
Prov 26:11 . . . As a *d* returns to its
Eccl 9:4 . . . to be a live *d* than a dead
Matt 15:26 . . . throw it to the *d-s.*
Phil 3:2 . . . Watch out for those *d-s,*
2 Pet 2:22 . . . this proverb: "A *d* returns to

**DONKEY (n)** a domestic mammal smaller than the horse and having long ears
Num 22:30 . . . same *d* you have ridden
Matt 21:5 . . . riding on a *d*—riding on a
2 Pet 2:16 . . . when his *d* rebuked him

**DOOR, DOORS (n)** a barrier by which an entry is closed and opened; a means of access or participation
Ps 24:7 . . . Open up, ancient *d-s,* and let
Matt 7:7 . . . the *d* will be opened to you.
Luke 13:24 . . . enter the narrow *d* to God's
Acts 14:27 . . . had opened the *d* of faith to
1 Cor 16:9 . . . is a wide-open *d* for a great
2 Cor 2:12 . . . opened a *d* of opportunity
Rev 3:20 . . . stand at the *d* and knock.

**DOUBT, DOUBTS (n)** uncertainty of belief or opinion; lack of confidence; distrust
Mark 11:23 . . . have no *d* in your heart.
Luke 24:38 . . . hearts filled with *d?*
Rom 14:23 . . . if you have *d-s* about whether

**DOUBT (v)** to distrust; to be uncertain
Matt 14:31 . . . Why did you *d* me?
Matt 21:21 . . . faith and don't *d,* you

**DRAGON (n)** a huge serpent
Rev 12:7 . . . fought against the *d* and his
Rev 20:2 . . . He seized the *d*—that old

**DREAM, DREAMS (n)** a strongly desired goal or purpose; a series of thoughts, images, or emotions occurring during sleep
Prov 13:12 . . . sick, but a *d* fulfilled is a
Prov 13:19 . . . pleasant to see *d-s* come true,
Eccl 5:3 . . . gives you restless *d-s;*

**DREAM (v)** to have a dream
Joel 2:28 . . . old men will *d* dreams,
Acts 2:17 . . . old men will *d* dreams.

**DRINK, DRINKING, DRINKS (v)** to swallow; to partake of alcoholic beverages
1 Sam 1:13 . . . she had been *d-ing.*
Isa 5:22 . . . who are heroes at *d-ing* wine
Isa 12:3 . . . you will *d* deeply from
Matt 26:27 . . . Each of you *d* from it,
Mark 16:18 . . . *d* anything poisonous,
John 4:13 . . . Anyone who *d-s* this water will
John 6:54 . . . my flesh and *d-s* my blood has
Rom 14:17 . . . we eat or *d,* but of living a
1 Cor 11:27 . . . this bread or *d-s* this cup of
Rev 14:10 . . . *d* the wine of God's anger.
Rev 22:17 . . . who desires *d* freely from

**DRINKER, DRINKERS (n)** a person who drinks alcoholic beverages
1 Tim 3:3 . . . not be a heavy *d* or be violent.
1 Tim 3:8 . . . not be heavy *d-s* or dishonest
Titus 2:3 . . . or be heavy *d-s.*

**DROWNED (v)** to suffocate by submersion especially in water
Exod 15:4 . . . officers are *d* in the Red
Matt 18:6 . . . neck and be *d* in the depths
Heb 11:29 . . . they were all *d.*

**DRUNK (adj)** having the faculties impaired by alcohol; intoxicated
Acts 2:15 . . . These people are not *d,* as

**DRUNKARD, DRUNKARDS (n)** one who is habitually drunk
Prov 23:20 . . . not carouse with *d-s* or feast
Matt 11:19 . . . glutton and a *d,* and a friend
1 Cor 5:11 . . . or is a *d,* or cheats people.
1 Cor 6:10 . . . greedy people, or *d-s,* or are

**DRY (adj)** free or relatively free from a liquid and especially water
Gen 1:9 . . . so *d* ground may appear.
Exod 14:16 . . . of the sea on *d* ground.
Josh 3:17 . . . Covenant stood on *d* ground
Isa 53:2 . . . a root in *d* ground.

**DUST (n)** specks or clumps of earthy matter; ground or earth
Gen 2:7 . . . man from the *d* of the ground.
Gen 3:19 . . . were made from *d,* and to *d*
Ps 22:15 . . . laid me in the *d* and left me
Eccl 3:20 . . . they return to *d.*
Matt 10:14 . . . shake its *d* from your feet
1 Cor 15:47 . . . from the *d* of the earth,

**EAGLE, EAGLES (n)** any of various large diurnal birds of prey noted for their strength, size, keenness of vision, and powers of flight
Deut 32:11 . . . Like an *e* that rouses her chicks
Isa 40:31 . . . soar high on wings like *e-s.*
Rev 4:7 . . . was like an *e* in flight.
Rev 12:14 . . . wings like those of a great *e*

**EARNEST (adj)** characterized by or proceeding from an intense and serious state of mind; ardent or fervent
Jas 5:16 . . . The *e* prayer of a righteous
1 Pet 4:7 . . . be *e* and disciplined

**EARNESTLY (adv)** in a manner that is intense and serious; fervently
2 Chr 15:15 . . . they *e* sought after God,
Col 4:12 . . . He always prays *e* for you,

**EARS (n)** the external organ for hearing, expressing the entire faculty of understanding
Prov 2:2 . . . Tune your *e* to wisdom,

Eccl 5:1 . . . your *e* open and your mouth shut.
2 Tim 4:3 . . . whatever their itching *e* want

**EARTH (n)**  the planet on which we live
Gen 1:1 . . . created the heavens and the *e.*
Gen 7:24 . . . floodwaters covered the *e*
Gen 14:19 . . . Creator of heaven and *e.*
Job 26:7 . . . and hangs the *e* on nothing.
Job 38:4 . . . I laid the foundations of the *e?*
Ps 108:5 . . . your glory shine over all the *e.*
Prov 8:23 . . . first, before the *e* began.
Prov 8:26 . . . had made the *e* and fields
Isa 6:3 . . . The whole *e* is filled with his glory!
Isa 40:22 . . . God sits above the circle of the *e.*
Isa 44:23 . . . O depths of the *e!*
Isa 55:9 . . . higher than the *e,* so my ways
Isa 65:17 . . . new heavens and a new *e,*
Isa 66:1 . . . and the *e* is my footstool.
Jer 23:24 . . . in all the heavens and *e?*
Hab 2:20 . . . Let all the *e* be silent
Matt 5:18 . . . until heaven and *e* disappear, not
Matt 5:35 . . . do not say, 'By the *e!'*
Matt 6:10 . . . your will be done on *e,*
Matt 16:19 . . . Whatever you forbid on *e*
Matt 28:18 . . . in heaven and on *e.*
Luke 2:14 . . . and peace on *e*
Acts 4:24 . . . Creator of heaven and *e,*
Acts 7:49 . . . the *e* is my footstool.
Rom 8:39 . . . or in the *e* below—
1 Cor 10:26 . . . the *e* is the Lord's,
Eph 3:15 . . . in heaven and on *e.*
Phil 2:10 . . . in heaven and on *e* and under
Col 3:2 . . . not the things of *e.*
Heb 1:10 . . . laid the foundation of the *e*
2 Pet 3:13 . . . and new *e* he has promised,
Rev 20:11 . . . The *e* and sky fled
Rev 21:1 . . . a new heaven and a new *e,*
Rev 21:1 . . . the old *e* had disappeared.

**EAST (n)**  the direction toward the right of one
facing north
Gen 2:8 . . . a garden in Eden in the *e,*
Ps 103:12 . . . far from us as the *e* is from

**EAT, EATEN, EATING, EATS (v)**  to ingest, chew,
and swallow in turn
Gen 2:16 . . . You may freely *e* the fruit
Gen 3:11 . . . Have you *e-en* from the tree
Deut 14:4 . . . the animals you may *e:*
Isa 65:25 . . . The lion will *e* hay
Jer 31:29 . . . parents have *e-en* sour grapes,
Matt 26:26 . . . Take this and *e* it,
Luke 15:2 . . . sinful people—even *e-ing* with
John 6:52 . . . give us his flesh to *e?*
John 6:54 . . . anyone who *e-s* my flesh and
Acts 10:13 . . . kill and *e* them.
Acts 10:14 . . . I have never *e-en* anything
Rom 14:15 . . . Don't let your *e-ing* ruin
1 Cor 8:4 . . . So, what about *e-ing* meat that
1 Cor 8:10 . . . *e-ing* in the temple of an idol,
1 Cor 10:31 . . . So whether you *e* or drink,
1 Cor 11:26 . . . every time you *e* this bread
1 Cor 11:27 . . . anyone who *e-s* this bread or

**EDEN (n)**  the garden where Adam and Eve first
lived
Gen 2:8 . . . a garden in *E* in the east,
Ezek 28:13 . . . in *E,* the garden of God.

**EDIFY, EDIFYING (KJV)**
1 Cor 10:23 . . . but not everything is *beneficial*
1 Cor 14:5 . . . will be *strengthened*
1 Cor 14:17 . . . won't *strengthen* the people
Eph 4:12 . . . work and *build up* the church,

**ELECT (KJV)**
Isa 42:1 . . . my *chosen one,* who pleases me
Matt 24:31 . . . gather his *chosen ones* from all
Rom 8:33 . . . *us whom God has chosen* for his
Col 3:12 . . . *chose* you to be the holy people
2 Tim 2:10 . . . Jesus to *those God has chosen*

**ELIJAH**  Powerful prophet in Israel (Northern
Kingdom); proclaimed drought (1 Kgs 17:1; Jas
5:17); hid and was fed by ravens (1 Kgs 17:2-6);
performed miracles for widow (1 Kgs 17:8-24;
Luke 4:25); proclaimed truth to King Ahab
(1 Kgs 18:1-15); defeated Baal and his prophets
on Mount Carmel (1 Kgs 18:16-40); brought
rain (1 Kgs 18:41-46; Jas 5:17); ran for his life
(1 Kgs 19:3); served by angels (1 Kgs 19:1-9);
given assurance by God (1 Kgs 19:9-18); put
mantle on Elisha (1 Kgs 19:19-21); condemned
by Ahab (1 Kgs 21:17-29); whirlwind and fire
took him into heaven (2 Kgs 2:11); return
prophesied and expected (Mal 4:5-6; Matt
11:14; Luke 1:17; John 1:25); compared to John
the Baptist (Matt 17:9-13; Mark 9:9-13; Luke
1:17); appeared at Jesus' Transfiguration (Matt
17:1-8; Mark 9:1-8).

**ELISHA**  Powerful prophet in Israel (Northern
Kingdom) who replaced Elijah (1 Kgs 19:16-21);
inherited Elijah's cloak (2 Kgs 2:1-18); asked for
double measure of spirit (2 Kgs 2:9); witnessed
Elijah's departure (2 Kgs 2:11-12); healed bad
water (2 Kgs 2:19-22); cursed 42 mockers
(2 Kgs 2:23-25); prophesied victory over Moab
(2 Kgs 3:11-27); provided abundant oil for
widow (2 Kgs 4:1-7); raised child to life (2 Kgs
4:32-37); made stew edible (2 Kgs 4:38-41); fed
a multitude with few loaves (2 Kgs 4:42-44);
healed Namaan's leprosy (2 Kgs 5:14-15); made
an ax head float (2 Kgs 6:1-7); prophesied the
availability of food (2 Kgs 7:1); prophesied
death of Ben-hadad (2 Kgs 8:7-15); died (2 Kgs
13:20); bones produced miracle after death
(2 Kgs 13:21).

**EMPTY (adj)**  containing nothing; having no
purpose or result; destitute of effect or force
Gen 1:2 . . . formless and *e,* and darkness
Deut 32:47 . . . not *e* words—they are your life!
Job 26:7 . . . the northern sky over *e* space
Isa 45:18 . . . not to be a place of *e* chaos.
Jer 4:23 . . . and it was *e* and formless.
Luke 1:53 . . . the rich away with *e* hands.
1 Cor 14:9 . . . be talking into *e* space.
1 Pet 1:18 . . . to save you from the *e* life
2 Pet 2:18 . . . with *e,* foolish boasting.

**ENCOURAGE, ENCOURAGED, ENCOURAGES,
ENCOURAGING (v)**  to inspire with courage,
spirit, or hope; to spur on
Isa 41:7 . . . The carver *e-s* the goldsmith,
Acts 11:23 . . . and he *e-d* the believers
Acts 15:32 . . . length to the believers, *e-ing*
Acts 20:1 . . . sent for the believers and *e-d*
Acts 28:15 . . . he was *e-d* and thanked God.
Rom 1:12 . . . I also want to be *e-d* by yours.
Rom 12:8 . . . your gift is to *e* others,
1 Cor 8:12 . . . other believers by *e-ing*
1 Cor 14:3 . . . strengthens others, *e-s* them,
2 Cor 7:6 . . . who *e-s* those who are
2 Cor 7:6 . . . *e-d* us by the arrival of Titus.
2 Cor 7:13 . . . have been greatly *e-d* by this.
Eph 6:22 . . . how we are doing and to *e*
Col 4:8 . . . how we are doing and to *e* you.

1 Thes 2:12 . . . pleaded with you, *e-d* you,
1 Thes 3:2 . . . to strengthen you, to *e* you
1 Thes 3:7 . . . we have been greatly *e-d* in
1 Thes 5:11 . . . So *e* each other
1 Thes 5:14 . . . *E* those who are timid.
Titus 1:9 . . . he will be able to *e* others
Heb 12:5 . . . you forgotten the *e-ing* words
1 Pet 5:12 . . . purpose in writing is to *e* you
2 Jn 1:11 . . . Anyone who *e-s* such people

**ENCOURAGEMENT (n)**  the act of encouraging;
the state of being encouraged
Rom 15:5 . . . who gives this patience and *e,*
1 Cor 16:18 . . . a wonderful *e* to me,
2 Cor 7:13 . . . In addition to our own *e,*
Eph 4:29 . . . an *e* to those who hear them.
Phil 2:1 . . . any *e* from belonging to Christ?
Phlm 20 . . . Give me this *e* in Christ.

**END, ENDS (n)**  the point where something
ceases to exist; death and destruction; goal or
result toward which some action or agent is
heading
Ps 65:8 . . . live at the *e-s* of the earth stand
Eccl 3:11 . . . work from beginning to *e.*
Isa 30:8 . . . stand until the *e* of time
Isa 49:6 . . . bring my salvation to the *e-s*
Matt 24:13 . . . the one who endures to the *e*
Matt 24:14 . . . and then the *e* will come.
Matt 24:31 . . . farthest *e-s* of the earth
1 Cor 15:24 . . . After that the *e* will come,
Phil 3:14 . . . press on to reach the *e* of
Rev 21:6 . . . the Beginning and the *E.*
Rev 22:13 . . . the Beginning and the *E.*

**END, ENDING, ENDS (v)**  to come to an end; to
die
1 Sam 12:23 . . . sin against the LORD by *e-ing*
Prov 14:12 . . . but it *e-s* in death.
Prov 14:13 . . . the laughter *e-s,* the grief
Prov 29:23 . . . Pride *e-s* in humiliation,
Isa 9:7 . . . its peace will never *e.*
Eph 2:15 . . . by *e-ing* the system of law

**ENDURANCE (n)**  the ability to withstand
hardship or adversity
*see also* PERSEVERANCE
Rom 5:3 . . . they help us develop *e.*
Col 1:11 . . . have all the *e* and patience
2 Thes 1:4 . . . your *e* and faithfulness
Heb 12:1 . . . let us run with *e* the race
Jas 1:3 . . . when your faith is tested, your *e*
2 Pet 1:6 . . . self-control with patient *e,*
Rev 1:9 . . . in the patient *e* to which Jesus

**ENDURE, ENDURED, ENDURES, ENDURING
(v)**  to withstand, suffer, or persevere
*see also* PERSEVERE
Ps 89:2 . . . Your faithfulness is as *e-ing* as
Ps 136:1 . . . faithful love *e-s* forever.
Matt 10:22 . . . everyone who *e-s* to the end
Mark 13:13 . . . one who *e-s* to the end
1 Cor 13:7 . . . *e-s* through every
2 Cor 1:6 . . . Then you can patiently *e*
2 Cor 6:4 . . . patiently *e* troubles and
2 Tim 2:3 . . . *E* suffering along with me,
2 Tim 2:12 . . . If we *e* hardship,
2 Tim 3:11 . . . suffering I have *e-d.*
Heb 12:2 . . . he *e-d* the cross,
Heb 12:3 . . . hostility he *e-d* from sinful
Heb 12:7 . . . As you *e* this divine discipline,
Jas 1:12 . . . who patiently *e* testing and
Jas 5:11 . . . those who *e* under suffering.

1 Pet 2:19 . . . patiently *e* unfair treatment.
Rev 13:10 . . . must *e* persecution patiently

**ENEMY, ENEMIES (n)** foe—personal, national, or spiritual
Ps 23:5 . . . the presence of my *e-ies.*
Ps 62:7 . . . a rock where no *e* can reach me.
Prov 16:7 . . . even their *e-ies* are at peace
Prov 24:17 . . . rejoice when your *e-ies* fall;
Prov 25:21 . . . If your *e-ies* are hungry,
Prov 27:6 . . . than many kisses from an *e.*
Isa 51:13 . . . fear the anger of your *e-ies?*
Isa 59:18 . . . repay his *e-ies* for their evil
Matt 5:44 . . . love your *e-ies!* Pray for those
Luke 6:35 . . . Love your *e-ies!* Do good to
Luke 10:19 . . . over all the power of the *e,*
Rom 5:10 . . . while we were still his *e-ies,*
Rom 12:20 . . . If your *e-ies* are hungry,
1 Cor 15:25 . . . until he humbles all his *e-ies*
1 Cor 15:26 . . . the last *e* to be destroyed
Phil 3:18 . . . they are really *e-ies* of the cross
Jas 4:4 . . . makes you an *e* of God?
1 Pet 5:8 . . . Watch out for your great *e,*

**ENTER, ENTERED, ENTERING, ENTERS (v)** to go or come in;
Ps 100:4 . . . *E* his gates
Matt 5:20 . . . you will never *e* the Kingdom
Matt 7:13 . . . *e* God's Kingdom only
Matt 19:23 . . . rich person to *e* the
Mark 9:43 . . . *e* eternal life with only
Mark 10:23 . . . for the rich to *e* the
Luke 11:52 . . . prevent others from *e-ing.*
Luke 13:24 . . . Work hard to *e* the narrow
Luke 18:17 . . . like a child will never *e* it.
John 3:5 . . . no one can *e* the Kingdom
John 10:2 . . . who *e-s* through the gate
Rom 5:12 . . . When Adam sinned, sin *e-ed*
Heb 3:11 . . . will never *e* my place of rest.
Heb 4:1 . . . God's promise of *e-ing* his rest
Heb 4:11 . . . do our best to *e* that rest.
Heb 9:12 . . . of goats and calves—he *e-ed*

**ENTHRONED (v)** to seat ceremonially on a throne or in a place associated with power and authority
1 Sam 4:4 . . . *e* between the cherubim.
2 Kgs 19:15 . . . *e* between the mighty
1 Chr 13:6 . . . *e* between the cherubim.
Ps 22:3 . . . you are holy, *e* on the praises
Ps 113:5 . . . God, who is *e* on high?
Isa 37:16 . . . God of Israel, you are *e*

**ENTHUSIASM (n)** strong excitement of feeling; zeal, fervor, passion
Neh 4:6 . . . the people had worked with *e.*
Prov 19:2 . . . *E* without knowledge
Rom 10:2 . . . I know what *e* they have
2 Cor 8:7 . . . your *e,* and your love
2 Cor 8:16 . . . Titus the same *e* for you
2 Cor 9:2 . . . your *e* that stirred up
Eph 6:7 . . . Work with *e,*

**ENTHUSIASTIC (adj)** filled with or marked by zeal, fervor, or passion
Ps 45:15 . . . a joyful and *e* procession
Acts 18:25 . . . about Jesus with an *e* spirit
Rom 15:17 . . . I have reason to be *e* about

**ENTRUST, ENTRUSTED (v)** to commit to another with confidence
Ps 31:5 . . . I *e* my spirit into your hand.
Luke 12:48 . . . has been *e-ed* with much,
Luke 23:46 . . . I *e* my spirit into your

Acts 15:40 . . . left, the believers *e-ed* him
Acts 20:32 . . . And now I *e* you to God
Rom 3:2 . . . Jews were *e-ed* with the whole
1 Thes 2:4 . . . to be *e-ed* with the Good News.
1 Tim 1:11 . . . Good News *e-ed* to me
2 Tim 1:14 . . . truth that has been *e-ed* to you.
1 Pet 5:2 . . . flock that God has *e-ed* to you.

**ENVY (n)** discontent or resentment because of another's success, advantages, or superiority
*see also* JEALOUSY
Mark 7:22 . . . lustful desires, *e,* slander,
Rom 1:29 . . . sin, greed, hate, *e,* murder,
Gal 5:21 . . . *e,* drunkenness, wild parties,
Titus 3:3 . . . full of evil and *e,* and we hated
Jas 4:5 . . . within us is filled with *e?*

**ENVY (v)** to feel or show envy; to begrudge
Prov 3:31 . . . Don't *e* violent people
Prov 24:1 . . . Don't *e* evil people

**EPILEPTIC (adj)** relating to, affected with, or having characteristics of epilepsy
Matt 4:24 . . . were demon-possessed or *e* or

**EQUIP (v)** to prepare; to furnish for service or action
Eph 4:12 . . . to *e* God's people to do
2 Tim 3:17 . . . to prepare and *e* his people
Heb 13:21 . . . *e* you with all you need

**ESCAPE, ESCAPED, ESCAPING (v)** to avoid; to get free of or break away from
Ps 89:48 . . . can *e* the power of the grave.
Ps 139:7 . . . I can never *e* from your Spirit!
Matt 23:33 . . . will you *e* the judgment
1 Cor 3:15 . . . barely *e-ing* through a wall of
Heb 2:3 . . . think we can *e* if we ignore
Heb 12:25 . . . we will certainly not *e* if we
2 Pet 2:18 . . . those who have barely *e-d*
2 Pet 2:20 . . . *e* from the wickedness

**ETERNAL (adj)** having infinite duration; valid or existing at all times
*see also* EVERLASTING, FOREVER
Gen 9:16 . . . will remember the *e* covenant
Exod 3:15 . . . my *e* name, my name to
Lev 24:8 . . . a requirement of the *e*
Num 18:19 . . . an *e* and unbreakable
Ps 119:142 . . . Your justice is *e,*
Jer 50:5 . . . with an *e* covenant
Dan 4:34 . . . and his kingdom is *e.*
Dan 7:14 . . . His rule is *e*—
Matt 8:8 . . . better to enter *e* life with
Matt 19:16 . . . must I do to have *e* life?
Matt 25:41 . . . into the *e* fire
Matt 25:46 . . . away into *e* punishment,
Mark 3:29 . . . a sin with *e* consequences.
Luke 10:25 . . . should I do to inherit *e* life?
Luke 18:18 . . . should I do to inherit *e* life?
John 3:15 . . . in him will have *e* life.
John 3:16 . . . not perish but have *e* life.
John 3:36 . . . believes in God's Son has *e*
John 5:29 . . . will rise to experience *e* life,
John 5:39 . . . you think they give you *e* life.
John 6:68 . . . the words that give *e* life.
John 12:50 . . . his commands lead to *e* life;
John 17:2 . . . He gives *e* life
Rom 1:20 . . . *e* power and divine nature
Rom 5:21 . . . resulting in *e* life through
Rom 6:23 . . . free gift of God is *e* life
Rom 9:5 . . . is worthy of *e* praise! Amen.
Rom 16:26 . . . the *e* God has commanded,

Eph 3:11 . . . This was his *e* plan,
2 Thes 1:9 . . . punished with *e* destruction,
1 Tim 6:12 . . . Hold tightly to the *e* life
Titus 3:7 . . . we will inherit *e* life.
Heb 5:9 . . . source of *e* salvation
Heb 9:15 . . . *e* inheritance God has
Heb 13:20 . . . an *e* covenant with his blood—
1 Pet 1:23 . . . from the *e,* living word
1 Pet 5:10 . . . to share in his *e* glory
1 Jn 1:2 . . . he is the one who is *e* life.
1 Jn 2:25 . . . we enjoy the *e* life he
1 Jn 5:20 . . . and he is *e* life.
Jude 1:7 . . . the *e* fire of God's judgment.
Jude 1:21 . . . who will bring you *e* life.

**ETERNITY (n)** immortality; infinite time
Eccl 3:11 . . . has planted *e* in the human
Isa 57:15 . . . who lives in *e,* the Holy One,
John 12:25 . . . will keep it for *e.*

**EVERLASTING (adj)** continuing indefinitely
*see also* ETERNAL, FOREVER
Gen 17:7 . . . This is the *e* covenant:
Gen 48:4 . . . as an *e* possession.
2 Sam 23:5 . . . made an *e* covenant with
Ps 139:24 . . . lead me along the path of *e* life.
Isa 9:6 . . . God, *E* Father, Prince of Peace.
Isa 35:10 . . . crowned with *e* joy.
Isa 40:28 . . . The LORD is the *e* God,
Isa 54:8 . . . But with *e* love
Isa 55:3 . . . an *e* covenant with you.
Isa 60:19 . . . God will be your *e* light,
Isa 60:20 . . . the LORD will be your *e* light.
Isa 61:7 . . . and *e* joy will be yours.
Isa 61:8 . . . an *e* covenant with them.
Jer 10:10 . . . the living God and the *e* King!
Jer 31:3 . . . with an *e* love.
Ezek 16:60 . . . establish an *e* covenant with
Dan 4:34 . . . His rule is *e,*
Dan 9:24 . . . to bring in *e* righteousness,
Dan 12:2 . . . to *e* life and some to shame
Gal 6:8 . . . will harvest *e* life from the

**EVIL (adj)** bad, sinful, or morally reprehensible; of the Devil
Gen 6:5 . . . was consistently and totally *e.*
Exod 32:22 . . . know how *e* these people
Ps 51:4 . . . what is *e* in your sight.
Ps 140:8 . . . not let *e* people have their way.
Prov 15:26 . . . The LORD detests *e* plans,
Matt 6:13 . . . rescue us from the *e* one.
Matt 12:45 . . . spirits more *e* than itself,
Matt 15:19 . . . from the heart come *e*
Mark 7:21 . . . heart, come *e* thoughts,
Luke 11:24 . . . When an *e* spirit leaves
John 17:15 . . . them safe from the *e* one.
Acts 19:13 . . . casting out *e* spirits.
Rom 2:9 . . . keeps on doing what is *e*—
Rom 13:14 . . . to indulge your *e* desires.
1 Cor 5:13 . . . remove the *e* person from
Eph 5:16 . . . in these *e* days.
Col 3:5 . . . lust, and *e* desires.
2 Thes 3:3 . . . guard you from the *e* one.
1 Tim 6:4 . . . slander, and *e* suspicions.
2 Tim 3:13 . . . *e* people and impostors
1 Jn 2:13 . . . your battle with the *e* one.
1 Jn 3:12 . . . Cain, who belonged to the *e* one
1 Jn 5:18 . . . the *e* one cannot touch

**EVIL (n)** something that brings sorrow, distress, or misfortune
Gen 2:9 . . . of the knowledge of good and *e.*
Gen 3:5 . . . knowing both good and *e.*

Judg 6:1 . . . The Israelites did *e*
Ps 5:5 . . . for you hate all who do *e.*
Ps 14:4 . . . Will those who do *e* never learn?
Ps 34:13 . . . tongue from speaking *e*
Ps 37:27 . . . Turn from *e* and do good,
Ps 45:7 . . . You love justice and hate *e.*
Ps 53:4 . . . Will those who do *e* never learn?
Ps 92:15 . . . There is no *e* in him!
Ps 101:4 . . . and stay away from every *e.*
Ps 125:5 . . . with those who do *e.*
Prov 6:18 . . . a heart that plots *e,*
Prov 8:13 . . . fear the LORD will hate *e.*
Prov 11:27 . . . search for *e,* it will find you!
Prov 13:6 . . . but the *e* are misled by sin.
Prov 17:13 . . . repay good with *e, e* will
Prov 20:30 . . . cleanses away *e;* such
Isa 5:20 . . . those who say that *e* is good
Isa 13:11 . . . punish the world for its *e*
Jer 23:14 . . . who are doing *e* so that
Hab 1:13 . . . cannot stand the sight of *e.*
Mal 3:15 . . . those who do *e* get rich,
Matt 5:45 . . . to both the *e* and the good,
Luke 13:27 . . . all you who do *e.*
John 3:20 . . . All who do *e* hate the light
Rom 12:21 . . . Don't let *e* conquer you,
1 Cor 14:20 . . . babies when it comes to *e,*
1 Thes 5:15 . . . no one pays back *e* for *e,*
1 Thes 5:22 . . . away from every kind of *e.*
1 Tim 6:10 . . . the root of all kinds of *e.*
2 Tim 2:19 . . . must turn away from *e.*
Heb 1:9 . . . You love justice and hate *e.*
Jas 1:21 . . . get rid of all the filth and *e*
Jas 3:8 . . . It is restless and *e,*
1 Pet 2:16 . . . as an excuse to do *e.*
1 Pet 3:9 . . . Don't repay *e* for *e.*
1 Pet 3:11 . . . Turn away from *e* and do
3 Jn 1:11 . . . those who do *e* prove that they

**EVILDOERS (n)** one who does evil
Ps 92:7 . . . like weeds and *e* flourish,
Ps 92:9 . . . perish; all *e* will be scattered.
Ps 94:16 . . . will stand up for me against *e?*
Prov 21:15 . . . it terrifies *e.*
Prov 24:19 . . . Don't fret because of *e;*

**EXALT, EXALTED, EXALTING, EXALTS (v)** to
elevate; to glorify; to raise in rank or power
*see also* GLORIFY, HONOR
Exod 15:2 . . . and I will *e* him!
2 Sam 22:47 . . . of my salvation, be *e-ed!*
Neh 9:5 . . . May it be *e-ed* above all blessing
Job 36:7 . . . kings and *e-s* them forever.
Ps 18:46 . . . God of my salvation be *e-ed!*
Ps 30:1 . . . I will *e* you, LORD,
Ps 92:8 . . . O LORD, will be *e-ed* forever.
Ps 97:9 . . . you are *e-ed* far above all gods.
Ps 107:32 . . . Let them *e* him publicly
Ps 145:1 . . . I will *e* you, my God and King,
Dan 11:36 . . . as he pleases, *e-ing* himself
Luke 14:11 . . . those who *e* themselves will
Acts 2:33 . . . is *e-ed* to the place of highest
2 Thes 2:4 . . . He will *e* himself

**EXAMINE, EXAMINED, EXAMINES,
EXAMINING (v)** to test the condition of; to
inspect closely
1 Chr 29:17 . . . you *e* our hearts
Ps 11:4 . . . *e-ing* every person on earth.
Ps 11:5 . . . The LORD *e-s* both
Ps 17:3 . . . *e-d* my heart in the night.
Ps 139:1 . . . LORD, you have *e-d* my heart
Prov 5:21 . . . *e-ing* every path he takes.

Prov 21:2 . . . the LORD *e-s* their heart.
Jer 11:20 . . . you *e* the deepest thoughts
Jer 17:10 . . . and *e* secret motives.
Lam 3:40 . . . let us test and *e* our ways.
1 Cor 4:4 . . . Lord himself who will *e*
1 Cor 11:28 . . . you should *e* yourself
2 Cor 13:5 . . . *E* yourselves to see
1 Thes 2:4 . . . He alone *e-s* the motives

**EXAMPLE, EXAMPLES (n)** one that serves as a
pattern to be or not to be imitated
John 13:15 . . . given you an *e* to
1 Cor 10:11 . . . happened to them as *e-s* for
2 Thes 3:9 . . . give you an *e* to follow.
Titus 2:7 . . . *e* to them by doing good
Heb 13:7 . . . and follow the *e* of their faith.
Jas 5:10 . . . For *e-s* of patience in suffering,
1 Pet 2:21 . . . He is your *e,* and you must

**EXCUSE (n)** the apology or justification offered
John 15:22 . . . they have no *e* for their sin.
Rom 1:20 . . . no *e* for not knowing God.
Rom 2:1 . . . and you have no *e!*
1 Pet 2:16 . . . your freedom as an *e*

**EXCUSE (v)** to overlook, justify, or make an
apology for
Exod 34:7 . . . But I do not *e* the guilty.
Eph 5:6 . . . those who try to *e* these sins,

**EXHORT(ATION) (KJV)**
Rom 12:8 . . . If your gift is to *encourage*
1 Thes 2:3 . . . not *preaching* with any deceit
Heb 3:13 . . . You must *warn* each other

**EXORCISTS (n)** one who expels evil spirits
Luke 11:19 . . . what about your own *e?*

**EXPLAIN, EXPLAINED, EXPLAINS (v)** to make
plain or understandable; to give the reason or
cause
Gen 2:24 . . . This *e-s* why a man leaves his
Neh 8:8 . . . and clearly *e-ed* the meaning
Matt 19:5 . . . This *e-s* why a man leaves his
Acts 17:3 . . . He *e-ed* the prophecies
Acts 18:28 . . . *e-ed* to them that Jesus was
Eph 6:19 . . . *e* God's mysterious plan
2 Tim 2:15 . . . correctly *e-s* the word of
1 Pet 3:15 . . . always be ready to *e* it.

**EXPLOIT (v)** to make use of meanly or unfairly
for one's own advantage
Exod 22:22 . . . must not *e* a widow or an
  orphan.
Prov 22:22 . . . or *e* the needy in court.

**EXPLOITED (n)** one unfairly used for another's
advantage
Isa 11:4 . . . fair decisions for the *e.*

**EXTOL(LED) (KJV)**
Ps 30:1 . . . will *exalt* you, LORD, for you
Ps 66:17 . . . to him for help, *praising* him
Ps 68:4 . . . *Sing loud praises* to him who
Isa 52:13 . . . he will be *highly exalted*

**EYE, EYES (n)** organ of (physical and spiritual)
sight
Exod 21:24 . . . an *e* for an *e,*
Deut 16:19 . . . bribes blind the *e-s* of
Job 36:7 . . . never takes his *e-s* off the
Ps 119:18 . . . Open my *e-s* to see
Ps 119:37 . . . Turn my *e-s* from worthless
Ps 123:1 . . . I lift my *e-s* to you,
Prov 4:25 . . . and fix your *e-s* on what
Matt 5:29 . . . *e*—causes you to lust,
Matt 5:38 . . . An *e* for an *e,*

Matt 6:22 . . . When your *e* is good,
1 Cor 2:9 . . . when they say, "No *e* has seen,
Heb 12:2 . . . by keeping our *e-s* on Jesus,
2 Pet 1:16 . . . with our own *e-s*
Rev 21:4 . . . wipe every tear from their *e-s,*

**FACE (n)** in or into direct contact or
confrontation (as in "face to face"); countenance;
presence; the front part of the head
Gen 32:30 . . . I have seen God *f* to *f,*
Exod 33:11 . . . speak to Moses *f* to *f,*
Exod 34:29 . . . his *f* had become radiant
Num 12:8 . . . I speak to him *f* to *f,*
Deut 31:17 . . . hiding my *f* from them,
Judg 6:22 . . . angel of the LORD *f* to *f!*
2 Chr 7:14 . . . and seek my *f* and turn from
Ps 4:6 . . . Let your *f* smile on us,
Ps 17:15 . . . I will see you *f* to *f*
Ps 67:1 . . . May his *f* smile with favor on us.
Luke 9:29 . . . appearance of his *f* was
2 Cor 3:7 . . . For his *f* shone with the glory
Rev 1:16 . . . And his *f* was like the sun
Rev 22:4 . . . they will see his *f,*

**FACE, FACED, FACING (v)** to confront; to be
confronted by
Ps 112:8 . . . *f* their foes triumphantly.
Ps 116:6 . . . I was *f-ing* death, and he saved
2 Cor 6:5 . . . *f-d* angry mobs,

**FADE, FADING (v)** to lose freshness, strength,
or vitality
Isa 40:7 . . . and the flowers *f*
1 Cor 9:25 . . . to win a prize that will *f*
2 Cor 3:7 . . . brightness was already *f-ing*
2 Cor 3:13 . . . it was destined to *f* away.
Jas 1:11 . . . the rich will *f* away
1 Jn 2:17 . . . this world is *f-ing* away,

**FAIL, FAILED, FAILS (v)** to disappoint; to fall
short; to weaken; to miss performing an
expected service; to be unsuccessful
Num 23:19 . . . spoken and *f-ed* to act?
Deut 31:6 . . . He will neither *f* you
Josh 23:14 . . . Not a single one has *f-ed!*
1 Kgs 8:56 . . . Not one word has *f-ed*
Ps 77:8 . . . his promises permanently *f-ed?*
Luke 13:24 . . . try to enter but will *f.*
Luke 22:32 . . . faith should not *f.*
Rom 9:6 . . . has God *f-ed* to fulfill his promise
2 Cor 13:5 . . . if not, you have *f-ed* the test
2 Cor 13:6 . . . we have not *f-ed* the test
Heb 12:15 . . . none of you *f-s* to receive
Heb 13:5 . . . I will never *f* you.
1 Pet 4:19 . . . he will never *f* you.

**FAINT (adj)** lacking strength or vigor
Jon 4:8 . . . grew *f* and wished to die.

**FAINT (v)** to become weak or lose courage in
body or spirit
Isa 40:31 . . . will walk and not *f.*

**FAIR (adj)** free from self-interest, prejudice, or
favoritism; beautiful
Prov 1:3 . . . do what is right, just, and *f.*
Song 2:13 . . . away with me, my *f* one!
Isa 11:4 . . . make *f* decisions for the
Rom 3:25 . . . God was being *f* when he
Rom 3:26 . . . he himself is *f* and just,
Col 4:1 . . . be just and *f* to your slaves.

**FAIRNESS (n)** the quality of being free from
self-interest, prejudice, or favoritism

Ps 9:8 . . . rule the nations with *f*.
Ps 98:9 . . . and the nations with *f*.
Ps 99:4 . . . you have established *f*.
Isa 9:7 . . . will rule with *f* and justice

**FAITH (n)** reliance, loyalty, or complete trust in God; a system of religious beliefs
*see also* BELIEVE, TRUST
Exod 14:31 . . . They put their *f* in the LORD
Isa 7:9 . . . Unless your *f* is firm,
Matt 9:2 . . . Seeing their *f*, Jesus said
Matt 9:29 . . . Because of your *f*, it will
Matt 15:28 . . . your *f* is great.
Matt 17:20 . . . *f* even as small as a mustard
Matt 21:22 . . . if you have *f*, you will receive
Mark 10:52 . . . for your *f* has healed you.
Luke 5:20 . . . Seeing their *f*, Jesus said
Luke 7:50 . . . Your *f* has saved you;
Luke 8:48 . . . your *f* has made you well.
Luke 12:28 . . . Why do you have so little *f?*
Luke 17:6 . . . *f* even as small as a mustard
Luke 18:8 . . . find on the earth who have *f?*
John 16:1 . . . won't abandon your *f*.
Acts 6:5 . . . full of *f* and the Holy Spirit
Acts 14:9 . . . he had *f* to be healed.
Acts 14:27 . . . opened the door of *f* to the
Acts 16:5 . . . strengthened in their *f* and grew
Acts 24:24 . . . told them about *f* in Christ
Rom 1:8 . . . your *f* in him is being talked about
Rom 1:12 . . . to encourage you in your *f*,
Rom 1:17 . . . from start to finish by *f*.
Rom 1:17 . . . through *f* that a righteous
Rom 3:28 . . . right with God through *f*
Rom 3:30 . . . right with himself only by *f*,
Rom 3:31 . . . only when we have *f*
Rom 4:5 . . . because of their *f* in God
Rom 4:9 . . . because of his *f*.
Rom 4:12 . . . same kind of *f* Abraham had
Rom 4:13 . . . with God that comes by *f*.
Rom 4:14 . . . then *f* is not necessary
Rom 4:16 . . . the promise is received by *f*.
Rom 4:16 . . . if we have *f* like Abraham's.
Rom 4:19 . . . And Abraham's *f* did not weaken,
Rom 4:20 . . . In fact, his *f* grew stronger,
Rom 5:1 . . . made right in God's sight by *f*,
Rom 5:2 . . . Because of our *f*, Christ has
Rom 10:8 . . . message about *f* that we preach:
Rom 10:17 . . . So *f* comes from hearing,
Rom 12:6 . . . speak out with as much *f* as
Rom 14:1 . . . believers who are weak in *f*,
1 Cor 12:9 . . . gives great *f* to another,
1 Cor 13:13 . . . *f*, hope, and love—
1 Cor 15:14 . . . and your *f* is useless.
1 Cor 16:13 . . . Stand firm in the *f*.
2 Cor 1:24 . . . put your *f* into practice.
2 Cor 13:5 . . . failed the test of genuine *f*.
Gal 1:23 . . . the very *f* he tried to destroy!
Gal 3:9 . . . all who put their *f* in Christ
Gal 3:11 . . . *f* that a righteous person
Gal 3:12 . . . This way of *f* is very different
Gal 3:14 . . . Holy Spirit through *f*.
Gal 3:23 . . . the way of *f* in Christ was available
Gal 3:24 . . . made right with God through *f*.
Gal 3:25 . . . the way of *f* has come,
Gal 3:26 . . . children of God through *f* in Christ
Gal 5:5 . . . wait to receive by *f*
Eph 1:15 . . . heard of your strong *f* in the Lord
Eph 4:5 . . . one Lord, one *f*, one baptism,
Eph 6:16 . . . hold up the shield of *f*
Phil 1:25 . . . experience the joy of your *f*.
Phil 3:9 . . . righteous through *f* in Christ.

Col 1:4 . . . we have heard of your *f* in Christ
1 Thes 1:8 . . . telling us about your *f* in God.
1 Thes 3:5 . . . your *f* was still strong.
1 Thes 3:10 . . . fill the gaps in your *f*.
2 Thes 1:3 . . . because your *f* is flourishing
1 Tim 1:4 . . . live a life of *f* in God.
1 Tim 1:19 . . . Cling to your *f* in Christ,
1 Tim 3:9 . . . mystery of the *f* now
1 Tim 4:1 . . . will turn away from the true *f;*
1 Tim 6:10 . . . have wandered from the true *f*
1 Tim 6:12 . . . good fight for the true *f*.
2 Tim 1:5 . . . remember your genuine *f*,
2 Tim 2:18 . . . away from the *f*.
2 Tim 3:10 . . . You know my *f*, my patience,
Titus 1:1 . . . have been sent to proclaim *f*
Titus 1:13 . . . make them strong in the *f*.
Titus 2:2 . . . must have sound *f* and be filled
Phlm 5 . . . hearing about your *f* in the Lord
Phlm 6 . . . that comes from your *f*
Heb 4:2 . . . they didn't share the *f*
Heb 6:1 . . . and placing our *f* in God.
Heb 6:12 . . . because of their *f* and endurance.
Heb 10:38 . . . will live by *f*.
Heb 11:5 . . . It was by *f* that Enoch
Heb 11:7 . . . It was by *f* that Noah
Heb 11:8 . . . It was by *f* that Abraham
Heb 11:23 . . . It was by *f* that Moses' parents
Heb 11:29 . . . It was by *f* that the people
Heb 12:2 . . . perfects our *f*.
Jas 1:3 . . . when your *f* is tested,
Jas 2:5 . . . be rich in *f?*
Jas 2:14 . . . Can that kind of *f* save anyone?
Jas 2:17 . . . *f* by itself isn't enough.
Jas 2:18 . . . Some people have *f;*
Jas 2:20 . . . *f* without good deeds
Jas 2:22 . . . made his *f* complete.
Jas 2:24 . . . not by *f* alone.
Jas 2:26 . . . so also *f* is dead
Jas 5:15 . . . prayer offered in *f* will heal
1 Pet 1:21 . . . have placed your *f* and hope
2 Pet 1:1 . . . the same precious *f* we have.
Jude 1:3 . . . defend the *f* that God
Jude 1:20 . . . in your most holy *f*,

**FAITHFUL (adj)** firm in adherence, utterly loyal
*see also* LOYAL, TRUSTWORTHY
Deut 7:9 . . . He is the *f* God who keeps his
1 Sam 2:9 . . . will protect his *f* ones,
1 Sam 20:14 . . . me with the *f* love of the
2 Sam 22:26 . . . you show yourself *f;* to those
1 Kgs 8:61 . . . you be completely *f* to the
1 Kgs 15:14 . . . remained completely *f* to
2 Kgs 20:3 . . . have always been *f* to you
Ps 18:25 . . . you show yourself *f;* to those
Ps 71:22 . . . because you are *f* to your
Ps 89:8 . . . You are entirely *f*.
Ps 89:49 . . . with a *f* pledge.
Ps 143:1 . . . you are *f* and righteous.
Isa 38:3 . . . have always been *f* to you and
Hos 11:12 . . . God and is *f* to the Holy One.
Zech 8:3 . . . be called the *F* City;
Zech 8:8 . . . I will be *f* and just toward
Matt 24:45 . . . A *f*, sensible
Matt 25:21 . . . You have been *f* in handling
Matt 25:23 . . . my good and *f* servant.
Luke 12:42 . . . Lord replied, "A *f*, sensible
Luke 16:10 . . . If you are *f* in little
1 Cor 4:17 . . . my beloved and *f* child in the
2 Cor 1:18 . . . as God is *f*, our word to you
Eph 1:1 . . . who are *f* followers of Christ
Phil 2:17 . . . just like your *f* service is

Col 4:7 . . . brother and *f* helper who
Col 4:9 . . . Onesimus, a *f* and beloved
1 Thes 1:3 . . . we think of your *f* work,
1 Thes 5:24 . . . calls you is *f*.
2 Thes 3:3 . . . But the Lord is *f;* he will
1 Tim 3:2 . . . He must be *f* to his wife.
1 Tim 3:11 . . . and be *f* in everything they
1 Tim 5:9 . . . old and was *f* to her husband.
2 Tim 4:7 . . . I have remained *f*.
Heb 2:17 . . . merciful and *f* High Priest
Heb 3:2 . . . For he was *f* to God, who
Heb 8:9 . . . They did not remain *f* to my
Heb 13:4 . . . marriage, and remain *f* to one
1 Jn 1:9 . . . to him, he is *f* and just to
Rev 1:5 . . . He is the *f* witness to these
Rev 2:10 . . . But if you remain *f* even when
Rev 3:14 . . . is the Amen—the *f* and true
Rev 17:14 . . . chosen and *f* ones will be

**FAITHFULNESS (n)** the quality of steadfast loyalty or firm adherence to promises
Exod 34:6 . . . unfailing love and *f*.
Ps 25:10 . . . with unfailing love and *f*
Ps 36:5 . . . your *f* reaches beyond
Ps 57:10 . . . Your *f* reaches to the clouds.
Ps 92:2 . . . your *f* in the evening,
Ps 100:5 . . . *f* continues to each
Prov 14:22 . . . unfailing love and *f*.
Prov 16:6 . . . love and *f* make atonement
Prov 20:28 . . . love and *f* protect the king;
Isa 38:18 . . . no longer hope in your *f*.
Lam 3:23 . . . Great is his *f;*
Gal 5:22 . . . kindness, goodness, *f*,
Eph 6:23 . . . give you love with *f*.
2 Thes 1:4 . . . your endurance and *f*
2 Tim 2:22 . . . pursue righteous living, *f*,

**FALL, FALLEN, FALLING (v)** to collapse; to drop down (wounded or dead); to become lower in degree or level; to come by assignment or inheritance; to descend; to stumble or stray (morally)
2 Sam 1:19 . . . the mighty heroes have *f-en!*
Ps 37:24 . . . they will never *f*,
Ps 69:9 . . . those who insult you have *f-en* on
Prov 10:8 . . . babbling fools *f* flat on their
Prov 24:17 . . . when your enemies *f;*
Isa 14:12 . . . How you are *f-en* from heaven,
Matt 13:21 . . . They *f* away as soon as
Luke 10:18 . . . I saw Satan *f* from heaven
Rom 3:23 . . . we all *f* short of
Rom 14:13 . . . believer to stumble and *f*.
Gal 5:4 . . . have *f-en* away from God's grace.
2 Pet 1:10 . . . and you will never *f* away.
Jude 1:24 . . . able to keep you from *f-ing* away

**FALSE (adj)** intentionally untrue; dishonest; misleading; unwise; faithless
Prov 12:17 . . . a *f* witness tells lies.
Isa 44:25 . . . I expose the *f* prophets as
Matt 24:11 . . . And many *f* prophets will
Mark 13:22 . . . For *f* messiahs and *f*
2 Cor 11:13 . . . These people are *f* apostles.
Titus 1:11 . . . by their *f* teaching.
2 Pet 2:1 . . . were also *f* prophets in Israel,
1 Jn 4:1 . . . many *f* prophets in the world.
Rev 16:13 . . . and the *f* prophet.
Rev 19:20 . . . beast and his *f* prophet were
Rev 20:10 . . . the beast and the *f* prophet.

**FAMILY, FAMILIES (n)** a household unit of related people, as in a clan

Josh 24:15 . . . my *f,* we will serve the LORD.
Ps 68:6 . . . God places the lonely in *f-ies;*
Mark 3:25 . . . a *f* splintered by feuding
Luke 9:61 . . . let me say good-bye to my *f.*
Luke 12:52 . . . *f-ies* will be split apart,
Gal 6:10 . . . to those in the *f* of faith.
Eph 2:19 . . . members of God's *f.*
1 Tim 3:4 . . . manage his own *f* well,
Titus 1:11 . . . whole *f-ies* away from the truth
1 Jn 3:9 . . . who have been born into God's *f*

**FAST, FASTING (v)** to abstain from food
Ps 35:13 . . . denied myself by *f-ing* for
Joel 2:12 . . . Come with *f-ing,* weeping,
Matt 6:16 . . . when you *f,* don't make it
Acts 13:2 . . . worshiping the Lord and *f-ing,*
Acts 14:23 . . . prayer and *f-ing,* they turned

**FATHER, FATHERS (n)** male parent;
ancestor(s); characteristic of a mentor or
provider relationship; name and role for God in
relation to the children he fosters/adopts;
originator or creator
*see also* MOTHER, PARENT
Gen 2:24 . . . a man leaves his *f* and mother
Gen 17:4 . . . make you the *f* of a multitude
Exod 20:12 . . . Honor your *f* and mother.
Exod 21:15 . . . Anyone who strikes *f* or
Deut 32:6 . . . he your *F* who created you?
2 Sam 7:14 . . . I will be his *f,* and he
Ps 2:7 . . . Today I have become your *F.*
Ps 89:26 . . . You are my *F,* my God,
Prov 10:1 . . . wise child brings joy to a *f;*
Prov 23:22 . . . Listen to your *f,*
Isa 9:6 . . . Everlasting *F,* Prince of Peace.
Isa 63:16 . . . you would still be our *F.*
Jer 3:19 . . . forward to your calling me '*F, '*
Ezek 22:10 . . . sleep with their *f-s '* wives
Mal 2:10 . . . children of the same *F?*
Mal 4:6 . . . will turn the hearts of *f-s*
Matt 5:16 . . . will praise your heavenly *F.*
Matt 6:9 . . . Our *F* in heaven, may your
Matt 6:14 . . . heavenly *F* will forgive
Matt 10:37 . . . If you love your *f* or mother
Matt 11:27 . . . no one truly knows the *F*
Matt 15:4 . . . Honor your *f* and mother,
Matt 16:27 . . . in the glory of his *F*
Matt 19:5 . . . a man leaves his *f* and mother
Matt 19:29 . . . or *f* or mother or children
Matt 23:9 . . . is your spiritual *F.*
Luke 1:17 . . . hearts of the *f-s* to their
Luke 9:59 . . . and bury my *f.*
John 4:21 . . . you worship the *F* on this
John 5:17 . . . My *F* is always working,
John 5:20 . . . For the *F* loves the Son
John 6:44 . . . come to me unless the *F*
John 6:65 . . . unless the *F* gives them
John 8:19 . . . you don't know who my *F* is.
John 8:41 . . . God himself is our true *F.*
John 10:38 . . . understand that the *F* is in me,
John 14:6 . . . come to the *F* except through
John 14:21 . . . love me, my *F* will love
John 15:8 . . . brings great glory to my *F.*
John 15:23 . . . also hates my *F.*
John 20:17 . . . ascending to my *F* and
Acts 13:33 . . . Today I have become your *F.*
Rom 4:11 . . . Abraham is the spiritual *f*
Rom 4:16 . . . Abraham is the *f* of all who
Rom 8:15 . . . we call him, "Abba, *F. "*
2 Cor 6:18 . . . I will be your *F,* and you
Eph 5:31 . . . man leaves his *f* and mother
Eph 6:2 . . . Honor your *f* and mother.

Eph 6:4 . . . *F-s,* do not provoke
Phil 2:11 . . . to the glory of God the *F.*
Col 3:21 . . . *F-s,* do not aggravate
Heb 12:7 . . . is never disciplined by its *f?*
Heb 12:9 . . . earthly *f-s* who disciplined
1 Jn 1:3 . . . fellowship is with the *F* and
1 Jn 2:15 . . . the love of the *F* in you.
1 Jn 2:22 . . . who denies the *F* and the Son
1 Jn 3:1 . . . See how very much our *F* loves
Rev 3:21 . . . sat with my *F* on his throne.

**FAVOR, FAVORS (n)** gracious kindness;
approval from a superior; a special privilege or
right granted or conceded
*see also* GRACE
Gen 6:8 . . . Noah found *f* with the LORD.
Exod 34:9 . . . if it is true that I have found *f*
1 Sam 2:26 . . . and grew in *f* with the LORD
Prov 3:4 . . . you will find *f* with both God
Prov 18:22 . . . receives *f* from the LORD.
Prov 19:6 . . . Many seek *f-s* from a ruler;
Zech 11:7 . . . named one *F* and the other
Luke 1:30 . . . you have found *f* with God!
Luke 2:40 . . . and God's *f* was on him.
Luke 2:52 . . . and in *f* with God
Luke 4:19 . . . the time of the LORD's *f*
Rom 11:7 . . . have not found the *f* of God
Phil 1:7 . . . with me the special *f* of God,

**FAVOR, FAVORING (v)** to show partiality
toward
Lev 19:15 . . . justice in legal matters by *f-ing*
Jas 2:9 . . . But if you *f* some people over

**FAVORITE (adj)** having special favor or liking
Gen 27:4 . . . Prepare my *f* dish,

**FAVORITES (n)** a person specially loved,
trusted, or provided with favors
*see also* PARTIALITY
Job 32:21 . . . I won't play *f*
Matt 22:16 . . . and don't play *f.*
Gal 2:6 . . . for God has no *f.*
Eph 6:9 . . . he has no *f.*
Col 3:25 . . . For God has no *f.*

**FAVORITISM (n)** the showing of special favor;
partiality
*see also* DISCRIMINATION, PARTIALITY
Prov 24:23 . . . *f* when passing judgment.
Mal 2:9 . . . *f* in the way you carry out
Acts 10:34 . . . that God shows no *f.*
Rom 2:11 . . . God does not show *f.*
Jas 3:17 . . . It shows no *f* and is always

**FEAR, FEARS (n)** dread or alarm in facing
danger; profound reverence and awe
2 Sam 23:3 . . . who rules in the *f* of God,
Ps 2:11 . . . Serve the LORD with reverent *f,*
Ps 34:4 . . . freed me from all my *f-s.*
Prov 1:33 . . . untroubled by *f* of harm.
Heb 13:6 . . . will have no *f.*

**FEAR, FEARED, FEARING, FEARS (v)** to have
reverential awe of God; to be afraid or
apprhehensive
Deut 6:13 . . . You must *f* the LORD your
Deut 8:6 . . . walking in his ways and *f-ing*
Deut 13:4 . . . your God and *f* him alone.
Deut 31:12 . . . learn to *f* the LORD your God
Josh 4:24 . . . might *f* the LORD your God
1 Sam 12:14 . . . if you *f* and worship
2 Chr 26:5 . . . taught him to *f* God.
Neh 5:15 . . . But because I *f-ed* God,
Neh 7:2 . . . a faithful man who *f-ed* God

Job 1:1 . . . He *f-ed* God
Job 1:8 . . . He *f-s* God and stays away from
Ps 34:7 . . . and defends all who *f* him.
Ps 46:2 . . . not *f* when earthquakes come
Ps 61:5 . . . for those who *f* your name.
Ps 76:7 . . . you are greatly *f-ed!*
Ps 103:17 . . . with those who *f* him.
Ps 128:1 . . . joyful are those who *f* the
Prov 8:13 . . . All who *f* the LORD will
Prov 28:14 . . . those who *f* to do wrong,
Prov 31:30 . . . a woman who *f-s* the LORD
Isa 25:3 . . . nations will *f* you.
Jer 2:19 . . . your God and not to *f* him.
Mal 3:16 . . . those who *f-ed* the LORD spoke
Mal 4:2 . . . for you who *f* my name,
2 Cor 7:1 . . . because we *f* God.
Rev 11:18 . . . and all who *f* your name,

**FEAST (n)** an elaborate meal; banquet
Ps 23:5 . . . You prepare a *f* for me
Prov 15:15 . . . life is a continual *f.*
Luke 15:29 . . . goat for a *f* with my friends.

**FEAST, FEASTING (v)** to enjoy a good meal
Esth 9:17 . . . with a day of *f-ing* and
gladness.
Prov 17:1 . . . a house filled with *f-ing*—and
Prov 23:20 . . . or *f* with gluttons,
Isa 22:13 . . . You *f* on meat and drink wine.

**FEED, FEEDS (v)** to give food to; to eat; to
provide something essential to the development,
sustenance, maintenance, or operation of
Prov 15:14 . . . while the fool *f-s* on trash.
Prov 22:9 . . . because they *f* the poor.
Jer 50:19 . . . own land, to *f* in the fields
Matt 6:26 . . . your heavenly Father *f-s* them.
Matt 14:16 . . . you *f* them.
Matt 25:42 . . . and you didn't *f* me.
John 6:57 . . . anyone who *f-s* on me will live
John 21:15 . . . Then *f* my lambs,
John 21:17 . . . Then *f* my sheep.
Rom 12:20 . . . enemies are hungry, *f* them.

**FEET (n)** *see also* FOOT
Ps 22:16 . . . pierced my hands and *f.*
Ps 40:2 . . . He set my *f* on solid ground
Ps 73:2 . . . My *f* were slipping,
Ps 119:105 . . . a lamp to guide my *f*
Isa 52:7 . . . are the *f* of the messenger
Matt 10:14 . . . shake its dust from your *f*
Luke 24:39 . . . Look at my *f.*
John 13:5 . . . began to wash the disciples' *f,*
John 13:14 . . . wash each other's *f.*
Rom 10:15 . . . beautiful are the *f* of
Rom 16:20 . . . crush Satan under your *f.*
1 Cor 15:25 . . . his enemies beneath his *f.*
Heb 1:13 . . . a footstool under your *f.*
Heb 12:13 . . . a straight path for your *f*

**FELLOWSHIP (n)** friendship; association;
company; partnership
Gen 5:24 . . . walking in close *f* with God.
1 Cor 5:2 . . . remove this man from your *f.*
2 Cor 13:14 . . . and the *f* of the Holy Spirit
1 Jn 1:3 . . . you may have *f* with us.
1 Jn 1:3 . . . And our *f* is with the Father and
1 Jn 1:6 . . . we say we have *f* with God but
1 Jn 2:27 . . . remain in *f* with Christ.

**FIELD, FIELDS (n)** an open land area free of
woods and buildings; an area of cleared land
used for cultivation
Lev 19:9 . . . along the edges of your *f-s,*

Ruth 2:2 . . . into the harvest *f - s* to pick
Isa 40:6 . . . the flowers in a *f.*
Matt 6:28 . . . Look at the lilies of the *f*
Matt 13:44 . . . hidden in a *f.*
Luke 2:8 . . . staying in the *f - s* nearby,
John 4:35 . . . The *f - s* are already ripe
1 Cor 3:9 . . . And you are God's *f.*
1 Pet 1:24 . . . like a flower in the *f.*

**FIGHT, FIGHTS (n)**  a hostile encounter; a
struggle for a goal or an objective
Prov 15:18 . . . person starts *f - s;* a cool-
Prov 20:3 . . . Avoiding a *f* is a mark of
Prov 29:22 . . . An angry person starts *f - s;*
2 Tim 4:7 . . . fought the good *f,*
Jas 4:1 . . . causing the quarrels and *f - s*

**FIGHT, FIGHTING, FIGHTS (v)**  to actively
oppose or combat, as with weapons; to gain by
struggle
*see also* FOUGHT
Exod 14:14 . . . LORD himself will *f* for you.
Josh 23:10 . . . LORD your God *f - s* for you,
1 Sam 17:32 . . . I'll go *f* him!
1 Sam 25:28 . . . are *f - i n g* the LORD's battles.
Neh 4:20 . . . our God will *f* for us!
Prov 28:25 . . . Greed causes *f - i n g;*
Ps 35:1 . . . *F* those who *f* against me.
Isa 49:25 . . . I will *f* those who *f* you,
1 Cor 15:32 . . . value was there in *f - i n g* wild
Phil 1:27 . . . *f - i n g* together for the faith
1 Tim 6:12 . . . *F* the good fight
Jas 4:2 . . . so you *f* and wage war

**FILL, FILLED, FILLS (v)**  to occupy the whole
of; to supply fully; to spread through
Gen 1:28 . . . *F* the earth and govern it.
Exod 34:6 . . . *f - e d* with unfailing love
1 Kgs 8:11 . . . presence of the LORD *f - e d* the
Ps 81:10 . . . and I will *f* it with good things.
Ps 107:9 . . . the thirsty and *f - s* the hungry
Ps 119:64 . . . unfailing love *f - s* the earth;
Ps 123:3 . . . have had our *f* of contempt.
Isa 6:3 . . . whole earth is *f - e d* with his glory!
Joel 2:13 . . . and *f - e d* with unfailing love.
Jon 4:2 . . . and *f - e d* with unfailing love.
Hag 2:7 . . . I will *f* this place with glory,
Luke 1:15 . . . be *f - e d* with the Holy Spirit,
Luke 1:41 . . . was *f - e d* with the Holy Spirit.
Luke 1:67 . . . *f - e d* with the Holy Spirit
Luke 2:40 . . . He was *f - e d* with wisdom,
Luke 24:49 . . . Holy Spirit comes and *f - s*
Acts 2:4 . . . was *f - e d* with the Holy Spirit
Acts 2:28 . . . you will *f* me with the joy
Acts 4:8 . . . *f - e d* with the Holy Spirit,
Acts 4:31 . . . all *f - e d* with the Holy Spirit.
Acts 9:17 . . . be *f - e d* with the Holy Spirit.
Acts 13:9 . . . was *f - e d* with the Holy Spirit,
Rom 5:5 . . . Holy Spirit to *f* our hearts
Rom 15:13 . . . *f* you completely with joy
Eph 1:23 . . . by Christ, who *f - s* all things
Eph 5:18 . . . be *f - e d* with the Holy Spirit,
Col 3:16 . . . in all its richness, *f* your lives.

**FIND, FINDS (v)**  to attain or reach (a goal or
conclusion); to discover by searching or effort;
to experience
1 Chr 28:9 . . . seek him, you will *f* him.
Job 23:3 . . . knew where to *f* God,
Prov 3:13 . . . the person who *f - s* wisdom,
Prov 8:17 . . . who search will surely *f* me.
Prov 8:35 . . . For whoever *f - s* me *f - s* life
Prov 11:27 . . . you will *f* favor;

Prov 31:10 . . . Who can *f* a virtuous and
Isa 55:6 . . . while you can *f* him.
Jer 6:16 . . . will *f* rest for your souls.
Matt 7:7 . . . seeking, and you will *f.*
Matt 7:8 . . . Everyone who seeks, *f - s.*
Matt 10:39 . . . your life for me, you will *f* it.
Luke 11:9 . . . and you will *f.*
Luke 11:10 . . . Everyone who seeks, *f - s.*
Luke 15:4 . . . that is lost until he *f - s* it?
Luke 15:8 . . . search carefully until she *f - s* it?

**FINGER, FINGERS (n)**  any of the five
terminating members of the hand; figurative for
the power of God
Exod 8:19 . . . This is the *f* of God!
Exod 31:18 . . . written by the *f* of God.
Deut 9:10 . . . had written with his own *f*
Luke 16:24 . . . dip the tip of his *f* in water
John 8:6 . . . wrote in the dust with his *f.*
John 20:25 . . . in his hands, put my *f - s* into

**FIRE, FIRES (n)**  hot flame and burning light;
symbolic of hell; severe trial or ordeal
Exod 3:2 . . . *f* from the middle of a bush.
Exod 13:21 . . . a pillar of *f.*
Dan 3:25 . . . walking around in the *f*
Matt 3:11 . . . the Holy Spirit and with *f.*
Matt 5:22 . . . are in danger of the *f - s* of hell.
Mark 9:43 . . . the unquenchable *f - s* of hell
Matt 18:8 . . . be thrown into eternal *f*
Mark 9:49 . . . be tested with *f.*
Luke 3:16 . . . with the Holy Spirit and with *f.*
Acts 2:3 . . . tongues of *f* appeared and
1 Cor 3:13 . . . The *f* will show
Heb 12:29 . . . God is a devouring *f.*
Jas 3:6 . . . it is set on *f* by hell itself.

**FIRMAMENT (KJV)**
Gen 1:7 . . . this *space* to separate the waters
Ps 19:1 . . . *skies* display his craftsmanship
Ezek 1:22 . . . surface like the *sky,* glittering
Dan 12:3 . . . will shine as bright as the *sky*

**FIRST (adj)**  preceding all others in time, order,
or importance
Gen 1:5 . . . morning came, marking the *f* day.
Isa 44:6 . . . I am the *F* and the Last;
Isa 48:12 . . . God, the *F* and the Last.
Matt 22:38 . . . the *f* and greatest
Mark 9:35 . . . wants to be *f* must take last
Mark 13:10 . . . Good News must *f* be
Rom 1:16 . . . Jew *f* and also the Gentile.
Rom 2:9 . . . Jew *f* and also for the Gentile.
1 Cor 15:45 . . . The *f* man, Adam,
Eph 6:2 . . . the *f* commandment with a
1 Tim 2:13 . . . God made Adam *f,*
Heb 10:9 . . . He cancels the *f* covenant
1 Jn 4:19 . . . because he loved us *f.*
Rev 1:17 . . . I am the *F* and the Last.
Rev 22:13 . . . and the Omega, the *F* and the

**FIRSTBEGOTTEN (KJV)**
Heb 1:6 . . . his *supreme Son* into the world

**FIRSTBORN (n)**  eldest; the most prominent;
the rightful heir
Gen 25:34 . . . for his rights as the *f.*
Exod 11:5 . . . All the *f* sons will die
Exod 13:2 . . . every *f* among the Israelites.
Exod 34:19 . . . The *f* of every animal
Exod 34:20 . . . buy back every *f* son.
Ps 89:27 . . . I will make him my *f* son,
Mic 6:7 . . . sacrifice our *f* children to pay
Heb 12:23 . . . the assembly of God's *f*

**FIRSTFRUITS (KJV)**
Exod 23:16 . . . the *first crops* of your harvest
Exod 23:19 . . . bring the *very best* of
Lev 2:14 . . . *first portion* of your harvest
Lev 23:10 . . . you harvest its *first crops,*
Num 28:26 . . . the *first* of your new grain
Rev 14:4 . . . as a *special offering* to God

**FISH (n)**  any of numerous cold-blooded
aquatic vertebrates
Jon 1:17 . . . had arranged for a great *f*
Matt 12:40 . . . in the belly of the great *f*
Luke 9:13 . . . loaves of bread and two *f,*
John 6:9 . . . five barley loaves and two *f.*

**FISH, FISHED, FISHING (v)**  to attempt to
catch fish
Mark 1:16 . . . for they *f - e d* for a living.
Mark 1:17 . . . how to *f* for people!
Luke 5:10 . . . you'll be *f - i n g* for people!

**FISHERMEN (n)**  those who attempt to catch fish
Ezek 26:5 . . . a rock in the sea, a place for *f*

**FISHERS (KJV)**
Isa 19:8 . . . *fishermen* will lament for lack of
    work
Jer 16:16 . . . *fishermen* who will catch
Matt 4:19 . . . show you *how to fish* for people

**FLATTER (v)**  to praise excessively out of self-
interest
Job 32:21 . . . or try to *f* anyone.
Prov 29:5 . . . To *f* friends is
Dan 11:32 . . . He will *f* and win over those
Jude 1:16 . . . they *f* others to get what they want.

**FLATTERING (adj)**  characterized by excessive
praise out of self-interest
Ps 12:2 . . . speaking with *f* lips
Ps 12:3 . . . cut off their *f* lips
Prov 26:28 . . . and *f* words cause ruin.

**FLATTERY (n)**  insincere or excessive praise
Job 32:22 . . . For if I tried *f,* my Creator
Ps 5:9 . . . tongues are filled with *f.*
Prov 28:23 . . . criticism far more than *f.*
1 Thes 2:5 . . . try to win you with *f,*

**FLESH (n)**  the meaty part of animal and human
bodies
*see also* BODY, HUMAN
Gen 2:23 . . . and *f* from my *f!*
John 6:51 . . . so the world may live, is my *f.*
1 Cor 15:39 . . . different kinds of *f—*

**FLOCK, FLOCKS (n)**  a group of animals
assembled or herded together; a group under
the guidance of a leader
Isa 40:11 . . . feed his *f* like a shepherd.
Jer 10:21 . . . and their *f - s* are scattered.
Jer 31:10 . . . as a shepherd does his *f.*
Zech 11:17 . . . who abandons the *f!*
Matt 26:31 . . . the *f* will be scattered.
Luke 2:8 . . . guarding their *f - s* of sheep.
Luke 12:32 . . . don't be afraid, little *f.*
John 10:16 . . . one *f* with one shepherd.
Acts 20:28 . . . shepherd God's *f—*

**FLOOD, FLOODS (n)**  a rising and overflowing
of a body of water; the destruction of the world
by water during the time of Noah
Gen 7:7 . . . the boat to escape the *f—*
Prov 27:4 . . . cruel, and wrath is like a *f,*
Matt 24:38 . . . In those days before the *f,*
Luke 6:49 . . . the *f - s* sweep down against
2 Pet 2:5 . . . ungodly people with a vast *f.*

**FOLLOW, FOLLOWED, FOLLOWING, FOLLOWS (v)** to pursue or run after; to imitate; to obey
Deut 1:36 . . . because he has *f-ed* the LORD
Deut 5:32 . . . *f-ing* his instructions
Josh 14:14 . . . he wholeheartedly *f-ed* the
1 Kgs 3:3 . . . loved the LORD and *f-ed*
2 Chr 10:14 . . . and *f-ed* the counsel
Prov 4:27 . . . feet from *f-ing* evil.
Prov 10:9 . . . those who *f* crooked paths
Isa 57:2 . . . For those who *f* godly paths
Isa 65:2 . . . But they *f* their own evil paths
Matt 4:20 . . . at once and *f-ed* him.
Matt 7:24 . . . listens to my teaching and *f-s*
Matt 8:19 . . . I will *f* you wherever you go.
Matt 8:22 . . . *F* me now. Let the
Matt 9:9 . . . got up and *f-ed* him.
Matt 16:24 . . . take up your cross, and *f*
Matt 19:27 . . . given up everything to *f* you.
Matt 26:58 . . . Meanwhile, Peter *f-ed* him
Mark 1:17 . . . Come, *f* me, and I will show
Luke 9:23 . . . your cross daily, and *f* me.
Luke 17:23 . . . go out and *f* them.
Luke 18:43 . . . *f-ed* Jesus, praising God.
John 8:12 . . . If you *f* me, you won't have to
John 10:4 . . . they *f* him because they know
John 10:27 . . . know them, and they *f* me.
John 12:26 . . . to be my disciple must *f* me,
John 21:19 . . . Jesus told him, "*F* me."
1 Cor 1:12 . . . or "I *f* only Christ."
1 Cor 4:17 . . . of how I *f* Christ Jesus,
Gal 5:7 . . . you back from *f-ing* the truth?
Gal 5:25 . . . *f* the Spirit's leading
Phil 2:12 . . . you always *f-ed* my instructions
Phil 3:17 . . . those who *f* our example.
2 Thes 3:6 . . . and don't *f* the tradition
1 Pet 2:21 . . . must *f* in his steps.
Rev 14:4 . . . as virgins, *f-ing* the Lamb

**FOLLOWER, FOLLOWERS (n)** one who follows the teachings of another; a disciple
1 Kgs 18:3 . . . was a devoted *f* of the LORD.
Matt 10:42 . . . one of the least of my *f-s,*
Matt 18:20 . . . together as my *f-s,* I am there
Acts 9:21 . . . Jesus' *f-s* in Jerusalem?

**FOLLY (KJV)**
Prov 14:18 . . . clothed with *foolishness*
Prov 26:11 . . . a fool repeats his *foolishness*
Eccl 2:13 . . . Wisdom is better than *foolishness*
Isa 9:17 . . . they all speak *foolishness*
2 Tim 3:9 . . . recognize what *fools* they are

**FOOD (n)** something that nourishes, sustains, or supplies energy and vitality
*see also* BREAD
Lev 11:2 . . . the ones you may use for *f.*
Prov 25:21 . . . hungry, give them *f* to eat.
Isa 58:7 . . . Share your *f* with the hungry,
Dan 1:8 . . . defile himself by eating the *f*
Matt 6:11 . . . today the *f* we need,
Matt 6:25 . . . Isn't life more than *f,*
Mark 7:19 . . . every kind of *f* is acceptable
John 6:55 . . . my flesh is true *f,* and my
John 13:18 . . . eats my *f* has turned against
Acts 15:20 . . . abstain from eating *f*
Rom 14:6 . . . kind of *f* do so to honor
1 Tim 6:8 . . . have enough *f* and clothing,
Jas 2:15 . . . who has no *f* or clothing,

**FOOL, FOOLS (n)** one deficient in intellectual, practical, or moral sense
1 Sam 25:25 . . . He is a *f,* just as his name

Ps 14:1 . . . Only *f-s* say in their hearts,
Prov 6:32 . . . commits adultery is an utter *f,*
Prov 10:8 . . . babbling *f-s* fall flat on
Prov 10:23 . . . wrong is fun for a *f,*
Prov 17:7 . . . are not fitting for a *f;*
Prov 17:16 . . . to pay tuition to educate a *f,*
Prov 26:1 . . . associated with *f-s* than snow
Prov 26:7 . . . A proverb in the mouth of a *f*
Prov 29:11 . . . *F-s* vent their anger,
Prov 29:20 . . . more hope for a *f* than for
Rom 1:22 . . . became utter *f-s.*
1 Cor 3:18 . . . need to become a *f* to be
2 Cor 11:21 . . . I'm talking like a *f* again—
Eph 5:15 . . . Don't live like *f-s,*
2 Tim 3:9 . . . will recognize what *f-s* they are,

**FOOLISH (adj)** lacking in sense, judgment, or discretion; irreverent
Prov 26:4 . . . the *f* arguments of fools,
Prov 26:17 . . . else's argument is as *f*
Rom 1:28 . . . abandoned them to their *f*
1 Cor 1:18 . . . the cross is *f* to those who
1 Cor 1:27 . . . world considers *f* in order to
1 Cor 2:14 . . . It all sounds *f* to them
Eph 5:4 . . . Obscene stories, *f* talk,
1 Tim 6:20 . . . Avoid godless, *f* discussions
Titus 3:9 . . . not get involved in *f* discussions

**FOOT (n)** the end of the leg upon which an individual stands
*see also* FEET
Josh 1:3 . . . Wherever you set *f,*
Matt 18:8 . . . with only one hand or one *f*
Luke 4:11 . . . won't even hurt your *f*
1 Cor 12:15 . . . If the *f* says,
Rev 10:2 . . . and his left *f* on the land.

**FOOTSTOOL (n)** a low stool used to support the feet
Ps 110:1 . . . making them a *f* under
Isa 66:1 . . . throne, and the earth is my *f.*
Matt 5:35 . . . the earth is his *f.*
Acts 7:49 . . . the earth is my *f.*
Heb 1:13 . . . making them a *f* under
Heb 10:13 . . . and made a *f* under

**FORCE (n)** violence, compulsion, or constraint exerted upon or against a person or thing
Zech 4:6 . . . is not by *f* nor by strength,

**FORCE, FORCED (v)** to compel by physical, moral, or intellectual means
Matt 27:32 . . . soldiers *f-d* him to carry
John 6:15 . . . were ready to *f* him to be

**(FORE)FATHERS (KJV)**
Exod 10:6 . . . *ancestors* seen a plague like
Num 11:12 . . . swore to give their *ancestors*
Jer 11:10 . . . the sins of their *forefathers*
Matt 23:32 . . . what your *ancestors* started

**FOREHEAD, FOREHEADS (n)** the part of the face above the eyes
Exod 13:9 . . . on your hand or your *f.*
Deut 6:8 . . . wear them on your *f*
1 Sam 17:49 . . . in the *f.*
Rev 9:4 . . . seal of God on their *f-s.*
Rev 13:16 . . . right hand or on the *f.*
Rev 14:1 . . . written on their *f-s.*

**FOREIGNER, FOREIGNERS (n)** nonresident, alien, or sojourner
*see also* STRANGER
Exod 22:21 . . . not mistreat or oppress *f-s*
Exod 23:9 . . . must not oppress *f-s.*

Lev 24:22 . . . to the *f-s* living among you.
Neh 9:2 . . . separated themselves from all *f-s*
Ps 119:19 . . . I am only a *f* in the land
Hos 7:8 . . . mingle with godless *f-s,*
Luke 17:18 . . . glory to God except this *f?*
1 Cor 14:11 . . . I will be a *f* to someone
Eph 2:19 . . . no longer strangers and *f-s.*
1 Pet 1:1 . . . living as *f-s* in the provinces
1 Pet 2:11 . . . temporary residents and *f-s*

**FOREKNOW, FOREKNEW, FOREKNOWLEDGE (KJV)**
Acts 2:23 . . . God *knew what would happen*
Rom 8:29 . . . God *knew* his people *in advance*
Rom 11:2 . . . whom he *chose from the very beginning*
1 Pet 1:2 . . . Father *knew you and chose you long*

**FOREORDAINED (KJV)**
1 Pet 1:20 . . . *chose* him *as* your ransom

**FOREVER (adv)** for a limitless time; continually
*see also* ETERNAL, EVERLASTING
Gen 3:22 . . . they will live *f!*
Gen 17:8 . . . be their possession *f,*
2 Sam 7:26 . . . name be honored *f*
1 Chr 17:24 . . . be established and honored *f*
1 Chr 29:10 . . . be praised *f* and ever!
Ezra 9:12 . . . prosperity to your children *f.*
Ps 9:7 . . . the LORD reigns *f,*
Ps 21:4 . . . of his life stretch on *f.*
Ps 28:9 . . . in your arms *f.*
Ps 37:28 . . . keep them safe *f,*
Ps 61:8 . . . sing praises to your name *f*
Ps 73:26 . . . he is mine *f.*
Ps 79:13 . . . will thank you *f* and ever,
Ps 86:12 . . . glory to your name *f,*
Ps 92:8 . . . will be exalted *f.*
Ps 100:5 . . . unfailing love continues *f,*
Ps 103:17 . . . the LORD remains *f* with
Ps 107:1 . . . faithful love endures *f.*
Ps 110:4 . . . are a priest *f*
Ps 111:8 . . . They are *f* true,
Ps 112:9 . . . be remembered *f.*
Ps 119:152 . . . laws will last *f.*
Ps 146:6 . . . every promise *f.*
Isa 32:17 . . . and confidence *f.*
Isa 51:6 . . . but my salvation lasts *f.*
Isa 60:15 . . . make you beautiful *f,*
Isa 63:12 . . . making himself famous *f?*
Jer 25:5 . . . you and your ancestors *f.*
Dan 2:44 . . . and it will stand *f.*
Dan 4:3 . . . kingdom will last *f,* his rule
Dan 7:27 . . . kingdom will last *f,*
John 6:51 . . . eats this bread will live *f;*
1 Cor 13:8 . . . But love will last *f!*
1 Cor 13:13 . . . Three things will last *f—*
1 Cor 15:42 . . . will be raised to live *f.*
1 Cor 15:50 . . . inherit what will last *f.*
2 Cor 4:17 . . . and will last *f!*
2 Cor 4:18 . . . cannot see will last *f.*
1 Thes 4:17 . . . will be with the Lord *f.*
2 Thes 1:9 . . . destruction, *f* separated
Heb 5:6 . . . a priest *f* in the order
Heb 7:17 . . . a priest *f* in the order
Heb 7:24 . . . Jesus lives *f.*
Heb 9:12 . . . secured our redemption *f.*
Heb 13:8 . . . yesterday, today, and *f.*
1 Pet 1:25 . . . word of the Lord remains *f.*
1 Jn 2:17 . . . will live *f.*
Rev 22:5 . . . they will reign *f* and ever.

**FORGAVE (v)** *see* also FORGIVE
Ps 78:38 . . . was merciful and *f* their sins
Luke 7:42 . . . so he kindly *f* them both,
Eph 1:7 . . . his Son and *f* our sins.
Col 1:14 . . . our freedom and *f* our sins.
Col 2:13 . . . with Christ, for he *f* all our

**FORGIVE, FORGIVEN, FORGIVES,**
**FORGIVING (v)** to pardon or acquit of sins
*see also* FORGAVE
Gen 50:17 . . . Please *f* your brothers
Exod 23:21 . . . he will not *f* your rebellion.
Exod 34:7 . . . I *f* iniquity, rebellion,
Exod 34:9 . . . but please *f* our iniquity and
Num 14:18 . . . *f-ing* every kind of sin
Num 14:19 . . . just as you have *f-n* them
1 Sam 3:14 . . . never be *f-n* by sacrifices
1 Kgs 8:34 . . . hear from heaven and *f*
Ps 65:3 . . . by our sins, you *f* them all.
Ps 79:9 . . . Save us and *f* our sins
Ps 86:5 . . . so good, so ready to *f*,
Ps 103:3 . . . He *f-s* all my sins
Prov 17:9 . . . when a fault is *f-n*,
Isa 22:14 . . . you will never be *f-n* for this
Isa 38:17 . . . and *f-n* all my sins.
Isa 55:7 . . . for he will *f* generously.
Jer 31:34 . . . I will *f* their wickedness,
Dan 9:19 . . . O Lord, hear. O Lord, *f.*
Hos 14:2 . . . *F* all our sins and
Matt 6:12 . . . and *f* us our sins,
Matt 6:14 . . . If you *f* those who sin
Matt 6:15 . . . if you refuse to *f* others,
Matt 9:6 . . . authority on earth to *f* sins.
Matt 18:21 . . . how often should I *f*
Matt 26:28 . . . to *f* the sins of many.
Mark 2:7 . . . Only God can *f* sins!
Mark 2:10 . . . authority on earth to *f* sins.
Mark 3:29 . . . will never be *f-n.*
Mark 11:25 . . . first *f* anyone you are
Mark 11:25 . . . will *f* your sins,
Luke 5:21 . . . Only God can *f* sins!
Luke 5:24 . . . authority on earth to *f* sins.
Luke 6:37 . . . *F* others, and you will be
Luke 7:47 . . . a person who is *f-n* little
Luke 7:49 . . . he goes around *f-ing* sins?
Luke 11:4 . . . *f* us our sins, as we
Luke 17:3 . . . if there is repentance, *f.*
Luke 17:4 . . . asks forgiveness, you must *f.*
Luke 23:34 . . . Father, *f* them,
John 20:23 . . . If you *f* anyone's sins,
Acts 5:31 . . . repent of their sins and be *f-n.*
Acts 8:22 . . . Perhaps he will *f* your evil
Rom 4:5 . . . faith in God who *f-s* sinners.
Rom 4:7 . . . whose disobedience is *f-n*,
2 Cor 2:7 . . . time to *f* and comfort
2 Cor 2:10 . . . When you *f* this man,
Col 3:13 . . . so you must *f* others.
Heb 8:12 . . . I will *f* their wickedness,
1 Jn 1:9 . . . is faithful and just to *f* us

**FORGIVENESS (n)** acquittal or pardon of sins
*see also* ATONEMENT, MERCY
Neh 9:17 . . . you are a God of *f*,
Luke 24:47 . . . There is *f* of sins for all
Acts 13:38 . . . this man Jesus there is *f*
Rom 5:15 . . . his gift of *f* to many
Heb 9:22 . . . of blood, there is no *f.*
Jas 5:20 . . . bring about the *f* of many sins.

**FORMED (v)** to create, fashion, or give shape
to something
*see also* CREATE(D), MADE, MAKE

Gen 2:7 . . . the LORD God *f* the man
Gen 2:19 . . . LORD God *f* from the ground
Ps 94:9 . . . the one who *f* your eyes?
Isa 49:5 . . . the one who *f* me
Jer 1:5 . . . knew you before I *f* you
Heb 11:3 . . . universe was *f* at God's

**FORNICATION (KJV)**
Isa 23:17 . . . *be a prostitute* to all kingdoms
Matt 19:9 . . . wife has been *unfaithful*
1 Cor 5:1 . . . *sexual immorality* going on
1 Cor 6:18 . . . *sexual immorality* is a sin
Jude 1:7 . . . were filled with *immorality*

**FORTRESS (n)** a fortified place; a place of
security or survival
*see also* REFUGE
2 Sam 22:2 . . . my *f*, and my savior;
Ps 27:1 . . . The LORD is my *f*,
Ps 71:3 . . . my rock and my *f.*
Ps 144:2 . . . and my *f*, my tower of safety,
Prov 18:10 . . . LORD is a strong *f;*
Zeph 3:6 . . . devastating their *f* walls and

**FORTY (adj)** the number 40
Gen 7:4 . . . for *f* days and *f* nights,
Exod 16:35 . . . Israel ate manna for *f* years
Exod 24:18 . . . *f* days and *f* nights.
Num 14:34 . . . wilderness for *f* years—
Matt 4:2 . . . For *f* days and *f* nights
Acts 1:3 . . . the *f* days after his crucifixion,
Acts 13:18 . . . *f* years of wandering

**FOUGHT (v)** *see* also FIGHT
Gen 32:28 . . . because you have *f* with God
Josh 10:14 . . . Surely the LORD *f* for Israel
2 Tim 4:7 . . . I have *f* the good fight,

**FOUNDATION (n)** basis upon which
something is built, supported, or added to;
substructure
Prov 1:7 . . . Fear of the LORD is the *f*
Prov 9:10 . . . the LORD is the *f* of wisdom.
Isa 28:16 . . . placing a *f* stone in Jerusalem,
Luke 6:49 . . . a house without a *f.*
Eph 2:20 . . . built on the *f* of the apostles
1 Tim 3:15 . . . pillar and *f* of the truth.
2 Tim 2:19 . . . stands firm like a *f* stone
Heb 1:10 . . . you laid the *f* of the earth

**FOUNTAIN (n)** source; spring of water
Isa 12:3 . . . from the *f* of salvation!
Zech 13:1 . . . a *f* to cleanse them

**FREE (adj)** not bound, confined, or
detained by force; without restraint,
inhibition, or cost; possessing the rights
of citizenship
John 8:32 . . . the truth will set you *f.*
John 8:36 . . . sets you *f*, you are truly *f.*
Rom 6:7 . . . we were set *f* from the power
Rom 6:18 . . . you are *f* from your slavery
Gal 3:28 . . . slave or *f*, male and female.
Jas 1:25 . . . the perfect law that sets
you *f*,
1 Pet 2:16 . . . For you are *f*, yet

**FREE, FREED, FREES (v)** to relieve or rid
of what restrains, confines, restricts, or
embarrasses
Ps 116:16 . . . *f-d* me from my chains.
Ps 146:7 . . . The LORD *f-s* the prisoners.
Isa 61:1 . . . prisoners will be *f-d.*
Rom 3:24 . . . he *f-d* us from the penalty
1 Cor 1:30 . . . and he *f-d* us from sin.
Rev 1:5 . . . and has *f-d* us from our sins

**FREEDOM (n)** liberation from slavery, restraint,
or the power of another
Ps 119:45 . . . I will walk in *f*, for I have
2 Cor 3:17 . . . the Lord is, there is *f.*
Gal 2:4 . . . take away the *f* we have in Christ
Gal 4:5 . . . sent him to buy *f* for us
Gal 5:13 . . . don't use your *f* to satisfy
Eph 1:7 . . . purchased our *f* with the blood
1 Pet 2:16 . . . don't use your *f* as an excuse

**FRIEND, FRIENDS (n)** intimate associate; a
favored companion
Prov 16:28 . . . separates the best of *f-s.*
Prov 17:9 . . . on it separates close *f-s.*
Prov 20:6 . . . Many will say they are loyal *f-s*,
Prov 27:6 . . . Wounds from a sincere *f* are
Prov 28:7 . . . with wild *f-s* bring shame
Prov 29:5 . . . To flatter *f-s* is to lay a trap
Isa 41:8 . . . from Abraham my *f*,
Zech 13:6 . . . was wounded at my *f-s'* house!
John 11:3 . . . Lord, your dear *f* is very sick.
John 15:13 . . . one's life for one's *f-s.*
John 15:14 . . . You are my *f-s* if you do
John 15:15 . . . Now you are my *f-s*,
John 19:12 . . . you are no '*f* of Caesar.'
Jas 2:23 . . . even called the *f* of God.
Jas 4:4 . . . want to be a *f* of the world,

**FRIENDSHIP (n)** association of familiarity and
companionship
Prov 3:32 . . . he offers his *f* to the godly.
Rom 5:10 . . . since our *f* with God was
Jas 4:4 . . . you realize that *f* with the world

**FRUIT (n)** a product of plant growth; product
or result
Ps 1:3 . . . bearing *f* each season.
Isa 11:1 . . . new Branch bearing *f* from
Dan 4:12 . . . loaded with *f* for all to eat.
Matt 3:10 . . . not produce good *f* will be
Matt 7:20 . . . can identify a tree by its *f*,
Matt 12:33 . . . is bad, its *f* will be bad.
John 15:2 . . . that doesn't produce *f*,
John 15:16 . . . go and produce lasting *f*,
Gal 5:22 . . . produces this kind of *f*
Phil 1:11 . . . the *f* of your salvation—
2 Tim 2:6 . . . first to enjoy the *f*
Rev 22:2 . . . bearing twelve crops of *f*,

**FRUITFUL (adj)** bearing fruit (product of a tree
or plant); abundant (at producing work or in
bearing children)
Gen 1:22 . . . Be *f* and multiply.
Gen 9:1 . . . Be *f* and multiply.
Gen 35:11 . . . Be *f* and multiply.
Ps 128:3 . . . will be like a *f* grapevine,
Jer 2:7 . . . brought you into a *f* land
Phil 1:22 . . . do more *f* work for Christ.

**FULFILL, FULFILLED, FULFILLS (v)** to
complete or perform as promised; to measure
up or satisfy
Ps 57:2 . . . to God who will *f* his purpose
Dan 9:4 . . . You always *f* your covenant
Matt 2:15 . . . This *f-ed* what the Lord had
Matt 2:23 . . . This *f-ed* what the prophets
Matt 13:35 . . . *f-ed* what God had spoken
Matt 27:9 . . . This *f-ed* the prophecy of
Luke 4:21 . . . has been *f-ed* this very day!
Luke 24:44 . . . the Psalms must be *f-ed.*
John 18:9 . . . this to *f* his own statement:
John 19:28 . . . and to *f* Scripture he said,
Acts 1:16 . . . Scriptures had to be *f-ed*

Rom 3:31 . . . do we truly *f* the law.
Rom 13:8 . . . you will *f* the requirements
Rom 13:10 . . . love *f-s* the requirements
Eph 1:9 . . . plan to *f* his own good pleasure.

**FULL (adj)** possessing or containing a great
amount
Deut 34:9 . . . was *f* of the spirit of wisdom,
Luke 4:1 . . . Then Jesus, *f* of the Holy Spirit,
Acts 6:3 . . . *f* of the Spirit and wisdom.
Acts 6:5 . . . Stephen (a man *f* of faith and
Acts 7:55 . . . Stephen, *f* of the Holy Spirit,
Acts 11:24 . . . man, *f* of the Holy Spirit

**FULLNESS (n)** the quality or state of containing
all that is wanted, needed, or possible
Eph 3:19 . . . with all the *f* of life and
Col 1:19 . . . God in all his *f* was pleased
Col 2:9 . . . lives all the *f* of God

**FURNACE (n)** an enclosed structure in which
heat is produced
Dan 3:6 . . . be thrown into a blazing *f.*
Matt 13:42 . . . throw them into the fiery *f,*

**FURY (n)** wrath; fierceness; rage
Exod 15:7 . . . You unleash your blazing *f;*
Deut 29:28 . . . In great anger and *f*
Jer 32:37 . . . will scatter them in my *f.*

**FUTURE (adj)** existing or occurring at a later
time
Rom 8:19 . . . waiting eagerly for that *f* day

**FUTURE (n)** time that is to come; what is going
to happen
Num 24:14 . . . do to your people in the *f.*
Ps 31:15 . . . My *f* is in your hands.
Ps 37:37 . . . a wonderful *f* awaits those
Isa 42:9 . . . tell you the *f* before it happens.
Isa 46:10 . . . can tell you the *f* before it
Jer 29:11 . . . to give you a *f* and a hope.
Jer 31:17 . . . There is hope for your *f,*


**GAIN (n)** winnings or profits
Isa 56:11 . . . intent on personal *g.*

**GAIN, GAINED, GAINS (v)** to acquire or win; to
profit or increase
Prov 3:13 . . . one who *g-s* understanding.
Prov 11:16 . . . gracious woman *g-s* respect,
Mark 8:36 . . . *g* the whole world but lose your
Luke 9:25 . . . *g* the whole world but are
1 Cor 13:3 . . . I would have *g-ed* nothing.

**GALILEE (n)** a Roman province of Palestine
during the time of Jesus
Isa 9:1 . . . a time in the future when *G*
Matt 4:15 . . . beyond the Jordan River, in *G*
Matt 26:32 . . . I will go ahead of you to *G*
Matt 28:10 . . . my brothers to leave for *G,*

**GARDEN (n)** a planted area where fruits,
vegetables, and flowers are cultivated
Gen 2:8 . . . God planted a *g* in Eden
Gen 2:15 . . . God placed the man in the *G*
1 Kgs 4:25 . . . had its own home and *g.*
Song 4:12 . . . my private *g,* my treasure,
Isa 58:11 . . . will be like a well-watered *g,*
Jer 31:12 . . . life will be like a watered *g,*
Ezek 28:13 . . . in Eden, the *g* of God.

**GARDENER (n)** one who takes care of a garden
John 15:1 . . . my Father is the *g.*

**GATE, GATES (n)** opening in a (city) wall or
fence, consisting of a door and protected by

defensive structures (as towers); the place of
judicial decisions, town criers, and marketplace
trade; entrance
Esth 6:10 . . . sits at the *g* of the palace.
Ps 24:7 . . . Open up, ancient *g-s!*
Ps 100:4 . . . Enter his *g-s* with thanksgiving;
Isa 62:10 . . . Go out through the *g-s!*
Matt 7:13 . . . only through the narrow *g.*
John 10:1 . . . going through the *g,*
John 10:2 . . . who enters through the *g*
John 10:7 . . . I am the *g* for the sheep.
Heb 13:12 . . . died outside the city *g-s*
Rev 21:21 . . . *g-s* were made of pearls—
Rev 21:21 . . . each *g* from a single pearl!

**GAVE (v)**  *see* also GIVE
John 3:16 . . . he *g* his one and only Son,
Rom 8:32 . . . *g* him up for us all,
Gal 2:20 . . . loved me and *g* himself for me.
1 Tim 2:6 . . . He *g* his life to purchase

**GENERATION, GENERATIONS (n)** the whole
body of individuals born about the same time
(nation or racial group); the period of time
during which those individuals lived (also, age
or era); offspring
Gen 17:7 . . . from generation to *g.*
Exod 20:6 . . . love for a thousand *g-s*
Num 32:13 . . . the entire *g* that sinned
Judg 2:10 . . . After that *g* died,
1 Chr 16:15 . . . to a thousand *g-s.*
Ps 71:18 . . . your power to this new *g,*
Ps 100:5 . . . continues to each *g.*
Ps 102:12 . . . endure to every *g.*
Ps 102:18 . . . recorded for future *g-s,*
Ps 105:8 . . . to a thousand *g-s.*
Ps 119:90 . . . extends to every *g,*
Ps 145:4 . . . Let each *g* tell its children
Ps 146:10 . . . throughout the *g-s.*
Prov 27:24 . . . not be passed to the next *g.*
Isa 41:4 . . . summoning each new *g*
Lam 5:19 . . . from generation to *g.*
Joel 1:3 . . . down from *g* to generation.
Matt 12:39 . . . Only an evil, adulterous *g*
Mark 13:30 . . . this *g* will not pass
Luke 1:48 . . . all *g-s* will call me blessed.
Luke 11:29 . . . This evil *g* keeps asking me
Acts 2:40 . . . this crooked *g!*
Eph 3:5 . . . did not reveal it to previous *g-s,*
Eph 3:21 . . . through all *g-s* forever and ever!

**GENEROSITY (n)** the quality or fact of being
magnanimous, kindly, or openhanded;
abundance
Acts 2:46 . . . meals with great joy and *g*—
2 Cor 9:10 . . . a great harvest of *g* in you.
Eph 4:7 . . . through the *g* of Christ.
Phlm 6 . . . put into action the *g* that

**GENEROUS (adj)** magnanimous, kindly; liberal
in giving; abundant
Deut 15:8 . . . Instead, be *g* and lend
Ps 37:26 . . . godly always give *g* loans to
2 Cor 9:6 . . . will get a *g* crop.
1 Tim 6:18 . . . *g* to those in need,

**GENTILE, GENTILES (n)** non-Jewish
individuals or nations, often connoting heathens
or pagans
*see* also NATION(S)
Isa 49:6 . . . I will make you a light to the *G-s,*
Luke 21:24 . . . period of the *G-s* comes
Acts 10:45 . . . out on the *G-s,* too.
Acts 14:27 . . . faith to the *G-s,* too.

Acts 15:14 . . . God first visited the *G-s*
Acts 21:25 . . . As for the *G* believers,
Acts 28:28 . . . also been offered to the *G-s,*
Rom 1:16 . . . and also the *G.*
Rom 2:9 . . . and also for the *G.*
Rom 3:9 . . . all people, whether Jews or *G-s,*
Rom 3:29 . . . God of the *G-s?*
Rom 10:12 . . . Jew and *G* are the same
Rom 11:11 . . . available to the *G-s.*
Rom 15:9 . . . so that the *G-s* might give glory
Rom 15:27 . . . *G-s* received the spiritual
Gal 2:2 . . . preaching to the *G-s.*
Gal 2:8 . . . apostle to the *G-s.*
Gal 2:9 . . . keep preaching to the *G-s,*
Gal 3:8 . . . God would declare the *G-s* to be
Gal 3:14 . . . blessed the *G-s* with the same
Gal 3:28 . . . no longer Jew or *G,* slave or
Eph 3:8 . . . the privilege of telling the *G-s*
Col 3:11 . . . a Jew or a *G,* circumcised or

**GENTLE (adj)** kind; mild-mannered; soft
1 Kgs 19:12 . . . sound of a *g* whisper.
Prov 15:1 . . . A *g* answer deflects anger,
Prov 15:4 . . . *G* words are a tree of life;
Matt 11:29 . . . am humble and *g* at heart,
1 Cor 4:21 . . . love and a *g* spirit?
Eph 4:2 . . . be humble and *g.* Be patient
1 Tim 3:3 . . . must be *g,* not quarrelsome,
Titus 3:2 . . . be *g* and show true humility
Jas 3:17 . . . *g* at all times,

**GENTLENESS (n)** mildness of manners or
disposition
Gal 5:23 . . . *g,* and self-control.
Col 3:12 . . . kindness, humility, *g,* and
1 Tim 6:11 . . . perseverance, and *g.*

**GENUINE (adj)** actual, true, authentic, sincere
John 1:47 . . . here is a *g* son of Israel—
2 Cor 8:8 . . . I am testing how *g* your love
Phil 1:18 . . . motives are false or *g,*
2 Tim 1:5 . . . I remember your *g* faith,

**GETHSEMANE (n)** the garden where Jesus
often went for prayer, rest, or fellowship; the site
where Judas betrayed Jesus before the
crucifixion
Matt 26:36 . . . to the olive grove called *G,*
Mark 14:32 . . . to the olive grove called *G,*

**GIFT, GIFTS (n)** a present from people to
people (often a bribe); a sacrifice from people to
God; anything given voluntarily or at no cost;
that which is given from God, enabling or
empowering his people
Prov 18:16 . . . Giving a *g* can open doors;
Matt 2:11 . . . and gave him *g-s* of gold,
Luke 11:13 . . . how to give good *g-s* to your
Rom 4:16 . . . given as a free *g.*
Rom 5:15 . . . and God's gracious *g.*
Rom 6:23 . . . free *g* of God is eternal
Rom 11:29 . . . For God's *g-s* and his call
1 Cor 12:4 . . . kinds of spiritual *g-s,*
1 Cor 12:7 . . . A spiritual *g* is given
1 Cor 12:31 . . . the most helpful *g-s.*
2 Cor 9:5 . . . I want it to be a willing *g,*
2 Cor 9:15 . . . Thank God for this *g*
Gal 2:9 . . . recognized the *g* God had
Eph 2:8 . . . it is a *g* from God.
Eph 4:8 . . . and gave *g-s* to his people.
2 Tim 1:6 . . . the spiritual *g* God gave you
Heb 2:4 . . . *g-s* of the Holy Spirit
1 Pet 3:7 . . . equal partner in God's *g*
1 Pet 4:10 . . . of spiritual *g-s.*

**GIVE, GIVEN, GIVES, GIVING (v)** to grant, bestow, convey, offer, provide, or designate; to yield or produce; to suffer the loss of (life)
Exod 30:15 . . . poor must not *g* less.
1 Sam 1:28 . . . *g-ing* him to the LORD,
Ps 112:9 . . . share freely and *g* generously
Ps 119:130 . . . your word *g-s* light,
Prov 21:26 . . . love to *g!*
Prov 23:26 . . . O my son, *g* me your heart.
Isa 9:6 . . . a son is *g-n* to us.
Matt 7:11 . . . heavenly Father *g* good gifts
Matt 16:19 . . . And I will *g* you the keys
Matt 22:30 . . . marry nor be *g-n* in marriage.
Mark 6:7 . . . by two, *g-ing* them authority
Luke 11:13 . . . know how to *g* good gifts to
Luke 14:33 . . . my disciple without *g-ing* up
Luke 22:19 . . . body, which is *g-n* for you.
John 1:17 . . . the law was *g-n* through Moses,
John 5:21 . . . so the Son *g-s* life to anyone
John 13:34 . . . So now I am *g-ing* you a new
John 14:27 . . . And the peace I *g* is a gift
Acts 5:32 . . . Spirit, who is *g-n* by God
Acts 14:3 . . . was true by *g-ing* them power
Acts 15:8 . . . Gentiles by *g-ing* them the Holy
Acts 20:35 . . . is more blessed to *g* than to
Rom 2:7 . . . He will *g* eternal life
Rom 5:5 . . . because he has *g-n* us the Holy
Rom 8:32 . . . won't he also *g* us everything
Rom 10:12 . . . Lord, who *g-s* generously
Rom 12:8 . . . is giving, *g* generously.
Rom 14:12 . . . each of us will *g* a personal
1 Cor 9:17 . . . God has *g-n* me this sacred
1 Cor 11:24 . . . body, which is *g-n* for you.
1 Cor 15:57 . . . thank God! He *g-s* us victory
2 Cor 3:6 . . . the Spirit *g-s* life.
2 Cor 8:6 . . . this ministry of *g-ing.*
2 Cor 9:7 . . . how much to *g.*
Eph 4:7 . . . However, he has *g-n* each one of
Eph 4:28 . . . and then *g* generously to
1 Thes 4:8 . . . rejecting God, who *g-s*
1 Tim 6:17 . . . God, who richly *g-s* us all we
1 Jn 4:13 . . . And God has *g-n* us his Spirit

**GLAD (adj)** joyful or happy, often with shouts
Ps 16:9 . . . my heart is *g,* and I rejoice.
Ps 32:11 . . . LORD and be *g,* all you who
Ps 69:32 . . . at work and be *g.*
Ps 97:1 . . . coastlands be *g.*
Ps 104:15 . . . wine to make them *g,*
Ps 118:24 . . . will rejoice and be *g* in it.
Prov 10:8 . . . The wise are *g* to be
Prov 27:11 . . . make my heart *g.*
Isa 35:1 . . . and desert will be *g*
Zeph 3:14 . . . O Israel! Be *g* and rejoice
Matt 5:12 . . . Be very *g!*
John 11:15 . . . for your sakes, I'm *g* I wasn't
Acts 13:48 . . . they were very *g*
1 Cor 12:26 . . . the parts are *g.*
2 Cor 2:2 . . . will make me *g?*
Rev 19:7 . . . Let us be *g* and rejoice,

**GLORIFY, GLORIFIED, GLORIFIES, GLORIFYING (v)** to bestow honor or praise (as in worship); to magnify
*see also* EXALT, HONOR
Ps 147:12 . . . *G* the LORD,
Isa 26:8 . . . desire is to *g* your name.
Isa 42:12 . . . the whole world *g* the LORD;
Dan 4:37 . . . praise and *g* and honor the
Luke 2:20 . . . flocks, *g-ing* and praising
John 8:50 . . . no wish to *g* myself, God is
John 13:31 . . . God will be *g-ied*

John 17:1 . . . *G* your Son so
John 21:19 . . . of death he would *g* God.
2 Cor 8:19 . . . a service that *g-ies* the Lord
Eph 1:14 . . . would praise and *g* him.
Rev 15:4 . . . you, Lord, and *g* your name?

**GLORIOUS (adj)** possessing or deserving special honor; splendid or magnificent
Exod 15:6 . . . O LORD, is *g* in power.
Exod 33:18 . . . show me your *g* presence.
Deut 32:3 . . . the LORD; how *g* is our God!
1 Chr 16:28 . . . the LORD is *g* and strong.
Neh 9:5 . . . prayed: "May your *g* name be
Job 37:5 . . . God's voice is *g* in the
Ps 45:3 . . . You are so *g,* so majestic!
Ps 76:4 . . . You are *g* and more majestic
Ps 96:3 . . . Publish his *g* deeds among the
Ps 149:9 . . . This is the *g* privilege of
Isa 55:5 . . . of Israel, have made you *g.*
Isa 63:15 . . . from your holy, *g* home,
Dan 8:9 . . . east and toward the *g* land of
Dan 11:45 . . . between the *g* holy mountain
Matt 19:28 . . . sits upon his *g* throne,
Acts 2:20 . . . that great and *g* day of the
Acts 7:2 . . . Our *g* God appeared to
Rom 1:23 . . . worshiping the *g,* ever-living
Rom 3:23 . . . of God's *g* standard.
Rom 8:21 . . . children in *g* freedom from
2 Cor 3:9 . . . how much more *g* is the new
2 Cor 3:10 . . . first glory was not *g* at all
2 Cor 3:18 . . . into his *g* image.
Eph 1:6 . . . God for the *g* grace he has
Eph 1:17 . . . asking God, the *g* Father of
Eph 3:16 . . . that from his *g,* unlimited
Eph 5:27 . . . himself as a *g* church without
Phil 3:21 . . . them into *g* bodies like his
Phil 4:19 . . . from his *g* riches, which have
Col 1:11 . . . with all his *g* power so you
Jas 2:1 . . . faith in our *g* Lord Jesus
1 Pet 1:8 . . . with a *g,* inexpressible joy.
1 Pet 4:14 . . . for then the *g* Spirit of God
Jude 1:24 . . . into his *g* presence without a

**GLORY (n)** honor bestowed; splendor or magnificence; a distinguishing quality, asset, or attribute; eternity
Exod 16:10 . . . awesome *g* of the LORD
Num 14:21 . . . filled with the LORD's *g,*
Josh 7:19 . . . My son, give *g* to the LORD,
1 Sam 4:21 . . . said, "Israel's *g* is gone."
Ps 8:5 . . . them with *g* and honor.
Ps 19:1 . . . proclaim the *g* of God.
Ps 29:1 . . . LORD for his *g* and strength.
Ps 44:8 . . . O God, we give *g* to you
Ps 57:11 . . . May your *g* shine over all the
Ps 71:8 . . . I declare your *g* all day
Ps 86:12 . . . I will give *g* to your name
Ps 108:5 . . . May your *g* shine over all the
Ps 145:12 . . . the majesty and *g* of your
Prov 16:31 . . . is a crown of *g;* it is gained
Isa 6:3 . . . earth is filled with his *g!*
Isa 24:16 . . . songs that give *g* to the
Isa 35:2 . . . display his *g,* the splendor
Isa 42:8 . . . not give my *g* to anyone else,
Isa 48:11 . . . not share my *g* with idols!
Isa 66:11 . . . Drink deeply of her *g* even
Isa 66:19 . . . they will declare my *g* to the
Ezek 44:4 . . . saw that the *g* of the LORD
Matt 16:27 . . . angels in the *g* of his Father
Matt 25:31 . . . comes in his *g,* and all the
Mark 13:26 . . . great power and *g.*
Luke 2:14 . . . *G* to God in highest heaven,

Luke 9:26 . . . and in the *g* of the Father
Luke 9:32 . . . they saw Jesus' *g* and the two
Luke 21:27 . . . power and great *g.*
John 1:14 . . . have seen his *g,* the glory of
John 7:39 . . . not yet entered into his *g.*
John 11:40 . . . you would see God's *g* if
John 12:23 . . . enter into his *g.*
John 12:41 . . . the Messiah's *g.*
John 14:13 . . . the Son can bring *g* to the
John 16:14 . . . will bring me *g* by telling
John 17:22 . . . given them the *g* you gave
Acts 3:13 . . . who has brought *g* to his
Rom 2:7 . . . seeking after the *g* and honor
Rom 2:10 . . . there will be *g* and honor and
Rom 3:7 . . . and brings him more *g?*
Rom 4:20 . . . in this he brought *g* to God.
Rom 8:17 . . . heirs of God's *g.*
Rom 8:18 . . . compared to the *g* he will
Rom 8:30 . . . gave them his *g.*
Rom 9:4 . . . God revealed his *g* to them.
Rom 9:23 . . . riches of his *g* shine even
Rom 9:23 . . . in advance for *g.*
Rom 15:6 . . . giving praise and *g* to God,
Rom 15:9 . . . Gentiles might give *g* to God
Rom 16:27 . . . All *g* to the only
1 Cor 2:7 . . . for our ultimate *g* before the
1 Cor 10:31 . . . all for the *g* of God.
1 Cor 15:43 . . . will be raised in *g.*
2 Cor 1:20 . . . to God for his *g.*
2 Cor 3:7 . . . shone with the *g* of God, even
2 Cor 3:10 . . . In fact, that first *g* was not
2 Cor 4:4 . . . about the *g* of Christ, who is
2 Cor 4:17 . . . for us a *g* that vastly
Eph 1:12 . . . bring praise and *g* to God.
Phil 1:11 . . . will bring much *g* and praise
Phil 2:11 . . . is Lord, to the *g* of God the
Phil 4:20 . . . Now all *g* to God our
1 Thes 2:12 . . . Kingdom and *g.*
2 Thes 2:14 . . . share in the *g* of our Lord
1 Tim 1:17 . . . All honor and *g* to God
1 Tim 3:16 . . . to heaven in *g.*
2 Tim 4:18 . . . All *g* to God forever
Titus 2:13 . . . when the *g* of our great God
Heb 1:3 . . . God's own *g* and expresses the
Heb 2:9 . . . crowned with *g* and honor.
Heb 3:3 . . . far more *g* than Moses, just
1 Pet 1:7 . . . much praise and *g* and honor
1 Pet 1:21 . . . gave him great *g.*
1 Pet 5:4 . . . of never-ending *g* and honor.
2 Pet 1:3 . . . means of his marvelous *g* and
2 Pet 1:17 . . . from the majestic *g* of God
Jude 1:25 . . . All *g,* majesty, power,
Rev 4:9 . . . beings give *g* and honor and
Rev 4:11 . . . God, to receive *g* and honor
Rev 5:12 . . . honor and *g* and blessing.
Rev 5:13 . . . and honor and *g* and power
Rev 11:13 . . . terrified and gave *g* to the
Rev 16:9 . . . God and give him *g.*
Rev 21:11 . . . shone with the *g* of God and
Rev 21:23 . . . for the *g* of God
Rev 21:26 . . . will bring their *g* and honor

**GNAT, GNATS (n)** any of various small usually biting dipteran flies
Exod 8:16 . . . swarms of *g-s* throughout the
Matt 23:24 . . . swallow a *g,* but you swallow

**GOD, GODS (n)** eternal, infinite Spirit; Creator, Redeemer, sovereign Lord; impotent pagan diety; image of pagan diety (made of wood, metal, or stone)
*see also* IDOL(S)

Gen 1:1 . . . In the beginning *G* created
Gen 1:27 . . . In the image of *G* he created
Gen 3:1 . . . Did *G* really say you must not
Gen 6:2 . . . The sons of *G* saw the
Gen 14:18 . . . a priest of *G* Most High,
Gen 17:1 . . . El-Shaddai—'*G* Almighty.'
Gen 22:12 . . . I know that you truly fear *G.*
Gen 50:20 . . . *G* intended it all for good.
Exod 20:5 . . . am a jealous *G* who will not
Exod 22:28 . . . must not dishonor *G* or curse
Exod 32:4 . . . these are the *g-s* who brought
Exod 34:6 . . . The *G* of compassion
Deut 6:4 . . . LORD is our *G,* the LORD
Deut 23:5 . . . LORD your *G* loves you.
Deut 32:16 . . . by worshiping foreign *g-s;* they
Deut 32:39 . . . There is no other *g* but me!
Deut 33:27 . . . The eternal *G* is
Josh 24:19 . . . a holy and jealous *G.*
1 Kgs 8:23 . . . there is no *G* like you
1 Kgs 18:21 . . . if Baal is *G,* then follow
2 Kgs 19:15 . . . You alone are *G* of all
Ezra 9:9 . . . unfailing love our *G* did not
Neh 1:5 . . . awesome *G* who keeps
Ps 19:1 . . . proclaim the glory of *G.*
Ps 22:1 . . . My *G,* my *G,* why have
Ps 42:2 . . . I thirst for *G,* the living *G.*
Ps 42:8 . . . praying to *G* who gives
Ps 51:10 . . . a clean heart, O *G.*
Ps 82:6 . . . say, 'You are *g-s;* you are all
Ps 100:3 . . . the LORD is *G!*
Ps 139:23 . . . Search me, O *G,* and know
Prov 24:12 . . . For *G* understands all
Eccl 12:13 . . . conclusion: Fear *G* and obey
Isa 9:6 . . . Mighty *G,* Everlasting Father,
Isa 43:10 . . . I alone am *G.*
Dan 6:16 . . . May your *G,* whom you
Jon 4:2 . . . compassionate *G,* slow to
Mic 6:8 . . . walk humbly with your *G.*
Mic 7:18 . . . Where is another *G* like you,
Nah 1:2 . . . a jealous *G,* filled with
Mark 2:7 . . . Only *G* can forgive
Mark 3:35 . . . Anyone who does *G*'s will is
Mark 15:34 . . . My *G,* my *G,* why
Luke 2:14 . . . Glory to *G* in highest
Luke 10:9 . . . The Kingdom of *G* is near
Luke 16:13 . . . cannot serve both *G* and
Luke 20:38 . . . So he is the *G* of the living,
John 1:1 . . . Word was with *G*
John 1:18 . . . who is himself *G,* is near
John 1:29 . . . The Lamb of *G* who
John 3:16 . . . For *G* loved the world so
John 10:34 . . . I say, you are *g-s!*
John 14:1 . . . Trust in *G,* and trust also
Acts 5:29 . . . We must obey *G* rather than
Acts 12:24 . . . word of *G* continued to
Acts 19:26 . . . aren't really *g-s* at all.
Rom 1:16 . . . the power of *G* at work,
Rom 3:23 . . . short of *G*'s glorious
Rom 5:1 . . . have peace with *G* because
Rom 5:5 . . . know how dearly *G* loves us,
Rom 6:23 . . . free gift of *G* is eternal
Rom 8:17 . . . are heirs of *G*'s glory.
Rom 12:2 . . . learn to know *G*'s will for you,
1 Cor 1:18 . . . the very power of *G.*
1 Cor 1:25 . . . foolish plan of *G* is wiser
1 Cor 6:20 . . . you must honor *G* with your
1 Cor 14:33 . . . not a *G* of disorder but
2 Cor 10:4 . . . We use *G*'s mighty weapons,
Gal 3:6 . . . believed *G,* and *G* counted him
Eph 2:10 . . . For we are *G*'s masterpiece.

Eph 5:1 . . . Imitate *G,* therefore, in
Phil 2:6 . . . equality with *G* as something
Phil 4:7 . . . you will experience *G*'s peace,
Col 2:9 . . . the fullness of *G* in a human
1 Thes 5:18 . . . for this is *G*'s will
1 Tim 2:5 . . . is only one *G* and one
Titus 1:2 . . . *G*—who does not lie—
Heb 6:18 . . . is impossible for *G* to lie.
Heb 7:19 . . . we draw near to *G.*
Heb 11:6 . . . believe that *G* exists
Jas 2:19 . . . there is one *G.*
Jas 2:23 . . . Abraham believed *G,* and *G*
Jas 4:8 . . . Come close to *G,* and *G*
1 Pet 2:15 . . . It is *G*'s will that your
1 Pet 5:5 . . . for "*G* opposes the proud
1 Jn 1:5 . . . declare to you: *G* is light,
1 Jn 4:21 . . . Those who love *G* must also
Rev 19:6 . . . the Lord our *G,* the Almighty,
Rev 21:23 . . . glory of *G* illuminates the

**GOD-BREATHED (KJV)**
2 Tim 3:16 . . . Scripture is *inspired by God*

**GODLINESS (n)**   devotion to God; piety
*see also* RIGHTEOUSNESS
Prov 16:8 . . . Better to have little, with *g,*
1 Tim 4:8 . . . but training for *g* is much
1 Tim 5:4 . . . to show *g* at home
1 Tim 6:6 . . . Yet true *g* with contentment

**GODLY (adj)**   marked by or showing reverence
for God and devotion to worship
*see also* RIGHTEOUS, UPRIGHT
Ps 31:23 . . . LORD, all you *g* ones!
Ps 34:9 . . . LORD, you his *g* people,
Prov 16:31 . . . by living a *g* life.
Prov 23:24 . . . The father of *g* children has
Acts 22:12 . . . He was a *g* man, deeply
Gal 6:1 . . . you who are *g* should gently
1 Tim 6:3 . . . promote a *g* life.
2 Tim 3:12 . . . to live a *g* life in Christ
Titus 1:1 . . . how to live *g* lives.
2 Pet 2:9 . . . how to rescue *g* people from
2 Pet 3:11 . . . what holy and *g* lives you

**GODLY (n)**   people who are righteous or devout
Ps 1:5 . . . no place among the *g.*
Ps 37:21 . . . but the *g* are generous givers.
Ps 37:30 . . . The *g* offer good counsel;
Ps 68:3 . . . But let the *g* rejoice.
Ps 118:20 . . . LORD, and the *g* enter there.
Prov 3:32 . . . friendship to the *g.*
Prov 10:11 . . . The words of the *g* are a
Prov 10:20 . . . The words of the *g* are like
Prov 10:28 . . . The hopes of the *g* result in
Prov 11:5 . . . The *g* are directed by
Prov 11:28 . . . But the *g* flourish like
Prov 13:9 . . . The life of the *g* is full of
Prov 20:7 . . . The *g* walk with
Prov 21:15 . . . Justice is a joy to the *g,*
Prov 28:1 . . . the *g* are as bold as lions.

**GOLD (n)**   a valuable yellow malleable metal
especially used in coins and jewelry
1 Kgs 20:3 . . . Your silver and *g* are mine,
Ps 19:10 . . . more desirable than *g,*
Ps 119:127 . . . even the finest *g.*
Prov 3:14 . . . are better than *g.*
Matt 2:11 . . . gifts of *g,* frankincense,
Rev 3:18 . . . advise you to buy *g* from me—

**GOLGOTHA (n)**   a hill just outside Jerusalem;
the place where Jesus was crucified
Matt 27:33 . . . a place called *G*

Mark 15:22 . . . a place called *G*
John 19:17 . . . (in Hebrew, *G*).

**GOOD (adj)**   kind; profitable; excellent; fitting
or appropriate; morally right
*see also* NEWS
Gen 1:4 . . . that the light was *g.*
Gen 1:31 . . . it was very *g!*
Gen 2:18 . . . It is not *g* for the man to
2 Chr 7:3 . . . He is *g!* His faithful
2 Chr 31:20 . . . was pleasing and *g* in the
Ps 34:8 . . . see that the LORD is *g.*
Ps 119:68 . . . You are *g* and do only
Eccl 7:20 . . . earth is always *g* and never
Isa 5:20 . . . that evil is *g* and *g* is
Isa 45:7 . . . I send *g* times and
Mic 6:8 . . . told you what is *g,* and this is
Matt 5:29 . . . eye—even your *g* eye—causes
Matt 19:17 . . . One who is *g.*
Matt 22:10 . . . they could find, *g* and bad
Matt 25:21 . . . Well done, my *g* and
Mark 3:4 . . . the law permit *g* deeds on the
Mark 10:18 . . . God is truly *g.*
Luke 6:45 . . . person produces *g* things from
Luke 6:45 . . . treasury of a *g* heart,
Luke 8:15 . . . seeds that fell on the *g* soil
Luke 14:34 . . . Salt is *g* for seasoning.
Luke 18:19 . . . God is truly *g.*
Luke 19:17 . . . You are a *g* servant.
John 10:11 . . . I am the *g* shepherd.
Rom 7:12 . . . and right and *g.*
Rom 7:16 . . . that the law is *g.*
Rom 7:18 . . . know that nothing *g* lives in
Rom 7:19 . . . do what is *g,* but I don't.
Rom 12:2 . . . you, which is *g* and pleasing
Rom 12:9 . . . Hold tightly to what is *g.*
1 Cor 6:12 . . . not everything is *g* for you.
1 Cor 7:1 . . . Yes, it is *g* to abstain
1 Cor 15:33 . . . corrupts *g* character.
Gal 6:9 . . . doing what is *g.*
Phil 1:6 . . . who began the *g* work within
1 Thes 5:21 . . . to what is *g.*
1 Tim 4:4 . . . everything God created is *g,*
1 Tim 6:12 . . . Fight the *g* fight
2 Tim 3:17 . . . people to do every *g* work.
2 Tim 4:7 . . . I have fought the *g* fight,
Titus 3:8 . . . These teachings are *g*
Heb 10:24 . . . of love and *g* works.
Heb 12:10 . . . is always *g* for us,
Jas 2:8 . . . indeed, it is *g* when you obey

**GOOD (n)**   something that is excellent,
profitable, or morally right; advancement of
prosperity or well-being; something useful or
beneficial
Gen 2:9 . . . the knowledge of *g* and evil.
Gen 3:22 . . . knowing both *g* and evil.
Gen 50:20 . . . God intended it all for *g.*
1 Sam 26:23 . . . reward for doing *g* and for
Ps 14:1 . . . not one of them does *g!*
Ps 53:3 . . . No one does *g,* not a single
Prov 3:27 . . . Do not withhold *g* from those
Prov 11:27 . . . If you search for *g,* you will
Prov 31:12 . . . She brings him *g,* not harm,
Isa 55:2 . . . does you no *g?*
Jer 13:23 . . . you start doing *g,* for you
Jer 32:39 . . . for their own *g* and for the
Matt 5:45 . . . evil and the *g,* and he sends
Rom 3:12 . . . No one does *g,* not a single
Rom 8:28 . . . together for the *g* of those
Rom 13:4 . . . sent for your *g.*
1 Cor 10:24 . . . but for the *g* of others.

Gal 6:10 . . . we should do *g* to everyone—
Eph 2:10 . . . so we can do the *g* things he
Eph 6:8 . . . each one of us for the *g* we do,
1 Tim 5:10 . . . because of the *g* she has
Heb 13:16 . . . forget to do *g* and to share
1 Pet 2:20 . . . suffer for doing *g* and endure
1 Pet 3:17 . . . suffer for doing *g*, if that

**GOODNESS (n)** the beneficial quality of
something; kindness
Ps 145:7 . . . the story of your wonderful *g*;
Isa 63:7 . . . in his great *g* to Israel,
Rom 14:17 . . . a life of *g* and peace and joy
Rom 15:14 . . . that you are full of *g*.

**GOSPEL (KJV)**
Mark 1:1 . . . the *Good News* about Jesus
Luke 4:18 . . . anointed me to bring *Good News*
Rom 1:16 . . . not ashamed of this *Good News*
Rom 10:15 . . . feet of messengers who bring
   *good news*
Gal 3:8 . . . God proclaimed this *good news*

**GOSSIP (n)** rumor or report revealing personal
or sensational facts about others
Prov 16:28 . . . of strife; *g* separates the
Prov 26:20 . . . disappear when *g* stops.
2 Cor 12:20 . . . slander, *g*, arrogance,

**GOSSIP, GOSSIPING (v)** to relate rumors or
reports about others
Ps 15:3 . . . who refuse to *g* or harm their
1 Tim 5:13 . . . spend their time *g-ing*

**GOVERNMENT (n)** the organization or agency
through which a political unit exercises authority
Isa 9:6 . . . The *g* will rest on his
Rom 13:6 . . . For *g* workers need
Titus 3:1 . . . to submit to the *g* and its

**GRACE (n)** God's free and unmerited favor
toward sinful humanity
*see also* FAVOR
Acts 6:8 . . . full of God's *g* and power,
Acts 14:3 . . . about the *g* of the Lord.
Acts 15:11 . . . by the undeserved *g* of the
Acts 20:32 . . . message of his *g* that is able
Rom 5:15 . . . is God's wonderful *g* and his
Rom 5:21 . . . now God's wonderful *g* rules
Rom 6:1 . . . of his wonderful *g*?
Rom 11:5 . . . of God's *g*—his undeserved
Rom 12:6 . . . In his *g*, God has
1 Cor 3:10 . . . Because of God's *g* to me,
1 Cor 16:23 . . . May the *g* of the Lord
2 Cor 4:15 . . . And as God's *g* reaches more
2 Cor 9:14 . . . of the overflowing *g* God has
Gal 1:15 . . . by his marvelous *g*,
Gal 2:21 . . . do not treat the *g* of God as
Gal 5:4 . . . away from God's *g*.
Eph 1:7 . . . in kindness and *g* that he
Eph 2:5 . . . only by God's *g* that you have
Eph 2:7 . . . wealth of his *g* and kindness
Eph 2:8 . . . saved you by his *g* when you
Eph 3:2 . . . of extending his *g* to you
Eph 3:7 . . . By God's *g* and mighty
Phil 4:23 . . . May the *g* of the Lord
2 Thes 1:12 . . . because of the *g* of our God
2 Thes 2:16 . . . and by his *g* gave us eternal
1 Tim 1:2 . . . Lord give you *g*, mercy,
2 Tim 1:9 . . . show us his *g* through Christ
2 Tim 2:1 . . . strong through the *g* that God
2 Tim 4:22 . . . And may his *g* be with all of
Titus 2:11 . . . For the *g* of God has
Titus 3:7 . . . Because of his *g* he declared

Titus 3:15 . . . May God's *g* be with you
Heb 4:16 . . . and we will find *g* to help us
Heb 12:15 . . . to receive the *g* of God.
Heb 13:9 . . . comes from God's *g*, not from
Heb 13:25 . . . May God's *g* be with you all.
Jas 4:6 . . . gives us even more *g* to stand
1 Pet 5:12 . . . Stand firm in this *g*.
2 Pet 3:18 . . . grow in the *g* and knowledge
Rev 22:21 . . . May the *g* of the Lord

**GRACIOUS (adj)** abounding in grace and
kindness; merciful, compassionate
2 Kgs 13:23 . . . the LORD was *g* and merciful
Ps 145:13 . . . he is *g* in all he
Prov 11:16 . . . A *g* woman gains
John 1:16 . . . received one *g* blessing after
2 Cor 8:7 . . . also in this *g* act of giving.
Col 4:6 . . . your conversation be *g* and
1 Tim 1:14 . . . and *g* our Lord
1 Pet 1:10 . . . about this *g* salvation
1 Pet 1:13 . . . to the *g* salvation that will

**GRAPEVINE (n)** the vine on which grapes grow
Ps 128:3 . . . a fruitful *g*, flourishing
Isa 36:16 . . . from your own *g* and fig tree
John 15:1 . . . am the true *g*, and my Father

**GRASS (n)** green plants that grow from the
ground and are suitable for grazing animals
Isa 40:6 . . . people are like the *g*.
1 Pet 1:24 . . . The *g* withers and

**GRAVE, GRAVES (n)** burial place; euphemism
for Hades, hell, or Sheol
Ps 5:9 . . . from an open *g*.
Ps 49:15 . . . power of the *g*.
John 5:28 . . . dead in their *g-s* will hear the
Acts 2:27 . . . rot in the *g*.
Rom 3:13 . . . from an open *g*.
Rev 20:13 . . . death and the *g* gave up their

**GREED (n)** a selfish and excessive desire for
more of something (as money) than is needed
Prov 15:27 . . . G brings grief
Rom 1:29 . . . of wickedness, sin, *g*, hate,
2 Pet 2:3 . . . In their *g* they will make up
2 Pet 2:14 . . . well trained in *g*.

**GREEDY (adj)** having or showing a selfish
desire for wealth and possessions
1 Sam 8:3 . . . for they were *g* for money.
Prov 1:19 . . . all who are *g* for money;
Prov 21:26 . . . people are always *g*
1 Cor 6:10 . . . are thieves, or *g* people,
Eph 5:5 . . . For a *g* person is an
Col 3:5 . . . Don't be *g*, for a *g*

**GRIEF (n)** deep and poignant distress due to
bereavement; a cause of suffering
Job 16:5 . . . take away your *g*.
Ps 10:14 . . . the trouble and *g* they cause.
Prov 10:1 . . . a foolish child brings *g* to a
Prov 15:27 . . . Greed brings *g* to the
John 16:20 . . . your *g* will suddenly turn
Rom 9:2 . . . sorrow and unending *g*

**GRIEVE, GRIEVED (v)** to feel, show, or cause
distress, vexation, sorrow, or regret
Eccl 3:4 . . . A time to *g* and a time
Isa 63:10 . . . rebelled against him and *g-d*
Lam 3:20 . . . time, as I *g* over my loss.
1 Thes 4:13 . . . so you will not *g* like people

**GROAN, GROANINGS (n)** a deep moan
indicative of pain, grief, or annoyance
Ps 90:9 . . . years with a *g*.
Rom 8:26 . . . for us with *g-ings* that cannot be

**GROUND (n)** soil, earth, or territory
Gen 1:10 . . . called the dry *g* "land" and
Gen 3:17 . . . the *g* is cursed because of you.
Gen 4:2 . . . Cain cultivated the *g*.
Gen 4:10 . . . cries out to me from the *g*!
Exod 3:5 . . . standing on holy *g*.
Exod 15:19 . . . sea on dry *g*!
Isa 53:2 . . . like a root in dry *g*.
Matt 10:29 . . . fall to the *g* without your

**GROW, GROWING, GROWS (v)** to become; to
spring up and develop to maturity
Isa 40:31 . . . run and not *g* weary.
1 Cor 3:6 . . . God who made it *g*.
Eph 4:16 . . . is healthy and *g-ing* and full of
Phil 1:25 . . . all of you *g* and experience
Col 2:19 . . . it *g-s* as God nourishes it.
2 Thes 1:3 . . . one another is *g-ing*.
Jas 1:15 . . . when sin is allowed to *g*,
2 Pet 3:18 . . . Rather, you must *g* in the

**GRUMBLE (v)** to mutter in discontent
1 Cor 10:10 . . . And don't *g* as some
Jas 5:9 . . . Don't *g* about each other

**GRUMBLERS (n)** one who mutters in discontent
Jude 1:16 . . . people are *g* and complainers,

**GUARD (adj)** defensively watchful; alert
2 Pet 3:17 . . . Be on *g* so that you

**GUARD, GUARDING, GUARDS (v)** to protect
by watchful attention; to watch over
*see also* KEEP
Prov 4:23 . . . G your heart
Prov 7:2 . . . as you *g* your own eyes.
Prov 24:12 . . . He who *g-s* your soul knows
Luke 2:8 . . . fields nearby, *g-ing* their flocks
Phil 4:7 . . . His peace will *g* your hearts
2 Thes 3:3 . . . and *g* you from

**GUARDIAN (n)** one who has the care of the
person or property of another
Gen 4:9 . . . Am I my brother's *g*?
Gal 3:25 . . . the law as our *g*.
1 Pet 2:25 . . . your Shepherd, the *G* of your

**GUIDANCE (n)** direction or counsel provided by
another person
2 Chr 26:5 . . . as the king sought *g* from
Prov 24:6 . . . go to war without wise *g*;
Prov 29:18 . . . do not accept divine *g*,

**GUIDE, GUIDED, GUIDES, GUIDING (v)** to
direct, supervise, or influence usually to a
particular end
Exod 13:21 . . . He *g-d* them during the
Exod 15:13 . . . In your might, you *g* them
Deut 1:33 . . . *g-ing* you with a pillar of fire
Ps 16:7 . . . bless the LORD who *g-s* me;
Ps 23:3 . . . He *g-s* me along
Ps 32:8 . . . I will *g* you along
Ps 139:10 . . . your hand will *g* me,
John 16:13 . . . he will *g* you into all
Gal 5:16 . . . let the Holy Spirit *g* your lives.

**GUILT (n)** the state or feeling of one who has
committed an offense
Job 6:29 . . . Stop assuming my *g*, for I
Ps 32:2 . . . the LORD has cleared of *g*,
Ps 38:4 . . . My *g* overwhelms me—
Ps 51:2 . . . Wash me clean from my *g*.
Isa 6:7 . . . Now your *g* is removed,
Dan 9:24 . . . atone for their *g*, to bring

**GUILTY (adj)** justly chargeable with
wrongdoing

Lev 19:17 . . . not be held *g* for their sin.
Rom 3:19 . . . entire world is *g* before God.
1 Cor 11:27 . . . *g* of sinning against
1 Jn 3:20 . . . if we feel *g,* God is greater
1 Jn 3:21 . . . we don't feel *g,* we can come

**HAIR, HAIRS (n)** a slender threadlike outgrowth of the skin of an animal or human
Lev 19:27 . . . Do not trim off the *h* on your
2 Sam 18:9 . . . his *h* got caught in the tree.
Matt 10:30 . . . And the very *h-s* on your head
1 Cor 11:6 . . . to have her *h* cut or her head
1 Cor 11:14 . . . man to have long *h?*
1 Cor 11:15 . . . And isn't long *h* a woman's
Rev 1:14 . . . His head and his *h* were white

**HALLELUJAH (KJV)**
Rev 19:1 . . . shouting, *"Praise the Lord!*
Rev 19:3 . . . voices rang out: *"Praise the Lord!*
Rev 19:4 . . . *"Amen! Praise the Lord!"*
Rev 19:6 . . . *"Praise the Lord! For the Lord*

**HALLOW(ED) (KJV)**
Exod 20:11 . . . Sabbath day and *set it apart as holy*
Lev 25:10 . . . *Set* this year *apart as holy*
1 Kgs 9:3 . . . *set* this Temple *apart to be holy*
Matt 6:9 . . . *may* your name *be kept holy*

**HAND, HANDS (n)** the end of the arm that serves as a grasping and handling tool for humans; symbolic of power
Gen 47:29 . . . Put your *h* under my
Exod 15:6 . . . Your right *h,* O LORD,
Exod 29:10 . . . will lay their *h-s* on its head.
Exod 33:22 . . . cover you with my *h* until
1 Kgs 13:4 . . . king's *h* became paralyzed
Ps 22:16 . . . have pierced my *h-s* and feet.
Ps 24:4 . . . Only those whose *h-s* and hearts
Ps 32:4 . . . your *h* of discipline
Ps 44:3 . . . It was your right *h* and
Ps 63:4 . . . lifting up my *h-s* to you in prayer.
Ps 75:8 . . . a cup in his *h* that is full
Ps 110:1 . . . at my right *h* until I humble
Ps 137:5 . . . let my right *h* forget how to
Ps 145:16 . . . you open your *h,* you satisfy
Isa 40:12 . . . the oceans in his *h?*
Isa 41:13 . . . by your right *h*—I, the LORD
Isa 55:12 . . . will clap their *h-s!*
Isa 64:8 . . . formed by your *h.*
Dan 10:10 . . . Just then a *h* touched me
Matt 5:30 . . . And if your *h*—even your
Matt 6:3 . . . don't let your left *h* know what
Matt 18:8 . . . with only one *h* or one foot
Matt 26:64 . . . at God's right *h* and coming
Mark 12:36 . . . at my right *h* until I humble
Acts 6:6 . . . they laid their *h-s* on them.
Acts 7:55 . . . at God's right *h.*
Acts 8:18 . . . laid their *h-s* on people,
Acts 13:3 . . . men laid their *h-s* on them
Acts 19:6 . . . Paul laid his *h-s* on them,
Acts 28:8 . . . and laying his *h-s* on him,
1 Thes 4:11 . . . working with your *h-s,*
1 Tim 2:8 . . . pray with holy *h-s* lifted up
1 Tim 4:14 . . . church laid their *h-s* on you.
2 Tim 1:6 . . . when I laid my *h-s* on you.
Heb 1:13 . . . at my right *h* until I humble
Rev 13:16 . . . mark on the right *h* or on the

**HAPPINESS (n)** a state of well-being and contentment; joy
Deut 24:5 . . . *h* to the wife he has married.

Job 7:7 . . . never again feel *h.*
Job 9:25 . . . a glimpse of *h.*
Ps 86:4 . . . Give me *h,* O LORD,
Ps 119:35 . . . that is where my *h* is found.
Eccl 8:15 . . . *h* along with all the hard work
Isa 65:18 . . . Jerusalem as a place of *h.*
Luke 6:24 . . . you have your only *h* now.

**HAPPY (adj)** expressing, reflecting, or suggestive of happiness
*see also* BLESSED
Deut 16:14 . . . festival will be a *h* time
Ps 113:9 . . . making her a *h* mother.
Prov 15:13 . . . A glad heart makes a *h* face;
Prov 15:15 . . . for the *h* heart, life is
Prov 23:25 . . . she who gave you birth be *h.*
Eccl 9:7 . . . drink your wine with a *h* heart,
Zech 10:7 . . . will be made *h* as if by wine.
Rom 12:15 . . . Be *h* with those who are *h,*
Phil 2:2 . . . make me truly *h* by agreeing
Jas 5:13 . . . Are any of you *h?*

**HARD (adj)** lacking in responsiveness; unfeeling; demanding the exertion of energy
Rom 11:25 . . . of Israel have *h* hearts,
Rev 2:2 . . . I have seen your *h* work and

**HARD, HARDER (adv)** with great or utmost effort or energy
Prov 13:4 . . . those who work *h*
Acts 20:35 . . . in need by working *h.*
Rom 16:12 . . . has worked so *h*
1 Cor 15:10 . . . worked *h-er* than any of
2 Cor 11:23 . . . worked *h-er,* been put in
1 Thes 5:12 . . . They work *h* among you
2 Thes 3:8 . . . We worked *h* day and night

**HARDEN, HARDENED (v)** to make callous or unfeeling
Exod 4:21 . . . But I will *h* his heart
Exod 10:20 . . . Lord *h-ed* Pharaoh's heart
Ps 95:8 . . . Don't *h* your hearts as Israel did
Isa 6:10 . . . *H* the hearts of these people.
Matt 13:15 . . . hearts of these people are *h-ed,*
John 12:40 . . . and *h-ed* their hearts—
Eph 4:18 . . . minds and *h-ed* their hearts
Heb 3:8 . . . don't *h* your hearts as Israel did

**HARLOT (KJV)**
Gen 38:15 . . . thought she was a *prostitute*
Josh 2:1 . . . a *prostitute* named Rahab
Hos 4:15 . . . you, Israel, are a *prostitute*
Matt 21:31 . . . *prostitutes* will get into the Kingdom
Rev 17:5 . . . Mother of All *Prostitutes* and

**HARMONY (n)** tranquility; agreement; unity
Zech 6:13 . . . will be perfect *h* between his
Rom 12:16 . . . Live in *h* with each other.
Rom 14:19 . . . aim for *h* in the church
Rom 15:5 . . . live in complete *h* with each
1 Cor 12:25 . . . This makes for *h*
2 Cor 6:15 . . . What *h* can there be
2 Cor 13:11 . . . Live in *h* and peace.
Col 3:14 . . . together in perfect *h.*

**HARVEST, HARVESTS (n)** the time or fruit of reaping or gathering in a crop—physically or spiritually
Deut 16:15 . . . blesses you with bountiful *h-s*
Matt 9:37 . . . The *h* is great, but
John 4:35 . . . fields are already ripe for *h.*
1 Cor 15:23 . . . raised as the first of the *h;*
2 Cor 9:10 . . . great *h* of generosity

Gal 6:9 . . . we will reap a *h* of blessing
Heb 12:11 . . . peaceful *h* of right living
Jas 3:18 . . . reap a *h* of righteousness.
Rev 14:15 . . . the time of *h* has come;

**HARVEST, HARVESTS (v)** to gather in (a crop); to reap
Gen 8:22 . . . there will be planting and *h,*
Job 4:8 . . . and cultivate evil will *h*
Prov 10:5 . . . wise youth *h-s* in the summer,
Gal 6:8 . . . sinful nature will *h* decay and

**HARVESTER, HARVESTERS (n)** one who gathers in (a crop)
Ruth 2:3 . . . to gather grain behind the *h-s.*
John 4:36 . . . planter and the *h* alike!

**HATE, HATED, HATES, HATING (v)** to feel extreme enmity toward; to have a strong aversion to
Ps 45:7 . . . love justice and *h* evil.
Prov 1:22 . . . you fools *h* knowledge?
Prov 6:16 . . . six things the Lord *h-s*—
Prov 13:5 . . . The godly *h* lies;
Prov 15:27 . . . those who *h* bribes will live.
Prov 26:28 . . . A lying tongue *h-s* its victims,
Prov 28:16 . . . but one who *h-s* corruption
Mal 2:16 . . . "For I *h* divorce!"
Matt 5:43 . . . and *h* your enemy.
Matt 24:9 . . . be *h-d* all over the world
Luke 6:22 . . . when people *h* you
John 3:20 . . . All who do evil *h* the light
John 15:18 . . . remember that it *h-d* me
2 Tim 3:3 . . . be cruel and *h* what is good.
Heb 1:9 . . . You love justice and *h* evil.
1 Jn 2:9 . . . *h-s* a Christian brother or sister,
1 Jn 4:20 . . . *h-s* a Christian brother or sister,
Jude 1:23 . . . *h-ing* the sins that contaminate

**HATRED (n)** strong emotional aversion
Lev 19:17 . . . Do not nurse *h* in your heart
Prov 26:24 . . . People may cover their *h*

**HEAD, HEADS (n)** top part of the body that contains the brain; one in charge; person, individual
Gen 3:15 . . . He will strike your *h,* and
Lev 26:13 . . . walk with your *h-s* held high.
Ps 22:7 . . . shake their *h-s,* saying,
Ps 23:5 . . . by anointing my *h* with oil.
Ps 133:2 . . . over Aaron's *h,* that ran
Prov 25:22 . . . coals of shame on their *h-s,*
Matt 27:39 . . . shaking their *h-s* in mockery.
John 19:2 . . . thorns and put it on his *h,*
Acts 18:6 . . . your own *h-s*—I am innocent.
Rom 12:20 . . . coals of shame on their *h-s.*
Eph 1:22 . . . and *h*as made him *h* over all
Eph 5:23 . . . as Christ is the *h* of the
Rev 4:4 . . . crowns on their *h-s.*
Rev 14:14 . . . He had a gold crown on his *h*
Rev 19:12 . . . on his *h* were many crowns.

**HEAL, HEALED, HEALING, HEALS (v)** to mend, cure, make whole; to restore to health
Gen 20:17 . . . and God *h-ed* Abimelech,
Exod 15:26 . . . I am the Lord who *h-s* you.
Num 12:13 . . . I beg you, please *h* her!
Deut 32:39 . . . one who wounds and *h-s;*
2 Chr 30:20 . . . prayer and *h-ed* the people.
Job 5:18 . . . his hands also *h.*
Ps 6:2 . . . *H* me, Lord,
Ps 103:3 . . . and *h-s* all my diseases.
Ps 107:20 . . . his word and *h-ed* them,
Prov 3:8 . . . will have *h-ing* for your body

Prov 13:17 . . . messenger brings *h-ing.*
Isa 6:10 . . . and turn to me for *h-ing.*
Isa 30:26 . . . Lord begins to *h* his people
Isa 57:18 . . . but I will *h* them anyway!
Isa 57:19 . . . the Lord, who *h-s* them.
Jer 8:18 . . . My grief is beyond *h-ing;*
Jer 17:14 . . . O Lord, if you *h* me, I will
Jer 17:14 . . . I will be truly *h-ed;*
Jer 30:13 . . . No medicine can *h* you.
Hos 6:1 . . . now he will *h* us.
Hos 7:1 . . . I want to *h* Israel, but its
Hos 14:4 . . . Then I will *h* you of your
Zech 11:16 . . . nor *h* the injured,
Mal 4:2 . . . with *h-ing* in his wings.
Matt 4:23 . . . And he *h-ed* every kind
Matt 8:7 . . . will come and *h* him.
Matt 8:16 . . . and he *h-ed* all the sick.
Matt 9:35 . . . he *h-ed* every kind of disease
Matt 10:8 . . . *H* the sick, raise the
Matt 15:30 . . . Jesus, and he *h-ed* them all.
Matt 17:16 . . . they couldn't *h* him.
Mark 1:34 . . . So Jesus *h-ed* many people
Mark 3:2 . . . If he *h-ed* the man's
Mark 3:10 . . . He had *h-ed* many people
Mark 5:28 . . . touch his robe, I will be *h-ed.*
Mark 6:5 . . . sick people and *h* them.
Mark 6:13 . . . and *h-ed* many sick
Mark 6:56 . . . who touched him were *h-ed.*
Mark 10:52 . . . your faith has *h-ed* you.
Luke 4:23 . . . Physician, *h* yourself
Luke 4:40 . . . his hand *h-ed* every one.
Luke 6:7 . . . If he *h-ed* the man's
Luke 8:50 . . . faith, and she will be *h-ed.*
Luke 10:9 . . . *H* the sick, and tell them
Luke 13:14 . . . indignant that Jesus had *h-ed*
Luke 14:3 . . . *h* people on the Sabbath
Luke 14:4 . . . the sick man and *h-ed* him
Luke 17:19 . . . Your faith has *h-ed* you.
Luke 18:42 . . . Your faith has *h-ed* you.
Luke 22:51 . . . man's ear and *h-ed* him.
John 4:47 . . . to Capernaum to *h* his son,
John 7:23 . . . angry with me for *h-ing* a man
John 12:40 . . . and have me *h* them.
Acts 3:16 . . . this man was *h-ed*—
Acts 4:9 . . . want to know how he was *h-ed?*
Acts 4:14 . . . see the man who had been *h-ed*
Acts 4:22 . . . sign—the *h-ing* of a man
Acts 8:7 . . . or lame were *h-ed.*
Acts 9:34 . . . Jesus Christ *h-s* you! Get up,
Acts 10:38 . . . and *h-ing* all who were
Acts 28:8 . . . his hands on him, he *h-ed*
Acts 28:27 . . . turn to me and let me *h*
1 Cor 12:28 . . . the gift of *h-ing,*
1 Cor 12:30 . . . have the gift of *h-ing?*
Jas 5:16 . . . so that you may be *h-ed.*
1 Pet 2:24 . . . By his wounds you are *h-ed.*
Rev 13:3 . . . fatal wound was *h-ed!*
Rev 13:12 . . . wound had been *h-ed.*

**HEALING (adj)**  marked by restoring to original purity or integrity
Luke 6:19 . . . *h* power went out from him,
Acts 4:30 . . . your hand with *h* power;

**HEALTH (n)**  the general condition of the body
Ps 38:3 . . . my *h* is broken because of
Ps 38:7 . . . and my *h* is broken.
Prov 15:30 . . . makes for good *h.*
Isa 38:16 . . . You restore my *h*
Jer 30:17 . . . I will give you back your *h*

**HEALTHY, HEALTHIER (adj)**  enjoying good health and vigor of body, mind, or spirit
Ps 73:4 . . . bodies are so *h* and strong.
Prov 16:24 . . . the soul and *h* for the body.
Dan 1:15 . . . friends looked *h-ier* and better
Zech 11:16 . . . nor feed the *h.* Instead,
Matt 9:12 . . . he said, "*H* people don't need
Mark 2:17 . . . *H* people don't need
Luke 5:31 . . . answered them, "*H* people
Eph 4:16 . . . whole body is *h* and growing
3 Jn 1:2 . . . that you are as *h* in body as

**HEAR, HEARD, HEARING (v)**  to perceive sound; to listen with attention; to be informed of; to take testimony from and make a legal decision
*see also* LISTEN
Gen 3:8 . . . and his wife *h-d* the Lord God
Exod 2:24 . . . God *h-d* their groaning,
Deut 1:16 . . . judges, 'You must *h* the cases
Josh 7:9 . . . people living in the land *h*
1 Kgs 8:30 . . . May you *h* the humble
2 Chr 7:14 . . . I will *h* from heaven and will
Neh 1:11 . . . O Lord, please *h* my prayer!
Ps 5:1 . . . O Lord, *h* me as I pray;
Ps 89:1 . . . Young and old will *h* of your
Isa 29:18 . . . the deaf will *h* words read
Isa 30:21 . . . own ears will *h* him.
Isa 40:28 . . . Have you never *h-d?*
Isa 59:1 . . . too deaf to *h* you call.
Dan 10:12 . . . has been *h-d* in heaven.
Matt 5:21 . . . have *h-d* that our ancestors
Matt 5:43 . . . You have *h-d* the law
Matt 11:5 . . . cured, the deaf *h,* the dead
Matt 13:14 . . . When you *h* what I say,
Mark 4:12 . . . When they *h* what I say,
Luke 7:22 . . . cured, the deaf *h,* the dead
John 8:26 . . . what I have *h-d* from the one
Acts 2:6 . . . When they *h-d* the loud noise,
Acts 13:7 . . . he wanted to *h* the word of
Rom 10:14 . . . how can they *h* about him
Rom 10:17 . . . faith comes from *h-ing,*
1 Cor 2:9 . . . no ear has *h-d,* and no mind
1 Cor 12:17 . . . how would you *h?*
Heb 3:7 . . . Today when you *h* his voice,
2 Jn 1:6 . . . just as you *h-d* from the
Rev 3:20 . . . If you *h* my voice and
Rev 22:8 . . . I, John, am the one who *h-d*

**HEART, HEARTS (n)**  figuratively, the seat of emotions, thoughts, and intentions; personality, disposition; courage; love, affection; central or most vital part of something
Gen 6:6 . . . It broke his *h.*
Exod 4:21 . . . will harden his *h* so he
Exod 35:21 . . . All whose *h-s* were stirred
Deut 6:5 . . . Lord your God with all your *h,*
Deut 9:10 . . . from the *h* of the fire
Deut 20:3 . . . Do not lose *h* or panic
Deut 28:65 . . . will cause your *h* to tremble,
Josh 22:5 . . . with all your *h* and all your
Josh 23:14 . . . Deep in your *h-s* you know
1 Sam 1:15 . . . pouring out my *h*
1 Sam 10:9 . . . God gave him a new *h,*
1 Sam 12:20 . . . the Lord with all your *h,*
1 Sam 13:14 . . . a man after his own *h.*
1 Sam 16:7 . . . but the Lord looks at the *h.*
1 Kgs 8:48 . . . with their whole *h* and soul
1 Kgs 11:2 . . . turn your *h-s* to their gods.
1 Kgs 11:3 . . . turn his *h* away from the Lord.
1 Kgs 14:8 . . . followed me with all his *h*
2 Kgs 23:3 . . . with all his *h* and soul.

1 Chr 22:19 . . . God with all your *h* and soul.
2 Chr 6:38 . . . with their whole *h* and soul
2 Chr 22:9 . . . sought the Lord with all his *h.*
2 Chr 34:31 . . . with all his *h* and soul.
Ezra 1:5 . . . God stirred the *h-s* of the priests
Job 4:5 . . . when trouble strikes, you lose *h.*
Ps 9:1 . . . praise you, Lord, with all my *h;*
Ps 14:1 . . . say in their *h-s,* "There is no
Ps 19:14 . . . meditation of my *h*
Ps 24:4 . . . whose hands and *h-s* are pure,
Ps 27:8 . . . my *h* responds, "Lord,
Ps 36:1 . . . within their *h-s.* They have no
Ps 42:11 . . . Why is my *h* so sad?
Ps 45:1 . . . Beautiful words stir my *h.*
Ps 51:10 . . . Create in me a clean *h,* O God.
Ps 57:7 . . . my *h* is confident.
Ps 73:7 . . . everything their *h-s* could ever
Ps 73:26 . . . the strength of my *h;*
Ps 108:1 . . . with all my *h!*
Ps 111:1 . . . thank the Lord with all my *h*
Ps 119:2 . . . with all their *h-s.*
Ps 119:11 . . . hidden your word in my *h,*
Ps 119:58 . . . With all my *h* I want your
Ps 119:145 . . . I pray with all my *h;*
Ps 139:23 . . . and know my *h;* test me and
Prov 3:3 . . . deep within your *h.*
Prov 4:23 . . . Guard your *h* above all else,
Prov 13:12 . . . deferred makes the *h* sick,
Prov 14:30 . . . A peaceful *h* leads to a
Prov 15:13 . . . a broken *h* crushes the
Prov 15:30 . . . look brings joy to the *h;*
Prov 17:22 . . . A cheerful *h* is good
Prov 20:9 . . . have cleansed my *h;* I am pure
Prov 23:15 . . . wise, my own *h* will rejoice!
Prov 27:23 . . . and put your *h* into caring
Song 4:9 . . . captured my *h,* my treasure,
Song 5:2 . . . I slept, but my *h* was awake,
Song 5:4 . . . and my *h* thrilled within me.
Song 8:6 . . . Place me like a seal over your *h,*
Isa 1:5 . . . and your *h* is sick.
Isa 6:10 . . . Harden the *h-s* of these people.
Isa 42:4 . . . or lose *h* until justice
Jer 3:15 . . . shepherds after my own *h,*
Jer 3:22 . . . your wayward *h-s.*
Jer 9:26 . . . have uncircumcised *h-s.*
Jer 20:9 . . . burns in my *h* like a fire.
Jer 32:39 . . . will give them one *h* and one
Ezek 44:7 . . . who have no *h* for God.
Joel 2:12 . . . Give me your *h-s.* Come with
Matt 5:8 . . . those whose *h-s* are pure,
Matt 5:28 . . . adultery with her in his *h.*
Matt 11:29 . . . I am humble and gentle at *h,*
Matt 12:34 . . . whatever is in your *h*
Matt 15:19 . . . For from the *h* come evil
Matt 18:35 . . . from your *h.*
Matt 22:37 . . . God with all your *h,* all your
Mark 11:23 . . . have no doubt in your *h.*
Mark 12:30 . . . God with all your *h,* all your
Mark 12:33 . . . love him with all my *h* and
Luke 6:45 . . . treasury of a good *h,*
Luke 10:27 . . . God with all your *h,* all your
Luke 12:34 . . . desires of your *h* will also
Luke 24:38 . . . Why are your *h-s* filled with
John 5:38 . . . your *h-s,* because you do not
Acts 1:24 . . . you know every *h.* Show us
Acts 4:32 . . . were united in *h* and mind.
Acts 8:21 . . . this, for your *h* is not right
Acts 15:8 . . . God knows people's *h-s,* and
Acts 16:14 . . . Lord opened her *h,* and she
Acts 28:27 . . . hear, and their *h-s* cannot

Rom 1:9 . . . with all my *h* by spreading
Rom 2:15 . . . written in their *h-s*, for their
Rom 2:29 . . . changed *h* seeks praise
Rom 10:9 . . . believe in your *h* that God
2 Cor 2:4 . . . with a troubled *h* and many
2 Cor 7:2 . . . Please open your *h-s* to us.
2 Cor 9:7 . . . decide in your *h* how much to
Eph 1:18 . . . I pray that your *h-s* will be
Eph 3:13 . . . don't lose *h* because of my
Eph 5:19 . . . music to the Lord in your *h-s.*
Eph 6:6 . . . of God with all your *h.*
Phil 1:7 . . . place in my *h.* You share with
1 Tim 1:5 . . . comes from a pure *h,* a clear

**HEAVEN, HEAVENS (n)** sky and stars above;
God's dwelling place; abode of eternal bliss
Deut 30:12 . . . is not kept in *h,* so distant
Job 41:11 . . . Everything under *h* is mine.
Ps 18:16 . . . down from *h* and rescued me;
Ps 71:19 . . . to the highest *h-s.* You have
Ps 108:4 . . . than the *h-s.* Your faithfulness
Matt 11:25 . . . Father, Lord of *h* and earth,
Matt 24:30 . . . appear in the *h-s,* and there
Rom 10:6 . . . 'Who will go up to *h?'*
2 Cor 12:2 . . . to the third *h* fourteen years
Heb 9:24 . . . He entered into *h* itself to

**HELL (n)** abode of the dead; place of punish-
ment; personification of evil; lowest place one
can go
Matt 5:22 . . . of the fires of *h.*
Matt 16:18 . . . all the powers of *h* will not
Matt 23:33 . . . judgment of *h?*
Mark 9:43 . . . fires of *h* with two hands.
Luke 12:5 . . . throw you into *h.*
Jas 3:6 . . . on fire by *h* itself.
2 Pet 2:4 . . . threw them into *h,* in gloomy

**HELMET (n)** any of various protective head
coverings usually made of hard metal
Isa 59:17 . . . and placed the *h* of salvation
Eph 6:17 . . . salvation as your *h,* and take

**HELP (n)** aid, assistance
2 Sam 22:36 . . . your *h* has made me great.
Ps 30:2 . . . I cried to you for *h,* and you
Ps 33:20 . . . He is our *h* and our shield.
Ps 108:12 . . . for all human *h* is useless.
Isa 30:18 . . . wait for his *h.*
Isa 38:14 . . . looking to heaven for *h.* I am
Phil 4:16 . . . you sent *h* more than once.

**HELP, HELPED, HELPING, HELPS (v)** to give
assistance or support; to rescue or save
Exod 23:5 . . . Instead, stop and *h.*
Deut 2:36 . . . our God also *h-ed* us conquer
1 Sam 7:12 . . . the LORD has *h-ed* us!
Ps 46:1 . . . always ready to *h* in times of
Ps 72:12 . . . he will *h* the oppressed,
Ps 145:14 . . . The LORD *h-s* the fallen
Prov 11:4 . . . Riches won't *h* on the
Prov 14:31 . . . their Maker, but *h-ing* the poor
Prov 19:17 . . . If you *h* the poor,
Isa 41:10 . . . strengthen you and *h* you.
Isa 44:10 . . . that cannot *h* him one bit?
Jer 51:9 . . . We would have *h-ed* her if we
Lam 4:16 . . . he no longer *h-s* them.
Mark 9:24 . . . but *h* me overcome
Acts 9:36 . . . for others and *h-ing* the poor.
Acts 16:9 . . . to Macedonia and *h* us!
Rom 12:13 . . . be ready to *h* them.
1 Cor 12:28 . . . those who can *h* others,
2 Cor 6:2 . . . salvation, I *h-ed* you.
Gal 6:1 . . . and humbly *h* that person back

1 Tim 5:10 . . . Has she *h-ed* those who
2 Tim 2:7 . . . Lord will *h* you understand
Heb 10:33 . . . you *h-ed* others who
1 Pet 4:11 . . . the gift of *h-ing* others?

**HELPER (n)** one who gives aid; co-worker
Gen 2:18 . . . I will make a *h* who is just
Ps 70:5 . . . You are my *h* and my savior;
Ps 115:9 . . . He is your *h* and your shield.
Heb 13:6 . . . The LORD is my *h,* so I will

**HELPLESS (adj)** without any aid, comfort,
protection, or chance of success
Ps 9:12 . . . cares for the *h.* He does not
Ps 10:12 . . . not ignore the *h!*
Ps 34:2 . . . let all who are *h* take heart.
Ps 35:10 . . . Who else protects the *h*
Amos 2:7 . . . They trample *h* people in the
Matt 9:36 . . . confused and *h,* like sheep
Rom 5:6 . . . were utterly *h,* Christ came

**HID, HIDDEN (v)** *see also* HIDE
Ps 119:11 . . . I have *h-den* your word
Matt 13:35 . . . explain things *h-den* since the
Matt 13:44 . . . discovered *h-den* in a field.
Matt 13:44 . . . he *h* it again and
Matt 25:25 . . . your money, so I *h* it in the
Mark 4:22 . . . that is *h-den* will eventually be
1 Cor 2:7 . . . was previously *h-den,* even
Col 3:3 . . . real life is *h-den* with Christ in
Heb 11:23 . . . that Moses' parents *h* him

**HIDE, HIDING (v)** to shield; to seek protection;
to put or remain out of sight
*see also* HID
Deut 31:17 . . . abandon them, *h-ing* my face
1 Sam 10:22 . . . "He is *h-ing* among the
Ps 27:5 . . . he will *h* me in his
Ps 57:1 . . . I will *h* beneath the shadow
Ps 143:9 . . . run to you to *h* me.
Jer 16:17 . . . cannot hope to *h* from me.
Matt 11:25 . . . thank you for *h-ing* these

**HOLINESS (n)** sanctity or purity
Exod 15:11 . . . glorious in *h,* awesome in
Deut 32:51 . . . to demonstrate my *h* to the
Ps 29:2 . . . the splendor of his *h.*
Luke 1:75 . . . in *h* and righteousness for
1 Cor 7:14 . . . wife brings *h* to her
2 Cor 1:12 . . . a God-given *h* and sincerity
1 Thes 4:4 . . . and live in *h* and honor—
1 Tim 2:15 . . . faith, love, *h,* and modesty.
Heb 12:10 . . . share in his *h.*

**HOLY (adj)** consecrated or set aside for sacred
use (as opposed to pagan or common use);
standing apart from sin and evil; characteristic
of God, especially the third person of the Trinity
*see also* PURE
Gen 2:3 . . . and declared it *h,* because it
Exod 3:5 . . . are standing on *h* ground.
Exod 19:6 . . . priests, my *h* nation.
Exod 26:33 . . . separate the *H* Place
Exod 29:37 . . . be absolutely *h,*
Exod 30:10 . . . LORD's most *h* altar.
Exod 31:13 . . . the LORD, who makes you *h.*
Lev 11:45 . . . you must be *h* because I am
Lev 19:8 . . . for defiling what is *h* to the
Lev 20:7 . . . set yourselves apart to be *h,*
Lev 20:26 . . . You must be *h* because I,
Lev 21:12 . . . for he has been made *h* by the
Lev 22:32 . . . the LORD who makes you *h.*
Lev 27:9 . . . LORD will be considered *h.*
Deut 5:12 . . . by keeping it *h,* as the LORD

Josh 5:15 . . . where you are standing is *h.*
Josh 24:19 . . . he is a *h* and jealous God.
1 Chr 16:35 . . . we can thank your *h* name
Neh 11:1 . . . in Jerusalem, the *h* city.
Ps 22:3 . . . Yet you are *h,* enthroned on
Ps 30:4 . . . Praise his *h* name.
Ps 99:3 . . . Your name is *h!*
Ps 105:3 . . . Exult in his *h* name; rejoice,
Ps 111:9 . . . What a *h,* awe-inspiring name
Prov 9:10 . . . of the *H* One results in good
Isa 6:3 . . . to each other, "*H,* holy, holy
Isa 40:25 . . . my equal?" asks the *H* One.
Isa 54:5 . . . your Redeemer, the *H* One of
Isa 66:20 . . . them to my *h* mountain in
Dan 7:18 . . . But in the end, the *h* people
Dan 9:24 . . . anoint the Most *H* Place.
Zech 14:5 . . . and all his *h* ones with him.
Matt 24:15 . . . in the *H* Place.
Mark 1:24 . . . —the *H* One of God!
Luke 1:35 . . . baby to be born will be *h,*
Luke 1:49 . . . Mighty One is *h,* and he has
Luke 4:34 . . . you are—the *H* One of God!
Luke 11:2 . . . may your name be kept *h.*
John 6:69 . . . you are the *H* One of God.
John 17:17 . . . Make them *h* by your
Acts 13:35 . . . not allow your *H* One to rot
Rom 7:12 . . . the law itself is *h,* and its
Rom 14:5 . . . day is more *h* than another
Rom 15:16 . . . made *h* by the *H* Spirit.
1 Cor 1:2 . . . be his own *h* people.
1 Cor 1:30 . . . made us pure and *h,*
1 Cor 3:17 . . . God's temple is *h,* and you
1 Cor 6:11 . . . you were made *h;* you were
1 Cor 7:14 . . . children would not be *h,* but
2 Cor 5:5 . . . given us his *H* Spirit.
Eph 1:4 . . . in Christ to be *h* and without
Eph 2:21 . . . becoming a *h* temple for
Eph 4:24 . . . righteous and *h.*
Eph 5:26 . . . to make her *h* and clean,
Col 1:22 . . . and you are *h* and blameless
1 Thes 3:13 . . . blameless, and *h* as you
1 Thes 4:7 . . . called us to live *h* lives,
1 Thes 5:23 . . . make you *h* in every
2 Thes 1:10 . . . from his *h* people—praise
1 Tim 2:8 . . . to pray with *h* hands lifted
2 Tim 1:9 . . . called us to live a *h* life.
2 Tim 3:15 . . . taught the *h* Scriptures from
Heb 2:11 . . . ones he makes *h* have the same
Heb 10:14 . . . those who are being made *h.*
Heb 10:19 . . . heaven's Most *H* Place
Heb 10:29 . . . which made us *h,* as if it
Heb 13:12 . . . make his people *h* by means
1 Pet 1:16 . . . You must be *h* because I am
1 Pet 2:5 . . . you are his *h* priests.
1 Pet 2:9 . . . priests, a *h* nation, God's
1 Pet 3:5 . . . is how the *h* women of old
2 Pet 1:18 . . . on the *h* mountain.
2 Pet 2:21 . . . to live a *h* life.
2 Pet 3:11 . . . like this, what *h* and godly
Rev 3:7 . . . one who is *h* and true,
Rev 4:8 . . . on saying, "Holy, *h,* holy is
Rev 15:4 . . . you alone are *h.* All nations
Rev 20:6 . . . Blessed and *h* are those who
Rev 22:11 . . . continue to be *h.*

**HOLY GHOST (KJV)**
Matt 1:18 . . . the power of the *Holy Spirit*
Matt 3:11 . . . baptize you with the *Holy Spirit*
Matt 28:19 . . . the Son and the *Holy Spirit*
Luke 3:22 . . . *Holy Spirit,* in bodily form,
1 Jn 5:7-8 . . . three witnesses—the *Spirit*

## HOLY SPIRIT (KJV)
Luke 11:13 . . . give the *Holy Spirit* to those
Eph 1:13 . . . *Holy Spirit,* whom he promised
Eph 4:30 . . . sorrow to God's *Holy Spirit*
1 Thes 4:8 . . . gives his *Holy Spirit* to you

## HOME (n)  one's place of residence; place of origin, destiny, or comfort; family-style social unit
*see also* HOUSE
Deut 11:19 . . . when you are at *h* and
1 Chr 16:43 . . . turned and went *h* to bless
Ps 46:4 . . . God, the sacred *h* of the Most
Prov 3:33 . . . but he blesses the *h* of the
Prov 27:8 . . . person who strays from *h*
Matt 10:11 . . . stay in his *h* until you leave
Luke 10:7 . . . move around from *h*
Luke 19:9 . . . has come to this *h* today,
John 14:2 . . . in my Father's *h.* If this
John 14:23 . . . make our *h* with each
Acts 16:15 . . . stay at my *h.*
Rom 16:5 . . . meets in their *h.* Greet my
Eph 3:17 . . . will make his *h* in your
1 Tim 5:4 . . . show godliness at *h*
Heb 13:14 . . . not our permanent *h;* we are
1 Pet 4:9 . . . share your *h* with those who

## HOMOSEXUALITY (n)  erotic activity with another of the same sex
1 Cor 6:9 . . . prostitutes, or practice *h,*
1 Tim 1:10 . . . or who practice *h,* or are

## HONEST (adj)  truthful; genuine; reputable; marked by integrity
Exod 18:21 . . . some capable, *h* men
2 Kgs 12:15 . . . were *h* and trustworthy
Ps 37:37 . . . those who are *h* and good,
Prov 12:17 . . . An *h* witness tells
Prov 28:6 . . . Better to be poor and *h* than
Jer 5:1 . . . find even one just and *h* person,
Matt 22:16 . . . we know how *h* you are.
1 Thes 2:10 . . . devout and *h* and faultless

## HONESTY (n)  fairness and straightforwardness of conduct; sincerity
Ps 51:6 . . . But you desire *h* from the
Prov 11:5 . . . are directed by *h;* the wicked
Jer 5:3 . . . searching for *h.* You struck

## HONEY (n)  a sweet liquid substance produced by bees; symbolic of abundance or delight in God's word
Exod 3:8 . . . with milk and *h*—the land
1 Sam 14:26 . . . dare touch the *h*
Ps 19:10 . . . sweeter than *h,* even honey
Ps 119:103 . . . they are sweeter than *h.*
Isa 7:15 . . . yogurt and *h.*
Rev 10:9 . . . be sweet as *h* in your mouth,

## HONEYCOMB (n)  a mass of hexagonal wax cells in a honeybee nest that stores honey
Song 5:1 . . . and eat *h* with my honey.

## HONOR, HONORS (n)  having a renowned reputation or social standing; physical or spiritual blessing (from God); a showing of merited respect
Ps 8:5 . . . crowned them with glory and *h.*
Ps 104:1 . . . are robed with *h* and majesty.
Prov 3:35 . . . The wise inherit *h,* but fools
Prov 15:33 . . . humility precedes *h.*
Prov 25:27 . . . not good to seek *h–s*
Isa 53:12 . . . I will give him the *h–s* of a
Isa 55:13 . . . will bring great *h* to the
Luke 14:8 . . . don't sit in the seat of *h.*
Eph 1:20 . . . the place of *h* at God's right

Heb 13:4 . . . Give *h* to marriage,
1 Pet 2:6 . . . chosen for great *h,* and
1 Pet 2:12 . . . they will give *h* to God when
1 Pet 3:7 . . . husbands must give *h* to
2 Pet 1:17 . . . when he received *h* and glory
Rev 4:9 . . . give glory and *h* and thanks
Rev 19:7 . . . and let us give *h* to him.

## HONOR, HONORED, HONORING, HONORS (v)  of God, to reverence his majesty; of man, to respect or esteem; to confer honor upon
Exod 20:12 . . . *H* your father and mother.
1 Kgs 8:43 . . . Temple I have built *h–s*
Neh 1:11 . . . who delight in *h–ing* you.
Ps 29:1 . . . *H* the LORD, you
Ps 45:11 . . . *h* him, for he is your LORD.
Ps 46:10 . . . I will be *h–ed* by every nation.
Ps 47:9 . . . He is highly *h–ed* everywhere.
Prov 14:31 . . . helping the poor *h–s* him.
Isa 66:5 . . . the LORD be *h–ed!*
Matt 15:4 . . . God says, '*H* your father and
Mark 6:4 . . . A prophet is *h–ed* everywhere
Luke 16:15 . . . What this world *h–s*
John 5:23 . . . that everyone will *h* the Son,
John 12:26 . . . the Father will *h* anyone who
Rom 12:10 . . . delight in *h–ing* each other.
Rom 13:3 . . . and they will *h* you.
1 Cor 6:20 . . . So you must *h* God with your
1 Cor 12:26 . . . if one part is *h–ed,* all the
Eph 6:2 . . . *H* your father and mother
Col 1:10 . . . the way you live will always *h*
1 Thes 5:12 . . . and sisters, *h* those who are
2 Thes 1:12 . . . be *h–ed* along with him.
Titus 2:3 . . . a way that *h–s* God.

## HOPE, HOPES (n)  confident trust with the expectation of fulfillment
1 Sam 9:20 . . . focus of all Israel's *h–s.*
Job 31:16 . . . crushed the *h–s* of widows?
Ps 10:17 . . . LORD, you know the *h–s* of the
Ps 42:5 . . . I will put my *h* in God!
Ps 112:10 . . . slink away, their *h–s* thwarted.
Ps 119:49 . . . to me; it is my only *h.*
Ps 119:74 . . . I have put my *h* in your word.
Prov 10:24 . . . the *h–s* of the godly will be
Prov 13:12 . . . *H* deferred makes the heart
Zech 9:12 . . . prisoners who still have *h!*
Rom 5:4 . . . our confident *h* of salvation.
Rom 8:20 . . . curse. But with eager *h,*
Rom 12:12 . . . Rejoice in our confident *h.*
Rom 15:4 . . . give us *h* and encouragement
Rom 15:13 . . . God, the source of *h,* will
1 Cor 13:13 . . . faith, *h,* and love—
1 Cor 15:19 . . . And if our *h* in Christ is
Eph 2:12 . . . without God and without *h.*
1 Thes 1:3 . . . and the enduring *h* you have
1 Tim 4:10 . . . struggle, for our *h* is in the
Heb 10:23 . . . wavering to the *h* we affirm,
1 Pet 3:15 . . . about your Christian *h,*

## HORSE (n)  a large solid-hoofed herbivorous mammal often used for working or riding
Ps 147:10 . . . strength of a *h* or in human
Prov 26:3 . . . Guide a *h* with a
Zech 1:8 . . . on a red *h* that was standing
Rev 6:2 . . . saw a white *h* standing there.
Rev 6:4 . . . Then another *h* appeared,
Rev 6:5 . . . saw a black *h,* and its rider
Rev 6:8 . . . and saw a *h* whose color was
Rev 19:11 . . . and a white *h* was standing

## HOSANNA (KJV)
Matt 21:9 . . . *Praise God* in highest heaven!

Matt 21:15 . . . *Praise God* for the Son of David
Mark 11:9 . . . *Praise God!* Blessings on the one
Mark 11:10 . . . *Praise God* in highest heaven
John 12:13 . . . *Praise God!* Blessings on the

## HOSPITALITY (n)  generous and cordial treatment, reception, or disposition
Matt 25:38 . . . and show you *h?*
Luke 10:7 . . . Don't hesitate to accept *h,*
Rom 12:13 . . . be eager to practice *h.*

## HOSTILITY (n)  deep-seated ill will; enmity
Gen 3:15 . . . I will cause *h* between you
Lev 26:28 . . . I will give full vent to my *h.*
Gal 5:20 . . . sorcery, *h,* quarreling,
Eph 2:14 . . . the wall of *h* that separated
Eph 2:16 . . . our *h* toward each other was
Heb 12:3 . . . of all the *h* he endured from

## HOUSE, HOUSES (n)  living quarters; a family including ancestors, descendants, and kindred extended family unit, including ancestors and descendants
*see also* HOME, TEMPLE
Exod 12:22 . . . doorframes of your *h–s.*
Exod 12:27 . . . he passed over the *h–s* of the
Exod 20:17 . . . your neighbor's *h.*
2 Sam 7:11 . . . he will make a *h* for you—
Ps 23:6 . . . live in the *h* of the LORD
Ps 27:4 . . . to live in the *h* of the LORD
Ps 69:9 . . . for your *h* has consumed me,
Ps 127:1 . . . Unless the LORD builds a *h,*
Isa 54:2 . . . Enlarge your *h;*
Amos 5:11 . . . beautiful stone *h–s,* you will
Matt 7:24 . . . who builds a *h* on solid rock.
Matt 19:29 . . . given up *h–s* or brothers or
Mark 11:17 . . . be called a *h* of prayer for
John 2:17 . . . for God's *h* will consume me.

## HOUSEHOLD (n)  a social unit composed of those living together in the same dwelling; family
*see also* FAMILY
Exod 12:3 . . . one animal for each *h.*
Acts 16:31 . . . everyone in your *h.*
1 Tim 3:5 . . . manage his own *h,*
1 Tim 3:12 . . . children and *h* well.
1 Tim 3:15 . . . themselves in the *h* of God.
1 Pet 4:17 . . . begin with God's *h.*

## HUMAN (adj)  of, relating to, or characteristic of men and women collectively; mortal; finite
Gen 1:26 . . . Let us make *h* beings in our
Gen 3:22 . . . Look, the *h* beings have
Gen 9:6 . . . If anyone takes a *h* life,
Ps 9:20 . . . they are merely *h.*
Ps 33:13 . . . sees the whole *h* race.
Ps 89:47 . . . futile this *h* existence!
John 1:14 . . . So the Word became *h*
John 2:24 . . . because he knew *h* nature.
John 8:15 . . . judge me by *h* standards,
Rom 6:19 . . . weakness of your *h* nature,
1 Cor 2:5 . . . trust not in *h* wisdom but in
1 Cor 2:13 . . . come from *h* wisdom.
2 Cor 3:3 . . . of stone, but on *h* hearts.
2 Cor 10:3 . . . We are *h,* but we
Gal 3:3 . . . by your own *h* effort?
Col 2:9 . . . of God in a *h* body.
1 Thes 2:13 . . . words as mere *h* ideas.
Heb 7:28 . . . limited by *h* weakness.
2 Pet 1:21 . . . or from *h* initiative.

## HUMAN, HUMANS (n)  a homo sapien; mankind
Gen 6:3 . . . Spirit will not put up with *h–s*
Isa 2:22 . . . trust in mere *h–s.* They are as
Jer 17:5 . . . trust in mere *h–s,* who rely on

**HUMBLE (adj)**  not proud or haughty; can imply lower social or economic status; meek or gentle
Num 12:3 . . . Moses was very *h*—
Ps 138:6 . . . cares for the *h*, but he keeps
Ps 149:4 . . . he crowns the *h* with victory.
Zech 9:9 . . . yet he is *h*, riding on a
Matt 5:5 . . . those who are *h*,
Matt 11:29 . . . I am *h* and gentle at
Matt 21:5 . . . He is *h*, riding on a
Eph 4:2 . . . Always be *h* and gentle.
Phil 2:3 . . . Be *h*, thinking of
Jas 4:6 . . . but favors the *h*.
1 Pet 3:8 . . . and keep a *h* attitude.

**HUMBLE, HUMBLED, HUMBLES (v)**  to not think too highly of oneself; to bring low or prostrate
Isa 26:5 . . . He *h-s* the proud and
Luke 14:11 . . . themselves will be *h-d*,
Luke 18:14 . . . will be *h-d*, and those who
2 Cor 11:7 . . . wrong when I *h-d* myself
Phil 2:8 . . . he *h-d* himself in obedience
Jas 1:10 . . . that God has *h-d* them.
Jas 4:10 . . . *H* yourselves before the Lord,
1 Pet 5:6 . . . So *h* yourselves under

**HUMILIATE, HUMILIATED (v)**  to shame or mortify
Deut 21:14 . . . for you have *h-ed* her.
2 Sam 22:28 . . . watch the proud and *h*
Ps 18:27 . . . but you *h* the proud

**HUMILITY (n)**  show of submission or meekness; quality or state of being humble
Prov 11:2 . . . but with *h* comes wisdom.
Prov 15:33 . . . *h* precedes honor.
Prov 22:4 . . . True *h* and fear
Col 3:12 . . . kindness, *h*, gentleness,
Jas 3:13 . . . works with the *h* that comes
1 Pet 5:5 . . . each other in *h*, for "God

**HUNGER (n)**  a craving or urgent need for food
Ps 145:16 . . . you satisfy the *h* and thirst

**HUNGRY (adj)**  feeling a strong desire for food; a craving for anything
Prov 25:21 . . . If your enemies are *h*,
Matt 15:32 . . . to send them away *h*,
Matt 25:35 . . . For I was *h*, and you fed me.
Luke 1:53 . . . He has filled the *h* with good
Luke 6:21 . . . you who are *h* now, for you
John 6:35 . . . never be *h* again.
Rom 8:35 . . . or are persecuted, or *h*, or
Rom 12:20 . . . enemies are *h*, feed them.
Rev 7:16 . . . never again be *h* or thirsty;

**HUSBAND, HUSBANDS (n)**  male partner in a marriage; head of family; protector and provider; figurative of Christ
Ruth 1:11 . . . could grow up to be your *h-s?*
Prov 12:4 . . . is a crown for her *h*,
Prov 31:28 . . . Her *h* praises her:
Jer 3:20 . . . wife who leaves her *h*.
Rom 7:2 . . . binds her to her *h* as long as
1 Cor 7:3 . . . The *h* should fulfill
1 Cor 7:10 . . . not leave her *h*.
1 Cor 7:39 . . . is bound to her *h* as long as
2 Cor 11:2 . . . bride to one *h*—Christ.
Gal 4:27 . . . lives with her *h!*
Eph 5:22 . . . means submit to your *h-s* as to
Eph 5:23 . . . For a *h* is the head
Eph 5:25 . . . For *h-s*, this means
Eph 5:28 . . . the same way, *h-s* ought to love
Col 3:18 . . . submit to your *h-s*, as is

Col 3:19 . . . *H-s*, love your
1 Tim 5:9 . . . faithful to her *h*.
Titus 2:4 . . . to love their *h-s* and their
1 Pet 3:1 . . . the authority of your *h-s*.
1 Pet 3:7 . . . same way, you *h-s* must give

**HYMN, HYMNS (n)**  a song of praise to God
Ps 40:3 . . . to sing, a *h* of praise to our
Matt 26:30 . . . they sang a *h* and went out
Mark 14:26 . . . they sang a *h* and went out
Acts 16:25 . . . praying and singing *h-s*
Eph 5:19 . . . psalms and *h-s* and spiritual
Col 3:16 . . . psalms and *h-s* and spiritual

**HYPOCRISY (n)**  feigning to be what one is not; pretense of piety
Matt 23:28 . . . your hearts are filled with *h*
Mark 12:15 . . . saw through their *h*
Gal 2:13 . . . followed Peter's *h*, and even
Gal 2:13 . . . led astray by their *h*.
1 Pet 2:1 . . . all deceit, *h*, jealousy,

**HYPOCRITE, HYPOCRITES (n)**  a person who portrays a false appearance of religion; a person who acts in contradiction to his or her stated beliefs; pretender
Matt 6:16 . . . make it obvious, as the *h-s*
Matt 7:5 . . . *H!* First get rid of the log
Matt 23:13 . . . and you Pharisees. *H-s!*
Luke 6:42 . . . the log in your own eye? *H!*
Luke 13:15 . . . Lord replied, "You *h-s!*
1 Tim 4:2 . . . These people are *h-s* and liars,

**IDOL, IDOLS (n)**  a representation or symbol of a false god
Exod 20:4 . . . make for yourself an *i*
Deut 27:15 . . . who carves or casts an *i*
1 Sam 15:23 . . . as bad as worshiping *i-s*.
Isa 40:19 . . . Can he be compared to an *i*
Isa 44:9 . . . who worship *i-s* don't know
Isa 44:15 . . . makes an *i* and bows down
Isa 44:17 . . . and makes his god: a carved *i!*
Isa 44:19 . . . who made the *i* never stops to
Hab 2:18 . . . What good is an *i* carved
Acts 15:20 . . . eating food offered to *i-s*,
Rom 1:23 . . . worshiped *i-s* made to look
1 Cor 6:9 . . . or who worship *i-s*, or commit
1 Cor 8:1 . . . has been offered to *i-s*.
1 Cor 8:4 . . . an *i* is not really a god
Rev 2:14 . . . sin by eating food offered to *i-s*

**IDOLATRY (n)**  the worship of a physical object as a god; immoderate attachment or devotion to something
Gal 5:20 . . . pleasures, *i*, sorcery,

**IMAGE (n)**  a God-given likeness or reflection; a tangible or visible representation
Gen 1:26 . . . make human beings in our *i*,
Gen 1:27 . . . human beings in his own *i*.
Gen 9:6 . . . made human beings in his own *i*.
Col 1:15 . . . Christ is the visible *i* of the
Jas 3:9 . . . have been made in the *i* of God.

**IMITATE, IMITATED (v)**  to follow as a pattern, model, or example; to resemble; to mimic
1 Cor 4:16 . . . I urge you to *i* me.
1 Cor 11:1 . . . should *i* me, just as I *i*
1 Thes 1:6 . . . In this way, you *i-d* both us and
1 Thes 2:14 . . . you *i-d* the believers
2 Thes 3:7 . . . that you ought to *i* us.

**IMMANUEL (n)**  Hebrew name meaning "God is with us"

Isa 7:14 . . . to a son and will call him *I*
Isa 8:8 . . . one end to the other, O *I*.
Matt 1:23 . . . a son, and they will call him *I*,

**IMMATURE (adj)**  lacking complete growth, development, or maturity
Eph 4:14 . . . no longer be *i* like children.

**IMMORAL (adj)**  characterized by conflicting with traditionally (biblically) held moral principles; sinful or impure
Prov 2:16 . . . save you from the *i* woman,
Prov 6:24 . . . keep you from the *i* woman,
Prov 22:14 . . . an *i* woman is a dangerous
Luke 7:37 . . . a certain *i* woman from
Rom 13:13 . . . promiscuity and *i* living,
Eph 5:5 . . . be sure that no *i*, impure,
1 Tim 1:10 . . . people who are sexually *i*,
Jude 1:4 . . . grace allows us to live *i* lives.
Rev 22:15 . . . the sorcerers, the sexually *i*,

**IMMORALITY (n)**  the quality or state of being immoral; an immoral act or practice
Matt 15:19 . . . all sexual *i*, theft, lying,
Acts 15:29 . . . animals, and from sexual *i*.
1 Cor 6:13 . . . made for sexual *i*.
1 Cor 6:18 . . . *i* is a sin against
1 Cor 7:2 . . . there is so much sexual *i*,
Gal 5:19 . . . very clear: sexual *i*, impurity,
2 Pet 2:7 . . . who was sick of the shameful *i*
Jude 1:7 . . . towns, which were filled with *i*

**IMPARTIAL (adj)**  not partial or biased; treating all equally
Deut 1:17 . . . and *i* in your judgments.
Matt 22:16 . . . *i* and don't play favorites.

**IMPOSSIBLE (adj)**  incapable of being or occurring
Zech 8:6 . . . this may seem *i* to you now,
Luke 1:37 . . . For nothing is *i* with God.
Heb 6:4 . . . it is *i* to bring back
Heb 11:6 . . . it is *i* to please God

**INDULGE, INDULGED, INDULGES (v)**  to take unrestrained pleasure in
Rom 1:26 . . . *i-d* in sex with each other.
Rom 13:14 . . . ways to *i* your evil desires.
1 Cor 5:9 . . . people who *i* in sexual sin.
1 Cor 5:11 . . . claims to be a believer yet *i-s*

**INFANTS (n)**  a child in the first period of (physical or spiritual) life
Ps 8:2 . . . and *i* to tell of your strength,
Matt 21:16 . . . and *i* to give you praise.
1 Cor 3:1 . . . were *i* in the Christian life.

**INHERIT, INHERITED (v)**  to receive as a legacy or promise; to take possession as a rightful heir
Matt 5:5 . . . they will *i* the whole earth.
Matt 25:34 . . . *i* the Kingdom prepared
Mark 10:17 . . . I do to *i* eternal life?
1 Cor 6:9 . . . will not *i* the Kingdom
Eph 3:6 . . . share equally in the riches *i-ed*
Eph 5:5 . . . impure, or greedy person will *i*
Rev 21:7 . . . All who are victorious will *i*

**INHERITANCE (n)**  the acquisition of a possession, condition, or trait from past generations; something that is or may be inherited
Ps 16:6 . . . What a wonderful *i!*
Ps 33:12 . . . people he has chosen as his *i*.
Ps 61:5 . . . an *i* reserved for those who fear
Gal 4:30 . . . will not share the *i*
Eph 1:14 . . . give us the *i* he promised

Col 3:24 . . . give you an *i* as your reward,
Heb 9:15 . . . receive the eternal *i* God has

**INIQUITY, INIQUITIES (KJV)**
Ps 51:9 . . . Remove the stain of my *guilt*
Isa 6:7 . . . your *guilt* is removed,
Isa 53:6 . . . laid on him the *sins* of us all.
1 Cor 13:6 . . . not rejoice about *injustice*
Rev 18:5 . . . God remembers her *evil deeds*

**INNOCENCE (n)** freedom from guilt or sin through being unacquainted with evil; blamelessness
Gen 20:5 . . . I acted in complete *i!*
2 Sam 22:25 . . . He has seen my *i.*
Hos 8:5 . . . will you be incapable of *i?*

**INNOCENT (adj)** regarded as righteous; free from guilt or sin; unaware or ignorant
Job 13:18 . . . I will be proved *i.*
Job 34:5 . . . Job also said, 'I am *i,*
Ps 7:8 . . . for I am *i,* O Most High!
Ps 26:1 . . . Declare me *i,* O LORD, for I
Ps 143:2 . . . no one is *i* before you.
Matt 27:4 . . . I have betrayed an *i* man.
Matt 27:24 . . . I am *i* of this man's blood.
Rom 16:18 . . . they deceive *i* people.

**INSIGHT (n)** the power or act of seeing into a situation; discernment
Ps 19:8 . . . are clear, giving *i* for living.
Prov 7:4 . . . make *i* a beloved member
Eph 1:17 . . . and *i* so that you might grow

**INSPIRED (adj)** to influence, move, or guide by divine influence
2 Tim 3:16 . . . All Scripture is *i* by God

**INSTRUCT, INSTRUCTED, INSTRUCTS (v)** to provide with authoritative information or advice; to teach, train, or direct
Exod 4:12 . . . I will *i* you in what to say.
Deut 2:1 . . . just as the LORD had *i-ed* me,
Deut 4:36 . . . so he could *i* you.
Josh 11:9 . . . chariots, as the LORD had *i-ed.*
Josh 11:23 . . . as the LORD had *i-ed* Moses.
Ps 105:22 . . . He could *i* the king's aides
Prov 9:9 . . . *i* the wise, and they will be even
Prov 10:8 . . . The wise are glad to be *i-ed,*
Prov 21:11 . . . if you *i* the wise,
Acts 8:31 . . . unless someone *i-s* me?
2 Tim 2:25 . . . Gently *i* those who oppose
Titus 2:12 . . . *i-ed* to turn from godless living

**INSTRUCTION, INSTRUCTIONS (n)** a command or principle intended especially as a general rule of action; an order; directions; the action, practice, or profession of teaching *see also* COMMANDMENT(S), LAW(S)
Exod 34:32 . . . Moses gave them all the *i-s*
Deut 31:11 . . . you must read this Book of *I*
Josh 1:7 . . . Be careful to obey all the *i-s*
Josh 1:8 . . . Study this Book of *I*
Ps 19:7 . . . The *i-s* of the LORD are perfect,
Ps 40:8 . . . your *i-s* are written on my heart.
Ps 119:97 . . . Oh, how I love your *i-s!*
Prov 4:13 . . . Take hold of my *i-s;*
Prov 7:2 . . . Guard my *i-s* as you guard
Prov 8:33 . . . Listen to my *i* and be wise.
Prov 23:12 . . . Commit yourself to *i;*
Isa 40:14 . . . need *i* about what is good?
Jer 31:33 . . . put my *i-s* deep within
Zech 7:12 . . . they could not hear the *i-s*
1 Tim 1:5 . . . purpose of my *i* is that all
1 Tim 1:18 . . . here are my *i-s* for you,

**INSULT, INSULTS (n)** a gross indignity
Job 20:3 . . . I've had to endure your *i-s,*
Ps 69:7 . . . For I endure *i-s* for your sake;
Ps 69:9 . . . the *i-s* of those who insult you
Ps 69:20 . . . Their *i-s* have broken my heart,
Prov 9:7 . . . will get an *i* in return.
Prov 22:10 . . . and *i-s* will disappear.
Rom 15:3 . . . The *i-s* of those who insult you,
2 Cor 12:10 . . . and in the *i-s,* hardships,
Jude 1:15 . . . all the *i-s* that ungodly sinners

**INSULT, INSULTED (v)** to treat with insolence, indignity, or contempt
Prov 12:16 . . . stays calm when *i-ed.*
Prov 20:20 . . . *i* your father or mother,
Prov 30:9 . . . and thus *i* God's holy name.
Heb 10:29 . . . have *i-ed* and disdained
1 Pet 2:23 . . . not retaliate when he was *i-ed,*
1 Pet 3:9 . . . insults when people *i* you.
1 Pet 4:14 . . . be happy when you are *i-ed*

**INTEGRITY (n)** honesty; without compromise or corruption
Job 2:3 . . . a man of complete *i.*
Job 2:9 . . . still trying to maintain your *i?*
Job 27:5 . . . I will defend my *i* until I die.
Ps 25:21 . . . May *i* and honesty protect me,
Ps 26:11 . . . I live with *i.* So redeem
Ps 111:8 . . . faithfully and with *i.*
Ps 119:1 . . . Joyful are people of *i,*
Prov 2:7 . . . shield to those who walk with *i.*
Prov 10:9 . . . People with *i* walk safely,
Titus 2:7 . . . you do reflect the *i*

**INTERCEDE, INTERCEDED (v)** to mediate or plead another's case for justice or mercy
Isa 53:12 . . . of many and *i-d* for rebels.
1 Tim 2:1 . . . *i* on their behalf, and
Heb 7:25 . . . lives forever to *i* with God

**INTERPRET, INTERPRETS (v)** to explain; to translate
Gen 41:15 . . . a dream you can *i* it.
Matt 16:3 . . . how to *i* the weather
1 Cor 12:30 . . . to *i* unknown languages?
1 Cor 14:5 . . . unless someone *i-s* what you
1 Cor 14:13 . . . *i* what has been said.
1 Cor 14:26 . . . another will *i* what is said.
1 Cor 14:27 . . . must *i* what they say.
1 Cor 14:28 . . . is present who can *i,*

**INVISIBLE (adj)** hidden; imperceptible
Rom 1:20 . . . see his *i* qualities—
Col 1:15 . . . visible image of the *i* God.
Heb 11:27 . . . his eyes on the one who is *i.*

**IRON (n)** metal used in instruments of war, farming, and building; symbolic of strength for both security and destruction
Ps 2:9 . . . break them with an *i* rod
Prov 27:17 . . . As *i* sharpens *i,* so
Dan 2:33 . . . its legs were *i,* and its feet
Rev 2:27 . . . rule the nations with an *i* rod
Rev 12:5 . . . nations with an *i* rod.
Rev 19:15 . . . rule them with an *i* rod.

**ISAAC** Patriarch, son of Abraham; promised by God (Gen 17:16-22; 18:14); born (Gen 21:1-7; 1 Chr 1:28; Acts 7:8); recipient of divine covenant (Gen 17:21; 26:2-5); offered to God by Abraham (Gen 22:1-19; Heb 11:17-19); took Rebekah as wife (Gen 24:67); inherited wealth (Gen 25:5); prayed for wife to have children (Gen 25:20-21); father of twins, Esau and Jacob (Gen 25:24; 1 Chr 1:34); preferred Esau (Gen

25:28); dealings with Abimelech (Gen 26:1-31); tricked into blessing Jacob (Gen 27:1-29); died (Gen 35:27-29); father of a nation (Deut 29:13; Rom 9:7, 10); often mentioned in NT (Luke 3:34; Gal 4:28; Heb 11:9, 17-20; Jas 2:21).

**ISRAEL**
1. Another name for Jacob (Gen 32:28); *see* JACOB.
2. The United Kingdom of Israel, including all twelve tribes, as ruled by Saul, David, and Solomon.
3. The Northern Kingdom of Israel, including the ten northern tribes, in contrast to Judah (Southern Kingdom) (*see* 2 Sam 19:41-43).
Exod 3:9 . . . cry of the people of *I* has
Exod 12:37 . . . *I* left Rameses and started
Exod 16:1 . . . *I* set out from Elim
Exod 28:29 . . . *I* on the sacred chestpiece
Exod 31:16 . . . *I* must keep the Sabbath day
Exod 39:42 . . . *I* followed all of the LORD's
Lev 25:55 . . . the people of *I* belong to me.
Num 6:23 . . . *I* with this special blessing:
Num 9:17 . . . *I* would break camp and follow
Num 20:22 . . . community of *I* left Kadesh
Num 27:12 . . . I have given the people of *I.*
Num 35:10 . . . instructions to the people of *I.*
Deut 10:12 . . . *I,* what does the LORD your
Josh 21:3 . . . *I* gave the Levites the following
Judg 17:6 . . . In those days *I* had no king;
1 Sam 3:20 . . . And all *I,* from Dan
1 Sam 4:21 . . . said, "*I*'s glory is gone."
1 Sam 15:26 . . . rejected you as king of *I.*
1 Sam 18:16 . . . all *I* and Judah loved David
2 Sam 14:25 . . . handsome man in all *I.*
1 Kgs 1:35 . . . him to be ruler over *I*
1 Kgs 12:1 . . . *I* had gathered to make him king.
1 Kgs 19:18 . . . preserve 7,000 others in *I*
2 Kgs 17:24 . . . replacing the people of *I.*
1 Chr 11:4 . . . and all *I* went to Jerusalem
1 Chr 21:1 . . . Satan rose up against *I*
2 Chr 9:8 . . . Because God loves *I*
Ps 73:1 . . . Truly God is good to *I,*
Ps 98:3 . . . to love and be faithful to *I,*
Isa 44:6 . . . says—*I*'s King and Redeemer,
Isa 44:21 . . . you are my servant, O *I.*
Jer 2:3 . . . In those days *I* was holy
Jer 31:2 . . . I will give rest to the people of *I.*
Jer 31:9 . . . For I am *I*'s father,
Jer 31:31 . . . covenant with the people of *I*
Ezek 3:17 . . . as a watchman for *I.*
Hos 1:10 . . . *I*'s people will be like the sands
Hos 3:1 . . . LORD still loves *I,* even though
Amos 4:12 . . . in judgment, you people of *I!*
Amos 8:2 . . . Like this fruit, *I* is ripe
Mic 5:2 . . . a ruler of *I* will come from you,
Mal 1:5 . . . far beyond *I*'s borders!
Matt 2:6 . . . the shepherd for my people *I.*
Matt 10:6 . . . people of *I*—God's lost sheep.
Matt 15:24 . . . lost sheep—the people of *I.*
Mark 12:29 . . . Listen, O *I!*
Acts 1:6 . . . time come for you to free *I*
Acts 9:15 . . . as well as to the people of *I.*
Rom 9:4 . . . *I,* chosen to be God's adopted
Rom 9:6 . . . *I* are truly members of God's
Rom 9:27 . . . *I* are as numerous as the sand
Rom 9:31 . . . *I,* who tried so hard to get
Rom 10:1 . . . the people of *I* to be saved.
Rom 11:7 . . . *I* have not found the favor of God
Rom 11:26 . . . And so all *I* will be saved.

Eph 2:12 . . . citizenship among the people of *I*,
Heb 8:8 . . . covenant with the people of *I*
Rev 7:4 . . . sealed from all the tribes of *I:*
Rev 21:12 . . . *I* were written on the gates.

**JACOB** Patriarch, son of Isaac, grandson of
Abraham; younger twin son of Issac and
Rebekah (Gen 25:23–35:26; 48–49); also known
as "Israel" (Gen 32:28); favored by Rebekah
(Gen 25:28); bought Esau's birthright for a meal
(Gen 25:29-34); deceived Isaac to receive his
blessing (Gen 27:1-29); fled from Esau (Gen
27:41-45); married inside of clan (Gen 28:1-5);
Jacob's ladder (Gen 28:12); covenant extended
to Jacob in a dream (Gen 28:13-15); wives and
concubines, Rachel favored (Gen 29:1-30);
children (Gen 29:31–30:24; 35:16-26);
prospered at his uncle Laban's expense (Gen
30:25-43); fled from Laban (Gen 31); name
changed to "Israel" (Gen 32:22-32); reconciled
with Esau (Gen 33); favored Rachel's oldest son
Joseph (Gen 37:3); overwhelmed by loss of
Joseph (Gen 37:33-35); migrated to Egypt (Gen
46:5-7); blessed Joseph's sons (Gen 48);
blessed his own sons (Gen 49:1-28); died (Gen
49:33); buried (Gen 50:1-14); often mentioned
in NT (John 4:5-6, 12; Acts 7:8-15; Rom 9:13;
Heb 11:20-21).

**JAMES**
1. One of the 12 disciples, brother of John, son
   of Zebedee (Matt 10:2; Mark 3:17); called by
   Jesus (Matt 4:21; Luke 5:10); zealous for the
   Lord (Luke 9:54); wanted honor (Mark
   10:35-45); witnessed the Transfiguration
   (Matt 17:1-9; Mark 9:2-8; Luke 9:28-36);
   killed by Herod Agrippa I (Acts 12:2).
2. One of the 12 disciples, son of Alphaeus
   (Matt 10:3; Mark 3:18; Luke 6:15); called
   "the younger" (Mark 15:40).
3. Half-brother of Jesus (Matt 13:55; Mark 6:3;
   Luke 24:10; Gal 1:19; 2:9, 12; 1 Cor 15:7),
   brother of Jude (Jude 1:1); leader of Jerusalem Council (Acts 15:13; 21:18); with select
   group before Pentecost (Acts 1:13); wrote
   letter (Jas 1:1).
4. Father of the apostle Judas, not Iscariot
   (Luke 6:16).
5. Son of a certain Mary, perhaps the same as
   the "son of Alphaeus" (Matt 27:56).

**JEALOUS (adj)** intolerant of rivalry or
unfaithfulness; hostile toward a rival
Exod 20:5 . . . am a *j* God who will not
Exod 34:14 . . . whose very name is *J*,
Prov 6:34 . . . *j* husband will be furious,
Nah 1:2 . . . a *j* God, filled with vengeance
Rom 11:14 . . . *j* of what you Gentiles have,
1 Cor 13:4 . . . Love is not *j* or boastful
Gal 5:26 . . . provoke one another, or be *j*
Jas 3:14 . . . if you are bitterly *j* and there is

**JEALOUSY (n)** a jealous feeling, disposition, or
attitude
Prov 27:4 . . . but *j* is even more dangerous.
Rom 10:19 . . . I will rouse your *j*
Rom 13:13 . . . or in quarreling and *j*.
1 Cor 10:22 . . . dare to rouse the Lord's *j?*
2 Cor 11:2 . . . you with the *j* of God
Gal 5:20 . . . *j*, outbursts of anger,
1 Tim 6:4 . . . arguments ending in *j*,
1 Pet 2:1 . . . with all deceit, hypocrisy, *j*,

**JEHOVAH (KJV)**
Exod 6:3 . . . did not reveal my name, *Yahweh*,
Ps 83:18 . . . you alone are called *the* LORD
Isa 12:2 . . . The LORD GOD is my strength
Isa 26:4 . . . the LORD GOD is the eternal

**JERICHO (n)** a city in the plain of the Jordan
Valley at the foot of the ascent to the Judean
mountains
Num 22:1 . . . across from *J*.
Josh 3:16 . . . near the town of *J*.
Josh 5:10 . . . at Gilgal on the plains of *J*,
Luke 10:30 . . . from Jerusalem down to *J*,
Heb 11:30 . . . around *J* for seven days,

**JERUSALEM (n)** sacred city and well-known
capital of Palestine during Bible times
Josh 10:1 . . . Adoni-zedek, king of *J*, heard that
Josh 15:8 . . . where the city of *J* is located.
Judg 1:8 . . . Judah attacked *J* and captured it,
2 Sam 5:5 . . . *J* he reigned over all Israel
2 Sam 11:1 . . . David stayed behind in *J*.
1 Kgs 9:15 . . . terraces, the wall of *J*,
1 Kgs 10:26 . . . and some near him in *J*.
1 Kgs 14:25 . . . came up and attacked *J*.
2 Kgs 8:17 . . . he reigned in *J* eight years.
2 Kgs 12:1 . . . He reigned in *J* forty years.
2 Kgs 14:2 . . . reigned in *J* twenty-nine years.
2 Kgs 15:2 . . . he reigned in *J* fifty-two years.
2 Kgs 16:2 . . . he reigned in *J* sixteen years.
2 Kgs 18:2 . . . reigned in *J* twenty-nine years.
2 Kgs 19:31 . . . will spread out from *J*,
2 Kgs 21:12 . . . I will bring such disaster on *J*
2 Kgs 22:1 . . . he reigned in *J* thirty-one years.
2 Kgs 23:31 . . . he reigned in *J* three months.
2 Kgs 24:8 . . . he reigned in *J* three months.
2 Kgs 24:14 . . . Nebuchadnezzar took all of *J*
2 Kgs 24:20 . . . anger against the people of *J*
2 Kgs 25:9 . . . and all the houses of *J*.
1 Chr 21:16 . . . reaching out over *J*.
2 Chr 3:1 . . . the Temple of the LORD in *J*
2 Chr 9:1 . . . she came to *J* to test him
2 Chr 20:15 . . . all you people of Judah and *J!*
2 Chr 29:8 . . . has fallen upon Judah and *J*.
2 Chr 36:19 . . . tore down the walls of *J*,
Ezra 2:1 . . . but now they returned to *J*
Ezra 4:12 . . . who came here to *J* from Babylon
Ezra 6:12 . . . who has chosen the city of *J*
Ezra 9:9 . . . a protective wall in Judah and *J*.
Neh 1:3 . . . The wall of *J* has been torn
Neh 3:8 . . . They left out a section of *J*
Neh 11:1 . . . of the people were living in *J*,
Neh 12:43 . . . joy of the people of *J* could be
Ps 9:11 . . . the LORD who reigns in *J*.
Ps 51:18 . . . rebuild the walls of *J*.
Ps 74:2 . . . remember *J*, your home here
Ps 79:1 . . . made *J* a heap of ruins.
Ps 87:2 . . . He loves the city of *J* more than
Ps 102:13 . . . arise and have mercy on *J*—
Ps 122:2 . . . standing inside your gates, O *J*.
Ps 122:6 . . . Pray for peace in *J*.
Ps 125:2 . . . *J*, so the LORD surrounds
Ps 128:5 . . . May you see *J* prosper
Ps 137:3 . . . Sing us one of those songs of *J!*
Ps 137:5 . . . If I forget you, O *J*,
Ps 147:2 . . . The LORD is rebuilding *J*
Ps 147:12 . . . Glorify the LORD, O *J!*
Isa 1:1 . . . saw concerning Judah and *J*.
Isa 3:1 . . . take away from *J* and Judah
Isa 4:3 . . . who survive the destruction of *J*
Isa 27:13 . . . return to *J* to worship the LORD
Isa 31:5 . . . will hover over *J* and protect it

Isa 40:2 . . . Speak tenderly to *J*.
Isa 51:11 . . . They will enter *J* singing,
Isa 52:1 . . . beautiful clothes, O holy city of *J*,
Isa 52:8 . . . they see the LORD returning to *J*.
Isa 62:7 . . . he makes *J* the pride of the earth.
Jer 2:2 . . . Go and shout this message to *J*.
Jer 4:5 . . . Shout to Judah, and broadcast to *J!*
Jer 6:6 . . . siege ramps against the walls of *J*.
Jer 9:11 . . . I will make *J* into a heap of ruins,
Jer 23:14 . . . the prophets of *J* are even worse!
Jer 26:18 . . . *J* will be reduced to ruins!
Jer 39:1 . . . came with his army to besiege *J*.
Jer 51:50 . . . think about your home in *J*.
Lam 1:7 . . . *J* remembers her ancient splendor.
Dan 6:10 . . . windows open toward *J*.
Dan 9:2 . . . *J* must lie desolate for seventy
Dan 9:12 . . . a disaster as happened in *J*.
Dan 9:25 . . . command is given to rebuild *J*
Joel 3:16 . . . from Zion and thunder from *J*,
Amos 2:5 . . . fortresses of *J* will be destroyed.
Obad 1:11 . . . and cast lots to divide up *J*,
Mic 4:2 . . . his word will go out from *J*.
Zeph 3:16 . . . the announcement to *J* will be,
Zech 1:17 . . . Zion and choose *J* as his own.
Zech 2:4 . . . *J* will someday be so full
Zech 8:8 . . . home again to live safely in *J*.
Zech 8:22 . . . nations will come to *J* to seek
Zech 9:10 . . . and the warhorses from *J*.
Zech 12:10 . . . and on the people of *J*.
Zech 14:8 . . . waters will flow out from *J*,
Matt 20:18 . . . going up to *J*, where the Son
Matt 21:10 . . . city of *J* was in an uproar
Matt 23:37 . . . *J*, the city that kills the
Mark 10:33 . . . going up to *J*, where the Son
Luke 2:22 . . . parents took him to *J*
Luke 2:41 . . . Jesus' parents went to *J*
Luke 4:9 . . . Then the devil took him to *J*,
Luke 9:31 . . . about to be fulfilled in *J*,
Luke 13:34 . . . O *J*, the city that kills
Luke 18:31 . . . to *J*, where all the predictions
Luke 21:20 . . . you see *J* surrounded
Luke 24:47 . . . nations, beginning in *J*:
Acts 1:8 . . . about me everywhere—in *J*,
Acts 6:7 . . . believers greatly increased in *J*,
Acts 20:22 . . . bound by the Spirit to go to *J*.
Acts 23:11 . . . a witness to me here in *J*,
Rom 9:33 . . . I am placing a stone in *J*
Rom 11:26 . . . rescues will come from *J*,
Rom 15:19 . . . from *J* all the way to Illyricum.
Gal 4:25 . . . *J* is just like Mount Sinai
Gal 4:26 . . . Sarah, represents the heavenly *J*.
Heb 12:22 . . . living God, the heavenly *J*,
Rev 21:10 . . . he showed me the holy city, *J*,

**JESUS** *see* also CHRIST, MESSIAH
Family line (Matt 1:1-17; Luke 3:23-38); birth
announced (Matt 1:18-25; Luke 1:26-38); born
in Bethlehem (Luke 2:1-20); circumcised, officially named, and presented at Temple (Luke
2:21-40); visited by Magi (Matt 2:1-12); escape
to and return from Egypt (Matt 2:13-23); amazed
the Temple scholars (Luke 2:41-50); summary of
youth (Luke 2:51-52); baptized by John (Matt
3:13-17; Mark 1:9-11; Luke 3:21-22; John 1:32-
34); tempted by Satan (Matt 4:1-11; Mark 1:12-
13; Luke 4:1-13); ministered in Galilee (Matt
4:12–18:35; Mark 1:14–9:50); transfigured on
a mountain (Matt 17:1-13; Mark 9:2-13; Luke
9:28-36; 2 Pet 1:16-18); triumphal entry (Matt
21:1-11; Mark 11:1-11; Luke 19:28-44; John
12:12-19); the Last Supper (Matt 26:17-35;

Mark 14:12-31; Luke 22:7-38; John 13–17); betrayed and tried (Matt 26:36–27:31; Mark 14:32–15:20; Luke 22:39–23:25; John 18:1–19:16); crucified, died, and was buried (Matt 27:32-66; Mark 15:21-47; Luke 23:26-56; John 19:17-42); rose again and appeared to followers (Matt 28; Mark 16; Luke 24; John 20–21; Acts 1:1-11; 7:55-56; 9:3-6; 1 Cor 15:1-8; Rev 1:1-20); ascended to heaven (Mark 16:19; Luke 24:50-53; John 1:51; Acts 1:9; Eph 4:8).

**JOHN**

1. The Baptist, son of Zechariah and Elizabeth (Luke 1:5-25, 57-80); called to prepare the way for the Messiah (Isa 40:3-5; Luke 3:1-6; John 1:19-28); called to preach and baptize (Matt 3:1-12; Mark 1:1-8); preached repentance (Luke 3:7-20); baptized Jesus (Matt 3:13-17; Luke 3:21-22); confirmed Jesus' ministry (Matt 3:11-12; Mark 1:7-8; Luke 3:15-18; John 3:22-36; 5:33); ministry compared to Elijah (Mal 4:5; Matt 11:11-19; Mark 9:11-13; Luke 7:24-35); arrested and beheaded by Herod Antipas (Matt 14:1-12; Mark 6:14-29; Luke 9:7-9).

2. One of the 12 disciples, brother of James, son of Zebedee (Matt 10:2; Mark 3:17); witnessed the Transfiguration (Matt 17:1-9; Mark 9:2-8; Luke 9:28-36); inner circle of Jesus' followers (Matt 17:1; Mark 5:37; 9:2; 13:3; Luke 8:51; 9:28; Gal 2:9); with Peter, healed a man and was arrested (Acts 3–4); with Peter, rebuked sorcerer (Acts 8:14-25); wrote fourth Gospel (John 13:23-25; *see also* 20:2; 21:20-25), letters of John (the "elder," 2 Jn 1:1; 3 Jn 1:1), and Revelation (the "servant," Rev 1:1, 9; 22:8).

**JOIN, JOINED, JOINS (v)** to put or bring into close association or relationship; to take part in a collective activity

Ps 26:5 . . . I refuse to *j* in with the wicked.
Dan 11:34 . . . who *j* them will not be sincere.
Zech 2:11 . . . will *j* themselves to the LORD
Matt 19:6 . . . what God has *j - e d* together.
Mark 10:9 . . . what God has *j - e d* together.
Rom 6:3 . . . *j - e d* with Christ Jesus in baptism,
Rom 8:16 . . . his Spirit *j - s* with our spirit
Rom 15:30 . . . *j* in my struggle by praying
1 Cor 6:16 . . . if a man *j - s* himself to
Eph 2:21 . . . carefully *j - e d* together in him,

**JOY, JOYS (n)** the emotion evoked by well-being, success, or good fortune

Deut 16:15 . . . be a time of great *j* for all.
1 Sam 18:6 . . . danced for *j* with tambourines
1 Chr 16:27 . . . and *j* fill his dwelling.
1 Chr 29:22 . . . with great *j* that day.
Ezra 3:12 . . . however, were shouting for *j.*
Neh 8:10 . . . *j* of the LORD is your strength!
Neh 8:17 . . . they were all filled with great *j!*
Esth 9:22 . . . and their mourning into *j.*
Job 3:22 . . . filled with *j* when they finally die,
Job 8:21 . . . your lips with shouts of *j.*
Ps 1:1 . . . *j - s* of those who do not follow the
Ps 2:12 . . . *j* for all who take refuge in him!
Ps 9:2 . . . filled with *j* because of you.
Ps 19:8 . . . are right, bringing *j* to the heart.
Ps 21:1 . . . He shouts with *j*
Ps 28:7 . . . my heart is filled with *j.*
Ps 30:11 . . . and clothed me with *j,*

Ps 32:2 . . . what *j* for those whose record
Ps 33:12 . . . *j* for the nation whose God
Ps 41:1 . . . *j - s* of those who are kind
Ps 42:4 . . . singing for *j* and giving thanks
Ps 45:7 . . . pouring out the oil of *j* on you
Ps 46:4 . . . A river brings *j* to the city
Ps 51:12 . . . to me the *j* of your salvation,
Ps 65:8 . . . you inspire shouts of *j.*
Ps 65:13 . . . They all shout and sing for *j*
Ps 71:23 . . . I will shout for *j* and sing
Ps 92:4 . . . I sing for *j* because of what
Ps 98:4 . . . in praise and sing for *j!*
Ps 105:43 . . . his people out of Egypt with *j,*
Ps 106:5 . . . Let me rejoice in the *j*
Ps 119:92 . . . hadn't sustained me with *j,*
Ps 126:2 . . . with laughter, and we sang for *j.*
Ps 132:9 . . . loyal servants sing for *j.*
Ps 132:16 . . . servants will sing for *j.*
Ps 145:7 . . . with *j* about your righteousness.
Prov 10:1 . . . A wise child brings *j*
Prov 11:10 . . . shout for *j* when the wicked die.
Prov 14:10 . . . no one else can fully share its *j.*
Prov 15:20 . . . Sensible children bring *j* to
Prov 21:15 . . . Justice is a *j* to the godly,
Prov 23:25 . . . your father and mother *j!*
Prov 29:6 . . . righteous escape, shouting for *j.*
Isa 12:6 . . . shout his praise with *j!*
Isa 16:9 . . . no more shouts of *j* over your
Isa 16:10 . . . gone the *j* of harvest.
Isa 26:19 . . . will rise up and sing for *j!*
Isa 35:10 . . . crowned with everlasting *j.*
Isa 42:11 . . . Let the people of Sela sing for *j;*
Isa 49:13 . . . Sing for *j,* O heavens!
Isa 51:11 . . . filled with *j* and gladness.
Isa 52:8 . . . watchmen shout and sing with *j,*
Isa 56:7 . . . fill them with *j* in my house
Isa 60:15 . . . beautiful forever, a *j* to all
Isa 61:7 . . . everlasting *j* will be yours.
Isa 65:14 . . . My servants will sing for *j,* but
Jer 31:13 . . . young women will dance for *j,*
Jer 31:13 . . . turn their mourning into *j.*
Jer 33:11 . . . the sounds of *j* and laughter.
Jer 48:33 . . . treads the grapes with shouts of *j.*
Jer 49:25 . . . a city of *j,* will be forsaken!
Joel 1:12 . . . And the people's *j* has dried up
Matt 2:10 . . . they were filled with *j!*
Matt 28:8 . . . but also filled with great *j,*
Mark 1:11 . . . Son, and you bring me great *j.*
Mark 4:16 . . . and immediately receive it with *j.*
Luke 1:14 . . . have great *j* and gladness,
Luke 1:44 . . . in my womb jumped for *j.*
Luke 2:10 . . . bring great *j* to all people.
Luke 6:23 . . . be happy! Yes, leap for *j!*
Luke 10:21 . . . with the *j* of the Holy Spirit,
Luke 24:41 . . . filled with *j* and wonder.
John 15:11 . . . you will be filled with my *j.*
John 16:20 . . . turn to wonderful *j.*
John 16:24 . . . and you will have abundant *j.*
John 20:20 . . . *j* when they saw the Lord!
Acts 2:28 . . . you will fill me with the *j*
Acts 2:46 . . . their meals with great *j*
Acts 11:23 . . . he was filled with *j,*
Acts 13:52 . . . believers were filled with *j*
Acts 15:3 . . . everyone's *j*—that the Gentiles,
Rom 14:17 . . . and *j* in the Holy Spirit.
Rom 15:13 . . . with *j* and peace because
2 Cor 1:24 . . . so you will be full of *j,*
2 Cor 2:3 . . . ought to give me the greatest *j.*
2 Cor 2:3 . . . *j* comes from your being *j*ful.
2 Cor 6:10 . . . but we always have *j.*

2 Cor 7:7 . . . I was filled with *j!*
Gal 5:22 . . . fruit in our lives: love, *j,* peace,
Phil 1:4 . . . requests for all of you with *j,*
Phil 1:25 . . . experience the *j* of your faith.
Phil 4:1 . . . you are my *j* and the crown I
1 Thes 1:6 . . . received the message with *j*
1 Thes 2:19 . . . what gives us hope and *j,*
1 Thes 2:20 . . . Yes, you are our pride and *j.*
1 Thes 3:9 . . . we have great *j*
2 Tim 1:4 . . . with *j* when we are together
Heb 10:34 . . . you accepted it with *j.*
Heb 12:2 . . . Because of the *j* awaiting him,
Heb 13:17 . . . reason to do this with *j*
Jas 1:2 . . . it an opportunity for great *j.*
1 Pet 1:8 . . . a glorious, inexpressible *j.*
1 Pet 4:13 . . . the wonderful *j* of seeing his
1 Jn 1:4 . . . you may fully share our *j.*

**JUDAH**

1. Fourth son of Jacob and Leah (Gen 29:35), who gave his name to a tribe of Israel; interceded for Joseph (Gen 37:26-27); failed to uphold daughter-in-law Tamar's rights (Gen 38:1-30); offered himself as slave and ransom (Gen 44:18-34); given the family birthright by Jacob (Gen 49:3-10); his tribe was numbered (Num 1:26-27), allotted land and cities (Josh 15:1-63), led the conquest of Canaan (Judg 1:2); 12,000 to be marked by God (Rev 7:7).

2. The Southern Kingdom of Judah, including the tribes of Judah and Benjamin, in contrast to Israel (Northern Kingdom) (*see also* 2 Sam 12:8).

**JUDEA (n)** the Greco-Roman name for the land of Judah

Matt 2:1 . . . was born in Bethlehem in *J,*
Matt 24:16 . . . in *J* must flee to the hills.
Luke 3:1 . . . Pilate was governor over *J;*
Acts 1:8 . . . throughout *J,* in Samaria,
Acts 9:31 . . . had peace throughout *J,*
1 Thes 2:14 . . . in God's churches in *J*

**JUDGE, JUDGES (n)** a public official authorized to decide issues brought before a court; one of a cycle of charismatic deliverers of ancient Israel

Deut 17:12 . . . to reject the verdict of the *j*
Judg 2:16 . . . LORD raised up *j - s* to rescue
Judg 2:18 . . . the LORD raised up a *j*
1 Sam 7:6 . . . Samuel became Israel's *j.* )
1 Sam 7:15 . . . continued as Israel's *j*
Ps 50:6 . . . God himself will be the *j.*
Isa 33:22 . . . the LORD is our *j,* our lawgiver,
Acts 7:35 . . . you a ruler and *j* over us?
Acts 10:42 . . . *j* of all—the living and
Rev 14:7 . . . he will sit as *j.*

**JUDGE, JUDGED, JUDGES, JUDGING (v)** to form an evaluation of; to decide as a judge; to govern or rule; to punish or condemn; to form a negative opinion about

1 Sam 16:7 . . . Don't *j* by his appearance or
1 Sam 24:12 . . . the LORD *j* between us.
2 Chr 19:7 . . . *j* with integrity, for the LORD
Ps 7:8 . . . The LORD *j - s* the nations.
Ps 9:4 . . . For you have *j - d* in my favor;
Ps 9:8 . . . He will *j* the world
Ps 82:8 . . . Rise up, O God, and *j* the earth,
Ps 96:10 . . . He will *j* all peoples fairly.
Ps 96:13 . . . He will *j* the world with justice,
Prov 16:10 . . . he must never *j* unfairly.
Prov 29:14 . . . If a king *j - s* the poor fairly,
Isa 11:3 . . . He will not *j* by appearance

Isa 66:16 . . . He will *j* the earth,
Matt 7:1 . . . Do not *j* others, and you
Matt 16:27 . . . will *j* all people according
Matt 19:28 . . . thrones, *j-ing* the twelve
John 3:18 . . . been *j-d* for not believing
John 5:22 . . . the Father *j-s* no one.
John 5:22 . . . absolute authority to *j*,
John 5:27 . . . authority to *j* everyone
John 5:30 . . . I *j* as God tells me.
John 12:31 . . . time for *j-ing* this world
John 12:47 . . . not *j* those who hear me
Acts 17:31 . . . he has set a day for *j-ing*
Rom 2:16 . . . Jesus, will *j* everyone's secret
Rom 3:6 . . . be qualified to *j* the world?
1 Cor 6:2 . . . we believers will *j* the world?
1 Cor 11:31 . . . we would not be *j-d*
2 Cor 5:10 . . . stand before Christ to be *j-d.*
2 Tim 4:1 . . . Jesus, who will someday *j*
Heb 10:30 . . . The LORD will *j* his own
Heb 13:4 . . . *j* people who are immoral
Jas 2:13 . . . God will be merciful when he *j-s*
Jas 3:1 . . . we who teach will be *j-d* more
Jas 4:11 . . . criticizing and *j-ing* God's law.
Jas 4:12 . . . So what right do you have to *j*
1 Pet 1:17 . . . He will *j* or reward you
1 Pet 2:23 . . . God, who always *j-s* fairly.
Rev 19:11 . . . *j-s* fairly and wages a righteous
Rev 20:4 . . . given the authority to *j.*
Rev 20:12 . . . the dead were *j-d* according to

**JUDGMENT, JUDGMENTS (n)** a ruling or moral decision by a ruler (often God), a judge, or an individual; the process of forming an opinion or evaluation by discerning and comparing
*see also* JUSTICE
Deut 1:17 . . . impartial in your *j-s.*
1 Sam 3:13 . . . warned him that *j* is coming
Ps 1:5 . . . be condemned at the time of *j.*
Ps 37:13 . . . he sees their day of *j* coming.
Ps 51:4 . . . your *j* against me is just.
Prov 4:1 . . . Pay attention and learn good *j*,
Prov 4:7 . . . else you do, develop good *j.*
Prov 9:10 . . . results in good *j.*
Isa 3:14 . . . comes forward to pronounce *j*
Jer 11:20 . . . you make righteous *j-s*,
Jer 25:31 . . . His cry of *j* will reach
Dan 9:11 . . . curses and *j-s* written in
Hos 6:5 . . . with *j-s* as inescapable as light.
Joel 3:12 . . . LORD, will sit to pronounce *j*
Matt 5:21 . . . murder, you are subject to *j.*
Matt 11:24 . . . will be better off on *j* day
Matt 12:36 . . . on *j* day for every idle word
Matt 12:41 . . . this generation on *j* day
John 5:30 . . . *j* is just, because I carry out
John 8:16 . . . if I did, my *j* would be correct
John 16:8 . . . and of the coming *j.*
Acts 24:25 . . . coming day of *j*,
1 Cor 4:3 . . . I don't even trust my own *j*
1 Cor 4:5 . . . don't make *j-s* about anyone
1 Cor 11:29 . . . eating and drinking God's *j*
2 Thes 1:8 . . . *j* on those who don't know
Heb 9:27 . . . and after that comes *j*,
1 Pet 4:17 . . . And if *j* begins with us,
2 Pet 2:9 . . . until the day of final *j.*
2 Pet 3:7 . . . being kept for the day of *j*,
Jude 1:6 . . . waiting for the great day of *j.*
Rev 16:7 . . . your *j-s* are true and just.

**JUST (adj)** conforming to a standard of correctness; faithful to the original design; honest, fair, upright
*see also* RIGHT, RIGHTEOUS

Gen 18:19 . . . by doing what is right and *j.*
Deut 32:4 . . . Everything he does is *j*
2 Sam 8:15 . . . did what was *j* and right
Neh 9:13 . . . and instructions that were *j*,
Job 37:23 . . . he is *j* and righteous,
Ps 33:5 . . . He loves whatever is *j* and good;
Ps 92:15 . . . The LORD is *j!* He is
Ps 119:121 . . . I have done what is *j*
Prov 1:3 . . . do what is right, *j*, and fair.
Prov 2:9 . . . will understand what is right, *j*,
Prov 12:5 . . . The plans of the godly are *j;*
Isa 16:5 . . . He will always do what is *j*
Isa 59:8 . . . or what it means to be *j*
Jer 22:3 . . . Be fair-minded and *j.*
Ezek 18:5 . . . and does what is *j* and right.
Dan 4:37 . . . All his acts are *j* and true,
Matt 5:45 . . . rain on the *j* and the unjust
1 Cor 11:1 . . . imitate me, *j* as I imitate
1 Jn 1:9 . . . he is faithful and *j* to forgive
Rev 15:3 . . . *J* and true are your ways,
Rev 16:5 . . . You are *j*, O Holy One,
Rev 16:7 . . . your judgments are true and *j.*
Rev 19:2 . . . His judgments are true and *j.*

**JUSTICE (n)** the administration of law that determines what is right, based on principles of equity and correctness, and rewards accordingly; the quality of being just, impartial, or fair
*see also* JUDGMENT, RIGHTEOUSNESS
Exod 23:2 . . . by the crowd to twist *j.*
Lev 19:15 . . . Do not twist *j* in legal matters
Deut 16:19 . . . never twist *j*
Deut 32:36 . . . LORD will give *j* to his
1 Sam 8:3 . . . bribes and perverted *j.*
1 Kgs 3:11 . . . governing my people with *j*
1 Kgs 7:7 . . . Hall of *J*, where he sat to hear
2 Chr 9:8 . . . so you can rule with *j*
Job 8:3 . . . Does God twist *j?*
Job 19:7 . . . I protest, but there is no *j.*
Job 31:6 . . . weigh me on the scales of *j*,
Job 34:17 . . . God govern if he hated *j?*
Ps 9:8 . . . He will judge the world with *j*
Ps 10:18 . . . You will bring *j* to the orphans
Ps 36:6 . . . your *j* like the ocean depths.
Ps 45:4 . . . defending truth, humility, and *j.*
Ps 45:7 . . . You love *j* and hate evil.
Ps 72:1 . . . Give your love of *j* to the king,
Ps 82:3 . . . Give *j* to the poor
Ps 96:13 . . . He will judge the world with *j*,
Ps 98:9 . . . *j*, and the nations with fairness.
Ps 99:4 . . . You have acted with *j*
Ps 103:6 . . . *j* to all who are treated
Ps 146:7 . . . He gives *j* to the oppressed
Prov 16:12 . . . his rule is built on *j.*
Prov 19:28 . . . makes a mockery of *j;*
Prov 29:26 . . . but *j* comes from the LORD.
Prov 31:9 . . . and see that they get *j.*
Isa 1:17 . . . Seek *j.* Help the oppressed.
Isa 1:27 . . . Zion will be restored by *j;*
Isa 5:16 . . . will be exalted by his *j.*
Isa 10:2 . . . They deprive the poor of *j*
Isa 28:17 . . . with the measuring line of *j*
Isa 33:5 . . . make Jerusalem his home of *j*
Isa 42:1 . . . He will bring *j* to the nations.
Isa 51:4 . . . my *j* will become a light
Isa 59:9 . . . there is no *j* among us,
Isa 59:14 . . . *j* is nowhere to be found.
Isa 61:8 . . . I, the LORD, love *j.*
Jer 4:2 . . . you could do so with truth, *j*,
Jer 9:24 . . . who brings *j* and righteousness

Jer 21:12 . . . Give *j* each morning
Jer 30:11 . . . discipline you, but with *j;*
Lam 3:36 . . . if they twist *j* in the courts—
Hos 2:19 . . . righteousness and *j*,
Amos 5:7 . . . You twist *j*, making it a bitter
Amos 5:15 . . . courts into true halls of *j.*
Amos 6:12 . . . when you turn *j* into poison
Mic 3:8 . . . I am filled with *j* and strength
Hab 1:4 . . . there is no *j* in the courts.
Zeph 3:5 . . . Day by day he hands down *j*,
Mal 2:17 . . . Where is the God of *j?*
Matt 5:6 . . . who hunger and thirst for *j*,
Matt 12:18 . . . proclaim *j* to the nations.
Matt 23:23 . . . aspects of the law—*j*,
Luke 11:42 . . . ignore *j* and the love of God.
Luke 18:3 . . . Give me *j* in this dispute
Acts 8:33 . . . humiliated and received no *j.*
Acts 17:31 . . . *j* by the man
Rom 2:2 . . . God, in his *j*, will punish
2 Thes 1:5 . . . persecution to show his *j*
2 Thes 1:6 . . . In his *j* he will pay back
Heb 1:8 . . . You rule with a scepter of *j.*
Heb 7:2 . . . Melchizedek means "king of *j*,"
Heb 11:33 . . . ruled with *j*,

**JUSTIFY, JUSTIFIED (v)** to prove to be just, right, or reasonable; to acquit or absolve
*see also* RIGHT, RIGHTEOUS
Luke 10:29 . . . wanted to *j* his actions,
Luke 18:14 . . . returned home *j-ied*
2 Cor 8:24 . . . boasting about you is *j-ied.*

**KEEP, KEEPING, KEEPS, KEPT (v)** to be faithful to; to have in control; to refrain from granting, giving, or allowing; to cause to remain in a given place, situation, or condition; to refrain from revealing; to maintain or preserve
*see also* GUARD, OBEY, PROTECT
Exod 12:42 . . . the LORD *k-pt* his promise
Exod 20:8 . . . Sabbath day by *k-ing* it holy.
Exod 31:13 . . . Be careful to *k* my Sabbath
Deut 5:12 . . . Sabbath day by *k-ing* it holy,
Deut 7:8 . . . *k-ing* the oath he had sworn
Deut 7:9 . . . God who *k-s* his covenant for a
Deut 7:12 . . . your God will *k* his covenant
2 Chr 6:14 . . . You *k* your covenant
2 Chr 34:31 . . . to obey the LORD by *k-ing*
Neh 1:5 . . . God who *k-s* his covenant of
Ps 15:4 . . . *k* their promises even when
Ps 116:14 . . . I will *k* my promises to
Ps 119:100 . . . *k-pt* your commandments.
Ps 121:7 . . . The LORD *k-s* you from
Ps 130:3 . . . if you *k-pt* a record of
Ps 146:6 . . . He *k-s* every promise
Prov 10:19 . . . and *k* your mouth
Prov 15:3 . . . *k-ing* his eye on
Prov 21:23 . . . your tongue and *k*
Eccl 3:6 . . . A time to *k* and a time to
John 17:6 . . . and they have *k-pt* your word.
Acts 2:24 . . . death could not *k* him in its
Rom 10:3 . . . by trying to *k* the law.
Rom 14:22 . . . *k* it between yourself
1 Cor 1:8 . . . He will *k* you strong
1 Cor 7:19 . . . *k* God's commandments.
1 Cor 13:5 . . . it *k-s* no record
Eph 4:3 . . . effort to *k* yourselves united
1 Tim 5:22 . . . *K* yourself pure.
2 Tim 4:5 . . . But you should *k* a clear mind
Heb 11:27 . . . going because he *k-pt* his eyes
Jas 2:10 . . . the person who *k-s* all of the
1 Pet 1:4 . . . *k-pt* in heaven for you, pure and

1 Jn 5:3 . . . means *k-ing* his commandments,
Jude 1:21 . . . *k* yourselves safe in God's love.
Rev 12:17 . . . *k* God's commandments

**KILL, KILLED, KILLING, KILLS (v)** to take or deprive of life
Gen 4:8 . . . Abel, and *k-ed* him.
Exod 2:12 . . . Moses *k-ed* the Egyptian
Exod 21:12 . . . assaults and *k-s* another
Lev 24:21 . . . whoever *k-s* another person
2 Sam 2:26 . . . always be *k-ing* each other?
Neh 9:26 . . . they *k-ed* your prophets
Job 13:15 . . . God might *k* me, but I
Ps 44:22 . . . for your sake we are *k-ed*
Prov 6:17 . . . hands that *k* the innocent,
Eccl 3:3 . . . A time to *k* and a time to
Matt 10:28 . . . who want to *k* your body;
Matt 16:21 . . . He would be *k-ed,*
Mark 10:34 . . . flog him with a whip, and *k*
Luke 11:48 . . . They *k-ed* the prophets,
Acts 3:15 . . . You *k-ed* the author
Rom 8:36 . . . For your sake we are *k-ed*
1 Tim 1:9 . . . who *k* their father or mother
1 Jn 3:12 . . . evil one and *k-ed* his brother.

**KIND (adj)** affectionate, loving; of a sympathetic or helping nature; gentle
Luke 6:35 . . . for he is *k* to those who are
1 Cor 13:4 . . . is patient and *k.* Love is not
Eph 4:32 . . . Instead, be *k* to each other,
2 Tim 2:24 . . . but must be *k* to everyone,

**KIND, KINDS (n)** nature, family, type, or category
Gen 1:12 . . . and trees of the same *k.*
1 Cor 12:4 . . . different *k-s* of spiritual gifts,
1 Tim 6:10 . . . root of all *k-s* of evil.

**KINDNESS (n)** a kind deed; affection; the quality or state of being kind
Ps 106:7 . . . his many acts of *k* to them.
Rom 2:4 . . . his *k* is intended to turn you
Rom 3:24 . . . with undeserved *k,* declares
Rom 12:8 . . . gift for showing *k* to others,
2 Cor 6:1 . . . marvelous gift of God's *k*
2 Cor 8:1 . . . God in his *k* has done through
2 Cor 10:1 . . . gentleness and *k* of Christ—
Gal 5:22 . . . peace, patience, *k,* goodness,
Eph 2:7 . . . his grace and *k* toward us,
Col 3:12 . . . mercy, *k,* humility,
Titus 3:4 . . . revealed his *k* and love,
1 Pet 2:3 . . . a taste of the Lord's *k.*

**KINGDOM (n)** rule or realm; dominion of a king
Exod 19:6 . . . will be my *k* of priests,
1 Kgs 11:31 . . . to tear the *k* from the hand
1 Chr 28:7 . . . make his *k* last forever.
Ps 145:11 . . . glory of your *k;*
Matt 3:2 . . . for the *K* of Heaven is near.
Matt 4:23 . . . Good News about the *K.*
Matt 5:10 . . . right, for the *K* of Heaven is
Matt 5:19 . . . great in the *K* of Heaven.
Matt 6:10 . . . May your *K* come soon.
Matt 7:21 . . . will enter the *K* of Heaven.
Matt 8:12 . . . whom the *K* was prepared—
Matt 10:7 . . . them that the *K* of Heaven is
Matt 11:12 . . . until now, the *K* of Heaven
Matt 12:26 . . . His own *k* will not
Matt 13:11 . . . secrets of the *K* of Heaven,
Matt 13:38 . . . represents the people of the *K.*
Matt 13:43 . . . their Father's *K.* Anyone with
Matt 13:45 . . . Again, the *K* of Heaven is
Matt 13:52 . . . a disciple in the *K* of Heaven
Matt 16:28 . . . Son of Man coming in his *K.*

Matt 18:4 . . . greatest in the *K* of Heaven.
Matt 19:12 . . . sake of the *K* of Heaven.
Matt 19:23 . . . to enter the *K* of Heaven.
Matt 20:1 . . . For the *K* of Heaven is
Matt 21:43 . . . I tell you, the *K* of God will
Matt 23:13 . . . shut the door of the *K* of Heaven
Matt 24:14 . . . Good News about the *K* will be
Matt 25:34 . . . inherit the *K* prepared for
Mark 3:24 . . . A *k* divided by
Mark 4:11 . . . secret of the *K* of God.
Mark 4:30 . . . I describe the *K* of God?
Mark 9:1 . . . they see the *K* of God arrive
Mark 10:15 . . . doesn't receive the *K* of God
Mark 10:24 . . . to enter the *K* of God.
Mark 11:10 . . . on the coming *K* of our
Mark 13:8 . . . and *k* against *k.*
Mark 15:43 . . . waiting for the *K* of God to
Luke 4:43 . . . Good News of the *K* of God in
Luke 7:28 . . . least person in the *K* of God
Luke 8:10 . . . secrets of the *K* of God.
Luke 9:11 . . . taught them about the *K* of God,
Luke 9:60 . . . preach about the *K* of God.
Luke 10:9 . . . tell them, 'The *K* of God is
Luke 10:11 . . . know this—the *K* of God is
Luke 11:17 . . . he said, "Any *k* divided
Luke 11:20 . . . the *K* of God has arrived
Luke 12:31 . . . Seek the *K* of God
Luke 13:18 . . . What is the *K* of God like?
Luke 14:15 . . . a banquet in the *K* of God!
Luke 17:20 . . . When will the *K* of God
Luke 17:21 . . . For the *K* of God is
Luke 18:24 . . . to enter the *K* of God!
Luke 18:29 . . . for the sake of the *K* of God,
Luke 21:10 . . . and *k* against *k.*
Luke 22:16 . . . fulfilled in the *K* of God.
Luke 22:29 . . . granted me a *K,* I now grant
Luke 23:42 . . . come into your *K.*
John 3:3 . . . you cannot see the *K* of God.
John 3:5 . . . no one can enter the *K* of God
John 18:36 . . . But my *K* is not of
Acts 1:3 . . . talked to them about the *K* of God.
Acts 1:6 . . . restore our *k?*
Acts 8:12 . . . News concerning the *K* of God
Acts 19:8 . . . about the *K* of God.
Acts 28:23 . . . testified about the *K* of God
Rom 14:17 . . . For the *K* of God is
1 Cor 4:20 . . . For the *K* of God is
1 Cor 6:10 . . . will inherit the *K* of God.
1 Cor 15:24 . . . will turn the *K* over to God
1 Cor 15:50 . . . cannot inherit the *K* of God.
Gal 5:21 . . . will not inherit the *K* of God.
Eph 5:5 . . . will inherit the *K* of Christ
Col 4:11 . . . with me here for the *K* of God.
1 Thes 2:12 . . . to share in his *K* and glory.
2 Thes 1:5 . . . worthy of his *K,* for which
2 Tim 4:18 . . . his heavenly *K.* All glory to
Heb 12:28 . . . we are receiving a *K* that is
Jas 2:5 . . . inherit the *K* he promised to
2 Pet 1:11 . . . into the eternal *K* of our
Rev 1:6 . . . made us a *K* of priests for
Rev 5:10 . . . to become a *K* of priests for
Rev 11:15 . . . now become the *K* of our Lord
Rev 12:10 . . . power and the *K* of our God,
Rev 16:10 . . . his *k* was plunged into darkness.

**KISS, KISSES (n)** a greeting or caress with the lips; an expression of affection
Prov 27:6 . . . better than many *k-es* from an
Song 7:9 . . . May your *k-es* be as
Mark 14:45 . . . and gave him the *k.*
Luke 22:48 . . . the Son of Man with a *k?*

**KISS, KISSING (v)** to caress with the lips
Song 1:2 . . . *K* me and *k* me again,
Song 8:1 . . . Then I could *k* you no matter
Luke 7:38 . . . Then she kept *k-ing* his feet and

**KNEE, KNEES (n)** the joint in the middle part of the leg; when bent, symbolic of submission or defeat
Isa 35:3 . . . those who have weak *k-s.*
Isa 45:23 . . . Every *k* will bend to me,
Luke 5:8 . . . he fell to his *k-s* before Jesus
Rom 14:11 . . . every *k* will bend to me,
Eph 3:14 . . . I fall to my *k-s* and pray to
Phil 2:10 . . . at the name of Jesus every *k*
Heb 12:12 . . . strengthen your weak *k-s.*

**KNEEL, KNELT (v)** to bend the knee; to fall or rest on the knees; usually a gesture of submission, defeat, or reverence
2 Chr 6:13 . . . then he *k-lt* in front of
Ps 95:6 . . . Let us *k* before the LORD
Dan 6:10 . . . went home and *k-lt* down
Matt 8:2 . . . approached him and *k-lt*
Matt 9:18 . . . came and *k-lt* before him.
Matt 17:14 . . . came and *k-lt* before Jesus
Matt 27:29 . . . *k-lt* before him in mockery
Luke 22:41 . . . stone's throw, and *k-lt* down
Acts 20:36 . . . speaking, he *k-lt* and prayed
Acts 21:5 . . . There we *k-lt,* prayed,

**KNEW (v)** *see also* KNOW
Matt 7:23 . . . reply, 'I never *k* you.
John 2:24 . . . because he *k* human nature.
John 19:28 . . . Jesus *k* that his mission
Acts 2:23 . . . But God *k* what would
Rom 1:21 . . . Yes, they *k* God,
Rom 8:29 . . . God *k* his people in advance,
1 Pet 1:2 . . . God the Father *k* you and

**KNOCK, KNOCKING, KNOCKS (v)** to strike sharply
Matt 7:7 . . . Keep on *k-ing,* and the door
Matt 7:8 . . . to everyone who *k-s,* the door
Luke 11:9 . . . Keep on *k-ing,* and the door
Rev 3:20 . . . I stand at the door and *k.*

**KNOW, KNOWING, KNOWN, KNOWS (v)** to be intimately familiar with; to discern, recognize, regard, acknowledge, pay heed to, approve, learn
Gen 3:5 . . . be like God, *k-ing* both good and
Gen 3:22 . . . become like us, *k-ing* both good
Gen 22:12 . . . for now I *k* that you truly
Exod 6:7 . . . Then you will *k* that I am the
Deut 18:21 . . . How will we *k* whether or not
Deut 29:29 . . . God has secrets *k-n* to no
Josh 23:14 . . . Deep in your hearts you *k* that
Job 19:25 . . . for me, I *k* that my Redeemer
Ps 9:10 . . . Those who *k* your name trust
Ps 19:2 . . . after night they make him *k-n.*
Ps 44:21 . . . for he *k-s* the secrets of
Ps 46:10 . . . Be still, and *k* that I am
Ps 94:10 . . . doesn't he also *k* what you
Ps 94:11 . . . The LORD *k-s* people's thoughts;
Ps 103:14 . . . For he *k-s* how weak we are;
Ps 119:168 . . . you *k* everything I do.
Ps 139:2 . . . You *k* when I sit
Ps 139:23 . . . O God, and *k* my heart;
Isa 12:4 . . . Let them *k* how mighty
Jer 9:24 . . . that they truly *k* me and
Jer 31:34 . . . will *k* me already,
Dan 11:32 . . . the people who *k* their God
Matt 6:3 . . . don't let your left hand *k* what
Matt 10:29 . . . without your Father *k-ing* it.
Matt 11:27 . . . no one truly *k-s* the Father

Mark 12:24 . . . you don't *k* the Scriptures,
Luke 11:13 . . . if you sinful people *k* how to
Luke 13:25 . . . will reply, 'I don't *k* you
Luke 16:15 . . . but God *k-s* your hearts.
Luke 23:34 . . . they don't *k* what they are
John 3:11 . . . you what we *k* and have seen,
John 4:42 . . . Now we *k* that he
John 6:69 . . . we *k* you are the Holy One
John 7:28 . . . Yes, you *k* me, and you
John 8:14 . . . For I *k* where I came
John 8:32 . . . And you will *k* the truth,
John 10:4 . . . because they *k* his voice.
John 10:27 . . . I *k* them, and they follow
John 13:17 . . . Now that you *k* these things,
John 14:7 . . . If you had really *k-n* me,
John 16:30 . . . we understand that you *k*
John 17:23 . . . the world will *k* that you sent
John 21:15 . . . Peter replied, "you *k* I love
Acts 1:24 . . . O Lord, you *k* every heart.
Rom 1:19 . . . They *k* the truth
Rom 7:18 . . . And I *k* that nothing good
Rom 8:26 . . . we don't *k* what God wants us
Rom 8:27 . . . the Father who *k-s* all hearts
Rom 11:34 . . . For who can *k* the LORD's
Rom 12:16 . . . And don't think you *k* it all!
Rom 16:26 . . . message is made *k-n* to all
1 Cor 2:11 . . . no one can *k* God's thoughts
1 Cor 13:12 . . . All that I *k* now is partial
2 Cor 4:6 . . . so we could *k* the glory of
Gal 4:9 . . . now that you *k* God (or should
Phil 3:10 . . . I want to *k* Christ and
Col 1:10 . . . you learn to *k* God better and
1 Thes 3:3 . . . But you *k* that we
1 Thes 5:2 . . . For you *k* quite well
2 Thes 1:8 . . . on those who don't *k* God
1 Tim 1:7 . . . but they don't *k* what they
1 Tim 3:15 . . . you will *k* how people must
2 Tim 1:12 . . . I *k* the one in whom I trust,
2 Tim 2:19 . . . The LORD *k-s* those who are
Heb 8:11 . . . greatest, will *k* me already.
Heb 11:8 . . . He went without *k-ing* where he
Jas 1:3 . . . For you *k* that when your faith
Jas 4:14 . . . How do you *k* what your life
Jas 4:17 . . . it is sin to *k* what you ought
1 Pet 2:19 . . . do what you *k* is right and
2 Pet 2:21 . . . they had never *k-n* the way to
1 Jn 2:3 . . . we can be sure that we *k* him
1 Jn 2:4 . . . claims, "I *k* God," but
1 Jn 2:5 . . . is how we *k* we are living in
1 Jn 2:11 . . . person does not *k* the way to
1 Jn 2:29 . . . Since we *k* that Christ
1 Jn 3:1 . . . they don't *k* him.
1 Jn 3:2 . . . But we do *k* that we will be
1 Jn 3:24 . . . And we *k* he lives in us
1 Jn 4:6 . . . is how we *k* if someone has
1 Jn 4:7 . . . is a child of God and *k-s* God.
1 Jn 4:8 . . . does not *k* God, for God
1 Jn 5:13 . . . that you may *k* you have eternal
1 Jn 5:15 . . . And since we *k* he hears us
1 Jn 5:20 . . . And we *k* that the Son of
Rev 3:15 . . . I *k* all the things you do,

**KNOWLEDGE (n)** the fact or condition of being aware of something, of having information, or of being learned; information, wisdom
Gen 2:9 . . . the tree of the *k* of good and
Gen 2:17 . . . the tree of the *k* of good and
Prov 1:7 . . . foundation of true *k,* but fools
Prov 2:6 . . . From his mouth come *k* and
Prov 3:20 . . . By his *k* the deep
Prov 8:10 . . . *k* rather than pure gold.

Prov 14:6 . . . *k* comes easily to those with
Prov 18:15 . . . Their ears are open for *k.*
Isa 11:2 . . . the Spirit of *k* and the fear
Luke 11:52 . . . the key to *k*
Rom 2:20 . . . gives you complete *k*
1 Cor 12:8 . . . gives a message of special *k.*
1 Cor 13:2 . . . and possessed all *k,*
1 Cor 13:9 . . . Now our *k* is partial
2 Cor 2:14 . . . to spread the *k* of Christ
Eph 1:17 . . . grow in your *k* of God.
Eph 4:13 . . . our faith and *k* of God's Son
Phil 1:9 . . . will keep on growing in *k* and
Col 1:9 . . . to give you complete *k* of his
Col 2:3 . . . treasures of wisdom and *k.*
Heb 10:26 . . . we have received *k* of the
2 Pet 1:5 . . . and moral excellence with *k,*
2 Pet 1:8 . . . *k* of our Lord Jesus Christ.
2 Pet 3:18 . . . the grace and *k* of our Lord

**LAID (v)** *see also* LAY
Isa 53:6 . . . Yet the LORD *l* on him the
Acts 6:6 . . . as they *l* their hands on them.
Acts 8:18 . . . the apostles *l* their hands on
1 Tim 4:14 . . . elders of the church *l* their
2 Tim 1:6 . . . when I *l* my hands on

**LAKE (n)** a considerable inland body of standing water
Matt 8:24 . . . a fierce storm struck the *l,*
Luke 8:33 . . . into the *l* and drowned.
John 6:25 . . . on the other side of the *l*
Rev 19:20 . . . into the fiery *l* of burning
Rev 20:14 . . . This *l* of fire is

**LAMB, LAMBS (n)** a young sheep that is less than one year old
Exod 12:21 . . . pick out a *l* or young goat
Isa 53:7 . . . He was led like a *l* to the
Mark 14:12 . . . the Passover *l* is sacrificed,
John 1:29 . . . and said, "Look! The *L* of God
John 21:15 . . . "Then feed my *l-s,*" Jesus
Luke 10:3 . . . out as *l-s* among wolves.
Acts 8:32 . . . And as a *l* is silent before
1 Pet 1:19 . . . sinless, spotless *L* of God.
Rev 5:6 . . . Then I saw a *L* that looked as
Rev 5:12 . . . Worthy is the *L* who was
Rev 7:14 . . . robes in the blood of the *L*
Rev 15:3 . . . the song of the *L:*
Rev 17:14 . . . to war against the *L,* but the
Rev 19:9 . . . to the wedding feast of the *L.*
Rev 21:23 . . . and the *L* is its light.

**LAME (adj)** having a disabled body part as to impair freedom of movement
Isa 33:23 . . . Even the *l* will take
Isa 35:6 . . . The *l* will leap like a
Matt 11:5 . . . blind see, the *l* walk,
Matt 15:31 . . . the *l* were walking,
Luke 14:21 . . . the blind, and the *l.*
Heb 12:13 . . . weak and *l* will not fall

**LAMP, LAMPS (n)** a source of intellectual or spiritual illumination; any of various devices for producing light
2 Sam 22:29 . . . O LORD, you are my *l.*
Ps 18:28 . . . You light a *l* for me.
Ps 119:105 . . . Your word is a *l* to guide my
Prov 6:23 . . . For their command is a *l*
Prov 31:18 . . . her *l* burns late
Matt 6:22 . . . Your eye is a *l* that
Matt 25:1 . . . who took their *l-s*
Matt 25:7 . . . got up and prepared their *l-s.*

Luke 8:16 . . . No one lights a *l* and then
Luke 12:35 . . . and keep your *l-s* burning,
Rev 22:5 . . . no need for *l-s* or sun—for the

**LAMPSTAND, LAMPSTANDS (n)** a support that holds a lamp
Exod 25:31 . . . Make the entire *l* and its
2 Chr 4:7 . . . cast ten gold *l-s* according to
Zech 4:2 . . . a solid gold *l* with a bowl of
Zech 4:11 . . . on each side of the *l,*
Heb 9:2 . . . In the first room were a *l,*
Rev 1:12 . . . I saw seven gold *l-s.*
Rev 1:20 . . . the seven gold *l-s:*
Rev 2:5 . . . and remove your *l* from its

**LAND (n)** the solid part of the surface of the earth; a portion of the earth's solid surface distinguishable by boundaries or ownership
Gen 1:10 . . . the dry ground "*l*" and the
Gen 15:18 . . . I have given this *l* to your
Exod 6:8 . . . you into the *l* I swore to
Deut 8:7 . . . you into a good *l* of flowing
Ps 37:11 . . . will possess the *l* and will

**LANGUAGE, LANGUAGES (n)** audible, meaningful sound; dialect or manner of speech peculiar to a certain people; a special language gift given by the Holy Spirit
*see also* TONGUE(S)
Gen 11:9 . . . the people with different *l-s.*
Isa 28:11 . . . speak a strange *l!*
Mark 16:17 . . . they will speak in new *l-s.*
Acts 2:4 . . . speaking in other *l-s,* as the
1 Cor 12:28 . . . speak in unknown *l-s.*
1 Cor 12:30 . . . to interpret unknown *l-s?*
1 Cor 13:8 . . . in unknown *l-s* and special
1 Cor 14:19 . . . in an unknown *l.*
Eph 4:29 . . . or abusive *l.* Let everything
Col 3:8 . . . slander, and dirty *l.*
Rev 5:9 . . . every tribe and *l* and people
Rev 7:9 . . . and tribe and people and *l,*
Rev 14:6 . . . nation, tribe, *l,* and people.

**LASCIVIOUSNESS (KJV)**
Mark 7:22 . . . deceit, *lustful desires,* envy,
2 Cor 12:21 . . . and *eagerness for lustful pleasure*
Gal 5:19 . . . impurity, *lustful pleasures*
Eph 4:19 . . . They live for *lustful pleasure*
1 Pet 4:3 . . . their *immorality* and lust,

**LAST, LASTING (adj)** following all the rest; being the only remaining; belonging to the final stage; of or relating to being continuous in time; existing or continuing a long while
Prov 10:25 . . . have a *l-ing* foundation.
Isa 41:4 . . . First and the *L.* I alone
Isa 44:6 . . . First and the *L;* there is no
Isa 48:12 . . . God, the First and the *L.*
John 15:16 . . . to go and produce *l-ing* fruit,
Acts 2:17 . . . 'In the *l* days,' God says,
1 Cor 15:26 . . . And the *l* enemy to be
1 Cor 15:52 . . . *l* trumpet is blown.
2 Tim 3:1 . . . that in the *l* days there will
2 Pet 3:3 . . . that in the *l* days scoffers
Jude 1:18 . . . you that in the *l* times there
Rev 1:17 . . . I am the First and the *L.*
Rev 22:13 . . . the Omega, the First and the *L,*

**LASTS (v)** to continue in time
Ps 30:5 . . . For his anger *l* only a moment,

**LAUGH, LAUGHED, LAUGHS (v)** to show mirth or joy or to despise or mock something with a chuckle or explosive vocal sound

Gen 17:17 . . . *I-ed* to himself in disbelief.
Gen 18:12 . . . So she *I-ed* silently to herself
Ps 2:4 . . . the one who rules in heaven *I-s.*
Ps 37:13 . . . the LORD just *I-s,* for he sees
Ps 59:8 . . . But LORD, you *I* at them.
Prov 31:25 . . . and she *I-s* without fear of
Eccl 3:4 . . . and a time to *I.* A time to
Luke 6:21 . . . for in due time you will *I.*
Luke 6:25 . . . awaits you who *I* now,

**LAUGHTER (n)** a chuckle or explosive vocal sound; cause for merriment
Gen 21:6 . . . God has brought me *I.*
Ps 126:2 . . . We were filled with *I,* and we
Eccl 2:2 . . . So I said, "*L* is silly.
Jer 7:34 . . . happy singing and *I* in the
Jas 4:9 . . . instead of *I,* and gloom

**LAW, LAWS (n)** words of Moses; a binding decree; a universal principle; governing authority
*see also* COMMANDMENT(S), INSTRUCTION(S), REGULATIONS, TEACHING(S)
2 Chr 17:9 . . . the Book of the *L*
Ps 1:2 . . . delight in the *I* of the LORD,
Ps 93:5 . . . Your royal *I-s* cannot be
Ps 119:14 . . . rejoiced in your *I-s* as much as
Ps 119:36 . . . for your *I-s* rather than a love
Ps 119:125 . . . I will understand your *I-s.*
Ps 119:152 . . . days that your *I-s* will last
Matt 5:17 . . . to abolish the *I* of Moses or
Matt 5:19 . . . who obeys God's *I-s*
Matt 22:40 . . . The entire *I* and all the
Matt 23:23 . . . of the *I*—justice, mercy,
Mark 7:8 . . . ignore God's *I* and substitute
Luke 11:52 . . . experts in religious *I!*
Luke 23:56 . . . rested as required by the *I.*
Luke 24:44 . . . written about me in the *I*
John 1:17 . . . For the *I* was given
Rom 2:12 . . . be judged by that *I* when they
Rom 2:15 . . . that God's *I* is written in
Rom 2:20 . . . that God's *I* gives you
Rom 2:25 . . . if you don't obey God's *I,*
Rom 3:19 . . . Obviously, the *I* applies to
Rom 3:21 . . . requirements of the *I,* as was
Rom 3:28 . . . not by obeying the *I.*
Rom 4:13 . . . his obedience to God's *I,*
Rom 4:16 . . . according to the *I* of Moses,
Rom 5:13 . . . was not yet any *I* to break.
Rom 6:15 . . . has set us free from the *I,*
Rom 7:4 . . . power of the *I* when you died
Rom 7:5 . . . the *I* aroused these evil desires
Rom 7:8 . . . If there were no *I,* sin would
Rom 7:12 . . . But still, the *I* itself is
Rom 7:22 . . . I love God's *I* with all my
Rom 7:25 . . . I really want to obey God's *I,*
Rom 8:3 . . . did what the *I* could not do.
Rom 8:4 . . . requirement of the *I* would be
Rom 8:7 . . . did obey God's *I-s,* and it
Rom 9:4 . . . gave them his *I.* He gave them
Rom 9:31 . . . with God by keeping the *I,*
Rom 10:4 . . . for which the *I* was given.
Rom 13:10 . . . requirements of God's *I.*
1 Cor 9:9 . . . For the *I* of Moses
1 Cor 9:21 . . . I obey the *I* of Christ.
2 Cor 3:6 . . . not of written *I-s,* but of the
Gal 2:16 . . . by obeying the *I.* And we have
Gal 2:19 . . . So I died to the *I*—I stopped
Gal 3:2 . . . by obeying the *I* of Moses?
Gal 3:5 . . . because you obey the *I?*
Gal 3:11 . . . by trying to keep the *I.*
Gal 3:19 . . . But the *I* was designed

Gal 3:21 . . . If the *I* could give us
Gal 3:23 . . . placed under guard by the *I.*
Gal 4:21 . . . live under the *I,* do you know
Gal 5:3 . . . in the whole *I* of Moses.
Gal 5:14 . . . the whole *I* can be summed
Gal 6:2 . . . this way obey the *I* of Christ.
Eph 2:15 . . . the system of *I* with its
Phil 3:6 . . . I obeyed the *I* without fault.
1 Tim 1:8 . . . know that the *I* is good when
Heb 10:1 . . . under the *I* of Moses
Jas 1:25 . . . into the perfect *I* that sets
Jas 2:8 . . . obey the royal *I* as found in
Jas 2:10 . . . all of the *I-s* except one is as

**LAWLESSNESS (n)** the quality or state of not being restrained or controlled by law
2 Thes 2:3 . . . the man of *I* is revealed—
2 Thes 2:7 . . . For this *I* is already
2 Thes 2:8 . . . Then the man of *I* will be

**LAWSUITS (n)** an act or instance of suing
1 Cor 6:7 . . . Even to have such *I* with one

**LAY, LAYING (v)** to put or set down
*see also* LAID
Exod 29:10 . . . his sons will *I* their hands
Lev 1:4 . . . *L* your hand on
Lev 4:15 . . . must then *I* their hands on
Num 8:10 . . . of Israel must *I* their hands
Num 27:18 . . . in him, and *I* your hands on
Acts 8:19 . . . so that when *I* my hands on
Heb 6:2 . . . the *I-ing* on of hands,
Rev 4:10 . . . And they *I* their crowns

**LAZINESS (n)** a disinclination to activity or exertion
Prov 31:27 . . . suffers nothing from *I.*
Ezek 16:49 . . . gluttony, and *I,* while the

**LAZY (adj)** disinclined to activity or exertion; not energetic or vigorous
Prov 12:27 . . . *L* people don't
Prov 20:4 . . . Those too *I* to plow in the
Rom 12:11 . . . Never be *I,* but work
1 Tim 5:13 . . . they will learn to be *I*
Titus 1:12 . . . animals, and *I* gluttons.

**LEAD, LEADING, LEADS (v)** to guide by direction or example; to go at the head of; to result in
*see also* LED
Deut 27:18 . . . anyone who *I-s* a blind
Deut 31:2 . . . no longer able to *I* you.
Josh 1:6 . . . one who will *I* these people
2 Chr 1:10 . . . knowledge to *I* them
Ps 25:9 . . . He *I-s* the humble in
Ps 73:24 . . . with your counsel, *I-ing* me to a
Prov 6:22 . . . counsel will *I* you.
Prov 14:30 . . . A peaceful heart *I-s* to a
Prov 19:23 . . . Fear of the LORD *I-s* to life,
Isa 11:6 . . . little child will *I* them all.
Matt 15:14 . . . blind guides *I-ing* the blind,
John 10:3 . . . by name and *I-s* them out.
Rom 6:16 . . . to sin, which *I-s* to death,
Rom 6:22 . . . things that *I* to holiness and
1 Tim 5:24 . . . *I-ing* them to certain judgment.
Rev 7:17 . . . He will *I* them to

**LEADER, LEADERS (n)** a person who has commanding authority or influence; chief among others
1 Sam 13:14 . . . to be the *I* of his people,
Prov 17:26 . . . to flog *I-s* for being honest.
Jer 51:46 . . . *I-s* fight against each other.
Matt 20:26 . . . a *I* among you must be

Mark 10:43 . . . a *I* among you must be
Luke 22:26 . . . *I* should be like a servant.
Acts 13:27 . . . Jerusalem and their *I-s* did not
1 Thes 5:12 . . . who are your *I-s* in the Lord's
Heb 13:7 . . . Remember your *I-s* who taught
Heb 13:17 . . . Obey your spiritual *I-s,* and do
3 Jn 1:9 . . . to be the *I,* refuses to have

**LEADERSHIP (n)** the office or position of a leader; capacity to lead
Num 33:1 . . . under the *I* of Moses
1 Cor 12:28 . . . those who have the gift of *I,*

**LEARN, LEARNED, LEARNS (v)** to come to know or realize; to acquire knowledge, skill, or behavioral tendency
Deut 4:10 . . . Then they will *I* to fear me
Deut 5:1 . . . so you may *I* them and obey
Prov 9:9 . . . and they will *I* even more.
Prov 18:15 . . . are always ready to *I.*
Isa 1:17 . . . *L* to do good.
Isa 26:9 . . . will people *I* what is right.
Isa 29:13 . . . man-made rules *I-ed* by rote.
Matt 2:7 . . . and he *I-ed* from them the time
John 6:45 . . . listens to the Father and *I-s*
Phil 4:9 . . . all you *I-ed* and received from
Phil 4:11 . . . have *I-ed* how to be content
Col 1:10 . . . grow as you *I* to know God
1 Tim 2:11 . . . Women should *I* quietly and
2 Tim 1:13 . . . teaching you *I-ed* from me—
Heb 5:8 . . . he *I-ed* obedience from the

**LEAVEN (KJV)**
Exod 12:20 . . . anything made with *yeast*
Exod 13:7 . . . any *yeast* at all found within
Matt 13:33 . . . of Heaven is like the *yeast*
Matt 16:6 . . . the *yeast* of the Pharisees
1 Cor 5:6 . . . this sin is like a little *yeast*

**LED (v)** *see also* LEAD
Ps 68:18 . . . the heights, you *I* a crowd of
Isa 53:7 . . . He was *I* like a lamb
Jer 11:19 . . . like a lamb being *I* to the
Luke 4:1 . . . He was *I* by the Spirit
Acts 8:32 . . . He was *I* like a sheep
Rom 8:14 . . . all who are *I* by the Spirit
Eph 4:8 . . . the heights, he *I* a crowd of

**LEFT (adj)** of, relating to, situated on, or being the side of the body in which the heart is mostly located
Matt 6:3 . . . don't let your *I* hand know

**LEFT (n)** the location or direction of the left side
Josh 1:7 . . . or to the *I.* Then you will be
Josh 23:6 . . . either to the right or to the *I.*
Isa 30:21 . . . to the right or to the *I.*
Matt 25:33 . . . and the goats at his *I.*
Matt 25:41 . . . those on the *I* and say, 'Away

**LEGION (n)** a very large number; multitude
Mark 5:9 . . . My name is *L,* because there

**LEND, LENDING (v)** to give for temporary use on condition that the same or its equivalent be returned
Lev 25:37 . . . interest on money you *I*
Deut 15:8 . . . and *I* them whatever
Ps 15:5 . . . Those who *I* money without
Prov 19:17 . . . you are *I-ing* to the LORD—
Luke 6:34 . . . Even sinners will *I* to other

**LENDER, LENDERS (n)** one who loans to another
Exod 22:25 . . . as a money *I* would.

Prov 22:7 . . . borrower is servant to the *l.*
Isa 24:2 . . . and sellers, *l-s* and borrowers,

**LEPERS (n)** one who suffers from a severe
contagious skin and nerve disease
Matt 11:5 . . . lame walk, the *l* are cured,
Luke 17:12 . . . ten *l* stood at a distance,

**LEPROSY (n)** a chronic infectious disease
affecting the skin and peripheral nerves which
causes loss of sensation, paralysis, and
deformities
Num 12:10 . . . as white as snow from *l.*
2 Kgs 5:1 . . . he suffered from *l.*
2 Kgs 7:3 . . . four men with *l* sitting at
2 Chr 26:21 . . . King Uzziah had *l* until the

**LIAR, LIARS (n)** a person who deceives by
telling untruths or falsehoods
Ps 63:11 . . . while *l-s* will be silenced.
Ps 116:11 . . . These people are all *l-s!*
Prov 17:4 . . . *l-s* pay close attention to
Prov 29:12 . . . pays attention to *l-s,* all his
Prov 30:6 . . . expose you as a *l.*
Isa 57:4 . . . of sinners and *l-s!*
Rom 3:4 . . . everyone else is a *l,* God is true.
1 Tim 1:10 . . . are slave traders, *l-s,* promise
Titus 1:12 . . . are all *l-s,* cruel animals,
1 Jn 1:10 . . . calling God a *l* and showing
1 Jn 2:4 . . . that person is a *l* and is not
1 Jn 4:20 . . . that person is a *l;* for if we
1 Jn 5:10 . . . calling God a *l* because they
Rev 3:9 . . . synagogue—those *l-s* who say
Rev 21:8 . . . and all *l-s*—their fate is in

**LIE, LIES (n)** an untrue or inaccurate
statement; something that misleads or deceives
Ps 7:14 . . . give birth to *l-s.*
Ps 24:4 . . . and never tell *l-s.*
Ps 34:13 . . . lips from telling *l-s!*
Prov 12:17 . . . a false witness tells *l-s.*
Prov 30:8 . . . never to tell a *l.*
John 8:44 . . . the father of *l-s.*
Rom 1:25 . . . about God for a *l.*
Rom 3:13 . . . filled with *l-s.*
Eph 4:14 . . . to trick us with *l-s* so clever
Eph 4:25 . . . So stop telling *l-s.*
2 Thes 2:11 . . . they will believe these *l-s.*
1 Pet 3:10 . . . and your lips from telling *l-s.*
2 Pet 2:3 . . . make up clever *l-s* to get hold
1 Jn 2:21 . . . between truth and *l-s.*
Rev 14:5 . . . They have told no *l-s;*

**LIE, LIED, LIES (v)** to make an untrue
statement with intent to deceive; to create a
false or misleading impression
*see also* LYING
Lev 6:3 . . . lost property and *l* about it,
Job 31:5 . . . Have I *l-d* to anyone or
Ps 58:3 . . . even from birth they have *l-d*
Ps 89:35 . . . in my holiness I cannot *l:*
Prov 24:28 . . . don't *l* about them.
Prov 26:19 . . . who *l-s* to a friend
Jer 7:9 . . . commit adultery, *l,* and burn
Matt 5:11 . . . persecute you and *l*
Col 3:9 . . . Don't *l* to each other,
Titus 1:2 . . . God—who does not *l*

**LIFE (n)** the quality that distinguishes a vital
and functional being from a dead body; period
from birth to death; a way or manner of living;
spiritual existence transcending death; salvation
Gen 1:30 . . . everything that has *l.*
Gen 2:7 . . . He breathed the breath of *l*

Gen 2:9 . . . the tree of *l* and the tree of
Gen 9:5 . . . who takes another person's *l.*
Gen 9:6 . . . a human *l,* that person's life
Exod 21:23 . . . the injury: a *l* for a life,
Num 35:31 . . . payment for the *l* of someone
Deut 19:21 . . . be life for *l,* eye for eye,
Deut 30:19 . . . choice between *l* and death,
Deut 32:39 . . . kills and gives *l;* I am the
1 Sam 2:6 . . . both death and *l;* he brings
Ps 23:6 . . . the days of my *l,* and I will
Ps 69:28 . . . the Book of *L;* don't let them
Ps 91:16 . . . with a long *l* and give them
Ps 139:24 . . . the path of everlasting *l.*
Prov 3:2 . . . your *l* will be satisfying.
Prov 6:26 . . . will cost you your *l.*
Prov 13:3 . . . have a long *l;* opening your
Prov 15:4 . . . Gentle words are a tree of *l;*
Prov 21:21 . . . will find *l,* righteousness,
Prov 28:16 . . . will have a long *l.*
Isa 53:8 . . . that his *l* was cut short in
Isa 55:3 . . . you will find *l.* I will make
Lam 3:58 . . . you have redeemed my *l.*
Dan 12:2 . . . to everlasting *l* and some to
Matt 7:14 . . . But the gateway to *l* is very
Matt 18:8 . . . to enter eternal *l* with only
Matt 20:28 . . . and to give his *l* as a ransom
Mark 8:35 . . . to hang on to your *l,*
Mark 10:45 . . . and to give his *l* as a ransom
Luke 6:9 . . . a day to save *l* or to destroy
Luke 9:24 . . . give up your *l* for my sake,
Luke 12:25 . . . single moment to your *l?*
John 1:4 . . . The Word gave *l* to everything
John 3:15 . . . will have eternal *l.*
John 4:14 . . . giving them eternal *l.*
John 5:24 . . . passed from death into *l.*
John 5:39 . . . they give you eternal *l.*
John 6:27 . . . the eternal *l* that the Son of
John 6:35 . . . I am the bread of *l.*
John 6:47 . . . who believes has eternal *l.*
John 6:53 . . . have eternal *l* within you.
John 6:68 . . . the words that give eternal *l.*
John 10:10 . . . a rich and satisfying *l.*
John 10:15 . . . So I sacrifice my *l* for the
John 10:28 . . . give them eternal *l,* and they
John 12:25 . . . nothing for their *l* in this
John 14:6 . . . the truth, and the *l.*
John 17:2 . . . He gives eternal *l* to each
John 20:31 . . . you will have *l* by the power
Acts 3:15 . . . You killed the author of *l,*
Rom 1:17 . . . a righteous person has *l.*
Rom 2:7 . . . will give eternal *l* to those
Rom 4:25 . . . he was raised to *l* to make us
Rom 5:10 . . . be saved through the *l* of his
Rom 5:18 . . . God and new *l* for everyone.
Rom 5:21 . . . in eternal *l* through Jesus
Rom 6:11 . . . now you have new *l.*
Rom 6:22 . . . result in eternal *l.*
Rom 6:23 . . . is eternal *l* through Christ
Rom 8:6 . . . mind leads to *l* and peace.
Rom 8:11 . . . he will give *l* to your mortal
Rom 8:38 . . . death nor *l,* neither angels
2 Cor 3:6 . . . the Spirit gives *l.*
2 Cor 4:10 . . . so that the *l* of Jesus may
Gal 3:11 . . . a righteous person has *l.*
Gal 3:21 . . . give us new *l,* we could be
Gal 6:8 . . . harvest everlasting *l* from
Eph 2:5 . . . he gave us *l* when he raised
Eph 4:1 . . . to lead a *l* worthy of your
Phil 2:16 . . . Hold firmly to the word of *l;*
Phil 4:3 . . . written in the Book of *L.*

Col 3:3 . . . and your real *l* is hidden
1 Tim 1:16 . . . and receive eternal *l.*
1 Tim 4:8 . . . and in the *l* to come.
1 Tim 6:19 . . . may experience true *l.*
2 Tim 1:9 . . . called us to live a holy *l.*
2 Tim 3:12 . . . to live a godly *l* in Christ
Titus 3:5 . . . new *l* through the Holy Spirit.
Heb 7:16 . . . power of a *l* that cannot be
Jas 1:12 . . . the crown of *l* that God has
1 Pet 3:7 . . . God's gift of new *l.*
1 Pet 3:10 . . . want to enjoy *l* and see many
1 Pet 3:16 . . . see what a good *l* you live
2 Pet 1:3 . . . for living a godly *l.*
1 Jn 1:1 . . . He is the Word of *l.*
1 Jn 3:14 . . . have passed from death to *l.*
1 Jn 3:16 . . . gave up his *l* for us.
1 Jn 5:20 . . . is eternal *l.*
Jude 1:21 . . . bring you eternal *l.*
Rev 3:5 . . . their names from the Book of *L,*
Rev 13:8 . . . in the Book of *L* before the
Rev 17:8 . . . in the Book of *L* before the
Rev 20:12 . . . the Book of *L.* And the dead
Rev 21:27 . . . in the Lamb's Book of *L.*
Rev 22:1 . . . with the water of *l,* clear as
Rev 22:2 . . . a tree of *l,* bearing twelve
Rev 22:14 . . . eat the fruit from the tree of *l.*
Rev 22:17 . . . from the water of *l.*
Rev 22:19 . . . in the tree of *l* and in the

**LIFT, LIFTED, LIFTING, LIFTS (v)** to raise from
a lower to a higher position; to raise in rank or
condition
Lev 23:11 . . . the priest will *l* it up
1 Sam 2:7 . . . some down and *l-s* others up.
Neh 8:6 . . . Amen!" as they *l-ed* their hands.
Ps 28:2 . . . I *l* my hands toward your holy
Ps 63:4 . . . *l-ing* up my hands to you in prayer.
Ps 89:13 . . . Your right hand is *l-ed* high in
Ps 113:7 . . . He *l-s* the poor from the dust
Ps 123:1 . . . I *l* my eyes to
Ps 134:2 . . . *L* up holy hands
Lam 1:9 . . . no one to *l* her out.
Lam 3:41 . . . Let us *l* our hearts and
John 3:14 . . . Son of Man must be *l-ed* up,
John 8:28 . . . When you have *l-ed* up the Son
John 12:32 . . . And when I am *l-ed* up
1 Tim 2:8 . . . with holy hands *l-ed* up to God,
Jas 4:10 . . . he will *l* you up in honor.
1 Pet 5:6 . . . he will *l* you up in honor.

**LIGHT, LIGHTS (n)** daylight; brightness;
illumination; celestial body; spiritual
enlightenment; exposure to the truth and justice
Gen 1:3 . . . "Let there be *l,* " and there
Gen 1:14 . . . God said, "Let *l-s* appear
Exod 13:21 . . . and he provided *l* at night
Job 38:19 . . . Where does *l* come from,
Ps 27:1 . . . The LORD is my *l* and my
Ps 56:13 . . . in your life-giving *l.*
Ps 119:105 . . . my feet and a *l* for my path.
Ps 132:17 . . . will be a *l* for my people.
Ps 139:12 . . . Darkness and *l* are the
Isa 2:5 . . . us walk in the *l* of the LORD!
Isa 42:6 . . . you will be a *l* to guide the
Isa 45:7 . . . I create the *l* and make the
Isa 49:6 . . . make you a *l* to the Gentiles,
Matt 5:14 . . . You are the *l* of the world—
Luke 2:32 . . . He is a *l* to reveal God to
Luke 11:33 . . . its *l* can be seen by all
John 1:4 . . . life brought *l* to everyone.
John 1:9 . . . who is the true *l,* who gives
John 3:20 . . . All who do evil hate the *l*

John 3:21 . . . come to the *l* so others can
John 8:12 . . . I am the *l* of the world.
John 9:5 . . . I am the *l* of the world.
John 12:46 . . . I have come as a *l* to shine
Acts 13:47 . . . made you a *l* to the Gentiles,
2 Cor 4:6 . . . said, "Let there be *l* in the
2 Cor 6:14 . . . can *l* live with darkness?
2 Cor 11:14 . . . as an angel of *l.*
Eph 1:18 . . . be flooded with *l* so that you
Eph 5:8 . . . live as people of *l!*
Phil 2:15 . . . like bright *l-s* in a world
1 Thes 5:5 . . . children of the *l* and of the
1 Tim 6:16 . . . he lives in *l* so brilliant
1 Pet 2:9 . . . into his wonderful *l.*
1 Jn 1:5 . . . God is *l,* and there is
1 Jn 1:7 . . . living in the *l,* as God is in
1 Jn 2:9 . . . I am living in the *l,*
Rev 21:23 . . . city, and the Lamb is its *l.*

**LIGHT, LIGHTS (v)** to brighten; to ignite
something
Ps 18:28 . . . The LORD, my God, *l-s* up my
Luke 8:16 . . . No one *l-s* a lamp and

**LIGHTNING (n)** the flashing of light produced
by a discharge of atmospheric electricity
Exod 9:23 . . . *l* flashed toward the earth.
Exod 20:18 . . . saw the flashes of *l* and the
Dan 10:6 . . . face flashed like *l,* and his
Matt 24:27 . . . For as the *l* flashes in the
Matt 28:3 . . . face shone like *l,* and his
Luke 10:18 . . . from heaven like *l!*
Rev 4:5 . . . came flashes of *l* and the

**LION, LIONS (n)** a wild beast with a
threatening roar; symbolic of a strong and fierce
enemy
Isa 11:7 . . . The *l* will eat hay like a cow.
Isa 65:25 . . . The *l* will eat hay like a cow.
Dan 6:7 . . . thrown into the den of *l-s.*
Dan 7:4 . . . was like a *l* with eagles'
1 Pet 5:8 . . . like a roaring *l,* looking for
Rev 5:5 . . . Look, the *L* of the tribe of

**LIPS (n)** the fleshy, muscular folds that
surround the mouth; symbolic of speech
Ps 140:3 . . . drips from their *l.*
Prov 12:22 . . . The LORD detests lying *l,*
Isa 6:5 . . . I have filthy *l,* and I live
Matt 15:8 . . . honor me with their *l,*
Rom 3:13 . . . venom drips from their *l.*
1 Pet 3:10 . . . evil and your *l* from telling

**LISTEN, LISTENED, LISTENING (v)** to hear
something with thoughtful attention
*see also* HEAR
Deut 6:4 . . . *L,* O Israel! The LORD
Deut 18:15 . . . You must *l* to him.
1 Sam 3:9 . . . LORD, your servant is *l-ing.*
Neh 8:3 . . . All the people *l-ed* closely to
Ps 95:7 . . . If only you would *l* to his voice
Prov 12:15 . . . but the wise *l* to others.
Prov 18:13 . . . Spouting off before *l-ing* to
Isa 6:9 . . . to this people, '*L* carefully,
Dan 9:6 . . . We have refused to *l* to your
Mark 9:7 . . . dearly loved Son. *L* to him.
Luke 10:39 . . . the Lord's feet, *l-ing* to
Luke 16:31 . . . If they won't *l* to Moses and
John 10:27 . . . My sheep *l* to my
John 15:20 . . . And if they had *l-ed* to me,
Rom 2:13 . . . For merely *l-ing* to the law
1 Tim 2:12 . . . Let them *l* quietly.
Jas 1:19 . . . be quick to *l,* slow to speak,

1 Jn 4:6 . . . they do not *l* to us.
Rev 1:3 . . . he blesses all who *l* to its
Rev 2:7 . . . to hear must *l* to the Spirit

**LIVE, LIVED, LIVES, LIVING (v)** to be alive or
come to life; to endure a period of time (a life
span); to attain eternal life; to dwell; to subsist;
to continue alive; to conduct or pass one's life
Gen 3:22 . . . Then they will *l* forever!
Exod 20:12 . . . Then you will *l* a long, full
Lev 26:11 . . . I will *l* among you,
Deut 6:2 . . . as long as you *l.*
Deut 8:3 . . . that people do not *l* by bread
Job 14:14 . . . Can the dead *l* again?
Job 19:25 . . . that my Redeemer *l-s,* and he
Ps 23:6 . . . and I will *l* in the house of
Ps 37:3 . . . Then you will *l* safely in the
Ps 61:4 . . . Let me *l* forever in your
Ps 104:33 . . . as long as I *l.* I will praise
Prov 21:19 . . . It's better to *l* alone in the
Isa 33:14 . . . Who can *l* with this
Isa 45:18 . . . He made the world to be *l-d* in,
Amos 5:6 . . . to the LORD and *l!*
Hab 2:4 . . . the righteous will *l* by their
Matt 4:4 . . . People do not *l* by bread
John 14:19 . . . Since I *l,* you also will *l.*
Acts 17:28 . . . For in him we *l* and move
Rom 2:8 . . . on those who *l* for themselves,
Rom 6:10 . . . he lives, he *l-s* for the glory
Rom 8:11 . . . same Spirit *l-ing* within you.
Rom 13:13 . . . we must *l* decent lives
Rom 14:7 . . . For we don't *l* for ourselves
1 Cor 3:16 . . . Spirit of God *l-s* in you?
2 Cor 5:7 . . . For we *l* by believing
2 Cor 6:16 . . . said: "I will *l* in them and
Gal 2:20 . . . no longer I who *l,* but Christ
Gal 5:25 . . . Since we are *l-ing* by the Spirit,
Col 1:19 . . . was pleased to *l* in Christ,
Col 2:5 . . . that you are *l-ing* as you should
1 Thes 4:11 . . . your goal to *l* a quiet life,
1 Thes 5:13 . . . And *l* peacefully with
1 Tim 2:2 . . . so that we can *l* peaceful and
1 Tim 4:16 . . . close watch on how you *l*
2 Tim 3:12 . . . who wants to *l* a godly life
Heb 10:38 . . . righteous ones will *l* by faith.
Heb 12:14 . . . and work at *l-ing* a holy life,
1 Pet 1:17 . . . So you must *l* in reverent
1 Jn 1:7 . . . But if we are *l-ing* in the light,
1 Jn 4:16 . . . God, and God *l-s* in them.

**LIVES (n)** *see also* LIFE
Exod 23:26 . . . I will give you long, full *l.*
1 Thes 2:8 . . . but our own *l,* too.
1 Tim 2:2 . . . and quiet *l* marked by
1 Pet 3:2 . . . pure and reverent *l.*
1 Pet 4:2 . . . rest of your *l* chasing your

**LOAN, LOANS (n)** money lent at interest
Deut 15:2 . . . must cancel the *l-s* they have
Deut 15:9 . . . refuse someone a *l*
Deut 24:6 . . . as security for a *l,* for the
Ps 37:26 . . . give generous *l-s* to others,

**LOANED (v)** to lend
Luke 7:41 . . . A man *l* money to two

**LOAVES (n)**
Mark 6:41 . . . took the five *l* and two fish,
Mark 8:6 . . . took the seven *l,* thanked God
Luke 11:5 . . . to borrow three *l* of bread.

**LOCUSTS (n)** a short-horned grasshopper
Exod 10:4 . . . a swarm of *l* on your country.

Joel 2:25 . . . and the cutting *l.* It was I
Matt 3:4 . . . he ate *l* and wild honey.
Rev 9:3 . . . Then *l* came from

**LOG (n)** a usually bulky piece or length of a
tree
Matt 7:3 . . . you have a *l* in your own?
Luke 6:41 . . . you have a *l* in your own?

**LONGSUFFERING (KJV)**
Exod 34:6 . . . I am *slow to anger* and filled
Num 14:18 . . . LORD is *slow to anger*
Ps 86:15 . . . mercy, *slow to get angry*
Gal 5:22 . . . love, joy, peace, *patience,*
Eph 4:2 . . . Be *patient* with each other

**LOOK (n)** glance
Prov 15:30 . . . A cheerful *l* brings joy to

**LOOK, LOOKED, LOOKING, LOOKS (v)** to
direct the eyes; to examine; to see; to make sure
or take care (that something is done); to regard
with contempt; to seem; to search
Gen 19:17 . . . And don't *l* back or
Gen 19:26 . . . But Lot's wife *l-ed* back as she
Exod 3:6 . . . was afraid to *l* at God.
1 Sam 6:19 . . . they *l-ed* into the Ark
1 Sam 16:7 . . . LORD *l-s* at the heart.
Ps 34:5 . . . Those who *l* to him for
Ps 113:6 . . . He stoops to *l* down on heaven
Ps 123:2 . . . We keep *l-ing* to the LORD
Isa 65:1 . . . but no one was *l-ing* for me.
Dan 10:5 . . . I *l-ed* up and saw a man
Hab 3:6 . . . When he *l-s,* the nations
Zech 12:10 . . . They will *l* on me
Matt 5:28 . . . who even *l-s* at a woman
Mark 16:6 . . . You are *l-ing* for Jesus
Luke 9:62 . . . plow and then *l-s* back is not
Luke 22:61 . . . turned and *l-ed* at Peter.
John 4:23 . . . The Father is *l-ing* for those
John 17:1 . . . Jesus *l-ed* up to heaven
Rom 14:10 . . . Why do you *l* down
Phil 2:4 . . . Don't *l* out only
Heb 11:16 . . . they were *l-ing* for a better
Jas 1:25 . . . But if you *l* carefully into
2 Pet 3:12 . . . *l-ing* forward to the day
Rev 5:6 . . . I saw a Lamb that *l-ed* as if it

**LORD (n)** traditionally rendered Jehovah
(Hebrew *Yahweh);* the sovereign God Almighty
*see also* YAHWEH
Gen 2:4 . . . When the *L* God made
Gen 4:4 . . . The *L* accepted Abel
Gen 15:6 . . . Abram believed the *L,* and
Gen 22:14 . . . "the *L* will provide"
Gen 31:49 . . . May the *L* keep watch
Exod 6:2 . . . I am Yahweh—'the *L.* '
Exod 15:26 . . . I am the *L* who heals you.
Exod 40:34 . . . the glory of the *L* filled
Lev 20:26 . . . because I, the *L,* am holy.
Lev 23:4 . . . these are the *L's* appointed
Num 6:24 . . . May the *L* bless you and
Num 14:18 . . . The *L* is slow to anger
Num 14:21 . . . filled with the *L's* glory,
Num 14:41 . . . disobeying the *L's* orders
Deut 5:9 . . . I, the *L* your God, am a jealous
Deut 6:5 . . . love the *L* your God with all
Deut 6:18 . . . good in the *L's* sight,
Deut 10:13 . . . obey the *L's* commands
Deut 10:20 . . . must fear the *L* your God
Deut 11:1 . . . must love the *L* your God
Deut 29:29 . . . The *L* our God has secrets
Deut 30:20 . . . obey the *L,* you will live
Josh 23:11 . . . to love the *L* your God.

2 Sam 22:2 . . . sang: "The *L* is my rock,
2 Sam 22:31 . . . All the *L*'s promises prove
2 Kgs 22:2 . . . pleasing in the *L*'s sight
2 Kgs 22:8 . . . Law in the *L*'s Temple!
1 Chr 17:1 . . . Ark of the *L*'s Covenant is
2 Chr 16:9 . . . The eyes of the *L* search
Neh 9:6 . . . You alone are the *L*.
Job 38:1 . . . Then the *L* answered Job
Ps 1:6 . . . For the *L* watches over
Ps 12:6 . . . The *L*'s promises are pure,
Ps 18:30 . . . All the *L*'s promises prove
Ps 23:1 . . . The *L* is my shepherd;
Ps 24:1 . . . The earth is the *L*'s,
Ps 34:3 . . . tell of the *L*'s greatness;
Ps 34:8 . . . see that the *L* is good.
Ps 89:1 . . . sing of the *L*'s unfailing love
Ps 92:13 . . . to the *L*'s own house.
Ps 95:6 . . . kneel before the *L* our maker,
Ps 97:1 . . . The *L* is king!
Ps 99:5 . . . Exalt the *L* our God!
Ps 100:5 . . . For the *L* is good.
Ps 107:1 . . . thanks to the *L*, for he is
Ps 118:8 . . . better to take refuge in the *L*
Ps 118:23 . . . This is the *L*'s doing,
Ps 121:2 . . . help comes from the *L*, who
Ps 145:3 . . . Great is the *L*!
Ps 145:17 . . . The *L* is righteous
Ps 146:7 . . . The *L* frees the prisoners.
Ps 147:11 . . . No, the *L*'s delight is
Prov 3:5 . . . Trust in the *L* with all your
Prov 3:9 . . . Honor the *L* with your
Prov 3:11 . . . reject the *L*'s discipline,
Prov 12:22 . . . The *L* detests lying
Prov 15:33 . . . Fear of the *L*
Prov 19:21 . . . the *L*'s purpose will prevail.
Prov 21:2 . . . the *L* examines their heart.
Prov 31:30 . . . a woman who fears the *L* will
Isa 6:3 . . . holy is the *L* of Heaven's
Isa 24:14 . . . praise the *L*'s majesty.
Isa 30:9 . . . to the *L*'s instructions.
Isa 42:8 . . . I am the *L*; that is my name!
Isa 43:11 . . . I, am the *L*, and there is
Isa 49:4 . . . leave it all in the *L*'s hand;
Isa 53:6 . . . Yet the *L* laid on him
Isa 53:10 . . . was the *L*'s good plan
Isa 55:13 . . . honor to the *L*'s name;
Isa 61:2 . . . time of the *L*'s favor
Isa 66:15 . . . See, the *L* is coming
Jer 8:7 . . . do not know the *L*'s laws.
Jer 17:10 . . . But I, the *L*, search all
Jer 31:11 . . . For the *L* has redeemed
Jer 48:10 . . . to do the *L*'s work,
Jer 51:7 . . . cup in the *L*'s hands,
Ezek 7:19 . . . day of the *L*'s anger.
Ezek 44:4 . . . the glory of the *L* filled
Joel 1:15 . . . The day of the *L* is near,
Joel 3:18 . . . from the *L*'s Temple, watering
Jon 2:9 . . . salvation comes from the *L*
Mic 4:1 . . . mountain of the *L*'s house
Mic 6:2 . . . listen to the *L*'s complaint!
Nah 1:2 . . . The *L* is a jealous God,
Nah 1:7 . . . The *L* is good, a strong
Hab 2:16 . . . cup in the *L*'s judgment,
Zeph 2:3 . . . yet the *L* will protect
Matt 3:3 . . . way for the *L*'s coming!
Matt 4:7 . . . not test the *L* your God.
Matt 4:10 . . . must worship the *L* your God
Matt 22:37 . . . must love the *L* your God
Mark 1:3 . . . way for the *L*'s coming!
Mark 12:11 . . . This is the *L*'s doing,

John 1:23 . . . way for the *L*'s coming!
Acts 2:21 . . . name of the *L* will be saved.
Rom 10:13 . . . name of the *L* will be saved.
Rom 11:34 . . . can know the *L*'s thoughts?
1 Cor 10:26 . . . the earth is the *L*'s,
Heb 12:5 . . . of the *L*'s discipline,

**LORD (n)** honored one or a superior; master
(to a slave); king or ruler; God or Jesus
*see also* LORD
Deut 10:17 . . . of gods and *L* of lords.
Neh 4:14 . . . Remember the *L*, who is
Isa 6:1 . . . I saw the *L*. He was sitting
Dan 9:19 . . . O *L*, listen and act!
Matt 12:8 . . . Son of Man is *L*, even
Luke 1:38 . . . I am the *L*'s servant.
Acts 10:36 . . . Christ, who is *L* of all.
Acts 16:31 . . . Believe in the *L* Jesus
Rom 10:9 . . . that Jesus is *L* and believe
1 Cor 8:6 . . . only one *L*, Jesus Christ,
1 Cor 11:26 . . . announcing the *L*'s death
1 Cor 12:3 . . . say Jesus is *L*, except
Eph 4:5 . . . There is one *L*, one faith,
Phil 2:11 . . . Jesus Christ is *L*,
Col 2:6 . . . Jesus as your *L*, you must
1 Thes 5:2 . . . day of the *L*'s return
1 Tim 6:15 . . . kings and *L* of all lords.
Jas 5:8 . . . the coming of the *L* is near.
1 Pet 2:3 . . . taste of the *L*'s kindness.
1 Pet 3:15 . . . worship Christ as *L* of
Rev 4:8 . . . holy, holy is the *L* God,
Rev 4:11 . . . are worthy, O *L* our God,
Rev 19:16 . . . kings and *L* of all lords.
Rev 22:20 . . . Amen! Come, *L* Jesus!

**LOSE, LOSES (v)** to fail to keep, sustain, or
maintain; to damn
Matt 10:39 . . . cling to your life, you will *l*
Mark 8:36 . . . whole world but *l* your own
Luke 15:8 . . . silver coins and *l-s* one.
Luke 17:33 . . . cling to your life, you will *l*
John 6:39 . . . I should not *l* even one of
2 Jn 1:8 . . . you do not *l* what we have

**LOST (adj)** no longer possessed or known;
lacking assurance of eternal salvation
Jer 50:6 . . . have been *l* sheep.
Ezek 34:16 . . . will search for my *l* ones
Luke 15:4 . . . and one of them gets *l*,
Luke 15:6 . . . I have found my *l* sheep.
Luke 15:9 . . . have found my *l* coin.

**LOST (v)** to wander or go astray from
Luke 15:24 . . . He was *l*, but now he

**LOVE (n)** the ultimate expression of God's
loyalty, purity, and mercy extended toward his
people—to be reflected in human relationships
of brotherly concern, marital fidelity, and
adoration of God; a beloved person
Gen 24:12 . . . unfailing *l* to my master,
Gen 32:10 . . . unfailing *l* and faithfulness
Gen 34:3 . . . he fell in *l* with her, and he
Gen 39:21 . . . showed him his faithful *l*.
Exod 20:6 . . . unfailing *l* for a thousand
Exod 34:6 . . . filled with unfailing *l* and
Num 14:18 . . . with unfailing *l*, forgiving
Num 14:19 . . . unfailing *l*, please pardon
Deut 5:10 . . . unfailing *l* for a thousand
Deut 7:9 . . . his unfailing *l* on those who
Deut 10:15 . . . the objects of his *l*.
Deut 10:18 . . . He shows *l* to the
Deut 10:19 . . . must show *l* to foreigners,
Judg 16:4 . . . Samson fell in *l* with a woman

1 Sam 18:20 . . . had fallen in *l* with David,
1 Kgs 8:23 . . . and show unfailing *l* to all
1 Kgs 10:9 . . . LORD's eternal *l* for Israel,
1 Chr 16:41 . . . for "his faithful *l* endures
1 Chr 29:18 . . . See to it that their *l*
2 Chr 5:13 . . . His faithful *l* endures
2 Chr 20:21 . . . faithful *l* endures forever!
Ezra 3:11 . . . His faithful *l* for Israel
Job 37:13 . . . to show his unfailing *l*.
Ps 6:4 . . . because of your unfailing *l*.
Ps 13:5 . . . I trust in your unfailing *l*.
Ps 18:50 . . . you show unfailing *l* to your
Ps 21:7 . . . The unfailing *l* of the
Ps 23:6 . . . and unfailing *l* will pursue
Ps 25:6 . . . and unfailing *l*, which you
Ps 25:10 . . . leads with unfailing *l* and
Ps 26:3 . . . of your unfailing *l*, and I
Ps 31:7 . . . in your unfailing *l*, for you
Ps 31:16 . . . your unfailing *l*, rescue me.
Ps 32:10 . . . but unfailing *l* surrounds
Ps 33:5 . . . the unfailing *l* of the
Ps 33:18 . . . who rely on his unfailing *l*.
Ps 33:22 . . . your unfailing *l* surround us,
Ps 36:5 . . . Your unfailing *l*, O LORD, is
Ps 36:10 . . . Pour out your unfailing *l* on
Ps 40:10 . . . of your unfailing *l* and
Ps 40:11 . . . Let your unfailing *l* and
Ps 42:8 . . . his unfailing *l* upon me,
Ps 48:9 . . . on your unfailing *l* as we
Ps 51:1 . . . your unfailing *l*. Because of
Ps 57:3 . . . send forth his unfailing *l* and
Ps 57:10 . . . For your unfailing *l* is as
Ps 59:10 . . . In his unfailing *l*, my God
Ps 59:16 . . . your unfailing *l*. For you
Ps 59:17 . . . shows me unfailing *l*.
Ps 62:12 . . . unfailing *l*, O LORD, is yours.
Ps 66:20 . . . his unfailing *l* from me.
Ps 69:16 . . . LORD, for your unfailing *l* is
Ps 77:8 . . . his unfailing *l* gone forever?
Ps 85:7 . . . us your unfailing *l*, O LORD,
Ps 86:5 . . . full of unfailing *l* for all
Ps 86:15 . . . filled with unfailing *l* and
Ps 88:11 . . . your unfailing *l*?
Ps 89:1 . . . LORD's unfailing *l* forever!
Ps 89:14 . . . Unfailing *l* and truth
Ps 89:49 . . . is your unfailing *l*?
Ps 90:14 . . . with your unfailing *l*, so we
Ps 92:2 . . . your unfailing *l* in the
Ps 100:5 . . . His unfailing *l* continues
Ps 101:1 . . . sing of your *l* and justice,
Ps 103:4 . . . crowns me with *l* and tender
Ps 103:11 . . . his unfailing *l* toward those
Ps 103:17 . . . But the *l* of the LORD
Ps 106:1 . . . His faithful *l* endures
Ps 106:45 . . . because of his unfailing *l*.
Ps 107:31 . . . for his great *l* and for the
Ps 107:43 . . . the faithful *l* of the LORD.
Ps 108:4 . . . your unfailing *l* is higher
Ps 109:26 . . . because of your unfailing *l*.
Ps 115:1 . . . for your unfailing *l* and
Ps 118:1 . . . His faithful *l* endures
Ps 119:41 . . . give me your unfailing *l*,
Ps 119:76 . . . let your unfailing *l* comfort
Ps 119:124 . . . deal with me in unfailing *l*,
Ps 130:7 . . . LORD there is unfailing *l*.
Ps 138:2 . . . your unfailing *l* and faithfulness;
Ps 143:12 . . . your unfailing *l*, silence all
Ps 147:11 . . . put their hope in his unfailing *l*.
Prov 5:19 . . . be captivated by her *l*.
Prov 14:22 . . . will receive unfailing *l* and

Prov 16:6 . . . Unfailing *l* and
Prov 20:28 . . . is made secure through *l.*
Prov 21:21 . . . and unfailing *l* will find
Prov 27:5 . . . better than hidden *l!*
Song 1:4 . . . We praise your *l* even more
Song 1:7 . . . Tell me, my *l,* where are you
Song 1:16 . . . so handsome, my *l,* pleasing
Song 2:7 . . . not to awaken *l* until the
Song 2:17 . . . to me, my *l,* like a gazelle
Song 3:4 . . . I found my *l!*
Song 4:10 . . . Your *l* delights me,
Song 4:16 . . . your garden, my *l; * taste its
Song 5:5 . . . door for my *l,* and my hands
Song 5:8 . . . tell him I am weak with *l.*
Song 7:6 . . . How pleasing, my *l,* how full
Song 7:12 . . . will give you my *l.*
Song 8:4 . . . not to awaken *l* until the
Song 8:7 . . . cannot quench *l,* nor can
Song 8:14 . . . Come away, my *l!*
Isa 55:3 . . . the unfailing *l* I promised to
Isa 63:7 . . . Lord's unfailing *l.*
Isa 63:9 . . . In his *l* and mercy he
Jer 2:25 . . . I'm in *l* with these
Jer 9:24 . . . demonstrates unfailing *l* and
Jer 16:5 . . . taken away my unfailing *l*
Jer 31:3 . . . with an everlasting *l.*
Jer 33:11 . . . His faithful *l* endures
Lam 3:22 . . . The faithful *l* of the
Lam 3:32 . . . the greatness of his unfailing *l.*
Dan 9:4 . . . of unfailing *l* to those who
Hos 1:7 . . . I will show *l* to the people
Hos 2:19 . . . and justice, unfailing *l* and
Hos 2:23 . . . I will show *l* to those I
Hos 6:4 . . . For your *l* vanishes like the
Hos 6:6 . . . want you to show *l,* not offer
Hos 11:4 . . . my ropes of kindness and *l.*
Hos 12:6 . . . Act with *l* and justice,
Joel 2:13 . . . filled with unfailing *l.*
Jon 4:2 . . . filled with unfailing *l.*
Zeph 3:17 . . . With his *l,* he will
Zech 8:17 . . . Stop your *l* of telling
Mark 10:21 . . . Jesus felt genuine *l* for him.
John 5:42 . . . have God's *l* within you.
John 15:9 . . . Remain in my *l.*
John 15:10 . . . remain in his *l.*
John 15:13 . . . is no greater *l* than to lay
John 17:26 . . . Then your *l* for me will
Rom 5:5 . . . fill our hearts with his *l.*
Rom 5:8 . . . showed his great *l* for us by
Rom 8:35 . . . us from Christ's *l?*
Rom 8:39 . . . us from the *l* of God that is
Rom 13:10 . . . *L* does no wrong
Rom 13:10 . . . to others, so *l* fulfills the
Rom 14:15 . . . not acting in *l* if you eat
Rom 15:30 . . . because of your *l* for me,
1 Cor 4:21 . . . I come with *l* and a gentle
1 Cor 8:1 . . . it is *l* that strengthens the
1 Cor 13:13 . . . faith, hope, and *l*—and the
1 Cor 13:13 . . . greatest of these is *l.*
2 Cor 2:4 . . . know how much *l* I have for
2 Cor 2:8 . . . to reaffirm your *l* for him.
2 Cor 5:14 . . . Either way, Christ's *l* controls
2 Cor 8:7 . . . and your *l* from us—I want
2 Cor 8:24 . . . show them your *l,* and prove
Gal 5:22 . . . *l,* joy, peace, patience,
Eph 1:15 . . . Jesus and your *l* for God's
Eph 3:17 . . . down into God's *l* and keep
Eph 3:18 . . . how deep his *l* is.
Eph 4:15 . . . the truth in *l,* growing in
Eph 5:2 . . . filled with *l,* following the

Eph 6:23 . . . give you *l* with faithfulness.
Phil 1:9 . . . that your *l* will overflow
Col 1:4 . . . Jesus and your *l* for all of
Col 1:8 . . . told us about the *l* for others
Col 2:2 . . . strong ties of *l.*
1 Thes 3:6 . . . your faith and *l.*
1 Thes 3:12 . . . the Lord make your *l* for one
1 Thes 5:13 . . . and wholehearted *l* because of
2 Thes 3:5 . . . expression of the *l* of God
1 Tim 1:5 . . . be filled with *l* that comes
1 Tim 2:15 . . . in faith, *l,* holiness,
1 Tim 4:12 . . . live, in your *l,* your faith,
1 Tim 6:10 . . . For the *l* of money is the
1 Tim 6:11 . . . with faith, *l,* perseverance,
2 Tim 1:7 . . . but of power, *l,* and
2 Tim 1:13 . . . the faith and *l* that you have
2 Tim 2:22 . . . living, faithfulness, *l,* and
2 Tim 3:10 . . . my patience, my *l,* and my
Titus 2:2 . . . filled with *l* and patience.
Titus 3:4 . . . revealed his kindness and *l,*
Heb 10:24 . . . to acts of *l* and good works.
1 Pet 4:8 . . . for *l* covers a multitude
1 Pet 5:14 . . . with Christian *l.*
1 Jn 3:14 . . . who has no *l* is still dead.
1 Jn 3:16 . . . know what real *l* is because
1 Jn 4:7 . . . for *l* comes from God.
1 Jn 4:8 . . . for God is *l.*
1 Jn 4:10 . . . This is real *l*—not that we
1 Jn 4:16 . . . put our trust in his *l.*
1 Jn 4:16 . . . God is *l,* and all who
1 Jn 4:17 . . . live in God, our *l* grows more
1 Jn 4:18 . . . because perfect *l* expels all
Jude 1:12 . . . commemorating the Lord's *l,*
Jude 1:21 . . . safe in God's *l.*
Rev 2:19 . . . have seen your *l,* your faith,

**LOVE, LOVED, LOVES, LOVING (v)** to hold
dear; to feel a lover's passion, devotion, or
tenderness for; to feel affection or experience
desire; to like or desire actively
Gen 22:2 . . . Isaac, whom you *l* so much—
Gen 29:32 . . . my husband will *l* me.
Exod 21:5 . . . may declare, 'I *l* my master,
Lev 19:34 . . . as you *l* yourself.
Deut 4:37 . . . Because he *l-d* your ancestors,
Deut 6:5 . . . And you must *l* the Lord your
Deut 7:8 . . . that the Lord *l-s* you, and he
Deut 7:13 . . . He will *l* you and
Deut 11:13 . . . and if you *l* the Lord your
Deut 13:3 . . . if you truly *l* him with all
Deut 15:16 . . . because he *l-s* you and
Deut 21:15 . . . son of the wife he does not *l.*
Deut 23:5 . . . Lord your God *l-s* you.
Deut 30:6 . . . that you will *l* him with all
Deut 30:16 . . . to *l* the Lord
Deut 30:20 . . . this choice by *l-ing* the Lord
Deut 30:20 . . . And if you *l* and obey the
Deut 33:3 . . . Indeed, he *l-s* his people;
Josh 23:11 . . . be very careful to *l* the Lord
Judg 14:16 . . . said, "You don't *l* me;
Judg 16:15 . . . tell me, 'I *l* you,' when you
1 Sam 18:1 . . . for Jonathan *l-d* David.
2 Sam 12:24 . . . The Lord *l-d* the child
2 Sam 19:6 . . . You seem to *l* those who hate
1 Kgs 3:3 . . . Solomon *l-d* the Lord and
1 Kgs 11:1 . . . King Solomon *l-d* many foreign
2 Chr 2:11 . . . the Lord *l-s* his people
2 Chr 19:2 . . . the wicked and *l* those who
Neh 1:5 . . . with those who *l* him and obey
Neh 13:26 . . . *l-d* him and made him king
Ps 11:5 . . . those who *l* violence.

Ps 11:7 . . . righteous Lord *l-s* justice.
Ps 18:1 . . . I *l* you, Lord;
Ps 26:8 . . . I *l* your sanctuary,
Ps 36:10 . . . on those who *l* you;
Ps 40:16 . . . those who *l* your salvation
Ps 44:3 . . . helped them, for you *l-d* them.
Ps 45:7 . . . You *l* justice and
Ps 52:3 . . . You *l* evil more
Ps 52:4 . . . You *l* to destroy
Ps 70:4 . . . those who *l* your salvation
Ps 78:68 . . . Mount Zion, which he *l-d.*
Ps 89:28 . . . I will *l* him and be
Ps 89:33 . . . I will never stop *l-ing* him nor
Ps 91:14 . . . rescue those who *l* me.
Ps 97:10 . . . You who *l* the Lord,
Ps 98:3 . . . his promise to *l* and be
Ps 119:48 . . . I honor and *l* your commands.
Ps 119:97 . . . how I *l* your instructions!
Ps 119:113 . . . but I *l* your instructions.
Ps 119:119 . . . no wonder I *l* to obey your
Ps 119:127 . . . I *l* your commands more
Ps 119:140 . . . that is why I *l* them so much.
Ps 122:6 . . . May all who *l* this city
Ps 145:20 . . . all those who *l* him, but he
Ps 146:8 . . . The Lord *l-s* the godly.
Prov 3:12 . . . corrects those he *l-s,* just as
Prov 8:17 . . . *l* all who *l* me.
Prov 8:21 . . . Those who *l* me inherit
Prov 8:36 . . . All who hate me *l* death.
Prov 9:8 . . . and they will *l* you.
Prov 12:1 . . . you must *l* discipline; it is
Prov 15:17 . . . with someone you *l* is better
Prov 17:19 . . . Anyone who *l-s* to quarrel
Prov 18:21 . . . those who *l* to talk
Prov 19:8 . . . wisdom is to *l* oneself;
Prov 21:17 . . . Those who *l* pleasure
Prov 22:11 . . . Whoever *l-s* a pure
Prov 30:19 . . . how a man *l-s* a woman.
Eccl 3:8 . . . A time to *l* and a time
Eccl 9:9 . . . the woman you *l* through all
Song 1:3 . . . the young women *l* you!
Song 3:2 . . . search for the one I *l.*
Song 3:3 . . . Have you seen the one I *l?*
Isa 1:23 . . . All of them *l* bribes and
Isa 56:6 . . . serve him and *l* his name, who
Isa 61:8 . . . I, the Lord, *l* justice.
Jer 2:2 . . . long ago, how you *l-d* me and
Jer 8:2 . . . my people have *l-d,* served,
Jer 31:20 . . . but I still *l* him.
Hos 2:1 . . . The ones I *l.*
Hos 2:4 . . . I will not *l* her children,
Hos 2:23 . . . to those I called 'Not *l-d.* '
Hos 9:15 . . . I will *l* them no
Hos 11:1 . . . was a child, I *l-d* him, and I
Hos 12:7 . . . scales—they *l* to cheat.
Amos 4:5 . . . you Israelites *l* to do," says
Amos 5:15 . . . Hate evil and *l* what is good;
Mic 6:8 . . . is right, to *l* mercy, and to
Mal 1:2 . . . "I have always *l-d* you," says
Matt 5:43 . . . that says, '*L* your neighbor'
Matt 5:44 . . . But I say, *l* your enemies!
Matt 5:46 . . . If you *l* only those
Matt 6:24 . . . hate one and *l* the other;
Matt 10:37 . . . If you *l* your father or
Matt 19:19 . . . *L* your neighbor
Matt 22:37 . . . You must *l* the Lord your
Mark 12:6 . . . his son whom he *l-d* dearly.
Mark 12:30 . . . you must *l* the Lord your
Mark 12:33 . . . it is important to *l* him with
Mark 12:33 . . . and to *l* my neighbor as

Luke 6:27 . . . I say, *I* your enemies!
Luke 6:32 . . . If you *I* only those who
Luke 6:35 . . . *L* your enemies!
Luke 10:27 . . . You must *I* the LORD your
Luke 10:27 . . . And, '*L* your neighbor
Luke 16:13 . . . hate one and *I* the other;
John 3:16 . . . For God *I-d* the world so
John 3:35 . . . The Father *I-s* his Son
John 5:20 . . . For the Father *I-s* the Son and
John 8:42 . . . you would *I* me, because I
John 10:17 . . . The Father *I-s* me because I
John 11:36 . . . See how much he *I-d* him!
John 12:25 . . . Those who *I* their life
John 12:43 . . . For they *I-d* human praise more
John 13:1 . . . He had *I-d* his disciples during
John 13:34 . . . *L* each other.
John 13:34 . . . as I have *I-d* you, you should
John 14:21 . . . are the ones who *I* me.
John 14:28 . . . If you really *I-d* me, you
John 14:31 . . . know that I *I* the Father.
John 17:23 . . . and that you *I* them as much
John 17:24 . . . gave me because you *I-d* me
John 19:26 . . . beside the disciple he *I-d*,
John 20:2 . . . one whom Jesus *I-d*.
John 21:15 . . . do you *I* me more than
John 21:16 . . . son of John, do you *I* me?
John 21:20 . . . the disciple Jesus *I-d*—the one
Rom 8:28 . . . of those who *I* God and are
Rom 8:37 . . . through Christ, who *I-d* us.
Rom 9:13 . . . Scriptures, "I *I-d* Jacob, but I
Rom 9:25 . . . And I will *I* those whom I did
Rom 12:10 . . . *L* each other with genuine
1 Cor 2:9 . . . for those who *I* him.
1 Cor 13:2 . . . but didn't *I* others, I would
1 Cor 16:22 . . . anyone does not *I* the Lord,
2 Cor 9:7 . . . For God *I-s* a person
2 Cor 12:15 . . . the more I *I* you, the less
Gal 2:20 . . . of God, who *I-d* me and gave
Eph 1:4 . . . God *I-d* us and chose us
Eph 2:4 . . . mercy, and he *I-d* us so much,
Eph 5:25 . . . this means *I* your wives, just
Eph 5:25 . . . just as Christ *I-d* the church.
Eph 5:28 . . . their wives as they *I* their own
Eph 5:28 . . . a man who *I-s* his wife actually
Eph 5:33 . . . love his wife as he *I-s* himself,
Phil 1:16 . . . preach because they *I* me,
Phil 2:2 . . . each other, *I-ing* one another,
1 Thes 1:4 . . . God *I-s* you and has chosen
1 Thes 4:10 . . . urge you to *I* them even
2 Thes 2:10 . . . they refuse to *I* and accept
2 Thes 2:16 . . . our Father, who *I-d* us and
1 Tim 3:3 . . . and not *I* money.
1 Tim 6:2 . . . believers who are well *I-d*.
2 Tim 3:2 . . . people will *I* only themselves
Titus 1:8 . . . and he must *I* what is good.
Titus 2:4 . . . women to *I* their husbands
Titus 3:15 . . . believers—all who *I* us.
Heb 12:6 . . . disciplines those he *I-s*,
Heb 13:1 . . . Keep on *I-ing* each other as
Heb 13:5 . . . Don't *I* money;
Jas 2:5 . . . to those who *I* him?
1 Pet 1:8 . . . You *I* him even though
1 Pet 2:17 . . . Respect everyone, and *I* your
1 Pet 3:8 . . . *L* each other
2 Pet 2:15 . . . *I-d* to earn money by doing
1 Jn 2:5 . . . how completely you *I* him.
1 Jn 2:10 . . . Anyone who *I-s* another brother
1 Jn 3:1 . . . how very much our Father *I-s* us,
1 Jn 3:14 . . . If we *I* our Christian
1 Jn 4:9 . . . how much he *I-d* us by sending

1 Jn 4:10 . . . not that we *I-d* God, but that
1 Jn 4:11 . . . since God *I-d* us that much,
1 Jn 4:11 . . . surely ought to *I* each other.
1 Jn 4:19 . . . We *I* each other
1 Jn 4:19 . . . because he *I-d* us first.
1 Jn 4:20 . . . someone says, "I *I* God," but
1 Jn 4:20 . . . how can we *I* God, whom we
1 Jn 5:1 . . . And everyone who *I-s* the Father
Jude 1:1 . . . God the Father, who *I-s* you and
Rev 1:5 . . . glory to him who *I-s* us and has
Rev 3:9 . . . you are the ones I *I*.
Rev 3:19 . . . discipline everyone I *I*.
Rev 12:11 . . . they did not *I* their lives so
Rev 22:15 . . . and all who *I* to live a lie.

**LOVE, LOVED, LOVING (adj)** of or relating to a
strong affection for another; affectionate,
painstaking
Ps 88:18 . . . my companions and *I-d* ones.
Ps 127:2 . . . gives rest to his *I-d* ones.
Ezek 33:32 . . . who sings *I* songs with a
Mark 1:11 . . . are my dearly *I-d* Son, and you
Mark 9:7 . . . is my dearly *I-d* Son.
1 Thes 1:3 . . . work, your *I-ing* deeds, and the

**LOVINGKINDNESS (KJV)**
Ps 25:6 . . . *unfailing love*, which you have
Ps 40:11 . . . Let your *unfailing love* and
Ps 63:3 . . . *unfailing love* is better than life
Ps 143:8 . . . your *unfailing love* each morning
Isa 63:7 . . . according to his *mercy and love*

**LOYAL (adj)** unswerving in allegiance; faithful
*see also* FAITHFUL, TRUSTWORTHY
1 Sam 26:23 . . . and for being *I*,
2 Sam 2:6 . . . May the LORD be *I* to you in
1 Chr 12:33 . . . and completely *I* to David.
Ps 31:23 . . . those who are *I* to him,
Ps 51:10 . . . Renew a *I* spirit within
Prov 17:17 . . . A friend is always *I*, and a
Prov 20:6 . . . say they are *I* friends,

**LOYALTY, LOYALTIES (n)** the quality or stat
an instance of being loyal
Judg 8:35 . . . Nor did they show any *I* to
Ps 119:113 . . . I hate those with divided *I-i*
Prov 19:22 . . . *L* makes a person

**LUST, LUSTS (n)** usually intense or unbrid
sexual desire; an intense longing
1 Cor 7:9 . . . than to burn with *I*.
Eph 4:22 . . . corrupted by *I* and deception.
Col 3:5 . . . immorality, impurity, *I*, and
2 Tim 2:22 . . . stimulates youthful *I-s*.
Titus 3:3 . . . to many *I-s* and pleasures.

**LUST, LUSTED (v)** to have an intense (se
desire or need
Prov 6:25 . . . Don't *I* for her
Ezek 23:5 . . . Then Oholah *I-ed* after oth

**LUSTFUL (adj)** excited by lust; lecherou
Mark 7:22 . . . deceit, *I* desires, envy,
Gal 5:19 . . . impurity, *I* pleasures,
Eph 4:19 . . . They live for *I* pleasure and

**LYING (adj)** marked by or containing
falsehoods; false
Prov 6:17 . . . haughty eyes, a *I* tongue,
Prov 12:22 . . . The LORD detests *I* lips,
Prov 21:6 . . . Wealth created by a *I* ton
Prov 26:28 . . . A *I* tongue hates

**LYING (v)** *see also* LIE
Mic 6:12 . . . are so used to *I* that their
Matt 15:19 . . . immorality, theft, *I*, an

Acts 5:4 . . . You weren't *I* to us but
1 Cor 15:15 . . . would all be *I* about God—

**MADE (v)** *see also* CREATE(D), FORMED, MAKE
Gen 1:7 . . . God *m* this space to separate
Gen 1:16 . . . He also *m* the stars.
Gen 1:25 . . . *m* all sorts of wild animals,
Gen 1:31 . . . God looked over all he had *m*,
Gen 2:4 . . . LORD God *m* the earth and
Gen 2:22 . . . LORD God *m* a woman
Gen 6:6 . . . LORD was sorry he had ever *m*
Gen 9:6 . . . God *m* human beings in his
Exod 20:11 . . . the LORD *m* the heavens,
Deut 32:6 . . . Has he not *m* you and
2 Chr 2:12 . . . *m* the heavens and
Job 10:9 . . . that you *m* me from dust—
Ps 95:5 . . . sea belongs to him, for he *m* it.
Ps 115:15 . . . who *m* heaven and earth.
Prov 22:2 . . . The LORD *m* them both.
Eccl 3:11 . . . God has *m* everything
Isa 27:11 . . . the one who *m* them will
Isa 43:7 . . . I have *m* them for my glory.
Isa 57:16 . . . all the souls I have *m*.
Jer 51:15 . . . The LORD *m* the earth
Jon 1:9 . . . God of heaven, who *m* the sea
Matt 19:4 . . . *m* them male and female.
Matt 19:28 . . . when the world is *m* new
Rom 9:22 . . . who were *m* for destruction.
1 Cor 11:9 . . . man was not *m* for woman,
2 Cor 5:1 . . . an eternal body *m* for us by
1 Tim 2:13 . . . For God *m* Adam first,
Heb 4:3 . . . since he *m* the world.
Rev 13:8 . . . before the world was *m*—
. . . *m* the heavens,

John 5:18 . . . *m-ing* himself equal with God.
Rom 14:20 . . . it *m-s* another person stumble.
1 Cor 3:7 . . . that God *m-s* the seed grow.
Heb 8:5 . . . you *m* everything according to
1 Pet 2:8 . . . stone that *m-s* people stumble,

**MAKER (n)** one who makes; God
*see also* CREATOR
Ps 95:6 . . . before the LORD our *m,*
Ps 149:2 . . . Israel, rejoice in your *M.*
Prov 17:5 . . . mock the poor insult their *M;*
Isa 45:9 . . . clay pot argue with its *m?*
Hos 8:14 . . . Israel has forgotten its *M*

**MAMMON (KJV)**
Matt 6:24 . . . serve both God and *money*
Luke 16:9 . . . your *worldly resources* to
  benefit
Luke 16:11 . . . untrustworthy about *worldly
  wealth,*

**MAN (n)** an adult male human; individual,
person
Gen 2:7 . . . the *m* from the dust
Gen 2:15 . . . the *m* in the Garden
Gen 2:18 . . . for the *m* to be alone.
Gen 2:23 . . . she was taken from '*m.*'
Gen 2:25 . . . *m* and his wife were both
Gen 3:9 . . . God called to the *m,* "Where
Isa 53:3 . . . rejected—a *m* of sorrows,
1 Cor 11:3 . . . of every *m* is Christ,
1 Cor 11:3 . . . the head of woman is *m,*
1 Cor 15:45 . . . The first *m,* Adam,
Eph 5:31 . . . A *m* leaves his father and
1 Tim 2:5 . . . the *m* Christ Jesus.

**MANAGE, MANAGING (v)** to handle or direct
with a degree of skill
Luke 12:42 . . . of *m-ing* his other household
1 Tim 3:4 . . . *m* his own family well,
1 Tim 3:12 . . . he must *m* his children

**MANAGER (n)** a person who conducts
business or household affairs
Luke 16:1 . . . a *m* handling his affairs.
1 Cor 4:2 . . . as a *m* must be faithful.
Titus 1:7 . . . a *m* of God's household,

**MANGER (n)** a trough or open box in a stable
designed to hold feed for livestock
Luke 2:7 . . . cloth and laid him in a *m,*
Luke 2:12 . . . strips of cloth, lying in a *m.*

**MANNA (n)** in Hebrew, the word means
"What is it?"; miraculous supply of food given
to Israel in the wilderness; symbolic of spiritual
nourishment
Exod 16:31 . . . Israelites called the food *m.*
Deut 8:16 . . . He fed you with *m* in the
John 6:49 . . . Your ancestors ate *m* in the
Rev 2:17 . . . some of the *m* that has been

**MARRIAGE (adj)** of or relating to marriage
Gen 49:4 . . . you defiled my *m* couch.
Mal 2:14 . . . the wife of your *m* vows.

**MARRIAGE (n)** the state of being lawfully
united to a person of the opposite sex as
husband or wife; an act of marrying
Matt 22:30 . . . marry nor be given in *m.*
Rom 7:2 . . . laws of *m* no longer apply
1 Cor 7:14 . . . brings holiness to her *m,*
1 Cor 7:27 . . . do not seek to end the *m.*
Heb 13:4 . . . Give honor to *m,* and remain

**MARRY, MARRIED, MARRIES, MARRYING (v)**
to take a spouse according to law or custom

Exod 21:10 . . . who has *m-ied* a slave wife
Deut 24:4 . . . first husband may not *m* her
Deut 24:5 . . . newly *m-ied* man must not be
Deut 25:5 . . . husband's brother should *m*
Ezra 10:10 . . . By *m-ing* pagan women,
Hos 1:2 . . . Go and *m* a prostitute, so that
Matt 1:18 . . . to be *m-ied* to Joseph.
Matt 19:9 . . . divorces his wife and *m-ies*
Matt 22:30 . . . will neither *m* nor be given
Mark 12:23 . . . all seven were *m-ied* to her.
Luke 16:18 . . . his wife and *m-ies* someone
Rom 7:2 . . . when a woman *m-ies,* the law
1 Cor 7:9 . . . better to *m* than to burn
1 Cor 7:28 . . . if you do get *m-ied,* it is not
1 Cor 7:33 . . . a *m-ied* man has to think
1 Tim 5:14 . . . these younger widows to *m*

**MARY**
1. Mother of Jesus, the foretold virgin (Matt
   1:16-25; Luke 1:26-38); psalmist of the
   Magnificat (Luke 1:46-56); gave birth in
   Bethlehem (Luke 2:5-20); at first sign (miracle) of Jesus (John 2:1-5); at the cross (John
   19:25-27); in upper room after the ascension
   (Acts 1:14); Jesus assigned her care to John
   (John 19:25-27).
2. Mary Magdalene, former demoniac,
   supporter of Jesus (Luke 8:1-3); was at the
   cross and Jesus' burial (Matt 27:55-61; Mark
   15:40-47; John 19:25); saw angel after
   resurrection (Matt 28:1-10; Mark 16:1-9;
   Luke 24:10); saw Jesus after resurrection
   (John 20:1-18).
3. Sister of Martha and Lazarus (Luke 10:38-42;
   John 11; 12:1-8).
4. Mother of James and Joseph (Matt 27:56;
   Mark 15:40, 47; 16:1).
5. Mother of John Mark (Acts 12:12).
6. A woman greeted by Paul in Rome (Rom
   16:6).

**MASTER, MASTERS (n)** one in authority or
leadership; employer; teacher; lord or Lord
Jer 3:14 . . . the LORD, "for I am your *m.*
Matt 10:24 . . . are not greater than their *m.*
Luke 16:13 . . . No one can serve two *m-s.*
Rom 6:14 . . . Sin is no longer your *m,*
Eph 6:5 . . . obey your earthly *m-s* with deep
Col 3:22 . . . Slaves, obey your earthly *m-s*
1 Tim 6:1 . . . full respect for their *m-s*
1 Tim 6:2 . . . If the *m-s* are believers,
2 Tim 2:21 . . . ready for the *M* to use you
Titus 2:9 . . . always obey their *m-s* and do
1 Pet 2:18 . . . the authority of your *m-s*
2 Pet 2:1 . . . deny the *M* who bought them.
Jude 1:4 . . . denied our only *M* and Lord,

**MATURE (adj)** of or relating to a condition of
full development or to attaining a desired or final
state
1 Cor 2:6 . . . I am among *m* believers,
1 Cor 14:20 . . . but be *m* in understanding
2 Cor 13:9 . . . that you will become *m.*
Eph 4:13 . . . we will be *m* in the Lord,
Phil 3:15 . . . all who are spiritually *m* agree
Heb 6:1 . . . *m* in our understanding.
1 Jn 2:13 . . . who are *m* in the faith

**MATURITY (n)** the quality or state of being fully
developed
Luke 8:14 . . . And so they never grow into *m.*
2 Cor 13:11 . . . Grow to *m.* Encourage each

**MEASURE, MEASURED, MEASURING (v)** to
gauge or regulate the specific dimensions of; to
have a specified measurement; to regulate by a
standard
Ps 145:3 . . . No one can *m* his greatness.
Isa 40:28 . . . No one can *m* the depths
Jer 31:37 . . . heavens cannot be *m-d* and
Ezek 45:3 . . . area, *m* out a portion of land
Dan 5:27 . . . balances and have not *m-d* up.
Zech 2:2 . . . I am going to *m* Jerusalem,
Luke 12:15 . . . Life is not *m-d* by how much
Eph 4:13 . . . mature in the Lord, *m-ing* up
Rev 11:1 . . . Go and *m* the Temple

**MEDIATE, MEDIATES (v)** to act as an
intermediary agent; to interpose
Job 16:21 . . . to *m* between God and me,
Isa 2:4 . . . LORD will *m* between nations
Heb 8:6 . . . the one who *m-s* for us a far
Heb 9:15 . . . who *m-s* a new covenant
Heb 12:24 . . . Jesus, the one who *m-s*

**MEDIATOR (n)** one who mediates
Job 9:33 . . . If only there were a *m* between
1 Tim 2:5 . . . one God and one *M* who can

**MEDICINE (n)** a substance or preparation used
in treating disease; something that affects well-
being
Prov 17:22 . . . A cheerful heart is good *m,*
Jer 8:22 . . . Is there no *m* in Gilead?
Rev 22:2 . . . The leaves were used for *m*

**MEDITATE, MEDITATING (v)** to contemplate,
reflect, or ponder
*see also* THINK
Gen 24:63 . . . walking and *m-ing* in the
  fields,
Ps 1:2 . . . LORD, *m-ing* on it day and night.
Ps 48:9 . . . O God, we *m* on your unfailing
Ps 63:6 . . . *m-ing* on you through the night.
Ps 119:23 . . . but I will *m* on your decrees.
Ps 119:27 . . . *m* on your wonderful deeds.
Ps 119:48 . . . I *m* on your decrees.
Ps 145:5 . . . I will *m* on your majestic,

**MEDITATION (n)** the act or process of
meditating
Ps 19:14 . . . words of my mouth and the *m*

**MERCIFUL (adj)** compassionate; forgiving
Deut 4:31 . . . your God is a *m* God;
Ps 78:38 . . . Yet he was *m* and forgave
Dan 4:27 . . . and be *m* to the poor.
Dan 9:9 . . . our God is *m* and forgiving,
Matt 5:7 . . . God blesses those who are *m,*
Luke 1:54 . . . and remembered to be *m.*
Heb 2:17 . . . *m* and faithful High Priest
Jas 2:13 . . . God will be *m* when he judges

**MERCY, MERCIES (n)** a blessing that is an
act of divine favor or compassion; withholding
of the punishment or judgment our sins deserve
*see also* COMPASSION, FORGIVENESS
Exod 34:6 . . . God of compassion and *m!*
2 Sam 24:14 . . . for his *m* is great.
Neh 9:27 . . . In your great *m,* you sent
Job 41:3 . . . beg you for *m* or implore
Ps 28:6 . . . he has heard my cry for *m.*
Ps 103:4 . . . me with love and tender *m-ies.*
Ps 119:77 . . . with your tender *m-ies* so I
Ps 119:156 . . . how great is your *m;*
Isa 14:1 . . . LORD will have *m* on
Isa 49:10 . . . LORD in his *m* will lead
Isa 60:10 . . . I will now have *m* on you

Lam 3:22 . . . His *m-ies* never cease.
Dan 9:18 . . . because of your *m.*
Jon 2:8 . . . their backs on all God's *m-ies.*
Mic 6:8 . . . do what is right, to love *m,*
Matt 5:7 . . . for they will be shown *m.*
Matt 9:13 . . . I want you to show *m,*
Matt 18:33 . . . just as I had *m* on you?
Matt 23:23 . . . law—justice, *m,* and faith.
Rom 9:15 . . . I will show *m* to anyone
Rom 9:18 . . . God chooses to show *m*
Rom 11:32 . . . have *m* on everyone.
2 Cor 4:1 . . . God in his *m* has given us
Gal 1:6 . . . through the loving *m* of Christ.
Eph 2:4 . . . But God is so rich in *m,* and
1 Tim 1:13 . . . But God had *m* on me
Titus 3:5 . . . but because of his *m.*
Heb 4:16 . . . we will receive his *m,*
Heb 10:29 . . . who brings God's *m* to us.
Jas 2:13 . . . will be no *m* for those
Jas 3:17 . . . It is full of *m* and good
1 Pet 1:3 . . . by his great *m* that we
Jude 1:22 . . . show *m* to those whose faith

**MESSENGER, MESSENGERS (n)** one who
bears a message or does an errand
Prov 13:17 . . . a reliable *m* brings healing.
Prov 25:13 . . . Trustworthy *m-s* refresh like
Isa 52:7 . . . feet of the *m* who brings good
Isa 66:19 . . . who survive to be *m-s* to the
Mal 3:1 . . . my *m,* and he will prepare
Matt 11:10 . . . am sending my *m* ahead
Rom 10:15 . . . feet of *m-s* who bring good
Rom 15:16 . . . a special *m* from Christ
2 Cor 12:7 . . . *m* from Satan to torment
Phil 2:25 . . . he was your *m* to help me
1 Thes 2:4 . . . speak as *m* approved by God
Heb 3:1 . . . to be God's *m* and High Priest.

**MESSIAH, MESSIAHS (n)** the one anointed by
God to deliver His people and establish His
kingdom
*see also* CHRIST, JESUS
Matt 24:24 . . . false *m-s* and false
Mark 13:22 . . . false *m-s* and false
John 1:41 . . . him, "We have found the *M*"
John 4:25 . . . I know the *M* is coming—

**MIGHTY, MIGHTIER, MIGHTIEST (adj)**
powerful; great or imposing in size or extent
Gen 49:24 . . . hands of the *M* One of Jacob,
Deut 10:17 . . . God, the *m* and awesome
Deut 34:12 . . . With *m* power, Moses
2 Sam 23:8 . . . David's *m-iest* warriors.
2 Chr 20:6 . . . You are powerful and *m;*
Neh 9:32 . . . and *m* and awesome God,
Job 9:4 . . . For God is so wise and so *m.*
Job 36:5 . . . He is *m* in both power and
Ps 24:8 . . . LORD, strong and *m;*
Ps 47:5 . . . ascended with a *m* shout.
Ps 50:1 . . . LORD, the *M* One, is God,
Ps 71:16 . . . I will praise your *m* deeds,
Ps 77:12 . . . thinking about your *m* works.
Ps 89:27 . . . son, the *m-iest* king on earth.
Ps 93:4 . . . But *m-ier* than the violent raging
Ps 93:4 . . . LORD above is *m-ier* than these!
Ps 95:4 . . . and the *m-iest* mountains.
Ps 145:4 . . . children of your *m* acts;
Ps 145:12 . . . will tell about your *m* deeds
Ps 150:2 . . . Praise him for his *m* works;
Prov 24:5 . . . wise are *m-ier* than the strong,
Isa 9:6 . . . Wonderful Counselor, *M* God,
Isa 60:16 . . . your Redeemer, the *M* One of

Zeph 3:17 . . . He is a *m* savior.
Eph 1:19 . . . This is the same *m* power
Eph 6:10 . . . in the Lord and in his *m*
Heb 1:3 . . . sustains everything by the *m*
1 Pet 5:6 . . . yourselves under the *m*
Jude 1:9 . . . Michael, one of the *m-iest* of the
angels,

**MILK (n)** from goats, used for food and drink;
figurative of abundant produce, prosperity,
spiritual food, or salvation
Exod 3:8 . . . flowing with *m* and honey—
1 Cor 3:2 . . . feed you with *m,* not with
1 Pet 2:2 . . . must crave pure spiritual *m*

**MIND, MINDS (n)** the part of humans that
engages in conscious thinking, feeling, and
decision making; in the Bible, mind is akin to the
heart, not the brain
Num 23:19 . . . he does not change his *m.*
1 Sam 15:29 . . . nor will he change his *m,*
Mark 12:30 . . . all your soul, all your *m,*
Luke 24:45 . . . opened their *m-s*
Acts 4:32 . . . were united in heart and *m.*
Rom 8:6 . . . Spirit control your *m*
1 Cor 1:10 . . . be of one *m,* united in
1 Cor 2:9 . . . heard, and no *m* has imagined
Col 2:18 . . . sinful *m-s* have made them
2 Cor 4:4 . . . has blinded the *m-s* of those
2 Tim 4:5 . . . clear *m* in every situation.
Heb 8:10 . . . I will put my laws in their *m-s,*
Heb 10:16 . . . I will write them on their *m-s.*

**MIRACLE, MIRACLES (n)** an extraordinary
event manifesting divine intervention in human
affairs
Exod 3:20 . . . performing all kinds of *m-s*
Exod 7:9 . . . demand, 'Show me a *m.*'
Deut 13:1 . . . they promise you signs or *m-s,*
Job 9:10 . . . He performs countless *m-s.*
Ps 105:5 . . . he has performed, his *m-s,*
Ps 106:2 . . . the glorious *m-s* of the LORD?
Jer 32:19 . . . and do great and mighty *m-s.*
Matt 7:22 . . . and performed many *m-s*
Matt 13:54 . . . and the power to do *m-s?*
Mark 6:2 . . . power to perform such *m-s?*
Mark 9:39 . . . No one who performs a *m*
Luke 19:37 . . . wonderful *m-s* they had
Luke 23:8 . . . to see him perform a *m.*
John 7:21 . . . I did one *m* on the Sabbath,
Acts 2:22 . . . by doing powerful *m-s,*
Acts 8:13 . . . *m-s* Philip performed.
Acts 19:11 . . . to perform unusual *m-s.*
1 Cor 12:28 . . . those who do *m-s,* those
2 Cor 12:12 . . . and *m-s* among you.
Gal 3:5 . . . Spirit and work *m-s* among you
Heb 2:4 . . . and various *m-s* and gifts of

**MIRROR (n)** a polished or smooth surface (as
of glass) that forms images by reflection
1 Cor 13:12 . . . puzzling reflections in a *m,*
Jas 1:23 . . . glancing at your face in a *m.*

**MONEY (n)** officially coined or stamped metal
or paper currency
*see also* POSSESSION(S), RICHES, TREASURE(S),
WEALTH
2 Chr 24:10 . . . gladly brought their *m* and
Eccl 5:10 . . . who love *m* will never have
Matt 6:24 . . . serve both God and *m.*
Luke 3:14 . . . Don't extort *m* or make false
1 Tim 3:3 . . . and not love *m.*
1 Tim 6:10 . . . love of *m* is the root of all

1 Tim 6:17 . . . and not to trust in their *m,*
1 Jn 3:17 . . . If someone has enough *m*

**MOON (n)** a celestial body that orbits the earth
Josh 10:13 . . . and the *m* stayed in place
Ps 121:6 . . . harm you by day, nor the *m* at
Ps 148:3 . . . Praise him, sun and *m!*
Joel 2:31 . . . the *m* will turn blood red
Hab 3:11 . . . The sun and *m* stood still
Matt 24:29 . . . the *m* will give no light,
Acts 2:20 . . . the *m* will turn blood red
Col 2:16 . . . or new *m* ceremonies
Rev 21:23 . . . city has no need of sun or *m,*

**MORNING (n)** the time from sunrise to noon
Gen 1:5 . . . evening passed and *m* came,
Ps 5:3 . . . Listen to my voice in the *m,*
Lam 3:23 . . . mercies begin afresh each *m.*

**MORTAL (adj)** subject to death
Gen 6:3 . . . for they are only *m* flesh.
Rom 8:11 . . . will give life to your *m* bodies
1 Cor 15:53 . . . our *m* bodies must be

**MORTALS (n)** a human being
Ps 8:4 . . . mere *m* that you should think
Ps 144:3 . . . mere *m* that you should think

**MOSES** Deliverer of Israel from Egypt, Lawgiver, servant of God; "drawn out" of the Nile,
raised in Pharaoh's house (Exod 2:1-10); killed
an Egyptian and fled to Midian (Exod 2:11-15;
Acts 7:24); married Zipporah and had a child
(Exod 2:16-22); saw the LORD at the burning
bush (Exod 3:1–4:17); returned to Egypt (Exod
4:18-31); conflict with Pharaoh and the 10
plagues (Exod 5–11); brother of Aaron and
Miriam (1 Chr 6:3); Passover and the Exodus
(Exod 12–14; 1 Cor 10:2); song of salvation and
praise (Exod 15:1-21; Rev 15:3); heavenly
provisions (Exod 15:22–17:7); raised arms to
defeat enemies (Exod 17:8-16); delegated
judgeships (Exod 18); received the Law at Sinai
(Exod 19–23; John 1:17; Heb 12:21); received
Tabernacle plans (Exod 25–31); broke tablets at
gold calf incident (Exod 32); received new tablets
(Exod 33–34); face glowed with the LORD's glory
(Exod 34:29-35; 2 Cor 3:13-15); directed the
building of the Tabernacle (Exod 35–40);
anointed Tabernacle and Aaronic priesthood (Lev
8–9); opposed by Aaron and Miriam, interceded
for sister (Num 12); interceded for Israel when
they refused to enter Canaan (Num 14:11-25);
Korah's rebellion (Num 16); water at Meribah
(Num 20:1-13); denied entrance to Promised
Land (Num 20:12; Deut 1:37; 3:23-28); bronze
snake healed (Num 21:4-9; John 3:14);
succeeded by Joshua (Num 27:12-23; Deut
31:1-8); received additional laws (Num 28–30);
gave concluding messages to Israel (Deut 1–33);
gave final blessings to the tribes (Deut 33; *see
also* Gen 49); died and was exalted (Deut 34;
Heb 3:2); wrote a psalm (Ps 90); recorded book
of the Law (Ezra 3:2; Neh 13:1; Luke 24:44).

**MOTHER (n)** a female parent; a woman in
authority
*see also* PARENT
Gen 2:24 . . . a man leaves his father and *m*
Gen 3:20 . . . she would be the *m* of all who
Exod 20:12 . . . Honor your father and *m.*
Deut 21:18 . . . not obey his father or *m,*
Judg 5:7 . . . Deborah arose as a *m*
Prov 10:1 . . . brings grief to a *m.*

Prov 23:22 . . . don't despise your *m*
Isa 66:13 . . . as a *m* comforts her child.
Matt 10:35 . . . a daughter against her *m,*
Matt 10:37 . . . father or *m* more than you
Matt 12:48 . . . Who is my *m?*
Mark 10:19 . . . Honor your father and *m.*
John 19:27 . . . disciple, "Here is your *m."*
Eph 5:31 . . . A man leaves his father and *m*
Eph 6:2 . . . Honor your father and *m.*

**MOTIVES (n)** something (as a need or desire) that causes a person to act
1 Chr 29:17 . . . all this with good *m,*
Ps 26:2 . . . Test my *m* and my heart.
Prov 16:2 . . . LORD examines their *m.*
Jer 17:10 . . . hearts and examine secret *m.*
1 Cor 4:5 . . . will reveal our private *m.*
Phil 1:18 . . . Whether their *m* are false or
1 Thes 2:3 . . . with any deceit or impure *m*
1 Thes 2:4 . . . He alone examines the *m* of
Jas 4:3 . . . because your *m* are all wrong—

**MOUNTAIN, MOUNTAINS (n)** a landmass that projects conspicuously above its surroundings and is higher than a hill
Exod 24:18 . . . on the *m* forty days
Deut 5:4 . . . At the *m* the LORD
Ps 36:6 . . . is like the mighty *m-s,*
Ps 121:1 . . . I look up to the *m-s—*
Isa 14:13 . . . preside on the *m* of the gods
Matt 17:20 . . . say to this *m,* 'Move
Mark 9:2 . . . led them up a high *m*
Mark 9:9 . . . went back down the *m,*
Luke 23:30 . . . beg the *m-s,* 'Fall on us,'
1 Cor 13:2 . . . faith that I could move *m-s,*
2 Pet 1:18 . . . with him on the holy *m.*
Rev 6:16 . . . they cried to the *m-s* and

**MOURN, MOURNING (v)** to feel or express grief or sorrow
Gen 50:11 . . . watched them *m*
Zech 12:10 . . . have pierced and *m*
Matt 5:4 . . . God blesses those who *m,*

**MOURNING (n)** the act of sorrowing; a period of time during which signs of grief are shown
Ps 30:11 . . . my clothes of *m* and clothed
Isa 60:20 . . . Your days of *m* will come to
Isa 61:3 . . . instead of *m,* festive praise
Jer 31:13 . . . I will turn their *m* into joy.
Zech 8:19 . . . times of *m* you have kept

**MOUTH, MOUTHS (n)** the natural opening through which food passes into the body of an animal; voice, speech
Ps 10:7 . . . Their *m-s* are full of cursing,
Ps 19:14 . . . words of my *m* and
Prov 13:3 . . . opening your *m* can ruin
Isa 51:16 . . . have put my words in your *m*
Isa 53:7 . . . he did not open his *m.*
Isa 59:3 . . . and your *m* spews corruption.
Jer 31:29 . . . their children's *m-s* pucker
Matt 4:4 . . . word that comes from the *m*
Rom 3:14 . . . Their *m-s* are full of cursing
Rom 10:9 . . . *m* that Jesus is Lord
Rev 2:16 . . . with the sword of my *m.*

**MOVE, MOVED, MOVES, MOVING (v)** to change the place or position of; to go from one place to another in continuous motion; to carry on one's life or activities in a specified environment; to stir the emotions or passions of; to prompt to the doing of something
Exod 35:21 . . . and whose spirits were *m-d*

Deut 19:14 . . . steal anyone's land by *m-ing*
Deut 23:14 . . . LORD your God *m-s* around
Prov 4:15 . . . Turn away and keep *m-ing.*
Prov 23:10 . . . cheat your neighbor by *m-ing*
Isa 54:10 . . . For the mountains may *m*
Acts 17:28 . . . For in him we live and *m*
1 Cor 13:2 . . . faith that I could *m*
2 Pet 1:21 . . . were *m-d* by the Holy Spirit,

**MURDER (n)** the personal, intentional killing of another person
Matt 5:21 . . . If you commit *m,*
Rom 1:29 . . . hate, envy, *m,* quarreling,

**MURDER, MURDERED, MURDERS (v)** to kill (a human being) unlawfully and with premeditated malice
Gen 9:5 . . . *m-s* a fellow human must die.
Exod 20:13 . . . You must not *m.*
Deut 5:17 . . . You must not *m.*
Matt 23:31 . . . who *m-ed* the prophets.
Acts 7:52 . . . whom you betrayed and *m-ed.*
Rom 13:9 . . . You must not *m.*
Jas 2:11 . . . You must not *m.*

**MURDERER, MURDERERS (n)** one who commits the crime of murder
Num 35:16 . . . *m* must be executed.
Ps 5:6 . . . LORD detests *m-s* and deceivers.
Ps 26:9 . . . condemn me along with *m-s.*
Ps 59:2 . . . save me from these *m-s.*
Ezek 18:10 . . . a robber or *m* and refuses
1 Jn 3:15 . . . brother or sister is really a *m*
Rev 21:8 . . . the corrupt, *m-s,* the immoral,
Rev 22:15 . . . the sexually immoral, the *m-s,*

**MUSIC (n)** vocal, instrumental, or mechanical sounds having rhythm, melody, or harmony
Judg 5:3 . . . I will make *m* to the LORD,
1 Chr 6:31 . . . lead the *m* at the house of
Neh 12:27 . . . and with the *m* of cymbals,
Ps 45:8 . . . the *m* of strings entertains
Amos 5:23 . . . to the *m* of your harps.
Eph 5:19 . . . and making *m* to the Lord

**MUSTARD (n)** a plant whose seeds are used as a condiment and for oil; in Jesus' time, the smallest seed known
Matt 13:31 . . . is like a *m* seed planted
Matt 17:20 . . . as small as a *m* seed,
Mark 4:31 . . . is like a *m* seed planted

**MUZZLE (v)** to fit with a fastening or covering for the mouth of an animal to prevent eating or biting
Deut 25:4 . . . You must not *m* an ox
1 Tim 5:18 . . . You must not *m* an ox

**MYSTERIOUS (adj)** exciting wonder, curiosity, or surprise while baffling efforts to comprehend or identify; of, relating to, or constituting mystery
1 Cor 14:2 . . . Spirit, but it will all be *m.*
Eph 1:9 . . . now revealed to us his *m* plan
Eph 3:3 . . . revealed his *m* plan to me.
Eph 6:19 . . . explain God's *m* plan that the
Col 2:2 . . . they understand God's *m* plan,
Col 4:3 . . . about his *m* plan concerning
Rev 10:7 . . . God's *m* plan will be fulfilled.

**MYSTERY, MYSTERIES (n)** something not understood or beyond understanding; a religious truth that one can know only by revelation and cannot fully understand
*see also* SECRET(S)

Dan 4:9 . . . and that no *m* is too great
Rom 11:25 . . . to understand this *m,*
1 Cor 2:7 . . . speak of is the *m* of God—
1 Cor 4:1 . . . explaining God's *m-ies.*
1 Tim 3:9 . . . to the *m* of the faith
1 Tim 3:16 . . . the great *m* of our faith:
Rev 1:20 . . . the *m* of the seven stars
Rev 17:7 . . . tell you the *m* of this woman

**NAIL, NAILED, NAILING (v)** to fasten with or as if with a nail
Matt 27:35 . . . had *n-ed* him to the cross,
Mark 15:24 . . . soldiers *n-ed* him to the
Acts 2:23 . . . you *n-ed* him to a cross
Col 2:14 . . . away by *n-ing* it to the cross.
Heb 6:6 . . . are *n-ing* him to the cross

**NAKED (adj)** not covered by clothing; nude
Gen 2:25 . . . man and his wife were both *n,*
Job 1:21 . . . and I will be *n* when I leave.
Eccl 5:15 . . . the end of our lives as *n*

**NAME, NAMES (n)** a word or phrase that constitutes the distinctive designation of a person or thing; reputation
*see also* REPUTATION
Gen 2:19 . . . the man chose a *n* for each
Exod 3:15 . . . my *n* to remember
Exod 28:9 . . . on them the *n-s* of the tribes
Exod 34:14 . . . whose very *n* is Jealous,
Lev 24:11 . . . blasphemed the *n*
Deut 18:5 . . . minister in the LORD's *n*
Deut 28:58 . . . awesome *n* of the LORD
1 Chr 17:8 . . . will make your *n* as famous
2 Chr 7:14 . . . called by my *n* will humble
Ps 8:1 . . . your majestic *n* fills the earth!
Ps 23:3 . . . paths, bringing honor to his *n.*
Ps 34:3 . . . let us exalt his *n* together.
Ps 66:2 . . . Sing about the glory of his *n!*
Ps 103:1 . . . I will praise his holy *n.*
Ps 138:2 . . . I praise your *n* for your
Ps 147:4 . . . stars and calls them all by *n.*
Isa 40:26 . . . calling each by its *n.*
Isa 42:8 . . . I am the LORD; that is my *n!*
Jer 15:16 . . . I bear your *n,* O LORD
Dan 12:1 . . . people whose *n* is written in
Joel 2:32 . . . calls on the *n* of the LORD
Mic 5:4 . . . majesty of the *n* of the LORD
Zech 14:9 . . . one LORD—his *n* alone
Mal 1:6 . . . have shown contempt for my *n!*
Matt 24:5 . . . come in my *n,* claiming, 'I am
Matt 28:19 . . . baptizing them in the *n* of
Luke 10:20 . . . your *n-s* are registered
Luke 11:2 . . . may your *n* be kept holy.
John 16:24 . . . Ask, using my *n,* and you
Acts 2:21 . . . calls on the *n* of the LORD
Acts 4:12 . . . no other *n* under heaven
Rom 10:13 . . . calls on the *n* of the LORD
Phil 2:9 . . . gave him the *n* above all
Phil 2:10 . . . that at the *n* of Jesus every
Phil 4:3 . . . whose *n-s* are written in the Book
Heb 12:23 . . . *n-s* are written in heaven.
Jas 5:14 . . . with oil in the *n* of the Lord.
Rev 2:17 . . . stone will be engraved a new *n*
Rev 3:5 . . . erase their *n-s* from the Book
Rev 3:12 . . . write on them the *n*
Rev 20:15 . . . whose *n* was not found
Rev 21:27 . . . *n-s* are written in the Lamb's

**NARROW (adj)** of slender width
Matt 7:13 . . . only through the *n* gate.
Matt 7:14 . . . the gateway to life is very *n*

**NATION, NATIONS (n)** group of people defined by geography or ethnicity
*see also* GENTILE(S), PEOPLE(S)
Gen 12:2 . . . I will make you into a great *n.*
Gen 17:4 . . . father of a multitude of *n-s!*
Gen 17:16 . . . the mother of many *n-s.*
Gen 25:23 . . . will become two *n-s.*
Gen 28:3 . . . multiply and become many *n-s!*
Exod 19:6 . . . of priests, my holy *n.*
Deut 15:6 . . . You will rule many *n-s,* but
Deut 28:10 . . . the *n-s* of the world will see
Ps 2:8 . . . you the *n-s* as your inheritance,
Ps 22:28 . . . He rules all the *n-s.*
Ps 46:10 . . . I will be honored by every *n.*
Ps 66:7 . . . every movement of the *n-s;*
Ps 68:30 . . . Scatter the *n-s* that delight in
Ps 87:6 . . . the LORD registers the *n-s.*
Ps 99:2 . . . exalted above all the *n-s.*
Ps 113:4 . . . LORD is high above the *n-s;*
Prov 14:34 . . . Godliness makes a *n* great,
Isa 11:10 . . . The *n-s* will rally to him,
Isa 34:1 . . . listen, O *n-s* of the earth.
Isa 40:15 . . . for all the *n-s* of the world
Isa 42:1 . . . He will bring justice to the *n-s.*
Isa 52:15 . . . And he will startle many *n-s.*
Isa 56:7 . . . a house of prayer for all *n-s.*
Isa 60:12 . . . the *n-s* that refuse to serve
Isa 66:8 . . . Has a *n* ever been born in a
Ezek 37:22 . . . divided into two *n-s* or into
Joel 3:2 . . . my people among the *n-s,*
Amos 9:12 . . . *n-s* I have called to be mine.
Mic 4:3 . . . disputes between strong *n-s*
Mic 5:7 . . . take their place among the *n-s.*
Zeph 3:8 . . . stand and accuse these evil *n-s.*
Hag 2:7 . . . I will shake all the *n-s,*
Zech 8:13 . . . Among the other *n-s,* Judah
Zech 12:2 . . . makes the nearby *n-s* stagger
Matt 12:18 . . . proclaim justice to the *n-s.*
Matt 24:14 . . . so that all *n-s* will hear it;
Matt 28:19 . . . make disciples of all the *n-s,*
Mark 11:17 . . . house of prayer for all *n-s.*
Acts 4:25 . . . Why were the *n-s* so angry?
Gal 3:8 . . . All *n-s* will be blessed through
1 Pet 2:9 . . . royal priests, a holy *n,*
Rev 5:9 . . . and language and people and *n.*
Rev 14:6 . . . to every *n,* tribe, language,
Rev 21:24 . . . The *n-s* will walk in its light,
Rev 22:2 . . . for medicine to heal the *n-s.*

**NATURE (n)** inherent character or essence; given by God at birth
Rom 1:20 . . . eternal power and divine *n.*
Rom 8:4 . . . follow our sinful *n*
Rom 8:7 . . . For the sinful *n* is always
Gal 5:19 . . . the desires of your sinful *n,*
Gal 5:24 . . . desires of their sinful *n* to
2 Pet 1:4 . . . share his divine *n* and escape

**NEED, NEEDS (n)** a condition requiring supply or relief; poverty; obligation; a lack of something requisite, desirable, or useful
1 Kgs 8:59 . . . according to each day's *n-s.*
Ps 79:8 . . . compassion quickly meet our *n-s,*
Ps 112:9 . . . give generously to those in *n.*
Prov 11:26 . . . who sells in time of *n.*
Prov 30:8 . . . just enough to satisfy my *n-s.*
Matt 6:2 . . . give to someone in *n,*
Acts 2:45 . . . the money with those in *n.*
Acts 20:35 . . . you can help those in *n* by
Rom 12:13 . . . God's people are in *n,*
1 Cor 7:3 . . . fulfill his wife's sexual *n-s,*
Eph 4:28 . . . give generously to others in *n.*

Phil 4:19 . . . will supply all your *n-s* from his
Titus 3:14 . . . by meeting the urgent *n-s*

**NEED, NEEDED, NEEDING (v)** to require; to be necessary; to be in want
Ps 34:9 . . . fear him will have all they *n.*
Ps 119:75 . . . disciplined me because I *n-ed*
Phil 4:6 . . . Tell God what you *n,* and
Heb 4:16 . . . grace to help us when we *n* it
Jas 1:4 . . . complete, *n-ing* nothing.
Jas 1:5 . . . If you *n* wisdom, ask our

**NEEDY (adj)** poverty-stricken; marked by want of affection, attention, or emotional support
1 Sam 2:8 . . . *n* from the garbage dump.
Ps 9:18 . . . the *n* will not be ignored
Ps 68:10 . . . you provided for your *n*
Ps 69:33 . . . LORD hears the cries of the *n;*
Prov 22:22 . . . or exploit the *n* in court.
Prov 31:20 . . . opens her arms to the *n.*

**NEIGHBOR, NEIGHBORS (n)** one living or located near another; fellow man
Lev 19:18 . . . but love your *n* as yourself.
Ps 15:3 . . . to gossip or harm their *n-s*
Prov 24:28 . . . your *n-s* without cause;
Prov 27:10 . . . better to go to a *n* than
Jer 31:34 . . . not need to teach their *n-s,*
Mark 12:31 . . . Love your *n* as yourself.
Luke 10:29 . . . And who is my *n?*
Rom 13:8 . . . If you love your *n,* you will
Gal 5:14 . . . Love your *n* as yourself.
Eph 4:25 . . . Let us tell our *n-s* the truth,
Heb 8:11 . . . not need to teach their *n-s,*
Jas 2:8 . . . Love your *n* as yourself.

**NEW (adj)** fresh; original; different than before; unfamiliar
Ps 98:1 . . . Sing a *n* song to the LORD,
Jer 31:31 . . . I will make a *n* covenant with
Ezek 36:26 . . . I will give you a *n* heart,
Mark 16:17 . . . will speak in *n* languages.
Luke 22:20 . . . cup is the *n* covenant
Rom 6:4 . . . we also may live *n* lives.
Rom 12:2 . . . you into a *n* person
1 Cor 11:25 . . . cup is the *n* covenant
2 Cor 3:6 . . . but under the *n* covenant,
2 Cor 5:17 . . . is gone; a *n* life has begun!
Gal 6:15 . . . into a *n* creation.
Eph 4:24 . . . Put on your *n* nature,
Col 3:10 . . . Put on your *n* nature,
Heb 8:8 . . . when I will make a *n* covenant
Heb 9:15 . . . mediates a *n* covenant
Heb 12:24 . . . the *n* covenant
2 Pet 3:13 . . . new heavens and *n* earth he
Rev 2:17 . . . a *n* name that no one
Rev 21:1 . . . *n* heaven and a *n* earth,

**NEWBORN (adj)** recently born
1 Pet 2:2 . . . Like *n* babies, you must crave

**NEWS (n)** a report of recent events; "Good News": the Gospel of Jesus Christ
Isa 40:9 . . . of good *n,* shout from the
Matt 4:23 . . . the Good *N* about
Mark 1:15 . . . sins and believe the Good *N!*
Luke 4:43 . . . I must preach the Good *N*
Acts 13:32 . . . to bring you this Good *N.*
Acts 14:21 . . . preaching the Good *N*
Rom 1:16 . . . not ashamed of this Good *N*
Rom 10:17 . . . the Good *N* about Christ.
Rom 15:16 . . . I bring you the Good *N*
Rom 16:25 . . . just as my Good *N* says.
1 Cor 1:17 . . . to preach the Good *N—*

1 Cor 9:12 . . . an obstacle to the Good *N*
1 Cor 9:16 . . . preach the Good *N!*
1 Cor 9:23 . . . to spread the Good *N*
1 Cor 15:1 . . . the Good *N* I preached
2 Cor 4:4 . . . glorious light of the Good *N.*
2 Cor 9:13 . . . obedient to the Good *N*
2 Cor 11:7 . . . preaching God's Good *N*
Gal 1:7 . . . is not the Good *N* at all.
Eph 6:15 . . . comes from the Good *N*
Phil 1:27 . . . worthy of the Good *N*
Col 1:5 . . . heard the truth of the Good *N.*
Col 1:23 . . . Good *N* has been preached
1 Thes 2:4 . . . entrusted with the Good *N.*
2 Thes 1:8 . . . obey the Good *N* of our Lord
2 Tim 1:10 . . . through the Good *N.*
2 Tim 4:5 . . . telling others the Good *N,*
Rev 14:6 . . . the eternal Good *N*

**NIGHT, NIGHTS (n)** period of darkness between sunset and sunrise; figurative of suffering and sorrow or the reign of sin and immorality
Gen 1:16 . . . smaller one to govern the *n.*
Exod 13:21 . . . provided light at *n*
Job 35:10 . . . who gives songs in the *n?*
Ps 1:2 . . . meditating on it day and *n.*
Ps 19:2 . . . *n* after *n* they make him
Ps 77:6 . . . my *n-s* were filled with joyful
Jon 1:17 . . . fish for three days and three *n-s.*
Matt 4:2 . . . days and forty *n-s* he fasted
Matt 12:40 . . . for three days and three *n-s.*
Luke 2:8 . . . That *n* there were shepherds
2 Cor 6:5 . . . endured sleepless *n-s,* and gone
1 Thes 5:2 . . . like a thief in the *n.*
1 Thes 5:5 . . . belong to darkness and *n.*
Rev 21:25 . . . there is no *n* there.

**NINETY-NINE (n)** the number 99
Matt 18:13 . . . than over the *n* that didn't
Luke 15:7 . . . to God than over *n* others

**NOAH** Builder of great boat, survivor of the Flood (Gen 6–9; Matt 24:37-38; Luke 17:26-27; Heb 11:7; 1 Pet 3:20; 2 Pet 2:5); family line (Gen 5:25-32); found favor with God (Gen 6:8); enacted covenant between God and all creatures (Gen 9:1-17); made wine and became drunk (Gen 9:18-23); gave blessings and curse to descendants (Gen 9:24-27); considered righteous (Ezek 14:14, 20).

**OATH (n)** an appeal to God to witness the truth of some statement
Ps 95:11 . . . in my anger I took an *o:*
Ps 110:4 . . . LORD has taken an *o*
Ezek 20:42 . . . I promised with a solemn *o*
Heb 6:16 . . . people take an *o,* they call
Heb 7:20 . . . established with a solemn *o.*
Heb 7:21 . . . was an *o* regarding Jesus.
Jas 5:12 . . . never take an *o,* by heaven

**OBEDIENCE (n)** an act or instance of obeying; the quality or state of being obedient
Judg 2:17 . . . who had walked in *o* to the
1 Sam 15:22 . . . *O* is better than sacrifice,
Phil 2:8 . . . he humbled himself in *o* to God
Heb 5:8 . . . learned *o* from the things he

**OBEDIENT (adj)** submissive to authority; willing to obey
Luke 2:51 . . . with them and was *o* to them.
Rom 16:19 . . . that you are *o* to the Lord.
2 Cor 9:13 . . . that you are *o* to the Good

2 Cor 10:6 . . . you have become fully *o,*
1 Pet 1:14 . . . as God's *o* children.

**OBEY, OBEYED, OBEYING, OBEYS (v)** to
follow the commands or guidance of; to
conform to or comply with
*see also* KEEP
Gen 22:18 . . . because you have *o-ed* me.
Exod 20:6 . . . love me and *o* my commands.
Lev 18:4 . . . be careful to *o* my decrees,
Lev 25:18 . . . decrees and *o* my regulations.
Deut 4:2 . . . Just *o* the commands of the
Deut 5:27 . . . we will listen and *o.*
Deut 6:17 . . . diligently the commands of
Deut 6:25 . . . when we *o* all the commands
Deut 11:1 . . . and *o* all his requirements,
Deut 11:22 . . . Be careful to *o* all these
Deut 13:4 . . . *O* his commands, listen to his
Deut 26:16 . . . to *o* them wholeheartedly.
Deut 28:1 . . . If you fully *o* the LORD
Deut 30:2 . . . if you *o* with all your heart
Deut 30:12 . . . so we can hear it and *o?*
Deut 30:20 . . . love and *o* the LORD,
Josh 1:7 . . . to *o* all the instructions Moses
Josh 22:5 . . . all his ways, *o* his commands,
1 Sam 7:3 . . . to *o* only the LORD;
1 Kgs 8:61 . . . May you always *o* his decrees
2 Kgs 17:13 . . . *O* my commands and
2 Kgs 18:6 . . . *o-ed* all the commands
2 Kgs 23:3 . . . pledged to *o* the LORD
Neh 1:5 . . . love him and *o* his commands,
Job 36:11 . . . they listen and *o* God,
Ps 111:10 . . . All who *o* his commandments
Ps 119:17 . . . I may live and *o* your word.
Ps 119:129 . . . No wonder I *o* them!
Eccl 8:2 . . . *O* the king since you vowed
Eccl 12:13 . . . and *o* his commands,
Isa 11:3 . . . delight in *o-ing* the LORD.
Jer 32:33 . . . not receive instruction or *o.*
Jer 42:6 . . . For if we *o* him, everything
Jer 43:4 . . . refused to *o* the LORD's
Dan 9:4 . . . love you and *o* your commands.
Dan 9:10 . . . We have not *o-ed* the LORD
Jon 3:3 . . . This time Jonah *o-ed* the LORD's
Mic 5:15 . . . nations that refuse to *o* me.
Matt 5:19 . . . anyone who *o-s* God's laws
Matt 8:27 . . . the winds and waves *o* him!
Matt 19:20 . . . *o-ed* all these commandments,
Matt 28:20 . . . to *o* all the commands
Luke 8:21 . . . hear God's word and *o* it.
John 3:36 . . . who doesn't *o* the Son
John 8:51 . . . anyone who *o-s* my teaching
John 14:15 . . . *o* my commandments.
Acts 4:19 . . . to *o* you rather than him?
Acts 5:29 . . . We must *o* God rather than
Rom 1:5 . . . believe and *o* him,
Rom 2:27 . . . possess God's law but don't *o*
Rom 3:28 . . . and not by *o-ing* the law.
Rom 6:16 . . . of whatever you choose to *o?*
Rom 6:17 . . . wholeheartedly *o* this
Rom 15:31 . . . in Judea who refuse to *o* God.
2 Cor 10:5 . . . teach them to *o* Christ.
Gal 2:16 . . . Christ, not by *o-ing* the law.
Gal 3:2 . . . by *o-ing* the law of Moses?
Gal 3:10 . . . and *o* all the commands
Eph 2:2 . . . who refuse to *o* God.
Eph 6:1 . . . Children, *o* your parents
Eph 6:5 . . . Slaves, *o* your earthly masters
2 Thes 3:14 . . . who refuse to *o* what we
1 Tim 3:4 . . . who respect and *o* him.
Titus 2:9 . . . Slaves must always *o* their

Heb 11:8 . . . that Abraham *o-ed* when God
Heb 11:31 . . . who refused to *o* God.
Jas 2:8 . . . good when you *o* the royal law
1 Pet 1:2 . . . you have *o-ed* him and have
1 Pet 1:22 . . . when you *o-ed* the truth,
1 Pet 2:8 . . . they do not *o* God's word,
1 Jn 3:22 . . . because we *o* him and do
Rev 22:7 . . . Blessed are those who *o* the

**OFFER, OFFERED, OFFERING (v)** to present
for acceptance as an act of worship or devotion;
to sacrifice
Ps 4:5 . . . *O* sacrifices in the right spirit,
Ps 116:12 . . . What can I *o* the LORD
Mic 6:7 . . . Should we *o* him thousands of
1 Cor 10:20 . . . sacrifices are *o-ed* to demons,
Eph 5:2 . . . He loved us and *o-ed* himself
Heb 7:27 . . . when he *o-ed* himself
Heb 9:14 . . . Christ *o-ed* himself to God
Heb 9:25 . . . to *o* himself again and again,
Heb 10:11 . . . *o-ing* the same sacrifices again
Heb 11:17 . . . that Abraham *o-ed* Isaac
Heb 13:15 . . . let us *o* through Jesus
Jas 5:15 . . . a prayer *o-ed* in faith will heal

**OFFERING, OFFERINGS (n)** a sacrifice
ceremonially offered as a part of worship;
a contribution to the support of a church
Gen 22:8 . . . a sheep for the burnt *o,*
1 Sam 13:9 . . . Bring me the burnt *o*
1 Sam 15:22 . . . burnt *o-s* and sacrifices
Ps 40:6 . . . no delight in sacrifices or *o-s.*
Ps 141:2 . . . hands as an evening *o.*
Isa 53:10 . . . his life is made an *o* for sin,
Hos 6:6 . . . more than I want burnt *o-s.*
Mal 3:8 . . . cheated me of the tithes and *o-s*
Mark 12:33 . . . all of the burnt *o-s*
Rom 15:26 . . . taken up an *o* for the poor
Phil 2:17 . . . faithful service is an *o*
Heb 10:5 . . . animal sacrifices or sin *o-s.*
Heb 10:14 . . . that one *o* he forever made
Heb 11:4 . . . Abel's *o* gave evidence that he

**OIL (n)** a liquid substance produced from
olives used in biblical times for lamp fuel,
anointing, trade, and dressing wounds; often
symbolic of the Holy Spirit
Exod 29:7 . . . anointing *o* over his head.
Exod 30:25 . . . to make a holy anointing *o.*
1 Sam 10:1 . . . *o* and poured it over Saul's
1 Sam 16:13 . . . *o* he had brought and
Ps 23:5 . . . anointing my head with *o.*
Ps 133:2 . . . as precious as the anointing *o*
Heb 1:9 . . . pouring out the *o* of joy

**OLIVE, OLIVES (n)** a Mediterranean evergreen
tree with berries that ripen black; the berries of
an olive tree
Gen 8:11 . . . evening with a fresh *o* leaf
Jer 11:16 . . . a thriving *o* tree, beautiful
Zech 4:3 . . . And I see two *o* trees,
Zech 4:4 . . . the Mount of *O-s* will split
Matt 24:3 . . . Jesus sat on the Mount of *O-s.*
Rom 11:17 . . . of God's special *o* tree.
Rom 11:24 . . . cut from a wild *o* tree.
Jas 3:12 . . . Does a fig tree produce *o-s,* or
Rev 11:4 . . . prophets are the two *o* trees

**OPPOSE, OPPOSED, OPPOSES (v)** to set
onself against or opposite someone or
something; to resist
Exod 23:22 . . . *o* those who *o* you.
Ps 8:2 . . . enemies and all who *o* you.
Ps 35:1 . . . *o* those who *o* me.

Acts 26:11 . . . was so violently *o-d* to them
Gal 2:11 . . . I had to *o* him to his face,
1 Tim 6:20 . . . with those who *o*
2 Tim 2:25 . . . instruct those who *o*
Titus 1:9 . . . show those who *o* it
Titus 2:8 . . . who *o* us will be ashamed
Jas 4:6 . . . God *o-s* the proud but favors
1 Pet 5:5 . . . God *o-s* the proud but favors

**OPPRESS, OPPRESSED, OPPRESSES,
OPPRESSING (v)** to crush or burden by abuse
of power or authority
Exod 22:21 . . . not mistreat or *o* foreigners
Ps 9:9 . . . a shelter for the *o-ed,* a refuge
Ps 14:6 . . . frustrate the plans of the *o-ed,*
Ps 82:3 . . . uphold the rights of the *o-ed* and
Ps 146:7 . . . He gives justice to the *o-ed*
Prov 22:16 . . . gets ahead by *o-ing* the
poor
Prov 28:16 . . . no understanding will *o*
Prov 31:5 . . . not give justice to the *o-ed.*
Isa 1:17 . . . Seek justice. Help the *o-ed.*
Isa 3:5 . . . People will *o* each other—
Isa 58:3 . . . you keep *o-ing* your workers.
Ezek 18:12 . . . *o-es* the poor and helpless,
Dan 7:25 . . . defy the Most High and *o* the
Amos 2:7 . . . shove the *o-ed* out of the way.
Amos 5:12 . . . *o* good people by taking
Zech 7:10 . . . Do not *o* widows, orphans,
Luke 4:18 . . . that the *o-ed* will be set free,
Jas 2:6 . . . the rich who *o* you and drag

**OPPRESSION (n)** unjust or cruel exercise of
power or authority
Judg 2:18 . . . burdened by *o* and suffering.
Ps 72:14 . . . redeem them from *o* and
Ps 119:134 . . . Ransom me from the *o* of
Isa 58:9 . . . Remove the heavy yoke of *o.*
Heb 11:25 . . . chose to share the *o* of God's

**ORPHAN, ORPHANS (n)** a child deprived by
death of one or (usually) both parents
Exod 22:22 . . . not exploit a widow or an *o.*
Deut 10:18 . . . *o-s* and widows receive
Deut 24:17 . . . among you and to *o-s,*
Deut 24:19 . . . *o-s,* and widows.
Ps 10:14 . . . in you. You defend the *o-s.*
Ps 82:3 . . . justice to the poor and the *o;*
Prov 23:10 . . . the land of defenseless *o-s.*
John 14:18 . . . will not abandon you as *o-s*—
Jas 1:27 . . . caring for *o-s* and widows in

**OVERSEER(S) (KJV)**
2 Chr 2:18 . . . and 3,600 as *foremen*
Neh 11:22 . . . *chief officer* of the Levites
Prov 6:7 . . . or *governor* or ruler to make
Acts 20:28 . . . appointed you as *elders*
1 Tim 3:1 . . . an *elder* must be a man whose
1 Pet 2:25 . . . Shepherd, the *Guardian* of

**OWE (v)** to be under obligation to pay or repay
in return for something received
Rom 13:7 . . . Give to everyone what you *o*
Phlm 19 . . . that you *o* me your very soul!

**OWN (adj)** belonging to oneself or itself
Luke 18:9 . . . in their *o* righteousness
1 Cor 13:5 . . . does not demand its *o* way.
Titus 2:14 . . . to make us his very *o* people,

**OWN (v)** to have or hold as property
Gen 28:4 . . . May you *o* this land

**OX, OXEN (n)** a domestic bovine mammal
Deut 25:4 . . . not muzzle an *o* to keep it
1 Kgs 7:25 . . . base of twelve bronze *o-en,*

1 Kgs 19:20 . . . Elisha left the *o-en*
Isa 1:3 . . . *o* knows its owner, and a
Ezek 1:10 . . . the face of an *o* on the left
1 Cor 9:9 . . . not muzzle an *o* to keep it
1 Tim 5:18 . . . not muzzle an *o* to keep it
Rev 4:7 . . . the second was like an *o;*

**PAGAN (adj)** of or relating to a pagan
1 Sam 17:26 . . . Who is this *p* Philistine

**PAGAN, PAGANS (n)** a follower of a false god
or a heathen religion; one who delights in
sensual pleasures and material goods
Ps 106:35 . . . they mingled among the *p-s*
Isa 2:6 . . . have made alliances with *p-s.*
Matt 5:47 . . . Even *p-s* do that.
Matt 18:17 . . . treat that person as a *p*
1 Cor 5:1 . . . something that even *p-s* don't
1 Cor 12:2 . . . when you were still *p-s*, you

**PAID (v)** *see* also PAY
1 Cor 7:23 . . . God *p* a high price for you,
Col 3:25 . . . be *p* back for the wrong
1 Tim 5:17 . . . should be respected and *p*

**PAIN, PAINS (n)** physical, mental, or emotional
suffering; the spasms of childbirth
Job 6:10 . . . Despite the *p,* I have not
Ps 73:14 . . . every morning brings me *p.*
Jer 4:19 . . . my heart—I writhe in *p!*
Matt 24:8 . . . only the first of the birth *p-s,*
John 16:21 . . . suffering the *p-s* of labor.
Rom 8:22 . . . in the *p-s* of childbirth
Gal 4:19 . . . going through labor *p-s* for
you
1 Thes 5:3 . . . woman's labor *p-s* begin.
Heb 13:3 . . . as if you felt their *p* in your
Rev 21:4 . . . death or sorrow or crying or *p.*

**PAINFUL (adj)** feeling or giving pain
Gen 5:29 . . . the *p* labor of farming
Prov 17:21 . . . *p* to be the parent of a fool;
2 Cor 2:1 . . . grief with another *p* visit.
Heb 12:11 . . . while it is happening—it's *p!*

**PANIC (n)** a sudden unreasoning terror often
accompanied by mass flight
1 Sam 14:15 . . . Suddenly, *p* broke out
Zech 14:13 . . . by the LORD with great *p.*

**PANIC (v)** to be affected with panic
Deut 20:3 . . . Do not lose heart or *p*
Mark 13:7 . . . threats of wars, but don't *p.*

**PARABLE, PARABLES (n)** a brief narrative
story told with earthly analogies to illustrate a
spiritual truth
Ps 78:2 . . . I will speak to you in a *p.*
Matt 13:35 . . . I will speak to you in *p-s.*
Luke 8:10 . . . I use *p-s* to teach the

**PARADISE (n)** an intermediate place where the
souls of the righteous await resurrection and the
final judgment
Luke 23:43 . . . you will be with me in *p.*
2 Cor 12:4 . . . that I was caught up to *p*

**PARALYZED (adj)** characterized by the inability
to move
Matt 9:2 . . . Jesus said to the *p* man,
Mark 2:3 . . . men arrived carrying a *p* man
John 5:3 . . . blind, lame, or *p*—

**PARDON, PARDONED (v)** to allow (an offense)
to pass without punishment; to forgive
Num 14:19 . . . *p* the sins of this people,

Deut 29:20 . . . LORD will never *p* such
2 Kgs 5:18 . . . may the LORD *p* me
2 Chr 30:18 . . . LORD, who is good, *p*
Isa 40:2 . . . gone and her sins are *p-ed.*
Jer 5:7 . . . How can I *p* you?
Joel 3:21 . . . I will *p* my people's crimes,
Joel 3:21 . . . which I have not yet *p-ed;*

**PARENT, PARENTS (n)** one that produces and
cares for offspring
*see also* FATHER, MOTHER
Exod 20:5 . . . I lay the sins of the *p-s* upon
Prov 13:1 . . . child accepts a *p*'s discipline;
Jer 31:29 . . . *p-s* have eaten sour grapes,
Ezek 18:19 . . . child pay for the *p*'s sins?
Matt 10:21 . . . will rebel against their *p-s*
Rom 1:30 . . . and they disobey their *p-s.*
Eph 6:1 . . . Children, obey your *p-s*
Col 3:20 . . . always obey your *p-s,*

**PARTIAL (adj)** inclined to favor one party more
than the other; of or relating to a part rather than
the whole
Lev 19:15 . . . or being *p* to the rich
1 Cor 13:10 . . . *p* things will become

**PARTIALITY (n)** the quality or state of being
partial
*see also* FAVORITES, FAVORITISM
Deut 10:17 . . . God, who shows no *p* and
Deut 16:19 . . . twist justice or show *p.*
2 Chr 19:7 . . . perverted justice, *p,*

**PARTNER, PARTNERS (n)** a person with whom
one shares an intimate relationship; one
associated with another especially in action
Mal 2:14 . . . she remained your faithful *p,*
2 Cor 6:14 . . . can righteousness be a *p*
Phil 1:5 . . . *p-s* in spreading the Good
1 Pet 3:7 . . . but she is your equal *p* in
1 Pet 4:13 . . . trials make you *p-s* with
3 Jn 1:8 . . . be their *p-s* as they teach
Rev 1:9 . . . your *p* in suffering and in God's

**PASSION, PASSIONS (n)** intense, driving, or
overmastering feeling or conviction; ardent
affection; sexual desire
Isa 59:17 . . . himself in a cloak of divine *p.*
Zech 8:2 . . . with *p* for Jerusalem!
1 Cor 7:37 . . . he can control his *p,* he does
Gal 5:24 . . . Jesus have nailed the *p-s*
1 Thes 4:5 . . . lustful *p* like the pagans

**PASSIONATE (adj)** capable of, affected by, or
expressing intense feeling
2 Kgs 19:31 . . . *p* commitment of the LORD
Isa 9:7 . . . *p* commitment of the LORD
Isa 37:32 . . . *p* commitment of the LORD
Zech 1:14 . . . Mount Zion is *p* and strong.
Zech 8:2 . . . Mount Zion is *p* and strong;

**PASSOVER (n)** a festival that commemorated
the Hebrew departure from Egypt in haste
Num 9:2 . . . celebrate the *P*
Deut 16:1 . . . celebrate the *P* each year
Ezra 6:19 . . . returned exiles celebrated *P.*
Mark 14:12 . . . *P* lamb is sacrificed,
Heb 11:28 . . . to keep the *P* and to sprinkle

**PASTORS (n)** a spiritual overseer
Eph 4:11 . . . and the *p* and teachers.

**PATH, PATHS (n)** course, route; a way of life,
conduct, or thought
1 Kgs 8:36 . . . follow the right *p,*
Ps 23:3 . . . He guides me along right *p-s,*

Ps 27:11 . . . Lead me along the right *p,*
Prov 2:13 . . . to walk down dark *p-s.*
Prov 3:6 . . . show you which *p* to take.
Prov 5:21 . . . examining every *p* he takes.
Prov 8:20 . . . in *p-s* of justice.
Prov 14:12 . . . a *p* before each person that
Isa 48:17 . . . leads you along the *p-s*
Hos 14:9 . . . *p-s* of the LORD are true
2 Tim 2:18 . . . have left the *p* of truth,
Heb 12:13 . . . Mark out a straight *p*

**PATIENCE (n)** the power or capacity to endure
without complaint something difficult or
disagreeable; forbearance, longsuffering
Rom 15:5 . . . May God, who gives this *p*
Gal 5:22 . . . joy, peace, *p,* kindness,
Col 1:11 . . . endurance and *p* you need.
Col 3:12 . . . humility, gentleness, and *p.*
2 Tim 3:10 . . . my faith, my *p,* my love,
Titus 2:2 . . . and be filled with love and *p.*
Jas 5:10 . . . examples of *p* in suffering,
2 Pet 3:15 . . . Lord's *p* gives people time

**PATIENT (adj)** bearing pains or trials calmly or
without complaint; steadfast despite opposition,
difficulty, or adversity; not hasty or impetuous
Rom 2:4 . . . and *p* God is with you?
Rom 12:12 . . . Be *p* in trouble,
1 Cor 4:12 . . . We are *p* with those who
1 Cor 13:4 . . . Love is *p* and kind.
1 Thes 5:14 . . . Be *p* with everyone.
Jas 5:8 . . . You, too, must be *p.*

**PATIENTLY (adv)** in a patient manner
Ps 40:1 . . . I waited *p* for the LORD
1 Pet 3:20 . . . God waited *p* while Noah
Rev 14:12 . . . endure persecution *p,*

**PAUL** Pharisee and Roman citizen (Acts 22:3);
from city of Tarsus (Acts 9:11; Phil 3:5); became
apostle (Gal 1) to the Gentiles (Rom 11:13); also
known as "Saul" (Acts 7:58; 13:9); supported
stoning of Stephen (Acts 8:1); attacked early
Christians (Acts 8:1-3; 9:1-2; Gal 1:13);
converted on road to Damascus (Acts 9:1-9;
22:6-16; 26:12-18); preached in Damascus
(Acts 9:20-22); escaped over the wall in basket
(Acts 9:23-25); escaped to Jerusalem, on to
Tarsus (Acts 9:26-30); saw visions in Arabia
(Gal 1:17); with Barnabas in Antioch (Acts
11:22-26); sent to Jerusalem (Acts 11:27-30);
first missionary journey: Cyprus and Galatia
(Acts 13–14); advocate for Gentile believers
(Acts 15:1-5); testified at Jerusalem Council
(Acts 15:12); split with Barnabas over John
Mark (Acts 15:36-41); second missionary
journey with Silas: northern and southern
Greece, western Asia (Acts 15:36–18:22);
received call to Macedonia (Acts 16:6-10);
Philippi, Thessalonica, Berea (Acts 16–17);
Athens, Corinth (Acts 17–18); third missionary
journey: returned to northern and southern
Greece, western Asia (Acts 18:23–21:14);
Corinth, Ephesus, Macedonia, Troas—to
Jerusalem (Acts 18–21); farewell to Ephesian
elders (Acts 20:13-38); journey to Rome (Acts
21–28); falsely arrested and in hands of mob
(Acts 21:26–22:21); saved by Roman custody
(Acts 22:22-29; 23:10); before the Jewish high
council (Acts 23:1-11); relocated to Caesarea
(Acts 23:12-35); trial before Felix (Acts 24);
appealed to Caesar before Festus (Acts 25:1-
12), before Herod Agrippa (Acts 25:13–26:32);

sailed to Rome, was shipwrecked (Acts 27); arrived in Rome (Acts 28); pattern of self-denial (1 Cor 9); his gospel message (Rom 1–5; Gal 3–6); catalog of trials (2 Cor 11:22-33); his goal (Phil 3:7-15); last known written words of (2 Tim 4); intervened for returning slave (Phlm 8-22); wrote letters: Romans through Philemon (see verse 1 of each book).

**PAY (n)** something paid for a purpose and especially as a salary or wage
1 Tim 5:18 . . . who work deserve their *p!*

**PAY, PAYS (v)** to suffer the consequences of an act; to requite according to what is deserved; to make due return to for services or goods rendered
Exod 22:3 . . . A thief who is caught must *p*
Deut 32:35 . . . I will *p* them back.
Ps 137:8 . . . Happy is the one who *p-s* you
Matt 22:17 . . . to *p* taxes to Caesar or not?
Rom 12:19 . . . I will *p* them back,
1 Thes 5:15 . . . no one *p-s* back evil
2 Thes 1:6 . . . he will *p* back those who

**PAYMENT (n)** the act of paying; something that is paid
Deut 15:2 . . . must not demand *p*
Deut 27:25 . . . anyone who accepts *p*
Hos 9:7 . . . the day of *p* is here.

**PEACE (n)** a state of tranquility or quiet; a pact or agreement to end hostilities between those who have been at war or in a state of enmity; harmony in personal relations, especially with God; a state of security or order within a community; freedom from disquieting or oppressive thoughts or emotions
Exod 20:24 . . . and *p* offerings, your sheep
Lev 26:6 . . . I will give you *p* in the land,
Num 6:26 . . . his favor and give you his *p.*
Deut 20:10 . . . offer its people terms for *p*
1 Sam 7:14 . . . there was *p* between Israel
1 Kgs 5:4 . . . God has given me *p* on every
1 Chr 22:9 . . . a son who will be a man of *p.*
2 Chr 14:7 . . . has given us *p* on every side.
Job 3:26 . . . I have no *p,* no quietness.
Job 25:2 . . . He enforces *p* in the heavens.
Ps 34:14 . . . Search for *p,* and work to
Ps 37:37 . . . awaits those who love *p.*
Ps 120:7 . . . I search for *p;*
Ps 147:14 . . . He sends *p* across your nation
Prov 12:20 . . . hearts that are planning *p!*
Eccl 3:8 . . . for war and a time for *p.*
Isa 9:6 . . . Everlasting Father, Prince of *P.*
Isa 32:17 . . . righteousness will bring *p.*
Isa 48:22 . . . there is no *p* for the wicked.
Isa 52:7 . . . good news of *p* and salvation,
Jer 6:14 . . . They give assurances of *p* when
Jer 46:27 . . . return to a life of *p* and quiet,
Ezek 34:25 . . . I will make a covenant of *p*
Zech 8:19 . . . So love truth and *p.*
Matt 5:9 . . . blesses those who work for *p,*
Mark 9:50 . . . live in *p* with each other.
Luke 1:79 . . . guide us to the path of *p.*
John 16:33 . . . you may have *p* in me.
Rom 5:1 . . . by faith, we have *p* with God
Rom 8:6 . . . your mind leads to life and *p.*
1 Cor 14:33 . . . God of disorder but of *p,*
Gal 5:22 . . . love, joy, *p,* patience,
Eph 2:14 . . . Christ himself has brought *p*
Eph 2:15 . . . made *p* between Jews and
Eph 2:17 . . . Good News of *p* to you Gentiles

Eph 6:15 . . . put on the *p* that comes from
Phil 4:7 . . . experience God's *p,*
1 Thes 5:23 . . . God of *p* make you holy
2 Thes 3:16 . . . Lord of *p* himself give you
2 Tim 2:22 . . . faithfulness, love, and *p.*
Heb 13:20 . . . the God of *p*—who brought
Jas 3:17 . . . It is also *p* loving, gentle
1 Pet 3:11 . . . Search for *p,* and work to

**PEACEFUL (adj)** quiet, tranquil; devoid of violence or force; of or relating to a state or time of peace
Ps 23:2 . . . leads me beside *p* streams.
Prov 14:30 . . . A *p* heart leads to a healthy
1 Thes 5:3 . . . Everything is *p* and secure,
1 Tim 2:2 . . . we can live *p* and quiet lives
Heb 12:11 . . . a *p* harvest of right living
2 Pet 3:14 . . . effort to be found living *p*

**PEACEMAKER, PEACEMAKERS (n)** one who makes peace especially by reconciling parties at variance
Acts 7:26 . . . He tried to be a *p.*
Jas 3:18 . . . *p-s* will plant seeds of peace

**PEARL, PEARLS (n)** a white translucent jewel created within certain species of mollusks
Matt 7:6 . . . throw your *p-s* to pigs!
1 Tim 2:9 . . . or by wearing gold or *p-s*
Rev 21:21 . . . were made of *p-s*—
Rev 21:21 . . . each gate from a single *p!*

**PENNY (n)** the smallest monetary unit equal to 1/100 of a dollar
Matt 5:26 . . . you have paid the last *p.*
Luke 12:59 . . . paid the very last *p.*

**PENTECOST (n)** a Jewish feast celebrated on the 50th day after the Feast of Unleavened Bread; the day God sent the Holy Spirit after Christ's resurrection
Acts 2:1 . . . the day of *P* all the believers
Acts 20:16 . . . in time for the Festival of *P.*
1 Cor 16:8 . . . until the Festival of *P.*

**PEOPLE, PEOPLES (n)** human beings making up a group or assembly or linked by a common interest; clan or nation; humanity
*see also* NATION(S)
Exod 5:1 . . . says: Let my *p* go
Exod 8:23 . . . between my *p* and your
Exod 9:5 . . . among all the *p-s* on earth;
Exod 19:8 . . . all the *p* responded together,
Exod 33:13 . . . nation is your very own *p.*
Lev 26:12 . . . and you will be my *p.*
Num 14:11 . . . How long will these *p*
Deut 7:6 . . . you are a holy *p,* who belong
Deut 14:1 . . . are the *p* of the LORD
Deut 32:9 . . . For the *p* of Israel belong
Deut 33:29 . . . *p* saved by the LORD?
Ruth 1:16 . . . Your *p* will be my people,
2 Chr 7:20 . . . uproot the *p* from this land
Neh 1:10 . . . The *p* you rescued by your
Neh 8:1 . . . the *p* assembled with a unified
Ps 33:12 . . . whose *p* he has chosen
Ps 53:6 . . . When God restores his *p,*
Ps 94:14 . . . will not reject his *p;*
Ps 96:10 . . . He will judge all *p-s* fairly.
Ps 135:14 . . . will give justice to his *p*
Isa 2:2 . . . *p* from all over the world
Isa 6:10 . . . Harden the hearts of these *p.*
Isa 40:1 . . . Comfort, comfort my *p,*
Isa 49:13 . . . LORD has comforted his *p*
Isa 52:6 . . . I will reveal my name to my *p,*

Isa 53:8 . . . for the rebellion of my *p.*
Isa 55:4 . . . my power among the *p-s.*
Jer 2:11 . . . Yet my *p* have exchanged their
Jer 2:32 . . . my *p* have forgotten me.
Jer 7:16 . . . Pray no more for these *p,*
Jer 32:27 . . . of all the *p-s* of the world.
Dan 8:24 . . . and devastate the holy *p.*
Dan 9:24 . . . decreed for your *p*
Hos 1:10 . . . You are not my *p,*
Hos 2:23 . . . Now you are my *p.*
Mic 4:1 . . . *p* from all over the world
Mic 4:3 . . . LORD will mediate between *p-s*
Matt 4:19 . . . show you how to fish for *p!*
Mark 7:6 . . . *p* honor me with their lips,
Mark 8:27 . . . Who do *p* say I am?
Luke 1:68 . . . visited and redeemed his *p.*
John 11:50 . . . should die for the *p*
John 18:14 . . . should die for the *p.*
Rom 9:25 . . . Those who were not my *p,*
Rom 11:1 . . . *p,* the nation of Israel?
2 Cor 6:16 . . . and they will be my *p.*
Gal 6:16 . . . they are the new *p* of God.
Eph 1:14 . . . purchased us to be his own *p.*
Eph 1:18 . . . he called—his holy *p*
Eph 2:15 . . . creating in himself one new *p*
Eph 4:8 . . . and gave gifts to his *p.*
2 Tim 2:2 . . . trustworthy *p* who will
2 Tim 3:17 . . . and equip his *p* to do every
Titus 2:11 . . . bringing salvation to all *p.*
Titus 2:14 . . . make us his very own *p,*
Heb 4:9 . . . waiting for the *p* of God.
1 Pet 2:9 . . . for you are a chosen *p.*
1 Pet 2:10 . . . now you are God's *p.*
Rev 5:8 . . . prayers of God's *p.*
Rev 10:11 . . . again about many *p-s,*
Rev 18:4 . . . from her, my *p.*
Rev 19:8 . . . of God's holy *p.*
Rev 21:3 . . . home is now among his *p!*

**PERFECT (adj)** being entirely without fault or defect; corresponding to an ideal standard or abstract concept; mature, pure, complete
Deut 32:4 . . . the Rock; his deeds are *p.*
Ps 19:7 . . . instructions of the LORD are *p,*
Ps 119:138 . . . laws are *p* and completely
Matt 5:48 . . . you are to be *p,* even as
John 17:23 . . . experience such *p* unity
Gal 3:3 . . . become *p* by your
Col 4:12 . . . God to make you strong and *p,*
Heb 2:10 . . . suffering, a *p* leader,
Heb 5:9 . . . as a *p* High Priest,
Heb 7:19 . . . law never made anything *p.*
Heb 9:11 . . . greater, more *p* Tabernacle
Heb 9:14 . . . as a *p* sacrifice for our sins.
Heb 10:14 . . . he forever made *p* those
Heb 12:23 . . . who have now been made *p.*
Jas 1:25 . . . look carefully into the *p* law
1 Jn 4:18 . . . because *p* love expels all fear.

**PERFECT, PERFECTED, PERFECTS (v)** to bring to final form; to refine or improve
Ezek 16:14 . . . splendor and *p-ed* your beauty,
Heb 12:2 . . . champion who initiates and *p-s*

**PERFECTION (n)** flawlessness; maturity; an exemplification of supreme excellence
Job 37:16 . . . with wonderful *p* and skill?
Ps 50:2 . . . Mount Zion, the *p* of beauty,
1 Cor 13:10 . . . when the time of *p* comes,
Phil 3:12 . . . I have already reached *p.*
Heb 7:11 . . . achieved the *p* God intended,
Heb 11:40 . . . not reach *p* without us.

**PERFUME (n)**  a substance that emits a pleasant odor
Eccl 7:1 . . . more valuable than costly *p*.
Mark 14:3 . . . and poured the *p* over his head.
2 Cor 2:14 . . . everywhere, like a sweet *p*.
2 Cor 2:16 . . . saved, we are a life-giving *p*.

**PERISH, PERISHING (v)**  to become destroyed or ruined physically or spiritually; to die
*see also* DESTROY, DIE
Ps 102:26 . . . They will *p*, but you remain
John 3:16 . . . believes in him will not *p* but
John 10:28 . . . they will never *p*.
2 Cor 2:15 . . . by those who are *p-ing*.
2 Cor 4:3 . . . from people who are *p-ing*.
Jude 1:11 . . . they *p* in their rebellion.

**PERSECUTE, PERSECUTED, PERSECUTING (v)**  to harass or punish in a manner designed to injure, grieve, or afflict; to cause to suffer because of belief
Ps 140:12 . . . help those they *p*;
Matt 5:10 . . . blesses those who are *p-d*
Matt 5:11 . . . when people mock you and *p*
Matt 5:12 . . . prophets were *p-d*
Matt 5:44 . . . Pray for those who *p* you!
Matt 13:21 . . . *p-d* for believing God's
John 15:20 . . . they *p-d* me, naturally
John 15:20 . . . they will *p* you.
Acts 9:4 . . . Why are you *p-ing* me?
Rom 8:35 . . . or are *p-d*, or hungry,
Rom 12:14 . . . Bless those who *p* you.
1 Cor 15:9 . . . the way I *p-d* God's church.
2 Thes 1:7 . . . for you who are being *p-d*

**PERSECUTION, PERSECUTIONS (n)**  the condition of being persecuted, harassed, or annoyed
Mark 10:30 . . . along with *p*.
2 Cor 12:10 . . . insults, hardships, *p-s*,
2 Thes 1:4 . . . all the *p-s* and hardships
2 Thes 1:5 . . . God will use this *p* to show
2 Tim 3:11 . . . You know how much *p* and
2 Tim 3:12 . . . in Christ Jesus will suffer *p*.
Rev 13:10 . . . must endure *p* patiently

**PERSEVERANCE (n)**  enduring hardships with patience; steadfastness
*see also* ENDURANCE
1 Tim 6:11 . . . along with faith, love, *p*, and

**PERSEVERE (v)**  to persist in a state, enterprise, or undertaking in spite of counterinfluences, opposition, or discouragement
*see also* ENDURE
Rev 3:10 . . . obeyed my command to *p*,

**PETER**  Leader of the 12 disciples, also known as "Simon son of John" (John 21:17) and "Cephas" (John 1:42); called to "fish for people" (Matt 4:18-20; Mark 1:16-20; Luke 5:1-11; *see also* John 21:3); mother-in-law healed (Matt 8:14-15; Mark 1:29-31; Luke 4:38-39); called to preach (Mark 1:36-39); brother of Andrew (Mark 3:16; Matt 10:2; Luke 6:14; Acts 1:13); present at raising of the dead (Mark 5:37; Luke 8:51); walked on water (Matt 14:22-33; Mark 6:45-52; John 6:15-21); identified Jesus as the Christ (Mark 8:27-30; Matt 16:13-20; Luke 9:18-20; *see also* John 6:68-69); rebuked by Jesus for lack of heavenly perspective (Matt 16:21-23; Mark 8:32-33; *see also* John 13:6-11); witnessed the Transfiguration (Matt 16:28–17:8; Mark 9:1-13; Luke 9:28-36; 2 Pet 1:16-20);

noticed the withered fig tree (Mark 11:21; *see also* Matt 21:20); his denial predicted by Jesus (Matt 26:31-35; Mark 14:27-31; Luke 22:31-34; John 13:36-38); in Gethsemane (Matt 26:36-46; Mark 14:32-42; Luke 22:39-46); cut off ear of Malchus (Matt 26:51; Mark 14:47; Luke 22:50); denied Jesus—then wept (Matt 26:69-75; Mark 14:66-72; Luke 22:54-62; John 18:15-27); visited empty tomb (Luke 24:12; John 20:1-10; *see also* Matt 28:1-8); saw Jesus (Luke 24:34; 1 Cor 15:5); told by Jesus to shepherd his flock (John 21:15-19); in upper room before Pentecost (Acts 1:13); preached at Pentecost (Acts 2); performed miracles (Acts 3:1-10; 5:14-16; 9:32-43); preached at Temple (Acts 3:11-26); preached before Jewish high council (Acts 4:1-22); prophesied death of Ananias and Sapphira (Acts 5:1-11); preached again before Jewish high council (Acts 5:29-32); rebuked power seeker (Acts 8:14-25); healed sick (Acts 9:32-34); raised dead (Acts 9:36-43); introduced Gentiles to gospel (Acts 10–11); rescued by angel from prison (Acts 12:3-19); preached grace at Jerusalem Council (Acts 15); became pillar of the church (Gal 2:9); was correctable (Gal 2:14); wrote letters (1 Pet 1:1; 2 Pet 1:1); had believing wife (1 Cor 9:5).

**PHARISEE, PHARISEES (n)**  a religious and political party in Palestine in New Testament times known for strict observance of rites and ceremonies of the written law and for insistence on the validity of their own oral traditions concerning the law
Matt 5:20 . . . *P-s*, you will never enter
Matt 16:6 . . . of the yeast of the *P-s*
Matt 23:13 . . . and you *P-s*. Hypocrites!
John 3:1 . . . religious leader who was a *P*.
Acts 23:6 . . . *P*, as were my ancestors!

**PHYSICAL (adj)**  having material existence; of or relating to the body
John 1:13 . . . reborn—not with a *p* birth
Col 1:22 . . . of Christ in his *p* body.
1 Tim 4:8 . . . *P* training is good, but
1 Tim 5:11 . . . *p* desires will overpower
1 Jn 2:16 . . . a craving for *p* pleasure

**PIERCE, PIERCED (v)**  to make a hole through; to stab
Exod 21:6 . . . and publicly *p* his ear
Ps 22:16 . . . have *p-d* my hands and feet.
Zech 12:10 . . . me whom they have *p-d*
Luke 2:35 . . . sword will *p* your very soul.
John 19:37 . . . look on the one they *p-d*.
Rev 1:7 . . . even those who *p-d* him.

**PIG, PIGS (n)**  a wild or domestic swine
Matt 7:6 . . . Don't throw your pearls to *p-s*!
Mark 5:11 . . . a large herd of *p-s* feeding
Luke 15:15 . . . his fields to feed the *p-s*.
2 Pet 2:22 . . . washed *p* returns to the mud.

**PILGRIM(S) (KJV)**
Heb 11:13 . . . *nomads* here on earth
1 Pet 2:11 . . . as "temporary residents and foreigners"

**PILLAR, PILLARS (n)**  a column or shaft standing alone as a monument or supporting a superstructure; miraculous cloud by day and fire by night; memorial pile of stones; a supporting, integral, or upstanding member of a group
Gen 19:26 . . . she turned into a *p* of salt.
Exod 13:21 . . . night with a *p* of fire.

Exod 24:4 . . . set up twelve *p-s*, one for
Deut 1:33 . . . by night and a *p* of cloud by
Judg 16:26 . . . my hands against the *p-s*
Gal 2:9 . . . known as *p-s* of the church,
1 Tim 3:15 . . . *p* and foundation of
Rev 3:12 . . . victorious will become *p-s*

**PIOUS (adj)**  marked by or showing reverence for God and devotion to worship; religious
Isa 58:2 . . . Yet they act so *p!*
Col 2:18 . . . insisting on *p* self-denial
Col 2:23 . . . strong devotion, *p* self-denial,

**PITY (n)**  sympathetic sorrow for one suffering, distressed, or unhappy
Judg 2:18 . . . For the LORD took *p* on
Ps 17:10 . . . They are without *p*.
Ps 69:20 . . . would show some *p*;
Ps 72:13 . . . He feels *p* for the weak
Isa 27:11 . . . show them no *p* or mercy.
Hos 13:14 . . . I will not take *p* on them.

**PLAGUE, PLAGUES (n)**  a disastrous evil, affliction, or epidemic of infectious disease, issued by God in judgment
2 Chr 6:28 . . . or a *p* or crop disease
Luke 21:11 . . . will be famines and *p-s*
Rev 21:9 . . . the seven last *p-s* came
Rev 22:18 . . . add to that person the *p-s*

**PLAGUED (v)**  to smite, infest, or afflict with disease, calamity, or natural evil
Ps 73:5 . . . they're not *p* with problems

**PLAN, PLANS (n)**  a detailed formulation of a program of action; goal, aim
*see also* PURPOSE
Ps 2:1 . . . waste their time with futile *p-s?*
Ps 33:10 . . . frustrates the *p-s* of the
Ps 40:5 . . . *p-s* for us are too numerous
Isa 30:1 . . . You make *p-s* that are contrary
Isa 32:6 . . . and make evil *p-s*.
Jer 29:11 . . . I know the *p-s* I have for you,
Acts 2:23 . . . his prearranged *p* was carried
Acts 4:25 . . . waste their time with futile *p-s?*
Acts 7:44 . . . according to the *p* God had
Rom 16:25 . . . *p* kept secret from
Eph 3:9 . . . this mysterious *p* that God,
Eph 3:11 . . . This was his eternal *p*,
2 Tim 1:9 . . . *p* from before the beginning

**PLAN, PLANNED, PLANNING (v)**  to devise or project the realization or achievement of
Prov 12:20 . . . hearts that are *p-n-ing* peace!
Isa 25:1 . . . You *p-ned* them long ago,
Jer 23:20 . . . has finished all he has *p-ned*.
Eph 2:10 . . . do the good things he *p-ned*

**PLANT (n)**  a young tree, vine, shrub, or herb planted or suitable for planting
Matt 15:13 . . . *p* not planted by
1 Cor 15:36 . . . it doesn't grow into a *p*

**PLANT, PLANTED, PLANTING, PLANTS (v)**  to put or set (seeds or plants) in the ground for growth; to establish or settle
Gen 2:8 . . . the LORD God *p-ed* a garden
Gen 8:22 . . . there will be *p-ing* and harvest,
Ps 1:3 . . . like trees *p-ed* along the riverbank,
Ps 126:5 . . . who *p* in tears will harvest
Prov 22:8 . . . who *p* injustice will harvest
Prov 31:16 . . . earnings she *p-s* a vineyard.
Hos 10:12 . . . *P* the good seeds
Amos 9:15 . . . I will firmly *p* them there
Matt 6:26 . . . They don't *p* or harvest or
Matt 13:3 . . . A farmer went out to *p* some

Matt 13:18 . . . about the farmer *p-ing*
1 Cor 3:6 . . . *p-ed* the seed in your hearts,
1 Cor 3:7 . . . who does the *p-ing*,
1 Cor 9:7 . . . What farmer *p-s* a vineyard
1 Cor 15:42 . . . earthly bodies are *p-ed*
2 Cor 9:6 . . . a farmer who *p-s* only a few
Jas 1:21 . . . accept the word God has *p-ed*
Jas 3:18 . . . will *p* seeds of peace

**PLEASANT (adj)** having qualities that tend to
give pleasure; agreeable
Gen 49:15 . . . and how *p* the land,
Ps 16:6 . . . given me is a *p* land.
Prov 16:21 . . . and *p* words are persuasive.
Isa 5:7 . . . of Judah are his *p* garden.

**PLEASE, PLEASED, PLEASES (v)** to make
glad; to satisfy; to like or wish; to be the will or
pleasure of
Deut 12:25 . . . doing what *p-s* the LORD.
Ps 135:6 . . . The LORD does whatever *p-s*
Prov 16:7 . . . people's lives *p* the LORD,
Isa 42:1 . . . my chosen one, who *p-s* me.
Matt 12:18 . . . my Beloved, who *p-s* me.
Luke 2:14 . . . those with whom God is *p-d*.
Luke 10:21 . . . Yes, Father, it *p-d* you to do
John 8:29 . . . I always do what *p-s* him.
Rom 8:8 . . . sinful nature can never *p* God.
Rom 14:18 . . . this attitude, you will *p* God,
2 Cor 5:9 . . . our goal is to *p* him.
Gal 6:8 . . . live to *p* the Spirit will harvest
Eph 5:10 . . . determine what *p-s* the
Phil 2:13 . . . power to do what *p-s* him.
Col 1:10 . . . always honor and *p* the Lord,
Col 1:19 . . . God in all his fullness was *p-d*
1 Thes 2:4 . . . Our purpose is to *p* God,
1 Thes 2:15 . . . They fail to *p* God
1 Tim 2:3 . . . is good and *p-s* God our
1 Tim 5:4 . . . is something that *p-s* God.
Heb 10:6 . . . not *p-d* with burnt offerings
Heb 11:6 . . . to *p* God without faith.
Heb 13:16 . . . sacrifices that *p* God.
1 Pet 2:19 . . . God is *p-d* with you when
1 Jn 2:17 . . . does what *p-s* God will live
Rev 4:11 . . . you created what you *p-d*.

**PLEASURE, PLEASURES (n)** desire, inclination;
a source of delight or joy; sensual gratification
Ps 5:4 . . . you take no *p* in wickedness;
Ps 16:3 . . . I take *p* in them!
Ps 16:11 . . . the *p-s* of living with you
Isa 1:11 . . . I get no *p* from the blood of
Luke 8:14 . . . cares and riches and *p-s*
Eph 1:9 . . . a plan to fulfill his own good *p*.
1 Tim 5:6 . . . widow who lives only for *p*
2 Tim 3:4 . . . and love *p* rather than God.
Titus 2:12 . . . living and sinful *p-s*.
Titus 3:3 . . . slaves to many lusts and *p-s*.
Heb 11:25 . . . the fleeting *p-s* of sin.
Jas 4:3 . . . want only what will give you *p*.

**PLOWS (v)** to turn, break up, or work with a
plow
1 Cor 9:10 . . . the one who *p* and the one

**PLOWSHARES (n)** a part of a plow that cuts
the furrow
Isa 2:4 . . . will hammer their swords into *p*
Joel 3:10 . . . Hammer your *p* into swords
Mic 4:3 . . . hammer their swords into *p*

**POISON (n)** a substance that usually kills,
injures, or impairs an organism; something
destructive or harmful

2 Kgs 4:40 . . . there's *p* in this stew!
Jas 3:8 . . . and evil, full of deadly *p*.

**POISONOUS (adj)** destructive, harmful;
venomous
Mark 16:18 . . . *p*, it won't hurt them.

**POOR (adj)** characterized by poverty or
insufficient resources; humble
Lev 19:10 . . . Leave them for the *p*
Deut 15:4 . . . should be no *p* among you,
Deut 15:11 . . . some in the land who are *p*.
Deut 24:12 . . . If your neighbor is *p*
1 Sam 2:7 . . . The LORD makes some *p*
Job 5:16 . . . at last the *p* have hope,
Ps 35:10 . . . protects the helpless and *p*
Ps 41:1 . . . those who are kind to the *p!*
Ps 82:3 . . . Give justice to the *p* and the
Prov 10:4 . . . Lazy people are soon *p*;
Prov 13:7 . . . Some who are *p* pretend
Prov 14:21 . . . those who help the *p*.
Prov 17:5 . . . mock the *p* insult
Prov 21:13 . . . cries of the *p* will be ignored
Prov 22:2 . . . rich and *p* have this
Prov 22:22 . . . Don't rob the *p* just because
Prov 28:27 . . . Whoever gives to the *p* will
Prov 31:20 . . . helping hand to the *p*
Isa 3:14 . . . things stolen from the *p*.
Isa 14:30 . . . I will feed the *p* in my pasture;
Isa 32:7 . . . They lie to convict the *p*,
Isa 61:1 . . . to bring good news to the *p*.
Jer 22:16 . . . help to the *p* and needy,
Amos 4:1 . . . who oppress the *p* and crush
Amos 5:11 . . . trample the *p*, stealing their
Zech 7:10 . . . foreigners, and the *p*.
Matt 11:5 . . . is being preached to the *p*.
Matt 19:21 . . . and give the money to the *p*,
Mark 12:42 . . . Then a *p* widow came and
Mark 14:7 . . . You will always have the *p*
Luke 4:18 . . . to bring Good News to the *p*.
Luke 14:13 . . . Instead, invite the *p*, the
John 12:8 . . . You will always have the *p*
Rom 15:26 . . . an offering for the *p* among
2 Cor 8:9 . . . for your sakes he became *p*,
Jas 2:2 . . . another comes in who is *p*
Jas 2:6 . . . you dishonor the *p!*

**POSSESS, POSSESSED (v)** to seize, gain, or
take (control of); to own
Ps 37:11 . . . The lowly will *p* the land
Ps 37:29 . . . The godly will *p* the land
John 7:20 . . . You're demon *p-ed!*
John 8:48 . . . you were *p-ed* by a demon?
John 8:52 . . . you are *p-ed* by a demon.
John 10:20 . . . He's demon *p-ed* and out
John 10:21 . . . like a man *p-ed* by a demon!
Phil 3:12 . . . press on to *p* that perfection

**POSSESSION, POSSESSIONS (n)** something
owned, occupied, or controlled
*see also* INHERITANCE, RICHES, TREASURE(S),
   WEALTH
Exod 6:8 . . . as your very own *p*.
Deut 4:20 . . . and his special *p*,
Deut 32:9 . . . is his special *p*.
Zech 2:12 . . . the LORD's special *p*
Matt 19:21 . . . sell all your *p-s* and
Mark 10:22 . . . for he had many *p-s*.
1 Pet 2:9 . . . God's very own *p*.

**POSSIBLE (adj)** being within the limits of
ability, capacity, or realization
Matt 19:26 . . . with God everything is *p*.

Matt 26:39 . . . *p*, let this cup of suffering
Mark 9:23 . . . Anything is *p* if a person
Mark 10:27 . . . Everything is *p* with God.
Mark 14:35 . . . if it were *p*, the awful hour
Heb 10:4 . . . it is not *p* for the blood

**POTTER (n)** one who makes pottery
Isa 29:16 . . . *p* who made me is stupid"?
Isa 64:8 . . . the clay, and you are the *p*.
Zech 11:13 . . . threw them to the *p*

**POUR, POURED, POURING, POURS (v)** to
move or come continuously; to supply or
produce freely
Ps 42:8 . . . LORD *p-s* his unfailing love
Ps 45:7 . . . *p-ing* out the oil of joy on
Isa 32:15 . . . Spirit is *p-ed* out on us
Isa 44:3 . . . I will *p* out my Spirit
Ezek 39:29 . . . I will *p* out my Spirit
Joel 2:28 . . . I will *p* out my Spirit
Zech 12:10 . . . I will *p* out a spirit of
Mal 3:10 . . . I will *p* out a blessing
Luke 22:20 . . . blood, which is *p-ed* out
Acts 2:17 . . . I will *p* out my Spirit
Acts 2:33 . . . the Holy Spirit to *p* out
Acts 10:45 . . . Holy Spirit had been *p-ed*
Eph 1:6 . . . grace he has *p-ed* out on us
Phil 2:17 . . . *p-ing* it out like a liquid
Titus 3:6 . . . generously *p-ed* out the Spirit

**POVERTY (n)** the state of one who lacks money
or material possessions
Prov 6:11 . . . *p* will pounce on you like
Prov 13:18 . . . end in *p* and disgrace;
Prov 21:5 . . . hasty shortcuts lead to *p*.
Prov 24:34 . . . *p* will pounce on you like
Prov 31:7 . . . drink to forget their *p*
2 Cor 8:9 . . . by his *p* he could make you
Rev 2:9 . . . your suffering and your *p*—

**POWER, POWERS (n)** ability to act or produce
an effect; possession of control, authority, or
influence over others; physical might; mental or
moral efficacy; a controlling group
*see also* STRENGTH
Exod 15:6 . . . LORD, is glorious in *p*.
Deut 8:18 . . . one who gives you *p* to be
Ps 89:7 . . . angelic *p-s* stand in awe of God.
Isa 40:26 . . . great *p* and incomparable
Jer 9:23 . . . the powerful boast in their *p*,
Mic 3:8 . . . I am filled with *p*—
Matt 16:18 . . . all the *p-s* of hell will not
Matt 22:29 . . . don't know the *p* of God.
Luke 1:35 . . . the *p* of the Most High will
Luke 4:14 . . . the Holy Spirit's *p*.
Luke 9:1 . . . gave them *p* and authority
Luke 10:19 . . . over all the *p* of the enemy,
Luke 11:20 . . . demons by the *p* of God,
Acts 1:8 . . . receive *p* when the Holy Spirit
Rom 1:16 . . . the *p* of God at work,
Rom 1:20 . . . his eternal *p* and divine
Rom 6:9 . . . Death no longer has any *p* over
Rom 7:23 . . . another *p* within me that is
Rom 8:38 . . . not even the *p-s* of hell can
Rom 15:13 . . . the *p* of the Holy Spirit.
1 Cor 1:18 . . . is the very *p* of God.
1 Cor 6:14 . . . from the dead by his *p*,
1 Cor 15:24 . . . ruler and authority and *p*.
2 Cor 4:7 . . . our great *p* is from God,
2 Cor 13:4 . . . now lives by the *p* of God.
Eph 6:10 . . . Lord and in his mighty *p*.
Phil 3:10 . . . and experience the mighty *p*
Col 1:11 . . . with all his glorious *p*

Col 1:29 . . . depending on Christ's mighty *p*
1 Thes 1:5 . . . words but also with *p,*
2 Tim 1:7 . . . but of *p,* love, and
2 Tim 3:5 . . . reject the *p* that could make
Heb 2:14 . . . break the *p* of the devil,
Jas 5:16 . . . righteous person has great *p*
1 Pet 1:5 . . . is protecting you by his *p*
1 Pet 3:22 . . . *p-s* accept his authority.
1 Pet 4:11 . . . All glory and *p* to him
2 Pet 1:3 . . . *p,* God has given us everything
Jude 1:25 . . . majesty, *p,* and authority are his
Rev 4:11 . . . receive glory and honor and *p.*
Rev 5:12 . . . receive *p* and riches and
Rev 19:1 . . . glory and *p* belong to our God.
Rev 20:6 . . . the second death holds no *p,*

**POWERFUL (adj)** having great power, prestige,
or influence
Exod 6:6 . . . will redeem you with a *p* arm
Deut 5:15 . . . strong hand and *p* arm.
Job 25:2 . . . God is *p* and dreadful.
Ps 29:4 . . . the LORD is *p;*
Ps 136:12 . . . strong hand and *p* arm.
Jer 9:23 . . . the *p* boast in their power,
Jer 27:5 . . . my great strength and *p* arm
Luke 24:19 . . . who did *p* miracles,
1 Cor 1:27 . . . to shame those who are *p.*

**PRAISE, PRAISES (n)** worship;
commendation; value, merit
Deut 26:19 . . . *p,* honor, and renown.
2 Sam 22:4 . . . LORD, who is worthy of *p,*
2 Chr 29:30 . . . So they offered joyous *p*
Ps 7:17 . . . I will sing *p* to the name
Ps 18:49 . . . I will sing *p-s* to your name.
Ps 34:1 . . . will constantly speak his *p-s.*
Ps 81:1 . . . Sing *p-s* to God,
Ps 108:1 . . . your *p-s* with all my heart!
Ps 145:3 . . . He is most worthy of *p!*
Ps 149:6 . . . Let the *p-s* of God be in
John 12:43 . . . loved human *p* more than
Rom 2:29 . . . heart seeks *p* from God,
Rom 15:9 . . . will sing *p-s* to your name.
1 Thes 2:6 . . . As for human *p,*
2 Thes 1:10 . . . his holy people—*p* from all
Jas 5:13 . . . You should sing *p-s.*

**PRAISE, PRAISED, PRAISES, PRAISING (v)** to
worship, commend, or give honor to
Exod 15:2 . . . and I will *p* him—
1 Chr 16:35 . . . name and rejoice and *p* you.
2 Chr 5:13 . . . together in unison to *p* and
2 Chr 20:21 . . . *p-ing* him for his holy
Neh 9:5 . . . Stand up and *p* the LORD
Ps 9:1 . . . I will *p* you, LORD,
Ps 12:8 . . . evil is *p-d* throughout the land.
Ps 34:1 . . . I will *p* the LORD
Ps 42:5 . . . I will *p* him again—
Ps 45:17 . . . nations will *p* you forever
Ps 51:15 . . . my mouth may *p* you.
Ps 63:3 . . . how I *p* you!
Ps 71:8 . . . why I can never stop *p-ing* you;
Ps 71:14 . . . I will *p* you more and
Ps 74:21 . . . and needy *p* your name.
Ps 89:5 . . . angels will *p* you for your
Ps 96:2 . . . LORD; *p* his name.
Ps 102:18 . . . not yet born will *p* the
Ps 104:1 . . . all that I am *p* the
Ps 115:18 . . . But we can *p* the LORD
Ps 135:20 . . . LORD, *p* the LORD!
Ps 144:1 . . . *P* the LORD, who is
Ps 148:13 . . . Let them all *p* the name

Ps 150:2 . . . *p* his unequaled greatness!
Prov 27:2 . . . Let someone else *p* you,
Prov 27:21 . . . person is tested by being *p-d.*
Isa 63:7 . . . I will *p* the LORD
Dan 2:19 . . . Daniel *p-d* the God of heaven.
Dan 2:20 . . . He said, "*P* the name
Dan 4:34 . . . *p-d* and worshiped the Most
Matt 5:16 . . . will *p* your heavenly Father.
Mark 11:9 . . . were shouting, "*P* God!
Luke 1:46 . . . how my soul *p-s* the Lord.
Luke 2:13 . . . armies of heaven—*p-ing* God
Luke 2:20 . . . glorifying and *p-ing* God for
Luke 19:37 . . . *p-ing* God for all the wonderful
Luke 18:43 . . . all who saw it *p-d* God, too.
Acts 2:47 . . . all the while *p-ing* God
Acts 10:46 . . . in other tongues and *p-ing* God
1 Cor 14:16 . . . if you *p* God only in
Gal 1:24 . . . they *p-d* God because of me.
Eph 1:6 . . . we *p* God for the glorious
Jas 3:9 . . . Sometimes it *p-s* our Lord
Rev 19:1 . . . heaven shouting, "*P* the LORD!

**PRAY, PRAYED, PRAYING, PRAYS (v)** to
address God with adoration, confession,
supplication, or thanksgiving; to intercede
Gen 24:45 . . . I had finished *p-ing* in my
1 Sam 1:12 . . . she was *p-ing* to the LORD,
2 Chr 7:14 . . . humble themselves and *p* and
2 Chr 30:18 . . . King Hezekiah *p-ed* for
Neh 4:9 . . . we *p-ed* to our God and
Job 42:8 . . . servant Job will *p* for you,
Job 42:10 . . . When Job *p-ed* for his friends,
Ps 5:2 . . . I *p* to no one but you.
Ps 32:6 . . . all the godly *p* to you
Ps 34:6 . . . In my desperation I *p-ed,*
Dan 6:10 . . . He *p-ed* three times a day,
Dan 9:4 . . . I *p-ed* to the LORD
Jon 2:1 . . . Jonah *p-ed* to the LORD
Matt 6:5 . . . When you *p,* don't be like
Matt 26:39 . . . face to the ground, *p-ing,*
Mark 11:24 . . . you can *p* for anything,
Mark 11:25 . . . when you are *p-ing,* first
Luke 3:21 . . . *p-ing,* the heavens opened,
Luke 9:29 . . . he was *p-ing,* the appearance
Luke 11:1 . . . teach us to *p,*
Luke 22:41 . . . and knelt down and *p-ed,*
John 17:20 . . . I am *p-ing* not only for these
Acts 6:6 . . . apostles, who *p-ed* for them
Acts 9:11 . . . He is *p-ing* to me right now.
Acts 16:25 . . . Paul and Silas were *p-ing*
Rom 8:26 . . . the Holy Spirit *p-s* for us
Rom 12:12 . . . and keep on *p-ing.*
Rom 15:30 . . . join in my struggle by *p-ing*
1 Cor 14:14 . . . For if I *p* in tongues,
1 Cor 14:14 . . . my spirit is *p-ing,*
2 Cor 13:9 . . . We *p* that you will become
Eph 1:18 . . . I *p* that your hearts will be
Eph 3:16 . . . I *p* that from his glorious,
Phil 4:6 . . . instead, *p* about everything.
1 Thes 1:3 . . . As we *p* to our God and
1 Thes 5:17 . . . Never stop *p-ing.*
2 Thes 1:11 . . . we keep on *p-ing* for you,
1 Tim 2:8 . . . to *p* with holy hands
Jas 5:13 . . . You should *p.*
Jas 5:16 . . . *p* for each other so that
Jude 1:20 . . . *p* in the power of the Holy

**PRAYER, PRAYERS (n)** conversation with
God—in praise, thanksgiving, or intercession
2 Chr 30:27 . . . God heard their *p* from
Ps 4:1 . . . mercy on me and hear my *p.*
Ps 17:1 . . . Pay attention to my *p,*

Ps 20:5 . . . LORD answer all your *p-s.*
Ps 86:6 . . . Listen closely to my *p,*
Prov 15:8 . . . in the *p-s* of the upright.
Isa 1:15 . . . Though you offer many *p-s,*
Isa 56:7 . . . will be called a house of *p*
Matt 11:25 . . . Jesus prayed this *p:*
John 17:9 . . . My *p* is not for the world,
Acts 1:14 . . . were constantly united in *p,*
Acts 4:31 . . . After this *p,* the meeting
Acts 6:4 . . . can spend our time in *p*
Acts 10:31 . . . your *p* has been heard,
Acts 13:3 . . . So after more fasting and *p,*
Eph 6:18 . . . persistent in your *p-s* for all
Col 4:2 . . . Devote yourselves to *p* with an
1 Pet 3:7 . . . your *p-s* will not be hindered.
1 Pet 3:12 . . . ears are open to their *p-s.*
Rev 5:8 . . . are the *p-s* of God's people.

**PREACH, PREACHED, PREACHES,
PREACHING (v)** to deliver a sermon; to exhort
an idea or course of action
*see also* PROCLAIM, TEACH
Luke 9:6 . . . *p-ing* the Good News and
Luke 9:60 . . . go and *p* about the Kingdom
Acts 5:42 . . . teach and *p* this message:
Acts 9:20 . . . he began *p-ing* about Jesus
Acts 16:10 . . . to *p* the Good News
Acts 18:5 . . . all his time *p-ing* the word.
Rom 1:15 . . . to *p* the Good News.
1 Cor 2:4 . . . my message and my *p-ing*
1 Cor 9:27 . . . I fear that after *p-ing* to
1 Cor 15:1 . . . Good News I *p-ed* to you
2 Cor 4:5 . . . We *p* that Jesus Christ is Lord,
2 Cor 11:4 . . . Jesus than the one we *p,*
Gal 1:8 . . . *p-es* a different kind of Good
Gal 1:8 . . . than the one we *p-ed* to you.
Gal 1:9 . . . *p-es* any other Good News
Gal 5:11 . . . no longer *p-ing* salvation
Phil 1:18 . . . Christ is being *p-ed* either way,
Col 1:23 . . . Good News has been *p-ed* all
1 Tim 5:17 . . . work hard at both *p-ing* and
2 Tim 4:17 . . . might *p* the Good News
1 Pet 1:25 . . . Good News that was *p-ed* to
1 Pet 3:19 . . . went and *p-ed* to the spirits

**PREACHER (n)** one who delivers sermons or
proclaims the gospel
1 Tim 2:7 . . . chosen as a *p* and apostle
2 Tim 1:11 . . . God chose me to be a *p,*

**PRECEPTS (KJV)**
Ps 119:15 . . . study your *commandments* and
Ps 119:159 . . . how I love your
   *commandments,*
Mark 10:5 . . . this *commandment* only as a
Heb 9:19 . . . each of God's *commandments*

**PREDICTED (v)** to declare or indicate in
advance; to foretell
Isa 43:12 . . . First I *p* your rescue,
John 12:38 . . . the prophet had *p:*
Acts 7:52 . . . *p* the coming of

**PREDICTIONS (n)** something that is predicted;
forecast
Isa 44:26 . . . I carry out the *p* of my
Jer 28:9 . . . Only when his *p* come true

**PREGNANCY (n)** the condition of being
pregnant
Gen 3:16 . . . sharpen the pain of your *p,*

**PREGNANT (adj)** containing a developing
unborn offspring within the body
Gen 11:30 . . . was unable to become *p*

Matt 24:19 . . . How terrible it will be for *p*
1 Thes 5:3 . . . as a *p* woman's labor

**PREPARE, PREPARED (v)** to make ready beforehand for some purpose, use, or activity; to get ready
Exod 23:20 . . . to the place I have *p-d* for
Ps 23:5 . . . You *p* a feast for me
Zeph 1:7 . . . LORD has *p-d* his people
Mal 3:1 . . . he will *p* the way before me.
Matt 25:34 . . . inherit the Kingdom *p-d*
John 14:2 . . . I am going to *p* a place
1 Cor 2:9 . . . has *p-d* for those who love
2 Cor 5:5 . . . God himself has *p-d* us for
2 Tim 4:2 . . . the word of God. Be *p-d,*

**PRESBYTERY (KJV)**
1 Tim 4:14 . . . *elders of the church* laid their hands

**PRESENT (adj)** being in view or at hand; now existing or in progress
Lev 16:2 . . . I myself am *p* in the cloud
1 Cor 7:26 . . . Because of the *p* crisis,

**PRESENT, PRESENTED, PRESENTING (v)** to give or bestow formally
Gen 28:22 . . . I will *p* to God a tenth
Matt 5:23 . . . you are *p-ing* a sacrifice
Rom 3:25 . . . *p-ed* Jesus as the sacrifice
Rom 15:19 . . . fully *p-ed* the Good News
Eph 5:27 . . . did this to *p* her to himself
2 Tim 2:15 . . . Work hard so you can *p*

**PRESERVE, PRESERVES (v)** to keep safe from injury, harm, or destruction
*see also* SAVE
Gen 45:5 . . . ahead of you to *p* your lives.
Deut 33:12 . . . *p-s* them from every harm.
1 Kgs 19:18 . . . I will *p* 7,000 others
Jer 10:12 . . . he *p-s* it by his wisdom.

**PRETEND, PRETENDED (v)** to give a false appearance of being, possessing, or performing
1 Sam 21:13 . . . So he *p-ed* to be insane,
Zech 13:4 . . . No one will *p* to be a prophet
Rom 12:9 . . . Don't just *p* to love

**PRICE (n)** the quantity of one thing that is exchanged or demanded in barter or sale for another
Job 28:18 . . . *p* of wisdom is far above
1 Cor 6:20 . . . bought you with a high *p.*

**PRIDE (n)** inordinate self-esteem or conceit; disdainful behavior or treatment of others
Ps 101:5 . . . will not endure conceit and *p.*
Prov 6:3 . . . Now swallow your *p;*
Prov 8:13 . . . I hate *p* and arrogance.
Mark 7:22 . . . envy, slander, *p,*
1 Jn 2:16 . . . *p* in our achievements and

**PRIEST, PRIESTS (n)** one authorized to perform the sacred rites of sacrifice and worship; a mediator between God and humans
Exod 19:6 . . . will be my kingdom of *p-s,*
Ps 110:4 . . . You are a *p* forever
Mal 1:6 . . . Armies says to the *p-s:*
Heb 4:14 . . . since we have a great High *P*
Heb 5:6 . . . You are a *p* forever
Heb 6:20 . . . our eternal High *P*
Heb 8:1 . . . a High *P* who sat down
1 Pet 2:5 . . . you are his holy *p-s.*
1 Pet 2:9 . . . You are royal *p-s,*
Rev 5:10 . . . Kingdom of *p-s* for our God.
Rev 20:6 . . . but they will be *p-s* of God

**PRISON, PRISONS (n)** a state of confinement or captivity; jail
Ps 142:7 . . . Bring me out of *p*
Isa 42:7 . . . will free the captives from *p,*
Matt 25:36 . . . I was in *p,* and you visited
2 Cor 11:23 . . . been put in *p* more often,
Heb 11:36 . . . were chained in *p-s.*
Heb 13:3 . . . Remember those in *p,*
1 Pet 3:19 . . . preached to the spirits in *p*—
Jude 1:6 . . . chained in *p-s* of darkness,
Rev 20:7 . . . Satan will be let out of his *p.*

**PRISONER, PRISONERS (n)** a person deprived of liberty and kept under involuntary restraint, confinement, or custody
Ps 79:11 . . . to the moaning of the *p-s.*
Ps 146:7 . . . The LORD frees the *p-s.*
Zech 9:12 . . . you *p-s* who still have hope!
Gal 3:22 . . . we are all *p-s* of sin,
Eph 3:1 . . . I, Paul, a *p* of Christ Jesus

**PRIZE (n)** something offered or striven for in competitions or in contests
1 Cor 9:24 . . . one person gets the *p?*
1 Cor 9:25 . . . we do it for an eternal *p.*
Phil 3:14 . . . heavenly *p* for which God,
2 Tim 2:5 . . . cannot win the *p* unless
2 Tim 4:8 . . . *p* awaits me—the crown

**PROCLAIM, PROCLAIMING, PROCLAIMS (v)** to declare publicly
*see also* PREACH
Lev 25:10 . . . a time to *p* freedom
Deut 32:3 . . . I will *p* the name of
1 Chr 16:8 . . . and *p* his greatness.
Ps 2:7 . . . king *p-s* the LORD's decree:
Ps 50:6 . . . heavens *p* his justice,
Ps 97:6 . . . heavens *p* his righteousness;
Ps 145:4 . . . let them *p* your power.
Isa 61:1 . . . to *p* that captives will be
Acts 28:31 . . . *p-ing* the Kingdom of God
Col 1:25 . . . *p-ing* his entire message to you.
1 Thes 3:2 . . . in *p-ing* the Good News
Titus 1:1 . . . I have been sent to *p* faith
1 Jn 1:1 . . . *p* to you the one who existed

**PRODUCE, PRODUCES (v)** to yield, make, or manufacture
Prov 3:9 . . . best part of everything you *p.*
Isa 55:11 . . . and it always *p-s* fruit.
Matt 7:18 . . . good tree can't *p* bad fruit,
Luke 3:9 . . . tree that does not *p* good fruit
John 15:8 . . . When you *p* much fruit,
John 15:16 . . . to go and *p* lasting fruit,
Rom 7:4 . . . *p* a harvest of good deeds
Eph 5:9 . . . light within you *p-s* only what
Col 1:10 . . . lives will *p* every kind of good
Jas 2:17 . . . Unless it *p-s* good deeds, it is

**PROMISCUITY (n)** miscellaneous mingling or selection of persons
*see also* IMMORALITY
Rom 13:13 . . . *p* and immoral living,

**PROMISCUOUS (adj)** not restricted to one sexual partner
Prov 23:27 . . . a *p* woman is as dangerous

**PROMISE, PROMISES (n)** a declaration that one will do or refrain from doing something specified
*see also* COVENANT, VOW
2 Sam 7:25 . . . a *p* that will last forever.
Neh 5:13 . . . If you fail to keep your *p,*
Ps 91:4 . . . faithful *p-s* are your armor

Ps 116:14 . . . keep my *p-s* to the LORD
Ps 145:13 . . . LORD always keeps his *p-s;*
Ps 146:6 . . . He keeps every *p* forever.
Rom 4:20 . . . in believing God's *p.*
Rom 9:4 . . . receiving his wonderful *p-s.*
Rom 15:4 . . . patiently for God's *p-s* to be
2 Cor 1:20 . . . *p-s* have been fulfilled
2 Cor 7:1 . . . Because we have these *p-s,*
Eph 2:12 . . . covenant *p-s* God had made
Heb 6:13 . . . God's *p* to Abraham,
Heb 8:6 . . . based on better *p-s.*
Heb 10:23 . . . be trusted to keep his *p.*
Heb 11:11 . . . that God would keep his *p.*
2 Pet 3:4 . . . *p* that Jesus is coming again?
2 Pet 3:9 . . . being slow about his *p,*

**PROMISE, PROMISED, PROMISES, PROMISING (v)** to pledge to do, bring about, or provide
Exod 3:17 . . . I have *p-d* to rescue you
Deut 15:6 . . . bless you as he has *p-d.*
Josh 23:15 . . . the good things he *p-d,*
Luke 24:49 . . . as my Father *p-d.*
Acts 1:4 . . . sends you the gift he *p-d,*
Rom 4:21 . . . able to do whatever he *p-s.*
Gal 3:14 . . . blessing he *p-d* to Abraham,
1 Tim 4:8 . . . *p-ing* benefits in this life
Titus 1:2 . . . God—who does not lie—*p-d*
Heb 10:36 . . . receive all that he has *p-d.*
Jas 1:12 . . . of life that God has *p-d*
Jas 2:5 . . . inherit the Kingdom he *p-d*
2 Pet 3:13 . . . new earth he has *p-d,*
1 Jn 2:25 . . . eternal life he *p-d* us.

**PROPHECY, PROPHECIES (n)** the spoken or written word from God; to forthtell (consoling or corrective material) and foretell (predicative material)
Matt 13:14 . . . fulfills the *p* of Isaiah
Acts 13:29 . . . all that the *p-ies* said about
Acts 17:3 . . . *p-ies* and proved that the Messiah
Acts 21:9 . . . who had the gift of *p.*
Acts 21:10 . . . who also had the gift of *p,*
1 Cor 13:2 . . . If I had the gift of *p,*
1 Cor 13:9 . . . gift of *p* reveals only part
1 Cor 14:6 . . . knowledge or *p* or teaching,
Rev 22:18 . . . words of *p* written in

**PROPHESY, PROPHESIED, PROPHESIES, PROPHESYING (v)** to issue a prophecy
Num 11:25 . . . upon them, they *p-ied.*
1 Sam 19:24 . . . day and all night, *p-ing* in
Isa 42:9 . . . Everything I *p-ied* has come true,
Joel 2:28 . . . sons and daughters will *p.*
Matt 7:22 . . . We *p-ied* in your name and
Acts 2:17 . . . sons and daughters will *p.*
Acts 19:6 . . . in other tongues and *p-ied.*
Rom 12:6 . . . the ability to *p,*
1 Cor 11:4 . . . head while praying or *p-ing.*
1 Cor 12:10 . . . the ability to *p.*
1 Cor 14:1 . . . the ability to *p.*
1 Cor 14:3 . . . one who *p-ies* strengthens
1 Cor 14:39 . . . be eager to *p,*

**PROPHET, PROPHETS (n)** an interpreter of the times and of people's hearts; one who issues divinely inspired revelations
Exod 7:1 . . . Aaron, will be your *p.*
Exod 15:20 . . . Miriam the *p,* Aaron's
Deut 13:1 . . . there are *p-s* among you
Deut 18:18 . . . I will raise up a *p* like you
1 Sam 9:9 . . . *p-s* used to be called seers.

1 Kgs 18:36 . . . Elijah the *p* walked up to
2 Kgs 5:8 . . . a true *p* here in Israel.
2 Kgs 6:12 . . . Elisha, the *p* in Israel,
Isa 44:26 . . . the predictions of my *p-s!*
Hos 9:7 . . . you say, "The *p-s* are crazy
Amos 7:14 . . . I'm not a professional *p,*
Hab 1:1 . . . that the *p* Habakkuk received
Zech 7:12 . . . through the earlier *p-s.*
Mal 4:5 . . . the *p* Elijah before the great
Matt 5:17 . . . or the writings of the *p-s.*
Matt 7:12 . . . in the law and the *p-s.*
Matt 10:41 . . . the same reward as a *p.*
Matt 11:9 . . . Yes, and he is more than a *p.*
Matt 12:39 . . . sign of the *p* Jonah.
Matt 23:37 . . . the city that kills the *p-s*
Matt 26:56 . . . fulfill the words of the *p-s*
Luke 4:24 . . . no *p* is accepted in his own
Luke 7:16 . . . A mighty *p* has risen
Luke 11:49 . . . will send *p-s* and apostles
Luke 24:19 . . . *p* who did powerful
Luke 24:25 . . . all that the *p-s* wrote in
Luke 24:44 . . . law of Moses and the *p-s*
John 1:21 . . . you the *P* we are expecting?
Acts 7:37 . . . a *P* like me from among your
Acts 10:43 . . . all the *p-s* testified about,
Acts 13:1 . . . Among the *p-s* and teachers
Rom 1:2 . . . long ago through his *p-s*
Rom 3:21 . . . Moses and the *p-s* long ago.
Rom 11:3 . . . they have killed your *p-s*
1 Cor 12:28 . . . second are *p-s,* third are
1 Cor 14:37 . . . If you claim to be a *p* or
Eph 2:20 . . . of the apostles and the *p-s.*
Eph 3:5 . . . to his holy apostles and *p-s.*
Eph 4:11 . . . the apostles, the *p-s,* the
1 Pet 1:10 . . . the *p-s* wanted to know
2 Pet 1:19 . . . proclaimed by the *p-s.*
2 Pet 1:21 . . . those *p-s* were moved by
2 Pet 3:2 . . . what the holy *p-s* said long
Rev 11:10 . . . death of the two *p-s* who
Rev 18:20 . . . God and apostles and *p-s!*

**PROPITIATION (KJV)**
Rom 3:25 . . . Jesus as the *sacrifice* for sin
1 Jn 2:2 . . . the *sacrifice that atones*
1 Jn 4:10 . . . *sacrifice to take away* our sins

**PROSPER, PROSPERS (v)** to achieve economic
success; to become strong and flourishing
Deut 28:63 . . . pleasure in causing you to *p*
Ps 37:3 . . . safely in the land and *p.*
Ps 73:3 . . . *p* despite their wickedness.
Prov 16:20 . . . listen to instruction will *p;*
Prov 17:9 . . . Love *p-s* when a fault is forgiven,
Prov 19:8 . . . cherish understanding will *p.*
Isa 53:10 . . . LORD's good plan will *p*
Isa 55:11 . . . it will *p* everywhere I send it.
Dan 4:27 . . . then you will continue to *p.*

**PROSPERITY (n)** the condition of being
successful or thriving
Gen 41:29 . . . will be a period of great *p*
Deut 28:11 . . . LORD will give you *p*
Deut 30:15 . . . life and death, between *p*
1 Sam 25:6 . . . Peace and *p* to you,
Ps 41:2 . . . He gives them *p* in the land
Prov 21:5 . . . and hard work lead to *p,*
Prov 28:25 . . . trusting the LORD leads to *p.*
Jer 33:6 . . . give it *p* and true peace.
Mic 4:4 . . . will live in peace and *p,*

**PROSPEROUS (adj)** marked by success or
economic well-being; flourishing
Deut 5:33 . . . live long and *p* lives

Ps 30:6 . . . When I was *p,* I said,
Ps 34:12 . . . a life that is long and *p?*
Ps 128:2 . . . How joyful and *p* you will be!
Ps 132:15 . . . bless this city and make it *p;*
Jer 12:1 . . . Why are the wicked so *p?*

**PROSTITUTE, PROSTITUTES (n)** a person who
engages in promiscuous sexual relations,
especially for money
Josh 6:17 . . . Rahab the *p* and
Prov 6:26 . . . a *p* will bring you to poverty,
Prov 29:3 . . . hangs around with *p-s,*
Ezek 16:15 . . . as a *p* to every man
Ezek 23:3 . . . They became *p-s* in Egypt.
Matt 21:31 . . . *p-s* will get into the
Luke 15:30 . . . your money on *p-s,*
1 Cor 6:16 . . . if a man joins himself to a *p,*
Rev 17:1 . . . going to come on the great *p,*

**PROSTITUTION (n)** the act or practice of
engaging in promiscuous sexual relations
especially for money
Lev 20:6 . . . who commit spiritual *p* by
Hos 3:3 . . . days and stop your *p.*

**PROTECT, PROTECTED, PROTECTING,
PROTECTS (v)** to cover or shield from expo-
sure, injury, damage, or destruction; to defend
*see also* KEEP
Gen 15:1 . . . for I will *p* you,
Num 6:24 . . . bless you and *p* you.
Josh 6:17 . . . for she *p-ed* our spies.
1 Sam 2:9 . . . He will *p* his faithful ones,
Ps 23:4 . . . your staff *p* and comfort me.
Ps 27:1 . . . fortress, *p-ing* me from danger,
Ps 41:2 . . . LORD *p-s* them and keeps
Ps 116:6 . . . LORD *p-s* those of childlike
Ps 127:1 . . . Unless the LORD *p-s* a city,
Ps 145:20 . . . LORD *p-s* all those who love
Ps 146:9 . . . LORD *p-s* the foreigners
Prov 2:8 . . . *p-s* those who are faithful
Isa 31:5 . . . like a bird *p-ing* its nest.
Isa 57:1 . . . God is *p-ing* them from the
John 17:11 . . . now *p* them by the power of
Acts 26:22 . . . But God has *p-ed* me
Gal 3:24 . . . *p-ed* us until we could be
1 Pet 1:5 . . . God is *p-ing* you by his power
Rev 3:10 . . . I will *p* you from the great

**PROTECTION (n)** the act of protecting; the
state of being protected
*see also* REFUGE
2 Sam 22:3 . . . my rock, in whom I find *p.*
2 Sam 22:31 . . . look to him for *p.*
Ps 5:11 . . . Spread your *p* over them,
Ps 31:2 . . . Be my rock of *p,*
Ps 71:1 . . . I have come to you for *p;*
Ps 91:4 . . . promises are your armor and *p.*
Prov 19:23 . . . security and *p* from harm.

**PROUD (adj)** having or displaying excessive
self-esteem
Ps 5:5 . . . *p* may not stand in your presence,
Prov 16:5 . . . LORD detests the *p;*
Prov 21:4 . . . Haughty eyes, a *p* heart,
Dan 4:37 . . . he is able to humble the *p.*
Rom 1:30 . . . haters of God, insolent, *p,*
1 Cor 13:4 . . . not jealous or boastful or *p*
1 Tim 3:6 . . . he might become *p,*
1 Tim 6:17 . . . rich in this world not to be *p*
2 Tim 3:2 . . . They will be boastful and *p,*
Jas 4:6 . . . God opposes the *p* but favors
1 Pet 5:5 . . . God opposes the *p* but favors

**PROVIDE, PROVIDED, PROVIDES (v)** to
furnish or supply, implying foresight in making
provision for the future
Gen 22:8 . . . God will *p* a sheep
Gen 22:14 . . . means "the LORD will *p* "
Ps 68:10 . . . O God, you *p-d* for your needy
Isa 4:5 . . . the LORD will *p* shade
Jer 5:28 . . . refuse to *p* justice to orphans
Ezek 18:7 . . . and *p-s* clothes for the needy.
2 Cor 9:8 . . . God will generously *p* all you
2 Cor 9:10 . . . he will *p* and increase your

**PRUDENT (adj)** marked by wisdom or
judiciousness; discreet
Prov 14:8 . . . *p* understand where they are
Prov 14:18 . . . the *p* are crowned with
Prov 22:3 . . . A *p* person foresees danger

**PUBLICAN(S) (KJV)**
Matt 5:46 . . . Even *corrupt tax collectors*
Matt 9:10 . . . with many *tax collectors*
Matt 10:3 . . . Matthew (the *tax collector*),
Luke 5:30 . . . and drink with *such scum?*
Luke 18:11 . . . not like that *tax collector*

**PUNISH, PUNISHED, PUNISHES, PUNISHING
(v)** to impose a penalty to fit the crime: from
corrective measures (fines or scolding) and
corporal punishment (spanking or whipping) to
capital punishment and eternal damnation
Gen 15:14 . . . But I will *p* the nation
1 Kgs 8:32 . . . *P* the guilty as they deserve.
Prov 11:21 . . . people will surely be *p-ed,*
Jer 25:14 . . . I will *p* them in proportion
Lam 3:39 . . . when we are *p-ed* for our sins?
Mark 12:40 . . . will be more severely *p-ed.*
Acts 7:7 . . . But I will *p* the nation
Rom 2:2 . . . God, in his justice, will *p*
Rom 13:4 . . . they have the power to *p* you.
Rom 13:4 . . . the very purpose of *p-ing*
2 Thes 1:9 . . . *p-ed* with eternal destruction,
Heb 2:2 . . . act of disobedience was *p-ed.*
Heb 12:6 . . . he *p-es* each one he accepts
1 Pet 2:14 . . . sent them to *p* those who
Rev 19:2 . . . has *p-ed* the great prostitute

**PUNISHMENT (n)** suffering, pain, or loss that
serves as retribution
Isa 53:4 . . . troubles were a *p* from God,
Jer 2:19 . . . will bring its own *p.*
Jer 4:18 . . . This *p* is bitter, piercing
Hos 5:9 . . . On your day of *p,* you will
Matt 25:46 . . . will go away into eternal *p,*
Rom 13:5 . . . not only to avoid *p,* but also
2 Pet 2:9 . . . keeping the wicked under *p*

**PURCHASE, PURCHASED (v)** to gain or
acquire; to buy
*see also* REDEEM
Acts 20:28 . . . *p-d* with his own blood—
Eph 1:7 . . . *p-d* our freedom with the
Eph 1:14 . . . *p-d* us to be his own people.
Col 1:14 . . . who *p-d* our freedom
1 Tim 2:6 . . . gave his life to *p* freedom
Rev 14:4 . . . have been *p-d* from among

**PURE (adj)** free of contamination or impurities;
ritually clean; guileless; faultless; guiltless; chaste
*see also* CLEAN, HOLY
Ps 19:9 . . . Reverence for the LORD is *p,*
Prov 20:9 . . . I am *p* and free
Matt 5:8 . . . those whose hearts are *p,*
1 Cor 1:30 . . . he made us *p* and holy,
Phil 4:8 . . . right, and *p,* and lovely,

1 Tim 5:22 . . . Keep yourself *p.*
2 Tim 2:21 . . . If you keep yourself *p,*
Titus 1:15 . . . Everything is *p* to those
Titus 2:5 . . . to live wisely and be *p,*
Jas 1:27 . . . *P* and genuine religion
1 Pet 3:2 . . . your *p* and reverent
2 Pet 3:14 . . . are *p* and blameless
1 Jn 3:3 . . . will keep themselves *p,* just as

**PURIFY, PURIFIED (v)** to make pure or remove (physical or moral) blemishes; to make ritually clean
*see also* CLEANSE
Exod 30:10 . . . offering made to *p* the people
Exod 30:15 . . . given to the LORD to *p*
Num 25:13 . . . *p-ied* the people of Israel,
1 Chr 15:12 . . . You must *p* yourselves and
2 Chr 30:17 . . . had not *p-ied* themselves,
Neh 12:30 . . . Levites first *p-ied* themselves;
Isa 52:11 . . . and *p* yourselves,
John 15:3 . . . pruned and *p-ied* by the
Heb 9:14 . . . Christ will *p* our consciences
Heb 9:22 . . . everything was *p-ied* with blood.
Jas 4:8 . . . you sinners; *p* your hearts,

**PURITY (n)** the quality or state of being pure
Job 14:4 . . . Who can bring *p* out of an
Ps 86:11 . . . Grant me *p* of heart,
2 Cor 6:6 . . . by our *p,* our understanding,
1 Tim 4:12 . . . love, your faith, and your *p.*
1 Tim 5:2 . . . younger women with all *p*

**PURPOSE, PURPOSES (n)** something set up as an object or end to be attained; resolution, determination
*see also* PLAN
Exod 9:16 . . . I have spared you for a *p*—
Prov 19:21 . . . the LORD's *p* will prevail.
Rom 8:28 . . . according to his *p* for them.
Rom 9:11 . . . according to his own *p-s;*
Rom 9:17 . . . for the very *p* of displaying
1 Cor 3:8 . . . with the same *p.*
1 Cor 9:26 . . . I run with *p* in every step.
Phil 2:2 . . . together with one mind and *p.*

**PURSUE, PURSUES (v)** to follow in order to overtake, capture, kill, or defeat; to seek
Ps 23:6 . . . unfailing love will *p* me
Ps 119:32 . . . I will *p* your commands,
Prov 15:9 . . . those who *p* godliness.
Prov 21:21 . . . Whoever *p-s* righteousness
1 Tim 6:11 . . . *P* righteousness and a godly
2 Tim 2:22 . . . Instead, *p* righteous living, Q

**QUARREL, QUARRELS (n)** a usually verbal conflict between antagonists
Prov 10:12 . . . Hatred stirs up *q-s,*
Prov 17:14 . . . Starting a *q* is like opening
Prov 26:20 . . . *q-s* disappear when gossip
Prov 30:33 . . . anger causes *q-s.*
Titus 3:9 . . . *q-s* and fights about
Jas 4:1 . . . causing the *q-s* and fights

**QUARREL, QUARRELING (v)** to find fault; to contend or dispute actively
Prov 17:19 . . . Anyone who loves to *q* loves
Prov 20:3 . . . fools insist on *q-ing.*
Rom 13:13 . . . or in *q-ing* and jealousy.
1 Cor 3:3 . . . and *q* with each other.
2 Cor 12:20 . . . will find *q-ing,* jealousy,

**QUARRELSOME (adj)** apt or disposed to quarrel in an often petty manner; contentious
Prov 19:13 . . . *q* wife is as annoying as
Prov 21:9 . . . than with a *q* wife in a lovely

Prov 26:21 . . . A *q* person starts fights
1 Tim 3:3 . . . He must be gentle, not *q,*

**QUIET (adj)** calm; gentle; peaceful; still; free from noise
Prov 11:12 . . . a sensible person keeps *q.*
Eccl 3:7 . . . A time to be *q* and a time
Eccl 9:17 . . . to hear the *q* words of a wise
Luke 19:40 . . . If they kept *q,* the stones
1 Thes 4:11 . . . to live a *q* life,
1 Tim 2:2 . . . peaceful and *q* lives marked

**QUIETNESS (n)** the state of being quiet; calmness; stillness
Eccl 4:6 . . . one handful with *q* than two
Isa 30:15 . . . *q* and confidence is
Isa 32:17 . . . it will bring *q* and confidence

**RABBI (n)** a title of honor and respect given by the Jews to a teacher of the Law
Matt 23:8 . . . anyone call you '*R,*'
John 3:2 . . . "*R,*" he said, "we all know

**RACE (n)** an athletic contest; an ethnic classification
Ps 19:5 . . . athlete eager to run the *r.*
Eccl 9:11 . . . doesn't always win the *r,*
Dan 7:14 . . . people of every *r* and nation
1 Cor 9:24 . . . that in a *r* everyone runs,
Gal 2:2 . . . running the *r* for nothing.
Gal 5:7 . . . were running the *r* so well.
2 Tim 4:7 . . . I have finished the *r,*
Heb 12:1 . . . run with endurance the *r* God

**RACE (v)** to go, move, or function at top speed or out of control
Prov 6:18 . . . feet that *r* to do wrong,

**RADIANCE (n)** the quality or state of being radiant
Isa 60:3 . . . will come to see your *r.*
Luke 2:9 . . . and the *r* of the Lord's

**RADIANT (adj)** vividly bright and shining; marked by or expressive of love, confidence, or happiness
Exod 34:29 . . . face had become *r* because
Ps 34:5 . . . help will be *r* with joy;
Ps 80:1 . . . display your *r* glory

**RAGS (n)** clothes usually in poor or ragged condition
Isa 64:6 . . . are nothing but filthy *r.*

**RAIN, RAINS (n)** water falling in drops from the sky
Deut 11:14 . . . will send the *r-s* in their
1 Kgs 17:1 . . . no dew or *r* during the next
1 Kgs 18:1 . . . that I will soon send *r!*
Prov 16:15 . . . refreshes like a spring *r.*
Matt 5:45 . . . and he sends *r* on the just
Jas 5:17 . . . earnestly that no *r* would fall,
Jude 1:12 . . . land without giving any *r.*

**RAINBOW (n)** an arch of colors in the sky caused by light passing through moisture in the air
Gen 9:13 . . . I have placed my *r* in the

**RAISE, RAISED (v)** to recall from death
*see also* RESURRECTION
Luke 7:22 . . . the dead are *r-d* to life,
John 6:39 . . . that I should *r* them up
Acts 2:32 . . . God *r-d* Jesus from the dead,
Acts 24:15 . . . that he will *r* both the
Rom 1:4 . . . he was *r-d* from the dead
Rom 6:5 . . . we will also be *r-d* to life

Rom 10:9 . . . God *r-d* him from the dead,
1 Cor 15:4 . . . he was *r-d* from the dead
Phil 3:10 . . . mighty power that *r-d* him
1 Thes 4:14 . . . died and was *r-d* to life
1 Pet 1:3 . . . because God *r-d* Jesus Christ

**RAM, RAMS (n)** a male sheep
Gen 22:13 . . . he took the *r* and sacrificed
1 Sam 15:22 . . . offering the fat of *r-s.*
Dan 8:3 . . . I saw a *r* with two long
Mic 6:7 . . . him thousands of *r-s* and ten

**RANSOM (n)** price paid or demanded to release someone or something from captivity
Matt 20:28 . . . his life as a *r* for many.
Mark 10:45 . . . his life as a *r* for many.
1 Pet 1:18 . . . that God paid a *r* to save

**RANSOM, RANSOMED (v)** to deliver especially from sin or its penalty; to free from captivity or punishment by paying a price
*see also* REDEEM(ED)
Ps 44:26 . . . Help us! *R* us because of
Ps 71:23 . . . for you have *r-ed* me.
Isa 35:10 . . . have been *r-ed* by the LORD
Hos 13:14 . . . Should I *r* them from
Rev 5:9 . . . your blood has *r-ed* people

**READ, READING, READS (v)** to receive and interpret letters or symbols by sight; to utter aloud the printed or written words of
Deut 17:19 . . . with him and *r* it daily
Josh 8:34 . . . Joshua then *r* to them
2 Kgs 23:2 . . . There the king *r* to them
Acts 8:28 . . . carriage, he was *r-ing* aloud
2 Cor 3:2 . . . everyone can *r* it and
1 Tim 4:13 . . . focus on *r-ing* the Scriptures
Rev 1:3 . . . the one who *r-s* the words of

**REAP (v)** *see also* HARVEST
Gal 6:9 . . . will *r* a harvest of blessing
Jas 3:18 . . . *r* a harvest of righteousness.

**REAPERS (KJV)**
Ruth 2:3 . . . grain behind the *harvesters*
2 Kgs 4:18 . . . working with the *harvesters*
Matt 13:30 . . . the *harvesters* to sort out
Matt 13:39 . . . the *harvesters* are the angels

**REBEL, REBELLED, REBELLING, REBELS (v)** to oppose or disobey one in authority or control
Num 14:9 . . . Do not *r* against the
Num 27:14 . . . of Israel *r-led,* you failed to
1 Sam 12:14 . . . if you do not *r* against the
Ps 78:56 . . . testing and *r-ling* against God
Isa 63:10 . . . But they *r-led* against him
Matt 10:21 . . . children will *r* against their
Rom 13:2 . . . So anyone who *r-s* against

**REBELLION (n)** opposition to one in authority or dominance; defiance
Exod 34:7 . . . forgive iniquity, *r,* and sin.
Ps 32:5 . . . I will confess my *r* to the
Ps 39:8 . . . Rescue me from my *r.*
Ps 51:3 . . . I recognize my *r;* it haunts
Isa 53:5 . . . was pierced for our *r,*
Isa 53:8 . . . for the *r* of my people.
Dan 9:24 . . . to finish their *r,* to put an
2 Thes 2:3 . . . is a great *r* against God

**REBELLIOUS (adj)** given to or engaged in rebellion
Isa 65:2 . . . opened my arms to a *r* people.
Luke 1:17 . . . those who are *r* to accept
Rom 10:21 . . . were disobedient and *r.*
1 Tim 1:9 . . . people who are lawless and *r,*
Titus 1:6 . . . reputation for being wild or *r.*

**REBELS (n)** those who rebel or participate in a rebellion
Ps 51:13 . . . will teach your ways to *r,*
Isa 53:12 . . . He was counted among the *r.*
Luke 22:37 . . . was counted among the *r.*
Rom 11:30 . . . Gentiles were *r* against God,
Rom 11:31 . . . they are the *r,* and God's

**REBUKE (n)** an expression of strong disapproval; reprimand
*see also* CORRECT, DISCIPLINE
Prov 17:10 . . . A single *r* does more for
Prov 27:5 . . . An open *r* is better than

**REBUKE, REBUKED (v)** to criticize sharply; to reprimand
Prov 30:6 . . . or he may *r* you and expose
Mark 16:14 . . . He *r-d* them for their
Luke 17:3 . . . believer sins, *r* that person;
2 Tim 4:2 . . . Patiently correct, *r,* and
Jas 1:5 . . . He will not *r* you for asking.

**RECEIVE, RECEIVED, RECEIVES (v)** to acquire or take possession of; to welcome
Matt 7:8 . . . For everyone who asks, *r-s.*
Matt 19:17 . . . you want to *r* eternal life,
John 20:22 . . . said, "*R* the Holy Spirit.
Acts 1:8 . . . But you will *r* power when the
Acts 2:38 . . . Then you will *r* the gift of
Acts 8:17 . . . they *r-d* the Holy Spirit.
Acts 10:47 . . . they have *r-d* the Holy
Acts 19:2 . . . Did you *r* the Holy Spirit
Rom 8:15 . . . Instead, you *r-d* God's Spirit
1 Tim 1:16 . . . in him and *r* eternal life.
Rev 4:11 . . . our God, to *r* glory and honor

**RECONCILE, RECONCILED, RECONCILING (v)** to restore to friendship or harmony, especially between God and human beings
2 Cor 5:18 . . . task of *r-ing* people to him.
Eph 2:16 . . . Christ *r-d* both groups to God
Col 1:20 . . . God *r-d* everything to himself.
Col 1:22 . . . now he has *r-d* you to himself

**RECONCILIATION (n)** the action of reconciling; the state of being reconciled
Prov 14:9 . . . acknowledge it and seek *r.*
2 Cor 5:19 . . . this wonderful message of *r.*

**RED (adj)** of the color red
Exod 15:4 . . . are drowned in the *R* Sea.
Ps 106:9 . . . He commanded the *R* Sea to
Prov 23:31 . . . wine, seeing how *r* it is,
Isa 1:18 . . . they are *r* like crimson,
Isa 63:1 . . . with his clothing stained *r?*

**REDEEM, REDEEMED, REDEEMS (v)** to buy back; to save by payment of a ransom; to free from the consequences of sin
*see also* PURCHASE, RANSOM, RESCUE
Exod 6:6 . . . I will *r* you with a powerful
2 Sam 7:23 . . . have you *r-ed* from slavery
Ps 34:22 . . . the LORD will *r* those
Ps 49:15 . . . God will *r* my life.
Ps 74:2 . . . the tribe you *r-ed* as your own
Ps 103:4 . . . He *r-s* me from death and
Ps 107:2 . . . Has the LORD *r-ed* you?
Ps 130:8 . . . He himself will *r* Israel from
Isa 35:9 . . . Only the *r-ed* will walk
Isa 63:9 . . . love and mercy he *r-ed* them.
Hos 7:13 . . . I wanted to *r* them, but they

**REDEEMER (n)** one who frees or delivers another from difficulty, danger, or bondage, usually by the payment of a ransom price

Ruth 3:9 . . . for you are my family *r.*
Ruth 4:14 . . . has now provided a *r* for
Job 19:25 . . . I know that my *R* lives,
Ps 19:14 . . . LORD, my rock and my *r.*
Prov 23:11 . . . For their *R* is strong;
Isa 44:6 . . . Israel's King and *R,* the LORD
Isa 48:17 . . . your *R,* the Holy One of Israel:
Isa 59:20 . . . The *R* will come to Jerusalem

**REDEMPTION (n)** the act, process, or an instance of redeeming
Ps 130:7 . . . love. His *r* overflows.
Eph 4:30 . . . be saved on the day of *r.*
Heb 9:12 . . . and secured our *r* forever.

**REFUGE (n)** shelter or protection from danger or distress
*see also* FORTRESS, PROTECTION, SHELTER
Deut 33:27 . . . eternal God is your *r,*
2 Sam 22:3 . . . He is my *r,* my savior,
Ps 2:12 . . . for all who take *r* in him!
Ps 5:11 . . . But let all who take *r* in you
Ps 17:7 . . . those who seek *r* from their
Ps 34:8 . . . those who take *r* in him!
Ps 46:1 . . . God is our *r* and strength,
Ps 91:2 . . . He alone is my *r,* my place

**REGENERATION (KJV)**
Matt 19:28 . . . world is *made new* and the
Titus 3:5 . . . giving us a *new birth* and new

**REGULATIONS (n)** authoritative rules dealing with details or procedure
*see also* LAW(S)
Exod 21:1 . . . These are the *r* you must
Deut 33:10 . . . They teach your *r* to Jacob;
Ps 119:30 . . . determined to live by your *r.*
Ps 119:43 . . . for your *r* are my only hope.
Ps 119:120 . . . I stand in awe of your *r.*
Ps 119:164 . . . because all your *r* are just.
Ps 119:175 . . . and may your *r* help me.

**REIGN, REIGNED, REIGNING, REIGNS (v)** to possess or exercise sovereign power; to rule
Exod 15:18 . . . The LORD will *r* forever
Ps 9:7 . . . But the LORD *r-s* forever,
Ps 29:10 . . . LORD *r-s* as king forever.
Ps 96:10 . . . The LORD *r-s!*
Ps 146:10 . . . The LORD will *r* forever.
Isa 52:7 . . . that the God of Israel *r-s!*
1 Cor 4:8 . . . then we would be *r-ing* with you.
1 Cor 15:25 . . . For Christ must *r* until he
Rev 5:10 . . . And they will *r* on the earth.
Rev 11:15 . . . and he will *r* forever
Rev 19:6 . . . our God, the Almighty, *r-s.*
Rev 20:4 . . . again, and they *r-ed* with Christ
Rev 22:5 . . . And they will *r* forever

**REIGNS (n)** the time during which one (as a sovereign) rules
Dan 2:44 . . . During the *r* of those kings,

**REJECT, REJECTED, REJECTING (v)** to refuse to accept, consider, submit to, or take for some purpose, or use; to refuse to hear, receive, or admit
1 Sam 8:7 . . . me they are *r-ing,* not you.
Ps 51:17 . . . not *r* a broken and repentant
Ps 118:22 . . . stone that the builders *r-ed*
Prov 3:11 . . . My child, don't *r* the LORD's
Mal 1:3 . . . but I *r-ed* his brother,
Matt 21:42 . . . stone that the builders *r-ed*
Luke 10:16 . . . who *r-s* me is *r-ing* God,
John 6:37 . . . I will never *r* them.
John 12:48 . . . But all who *r* me and my

Rom 9:13 . . . loved Jacob, but I *r-ed* Esau.
1 Thes 4:8 . . . teaching but is *r-ing* God,
1 Tim 4:4 . . . we should not *r* any of it
2 Tim 3:5 . . . but they will *r* the power
Heb 6:6 . . . by *r-ing* the Son of God, they
1 Pet 2:4 . . . He was *r-ed* by people,
1 Pet 2:7 . . . stone that the builders *r-ed*

**REJOICE, REJOICED, REJOICES, REJOICING (v)** to feel joy or great delight; to gladden
1 Chr 16:31 . . . glad, and the earth *r!*
1 Chr 29:17 . . . *r* when you find integrity
Esth 8:17 . . . decree arrived, the Jews *r-d*
Ps 5:11 . . . who take refuge in you *r;*
Ps 13:5 . . . I will *r* because you
Ps 35:9 . . . I will *r* in the LORD.
Ps 48:2 . . . the whole earth *r-s* to see it!
Ps 58:10 . . . The godly will *r* when they
Ps 66:6 . . . There we *r-d* in him.
Ps 68:4 . . . LORD—*r* in his presence!
Ps 119:14 . . . I have *r-d* in your laws
Ps 119:162 . . . I *r* in your word like one
Prov 8:31 . . . I *r-d* with the human family!
Prov 17:5 . . . who *r* at the misfortune
Prov 29:2 . . . in authority, the people *r.*
Isa 9:3 . . . and its people will *r.*
Isa 35:1 . . . wasteland will *r* and blossom
Isa 62:5 . . . *r* over you as a bridegroom *r-s*
Jer 51:48 . . . the heavens and earth will *r,*
Lam 4:21 . . . Are you *r-ing* in the land
Hab 1:15 . . . while they *r* and celebrate?
Zeph 3:17 . . . He will *r* over you
Zech 2:10 . . . Shout and *r,* O beautiful
Luke 1:14 . . . and many will *r* at his birth,
Luke 1:47 . . . How my spirit *r-s* in God my
Luke 1:58 . . . everyone *r-d* with her.
Luke 10:20 . . . But don't *r* because evil
Luke 13:17 . . . but all the people *r-d* at the
Acts 5:41 . . . high council *r-ing* that God
Acts 16:34 . . . his entire household *r-d*
1 Cor 13:6 . . . *r* about injustice but *r-s*
Phil 2:18 . . . you should *r,* and I will
Phil 3:1 . . . and sisters, *r* in the Lord.
Phil 4:4 . . . I say it again—*r!*
Col 2:5 . . . I *r* that you are living as
Rev 19:7 . . . Let us be glad and *r,* and

**RELIABLE (adj)** dependable
1 Chr 9:22 . . . they were *r* men.
Prov 13:17 . . . but a *r* messenger brings
Prov 20:6 . . . find one who is truly *r?*
2 Tim 2:2 . . . by many *r* witnesses.

**RELIGION, RELIGIONS (n)** a personal set or institutionalized system of religious attitudes, beliefs, and practices; the service and worship of God or the supernatural
Matt 6:7 . . . as people of other *r-s* do.
Acts 25:19 . . . something about their *r* and
Acts 26:5 . . . the strictest sect of our *r.*
Gal 1:13 . . . I followed the Jewish *r*—
Jas 1:26 . . . and your *r* is worthless.

**RELIGIOUS (adj)** relating to or manifesting faithful devotion to God or a god
Luke 11:46 . . . with unbearable *r* demands,
Acts 13:50 . . . the influential *r* women and
Jas 1:26 . . . you claim to be *r* but don't

**REMAIN, REMAINED, REMAINS (v)** to stay in the same place or with the same person or group; to continue unchanged
2 Kgs 18:6 . . . He *r-ed* faithful to the LORD
John 15:7 . . . But if you *r* in me and my

John 15:9 . . . loved me. *R* in my love.
Rom 11:5 . . . of Israel have *r-ed* faithful
2 Tim 2:13 . . . unfaithful, he *r-s* faithful,
2 Tim 3:14 . . . But you must *r* faithful
2 Tim 4:7 . . . and I have *r-ed* faithful.
Heb 7:3 . . . He *r-s* a priest forever,
Heb 10:32 . . . how you *r-ed* faithful even
Heb 13:4 . . . and *r* faithful to one another
1 Pet 1:25 . . . word of the Lord *r-s*
1 Jn 2:27 . . . *r* in fellowship with Christ.

**REMEMBER, REMEMBERED, REMEMBERING, REMEMBERS (v)** to bring to mind or think of again; to keep in mind for attention or consideration; to retain in the memory
Gen 9:15 . . . I will *r* my covenant with
Exod 2:24 . . . *r-ed* his covenant promise
1 Chr 16:12 . . . *R* the wonders he has
Ps 49:13 . . . though they are *r-ed* as being
Ps 103:14 . . . he *r-s* we are only dust.
Ps 106:45 . . . *r-ed* his covenant with them
Ps 111:5 . . . he always *r-s* his covenant.
Ps 136:23 . . . He *r-ed* us in our weakness.
Jer 31:34 . . . never again *r* their sins.
Jer 32:20 . . . things still *r-ed* to this day!
Hab 3:2 . . . in your anger, *r* your mercy.
Matt 26:13 . . . will be *r-ed* and discussed.
Luke 1:72 . . . *r-ing* his sacred covenant—
Luke 22:19 . . . Do this to *r* me.
1 Cor 11:24 . . . Do this to *r* me.
2 Tim 2:8 . . . Always *r* that Jesus
Heb 8:12 . . . never again *r* their sins.
2 Pet 1:15 . . . you always *r* these things

**REMISSION (KJV)**
Matt 26:28 . . . as a sacrifice *to forgive*
Acts 10:43 . . . *forgiven* through his
Rom 3:25 . . . he *held back and did not punish*
Heb 9:22 . . . blood, there is no *forgiveness*

**REMNANT (n)** a usually small part, member, or trace remaining; the few people left who gathered together after God scattered them into exile
Ezra 9:8 . . . few of us to survive as a *r.*
Isa 6:13 . . . a tenth—a *r*—survive,
Isa 11:11 . . . to bring back the *r* of his
Jer 23:3 . . . gather together the *r* of my
Zech 8:12 . . . will cause the *r* in Judah

**RENEW, RENEWED, RENEWS (v)** to restore to freshness, vigor, or perfection; to make new spiritually
Ps 23:3 . . . He *r-s* my strength.
Ps 51:10 . . . *R* a loyal spirit within me.
Isa 57:10 . . . Desire gave you *r-ed* strength,
Eph 4:23 . . . let the Spirit *r* your thoughts
Col 3:10 . . . be *r-ed* as you learn to know

**RENOWN (KJV)**
Gen 6:4 . . . the *heroes* and famous warriors
Isa 14:20 . . . will never again *receive honor*
Ezek 16:14 . . . *fame* soon spread
Ezek 39:13 . . . a *glorious victory* for Israel

**REPAY, REPAYS (v)** to give or inflict in return or requital; to pay back (money)
Ps 62:12 . . . Surely you *r* all people
Prov 17:13 . . . If you *r* good with evil,
Prov 19:17 . . . and he will *r* you!
Jer 51:6 . . . he will *r* her in full.
Jer 51:56 . . . he always *r-s* in full.
Luke 6:34 . . . to those who can *r* you,
Luke 7:42 . . . neither of them could *r* him,

1 Tim 5:4 . . . *r* their parents by taking
1 Pet 3:9 . . . Don't *r* evil for evil.

**REPENT, REPENTED, REPENTING, REPENTS (v)** to turn from sin and change one's heart and behavior; to feel regret and contrition
Matt 3:2 . . . *R* of your sins and turn
Matt 3:8 . . . that you have *r-ed* of your sins
Matt 4:17 . . . began to preach, "*R* of your
Matt 11:21 . . . people would have *r-ed* of
Luke 3:8 . . . that you have *r-ed* of your sins
Luke 15:7 . . . sinner who *r-s* and returns
Luke 15:10 . . . when even one sinner *r-s.*
Acts 2:38 . . . you must *r* of your sins,
Acts 17:30 . . . everywhere to *r* of their sins
Acts 20:21 . . . necessity of *r-ing* from sin
Heb 6:1 . . . importance of *r-ing* from evil
2 Pet 3:9 . . . but wants everyone to *r.*
Rev 2:5 . . . If you don't *r,* I will come

**REPENTANCE (n)** a turning away from sin, disobedience, or rebellion, and a turning back to God
1 Kgs 8:47 . . . to you in *r* and pray,
Job 42:6 . . . dust and ashes to show my *r.*
Luke 17:3 . . . if there is *r,* forgive.
2 Cor 7:10 . . . sorrow, which lacks *r,*

**REPUTATION (n)** overall quality or character as seen or judged by people in general
*see also* NAME
Ps 109:21 . . . the sake of your own *r!*
Prov 3:4 . . . you will earn a good *r.*
Prov 22:1 . . . Choose a good *r* over great
Eccl 7:1 . . . A good *r* is more valuable
1 Tim 3:2 . . . wisely, and have a good *r.*
Heb 11:39 . . . good *r* because of their

**RESCUE, RESCUED, RESCUES, RESCUING (v)** to save or deliver
*see also* REDEEM, SAVE
2 Kgs 13:5 . . . someone to *r* the Israelites
Ps 9:14 . . . rejoice that you have *r-d* me.
Ps 17:7 . . . mighty power you *r* those who
Ps 22:8 . . . let the LORD *r* him!
Ps 31:2 . . . listen to me; *r* me quickly.
Ps 37:39 . . . The LORD *r-s* the godly;
Ps 37:40 . . . LORD helps them, *r-ing* them
Ps 68:20 . . . The Sovereign LORD *r-s* us
Ps 72:12 . . . He will *r* the poor when
Ps 145:19 . . . cries for help and *r-s* them.
Prov 11:8 . . . godly are *r-d* from trouble,
Isa 56:1 . . . coming soon to *r* you and
Dan 6:27 . . . He *r-s* and saves his people;
Zech 8:7 . . . that I will *r* my people from
Matt 6:13 . . . but *r* us from the evil one.
Rom 11:26 . . . The one who *r-s* will come
2 Cor 1:10 . . . And he did *r* us from mortal
Gal 1:4 . . . in order to *r* us from this
Gal 3:13 . . . But Christ has *r-d* us from the
Col 1:13 . . . For he has *r-d* us from the
1 Thes 1:10 . . . the one who has *r-d* us
2 Pet 2:9 . . . knows how to *r* godly people

**RESIST (v)** to withstand the force or effect of; to counteract or defeat
Dan 11:32 . . . will be strong and will *r* him.
Matt 5:39 . . . do not *r* an evil person!
Jas 4:7 . . . *R* the devil, and he will flee

**RESPECT (n)** a high or special regard; esteem
*see also* AWE, REVERENCE
Prov 11:16 . . . A gracious woman gains *r,*
Mal 1:6 . . . the honor and *r* I deserve?

Titus 2:2 . . . be worthy of *r,* and to live

**RESPECT, RESPECTED (v)** to consider worthy of high regard; to esteem
Eph 5:33 . . . the wife must *r* her husband.
1 Tim 3:4 . . . children who *r* and obey him.
1 Tim 3:8 . . . deacons must be well *r-ed*
1 Tim 3:11 . . . their wives must be *r-ed*
1 Tim 5:17 . . . work well should be *r-ed*
1 Pet 2:17 . . . Fear God, and *r* the king.

**RESPONSIBLE (adj)** marked by or involving responsibility or accountability; liable to be called to account as the primary cause, motive, or agent
Exod 32:34 . . . hold them *r* for their sins.
Num 1:53 . . . The Levites are *r* to stand
Ezek 33:6 . . . he is *r* for their captivity.
Jon 1:14 . . . And don't hold us *r* for his
Gal 6:5 . . . For we are each *r* for our own

**REST (n)** freedom from activity or labor; peace of mind or spirit; repose, sleep
*see also* SABBATH
Exod 31:15 . . . day of complete *r,* a holy
Exod 33:14 . . . and I will give you *r*—
Ps 91:1 . . . Most High will find *r* in the
Ps 127:2 . . . for God gives *r* to his loved
Jer 6:16 . . . you will find *r* for your
Matt 11:28 . . . and I will give you *r.*
2 Thes 1:7 . . . God will provide *r* for you
Heb 4:3 . . . even though this *r* has been
Heb 4:9 . . . a special *r* still waiting
Heb 4:10 . . . who have entered into God's *r*

**REST, RESTED, RESTING, RESTS (v)** to sit or lie on; to cease from action or motion; to take relief or respite
Gen 2:2 . . . of creation, so he *r-ed* from all
Ps 16:9 . . . My body *r-s* in safety.
Ps 23:2 . . . He lets me *r* in green
Isa 11:2 . . . Spirit of the LORD will *r*
Isa 30:15 . . . and *r-ing* in me will you
John 1:32 . . . from heaven and *r-ing* upon
Heb 4:4 . . . seventh day God *r-ed* from all
Rev 14:13 . . . will *r* from their hard work;

**RESTITUTION (n)** a making good of or giving an equivalent for some injury
Lev 6:5 . . . You must make *r* by paying
Num 5:8 . . . relatives to whom *r* can be

**RESTORE, RESTORED, RESTORES, RESTORING (v)** to give back, return; to renew
Ps 14:7 . . . When the LORD *r-s* his people,
Ps 30:2 . . . and you *r-d* my health.
Isa 58:11 . . . are dry and *r-ing* your strength.
Jer 30:3 . . . when I will *r* the fortunes of
Jer 30:18 . . . from captivity and *r* their
Jer 31:18 . . . Turn me again to you and *r*
Hos 6:2 . . . a short time he will *r* us,
Nah 2:2 . . . but he will *r* its splendor.
Rom 5:10 . . . friendship with God was *r-d*
1 Pet 5:10 . . . he will *r,* support,

**RESURRECTION (n)** the state of one risen from the dead; the rising again to life of all the human dead before the final judgment
*see also* RAISE, RISE
Matt 27:53 . . . cemetery after Jesus' *r,*
Mark 12:23 . . . will she be in the *r?*
Luke 20:36 . . . children of the *r.*
John 11:25 . . . I am the *r* and the life.
Acts 1:22 . . . as a witness of Jesus' *r.*
Acts 2:31 . . . speaking of the Messiah's *r.*

Acts 4:2 . . . there is a *r* of the dead.
Acts 4:33 . . . powerfully to the *r* of
Acts 17:32 . . . Paul speak about the *r* of
1 Cor 15:13 . . . if there is no *r* of the
1 Cor 15:42 . . . way with the *r* of the dead.
Phil 3:11 . . . experience the *r* from the
2 Tim 2:18 . . . claiming that the *r* of the
Heb 6:2 . . . of hands, the *r* of the dead,
Heb 11:35 . . . a better life after the *r*.
1 Pet 3:21 . . . because of the *r* of Jesus
Rev 20:5 . . . This is the first *r*.

**REVEAL, REVEALED (v)** to make known
through divine inspiration; to make (something
secret or hidden) publicly or generally known; to
display
Exod 6:3 . . . did not *r* my name, Yahweh,
Deut 29:29 . . . all that he has *r-ed* to us,
Isa 40:5 . . . the LORD will be *r-ed*,
Isa 53:1 . . . the LORD *r-ed* his powerful
Matt 10:26 . . . is covered will be *r-ed*,
Matt 11:27 . . . Son chooses to *r* him.
Luke 2:32 . . . He is a light to *r* God
John 12:38 . . . the LORD *r-ed* his powerful
John 14:21 . . . love them and *r* myself
John 17:6 . . . I have *r-ed* you to the
Rom 8:18 . . . glory he will *r* to us
Rom 16:25 . . . Christ has *r-ed* his plan
1 Cor 2:10 . . . that God *r-ed* these things
Gal 1:16 . . . to *r* his Son to me so that
Gal 2:2 . . . because God *r-ed* to me
Eph 3:3 . . . himself *r-ed* his mysterious
Col 1:26 . . . it has been *r-ed* to God's
2 Thes 2:3 . . . man of lawlessness is *r-ed*
Titus 2:13 . . . Christ, will be *r-ed*.
Heb 9:8 . . . the Holy Spirit *r-ed* that
1 Pet 1:7 . . . when Jesus Christ is *r-ed*

**REVELATION, REVELATIONS (n)** something
that is revealed by God to humans; an act of
revealing or communicating divine truth
1 Cor 14:6 . . . bring you a *r* or some
1 Cor 14:30 . . . person receives a *r* from
2 Cor 12:1 . . . visions and *r-s* from the
2 Cor 12:7 . . . wonderful *r-s* from God.
Gal 1:12 . . . by direct *r* from Jesus
Rev 1:1 . . . This is a *r* from Jesus

**REVELRY (n)** noisy partying or merrymaking
Exod 32:6 . . . they indulged in pagan *r*.
1 Cor 10:7 . . . they indulged in pagan *r*.

**REVENGE (n)** an act or instance of retaliating in
order to get even
Lev 19:18 . . . Do not seek *r* or bear
Num 31:3 . . . war of *r* against Midian.
Deut 32:35 . . . I will take *r;* I will
Josh 20:3 . . . relatives seeking *r* for
Judg 20:10 . . . will take *r* on Gibeah
Isa 34:8 . . . day of the LORD's *r*,
Heb 10:30 . . . I will take *r*. I will

**REVERENCE (n)** profound, adoring, awed
respect
*see also* AWE, FEAR, RESPECT
Lev 19:30 . . . of rest, and show *r* toward
Job 15:4 . . . fear of God, no *r* for him?
Job 37:24 . . . who are wise show him *r*.
Eph 5:21 . . . another out of *r* for Christ.
Heb 5:7 . . . of his deep *r* for God.

**REVERENT (adj)** expressing or characterized
by reverence; worshipful
Col 3:22 . . . because of your *r* fear

1 Pet 1:17 . . . must live in *r* fear
1 Pet 3:2 . . . your pure and *r* lives.

**REWARD, REWARDS (n)** something that is
given in return for good or evil done or received
or that is offered or given for some service or
attainment
Gen 15:1 . . . and your *r* will be
1 Sam 26:23 . . . gives his own *r* for doing
Prov 12:14 . . . and hard work brings *r-s.*
Isa 49:4 . . . I will trust God for my *r.*
Matt 5:12 . . . For a great *r* awaits you
Matt 6:5 . . . all the *r* they will ever
Luke 6:23 . . . For a great *r* awaits you
Luke 6:35 . . . your *r* from heaven will
Phil 4:17 . . . you to receive a *r* for your
1 Thes 2:19 . . . be our proud *r* and crown
Heb 10:35 . . . the great *r* it brings you!
1 Pet 1:9 . . . The *r* for trusting him

**REWARD, REWARDED, REWARDS (v)** to give
a reward to; to recompense
2 Sam 22:21 . . . The LORD *r-ed* me for
Prov 13:21 . . . while blessings *r* the
Prov 25:22 . . . the LORD will *r* you.
Jer 31:16 . . . for I will *r* you," says
Matt 6:18 . . . sees everything, will *r* you.
Luke 12:37 . . . for his return will be *r-ed.*
Luke 14:14 . . . God will *r* you for
1 Cor 3:8 . . . both will be *r-ed* for their
Eph 6:8 . . . the Lord will *r* each one
1 Tim 3:13 . . . will be *r-ed* with respect
Heb 11:6 . . . that he *r-s* those who
Rev 11:18 . . . the dead and *r* your servants

**RICH (adj)** having abundant possessions and
especially material wealth
Job 34:19 . . . no more attention to the *r*
Ps 49:16 . . . the wicked grow *r* and
Prov 10:4 . . . poor; hard workers get *r.*
Prov 11:18 . . . Evil people get *r* for
Prov 13:7 . . . are poor pretend to be *r;*
Prov 21:17 . . . and luxury will never be *r.*
Prov 22:2 . . . The *r* and poor have this
Prov 23:4 . . . yourself out trying to get *r.*
Prov 28:6 . . . than to be dishonest and *r.*
Prov 28:22 . . . Greedy people try to get *r*
Eccl 5:12 . . . But the *r* seldom get a
Isa 53:9 . . . put in a *r* man's grave.
Matt 19:23 . . . hard for a *r* person to enter
Luke 1:53 . . . and sent the *r* away with
Luke 6:24 . . . you who are *r*, for you have
Luke 16:1 . . . was a certain *r* man who had
Luke 21:1 . . . watched the *r* people
2 Cor 8:9 . . . Though he was *r*, yet for your
1 Tim 6:9 . . . who long to be *r* fall into
1 Tim 6:17 . . . who are *r* in this world
Jas 1:10 . . . those who are *r* should boast
Jas 2:3 . . . seat to the *r* person, but you
Jas 5:1 . . . Look here, you *r* people:

**RICHES (n)** things that make one rich; wealth
*see also* MONEY, POSSESSION(S), TREASURE(S),
WEALTH
2 Chr 1:11 . . . ask for wealth, *r*, fame,
Ps 49:6 . . . wealth and boast of great *r.*
Prov 27:24 . . . for *r* don't last forever,
Eccl 5:13 . . . Hoarding *r* harms the
Jer 9:23 . . . rich boast in their *r.*
Luke 8:14 . . . cares and *r* and pleasures
Rom 11:33 . . . great are God's *r* and
2 Cor 6:10 . . . give spiritual *r* to others.
Col 1:27 . . . know that the *r* and glory

**RIGHT (adj)** being in accordance with what
is good, just, or proper; being in a correct or
proper state; located opposite of left; acting or
judging in accordance with truth or fact
*see also* JUST, JUSTIFY, RIGHTEOUS, UPRIGHT
Gen 4:7 . . . do what is *r*, then watch out!
Gen 18:19 . . . by doing what is *r* and just.
Exod 15:26 . . . do what is *r* in his sight,
Num 25:13 . . . making them *r* with me.
Deut 6:18 . . . Do what is *r* and good
Deut 25:1 . . . that one is *r* and the other
Josh 1:7 . . . either to the *r* or to the
Judg 17:6 . . . whatever seemed *r* in their
1 Sam 12:23 . . . what is good and *r*.
1 Kgs 3:9 . . . difference between *r* and
2 Chr 12:6 . . . The LORD is *r* in doing
Ps 19:8 . . . LORD are *r*, bringing joy
Ps 24:5 . . . have a *r* relationship with
Ps 25:8 . . . does what is *r;* he shows the
Ps 37:30 . . . they teach *r* from wrong.
Ps 64:10 . . . do what is *r* will praise him.
Ps 71:2 . . . do what is *r.* Turn your ear
Ps 84:11 . . . from those who do what is *r.*
Ps 97:11 . . . on those whose hearts are *r.*
Ps 106:3 . . . and always do what is *r.*
Ps 119:144 . . . laws are always *r;* help me
Prov 1:3 . . . do what is *r*, just, and fair.
Prov 2:13 . . . men turn from the *r* way
Prov 14:2 . . . who follow the *r* path
Prov 14:12 . . . person that seems *r*, but
Prov 15:21 . . . stays on the *r* path.
Prov 15:23 . . . to say the *r* thing at the
Prov 18:17 . . . in court sounds *r*—until
Eccl 8:5 . . . and a way to do what is *r*,
Eccl 9:11 . . . being in the *r* place at the
Isa 7:15 . . . choose what is *r* and reject
Isa 16:5 . . . be eager to do what is *r.*
Isa 26:7 . . . who does what is *r*, and you
Jer 23:5 . . . is just and *r* throughout the
Ezek 18:5 . . . and does what is just and *r.*
Ezek 18:21 . . . and do what is just and *r*,
Hos 14:9 . . . are true and *r*, and righteous
Mic 3:1 . . . to know *r* from wrong,
Mic 6:8 . . . do what is *r*, to love mercy,
Zeph 2:3 . . . to do what is *r* and to live
Matt 6:3 . . . hand know what your *r* hand is
Matt 22:44 . . . of honor at my *r* hand until
Acts 2:34 . . . the place of honor at my *r* hand
Acts 7:55 . . . honor at God's *r* hand.
Acts 13:39 . . . is declared *r* with God—
Rom 1:17 . . . God makes us *r* in his sight.
Rom 2:13 . . . doesn't make us *r* with God.
Rom 3:4 . . . will be proved *r* in what you
Rom 3:20 . . . ever be made *r* with God by
Rom 3:22 . . . We are made *r* with God by
Rom 3:28 . . . So we are made *r* with God
Rom 3:30 . . . makes people *r* with himself
Rom 4:13 . . . but on a *r* relationship with
Rom 4:25 . . . life to make us *r* with God.
Rom 5:1 . . . we have been made *r* in God's
Rom 5:16 . . . being made *r* with God,
Rom 6:13 . . . to do what is *r* for the glory
Rom 8:10 . . . have been made *r* with God.
Rom 8:30 . . . given them *r* standing,
Rom 9:30 . . . they were made *r* with God.
Rom 10:3 . . . way of getting *r* with God by
Rom 10:10 . . . you are made *r* with God,
1 Cor 6:11 . . . you were made *r* with God
2 Cor 3:9 . . . which makes us *r* with God!
2 Cor 5:21 . . . be made *r* with God

Gal 2:16 . . . person is made *r* with God by
Gal 2:17 . . . to be made *r* with God through
Gal 2:21 . . . law could make us *r* with God,
Gal 3:11 . . . can be made *r* with God by
Gal 3:21 . . . could be made *r* with God by
Gal 3:24 . . . could be made *r* with God
Gal 5:4 . . . to make yourselves *r* with God
Eph 5:9 . . . what is good and *r* and true.
Phil 4:8 . . . honorable, and, *r*, and pure,
2 Tim 3:16 . . . teaches us to do what is *r*.
Heb 2:10 . . . it was only *r* that he should
Heb 12:11 . . . harvest of *r* living for those
Jas 2:24 . . . are shown to be *r* with God by
1 Jn 2:29 . . . who do what is *r* are God's

**RIGHT, RIGHTS (n)** correct or moral behavior;
something to which one has a just claim
Job 27:2 . . . has taken away my *r-s,* by
Ps 25:9 . . . in doing *r,* teaching them his
Ps 34:15 . . . those who do *r;* his ears are
Ps 82:3 . . . the *r-s* of the oppressed
Prov 29:7 . . . about the *r-s* of the poor;
Isa 1:17 . . . Fight for the *r-s* of widows.
Isa 10:2 . . . and deny the *r-s* of the needy
Lam 3:35 . . . others of their *r-s* in
Matt 5:10 . . . for doing *r,* for the Kingdom
John 1:12 . . . he gave the *r* to become
Rom 9:21 . . . he have a *r* to use the same
1 Cor 9:4 . . . have the *r* to live in your
1 Pet 3:12 . . . those who do *r,* and his ears

**RIGHTEOUS (adj)** acting in accord with divine
or moral law; free from guilt or sin; morally right
or justifiable
*see also* JUST, JUSTIFY, RIGHT, UPRIGHT
Gen 6:9 . . . Noah was a *r* man, the only
Gen 15:6 . . . counted him as *r* because of
Gen 18:23 . . . sweep away both the *r* and
Ps 7:8 . . . Declare me *r,* O LORD, for
Ps 17:15 . . . Because I am *r,* I will see
Ps 106:31 . . . regarded as a *r* man ever
Ps 119:7 . . . I learn your *r* regulations,
Ps 119:137 . . . O LORD, you are *r,*
Ps 145:17 . . . The LORD is *r* in everything
Prov 4:18 . . . The way of the *r* is like the
Prov 9:9 . . . Teach the *r,* and they
Prov 29:6 . . . but the *r* escape, shouting
Isa 26:2 . . . to all who are *r;* allow the
Isa 42:21 . . . Because he is *r,* the LORD
Isa 64:6 . . . we display our *r* deeds,
Jer 11:20 . . . you make *r* judgments, and
Jer 23:5 . . . raise up a *r* descendant from
Ezek 3:20 . . . None of their *r* acts will be
Amos 5:24 . . . river of *r* living.
Hab 2:4 . . . But the *r* will live
Mal 3:18 . . . between the *r* and the wicked,
Matt 9:13 . . . think they are *r,* but those
Matt 13:43 . . . Then the *r* will shine
Matt 25:37 . . . Then these *r* ones will
Luke 1:6 . . . and Elizabeth were *r* in God's
Luke 16:15 . . . like to appear *r* in public,
Rom 1:17 . . . faith that a *r* person has
Rom 3:5 . . . people see how *r* God is.
Rom 3:10 . . . No one is *r*—not even one.
Rom 4:3 . . . counted him as *r* because of
Rom 4:6 . . . who are declared *r* without
Rom 4:22 . . . God counted him as *r.*
Rom 6:19 . . . be slaves to *r* living so that
Gal 3:6 . . . counted him as *r* because of
Eph 4:24 . . . like God—truly *r* and holy.
Phil 1:11 . . . salvation—the *r* character
2 Tim 2:22 . . . Instead, pursue *r* living,

Titus 3:7 . . . he declared us *r* and gave us
Jas 2:23 . . . counted him as *r* because of
Jas 5:16 . . . prayer of a *r* person has
1 Jn 2:1 . . . the one who is truly *r.*
1 Jn 3:7 . . . that they are *r,* even as

**RIGHTEOUSNESS (n)** the state or quality of
being righteous
*see also* GODLINESS, JUSTICE
Ps 36:6 . . . Your *r* is like the mighty
Ps 71:15 . . . tell everyone about your *r.*
Ps 85:10 . . . *R* and peace have kissed!
Ps 98:2 . . . has revealed his *r* to every
Ps 111:3 . . . His *r* never fails.
Prov 21:21 . . . Whoever pursues *r* and
Isa 11:5 . . . He will wear *r* like a belt
Isa 42:6 . . . you to demonstrate my *r.*
Isa 45:8 . . . so salvation and *r* can sprout
Isa 56:1 . . . to display my *r* among you.
Isa 59:17 . . . He put on *r* as his body
Jer 9:24 . . . brings justice and *r* to the
Jer 23:6 . . . LORD Is Our *R.*
Hos 10:12 . . . come and shower *r* upon
Mic 7:9 . . . and I will see his *r.*
Mal 4:2 . . . the Sun of *R* will rise
Matt 5:20 . . . unless your *r* is better
John 16:8 . . . and of God's *r,* and of the
Acts 24:25 . . . about *r* and self-control
Rom 3:26 . . . to demonstrate his *r,* for he
Rom 5:18 . . . one act of *r* brings a right
2 Cor 6:7 . . . the weapons of *r* in the
Eph 6:14 . . . the body armor of God's *r.*
Phil 3:6 . . . And as for *r,* I obeyed the
2 Tim 4:8 . . . the crown of *r,* which
Heb 11:7 . . . he received the *r* that comes
Jas 3:18 . . . and reap a harvest of *r.*
2 Pet 3:13 . . . filled with God's *r.*

**RISE, RISEN, RISES (v)** to ascend or extend
above other objects; to return from death; to
assume an upright position
*see also* RESURRECTION
Num 24:17 . . . A star will *r* from Jacob;
Isa 26:19 . . . bodies will *r* again!
Mal 4:2 . . . of Righteousness will *r* with
Matt 22:30 . . . when the dead *r,* they will
Matt 27:63 . . . I will *r* from the dead.
Matt 28:6 . . . He is *r-n* from the dead,
Mark 8:31 . . . later he would *r* from the
Mark 16:6 . . . He is *r-n* from the dead!
Luke 18:33 . . . day he will *r* again.
Luke 24:34 . . . The Lord has really *r-n!*
John 5:29 . . . and they will *r* again.
John 11:24 . . . when everyone else *r-s,* at
John 20:9 . . . said Jesus must *r* from the
Acts 17:3 . . . must suffer and *r* from the
1 Thes 4:16 . . . have died will *r* from

**ROCK (n)** a stone; a cliff; foundation, support;
refuge
Exod 17:6 . . . Moses struck the *r* as he was
Num 20:8 . . . speak to the *r* over there,
Deut 32:13 . . . honey from the *r* and olive
2 Sam 22:2 . . . LORD is my *r,* my
Ps 18:2 . . . God is my *r,* in whom I
Ps 19:14 . . . LORD, my *r* and my redeemer.
Ps 61:2 . . . to the towering *r* of safety,
Ps 62:7 . . . my refuge, a *r* where no enemy
Ps 92:15 . . . He is my *r!*
Isa 26:4 . . . GOD is the eternal *R.*
Matt 7:24 . . . builds a house on solid *r.*
Matt 16:18 . . . upon this *r* I will build

Rom 9:33 . . . stumble, a *r* that makes them
1 Cor 10:4 . . . and that *r* was Christ.
1 Pet 2:8 . . . stumble, the *r* that makes

**ROD, RODS (n)** a straight, slender stick used
as a walking stick, a club or weapon, a shepherd's crook, a paddling stick, a royal scepter, or
a measuring stick; figurative of divine authority
*see also* STAFF
2 Sam 7:14 . . . him with the *r,* like any
Ps 2:9 . . . will break them with an iron *r*
Ps 23:4 . . . Your *r* and your staff
Prov 13:24 . . . spare the *r* of discipline
2 Cor 11:25 . . . times I was beaten with *r-s.*
Rev 2:27 . . . the nations with an iron *r*
Rev 12:5 . . . rule all nations with an iron *r.*
Rev 19:15 . . . rule them with an iron *r.*

**ROOSTER (n)** an adult male domestic chicken
Matt 26:34 . . . before the *r* crows, you will

**ROOT, ROOTS (n)** the part of a plant usually
found underground; something that is an origin
or source (as of a condition or quality)
Isa 11:1 . . . bearing fruit from the old *r.*
Isa 53:2 . . . green shoot, like a *r* in dry
Matt 3:10 . . . to sever the *r-s* of the trees.
Matt 13:21 . . . don't have deep *r-s,* they
Eph 3:17 . . . Your *r-s* will grow down
1 Tim 6:10 . . . money is the *r* of all kinds
Jude 1:12 . . . have been pulled up by the *r-s.*

**RUDDER (n)** an underwater blade that steers a
boat or ship
Jas 3:4 . . . a small *r* makes a huge ship

**RUIN (n)** physical, moral, economic, or social
collapse
Eccl 4:5 . . . idle hands, leading them to *r.*
1 Tim 6:9 . . . them into *r* and destruction.

**RUIN, RUINED, RUINING, RUINS (v)** to
damage irreparably; to subject to frustration,
failure, or disaster
Prov 19:3 . . . People *r* their lives by
Prov 19:18 . . . you will *r* their lives.
Prov 22:23 . . . He will *r* anyone who *r-s*
Isa 3:14 . . . You have *r-ed* Israel,
Matt 9:17 . . . the wine and *r-ing* the skins.
2 Tim 2:14 . . . they can *r* those who hear

**RULE, RULES (n)** a prescribed guide for
conduct or action
Isa 29:13 . . . but man-made *r-s* learned by
2 Tim 2:5 . . . unless they follow the *r-s.*
Heb 13:9 . . . not from *r-s* about food,

**RULE, RULED, RULES (v)** to exert control,
direction, or influence on; to exercise authority
or power over
Gen 3:16 . . . but he will *r* over you.
Ps 2:4 . . . But the one who *r-s* in heaven
Ps 11:4 . . . LORD still *r-s* from heaven.
Ps 55:19 . . . God, who has *r-d* forever,
Ps 66:7 . . . great power he *r-s* forever.
Ps 89:9 . . . You *r* the oceans.
Ps 103:19 . . . there he *r-s* over everything.
Prov 17:2 . . . wise servant will *r* over the
Isa 9:7 . . . He will *r* with fairness
Isa 40:10 . . . He will *r* with a powerful
Jer 23:5 . . . a King who *r-s* with wisdom.
Zech 6:13 . . . honor and will *r* as king
Rom 5:21 . . . as sin *r-d* over all people
Rom 15:12 . . . come, and he will *r* over
Col 3:15 . . . comes from Christ *r* in your
Rev 19:15 . . . He will *r* them with

**RULER, RULERS (n)**   person with authority; tribal chief; prince or king; city magistrate; powerful spiritual beings; God himself
Judg 8:22 . . . to Gideon, "Be our *r!*
1 Sam 10:1 . . . to be the *r* over Israel,
Prov 19:6 . . . favors from a *r;* everyone is
Prov 23:1 . . . with a *r,* pay attention to
Jer 30:21 . . . have their own *r* again,
Dan 7:27 . . . all *r-s* will serve and obey him.
Dan 9:25 . . . until a *r*—the Anointed One—
Mic 5:2 . . . a *r* of Israel will come from
Matt 2:6 . . . for a *r* will come from
Matt 20:25 . . . that the *r-s* in this world
John 12:31 . . . when Satan, the *r* of this
1 Cor 2:6 . . . or to the *r-s* of this world,
Eph 1:21 . . . far above any *r* or authority
Eph 3:10 . . . the unseen *r-s* and authorities
Eph 6:12 . . . but against evil *r-s* and
Col 1:16 . . . as thrones, kingdoms, *r-s,* and
Col 2:15 . . . disarmed the spiritual *r-s* and
Rev 1:5 . . . and the *r* of all the kings

**RUMORS (n)**   a statement or report without known authority for its truth
Exod 23:1 . . . must not pass along false *r.*
Prov 18:8 . . . *R* are dainty morsels that
Jer 51:46 . . . For *r* will keep coming year

**RUN, RUNNING (v)**   to go faster than a walk; to flee
Ps 19:5 . . . athlete eager to *r* the race.
Prov 4:12 . . . when you *r,* you won't
Isa 40:31 . . . will *r* and not grow weary.
1 Cor 9:26 . . . So I *r* with purpose in
Gal 2:2 . . . and I was *r-ning* the race for
Gal 5:7 . . . You were *r-ning* the race so
Phil 2:16 . . . that I did not *r* the race in
1 Tim 6:11 . . . so *r* from all these evil
2 Tim 2:22 . . . *R* from anything that
Heb 12:1 . . . let us *r* with endurance

**RUNNER (n)**   a messenger
Hab 2:2 . . . so that a *r* can carry

**RUST (n)**   the reddish brittle coating formed on iron
Matt 6:19 . . . them and *r* destroys them,

**SABAOTH (KJV)**
Rom 9:29 . . . LORD of *Heaven's Armies* had not
Jas 5:4 . . . the LORD of *Heaven's Armies*

**SABBATH, SABBATHS (n)**   cessation of activity; a holy day set aside to honor God through rest and worship
*see also* REST
Exod 20:8 . . . to observe the *S* day by
Exod 31:14 . . . must keep the *S* day, for it
Lev 25:2 . . . must observe a *S* rest before
Deut 5:12 . . . Observe the *S* day by
2 Chr 2:4 . . . morning and evening, on the *S-s,*
Isa 56:2 . . . who honor my *S* days of rest
Isa 56:6 . . . do not desecrate the *S* day
Isa 58:13 . . . Honor the *S* in everything
Matt 12:1 . . . some grainfields on the *S.*
Luke 13:10 . . . One *S* day as Jesus was
Col 2:16 . . . or new moon ceremonies or *S-s.*

**SACRIFICE, SACRIFICES (n)**   worship or atonement offering; something given up or lost
Exod 12:27 . . . It is the Passover *s* to the
1 Sam 15:22 . . . Obedience is better than *s,*
Ps 40:6 . . . no delight in *s-s* or offerings.
Ps 51:16 . . . do not desire a *s,* or I would

Ps 51:17 . . . The *s* you desire is
Ps 107:22 . . . offer *s-s* of thanksgiving
Prov 15:8 . . . LORD detests the *s* of
Hos 6:6 . . . to show love, not offer *s-s.*
Matt 9:13 . . . to show mercy, not offer *s-s.*
Rom 3:25 . . . Jesus as the *s* for sin.
Rom 8:3 . . . Son as a *s* for our sins.
Rom 12:1 . . . a living and holy *s*—the
Eph 5:2 . . . himself as a *s* for us,
Heb 5:3 . . . he must offer *s-s* for his own
Heb 7:27 . . . need to offer *s-s* every day.
Heb 9:28 . . . time as a *s* to take away
Heb 10:5 . . . did not want animal *s-s* or sin
Heb 10:10 . . . holy by the *s* of the body of
Heb 13:15 . . . Jesus a continual *s* of praise
Heb 13:16 . . . These are the *s-s* that please
1 Pet 2:5 . . . offer spiritual *s-s* that please
1 Jn 2:2 . . . himself is the *s* that atones
1 Jn 4:10 . . . his Son as a *s* to take away

**SACRIFICE, SACRIFICED, SACRIFICES (v)**   to suffer loss of, give up, renounce, injure, kill, or destroy, especially for an ideal, belief, or end
Gen 22:2 . . . Go and *s* him as a
John 10:11 . . . good shepherd *s-s* his life
John 10:15 . . . I *s* my life for the sheep.
1 Cor 5:7 . . . Lamb, has been *s-d* for us.
1 Cor 13:3 . . . poor and even *s-d* my body,

**SAFE (adj)**   free from harm or risk; secure from threat of danger, harm, or loss
Deut 29:19 . . . I am *s,* even though I am
1 Sam 30:23 . . . has kept us *s* and helped
Ps 4:8 . . . O LORD, will keep me *s.*
Ps 28:8 . . . He is a *s* fortress for his
Prov 2:11 . . . will keep you *s.*
Prov 4:26 . . . stay on the *s* path.
Prov 18:10 . . . run to him and are *s.*
Prov 28:26 . . . who walks in wisdom is *s.*
John 17:15 . . . keep them *s* from the evil

**SAFETY (n)**   the condition of being safe from undergoing or causing hurt, injury, or loss
Deut 33:12 . . . and live in *s* beside him.
2 Sam 23:5 . . . ensure my *s* and success.
Ps 16:9 . . . My body rests in *s.*
Ps 59:16 . . . my refuge, a place of *s*
Prov 11:14 . . . is *s* in having many advisers.
Prov 29:25 . . . trusting the LORD means *s.*
Hos 2:18 . . . live unafraid in peace and *s.*

**SAINTS (KJV)**
Ps 34:9 . . . you his *godly people,* for
Ps 97:10 . . . the lives of his *godly people*
Dan 7:18 . . . *holy people* of the Most High
1 Cor 6:2 . . . *we believers* will judge the
Rom 8:27 . . . Spirit pleads for *us believers*

**SALT (n)**   the mineral sodium chloride used mainly for seasoning and as a preservative
Gen 19:26 . . . she turned into a pillar of *s.*
Matt 5:13 . . . You are the *s* of the earth.

**SALVATION (n)**   deliverance from the power and effects of sin, danger, or difficulty by God's intervention
*see also* SAVE
2 Sam 22:47 . . . Rock of my *s,* be exalted!
2 Chr 6:41 . . . be clothed with *s;* may your
Ps 18:46 . . . God of my *s* be exalted!
Ps 27:1 . . . light and my *s*—so why should
Ps 40:16 . . . love your *s* repeatedly shout,
Ps 51:12 . . . joy of your *s,* and make me
Ps 62:2 . . . rock and my *s,* my fortress

Ps 69:13 . . . my prayer with your sure *s.*
Ps 74:12 . . . ages past, bringing *s* to
Ps 85:4 . . . us again, O God of our *s.*
Ps 89:26 . . . and the Rock of my *s.*
Ps 91:16 . . . long life and give them my *s.*
Ps 95:1 . . . joyfully to the Rock of our *s.*
Isa 25:9 . . . rejoice in the *s* he brings!
Isa 26:18 . . . We have not given *s* to the
Isa 33:6 . . . rich store of *s,* wisdom,
Isa 45:8 . . . wide so *s* and righteousness
Isa 45:22 . . . the world look to me for *s!*
Isa 49:6 . . . will bring my *s* to the ends
Isa 51:6 . . . but my *s* lasts forever.
Isa 52:7 . . . of peace and *s,* the news that
Isa 59:17 . . . the helmet of *s* on his head.
Isa 62:1 . . . dawn, and her *s* blazes like
Lam 3:26 . . . wait quietly for *s* from the
Jon 2:9 . . . For my *s* comes from the
Luke 1:77 . . . to find *s* through forgiveness
Luke 2:30 . . . I have seen your *s,*
Luke 3:6 . . . will see the *s* sent from
Luke 21:28 . . . up, for your *s* is near!
John 4:22 . . . him, for *s* comes through the
Acts 13:26 . . . this message of *s* has been
Acts 13:47 . . . Gentiles, to bring *s* to the
Acts 28:28 . . . know that this *s* from God
Rom 11:11 . . . so God made *s* available to
Rom 13:11 . . . for our *s* is nearer now
2 Cor 6:2 . . . the day of *s,* I helped you.
2 Cor 7:10 . . . from sin and results in *s.*
Eph 6:17 . . . Put on *s* as your helmet,
Phil 2:12 . . . show the results of your *s,*
2 Thes 2:13 . . . to experience *s*—a *s*
Titus 2:11 . . . bringing *s* to all people.
Heb 2:3 . . . if we ignore this great *s* that
Heb 5:9 . . . source of eternal *s* for all
Heb 9:28 . . . but to bring *s* to all who
1 Pet 1:9 . . . will be the *s* of your souls.
1 Pet 1:13 . . . to the gracious *s* that will
1 Pet 2:2 . . . into a full experience of *s.*
Rev 7:10 . . . a great roar, "*S* comes from

**SAMARITAN (n)**   a native or inhabitant of Samaria
Luke 10:33 . . . a despised *S* came along,
Luke 17:16 . . . man was a *S.*
John 4:5 . . . he came to the *S* village of
John 4:7 . . . a *S* woman came to draw

**SAMUEL**   Judge and prophet of Israel (Heb 11:32); prophet's birth and dedication (1 Sam 1); raised by Eli in the Temple (1 Sam 2:11, 18-21); called as a prophet (1 Sam 3); served as judge over Israel (1 Sam 7:15); warned Israel of the tyranny of kingship (1 Sam 8:10-18); anointed Saul (1 Sam 10:1); rejected Saul (1 Sam 15:23); anointed David (1 Sam 16:13); protected David from Saul (1 Sam 19:18-24); died (1 Sam 25:1); ghost of Samuel rebuked Saul (1 Sam 28:14-19).

**SANCTIFY, SANCTIFIED (KJV)**
Gen 2:3 . . . and *declared it holy*
Exod 31:13 . . . LORD, who *makes you holy*
Deut 5:12 . . . Sabbath day by *keeping it holy*
John 17:19 . . . myself as a *holy sacrifice*
Heb 10:10 . . . for us to be *made holy* by

**SANCTUARY (n)**   a holy place set apart for worship of God or refuge from danger
*see also* TABERNACLE, TEMPLE
Exod 25:8 . . . build me a holy *s* so I can
Lev 19:30 . . . show reverence toward my *s.*

Ps 27:5 . . . he will hide me in his *s*.
Ps 63:2 . . . you in your *s* and gazed upon
Ps 68:35 . . . God is awesome in his *s*.
Ps 150:1 . . . Praise God in his *s; praise
Heb 6:19 . . . curtain into God's inner *s*.

**SAND (n)** fine grains of rock which are worn
away by wind and rain
Gen 22:17 . . . in the sky and the *s* on
Matt 7:26 . . . who builds a house on *s*.

**SANDAL, SANDALS (n)** a shoe consisting of a
sole strapped to the foot
Exod 3:5 . . . Take off your *s-s*, for you are
Exod 12:11 . . . wear your *s-s*, and carry
Deut 25:9 . . . elders, pull his *s* from his
Josh 5:15 . . . Take off your *s-s*, for the
Ruth 4:7 . . . to remove his *s* and hand it
Matt 3:11 . . . his slave and carry his *s-s*.

**SANG (v)** *see also* SING
Exod 15:1 . . . people of Israel *s* this
Exod 15:21 . . . And Miriam *s* this song:
Num 21:17 . . . the Israelites *s* this song:
Judg 5:1 . . . son of Abinoam *s* this song:
2 Sam 22:1 . . . David *s* this song to
Ezra 3:11 . . . and thanks, they *s* this song
Job 38:7 . . . morning stars *s* together and
Ps 106:12 . . . Then they *s* his praise.
Matt 26:30 . . . Then they *s* a hymn
Rev 5:9 . . . And they *s* a new song
Rev 5:13 . . . They *s*: "Blessing and
Rev 14:3 . . . great choir *s* a wonderful

**SARAH (SARAI)** Wife of Abraham (Abram)
(Gen 11:30-31); was infertile (Gen 11:30; Rom
4:19) and very beautiful (Gen 12:11); with
Abraham, deceived Pharaoh (Gen 12:10-20);
dealings with Hagar and Ishmael (Gen 16);
name changed (Gen 17:15); Isaac promised
(Gen 18:10-15; Rom 9:9); example of faith (Heb
11:11); with Abraham, deceived Abimelech (Gen
20); Isaac born (Gen 21:1-7); Hagar and
Ishmael sent away (Gen 21:8-21); died and was
buried (Gen 23); Paul's analogy using Sarah and
Hagar (Gal 4:25-26).

**SATAN (n)** "adversary" of God and man; the
personal name of the devil
*see also* DEVIL
Job 1:6 . . . and the Accuser, *S*, came with
Zech 3:2 . . . your accusations, *S*. Yes,
Matt 12:26 . . . if *S* is casting out *S*, he
Matt 16:23 . . . Get away from me, *S!*
Mark 4:15 . . . only to have *S* come at once
Luke 10:18 . . . told them, "I saw *S* fall from
Luke 22:3 . . . Then *S* entered into Judas
Rom 16:20 . . . soon crush *S* under your
1 Cor 5:5 . . . him over to *S* so that his
2 Cor 11:14 . . . Even *S* disguises himself as
2 Cor 12:7 . . . from *S* to torment
1 Tim 1:20 . . . them over to *S* so they might
Rev 12:9 . . . the devil, or *S*, the one
Rev 20:2 . . . is the devil, *S*—and bound
Rev 20:7 . . . come to an end, *S* will be let

**SAVE, SAVED, SAVES, SAVING (v)** to rescue
or deliver from danger or harm; to deliver from
sin; to preserve or guard from injury,
destruction, or loss; to maintain or preserve
*see also* PRESERVE, RESCUE, SALVATION
2 Sam 22:3 . . . the power that *s-s* me,
1 Chr 16:23 . . . good news that he *s-s*.
Ps 7:10 . . . is my shield, *s-ing* those whose

Ps 18:48 . . . you *s* me from violent
Ps 22:8 . . . let the LORD *s* him!
Ps 25:5 . . . you are the God who *s-s* me.
Ps 33:16 . . . army cannot *s* a king, nor
Ps 34:6 . . . LORD listened; he *s-d* me
Ps 44:6 . . . not count on my sword to *s*
Ps 68:20 . . . Our God is a God who *s-s!*
Ps 109:31 . . . the needy, ready to *s* them
Ps 116:6 . . . death, and he *s-d* me.
Prov 2:16 . . . Wisdom will *s* you from
Prov 10:2 . . . right living can *s* your
Isa 25:9 . . . trusted in him, and he *s-d* us!
Isa 30:15 . . . resting in me will you be *s-d.*
Isa 35:4 . . . He is coming to *s* you.
Isa 59:1 . . . arm is not too weak to *s*
Isa 63:1 . . . who has the power to *s!*
Jer 4:14 . . . your heart that you may be *s-d.*
Jer 17:14 . . . if you *s* me, I will
Jer 51:9 . . . nothing can *s* her now.
Dan 3:17 . . . we serve is able to *s* us.
Joel 2:32 . . . name of the LORD will be *s-d,*
Mic 7:7 . . . wait confidently for God to *s*
Zeph 1:18 . . . gold will not *s* you
Matt 1:21 . . . he will *s* his people
Matt 16:25 . . . my sake, you will *s* it.
Matt 24:13 . . . to the end will be *s-d.*
Luke 17:33 . . . life go, you will *s* it.
Luke 19:10 . . . seek and *s* those who are
John 10:9 . . . in through me will be *s-d.*
John 12:47 . . . I have come to *s* the world
Acts 2:21 . . . name of the LORD will be *s-d.*
Acts 4:12 . . . by which we must be *s-d.*
Acts 15:11 . . . we are all *s-d* the same way,
Acts 16:30 . . . what must I do to be *s-d?*
Rom 1:16 . . . God at work, *s-ing* everyone
Rom 5:9 . . . he will certainly *s* us from
Rom 10:9 . . . the dead, you will be *s-d.*
Rom 10:13 . . . of the LORD will be *s-d.*
1 Cor 1:18 . . . we who are being *s-d* know
1 Cor 5:5 . . . himself will be *s-d* on the
1 Cor 7:16 . . . wives might be *s-d* because
1 Cor 10:33 . . . so that many may be *s-d.*
1 Cor 15:2 . . . this Good News that *s-s*
Eph 1:13 . . . Good News that God *s-s* you.
1 Thes 5:9 . . . God chose to *s* us through
1 Tim 1:15 . . . the world to *s* sinners
1 Tim 2:4 . . . wants everyone to be *s-d* and
1 Tim 2:15 . . . women will be *s-d* through
2 Tim 1:9 . . . For God *s-d* us and called
Titus 3:5 . . . he *s-d* us, not because of the
Heb 7:25 . . . and forever, to *s* those who
Jas 5:20 . . . sinner back will *s* that person
2 Pet 3:15 . . . gives people time to be *s-d.*

**SAVING (adj)** of or relating to delivering or
rescuing
Ps 40:10 . . . faithfulness and *s* power.
Ps 67:2 . . . the earth, your *s* power
Ps 69:29 . . . God, by your *s* power.
Ps 71:15 . . . proclaim your *s* power,
Ps 98:1 . . . has shown his *s* power!

**SAVIOR (n)** one who delivers from trouble, sin,
or judgment
2 Sam 22:2 . . . my fortress, and my *s;*
Ps 38:22 . . . help me, O LORD my *s*.
Ps 40:17 . . . You are my helper and my *s.*
Ps 106:21 . . . They forgot God, their *s*,
Isa 43:11 . . . and there is no other *S.*
Isa 45:21 . . . a righteous God and *S.*
Isa 49:26 . . . the LORD, am your *S* and
Isa 62:11 . . . Look, your *S* is coming.

Jer 14:8 . . . Hope of Israel, our *S* in
Hos 13:4 . . . for there is no other *s*.
Zeph 3:17 . . . He is a mighty *s*.
Luke 1:47 . . . rejoices in God my *S!*
Luke 1:69 . . . He has sent us a mighty *S*
John 4:42 . . . he is indeed the *S* of the
Acts 5:31 . . . right hand as Prince and *S.*
Acts 13:23 . . . God's promised *S* of Israel!
Eph 5:23 . . . He is the *S* of his body,
1 Tim 2:3 . . . good and pleases God our *S,*
1 Tim 4:10 . . . who is the *S* of all people
Titus 2:10 . . . about God our *S* attractive
Titus 3:4 . . . When God our *S* revealed his
2 Pet 3:2 . . . Lord and *S* commanded
1 Jn 4:14 . . . Son to be the *S* of the world.

**SCAPEGOAT (n)** a goat upon whose head are
symbolically placed the sins of the people, after
which he is sent into the wilderness on the Day
of Atonement
Lev 16:10 . . . other goat, the *s* chosen by

**SCARLET (adj)** of the color of any various
bright reds
Josh 2:21 . . . leaving the *s* rope hanging
Isa 1:18 . . . sins are like *s*, I will make
Matt 27:28 . . . and put a *s* robe on him.

**SCATTER, SCATTERED (v)** to separate and go
in various directions; to disperse
Deut 4:27 . . . the LORD will *s* you
Neh 1:8 . . . to me, I will *s* you among
Isa 11:12 . . . will gather the *s-ed* people
Jer 9:16 . . . I will *s* them around
Jer 30:11 . . . where I have *s-ed* you, but I
Jer 31:10 . . . LORD, who *s-ed* his people,
Ezek 34:21 . . . flock until you *s-ed* them to
Zech 2:6 . . . for I have *s-ed* you to the four
Zech 10:9 . . . Though I have *s-ed* them like
Zech 13:7 . . . sheep will be *s-ed*, and I will
Matt 26:31 . . . of the flock will be *s-ed*
John 11:52 . . . children of God *s-ed* around
Acts 8:4 . . . were *s-ed* preached the Good
Jas 1:1 . . . Jewish believers *s-ed* abroad.

**SCEPTER (n)** the official staff of a ruler,
symbolizing his authority and power
Gen 49:10 . . . The *s* will not depart from
Num 24:17 . . . a *s* will emerge from Israel.
Heb 1:8 . . . rule with a *s* of justice.

**SCOFF, SCOFFING (v)** to show contempt by
derisive acts or language; to mock
Lam 2:15 . . . They *s* and insult
Ps 123:4 . . . fill of the *s-ing* of the proud
1 Thes 5:20 . . . Do not *s* at prophecies,
2 Pet 2:12 . . . They *s* at things they do not
Jude 1:8 . . . defy authority, and *s* at

**SCORN (n)** open dislike, disrespect, or derision
often mixed with indignation
Ps 109:25 . . . they shake their heads in *s*.
Isa 51:7 . . . not be afraid of people's *s*,

**SCORN, SCORNED (v)** to reject or dismiss as
contemptible or unworthy
Ps 22:6 . . . I am *s-ed* and despised by all!
Ps 119:22 . . . Don't let them *s* and insult
Prov 9:12 . . . If you *s* wisdom, you will
Jer 6:10 . . . They *s* the word of the LORD.

**SCRIPTURE, SCRIPTURES (n)** the Law; the
writings of Moses; the entire collection of
sacred books
Matt 21:16 . . . you ever read the *S-s?*

Matt 22:29 . . . you don't know the **S-s,**
Luke 24:27 . . . from all the **S-s** the things
Luke 24:45 . . . to understand the **S-s.**
John 2:22 . . . believed both the **S-s** and
John 5:39 . . . You search the **S-s** because
John 7:42 . . . the **S-s** clearly state that
John 10:35 . . . know that the **S-s** cannot
Acts 8:32 . . . The passage of **S** he had
1 Cor 4:6 . . . quoted from the **S-s,** you
    won't
1 Tim 4:13 . . . focus on reading the **S-s** to
2 Tim 3:16 . . . All **S** is inspired by God
Heb 10:7 . . . written about me in the **S-s.**
2 Pet 1:20 . . . no prophecy in **S** ever came
2 Pet 3:16 . . . do with other parts of **S.**

**SCROLL (n)**  a roll (as of papyrus, leather,
or parchment) for writing a document
Isa 34:4 . . . disappear like a rolled-up **s.**
Ezek 3:1 . . . giving you—eat this **s!**
Rev 6:14 . . . sky was rolled up like a **s,**
Rev 10:8 . . . take the open **s** from the hand

**SEA, SEAS (n)**  a great body of salt water that
covers much of the earth
Exod 14:16 . . . middle of the **s** on dry
Deut 30:13 . . . not kept beyond the **s,**
Job 11:9 . . . and wider than the **s.**
Ps 93:4 . . . violent raging of the **s-s,**
Ps 95:5 . . . The **s** belongs to him,
Eccl 11:1 . . . your grain across the **s-s,**
Isa 57:20 . . . like the restless **s,** which
Jon 1:4 . . . wind over the **s,** causing a
Hab 2:14 . . . waters fill the **s,** the earth
Matt 18:6 . . . in the depths of the **s.**
Jas 1:6 . . . wave of the **s** that is blown
Jude 1:13 . . . waves of the **s,** churning up
Rev 10:2 . . . right foot on the **s** and
Rev 13:1 . . . rising up out of the **s.**
Rev 20:13 . . . The **s** gave up its dead,
Rev 21:1 . . . And the **s** was also gone.

**SEARCH, SEARCHES (v)**  to investigate or
examine thoroughly in an effort to find or verify
something
Ps 34:14 . . . **S** for peace, and work
Ps 139:23 . . . **S** me, O God, and know
Eccl 3:6 . . . A time to **s** and a time to
Jer 17:10 . . . I, the LORD, **s** all hearts
1 Cor 2:10 . . . Spirit **s-es** out everything
1 Pet 3:11 . . . **S** for peace, and work

**SEAT, SEATS (n)**  a chair, stool, or bench
intended to be sat in or on
Luke 11:43 . . . to sit in the **s-s** of honor
Luke 14:9 . . . to take whatever **s** is left

**SEATED (v)**  to put into a sitting position; to take
one's seat or place
Matt 26:64 . . . Son of Man **s** in the place
Luke 22:69 . . . of Man will be **s** in the place
Eph 1:20 . . . the dead and **s** him in the
Eph 2:6 . . . with Christ and **s** us with him
Heb 12:2 . . . Now he is **s** in the place of
Rev 14:14 . . . a white cloud, and **s** on the

**SECRET (adj)**  kept from knowledge or view;
hidden
Ps 90:8 . . . before you—our **s** sins—
Jer 23:24 . . . me in a **s** place?
Matt 10:26 . . . all that is **s** will be
Rom 2:16 . . . judge everyone's **s** life.
Rom 16:25 . . . a plan kept **s** from the
1 Cor 13:2 . . . all of God's **s** plans

1 Cor 14:25 . . . their **s** thoughts will be
Col 1:26 . . . was kept **s** for centuries and

**SECRET, SECRETS (n)**  something kept hidden
or unexplained; something kept from the
knowledge of others or shared only
confidentially with a few
*see also* MYSTERY
Deut 29:29 . . . God has **s-s** known to no
Judg 16:15 . . . don't share your **s-s** with
Ps 44:21 . . . he knows the **s-s** of every
Prov 11:13 . . . goes around telling **s-s,**
Dan 2:28 . . . heaven who reveals **s-s,** and
Dan 2:29 . . . who reveals **s-s** has shown
Mark 4:11 . . . to understand the **s**
Mark 4:22 . . . and every **s** will be brought
Luke 8:10 . . . to understand the **s-s** of
1 Cor 15:51 . . . reveal to you a wonderful **s.**
Phil 4:12 . . . have learned the **s** of living
Col 1:27 . . . the **s:** Christ lives in you.

**SEE, SEEING, SEES (v)**  to perceive by the eye;
to understand or recognize; to come to know
Ps 34:8 . . . Taste and **s** that the
Ps 36:2 . . . they cannot **s** how wicked
Ps 90:8 . . . sins—and you **s** them
Ps 119:82 . . . straining to **s** your promises
Prov 5:21 . . . For the LORD **s-s** clearly
Prov 13:19 . . . pleasant to **s** dreams come
Eccl 3:11 . . . people cannot **s** the whole
Matt 6:18 . . . Father, who **s-s** everything,
John 12:45 . . . you are **s-ing** the one who
Rom 1:20 . . . can clearly **s** his invisible
Rom 7:13 . . . So we can **s** how terrible sin
1 Cor 13:12 . . . we will **s** everything with
2 Cor 4:18 . . . things we cannot **s** will last
2 Cor 5:7 . . . by believing and not by **s-ing.**
2 Cor 8:21 . . . everyone else to **s** that we
Phil 4:5 . . . Let everyone **s** that you are
Col 1:16 . . . things we can't **s**—such as
Rev 1:7 . . . everyone will **s** him—even

**SEED, SEEDS (n)**  the grains of plants used for
sowing
Gen 1:11 . . . These **s-s** will then produce
Prov 11:30 . . . The **s-s** of good deeds
Matt 13:3 . . . went out to plant some **s-s.**
Matt 13:31 . . . like a mustard **s** planted in
Matt 17:20 . . . as a mustard **s,** you could say
Mark 4:15 . . . The **s** that fell on
Luke 8:12 . . . The **s-s** that fell on
1 Cor 3:6 . . . I planted the **s** in your
2 Cor 9:6 . . . few **s-s** will get a small
2 Cor 9:10 . . . one who provides **s** for the

**SEEK, SEEKING, SEEKS (v)**  to go in search of;
to ask for; to try to acquire or gain
2 Chr 7:14 . . . pray and **s** my face and
2 Chr 15:2 . . . Whenever you **s** him,
Prov 3:6 . . . **S** his will in all you do,
Prov 25:27 . . . not good to **s** honors
Prov 29:26 . . . Many **s** the ruler's favor,
Isa 55:6 . . . **S** the LORD while you can
Hos 10:12 . . . time to **s** the LORD,
Zeph 2:3 . . . **S** the LORD, all who are
Matt 6:33 . . . **S** the Kingdom of God above
Matt 7:7 . . . Keep on **s-ing,** and you
Matt 7:8 . . . Everyone who **s-s,** finds.
Luke 12:31 . . . **S** the Kingdom of God
Luke 19:10 . . . Son of Man came to **s** and
Rom 3:11 . . . no one is **s-ing** God.
1 Cor 7:27 . . . have a wife, do not **s** to get
Heb 11:6 . . . those who sincerely **s** him.

**SELF-CONTROL (n)**  restraint exercised over
one's own impulses, emotions, or desires
Prov 5:23 . . . He will die for lack of **s;**
Prov 16:32 . . . better to have **s** than to
Acts 24:25 . . . righteousness and **s** and the
Gal 5:23 . . . gentleness, and **s.** There is no
1 Tim 3:2 . . . must exercise **s,** live wisely,
1 Tim 3:11 . . . They must exercise **s** and be
Titus 2:2 . . . older men to exercise **s,**
1 Pet 1:13 . . . think clearly and exercise **s.**
2 Pet 1:6 . . . and knowledge with **s,** and

**SELF-DISCIPLINE (n)**  correction or regulation
of oneself for the sake of improvement
2 Tim 1:7 . . . but of power, love, and **s.**

**SELFISH (adj)**  seeking or concentrating on
one's own advantage, pleasure, or well-being
without regard for others
Matt 16:24 . . . turn from your **s** ways,
Luke 9:23 . . . turn from your **s** ways,
Gal 5:20 . . . of anger, **s** ambition,
Phil 1:17 . . . They preach with **s** ambition,
Jas 3:14 . . . and there is **s** ambition in
Jas 3:16 . . . is jealousy and **s** ambition,

**SELL, SELLING (v)**  to give up (property) to
another for something of value (as money)
Prov 23:23 . . . truth and never **s** it;
Prov 31:24 . . . and sashes to **s** to the
Mark 10:21 . . . and **s** all your possessions
Luke 17:28 . . . buying and **s-ing,** farming and
Rev 13:17 . . . could buy or **s** anything

**SEND, SENDING (v)**  to direct, order, or request
to go
*see also* SENT
Isa 6:8 . . . Here I am. **S** me.
Isa 55:11 . . . with my word. **S** it out,
Mal 3:1 . . . I am **s-ing** my messenger,
Matt 9:38 . . . ask him to **s** more workers
Mark 1:2 . . . I am **s-ing** my messenger
1 Cor 1:17 . . . For Christ didn't **s** me to

**SENSE (n)**  sound and prudent judgment based
on a simple perception of the situation or facts;
intelligence
Prov 3:21 . . . common **s** and discernment.
Prov 8:14 . . . Common **s** and success
Prov 12:11 . . . chases fantasies has no **s.**
Prov 15:21 . . . brings joy to those with no **s;**
Prov 18:1 . . . they lash out at common **s.**
Prov 24:30 . . . of one with no common **s.**

**SENSIBLE (adj)**  having, containing, or
indicative of good sense or reason; rational,
reasonable
Prov 10:23 . . . brings pleasure to the **s.**
Prov 11:12 . . . a **s** person keeps quiet.
Prov 15:21 . . . **s** person stays on the right
Matt 24:45 . . . A faithful, **s** servant is one

**SENT (v)**  *see* also SEND
Exod 3:14 . . . I AM has **s** me.
Matt 10:40 . . . the Father who **s** me.
Luke 10:16 . . . God, who **s** me.
John 3:17 . . . God **s** his Son into the
John 20:21 . . . As the Father has **s** me, so
Rom 8:3 . . . He **s** his own Son in a
Rom 10:15 . . . them without being **s?**
Gal 4:4 . . . time came, God **s** his Son,

**SEPARATE, SEPARATED, SEPARATES (v)**  to
set or keep apart; to sort
Prov 17:9 . . . on it **s-s** close friends.

Matt 25:32 . . . a shepherd *s-s* the sheep
Rom 8:35 . . . Can anything ever *s* us
Eph 2:14 . . . of hostility that *s-d* us.
Col 1:21 . . . his enemies, *s-d* from him

**SERAPHIM (n)** six-winged angels standing in the presence of God
Isa 6:2 . . . were mighty *s,* each having
Isa 6:6 . . . Then one of the *s* flew to me

**SERPENT (n)** a snake or crawling reptile often associated with temptation, sin, and evil; Satan
Gen 3:1 . . . The *s* was the shrewdest of
Isa 27:1 . . . *s,* the coiling, writhing *s.*
2 Cor 11:3 . . . the cunning ways of the *s.*
Rev 12:9 . . . the ancient *s* called the devil,
Rev 20:2 . . . that old *s,* who is the devil,

**SERVANT, SERVANTS (n)** one who performs tasks under the direction of another
*see also* SLAVE(S)
Exod 14:31 . . . LORD and in his *s* Moses.
Lev 25:55 . . . They are my *s-s,* whom I
1 Sam 3:10 . . . Speak, your *s* is listening.
2 Kgs 17:13 . . . my *s-s* the prophets.
Job 1:8 . . . Have you noticed my *s* Job?
Ps 19:13 . . . Keep your *s* from deliberate
Ps 31:16 . . . your favor shine on your *s.*
Ps 89:3 . . . with David, my chosen *s.*
Ps 104:4 . . . flames of fire are your *s-s.*
Prov 14:35 . . . king rejoices in wise *s-s*
Prov 17:2 . . . A wise *s* will rule
Prov 22:7 . . . so the borrower is *s* to the
Prov 31:15 . . . work for her *s* girls.
Eccl 7:21 . . . may hear your *s* curse you.
Eccl 10:7 . . . seen *s* riding horseback
Isa 53:11 . . . my righteous *s* will make it
Isa 65:8 . . . I still have true *s-s* there.
Zech 3:8 . . . to bring my *s,* the Branch.
Mal 1:6 . . . father, and a *s* respects his
Matt 20:26 . . . among you must be your *s,*
Matt 24:45 . . . faithful, sensible *s* is one
Luke 1:48 . . . of his lowly *s* girl, and
Luke 17:10 . . . We are unworthy *s-s* who
Luke 22:26 . . . leader should be like a *s.*
John 12:26 . . . because my *s-s* must be
Rom 13:4 . . . authorities are God's *s-s,*
1 Cor 3:5 . . . are only God's *s-s* through
Col 1:23 . . . God's *s* to proclaim it.
1 Tim 4:6 . . . be a worthy *s* of Christ
Heb 1:7 . . . his *s-s* like flames of fire.
Heb 1:14 . . . angels are only *s-s*—spirits

**SERVE, SERVED, SERVES, SERVING (v)** to meet the needs of and subject one's will to that of another
Deut 10:12 . . . love him and *s* him with
Deut 11:13 . . . your God and *s* him with
Deut 28:47 . . . If you do not *s* the LORD
Deut 30:17 . . . drawn away to *s* and
Josh 24:15 . . . family, we will *s* the LORD.
2 Chr 12:8 . . . between *s-ing* me and
Ps 34:22 . . . redeem those who *s* him.
Ps 101:6 . . . be allowed to *s* me.
Ps 103:21 . . . of angels who *s* him and do
Isa 38:3 . . . have *s-d* you single-mindedly
Dan 3:17 . . . the God whom we *s* is able to
Matt 4:10 . . . your God and *s* only him.
Matt 6:24 . . . No one can *s* two masters.
Matt 20:28 . . . not to be *s-d* but to *s*
Luke 22:27 . . . among you as one who *s-s.*
John 12:2 . . . Martha *s-d,* and Lazarus was

John 12:26 . . . honor anyone who *s-s* me.
Acts 17:25 . . . hands can't *s* his needs—
Rom 1:25 . . . worshiped and *s-d* the things
Rom 12:7 . . . your gift is *s-ing* others, *s*
Rom 12:11 . . . work hard and *s* the Lord
Rom 13:6 . . . They are *s-ing* God in what
Rom 14:18 . . . If you *s* Christ with
Rom 16:18 . . . people are not *s-ing* Christ
1 Cor 16:18 . . . to all who *s* so well.
Gal 5:13 . . . your freedom to *s* one another
Col 3:24 . . . Master you are *s-ing* is Christ.
1 Tim 5:10 . . . kind to strangers and *s-d* other
1 Pet 5:5 . . . all of you, *s* each other in

**SEVEN (adj)** of or relating to the number 7
Josh 6:4 . . . around the town *s* times, with
Prov 6:16 . . . LORD hates—no, *s* things
Prov 24:16 . . . godly may trip *s* times,
Isa 4:1 . . . so few men will be left that *s*
Luke 11:26 . . . spirit finds *s* other spirits
Rev 1:4 . . . John to the *s* churches in the
Rev 6:1 . . . first of the *s* seals on the
Rev 8:2 . . . were given *s* trumpets.
Rev 10:4 . . . what the *s* thunders said,
Rev 15:7 . . . handed each of the *s* angels

**SEXUAL (adj)** of, relating to, or associated with sex or the sexes; having or involving sex
Exod 22:19 . . . who has *s* relations with
Lev 18:6 . . . never have *s* relations with
Num 25:1 . . . by having *s* relations with
Matt 1:25 . . . did not have *s* relations with
Matt 15:19 . . . adultery, all *s* immorality,
Acts 15:20 . . . to idols, from *s* immorality,
1 Cor 5:1 . . . about the *s* immorality going
1 Cor 5:11 . . . yet indulges in *s* sin
1 Cor 6:9 . . . who indulge in *s* sin, or who
1 Cor 6:18 . . . Run from *s* sin! No other
1 Cor 7:1 . . . to abstain from *s* relations.
1 Cor 10:8 . . . not engage in *s* immorality
2 Cor 12:21 . . . impurity, *s* immorality,
Eph 5:3 . . . be no *s* immorality, impurity,
Col 3:5 . . . nothing to do with *s* immorality,
1 Thes 4:3 . . . stay away from all *s* sin
2 Pet 2:10 . . . own twisted *s* desire, and
2 Pet 2:18 . . . to twisted *s* desires,
Rev 2:14 . . . and by committing *s* sin.
Rev 2:20 . . . teaches them to commit *s* sin

**SHADOW, SHADOWS (n)** shelter from danger or observation; an imperfect and faint representation; partial darkness or obscurity within a part of space
Ps 17:8 . . . me in the *s* of your wings.
Ps 36:7 . . . shelter in the *s* of your
Ps 39:6 . . . are merely moving *s-s,* and
Ps 91:1 . . . find rest in the *s* of the
Col 2:17 . . . these rules are only *s-s* of
Heb 8:5 . . . only a copy, a *s* of the real
Heb 10:1 . . . was only a *s,* a dim preview

**SHAME (n)** a condition or feeling of humiliating disgrace or disrepute; something that brings censure and reproach
Lev 19:12 . . . Do not bring *s* on the name
Ps 34:5 . . . no shadow of *s* will darken
Prov 28:7 . . . wild friends bring *s* to
Dan 12:2 . . . some to *s* and everlasting
Titus 2:5 . . . not bring *s* on the word
Heb 6:6 . . . holding him up to public *s.*
1 Jn 2:28 . . . shrink back from him in *s.*

**SHAME (v)** to disgrace
1 Cor 1:27 . . . in order to *s* those who
1 Cor 11:22 . . . church and *s* the poor?

**SHAMEFUL (adj)** bringing shame
Prov 18:13 . . . facts is both *s* and foolish.
Hab 2:15 . . . over their *s* nakedness.
Rom 1:24 . . . do whatever *s* things their
Rom 1:27 . . . Men did *s* things with
2 Cor 4:2 . . . We reject all *s* deeds
2 Pet 2:2 . . . teaching and *s* immorality.

**SHARE (n)** a portion belonging to or due to
Deut 10:9 . . . Levites have no *s* of property
2 Kgs 2:9 . . . inherit a double *s* of your
Matt 21:34 . . . to collect his *s* of the crop.
Rev 22:19 . . . remove that person's *s* in

**SHARE, SHARED, SHARING (v)** to grant or give a share in; to partake of, use, experience, occupy, or enjoy with others; to have in common
Gen 21:10 . . . to *s* the inheritance
1 Sam 30:24 . . . We *s* and *s* alike—
Ps 41:9 . . . the one who *s-d* my food,
Luke 3:11 . . . If you have food, *s* it with
Acts 2:42 . . . fellowship, and to *s-ing* in
Acts 2:45 . . . possessions and *s-d* the
Rom 8:17 . . . we must also *s* his suffering.
Rom 11:31 . . . they, too, will *s* in God's
1 Cor 10:16 . . . aren't we *s-ing* in the blood
1 Cor 12:13 . . . we all *s* the same Spirit.
2 Cor 1:7 . . . as you *s* in our sufferings,
2 Cor 9:8 . . . left over to *s* with others.
Gal 4:30 . . . will not *s* the inheritance
Gal 6:6 . . . teachers, *s-ing* all good things
Phil 3:10 . . . suffer with him, *s-ing* in his
Col 1:12 . . . has enabled you to *s* in the
1 Thes 2:8 . . . much that we *s-d* with you
2 Thes 2:14 . . . you can *s* in the glory
1 Tim 6:18 . . . ready to *s* with others.
Heb 6:4 . . . and *s-d* in the Holy Spirit,
Heb 12:10 . . . we might *s* in his holiness.
Heb 13:16 . . . to *s* with those in need.
Rev 3:20 . . . and we will *s* a meal together

**SHEARERS (n)** one who cuts or clips (as hair or wool) from someone or something
Isa 53:7 . . . silent before the *s,* he did
Acts 8:32 . . . silent before the *s,* he did

**SHEEP (n)** a small domesticated animal, representing wealth and livelihood for many Israelites; figurative of God's people
Gen 22:8 . . . God will provide a *s* for
Num 27:17 . . . not be like *s* without a
Deut 17:1 . . . defective cattle, *s,* or
1 Sam 15:14 . . . bleating of *s* and goats
Ps 44:22 . . . being slaughtered like *s.*
Ps 78:52 . . . people like a flock of *s,*
Ps 100:3 . . . We are his people, the *s*
Ps 119:176 . . . wandered away like a lost *s;*
Isa 53:7 . . . as a *s* is silent before
Jer 50:6 . . . people have been lost *s.*
Matt 7:15 . . . disguised as harmless *s* but
Matt 9:36 . . . like *s* without a shepherd.
Matt 10:16 . . . you out as *s* among wolves.
Matt 12:11 . . . a *s* that fell into a well
Matt 25:32 . . . separates the *s* from the
John 10:3 . . . calls his own *s* by name
John 10:7 . . . I am the gate for the *s.*
John 10:15 . . . sacrifice my life for the *s.*
John 21:17 . . . Then feed my *s.*
1 Pet 2:25 . . . were like *s* who wandered

**SHELTER, SHELTERS (n)** something that covers or affords protection
*see also* REFUGE
Lev 23:34 . . . the Festival of *S-s* on the
Deut 16:16 . . . the Festival of *S-s.*
Ps 9:9 . . . LORD is a *s* for the
Ps 31:20 . . . hide them in the *s* of your
Ps 36:7 . . . All humanity finds *s* in the
Ps 61:4 . . . safe beneath the *s* of your
Isa 4:6 . . . will be a *s* from daytime heat
Isa 32:2 . . . be like a *s* from the wind
Isa 58:7 . . . give *s* to the homeless.
Zech 14:16 . . . the Festival of *S-s.*

**SHEPHERD, SHEPHERDS (n)** a person who tends sheep; figurative of political and religious leaders, especially those who care for God's people
Gen 48:15 . . . has been my *s* all my life,
Gen 49:24 . . . by the *S,* the Rock of Israel.
Num 27:17 . . . be like sheep without a *s.*
2 Sam 7:7 . . . tribal leaders, the *s-s* of my
1 Kgs 22:17 . . . like sheep without a *s.*
Ps 23:1 . . . The LORD is my *s;*
Ps 28:9 . . . Lead them like a *s,* and
Isa 40:11 . . . feed his flock like a *s.*
Jer 23:1 . . . my people—the *s-s* of my
Jer 31:10 . . . as a *s* does his flock.
Ezek 34:5 . . . scattered without a *s,* and
Ezek 34:8 . . . you were my *s-s,* you didn't
Ezek 34:12 . . . like a *s* looking for his
Zech 11:9 . . . won't be your *s* any longer.
Zech 13:7 . . . Strike down the *s,* and
Matt 2:6 . . . will be the *s* for my people
Matt 9:36 . . . like sheep without a *s.*
Matt 26:31 . . . God will strike the *S,*
John 10:11 . . . I am the good *s.*
Acts 20:28 . . . Feed and *s* God's flock—
Heb 13:20 . . . Jesus, the great *S* of the
Jude 1:12 . . . are like shameless *s-s* who care
Rev 7:17 . . . on the throne will be their *S.*

**SHIELD (n)** a broad piece of defensive armor carried on the arm; one that protects or defends
2 Sam 22:3 . . . He is my *s,* the power that
2 Sam 22:36 . . . me your *s* of victory;
Ps 3:3 . . . LORD, are a *s* around me;
Ps 5:12 . . . them with your *s* of love.
Ps 7:10 . . . God is my *s,* saving those
Ps 18:2 . . . He is my *s,* the power that
Ps 28:7 . . . LORD is my strength and *s.*
Ps 33:20 . . . is our help and our *s.*
Ps 35:2 . . . armor, and take up your *s.*
Ps 84:11 . . . God is our sun and our *s.*
Ps 119:114 . . . are my refuge and my *s;*
Ps 144:2 . . . He is my *s,* and I take refuge
Prov 2:7 . . . He is a *s* to those who walk
Eph 6:16 . . . hold up the *s* of faith

**SHINE, SHINES, SHINING (v)** to emit rays of light; to be eminent, conspicuous, or distinguished; to have a bright, glowing appearance
Ps 37:6 . . . of your cause will *s* like
Ps 50:2 . . . God *s-s* in glorious radiance.
Ps 112:4 . . . Light *s-s* in the darkness for
Ps 118:27 . . . LORD is God, *s-ing* upon us.
Isa 60:1 . . . Let your light *s* for all
Ezek 1:27 . . . like a burning flame, *s-ing*
Dan 2:31 . . . you a huge, *s-ing* statue of a
Dan 12:3 . . . righteousness will *s* like
Matt 13:43 . . . the righteous will *s* like

John 1:5 . . . The light *s-s* in the darkness,
Rom 13:12 . . . put on the *s-ing* armor of
2 Cor 4:6 . . . has made this light *s* in
Phil 2:15 . . . of God, *s-ing* like bright lights

**SHORT (adj)** brief; not coming up to a measure or requirement
Ps 89:47 . . . Remember how *s* my life is,
Rom 3:23 . . . all fall *s* of God's glorious
1 Cor 7:29 . . . time that remains is very *s.*

**SHOULDERS (n)** the place on the human body where the arm is joined to the trunk
Isa 9:6 . . . government will rest on his *s.*
Luke 15:5 . . . carry it home on his *s.*

**SHOUT, SHOUTED, SHOUTING (v)** to utter a loud cry or in a loud voice
Job 38:7 . . . all the angels *s-ed* for joy?
Ps 95:1 . . . Let us *s* joyfully to
Ps 100:1 . . . *S* with joy to the LORD,
Isa 12:6 . . . people of Jerusalem *s* his
Isa 40:3 . . . someone *s-ing,* "Clear the way
Isa 40:9 . . . news, *s* from the mountaintops!
Isa 42:2 . . . He will not *s* or raise his
Zech 9:9 . . . people of Zion! *S* in triumph,
Matt 3:3 . . . a voice *s-ing* in the wilderness,
Matt 10:27 . . . *s* from the housetops for

**SHOW (n)** an impressive display
Matt 23:5 . . . Everything they do is for *s.*

**SHOW, SHOWED, SHOWN, SHOWS (v)** to cause or permit to be seen; to point out; to reveal or demonstrate; to bestow
Exod 33:18 . . . Then *s* me your glorious
2 Sam 22:26 . . . To the faithful you *s*
Neh 9:19 . . . pillar of fire *s-ed* them the
Ps 4:6 . . . Who will *s* us better times?
Ps 16:11 . . . You will *s* me the way
Ps 119:132 . . . Come and *s* me your
Prov 3:6 . . . he will *s* you which path
Prov 24:23 . . . wrong to *s* favoritism
Eccl 9:1 . . . God will *s* them favor.
Isa 30:18 . . . so he can *s* you his love
Hos 6:6 . . . I want you to *s* love, not
Zech 7:9 . . . Judge fairly, and *s* mercy
Luke 24:40 . . . *s-ed* them his hands and his
Acts 2:28 . . . You have *s-n* me the way
Acts 10:34 . . . that God *s-s* no favoritism.
Rom 3:20 . . . The law simply *s-s* us how
Rom 3:21 . . . But now God has *s-n* us a way
Rom 5:8 . . . God *s-ed* his great love for us
Rom 9:22 . . . the right to *s* his anger
Eph 2:7 . . . as *s-n* in all he has done
Jas 2:18 . . . I will *s* you my faith
1 Jn 4:9 . . . God *s-ed* how much he loved

**SHUT (v)** to close
Isa 6:10 . . . their ears and *s* their eyes.
Dan 6:22 . . . his angel to *s* the lions'
Amos 5:13 . . . keep their mouths *s,* for it
Heb 11:33 . . . They *s* the mouths of lions,

**SICK (adj)** affected with disease or ill health; lacking vigor
Ps 41:3 . . . when they are *s* and restores
Prov 13:12 . . . deferred makes the heart *s,*
Matt 9:12 . . . need a doctor—*s* people do.
Matt 10:8 . . . Heal the *s,* raise the dead,
Matt 25:36 . . . I was *s,* and you cared for
Mark 3:10 . . . all the *s* people eagerly
1 Cor 11:30 . . . many of you are weak and *s*
Jas 5:14 . . . Are any of you *s?*

**SICKNESS, SICKNESSES (n)** a disordered, weakened, or unsound condition; illness
Matt 4:24 . . . whatever their *s* or disease,
Matt 8:17 . . . He took our *s-es* and removed

**SIGN, SIGNS (n)** something indicating the presence or existence of something else; something material or external that stands for or signifies something spiritual
Gen 9:12 . . . you a *s* of my covenant
Gen 17:11 . . . your foreskin as a *s* of
Ps 105:27 . . . performed miraculous *s-s*
Isa 55:13 . . . be an everlasting *s* of
Dan 6:27 . . . he performs miraculous *s-s* and
Matt 12:38 . . . a miraculous *s* to prove
Matt 24:3 . . . What *s* will signal your
Matt 24:30 . . . the *s* that the Son of Man
Mark 16:17 . . . These miraculous *s-s* will
Luke 11:29 . . . them is the *s* of Jonah.
John 3:2 . . . Your miraculous *s-s* are
John 20:30 . . . do many other miraculous *s-s*
1 Cor 14:22 . . . in tongues is a *s,* not for
2 Cor 12:12 . . . did many *s-s* and wonders
2 Thes 2:9 . . . counterfeit power and *s-s*

**SILENCE (n)** absence of speech, sound, or noise
Ps 39:2 . . . I stood there in *s*—not even
Rev 8:1 . . . there was *s* throughout heaven

**SILENCE, SILENCED, SILENCING (v)** to compel or reduce to silence; to cause to cease criticism
Ps 8:2 . . . your strength, *s-ing* your enemies
Titus 1:11 . . . They must be *s-d,* because they
1 Pet 2:15 . . . honorable lives should *s*

**SILENT (adj)** mute, speechless; still
Ps 30:12 . . . praises to you and not be *s.*
Isa 53:7 . . . as a sheep is *s* before the
Isa 62:1 . . . Jerusalem, I cannot remain *s.*
Hab 2:20 . . . the earth be *s* before him.
Acts 8:32 . . . And as a lamb is *s* before
Acts 18:9 . . . Speak out! Don't be *s!*
1 Cor 14:34 . . . Women should be *s* during

**SILVER (adj)** made of silver
Prov 25:11 . . . apples in a *s* basket.
Dan 2:32 . . . and arms were *s,* its belly

**SILVER (n)** a silvery-white metal valued next to gold, capable of a high polish; coin made of silver
Ps 66:10 . . . have purified us like *s.*
Prov 3:14 . . . is more profitable than *s,*
Prov 8:10 . . . instruction rather than *s,*
Prov 22:1 . . . is better than *s* or gold.
Isa 48:10 . . . but not as *s* is refined.
Zech 11:12 . . . wages thirty pieces of *s.*
Zech 13:9 . . . refine them like *s* and
Matt 25:15 . . . two bags of *s* to another,
Matt 26:15 . . . gave him thirty pieces of *s.*
Luke 7:41 . . . 500 pieces of *s* to one
Acts 3:6 . . . don't have any *s* or gold
1 Cor 3:12 . . . materials—gold, *s,* jewels,

**SIMPLE (n)** a person lacking in knowledge or expertise
Ps 19:7 . . . trustworthy, making wise the *s.*

**SIMPLEMINDED (adj)** foolish
Prov 19:25 . . . the *s* will learn a lesson;

**SIN, SINS (n)** moral evil; transgression of or rebellion against God's laws
Gen 4:7 . . . *S* is crouching at the door,

Lev 5:5 . . . ways, you must confess your *s.*
Num 32:23 . . . be sure that your *s* will find
Deut 24:16 . . . to death for the *s-s* of their
Ps 19:13 . . . servant from deliberate *s-s!*
Ps 32:1 . . . whose *s* is put out of sight!
Ps 38:18 . . . I confess my *s-s;* I am deeply
Ps 51:1 . . . blot out the stain of my *s-s.*
Ps 51:2 . . . Purify me from my *s.*
Ps 65:3 . . . we are overwhelmed by our *s-s,*
Ps 79:9 . . . Save us and forgive our *s-s*
Ps 103:12 . . . removed our *s-s* as far from
Prov 5:22 . . . held captive by his own *s-s;*
Prov 10:19 . . . Too much talk leads to *s.*
Prov 14:21 . . . *s* to belittle one's neighbor;
Prov 17:19 . . . who loves to quarrel loves *s;*
Prov 28:13 . . . who conceal their *s-s* will
Prov 29:22 . . . commits all kinds of *s.*
Isa 1:18 . . . your *s-s* are like scarlet,
Isa 53:6 . . . laid on him the *s-s* of us all.
Isa 59:2 . . . Because of your *s-s,* he has
Jer 31:30 . . . die for their own *s-s—*
Jer 31:34 . . . again remember their *s-s.*
Ezek 18:19 . . . pay for the parent's *s-s?*
Matt 1:21 . . . save his people from their *s-s.*
Matt 6:12 . . . forgive us our *s-s,* as we
Matt 26:28 . . . to forgive the *s-s* of many.
Mark 3:29 . . . This is a *s* with eternal
Luke 5:24 . . . on earth to forgive *s-s.*
John 1:29 . . . takes away the *s* of the world!
John 20:23 . . . forgive anyone's *s-s,* they
Acts 2:38 . . . repent of your *s-s* and turn to
Rom 4:25 . . . because of our *s-s,* and he
Rom 6:2 . . . we have died to *s,* how can
Rom 6:11 . . . the power of *s* and alive to
Rom 6:23 . . . the wages of *s* is death,
Rom 7:7 . . . law that showed me my *s.*
Rom 7:25 . . . nature I am a slave to *s.*
1 Cor 6:18 . . . is a *s* against your own body.
1 Cor 15:3 . . . died for our *s-s,* just as
1 Cor 15:56 . . . the law gives *s* its power.
Gal 1:4 . . . gave his life for our *s-s,* just
Gal 6:1 . . . believer is overcome by some *s,*
Eph 2:5 . . . were dead because of our *s-s,*
1 Tim 5:22 . . . share in the *s-s* of others.
Heb 2:17 . . . would take away the *s-s* of
Heb 9:28 . . . to take away the *s-s* of many
Heb 10:12 . . . sacrifice for *s-s,* good for
Heb 12:1 . . . the *s* that so easily trips
Jas 1:15 . . . when *s* is allowed to grow,
Jas 4:17 . . . is *s* to know what you ought
Jas 5:16 . . . Confess your *s-s* to each other
1 Pet 2:24 . . . carried our *s-s* in his body
1 Pet 3:18 . . . suffered for our *s-s* once for
1 Jn 1:8 . . . claim we have no *s,* we are
1 Jn 1:9 . . . to forgive us our *s-s* and to
1 Jn 2:1 . . . if anyone does *s,* we have
1 Jn 3:5 . . . take away our *s-s,* and
1 Jn 3:5 . . . there is no *s* in him.
1 Jn 5:16 . . . a *s* that leads to death,
Rev 1:5 . . . from our *s-s* by shedding his

**SIN, SINNED, SINNING, SINS (v)** to commit an offense or fault against God; to break God's law
Exod 20:20 . . . will keep you from *s-ning!*
2 Sam 12:13 . . . I have *s-ned* against the
2 Chr 6:37 . . . We have *s-ned,* done evil,
Job 1:5 . . . my children have *s-ned*
Ps 51:4 . . . and you alone, have I *s-ned;*
Ps 119:11 . . . I might not *s* against you.
Jer 14:20 . . . all have *s-ned* against you.

Dan 9:5 . . . have *s-ned* and done wrong.
Mark 9:43 . . . causes you to *s,* cut it off.
Luke 15:18 . . . I have *s-ned* against both
Luke 17:3 . . . another believer *s-s,* rebuke
John 8:7 . . . who has never *s-ned* throw
John 8:11 . . . Go and *s* no more.
Rom 1:30 . . . invent new ways of *s-ning,*
Rom 3:23 . . . everyone has *s-ned;* we all
Rom 5:12 . . . When Adam *s-ned, s* entered
Rom 14:23 . . . is not right, you are *s-ning.*
1 Cor 15:34 . . . is right, and stop *s-ning.*
Heb 4:15 . . . we do, yet he did not *s.*
Heb 10:26 . . . deliberately continue *s-ning*
1 Pet 2:22 . . . He never *s-ned,* nor ever
1 Jn 1:10 . . . we have not *s-ned,* we are
1 Jn 3:6 . . . who keeps on *s-ning* does not
1 Jn 5:18 . . . not make a practice of *s-ning,*

**SINFUL (adj)** tainted with, marked by, or full of sin; wicked
Lev 5:1 . . . is *s* to refuse to testify,
1 Sam 15:23 . . . is as *s* as witchcraft,
Luke 11:13 . . . So if you *s* people know
Rom 5:20 . . . could see how *s* they were.
Rom 7:5 . . . harvest of *s* deeds, resulting
Rom 7:18 . . . is, in my *s* nature.
Rom 7:25 . . . because of my *s* nature I am
Rom 8:4 . . . follow our *s* nature but
Rom 8:13 . . . deeds of your *s* nature,
Gal 5:13 . . . to satisfy your *s* nature.
Col 2:11 . . . away of your *s* nature.

**SING, SINGING (v)** to produce musical tones by means of the voice
Exod 15:1 . . . I will *s* to the LORD,
Ps 5:11 . . . let them *s* joyful praises
Ps 13:6 . . . I will *s* to the LORD
Ps 47:6 . . . to our King, *s* praises!
Ps 51:14 . . . I will joyfully *s* of
Ps 63:7 . . . my helper, I *s* for joy
Ps 69:30 . . . praise God's name with *s-ing,*
Ps 89:1 . . . I will *s* of the
Ps 95:1 . . . let us *s* to the LORD!
Ps 96:1 . . . *S* a new song to the LORD!
Ps 98:4 . . . praise and *s* for joy!
Ps 100:2 . . . Come before him, *s-ing* with
Ps 101:1 . . . I will *s* of your love
Ps 108:1 . . . can *s* your praises with all
Ps 147:1 . . . How good to *s* praises to
Isa 35:10 . . . enter Jerusalem *s-ing*
Jer 16:9 . . . to the happy *s-ing* and laughter
Acts 16:25 . . . praying and *s-ing* hymns
1 Cor 14:15 . . . I will also *s* in words
1 Cor 14:26 . . . one will *s,* another will
Col 3:16 . . . *S* psalms and hymns and
Rev 15:3 . . . And they were *s-ing* the song

**SINNER, SINNERS (n)** those guilty of sin
Ps 51:5 . . . I was born a *s*—yes,
Prov 1:10 . . . if *s-s* entice you, turn
Prov 23:17 . . . Don't envy *s-s,* but
Eccl 9:18 . . . one *s* can destroy much that
Isa 59:12 . . . we know what *s-s* we are.
Isa 64:5 . . . We are constant *s-s;* how
Matt 9:13 . . . who know they are *s-s.*
Luke 5:8 . . . I'm too much of a *s* to be
Luke 15:7 . . . over one lost *s* who repents
Luke 18:13 . . . to me, for I am a *s.*
Rom 4:5 . . . faith in God who forgives *s-s.*
Rom 5:6 . . . time and died for us *s-s.*
1 Tim 1:15 . . . into the world to save *s-s*
Jas 5:20 . . . whoever brings the *s* back
1 Pet 3:18 . . . he died for *s-s* to bring

**SKIES, SKY (n)** the upper atmosphere appearing as a great vault or arch above the earth
Gen 1:8 . . . God called the space "*s.* "
Deut 33:26 . . . across the *s-ies* in majestic
Ps 19:1 . . . *s-ies* display his craftsmanship.
Prov 30:19 . . . eagle glides through the *s,*
Isa 34:4 . . . fall from the *s* like withered
Jer 33:22 . . . the stars of the *s* cannot
Matt 24:29 . . . will fall from the *s,*
Rev 20:11 . . . The earth and *s* fled from

**SLANDER (n)** the utterance of false charges or misrepresentations which defame and damage another's reputation
Matt 15:19 . . . theft, lying, and *s.*
Mark 7:22 . . . desires, envy, *s,* pride,
2 Cor 12:20 . . . selfishness, *s,* gossip,
Eph 4:31 . . . harsh words, and *s,* as
Col 3:8 . . . malicious behavior, *s,*

**SLANDER, SLANDERED, SLANDERING (v)** to utter slander; to malign or defame
Prov 10:18 . . . *s-ing* others makes you a
1 Tim 3:11 . . . must not *s* others.
2 Tim 3:3 . . . they will *s* others
Titus 2:3 . . . They must not *s* others
Titus 3:2 . . . They must not *s* anyone
2 Pet 2:2 . . . way of truth will be *s-ed.*

**SLAUGHTER (n)** the butchering of livestock for market or sacrifice
Isa 53:7 . . . led like a lamb to the *s.*
Jer 11:19 . . . lamb being led to the *s.*
Acts 8:32 . . . led like a sheep to the *s.*

**SLAUGHTER, SLAUGHTERED (v)** to discredit, defeat, or demolish completely; to kill in a bloody or violent manner
Hos 6:5 . . . to *s* you with my words,
Rev 5:6 . . . looked as if it had been *s-ed,*
Rev 5:12 . . . Lamb who was *s-ed*—to receive

**SLAVE, SLAVES (n)** a person bound in servitude; one who has lost his liberty and has no rights
*see also* SERVANT(S)
Matt 20:27 . . . must become your *s.*
John 8:34 . . . who sins is a *s* of sin.
John 15:15 . . . longer call you *s-s,* because
Rom 1:1 . . . is from Paul, a *s* of Christ
Rom 6:6 . . . are no longer *s-s* to sin.
Rom 6:16 . . . you become the *s* of whatever
Rom 6:22 . . . and have become *s-s* of God.
Rom 7:23 . . . makes me a *s* to the sin
1 Cor 6:12 . . . not become a *s* to anything.
1 Cor 9:19 . . . have become a *s* to all
1 Cor 12:13 . . . some are *s-s,* and some
Gal 3:28 . . . Jew or Gentile, *s* or free,
Gal 4:7 . . . no longer a *s* but God's own
Gal 4:8 . . . you were *s* to so-called gods
Gal 4:30 . . . rid of the *s* and her son,
Eph 6:5 . . . *S-s,* obey your earthly masters
Phil 2:7 . . . position of a *s* and was born
Col 3:11 . . . barbaric, uncivilized, *s,* or
Col 4:1 . . . be just and fair to your *s-s.*
1 Tim 1:10 . . . or are *s* traders, liars,
Titus 3:3 . . . became *s-s* to many lusts
Phlm 16 . . . no longer like a *s* to you.
2 Pet 2:19 . . . For you are a *s* to whatever

**SLAVERY (n)** submission to a dominating influence; the practice of slaveholding
Exod 2:23 . . . under their burden of *s.*
Rom 6:19 . . . the illustration of *s* to help

**SLEEP (n)**  natural or induced state of rest; a state of lazy inactivity
Gen 2:21 . . . man to fall into a deep *s*.
Gen 15:12 . . . Abram fell into a deep *s*,
Prov 20:13 . . . If you love *s*, you will
Prov 23:21 . . . too much *s* clothes them
Rom 11:8 . . . has put them into a deep *s*.

**SLEEP, SLEEPING, SLEEPS (v)**  to rest in a state of natural unconsciousness
Gen 28:11 . . . against and lay down to *s*.
Ps 4:8 . . . peace I will lie down and *s*,
Ps 121:4 . . . Israel never slumbers or *s-s*.
Prov 6:9 . . . how long will you *s*?
Eccl 5:12 . . . who work hard *s* well,
Mark 13:36 . . . find you *s-ing* when he

**SLOTHFUL(NESS) (KJV)**
Prov 15:19 . . . *lazy* person's way is blocked
Prov 21:25 . . . the *lazy* will come to ruin
Eccl 10:18 . . . *Laziness* leads to a sagging roof
Rom 12:11 . . . Never be *lazy*, but work hard
Heb 6:12 . . . *spiritually dull and indifferent*

**SLUGGARD (KJV)**
Prov 6:6 . . . a lesson from the ants, you *lazybones*
Prov 10:26 . . . *Lazy people* irritate their employers
Prov 13:4 . . . *Lazy people* want much but
Prov 20:4 . . . *Those too lazy* to plow
Prov 26:16 . . . *Lazy people* consider themselves smarter

**SMILE (v)**  to bestow approval
Num 6:25 . . . May the LORD *s* on you and
Ps 4:6 . . . Let your face *s* on us, LORD.
Ps 67:1 . . . May his face *s* with favor on

**SMOKE (n)**  the gaseous products of burning materials
Exod 19:18 . . . The *s* billowed into the sky
Isa 6:4 . . . building was filled with *s*.
Joel 2:30 . . . and fire and columns of *s*.
Acts 2:19 . . . and fire and clouds of *s*.
Rev 9:2 . . . air turned dark from the *s*.
Rev 15:8 . . . filled with *s* from God's

**SMOKE (v)**  to emit smoke
Ps 104:32 . . . the mountains *s* at his touch.

**SNAKE, SNAKES (n)**  any of numerous limbless scaled reptiles; a worthless or treacherous person
Num 21:8 . . . replica of a poisonous *s* and
Prov 23:32 . . . it bites like a poisonous *s*;
Matt 10:16 . . . shrewd as *s-s* and harmless
Luke 3:7 . . . You brood of *s-s!* Who warned
John 3:14 . . . lifted up the bronze *s* on a
Rom 3:13 . . . *S* venom drips from their

**SNOW (n)**  precipitation in the form of small white ice crystals
Prov 25:13 . . . refresh like *s* in summer.
Isa 1:18 . . . will make them as white as *s*.
Dan 7:9 . . . clothing was as white as *s*,

**SODOM (n)**  a city at the southern end of the Dead Sea destroyed because of its wickedness
Gen 13:12 . . . to a place near *S* and settled
Gen 19:24 . . . the sky on *S* and Gomorrah.
Isa 1:9 . . . have been wiped out like *S*,
Luke 10:12 . . . you, even wicked *S* will be
Rom 9:29 . . . have been wiped out like *S*,
Rev 11:8 . . . figuratively called "*S*"

**SOLDIER (n)**  one engaged in military service
1 Cor 9:7 . . . What *s* has to pay his own
2 Tim 2:3 . . . a good *s* of Christ Jesus.

**SOLOMON**  King of Israel (United Kingdom), second son of David and Bathsheba (2 Sam 12:24-25); chosen as successor by David (1 Kgs 1:28-40); given final advice by David (1 Kgs 2:1-9); enemies of his rule removed (1 Kgs 2:13-46); prayed for wisdom (1 Kgs 3:3-15; 4:29-34); demonstrated wisdom (1 Kgs 3:16-28); built and dedicated the Temple (1 Kgs 5–8); the LORD's second appearance (1 Kgs 9:1-9); became famous and powerful (9:10–10:29); visited by the queen of Sheba (1 Kgs 10:1-13); practiced idolatry and warned by God (1 Kgs 11:1-13); troubled by enemies (1 Kgs 11:14-40); died (1 Kgs 11:41-43); wrote many things (1 Kgs 4:32; Ps 72; 127; Prov 1:1; 10:1; 25:1; Eccl 1:1; Song 1:1); often mentioned in NT (Matt 6:29; 12:42; Luke 11:31; 12:27; Acts 7:47).

**SON, SONS (n)**  a parent's male child or descendant further removed; spiritual heir (of Christ); relationship of Jesus to the heavenly Father
*see also* CHILD(REN)
Gen 17:19 . . . birth to a *s* for you.
Gen 21:10 . . . slave-woman and her *s*.
Gen 22:2 . . . Take your *s*, your only
Ruth 4:15 . . . better to you than seven *s-s!*
Ps 2:7 . . . You are my *s*. Today I have
Isa 7:14 . . . birth to a *s* and will call
Dan 7:13 . . . someone like a *s* of man
Hos 11:1 . . . I called my *s* out of Egypt.
Joel 2:28 . . . *s-s* and daughters will
Matt 1:21 . . . will have a *s*, and you are
Matt 2:15 . . . I called my *S* out of Egypt.
Matt 3:17 . . . my dearly loved *S*, who brings
Matt 4:3 . . . you are the *S* of God, tell
Matt 11:27 . . . truly knows the *S* except the
Matt 13:55 . . . the carpenter's *s*, and we
Matt 14:33 . . . really are the *S* of God!
Matt 16:16 . . . are the Messiah, the *S* of
Matt 17:5 . . . my dearly loved *S*, who brings
Matt 21:9 . . . God for the *S* of David!
Matt 27:54 . . . truly was the *S* of God!
Matt 28:19 . . . Father and the *S* and the
Mark 14:62 . . . will see the *S* of Man seated
Luke 1:32 . . . be called the *S* of the Most
Luke 2:7 . . . first child, a *s*. She wrapped
Luke 9:35 . . . This is my *S*, my Chosen One.
Luke 12:8 . . . on earth, the *S* of Man will
Luke 15:20 . . . ran to his *s*, embraced him,
John 3:16 . . . his one and only *S*, so that
John 3:36 . . . doesn't obey the *S* will never
John 17:1 . . . Glorify your *S* so he
Acts 13:33 . . . You are my *S*. Today I have
Rom 1:4 . . . shown to be the *S* of God
Rom 5:10 . . . death of his *S* while we
Rom 8:3 . . . He sent his own *S* in a body
Rom 8:29 . . . to become like his *S*, so
Rom 8:32 . . . even his own *S* but gave him
1 Cor 15:28 . . . who gave his *S* authority
2 Cor 6:18 . . . be my *s-s* and daughters,
Gal 4:4 . . . God sent his *S*, born of a
Gal 4:30 . . . slave and her *s*, for the son
Heb 1:2 . . . and through the *S* he created
Heb 1:5 . . . You are my *S*. Today I have
Heb 7:28 . . . God appointed his *S* with an
Heb 10:29 . . . trampled on the *S* of God,
1 Jn 2:23 . . . acknowledges the *S* has the

1 Jn 4:9 . . . one and only *S* into the world
1 Jn 5:5 . . . Jesus is the *S* of God.
Rev 1:13 . . . someone like the *S* of Man.

**SONG, SONGS (n)**  a short musical composition of words and music; the act of singing
Exod 15:2 . . . my strength and my *s*;
Job 35:10 . . . who gives *s-s* in the night?
Ps 40:3 . . . given me a new *s* to sing,
Ps 63:5 . . . praise you with *s-s* of joy.
Ps 96:1 . . . Sing a new *s* to the LORD!
Ps 119:54 . . . theme of my *s-s* wherever
Ps 137:3 . . . of those *s-s* of Jerusalem!
Ps 149:1 . . . Sing to the LORD a new *s*.
Isa 49:13 . . . Burst into *s*, O mountains!
Isa 55:12 . . . and hills will burst into *s*,
Rev 5:9 . . . they sang a new *s* with these
Rev 15:3 . . . God, and the *s* of the Lamb:

**SORCERER, SORCERERS (n)**  a person who practices sorcery
Exod 7:11 . . . his own wise men and *s-s*,
Acts 8:9 . . . a *s* there for many years,
Acts 13:6 . . . a Jewish *s*, a false prophet
Rev 22:15 . . . the dogs—the *s*, the sexually

**SORCERY (n)**  the use of power gained from the assistance or control of evil spirits, especially for divining
Gal 5:20 . . . idolatry, *s*, hostility, quarreling,

**SORROW, SORROWS (n)**  deep distress, sadness, or regret
Ps 116:3 . . . I saw only trouble and *s*.
Isa 65:14 . . . will cry in *s* and despair.
Jer 31:12 . . . all their *s-s* will be gone.
Ezek 34:2 . . . What *s* awaits you
Amos 5:18 . . . What *s* awaits you
Matt 18:7 . . . What *s* awaits the
Matt 23:13 . . . What *s* awaits you
Luke 11:46 . . . what *s* also awaits
Rom 9:2 . . . with bitter *s* and unending
2 Cor 7:10 . . . the kind of *s* God wants
Eph 4:30 . . . do not bring *s* to God's Holy
1 Tim 6:10 . . . themselves with many *s-s*.
Heb 13:17 . . . with joy and not with *s*.
Jude 1:11 . . . What *s* awaits them!
Rev 21:4 . . . more death or *s* or crying

**SORRY (adj)**  feeling sorrow, regret, or penitence; inspiring pity
Gen 6:6 . . . So the LORD was *s* he had
2 Chr 21:20 . . . No one was *s* when he died.
Ps 38:18 . . . I am deeply *s* for what I have
Mal 3:14 . . . that we are *s* for our sins?
Matt 15:32 . . . I feel *s* for these people.
Matt 20:34 . . . Jesus felt *s* for them and
Mark 8:2 . . . I feel *s* for these people.

**SOUL, SOULS (n)**  the inner life of a human being, the seat of emotions, and the center of human personality
Deut 6:5 . . . heart, all your *s*, and all
Deut 28:65 . . . fail, and your *s* to despair.
Deut 30:6 . . . your heart and *s* and so you
Josh 22:5 . . . all your heart and all your *s*.
2 Kgs 23:25 . . . heart and *s* and strength,
Prov 3:22 . . . for they will refresh your *s*.
Prov 16:24 . . . sweet to the *s* and healthy
Jer 6:16 . . . you will find rest for your *s-s*.
Matt 10:28 . . . can destroy both *s* and body
Matt 11:29 . . . you will find rest for your *s-s*.
Matt 22:37 . . . all your heart, all your *s*,

Mark 8:37 . . . worth more than your *s?*
Mark 12:30 . . . heart, all your *s,* all your
Luke 16:23 . . . his *s* went to the place of
Luke 21:19 . . . firm, you will win your *s-s.*
John 12:27 . . . my *s* is deeply troubled.
Heb 4:12 . . . cutting between *s* and spirit,

**SOW(ED), SOWING (KJV)**
Lev 25:3 . . . you may *plant* your fields
Ps 126:5 . . . Those who *plant* in tears
Matt 13:4 . . . As he *scattered* them across
Luke 12:24 . . . the ravens. They don't *plant*
Luke 19:21 . . . crops you didn't *plant*

**SOWER (KJV)**
Isa 55:10 . . . producing seed for the *farmer* and
Jer 50:16 . . . all *those who plant crops*
Matt 13:18 . . . parable about the *farmer*
    *planting seeds*
2 Cor 9:10 . . . provides seed for the *farmer*

**SPANK (n)** to strike especially on the buttocks
with the open hand
Prov 23:13 . . . won't die if you *s* them.

**SPARE, SPARED, SPARES (v)** to hold back
from destroying, punishing, or harming; to have
left over or as margin; to rescue from the
necessity of doing or undergoing something
Esth 7:3 . . . lives of my people will be *s-d.*
Prov 13:24 . . . Those who *s* the rod of
Isa 54:2 . . . your home, and *s* no expense!
Mal 3:17 . . . as a father *s-s* an obedient
Rom 8:32 . . . did not *s* even his own Son
Rom 11:21 . . . if God did not *s* the original
2 Pet 2:4 . . . God did not *s* even the angels
2 Pet 2:5 . . . And God did not *s* the ancient

**SPEAK, SPEAKING, SPEAKS (v)** to express
thoughts, opinions, or feelings orally; to talk
Deut 18:22 . . . If the prophet *s-s* in the
Ps 15:3 . . . or *s* evil of their friends.
Ps 78:2 . . . will *s* to you in a parable.
Isa 3:8 . . . because they *s* out against
Isa 32:4 . . . stammer will *s* out plainly.
Matt 12:34 . . . men like you *s* what is good
Matt 15:18 . . . the words you *s* come from
Acts 2:11 . . . hear these people *s-ing* in our
1 Cor 14:2 . . . ability to *s* in tongues,
1 Cor 14:19 . . . I would rather *s* five
1 Pet 3:16 . . . if people *s* against you,

**SPEECH (n)** the communication or expression
of thoughts in spoken words
Prov 16:23 . . . a wise mind comes wise *s;*
Prov 22:11 . . . gracious *s* will have the king
Prov 25:15 . . . soft *s* can break bones.
Zeph 3:9 . . . I will purify the *s* of all
1 Cor 1:17 . . . not with clever *s,* for

**SPEND, SPENT (v)** to use up or pay out; to
exhaust or wear out
Prov 21:20 . . . but fools *s* whatever they
Isa 55:2 . . . Why *s* your money on food that
Mark 5:26 . . . she had *s-t* everything she had
2 Cor 12:15 . . . I will gladly *s* myself

**SPIRIT, SPIRITS (n)** "wind" or "breath"; a
supernatural being; the third member of the
Trinity, with God the Father and Jesus the Son;
an attitude, mood, or disposition; an evil
presence that can possess or influence a
person; invisible, nonmaterial part of humans
(as opposed to body or flesh)
*see also* ADVOCATE

Gen 1:2 . . . the *S* of God was hovering
Gen 6:3 . . . My *S* will not put up with
Exod 31:3 . . . filled him with the *S* of God,
Num 11:25 . . . *S* rested upon them, they
Deut 34:9 . . . full of the *s* of wisdom,
Judg 13:25 . . . And the *S* of the LORD
1 Sam 16:13 . . . And the *S* of the LORD
1 Sam 16:14 . . . a tormenting *s* that filled
2 Kgs 2:9 . . . double share of your *s* and
Job 33:4 . . . the *S* of God has made me,
Ps 31:5 . . . I entrust my *s* into your
Ps 34:18 . . . those whose *s-s* are crushed.
Ps 51:10 . . . Renew a loyal *s* within me.
Ps 51:17 . . . you desire is a broken *s.*
Ps 139:7 . . . can never escape from
    your *S!*
Isa 11:2 . . . *S* of the LORD will rest
Isa 44:3 . . . I will pour out my *S* on your
Isa 63:10 . . . him and grieved his Holy *S.*
Ezek 11:19 . . . put a new *s* within them.
Joel 2:28 . . . I will pour out my *S* upon all
Zech 4:6 . . . by my *S,* says the LORD
Matt 3:11 . . . baptize you with the Holy *S*
Matt 3:16 . . . and he saw the *S* of God
Matt 4:1 . . . was led by the *S* into the
Matt 28:19 . . . and the Son and the Holy *S.*
Mark 1:8 . . . baptize you with the Holy *S!*
Mark 5:12 . . . pigs," the *s-s* begged.
Luke 1:35 . . . The Holy *S* will come upon
John 3:5 . . . born of water and the *S.*
John 6:63 . . . *S* alone gives eternal life.
John 14:26 . . . the Holy *S*—he will teach
John 16:13 . . . When the *S* of truth comes,
Acts 1:8 . . . when the Holy *S* comes
Acts 2:4 . . . as the Holy *S* gave them this
Acts 2:17 . . . will pour out my *S* upon all
Acts 5:3 . . . You lied to the Holy *S,* and
Acts 6:3 . . . full of the *S* and wisdom.
Acts 8:15 . . . to receive the Holy *S.*
Acts 9:17 . . . and be filled with the Holy *S.*
Acts 11:16 . . . be baptized with the Holy *S.*
Acts 19:2 . . . receive the Holy *S* when you
Rom 8:5 . . . controlled by the Holy *S* think
Rom 8:9 . . . do not have the *S* of Christ
Rom 8:26 . . . the Holy *S* prays for us
1 Cor 2:10 . . . For his *S* searches out
1 Cor 12:1 . . . abilities the *S* gives us.
1 Cor 12:13 . . . one body by one *S,* and we
1 Cor 14:1 . . . abilities the *S* gives—
2 Cor 3:6 . . . covenant, the *S* gives life.
2 Cor 3:17 . . . and wherever the *S* of the
2 Cor 5:3 . . . not be *s-s* without bodies.
Gal 3:2 . . . receive the Holy *S* by obeying
Gal 5:22 . . . But the Holy *S* produces this
Eph 4:4 . . . body and one *S,* just as you
Eph 4:30 . . . to God's Holy *S* by the way
Eph 6:12 . . . and against evil *s-s* in the
Eph 6:17 . . . sword of the *S,* which is the
1 Thes 5:19 . . . Do not stifle the Holy *S.*
1 Tim 3:16 . . . vindicated by the *S.*
2 Tim 1:7 . . . not given us a *s* of fear
1 Pet 3:4 . . . gentle and quiet *s,* which
1 Jn 4:1 . . . who claims to speak by the *S.*

**SPIRITUAL (adj)** having to do with the spirit,
usually God's Spirit
Jon 4:11 . . . living in *s* darkness, not
Rom 7:14 . . . for it is *s* and good.
1 Cor 2:14 . . . who are *s* can understand
1 Cor 14:37 . . . think you are *s,* you should
1 Cor 15:44 . . . there are also *s* bodies.

Eph 5:19 . . . and hymns and *s* songs among
1 Pet 2:5 . . . you offer *s* sacrifices that

**SPLENDOR (n)** great brightness or luster;
magnificence
2 Chr 20:21 . . . him for his holy *s.*
Ps 29:2 . . . the LORD in the *s* of
Ps 145:5 . . . majestic, glorious *s* and
Prov 20:29 . . . experience is the *s* of
Isa 33:17 . . . see the king in all his *s,*
Hab 3:3 . . . brilliant *s* fills the heavens,

**SPOT, SPOTS (n)** a small area visibly different
(as in color, finish, or material) from the
surrounding area; a taint on character or
reputation
Jer 13:23 . . . leopard take away its *s-s?*
Eph 5:27 . . . church without a *s* or wrinkle

**SPOTLESS (adj)** free from impurity;
unblemished
1 Pet 1:19 . . . the sinless, *s* Lamb of God.

**STAFF (n)** a long stick used for walking or a
weapon, often a symbol of authority and
protection
*see also* ROD
Gen 49:10 . . . nor the ruler's *s* from his
Exod 7:12 . . . then Aaron's *s* swallowed up
Num 17:6 . . . Aaron, brought Moses a *s.*
2 Kgs 4:29 . . . travel; take my *s* and go!
Ps 23:4 . . . Your rod and your *s* protect

**STAND, STANDING, STANDS (v)** to remain
stationary; to remain erect; to maintain one's
position; to endure successfully
*see also* STOOD
Exod 3:5 . . . you are *s-ing* on holy ground.
Josh 5:15 . . . where you are *s-ing* is holy.
Josh 10:12 . . . Let the sun *s* still
2 Chr 20:17 . . . then *s* still and
Ps 24:3 . . . Who may *s* in his holy
Ps 33:11 . . . LORD's plans *s* firm
Ps 76:7 . . . Who can *s* before you
Ps 119:89 . . . word, O LORD, *s-s* firm
Prov 12:7 . . . family of the godly *s-s* firm.
Isa 40:8 . . . word of our God *s-s* forever.
Mal 3:2 . . . be able to *s* and face him
Luke 6:48 . . . that house, it *s-s* firm because
Rom 14:10 . . . all *s* before the judgment
1 Cor 10:12 . . . think you are *s-ing* strong,
1 Cor 10:13 . . . to be more than you can *s.*
2 Cor 5:10 . . . we must all *s* before Christ
Eph 6:14 . . . *S* your ground, putting on the
Phil 1:27 . . . you are *s-ing* together
2 Tim 2:19 . . . But God's truth *s-s* firm like
1 Pet 5:9 . . . *S* firm against him, and
Rev 3:20 . . . I *s* at the door and knock.

**STANDING (n)** a position or condition
Rom 8:33 . . . us right *s* with himself.

**STAR, STARS (n)** a natural luminous body
visible in the sky especially at night; sometimes
symbolic for angels
Gen 1:16 . . . He also made the *s-s.*
Num 24:17 . . . A *s* will rise from Jacob;
Job 38:7 . . . morning *s-s* sang together
Isa 14:12 . . . O shining *s,* son of the
Dan 12:3 . . . shine like the *s-s* forever.
Matt 2:2 . . . We saw his *s* as it rose,
2 Pet 1:19 . . . the Morning *S* shines in
Rev 2:28 . . . also give them the morning *s!*
Rev 22:16 . . . I am the bright morning *s.*

**STATUTES (KJV)**
Exod 15:26 . . . keeping all his *decrees*
Deut 4:40 . . . If you obey all the *decrees* and
1 Kgs 3:14 . . . *decrees* and my commands
Ps 19:8 . . . *commandments* of the LORD
Ps 119:112 . . . to keep your *decrees*

**STEDFAST (KJV)**
Ps 78:37 . . . They did not *keep* his covenant
1 Cor 15:58 . . . be *strong* and immovable.
Heb 3:14 . . . if we are *faithful* to the end,
1 Pet 5:9 . . . and be *strong* in your faith

**STEAL, STEALING, STEALS (v)** to take the property of another wrongfully
Exod 20:15 . . . You must not *s.*
Lev 19:11 . . . Do not *s.*
Deut 5:19 . . . You must not *s.*
Prov 28:24 . . . who *s-s* from his father
Matt 19:18 . . . You must not *s.*
Matt 27:64 . . . coming and *s-ing* his body
Rom 13:9 . . . You must not *s.*
Eph 4:28 . . . If you are a thief, quit *s-ing.*
1 Pet 4:15 . . . not be for murder, *s-ing,*

**STEPS (n)** course, way
Ps 37:23 . . . LORD directs the *s* of
Prov 20:24 . . . LORD directs our *s,*
1 Pet 2:21 . . . you must follow in his *s.*

**STIFFNECKED (KJV)**
Exod 32:9 . . . how *stubborn and rebellious*
Exod 34:9 . . . *stubborn and rebellious* people
Deut 10:16 . . . stop being *stubborn*
2 Chr 30:8 . . . not be *stubborn,* as they
Acts 7:51 . . . You *stubborn* people! You are

**STIFFHEARTED (KJV)**
Ezek 2:4 . . . stubborn and *hard-hearted*

**STILL (adj)** devoid of or abstaining from motion; quiet, calm
Ps 46:10 . . . Be *s,* and know that I am
Isa 57:20 . . . never *s* but continually
Mark 4:39 . . . Silence! Be *s!*

**STILL (adv)** without motion
Exod 14:13 . . . Just stand *s* and watch
Josh 10:13 . . . sun stood *s* and the moon
2 Chr 20:17 . . . then stand *s* and watch

**STING (n)** a wound or pain caused by or as if by stinging
1 Cor 15:55 . . . where is your *s?*

**STONE (adj)** of, relating to, or made of stone
Deut 4:13 . . . he wrote on two *s* tablets.

**STONE, STONES (n)** hardened mineral or rock; figurative of Christ or of hardened hearts
Exod 28:10 . . . Six names will be on each *s,*
Josh 4:3 . . . Take twelve *s-s* from the very
1 Sam 17:40 . . . picked up five smooth *s-s*
Ps 91:12 . . . even hurt your foot on a *s.*
Ps 118:22 . . . *s* that the builders rejected
Isa 8:14 . . . a *s* that makes people stumble,
Isa 28:16 . . . a foundation *s* in Jerusalem,
Isa 50:7 . . . face like a *s,* determined to
Jer 51:26 . . . Even your *s-s* will never again
Matt 3:9 . . . Abraham from these very *s-s.*
Matt 7:9 . . . give them a *s* instead?
Matt 21:42 . . . *s* that the builders rejected
Matt 24:2 . . . Not one *s* will be left
Mark 16:3 . . . roll away the *s* for us from
Luke 4:3 . . . tell this *s* to become a loaf of
John 8:7 . . . sinned throw the first *s!*
1 Pet 2:5 . . . you are living *s-s* that God

**STONED, STONING (v)** to kill by pelting with stones
2 Cor 11:25 . . . with rods. Once I was *s.*
Heb 11:37 . . . Some died by *s-ing,* some were

**STONY (adj)** insensitive to pity or human feeling
Ezek 11:19 . . . away their *s,* stubborn heart

**STOOD (v)** *see also* STAND
Josh 10:13 . . . So the sun *s* still and
2 Tim 4:17 . . . But the Lord *s* with me

**STOP, STOPS (v)** to cease activity or operation; to pause or hesitate; to restrain or prevent
Job 37:14 . . . *S* and consider the wonderful
Prov 15:18 . . . cool-tempered person *s-s*
Jer 7:5 . . . only if you *s* your evil
Jer 32:40 . . . I will never *s* doing good
Lam 3:49 . . . flow endlessly; they will not *s*
Dan 4:35 . . . No one can *s* him or say to
Matt 19:14 . . . come to me. Don't *s* them!
Eph 6:16 . . . shield of faith to *s* the

**STORE (n)** a large quantity, supply, or number
Isa 33:6 . . . a rich *s* of salvation,

**STORE, STORED (v)** to lay away; to accumulate
Matt 6:19 . . . Don't *s* up treasures
Matt 6:26 . . . plant or harvest or *s* food
Luke 2:51 . . . And his mother *s-d* all these

**STORM (n)** a heavy fall of rain, snow, or hail sometimes accompanied by thunder and lightning; a disturbed or agitated state
*see also* WHIRLWIND
Ps 50:3 . . . and a great *s* rages around
Ps 55:8 . . . from this wild *s* of hatred.
Ps 107:29 . . . He calmed the *s* to a whisper
Luke 8:24 . . . *s* stopped and all was calm.

**STRANGER, STRANGERS (n)** a person who is unknown or with whom one is unacquainted
*see also* FOREIGNER(S)
Job 31:32 . . . turned away a *s* but have
Matt 25:35 . . . I was a *s,* and you invited
John 10:5 . . . They won't follow a *s;*
1 Tim 5:10 . . . been kind to *s-s* and served
Heb 13:2 . . . to show hospitality to *s-s,* for

**STRAYED (v)** to wander
Isa 53:6 . . . like sheep, have *s* away.
Ezek 34:16 . . . lost ones who *s* away, and

**STREAMS (n)** a body of running water (as a river or brook)
Ps 23:2 . . . leads me beside peaceful *s.*
Jer 31:9 . . . walk beside quiet *s* and

**STRENGTH (n)** capacity for exertion or endurance; support; the power of a person or of God, measured variously in terms of wealth, wisdom, military might, or physical prowess
Exod 15:2 . . . LORD is my *s* and my
Deut 6:5 . . . your soul, and all your *s.*
2 Kgs 23:25 . . . his heart and soul and *s,*
1 Chr 16:11 . . . LORD and for his *s;*
Neh 8:10 . . . of the LORD is your *s!*
Ps 23:3 . . . He renews my *s.* He guides me
Ps 28:7 . . . LORD is my *s* and shield.
Ps 33:16 . . . nor is great *s* enough to save
Ps 46:1 . . . God is our refuge and *s,*
Ps 59:17 . . . O my *S,* to you I sing
Ps 65:6 . . . armed yourself with mighty *s.*
Ps 84:5 . . . for those whose *s* comes from
Ps 139:10 . . . your *s* will support me.
Isa 31:1 . . . depending on the *s* of human

Isa 40:26 . . . power and incomparable *s,*
Jer 27:5 . . . With my great *s* and powerful
Mic 5:4 . . . with the LORD's *s,* in
Hab 3:19 . . . LORD is my *s!*
Zech 4:6 . . . nor by *s,* but by my Spirit,
Mark 12:30 . . . your mind, and all your *s.*
1 Cor 1:25 . . . the greatest of human *s.*
Phil 4:13 . . . Christ, who gives me *s.*
Heb 11:34 . . . weakness was turned to *s.*
Heb 13:9 . . . Your *s* comes from God's

**STRENGTHEN, STRENGTHENED, STRENGTHENS (v)** to make or become stronger
2 Chr 16:9 . . . in order to *s* those whose
Isa 41:10 . . . I will *s* you and help you.
1 Cor 8:1 . . . is love that *s-s* the church.
1 Cor 14:4 . . . in tongues is *s-ed* personally,
1 Cor 14:4 . . . word of prophecy *s-s*
1 Cor 14:5 . . . whole church will be *s-ed.*
1 Cor 14:12 . . . seek those that will *s* the
1 Cor 14:17 . . . but it won't *s* the people
1 Cor 14:26 . . . is done must *s* all of you.
2 Cor 13:10 . . . has given me to *s* you, not
Heb 12:12 . . . tired hands and *s* your weak
1 Pet 5:10 . . . support, and *s* you, and he

**STRONG, STRONGER, STRONGEST (adj)** having or marked by great physical power, moral or intellectual power, or great resources (as of wealth or talent); firm
Exod 6:1 . . . force of my *s* hand, he
Deut 5:15 . . . you out with his *s* hand
Deut 7:8 . . . with such a *s* hand from your
Deut 31:6 . . . So be *s* and courageous!
Josh 1:6 . . . Be *s* and courageous,
Judg 16:5 . . . makes him so *s* and how he
2 Sam 22:33 . . . God is my *s* fortress, and
1 Kgs 8:42 . . . and your *s* hand and your
1 Chr 28:20 . . . Be *s* and courageous, and
Ezra 10:4 . . . so be *s* and take action.
Ps 24:8 . . . The LORD, *s* and mighty;
Ps 96:7 . . . LORD is glorious and *s.*
Prov 18:10 . . . LORD is a *s* fortress;
Prov 24:5 . . . wise are mightier than the *s,*
Prov 30:25 . . . Ants—they aren't *s,* but
Prov 31:17 . . . She is energetic and *s,* a
Eccl 9:11 . . . *s-est* warrior doesn't always
Isa 35:4 . . . Be *s,* and do not fear,
Jer 50:34 . . . one who redeems them is *s.*
Zeph 1:14 . . . when even *s* men will cry
Luke 1:80 . . . and became *s* in spirit.
Luke 2:40 . . . grew up healthy and *s.*
Luke 11:22 . . . someone even *s-er* attacks
1 Cor 1:8 . . . keep you *s* to the end
1 Cor 1:25 . . . God's weakness is *s-er* than
1 Cor 16:13 . . . Be courageous. Be *s.*
Eph 6:10 . . . final word: Be *s* in the Lord
1 Thes 3:13 . . . your hearts *s,* blameless,
2 Tim 2:1 . . . dear son, be *s* through the

**STRUGGLE (n)** strife; a violent effort or exertion
Rom 15:30 . . . to join in my *s* by praying
Heb 12:4 . . . lives in your *s* against sin.

**STRUGGLE (v)** to proceed with difficulty or with great effort; to make strenuous or violent efforts in the face of difficulties or opposition
Gen 3:17 . . . will *s* to scratch a living
Col 1:29 . . . why I work and *s* so hard,
1 Tim 4:10 . . . and continue to *s,* for our

**STUBBORN (adj)** unreasonably or perversely unyielding

Exod 33:5 . . . You are a *s* and rebellious
Exod 34:9 . . . this is a *s* and rebellious
Lev 26:41 . . . at last their *s* hearts will
Deut 10:16 . . . hearts and stop being *s.*
2 Chr 36:13 . . . a hard and *s* man, refusing
Ps 78:8 . . . ancestors—*s*, rebellious,
Prov 28:14 . . . the *s* are headed for serious
Ezek 36:26 . . . out your stony, *s* heart and
Rom 2:5 . . . because you are *s* and refuse

**STUDY (n)** application of the mental faculties to the acquisition of knowledge

Eccl 12:12 . . . and much *s* wears you

**STUDY (v)** to read in detail, especially with the intention of learning

Josh 1:8 . . . *S* this Book of Instruction
Ezra 7:10 . . . had determined to *s* and obey

**STUMBLE, STUMBLES, STUMBLING (v)** to trip or walk unsteadily; to fall into sin or waywardness

Lev 19:14 . . . or cause the blind to *s.*
Ps 37:24 . . . Though they *s*, they will
Ps 66:9 . . . he keeps our feet from *s-ing.*
Ps 119:165 . . . great peace and do not *s.*
Ps 121:3 . . . He will not let you *s;*
Prov 3:23 . . . and your feet will not *s.*
Prov 24:17 . . . don't be happy when they *s.*
Isa 8:14 . . . stone that makes people *s*,
Jer 13:16 . . . causing you to *s* and fall
Hos 14:9 . . . paths sinners *s* and fall.
Mal 2:8 . . . caused many to *s* into sin.
Matt 21:44 . . . Anyone who *s-s* over that
John 11:10 . . . is danger of *s-ing* because
Rom 9:33 . . . that makes people *s*,
Rom 14:13 . . . believer to *s* and fall.
Rom 14:20 . . . makes another person *s.*
1 Cor 8:9 . . . weaker conscience to *s.*
2 Cor 6:3 . . . no one will *s* because of us,
1 Jn 2:10 . . . does not cause others to *s.*

**STUMP (n)** the part of a tree remaining attached to the root after the trunk is cut

Isa 6:13 . . . so Israel's *s* will be a
Isa 11:1 . . . Out of the *s* of David's

**STUPID (adj)** lacking intelligence or reason

Ps 119:70 . . . hearts are dull and *s*,
Prov 12:1 . . . is *s* to hate correction.

**SUBMISSIVE (adj)** submitting to others

1 Cor 14:34 . . . They should be *s*, just
Titus 2:5 . . . be *s* to their husbands.

**SUBMIT, SUBMITS (v)** to yield to authority or be accountable to another—God, society, or fellow believers

Ps 2:12 . . . *S* to God's royal son,
Rom 13:1 . . . Everyone must *s* to governing
Rom 13:5 . . . So you must *s* to them, not
Eph 5:21 . . . *s* to one another out of
Eph 5:24 . . . As the church *s-s* to Christ,
Col 3:18 . . . Wives, *s* to your husbands,
Heb 12:9 . . . shouldn't we *s* even more

**SUCCEED (v)** to turn out well; to attain a desired end

Gen 39:23 . . . everything he did to *s.*
Josh 1:8 . . . prosper and *s* in all you
1 Sam 2:9 . . . No one will *s* by strength
1 Sam 18:14 . . . continued to *s* in
2 Chr 20:20 . . . prophets, and you will *s.*

Ps 20:4 . . . and make all your plans *s.*
Prov 11:10 . . . celebrates when the godly *s;*
Prov 13:13 . . . respect a command will *s.*
Prov 16:3 . . . and your plans will *s.*
Prov 20:18 . . . Plans *s* through good
Prov 28:12 . . . When the godly *s*, everyone
Eccl 10:10 . . . wisdom; it helps you *s.*

**SUCCESS (n)** the attainment of wealth, favor, or eminence; favorable or desired outcome

1 Chr 12:18 . . . and *s* to all who help
2 Chr 26:5 . . . LORD, God gave him *s.*
Prov 15:22 . . . many advisers bring *s.*

**SUCCESSFUL (adj)** resulting or terminating in success; gaining or having gained success

Deut 8:18 . . . gives you power to be *s*,
Deut 30:9 . . . make you *s* in everything
1 Kgs 2:3 . . . that you will be *s* in all
2 Kgs 18:7 . . . Hezekiah was *s* in
1 Chr 22:13 . . . For you will be *s* if you
2 Chr 31:21 . . . result, he was very *s.*
Ps 90:17 . . . and make our efforts *s.*
Prov 1:3 . . . disciplined and *s* lives,
Eccl 9:11 . . . don't always lead *s* lives.

**SUES (v)** to seek justice or right from (a person) by legal process

1 Cor 6:6 . . . one believer *s* another—

**SUFFER, SUFFERED, SUFFERING, SUFFERS (v)** to endure death, pain, distress, or loss

Job 36:15 . . . rescues those who *s.*
Mark 8:31 . . . Son of Man must *s* many
Luke 24:26 . . . would have to *s* all these
Luke 24:46 . . . Messiah would *s* and die
Rom 8:18 . . . Yet what we *s* now is nothing
1 Cor 12:26 . . . If one part *s-s*, all the parts
2 Cor 1:5 . . . the more we *s* for Christ,
2 Cor 12:10 . . . troubles that I *s* for Christ,
Phil 3:10 . . . I want to *s* with him, sharing
2 Thes 1:4 . . . and hardships you are *s-ing.*
Heb 11:26 . . . better to *s* for the sake
1 Pet 2:21 . . . just as Christ *s-ed* for you.
1 Pet 4:1 . . . since Christ *s-ed* physical pain,
1 Pet 4:16 . . . is no shame to *s* for being
1 Pet 5:10 . . . So after you have *s-ed* a little
Rev 2:3 . . . You have patiently *s-ed* for me

**SUFFERING, SUFFERINGS (n)** the state or experience of one that suffers; pain, distress

Deut 16:3 . . . the bread of *s*—so that
Job 36:15 . . . means of their *s*, he rescues
Ps 119:71 . . . My *s* was good for me,
Isa 48:10 . . . you in the furnace of *s.*
Isa 49:13 . . . on them in their *s.*
Lam 1:12 . . . if there is any *s* like mine,
Luke 22:15 . . . you before my *s* begins.
2 Cor 1:7 . . . as you share in our *s-s*, you
Phil 1:29 . . . the privilege of *s* for him.
Col 1:24 . . . participating in the *s-s* of
2 Tim 2:3 . . . Endure *s* along with me,
2 Tim 4:5 . . . afraid of *s* for the Lord.
Heb 2:10 . . . through his *s*, a perfect
Heb 2:18 . . . gone through *s* and testing,
1 Pet 1:11 . . . about Christ's *s* and his
1 Pet 4:13 . . . Christ in his *s*, so that

**SUN (n)** a star that sustains life on the earth, being the source of heat and light;

Josh 10:13 . . . So the *s* stood still and
Judg 5:31 . . . rise like the *s* in all its
Ps 84:11 . . . God is our *s* and our shield.
Ps 121:6 . . . The *s* will not harm you

Ps 136:8 . . . the *s* to rule the day,
Eccl 1:9 . . . Nothing under the *s* is truly
Isa 60:19 . . . you need the *s* to shine by
Mal 4:2 . . . name, the *S* of Righteousness
Matt 13:43 . . . shine like the *s* in their
Matt 17:2 . . . shone like the *s*, and his
Luke 23:45 . . . light from the *s* was gone.
Eph 4:26 . . . Don't let the *s* go down while
Rev 1:16 . . . was like the *s* in all its
Rev 21:23 . . . has no need of *s* or moon,

**SUSTAINS (v)** to keep up or prolong

Heb 1:3 . . . God, and he *s* everything by

**SWADDLED, SWADDLING (KJV)**

Ezek 16:4 . . . salt, and *wrapped in cloth*
Luke 2:7 . . . wrapped him *snugly in strips of cloth*
Luke 2:12 . . . a baby *wrapped snugly*

**SWALLOW, SWALLOWED (v)** to take through the mouth and esophagus into the stomach; to envelop or absorb

Isa 25:8 . . . He will *s* up death
Jon 1:17 . . . a great fish to *s* Jonah.
Hab 1:13 . . . while the wicked *s* up people
Matt 23:24 . . . a gnat, but you *s* a camel!
1 Cor 15:54 . . . fulfilled: "Death is *s-ed* up
2 Cor 5:4 . . . bodies will be *s-ed* up by life.

**SWORD, SWORDS (n)** a handheld weapon with a long blade; figurative of war or persecution by government, also of God's word in spiritual warfare

Gen 3:24 . . . a flaming *s* that flashed
Deut 32:41 . . . my flashing *s* and begin
1 Sam 17:45 . . . come to me with *s*, spear,
1 Sam 31:4 . . . Take your *s* and kill me
2 Sam 12:10 . . . live by the *s* because you
1 Kgs 20:11 . . . putting on his *s* for battle
Ps 44:6 . . . not count on my *s* to save me.
Ps 45:3 . . . Put on your *s*, O mighty
Ps 64:3 . . . their tongues like *s-s* and aim
Joel 3:10 . . . plowshares into *s-s* and your
Amos 9:4 . . . I will command the *s* to kill
Mic 4:3 . . . will hammer their *s-s* into
Matt 10:34 . . . not to bring peace, but a *s.*
Matt 26:52 . . . who use the *s* will die by
Luke 2:35 . . . a *s* will pierce your very
Eph 6:17 . . . take the *s* of the Spirit,
Heb 4:12 . . . sharpest two-edged *s*, cutting
Rev 1:16 . . . sharp two-edged *s* came
Rev 19:15 . . . came a sharp *s* to strike

**SYNAGOGUE (n)** the house of worship and communal center of a Jewish congregation

Luke 4:16 . . . to the *s* on the Sabbath
Acts 17:2 . . . he went to the *s* service,

**TABERNACLE (n)** portable shrine or tent designated for the worship of God; metaphor for God dwelling among his people

*see also* SANCTUARY, TEMPLE

Exod 27:21 . . . stand in the *T*, in front of
Exod 40:2 . . . Set up the *T* on the first
Exod 40:34 . . . cloud covered the *T*, and
Exod 40:34 . . . of the LORD filled the *T.*
Num 3:29 . . . area south of the *T* for their
Heb 8:5 . . . to build the *T*, God gave him
Heb 9:11 . . . more perfect *T* in heaven,
Heb 9:21 . . . blood on the *T* and on
Rev 15:5 . . . heaven, God's *T*, was thrown

**TABLETS (n)** a flat slab or plaque suited for or bearing an inscription
Exod 31:18 . . . two stone *t* inscribed with
Deut 10:5 . . . and placed the *t* in the Ark
2 Cor 3:3 . . . carved not on *t* of stone,

**TAME (v)** to reduce from a wild to a domestic state; to harness
Jas 3:7 . . . People can *t* all kinds of
Jas 3:8 . . . no one can *t* the tongue.

**TASTE (n)** the act of tasting; a sample experience
Prov 24:13 . . . honeycomb is sweet to the *t.*
1 Pet 2:3 . . . a *t* of the Lord's kindness.

**TASTE, TASTED, TASTES (v)** to become acquainted with by experience; to ascertain the flavor of by taking a little into the mouth
Ps 34:8 . . . *T* and see that the LORD
Prov 9:17 . . . eaten in secret *t-s* the best!
Song 2:3 . . . and *t* his delicious fruit.
Ezek 3:3 . . . I ate it, it *t-d* as sweet as
Col 2:21 . . . Don't handle! Don't *t!*

**TAX, TAXES (n)** a charge usually of money imposed by authority on persons or property for public purposes
Matt 11:19 . . . a friend of *t* collectors
Matt 17:24 . . . teacher pay the Temple *t?*
Matt 22:17 . . . right to pay *t-es* to Caesar
Rom 13:7 . . . Pay your *t-es* and

**TEACH, TEACHES, TEACHING (v)** to cause to know something; to instruct by precept, example, or experience
*see also* INSTRUCT, PREACH, TRAIN
Lev 10:11 . . . you must *t* the Israelites
Deut 6:1 . . . commanded me to *t* you.
2 Chr 17:9 . . . of Judah, *t-ing* the people.
Job 21:22 . . . who can *t* a lesson to God,
Ps 37:30 . . . they *t* right from wrong.
Ps 51:13 . . . Then I will *t* your ways
Prov 15:33 . . . the LORD *t-es* wisdom;
Isa 2:3 . . . he will *t* us his ways,
Matt 5:19 . . . obeys God's laws and *t-es*
Matt 11:29 . . . Let me *t* you, because
Matt 15:9 . . . they *t* man-made ideas
Matt 22:16 . . . You *t* the way of God
Matt 28:20 . . . *T* these new disciples to
Mark 10:1 . . . as usual he was *t-ing* them.
Luke 11:1 . . . Lord, *t* us to pray,
Luke 12:12 . . . Holy Spirit will *t* you
John 14:26 . . . he will *t* you everything
Acts 6:4 . . . in prayer and *t-ing* the word.
Rom 15:4 . . . Scriptures long ago to *t*
Rom 15:14 . . . you can *t* each other all
1 Cor 2:16 . . . knows enough to *t* him?
1 Cor 14:26 . . . another will *t,* another
1 Tim 2:12 . . . do not let women *t* men
1 Tim 3:2 . . . he must be able to *t.*
2 Tim 3:16 . . . is useful to *t* us what
2 Tim 3:16 . . . *t-es* us to do what is right.
Titus 2:15 . . . You must *t* these things
Heb 5:12 . . . you ought to be *t-ing* others.
1 Jn 2:27 . . . need anyone to *t* you what

**TEACHER, TEACHERS (n)** one who teaches
Job 36:22 . . . Who is a *t* like him?
Prov 5:13 . . . didn't I listen to my *t-s?*
Eccl 1:1 . . . words of the *T,* King David's
Matt 10:24 . . . not greater than their *t,*
Matt 23:10 . . . only one *t,* the Messiah.
Luke 6:40 . . . will become like the *t.*

Luke 20:46 . . . these *t-s* of religious law!
John 13:14 . . . Lord and *T,* have washed
Rom 12:7 . . . If you are a *t,* teach well.
1 Cor 12:28 . . . third are *t-s,* then those
Gal 6:6 . . . should provide for their *t-s,*
Eph 4:11 . . . and the pastors and *t-s.*
2 Tim 4:3 . . . look for *t-s* who will tell
Jas 3:1 . . . of you should become *t-s*
3 Jn 1:10 . . . the traveling *t-s,* he also

**TEACHING, TEACHINGS (n)** something taught; doctrine
*see also* INSTRUCTION(S), LAW(S)
Isa 8:20 . . . to God's instructions and *t-s!*
Luke 6:47 . . . listens to my *t,* and then
John 7:17 . . . whether my *t* is from God
John 8:31 . . . remain faithful to my *t-s.*
Acts 2:42 . . . themselves to the apostles' *t,*
Eph 4:14 . . . about by every wind of new *t.*
1 Thes 4:8 . . . not disobeying human *t* but
2 Thes 2:15 . . . grip on the *t* we passed on
1 Tim 1:3 . . . those whose *t* is contrary to
1 Tim 1:10 . . . contradicts the wholesome *t*
1 Tim 4:6 . . . and the good *t* you have
1 Tim 4:16 . . . how you live and on your *t.*
1 Tim 6:3 . . . people may contradict our *t,*
2 Tim 4:2 . . . your people with good *t.*
Titus 1:9 . . . with wholesome *t* and show
Titus 3:8 . . . insist on these *t-s* so that
Heb 6:1 . . . stop going over the basic *t-s*

**TEAR, TEARS (n)** a drop of clear saline fluid secreted from the eye
Job 16:20 . . . I pour out my *t-s* to God.
Isa 25:8 . . . will wipe away all *t-s.*
Rev 7:17 . . . will wipe every *t* from their
Rev 21:4 . . . will wipe every *t* from their

**TEMPER (n)** disposition; characteristic state of mind or an emotion; proneness to anger
Ps 37:8 . . . Do not lose your *t*—it only
Prov 14:29 . . . *t* shows great foolishness.
Prov 19:11 . . . people control their *t;*
Eccl 7:9 . . . Control your *t,* for anger

**TEMPLE, TEMPLES (n)** first built in Solomon's reign as a permanent worship center, which was destroyed then rebuilt under Herod's reign; figurative of the human body and of Christ
*see also* HOUSE, SANCTUARY, TABERNACLE
1 Kgs 6:1 . . . to construct the *T* of the
1 Kgs 8:10 . . . cloud filled the *T* of the
1 Chr 29:16 . . . to build a *T* to honor your
2 Chr 36:19 . . . his army burned the *T*
Ps 27:4 . . . meditating in his *T.*
Isa 6:1 . . . train of his robe filled the *T.*
Jer 7:8 . . . suffer because the *T* is here.
Joel 3:18 . . . forth from the LORD's *T,*
Hab 2:20 . . . LORD is in his holy *T.*
Hag 2:18 . . . of the LORD's *T* was laid.
Matt 12:6 . . . is even greater than the *T!*
Matt 26:61 . . . able to destroy the *T* of God
Matt 27:51 . . . sanctuary of the *T* was torn
Luke 21:5 . . . stonework of the *T* and the
John 2:14 . . . the *T* area he saw merchants
Acts 5:20 . . . Go to the *T* and give the
Acts 17:24 . . . live in man-made *t-s,*
1 Cor 3:16 . . . together are the *t* of God
1 Cor 6:19 . . . body is the *t* of the Holy
Eph 2:21 . . . becoming a holy *t* for the
1 Pet 2:5 . . . building into his spiritual *t.*
Rev 21:22 . . . and the Lamb are its *t.*

**TEMPT, TEMPTED, TEMPTING (v)** to entice to do wrong by promise of pleasure or gain; to test
Isa 13:17 . . . They cannot be *t-ed* by silver
Matt 4:1 . . . wilderness to be *t-ed* there by
Luke 4:2 . . . where he was *t-ed* by the devil
Luke 4:13 . . . finished *t-ing* Jesus, he left
1 Cor 7:5 . . . be able to *t* you because
1 Cor 10:13 . . . When you are *t-ed,* he will
Jas 1:13 . . . you are being *t-ed,* do not say,
Jas 1:13 . . . God is never *t-ed* to do wrong,

**TEMPTATION, TEMPTATIONS (n)** a cause or occasion of enticement
Matt 6:13 . . . don't let us yield to *t,*
Matt 18:7 . . . *T-s* are inevitable, but what
Matt 26:41 . . . will not give in to *t.*
Luke 8:13 . . . fall away when they face *t.*
1 Cor 10:13 . . . The *t-s* in your life are
1 Cor 10:13 . . . not allow the *t* to be
Gal 6:1 . . . fall into the same *t* yourself.
1 Tim 6:9 . . . to be rich fall into *t* and
Jas 1:12 . . . endure testing and *t.*

**TEN (n)** the number 10
Exod 34:28 . . . the *T* Commandments—
Deut 10:4 . . . wrote the *T* Commandments on
Luke 15:8 . . . a woman has *t* silver coins
Rev 12:3 . . . seven heads and *t* horns, with

**TENDERHEARTED (adj)** easily moved to love, pity, or sorrow; compassionate
Deut 28:54 . . . The most *t* man among you
Eph 4:32 . . . each other, *t,* forgiving one
Col 3:12 . . . yourselves with *t* mercy,

**TENDERNESS (n)** the quality or state of being gentle, fond, or loving
Jas 5:11 . . . is full of *t* and mercy.

**TENTH (n)** one-tenth of any property or produce
*see also* TITHE
Gen 14:20 . . . gave Melchizedek a *t* of all
Heb 7:2 . . . Abraham took a *t* of all he

**TERRIBLE (adj)** extremely bad; terrifying
Jer 8:6 . . . What a *t* thing I have done
Zeph 1:15 . . . a day of *t* distress and
Heb 10:31 . . . It is a *t* thing to fall into

**TERRIFY, TERRIFIED, TERRIFIES (v)** to scare, deter, or intimidate; to fill with terror
Deut 2:25 . . . the earth *t-ied* because of you.
Deut 28:67 . . . you will be *t-ied* by the awful
1 Sam 12:18 . . . were *t-ied* of the LORD
Prov 21:15 . . . but it *t-ies* evildoers.
Isa 13:8 . . . and people are *t-ied.* Pangs of
Zeph 2:11 . . . The LORD will *t* them
Matt 14:26 . . . on the water, they were *t-ied.*
Matt 17:6 . . . disciples were *t-ied* and fell
Matt 27:54 . . . the crucifixion were *t-ied*
Mark 4:41 . . . disciples were absolutely *t-ied.*
Luke 21:26 . . . will be *t-ied* at what they

**TERRIFYING (adj)** causing terror or apprehension
Deut 4:34 . . . powerful arm, and *t* acts?
Deut 34:12 . . . Moses performed *t* acts in the
Judg 13:6 . . . of God's angels, *t* to see.

**TERROR, TERRORS (n)** a state of intense fear; a frightening aspect
Deut 7:19 . . . Remember the great *t-s* the
Job 9:34 . . . no longer live in *t* of his
Ps 53:5 . . . will grip them, *t* like they
Ps 91:5 . . . afraid of the *t-s* of the night,

Prov 22:8 . . . their reign of *t* will come to
Isa 51:17 . . . the cup of *t*, tipping out its
Mic 7:17 . . . trembling in *t* at his
Luke 9:34 . . . them, and *t* gripped them
Acts 7:32 . . . Moses shook with *t* and did

**TEST, TESTINGS, TESTS (n)** a critical examination, observation, or evaluation
*see also* TRIAL(S), TROUBLE(S)
Deut 29:3 . . . all the great *t-s* of strength,
1 Cor 10:9 . . . should we put Christ to the *t*,
1 Tim 3:10 . . . If they pass the *t*, then let
Heb 4:15 . . . of the same *t-ings* we do, yet

**TEST, TESTED, TESTING, TESTS (v)** to put to test or proof
Gen 22:1 . . . God *t-ed* Abraham's faith.
Deut 6:16 . . . You must not *t* the LORD your
Judg 3:1 . . . land to *t* those Israelites
1 Kgs 10:1 . . . she came to *t* him with hard
Job 23:10 . . . when he *t-s* me, I will come
Ps 17:3 . . . You have *t-ed* my thoughts
Ps 66:10 . . . You have *t-ed* us,
Ps 78:18 . . . They stubbornly *t-ed* God in
Ps 106:14 . . . ran wild, *t-ing* God's patience
Ps 139:23 . . . *t* me and know my anxious
Prov 17:3 . . . the LORD *t-s* the heart.
Luke 4:12 . . . You must not *t* the LORD your
Acts 5:9 . . . of conspiring to *t* the Spirit
1 Thes 5:21 . . . but *t* everything that is said.
Heb 2:18 . . . suffering and *t-ing*, he is able
Heb 2:18 . . . us when we are being *t-ed*.
Heb 3:8 . . . they *t-ed* me in the wilderness.
Heb 11:17 . . . when God was *t-ing* him.
Jas 1:3 . . . when your faith is *t-ed*, your
Jas 1:12 . . . who patiently endure *t-ing* and
1 Pet 1:7 . . . It is being *t-ed* as fire tests
1 Jn 4:1 . . . You must *t* them to see if
Rev 2:10 . . . you into prison to *t* you.
Rev 3:10 . . . great time of *t-ing* that will

**TESTIFY, TESTIFIED, TESTIFIES, TESTIFYING (v)** to make a statement based on personal knowledge or belief; to give evidence or proof
Exod 20:16 . . . must not *t* falsely against
Deut 5:20 . . . must not *t* falsely against
Prov 24:28 . . . Don't *t* against your
Luke 18:20 . . . You must not *t* falsely.
John 1:34 . . . Jesus, so I *t* that he is
John 5:32 . . . else is also *t-ing* about me,
John 15:26 . . . Father and will *t* all about
John 18:37 . . . the world to *t* to the truth.
John 21:24 . . . one who *t-ies* to these events
Acts 4:33 . . . The apostles *t-ied* powerfully
Acts 10:43 . . . the prophets *t-ied* about,
1 Jn 4:14 . . . own eyes and now *t* that the

**TESTIMONY (n)** the evidence given by a witness
*see also* TESTIFY
Num 35:30 . . . to death on the *t* of only
John 1:7 . . . might believe because of his *t*.
1 Tim 6:13 . . . gave a good *t* before Pontius
1 Jn 5:9 . . . Since we believe human *t*,
Rev 12:11 . . . of the Lamb and by their *t*.

**THANK, THANKING (v)** to express gratitude to; to acknowledge God's goodness
Ps 35:18 . . . Then I will *t* you in front
Ps 79:13 . . . pasture, will *t* you forever
Ps 145:10 . . . works will *t* you, LORD,
Isa 12:4 . . . sing: "*T* the LORD!
1 Cor 10:30 . . . If I can *t* God for the food
Phil 4:6 . . . and *t* him for all he has done.

1 Thes 2:13 . . . we never stop *t-ing* God
1 Thes 3:9 . . . How we *t* God for you!

**THANKFUL (adj)** conscious of benefit received; expressive of thanks
Col 3:15 . . . And always be *t*.
Col 3:16 . . . to God with *t* hearts.
1 Thes 5:18 . . . Be *t* in all circumstances,
Heb 12:28 . . . let us be *t* and please God by

**THANKS (n)** kindly or grateful thoughts; gratitude
1 Chr 16:4 . . . to give *t*, and to praise
Ps 30:12 . . . I will give you *t* forever!
Ps 107:1 . . . Give *t* to the LORD,
Rom 1:21 . . . as God or even give him *t*.
1 Cor 11:24 . . . gave *t* to God for it.
Phil 1:3 . . . of you, I give *t* to my God.
1 Tim 2:1 . . . behalf, and give *t* for them.
1 Tim 4:3 . . . be eaten with *t* by faithful
Rev 4:9 . . . and honor and *t* to the one

**THANKSGIVING (n)** a prayer expressing gratitude; a public acknowledgment or celebration of God's goodness
Ps 26:7 . . . singing a song of *t* and telling
Ps 28:7 . . . I burst out in songs of *t*.
Ps 100:4 . . . Enter his gates with *t*; go
Isa 51:3 . . . Songs of *t* will fill the air.

**THIEF, THIEVES (n)** one that steals, especially stealthily or secretly
Prov 6:30 . . . might be found for a *t*
Prov 29:24 . . . If you assist a *t*, you only
Jer 7:11 . . . has become a den of *t-ves?*
Matt 6:19 . . . where *t-ves* break in and steal.
Luke 19:46 . . . turned it into a den of *t-ves*.
John 10:1 . . . surely be a *t* and a robber!
John 10:8 . . . me were *t-ves* and robbers.
1 Cor 6:10 . . . or are *t-ves*, or greedy people,
1 Thes 5:2 . . . unexpectedly, like a *t* in the
Rev 16:15 . . . as unexpectedly as a *t!*

**THINK, THINKING, THINKS (v)** to reflect, ponder, or remember; to subject to the processes of logical thought; to have as an opinion; to conceive or reason
*see also* MEDITATE, THOUGHT
1 Sam 12:24 . . . *T* of all the wonderful
2 Chr 19:6 . . . Always *t* carefully before
Ps 8:4 . . . you should *t* about them,
Ps 63:6 . . . I lie awake *t-ing* of you,
Ps 77:12 . . . I cannot stop *t-ing* about your
Ps 119:97 . . . I *t* about them all day long.
Ps 119:148 . . . the night, *t-ing* about your
Prov 13:16 . . . Wise people *t* before they
Prov 15:28 . . . godly *t-s* carefully before
Prov 21:29 . . . the virtuous *t* before they
Prov 23:7 . . . are always *t-ing* about how
Prov 29:20 . . . who speaks without *t-ing*.
Isa 44:18 . . . are shut, and they cannot *t*.
Matt 22:42 . . . What do you *t* about the
Rom 11:20 . . . So don't *t* highly of
Phil 1:3 . . . Every time I *t* of you, I give
Phil 2:3 . . . Be humble, *t-ing* of others as
Phil 3:19 . . . they *t* only about this life
Heb 10:24 . . . Let us *t* of ways to motivate
1 Pet 1:13 . . . So *t* clearly and exercise

**THIRST (v)** to crave vehemently and urgently
Ps 42:2 . . . I *t* for God, the living God.
Matt 5:6 . . . who hunger and *t* for justice,

**THIRSTY (adj)** feeling a desire for liquids; having a strong desire

Ps 107:9 . . . he satisfies the *t* and fills
Prov 25:21 . . . If they are *t*, give them
Isa 55:1 . . . Is anyone *t?* Come and drink—
Matt 25:35 . . . I was *t*, and you gave
John 4:14 . . . will never be *t* again.
Rom 12:20 . . . If they are *t*, give them
2 Cor 11:27 . . . been hungry and *t* and
Rev 7:16 . . . never again be hungry or *t*;
Rev 22:17 . . . Let anyone who is *t* come.

**THORN, THORNS (n)** a woody plant bearing sharp impeding prickles or spines; something that causes distress or irritation
Gen 3:18 . . . It will grow *t-s* and thistles
Num 33:55 . . . in your eyes and *t-s* in your
Matt 13:7 . . . seeds fell among *t-s* that
Matt 27:29 . . . wove *t* branches into a
2 Cor 12:7 . . . I was given a *t* in my flesh,
Heb 6:8 . . . a field bears *t-s* and thistles,

**THORNBUSHES (n)** any of various spiny or thorny shrubs or small trees
Luke 6:44 . . . Figs are never gathered from *t*,

**THOUGHT, THOUGHTS (n)** the action or process of thinking; a developed intention or plan; recollection, remembrance
Ps 77:12 . . . They are constantly in my *t-s*.
Ps 92:5 . . . And how deep are your *t-s*.
Ps 94:11 . . . LORD knows people's *t-s*;
Ps 104:34 . . . May all my *t-s* be pleasing
Ps 139:23 . . . and know my anxious *t-s*.
Ps 142:4 . . . no one gives me a passing *t!*
Isa 26:3 . . . whose *t-s* are fixed on you!
Isa 55:8 . . . My *t-s* are nothing like your
Matt 9:4 . . . you have such evil *t-s* in your
Matt 15:19 . . . heart come evil *t-s*, murder,
1 Cor 14:25 . . . their secret *t-s* will be
Eph 4:23 . . . renew your *t-s* and attitudes.
Rev 2:23 . . . searches out the *t-s* and

**THOUSAND (adj)** of the number 1,000
Ps 90:4 . . . For you, a *t* years are as
Rev 20:7 . . . When the *t* years come to an

**THOUSANDS (n)** a very large number
Joel 3:14 . . . Thousands upon *t* are waiting

**THREE (adj)** the number 3
Deut 19:15 . . . of two or *t* witnesses.
Jon 1:17 . . . three days and *t* nights.
Matt 12:40 . . . three days and *t* nights,
Matt 18:20 . . . where two or *t* gather
Matt 26:34 . . . you will deny *t* times that
Mark 8:31 . . . but *t* days later he would rise
1 Jn 5:7 . . . have these *t* witnesses—

**THRONE, THRONES (n)** seat of power for a king or deity; symbolic of royal authority and the king's role as a judge
Deut 17:18 . . . he sits on the *t* as king,
2 Sam 7:16 . . . and your *t* will be secure
1 Chr 17:12 . . . will secure his *t* forever.
Job 36:7 . . . sets them on *t-s* with kings
Ps 45:6 . . . Your *t*, O God, endures
Ps 47:8 . . . nations, sitting on his holy *t*.
Ps 89:14 . . . are the foundation of your *t*.
Ps 99:1 . . . He sits on his *t* between the
Ps 102:12 . . . sit on your *t* forever.
Ps 103:19 . . . has made the heavens his *t*;
Isa 6:1 . . . He was sitting on a lofty *t*,
Isa 66:1 . . . Heaven is my *t*, and the
Dan 7:9 . . . on a fiery *t* with wheels
Matt 19:28 . . . upon his glorious *t*, you who
Matt 19:28 . . . sit on twelve *t-s*, judging

Acts 7:49 . . . Heaven is my *t,* and the
Rom 15:12 . . . heir to David's *t* will come,
Col 1:16 . . . such as *t-s,* kingdoms, rulers,
Heb 12:2 . . . place of honor beside God's *t.*
Rev 3:21 . . . sat with my Father on his *t.*
Rev 4:2 . . . and I saw a *t* in heaven
Rev 4:4 . . . Twenty-four *t-s* surrounded
Rev 5:5 . . . heir to David's *t,* has won
Rev 20:11 . . . a great white *t* and the
Rev 22:3 . . . the *t* of God and of the Lamb

**TIME, TIMES (n)** occasion; an opportune or suitable moment; an appointed, fixed, or customary moment or hour for something to happen, begin, or end; duration; conditions at present or at some specified period; added or accumulated quantities or instances
Esth 4:14 . . . keep quiet at a *t* like this,
Ps 9:9 . . . a refuge in *t-s* of trouble.
Ps 62:8 . . . trust in him at all *t-s.*
Eccl 3:1 . . . a *t* for every activity under
Eccl 7:14 . . . when hard *t-s* strike,
Eccl 8:5 . . . wise will find a *t* and a way
Dan 12:7 . . . times, and half a *t.*
Hos 10:12 . . . for now is the *t* to seek the
Amos 5:13 . . . shut, for it is an evil *t.*
Matt 16:3 . . . interpret the signs of the *t-s!*
Matt 18:21 . . . sins against me? Seven *t-s?*
Luke 12:40 . . . ready all the *t,* for the Son
John 4:53 . . . was the very *t* Jesus had told
John 12:23 . . . the *t* has come for the Son
Acts 1:7 . . . those dates and *t-s,* and they
Acts 18:5 . . . spent all his *t* preaching
1 Cor 7:29 . . . The *t* that remains is very
2 Cor 6:2 . . . the "right *t*" is now.
Gal 6:9 . . . just the right *t* we will reap
2 Tim 1:9 . . . the beginning of *t*—to show
Heb 9:28 . . . once for all *t* as a sacrifice
Heb 10:12 . . . for sins, good for all *t.*
1 Pet 4:17 . . . For the *t* has come for
Rev 12:14 . . . for a time, *t-s,* and half a

**TIRED (adj)** drained of strength and energy
Exod 17:12 . . . became so *t* he could no
Isa 35:3 . . . those who have *t* hands,
Gal 6:9 . . . let's not get *t* of doing what
2 Thes 3:13 . . . never get *t* of doing good.
Heb 12:12 . . . new grip with your *t* hands

**TITHE, TITHES (n)** one-tenth of any property or produce
*see also* TENTH
Num 18:21 . . . give them the *t-s* from the
Deut 12:17 . . . neither the *t* of your grain
2 Chr 31:12 . . . brought all the *t-s* and
Amos 4:4 . . . bring your *t-s* every three
Mal 3:8 . . . of the *t-s* and offerings due
Mal 3:10 . . . Bring all the *t-s* into the

**TITHE (v)** to pay or give a tenth of as an offering to God
Matt 23:23 . . . You should *t,* yes,
Luke 11:42 . . . you are careful to *t* even the

**TODAY (adv)** on or for this day; at the present time
Ps 2:7 . . . *T* I have become your Father.
Ps 95:7 . . . listen to his voice *t!*
Matt 6:11 . . . Give us *t* the food we
Luke 2:11 . . . born *t* in Bethlehem,
Luke 23:43 . . . I assure you, *t* you will be
Heb 1:5 . . . *T* I have become your Father.
Heb 3:7 . . . *T* when you hear his voice,
Heb 13:8 . . . is the same yesterday, *t,* and

**TOMORROW (n)** the day after the present; the future
Prov 27:1 . . . Don't brag about *t,* since you
Isa 22:13 . . . and drink, for *t* we die!
Rom 8:38 . . . our worries about *t*—not even
1 Cor 15:32 . . . and drink, for *t* we die!

**TONGUE, TONGUES (n)** part of the mouth that enables speech; dialect or language of a people; a special gift of speech given by the Holy Spirit
*see also* LANGUAGE(S)
Ps 5:9 . . . Their *t-s* are filled
Ps 34:13 . . . keep your *t* from speaking
Ps 39:1 . . . I will hold my *t* when
Ps 45:1 . . . king, for my *t* is like
Ps 78:36 . . . lied to him with their *t-s.*
Ps 119:172 . . . Let my *t* sing about
Ps 137:6 . . . May my *t* stick to the
Prov 13:3 . . . who control their *t* will have
Prov 15:4 . . . a deceitful *t* crushes the
Prov 17:20 . . . the lying *t* tumbles into
Prov 21:23 . . . Watch your *t* and keep
Luke 16:24 . . . in water and cool my *t.*
Acts 2:3 . . . like flames or *t-s* of fire
Acts 10:46 . . . speaking in other *t-s* and praising
Acts 19:6 . . . in other *t-s* and prophesied.
Rom 14:11 . . . me, and every *t* will confess
1 Cor 14:2 . . . to speak in *t-s,* you will
1 Cor 14:4 . . . speaks in *t-s* is strengthened
1 Cor 14:5 . . . speak in *t-s,* but even more
1 Cor 14:13 . . . speaks in *t-s* should pray
1 Cor 14:18 . . . I speak in *t-s* more than
1 Cor 14:27 . . . three should speak in *t-s.*
1 Cor 14:39 . . . forbid speaking in *t-s.*
Phil 2:11 . . . and every *t* confess that
Jas 3:2 . . . if we could control our *t-s,* we
Jas 3:5 . . . same way, the *t* is a small

**TOOTH (n)** a bonelike structure in the mouth used for chewing
Exod 21:24 . . . eye for an eye, a *t* for a *t,*
Matt 5:38 . . . eye for an eye, and a *t* for a *t.*

**TORTURED (v)** to punish or coerce by inflicting excruciating pain
Matt 18:34 . . . prison to be *t* until he
Heb 11:35 . . . others were *t,* refusing to

**TOUCH, TOUCHED, TOUCHES (v)** to reach out or come in contact with; to lay hands upon; to have an influence upon
Gen 3:3 . . . must not eat it or even *t* it;
Exod 19:12 . . . or even *t* its boundaries.
Exod 19:12 . . . Anyone who *t-es* the mountain
Isa 6:7 . . . this coal has *t-ed* your lips.
Matt 9:21 . . . If I can just *t* his robe,
Matt 14:36 . . . who *t-ed* him were healed.
Luke 8:45 . . . "Who *t-ed* me?" Jesus asked.
Luke 18:15 . . . so he could *t* and bless
Luke 24:39 . . . *T* me and make sure that
2 Cor 6:17 . . . Don't *t* their filthy things,
Col 2:21 . . . Don't taste! Don't *t!* "?
1 Jn 1:1 . . . *t-ed* him with our own hands.
1 Jn 5:18 . . . evil one cannot *t* them.

**TRADE, TRADED (v)** to give one thing in exchange for another
Gen 25:31 . . . Jacob replied, "but *t* me your
Ps 106:20 . . . They *t-d* their glorious God
Rom 1:25 . . . They *t-d* the truth about God

**TRADITION, TRADITIONS (n)** an inherited, customary, or established pattern of thought, action, or behavior

Matt 15:6 . . . for the sake of your own *t.*
Mark 7:5 . . . disciples follow our age-old *t?*
Mark 7:8 . . . law and substitute your own *t.*
Mark 7:13 . . . to hand down your own *t.*
Gal 1:14 . . . in my zeal for the *t-s* of my

**TRAIN (n)** a part of a gown that trails behind the wearer
Isa 6:1 . . . throne, and the *t* of his robe

**TRAIN, TRAINED (v)** to form by or undergo instruction, discipline, or drill
*see also* TEACH
Isa 2:4 . . . against nation, nor *t* for war
Luke 6:40 . . . who is fully *t-ed* will become
John 7:15 . . . when he hasn't been *t-ed?*
Acts 22:3 . . . I was carefully *t-ed* in our
1 Tim 4:7 . . . *t* yourself to be godly.
Titus 2:4 . . . women must *t* the younger
Heb 12:11 . . . those who are *t-ed* in this way.

**TRAITORS (n)** one who betrays another's trust, is false to an obligation or duty, or commits treason
Ps 59:5 . . . Show no mercy to wicked *t.*
Ps 119:158 . . . Seeing these *t* makes me

**TRAMPLE, TRAMPLED (v)** to crush, injure, or destroy by or as if by treading
Ps 60:12 . . . for he will *t* down our foes.
Ps 91:13 . . . You will *t* upon lions
Amos 5:11 . . . You *t* the poor,
Amos 8:4 . . . rob the poor and *t* down the
Mic 4:13 . . . so you can *t* many nations to
Mic 7:19 . . . You will *t* our sins under
Matt 7:6 . . . They will *t* the pearls,
Luke 21:24 . . . Jerusalem will be *t-d* down
Heb 10:29 . . . who have *t-d* on the Son
Rev 14:20 . . . The grapes were *t-d* in the

**TRANSFIGURED (KJV)**
Matt 17:2 . . . Jesus' appearance was *transformed*
Mark 9:2 . . . Jesus' appearance was *transformed*

**TRANSFORM, TRANSFORMED (v)** to change the outward appearance of; to change in character or condition
*see also* CHANGE(D)
Matt 17:2 . . . appearance was *t-ed* so that
Rom 12:2 . . . let God *t* you into a new
1 Cor 15:51 . . . but we will all be *t-ed!*

**TRANSGRESSED, TRANSGRESSION (KJV)**
Josh 7:11 . . . and *broken* my covenant
1 Chr 5:25 . . . tribes were *unfaithful*
1 Chr 10:13 . . . because he was *unfaithful*
Rom 4:15 . . . to avoid *breaking* the law
1 Jn 3:4 . . . sin is *contrary to* the law

**TRAP, TRAPS (n)** something by which one is caught or stopped unawares; a position or situation from which it is difficult or impossible to escape; a device for taking game or other animals
Deut 7:25 . . . will become a *t* to you,
Deut 12:30 . . . fall into the *t* of following
Ps 91:3 . . . you from every *t* and protect
Prov 1:17 . . . a bird sees a *t* being set,
Prov 3:26 . . . foot from being caught in a *t.*
Prov 28:10 . . . into their own *t,* but the
Prov 29:5 . . . is to lay a *t* for their feet.
Prov 29:25 . . . a dangerous *t,* but trusting
Isa 8:14 . . . he will be a *t* and a snare.

Isa 24:17 . . . Terror and *t-s* and snares will
Matt 16:23 . . . are a dangerous *t* to me.
Rom 11:9 . . . a snare, a *t* that makes them
1 Tim 3:7 . . . into the devil's *t.*
2 Tim 2:26 . . . from the devil's *t.*

**TRAP, TRAPPED, TRAPS (v)** to catch or take in
or as if in a trap
Ps 7:15 . . . a deep pit to *t* others, then
Ps 9:16 . . . wicked are *t-ped* by their own
Prov 6:2 . . . if you have *t-ped* yourself by
Prov 12:13 . . . wicked are *t-ped* by their
Prov 18:7 . . . they *t* themselves with
Matt 22:15 . . . to plot how to *t* Jesus into
1 Cor 3:19 . . . He *t-s* the wise in the snare
1 Tim 6:9 . . . temptation and are *t-ped* by

**TREAD, TREADING, TREADS (v)** to beat or
press with the feet
Deut 25:4 . . . eating as it *t-s* out the grain.
Isa 63:2 . . . have been *t-ing* out grapes?
Joel 3:13 . . . Come, *t* the grapes,
1 Cor 9:9 . . . from eating as it *t-s* out
1 Tim 5:18 . . . from eating as it *t-s* out

**TREASURE, TREASURES (n)** wealth or a
collection of precious things; something of great
value
Exod 19:5 . . . my own special *t* from
Deut 7:6 . . . to be his own special *t.*
1 Chr 29:3 . . . my own private *t-s* of gold
Ps 119:111 . . . Your laws are my *t;* they
Ps 135:4 . . . Israel for his own special *t.*
Prov 2:4 . . . seek them like hidden *t-s.*
Prov 18:22 . . . finds a wife finds a *t,*
Song 4:10 . . . delights me, my *t,* my bride.
Isa 10:3 . . . Where will your *t-s* be safe?
Hag 2:7 . . . the *t-s* of all the nations
Mal 3:17 . . . they will be my own special *t.*
Matt 6:19 . . . Don't store up *t-s* here on
Matt 6:21 . . . Wherever your *t* is, there the
Matt 13:44 . . . Heaven is like a *t* that a man
Luke 12:33 . . . will store up *t* for you in
2 Cor 4:7 . . . jars containing this great *t.*
Eph 3:8 . . . the endless *t-s* available to
Col 2:3 . . . hidden all the *t-s* of wisdom
1 Tim 6:19 . . . storing up their *t* as a good
Heb 11:26 . . . to own the *t-s* of Egypt, for

**TREASURE, TREASURED (v)** to hold or keep
as precious
Job 23:12 . . . but have *t-d* his words more
Prov 2:1 . . . I say, and *t* my commands.
Prov 7:1 . . . always *t* my commands.
Prov 10:14 . . . Wise people *t* knowledge,

**TREASURY (n)** a place in which stores of
wealth are kept
Deut 28:12 . . . time from his rich *t* in the
Luke 6:45 . . . things from the *t* of a good

**TREE, TREES (n)** woody perennial plants,
many of which produce crops; highly treasured
natural resource; often linked with worship of
pagan gods; symbolic of a growing believer
Gen 2:9 . . . he placed the *t* of life and
Deut 21:23 . . . from the *t* overnight.
Judg 9:8 . . . the *t-s* decided to choose
2 Sam 18:9 . . . got caught in the *t.*
1 Kgs 14:23 . . . and under every green *t.*
Ps 1:3 . . . They are like *t-s* planted along
Ps 52:8 . . . like an olive *t,* thriving in
Ps 92:12 . . . like palm *t-s* and grow
Ps 96:12 . . . Let the *t-s* of the forest

Prov 3:18 . . . Wisdom is a *t* of life to
Prov 11:30 . . . deeds become a *t* of life;
Isa 55:12 . . . and the *t-s* of the field
Isa 65:22 . . . people will live as long as *t-s,*
Jer 17:8 . . . They are like *t-s* planted along
Dan 4:10 . . . saw a large *t* in the middle
Mic 4:4 . . . and fig *t-s,* for there will be
Matt 3:10 . . . sever the roots of the *t-s.*
Matt 3:10 . . . every *t* that does not produce
Matt 12:33 . . . *t* is identified by its fruit.
Mark 8:24 . . . look like *t-s* walking
Luke 19:4 . . . a sycamore-fig *t* beside the
Rom 11:24 . . . cut from a wild olive *t.*
Gal 3:13 . . . everyone who is hung on a *t.*
Jas 3:12 . . . Does a fig *t* produce olives,
Jude 1:12 . . . They are like *t-s* in autumn
Rev 22:2 . . . the river grew a *t* of life,
Rev 22:14 . . . the fruit from the *t* of life.
Rev 22:19 . . . share in the *t* of life and

**TREMBLE, TREMBLED, TREMBLES,
TREMBLING (v)** to be affected with great fear
or anxiety; to shake involuntarily
Exod 15:14 . . . hear and *t;* anguish grips
Exod 19:16 . . . horn, and all the people *t-d.*
Exod 20:18 . . . a distance, *t-ing* with fear.
2 Sam 22:8 . . . the earth quaked and *t-d.*
1 Chr 16:30 . . . all the earth *t* before him.
Ps 2:11 . . . fear, and rejoice with *t-ing.*
Ps 97:4 . . . The earth sees and *t-s.*
Ps 102:15 . . . the earth will *t* before his
Ps 104:32 . . . The earth *t-s* at his glance;
Isa 66:2 . . . contrite hearts, who *t* at my
Jer 10:10 . . . whole earth *t-s* at his anger.
Dan 10:10 . . . and lifted me, still *t-ing,*
Joel 2:1 . . . Let everyone *t* in fear
Nah 1:5 . . . hills melt away; the earth *t-s,*
Hab 3:6 . . . the nations *t.* He shatters
Heb 4:1 . . . we ought to *t* with fear that
Heb 12:21 . . . I am terrified and *t-ing.*

**TRESPASS(ES) (KJV)**
Lev 19:21 . . . a ram as a *guilt* offering
2 Chr 24:18 . . . Because of this *sin,* divine
Matt 6:15 . . . Father will not forgive your *sins*
Matt 18:15 . . . believer *sins* against you,
Eph 2:1 . . . because of your *disobedience*

**TRIAL, TRIALS (n)** a legal proceeding based in
court; a test of faith, patience, or stamina
through subjection to suffering or temptation
*see also* TEMPTATION(S), TEST(S), TROUBLE(S)
Job 42:11 . . . all the *t-s* the LORD had
Ps 26:2 . . . Put me on *t,* LORD,
Ps 37:33 . . . when they are put on *t.*
Ps 143:2 . . . Don't put your servant on *t,*
Mark 13:11 . . . and stand *t,* don't worry in
Luke 22:28 . . . with me in my time of *t.*
John 16:33 . . . have many *t-s* and sorrows.
Rom 5:3 . . . into problems and *t-s,* for we
1 Pet 1:7 . . . through many *t-s,* it will
1 Pet 4:12 . . . the fiery *t-s* you are going
2 Pet 2:9 . . . from their *t-s,* even while

**TRIBULATION (n)** a period of unparalleled
suffering in the last days
Rev 7:14 . . . who died in the great *t.*

**TRICK, TRICKED (v)** to deceive or cheat
Gen 27:35 . . . and he *t-d* me
Gen 29:25 . . . Why have you *t-d* me
Jer 29:31 . . . has *t-d* you into believing
2 Cor 4:2 . . . We don't try to *t* anyone

Eph 4:14 . . . people try to *t* us with lies

**TRICKERY (n)** deception
Isa 29:21 . . . those who use *t* to pervert
2 Cor 12:16 . . . advantage of you by *t.*

**TROUBLE, TROUBLES (n)** a state, condition, or
cause of distress, annoyance, difficulty, or
inconvenience
*see also* TEST(S), TRIAL(S)
Gen 41:51 . . . made me forget all my *t-s*
Josh 7:25 . . . have you brought *t* on us?
2 Chr 15:4 . . . they were in *t* and turned
Job 5:7 . . . are born for *t* as readily as
Ps 7:14 . . . they are pregnant with *t*
Ps 9:9 . . . a refuge in times of *t.*
Ps 10:14 . . . you see the *t* and grief
Ps 22:11 . . . from me, for *t* is near,
Ps 27:5 . . . me there when *t-s* come;
Ps 32:7 . . . you protect me from *t.*
Ps 34:17 . . . them from all their *t-s.*
Ps 37:39 . . . their fortress in times of *t.*
Ps 40:12 . . . For *t-s* surround me—
Ps 41:1 . . . them when they are in *t.*
Ps 46:1 . . . ready to help in times of *t.*
Ps 49:5 . . . I fear when *t* comes, when
Ps 50:15 . . . when you are in *t,* and I will
Ps 54:7 . . . have rescued me from my *t-s*
Ps 55:3 . . . They bring *t* on me
Ps 66:14 . . . I was in deep *t.*
Ps 81:7 . . . cried to me in *t,* and
Ps 86:7 . . . whenever I'm in *t,* and
Ps 91:15 . . . I will be with them in *t.*
Ps 107:6 . . . they cried in their *t,*
Ps 107:41 . . . rescues the poor from *t*
Ps 116:3 . . . I saw only *t* and sorrow.
Ps 120:1 . . . took my *t-s* to the LORD;
Ps 138:7 . . . I am surrounded by *t-s,* you
Prov 6:14 . . . they constantly stir up *t.*
Prov 10:10 . . . who wink at wrong cause *t,*
Prov 11:8 . . . godly are rescued from *t,*
Prov 11:29 . . . Those who bring *t* on their
Prov 12:13 . . . the godly escape such *t.*
Prov 12:21 . . . wicked have their fill of *t.*
Prov 13:20 . . . with fools and get in *t.*
Prov 25:19 . . . in times of *t* is like chewing
Eccl 4:10 . . . falls alone is in real *t.*
Isa 38:14 . . . I am in *t,* LORD. Help me!
Isa 53:4 . . . And we thought his *t-s* were
Isa 58:10 . . . and help those in *t.*
Hos 5:15 . . . as soon as *t* comes, they
Nah 1:7 . . . strong refuge when *t* comes.
Matt 6:34 . . . Today's *t* is enough
Rom 8:35 . . . if we have *t* or calamity,
1 Cor 7:28 . . . at this time will have *t-s,*
2 Cor 4:17 . . . our present *t-s* are small
2 Cor 6:4 . . . We patiently endure *t-s* and
2 Cor 7:4 . . . me happy despite all our *t-s.*
2 Cor 8:2 . . . being tested by many *t-s,*
1 Thes 3:3 . . . shaken by the *t-s* you were
1 Tim 6:5 . . . These people always cause *t.*
Jas 1:2 . . . when *t-s* come your way,
Jas 5:1 . . . all the terrible *t-s* ahead

**TRUE (adj)** fully realized or fulfilled; accurate;
properly so called; steadfast, loyal, honest,
and just; ideal, essential; being in accordance
with the actual state of affairs; legitimate,
rightful
Num 11:23 . . . my word comes *t!*
Deut 18:22 . . . does not happen or come *t,*
Josh 23:14 . . . your God has come *t.*

1 Sam 9:6 . . . everything he says comes *t.*
1 Kgs 10:6 . . . and wisdom is *t!*
2 Chr 15:3 . . . without the *t* God,
Ps 7:10 . . . hearts are *t* and right.
Ps 19:9 . . . laws of the LORD are *t;*
Ps 119:142 . . . instructions are perfectly *t.*
Ps 119:151 . . . your commands are *t.*
Isa 45:19 . . . speak only what is *t* and
Jer 10:10 . . . is the only *t* God.
Jer 26:15 . . . it is absolutely *t* that
Jer 28:9 . . . when his predictions come *t*
Luke 16:11 . . . the *t* riches of heaven?
Luke 18:31 . . . Son of Man will come *t.*
John 1:9 . . . one who is the *t* light,
John 3:33 . . . can affirm that God is *t.*
John 4:23 . . . *t* worshipers will worship
John 6:32 . . . offers you the *t* bread
John 6:55 . . . my flesh is *t* food, and
John 7:28 . . . one who sent me is *t,*
John 15:1 . . . I am the *t* grapevine,
John 17:3 . . . know you, the only *t* God,
Rom 3:4 . . . else is a liar, God is *t.*
Rom 15:8 . . . God is *t* to the promises
Eph 5:9 . . . is good and right and *t.*
Phil 4:1 . . . stay *t* to the Lord.
Phil 4:8 . . . thoughts on what is *t,*
Jas 1:18 . . . giving us his *t* word.
1 Jn 2:8 . . . the *t* light is already
1 Jn 2:27 . . . to teach you what is *t.*
1 Jn 5:20 . . . He is the only *t* God,
Rev 19:9 . . . These are *t* words that come
Rev 22:6 . . . seen is trustworthy and *t.*

**TRUMPET, TRUMPETS (n)**  a wind instrument
made of metal or an animal horn used to rally
troops on the battlefield or by priests during
sacrifices
Isa 27:13 . . . the great *t* will sound.
Matt 24:31 . . . blast of a *t,* and they will
1 Cor 15:52 . . . when the last *t* is blown.
1 Thes 4:16 . . . with the *t* call of God.
Rev 8:2 . . . they were given seven *t-s.*
Rev 8:7 . . . angel blew his *t,* and hail
Rev 18:22 . . . flutes, and *t-s* will never

**TRUST (n)**  assured reliance on the character,
ability, strength, or truth of someone or
something; hope
*see also* BELIEVE, FAITH
Job 31:24 . . . Have I put my *t* in money
Ps 40:3 . . . put their *t* in the LORD.
Ps 56:3 . . . I will put my *t* in you.
Isa 2:22 . . . Don't put your *t* in mere
Jer 13:25 . . . putting your *t* in false
Jer 17:5 . . . who put their *t* in mere
John 12:46 . . . who put their *t* in me
Heb 2:13 . . . will put my *t* in him,
1 Jn 4:16 . . . have put our *t* in his love.

**TRUST, TRUSTED, TRUSTING, TRUSTS (v)**  to
place confidence or depend; to commit or place
in one's care or keeping; to rely on the
truthfulness or accuracy of
*see also* BELIEVE, FAITH
Gen 39:8 . . . master *t-s* me with everything
Deut 1:32 . . . refused to *t* the LORD
Deut 28:52 . . . walls you *t-ed* to protect
2 Kgs 18:5 . . . Hezekiah *t-ed* in the
2 Kgs 18:19 . . . What are you *t-ing* in that
1 Chr 5:20 . . . because they *t-ed* in him.
2 Chr 13:18 . . . they *t-ed* in the LORD,
Job 4:18 . . . God does not *t* his own angels

Job 15:31 . . . fool themselves by *t-ing* in
Ps 13:5 . . . I *t* in your unfailing love.
Ps 21:7 . . . the king *t-s* in the LORD.
Ps 25:2 . . . I *t* in you, my God!
Ps 25:3 . . . No one who *t-s* in you will ever
Ps 31:14 . . . I am *t-ing* you, O LORD,
Ps 33:4 . . . we can *t* everything he
Ps 37:3 . . . *T* in the LORD and do
Ps 41:9 . . . the one I *t-ed* completely,
Ps 44:6 . . . I do not *t* in my bow;
Ps 55:23 . . . but I am *t-ing* you to save
Ps 62:8 . . . O my people, *t* in him at
Ps 71:5 . . . I've *t-ed* you, O LORD,
Ps 84:12 . . . for those who *t* in you.
Ps 86:2 . . . serve you and *t* you.
Ps 112:7 . . . confidently *t* the LORD
Ps 115:8 . . . as are all who *t* in them.
Ps 118:8 . . . LORD than to *t* in
Ps 119:42 . . . for I *t* in your word.
Prov 3:5 . . . *T* in the LORD with
Prov 21:22 . . . fortress in which they *t.*
Prov 28:25 . . . *t-ing* the LORD leads to
Prov 28:26 . . . who *t* their own insight
Prov 29:25 . . . *t-ing* the LORD means safety.
Prov 31:11 . . . Her husband can *t* her,
Isa 12:2 . . . I will *t* in him and
Isa 25:9 . . . We *t-ed* in him, and he saved
Isa 26:3 . . . peace all who *t* in you,
Isa 31:1 . . . for help, *t-ing* their horses,
Isa 40:31 . . . who *t* in the LORD
Jer 7:14 . . . this Temple that you *t* in
Jer 12:6 . . . Do not *t* them, no matter
Jer 48:7 . . . Because you have *t-ed* in your
Dan 3:28 . . . his servants who *t-ed* in him.
Dan 6:23 . . . for he had *t-ed* in his God.
Nah 1:7 . . . to those who *t* in him.
Hab 2:4 . . . They *t* in themselves,
Hab 2:18 . . . foolish to *t* in your own
Matt 18:6 . . . little ones who *t-s* in me to
John 2:24 . . . Jesus didn't *t* them,
John 12:44 . . . you are *t-ing* not only me,
John 14:1 . . . in God, and *t* also in me.
Rom 9:32 . . . instead of by *t-ing* in him.
Rom 9:33 . . . But anyone who *t-s* in him will
Rom 10:11 . . . Anyone who *t-s* in him will
Rom 15:13 . . . peace because you *t* in
1 Cor 2:5 . . . so you would *t* not in
1 Cor 7:25 . . . wisdom that can be *t-ed,*
Eph 3:17 . . . hearts as you *t* in him.
Phil 1:29 . . . the privilege of *t-ing* in Christ
Col 2:12 . . . because you *t-ed* the mighty
1 Tim 6:17 . . . not to *t* in their money,
2 Tim 1:12 . . . the one in whom I *t,*
2 Tim 3:15 . . . that comes by *t-ing* in Christ
Heb 10:22 . . . hearts fully *t-ing* him.
Heb 10:23 . . . God can be *t-ed* to keep his
1 Pet 1:9 . . . reward for *t-ing* him will be
1 Pet 2:6 . . . anyone who *t-s* in him will
1 Pet 2:7 . . . you who *t* him recognize

**TRUSTWORTHY (adj)**  worthy of confidence;
dependable
*see also* FAITHFUL, LOYAL
2 Kgs 22:7 . . . honest and *t* men.
Ps 19:7 . . . of the LORD are *t,*
Ps 119:86 . . . All your commands are *t.*
Ps 119:138 . . . perfect and completely *t.*
Prov 11:13 . . . those who are *t* can keep
Dan 6:4 . . . responsible, and completely *t.*
Titus 2:10 . . . to be entirely *t* and good.
Heb 6:19 . . . a strong and *t* anchor

**TRUTH, TRUTHS (n)**  the property (as of a
statement) of being in accord with fact or reality
(natural and spiritual); sincerity in action,
character, and utterance
Ps 15:2 . . . speaking the *t* from sincere
Ps 25:5 . . . Lead me by your *t* and teach
Ps 26:3 . . . lived according to your *t.*
Ps 43:3 . . . light and your *t;* let them
Ps 45:4 . . . defending *t,* humility, and
Ps 86:11 . . . live according to your *t!*
Ps 119:160 . . . essence of your words is *t;*
Prov 8:7 . . . for I speak the *t* and detest
Prov 12:17 . . . honest witness tells the *t;*
Prov 12:22 . . . in those who tell the *t.*
Prov 23:23 . . . Get the *t* and never sell
Isa 45:23 . . . I have spoken the *t,*
Isa 59:15 . . . Yes, *t* is gone,
Jer 4:2 . . . do so with *t,* justice,
Jer 9:3 . . . to stand up for the *t.*
Dan 10:21 . . . written in the Book of *T.*
Dan 11:2 . . . I will reveal the *t* to you.
Amos 5:10 . . . people who tell the *t!*
Zech 8:16 . . . Tell the *t* to each other.
Zech 8:19 . . . So love *t* and peace.
Luke 1:4 . . . can be certain of the *t*
John 4:23 . . . Father in spirit and in *t.*
John 7:18 . . . him speaks *t,* not lies.
John 8:32 . . . the *t* will set you free.
John 8:44 . . . there is no *t* in him.
John 14:6 . . . way, the *t,* and the life.
John 14:17 . . . who leads into all *t.*
John 15:26 . . . Advocate—the Spirit of *t.*
John 16:13 . . . the Spirit of *t* comes,
John 17:17 . . . your word, which is *t.*
John 18:37 . . . to testify to the *t.*
Acts 20:30 . . . distort the *t* in order
Acts 21:34 . . . find out the *t* in all
Acts 24:8 . . . can find out the *t* of our
Rom 1:18 . . . who suppress the *t* by their
Rom 1:25 . . . They traded the *t* about God
Rom 2:8 . . . to obey the *t* and instead
Rom 2:20 . . . complete knowledge and *t.*
1 Cor 2:13 . . . to explain spiritual *t-s.*
2 Cor 6:7 . . . We faithfully preach the *t.*
2 Cor 13:8 . . . always stand for the *t.*
Gal 2:5 . . . wanted to preserve the *t*
Gal 5:7 . . . back from following the *t?*
Eph 1:13 . . . also heard the *t,* the Good
Eph 4:15 . . . will speak the *t* in love,
Eph 6:14 . . . the belt of *t* and the body
2 Thes 2:10 . . . *t* that would save them.
2 Thes 2:12 . . . rather than believing the *t.*
1 Tim 2:4 . . . and to understand the *t.*
1 Tim 3:15 . . . and foundation of the *t.*
1 Tim 4:3 . . . people who know the *t.*
1 Tim 6:5 . . . their backs on the *t.*
2 Tim 2:15 . . . explains the word of *t.*
2 Tim 3:7 . . . able to understand the *t.*
Titus 1:14 . . . turned away from the *t.*
Heb 10:26 . . . received knowledge of the *t,*
Jas 3:14 . . . don't cover up the *t* with
Jas 5:19 . . . wanders away from the *t*
1 Pet 1:22 . . . you obeyed the *t,* so now
2 Pet 1:12 . . . standing firm in the *t*
2 Pet 2:2 . . . the way of *t* will be
1 Jn 1:8 . . . and not living in the *t.*
1 Jn 2:20 . . . all of you know the *t.*
1 Jn 3:19 . . . belong to the *t,* so we
1 Jn 4:6 . . . Spirit of *t* or the spirit
1 Jn 5:6 . . . Spirit, who is *t,* confirms

2 Jn 1:2 . . . because the *t* lives
2 Jn 1:3 . . . who live in *t* and love.
3 Jn 1:3 . . . living according to the *t.*
3 Jn 1:8 . . . partners as they teach the *t.*

**TURN, TURNED, TURNING, TURNS (v)** to convert or change allegiance; to return or change direction; to face toward or away; to divert one's attention from; to become or transform; to shape or bend
Deut 28:14 . . . You must not *t* away from
Deut 30:10 . . . if you *t* to the LORD
1 Kgs 11:4 . . . old age, they *t-ed* his heart
2 Chr 7:14 . . . seek my face and *t* from
2 Chr 34:33 . . . they did not *t* away from
Esth 9:22 . . . sorrow was *t-ed* into gladness
Ps 14:3 . . . no, all have *t-ed* away; all
Ps 30:11 . . . You have *t-ed* my mourning
Ps 40:1 . . . and he *t-ed* to me and
Ps 119:59 . . . I *t-ed* to follow your
Ps 119:102 . . . I haven't *t-ed* away from
Prov 3:7 . . . fear the LORD and *t* away
Prov 28:13 . . . confess and *t* from them,
Isa 17:7 . . . Creator and *t* their eyes to
Isa 54:8 . . . anger I *t-ed* my face away
Isa 55:7 . . . Let them *t* to the LORD
Isa 59:2 . . . he has *t-ed* away and will
Jer 14:7 . . . We have *t-ed* away from you
Jer 31:13 . . . I will *t* their mourning into
Jer 31:19 . . . I *t-ed* away from God,
Lam 3:40 . . . Let us *t* back to the LORD.
Mal 4:6 . . . preaching will *t* the hearts
Matt 3:8 . . . your sins and *t-ed* to God.
Matt 18:3 . . . truth, unless you *t* from your
Mark 4:12 . . . Otherwise, they will *t* to me
Mark 8:34 . . . must *t* from your selfish
Luke 1:17 . . . He will *t* the hearts of
Luke 22:32 . . . you have repented and *t-ed*
John 12:40 . . . and they cannot *t* to me
John 16:20 . . . will suddenly *t* to wonderful
Acts 3:19 . . . of your sins and *t* to God,
Acts 7:42 . . . Then God *t-ed* away from
Acts 26:18 . . . so they may *t* from darkness
Rom 1:26 . . . Even the women *t-ed* against
Rom 2:4 . . . to *t* you from your sin?
Rom 3:12 . . . All have *t-ed* away;
Gal 1:6 . . . that you are *t-ing* away so
2 Tim 2:19 . . . LORD must *t* away from
Titus 2:12 . . . instructed to *t* from godless
Heb 10:38 . . . in anyone who *t-s* away.
1 Pet 2:25 . . . But now you have *t-ed* to

**TWELVE (adj)** of or relating to the number 12
Gen 35:22 . . . names of the *t* sons of Jacob:
Gen 49:28 . . . These are the *t* tribes of
Matt 10:1 . . . Jesus called his *t* disciples
Luke 9:17 . . . picked up *t* baskets of
Rev 21:12 . . . names of the *t* tribes of
Rev 21:14 . . . names of the *t* apostles of
Rev 21:21 . . . The *t* gates were made of

**UNBELIEF (n)** incredulity or skepticism in matters of religious truth
Matt 13:58 . . . there because of their *u.*
Mark 6:6 . . . he was amazed at their *u.*
Mark 9:24 . . . help me overcome my *u!*
Mark 16:14 . . . them for their stubborn *u*
Rom 11:23 . . . Israel turn from their *u,*
1 Tim 1:13 . . . it in ignorance and *u.*
Heb 3:19 . . . because of their *u* they

**UNBELIEVER, UNBELIEVERS (n)** one who does not believe; a non-Christian
Matt 6:32 . . . dominate the thoughts of *u-s,*
Luke 12:30 . . . the thoughts of *u-s* all over
1 Cor 6:6 . . . right in front of *u-s!*
1 Cor 14:22 . . . for believers, but for *u-s.*
2 Cor 6:15 . . . a partner with an *u?*
1 Tim 5:8 . . . people are worse than *u-s.*
Rev 21:8 . . . But cowards, *u-s,* the corrupt,

**UNCLEAN (adj)** morally or spiritually impure; prohibited by ritual law for use or contact
Lev 10:10 . . . is ceremonially *u* and what is
Lev 11:4 . . . it is ceremonially *u* for you.
Lev 17:15 . . . remain ceremonially *u* until
Lev 27:11 . . . vow involves an *u* animal—
Isa 52:11 . . . everything you touch is *u.*
Acts 10:14 . . . have declared impure and *u.*
Acts 10:15 . . . not call something *u* if God

**UNDERSTAND (v)** to grasp the meaning or reasonableness of; to be thoroughly familiar with
Job 5:9 . . . things too marvelous to *u.*
Job 36:26 . . . is greater than we can *u.*
Ps 73:16 . . . tried to *u* why the wicked
Ps 119:27 . . . Help me *u* the meaning of
Ps 119:125 . . . then I will *u* your laws.
Ps 119:130 . . . so even the simple can *u.*
Prov 2:5 . . . will *u* what it means to fear
Prov 2:9 . . . you will *u* what is right,
Prov 28:5 . . . the LORD *u* completely.
Prov 30:18 . . . things that I don't *u:*
Eccl 7:25 . . . and to *u* the reason
Isa 6:9 . . . carefully, but do not *u.*
Isa 40:21 . . . you heard? Don't you *u?*
Jer 9:24 . . . truly know me and *u* that
Hos 14:9 . . . who are wise *u* these things.
Matt 13:11 . . . permitted to *u* the secrets
Matt 13:23 . . . truly hear and *u* God's
Luke 19:42 . . . people would *u* the way
Luke 24:45 . . . minds to *u* the Scriptures.
Acts 8:30 . . . Do you *u* what you are
Rom 7:15 . . . I don't really *u* myself,
Rom 15:21 . . . never heard of him will *u.*
1 Cor 2:14 . . . and they can't *u* it,
1 Cor 14:14 . . . but I don't *u* what I am
2 Cor 3:14 . . . they cannot *u* the truth.
Gal 1:11 . . . you to *u* that the gospel
Eph 1:18 . . . you can *u* the confident
Eph 5:17 . . . thoughtlessly, but *u* what
Phil 1:10 . . . want you to *u* what really
Phil 4:7 . . . exceeds anything we can *u.*
Col 2:2 . . . that they *u* God's mysterious
1 Tim 2:4 . . . saved and to *u* the truth.
2 Tim 2:7 . . . will help you *u* all these
Heb 11:3 . . . By faith we *u* that the entire
2 Pet 3:16 . . . are hard to *u,* and those

**UNITED (v)** to become one or as if one; in one accord or spirit
Gen 2:24 . . . the two are *u* into one.
Mark 10:8 . . . the two are *u* into one.
Rom 6:5 . . . we have been *u* with him
Rom 7:4 . . . now you are *u* with the one
1 Cor 6:16 . . . The two are *u* into one.
Eph 4:3 . . . to keep yourselves *u* in the

**UNITY (n)** the quality or state of oneness or harmony
John 17:23 . . . perfect *u* that the world
Eph 4:13 . . . come to such *u* in our faith

**UNWORTHILY (adv)** in an undeserving manner
1 Cor 11:27 . . . this cup of the Lord *u*

**UPRIGHT (adj)** marked by strong moral integrity
*see also* GODLY, RIGHT, RIGHTEOUS
Deut 32:4 . . . how just and *u* he is!
Prov 3:33 . . . blesses the home of the *u.*
Prov 15:8 . . . in the prayers of the *u.*

**USEFUL (adj)** serviceable for an end or purpose
2 Tim 3:16 . . . inspired by God and is *u* to
2 Pet 1:8 . . . productive and *u* you will be

**USELESS (adj)** having or being of no use; ineffectual, inept
Acts 26:14 . . . It is *u* for you to fight
1 Cor 13:8 . . . knowledge will become *u.*
1 Cor 15:14 . . . *u,* and your faith is *u.*
1 Cor 15:58 . . . do for the Lord is ever *u.*
2 Tim 2:14 . . . Such arguments are *u,* and
Titus 1:10 . . . who engage in *u* talk and
Heb 7:18 . . . because it was weak and *u.*

**VALLEY, VALLEYS (n)** a depression in the earth's surface between ranges of mountains, hills, or other uplands
Ps 23:4 . . . through the darkest *v,* I will
Song 2:1 . . . lily of the *v.*
Isa 40:4 . . . Fill in the *v-s,* and level
Joel 3:14 . . . waiting in the *v* of decision.
Luke 3:5 . . . The *v-s* will be filled, and

**VALUABLE (adj)** having desirable or esteemed characteristics or qualities; of great use or service
Job 28:17 . . . Wisdom is more *v* than gold
Ps 119:72 . . . instructions are more *v*
Prov 8:11 . . . is far more *v* than rubies.
Prov 20:15 . . . words are more *v* than
Matt 10:31 . . . you are more *v* to God than
Luke 12:24 . . . are far more *v* to him than
Phil 3:7 . . . these things were *v,* but now

**VALUE (n)** monetary worth of something; relative worth, utility, or importance
Matt 13:46 . . . a pearl of great *v,* he sold
1 Cor 3:13 . . . a person's work has any *v.*
Phil 3:8 . . . the infinite *v* of knowing

**VEIL (n)** a facial covering
Exod 34:33 . . . covered his face with a *v.*
2 Cor 3:14 . . . same *v* covers their minds
2 Cor 3:18 . . . have had that *v* removed can

**VENGEANCE (n)** punishment inflicted in retaliation for an injury or offense
1 Sam 25:26 . . . taking *v* into your own
1 Sam 25:33 . . . carrying out *v* with my
Ps 94:1 . . . O LORD, the God of *v,*
Isa 66:6 . . . the LORD taking *v* against
Luke 21:22 . . . be days of God's *v,* and the

**VICTORY, VICTORIES (n)** the overcoming of an enemy, antagonist, or struggle
Exod 15:2 . . . he has given me *v.*
2 Sam 22:51 . . . You give great *v-ies* to your
Ps 18:50 . . . You give great *v-ies* to your
Ps 20:5 . . . we hear of your *v* and
Ps 21:1 . . . because you give him *v.*
Ps 35:3 . . . I will give you *v!*
Ps 44:4 . . . You command *v-ies* for Israel.
Ps 45:4 . . . majesty, ride out to *v,*
Ps 48:10 . . . right hand is filled with *v.*

Ps 62:1 . . . for my **v** comes from him.
Ps 98:3 . . . have seen the **v** of our God.
Ps 118:14 . . . he has given me **v.**
Ps 149:4 . . . crowns the humble with **v.**
Isa 12:2 . . . he has given me **v.**
Isa 52:10 . . . see the **v** of our God.
Rom 8:37 . . . overwhelming **v** is ours
1 Cor 15:54 . . . Death is swallowed up in **v.**
Col 2:15 . . . publicly by his **v** over them
Rev 5:5 . . . David's throne, has won the **v.**

**VINEYARD (n)** a plantation of grapevines
1 Kgs 21:1 . . . who owned a **v** in Jezreel
Prov 31:16 . . . earnings she plants a **v.**
Song 1:6 . . . for myself—my own **v.**
Isa 5:1 . . . beloved had a **v** on a rich
1 Cor 9:7 . . . farmer plants a **v** and

**VIOLATE, VIOLATED, VIOLATES, VIOLATING
(v)** to do harm to the person or especially the
chastity of; to fail to show proper respect for; to
break or disregard
Lev 18:7 . . . Do not **v** your father
Lev 18:8 . . . for this would **v** your father.
Lev 18:10 . . . this would **v** yourself.
Lev 18:14 . . . Do not **v** your uncle.
Lev 18:16 . . . this would **v** your brother.
Lev 20:11 . . . If a man **v-s** his father by
Lev 20:20 . . . he has **v-d** his uncle.
Lev 20:21 . . . He has **v-d** his brother, and
Num 15:30 . . . who brazenly **v** the LORD's
Deut 22:30 . . . for this would **v** his father.
Deut 27:20 . . . for he has **v-d** his father.
Isa 24:5 . . . instructions, **v-d** his laws,
Mal 2:10 . . . each other, **v-ing** the covenant

**VIOLENCE (n)** exertion of physical force so as
to injure or abuse
Gen 6:11 . . . and was filled with **v.**
Ps 12:5 . . . I have seen **v** done to the
Ps 72:14 . . . them from oppression and **v,**
Isa 60:18 . . . **V** will disappear from your
Jon 3:8 . . . and stop all their **v.**
Mic 2:2 . . . take it by fraud and **v.**

**VIOLENT (adj)** emotionally agitated to the point
of loss of self-control
1 Tim 3:3 . . . a heavy drinker or be **v.**
Titus 1:7 . . . not be a heavy drinker, **v,**

**VIRGIN (n)** an unmarried woman who has not
had sexual intercourse
Gen 24:16 . . . but she was still a **v.**
Isa 7:14 . . . The **v** will conceive a child!
Matt 1:18 . . . while she was still a **v,** she
Matt 1:23 . . . The **v** will conceive a child!
Luke 1:34 . . . this happen? I am a **v.**

**VIRGINITY (n)** the quality or state of being
virgin
Deut 22:15 . . . proof of her **v** to the elders

**VIRTUOUS (adj)** morally excellent; righteous
Ruth 3:11 . . . you are a **v** woman.
Prov 21:29 . . . but the **v** think before they
Prov 31:10 . . . Who can find a **v** and
Prov 31:29 . . . There are many **v** and

**VOICE (n)** verbal communication by human
and divine means
Isa 40:3 . . . the **v** of someone shouting,
Mark 1:3 . . . He is a **v** shouting in the
John 10:3 . . . sheep recognize his **v** and
John 12:28 . . . a **v** spoke from heaven,
Rev 3:20 . . . If you hear my **v** and open

**VOMIT (n)** matter disgorged from the stomach
Prov 26:11 . . . returns to its **v,** so a fool
2 Pet 2:22 . . . A dog returns to its **v.**

**VOMIT (v)** to eject violently or abundantly
Lev 18:28 . . . it will **v** out the people

**VOW, VOWS (n)** a binding promise or pledge
*see also* COVENANT, PROMISE
Num 6:2 . . . the special **v** of a Nazirite,
Judg 11:30 . . . Jephthah made a **v** to the
Ps 110:4 . . . and will not break his **v:**
Matt 5:34 . . . do not make any **v-s!**
Heb 7:21 . . . and will not break his **v:**

**VOWED (v)** to promise solemnly
Eccl 8:2 . . . since you **v** to God that
Mark 7:11 . . . For I have **v** to give to

**WAGE, WAGES (n)** payment for labor or
services; compensation
Hag 1:6 . . . Your **w-s** disappear as though
Zech 11:12 . . . give me my **w-s,** whatever
Mal 3:5 . . . cheat employees of their **w-s,**
Matt 20:2 . . . the normal daily **w** and
Rom 4:4 . . . their **w-s** are not a gift,
Rom 6:23 . . . For the **w-s** of sin is death,

**WAIT, WAITED, WAITING (v)** to look forward
expectantly; to stay in place in expectation of
Ps 40:1 . . . I **w-ed** patiently for the LORD
Ps 62:5 . . . that I am **w** quietly before
Ps 69:3 . . . **w-ing** for my God to help me.
Isa 30:18 . . . Blessed are those who **w** for
Mic 7:7 . . . I **w** confidently for God to
Hab 3:16 . . . I will **w** quietly for the
Luke 12:37 . . . who are ready and **w-ing**
Rom 8:19 . . . all creation is **w-ing** eagerly
Rom 8:23 . . . We, too, **w** with eager hope
Heb 9:28 . . . are eagerly **w-ing** for him.

**WALK, WALKED, WALKING (v)** to roam,
traverse, or advance by steps; to pursue a
course of action or way of life
Gen 3:8 . . . God **w-ing** about in the garden.
Lev 26:12 . . . I will **w** among you;
Deut 11:22 . . . God by **w-ing** in his ways
Deut 26:17 . . . promised to **w** in his ways,
Josh 22:5 . . . God, **w** in all his ways,
Ps 23:4 . . . when I **w** through the
Ps 89:15 . . . they will **w** in the light
Prov 4:12 . . . When you **w,** you won't
Prov 6:22 . . . When you **w,** their counsel
Isa 2:3 . . . we will **w** in his paths.
Isa 40:31 . . . They will **w** and not
Isa 43:2 . . . When you **w** through the
Jer 6:16 . . . godly way, and **w** in it.
Dan 3:25 . . . **w-ing** around in the fire
Amos 3:3 . . . two people **w** together
Mic 6:8 . . . to **w** humbly with your God.
Mal 2:6 . . . they **w-ed** with me, living good
Matt 14:29 . . . boat and **w-ed** on the water
Mark 2:9 . . . pick up your mat, and **w**
John 8:12 . . . have to **w** in darkness,

**WANDER, WANDERED, WANDERS (v)** to
follow a winding course; to stray
Num 32:13 . . . them **w** in the wilderness
Ps 119:10 . . . don't let me **w** from your
Ps 119:67 . . . I used to **w** off until you
Ps 119:176 . . . I have **w-ed** away like a
Matt 18:12 . . . one of them **w-s** away
Eph 4:18 . . . **w** far from the life God
1 Tim 6:10 . . . have **w-ed** from the true

Jas 5:19 . . . someone among you **w-s**
1 Pet 2:25 . . . like sheep who **w-ed** away.
2 Pet 2:15 . . . They have **w-ed** off the

**WAR, WARS (n)** armed conflict with an
opposing military force; a state of hostility,
conflict, or antagonism
Josh 11:23 . . . finally had rest from **w.**
Ps 46:9 . . . He causes **w-s** to end
Ps 68:30 . . . nations that delight in **w.**
Ps 120:7 . . . peace, they want **w!**
Ps 144:1 . . . He trains my hands for **w**
Isa 2:4 . . . nor train for **w** anymore.
2 Cor 10:3 . . . we don't wage **w** as humans
1 Pet 2:11 . . . that wage **w** against your
Rev 12:7 . . . Then there was **w** in heaven.
Rev 19:11 . . . and wages a righteous **w.**

**WARN, WARNED, WARNING (v)** to give notice
to beforehand especially of danger or evil; to
counsel
Gen 2:16 . . . God **w-ed** him, "You may freely
Gen 31:24 . . . told him, "I'm **w-ing** you—
Gen 31:29 . . . to me last night and **w-ed** me,
Exod 19:21 . . . down and **w** the people
Num 16:40 . . . This would **w** the Israelites
1 Sam 8:9 . . . but solemnly **w** them about
1 Kgs 2:42 . . . LORD and **w** you not to
2 Kgs 17:13 . . . and seers to **w** both Israel
2 Chr 19:10 . . . must **w** them not to sin
Ezek 3:18 . . . If I **w** the wicked,
Ezek 33:3 . . . the alarm to **w** the people.
Luke 16:28 . . . I want him to **w** them so
Matt 16:6 . . . "Watch out!" Jesus **w-ed** them.
Acts 4:17 . . . must **w** them not to speak
1 Cor 4:14 . . . to **w** you as my beloved
1 Cor 10:11 . . . written down to **w** us who
Col 1:28 . . . **w-ing** everyone and teaching
1 Thes 4:6 . . . solemnly **w-ed** you before.
1 Thes 5:14 . . . urge you to **w** those who
2 Thes 3:15 . . . but **w** them as you would
Heb 3:13 . . . You must **w** each other

**WARNING, WARNINGS (n)** something that
warns or serves to warn; the act of warning
Ps 19:11 . . . They are a **w** to your servant,
Ps 81:8 . . . while I give you stern **w-s.**
Jer 6:8 . . . Listen to this **w,** Jerusalem,
Jer 42:19 . . . Don't forget this **w** I have
Zeph 3:7 . . . they will listen to my **w-s.**
1 Cor 10:6 . . . happened as a **w** to us,
1 Tim 5:20 . . . as a strong **w** to others.
Titus 3:10 . . . give a first and second **w.**

**WARRIOR, WARRIORS (n)** a man engaged or
experienced in warfare
Gen 6:4 . . . and famous **w-s** of ancient
Exod 15:3 . . . LORD is a **w;** Yahweh
Josh 1:14 . . . strong **w-s,** fully armed,
1 Chr 28:3 . . . for you are a **w** and
Ps 45:3 . . . your sword, O mighty **w!**
Jer 20:11 . . . beside me like a great **w.**

**WASH, WASHED (v)** to cleanse—of physical,
ceremonial, or spiritual significance
*see also* BAPTIZE(D), CLEANSE
Ps 51:7 . . . **w** me, and I will be whiter
John 13:5 . . . he began to **w** the disciples'
John 13:10 . . . does not need to **w,** except
Acts 22:16 . . . Have your sins **w-ed** away
Eph 5:26 . . . holy and clean, **w-ed** by the
Titus 3:5 . . . He **w-ed** away our sins,
Heb 10:22 . . . bodies have been **w-ed**

Jas 4:8 . . . *W* your hands, you sinners;
2 Pet 2:22 . . . *w-ed* pig returns to the mud.
Rev 7:14 . . . They have *w-ed* their robes in
Rev 22:14 . . . those who *w* their robes.

**WASTE, WASTED (v)** to spend or use carelessly or inefficiently
Ps 127:1 . . . work of the builders is *w-d.*
Prov 29:3 . . . prostitutes, his wealth is *w-d.*
Prov 31:3 . . . do not *w* your strength
Luke 15:13 . . . there he *w-d* all his money
John 6:12 . . . so that nothing is *w-d.*
Gal 2:2 . . . all my efforts had been *w-d*

**WATCH (n)** the act of keeping awake to guard, protect, or attend
Matt 24:42 . . . you, too, must keep *w!*
Acts 20:31 . . . my constant *w* and care

**WATCH, WATCHES, WATCHING (v)** to diligently wait or keep guard; to observe closely
Judg 18:6 . . . the LORD is *w-ing* over
Job 14:16 . . . my steps, instead of *w-ing*
Job 34:21 . . . God *w-es* how people live;
Ps 1:6 . . . For the LORD *w-es* over the
Ps 17:11 . . . and surround me, *w-ing* for
Ps 61:7 . . . faithfulness *w* over him.
Ps 121:3 . . . one who *w-es* over you will
Prov 2:11 . . . Wise choices will *w* over
Prov 31:27 . . . carefully *w-es* everything
Eccl 11:4 . . . If they *w* every cloud,
Jer 24:6 . . . I will *w* over and care for
Jer 31:10 . . . gather them and *w* over
Acts 1:9 . . . while they were *w-ing,* and
Eph 6:6 . . . just when they are *w-ing* you.
Heb 13:17 . . . is to *w* over your souls,
1 Pet 1:12 . . . eagerly *w-ing* these things
1 Pet 3:12 . . . eyes of the Lord *w* over

**WATER, WATERS (n)** precious resource for drink and irrigation, usually associated with blessing; a body of water
Exod 7:20 . . . struck the *w* of the Nile.
Exod 17:1 . . . there was no *w* there for
Num 20:2 . . . was no *w* for the people
2 Sam 23:15 . . . good *w* from the well
Ps 42:1 . . . streams of *w,* so I long
Prov 25:21 . . . give them *w* to drink.
Song 8:7 . . . Many *w-s* cannot quench
Isa 11:9 . . . for as the *w-s* fill the sea,
Isa 32:2 . . . like streams of *w* in the
Isa 43:2 . . . through deep *w-s,* I will be
Isa 49:10 . . . lead them beside cool *w-s.*
Jer 17:8 . . . reach deep into the *w.*
Jon 2:3 . . . The mighty *w-s* engulfed me;
Hab 2:14 . . . For as the *w-s* fill the sea,
Zech 14:8 . . . life-giving *w-s* will flow
Matt 14:25 . . . them, walking on the *w.*
John 3:5 . . . born of *w* and the Spirit.
John 4:10 . . . would give you living *w.*
John 7:38 . . . Rivers of living *w* will
1 Jn 5:6 . . . his baptism in *w* and by
Rev 7:17 . . . springs of life-giving *w.*
Rev 21:6 . . . springs of the *w* of life.

**WAY, WAYS (n)** characteristic, regular, or habitual manner or mode of being, behaving, or happening; manner or method of doing or happening; a course of action; route
Exod 33:13 . . . let me know your *w-s*
Deut 26:17 . . . to walk in his *w-s,* and
Deut 30:16 . . . by walking in his *w-s.*
Josh 22:5 . . . walk in all his *w-s,* obey

2 Sam 22:31 . . . God's *w* is perfect.
Ps 77:13 . . . O God, your *w-s* are holy.
Ps 86:11 . . . Teach me your *w-s,* O LORD,
Prov 2:9 . . . find the right *w* to go.
Prov 4:11 . . . teach you wisdom's *w-s*
Eccl 8:6 . . . and a *w* for everything,
Isa 2:3 . . . teach us his *w-s,* and we will
Isa 40:3 . . . Clear the *w* through the
Jer 6:16 . . . old, godly *w,* and walk in
Mic 4:2 . . . teach us his *w-s,* and we will
Mal 3:1 . . . prepare the *w* before me.
Matt 3:3 . . . Prepare the *w* for the
Matt 3:8 . . . Prove by the *w* you live
Luke 7:27 . . . prepare your *w* before you.
John 14:6 . . . I am the *w,* the truth,
Acts 9:2 . . . followers of the *W* he
Acts 24:14 . . . I follow the *W,* which
Rom 1:30 . . . invent new *w-s* of sinning,
1 Cor 10:13 . . . will show you a *w* out
1 Cor 12:31 . . . show you a *w* of life
Col 1:10 . . . Then the *w* you live will
Heb 10:20 . . . and life-giving *w* through

**WEAK, WEAKER, WEAKEST (adj)** lacking strength; not able to withstand temptation or persuasion
Ps 72:13 . . . pity for the *w* and the
Ps 103:14 . . . he knows how *w* we are;
Isa 59:1 . . . arm is not too *w* to save
Matt 12:20 . . . will not crush the *w-est* reed
Matt 26:41 . . . but the body is *w!*
Rom 14:1 . . . who are *w* in faith,
1 Cor 8:9 . . . others with a *w-er* conscience
1 Cor 9:22 . . . bring the *w* to Christ.
1 Cor 11:30 . . . many of you are *w* and
1 Cor 12:22 . . . of the body that seem *w-est*
2 Cor 12:10 . . . For when I am *w,* then
1 Thes 5:14 . . . care of those who are *w.*

**WEAKNESS, WEAKNESSES (n)** the quality or state of being weak
Ps 136:23 . . . He remembered us in our *w.*
Isa 53:4 . . . it was our *w-es* he carried;
Rom 8:3 . . . the *w* of our sinful nature.
Rom 8:26 . . . Spirit helps us in our *w.*
1 Cor 1:25 . . . God's *w* is stronger than
1 Cor 2:3 . . . I came to you in *w*—timid
2 Cor 12:5 . . . boast only about my *w-es.*
2 Cor 12:10 . . . take pleasure in my *w-es,*
2 Cor 13:4 . . . he was crucified in *w,*
Heb 5:2 . . . is subject to the same *w-es.*

**WEALTH (n)** abundance of valuable material possessions or resources
*see also* MONEY, POSSESSION(S), RICHES, TREASURE(S)
2 Chr 1:11 . . . not ask for *w,* riches,
Job 36:18 . . . you may be seduced by *w.*
Ps 39:6 . . . We heap up *w,* not knowing
Ps 62:10 . . . if your *w* increases, don't
Prov 3:9 . . . the LORD with your *w*
Prov 10:2 . . . Tainted *w* has no lasting
Prov 13:11 . . . *w* from hard work grows
Prov 21:20 . . . wise have *w* and luxury,
Prov 29:3 . . . prostitutes, his *w* is wasted.
Eccl 4:8 . . . gain as much *w* as he can.
Luke 19:8 . . . give half my *w* to the poor,
Eph 2:7 . . . of the incredible *w* of his
1 Tim 6:6 . . . contentment is itself great *w.*
Jas 5:3 . . . The very *w* you were counting

**WEALTHY (adj)** characterized by abundance
Prov 11:24 . . . freely and become more *w;*

Eccl 2:26 . . . sinner becomes *w,* God takes
1 Cor 1:26 . . . or *w* when God called you.

**WEAPON, WEAPONS (n)** something used to injure, defeat, or destroy
Prov 26:18 . . . shooting a deadly *w*
Eccl 9:18 . . . have wisdom than *w-s* of war,
2 Cor 6:7 . . . use the *w-s* of righteousness

**WEARY (adj)** exhausted in strength, endurance, or vigor
Isa 40:31 . . . They will run and not grow *w.*
Isa 50:4 . . . know how to comfort the *w.*
Matt 11:28 . . . you who are *w* and carry
2 Cor 5:2 . . . We grow *w* in our present
Heb 12:3 . . . won't become *w* and give up.

**WEDDING, WEDDINGS (n)** a marriage ceremony usually with its accompanying festivities
Matt 11:17 . . . We played *w* songs, and
Matt 22:11 . . . the proper clothes for a *w.*
Matt 24:38 . . . parties and *w-s* right up
Rev 19:7 . . . for the *w* feast of the Lamb,

**WEEP, WEEPING (v)** to cry aloud, often linked with prayer and repentance
2 Sam 1:26 . . . How I *w* for you,
Ps 126:6 . . . They *w* as they go to
Jer 31:15 . . . deep anguish and bitter *w-ing.*
Jer 31:16 . . . Do not *w* any longer,
Jer 50:4 . . . will come *w-ing* and seeking
Matt 2:18 . . . heard in Ramah—*w-ing* and
Matt 8:12 . . . will be *w-ing* and gnashing
Luke 6:21 . . . blesses you who *w* now,
Luke 22:62 . . . the courtyard, *w-ing* bitterly.
Luke 23:28 . . . don't *w* for me, but *w*
Rom 12:15 . . . and *w* with those who *w.*

**WEST (n)** the general direction of the sunset
Ps 103:12 . . . as the east is from the *w.*
Ps 107:3 . . . from east and *w,* from north

**WHEAT (n)** a cereal grain that yields a fine white flour
Matt 3:12 . . . gathering the *w* into his barn
Matt 13:25 . . . among the *w,* then slipped
Mark 4:28 . . . the heads of *w* are formed,
Luke 22:31 . . . sift each of you like *w.*
John 12:24 . . . a kernel of *w* is planted in

**WHIRLWIND (n)** a small rotating windstorm, sometimes violent and destructive
*see also* STORM
2 Kgs 2:1 . . . to heaven in a *w,*
Job 38:1 . . . answered Job from the *w:*
Hos 8:7 . . . and will harvest the *w.*
Nah 1:3 . . . in the *w* and the storm.

**WHISPER (n)** a minor or softer reflection of the original noise; hint, trace
1 Kgs 19:12 . . . sound of a gentle *w.*
Job 26:14 . . . merely a *w* of his power.
Ps 107:29 . . . calmed the storm to a *w*

**WHISPER (v)** to speak softly with little or no vibration of the vocal cords
Matt 10:27 . . . What I *w* in your ear,

**WHITE, WHITER (adj)** free from color; of the color white
Ps 51:7 . . . I will be *w-r* than snow.
Isa 1:18 . . . make them as *w* as snow,
Dan 7:9 . . . clothing was as *w* as snow,
Matt 28:3 . . . clothing was as *w* as snow.
Rev 1:14 . . . like wool, as *w* as snow.
Rev 6:2 . . . saw a *w* horse standing

Rev 19:11 . . . a **w** horse was standing
Rev 20:11 . . . saw a great **w** throne

**WHITE (n)**  the absence of color; free from spot or blemish
Rev 3:4 . . . will walk with me in **w**,
Rev 7:13 . . . who are clothed in **w?**

**WHITEWASHED (adj)**  glossed over with whitewash
Matt 23:27 . . . are like **w** tombs—

**WHOLE (adj)**  entire; complete, unmodified; undivided
1 Sam 1:28 . . . LORD his **w** life.
1 Sam 17:46 . . . the **w** world will know
1 Chr 28:9 . . . him with your **w** heart
Ps 72:19 . . . Let the **w** earth be filled
Ps 103:1 . . . with my **w** heart, I will
Prov 4:22 . . . healing to their **w** body.
Eccl 12:13 . . . That's the **w** story.
Isa 6:3 . . . The **w** earth is filled
Isa 14:26 . . . plan for the **w** earth,
Dan 2:35 . . . covered the **w** earth.
Zeph 1:18 . . . For the **w** land will be
Matt 6:22 . . . eye is good, your **w** body
Matt 16:26 . . . gain the **w** world but lose
Matt 24:14 . . . throughout the **w** world,
John 21:25 . . . I suppose the **w** world
Acts 17:26 . . . throughout the **w** earth.
1 Cor 12:17 . . . Or if your **w** body were
Gal 5:3 . . . regulation in the **w** law of

**WHORE (KJV)**
Lev 21:7 . . . a woman *defiled by prostitution*
Deut 23:18 . . . from the earnings of a *prostitute*
Prov 23:27 . . . A *prostitute* is a dangerous trap
Hos 4:14 . . . sinning with *whores*
Rev 17:1 . . . *prostitute*, who rules over

**WICKED (adj)**  morally very bad
Gen 13:13 . . . area were extremely **w** and
2 Sam 22:27 . . . but to the **w** you show
Ps 1:1 . . . the advice of the **w**, or stand
Ps 7:9 . . . those who are **w**, and defend
Ps 10:13 . . . Why do the **w** get away with
Ps 12:8 . . . though the **w** strut about,
Ps 14:6 . . . The **w** frustrate the plans
Ps 18:26 . . . but to the **w** you show
Ps 37:1 . . . worry about the **w** or envy
Ps 82:2 . . . by favoring the **w?**
Ps 101:8 . . . ferret out the **w** and free
Ps 139:19 . . . you would destroy the **w!**
Ps 146:9 . . . the plans of the **w**.
Prov 4:14 . . . Don't do as the **w** do,
Prov 9:7 . . . who corrects the **w** will
Prov 10:7 . . . name of a **w** person rots
Prov 10:28 . . . expectations of the **w** come
Prov 11:10 . . . joy when the **w** die.
Prov 12:5 . . . of the **w** is treacherous.
Prov 26:23 . . . may hide a **w** heart, just
Prov 29:7 . . . the **w** don't care at all.
Isa 5:23 . . . to let the **w** go free,
Isa 11:4 . . . mouth will destroy the **w**.
Isa 26:10 . . . the **w** keep doing wrong
Isa 48:22 . . . no peace for the **w**,
Jer 35:15 . . . Turn from your **w** ways,
Ezek 18:21 . . . But if **w** people turn away
Ezek 21:25 . . . you corrupt and **w** prince
Ezek 33:8 . . . that some **w** people are sure
Hos 10:9 . . . not right that the **w** men of
Jon 1:2 . . . I have seen how **w** its people
Mal 4:1 . . . arrogant and the **w** will be

Luke 6:35 . . . who are unthankful and **w**.
1 Jn 5:17 . . . All **w** actions are sin,

**WICKEDNESS (n)**  the quality or state of being wicked; something wicked
Lev 16:21 . . . it all the **w**, rebellion,
Lev 19:29 . . . with prostitution and **w**.
Deut 9:4 . . . because of the **w** of the other
Ps 73:3 . . . them prosper despite their **w**.
Jer 3:2 . . . your prostitution and your **w**.
Jer 14:16 . . . out their own **w** on them.
Jer 14:20 . . . we confess our **w** and that
Ezek 33:19 . . . turn from their **w** and do
Luke 11:39 . . . of greed and **w!**
Rom 1:18 . . . the truth by their **w**.
Rom 1:29 . . . every kind of **w**, sin, greed,
Rom 2:8 . . . and instead live lives of **w**.
2 Cor 6:14 . . . be a partner with **w?**
Heb 8:12 . . . I will forgive their **w**,

**WIDOW, WIDOWS (n)**  a woman whose husband has died
Deut 10:18 . . . orphans and **w-s** receive
Ps 68:5 . . . defender of **w-s**—this is God,
Ps 146:9 . . . for the orphans and **w-s**, but
Isa 1:17 . . . Fight for the rights of **w-s**.
Luke 21:2 . . . Then a poor **w** came by and
Acts 6:1 . . . that their **w-s** were being
1 Cor 7:8 . . . aren't married and to **w-s**—
1 Tim 5:3 . . . Take care of any **w** who
1 Tim 5:16 . . . care for the **w-s** who are
Jas 1:27 . . . for orphans and **w-s** in their

**WIFE (n)**  the female partner in a marriage
*see also* WIVES
Gen 2:24 . . . and is joined to his **w**,
Gen 19:26 . . . But Lot's **w** looked back
Exod 20:17 . . . covet your neighbor's **w**,
Lev 20:10 . . . his neighbor's **w**, both
Deut 5:21 . . . not covet your neighbor's **w**.
Deut 24:5 . . . happiness to the **w** he has
Prov 5:18 . . . Rejoice in the **w** of your
Prov 12:4 . . . A worthy **w** is a crown
Prov 18:22 . . . man who finds a **w**
Prov 19:13 . . . a quarrelsome **w** is as
Prov 21:9 . . . a quarrelsome **w** in a
Prov 31:10 . . . a virtuous and capable **w?**
Mal 2:14 . . . vows you and your **w** made
Matt 1:20 . . . to take Mary as your **w**.
Matt 19:3 . . . to divorce his **w** for just
Luke 17:32 . . . happened to Lot's **w!**
Luke 18:29 . . . up house or **w** or brothers
1 Cor 7:2 . . . should have his own **w**,
1 Cor 7:15 . . . the husband or **w** who isn't
1 Cor 7:33 . . . and how to please his **w**.
Eph 5:23 . . . head of his **w** as Christ
Eph 5:33 . . . love his **w** as he loves
1 Tim 3:12 . . . be faithful to his **w**,
Titus 1:6 . . . be faithful to his **w**,
1 Pet 3:7 . . . Treat your **w** with
Rev 21:9 . . . bride, the **w** of the Lamb.

**WILDERNESS (n)**  any desolate, barren, or unpopulated area, usually linked with danger
*see also* DESERT
Num 16:13 . . . kill us here in this **w**,
Num 26:65 . . . all die in the **w**.
Num 32:13 . . . wander in the **w** for forty
Deut 8:16 . . . manna in the **w**, a food
Deut 29:5 . . . led you through the **w**,
Ps 78:19 . . . give us food in the **w**.
Ps 78:52 . . . safely through the **w**.
Isa 32:15 . . . **w** will become a fertile

Isa 35:6 . . . will gush forth in the **w**,
Matt 3:3 . . . the **w**, 'Prepare the way
Luke 5:16 . . . withdrew to the **w** for
Rev 12:6 . . . fled into the **w**, where God

**WILDFLOWERS (n)**  the flower of a wild or uncultivated plant
Ps 103:15 . . . like grass; like **w**, we bloom
Matt 6:30 . . . so wonderfully for **w** that are

**WILL (n)**  desire, wish
Ps 40:8 . . . in doing your **w**, my God,
Ps 143:10 . . . me to do your **w**, for you
Prov 3:6 . . . Seek his **w** in all you do,
Matt 6:10 . . . May your **w** be done on
Matt 7:21 . . . who actually do the **w**
Matt 12:50 . . . does the **w** of my Father
Matt 18:14 . . . heavenly Father's **w** that
Matt 26:39 . . . want your **w** to be done,
Matt 26:42 . . . I drink it, your **w** be done.
John 5:30 . . . carry out the **w** of the one
John 6:38 . . . heaven to do the **w** of God
1 Thes 5:18 . . . this is God's **w** for you
Heb 10:7 . . . come to do your **w**, O God—
Heb 13:21 . . . need for doing his **w**.
1 Pet 4:2 . . . to do the **w** of God.

**WINE (n)**  the fermented juice of grapes, linked positively with blessings and negatively with strong drink
Ps 104:15 . . . **w** to make them glad,
Prov 31:6 . . . and **w** for those in bitter
Song 1:2 . . . love is sweeter than **w**.
Isa 28:7 . . . who reel with **w** and stagger
Mark 15:36 . . . with sour **w**, holding it
John 2:3 . . . The **w** supply ran out
Rom 14:21 . . . to eat meat or drink **w**
Eph 5:18 . . . Don't be drunk with **w**,
1 Tim 5:23 . . . drink a little **w** for
Rev 16:19 . . . was filled with the **w**

**WINEBIBBER(S) (KJV)**
Prov 23:20 . . . not carouse with *drunkards*
Matt 11:19 . . . glutton and a *drunkard,* and
Luke 7:34 . . . glutton and a *drunkard,* and

**WINESKINS (n)**  a bag used for holding wine, made from the skin of an animal
Matt 9:17 . . . stored in new **w** so that
Luke 5:37 . . . new wine into old **w**.

**WINGS (n)**  feathered appendage of a bird, figurative of freedom, strength, and protection from God
Exod 19:4 . . . carried you on eagles' **w**
Ps 17:8 . . . in the shadow of your **w**.
Ps 91:4 . . . shelter you with his **w**.
Isa 6:2 . . . each having six **w**.
Isa 40:31 . . . high on **w** like eagles.
Mal 4:2 . . . rise with healing in his **w**.
Luke 13:34 . . . chicks beneath her **w**,
Rev 4:8 . . . living beings had six **w**,

**WISDOM (n)**  knowledge, insight, judgment
Gen 3:6 . . . she wanted the **w** it would
1 Kgs 4:29 . . . gave Solomon very great **w**
1 Kgs 10:24 . . . to hear the **w** God had
2 Chr 1:10 . . . Give me the **w** and
Job 11:6 . . . **w**, for true **w** is not
Job 42:3 . . . that questions my **w** with such
Ps 51:6 . . . teaching me **w** even there.
Prov 2:6 . . . the LORD grants **w!**
Prov 3:13 . . . the person who finds **w**,
Prov 8:11 . . . **w** is far more valuable
Prov 11:2 . . . with humility comes **w**.

Prov 16:16 . . . better to get *w* than gold,
Prov 23:23 . . . also get *w,* discipline,
Prov 29:3 . . . man who loves *w* brings joy
Eccl 10:10 . . . the value of *w;* it helps
Isa 11:2 . . . on him—the Spirit of *w*
Isa 50:4 . . . me his words of *w,* so that
Luke 2:52 . . . Jesus grew in *w* and in
Acts 6:3 . . . full of the Spirit and *w.*
1 Cor 1:21 . . . him through human *w,* he
Eph 1:17 . . . you spiritual *w* and insight
Col 2:3 . . . treasures of *w* and knowledge.
Col 3:16 . . . with all the *w* he gives.
2 Tim 3:15 . . . given you the *w* to receive
Titus 2:12 . . . world with *w,* righteousness,
Jas 1:5 . . . If you need *w,* ask our
Rev 5:12 . . . riches and *w* and strength

**WISE, WISER, WISEST (adj)** marked by deep understanding, keen discernment, and a capacity for sound judgment
1 Kgs 3:12 . . . you a *w* and understanding
Job 9:4 . . . God is so *w* and so mighty.
Ps 14:2 . . . anyone is truly *w,* if anyone
Ps 19:7 . . . are trustworthy, making *w* the
Ps 119:100 . . . I am even *w-r* than my
Prov 4:7 . . . wisdom is the *w-st* thing
Prov 9:8 . . . correct the *w,* and they
Prov 10:1 . . . A *w* child brings joy to
Prov 11:30 . . . a *w* person wins friends.
Prov 12:16 . . . a *w* person stays calm
Prov 12:18 . . . of the *w* bring healing.
Prov 13:1 . . . A *w* child accepts a parent's
Prov 13:10 . . . who take advice are *w.*
Prov 13:20 . . . Walk with the *w* and
Prov 15:5 . . . learns from correction is *w.*
Prov 16:23 . . . From a *w* mind comes *w*
Prov 18:4 . . . wisdom flows from the *w*
Prov 19:25 . . . they will be all the *w-r.*
Prov 24:5 . . . *w* are mightier than the
Prov 28:7 . . . who obey the law are *w;*
Eccl 8:5 . . . who are *w* will find a time
Eccl 9:17 . . . quiet words of a *w* person
Matt 2:1 . . . some *w* men from eastern
Matt 11:25 . . . who think themselves *w*
Matt 25:2 . . . foolish, and five were *w.*
Rom 3:11 . . . No one is truly *w;* no one
1 Cor 1:19 . . . wisdom of the *w* and
1 Cor 1:25 . . . plan of God is *w-r* than
1 Cor 12:8 . . . ability to give *w* advice;
Jas 3:13 . . . If you are *w* and understand

**WITCHCRAFT (n)** the use of sorcery or magic
Lev 19:26 . . . practice fortune-telling or *w.*
Deut 18:10 . . . omens, or engage in *w,*
Rev 21:8 . . . those who practice *w,* idol

**WITHER, WITHERS (v)** to shrivel and lose vitality, force, or freshness
Job 14:2 . . . like a flower and then *w.*
Ps 1:3 . . . leaves never *w,* and they
Isa 40:7 . . . grass *w-s* and the flowers
Isa 64:6 . . . autumn leaves, we *w* and fall,
1 Pet 1:24 . . . grass *w-s* and the flower

**WITNESS, WITNESSES (n)** a person who gives testimony; one asked to be present at a transaction so as to be able to testify to its having taken place
Deut 19:15 . . . of two or three *w-es.*
Prov 19:5 . . . A false *w* will not go
Prov 21:28 . . . but a credible *w* will be
Matt 18:16 . . . by two or three *w-es.*
John 1:8 . . . simply a *w* to tell about

Acts 1:8 . . . will be my *w-es,* telling people
1 Tim 5:19 . . . by two or three *w-es.*
1 Jn 5:7 . . . we have these three *w-es*—

**WITNESSED (v)** to have personal or direct cognizance of
Mal 2:14 . . . the LORD *w* the vows

**WIVES (n)** *see also* WIFE
Eph 5:22 . . . For *w,* this means submit
Eph 5:25 . . . this means love your *w,*
1 Pet 3:1 . . . way, you *w* must accept

**WOE (KJV)**
Isa 6:5 . . . *It's all over!* I am doomed
Matt 18:7 . . . *What sorrow awaits* the world
Matt 23:13 . . . *What sorrow awaits* you
1 Cor 9:16 . . . *How terrible* for me if I didn't
Rev 8:13 . . . *Terror, terror, terror* to all who

**WOLVES (n)** any of several predatory animals that resemble large dogs
Matt 7:15 . . . but are really vicious *w.*
Matt 10:16 . . . you out as sheep among *w.*

**WOMAN (n)** an adult female person
*see also* WOMEN
Gen 2:22 . . . God made a *w* from the rib,
Gen 3:6 . . . The *w* was convinced.
Gen 3:12 . . . It was the *w* you gave me
Gen 3:16 . . . he said to the *w,* "I will
Exod 3:22 . . . Every Israelite *w* will ask
Lev 12:2 . . . If a *w* becomes pregnant
Lev 15:19 . . . a *w* has her menstrual
Lev 15:25 . . . a *w* has a flow of blood
Num 5:29 . . . If a *w* goes astray and defiles
Judg 4:9 . . . be at the hands of a *w.*
Judg 16:4 . . . love with a *w* named Delilah,
Ruth 3:11 . . . knows you are a virtuous *w.*
2 Sam 11:2 . . . he noticed a *w* of unusual
2 Sam 20:16 . . . But a wise *w* in the town
Prov 11:16 . . . A gracious *w* gains respect,
Prov 11:22 . . . A beautiful *w* who lacks
Prov 14:1 . . . A wise *w* builds her
Prov 30:19 . . . how a man loves a *w.*
Prov 30:23 . . . a bitter *w* who finally gets
Prov 31:30 . . . *w* who fears the LORD
Matt 5:28 . . . looks at a *w* with lust
Matt 9:20 . . . Just then a *w* who had
Matt 26:7 . . . was eating, a *w* came in
Mark 7:25 . . . Right away a *w* who had
Luke 7:39 . . . what kind of *w* is touching
John 4:7 . . . Soon a Samaritan *w* came to
John 8:3 . . . Pharisees brought a *w* who
Rom 7:2 . . . when a *w* marries, the law
1 Cor 7:2 . . . and each *w* should have
1 Cor 7:34 . . . a married *w* has to think
1 Cor 11:3 . . . the head of *w* is man, and
1 Cor 11:6 . . . shameful for a *w* to have
1 Cor 11:13 . . . it right for a *w* to pray
Gal 4:4 . . . born of a *w,* subject to the
Gal 4:31 . . . are children of the free *w.*
Rev 12:1 . . . I saw a *w* clothed with the
Rev 12:13 . . . he pursued the *w* who had
Rev 17:3 . . . There I saw a *w* sitting on a

**WOMB (n)** uterus
Ps 139:13 . . . together in my mother's *w.*
Prov 31:2 . . . O son of my *w,* O son
Jer 1:5 . . . you in your mother's *w.*
Luke 1:44 . . . baby in my *w* jumped for joy.
John 3:4 . . . into his mother's *w* and be

**WOMEN (n)** *see also* WOMAN
Gen 6:2 . . . saw the beautiful *w* and took

Song 1:3 . . . all the young *w* love you!
Mark 15:41 . . . Many other *w* who had
Luke 1:42 . . . you above all *w,* and your
Luke 23:27 . . . many grief-stricken *w.*
Rom 1:26 . . . Even the *w* turned against
1 Cor 7:25 . . . the young *w* who are not
1 Tim 2:9 . . . I want *w* to be modest in
2 Tim 3:6 . . . of vulnerable *w* who are
Titus 2:3 . . . teach the older *w* to live in
Titus 2:4 . . . train the younger *w* to love
1 Pet 3:5 . . . how the holy *w* of old made

**WONDERFUL (adj)** marked by a marvelous, amazing, or extraordinary quality
1 Chr 16:9 . . . about his *w* deeds.
Job 37:14 . . . consider the *w* miracles
Ps 16:6 . . . What a *w* inheritance!
Ps 17:7 . . . unfailing love in *w* ways.
Ps 71:17 . . . about the *w* things you
Ps 72:18 . . . does such *w* things.
Ps 75:1 . . . tell of your *w* deeds.
Ps 105:2 . . . about his *w* deeds.
Ps 118:23 . . . it is *w* to see.
Ps 119:18 . . . to see the *w* truths in
Ps 119:27 . . . meditate on your *w* deeds.
Ps 119:129 . . . Your laws are *w.*
Ps 139:6 . . . knowledge is too *w* for
Ps 145:5 . . . and your *w* miracles.
Eccl 11:9 . . . Young people, it's *w* to be
Isa 9:6 . . . be called: *W* Counselor,
Isa 12:5 . . . he has done *w* things.
Isa 25:1 . . . You do such *w* things!
Matt 21:15 . . . saw these *w* miracles
Matt 21:42 . . . and it is *w* to see.
Luke 13:17 . . . rejoiced at the *w* things
Acts 2:11 . . . about the *w* things God has
Acts 20:24 . . . News about the *w* grace of
2 Cor 10:12 . . . we are as *w* as these
Titus 2:13 . . . hope to that *w* day when

**WONDERS (n)** mighty works, miracles
1 Chr 16:12 . . . Remember the *w* he has
Ps 26:7 . . . and telling of all your *w.*
Ps 31:21 . . . has shown me the *w* of his
Ps 77:14 . . . are the God of great *w!*
Ps 89:5 . . . your great *w,* LORD;
Mark 13:22 . . . perform signs and *w* so
Acts 2:19 . . . will cause *w* in the heavens
Acts 5:12 . . . signs and *w* among the people.
2 Cor 12:12 . . . signs and *w* and miracles
Heb 2:4 . . . signs and *w* and various

**WORD, WORDS (n)** something that is said; special revelation from God; commands
Deut 8:3 . . . live by every *w* that comes
Deut 11:18 . . . to these *w-s* of mine. Tie
Job 38:2 . . . with such ignorant *w-s?*
Ps 19:3 . . . speak without a sound or *w;*
Ps 52:4 . . . others with your *w-s,* you liar!
Ps 119:9 . . . pure? By obeying your *w.*
Ps 119:11 . . . hidden your *w* in my heart,
Ps 119:103 . . . How sweet your *w-s* taste
Ps 119:160 . . . essence of your *w-s* is
Ps 119:162 . . . I rejoice in your *w*
Prov 12:19 . . . Truthful *w-s* stand the test
Prov 12:25 . . . an encouraging *w* cheers
Prov 16:24 . . . Kind *w-s* are like honey—
Prov 17:27 . . . wise person uses few *w-s;*
Prov 26:23 . . . Smooth *w-s* may hide a
Isa 40:21 . . . deaf to the *w-s* of God—
Jer 15:16 . . . your *w-s,* I devoured
Jer 23:29 . . . Does not my *w* burn like

Amos 8:13 . . . for the LORD's *w.*
Matt 4:4 . . . but by every *w* that comes
Matt 15:6 . . . you cancel the *w* of God
Matt 24:35 . . . *w-s* will never disappear.
John 1:1 . . . the beginning the *W* already
John 6:68 . . . the *w-s* that give eternal life.
John 15:7 . . . and my *w-s* remain in you,
John 17:17 . . . teach them your *w,* which
Rom 10:18 . . . the *w-s* to all the world.
1 Cor 2:1 . . . use lofty *w-s* and impressive
1 Cor 2:13 . . . do not use *w-s* that come
1 Cor 14:9 . . . to people in *w-s* they don't
1 Cor 14:19 . . . than ten thousand *w-s* in
2 Cor 2:17 . . . We preach the *w* of God
2 Cor 4:2 . . . or distort the *w* of God.
Eph 6:17 . . . which is the *w* of God.
Phil 2:16 . . . firmly to the *w* of life;
2 Tim 2:15 . . . explains the *w* of truth.
Titus 2:5 . . . shame on the *w* of God.
Heb 4:12 . . . For the *w* of God is
Heb 5:12 . . . things about God's *w.*
Jas 1:22 . . . listen to God's *w.*
1 Pet 1:23 . . . eternal, living *w* of God.
1 Pet 2:8 . . . not obey God's *w,* and so
1 Pet 3:1 . . . to them without any *w-s.*
2 Pet 3:5 . . . the heavens by the *w* of
Rev 19:13 . . . title was the *W* of God.
Rev 22:19 . . . of the *w-s* from this book

**WORK, WORKS (n)** one's occupation; physical
or creative effort
*see also* DEEDS
Gen 2:2 . . . finished his *w* of creation,
Exod 20:9 . . . week for your ordinary *w,*
Deut 5:13 . . . week for your ordinary *w,*
Ps 77:12 . . . about your mighty *w-s.*
Ps 107:24 . . . impressive *w-s* on the
Ps 127:1 . . . *w* of the builders is wasted.
Ps 150:2 . . . Praise him for his mighty *w-s;*
Prov 21:5 . . . planning and hard *w* lead
Eccl 2:19 . . . my skill and hard *w* under
Eccl 5:19 . . . To enjoy your *w* and accept
John 4:34 . . . and from finishing his *w.*
John 5:36 . . . Father gave me these *w-s* to
John 10:32 . . . have done many good *w-s.*
Acts 13:2 . . . for the special *w* to which
Acts 20:24 . . . finishing the *w* assigned
Rom 4:5 . . . not because of their *w,* but
1 Cor 3:5 . . . the *w* the Lord gave us.
Gal 6:4 . . . attention to your own *w,* for
Eph 4:12 . . . people to do his *w* and build
Eph 4:16 . . . part does its own special *w,*
Eph 4:28 . . . your hands for good hard *w,*
Phil 1:6 . . . began the good *w* within you,
1 Tim 6:18 . . . rich in good *w-s* and
2 Tim 3:17 . . . people to do every good *w.*
Heb 10:24 . . . acts of love and good *w-s.*
Jas 2:26 . . . faith is dead without good *w-s.*
Rev 15:3 . . . marvelous are your *w-s,* O

**WORK, WORKED, WORKING (v)** to exert
oneself physically or mentally
Prov 13:4 . . . but those who *w* hard will
Eccl 5:12 . . . who *w* hard sleep well,
Matt 6:28 . . . They don't *w* or make their
Matt 12:30 . . . anyone who isn't *w-ing* with
Luke 10:7 . . . who *w* deserve their pay.
Luke 13:24 . . . *W* hard to enter the narrow
Rom 4:6 . . . righteous without *w-ing* for
Rom 8:28 . . . to *w* together for the good
Rom 12:11 . . . Never be lazy, but *w* hard
1 Cor 15:10 . . . I have *w-ed* harder than

1 Cor 15:58 . . . Always *w* enthusiastically
2 Cor 11:27 . . . I have *w-ed* hard and
Eph 6:7 . . . you were *w-ing* for the Lord
1 Thes 4:11 . . . and *w-ing* with your hands,
2 Thes 3:10 . . . unwilling to *w* will not
1 Tim 5:18 . . . Those who *w* deserve their
1 Tim 6:2 . . . slaves should *w* all the harder
Heb 6:10 . . . how hard you have *w-ed* for
2 Pet 1:10 . . . *w* hard to prove that you

**WORLD (n)** the earth and its inhabitants; the
human race; the current age and its value system
Ps 33:9 . . . he spoke, the *w* began!
Ps 50:12 . . . for all the *w* is mine
Ps 96:13 . . . judge the *w* with justice,
Isa 13:11 . . . will punish the *w* for its
Matt 16:26 . . . you gain the whole *w* but
John 1:29 . . . away the sin of the *w!*
John 3:16 . . . God loved the *w* so much
John 8:12 . . . I am the light of the *w.*
John 13:35 . . . prove to the *w* that you
John 16:33 . . . I have overcome the *w.*
John 17:5 . . . shared before the *w* began.
John 17:14 . . . And the *w* hates them
John 18:36 . . . Kingdom is not of this *w.*
Rom 3:19 . . . the entire *w* is guilty
1 Cor 1:27 . . . things the *w* considers
1 Cor 2:7 . . . glory before the *w* began.
1 Cor 3:1 . . . you belonged to this *w* or
1 Cor 3:19 . . . of this *w* is foolishness
1 Cor 6:2 . . . to judge the *w,* can't you
2 Cor 5:19 . . . reconciling the *w* to himself,
Eph 2:12 . . . lived in this *w* without God
Eph 4:9 . . . also descended to our lowly *w.*
Phil 2:15 . . . lights in a *w* full of crooked
Titus 1:2 . . . them before the *w* began.
Heb 9:26 . . . ever since the *w* began.
Jas 2:5 . . . poor in this *w* to be rich
Jas 4:4 . . . a friend of the *w,* you make
1 Jn 2:2 . . . the sins of all the *w.*
1 Jn 2:15 . . . Do not love this *w* nor
1 Jn 5:4 . . . defeats this evil *w,* and

**WORRY, WORRIES (n)** mental distress or
agitation resulting from concern; anxiety
Prov 12:25 . . . *W* weighs a person down;
Matt 6:27 . . . Can all your *w-ies* add a single
Luke 21:34 . . . and by the *w-ies* of this life.
1 Pet 5:7 . . . Give all your *w-ies* and cares

**WORRY, WORRIED, WORRYING (v)** to feel or
experience concern or anxiety
Deut 20:8 . . . anyone here afraid or *w-ied?*
Ps 37:1 . . . Don't *w* about the wicked
Isa 7:4 . . . Tell him to stop *w-ing.*
Matt 6:25 . . . I tell you not to *w* about
Matt 10:19 . . . don't *w* about how to
Luke 6:41 . . . And why *w* about a speck in
Acts 27:33 . . . You have been so *w-ied* that
Phil 4:6 . . . Don't *w* about anything;

**WORSHIP (n)** reverent devotion and allegiance
pledged to God or a god
1 Cor 10:14 . . . flee from the *w* of idols.

**WORSHIP, WORSHIPED, WORSHIPING,
WORSHIPS (v)** to regard with great
extravagant respect, honor, or devotion
Gen 12:8 . . . and he *w-ed* the LORD.
Gen 13:4 . . . and there he *w-ed* the LORD
Gen 21:33 . . . and there he *w-ed* the LORD,
Gen 26:25 . . . there and *w-ed* the LORD.
Deut 12:30 . . . and *w-ing* their gods.
2 Kgs 17:36 . . . But *w* only the LORD,

Ps 29:2 . . . *W* the LORD in the splendor
Ps 95:6 . . . Come, let us *w* and bow down.
Ps 105:3 . . . rejoice, you who *w* the LORD.
Isa 44:19 . . . bow down to *w* a piece of
Jer 16:11 . . . *w-ed* other gods and served
Dan 3:28 . . . die rather than serve or *w* any
Hos 9:1 . . . like prostitutes, *w-ing* other
Hos 9:10 . . . as vile as the god they *w-ed.*
Hos 13:1 . . . Ephraim sinned by *w-ing* Baal
Zeph 3:9 . . . everyone can *w* the LORD
Zech 14:17 . . . to Jerusalem to *w* the King,
Matt 2:2 . . . we have come to *w* him.
Matt 4:9 . . . kneel down and *w* me.
Matt 15:25 . . . she came and *w-ed* him,
Matt 28:9 . . . grasped his feet, and *w-ed*
Luke 23:47 . . . he *w-ed* God and said,
John 4:24 . . . *w* in spirit and in truth.
1 Cor 5:11 . . . is greedy, or *w-s* idols,
Heb 9:14 . . . we can *w* the living God.

**WORTHLESS (adj)** valueless, useless,
contemptible
1 Sam 12:21 . . . worshiping *w* idols that
Prov 6:12 . . . *w* and wicked people
1 Cor 3:20 . . . he knows they are *w.*
Eph 5:11 . . . part in the *w* deeds of evil
Titus 1:16 . . . *w* for doing anything good.
Jas 5:3 . . . and silver have become *w.*

**WORTHY (adj)** having sufficient merit or
importance; estimable, honorable
Gen 32:10 . . . I am not *w* of all the
Prov 12:4 . . . A *w* wife is a crown
Matt 8:8 . . . Lord, I am not *w* to have
Matt 10:37 . . . are not *w* of being mine;
Matt 22:8 . . . I invited aren't *w* of the
Luke 15:19 . . . I am no longer *w* of being
1 Cor 15:9 . . . I'm not even *w* to be called
Eph 4:1 . . . lead a life *w* of your calling,
Phil 1:27 . . . a manner *w* of the Good News
Rev 5:5 . . . He is *w* to open the scroll

**WOUNDS (n)** an injury to the body
Isa 30:26 . . . and cure the *w* he gave them.
Zech 13:6 . . . what about those *w* on your
John 20:20 . . . he showed them the *w* in
1 Pet 2:24 . . . By his *w* you are healed.

**WRATH (n)** extreme displeasure, anger, or
hostility; God's response to sin
Isa 13:13 . . . Armies displays his *w* in
Rev 6:16 . . . and from the *w* of the Lamb.
Rev 16:19 . . . the wine of his fierce *w.*

**WRITE, WRITING (v)** to inscribe or engrave; to
record
*see also* WRITTEN
Deut 10:2 . . . I will *w* on the tablets
Prov 3:3 . . . *W* them deep within your
Prov 7:3 . . . *W* them deep within your
Eccl 12:12 . . . for *w-ing* books is endless,
Jer 31:33 . . . I will *w* them on their hearts.
1 Tim 3:14 . . . I am *w-ing* these things to
Heb 8:10 . . . I will *w* them on their hearts.
Rev 3:12 . . . I will *w* on them the name of

**WRITTEN (v)** *see* also WRITE
Deut 28:58 . . . that are *w* in this book,
Josh 1:8 . . . to obey everything *w* in it.
Isa 49:16 . . . See, I have *w* your name
Dan 12:1 . . . whose name is *w* in the book
Mal 3:16 . . . scroll of remembrance was *w*
Luke 24:44 . . . everything *w* about me in
John 20:31 . . . these are *w* so that you

John 21:25 . . . the books that would be **w.**
Rom 2:15 . . . law is **w** in their hearts,
1 Cor 10:11 . . . They were **w** down to warn
Heb 12:23 . . . names are **w** in heaven.
Rev 21:27 . . . whose names are **w** in the

**WRONG (adj)** incorrect, sinful, immoral, or improper
Prov 14:2 . . . who take the **w** path
Rom 7:19 . . . don't want to do what is **w,**
Rom 12:9 . . . Hate what is **w.** Hold tightly
Rom 14:14 . . . of itself, is **w** to eat.
2 Tim 3:16 . . . make us realize what is **w**

**WRONG (adv)** in an unsuccessful or unfortunate way
Prov 15:22 . . . Plans go **w** for lack

**WRONG (n)** an injurious, unfair, or unjust act; something wrong, immoral, or unethical
Exod 23:2 . . . the crowd in doing **w.**
Deut 32:4 . . . faithful God who does no **w;**
Job 34:10 . . . The Almighty can do no **w.**
Ps 141:9 . . . snares of those who do **w.**
Isa 53:9 . . . done no **w** and had never
Rom 13:10 . . . Love does no **w** to others,
Rom 16:19 . . . to stay innocent of any **w.**
1 Cor 6:9 . . . those who do **w** will not
Jas 1:13 . . . God is never tempted to do **w,**
1 Pet 3:17 . . . to suffer for doing **w!**

**WRONGED (v)** to injure or harm; to malign or discredit
Num 5:7 . . . to the person who was **w.**

Isa 42:3 . . . to all who have been **w.**
1 Cor 13:5 . . . keeps no record of being **w.**

**YAHWEH (n)** "I AM WHO I AM" or "I WILL BE WHAT I WILL BE"; the personal name of God revealed to Moses in the burning bush
*see also* LORD
Gen 22:14 . . . named the place **Y**-Yireh
Exod 3:15 . . . **Y,** the God of your ancestors
Exod 6:2 . . . I am **Y**—'the LORD'
Exod 15:3 . . . warrior; **Y** is his name!
Exod 17:15 . . . there and named it **Y**-nissi
Exod 33:19 . . . I will call out my name, **Y,**
Exod 34:5 . . . called out his own name, **Y.**
Judg 6:24 . . . there and named it **Y**-Shalom

**YEAR, YEARS (n)** the period of about 365 days; a period having special significance; a measure of age or duration
Gen 1:14 . . . the seasons, days, and **y-s.**
Exod 12:40 . . . lived in Egypt for 430 **y-s.**
Exod 16:35 . . . manna for forty **y-s** until
Exod 34:23 . . . Three times each **y** every
Lev 16:34 . . . the LORD once each **y.**
Lev 25:11 . . . During that **y** you must
Job 36:26 . . . His **y-s** cannot be counted.
Ps 90:4 . . . a thousand **y-s** are as a
Luke 3:23 . . . about thirty **y-s** old when
Heb 10:1 . . . again and again, **y** after **y,**
Heb 10:3 . . . of their sins **y** after **y.**
2 Pet 3:8 . . . like a thousand **y-s** to the
Rev 20:2 . . . in chains for a thousand **y-s.**

**YEAST (n)** a fungus used for making alcoholic liquors and bread
Exod 12:8 . . . and bread made without **y.**
Exod 12:15 . . . bread made with **y** during
Matt 16:6 . . . Beware of the **y** of the
1 Cor 5:6 . . . a little **y** that spreads

**YOKE (n)** a wooden crossbar linking two load-pulling animals together; figurative of bondage or linkage between people
Hos 11:4 . . . lifted the **y** from his neck,
Matt 11:29 . . . Take my **y** upon you.

**YOUNG, YOUNGER (adj)** being in the first or an early stage of life, growth, or development
2 Chr 10:14 . . . counsel of his **y-er** advisers.
Ps 119:9 . . . How can a **y** person stay pure?
Prov 20:29 . . . The glory of the **y** is their
Joel 2:28 . . . your **y** men will see visions.
Acts 2:17 . . . Your **y** men will see visions,
Acts 7:58 . . . feet of a **y** man named Saul.
1 Tim 5:1 . . . Talk to **y-er** men as you
Titus 2:4 . . . must train the **y-er** women to
Titus 2:6 . . . encourage the **y** men to live
1 Pet 5:5 . . . same way, you **y-er** men must
1 Jn 2:13 . . . you who are **y** in the faith

**ZEAL (n)** eagerness and ardent interest in pursuit of something
Num 25:13 . . . in his **z** for me, his God,
Rom 10:2 . . . but it is misdirected **z.**

- City
- ○ City (modern name)
- ▲ Mountain peak

*River*

Beirut ○

LEBANON MTS.

ANTI-LEBANON MTS.

*Orontes*

Sidon ●

Damascus ●

*River*

▲ *Mt. Hermon*

GALILEAN MTS.

Acco ●

Haifa ○

*Sea of Galilee*

JEZREEL VALLEY

*Yarmuk River*

*Mt. Carmel* ▲

Nazareth ●

Megiddo ●

Beth-shan ●

*Mediterranean Sea (Great Sea)*

Mount Gilboa

EPHRAIM MTS.

*Jordan*

GILEAD

*Jabbok River*

*Mt. Ebal* ▲  Shechem ●

DOME

*Mt. Gerizim* ▲

Amman ●

Tel-Aviv ○

BENJAMIN MTS.

*River*

Jericho ●

Jerusalem ● ▲ *Mt. of Olives*

▲ *Mt. Nebo*

JUDEAN MTS.

ABARIM MTS.

Hebron ●

JUDEAN WILDERNESS

*Dead Sea*

Gaza ●

*Amon River*

*Besor Brook*

Beersheba ●

NEGEV

*Zered Brook*

Mitzpeh Ramon ○

ARABAH

Petra ●

## TOPOGRAPHY OF PALESTINE

*Direction of view*

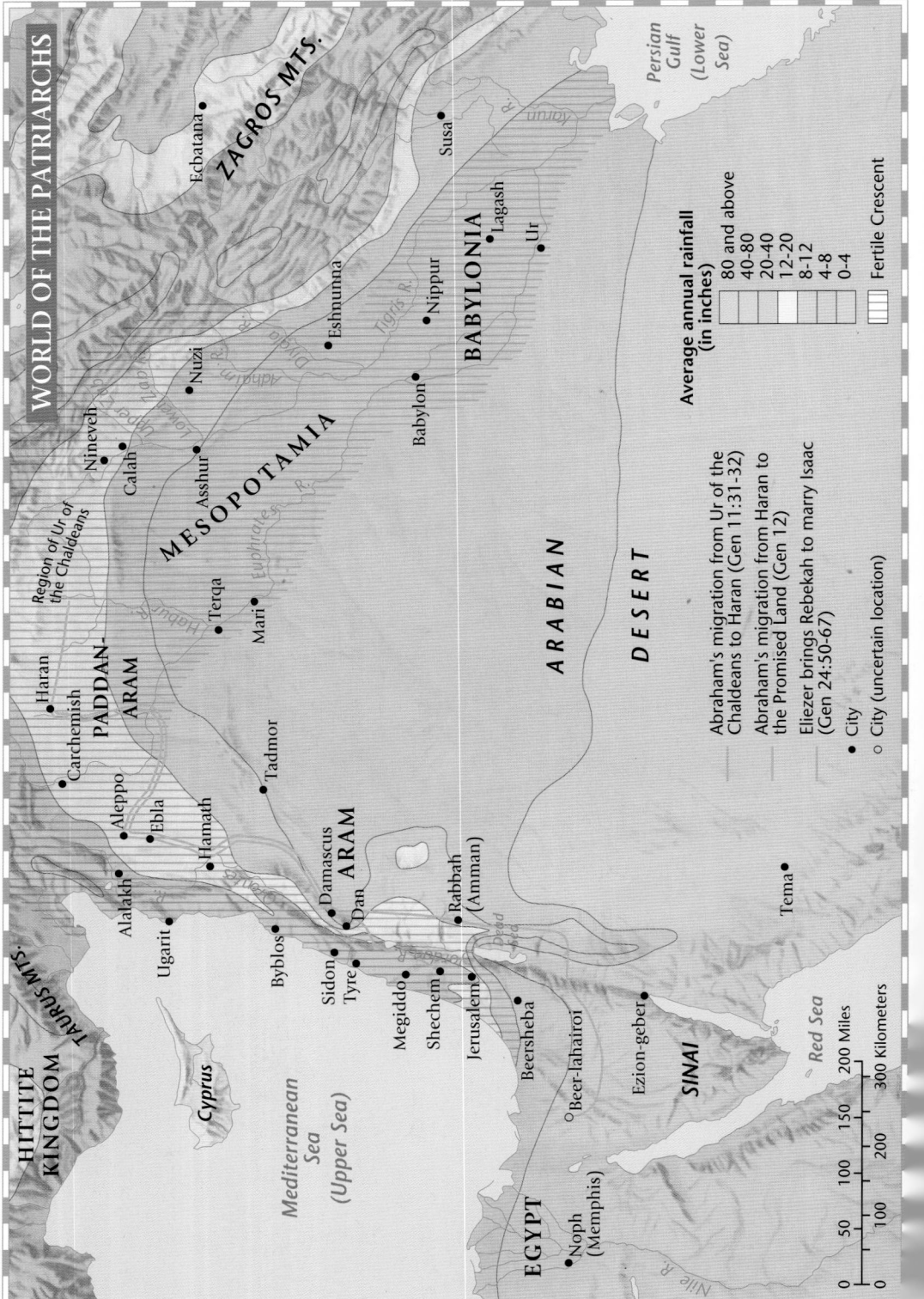

# WORLD OF THE PATRIARCHS

HITTITE KINGDOM

TAURUS MTS.

ZAGROS MTS.

Ecbatana

Nineveh

Calah

Asshur

Nuzi

Eshnunna

MESOPOTAMIA

Susa

Persian Gulf (Lower Sea)

Nippur

Lagash

BABYLONIA

Ur

Babylon

Region of Ur of the Chaldeans

Haran

Carchemish

PADDAN-ARAM

Terqa

Mari

Tadmor

Aleppo

Ebla

Hamath

Alalakh

Ugarit

Byblos

Damascus

ARAM

Dan

Sidon

Tyre

Megiddo

Shechem

Jerusalem

Rabbah (Amman)

ARABIAN

DESERT

Tema

Beersheba

Beer-lahai-roi

Ezion-geber

SINAI

Red Sea

EGYPT

Noph (Memphis)

Cyprus

Mediterranean Sea (Upper Sea)

Average annual rainfall (in inches)

80 and above
40-80
20-40
12-20
8-12
4-8
0-4

Fertile Crescent

Abraham's migration from Ur of the Chaldeans to Haran (Gen 11:31-32)

Abraham's migration from Haran to the Promised Land (Gen 12)

Eliezer brings Rebekah to marry Isaac (Gen 24:50-67)

• City

○ City (uncertain location)

0    50    100   150   200 Miles
0  100  200  300 Kilometers

Copyright © 1996 Tyndale House Publishers, Inc.

City
City (modern name)
Mountain peak
(possible sites for
Mount Sinai)

Route from Egypt to Mt. Sinai
Route from Mt. Sinai to Kadesh-barnea
Route from Kadesh-barnea to Abel-shittim
Ancient roadway

Direction
of view

*Cyprus*          Larnaca

*Mediterranean Sea
(Great Sea)*

Antioch

Beirut          Lebo-
hamath
Damascus

Acco          Coastal Road
Megiddo                    Great Trunk Road

Amman
Abel-shittim
Jerusalem   Heshbon
Gaza          *PHILISTIA*          Dibon
Beersheba          *NEGEV*          **MOAB**

*Lake
Menzaleh*          *Lake
Sirbonis*          *Dead Sea*

Zoan
(San el-
Hagar)          Way to the Land of the Philistines          *WILDERNESS
OF ZIN*
Raamses                              Punon
**GOSHEN**   Ismalia   Way to Shur          Kadesh-barnea          **EDOM**
Pithom   Succoth   *WILDERNESS
OF SHUR*          Petra

*Great Bitter
Lake*   *Little Bitter
Lake*          Darb el-Hajj          *WILDERNESS
OF
PARAN*   Timna          King's Highway

Suez          *Brook of Egypt*

*S I N A I*          Taba   Ezion-geber

Serabit
el-Khadim          Nuweiba          *M I D I A N*

Abu Zeneimeh          Ain Khadra

*WILDERNESS
OF SIN*          *Gulf of Aqaba*

*Gulf of Suez*          *Ras Safsaf*
▲ Jebel Serbal   ▲ Jebel Musa          Dahab
▲ Jebel
Katarina

Ras Gharib

*Tiran*          *Darb el-Hajj*

Sharm el-Sheikh
Ras Muhammad

*Red Sea*

Bur Safagah

**EXODUS FROM EGYPT**

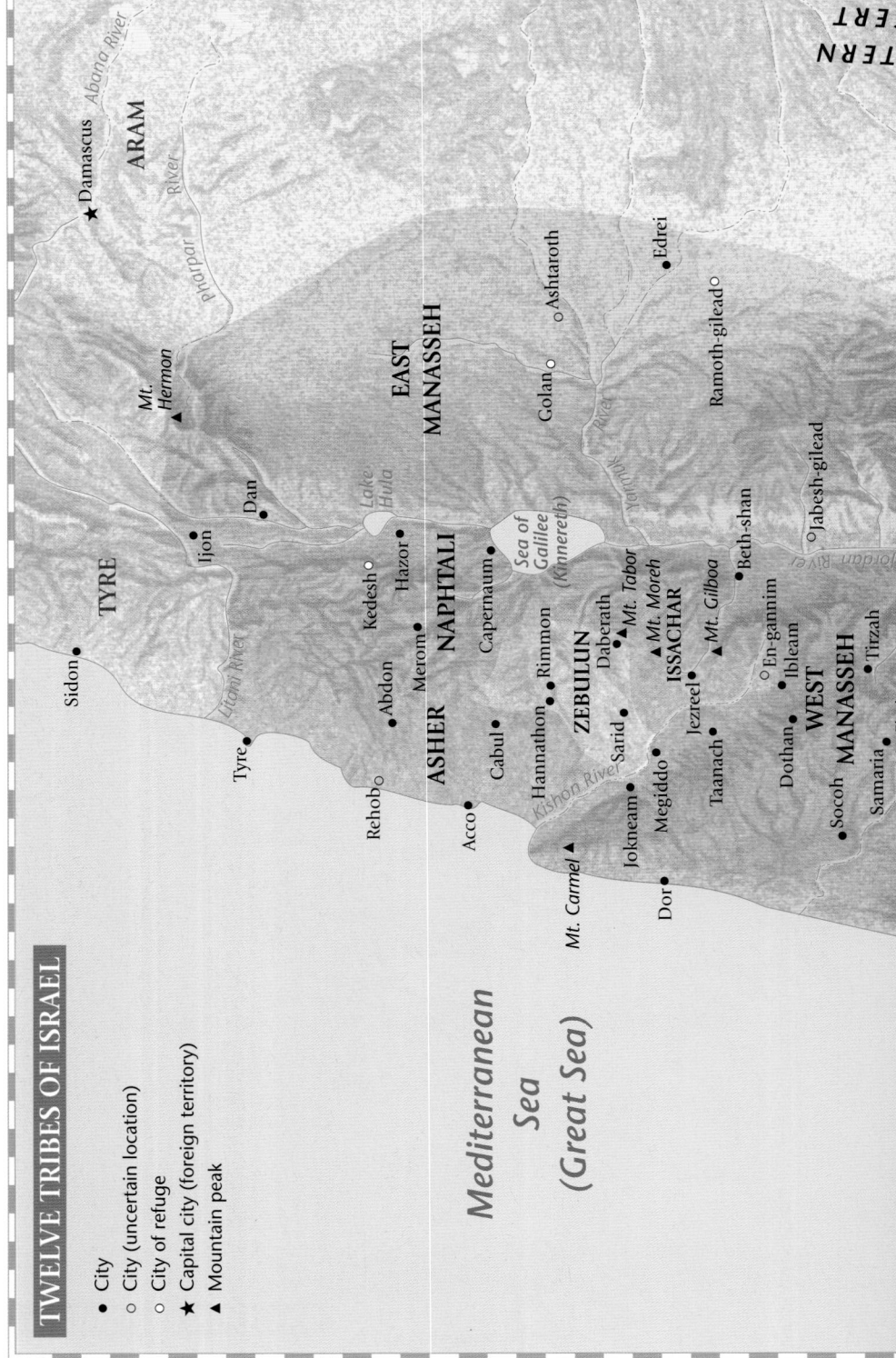

# TWELVE TRIBES OF ISRAEL

- • City
- ○ City (uncertain location)
- ◎ City of refuge
- ★ Capital city (foreign territory)
- ▲ Mountain peak

Mediterranean Sea (Great Sea)

ARAM

★ Damascus

*Abana River*

*Pharpar River*

ASTERN
DESERT

AMM

EAST MANASSEH

○ Ashtaroth

○ Edrei

○ Mahanaim

Golan ○

Ramoth-gilead ○

*Yarmuk River*

Mt. Hermon ▲

Dan •

Ijon •

*Lake Hula*

TYRE

Kedesh ◎

Hazor •

NAPHTALI

Merom •

Capernaum •

*Sea of Galilee (Kinnereth)*

Beth-shan •

○ Jabesh-gilead

Penuel ○

Abdon •

Sidon •

*Litani River*

Tyre •

ASHER

Cabul •

Hannathon •

Rimmon •

ZEBULUN

Sarid •

*Kishon River*

Daberath •

Mt. Tabor ▲

Mt. Moreh ▲

ISSACHAR

Jezreel •

Mt. Gilboa ▲

En-gannim ○

Ibleam •

Dothan •

*Jordan River*

Rehob ○

Acco •

Jokneam •

Megiddo •

Taanach •

WEST MANASSEH

Tirzah •

Samaria •

Socoh •

Mt. Ebal ▲

Dor •

Mt. Carmel ▲

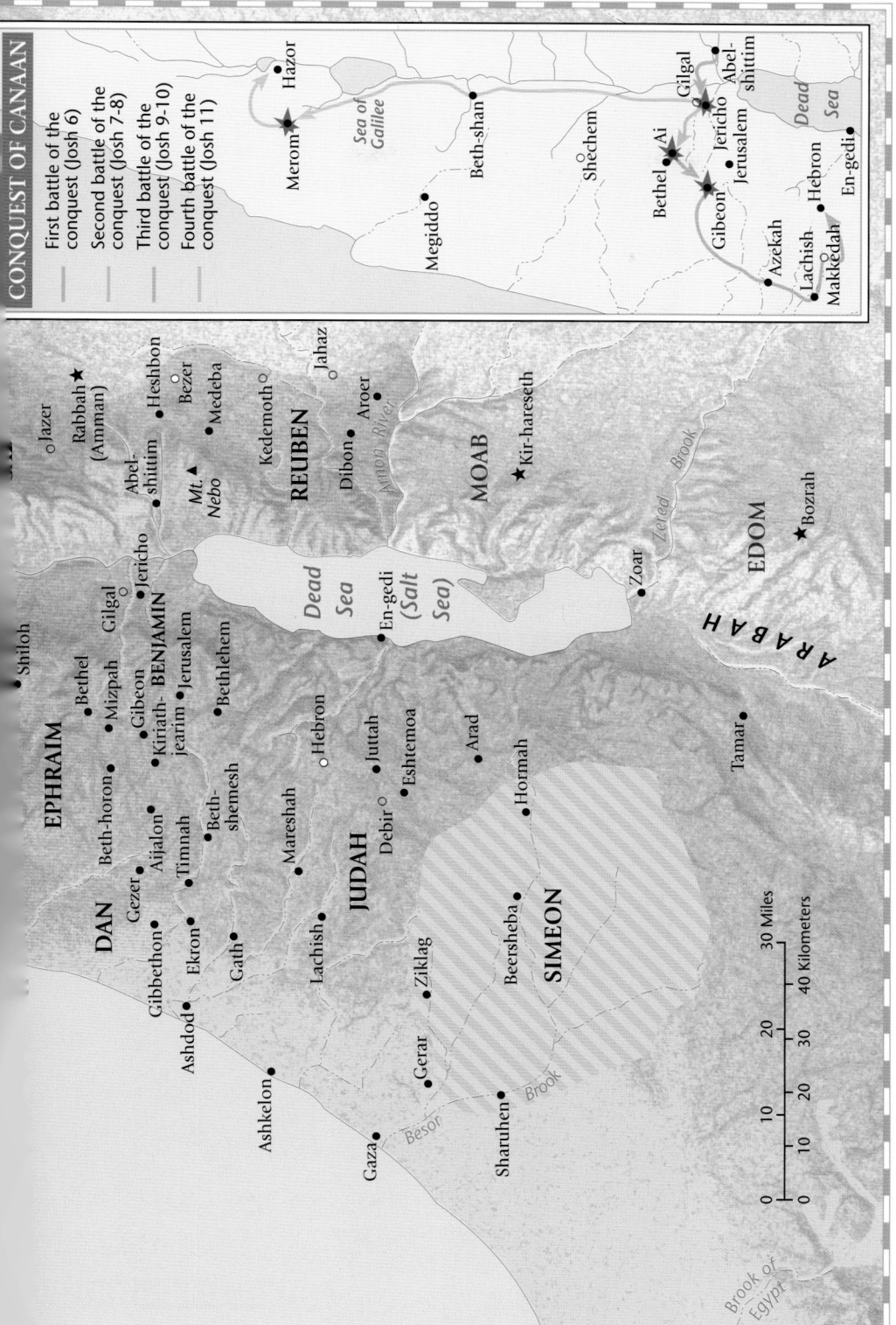

## CONQUEST OF CANAAN

—— First battle of the
conquest (Josh 6)
—— Second battle of the
conquest (Josh 7-8)
—— Third battle of the
conquest (Josh 9-10)
—— Fourth battle of the
conquest (Josh 11)

Hazor

Merom

Sea of
Galilee

Beth-shan

Shechem

Megiddo

Gilgal

Abel-
shittim

Jericho

Bethel • Ai

Jerusalem

Dead
Sea

Gibeon

Azekah

Lachish

Makkedah

Hebron

En-gedi

---

EPHRAIM

DAN

Shiloh

Bethel

Mizpah

Beth-horon

Ajalon

Gezer

Timnah

Beth-
shemesh

Gibeon

Kiriath-
jearim

BENJAMIN

Jericho

Gilgal

Jerusalem

Bethlehem

Dead
Sea

En-gedi

(Salt
Sea)

Gibbethon

Ekron

Gath

Ashdod

Lachish

Mareshah

Hebron

JUDAH

Debir

Juttah

Eshtemoa

Arad

Hormah

Ashkelon

Gerar

Ziklag

Beersheba

SIMEON

Gaza

Sharuhen

Brook

Besor

Brook of
Egypt

Tamar

A R A B A H

EDOM

Bozrah

Zoar

Kir-hareseth

MOAB

Zered Brook

Dibon

Aroer

Jahaz

Kedemoth

Arnon River

REUBEN

Mt.
Nebo

Medeba

Bezer

Heshbon

Abel-
shittim

Jazer

Rabbah
(Amman)

0    10    20    30 Miles
0    10  20    30    40 Kilometers

0    40 Miles
0    40 Kilometers

Aleppo
YAMHAD
Tiphsah
Cyprus
Hamath
HAMATH
Arvad
Tadmor
Byblos
Lebo-hamath
PHOENICIA
Mediterranean
Sea
(Great Sea)
Damascus
ARAM
Tyre
Dan
Hazor
Sea of Galilee (Kinnereth)
Dor
EASTERN DESERT
Megiddo
Shechem
AMMON
Joppa
Gezer
Rabbah
(Amman)
PHILISTIA
Jerusalem
Gaza
Dead Sea
MOAB
Raphia
Beersheba
(Salt Sea)
AMALEK
Petra
EDOM
Kadesh-
barnea
Ezion-
geber
Gulf of
Aqaba
SINAI

Kingdom of Saul
Kingdom of David
Kingdom of Solomon

UNITED KINGDOM

0   25   50 Miles
0   25   50 Kilometers

AMURRU
Great Trunk Road
Euphrates R.
Hamath
HAMATH
Qatna
Mediterranean
Sea
(Great Sea)
Arvad
Kadesh
Orontes R.
Sadad
Byblos
Road
PHOENICIA
Lebo-
hamath
Berothai
Coastal
Sidon
Damascus
Tyre
Litani R.
Dan
ARAM
Kedesh
Hazor
Sea of
Galilee
(Kinnereth)
Acco
Ashtaroth
Dor
Ramoth-
Salecah
Megiddo
gilead
Beth-
shan
Jabbok R.
Jordan R.
Shechem
ISRAEL
Joppa
Rabbah
(Amman)
Gezer
Gibeah
AMMON
Ashdod
Jerusalem
Medeba
Road
Gath
Lachish
Dead Sea (Salt Sea)
Aroer
Gaza
Hebron
Highway
Raphia
JUDAH
MOAB
Great
Beersheba
Kir-hareseth (Kir-moab)
PHILISTIA
NEGEV
Trunk
King's
Brook of Egypt
Kadesh-
barnea
Bozrah
Petra
EDOM
Territory
periodically
contested by
Edom and Judah
WILDERNESS
OF ZIN
EASTERN DESERT
Ezion-
geber
Gulf of
Aqaba
SINAI

DIVIDED KINGDOM

# ASSYRIAN AND BABYLONIAN EMPIRES

*Black Sea*

Byzantium

LYDIA

*Lake Tuz*

URARTU

*Araxes R.*

*Caspian Sea*

*Lake Van*

*Lake Urmia*

Carchemish

Tarsus • KUE

Haran

*Cyprus*

Aleppo

Nineveh • Calah

Asshur • Arrapha

MEDIA

Ecbatana

Riblah

Tadmor

*Mediterranean Sea (Great Sea)*

Tyre

Damascus

KEDAR

Samaria

*Euphrates*

*Tigris*

Sippar

Babylon • Nippur

Jerusalem

*SAHARA DESERT*

Memphis

Ezion-geber

Dumah

*ARABIAN DESERT*

Erech (Uruk)

Ur

Susa

ELAM

PERSIA

*Persian Gulf*

*Nile R.*

Assyria around 700 B.C.

Babylonia around 600 B.C.

*Red Sea*

Tema

| 0 | 100 | 200 Miles |
| 0 | 150 | 300 Kilometers |

# GREEK EMPIRE

*Danube R.*

MACEDONIA

THRACE

*Black Sea*

Sinope

CAUCASUS MTS.

*Caspian Sea*

Pella

Athens

*Lake Tuz*

ASIA

ARMENIA

HELLAS

Ephesus

*Lake Van*

*Lake Urmia*

Sparta

Tarsus

Carchemish

Haran

Gaugamela

*Crete*

*Cyprus*

Aleppo

*Euphrates*

Arbela

MEDIA

Ecbatana

*Mediterranean Sea (Great Sea)*

Tadmor

*Tigris*

Opis

Cyrene

Tyre

Damascus

BABYLONIA

LIBYA

Alexandria

Jerusalem

Babylon

Susa

EGYPT

Ezion-geber

NABATEA

Erech (Uruk)

Ur

Memphis

*Persian Gulf*

*SAHARA DESERT*

*Nile R.*

*ARABIAN DESERT*

Extent of Alexandrian empire

Ptolemaic realm

Seleucid realm

Antigonid realm

Minor Hellenistic provinces

*Red Sea*

Thebes

| 0 | 200 | 400 Miles |
| 0 | 250 | 500 Kilometers |

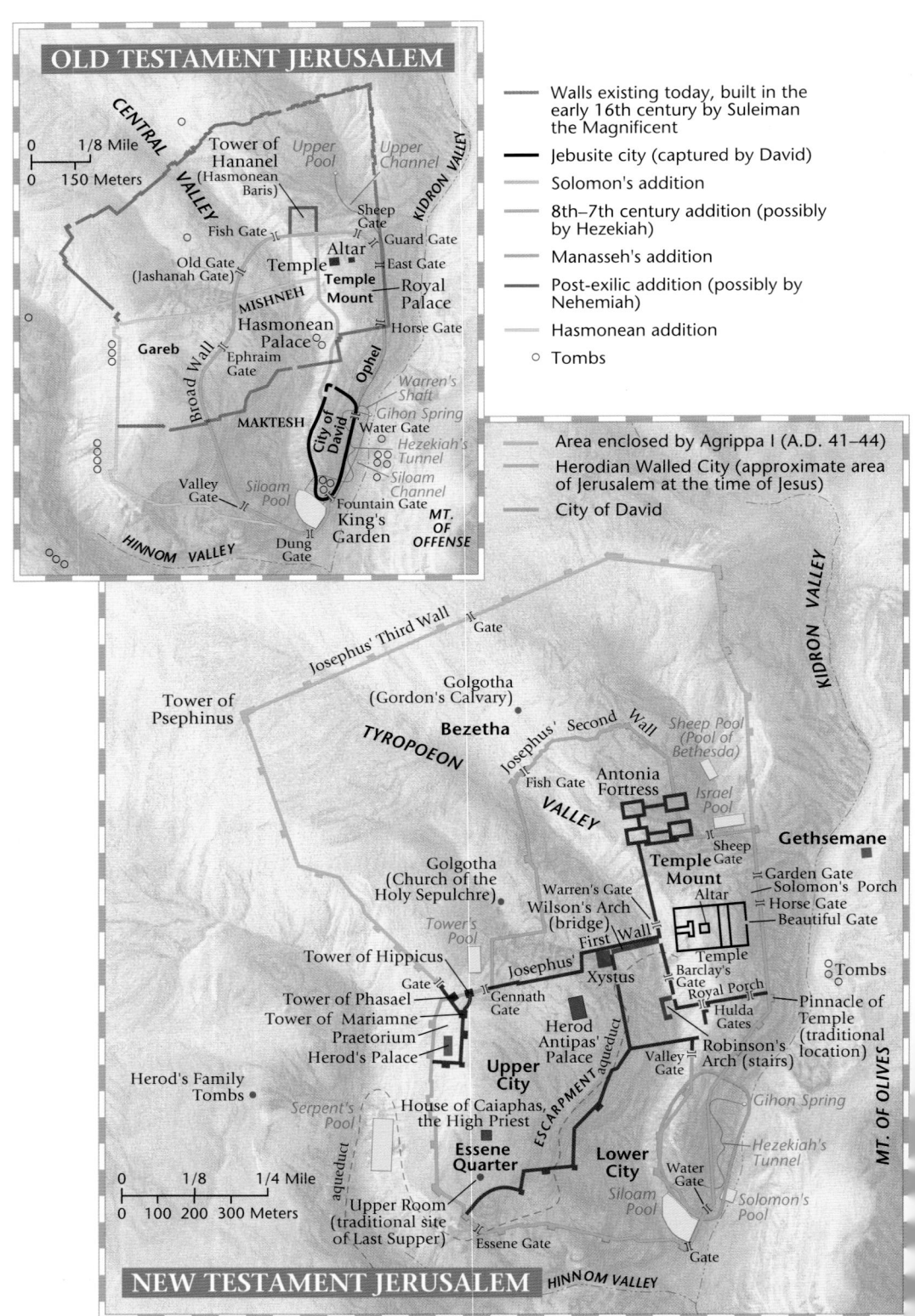

# OLD TESTAMENT JERUSALEM

CENTRAL VALLEY

KIDRON VALLEY

0   1/8 Mile
0   150 Meters

Tower of Hananel (Hasmonean Baris)
Upper Pool
Upper Channel
Sheep Gate
Fish Gate
Guard Gate
Old Gate (Jashanah Gate)
Altar
East Gate
Temple
Temple Mount
Royal Palace
MISHNEH
Hasmonean Palace
Horse Gate
Gareb
Broad Wall
Ephraim Gate
Ophel
Warren's Shaft
MAKTESH
City of David
Water Gate
Gihon Spring
Hezekiah's Tunnel
Siloam Channel
Valley Gate
Siloam Pool
King's Garden
Fountain Gate
MT. OF OFFENSE
HINNOM VALLEY
Dung Gate

Walls existing today, built in the early 16th century by Suleiman the Magnificent
Jebusite city (captured by David)
Solomon's addition
8th–7th century addition (possibly by Hezekiah)
Manasseh's addition
Post-exilic addition (possibly by Nehemiah)
Hasmonean addition
○ Tombs

Area enclosed by Agrippa I (A.D. 41–44)
Herodian Walled City (approximate area of Jerusalem at the time of Jesus)
City of David

KIDRON VALLEY

Josephus' Third Wall
Gate
Golgotha (Gordon's Calvary)
Tower of Psephinus
TYROPOEON
Bezetha
Josephus' Second Wall
Sheep Pool (Pool of Bethesda)
Fish Gate
VALLEY
Antonia Fortress
Israel Pool
Sheep Gate
Temple Mount
Gethsemane
Golgotha (Church of the Holy Sepulchre)
Garden Gate
Solomon's Porch
Warren's Gate
Horse Gate
Beautiful Gate
Wilson's Arch (bridge)
Altar
Tower's Pool
First Wall
Temple
Tombs
Tower of Hippicus
Josephus'
Xystus
Barclay's Gate
Royal Porch
Gate
Gennath Gate
Pinnacle of Temple (traditional location)
Tower of Phasael
Tower of Mariamne
Hulda Gates
Praetorium
Herod Antipas' Palace
Valley Gate
Robinson's Arch (stairs)
Herod's Palace
Upper City
aqueduct
ESCARPMENT
Herod's Family Tombs
Serpent's Pool
Gihon Spring
House of Caiaphas, the High Priest
Lower City
MT. OF OLIVES
Essene Quarter
Water Gate
Hezekiah's Tunnel
aqueduct
Siloam Pool
Solomon's Pool
Upper Room (traditional site of Last Supper)
Essene Gate
Gate

# NEW TESTAMENT JERUSALEM
HINNOM VALLEY

Copyright © 1996 Tyndale House Publishers, Inc.

# ROMAN DIVISION OF PALESTINE

0    10    20    30 Miles
0    10    20    30    40 Kilometers

*Mediterranean
Sea
(Great Sea)*

**PHOENICIA**

**ABILENE**
• Abila

**ITUREA**
*Mt.
Hermon* ▲

○ Damascus
*Abana R.*

**SYRIA**
*Pharpar R.*

Sidon •

*Road*
*Litani*

Tyre •

*Coastal Road*

Caesarea
Philippi •

**GAULANITIS**

**TRACHONITIS**
• Raphana

Cadasa
(Kedesh) •

*Lake Hula*

Mt. Meron ▲  • Thella

**GALILEE**

Korazin •

Capernaum •    • Bethsaida
Gennesaret •              • Gergesa
Magdala •    *Sea
of
Galilee
(Kinnereth)*    ○ Hippus

Tiberias •
*Mt.
Tabor* ▲

**BATANEA**

Ptolemais
(Acco) •

*Mt.
Carmel* ▲

□ Gebae

*Kishon R.*

• Nain

Gadara •    • Abila

*Yarmuk R.*

• Edrei
**AURANITIS**

Dora •

Caesarea •

*Great Trunk Road*

Dothan •    Scythopolis
(Beth-shan) •

○ Pella

• Dion

**DECAPOLIS**

○ Gerasa

**SAMARIA**

Sebaste •
(Samaria)

*Mt. Ebal* ▲
• Sychar
▲ *Mt.
Gerizim*

Alexandrium □

□ Amathus
*Jabbok R.*

*Jordan R.*

**PEREA**

Joppa •

Antipatris •
(Aphek)

*Yarkon R.*

Lydda •
(Lod)

Bethel •

• Ephraim

Tyrus □

Philadelphia
(Amman) •

Azotus •
(Ashdod)    • Jamnia

Jerusalem •
*Mt. of Olives* ▲  • Bethany

Jericho □
• Cyprus

• Abila

Esbus □
(Heshbon)

• Medeba

Ascalon •

Bethlehem •
**JUDEA**
Marisa •

□ Hyrcania

□ Herodium

Machaerus □

**NABATEA**

Adora •  • Hebron

En-gedi •

*Dead
Sea
(Salt Sea)*

*Arnon R.*

*King's Highway*

• Gaza

• Raphia

*Besor Brook*

Arad •  Masada
□

Beersheba •
**IDUMEA**
□
• Malatha

## Division of Herod's Kingdom
## to his three sons

Territory of Archelaus
Territory of Herod Antipas
Territory of Philip
Territory of the
Proconsul of Syria

• City
○ Decapolis city
□ Herodian fortress
○ Decapolis city (uncertain location)
▲ Mountain peak
— Extent of Herod the Great's kingdom

# MINISTRY OF JESUS

Chronologically speaking, it is not possible to sequentially arrange the events in the life of Christ in any definitive way; none of the New Testament gospels follows an overtly chronological pattern. Accordingly, the arrangement here follows a geographic order, basically proceeding from north to south on the map. Because the gospel of Matthew most frequently contains information cited here, and because it is the most geographically particularistic gospel, synoptic passages are keyed to the book of Matthew, except where they are unattested there or where more pertinent information about the event cited is available in another gospel.

A. *Region of Tyre:* Gentile woman's daughter healed (Mt 15:21-28)

B. *Caesarea Philippi:* Peter's great declaration (Mt 16:13-20)

C. *Mt. Meron/Mt. Tabor/Mt. Hermon:* (1) possible location of Transfiguration (Mt 17:1-13); (2) demon-possessed boy healed nearby (Mt 17:14-21)

D. *Cana of Galilee:* (1) water changed to wine (Jn 2:1-11); (2) Capernaum official's son healed (Jn 4:46-54)

E. *Gennesaret:* (1) possible location of feeding of multitudes (Mt 14:13-21; 15:32-39); (2) many healings (Mk 6:53-56)

F. *Area of Korazin:* (1) judgment pronounced on the cities of Korazin, Bethsaida, and Capernaum (Mt 11:20-24); (2) possible area of Sermon on the Mount (Mt 5-7)

G. *Capernaum:* (1) catch of fish (Lk 5:1-11); (2) evil spirit cast out (Mk 1:21-28); (3) Sermon on the Mount (Mt 5-7); (4) Peter's mother-in-law healed (Mt 8:5-13); (5) Roman officer's servant healed (Mt 8:5-13); (6) paralyzed man healed (Mk 2:1-12); (7) woman with a hemorrhage healed (Mk 5:25-34); (8) Jairus's daughter raised (Lk 8:40-56); (9) two blind men healed (Mt 9:27-31); (10) a mute, demon-possessed man healed (Mt 9:32-34); (11) the twelve apostles sent out (Mt 10:1-15); (12) man with deformed hand healed (Mt 12:9-13); (13) another demon-possessed man healed (Mt 12:22-37); (14) Temple tax provided (Mt 17:24-27); (15) Bread of Life discourse (Jn 6:22-59)

H. *Bethsaida:* (1) possible location of feeding of multitudes (Mt 14:13-21; 15:32-39); (2) blind man healed (Mk 8:22-26)

I. *Sea of Galilee near Bethsaida:* walking on water (Mt 14:22-33)

J. *Sea of Galilee:* storm quieted (Mt 8:23-27)

K. *Gergesa/Gadara:* possible location of casting out demons, which enter pigs; the pigs then rush down a steep bank and drown (Lk 8:26-39)

L. *Nazareth:* (1) childhood home (Mt 2:19-23); (2) rejected by townspeople (Lk 4:16-30)

M. *Nain:* widow's son raised (Lk 7:11-17)

N. *Region of Galilee:* (1) leper cleansed (Mk 1:40-45); (2) post-resurrection appearances to the disciples (Mt 28:16-20)

O. *Region of Ten Towns:* many healings (Mt 15:29-31; Mk 7:31-37)

P. *Region between Galilee and Samaria:* (1) refused entry into village (Lk 9:51-56); (2) ten lepers healed (Lk 17:11-19)

Q. *Sychar:* woman at the well of Samaria (Jn 4:1-42)

R. *Ephraim:* enters into seclusion with the disciples (Jn 11:54)

S. *Region of Perea:* (1) teaching on marriage (Mt 19:1-12); (2) possible location of healing of woman with infirmity (Lk 13:10-13); (3) possible location of healing of man with swollen limbs (Lk 14:1-6); (4) possible location of the rich young ruler (Lk 18:18-30)

T. *Jericho:* (1) Bartimaeus healed (Mk 10:46-52); (2) Zacchaeus converted

## Map labels

to Mt. Hermon — C

Caesarea Philippi (Paneas) — B

Lake Hula

GAULANITIS

Tyre — A

TYRE

UPPER GALILEE

Gischala

Mt. Meron (Jebel Jarmuk) — C

Korazin — F

Bethsaida — H

Capernaum

Sea of Galilee (Sea of Kinnereth) — G

Gennesaret — E

Gergesa — K

Hippus

Magdala

Yarmuk River

Gadara — K

Bethany beyond Jordan (possible site)

Pella

DECAPOLIS — O

Gerasa

Ptolemais (Acco)

LOWER GALILEE

Jotapata

Sepphoris

Cana — D

Nazareth — L

Tiberias — I

Mt. Tabor — C

Nain — M

Jordan River

Kishon

ESDRAELON VALLEY

Scythopolis (Beth-shan)

Aenon

Salim

Dora

Caesarea

SAMARIA

Sebaste (Samaria)

Mt. Ebal

Mt. ▲ Sychar — P

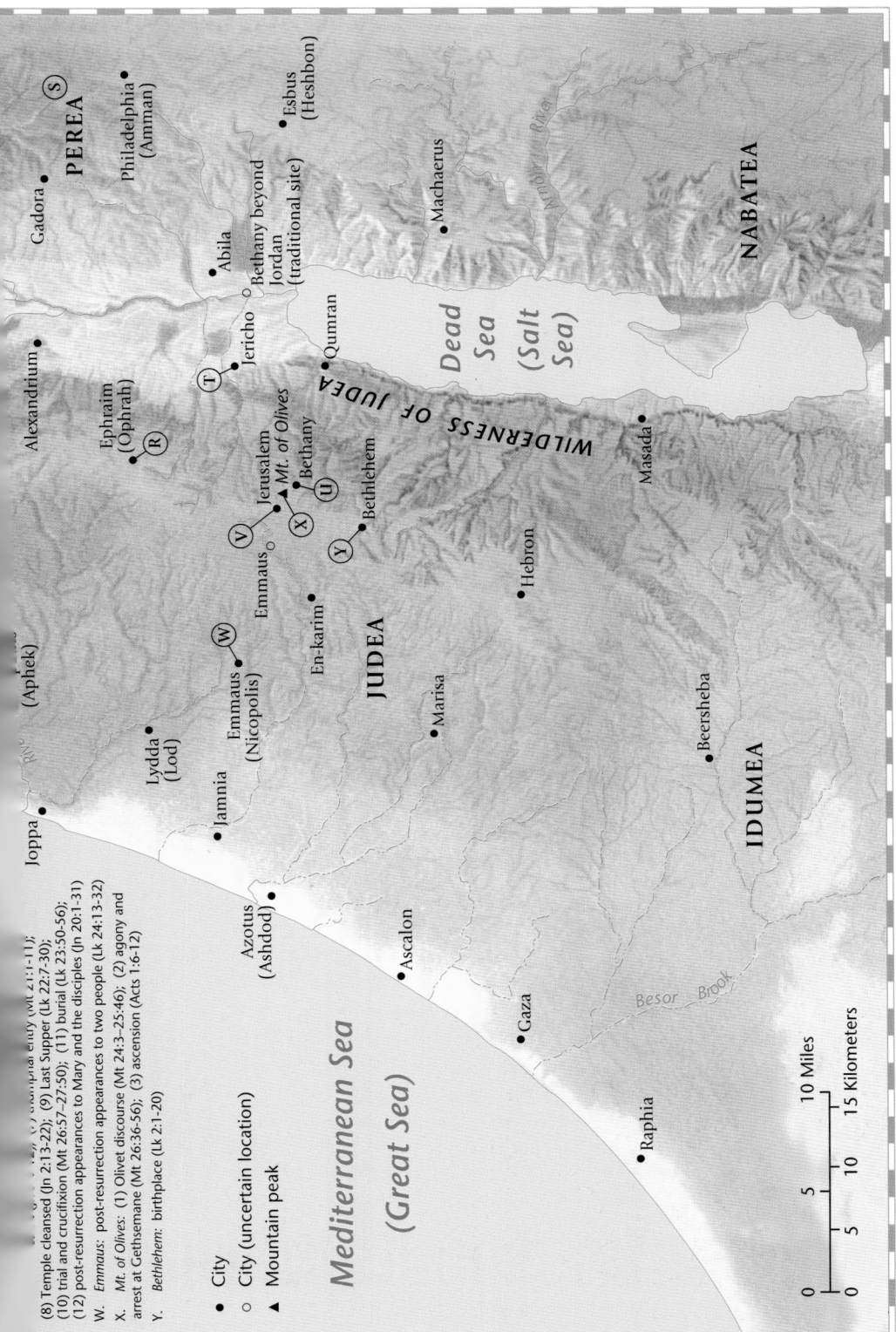

(8) Temple cleansed (Jn 2:13-22); (9) Last Supper (Lk 22:7-30);
(10) trial and crucifixion (Mt 26:57–27:50); (11) burial (Lk 23:50-56);
(12) post-resurrection appearances to the disciples (Jn 20:1-31)

W. *Emmaus:* post-resurrection appearances to two people (Lk 24:13-32)

X. *Mt. of Olives:* (1) Olivet discourse (Mt 24:3–25:46); (2) agony and
   arrest at Gethsemane (Mt 26:36-56); (3) ascension (Acts 1:6-12)

Y. *Bethlehem:* birthplace (Lk 2:1-20)

● City
○ City (uncertain location)
▲ Mountain peak

*Mediterranean Sea*
*(Great Sea)*

0  5  10 Miles
0  5  10  15 Kilometers

PEREA  Ⓢ

Gadora ●

Philadelphia ●
(Amman)

Esbus ●
(Heshbon)

NABATEA

Alexandrium ●

Abila ●

Machaerus ●

Bethany beyond
Jordan ○
(traditional site)

Ephraim
(Ophrah) Ⓡ

Ⓣ

Jericho ●

Qumran ●

*Dead*
*Sea*
*(Salt*
*Sea)*

WILDERNESS OF JUDEA

Jerusalem ●
*Mt. of Olives*
Ⓥ Ⓧ Bethany Ⓤ

Emmaus ○   Ⓨ Bethlehem ●

En-karim ●

Masada ●

(Aphek)

Ⓦ

Emmaus ●
(Nicopolis)

Lydda ●
(Lod)

Jamnia ●

JUDEA

Marisa ●

Hebron ●

Beersheba ●

IDUMEA

Joppa ●

Azotus ●
(Ashdod)

Ascalon ●

*Besor Brook*

Gaza ●

Raphia ●

Copyright © 1996 Tyndale House Publishers, Inc.

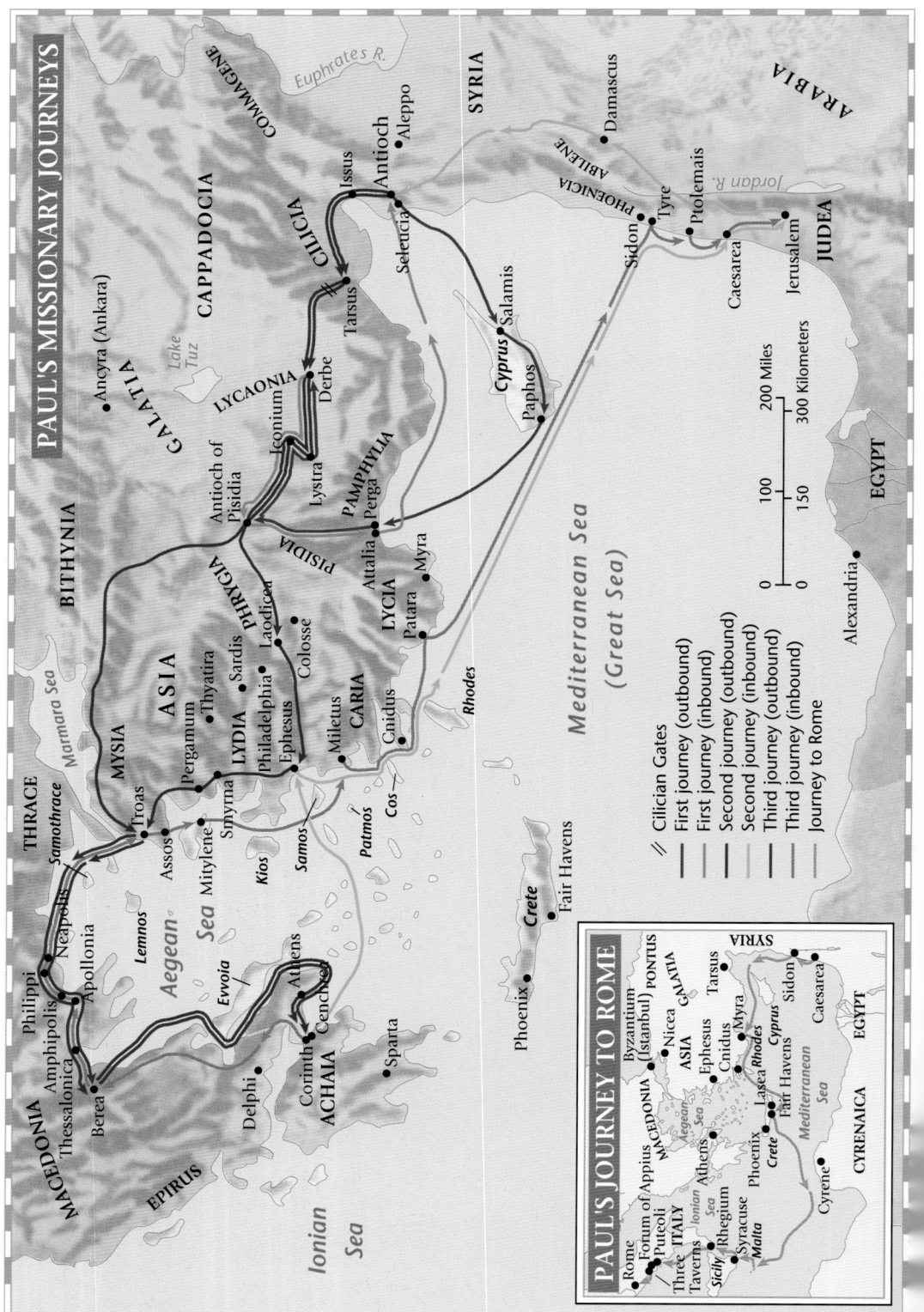

# PAUL'S MISSIONARY JOURNEYS

SYRIA

COMMAGENE

Euphrates R.

Damascus

Aleppo

ABILENE

Antioch

Issus

PHOENICIA

CILICIA

Seleucia

Tyre

Ptolemais

Jordan R.

Sidon

Caesarea

JUDEA

Tarsus

Salamis

Jerusalem

Cyprus

Derbe

Paphos

LYCAONIA

Iconium

Ancyra (Ankara)

GALATIA

Lake Tuz

CAPPADOCIA

Antioch of Pisidia

Lystra

PAMPHYLIA

Perga

Attalia

PISIDIA

Myra

LYCIA

Patara

BITHYNIA

PHRYGIA

Laodicea

Colosse

Thyatira

Sardis

ASIA

Philadelphia

LYDIA

Ephesus

CARIA

Miletus

Cnidus

Rhodes

Mediterranean Sea
(Great Sea)

200 Miles

100

300 Kilometers

150

0

EGYPT

Alexandria

Pergamum

MYSIA

Smyrna

Troas

Kios

Assos

Samos

Mitylene

Patmos

Cos

THRACE

Samothrace

Lemnos

Aegean
Sea

Evvoia

Fair Havens

Marmara Sea

MACEDONIA

Neapolis

Apollonia

Philippi

Amphipolis

Thessalonica

Berea

Athens

Cenchrea

Corinth

ACHAIA

Delphi

Sparta

EPIRUS

Ionian
Sea

Phoenix

Crete

## Legend

⫻ Cilician Gates
First journey (outbound)
First journey (inbound)
Second journey (outbound)
Second journey (inbound)
Third journey (outbound)
Third journey (inbound)
Journey to Rome

## PAUL'S JOURNEY TO ROME

Rome

Forum of Appius

Three Taverns

Puteoli

ITALY

Rhegium

Sicily

Syracuse

Malta

Byzantium (Istanbul)

PONTUS

Nicea

GALATIA

ASIA

Tarsus

Ephesus

Cnidus

Myra

Rhodes

Cyprus

SYRIA

Sidon

Caesarea

EGYPT

MACEDONIA

Athens

Lasea

Phoenix

Crete

Fair Havens

Mediterranean
Sea

Aegean
Sea

Ionian
Sea

Cyrene

CYRENAICA

# ROMAN EMPIRE AND SPREAD OF CHRISTIANITY

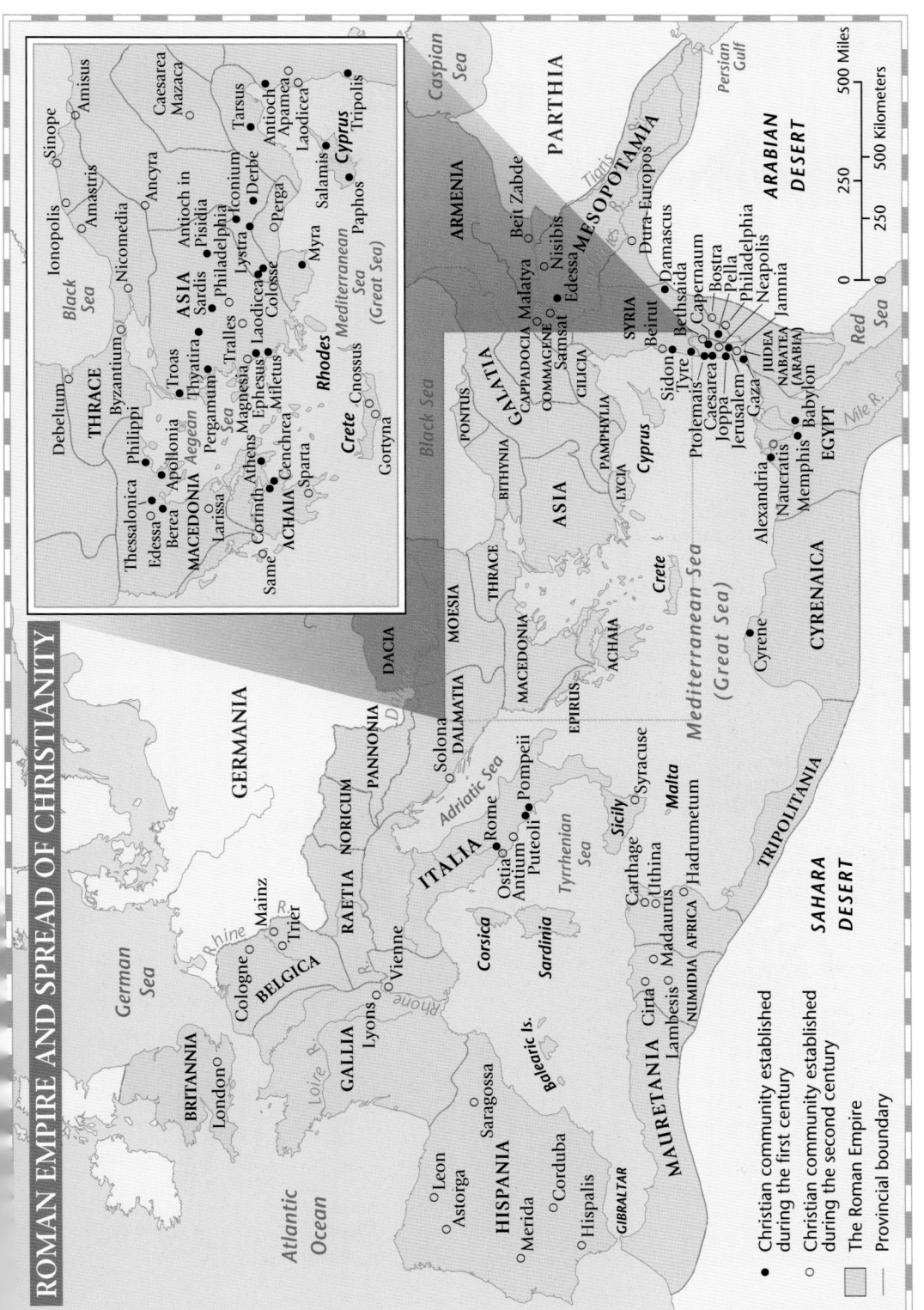

**Inset map labels:**

Sinope, Amisus, Caesarea Mazaca, Ionopolis, Amastris, Ancyra, Nicomedia, Byzantium, Tarsus, Antioch, Apamea, Laodicea, Tripolis, Antioch in Pisidia, Iconium, Derbe, Perga, Salamis, *Cyprus*, Paphos, THRACE, Debeltum, Philippi, Apollonia, Troas, Pergamum, Thyatira, Sardis, Philadelphia, ASIA, *Aegean Sea*, Magnesia, Ephesus, Miletus, Laodicea, Colosse, Myra, *Rhodes*, Thessalonica, Edessa, Berea, MACEDONIA, Larissa, Athens, Cenchrea, Corinth, ACHAIA, Sparta, Same, *Crete*, Cnossus, Gortyna, *Mediterranean Sea (Great Sea)*

**Main map labels:**

*Caspian Sea*, PARTHIA, ARMENIA, MESOPOTAMIA, *Persian Gulf*, ARABIAN DESERT, Beit Zabde, Nisibis, Edessa, Dura-Europos, Damascus, Malatya, Samsat, CAPPADOCIA, COMMAGENE, CILICIA, SYRIA, Beirut, Sidon, Tyre, Bethsaida, Capernaum, Bostra, Pella, Philadelphia, Neapolis, Jamnia, Ptolemais, Caesarea, Joppa, Jerusalem, Gaza, JUDEA, NABATEA (ARABIA), Babylon, Memphis, Naucratis, Alexandria, EGYPT, *Nile R.*, *Red Sea*, GALATIA, PONTUS, BITHYNIA, PAMPHYLIA, LYCIA, *Cyprus*, ASIA, *Black Sea*, THRACE, MOESIA, MACEDONIA, EPIRUS, ACHAIA, *Crete*, *Mediterranean Sea (Great Sea)*, Cyrene, CYRENAICA, GERMANIA, DACIA, PANNONIA, NORICUM, DALMATIA, Solona, *Adriatic Sea*, Pompeii, Rome, Ostia, Antium, Puteoli, ITALIA, *Tyrrhenian Sea*, Syracuse, *Sicily*, *Malta*, Carthage, Uthina, Madaurus, Hadrumetum, AFRICA, NUMIDIA, Cirta, Lambesis, *Corsica*, *Sardinia*, RAETIA, BELGICA, Mainz, Trier, Cologne, *R. Rhine*, Vienne, Lyons, GALLIA, *Loire R.*, *Rhône R.*, BRITANNIA, London, *German Sea*, *Atlantic Ocean*, HISPANIA, Leon, Astorga, Saragossa, Merida, Corduba, Hispalis, GIBRALTAR, *Balearic Is.*, MAURETANIA, TRIPOLITANIA, SAHARA DESERT, *Tigris*, *Danube*

**Scale:**

500 Miles — 250 — 0
500 Kilometers — 250 — 0

**Legend:**

- ● Christian community established during the first century
- ○ Christian community established during the second century
- The Roman Empire
- — Provincial boundary

c. 2170
(or c. 2000 B.C.)
*Abraham leaves Ur*

c. 1880
(or c. 1720 B.C.)
*Entry into Egypt*

The
Patriarchs

Wilderness
Wanderings

ASHER
BENJAMIN
DAN
EPHRAIM
GAD
ISSACHAR
JUDAH
MANASSEH
NAPHTALI
REUBEN
SIMEON
ZEBULUN

Judges of the
Twelve Tribes

Egyptian
Sojourn

c. 1450 B.C.
(or c. 1280 B.C.)
*Exodus*

c. 1410 B.C.
(or c. 1240 B.C.)
*Entry into Canaan*

c. 1050 B.C.
*Saul anointed king*

United
Monarchy

Northern
Tribes
of
Israel

586 B.C.
*Fall of Jerusalem;
Judah exiled
to Babylon*

Judah

930 B.C.
*Division
of kingdom*

538 B.C.
*Jewish exiles
return to
Jerusalem*

722 B.C.
*Fall of Samaria;
end of northern kingdom*

E X I L E

Restoration
under
Persian Empire

515 B.C.
*Temple is rebuilt*

Syrian
Rule

6 B.C.
*Birth of Jesus Christ*

Empire of
Alexander the
Great

Egyptian Rule

Roman
Empire

A.D. 70
*Temple is
destroyed*

Maccabean
Dynasty

Terrace

Beautiful
Gate

Store
(Oil, wine)

Court of
the Women

Where the
Levites sang

Store
(Wood)

Great Gate

Court of the
Israelites

Slaughtering
Place

Terrace

Altar

Porch

Most Holy Place

Holy Place

Court of the Priests

Barrier

North
Gate

Antonia
Fortress

Golden
Gate

Court of
the Gentiles

Solomon's Porch

Passages to court

## THE TEMPLE IN NEW TESTAMENT TIMES

ISRAEL AND THE MIDDLE EAST TODAY

ROMANIA
Odessa
Bucharest
UKRAINE
Sofia
BULGARIA
Black Sea
RUSSIA
KAZAKSTAN
UZBEKISTAN
GEORGIA
Caspian
Sea
Istanbul
GREECE
Ankara
ARMENIA
AZERBAIJAN
Baku
Oxus R.
TURKMENISTAN
Mt. Ararat
Izmir
(Smyrna)
Hal's R.
TURKEY
Tabriz
Maimana
Tehran
AFGHANISTAN
Aleppo
CYPRUS
SYRIA
Mosul
Tigris R.
IRAN
PAKISTAN
LEBANON
Beirut
Mediterranean
Sea
Damascus
Euphrates R.
Baghdad
Jerusalem
Amman
IRAQ
JORDAN
Basra
Alexandria
Cairo
SINAI
Kuwait
Shiraz
Bandar
Abbas
KUWAIT City
Persian Gulf
SAHARA
DESERT
EGYPT
Nile R.
SAUDI ARABIA
Doha
QATAR
Riyadh
Arabian
Sea
Aswan
Red
Sea
Medina

SUDAN
Khartoum
ERITREA
0   200   400 Miles
0   200   400   600 Kilometers
ETHIOPIA

Copyright © 1996
Tyndale House Publishers, Inc.

AL   GA   SC
Atlantic
Ocean
FL
Gulf of
Mexico

Note the comparative size of
Israel to the state of Florida

LEBANON   Mt. Hermon
Tyre
SYRIA
Kiryat Shemona
GOLAN
HEIGHTS
Acco
Safed
Mediterranean
Sea
Haifa
Tiberias
Sea of Galilee
Megiddo
Nazareth
Jenin
Beth-shan
Netanya
Tulkarm
Jordan R.
Nablus
Tel Aviv
WEST BANK
Amman
Ramallah
Jericho
Jerusalem
Qumran
Gaza
Hebron
Dead Sea
Khan Yunis
GAZA
STRIP
Beersheba
En-gedi
El-Arish
Dimona
ISRAEL
JORDAN
Mizpe Ramon
EGYPT
Petra
SINAI
Eilat
Red Sea